CW01080690

PEOPLE OF TODAY

Anno MMXVII

Editor

Lucy Hume

Senior Designer

John Scott

Debrett's Board

Darryl Eales (Chairman)

Joanne Milner (Chairman)

Richard Thompson (Chairman, *People of Today*)

Renée Kuo (Co-Managing Director)

Louise Ruell (Co-Managing Director)

Debrett's would like to thank the members of the *People of Today*
Nominations Panel for their invaluable help in recommending the inspiring,
influential and high achieving new entrants for this year's edition.

Debrett's *People of Today* 2017

Published by Debrett's Limited

4 Cavendish Square, London W1G 0PG

Tel: +44 (0) 20 3786 7420

E-mail: people@debretts.com Website: www.debretts.com

Database typesetting by David Lewis XML Associates Ltd, Bungay, Suffolk

Printed and bound by CPI William Clowes, Beccles, Suffolk

CONTENTS

FOREWORD BY KAREN BLACKETT, OBE   IV

THE ROYAL FAMILY   V

A READER'S GUIDE   IX

ABBREVIATIONS   X

DEBRETT'S PEOPLE OF TODAY: BIOGRAPHICAL ENTRIES   1

FOREWORD

I HAVE THE IMMENSE PRIVILEGE of being asked to write the foreword for the 2017 edition of *People of Today*. This comes at a time when I am taking a well-earned three-month sabbatical from my employment at MediaCom, and have spent the summer travelling around California and Hawaii with my six-year-old son, learning to surf and exploring volcanoes! My travels have allowed me to reflect on the year that has passed, which has included some unique events which I am sure will never be repeated in my lifetime.

When I was chatting to a close friend recently, she quite rightly pointed out that if someone had been in a coma for the time that I have been on my sabbatical, and then woke up to be updated on news in the UK, they wouldn't quite believe it. As a nation we have decided to part company with the European Union – a bold decision and a leap into new and uncharted territory. We have a female prime minister, only the second one in our country's history, a new London mayor who is Muslim, and we have had our best ever Olympics with 67 medals overall, finishing second in the medal table behind the USA. Oh, and Leicester City won the Premiership.

No one expected that. And no one – or certainly none of the supposedly informed commentators – expected the Brexit vote.

It has been an extraordinary few months.

As I travelled around California, I was acutely aware of the Black Lives Matter movement, and the campaign against violence and systematic racism towards black people. This is especially pertinent as my son is black, as is his male nanny (or Manny), as am I. What I experienced was a country that is welcoming, and truly multicultural. Hawaii has become my favourite American state. Of course the sun was shining, I learned to surf (sort of), and the islands contain amazing contrasting landscapes – lush and tropical, lava fields and arid, amazing coloured beaches – but I also enjoyed the inclusive culture created by the diversity of the people living there. Asian, Polynesian, White and Afro-American were all living and working together – collaborative and integrated. I felt relaxed, happy and welcomed.

As one of the few black women in a senior media role, I have a burning passion to ensure my industry embraces diversity of all types. Aside from the fact that it is clearly morally correct, I firmly believe it is essential to the continued success of advertising and media agencies. I can't help but have a busman's holiday when away from work, so I do look at the media, and especially the adverts, to compare with my craft in the UK. The US ads are diverse. What I see on screen in terms of TV presenters is diverse, and it doesn't seem contrived. I see gender representation, ethnic representation, and all ages, but interestingly, not all physical abilities, same-sex couples, or blended families.

When I compare a snapshot of one part of America (California and Hawaii) with the UK, there is no doubt that the UK is a nation that is inclusive, and I hope will continue to be so. The immediate after-effects of the decision to leave the EU saw a surge in anti-immigrant hate crime in those areas that voted Leave. The National Police Chiefs' Council reported a 57% nationwide increase in hate crimes in the UK in the aftermath of the referendum. The narrow-minded and hateful few seemed to feel vindicated by the referendum result, which was a shock, and extremely disappointing. But this is not the UK that I know and love.

The Black and Ethnic Minority population in England and Wales stands at 14%, and according to the Institute of Practitioners in Advertising's *Multicultural Britain* report, England and Wales will be as diverse as London is now (with around 40% of the population from a Black, Asian or Minority Ethnic background) by 2051. Our triumphant team representing Great Britain at the Rio 2016 Olympics offered a snapshot of the brilliant diversity and inclusivity that our nation has to offer. We are a wonderful fruit salad of talented, achieving people.

People of Today 2017 is a snapshot of the most influential people in Britain today. It showcases the huge breadth of people who have achieved, and who continue to do so, in our country. Our country is full of talent and diversity of thought. This book contains almost 300 entrants from a wide range of sectors. It includes many businesswomen who cheerlead other working women and act as amazing role models to people like myself: I doff my cap to you Dame Carolyn McCall! The list includes cabinet ministers, as one might expect, but also authors such as J K Rowling, Hilary Mantel and Salman Rushdie, entrepreneurs, sports stars, head teachers, media professionals, architects and journalists.

The UK is talented. The people of the UK are diverse. We are a nation united by values such as democracy, free speech, mutual respect and opportunity for all. We are the sum of all our parts – a proud, diverse society.

This book has evolved from year to year to reflect that diversity, and I'm sure will continue to do so. I believe that in years to come, when my son is older, he will be able to look to this list to see people like himself and be inspired.

Karen Blackett is chairwoman of media buying and planning agency MediaCom and a government expert adviser on diversity. Appointed OBE in 2014, she was named the UK's most influential black person in the 2015 PowerList.

THE ROYAL FAMILY

For further details, see Debrett's *Peerage & Baronetage*.
All references are to the 2015 edition unless otherwise stated.
Army units are listed in order of precedence.

THE ORDER OF SUCCESSION TO THE THRONE

PRINCE OF WALES

DUKE OF CAMBRIDGE

PRINCE GEORGE OF CAMBRIDGE

PRINCESS CHARLOTTE OF CAMBRIDGE

PRINCE HENRY OF WALES

DUKE OF YORK

PRINCESS BEATRICE OF YORK

PRINCESS EUGENIE OF YORK

EARL OF WESSEX

VISCOUNT SEVERN

LADY LOUISE MOUNTBATTEN-WINDSOR

PRINCESS ROYAL

PETER PHILLIPS

SAVANNAH PHILLIPS

ISLA PHILLIPS

ZARA TINDALL

MIA TINDALL

VISCOUNT LINLEY

HON CHARLES ARMSTRONG-JONES

HON MARGARITA ARMSTRONG-JONES

LADY SARAH CHATTO

SAMUEL CHATTO

ARTHUR CHATTO

HM THE QUEEN; Elizabeth Alexandra Mary; declared in Council 9 April 1952 that she and her children would be styled and known as the House and Family of Windsor and 8 Feb 1960 that her descendants other than those enjoying the style, title or attribute of HRH and the titular dignity of Prince or Princess and female descendants who marry and their descendants should bear the name Mountbatten-Windsor, though this declaration overridden when Lady Louise Windsor b 2003 (*see below*); proclaimed Queen 8 Feb 1952; style in the United Kingdom: Elizabeth II, by the Grace of God, of the United Kingdom of Great Britain and Northern Ireland, and of Her Other Realms and Territories, Queen, Head of the Commonwealth, Defender of the Faith; crowned Westminster Abbey 2 June 1953; celebrated: Silver Jubilee 1977, Golden Jubilee 2002, Diamond Jubilee 2012; er da of HM King George VI (d 6 Feb 1952), and Lady Elizabeth Angela Marguerite Bowes-Lyon (HM Queen Elizabeth The Queen Mother; d 2002), da of 14 Earl of Strathmore and Kinghorne (*see Debrett's Peerage & Baronetage*); *b* 21 April 1926; *Educ* privately; *m* 20 Nov 1947, HRH The Prince Philip, Duke of Edinburgh, KG, KT, OM, GBE, AC, QSO, PC, *qv*, 3 s, 1 da (*see below*), who all by letters patent 22 Oct 1948 take style HRH and titular dignity of Prince/Princess; *Heir* eld s, Prince of Wales, *qv*; WWII as Subaltern then Jr Cdr ATS, LG 1947, Lord High Adm of the United Kingdom 1964–2011; Col-in-Chief (UK): Life Gds 1952–, Blues and Royals (Royal Horse Gds and 1 Dragoons) 1969–, Royal Scots Dragoon Gds (Carabiniers and Greys) 1971–, Royal Lancers 2015–, Royal Tank Regt 1953–, RE 1952–, Grenadier Gds (which HM inspected on her 16th birthday, it being her first official engagement) 1952–, Coldstream Gds 1952–, Scots Gds 1952–, Irish Gds 1952–, Welsh Gds 1952–, Royal Welch Fus 1953, The Royal Welsh 2006–, The Royal Regt of Scotland 2006–, The Duke of Lancasters Regt 2006–, Adj Gen's Corps 1992–, Royal Mercian and Lancastrian Yeo 1994–; Colin-Chief (Commonwealth): Govr Gen's Horse Gds (Canada) 1953–, Canadian Forces Mil Engrs Branch 1977–, King's Own Calgary Regt 1953–, Royal 22e Regt (Canada) 1953–, Govr-Gen's Foot Gds (Canada) 1953–, Canadian Grenadier Gds 1953–, Le Régiment de la Chaudière (Canada) 1947–, Royal New Brunswick Regt 1956–, 48 Highlanders Canada 1947–, Argyll and Sutherland Highlanders Canada (Princess Louise's) 1950–, Royal Canadian Ordnance Corps 1958–, Calgary Highlanders 1981–, Royal Australian Engrs 1953–, Royal Australian Inf Corps 1953–, Royal Australian Army Ordnance Corps 1953–, Royal Australian Army Nursing Corps 1953–, Corps of Royal New Zealand Engrs 1953–, Royal New Zealand Inf Regt 1964–, Malawi Rifles 1964–; Affiliated Col-in-Chief Queen's Gurkha Engrs; Royal Col The Argyll and Sutherland Highlanders 15th Battalion, Royal Regt of Scotland 2006–; Capt-Gen: RA 1952–, HAC 1952–, CCF 1953–, Royal Regt of Canadian Artillery 1952–, Royal Regt of Australian Artillery 1953–, Royal Regt of New Zealand Artillery 1953–, Royal New Zealand Armoured Corps 1953–; patron Royal Army Chaplains' Dept; Air Cdre-in-Chief: RAuxAF, RAF Regt, Air Reserve Canada, RAAF Reserve, Territorial Air Force (New Zealand); Cmdt-in-Chief RAF Coll Cranwell; Royal Hon Air Cdre: RAF Marham, 603 (City of Edinburgh) Sqdn RAuxAF, Cmmrin-Chief RCMP 2012; Sovereign of all British Orders of Knighthood, Order of Merit, Royal Order of Victoria and Albert, Order of Crown of India, Order of Companions of Honour, Order of Canada, Distinguished Service Order and Imperial Service Order; Sovereign Head of Order of Hosp of St John of Jerusalem, Order of Australia and Queen's Service Order of New Zealand; Hon BAFTA 2013; Freedom: City London, Edinburgh 1947; FRS 1947; racehorse owner (colours: purple body with gold braid, scarlet sleeves, black velvet cap with gold fringe), as which presented with Cartier Millennium Award 2000 honouring achievements as owner-breeder and patron of the Turf; major races won incl: King George VI Chase 1950 (Manicou), Coronation Cup 1954 (Aureole), King George VI & Queen Elizabeth Diamond Stakes 1954 (Aureole, champion 4–year old 1954), Sussex Stakes 1954 (Landau), Norfolk Stakes 1957 (Pall Mall), Oaks 1957 (Carozza), Yorkshire Oaks 1957 (Almeria), Two Thousand Guineas 1958 (Pall Mall, first win by a horse bred by HM), Coronation Stakes 1961 (Aiming High), Eclipse Stakes 1965 (Canisbay), Goodwood Cup 1965 (Apprentice), Goodwood Cup 1966 (Gaulois), One Thousand Guineas 1974 (Highclere, first filly also to win French Oaks), Oaks 1977 (Dunfermline), St Leger 1977 (Dunfermline), Royal Ascot Gold Cup 2013 (Estimate); *Style*— HM The Queen; *Residences* Buckingham Palace, London SW1A 1AA; Windsor Castle, Berkshire SL4 1NJ; Palace of Holyroodhouse, Canongate, Edinburgh EH8 8DX; Balmoral Castle, Aberdeenshire AB35 5TB; Sandringham House, Norfolk PE35 6EN

EDINBURGH, HRH I Duke of (UK 1947); Philip; KG (1947), KT (1952), OM (1968), GBE (Mil 1953), AK (2015, AC 1988), QSO (1981), PC (1951, Canada 1957); Royal Victorian Chain (2007); also Baron Greenwich and Earl of Merioneth (UK 1947); naturalised a British subject and adopted surname of Mountbatten (dropped f's name 'of Greece and Denmark', renouncing right of succession to those countries' crowns) 1947; granted title, style and attribute of HRH 19 Nov 1947; granted precedence next to HM The Queen except where otherwise provided by Act of Parliament (Royal Warrant 18 Sept 1952); granted style and titular dignity of Prince of United Kingdom 1957; only s of HRH Prince Andrew of Greece and Denmark, GCVO (d 1944), and HRH Princess (Victoria) Alice Elizabeth Julia Marie (d 1969), da of 1 Marquess of Milford Haven (*see* Debrett's *Peerage & Baronetage 2008* descendant of Queen Victoria); *b* 10 June 1921; *Educ* Salem Sch Baden, Gordonstoun (head of sch, capt cricket and hockey), RNC Dartmouth (King's Dirk, prize as best cadet of his entry); *m* 20 Nov 1947, Princess Elizabeth (later HM The Queen, *qv*); 3 s, 1 da (*see below*); *Heir* (to peerages, but not titular dignity of Prince) eld s, Prince of Wales, *qv*; *Career* WWII: Midshipman 1940, as which served HMS Ramillies Indian Ocean 1940 and Valiant Mediterranean Fleet 1941 (despatches and Greek War Cross of Valour following Battle of Cape Matapan 1941, in which i/c Valiant's searchlight unit), Sub-Lt 1941, Lt July 1942, 1 Lt (2 i/c) HMS Wallace 1942 (participated Sicily landings 1943) then HMS Whelp 27 Destroyer Flotilla British Pacific Fleet Indian Ocean and Pacific, Instr Petty Offrs' Sch, attended RN Staff Coll Greenwich, 1 Lt HMS Chequers 1949 (Leader 1 Destroyer Flotilla Mediterranean Fleet), Lt-Cdr 1950, cmd HMS Magpie (frigate), Cdr 1952; 1939–45, Atlantic, Africa, Burma (with Pacific Rosette) and Italy Stars; War Medal 1939–45 (with oak leaf), Greek War Cross 1950 and French Croix de Guerre (with palm); Personal ADC to HM King George VI 1948; Lord High Adm of the UK 2011; Adm of the Fleet: RN, RAN, RNZN, Royal Canadian Sea Cadets; Capt-Gen RM, Lord High Adm of the UK 2011; Field Marshal: United Kingdom 1953, Australian Mil Forces 1954, New Zealand Army 1977; Col-in-Chief (UK): Queen's Royal Hussars 2002–, The Rifles 2007–, REME 1969–, Intelligence Corps 1977–, ACF 1953–; Col-in-Chief (Commonwealth): Royal Canadian Regt 1953–, Royal Hamilton LI (Wentworth Regt of Canada) 1978–, Cameron Highlanders Ottawa 1967–, Queen's Own Cameron Highlanders Canada 1967–, Seaforth Highlanders Canada 1967–, Royal Canadian Army Cadets 1953–, Royal Australian Corps Electrical and Mech Engrs 1959–, Australian Army Cadet Corps 1963–; Col Grenadier Gds 1975–; Royal Col Highlanders 4th Battalion, Royal Regiment of Scotland; Royal Hon Col: City of Edinburgh Univs OTC 1965–, Trinidad and Tobago Regt 1964–; Marshal: RAF, RAAF, RNZF; Air Cdre-in-Chief: ATC, Royal Canadian Air Cadets; Royal Hon Air Cdre: RAF Kinloss, RAF Northolt 2012; Adm Royal Yacht Sqdn, Hon Gen and Hon Adm Canadian Armed Forces 2011; chllr: Univ of Wales 1948–76, Univ of Edinburgh 1952–2010, Univ of Salford 1967–91, Univ of Cambridge 1976–2011; life govr KCL; pres: CCPR 1951–, BAAS 1952, FEI 1964–86 (hon pres 1986–); as pres FEI instrumental in founding Nations Cup Series, estab ctee to examine introduction of carriage driving (specifically four-in-hand driving) as FEI event 1969 (instituted 1970); competed in six World Championships: team Bronze medal 1978, 1982 and 1984, team Gold medal 1980, individual sixth place 1982; memb British team at three European Championships; fndr memb British Equestrian Centre, memb Horse Driving Trials Assoc, memb Equestrian Hall of Fame 2007, Br Horse Soc Queen's Award for Equestrianism 2008; hon memb: BHS, USA Equestrian Assoc, Canadian Horse Cutting Assoc; past pres MCC (twice); pres emeritus WWF first (fndr) pres 1961–82, int pres 1981–96); patron: Duke of Edinburgh's Award 1956– (chm of tstees 1956–2001), Industrial Soc, London Guildhall Univ; Grand Master Guild of Air Pilots and Air Navigators; Master Trinity House 1969–2011 (Er Bro 1952–69); King George VI 1937 and Queen Elizabeth II 1953 Coronation Medals, Silver Jubilee Medal 1977, Queen's Gold Jubilee Medal 2002, Queen's Diamond Jubilee Medal 2012, Order of Canada 2013, Order of Military Merit 2013; Order of Australia 1988, Order of NZ 2012; Canadian Forces Decoration (four bars), Queen's Service Order NZ, NZ Commemoration Medal 1990, Malta George Cross 50th Anniversary Medal 1992; Grand Master and First or Princ Knight Order of the British Empire 1953; FRS 1951; *Style—* HRH The Prince Philip, Duke of Edinburgh, KG, KT, OM, GBE, AC, QSO, PC

WALES, HRH The Prince of; Charles Philip Arthur George; KG (1958, invested and installed 1968), KT (1977), GCB and Great Master Order of the Bath (1975), OM (2002), AK (1981), CD (1982), QSO (1983), PC (1977), PC Canada (2014); cr Prince of Walesand Earl of Chester 1958 (invested 1969); also Duke of Cornwall, Duke of Rothesay, Earl of Carrick, Baron of Renfrew, Lord of the Isles and Prince and Great Steward of Scotland; eld s and h of HM The Queen, *qv*; *b* 14 Nov 1948; *Educ* Gordonstoun, Geelong GS Australia, Trinity Coll Cambridge (MA, Polo half blue), UCW Aberystwyth; *m* 1, 29 July 1981 (m dis 1996), Lady Diana Frances Spencer (d 1997), 3 da of 8 Earl Spencer (*see* Debrett's *Peerage & Baronetage*); 2 s (*see below*); *m* 2, 9 April 2005, Mrs Camilla Rosemary Parker Bowles, GCVO (Col 4th Battlion The Rifles 2006–; Cdre-in-Chief Naval Medical Services 2006–; Hon Air Cdre RAF Halton and RAF Leeming 2008–; Col-in-Chief Royal Australian Military Corps 2012; chllr Univ of Aberdeen 2013–; for a list of her charities see http://www.princeofwales.gov.uk), da of late Maj Bruce Middleton Hope Shand, MC (*see* Debrett's *Peerage & Baronetage* Ashcombe, B), and formerly w of Brig Andrew Henry Parker Bowles, OBE (*see* Debrett's *Peerage & Baronetage* Macclesfield, E); *Heir* er s, HRH Prince William of Wales, *qv*; *Career* RN: served HMS Norfolk 1971–72, HMS Minerva 1972–73 and HMS Jupiter 1974, helicopter pilot trg RNAS Yeovilton 1974–75, pilot with 845 NAS aboard HM Hermes 1975, cmd HMS Bronington (minehunter) as Cdr 1976, Capt 1988, RearAdm 1998, Vice Adm 2002, Adm 2006, Adm of the Fleet 2012; Adm of the Fleet RNZN 2015; Cdre-in-Chief Plymouth 2006–, Gen 2006 (Lt-Gen 2002, Maj-Gen 1998), Field Marshal 2012; Col-in-Chief (UK): 1st Queen's Dragoon Gds 2003–, Royal Dragoon Gds 1992–, Parachute Regt 1977–, Royal Gurkha Rifles 1994–, Army Air Corps 1992–; Royal Col: The Black Watch 3rd Battalion 2006–, The Royal Regt of Scotland, 51st Highland 7th Battalion, The Royal Regt of Scotland 2006–, The Mercian Regt 2007–, Col-in-Chief (Commonwealth): Royal Canadian Dragoons 1985–, Lord Strathcona's Horse (Royal Canadians) 1977–, Royal Regt of Canada 1977–, Royal Winnipeg Rifles 1977–, Royal Australian Armoured Corps 1977–, 2 Bn Royal Pacific Islands Regt 1984–, Black Watch (Royal Highland Regt) Canada 2004–, Toronto Canada Regt 1977–, Air Reserve Gp Air Cmd Canada 1977–,Toronto Scottish Regt (Queen Elizabeth The Queen Mother's Own) 2005–; Dep Col-in-Chief Highlanders (Seaforth, Gordons and Camerons) 1994–; Field Marshal RNZA 2015; Personal ADC to HM The Queen 1973–; Col Welsh Gds 1975–; Royal Hon Col Queen's Own Yeo 2000-; RAF: Marshal 2012 (Wing Cdr 1976, Gp Capt 1988, Air Vice Marshal 1998, Air Marshal 2002, Air Chief Marshal 2006), Hon Air Cdre RAF Valley 1977–; Air Cdre-in-Chief RNZAF 1993–; Vice-Adm Canadian Forces Maritime Command 2009–; Lt-Gen Canadian Forces Land Command 2009; Lt-Gen Canadian Forces Air Command 2009–; Hon Cmmr RCMP 2012; chllr Univ of Wales 1976–; for a list of his charities see www.princeofwales.gov.uk; hon bencher Gray's Inn 1975; hon fell Trinity Coll Cambridge 1988; Coronation Medal 1953, Queen's Silver Jubilee Medal 1977, Queen's Golden Jubilee Medal 2002, Queen's Diamond Jubilee Medal 2012; NZ Commemoration Medal 1990, Order of Merit Saskatchewan 2001, RHS Medal of Honour 2009, Hon Confedn Centre of Arts Symons Medal 2014; FRS 1978; *Publications* The Old Man of Lochnagar (1980, illustrations Sir Hugh Casson, dramatised Aberdeen and London West End 1986, also TV production for Channel 4, DVD 1999), A Vision of Britain (1989); *Style—* HRH The Prince of Wales, KG, KT, GCB, OM, AK, CD, QSO, PC; *Residences* Clarence House, London SW1A 1BA; Highgrove House, Doughton, Tetbury, Glos GL8 8TN

CAMBRIDGE, HRH Duke of (UK 2011); William Arthur Philip Louis; KG (2008), KT (2012); also Baron Carrickfergus and Earl of Strathearn (UK 2011); s and h of HRH The Prince of Wales, *qv*; *b* 21 June 1982; *Educ* Eton, Univ of St Andrews (MA), RMA Sandhurst, RAF Cranwell, RAF Shawbury, RAF Valley Angelsey; *m* 29April 2011, Catherine Elizabeth (patron: Royal Fedn of the Duke and Duchess of Cambridge and Prince Harry 2011–, The Art Room 2012–, Nat Portrait Gallery 2012–, Action in Addiction 2012–, East Anglian Children's Hospices 2012–, Place 2 Be 2013–, Sports Aid 2013–, Natural History Museum 2013–), da of Michael Francis Middleton, and Carole Elizabeth Goldsmith; 1 s, 1 da (*see below*); *Career* ADC to HM The Queen 2013–; helicopter pilot E Anglian Air Ambulance Service 2015–; Queen's Golden Jubilee Medal 2002, Queen's Diamond Jubilee Medal 2012; Cdre-in-Chief Scotland and Submarines 2006–; 2nd Lt, Blues and Royals 2006, Lt 2007–13, Royal Col Irish Guards 2011; flying offr RAF 2008; Sub-Lt, RN 2008; Hon Air Cmdt RAF Coningsby 2008; hon barr and bencher Middle Temple 2009; Hon Canadian Ranger 2009; FRS 2010; pres: The Football Assoc 2006, Royal Marsden Hosp 2007–, BAFTA 2010–; patron: Centrepoint 2005–, The Tusk Trust 2005–, English Swimming Sch's Assoc 2007–, Mountain Rescue 2007–, Royal Marsden Hosp 2007–, Lord Mayor's Appeal 2008, HMS Alliance Conservation Appeal 2008–, A Positive View 2010 2008–, RAF Battle of Britain Meml Flight 2008–, Still Force 2009, Child Bereavement Charity 2009, Nat Meml Arboretum Future Fndns Appeal Fund 2009–, Queen Elizabeth II Fields Challenge 2010–, Univ of St Andrews 600th Anniversary Appeal 2011–, St Giles Trust 2012, Fields in Trust 2013–, Br Sub Aqua Club 2014–; vice-patron Welsh Rugby Union 2007–; jt patron: City Salute 2008, Henry van Straubenzee Meml Fund 2009–, Royal Fndn of the Duke and Duchess of Cambridge and Prince Harry 2009–; jt pres Patron's Lunch on the Mall 2015; *Style—* HRH The Duke of Cambridge, KG, KT; *Residences* Kensington Palace, London W8 4PU; Anmer Hall, Norfolk PE31 6RW

CAMBRIDGE, HRH Prince George of; George Alexander Louis; s of HRH The Duke of Cambridge, *qv*; *b* 22 July 2013; *Style—* HRH Prince George of Cambridge

CAMBRIDGE, HRH Princess Charlotte of; Charlotte Elizabeth Diana; da of HRH The Duke of Cambridge, *qv*; *b* 2 May 2015; *Style—* HRH Princess Charlotte of Cambridge

WALES, HRH Prince Henry of; Henry Charles Albert David (Harry); KCVO (2015); yr s of HRH The Prince of Wales, *qv*; *b* 15 Sept 1984; *Educ* Eton, RMA Sandhurst, RAF Barkston Heath, RAF Shawbury, AAC Middle Wallop; Queen's Golden Jubilee Medal 2002, Afghanistan Operational Service Medal 2008, Golden Heart from a Heart of a Child Berlin 2010, Queen's Diamond Jubilee Medal 2012; Cdre-in-Chief, Small Ships and Diving 2006–; Blues and Royals 2006–15: 2nd Lt 2006, Lt 2008, Capt 2011; Hon Air Cmdt RAF Honington 2008–, Hon Canadian Ranger 2009; patron: Sentebale 2006–, Dolen Cymru 2007–, MapAction 2007–, WellChild 2007–, Khumbu Challenge 09 2008–, Walking with the Wounded 2010, HALO Trust 25th Anniversary Appeal 2013–, Rugby Football Union's All Schools Programme 2013–, Invictus Fndn 2014–; vice-patron: RFU 2010, Injured Players Fndn 2010; jt patron: City Salute Appeal 2008, Henry van Straubenzee Meml Fund 2009–, Royal Fndn of the Duke and Duchess of Cambridge and Prince Harry 2009–; jt pres Patron's Lunch on the Mall 2015, hon pres Rugby World Cup 2015; *Style—*HRH The Prince Henry of Wales; *Residence* Nottingham Cottage, Kensington Palace, London W8 4PZ

YORK, HRH 1 Duke of (UK 1986); Andrew Albert Christian Edward; KG (2006), GCVO (2011, KCVO 2003, CVO 1979), CD (2001); also Baron Killyleagh and Earl of Inverness (UK 1986); 2 s of HM The Queen, *qv*; *b* 19 Feb 1960; *Educ* Gordonstoun, Lakefield Coll Sch Canada, RNC Dartmouth; *m* 23 July 1986 (m dis 1996), Sarah Margaret, da of Maj Ronald Ivor Ferguson (d 2003; *see* Debrett's *Peerage & Baronetage* Hampden, V), by his 1 w Susan Mary, da of FitzHerbert Wright (*see* Debrett's *Peerage & Baronetage* (1990 edn) Powerscourt, V), later Mrs Hector Barrantes (d 1998); 2 da (*see below*); Career RN: joined 1979 as Seaman Offr, helicopter pilot HMS Invincible S Atlantic Campaign 1982 (Campaign Medal 1982), Lt 1984, Lt Cdr 1992, cmd HMS Cottesmore (minehunter) 1993–94, Cdr 1998, left RN 2001, Hon Capt 2005, Hon Rear-Adm 2010, Vice-Adm 2015; Adm

Sea Cadet Corps 1992–; Cdre-in-Chief Fleet Air Arm 2006–, Rear-Adm 2010; Col-in-Chief (UK): 9/12 Royal Lancers 2003–15, Royal Irish Regt 1992–, Small Arms Sch Corps 2003–; Royal Col: Royal Highland Fus, 2nd Battalion, The Royal Regt of Scotland 2006–, Yorkshire Regt 2006–; Col-in-Chief (Commonwealth): Canadian Airborne Regt 1991–, Queen's York Rangers (1 American Regt) 1997–, Royal Highland Fus of Canada 2003–, Princess Louise Fus 2005–, Royal NZ Army Logistic Regt 1997–; Hon Air Cdre RAF Lossiemouth 1996–; Personal ADC to HM The Queen 1984–; UK special rep Int Trade and Investment 2001–11; Queen's Silver Jubilee Medal 1977, Grand Cross of the Royal Norwegian Order of St Olav 1988, NZ Commemoration Medal 1990, Canadian Forces Decoration 2001, Queen's Golden Jubilee Medal 2002, Commemorative Medal for the Centennial of Saskatchewan 2005, Order of the Federation (UAE) 2010, Queen's Diamond Jubilee Medal 2012; Cdre Royal Thames Yacht Club 1986–; pres: Royal Aero Club of GB 1982–; patron: Greenwich Hospital 1994–, Nat Maritime Museum 1995, English Nat Ballet 2001–, Royal Philharmonic Orch 2003–,Tall Ships Youth Trust 2005–, Ludder for London 2012–, Metropolitan Univ 2013–, Univ of Huddersfield 2013–; FRS 2013; *Books* Photographs (1985); *Style*— HRH The Duke of York, GCVO, CD; *Residences* Buckingham Palace, London SW1A 1AA; Royal Lodge, Windsor SL4 2BU

YORK, HRH Princess Beatrice of; Beatrice Elizabeth Mary; er da of HRH The Duke of York, *qv*; *b* 8 Aug 1988; *Educ* St George's Sch Ascot, Goldsmiths Coll London; with Cabot Square Capital 2012, with Sony Pictures 2014, with Sandbridge Capital 2015-16; patron: York Musical Soc 2012–, Helen Arkell Dyslexia Centre 2013–, Forget Me Not Children's Hospice 2013–; *Style*— HRH Princess Beatrice of York; *Residence* St James's Palace, London SW1 1BW

YORK, HRH Princess Eugenie of; Eugenie Victoria Helena; yr da of HRH The Duke of York, *qv*, *b* 23 March 1990; *Educ* St George's Sch Windsor, Marlborough, Newcastle Univ; benefit auctions mangr Paddle8 Auctioneers New York 2013–15, assoc dir Hauser and Wirth Gallery London 2015–; patron Nat Orthopaedic Hosp Redevelopment Appeal 2012–; *Style*— HRH Princess Eugenie of York; *Residence* St James's Palace, London SW1 1BW

WESSEX, HRH 1 Earl of (UK 1999); Edward Antony Richard Louis; KG (2006), GCVO (2011, KCVO 2003, CVO 1989); also Viscount Severn (UK 1999); 3 s of HM The Queen, *qv*, *b* 10 March 1964; *Educ* Gordonstoun, Jesus Coll Cambridge; er house tutor and jr master Wanganui Collegiate Sch New Zealand; *m* 19 June 1999, Sophie Helen (GCVO 2010, DJStJ 2005, Col-in-Chief Queen Alexandra's Royal Army Nursing Corps 2003–; The Lincoln and Welland Regt 2004–05, Alberta Light Horse 2005–, Corps of Army Music 2007–; Royal Col 5th Batalion The Rifles 2007–; Hon Air Cdre RAF Wiltering 2008–; pres Girlguiding UK 2003–, global ambass Duke of Edinburgh's Int Award Fndn 2013–; Hon FRCOG 2006), only da of Christopher Bourne Rhys-Jones (*see* Debrett's *Peerage & Baronetage* Molesworth, V); 1 da, 1 s (*see below*); *Career* 2 Lt RM 1983 (resigned 1987); Cdre-in-Chief Royal Fleet Auxiliary 2006–; Col-in-Chief: Hastings and Prince Edward Regt 2002–, Saskatchewan Dragoons 2003–, Prince Edward Island Regt 2003–; Royal Col 2nd Battalion The Rifles 2007–; Royal Hon Col Royal Wessex Yeo 2003–, The London Regt 2011; Hon Air Cdre RAF Waddington 2008–, Hon Dep Cmmr Royal Canadian Mounted Police 2007-; Personal ADC to HM The Queen 2004–; film/TV prodr as Edward Windsor, dir Ardent Productions 1993–2002; Lord High Cmmr to the Gen Assembly of the Church of Scotland 2014; tstee: Duke of Edinburgh's Int Award Fndn 1987–, Duke of Edinburgh's Award 1988–; vice-patron Commonwealth Games Federation 2006; chllr Univ of Bath 2013; pres Children's Film Unit 1992–; hon memb Incorporation of the Coopers of Glasgow 2008; Queen's Silver Jubilee Medal 1977, Queen's Golden Jubilee Medal 2002, Queen's Diamond Jubilee Medal 2012, New Zealand Commemorative Medal 1990, Order of Merit of Saskatchewan 2005; *Style*— HRH The Earl of Wessex, KG, GCVO; *Residence* Bagshot Park, Bagshot, Surrey GU19 5PJ

SEVERN, Viscount; James Alexander Philip Theo; only s of HRH The Earl of Wessex, *qv*, *b* 17 Dec 2007; *Style*— Viscount Severn

MOUNTBATTEN-WINDSOR, Lady Louise Alice Elizabeth Mary; only da of HRH The Earl of Wessex, *qv*, *b* 8 Nov 2003; *Style*— Lady Louise Windsor

HRH THE PRINCESS ROYAL; Anne Elizabeth Alice Louise; KG (1994), KT (2000), GCVO (1974), CD (1990), QSO (1990); declared Princess Royal 13 June 1987; only da of HM The Queen, *qv*, *b* 15 Aug 1950; *Educ* Benenden; *m* 1, 14 Nov 1973 (m dis 1992), Capt Mark Anthony Peter Phillips, CVO, ADC(P) (*see main text*); 1s, 1 da (*see below*); *m* 2, 12 Dec 1992, Vice-Adm Sir Timothy James Hamilton Laurence, CB, KCVO, MVO, RN (*see main text*); *Career* equestrian, individual winner European Three-Day Event Burghley 1971 (Sportswoman of the Year Sports Writers' Assoc, Daily Express and World Sport (BOA jl), BBC Sports Personality of the Year), memb three-day event team Olympic Games Montreal 1976, fndr and course designer Gatcombe Park One-Day Event 1995; UK memb (one of two) IOC 1988–; Cdre-in-Chief Portsmouth 2006–; Col-in-Chief (UK): King's Royal Hussars 1992–, Royal Corps of Signals 1977–, Royal Logistic Corps 1993–, Royal Army Veterinary Corps 2003–; Col-in-Chief (Commonwealth): 8 Canadian Hussars (Princess Louise's) 1972–, Canadian Forces Communications and Electronics Branch 1977–, Grey and Simcoe Foresters (Royal Canadian Armoured Corps) 1972–, Royal Regina Rifle Regt 1982–, Canadian Forces Medical Branch, Royal Australian Corps Signals 1977–, Royal New Zealand Corps of Signals 1977–, Royal New Zealand Nursing Corps 1977–, Royal Newfoundland Regt; Affiliated Col-in-Chief: Queen's Gurkha Signals 1993–, Queen's Own Gurkha Signals 1993–; Col Blues and Royals (Royal Horse Gds and 1 Dragoons) 1998–; Royal Col: Scots Borderers 1st Battalion 2006–; 52nd Lowland 6th Battalion, The Royal Regt of Scotland 2006–; Royal Hon Col Univ of London OTC 1989–; Royal Hon Air Cdre: RAF Lyneham 1977–, London University Air Sqdn 993–; Cmdt-in-Chief First Aid Nursing Yeo (Princess Royal's Vol Corps) 1981–; Rear Adm and Chief Cmdt Women in the RN 1993–, Vice-Adm 2009, Adm 2012; sponsor: HMS Albion, HMS Talent; pres Nat Equine Forum 2009–, RSA 2011–; Master Trinity House 2011–; patron Save the Children Fund 1970–, and other charities; chllr: Univ of London 1981–, Univ of Edinburgh 2011, Univ of the Highlands and Islands 2012–, Harper Adams Univ 2013–; Renter Asst The Butchers' Co 2009; FRS 1987; Queen's Silver Jubilee Medal 1977, New Zealand Commemorative Medal 1990, Queen's Golden Jubilee Medal 2002, Queen's Diamond Jubilee Medal 2012; GCStJ; *Books* Riding Through My Life (1991); *Style*— HRH The Princess Royal, KG, KT, GCVO, QSO; *Residences* St James's Palace, London SW1 1BW; Buckingham Palace, London SW1A 1AA; Gatcombe Park, Minchinhampton, Glos GL6 9AT

PHILLIPS, Peter Mark Andrew; only s of HRH The Princess Royal, *qv*, *b* 15 Nov 1977; *Educ* Gordonstoun (head boy, memb Scottish Schs Rugby Team 1996), Univ of Exeter (BSc); *m* 17 May 2008, Autumn Patricia, da of Brian Kelly, and Kathleen (Kitty) McCarthy (Mrs Ron Magus); 2 da (Savannah Kathleen Anne b 9 Dec 2010, Isla Elizabeth b 29 March 2012); *Career* events mangr (corporate hospitality) Jaguar Formula One Team 2001–02, account mangr Williams F1 2003–05, with Royal Bank of Scotland 2005–12, md SEL Ltd 2012–; *Style*— Peter Phillips, Esq

TINDALL, Zara Anne Elizabeth; MBE (2006); only da of HRH The Princess Royal, *qv*, *b* 15 May 1981; *Educ* Gordonstoun, Univ of Exeter; *m* 30 July 2011, Michael James Tindall, MBE (*see main text*); 1 da (Mia Grace b 17 Jan 2014); *Career* qualified equine physiotherapist 2002; professional equestrian, sponsored by Cantor Index (spread betting firm) 2003–; achievements incl: Silver medal European Young Riders Championship 2002, second place Burgley Horse Trials 2003, winner Military Trophy Gatcombe Park One-Day Event 2004, third place Festival of British Eventing Gatcombe 2005, memb British team European Three-Day Event Championship 2005, European Eventing Champion 2005, World Eventing Champion 2006, Equestrian of the Year 2006, BBC Sports Personality of the Year 2006, Olympic silver medalist in equestrian team event 2012; pres Club 16–24 (Cheltenham young racegoers gp) 2000–05; memb Cheltenham Ladies Hockey Club; *Style*— Mrs Michael Tindall, MBE; *Residence* The Bothy, Gatcombe Park, Minchinhampton, Gloucestershire GL6 9AT

LINLEY, Viscount; David Albert Charles Armstrong-Jones; only s of HRH The Princess Margaret (d 2002), and s and h of 1 Earl of Snowdon (*see main text*); *b* 3 Nov 1961; *Educ* Bedales, John Makepeace Sch of Woodcraft Beaminster; *m* 8 Oct 1993, Hon Serena Alleyne Stanhope, only da of Viscount Petersham; 1 s (Hon Charles Patrick Inigo b 1 July 1999), 1 da (Hon Margarita Elizabeth Rose Alleyne b 14 May 2002); *Career* furniture designer; chm: David Linley Furniture Ltd 1985–, David Linley Co 1998–; dir Christie Intl 2005–, chm Christie's UK 2006; *Books* Classical Furniture (1993, 2nd ed 1998), Extraordinary Furniture (1993), Design and Detail in the Home (2000); *Style*— Viscount Linley

CHATTO, Lady Sarah Frances Elizabeth; née Armstrong-Jones; only da of HRH The Princess Margaret (d 2002), and 1 Earl of Snowdon (*see main text*); *b* 1 May 1964; *Educ* Bedales, Camberwell Coll of Art, Royal Acad Sch; *m* 14 July 1994, Daniel Chatto, yr s of late Thomas Chatto; 2 s (Samuel David Benedict b 28 July 1996, Arthur Robert Nathaniel b 5 Feb 1999); *Style*— Lady Sarah Chatto

GLOUCESTER, HRH 2 Duke of (UK 1928); Richard Alexander Walter George; KG (1997), GCVO (1974); also Earl of Ulster and Baron Culloden (UK 1928); yr but only surviving s of HRH Prince Henry, 1 Duke of Gloucester (3 s of King George V; d 1974), and Princess Alice, Duchess of Gloucester (d 2004), da of 7 Duke of Buccleuch; *b* 26 Aug 1944; *Educ* Eton, Magdalene Coll Cambridge (MA, DipArch, including one year practical experience with Offices Devpt Gp Ministry Public Building and Works); *m* 8 July 1972, Birgitte Eva, GCVO, GCStJ (Col-in-Chief: Royal Army Dental Corps 1977–, Royal Australian Army Educational Corps 1977–, Royal New Zealand Army Educational Corps 1985–, Bermuda Regt 2003–, Royal Canadian Dental Corps 2006–; Dep Col-in-Chief Adj-Gen's Corps 1992–; Royal Col 7th Battalion The Rifles 2007–; sponsor: HMS Gloucester (guided missile destroyer), HMS Sandown (minesweeper), da of Asger Preben Wissing Henriksen, lawyer, of Odense, Denmark, by his 1 w Vivian, da of Waldemar Oswald van Deurs, whose surname Birgitte assumed; 1 s, 2 da (*see below*); *Heir* s, Earl of Ulster; *Career* architect in private practice 1969–72, corporate memb RIBA 1972–; Col-in-Chief: Royal Army Medical Corps 2003–, The Royal Anglian Regt 2006; Dep Col-in-Chief: Royal Logistic Corps 1993–; Royal Col 6th Battalion The Rifles 2007–; Royal Hon Col Royal Monmouthshire RE (Militia) 1977–; RAF: Hon Air Marshal 1996–, Royal Hon Air Cdre RAF Odiham and No 501 (County of Gloucester) Sqdn RAuxAF 1993–; chllr Univ of Worcester 2008–; pres: British-Nepal Soc, British Expertise, British Leprosy Relief Assoc, Christ's Hosp, London Soc, National Assoc of Clubs for Young People, Pevsner Memorial Tst, Public Monument and Sculpture Assoc, Royal Smithfield Club, St Bartholomew's Hosp, Soc of Architect-Artists, Victorian Soc; jt-pres Cancer Research UK; patron: American Friends of English Heritage, Architects Benevolent Soc, Assoc for Smoking and Health (ASH) 1974–, British Assoc of Friends of Museums 1976–, British Homeopathic Assoc, British Limbless Ex Service Assoc, British-Mexican Soc, British Museum, Canine Partners, Construction Industry Tst for Youth, Cncl for Educn in World Citizenship, Fenland Archaeological Tst, Friends of Gloucester and Peterborough Cathedrals, Habitat for Humanity GB, Inner London Probation Service, Islington and Hackney Housing Assoc, Japan Soc, League of Friends of Royal National Orthopaedic Hosp, London Chorus, Magdalene Australia Soc,

Normandy Veterans Assoc, Oriental Ceramic Soc, Pestalozzi Children's Village Tst, Richard III Soc, Royal Acad of Schs, Royal Anthropological Inst, Severn Valley Railway, Soc of Antiquaries of London, Tramway Museum; fell Inst of Clerks of Works for GB Inc; FIStructE, FRIAS, FRSA, GCStJ 1975, Grand Prior StJ, Coronation Medal 1953, Queen's Silver Jubilee Medal 1977, Queen's Golden Jubilee Medal 2002, Queen's Diamond Jubilee Medal 2012; Grand Cross Order of St Olav (Norway) 1973, Royal Order of the Northern Star (Sweden) 1975, Solomon Islands Independence Medal 1978, Nepal Coronation Medal 1980, Vanuatu Independence Medal 1980, Kt Grand Cross Order of Tonga 2008, Order of the Star of The Solomon Islands 2008; *Style*— HRH The Duke of Gloucester, KG, GCVO; *Residence* Kensington Palace, London W8 4PU

ULSTER, Earl of; Alexander Patrick Gregers Richard Windsor; only s and h of HRH 2 Duke of Gloucester, GCVO, *qv*; *b* 24 Oct 1974; *Educ* Eton, King's Coll London (BA), RMA Sandhurst; *m* 22 June 2002, Dr Claire Alexandra Booth, da of Robert Booth; 1 s (Baron Culloden), 1 da (Lady Cosima Windsor); *Heir* s, Baron Culloden; *Career* King's Royal Hussars: 1998–2008, Capt 2000, served Kosovo 200 2 and Iraq 2007; prog mangr TransnationalCrisis Project 2008–; *Style*—Earl of Ulster

LEWIS, Lady Davina Elizabeth Alice Benedikte; née Windsor; er da of HRH 2 Duke of Gloucester, GCVO, *qv*; *b* 19 Nov 1977; *Educ* St George's Sch Ascot, Univ of the West of England Bristol; *m* 31 July 2004, Gary Christie Lewis, eld s of Larry Lewis, of Gisborne, New Zealand, and Viki, née Smiler; 1 da (Senna Kowhai b 22 June 2010), 1 s (Tane Mahuta b 25 May 2012); *Style*— Lady Davina Lewis

GILMAN, Lady Rose Victoria Birgitte Louise; yr da of HRH 2 Duke of Gloucester, GCVO, *qv*; *b* 1 March 1980; *Educ* St George's Sch Ascot; *m* 19 July 2008, George Gilman; 1 da (Lyla Beatrix Christabel b 30 May 2010), 1 s (Rufus Frederick Montagu b 2 Nov 2012); *Style*— Lady Rose Gilman

KENT, HRH 2 Duke of (UK 1934); Edward George Nicholas Paul Patrick; KG (1985), GCMG (1967), GCVO (1960); also Earl of St Andrews and Baron Downpatrick (UK 1934); er s of HRH 1 Duke of Kent, KG, KT, GCMG, GCVO, PC (4 s of King George V; k on active service 1942), and HRH Princess Marina, CI, GCVO, GBE (d 1968), yst da of HRH Prince Nicholas of Greece and Denmark (d 1938); *b* 9 Oct 1935; *Educ* Eton, Le Rosey Switzerland, RMA Sandhurst (Sir JamesMoncrieff Grierson languages prize, qualified French interpreter, Company Instr 1968–70); *m* 8 June 1961, Katharine Lucy Mary, GCVO, only da of Sir William Arthington Worsley, 4 Bt (*see* Debrett's *Peerage & Baronetage*); 2 s, 1 da (*see below*); *Heir* er s, Earl of St Andrews; *Career* Army: 2 Lt Royal Scots Greys 1955, Personal ADC to HM The Queen 1966–, GSO II E Cmd 1966–68, Cmd C Sqdn Royal Scots Greys 1970–71,GSO I, MOD 1972-76, ret as Lt-Col 1976, Maj-Gen 1983, Field Marshal 1993; Col-in-Chief: Royal Regt of Fus 1969–, Lorne Scots (Peel, Dufferin and Hamilton Regt) 1977–; Dep Col-in-Chief Scots Dragoon Gds 1993–, Col Scots Gds 1974–; Royal Col 1st Battalion The Rifles 2007–; Hon Air Chief Marshal RAF 1998, Royal Hon Air Cdre RAF Leuchars; Grand Master United Grand Lodge Freemasons of England, Grand Master Order of St Michael and St George 1967; pres: Commonwealth War Graves Cmmn, RAF Benevolent Fund, RNLI, Stroke Assoc, All England Lawn Tennis and Croquet Club, UK Scout Assoc; pres-in-chief British Racing Drivers' Club; patron: Hanover Band, LPO, Opera North, S Bank Fndn, Trinity Coll of Music; chllr Univ of Surrey 1977–, visitor Cranfield Univ; hon degrees: Univ of Durham, Univ of Leeds, Univ of York; FRS 1990; Dresden Prize for Anglo-German reconciliation 2015; King George VI and Queen Elizabeth Coronation Medal 1937, Queen's Silver Jubilee Medal 1977, Queen's Golden Jubilee Medal 2002, Queen's Diamond Jubilee Medal 2012, Order of Merit Free State of Saxony 2015; *Books* On Public View (1970), The Face of London (1975), Oxford and Cambridge (1980); *Style*— HRH The Duke of Kent, KG, GCMG, GCVO; *Residence* Wren House, Palace Green, London W8 4PY

ST ANDREWS, Earl of; George Philip Nicholas Windsor; er s and h of HRH 2 Duke of Kent, KG, GCMG, GCVO, *qv*; *b* 26 June 1962; *Educ* Eton, Downing Coll Cambridge; *m* 9 Jan 1988, Sylvana Palma, da of Maximilian Karl Tomaselli, and formerly w of John Paul Jones; 1 s (Edward Edmund Maximilian George, Lord Downpatrick b 2 Dec 1988, converted Roman Catholic 2003, hence excluded from succession to throne), 2 da (Lady Marina-Charlotte Alexandra Katharine Helen b 30 Sept 1992 (converted to Roman Catholicism 2008, hence excluded from succession to throne), Lady Amelia Sophia Theodora Mary Margaret b 24 Aug 1995); *Career* FCO 1987–88, Books and Manuscripts Dept Christie's 1996–98; trustee: GBSasakawa Fndn 1995– (chm 2005–), SOS Children's Village UK 1999–, Golden Web Fndn 2003– (chm 2006), Pirnce George Galitzine Meml Lib 2005–, Next Century Fndn 2012–; patron: Assoc for Int Cancer Research 1995–, Princess Margarita of Romania Trust 1997–, Friends of the Mongolia and Inner Asia Studies Unit 2012–; *Style*— Earl of St Andrews

WINDSOR, Lord Nicholas Charles Edward Jonathan; yr s of HRH 2 Duke of Kent, KG, GCMG, GCVO, *qv*; converted Roman Catholic 2001, hence excluded

from succession to throne; *b* 25 July 1970; *Educ* Harrow; *m* 19 Oct 2006 (civil) and 4 Nov 2006 (religious), Paola, da of Don Louis Doimi de Frankopan, and Ingrid, née Detter; 3 s (Albert Louis Philip Edward b 22 Sept 2007, Leopold Ernest Augustus Guelph b 8 Sept 2009, Louis Arthur Nicholas Felix b 29 May 2014); patron Bromley Mind 2007–, patron Church Heritage Centre at Stonyhurst, tstee Catholic Nat Lib and Right to Life Charitable Trust, dir Dignitas Humanae Inst; *Style*— Lord Nicholas Windsor

TAYLOR, Lady Helen Marina Lucy; née Windsor; only da of HRH 2 Duke of Kent, KG, GCMG, GCVO, *qv*; *b* 28 April 1964; *Educ* St Mary's Wantage, Gordonstoun; *m* 18 July 1992, Timothy Verner (Tim) Taylor, art dealer, eld s of Cdr Michael Verner Taylor, RN, of Stoke St Gregory, Somerset, and Mrs Colin Walkinshaw; 2 s (Columbus George Donald b 6 Aug 1994, Cassius Edward b 26 Dec 1996), 2 da (Eloise Olivia Katherine b 2 March 2003, Estella Olga Elizabeth b 21 Dec 2004); *Style*— Lady Helen Taylor

KENT, HRH Prince Michael of; Michael George Charles Franklin; GCVO (2003, KCVO 1992); yr bro of 2 Duke of Kent, *qv*; *b* 4 July 1942; *Educ* Eton, RMA Sandhurst (qualified Russian interpreter); *m* 30 June 1978, Baroness Marie-Christine Agnes Hedwig Ida, da of Baron Günther Hubertus von Reibnitz, by his w Countess Marianne Szapáry de Mura-szombath, Széchysziget et Szapár, and formerly w of Thomas Troubridge (see Debrett's *Peerage & Baronetage* Troubridge, Bt); 1 s, 1 da (*see below*); *Career* Army: cmmnd 11 Hussars (Prince Albert's Own) 1963, MOD 1968–70, UN Force Cyprus 1971, Def Intelligence Service 1974–76, GSO Def 1974–76, Army Recruiting Directorate 1976–78, GSO Def Intelligence Staff 1978–81, ret as Maj 1981, Hon Col 2010; Col-in-Chief Essex and Kent Scottish Regt Ontario 2002–, Royal Hon Col Artillery Co 2012; Hon Rear Adm RNR 2004 (Hon Cdre 1994); Cdre-in-Chief Maritime Reserves 2006–; liveryman Guild of Air Pilots and Air Navigators; Adm Royal Naval volunteer Reserve Yacht Club; memb HAC; Royal Hon Air Cdre RAF Benson 2002, Air Marshal RAF 2012; hon mem Air Sqdn; fellow: Inst of Motor Industry, Royal Aeronautical Soc; pres: Dogs' and Cats' Home Battersea, Inst of Road Safety, Kennel Club, National Eye Research Centre, RAC Fndn, SSAFA Forces Help, Royal Patriotic Fund; Commonwealth pres RLSS; fndr patron Pan-European Genesis Initiative; patron: Battle of Britaim Memorial Tst, Brooklands Museum Tst, Chatham Historic Dockyard Volunteer Service, Children's Fire and Burns Tst, First Gear, Harefield Research Fndn, Museum of Army Flying, Russo-British C of C, World Monuments Fund (UK); dir Cantium Services; memb British team in international bobsleigh events (reserve Winter Olympics Sapporo 1972); memb team 1929 Bentley Special Millbrook 1992 (1,000-mile record for cars over 5,000 cc); Hon Dr Plekhanov Economics Acad Moscow; Coronation Medal 1953, UN Peacekeeping Medal 1971, Queen's Silver Jubilee Medal 1977, Queen's Golden Jubilee Medal 2002, Queen's Diamond Jubilee Medal 2012; Russian Order of Friendship 2009; KJStJ 2000; *Style*— HRH Prince Michael of Kent, GCVO; *Residence* Kensington Palace, London W8 4PU.

WINDSOR, Lord Frederick Michael George David Louis (Freddie); *b* 6 April 1979; *Educ* Eton (Oppidan scholar), Magdalen Coll Oxford; *m* 12 Sept 2009, Sophie, da of Barry Lester David Winkleman; 2 da (Maud Elizabeth Daphne Marina b 15 Aug 2013, Isabella Alexandra May b 16 Jan 2016); *Career* trainee barrister until 2004, with film co Brass Hat Prodns 2004, banker JPMorgan 2006– (vice-pres 2010-); *Style*— Lord Frederick Windsor

WINDSOR, Lady Gabriella Marina Alexandra Ophelia (Ella); *b* 23 April 1981; *Educ* Downe House Sch, Brown Univ RI, Linacre Coll Oxford; *Career* journalist, contrib Night & Day (Mail on Sunday colour supplement); *Style*— Lady Gabriella Windsor

HRH Princess Alexandra, The Hon Lady Ogilvy; Alexandra Helen Elizabeth Olga Christabel Ogilvy; KG (2003), GCVO (1960); sis of 2 Duke of Kent, *qv*; *b* 25 Dec 1936; *Educ* Heathfield Sch Ascot, finishing sch Paris; *m* 24 April 1963, Sir Angus James Bruce Ogilvy, KCVO, PC (d 2004), 2 s of 12 Earl of Airlie, KT, GCVO, MC (*see* Debrett's *Peerage & Baronetage*); 1 s, 1 da; Col-in-Chief (Commonwealth): Queen Own Rifles 1960–2010, Canadian Scottish Regt (Princess Mary's) 1977–; Dep Colin- Chief Queen's Royal Lancers 1993–; Royal Col 3rd Battalion The Rifles 2007–; Hon Royal Col Royal Yeo 2002–; Dep Royal Hon Col The King's Own Yorkshire Yeo 1996–, Hon Col North Irish Horse 1957–; pres: Royal Patriotic Fund Corp, Star and Garter Home for Disabled Sailors, Soldiers and Airmen, Alexandra Rose Day, SightSavers Int; jt-pres Cancer Research UK; vice-pres British Red Cross Soc; patron: Queen Alexandra's Royal Naval Nursing Service, Alexandra House, Alzheimer's Soc, St Christopher's Hospice, Guide Dogs for the Blind Assoc; patron and Air Chief Cmdt Princess Mary's RAF Nursing Service; Hon Cmdt Women's Royal Australian Naval Service 1966–; Hon Dr: Univ of Hong Kong, Univ of Liverpool, Univ of Mauritius, Univ of Queensland; Hon DMus Univ of Lancaster; Hon FRCPS, Hon FRCA; King George VI and Queen Elizabeth Coronation Medal 1937, Coronation Medal 1953, Queen's Silver Jubilee Medal 1977, Queen's Golden Jubilee Medal 2003, Queen's Diamond Jubilee Medal 2012; *Style*— HRH Princess Alexandra, The Hon Lady Ogilvy, KG, GCVO; *Residence* Thatched House Lodge, Richmond Park, Surrey TW10 5HP

A READER'S GUIDE

The following notes should be borne in mind when reading an entry in Debrett's *People of Today*.

Surnames are listed by the initial letter; double-barrelled and hyphenated names, as well as those prefixed 'de' and 'von', are thus listed by their first part. 'Mac_____' and 'Mc_____' are listed together, as if they were all spelt 'Mac_____'.

Brackets around entrants' first forenames indicate names not used, while brackets around later forenames denote nicknames by which they are generally known. If clarification is needed, see the Style section towards the end of each entry.

It is standard genealogical practice to list sons first, followed by daughters. In recent times the editors have felt it appropriate to relax this rule and entries will predominantly list daughters first if an entrant's first-born child was female.

Careers generally begin by detailing the entrant's main professional career, including military service where applicable, in chronological order. This will typically be followed by involvement with other career-related organisations, then any charitable, public or other appointments. Honours, distinctions and awards are listed next, with the section concluding with memberships or fellowships of professional bodies. Because of the wide range of entrants' activities in Debrett's *People of Today*, there is necessarily considerable variation in the way career information is presented. With the exception of Armed Forces and Police Service related careers, job titles are largely styled lower case.

Clubs are generally in London unless otherwise stated. The word 'Club' is normally omitted from their names.

The entrant's style is the preferred way to address him or her in correspondence, in line with commonly accepted correct form and as agreed by the entrant. The styles given in Debrett's *People of Today* do not generally include professional qualifications or academic distinctions after an entrant's name, though it may be appropriate to do so in correspondence pertaining to the entrant's particular profession (see Debrett's *Handbook* for further information).

Addresses and telephone numbers are given as required for writing or dialling from within the United Kingdom.

DISCLAIMER

Debrett's Limited makes every effort to check and update the extensive information contained in this publication. Any errors or omissions are unintentional, and no liability of any kind is accepted by the publisher or distributor in respect of them. Such errors or omissions should be drawn to the attention of Debrett's Limited for correction in future editions.

ABBREVIATIONS

A

AA	Automobile Association; Architectural Association; Anti-Aircraft
AAA	Amateur Athletic Association (now BAF)
AAAS	American Association for the Advancement of Science
AABC	Architect Accredited in Building Conservation
AAC	Army Air Corps
AACCA	Associate, Association of Certified and Corporate Accountants
AADipl	Diploma of the Architectural Association
A&AEE	Aeroplane and Armament Experimental Establishment
AAF	Auxiliary Air Force
AAFCE	Allied Air Forces Central Europe
AAG	Assistant Adjutant-General
AAGBI	Associate, Anaesthetists of Great Britain and Ireland
AAI	Associate, Chartered Auctioneers' and Estate Agents' Institute
AALPA	Association of Incorporated Auctioneers and Landed Property Agents
AAM	Association of Assistant Mistresses in Secondary Schools
AAPG	American Association of Petroleum Geologists
AA&QMG	Assistant Adjutant & Quartermaster-General
AASA	Associate, Australian Society of Accountants
AAT	Association of Accounting Technicians
AB	Bachelor of Arts (USA); Able-bodied Seaman
ABA	Associate of the British Archaeological Association; Antiquarian Booksellers' Association; Amateur Boxing Association
ABCC	Association of British Chambers of Commerce
ABI	Association of British Insurers
ABIA	Associate, Bankers' Institute of Australia; Association of British Introduction Agencies
ABIBA	Associate, British Institute of Brokers Association
ABIM	Associate, British Institute of Management (now ACMI)
ABIPP	Associate, British Institute of Professional Photographers
ABP	Associated British Ports (formerly BTDB)
ABPS	Associate, British Psychological Society
ABRC	Advisory Board for the Research Councils
ABSA	Association for Business Sponsorship of the Arts
ABTA	Association of British Travel Agents
AC	Companion of the Order of Australia
ACA	Associate, Institute of Chartered Accountants
Acad	Academy
ACARD	Advisory Council for Applied Research and Development
ACAS	Advisory, Conciliation and Arbitration Service
ACBSI	Associate, Chartered Building Societies Institute
ACC	Association of County Councils
ACCA	Associate, Chartered Association of Certified Accountants
ACCM	Advisory Council for the Church's Ministry
ACCS	Associate, Corporation of Secretaries
AcDipEd	Academic Diploma in Education
ACDS	Assistant Chief of Defence Staff
ACE	Association of Consulting Engineers
ACENVO	Association of Chief Executives of National Voluntary Organisations (now ACEVO)
ACEVO	Association of Chief Executives of Voluntary Organisations
ACF	Army Cadet Force
ACFA	Army Cadet Forces Association
ACG	Assistant Chaplain General
ACGI	Associate, City and Guilds of London Institute
ACGS	Assistant Chief of General Staff
ACIArb	Associate, Chartered Institute of Arbitrators
ACIB	Associate, Chartered Institute of Bankers
ACII	Associate, Chartered Insurance Institute
ACInstT	Associate, Chartered Institute of Taxation (formerly AInstT)
ACIOB	Associate, Chartered Institute of Building
ACIS	Associate, Institute of Chartered Secretaries (now ICSA)
ACMA	Associate, Institute of Cost and Management Accountants
ACMI	Associate, Chartered Management Institute
ACNS	Assistant Chief of Naval Staff
ACORD	Advisory Committee on Research and Development
ACOS	Assistant Chief of Staff
ACOST	Advisory Council on Science and Technology
ACP	Association of Clinical Pathologists; Associate, College of Preceptors
ACPO	Association of Chief Police Officers
ACPOS	Association of Chief Police Officers in Scotland
ACRE	Action with Rural Communities in England
ACS	American Chemical Society
ACSEA	Allied Command South East Asia
AcSS	Academician, Academy for the Learned Societies in the Social Sciences (now FAcSS)
ACT	Australian Capital Territory; Australian College of Theology; Association of Corporate Treasurers
actg	acting
ACTT	Association of Cinematograph, Television and Allied Technicians
ACVO	Assistant Chief Veterinary Officer
ACWA	Associate, Institute of Cost and Works Accountants
ADAS	Agricultural Development and Advisory Service (MAFF)
ADB	Associate of the Drama Board
ADC	Aide-de-Camp
AD	Corps Army Dental Corps
ADC(P)	Personal Aide-de-Camp to HM The Queen
Adj	Adjutant
Adj-Gen	Adjutant-General
Adm	Admiral
admin	administration; administrative; administrator
ADMS	Assistant Director of Medical Services
Admty	Admiralty
ADNI	Assistant Director of Naval Intelligence
ADOS	Assistant Director of Ordnance Service
ADP	Automatic Data Processing
ADPR	Assistant Director of Public Relations
ADS&T	Assistant Director of Supplies and Transport
Adv-Gen	Advocate-General
ADVS	Assistant Director of Veterinary Services
advsr	advisor
advsy	advisory
advtg	advertising
A&E	Accident and Emergency
AE	Air Efficiency Award
AEA	Air Efficiency Award; Atomic Energy Authority
AEAF	Allied Expeditionary Air Force
AEC	Army Educational Corps (now RAEC); Agricultural Executive Committee
AED	Air Efficiency Decoration
AEEU	Amalgamated Engineering and Electrical Union (now AMICUS)
AEF	Amalgamated Union of Engineering and Foundry Workers
AEM	Air Efficiency Medal
AER	Air Emergency Reserve
AERE	Atomic Energy Research Establishment
AEU	Amalgamated Engineering Union
AF	Air Force
AFAEP	Association of Fashion, Advertising and Editorial Photographers (now Association of Photographers)
AFAIM	Associate Fellow, Australian Institute of Management
AFB	Air Force Base (USA)
AFBPsS	Associate Fellow, British Psychological Society
AFC	Air Force Cross; Association Football Club
AFCENT	Allied Forces Central Europe
affrs	affairs
AFHQ	Allied Forces Headquarters
AFI	Associate, Faculty of Insurance; American Film Institute
AFIMA	Associate Fellow, Institute of Mathematics and its Applications
AFM	Air Force Medal
AFOM	Associate, Faculty of Occupational Medicine
AFRAeS	Associate Fellow, Royal Aeronautical Society
AFRC	Agricultural and Food Research Council (now BBSRC)
AFS	Auxiliary Fire Service
AFV	Armoured Fighting Vehicles
AFVPA	Advertising, Film and Video Producers' Association
AG	Attorney-General

Agent-Gen	Agent-General
AGI	Alliance Graphique Internationale
AGRA	Association of Genealogists and Researchers in Archives (formerly Association of Genealogists and Record Agents)
agric	agriculture; agricultural
AGSM	Associate, Guildhall School of Music and Drama
AHA	Area Health Authority
AHA(T)	Area Health Authority (Teaching)
AHQ	Army Headquarters
AHRB	Arts and Humanities Research Board (now AHRC)
AHRC	Arts and Humanities Research Council (formerly AHRB)
AHSM	Associate, Institute of Health Services Management
AIA	American Institute of Architects; Associate, Institute of Actuaries; Association of International Artists
AIAA	Associate, Institute of Administrative Accountants
AIAC	Associate, Institute of Company Accountants
AIAS	Associate Surveyor Member, Incorporated Association of Architects and Surveyors
AIB	Associate, Institute of Banking
AIBD	Associate, Institute of British Decorators
AICA	Associate Member, Commonwealth Institute of Accountants
AICE	Associate, Institute of Civil Engineers
AIChor	Associate, Institute of Choreography
AICS	Associate, Institute of Chartered Shipbuilders
AICTM	Associate, Imperial College of Tropical Medicine
AIEE	Associate, Institution of Electrical Engineers
AIF	Australian Imperial Forces
AIG	Adjutant-Inspector-General
AIIA	Associate, Institute of Industrial Administration
AIIMR	Associate, Institute of Investment Management and Research
AIL	Associate, Institute of Linguists
AIM	Associate, Institution of Metallurgists
AIMarE	Associate, Institute of Marine Engineers
AIMarEst	Associate, Institute of Marine Engineering, Science and Technology
AIMgt	Associate, Institute of Management (now ACMI)
AIMSW	Associate, Institute of Medical Social Workers
AINA	Associate, Institute of Naval Architects
AInstM	Associate Member, Institute of Marketing
AInstP	Associate, Institute of Physics
AInstT	Associate, Institute of Taxation (now ACInstT)
AInstTport	Associate, Institute of Transport
AIP	Association of Independent Producers
AIPM	Associate, Institute of Personnel Management
AIRC	Association of Independent Radio Contractors
Air Cdre	Air Commodore
AIRMIC	Associate, Insurance and Risk Managers in Industry and Commerce
AISVA	Associate, Incorporated Society of Valuers and Auctioneers
AK	Knight of the Order of Australia; Alaska
aka	also known as
AKC	Associate, King's College London
AL	Alabama
ALA	Associate, Library Association
ALAM	Associate, London Academy of Music and Dramatic Art
ALAS	Associate Member of Chartered Land Agents' Society
ALCD	Associate, London College of Divinity
ALCM	Associate, London College of Music
ALCS	Authors' Licensing and Collecting Society
ALFSEA	Allied Land Forces South East Asia
ALI	Argyll Light Infantry; Associate, Landscape Institute
ALIA	Associate, Life Insurance Association
ALL	Association of Language Learning
ALLC	Association for Literary and Linguistic Computing
Alta	Alberta
AM	Member of the Order of Australia; Albert Medal; Master of Arts (USA); Alpes Maritimes; Member, National Assembly for Wales; Member, London Assembly
AMA	Associate, Museum Association; Association of Metropolitan Authorities
ambass	ambassador
AMBIM	Associate, Member of the British Institute of Management
AMCT	Associate, Manchester College of Technology
AMEC	Association of Management Education for Clinicians
AMEI	Associate Member, Energy Institute
AMEME	Association of Mining, Electrical and Mechanical Engineers
AMF	Australian Military Forces
AMI	Association of Media Independents
AMICE	Associate Member, Institution of Civil Engineers
AMIChemE	Associate Member, Institution of Chemical Engineers
AMICUS	Amalgamated Engineering and Electrical Union (formerly AEEU)
AMIEE	Associate Member, Institution of Electrical Engineers
AMIEEIE	Associate Member, Institution of Electronic and Electrical Incorporated Engineers
AMIMechE	Associate Member, Institution of Mechanical Engineers
AMIMinE	Associate Member, Institution of Mining Engineers
AMIPE	Associate Member, Institution of Production Engineers
AMIStructE	Associate Member, Institution of Structural Engineers
AMP	Air Ministry Personnel; Advanced Management Programme
AMPAS	Academy of Motion Picture Arts and Sciences
AMRAeS	Associate Member, Royal Aeronautical Society
AMRINA	Associate Member, Royal Institution of Naval Architects
AMS	Army Medical Service; Assistant Military Secretary
AMSI	Associate Member, Securities Institute
AMSO	Air Member for Supply and Organisation
AMTPI	Association of the Town Planning Institution
AnalaR	Analytical Reagents
ANU	Australian National University
AO	Air Officer; Officer of the Order of Australia
AOA	Air Officer in Charge of Administration
AOC	Air Officer Commanding
AOC-in-C	Air Officer Commanding-in-Chief
AOD	Army Ordnance Department
AOEng	Air Officer Engineering
AOM	Air Officer Maintenance
AOP	Association of Photographers
APA	American Psychiatric Association
APEX	Association of Professional, Executive, Clerical and Computer Staffs
APM	Assistant Provost Marshal
APP	Associate of Psychoanalytic Psychotherapy
APPG	All-Party Parliamentary Group
appt	appointment
APR	Accredited Public Relations Practitioner
APRA	Association of Political Risks Analysts
APS	American Physical Society
APU	Anglia Polytechnic University
AQ	Administration and Quartering
AQH	Association of Quality Assurance in Healthcare
AQMG	Assistant Quartermaster-General
AR	Arkansas
A&R	Artistes and Repertoire
ARA	Associate, Royal Academy; Amateur Rowing Association
ARAD	Associate, Royal Academy of Dancing
ARAeS	Associate, Royal Aeronautical Society
ARAgS	Associate, Royal Agricultural Societies
ARAM	Associate, Royal Academy of Music
ARB	Architects' Registration Board (formerly ARCUK); Airworthiness Requirements Board
ARBA	Associate, Royal Society of British Artists
ARBS	Associate, Royal Society of British Sculptors
ARC	Agricultural Research Council
ARCA	Associate, Royal College of Art
ARCM	Associate, Royal College of Music
ARCO	Associate, Royal College of Organists
ARCS	Associate, Royal College of Science
ARCST	Associate, Royal College of Science and Technology
ARCUK	Architects' Registration Council of the UK (now ARB)
ARCVS	Associate, Royal College of Veterinary Surgeons
ARE	Associate, Royal Society of Painter-Etchers and Engravers
ARELS	Association of Recognised English Language Schools
ARIAS	Associate, Royal Incorporation of Architects in Scotland
ARIBA	Associate, Royal Institute of British Architects
ARIC	Associate, Royal Institute of Chemistry
ARICS	Associate, Royal Institution of Chartered Surveyors
ARINA	Associate, Royal Institution of Naval Architects
ARMCM	Associate, Royal Manchester College of Music
armd	armoured
ARP	Air Raid Precautions
ARPS	Associate, Royal Photographic Society
ARRC	Associate, Royal Red Cross
ARSA	Associate, Royal Scottish Academy
ARSM	Associate, Royal School of Mines
ARTC	Associate, Royal Technical College
ARWS	Associate, Royal Society of Painters in Water Colours
ASA	Associate Member, Society of Actuaries; Australian Society of Accountants; Army Sailing Association; Advertising Standards Authority
ASAA	Associate, Society of Incorporated Accountants and Auditors
ASC	Army Service Corps
ASCAP	American Society of Composers, Authors and Publishers
ASCL	Association of School and College Leaders (formerly SHA)
ASD	Armament Supply Department
ASEAN	Association of South East Asian Nations

ASFA	Associate, Institute of Shipping and Forwarding Agents
A&SH	Argyll and Sutherland Highlanders
ASIAD	Associate, Society of Industrial Artists and Designers
ASIP	Associate, Society of Investment Professionals
ASLIB	Association of Special Libraries and Information Bureaux
ASM	Association of Senior Members
ASME	American Society of Mechanical Engineers; Association for the Study of Medical Education
ASO	Air Staff Officer
assas	assassinated
ASSC	Accounting Standards Steering Committee
assoc	association; associate; associated
asst	assistant
Assur	Assurance
ASTD	Associate Member, Society of Typographic Designers
ASTMS	Association of Scientific, Technical and Managerial Staff (now MSF)
ASWE	Admiralty Surface Weapons Establishment
ATA	Air Transport Auxiliary
ATAF	Allied Tactical Air Force
ATC	Air Training Corps; Art Teachers' Certificate
ATCL	Associate, Trinity College of Music, London
ATD	Art Teachers' Diploma
ATI	Associate, Textile Institute
ATII	Associate Member, Institute of Taxation
ATO	Ammunitions Technical Officer
ATS	Auxiliary Territorial Service
AUEW	Amalgamated Union of Engineering Workers
Aust	Australian; Australia
AUT	Association of University Teachers
Authy	Authority
Aux	Auxiliary
Ave	Avenue
AVR	Army Volunteer Reserve
AWeldI	Associate of the Welding Institute
AWRE	Atomic Weapons Research Establishment
AZ	Arizona

B

b	born
BA	Bachelor of Arts; British Airways
BAAB	British Amateur Athletics Board
BAAL	British Association for Applied Linguistics
BAAS	British Association for the Advancement of Science
BAc	Bachelor in Acupuncture
BAC	Battersea Arts Centre; British Aircraft Corporation
BACB	British Association of Communicators in Business (formerly BAIE)
Bacc	Baccalauréate
BAcc	Bachelor of Accountancy
BADA	British Antique Dealers' Association
BAEM	British Association for Accident and Emergency Medicine
BAF	British Athletic Federation (formerly AAA)
BAFO	British Air Forces Occupation
BAFSEA	British Air Forces South East Asia
BAFTA	British Academy of Film and Television Arts
BAgric	Bachelor of Agriculture
BAI	Baccalarius in Arte Ingeniaria
BAIE	British Association of Industrial Editors (now BACB)
BALPA	British Airline Pilots' Association
BAO	Bachelor of Obstetrics
BAOL	British Association of Otolaryngologists
BAOMS	British Association of Oral and Maxillo-Facial Surgeons
BAOR	British Army of the Rhine
BARB	Broadcasters' Audience Research Board
BARC	British Automobile Racing Club
BArch	Bachelor of Architecture
BARR	British Association of Rheumatology Rehabilitation (now BSR)
barr	barrister
Bart's	St Bartholomew's Hospital
BAS	Bachelor in Agricultural Science
BASc	Bachelor of Applied Science
BASC	British Association of Shooting and Conservation
BASCA	British Academy of Songwriters, Composers and Authors
Batty	Battery
BBA	British Bankers' Association; Bachelor of Business Administration
BBC	British Broadcasting Corporation
BBFC	British Board of Film Classification
BBS	Bachelor of Business Studies
BBSRC	Biotechnology and Biological Sciences Research Council (formerly AFRC)
BC	British Columbia; Borough Council

BCC	British Council of Churches
BCE	Bachelor of Civil Engineering
BCh	Bachelor of Surgery
BChir	Bachelor of Surgery
BCL	Bachelor in Civil Law
BCom	Bachelor of Commerce
BComm	Bachelor of Commerce
BCS	British Computer Society; Bengal Civil Service
BCU	British Canoeing Union
BD	Bachelor in Divinity
Bd	Board
BDA	British Dental Association; Broadcasting Design Association
Bde	Brigade
BDes	Bachelor of Design
BDMA	British Direct Marketing Association (now DMA)
BDS	Bachelor of Dental Surgery
BE	Bachelor of Engineering
BEA	British European Airways
BEAMA	Federation of British Electrotechnical and Allied Manufacturers Association
BEC	Business Education Council (now BTEC)
BEcon	Bachelor of Economics
BECTU	Broadcast Entertainment Cinematograph and Theatre Union
BEd	Bachelor of Education
Beds	Bedfordshire
BEE	Bachelor of Electrical Engineering
BEF	British Expeditionary Force
BEM	British Empire Medal
BEng	Bachelor of Engineering
BERA	British Educational Research Association
Berks	Berkshire
BESO	British Executive Services Overseas
BFBS	British Forces Broadcasting Service
BFI	British Film Institute
BFME	British Forces Middle East
BFPO	British Forces Post Office
BFSS	British Field Sports Society
BGGS	Brigadier-General, General Staff
BGS	Brigadier, General Staff
BHA	British Hoteliers' Association (formerly BHRCA)
BHRA	British Hydromechanics Research Association
BHRCA	British Hotel, Restaurant and Catering Association (now BHA)
BHS	British Horse Society
BIBA	British Insurance Brokers' Association
BICC	British Insulated Callender's Cables
BIEE	British Institute of Energy Economics
BIFU	Banking, Insurance and Finance Union
BIIBA	British Insurance and Investment Brokers' Association
BIID	British Institute of Interior Design
BIM	British Institute of Management
BIPP	British Institute of Professional Photographers
BIR	British Institute of Radiology
BIS	Department for Business, Innovation and Skills
BJSM	British Joint Service Mission
BJur	Bachelor in Jurisprudence
BJuris	Bachelor in Jurisprudence
BL	Bachelor of Law; British Leyland
BLA	British Army of Liberation
bldg	building
BLESMA	British Limbless Ex-Servicemen's Association
BLitt	Bachelor of Letters
BM	Bachelor of Medicine (Oxford); Brigade Major
BMA	British Medical Association
BMedBiol	Bachelor of Medical Biology
BMedSci	Bachelor of Medical Science
BMet	Bachelor of Metallurgy
BMH	British Military Hospital
BMJ	British Medical Journal
BMus	Bachelor of Music
Bn	Battalion
BN	Bachelor of Nursing
BNA	British Neuroscience Association
BNAF	British North Africa Force
BNC	Brasenose College (Oxford)
BNES	British Nuclear Energy Society
BNF	British Nuclear Fuels
BNFL	British Nuclear Fuels Ltd
BNSC	British National Space Centre
BOA	British Olympic Association
BOAC	British Overseas Airways Corporation
BOAG	British Overseas Aid Group
BOT	Board of Trade

BOTB	British Overseas Trade Board
BP	British Petroleum
BPA	British Paediatric Association
BPG	Broadcasting Press Guild
BPharm	Bachelor of Pharmacy
BPhil	Bachelor of Philosophy
BPI	British Phonographic Industry
BPIF	British Printing Industries' Federation
BPMF	British Postgraduate Medical Federation
BPNA	British Paediatric Neurology Association
Br	British
BR	British Rail
BRCS	British Red Cross Society
BRDC	British Racing Drivers' Club
Brig	Brigadier
BRNC	Britannia Royal Naval College
bro	brother
BS	Bachelor of Surgery; Bachelor of Science (USA)
BSA	Building Societies Association
BSAC	British Screen Advisory Council; British Sub-Aqua Club
BSACI	British Society for Allergy and Clinical Immunology
BSc	Bachelor of Science
BSC	British Steel Corporation; British Society of Cinematographers
BSCC	British-Soviet Chamber of Commerce
BSDA	British Soft Drinks Association
BSI	British Standards Institution; British Society for Immunology
BSJ	Bachelor of Science in Journalism
BSME	British Society of Magazine Editors
BSocSc	Bachelor of Social Science
BSocSci	Bachelor of Social Science
BSR	British Society of Rheumatology (formerly BARR)
BSS	Bachelor of Social Sciences (USA)
Bt	Baronet
BT	British Telecom
BTA	British Troops in Austria; British Tourist Authority; British Theatre Association
Bt-Col	Brevet-Colonel
Btcy	Baronetcy
BTDB	British Transport Docks Board (now ABP)
BTEC	Business and Technicians Education Council (formerly BEC)
BTh	Bachelor of Theology
Btss	Baroness
Bucks	Buckinghamshire
BUPA	British United Provident Association
BV	Besloten Vennootschap (Netherlands)
BVA	British Veterinary Association
BVetMed	Bachelor of Veterinary Medicine
BVMS	Bachelor of Veterinary Medicine and Surgery
BVSc	Bachelor of Veterinary Science
BWI	British West Indies
BWM	British War Medal
BWS	Member, British Watercolour Society

C

c	children
C	Conservative
ca	circa
CA	Chartered Accountant; County Alderman; California
CAA	Civil Aviation Authority
CAABU	Council for the Advancement of Arab and British Understanding
CAB	Citizens Advice Bureau
CACA	Chartered Association of Certified Accountants
CAFOD	Catholic Agency for Overseas Development
Calif	California
Caltech	California Institute of Technology
CAM	Communications, Advertising and Marketing
Cambs	Cambridgeshire
CAMRA	Campaign for Real Ale
Cantab	of Cambridge
Capt	Captain
CARE	Cottage and Rural Enterprises
CAS	Chief of Air Staff
CB	Companion of the Order of the Bath
CBA	Council for British Archaeology
CBC	County Borough Council
CBE	Commander of the Order of the British Empire
CBI	Confederation of British Industry
CBIM	Companion, British Institute of Management (now CIMgt)
CBiol	Chartered Biologist
CBIREE	Companion, British Institute of Radio and Electronic Engineers

CBSO	City of Birmingham Symphony Orchestra
CC	County Council; Companion of the Order of Canada; Cricket Club
CCA	County Councils' Association
CCAB	Consultative Committee of Accounting Bodies
CCBE	Consultative Council of European Bars and Law Societies (Commission Consultative des Barreaux de la Communant Européene)
CCBI	Council of Churches for Britain and Ireland
CCC	Corpus Christi College (Oxford and Cambridge); County Cricket Club
CCF	Combined Cadet Force
CCG(BE)	Control Commission, Germany (British Element)
CChem	Chartered Chemist
CCHMS	Central Committee for Hospital and Medical Services
CCIBS	Companion, Chartered Institute of Building Services
CCIPD	Companion, Chartered Institute of Personnel and Development
CCMI	Companion, Chartered Management Institute
CCncllr	County Councillor
CCO	Conservative Central Office
CCPR	Central Council of Physical Recreation
CCRA	Commander Corps of Royal Artillery
CCRE	Commander Corps of Royal Engineers
CCRSigs	Commander Corps of Royal Signals
CCS	Casualty Clearing Station
CCSC	Central Consultants and Specialists Committee
CD	Canadian Forces Decorations; Compact Disc
CDipAF	Certified Diploma in Accounting and Finance
CDir	Chartered Director
Cdr	Commander
Cdre	Commodore
CD-ROM	Compact Disc Read-Only Memory
CDS	Chief of Defence Staff
CE	Chief Engineer; Church of England
CEDEP	Centre Européen d'Education Permanente
CEDR	Centre for Dispute Resolution
CEFIC	Conseil Européen des Federations de l'Industrie Chimique
CEGB	Central Electricity Generating Board
CEI	Council of Engineering Institutions
CEng	Chartered Engineer
CEnv	Chartered Environmentalist
ceo	chief executive officer
CERI	Centre d'Etudes et de Recherches Internationales (Paris)
CERN	Conseil (now Organisation) Européenne pour la Recherche Nucléaire
Cert	Certificate
CertEd	Certificate of Education
CertHE	Certificate of Higher Education
CertTheol	Certificate of Theology
CF	Chaplain to the Forces
CFBOA	Companion Fellow, British Orthopaedic Association
CFM	Canadian Forces Medal
CFR	Commander, Order of the Federal Republic of Nigeria
CFS	Central Flying School
CFTC	Commonwealth Fund for Technical Co-operation
C&G	City and Guilds of London Institute (formerly CGLI)
CGA	Country Gentlemen's Association
CGC	Conspicuous Gallantry Cross
CGeog	Chartered Geographer
CGeol	Chartered Geologist
CGIA	City and Guilds of London Insignia Award
CGLI	City and Guilds of London Institute (now C&G)
CGMA	Chartered Global Management Accountant
CGS	Chief of the General Staff
CH	Companion of Honour
ChB	Bachelor of Surgery
CHB	Companion of Honour Barbados
CHC	Community Health Council
ChCh	Christ Church (Oxford)
chem	chemical
Chev	Chevalier
chllr	chancellor
chm	chairman
ChM	Mastery of Surgery
ChStJ	Chaplain of the Order of St John of Jerusalem
CI	Order of the Crown of India; Channel Islands
CIAgrE	Companion, Institute of Agricultural Engineers
CIArb	Chartered Institute of Arbitrators
CIBS	Chartered Institute of Building Services
CIBSE	Chartered Institution of Building Services Engineers
CIC	Construction Industry Council
CICAP	Criminal Injuries Compensation Appeal Panel

CICeram	Companion, Institute of Ceramics
CICHE	Committee for International Co-operation in Higher Education
CID	Criminal Investigation Department
CIE	Companion of the Order of the Indian Empire
CIEE	Companion, Institution of Electrical Engineers
CIGE	Companion, Institution of Gas Engineers
CIGRE	Conference Internationale des Grands Réseaux Electriques
CIGS	Chief of the Imperial General Staff
CIHM	Companion, Institute of Healthcare Management
CII	Chartered Insurance Institute
CILIP	Chartered Institute of Library and Information Professionals
CILT	Chartered Institute of Logistics and Transport (former CIT)
CIM	Chartered Institute of Marketing
CIMA	Chartered Institute of Management Accountants
CIMarE	Companion, Institute of Marine Engineers
CIMarEst	Companion, Institute of Marine Engineering, Science and Technology
CIMechE	Companion, Institution of Mechanical Engineers
CIMgt	Companion, Institute of Management (formerly CBIM)
C-in-C	Commander-in-Chief
CInstE	Companion, Institute of Energy
CInstSMM	Companion, Institute of Sales and Marketing Management
CIOB	Chartered Institute of Building
CIOJ	Chartered Institute of Journalists
CIPD	Companion, Institute of Personnel and Development (formerly CIPM)
CIPFA	Chartered Institute of Public Finance and Accountancy
CIPM	Companion, Institute of Personnel Management (now CIPD)
CIPR	Chartered Institute of Public Relations (formerly IPR)
CIRIA	Construction Industry Research and Information Association
CISI	Chartered Institute for Securities and Investment
CIT	Chartered Institute of Transport (now CILT)
CITP	Certified Information Technology Professional; Chartered Information Technology Professional
CLA	Country Landowners' Association (now Country Land and Business Association)
CLit	Companion of Literature
CLP	Constituency Labour Party
CM	Member of the Order of Canada; Master of Surgery
CMA	Cost and Management Accountant (NZ)
CMath	Chartered Mathematician
CMC	Certified Management Consultant
cmd	commanded; command
cmdg	commanding
Cmdt	Commandant
CMF	Commonwealth Military Forces; Central Mediterranean Force
CMG	Companion of the Order of St Michael and St George
CMI	Chartered Management Institute
cmmn	commission
cmmnd	commissioned
cmmr	commissioner
CMO	Chief Medical Officer
CMP	Corps of Military Police
CMS	Church Missionary Society
CNAA	Council for National Academic Awards
Cncl	Council
cncllr	councillor
CND	Campaign for Nuclear Disarmament
CNRS	Centre Nationale de la Recherche Scientifique
CNS	Chief of Naval Staff
cnsllr	counsellor
CNZM	Companion of the New Zealand Order of Merit
CO	Commanding Officer; Colorado
Co	Company; County
COD	Communications and Operations Department (FO)
C of C	Chamber of Commerce
C of E	Church of England
COGS	Chief of General Staff
COHSE	Confederation of Health Service Employees
COI	Central Office of Information
Co L	Coalition Liberal
Col	Colonel
Coll	College
Comp	Comprehensive
Conf	Conference
Confedn	Confederation
Conn	Connecticut
Cons	Conservative
conslt	consultant
consltg	consulting
contrib	contributor; contributed; contribution
Co-op	Co-operative

Corp	Corporation; corporate
Corpl	Corporal
corr	correspondent
COS	Chief of Staff
COSIRA	Council for Smaller Industries in Rural Areas
cous	cousin
CP	Captain of a Parish (IOM)
CPA	Commonwealth Parliamentary Association; Chartered Patent Agent
CPC	Conservative Political Centre
CPE	Common Professional Examination (of the Law Society)
CPFA	Member/Associate, Chartered Institute of Public Finance and Accountancy
CPhys	Chartered Physicist
CPL	Chief, Personnel & Logistics
CPM	Colonial Police Medal
CPRE	Council for the Protection of Rural England
CPRS	Central Policy Review Staff
CPS	Crown Prosecution Service; Canadian Pacific Steamships
CPSA	Civil and Public Services Association
CPsychol	Chartered Psychologist
CPU	Commonwealth Press Union
CQSW	Certificate of Qualification in Social Work
cr	created
CRA	Commander Royal Artillery
CRAC	Careers Research and Advisory Council
CRAeS	Companion, Royal Aeronautical Society
CRASC	Commander, Royal Army Service Corps
CRC	Community Relations Commission
CRD	Conservative Research Department
CRE	Commanding Royal Engineers
CRMP	Corps of Royal Military Police
CRO	Commonwealth Relations Office
CS	Clerk to the Signet
CSA	Commonwealth Society of Artists; Chair, Schools Association
CSCE	Conference on Security and Co-operation in Europe
CSci	Chartered Scientist
CSD	Chartered Society of Designers
CSERB	Computer Systems and Electronics Requirements Board
CSI	Companion of the Order of the Star of India; Council for the Securities Industries
CSIR	Council for Scientific and Industrial Research
CSIRO	Commonwealth Scientific and Industrial Research Organisation
CSO	Chief Signal Officer; Chief Staff Officer; Chief Scientific Officer; Central Statistical Office
CSS	Council for Science and Society
CStat	Chartered Statistician (formerly FSS)
CSTI	Council of Science and Technology Institutes
CStJ	Commander of the Order of St John of Jerusalem
CSV	Community Service Volunteers
Ct	Court
CT	Connecticut
CTA	Chartered Tax Advisor
CTA(Fell)	Fellow, Institute of Taxation (formerly FTII)
CTBI	Churches Together in Britain and Ireland
CTC	City Technology College
Ctee	Committee
CText	Chartered Textile Technologist
CUBC	Cambridge University Boat Club
CUF	Common University Fund
CUP	Cambridge University Press
CVCP	Committee of Vice-Chancellors and Principals of the UK
CVL	Central Veterinary Laboratory
CVO	Commander of the Royal Victorian Order
CWA	Crime Writers' Association
Cwlth	Commonwealth

D

d	died; death
D(Th)	Doctor of Theology
da	daughter
DA	Diploma in Anaesthetics; Diploma in Art
DAAG	Deputy Assistant-Adjutant-General
DAA&QMG	Deputy Assistant-Adjutant and Quartermaster-General
DACG	Deputy Assistant Chaplain-General
DACOS	Deputy Assistant Chief of Staff
D&AD	Designers & Art Directors' Association
DAD	Deputy Assistant Director

DADGMS	Deputy Assistant Director-General of Medical Services
DADMS	Deputy Assistant Director of Medical Services
DADOS	Deputy Assistant Director of Ordnance Services
DADR	Deputy Assistant Director of Remounts
DADST	Deputy Assistant Director of Supplies and Transport
DAG	Deputy Adjutant-General
DAMS	Deputy Assistant Military Secretary
DAPM	Deputy Assistant Provost Marshal
DAPS	Director of Army Postal Services
DA&QMG	Deputy Adjutant and Quartermaster-General
DAQMG	Deputy Assistant Quartermaster-General
DAvMed	Diploma in Aviation Medicine
DBA	Doctor of Business Administration; Design Business Association
DBE	Dame Commander of the Order of the British Empire
DBO	Diploma of British Orthoptics
DC	District Council; Doctor in Chiropractics; District of Columbia
DCA	Department for Constitutional Affairs
DCAe	Diploma of the College of Aeronautics
DCAS	Deputy Chief of Air Staff
DCB	Dame Commander of the Order of the Bath
DCDS	Deputy Chief of Defence Staff
DCGS	Deputy Chief of General Staff
DCH	Diploma in Child Health
DCL	Doctor of Civil Law
DCLI	Duke of Cornwall's Light Infantry
DCM	Distinguished Conduct Medal
DCMG	Dame Commander of the Order of St Michael and St George
DCMS	Deputy Commissioner Medical Services; Department for Culture, Media and Sport
DCom	Doctor of Communications
DCPO	Dame Commander of the Order of Puis IX
DCSF	Department for Children, Schools and Families
DCSG	Dame Commander of the Order of St Gregory the Great
DCSO	Deputy Chief Scientific Officer
DCSS	Dame Commander of the Order of Pope St Sylvester
DCVO	Dame Commander Royal Victorian Order
DD	Doctor of Divinity
DDDS	Deputy Director of Dental Services
DDes	Doctor of Design
DDME	Deputy Director of Mechanical Engineering
DDMS	Deputy Director of Medical Services
DDO	Diploma in Dental Orthopaedics
DDOS	Deputy Director of Ordnance Services
DDPS	Deputy Director of Personal Services
DDR	Deputy Director of Remounts
DDS	Doctor of Dental Surgery; Director of Dental Services
DDSD	Deputy Director of Staff Duties
DDS&T	Deputy Director Supplies and Transport
DDVS	Deputy Director of Veterinary Services
DDWE&M	Deputy Director of Works, Electrical and Mechanical
DE	Doctor of Engineering (USA); Delaware
DEA	Department of Economic Affairs
DEC	Disasters Emergency Committee
decd	deceased
DEd	Doctor of Education
Def	Defence
DEFRA	Department for Environment, Food and Rural Affairs
DèsL	Docteur ès Lettres
delg	delegate
delgn	delegation
Dem	Democrat
DEM	Diploma in Education Management
DEME	Director of Electrical and Mechanical Engineering
DEng	Doctor of Engineering
dep	deputy
Dept	Department
Derbys	Derbyshire
DES	Department of Education and Science
DesRCA	Designer, Royal College of Art
DETR	Department of the Environment, Transport and the Regions
Devpt	Development
DFA	Doctor of Fine Arts
DFC	Distinguished Flying Cross
DFE	Department for Education
DfEE	Department for Education and Employment
DfES	Department for Education and Skills
DFFP	Diploma, Faculty of Family Planning and Reproductive Health (now DFRSH)
DFH	Diploma of the Faraday House
DFID	Department for International Development
DFM	Distinguished Flying Medal; Diploma in Forensic Medicine
DFRSH	Diploma, Faculty of Reproductive and Sexual Health (formerly DFFP)
DG	Director-General
DGAMS	Director-General of Army Medical Services
DGCStJ	Dame Grand Cross of the Order of St John of Jerusalem
DGDP	Diploma in General Dental Practice
DGMS	Director-General of Medical Services
DGS	Diploma in Graduate Studies
DGStJ	Dame of Grace of the Order of St John of Jerusalem
DH	Doctor of Humanities
DHA	District Health Authority
DHL	Doctor of Humane Letters; Doctor of Hebrew Literature
DHMSA	Diploma in the History of Medicine (Society of Apothecaries)
DHQ	District Headquarters
DHSS	Department of Health and Social Security
DHy	Doctor of Hygiene
DIC	Diploma of the Imperial College
DIH	Diploma in Industrial Health
Dio	Diocese
Dip	Diploma; Diplomatic
DipAD	Diploma in Art and Design
DipAg	Diploma in Agriculture
DipArch	Diploma in Architecture
DipAvMed	Diploma in Aviation Medicine
DipBA	Diploma in Business Administration
DipCAM	Diploma in Communications, Advertising and Marketing of the CAM Foundation
DipCD	Diploma in Civic Design
DipCThandM	Diploma in Christian Theology and Ministry
DipEd	Diploma in Education
DipEE	Diploma in Electrical Engineering
DipESL	Diploma in English as a Second Language
DipFM	Diploma in Forensic Medicine
DipHA	Diploma in Hospital Administration
DipHSM	Diploma in Health Services Management
DipLA	Diploma in Landscape Architecture
DiplArch	Diploma in Architecture
DipLD	Diploma in Landscape Design
DipLP	Diploma in Legal Practice
DipM	Diploma in Marketing
DipMRS	Diploma of the Market Research Society
DipN	Diploma in Nursing
DipOrthMed	Diploma in Orthopaedic Medicine
DipRAM	Diploma of the Royal Academy of Music
DipTh	Diploma in Theology
DipTP	Diploma in Town Planning
dir	director
dis	dissolved (marriage)
Dist	District
Div	Division
Divnl	Divisional
DJ	disc jockey
DJAG	Deputy Judge Advocate-General
DJStJ	Dame of Justice of the Order of St John of Jerusalem
DK	Most Esteemed Family Order of Brunei
DL	Deputy Lieutenant; Doctor of Laws
DLC	Diploma Loughborough College
DLI	Durham Light Infantry
DLit	Doctor of Literature
DLitt	Doctor of Letters
DLO	Diploma in Laryngology and Otology/ Otorhinolaryngology; Defence Logistics Organisation
DM	Doctor of Medicine
DMA	Direct Marketing Association (formerly BDMA); Diploma in Municipal Administration
DMD	Doctor in Dental Medicine
DME	Director of Mechanical Engineering
DMI	Director Military Intelligence
DMJ	Diploma in Medical Jurisprudence
DMO&I	Director Military Operations and Intelligence
DMRD	Diploma in Medical Radiological Diagnosis
DMRE	Diploma in Medical Radiology and Electrology
DMRT	Diploma in Medical Radiotherapy
DMS	Director of Medical Services; Diploma in Management Studies
DMSI	Director of Management and Support Intelligence
DMT	Director of Military Training
DMus	Doctor of Music
DNB	Dictionary of National Biography
DNI	Director of Naval Intelligence
DNO	Director of Naval Ordnance
DO	Divisional Officer; Diploma in Ophthalmology; Diploma in Osteopathy

DOAE	Defence Operational Analysis Establishment
DObstRCOG	Diploma Royal College of Obstetricians and Gynaecologists
DOC	District Officer Commanding
DOE	Department of Environment
DOI	Department of Industry
DOMS	Diploma in Ophthalmic Medicine
DOR	Director of Operational Requirements
DOrthRCS	Diploma in Orthodontics Royal College of Surgeons
DOS	Director of Ordnance Services
DPA	Diploma in Public Administration
DPCP	Department of Prices and Consumer Protection
DPH	Diploma in Public Health
DPhil	Doctor of Philosophy
DPL	Director of Pioneers and Labour
DPM	Diploma in Psychological Medicine
DPMO	Deputy Principal Medical Officer
DPP	Director of Public Prosecutions
DPR	Director of Public Relations
DPS	Director of Personal Services
DQMG	Deputy Quartermaster-General
Dr	Doctor
DRA	Defence Research Agency
DRC	Diploma of the Royal College of Science and Technology, Glasgow
DRCOG	Doctor, Royal College of Obstetricians and Gynaecologists
DRD	Diploma in Restorative Dentistry
Dr jur	Doctor of Laws
DrPA	Doctor of Public Administration (USA)
DRSAMD	Diploma of the Royal Scottish Academy of Music and Drama
DrScNat	Doctor of Natural Sciences
DRVO	Deputy Regional Veterinary Officer
DS	Directing Staff
DSA	Diploma in Social Administration
DSAC	Defence Scientist Advisory Committee
DSAO	Diplomatic Service Administration Office
DSC	Distinguished Service Cross
DSc	Doctor of Science
DSCHE	Diploma of the Scottish Council for Health Education
DSD	Director of Staff Duties
DSG	Dame of the Order of St Gregory the Great
DSIR	Department of Scientific and Industrial Research
DSLitt	Doctor of Sacred Letters
DSM	Distinguished Service Medal (USA)
DSO	Companion of the Distinguished Service Order
DSocSc	Doctor of Social Sciences
dsp	decessit sine prole (died without issue)
DSP	Docteur en Sciences Politiques (Montreal)
DSS	Department of Social Security; Dame of the Order of Pope St Sylvester
DSSc	Doctor of Social Sciences
DSSS	Doctor of Science in Social Sciences
DS&T	Director of Supplies and Transport
DStJ	Dame of Grace of the Order of St John of Jerusalem
DTech	Doctor of Technology
DTh	Doctor of Theology
DTI	Department of Trade and Industry
DTLR	Department of Transport, Local Government and the Regions
DTM	Diploma in Tropical Medicine
DTM&H	Diploma in Tropical Medicine and Hygiene
DUniv	Doctor of the University
DUP	Democratic Unionist Party
DVD	Digital Versatile Disc
DVFS	Director, Veterinary Field Services
DVM	Doctor of Veterinary Medicine
DVMS	Doctor of Veterinary Medicine and Surgery
DVO	Divisional Veterinary Officer
DVS	Director of Veterinary Services
DVSM	Diploma of Veterinary State Medicine
DWP	Department for Work and Pensions
DX	Document Exchange

E

E	East; Earl; England
EAMBES	European Alliance for Medical and Biological Engineering and Sciences
EASA	Ecclesiastical Architects and Surveyors' Association
EBRD	European Bank for Reconstruction and Development
EBU	European Broadcasting Union
EC	European Commission, European Community
ECB	England and Wales Cricket Board (formerly TCCB)

ECFMG	Educational Council for Foreign Medical Graduates
ECGD	Export Credit Guarantee Department
Econ	Economic
ed	editor; edited
ED	Efficiency Decoration; European Democratic (Group)
EDC	Economic Development Committee
EdD	Doctor of Education
EDG	European Democratic Group (UK Conservative Group, European Parliament)
edn	edition
Educn	Education
educnl	educational
EEA	European Economic Area
EEF	Engineering Employers' Federation
EETPU	Electrical, Electronic, Telecommunications and Plumbing Union (now AEEU)
EFTA	European Free Trade Association
EIU	Economist Intelligence Unit
eld	eldest
ELT	English Language Teaching
EMBL	European Molecular Biology Laboratory
EMBO	European Molecular Biology Organisation
EMEA	Europe, Middle East and Africa
EMS	Emergency Medical Service
EN (G)	Enrolled Nurse (General)
Eng	English; England
engr	Engineer
engrg	Engineering
ENO	English National Opera
ENSA	Entertainments National Services Association
ENT	Ear, Nose and Throat
ENWFC	England North West Film Commission
EP	European Parliament
EPLP	European Parliamentary Labour Party
EPP	European People's Party
EPSRC	Engineering and Physical Sciences Research Council (formerly SERC)
er	elder
ERA	Electrical Research Association
ERD	Emergency Reserve Decoration
Esq	Esquire
ESRC	Economic and Social Research Council
ESRO	European Space Research Organisation
estab	established; establishment
ESU	English Speaking Union
ETH	Eidgenössische Technische Hochschule
EU	European Union (formerly European Community)
EurGeol	European Geologist
Eur Ing	European Engineer
Euro	European
exec	executive
exhbn	exhibition
expdn	expedition
ext	extinct; extension

F

f	father
FA	Football Association
FAA	Fellow, Australian Academy of Science
FAAAS	Fellow, American Academy of Arts & Sciences
FAAO	Fellow, American Academy of Optometry
FAAP	Fellow, American Academy of Paediatrics
FAAV	Fellow, Central Association of Agricultural Valuers
FABRP	Fellow, Association of Business Recovery Professionals (formerly FSPI)
FAcadMEd	Fellow, Academy of Medical Educators
FACC	Fellow, American College of Cardiology
FACCA	Fellow, Association of Certified and Corporate Accountants
FACD	Fellow, American College of Dentistry
FACE	Fellow, Australian College of Education
FACM	Fellow, Association of Computing Machines
FACOG	Fellow, American College of Obstetricians and Gynaecologists
FACP	Fellow, American College of Physicians
FACS	Fellow, American College of Surgeons
FAcSS	Fellow, Academy for the Learned Societies in Social Sciences (formerly AcSS)
FACT	Fellow, Association of Corporate Treasurers
FACVT	Fellow, American College of Veterinary Toxicology
FAE	Fellow, Academy of Experts (formerly FBAE)

FAES	Fellow, Audio Engineering Society	FCIOB	Fellow, Chartered Institute of Building
FAI	Fellow, Chartered Auctioneers' and Estate Agents' Institute; Fellow, Financial Accountants' Institute	FCIOL	Fellow, Chartered Institute of Linguistics
		FCIPA	Fellow, Chartered Institute of Patent Agents (now CPA)
FAIA	Fellow, American Institute of Architects	FCIPD	Fellow, Chartered Institute of Personnel and Development
FAIE	Fellow, British Association of Industrial Editors (now FCB)	FCIPR	Fellow, Chartered Institute of Public Relations
FAIM	Fellow, Australian Institute of Management	FCIPS	Fellow, Chartered Institute of Purchasing and Supply
FAIP	Fellow, Australian Institute of Physics	FCIS	Fellow, Institute of Chartered Secretaries and Administrators
FAIRE	Fellow, Australian Institute of Radio Engineers	FCISI	Fellow, Chartered Institute for Securities and Investment (formerly FCSI)
FAM	Fellow, Academy of Marketing		
FAMGP	Fellow, Association of Managers in General Practice	FCIT	Fellow, Chartered Institute of Transport (now FCILT)
FAMS	Fellow, Ancient Monuments Society	FCIWEM	Fellow, Chartered Institution of Water and Environmental Management (formerly FIWEM)
FANY	First Aid Nursing Yeomanry		
FANZCA	Fellow, Australian and New Zealand College of Anaesthetists	FCIWM	Fellow, Chartered Institute of Waste Management
FAO	Food and Agriculture Organisation of the United Nations	FCMA	Fellow, Institute of Cost and Management Accountants; Fellow, Communications Management Association
FAPA	Fellow, American Psychiatric Association		
FAPM	Fellow, Association of Project Managers	FCMC	Fellow grade Certified Management Consultant (Institute of Management Consultancy)
FAQMC	Fellow, Association of Quality Management Consultants		
FARELF	Far East Land Forces	FCMI	Fellow, Chartered Management Institute (formerly FIMgt)
FAS	Fellow, Antiquarian Society	FCMSA	Fellow, College of Medicine of South Africa
FASA	Fellow, Australian Society of Accountants	FCO	Foreign & Commonwealth Office
FASCE	Fellow, American Society of Civil Engineers	FCOG	Fellow, College of Obstetrics and Gynaecology
FASI	Fellow, Architects and Surveyors' Institute	FCollP	Ordinary Fellow, College of Preceptors
FASME	Fellow, American Society of Mechanical Engineers	FCollT	Fellow, College of Teachers (formerly FCP)
FBA	Fellow, British Academy	FConsE	Fellow, Association of Consulting Engineers
FBAA	Fellow, British Acupuncture Association; Fellow, British Archaeological Association	FCOphth	Fellow, College of Ophthalmology (now FRCOphth)
		FCOptom	Fellow, College of Optometrists (formerly FBCO)
FBAE	Fellow, British Academy of Experts (now FAE)	FCP	Academic Fellow, College of Preceptors (now FCollT)
FBAM	Fellow, British Academy of Management	FCPA	Fellow, Australian Society of Certified Practising Accountants
FBCO	Fellow, British College of Opticians (now FCOptom)	FCPS	Fellow, College of Physicians and Surgeons
FBCS	Fellow, British Computer Society	FCSI	Fellow, Chemical Society; Federation of Conservative Students (now Conservative Collegiate Forum)
FBEC(S)	Fellow, Business Education Council (Scotland)		
FBEng	Fellow, Association of Building Engineers	FCSD	Fellow, Chartered Society of Designers
FBHI	Fellow, British Horological Institute	FCS	Fellow, Chartered Securities Institute (now FCISI)
FBI	Federation of British Industries	FCT	Fellow, Institute of Corporate Treasurers
FBIAC	Fellow, British Institute of Agricultural Consultants	FCWA	Fellow, Institute of Cost and Works Accountants
FBIBA	Fellow, British Insurance Brokers' Association	FDI	Fédération Dentaire Internationale
FBID	Fellow, British Institute of Interior Design	FDR	Federalische Deutsche Republik
FBIEE	Fellow, British Institute of Energy Economists	FDS	Fellow in Dental Surgery
FBIM	Fellow, British Institute of Management (now FIMgt)	FDSRCPS	Fellow in Dental Surgery, Royal College of Physicians and Surgeons
FBIPP	Fellow, British Institute of Professional Photographers		
FBIS	Fellow, British Interplanetary Society	FDSRCS	Fellow in Dental Surgery, Royal College of Surgeons of England
FBISA	Fellow, British Institute of Sports Administration		
FBKSTS	Fellow, British Kinematograph, Sound and Television Society	FDSRCSE	Fellow in Dental Surgery, Royal College of Surgeons of Edinburgh
FBOA	Fellow, British Optical Association; Fellow, British Orthopaedic Association	FDSRCSI	Fellow in Dental Surgery, Royal College of Surgeons in Ireland
		FE	Further Education
FBPsS	Fellow, British Psychological Society	FEA	Fellow, English Association
FBSG	Fellow, British Society for Geomorphology	FEAF	Far East Air Force
FBSI	Fellow, Boot and Shoe Industry	FEBU	Fellowship of European Boards of Urology
FC	Football Club	Fed	Federal
FCA	Fellow, Institute of Chartered Accountants, Financial Conduct Authority	Fedn	Federation
		FEFC	Further Education Funding Council
FCAI	Fellow, Canadian Aeronautical Institute	FEI	International Equestrian Federation; Fellow, Energy Institute
FCAM	Fellow, Communications Advertising and Marketing Educational Foundation	FEIS	Fellow, Educational Institute of Scotland
		fell	fellow
FCAnaes	Fellow, College of Anaesthetists	FESC	Fellow, European Society of Cardiology
FCB	Fellow, British Association of Communicators in Business (formerly FAIE)	FFA	Fellow, Faculty of Actuaries (Scotland); Fellow, Institute of Financial Accountants
		FFAEM	Fellow, Faculty of Accident & Emergency Medicine
FCBSI	Fellow, Chartered Building Societies Institute	FFARACS	Fellow, Faculty of Anaesthetists Royal Australasian College of Surgeons
FCCA	Fellow, Chartered Association of Certified Accountants		
FCCS	Fellow, Corporation of Certified Secretaries	FFARCS	Fellow, Faculty of Anaesthetists, Royal College of Surgeons (now FRCA)
FA	Football Association		
FCEC	Federation of Civil Engineering Contractors	FFARCSI	Fellow, Faculty of Anaesthetists Royal College of Surgeons of Ireland
FCEM	Fellow, College of Emergency Medicine (now FRCEM)		
FCFA	Fellow, Cookery and Food Association	FFAS	Fellow, Faculty of Architects and Surveyors
FCFI	Fellow, Clothing and Footwear Institute	FFB	Fellow, Faculty of Building
FCGI	Fellow, City and Guilds of London Institute	FFCM	Fellow, Faculty of Community Medicine (now FFPH)
FCIA	Fellow, Corporation of Insurance Agents	FFCS	Founding Fellow, Institute of Contemporary Scotland
FCIArb	Fellow, Chartered Institute of Arbitrators	FFDRCSI	Fellow, Faculty of Dentistry, Royal College of Surgeons in Ireland
FCIB	Fellow, Corporation of Insurance Brokers; Fellow, Chartered Institute of Bankers		
		FFFP	Fellow, Faculty of Family Planning (of the RCOG)
FCIBS	Fellow, Chartered Institution of Building Services; Fellow, Chartered Institute of Bankers of Scotland	FFGDP	Fellow, Faculty of General Dental Practice
		FFHom	Fellow, Faculty of Homeopathy
FCIBSE	Fellow, Chartered Institution of Building Service Engineers	FFOHM	Fellow, Faculty of Occupational Health Medicine
FCIHort	Fellow, Chartered Institute of Horticulture	FFOM	Fellow, Faculty of Occupational Medicine
FCIHT	Fellow, Chartered Institution of Highways and Transportation	FFPathRCPI	Fellow, Faculty of Pathology Royal College of Physicians of Ireland
FCII	Fellow, Chartered Insurance Institute		
FCILT	Fellow, Chartered Institute of Logistics and Transport (formerly FCIT)	FFPH	Fellow, Faculty of Public Health (formerly FFPHM)
		FFPHM	Fellow, Faculty of Public Health Medicine (formerly FFCM, now FFPH)
FCIM	Fellow, Chartered Institute of Marketing (formerly FInstM)		
FCInstCES	Fellow, Chartered Institution of Civil Engineering Surveyors (formerly FInstCES)		
FCInstT	Fellow, Chartered Institute of Taxation (formerly FInstT)		

FFPHMI	Fellow, Faculty of Public Health Medicine Royal College of Physicians of Ireland
FFPM	Fellow, Faculty of Pharmaceutical Medicine
FFR	Fellow, Faculty of Radiologists
FFRRCSI	Fellow, Faculty of Radiologists, Royal College of Surgeons in Ireland
FFSSoc	Fellow, Forensic Science Society
FFY	Fife and Forfar Yeomanry
FGA	Fellow, Gemmological Association
FGCM	Fellow, Guild of Church Musicians
FGDP	Faculty of General Dental Practitioners
FGS	Fellow, Geological Society
FGSM	Fellow, Guildhall School of Music
FHCIMA	Fellow, Hotel Catering and Institutional Management Association (now FIH)
FHEA	Fellow, Higher Education Academy
FHG	Fellow in Heraldry and Genealogy
FHKCPath	Fellow, Hong Kong College of Pathologists
FHKIE	Fellow, Hong Kong Institute of Engineers
FHS	Fellow, Heraldry Society; Forces Help Society
FHSA	Family Health Services Authority
FHSM	Fellow, Institute of Health Services Management
FIA	Fellow, Institute of Actuaries; Fédération Internationale de l'Automobile
FIAA	Fellow, Institute of Administrative Accountants
FIAC	Fellow, Institute of Company Accountants
FIAcadE	Fellow, Irish Academy of Engineering
FIAeS	Fellow, Institute of Aeronautical Sciences
FIAgrE	Fellow, Institution of Agricultural Engineers
FIAgrM	Fellow, Institution of Agricultural Management
FIAL	Fellow, International Institute of Arts and Letters
FIAM	Fellow, International Academy of Management
FIAP	Fellow, Institute of Analysts and Programmers
FIArb	Fellow, Institute of Arbitration
FIAS	Fellow, Institute of Aeronautical Sciences (USA); Fellow, Incorporated Society of Architects
FIB	Fellow, Institute of Bankers (now FCIB)
FIBA	Fellow, Institute of Business Advisers (formerly FIBC)
FIBC	Fellow, Institute of Business Counsellors (now FIBA)
FIBF	Fellow, Institute of British Foundrymen
FIBiol	Fellow, Institute of Biology (now FSB)
FIBM	Fellow, Institute of Builders' Merchants
FIBMS	Fellow, Institute of Biomedical Science (formerly FIMLS)
FIBrew	Fellow, Institute of Brewing
FIBScot	Fellow, Institute of Bankers in Scotland
FICA	Fellow, Institute of Chartered Accountants in England and Wales (now FCA); Fellow, Independent Consultants' Association
FICAI	Fellow, Institute of Chartered Accountants in Ireland
FICAS	Fellow, Institute of Chartered Accountants in Scotland
FICD	Fellow, Institute of Civil Defence
FICE	Fellow, Institution of Civil Engineers
FICeram	Fellow, Institute of Ceramics
FICFor	Fellow, Institute of Chartered Foresters
FIChemE	Fellow, Institution of Chemical Engineers
FICM	Fellow, Institute of Credit Management
FICMA	Fellow, Institute of Cost and Management Accountants
FICorrST	Fellow, Institute of Corrosion Science and Technology
FICPD	Fellow, Institute of Continuing Professional Development
FICS	Fellow, Institute of Chartered Shipbrokers; Fellow, International College of Surgeons
FICSA	Fellow, Institute of Chartered Secretaries and Administrators
FIDE	Fédération Internationale des Échecs; Fellow, Institute of Design Engineers; Fédération Internationale pour le Droit Européen
FIDM	Fellow, Institute of Direct Marketing
FIDPM	Fellow, Institute of Data Processing Management
FIE(Aust)	Fellow, Institution of Engineers (Australia)
FIED	Fellow, Institution of Engineering Design
FIEE	Fellow, Institution of Electrical Engineers
FIEEE	Fellow, Institution of Electrical and Electronics Engineers (USA)
FIEI	Fellow, Institution of Engineers of Ireland
FIElecIE	Fellow, Institution of Electronic Incorporated Engineers
FIERE	Fellow, Institution of Electronics and Radio Engineers
FIET	Fellow, Intitute of Engineering and Technology
FIEx	Fellow, Institute of Export
FIFF	Fellow, Institute of Freight Forwarders (now FIFP)
FIFireE	Fellow, Institute of Fire Engineers
FIFM	Fellow, Institute of Fisheries Management
FIFor	Fellow, Institute of Forestry
FIFP	Fellow, Institute of Freight Professionals
FIFST	Fellow, Institute of Food Science and Technology
FIGasE	Fellow, Institution of Gas Engineers
FIGD	Fellow, Institute of Grocery Distribution
FIGEM	Fellow, Institute of Gas Engineers and Managers (formerly FIGasE)
FIGeol	Fellow, Institute of Geology
FIH	Fellow, Institute of Hospitality (formerly FHCIMA)
FIHE	Fellow, Institute of Health Education
FIHort	Fellow, Institute of Horticulture (now FCIHort)
FIHospE	Fellow, Institute of Hospital Engineering
FIHSM	Fellow, Institute of Health Service Managers
FIHT	Fellow, Institute of Highways and Transportation
FIHVE	Fellow, Institution of Heating and Ventilating Engineers
FIIA	Fellow, Institute of Internal Auditors
FIIB	Fellow, International Institute of Biotechnology
FIIE	Fellow, Institution of Incorporated Engineers
FIIM	Fellow, Institute of Industrial Managers
FIInfSc	Fellow, Institute of Information Scientists (now FCLIP)
FIInst	Fellow, Imperial Institute
FIL	Fellow, Institute of Linguists
FILA	Fellow, Institute of Landscape Architects
FILDM	Fellow, Institute of Logistics and Distribution Management
FilDr	Doctor of Philosophy
FILog	Fellow, Institute of Logistics
FILT	Fellow, Institute of Logistics and Transport
FIM	Fellow, Institute of Materials (formerly Institute of Metals)
FIMA	Fellow, Institute of Mathematics and its Applications
FIMarE	Fellow, Institute of Marine Engineers
FIMarEst	Fellow, Institute of Marine Engineering, Science and Technology
FIMBRA	Financial Intermediaries, Managers and Brokers Regulatory Association
FIMC	Fellow, Institute of Management Consultants
FIMechE	Fellow, Institution of Mechanical Engineers
FIMF	Fellow, Institute of Metal Finishing
FIMfgE	Fellow, Institution of Manufacturing Engineers
FIMFT	Fellow, Institute of Maxillo-Facial Technology
FIMgt	Fellow, Institute of Management
FIMH	Fellow, Institute of Material Handling; Fellow, Institute of Military History
FIMI	Fellow, Institute of Motor Industry
FIMinE	Fellow, Institute of Mining Engineers
FIMIT	Fellow, Institute of Musical Instrument Technology
FIMLS	Fellow, Institute of Medical and Laboratory Sciences (now FIBMS)
FIMM	Fellow, Institution of Mining and Metallurgy
FIMMM	Fellow, Institute of Materials, Minerals and Mining
FIMS	Fellow, Institute of Mathematical Statistics
FIMT	Fellow, Institute of the Motor Trade
FIMTA	Fellow, Institute of Municipal Treasurers and Accountants
fin	finance; financial
FInstAA	Fellow, Institute of Administrative Accountants
FInstAM	Fellow, Institute of Administrative Management
FInstCES	Fellow, Institution of Civil Engineering Surveyors (now FCInstCES)
FInstCS	Fellow, Institute of Chartered Secretaries
FInstD	Fellow, Institute of Directors (now FIoD)
FInstE	Fellow, Institute of Energy (formerly FInstF)
FInstF	Fellow, Institute of Fuel (now FInstE)
FInstFF	Fellow, Institute of Freight Forwarders
FInstGasE	Fellow, Institution of Gas Engineers
FInstGeol	Fellow, Institute of Geologists
FInstHE	Fellow, Institution of Highway Engineers
FInstLEx	Fellow, Institute of Legal Executives
FInstLM	Fellow, Institute of Leadership and Management
FInstM	Fellow, Institute of Marketing (now FCIM)
FInstMC	Fellow, Institute of Measurement and Control
FInstMSM	Fellow, Institute of Marketing and Sales Management
FInstNDT	Fellow, Institute of Non-Destructive Testing
FInstP	Fellow, Institute of Physics
FInstPet	Fellow, Institute of Petroleum
FInstPS	Fellow, Institute of Purchasing and Supply (now FCIPS)
FInstSMM	Fellow, Institute of Sales and Marketing Management
FInstT	Fellow, Institute of Taxation (now FCInstT)
FInstTT	Fellow, Institute of Travel and Tourism
FNucE	Fellow, Institute of Nuclear Engineers (now FNucI)
FIOA	Fellow, Institute of Acoustics
FIOB	Fellow, Institute of Building
FIoD	Fellow, Institute of Directors (formerly FInstD)
FIOP	Fellow, Institute of Printing
FIOSc	Fellow, Institute of Optical Science
FIOSH	Fellow, Institute of Occupational Safety and Health
FIP	Fellow, Institute of Packaging; Fellow, Australian Institute of Petroleum

FIPA	Fellow, Institute of Public Administration; Fellow, Institute of Practitioners in Advertising; Fellow, Insolvency Practitioners' Association
FIPD	Fellow, Institute of Personnel and Development (now FCIPD)
FIPG	Fellow, Institute of Professional Goldsmiths
FIPHE	Fellow, Institution of Public Health Engineers
FIPI	Fellow, Institute of Professional Investigators
FIPlantE	Fellow, Institute of Plant Engineers
FIPM	Fellow, Institute of Personnel Management (now FCIPD)
FIPR	Fellow, Institute of Public Relations
FIProdE	Fellow, Institute of Production Engineers (now FIEE)
FIPS	Fellow, Institute of Purchasing and Supply
FIPSM	Fellow, Institute of Physical Sciences in Medicine
FIQ	Fellow, Institute of Quarrying
FIQA	Fellow, Institute of Quality Assurance
FIRE	Fellow, Institution of Radio Engineers
FIRI	Fellow, Institution of the Rubber Industry
FIRM	Fellow, Institute of Risk Management
FIRSE	Fellow, Institute of Railway Signalling Engineers
FIRTE	Fellow, Institute of Road Transport Engineers
FIS	Fellow, Institute of Stationers
FISA	Fédération Internationale des Sociétés d'Aviron
FISE	Fellow, Institute of Sanitary Engineers
FISITA	Fédération Internationale des Sociétés d'Ingénieurs des Techniques de l'Automobile
FISM	Fellow, Institute of Supervisory Managers
FISP	Fellow, Institute of Sales Promotion
FISTC	Fellow, Institute of Scientific and Technical Communicators
FISTD	Fellow, Imperial Society of Teachers of Dancing
FIStructE	Fellow, Institution of Structural Engineers
FISVA	Fellow, Incorporated Society of Valuers and Auctioneers
FITA	Fellow, International Archery Federation
FITD	Fellow, Institute of Training and Development (now FIPD)
FIWEM	Fellow, Institution of Water and Environmental Management (now FCIWEM)
FIWES	Fellow, Insititute of Water Engineers and Scientists
FIWSc	Fellow, Institute of Wood Science
FKC	Fellow, King's College London
FL	Florida
FLA	Fellow, Library Association (now FCLIP)
FLAS	Fellow, Land Agents Society
FLCM	Fellow, London College of Music
FLCOM	Fellow, London College of Osteopathic Medicine
FLI	Fellow, Landscape Institute
FLIA	Fellow, Life Insurance Association
FLS	Fellow, Linnean Society
FLSW	Fellow, Learned Society of Wales
Flt	Flight
Flt Lt	Flight Lieutenant
FMA	Fellow, Museums Association
FMedSci	Fellow, Academy of Medical Sciences
FMES	Fellow, Minerals Engineering Society
FMPA	Fellow, Master Photographers Association
FMS	Fellow, Institute of Management Services; Fellow of the Medical Society; Fellow, Manorial Society
FNAEA	Fellow, National Association of Estate Agents
Fndn	Foundation
fndr	founder
FNI	Fellow, Nautical Institute
FNIAB	Fellow, National Institute of Agricultural Botany
FNucI	Fellow, Nuclear Institute (formerly FINucE)
FO	Foreign Office
FODA	Fellow, Overseas Doctors' Association
FOR	Fellowship of Operational Research
FPA	Family Practitioners' Association
FPC	Family Practitioner Committee
FPCA	Fellow of Practising and Commercial Accountants
FPCS	Fellow, Property Consultants' Society
FPEA	Fellow, Physical Education Association
FPhS	Fellow, Philosophical Society of England
FPMI	Fellow, Pensions Management Institute
FPMS	Institution of Professionals, Managers and Specialists
FPRI	Fellow, Plastics and Rubber Institute
FPS	Fellow, Philological Society of Great Britain
FPWI	Fellow, Permanent Way Institution
FRACDS	Fellow, Royal Australian College of Dental Surgeons
FRACGP	Fellow, Royal Australian College of General Practitioners
FRACI	Fellow, Royal Australian Chemical Institute
FRACMA	Fellow, Royal Australian College of Medical Administrators
FRACO	Fellow, Royal Australian College of Ophthalmologists
FRACP	Fellow, Royal Australasian College of Physicians
FRACR	Fellow, Royal Australasian College of Radiologists
FRACS	Fellow, Royal Australasian College of Surgeons
FRAD	Fellow, Royal Academy of Dancing
FRAeS	Fellow, Royal Aeronautical Society
FRAgS	Fellow, Royal Agricultural Societies
FRAI	Fellow, Royal Anthropological Institute
FRAIA	Fellow, Royal Australian Institute of Architects
FRAIC	Fellow, Royal Architectural Institute of Canada
FRAM	Fellow, Royal Academy of Music
FRANZCP	Fellow, Royal Australian and New Zealand College of Psychiatrists
FRANZCR	Fellow, Royal Australian and New Zealand College of Radiologists
FRAS	Fellow, Royal Astronomical Society; Fellow, Royal Asiatic Society
FRASE	Fellow, Royal Agricultural Society of England
FRBS	Fellow, Royal Botanic Society; Fellow, Royal Society of British Sculptors
FRCA	Fellow, Royal College of Art; Fellow, Royal College of Anaesthetists (formerly FFARCS)
FRCD(C)	Fellow, Royal College of Dentists of Canada
FRCEM	Fellow, Royal College of Emergency Medicine (formerly FCEM)
FRCGP	Fellow, Royal College of General Practitioners
FRCM	Fellow, Royal College of Music
FRCN	Fellow, Royal College of Nursing
FRCO	Fellow, Royal College of Organists
FRCO(CHM)	Fellow, Royal College of Organists with Diploma in Choir Training
FRCOG	Fellow, Royal College of Obstetricians and Gynaecologists
FRCOphth	Fellow, Royal College of Ophthalmologists (formerly FCOphth)
FRCP	Fellow, Royal College of Physicians
FRCPA	Fellow, Royal College of Pathologists of Australia
FRCPath	Fellow, Royal College of Pathologists
FRCP(C)	Fellow, Royal College of Physicians of Canada
FRCPCH	Fellow, Royal College of Paediatrics and Child Health
FRCPE	Fellow, Royal College of Physicians of Edinburgh
FRCPEd	Fellow, Royal College of Physicians of Edinburgh
FRCPGlas	Fellow, Royal College of Physicians and Surgeons of Glasgow
FRCPI	Fellow, Royal College of Physicians in Ireland
FRCPS	Fellow, Royal College of Physicians and Surgeons
FRCPsych	Fellow, Royal College of Psychiatrists
FRCR	Fellow, Royal College of Radiologists
FRCS	Fellow, Royal College of Surgeons; Fellow, Royal Commonwealth Society (formerly Royal Empire Society)
FRCSEd	Fellow, Royal College of Surgeons Edinburgh
FRCSGlas	Fellow, Royal College of Physicians and Surgeons of Glasgow
FRCSI	Fellow, Royal College of Surgeons in Ireland
FRCVS	Fellow, Royal College of Veterinary Surgeons
FREconS	Fellow, Royal Economic Society
FREng	Fellow, Royal Academy of Engineering
FRES	Fellow, Royal Entomological Society
FRG	Federal Republic of Germany
FRGS	Fellow, Royal Geographical Society
FRHistS	Fellow, Royal Historical Society
FRHS	Fellow, Royal Horticultural Society
FRI	Fellow, Royal Institution
FRIA	Fellow, Royal Institute of Arbitrators
FRIAS	Fellow, Royal Incorporation of Architects in Scotland
FRIBA	Fellow, Royal Institute of British Architects
FRIC	Fellow, Royal Institute of Chemistry (now FRSC)
FRICS	Fellow, Royal Institute of Chartered Surveyors
FRIN	Fellow, Royal Institute of Navigation
FRINA	Fellow, Royal Institution of Naval Architects
FRIPH	Fellow, Royal Institute of Public Health
FRIPHH	Fellow, Royal Institute of Public Health and Hygiene
FRMetS	Fellow, Royal Meteorological Society
FRMS	Fellow, Royal Microscopical Society
FRNCM	Fellow, Royal Northern College of Music
FRNS	Fellow, Royal Numismatic Society
FInstMSM	Fellow, Institute of Marketing and Sales Management
FRPharmS	Fellow, Royal Pharmaceutical Society
FRPI	Fellow, Institute of Rubber and Plastics Industry
FRPMS	Fellow, Royal Postgraduate Medical School
FRPS	Fellow, Royal Photographic Society
FRPSL	Fellow, Royal Philatelic Society, London
FRS	Fellow, Royal Society
FRSA	Fellow, Royal Society of Arts
FRSAIre	Fellow, Royal Society of Antiquaries of Ireland
FRSAMD	Fellow, Royal Scottish Academy of Music and Drama
FRSB	Fellow, Royal Society of Biology (formerly FSB)
FRSBS	Fellow, Royal Society of British Sculptors
FRSC	Fellow, Royal Society of Canada; Fellow, Royal Society of Chemistry
FRSCM	Fellow, Royal School of Church Music
FRSE	Fellow, Royal Society of Edinburgh
FRSGS	Fellow, Royal Scottish Geographical Society
FRSH	Fellow of the Royal Society of Health

FRSL	Fellow, Royal Society of Literature
FRSM	Fellow, Royal Society of Medicine
FRSNZ	Fellow, Royal Society of New Zealand
FRSPH	Fellow, Royal Society for Public Health
FRSS	Fellow, Royal Statistical Society
FRSSA	Fellow, Royal Scottish Society of Arts (Science and Technology)
FRSTM&H	Fellow, Royal Society of Tropical Medicine and Health
FRTPI	Fellow, Royal Town Planning Institute
FRTS	Fellow, Royal Television Society
FRVA	Fellow, Rating and Valuation Association
FRVC	Fellow, Royal Veterinary College
FRZS	Fellow, Royal Zoological Society
FSA	Fellow, Society of Antiquaries; Financial Services Authority (formerly SIB)
FSA	Scot Fellow, Society of Antiquaries of Scotland
FSAA	Fellow, Society of Incorporated Accountants and Auditors
FSAE	Fellow, Society of Arts Education
FSAI	Fellow, Society of Architectural Illustrators
FSALS	Fellow, Society of Advanced Legal Studies
FSB	Fellow, Society of Biology (formerly FIBiol, now FRSB)
FSCA	Fellow, Society of Company and Commercial Accountants
FScotvec	Fellow, Scottish Vocational Educational Council
FSDC	Fellow, Society of Dyers and Colourists
FSE	Fellow, Society of Engineers
FSF	Fellow, Institute of Shipping and Forwarding Agents
FSG	Fellow, Society of Genealogists
FSGD	Fellow, Society of Garden Designers
FSI	Fellow, Royal Institution of Chartered Surveyors (see also FRICS); Fellow, Securities Institute (now FCISI)
FSIA	Fellow, Society of Industrial Artists
FSIAD	Fellow, Society of Industrial Artists and Designers (now FCSD)
FSLAET	Fellow, Society of Licensed Aircraft Engineers and Technologists
FSLGD	Fellow, Society for Landscape and Garden Designs
FSME	Fellow, Society of Mechanical Engineering
FSMPTE	Fellow, Society of Motion Pictures and Television Engineers (USA)
FSNAME	Fellow, American Society of Naval Architects and Marine Engineers
FSPI	Fellow, Society of Practitioners of Insolvency (now FABRP)
FSRP	Fellow, Society for Radiological Protection
FSS	Fellow, Royal Statistical Society (now CStat)
FSSP	Priestly Fraternity of St Peter
FSTD	Fellow, Society of Typographical Designers
FSUT	Fellow, Society for Underwater Technology
FSVA	Fellow, Incorporated Society of Valuers and Auctioneers
FT	Financial Times
FTC	Flying Training Command
FTCL	Fellow, Trinity College of Music, London
FTI	Fellow, Textile Institute
FTII	Fellow, Institute of Taxation (now CTA (Fell))
FTMA	Fellow, Telecommunications Managers' Association (now FCMA)
FTS	Fellow, Tourism Society
Fus	Fusiliers
FVI	Fellow, Valuers Institution
FWA	Fellow, World Academy of Arts and Sciences
FWCMD	Fellow, Welsh College of Music and Drama
FWeldI	Fellow, Welding Institute
FZS	Fellow, Zoological Society

G

g	great
Ga	Georgia
GA	Geologists' Association; Georgia
Gall	Gallery
GAPAN	Guild of Air Pilots and Air Navigators
GATT	General Agreement on Tariffs and Trade
GB	Great Britain
GBA	Governing Bodies Association
GBE	Knight/Dame Grand Cross of the Order of the British Empire
GBSM	Graduate, Birmingham and Midland Institute School of Music
GC	George Cross
GCB	Knight/Dame Grand Cross of the Order of the Bath
GCBS	General Council of British Shipping
GCGI	Graduate, City and Guilds of London Institute
GCH	Knight Grand Cross of the Hanoverian Order
GCHQ	Government Communications Headquarters
GCIE	Knight/Dame Grand Commander of the Order of the Indian Empire
GCLJ	Grand Cross of St Lazarus of Jerusalem
GCMG	Knight/Dame Grand Cross of the Order of St Michael and St George

GCON	Grand Cross of the Order of the Niger
GCPO	Knight/Dame Grand Cross of the Order of Pius IX
GCSE	General Certificate in Secondary Education
GCSG	Knight Grand Cross of the Order of St Gregory the Great
GCSI	Knight Grand Commander of the Order of the Star of India
GCSJ	Knight Grand Cross of Justice of the Order of St John of Jerusalem
GCSS	Knight/Dame Grand Cross of the Order of Pope St Sylvester
GCStJ	Bailiff/Dame Grand Cross of the Order of St John of Jerusalem
GCVO	Knight/Dame Grand Cross of the Royal Victorian Order
gda	granddaughter
GDBA	Guide Dogs for the Blind Association
GDC	General Dental Council
gdns	gardens
GDPA	General Dental Practitioners' Association
GDR	German Democratic Republic
Gds	Guards
GDST	Girls' Day School Trust (formerly GPDST)
Gen	General
Ger	Germany
gf	grandfather
ggda	great granddaughter (and so forth)
ggs	great grandson (and so forth)
GHQ	General Headquarters
GIFireE	Graduate, Institute of Fire Engineers
GIMechE	Graduate, Institution of Mechanical Engineers
GKT	Guy's, King's College and St Thomas' Hospitals Medical and Dental School (formerly UMDS)
GLA	Greater London Authority
GLAA	Greater London Arts Association (now GLAB)
GLAB	Greater London Arts Board (formerly GLAA)
GLC	Greater London Council
Glos	Gloucestershire
GLR	Greater London Radio
GM	George Medal; genetically modified
gm	grandmother
GMB	Great Master of the Bath; (Union for) General, Municipal, Boilermakers
GMBATU	General Municipal Boilermakers and Allied Trade Unions (now GMB)
GMC	General Medical Council
GME	General Ministerial Examination
GMIE	Grand Master of the Order of the Indian Empire
GMMG	Grand Master of the Order of St Michael and St George
GMSI	Grand Master of the Order of the Star of India
GMWU	General and Municipal Workers' Union (now GMB)
gn	great nephew; great niece
GO	Grand Officier (de la Légion d'Honneur)
GOC	General Officer Commanding
GOC-in-C	General Officer Commanding-in-Chief
govr	governor
Govt	Government
GP	General Practitioner; General Practice
gp	group
Gp	Capt Group Captain
GPDST	Girls' Public Day School Trust (now GDST)
GPMU	Graphical, Paper and Media Union
GPO	General Post Office
grad	graduate; graduated
GRCM	Graduate, Royal College of Music
GRSM	Graduate, Royal Schools of Music
GS	General Staff; Grammar School
gs	grandson
GSA	Girls' Schools Association
GSM	General Service Medal; Guildhall School of Music and Drama
GSO	General Staff Officer
Gt	Great
GTCL	Graduate, Trinity College of Music, London
Gtr	Greater
Guy's	Guy's Hospital
GWR	Great Western Railway

H

h	heir
ha	heir apparent
HA	Health Authority; Historical Association
HAA	Heavy Anti-Aircraft
HAC	Honourable Artillery Company
Hants	Hampshire
HBM	His/Her Britannic Majesty

hc	honoris causa
HCF	Hon Chaplain to the Forces
HCIMA	Hotel, Catering and Institutional Management Association
HCITB	Hotel and Catering Industry Training Board
HD	home defence; honourable discharge; (51st) Highland Division
HDE	Higher Diploma in Education
HDipEd	Higher Diploma in Education
HDip in Ed	Honorary Diploma in Education
HE	His/Her Excellency; Higher Education
HEFCE	Higher Education Funding Council of England
HEQC	Higher Education Quality Council
Herefords	Herefordshire
Herts	Hertfordshire
HESIN	Higher Education Support for Industry in the North
HFEA	Human Fertilisation and Embryology Authority
HG	Home Guard
HGTAC	Home Grown Timber Advisory Committee
HH	His/Her Highness; His Holiness
HHA	Historic Houses Association
HI	Hawaii
high cmmr	high commissioner
HIH	His/Her Imperial Highness
HIIIH	His/Her Illustrious Highness
HIM	His/Her Imperial Majesty
Hist	Historical
HKIA	Member, Hong Kong Institute of Architects
Hldgs	Holdings
HLI	Highland Light Infantry
HM	His/Her Majesty
HMAS	His/Her Majesty's Australian Ship
HMC	Headmasters' and Headmistresses' Conference; Hospital Management Committee
HMEH	His/Her Most Eminent Highness
HMHS	His/Her Majesty's Hospital Ship
HMI	His/Her Majesty's Inspectorate
HMMTB	His/Her Majesty's Motor Torpedo Boat
HMOCS	His/Her Majesty's Overseas Civil Service
HMP	His/Her Majesty's Prison
HMS	His/Her Majesty's Ship
HMSO	His/Her Majesty's Stationery Office
HMY	His/Her Majesty's Yacht
HNC	Higher National Certificate
HND	Higher National Diploma
Hon	Honourable; Honour (Judges); Honorary
Hons	Honours
hort	horticulture; horticultural
Hosp	Hospital
hp	heir presumptive
HQ	Headquarters
HR	Human Resources
HRE	Holy Roman Empire
HRH	His/Her Royal Highness
HRHA	Honorary Member, Royal Hibernian Academy
HRI	Hon Member, Royal Institute of Painters in Water Colours
HRSA	Hon Member, Royal Scottish Academy
HS	High School
HSE	Health and Safety Executive
HSH	His/Her Serene Highness
HSM	Health Service Management
Hunts	Huntingdonshire
husb	husband
HVCert	Health Visitors' Certificate

I

I	Ireland
IA	Indian Army; Iowa
IAA	International Advertising Association
IAAF	International Amateur Athletics Federation
IAB	Brazilian Institute of Architects
IABSE	International Association of Bridge and Structural Engineering
IAC	Indian Armoured Corps; Institute of Amateur Cinematographers
IACP	International Association of Chiefs of Police (USA)
IADR	International Association for Dental Research
IAEA	International Atomic Energy Agency
IAF	Indian Air Force; Indian Auxiliary Force
IAM	Institute of Advanced Motorists; Institute of Aviation Medicine
IAMC	Indian Army Medical Corps
IAOC	Indian Army Ordnance Corps
IAOMS	International Association of Oral and Maxillo-Facial Surgeons

IAP	Institute of Analysts and Programmers
IAPS	Incorporated Association of Preparatory Schools
IAPSO	International Association for the Physical Sciences of the Ocean
IARO	Indian Army Reserve of Officers
IAS	Indian Administrative Service
IASC	Indian Army Service Corps
IATA	International Air Transport Association
IATEFL	International Association of Teachers of English as a Foreign Language
IAU	International Astronomical Union
IBA	Independent Broadcasting Authority
IBF	International Boxing Federation
IBG	Institute of British Geographers
IBP	Institute of British Photographers
IBPA	International Bridge Players' Association
IBRC	Insurance Brokers' Registration Council
IBRD	International Bank for Reconstruction and Development (World Bank)
IBRO	International Brain Research Organisation
i/c	in charge of
ICA	Institute of Contemporary Arts; Institute of Chartered Accountants
ICAA	Invalid Children's Aid Association
ICAEW	Institute of Chartered Accountants of England and Wales
ICAS	Institute of Chartered Accountants of Scotland
ICC	International Chamber of Commerce
ICCROM	International Centre for Conservation at Rome
ICE	Institution of Civil Engineers
ICEF	International Federation of Chemical, Energy and General Workers' Unions
ICF	International Canoe Federation
ICFC	Industrial and Commercial Finance Corporation
IChemE	Institution of Chemical Engineering
ICI	Imperial Chemical Industries
ICJ	International Commission of Jurists; International Court of Justice
ICL	International Computers Ltd
ICMA	Institute of Cost and Management Accountants (now CIMA)
ICOM	International Council of Museums
ICPO	International Criminal Police Organisation (Interpol)
ICRA	International Centre for Research in Accounting
ICRF	Imperial Cancer Research Fund (now Cancer Research UK)
ICS	Indian Civil Service
ICSA	Institute of Chartered Secretaries and Administrators
ICSID	International Council of Societies of Industrial Design
ICSTM	Imperial College of Science, Technology and Medicine (London)
ICT	Information and Communications Technology
ID	Idaho
idc	has completed a course at, or served for a year on the staff of, The Imperial Defence College
IDC	Imperial Defence College
IDM	Institute of Direct Marketing
IDS	Institute of Development Studies
IEA	Institute of Economic Affairs
IEC	International Electrotechnical Commission
IEE	Institution of Electrical Engineers
IEEE	Institute of Electrical and Electronic Engineers (USA)
IEF	Indian Expeditionary Force
IEng	Incorporated Engineer
IERE	Institute of Electronic and Radio Engineers (now part of IEE)
IFAC	International Federation of Automatic Control
IFAD	International Fund for Agricultural Development (UN)
IFAW	International Fund for Animal Welfare
IFC	International Finance Corporation
IFLA	International Federation of Library Associations
IFPA	Industrial Fire Protection Association
IFPI	International Federation of the Phonographic Industry
IG	Instructor in Gunnery
IGasE	Institution of Gas Engineers
IGD	Institute of Grocery Distribution
IHA	Institute of Health Service Administrators
IHBC	Institute of Historic Building Conservation
IHSM	Institute of Health Services Management
IIC	International Institute of Communicators; International Institute of Conservation
IIEP	International Institute for Educational Planning
IIM	Institution of Industrial Managers
IIMR	Institute of Investment Management and Research
IIP	Institute of Incorporated Photographers
IISI	International Iron and Steel Institute
IISS	International Institute of Strategic Studies

IIT	Indian Institute of Technology
IL	Illinois
ILAM	Institution of Landscape and Amenity Management
ILEA	Inner London Education Authority
Ill	Illinois
ILO	International Labour Office
ILP	Independent Labour Party
ILR	Independent Local Radio
ILT	Institute of Logistics and Transport
ILTM	Member, Institute of Learning and Teaching
IMA	International Music Association; Institute of Mathematics and its Applications
IMarE	Institute of Marine Engineers (now IMarEst)
IMarEst	Institute of Marine Engineering, Science and Technology (formerly IMarE)
IMCB	International Management Centre, Buckingham
IMechE	Institution of Mechanical Engineers
IMEDE	Institut pour l'Etude des Méthodes de Direction de l'Enterprise
IMER	Institute of Marine Environmental Research
IMF	International Monetary Fund
IMM	Institute of Mining and Metallurgy (now IMMM)
IMMM	Institute of Materials, Minerals and Mining (formerly IMM)
Imp	Imperial
IMRO	Investment Management Regulatory Organisation
IMS	Indian Medical Service; International Military Services
IN	Indiana
Inc	Incorporated
incl	include; including
ind	independent
Inf	Infantry
info	information
INSEAD	Institut Européen d'Administration des Affaires
inspr	inspector
Inst	Institute
Instn	Institution
instr	instructor
Insur	Insurance
int	international
IOC	International Olympic Committee
IOD	Institute of Directors
IOM	Isle of Man
IOW	Isle of Wight
IPA	Institute of Practitioners in Advertising; Insolvency Practitioners' Association
IPC	International Publishing Corporation
IPCS	Institution of Professional Civil Servants
IPFA	Member/Associate, Chartered Institute of Public Finance and Accountancy
IPG	Independent Publishers' Guild; Industrial Painters' Group
IPHE	Institution of Public Health Engineers
IPI	Institute of Patentees and Inventors
IPM	Institute of Personnel Management
IPMS	Institute of Professionals, Managers and Specialists (formerly IPCS)
IPPA	Independent Programme Producers' Association
IPPF	International Planned Parenthood Federation
IPPR	Institute of Public Policy Research
IPR	Institute of Public Relations (now CIPR)
IPRA	International Public Relations Association
IProdE	Institute of Production Engineers
IPS	Indian Political Service
IPSA	International Political Science Association
IPT	Industry and Parliament Trust
IPU	Inter-Parliamentary Union
IQA	Institute of Quality Assurance
Ir	Irish
IRA	Irish Republican Army
IRC	Industrial Re-organisation Corporation
IRE	Indian Corps of Royal Engineers; Institute of Radio Engineers (USA)
IRN	Independent Radio News
IRRV	Institute of Revenues, Rating and Valuation
Is	Island(s)
ISBA	Incorporated Society of British Advertisers
ISC	Indian Staff Corps; Imperial Service College; Independent Schools' Council (formerly ISJC)
ISCO	Independent Schools Careers Organisation
ISE	Indian Service of Engineers
ISI	International Statistical Institute
ISID	International Society of Interior Design
ISIS	Independent Schools Information Service
ISJC	Independent Schools Joint Council (now ISC)

ISM	Imperial Service Medal; (Member/Associate) Incorporated Society of Musicians
ISO	Imperial Service Order; International Standards Organisation
ISOCARP	International Society of City and Regional Planning
ISP	Institute of Sales Promotion; International Study Programme
ISPP	International Society of Political Psychology
ISSC	International Social Science Council
IStructE	Institution of Structural Engineers
ISVA	Incorporated Society of Valuers and Auctioneers
IT	Information Technology
ITA	Independent Television Authority
ITC	Independent Television Commission
ITCA	Independent Television Companies Association
ITN	Independent Television News
ITU	International Telecommunications Union
ITV	Independent Television
ITVA	Independent Television Association
IUCN	International Union for the Conservation of Nature and Natural Resources
IUPAC	International Union of Pure and Applied Chemistry
IUPAP	International Union of Pure and Applied Physics
IUTAM	International Union of Theoretical and Applied Mechanics
IVF	In Vitro Fertilisation
IWEM	Institution of Water and Environmental Management
IWS	International Wool Secretariat
IY	Imperial Yeomanry
IYRU	International Yacht Racing Union

J

JACT	Joint Association of Classical Teachers
JAG	Judge Advocate General
JCD	Doctor of Canon Law (Juris Canonici Doctor)
JCR	Junior Common Room; Junior Combination Room (Cambridge)
JD	Doctor of Jurisprudence
JDipMA	Joint Diploma in Management Accounting Services
JETRO	Japan External Trade Organisation
JI	Journal
JMB	Joint Matriculation Board
JMN	Johan Mangku Negara (Malaysia)
JP	Justice of the Peace
jr	junior
JSDC	Joint Services Defence College
jsdc	Qualified at Joint Service Defence College
JSM	Johan Seita Mahkota (Malaysia)
JSSC	Joint Services Staff College
jssc	Qualified at Joint Services Staff College
jt	joint
jtly	jointly

K

k	killed
ka	killed in action
KAR	King's African Rifles
KASG	Knightly Association of St George the Martyr
KBE	Knight Commander of the Order of the British Empire
KC	King's Counsel
KCB	Knight Commander of the Order of the Bath
KCH	King's College Hospital
KCHS	Knight Commander of the Order of the Holy Sepulchre
KCIE	Knight Commander of the Order of the Indian Empire
KCL	King's College London
KCMG	Knight Commander of the Order of St Michael and St George
KCPO	Knight Commander of the Order of Pius IX
KCS	King's College School
KCSG	Knight Commander of the Order of St Gregory the Great
KCSI	Knight Commander of the Order of the Star of India
KCSS	Knight of the Order of Pope St Sylvester
KCVO	Knight Commander of the Royal Victorian Order
KDG	King's Dragoon Guards
KEH	King Edward's Horse (Regiment)
KEO	King Edward's Own
KG	Knight of the Order of the Garter
KGStJ	Knight of Grace of the Order of St John of Jerusalem
KGVO	King George V's Own
KHC	Honorary Chaplain to the King
KHDS	Honorary Dental Surgeon to the King
KHP	Honorary Physician to the King

KHS	Honorary Surgeon to the King; Knight of the Order of the Holy Sepulchre
K-i-H	Kaisar-i-Hind (Emperor of India, medal)
KJStJ	Knight of Justice of the Order of St John of Jerusalem
KM	Knight of Malta
KMCO	Knight of Merit of the Sacred Military Constantinian Order of St George
KMN	Kesatria Mangku Negara (Malaysian decoration)
KORR	King's Own Royal Regiment
KOSB	King's Own Scottish Borderers
KOYLI	King's Own Yorkshire Light Infantry
KP	Knight of the Order of St Patrick
KPFSM	King's Police and Fire Service Medal
KPM	King's Police Medal
KRI	King's Royal Irish
KRRC	King's Royal Rifle Corps
KS	Kansas
KSG	Knight of the Order of St Gregory the Great
KSLI	King's Shropshire Light Infantry
KSS	Knight of the Order of Pope St Sylvester
KStJ	Knight of the Order of St John of Jerusalem
KT	Knight of the Order of the Thistle
kt	knighted (Knight Bachelor)
KY	Kentucky

L

L	Labour
LA	Los Angeles; Louisiana
La	Louisiana
LAA	Light Anti-Aircraft
Lab	Labour; Laboratory
Lab Co-op	Labour and Co-operative
LAC	Leading Aircraftsman
LACOTS	Local Authorities' Co-ordination of Trading Standards Committee
LACSAB	Local Authorities' Conditions of Service Advisory Board
LAH	Licentiate, Apothecaries Hall, Dublin
LAMDA	London Academy of Music and Dramatic Art
LAMSAC	Local Authorities' Management Services and Computer Committee
LAMTPI	Legal Association Member, Town Planning Institute (now LMRTPI)
Lancs	Lancashire
LAPADA	London and Provincial Antique Dealers' Association
LBC	London Broadcasting Company
LBIPP	Licentiate, British Institute of Professional Photographers
LCC	London County Council
LCDS	London Contemporary Dance Studio
LCDT	London Contemporary Dance Theatre
LCGI	Licentiate, City and Guilds of London Institute
LCh	Licentiate in Surgery
LCJ	Lord Chief Justice
LCP	Licentiate, College of Preceptors
LDDC	London Docklands Development Corporation
ldr	leader
LDS	Licentiate in Dental Surgery
LDSRCS	Licentiate in Dental Surgery, Royal College of Surgeons
LDV	Local Defence Volunteers
LEA	Local Education Authority
LEB	London Electricity Board
lectr	lecturer
Leics	Leicestershire
LEPRA	Leprosy Relief Association
LèsL	Licencié ès Lettres
LF	Land Forces
LG	Life Guards; Lady Companion of the Order of the Garter
LGSM	Licentiate, Guildhall School of Music and Drama
LH	Light Horse
LHD	Litterarum Humaniorum Doctor
LHSM	Licentiate, Institute of Health Services Management
LI	Light Infantry
Lib	Liberal
LIBC	Lloyd's Insurance Brokers' Committee
Lib Dem	Liberal Democrat
Lieut	Lieutenant
LIFFE	London International Financial Futures and Options Exchange
Lincs	Lincolnshire
LIOB	Licentiate, Institute of Building
lit	literature
LittD	Doctor of Letters (Cambridge and Dublin)
LLA	Lady Literate in Arts
LLB	Bachelor of Laws

LLC	Limited Liability Company
LLCM	Licentiate, London College of Music
LLD	Doctor of Laws
LLL	Licenciate in Laws
LLM	Master of Laws
LLP	Limited Liability Partnership
LM	Licentiate in Midwifery
LMA	League Managers' Association
LMBC	Lady Margaret Boat Club (St John's College, Cambridge)
LMCC	Licentiate of Medical Council of Canada
LMH	Lady Margaret Hall (Oxford)
LMRTPI	Legal Member, Royal Town Planning Institute
LMSSA	Licentiate in Medicine and Surgery, Society of Apothecaries
LNat&U	Liberal National and Unionist
LNER	London and North East Railway
LOCOG	London Organising Committee of the Olympic Games
LPh	Licentiate in Philosophy
LPO	London Philharmonic Orchestra
LPTB	London Passenger Transport Board
LRAM	Licentiate, Royal Academy of Music
LRCP	Licentiate, Royal College of Physicians
LRCPE	Licentiate, Royal College of Physicians of Edinburgh
LRCPI	Licentiate, Royal College of Physicians of Ireland
LRCS	Licentiate, Royal College of Surgeons of England; League of Red Cross Societies
LRCSE	Licentiate, Royal College of Surgeons of Edinburgh
LRCSI	Licentiate, Royal College of Surgeons in Ireland
LRFPS	Licentiate, Royal Faculty of Physicians and Surgeons (Glasgow)
LRIBA	Licentiate, Royal Institute of British Architects
LRPS	Licentiate, Royal Photographic Society
LRSC	Licentiate, Royal Society of Chemistry
LRT	London Regional Transport
LSA	Licentiate, Society of Apothecaries
LSC	Learning and Skills Council
LSCA	London Society of Chartered Accountants
LSE	London School of Economics
LSHTM	London School of Hygiene and Tropical Medicine
LSO	London Symphony Orchestra
Lt	Lieutenant
LT	Lady of the Order of the Thistle
LTA	Lawn Tennis Association
LTC	Lawn Tennis Club; Low Temperature Carbonization
LTCL	Licentiate, Trinity College of Music, London
Lt-Col	Lieutenant-Colonel
Ltcy	Lieutenancy
Ltd	Limited
LTE	London Transport Executive (now LRT)
Lt-Gen	Lieutenant-General
LTh	Licentiate in Theology
LU	Liberal Unionist
LVO	Lieutenant of the Royal Victorian Order
LWT	London Weekend Television

M

m	married; marriage
M&A	Mergers and Acquisitions
MA	Master of Arts; Military Assistant; Massachusetts
MAAEM	Member, American Association of Electrodiagnostic Medicine
MAAF	Mediterranean Allied Air Forces
MAAT	Member, Association of Accounting Technicians
MABRP	Member, Association of Business Recovery Professionals
MAcadMEd	Member, Academy of Medical Educators
MACC	Member, American College of Cardiology
MACE	Member, Association of Conference Executives; Member, Association of Consulting Engineers
MACM	Member, Association of Computing Machines
MACP	Member, Association of Child Psychotherapists
MACS	Member, American Chemical Society
MAE	Member, Academy of Experts (formerly MBAE)
MAFF	Ministry of Agriculture, Fisheries and Food
MAI	Master of Engineering
MAIAA	Member, American Institute of Aeronautics and Astronautics
MAIE	Member, British Association of Industrial Editors (now MCB)
Maj	Major
Maj-Gen	Major-General
mangr	manager
MAP	Ministry of Aircraft Production
MAPM	Member, Association of Project Managers
MaPS	Member, Association of Planning Services
MArch	Master of Architecture

Marq	Marquess
MASAE	Member, American Society of Agricultural Engineers
MASCE	Member, American Society of Civil Engineers
MASME	Member, American Society of Mechanical Engineers
Mass	Massachusetts
MB	Bachelor of Medicine
MBA	Master of Business Administration
MBAC	Member, British Association of Chemists
MBAE	Member, British Academy of Experts (now MAE)
MBC	Metropolitan/Municipal Borough Council
MBCS	Member, British Computer Society
MBE	Member of the Order of the British Empire
MBEDA	Member, Bureau of European Design
MBFR	Mutual and Balanced Force Reductions
MBHI	Member, British Horological Institute
MBIM	Member, British Institute of Management (now MIMgt)
MBIPP	Member, British Institute of Professional Photography
MBISC	Member, British Institute of Sports Coaches
MBKS	Member, British Kinematograph Society
MBO	Management Buyout
MBOU	Member, British Ornithologists' Union
MBPsS	Member, British Psychological Society
MBSG	Member, British Society of Gastroenterology
MC	Military Cross
MCAM	Member, Institute of Communications, Advertising and Marketing
MCB	Master of Clinical Biochemistry; Member, British Association of Communicators in Business (formerly MAIE)
MCC	Marylebone Cricket Club; Metropolitan County Council
MCCI	Manchester Chamber of Commerce and Industry
MCD	Master of Civic Design
MCFA	Member, Cookery and Food Association
MCGI	Member, City and Guilds of London Institute
MChir	Master in Surgery
MChOrth	Master of Orthopaedic Surgery
MCIA	Member, Chartered Institute of Arbitrators
MCIArb	Member, Chartered Institute of Arbitrators
MCIB	Member, Chartered Institute of Banking
MCIBSE	Member, Chartered Institution of Building Services Engineers
MCIH	Member, Chartered Institute of Housing (formerly MIH)
MCIHort	Member, Chartered Institute of Horticulture (formerly MIHort)
MCII	Member, Chartered Insurance Institute
MCIJ	Member, Chartered Institute of Journalists
MCIM	Member, Chartered Institute of Marketing
MCIOB	Member, Chartered Institute of Building
MCIPD	Member, Chartered Institute of Personnel and Development
MCIPR	Member, Chartered Institute of Public Relations
MCIPS	Member, Chartered Institute of Purchasing and Supply
MCIT	Member, Chartered Institute of Transport
MCIWEM	Member, Chartered Institution of Water and Environmental Management (formerly MIWEM)
MCLIP	Member, Chartered Institute of Library and Information Professionals
MCMB	Molecular and Cellular Medicine Board
MCMI	Member, Chartered Institute of Management (formerly MIMgt)
MCom	Master of Commerce
MConsE	Member, Association of Consulting Engineers
MCOphth	Member, College of Ophthalmologists (formerly Faculty of Ophthalmologists, FacOph, and Ophthalmic Society of UK, OSUK)
MCP	Member of Colonial Parliament; Member, College of Preceptors
MCPath	Member, College of Pathologists
MCPCH	Member, College of Paediatrics and Child Health
MCPS	Member, College of Physicians and Surgeons
MCSD	Member, Chartered Society of Designers
MCSP	Member, Chartered Society of Physiotherapy
MCT	Member, Association of Corporate Treasurers
MD	Doctor of Medicine; Maryland
md	managing director
MDC	Metropolitan District Council
MDes	Master of Design
m dis	marriage dissolved
MDiv	Master of Divinity
MDS	Master of Dental Surgery
ME	Middle East; Maine
MEAF	Middle East Air Force
MEC	Member, Executive Council
MECAS	Middle East Centre for Arab Studies
mech	mechanical; mechanised
MECI	Member, Institute of Employment Consultants
MEd	Master of Education
Med	medical; medicine; Mediterranean
MEF	Mediterranean Expeditionary Force
MEI	Member, Energy Institute
MEIC	Member, Engineering Institute of Canada
MELF	Middle East Land Forces
memb	member
Meml	Memorial
MENCAP	Royal Society for Mentally Handicapped Children and Adults
MEng	Masters of Engineering
MEP	Member of the European Parliament
MESC	Member, European Society of Cardiology
Met	Metropolitan
MFA	Master of Fine Arts (USA)
MFARCS	Member, Faculty of Anaesthetists, Royal College of Surgeons
MFB	Member, Faculty of Building
MFC	Mastership in Food Control
MFCM	Member, Faculty of Community Medicine (now MFPHM)
MFGDP	Member, Faculty of General Dental Practitioners
MFH	Master of Foxhounds
MFHom	Member, Faculty of Homeopathy
MFOM	Member, Faculty of Occupational Medicine
MFPH	Member, Faculty of Public Health (formerly MFPHM)
MFPHM	Member, Faculty of Public Health Medicine (now MFPH)
MFPHMI	Member, Faculty of Public Health Medicine Royal College of Physicians of Ireland
mfr	manufacturer
mfrg	manufacturing
MGC	Machine Gun Corps
MGDS RCS	Member in General Dental Surgery, Royal College of Surgeons
MGGS	Major-General General Staff
mgmnt	management
MGO	Master-General of the Ordnance
Mgr	Monsignor
MGRA	Major-General Royal Artillery
MH	Military Hospital
MHCIMA	Member, Hotel Catering and Institutional Management Association
MHK	Member of the House of Keys (IOM)
MHM	Masters in Health Management
MHR	Member of the House of Representatives (USA and Australia)
MHRA	Modern Humanities Research Association
MHSM	Member, Institute of Health Services Management
MI	Military Intelligence; Michigan
MIAA	Member, International Advertising Association
MIAeE	Member, Institute of Aeronautical Engineers
MIAM	Member, Institute of Administrative Management
MIBE	Member, Institution of British Engineers
MIBG	Member, Institute of British Geographers
MIBiol	Member, Institute of Biology (now MSB)
MICAS	Member, Institute of Chartered Accountants of Scotland
MICE	Member, Institution of Civil Engineers
MICEI	Member, Institution of Civil Engineers of Ireland
MICFM	Member, Institute of Charity Fundraising Managers
MIChemE	Member, Institution of Chemical Engineers
MICM	Member, Institute of Credit Management
MIConsE	Member, Institute of Consulting Engineers
Middx	Middlesex
MIDM	Member, Institute of Direct Marketing
MIDPM	Member, Institute of Data Processing Management
MIED	Member, Institution of Engineering Design
MIEE	Member, Institution of Electrical Engineers
MIEEE	Member, Institute of Electrical and Electronics Engineers (USA)
MIEI	Member, Institute of Engineering Inspection
MIEIE	Member, Institute of Electronic Incorporated Engineers
MIERE	Member, Institution of Electronic and Radio Engineers
MIES	Member, Institution of Engineers and Shipbuilders, Scotland
MIEx	Member, Institute of Export
MIFA	Member, Institute of Field Archaeologists
MIFireE	Member, Institute of Fire Engineers
MIH	Member, Institute of Housing (now MCIH)
MIHE	Member, Institute of Health Education
MIHort	Member, Institute of Horticulture (now MCIHort)
MIHT	Member, Institute of Highways and Transportation
MIIA	Member, Institute of Internal Auditors
MIIExE	Member, Institute of Incorporated Executive Engineers
MIIM	Member, Institute of Industrial Managers
MIInfSc	Member, Institute of Information Sciences (now MCLIP)
MIL	Member, Institute of Linguists
Mil	Military
MILDM	Member, Institute of Logistics and Distribution Management
MILE	Member, Institution of Locomotive Engineers
MILog	Member, Institute of Logistics
MIM	Member, Institute of Materials (formerly Institute of Metals)
MIMarE	Member, Institute of Marine Engineers (now MIMarEst)

MIMarEst	Member, Institute of Marine Engineering, Science and Technology (formerly MIMarE)	MOMA	Museum of Modern Art
MIMC	Member, Institute of Management Consultants	MOP	Ministry of Power
MIMCE	Member, Institute of Municipal and County Engineers	MOS	Ministry of Supply
MIMechE	Member, Institution of Mechanical Engineers	MP	Member of Parliament
MIMfgE	Member, Institution of Manufacturing Engineers	MPA	Master of Public Administration
MIMgt	Member, Institute of Management	MPBW	Ministry of Public Building Works
MIMI	Member, Institute of the Motor Industry	MPH	Master of Public Health
MIMinE	Member, Institution of Mining Engineers	MPhil	Master of Philosophy
MIMM	Member, Institution of Mining and Metallurgy	MPO	Management and Personnel Office
min	minister	MPS	Member, Pharmaceutical Society of Great Britain
MIngF	Member, Danish Engineers' Association	MR	Master of the Rolls
MInstB	Member, Institute of Bankers	MRAC	Member, Royal Agricultural College
MInstD	Member, Institute of Directors	MRAD	Member, Royal Academy of Dancing
MInstE	Member, Institute of Energy	MRad	Master of Radiology
MInstEnvSci	Member, Institute of Environmental Sciences	MRAeS	Member, Royal Aeronautical Society
MInstF	Member, Institute of Fundraising	MRAS	Member, Royal Asiatic Society
MInstGasE	Member, Institution of Gas Engineers	MRC	Medical Research Council
MInstHE	Member, Institution of Highway Engineers	MRCGP	Member, Royal College of General Practitioners
MInstM	Member, Institute of Marketing	MRCOG	Member, Royal College of Obstetricians and Gynaecologists
MInstMC	Member, Institute of Measurement and Control	MRCP	Member, Royal College of Physicians
MInstMet	Member, Institute of Metals	MRCPath	Member, Royal College of Pathologists
MInstP	Member, Institute of Physics	MRCPGlas	Member, Royal College of Physicians and Surgeons of Glasgow
MInstPet	Member, Institute of Petroleum	MRCPI	Member, Royal College of Physicians of Ireland
MInstPS	Member, Institute of Purchasing and Supply (now MCIPS)	MRCPsych	Member, Royal College of Psychiatrists
MInstR	Member, Institute of Refrigeration	MRCR	Member, Royal College of Radiologists
MInstRE	Member, Institution of Royal Engineers	MRCS	Member, Royal College of Surgeons
MInstTT	Member, Institute of Travel and Tourism	MRCVS	Member, Royal College of Veterinary Surgeons
MINucE	Member, Institution of Nuclear Engineers	MRI	Member, Royal Institution
Miny	Ministry	MRIA	Member, Royal Irish Academy
MIOB	Member, Institute of Building	MRIAI	Member, Royal Institute of the Architects of Ireland
MIOSH	Member, Institution of Occupational Safety and Health	MRIC	Member, Royal Institute of Chemistry
MIPA	Member, Institution of Practitioners in Advertising; Member, Insolvency Practitioners' Association	MRICS	Member, Royal Institution of Chartered Surveyors
		MRIN	Member, Royal Institute of Navigation
		MRINA	Member, Royal Institution of Naval Architects
MIPD	Member, Institute of Personnel and Development	MRIPHH	Member, Royal Institute of Public Health and Hygiene
MIPharmM	Member, Institute of Pharmacy Management	MRO	Member, Register of Osteopaths
MIPHE	Member, Institute of Public Health Engineers	MRPharmS	Member, Royal Pharmaceutical Society
MIPlantE	Member, Institute of Plant Engineers	MRS	Market Research Society; Medical Research Society
MIPM	Member, Institute of Personnel Management	MRSC	Member, Royal Society of Chemistry
MIPR	Member, Institute of Public Relations	MRSH	Member, Royal Society of Health
MIProdE	Member, Institute of Production Engineers (now MIMfgE)	MRST	Member, Royal Society of Teachers
MIQ	Member, Institute of Quarrying	MRTPI	Member, Royal Town Planning Institute
MIRA	Motor Industry Research Association	MRUSI	Member, Royal United Service Institute for Defence Studies
MIRS	Member, Investor Relations Society	MRVA	Member, Rating and Valuation Association
MIS	Member, Institute of Statisticians	MS	Master of Surgery; Manuscript; Master of Science (USA); Mississippi
misc	miscellaneous		
MISI	Member, Iron and Steel Institute	MSAE	Member, Society of Automotive Engineers (USA)
Miss	Mississippi	MSB	Member, Society of Biology (formerly MIBiol)
MIStructE	Member, Institution of Structural Engineers	MSC	Manpower Services Commission; Meritorious Service Cross (Canada)
MIT	Massachusetts Institute of Technology (USA)		
MITD	Member, Institute of Training and Development (now MIPD)	MSc	Master of Science
MITI	Member, Institute of Translation and Interpreting	MScD	Master of Dental Science
MIWEM	Member, Institution of Water and Environmental Management (now MCIWEM)	MSCI	Member, Society of Chemical Industry
		MScL	Member, Society of Construction Law
		MSE	Member, Society of Engineers; Master of Science in Engineering (USA)
mktg	marketing		
MLA	Member, Legislative Assembly (Northern Ireland); Modern Language Association; Master in Landscape Architecture	MSEE	Member, Society of Environmental Engineers
		MSF	Manufacturing, Science and Finance Union (formerly ASTMS)
MLC	Member, Legislative Council	MSI	Member, Securities Institute (formerly member of the Stock Exchange)
MLI	Member, Landscape Institute		
MLIA	Member, Life Insurance Association	MSIA	Member, Society of Industrial Artists
MLib	Master of Library Science	MSIAD	Member, Society of Industrial Artists and Designers
MLitt	Master of Letters	MSM	Meritorious Service Medal
MLO	Military Liaison Officer	MSocIS	Member, Societé des Ingenieurs et Scientifiques de France
MLS	Master of Library Science	MSocSci	Master of Social Sciences
MM	Military Medal	MSP	Member of Scottish Parliament
MMC	Monopolies and Mergers Commission	MSPI	Member, Society of Practitioners of Insolvency
MMet	Master of Metallurgy	MSR	Member, Society of Radiographers
MMIM	Member, Malaysian Institute of Management	MSSCC	Member, Scottish Society of Contamination Control
MMin	Master of Ministry	MSST	Member, Society of Surveying Technicians
MMRS	Member, Market Research Society	MSt	Master of Studies
MMS	Master of Management Services; Member, Institute of Management Services	MSTD	Member, Society of Typographic Designers
		MT	Montana
MMSA	Master of Midwifery, Society of Apothecaries	MTAI	Member, Institute of Travel Agents
MMus	Master of Music	MTB	Motor Torpedo Boat
MN	Merchant Navy; Minnesota	MTh	Master of Theology
MNECInst	Member, North East Coast Institution of Engineers and Shipbuilders	MTPI	Member, Town Planning Institute
		MUniv	Master of the University
MNI	Member, Nautical Institute	MusB	Bachelor of Music
MO	Medical Officer; Missouri	MusD	Doctor of Music (Cambridge)
MOD	Ministry of Defence	MusM	Master of Music
MOH	Medical Officer of Health	MV	Motor Vessel
MOI	Ministry of Information; Ministry of the Interior		

MVO	Member of the Royal Victorian Order	Northants	Northamptonshire
MVSc	Master of Veterinary Science	Notts	Nottinghamshire
MW	Master of Wine	NP	Notary Public
MWB	Metropolitan Water Board	NPQH	National Professional Qualification for Headship
MWeldI	Member, Welding Institute	NRA	National Rifle Association
MY	Motor Yacht	NRDC	National Research Development Corporation

N

		NRPB	National Radiological Protection Board
		ns	Graduate of the Royal Naval Staff College, Greenwich
N	North; Nationalist	NS	Nova Scotia
n	nephew; niece	NS&I	National Savings and Investments
NAAFI	Navy, Army, and Air Force Institutes	NsgMD	Nursing Management Diploma
NABC	National Association of Boys' Clubs	NSPCC	National Society for the Prevention of Cruelty to Children
NAC	National Agriculture Centre	NSW	New South Wales
NACF	National Art Collectors' Fund	NT	National Theatre
NACRO	National Association for the Care and Resettlement of Offenders	NTDA	National Trade Development Association
NADFAS	National Association of Decorative and Fine Arts Societies	NTO	National Training Organisation
NAEB	National Association of Educational Broadcasters	NUBE	National Union of Bank Employees (now BIFU)
NAG	Northern Army Group	NUGMW	National Union of General and Municipal Workers
NAHAT	National Association of Health Authorities and Trusts	NUI	National University of Ireland
NAHT	National Association of Head Teachers	NUJ	National Union of Journalists
NALGO	National and Local Government Officers' Association	NUM	National Union of Mineworkers
NAMH	National Association for Mental Health	NUMAST	National Union of Marine, Aviation, and Shipping Transport Officers
NAO	National Audit Office	NUPE	National Union of Public Employees
NAPE	National Association of Primary Education	NUR	National Union of Railwaymen
NAQA	National Association of Quality Assurance in Healthcare (now AQM)	NUS	National Union of Students
		NUT	National Union of Teachers
NAS	Naval Air Squadron	NV	Naamloze Vennootschap (Netherlands); Nevada
NASDAQ	National Association of Securities Dealers Automated Quotations (USA)	NVQ	National Vocational Qualification
		NW	North West
NASUWT	National Association of Schoolmasters/Union of Women Teachers	NWFP	North West Frontier Province
nat	national	NY	New York
NATCS	National Air Traffic Control Services	NYC	New York City
NATFHE	National Association of Teachers in Further and Higher Education	NYSE	New York Stock Exchange
		NYU	New York University
Nat Lib	National Liberal	NZ	New Zealand
NATO	North Atlantic Treaty Organisation	NZEF	New Zealand Expeditionary Force
NBL	National Book League		

O

NBPI	National Board for Prices and Incomes		
NC	Nautical College; North Carolina		
NCA	National Cricket Association; National Certificate of Agriculture	o	only
NCB	National Coal Board	OA	Officier d'Académie
NCCI	National Committee for Commonwealth Immigrants	OAS	Organisation of American States
NCCL	National Council for Civil Liberties	OB	Order of Barbados
NCLC	National Council of Labour Colleges	OBE	Officer of the Order of the British Empire
NCO	Non-Commissioned Officer	OBStJ	Officer Brother of the Order of St John of Jerusalem
NCRI	National Cancer Research Institute (formerly UKCCCR)	OC	Officer Commanding; Officer of the Order of Canada
NCTJ	National Council for the Training of Journalists	OCF	Officiating Chaplain to the Forces
NCVCCO	National Council for Voluntary Child Care Organisations	OCR	Oxford and Cambridge and RSA Examination Board
NCVQ	National Council for Vocational Qualifications	OCS	Officer Cadet School
ND	Diploma in Naturopathy; North Dakota	OCTU	Officer Cadet Training Unit
NDA	National Diploma in Agriculture	ODA	Overseas Development Administration
NDC	National Defence College	ODI	Overseas Development Institute
NDD	National Diploma in Dairying; National Diploma in Design	ODM	Ministry of Overseas Development
NE	Nebraska; North East	ODPM	Office of the Deputy Prime Minister
NEAC	New English Art Club	OE	Order of Excellence (Guyana)
NEAF	Near East Air Force	OECD	Organisation for Economic Co-operation and Development
NEC	National Executive Committee	OEEC	Organisation for European Economic Co-operation
NEDC	National Economic Development Council	OER	Officers' Emergency Reserve
NEDO	National Economic Development Office	offr	officer
NERC	Natural Environment Research Council	OFMCap	Order of Friars Minor Capuchin (Franciscans)
NESTA	National Endowment for Science, Technology and the Arts	OFMConv	Order of Friars Minor Conventual (Franciscans)
NFER	National Foundation for Educational Research	OFT	Office of Fair Trading
NFS	National Fire Service	OGS	Order of the Good Shepherd
NFU	National Farmers' Union	OH	Ohio
NFWI	National Federation of Women's Institutes	OIC	Officer in Charge
NGO	Non-Governmental Organisation	OJ	Order of Jamaica
NH	New Hampshire	OK	Oklahoma
NHS	National Health Service	OM	Order of Merit
NI	Northern Ireland	O&M	Organisation and Method
NICE	National Institute for Health and Clinical Excellence	OMC	Oxford Military College
NICS	Northern Ireland Civil Service	ON	Order of the Nation (Jamaica)
NID	Naval Intelligence Department	ONC	Ordinary National Certificate
NIESR	National Institute of Economic and Social Research	OND	Ordinary National Diploma
NIH	National Institute of Health (USA)	ONZ	Order of New Zealand
NIHR	National Institute for Health Research	O&O	Oriental and Occidental Steamship Company
NILP	Northern Ireland Labour Party	OP	Observation Post
NJ	New Jersey	OPB	Occupational Pensions Board
NLF	National Liberal Federation	oppn	opposition
NM	New Mexico	ops	operations
NMCU	National Meteorological Co-ordinating Unit Committee	OR	Order of Roraima (Guyana); Oregon
NN	The Niadh Nask (Military Order of the Golden Chain)		

Orch Orchestra
Orgn Organisation
ORS Operational Research Society
ORT Organisation for Rehabilitation by Training
OSB Order of St Benedict (Benedictines)
OSC Graduate of Overseas Staff College
OSCE Organization for Security and Co-operation in Europe
OSNC Orient Steam Navigation Company
OSRD Office of Scientific Research and Development
OStJ Officer of the Order of St John of Jerusalem
OTC Officers' Training Corps
OUAC Oxford University Athletics Club
OUBC Oxford University Boat Club
OUCA Oxford University Conservative Association
OUDS Oxford University Dramatic Society
OUP Oxford University Press
Oxon Oxfordshire; of Oxford

P

PA Personal Assistant; Pennsylvania
pa per annum
Pa Pennsylvania
pac Passed final exam of advanced class Military College of Science
PACT Producers' Alliance for Cinema and Television
Paiforce Palestine and Iraq Force
PAO Prince Albert's Own
Parl Parliament
Parly Parliamentary
PBWS President, British Watercolour Society
PC Privy Counsellor; Peace Commissioner (Ireland); Parish Council
PCC Parochial Church Council; Press Complaints Commission
PCFC Polytechnics and Colleges Funding Council
PCL Polytechnic of Central London
PCT Primary Care Trust
PDSA People's Dispensary for Sick Animals
PDTC Professional Dancers' Training Course Diploma
PE Procurement Executive; Physical Education
PEI Prince Edward Island
PEN International Association of Poets, Playwrights, Editors, Essayists, and Novelists
PEng Registered Professional Engineer (Canada); Member, Society of Professional Engineers
PEP Political and Economic Planning
perm permanent
PFA Professional Footballers' Association
PFI Private Finance Initiative
PGA Professional Golfers' Association
PGCE Postgraduate Certificate of Education
PGCert Postgraduate Certificate
PGDip Postgraduate Diploma
PHAB Physically Handicapped and Able-Bodied
PhC Pharmaceutical Chemist
PhD Doctor of Philosophy
PhL Licentiate of Philosophy
PIA Personal Investment Authority
PIARC Permanent International Association of Road Congresses
PID Political Intelligence Department
PIRA Paper Industries Research Association
PLA Port of London Authority
plc public limited company
PLP Parliamentary Labour Party
PM Prime Minister
PMD Program for Management Development (USA)
PMG Postmaster-General
PMN Panglima Mangku Negara (Malaysia)
PMO Principal Medical Officer
PNEU Parents' National Educational Union
PNG Papua New Guinea
PO Pilot Officer; Post Office
POD Personnel Operations Department
POEU Post Office Engineering Union
Poly Polytechnic
P&OSNCo Peninsular and Oriental Steam Navigation Company
postgrad postgraduate
POUNC Post Office Users' National Council
POW Prisoner of War
PPA Periodical Publishers Association
PPARC Particle Physics and Astronomy Research Council (formerly SERC)
PPE Philosophy, Politics and Economics
PPL Private Pilot's Licence
PPRA Past President, Royal Academy
PPRIBA Immediate Past President, Royal Institute of British Architects
PPRSA Past President, Royal Scottish Academy
PPS Parliamentary Private Secretary
PR Public Relations
PRA President, Royal Academy
PRC People's Republic of China
PRCA Public Relations Consultants Association
PRCS President, Royal College of Surgeons
PRE President, Royal Society of Painters, Etchers and Engravers
Preb Prebendary
Prep Preparatory
pres president
prev previously
PRI Plastics and Rubber Institute (now part of Inst of Materials)
princ principal
PRO Public Relations Officer; Public Records Office
prodn production
prodr producer
prods products
prof professor
prog programme
prop proprietor
Prov Provost; Provincial
PRS President, Royal Society
PRWS President, Royal Society of Painters in Water Colours
PS Pastel Society
psa Graduate of RAF Staff College
PSA President, Society of Antiquaries; Property Services Agency
psc Staff College Graduate
PSD Petty Session Division
PSI Policy Studies Institute
psm Certificate of the Military School of Music
PSM President, Society of Miniaturists
PSNC Pacific Steam Navigation Company
PSO Principal Staff Officer
PSPA Professional Sports Photographers' Association
pt part
PT Physical Training
PTA Parent-Teacher Association
PTE Passenger Transport Executive
ptnr partner
ptsc passed Technical Staff College
pt/t part time
Pty Proprietary; Party
pub public
pubns publications
PWD Public Works Department
PWO Prince of Wales' Own
PWR Pressurised Water Reactor
PYBT Prince's Youth Business Trust

Q

QAIMNS Queen Alexandra's Imperial Military Nursing Service
QALAS Qualified Associate of Land Agents' Society
QARANC Queen Alexandra's Royal Army Nursing Corps
QARNNS Queen Alexandra's Royal Naval Nursing Service
QC Queen's Counsel
QCB Queen's Commendation for Bravery
QCVSA Queen's Commendation for Valuable Service in the Air
QDR Qualified Dispute Resolver
QFSM Queen's Fire Service Medal for Distinguished Service
QGM Queen's Gallantry Medal
QHC Honorary Chaplain to The Queen
QHDS Honorary Dental Surgeon to The Queen
QHNS Honorary Nursing Sister to The Queen
QHP Honorary Physician to The Queen
QHS Honorary Surgeon to The Queen
Qld Queensland
QMAAC Queen Mary's Army Auxiliary Corps
QMC Queen Mary College, London
QMG Quartermaster-General
QO Qualified Officer
QOH Queen's Own Hussars
QPM Queen's Police Medal
qqv qua vide (which see, plural)
QRIH Queen's Royal Irish Hussars
QS Quarter Sessions
QSM Queen's Service Medal (NZ)

QSO	Queen's Service Order (NZ)
QUB	Queen's University Belfast
qv	quod vide (which see)
QVRM	Queen's Volunteer Reserves Medal

R

(R)	Reserve
R&A	Royal and Ancient Club (St Andrews)
RA	Royal Artillery; Royal Academician
RAAF	Royal Australian Air Force
RAAMC	Royal Australian Army Medical Corps
RAC	Royal Armoured Corps; Royal Automobile Club; Royal Agricultural College (now Royal Agricultural University, Cirencester)
RACGP	Royal Australian College of General Practitioners
RAChD	Royal Army Chaplains' Department
RACI	Royal Australian Chemical Institute
RACP	Royal Australasian College of Physicians
RACS	Royal Australasian College of Surgeons
RADA	Royal Academy of Dramatic Art
RADC	Royal Army Dental Corps
RAE	Royal Australian Engineers; Royal Aircraft Establishment
RAEC	Royal Army Educational Corps
RAeS	Royal Aeronautical Society
RAF	Royal Air Force
RAF(H)	Royal Air Force Hospital
RAFA	Royal Air Force Association
RAFO	Reserve of Air Force Officers
RAFRO	Royal Air Force Reserve of Officers
RAFVR	Royal Air Force Volunteer Reserve
RAI	Royal Anthropological Institute
RAIA	Royal Australian Institute of Architects
RAIC	Royal Architectural Institute of Canada
RAM	(Member) Royal Academy of Music
RAMC	Royal Army Medical Corps
RAN	Royal Australian Navy
RANR	Royal Australian Naval Reserve
RANVR	Royal Australian Naval Volunteer Reserve
RAOC	Royal Army Ordnance Corps
RAPC	Royal Army Pay Corps
RARDE	Royal Armament Research and Development Establishment
RARO	Regular Army Reserve of Officers
RAS	Royal Agricultural Society; Royal Astronomical Society; Royal Asiatic Society
RASC	Royal Army Service Corps (now RCT)
RASE	Royal Agricultural Society of England
RAU	Royal Agricultural University, Cirencester (formerly Royal Agricultural College)
RAuxAF	Royal Auxiliary Air Force
RAVC	Royal Army Veterinary Corps
RB	Rifle Brigade
RBA	(Member) Royal Society of British Artists
RBC	Royal British Colonial Society of Artists
RBK&C	Royal Borough of Kensington and Chelsea
RBS	Royal Society of British Sculptors
RC	Roman Catholic
RCA	Royal College of Art
RCAC	Royal Canadian Armoured Corps
RCAF	Royal Canadian Air Force
RCAMC	Royal Canadian Army Medical Corps
RCDS	Royal College of Defence Studies
RCGP	Royal College of General Practitioners
RCHA	Royal Canadian Horse Artiller
RCM	(Member) Royal College of Music
RCN	Royal College of Nursing; Royal Canadian Navy
RCNC	Royal Corps of Naval Constructors
RCNR	Royal Canadian Naval Reserve
RCNVR	Royal Canadian Naval Volunteer Reserve
RCO	Royal College of Organists
RCOG	Royal College of Obstetricians and Gynaecologists
RCP	Royal College of Physicians
RCPath	Royal College of Pathologists
RCPCH	Royal College of Paediatrics and Child Health
RCPEd	Royal College of Physicians of Edinburgh
RCPI	Royal College of Physicians of Ireland
RCPSGlas	Royal College of Physicians and Surgeons of Glasgow
RCPsych	Royal College of Psychiatrists
RCR	Royal College of Radiologists
RCS	Royal College of Surgeons of England; Royal Corps of Signals; Royal College of Science
RCS(Ed)	Royal College of Surgeons of Edinburgh
RCSI	Royal College of Surgeons in Ireland
RCST	Royal College of Science and Technology
RCT	Royal Corps of Transport
RCVS	Royal College of Veterinary Surgeons
Rd	Road
RD	Royal Naval Reserve Officers' Decoration
R&D	Research and Development
RDA	Regional Development Agency; Royal Defence Academy
RDC	Rural District Council
RDF	Royal Dublin Fusiliers
RDI	Royal Designer for Industry (RSA)
RDS	Royal Dublin Society
RE	Royal Engineers; Fellow, Royal Society of Painter-Etchers and Engravers
Rear Adm	Rear Admiral
rec	recorder
reg	regular
regnl	regional
Regt	Regiment
Regtl	Regimental
rels	relations
REME	Royal Electrical and Mechanical Engineers
REngDes	Registered Engineering Designer
rep	representative; repertory
Repub	Republican; Republic
RERO	Royal Engineers Reserve of Officers
res	reserve; research; resident
RES	Royal Empire Society (now Royal Commonwealth Society)
ret	retired
Rev	Reverend
RFA	Royal Field Artillery
RFC	Royal Flying Corps; Rugby Football Club
RFCA	Reserve Forces and Cadets Association
RFS	Royal Forestry Society
RFU	Rugby Football Union
RGA	Royal Garrison Artillery
RGI	Royal Glasgow Institute of the Fine Arts
RGN	Registered General Nurse
RGS	Royal Geographical Society
RHA	Royal Horse Artillery; Royal Hibernian Academy; Regional Health Authority
RHB	Regional Hospital Board
RHF	Royal Highland Fusiliers
RHG	Royal Horse Guards
RHR	Royal Highland Regiment
RHS	Royal Horticultural Society
RI	(Member) Royal Institute of Painters in Water Colours; Rhode Island, Royal Institution
RIAI	Royal Institute of the Architects of Ireland
RIAS	Royal Incorporation of Architects in Scotland
RIASC	Royal Indian Army Service Corps
RIBA	(Member) Royal Institute of British Architects
RIC	Royal Irish Constabulary
RICS	Royal Institution of Chartered Surveyors
RIF	Royal Irish Fusiliers
RIIA	Royal Institute of International Affairs
RIM	Royal Indian Marine
RIN	Royal Indian Navy
RINA	Royal Institute of Naval Architects
RINVR	Royal Indian Navy Volunteer Reserve
RIOP	Royal Institute of Oil Painters
RIPA	Royal Institute of Public Administration
RIPH	Royal Institute of Public Health
RIPHH	Royal Institute of Public Health and Hygiene
RIrR	Royal Irish Rifles
RL	Retired List
RLFC	Rugby League Football Club
RLSS	Royal Life Saving Society
RM	Royal Marines
RMA	Royal Military Academy; Royal Marine Artillery; Royal Musical Association
RMC	Royal Military College, Sandhurst (now Royal Military Academy)
RMCS	Royal Military College of Science
RMFVR	Royal Marine Forces Volunteer Reserve
RMLI	Royal Marine Light Infantry
RMN	Registered Mental Nurse
RMO	Resident Medical Officer
RMP	Royal Military Police
RMPA	Royal Medico-Psychological Association
RMR	Royal Marine Reserve
RMS	Royal Meteorological Society

RMT	National Union of Rail, Maritime and Transport Workers
RN	Royal Navy
RNAS	Royal Naval Air Service; Royal Naval Air Station
RNC	Royal Nautical College; Royal Naval College
RNCM	(Member) Royal Northern College of Music
RND	Royal Naval Division
RNEC	Royal Naval Engineering College
RNH	Royal Naval Hospital
RNIB	Royal National Institute for the Blind
RNID	Royal National Institute for Deaf People
RNLI	Royal National Lifeboat Institution
RNR	Royal Naval Reserve
RNSA	Royal Naval Sailing Association
RNSD	Royal Naval Store Department
RNT	Royal National Theatre; Registered Nurse Tutor
RNVR	Royal Naval Volunteer Reserve
RNVSR	Royal Naval Volunteer Supplementary Reserve
RNZADC	Royal New Zealand Army Dental Corps
RNZAF	Royal New Zealand Air Force
RNZN	Royal New Zealand Navy
RNZNVR	Royal New Zealand Naval Volunteer Reserve
ROC	Royal Observer Corps
R of O	Reserve of Officers
ROH	Royal Opera House
ROI	Member, Royal Institute of Painters in Oils
RORC	Royal Ocean Racing Club
RoSPA	Royal Society for the Prevention of Accidents
RP	Member, Royal Society of Portrait Painters
RPC	Royal Pioneer Corps
RPMS	Royal Postgraduate Medical School
RPO	Royal Philharmonic Orchestra
RPS	Royal Photographic Society
RPSGB	Royal Pharmaceutical Society of Great Britain
RR	Royal Regiment
RRC	Royal Red Cross
RRF	Royal Regiment of Fusiliers
RSA	Royal Scottish Academician; Royal Society of Arts
RSAA	Royal Society for Asian Affairs
RSAC	Royal Scottish Automobile Club
RSAMD	(Diploma of) Royal Scottish Academy of Music and Drama
RSBA	Royal Society of British Artists
RSBS	Royal Society of British Sculptors
RSC	Royal Shakespeare Company; Royal Society of Canada; Royal Society of Chemistry
RSCM	Royal Society of Church Music
RSCN	Registered Sick Children's Nurse
RSE	Royal Society of Edinburgh
RSF	Royal Scots Fusiliers
RSGS	Royal Scottish Geographical Society
RSL	Royal Society of Literature; Returned Services League (Australia)
RSM	Royal Society of Medicine; Royal Society of Music; Regimental Sergeant Major
RSMA	Royal Society of Marine Artists
RSME	Royal School of Military Engineers
RSNC	Royal Society for Nature Conservation
RSPB	Royal Society for the Protection of Birds
RSPCA	Royal Society for the Prevention of Cruelty to Animals
RSPP	Royal Society of Portrait Painters
RSRE	Royal Signals and Radar Establishment
RSS	Royal Statistical Society
RSSPCC	Royal Scottish Society for the Prevention of Cruelty to Children
RSW	(Member) Royal Scottish Society of Painters in Water Colours
Rt	Right
RTC	Royal Tank Corps
RTE	Radio Telefis Eireann
Rt Hon	Right Honourable
RTO	Railway Transport Officer
RTPI	Royal Town Planning Institute
RTR	Royal Tank Regiment
Rt Rev	Right Reverend
RTS	Royal Television Society
RUA	Royal Ulster Academy
RUC	Royal Ulster Constabulary
RUFC	Rugby Union Football Club
RUI	Royal University of Ireland
RUKBA	Royal United Kingdom Beneficent Association
RUR	Royal Ulster Regiment
RUSI	Royal United Services Institute for Defence Studies (formerly Royal United Services Institution)
RVC	Royal Veterinary College
RVO	Regional Veterinary Officer
RWAFF	Royal West African Frontier Force

RWAR	Royal West African Regiment
RWEA	(Member) Royal West of England Academy
RWF	Royal Welch Fusiliers
RWS	Royal Society of Painters in Water Colours
RYA	Royal Yachting Association
RYS	Royal Yacht Squadron
RZS	Royal Zoological Society

S

s	son
S	South; Scotland, Scottish (Peerages)
S4C	Sianel Pedwar Cymru (Channel 4 Wales)
SA	South Africa; South Australia; Société Anonyme; Sociedad Anónima
SAAF	South African Air Force
sac	Qualified at Small Arms Technical Long Course
SAC	Senior Aircraftsman; Scientific Advisory Committee
SACEUR	Supreme Allied Commander Europe
SACLANT	Supreme Allied Commander Atlantic
SACRO	Scottish Association for the Care and Resettlement of Offenders
SACSEA	Supreme Allied Commander, South East Asia
SADG	Société des Architectes Diplômés par le Gouvernement
Salop	Shropshire
SAS	Special Air Service
Sask	Saskatchewan
SASO	Senior Air Staff Officer
SAT	Senior Member Association of Accounting Technicians
SATRO	Science and Technology Regional Organisation
SBAC	Society of British Aircraft Constructors (now Society of British Aerospace Companies)
SBNO	Senior British Naval Officer
SBStJ	Serving Brother of the Order of St John of Jerusalem
SBTD	Society of British Theatre Designers
sc	Student at the Staff College
SC	Senior Counsel (Australia, Guyana, Ireland, South Africa); South Carolina
SCAR	Scientific Commission for Antarctic Research
ScD	Doctor of Science (Cambridge and Dublin)
SCF	Senior Chaplain to the Forces
SCGB	Ski Club of Great Britain
Sch	School
sci	science
SCI	Society of Chemical Industry
SCL	Student in Civil Law
SCM	State Certified Midwife
SCONUL	Standing Conference of National and University Libraries
Scot	Scotland; Scottish
SCR	Senior Common Room; Senior Combination Room (Cambridge)
SCUA	Scottish Conservative Unionist Association
SD	South Dakota
SDA	Scottish Diploma in Agriculture
SDLP	Social Democratic and Labour Party
SDP	Social Democratic Party
SE	South East
SEAC	South East Asia Command
SEATAG	South East Asia Trade Advisory Group
sec	secretary
Secdy	Secondary
sec-gen	secretary-general
Sen	Senator
SEN	State Enrolled Nurse
sep	separated
SERC	Science and Engineering Research Council (now EPSRC and PPARC)
SERT	Society of Electronic and Radio Technicians
Serv	Service
SFA	Securities and Futures Authority
SFInstE	Senior Fellow Institute of Energy
SFTA	Society of Film and Television Arts
SG	Solicitor-General
SGM	Sea Gallantry Medal
Sgt	Sergeant
SHA	Secondary Heads Association (now ASCL)
SHAEF	Supreme Headquarters, Allied Expeditionary Force
SHAPE	Supreme Headquarters, Allied Powers Europe
SHHD	Scottish Home and Health Department
SHMIS	The Society of Headmasters and Headmistresses of Independent Schools
SHO	Senior House Officer
SIAD	Society of Industrial Artists and Designers

SIB	Securities and Investments Board (now FSA)
SICOT	Société Internationale de Chirurgie Orthopédique et de Traumatologie
sis	sister
SJ	Society of Jesus (Jesuits)
SJD	Doctor of Juristic Science
SLAET	Society of Licensed Aircraft Engineers and Technologists
SLD	Social and Liberal Democrats
SLDP	Social, Liberal and Democratic Party
slr	solicitor
SM	Service Medal of the Order of Canada; Master of Science (USA); Member, Society of Miniaturists
SME	School of Military Engineering
SMIEEE	Senior Member, Institute of Electrical and Electronic Engineers (USA)
SMMT	Society of Motor Manufacturers and Traders
SMN	Seri Maharaja Mangku Negara (Malaysia)
SMO	Senior Medical Officer; Sovereign Military Order
SMOM	Sovereign Military Order of Malta
SNO	Senior Naval Officer
SNP	Scottish Nationalist Party
SNTS	Society for New Testament Studies
SO	Scottish Office; Staff Officer
SOAS	School of Oriental and African Studies
Soc	Society
SOE	Special Operations Executive
SOGAT	Society of Graphical and Allied Trades
SOLACE	Society of Local Authority Chief Executives
SOLT	Society of London Theatres (formerly SWET)
Som	Somerset
SOTS	Society for Old Testament Studies
Sov	Sovereign
sp	sine prole (without issue)
SPAB	Society for the Protection of Ancient Buildings
SPCK	Society for Promoting Christian Knowledge
SPG	Society for the Propagation of the Gospel
SPNM	Society for the Promotion of New Music
SPSO	Senior Personnel Staff Officer
SPTL	Society of Public Teaching of Law
SPUC	Society for the Protection of the Unborn Child
Sq	Square
Sqdn	Squadron
Sqdn Ldr	Squadron Leader
sr	senior
SR	Special Reserve; Southern Railway; Southern Region
SRC	Science Research Council
SRDE	Signals Research and Development Establishment
SRHE	Society for Research in Higher Education
SRN	State Registered Nurse
SRO	Supplementary Reserve of Officers
SRP	State Registered Physiotherapist
SRR	State Registered Radiographer
SSA	Society of Scottish Artists
SSAFA	Soldiers', Sailors', and Airmen's Families Association
SSC	Solicitor, Supreme Court (Scotland); Short Service Commission
SSEES	School of Slavonic and East European Studies
SSM	Self-Supporting Minister
SSMLL	Society for the Study of Modern Languages and Literature
SSO	Senior Supply Officer
SSRC	Social Science Research Council
SSStJ	Serving Sister of the Order of St John of Jerusalem
STA	Society of Technical Analysts
Staffs	Staffordshire
STC	Senior Training Corps
STD	Doctor of Sacred Theology
STFC	Science and Technology Facilities Council
STh	Scholar in Theology
STL	Licentiate of Sacred Theology
STM	Master of Sacred Theology
STSO	Senior Technical Staff Officer
Subalt	Subaltern
Subs	Submarines (RN)
subseq	subsequent; subsequently
subsid	subsidiary
suc	succeeded
SUNY	The State University of New York
sup	supérieure
supp	supplementary
Supt	Superintendent
surgn	surgeon
survg	surviving
SW	South West

SWA	Sports Writers' Association
SWB	South Wales Borderers
SWEB	South Western Electricity Board
SWET	Society of West End Theatres (now SOLT)

T

TA	Territorial Army
TAA	Territorial Army Association; Tropical Agriculture Association
TAF	Tactical Air Force
T&AFA	Territorial and Auxiliary Forces' Association
TANS	Territorial Army Nursing Service
TARO	Territorial Army Reserve of Officers
TAS	Torpedo and Anti-Submarine Course
Tas	Tasmania
T&AVR	Territorial and Army Volunteer Reserve
TAVRA	Territorial Auxiliary and Volunteer Reserve Association (now RFCA)
Tbnl	Tribunal
TC	Order of the Trinity Cross (Trinidad and Tobago)
TCCB	Test and County Cricket Board (now ECB)
TCD	Trinity College Dublin
TD	Territorial Officers' Decoration; Teachta Dala (member of the Dáil, Parliament of Ireland)
TEC	Training and Enterprise Council
tech	technical
technol	technology; technological
TEFL	Teaching English as a Foreign Language
TEM	Territorial Efficiency Medal
temp	temporary
temp	tempore (in the time of)
TEP	Member, Society of Trust and Estate Practitioners
TES	Times Educational Supplement
TF	Territorial Force
TfL	Transport for London
TGWU	Transport and General Workers' Union
ThD	Doctor of Theology
Theol	Theological
ThM	Master of Theology
ThSchol	Scholar of Theology
TLS	Times Literary Supplement
TMA	Theatre Managers' Association
TN	Tennessee
tport	transport
trans	translation; translated; translator
TRE	Telecommunications Research Establishment
treas	treasurer
Treasy	Treasury
trg	training
TRH	Their Royal Highnesses
TRIC	Television and Radio Industries' Club
Tst	Trust
tstee	trustee
TUC	Trades Union Congress
TUV	Traditional Unionist Voice
TV	Television
TVEI	Technical and Vocational Educational Initiative
TX	Texas

U

U	Unionist
UAE	United Arab Emirates
UAR	United Arab Republic
UAU	Universities' Athletic Union
UC	University College
UCAS	Universities and Colleges Admissions Service
UCATT	Union of Construction, Allied Trades and Technicians
UCCA	Universities' Central Council on Admissions
UCD	University College Dublin
UCE	University of Central England
UCH	University College Hospital (now UCHL)
UCHL	University College Hospital, London
UCL	University College London
UCLA	University of California at Los Angeles
UCNS	Universities' Council for Non-Academic Staff
UCNW	University College of North Wales
UCS	University College School
UCUNF	Ulster Conservatives and Unionists - New Force
UCW	University College of Wales

UDC	Urban District Council
UDF	Union Defence Force; Ulster Defence Force
UDR	Ulster Defence Regiment
UDS	United Drapery Stores
UDUP	Ulster Democratic Unionist Party
UEA	University of East Anglia
UFAW	Universities' Federation of Animal Welfare
UFC	Universities' Funding Council
UFO	Unidentified Flying Object
UGC	University Grants Committee
UHS	University High School
UK	United Kingdom
UKAEA	United Kingdom Atomic Energy Authority
UKCC	United Kingdom Central Council for Nurses, Midwives and Health Visitors
UKCCCR	United Kingdom Co-ordinating Committee on Cancer Research (now NCRI)
UKIP	United Kingdom Independence Party
UKLF	United Kingdom Land Forces
UKMIS	UK Mission
UKREP	United Kingdom Permanent Representation to the European Union
UMDS	United Medical and Dental Schools of Guy's and St Thomas' Hospitals (now GKT)
UMIST	University of Manchester Institute of Science and Technology
UN	United Nations
UNA	United Nations Association
unc	uncle
UNCTAD	United Nations Conference on Trade and Development
undergrad	undergraduate
UNDP	United Nations Development Programme
UNESCO	United Nations Educational, Scientific and Cultural Organisation
UNFAO	United Nations Food and Agricultural Organisation (now FAO)
UNHCR	United Nations High Commissioner for Refugees
UNHQ	United Nations Headquarters
UNIC	United Nations Information Centre
UNICE	Union des Industries de la Communauté Européenne
UNICEF	United Nations International Children's Emergency Fund (now United Nations Children's Fund)
UNIDO	United Nations Industrial Development Organisation
UNIDROIT	Institut International pour l'Unification du Droit Privé
UNIPEDE	Union Internationale des Producteurs et Distributeurs d'Énergie Électrique
Univ	University
UNO	United Nations Organisation
UNRRA	United Nations Relief and Rehabilitation Administration
UP	Uttar Pradesh; United Provinces; United Presbyterian
UPNI	Unionist Party of Northern Ireland
URSI	Union Radio-Scientifique Internationale
US	United States
USA	United States of America
USAF	United States Air Force
USDAW	Union of Shop, Distributive, and Allied Workers
USM	Unlisted Securities Market
USMC	United States Military College
USN	United States Navy
USNR	United States Naval Reserve
USPG	United Society for the Propagation of the Gospel
USSR	Union of Soviet Socialist Republics
UT	Utah
UTC	University Training Corps
UU	Ulster Unionist
UUK	Universities United Kingdom
UUP	Ulster Unionist Party
UWE	University of the West of England
UWIST	University of Wales Institute of Science and Technology

V

v	versus
V&A	Victoria and Albert (Museum)
VA	Lady of the Order of Victoria and Albert; Virginia
Va	Virginia
VAD	Voluntary Aid Detachment
VAT	Value Added Tax
VBF	Veterinary Benevolent Fund
VC	Victoria Cross
VCAS	Vice-Chief of the Air Staff
VCC	Vintage Car Club
VD	Volunteer Officers' Decoration (now VRD); Venereal Disease
VDC	Volunteer Defence Corps

Ven	Venerable
Very Rev	Very Reverend
vet	veterinary
VHF	Very High Frequency
Visc	Viscount
VM	Victory Medal
VMH	Victoria Medal of Honour (Royal Horticultural Society)
VO	Veterinary Officer
vol	volunteer; volume
VPRWS	Vice-President, Royal Society of Painters in Water Colours
VRD	Volunteer Reserve Officers Decoration
VSCC	Vintage Sports Car Club
VSO	Voluntary Service Overseas
VT	Vermont

W

w	wife
W	West
WA	Western Australia; Washington
WAAA	Women's Amateur Athletics Association
WAAF	Women's Auxiliary Air Force (later WRAF)
WACL	Women in Advertising and Communications London
Warks	Warwickshire
WBA	World Boxing Association
WBC	World Boxing Council
WBO	World Boxing Organisation
WEA	Workers' Educational Association
WEU	Western European Union
WFTU	World Federation of Trade Unions
WHO	World Health Organisation
WI	West Indies; Wisconsin; Women's Institute
wid	widow
Wilts	Wiltshire
WIPO	World Intellectual Property Organisation
WIS	Wales Information Society
Wm	William
WNO	Welsh National Opera
WNSM	Welsh National School of Medicine
WO	War Office
Worcs	Worcestershire
WRAC	Women's Royal Army Corps
WRAF	Women's Royal Air Force (formerly WAAF)
WRNR	Women's Royal Naval Reserve
WRNS	Women's Royal Naval Service
WRVS	Women's Royal Voluntary Service (formerly WVS)
w/s	war substantive
WS	Writer to the Signet
WV	West Virginia
WVS	Women's Voluntary Service
WWF	World Wide Fund for Nature (formerly World Wildlife Fund)
WWI	First World War
WWII	Second World War
WY	Wyoming

Y

YCs	Young Conservatives
Yeo	Yeomanry
YHA	Youth Hostels Association
YMCA	Young Men's Christian Association
YOI	Young Offenders Institution
Yorks	Yorkshire
yr	younger
yst	youngest
YTS	Youth Training Scheme
YWCA	Young Women's Christian Association

DEBRETT'S
LONDON 1769

PEOPLE OF TODAY
BIOGRAPHICAL ENTRIES

A

A

à BRASSARD, Nigel Courtenay; s of late Maj Herbert Forbes à Brassard, of Oxfordshire, and Elisabeth Kane, *née* McCue; *b* 7 June 1955, London; *Educ* Cheltenham Coll, KCL (BA), De Montfort Univ (MA); *m* 16 March 1996 (m dis 2015), Adèle, da of Dr and Mrs Herman Dexter Webster, of New Orleans, Louisiana; 2 s (Louis Forbes b 20 Dec 1996, William Claiborne b 5 Oct 1999), 1 da (Celeste Ninette b 22 Sept 2001); *Career* Samuel Montagu Co Ltd London 1977–86, seconded to Dominguez Barry Samuel Montagu Ltd Sydney 1984–85; md Dresdner Kleinwort Benson Ltd 1986–2001, dir Dresdner Kleinwort Benson Iberfomento SA, global head equity capital markets, head of M&A and head of corp fin Dresdner Kleinwort Benson North America 2001–, md Lenox Hill Investments Ltd 2001–; conslt London Bridge Capital 2007–08, chm and fndr Four Elements Capital Ltd 2008–, dir and fndr Clarendon Academies Ltd 2009–; ambass FIP (Int Polo Fedn), memb Fin Ctee Hurlingham Polo Assoc; *Publications* Modern Merchant Banking, SCP Guide for Issuers and Investors, A Glorious Victory – A Glorious Defeat, A Posthumous Life – Keats in Rome, Tommy Hitchcock – A Tribute, Profiles in Polo; *Recreations* polo, cricket, real tennis, stické tennis; *Clubs* Buck's, Hurlingham, Pilgrims, Cirencester Park Polo, MCC, Sydney Cricket Ground, Winchester House, Krewe d'Etat, Shuttlecock, Radley Coll Real Tennis, The Cook Soc, Hartham Park Stické Tennis; *Style*— Nigel à Brassard, Esq

AARONS, Elaine; da of Lionel Freedman, of Manchester, and Freda Freedman; *b* 7 February 1958, Manchester; *Educ* Manchester HS for Girls, KCL (LLB); *m* 28 June 1977, Dr Stephen Aarons; 2 da (Elizabeth Ruth b 12 Jan 1985, Abigail Rivka b 27 April 1991), 1 s (Robert Joshua b 24 April 1987); *Career* admitted slr 1982; slr specialising in employment law; asst slr Norton Rose 1980–89, ptnr Eversheds 1989–2006, princ Withers LLP 2006–; memb Editorial Bd Complinet HR; memb Mgmnt Ctee Employment Lawyers' Assoc 1992–2001 (sometime trg co-ordinator, chair Legislative and Policy Ctee and co sec), chair Employers Forum on Social Policy 1997–, vice-chair Employment Law Sub-Ctee London Law Soc 2003–; govr Hasmonean HS 2002–03, fndr N London Learning Prog for Girls 2003; *Publications* Tolleys Termination of Employment (gen ed); *Recreations* entertaining, charitable events; *Style*— Mrs Elaine Aarons

AARONSON, Graham Raphael; QC (1982); s of Jack Aaronson (d 1973), of London, and Dora, *née* Franks (d 2007); *b* 31 December 1944; *Educ* City of London Sch, Trinity Hall Cambridge (MA); *m* 1 (m dis 1992); 2 s (Oran b 1968, Avi b 1974), 1 da (Orit b 1970); m 2, 12 May 1993, Pearl Isobel, da of Harold Rose (d 2011), and Berta Rose (d 2001); 2 step s (Adam b 1976, Simon b 1986), 1 step da (Sara b 1978); *Career* called to the Bar Middle Temple 1966 (bencher 1991); md Worldwide Plastics Development Ltd 1973–77, fndr Standford Grange Rehabilitation Centre for Ex-Offenders, advsr on taxation Treasy Israel 1986–92; chm: Tax Law Review Ctee 1994–98, Revenue Bar Assoc 1995–98, Dietary Res Fndn 1989–91; ldr UK Treasy GAAR Study 2011; *Style*— Graham Aaronson, Esq, QC; ✉ Joseph Hage Aaronson LLP, 280 High Holborn, London WC1V 7EE (☎ 020 7851 8888, website www.jha.com)

AARONSON, Sir Michael John (Mike); kt (2006), CBE (2000); s of late Edward John (Jack) Aaronson, of Bishops Cannings, Wilts, and late Marian, *née* Davies; *b* 8 September 1947; *Educ* Merchant Taylors' Sch Northwood, St John's Coll Oxford (Sir Thomas White scholar, Trevelyan scholar, MA); *m* 27 Aug 1988, Andrene Margaret Dundas, da of late John Sutherland; 1 da (Katherine Sara Dundas b 22 Feb 1989), 2 s (Benedict Lodwick MacGregor b 24 Aug 1991, Nathanael Aeron Sutherland b 10 Feb 1994); *Career* field co-ordinator Nigeria Save the Children Fund 1969–71; HM Dip Serv 1972–88: third, second and first sec Paris 1973–77, Lagos 1981–83, Rangoon 1987–88; Save the Children Fund: overseas dir 1988–95, DG 1995–2005; dir Oxford Policy Mgmnt Ltd 2006–; UK rep EC NGO Liaison Ctee 1994–2000, pres EC NGO Liaison Ctee 1998–2000; govr Westminster Fndn for Democracy 2001–07 (vice-chair 2006–07), chair Centre for Humanitarian Dialogue Geneva 2001–08; visiting fell Nuffield Coll Oxford 2004–12 (hon fell 2012–), hon visiting prof Univ of Surrey 2008–11 and 2015–, professorial research fell 2011–15; Civil Serv cmmr 2007–12, sr advsr NATO 2006–12; chm Frimley Health NHS Fndn Tst (formerly Frimley Park Hosp NHS Fndn Tst) 2006–16; non-exec dir Nat Sch of Govt Int (NSGI) 2012–15, chair RCUK Strategic Advsy Gp Global Challenge Research Fund 2016–; Freeman: City of London, Worshipful Co of Merchant Taylors; Hon DUniv Surrey 2011; FRSA; *Books* Precision Strike Warfare and International Intervention (ed, with Wali Aslam, Tom Dyson and Regina Rauxloh, 2015); *Recreations* sports, the performing arts; *Clubs* MCC; *Style*— Sir Michael Aaronson, CBE; ✉ e-mail aaronson@hiboulimited.co.uk

AARONSON, Robin Hugh; s of Edward John (Jack) Aaronson, of Bishop's Cannings, Wilts, and Marian, *née* Davies; *b* 7 July 1951; *Educ* Merchant Taylors', Balliol Coll Oxford (MA, OU Prize for Comparative Philology, pres Dramatic Soc), LSE (MSc, Eli Devons Prize for Economics), Metanoia Inst (BA); *m* 1 (m dis), Janet Charmian Christabel, da of Joseph Evans; m 2, Veronica Fay, da of Ronald Feltham; 1 s (Matthew John), 3 step c; *Career* admin trainee MOD 1974–80 (on secondment to LSE 1978–80), economic advsr HM Treasy 1980–86 (speechwriter to Chancellor of the Exchequer, advsr on economic effects of tax changes), sr economic advsr Monopolies and Mergers Cmmn 1986–89 (advsr on numerous investigations); PricewaterhouseCoopers (formerly Coopers & Lybrand before merger): joined as mangr 1989, ptnr responsible for competition policy advice servs 1993–98; dir: LECG Ltd 1998–2009, Akousis Counselling Ltd 2003–, Forest of Dreams Ltd 2007–; visiting lectr on Euro competition policy Centre des Études Européennes Strasbourg 1994–97, specialist advsr House of Commons Trade and Industry Ctee 1991; memb Bd Countrywide Workshops Charitable Tst 1998–2001; memb PO Users Nat Cncl 1998–2000, memb Postal Services Cmmn 2000–06, memb Competition and Markets Authy (formerly Competition Cmmn) 2009–; *Recreations* mountains, photography, gardening; *Style*— Robin Aaronson, Esq; ✉ Akousis, 1 Fairlawn Road, Bristol BS6 5JR (☎ 0117 924 7154, e-mail robin@akousis.co.uk or grandvizier51@gmail.com)

ABBESS, Lynne Margaret; da of Lawrence Peter Abbess (d 2003), and Margaret Thelma, *née* Scott (d 1986); *b* 1956, Kent; *Educ* Newstead Wood Sch for Girls, Kingston Univ (LLB), Coll of Law Guildford; *Career* admitted slr 1982; Hempsons Slrs: articled clerk 1980, ptnr 1985–; fndr and creator LandlordAssurance.com; memb: Law Soc 1982, Assoc of Partnership Practitioners (former hon sec); jt chair Primary Care Premises Forum, memb Lloyds Bank Healthcare Forum; *Publications* The Law and General Practice: Partnership Agreements (contrib), Making Sense of Partnerships: When Partners Fall Out – Legal Remedies (contrib), A Practitioner's Guide to Partnership and LLP Law and Regulation (contrib), Primary Healthcare Premises: An Expert Guide (co-ed); regular columnist GP and Medeconomics; *Style*— Miss Lynne Abbess; ✉ e-mail lmabbess@icloud.com; Hempsons, Hempsons House, 40 Villiers Street, London WC2N 6NJ (☎ 020 7484 7626, e-mail l.abbess@hempsons.co.uk)

ABBISS, Jim; *Career* music prodr; albums incl: Kasabian (Kasabian) 2004, The Back Room (Editors) 2005, Whatever People Say I Am, That's What I'm Not (Arctic Monkeys) 2006 (UK no 1, Mercury Music Prize 2006), Empire (Kasabian) 2006 (UK no 1), 19 (Adele) 2008 (UK no 1), Tiger Suit (KT Tunstall) 2010, 21 (Adele) 2011 (UK no 1, US no 1); *Style*— Jim Abbiss, Esq

ABBOTT, Diane Julie; MP; *b* 27 September 1953; *Educ* Harrow County Girls' GS, Newnham Coll Cambridge; *Children* 1 s (James Alexander Abbott-Thompson b 21 Oct 1991); *Career* successively: admin trainee Home Office, race relations offr NCCL, researcher Thames TV, reporter TV-am, equality offr ACTT, press and PR offr GLC, princ press offr Lambeth BC; MP (Lab) Hackney North and Stoke Newington 1987–, shadow min for int devpt 2015–16, shadow sec of state for health 2016, shadow home sec 2016–; memb: Treasy Select Ctee 1989–97, Foreign Affrs Select Ctee 1997–2001; joined Lab Pty 1971, memb Lab Pty Nat Exec, sec Campaign Gp of Lab MPs 1992–; memb Westminster City Cncl 1982–86; *Style*— Ms Diane Abbott, MP; ✉ House of Commons, London SW1A 0AA (☎ 020 7219 4426, fax 020 7219 4964)

ABBOTT, Stephen (Steve); s of Wilfrid Lockley Abbott (d 2006), of Bradford, W Yorks, and Lily Templeton, *née* Limbert; *b* 28 July 1954, Bradford, Yorks; *Educ* Bradford GS, CCC Cambridge (MA); *m* 1992 (m dis 1998), Karen Lesley Lewis; 1 da (Francesca b 1986), 1 s (James Alexander b 1989); *Career* film and television producer; Price Waterhouse London 1976–79, Hand Made Films London 1979–81, Mayday Management Ltd 1981–, chm Prominent Features Ltd 1989– (md 1986–89), dir Prominent Television 1992– (exec prodr Himalaya 2004, New Europe 2007, Around the World in 20 Years 2008 and Brazil 2012 (all with Michael Palin)); dir Nat Film Tstee Co Ltd 2002–06; chair Screen Yorkshire 2002–, tstee Training and Performance Showcase 2001–06, chair Bradford City of Film 2007–; ambass to City of Bradford 1997; hon treas Belsize Square Synagogue 2012–13; hon fell Bradford Coll 2012; memb: AMPAS, BAFTA, EFA (Euro Film Acad), RTS; Hon DLitt Univ of Bradford 1998; FCA 1990 (ACA 1979), FRSA 1999; *Films* exec prodr: A Fish Called Wanda 1988, Fierce Creatures 1995 (released 1997); prodr: American Friends 1990, Blame It On the Bellboy 1991, Brassed Off 1996; *Recreations* Bradford City AFC; *Clubs* Hospital, Quo Vadis; *Style*— Steve Abbott, Esq; ✉ Prominent Television Ltd, 34 Tavistock Street, London WC2E 7PB (☎ 020 7497 1100)

ABBOTT-WATT, Thorhilda Mary Vivia (Thorda); da of Samuel Abbott-Watt, and Elva Mary, *née* Clare Gibson; *b* 11 February 1955, London; *Educ* Stonar Sch, Atworth; *Partner* Reef Talbot Hogg; *Career* joined HM Dip Serv 1974, third sec FCO 1974–79, temporary duty tours Latin America and Far and Middle East 1979–80, vice-consul Paris 1981–84, third sec (Chancery) UK Representation to EU 1984–86, second sec FCO 1986–88, second sec Bonn 1988–81, first sec EU and Western Europe Depts FCO 1991–95, first sec and head Commercial Section Kiev 1995–98, first sec Belgrade 1998–99, first sec and head Visa Policy Section Jt Entry Clearance Unit 1999–2001, chargee d'affaires Dushanbe 2001–02, ambass to Armenia 2003–06, FCO 2006, head political/mil section Kabul 2006, FCO 2007–08, chargee d'affaires Ulaanbaatar 2008, ambass to Mongolia 2008–09, Finance Directorate FCO 2009–10, int liaison MOD 2010–11, ambass to Mongolia 2011–12, dep then head Projects Task Force FCO 2013–15, ambass to Turkmenistan 2016–; *Recreations* riding, reading, theatre; *Clubs* Art Fund (life memb); *Style*— Miss Thorda Abbott-Watt; ✉ c/o Foreign & Commonwealth Office, King Charles Street, London SW1A 2AH

ABBS, Prof Peter Francis; s of Eric Charles Abbs (d 1987), and Mary Bertha, *née* Bullock (d 1994); *b* 22 February 1942; *Educ* Norwich Tech Coll, Univ of Bristol (BA), Univ of Sussex (PhD); *m* (m dis 2002) Barbara Ann, da of Jack Beazeley; 2 da (Annabel b 20 Oct 1964, Miranda b 22 July 1966), 1 s (Theodore b 29 March 1973); *Career* English teacher Bristol 1966–70, res asst Univ of Wales 1970–76; Univ of Sussex: reader in educn 1976–, prof of creative writing 1999–; has lectured widely in USA, Aust, India, Denmark, Ireland, Belgium and elsewhere; memb: Soc of Authors, Assoc of Univ Teachers; fndr memb New Metaphysical Art 1996; fell English Assoc; *Poetry* For Man and Islands, Songs of a New Taliesin, Icons of Time, Personae, Angelic Imagination, Love After Sappho, Earth Songs, Selected Poems, Viva la Vida, Flowering of Flint: Selected Poems, Voyaging Out, The Greater Journey; *Non-Fiction* English For Diversity, Root and Blossom: The Philosophy, Practice and Politics of English Teaching, English Within the Arts, The Forms of Poetry, The Forms of Narrative, Autobiography in Education, Proposal for a New College (with Graham Carey), Reclamations Essays on Culture, Mass-Culture and the Curriculum, A is for Aesthetic: Essays on Creative and Aesthetic Education, The Educational Imperative, The Polemics of Imagination: Selected Essays on Art, Culture and Society; ed: The Black Rainbow: Essays on the Present Breakdown of Culture, Living Powers: The Arts in Education, The Symbolic Order: A Contemporary Reader on the Arts Debate, Against the Flow: The Arts, Postmodern Culture and Education; *Recreations* swimming, walking, film, music; *Style*— Prof Peter Abbs; ✉ English Department, Arts Building B, University of Sussex, Falmer, Brighton BN1 9QN (☎ 01273 872597, fax 01273 625972, e-mail p.f.abbs@sussex.ac.uk, website www.peterabbs.net)

ABDELA, Lesley Julia; MBE (1990); da of Frederick Abdela (d 1985), and Henrietta, *née* Hardy (d 1959); *b* 17 November 1945; *Educ* Glendower London, Queen Anne's Caversham, Châtelard Sch Les Avants Switzerland, Queen's Coll Harley St, Hammersmith Coll of Art, London Coll of Printing; *m* 1972 (m dis); 1 s (Nicholas b 1973); *Career* int conslt on equal opportunities and trainer in democratic skills (primary clients EU, UNDP, Br Cncl, Harvard, DfID, FCO), feature writer, author, TV and radio bdcaster on politics; formerly advtg exec Royds London, researcher House of Commons and House of Lords 1976–77, Parly candidate (Lib) Herts E 1979, fndr All-Party 300 Gp for Women in Politics 1980, USA Leader Grant visiting Washington DC, LA and Seattle 1983, studied Third World by residence in the Gambia 1984–86, currently sr ptnr Eyecatcher Associates (journalism, copywriting, research, conference speakers) and sr ptnr Shevolution; conslt on women and politics in East and Central Europe Project Liberty Kennedy Sch of Government Harvard Univ 1992–98, political ed Cosmopolitan 1993–96, accredited journalist UN 4th World Conf on Women Beijing 1995, chief exec Project Parity 1996–, dep dir for democratisation for OSCE Mission in Kosovo 1999–2000; vice-pres Electoral Reform Soc 1995–; memb: Bd International Inst for Environment and Devpt 1992–96, Bd of Govrs Westminster Fndn for Democracy 1996–97, Bd of Govrs Br Cncl; experience of gender issues in post-conflict reconstruction and peace-building ops in Aceh, Iraq, Afghanistan, Sierra Leone and Kosovo, conducts bi-annual workshops on implementation of UN Security Cncl Resolution 1325 (mainstreaming gender into peace ops and civil military cooperation) Swedish Armed Forces Int Centre, ldr workshops for NATO sr civil servants on gender and culture in Afghanistan NATO HQ Brussels 2006 and 2007, sr gender advsr to UN OCHA Chief Humanitarian Coordinator Kathmandu 2007–08, a princ speaker NATO Conf – Women in Armed Conflicts – The Implementation of UN Security Cncl Resolution 1325 Vienna 2008, plenary speaker SOLON War Crimes Conf Inst for Advanced Legal Studies Univ of London 2009; govr Nottingham Trent Univ 1997–2000; appeared on Great Lives (BBC Radio 4) 2008 (discussing Millicent Fawcett); winner EC's UK Woman of Europe Award (for servs to EU) 1995, listed thirty-fourth in New Statesman's Top 50 Heroes of Our Time 2006, Woman Political Journalist of the Year Dods & Scottish Widows Women In Public Life Award 2009; Hon DLitt Nottingham Trent Univ 1996; FRGS, FRSA 1991; *Books* Women with X Appeal (1989), Breaking Through The Glass Ceilings (Met Authys Recruitment Agency guide, 1991), What Women Want, 1993–2000 (ed, 1993), DO IT! – Walk the Talk (1994); *Recreations* travel, painting; *Style*— Ms Lesley Abdela, MBE; ✉ e-mail lesley.abdela@shevolution.com

ABDU'ALLAH, Faisal; *b* 5 August 1969, London; *Educ* Central St Martins Coll (BA), Massachusetts Coll of Art, RCA (MA); *Career* artist; sr lectr Univ of East London, visiting lectr RCA; Serpentine Gallery artist-in-residence at N Westminster Community Sch; Individual Artist Award London Arts Board 1995; *Solo Exhibitions* Censored, Nigger to Nubian (198 Gallery London) 1993, Revelations (Bonnington Gallery Nottingham and 198 Gallery London) 1995, Heads of State (Margaret Harvey Gallery Herts, Standpoint Gallery London and Middlesbrough Art Gallery) 1997–98, The Collection (The Agency Contemporary Art London) 2000, The Agency Contemporary Art London 2000, 2001, 2002 and 2004, Horniman Museum London 2001, Chisenhale Gallery London 2002; *Group Exhibitions* African Themes (V&A) 1993, Borderless Print (Rochdale Art Gallery) 1993, Presences (Photographers' Gallery London) 1993, Us An' Dem (Storey Inst Lancs and Art '94 London) 1994, Different Stories (Netherlands Photo Inst Rotterdam) 1994, Make Believe (RCA) 1995, The Impossible Science of Being (Photographers' Gallery London, Leeds Museum Gallery and Brighton Museum) 1996, Radical Images (Neue Galerie Austria and Szombatheley Art Gallery Hungary) 1996, The 90's: Family of Man (Forum de l'Art Contemporain Luxembourg) 1997–98, On the Bright Side of Life (NGBK Berlin) 1997–98, Transforming the Crown (Studio Museum Harlem NYC) 1997–98, Out of the Blue (MOMA Glasgow) 1997–99, In Visible Light (MOMA Oxford and tour) 1997–99, They don't know me but, (De la Warr Pavillion Brighton, Winchester Art Gallery and Pitshanger Manor London) 1998, LKW (OK Centre for Contemporary Art Linz) 1999, Basel Liste 99 1999, Holland Festival Rotterdam 1999, Missing Link (Kunstmuseum Bern) 1999, Hackney Empire Benefit Auction London 1999, film screening London 1999, Project X (S London Gallery) 1999, Cologne Artfair (The Agency Cologne) 1999 and 2000, Warningshots (Royal Armouries Leeds) 2000, Tirannicidi (Calcografia Nat Gallery Rome and Archivio de Stato Turin) 2000, LKW (Kunstverein Bregenz) 2000, Ecce Homo (Kunsthal Rotterdam) 2000, Aesthetic Terrorism (The Agency Contemporary Art London) 2001, ARCO Artfair Madrid 2001, Nat Maritime Museum London 2001, BIG Torino Biennial Turin 2002, Sharjah International Biennale (UAE) 2003, Aspex Gallery Portsmouth (with David Adjaye) 2003, Independence (South London Gallery) 2003, The Veil (touring exhbn, venues incl Stockholm and Modern Art Oxford) 2003–04, Britannia Works Athens 2004; *Style*— Faisal Abdu'Allah, Esq

ABEL SMITH, David Francis; s of Sir Alexander Abel Smith, KCVO, TD, JP (d 1980), of Quenington Old Rectory, Cirencester, Glos, and Elizabeth, *née* Morgan (d 1948); *b* 3 February 1940; *Educ* Gordonstoun, Stockton and Billingham Tech Coll; *m* 18 Nov 1982, Lucy Marie, da of Col Sir Bryce Muir Knox, KCVO, MC, TD (former Lord Lt of Ayr and Arran); 1 da (Eliza Violet Daria b 15 March 1991); *Career* exec dir The Delta Group plc 1974–82 (joined 1961), md Benjamin Priest Group plc 1983–91, chief exec Marling Industries plc 1992–97; exec chm Majorlift Hldgs Ltd 2003–, Zimbabwe Agricultural Tst 2006–12; non-exec chm: Equitalk Ltd 1999–2006, VectorCommand Ltd 2000–03, Permali Gloucester Ltd 2001–10, Brandauer Holdings Ltd 2001–05, Mosandam Ltd 2004–06; non-exec dir Metalwash Ltd 2000–04; chm: The Cotswold Arcadians 1998–2001, Cobalt Appeal Fund 2008–14; collector, cmmr and promoter of contemporary applied arts incl glass, ceramics and furniture, co-fndr and tstee Quenington Sculpture Tst 1998–; memb Quenington Parish Cncl 1987–93; Freeman City of London, memb Worshipful Co of Fishmongers; *Recreations* country sports; *Clubs* Pratt's, The Pilgrims; *Style*— David Abel Smith, Esq; ✉ Quenington Old Rectory, Cirencester, Gloucestershire GL7 5BN

ABELL, Prof Christopher (Chris); *b* 11 November 1957; *Educ* St John's Coll Cambridge; *m* 1981, Katherine; 1 s (Daniel Jonathan b 1989); *Career* SERC overseas postdoctoral fell Brown Univ RI 1982–83, research fell King's Coll Cambridge 1983–86; Dept of Chemistry Univ of Cambridge: demonstrator 1984–88, lectr 1988–99, reader in chemical biology 1999–2002, prof of biological chemistry 2002–, dir of postdoctoral affrs 2013–15; pro-vice-chllr for research Univ of Cambridge 2016–; Todd Hamied fell Christ's Coll Cambridge; Iberdrola visiting prof Santiago de Compostela Spain 1999–2000, Erskine fell Univ of Canterbury Christchurch NZ 2000, David P Craig visiting prof ANU Canberra 2003, visiting prof Université Paul Sabatier Toulouse 2008–09, BIC int fell Univ of Canterbury Christchurch NZ 2011; author of over 275 scientific papers; fndr: Astex Therapeutics 1999, Akubio 2002, Sphere Fluidics 2010, Aqdot 2013; Hickenbottom Award 1991–92, ICI Prize in Organic Chemistry 1992; FMedSci 2012, FRSC 2015; *Recreations* running; *Style*— Prof Chris Abell; ✉ Department of Chemistry, University Chemical Laboratory, Lensfield Road, Cambridge CB2 1EW (website http://www-abell.ch.cam.ac.uk)

ABELL, (John) David; s of Leonard Abell, and Irene Craig, *née* Anderson; *b* 15 December 1942; *Educ* Univ of Leeds (BA), LSE (Dip Business Admin); *m* 1, 1967 (m dis), Anne Janette, *née* Priestley; 3 s; m 2, 1981 (m dis), Sandra Dawn, *née* Atkinson; 1 s, 1 da; m 3, 1988, Juliana, da of late Prof John Lister Illingworth Fennell, of Oxford; *Career* Ford Motor Co 1962–65, AEI 1965–67, various appts British Leyland 1968–72 and 1974–81 (incl md Trucks and Buses and dir), First National Finance Corp 1972–73, chm and chief exec Suter plc 1981–96, exec chm Jourdan plc 1997–; CIMgt; *Recreations* Rugby Union (dir, Leicester Tigers), racing (flat and nat hunt); *Clubs* Leicester Tigers (dir); *Style*— J David Abell, Esq; ✉ The Old Rectory, Branston-by-Belvoir, Grantham, Lincolnshire NG32 1RU

ABERCORN, 5 Duke of (I 1868); Sir James Hamilton; 15 Bt (I 1660), KG (1999); also Lord Paisley (S 1578), Lord Abercorn (S 1603), Earl of Abercorn and Lord Paisley, Hamilton, Mountcastell, and Kilpatrick (S 1606), Baron of Strabane (I 1617), Baron Mountcastle and Viscount Strabane (I 1701), Viscount Hamilton (GB 1785), Marquess of Abercorn (GB 1790 – title in House of Lords), and Marquess of Hamilton (I 1868); s of 4 Duke of Abercorn (d 1979), and Lady Kathleen Mary, GCVO, *née* Crichton (d 1990), sis of 5 Earl of Erne; *b* 4 July 1934; *Educ* Eton, RAC Cirencester; *m* 1966, Alexandra Anastasia, da of Lt-Col Harold Pedro Phillips (d 1980), of Checkendon Court, Berks, also sis of Duchess of Westminster and gda through her m, Georgina, of late Sir Harold Wernher, 3 Bt, GCVO, TD, DL, by his w, late Lady Zia, CBE, *née* Countess Anastasia Mikhailovna (er da of HIH Grand Duke Mikhail Mikhailovitch of Russia, himself gs of Tsar Nicholas I); 2 s (James, Marquess of Hamilton b 1969, Lord Nicholas b 1979), 1 da (Lady Sophia b 1973); *Heir* s, Marquess of Hamilton; *Career* 2 Lt Grenadier Gds; MP (UUP) Fermanagh and S Tyrone 1964–70; dir Local Enterprise Devpt Unit 1971–77; chm Laganside Devpt Corp 1989–96, dir Northern Bank Ltd 1970–97; pres: RUKBA 1979–2013, Building Socs Assoc 1986–92, NI Concrete Soc 1991–, NI Business in the Community 1992–; dir: NI Industrial Devpt Bd 1982–87, Inter Trade Ireland 1993–2003, Nat Gallery of Ireland 2003–07; memb: Cncl of Europe 1968–70, Economic and Social Ctee EEC 1973–78; tstee: Winston Churchill Meml Tst 1991–2002, Omagh Fund 1998–2003; patron Royal Ulster Agric Soc 1990–95; chllr Order of the Garter 2013–; High Sheriff Co Tyrone 1970, HM Lord-Lt Co Tyrone 1987–2009; Lord Steward of HM's Household 2001–09; Col Irish Gds 2000–08; Hon LLB Queen's Univ Belfast 1997; *Recreations* shooting; *Clubs* Brooks's; *Style*— His Grace the Duke of Abercorn; ✉ Barons Court, Omagh, Co Tyrone BT78 4EZ (☎ 028 816 61470, e-mail duke.baronscourt@talk21.com); Barons Court Estate Office, Omagh, Co Tyrone BT78 4EZ (☎ 028 8166 1683, fax 028 8166 2231)

ABERCROMBIE, Sheriff Principal Ian Ralph; QC (Scot 1994); s of Ralph Abercrombie (d 2002), and Jean Hamilton Brown Lithgow (d 1992); *b* 7 July 1955; *Educ* Milton HS Bulawayo, Univ of Edinburgh (LLB); *Career* admitted to Faculty of Advocates 1981; Sheriff of Grampian Highlands & Islands at Inverness 2009–12, Sheriff of Tayside, Central & Fife at Dunfermline 2012–14, Sheriff Principal South Strathclyde Dumfries & Galloway 2015; *Style*— Sheriff Principal I R Abercrombie, QC; ✉ Sheriff Principals' Chambers, Airdrie Sheriff Court, Graham Street, Airdrie

ABERCROMBIE, Prof Nicholas; s of Michael Abercrombie (d 1978), and Jane Abercrombie (d 1984); *b* 13 April 1944; *Educ* UCS, The Queen's Coll Oxford (BA), LSE (MSc), Lancaster Univ (PhD); *m* 1969, Brenda, da of Harry Patterson; 2 s (Robert b 1971, Joseph b 1974); *Career* hon research asst UCL 1968–70; Lancaster Univ: lectr in sociology 1970–83, sr lectr 1983–88, reader 1988–90, prof of sociology 1990–, dean of undergraduate studies 1992–95, pro-vice-chllr 1995–98, dep vice-chllr 1998–2004; memb British Sociological Soc 1968; FRSA 1999; *Books* incl: The Dominant Ideology Thesis (with S Hill and B Turner, 1980), The Penguin Dictionary of Sociology (with S Hill and B Turner, 1984, 4 edn 2000), Sovereign Individuals of Capitalism (with S Hill and B Turner, 1986), Contemporary British Society (jtly, 1988, 3 edn 2000), Television and Society (1996), Audiences (with B Longhurst, 1998), Sociology (2004); also author of numerous articles in learned jls; *Recreations* gardening, walking; *Style*— Prof Nicholas Abercrombie; ✉ 12 Mount Road, Lansdown, Bath BA1 5PW (☎ 01225 471241, e-mail nick.abercrombie@btinternet.com)

ABERDARE, 5 Baron (UK 1873); Alastair John Lyndhurst Bruce; DL (Dyfed, 2009); s of 4 Baron Aberdare, KBE, PC, DL (d 2005); *b* 2 May 1947, London; *Educ* Eton, ChCh Oxford; *m* 1971, Elizabeth Mary Culbert, da of John F Foulkes; 1 s, 1 da; *Heir* s, Hon Hector Bruce; *Career* IBM UK Ltd 1969–91; ptnr Bruce Naughton Wade Public Affairs Mgmnt Conslts 1991–99; dir: ProbusBNW Ltd Corporate Reputation Conslts 1999–2009, TWIST Partnership 2007–12, WALTZ Progs Ltd 2009–13; elected memb House of Lords 2009; tstee: Nat Botanical Garden of Wales 1994–2006, St John Cymru Wales 2008–, Nat Library of Wales 2012–; chm Berlioz Soc 2014– (tstee 2008–); hon fell Univ of Cardiff 2008; FRSA, FRGS; *Books* The Musical Madhouse (2003), Berlioz: Scenes from the Life and Work (contrib, 2008); *Recreations* music (especially Berlioz), Wales, crosswords; *Clubs* MCC; *Style*— The Rt Hon the Lord Aberdare, DL; ✉ 16 Beverley Road, London SW13 0LX

ABERDEEN AND TEMAIR, 7 Marquess of (UK 1915); Alexander George Gordon; DL (Aberdeenshire 1998); s of 6 Marquess of Aberdeen and Temair (d 2002); *b* 31 March 1955; *Educ* Harrow, Poly of Central London (Dip Bldg Econs); *m* 30 May 1981, Joanna Clodagh, da of late Maj Ian George Henry Houldsworth, of Forres, Moray; 3 s (George Ian Alastair, Earl of Haddo b 4 May 1983, Lord Sam Dudley b 25 Oct 1985, Lord Charles David b 8 June 1990), 1 da (Lady Anna Katharine b 2 Sept 1988); *Heir* s, Earl of Haddo; *Career* London & Edinburgh Trust plc 1986–94, chm Kellie Estates Ltd 1995–2008, dir Gordon Enterprise Tst Ltd 1998–2002, chm Gordon Land Ltd 2000–, chm Braiklay Estates Ltd 2006–; landowner (7,000 acres); ARICS 1979–96; *Recreations* sport, music, art; *Clubs* MCC, Royal Aberdeen Golf, Meldrum House Golf, New (Edinburgh); *Style*— The Most Hon the Marquess of Aberdeen and Temair, DL; ✉ House of Formartine, Methlick, Ellon, Aberdeenshire AB41 7EQ; Estate Office, Mains of Haddo, Tarves, Aberdeenshire (☎ 01651 851664)

ABERNETHY, Rt Hon Lord; (John) Alastair Cameron; PC (2005); s of William Philip Legerwood Cameron (d 1977), and Kathleen Milthorpe, *née* Parker (d 1966); *b* 1 February 1938; *Educ* Clergy House Sch Khartoum, St Mary's Sch Melrose, Glenalmond Coll Perth, Pembroke Coll Oxford (MA); *m* 1968, Elspeth Mary Dunlop, da of James Bowie Miller (d 1994), of E Lothian; 3 s (Hamish b 1970, Neil b 1972, Iain b 1975); *Career* Nat Serv 2 Lt RASC Aldershot & Malta 1956–58; called to the Bar Inner Temple 1963, advocate 1966, advocate depute 1972–75, vice-dean Faculty of Advocates 1983–92; standing jr counsel to: Dept of Energy 1976–79, Scot Devpt Dept 1978–79; QC Scotland 1979; pres Pensions Appeal Tbnls for Scotland 1985–92 (legal chm 1979–85), chm Faculty Services Ltd 1983–89 (dir 1979–89), cmmr NI (Remission of Sentences) Act 1995 2008–; Lord of Session (Senator of the College of Justice) 1992–2007, Justice of Appeal Botswana 2009–, Judge of Interim Independent Constitutional Dispute Resolution Court Kenya 2010; Int Bar Assoc: chm Judges' Forum 1994–98 (vice-chm 1993–94), memb Cncl Section on Legal Practice 1998–2002, memb Cncl Human Rights Inst 1998–2000 and 2002–05; pres The Scottish Medico-Legal Soc 1996–2000, memb Int Legal Assistance Consortium 2002–, tstee Southern African Litigation Centre 2008–15; memb Exec Ctee Soc for the Welfare and Teaching of the Blind (Edinburgh and SE Scotland) 1979–92; chm Arthur Smith Meml Tst 1990–2001 (tstee 1975–2001), tstee Faculty of Advocates 1985 Charitable Tst 1985–; govr Sr Mary's Sch Melrose 1998–2012 (vice-chm 2004–12); hon fell Pembroke Coll Oxford 1993–; *Publications* Medical Negligence: An Introduction (1983), contrib to Reproductive Medicine and the Law (ed A A Templeton and D J Cusine, 1990); *Recreations* travel, Africana, nature conservation; *Clubs* New (Edinburgh); *Style*— The Rt Hon Lord Abernethy; ✉ 4 Garscube Terrace, Edinburgh EH12 6BQ (☎ 0131 337 3460, fax 0131 240 6711)

ABINGDON, Earl of; *see:* Lindsey and Abingdon, Earl of

ABINGER, 9 Baron (UK 1835); James Harry Scarlett; s of 8 Baron (d 2002); *b* 28 May 1959, London; *Educ* Univ of Aberdeen (BSc), Univ of Cambridge (MPhil); *m* 15 Aug 1995, Tracy Lee, *née* Cloutier; 1 s (Hon Louis William Shelley b 1 Nov 2000 (twin)), 1 da (Xanthe Ryoko Cloutier b 1 Nov 2000 (twin)); *Heir* Hon Louis Scarlett; *Career* author; fndr A-Music 2005; rep Audio Network in Europe; FRGS, FLS; *Recreations* playing cello in the Soissons Symphony Orch; *Clubs* MCC; *Style*— The Rt Hon the Lord Abinger; ✉ e-mail contact@a-music.fr, website www.a-music.fr

ABLE, Graham George; s of George Jasper Able, and Irene Helen, *née* Gaff; *b* 28 July 1947; *Educ* Worksop Coll, Trinity Coll Cambridge (MA, PGCE), Univ of Durham (MA); *m* Mary Susan, da of John Sidney Thomas Munro; 1 s (Richard Graham Munro b 10 May 1973), 1 da (Lisa Maria b 17 June 1976); *Career* Sutton Valence Sch: teacher of chemistry 1969–83, cricket master 1971–76 and 1980–83, hockey master 1972–83, boarding housemaster 1976–83; second master Barnard Castle Sch 1983–88, headmaster Hampton Sch 1988–96, master Dulwich Coll 1997–2009; ceo Alpha Plus Gp 2009–14 (dep chm 2014–); fndr memb Kent Schs Sports Cncl 1976–83; chm of Conf Ctee BSA Housemasters' and Housemistresses' Conf 1980 and 1981; HMC: memb 1988–, chm 2003, memb Sports Sub-Ctee 1989–91, memb Assisted Places Working Pty 1991–96, chm London Div 1993–94, chm Acad Policy Ctee 1998–2001 (memb 1995–2001); memb: Assisted Places Ctee

ISJC 1991–96, Assoc for Science Educn 1968–88, SHA 1988–2009, Cncl Imperial Coll 1999–2006, Fin Ctee EDEXCEL 1998–2003, Ct of Imperial Coll London 1998–2006, Cncl of Roedean 2000–09; pres Int Boys Schs Coalition 2006–09; sr vice-pres (educn) Dulwich Coll Mgmnt Int Ltd 2009–, chm ExEd UK 2013–; govr: Beeston Hall Sch 2012–, Gresham's Sch 2013–; MInstD, FRSA 1994; *Recreations* cricket and golf, sailing, contract bridge, the theatre; *Clubs* East India & Public Schools (hon memb), MCC; *Style*— Graham Able, Esq

ABLEMAN, Sheila; da of late Dennis Hutton-Fox, of Hove, E Sussex, and late Rosamund Alice Evelyn, *née* Tapsell; *b* 3 February 1949; *Educ* Cheam Co Sch for Girls, Epsom Art Sch, Cambridge Art Sch, Queen Mary Coll London (BA); *m* 1978, Paul Victor Ableman, novelist and playwright (d 2006); 1 s (Thomas Mark b 7 July 1981); *Career* designer's asst Weidenfeld & Nicolson Ltd 1970, editorial asst Victor Gollancz 1976–78; BBC Books: commissioning ed 1978–90, editorial dir 1990–99, literary agent 2000–; *Style*— Mrs Sheila Ableman; ✉ Sheila Ableman Literary Agency, 36 Duncan House, 7–9 Fellows Road, London NW3 3LZ

ABOUD, Alan Kieran; s of Kibon M Aboud, and Mary, *née* Neylon; *b* 13 May 1966, Dublin; *Educ* Belvedere Coll Dublin, Nat Coll of Art and Design Dublin, St Martin's Sch of Art (BA); *Family* 2 s (Victor Sylvester, Milo Van (twins) b 2 June 1995); *Career* designer; estab ABOUD SODANO with Sandro Sodano, *qv*, 1990 (currently creative dir), estab ABOUD Creative 2008; *Awards* Citation for Typographic Excellence NY Type Dirs' Club 1992, Silver Bell Award Irish Inst of Creative Advtg and Design 1994, Br D&AD Silver Award 1997 and 2002, Silver Cube Award NY Art Dirs' Club 2002, Gold Award Art Dirs' Club of Europe 2002; Growing (1995), The End (2002), Above All Else (2011); *Recreations* music, music video, film, armchair football supporter; *Style*— Alan K Aboud; ✉ ABOUD Creative, Studio 26, Pall Mall Deposit, 124–128 Barlby Road, London W10 6BL (✆ 020 8968 6142, fax 020 8968 6143, e-mail mail@aboud-creative.com, website www.aboud-creative.com)

ABRAHAM, David; *b* Waddington, Lincs; *Educ* Magdalen Coll Oxford; *Career* account mangr and dir Benton&Bowles and CDP advertising agencies 1984–90, account dir and dep md Chiat Day 1990–95, fndr and chief operating offr St Luke's 1995–2000, gen mangr Discovery Networks UK 2001–04, pres The Learning Channel USA 2005–07; chief exec: UKTV 2007–10, Channel 4 2010–; memb: Bd Creative Skillset, BAFTA, RTS; *Style*— David Abraham, Esq; ✉ Channel 4 Television, 124 Horseferry Road, London SW1P 2TX

ABRAHAM, Neville Victor; CBE; s of Solomon Abraham (d 1991), and Sarah Raphael (d 1999); *b* 22 January 1937, Calcutta, India; *Educ* Brighton Coll, Univ of London, LSE (BSc); *m* Nicola Leach; *Career* sr princ Board of Trade and private sec to Min of State 1963–71; corporate policy advsr Whitehead Consulting Group 1971–76; fndr chm and md Amis du Vin Gp and Les Amis du Vin Ltd 1974–86; gp exec dir Kennedy Brookes plc 1984–86, dir Creative Business Communications plc 1986–91; fndr chm and chief exec: Groupe Chez Gérard Restaurants Ltd 1986–99, Groupe Chez Gérard plc 1994–2003 (exec chm 1999–2000 and 2002–03, non-exec chm 2000–02); non-exec chm Liberty Wines Ltd 2003–; non-exec dir Draft House Hldg Ltd 2009–; exec chm Metabolic Services Ltd 2013–; visiting lectr at leading business schs 1974–83; jt exec chm BOC Covent Garden Festival 1991–99, chm London String Quartet Fndn 2000–06; vice-chm Restaurateurs Assoc of GB 1994–99; govr Brighton Coll 2006–; *Books* Big Business and Government: The New Disorder (1974); *Recreations* music, wine and food, sport; *Clubs* RAC, MCC, Home House; *Style*— Neville Abraham, CBE

ABRAHAM, Prof Raymond John; s of Judah H Abraham (d 1989), and Elizabeth, *née* Harrop (d 2006); *b* 26 November 1933; *Educ* Magnus GS Newark, Univ of Birmingham (BSc, PhD, DSc); *m* 1, 16 Aug 1958 (m dis 1986), June Roslyn; 1 da (Susan Elizabeth b 8 Sept 1959), 2 s (David Joseph b 3 Sept 1962, Simon Douglas b 27 Oct 1969); m 2, 17 Sept 1988, Barbara Ann, da of Henry Broadbent (d 1982); *Career* postdoctoral fell NRC Canada 1957–59, sr fell Nat Physical Lab 1959–61, Univ of Liverpool 1961– (lectr, sr lectr, reader, prof 2001–, emeritus prof); visiting prof: Carnegie-Mellon Univ Pittsburgh 1966–67, Univ of Calif 1981–89; Ciba-Geigy fell Univ of Trondheim 1979; *Books* The Analysis of NMR Spectra (1971), Proton and Carbon 13 NMR Spectroscopy (with P Loftus, 1978), Introduction to NMR Spectroscopy (with J Fisher and P Loftus, 1988), Modelling 1H NMR Spectra of Organic Compounds (with M Mobli, 2008); *Recreations* golf, gardening, theatre; *Style*— Prof Raymond Abraham; ✉ 11 Lawns Avenue, Raby Mere, Wirral CH63 0NF (✆ 0151 3342188); The Chemistry Department, The University of Liverpool, Crown Street, Liverpool L69 7ZP (e-mail rabraham@liv.ac.uk)

ABRAHAMI, Natalie; *Career* artistic dir Gate Theatre 2007–; *Style*— Ms Natalie Abrahami; ✉ The Gate Theatre, 11 Pembridge Road, London W11 3HQ

ABRAHAMS, Col (Sidney) Anthony George; TD, DL; s of Anthony Claude Walter Abrahams (d 2011), and Laila, *née* Myking; *b* 30 October 1951; *Educ* Bedford Sch, Nottingham Law Sch, MBA; *m* 6 Oct 1979, Kathryn Helen Anne, da of Humphrey John Patrick Chetwynd-Talbot, of Southoe, Beds; 2 da (Annika b 1983, Harriett b 1988), 1 s (Thomas b 1985); *Career* cmmnd 1976, Lt-Col 1994 rising to Col, Royal Green Jackets (V); admitted slr 1978; Wade-Gery and Brackenbury 1980–84, Alexander Farr and Son 1984–88, Pictons 1988–2000 (head slr 2000), ptnr Heald Heffron 2000–07, md Kain Knight Gp plc 2009–11, ceo Charter Chambers 2011–12, DG Chartered Inst of Arbitrators 2012–; Chief of Mil Ops Office of the Staff Judge Advocate Multi-Nat Corps Iraq 2006–07; dep district judge Co Court 1989–; memb Law Soc; Freeman City of London 1985, Liveryman Worshipful Co of Glaziers and Painters of Glass 1985; *Recreations* TA, tennis, food and drink, sailing; *Clubs* Army and Navy; *Style*— Col Anthony Abrahams, TD, DL; ✉ Woodfield, Honeydon Road, Colmworth, Bedfordshire MK44 2LZ (✆ 01234 378132, e-mail aa2abrahams@yahoo.co.uk)

ABRAHAMS, Debbie Angela; MP; *b* 1960, Sheffield; *Educ* Univ of Salford, Univ of Liverpool; *m* John; 2 da (Victoria, Dawn); *Career* chair Rochdale PCT 2002–06, dir Int Health Impact Assessment Consortium Univ of Liverpool 2006–10; MP (Lab) Oldham East and Saddleworth 2011–, PPS to Rt Hon Andy Burnham, MP, *qv* (as Shadow Health Sec) until 2015, shadow min for disabled people 2015–16, shadow sec of state for work and pensions 2016–; FFPH; *Style*— Ms Debbie Abrahams; ✉ House of Commons, London SW1A 0AA (✆ 020 7219 1041, e-mail abrahamsd@parliament.uk, website www.debbieabrahams.org.uk, Twitter @debbie_abrahams)

ABRAHAMS, Mark Simon; s of Robert Abrahams; *b* 24 February 1955; *Educ* Wanstead Co HS, Trinity Coll Cambridge (MA); *m* 24 Aug 1991, Lucia Mary Caitriona; *Career* fin dir Coloroll Carpets/Edinburgh Crystal 1987–90; Fenner plc: gp fin dir 1990–94, chief exec 1994–2011, chm 2011–; non-exec chm: Darby Gp plc 1999–2003, Inditherm plc 2001–; vice-chm Leeds Teaching Hosps Tst 2009–15; chm Inspiration Healthcare Gp plc 2015–; memb Econ Affrs Ctee CBI; FCA 1979; *Recreations* travel, bridge, opera, fine wine; *Clubs* Oxford and Cambridge; *Style*— Mark Abrahams, Esq; ✉ Fenner plc, Hesslewood Country Office Park, Ferriby Road, Hessle HU13 0PW (✆ 01482 626501, fax 01482 626502, e-mail mark.abrahams@fenner.com)

ABRAHAMS, Michael David; CBE 1994 (MBE 1988), DL (N Yorks 1994); s of Alexander Abrahams, and Anne, *née* Sokoloff; *b* 23 November 1937; *Educ* Shrewsbury, Worcester Coll Oxford; *m* 1967, Amanda, *née* Atha; 2 da (Emily, Victoria), 1 s (Rupert); *Career* cmmnd Royal Marines; md A W (Securities) Ltd 1968–73; dir: John Waddington plc 1984–2000, Drummond Group plc 1989–; chm Cavaghan and Gray Group plc (formerly Dalepak Foods plc) 1992–97 (dir 1987–97); non-exec chm: Kingston Communications plc 1999–2009, Ferrexpo plc 2007–, I M Jack plc (formerly Amteus plc) 2008–11; dep chm: York Trust plc 1985–88, John Crowther plc 1985–88, Prudential Corporation plc 1991–2001 (dir 1984–2001); non-exec chm Minorplanet Systems plc 1997–2004; dir The Rank Fndn 1992–2007; pres British Carpet Manufacturers' Assoc 1979–80; chm: Ripon Improvement Tst 1994–2009, Nat Tst Regl Ctee for Yorks 1996–2002, The London Clinic 1996–2012 (govr 1990–2012); dep chm Cncl Prince of Wales's Inst of Architecture 1991–99; High Sheriff N Yorks 1993–94; jt master and huntsman West of Yore Hunt 1970–81, jt master Bedale Hunt 1971–79; Hon Freeman City of Ripon 2002; Master Worshipful Co of Woolmen 1996; *Recreations* reading, architecture; *Clubs* Garrick, Pratt's; *Style*— Michael Abrahams, Esq, CBE, DL; ✉ Newfield, Mickley, Ripon, North Yorkshire HG4 3JH (e-mail mda@newfield.uk.net)

ABRAHAMS, Paul Richard; s of Anthony Claud Walter Abrahams, of London, and Laila, *née* Myking; *b* 20 April 1962; *Educ* Radley, Downing Coll Cambridge (BA, MA), Darwin Coll Cambridge (PhD, Fencing half blue); *m* 1997, Abby Deveney; 1 da (Sophie Eleanor Deveney Abrahams b 1997), 1 s (Matthew Paul Deveney Abrahams b 2000); *Career* FT: technol corr 1988–89, dep defence and aerospace corr 1989–91, chemicals and pharmaceuticals corr 1991–94, Lex columnist 1994–95, int cos ed 1995–97, bureau chief Tokyo 1997–2000, bureau chief Silicon Valley 2000–03; md Waggener Edstrom Ltd 2003–06, dir of communications Europe Nomura 2006–; *Publications* La Haute-Savoie contre elle-même: 1939–45 (2006); *Recreations* skiing, fencing; *Clubs* Garrick, Lansdowne, Ski Club of GB; *Style*— Paul Abrahams, Esq

ABRAM, Prof Richard Arthur; s of Richard Abram (d 1991), and Kathleen Lilian, *née* Radbourne (d 1989); *b* 25 March 1947, Southport, Lancs; *Educ* Chiswick Co GS for Boys, Univ of Manchester (BSc, Dip Advanced Studies in Science, PhD); *m* 29 Dec 1973, Jane, da of Dennis Cuppello (d 2004), of Ashton-under-Lyne, Lancs; 1 s (Edward John b 17 July 1976), 2 da (Anna Christabel b 6 Oct 1979, Francesca Clare b 12 July 1985); *Career* sr scientist rising to princ scientist Plessey Research (Caswell) Ltd 1972–78, conslt GEC-Marconi Materials Technol Ltd 1978–94; Univ of Durham: lectr in applied physics 1978–85, sr lectr in applied physics 1985–92, reader in physics 1992–95, prof of physics 1995–2013 (emeritus prof 2013–), head Dept of Physics 2003–09, dir of educn Dept of Physics 2011–12, dir of postgrad studies Dept of Physics 2011–12; chm Semiconductor Physics Gp Inst of Physics 1999–2003 (memb Ctee 1987–91); memb: Electronic Materials Ctee SERC 1992–94, Physics Ctee SERC 1993–94, EPSRC Peer Review Coll 1995–2014, Advsy Bd Inst of Physics Jl of Physics: Condensed Matter 2000–03; author of numerous research papers in scientific jls; memb Senate Durham Univ 2003–09; CEng, CPhys, FInstP, FHEA, FRSA; *Style*— Prof Richard Abram; ✉ Department of Physics, Durham University, Durham DH1 3LE (✆ 0191 334 3581, e-mail r.a.abram@durham.ac.uk)

ABRAMOVICH, Solomon; s of Dr Jacob Abramovich, MD (d 1977), and Bronia, *née* Maizel (d 1980); *b* Vilnius. Lithuania; *Educ* Sch of Music, Kaunas Med Sch (MSc, MB BS); *m* Gillian; 1 s (Alexander Jacob b 5 Jan 1992), 2 da (Natalia Bronia b 6 Jan 1996, Katerina Rachel b 31 July 2000); *Career* Radcliffe Infirmary Oxford 1974–75, Hammersmith Hosp London 1975, UCH 1976–78, King's Coll Hosp 1979, clinical fell Univ of Toronto 1983, St Bartholomew's and Nat Hosp for Neurology and Neurosurgery London 1982, conslt ENT surgn St Mary's Hosp London and Central Middlesex Hosp 1988; hon clinical sr lectr ICSTM 1989, hon conslt Royal London Hosp, hon conslt Charing Cross Hosp London, hon conslt to Gibraltar; journalist with J McGinty on scientific film Early Detection of Hearing Loss in Children (ITN, Glaxo Fellowship Prize for best popular scientific film 1984); memb: Int Barany Soc, Int Maniere's Soc, Br Assoc of Otorhinolaryngology and Head and Neck Surgery; fndr memb: Standing Ctee Euro Acad of Otology, Cochlear Implant Gp; memb Ctee Politzer Otology Soc 2006–09; FRSM (memb Cncl), FRCS (MRCS), LRCP; *Books* Electric Response Audiometry in Clinical Practice (1991, electronic edn 2013), Clinical Surgery Textbook (contrib, 2001, 2 edn 2005 (BMA Award), 3 edn 2012), Smuggled in Potato Sacks (ed, 2011, 2 edn 2014); *Recreations* tennis, skiing, playing the violin; *Clubs* Athenaeum; *Style*— Solomon Abramovich, Esq; ✉ 73 Harley Street, London W1G 8QJ (✆ 020 7935 0604, fax 020 7627 2205, e-mail solomon@abramovich.org.uk, website www.abramovich.org.uk)

ABRAMSKY, Dame Jennifer (Jenny); DBE (2009, CBE 2001); da of Chimen Abramsky, and Miriam, *née* Nirenstein (d 1997); *b* 7 October 1946; *Educ* Holland Park Sch, UEA (BA); *m* Alasdair D MacDuff Liddell, CBE, *qv*; 1 s, 1 da; *Career* BBC: joined 1969 as progs ops asst, prodr The World At One 1973 (ed 1981), jt prodr special prog on Nixon 1974, ed PM 1978, prodr Radio 4's Budget progs 1979–86, ed Today Prog 1986–87, ed News and Current Affrs Radio 1987–93 (set up Radio 4 Gulf FM for duration of Gulf War), controller Radio 5 Live and head of Ceefax 1994–96, dir Continuous News 1996–98, dir BBC Radio 1998–2000, dir BBC Audio and Music 2000–08; dep chair Digital Radio Devpt Bureau (DRDB) 2002–; special award for Radio 5 Live Sony Radio Awards 1995, UK Station of the Year Sony Radio Awards 1996; Woman of Distinction award (Jewish Care) 1990; appointed to ESRC 1992–96; News Int visiting prof of broadcast media Univ of Oxford 2002, hon prof Thames Valley Univ 1994; dir Rajar 1995–, chm Hampstead Theatre 2005 (dir 2003–05); fell Radio Acad 1998; *Recreations* theatre, music; *Style*— Dame Jenny Abramsky, DBE

ABRAMSKY, Prof Samson; *Educ* Univ of Cambridge (MA, Dip Computer Science), Univ of London (PhD); *Career* programmer GEC Computers Ltd 1976–78, lectr Dept of Computer Science and Statistics QMC London 1980–83 (research student 1978–80); Dept of Computing ICSTM London: lectr 1983–88, reader in computing science 1988–90, prof of computing science and head Theory and Formal Methods Section 1990–95; prof of theoretical computer science Univ of Edinburgh 1995–2000, Christopher Strachey prof of computing science Univ of Oxford 2000–, fell Wolfson Coll Oxford 2000–; visiting prof: Univ of Nijmegen 1986, Univ of Pennsylvania 1998 (visiting assoc prof 1989), Univ of Paris VII and CNRS Lab PPS 2001; visiting lectr Programming Methodology Gp Chalmers Univ Gothenberg 1984, visiting research Kestrel Inst Palo Alto 1998 and 2000; conslt to GEC Hirst Research Centre 1985–88; gen chair Logic in Computer Science (LiCS) IEEE Symposium 2000–03, memb Scientific Steering Ctee Isaac Newton Inst for the Mathematical Sciences 2003–06; memb Editorial Bd: Cambridge Series of Tracts in Theoretical Computer Science, Studies in Logic and the Foundations of Mathematics, Jl of Logic and Computation, Jl of Mathematical Structures in Computer Science; Nuffield science research fell 1988–89; MA (by incorporation) Univ of Oxford 2001; memb Academia Europaea 1993, FRSE 2000, FRS 2004; *Style*— Prof Samson Abramsky; ✉ Computing Laboratory, Wolfson Building, Parks Road, Oxford OX1 3QD

ABULAFIA, Prof David Samuel Harvard; s of Leon Abulafia (d 1963), and Rachel Abulafia (d 1997); *b* 12 December 1949, Twickenham; *Educ* St Paul's, King's Coll Cambridge (BA), Gonville & Caius Coll Cambridge (MA, PhD, LittD); *m* 12 Dec 1979, Prof Anna Sapir Abulafia; 2 da (Bianca Susanna b 15 Nov 1984, Rosa Alexandra b 6 March 1987); *Career* fell Gonville & Caius Coll Cambridge 1974– (tutor for grad students 1984–91, Papathomas professorial fell 2014–); Univ of Cambridge: lectr in history 1983–91 (asst lectr 1978–83), reader in Mediterranean history 1991–2000, prof of Mediterranean history 2000–, chm Faculty of History 2003–; Rome scholar Br Sch at Rome 1972–74; delivered guest lectures at Nat Gall of Art Washington, Bibliotheca Alexandrina Egypt and numerous univs (incl: Tokyo, Kyoto, Jerusalem, Tel Aviv, Aix, Naples, Pisa, Barcelona); Crossroads Inaugural Lecture Univ of N Carolina at Chapel Hill 2008, Mountbatten Literary Award 2011, Br Acad Medal 2013; memb: Review Ctee Ben Gurion Univ of Negev 1999–2000, Academic Bd Gibraltar Univ 2015–, Cncl Br Acad 2015–; project co-ordinator EU Culture 2000 2000–03; govr Perse Sch Cambridge 2002–11, chm Historians for Britain 2014–; memb Academia Europaea 2002–; FRHistS 1981, FBA 2010, FSA 2010, fell Legatum Inst 2011–; Commendatore dell'Ordine della Stella della Solidarietà Italiana

2003; *Books* incl: The Two Italies (1977), Italy, Sicily and the Mediterranean (1987), Frederick II (1988, 3 edn 2002), Spain and 1492 (1992), Church and City (jt ed, 1992), Commerce and Conquest in the Mediterranean (1993), A Mediterranean Emporium (1994), The French Descent into Renaissance Italy (ed, 1995), The Western Mediterranean Kingdoms (1997), En las costas del Mediterráneo Occidental (jt ed, 1997), The New Cambridge Medieval History vol 5 (ed, 1999), Mediterranean Encounters (2000), Medieval Frontiers (jt ed, 2002), The Mediterranean in History (ed, 2003), Italy in the Central Middle Ages (ed, 2004), The Discovery of Mankind (2008), The Great Sea (2011); *Recreations* travel; *Clubs* Athenaeum; *Style*— Prof David Abulafia; ✉ Gonville & Caius College, Cambridge CB2 1TA (☎ 01223 332400, fax 01223 332456, e-mail dsa1000@hermes.cam.ac.uk)

ACHER, Sir Gerald; kt (2012), CBE (1999), LVO (2002); s of David Acher (d 1979), and Andrée Diana, *née* Laredo (d 2007); *b* 30 April 1945, Wimbledon, London; *Educ* KCS Wimbledon; *m* 18 July 1970, Joyce Kathleen, *née* White; 2 s (James David b 4 July 1973, Mark Gerald b 3 Jan 1976); *Career* articled clerk Bird Potter & Co 1961–66; KPMG (and predecessor firms): asst mangr 1967–73, mangr 1973–75, sr mangr 1975–80, ptnr 1980–2001, memb UK Bd 1987–2001, head Corp Fin 1990–93, UK head Audit and Accounting 1993–98, chm World-Wide Audit and Accounting Ctee 1995–98, chm Client Service Bd 1998–2001, sr ptnr London 1998–2001; non-exec dir BPB plc 2002–05, dep chm Camelot Group plc 2002–15 (interim chm 2004); chm London Mayoral Cmmn into an Int Convention Centre for London, chm Cobham Conservation and Heritage Tst 2005–, chm London Climate Change Partnership 2005–13, chm Heart of the City 2006–12, dep chm Imperial Coll Healthcare NHS Tst 2016–; chm Cobham Conservation and Heritage Tst 2005–, chm Cobham Community Bus CIC 2014–, chm Brooklands Museum Tst 2015–; pres Young Epilepsy 2011–; non-exec dir and chm Audit, Risk and Governance Ctee Imperial Coll Healthcare NHS Tst 2012–; memb: Cncl and chm Audit Faculty ICAEW 1995–2001, Bd London First Centre 1998–2001, Advsy Ctee for Business and the Environment 1998–2002, Bd and dep chm London First 1999–2004; govr and vice-chm Motability, tstee Motability 10th Anniversary Tst 1989–; chm of govrs Milbourne Lodge Jr Sch 1986–2007; William Quilter Prize, Plender Prize for Auditing ICA 1966; memb Ct of Assts Worshipful Co of Chartered Accountants (Master 2003–04); FCA 1977 (ACA 1967), fell Securities Industries Assoc, life fell RSA (tstee 1999–2009, memb Cncl, sr treas, chm 2006–09); *Recreations* mountain walking, rallying, vintage cars, opera and music, gardening; *Clubs* Travellers; *Style*— Sir Gerald Acher, CBE, LVO

ACKFORD, Paul John; *b* 26 February 1958; *m* Suzie Mummé; *Career* former rugby union player (lock); clubs: Plymouth Albion, Rosslyn Park, Metropolitan Police, Harlequins; England: B debut 1979, full debut v Aust 1988, Five Nations debut v Scotland 1989, memb Grand Slam winning team 1991, memb World Cup runners-up team 1991, 22 caps; 3 test appearances Br Lions 1989; memb: RFU Ctee 1992–94, Surrey RFU Ctee 1992–94; former police offr; currently rugby corr The Sunday Telegraph; *Recreations* cooking, entertaining, golf; *Style*— Paul Ackford, Esq

ACKLAND, Joss (Sidney Edmond Jocelyn); CBE (2001); s of Maj Sidney Norman Ackland (d 1981), and Ruth, *née* Izod (d 1957); *b* 29 February 1928; *Educ* Dame Alice Owens Sch, Central Sch of Speech Training and Dramatic Art; *m* 18 Aug 1951, Rosemary Jean (d 2002), da of Capt Robert Hunter Kirkcaldy (d 1954); 5 da (Melanie b 1952, Antonia b 1956, Penelope b 1958, Samantha b 1962, Kirsty b 1963), 2 s (Paul b 1953 d 1982, Toby b 1966); *Career* actor; worked in theatre since 1945, tea planter Central Africa 1954–55, disc jockey in Cape Town 1955–57; memb: Drug Helpline, Amnesty International, Covent Garden Community Assoc; *Theatre* rep work incl: Stratford-on-Avon, Arts Theatre, Buxton, Croydon, The Embassy Coventry, Oxford, Pitlochry; Old Vic Theatre Co 1958–61, roles incl: Toby Belch, Caliban, Pistol, Lord Froth in The Double Dealer, Aegisthus in The Oresteia and Falstaff in Henry IV part 1, The Merry Wives of Windsor; artistic dir Mermaid Theatre 1961–63; roles incl: Galileo, Long John Silver, Bluntschli in Arms and the Man, Scrofulovsky in The Bedbug, Kirilov in the Possessed; dir Plough and the Stars; *West End* roles incl: Professor in The Professor, Gus in Hotel in Amsterdam, Come As You Are, Sam in The Collaborators, Mitch in A Streetcar Named Desire, Brassbound in Captain Brassbound's Conversion, Stewart in A Pack of Lies, Clarence Darrow in Never the Sinner, Weller Martin in The Gin Game, King George V in The King's Speech; *Other* roles incl: Gaev in The Cherry Orchard (Chichester), Petruchio in The Taming of the Shrew, Sir in The Dresser (both nat tours), Eustace Perrin State in The Madras House, Romain Gary in Jean Seburg (both NT); Opening of the Barbican Theatre: Falstaff in Henry IV Parts 1 and 2, Captain Hook and Mr Darling in Peter Pan; most recently Alfred Ill in The Visit (Chichester) 1995, John Tarleton in Misalliance (Chichester) 1997, Captain Shotover in Heartbreak House (Chichester) 2000, King Lear (charity gala, St James Theatre) 2013; *West End Musicals* incl: Squeezum in Lock Up Your Daughters, title role in Jorrocks, Fredrik in A Little Night Music, Peron in Evita, Captain Hook and Mr Darling in Peter Pan – The Musical; *Television* numerous appearances incl: Kipling in the Kipling series, D'Artagnan in Twenty Years After, Barrett in The Barretts of Wimpole Street, C S Lewis in Shadowlands, Clarence Darrow in Never the Sinner, Terence Fielding in A Murder of Quality, Archie in Voices in the Garden, Alan Holly in First and Last, Bondarchuk in Citizen X, Henry VII in Henry VIII, Mustrum Ridcully in The Hogfather; mini-series incl: Heat of the Sun, Herman Goering in The Man Who Lived at The Ritz, Sir Burton in Queenie, Onassis in A Woman Named Jackie, Winston Churchill in Above and Beyond, Sir Freddie Buller in Midsomer Murders, John Narbutowiz in Kingdom, Judge Jefferies in Crusoe, Master Ciliegia in Pinocchio; *Radio* roles incl: God, Macbeth, Falstaff, Flashman, Kafka's Dog, Victor Hugo, Socrates, Big Daddy, Honore L'Achailles in Gigi, The King in The King and I; *Film* incl: Seven Days to Noon, Forbush and the Penguins, The House that Dripped Blood, Villain, Crescendo, The Happiness Cage, England Made Me, Hitler – The Last Ten Days, The Black Windmill, The Little Prince, S-P-Y-S, Royal Flash, One of our Dinosaurs is Missing, Operation Daybreak, Silver Bears, Watership Down, Who is Killing the Great Chefs of Europe?, Saint Jack, The Apple, Rough Cut, Lady Jane, A Zed and Two Noughts, It Couldn't Happen Here, Don Masino in The Sicilian, The Colonel in To Kill a Priest, Sir Jock Delves Broughton in White Mischief, Arjen Rudd in Lethal Weapon 2, Russian Ambassador in The Hunt for Red October, The Man of Power in The Palermo Connection, Tre Colonne in Cronaca, The Object of Beauty, The Sheltering Desert, The Bridge, Georgino, Brando in Occhio Pinocchio, Hale in Nowhere to Run, Isaac in The Bible, Miracle on 34th Street, Stringer in Mad Dogs and Englishmen, Gerald Carmody in Daisies in December, King Francis in Till the End of Time, King Arthur in A Kid at the Court of King Arthur, Mighty Ducks 1 & 3, Matisse in Surviving Picasso, The Captain in Deadly Voyage, Lord Claire in Firelight, Swaffer in Amy Foster, Bennett in Hall of Mirrors, Lord Wyndham in Son of Sandokarn, Milk, Passion of Mind, Mumbo Jumbo, Defense Min Malinovsky in K19 the Widowmaker, Mr Quarre in The House on Turk Street, Evil Edmonds in I'll Be there, Randolph Caulffield in A Different Loyalty, Jack Straffen in Asylum, The Icon in Icon, Charlie in These Foolish Things, Tolstoy in Moscow Zero, Sir Milton Kendrick Ashtoncroft in Flawless, Donald Vanston in How About You; *Books* I Must Be in There Somewhere (autobiography, 1989), My Better Half and Me (2009); *Recreations* writing, painting, reading, 33 grandchildren, 14 great grandchildren; *Style*— Joss Ackland, Esq; ✉ c/o Paul Pearson, 18 Leamore Street, London W6 0JZ (☎ 020 8748 1478)

ACKROYD, Jane Victoria Macleod; da of late Sir John Robert Whyte Ackroyd, 2 Bt, and Jennifer Eileen Macleod, *née* Bishop; *b* 25 February 1957; *Educ* Godolphin & Latymer Sch, St Martin's Sch of Art (BA), Royal Coll of Art (MA); *m* (m dis 2001), David Robert Ewart Annesley; 1 s (William Harry Macleod b 31 August 1992); *Career* artist and sculptor; exhibitions incl: The Albert Exhibition 1983, Anti-thesis (Angela Flowers Gallery) 1986, Anderson O'Day summer exhibition 1987 and 1988, The Royal Academy Summer Exhibition 1988, 1989, 1997, 1998, 2001 2002 and 2005; solo exhibitions incl: Kingsgate Workshops Gallery 1984, 1985, 1986, 1987 and 2002, Anderson O'Day Gallery 1988 and 1991, Provost's Garden Worcester Coll Oxford (major retrospective exhibition) 1997, Lynne Gould's 102 2004; work in public and private collections incl: The Arts Cncl of GB, The Contemporary Arts Soc, The Harlow Arts Tst; cmmn: Moonlight Ramble (Haymarket) 1992, Limehouse Narrow Street (Herring Gull) 1994, Beaulieu Park Chelmsford (for Countryside plc); Pollock/Krasner Fndn Award USA 1995; Freeman: City of London 1980, Worshipful Co of Carpenters; *Recreations* tennis, walking, music; *Style*— Miss Jane Ackroyd; ☎ 07931 543426, e-mail jane.ackroyd@blueyonder.co.uk, website www.janeackroyd.com

ACKROYD, Peter; CBE (2003); s of Graham Ackroyd, and Audrey, *née* Whiteside; *b* 5 October 1949; *Educ* Clare Coll Cambridge, Yale Univ; *Career* writer; The Spectator: lit ed 1971–77, managing ed 1977–81; chief book reviewer The Times 1986–; Somerset Maugham Prize 1984, The Guardian Fiction Award 1985, Whitbread Prize for Best Biography 1984/85; Hon DLitt: Univ of Exeter 1992, City Univ 1997, Univ of London 2001; FRSL; *Poetry* London Lickpenny (1973), Country Life (1978), The Diversions of Purley (1987); *Non-Fiction* Notes for a New Culture (1976), Ezra Pound and His World (1980), T S Eliot (1984), Dickens (1990), Introduction to Dickens (1991), Blake (1995), The Life of Thomas More (1998), London: The Biography (2000), The Collection (2001), Albion: The Origins of the English Imagination (2002), Chaucer (2004), Shakespeare: The Biography (2005), Thames: Sacred River (2007), The English Ghost: Spectres Through Time (2010), London Under (2011), Wilkie Collins (2012), Foundation: A History of England Vol I (2011); *Novels* The Great Fire of London (1982), The Last Testament of Oscar Wilde (1983), Hawksmoor (1985), Chatterton (1987), First Light (1989), English Music (1992), The House of Doctor Dee (1993), Dan Leno and the Limehouse Golem (1994), Milton in America (1996), The Plato Papers (1999), The Clerkenwell Tales (2003), The Lambs of London (2004), The Casebook of Victor Frankenstein (2008), The Canterbury Tales: A Retelling (2009), The Death of King Arthur: The Immortal Legend (2010); *Style*— Peter Ackroyd, Esq, CBE, FRSL

ACKROYD, Sir Timothy Robert Whyte; 3 Bt (UK 1956), of Dewsbury, W Riding of Yorks; s of Sir John Robert Whyte Ackroyd, 2 Bt (d 1995), and Jennifer Eileen MacLeod, *née* Bishop (d 1997); *b* 7 October 1958; *Educ* Bradfield, LAMDA; *Heir* bro, Andrew Ackroyd; *Career* actor; dir Martingale Productions 1985–, fndr Archview Film Prodns, dir LISA 1991–; conslt Hotspur Fim Prodns and 11th Duke of Northumberland; artistic dir Ragamuffin Prodns 2010; hon memb Theatre of Comedy 1984, fndr tstee and hon vice-pres of charity Tusk Tst 1989, tstee: Marjorie & Dorothy Whyte Memorial Fund 1992, The Ackroyd Tst 1994, Ackroyd/Pullan Prodns 1994, Ackroyd & Co 2004, Mane Chance Sanctuary 2012; memb: Exec Ctee Earth 2000, Ctee Have-A-Go-Holidays, cultural advsr on the art of language Today Translations; Freeman City of London, Liveryman Worshipful Co of Carpenters 1982; *Theatre* incl: Agamemnon (West End Theatre Critics' Award nomination Most Promising Newcomer) 1976, On Approval 1979, Much Ado About Nothing 1980, A Month in the Country 1981, Man and Superman 1982, A Sleep of Prisoners 1983, Pygmalion 1984, Another Country 1986, No Sex Please – We're British 1987, Black Coffee 1988, The Reluctant Debutante 1989, Jeffrey Bernard is Unwell 1989–91, Journey's End 1993, The Bad Soldier Smith 1995, Super-Beasts 1997, A Step Out of Time 1998, Jeffrey Bernard is Unwell 1999, The Rivals 2000, A Step Out of Time 2000 (USA 2001), Village Wooing 2002, You're Alright – How Am I 2002, Henry IV Part I 2003, Les Parents Terribles 2004, A Compassionate Satirist 2005 and 2006; *Films and Television* incl: Jack Be Nimble 1979, Martin Luther – Heretic 1983, Creator 1984 (Hollywood), Man and Superman 1985, That Has Such People In It 1987, Pied Piper 1989, Bullseye 1989, The Wildlands (Kenya) 1992, A Royal Scandal 1996, The Mummy's Curse 1998, The New Avengers 1998, Timewatch 2003; *Radio* Jakob Beer in Fugitive Pieces 1998, Life Story 2003, Beau Geste 2010, The Signalman 2010, A Christmas Carol 2012, Three Men in a Boat 2013, Dracula 2013; *Publications* Ackroyd's Ark (2004), Tripe (poems, 2008), Ackroyd's Ark: Two by Two (2010); *Recreations* rugby, literature, history, sumo wrestling; *Clubs* MCC, Garrick; *Style*— Sir Timothy Ackroyd, Bt; ✉ website www.sirtimothyackroyd.com, Twitter @SirTimAckroyd

ACLAND, Lt-Col Sir (Christopher) Guy Dyke; 6 Bt (UK 1890), of St Mary Magdalen, Oxford; LVO (1999, MVO 1990), DL (Isle of Wight 2002); s of Sir Antony Acland, 5 Bt (d 1983), and Margaret Joan, *née* Rooke (d 2010); *b* 24 March 1946; *Educ* Allhallows Sch, RMA Sandhurst; *m* 1971, Christine Mary Carden, da of late John William Brodie Waring; 2 s (Alexander b 1973, Hugh b 1976); *Heir* s, Alexander Acland; *Career* cmmnd RA 1966, served UK, Germany and Hong Kong, 2 i/c 1 RHA 1985–88, Equerry to HRH The Duke of Edinburgh 1988–90, Lt-Col 1990, SO1 Mgmnt Servs (Org 3) MOD 1990–92, cmd Southampton UOTC 1992–94, ret; Dep Master HM Household and Equerry to HM The Queen 1994–99, Extra Equerry to HM The Queen 1999–; administrator HSA Charitable Tst 2000–06; Vice Lord-Lt IOW 2006–; *Recreations* sailing, gardening, walking; *Clubs* Royal Artillery Yacht, Royal Solent Yacht; *Style*— Lt-Col Sir Guy Acland, Bt, LVO, DL

ACLAND HOOD GASS; *see:* Gass

ACTON, 5 Baron (UK 1869); Sir John Charles Ferdinand Harold Lyon-Dalberg-Acton; 12 Bt (E 1644); also a Patrician of Naples (1802); patron of one living (but being a Roman Catholic cannot present); eldest s of 4 Baron Acton (d 2010), and Hilary Juliet Sarah, *née* Cookson (d 1973); *b* 19 August 1966; *Educ* Winchester, Balliol Coll Oxford; *m* 1998, Lucinda Ann Forsyth, da of Brig James Percival, OBE; *Career* obituarist The Times 1995–98, freelance journalist 1995–, fndr and mktg dir Soup Works plc 1998–2001; *Books* author or co-author of 13 books incl: The Man Who Touched The Sky (2002), The Origin of Everyday Things (2006), The Duchy Originals Cookbook (2007), The Football Book (2009), Economy (2010); *Recreations* pig keeping; *Style*— The Lord Acton; ✉ 30 Lower Street, Stroud, Gloucestershire GL15 2HS

ACTON DAVIS, Jonathan James; QC (1996); s of Michael James Acton Davis (d 1994), of London, and Elizabeth Margaret; *b* 15 January 1953; *m* Lindsay Alice Boswell, QC, *qv*; 1 s (Matthew James Acton Davis); *Career* called to the Bar Inner Temple 1977 (bencher 1995, master of house 1999–2005); asst recorder 1997–2000, recorder 2000–, dep judge of the High Court 2008–; memb Gen Cncl of the Bar 1993–98; chm Professional Conduct and Complaints Ctee 2001–02 (vice-chm 1999–2000), memb Legal Services Consultative Panel 2004–09; *Recreations* cricket, walking, South West France; *Clubs* MCC, Garrick, Beefsteak, Chelsea Arts; *Style*— Jonathan Acton Davis, Esq, QC; ✉ Atkin Chambers, 1 Atkin Building, Gray's Inn, London WC1R 5AT (☎ 020 7404 0102, fax 020 7405 7456, e-mail jadavis@atkinchambers.com)

ACTON SMITH, Michael; OBE (2014); s of Charles Smith, and Colette Smith; *b* 3 September 1974, London; *Educ* Univ of Birmingham (BSc); *Career* co-fndr Firebox.com 1998 (currently non-exec chm), fndr and ceo Mind Candy 2004–; *Clubs* Soho House, Paramount, The Hospital; *Style*— Michael Acton Smith, Esq, OBE; ✉ Mind Candy Ltd, Floor 4, 15 Bonhill Street, London EC2A 4DN (Twitter @acton)

ADAM; *see also:* Forbes Adam

ADAM, Prof Andreas; CBE (2012); s of Constantinos Adam, and Hera, *née* Spanou; *b* 4 May 1951, Nicosia, Cyprus; *Educ* Middlesex Hosp (MB BS); *m* 1977, Dr Jane Adam; 2 c (Sophie b 18 June 1985, Clio b 16 Sept 1989); *Career* Royal Postgrad Medical Sch: sr lectr 1987–91, reader 1991–92; currently prof of interventional radiology Guy's, King's and St Thomas' Sch of Medicine KCL; pres: Soc for Minimally Invasive Therapy 1996–97, Br Soc of Interventional Radiologists 1997–99, Br Inst of Radiology 1998–99, Int Soc of Hepatobiliary Radiology 1998–99, Cardiovascular and Interventional Radiological Soc of Europe 2005–07, European Congress of Radiology 2006, European Soc of Radiology 2006–07, Soc of Gastrointestinal Intervention 2007, Royal Coll of Radiologists 2007–10; Russian Acad of Medical Sciences Medal 2004, Br Soc of Interventional Radiologists Gold Medal 2005, Royal Coll of Radiologists Gold Medal 2006, Cardiovascular and Interventional Radiological Soc of Europe Gold Medal 2007, Soc of Interventional Radiology Gold Medal 2009, European Soc of Radiology Gold Medal 2010; Hon PhD Univ of Crete 2012; hon memb: Turkish Radiological Soc 1997, Royal Belgian Soc of Radiology 2000, Japanese Soc of Radiology 2002, Radiological Soc of N America 2006, Greek Radiological Soc 2006, French Soc of Radiology 2008; hon fell: Royal Australian and NZ Coll of Radiologists 2007,Greek Soc of Interventional Radiology 2007, German Soc of Interventional Radiology 2008, American Coll of Radiology 2011; hon fell and distinguished academician Singapore Acad of Medicine 2009; fell: Soc of Cardiovasular and Intervensional Radiology (USA) 1993, European Soc of Gastrointestinal and Abdominal Radiology 1998, Br Inst of Radiology 2007, Faculty of Radiologists Royal Coll of Surgeons of Ireland 2007, Acad of Medical Sciences 2008; FRCR 1985, FRCP 1994, FRCS 1998; *Publications* numerous scientific articles and twelve books on interventional radiology; *Recreations* reading history; *Clubs* Athenaeum; *Style*— Prof Andreas Adam, CBE; ✉ Department of Radiology, 1st Lambeth Wing, St Thomas Hospital, Westminster Bridge Road, London SE1 7EH (✆ 020 7188 5550, e-mail andy.adam@kcl.ac.uk)

ADAM, Ian Clark; s of George Adam (d 1976), of Dundee, and Natalie Jane Gibson, *née* Clark (d 1997); *b* 2 September 1943; *Educ* Harris Acad; *m* 25 Sept 1967, Betty Anne, da of Norman James McKie Crosbie; 1 da (Allison Jane b 26 July 1968), 1 s (Garry Clark b 19 Dec 1970); *Career* trainee accountant Henderson & Logie 1962–67; Price Waterhouse: audit sr and asst mangr (Rio de Janeiro) 1967–70, mangr Bristol 1970–76, ptnr Edinburgh 1976–86, sr ptnr Scotland 1986–95; fin dir Christian Salvesen plc 1995–98; non-exec dir: Fishers Holdings Ltd 1996–2004, Britannia Building Society 1998–2008 (non-exec chm 2004–08); memb Cncl Scottish Further and Higher Educn Funding Cncl 2003–11; chm Columba's Hospice, govr St Leonards Sch St Andrews; Old Master Co of Merchants of the City of Edinburgh; memb High Constable City of Edinburgh; MICAS 1967; *Recreations* reading, golf, gardening, travel; *Clubs* Royal Burgess Golfing Soc of Edinburgh, Royal & Ancient; *Style*— Ian C Adam, Esq; ✉ Gowanfield, 2 Cammo Road, Edinburgh EH4 8EB (✆ 0131 339 6401)

ADAM, Prof Robert; s of Wilson Adam, and Margaret Adam; *b* 10 April 1948; *Educ* Univ of Westminster; *m* 1970, Sarah; 1 s, 1 da; *Career* architect; dir Robert Adam Architects (became ADAM Architecture 2010) 1977–; fndr and chm Popular Housing Group 1995–2003 (now Design for Homes (dir 2004–08)), chm Coll of Chapters INTBAU 2000–12, chair INTBAU UK 2009–; RIBA: memb Planning and Urban Design Gp 1995–2012, chm Pres Special Working Party 1995, cncllr 1999–2005, hon sec 2001–03; British Sch at Rome: chm Faculty of Fine Art 1993–97 (memb 1989), vice-chm Cncl 1997–99; memb: Architecture Club Ctee 1987–, Eng Heritage London Advsy Gp 1996–2002, DOE Good Practice Guidance on Design in the Planning System Project Sounding Bd 1997, Design Review Panel CABE London 2012–; design advsr Cmmn for Architecture and the Built Environment (CABE) 1999–2004; visiting prof Univ of Strathclyde; lectr incl tours in USA and Russia; Bro of the Art Worker's Guild 1982; academician Acad of Urbanism 2006, sr fell The Prince's Fndn for Building Community (Heritage) 2008–; RIBA, FRSA 1988, hon FRIAS 2014–; *Projects* new country houses: Hants, Cambridge, Yorks, S Oxon, Glos, Wilts, Bucks, Dorset, Cheshire; restaurant and display buildings Nagano Prefecture Japan, roof garden Daimaru Dept Store Osaka Japan, new villages for the Duchy of Cornwall in Shepton Mallet and Midsomer Norton, new town centre Rocester Staffs, village extension Trowse nr Norwich, master plan St Andrews Hosp Northampton, mental health facility Northampton, new district Leith masterplans, new co HQ Dogmersfield Park, Humanities Library Univ of Oxford, new gallery Ashmolean Museum Oxford, Solar House W Sussex, Millennium Temple Private Estate Hants, new offices Piccadilly London; *Exhibitions* RIBA Heinz Gall 1990, Sculpture in the Garden Wimborne Dorset 1991, Ruskin, Tradition and Architecture (Peter Scott Gall Lancaster Univ) 1992, Visions of Europe Bologna 1992, The Eye of the Architect (RIBA) 1993, Contemporary British Architecture USA 1994, Models Trial Exhibition London 1996, Vision of Europe (Urban Renaissance) 1996, Royal Acad Summer Exhibition 1993, 1996 and 1997, Art Workers Guild Integrity and Craftsmanship London Festival of Architecture 2008, New Palladians exhbn (The Prince's Fndn for the Built Environment) 2008, Buildings by Hand (The Prince's Fndn for Building Community) 2013; *Work in Public Collections* V&A Contemporary Furniture Collection (Pembroke table for Alma Furniture Co), RIBA Drawings Collection Tower of the Orders; *Awards* commendation London Borough of Richmond-upon-Thames Conservation and Design Awards Scheme 1991, winner Copper Roofing Competition Copper Devpt Assoc 1995, Elmbridge BC Design/Conservation Award 1998, RIBA Southern Regn Nat Housebuilder Design Award, Best Partnership Devpt Commendation for Roman Ct Rocester 2000, Marsh Country Life Awards 2001, Award for New Building in the Classical Tradition Georgian Gp Awards 2007, Award of Excellence CNU 2008 (for Masterplan, Edinburgh), Giles Worsley Award for a new building in a Georgian context 2014; *Publications* Classical Architecture – A Complete Handbook (1990), Buildings By Design (1994), Tradition Today (ed, 2008), The 7 Sins of Architects (2010), New Classicists: Robert Adam, The Search for a Modern Classicism (2010), Urban Identity Learning from Place (contrib, 2011) The Globalisation of Modern Architecture (2012), Doha, Qatar – Architecture and Globalisation in the Persian Gulf Region (2013), Identifying trends in masterplanning: A typographical classification system (in Urban Design International 2013), Building the Capriccio – The Architectural Capriccio (2014); author of numerous articles for pubns incl nat and int newspapers, magazines and jls; contrib to numerous TV and radio progs; *Style*— Prof Robert Adam; ✉ ADAM Architecture, Old Hyde House, 75 Hyde Street, Winchester, Hampshire SO23 7DW (✆ 01962 843843, e-mail contact@adamarchitecture.com)

ADAMS, Aubrey John; s of John William Lane Adams (d 1999), and Nichole, *née* Stevenson (d 2000); *b* 16 October 1949; *Educ* Univ of Cambridge (MA); *m* 6 May 1972, Angela Mary, *née* Stevens; 3 da (Katie b 1975, Sara b 1978, Felicity b 1983); *Career* with Price Waterhouse (later Price Waterhouse Associates) 1970–78, fin dir Peachey Property Corp plc 1978–89; Savills plc: md 1990–2000, gp chief exec 2000–08; chm: Air Partner plc 2008–, Max Property Gp plc 2009–; non-exec dir: Unitech Corporate Parks plc 2006–, Br Land Co plc; tstee Wigmore Hall; *Recreations* golf, gardening, music; *Style*— Aubrey Adams, Esq; ✉ Vines Farm, Kidmore End, Reading, Berkshire RG4 9AP (✆ 0118 972 2004)

ADAMS, Colin; CBE (1995), AFC (1973); s of Maj Ronald Adams, RAC and Chindits (ka Burma 1944), of Bury, W Sussex, and Margaret, *née* Carne (d 1987); *b* 1 April 1940; *Educ* Christ's Hosp, RAF Coll Cranwell; *m* Josephine (Jo) Adams, da of Herbert Colton; 2 da (Sophie b 1 Nov 1965, Pip b 23 April 1967), 1 s (Nick b 23 May 1969); *Career* cmmnd RAF 1961, served in various reconnaissance flying appts UK, Middle East, Far East, Malta and Cyprus, flying instr, RN Staff Coll 1974, memb Tornado Aircraft Project Team Munich 1977–81, dep dir RAF Personnel Mgmnt 1983–86, CO RAF Akrotiri Cyprus

1986–88, project dir RAF Estate Rationalisation 1989–90, Defence Attaché Br Embassy Paris 1990–95, ret RAF 1995 (Air Commodore); chief exec BCCB (British Consultants and Construction Bureau, formerly BCB) 1995–2004, dir Colin Adams Int Consultancy (CAIC) Ltd 2004–09 (conslt to Shadbolt and Co LLP, JLT Risk Solutions Ltd, Rotary Int Gp Ltd and Chinese construction cos), conslt MMC Gp 2009–12; memb: Sydney 2000 Olympics Task Force DTI 1995–98, London Chamber Int Cmmn 1996–2000, Worldaware Business Gp DfID 1996–2000, Br Trade Int Sectors and Projects Gp 1997–2000, Int Ctee CBI 1998–2003, UK Public/Private Sector Task Forces Kosovo 1999, Serbia 2001 and Iraq 2003, Trade Partners UK Business Advsy Panel 2001–04, memb Bd BOND 1998–2004, Cncl and Exec Ctee Union Jack Club 2002–; FIPD 1989; Hon Cdr Ordre National du Mérite (France) 1992, Humanitarian Gold Medal (France) 1993; *Books* The International Guide to Management Consultancy (contrib); *Recreations* offshore sailing, skiing, visual arts, gardening, walking and visiting children and grandchildren in Canada; *Clubs* RAF; *Style*— Colin Adams, CBE, AFC; ✉ mobile 07768 685982

ADAMS, David; *Educ* MA; *Career* finance dir Texas Homecare then gp finance dir Asprey plc until 1997, dep chief exec and finance dir House of Fraser plc 1997–2006, chm Jessops plc 2007–12; sr ind dir JJB Sports plc; non-exec dir: Alexon plc, Halfords plc; dir and tstee Walk The Walk; FCMA; *Style*— David Adams, Esq

ADAMS, Prof David; s of Richard Adams, and Sylvia Mary, *née* Wolf; *b* 10 September 1954; *Educ* Rossall Sch, Univ of Liverpool (MCD), Univ of Cambridge (MA, PhD); *m* 11 March 1989, Judith; 1 s (Daniel Stuart b 10 Jan 1995), 1 da (Eleanor Mary b 10 Aug 1996); *Career* planning asst Leeds City Cncl 1978–83; research asst Univ of Reading 1983–84; lectr in urban planning and devpt Univ of Manchester 1984–93; Univ of Aberdeen: sr lectr in land economy 1993–95, reader in land economy 1995–97, prof of land economy 1997–2004; Ian Mactaggart prof of property and urban studies Univ of Glasgow 2004–; FRICS, FRTPI, FRSA, FAcSS; *Publications* Urban Planning and the Development Process (1994), Land for Industrial Development (with L Russell and C Taylor-Russell, 1994), Greenfields, Brownfields and Housing Development (with C Watkins, 2002), Planning, Public Policy and Property Markets (with C Watkins and M White, 2005), Urban Design in the Real Estate Development Process (with S Tiesdell, 2011), Shaping Places: Urban Planning Design and Development (with S Tiesdell, 2013); author of over 100 chapters, papers and articles on urban planning, land development and related subjects; *Recreations* walking, listening to classical music; *Style*— Prof David Adams; ✉ Urban Studies, School of Social and Political Sciences, University of Glasgow, 25 Bute Gardens, Glasgow G12 8RS (✆ 0141 330 6280, fax 0141 330 6032, e-mail david.adams@glasgow.ac.uk, website www.gla.ac.uk/schools/socialpolitical/staff/davidadams)

ADAMS, Gerard (Gerry); TD; s of Gerard Adams (d 2003); *b* 6 October 1948; *Educ* St Mary's GS Belfast; *m* 1971, Colette McArdle; 1 s; *Career* fndr memb Northern Ireland Civil Rights Assoc; interned by British Govt 1971, released for talks with Govt 1972, re-interned 1973; sentenced to 18 months imprisonment for attempted escape; released 1977; charged with IRA membership 1978, but charges unproven and released after seven months; elected to: Northern Ireland Assembly 1982–2011, Stormont Assembly 1998; MP (Sinn Féin) Belfast W 1983–92 and 1997–2011, TD 2011–; pres Sinn Féin 1983– (vice-pres 1978–83); fndg memb and dir Féile an Phobail 1988–; *Books* Peace In Ireland, Politics of Irish Freedom, Pathway to Peace, Falls Memories, Cage 11, The Street and Other Stories, Free Ireland: Towards A Lasting Peace, Before the Dawn: An Autobiography, An Irish Voice: The Quest for Peace, An Irish Journal, Hope and History, The New Ireland: A Vision for the Future, An Irish Eye; *Style*— Gerry Adams, Esq, TD

ADAMS, Dr James Noel; CBE (2015); *b* 24 September 1943; *Educ* North Sydney Boys' HS, Univ of Sydney (BA, Univ medal), BNC Oxford (DPhil); *m* 1, 22 March 1971 (m dis 2000), Geneviève Lucienne, *née* Baudon; 1 s (Nicholas James b 20 July 1976); *m* 2, 28 Sept 2001, Iveta, *née* Mednikarova; 1 da (Elena Rosemary b 16 Dec 2002); *Career* teaching fell Dept of Latin Univ of Sydney 1965–67, Rouse res fell in classics Christ's Coll Cambridge (MA on election) 1970–72; Univ of Manchester: lectr 1972–78, sr lectr 1978–82, reader 1982–93, prof of Latin 1993–95, prof research fell 2013–14; prof of Latin Univ of Reading 1995–97, sr research fell All Souls Coll Oxford (MA on election) 1998–2010; visiting sr research fell St John's Coll Oxford 1994–95, hon fell BNC Oxford 2012–; Kenyon Medal Br Acad 2009; memb Philological Soc 1972; FBA 1992, fell Australian Acad of the Humanities 2002, memb Academia Europaea 2007; *Books* The Text and Language of a Vulgar Latin Chronicle (1976), The Vulgar Latin of the Letters of Claudius Terentianus (1977), The Latin Sexual Vocabulary (1982), Wackernagel's Law and the Placement of the Copula esse in Classical Latin (1994), Pelagonius and Latin Veterinary Terminology in the Roman Empire (1995), Bilingualism and the Latin Language (2003), The regional Diversification of Latin 200 BC – AD 600 (2007), Social Variation and the Latin Language (2013), An Anthology of Informal Latin, 200 BC – AD 900 (2016); *Recreations* cricket; *Style*— Dr J N Adams, CBE, FBA; ✉ All Souls College, Oxford OX1 4AL

ADAMS, Jennifer; LVO (1993), OBE (2008); da of Arthur Roy Thomas Crisp, and Joyce Muriel, *née* Davey; *b* 1 February 1948; *Educ* City of London Sch for Girls, IPRA Staff Coll; *m* 21 Sept 1968, Terence William Adams; *Career* mangr Central Royal Parks 1983–97 (actg bailiff 1990–92), head of inner parks and commerce Royal Parks Agency 1997–2001, dir of open spaces Corp of London 2001–08; pres Inst of Horticulture 1996–98 (pres-elect 1994–96); Liveryman Worshipful Co of Gardners; assoc of honour RHS 1999; FILAM, Dip PRA, FIHort; *Style*— Mrs Jennifer Adams, LVO, OBE, FILAM, FIHort; ✉ Open Spaces Department, PO Box 270, Guildhall, London EC2P 2EJ (✆ 020 7332 3033, fax 020 7332 3522)

ADAMS, Prof Judith Elizabeth; *née* Lockyer; da of late Percy Charles Lockyer, of Hale, Cheshire, and Barbara, *née* Bailey; *b* 16 May 1945; *Educ* Roedean, UCH London (MB BS); *m* 16 Sept 1972, Prof Peter Harold Adams, s of late Alfred Adams, of Penarth, Wales; 2 s (Charles Edward b 25 Dec 1978, James Lindsay b 26 Jan 1983); *Career* prof of diagnostic radiology Univ of Manchester 1993– (lectr 1976–79, sr lectr 1979–), hon conslt radiologist Royal Infirmary Manchester 1978–, dean Faculty of Clinical Radiology RCR 1993– (vice-pres RCR 1994–95), acad gp ldr Imaging Sci and Biomedical Engrg 1998–; clinical dir of radiology Central Manchester Healthcare Tst (CMHT) 1997–2000; chm Examining Bd pt 1 FRCR 1984–89 (examiner 1980–84); memb: Editorial Bd British Journal of Radiology 1984–89, Editorial Bd Skeletal Radiology 1987–95, Int Skeletal Soc 1987–, Bd of Dirs Int Bone Mineral Soc 2009; non-exec memb Manchester Health Authy 1995–98, chm Congress Ctee Radiology UK 1997 and 1998; tstee Nat Osteoporosis Soc 2001–09; hon sec Br Assoc Clinical Anatomists 1990–93; Gold Medal Int Skeletal Soc 2007, Clinician of the Year Int Soc of Clinical Densitometry 2009; FRCR 1975, FRCP (MRCP) 1988, fell BIR 2007; *Publications* 169 peer-reviewed pubns, 23 invited reviews, 24 chapters in books and 6 invited editorships; *Recreations* embroidery, flower arranging, sewing, swimming, gardening; *Style*— Prof Judith Adams, MBBS, FRCP, FRCR, FBIR; ✉ Department of Clinical Radiology, Central Manchester University Hospitals NHS Foundation Trust, The Royal Infirmary, Oxford Road, Manchester M13 9WL (✆ 0161 701 6200, fax 0161 276 8916)

ADAMS, Prof Mac; *b* Brynmawr, S Wales; *Educ* Cardiff Coll of Art (NDD, ATD), Rutgers Univ (MFA); *Career* artist, sculptor and photographer; assoc prof SUNY, distinguished teaching prof SUNY Coll at Old Westbury; *Solo Exhibitions* incl: Farideh Cadot Gallery NY 1990, Gracie Mansion Gallery NY 1990, Sable/Castelli Gallery Toronto 1990, Yoshiaki Inoue Gallery Osaka 1992, John Gibson Gallery NY 1992, Jersey City Museum NJ 1993,

Art Awareness Lexington NY 1993, Galerie Froment and Putman Paris 1994, Exposition Monographique (Mai de Reims) 1996, Stux gallery NY 1997, Todd Gallery London 1997, Silence of Shadows (touring exhbn UK) 1998–2000, Serge Aboukrat Gallery Paris 2000, One Hundred Eyes (Center Photgraphique D'Ile-de-France) 2001, G/B Agency Paris 2002–03 and 2007, Musees de Chateauroux 2004, Mens Rea (CEAAC Strasbourg) 2006, Illuminated Perception, Explorations of Light and Shadow (Univ of Iowa Ames) 2013 and 2014, Crimes of Perception (Elizabeth Dee Gallery NY) 2013, Dialogues and Erasure (Galerie GB Agency Paris) 2014; *Group Exhibitions* incl: Des Images Comme des Oiseaux (La Friche La Belle de Mai Marseille-Provence) 2013, Doing and Undoing (Columbia Univ NY) 2013, Fixing Shadows (Le Granite Belfort France) 2013, Projecting an Exhibition (Jeu De Paume Paris) 2013, J'Ouvre Les Yeux et Tues La (Mudam Luxembourg) 2013, Trapping Lions in the Scottish Highlands (Museum of Art Aspen) 2013, Bad Thoughts (Stedelijk Museum) 2014, Art and Crime (Museum of Contemporary Art Krakow) 2014; *Public Commissions* Sweptaway (N Princeton Developmental Center NJ), Serpent Bearer (Montclair State Coll NJ), New York Korean War Memorial (Battery Park NY) 1991, Meditation (Botanical Gardens Louis Pasteur Univ Strasbourg) 1996, Mustangs at Noon (Henry Gonzalez Convention Center San Antonio) 1998, Solar Pavilion (belvedere, Penarth Haven Park) 1999, Wings and Wheels (solar pavilion, Dept of Transportation Cherry Hill NJ) 2001, Apparitions (Castle Blois France) 2002, Wetlands (photo mosaics, Secausus Transfer Railway Station NJ) 2003, Life Force (aluminium sculpture, NJ Sch of Medicine and Dentistry Newark) 2005, The Falls (glass and stone mosaic, Richard Stockton Coll NJ) 2006, Glass Tapestry (window, Rutgers Univ Law Sch NJ) 2007; *Public Collections* incl: Musée National d'Art Modern Center Pompidou Paris, Musée Nicephore Niepce Chalon sur Saone, Getty Musuem of Art LA, Fonds Regnl d'Art Contemporain (FRAC) Basse-Normandie, Microsoft Corp, Maison Europeenne de la Photographie Paris, DG Bank Frankfurt, Welsh Nat Museum, Goldman Sachs Investment Co, Harvard Univ, Fonds Regnl d'Art Contemporain (FRAC) Limousin, Fonds Nat d'Art Contemporain (FNAC) Paris, Caisse des Depots Paris, Lhoist Collection Belgium, Museum of Fine Arts Houston, MOMA NY, LA County Museum, Brooklyn Museum, First Nat Bank of Chicago, La Jolla Museum of Contemporary Art CA, Guggenheim Museum NY, Jersey City Museum NJ, Jane Voorhees-Zimmerli Art Museum Rutgers Univ, New Jersey State Cncl for the Arts, Ludwig Museum Cologne, Hamilton Art Gallery Ontario, Univ of Iowa Museum, Georgia Museum of Art, Welsh Arts Cncl Cardiff, Commodities Corp of New Jersey, V&A, Chase Manhattan Bank NY, Musée de Toulon, Morton Neumann Family Collection Chicago; *Awards* Nat Endowment Fellowship for the arts 1976, 1980 and 1982, Berlin Deutscher Akademischer Austauschdienst Berliner Kunstlerprogram 1981, NY State Fellowship for the Arts 1988, Chllr's Research Award for Excellence in the Arts and Humanities NY State Univ 2002; *Publications* Art and Crime, Le Regardeur la collection neuflize vie, Trapping Lions in the Scottish Highlands (text by Jacob Prockor), Illuminated Perception, explorations of light and shadow by Mac Adams (text by Emily Morgan); work in periodicals incl: Artforum (2013), NYCgo (2013), Westbury Times (text by Betsy Abraham, 2013), Des Moines Register (2013); *Style*— Prof Mac Adams; ✉ 18 Llewllyn Road, Montclair, NJ 07042, USA (✆ and fax 00 1 973 746 2761, e-mail mbadams2@aol.com, website www.macadamsstudio.com)

ADAMS, Nigel; MP; *b* 30 November 1966; *Educ* Selby GS; *m* Claire; 4 c; *Career* founding md Advances Digital Telecom Ltd 1993–99, dir JWE Telecom plc 1999, non-exec chm Pareto Law plc 2001–02, dir Ebor Events Ltd 2003–05, dir NGC Networks Ltd 2006–; MP (Cons) Selby and Ainsty 2010–, PPS to Ldr of the House of Lords and Chllr of the Duchy of Lancaster 2010–; *Style*— Nigel Adams, Esq, MP; ✉ House of Commons, London SW1A 0AA

ADAMS, Paul Michael; s of Michael Adams, of Budleigh Salterton, Devon, and Celia, *née* Pridham; *b* 21 March 1961, Beirut, Lebanon; *Educ* Sevenoaks Sch, Univ of York (BA); *m* Susanna Berry; 2 s (William b 1999, Felix b 2002); *Career* English teacher Br Cncl Yemen 1983–85; BBC: Arabic service World Service 1989, Jerusalem corr 1989–92, Belgrade corr 1993–95, reporter World TV 1995–97, Middle East corr 1997–2001, defence corr 2001–04, chief dip corr BBC News 24 2004–09, Washington corr BBC World Service 2009–, world affrs corr 2013–15, diplomatic corr 2015–; winner Amnesty Int TV News Award 2001; MRUSI, memb Chatham House; *Books* The Battle for Iraq (contrib, 2003); *Recreations* walking, photography, birdwatching, cinema; *Style*— Paul Adams, Esq; ✉ e-mail paul.adams@bbc.co.uk

ADAMS, Paul Nicholas; s of Peter Charles Adams (d 2001), and Joan, *née* Smith; *b* 12 March 1953; *Educ* Culford Sch Bury St Edmunds, Ealing Coll London (BA); *m* 26 Aug 1978, Gail Edwina, da of Emil Keith McCann; 1 s (Maximilian James b 8 April 1987), 2 da (Francesca Lindsay b 20 May 1989, Georgia Lucy b 25 Nov 1994); *Career* mktg dir Beecham Products Int 1983–86, European mktg vice-pres Pepsi Int 1986–91; British American Tobacco plc: regnl dir Asia-Pacific 1991–98, regnl dir Europe 1999–2001, dep md 2001, md 2002–03, chief exec 2004–11; non-exec dir Allied Domecq plc 2003–05; *Recreations* reading, walking, country pursuits; *Style*— Paul Adams

ADAMS, Ralph Gange; s of Ralph Noel Adams (d 1988), and Catherine Anne, *née* Reid (d 1988); *b* 30 October 1955; *Educ* Trinity Coll Glenalmond, Univ of Dundee (LLB); *m* 3 Aug 1989, Kirstine Mary Park, da of Rev Keith Campbell (d 1994); 2 da (Catherine Christine Campbell b 27 May 1992, Mairi Kirstine Reid b 17 May 1999), 2 s (Angus Keith Gange b 5 May 1994, Gavin Graham McFarlane b 11 March 1996); *Career* Deloitte LLP: indentured student 1976–79, qualified chartered accountant 1979, seconded to Melbourne 1980, seconded to Bank of Scotland 1984–85, ptnr (specialist in corp fin) 1986–, ptnr i/c Edinburgh office 1989–93, ptnr i/c Scotland and NI offices 1993–99, memb UK Bd of Ptnrs 1993–99, managing ptnr Global Fin Advsy Servs 1999–2007; Deloitte Touche Tohmatsu: managing ptnr global fin advsy services and corp fin 1999–2007, memb Global Mgmnt Ctee 1999–2007; vice-chm Deloitte UK 2008–; MICAS 1979; *Recreations* golf; *Clubs* Prestwick Golf, Golf House (Elie), Bruntsfield Golf (Edinburgh); *Style*— Ralph Adams, Esq; ✉ Deloitte LLP, Saltire Court, 20 Castle Terrace, Edinburgh EH1 2DB (✆ 0131 221 0002, fax 0131 535 7301)

ADAMS, Sheenagh; da of James Adams (d 2014), and Isabella, *née* Ross (d 2010); *b* 31 August 1957, Dundee; *Educ* Harris Acad Dundee, Univ of St Andrews (MA); *m* 3 June 1997, Peter Craig; 2 da (Caroline b 17 July 1994, Lyndsey b 5 Dec 1996); *Career* Registers of Scotland: md until 2009, keeper 2009–; tstee New Lanark Tst; *Recreations* cinema, reading, travel; *Style*— Ms Sheenagh Adams; ✉ Registers of Scotland, Meadowbank House, 153 London Road, Edinburgh EH8 7AU

ADAMS-JONES, Fiona; *Career* dir Wales Office; *Style*— Ms Fiona Adams-Jones; ✉ The Wales Office, Gwydyr House, Whitehall, London SW1A 2NP

ADAMSON, Clare Anne; MSP; da of George Pickering, and Eileen, *née* Daly; *b* 1 August 1967, Motherwell, Lanarkshire; *Educ* Glasgow Caledonian Univ (BSc); *m* 30 Sept 2002, John Adamson; 1 s (Aidan Michael b 6 Aug 1997); *Career* IT professional 1989–2003, project mangr SNP HQ Edinburgh 2003–07, cncllr N Lanarkshire Cncl 2007–11, MSP (SNP) Central Scotland 2011–; vice-chair Scottish Accident Prevention Cncl Home Safety Ctee, memb Bd Lanarkshire Leisure Tst, memb Lanarkshire Int Children's Games Organising Ctee; MBCS 2004; *Style*— Cncllr Clare Adamson, MSP; ✉ The Scottish Parliament, Edinburgh EH99 1SP

ADAMSON, (Ronald) Crawfurd; s of Ronald Adamson, of Edinburgh, and Janette Elizabeth Minna, *née* Bauermeister, of Edinburgh; *b* 24 March 1953; *Educ* Duncan of Jordanstone Coll of Art Dundee (Scottish Educn Dept travelling scholar, postgrad commendation), Elizabeth Greenshields Fndn Canada; *m* 1974, Mary Ann Elizabeth, da of Andrew Alexander Hansen Phimister; 1 s (Matthew Andrew b 1978), 1 da (Cassie Francesca b 1981); *Career* artist; gave up teaching to paint full time 1983; invited artist Salon d'Automne Paris 1993; works in numerous collections incl Met Museum of Art NYC; First Prize for Most Outstanding Work and Schmincke Pastel Award Pastel Soc London 2012; *Solo Exhibitions* incl: Cylinder Gallery London 1984 and 1985, Trinity Arts Centre Kent 1985, Scottish Gallery Edinburgh 1987, 1988 and 1989, Thumb Gallery London 1988, Scottish Gallery London 1989, Parnham House Dorset 1991, Jill George Gallery London 1991, 1993, 1995 and 1997, Château de la Muette Paris 1993, Art First London 1999, Schoeni Gallery Hong Kong 2001, Broderick Gallery Portland OR 2001, 2002, 2003 and 2004, Bohun Gallery Henley-on-Thames 2002, Broderick Gallery OR 2008, Flying Colours Gallery 2015; *Group Exhibitions* incl: Soc of Scottish Artists 1978 and 1979, Royal Scottish Acad 1979, Prix International d'Art Contemporain de Monte-Carlo 1984 and 1993, Contemporary Scottish Art (touring Japan, 1990), Scottish Art in the 20th Century (Royal W of England Acad Bristol) 1991; *Recreations* woodworking, music; *Style*— Crawfurd Adamson, Esq; ✉ 14 Sedlescombe Road South, St Leonards on Sea, East Sussex TN38 0TA

ADAMSON, Dr Donald; JP; s of Donald Adamson (d 1982), of Lymm, Cheshire, and Hannah Mary Adamson, *née* Booth (d 1994); *b* 30 March 1939; *Educ* Manchester GS, Magdalen Coll Oxford (Heath Harrison travelling scholar, Zaharoff travelling scholar), Univ of Paris (MA, MLitt, DPhil); *m* 24 Sept 1966, Helen Freda, da of (Frederick) Percival Griffiths, TD (d 1970), of Mossley Hill, Liverpool; 2 s (Richard Henry Egerton b 17 Jan 1970, John Daniel b 21 April 1971); *Career* author and historian; recognised teacher Univ of London 1971–89 (chm Bd of Examiners 1983–86), visiting scholar Wolfson Coll Cambridge 1981 (visiting fell 1989–90, fell 1990); chm Bow Group Research Ctee Museums and Libraries Policy 1969–71, fndr and sec Bow Group Standing Ctee on the Arts 1975–80; judge Museum of the Year Awards 1979–83, memb Exec Ctee Nat Heritage 1980–92; JP: City of London 1983–92, Cornwall 1993–2009; Lord of the Manor of Dodmore; Liveryman: Worshipful Co of Haberdashers 1976, Worshipful Co of Curriers 1991 (Renter Warden 2010, Upper Warden 2011, Master 2012); FSA 1979, FRSL 1983, FCIL 1989, FRHistS 2007; Order of St John: OStJ 1985, CStJ 1992, KStJ 1998, ceremonial dir Essex 1992–2010, asst dir of ceremonies Order of St John Grand Priory 1995–99, Priory of England and the Islands 1999–2007 (dep dir 2007–08); Chevalier dans l'Ordre des Palmes Académiques (France) 1986, Chevalier du Tastevin 2005, Cross of Merit Order Pro Merito Melitensi 2013; *Books* The Genesis of Le Cousin Pons (1966), Dusty Heritage (1971), T S Eliot: A Memoir (ed, 1971), The House of Nell Gwyn (jtly, 1974), A Rescue Policy for Museums (1980), Balzac: Illusions Perdues (1981), Les Romantiques français devant la peinture espagnole (1989), Blaise Pascal: Mathematician, Physicist, and Thinker about God (1995, 2 edn 2001), Rides Round Britain, The Travel Journals of John Byng, 5th Viscount Torrington (ed, 1996), The Curriers' Company: A Modern History (2000); Balzac and the Tradition of the European Novel (online, 2001); translations of works by Balzac (1970 and 1976) and Maupassant (1993), numerous French literature, historical and political articles, incl articles on the history of Cornwall and of the Sovereign Military Order of Malta and on Cyprus; *Recreations* personal training, swimming, travel, collecting, genealogy; *Clubs* National Liberal, Beefsteak, City Livery; *Style*— Dr Donald Adamson, JP; ✉ Dodmore House, The Street, Meopham, Kent DA13 0AJ; Topple Cottage, Polperro, Cornwall PL13 2RS (mobile 07747 733931 or 07890 824213, e-mail aimsworthy@aol.com, website www.dodmore.co.uk)

ADAMSON, Dr (Samuel) Ian Gamble; OBE (1998); s of John Gamble Sloan Adamson (d 1985), and Jane Gamble Sloan, *née* Kerr (d 2009); *b* 28 June 1944, Bangor, Co Down; *Educ* Bangor GS, Queen's Univ Belfast (MB, BCh, BAO), DCH RCSI, DCH RCPSGlas; *m* 1998, Kerry Christian, da of Douglas David Patrick Carson; *Career* doctor; registrar in paediatrics: Royal Belfast Hosp for Sick Children 1974–76, Ulster Hosp Dundonald 1976–77; specialist in community child health and travel med N and W Belfast HSS Tst 1981–2004; memb (UUP) Belfast City Cncl 1989–2011, Lord Mayor of Belfast 1996–97; MLA (UUP) Belfast E 1998–2003; former personal physician and advsr on history and culture to late Dr Ian Paisley (First Min of NI 2007–08; now Lord Bannside); co-dir Pretani Assocs 2012–; pres Belfast Civic Tst 2001–; chm Farset Youth and Community Devpt 1988–90; fndr chm: Somme Assoc 1989–2015, Ulster-Scots Language Soc 1992–2002 (vice-pres 2002–08); fndr pres Ullans Acad 1992–, fndr rector Ulster-Scots Acad 1994 (chm 1994–2004); fndr memb: Cultural Traditions Gp NI CRC 1988, Ultach Tst 1990; chm: Imported Foods and Feeds Ctee 2006–, Health and Environment Services Ctee Belfast City Cncl 2010–11; memb: Ulster-Scots Agency 2003–12, Ulster-Scots Acad Implementation Gp 2005–, Faculty of Community Health (MFCH), Bd Assoc of Port Health Authorities 2005–11 (chm Border Inspection Ctee 2005–06, memb Imported Food Ctee 2006); patron Dalaradia 2012–; High Sheriff Belfast 2011; fndr memb Ulster Soc 1985–; FRIPH; holds Wisdom-Keeper status among Lakota (Sioux) nation; OStJ 1998 (librarian and serving offr Commandery of the Ards); *Publications* The Cruthin (1974, 6 edn 2014), Bangor: light of the world (1979, 3 edn 2015), The Battle of Moira (1980), The Identity of Ulster (1982, 4 edn 1995), Colonel Paddy (1983, 2 edn 2013), The Ulster People (1991), 1690: William and the Boyne (1995), Dalaradia: kingdom of the Cruthin (1998, 2 edn 2003), Stormont: The House on the Hill (2008), Bombs on Belfast (2011), Ulster Scots A Short Reference Grammar (2012), Towards Commemoration: Ireland in War and Revolution 1912–23 (2013), Ulster – Scots in Northern Ireland Today: Language, Culture and Community (2013), The Old Testament in Scots, Vols 1&2 (2014), The Old Testament in Scots, Vols 3&4 (2016), The Voyage of Bran (2016); *Recreations* oil painting, theatre, travel; *Clubs* Ulster Reform Belfast, Clandeboye Golf; *Style*— Dr Ian Adamson, OBE; ✉ Members' Room, City Hall, Belfast BT1 5GS (✆ and fax 028 9042 1005, e-mail ian@pretani.co.uk, website www.ianadamson.net)

ADAMSON, James; CBE (1997, OBE 1970); s of Charles Adamson (d 1980), and Magdalene Adamson (d 1964); *b* 25 May 1941, Rosyth; *Educ* Kings Road Secdy Sch (Dux, Tech Cert), Royal Dockyards Tech Coll (ONC, HNC); *m* 24 Oct 1964, Ann May, da of George Gargett; 2 s (James b 10 May 1965, Joseph b 16 Oct 1966), 2 da (Rachel b 5 May 1970, Rebecca b 1 Jan 1978); *Career* civilian tech offr RN; various posts: Honeywell, AT&T, ITT, GEC; vice-chm NCR Financial Systems Ltd, fndr and chm amf INSIGHT 1998–; non-exec dir: East Bd Royal Bank of Scotland, First Banking Systems; memb Advsy Cncl Scottish Cncl for Devpt and Industry; hon pres Fife Soc for the Blind, tech advsr RNIB; hon fell Univ of Abertay Dundee, Hon Dr Heriot-Watt Univ, Hon Dr Univ of Dundee (also visiting prof); FRSA, FRSE; *Recreations* sailing, singing; *Style*— Mr James Adamson, CBE

ADAMSON, Paul Edward; OBE (2012); *b* Chester, Cheshire; *Educ* European Univ Inst Florence, Institut d'Etudes Politiques Grenoble, Kingston Univ; *m* 1978, Denyse Molaro; 1 da (Tessa b 1986), 1 s (William b 1989); *Career* res aide to MEPs 1979; former head European affrs BSMG Worldwide (co-chair global public affrs practice), ceo Adamson BSMG Worldwide Brussels, chm WeberShandwick Adamson; currently sr European policy advsr Covington and Burling; formerly: fndr Adamson Assoc (sold to WeberShandwick), fndr and chm The Centre (sold to Edelman); memb: Advsy American Security Project, Rand Europe Cncl of Advsrs, Advsy Bd Washington European Soc, Advsy Bd YouGov-Cambridge, Advsy Gp British Influence; tstee Citizenship Fndn; patron Univ Assoc of Contemporary European Studies (UACES); founding publisher and ed-in-chief E! Sharp (European affrs magazine); regular writer and speaker on European affrs; FAcSS; *Style*— Paul Adamson, Esq, OBE; ✉ 11 avenue Juliette, 1180 Brussels, Belgium

ADCOCK, Fleur; OBE (1996); da of Cyril John Adcock, and Irene, *née* Robinson; *b* 10 February 1934; *Educ* Wellington Girls' Coll NZ, Victoria Univ of Wellington (MA); *m* 1, 1952 (m dis 1958), Alistair Teariki Campbell; 2 s (Gregory Stuart b 1954, Andrew Robert Teariki b 1957); m 2, 1962 (m dis 1966), Barry Crump; *Career* poet; asst librarian: Univ of Otago 1959–61 (asst lectr 1958), Alexander Turnbull Library 1962, FCO 1963–79; freelance writer 1979–; Northern Arts Fellowship in Literature Univs of Newcastle upon Tyne and Durham 1979–81, Eastern Arts Fellowship UEA 1984, writer in residence Univ of Adelaide 1986; FRSL 1984; *Awards* Buckland Award 1967 and 1979, Jessie MacKay Award 1968 and 1972, Cholmondeley Award 1976, NZ Book Award 1984, Arts Cncl Bursaries 1982 and 1988, Queen's Gold Medal for Poetry 2006; *Books* The Eye of the Hurricane (1964), Tigers (1967), High Tide in the Garden (1971), The Scenic Route (1974), The Inner Harbour (1979), Below Loughrigg (1979), The Oxford Book of Contemporary NZ Poetry (1982), Selected Poems (1983), The Virgin and the Nightingale: medieval Latin poems (1983), Hotspur: a ballad for music (1986), The Incident Book (1986), The Faber Book of 20th Century Woman's Poetry (1987), Orient Express: poems by Grete Tartler (trans, 1989), Time Zones (1991), Letters from Darkness: poems by Daniela Crasnaru (trans, 1991), Hugh Primas and the Archpoet (ed and trans, 1994), The Oxford Book of Creatures (ed with Jacqueline Simms, 1995), Looking Back (1997), Poems 1960–2000 (2000), Dragon Talk (2010), Glass Wings (2013), The Land Ballot (2015); *Style*— Ms Fleur Adcock, OBE, FRSL; ✉ 14 Lincoln Road, London N2 9DL

ADEBOWALE, Dr Olutayo Omonitan (Tayo); *b* 28 August 1963, Huddersfield; *Educ* Manchester Met Univ (BSc), Univ of Manchester (PhD); *Career* project mangr UMIST Environmental 1989–93, sr environmental scientist Jacob Gp 1993–97, sr conslt Environmental Resources Management 1997–2002, dir Cirkadia 2003–; assoc lectr Open Univ 1988–2001, lectr Environmental Policy and Legislation module Liverpool John Moores Univ, non-exec GB forestry cmmr 2006–12, non-exec memb Countryside Agency Bd 2003–06 (memb: Audit & Risk Ctee, Landscape Access & Recreation Task Gp, Natural England Steering Gp); nominee NW Business Environment Award 2005; memb: Inst of Leadership and Mgmnt, Int Assoc of Water Quality, Chartered Inst of Water and Environmental Mgmnt (chair N Western and N Wales Branch 2004–05), Canal and River Tst Manchester and Pennines Partnership 2012–, Environment Agency NW Regional Flood and Coastal Ctee 2012–; chartered environmentalist, chartered water and environmental mangr; *Style*— Dr Tayo Adebowale; ✉ Cirkadia, PO Box 215, Manchester M13 1WX (☎ 01942 882134, e-mail tayoadebowale@cirkadia.co.uk)

ADEBOWALE, Baron (Life Peer UK 2001), of Thornes in the County of West Yorkshire; Victor Olufemi Adebowale; CBE (2000); s of E O Adebowale, and Grace Adebowale; *b* 21 July 1962; *Educ* Thornes House Wakefield, Poly of E London, City Univ (MA), Tavistock Inst (Dip); *Children* 1 s (Hon Adam b 1994), 1 da (Isabella b 2005); *Career* London Borough of Newham: private sector repairs admin 1983, estate offr 1983–84, sr estate mangr 1984–86; permanent property mangr Patchwork Community Housing Assoc 1986–88, regnl dir Ujima Housing Assoc 1988–90, dir Alcohol Recovery Project 1990–95; chief exec Centrepoint 1995–2001, ceo Turning Point 2001–; non-exec dir: 360 Advsy Ltd, TSIP Ltd, THP Ltd; chair: IPPR Review of Social Housing 1999, Fabian Soc/Barrow Cadbury Tst Review of Life Chances and Poverty 2003–04, Advsy Panel on Race Impact Assessment ODPM, Stop and Search Community Panel 2005–08, All-Pty Parly Gp on Complex Needs, Urban Devpt Youth Music, London Fairness Cmmn 2015; dir www.IOcom.com; co-chair: Mental Health Steering Gp Dept of Health 2002–, Black and Minority Ethnic Mental Health Steering Gp 2003–; pres Community Practitioners and Health Visitors Assoc; memb: New Deal Task Force, Policy Action Team 12 on Young People Social Exclusion Unit, Advsy Cncl Demos, Nat Employment Panel until 2007, Cncl Inst of Fiscal Studies 2002–07, Bd Places for People until 2007, Bd Nat Sch of Govt (also fell), Bd Audit Cmmn, Employment and Trg Cmmn, NHS Future Forum, NHS Quality Bd, Audit Cmmn until 2012, Bd Co-Operative Gp 2016–, Bd NHS England; dir Leadership in Mind; tstee: RNID until 2006, Nat Economics Fndn until 2007; patron: Nurse Trg Cncl on Alcohol, Centre for Inclusion and Diversity Univ of Bradford; hon fell South Bank Univ (chair Inst for Collaborative Practice 2012), assoc Health Servs Mgmnt Centre Univ of Birmingham, hon visiting prof and chllr Lincoln Univ, fell Sunningdale Inst; Hon PhD Univ of Central Eng, Hon PhD Univ of East London, Hon DLitt Lincoln Univ, Hon Dr Univ of Bradford; FRSA; *Publications* incl: Alcohol Problems in the Community: Drinking Problems Among Black Communities (1996), New Deal and the Disadvantaged (1999), Review of Social Housing (2000), Review of the Most Disadvantaged: Scond report (2003); contrib: Community Care, Voluntary Voice, Mental Health Today, Community Practitioner, Mental Health Review Jl, Public Policy Research; *Recreations* kite flying, reading, writing poetry, music; *Style*— The Rt Hon the Lord Adebowale, CBE; ✉ e-mail victor@leadershipinmind.co.uk

ADEBOWALE-SCHWARTE, Maria Seun; *Educ* Univ of Lancaster (BA), Huddersfield Poly (CPE), De Montfort Univ, SOAS (LLM), Univ of East London (PGCert); *Career* dir Environmental Law Fndn 1998–2001, fndr and dir Capacity Global 2001–14, dir Living Space Project 2014–; visiting fell School of Built Environment South Bank Univ 2001–02, research fell Centre for Sustainable Devpt Sch of Architecture and the Built Environment 2003–04; memb: UK Sustainable Devpt Cmmn 2000–03, Information and Communication Ctee ESRC 2004–07, Science Funding Grants Panel Science Wise DTI 2004–06, Advsy Panel Sustainable Business The Guardian; cmmr English Heritage 2003–11, chair Waterwise 2005–10, tstee Allavida 2006–10, tstee Shared Assets 2013–16, tstee Tst for Conservation Volunteers 2014–, chair SE Ctee Heritage Lottery Fndn 2016; Clore social leadership environment fell 2014; matron Women's Environment Network; listed in Independent on Sunday Top 100 Green List 2008, London Ldr Award 2011; FRSA 2001; *Style*— Ms Maria Adebowale-Schwarte; ✉ e-mail hello@livingspaceproject.com

ADEFARASIN, Remi; OBE (2012); *b* 2 February 1948, London; *m* Jaya Adefarasin; 3 s (René b 29 June 1976, John b 26 May 1979, Benjamin b 28 May 1981); *Career* cinematographer; memb: BSC 1992, AMPAS 1999; *Film* incl: Truly Madly Deeply, Sliding Doors, Elizabeth (Best Cinematography BAFTA 1998, Golden Frog, Best Cinematography BSC Award), Onegin, House of Mirth, About A Boy, Match Point, Scoop, Amazing Grace, Elizabeth: The Golden Age, Cemetery Junction, The Cold Light of Day, Molly Moon, Pride and Prejudice and Zombies, Me Before You, David Brent: Life On The Road; *Television* incl: Christabel, Lost Language of Cranes, Memento Mori, Sweet As You Are, The Buccaneers, Cold Lazarus, Arabian Nights, Band of Brothers, The Pacific; *Style*— Remi Adefarasin, Esq, OBE, BSC; ✉ c/o Lynda Mamy, United Agents (☎ 020 3214 0895, e-mail lmamy@unitedagents.co.uk, website www.unitedagents.co.uk)

ADER, His Hon Judge Peter Charles; s of Max Ader (d 1978), and Inge, *née* Nord (d 2006); *b* 14 May 1950, London; *Educ* Highgate Sch, Univ of Southampton (LLB); *m* 30 June 1979 (m dis 2005), Margaret Taylor; 2 da (Caroline Sarah b 1985, Catherine Elizabeth b 1993), 1 s (David Max b 1989); *Career* called to the Bar Middle Temple 1973; in private practice (specialising in criminal law) 1974–99, circuit judge (SE Circuit) 1999–; *Recreations* squash, tennis, skiing, golf, travel; *Clubs* Hampstead Golf; *Style*— His Hon Judge Ader; ✉ Wood Green Crown Court, Lordship Lane, London N22 5LF (☎ 020 8826 4100)

ADERIN-POCOCK, Dr Margaret (Maggie); MBE (2009); da of Justus Bayo Aderin, and Carol Phillips; *b* 9 March 1968, London; *Educ* La Sainte Union Convent Sch London, Imperial Coll London (BSc, PhD); *m* 06 July 2002, Dr Martin Pocock; 1 da (Lauren b 27 March 2010); *Career* MOD (Science) 1994–99, Mullard Space Science Laboratory UCL 1999–2004, Surrey Satellites Technol Ltd 2004–06, Astrium Space 2006–10; md Science Innovation Ltd 2006–; research fell Dept of Science and Technol Studies UCL 2006–, hon research assoc Dept of Physics and Astronomy UCL; co-presenter The Sky at Night; fell Br Science Assoc, FInstP; *Books* The Knowledge: Stargazing (2015); *Recreations* cinema, fashion, travel, walking; *Style*— Dr Maggie Aderin-Pocock, MBE; ✉ c/o Vicki McIvor, Take 3 Management, 110 Gloucester Avenue, Primrose Hill, London NW1 8HX (☎ 020 7209 3777, e-mail vicki@take3management.com, website www.take3management.co.uk)

ADÈS, Prof (Josephine) Dawn; CBE (2013, OBE 2002); da of A E Tylden-Pattenson, CSI (d 1955), and Ruth, *née* Morton (later Mrs Breakwell, d 1993); *b* 6 May 1943; *Educ* Guildford HS, Cheltenham Ladies' Coll, St Hilda's Coll Oxford (BA), Courtauld Inst of Art London (MA); *m* 9 July 1966, Timothy Adès; 3 s (Thomas b 1971, Harry b 1973, Robert b 1981); *Career* prof of history and theory of art Univ of Essex 1990–2014 (lectr 1978–); dir: Burlington Magazine 1996–, AHRC Research Centre for Studies of Surrealism and its Legacies 2002–07; tstee: Tate 1995–2005, Nat Gallery 1998–2005, Elephant Tst 2000–, Freud Museum 2000–, Henry Moore Fndn 2003–13; memb: Bd Canning House 2002–08, Collections Cncl Tate 2005–12; prof of history of art Royal Acad London 2009–, Slade prof of the history of art Univ of Oxford 2010, prof emerita Univ of Essex 2014–; FBA 1995; *Exhibitions* curator: Art in Latin America: the modern era 1820–1980 (Hayward Gallery London) 1989, Dalí's Optical Illusions (Wordsworth Atheneum Hartford CT) 2000, Undercover Surrealism (Hayward Gallery London) 2006 (AXA/Art Newspaper Award for Best Exhibition Catalogue 2006), The Colour of my Dreams: The Surrealist Revolution in Art (Vancouver Art Gallery) 2011; co-curator: Dada and Surrealism Reviewed (Arts Cncl of GB) 1978, Art and Power: Europe under the Dictators 1930–45 (Hayward Gallery London) 1995, Dali (Palazzo Grassi Venice and Philadelphia Museum of Art) 2004; *Books* Dada and Surrealism Reviewed (1978), Salvador Dalí (1982), Photomontage (1986), Art in Latin America (1989), André Masson (1994), Siron Franco (1995), Surrealist Art (1997), Marcel Duchamp (with Cox and Hopkins, 1999), Close-Up: Proximity and Defamiliarisation in Art, Film and Photography (jtly, 2008), Dawn Adès: Writings on Art and Anti-Art (2015); *Style*— Prof Dawn Adès, CBE, FBA; ✉ School of Philosophy and Art History, University of Essex, Colchester CO4 3SQ (☎ 01206 872200, mobile 07850 152055, e-mail dawnadesemail@gmail.com)

ADÈS, Thomas Joseph Edmund; s of Timothy Raymond Ades, of London, and Prof Dawn Ades, *née* Tylden-Pattenson; *b* 1 March 1971; *Educ* Univ Coll Sch, Guildhall Sch of Music, King's Coll Cambridge, St John's Coll Cambridge; *Partner* Tal Rosner (civil partnership 2006); *Career* composer, pianist, conductor; composer-in-residence Hallé Orch 1993–95, fell commoner in creative arts Trinity Coll Cambridge 1995–97, Benjamin Britten prof of music RAM 1997–2000, music dir Birmingham Contemporary Music Gp 1998–2001, artistic dir Aldeburgh Festival 1999–2008, composer in residence Ojai Festival Calif 2000; subject of retrospective festival Barbican London 2007; several CD releases of performances and compositions; Editor's Choice Gramophone Award 1998, Munich Ernst von Siemens Prize for Young Composers 1999, Grawemeyer Award 2000; Hon Dr Univ of Essex 2004; hon FGS; *Compositions* Five Eliot Landscapes 1990, O thou who didst with pitfall and gin (choral) 1990, Chamber Symphony 1990, Catch (chamber ensemble) 1991, Still Sorrowing (piano) 1991–92, Under Hamelin Hill (chamber organ) 1992, Fool's Rhymes (choral) 1992, ...but all shall be well (orchestral) 1993, Sonata da Caccia (chamber ensemble) 1993, Life Story (soprano and chamber ensemble) 1993, Living Toys (chamber ensemble) 1993 (Paris Int Rostrum of Composers 1994), Arcadiana (string quartet) 1994 (Elise L Stoeger Prize 1998, Salzburg Easter Festival Composition Prize 1999), The Origin of the Harp (chamber ensemble) 1994, Les baricades mistérieuses (chamber ensemble) 1994, Powder Her Face (chamber opera) 1995, Traced Overhead (piano) 1996, These Premises are Alarmed (orchestral) 1996, Asyla (orchestral) 1997 (Royal Philharmonic Society Prize 1997, Grawemeyer Prize 2000), Concerto Conciso (piano and chamber ensemble) 1997–98, America (mezzo-soprano, orchestra, and chorus) 1998–99, Piano Quintet 2000, Brahms (baritone and orchestra) 2001, The Tempest (opera) 2003–04 (Royal Philharmonic Soc Prize 2004), Concentric Paths (violin concerto) 2005, Three Studies from Couperin (chamber orchestra) 2006, Tevot 2007 (Royal Philharmonic Soc Prize 2007), In Seven Days (piano concerto with moving image) 2008, Lieux Retrouvés (cello and piano) 2009; *Clubs* Black's; *Style*— Thomas Adès; ✉ c/o Liz Lomas, Faber Music, Bloomsbury House, 74–77 Great Russell Street, London WC1B 3DA

ADGEY, Prof (Agnes Anne) Jennifer; CBE (2002); da of Robert Henry Adgey (d 1973), of Newtownards, Co Down, and Sarah Jane, *née* Menown (d 1990); *b* 2 October 1941; *Educ* Regent House Sch Newtownards Co Down, Queen's Univ Belfast (MB, MD); *Career* res fell in cardiology Presbyterian Med Centre San Francisco 1967–68; Royal Victoria Hosp Belfast: jr house offr 1964–65, sr house offr and registrar 1965–67, sr registrar in cardiology 1968–71, conslt cardiologist 1971–, prof of cardiology 1991–; examiner and censor RCP London, expert Advsy Panel on Cardiovascular Diseases WHO, examiner RCP Ireland 1988; memb: Cncl Br Cardiac Soc 1995–, Cncl Med Defence Union 1995–; memb: Br Cardiac Soc 1973, Assoc of Physicians of GB and Ireland 1980, NY Acad of Sci 1983, Resuscitation Cncl UK 1987, GMC 2010; fell American Coll of Cardiology 1975; Hon DSc Univ of Ulster 2007; FRCP 1978 (MRCP 1967), FESC 1995; *Books* The Acute Coronary Attack (with J F Pantridge, J S Geddes and S W Webb, 1975), Developments in Cardiovascular Medicine (1982), Acute Phase of Ischemic Heart Disease and Myocardial Infarction (ed), numerous papers on cardiology; *Recreations* piano and classical music; *Style*— Prof Jennifer Adgey, CBE; ✉ Mossvale House, 71 Ballyskeagh Road, Lisburn, Co Antrim BT27 5TE (☎ 028 9062 9773); Regional Medical Cardiology Centre, Royal Victoria Hospital, Belfast BT12 6BA (☎ 028 9063 2171, fax 028 9031 2907)

ADIE, Kathryn (Kate); OBE (1993); d of Babe Dunnet, *née* Issitt, and adopted da of John Wilfrid Adie (d 1993), and Maud, *née* Fambely (d 1990); *b* 19 September 1945; *Educ* Sunderland Church HS, Univ of Newcastle upon Tyne (BA); *Career* technician and prodr BBC local radio 1969–76, reporter BBC TV South 1977–78; BBC TV News: reporter 1979–81, corr 1982, chief news corr 1989–2003; presenter From Our Own Correspondent (BBC Radio 4) 1998–; hon prof broadcasting and journalism Univ of Sunderland 1995; Hon MA: Univ of Bath 1987, Univ of Newcastle upon Tyne 1990; Hon DLitt: City Univ 1989, Loughborough Univ 1991, Univ of Sunderland 1993, Robert Gordon Univ 1996, Univ of Nottingham 1998, Nottingham Trent Univ 1998; Hon DUniv: Oxford Brookes 2002, Anglia Poly 1999; Hon LLD Univ of St Andrews 2010, Hon LLD Univ of Bristol 2012; hon fell: Royal Holloway Univ of London 1996, Univ of Central Lancashire 2002, Univ of Cardiff 2004, York St John Univ 2006; visiting fell Bournemouth Univ 1998; RTS: News Award 1981 and 1987, Judges' Award 1989; Monte Carlo Int TV News Award 1981 and 1990, BAFTA Richard Dimbleby Award 1989; Freedom of City of Sunderland, Hon Freeman City of London 1995, memb Worshipful Co of Glaziers 1996; The Kindness of Strangers (memoirs 2002), Corsets to Camouflage: Women and War (2003), Nobodys Child : Who Are You When You Don't Know Your Past? (2005), Into Danger (2008); *Style*— Ms Kate Adie, OBE; ✉ c/o PO Box 317, Brentford TW8 8WX

ADJAYE, David; OBE (2007); s of Affram Adjaye, and Cecilia Adjaye; *b* 22 September 1966, Tanzania; *Educ* South Bank Univ (BA), RCA (MA); *Career* architect; Chassay Architects 1988–90, David Chipperfield Architects 1991, Eduardo Souto de Moura Architects Portugal 1991, founding ptnr Adjaye & Russell 1994–2000, princ Adjaye/Associates 2000–; projects: Idea Store Chrisp Street London 2004, Nobel Peace Centre Oslo 2005, Idea Store Whitechapel London 2005, Rivington Place London 2007, Bernie Grant Centre London 2007, Stephen Lawrence Centre London 2007, Museum of Contemporary Art USA 2007, William O Lockridge Bellevue Neighborhood Library Washington DC 2012,

Francis A Gregory Neighborhood Library Washington DC 2012; presenter Building Africa: Architecture of a Continent, co-presenter of two television series Dreamspaces (BBC); lectr: South Bank Univ 1993–98, RCA 1998–2002; first Louis Khan visiting prof Univ of Pensylvania, tutor AA, Kenzo Tange prof in architecture Harvard Grad Sch of Design, visiting prof Princeton Univ Sch of Architecture; delivered numerous talks and lectures worldwide; sr fell Royal Coll of Art 2007, hon fell AIA NY 2008; Hon Dr Arts Univ of E London 2007; RIBA, ARB; *Exhibitions* Sumi (Kyoto Geidai Gallery Japan) 1993, Papers (Architecture Foundation London) 1995, Tasty (Selfridges London) 1997, Outside/In: London Architecture (Architeckturforum Innsbruck) 2000, Adjaye/Associates Recent Work (Hanover Univ) 2001, David Adjaye Making Public Buildings (Whitechapel Gall) 2006; *Awards* First Prize Housing British Gas Student Competition 1992, First Prize Bronze Medal RIBA 1993, Highly Commended Phoenix Meml Competition 1993, First Prize Lewes Ideas Competition 1993, RIBA Building Award 2005 (for Idea Store Chrisp Street), RIBA Accessibility Award 2005 (for Idea Store Whitechapel), nomination RIBA Stirling Prize 2006, RIBA London Awards (Art and Culture) 2008 (for Rivington Place), Designs of the Year Design Museum 2008 (for Stephen Lawrence Centre), Elle Decoration Award 2008 (for Rivington Place), RIBA Int Award 2008 (for Museum of Contemporary Art), Design Miami Designer of the Year Award 2011, First Prize IX Int Architecture Award in the category Public Building 2011, Condé Nast Innovation and Design Award 2011 (for Genesis Pavilion), awarded top place in Guardian's Powerlist 2013, RIBA Int Award 2013 (for Francis A Gregory Neighborhood Library), RIBA Int Award 2013 (for William O Lockridge Bellevue Neighborhood Library); *Style*— David Adjaye, Esq, OBE; ✉ Adjaye/Associates, Edison House, 223–231 Old Marylebone Road, London NW1 5QT (☎ 020 7258 6140 or 020 7258 6148, e-mail mediaenquiries@adjaye.com)

ADKINS, Richard David; QC (1995); s of Walter David Adkins, and Patricia, *née* Chimes; *b* 21 October 1954, Royal Leamington Spa, Warks; *Educ* Leamington Coll for Boys, Hertford Coll Oxford (MA); *m* 1977, Jane Margaret, da of Derek and Ella Sparrow; 2 s, 1 da; *Career* admitted slr 1978; called to the Bar Middle Temple 1982; memb Ctee Chancery Bar Assoc 1991–93; *Publications* Encyclopaedia of Forms and Precedents (Vol 3, 1985), Company Receivers: A New Status? (1988), Gore-Browne on Companies (contrib, 44 edn, 1992–2008); *Recreations* opera; *Style*— Richard Adkins, Esq, QC; ✉ 3–4 South Square, Gray's Inn, London WC1R 5HP (☎ 020 7696 9900, fax 020 7696 9911, e-mail richardadkins@southsquare.com)

ADLAM, Lance Edward Stott; s of Edward Douglas Stott Adlam (d 1991), of Cotleigh, Devon, and Margaret Elsie, *née* May-Arrindell (d 1996); *b* 3 April 1944; *Educ* Acton Central Sch, The Elms Secdy Sch Acton, Chiswick Poly, Thames Poly (formerly Hammersmith Coll of Art & Building), Poly of Central London; *m* 1 July 1967, Angela Marie, da of Vivian Egerton Saunders; 2 s (Mark Edward Vivian b 1970, Paul Andrew John b 1972); *Career* architect: Fitzroy Robinson & Partners 1960–71, Bucks Co Architects' Dept 1971–78, Architects' Dept Ind Coope Ltd 1978–80, Fitzroy Robinson Partnership 1980–83; ptnr T P Bennett Partnership (formerly T P Bennett & Son) 1989–93 (assoc 1983–89), princ Lance Adlam Architects 1993–; chm: Princes Risborough Chamber of Trade 1998–2005, Princes Risborough Town Forum 1999–2007; pres Risborough Area Business Gp 2005–13; ARB 1974, RIBA 1974; A Triumph of Restoration (with Bill Simpson, 2008), Oxford Archaeological Unit, Paper 16 (contrib 2007); *Recreations* bowls, railway modelling, railway history, philately, music, reading; *Clubs* Princes Risborough Bowls (chm 2005–07), Great Western Soc, Quainton Railway Soc, Chinnor and Princes Risborough Railway Assoc, N Gauge Soc, Buckinghamshire Family History Soc, Buckinghamshire Genealogical Soc; *Style*— Lance Adlam, Esq; ✉ 6 Salisbury Close, Princes Risborough, Buckinghamshire HP27 0JF (☎ 01844 345423, e-mail l.adlam@lance-adlam-architects.org.uk)

ADLARD, David Boyd; s of Clifford Boyd Adlard (d 1985), of Norwich, and Elsie Lawrence, *née* Fielder (d 1990); *b* 13 June 1944; *Educ* Gresham's, Univ of Sussex (BSc), Middlesex Poly (Dip Mgmnt Studies), Kilburn Poly (Catering Studies); *m* Aug 1984 (m dis 1999), Mary Ellen, da of Edward Patrick Healy, of North Worcester, Mass; 1 da (Lucy Elizabeth b Nov 1987), 1 s (Matthew John Boyd b Aug 1991); partner, Diana Lowe; *Career* work study engr then prodn mangr Alcan Industries Ltd 1966–73, prodn mangr Cape Universal Building Products 1973–74; chef: various hotels and restaurants 1975–77, Connaught Hotel Mayfair 1978–81; chef tournant Le Talbooth Restaurant Dedham Colchester Essex 1981–82, pastry chef and asst to Maître D'Hotel Castle Restaurant Leicester Mass USA 1982, restaurant mangr The Terrace Restaurant Dedham Vale Hotel Dedham Colchester Essex 1982, prop Adlard's Restaurant Wymondham Norfolk 1983–2007 (moved restaurant to 79 Upper St Giles St Norwich 1989), co-prop (with Diana Lowe) Adlards in the Country W Somerton (Focus on Food) 2007–; contrib Taste magazine; *Awards* (for Adlard's restaurant) Michelin one rosette (first one in East Anglia) 1987–92 and 1995–2005, winner Glenfiddich Food & Drink Awards Regional Writer 2001, Outstanding Achievement Award Eastern Daily Press Food Awards 2005; *Recreations* wine, gardening; *Style*— David Adlard, Esq; ✉ Adlards In The Country, White House Farm, The Street, West Somerton, Norfolk NR29 4EA (☎ 01493 393991, e-mail info@adlardsinthecountry.co.uk)

ADLINGTON, Jonathan Peter Nathaniel; s of Sidney Roy Adlington, JP (d 1982), of Mylor, Cornwall, and Patricia, *née* Moxon (d 1998); *b* 26 April 1949; *Educ* Downside, Univ of Liverpool (LLB); *m* 2 June 1973, Carolyn Patricia Lilian Marie, da of Brian B W Bromley, of Crowborough, E Sussex; 2 da (Emily b 3 May 1975, Tamsin b 19 Sept 1976), 1 s (Edward b 25 Dec 1983); *Career* admitted slr 1973; sr ptnr Trowers & Hamlins 2000–13 (articled clerk 1971–73, ptnr 1976–13); memb Law Soc; *Recreations* sailing; *Clubs* RAC; *Style*— Jonathan Adlington, Esq

ADORNO-S, Jesus Antonio; s of Luciano Adorno Rolon (d 1958), of Santa Cruz, Bolivia, and Maria Sanabria Osorio (d 2002); *b* Santa Cruz, Bolivia; *Educ* Gaston Guillaux Coll Santa Cruz; *m* (m dis); 2 da (Diana Luz b 16 May 1985, Monica Maria b 4 March 1987); *Career* waiter: Fredericks Restaurant 1974–75, Jardin des Gourmet 1974–76, Inigo Jones 1977–81; head waiter rising to restaurant mangr Le Caprice 1981–, dir Caprice Holdings 1990–, dir Daphne's Restaurant 1992–; freelance journalist: The Telegraph, The Mail on Sunday, Orient Express Magazine; Fashion Restaurant of the Year 2000; supporter Anglo-Bolivian Soc; *Recreations* football, walking, snorkling, cricket; *Clubs* Destroyers (Bolivia), Tottenham Hotspur; *Style*— Jesus Adorno-S, Esq; ✉ Le Caprice, Arlington House, Arlington Street, London SW1A 1RT (☎ 020 7629 2239, fax 020 7493 9040)

ADRIANO, Dino; s of Dante Adriano, and Yole Adriano; *b* 24 April 1943; *Educ* Highgate Coll, Strand GS; *m* 1966, Susan Rivett; 2 da; *Career* articled clerk George W Spencer & Co 1959–64; J Sainsbury plc: joined as accountant 1964, gen mangr Homebase 1981–86, area dir 1986–89, md Homebase 1989–95 (chm 1991–96), main bd dir 1990–2000, chm Shaw's Supermarkets Inc 1994–96 (dep chm 1993–94), dir Giant Food Inc 1994–96, asst md 1995–96, dep chief exec 1996–97, chm and chief exec Sainsbury's Supermarkets Ltd 1997–2000 (dep chief exec 1996-March 1997), gp chief exec J Sainsbury plc 1998–2000; dir Laura Ashley plc 1996–98; tstee: Oxfam 1990–96 and 1998–2004 (vice-chm 2001–04, advsr 1996–98 and 2004–07), WRVS 2001–07, Sainsbury Archive 2007–, Sainsbury Veterans Welfare Scheme 2008–; chair of govrs Thames Valley Univ 2004–09; Hon DUniv Thames Valley 2009; FCCA 1980 (ACCA 1965), FCIM 2011 (tstee 2015–); *Style*— Dino Adriano, Esq

ADSETTS, Sir (William) Norman; kt (1999), OBE (1988); s of Ernest Norman Adsetts (d 1992), and Hilda Rachael, *née* Wheeler (d 1986); *b* 6 April 1931; *Educ* King Edward VII Sch Sheffield, The Queen's Coll Oxford (MA); *m* 20 Oct 1956, Eve, da of Eric Stefanuti (d 1985); 1 da (Helen Eve b 1957), 1 s (Philip Norman b 1959); *Career* Nat Serv flying offr Equipment Branch RAF 1950–52; appts in sales and mktg and product devpt Fibreglass Ltd 1955–66; chm: Sheffield Insulating Co Ltd 1985–89 (dir 1966, md 1970), SIG plc 1989–96 (pres 1996–), Sheffield Partnerships Ltd 1988–93, South Yorkshire Supertram Tst Ltd 1993–98, Adsetts Partnership 2012–; non-exec dir Sheffield Theatres Ltd 1988–94, dep chm Sheffield Devpt Corp 1991–97 (memb Bd 1988–91); chm: Kelham Island Museum Ltd (renamed Sheffield Industrial Museums Tst in 1997) 1994–98 (pres 2014–), Sheffield Theatres Tst 1996–2005 (pres 2005–), Kelham Riverside Devpt Agency 1998–2001; vice-pres Assoc for the Conservation of Energy Ltd 1990– (chm 1985–90 and 1993–95); pres Sheffield C of C 1988–89; chm: CBI Yorkshire and Humberside 1989–91, Sheffield First for Investment 1999–2001, Bd of Govrs Sheffield Hallam Univ 1993–99, Autism Plus 2008–12 (pres 2014–); tstee: Hillsborough Disaster Appeal 1989–95, Research Autism 2006–14; memb: Advsy Ctee on Business and the Environment 1991–93, Yorkshire and Humberside Arts Bd 1991–94, Bd Opera North Ltd 1991–94, Fin Bd RC Diocese of Hallam 1998–2004, Nat Cncl of Arts Cncl of England 2002–05; chm of govrs Mount St Mary's Coll 1999–2008 (pres 2011–); Campion Medal of Society of Jesus 2008; *Recreations* reading, local history, grandchildren; *Style*— Sir Norman Adsetts, OBE; ✉ Danes Balk, 8 Rotherham Road, Eckington, Sheffield S21 4FH (☎ 01246 431008, e-mail sirnormanadsetts@icloud.com)

ADSHEAD, Dr Fiona; *Career* previously: conslt in public health medicine Camden and Islington Health Authy 2002, dir of public health Camden PCT 2002, policy advsr Faculty of Public Health, registrar then sr registrar Croydon Health Authy, lectr St George's Hosp Medical Sch; latterly dep chief medical offr and DG of health improvement Dept of Health, currently govt advsr on health inequalities; tstee Nat Heart Forum; *Style*— Dr Fiona Adshead; ✉ Department of Health, 79 Whitehall, London SW1A 2NS

AFRIYIE, Adam; MP; *b* 4 August 1965, Wimbledon, London; *Educ* Addey and Stanhope GS, Imperial Coll London (BSc); *m* Aug 2005, Tracy-Jane Newall; 3 s, 1 da, 1 step-s; *Career* founding dir Connect Support Services 1993–, former chm DeHallivand Info Services plc, chm Adfero; MP (Cons) Windsor 2005–; Parly Office of Science and Technology 2005–; dir Policy Exchange, former govr Museum of London, patron Young Enterprise Berks; *Style*— Adam Afriyie, Esq, MP; ✉ House of Commons, London SW1A 0AA

AFSHAR, Farhad; s of Aziz Afshar Yazdi, and Btoul, *née* Ameli; *b* 4 December 1941; *Educ* Lord Wandsworth Coll, London Hosp Med Coll (BSc, MB BS, MD); *m* 1, 23 Aug 1968 (m dis 1983), Lucille Anne, da of William E Goodfellow (d 1985); 3 s (Iain b 1970, Daniel b 1973, Brett b 1974), 1 da (Nina b 1977); *Career* fell in neurosurgery Ohio State Univ 1974–75, conslt neurosurgeon and sr lectr in neurosurgery London Hosp 1975–85, sr registrar in neurosurgery London Hosp and Bart's 1977, conslt neurosurgeon Bart's 1985–2010, currently sr conslt neurosurgeon, chm of neurosciences and chm of neuro-cyberknife radio-surgery The London Clinic and conslt neurosurgeon Nicosia Gen Hosp Cyprus; former sr conslt neurosurgeon Royal London Hosp; author of numerous chapters and scientific papers on neurosurgery, examiner in surgery Univ of London; memb: Soc of Br Neurosurgeons, Congress of American Neurosurgeons, Euro and World Sterotaxic Surgns, World Pituitary Surgns; FRSM, LRCP, FRCS (MRCS); *Books* Stereotaxic Atlas of Human Brain Stem and Cerebellar Nuclei (1978); *Recreations* photography, natural history, walking; *Style*— Farhad Afshar, Esq; ✉ e-mail faryafshar@hotmail.com

AFSHAR, Baroness (Life Peer 2007), of Heslington in the County of North Yorkshire; Prof Haleh Afshar; OBE; da of Hassan Afshar; *b* 1944; *Educ* Ecole Jean d'Arc Tehran, St Martin's Sch Solihull, Davis's Sch Brighton, Univ of York (BA), Univ of Strasbourg, Univ of Cambridge (PhD); *m* 1974, Maurice Dodson; 1 s, 1 da; *Career* feature writer Kayhan Int Tehran 1971–74, lectr Univ of Bradford 1976–85, lectr Univ of York 1985– (prof of politics and women's studies 1999–); fnd and pres Muslim Women's Network 2002, govt policy advsr on Muslim women and Islamic law; memb: Working Gp on Ethics and Pharmacogenetics Nuffield Cncl on Bioethics 2002, UK Drug Policy Cmmn 2006; AcSS 2009; *Publications* lauched Democracy Series Hansard Soc 2006; ed and author of many learned pubns on Iran, Women and the Third World; *Style*— Prof the Baroness Afshar, OBE, AcSS; ✉ Department of Politics, York University, York YO10 5DD; House of Lords, London SW1A 0PW

AGA KHAN (IV), HH The; Prince Karim; KBE (2004), Hon CC (2004); s of late Prince Aly Khan, and Hon Joan, *née* Yarde-Buller (later Viscountess Camrose d 1997), da of 3 Baron Churston, MVO, OBE; gs of late Sir Sultan Mahomed Shah Aga Khan (III) (d 1957); *b* 13 December 1936; *Educ* Le Rosey Switzerland, Harvard Univ (BA); *m* 1, 1969 (m dis 1995), Sarah Frances (Sally), *née* Croker-Poole; 2 s (Prince Rahim b 1971, Prince Hussain b 1974), 1 da (Princess Zahra (Mrs Mark Boyden) b 1970); *m* 2, 1998 (m dis 2004), Princess Gabriele zu Leiningen; 1 s (Prince Aly Muhammad b 2000); *Career* Spiritual Leader and Imam of Ismaili Muslims 1975–, granted title HH by HM The Queen 1957, and HRH by late Shah of Iran 1959; philanthropist; fndr: Aga Kham Devpt Network; fndr and chm: Aga Khan Fndn Switzerland 1967 (branches/affiliates in Bangladesh, Canada, India, Kenya, Pakistan, Portugal, Tajikistan, Tanzania, Uganda, UK and USA), Aga Khan Award for Architecture 1977, Inst of Ismaili Studies London 1977, Aga Khan Fund for Econ Devpt 1984, Aga Khan Tst for Culture Switzerland 1988, Aga Khan Agency for Micro-finance 2005; fndr and chllr: Aga Khan Univ Pakistan 1983, Univ of Central Asia (by treaty with Kurgyzstan, Tajikistan and Kazakhstan) 2000; leading owner and breeder of race horses in France, Ireland and UK; winner Derby: 1981 (Shergar), 1986 (Shahrastani), 1988 (Kahyasi), 2000 (Sinndar); winner Irish Derby: 1981 (Shergar), 1986 (Shahrastani), 1988 (Kahayasi), 2000 (Sinndar), 2003 (Alamshar); winner Prix de L'Arc de Triomphe: 1982 (Akiyda), 2000 (Sinndar), 2003 (Dalakhani); winner Prix de Jockey Club: 1960 (Charlottesville), 1979 (Top Ville), 1984 (Darshaan), 1985 (Mouktar), 1987 (Natroun), 2003 (Dalakhani); winner Prix de Diane: 1993 (Shemaka), 1997 (vereva), 1998 (Zainta), 1999 (Daryaba); Dr of Laws (hc): Peshawar Univ Pakistan 1967, Sind Univ Pakistan 1970, McGill Univ Canada 1983, McMaster Univ Canada 1987, Univ of Wales 1993, Brown Univ USA 1996, Univ of Toronto Canada 2004; DLitt (hc) Univ of London 1989, Dr of Humane Letters (hc) American Univ of Beirut 2005; hon prof Univ of Osh Kyrgyzstan 2002; foreign hon memb American Acad of Arts and Sciences; Thomas Jefferson Meml Fndn Medal in Architecture 1984, American Inst of Architects Honor 1984, Medalla de Oro Consejo Superior de Colegios de Arquitectos Spain 1987, Huésped de Honor de Granada Spain 1991, Hon FRIBA 1991, Medaille d'Argent Académie d'Architecture France 1991, Gold Medal City of Granada 1998, Insignia of Honour Int Union of Architects France 2001; hon memb: American Inst of Architects 1992, Hadrian Awards World Monuments Fund; Vincent Scully Prize USA 2005; Commandeur Ordre du Mérite Mauritanien 1960; Grand-croix: Order of Prince Henry Portugal 1960, Ordre National de la Côte d'Ivoire 1965, Ordre National de la Haute-Volta 1965, Ordre Malgache 1966, Ordre du Croissant Vert des Comores 1966; Grand Cordon Order of the Tadj Iran 1967, Nishan-i-Imtiaz Pakistan 1970, Cavaliere di Gran Croce dell'Ordine al Merito della Repubblica Italy 1977, Grand Officier Ordre National du Lion Sénégal 1982, Nishan-e-Pakistan 1983, Grand Cordon Ouissam-al Arch Morocco 1986, Cavaliere del Lavoro Italy 1988, Cdr de la Légion d'Honneur France 1990, Gran Cruz de la Orden del Merito Civil Spain 1991, Grand-croix Order of Merit Portugal 1998, Order of Friendship Tajikistan 1998; State Award of Peace and Progress Kazakhstan 2002; hon citizen Islamic Ummah of Timbuktu Mali 2003; Order of Bahrain (first class) 2003; *Recreations* yachting, skiing; *Clubs* Royal Yacht Squadron, Yacht Club Costa Smeralda (Sardinia, fndr and pres); *Style*— His Highness the Aga Khan; ✉ Aiglemont, 60270 Gouvieux, France

AGBAJE, Bola; da of Agbaje Olakunle, and Agbaje Sikirat, *née* Adio; *b* 8 June 1981, London; *Career* playwright; dir 2 Far Media Ltd; Woman of the Future Award 2010, Red Magazine Hot Woman to Watch 2010; *Plays* Gone Too Far! (Royal Court, Albany Theatre and Hackney Empire) 2007–08 (Outstanding Achievement in an Affiliated Theatre Laurence Olivier Award 2008), Detaining Justice (Tricycle Theatre) 2009, Off the Endz (Royal Court) 2010, Belong (Royal Court) 2012; *Recreations* cinema, gardening, horse racing, motorsport, music, opera, reading, sailing, shooting, skiing, travel, walking; *Style—* Ms Bola Agbaje; ✉ c/o United Agents, 12–26 Lexington Street, London W1F 0LE (☎ 020 3214 0800, e-mail gsmart@unitedagents.co.uk, Twitter @bolaagbaje)

AGGAR, Tom; *b* 24 May 1984, London; *Educ* Queen Elizabeth Boys' Sch, Univ of Warwick (BSc); *Career* Paralympic rower; achievements incl: Gold medal men's single sculls World Rowing Championships 2007, 2009, 2010 and 2011, Gold medal men's single sculls Paralympics Beijing 2008; *Style—* Tom Aggar, Esq

AGGISS, Emeritus Prof Liz; da of James Henry Aggiss, of Terling, Essex (d 2004), and Marie Elizabeth, *née* Chamberlain (d 1975); *b* 28 May 1953; *Educ* Hornchurch GS, Madeley Coll, Nikolais/Louis Dance Theatre NY; *Career* choreographer, dancer, performer, film maker; artistic dir Divas Dance Theatre (in collaboration with Billy Cowie) 1980–2006, prof of visual performance Univ of Brighton 2002– (subject ldr BA Hons Dance Visual Art 1993–2002), artistic dir SE Dance Agency 1997–98; contrib dance entries Fontana Dictionary of Modern Thought (1988); memb The Wild Wigglers (formed 1982, touring worldwide); work with Divas Dance Co (formed 1985, touring worldwide) incl: Torei en Veran Veta Arnold! 1986–87, Eleven Executions 1988, Dorothy and Klaus 1989–91, Die Orchidee im Plastik Karton 1989–91, Drool and Drivel They Care 1990–91, La Petite Soupe 1990–91, La Chanson Bien Douce 1991; solo performances incl: Grotesque Dancer 1986–89, Stations of the Angry 1989, Tell Tale Heart 1989, El Puñal Entra En El Corazón 1991, Vier Tänze (reconstructions from the 1920s and '30s by Hilde Holger) 1992, Falling Apart at the Seams (So it Seems) 1993, No Man's Land 1993, Absurditties 1994, Hi Jinx 1995, The Fetching Bride 1995, Divagate (cmmnd by Gardner Arts and Royal Festival Hall) 1997; solo choreographic work: Guerrilla Dances 2008, Double Vision (in collaboration with Charlotte Vincent AD Vincent Dance Theatre) 2009 and Survival Tactics 2009–11, The English Channel 2013, Slap and Tickle 2015; cmmns incl: Dead Steps/Die Totenschritte (for Extemporary Dance Theatre) 1988–89, Banda Banda and La Soupe (for Carousel) 1989–90, Bird in A Ribcage (for Transitions Dance Co) 1994, Taped Up Sea of Heads Film for TVS 1997, The 38 Steps (for Intoto Dance Co), The Surgeon's Waltz (for Carousel) 2000, Rice Rain (for Carousel) 2001, Don't Put Your Daughter on the Stage (for Mapdance Co) 2008, Cut with the Kitchen Knife (for Mapdance Co) 2014, History Repeating (for Mapdance Co) 2016, Bloody Nora (for NORA) 2016; hon doctorate Univ of Gothenburg Sweden; *Awards* Colorado Coll scholarship to study with Hanya Holm 1980, Brighton Festival Special Award 1989, Brighton Festival Zap Award for Dance 1989, Brighton Festival BBC Radio Award 1990, Alliance and Leicester Award 1990 and 1992, Time Out/Dance Umbrella Award 1990, Arts Cncl and BBC2 Dance for Camera Award 1992 (Beethoven in Love) and 2000, Bonnie Bird Choreography Award 1994, BBC/Arts Cncl Dance for Camera 2000 (Motion Control), Arts Cncl Ind Dance Fellowship 2002, Capture 2002 (film award, Anarchic Varitations), Capture Award 2003 (The Men in the Wall), Czech Crystal Award Golden Prague Int TV Awards 2002, Special Jury Golden Award World Film Festival Houston 2003, Best Woman Film Mediawave Hungary 2003, Romanian Nat Office of Cinematography Prize 2003, Capture 2004 and New Art Gall Walsall Cmmn (Doppelgänger) 4Dance Channel 4 Cmmn (Break), Dance Camera West LA Award for Innovation in the Field of Dance Media (for Men in the Wall), Hong Kong Jumping Frames Screen Dance Award 2008 (for Diva), Beach Party Animal South East Dance Screen Dance Cmmn 2011; *Publications* The Rough Guide to Reconstruction (animated magazine) 1999, Juggling not Struggling (Dance Theatre Jl Vol 15 No 4) 2000, Outsider Performance (animated magazine) 2001, Being There (animated magazine, 2003), Anarchic Dance (jtly with Billy Cowe and Ian Bramley, 2006), Zap: 25 Years of Innovation (contrib); *Recreations* music, cinema; *Style—* Emeritus Prof Liz Aggiss; ✉ websites www.lizaggiss.com and http://arts.brighton.ac.uk/staff/liz-aggiss

AGIS, Gaby; *b* 1960; *Career* independent choreographer 1983–; choreographer in residence Riverside Studios 1984–86, launched own co 1985; progs incl: Close Streams 1983, Crossing Under Upwards 1983, Surfacing 1984, Borders 1984, Shouting Out Loud 1984, Between Public Places 1985, Undine and the Still 1985, This Is, What, Where 1985, In Anticipation of Surrender 1986, Fow Fold 1986, Lying On the Warm Concrete 1986, Trail 1986, Kin 1987, Freefall 1988, Don't Trash My Altar/Don't Alter My Trash 1988, Mlada (LSO) 1989, Hess Is Dead (RSC) 1989, Dark Hours And Finer Moments 1989, Pale Shelter 1990, Cold Dark Matter 1991, The Family 1994, Beyond the Edges (AA) 1997, Silver for Boty (Union Chapel) 1998, Doctor Oxo's Experiment (ENO) 1998, touch Unsited (AA) 2000, Tamar's Revenge (RSC) 2004, Explicit Faith 2004; performance art venues incl: Tate Gallery Liverpool, Chisenhale Gallery, Whitechapel Art Gallery, Riverside Studios Gallery, MOMA Oxford, Cornerhouse Gallery Manchester; TV and film appearances incl: Hail the New Puritan 1985, Imaginary Women 1986, Freefall 1988, Dark Hours and Finer Moments 1994; awards incl Distinguished Visitors award of US Govt 1986; *Style—* Ms Gaby Agis; ✉ c/o Bolton & Quinn, 10 Pottery Lane, London W11 4LZ (☎ 020 7221 5000, fax 020 7221 8100)

AGIUS, Marcus Ambrose Paul; s of Lt-Col Alfred Victor Louis Benedict Agius, MC, TD (d 1969), and Ena Eleanora, *née* Hueffer (d 2000); *b* 22 July 1946; *Educ* St George's Coll Weybridge, Trinity Hall Cambridge (MA), Harvard Business Sch (MBA); *m* 1971, Kate Juliette, da of Maj Edmund Leopold de Rothschild, TD, CBE, of Hants; 2 da (Marie-Louise Eleanor b 1977, Lara Sophie Elizabeth b 1980); *Career* Lazard: joined 1972, dir 1981–85, md 1985–90, vice-chm 1990–2001, chm 2001–06, dep chm Lazard LLC 2002–06; chm: BAA plc 2002–2006 (non-exec dir 1995–, dep chm 1998–2002), Barclays plc 2007–12 (non-exec dir 2006–12); chm Br Bankers' Assoc 2010; Br business ambass 2010; non-exec dir: Exbury Gardens Ltd 1977–, Exbury Gardens Retail Ltd 1998; sr ind dir BBC 2006–; memb Advsy Cncl TheCityUK 2010, memb Exec Ctee Institut International d'Etudes Bancaires (IIEB) 2010, memb The Takeover Panel 2010; chm Fndn and Friends of the Royal Botanic Gardens Kew 2004, tstee Royal Botanic Gardens Kew 2006– (chm Bd of Tstees 2009–); *Recreations* gardening, shooting, skiing, sailing; *Clubs* White's, Swinley Forest; *Style—* Marcus Agius, Esq

AGNEW, Christine; QC (2015); *Career* called to the Bar 1992; *Style—* Ms Christine Agnew, QC; ✉ The Chambers of William Clegg QC, 2 Bedford Row, London WC1R 4BU

AGNEW, Jonathan Geoffrey William; s of late Sir Geoffrey Agnew, and late Hon Doreen, da of 1 Baron Jessel, CB, CMG; *b* 30 July 1941; *Educ* Eton, Trinity Coll Cambridge (MA); *m* 1966 (m dis 1986), Hon Agneta Joanna Middleton (d 2002), yr da of Baron Campbell of Eskan (Life Peer, d 1994); 1 s (Caspar Jonathan William b 1967), 2 da (Lara Joanna b 1969, Katherine Agneta b 1971); m 2, 1990, Marie-Claire, er da of Bernard Dreesmann; 1 da (Clarissa Virginia b 1992), 1 s (George Jonathan Henry b 1999); *Career* The Economist 1964–65, World Bank 1965–67, Hill Samuel & Co 1967–73 (dir 1971), Morgan Stanley & Co 1973–82 (md 1977), J G W Agnew & Co 1983–86, gp chief exec Kleinwort Benson Group plc 1989–93 (joined 1987); chm: Henderson Geared Income and Growth Trust plc 1995–2003, Limit plc 1993–2000, Gerrard Gp plc 1998–2000, Nationwide Building Soc 2002–07 (non-exec dir 1997–2007, dep chm 1999–2002), Beazley plc 2003–12 (non-exec dir 2002–12), The Cayenne Tst plc 2006–15, LMS Capital plc 2006–11, Ashmore Global Opportunities Ltd 2007–12; Fleet Mortgages Ltd 2014–; dir: Thos Agnew and Sons Hldgs Ltd 1969–2013, Rightmove plc 2006–15;; *Clubs* White's, Automobile (Paris); *Style—* Jonathan Agnew, Esq

AGNEW, Jonathan Philip; s of Philip Agnew, of Ketton, Lincs, and Margaret, *née* McConnell; *b* 4 April 1960; *Educ* Uppingham; *m* 1, 8 Oct 1983 (m dis 1994), Beverley Measures; 2 da (Jennifer Ann b 31 Oct 1985, Rebecca Louise b 18 Sept 1988); m 2, 4 May 1996, Emma Norris; *Career* former cricketer (bowler); joined Leics CCC 1978, took 101 wickets 1987 season, ret 1990; played for Eng 1984 and 1985 (3 tests, 3 one day ints); cricket corr Today 1990–91, BBC cricket corr 1991–; Radio Acad Best Sports Reporter Sony Radio Awards 1993; *Books* 8 Days a Week (1988), Over to You, Aggers (1997); *Recreations* golf, gardening; *Style—* Jonathan Agnew, Esq

AGNEW, (Morland Herbert) Julian; yr s of Sir Geoffrey William Gerald Agnew (d 1986), and Hon Doreen Maud Jessel, da of 1 Baron Jessel, CB, CMG; *b* 1943; *Educ* Eton, Trinity Coll Cambridge (scholar and sr scholar, MA); *m* 1, 1973 (m dis), Elizabeth Margaret, yst da of William B Mitchell, of Blanefield, Stirlingshire; 1 s (Thomas Julian Noel b 1975), 2 da (Amelia Elizabeth b 1979, Georgina Helen b 1982); m 2, 4 Sept 1993, Victoria, 2 da of Maj (Henry) Ronald Burn Callander, MC, and Penelope, Countess of Lindsay; 1 s (Benjamin Geoffrey David Callander b 6 Oct 1996); *Career* Agnew's: joined 1965, dir 1968, md 1987, chm 1992–; pres BADA 1979–81, chm Soc of London Art Dealers 1986–90, chm Friends of the Courtauld Inst 2002–05 (tstee 2006–), pres Evelyn Tst Cambridge; *Recreations* grand opera, music, books, golf; *Style—* Julian Agnew, Esq; ✉ Thomas Agnew & Sons Ltd, 35 Albemarle Street, London W1S 4JD (☎ 020 7290 9250, fax 020 7629 4359, e-mail julianagnew@agnewsgallery.co.uk, website www.agnewsgallery.co.uk)

AGNEW, Steven; MLA; *b* 12 October 1979, Dundonald, Co Down; *Educ* Grosvenor GS Belfast, Queen's Univ Belfast; *Career* homeless support worker 2002–07, research offr for Brian Wilson MLA 2007–11, MLA (Green) N Down 2011–, ldr Green Pty NI 2011–; *Style—* Steven Agnew, Esq, MLA; ✉ Northern Ireland Assembly, Parliament Buildings, Belfast BT4 3XX

AGNEW, (John) Stuart; MEP; *Career* MEP (UKIP) East of England 2009–; *Style—* Stuart Agnew, MEP; ✉ Rochester House, 145 New London Road, Chelmsford, Essex CM2 0QT (☎ 01245 266466, fax 01245 252071, e-mail stuartagnewmep@ukip.org)

AGNEW OF LOCHNAW, Sir Crispin Hamlyn; 11 Bt (NS 1629), of Lochnaw, Wigtownshire; QC (Scot 1995); Chief of the Clan Agnew; Hereditary Sheriff of Wigton; s of Sir Fulque Melville Gerald Noel Agnew of Lochnaw, 10 Bt (d 1975), and Swanzie (d 2000), da of Maj Esme Nourse Erskine, CMG, MC (descended from the Earls of Buchan), late Consular Serv; *b* 13 May 1944, Edinburgh; *Educ* Uppingham, RMA Sandhurst; *m* 27 Sept 1980, Susan Rachel Strang, da of late Jock Wykeham Strang Steel of Logie (2 s of Sir Samuel Strang Steel of Philiphaugh, 1 Bt, TD, DL, and Vere Mabel, 2 da of 1 Baron Cornwallis) and Lesley (da of Lt-Col Sir John Graham of Larbert, Bt, VC, OBE, and Rachel, 5 da of Col Sir Alexander Sprot of Stravithie, 1 Bt, CMG); 3 da (Isabel Sevilla Wilhelmina b 1984, Emma Rachel Elizabeth b 1986, Roseanna Celia Nancy b 1989), 1 s (Mark Douglas Noel of Lochnaw, yr b 1991); *Heir* s, Mark Agnew of Lochnaw, yr; *Career* Maj RHF (ret 1981); admitted Faculty of Advocates 1982; Slains Pursuivant of Arms to the Lord High Constable of Scotland (The Earl of Erroll) 1978–81, Unicorn Pursuivant of Arms 1981–86, Rothesay Herald of Arms 1986–; dep social security and child support cmmr 2000–08, pt/t chm Pensions Appeal Tbn 2002–12, dep judge Upper Tbnl 2008–; ldr of expeditions to: Greenland 1968, Patagonia 1972, Api Himal 1980; memb of expeditions to: Greenland 1966, Elephant Island, Antarctica 1970, Nuptse Himal 1975, Everest 1976; tstee John Muir Tst 1989–2005, memb Cncl Scottish Youth Hostels Assoc 2008–12 (memb Bd 2010–12), patron UK Environmental Law Assoc 2010–; *Books* The Licensing (Scotland) Act 1976 (co-author with Heather Baillie, 2 edn 1989, 5 edn 2002), Connell on the Agricultural Holdings (Scotland) Act (co-author with Donald Rennie, OBE, 7 edn, 1996), Agricultural Law in Scotland (1996), Variation & Discharge of Land Obligations (1999), Crofting Law (2000); *Recreations* yachting (yacht 'Pippa's Song'), mountain biking; *Style—* Sir Crispin Agnew of Lochnaw, Bt, QC; ✉ 6 Palmerston Road, Edinburgh EH9 1TN (☎ 0131 668 3792, fax 0131 668 4357)

AGUTTER, Jennifer Ann (Jenny); OBE (2012); da of Derek Brodie Agutter, OBE, of London, and Catherine (Kit), *née* Lynam; *b* 20 December 1952; *Educ* Elmhurst Ballet Sch Camberley; *m* 4 Aug 1990, Johan Carl Sebastian Tham; 1 s (Jonathan Volrath Sebastian b 25 Dec 1990); *Career* actress; Hon DLitt Univ of Bradford 2004; *Theatre* incl: School for Scandal 1972, Rooted 1973, The Ride Across Lake Constance, Arms and the Man 1973, The Tempest (NT) 1974, Spring Awakening (NT) 1974, The Unified Field LA 1987, Breaking the Code (Neil Simon Theatre, NY) 1987; RSC 1982–83, 1985 and 1995–96: Fontanelle in Lear, Regan in King Lear, Alice Arden in Arden of Faversham, Grace in the Body, Breaking the Silence 1985, Love's Labour's Lost 1995, English Places English Faces 1996, Mothers and Daughters 1996; Peter Pan (RNT) 1997, Equus 2007; *Television* incl: Long After Summer 1967, The Wild Duck 1971, The Snow Goose 1971, A Legacy 1971, A War of Children 1972, Amy 1980, Love's Labour's Lost 1984, Silas Marner 1985, Murder She Wrote 1986, The Equaliser 1988, Not a Penny More Not a Penny Less 1989, TECX 1990, Boon 1991, The Good Guys 1991, Love Hurts 1994, Heartbeat (ITV) 1994, The Buccaneers (BBC) 1995, September 1995, Alexis Sayle Show 1995, Connie in And The Beat Goes On (Channel 4) 1996, Heartbeat 1996, A Respectable Trade 1997, Bramwell 1998, The Railway Children (ITV) 2000, Spooks (BBC) 2002, Alan Clark Diaries (BBC) 2004, Poirot: After the Flood 2006, Diamond Geezer II 2007, The Invisibles (BBC) 2008, Monday Monday (ITV Talkback Thames) 2009; *Radio* incl: Jamaica Inn (BBC) 1996, Silas Marner (USA) 2000, Lunch In Fairyland (BBC) 2002, My Love Must Wait (BBC) 2005; *Films* incl: East of Sudan (debut) 1964, Ballerina 1964, Gates of Paradise 1967, Star! 1968, I Start Counting, Walkabout 1969, The Railway Children 1970, Logan's Run 1975, The Eagle Has Landed 1976, The Man in the Iron Mask 1976, Equus 1976, Dominique 1977, China 9 Liberty 37 1978, Riddle of the Sands, Sweet William, The Survivor 1980, An American Werewolf in London 1981, Secret Places 1983, Dark Tower 1987, King of the Wind 1989, Child's Play II 1989, The Dark Man 1990, Freddie as Fro7 1992, Blue Juice 1995, The Parole Officer 2001, At Dawning 2001, The Lonely Troll 2003, Act of God 2006, Irina P 2006, 1939 2009; *Awards* incl: Royal Variety Club Most Promising Artist 1971, Emmy Award Best Supporting Actress (for The Snow Goose) 1971, BAFTA Award Best Supporting Actress (for Equus) 1976; *Books* Snap (1984); *Style—* Miss Jenny Agutter, OBE; ✉ c/o Ken McReddie Associates Ltd, 11 Connaught Place, London W2 2ET

AHLÅS, (Lars) Peter Richard; *b* 22 September 1948; *Educ* Högre Allmana Laroverket å Kungsholmen Stockholm, Royal Swedish Naval Acad, London Sch of Foreign Trade (Dip Shipping & Marine Insur); *m* 1973, Sian Fiona, *née* Holford-Walker; 2 da; *Career* Lt Cdr Royal Swedish Navy 1969–71, Res 1971–; marine insurance broker; W K Webster 1971–73, gen mangr Liberian Insurance Agency 1973–74, broker Bland Payne 1974–78; dir: Jardine Glanvill Marine 1978–86, Gibbs Insurance Holdings Ltd 1986–, HSBC Shipping Services Ltd 2000–, Maritime London; HSBC Insurance Brokers Ltd (formerly Gibbs Hartley Cooper Ltd): chief exec Marine Cargo and Aviation Divs 1986–, chm global marine practice 2006–; mgmnt conslt in the shipping and marine insurance sector 2007–, sr advsr Park Partners Ltd; chm: C Solutions Ltd, C J Coleman Ltd; non-exec dir HSBC Shipping Services Ltd; memb Advsy Bd Svenska Bostadsfonden; tstee Maritime London Cadet Scholarship Tst; memb IBRC; Freeman City of London, Liveryman Worshipful Co of Shipwrights; *Recreations* shooting, polo, riding; *Clubs* SOSS; *Style—* Peter Ahlås, Esq; ✉ e-mail peter.ahlas@btinternet.com

AHMAD OF WIMBLEDON, Baron (Life Peer UK 2011), of Wimbledon in the London Borough of Merton; Tariq Mahmood Ahmad; s of Mansoor Ahmad (Chief Justice of Himachal Pradesh High Court), and Amtul Matin, *née* Mir; *b* 3 April 1968, London; *m* Lady Siddiquea, *née* Masud; 1 da (Hon Shaista b 2006), 2 s (Hon Mansoor b 2012, Hon Faris b 2014); *Career* NatWest Gp 1991–2000, dir Alliance Capital 2000–03, dir Sucden Financial 2004–12; London Borough of Merton: cncllr 2002–12, cabinet memb for environment and tport 2006–08, cabinet memb for community safety and engagement 2008–; whip and Govt spokesman on justice 2012–13, whip and Govt spokesman on univs and science 2013–14, communities min and under-sec of state Dept for Communities and Local Govt 2014–15, min for aviation security and London Dept of Tport 2015–, min for countering extremism Home Office 2015–; dep chm Wimbledon Cons Assoc 1997–2002, dep chm Tport and Environment Ctee London Cncls 2006–08, vice-chm Cons Pty 2008–; Lord in Waiting to HM The Queen 2012–13; MInstD, assoc Inst of Financial Servs, ACIB; *Recreations* gardening, reading, travel; *Style*— The Lord Ahmad of Wimbledon; ✉ House of Lords, London SW1A 0PW (☎ 020 7944 4484, e-mail ahmadt@parliament.uk, Twitter @TariqAhmadBt)

AHMED, Ajaz Quoram Khowaj; s of Khowaj Ahmed, of India; *b* 1 May 1973, Taplow, Bucks; *Career* at Apple until 1995, fndr, chm and ceo AKQA (ideas and innovation co) 1995–; reviewer MIT, mentor Said Business Sch Univ of Oxford 2003; Forbes Media Innovator of the Year 1998; Hon Dr Oxford Brookes Univ 2002; FRSA 2005; *Publications* Velocity – The Seven New Laws for a World Gone Digital (2012), Limitless – Leadership That Endures (2015); *Recreations* swimming, sailing; *Style*— Ajaz Ahmed, Esq; ✉ website www.akqa.com/ajaz, Twitter @ajaz, Instagram @ajazahmed; AKQA Limited, 1 St John's Lane, London EC1M 4BL (website www.akqa.com)

AHMED, Javed; *b* 10 February 1960; *Educ* Williams Coll MA USA, Stanford Grad Sch of Business USA (MBA); *Career* numerous sr positions Reckitt Benckiser plc 1992–2009, chief exec Tate & Lyle plc 2009–; *Style*— Javed Ahmed, Esq; ✉ Tate & Lyle plc, 1 Kingsway, London WC2B 6AT

AHMED, Muquim Uddin; s of Haji Mubarak Ahmed (d 1992), and Omar Jan (d 2002); *b* 1 September 1954, Dhaka, Bangladesh; *Educ* SE London Coll (HND); *m* 15 Oct 1976, Rashmi, *née* Bakshi; 1 s (Miraj b 16 Jan 1991), 1 da (Monique b 30 Aug 1993); *Career* early career with family business importing goods (incl electrical appliances, Bedford trucks and re-conditioned cars) into Bangladesh, fndr travel agency (largest UK operator for Bangladesh Airlines) 1977, fndr record business for Bangladeshi artists 1978, owner Naz cinema Brick Lane (importing Bangladeshi films, also distributing videos) 1980, fndr MILFA properties, owner Sylto Cash and Carry and Asian Foods Ltd, owner Cafe Naz Brick Lane (now part of restaurant chain) 1996, estab ready meals business 2006; md Notun Din newspaper; vice-chm Bethnal Green and Bow Cons Assoc; Bangladesh Br C of C: pres London region 1991–2001, chm 2001–05, dir 2006–; nominated Asian Jewel Awards 2005; *Recreations* gardening; *Style*— Muquim Ahmed, Esq; ✉ Asian Foods Limited, Caxton Street North, London E16 1JL (☎ 020 7476 6969, fax 020 7476 8555, e-mail muquim@aol.com)

AHMED, Baron (Life Peer UK 1998), of Rotherham in the County of South Yorkshire; Nazir Ahmed; JP (Rotherham 1992); s of Haji Mohammed (d 1989), and Rashim Bibi; *b* 24 April 1957; *Educ* Spurley Hey Secdy Sch, Thomas Rotherham Coll, Sheffield Hallam Univ; *m* 1974, Sakina, da of Chaudhary Manga Khan; 1 da (Hon Maryam b 26 Nov 1977), 2 s (Hon Ahmar b 22 Feb 1979, Hon Babar b 1 Sept 1982); *Career* shop mangr 1978–82, petrol station mangr 1982–84, with marble mining indust 1984–87, business devpt mangr 1987–; cncllr Met Borough of Rotherham 1990–2000; chm South Yorks Met Lab Pty 1993–2000; vice-chm: South Yorks Euro-constituency, Policy Bd Housing and Environmental Health Bd Rotherham Met Borough Cncl, Ferham Advice Centre; fndr and convenor Nat Forum of Br Muslim Councillors; first Muslim male in the House of Lords; former chm All Pty Libya Gp, co-chm Forced Marriage Working Gp, chm All Pty Interfaith Interreligions Gp, chm All Pty Entrepreneurship Gp, chm All Pty Parly Gp on Kashmir, fndr All Pty Parly Gp on Interfaith; interested in human rights conflict resolution; led first European Parly delgn to Gaza via sea 2008, negotiated the release of a Br sch teacher Gillian Gibbons 2009; chm 7/7 Working Gp on Imams and Mosques; ldr Muslim Peace and Reconcilliation Initiative for Darfur; memb Br Inst of Technol and E-Commerce; chm Blackhorn Ltd; memb: Amnesty Int, Kashmir Policy Gp, Rotherham Racial Equality Cncl 1976–98, Standing Advsy Cncl of Religious Educn 1976–2000, USDAW, Cncl Br Heart Fndn 2007–12; pres S Yorks Victim Support 2006–09; runs charity sch in Kashmir; JP 1992–2000; *Recreations* volleyball; *Style*— The Rt Hon Lord Ahmed; ✉ House of Lords, London SW1A 0PW (☎ 020 7219 1396, e-mail ahmedn@parliament.uk); website www.abettertomorrowschool.org

AHMED, Rizwan (Riz); s of Javed Ahmed, of London and Nusrat, *née* Hashmi; *b* 1 December 1982, London; *Educ* Merchant Taylors' Sch, ChCh Oxford (BA), Central Sch of Speech and Drama (Dip); *Career* actor and musician; solo artist (as Riz MC) and jazz vocalist with band; singles incl: Post 911 Blues 2006, People like People 2006; Jump Off MC Battle finalist 2005, winner Bombay Bronx MC Battle Competition 2005, winner One Music BattleScars MC Competition 2005, Best MC UK Asian Awards 2006; emerging artist in residence Royal Festival Hall 2007; *Television* Banglatown Banquet, Rejkjavik (The Play's The Thing, Channel 4), Berry's Way, Sohail in Britz (Channel 4) 2007, Dead Set (Channel 4) 2008, Free Fall 2009; *Theatre* Julius Caesar (Thelma Holt Japan Tour) 2004, Prayer Room (Birmingham Rep and Lyceum Edinburgh) 2005, Borderline (Royal Court Theatre), Gaddafi: A Living Myth (ENO) 2006, A Disappearing Number (Complicité); *Film* Shafiq Rasul in The Road To Guantanamo 2005, Shifty in Shifty 2007, Four Lions 2009, Rage 2009, Centurion 2010, Trishna 2011, Black Gold 2011, Ill Manors 2012, The Reluctant Fundamentalist 2013; script writer Life 'n Lyrics; *Radio* Farooq in Midnight's Children (BBC World Service); *Style*— Rizwan Ahmed, Esq; ✉ c/o Michael Symons, Hamilton Hodell, 5th Floor, 60–68 Margaret Street, London W1W 8SR (☎ 020 7636 1221, fax 020 7636 1226, e-mail michael@hamiltonhodell.co.uk)

AHRENDS, Peter; s of Steffen Bruno Ahrends, and Margarete Maria Sophie Ahrends; *b* 30 April 1933, Berlin; *Educ* AA Sch of Architecture (AADipl); *m* 1954, Elizabeth Robertson; 2 da; *Career* architect; fndr ptnr and dir Ahrends Burton & Koralek (now ABK Architects) 1961–; princ works incl buildings and devpt plans in areas such as educn, housing, health, govt, public tport, museums, industrial and retail; memb: Cncl AA 1965–67, Design Cncl 1988–93; chm UK Architects Against Apartheid 1988–93, chm Architect's Support Gp (South Africa); visiting prof of architecture Kingston Poly 1984–85, prof of architecture Bartlett Sch of Architecture and Planning UCL 1986–89; pt/t teaching posts, external examiner and workshops UK, Africa, HK and Canada; exhibitions of drawings and works incl: RIBA Heinz Gallery 1980, Douglas Hyde Gallery Dublin 1981, Alvar Aalto Museum Finland 1982, AA HQ Oslo 1983; RIBA 1959; *Publications* Monograph on Ahrends Burton & Koralek (1991), Collaborations: The Architecture of ABK (2002), Ahrends, Burton and Koralek (2012), A3, Threads and Connections (2015), and various pubns in the architectural press internationally; *Style*— Mr Peter Ahrends; ☎ 020 7485 7570, e-mail pahrends@gmail.com

AICHROTH, Prof Paul Michael; s of Gerald Paul Aichroth, of Vancouver, Canada, and Elsie, *née* Webb; *b* 30 April 1936; *Educ* Alleyn's Sch Dulwich, KCL, Westminster Med Sch (MB BS, MS); *m* 17 June 1961, Angela, da of Frederick Gordon Joslin, of Bournemouth, Dorset; 1 s (Mark Jonathan Paul); *Career* conslt orthopaedic surgn Chelsea and Westminster Hosp and Wellington Hosp 1971–; visiting prof Dept of Surgery Imperial Coll London 2002; author of various papers and theses on knee disorders; Hunterian prof RCS 1973, Robert Jones Gold medallist 1973, annual orator London Med Soc 1991–, orator Hunterian Soc 2000; pres Br Assoc for Surgery of the Knee 1992, hon memb Arthroscopy Assoc of N America 2004; memb: Br Orthopaedic Assoc, RSM, BMA 1963; Master of Surgery (Univ of London) 1972; FRCS 1965; *Books* Harris's Orthopaedics (contrib, 1975 and 1995), Operative Surgery (contrib, 1990), Insall Knee Surgery (contrib, 1992), Knee Surgery: Current Practice (1992), Interactive Knee (2000); *Recreations* boats, countryside, Mozart, claret; *Clubs* Athenaeum; *Style*— Prof Paul Aichroth, FRCS; ✉ Church Cottage, 47 Church Lane, Holybourne, Alton, Hampshire GU34 4HD (e-mail aichroth.paul@gmail.com)

AIKEN, Alex; *Educ* Dame Alice Owen's Sch, LSE; *Career* sr posts Cons Central Office 1995–2000, dir of communications and strategy Westminster City Cncl 2000–12, exec dir for Govt communications 10 Downing St 2012–; *Style*— Alex Aiken, Esq; ✉ Downing Street Press Office, 10 Downing Street, London SW1A 2AA (Twitter @AlexanderAiken)

AIKENS, Rt Hon Sir Richard John Pearson; kt (1999), PC (2008); s of Maj Basil Aikens (d 1983), and Jean Eleanor, *née* Pearson (d 2009); *b* 28 August 1948; *Educ* Norwich Sch, St John's Coll Cambridge (MA); *m* 3 March 1979, Penelope Anne Hartley, da of Hartley Baker (d 1961); 2 s (Christopher b 1979, Nicholas b 1981), 2 step da (Jessica b 1964, Anna b 1966); *Career* called to the Bar Middle Temple 1973 (bencher 1994); in practice 1974–99, a jr counsel to the Crown common law 1981–86, QC 1986, recorder of the Crown Court 1993–99, judge of the High Court of Justice (Queen's Bench Div) 1999–2008, presiding judge SE Circuit 2001–04, judge i/c Commercial Court 2005–06, a Lord Justice of Appeal 2008–15, ret; visiting prof of law KCL 2016–; memb Supreme Court Rules Ctee 1984–88; dir: Bar Mutual Indemnity Fund Ltd 1988–2000 (chm 1998–99), ENO 1995–2004, Temple Music Fndn 2003– (chm); govr Sedbergh Sch 1988–97; hon fell St John's Coll Cambridge 2005; *Books* Bullen and Leake on Pleadings and Practice (contributing ed, 13 edn 1991), Bills of Lading (jtly, 2006, 2 edn 2015), Reforming Marine and Commercial Insurance Law (contrib, 2008), Tom Bingham and the Transformation of the Law: x liber amicorum (contrib, 2009), Law and Soc: Which is to be Master (jt ed, 2011); *Recreations* music, the country, Le Pays Basque, cycling; *Clubs* Leander, Groucho; *Style*— The Rt Hon Sir Richard Aikens; ✉ Brick Court Chambers, 7–8 Essex Street, London WC2R 3LD

AIKENS, Tom; s of Kevin Aikens, and Tania, *née* Chaloner; *b* 7 February 1970, Norwich; *Educ* Norwich City Coll; *m* 14 June 2007 (sep), Amber Louise, *née* Nuttall; partner Justine Dobbs-Higginson; 2 da (Violette, Josephine); *Career* chef; worked with Joel Robuchon in Paris 1993–94 and Gerard Boyeren in Champagne 1994–95, head chef and co-prop Pied á Terre 1995–2000 (two Michelin stars); chef and prop: Tom Aikens Restaurant London 2003–14, Tom's Kitchen Chelsea 2006, Tom's Kitchen Somerset House 2010, Tom's Kitchen Canary Wharf 2013, Tom's Kitchen Istanbul 2013, Tom's Kitchen St Katherine's Dock 2014; two restaurants in Hong Kong (The Pawn 2014 and The Fat Pig 2015), one new restaurant in Dubai 2015; conslt Soho Farmhouse 2015; awards for Tom Aikens Restaurant: one Michelin star 2004–14 (awarded 'rising two' status 2008), Caterer & Hotelkeeper Catey Best Newcomer of the Year 2004, Vintage Year Award and Top London Restaurant Award Tio Pepe ITV London Restaurant Awards 2004, three stars Egon Ronay's Guide 2006, five AA Rosettes 2007; supporter: Environment Justice Fndn, Marine Conservation Soc, Marine Stewardship Cncl, WWF, Greenpeace; *Books* Tom Aikens: Cooking (2006), Tom Aikens: Fish (2008), Easy Cooking (2010); *Recreations* cycling (cycled LEtape du Tour 2009 and Marmotte 2010), horse riding, running (completed Marathon des Sables 2011); *Style*— Tom Aikens, Esq; ✉ www.facebook.com/tomaikens, Twitter @tomaikens, Instagram tomaikens

AIKIN, Olga Lindholm (Mrs J M Driver); CBE (1997); da of late Sidney Richard Daly, of Buckley, Clwyd, and Lilian May, *née* Lindholm (d 1966); *b* 10 September 1934; *Educ* Ilford Co HS for Girls, LSE (LLB), KCL, London Business Sch; *m* 1, 1959 (m dis 1979), Ronald Sidney Aikin; 1 da (Gillian); m 2, 1982, John Michael Driver; 1 step da (Katie); *Career* called to the Bar Gray's Inn 1956; lectr: KCL 1956–59, LSE 1959–70, London Business Sch 1971–90; dir gen Law Div Lion Int 1985–90, ptnr Aikin Driver Partnership 1988–; ed Law & Employment series Inst of Personnel Mgmnt; chm Bd of Mgmnt Nat Conciliation Service Qualitas Furnishing Standards Ltd 1992–94, memb Cncl ACAS 1982–95; *Books* Employment, Welfare and Safety at Work (1971), Legal Problems of Employment (1990), Contracts (1992); *Recreations* collecting cookery books and glass; *Style*— Mrs Olga Aikin, CBE; ✉ Aikin Driver Partnership, 22 St Lukes Road, London W11 1DP (☎ 020 7727 9791, website www.aikindriver.com)

AINSCOW, Prof Mel; CBE (2012); *Career* prof of educn and co-dir Centre for Equity in Educn Univ of Manchester; *Publications* Improving Urban Schools: Leadership and Collaboration (jt ed, 2006), Improving Schools, Developing Inclusion (jtly, 2006), Responding to Diversity in Schools (jt ed, 2011), Developing Equitable Education Systems (jtly, 2011); author of numerous jl articles; *Style*— Prof Mel Ainscow, CBE; ✉ School of Education, Ellen Wilkinson Building, The University of Manchester, Oxford Road, Manchester M13 9PL

AINSLEY, David Edwin; s of Edwin Ainsley (d 2004), of Bebington, Merseyside, and Gertrude Mary, *née* Fletcher (d 1978); *b* 13 September 1944, Ripon, Yorks; *Educ* Portsmouth GS, Sch of Architecture Univ of Liverpool (BArch), Columbia Pacific Univ (MA); *m* 1 (m dis 1984), Pauline Elisabeth, da of Aubrey Highton; 2 s (Sam b 21 Sept 1975, Christian b 24 May 1978); m 2, Beatrix Hinchliffe Parry, da of William Ellis, of Oxton, Merseyside; 2 step s (Nathan b 22 Dec 1971, Benjamin b 7 Feb 1976); *Career* dir Ainsley Gommon Architects 1979–2009; winner of thirty-five national and international design awards incl: Royal Town Planning Inst commendation, Housing Centre Tst Award, Liverpool Int Garden Festival Best Home Garden, twice winner of RIBA Community Enterprise Scheme Award, RIBA Housing Design Awards, three Civic Tst commendations, Welsh Nat Eisteddfod Architecture Prize; dir Denbighshire Foyer Ltd 1997–2000; assessor Civic Tst Award 2008–; memb: Cncl Liverpool Architectural Soc 1988–97 (pres 1993–94), Cncl Liverpool C of C and Industry 1993–95; vice-chair Liverpool Architecture and Design Tst 1997–2005; memb Stoke Urban Vision Design Review Panel 2005–13, RIBA client design advsr 2007; tstee Artsworks Wirral Arts Devpt Agency 1994–98, tstee LADT Trg 1999–2003; fndr memb and former chm Oxton Soc; co-fndr Tst for the Encouragement of Pastoralist Educn in Africa (TEPEA); memb Cncl Merseyside Civic Soc 1999–2002, memb Exec Ctee Hopes (Liverpool Hope Street Quarter Assoc) 2000–02, memb Bd Liverpool Habitat for Humanity 2005–10; govr Christchurch C of E Primary Sch Birkenhead 1992–98 (chair Fin Ctee 1997–98), memb Ctee Friends of the Williamson Art Gallery; RIBA, FRSA; *Recreations* music (keyboard and saxophone), Orange Zebra, Low Flier, walking, cycling, gardening, painting; *Style*— David Ainsley, Esq; ✉ Architect and Client Design Advisor, 10 South Bank, Oxton, Prenton, Merseyside CH43 5UP (☎ 0151 652 4064, mobile 07894 077917, e-mail dadesignadvisor@gmail.com)

AINSLEY, John Mark; s of John Alwyn Ainsley, of Maidenhead, and (Dorothy) Sylvia *née* Anderson; *b* 9 July 1963; *Educ* Nunnery Wood Secdy Modern Worcester, Worcester Royal GS, Magdalen Coll Oxford; *Career* tenor; lay clerk ChCh Oxford 1982–84; currently studies with Diane Forlano, professional debut singing Stravinsky's Mass (Royal Festival Hall under Simon Rattle) 1984, operatic debut in Scarlatti's Gli Equivoci nel Sembiante (Innsbruck Festival) 1988; former memb Deller Consort, former memb Gothic Voices, has sung with all major Baroque ensembles, also soloist in later repertoire; performed with numerous orchs incl: London Philharmonic, Royal Liverpool Philharmonic, BBC Symphony, City of Birmingham Symphony, English Chamber, Scottish Chamber,

Bournemouth Symphony, London Classical Players, Berlin Philharmonic, Montreal Symphony; appeared at numerous international venues incl: Konzerthaus Vienna, Musikverein Vienna, Philharmonic Berlin, Gewandhaus Leipzig, Stuttgart Festival, Göttingen Festival, others in New York, Boston, France, Holland and Switzerland; *Performances* operatic roles incl: Return of Ulysses (ENO) 1989, Fenton in Falstaff (Scottish Opera), Idamantes in Idomeneo (WNO under Sir Charles Mackerras and Munich), Don Ottavio in Don Giovanni (Lyon Opera and Aix en Provence Festival, Glyndebourne Festival and San Francisco), Ferrando in Cosi fan Tutte (Glyndebourne Festival, La Monnaie Brussels) 1992; concert performances incl world première of Tavener's We Shall See Him as He Is (Chester Festival, later BBC Proms) 1992, Bach Mass in B minor (with The English Concert under Trevor Pinnock, BBC Proms) 1997; *Recordings* incl: Handel's Nisi Dominus (with Choir of Westminster Abbey under Simon Preston, Deutsche Grammophon), Purcell's Odes (with English Concert under Trevor Pinnock, Deutsche Grammophon), Mozart's C Minor Mass and Handel's Acis and Galatea (with Acad of Ancient Music under Christopher Hogwood, Decca), Handel's Saul (under John Eliot Gardiner, Philips), Handel's Acis and Galatea and Joshua (under King, Hyperion), title role in Monteverdi's Orfeo (Decca), Mozart's Requiem (under Roger Norrington, EMI), Charlie in Brigadoon (EMI), Ottavio in Mozart's Don Giovanni (under Roger Norrington, EMI) Frederic in Gilbert and Sullivan's Pirates of Penzance (Mackerras/Telare), Mendelssohn's Elijah (under Herrewege, Harmonia Mundi), Berlioz's Les Troyens (under Dutoit, Decca), various works by Britten for EMI, Decca and Philips, Haydn's Die Schöpfung (under Brüggen, Philips), Purcell's Odes (under Trevor Pinnock, DG Archiv), Quilter Songs (with Malcolm Martineau on piano, Hyperion), Complete Schubert Edition (with Graham Johnson on piano, Hyperion), Stravinsky's Oedipus Rex (under Welser-Möst, EMI), Stravinsky's Pulcinella (under Bernard Haitink, Philips), Finzi's Dies Natalis/Intimations of Immortality (under Best, Hyperion), Vaughan Williams's Serenade to Music (under Roger Norrington, Decca); *Recreations* chocolate, early Flemish painting; *Style*— John Mark Ainsley, Esq; ✉ c/o Askonas Holt Limited, Lincoln House, 300 High Holborn, London WC1V 7JH (website www.askonasholt.co.uk)

AINSLIE, Sir (Charles) Benedict (Ben); kt (2013), CBE (2008, OBE 2005, MBE 2001); s of Roderick (Roddy) Ainslie (skipper Second Life in first Whitbread Round the World Race 1973–74), and Susan Ainslie; *b* 5 February 1977, Macclesfield, Cheshire; *Educ* Peter Symonds Coll Winchester, Truro Sch; *m* 2014, Georgie Thompson; *Career* yachtsman; achievements in Laser class incl: Gold medal World Youth Championships 1995, Gold medal European Championships 1996, 1998, 1999 and 2000 (Bronze medal 1997), Silver medal Olympic Games Atlanta 1996, Gold medal World Championships 1998 and 1999 (Bronze medal 1996, 1997 and 2000), Gold medal Olympic Games Sydney 2000; transferred to Finn class 2001; achievements in Finn class incl: Gold medal European Championships 2002, 2003, 2005 and 2008, Gold medal World Championships (Finn Gold Cup) 2002, 2003, 2004, 2005 and 2008, Gold medal Pre-Olympics Athens 2003, Gold medal Olympic Games Athens 2004, Gold medal Qingdao Int Regatta (Pre-Olympics) 2006 and 2007, Gold medal Olympic Games Beijing (Qingdao) 2008, Gold medal Princess Sofia Regatta Palma 2011, Gold medal Olympic Class Week Hyeres 2011, Gold medal Sail for Gold Olympic Class Regatta 2011, Gold medal Olympic Games 2012; ISAF World Match Racing Champion 2010; B-Team helmsman Team NZ America's Cup challenger series 2005–07, Br campaign skipper Team Origin America's Cup challenger series 2007–10; British Young Sailor of the Year 1995, British Yachtsman of the Year 1995, 1999, 2000, 2002 and 2008, Sports Writers' Assoc Best Int Newcomer 1996, Int Sailing Fedn World Sailor of the Year 1998, 2002 and 2008; *Books* Close to the Wind (2008); *Recreations* flying; *Clubs* Royal Lymington Yacht, Royal Yacht Squadron, Mark's; *Style*— Sir Ben Ainslie, CBE; ✉ website www.benainslie.com; c/o Into the Blue, One The Parade, Cowes, Isle of Wight PO31 7QJ (website www.intotheblue.biz); c/o Mission Media, 32 Shelton Street, London WC2H 9JE

AINSLIE, David Galbraith; s of Patrick David Lafone Ainslie (d 1999), and Agnes Ursula, *née* Galbraith; *b* 13 October 1947; *Educ* Wellington, Pembroke Coll Cambridge (MA); *m* 16 July 1993, Catherine Mary Ruth, *née* Green; 2 s (Jonathan David Alexander b 6 April 1996, Richard Hugh Campbell b 22 August 1998); *Career* admitted slr 1973; joined Dawson & Co 1969; ptnr: Lovell White & King 1981–83 (joined 1976), Towry Group (ind fin advsrs) 1983–2002, Pitmans, Slrs 2003–05, Horsey Lightly Fynn, Slrs 2006–08, Stone King Slrs 2008–13, Pitmans Slrs 2013–; tstee Towry Law Charitable Tst 1997–2008; memb Bank of England Money Laundering Working Party 1994–96; memb: UK Falkland Islands Ctee 1973–, Exec Ctee Falkland Islands Assoc 1977–, Exec Ctee Philanthropy Advsrs Forum 2011–12; tstee UK Falkland Islands Tst 1981– (chm 2008–), tstee Falklands Maritime Heritage Tst 2014–; tstee Berks Community Fndn 1999–2005 (vice-chm 2002–05); memb Law Soc 1971; Freeman City of London, Liveryman Worshipful Co of Haberdashers 1971; *Books* Practical Tax Planning with Precedents (contrib, 1987–2002); *Recreations* fishing, shooting; *Clubs* London Rowing; *Style*— David Ainslie, Esq; ✉ Watermeadow Lodge, Forge Hill, Hampstead Norreys, Thatcham, Berkshire RG18 0TE (☎ 01635 201355); Pitmans LLP, 47 Castle Street, Reading, Berkshire RG1 7SR (☎ 0118 958 0224, e-mail dainslie@pitmans.com)

AINSWORTH, Sir Anthony Thomas Hugh; 5 Bt (UK 1916), of Ardanaiseig, Co Argyll; s of Sir (Thomas) David Ainsworth, 4 Bt (d 1999); *b* 30 March 1962; *Educ* Harrow; *Children* 1 da (Anna Alexandra b 6 April 2006); *Heir* bro, Charles Ainsworth; *Career* Lt Royal Hussars (PWO) 1982–85; dir Richard Glynn Consultants 2000–, dir IIC Partners 2002–06; *Style*— Sir Anthony Ainsworth, Bt

AINSWORTH, (Mervyn) John; OBE (2008); s of Gordon John Ainsworth (d 1974), and Eileen, *née* MacDonald (d 2010); *b* 28 January 1947; *Educ* Stanfield HS Stoke-on-Trent, Goldsmiths Coll London (CertEd, DipEd); *m* Marta Christina, o da of Piotr Marmolak (d 1973); 2 s (Andrew Edward John b 5 Dec 1975, Peter Gordon John b 10 July 1983), 1 da (Stefanie Mary b 28 Sept 1978); *Career* asst clerk to the Governors and Bursar Dulwich Coll 1969–74, princ asst CEGB 1974–77, secretarial asst and mangr Secretariat Servs BTDB (now ABP) 1977–78; BPIF: sec 1978–84, fin dir 1983–84; sec-gen Inst of Admin Mgmnt 1984–90, chief exec and sec Inst of Chartered Secretaries and Administrators 1990–2007; special advsr Assets Reunited LLP 2008–11; sec Shepway Economic Redevelopment Partnership 2010–14; chm Open and Distance Learning Quality Cncl 1999–2016; govr Rokeby Sch London E16 2010– (vice-chair 2014, chair 2016–); Hon DBA Bournemouth Univ 1997, Hon DUniv Anglia Ruskin Univ 2006; Freeman City of London, Liveryman Worshipful Co of Chartered Secs and Admins; FIMgt 1978, FCIS 1980, FInstAM 1983, hon fell Canadian Inst of Certified Admin Mangrs 1987, hon memb C&G 2006; *Recreations* golf, motorsport, travel; *Style*— John Ainsworth, Esq, OBE; ✉ 2 Aspen House, Folkestone, Kent CT20 1TH

AINSWORTH, Paul; s of David Ainsworth, and Annabelle, *née* Bacari; *b* 21 May 1979, Southampton, Hants; *Educ* Southampton City Coll; *m* 10 Oct 2009, Emma, *née* Simpson; *Career* chef; formerly at: Rhodes in the Square London, Royal Hospital Road London, Petrus London, Berkeley Hotel London; chef proprietor Number 6 Padstow 2005– (Michelin star 2013–); television appearances incl Great British Menu (BBC 2) 2011 (winner, cooked dessert for the People's Banquet); *Style*— Paul Ainsworth, Esq; ✉ Number 6, 6 Middle Street, Padstow, Cornwall PL28 8AP (email paul@number6inpadstow.co.uk, website www.number6inpadstow.co.uk, Twitter @paulainsw6rth)

AINSWORTH, Peter; s of Lt Cdr Michael Lionel Yeoward Ainsworth (d 1978), and Patricia Mary, *née* Bedford; *b* 16 November 1956; *Educ* Bradfield Coll, Lincoln Coll Oxford; *m* 1981, Claire, *née* Burnett; 1 s, 2 da; *Career* res asst to Sir John Stewart-Clark MEP 1979–81, investment analyst Laing & Cruickshank 1981–85, dir S G Warburg Securities 1989–92 (joined as investment analyst 1985); MP (Cons) Surrey E 1992–2010; memb Environment Select Ctee 1993–94, PPS to Jonathan Aitken as chief sec to the Treasy 1994–95, PPS to Virginia Bottomley as sec of state for Nat Heritage 1995–96, asst Govt whip 1996–97, oppn dep chief whip 1997–98, shadow sec of state Culture, Media and Sport 1998–2001, shadow sec of state for the environment, food and rural affrs 2001–02, chm Environmental Audit Ctee 2003–05, shadow sec of state for environment, food and rural affrs 2005–09; memb Culture, Media and Sport Select Ctee, memb Speaker's Advsy Ctee on Works of Art, chair All Pty Parly Gp for the Environment, chair All Pty Parly Gp for Sustainable Aviation, treas All Pty Parly Climate Change Gp; cncllr London Borough of Wandsworth 1986–92 (sometime chm Cons Gp); founding ptnr Robertsbridge Gp 2010–; cmmr London Sustainable Devpt Cmmn 2015–; memb Bow Gp 1983– (memb Cncl 1984–86); chm Bd Plantlife Int 2010– (tstee), vice-pres Arthur Bliss Soc, chm Elgar Fndn 2005–13, chair Big Lottery Fund 2011–, memb Bd Environment Agency 2012–; memb: MCC, Friends of the Earth, Greenpeace 2012–; patron Coll of St Barnabas 2010–; presenter Discord: Music and Dissent (Radio 4) 2000; hon fell: Soc for the Environment 2013–, Chartered Inst of Wastes Mgmnt; *Recreations* family, music, writing; *Clubs* MCC, Garrick; *Style*— Peter Ainsworth, Esq; ✉ Big Lottery Fund, 1 Plough Place, London EC4A 1DE

AINSWORTH, Rt Hon Robert (Bob); PC (2005); s of late Stanley Ainsworth, and Pearl Ainsworth; *b* 19 June 1952; *Educ* Foxford Comp Sch Coventry; *m* 22 June 1974, Gloria, *née* Sandall; 2 da; *Career* sheet metal worker Jaguar Cars Ltd Coventry 1971–91, MP (Lab) Coventry NE 1992–2015; oppn whip 1995–97, a Lord Cmmr of HM Treasy (Govt whip) 1997–2001; Parly under sec of state: DETR 2001, Home Office 2001–03; treas HM Household (Govt dep chief whip) 2003–07, min of state for the Armed Forces 2007–09, sec of state for defence 2009–10; MSF (formerly TGWU): shop steward 1974–80, sr steward 1980–91, sec jt shop stewards 1980–91, branch pres 1983–87; Coventry City Cncl: cncllr 1984–92, dep ldr 1988–91, chm Fin Ctee 1989–92; *Recreations* walking, chess, reading, cycling; *Style*— The Rt Hon Bob Ainsworth; ✉ House of Commons, London SW1A 0AA (☎ 020 7219 4047, constituency ☎ 024 76226707, fax 024 76226707, e-mail ainsworthr@parliament.uk)

AINSWORTH, William Robert; OBE (1998); s of William Murray Ainsworth (d 1964), of Stockton-on-Tees, Co Durham, and Emma Laura Mary, *née* Easley (d 1981); *b* 24 June 1935; *Educ* Holy Trinity Sch Stockton-on-Tees, Stockton GS, Sch of Architecture Univ of Durham (BArch); *m* 7 Nov 1959, Sylvia Vivian, da of Norman Brown, of Buenos Aires, Argentina; 3 da (Graciela Glenn b 1960, Anita Susan b 1964, Lucia Emma b 1977); *Career* chartered architect, designer and urban planner; fndr ptnr Ainsworth Spark Assocs 1963– (completed over 4,500 projects throughout UK and Europe for local, nat and int companies); working tours of: S America, USA, and Europe; external examiner: Sch of Architecture, Coll of Arts and Technol Newcastle upon Tyne; RIBA: chm Northern Region 1972–73, fndr chm Nat Ctee for Environmental Educn 1977, dir Bd of Servs Ltd London, memb and vice-pres Nat Cncl 1980–82; vice-pres and hon librarian Br Architectural Library 1987–90; bd govr Coll of Arts and Technol 1984–86, chm Bd of Govrs Newcastle Coll 1999–2000 (vice-chm 1996–99, memb Bd and govr 1991–); initiator of World Day of Architecture in UK 1989, chm Int Conf UIA/UNESCO (Art and Architecture) 1997; chm Sculpture Tst Northern Arts 1981– (fndr), memb Bd Arts Resources 1995–2000; fndr chm Northumberland and Durham Lord's Taverners; memb Union of Int Architects (UIA); FRIBA 1967, MCSD 1977, IOB 1980, FRSA 1985; *Recreations* cricket, golf, gardening (lifetime project building quarry garden), reading, painting (watercolours), music (guitar); *Clubs* Northumberland Golf, Durham CCC; *Style*— William Ainsworth, Esq, OBE; ✉ Ainsworth Spark Associates, Summerhill House, 9 Summerhill Terrace, Newcastle upon Tyne NE4 6EB (☎ 0191 232 3434, fax 0191 261 0628, e-mail bill@ainsworthspark.com, website www.ainsworthspark.com)

AIRD, Sir (George) John; 4 Bt (UK 1901), of Hyde Park Terrace, Paddington, Co London; s of Col Sir John Renton Aird, 3 Bt, MVO, MC, JP, DL (d 1973), equerry to the Prince of Wales later Edward VIII 1929–36, sometime extra equerry to King George VI and to HM The Queen, of Forest Lodge, Windsor Great Park, and Lady Priscilla, *née* Heathcote-Drummond-Willoughby (d 2002), yr da of 2 Earl of Ancaster; *b* 30 January 1940; *Educ* Eton, ChCh Oxford (MA), Harvard Univ (MBA); *m* 1, 31 Aug 1968, Margaret Elizabeth (d 2010), yr da of Sir John Harling Muir, 3 Bt, TD, DL; 2 da (Rebecca b 1970, Belinda Elizabeth b 1972), 1 s (James John b 1978); *m* 2, 12 Aug 2011, Xiao Fen, da of Jin Fen Wang, of Beijing, China; *Heir* s, James Aird; *Career* page of honour to HM The Queen 1955–57; engr Sir Alexander Gibb & Partners 1961–65, mangr John Laing & Co 1967–69, chm and md Sir John Aird & Co 1969–96; chm: Matcon Gp Ltd 1981–2012, Healthcare Devpt Services 1995–2006; Liveryman Worshipful Co of Drapers; MICE 1965; *Recreations* skiing, hunting, tennis; *Style*— Sir John Aird, Bt; ✉ Two Leys, Evenlode, Moreton-in-Marsh, Gloucestershire GL56 0NT (☎ 01608 650607, e-mail johnaird@aol.com)

AIREY, Dawn Elizabeth; da of Clifford Airey, *qv*, and Maureen Airey; *b* 1960; *Educ* Girton Coll Cambridge; *m* 2014, Jacqueline Lawrence; 2 da (Dulcie b 9 March 2007, Matilda b 2 May 2010); *Career* controller then dir of prog planning Central Independent Television until 1992 (joined as mgmnt trainee 1985), controller of daytime and children's progs ITV Network Centre 1993–94, controller of arts and entertainment Channel Four Television 1994–96; Channel 5 Broadcasting: dir of progs 1996–2000, ceo 2000–02; British Sky Broadcasting: md Sky Networks 2003–07, md of channels and servs 2006–07; chief exec Iostar 2007, dir of global content ITV plc 2007–08; chm and chief exec Channel 5 2008–10, pres UK TV RTL 2010–13, sr vice-pres Yahoo EMEA 2013–; exec chair Media Guardian Edinburgh Int TV Festival 2002–05, memb bd Int Acad of TV Arts 2002–, chair Nat Youth Theatre 2011–, chair Grierson Tst 2010–13; non-exec dir: Easyjet 2004–08, Taylor Nelson Sofres plc 2007, Thomas Cook Ltd 2010–; FRTS 1998, FRSA 1998; *Style*— Ms Dawn Airey

AIRS, Graham John; s of George William Laurence Airs (d 1999), and Marjorie, *née* Lewis (d 1967); *b* 8 August 1953; *Educ* Newport GS Essex, Emmanuel Coll Cambridge (MA, LLB); *m* 4 April 1981, Stephanie Annette, da of William Henry Marshall; *Career* admitted slr 1978; Slaughter and May 1976–80; ptnr: Airs Dickinson 1980–84, Slaughter and May 1987– (rejoined as asst slr 1984–87); memb Law Soc; *Style*— Graham Airs, Esq; ✉ Slaughter and May, 1 Bunhill Row, London EC1Y 8YY (☎ 020 7600 1200, direct line 020 7090 5050, fax 020 7090 5000, e-mail graham.airs@slaughtermay.com)

AITCHISON, Prof Jean Margaret; da of John Frederick Aitchison (d 1997), of Debden Green, Essex, and Joan Eileen, *née* Chivers (d 1994); *b* 3 July 1938; *Educ* Wimbledon HS GPDST, Girton Coll Cambridge (MA), Radcliffe Coll Harvard (AM); *m* 3 July 2000, John Robert Ayto; *Career* asst lectr in Greek Bedford Coll London 1961–65, lectr, sr lectr and reader in linguistics LSE 1965–92, Rupert Murdoch prof of language and communication Univ of Oxford 1993–2003, professorial fell Worcester Coll Oxford 1993–2003 (emeritus 2003–); BBC Reith lectr 1996; *Books* Linguistics (1973, 7 edn 2010 (under title Aitchison's Linguistics)), The articulate mammal: An introduction to psycholinguistics (1976, Routledge Classics edn 2011), Language change: Progress or decay? (1981, 4 edn 2013), Words in the mind: An introduction to the mental lexicon (1987, 4 edn 2012), Introducing language and mind (1992, new edn 2003), Language Joyriding (1994), The seeds of speech: Language origin and evolution (1996, extended edn 2000), The language web: The power and problem of words (1997), New media language (ed jtly, 2003), The word weavers: Newshounds and wordsmiths (2007), Linguistics Made Easy (2012); *Recreations* gardening; *Style*— Prof Jean Aitchison; ✉ 45 Malvern Road, London E8 3LP (☎ 020 7249 3734, e-mail jean.aitchison@worc.ox.ac.uk)

AITKEN, Gill; *Career* slr and DG Law and HR DEFRA; *Style*— Ms Gill Aitken; ✉ Department for Work and Pensions, Caxton House, Tothill Street, London SW1H 9NA

AITKEN, Gillon Reid; s of James Aitken (d 1954), and Margaret Joane, *née* Simpson (d 1982); *Educ* Charterhouse, privately; *Career* with Stuart's Advtg Agency 1958–59, ed Chapman & Hall Ltd 1959–66, ed Hodder & Stoughton Ltd 1966–67, dir Anthony Sheil Assocs Ltd 1967–71, md Hamish Hamilton Ltd 1971–74, vice-pres Wallace, Aitken & Sheil Inc (NY) 1974–77; chm: Gillon Aitken Associates Ltd (now Aitken Alexander Associates) 1977–, Christy & Moore Ltd 1977–, Hughes Massie Ltd 1985–; *Books* The Captain's Daughter and Other Stories (by A S Pushkin, trans, 1962), The Complete Prose Tales of A S Pushkin (trans, 1966), One Day in the Life of Ivan Denisovich (by Aleksandr Solzhenitsyn, trans, 1970); *Recreations* crossword puzzles, ping-pong; *Style*— Gillon Aitken, Esq; ✉ Garden Flat, 4 The Boltons, London SW10 9TB (☎ and fax 020 7373 7438); Aitken Alexander Associates, 18–21 Cavaye Place, London SW10 9PG (☎ 020 7373 8672, fax 020 7373 6002, e-mail gillon@aitkenalexander.co.uk)

AITKEN, Robin Peter; MBE (2014); s of William Ferguson Kent Aitken, and Dorothy Fane Brown; *b* 24 November 1952, Hereford; *Educ* Prior Park Coll Bath, Univ of Bristol; *m* 1978, Sarah Anne Nagle; 2 da (Nancy Mary b 18 May 1981, Alice Sarah b 3 Nov 1983); *Career* reporter; trained West Midlands Press Ltd 1973–76; BBC: joined 1978, worked on successively Radio Brighton, BBC Scotland, BBC Radio News, Money Programme, BBC Breakfast, On The Record, Today Programme, left 2006; co-fndr Oxford Food Bank 2009; *Books* Can We Trust the BBC? (2007, republished as Can We Still Trust the BBC? 2013); *Recreations* walking, reading history, skiing, gardening, rugby; *Style*— Robin Aitken, Esq, MBE; ✉ e-mail robinait@aol.com

AITMAN, David Charles; s of Gabriel Aitman, and Irene Bertha, *née* Polack; *b* 11 April 1956; *Educ* Clifton, Univ of Sheffield (BA); *m* 26 March 1983, Marianne Lucille, da of Edward Atherton; 1 s (Marcus), 2 da (Lauren, Polly); *Career* admitted slr 1982; ptnr: Denton Wilde Sapte 1988–2001, Freshfields Bruckhaus Deringer 2001– (departmental managing ptnr 2003–06, global practice ldr 2006–10, global managing ptnr 2014–); memb Law Soc; LRAM; *Books* Butterworth's Encyclopaedia of Competition Law (chapter on intellectual property licensing, 1991), Practical Intellectual Property (chapter on competition law), Yearbook of Media Law (chapter on competition law), Bellamy & Child's European Community Law of Competition (chapter on telecommunications); *Recreations* tennis, wind surfing, music (performing and concert going); *Style*— David Aitman, Esq

AKAM, Prof Michael Edwin; s of William Edwin Akam (d 2010), and Evelyn Warriner, *née* Thorne (d 1996); *b* 19 June 1952, Bromley, Kent; *Educ* Eltham Coll, Kings Coll Cambridge (BA), Magdalen Coll Oxford (DPhil); *m* 21 April 1979, Dr Margaret Madeline Bray; 2 s (Thomas Edwin b 18 July 1983, Simon Hugh b 18 July 1985); *Career* coll lectr in zoology Magdalen Coll Oxford 1978, MRC res fell Lab of Molecular Biology Cambridge 1978–79, Damon Runyan res fell Dept of Biochemistry Stanford Univ Calif 1979–81, MRC sr fell Dept of Genetics Univ of Cambridge 1982–1990, Wellcome princ fell and founding staff memb Wellcome/CRC Inst Cambridge 1990–97, res prof of developmental genetics Univ of Cambridge 1997, 1866 prof of zoology Univ of Cambridge 1997– (head Dept of Zoology 2010–16), dir Univ Museum of Zoology Cambridge 1997–2010; professorial fell Darwin Coll Cambridge 2006–, hon research fell Natural History Museum 2010–; chm Br Soc of Developmental Biology 1989–94; Waddington Medal Br Soc for Developmental Biology 2005, Kowalevsky Medal St Petersburg Soc of Naturalists 2007, Linnean Medal for Zoology 2009, FRINK Medal ZSL 2014; memb European Molecular Biology Orgn (EMBO) 1987; FLS 1999, FRS 2000, fell American Assoc for Advancement of Science 2006; The Evolution of Developmental Mechanisms (co-ed, 1994); numerous articles published in learned jls; *Recreations* the living world; *Style*— Prof Michael Akam; ✉ Department of Zoology, Downing Street, Cambridge CB2 3EJ (☎ 01223 336600)

AKENHEAD, Hon Mr Justice; Sir Robert Akenhead; kt (2008); s of Lt-Col Edmund Akenhead, TD (d 1990), and Angela Miriam, *née* Cullen; *b* 15 September 1949; *Educ* Rugby, Univ of Exeter (LLB); *m* 9 Dec 1972, Elizabeth Anne, da of Capt Frederick Hume Jackson, CMG, OBE, of Tonbridge, Kent; 1 s (Edmund b 1983), 3 da (Eleanor b 1978, Isobel b 1980, Rosalind b 1985); *Career* called to the Bar Inner Temple 1972 (bencher 1997), QC 1989, recorder of the Crown Court 1994–2007 (asst recorder 1991–94), judge of the High Court of Justice (Queen's Bench Division) 2007–, judge in charge Technol and Construction Court 2010–13; *Books* Building Law Reports (jt ed), Site Investigation and the Law (with J Cottington, 1984), Technology and Construction Court Practice and Procedure (with M Davis, 2007); *Recreations* cricket, skiing, theatre, golf; *Style*— The Hon Mr Justice Akenhead; ✉ Royal Courts of Justice, Strand, London WC2A 2LL

AKERS, Sue; CBE (2013), QPM (2007); *Career* Met Police; joined 1976, Cdr Barnet 2001–04, Dep Asst Cmmr Confidential and Sensitive Investigations Specialist Crime Directorate 2011–12, ret; has led the investigations into phone hacking and corruption in the newspaper industry; *Recreations* golf, skiing, walking; *Style*— Ms Sue Akers, CBE, QPM; ✉ Twitter @sueakers2000

AKERS-DOUGLAS, Francis Alexander Moreton (Frank); s of Anthony George Akers-Douglas (d 1991), and Dorothy Louise, *née* Gage (d 2010); *b* 23 September 1948; *Educ* Eton, Brown Univ USA; *m* 1, 1974 (m dis 1997), Hon Julian Mary, eld da of 2 Baron Bruntisfield, *qv*; 2 s (Joseph Michael Aretas b 1979, James George b 1989); m 2, 1998, Lorna Farquharson; 1 s (Maxwell Alastair Edward b 1998), 1 da (Emma Claire b 2000); *Career* Binder Hamlyn: articled clerk 1967, ptnr 1978–97, head Private Client Servs 1980–97; ptnr Smith & Williamson 1997–; memb: ICAEW, Soc of Trust and Estate Practitioners 1993; FCA 1971; *Books* Butterworths: Self Assessment and Simplification (1994), Corporal Haggis (1996); *Recreations* tennis, cricket, woodlands management; *Clubs* Boodles; *Style*— Frank Akers-Douglas, Esq; ✉ Smith & Williamson, 25 Moorgate, London EC2R 6AY (☎ 020 7131 4232, e-mail fad@smith-williamson.co.uk)

AKHTAR, Prof Muhammad; s of Muhammad Azeem Chaudhry; *b* 23 February 1933; *Educ* Punjab Univ Pakistan (MSc), Imperial Coll London (PhD, DIC); *m* 3 Aug 1963, Monika E, *née* Schurmann; 2 s (Marcus, Daniel); *Career* res scientist Res Inst for Med and Chemistry Cambridge USA 1959–63; Univ of Southampton: lectr 1963–, sr lectr then reader, prof of biochemistry 1973–98, head Dept of Biochemistry 1978–93, chm Sch of Biochemical and Physiological Sciences 1983–87, chm Inst of Biomolecular Sciences 1989–91, emeritus prof 1998–; distinguished nat prof and DG Sch of Biological Sciences Univ of the Punjab Lahore Pakistan 2002–; dir SERC Centre for Molecular Recognition 1990–94; author of articles in learned jls; founding fell Third World Acad of Sci 1984 (vice-pres 1998–2003, treas 1993–98, lectr 1996), hon fell UCL 2010; memb: Royal Soc of Chemistry, American Chem Soc, Biochemical Soc; award of Sitara-I-Imtiaz by Govt of Pakistan 1981, Flintoff medal 1993; Hon DSc Univ of Karachi 2000; FRS (memb Cncl 1983–85); *Style*— Prof Muhammad Akhtar, FRS; ✉ Centre of Biological Sciences, The University, Life Sciences Building 85, Southampton SO17 1BJ

AKINSANYA, David O; *b* Chelmsford, Essex; *Career* broadcaster, freelance journalist/ reporter and campaigner; began broadcasting career at BBC Radio 1, freelancer on progs incl Kilroy (BBC), Gloria Live (ITV), The Cook Report (ITV), Sex Talk (Channel 4) and The Sky Book Show (Sky), reporter current affairs BBC News 1997–2005, currently freelancer; presenting/reporting projects incl: Heaven and Earth Show (BBC 1), Inside Out (BBC 1), Real Story Special: Becky's Story (BBC 1), Sad to be Gay (BBC 2), This World (BBC 2), Black Britain (BBC 2), 4x4 (BBC 1), Raised by the State (BBC 2), Correspondent (BBC 2), Rubberman (BBC 3), Tales from the Towpath (BBC Radio 4), The Battle for Lozell's (BBC Radio 4), Find Me A Family (Channel 4); regular contrib to 5 Live, Sky News, Inside Out and BBC Radio London; ran hostel for young single homeless people for 15 years, currently provides respite care to 'looked after' young people in various local authorities and acts as a mentor to many more; ambass: Prince's Tst (former memb Bd), PACT (Parents and Children Together), Who Cares? magazine; winner of numerous awards for youth and community work; pres-elect Basildon Boys FC; *Recreations* cycling, canoeing, camping; *Style*— David O Akinsanya, Esq

AL FAYED, Mohamed Abdel Moneim; *b* 27 January 1933, Alexandria, Egypt; *m*; 4 c; *Career* owner: L'Hotel Ritz Paris 1978–, House of Fraser 1985 (floated on London Stock Exchange 1994), Harrods 1985–2010 (hon chm 2010–), Turnbull and Asser, Fulham FC 1997–; jt prodr Chariots of Fire 1980 (4 Academy Awards); fndr Liberty Publishing, relaunched Punch magazine 1996; La Grande Médaille de la Ville de Paris 1985, Plaque de Paris, Offr Légion d'Honneur (France) 1993 (Légion d'Honneur 1986), Commendatore Order of Merit (Italy) 1990; *Style*— Mr Mohamed Al Fayed; ✉ Harrods Limited, 87–135 Brompton Road, London SW1X 7XL

AL JABER, Sheikh Mohamed Bin Issa; *b* 17 January 1959, Jeddah, Kingdom of Saudi Arabia; *Educ* Univ of Westminster (DLitt); *Career* businessman and philanthropist; Jadawel Int Construction and Devpt 1982–89, JJW Hotels and Resorts 1989–92, AJWA Gp for Agriculture and Food Industries 1992–2000, fndr MBI Tst SOAS 2000, fndr, chm and ceo MBI International & Partner 2002–; fndr and chm MBI Al Jaber Fndn 2006–; UNESCO special envoy for education, tolerance and cultures 2004–, UN spokesperson for global forums on reinventing govt 2007–; senator Modul Univ Vienna 2013; Medaille D'Or du Tourisme France 2005, UNESCO 60th Anniversary Medal 2005, UNESCO Gold Medal 2007, Gold Medal Arab League Educational, Cultural and Scientific Organisation (ALESCO) 2007, Gold Medal City of Vienna 2009, Gold Medal Islamic Educational, Cultural and Scientific Organisation (ISESCO) 2012; hon fell: SOAS 2002, UCL 2012; Hon DLitt Univ of Westminster 2004, Hon DSc City Univ 2004; *Publications* Yes the Arabs Can Too (Arabic 2009, English 2013, German 2015, French 2016); *Recreations* poetry, history, reading; *Style*— Sheikh Mohamed Bin Issa al Jaber; ✉ MBI Group, 78 Wigmore Street, London W1U 2SJ (☎ 020 7935 5859, website www.mbialjaber.com)

AL MUHAIRI, Dr Abdul Rahman; *b* 7 October 1964, UAE; *Educ* Univ of London (MSc, PhD), Univ of Hull (MBA); *m* ; 3 c; *Career* registrar in nuclear medicine Hammersmith Hosp London 1994–96, registrar then specialist registrar in nuclear medicine St Bart's 1996–2000, hon conslt of nuclear medicine and sr lectr in nuclear medicine Dept of Nuclear Medicine London Univ 2002–; Cromwell Hosp London: sr physician in nuclear medicine 2002–, exec bd dir 2002–, co sec 2003–06, dep ceo 2003–05, acting ceo 2005–06, pres 2006–; pres Healthcare Investment Holdings UAE, vice-chm Injaz UAE, memb Bd Life Bridge Germany; co-author of many publications in medical jls; memb: Br Nuclear Medicine Soc, European Assoc of Nuclear Medicine, Soc of Nuclear Medicine USA, American Soc of Nuclear Cardiology, Br Nuclear Cardiology Soc; *Style*— Dr Abdul Al Muhairi; ✉ Cromwell Hospital, Cromwell Road, London SW5 0TU (☎ 020 7460 5517, fax 020 7460 5833)

AL-DUWAISAN, HE Khaled; Hon GCVO; *b* 15 August 1947; *Educ* Cairo Univ (BA), Univ of Kuwait (business admin dipl); *m*; 2 c; *Career* Kuwaiti diplomat; researcher Miny of Foreign Affairs 1970–71, diplomatic attaché 1971–72, third sec 1972–74, second sec 1974–76, joined Embassy of Kuwait in Washington DC 1975, first sec 1976–80, counsellor 1980–84, ambass extraordinary and plenipotentiary to the Netherlands 1984–90, appointed non-resident ambass to Romania 1988, ambass to the Ct of St James's 1993– (Doyen of Diplomatic Corps 2003); non-resident ambass: Denmark, Norway and Sweden 1994–95, Republic of Ireland 1995–; memb: Advsy Bd Centre of Near and and ME Studies SOAS 1998–, Management of Public Sector Projects and facilities: an Executive Program for Kuwait Harvard Univ 2005–; co-ordinator with UN during creation of the demilitarised zone and with UN ctee for return of missing and stolen property 1992; Award of Excellence Br Business Forum 2009, Lifetime Contribution to Diplomacy in London Diplomat Magazine 2009, Three Faiths Forum Gold Medallion 2010, UN Assoc Annual Award for Exceptional Service to the Int Community 2011, Lifetime Achievement as a Diplomat Ben TV Diplomatic Award 2011, Diplomat of the Year for Middle East Diplomat Magazine 2014, Policy Driver Award 2015 (awarded by sec-gen of the Arab League in recogniton of outstanding role and exceptional services in promoting and supporting Arab issues in the UK); Freeman City of London 2001; hon doctorate Univ of E Anglia 2012; memb: IOD, RIIA; *Clubs* Queen's Tennis; *Style*— HE Mr Khaled Al-Duwaisan, GCVO; ✉ Embassy of the State of Kuwait, 2 Albert Gate, London SW1X 7JU (☎ 020 7590 3400)

AL-HASSANI, Prof Salim T S; *b* 23 July 1941; *Educ* Victoria Univ of Manchester (BSc, MSc, PhD); *Career* prof of high energy rate engrg UMIST (now Univ of Manchester); tech dir: Reverse Engrg Ltd UK, EROS project; chm Fndn for Science, Technol and Civilisation; conslt: BP, John Brown, MOBIL, HEREEMA, Br Gas, AMOCO, BUKOM; expert witness on explosion damage in process plants, aircraft and offshore facilities; NYSci Award for Global Science 2010; MInstD, FInstPet, fell Br Sci Assoc 2009; *Publications* 1001 Inventions: Muslim Heritage in our World (ed-in-chief), author of over 200 scientific papers in int jls and books; *Style*— Prof S T S Al-Hassani; ✉ Foundation for Science Technology and Civilisation, FSTC House, 9 Conyngham Road, Manchester M14 5DX (☎ 0161 248 7877, fax 0161 224 6711, websites www.fstc.org.uk and www.1001inventions.com)

ALAGIAH, George Maxwell; OBE (2008); *b* 22 November 1955, Sri Lanka; *Educ* St John's Coll Southsea, Univ of Durham; *m*; 2 s; *Career* South Magazine London 1981–89; BBC: joined 1989, foreign affrs corr 1989–94, Africa corr 1995–98, presenter BBC News 24 1998, presenter BBC TV News 1999–; BBC assignments incl news reports/documentaries on: trade in human organs India, street children Brazil, civil war in Liberia, famine and civil war in Somalia, persecution of Kurds in Iraq, effects on developing countries of GATT Agreement, ethnic conflict in Burundi, civil war in Afghanistan, genocide in Rwanda, Kosovo Crisis, East Timor, Asian tsunami; *Awards* Monte Carlo TV Festival and RTS awards for Somalia reports 1993, BAFTA commendation for Newsnight Kurdistan reports 1994, Amnesty International Press Awards Journalist of the Year 1994, Broadcasting Press Guild Journalist of the Year 1994, James Cameron Memorial Tst Award 1995, One World Broadcasting Tst TV News Premier Award 1995, Bayeux War Reporting Award 1996, Ethnic Minority Media Awards Media Personality of the Year 1998, Asian Film and TV Best TV Journalist 1999; *Books* A Passage to Africa (2001), A Home from Home (2006); *Style*— George Alagiah, OBE; ✉ BBC, MediaCityUK, Salford M50 2EQ (☎ 020 8624 9999, e-mail george.alagiah@bbc.co.uk)

ALAMBRITIS, Stephen; s of Andreas Alambritis (d 2011), and Christina, *née* Skardashi (d 1995); *b* 22 February 1957; *Educ* Elliott Sch Putney, Birmingham Poly (BA), LSE (MSc), City Poly (MA); *m* 11 Oct 1987, Athanasia, *née* Georgiou; 1 da (Maria b 20 Jan 1989), 1 s (Andreas b 14 Oct 1992); *Career* researcher Assoc of Ind Businesses 1984–88, head of public affairs Fedn of Small Businesses 1988–2010; memb: Rural Affrs Task Force DEFRA 2001–02, Better Regulation Task Force Cabinet Office 1998–2001, Consumer Advsy Panel DCA 2005–09, Bd South London Business 2010–13, Bd Sutton Croydon and Merton Credit Union Ltd 2010–13; cmmr Disability Rights Cmmn 2004–07, cmmr Equality and Human Rights Cmmn 2009–12; tstee Enterprise UK 2005–10, memb Bd London Pensions Fund Authy 2010–, memb Ctee of the Regions EU; cncllr (Lab)

Ravensbury Ward London Borough of Merton 2003– (ldr 2010–); memb: NUJ 1985–2010, UNITE 1999–2010, CAMRA 1995, GMB 2008, Fedn of Small Businesses 2010; FCIPR 1990; *Recreations* FA referee grade I; *Style—* Stephen Alambritis, Esq; ✉ 10 Woodland Way, Morden, Surrey SM4 4DS (☎ 020 8543 6003, e-mail stephen.alambritis@btinternet.com); London Borough of Merton, Merton Civic Centre, London Road, Morden, Surrey SM4 5DX (☎ 020 8545 3424, mobile 07958 139498, e-mail stephen.alambritis@merton.gov.uk)

ALBARN, Damon; OBE (2016); *b* 23 March 1968; *Career* singer; memb Blur 1990–, co-creator Gorillaz 2000–; singles with Blur incl: There's No Other Way, Girls & Boys, To The End, Parklife, End Of A Century, Country House (UK no 1, Aug 1995), The Universal, Stereotypes, Charmless Man, Beetlebum (UK no 1, Jan 1997), Song 2, On Your Own, MOR, Tender, Coffee & TV, No Distance Left to Run, Music Is My Radar; albums with Blur: Leisure (UK no 7, Gold), Modern Life Is Rubbish (UK no 15, Gold), Parklife (UK no 1, 4 x Platinum) 1994, The Great Escape (UK no 1, Triple Platinum) 1995, Live at the Budokan 1996, Blur (UK no 1, Platinum) 1997, 13 (UK no 1, Platinum), Bustin' + Dronin' (remixes) 1998, 13 1999, The Best of Blur 2000, Think Tank 2003, The Magic Whip (UK no 1) 2015; albums with Gorillaz: Gorillaz (UK no 3) 2001, G-Sides 2002, Laika Come Home 2002, Demon Days (UK no 1) 2005; other albums: Democrazy (solo album) 2003, The Good, the Bad and the Queen 2007, Everyday Robots 2014; writer of original score for film 101 Reykjavik (with Einar Örn Benediktsson, 2000), co-prodr The Bravest Man in the Universe by Bobby Womack 2012; *Soundtracks* Ravenous (with Michael Nyman); Ordinary Decent Criminal (composed original score, 1999); appeared in film Face 1997; *Videos* Starshaped (1993), Showtime (1995) No Distance Left To Run (2000, DVD); *Awards* Best Band, Best Album, Best Video and Best Single (all for Parklife) BRIT Awards 1995, jt winner Songwriter of the Year Ivor Novello Awards 1996, Mercury Music Prize nomination 1999, Best Dance Artist (Gorillaz) MTV Europe Awards, Best Song (Clint Eastwood – Gorillaz) MTV Europe Awards 2001, Best Group (Gorillaz) MTV Europe Awards 2005, Best Band (Gorillaz) GQ Awards 2010, Outstanding Contribution to Music BRIT Award 2012 (with Blur), Award for Innovation NME Award 2014, nominated Mercury Music Prize (for Everyday Robots) 2014; *Style—* Damon Albarn, OBE

ALBEMARLE, 10 Earl of (E 1696); Rufus Arnold Alexis Keppel; also Baron Ashford and Viscount Bury (both E 1696); s of Viscount Bury (d 1968, eld s of 9 E of Albemarle, MC) and his 2 w, Marina, da of late Lt Cdr Count Serge Orloff-Davidoff, RNVR, and late Hon Elisabeth, *née* Scott-Ellis, 2 da of 8 Baron Howard de Walden; *b* 16 July 1965; *Educ* St Christopher Sch Letchworth, Central St Martins (BA); *m* 2001 (m dis), Sally Tadayon; 1 s (Augustus Sergei Darius, Viscount Bury b 8 Feb 2003); *Heir* s, Viscount Bury; *Career* designer; prop Albemarle Associates; *Style—* The Rt Hon the Earl of Albemarle; ✉ e-mail rufalb@mac.com

ALBERGE, Dalya; da of Maurice Ernest Alberge, and Ella Alberge; *Educ* S Hampstead HS, Trinity Coll of Music London (GTCL), Keele Univ (MA); *Career* asst ed Brevet Publishing magazines 1981–83, freelance journalist 1983, asst ed Classical Music Magazine 1984–86, art market corr and arts writer The Independent 1986–94, arts corr The Times 1994–2008, arts writer The Observer, Sunday Times, The Guardian, Financial Times and Daily Mail 2009–; memb Educn Advsy Bd Dulwich Picture Gallery 1991–2014, Arts Cncl adjudicator British Gas Working for Cities public art award 1992–93; judge UKIC Conservation Awards 2004; *Recreations* the arts; *Style—* Ms Dalya Alberge

ALBERT, Chris; *b* 30 January 1968, South Africa; *Career* md Vantage Property Gp 2003–07, head of product devpt and sales mgmnt Kleinwort Benson 2008–11, exec dir International Devpt Equiom Tst Co Ltd 2011, head Wealth Advsy 360 Service Canaccord Genuity Wealth Mgmnt UK and Europe 2011– (currently UK head of wealth planning); memb Chartered Inst of Securities 1996, memb CFA Inst 2008; *Recreations* cooking, travel, golf, music; *Style—* Chris Albert, Esq; ✉ (☎ 07557 345081, e-mail chrisalbert1@me.com)

ALBUM, Edward Jonathan Corcos; s of Harry Album (d 1988), of London, and Matilda, *née* Corcos (d 1999); *b* 8 September 1936; *Educ* Emanuel Sch, ChCh Oxford (MA); *m* 14 July 1970, Elizabeth Ann, da of Lancelot Ezra, of London; 1 s (Richard b 1974), 1 da (Victoria b 1977); *Career* Capt Res TA 1962–70; arbitrator, slr; dir: Macsteel International UK Ltd; chm Sanderling Ltd, vice-pres Settle & Carlisle Railway Tst; vice-pres Friends of the Settle-Carlisle Line; Liveryman Worshipful Co of Basketmakers, memb City of London Slrs' Co, memb Hon Artillery Co; FCIArb, FInstD, FCT; *Recreations* military history, ornithology, railway preservation; *Clubs* Sir Walter Scott (Edinburgh), Army and Navy, Oriental, AC Owners', AEC Soc; *Style—* Edward Album, Esq; ✉ 47 Lyndale Avenue, London NW2 2QB (☎ 020 7431 2942 or 020 8455 7653, e-mail ejca@mitgr.com); Sanderling House, High Street, Cley, Norfolk NR25 7RG (☎ 01263 740810)

ALBURY, Simon Albert; s of Cyril Lyon Albury (d 1971), and Eileen Palmer, *née* Lloyd-Jones (d 1986); *b* 9 February 1944; *Educ* West House Sch Birmingham, Clifton, Univ of Nottingham (BA), Brandeis Univ, Univ of Sussex (MA); *m* 14 Jan 1989, Phillida Bartels-Ellis; 1 s (David Kwamena Bartels b 25 March 1989); *Career* info offr Govt Social Survey 1967, res assoc American Psychological Assoc project on Scientific Info Exchange in Psychology 1968, reporter World in Action Granada Television 1969, with BBC Current Affrs Gp 1969–73, BBC Open Univ 1973–74, sr prodr Granada Television (progs incl: World in Action, What the Papers Say, End of Empire, The Outrageous Millie Jackson) 1974–89, dir Campaign for Quality Television 1989–90; dir of public affrs: Meridian Broadcasting Ltd 1991–99 (dir of strategy 1991), MAI Broadcasting 1994–95 (dir of strategy 1990), MAI Media 1995–96, United Broadcasting and Entertainment 1996–99; chief exec RTS 2000–12; presenter (as Sam Scott) gospel music show Hallelujah (Capital Radio) 1973–75; chair BSAC Ctee for Ethnic Minority Employment in Film 2000–07, memb Bd Int Broadcasting Convention 2001–12; tstee Meridian Broadcasting Charitable Tst 1993–99; chair Centre for Investigative Journalism 2005–08, special advsr Nafsiyat The Intercultural Therapy Centre 2001–08 (non-exec dir 2000–01), memb Advsy Bd Elizabeth R Fund 2002–03, chair DaCapo Music Fndn 2013–14, chair Campaign for Broadcasting Equality CIO 2014–; *Recreations* music, travel, ballet, opera; *Clubs* BAFTA; *Style—* Simon Albury, Esq; ✉ e-mail simon.albury@gmail.com

ALDCROFT, Prof Derek Howard; s of Leslie Howard Aldcroft, and Freda, *née* Wallen; *b* 25 October 1936; *Educ* Univ of Manchester (BA, PhD); *Career* lectr in economic history Univ of Leicester and Univ of Glasgow 1960–71, reader Univ of Leicester 1971–73, prof of economic history Univ of Sidney 1973–76, prof of economic history Univ of Leicester 1976–94, research prof in economic history Manchester Met Univ 1994–2001 (visiting prof 2001–), fell Univ of Leicester 2002–; visiting prof Anglia Poly Univ 1993–1999; series ed Modern Economic and Social History; memb Economic History Soc; *Books* incl: From Versailles to Wall Street (1977), The European Economy 1914–90 (1993), Full Employment: The Elusive Goal (1984), The British Economy 1920–51 (1986), Economic Change in Eastern Europe since 1918 (with Steven Morewood, 1995), Studies in the Interwar European Economy (1997), Exchange Rate Regimes in the Twentieth Century (with Michael Oliver, 1998); Trade Unions and the Economy 1870–2000 (with Michael Oliver, 2000), The European Economy 1914–2000 (1993, 4 ed 2001), Europe's Third World: The European Periphery in the Interwar Years (2006), Economic Disasters in the Twentieth Century (ed with Michael Oliver, 2007), The European Economy since 1914 (with Steven Morewood, 5 edn 2012); *Recreations* tennis, swimming, the Stock Exchange and gardening; *Style—* Prof Derek Aldcroft; ✉ 10 Linden Drive, Evington, Leicester LE5 6AH (☎ 0116 273 5951); School of History, University of Leicester, Leicester LE1 7RH

ALDEN, David; s of Jerome Alden (d 1997), and Barbara Gaye; *b* 1949, NYC; *Educ* Univ of Pennsylvania; *Career* opera dir; ENO prodns incl: Mazeppa, Simon Boccanegra, Un ballo in maschera, Ariodante, La Damnation de Faust, Tristan und Isolde, Jenufa (Best New Opera Prodn Olivier Award 2007); Bravarian State Opera prodns incl: Ariodante, Orlando, Rinaldo and Rodelinda, L'incoronazione di Poppea, Il ritorno d'Ulisse in patria, Tannhäuser, Der Ring des Nibelungen, La Calisto, La forza del destino, The Queen of Spades, Lulu; also prodr for WNO, Vienna Volksoper and Komische Oper Berlin; *Style—* David Alden, Esq; ✉ c/o Intermusica Artists' Management Ltd, 36 Graham Street, Crystal Wharf, London N1 8GJ

ALDENHAM (AND HUNSDON OF HUNSDON), 6 (and 4) Baron (UK 1896 and 1923 respectively); Vicary Tyser Gibbs; s of 5 Baron Aldenham and 3 Baron Hunsdon of Hunsdon (d 1986); *b* 9 June 1948; *Educ* Eton, Oriel Coll Oxford, RAC Cirencester; *m* 16 May 1980, Josephine Nicola, er da of John Richmond Fell, of Farnham, Surrey; 1 da (Hon Jessica Juliet Mary b 1984), 3 s (Hon Humphrey William Fell b 31 Jan 1989, Hon Thomas Antony John b 13 Oct 1992, Hon Theodore Harry Charles b 14 July 2000); *Heir* s, Hon Humphrey Gibbs; *Career* dir: Hundred Oaks Co 1978–, Montclare Shipping Co 1986–; chm Herts & Middx CLA 1995–98, chm Watling Chase Community Forest 1997–99; Liveryman Worshipful Co of Merchant Taylors 1979; *Style—* The Rt Hon Lord Aldenham

ALDER, Samuel George (Sam); s of George Parker Alder (d 1981), of Douglas, IOM, and Brenda Margaret, *née* Moore (d 1980); *b* 28 January 1944; *Educ* King Williams Coll IOM, Grey Coll Durham (BA); *m* 6 Sept 1983, Helen Mary, da of Dr Algernon Ivor Boyd, OBE, of St Johns, Antigua; 1 da (Alison Margaret b 16 Feb 1989), 1 s (Samuel Moore Boyd b 6 Oct 1991); *Career* Whinney Murray & Co (chartered accountants) 1966–71; chm and md EG Gp of Cos 1977– (fin dir 1971–77), sr ptnr Alder Dodsworth & Co (CAs) 1984–, chm and owner The Clypse Estate Ltd 1988–; chm: Villiers Gp plc 1981–, Yeoman Security Gp plc 1986–91, London Musici Orch 1997–98, The Athol Media Co plc 1988–, 3FM Ltd 2004–12; dir: Douglas Gas plc 1990–96, Sefton Gp plc 1997–2014, Woodard Corp 2010– (chm Governance Ctee 2010–), ISI Consultancy Ltd 2014–; mangr: Roxy Music 1972–83, King Crimson 1972–85; hon treas: Duke of Edinburgh's Award Int Project 1987, Duke of Edinburgh's Award Special Projects Gp 1988–92 (dep chm 1992–97), Appeal Ctee Museum of Garden History 1989–97; tstee: Bishop Barrow's Charity 1985–2015, British Record Industry Tst 1994–2007, The IOM Golden Jubilee Tst 2002–16; Nordoff-Robbins Music Therapy: hon treas Fund Raising Ctee 1975–81, sec and treas 1981–97, govr 1981–2007, tstee 1996–2007, chm Int Tst 1996–97, chm Bd of Govrs 1997–2007, dir Nordoff-Robbins Music Therapy in Scotland 1997–2007 (hon treas 2001–07); chm Exec Ctee IOM Milk Mktg Assoc 2004–07 (prodr memb 1998–, vice-chm 2001), prodr memb IOM Agricultural Mktg Soc 1998–2007, chm IOM Young Citizens Fund 2006–08, chm Bd of Dirs IOM Milk Mktg Assoc Ltd 2008–14, chm IOM Creamery Ltd 2008–14, dir IOM Agricultural Mktg Soc Ltd 2008–14; exec chm IOM Arts Cncl 2006–10 (memb 2003–10); dir The Sayle Gallery 2016–; hon sec and treas The Barrovian Soc 2004– (pres 2003–04), memb Cncl Bishop Barrow's Fndn 2015–; chm Bd of Govrs King William's Coll IOM 1997–2009 (govr 1991–2010), chm Bd Assoc of Governing Bodies of Ind Schs 2008–13 (memb 2001–14, jt dep chm 2007–08), dir ISC 2007–14 (chm Finance Ctee 2008–11, chm Audit Ctee 2011–14), dir ISI 2008–14, govr Lancing Coll 2009–14, pres King William's Coll Soc 2010–12; Hon Dr of Arts City Univ London 2009; FCA 1977 (ACA 1971); *Recreations* music, farming, history; *Clubs* RAC, Douglas Rotary (pres 2011–12); *Style—* S G Alder, Esq; ✉ Alder Dodsworth & Co, 22 Athol Street, Douglas, Isle of Man IM1 1JA (☎ 01624 622865, fax 01624 661410, e-mail sam.adco@manx.net)

ALDERDICE, David William; CBE (2008); s of William Alderdice (d 1982), and Ella Alderdice (d 1973); *b* 21 May 1955; *Educ* Sullivan Upper Sch Holywood, Univ of Ulster (BA), UCL (MA); *m* 7 March 1984, Nel Veenstra; 2 da (Caitlin b 20 Aug 1991, Josephine b 7 April 1994); *Career* Br Cncl: asst dir Bangladesh 1994–97, dep dir Thailand 1997–99, dep dir Argentina 1999–2002, dir Netherlands 2002–06, dir Iraq 2006–; *Recreations* rugby, football; *Style—* David Alderdice, Esq, CBE

ALDERDICE, Baron (Life Peer UK 1996), of Knock in the City of Belfast; John Thomas Alderdice; s of Rev David Alderdice (d 2011), and (Annie Margaret) Helena, *née* Shields (d 2013); *b* 28 March 1955, Lurgan, NI; *Educ* Ballymena Acad, Queen's Univ Belfast (MB BCh, BAO); *m* 30 July 1977, Dr Joan Margaret Hill, da of late James Hill, of Ballymena, NI; 2 s (Hon Stephen David b 6 Dec 1980, Hon Peter James b 7 Dec 1983), 1 da (Hon Joanna Margaret b 7 March 1988); *Career* conslt psychiatrist in psychotherapy E Health and Social Servs Bd 1988–2010, hon sr lectr in psychotherapy Queen's Univ Belfast 1999 (hon lectr 1990–99), exec med dir South and East Belfast Health & Social Servs Tst 1994–97, visiting prof Dept of Psychiatry Univ of Virginia USA 2006–10, sr research fell Harris Manchester Coll Oxford 2012–, clinical prof Dept of Psychiatry Univ of Maryland Baltimore USA 2016–; research assoc: Dept of Anthropology and Museum Ethnography Univ of Oxford 2013–, Dept of Politics and Int Relations Univ of Oxford 2013–; dir Centre for the Resolution of Intractable Conflict Harris Manchester Coll Oxford 2013–, chm Centre for Democracy and Peace Building Belfast 2014–; dir NI Inst of Human Rels 1990–95; Alliance Pty of NI: memb Exec Ctee 1984–98, vice-chm 1987, ldr 1987–98; Parly candidate 1987 and 1992, Euro Parly candidate 1989; cncllr (Victoria Area) Belfast City Cncl 1989–97; leader Alliance Delgns: to Inter-Party and Intergovernmental talks on the future of NI 1991–98, to Forum for Peace and Reconciliation Dublin Castle 1994–96; Liberal Int (LI): vice-pres 1992–99, bureau memb 1996–, chair Human Rights Ctee 1999–2005, dep pres 2000–05, pres 2005–09; treas Euro Lib Dem and Reform Party 1995–99 (vice-pres 1999–2003), elected memb NI Assembly 1998–2003 (Forum 1996–98), speaker NI Assembly 1998–2004; convener (chair) Lib Dem Parly Pty House of Lords 2010–14, ret; Lib Dem spokesman on NI 2015–; pres ARTIS Europe Ltd 2008–; memb Ind Monitoring Cmmn 2003–11; memb Cwlth Cmmn on Respect and Understanding 2006–07, memb UK Ctee on Standards in Public Life 2010–16; hon memb: Peruvian Psychiatric Assoc 2000, Br Psychoanalytical Soc 2001; hon prof Faculty of Med Univ of San Marcos Peru 1999; John F Kennedy Profile in Courage Award 1998, W Averell Harriman Award for Democracy 1998, Medal of Honor Coll of Medicine of Peru 1999, Int Psychoanalytic Assoc Extraordinary Meritorious Service to Psychoanalysis Award 2005, World Fedn of Scientists Ettore Majorana Erice Prize 2005, Prize for Freedom Liberal Int 2015, Presidente D'Honneur Liberal Int 2015–; Hon DLitt Univ of E London 2008, Hon LLD Robert Gordon Univ Aberdeen 2009, Hon DUniv Open Univ 2014; Hon FRCPI 1997, Hon FRCPsych 2001 (MRCPsych 1983, FRCPsych 1997); Knight Cdr of the Order of Frances I (KCFO) 2002; *Publications* pubns on the psychology of fundamentalism, terrorism and violent political conflict, political negotiation and parliamentary institutions and problems of First Nation peoples; *Recreations* reading, music, gastronomy; *Clubs* Ulster Reform (Belfast), National Liberal (memb Bd of Tstees, former chm of tstees); *Style—* The Rt Hon Lord Alderdice; ✉ House of Lords, London SW1A 0PW (☎ 020 7219 5050, e-mail alderdicej@parliament.uk, website www.lordalderdice.com/blog)

ALDERMAN, Prof Geoffrey; s of Samuel Alderman (d 1987), of London, and Lily, *née* Landau (d 2006); *b* 10 February 1944; *Educ* Grocers' Company's Sch Hackney, Lincoln Coll Oxford (open exhibitioner, MA, DPhil, DLitt); *m* 9 Sept 1973, Marion Joan, yr da of Eliezer and Stella Freed; 1 da (Naomi Alicia b 1974), 1 s (Eliot Daniel b 1978); *Career* res asst Dept of History UCL 1968–69, temp lectr Dept of Political Theory and Govt UC Swansea 1969–70, postdoctoral res fell Univ of Reading 1970–72; Royal Holloway Coll

London: lectr in politics 1972–84, reader in politics 1984–88, prof of politics and contemporary history 1988–94; Univ of London: chm Academic Cncl 1989–94, pro-vice-chllr for academic standards 1992–93, dean of arts 1992–94; Middlesex Univ: head of Academic Devpt and Quality Assurance Unit 1994–99, pro-vice-chllr 1996–99, emeritus prof 2002; Michael Gross prof of politics and contemporary history Univ of Buckingham 2007–; vice-pres for international programs Touro Coll NYC 2000–02 (emeritus prof 2002), sr vice-pres American Intercontinental Univ London 2004–06 (vice-pres 2002–04); visiting prof: Univ of Northumbria at Newcastle 1993–96, Sheffield Hallam Univ 1994–97; sr assoc Oxford Centre for Hebrew and Jewish Studies 1996–99, professorial research assoc SOAS Univ of London 1996–98, visiting res fell Inst of Historical Research Univ of London 2007–08, visiting fell Oxford Centre for HE Policy Studies 2010–, guest prof Ariel Univ Israel 2010–; govr Newham Coll 1998–99; tstee Huntleigh Fndn 1998–2003 (chm 1999–2000); memb Academic and Accreditation Advsy Ctee Global Alliance for Transnational Educn 2001–03, memb Race Ind Advsy Gp Met Police 2013–, memb and vice-chair Barnet Pension Fund Bd 2015–; Loewenstein-Wiener fell American Jewish Archives Cincinnati Ohio; memb Exec: Cncl of Validating Univs 1997–2000, Soc for Research into Higher Educn 1997–2000; memb Cncl Jewish Historical Soc of England 1997–99; Chaim Bermant Prize for Journalism 2011; FRHistS 1971, FRSA 1991, MCQI 1995, MCMI 1998, FICPD 1999; *Books* incl: The Railway Interest (1973), The Jewish Community in British Politics (1983), Pressure Groups and Government in Great Britain (1984), Modern Britain (1986), London Jewry and London Politics (1989), Modern British Jewry (1992, 2 edn 1998), Controversy and Crisis: Studies in the History of the Jews in Modern Britain (2008), The Communal Gadfly (2009), Hackney Downs 1876–1995: The Life and Death of a School (2012), British Jewry Since Emancipation (2014); *Recreations* music, reading; *Clubs* Athenaeum; *Style*— Prof Geoffrey Alderman; ✉ e-mail geoffreyalderman@gmail.com, website www.geoffreyalderman.com

ALDERMAN, Richard J; *Career* barr; HM Revenue and Customs: sr lawyer Sol's Office until 2003, dir Special Compliance Office 2003–05, dir of nat teams and special civil investigations 2005–08; dir Serious Fraud Office 2008–; *Style*— Richard Alderman, Esq; ✉ Serious Fraud Office, Elm House, 10–16 Elm Street, London WC1X 0BJ

ALDERSON, Prof Derek; s of late Frederick Alan Alderson, of Birtley, Co Durham, and Mary Annie, *née* Brown; *b* 18 January 1953; *Educ* Chester-le-Street GS, Univ of Newcastle upon Tyne (MB BS, MD); *m* 19 Oct 1975, Lyn Margaret, da of late Anthony Smith, of Pelton, Co Durham; 1 s (Kevin b 1979), 1 da (Helen b 1981); *Career* house offr Royal Victoria Infirmary Newcastle upon Tyne 1976–77, surgical registrar Newcastle AHA 1979–81, Wellcome surgical training fell 1981–83, sr registrar in surgery Northern RHA 1983–88, res fell Washington Univ St Louis USA 1985–86; Univ of Bristol: conslt sr lectr in surgery 1988–96, conslt surgn and chair of gastrointestinal surgery 1997–2005; conslt surgn and Barling prof of surgery Univ of Birmingham 2005–; memb: Soc Academic and Research Surgeons, Assoc of Surgns of GB and I, Br Assoc of Surgical Oncology, Br Soc of Gastroenterology, Pancreatic Soc of GB and I, past pres Assoc of Upper Gastrointestinal Surgns of GB and I; FRCS 1980 (memb Cncl 2009–); *Recreations* jogging, diving; *Style*— Prof Derek Alderson; ✉ University Department of Surgery, Room 29, 4th Floor, Queen Elizabeth Hospital, Birmingham B15 2TH (☎ 0121 627 2276, fax 0121 472 1230, e-mail d.alderson@bham.ac.uk)

ALDERSON, Matti; *b* 20 December 1951; *Educ* Bearsden Acad, Open Univ (BA); *Career* DG Advtg Standards Authy 1990–2000 (joined 1975), md FireHorses Ltd 2000–; UN advsr to Vietnam 2012; sec Ctee of Advtg Practice 1990–99, vice-chm Euro Advtg Standards Alliance Brussels 1991–2000, chm Direct Mktg Cmmn 2007–10, Removals Ombudsman 2008–11; memb: Food Advsy Ctee MAFF 1997–2002, Doctors' and Dentists' Pay Review Body 1998–2001, Bd Better Regulation Task Force 1998–2004, Bd PCC 2002–11 (memb Audit Ctee), Bd PhonepayPlus 2008–14 (memb Governance Ctee and chm HR Ctee), Bd IMCB 2008–14; vice-chm Chernobyl Children Lifeline (Chiltern) 1996–2015; memb IAM (sec High Wycombe Region 2016–); FRSA 1993, FCAM 1993, CCMI 2011; *Recreations* design, reading, travelling, driving; *Clubs* ROSL; *Style*— Matti Alderson; ✉ Raglan House, 23 Windsor Road, Gerrards Cross, Buckinghamshire SL9 7ND (☎ 01753 885445, mobile 07801 769270, e-mail matti@firehorses.com)

ALDERTON, Clive; LVO (2013); *m* Catriona Canning; 1 da (b 1998), 1 s (b 2000); *Career* diplomat; UKRep Brussels 1990–93; FCO: desk offr Far Eastern Dept 1993–96, head Indo-China Section SE Asia Dept 1996–98; head of chancery and dep head of mission Singapore 1998–2003, consul-gen Lille 2004–06, private sec to TRH the Prince of Wales and the Duchess of Cornwall 2006–12, ambass to Kingdom of Morocco and non-res ambass to Islamic Repub of Mauritiania 2012–15, princ private sec to TRH the Prince of Wales and the Duchess of Cornwall 2015–; *Style*— Mr Clive Alderton, LVO

ALDINGTON, 2 Baron (UK 1962) Charles Harold Stuart Low; s of 1 Baron Aldington, KCMG, CBE, DSO, TD, PC, DL (d 2000), and Araminta, *née* MacMichael; bro of Hon (Priscilla) Jane Stephanie (Hon Lady Roberts, CVO, *qv*); *b* 22 June 1948; *Educ* Winchester, New Coll Oxford, INSEAD; *m* 16 Sept 1989, Regine, da of late Erwin von Csongrady-Schopf; 1 s (Hon Philip Toby Augustus b 1 Sept 1990), 2 da (Hon Louisa Charlotte Patience, Hon Marie-Therese Sophie Araminta (twins) b 8 July 1992); *Heir* s, Hon Philip Low; *Career* formerly with Citibank and Grindlays Bank; md Deutsche Bank AG London 1988–2002, chm Deutsche Bank London 2002–09, sr advsr Deutsche Bank 2009–; dir GTT Duisburg 1986–87; chm: Euro Vocational Coll 1993–96, Centec 1995–96, Focus Central London 1996–99, Stramongate Ltd 2007–11; memb Cncl German Br C of C 1994–2008; tstee: English Int 1979–86, Whitechapel Art Gallery Fndn 1992–96, Royal Acad Tst 2003– (dep chm 2007–, chm Investment Ctee), Inst of Philanthropy 2008–; vice-pres Nat Churches Tst 2008–; memb: Oxford Univ Ct of Benefactors 1990–, Said Business Sch Business Advsy Forum, LIBA Chm's Ctee 2002–09, Bd BBA until 2009, EU Advsy Ctee City of London until 2009; govr Ditchley Fndn 2006–, chair New Coll Ctee 2010–; Liveryman Worshipful Co of Grocers; *Clubs* Brooks's, Hong Kong; *Style*— The Lord Aldington; ✉ Deutsche Bank AG London, 1 Great Winchester Street, London EC2N 2DB (☎ 020 7545 7505, fax 020 7545 7844)

ALDISS, Brian Wilson; OBE (2005); s of Stanley Aldiss, and May, *née* Wilson; *b* 18 August 1925; *Educ* Framlingham Coll, West Buckland Sch; *m* 1, 1949 (m dis 1965); 1 s (Clive b 1955), 1 da (Wendy b 1959); m 2, 11 Dec 1965, Margaret Christie, da of John Manson (d 1997); 1 s (Tim b 1967), 1 da (Charlotte b 1969); partner, Alison Soskice; *Career* author, critic, artist and poet; served RCS 1943–47, India, Assam, Burma, Sumatra, Singapore, Hong Kong; bookseller Oxford 1948–56, lit ed Oxford Mail 1956–71; pres Br Science Fiction Assoc 1960–64, ed SF Horizons 1964–70, chm Oxford Branch Conservation Soc 1968–69, vice-pres The Stapledon Soc 1975–, jt pres Euro SF Ctees 1976–79, pres World SF 1982–84 (fndr memb); Soc of Authors: memb Ctee of Mgmnt 1976–78, chm 1978, chm Cultural Exchanges Ctee 1979–; memb: Arts Cncl (Lit Panel) 1978–80, Cncl for Posterity 1990–97; vice-pres West Buckland Sch 1997–; Grand Master of Science Fiction 2000; prolific lectr, contrib articles to newspapers and jls; Observer Book Award for Science Fiction 1956, Ditmar Award for Best Contemporary Writer of Science Fiction 1969, James Blish Award for SF Criticism (only recipient) 1977, Pilgrim Award 1978, Award for Distinguished Scholarship Int Assoc for the Fantastic in the Arts (first recipient) 1986; Hon DLitt Univ of Reading 2000; FRSL 1990; Vision Award (Macedonia) 2001; *Books* novels incl: The Brightfount Diaries (1955), Non-Stop (1958), Hothouse (1962 and 2008), Greybeard (1964), Barefoot in the Head (1969), The Hand-Reared-Boy (1970), Soldier Erect (1971), Frankenstein Unbound (1973), The Malacia Tapestry (1976), A Rude Awakening (1978), Life in the West (1980), The Helliconia Trilogy (1982–85), Forgotten Life (1988), Dracula Unbound (1990), Remembrance Day (1993), Somewhere East of Life (1994), White Mars (with Roger Penrose) 1999, Super-State (2002), Affairs at Hampden Ferrers (2004), Jocasta (2005), Sanity and the Lady (2005), Harm (2008), Walcot (2009); short stories collections incl: Space, Time and Nathaniel (1957), The Canopy of Time (1959), The Saliva Tree (1966), Intangibles Inc (1969), The Moment of Eclipse (1970), Last Orders (1977), Seasons in Flight (1984), Best Science Fiction Stories of Brian W Aldiss (1988), A Romance of the Equator (1989), A Tupolev Too Far (1993), The Secret of This Book (1995), Supertoys Last All Summer Long (2001), Cultural Breaks (short stories, 2005), Finches of Mars (2013), Comfort Zone (2013); non-fiction incl: Cities and Stones (travel, 1966), The Shape of Further Things (1970), Billion Year Spree (1973), Trillion Year Spree (update, 1986), Bury My Heart at W H Smiths (1990), The Detached Retina (1995), Twinkling of an Eye (autobiography, 1998), When the Feast is Finished (1999), Penguin Books Science Fiction Omnibus (2008); poetry incl: At the Caligula Hotel (1995), The Poems of Makhtumkuli (1996), A Prehistory of Mind (2008), Mortal Morning (2011), An Exile on Planet Earth (2012), The Invention of Happiness (2013); *Recreations* amateur theatricals, painting; *Style*— Brian Aldiss, Esq, OBE, FRSL; ✉ Hambleden, 39 St Andrews Road, Old Headington, Oxford OX3 9DL (☎ 01865 762464, fax 01865 744435, e-mail aldiss.brian@gmail.com, website www.brianwaldiss.com)

ALDOUS, Hugh Graham Cazalet; s of Maj Hugh Francis Travers Aldous (d 1979), and Emily, *née* Watkinson; *b* 1 June 1944; *Educ* Scarborough HS, Univ of Leeds (BCom); *m* 25 Aug 1967, Christabel, da of Alan Marshall (d 1974); *Career* accountant; Grant Thornton UK LLP (formerly RSM Robson Rhodes): ptnr 1976, seconded to Dept of Tport 1976–79, head corp fin consultancy 1983–85, dep managing ptnr 1985–87, managing ptnr 1987–97; DTI: inspr into affairs of House of Fraser Holdings plc 1987–88, inspr into TransTec 2002–03; dir: Freightliner Ltd 1979–84, Sealink UK Ltd 1981–84, The Eastern European Tst plc (formerly First Russian Frontiers Trust) 1995–2011, Elderstreet Millennium Venture Capital Tst plc (formerly Gartmore Venture Capital Trust plc) 1995–, RSM International (chm) 1996–2001, Asian Total Return Investment Co plc (formerly Henderson TR Pacific Investment Tst plc) 2003–14, Innospec Inc (formerly Octel Corp) 2005–, Melorio plc 2007–10, Polar Capital Hldgs 2007–; chm and dir Capita Sinclair Henderson Ltd 2007–15, chm SPL Guernsey ICC Ltd 2010–; memb: Br Waterways Bd 1983–86, Tech Directorate ICAEW 1995–98; chm CILNTEC 1994–97 (dir 1991–97), dep chm FOCUS 1996–98, memb Comp Cmmn 1998–2001; chm: Protocol Assoc BV 2000–02, Instem Ltd 2001–04, Craegmoor Ltd 2001–05; FCA 1979 (ACA 1970); *Publications* Investment Companies: Performance Fees (2008); *Recreations* walking, tennis, music; *Clubs* RAC; *Style*— Hugh Aldous, Esq

ALDOUS, Peter; MP; *b* Ipswich, Suffolk; *Career* chartered surveyor; MP (Cons) Waveney 2010–; *Style*— Peter Aldous, Esq, MP; ✉ House of Commons, London SW1A 0AA (☎ 020 7219 7182, e-mail peter.aldous.mp@parliament.uk)

ALDOUS, Rt Hon Sir William; kt (1988), PC (1995); s of Guy Travers Aldous, QC (d 1981), and Elizabeth Angela, *née* Paul; *b* 17 March 1936; *Educ* Harrow, Trinity Coll Cambridge (MA); *m* 1960, Gillian Frances, da of John Gordon Henson, CBE; 1 s, 2 da; *Career* called to the Bar Inner Temple 1960; memb jr counsel DTI 1972–76; QC 1976; chm Performing Right Tbnl 1987–88; judge of the High Court of Justice (Chancery Div) 1988–95, a Lord Justice of Appeal 1995–2003, Justice of Appeal Gibraltar 2005–15; *Recreations* horses; *Style*— The Rt Hon Sir William Aldous

ALDRED, Adam David Scott; s of Ian Alastair Scott, OBE (d 1982), and Brenda Marion Aldred, *née* Farthing (d 2014); step s of Peter Norman Aldred, DFC (d 2013); *b* 2 November 1962, Sydney, Aust; *Educ* Cranbrook Sch Sydney, Slrs' Admission Bd Sydney (Dip Law), Trinity Hall Cambridge (LLM); *m* 12 June 1993, Ruth Elizabeth, *née* Chatterton; 3 da (Sophie Elena b 30 July 1996, Emily Elizabeth b 18 Nov 1998, Lucy Eloise b 16 Sept 2006); *Career* admitted slr: NSW 1987, Eng & Wales 1991; admitted as slr advocate 2000; slr specialising in EU and competition law; Norton Rose 1989–93, Hammond Suddards Edge (now Squire Patton Boggs) 1994–2001, Addleshaw Goddard 2001–14, called to the Bar Gray's Inn 2014, practising barr Kings Chambers 2014–; accredited mediator ADR Net 1999, memb Br Inst of Int and Comparative Law; memb Law Soc 1991; Competition/Regulatory Team of the Year The Lawyer Awards 2006, Standout FT Innovative Lawyers Awards 2012; MCIArb 2016; *Publications* Cartels – Enforcement, Appeals and Damages Actions (jt author UK chapter, 2 edn 2014); *Recreations* family, water skiing, snow skiing, horses; *Clubs* White Rose Water Ski; *Style*— Adam Aldred, Esq; ✉ Kings Chambers, 5 Park Square, Leeds LS1 2NE (☎ 0345 034 3444, e-mail aaldred@kingschambers.com)

ALDRED, (Patricia) Margaret; CB (2009), CBE (1991); *b* 16 June 1954; *Career* various posts MOD 1975–88, private sec to Min of State for the Armed Forces 1988–90, head Policy Studies Secretariat MOD 1990–92, dir of defence policy MOD 1992–93, head Costs Review Secretariat MOD 1993–94, PPS to Defence Sec 1994–97, asst under sec (service personnel policy) MOD 1997–98, DG mgmnt and organisation MOD 1998–2000, dir Public Services Directorate HM Treasy 2001, DG resources and performance Home Office 2001–04, DG and dep head Foreign and Defence Policy Secretariat Cabinet Office 2004–09, sec Iraq Inquiry 2009–16; *Style*— Ms Margaret Aldred, CB, CBE

ALDRIDGE, Simon Anthony; s of Maj Anthony Harvey Aldridge, TD (d 1994), of Elstead, Surrey, and Betty Angela *née* Harbord (d 1998); *b* 12 April 1942; *Educ* Marlborough, Grenoble Univ; *m* 23 Feb 1968, Jennifer Roberta Anne, da of Maj Denzil Robert Noble Clarke (d 1986), of Wokingham, Surrey; 1 da (Victoria Helmore Elizabeth b 1 May 1969); *Career* md Savory Milln 1986–89 (ptnr 1969–86), co chm SBC Stockbroking 1988–89; dir: Baring Securities Ltd 1989–93, Baring Securities (Europe) Ltd 1991–93, Baring Securities Bourse SA 1992–93; md BZW Securities Ltd 1993–98, pres BZW Bourse SA 1997–98, dir Credit Suisse First Boston 1998, dir int sales Fauchier Partners 1999–2009, ptnr Cadogan Advsy Servs 2002–; dep chm Croissance Britannia Paris 1987–; Ordre Nationale du Mérite (France) 1989; *Recreations* art, golf, shooting, tennis; *Clubs* Cercle de l'Union Interalliée (Paris), City of London, Garrick; *Style*— Simon Aldridge, Esq; ✉ 31 Cadogan Street, London SW3 2PP (☎ 020 7589 3895)

ALESBURY, Alun; s of George Alesbury (d 2007), and Eveline, *née* Richards (d 2011); *b* 14 May 1949; *Educ* Fitzwilliam Coll Cambridge, Univ of Seville; *m* 26 June 1976, Julia Rosemary, 6 da of Herbert Archibald Graham Butt (d 1971), of Sibford Gower, Oxon; 1 s (Rupert b 1980), 2 da (Lucy b 1982, Katie b 1990); *Career* called to the Bar Inner Temple 1974, legal corr The Architect 1976–80, memb Panel of Jr Treasy Counsel (Lands Tbnl) 1978–, memb Supplementary Panel Common Law (Planning) 1991–2000; memb: Parly Bar Mess, Br-Spanish Law Assoc, Admin Law Bar Assoc, Ecclesiastical Law Soc; fndr memb Planning and Environment Bar Assoc 1986 (hon sec 1986–88); appointed to hold inquiry into: Palmeira Avenue fire Hove 1992, Lake Windermere speed limit inquiry 1994–95, Canbury Gardens Kingston 1998–99, Chardon LL (GM seed licensing) 2000–02, numerous village green registration inquiries; memb: South Downs Jt Ctee (formerly Sussex Downs Conservation Bd) 2001–11, South Downs Nat Park Authy 2010–; *Publications* incl: Highways (contrib 4 edn Halsburys Laws of England), articles on planning law; *Recreations* walking, travel, old buildings, reeling and Scottish country dancing; *Clubs* London Highland, Southsea Reel, Royal Scottish Country Dance Soc (London & Int branches), British-Spanish Soc; *Style*— Alun Alesbury, Esq; ✉ Cornerstone Barristers, 2–3 Gray's Inn Square, London WC1R 5JH (☎ 020 7242 4986, fax 020 7405 1166, e-mail)

ALESSI, Prof Dario Renato; *b* 23 December 1967, Strasbourg, France; *Educ* European Sch of Brussels II, Univ of Birmingham (BSc, PhD, Univ Undergraduate Prize, Science

Faculty Scholarship, Perry Prize, Wellcome Trust Prize Studentship); *Career* MRC Protein Phosphorylation Unit Univ of Dundee: MRC postdoctoral trg fell 1991–94, MRC scientist 1994–96, princ investigator 1997, dir; awarded career appt MRC 2000, hon prof Univ of Dundee 2001 (hon lectr 1997); advsr Biomedical Central Cancer; memb Scientific Advsy Bd: MRC Clinical Sciences Centre, Max Planck Inst for Molecular Physiology; dir Dundee Signal Transduction Therapy Unit; memb Editorial Bd: Biochemical Jl, Jl of Cell Science, EMBO, EMBO Reports, Jl of Cell Science, Jl of Molecular Cell Biology; vice-chair European Biochemical Jl, sr ed EMBO Molecular Medicine; author of numerous articles in learned jls, delivered lectures and seminars worldwide incl R D Lawrence lecture Diabetes UK 2004; Colworth Medal Biochemical Soc 1999, Eppendorf Young European Investigator Award 2000, Morgagni Young Investigator Prize 2002, Pfizer Academic Award 2002, Makdougall Brisbane Prize Royal Soc of Edinburgh 2002, Philip Leverhulme Prize 2002, Fedn of European Biochemical Socs (FEBS) Anniversary Prize 2003, Gold Medal EMBO 2005, Francis Crick lectr Royal Soc 2006; memb: Biochemical Soc, EMBO 2005; FRSE 2002, FRS 2008; *Style*— Prof Dario Alessi; ✉ MRC Protein Phosphorylation & Ubiquitylation Unit, Sir James Black Centre, University of Dundee, Dundee DD1 5EH (e-mail d.r.alessi@dundee.ac.uk)

ALEXANDER, Bill (ne Paterson); s of William Paterson, of Warton, Lancs, and Rosemary, *née* McCormack; *b* 23 February 1948; *Educ* St Lawrence Coll Ramsgate, Keele Univ (BA); *m* 1 June 1977, Juliet Linda, da of Michael Hedley Harmer, of Petworth, W Sussex; 2 da (Jessie b 1974, Lola b 1979); *Career* director; seasons with The Other Company, Bristol Old Vic and Royal Court 1972–78, hon assoc dir RSC 1991– (assoc dir RSC 1978–91), artistic dir Birmingham Rep Theatre 1992–2000; *Theatre* Bristol Old Vic incl: The Ride Across Lake Constance, Twelfth Night, Old Times, Butley, How the Other Half Loves; Royal Court incl: Sex and Kinship in a Savage Society 1976, Amy and the Price of Cotton 1977, Class Enemy 1978, Sugar and Spice 1979; RSC incl: Factory Birds 1977, Shout Across the River, The Hang of the Gaol, Captain Swing 1978, Men's Beano 1979, Bastard Angel 1980, Henry IV 1980 (tour), Accrington Pals 1981, Volpone 1983, Richard III 1984, The Merry Wives of Windsor 1985, A Midsummer Night's Dream 1986, Twelfth Night, The Merchant of Venice, Cymbeline 1987, Duchess of Malfi 1989, The Taming of the Shrew 1990 and 1992, Much Ado About Nothing 1991, The School of Night 1992, Titus Andronicus 2003, King Lear 2004; Birmingham Rep incl: Othello 1993, Volpone 1993, Old Times 1993, The Snowman 1993, Awake and Sing 1994, The Tempest 1994, The Servant 1995, Macbeth 1995, Way of the World 1995, Divine Right 1996, Dr Jekyll and Mr Hyde 1996, The Alchemist 1996, The Merchant of Venice 1997, The Snowman 1997, Frozen 1998, Hamlet 1998, The Four Alice Bakers 1999, Jumpers 1999, Nativity 1999, Quarantine 2000, Hamlet 2000, Twelfth Night 2000; LAMDA: Twelfth Night 2012, Summerfolk 2013, Measure for Measure 2013; other credits incl: Troilus and Cressida (Shakespeare Theatre Washington) 1992, The Importance of Being Earnest (Northampton) 2002, Mappa Mundi (RNT) 2002, Enemy of the People (Theatr Clwyd) 2002, Frozen (RNT) 2002, Henry IV parts 1 and 2 (Shakespeare Theatre Washington) 2004, A Midsummer Night's Dream (ballet) 2007, School of Night (Mark Taper Forum LA) 2008, Glamour (Nottingham Playhouse) 2009, Bette and Joan (Arts Theatre London) 2011 and (nat tour) 2012, Othello (NWCTC Portland OR) 2012; *Recreations* golf, tennis; *Clubs* Groucho; *Style*— Bill Alexander, Esq; ✉ Rose Cottage, Tunley, Cirencester, Gloucestershire GL7 6LP (☎ 01285 760555, e-mail bill2juliet@btinternet.com); c/o Nicki Stoddart, United Agents, 12–16 Lexington Street, London W1F 0LE (☎ 020 3214 0869, e-mail nstoddart@unitedagents.co.uk)

ALEXANDER, Rt Hon Sir Danny; kt (2015), PC (2010); *b* 15 May 1972; *Educ* Lochaber HS, Univ of Oxford; *m* 9 July 2005, Rebecca Louise; *Career* press offr Scottish Lib Dems 1993–95, dir of communications European Movement 1996–99, head of communications Br in Europe 1999–2004, head of communications Cairngorms Nat Park 2004–; MP (Lib Dem) Inverness, Nairn, Badenoch and Strathspey 2005–15, shadow minister for Social Exclusion 2007, shadow sec of state for work and pensions 2007–08, sec of state for Scotland 2010, chief sec to the Treasy 2010–15; *Style*— The Rt Hon Sir Danny Alexander; ✉ House of Commons, London SW1A 0AA (☎ 020 7219 2300, e-mail alexanderdg@parliament.uk)

ALEXANDER, Douglas; PC (2005); *b* 1967, Glasgow; *Educ* Univ of Edinburgh (chair Univ Labour Club, MA, LLB, Dip Legal Practice), Univ of Pennysylvania (scholar).; *Career* slr; MP (Lab): Paisley S 1997–2005 (by-election), Paisley and Renfrewshire S 2005–15; min of state for e-commerce and competitiveness 2001–02, min of state Cabinet Office 2002–03, min for the Cabinet Office and Chllr of the Duchy of Lancaster 2003–04, min of state for trade, investment and foreign affrs 2004–05, min of state for Europe FCO 2005–06, sec of state for tport 2006–07, sec of state for Scotland 2006–07, sec of state Int Devpt 2007–10, shadow sec for work and pensions 2010–11, shadow foreign sec 2011–15; memb Lab Pty 1981–; *Style*— The Rt Hon Douglas Alexander; ✉ House of Commons, London SW1A 0AA

ALEXANDER, Heidi; MP; s of Malcolm Alexander, and Elaine, *née* Lanham; *b* 17 April 1975, Swindon, Wilts; *Educ* Churchfields Sch Swindon, Univ of Durham (BA, MA); *m* 6 Aug 2011, Martin Ballantyne; *Career* researcher to Joan Ruddock, MP, *qv* 1999–2005, campaign mangr Clothes Aid 2005; cncllr Lewisham Borough Cncl 2004–10 (dep mayor and Cabinet memb for regeneration 2006–10); MP (Lab) Lewisham E 2010–; chair London Enterprise 2007–09; shadow health sec 2015–; *Style*— Ms Heidi Alexander, MP; ✉ House of Commons, London SW1A 0AA

ALEXANDER, Dame Helen Anne; DBE (2011, CBE 2004); da of Bernard Alexander (d 1990), and Tania von Benckendorff (d 2004); *b* 10 February 1957; *Educ* St Paul's Girls' Sch, Hertford Coll Oxford, INSEAD; *m* Feb 1985, Timothy Suter, s of Martin Edward Hayles Suter; 1 da, 2 s; *Career* Duckworth & Co 1978–79, Faber & Faber 1979–83, The Economist Newspaper Ltd 1985–93, md The Economist Intelligence Unit 1993–96; chief exec The Economist Group London 1997–2008; chm: Port of London Authy 2010–, UBM plc 2012–; dep chm esure plc 2011–; non-exec dir: Rolls-Royce plc 2007–, Grand Palais Paris; former non-exec dir: Northern Foods, BT, Centrica; former tstee Tate Gallery; chllr Univ of Southampton 2011–, dep chair Said Business Sch, dep chair St Paul's Girl's Sch; hon fell Hertford Coll Oxford; *Style*— Dame Helen Alexander, DBE; ✉ e-mail ha.alexander@btinternet.com

ALEXANDER, John Bernard Alexei; s of B G Alexander, of Great Haseley, Oxon, and T Alexander, *née* Benckendorff; *b* 23 August 1941; *Educ* Westminster, Balliol Coll Oxford; *m* 1 July 1969, Jacquelyn, da of John Bray, of Sydney, Aust; 2 s (Nicolas b 1971, Christopher b 1974); m 2, 14 April 1981, Judy, da of Maj Patrick Chilton, of West Ashling, W Sussex; 1 da (Tania b 1982); *Career* merchant banker; dir Hill Samuel & Co Ltd 1973–83, md Edmond de Rothschild Ltd 1984–2011; dir: Port of Bristol 1991–, Banque Privée Edmond de Rothschild Geneva 1994–2012, Sterling Insurance Group Ltd 1995–2015, La Compagnie Financière Edmond de Rothschild Banque Paris 1996–2012, Edmond de Rothschild Hldg SA 1996–2011; chm: CPRE Oxfordshire Buildings Preservation Trust Ltd 1995–, Assoc of Small Historic Towns and Villages of the UK (ASHTAV) 2004–, Pacific Alliance Asia Opportunity Fund Ltd; *Recreations* skiing, tennis, gardening; *Clubs* Brooks's; *Style*— John B Alexander, Esq; ✉ 71 Whitelands House, Cheltenham Terrace, London SW3 4QZ (☎ 07836 220704)

ALEXANDER, Dr John Huston (Ian); s of late John Alexander, of Bath, and late Agnes Margaret Crawford, *née* Huston; *b* 5 April 1941; *Educ* Campbell Coll Belfast, St Edmund Hall Oxford (BLitt, MA, DPhil); *m* 1970, Flora Munro, da of late Angus Ross, of Invergordon; 2 da (Ruth b 1971, Jane b 1974), 2 s (Mark b 1976, Patrick John b 1977); *Career* sessional lectr in English Univ of Saskatchewan Saskatoon Canada 1966–67, reader in English Univ of Aberdeen 1996–2001 (lectr in English 1968–84, sr lectr 1984–96); ed: The Scott Newsletter 1982–2001, Scottish Literary Journal 1991–95; gen ed Edinburgh Edn Waverley Novels 1984–2012; hon fell Assoc for Scottish Literary Studies 2013; *Books* Two Studies in Romantic Reviewing (1976), The Lay of the Last Minstrel: Three Essays (1978), The Reception of Scott's Poetry by his Correspondents (1979), Marmion: Studies in Interpretation and Composition (1981), Scott and His Influence (ed with David Hewitt, 1983), Reading Wordsworth (1987), The Tavern Sages: Selections from the Noctes Ambrosianae (ed, 1992), Scott in Carnival (ed with David Hewitt, 1993), Walter Scott: Kenilworth – A Romance (ed, 1993), Walter Scott: The Bride of Lammermoor and A Legend of the Wars of Montrose (ed, 1995), Walter Scott: Tales of a Grandfather: The History of France (second series, ed with William Baker, 1996), Walter Scott: Anne of Geierstein (ed, 2000), Walter Scott: Quentin Durward (ed with G A M Wood, 2001), Walter Scott: Count Robert of Paris (ed, 2006), Walter Scott: Castle Dangerous (ed, 2006), Walter Scott: The Siege of Malta and Bizarro (ed with Judy King and Graham Tulloch, 2008), Walter Scott: Woodstock (ed with Tony Inglis and others, 2009), Walter Scott: The Betrothed (ed with J B Ellis and David Hewitt, 2009), Walter Scott: The Talisman (ed with J B Ellis and others, 2009), Walter Scott: Introductions and Notes from The Magnum Opus (ed with P D Garside and Claire Lamont, 2012); *Recreations* music, walking; *Style*— Dr J H Alexander; ✉ 14 Holley Crescent, Headington, Oxford OX3 8AW (☎ 01865 764524, e-mail alexanderjohn998@yahoo.co.uk)

ALEXANDER, Lesley-Anne; CBE (2012); *Educ* MSc; *m*; 1 s; *Career* various positions rising to dir of housing Housing Dept London Borough of Enfield 1992–98, dir of ops Peabody Tst 1998–2003, chief exec RNIB 2004–; non-exec dir Royal Brompton & Harefield NHS Fndn Tst 2013–; tstee and chm ACEVO 2009–15; *Style*— Lesley-Anne Alexander, CBE; ✉ Royal National Institute of Blind People, 105 Judd Street, London WC1H 9NE (☎ 020 7388 1266)

ALEXANDER, Prof Michael Joseph; s of Joseph Brian Alexander, MBE, JP (d 1984), and Winifred, *née* Gaul (d 1985); *b* 21 May 1941; *Educ* Downside, Trinity Coll Oxford (MA); *m* 1, 1 Sept 1973, Eileen Mary (d 1986), da of Anthony Hamilton McCall; 2 da (Lucy b 1977, Flora b 1982), 1 s (Patrick b 1980); m 2, 11 July 1987, Mary Cecilia Sheahan; *Career* ed William Collins 1963, fell Princeton Graduate Sch 1965, lectr Univ of Calif 1966, ed André Deutsch 1967, lectr UEA 1968, reader Univ of Stirling 1985 (lectr 1969), Berry prof of Eng lit Univ of St Andrews 1985–2003 (now emeritus); rep Scotland Round Britain Quiz (BBC); *Books* verse translations incl: The Earliest English Poems (1966, 3 edn 1991), Beowulf (1973, 2 edn 2001), Old English Riddles from the Exeter Book (1980, 2 edn 2008), The First Poems in English (2008), The Wanderer (2013); other publications incl: Twelve Poems (1977), The Poetic Achievement of Ezra Pound (1979, new edn 1998), Macmillan Anthology of English Literature (jt ed, 1989), Beowulf (ed, 1995, 2 edn 2005), Sons of Ezra (jt ed, 1995), The Canterbury Tales: The First Fragment (ed, 1996), A History of English Literature (2000, 3 edn 2013), Medievalism: The Middle Ages in Modern England (2007), Geoffrey Chaucer (2012), Reading Shakespeare (2012); *Clubs* Athenaeum; *Style*— Prof Michael Alexander; ✉ 21 Stapleton Road, Headington, Oxford OX3 7LX (☎ 01865 741774); School of English, The University, St Andrews KY16 9AL (e-mail michael.j.alex@gmail.com)

ALEXANDER, Michael Richard; s of Pauline Alexander, *née* Parkinson; *b* 17 November 1947, Southport, Merseyside; *Educ* King George GS Southport, UMIST (BSc, MSc); *m* (m dis); 2 s (James Richard b 2 June 1977, Simon Elliot b 18 May 1981); *Career* BP plc 1966–91; British Gas (now Centrica plc following demerger): commercial mangr Exploration and Prodn 1991–93, dir CIS and Central Europe 1993, md British Gas Supply 1993–96, md British Gas Trading Ltd 1996–2002, exec dir Centrica plc 1997–2003, chief operating offr Centrica plc 2002–03; ceo British Energy plc 2003–05; non-exec dir: Energy Saving Tst 1994–2001, Associated British Foods 2002–07, Costain plc 2007–14, UK Payments Cncl 2007–14; chm: Assoc of Train Operating Cos 2008–09, TGE Marine AG 2008–09; dep chm and sr ind dir Russian Platinum 2011–14, sr ind dir Seplat Petroleum Devpt Co Ltd 2013–; European advsr Landis & Gyr 2008–; CEng, FIChemE, FIGasE, FIEE; *Recreations* squash, walking, dining; *Style*— Michael Alexander, Esq

ALEXANDER, Robert Manus O'Donel; OBE, JP (2010); s of Dr Conel Alexander, of Leicester (d 1992), and Lilias Margaret (Sue), *née* Munro; *b* 14 August 1964, Leicester; *Educ* Wyggeston Boys Sch Leicester, Univ Coll Durham (BA); *Career* asst info offr Central Office of Info 1988–90; FCO: joined 1990, visit offr 1990–92, head of visits Govt Hospitality Fund 1992–97, Southern European Dept 1997–99, head Govt Hospitality 1999–; *Recreations* gardening, cinema, theatre, music, food and drink, literature; *Style*— Robert Alexander, Esq, OBE, JP; ✉ Government Hospitality, Lancaster House, Stable Yard, St James's, London SW1A 1BB (☎ 020 7008 3231, e-mail robert.alexander@fco.gov.uk)

ALEXANDER, Roger Michael; s of Hyman Isador Alexander, of London, and Anna, *née* Blumberg; *b* 29 June 1942; *Educ* Dulwich Coll, Law Soc Coll of Law; *m* 26 June 1966, Monica Anne, da of Freddie Freedman; 2 da (Jessica Louise b 6 June 1969, Lucy Katharine b 27 Feb 1971); *Career* admitted slr 1965; Lewis Silkin: ptnr 1965, head Corporate Dept 1985–89, lead ptnr 1989–98, head of Mktg Servs Law Gp 1990–2005, sr ptnr 1998–2005, chm 2005–10; non-exec chm Walker Books Ltd 2010– (non-exec dir 1999–); non-exec dir: EDS Financial Services Div 1995–96, London String Quartet Fndn 2003–08, Central Sch of Speech and Drama 2005–14, Communications Agency Ltd 2010–13; advsr Bd of Strategy Investment Partners LLP 2010–; memb Devpt Strategy Ctee Dulwich Coll 2013–; hon slr London Marriage Guidance Cncl 1988 (memb Exec Cncl 1986–90); memb Law Soc 1965–2010; *Recreations* books, theatre, photography, gardening, travel, bridge; *Clubs* MCC; *Style*— Roger Alexander, Esq; ✉ e-mail roger.m.alexander@btinternet.com; Walker Books Ltd, London SE11 5HJ (e-mail roger.alexander@walker.co.uk)

ALEXANDER, Dr William John (Bill); CBE (2005); s of John Fryer Alexander, and Kathleen Mary, *née* Berry; *b* 15 February 1947, Dilston, Northumberland; *m* Dorothy (Dee), *née* Full; 1 s (Paul b 6 Aug 1972), 1 da (Sarah b 6 April1976); *Career* British Coal Corp (formerly NCB): joined as graduate trainee 1970, area mech engr Scotland 1982–83, chief engr Scottish Region 1983–86, chief mech engr HQ 1986–87, head of engrg 1987–89; Thames Water Utilities Ltd: engrg dir 1989–91, tech dir 1991–92, md 1992–94; Thames Water plc: exec main bd dir (incl responsibility for construction of Thames Water London Ring Main) 1994–96, group md 1995–97, chief exec 1997–2005; non-exec chm: Xansa 2004–07, Invesco Perpetual Income and Growth Investment Tst plc 2007–, Clearview Traffic Ltd 2007–09, Beyond Analysis Ltd 2008–; non-exec dir CBI 2005–08; former non-exec dir: RMC Gp plc, Laporte plc; former pres Inst of Mining Electrical and Mining Mechanical Engrs (IMEMME); chm Henley Music Festival 2003–11; Hon DSc: Univ of Reading 2002, Cranfield Univ 2003; CEng, FIMechE, FREng, Hon FIMMM, Hon FCIWEM; *Recreations* classic cars, tennis, golf; *Style*— Dr Bill Alexander, CBE, FREng; ✉ Beyond Analysis Ltd, 116 Putney Bridge Road, London SW15 2NQ

ALEXANDER OF TUNIS, Countess; Hon Davina Mary; LVO (1991); *née* Woodhouse; da of 4 Baron Terrington (d 1998); *b* 12 April 1955; *Educ* Hatherop Castle; *m* 1981, as his 2 w, 2 Earl Alexander of Tunis, *qv*; 2 da (Lady Rose Houssemayne Du Boulay b 1982, Lady Lucy (Viscountess Somerton) b 1984); *Career* lady in waiting to HRH the late Princess Margaret, Countess of Snowdon 1975–79; extra lady in waiting 1979–2002; party co-ordinator Alexander Events 1998–2014; conslt Debrett's Ltd; pres: SOS (stars orgn supporting action for people with cerebral palsy) 1992–95, Society of Stars (celebrity support for children and adults with cerebral palsy) 1996–99; memb Governing Cncl Friends of The Elderly 1986–2002; *Recreations* tennis, skiing, cooking; *Style—* The Rt Hon the Countess Alexander of Tunis, LVO; ✉ 28 Clonmel Road, London SW6 5BJ

ALEXANDER OF TUNIS, 2 Earl (UK 1952); Shane William Desmond Alexander; also Viscount Alexander of Tunis (UK 1946) and Baron Rideau (UK 1952); s of Field Marshal 1 Earl Alexander of Tunis, KG, GCB, OM, GCMG, CSI, DSO, MC, PC (3 s of 4 Earl of Caledon), and Lady Margaret Bingham, GBE, JP (d 1977), da of 5 Earl of Lucan (gs of the Crimean War commander); *b* 30 June 1935; *Educ* Harrow, Ashbury Coll Ottawa; *m* 1, 1971 (m dis 1976), Hilary, da of John van Geest, of Lincs; m 2, 1981, Hon Davina Woodhouse, LVO (Countess Alexander of Tunis), *qv* former Lady-in-Waiting to HRH The Princess Margaret, da of 4 Baron Terrington (d 1998); 2 da (Lady Rose Margaret b 23 April 1982, Lady Lucy Caroline b 20 Sept 1984); *Heir* bro, Hon Brian Alexander, CMG; *Career* Lt Irish Gds (res); Lord in Waiting to HM The Queen 1974; patron Br-Tunisian Soc 1975–99, dir: International Hospitals Group 1981–2013, Kyrgoil Corp (Canada) 1995–2013, Marketform Ltd 1996–2009; pres Br-American Canadian Assocs 1988–94, chm and tstee Canada Meml Fndn 1990–; Liveryman Worshipful Co of Mercers 1965; Order of Republic of Tunisia 1996; *Recreations* tennis, skiing, music; *Clubs* MCC, Stoke Park; *Style—* The Rt Hon Earl Alexander of Tunis; ✉ 28 Clonmel Road, London SW6 5BJ (e-mail swdalexander@btinternet.com)

ALI, Monica; *b* 1967, Dhaka, Bangladesh; *Educ* Wadham Coll Oxford; *m* Simon Torrance; 1 s, 1 da; *Career* novelist; formerly employed in publishing, design and branding; named in Granta Best of Young British Novelists list 2003; *Books* Brick Lane (2003, shortlisted Man Booker Prize for Fiction 2003, shortlisted Guardian First Book Award 2003, Debut Novel Award W H Smith People's Choice Awards 2004, Newcomer of the Year British Book Awards 2004), Alentejo Blue (2006); *Style—* Ms Monica Ali

ALIBHAI-BROWN, Yasmin; da of Kassam Damji (d 1970), and Jena Damji; *b* 10 December 1949; *Educ* Univ of Oxford (MPhil); *m* 1, 1972 (m dis 1990), Shiraz Alibhai; 1 s (Ari b 30 Jan 1978); m 2, 1990, Colin Brown; 1 da (Leila b 11 April 1993); *Career* journalist and broadcaster; contrib various newspapers incl: The Guardian, New Statesman, The Independent (columnist); research fell IPPR 1996–, sr fell Foreign Policy Centre; memb Home Office Race Forum, advsr on race matters; hon visiting prof in journalism Univ of Cardiff 2007–, visiting prof of journalism Univ of Lincoln 2008–, visiting prof Univ of the West of England 2008–, prof Middlesex Univ; pres Inst of Family Therapy, vice-pres UN Assoc (UK), special ambass Samaritans; govr RSC, one woman show (RSC, UK and int tour); George Orwell Prize for Politicial Journalism 2002, EMMA Award for Journalism 2004; hon degree Open Univ 1999, hon fell Liverpool John Moores Univ 2003, hon dr York St John Univ 2008; *Books* No Place Like Home, True Colours (1999), Who Do We Think We Are? (2000), After Multiculturalism (2000), Mixed Feelings (2001), Some of my Best Friends are... (2004), The Settler's Cookbook (2009), Exotic England; *Recreations* theatre, cookery; *Style—* Ms Yasmin Alibhai-Brown; ✉ c/o People Matter, 40 Bowling Green Lane, Clerkenwell, London EC1R 0NE

ALIDAD, (né Alidad Mahloudji); s of Khalil Mahloudji, of London, and Farzaneh Mahloudji; *b* 18 July 1954; *Educ* Tehran, Switzerland, Mill Hill Sch London, UCL (BSc); *Career* interior designer; dir Islamic Dept Sotheby's London 1977–84, estab Alidad Ltd 1985 and Studio Alidad 2013; cmmns for restoration of Nat Tst houses (incl saloon and music room at Buscot House Oxon) and many private residences in the UK and abroad; launched furniture collection 2004, launched fabric collection (for Pierre Frey) 2005 and the Bosphorus Collection (for Chelsea Textiles) 2008, lauched Medici collection for Chelsea Textiles 2011; exhibited Br Interior Design Exhbn 1988, 1989 and 1997 (Best Interior Designer The World of Interiors, House and Garden and Elle Decoration magazines 1997); articles and photographs published in numerous interior design magazines and books; memb: Br Inst of Interior Designers (formerly Br Interior Design Assoc) 1992–, Int Interior Design Assoc (IIDA) 1999–; Best Product of the Year Award World of Interiors 2004; memb charity ctees incl Chicken Shed Theatre Co; *Publications* Alidad: The Timeless Home (2013); *Clubs* Chelsea Arts; *Style—* Alidad; ✉ Alidad Ltd, Units 314–316 Harbour Yard, Chelsea Harbour, London SW10 0XD (☎ 020 7384 0121, e-mail info@alidad.com, website www.alidad.com and www.studioalidad.com, Twitter @alidadltd, Instagram alidad_ltd)

ALINEK, Ruth Susan; da of Dennis Alinek (d 1994), and Evelyn, *née* Fineman (d 2009); *b* 27 February 1953, London; *Educ* Heriots Wood GS Stanmore, Univ of Warwick (BA, MA), Garnett Coll Roehampton (PGCE); *m* 27 Nov 2004, David Wilkins; *Career* teacher of English Oakham Sch 1975–77, second in English Dept Aldenham Sch 1978–82, head of drama Haberdashers' Aske's Sch for Girls Elstree 1982–85, head of sixth form and sr teacher Chelmsford Co HS for Girls 1986–92, dep head (curriculum) Westcliff HS for Girls 1992–95, headmistress Southend HS for Girls 1995–2003, headmistress Aylesbury HS 2003–05, educnl leadership advsr and HR conslt 2006–; *Style—* Ms Ruth Alinek; ✉ e-mail rsalinek@yahoo.co.uk

ALISON, Fiona; *née* Widdup; da of Harry Widdup (d 1976), of Weymouth, Dorset, and Nell Roberts (d 1968); *b* 7 March 1939; *Educ* Weymouth GS, Weymouth Coll, Univ of London (CertEd); *m* 30 June 1962, Peter Alison (d 1995), s of Youssof Alison; 1 s (Julian Piers b 16 June 1969), 1 da (Elizabeth Charlotte b 10 Jan 1973); *Career* int child photographer 1980–; works incl: children's portraiture 1980–84, children's fashion and advertising photography GB 1984–87, photographic assignments and lectures worldwide 1988–; exhibition of work at Glaziers' Hall London 1983, numerous appearances on radio and TV, first woman judge BP Chemicals World Photographic Competition 1990, tutor Fuji Film UK Sch of Photography Cyprus and GB 1991, judge 1997 Fuji Awards, judge Southampton Int 90th Exhibition 2003, selector Royal Photographic Soc Int Exhibition 2005, photographic lecture tour China 2008–09, judge, lectr and TV prog in Gibraltar 2013, one month photographic lecture tour Sydney Australia and S Island NZ 2016; int speaker Nikon-PSS Master Photographer Seminar Singapore 2007; Afocier Agrupacio Foto-Cine Cardanyola-Ripollet Aqueducte 2004: 3 images retained for the Museum of Contemporary Photography; hon lifetime prof Nanjing (China) Inst of Visual Arts 2009, lifetime prof Quanzhou Huaguang Inst of Photography and Art 2009; RPS Int Print Exhbn Bronze Medal 2004; FBIPP 1988 (LBIPP 1981, ABIPP 1982), FRSA 1982, FRPS 1992 (Fellowship and Associateship Applied Distinctions Panel, 1993), FMPA 1995 (first woman pres 2006–07); *Awards* Kodak Nat Portrait Award winner (first woman to win) 1980, 3M Nat Portfolio Award winner (first woman to win) 1983, BIPP Peter Grugeon Award (first woman to win) 1988, Salon International de la Photographie Mayet Prix du Public Gold Award 2004, Silver Medal for Best Landscape Southampton Int Exhibition 2011; *Recreations* reading, theatre; *Clubs* London Portrait Gp; *Style—* Mrs Fiona Alison; ✉ Normandy Cottage, 14 Avon Park, Ashley, Ringwood, Hampshire BH24 2AT (e-mail fiona@littlepics.freeserve.co.uk)

ALLAM, Roger William; s of Rev William Sydney Allam (d 1977), of London, and Kathleen, *née* Service (d 1995); *b* 26 October 1953; *Educ* Christ's Hosp, Univ of Manchester (BA); *Career* actor; fndr memb Monstrous Regiment Theatre Co; repertory work in Manchester, Birmingham and Glasgow; author of contribs on Mercutio and Duke Vincentio in Players of Shakespeare II and III; *Theatre* roles incl: Angelo in Measure for Measure, title role in Macbeth, Macheath in Threepenny Opera, Dr Rock in The Doctor and The Devils; RSC (joined RSC 1981 (assoc artist 1990)) roles incl: Richmore in Twin Rivals, Conrad in Our Friends in The North, Theseus and Oberon in A Midsummer Night's Dream, Mercutio in Romeo and Juliet, Victor in Today, Ford in The Party, The Officer in The Dream Play, Javert in Les Miserables, Adrian in The Archbishop's Ceiling, Clarence in Richard III, Pimm in Heresies, Brutus in Julius Caesar, Sir Toby Belch in Twelfth Night, Duke Vincentio in Measure for Measure, Benedick in Much Ado About Nothing, Trigorin in The Seagull, Dr Jekyll in The Strange Case of Dr Jekyll and Mr Hyde, Macbeth; RNT roles incl: Mirabell in The Way of the World, Ulysses in Troilus and Cressida (Clarence Derwent Award), Graves in Money (Olivier Award), Bassov in Summer Folk (Olivier nomination), Hitler in Albert Speer, Lophakin in The Cherry Orchard, Willy Brandt in Democracy (Olivier nomination); other roles incl: Oberon in The Fairy Queen (Aix-en-Provence Festival) 1989, Angelo in Una Pooka (London) 1992, Philip Madras in The Madras House (London) 1992, Stone in City of Angels (London) 1993 (Olivier nomination), Bernard Nightingale in Arcadia (London) 1994, John Worthing in The Importance of Being Earnest (Birmingham Rep and Old Vic) 1995, Serge in Art (London) 1997, Marc in Art (London) 1998, Captain Terri in Privates on Parade (London) 2001 (Olivier Award for Best Actor 2002), What the Night is For (London) 2002, Abanazar in Aladdin (Old Vic) 2004 and 2005, Ray in Blackbird (Edinburgh) 2005 and (London) 2006, Lambert le Roux in Pravda (Chichester) 2006, Bernard in Boeing Boeing (London) 2007, Leonardo in The Giant, Max Reinhardt in Afterlife, Michel in The God of Carnage (Bath and tour) 2009, Albin in La Cages Aux Folles 2009, Falstaff in Henry IV (Globe Theatre) 2010 (Best Actor Laurence Olivier Award 2011), Vanya in Uncle Vanya (Chichester) 2012, Propsero in The Tempest (Globe Theatre) 2013, Leonard in Seminar (Hampstead) 2014, John Christie in The Moderate Soprano (Hampstead) 2015; *Television* incl: Who Bombed Birmingham?, Summerchild in A Landing on the Sun, Between the Lines, Morse, Charlie in The Creatives, Peter Mannion in The Thick of It, Mac in Ashes to Ashes, Inspector Thursday in Endeavour series 1, 2 and 3, General Campion in Parade's End, Game of Thrones, Major General Stone in The Missing; *Radio* incl: Jean Valjean in Les Miserables, Svengali in Trilby, Laughter in the Dark (Sony Award), Gilbert Harding, Henry Gosse in Father and Son, The Ring and the Book, Blithe Spirit, Cabin Pressure, How Does That Make You Feel?; *Film* incl: Stranded, The Roman Spring of Mrs Stone, A Cock and Bull Story, V for Vendetta, The Wind that Shakes the Barley, The Queen, Speed Racer, Tamara Drewe (Evening Standard Award), The Iron Lady, The Angels Share, A Royal Night Out, Mr Holmes, The Truth Commissioner, The Lady in the Van; *Recreations* playing and listening to music, cooking, drinking red wine; *Style—* Roger Allam, Esq; ✉ c/o Claire Maroussas, Independent Talent, 40 Whitfield St, London W1T 2RH (☎ 020 7636 6565)

ALLAN; *see also:* Havelock-Allan

ALLAN, HE Christopher; *b* 18 December 1975, Edinburgh; *Educ* George Watson's Coll Edinburgh, LSE (MSc), Pembroke Coll Cambridge (MA); *m* 17 July 2004, Alice Mary Edith, *née* Hackett; 2 da (Cara Rose b 2006, Sylvie Neve b 2008); *Career* diplomat; desk offr Environment Policy Dept FCO 2000–01, Japanese language trg 2002–03, first sec Tokyo 2004–06, ldr Nuclear and Missile Defence Team Security Policy Dept FCO 2006–09, dep head S Asia Gp FCO 2009, head S Asia Gp 2009–10, dep head of mission Addis Ababa 2011–14, Russian language trg 2015, ambass to Repub of Uzbekistan 2015–; *Recreations* music, travel, walking, football; *Style—* HE Christopher Allan

ALLAN, (Gordon) David; s of Joseph Allan (d 1981), of Banbury, Oxon, and Isobel Joyce, *née* Williams (d 1982); *b* 7 August 1940; *Educ* Bury GS; *m* 1972, Margaret Elizabeth, da of John Beresford Humphries; 2 s (Simon b 24 Oct 1978, Robin b 2 June 1981); *Career* country music disc jockey; gen factotum then asst stage mangr Manchester Library Theatre 1957–59, backstage jobs in various rep theatres incl Theatre Royal Windsor 1959–64, stage mgmnt in West End incl asst stage mangr for Barbra Streisand's Funny Girl 1964–67, disc jockey Radio 390 (pirate station) 1967–68, announcer/newsreader Anglia TV 1968–69; BBC TV and Radio: continuity announcer BBC2 1969–94, freelance country music broadcaster Radio 2 1969–, presenter/co-prodr TV coverage of annual Wembley Country Music Festival 1969–89; presenter: Sunday Early Show (Radio 2) 1988–92, internetcountryshow.com, Prime Time Radio 2004; continuity announcer The History Channel; currently doing voiceover work and columnist for Country Music People (monthly jl); hon citizen Nashville Tennessee 1978; memb Country Music Assoc of America 1970; *Awards* Disc Jockey of the Year Br Country Music Assoc 1977, 1978 and 1979, Most Popular Euro Country Music Disc Jockey (poll taken in 5 countries by Br Jl Country Music Roundup) 1990, Favourite Presenter UK Country Radio Awards 2001, Int Broadcaster Country Music Assoc 2002; *Recreations* photography, swimming, lying in the (preferably Spanish) sun; *Style—* David Allan, Esq; ✉ Twitter @davidallanvoice

ALLAN, Prof James Wilson; *b* 5 May 1945; *Educ* Marlborough, St Edmund Hall Oxford (MA, DPhil); *m* 1970, Jennifer Robin, *née* Hawksworth; 2 s, 2 da; *Career* Dept of Eastern Art Ashmolean Museum: asst keeper 1966–88, sr asst keeper 1988–91, keeper 1991–2005, prof of eastern art 1996–, dir Inter-Faith Exhbn Serv 2005–06; fell St Cross Coll 1990–2005 (emeritus fell 2005–); pres Br Inst of Persian Studies 2002–06; *Publications* Medieval Middle Eastern Pottery (1971), Persian Metal Technology 700–1300 AD (1978), Islamic Metalwork: Nuhad Es-Said Collection (1982), Nishapur: Metalwork of the Early Islamic Period (1982), Metalwork of the Islamic World: the Aron Collection (1986), A Short Account of Early Muslim Architecture (1989), Persian Steel: The Tanavoli Collection (with B Gilmour, 2000), Metalwork Treasures from the Islamic Courts (2002), The Art and Architecture of Twelver Shi'ism: Iraq, Iran and the Indian Sub-continent (2012); *Recreations* music, ornithology, walking, travel; *Style—* Prof James Allan

ALLAN, John; CBE (2005); *b* 20 August 1948; *Educ* Univ of Edinburgh (BSc); *Career* mktg trainee then brand mangr Lever Bros 1970–74, mktg appts Consumer Products Div Bristol-Myers 1974–77, various appts rising to mktg and buying dir Fine Fare 1977–85, main bd dir i/c business servs Europe and gp mktg dir BET plc 1985–94, chief exec Exel plc (formerly Ocean Group plc) 1994–2005, chief exec DHL Logisitics 2006–, gp chief fin offr and ceo global business servs Deutsche Post World Net 2007– (memb Mgmnt Bd 2006–); chm DSG Int plc 2009–; non-exec dir: Hamleys plc 1996–2001, Wolseley plc 1999–2004, PHS plc 2001–05, Nat Grid plc 2005–, Samsonite 2007–; pres Freight Tport Assoc 2003–05, chm Freight Forwarding Int 2006–; chm Tport Policy Ctee CBI 1998–2001; memb: Pres's Ctee CBI 2001–, Int Advsy Ctee Econ Devpt Bd Singapore 2002–07, Univ of Edinburgh Campaign Bd, Supervisory Bd Postbank 2008–, Supervisory Bd Lufthansa 2008–; *Style—* John Allan, Esq, CBE; ✉ Deutsche Post World Net Headquarters, Charles-de-Gaulle Street, 20 53113 Bonn, Germany (☎ 00 49 228 1820)

ALLAN, Lucy; MP; *Career* MP (Cons) Telford 2015–; *Style—* Ms Lucy Allan, MP; ✉ House of Commons, London SW1A 0AA

ALLAN, Richard Bellerby; *b* 2 August 1940; *Educ* Marlborough, Merton Coll Oxford (MA); *m* 17 Sept 1966, Diana Rosemary Cotton, QC, *qv*; 2 s (Jonathan Bellerby b 28 June 1972, Jeremy Richard b 7 Aug 1974), 1 da (Joanna Frances b 10 March 1977); *Career* KPMG (and predecessor firms): articled clerk 1962–65, qualified sr 1965–69, mangr 1969–77, ptnr 1977–96; tstee Toynbee Hall; Bodley fell Merton Coll Oxford; FRGS, FICAEW; *Recreations* cricket, golf, music, opera, walking; *Style—* Richard Allan, Esq; ✉ 8 Northampton Park, London N1 2PJ (☎ 020 7226 7440)

ALLAN, Stephen David; s of Gerry Allan, of London, and Sonja, *née* Geiringer; *b* 26 June 1963; *Educ* City of London Sch; *m* 21 March 1991, Hayley Sara, da of Jeffrey Frankel; *Career* mangr Fotofast 1981, trainee media exec Yershon Media 1981; The Media Business Group plc (floated 1995): media exec 1982, assoc dir 1986, bd dir holding co 1987, equity shareholder and md 1988– (merged with Mediacom 1998), first dir of new business 1989–93; Mediacom: joint md 1998–99, chief exec 1999–2004, vice-chm 2004–

08 (taken over by WPP 2005), worldwide chm and ceo 2008–; ceo Group M 2005–; MIPA 1988; *Recreations* golf, shooting, travel; *Clubs* Coombe Hill Golf; *Style—* Stephen Allan, Esq; ✉ 124 Theobald's Road, London WC1X 8RX (☎ 020 7158 5002, fax 020 7158 5003)

ALLAN, Timothy Neil (Tim); s of Dr Tom and Helen Allan, of Godalming; *b* 5 March 1970; *Educ* Royal GS Guildford, Godalming Coll, Sorbonne Paris, Pembroke Coll Cambridge (BA), INSEAD (MBA); *Partner* Ms Carey Scott; *Career* restaurant reviewer Paupers' Paris 1989, researcher for Rt Hon Tony Blair, MP 1992–94 (as oppn spokesman on home affrs), prodr A Week in Politics Channel Four TV 1994, press offr to Rt Hon Tony Blair, MP 1994–98 (as ldr of Oppn 1994–97 and Prime Minister 1997–98), dir of corp communications BSkyB 1998–2001; fndr Portland 2001–; *Recreations* golf, New York, wine tasting; *Clubs* Soho House, 67 Pall Mall, Oxford and Cambridge; *Style—* Tim Allan, Esq

ALLARDYCE, Sam; *b* 19 October 1954, Dudley; *Career* professional footballer and manager; clubs as player: Bolton Wanderers 1969–1980 (debut 1973, winners Second Division 1978), Sunderland 1980–81, Millwall 1981–83, Tampa Bay Rowdies (USA) 1983, Coventry City 1983–84, Huddersfield Town 1984–85, Bolton Wanderers 1985–86, Preston North End 1986–89; player-coach: West Bromwich Albion 1989–91, Preston North End 1992–93; mangr: Limerick (Ireland) 1993–94, Blackpool 1994–96, Notts County 1997–99 (winners Third Division 1998), Bolton Wanderers 1999–2007 (promoted to Premier League 2001), Newcastle United 2007–08, Blackburn Rovers 2008–10, West Ham United 2011–16, England 2016; *Style—* Mr Sam Allardyce; ✉ West Ham United FC, Boleyn Ground, Green Street, Upton Park, London E13 9AZ

ALLASON, Julian Edward; s of Lt-Col James Harry Allason, OBE, FRSA; *Educ* Downside, Univ of Sussex, Aix-en-Provence Univ, St John's Nottingham; *m* 1976 (m dis 1989), Jessica Marland, da of Richard Thomas Wingert, of Conn, USA; 2 s (James b 1980, Benjamin b 1984), 1 da (Chloe b 1982); m 2, 1999, Dr Sarah King; 2 s (Gabriel b 2000, Raphael b 2004); *Career* dir: Apricot Computers plc 1979–86, Sharp Technology Fund plc 1984–99; md The Blackthorn Gp 1989–; author; publisher Microcomputer Printout Magazine 1979–83; columnist: The Observer 1981–83, Daily Telegraph 1983–86; contrib ed Condé Nast magazines 1997–2002; contrib FT 1999–; JP Inner London 1973–78; memb Information Technol NEDC 1984–86; Knight SMOM 1985 (Cdr of Merit 1989); *Books* The Pet Companion (1981), English Legal Heritage (co-ed, 1979), Counselling and Happiness (1997), Ringside Seat (ed, 2006); *Recreations* photography, messing about in boats; *Clubs* White's, Jet; *Style—* Julian Allason, Esq; ✉ 7 High Holborn, London WC1V 6DR

ALLASON, Rupert William Simon; s of Lt-Col James Harry Allason, OBE, FRSA; *b* 8 November 1951, London; *Educ* Downside, Univ Hall Buckland, Univ of Lille, Univ of Grenoble; *m* 1, 1979 (m dis 1996), Nicole Jane, da of M L Van Moppes (d 1963), of Bermuda; 1 s (Thomas b 1980), 1 da (Alexandra b 1987); m 2, 2012, Nicola, da of David Loud, of Crouch End, London; *Career* author (pen name Nigel West); special constable 1975–82, BBC TV 1978–82, Euro ed Intelligence Quarterly 1985–; Parly candidate (Cons): Kettering 1979, Battersea 1983; MP (Cons) Torbay 1987–97; *Books* The Branch – A History of the Metropolitan Police Special Branch 1883–1983 (1983); as Nigel West: SPY! (with Richard Deacon, 1980), MI5 (1981), A Matter of Trust (1982), MI6 (1983), Unreliable Witness (1984), GARBO (with Juan Pujol, 1985), GCHQ (1986), Molehunt (1987), The Friends (1988), Games of Intelligence (1989), The Blue List (1989), Cuban Bluff (1990), Seven Spies (1991), Secret War (1992), The Faber Book of Espionage (ed, 1993), The Illegals (1993), The Faber Book of Treachery (1995), The Secret War for the Falklands (1997), Counterfeit Spies (1998), Crown Jewels (with Oleg Tsarev, 1998), Venona (1999), The Third Secret (2000), Mortal Crimes (2004), The Guy Liddell Diaries (2005), MASK (2005), The Historical Dictionary of British Intelligence (2005), At Her Majesty's Secret Service (2006), Historical Dictionary of Cold War Counter-Intelligence (2007), Historical Dictionary of International Intelligence (2006), Historical Dictionary of World War II Intelligence (2008), Historical Dictionary of Sexspionage (2009), TRIPLEX (with Oleg Tsarev, 2009), Historical Dictionary of Ian Fleming's James Bond (2009), Historical Dictionary of Naval Intelligence (2010), Historical Dictionary of Chinese Intelligence (2012), SNOW (with Madoc Roberts), Historical Dictionary of Signals Intelligence (2013), Historical Dictionary of World War I Intelligence (2014), MI5 in the Great War (2014), Double Cross in Cairo (2015); *Recreations* skiing, sailing; *Clubs* White's, Special Forces; *Style—* Rupert Allason, Esq; ✉ 36 Great Smith Street, London SW1P 3BU

ALLASON-JONES, Lindsay; OBE (2014); *Educ* BA, MLitt; *Career* chair Marc Fitch Fund; FSA, FSAScot, FMA, FRSA; *Style—* Ms Lindsay Allason-Jones, OBE; ✉ Centre for Interdisciplinary Artefact Studies, Newcastle University, Newcastle upon Tyne NE1 7RU

ALLCOCK, Anthony (Tony); MBE; s of Ernest Stacey Allcock (d 1999), and Joan Winifred Allcock (d 1986); *b* 11 June 1955; *Educ* Norwich City Coll; *Career* bowls player; world outdoor champion 1980, 1984 and 1988, world outdoor singles champion 1992 and 1996, world indoor singles champion 1986, 1987 and 2002, world indoor pairs champion (with David Bryant, CBE) 1986, 1987, 1989, 1990, 1991, 1992 and 1996, world pairs champion (with David A Holt) 2003; Eng Bowls Capt 1998–; chief exec: English Bowling Assoc 2003–08, Bowls England 2008–; patron Visually Impaired Bowls England (VIBE); hon fell Univ of Gloucestershire 2000; *Books* Improve your Bowls (1988), Step by Step Guide to Bowls (1988), End to End – a year in bowls (1989), Bowl to Win (1994); *Recreations* countryside, opera, horses, antiques, showing and breeding dogs; *Clubs* Cheltenham Bowling, Cotswold and Mid Glos; *Style—* Tony Allcock, Esq, MBE; ✉ Meadow View, Castlett Street, Guiting Power, Cheltenham, Gloucestershire GL54 5US

ALLDIS, Christopher John; s of John Henry Alldis (d 1981), and Isabel Marjorie, *née* Carter (d 1999); *b* 16 May 1947; *Educ* Birkenhead Sch, Emmanuel Coll Cambridge (MA, LLB); *m* 14 Sept 1985, Marcia Elizabeth, *née* Kidman; 2 da (Amy Elizabeth b 1987, Rebecca Isabel Amelia b 1989); *Career* called to the Bar Gray's Inn 1970; practising Northern Circuit, recorder of the Crown Court 1994–; *Recreations* gliding, light aviation, skiing, fishing; *Clubs* Naval and Military; *Style—* Christopher Alldis, Esq; ✉ Romsdal, 3 Prenton Lane, Birkenhead, Merseyside (☎ 0151 608 1828); Oriel Chambers, Water Street, Liverpool (☎ 0151 236 4321, fax 0151 236 3332, e-mail christopheralldis@compuserve.com)

ALLEN, Benedict; s of Colin Allen; *b* 1 March 1960, Macclesfield; *Educ* Bradfield Coll, UEA (BSc); *m* Lenka Flidrova; 2 da (Natalya Anna, Beatrice Klara), 1 s (Frederick St George); *Career* author and explorer; TV presenter and filmmaker, pioneer of the filming of arduous expeditions for TV; walked and canoed (with indigenous help) 600 miles across NE Amazonia 1983, made first contact with threatened Obini people (Irian Jaya), first outsider to undergo secret sacred Niowra male initiation ceremony Papua New Guinea 1984–85, investigated apemen stories Sumatra 1987, first contact with threatened Yaifo people Papua New Guinea, crossed Central Range of Papua New Guinea and (by small craft with two companions) Torres Strait from New Guinea to Aust to live with Aboriginals in Gibson Desert 1988–89, crossed (often alone on foot) Amazon Basin at widest point (5600 km), walked entire length (1000 miles) of Skeleton Coast/Namib Desert Namibia 1996 (first to be allowed to make this journey), 5.5 month trek by horse and camel through Mongolia (incl 6 week lone crossing of the Gobi Desert) 1997, obtained point-of-view of indigenous people accused of murder of Col Fawcett 1998, researched and filmed Last of the Medicine Men (first major TV documentary series on practises of shamans and medicine men) 2000, journeyed (with dogteams with assistance of Chukchi people) 1000 miles through Siberia 2001; patron: Save the Rhino, Environmental Justice Fndn; supporter: Survival Int, Orang Utan Fndn; FRAI 1985, FRGS 1985 (memb Cncl); *Television* Raiders of the Lost Lake 1995, Mombasa to the Mountains of the Moon 1996, The Skeleton Coast 1997, Edge of Blue Heaven 1998, The Bones of Colonel Fawcett 1998, Last of the Medicine Men 2000, Ice Dogs 2002, The Big Read: His Dark Materials 2003, Adventure for Boys: The Lost Worlds of Rider Haggard 2006, Travellers Century 2008, Unbreakable 2008, Travellers Century 2008; *Radio* Two Men and A Mule (with Hugh Thomson) 2015; *Publications* Mad White Giant (1985), Into the Crocodile Nest (1987), Hunting the Gugu (1989), The Proving Grounds (1991), Through Jaguar Eyes (1994), More Great Railway Journeys (jtly, 1996), The Skeleton Coast (1997), Edge of Blue Heaven (1998), Last of the Medicine Men (2000), The Faber Book of Exploration (2002), Into the Abyss (2006), Wilfred Thesiger in Africa (jtly, 2010); *Recreations* taking my children into the wild; *Style—* Benedict Allen, Esq; ✉ 28 Broadway Avenue, St Margaret's, Twickenham, Middlesex TW1 1RH (e-mail info@benedictallen.com, website www.benedictallen.com)

ALLEN, Dr Christopher Michael Colquhoun; s of Christopher Oswald Colquhoun Allen, of Kingsbridge, S Devon, and Barbara Louise, *née* Archer; *b* 1 December 1948, Valparai, India; *Educ* Eastbourne Coll, Christ's Coll Cambridge (MA, MD), Guy's Hosp Med Sch; *m* 28 July 1973, Susan Valerie, da of Alan Douglas Belcher (d 1971), of Sheffield; 2 da (Kate b 1978, Joanna b Dec 1979), 1 s (Samuel b 1982); *Career* sr house offr: renal medicine St Thomas' Hosp 1976–77, Nat Hosp for Nervous Diseases 1977; hon sr registrar Dept of Neurology Guy's Hosp 1979–82 (house offr Med Professorial Unit 1973–74, med registrar 1977–79), neurology registrar Middx Hosp 1982–84, sr registrar in neurology Charing Cross Hosp 1984–86, conslt neurologist Addenbrooke's Hosp Cambridge 1986–, dean Sch of Clinical Med Univ of Cambridge 1996–2003; fell Wolfson Coll Cambridge 1996–; FRCP; *Books* The Management of Acute Stroke (1988), contrib (with Dr C Luek) Diseases of the Nervous System in Davidson's Textbook of Medicine (1999); *Recreations* listening to Mozart, writing book reviews, windsurfing, sailing; *Style—* Dr Christopher Allen; ✉ 232 Hills Road, Cambridge CB2 8QE (☎ 01223 247694, fax 01223 414904, e-mail cmca100@cam.ac.uk); Department of Neurology, Addenbrooke's Hospital, Cambridge CB2 0QQ (☎ 01223 216301, fax 01223 336941)

ALLEN, Gary James; CBE (1991), DL (1993); s of late Alfred Allen, of Sutton Coldfield, W Midlands, and late Alice Jane Allen; *b* 30 September 1944; *Educ* King Edward VI GS Birmingham, Univ of Liverpool (BCom); *m* 10 Sept 1966, Judith Anne, da of William Nattrass (d 1961); 3 s (Andrew b 1969, Anthony b 1971, James b 1979); *Career* md IMI Range Ltd 1973–77; IMI plc: dir 1978–2005, asst md 1985–86, chief exec 1986–2000, chm 2001–05; chm Eley Ltd 1981–85; non-exec dir: NV Bekaert SA Belgium 1987–, Marley plc 1989–97 (dep chm 1993–97), Birmingham European Airways 1989–91, London Stock Exchange 1994–, The Nat Exhibition Centre Ltd 1989–, Temple Bar Investment Tst plc 2001–; memb Cncl: Birmingham Chamber of Industry and Commerce 1983–98 (pres 1991–92, memb Bd 1994–96), Univ of Birmingham 1985–90 (hon life memb Ct 1984–), CBI 1986–99 (W Midlands Regnl Cncl 1983–89); Midland Businessman of the Year 1989; pres W Midlands Region Lord's Taverners 1994– (chm 1987–93, memb Cncl 1995–2001, tstee 1995–2001); memb Bd Birmingham Royal Ballet 1993–2003, pres Midlands Club Cricket Conf 1995–96, tstee Industry in Educn 1998–, chm Birmingham Children's Hosp Appeal 1995–2000; High Sheriff W Midlands 2002–03; Freeman Worshipful Co of Gunmakers; Hon DSc Univ of Birmingham 2003; FCMA 1985, CIMgt 1986, FRSA 1988; Order of Leopold II (Belgium) 2002; *Recreations* sport, reading, gardening, cooking; *Clubs* Lord's Taverners, RAC; *Style—* Gary J Allen, Esq, CBE, DL

ALLEN, Graham William; MP; s of William Allen, and Edna, *née* Holt; *b* 11 January 1953; *Educ* Robert Shaw Primary, Forest Fields GS; *Career* warehouseman Nottingham 1971–72, Lab Pty res offr 1978–83, Local Govt offr GLC 1983–84, Trades Union nat co-ordinator Political Fund Ballots Campaign 1984–86, regnl res and educn offr GMBATU 1986–87, MP (Lab) Nottingham N 1987–; memb: Public Accounts Ctee 1988–90, Procedure Ctee, 1990 Fin Bill Ctee; chm PLP Treasy Ctee 1990–92; oppn frontbench spokesman on social security 1991–92, shadow min (democracy and the constitution) Home Office 1992–94, shadow min (media) Dept of Nat Heritage 1994–95, shadow min (buses, air and sea) Dept of Tport 1995–96, shadow min (health and safety) Dept of Environment 1996–97, a Lord Cmmr of HM Treasy (Govt whip) 1997–98, vice-chamberlain HM Household 1998–2001; *Publications* Reinventing Democracy (1995), The Last Prime Minister – Being Honest About the UK Presidency (2002), Early Intervention (with Rt Hon Iain Duncan Smith, MP, *qv*, 2008); *Recreations* painting, golf, cooking, cricket, walking, democratising the UK; *Clubs* Basford Hall Miners' Welfare, Strelley Social, Dunkirk Cricket, Beechdale Community Assoc, Lords and Commons Cricket; *Style—* Graham W Allen, Esq, MP; ✉ House of Commons, London SW1A 0AA

ALLEN, Heidi; MP; *née* Bancroft; *b* 18 January 1975, Keighley; *Career* MP (Cons) S Cambridgeshire 2015–; *Style—* Mrs Heidi Allen, MP; ✉ House of Commons, London SW1A 0AA

ALLEN, Isabel Clare; da of Very Rev John Edward Allen, and Eleanor Allen; *b* 30 May 1968; *Educ* Univ of Manchester (BA), Univ of Westminster (RIBA pt I), South Bank Univ (DipArch, RIBA pt II, RIBA dissertation prize); *Career* ed Architects Jl 1999–2007 (buildings ed 1996–99), design dir Happiness Architecture Beauty 2007–; memb Cncl AA; judge of various architectural awards incl RIBA Stirling Prize 2006; IBP Young Journalist of the Year 1997; *Publications* Structure as Design (2000); *Clubs* Architecture; *Style—* Ms Isabel Allen

ALLEN, Jeremy Roger; s of Guy Lancelot Allen (d 1990), and Joan Isobel Lingwood, *née* Wright (d 2005); *b* 5 July 1944, Bournemouth, Dorset; *Educ* Bedales, Coll of Law; *m* 24 Jan 1970, Margaret, *née* Gilbert; 2 s (Jonathan Guy b 5 March 1974, Nicholas William b 11 March 1982), 1 da (Charlotte Lucy b 16 March 1977); *Career* admitted slr 1970; articled Johnstone Sharp & Walker, with Raleigh Industries 1968–72, ptnr Hunt Dickins 1973–94 (asst slt 1972, managing ptnr 1987), co-fndr Poppleston Allen Licensing Slrs 1994; chm Inst of Licensing 2011–; memb: Magistrates' Court Rule Ctee 1982–2002, Cncl Law Soc 1986–92 (chm Criminal Law Ctee 1987–91), Lord Chllr's Efficiency Cmmn 1987–89, Advsy Ctee on Licensing Act DCMS; legal dir: Noctis, Br Beer and Pub Assoc; memb Law Soc; companion Br Inst of Innkeeping; *Recreations* reading, theatre, running, watching sport; *Clubs* Nottingham and Notts United Servs; *Style—* Jeremy Allen, Esq; ✉ 10 Pelham Crescent, The Park, Nottingham NG7 1AW (☎ 0115 947 3471); Poppleston Allen, 37 Stoney Street, The Lace Market, Nottingham NG1 1LS (☎ 0115 953 8500, fax 0115 953 8501, e-mail jeremy@popall.co.uk)

ALLEN, Keith Howell Charles; s of Edward Allen, and Mary Elizabeth, *née* John; *b* 2 September 1953; *Educ* Sir Anthony Browns Brentwood, Brune Park Comp Gosport; *Children* 1 da (Lily Rose b 2 May 1985), 1 s (Alfie b 11 Sept 1986); *Career* actor and writer; writer England World Cup Song (World in Motion) 1990 and Euro Cup Song (Englands Irie, with Black Grape) 1996, performed unofficial England World Cup Song (Vindaloo) 1998; *Theatre* acting credits incl: Street Trash (NT Studio), DC Barry Hooper in Murmuring Judges (RNT) 1993, Teddy in The Homecoming (RNT) 1997, The Room/Celebration (Almeida Theatre) 2000; as writer and performer: The Yob, The Bullshitters, Detectives on The Verge of a Nervous Breakdown, Whatever You Want, I Love Keith Allen; *Television* credits incl: Comic Strip Presents..., The Gatekeeper, Born to Run, Martin Chuzzlewit, Sharman, Dangerfield, A Very British Coup, The Life and Crimes of William Palmer, You Are Here, Roger Roger, Jack of Hearts, Bob Martin, Inspector Morse, Murder in Mind, The Runaway; *Films* incl: Shallow Grave, Trainspotting, Second Best, Loch Ness, Blue Juice, Scandal, Chicago Joe and the Showgirl, Kafka, Beyond

Bedlam, Preaching to the Perverted, Mauvaise passe, Rancid Aluminium, My Wife is an Actress, Bear's Kiss; *Clubs* The Colony Room, Groucho; *Style*— Keith Allen, Esq; ✉ c/o Harriet Robinson, Independent Talent Group, 40 Whitfield Street, London W1T 2RH

ALLEN, Kenton Paul Benbow; *b* 16 June 1965, Warks; *Educ* Grange Comp Stourbridge, King Edward VI Stourbridge; *m* Sept 1999, Imogen Edwards-Jones; 1 da (Allegra Carmen Elizabeth *b* May 2005), 1 s (Rafe Elliot Benbow *b* Sept 2009); *Career* prodr Granada TV 1995–2000, creative dir Shine Entertainment 2000–03, creative head of comedy BBC TV 2003–; ceo Big Talk Prodns 2008–; columnist Broadcast magazine 2005–; Best Comedy (The Royle Family) BAFTA Awards 2000, Best Live Action Short (Six Shooter) Oscars 2006; memb: BAFTA, RTS; *Recreations* sailing, fishing, hunting, sleeping; *Clubs* Soho House, Groucho, Ivy; *Style*— Kenton Allen, Esq; ✉ Big Talk Productions, 26 Nassau Street, London W1 (✆ 020 7255 1131, e-mail kenton.allen@mac.com, website www.bigtalkproductions.com, Twitter @kentonallen)

ALLEN, Leonard; s of Joseph Allen (d 1956), of Bournemouth, and Henrietta Emily, *née* Fowle; *b* 30 November 1930; *m* 1, 1955 (m dis 1969), Diana, *née* Love; m 2, 27 April 1970, Theodora Jane, da of John Russell (d 1984), of Caversham, Reading; 1 da (Henrietta Sophie *b* 1972); *Career* public affairs advsr; Nat Serv RTR 1949–50; Cons Central Office: agent Reading 1959–64, political educn offr Eastern Area 1964–67 (dep area agent 1967–74), dep dir and head Local Govt Dept 1974–77; chief exec Fedn of Recruitment and Employment Servs 1977–93, dep chm Machinery Users' Assoc 1995–98, dep chm MUA Management Services Ltd 1995–98; sec gen Int Confedn of Temp Work Businesses 1990–93 (currently advsr); conslt T L Dallas (City) Ltd 1995–, corp affrs dir Stirling Recruitment Group Ltd 1996–; policy advsr CBI 1998–; vice-chm Southern Region UNs Assoc 1955–57, chm Recruitment Soc 1982–84, memb Governing Body SPCK 1977–80, vice-chm Bow Gp 1959–64, memb DOE Advsy Ctee on Women's Employment 1980–92; govr Battle Abbey Sch 1983–88, churchwarden St Edmund's Anglo-Catholic Church Downham Market, lay chm Fincham & Feltwell Deanery Synod (Ely Diocese) 2010–; Freeman: City of London 1978, Worshipful Co of Woolmen; memb NUJ, MIPR, FRSA; *Recreations* conversation, music, reading, art galleries, dining out and in; *Clubs* West Norfolk Hunt Supporters', Athenaeum (before quiescent retirement), Carlton, City Livery, Arts Mortons; *Style*— Leonard Allen, Esq; ✉ 1 Cottage Farm Mews, The Street, Marham, King's Lynn, Norfolk PE33 9JQ (✆ 01760 338201, mobile 07913 332314, e-mail leoadvise@supanet.com)

ALLEN, Lisa; da of Ken Allen, and Cynthia, *née* Crane; *b* 29 April 1981, Lancaster; *Educ* Carnforth HS, Lancaster and Morecambe Coll; *Career* commis chef: Whitewalls Restaurant Lancaster 1997–99, Camp America NY 1999, Hest Bank Hotel Lancaster 1999–2000, Holbeck Ghyll Cumbria 2000, Le Champignon Sauvage Cheltenham 2000–01; Northcote Manor Lancs: demi chef de partie 2001–02, chef de partie 2002–03, jr sous chef 2003–04, sous chef 2004–05, head chef 2005–; Michelin Star, finalist Roux Scholarship 2006, Young Chef regnl finalist 2006, Acorn Award 2007; *Recreations* travelling, decorating, eating out; *Style*— Miss Lisa Allen; ✉ Northcote Manor, Northcote Road, Langho, Lancashire BB6 8BE (✆ 01254 240555, fax 01254 246568, e-mail lallen@northcotemanor.com)

ALLEN, Peter; *b* 4 February 1946; *Career* journalist with various newspapers in England and Australia 1965–73, political corr then political ed LBC/IRN 1973–83, political ed Granada TV 1983–86, chief political corr ITN 1986–93, political ed and prog presenter LWT 1993–94; presenter: 5 Live Breakfast BBC Radio 5 Live 1994–98, Drive Time BBC Radio 5 Live 1998–; Best News Presentation Sony Awards 1996, Best Breakfast Prog Sony Awards 1998, Best Radio Prog TRIC 1998, Sony News Broadcaster of the Year 2002, London Press Club Broadcaster of the Year 2010; *Recreations* golf, waiting for Spurs to be great again, bird-watching; *Style*— Peter Allen, Esq; ✉ BBC Radio 5 Live, BBC Broadcasting House, Portland Place, W1A 1AA

ALLEN, Peter William; s of Alfred William Allen (d 1987), of Sittingbourne, Kent, and Myra Nora, *née* Rogers (d 1982); *b* 22 July 1938; *Educ* Borden GS, Sidney Sussex Coll Cambridge (MA); *m* 1965, Patricia Mary, da of Joseph Frederick Dunk, of Sheffield; 3 da (Samantha, Joanna, Annabel); *Career* RAF 1957–59; Coopers & Lybrand: joined 1963, qualified CA 1966, ptnr 1973, chm Int Personnel Ctee 1975–78, ptnr i/c London Office 1983, managing ptnr 1984–90, memb UK Mgmnt Ctee 1984–90, memb Int Exec Ctee 1988–90 and 1992–94, dep chm Coopers & Lybrand 1990–94 (memb Bd 1990–94), chm Mgmnt Consulting Servs UK 1990–94; non-exec dir: Charter plc 1994–2001, Schroder Ventures Group 1994–, The Post Office 1995–98; memb Governing Bd Lister Inst of Preventive Med 1998–2005; memb Bd BRCS 1999–2000; Freeman City of London 1988, Liveryman Worshipful Co of Glaziers and Painters of Glass 1989–2003; FCA 1969, CIMgt 1993–2003; *Recreations* golf, painting; *Clubs* Reform; *Style*— Peter W Allen, Esq; ✉ Fordham House, Abbots Brook, Bourne End, Buckinghamshire SL8 5QS (✆ 01628 521923)

ALLEN, Prof Raymond William Kenneth (Ray); s of Raymond Kenneth Allen, of Bishopstoke, Hants, and Dee, *née* Powell; *b* 14 February 1948; *Educ* Portsmouth GS, UMIST (MSc), McGill Univ Montreal (PhD); *m* April 1978, Rosemarie; 3 da (Aemelia Catherine Payard *b* 1979, Hermione Sarah Payard *b* 1990, Beatrice Eleanor Payard *b* 1994), 1 s (Sebastian Alexander Payard *b* 1983); *Career* Harwell Res Laboratory: industry res fell 1975–95, head Environmental and Process Engrg Dept 1988–93, head Tech Area for Chemical and Process Engrg 1990–95, business devpt dir 1993–95; prof of chemical engrg Univ of Sheffield 1995– (head Dept of Chemical and Process Engrg 1995–2000), seconded DTI Innovation Unit 1995–98; visiting prof Dept of Chemical Engrg Univ of Newcastle upon Tyne 1989–93; tech ed Filtration and Separation Jl 1983–88; author of numerous technical pubns on chemical engrg; memb: Editorial Bd Jl of Separation Technol 1979–89, Chemicals Sector Foresight Panel 1996–99; memb Cncl Filtration Soc 1985–86 (chm 1985–86), chm Standing Conf of Chemical Engrg Profs 2000–06, pres Engrg Profs Cncl 2006–10; FIChemE 1986 (memb Cncl 1990–92 and 2000–02), FREng 1993; *Recreations* practical politics, fireworks, almost any activity with my family; *Style*— Prof Ray Allen, FREng; ✉ Department of Chemical and Biological Engineering, University of Sheffield, Mappin Street, Sheffield S1 3JD (✆ 0114 222 7600, fax 0114 276 2154, e-mail r.w.k.allen@sheffield.ac.uk)

ALLEN, Richard; s of Anthony Peter Allen (d 1997), and Janet Allen; *b* 18 May 1975, Solihull, W Midlands; *Educ* Bournemouth and Poole Coll of FE; *m* 12 May 2012, Leanne Perkins; 2 s (Lennon, Jackson); *Career* Dukes Hotel Bath 2004–07 (3 AA Rosettes), exec head chef Tassili Grand Jersey 2007– (3 AA Rosettes 2007–, 5 AA stars 2009–, Michelin star 2012–), currently Rockliffe Hall (5 Red Star); Catey's finalist 2010–11, Craft Guild of Chefs Restaurant Chef of the Year 2012, Catey's Chef of the Year 2012; *Recreations* Thai boxing, cycling; *Clubs* Darlington Martial Arts Acad; *Style*— Richard Allen, Esq; ✉ Rockliffe Hall, Hurworth-on-Tees, Darlington, County Durham DL2 2DU (e-mail richard.allen@rockliffehall.com, Twitter @orangerychef)

ALLEN, Prof Robert; *Educ* Carleton Coll MN (BA), Harvard Univ (MA, PhD); *Career* prof of economic history Univ of Oxford, professorial fell Nuffield Coll Oxford; FBA 2005; *Style*— Prof Robert Allen; ✉ Department of Economics, University of Oxford, Manor Road Building, Manor Road, Oxford OX1 3UQ

ALLEN, Robert Geoffrey Bruère (Robin); QC (1995); s of Rev Canon Ronald Edward Taylor Allen (d 1984), of Ludlow, Salop, and Isabel Edith Allen (d 1994); *b* 13 February 1951; *Educ* Rugby, UC Oxford (MA); *m* 3 Sept 1977, (Elizabeth) Gay, da of Dr Anthony James Moon, of Rickmansworth, Herts; 2 s; *Career* co-organiser Free Representation Unit 1973; called to the Bar Middle Temple 1974 (bencher 2004); in practice 1976–, employment

law advsr to Legal Action Gp 1978–80, legal advsr to Local Govt Gp Inst of PR 1988–90, asst recorder 1997–2000, recorder 2000–, head Cloisters Barristers' Chambers 2002–; expert advsr to EC on UK law affecting the most disadvantaged 1993; sec Lambeth Central Constituency Lab Party 1977; chm: London Youth Advsy Centre 1984–90, Bd of Govrs Eleanor Palmer Sch 1988–91, Brandon Centre 1991–93; Employment Law Bar Assoc: fndr ctee memb 1994–, vice-chm 1996, chm 1997–99; chm Bar Pro Bono Unit 2000–02 (vice-chm 1996–2000); memb Bar Cncl 1999–2001 and 2013–, chm Bar Conf 2002 (vice-chm 2001), chair Bar Equality and Diversity Ctee 2013–; memb Home Office Human Rights Task Force 1999–2001, special advsr to Disability Rights Cmmn 2002–07; conslt: Age Concern 2004–09, Age Europe 2004–10, Age UK 2012–15; dir London Emergencies Tst 2016–; tstee London Bombing Relief Charitable Fund 2005–08, patron Andrea Adams Tst 2008–09; FT Innovative Lawyer 2008, Chambers and Ptnrs Employment Law Silk 2008 and 2012, runner-up Lawyer Magazine Barrister of the Year 2010; *Television* The Great Ape Trial (Channel 4) 1995; *Books* How to Prepare a Case for an Industrial Tribunal (1987), Employment Law Manual (contrib, 1988), Civil Liberty (contrib, 1989), The Legal Framework and Social Consequences of Free Movement of Persons in the European Union (contrib, 1998), Women Work and Inequality, the Challenge of Equal Pay in a Deregulated Labour Market (contrib, 1999), Study Guide to Human Rights Act (ed, 2000), Bullen and Leake and Jacob's Precedents of Pleading (contrib, 2001), The Legal Regulation of the Employment Relationship (contrib, 2001), Human Rights and Employment Law (2002, 2 edn 2007), A proposal for a Council Directive implementing the principle of equal treatment in respect of Age (2006), Equality Law in an Enlarged Europe (contrib, 2007), Blackstone Guide to the Equality Act (2010, 2 edn 2016), Family Rights at Work (2012); *Recreations* family life, fishing, fireworks, singing, growing chrysanthemums; *Clubs* Vincents (Oxford); *Style*— Robin Allen, Esq, QC; ✉ Cloisters, 1 Pump Court, Temple, London EC4Y 7AA (✆ 020 7827 4000, fax 020 7827 4100)

ALLEN, Simon John Nicholas; s of Adrian Allen, of Sheffield, and Sheila, *née* Moore; *b* 6 August 1959, Preston, Lancs; *Educ* Preston Catholic Coll, De La Salle Coll Sheffield, Leicester Poly (BA), Chester Law Sch; *m* 4 Aug 1987, Rosalind Ann, *née* Howe; 2 da (Gabrielle Julia *b* 22 Oct 1989, Susannah Fiona *b* 1 April 1998), 1 s (Sebastian Charles *b* 12 March 1992); *Career* slr; Brian Thompson & Partners 1985–89 (ptnr 1988–89); Russell Jones & Walker: slr 1989, ptnr 1990–2012, jt head Personal Injury Dept 2005–12; nat practice gp ldr Slater and Gordon Lawyers 2012–15 (conslt 2015–16, ret); currently photographer (see website in contact info); memb: Law Soc (Personal Injury Panel assessor 2002), Sheffield Law Soc, Assoc of Trial Lawyers of America 1985; fell Assoc of Personal Injury Lawyers (APIL) 1986; *Publications* APIL Guide to Damages (2005, 2008 and 2014), Kemp & Kemp: Personal Injury Law Practice and Procedure (2006, updated annually), APIL Personal Injury Law Practice and Precedents (2006, updated annually); writer Personal Injury Update section Law Soc Gazette, memb Bd Jl of Personal Injury Law (JPIL) 2014–15; *Recreations* family, photography www.simonallenphotoworks.com), golf (memb Sickleholme GC, studying Italian, Japanese Studies; *Clubs* Sickleholme Golf (Bamford, Derbys), Hallamshire Tennis (Sheffield); *Style*— Simon Allen, Esq; ✉ 234 Millhouses Lane, Ecclesall, Sheffield S11 9JA (✆ 07540 70254, e-mail sjnallen@btinternet.com, website www.simonallenphotoworks.com)

ALLEN, Brig Simon Richard Burton; s of William Richard Burton Allen (d 1990), and Anne Frederica, *née* Thwaites (d 1985); *b* 5 November 1952; *Educ* Rugby, RMA Sandhurst; *m* 3 Sept 1976, Ferlina Diana, da of late Sir William Lindsay; 2 da (Claire Diana *b* 16 Sept 1978, Camilla Anne 26 March 1982), 1 s (Richard William Burton *b* 28 Aug 1984); *Career* cmmnd Royal Scots Dragoon Gds 1972, student Staff Coll 1984; Cdr RAC Demonstration Sqdn Warminster 1987–88, instr Staff Coll 1990–93, Cdr Royal Scots Dragoon Gds 1993–95, COS HQ Dir Royal Armoured Corps 1995–99, memb RCDS 1999, Cdr 51 Highland Bde 1999–2002, COS Kosovo Force 2002, pres The Regular Cmmns Bd 2003–06; self-employed conslt 2006–, currently chief operating offr Inform and Inspire, project dir Reconstruction Ops Centre 2008–; chm: Army Point to Point, Army Alpine Skiing; *Recreations* National Hunt racing, point to point racing, fishing; *Clubs* Cavalry and Guards'; *Style*— Brig Simon Allen; ✉ Inform & Inspire, Holly End, Bramshott Chase, Hampshire GU26 6DE (website www.informandinspire.org)

ALLEN, Steve James; s of James Arthur Allen (d 1998), of Manchester, and Doris, *née* Waters (d 1998); *b* 29 January 1953; *Educ* South Wythenshawe HS, Mid-Cheshire Coll of Art & Design; *Career* photographer; Wythenshawe Gen Hosp: trainee med photographer 1972–74, qualified med photographer 1974–76, head of dept med illustration 1976–83; company dir Photographic Images (Manchester) Ltd 1983–89, sr ptnr Steve Allen Photography 1989–; Qualified European Photographer (QEP); int judge and speaker at nat and int photographic events in UK, Ireland, Norway, Singapore, Indonesia, Cyprus, Malta, Tunisia and Belgium, contrib numerous articles in professional photographic magazines; FBIPP, FMPA, FBPPA (Master), fell Soc of Int Commercial and Industrial Photographers, fell Soc of Int Nature and Wildlife Photographers; *Recreations* photography, travel, reading; *Style*— Steve Allen, Esq; ✉ Steve Allen Photography, Lindon House, The Green, Slingsby, North Yorkshire YO62 4AA (✆ and fax 01653 628777, e-mail mail@steveallenphotography.com, website www.steveallenphotography.com)

ALLEN, Susan Jennifer (Susie); da of Henry Francis Metcalfe (d 1991), and Yolande, *née* Senior-Ellis (d 1999); *b* 12 May 1949; *Educ* Kingston Poly (BA), RCA (MA), Cite Int des Arts Paris (RCA travelling scholarship); *m* 1, 1969 (m dis 1985); m 2, 1990, Prof Paul Huxley, RA, *qv*; *Career* artist and curator; cmmnd to design sets and costumes IBIS Dance Co Theatre Royal Stratford East 1982; curator RCA Collection 1989–99 (Fine Art Devpt Office RCA 1994–99), dir Artwise Curators Ltd 1996–; pt/t and visiting lectr 1981–99: RCA, Wimbledon Sch of Art, Kingston Poly, Ruskin Sch of Drawing Univ of Oxford, Chelsea Coll of Art, Central/St Martin's Coll of Art, Edinburgh Coll of Art; contemporary art conslt: British Airways, NACF, CAS, Wedgwood, TI Group, Visa Int, Virgin Atlantic Airways, Absolut Vodka; recipient NACF Award for Outstanding Services to the Arts 1988–89; FRCA 1990, FRSA 2002; *Selected Exhibitions* New Contemporaries ICA 1978–79, Demarco Gallery Edinburgh 1979, Edinburgh City Art Gall 1980, Mulhouse Print Biennale France 1981, 35 printmakers RCA touring exhbn UK and France 1983–86, Raab Gallery 1987, Artist's Choice V&A 1987, RCA Anniversary exhbn Barbican Art Gall 1987, Homage to the Square Flaxman Gallery 1988, Galerie zur Alten Deutschen Schule Switzerland 1989, 1990, 1992, 1993 and 1995, Cabinet Paintings Gillian Jason Gallery London and touring 1991–92, Artistic Assocs Gillian Jason Gallery 1992, Gallery 7 Hong Kong 1995, Thinking Eye Gallery 7 Hong Kong 1996 (and curator); *Work in Public Collections* South London Art Gallery, Scottish Arts Cncl, British Cncl, Govt Art Collection, V&A; *Curator* British Art Britain in Vienna British Art Show for Contemporary Art Soc Vienna 1986, Exhbn Road Painters at the RCA 1988, 3 Ways British Cncl touring exhbn E Europe and Africa 1989–96, Absolut RCA 1995, An American Passion Contemporary Br Painting The Kasen/Summer Collection 1994–95, Absolut Secret 1995–98, Absolut Secret NY 1998, Decorative Forms Over the World – Edward Allington London and NY 1996–99; Artwise commissions incl: two wall drawings by Sol Le Witt, sculptures by Andy Goldsworthy, *qv*, David Nash and Janet Cardiff 1998–; Tribe Art cmmns by Julian Opie 2002 and Hussein Chalayan 2003; *Style*— Ms Susie Allen; ✉ 2 Dalling Road, Hammersmith, London W6 0JB (✆ 020 8563 9495, fax 020 8563 9578, e-mail mail@artwisecurators.com)

ALLEN, Sir Thomas Boaz; kt (1999), CBE (1989); s of Thomas Boaz Allen (d 1987), of Seaham, Co Durham, and Florence, *née* Hemmings (d 1990); *b* 10 September 1944; *Educ* Robert Richardson GS Ryhope, Royal Coll of Music (ARCM); *m* 1, 30 March 1968 (m dis 1986), Margaret, da of George Holley (d 1980), of Seaham, Co Durham; 1 s (Stephen Boaz b 31 Jan 1970); m 2, 12 March 1988, Jeannie Gordon Lascelles, da of Norman Gordon Farquharson, of Southbroom, Natal, SA; *Career* opera singer; princ baritone: WNO 1969–72, ROH Covent Garden 1972–77; celebrated 25 seasons at Covent Garden 1996; guest appearances: Metropolitan Opera NY (debut) 1981, Bayerische Staatsoper München 1985, Wiener Staatsoper, Paris Opera, La Scala Milan (opened 1987/88 season as Don Giovanni), ENO, San Francisco Opera, Chicago Lyric Opera, LA, Glyndebourne, Aldeburgh and Salzburg Festivals, BBC Proms, Last Night of the Proms Royal Albert Hall 2004; dir Albert Herring RCM 2002; patron Samling Fndn; Prince Consort prof RCM; chancellor Durham Univ 2011–; hon fell: Jesus Coll Oxford 2001, St Hilda's Coll Oxford; kammersänger Bayerische Staatsoper 2003; Hon MA Univ of Newcastle upon Tyne 1984, Hon DMus Univ of Durham 1988, Hon RAM 1988; FRCM 1988; *Books* Foreign Parts: A Singer's Journal; *Recreations* golf, drawing and painting, ornithology, fishing; *Clubs* Athenaeum; *Style*— Sir Thomas Allen, CBE; ✉ c/o Askonas Holt, Lincoln House, 300 High Holborn, London WC1V 7JH

ALLEN, Thomas Michael Chard; QC (2015); *Career* called to the Bar 1994; *Style*— Tom Allen, Esq, QC; ✉ 5 Paper Buildings, Temple, London EC4Y 7HB

ALLEN, Timothy James; s of John Edward Allen, of Uckfield, Kent, and Jean Dorothy Allen; *b* 26 May 1971; *Educ* Judd Sch Tonbridge, Univ of Leeds (BSc); *Career* photographer; environmental conslt Repub of Indonesia 1993–97, photographer Sunday Telegraph 1998–2000, photographer The Independent 2000–, chief photographer Independent on Sunday 2002–, photographer BBC Human Planet 2009–11; exhbns incl: Trade (Exposure) 1999, Karen, Burma's Forgotten Tribe (Exposure) 2000, Daily Press (Visa Pour L'Image International Photojournalism Festival) 2002; corporate campaigns incl Barclays Bank and Sky TV; memb NUJ, memb Br Press Photographers Assoc; *Awards* Internationaler Preis für Jungen Bildjournalismus 1999, Fuji Film Features Photographer of the Year 2001, finalist Br Press Awards Photographer of the Year 2002 and 2003, Fuji Film Arts Photographer of the Year 2002 and 2003, Lord Mayor's Award for Business and Industry Photographer of the Year 2003, BG Gp Magazine Photographer of the Year 2005, Nikon Celebrity Photgrapher of the Year 2005, commended The Guardian Weekend Photograph Prize 2006, First Prize Business Industry and Technol Press Photographers of the Year Awards 2007 (shortlisted: Photo Essay, News, Entertainment and News Features 2006, Portrait, Photo Essay and Sports Feature 2007, Photo Essay 2008), One Planet Many Lives Travel Photographer of the Year 2007; *Recreations* woodland owner, kite surfer; *Style*— Timothy Allen, Esq; ✉ Axiom Photographic Agency, The Saga Building, 326 Kensal Road, London W10 5BZ (☎ 020 8964 9970, fax 020 8964 8440, e-mail info@axiomphoto.co.uk and people@photojournal.co.uk, website http://timothyallen.blogs.bbcearth.com)

ALLEN, Prof William Richard (Twink); CBE (2002); *b* 29 August 1940; *Educ* Auckland GS, Univ of Auckland (Med Intermediate Cert), Univ of Sydney (BVSc), Univ of Cambridge (PhD, ScD); *Career* with large animal veterinary practice Kaitaia NZ 1965–66, principal veterinary research offr TBA Equine Fertility Unit Animal Research Station Cambridge 1972–89 (post-doctoral sci 1970–71), dir TBA Equine Fertility Unit Mertoun Paddocks Newmarket 1989–2007 (joined 1975), Jim Joel prof of equine reproduction Dept of Clinical Veterinary Med Univ of Cambridge 1995–2007 (assoc lectr 1990–95), professorial fell Robinson Coll Cambridge 1996; hon professorial fell Univ Coll of Wales Aberystwyth 1980–85, adjunct prof Faculty of Veterinary Microbiology Cornell Univ NY 1984–, special prof Depts of Physiology and Environmental Sci and Veterinary Medicine and Sci Univ of Nottingham 1994–; Hon DSc: Jagellonian Univ Krakow 1990, Univ of Gent 2007, Univ of Helsinki 2008; Hon FRAgS 1996, CBiol, FIBiol 1997, foreign memb Polish Acad of Sci 1999; *Clubs* East India; *Style*— Prof Twink Allen, CBE; ✉ The Paul Mellon Laboratory of Equine Reproduction, Brunswick, 18 Woodditton Road, Newmarket, Suffolk CB8 9BJ (☎ 01638 666930, e-mail pml@btinternet.com)

ALLEN OF KENSINGTON, Baron (Life Peer UK 2013), of Kensington in the Royal Borough of Kensington and Chelsea; Sir Charles Lamb Allen; kt (2012), CBE (2002); *b* 4 January 1957, Lanark, Scotland; *Career* accountant British Steel 1974–79, dep audit mangr TM Gp Galaghers plc 1979–82; Grand Metropolitan plc: dir GrandMet International Services Ltd 1982–85, gp md Compass Vending and Grand Metropolitan Innovations Ltd 1986–87, md GIS Middle East Ltd 1987–88; md Compass Group plc (following buyout from GrandMet) 1988–91; chm Leisure Div Granada Gp plc 1991–92, chief exec Granada TV 1992–96 (chm 1996–2000), chm Granada Leisure and Services to Business Div 1994–2000, chief exec LWT (following takeover by Granada) 1994–96 (chm 1996–), chief operating offr Granada Gp plc 1995–96, chief exec Granada Gp plc 1996–2000, chm Forte plc (following takeover by Granada) 1996–2000, chm GMTV 1996–2000 (dep chm 1994–96), chm Yorkshire Tyne Tees Television 1997–2000, dep chm Granada Compass plc 2000–01, exec chm Granada plc 2000–04, chief exec ITV plc 2004–07, chm EMI Music 2008–10; chm Global Radio Gp 2007–, non-exec dir Virgin Media 2008–13, dir Endemol 2008–14 (chair 2012), GET AS 2009–14, ptnr Xsequor Partners 2009–, chm 2 Sisters Food Gp 2011–, chair ISS AS 2013–; non-exec dir Tesco plc 1999–2010, memb Liberty Global European Advsy Cncl 2014; chief advsr Home Office 2006–08, sr advsr Goldman Sachs 2008–15, advsr Terra Firma 2010–11, advsy chm Moelis & Co 2015; Race for Opportunity 1997–2000; dir International Cncl; vice-pres RTS; dep chm Business in the Community 1997–2008; chm Br Hospitality Cncl 1998–2000, dir Br Hospitality Assoc 1998–2000, chm Manchester 2002 Commonwealth Games 2000–03, vice-chm London 2012 2003–05, dir LOCOG 2005–13, chm Join In Tst 2012–, memb Mgmnt Bd Lab Pty 2012–15, chair Br Red Cross 2013–14; memb Communications Ctee House of Lords 2016; HRH The Prince of Wales Ambassador Award 1999; Hon DBA Manchester Metropolitan Univ 1999, Hon DLitt Univ of Salford 2002, Hon DEcon Southampton Solent Univ 2006; fell Chartered Mgmnt Accountants (FCMA), FHCIMA, FRSA; *Recreations* visual and performing arts, international travel; *Clubs* Garrick; *Style*— The Lord Allen of Kensington, CBE

ALLEN-JONES, Charles Martin; s of Air Vice-Marshal John Ernest Allen-Jones, CBE (d 1999), of Dunmow, Essex, and Margaret Ena, *née* Rix (d 1974); *b* 7 August 1939; *Educ* Clifton; *m* 25 June 1966, Caroline, da of Keith Beale, OBE (d 1979), of Woodchurch, Kent; 1 s (Christof b 1968), 2 da (Nicola b 1970, Anna b 1972); *Career* articled to Clerk of the Justices Uxbridge Magistrates Ct 1958–60, articled to Vizard Oldham Crowder and Cash 1960–63; admitted slr 1963; Linklaters: joined 1964, ptnr 1968–2001, Hong Kong Office 1976–81, head Corporate Dept 1985–91, sr ptnr 1996–2001, co-chm Linklaters & Alliance 1998–2001; non-exec dir: Caledonia Investments plc 2001–15, Hongkong Land Holdings Ltd 2001–, Jardine Strategic Hldgs Ltd 2008–; memb: City Taxation Ctee 1973–75, Hong Kong Banking Advsy Ctee 1978–80, Financial Reporting Cncl 2001–07, Financial Reporting Review Panel 2005–11; memb: Barbican Advsy Cncl 1997–2005, Cncl RCA 2004–16 (vice-chm 2007–16), Ctee Hong Kong Assoc 2002–, Int Advsy Cncl SOAS 2007–10; tstee: Br Museum 2000–04, Asia House 2001–09 (chm 2005–06); hon FRCA 2016; *Recreations* gardening, tennis, travel, reading; *Clubs* Hong Kong, Brooks's; *Style*— Charles Allen-Jones, Esq

ALLENBY, 3 Viscount (UK 1919); Michael Jaffray Hynman Allenby; s of 2 Viscount Allenby (d 1984), s of Capt Frederick Allenby, CBE, JP, RN; n of 1 Viscount Allenby, GCB, GCMG, GCVO, and his 1 w (Gertrude) Mary Lethbridge, *née* Champneys (d 1988); *b* 20 April 1931; *Educ* Eton; *m* 29 July 1965, Sara Margaret, o da of Lt-Col Peter Milner Wiggin; 1 s (Hon Henry Jaffray Hynman b 29 July 1968); *Heir* s, Hon Henry Allenby; *Career* cmmnd 2 Lt 11 Hussars (PAO) 1951, served Malaya 1953–56, ADC to Govr Cyprus 1957–58, Bde Maj 51 Bde Hong Kong 1967–70, Lt-Col Royal Hussars, CO Royal Yeo 1974–77, GSO1 Instr Nigerian Staff Coll Kaduna 1977–79; chm Quickrest Ltd 1987–91, vice-pres The International League for the Protection of Horses 1999– (chm 1997–99); dep speaker and dep chm ctee House of Lords 1993–2009; *Clubs* Naval and Military; *Style*— The Viscount Allenby

ALLENDALE, 4 Viscount (UK 1911) Wentworth Peter Ismay Beaumont; s of 3 Viscount (d 2002); *b* 13 November 1948; *Educ* Harrow; *m* 1975, Theresa Mary Magdalene, da of Frank More O'Ferrall (d 1977); 1 s, 3 da; *Career* landowner; *Recreations* shooting, skiing, horseracing; *Clubs* Jockey, Northern Counties, White's; *Style*— The Rt Hon the Viscount Allendale; ✉ Bywell Castle, Stocksfield-on-Tyne, Northumberland NE43 7AB (☎ 01661 842450, office 01661 843296, fax 01661 842838, mobile 07703 367740); Flat 5G, Cliveden Place, London SW1W 8LA (☎ 020 7881 0820)

ALLERT, John Maxwell; s of Richard Hugh Allert, of Adelaide, Aust, and Barbara Milton, *née* Wilson; *b* 19 June 1969, Mt Gambier, Aust; *Educ* Pembroke Sch Adelaide, Univ of S Australia (BDes); *m* 13 March 1993, Rosslyn Jane, *née* Morgan; 2 da (Lily Mathilde b 18 Oct 1995, Rose Adelaide 27 July 1998), 1 s (Hugo William Morgan 31 Oct 2000); *Career* md Cato Design 1996, ceo Interbrand Australia 1998–2003, chief operating offr Interbrand UK Pte Ltd 2003–06, ceo Interbrand UK 2006–07, gp head of brand McLaren Gp 2007–; FRSA; *Recreations* wine, motor racing, art, family; *Clubs* Australian, South Australian Cricket Assoc, Australian Football League; *Style*— John Allert, Esq; ✉ McLaren Marketing Limited, McLaren Technology Centre, Chertsey Road, Woking, Surrey GU21 4YH (☎ 01483 267900, fax 01483 261902)

ALLFORD, Simon; s of David Allford, CBE (d 1997), and M B Allford, *née* Roebuck; *b* 27 July 1961; *Educ* Hampstead Comp, Univ of Sheffield (BA(Arch)), UCL (DipArch); *Career* architect; with Nicholas Grimshaw & Partners 1983–85, Building Design Partnership 1986–89, princ Allford Hall Monaghan Morris Architects 1989–; tutor: Bartlett School of Architecture 1988–, Univ of Nottingham 1992–94; involvement with projects incl numerous award-winning apartments, offices, masterplans, schs, univs and arts buildings around the world; columnist Architects' Jl 2004–; Architectural Assoc: memb Cncl 1996–, hon sec 2000–, hon treas 2003–, vice-pres 2005–; vice-pres of educn RIBA 2004–09; CABE Design Review Ctee 2004–09; awards incl: 23 RIBA Awards, 6 Civic Tst Awards, 8 Housing Design Awards, 3 times finalist Br PM Better Public Building, 3 American Inst Awards, Best Portfolio Nat House Builder Awards 2006, 4 Br Construction Industry Awards, 3 Building Better Healthcare Awards, Best Design for a Healthcare Project LIFT Award, Nat Homebuilder Design Award Best Portfolio 2006, BD Office Architects of the Year Award 2006, BD Richard Feilden Architect of the Year 2008, BD Affordable Housing of the Year Awards 2008, RIBA Stirling shortlist 2008 and 2009, Building Magazine Architectural Practice of the Year 2009, BD Healthcare Architect of the Year 2009, RIBA Stirling Prize 2015; RIBA 1988; *Recreations* travel, art, architecture and literature, following Sheffield Wednesday FC; *Clubs* The Bond, Architecture; *Style*— Simon Allford, Esq; ✉ Allford Hall Monaghan Morris, 5–23 Old Street, London EC1V 9HL (☎ 020 7251 5261, fax 020 7251 5123, website www.ahmm.co.uk)

ALLIANCE, Baron (Life Peer UK 2004), of Manchester in the County of Greater Manchester; Sir David Alliance; kt (1989), CBE (1984); *b* 15 June 1932, Iran; *Educ* Etehad Sch Kashan; *m* (m dis); 2 s, 1 da; *Career* Coats Viyella: chief exec 1975–90, chm 1989–99, acquired Thomas Houghton 1956, Spirella 1968, Vantona 1975, Carrington Viyella 1983 and Coats Paton and Nottingham Manufacturing 1985; chm: N Brown Gp plc 1968–2012 (non-exec dir 2012–), Tootal Group 1991–99; hon fell: UMIST 1988, Shenkar Israel 1990; Hon LLD: Victoria Univ of Manchester 1989, Univ of Liverpool 1996; Hon DSc Heriot-Watt Univ 1991, Hon DPhil Univ of Tel Aviv 2009; COMPTI 1984, CCMI (CBIM 1985), FRSA 1988, Hon FCGI 1991; *Recreations* art, Persian poetry and music, reading; *Style*— The Lord Alliance, CBE; ✉ House of Lords, London SW1A 0AA

ALLIES, Edgar Robin (Bob); OBE (2016); s of Edgar Martyn Allies, of Reading, Berks, and Lilian Maud, *née* Smith; *b* 5 September 1953, Singapore; *Educ* Reading Sch, Univ of Edinburgh (MA, DipArch); *m* 8 Nov 1991, Jill Anne, da of Cyril William Franklin; 1 s (Patrick), 1 da (Isabel); *Career* architect; co-fndr (with Graham Morrison, *qv*) Allies and Morrison 1984; architects to Royal Festival Hall 1994–98; projects incl: The Clove Bldg (RIBA Award 1991), Pierhead Liverpool, Sarum Hall Sch (RIBA Award 1996), Nunnery Square Sheffield (RIBA Award 1996), Rosalind Franklin Bldg Newnham Coll Cambridge (RIBA Award 1996), Br Embassy Dublin (RIBA Award 1997), Abbey Mills Pumping Station Stratford (RIBA Award 1997), Rutherford Info Servs Bldg Goldsmiths Coll London (RIBA Award 1998), Blackburn House London (RIBA Award 2000), Blackwell Cumbria (RIBA Award 2003), extension to Horniman Museum London (RIBA Award 2004), 85 Southwark St London (RIBA London Bldg of the Year Award 2004, nat winner Corporate Workplace Bldg British Cncl for Offices Awards 2004), One Piccadilly Gardens Manchester (RIBA Award 2004), BBC Media Village White City (RIBA Award 2005), court and theatre Fitzwilliam Coll Cambridge (RIBA Award 2005), library and archive Girton Coll Cambridge (RIBA Award 2006), Farnborough Business Park (RIBA Award 2007), Royal Festival Hall (RIBA Award 2008, RIBA Design for London Space Award finalist 2008, Stirling Prize finalist 2008), Royal Observatory Greenwich (RIBA Award 2008), Paradise Street Liverpool One (RIBA Award 2009), Charles Street Car Park Sheffield (RIBA Award 2009), One Vine Street, The Quadrant Regent Street (RIBA Award 2009), Bankside 123 (RIBA Award 2010), Highbury Square (RIBA Award 2010), Mint Hotel Leeds (RIBA Award 2011), masterplan London 2012 Stratford (RIBA Award 2013), RA Meml Museum Exeter (RIBA Award 2013), Simon Smith Building Brighton Coll (RIBA Award 2012), Brighton Coll Boarding House (RIBA Award 2014), Ash Court Cambridge (RIBA Award 2014), Rambert London (RIBA Award 2014), STAC London (RIBA Award 2015), Addenbrooke's Car Park Cambridge (RIBA Award 2015); exhibitions: New British Architecture (Japan) 1994, Retrospective (USA Schs of Architecture) 1996–98; lectr Univ of Cambridge 1984–88, George Simpson visiting prof Univ of Edinburgh 1995, visiting prof Univ of Bath 1996–99, Kea distinguished visiting prof Univ of Maryland 1999; chm Shape East Design Review Panel 2011–; memb: Faculty of Fine Arts Br Sch at Rome 1997–2002, Cncl AA 2004–07, Design Panel Cmmn for Architecture and the Built Environment 2005–, London Mayor's Design Advsy Gp 2012–; Edinburgh Architectural Assoc Medal for Architecture 1977, Rome Scholar in Architecture 1981–82, AJ120 Practice of the Year Award 2015; RIBA 1978, FRSA; *Publications* Model Futures (ICA, 1983), Allies and Morrison (Univ of Michigan Architectural Papers, 1996), Cultivating the City: London before and after 2012 (2009), Allies and Morrison 1 (2011), Fabric of Place (ed with Diane Haigh, 2014); *Recreations* contemporary music; *Style*— Bob Allies, Esq, OBE; ✉ 12 Well Road, London NW3 1LH (☎ 020 7443 9309); Allies and Morrison, 85 Southwark Street, London SE1 0HX (☎ 020 7921 0100, fax 020 7921 0101, e-mail boballies@alliesandmorrison.com)

ALLINGTON, Edward Thomas; s of Ralph Allington, of Troutbeck Bridge, Cumbria, and Evelyn Hewartson (d 1988); *b* 24 June 1951; *Educ* Lancaster Sch of Art, Central Sch of Art (DipAD), RCA (Herbert Read meml prize); *m* 1974 (sep 1981), Susan Jean Bradley (d 1984); partner, 1983, Julia Wood; 1 s (Harry Roland Allington Wood b 1991), 1 da (Thalia Evelyn Allington Wood b 1988); *Career* sculptor; *Solo Exhibitions* incl: 1B Kensington Church Walk London 1977, Spacex Gallery Exeter 1981, Exe Gallery Exeter 1982, Spectro Gallery Newcastle upon Tyne 1983, ICA London 1983–84, Lisson Gallery London 1984,

Midland Gp Arts Centre Nottingham 1984, Gallery Schmela Düsseldorf 1984, Riverside Studios London 1985, Lisson Gallery 1985, Northern Centre for Contemporary Art Sunderland 1985–86, Abbot Hall Art Gallery Kendal 1986, Diane Brown Gallery NY 1986, Galerie 565 Aalst Belgium 1986, Galerie Adrien Maeght Paris 1986, Galerie Montenay-Delsol Paris 1986, Marlene Eleini Gallery London 1987, Diane Brown Gallery NY 1987, Fuji TV Gallery Tokyo 1988, Gallery Face Tokyo 1988, Lisson Gallery 1990, Galerie Faust Geneva 1990, Vaughan and Vaughan Minneapolis, Kohji Ogura Gallery Nagoya; *Group Exhibitions* incl: Summer Show (Serpentine Gallery London) 1976, Objects and Sculpture (Arnolfini Gallery Bristol) 1981, London/NY 1982, Lisson Gallery 1982, Teme Celeste (Museo Civico D'Arte Contemporanea Gibellina Sicily) 1983, Beelden/sculpture 1983 (Rotterdam Arts Cncl) 1983, The Sculpture Show (Hayward and Serpentine Galleries London) 1983, Metaphor and/or Symbol (Nat MOMA Tokyo and Nat Museum of Osaka) 1984–85, Space Invaders (Mackenzie Art Gall Regina and tour Canada) 1985, Time after Time (Diane Brown Gallery NY) 1986, Britain in Vienna 1986, British Art (Künstlerhaus Vienna) 1986, 3eme Ateliers Internationaux FRAC Pays de la Loire 1986, Prospect 86 (Kunstverein Frankfurt) 1986, Vessel (Serpentine Gallery) 1987, Inside/Outside (Museum van Hedendaagse Kunst Antwerp) 1987, Die Grosse Oper (Bonner Kunstverein Bonn and tour) 1987–88, Britannia 30 Ans de Sculpture (Musée des Beaux Arts Brussels) 1988, British Now Sculpture et Autre Dessins (Musée D'Art Contemporain de Montreal) 1988–89, 2000 Jahre Die Gegenwart der Vergangenheit (Bonner Kunstverein Bonn) 1989; *Major works* His Favourite Was David Smith But She Preferred Dame Barbara Hepworth 1975, Ideal Standard Forms 1980, The Fruit of Oblivion 1982, We Are Time 1985, Building With Missing Columns 1986, Seated in Darkness 1987, Victory Boxed 1987, Light Temple PAS Heizcraftwerk Saarbrucken 1989, Inverted Architrave 1990, set for prodn of Apollon La Nuit 1990; *Awards* prizewinner John Moores 16 Liverpool Exhbn 1989, Gregory fell in Sculpture Univ of Leeds; *Style—* Edward Allington, Esq

ALLINSON, Richard John McNeill; s of late Deryck Edward Allinson, and late Edith Allinson; *b* Lichfield, Staffordshire; *Educ* Tudor Grange GS Solihull, Solihull Sixth Form Coll, Lancaster Univ (BA); *Career* broadcaster; Capital Radio 1980–97, BFBS Radio 1985–, BBC World Serv 1986–87, VH1 TV 1994–98, BBC Radio 2 1997–; judge: Olivier Theatre Awards 1988–89, Ivor Novello Awards, Sony Radio Awards; chm Commercial Radio Convention; dir Magnum Opus Broadcasting Ltd; Gold Award Sony Radio Awards 1993 (for National Music Day), Gold Award Sony Radio Awards 1997 (for Radio 2 Late Show); memb Radio Acad; music producers guild; chair: commercial radio convention; *Recreations* theatre, rediscovering my record collection, piano-playing, boating, cooking, tormenting the children..., music on vinyl, literature; *Style—* Richard Allinson; ✉ Nick Canham/Vivienne Clore, The Richard Stone Partnership (☎ 020749 70849)

ALLISON, (Samuel) Austin; s of Dr Samuel Allison, of Stedham, W Sussex (d 2003), and Helen Burns Brighton, *née* Wilson (d 2000); *b* 30 June 1947; *Educ* Liverpool Coll, Wadham Coll Oxford (BA, BCL); *m* 5 June 1971, June, da of late Henry Edward Brassington, of Crofton, Kent; 2 s (Giles b 1973, Jonathan b 1975); *Career* called to the Bar Middle Temple 1969 (bencher 2003); private practice at the Bar 1970–87, head of gp compliance Standard Chartered Bank 1987–95, dir West Merchant Bank 1996–98, dir compliance and legal affairs Westdeutsche Landesbank 1999–2000; head of compliance and legal affairs TT International 2000–11, ptnr TT International 2001– (gen counsel 2011–), dir TT International Funds plc; memb: Panel of Arbitrators City Disputes Panel, Gen Cncl of the Bar 1991–96; vice-pres Bar Assoc of Commerce Fin and Industry 1997–2012 and 2014– (chm 1995); accredited mediator Centre for Dispute Resolution, FCIArb, fell Indian Cncl of Arbitration, fell Indian Soc of Arbitrators; *Publications* Banking and the Financial Services Act (jtly, 1993), Banking and Financial Services Regulation (jtly, 3 edn 2003); *Recreations* the turf; *Style—* Austin Allison, Esq; ✉ 156 Kingston Lane, Teddington, Middlesex TW11 9HD; TT International, 62 Threadneedle Street, London EC2R 8HP (☎ 020 7509 1256, fax 020 7509 1281, e-mail allisona@ttint.com)

ALLISON, John; *Career* creative ptnr Fallon until 2012, head 4Creative Channel 4 2012–; *Style—* John Allison, Esq; ✉ 4Creative, Channel 4, 124 Horseferry Road, Westminster, London SW1P 2TX

ALLISON, Prof Robert John; s of Gordon Allison, and Elizabeth Anne, *née* Oman; *b* 4 February 1961; *Educ* Univ of Hull (BA), KCL (NERC funded research student, PhD); *Career* Addison Wheeler research fell Dept of Geography Univ of Durham 1986–89, lectr in engrg sedimentology UCL 1989–93; Univ of Durham: lectr in geography 1993–95, reader in geography 1995–99, prof of geography 1999–2006, chm Bd of Studies in Geography (head of dept) 2000–03, dean Faculty of Social Sciences and Health 2003–06; pro-vice-chllr and prof of geography Univ of Sussex 2006–12, vice-chllr and pres Loughborough Univ 2012–; tutor EPSRC Grad Schs Trg Prog 1996–, course/prog dir ESRC/NERC Grad Research Sch 1999; scientist: Oman Wahiba Sands Research Project RGS (with IBG) 1986, Kimberley Research Project RGS (with IBG) 1988; geomorphology prog dir Jordan Badia R&D Prog RGS (with IBG) 1992–2001, memb Jordan Steering Ctee Badia R&D Prog 1998–2001; gen sec Int Assoc of Geomorphologists 1993–97, hon sec RGS (with IBG) 1998–2001 (memb Cncl Exec Ctee 1999–2001), chair Exec Ctee Br Geomorphological Research Gp 2006–07 (memb 1989–92, jr vice-chair 2004–05, vice-chair 2005–06); convenor, keynote speaker and plenary lectr at int confs and symposia; hon canon Leicester Cathedral 2015–; govr Loughborough Endowed Schs, vice-pres Leicestershire Scouts, memb Bd Leicester and Leicestershire Enterprise Partnership, pres Charnwood Athletics; Jan De Ploey Prize Katholieke Universitat Leuven 1993, Charles Lyell Award BAAS 1995, Cuthbert Peek Award RGS (with IBG) 1997; *Publications* Landslides of the Dorset Coast (ed, 1990), The Coastal Landforms of West Dorset (ed, 1992), Landscape Sensitivity (jt ed, 1993), Applied Geomorphology: Theory and Practice (ed, 2002), Sediment Cascades: an integrated approach (jt ed, 2010); also author of articles in refereed jls and other pubns; *Style—* Prof Robert J Allison; ✉ Vice-Chancellor's Office, Loughborough University, Leicestershire LE11 3TU (☎ 01509 222001, e-mail r.j.allison@lboro.ac.uk, website www.lboro.ac.uk/admin/vc/who/vice-chancellor)

ALLISS, Peter; s of Percy Alliss (d 1975), of Sheffield, and Dorothy, *née* Rust (d 1973); *b* 28 February 1931; *Educ* Queen Elizabeth GS Wimborne, Crosby House Sch Winton; *m* 1, 1953 (m dis 1968), Joan; 1 s (Gary b 1954), 1 da (Carol b 1960); m 2, 1969, Jacqueline Anne, da of Col Geoffrey Bridgeman Grey, CB, CBE, TD, DL, of Birmingham; 2 da (Sara b 1972, Victoria b 1973 d 1982), 2 s (Simon b 1975, Henry b 1983); *Career* Nat Serv RAF Regt 1949–51; professional golfer 1946; played in 8 Ryder Cup matches and 10 Canada Cup (now World Cup) matches, winner of 21 maj events incl open championships of Spain, Portugal, Italy and Brazil; golf commentator/broadcaster and corr (for BBC and ABC) following retirement, also golf course designer; former pres: Br Greenkeepers' Assoc 1977–86, Ladies Professional Golfers' Assoc 1980–86; twice capt PGA 1962–87, pres Nat Assoc of Public Golf Courses; Hon Doc: Univ of Bournemouth, Univ of Humberside, Univ of St Andrews; *Books* Alliss in Wonderland (autobiography, 1964), Easier Golf (with Paul Trevillion, 1969), Bedside Golf (1980), Peter Alliss: An Autobiography (1981), Shell Book of Golf (1982), The Duke (1983), Play Golf with Peter Alliss (1983), The Who's Who of Golf (1983), The Open (with Michael Hobbs, 1984), Golfer's Logbook (1984), Lasting the Course (1984), More Bedside Golf (1984), Peter Alliss's Most Memorable Golf (1986), Yet More Bedside Golf (1986), Play Better Golf with Peter Alliss (1989), Peter Alliss's Best 100 Golfers (1989), The Best of Golf (with Bob Ferrier, 1989), A Golfer's Travels (1997), Peter Allis Golf Heroes (2002), My Life (autobiography, 2004), Golf, The Cure For A Grumpy Old Man (2009); *Recreations* conversation (with wine!); *Clubs* Lansdowne, Motcombs, Ritz, Crockfords; hon memb: R&A, Wentworth, Stoke Park, Royal Cinque Ports, Royal Porthcawl, Parkstone, Ferndown, Loch Lomond, Trevose, Moor Allerton, Peel Combe Hill, Muirfield Village Columbus OH, West Cornwall, Reigate Heath, Old Thorns, Royal Lytham and St Annes, Lahinch, Royal Dornech Golf, Canterbury Golf, Castlemartyr Golf (Co Cork Ireland); *Style—* Peter Alliss, Esq; ✉ Bucklands, Churt Road, Hindhead, Surrey GU26 6HY (☎ 01428 607253, e-mail jackie@alliss-promotions.co.uk)

ALLISTER, James Hugh (Jim); QC, MLA; s of Robert Allister (d 1998), and Mary Jane, *née* McCrory (d 1996); *b* 2 April 1953, Crossgar, Co Down; *Educ* Regent House GS, Queen's Univ Belfast (LLB); *m* 14 July 1978, Ruth Elizabeth, *née* McCullagh; 1 da (Karen Jane b 7 Sept 1982), 2 s (Graeme Alexander James b 23 Aug 1984, Philip Robert Andrew b 11 Nov 1986); *Career* called to the Bar: NI 1976, Inner Bar NI 2001; practising barr 1976–80, asst to Dr Ian Paisley MEP in the European Parl 1980–82, memb NI Assembly 1982–86 (also chief whip DUP Gp), practising barr specialising in criminal def work 1987–2004, MEP (DUP until 2007, subsequently Ind) NI 2004–09; memb Constitutional Affrs Ctee and Fisheries Ctee European Parl, substitute memb Traditional Unionist Agriculture Ctee; fndr and ldr TUV 2007–; MLA (TUV) N Antrim 2011–; author of various political pubns; *Style—* Jim Allister, Esq, QC, MLA; ✉ Northern Ireland Assembly, Parliament Buildings, Belfast BT4 3XX

ALLNER, Andrew James; s of Cedric George Allner (d 2002), and Jennifer Jane, *née* Swallow; *b* 16 December 1953, Northwich, Cheshire; *Educ* Bedford Sch, Exeter Coll Oxford (BA); *m* 25 April 1981, Susan Isabel, *née* McCann; 1 da (Elizabeth Kate b 14 March 1990), 1 s (James Stephen b 28 Oct 1995); *Career* Pricewaterhouse 1975–92 (ptnr 1987–92), Guinness plc 1992–96; gp finance dir: Nycomed Amersham 1996–98, Dalgety plc (latterly PIC Int Gp plc) 1998–2000; ceo Enodis plc 2000–03, gp finance dir RHM plc 2004–07; chm Fox Marble Hldgs plc 2011–; non-exec dir: Moss Bross plc 2001–05, Marshalls plc 2003– (chm 2010–), Northgate plc 2007–, CSR plc 2008–13, Go-Ahead Gp plc 2008– (chm 2013), AZ Electronic Materials SA 2010–14; FCA (ACA 1978); *Recreations* sailing, skiing, shooting; *Clubs* Royal Thames Yacht, Roehampton; *Style—* Andrew Allner, Esq

ALLSOP, Prof Richard Edward; OBE (1997); s of Edward James Allsop (d 2007), of Mackworth, Derbys, and Grace Ada, *née* Tacey (d 1984); *b* 2 May 1940, Derby; *Educ* Bemrose Sch Derby, Queens' Coll Cambridge (MA), UCL (PhD, DSc); *m* 23 June 1990, Frances Elizabeth, da of Henry James Killick (d 1978); *Career* sci offr Road Research Laboratory 1964–66, research fell UCL 1967–69, lectr in tport studies UCL 1970–72, dir Tport Ops Research Gp Univ of Newcastle upon Tyne 1973–76, prof of tport studies UCL 1976–2005, emeritus prof UCL 2005–; visitor to Traffic Gp Tport and Road Res Laboratory 1987–92, external research advsr Dept for Tport 1993–2015; dir Parly Advsy Cncl for Tport Safety 1995–2015, memb Bd European Tport Safety Cncl 2005–; memb: Road Traffic Law Review 1985–88, Road Safety Advsy Panel 2000–10, War on Want, Chiltern Soc, Northumberland and Newcastle Soc; visiting prof Univ of Karlsruhe 1977, visiting fell Univ of Osaka 1981, visiting Erskine fell Univ of Canterbury Christchurch 1997, visiting prof Univ of Natural Resources and Applied Life Sciences Vienna 2002, visiting prof Newcastle Univ 2006–, adjunct prof Queensland Univ of Technol 2006–10, visiting Choi Kin Chung fell Univ of Hong Kong 2012; hon prof: Technol Univ Cracow 2000, Moscow Automobile and Road Inst State Technol Univ 2001; Highways and Transportation Award 1997, Prince Michael Road Safety Award 2011, TRL Academy Award 2015; hon fell UCL (fell 2000); FCILT (FCIT 1981), FCIHT (FIHT 1983), CEng 1990–2015, FICE 1990, FREng 1996, fell Tport Research Fndn 1998, TPP 2009; *Publications* Transportation and Traffic Theory 2007 (jt ed, 2007); author of over 250 papers in learned jls and proceedings; *Recreations* photography, theatre, walking; *Style—* Prof Richard Allsop, OBE, FREng; ✉ Centre for Transport Studies, University College London, Gower Street, London WC1E 6BT (e-mail r.e.allsop@ucl.ac.uk)

ALLTHORPE-GUYTON, Dr Marjorie; da of Maurice Jack Allthorpe-Guyton, of Norwich, and Edith Florence, *née* Clark (d 1972); *b* 29 July 1948, Norwich; *Educ* Blyth GS Norwich, UEA (BA), Leverhulme scholarship, Courtauld Inst London; *m* 1, 12 Dec 1970 (m dis), Brian Collison; m 2, 27 Oct 1989 (m dis), John Mullis; 1 da (Elise Charlotte Allthorpe-Mullis b 30 Sept 1984), 1 s (Theodore Edmund Allthorpe-Mullis b 14 Feb 1991); m 3, 15 April 2000, Paul Dale; *Career* asst keeper Norwich Castle Museum 1969–79, researcher Norwich Sch of Art 1980–82, lectr Open Univ 1983, lectr London program Univ of Connecticut 1982–88, visiting lectr in theoretical studies Norwich Sch of Art 1985–88; co-selector Art Cncl British Art Show 1982–84; external assessor: BA and MA Fine Art Goldsmiths Coll London 1988–94, BA Fine Art Univ of Plymouth (formerly Poly SW) and Exeter Coll of Art 1989–93, Oxford Brookes Univ 1997–2000, City Univ London 2003–07, Univ of Oxford; examiner MA Painting Slade Sch of Art UCL 2010–14; memb Art and Design Research Assessment Exercise HEFCE 2008; UK contrib ed Flash Art 1987–89, ed Artscribe 1991–92 (assoc ed 1989–91), conslt VIART 1993, dir of visual arts Arts Cncl of England 1993–2006; assoc: Museums Assoc 1975, Art Historians' Assoc 1979; memb exec Ctee Int Assoc of Art Critics 1996 and 2008; Assoc of Art Critics: pres Br Section Int 2009–, chair Congress Cmmn 2012–14, sec-gen 2014–; Cncl Goldsmiths Coll London 1997–2006; tstee: Paintings in Hospitals 2007–14, City and Guilds of London Art Sch 2011–, Kenneth Armitage Fndn 2012–; Hon Dr Anglia Polytechnic Univ 2005; FRSA 1993, FRCA 1999, FRIBA 2003; *Publications* Ian McKeever (2009); several oeuvre catalogues, numerous articles for art jls and press, contrib to various exhbn catalogues; *Recreations* family, art, cooking, film (especially European), sailing, growing pomegranates; *Clubs* Chelsea Arts; *Style—* Dr Marjorie Allthorpe-Guyton; ✉ AICA Office International Association of Art Critics, 32 Rue Yves Toudic, Paris 75010, France (e-mail aica.office@gmail.com, websites www.aicainternational.org and www.aica.uk.org)

ALLUM, William Herbert; s of Herbert Edward Allum (d 1987), of Oxford, and Gladys Marion, *née* Bolton; *b* 9 February 1953; *Educ* St Edward's Sch Oxford, Univ of Birmingham (BSc, MB ChB, MD); *m* 23 April 1983, (Pamela) Anne, da of Joseph Anthony Collier (d 1995), of Stratford-upon-Avon; 3 s (Charles b 1985, Henry b 1987, James b 1990); *Career* house offr posts 1977–78, demonstrator in anatomy Univ of Southampton 1978–79, SHO in surgery Reading Hosps 1979–80; registrar in surgery: Central Birmingham 1980–82, Hereford Hosps 1982–83; lectr in surgery Univ of Birmingham 1985–88 (hon res fell 1983–85), sr lectr Univ of Leicester and hon conslt surgn Leicester Hosps 1988–90; conslt surgn: Bart's London 1991–93, Epsom Dist Gen Hosp 1993–2003, Royal Marsden Hosp 2001–; memb: Physiotherapists' Bd Cncl of Professions Supplimentary to Med, Specialist Advsy Ctee Jt Ctee on Higher Surgical Trg 2003–; hon sec Assoc of Upper Gastrointestinal Surgns; RCS: memb Ct of Examiners, regnl advsr; memb: Surgical Res Soc, Br Assoc of Surgical Oncology (nat ctee memb); FRCS 1982; *Books* Cancer of the Stomach – Clinical Cancer Monographs 1989 (co-author), Premalignancy and Early Cancer in General Surgery (co-author, 1996); *Recreations* golf, cricket; *Clubs* MCC, RAC, Walton Heath Golf; *Style—* William Allum, Esq; ✉ The Chestnuts, 21 Greville Park Road, Ashtead, Surrey KT21 2QU (☎ 01372 813318); Royal Marsden Hospital, Downs Road, Sutton, Surrey SM2 5PT (☎ 020 8661 3982)

ALLVEY, David Philip; s of Edgar Frederick Allvey, and Kathleen Beatrice, *née* Lamb; *b* 13 March 1945; *Educ* Lewes County GS, Univ of London; *m* 15 July 2000, Alison Cullen; 2 s from previous m (Mark James b 11 Dec 1979, Philip Duncan b 4 May 1982); *Career* various mgmnt positions in construction industry until 1972, articled clerk with accountancy firm, mangr International Tax Dept Price Waterhouse London until 1980; BAT Industries plc: joined as gp dep tax mangr 1980, fin dir gp cosmetic interests and fin advsr and taxation mangr British-American Tobacco Co Ltd 1984–86, head of Finance Dept BAT Industries 1986, gp fin dir 1989–98, dir various gp subsids incl Eagle Star and Allied Dunbar, memb Chief Exec's Ctee (formerly Chm's Policy Ctee) 1992–98; chief of corp operations Zurich Financial Services 1998–99; fin dir Barclays plc 1999–2001; non-exec dir McKechnie plc 1993–2000, Intertek 2000–, Costain 2001–, Resolution (formerly Britannic) 2002–, William Hill 2002–, My.Travel 2003–; memb UK Accounting Standards Bd 1993–2003, chm Fiscal Ctee Hundred Gp of Financial Dirs 1994–2001; FCA, ATII; *Recreations* golf; *Style*— David Allvey, Esq

ALLWEIS, His Hon Judge Martin Peter; s of Jack Allweis (d 1993), and Iris, *née* Mosco (d 2007); *b* 22 December 1947; *Educ* Manchester Grammar, Sidney Sussex Coll Cambridge (BA); *m* 1 April 1984, Tracy Ruth, da of late Hyam Barr, and Bernice Barr; 1 da, 1 s; *Career* called to the Bar Inner Temple 1970; in practice 1970–94, recorder 1990–94, circuit judge (Northern Circuit) 1994–, designated family judge for Gtr Manchester 1996–2005; *Recreations* family, football (Manchester City FC), squash; *Style*— His Hon Judge Allweis; ✉ c/o Manchester Family Court, Manchester Civil Justice Centre, 1 Bridge Street West, Manchester M3 3FX

ALMOND, Darren; *b* Wigan, 1971; *Educ* Winchester Sch of Art (BA); *Career* artist; winner Art & Innovation Prize 1996; *Solo Exhibitions* Crawford Art College Cork 1991, KN120 (Great Western Studios London) 1995, Jay Jopling/White Cube London 1997, Darren Almond (ICA London) 1997, Darren Almond (Galerie Max Hetzler Berlin) 1999, Darren Almond (The Renaissance Soc Chicago) 1999, Traction (Chisenhale Gallery London) 2000, Darren Almond (The Approach London) 2000, Darren Almond (Matthew Marks Gallery NY) 2000 and 2005, Night as a Day (Tate Britain) 2001, At Speed (Galerie Max Hetzler Berlin) 2002, A (Fourth Wall PADT London) 2002, Nightvision (Sommercontemporaryart Tel Aviv) 2003, 11 miles...from safety (White Cube London) 2003, If I Had You (Galerie Max Hetzler Berlin) 2004, Life Sentence (Lentos Museum of Modern Art Linz) 2004, Darren Almond (K21 Kuntstsammlung Nordhein-Westfalen Dusseldorf) 2005; *Group Exhibitions* incl: Southampton Quays Southampton 1992, Winchester Gallery Winchester 1993, A Small Shifting Sphere of Serious Culture (ICA London) 1996, Something Else (Exmouth Market London) 1996, Art & Innovation Prize (ICA London) 1996, Sensation (Royal Acad London) 1997, Delta (Musée d'Art Moderne de la Ville de Paris) 1998, View Four (Mary Boone Gallery NY) 1998, Hidden Desires and Images (Art Dynamics Tokyo) 1998, Art Crash (Arhus Kunstmuseum Denmark) 1999, Chronos and Kairos (Museum Fridericanum Kassel Germany) 1999, Seeing Time (San Francisco MOMA) 1999, Concrete Ashtray (Friedrich Petzel Gallery NY) 1999, Common People (Fondazione Sandretto Re Rebaundengo Turin) 1999, Diary (Cornerhouse Manchester) 2000, Out There (White Cube 2 London) 2000, Apocalypse (Royal Acad London) 2000, Geographies (Galerie Chantal Crousel Paris) 2000, Deliberate Living (Greene Naftali Gallery NY) 2001, Unreal Time Video (Fine Art Center The Korean Culture & Arts Fndn Seoul) 2001, Tracking (Kent & Vicki Logan Gallery Calif Coll of Arts and Crafts Oakland) 2001, Berlin Biennale 2001, Nature in Photography (Galerie Nachst St Stephan Vienna) 2001, Casino 2001 (SMAK and Bijlokenmuseum Ghent) 2001, 10th Anniversary Exhibition. 100 Drawings and Photographs (Matthew Marks Gallery NY) 2001, In the Freud Museum (Freud Museum London) 2002, Presentness is Grace – Experiencing the Suspended Moment (Spacex Gallery Exeter) 2002, The Rowan Collection. Contemporary British & Irish Art (Irish MOMA Dublin) 2002, Contextualize (Kunstverein Hamburg) 2002, The Hate U Give Little Infants Fucks Everyone (Smart Project Space Amsterdam) 2002, Video – Zone (1st International video-art biennal in Israel Tel Aviv) 2002, Melodrama (Centro José Guerrero and Palacio de los Condes de Gabia Granada) 2002, Video Acts (PS1 and Krammlich Collection NY) 2002, Breathing the Water (Galerie Hauser & Wirth & Presenhubera Zurich) 2003, Edén (La Colección Jumex Mexico City) 2003, Witness (Barbican Art Gallery and Curve Gallery London) 2003, La Biennale di Venezia 2003, Hot Summer in the City (Sean Kelly Gallery NY) 2003, Skulptur Biennale Münsterland (Stadtmuseum Beckum) 2003, Melodrama (MARCO Vigo) 2003, Other Times: Br Contemporary Art (City Art Gall Prague) 2004, Open Secrets (Imperial War Museum London) 2004, Universal Experience (Museum of Contemporary Art Chicago) 2005, The Mind is a Horse Part II (Bloomberg Space London) 2005; *Work in Public Collections* Art Inst Chicago, La Coleccion Jumex Mexico, DaimlerChrysler Berlin, Government Art Collection London, Imperial War Museum London, Met Museum of Art NY, Paine Webber Art Collection NY; *Style*— Darren Almond, Esq

ALMOND, David William; s of George Sydney Almond (d 1999), of Lymington, Hants, and Madge Lilian, *née* Skegg (d 1993); *b* 24 October 1945, Purley, Surrey; *Educ* Purley GS; *m* 6 June 1970, Elizabeth (Liz), da of Percy Thomas Bisby (d 1978), of Aldwick, W Sussex; 2 da (Amanda Jane b 25 Feb 1974, Juliette b 10 March 1977); *Career* CA; articles City of London 1962–67, ptnr Alliotts (formerly Evans Peirson) 1969–2002, chm Alliott Peirson Associates 1974–86; Alliott Gp: chm 1979–89, exec dir 1989–2010, exec dir North America 2007–12; ceo TEX-XL Solutions 2016–; pres Accountants' Club of N America Inc 2013–; dir Accounting Firms Associates Inc 1982–92; chm: Croydon Soc of CAs 1979–80 (sec 1975–79), Storrington Rural Preservation Soc 1995–99; Freeman City of London 1976, memb Ct of Assts Worshipful Co of Coachmakers and Coach Harness Makers 1977 (Master 2001); FCA 1967; *Recreations* sailing, travel, gardening and eating; *Clubs* Spicewood Lions Texas (pres 2014–); *Style*— David Almond, Esq; ✉ 5645 Fall Creek Road, Spicewood, Texas, 78669 USA

ALRED, David (Dave); MBE (2004); *b* 2 April 1948, London; *Educ* Loughborough Univ (PhD); *Career* rugby union coach; played for Bristol RUFC and Bath RUFC, also Minnesota Vikings (American football), Sheffield (rugby league), Blue Dragons (rugby league); coach: GB (rugby league) 1984, Bath RUFC 1990–92, St George Aust (rugby league) 1991–93, Bristol RUFC 1993–94, Newcastle RUFC, Aust 1993–94; asst (kicking) coach England 1998–2006 (winners Six Nations Championship 2000, 2001 and 2003 (Grand Slam 2003), winners World Cup Aust 2003), kicking coach Br and Irish Lions South Africa 1997, Aust 2001 and NZ 2005; awarded Mussabini medal; *Style*— Dave Alred, Esq, MBE; ✉ e-mail dave@davealred.com

ALSOP, Prof William Allen; OBE (1999); s of Francis John Alsop (d 1964), and Brenda Ethelwyn, *née* Hight (d 1998); *b* 12 December 1947; *Educ* Eaglehurst Coll Northampton, AA Sch of Architecture, Br Sch in Rome (Bernard Webb scholar); *m* 1972, Sheila Elizabeth, da of George Bean; 2 s (Oliver b 1977, Piers b 1984), 1 da (Nancy b 1980); *Career* architect; with: Maxwell Fry 1971, Cedric Price 1973–77, Rodrick Ham 1977–79; princ then conslt Alsop & Störmer (then Alsop, later SMC Alsop Architects) 1979–2009, princ RMJM 2009–11, dir aLL Design 2011–; tutor in sculpture Central St Martin's Coll of Art and Design 1973 (hon prof 1997), prof of architecture Tech Univ Vienna 1996–, prof of architecture Canterbury Sch of Architecture Univ for the Creative Arts Canterbury 2013–; memb Design Cncl 1994–1998, chm Architectural Fndn 2000–07, memb Urban Renaissance Panel Yorkshire Forward 2001–03, memb Int Design Ctee Thames Gateway 2004–, memb Kensington and Chelsea Architectural Advsy Bd 2009–; princ buildings incl: Hamburg Ferry Terminal, Cardiff Visitor Centre (RIBA Nat Award 1991), Cardiff Barrage, N Greenwich underground station, Tottenham Hale interchange station, Nat Museum Nuremberg, Govt HQ Marseilles (RIBA Nat Award 1997), Peckham Library (RIBA Stirling Prize 2000), Ontario Coll of Art and Design Toronto 2004 (RIBA World Award 2004), Sch of Medicine and Dentistry Queen Mary Westfield Coll 2004 (RIBA Edcn Award 2006, Civic Trust Award 2006), Fawood Children's Centre, Blizard Building, Palestra; other projects incl: Blackfriars London 2000, Calypso Rotterdam 2006, Clarke Quay Singapore, Raffles City Beijing, Gao Yang Shanghai 2009, Chips Manchester 2009, Michael Farraday Community Sch London 2010, RiversideOne Middlesbrough 2011, Finch West Station Toronto 2016 (in construction); hon fell: Sheffield Hallam Univ 2002, Univ Coll Northampton 2005, Queen Mary and Westfield Coll 2006; Hon Dr: Nottingham Trent Univ 2001, Ontario Coll of Art and Design Toronto 2004, UEA 2007, Ryerson Univ Toronto 2010; Hon DUniv Sheffield Hallam Univ 2001, Hon DDes Univ of Greenwich 2016; memb: Bundes Deutsches Architecten, AA 1968, SADG 1973, ARB 1978, RIBA 1978, Hamburgische Architektenkammer 1992, Russian Architectural Inst 1995, Russian Acad of Art 1995; FRSA 1981, Hon FRSBS 1996, RA 2000; *Books* City of Objects (1992), William Alsop Buildings and Projects (1992), William Alsop Architect, Four Projects (1993), Will Alsop and Jan Störmer, Architects (1993), Le Grand Blue-Marseille (1994), Will Alsop Book 1 (2001, Book 2 2002), Will Alsop – The Noise (by Tom Porter, 2010); *Recreations* architecture, painting, fishing, writing; *Style*— Prof William Alsop, OBE, RA; ✉ website www.all-worldwide.com

ALSTEAD, Brig (Francis) Allan Littlejohns; CBE (1984), DL (City of Edinburgh 1996); s of Prof Stanley Alstead, CBE (d 1992), of Dunblane, Perthshire, and his 1 w, Nora, *née* Sowden (d 1980); *b* 19 June 1935; *Educ* Glasgow Acad, RMA Sandhurst, UCW Aberystwyth (MPhil), Univ of Edinburgh (NATO res fell); *m* 4 April 1964, Joy Veronica, da of George Alexander Edwards (d 1991), of Carlisle, Cumbria; 2 s (Robert b 24 Dec 1965, Jonathan b 13 Nov 1968); *Career* cmmnd KOSB 1955, RN Staff Coll 1966, JSSC 1971, cmd 1 Bn KOSB 1974–76 (despatches 1976), MA to QMG 1976–79, ACOS Log Plans BAOR 1981–84, cmd 51 Highland Bde 1984–87; NATO reinforcement co-ordinator 1987–90; chief exec Scottish Sports Cncl 1990–99, chief exec SportScotland 1999–2000, Chef de Mission Scottish Cwlth Games Team Manchester 2002; md Alstead Consulting 2000–; chm Mercy Corps Europe 2001–08 (Mercy Corps Humanitarian Hero 2008), memb Bd Mercy Corps Int (USA) 2001–08; non-exec dir JRG Ltd 1996–2007; memb Exec Scottish Cncl for Devpt and Industry 1995–2000 and 2002–08; memb Queen's Body Guard for Scotland (Royal Co of Archers), Dep Hon Col City of Edinburgh Univs OTC 1990–99; regimental tstee KOSB; pres Edinburgh and Lothians SSAFA/Forces Help 2003–05 (pres Edinburgh and Midlothian 1991–98), chm Scottish Target Shooting Fedn 2011–15, memb Lowland Territorial and Volunteer Assoc 1995–; dir and tstee: Seagull Tst 1995–2008, Youth Sport Tst 1996–2000; tstee Cncl for the Advancement of Arts, Recreation and Education (CAARE) 2003–14; govr: Moray House Coll Edinburgh 1991–96, Glasgow Acad 1995–2001; memb: Gen Cncl Erskine Hosp 2001–, Cncl Nat Playing Fields Assoc (NPFA) 2001–08; Hon DUniv Glasgow Caledonian Univ; FCMI (FIMgt 1984), FCIPD (FIPD 1986), FCILT 1989, FInstAM 1990, FInstD 1992, FBISA 2000; *Books* Ten In Ten: The Reinforcement of Europe in Crisis and War (1991); *Recreations* archery, opera, ballet, classical music; *Style*— Brig Allan Alstead, CBE, DL; ✉ 49 Moray Place, Edinburgh EH3 6BQ

ALTHAM, His Hon Judge John Robert Carr; s of John Carr Altham, and Linda Margaret Altham; *b* 30 March 1966, Morecambe, Lancs; *Educ* Lancaster Royal GS, UCL (BA), Univ of Birmingham; *m* 15 Aug 1992, Fiona Aubrey; 2 da (Jodie b 3 Jan 1994, Sophie b 15 Jan 1996), 1 s (Ben b 7 March 2000); *Career* called to the Bar Gray's Inn 1993; jr of the Northern Circuit 1996, recorder 2008, circuit judge (Northern Circuit) 2011–; *Recreations* family, hiking, running, piano; *Style*— His Hon Judge Altham; ✉ Preston Crown Court, Openshaw Place, Preston PR1 2LL

ALTMAN, Brian; QC (2008); s of Stanley Altman (d 1999), and Pauline, *née* Bendon; *b* 16 August 1957; *Educ* KCL (LLB), Univ of Amsterdam (Dip); *m* 23 March 1996, Charlotte Ann, *née* Parkin; 2 s (Frederick b 8 Oct 1988, Hugo b 25 Oct 1999), 2 da (Georgina b 25 May 1990, Lydia b 19 July 1997); *Career* called to the Bar Middle Temple 1981 (bencher 2010); recorder 2003, currently memb of chambers 2 Bedford Row; Central Criminal Court: jr treasy counsel 1997–2002, sr treasy counsel 2002–10, first sr treasy counsel to the Crown 2010–13; *Style*— Brian Altman, Esq, QC; ✉ 2 Bedford Row, London WC1R 4 BU (☎ 020 7440 8888, e-mail baltman@2bedfordrow.co.uk, website www.2bedfordrow.co.uk)

ALTMAN, His Hon John; s of Lionel Altman (d 1987), of Leeds, and Vita, *née* Levi (d 1969); *b* 21 June 1944; *Educ* Moorlands Sch Leeds, Bootham Sch York, Univ of Bristol (LLB); *m* 25 Feb 1968, Elizabeth, da of Ralph and Helen Brown; 2 da (Claire Rose b 11 Aug 1973, Vivien Simone b 10 April 1976); *Career* called to the Bar Middle Temple 1967; practised at the Bar in London and N Eastern Circuit, chm Industrial Tbnls 1986–91 (pt/t chm 1983–86), recorder 1989–91 (asst recorder 1985–89), circuit judge: NE Circuit 1991–2001, SE Circuit 2001–; designated family judge: Milton Keynes 2003–07, Luton 2004, Oxford 2005–07, London 2007; sr circuit judge 2007–16, ret; past chm W Yorks Family Mediation Service, past pres The Leeds Jewish Historical Soc; memb Hon Soc of Middle Temple; *Recreations* reading, music, theatre, photography, gardening; *Style*— His Hon John Altman

ALTMANN, Baroness (Life Peer 2015), of Tottenham in the London Borough of Haringey; Ros; CBE (2014); da of Leo Altmann (d 1986), and Renate Altmann; *Educ* Henrietta Barnett Sch London, UCL (Hume-Lloyd scholar, BSc), Harvard Univ (Kennedy scholar), LSE (PhD); *m* 1982, Paul Richer; 1 s (Steven), 2 da (Lisa, Emma); *Career* fund mangr Prudential Assurance 1981–84, head of int equities Chase Manhattan Bank 1984–89, dir Rothschild Asset Mgmnt 1989–91, dir NatWest Investment Mgmnt 1991–93, and conslt on investment strategy, pensions and savings policy 1993–, DG Saga Gp 2010–13; conslt to HM Treasy on Myners Review of Institutional Investment April-Sept 2000, advsr on savings, pensions and retirement policy to 10 Downing St Policy Unit 2000–05, memb Lord Chllr's Strategic Investment Bd 2004–, appointed business champion for older workers by UK Govt 2014–, min of state for pensions UK Govt 2015–; author of numerous articles in newspapers, jls and industry magazines; govr and non-exec dir LSE 1989–, govr Pensions Policy Inst 2002–; tstee The Age Employment Network, advsr Bd of Int Longevity Centre; fell National Cncl of Women GB, memb Bd Ind Press Standards Orgn 2014; Hon DLitt Univ of Westminster 2009, Hon DCL Newcastle Univ 2015; MSI, MInstD, FRSA; *Recreations* charity fundraising, swimming, table-tennis; *Style*— The Baroness Altmann, CBE; ✉ e-mail altmannr@parliament.uk

ALTON, Roger; *Educ* Exeter Coll Oxford; *Career* Liverpool Post 1969–74; The Guardian: chief news sub ed 1976–81, dep sports ed 1981–85, arts ed 1985–90, ed Weekend Guardian 1990–93, features ed 1993–96, asst ed 1996–98; ed The Observer 1998–2008, ed The Independent 2008–10, exec ed The Times 2010–; Ed of the Year What the Papers Say Awards 2000, Ed of the Year GQ Men of the Year Awards 2005, Newspaper of the Year Br Press Awards 2007; *Recreations* skiing, climbing, films, sports; *Style*— Roger Alton, Esq

ALTON OF LIVERPOOL, Baron (Life Peer UK 1997), of Mossley Hill in the County of Merseyside; David Patrick Alton; s of late Frederick Alton, of Bow, London, and Bridget, *née* Mulroe; *b* 15 March 1951; *Educ* Campion Sch, Christ Coll Liverpool, Univ of St Andrews; *m* 23 July 1988, Elizabeth, *née* Bell; 1 da (Hon Marianne b 1989), 3 s (Hon Padraig b 1990, Hon Philip b 1992, Hon James b 1997); *Career* teacher 1972–74, teacher of children with special needs 1974–79; cnclr Liverpool City Cncl 1972–80 (dep ldr Cncl 1978–79, chm Housing Ctee 1978–79), nat pres Nat League of Young Liberals 1979; MP (Lib): Liverpool Edge Hill March 1979–83, Liverpool Mossley Hill 1983–97; chm Lib Pty Standing Ctee (Policy) 1980–81, memb Select Ctee on the Environment 1981–85, Lib chief whip 1985–87, Lib and Alliance spokesman on NI 1986–87; sits as Ind cross-bench peer in House of Lords; memb House of Commons Privileges Ctee 1994–96; chm: All-Pty Mersey Barrage Group 1990–97, All-Pty British-North Korea Gp; vice-chm: All-Pty Drug Abuse Group 1992–96, All-Pty Mental Health Gp 1995–97, All-Pty Tibet Gp, All-Pty Gp on Foreign Affrs, All-Pty Parly Gp on Freedom of Religion and Belief 2014–16; treas: All-Pty Pro-Life Gp 1996–2007, All-Pty Anti-Personnel Land Mines Gp 1996–99, All-Pty Gp Egypt 2014–; sec All Pty Sudan Gp; prof of citizenship Liverpool John Moores Univ 1997–, visiting fell Univ of St Andrews; co-fndr Movement for Christian Democracy 1990; nat vice-pres Life, vice-pres Assoc of Cncllrs; pres: Karen Aid; chm Merseyside Cncl for Voluntary Services 1997–2001; patron and co-fndr Jubilee Campaign and Jubilee Action 1986–; patron: Habitat for Humanity, Mersey Kidney Research, Jospice, Right to Life, Zoe's Place, Alert, Liverpool Sch of Tropical Medicine, G K Chesteron Inst, Motec Life (Ghana), Asylum Link Merseyside, Local Solutions, British Coptic Assoc; past chm Forget-me-Not Appeal; tstee Arise Fndn 2016–; treas All-Pty Friends of CAFOD; memb Bd of Aid to the Church in Need 2014; columnist: Catholic Pictorial 1982–95, The Universe 1989–2013, Liverpool Daily Post 1997–98; Michael Bell Meml Award, Korean Mystery of Life Award, Good Samaritan Award for Human Rights (Advocates Int US); hon fell Liverpool John Moores Univ 2016; Knight Order of Constantine and St George 2002, KCSG 2008; *Books* What Kind of Country (1987), Whose Choice Anyway? (1988), Faith in Britain (1991), Signs of Contradiction (1996), Life After Death (1997), Citizen Virtues (1999), Pilgrim Ways (2001), Citizen 21 (ed, 2001), Passion and Pain (2003), Euthanasia: Heart of the Matter (2005), Abortion: Heart of the Matter (2005), Building Bridges: Is there hope for North Korea (2013); *Recreations* gardening, books, walking; *Style*— The Rt Hon Lord Alton of Liverpool; ✉ Jacob's Ladder, Lower Road, Knowle Green, Lancashire PR3 2YN (☎ 01772 786551, website www.davidalton.net); House of Lords, London SW1A 0PW (☎ 020 7219 3551, e-mail altond@parliament.uk); c/o Barbara Mace, Roscoe Foundation for Citizenship, Egerton Court, 2 Rodney Street, Liverpool L3 5UX (☎ 0151 231 3852, e-mail b.mace@ljmu.ac.uk)

ALTY, Prof James Lenton; s of William Graham Alty (d 1959), of Haslingden, Lancs, and Annie Alty (d 1989); *b* 21 August 1939; *Educ* King Edward VII Sch Lytham, Univ of Liverpool (BSc, PhD); *m* 16 Jan 1965, Mary Eleanor, da of Thomas Roberts (d 1986), of Llanerchymedd, Anglesey; 2 s (Gareth Thomas b 1965, Graham James b 1971), 2 da (Carys Ann b 1967, Sian Cathryn b 1968); *Career* account exec IBM (UK) Ltd 1971–72 (sr systems engr 1968–71), dir Computer Laboratory Univ of Liverpool 1972–82 (Oliver Lodge res fell 1962–64, Leverhulme res fell 1966–68), exec dir Turing Inst 1984–90, BT prof of computer sci Univ of Strathclyde 1989–90 (prof of computer sci 1982–89, dir Scot HCI Centre 1984–90); Loughborough Univ: prof of computer sci 1990–, head Computer Science Dept 1991–2000, dean Faculty of Science 2001–04, prof emeritus 2004–; prof of human computer interaction Middlesex Univ 2004–06; over 100 pubns in academic jls and conf proceedings; memb: Computer Bd for Univs and Res Cncls 1975–81, Cncl Br Computer Soc 1981–84 (fell 1982); FBCS 1986, FRSA 1987, FIET 1993, CEng 1998; *Books* Computing Skills and the User Interface (with M J Coombs, 1982), Expert Systems: Concepts and Examples (with M J Coombs, 1984), Human Computer Interaction (with G R S Weir, 1990), Industrial Applications of Artificial Intelligence (with Mikulich, 1991), People and Computer VIII (with Diaper and Guest, 1993), The Thurcaston Carols (2013), On Course! (2015); *Recreations* skiing, musical composition, golf; *Clubs* National Liberal; *Style*— Prof James Alty; ✉ Loughborough University, Loughborough, Leicestershire LE11 3TU (☎ 01509 222681, fax 01509 211586, e-mail jamesalty1@gmail.com)

ALTY, John; CB (2010); *b* 2 December 1956, Liverpool; *Educ* Liverpool Coll; Univ of Oxford; *m* Jane; 3 s, 1 da; *Career* DG Fair Markets Gp Dept for Business, Innovation and Skills until 2010, ceo and comptroller gen Intellectual Property Office 2010–; *Recreations* Liverpool FC; *Style*— John Alty, Esq, CB; ✉ Intellectual Property Office, Concept House, Cardiff Road, Newport NP10 8QQ

AMANN, Prof Ronald; s of George James Amann, of Newcastle upon Tyne, and Elizabeth Clementson, *née* Towell (d 1983); *b* 21 August 1943; *Educ* Heaton GS Newcastle upon Tyne, Univ of Birmingham (MSocSci, PhD); *m* 28 Aug 1965, Susan Frances, da of Leslie Peters, of S Porcupine, Ontario, Canada; 2 s (Edmund b 1968, Timothy Francis b 1970), 1 da (Jessica Louise b 1974); *Career* conslt OECD 1965–68; Univ of Birmingham: asst lectr, lectr then sr lectr 1968–83, dir Centre for Russian and E European Studies 1983–89, prof of comparative politics 1985–2003 (emeritus prof 2003–), dean Faculty of Commerce and Social Sci 1989–91, pro-vice-chllr 1991–94; chief exec and dep chm ESRC 1994–99, DG Centre for Management and Policy Studies Cabinet Office 1999–2002; specialist advsr and witness Foreign Affrs Ctee and Ctee on Sci and Technol House of Commons; chm: Steering Ctee ESRC E-W Research Initiative, Advsy Bd Centre for Res on Innovation and Competition Univ of Manchester 2001–; memb: Cncl Sch of Slavonic and E Euro Studies Univ of London 1986–89, Nat Technol Foresight Steering Gp 1995–2000, Steering Ctee Centre for the Analysis of Risk and Regulation LSE 2000–; chm Protective Services Ctee ind memb W Midlands Police Authy 2007–12; AcSS 1999. FRSA; *Books* Science Policy in the USSR (with Berry and Davies, 1969), The Technological Level of Soviet Industry (with Cooper and Davies), Industrial Innovation in the Soviet Union (with Cooper, 1982), Technical Progress and Soviet Economic Development (with Cooper, 1986); *Recreations* walking, modern jazz, cricket; *Style*— Prof Ronald Amann

AMARATUNGA, Prof Gehan Anil Joseph; s of Carl Herman Joseph Amaratunga (d 1966), and Swarna Mallika, *née* Undugodage; *b* 6 April 1956; *Educ* Royal Coll Colombo Sri Lanka, Pelham Meml HS Westchester NY, UC Cardiff (BSc), Univ of Cambridge (PhD); *m* 19 Sept 1981, Praveen Dharshini, da of John Hitchcock; 1 s (Ravindran b 9 Oct 1985), 2 da (Minoli b 19 April 1989, Gitanjali b 1 July 1990); *Career* res fell Microelectronics Centre Univ of Southampton 1983–84, lectr Dept of Electronics and Computer Sci Univ of Southampton 1984–87; lectr Dept of Engrg Univ of Cambridge 1987–95; prof of electrical engrg Univ of Liverpool 1995–98; prof of engrg Univ of Cambridge 1998–, fell Churchill Coll Cambridge 1998– (and 1987–95); founding dir and chief scientific offr Cambridge Semiconductor Ltd 2000– (acquired by Power Integrations Jan 2015), co-fndr Enecsys Ltd 2003, chm Wind Technologies Ltd 2007, chief of research and innovation Sri Lanka Inst of Nanotechnology (SLINTEC) 2011, Camutronics Ltd 2012; Tan Chin Tuan centennial prof Nanyang Technol Univ Singapore 2012; RAE Research Award (Univ of Cambridge) 1979–82, IEE Prize 1979, Royal Acad of Engrg Overseas Secondment Award (Stanford Univ) 1989; FREng 2004 (Silver Medal 2007), FIET 2004, FRSA 2009; *Publications* over 500 academic publications in jls and symposia proceedings incl: Transactions of the IEEE, Physical Review, Nature, Jl of Applied Physics; *Recreations* jazz, cinema, vintage sports cars, cricket; *Style*— Prof Gehan Amaratunga; ✉ Department of Engineering, Electrical Engineering Division, 9 J J Thomson Avenue, Cambridge CB3 0FA (☎ 01223 748320, fax 01223 748322, e-mail gaja1@cam.ac.uk)

AMBROSE, Timothy Michael; s of Henry Ambrose, and Janet, *née* Millard; *b* 8 December 1949, Devizes, Wiltshire; *Educ* Dauntsey's Sch West Lavington, Univ of Southampton (BA, CertEd); *m* 21 Sept 1974, Hon Angela Francesca Hayward Blanch, 3 da of Rt Rev Baron Blanch, PC, DD (Life Peer, d 1994); 2 da (Bethany Beatrice Hayward b 24 July 1978, Emily Kate b 15 May 1981); *Career* res asst Univ of Oxford Inst of Archaeology and archivist Ashmolean Museum Library 1972–74, pubns asst DOE 1974–75, res asst in Euro archaeology Univ of Oxford 1975–77, asst keeper of archaeology Lincolnshire Museums 1977–82; Scottish Museums Cncl: dep dir 1982–86, dir 1986–94; sr res fell City Univ Dept of Arts Policy and Mgmnt 1994–96, head of practice Museum Resource Management (UK and int museum advsrs) 1994–99; chm Exec Bd ICOM UK 1992–98; assoc dir L & R Consulting 1996–99, dir Locum Destination Consulting 1999–2004, princ assoc Locum Consulting 2004–08, princ Timothy Ambrose Consulting 2004–, dir Metaphor 2008–09, princ assoc Colliers Int 2009–16, assoc Fourth Street 2016–; hon sr res fell Dept of Arts Policy and Management City Univ 1996–99; author of numerous reports, reviews and papers; FMA 1990 (AMA 1980), FSA 1993; *Books* New Museums – A Start-Up Guide (1987), Education in Museums, Museums in Education (1987), Working with Museums (1988), Presenting Scotland's Story (1989), Money, Money, Money and Museums (1991), Forward Planning – a Handbook (1991), Managing New Museums (1993), Museum Basics (1993, 3 edn 2012); *Recreations* gardening; *Style*— Timothy M Ambrose, Esq, FSA; ✉ Friars Cottage, The Street, Kingston, Lewes, East Sussex BN7 3PD

AMED, Imran; *b* 20 April 1975, Calgary, Canada; *Educ* Harvard Business Sch (MBA), McGill Univ (BCom); *Career* fashion business advsr, writer and entrepreneur; former mgmnt conslt McKinsey& Co, currently fndr and ed The Business of Fashion; assoc lectr Central St Martin's Coll of Art and Design; *Style*— Imran Amed, Esq; e-mail imran@businessoffashion.com, website www.businessoffashion.com, Twitter @imranamed

AMENT, Sharon Ann; da of Horace Cecil Ament (d 1969), and Pauline, *née* Anderson (d 1976); *b* 29 September 1962, London; *Educ* Univ of Leeds (BA); *m* 18 Aug 2006, Nick Lane; *Career* dir of public engagement Natural History Museum until 2012, dir Museum of London 2012–; fell: Noyce Leadership Inst, Salzburg Global Seminar; *Recreations* gardening, cycling, walking, wine; *Style*— Ms Sharon Ament; ✉ Museum of London, 150 London Wall, London EC2Y 5HN (☎ 020 7814 5700, e-mail director@museumoflondon.org.uk, website www.museumoflondon.org.uk, Twitter @sharonament)

AMESS, Sir David Anthony Andrew; kt (2015), MP; s of James Henry Valentine Amess (d 1986), and Maud Ethel, *née* Martin; *b* 26 March 1952; *Educ* St Bonaventures GS, Bournemouth Coll of Technol (BSc); *m* 1983, Julia Margaret Monica, da of Graham Harry Arnold, of Southend-on-Sea, Essex; 1 s, 4 da; *Career* teacher 1970–71, insurance underwriter Leslie & Godwin Agency 1974–76, sr conslt Accountancy Personnel 1976–80, ptnr Accountancy Aims Employment Agency 1981–87; chm: Accountancy Solutions 1987–90, Accountancy Aims Group 1990–96, 1912 Club 1996–; memb Cons Pty 1968–, Parly candidate (Cons) Forest Gate 1974 and 1978, GLC candidate Newham NW 1977, Parly candidate (Cons) Newham NW 1979; MP (Cons): Basildon 1983–97, Southend W 1997–; PPS at DHSS 1987 to: Edwina Currie, Michael Portillo, Lord Skelmersdale; PPS to Michael Portillo: as Min of State Dept of Tport 1988–90, at DOE 1990–92, as Chief Sec to the Treasy 1992–94, as Sec of State for Employment 1994–95, as Sec of State for Def 1995–97; dir Parly Broadcasting Unit 1997–99; memb: Broadcasting Select Ctee 1995–97, Health Select Ctee 1998–2008, Backbench Business Ctee 2012–15, Administration Select Ctee 2015–; chm Bd of Tstees Industry and Parliament Tst; chm All-Pty: Maldives Gp, Fire Safety Gp, Maternity Gp, Hepatology Gp; vice-pres Lotteries Cncl 1998–; Chm's Panel 2001–; Redbridge Cncl: elected 1982, vice-chm Housing Ctee 1981–85; *Publications* The Road to Basildon (1993), Conservatives Fight Back (1994), Basildon 1992: Against All Odds (2012), Party of Opportunity (2014, updated and expanded 2015); contrib to various magazines and pamphlets; *Recreations* reading, writing, sport, theatre, gardening, popular music; *Clubs* Kingswood Squash and Racketball (Basildon); *Style*— Sir David Amess, MP; ✉ House of Commons, London SW1A 0AA (☎ 020 7219 3452, fax 020 7219 2245, e-mail amessd@parliament.uk)

AMEY, Julian Nigel Robert; s of Robert Amey, of Barton Seagrave, Northants, and Diana, *née* Coles; *b* 19 June 1949; *Educ* Wellingborough Sch, Magdalene Coll Cambridge (MA); *m* 16 Dec 1972, Ann Victoria, da of Thomas Frank Brenchley, CMG, of London, and Edith, *née* Helfand; 3 da (Joanna b 9 Sept 1981, Frances b 12 Oct 1984, Charlotte b 7 Jan 1990); *Career* dir of int sales and marketing Longman Group Ltd 1985–89, exec dir BBC English World Service 1989–94, seconded to DTI 1994–96, DG Canning House (Hispanic and Luso Brazilian Cncl) 1996–2001; chief exec: CIBSE 2001–06, Trinity Coll London 2006–09, Imperial Soc of Teachers of Dancing 2009–11, Inst of Healthcare Engrg and Estate Mangrs 2012–; govr Bath Spa Univ; *Books* Spanish Business Dictionary (1979), Portuguese Business Dictionary (1981); *Recreations* cricket, travel; *Clubs* Hawks' (Cambridge), ESU, Rumford; *Style*— Julian Amey, Esq

AMIEL, Jonathan Michael (Jon); s of Barry Conrad Amiel (d 1978), of London, and Anita, *née* Barron; *b* 20 May 1948; *Educ* William Ellis Sch London, Univ of Cambridge (MA); *m* Tara, da of Lawrence Fuccella, and Sally Byrd; 4 s (Leo Barry, Jack Barry, Luke Barry, Max Barry); *Career* freelance director; admin Oxford & Cambridge Shakespeare Co 1970–73, literary mangr then assoc dir Hampstead Theatre Club 1973–76, asst then assoc dir Royal Shakespeare Co 1976–78, story ed BBC TV 1978–79; directed numerous prodns for BBC Play for Today 1980–85, incl: Preview, Lunch, A Sudden Wrench, Busted, Gates of Gold, Nobody's Property; other credits as dir incl: Tandoori Nights (series, Channel 4) 1985, Silent Twins (film) 1986, The Singing Detective (BBC) 1986, Queen of Hearts (feature film) 1988, Aunt Julia & The Scriptwriter (US title Tune In Tomorrow) 1990, Sommersby (with Richard Gere and Jodie Foster) 1993, Copycat (with Sigourney Weaver and Holly Hunter) 1995, The Man Who Knew Too Little (with Bill Murray) 1997, Entrapment (with Sean Connery and Catherine Zeta-Jones) 1999, The Core (with Aaron Eckhart, Hilary Swank and Stanley Tucci) 2002, Creation (with Jennifer Connelly and Paul Bettany) 2009; winner numerous awards for The Singing Detective, several festival awards for Queen of Hearts and Tune In Tomorrow; *Style*— Jon Amiel, Esq

AMIN, Prof Ash; CBE (2014); *b* 31 October 1955, Kampala, Uganda; *Educ* Univ of Reading (PhD); *m* Lynne; 3 c (Usha, Samir, Isla); *Career* Univ of Durham: prof of geography, head Dept of Geography 2002–05, exec dir Inst of Advanced Study 2006–11; chair in geography Dept of Geography Univ of Cambrige 2011–; fell Swedish Collegium of Advanced Study in the Social Sciences 1999 and 2011; visiting posts: Univ of Naples, Univ of Bologna, Univ of Copenhagen, Univ of Rotterdam; memb Research Priorities Bd ESRC 1997–2001, memb Cncl European Assoc for Evolutionary Political Economy until 2002; AcSS 2000, fell World Acad of Art and Science 2003, FBA 2007; *Books* Technological Change, Industrial Restructuring and Regional Development (jt ed, 1986), Towards a New Europe? (jt ed, 1991), Post-Fordism: A Reader (ed, 1994), Globalisation, Institutions and Regional Development in Europe (jt ed, 1994), Behind the Myth of European Union (jt ed, 1995), Beyond Market and Hierarchy: Interactive Governance and Social Complexity (jt ed, 1997), Cities for the Many not the Few (jtly, 2000), Placing the Social Economy (jtly, 2002), Cities: Reimaging the Urban (jtly, 2002), Decentering the Nation: A Radical Approach to Regional Inequality (jtly, 2003), Architectures of Knowledge: Firms, Capabilities and Communities (jtly, 2004), The Blackwell Cultural Economy Reader (jt ed, 2005), Thinking About Almost Everything: New Ideas to Light Up Minds (jt ed, 2009), The Social Economy: International Perspectives on Economic Solidarity (ed, 2009), Land of Strangers (2012); *Recreations* walking, cooking, music, gardening; *Style*— Prof Ash Amin, CBE

AMIN, Mohammed; MBE (2016); s of Shadi Mehrban (d 1987), and Riaban Mehrban (d 1992); *b* 29 October 1950, Kalyanpur, Pakistan; *Educ* Central GS Manchester, Clare Coll Cambridge (BA), Univ of Leeds (CertEd); *m* 1978, Tahara; 2 s (Ibrahim b 1980, Ismail b 1982), 2 da (Scheherazade b 1985, Khadijah b 1988); *Career* teacher Counthill Sch Oldham 1973–74, trainee accountant Graham H Wood & Co 1974–77, tax sr then tax mangr Arthur Andersen 1977–84, sr tax mangr then tax ptnr John Fairhurst & Co 1984–87, ptnr Price Waterhouse (now PricewaterhouseCoopers LLP) 1990–2009 (sr tax mangr 1987–90, memb UK Supervisory Bd 2003–09), Islamic finance conslt 2010–; chm Manchester Branch Inst of Taxation 1985–87, memb Cncl Chartered Inst of Taxation 2003–15, memb Technical Ctee ACT 2004–12; memb Conservative Muslim Forum v-chm 2007–12, dep chm 2012–14, chm 2014–; fndr memb Muslim Jewish Forum of Gtr

Manchester 2004– (co-chair 2013–), patron and chair of donors Curriculum for Cohesion 2011–, patron Monitoring Anti-Muslim Attacks 2012–15, memb Advsy Cncl Three Faiths Forum 2009–; memb Cncl Manchester and Dist Chess Assoc 1983–2014 (pres 1981–83), finance dir Br Chess Fedn 1985–89; memb Cncl Univ of Salford 2012–14; listed in: Asian Power 100 2005, Muslim Power 100 2007; Alumnus of the Year Clare Coll Cambridge 2014; assoc memb ACT 1995, FCA (ACA 1977), FCInstT 2000 (ATII 1978); *Publications* The Taxation of Equity Derivatives and Structured Products (contrib, 2002), Euromoney Encyclopedia of Islamic Finance (contrib, 2009), The Chancellor Guide to the Legal and Shari'a Aspects of Islamic Finance (contrib, 2009), Islamic Investment Banking: Emerging Trends, Developments and Opportunities (contrib, 2010), Global Growth, Opportunities and Challenges in the Sukuk Market (contrib, 2011), Cross Border Taxation of Islamic Finance in the MENA Region – Phase One (lead author, 2013); *Recreations* chess, go (Japanese board game), listening to classical and modern music, reading science fiction; *Clubs* Carlton; *Style*— Mohammed Amin, Esq, MBE; ☎ 07802 788357, e-mail mohammed.amin@btinternet.com, website www.mohammedamin.com

AMINI, Hossein; s of Iradj Amini and Vida Amini; *Educ* Bryanston, Wadham Coll Oxford (scholarship); *m* Alexandra; 2 da (Nina, Nieve); *Career* writer; *Film* incl: The Dying of the Light 1994 (TV film, BAFTA nomination Best Single Drama), Jude 1996 (Michael Powell Award for Best Br Film Edinburgh Film Festival, Best Film Dinard Film Festival), The Wings of the Dove 1997 (Oscar nomination Best Adapted Screenplay 1998, nomination Best Adapted Screenplay Writer's Guild of America 1998, nomination Best Adapted Screenplay BAFTA Awards 1998) 1997, In a Lonely Place 1997, Four Feathers 2000, Shanghai 2000, Gangs of New York (draft for Martin Scorsese) 2001, Mila 18 2002; *Publications* Jude (1996), Wings of the Dove (1998); *Style*— Hossein Amini, Esq; ✉ c/o Curtis Brown, Haymarket House, 28–29 Haymarket, London SW1Y 4SP (☎ 020 7396 6600, fax 020 7396 0110)

AMIS, Martin Louis; s of Sir Kingsley William Amis, CBE (d 1995), and his 1 w, Hilary Ann, *née* Bardwell; *b* 25 August 1949; *Educ* Exeter Coll Oxford (BA); *m* 1, (m dis 1996), Antonia; m 2, 1998, Isabel; *Career* writer; literary ed New Statesman 1977–79, special writer The Observer 1980–; tennis corr The New Yorker 1992–; Outstanding Achievement Award Galaxy Nat Book Award 2010; FRSL 1983; *Books* The Rachel Papers (1973, Somerset Maugham Award 1974), Dead Babies (1975), Success (1978), Other People: A Mystery Story (1981), Money (1984), The Moronic Inferno and Other Visits to America (1986), Einstein's Monsters (1987), London Fields (1989), Time's Arrow (1991), The Information (1995), Night Train (1997), Heavy Water and Other Stories (short stories, 1998), Experience (2000, James Tait Black Memorial Prize), The War Against Cliché: Essays and Reviews 1971–2000 (2001), Koba the Dread: Laughter and the Twenty Million (2002), Yellow Dog (2003), House of Meetings (2006), The Second Plane (2008), The Pregnant Widow (2010); *Style*— Martin Amis, Esq; ✉ c/o Wylie Agency, 17 Bedford Square, London WC1B 3JA (☎ 020 7908 5900)

AMORY; *see also:* HeathcoatAmory

AMOS, Gideon John; OBE (2009); s of Francis John Clarke Amos, CBE (d 2003), and Geraldine Amos, MBE, *née* Sutton (d 2014); *b* 16 January 1965, Liverpool; *Educ* Wells Cathedral Sch, Oxford Poly (BA), Oxford Brookes Univ (DipArch, DipUD, MA); *m* 6 May 1995, Caroline, da of David Ellis; *Career* dep pres Oxford Poly Students Union 1988–89, architectural asst R J Harrison Architects 1989–90, devpt designer WS Atkins 1994–97, dir Planning Aid for London 1997–2000; Town and Country Planning Assoc (TCPA): dir 2000–06, chief exec 2006–10, vice-pres 2011–; cmmr Infrastructure Planning Cmmn 2010–12; inspector Planning Inspectorate 2012–15; nat planning advsr GL Hearn 2015–; memb Bd Swan Housing Assoc 2007–; ptnr French Weir Affordable Homes 2011–; memb Planning Advsy Gp Dept for Communities and Local Govt 2003–10, chair DCLG Eco-Devpt Gp 2008–10; cncllr Oxford City Cncl 1992–96 (gp ldr 1995–96); govr Oxford Poly 1988–89; memb: Hackney Soc, Taunton Civic Soc; RIBA 1994, MRTPI 2004; *Publications* Programme for Sustainable Communities (co-author, 2001), Connecting England: A Framework for Regional Development (ed, 2006), Planning Policy Statement: Eco-Trowns – A supplement to PPS1 (contrib, 2009), Reports: Ipswich Rail Chord Order (2012), Triton Knoll Wind Farm Order (2013), East Anglia One Wind Farm Order (2014), Tidal Lagoon Swansea Bay Order (2015); *Clubs* Nat Lib; *Style*— Gideon Amos, Esq, OBE; ✉ National Liberal Club, 1 Whitehall Place, London SW1A 2HE (e-mail enquiries@infrastructure.gsi.gov.uk)

AMOS, Stephen K; *Career* comedian; stand-up incl: Stephen K Amos (Edinburgh Fringe Festival) 2001, 2003, 2004 and 2005, Amused Moose Comedy Star Seach Final (Edinburgh Fringe) 2004, Talk RadiO, Stephen K Amos & Guests: It Might Just Happen and All of Me (Edinburgh Fringe) 2006, Stephen K Amos: More of Me (Edinburgh Fringe) 2007, Britcom 2007 (Montreal Comedy Festival) 2007, Stephen K Amos: Weekend Talk Show (Edinburgh Fringe) 2007, Weekend Chat Show (Edinburgh Fringe) 2008, Stephen K Amos Gets Next To You (Melbourne Fringe Festival) 2008, Find The Funny (Prague Fringe Festival and Edinburgh Fringe) 2008, (UK tour) 2008–09, (Adelaide Fringe Festival) 2009; nominated Richard Pryor Award 2004, Best Stand-up Time Out Live Award 2004, nominated Best Compere Chortle Comedy Award 2004, 2007 and 2008, Spirit of the Festival Award NZ Comedy Festival 2005, Best Int Guest Comedian and Best Int Comedy NZ Comedy Guild Awards 2007; *Radio* Jon Richardson Radio Show (BBC6 Music), Stand Up on 7 (BBC Radio 7), The Odd Half Hour (BBC Radio 4), The Blame Game (BBCNI), Act Your Age (BBC Radio 4), 4 Stands Up (BBC Radio 4), Out To Lunch (BBC Radio 2), The Big Night In, Sean Lock and Friends at the Fringe, Hot Gossip (BBC Radio 2); *Television* appearances incl: The Royal Variety Show (ITV), Have I Got News For You (BBC), Live at the Apollo (BBC1), Mock The Week (BBC2), Newsnight (BBC), Stand Up Show (BBC), The 11 O'Clock Show (Channel 4); *Theatre* One Flew Over The Cuckoo's Nest (Assembly Rooms, Gielgud Theatre and Edinburgh Fringe Festival) 2004–05; *Film* Absolute Beginners, Hawks, Soweto, Young Soul Rebels, Downtown Largos; *Style*— Mr Stephen K Amos; ✉ c/o Lisa White, Glorious Management Ltd, Lower Ground Floor, 79 Noel Road, London N1 8HE (☎ 020 7704 6555, e-mail lisa@glorioustalent.co.uk)

AMOS, Baroness (Life Peer UK 1997), of Brondesbury, in the London Borough of Brent; Valerie Amos; PC (2003); *b* 13 March 1954; *Educ* Univ of Warwick (BA), Univ of Birmingham (MA), UEA; *Career* Lambeth Borough Cncl 1981–82, women's advsr London Borough of Camden 1983–85, head of mgmnt servs London Borough of Hackney 1987–89 (head of trg and devpt 1985–87); chief exec Equal Opportunities Cmmn 1989–94, md Quality and Equality 1994–95, dir Amos Fraser Bernard 1995–98; a Baroness in Waiting (Govt whip) 1998–2001, Parly under-sec of state FCO 2001–03, sec of state for International Devpt 2003, ldr House of Lords and Lord Pres of the Cncl 2003–07; high cmmr to Australia 2009–11; cmmr Fulbright Cmmn 2009–10; under sec gen humanitarian affrs UN 2010–; former non-exec dir UCLH; author and presenter numerous papers at nat and int confs; external examiner Univ of Liverpool 1991–97, hon prof Thames Valley Univ, memb Advsy Bd Global Health Gp Univ of Calif 2008–; former memb: Cncl Inst of Employment Studies, Cncl King's Fund; former dep chair Runnymede Tst; chair: Bd of Govrs RCN, AFIYA Tst (formerly), Royal African Soc 2008–; former dir Hampstead Theatre, former tstee Inst of Public Policy Research; Hon Dr jur Univ of Warwick, Hon Dr jur Univ of Staffordshire, Hon Dr jur Univ of Manchester; FRSA; *Style*— The Rt Hon Baroness Amos, PC; ✉ House of Lords, London SW1A 0PW

AMPHLETT, Philip Nicholas; s of Colin Bernard Amphlett, of Wootton Village, Oxon, and Hilda, *née* Price (d 1972); *b* 20 October 1948; *Educ* Winchester, Balliol Coll Oxford (BA); *m* 4 Aug 1969, Marjolein Erantha, da of Jan Cornelius de Vries (d 1952), of Eindhoven, Holland; 2 da (Jessica b 9 Jan 1970, Catherine b 14 Nov 1974), 1 s (Jan b 17 Aug 1972 d 2001); *Career* trainee mangr W H Brandts Sons and Co Ltd 1971–73, dir Henry Ansbacher and Co Ltd 1981–85 (joined 1973), sr vice-pres Bank Julius Baer and Co Ltd 1985–97; EFG Private Bank: exec dir 1997–2006, dep head of private banking 2006–; *Recreations* sailing, swimming, tennis; *Style*— Philip Amphlett, Esq; ✉ Howletts, Great Hallingbury, Bishop's Stortford, Hertfordshire CM22 7TR (☎ 01279 654563); Ballaminers Cottage, Little Petherick, Wadebridge, Cornwall PL27 7QT

AMSTELL, Simon Marc; *b* 29 November 1979, London; *Career* comedian, presenter, writer and actor; stand-up incl: Edinburgh Fringe Festival 2005, 2006, 2007 and 2009, Do Nothing (Royal Court Theatre) 2009 and (Vicar Street Dublin) 2010, Numb (UK and US tours) 2012; *Television* presenter: Popworld (Channel 4) 2000–06, Never Mind the Buzzcocks (BBC 2) 2006–09 (Best Entertainment Performance RTS Award 2006, Best Comedy Entertainment Personality Br Comedy Award 2007); actor and co-writer Grandma's House (BBC 2) 2010–; *DVD* Do Nothing (2010); *Style*— Mr Simon Amstell; ✉ c/o KBJ Management, 22 Rathbone Street, London W1T 1LA

AMYES, Prof Sebastian Giles Becket; s of Julian Charles Becket Amyes (d 1992), of London, and Katherine Anne Smith, *née* Allan (d 1999); *b* 6 May 1949, Cheshire; *Educ* Cranleigh Sch, UCL (BSc, PhD), Univ of Reading (MSc), Univ of London (DSc); *m* 1, 17 April 1976 (m dis 2006), Dorothy Mary, da of William Thomas Gregory; 1 s (Rupert William Becket b 26 May 1978), 1 da (Alexandra Katherine Becket b 15 Nov 1979); m 2, 15 May 2011, Hilary-Kay, da of John Whiteford Young; *Career* teaching fell Sch of Pharmacy Univ of London 1974–77; Univ of Edinburgh: lectr 1977–88, reader 1988–92, prof of microbial chemotherapy 1992–, head Medical Microbiology Dept 1997–2001; Annual Science award Royal Pharmaceutical Soc 1984, C L Oakley lectr Pathological Soc 1987; Dr (hc) Semmelweis Medical Univ 2004; hon memb Hungarian Microbiology Soc 2007; FRCPath 1995 (MRCPath 1985), FIBiol 1988; *Books* Antimicrobial Chemotherapy, Magic Bullets: Lost Horizons, Antibacterial Chemotherapy, Bacteria VSI, Bacteria A Very Short Introduction, Guide to Antioboitic Usage; author of 520 pubns; *Recreations* fishing, foreign exploration, antique maps, opera; *Style*— Prof Sebastian Amyes; ✉ Medical Microbiology, College of Medicine and Veterinary Medicine, Chancellors Building, 49 Little France Crescent, Edinburgh EH16 4SB (☎ 0131 242 6652, fax 0131 242 6611, e-mail s.g.b.amyes@ed.ac.uk)

ANAND, Rooney; *Career* Greene King plc: memb Bd 2001–, md Brewing Co 2001–05, chief exec 2005–; *Style*— Rooney Anand, Esq; ✉ Greene King plc, Westgate Brewery, Bury St Edmunds, Suffolk IP33 1QT

ANCASTER, Earl of ; *see:* Willoughby de Eresby, Baroness

ANCRAM, Rt Hon Michael; *see:* Lothian, 13 Marquess of

ANDERSON, Alexander Beveridge (Sandy); CBE (2015, OBE 2010), DL (1991); s of John Weir Anderson, of Methil, Fife, and Elizabeth Warrender, *née* Beveridge (d 1979); *b* 16 April 1944; *Educ* Buckhaven HS, Heriot-Watt Univ (BSc); *m* 1970, Mary Bell Scott, *née* Wemyss (d 2001); 3 s; *Career* general mangr ICI Teesside Operations 1989–94, dir of engrg ICI plc 1994–96, ops dir Tioxide Gp Ltd 1994–97, sr vice-pres of technology ICI plc 1997–2000, ret; dir Eutech Engineering Solutions Ltd 1994–2001, dir ICI Pakistan Ltd 1998–2000, chm Ensus UK 2005–11; chm: Teesside Training Enterprise 1990–94, Teesside Tomorrow Ltd 1990–94; dir: Teesside Devpt Co 1989–98, Teesside TEC 1991–94, Tees Valley LEP 2010–15; govr Durham Sch 2003–13, chm Bd of Govrs Univ of Teesside 2005–14; Hon LLD Univ of Teesside 2015; FIChemE 1990, FREng 1997; *Recreations* golf, reading, music, theatre, gardening; *Style*— Sandy Anderson, Esq, CBE, DL, FREng; ✉ Carperby Lodge, 39 Abbey Road, Darlington, County Durham DL3 8LR (☎ 01325 354386, fax 01325 360389, e-mail sandy_anderson@talk21.com)

ANDERSON, Dr Alun Mark; s of Peter Marchmont Anderson, of Denbigh, N Wales, and Jane Watkin James; *b* 27 May 1948; *Educ* Rhyl GS, Univ of Sussex (BSc), Univ of Edinburgh (PhD), Univ of Oxford (IBM res fell), Univ of Kyoto Japan (Royal Soc fell); *Career* Nature (Int Jl of Sci): news and views ed 1980–83, Tokyo bureau chief 1983–86, Washington bureau chief 1986–90, int ed Science 1991–92; New Scientist: ed 1992–2000, ed-in-chief and publishing dir 2000–05, sr conslt 2005–; dir IPC Magazines 1997–98, dir Xconomy.com 2007–; memb: Royal Soc Ctee on the Public Understanding of Science 1997–2000, Royal Soc Faraday Prize Ctee 1999–2004, Br Cncl Science, Engrg and Environment Ctee 2001–07, Cncl Royal Inst 2005–10, Cncl Soc for Experimental Biology 2008–15; tstee St Andrews Prize 1999–2016; Ed of the Year BSME 1993, 1995 and 1997, Eds' Ed of the Year 1997; memb Cncl Univ of Sussex 1998–2001; *Books* Science Technology In Japan (1984, 2 edn 1990), After the Ice: Death and Geopolitics in the New Arctic (2009). The Fast-Changing Arctic: Rethinking Arctic Security for a Warmer World (2013); *Recreations* mountain walking, photography; *Style*— Dr Alun Anderson; ✉ New Scientist, Lacon House, 84 Theobald's Road, London WC1X 8NS (☎ 020 7611 1204, e-mail alun.anderson@gmail.com)

ANDERSON, Clive Stuart; *Educ* Selwyn Coll Cambridge (MA, pres Cambridge Footlights); *Career* television presenter and barrister; called to the Bar Middle Temple 1976; host The Cabaret Upstairs (BBC Radio 4) 1986–88, chm Whose Line Is It Anyway? (Radio 4 1988, Channel 4 1988–98), host Clive Anderson Talks Back (Channel 4) 1989–95; presenter: Notes and Queries (BBC2) 1991–93, Great Railway Journeys of the World: Hong Kong to Outer Mongolia (BBC2) 1994, Our Man In... (documentary series, BBC2) 1995–96 and Our Man In Heaven & Hell 1996, Clive Anderson All Talk (BBC 1) 1996–1999, Unreliable Evidence (BBC Radio 4) 1998–, If I Ruled the World (BBC2) 1998–99, Clive Anderson Now (BBC1) 2001, CA Bites the Ballot (Radio 2), The Real..... (Radio 5), Clive Anderson's Chat Room (BBC Radio 2) 2004–, Back in the Day (Channel 4) 2005, Loose Ends (BBC Radio 4) 2008–; occasional presenter/guest numerous other progs; formerly scriptwriter: Weekending (BBC Radio 4), The Frankie Howerd Variety Show (Radio 2), Not the Nine O'Clock News (BBC2), Alas Smith & Jones (notably head-to-head dialogues, BBC2), Around Midnight (LWT), The World According to Smith & Jones (LWT); memb revue group An Evening Without (toured England, Scotland and Aust) 1979, numerous stand-up comedy appearances Comedy Store and other venues in early 1980s; author of various articles in The Times, The Observer and The Guardian, former regular columnist Sunday Correspondent, regular columnist Independent on Sunday; pres The Woodland Tst 2004–; *Awards* Comedy Presenter of the Year RTS Awards 1991, Top Channel 4 Presenter British Comedy Awards 1992; for Whose Line Is It Anyway?: Best Light Entertainment Prog RTS Awards 1990, Best International Comedy Series ACE Awards 1991, Best Light Entertainment Prog Br Academy Awards 1991 (also nominated 1990 and 1992), also nominated for Top Entertainment Series Br Comedy Awards 1991 and Best Popular Arts Prog International Emmy Awards 1991, TRIC Best ITV/Channel 4 TV Personality Award 1995; for The Real...: Sony Gold Award 2004; *Style*— Clive Anderson, Esq; ✉ Curtis Brown, Haymarket House, 28–29 Haymarket, London SW1Y 4SP (☎ 020 7393 4400, fax 020 7393 4401, e-mail cb@curtisbrown.co.uk)

ANDERSON, (Richard James) Colin; OBE (1997); s of Richard Henry Anderson (d 1979), and Roseina, *née* Blaney; *b* 11 May 1954; *Educ* Regent House GS, Univ of Ulster; *m* 18 May 1978, Hilary Ann, da of Wilson Somerville Smyth; 2 s (Kyle, Jeffrey), 1 da (Kelly); *Career* trainee Thomson Newspapers Orgn, fndr chm and princ shareholder ASG Ltd, chm Anderson Spratt Gp Holdings Ltd; co-chm Heenan Anderson Cmmn 2014–15; visiting prof Sch of Psychology and Communication Univ of Ulster; memb NI Tourist Bd 1988–94, pres NI C of C and Industry 1996–97 and 1997–98, dir NI Quality Centre 1993–96, chm NI Screen 2001–08, former memb Cncl NI Branch Inst of Mktg, memb

CBI NI Cncl; rugby rep for: Ulster, Ards Rugby Club, CIYMS Rugby Club; Duke of Edinburgh's Gold Award (memb Ctee NI 1989–92); MInstD, FCIM; *Recreations* yachting, skiing, golf, rugby; *Clubs* Royal Ulster Yacht, Killyleagh Yacht; *Style—* R J C Anderson, OBE; ✉ Anderson Spratt Group Holdings Ltd, Anderson House, Holywood Road, Belfast BT4 2GU (☎ 028 9080 2020, fax 028 9080 2021, e-mail canderson@asgh.com)

ANDERSON, David; MP; *b* 2 December 1953; *Educ* Maltby GS, Durham Tech Coll, Doncaster Tech Coll, Univ of Durham; *Career* former miner (active in 1984–85 strike), former care worker and lay trade union official; MP (Lab) Blaydon 2005–; PPS: DfES and DIUS 2006–08, FCO 2008–; shadow sec of state for NI 2016–, shadow sec of state for Scotland 2016–; memb: NEC Bd Unison, Gen Cncl TUC; *Style—* David Anderson, Esq, MP; ✉ House of Commons, London SW1A 0AA

ANDERSON, David Munro; s of late Alexander Anderson, and late Jessica Hope, *née* Vincent-Innes; *b* 15 December 1937; *Educ* Strathallan Sch; *m* 1, Veronica Jane, da of late Reginald Eric Stevens; 2 s (Angus b 1 Oct 1967, Duncan b 10 Nov 1968), 1 da (Lucy b 29 Sept 1973); m 2, Ruth, da of late Lt-Col E Lewis-Bowen (late RAVC); *Career* cmmnd: The Black Watch 1956–59, The London Scottish 1963–68; chm: Allingham Anderson Roll Ross Ltd 1990–96, Anderson Finance Ltd 1996–, Anderson Quantrend Ltd 1996–; dir Malcolm Innes Gallery 1990–2000; churchwarden Holy Innocents Lamarsh 1972–2007, tstee Friends of Lamarsh Church; MSI; *Recreations* shooting, skiing, gundog training, the arts; *Clubs* Caledonian; *Style—* David Anderson, Esq; ✉ The Old Gardens, Kersey, Ipswich, Suffolk IP7 6ED

ANDERSON, David William Kinloch; QC (1999); s of Sir Eric Anderson, KT, FRSE, *qv*, of Kingham, and Poppy, *née* Mason; *b* 5 July 1961, Edinburgh; *Educ* New Coll Oxford (open scholarship, MA), Downing Coll Cambridge (BA); *m* 1989, Margaret Elizabeth, *née* Beeton; 2 da (Frances Elizabeth b 1993, Isobel Kinloch b 1995); *Career* lawyer Covington & Burling, Washington DC 1985–86; stagiaire Cabinet of Lord Cockfield EC 1987–88; barrister Brick Court Chambers 1988–, recorder 2004–13, bencher Middle Temple 2007–, judge of the Courts of Appeal of Guernsey and Jersey 2014–; KCL: visiting lectr 1989–95, visiting fell 1995–99, visiting prof of law 1999–; tstee: Governing Body Br Assoc for Central and Eastern Europe 2002–08, Br Inst of Int and Comparative Law 2005–09; memb Advsy Bd Sch of Slavonic and E European Studies UCL 2007–10; ind reviewer of terrorism legislation 2011–; memb RIIA; *Publications* References to the European Court (1995, 2 edn 2002), A Question of Trust (2015), various articles in legal jls; *Recreations* mountain biking, sea kayaking, history; *Clubs* Alpine, Athenaeum; *Style—* David Anderson, Esq, QC; ✉ Brick Court Chambers, 7–8 Essex Street, London WC2R 3LD (☎ 020 7379 3550, website www.brickcourt.co.uk and https://terrorismlegislationreviewer.independent.gov.uk)

ANDERSON, Douglas Hardinge; s of James Alasdair Anderson (d 1982), of Tullichewan, and Lady Flavia Joan Lucy Anderson, *née* Giffard (d 1998); *b* 8 August 1934; *Educ* Eton; *m* 1, 1962 (m dis), Mary Jenkins; 1 da (Lucy Elizabeth b 1962), 1 s (James Henry Wallace b 1964); m 2, 1974, Veronica, da of John Markes; 1 da (Sophie Esme b 1977); *Career* portrait painter and wildlife artist; trained with Pietro Annigoni in Florence; exhbns in Florence, Munich, RA London, Royal Hibernian Acad Ireland, Gothenburg, Stockholm, New York and others; paintings in private collections in Europe, USA, etc; cmmnd for portraits of HM The Queen, HM Queen Elizabeth The Queen Mother and HRH The Princess of Wales (for The Royal Marsden Hosp); memb RSPP 1957; *Recreations* painting, gardening, orchids and cooking; *Style—* Douglas Anderson, Esq; ✉ Luthy Cottage, Recess, Co Galway, H91 WF2H Ireland (☎ 00 353 95 51076)

ANDERSON, Douglas Kinloch; OBE (1983); s of William James Kinloch Anderson, of Edinburgh, and Margaret, *née* Gowenlock Harper; *b* 19 February 1939; *Educ* George Watson's Coll Edinburgh, Univ of St Andrews (MA), Univ of Edinburgh; *m* 14 June 1962, Deirdre Anne, da of Leonard Walter Loryman (d 1985); 1 da (Claire Deirdre b 1964), 2 s (Peter Douglas b 1968, John William b 1972); *Career* Kinloch Anderson Ltd: dir 1962–72, md 1972–, chm 1980– (Queen's Award for Export Achievement 1979); chm Kinloch Anderson (Holdings) Ltd; dir: F&C Private Equity Tst plc; pres: Edinburgh Assoc of Royal Tradesmen 1986–88, Edinburgh C of C 1988–90, Royal Warrant Holders Assoc 1994–95; memb: Bd Scottish Tourist Bd 1986–92, Edinburgh Festival Cncl 1988–90, Scottish Ctee IOD; hon memb St Andrews Soc Washington DC 1985; Edinburgh Merchant Company: asst 1976–79, treas 1988–90, Master 1990–92, moderator 2010; Leith High Constables, Freeman City of London; *Recreations* fishing, golf, travel, reading; *Clubs* The Honourable Co of Edinburgh Golfers, Caledonian; *Style—* Douglas Kinloch Anderson, Esq, OBE; ✉ Brockham Green, 36A Kings Road, Longniddry, East Lothian EH32 0NN; Kinloch Anderson Ltd, Commercial Street/Dock Street, Leith, Edinburgh EH6 6EY (☎ 0131 555 1355, fax 0131 555 1392, e-mail douglaska@kinlochanderson.com)

ANDERSON, Eric George; s of Charles G Anderson (d 1984), of Alyth, Perthshire, and Margery Drysdale, *née* Taylor (d 1992); *b* 7 June 1940; *Educ* Dundee HS, Univ of St Andrews (MB ChB), Univ of Salford (MSc), Dip Sports Med (Jt Scottish Royal Colls); *m* 26 March 1966, Elizabeth Clare (Liz), da of Donald George Cracknell (d 1995), of Appin, Argyll; 1 s (Colin b 1967), 2 da (Fiona b 1969, Heather b 1973); *Career* sr registrar Robert Jones and Agnes Hunt Orthopaedic Hosp Oswestry and Birmingham Accident Hosp 1973–78, conslt orthopaedic surgn Western Infirmary and Gartnavel Gen Hosp Glasgow 1978–97, hon clinical sr lectr Univ of Glasgow 1978–97, clinical assoc Univ of Strathclyde 1979–2000, visiting lectr in surgery Glasgow Caledonian Univ 1994–2007; former: memb Surgical Faculty Coll of Podiatrists, hon med advsr Scot Amateur Swimming Assoc, pres Br Orthopaedic Foot Surgery Soc, dep ed Injury; sec-gen Int Fedn of Foot and Ankle Socs (fndr memb 1999), sec Euro Foot and Ankle Soc (emeritus memb 2001); memb Editorial Bd: Foot, Foot and Ankle Surgery; memb: Int Soc Prosthetics and Orthotics 1976, Br Orthopaedic Foot Surgery Soc 1981 (hon memb 2000); int memb American Orthopaedic Foot and Ankle Soc 1996; hon memb Société Française de Médecine et Chirurgie du Pied; Hon FChS, FRCSEd 1971, FRSM 1973, FBOA 1978, FRCSGlas 1981; *Books* contrib: Common Foot Disorders (1989), The Foot and its Disorders (1991), Airds Companion to Surgical Studies (1997), Atlas of Foot Surgery (1997); *Recreations* philately, modelling buses and tramways, music, golf; *Style—* Eric Anderson, Esq; ✉ 102 Prestonfield, Milngavie, Glasgow G62 7PZ (☎ 0141 956 3594, e-mail ericg.anderson@ntlworld.com)

ANDERSON, Dr Gordon; *b* 22 May 1954; *Educ* Univ of Dundee (BArch), Univ of Aberdeen (PhD); *m* Catherine Ann, *née* MacInnes; *Career* architect; various architectural appts in private and public sector Western Isles 1981–96, princ Anderson Associates Stornoway 1996–; memb: Assoc of Planning Supervisors, Assoc of Project Managers; RIBA, FRIAS 2001 (current memb Cncl); *Recreations* reading, art, gardening; *Style—* Dr Gordon Anderson; ✉ Tigh-na-Beinne, 68 Leurbost, Lochs, Isle of Lewis HS2 9NS (☎ 01851 860226); Anderson Associates, Chartered Architects, 20 North Beach, Stornoway, Isle of Lewis, Western Isles HS1 2XQ (☎ 01851 701500, fax 01851 701515, website www.andersonassociatesltd.com)

ANDERSON, Hamish; s of Dr James Anderson, of Plymouth, and Joan, *née* Caughey; *b* 12 July 1948; *Educ* Clifton Coll, Kingston Poly (LLB), UCL (LLM); *m* 1, 1972 (m dis); 1 s (James b 1975), 1 da (Bryony b 1977); m 2, 2002, Amanda Jane Le Page; *Career* admitted slr 1973; pt/t lectr in law and res asst Kingston Poly 1969–71, licensed insolvency practitioner 1987–; ptnr: Bond Pearce 1977–96 (joined 1971), Norton Rose Fulbright LLP 1996–2016 (conslt 2016–); hon prof Nottingham Trent Univ, visiting fell Kingston Univ; sometime memb Insolvency Practices Cncl, former vice-chm Jt Insolvency Examination Bd, former memb Cncl R3, former ed Recovery, memb Editorial Bd Insolvency Law & Practice, former publications offr Ctee J (creditor's rights) Int Bar Assoc, memb Int Insolvency Inst; past pres Insolvency Lawyers' Assoc; memb: Law Soc (memb Insolvency Sub-Ctee), City of London Law Soc (memb Insolvency Ctee (chm 2007–16)); Hon LLD Kingston; *Books* Administrators – Part II of the Insolvency Act 1986, Anderson's Notes on Insolvency Conveyancing, Agricultural Charges and Receivership, Commercial Aspects of Trusts and Fiduciary Obligations (contrib), Current Issues in Insolvency Law (contrib), Lightman and Moss: The Law of Receivers of Companies (jt ed), Tolley's Insolvency Law (contrib), Banks and Remedies (contrib), Practitioner's Guide to Cross-Border Insolvencies (contrib), Cross-Border Security and Insolvency (contrib), Practitioner's Guide to the Role of Directors and their Duties and Responsibilities (contrib), Transaction Avoidance in Insolvencies (conslt ed), Treatment of Contracts in Insolvency (contrib), Ranking and Priority of Creditors (contrib); *Style—* Hamish Anderson, Esq; ✉ Norton Rose Fulbright LLP, 3 More London Riverside, London SE1 2AQ (☎ 020 7283 6000, fax 020 7283 6500, e-mail hamish.anderson@nortonrosefulbright.com)

ANDERSON, Iain David; MBE (2014); *Educ* Univ of St Andrews (BSc), Univ of Manchester (MBChB, MD); *Career* conslt surgeon Hope Hosp Salford 1995–; tutor in surgical critical care RCS 1994–2007, hon sr lectr Univ of Manchester; dir Emergency Surgery Assoc of Surgeons of GB and I; Hallett Prize 1985, Assoc of Surgeons of GB and I Prize 1994, Hunterian Professorship 1996; FRCS, Hon FRACS 2014; *Publications* multiple pubns on emergency surgery and intestinal fistulae; *Recreations* gardening, golf, skiing; *Clubs* Bolton Golf, Lamlash Golf; *Style—* Iain Anderson, Esq, MBE; ✉ Salford Royal NHS Foundation Trust, Stott Lane, Salford M6 8HD; Spire Manchester Hospital, Russell Road, Whalley Range, Manchester M16 8AJ

ANDERSON, Prof Jack Maxwell; CBE (1999); *b* 2 June 1928, Ballymena, Co Antrim; *Career* architect: ptnr Rowell and Anderson 1960–71, conslt architect/designer 1972–79, conslt OECD Paris 1973–74, assoc BAP 1979–81, ptnr BAP London 1981–98, conslt architect/designer 1998–; princ lectr/dir of studies Mackintosh Sch of Architecture Univ of Glasgow 1969–74, prof and dean of faculty of architecture Univ of Manitoba 1974–79, visiting prof of architecture Univ of Manitoba 1979–83, visiting research prof Univ of Washington 1984, visiting prof Bartlett Sch of Architecture Univ Coll London 1997–; chm: Advsy Ctee CIRIA (Construction Industry Research and Info Assoc) 1984–89, UK Govt Building Standards Ctee 1990–2000; memb: Royal Glasgow Inst of Fine Arts 1981–, E&PS Research Cncl Coll of Assessors 1989–92; assessor Scottish Govt Building Standards Review 2000–01; vice-pres (Europe) Cwlth Assoc of Architects 1984–85; Freeman and Liveryman Worshipful Company of Chartered Architects; hon fell Royal Acad of Music; hon architect Royal Coll of Organists 1984–90, hon fell Inst of Building Control; FRIBA 1967 (memb Cncl 1983–86, chm Research Steering Ctee 1983–91), RIAS 1967, FCSD 1986; *Recreations* art, music, opera, theatre, walking; *Clubs* Athenaeum; *Style—* Prof Jack Anderson, CBE

ANDERSON, James Michael; OBE (2015); *b* 30 July 1982, Burnley, Lancs; *m* Daniella; *Career* cricketer; Lancashire CCC 2002–; England: 30 Test caps, over 100 one day appearances, 34 Twenty20 appearances, Test debut v Zimbabwe Lord's 2003, one day debut v Aust Melbourne 2002, memb squad World Cup 2003; NBC Denis Compton Award 2002; *Style—* James Anderson, Esq, OBE

ANDERSON, Jonathan (J W); *Educ* London Coll of Fashion; *Career* designer; launched J.W. Anderson 2008, creative dir Loewe 2013–; *Awards* Emerging Talent in Ready-To-Wear Br Fashion Awards 2012, The New Establishment Award Br Fashion Awards 2013, Designer of the Year GQ Spain 2014, Menswear Designer of the Year Br Fashion Awards 2014, Fashion Star Award Fashion Gp Int (FGI) 2015; *Style—* J W Anderson, Esq; ✉ J.W. Anderson Ltd, 97 Springfield House, 5 Tyssen Street, London E8 2LZ

ANDERSON, Keith David; s of Dr Redvers Edward Anderson (d 1947), of Luton, Beds, and Norah Mary Agnes, *née* Payne (d 1972); *b* 3 June 1939; *Educ* Alton Castle Sch, St Bernardine's Coll Buckingham; *m* 1, 27 July 1963 (m dis 1974), Sarah Jane, *née* Beddow; 1 s (Timothy Stuart b 26 Sept 1967), 1 da (Jane Ann b 24 May 1964); m 2, 21 March 1975, Susan Lesley, da of late Gordon Rodney Kent; 1 s (Stuart David b 20 July 1978); *Career* Nat Serv 1959–61, RAPC attached to RNF in 1 Gurkha Inf Bde; local govt offr Aylesbury 1954–64; BBC TV: mangr Alexandra Palace 1965–69, organiser Arts Dept 1970–74, prog planning mangr 1974–78, head prog planning resources 1978–82, gen mangr prog planning 1982–89, controller planning and prog servs 1989–92; md: Anderson Associates 1992–, Production Finance and Management Ltd (PFM) 1992–2000; dir: Stock Productions Ltd 2000–03, Windmill TV Productions Ltd 2000–04, Track Prodns Ltd 2000–06, Deleste Prodns Ltd 2000–; chm: Horsebridge Prodns Ltd 2001–10, Highpoint Productions Ltd 2006–08; advsr V Good Productions; memb BAFTA 2008–; FRTS 1991, MInstD; *Recreations* golf, squash; *Clubs* Groucho, Ellesborough Golf; *Style—* Keith Anderson, Esq

ANDERSON, Prof Malcolm; s of Wilfred Roy Anderson, and Frances Betty Anderson; *b* Leicestershire; *Educ* Univ of Nottingham (BSc), Univ of Cambridge (PhD), Univ of Bristol (DSc); *m* 1 April 1972, Elizabeth Ann Roger; 1 da (Rebecca Jane Anderson); *Career* sr research hydrologist US Corps Engrs Waterways Experiment Station Vicksburg MS, sr research geotechnical engr Geotechnical Control Office Hong Kong, pro-vice-chllr (research) Univ of Bristol 2005–09; sr landslide risk reduction specialist World Bank 2011–; Quarter Centenary visiting fell Emmanuel Coll Cambridge, visiting prof of hydrology Univ of Oxford 2010–14; fndr and ed-in-chief Hydrological Processes, fndr and jt series ed Advances in Hydrological Processes, memb Editorial Advsy Bd Water Science and Technol 1994–2014; memb Cncl NERC, memb Tech Opportunities Panel EPSRC; technical advsr Orgn of Eastern Caribbean States; Gill Meml Award for Research in Geomorphology RGS, Senior Science Fellowship Nuffield Fndn, Trevithick Premium Triennial Award ICE; life fell Indian Assoc of Hydrologists; FICE, CEng; *Publications* jt ed: Hydrological Forecasting (1985), Slope Stability: geotechnical engineering and geomorphology (1987), Modelling Geomorphological Systems (1988), Process Studies in Hillslope Hydrology (1990), Floodplain Processes (1996), Advances in Hillslope Processes (1996), Model Validation: perspectives in hydrological science (2001), Encyclopaedia of Hydrological Sciences (2005), Landslides: hazard and risk (2005); Community-based Landslide Risk Reduction: managing disasters in small steps (jt author, 2013); numerous research pubns in hydrological sciences and geotechnics; *Recreations* sailing; *Style—* Prof Malcolm Anderson; ✉ Senate House, University of Bristol, Tyndall Avenue, Bristol BS8 1TH

ANDERSON, Mark Andrew D'Arcy; s of Graham D'Arcy Anderson, of Inverness-shire, and Diana, *née* Hatch; *b* 10 July 1961, Dingwall, Ross and Cromarty; *Educ* Haileybury and ISC, RMA Sandhurst; *m* 26 Aug 1986, Lucy, *née* Page Ratcliff; 2 da (Holly Beatrice D'Arcy b 21 June 1993, Daisy Lucinda D'Arcy b 22 Sept 1995); *Career* HM Forces (Queen's Own Highlanders) 1982–89, resigned as Capt; Hamptons Int: joined 1990, appointed to Gp Ops Bd 1998, chief operating offr 2003, md residential agency 2004–; *Recreations* skiing, salmon fishing; *Clubs* Highland Brigade; *Style—* Mark Anderson, Esq; ✉ Hamptons International, 32 Grosvenor Square, London W1K 2HJ (☎ 020 7758 8488)

ANDERSON, Dr Robert Geoffrey William; er s of late Herbert Patrick Anderson, and Kathleen Diana, *née* Burns; *b* 2 May 1944; *Educ* Univ of Oxford (BSc, MA, DPhil); *m* 1, 1973 (m dis 2003), Margaret Elizabeth Callis, da of John Austin Lea; 2 s (William b 1979, Edward b 1984); m 2, 2005, Jane Virginia Portal; *Career* asst keeper: Royal Scottish

Museum 1970–75, Science Museum 1975–78; dep keeper Wellcome Museum of the History of Medicine 1978–80, keeper of chemistry Science Museum 1980–84 (sec Advsy Cncl 1978–80); dir: Royal Scottish Museum 1984–85 (formerly curator of the history of science), Nat Museums of Scotland 1985–92, British Museum 1992–2002; fell Inst for Advanced Study Princeton 2002–03, by-fell Churchill Coll Cambridge 2003–04, visiting fell CCC Cambridge 2004–05, fell Clare Hall Cambridge 2006– (vice-pres 2009–14); memb Cncl: Soc for the History of Alchemy and Chemistry 1978– (chm 2006–), Gp for Scientific Technological and Medical Collections 1979–83, Br Soc for the History of Sci 1981–84 (pres 1988–90), Scottish Museums 1984–91, Museums Assoc 1988–92; memb Editorial Bd: Annals of Sci 1981–, Annali di Storia della Scienza 1986–2006, Journal of the History of Collections 1993–; sec Royal Scottish Soc of Arts 1973–75, pres Scientific Instrument Cmmn Int Union of the History and Philosophy of Sci 1982–97, memb Br Nat Ctee for the Hist of Sci 1985–89, memb Bd Chemical Heritage Fndn Philadelphia 2006– (vice-chm 2012–); tstee Boerhaave Museum Leiden 1994–99, pres Assoc of Independent Libraries 2003–; Dexter Prize American Chemical Soc 1986, Paul Bunge Prize Gesellschaft Deutscher Chemiker 2016; Hon DSc: Edinburgh 1995, Durham 1998; hon fell St John's Coll Oxford 2002; FSA 1986, FRSE 1990, Hon FSA Scot 1991; Commandeur Ordre des Arts et des Lettres 2002; *Books* The Mariner's Astrolabe (1972), Edinburgh and Medicine (1976), The Early Years of the Edinburgh Medical School (1976), The Playfair Collection and the Teaching of Chemistry at the University of Edinburgh (1978), The History of Technology Vol VI (contrib, 1978), Science in India (1982), Science, Medicine and Dissent – Joseph Priestley 1733–1804 (ed, 1987), Joseph Black: A Bibliography (1992), Making Instruments Count (jt ed, 1993), The Great Court and the British Museum (2000), The Correspondence of Joseph Black (jt ed, 2012), Cradle of Chemistry (ed, 2015); *Recreations* collecting too many books; *Clubs* Athenaeum; *Style—* Dr R G W Anderson, FRSE, FSA; ✉ Clare Hall, Herschel Road, Cambridge CB3 9AL (e-mail rgwa2@cam.ac.uk)

ANDERSON, Prof Robert Henry; s of Henry Anderson (d 1981), and Doris Amy, *née* Callear (d 1977); *b* 4 April 1942; *Educ* Wellington GS, Univ of Manchester (BSc, MB ChB, MD); *m* 9 July 1966, Christine, da of Keith Ibbotson, of Grantham, Lincs; 1 da (Elizabeth b 1970), 1 s (John b 1972); *Career* travelling fell MRC Univ of Amsterdam 1973, sr res fell Br Heart Fndn Brompton Hosp 1974, Joseph Levy prof of paediatric cardiac morphology Nat Heart and Lung Inst (formerly Cardiothoracic Inst) Imperial Coll Sch of Med Univ of London 1979–99 (reader 1977) and Inst of Child Health UCL 1999–2007 (emeritus prof UCL 2007–), prof of paediatrics Medical Univ of S Carolina 2007–; visiting prof Univ of Pittsburgh 1984–2007, hon prof Univ of North Carolina 1984–2007, visiting prof Univ of Liverpool 1988–2007, visiting prof Univ of Newcastle 2007–, emeritus prof Univ of Manchester 2007–; hon conslt: Southampton Hosps NHS Tst 2014–, Birmingham Children's Hosp 2015–; Excerpta Medica Travel Award 1977, Br Heart Fndn Prize for Cardiovascular Res 1984; FRCPath 1986; *Publications* 850 articles, 280 chapters in books; 36 books incl: Cardiac Anatomy (1978), Cardiac Pathology (1983), Surgical Anatomy of the Heart (1985, 4 edn 2013), Paediatric Cardiology (3 edn 2010); *Recreations* music, golf, wine; *Clubs* Roehampton, Saintsbury, Walton Heath Golf; *Style—* Prof Robert Anderson; ✉ 60 Earlsfield Road, Wandsworth, London SW18 3DN (✆ 020 8870 4368, e-mail sejjran@ucl.ac.uk)

ANDERSON, Prof Sir Roy Malcolm; kt (2006); s of James Anderson, and Elizabeth, *née* Watson-Weatherburn; *b* 12 April 1947; *Educ* Duncombe Sch, Richard Hale Sch, Imperial Coll London (BSc, PhD, DIC); *m* 1, 16 Aug 1974 (m dis 1989), Mary Joan, da of Peter Mitchell; m 2, 21 July 1990 (m dis 2013), Claire, da of Rev Peter Baron; m 3, 9 April 2014, Janet Louise Meyrick; *Career* IBM research fell Univ of Oxford 1971–73, lectr Dept of Zoology KCL 1973–77; Dept of Biology Imperial Coll London: lectr 1977–80, reader 1980–82, prof 1982–93, head of dept 1984–93; dir Wellcome Centre for Parasite Infections 1989–93, dir Wellcome Tst Centre for the Epidemiology of Infectious Disease 1993–2000, Linacre prof of zoology and head of zoology Dept Univ of Oxford 1993–98, fell Merton Coll Oxford 1993–2000, prof of infectious disease epidemiology and head Dept of Infectious Disease Epidemiology Faculty of Med Imperial Coll London 2000–04, chief scientific advsr MOD 2004–07, rector Imperial Coll London 2008–10, dir London Centre for Neglected Tropical Disease Research 2010–; visiting prof Imperial Coll London 1993, Genentech distinguished prof Dept of Biostatistics Univ of Washington 1998; chm Advsy Bd Schistosomiasis Control Initiative 2000–, chair Science Advsy Bd WHO's Neglected Tropical Diseases Prog 2003–09, chm Sci Advsy Cncl DEFRA 2004–05, chair Baccalaureate Advsy Gp Pearson 2012–; non-exec dir Glaxo Smith Kline, memb Int Advsy Bd for Hakluyt and Co Ltd; memb: NERC 1988–91, Cncl Zoological Soc 1988–90, Advsy Cncl on Science and Technol 1989–91, Cncl Royal Soc 1989–91, Cncl RPMS Hammersmith 1992–95, Cncl LSHTM 1993–2000, Spongiform Encephalopathy Advsy Ctee 1997–2004, Bill and Melinda Gates Grand Challenges Advsy Bd 2003–08, Scientific Advsy Ctee Health Protection Agency 2004–06, Cncl EPSRC 2004–08, Cncl RUSI 2005–08, Cncl Royal Coll of Art, Advsy Bd Royal Soc Policy Centre, Advsy Bd Singapore Nat Research Fndn, Int Advsy Ctee Thailand Nat Science and Technol Devpt Agency 2009–, memb Malaysia BIO-Int Advsy Panel 2009–, Advsy Bd Partnership for Child Devpt 2012; govr The Wellcome Tst 1991–2000 (tstee 1991), tstee Natural History Museum; author of over 450 scientific jls and books; Huxley Meml medal 1981, Zoological Scientific medal 1982, C A Wright Meml medal 1986, David Starr Jordan prize 1987, Chalmers medal 1988, Weldon prize 1989, John Grundy Lecture medal 1990, Frink medal for Br Zoologists 1993; Storer lectr Univ of Calif Davis 1994, Croonian lectr Royal Soc 1994, Joseph Smadel lectr Univ of N Carolina 1994, P H Thiel lectr Boerhaave Course on Travel Med Leiden 1995, Thomas Francis meml lectr Univ of Michigan 1995, Nuffield lectr RSM 2002; hon fell Linacre Coll Oxford 1993; Hon DSc: UEA 1997, Univ of Stirling 1998, Univ of Aberdeen 2008; fell Academia Europaea 1998, foreign memb Inst of Med Nat Acad of Sciences USA 1999, foreign memb French Nat Acad of Sciences 2011; Hon MRCP 1991, Hon FRCPath 1999, FRS 1986, Hon FIA 2000, Hon FRSS 2002 (FRSS), Hon FRASE 2002, FIBiol, FMedSci, ARCS, Hon FRAgS 2002; *Books* Population Dynamics of Infectious Diseases (1982), Infectious Diseases of Humans: Dynamics and Control (jtly, 1990); *Recreations* croquet, hill walking, music, natural history; *Clubs* Athenaeum; *Style—* Prof Sir Roy Anderson, FRS

ANDERSON, Sarah Pia; da of Stewart Angus Anderson, and Eldina Pia Anderson; *b* 19 July 1952; *Educ* The Cedars Sch, Univ of Swansea (BA); *m* Pamela L Kling; *Career* theatre and television director; prof of cinema and digital media Univ of Calif Davis; memb: Dirs' Guild of GB, Dirs' Guild of America, Women in Film (UK), BAFTA LA, Directors UK, American Acad of Television Arts and Sciences; *Theatre* trained at Crucible Theatre Sheffield; prodns incl: Hello and Goodbye, What The Butler Saw, Ashes, The Caucasian Chalk Circle; prodns for Bush Theatre incl: Blisters, Gin Trap, First Blush Last Resort, The Estuary, These Men, The Nest; prodns for RSC incl: Indigo, Old Year's Eve, Across Oka, Mary and Lizzie; other prodns incl: Rosmersholm (NT, La Mama Theatre NY), Carthagians (Abbey and Hampstead), Mary Stuart and St Joan (Shakespeare Theatre Washington DC), The Winter's Tale (Santa Cruz Shakespeare Festival), Hedda Gabler (Roundabout Theatre NY); *Television* incl: Blisters, Stepping Out, Shaping Up, Pity in History, A Woman Calling (Samuel Beckett Award), Summers Awakening, This Is History Gran, The Bill (15 episodes), The Alleyn Mysteries, Dr Finlay (Scottish BAFTA for Best Series 1995), Prime Suspect (Emmy Award for Best Series 1993–94), The Profiler, ER (Best Series Emmy Awards 1996), Nothing Sacred (Prism Award for Directing 1998, Peabody Award 1998), Plastic Man, Ally McBeal (Emmy Award for Best Series 2000), Dead Like Me, Huff (Emmy Award), Ugly Betty (Golden Globe Award for Best Series and Best Leading Actress), Big Love (nominated Golden Globe Award), Grey's Anatomy (Best Series Emmy Awards 2007), Scott & Bailey (nominated Best Series RTS and BAFTA 2011); *Recreations* photography, swimming, cycling, scuba diving; *Style—* Ms Sarah Pia Anderson; ✉ e-mail spa1@earthlink.net, website www.sarahpiaanderson.com; c/o Andrea Simon Entertainment, 4230 Woodman Avenue, Sherman Oaks, CA 91423, USA (✆ 00 1 818 380 1901); c/o Bradley Glenn, Kaplan Stahler Agency, 8383 Wilshire Boulevard, Suite 923, Beverley Hills, CA 90211, USA (✆ 00 1 323 966 2760)

ANDERSON, Steve; *b* 9 May 1958; *m* 3 c; *Career* South Lancashire Newspapers 1974–78, Liverpool Daily Post and Echo 1978; researcher World in Action, news ed and prodr regnl magazine progs Granada TV Manchester 1978–84; BBC TV: BBC Network Features 1984–87, prodr and dir BBC Breakfast Time 1987, Newsnight 1987–92, prodr Election 92 and Election 97, sr prodr One O'Clock News and Six O'Clock News 1992–93, prodr and dir BBC News and Current Affrs Weekly Progs (progs incl Here and Now, Panorama) 1993–95, ed BBC Consumer Progs (progs incl Watchdog, Weekend Watchdog, Watchdog Healthcheck, Value for Money, Face Value, Computers Don't Bite) 1995–97; controller News, Current Affrs, Arts and Religion ITN Network Centre 1997–2004, currently creative dir Mentorn; *Style—* Steve Anderson, Esq

ANDERSON, Prof Thomas; s of Frederick Anderson (d 1992), and May, *née* Barrett (d 1987); *b* 24 July 1947, Blaydon on Tyne; *Educ* Blaydon GS, Univ of Newcastle upon Tyne (BSc, PhD); *m* 3 Aug 1968, Patricia, da of Robert Ormston; 1 s (Iain b 1972), 1 da (Claire b 1975); *Career* Newcastle Univ: dir Centre for Software Reliability 1982–2012, prof 1986–, head Computing Science Dept 1992–97, dean of science 1998–2004, dean of business devpt 2008–12; FBCS; *Books* Fault Tolerance – Principles and Practice (with P A Lee, 2 edn 1990), also ed 31 other volumes 1979–2016; *Recreations* fell walking, choral singing; *Style—* Prof Thomas Anderson; ✉ Centre for Software Reliability, Newcastle University, Newcastle upon Tyne NE1 7RU (✆ 0191 221 2222, fax 0191 208 7995, e-mail tom.anderson@newcastle.ac.uk)

ANDERSON OF SWANSEA, Baron (Life Peer UK 2005), of Swansea in the County of West Glamorgan; Donald Anderson; PC; s of David Robert Anderson (d 1954), of Swansea, and Eva, *née* Mathias (d 1994); *b* 17 June 1939; *Educ* Swansea GS, UC Swansea (BA), Inns of Court Sch of Law; *m* 28 Sept 1963, Dr Dorothy Mary, da of Rev Frank L Trotman (d 1970), of Bolivia; 3 s (Hon Robert b 24 Dec 1964, Hon Huw b 17 Nov 1967, Hon Geraint b 20 Sept 1972); *Career* called to the Bar Inner Temple 1969; HM Foreign Serv 1960–64 (third sec Br Embassy Budapest 1963–64); lectr in politics UC Swansea 1964–66; MP (Lab): Monmouth 1966–70, Swansea E 1974–2005; PPS to: Min of Defence 1969–70, Attorney Gen 1974–79; chm Select Ctee on Welsh Affairs 1981–83; oppn spokesman: foreign affairs 1983–92, defence 1993–94, legal affairs 1995–96; chm Select Ctee on Foreign Affairs 1997–2005; memb Chairmen's Panel 1995–97; chm: Welsh Lab Gp 1977–78, Br Zimbabwe Gp, Parly Christian Fellowship 1990–93, chm Br German Parly Gp 1994–97, Br French Parly Gp 1997–2001, Br Norwegian Gp (jtly) 1997–2005, Br South African Gp 1997–99, UK Branch CPA 1997–2001; memb: Assembly of Western EU 20008–11, Parly Assembly Cncl of Europe 2008– (chair ME Sub-Ctee 2014–); ldr UK delgn: to NATO Parly Assembly 1997–2001 (ldr Socialist Gp), to OSCE 1997; vice-chm and treas IPU 1986–90 (treas 1990–91 and 1993–95); cncllr Royal Borough of Kensington and Chelsea 1971–75; chm Nat Prayer Breakfast 1989, memb Bd World Vision of Britain 1991–94, pres The Boys' Brigade in Wales 1991–97, memb Bd Mercy Ships 2005–12; Freeman City and County of Swansea 2000; Parly fell St Antony's Coll Oxford 1999–2000; hon fell UC Swansea; Cdr's Cross Order of FRG for contrib to Br German Relations 1986, Legion of Honour France, honours from Slovakia and Hungary; *Style—* The Rt Hon the Lord Anderson of Swansea

ANDRÉ, Martin; *b* 10 December 1960; *Educ* Yehudi Menuhin Sch, Univ of Cambridge; *m* Karin; 2 da (Sophie, Emily), 1 s (Ben); *Career* conductor; sometime resident conductor WNO, freelance conductor, music dir English Touring Opera 1993–96; performances with WNO incl: chamber version of Aida (professional debut), Falstaff, Jenufa, Ernani, Rigoletto, Madama Butterfly, Un Ballo in Maschera, Eugene Onegin, Il Barbiere de Siviglia; freelance prodns incl: The Merry Widow and La Clemenza di Tito (Scottish Opera), The Love for Three Oranges and John Buller Bakxai (world première, ENO), Madama Butterfly (Opera North), Le Nozze di Figaro, Mozart Die Entführung aus dem Serail (Opera 80), Janácek From the House of the Dead (N American première for Vancouver Opera), Ariadne (Vancouver Opera), La Traviata (Opera Zuid Maastricht and Vancouver Opera), L'amour des Trois Oranges (Lisbon, Stuttgart and New Israeli Opera), Carmen (US debut, Seattle Opera), Un Ballo in Maschera (Royal Opera House debut), Christoph Rilke's Song of Love and Death (UK première, Glyndebourne Touring Opera), Don Pasquale (New Israeli Opera), Cunning Little Vixen (Scottish Opera), La Traviata (Opera NI), Cav and Pag (Staastheater Stuttgart), Makropulos Case (Glyndebourne Touring Opera), Aida (Opera NI), Julietta (Opera Zuid Holland), Macbeth, Madam Butterfly (Staatsoper Cologne), The Magic Flute (Opera NI), world premières by James MacMillan and Craig Armstrong Edinburgh Int Festival, Cosi fan Tutte, Orpheus and Euridice, La Bohème, Werther, Rigoletto (all for English Touring Opera); also performances with English Chamber Orch, Royal Scottish National Orch, Scottish Chamber Orch, BBC Concert Orch, Ulster Orch, New London Sinfonia, London Soloists Chamber Orch, London Concert Orch, City of London Chamber Orch, New Queen's Hall Orch, Northern Sinfonia, Jerusalem Symphony Orch and Philharmonia, Limburges Symphonie Orkest, Collegium Musicum Bergen, Bergen Filharmoniske Orkester, Tromsø Symfoniorkester, Queensland Philharmonic Orch, Tasmanian Symphony Orch, Orquestra Nacional do Porto, Remix Contemporary Ensemble Portugal, Peking Symphony Orch Macau; *Recreations* has season ticket for Arsenal FC; *Style—* Martin André, Esq

ANDREW, Charles Frederick (Charlie); s of Stuart Andrew, of Kent, and Ann Andrew (d 2005); *b* 18 November 1980, Pembury; *Educ* Bethany Sch, Univ of Surrey; *m* 11 June 2011, Kirsty, *née* Mangan; 1 da (Olive b 2015); *Career* music producer; runner Abbey Road 1999–2000, studio asst Abbey Road 2003–04, drummer The Laurel Collective 2004–, freelance record prodr 2008–, owner and md Square Leg Records 2015–, owner and md Big Tree Music Publishing 2015–; has worked with artists incl: Madness, Alt J, Matt Corby, Marika Hackman, Sivu; *Albums* incl: An Awesome Wave by Alt J 2012 (Barclycard Mercury Prize 2012), Oui Oui Si Si Ja Ja Da Da by Madness 2012, This is All Yours by Alt J 2014; *Awards* Breakthrough Producer of the Year Music Producers Guild Awards 2013, UK Producer of the Year Music Producers Guild Awards 2015, British Producer of the Year BRIT Awards 2016; *Recreations* cricket, music, skiing, travel, sports in general; *Style—* Charlie Andrew, Esq; ✉ c/o Hannah Management, Fulham Palace, Bishops Avenue, London SW6 6EA (✆ 07833 450460, e-mail gareth@hannahmanagement.co.uk, website www.hannahmanagement.co.uk)

ANDREW, Derek; MBE (2001); s of Harold Andrew, of Chadderton, Oldham, and Elisabeth, *née* Bogaard; *b* 14 October 1955, Oldham, Lancs; *Educ* Oldham Hulme GS, Univ of Newcastle upon Tyne (BA); *m* 6 June 1993, Rebecca, *née* Westwood; *Career* Marstons plc (formerly Wolverhampton and Dudley Breweries plc): joined 1980, managerial positions 1980–90, managed house ops controller 1990–91, md Cameron's Brewery Co 1991–97, main bd dir 1994–2012, gp sales dir 1997–2001, chm Cameron's Brewery Co 1997–2001, md Pathfinder Pubs 2001–; owner Opstat Consulting Ltd 2012–; chm Pathfinder Local Heroes Fndn 2001–; chm Midland Counties Br Beer and Pub Assoc 2000–03; govr Hartlepool Coll of FE 1993–97; chm Teeside TEC Investors in People

1994–97; *Recreations* music, sport, theatre, cars, horses; *Style*— Derek Andrew, Esq, MBE; ✉ Marstons plc, Marstons House, Marstons Road, Wolverhampton WV1 4JT

ANDREW, Hugh; s of Hubert and Elizabeth Andrew; *b* 8 April 1962, Paisley; *Educ* Magdalen Coll Oxford; *Career* md Birlinn Ltd 1992–; dir Compass Ind Publishing Services Ltd; chm Ossian Tst, tstee Great Tapestry of Scotland; FSA Scot; *Recreations* reading, music, travel, archaeology; *Clubs* Tuesday; *Style*— Hugh Andrew; ✉ West Newington House, 10 Newington Road, Edinburgh EH9 1QS (☎ 0131 668 4371, fax 0131 668 4466, e-mail hugh@birlinn.co.uk)

ANDREW, Dr Kenneth; s of late Arthur James Andrew, of Benfleet, Essex, and late Emily Sarah, *née* Elderkin; *b* 21 December 1944; *Educ* Enfield Coll of Technol (ONC), Imperial Coll London (MSc, DIC), Univ of Wales (BEng), Int Mgmnt Centre (MPhil); *m* 1, 21 July 1967, Elizabeth Honora (d 2002), da of late Dilwyn Thomas; 2 s; m 2, 19 Sept 2009, Pamela, da of late Frederick Neil Hope; *Career* apprentice draughtsman 1961–64, various posts including head of operational res, branch mgmnt City and West End London, head of mktg NatWest Bank plc 1969–84, gp markets dir Good Relations Group plc 1984–85, dir consumer mktg Europe The Chase Manhattan Bank NA 1985–87, gp dir strategy and mktg National & Provincial Building Society 1987–90, independent business conslt 1990–91; dir: DBS Management plc 1993–99, Manitous 1991–96, St James International 1995–98; chm: St James Business Centres 1995–99, Sherwood International Gp plc 1997–2003, Assuresoft Ltd 1998–99, Recall Gp plc 2001–02, Space 200 Ltd 2009–; sr vice-pres, chm and md Aetna UK 1991–93; industrial prof of fin servs mgmnt IMCB; dir Mount Vernon Watford Hosp NHS Tst 1994–97; chm Membs' Cncl Link Network 2004–, chm Link Scheme 2015–; Hon MPhil IMCB 1984; memb IOD; MIMgt, MBBA, MInstScB, FInstD, FRSA; *Books* The Bank Marketing Handbook (1986), The Financial Public Relations Handbook (1990), Bank Marketing in a Changing World (1991); *Recreations* swimming, reading, writing, travel; *Clubs* MCC, Carlton, Lansdowne; *Style*— Dr Kenneth Andrew; ✉ Space200 Ltd, 33 St James's Square, London SW1Y 4JS; mobile 07710 488282, e-mail andrewkenneth@mac.com

ANDREW, Prof Malcolm Ross; s of John Malcolm Young Andrew, of Latchley, nr Gunnislake, Cornwall, and Mary Lilian, *née* Faulkner; *b* 27 January 1945; *Educ* The Perse Sch Cambridge, St Catharine's Coll Cambridge (BA, MA), Simon Fraser Univ BC Canada (MA), Univ of York (DPhil); *m* 17 Aug 1968, Lena Margareta, da of Gustaf Bernström, of Göteborg, Sweden; 1 s (Christopher b 1980 d 2003), 1 da (Elizabeth b 1982); *Career* asst English master Haileybury Coll 1973–74, lectr then sr lectr Sch of English and American Studies UEA 1974–85; Queen's Univ Belfast: prof of English 1985–2007, head of dept then dir Sch of English 1986–92, dean Faculty of Arts 1992–96, provost of humanities 1993–98, pro-vice-chllr 1998–2002; memb: Steering Ctee Cncl for Univ English 1989–92, English Panel Humanities Research Bd 1995–98, Humanities Research Bd British Acad 1997–98, Arts and Humanities Research Bd 1998–2000; founding fell Eng Assoc 1999; DLit Queen's Univ Belfast 1995; *Books* On the Properties of Things, Book VII (1975), Poems of the Pearl Manuscript (with R Waldron, 1978), The Gawain-Poet: An Annotated Bibliography (1979), Two Early Renaissance Bird Poems (1984), Critical Essays on Chaucer's Canterbury Tales (1991), Variorum Chaucer: General Prologue to the Canterbury Tales (1993), Geoffrey Chaucer, The Canterbury Tales (ed with A C Cawley, 1996), Geoffrey Chaucer: Comic and Bawdy Tales (ed with A C Cawley, 1997), Geoffrey Chaucer: Three Tales about Marriage (ed with A C Cawley, 1998), Geoffrey Chaucer: Three Tales of Love and Chivalry (ed with A C Cawley, 2000), The Palgrave Literary Dictionary of Chaucer (2006), The Poems of the Pearl Manuscript in Modern English Prose Translation (with R Waldron, 2008); *Recreations* literature, art, architecture, music; *Style*— Prof Malcolm Andrew; ✉ The Red House, Down Road, Tavistock, Devon PL19 9AQ (☎ 01822 613874)

ANDREW, Nicholas Anthony Samuel; s of Samuel Ogden Lees Andrew (d 1966), of Hants, and Rosalind Molly Carlyon, *née* Evans (d 1984); *b* 20 December 1946; *Educ* Winchester, Queens' Coll Cambridge (MA); *m* 28 Nov 1981, Jeryl Christine, da of Col John George Harrison, OBE, TD, DL, of Devon; 2 da (Venetia b 1989, Olivia b 1992); *Career* chartered accountant; ptnr: Robson Rhodes 1986–90, Rawlinson & Hunter 1990–92; md Nicholas Andrew International Tax Consultancy and Family Office 1992–; *Books* Yuppies and their Money (1987), Robson Rhodes Personal Financial Planning Manual (jtly, 2–6 edns), How to Make Yourself Wealthy in the 1990's; *Recreations* golf, music, travel; *Clubs* MCC, RAC, Automobile (Monaco); *Style*— Nicholas A S Andrew, Esq; ✉ 49 Berkeley Square, London W1J 5AZ

ANDREW, (Christopher) Robert (Rob); MBE (1995); *b* 18 February 1963; *Educ* Barnard Castle, Univ of Cambridge (BA, Rugby blue, Cricket blue); *m* 18 Aug 1989, Sara (m diss 2014); 3 da (Emily b 5 July 1990, Beth b 29 March 1995, Iola b 6 June 2000); *Career* rugby union player (fly-half) and coach; amateur rugby player until 1995, professional player 1995–99, chartered surveyor until 1995 (latterly a dir Debenham Thorpe DTZ); clubs as player: Middlesbrough RUFC, Cambridge Univ 1981–84, Nottingham RFC 1984–87, Gordon RFC (Aust), Wasps FC 1987–91 and 1992–96, Toulouse 1991–92, Barbarians RFC; dir of rugby Newcastle RFC 1995–2006 (also player until 1999, promoted to First Division 1997, winners Tetley's Bitter Cup 2001 (finalists 1999) and Powergen Cup 2004), elite rugby dir RFU 2006–11, professional rugby dir RFU 2011–16; rep: North 1985 and 1987, London 1989, England B (debut 1988), Home Unions 1989 (capt v France); England: debut v Romania 1985, Five Nations debut v France 1985, memb World Cup squad (2 appearances) 1987, tour Aust & Fiji 1988 (3 test appearances), tour Romania 1989, memb Grand Slam winning team 1991, 1992 and 1995, memb runners-up team World Cup 1991, memb team semi-finalists World Cup 1995, tour to South Africa 1994, 71 caps, ret; kicked 6 penalties and scored 21 points v Wales 1986, record holder for drop goals in internationals, highest individual scoring mark (30 points v Canada, equalling world record) 1994; memb Br Lions tour Aust (2 tests) 1989; cricket: first class Yorkshire CCC 2nd XI, Cambridge Univ CC (capt 1985); *Style*— Rob Andrew, Esq, MBE; ✉ c/o RFU, Rugby House, 200 Whitton Road, Twickenham TW2 7BA

ANDREW, Stuart James; MP; s of James Edward Andrew, of Spain, and Maureen Catherine, *née* Gerrard; *b* 25 November 1971, Bangor, N Wales; *Educ* Ysgol David Hughes Anglesey; *Partner* Robin Michael Rogers; *Career* head of fundraising Martin House Children's Hospice 2003–10; cncllr Leeds City Cncl 2003–10, MP (Cons) Pudsey 2010–; *Style*— Stuart Andrew, Esq, MP; ✉ House of Commons, London SW1A 0AA (☎ 020 7219 7130, e-mail stuart.andrew.mp@parliament.uk, Twitter @stuartandrewmp)

ANDREWS, Anthony; *b* 12 January 1948; *Educ* Royal Masonic Sch; *m* Georgina, *née* Simpson; 1 s (Joshua), 2 da (Jessica, Amy-Samantha); *Career* actor and film producer; memb: Equity, Screen Actors Guild USA, BAFTA; *Theatre* incl: 2 seasons Chichester Festival Theatre, 40 Years On (Apollo), One of Us 1986, Coming Into Land (NT) 1987, Dragon Variation (Duke of York's), Time and the Conways, A Midsummer Night's Dream (The New Shakespeare Co), Romeo & Juliet (The New Shakespeare Co), Vertigo, Ghosts (Comedy Theatre London), Henry Higgins in My Fair Lady (Theatre Royal Drury Lane), A Woman in White (Palace Theatre) 2005, The Letter (Wyndhams Theatre) 2007, A Marvellous Year for Plums (Chichester Festival Theatre) 2012, My Fair Lady (Royal Albert Hall Prom) 2012, Bully Boy (St James' Theatre) 2012; *Television* incl: Brideshead Revisited, Danger UXB, Much Ado About Nothing, Romeo and Juliet, Jewels, Bluegrass, The Law Lord, Columbo Goes To The Guillotine, The Fortunes of Nigel, The Beast with Two Backs, Suspicion, Z For Zachariah, Burning Bridges, A Superstition, The Woman He Loved, Dixon of Dock Green, The Judge's Wife, Alma Mater, AD, Sparkling Cyanide, The Scarlet Pimpernel, Ivanhoe, La Ronde, Upstairs Downstairs, David Copperfield, The Pallisers, Follyfoot, A Day Out, French Without Tears, The Country Wife, London Assurance, QBVII, Woodstock, Doomwatch, The Duchess of Duke Street, Hands of a Murderer (USA), The Strange Case of Dr Jekyll and Mr Hyde (USA), Ruth Rendell's Heartstones, Mothertime, Love in a Cold Climate, The Cambridge Spies, Miss Marple, Birdsong; *Film* incl: The Scarlet Pimpernel, Under the Volcano, The Holcroft Covenant, Second Victory, The Light Horseman, Hannah's War, A War of Children, Take Me High, Operation Daybreak, Mistress of Paradise, Lost in Siberia (also prodr), Haunted (also prodr), The King's Speech; *Concerts* inc: A Celebration of Lerner and Loewe (with City of Birmingham Symphony Orch, Northern Sinfonia, Liverpool Philharmonic and RTE Dublin), My Fair Lady, Lerner and Loewe: Magic of the Musicals (with Northern Sinfonia and Liverpool Philharmonic), tribute concert for Bill Brohn (Drury Lane), meml tribute concert for Alan J Lerner; *Clubs* Garrick; *Style*— Anthony Andrews, Esq; ✉ c/o Lindy King, United Agents, 12–26 Lexington Street, London S1F 0LE (☎ 020 3214 0800, fax 020 3214 0802)

ANDREWS, Claire Marguerite; da of David Andrews, of Rugby, Warks, and Kathleen Andrews; *b* 25 October 1956, Newbold-on-Avon, Warks; *Educ* Rugby HS for Girls, Univ of Manchester (LLB); *m* 1; 1 s (Patrick b 4 Sept 1988); m 2, 16 March 1991, Paul Boyle; 2 da (Marguerite b 2 Dec 1992, Eleanor b 25 Nov 1994); *Career* called to the Bar 1979; memb of chambers 2 Harcourt Buildings 1980–84, with Home Office 1984–86, memb Gough Square Chambers 1986– (head of chambers with William Hibbert 2006); asst boundary cmmr; legal memb Mental Health Review Tbnl 1995–; memb: London Common Law and Commercial Bar Assoc, Administrative Law Bar Assoc; FCIArb; *Publications* The Enforcement of Regulatory Offences; *Recreations* tennis, painting; *Style*— Miss Claire Andrews; ✉ Gough Square Chambers, 6–7 Gough Square, London EC4A 3DE (☎ 020 7353 0924, fax 020 7353 2221, e-mail claire.andrews@goughsq.co.uk)

ANDREWS, Rev Clive Francis; s of Francis Edward Andrews (d 1966), of New Malden, Surrey, and Iris Emily Amelia, *née* Barton (d 1991); *b* 14 February 1950; *Educ* King's Coll Sch Wimbledon, KCL (BD, AKC, Tinniswood Prize), St George's Coll Jerusalem (Goldsmiths' Scholar), St Augustine's Coll Canterbury (pres), Open Univ Business Sch, ICSA; *m* 20 Feb 1982 (m dis 1992), Diana Ruth, da of Harry John Scrivener (d 1982), of Burstow, Surrey; 2 da (Siobhan b 1983, Caroline b 1986); *Career* exec offr Home Office 1968–69, curate Clapham Parish Church 1973–75, curate i/c St Nicholas Kidbrooke 1975–78, diocesan youth advsr Southwark 1979–84, vicar St Augustine's Honor Oak 1984–89, project conslt Harris City Technol Coll 1989–90, admin dir City Technol Colls Tst 1990–95 (also co sec 1991–95), self-employed business conslt 1995–96, charities asst Worshipful Co of Weavers 1996–98, ceo Royal Masonic Trust for Girls and Boys 2005–08 (asst sec 1998–2005), charity conslt 2008–; memb: Surrey Cncl for Voluntary Youth Orgns 1979–84, London Youth Ctee 1981–83, London S Ctee The Prince's Tst 1984–89 (vice-chm 1986–89); chm: Lewisham Youth Ctee 1982–84, Bacon's Sch Bermondsey 1985–91 (govr 1981–91); dir The English Dance Consort 1986–91; Freeman City of London 2000; FRSA 2007; *Publications* A Handbook of Parish Youth Work (1984), An End of All Education? Moral and spiritual development in secondary schools (1994); author of articles in various pubns; *Recreations* building restoration, keyboard playing, walking, spending time with my daughters and grandchildren, painting; *Style*— The Rev Clive Andrews

ANDREWS, Prof David; *Educ* Stationers' Co Sch Hornsey, UCL (BSc, MSc, PhD); *Career* awarded RCNC cadetship 1965, Constructor Lieut RCNC 1967–71; MOD Ship Dept Bath: submarine and ship design 1971–80, TRIDENT submarine project 1984–86, chief constructor (head of amphibious gp) 1986–90; head of concept design (naval) 1990–93, dir frigates and mine counter measures then integrated project team leader Future Surface Combatant Defence Procurement Agency 1998–2000; UCL: lectr in naval architecture 1980–84, MOD prof of naval architecture 1993–98, prof of engrg design Dept of Mechanical Engrg 2000–; RINA: chair Individual Case Exemption Panel 1991–, memb Cncl 1992–, memb Exec Ctee 1993–99 and 2006–11, chair Membership Ctee 1993–2000, chair Future Directions Ctee 2000–, vice-pres 2007–, memb Bd of Tstees 2012–; chair Design Methodology Panel IMDC 1995–, chair Int Ctee Int Marine Design Conference 2015–, memb RAE 2008 Sub Panel Engrg 2005–08; Freeman Worshipful Co of Engineers 2007; memb RCNC 1972; FRINA 1987, FRSA 1996, FREng 2000, FIMechE 2002; *Publications* Synthesis in Ship Design (PhD thesis, 1984), FE Analysis and Design of Thin Walled Ship Structures (book chapter, 1987), Technology, Shipbuilding and Future Combat Beyond 2020 (book chapter, 2001), Multi-Hull Vessels (book chapter, 2004), The View from Bath: A Naval Constructor's Perspective (book chapter, 2013); author of numerous papers on ship design to RINA, Royal Soc, conferences etc; *Recreations* painting and sketching, reading, cinema and theatre-going, re-exploring London; *Style*— Prof David Andrews; ✉ Department of Mechanical Engineering, University College London, Torrington Place, London WC1E 7JE (☎ 020 7679 3874, fax 020 7388 0180, e-mail d_andrews@meng.ucl.ac.uk, website www.mecheng.ucl.ac.uk)

ANDREWS, Prof Edgar Harold; s of Richard Thomas Andrews (d 1968); *b* 16 December 1932, Didcot, Berks; *Educ* Dartford GS, Univ of London (BSc, PhD, DSc); *m* 1961, Thelma Doris, da of Selby John Walker, of Watford, Herts; 1 da (Rachel b 1962), 1 s (Martyn b 1964); *Career* dean Faculty of Engrg Queen Mary Coll London 1971–74 (prof of materials 1968–98, emeritus 1998–); dir: QMC Industrial Research Ltd 1970–88, Denbyware Ltd 1971–81, Materials Technol Consultants Ltd 1974–, Evangelical Press 1975–2004, Fire and Materials Ltd 1985–88; ed Evangelical Times 1998–2008; recipient A A Griffith Silver Medal 1977; FInstP, FIMMM, CEng, CPhys; *Books* Fracture in Polymers (1968), From Nothing to Nature (1978), God, Science and Evolution (1980), The Promise of the Spirit (1982), Christ and the Cosmos (1986), Free in Christ (1996), A Glorious High Throne (2003), Preaching Christ (2005), Who Made God? (2009); *Recreations* writing, music, church work; *Style*— Prof Edgar Andrews; ✉ 25 Russellcroft Road, Welwyn Garden City, Hertfordshire AL8 6QX (☎ 01707 331680, e-mail edgarandrews@btinternet.com, website www.whomadegod.com)

ANDREWS, Hon Mrs Justice; Dame Geraldine Mary Andrews; DBE (2013), QC (2001); *Career* called to the Bar (Gray's Inn) 1981; recorder 2001, judge of the High Court of Justice (Queen's Bench Div) 2013–; *Style*— The Hon Mrs Justice Andrews; ✉ Royal Courts of Justice, Strand, London WC2A 2LL

ANDREWS, Sir Ian Charles Franklin; kt (2007), CBE (1992), TD (1989); s of Peter Harry Andrews, and Nancy Gwladys, *née* Franklin; *b* 26 November 1953; *Educ* Solihull Sch, Univ of Bristol (BSc); *m* 1985, Moira Fraser McEwan; 2 s, 1 da; *Career* MOD: joined 1975, private sec to Second Perm Under Sec of State 1979–81, short serv vol cmmn 1981–82, princ 1982, NATO Def Coll 1984–85, asst private sec to Sec of State for Def 1986–88, head Def Lands 1988–90, Resources and Prog (Army) 1990–93, civil sec Br Forces Germany/BAOR 1993–95, md (facilities) DERA 1995–97, chief exec Def Estates 1998–2002, second perm under sec of state for def 2002–08; chm Serious Organised Crime Agency 2009–13; non-exec dir Health and Social Care Information Centre 2013–; Maj TA 1972–93; FRGS 1996; *Recreations* travel, skiing; *Style*— Sir Ian Andrews, CBE, TD

ANDREWS, Prof John A; CBE (2000), JP (1975, supplemental list 1992); s of Arthur George Andrews (d 1980), of Newport, Gwent, and Hilda May Andrews (d 1989); *b* 29 January 1935; *Educ* Newport HS, Wadham Coll Oxford (MA, BCL); *m* 2 April 1960, Elizabeth Ann Mary, da of Frederick Edward Wilkes (d 1939), of King's Heath, Birmingham; 2 da (Carolyn Elizabeth b 1963, Susan Rebecca b 1966); *Career* called to the Bar Gray's Inn 1960 (bencher 1991); asst lectr Univ of Manchester 1957–58, lectr Univ of Birmingham 1958–67; Univ of Wales Aberystwyth: head Dept of Law 1970–92, prof of law 1967–92, vice-princ 1985–88, hon prof of law 1992–2000, emeritus prof 2000–; chief exec Further and Higher Educn Funding Cncls for Wales 1992–2000; visiting prof Univs of: Thessaloniki 1974 and 1990, Cracow 1978, Maryland 1983; ed Legal Studies 1981–93; chm: Cncl of Validating Univs 1987–90, Police Promotions Examinations Bd 1987–2002, Wales Advsy Body for Local Authy Higher Educn Standing Working Gp 1990–92, Agricultural Wages Bd 1999–2003, Gen Teaching Cncl for Wales 2000–04; memb Police Skills and Standards Orgn 2001–04; law advsr to the Universities Funding Cncl 1989–93; pres SPTL 1988–89; memb: Ct of Govrs Univ of Wales 1969–92 and 2000–04, Ct of Govrs Nat Library of Wales 1979–92, Police Trg Cncl 1987–2002 (acad advsr 1997–2002), Lord Chllr's Advsy Ctee on Legal Educn 1987–90, Welsh Economic Cncl 1994–96, SE Wales Economic Forum 1997–2000, Criminal Injuries Compensation Appeals Panel 2000–06, Cncl Univ of Cardiff 2000–08, Police Accreditation and Licensing Bd 2002–06, Cncl Univ of Wales Coll of Med 2000–04, Policing Ctee Justice Sector Skills Cncl 2004–06, Actuarial Profession Disciplinary Panel 2004–13, Ctee Action For Children Wales 2004–10, Bd of Dirs Royal Welsh Coll of Music and Drama 2006–14, Practice Assurance Ctee CIPFA 2007–15; Univ of S Wales (formerly Univ of Glamorgan): govr 2002–15, pro-chllr 2005–, vice-chm 2005–08, chm 2008–13; govr Llanishen HS 2005– (chm Bd of Govrs 2010–14); tstee: Hamlyn Tst 1969–2000, SPTL 1990–2005, AHRB 2001–05; hon fell: Univ of Wales Coll Newport 2000, Cardiff Univ 2008; Hon LLD Univ of South Wales 2016; FRSA 1992, FLSW 2014; *Books* Welsh Studies in Public Law (ed, 1970), Human Rights in Criminal Procedure (ed, 1982), The Welsh Language in the Courts (jtly, 1984), The International Protection of Human Rights (jtly, 1987), Criminal Evidence (jtly, 1987, 2 edn 1992), Criminal Evidence – Statutes and Materials (1990); numerous articles and notes on law and educn; *Recreations* walking, theatre, opera, food; *Clubs* Brynamlwg, Cardiff & County; *Style—* Prof John Andrews, CBE; ✉ The Croft, 110 Mill Road, Lisvane, Cardiff CF14 0UG (☎ 029 2075 3980, e-mail johnandr@talk21.com)

ANDREWS, Baroness (Life Peer UK 2000), of Southover in the County of East Sussex; (Elizabeth) Kay Andrews; OBE (1998); da of Thomas Clifford Andrews, of Tredegar, Gwent; *b* 16 May 1943; *Educ* Univ of Wales (BA), Univ of Sussex (MA, DPhil); *m* 1970 (m dis 1992), Prof Roy MacLeod; 1 s (Hon Alexander Roy David b 1975); *Career* Parly clerk Research Div House of Commons 1970–85, special advsr to Rt Hon Neil Kinnock as Ldr of Oppn 1985–92, fndr and dir Education Extra 1992–2002, a Baroness in Waiting (Govt whip for educn, health and social security) 2002–05, Parly sec ODPM 2005–06, Parly sec Dept for Communities and Local Govt 2006–09, chair English Heritage 2009–; *Style—* The Baroness Andrews, OBE; ✉ English Heritage, 1 Waterhouse Square, 138–142 Holborn, London EC1N 2ST

ANDREWS, Leighton; s of Thomas Leonard Andrews (d 1967), and Peggy, *née* Squires; *b* 11 August 1957, Cardiff; *Educ* Poole GS, Univ of Wales Bangor (BA), Univ of Sussex (MA); *m* 6 July 1996, Ann Beynon; 2 step c; *Career* vice-pres NUS 1980–81, parly offr Age Concern 1982–84, UK campaign dir UN Int Year of Shelter 1984–87, dir then md Sallingbury Casey 1988–91, dir then jt md Rowland Co 1991–93, head of public affrs BBC 1993–96, chm Political Context and Welsh Context 1996–99, dir then md Westminster Strategy 2000–02, md Smart Co 2001–02, lectr Univ of Cardiff Journalism Sch 2002–03, memb Nat Assembly for Wales (Lab) Rhondda 2003–16, dep min for social justice and public serv delivery with special responsibility for housing 2007, dep min for regeneration 2007–09, min for children, educn and lifelong learning 2009–11, min for educn and skills 2011–13, min for public skills 2014–16; visiting prof: Univ of Westminster 1997–2002, Cardiff Univ 2004–; memb Inst of Welsh Affrs; supporter Homeless Int; *Publications* Wales Says Yes (1999), Ministering to Education (2014); author of various chapters in books and academic articles; *Recreations* watching Cardiff City FC, reading, cinema, cooking; *Style—* Leighton Andrews, Esq; ✉ e-mail leighton4labour@gmail.com

ANDREWS, Prof Emeritus Malcolm Yardley; s of Francis Yardley Andrews (d 1980), and Marguerite Joan, *née* West (d 2012); *b* 1 September 1942, Talyllyn, Wales; *Educ* Lancing, Gonville & Caius Coll Cambridge (BA), London Institute of Education (PGCE), Birkbeck Coll London (PhD); *m* 1, 1967 (m dis 1973), Mildred, *née* Randolph; 1 s (Richard Randolph Yardley b 18 Feb 1971), 1 step da (Megan Jennifer Clarke b 5 Oct 1962); m 2, 1981, Kristin Avelda, *née* Wade; 2 s (Peter Nigel b 18 Dec 1982, Francis Hunter b 7 June 1984); *Career* lectr: Dept of English Univ of Guelph 1966–67, Dept of English Birkbeck Coll London 1969–70, Sch of English Univ of Kent 1971–2009 (prof 1996–); pres Dickens Soc USA 2003–04, ed The Dickensian jl 1991–; memb AHRC Peer Review Coll 2004–09; *Books* Dickens on England and the English (1979), The Search for the Picturesque: Landscape Aesthetics and Tourism in Britain, 1750–1800 (1989), Dickens and the Grown-up Child (1994), The Picturesque: Sources and Documents (ed, 3 vols, 1994), Landscape and Western Art (1999), Charles Dickens and His Performing Selves: Dickens and the Public Readings (2006), Dickensian Laughter: Essays on Dickens and Humour (2013); *Recreations* writing, reading, public readings of Dickens, Languedoc holidays and wines; *Style—* Prof Emeritus Malcolm Andrews; ✉ School of English, Rutherford College, University of Kent, Canterbury, Kent CT2 7NX (e-mail m.y.andrews@kent.ac.uk)

ANDREWS, Margaret; MBE (2013); *Career* chair NI Fishery Harbour Authy; *Style—* Ms Margaret Andrews, MBE; ✉ Northern Ireland Fishery Harbour Authority, 3 St Patricks Avenue, Downpatrick, Co Down BT30 6DW

ANDREWS, Mark Björnsen; s of Harry Field Andrews, of Reading, and Ruth Margaret, *née* Legge; *b* 12 July 1952; *Educ* Reading GS, Hertford Coll Oxford (BA); *m* 20 June 2003, Jane Mary Shillito; 2 step s (Matthew Redway, Robert Redway); *Career* admitted slr 1976; Wilde Sapte (now Dentons UKMEA LLP): ptnr 1979–2011, head of Restructuring and Insolvency Gp 1990–2010, sr ptnr 1996–2000, dep chm 2000–02, conslt 2011–; non-exec dir Healthcare Locums plc 2011–13, sr ind dir Zolfo Cooper LLP 2013–15, dir AI Scheme Ltd 2014–; dir Dulwich Picture Gallery Enterprises Ltd 2013–; chm of tstees Pimlico Opera 1995–2015, chm of tstees Grange Park Opera Endowment Fund 2005–14, tstee Dulwich Picture Gallery 2012–, tstee The Crescent 2013–; memb: Law Soc 1974, Assoc of Business Recovery Practioners 1991, City of London Slrs' Co 1994, Int Bar Assoc 1994, Int Insolvency Inst 2005; *Recreations* music, history, outdoor activities, ornithology, art; *Style—* Mark Andrews, Esq; ✉ e-mail m.bjornsen@hotmail.com

ANDREWS, Mark Canter; s of Peter J Andrews (d 1993), of Bristol, and Joyce, *née* Abbey; *b* 9 November 1954; *Educ* Bristol Cathedral Sch; *Career* trainee architect Moxley Jenner & Partners 1973–74; graphic designer: BBC Bristol 1974–76, ITV (ATV, HTV, Westward TV) 1976–78; prodr Freeman Mathews & Milne advtg agency 1978–80; Collett Dickenson Pearce & Partners: prodr 1980–86, bd dir/head of TV 1986–89, fndr chm Independent Image (subsid) 1989–92; fndr md Propaganda Films Europe (subsid of Polygram plc) 1992–95, md Rogue Films (subsid of Carlton plc) 1995–96, fndr md Tsunami Films Ltd 1996–2002, Manifesto Films 2002–, M-A-D-E Ltd (Mark Andrews Digital Emporium Ltd) 2004–, MADE In London Ltd 2011, MADE Other 2012; chm Pliatsky II Ctee 1994–95; former memb: ACTT, IPA; memb AFVPA 1992; *Recreations* skiing, wine, fly fishing, lunch, big hi-fi, Br Cwlth stamps; *Clubs* Soho House; *Style—* Mark Andrews, Esq; ✉ 25 Battersea Church Road, London SW11 3LY (☎ 07785 791429); M-A-D-E Ltd, 10–11 Charterhouse Square, London EC1M 6EH (e-mail mark@madeinlondon.biz, website www.m-a-d-e.net)

ANDREWS, Naveen William Sidney; s of Stanley Andrews, and Nirmala Andrews; *b* 17 January 1969, London; *Educ* GSM; *Children* 2 s (Jaisal, Joshua); *Career* actor; *Film* incl: The English Patient 1996, Bride and Prejudice 2004, Grindhouse 2007, The Brave One 2007, Caught in Flight 2013, Diana 2013; *Television* incl Lost 2004–10, Sinbad 2012; *Style—* Mr Naveen Andrews

ANDREWS, Peter John; QC (1991); s of Reginald Percy Andrews, of Sutton Coldfield, and Dora, *née* Carter; *b* 14 November 1946; *Educ* Bishop Veseys GS, Univ of Bristol (undergraduate scholar), Christ's Coll Cambridge; *m* 10 Sept 1976, (Hilary) Ann, da of Graham Chavasse (d 1978); 2 da (Emily Alice b 19 May 1979, Fleur Victoria b 17 May 1981); *Career* called to the Bar Lincoln's Inn 1970 (Hardwicke scholar; bencher 1999), barrister specialising in catastrophic personal injury and clinical negligence law, jr Midland & Oxford Circuit 1973–74, dir Birmingham Legal Advice Centre 1974–75, recorder of the Crown Court 1990–2012 (asst recorder 1986–90), chm Fountain Court Chambers Ltd 1994–2004, head of chambers 199 Strand 1997–2000, dep High Court judge 1998–2012; memb Professional Conduct Ctee GMC 2001–12, legal chm Mental Health Review Tbnl 2007–; *Books* Catastrophic Injuries: A Guide to Compensation (1997), Kemp & Kemp: The Quantum of Damages (contributing ed, 2004), Personal Injury Handbook (contrib, 2006), Guide to Catastrophic Injury Claims (contrib, 2010); *Style—* Peter Andrews, Esq, QC; ✉ 7 Bedford Row, London WC1R 4BS (☎ 020 7242 3555, fax 020 7242 2511, e-mail pandrews@7br.co.uk)

ANDREWS, Richard Edward; s of William Reginald Andrews (d 1983), and Agnes Ruby Whiffen (d 1994); *b* 15 August 1936, Cambridge; *Educ* Cambridgeshire HS, St Catharine's Coll Cambridge (scholar, MA, two Figgis Meml prizes); *m* 20 Aug 1982, Stephanie Elizabeth, da of Percy Craig, of Motueka, NZ; 1 s, 1 da; *Career* Fly Offr RAF 1955–57; sr conslt PA 1965–72, personnel mangr BLMC 1972–74, personnel dir Franklin Mint USA 1974–78, business mangr Cassells 1979, gp personnel dir Dixons Gp plc 1980–95; dir Dixons Bradford CTC Tst 1988–; memb: Industry In Educn 1994–97, Industrial Tbnls 1995–98; FIPD, FRSA; *Books* Linda Nham: My Story (jtly, 2015); *Publications* Selection and Assessment (1989), Ethics in Business (1995); various articles on pay and personnel mgmnt; *Recreations* playing bad golf, watching good rugby, surfing the net, sketching badly, trying to stop wine tasting turning into too much wine drinking; *Clubs* Maungakiekie Golf, Achilles; *Style—* Richard Andrews, Esq; ✉ 18 Golf Road, Epsom, Auckland, New Zealand (☎ 00 64 9 631 5562, e-mail dick@andrewsfamily.co.nz)

ANG, Dr Swee Chai; da of P L Ang, of Singapore, and L H Ang, *née* Lee; *b* 26 October 1948; *Educ* Raffles GS, Univ of Singapore (MB BS, MSc); *m* 29 Jan 1977, Francis Khoo, *qv*, s of Anthony T E Khoo (d 1972), of Singapore; *Career* orthopaedic surgn HS of Gaza Hosp Beirut 1982–, surgn UN Gaza Strip 1988–89, conslt surgn WHO Gaza and W Bank 1989, sr conslt orthopaedic surgn Newham Gen Hosp London 1994–96, conslt orthopaedic surgn Royal London Hosp 1996–; fndr memb Br Charity Medical Aid for Palestinians; memb BMA; FBOA, FRCS; *Books* From Beirut to Jerusalem (1989), Manual of War Surgery (1994); *Recreations* music, poetry; *Style—* Dr Swee Ang; ✉ Medical Aid for Palestinians, 33A Islington Park Street, London N1 1QB (☎ 020 7226 4114, fax 020 7226 0880)

ANGEL, Prof Heather; *née* Le Rougetel; da of Stanley Paul Le Rougel (d 2002), and Hazel Marie, *née* Sherwood (d 2010); *b* 21 July 1941, Fulmer, Bucks; *Educ* 14 schs in England and NZ, Univ of Bristol (BSc, MSc); *m* 3 Oct 1964, Martin Vivian Angel, s of Thomas Huber Angel; 1 s (Giles Philip b 25 May 1977); *Career* marine biologist, professional wildlife photographer, author and lectr; special prof Dept of Life Science Univ of Nottingham 1994–; columnist Amateur Photographer 1990–97; television appearances (demonstrating photographic techniques): Me and My Camera 1981 and 1983, Gardeners' World 1983 and 1991, Nature 1984, Nocon on Photography 1988; pres RPS 1984–86; RPS Hood medal 1975, Medaille de Salverte (Société Française de Photographie) 1984, Louise Schmidt Laureate 1998; Hon DSc Univ of Bath 1986; Hon FRPS 1986 (FRPS 1972), FBIPP 1972; *Solo Exhibitions* Kodak Exhibition The Natural History of Britain and Ireland (Science Museum) 1981, Nature in Focus (Nat Hist Museum) 1987, The Art of Wildlife Photography (Nature in Art Gloucester) 1989, Natural Visions (Dimbola Lodge Isle of Wight, Gilbert White's House Selborne, The Yard Gallery Nottingham and Nature in Art Gloucester) 2000, Natural Visions (Edinburgh Botanic Garden, Aberystwyth Arts Centre, Gosport Gallery, Bradford Design Exchange, Lynn Museum Kings Lynn, Booth Museum Brighton, Oxford Univ Museum, Astley Hall Museum Chorley, Royal Botanic Gardens Kew, Somerset County Museum Taunton, New Walk Museum Leicester, Grosvenor Museum Chester, Bristol Museum and Art Gallery, Haslemere Educational Museum, Kuala Lumpur, Cairo and Beijing) 2001–04; *Books* Nature Photography: Its Art and Techniques (1972), Photographing Nature (5 vols, 1975), Life in The Oceans (1977), The Book of Nature Photography (1983), Camera in the Garden (1984), The Book of Close-up Photography (1986), A View from a Window (1988), Nature in Focus (1988), Landscape Photography (1989), Animal Photography (1991), Kew: A World of Plants (1993), Photographing the Natural World (1994), Outdoor Photography: 101 Tips and Hints (1997), Pandas (1998), How to Photograph Flowers (1998), How to Photograph Water (1999), Natural Visions (2000), Giant Pandas (2006), Puffins (2007), Macro through a Nikon Lens (2007), Green China (2008), Snow Monkeys (2009), Living Dinosaurs (2009), Heather Angel's Wild Kew (2009), Exploring Natural China (2010), Digital Outdoor Photography: 101 Top Tips (2012); *Recreations* travelling to remote parts of the world to photograph wilderness areas and unusual aspects of animal behaviour; *Style—* Prof Heather Angel; ✉ e-mail heather@naturalvisions.co.uk, website www.heatherangel.co.uk, Twitter @angelantics

ANGEL, Marie Louise; da of Francis John Angel (d 1968), of Australia, and Thelma Lilie, *née* Schwab (d 1974); *b* 30 July 1953; *Educ* Methodist Ladies' Coll Adelaide; *m* 1985, David Charles Freeman, s of Howard Freeman; 1 da (Catherine Elinor b 13 May 1989), 1 s (Lachlan John b 28 Feb 1993); *Career* soprano; with Opera Factory London 1982–; winner Gulbenkian prize 1977, Countess of Munster prize 1977, Kammersägerin 1997; *Performances* with Opera Factory incl: Pretty Polly 1983, Donna Anna in Don Giovanni 1990 and 1992, Countess Almaviva in Don Giovanni 1992 (later filmed for Channel 4), Fiordiligi in Cosi fan Tutte 1986 (later filmed for Channel 4), Hannah in Yan Tan Thethera 1992, title role in L'Incoronazione di Poppea 1992, Sarajevo 1994 (several acting roles incl Cassandra in Trojan Women), Dido in Dido & Aeneas London and Zürich 1995; others incl: Oracle of the Dead in The Mask of Orpheus (ENO) 1986, Donna Anna (Melbourne State Opera) 1990, cr role Morgan le Fay in Gawain (Royal Opera House Covent Garden) 1991, cr role Esmerelda in Rosa (Peter Greenaway and Louis Andriessen, Netherlands Opera) 1994 (filmed 1998), cr role Ingrid in Lovendier Esmée Holland Festival 1995, Kagel's Aud Deutchland (1997), Countess in Soldaten (ENO) 1996 and (Basel Theatre) 1998–99, Fortunata in Satyricon (with Herbert Wernicke and Basel Theatre) 1998, title role in Lustige Witwe (Herbert Wernicke and Basel Theatre) 1999, Ottavia in L'Incoronazione di Poppea (Basel Theatre) 2003–04, one-woman show Til the Fat Lady Sings (Drill Hall London) 2007 and (tour Basel, Zurich and Australia) 2008, Silent Twins (Almeida) 2007; also appeared in Peter Greenaway's film Prospero's Books 1991, Facing Goya (throughout Spain) 2000–01, Kagel/Mozart Project (La Fenice, Venice) 2001, John Cage's Europera 5 2001–02, Sonetti Lussuriosi (written by Michael Nyman, world tour) 2007 and (world tour) 2007–09, Fast Forward Figaro (with Janis Kelly); *Recordings* Gawain (Grammy of the Year 1997), Mask of Orpheus 1997, Prospero's Books, Rosa 1999, Facing Goya 2002, Nyman World Tour of I Sonetti Lussuriosi 2008–09; *Videos/DVDs* Gawain, Rosa, Aus Deutchland, Cosi fan Tutte, Don Giovanni, The Marriage of Figaro, Seven Deadly Sins, Hotel de Pekin; *Recreations* gardening; *Style—* Ms Marie Angel; ✉ c/o Allied Artists' Agency, 42 Montpelier Square, London SW7 1JZ (☎ 020 7589 6243)

ANGELINI, Prof Gianni Davide; s of Marzio Angelini, of Siena, Italy, and Erina Angelini; *b* 29 January 1953, Siena, Italy; *Educ* Instituto T Sarrocchi Siena (Dip Mech Engrg), Univ of Siena Sch of Med (Lode Prize, MD), Univ of Wales Coll of Med (MCh); *m* 5 July 1985, Rosalind, da of Arthur John, and Megan John; 3 s (Jonathan b 7 Dec 1986, Timothy b 5 April 1988, Simon b 27 Dec 1994); *Career* Univ Hosp of Siena 1979–80 (latterly SHO in cardiovascular surgery); SHO: in cardiothoracic surgery Llandough Hosp Cardiff 1981, in gen surgery Univ Hosp of Wales Cardiff 1981–82, in casualty/accident Royal Gwent Hosp Newport 1982–83; registrar then sr registrar in cardiothoracic surgery Univ Hosp of Wales Cardiff 1983–88, sr registrar in cardiothoracic surgery Thoraxcenter Erasmus Univ Rotterdam 1988–89, lectr and Br Heart Fndn intermediate research fell in cardiothoracic surgery Univ Hosp of Wales Cardiff 1989, sr lectr and conslt in cardiothroacic surgery Univ of Sheffield 1989–92; currently: Br Heart Fndn prof of cardiac surgery Univ of Bristol, dir Bristol Heart, chair of cardiothoracic surgery and head of HNLI cardiac surgery Imperial Coll London 2010–; dir NIHR Biomedical Research Unit in Cardiovascular Medicine Bristol 2009, sr NIHR clinical investigator 2009; visiting prof: Univ of the WI 1992, Queen Alia Med Centre Amman 1995, Univ of Buffalo 1996, Chinese Univ of Hong Kong 1997 and 2013, European Hosp Paris 1997, Univ of Groningen 1997, Univ of Milan 1997 and 1999, Univ of Chieti 1998, St Luke's Hosp Thessaloniki 1999, Univ of Utrecht 2000, Hosp Univ Kebangsaan Malaysia 2001; regnl advsr to the Royal Colls NHS R&D Exec; expert assessor: Med Devices Directorate Dept of Health, Nat Inst for Clinical Excellence (NICE), Cardiosource; rep of profs of surgery Cardiothoracic SAC Jt Ctee of Higher Surgical Trg; memb Project Grant Ctee: Br Heart Fndn, EPSRC; memb: Br Soc for Cardiovascular Res (past chm), Br Cardiac Soc (exec memb Cncl), Soc of Cardiothoracic Surgeons of GB and I (exec memb Cncl Cardiothoracic Section), Int Soc for Heart Research, European Soc of Cardiology (exec memb Pathogenesis of Atherosclerosis Gp, memb Study Gp on Advanced Heart Failure), European Soc for Cardiothoracic Surgery, Br Atherosclerosis Soc, American Assoc for Thoracic Surgery; Young Research Workers Prize Br Cardiac Soc 1986, Peter Allen Prize Soc of Cardiothoracic Surgns of GB and I 1988, First Research Prize European Soc for Vascular Surgery 1990, David Cooper Prize Soc of Cardiothoracic Surgns of GB and I 1991; FRCSGlas 1986, fell European Bd of Thoracic and Cardiovascular Surgns (FETCS) 1998, FMedSci 2011; Cavaliere Merit Repubblica Italiana; *Recreations* jazz music, running; *Style*— Prof Gianni Angelini; ✉ Bristol Heart Institute, Bristol Royal Infirmary, Bristol BS2 8HW (☎ 0117 928 3145, fax 0117 929 9737, e-mail g.d.angelini@bristol.ac.uk)

ANGEST, Sir Henry; kt (2015); *Educ* Univ of Basel Switzerland (LLL); *Career* chm: Arbuthnot Banking Gp plc (also chief exec), Arbuthnot Latham & Co Ltd; dir Secure Trust Bank plc; Past Master Worshipful Co of Int Bankers; *Recreations* dendrology; *Clubs* City Swiss (hon pres), White's; *Style*— Sir Henry Angest; ✉ Arbuthnot Banking Group plc, Arbuthnot House, 7 Wilson Street, London EC2M 2SN (☎ 020 7012 2400, fax 020 7012 2401)

ANGIER, Carole; da of Jussi Brainin, and Liesl, *née* Kelsen; *b* 30 October 1943, London; *Educ* McGill Univ Montreal (BA), Univ of Oxford (MA), Univ of Cambridge (MLitt); *Children* 1 s (Thomas Peter Stephen b 22 May 1970); *Career* lectr in literature and philosophy: Univ of Cambridge and Univ of Sussex 1975, external studies depts Univ of Oxford and Univ of Bristol 1975–80, Open Univ 1975–85; Univ of Warwick: fndr and teacher of the practice of biography 2003–04, Royal Literary Fund Advsy fell 2003–05 (fell 1999–2003), project fell (teaching creative writing to refugees and asylum seekers in Oxford) 2004; teacher of life writing Birkbeck Coll Univ of London 2005–, assoc lectr MA in Creative Writing Oxford Brookes Univ 2011–13; mentor Arts Cncl Writers' Pool 2003–05, mentor Gold Dust 2006–12, fndr and mentor The Writer's Project 2013–; Royal Literary Fund fell Oxford Brookes Univ 2010–11; book reviewer The Spectator, New Statesman, The Independent, The Daily Telegraph, The Sunday Times and Literary Review 1975–; freelance journalist, articles in numerous publications incl: The Guardian, London Review of Books, London Magazine, Sight & Sound, Jewish Quarterly; wrote and presented Edgar Reitz for Omnibus (BBC2) 1991, wrote English subtitles for Edgar Reitz's Die Zweite Heimat 1991; Commonwealth Scholarship 1964–66, Canada Cncl Fellowship 1969–75; Writers Guild Non-Fiction Award 1991, Southern Arts Non-Fiction Award 1991, Winston Churchill Travelling Fellowship 1993, Arts Cncl Writers Award 1998; shortlisted Whitbread Biography Prize 1991; patron Nat Acad of Writing, vol worker and tstee Asylum Welcome Oxford (visitor to immigration detainees), message and tracing vol Red Cross, supporter Med Fndn for the Victims of Torture; memb: PEN, Writers in Oxford, Soc of Authors; FRSL 2002; *Books* Life of Margaret Hill (1978), Jean Rhys (1985), Jean Rhys: Life and Work (1990), The Double Bond: Primo Levi, A Biography (2002), The Story of my Life: Refugees Writing in Oxford (ed, 2005), Lyla and Majnon: poems by Hasan Bamyani (trans and ed, 2008), See How I Land: Oxford Poets and Exiled Writers (co-ed, 2009), Life Writing: A Writers' and Artists' Companion (jtly, 2010), series ed (jtly) 8 further Artists' and Writers' Companions 2012–15, currently working on a literary life of W G Sebald; *Recreations* walking, talking; *Style*— Carole Angier, FRSL; ✉ 13 High Street, Ascott-under-Wychwood, Oxfordshire OX7 6AW (☎ 01993 830414), c/o Rogers, Coleridge & White Ltd, 20 Powis Mews, London W11 1JN (☎ 020 7221 3717)

ANGIOLINI, Rt Hon Dame Elish Frances; DBE (2011), PC (2006), QC (2001), WS (2005); da of James McPhilomy (d 1981), and Mary McPhilomy; *b* 24 June 1960, Glasgow; *Educ* Notre Dame Sch Glasgow, Univ of Strathclyde (LLB, DipLP); *m* 14 Sept 1985, Domenico Angiolini; 2 s (Domenico b 16 Nov 1996, David b 4 April 2000); *Career* admitted slr 1985; early career as depute procurator fiscal Airdrie and with Mgmnt Servs Gp Crown Office, sr depute procurator fiscal then asst procurator fiscal Glasgow 1995–97, head of policy Crown Office 1997–2000, regnl procurator fiscal Grampian, Highlands and Islands 2000–01, slr gen for Scotland 2001–06, Lord Advocate of Scotland 2006–11, princ St Hugh's Coll Oxford 2012–, chllr Univ of West Scotland 2013; Hon LLD: Glasgow Caledonian Univ 2005, Univ of Strathclyde 2007, Univ of Aberdeen 2007; Hon DUniv Open Univ 2013, Hon DUniv Univ of Stirling 2013; FRSA; *Style*— The Rt Hon Dame Elish Angiolini, DBE, QC; ✉ St Hugh's College, St Margaret's Road, Oxford OX2 6LE

ANGUS, Jamie; *Career* ed The World at One (BBC Radio 4) 2009–10, acting dep ed Newsnight (BBC) until 2013, ed Today (BBC Radio 4) 2013–; *Style*— Jamie Angus, Esq; ✉ Today, BBC Radio 4, Broadcasting House, London W1A 1AA

ANGUS, Robin John; s of Ian Gordon Angus (d 1994), of Forres, Moray, and Morag Ann (Sally), *née* Macdonald; *b* 15 September 1952; *Educ* Forres Acad, Univ of St Andrews (MA), Peterhouse Cambridge; *m* 20 Aug 1977, Lorna Christine, da of James Smith Campbell (d 1986), of Drumlemble, Argyll; *Career* investment mangr Baillie Gifford & Co 1977–81, investment tst analyst Wood Mackenzie & Co 1981–85, asst dir Wood Mackenzie & Co Ltd 1985–88; dir: Personal Assets Tst plc 1984–, Hill Samuel Securities Ltd 1985–88, NatWest Securities Ltd (incorporating Wood Mackenzie & Co Ltd) 1988–91 (dir Equities 1991–98), Charlotte Marketing Services Ltd 1991–94, The Edinburgh Agency Ltd 1991–, Ivory & Sime Trustlink Ltd 1994–98, Collective Assets Tst plc 1998–2005; advsr Centre for Fin Markets Research Univ of Edinburgh 1995–2010; hon prof Sch of Mgmnt and Languages Heriot-Watt Univ 2010–; memb Gen Synod Scottish Episcopal Church 1987–91; memb Monks of St Giles 2004–; Grand Makar Von Poser Soc of Scotland 1997–, Laureate Edinburgh Morayshire Soc 1996–; hon DLitt Heriot-Watt Univ 2013; hon fell Faculty of Social Sciences Univ of Edinburgh 1999–2010; FCSI 2010; Knight of St Sylvester 2001; *Books* Independence – The Option for Growth (1989), Haec Olim – Exploring the World of Investment Trusts 1981–1991 (1991), Capital – A Moral Instrument? (contrib, 1992), Dictionary of Scottish Church History and Theology (contrib, 1993), Personal Assets Trust Quarterlies: The 1990s and Beyond (2002), 60 Not Out – Personal Assets Trust Quarterlies 2002–11 (2011); *Recreations* church work, politics (Scottish Nationalist), history, music, reading, writing verse; *Clubs* New (Edinburgh), Scottish Arts (Edinburgh), McSkate's (St Andrews); *Style*— Robin Angus, Esq; ✉ Personal Assets Trust plc, 10 Colme Street, Edinburgh EH3 6AA

ANHOLT, Catherine; da of Daniel Hogarty, and Diane, *née* Kelly; *b* 18 January 1958; *Educ* Stroud Girls' HS, Falmouth Sch of Art (BA), RCA (MA); *m* Laurence Anholt , *qv*; 1 s (Tom), 2 da (Claire, Maddy); *Career* illustrator of children's books for 30 years, now fine artist; involved with Bookstart (early years literacy campaign); *Books* Big Book of Families, What Makes me Happy?, Here Come the Babies, What I Like, Kids, The Twins, Two By Two, Bear and Baby, Come Back, Jack!, Baby's Things, First Words, Colours, Clothes, Can You Guess?, Chimp and Zee, Animals, Animals All Around, Look What I Can Do, Sun, Snow, Stars, Sky, One, Two, Three Count With Me, All About You, The Snow Fairy and the Spaceman, Tom's Rainbow Walk, When I Was A Baby, Aren't You Lucky!, Harry's Home, Billy and the Big New School, Good Days Bad Days, Going To Playgroup, Sophie and the New Baby, The New Puppy, Animal Friends, Bed Time, Busy Day, Play Time, A Kiss Like This, Little Copy Cub, Chimp and Zee and the Big Storm; *Awards* Right Start Toy and Book Award 1998 (three titles), overall winner Kid's Club Network Award 1999, Nestlé Smarties Gold Award 1999 and 2001, US CCBC Choices 2001 (two titles), Oppenheim Portfolio Gold Award (twice), The English Assoc 4–11 Awards (two titles); *Recreations* family life, cycling, fishing, walking; *Style*— Mrs Catherine Anholt; ✉ e-mail catherine@anholt.co.uk, website www.anholt.co.uk

ANHOLT, Laurence; s of Gerry Anholt, and Joan, *née* Pickford (d 2003); *Educ* Boxhill Sch, Epsom Sch of Art, Falmouth Sch of Art (BA), Royal Acad of Art (MA); *m* Catherine Anholt , *qv*; 1 s (Tom), 2 da (Claire, Maddy); *Career* carpenter, sch teacher, author and illustrator of children's books; involved with Bookstart (early years literacy campaign); *Books* author and illustrator: Camille and the Sunflowers, Degas and the Little Dancer, Picasso and the Girl With a Ponytail, Leonardo and the Flying Boy, The Forgotten Forest; illustrated by Catherine Anholt: Big Book of Families, What Makes me Happy?, Here Come the Babies, What I Like, Kids, The Twins, Two By Two, Bear and Baby, Come Back, Jack!, Baby's Things, First Words, Colours, Clothes, Can You Guess?, Chimp and Zee, Animals, Animals All Around, Look What I Can Do, Sun, Snow, Stars, Sky, One, Two, Three Count With Me, All About You, The Snow Fairy and the Spaceman, Tom's Rainbow Walk, When I Was A Baby, Aren't You Lucky!, Harry's Home, Billy and the Big New School, Good Days Bad Days, Going To Playgroup, Sophie and the New Baby, The New Puppy, Animal Friends, Bed Time, Busy Day, Play Time, A Kiss Like This, Little Copy Cub, Chimp and Zee and the Big Storm; Seriously Silly Stories (illustrated by Arthur Robins): Cinderboy, Daft Jack and the Beanstack, Rumply Crumply Stinky Pin, Billy Beast, The Emperor's Underwear, The Rather Small Turnip, The Fried Piper of Hamstring Town, Little Red Riding Wolf, Snow White and the Seven Aliens, Shampoozel, Eco Wolf and the Three Pig, Ghostyshocks and the Three Scares, Seriously Silly Stories – The Collection; The One and Only series (illustrated by Tony Ross): Harold the Hairiest Man, Ruby the Rudest Girl, Boris the Brainiest Baby, Polly the Most Poetic Person, Bruno the Bravest Man, Ben the Bendiest Boy, Tina the Tiniest Girl, Micky the Muckiest Boy; other books: The Superkid Handbook (illustrated by Martin Chatterton), Knee High Nigel (illustrated by Arthur Robins), The Magpie Song (illustrated by Dan Williams), Summerhouse (illustrated by Lynne Russell), I Like Me (illustrated by Adriano Gon), Stone Girl, Bone Girl (illustrated by Sheila Moxley); *Awards* Right Start Toy and Book Award 1998 (three titles), overall winner Kid's Club Network Award 1999, Nestlé Smarties Gold Award 1999 and 2001, US CCBC Choices 2001 (two titles), Oppenheim Portfolio Gold Award (twice), The English Assoc 4–11 Awards (two titles); *Recreations* a long soak in a warm book; *Style*— Laurence Anholt, Esq; ✉ e-mail info@anholt.co.uk, website www.anholt.co.uk

ANKARCRONA, Jan Gustaf Theodor Stensson; s of Sten Stensson Ankarcrona, RVO (d 1981), of Stockholm, Sweden, and Ebba, *née* Countess Mörner (d 1999); *b* 18 April 1940; *Educ* Östra Real Stockholm, Stockholm Sch of Econ (MBA), Univ of Calif Berkeley (MBA); *m* 1, 16 June 1968 (m dis 1978), E Margaretha Antonie, da of Erik von Eckermann (d 2004), of Ripsa, Sweden; 2 s (Johan b 1969, Edward b 1972); m 2, 6 March 1981, Sandra, da of E B Coxe (d 2007), of Hobe Sound, USA; 2 da (Aurore b 1983, Ariane b 1988); *Career* Royal Swedish Navy 1958–61, Lt-Cdr Royal Swedish Navy Reserve 1974; Stockholms Enskilda Bank Stockholm 1964–65, Gränges AB Stockholm 1966–69, American Express Securities SA Paris 1969–70, dep md Nordic Bank Ltd London 1971–83, md and chief exec Fennoscandia Bank Ltd London 1983–91, md Lexa UK Ltd London 1992–; non-exec dir: China Devpt Capital GP Ltd, Martin Currie ALTU Fund, China Healthcare Partnership, China Devpt Capital GP Ltd; chm China Absolute Fund Ltd; OStJ Sweden; *Recreations* shooting, sailing, tennis, music, history; *Clubs* Brooks's, Hurlingham, Nya Sällskapet Stockholm; *Style*— Jan Ankarcrona, Esq; ✉ 6 Stratford Studios, Stratford Road, London W8 6RG (☎ 020 7937 9438); Lexa UK Ltd, 14 Queen Anne's Gate, London SW1H 9AA (☎ 020 7222 0400, fax 020 7222 0125)

ANNANDALE AND HARTFELL, 11 Earl of (S, by Charter, 1662 with precedence of 1643); Patrick Andrew Wentworth Hope Johnstone of Annandale and of that Ilk; DL (Dumfriesshire 1987); also Lord of Johnstone (S 1662), Hereditary Steward of Stewartry of Annandale, Hereditary Keeper of Castle of Lochmaben, and Chief of Clan Johnstone; s of Maj Percy Wentworth Hope Johnstone, TD, JP, RA (TA), *de jure* 10 Earl (d 1983), by his 2 w, Margaret Jane Hunter-Arundell (Dowager Countess of Annandale and Hartfell) (d 1998); claim to Earldom (which had been dormant since 1792) admitted by Ctee for Privileges of House of Lords, and a writ issued summoning him to Parl in the Upper House 1986; *b* 19 April 1941; *Educ* Stowe, RAC Cirencester; *m* 1969, Susan, o da of Col Walter John Macdonald Ross, CB, OBE, TD, JP, Lord-Lt of the Stewartry, of Netherhall, Castle Douglas, Kirkcudbrightshire; 1 s (David Patrick Wentworth, Lord Johnstone and Master of Annandale and Hartfell b 13 Oct 1971), 1 da (Lady Julia Clare b 1974); *Heir* s, Lord Johnstone; *Career* underwriting memb Lloyd's 1976–2004; memb: Solway River Purification Bd 1970–86, Scottish Valuation Advsy Cncl to Sec of State for Scotland 1984–86, Annan Fishery Bd 1983–, Standing Cncl of Scottish Chiefs, various ctees Dumfries CC 1970–75, Dumfries & Galloway Regnl Cncl 1974–86; chm: Royal Jubilee and Prince's Tst for Dumfries and Galloway 1984–88, Royal Scottish Forestry Soc 1981–84; dir: Bowerings Members Agency 1985–88, Murray Lawrence Members Agency 1988–92; co-dir: The Maclay Group, Raehills Farms Ltd, Skairfield Ltd, River Annan Tst, Mattheus ONE; Vice Lord-Lt Dumfriesshire 1992–2016; *Recreations* golf; *Clubs* New, Puffin's (Edinburgh); *Style*— The Rt Hon the Earl of Annandale and Hartfell, DL; ✉ Annandale Estates Office, St Anns, Lockerbie, Dumfriesshire DG11 1HQ

ANNAS, Rt Rev Geoffrey Peter (Geoff); *see:* Stafford, Bishop of

ANNESLEY, (Arthur) Noël Grove; s of Edmund Patrick Grove Annesley, OBE (d 1975), of Annes Grove, Castletownroche, Co Cork, and Ruth, *née* Rushforth (d 2007); *b* 28 December 1941; *Educ* Harrow, Worcester Coll Oxford (open scholarship, MA); *m* 7 Sept 1968, Caroline Susan, da of Thomas Henry Waldore Lumley; 2 s (Marcus Robert Grove b 27 March 1972, James Alexander Grove b 22 May 1974); *Career* Christie, Manson & Woods Ltd: joined 1964, fndr Dept of Prints, Drawings and Watercolours, auctioneer 1967–, dep chm 1985–91 (dir 1969–91); dep chm Christie's International plc 1992–98 (dir 1989–98), dep chm Christie's Fine Art Ltd 1998–2000, chm Christie's Education 2000–

11, chm Christie's International Fine Art Specialist Group 2000–03, hon chm Christie's Int (UK) Ltd 2004–; holds world record prices for Old Master drawings (Michelangelo and Leonardo da Vinci) and Br watercolours (J M W Turner); an authority on Old Master drawings with discoveries incl drawings by Michelangelo, Sebastiano del Piombo, Raphael and Rubens; tstee: Dulwich Picture Gallery 1998–2010 (dep chm 2006–10), Michael Marks Charitable Tst 2006–, Advsy Panel Nat Heritage Meml Fund 2006–11; govr Yehudi Menuhin Sch 2000–; The Touch of the Artist: Master Drawings from the Woodner Collection (contrib, 1995), The Expert versus the Object (contrib, 2004); contribs to Burlington Magazine and other specialist art jls; *Recreations* music (esp chamber), gardening, exploring classical sites, Ireland; *Clubs* Brooks's, Garrick, MCC; *Style*— Noël Annesley, Esq; ✉ Christie's, 8 King Street, St James's, London SW1Y 6QT (☎ 020 7389 2241, fax 020 7389 2520, e-mail nannesley@christies.com)

ANSARI, Dr Joseph Mohammad Ayub; s of Hakim Mohammad Yusuf Ansari (d 1971), and Hasina Khatoan, *née* Kidwai (d 1971); *b* 25 June 1938; *Educ* Shia Degree Coll Lucknow India (BSc), King Edward VII Med Coll Lahore Pakistan (MB BS); *m* 26 May 1972, Ruth, da of William Haughton Hill (d 1975), of Merseyside; 1 s (Arif b 20 Oct 1974), 1 da (Sarah b 16 Jan 1977); *Career* Dept of Psychiatry Univ of Liverpool: lectr 1971–75, sr lectr 1975–76, clinical lectr 1976–; conslt in psychological med 1976, med dir Regnl Alcohol Unit Liverpool 1976–, supervisor for Sr Registrar Training in Psychiatry Merseyside 1986–89; sec and treas NW Div RCPsych, treas Liverpool Psychiatric Soc (former pres); memb: Nat Cncl of Alcohol 1980–, World Psychiatric Assoc 1985–, BMA 1988–; author of several contribs on psycho-sexual problems and mental illness in leading medical jls; DPM 1970, MPsyMed 1975, FRCPsych 1985, FRSM 1997; *Recreations* photography, painting and reading; *Clubs* Rotary (Prescot Merseyside); *Style*— Dr Joseph Ansari; ✉ 31 Rodney Street, Liverpool L1 9EH (☎ 0151 709 1978)

ANSBRO, David Anthony; s of David Thomas Ansbro (d 1963), and Kathleen Mary, *née* Mallett (d 2007); *b* 3 April 1945; *Educ* Xaverian Coll Manchester, Univ of Leeds (LLB), Coll of Law, Univ of Birmingham (Advanced Mgmnt Course); *m* 1967, Veronica Mary, *née* Auton; 2 da (Lucy b 10 Aug 1968, Kate b 10 Sept 1970); *Career* admitted slr 1969, dep dir of admin W Yorks CC 1977–81 (asst dir of admin 1973–77), town clerk and chief exec York City Cncl 1981–85; chief exec: Kirklees Cncl 1985–87, Leeds City Cncl 1988–91; Eversheds: ptnr Leeds 1991, managing ptnr Leeds 1994–95, managing ptnr Leeds and Manchester 1995–2000, nat managing ptnr 2000–03, conslt 2003–06; memb Local Govt Cmmn for England 1992–95, dir Leeds TEC 1990–99; chm: Leeds Renaissance Partnership 2005–10, SFL Ltd 2005–10; pro-chllr Univ of Leeds 2000–07; dir and tstee Nat Centre for Early Music 2003–09, tstee Henry Moore Fndn 2003–10, chm Airton Parish Meeting 2011–; awarded Papal Medal 1982; Hon LLD Univ of Leeds 2007; memb SOLACE 1981; Order of St Gregory 2008; *Recreations* golf, wine, sport of any kind (except synchronised swimming!), passionate supporter of Manchester City FC; *Clubs* Honley Cricket, Upper Wharfedale RUFC; *Style*— David Ansbro; ✉ The Green, Airton, Skipton, North Yorkshire BD23 4AH (☎ 01729 830451, mobile 07721 868684, e-mail david.ansbro@btinternet.com)

ANSELL, His Hon Judge Anthony Ronald Louis; s of Samuel Ansell (d 1974), of London, and Joan Teresa, *née* Berman; *b* 9 September 1946; *Educ* Dulwich Coll, UCL (LLB); *m* 28 June 1970, Karen Judith (Kaye); 1 s (Simon b 1 Jan 1978), 1 da (Naomi b 4 May 1979); *Career* called to the Bar Gray's Inn 1968, in practice until 1979, slr 1980–95, circuit judge (SE Circuit) 1995–, judge of Employment Appeal Tbnl 2002–; memb Sentencing Advsy Panel 2005–; vice-pres United Synagogue 1992–97; *Books* Kalms Review – A Time for Change (co-author, 1992); *Recreations* opera, music, theatre, walking, swimming, gardening; *Style*— His Hon Judge Ansell; ✉ Wood Green Crown Court, Woodall House, Lordship Lane, London N22 5LF (☎ 020 8881 1400)

ANSELL, Caroline; MP; *b* 1971; *Educ* MA, NPQH; *m* Nick, 3 s; *Career* MP (Cons) Eastbourne 2015–; *Style*— Mrs Caroline Ansell, MP; ✉ House of Commons, London SW1A 0AA

ANSON, Lady Elizabeth; *see:* Shakerley, Lady Elizabeth Georgiana

ANSTEE, Eric E; s of Reginald Thomas Anstee, and Margaret Doris Anstee; *b* 1 January 1951; *Educ* St Albans Sch; *m*; 4 c; *Career* audit trainee Keens Shay Keens & Co 1969–74, audit sr to mangr Turquand Barton Mayhew 1974–76, joined Ernst & Young 1976, advsr DTI (secondment to Industrial Devpt Unit/MAFF) 1976–77, sr mangr Ernst & Young (Singapore) 1977–80, fin and business advsr (secondment) Cambridge Instrument Co Ltd 1980–83, commercial accountancy advsr (secondment) H M Treasy 1983–86, ptnr i/c co-ordinating work in Public Sector Ernst & Young 1986–88; Ernst & Young Mgmnt Consultants: ptnr, dir World-wide Privatisation Servs and dir UK Utilities Servs 1988–92, memb Mgmnt Bd 1992–93; gp fin dir Eastern Gp plc 1993–97, fin dir The Energy Gp plc 1997–98, gp fin dir Old Mutual plc 1998–99, chief exec Old Mutual Financial Servs (UK) plc 2000–01, managing ptnr Anstee Associates 2002–03, chief exec ICAEW 2003–06 (memb Senate 1996); non-exec chm: Mansell plc 2002–03, CPPGroup plc 2015–; non-exec dir: Severn Trent 1999–2003, SSL Int plc 2002–03, Insight Investments 2006–, Insight Investment Management Ltd, One Savings Bank plc 2016–; non-exec dir and chair Audit Vocalink Hldgs Ltd 2015–; fndr bd memb Centre for the Study of Regulated Industries, memb UITF of Accounting Standards Bd 1997–2003, memb Takeover Panel Appeals Bd 2007–; visiting prof London Met Univ; FCA 1979 (ACA 1974); *Recreations* golf, tennis, gardening; *Clubs* Athenaeum; *Style*— E E Anstee, Esq

ANSTEE, Prof John Howard; DL (Durham 2003); s of Stanley George Anstee (d 1978), of Milford Haven, and Anne May, *née* Griffiths (d 1992); *b* 25 April 1943; *Educ* Milford Haven GS, Univ of Nottingham (BSc, PhD); *m* 18 July 1966, Angela June, da of Emlyn Havard Young; 1 s (Quentin Mark b 7 Feb 1973); *Career* Univ of Durham: sr demonstrator in zoology 1968–71, lectr 1971–81, sr lectr 1981–96, dean Faculty of Science 1994–97 (dep dean 1991–94), prof of biological sciences 1996–2004 (emeritus 2004–), pro-vice-chllr 1997–2004, subwarden 2000–04, chair Univ of Durham Business Sch 2007–08; NETPark scientific dir Co Durham Devpt Co 2004–09, dir of a number of cos; memb Cncl Durham Cathedral 2005– (chair Devpt Steering Ctee 2006–13); hon sec Soc for Experimental Biology 1990–94 (memb 1972); author of numerous articles on insect physiology and biochemistry; FRES (memb Cncl 1991–94), FZS 1967; *Recreations* cricket, dinghy sailing and rugby; *Style*— Prof John H Anstee, DL; ✉ 35 Albert Street, Western Hill, Durham DH1 4RJ (☎ and fax 0191 386 6630, e-mail johnanstee@btinternet.com)

ANSTEE, Dame Margaret Joan; DCMG (1994); da of Edward Curtis Anstee (d 1971), and Anne Adaliza, *née* Mills (d 1972); *b* 25 June 1926; *Educ* Chelmsford Co HS for Girls, Newnham Coll Cambridge (MA), Univ of London (BSc); *Career* lectr in Spanish Queen's Univ Belfast 1947–48, third sec FO 1948–52, admin offr UN Tech Assistance Bd Manila Philippines 1952–54, Spanish supervisor Univ of Cambridge 1955–56; UN Tech Assistance Bd: offr i/c Bogotá Colombia 1956–57, resident rep Uruguay 1957–59, dir Special Fund progs and UN Info Centre La Paz Bolivia 1960–65, resident rep UNDP Ethiopia 1965–67, liaison offr with UN Econ Cmmn for Africa 1965–67, sr econ advsr PM's UK 1967–68, sr asst to cmmr i/c of Study of Capacity of UN Devpt System 1968–69; resident rep UNDP: Morocco 1969–72, Chile and liaison offr with UN Econ Cmmn for Latin America 1972–74; dep to UN Under Sec-Gen i/c of UN relief operation to Bangladesh and dep co-ordinator of UN emergency assistance to Zambia 1973; UNDP NY: dep asst admin and dep regnl dir for Latin America 1974–76, dir Admins Unit for Special Assignments 1976, asst dep admin 1976, asst admin and dir Bureau for Prog Policy and Evaluation 1977–78, asst Sec-Gen UN Dept of Tech Co-operation for Devpt 1978–87, special rep of Sec-Gen for co-ordination of int assistance following Mexico earthquake 1985–87, chm Advsy Gp on review of UN World Food Cncl 1985–86, special co-ordinator of UN Sec-Gen to ensure implementation of Gen Assembly resolution on fin and admin reform of the UN 1986–87; special rep of UN Sec-Gen for Bolivia 1982–92, rep UN Sec-Gen at Conf for the Adoption of a Convention Against Illicit Traffic in Narcotic Drugs and Psychotropic Substances 1988, sec-gen Eighth UN Congress on the Prevention of Crime and the Treatment of Offenders Havana 1990, special rep of the UN Sec-Gen for Peru 1990–92, Sec-Gen's co-ordinator for addressing the effects of the Chernobyl disaster 1991–92, Sec-Gen's personal rep to co-ordinate UN efforts to counter impact of burning oilfields in Kuwait and region 1991–92; DG UN office Vienna, under sec gen UN, head Centre for Social Devpt and Humanitarian Affrs 1987–92, co-ordinator of all UN drug control related activities 1987–91, under sec-gen and special rep of UN Sec-Gen for Angola and head UN Angolan Verification Mission (UNAVEM II) 1992–93, ind conslt and advsr to Pres and Govt of Bolivia 1993–1997 and 2002–06, advsr to the UN Sec-Gen on peacekeeping, post-conflict peacebuilding and training troops for peacekeeping missions and to various govts 1994–2003; lectr and author; memb Bd of Tstees Help Age Int 1993–97, memb Advsy Cncl on UN Studies Yale Univ 1994–, memb Cncl of Advsrs Oxford Res Gp 1996–, chm Expert Advsy Gp to Lessons Learned Unit UN Dept Peacekeeping Operations 1996–2002, patron and memb Bd British-Angola Forum 1998–2009, memb Int Advsy Cncl UN Intellectual History Project 1999–2010, memb Strategic Devpt Bd Univ of Durham Global Security Inst 2011–; memb Jimmy Carter's Int Cncl for Conflict Prevention 2001–; vice-pres UK UN Assoc, hon life vice-pres Br Assoc of Former UN Civil Servants (BAFUNCS) 2010–; subject of documentary 'Nine Lives' BBC4 2002; Sir Brian Urquhart Award for Distinguished Services to the UN 2011; hon fell Newnham Coll Cambridge; Hon LLD: Univ of Essex 1994, Univ of Westminster 1996, Univ of Cambridge 2004; Hon DSc (Econ) Univ of London 1998; foreign honours: Commandeur Ouissam Alaouite (Morocco) 1972, Dama Gran Cruz Condor of the Andes (Bolivia) 1986, Das Grosse Goldene Ehrenzeichen am Bande (Austria) 1993, Reves Peace Prize William & Mary Coll USA 1993, Grand Offr Order of Bernardo O'Higgins 2006 (Chile); *Books* The Administration of International Development Aid (USA 1969), Gate of the Sun: a Prospect of Bolivia (1970, USA 1971), Africa and the World (ed with R K A Gardiner and C Patterson, 1970), Orphan of the Cold War: The Inside Story of the Collapse of the Angolan Peace Process 1992–93 (1996, UK, US and Portugal 1997), Never Learn to Type: A Woman at the United Nations (2003, 2 edn 2004), The House on the Sacred Lake, and Other Bolivian Dreams – and Nightmares (2009), JB: An Unlikely Spanish Don – The Life and Times of Professor John Brande Trend (2013); numerous articles and chapters in books on UN reform, peackeeping, economic and social development; *Recreations* writing, gardening, hill walking (preferably in the Andes), bird-watching, swimming; *Clubs* Oxford and Cambridge; *Style*— Dame Margaret J Anstee, DCMG; ✉ The Walled Garden Knill, Powys LD8 2PR (☎ 01544 267411)

ANSTRUTHER, Harriet Joan Campbell; da of Sir Ian Fife Campbell Anstruther, 8 Bt (d 2007), of London, and Susan Margaret, *née* Paten; *b* 24 March 1967, London; *Educ* Queen's Coll London, City & Guilds Sch of Art, Byam-Shaw Sch of Fine Art, Inchbald Sch of Design; *m* 1, 19 July 1991 (m dis), Hamish Howard Anthony Summers, s of Anthony Gilbert Summers; 1 da (Celestia Nell Campbell b 23 Aug 1993); m 2, 27 July 2002, Henry Bourne, s of Prof Kenneth Bourne; *Career* textile, interior and fashion designer and design conslt, stylist and art dir; fndr Hufitts (T-shirt design/wholesale business) 1991–92, fndr Harriet Anstruther (accessories, men's and women's ready to wear and furnishing fabrics) 1991–97, over 340 stockists worldwide; jt fndr Selina Blow, Harriet Anstruther, Lulu Guinness (shop in Elizabeth St SW1) 1995–, fndr Harriet Anstruther Design Consultancy (incorporating all areas of design and styling incl china, textile, furnishing fabric, wallpaper, set and interior design and illustrations, TV film design and consultation) 1996–, fndr Harriet Anstruther Studio Ltd (architectural interior design studio) 2010–; conslt Yohji Yamamoto & Design Museum, collaboration and curation for Christies; visiting lectr and tutor Sch of Architecture RCA; memb Devpt Advsy Bd: V&A Museum, Royal Acad, Museum of Br Folklore; tstee Museum of Br Folklore; Harriet Anstruther MA Prize for Excellence City & Guilds Sch of Art; *Books* Reveal – Interior Design as a Reflection of Who We Are (2014); *Recreations* gardening, music, art collecting, literature; *Style*— Ms Harriet Anstruther; ☎ 020 7584 4776, e-mail harriet@harrietanstruther.com, website www.harrietanstruther.com

ANSTRUTHER, Sir Sebastian Paten Campbell; 9 Bt (NS 1694), of Balcaskie, 14 Bt (NS 1700), of Anstruther; s of Sir Ian Fife Campbell Anstruther, 8 Bt (d 2007), and Susan Margaret Walker; *b* 13 September 1962, London; *Educ* Univ of Bristol (BA); *m* 14 Feb 1992, Pornpan (Goy) Pinitwong; 1 da (Penelope Julalak Pinitwong b 6 Aug 1992), 1 s (Maximilian Sengtawan Pinitwong b 26 Jan 1995); *Heir* s, Maximilian Sengtawan Pinitwong; *Career* farmer and landowner; dir: Barlavington Estates No 2 Ltd, Barlavington Estates No 3 Ltd; tstee: Fagus Anstruther Memorial Tst; ✉ The Barlavington Estate Office, Duncton Mill, Dye House Lane, Duncton, Petworth, West Sussex GU28 0LF

ANSTRUTHER-GOUGH-CALTHORPE, Sir Euan Hamilton; 3 Bt (UK 1929), of Elvetham Hall, Elvetham, Co Southampton; s of Niall Hamilton Anstruther-Gough-Calthorpe (d 1970), and Martha (who m 2, 1975, Sir Charles Nicholson, 3 Bt, *qv*), da of Stuart Warren Don (d 2009); suc gf, Brig Sir Richard Anstruther-Gough-Calthorpe, 2 Bt, CBE (d 1985); *b* 22 June 1966; *Educ* Harrow, Univ of Reading, RAC Cirencester; *m* 8 June 2002 (m dis 2016), Anna Joan, da of Christopher Wysock Wright, of Horsted Keynes, W Sussex; 2 s (Barnaby Charles b 28 Oct 2005, Frederick Christopher b 30 April 2009), 2 da (Flora Susan b 29 April 2007, Georgina Martha b 24 Oct 2010); *Career* co dir (real estate investment); Freeman Worshipful Co of Armourers & Brasiers; Hon DUniv Birmingham 2008; *Clubs* Brooks's; *Style*— Sir Euan Calthorpe, Bt

ANTHONY, David Gwilym; s of Ernest Anthony (d 1990), and Megan Euron, *née* Davies (d 2004); *b* 10 February 1947; *Educ* Hull GS, St Catherine's Coll Oxford (MA); *m* 8 June 1974, (Ellen) Brigid, da of Air Vice-Marshal W J Crisham (d 1987); 1 s (Peter b 1979), 1 da (Jane b 1980); *Career* Barton Mayhew (now Ernst & Young) 1969–73, Dymo Business Systems Ltd 1973–75, Slater Walker Finance Ltd 1975–77, Forward Trust (Ireland) Ltd 1977–82, md Hitachi Capital (UK) plc 1982–2010, chm Hitachi Capital Vehicle Solutions Ltd 1991–2010, chm Private and Commercial Finance plc 2011–; dir: Hitachi Capital Insurance Corp Ltd 1995–2010, Secure Tst Bank plc 2007–10, Private and Commercial Finance plc 2011–; cncllr S Bucks District Cncl 2011–; FCA 1973, FRSA 2007; *Books* Words to Say (2002), Talking to Lord Newborough (2004), Passing through the Woods (2012); *Recreations* fell walking, skiing, poetry, classic cars; *Style*— David G Anthony, Esq; ✉ Retreat, Church Lane, Stoke Poges, Buckinghamshire SL2 4NZ (☎ 01753 530895)

ANTHONY, Graham; s of Edward Herbert Claude Anthony (decd), and Hilda May, *née* Pohler (decd); *b* 26 March 1938; *Educ* Hamilton House Sch, Architectural Assoc (AA Dip Arch); *m* 1 (m dis), Sheila, *née* McGregor; 2 da (Lucinda Jane b 1964, Justine b 1966); m 2, Jacqueline Dorothy, *née* Miller (decd); 2 da (Lara Catherine b 1967, Alice b 1975); *Career* architect; Ahrends Burton Koralek 1966–72 and 1976–80, Wadley Anthony Architects 1972–76, Richard Rogers Partnership 1980–87, Graham Anthony Architects 1987–89; Sheppard Robson (architects, planners and interior designers) London: joined 1990, assoc 1996–97, design dir 1997–, ptnr 1998–2003, design conslt 2003–; projects incl: Central Plant facility for Glaxo Stevenage 1990–92, The Helicon EC2 for London and Manchester 1992–95 (RIBA Regnl Award for Architecture, Civic Tst Award commendation 1998), Motorola HQ Swindon 1996–98 (RIBA Regnl Award for

Architecture, Structural Steel Design Award 1999, High Commendation Br Construction Industry Award), Pfizer HQ Walton Oaks 1997 (RIBA Nat Award for Architecture, Br Cncl of Offices Award, Art and Work Award), Arup HQ London 2001–03; *Recreations* watercolouring, music, weight training, running; *Style*— Graham Anthony, Esq; ✉ Sheppard Robson, 77 Parkway, London NW1 7PU (☎ 020 7504 1700, fax 020 7504 1701, e-mail graham.anthony@sheppardrobson.com)

ANTHONY, His Hon Judge Michael Guy; s of Kenneth Anthony (d 1995), and June, *née* Gallifent (d 2007); *b* 5 March 1950, London; *Educ* St Paul's, Magdalen Coll Oxford (MA); *m* 1974, Jane Rosemary, da of Peter Farrer, MC; 1 s (Christopher b 4 Nov 1986); *Career* barr 1972–98, asst recorder 1989–93, recorder 1993–98, circuit judge (SE Circuit) 1998–; memb Mental Health Review Tbnl 2002–14; *Recreations* travel, reading, rugby and other sports, spending time with family; *Clubs* Army & Navy; *Style*— His Hon Judge Anthony; ✉ Lewes Combined Court, The Law Courts, High Street, Lewes, East Sussex BN7 1YB (☎ 01273 480400, fax 01273 485269)

ANTONIADES, Reno Michael; s of Michael Antoniades, and Joy, *née* Post; *b* 27 July 1966, London; *Educ* Alleyn's Sch Dulwich (head boy), Univ of Leicester (LLB); *m* 6 Sep 1997, Julie Cunningham; 1 da (Madeleine Anastasia b 29 June 2003), 1 s (Noah Michael Laurence b 20 Nov 2005); *Career* slr; Herbert Smith 1989–93, Olswang 1993–94, Lee & Thompson 1994–; memb: Law Soc 1991, BAFTA; *Recreations* cinema, golf, football (season ticket holder Tottenham Hotspur FC); *Clubs* Edward Alleyn, Soho House; *Style*— Reno Antoniades, Esq; ✉ Lee & Thompson LLP, 4 Gee's Court, St Christopher's Place, London W1U 1JD (☎ 020 3073 7600, fax 020 3073 7601, e-mail renoantoniades@leeandthompson.com)

ANTONOWICZ, Anton; s of Marian Antonowicz, of Brixworth, and Eileen, *née* Kelly; *b* 29 December 1950; *Educ* St Ignatius Coll Enfield, Univ of Warwick (BA); *m* 1979, Nasrin, *née* Abdollahi (d 1998); 1 da (Anna-Yasmin b 28 July 1981), 1 s (Stefan b 30 March 1983); *Career* chief feature writer The Mirror (joined 1977); memb: NUJ, BAJ; life memb Newspaper Press Fund; *Awards* Cudlipp Award 1986, 1987 and 2003, Foreign Reporter of the Year British Press Awards 1998, Newspaper Reporter of the Year Amnesty Int 2002; *Recreations* walking, tennis; *Style*— Anton Antonowicz, Esq; ✉ The Mirror, 1 Canada Tower, London E14 5AP (☎ 020 7293 3066, fax 020 7293 3834)

ANTRIM, 9 Earl of (I 1785); Alexander Randal Mark McDonnell; also Viscount Dunluce; s of 8 Earl of Antrim, KBE (d 1977), and Angela Christina, da of Col Sir Mark Sykes; *b* 3 February 1935; *Educ* Downside, ChCh Oxford, Ruskin Sch of Art; *m* 1, 1963 (m dis 1974), Sarah Elizabeth Anne, 2 da of St John Bernard Vyvyan Harmsworth (d 1995); 2 da (Lady Flora Mary (Lady Flora Pennybacker) b 1963, Lady Alice Angela Jane (Lady Alice Gwinn) b 1964), 1 s (Randal Alexander St John, Viscount Dunluce b 1967); m 2, 1977, Elizabeth, da of Michael Moses Sacher; 1 da (Lady Rachel Frances b 1978); *Heir* s, Viscount Dunluce, *qv*; *Career* Tate Gallery: restorer 1965–75, keeper of conservation 1975–90, head of collection servs 1990–93, dir of collection servs 1994–95; memb Art Advsy Ctee Nat Museums and Galleries of Wales 1995–2012; chm Rathlin Island Tst 1990–93, dir Northern Salmon Co (former chm), former dir Ulster TV, dir Antrim Estates Co, memb High Cncl of the Clan Donald 2001–; Prime Warden Hon Co of Fishmongers 1995–96; FRSA; *Recreations* vintage cars; *Clubs* Beefsteak; *Style*— The Rt Hon the Earl of Antrim; ✉ Deer Park Cottage, Glenarm, Co Antrim BT44 0BQ

ANWAR, Tariq Rafiq; s of Rafiq Anwar (d 1976), of Chiswick, and Edith Fordham, *née* Reich (d 1994); *b* 21 September 1945; *Educ* Walpole GS, Sir John Cass Coll London; *m* 29 Sept 1966, Shirley Natalie, da of John Richard Hills (d 1990), of Hainault, Essex; 1 s (Dominic b 1967), 1 da (Gabrielle b 1970); *Career* film ed with BBC; films incl: Madness of King George, The Crucible, Wings of the Dove, Tea with Mussolini, American Beauty, Stage Beauty, The Good Shepherd, Revolutionary Road, The King's Speech; Best Ed BAFTA Awards: Caught on a Train, Oppenheimer, American Beauty; Best Ed European Film Award for The King's Speech, Asian Voice Special Achievement Award in Film; BAFTA nominations: Monocled Mutineer, Fortunes of War, Summer's Lease, Madness of King George, The King's Speech; ACE (Cable) nomination for Tender is the Night; Oscar nominations: American Beauty, The King's Speech; ACE (Editors' Guild) nominations: American Beauty, The King's Speech; memb Motion Picture Editors Guild (MPEG); *Recreations* music, tennis; *Style*— Tariq Anwar, Esq; ✉ c/o United Agents Ltd, 12–26 Lexington Street, London W1F 0LE (☎ 020 3214 0800, fax 020 3214 0801, website www.unitedagents.co.uk)

APPIGNANESI, Dr Lisa; OBE (2013); da of Aron Borenstein (d 1981), and Hena Lipszyc (d 2001); *b* 4 January 1946, Poland; *Educ* McGill Univ Montreal (BA, MA), Univ of Sussex (PhD); *m* Prof John Forrester; 1 s (Joshua Appignanesi b 5 May 1975), 1 da (Katrina Forrester b 1 March 1986); *Career* univ lectr 1971–80, fndr memb Writers and Readers Publishing 1976–89, dep dir ICA 1981–90, freelance writer 1990–; gen ed Big Ideas series Profile Books 2007–11; visiting prof in literature and medical humanities KCL 2011–; pres English PEN 2007–10 (memb Prison Ctee 2003–, vice-pres 2004–07), chair No Offence campaign, chair Freud Museum London 2007–14; memb: Cncl ICA 1999–2007, Ctee on the Arts LSE 1999–2000, Mgmnt Ctee Soc of Authors 1996–99, Soc of Authors, PEN; judge: Betty Trask Prize 1993, Wingate Prize 2011, Orange Prize 2012; patron Writers in Exile; participant in numerous confs, int lectr and memb many panels; Wellcome Tst People Award; FRSL 2015; Chevalier de l'Ordre des Arts et des Lettres (France) 1988; *Television* exec prodr: No Place Quite Like It (BBC) 1987, Intruders at the Palace (BBC) 1988, The World of Gypsy Music (BBC) 1988, England's Henry Moore (Channel 4) 1991, Seductions (four short plays by Marina Warner, Jenny Diski, Geoff Dyer and Edmund White, Channel 4) 1991; series conslt Fin de Siècle (Channel 4) 1992, co-dir and author Rendez Vous à New York: Un portrait de Salman Rushdie (FR3) 1999, Salman Rushdie: Imagining India (Arte) 2011; series ed Writers in Conversation (ICA video) 1993–90; *Radio* writer and presenter: Cabaret (BBC Radio 4) 1978, The Case of Sigmund Freud (BBC Radio 4) 2000; presenter: Nightwaves (BBC Radio 3) 2002–03, Freudian Slips (Radio 4) 2005; contrib to numerous progs incl Routes of English, Kaleidoscope, Woman's Hour, Start the Week, BBC 4 Archive Hour, Saturday Review; *Publications* fiction incl: Memory and Desire (1991), Dreams of Innocence (1994), A Good Woman (1996), The Things We Do for Love (1997), The Dead of Winter (1999), Sanctuary (2000), Paris Requiem (2002, new edn 2005), Kicking Fifty (2003), The Memory Man (2004), Paris Requiem (2013), Sacred Ends (2014); non-fiction incl: Dialogue of Generations (1974), Femininity and the Creative Imagination: James, Proust and Musil (1974), Cabaret: The First Hundred Years (1976, new edn 1986, revised and enlarged edn 2004), Simone de Beauvoir (1988, new edn 2005), Freud's Women (with John Forrester, 1992, new edn 2005), Losing the Dead (1999, 2 edn 2013), Mad, Bad and Sad: A History of Women and the Mind Doctors from 1800 to the Present (2008, BMA Award for the Public Understanding of Science), All About Love: Anatomy of an Unruly Emotion (2011), Trials of Passion: Crimes in the Name of Love and Madness (2014); edited volumes: Science and Beyond (with Stephen Rose, 1986), The Rushdie File (with Sara Maitland, 1989), Dismantling Truth (with Hilary Lawson, 1989), Ideas from France (1989), Postmodernism (1989), Fifty Shades of Feminism (with Susie Orbach and Rachel Holmes, 2013); written and reviewed for newspapers incl: The Guardian, The Sunday Times, The Daily Telegraph, The Observer, The Independent; trans of pubns and books from French, Italian and German; *Style*— Dr Lisa Appignanesi, OBE; ✉ c/o Clare Alexander, Aitken Alexander Associates, 18–21 Cavaye Place, London SW10 9PT (☎ 020 7373 8672, fax 020 7373 6002, email matias@aitkenalexander.co.uk)

APPIO, Isabel Anne; da of Chief Gabriel Fenton Appio (d 1992), of Lagos, Nigeria, and Marguerite, *née* Lancaster-Cooper; *b* 30 June 1959; *Educ* Blackheath HS London, Central London Poly (BA); *Career* asst ed Caribbean Times newspaper 1981–83, asst music ed Time Out 1986–91, ed The Weekly Journal 1992–, chief editorial dir Voice Communications Group, dir Sugar Media; *Style*— Ms Isabel Appio; ☎ 020 7407 7747, fax 020 7407 6800, e-mail isabel@sugarmedia.co.uk

APPLEBY, (Lesley) Elizabeth (Mrs Michael Collins); QC (1979); o da of Arthur Leslie Appleby, and Dorothy Evelyn, *née* Edwards; *b* 12 August 1942; *Educ* Dominican Convent Brewood, Wolverhampton Girls' HS, Univ of Manchester (LLB); *m* 6 Jan 1978, Michael Kenneth Collins, OBE, BSc, MICE; 1 s (Andrew b 23 Jan 1980), 1 da (Emma b 13 Feb 1984); *Career* called to the Bar Gray's Inn 1965, ad eundem Lincoln's Inn 1975; in practice Chancery Bar 1966–; memb of Senate of Inns of Court and Bar 1977–80 and 1981–82; bencher Lincoln's Inn 1986, recorder of the Crown Court 1989–, dep judge of the High Ct, jt head of chambers; chm Ethics & Integrity Ctee Cons Pty; *Recreations* gardening, swimming; *Style*— Miss Elizabeth Appleby, QC; ✉ 4/5 Gray's Inn Square, Gray's Inn, London WC1R 5AY (☎ 020 7404 5252, fax 020 7242 7803)

APPLEBY, His Hon John Montague; s of Montague Eric Appleby (d 1983), and Carmen Irene Appleby (d 1993); *b* 8 November 1945; *Educ* Dauntsey's Sch West Lavington, Univ of Nottingham (LLB, pres Univ Law Students' Soc, capt Univ and UAU hockey); *m* 30 May 1970, Barbara Joan, da of Arthur Plumb; 1 s (Luke Justin b 17 July 1976); *Career* admitted slr 1970, asst slr Leicester 1970–72; Truman Close Kendall & Appleby (formerly Trumans & Appleby): joined 1972, ptnr 1974–88, managing ptnr (following merger of Truman & Appleby and Close Kendall & Co) 1988–98, memb Mgmnt Bd Nelsons (following merger of Trumans and Nelsons) 1999–2003; recorder 1999–2003 (asst recorder 1993–99), circuit judge (Northern Circuit) 2003–15, ret; sec Notts Young Slrs Gp 1973 (Nat Ctee rep 1976–82), chm Nat Ctee Young Slrs Gp 1980–81; pres Notts Law Soc 1997 (vice-pres 1996); Law Soc: memb 1970–, memb Regnl Cncl (for Lincs and Notts) 1984, memb Cncl 1984–99, chm Family Law Ctee 1987–90, chm Cts and Legal Servs Ctee 1990–93, memb Remuneration & Practice Devpt Ctee 1986–89, dir Slrs Indemnity Fund 1987–90, memb Practice Devpt Ctee 1993–96, memb Civil Litigation Ctee 1993–99, memb Trg Ctee 1996–2001; *Books* Professional Management of a Solicitors Practice (contrib); *Recreations* golf, travel, wine, theatre; *Clubs* Notts Hockey Assoc (pres 1994–96), Nottingham Hockey (vice-pres), Nottingham CC (vice-pres), Hale Golf; *Style*— His Hon John Appleby

APPLEBY, Keith David; s of Cornelius Appleby, of Amersham, Bucks, and Doreen Mary, *née* Briscoe; *b* 14 May 1953; *Educ* Bucks Coll of Higher Educn (BA), RCA (MA); *m* 1987, Margaret Ann, da of Anthony Lepps; 3 s (Frederick William b 25 March 1990, Noah Alexander b 21 April 1996, Joseph John b 22 October 1997); *Career* designer Habitat Designs Ltd 1978–81, sr designer Habitat-Mothercare plc 1981–84, assoc dir Storehouse plc 1984–88, mktg dir RSCG Conran Design 1993–96 (design dir 1988–93), design and mktg dir Dorma Gp Ltd 1998–2005, gp brands dir Royal Doulton 2005–07, global mktg dir Waterford Wedgwood Royal Doulton 2008–; *Style*— Keith Appleby, Esq

APPLEBY, Prof (James) Louis John; CBE (2006); s of James Appleby, of Livingston, W Lothian, and Doris, *née* Cooper; *b* 27 February 1955; *Educ* Bathgate Acad, Univ of Edinburgh (BSc, MB ChB, MD); *m* 26 Sept 1992, Juliet Elisabeth, *née* Haselden; 2 s (Matthew, Tom), 2 da (Michelle, Rebecca); *Career* trg Maudsley Hosp London 1983–86, lectr Inst of Psychiatry London 1986–91; Univ of Manchester: sr lectr 1991–96, prof of psychiatry 1996–; dir Nat Confidential Inquiry into Suicide and Homicide 1996–; Dept of Health: nat dir for mental health 2000–10, nat clinical dir for health and criminal justice 2010–; FRCP 1995 (MRCP 1983), FRCPsych 1997 (MRCPsych 1986); *Publications* A Medical Tour Through the Whole Island of Great Britain (1994); *Recreations* clarinet, family, astronomy, ornithology, Manchester United; *Style*— Prof Louis Appleby, CBE; ✉ The Department of Health, Richmond House, 79 Whitehall, London SW1A 2NS (e-mail louis.appleby@dh.gsi.gov.uk); University of Manchester, Oxford Road, Manchester M13 9PL

APPLEBY, Malcolm Arthur; MBE (2014); s of James William Appleby (d 1976), of West Wickham, Kent, and Marjory, *née* Stokes (d 1991); *b* 6 January 1946; *Educ* Hawesdown Co Secdy Modern Sch for Boys, Beckenham Sch of Art, Ravensbourn Coll of Art and Design, Central Sch of Arts and Crafts, Sir John Cass Sch of Art, Royal Coll of Art; *Children* 1 da (May); *Career* started career as engraver 1968, currently designer for silver and specialist gun engraver (developed gold fusing onto steel and created new silver engraving techniques); research into platinum engraving techniques for Ayrton Metals 1992 (resulting in a platinum and gold collection); external tutor Engraving for Bishopsland Educnl Tst; fndr chm Br Art Postage Stamp Soc, fndr memb Br Hand Engraving Soc; memb: Br Art Medal Soc, Butterfly Conservation Soc, SPAB, Silver Soc, Steering Ctee Highland Perthshire Communities Land Tst 2001–02, Br Designer Silversmiths; life memb: Nat Tst Scotland, British Dragonfly Soc, John Muir Tst, Maclaren Soc; hon memb Grandtully & Strathtay WRI, life memb Orkney Small Boat Museum; former memb: Crathes Drumoak and Durris Community Cncl (chm 1992), Grandtully Hall Ctee; life memb Butterfly Conservation; winner First Inches Carr Craft Bursary 1997, winner Silver Soc Prize Festival of Silver 2014; Liveryman Worshipful Co of Goldsmiths 1991; Hon DLitt Heriot-Watt Univ; *Work* incl: engraving orb on Prince of Wales's Coronet, King George VI Diamond Stakes trophy 1978, 500th anniversary silver cup for London Assay Office, V&A seal, condiment set destined for 10 Downing St, major silver cmmn (cup and cover) for Royal Museum of Scotland 1990, former designer to Holland & Holland Gunmaker, silver centre piece for the new Scottish Parliament, gold millennium casket for Worshipful Co of Goldsmiths, pair of tazzas for the Soc of Writers to Her Majesty's Signet, bell push as a 100th birthday present to HM The Queen Mother from a member of her family, RSE Royal Medal 2000, 22 carat gold medal for Gannochy Tst Innovation Award of RSE, The Muckle Buckle of Braemar, Trafalgar Medal, Annual Banchory Bangle for Children 1st, The George Heriot Sch Loving Cup, Grandtully Engraving Symposium, candlesticks for St Giles' Cathedral Edinburgh; *Collections* work in collections incl: Aberdeen Art Gallery Nat Museum of Scotland, Aland's Bay Maritime Museum, Nat Museum of Finland, South Aust Maritime Museum, Royal Armouries, V&A, Crafts Cncl, BR Museum, Contemporary Arts Soc, Goldsmiths' Co, Fitzwilliam Museum, Hunterian Museum, Perth Museum and Art Galleries, Ashmolean Museum, George Heriot's Sch; *Exhibitions* Br Cncl Crafts Exhibition to Japan, Sotheby's Contemporary Arts Exhibition to Japan, Chicago New Art Forms Exhibition (with the Scottish Gallery), one-man show Pier Arts Centre Stromness Orkney (prints and silver), major one-man show Aberdeen Art Gallery, Silversmiths Gallery Museet Pa Koldinghus Denmark, Inspirations (Goldsmiths Hall), Precious Statements (Goldsmiths Hall), Cutting Edge (Museums of Scotland), Raising the Bar (Dovecot Edinburgh), Collect (Saatchi Gallery), Made in Scotland (Fleming Collection), Malcolm Appleby: Maker (Scottish Gallery Edinburgh), Gold, Power and Allure (Goldsmiths Hall London), Passing It On (Scottish Gallery); *Recreations* work, standing in the garden, cups of herbal tea with friends and neighbours, low cholesterol diet, still darning my very old but colourful pullover, kissing daughter and kissing her mother even harder; *Style*— Malcolm Appleby, Esq, MBE; ✉ Aultbeag, Grandtully, Perthshire PH15 2QU (☎ 01887 840484)

APPLEGATE, Jessica-Jane; MBE (2013); da of Dawn Applegate; *b* 22 August 1996, Great Yarmouth, Norfolk; *Educ* Easton and Otley Coll, Nurture Unit Ormiston Venture Acad; *Career* Paralympic swimmer; achievements incl: Gold medal (200m freestyle) Br Championships 2012, Gold medal (200m freestyle) and 2 Silver medals (50m freestyle and 100m freestyle) Br Int Disablilty Swimming Championships 2012, Gold medal (200m freestyle) Paralympic Games 2012, Gold medal (200m freestlye), Silver medal (200m individual medley) and Bronze medal (100m backstroke) World Championships 2013, Silver medal (200m freestyle) and 2 Bronze medals (200m individual medley and 100m backstroke) European Championships 2014, Gold medal (100m backstroke) and 2 Silver medals (200m freestyle and 200m individual medley) World Championships 2015, 2 Silver medals (200m freestyle and 100m backstroke) European Championships 2016, 2 Silver medals (200m freestyle and 200m individual medley) and 1 Bronze medal (100m backstroke) Paralympics Rio 2016; runner-up BBC's Young Sports Personality of the Year, Para Athlete of the Year British Swimming 2015; ambass: Int Assoc Sport (INAS, promoting athletes with learning and intellectual disabilities worldwide), MENCAP, Norwich Community Sports Fndn; *Recreations* walking, rescue homes for animals; *Clubs* City of Norwich Swimming, Great Yarmouth Swimming (volunteer coach); *Style—* Ms Jessica-Jane Applegate, MBE; ✉ website www.jessicajaneapplegate.com, Twitter @jessica_jane96, Facebook Jessica Jane Applegate MBE, Instagram jessicajaneapplegate

APPLEYARD, Bryan Edward; s of Cyril John Snowdon Appleyard (d 1965), and Freda Bendelsen (d 1971); *b* 24 August 1951; *Educ* Bolton Sch, King's Coll Cambridge; *m* Christena Marie-Thérèse; 1 da (Charlotte Mary Freda b 26 June 1982); *Career* journalist; South London News Group 1972–75, United Newspapers City Office 1975–76, journalist The Times 1976– (financial news ed and dep arts ed 1981–84), freelance journalist and author 1985–; columnist: The Independent (The Bryan Appleyard Interview 1990–), The Times; weekly columnist The Sunday Times (Bryan Appleyard's Forum), also writer The Sunday Times Magazine; also contrib to: Vogue, Spectator, London Review of Books; TV critic The Tablet; British Press Awards: General Feature Writer of the Year 1986, commended Feature Writer of the Year 1992, Feature Writer of the Year 1996 and 2006, Interviewer of the Year Br Press Awards 2015 (shortlisted 2013, 2014); Brave New Worlds highly commended in the Br Med Assoc Med Books competition 1999, shortlisted Feature Writer of the Year Br Press Awards 2009; *Books* The Culture Club (1984), Richard Rogers – A Biography (1986), The Pleasures of Peace (1989), Understanding the Present – Science and the Soul of Modern Man (1992), The First Church of the New Millennium (1994), Brave New Worlds: Staying Human in the Genetic Future (1998), Aliens: Why They Are Here (2005), How to Live Forever or Die Trying: on the New Immortality (2007), Bedford Park: a Novel (2013), The Brain is Wider than the Sky: Why Simple Solutions Don't Work in a Complex World (2011); *Recreations* writing; *Clubs* Groucho, The Academy; *Style—* Bryan Appleyard, Esq; ✉ c/o (Agent) David Millers, Rogers, Coleridge & White, 20 Powys Mews, London W11 1JN (☎ 020 7221 3717, e-mail davidm@rcwlitagency.com)

APPLEYARD, Dr (William) James; s of Edward Rollo Appleyard (d 1937), and Maud Oliver, *née* Marshall (d 1979); *b* 25 October 1935; *Educ* Canford Sch, Exeter Coll Oxford, Guy's Hosp London, Univ of Louisville Sch of Med Kentucky (Alumnus award); *m* 1964, Elizabeth Anne, *née* Ward; 1 s (Richard James b 1966), 2 da (Lisa Jane b 1968, Suzanne Mary b 1970); *Career* SHO Hosp for Sick Children Gt Ormond St London 1967, Dyers' Co research registrar St Thomas' Hosp London 1968, sr paediatric registrar Guy's Hosp London 1969–71, conslt paediatrician Kent and Canterbury Hosp 1971–98 (hon consult paediatrician 1998–99), conslt Hope Medical Inst VA 2009–; dean of clinical studies (UK) St George's Univ Sch of Med Grenada WI 1995–97 (prof of paediatrics 1983–95); dean of clinical sciences Kigezi Int Sch of Med (Uganda) 2000–04; BMA: chm Representative Body 1993–95, hon treas 1996–2002, vice-pres 2003–; pres World Med Assoc 2003–04 (memb Cncl 1994–2005, chm Ethical Ctee 1996–99), treas Br Paediatric Assoc 1983–88, memb GMC 1984–2003; memb: Kent AHA 1974–79, Supra Regnl Servs Advsy Ctee Dept of Health 1990–95; vice-pres Int Assoc of Medical Colls NY 2011– (chair Ethics Ctee, memb Advsy Cncl, memb Expert Panel of Examiners 2005–, hon sec to Bd of Tstees 2007–11); hon life memb Kent Postgraduate Medical Centre 1998– (hon treas 1999), memb Int Coll of Person-Centered Medicine 2011– (pres 2013–), memb Editorial Bd Internal Jl of Person-Centered Medicine, chm East Kent Div BMA 2014–, pres Int Assoc of Med Colls 2015–; patron Dyspraxia Tst, chm of tstees St John's Hosp Canterbury 2012–; Liveryman Worshipful Soc of Apothecaries (memb Livery Ctee 2005–08 and 2009–12); Hon MD Univ of Kent 1999, Hon DHL Univ of St Georges, Grenada 2000; FRCP 1978, Hon FRCPCH 2002 (FRCPCH 1997); *Publications* articles in refereed based med jls on the newborn, disabled children, medical manpower and medical ethics; *Recreations* croquet, photography; *Clubs* Athenaeum, Oddfellows; *Style—* Dr James Appleyard; ✉ Thimble Hall, Blean Common, Kent CT2 9JJ

APPLEYARD, Sir Leonard Vincent; KCMG (1994, CMG 1986); s of Thomas William Appleyard (d 1979), of Cawood, W Yorks, and Beatrix, *née* Golton (d 1982); *b* 2 September 1938; *Educ* Read Sch Drax, Queens' Coll Cambridge (MA); *m* 1, 3 May 1964 (m dis), Elizabeth Margaret, da of John Lees West, of Grasmere, Cumbria; 2 da (Caroline b 1965, Rebecca b 1967); m 2, 27 Aug 1994, Joan Jefferson; *Career* FO 1962, third sec Hong Kong 1964, second sec Peking 1966, second (later first) sec FO 1969; first sec: Delhi 1971, Moscow 1975, HM Treasy 1978; fin cnsllr Paris 1979–82, head of Econ Rels Dept FCO 1982–84, princ private sec 1984–86, ambass to Hungary 1986–89, dep sec Cabinet Office 1989–91, political dir FCO 1991–94, ambass to China 1994–97; vice-chm Barclays Capital 1998–2003 (special advsr 2005–07); chm Farnham Castle 2003–07, pro-chllr Bournemouth Univ 2003–, visiting prof Southampton Univ 2009–; chm Cncl Winchester Cathedral 2007–12; *Recreations* music, reading, history; *Style—* Sir Leonard Appleyard, KCMG

APTED, Michael D; CMG (2008); *b* 10 February 1941; *Educ* Univ of Cambridge (BA); *Career* film director; began as researcher Granada TV; credits as TV dir incl: Coronation Street, The Lovers (Best Comedy Series BAFTA), Folly Foot (Best Children's Series BAFTA), Another Sunday and Sweet FA, Kisses at Fifty (Best Dramatic Dir BAFTA), The Collection, Stronger than the Sun, P'Tang Yang Kipperbang, Crossroads, Socrates, Rome; film dir: Triple Echo 1972, Stardust 1975, The Squeeze 1977, Agatha 1979, Coal Miner's Daughter 1980 (nominated Directors' Guild of America award), Continental Divide 1981, Gorky Park 1983, Kipperbang 1983 (BAFTA nomination), First Born 1984, Bring on the Night 1985 (Grammy award), Critical Condition 1987, Gorillas in the Mist 1988, The Long Way Home 1989, Class Action 1990, Incident at Oglala 1992, Thunderheart 1992, Blink 1993, Moving the Mountain 1993, Nell 1994, Extreme Measures 1996, Inspirations 1997, Always Outnumbered 1998, James Bond – The World is not Enough 1999, Me and Isaac Newton 1999, Enigma 2001, Enough, 2002, Amazing Grace 2007, The Chronicles of Narnia: The Voyage of the Dawn Treader 2010; exec prodr: Bram Stoker's Dracula, Strapped, Criminal Justice; dir on-going documentary series revisiting gp of 14 people every 7 years (began with 7 Up 1963), 28 Up (BAFTA Award, Int Emmy and Int Documentary awards), 35 Up (BAFTA Award); *Style—* Michael Apted, Esq, CMG; ✉ Michael Apted Film Co, 1901 Avenue of the Stars, Suite 1245, Los Angeles, CA 90067–6013, USA

ARAD, Ron; *b* 1951, Tel Aviv, Israel; *Educ* Jerusalem Acad of Art, AA Sch of Architecture; *Career* architect and furniture/product designer; jt fndr with Caroline Thorman: One Off Ltd (design studio, workshops and showroom) London 1981–93, Ron Arad Associates (architecture and design practice) 1989–, Ron Arad Studio Como 1994–99; prof of product design Hochschule Vienna 1994–97, prof of product design RCA 1997–2009; projects incl: The New Tel Aviv Opera foyer architecture 1989–94, Maserati HQ showroom 2002–03, Y's (Yohji Yamamoto) store Roppongi Hills 2003, Upper World Hotel Battersea Power Station London 2003, 7th Floor Hotel Puerto America Madrid 2005, Hotel Duomo Rimini 2005, Mediacité Liege Belgium 2009, Design Museum Holon 2009, designs for Alessi, Kartell, Cassina, Fiam, Moroso, Flos, Driade, Magis, Vitra International and Swarovski; exhibition designs incl: Winning the Design of Sport Glasgow 1999, Louisiana MOMA 1996; architectural projects incl: Belgo Centraal London 1995, Belgo Noord London 1994, Adidas Sports Cafe France 1996, Amiga House (private residence) London 1997, Alan Journo (boutique) Milan 1999, Windwand Canary Wharf London 1999, The Big Blue Canary Wharf London 2000, Selfridges Technology Hall 2001; Art guest ed 1994 Int Design Yearbook and Designer of the Year 1994; work featured in design/architectural books and magazines worldwide, subject of various monographs; one-man exhbns incl: Powerhouse Museum Sydney 1997, Gallery Mourmans 1999, Before and After Now (V&A) 2000, Not Made by Hand Not Made in China (Gió Marconi Milan) 2000, Delight in Dedark (Gió Marconi Milan) 2001, Two Floors (Gió Marconi Milan) 2002, Permetre's la Ilisertat (Centre d'Art Santa Monica Barcelona) 2003, Ron Arad: A Retrospective Exhibition (Barry Friedman Ltd NY) 2005, Ron Arad: Architectural Installations (Phillips de Pury & Co NY) 2005, There is no solution because there is no problem (Barry Friedman Gallery NY) 2006, Blo-Glo (Milan) 2006, The Dogs barked (de Pury & Luxembourg Zurich) 2006–07, Bodyguards (Milan) 2007, No Discipline (Centre Pompidou Paris) 2008 and (MOMA NY) 2009, Restless (Barbican) 2010, In Reverse (Design Museum Holon Israel) 2013; work in many public collections incl: Musée des Arts Decoratifs Paris and Musée National d'Art Moderne/Centre Georges Pompidou Paris, Metropolitan Museum of Art NY, V&A and Design Museum London, Stedelijk Museum Amersterdam, Tel Aviv Museum, Powerhouse Museum Aust, Montreal Museum of Decorative Arts, Vitra Design Museum Weil am Rhein, Design Museum Osaka; Barcelona Primavera International Award for Design 2001, Jerusalem Prize for Arts and Letters Bezalel Acad of Arts and Design Israel 2006, FX Magazine Designer of the Year 2005, Visionary Award Museum of Arts & Design NY 2006, London Design Week Medal 2011; hon doctorate Tel Aviv Univ 2010; RDI 2002, RA 2013; *Style—* Ron Arad; ✉ Ron Arad Associates Ltd, 62 Chalk Farm Road, London NW1 8AN (☎ 020 7284 4963, e-mail info@ronarad.com, website www.ronarad.com)

ARAKI, Mitsuhiro; *b* 11 October 1966, Japan; *m* Yoko Araki; 1 da (Manae Araki b 16 Feb 2000); *Career* owner and chef Araki Sushi Tokyo 2011–13 (3 Michelin stars), owner and chef The Araki London 2014– (2 Michelin stars 2015–); *Books* Edomae No Nigri (2003), Mitou (2011); *Recreations* cinema, fashion, opera, travel; *Style—* Mr Mitsuhiro Araki; ✉ The Araki, 12 New Burlington Street, London W1S 3BF (☎ 020 7287 2481, website www.the-araki.com)

ARAYA, Dr Negusse; s of Araya Tewoldemedhin (d 1982), and Haregewoin Misgina; *b* 16 January 1950; *Educ* Gelawdeos Secdy Sch Ethiopia, Haile Selassie I Univ Ethiopia (Dip), Addis Ababa Univ (BA), Humboldt Univ of Berlin (MA, PhD); *m* 4 Jan 1974, Gebriela, *née* Woldemariam; 4 c (Yoseph b 4 Dec 1975, Winta b 7 Jan 1978, Biniam b 1 Nov 1979, Samuel b 6 March 1984); *Career* teacher and dir of jr and secdy schs 1972–82; Univ of Asmara: lectr, asst prof and head Educn Unit 1988–91, dean Faculty of Social Scis 1991–92, dir Educn Prog 1992–93; dir Br Cncl Eritrea 1994–, resident rep BESO 1995–; chair Bd of dirs Haben (Eritrean community devpt NGO) 2000–, memb Prog Planning and Research Ctee Family Reproductive Health Assoc of Eritrea; memb Univ Teachers Assoc of Eritrea 1983– (pres 1992–93); *Recreations* visiting historical places, hiking, reading; *Style—* Dr Negusse Araya; ✉ PO Box 9217, Asmara, Eritrea (☎ 00 291 1 125777, fax 00 291 1 127230); The British Council, Lorenzo Tazaz Street, PO Box 997, Asmara, Eritrea (☎ 00 291 1 123415, fax 00 291 1 127230, e-mail negusse.araya@britishcouncil.org.er)

ARBOUR, Anthony Francis (Tony); JP (Richmond upon Thames 1975), AM; s of Charles Arbour, and Magdalen Arbour; *Educ* Surbiton Co GS, Kingston Coll of Tech (BSc), City Univ Business Sch (MBA); *Career* admitted Gray's Inn 1967; sr lectr 1968–2000: Kingston Coll of Technol, Kingston Poly, Kingston Univ Business Sch; visiting fell Kingston Univ 2000–07; memb London Borough of Richmond Cncl 1968– (ldr 2002–06), GLC (Cons) Surbiton 1983–86; GLA: memb London Assembly (Cons) South West 2000–, chm Planning Ctee 2000–03, chm Planning and Spatial Ctee 2005–; chm Hampton Wick United Charity 1978–; vice-chm Kingston & Richmond FHSA 1990–96; govr: Tiffin Sch 1990–94, Kingston Poly 1998–2000; memb Industrial Tbnl 1992–2013; *Recreations* book collecting, car booting, watching TV soap operas; *Clubs* Hounslow Cons; *Style—* Tony Arbour, AM; ✉ London Assembly, City Hall, Queens Walk, Southwark, London SE1 2AA (☎ 020 7983 4361)

ARBUTHNOT, Sir William Reierson; 2 Bt (UK 1964), of Kittybrewster, Aberdeen; s of Sir John Sinclair-Wemyss Arbuthnot, 1 Bt, MBE, TD (d 1992), and (Margaret) Jean, *née* Duff; *b* 2 September 1950; *Educ* Eton, Coll of Law; *m* 2010, Louise Alexandra Mary Barry, da of late Mr and Mrs Bruce Barry, of Weybridge; 1 da ((Thomasina) Lucy b 1998), 2 s (Henry William, John Walter b 21 March 2011 (twins)); *Heir* s, Henry William Arbuthnot; *Career* Scottish American Investment Co 1969–70, Arbuthnot Latham Holdings Ltd 1970–76, Joynson-Hicks & Co (slrs) 1978–81; dep chm High Premium Gp 1994–2010, dir ALM Ltd 1997–2005; memb Lloyd's 1971–; memb Families Need Fathers; Liveryman Worshipful Co of Grocers; *Recreations* genealogy; *Style—* Sir William Arbuthnot, Bt; ✉ 37 Cathcart Road, London SW10 9JG (☎ 020 7795 0707, e-mail wra@arbuthnot.org)

ARBUTHNOT OF ERDOM, Baron (Life Peer UK 2015), of Edrom in the County of Berwick; Rt Hon James Norwich Arbuthnot; PC (1998); yr s of Sir John Sinclair-Wemyss Arbuthnot, 1 Bt, MBE, TD (d 1992), and (Margaret) Jean, *née* Duff; bro Sir William Reierson Arbuthnot, 2 Bt, *qv*; *b* 4 August 1952; *Educ* Eton, Trinity Coll Cambridge (MA); *m* 6 Sept 1984, Emma Louise, da of (John) Michael Broadbent, of S Glos; 1 s (Alexander Broadbent b 1986), 3 da (Katherine Rose Joste b 1989, Leaf Sophie Duff b 1992, Alice Tempest Wemyss b 1998); *Career* called to the Bar Inner Temple 1975; practising barr 1977–92; cncllr Royal Borough of Kensington and Chelsea 1978–87; Parly candidate (Cons) Cynon Valley 1983 and May 1984; MP (Cons): Wanstead and Woodford 1987–97, Hants NE 1997–2015; asst whip 1992–94, Parly under sec of state DSS 1994–95, min of state (def procurement) MOD 1995–97, oppn chief whip in the House of Commons 1997–2001, shadow sec of state for Trade 2003–05; memb Intelligence and Security Ctee 2001–05, chm House of Commons Defence Select Ctee 2005–14; pres Cynon Valley Cons Assoc 1983–92, pres Hants NE Cons Assoc 2015–; *Recreations* skiing, guitar; *Clubs* Pratt's; *Style—* The Rt Hon the Lord Arbuthnot of Edrom; ✉ House of Lords, London SW1A 0PW (☎ 020 7219 3000)

ARBUTHNOTT, Prof Sir John Peebles; kt (1998); s of James Anderson Arbuthnott (d 1961), and Jean, *née* Kelly (d 1982); *b* 8 April 1939, Glasgow; *Educ* Hyndland Sr Secdy Sch, Univ of Glasgow (BSc, PhD), Trinity Coll Dublin (MA, ScD); *m* 2 July 1962, Elinor Rutherford, da of John Smillie (d 1986); 2 da (Anne b 6 March 1966, Alison b 11 Nov 1974), 1 s (Andrew b 10 Feb 1969); *Career* res fell Royal Soc 1968–72, sr lectr Dept of Microbiology Univ of Glasgow 1972–75 (asst lectr 1960–63, lectr 1963–67), bursar Trinity Coll Dublin 1983–86 (prof of microbiology 1976–88), prof of microbiology Univ of Nottingham 1988–91, princ and vice-chllr Univ of Strathclyde 1991–2000, sec and treas Carnegie Tst for the Univs of Scotland 2001–04; chm Jt Information Systems Ctee 1993–98, vice-chm CVCP 1997–99, convener Ctee of Scottish Higher Educn Princs 1994–96; author of many papers on bacterial toxins and microbial pathogenicity; memb Cncl Soc of Gen Microbiology 1981–86 (sr ed 1980–84, treas 1987–92), meetings sec Fedn of Euro Microbiology Socs 1986–90; chm: National Review of Allocation of Health Resources in Scotland 1997–99, Scottish Food Advsy Ctee 2000–02, Standing Ctee on Resource Allocation in NHS Scotland 2001–03, Health Bd NHS Gtr Glasgow and Clyde 2002–07, Cmmn on Boundary Changes and Voting Systems 2004–06, Clyde Valley Review 2008–09; ind chair Export Gp on Integration of Health and Social Care in Scotland 2010–11;

memb: Microbiological Safety of Food Ctee 1989–90, AFRC Animal Res Bd 1989–92, Public Health Laboratory Serv Bd 1991–97, DTI Multimedia Industry Advsy Gp 1994–96, Educn Counselling Serv Bd Br Cncl 1995–96, Glasgow Devpt Agency 1995–2000, Nat Ctee of Enquiry into Higher Educn 1996–97, Bd Food Standards Agency 2000–02; pres Scottish Assoc of Marine Science 2003–09; memb: Soc of Gen Microbiology 1968–2005, Glasgow Science Tst 1999–2001, Scottish Science Tst 1999–2004; chair Medical and Scientific Bd Lamellar Biomedical Ltd 2008–; fndr memb AfOx 2008–; tstee Lloyds TSB Fndn for Scotland 2008–; St Mungo Medal of City of Glasgow 2011; hon degree: Poly Univ Lodz, Queens Univ Belfast, Univ of Glasgow, Univ of Aberdeen, Univ of Strathclyde, Univ Techol Malaysia, Int Med Univ Kuala Lumpur, Glasgow Caledonian Univ, Queen Margaret UC; hon fell: TCD 1992, Univ of Durham 2007; hon princ fell Dept of Clinical Pharmacology Univ of Oxford 2008–; MRIA 1985, FIBiol 1988, FRSE 1993 (memb Cncl 2007–10, pres 2011–14), FIIB 1993, FRCPath 1995, Hon FRCPSGlas, FMedSci 1998; *Books* Isoelectric Focussing (jt ed, 1974), Determinants of Microbial Pathogenicity (jt ed, 1983), Foodborne Illness: a Lancet review (jtly, 1991), Fair Shares for All – Final Report (for the NHS in Scot, 2000), Breaking the Mould (autobiography, 2015); *Recreations* photography, bird watching; *Style*— Prof Sir John Arbuthnott, FRSE; ✉ 9 Curlinghall, Largs KA30 8LB (☎ 01475 689426, e-mail jarbuthnott@btinternet.com); 3 Priors Close, Bingham, Nottingham NG13 8EP (☎ 01949 831395, mobile 07968 217263, e-mail j.arbuthnott@btinternet.com)

ARBUTHNOTT, 17 Viscount of (S 1641); (John) Keith Oxley Arbuthnott; DL (Kincardineshire 2000); s and h of 16 Viscount of Arbuthnott, CBE, DSC (d 2012); *b* 18 July 1950; *Educ* Fettes, N Scotland Coll of Agric Aberdeen (HND, Dip Farm Business, Orgn and Mgmnt), Robert Gordon's Inst of Technol Aberdeen (Dip Mgmnt Studies); *m* 1974, Jill Mary, eld da of Capt Colin Farquharson, of Whitehouse, Aberdeenshire; 2 da (Clare Anne b 1974, Rachel Sarah b 1979), 1 s (Christopher Keith b 20 July 1977); *Career* owner/mangr Arbuthnott Estate, fndr and dir Arbuthnott Wood Pellets Ltd; vice-convenor Scottish Landowners' Fedn 2002–05, chm Scottish Rural Property and Business Assoc 2005–08; memb Grampian Health Bd 1993–97; *Recreations* family, photography; *Style*— The Viscount of Arbuthnott; ✉ Kilternan, Arbuthnott, Laurencekirk, Kincardineshire AB30 1NA (e-mail keith@arbuthnott.co.uk)

ARCHARD, Dr Graham Eric; MBE (2011); s of Eric Harry Archard, of Bournemouth, Dorset, and Irene Lilian Mary, *née* Etchell; *b* 31 March 1951, Winchester, Hampshire; *Educ* Canford Sch Wimborne, Univ of Leeds (BSc, MB ChB); *m* 24 Sept 1977, Honor, *née* Guy; 1 da (Elizabeth Honor b 5 Sept 1983), 1 s (Guy Graham Robin b 1 Aug 1985); *Career* princ in gen practice 1984–2011; jt chm S & E Dorset PCT 2003–07, vice-chm RCGP 2005–07; clinical governance lead NHS Alliance 2000–05; medical expert advsr GMC 2006–13; author of articles in professional jls; Jamieson Medal and Prize in practical anatomy 1978; memb: BMA, NHS Alliance; FRCGP; *Recreations* music (guitar and piano), walking, qualifications in wine tasting; *Clubs* Rotary (Boscombe and Southbourne); *Style*— Dr Graham Archard, MBE; ✉ Willowmarsh, St Catherine's Hill Lane, Christchurch, Dorset BH23 2NL (☎ 07768 910273, e-mail g.archard@doctors.org.uk)

ARCHER, David Birdwood; s of Geoffrey Archer, of Renson Mill, N Devon, and Hon Sonia, *née* Birdwood; *b* 18 June 1959, Montreal, Canada; *Educ* Cheltenham Coll, LSE (LLB); *m* 25 Feb 1984, Gwenyth, *née* Highley; 2 s (Thomas b 3 Sept 1988, James b 28 July 1990), 1 da (Isabel b 29 Sept 1992); *Career* slr: Norton Rose 1982–88, Baker & MacKenzie Aust 1988–90, Clifford Chance 1990–92, Pitmans 1992– (md Pitmans Trustees Limited 1994–); memb Law Soc 1982; *Clubs* Brooks'; *Style*— David Archer, Esq; ✉ Pitmans, 1 Crown Court, 66 Cheapside, London EC2V 6LR (☎ 020 7634 4651, e-mail darcher@pitmans.com)

ARCHER, Janet; *Educ* Welsh Coll of Music and Drama (Dip Theatre Studies), Rambert Sch, London Sch of Contemporary Dance; *Career* dancer, choreographer and dir; dancer Jumpers Dance Theatre 1981, freelance dir, choreographer and performer 1982–85 (credits incl: HTV, WNO, Nat Youth Theatre of Wales, Cardiff Univ, Sherman Theatre) 1982–85, dance ldr CATO Bridgend 1985–86, artistic dir Nexus Dance Co 1987–91, arts mangr Welwyn Hatfield Cncl 1989–91 (dance animateur 1986–89), artistic dir and ceo DanceCity Newcastle upon Tyne 1991–2007, dance dir Arts Cncl England 2007–13, chief exec Creative Scotland 2013–; memb Bd: Phoenix Dance Co (interim chm 2001), Dance UK, Dancers Career Devpt, Newcastle Arts Forum, Graingertown Arts Ctee; former memb Bd: Fndn for Community Dance, Diversions Dance Theatre, Nat Youth Dance Festival; judge Jerwood Award 2000; Cosmopolitan Young Dancer of the Year 1981, Digital Dance Award 1987, Northern Electric Arts Award 1992, British Gas Working for Cities Award 1993, Cosmoplitan Woman of the Year 1995; *Recreations* film, food, psychology, entertaining, books, spending time with my daughter; *Style*— Ms Janet Archer; ✉ Waverley Gate, 2–4 Waterloo Place, Edinburgh EH1 3EG

ARCHER, Malcolm David; s of Gordon and Joan Archer, of Bolton-le-Sands, Lancs; *b* 29 April 1952; *Educ* King Edward VII Sch Lytham, RCM (RJ Pitcher scholar, ARCM), Jesus Coll Cambridge (organ scholar, MA, CertEd), FRCO; *m* 1994, Alison Jane, *née* Robinson; 1 s (Nathaniel Luke b 27 Dec 1997), 1 da (Tabitha Jane b 5 Nov 1999); *Career* asst dir of music Magdalen Coll Sch Oxford 1976–78, asst organist Norwich Cathedral 1978–83, organist and master of the choristers Bristol Cathedral 1983–90, head of chapel music Clifton Coll 1994–96, freelance composer, conductor and organist 1990–96, organist and master of the choristers Wells Cathedral 1996–2004, organist and dir of music St Paul's Cathedral 2004–07, dir of chapel music Winchester Coll 2007–; fndr and musical dir City of Bristol Choir 1991–99, musical dir Wells Cathedral Oratorio Soc; memb: Cncl RCO 1996–, Cathedral Organists Assoc, Friends of Cathedral Music; Hon fell North and Midlands Sch of Music (Hon FNMSM), Hon FGCM, FRSCM 2009; *Publications* Love Unknown (1992), Requiem (1993), Nowell! Nowell! (2010); over 200 published works; *Recreations* swimming, cooking, travel, painting, classic cars; *Clubs* MG Car, Octagon Car, Austin Healey Drivers'; *Style*— Malcolm Archer, Esq

ARCHER, Prof Margaret Scotford; da of Ronald Archer (d 1964), and Elise, *née* Scotford; *b* 20 January 1943; *Educ* Sheffield HS for Girls, LSE (BSc, PhD), Ecole Pratique des Hautes Etudes Paris; *Children* 2 s (Kingsley b 1975, Marcus b 1979); *Career* lectr Univ of Reading 1966–73, prof Univ of Warwick 1979– (reader 1973–79); memb Br Sociological Assoc, pres Int Sociological Assoc; counsellor Pontifical Acad of Social Scis; *Books* Social Conflict and Educational Change in England and France 1789–1848 (with M Vaughan, 1971), Contemporary Europe, Class, Status and Power (ed with S Giner, 1971), Students, University and Society (ed, 1972), Contemporary Europe, Social Structures and Cultural Patterns (ed with S Giner, 1978), Social Origins of Educational Systems (1979), The Sociology of Educational Expansion (ed, 1982), Culture and Agency (1988), Realist Social Theory: the Morphogenetic Approach (1995), Rational Choice Theory: Resisting Colonization (ed with J Tritter, 2000), Being Human: the Problem of Agency (2000), Structure, Agency and the Internal Conversation (2003), Making Our Way Through the World: Human Reflexivity and Social Mobility (2007); *Recreations* equestrian; *Style*— Prof Margaret Archer

ARCHER OF WESTON-SUPER-MARE, Baron (Life Peer UK 1992), of Mark in the County of Somerset; Jeffrey Howard Archer; s of William Archer (d 1956), and Lola, *née* Cook; *b* 15 April 1940, London; *Educ* Wellington Sch Somerset, BNC Oxford (Athletics blues 1963–65, Gymnastics blue 1965, Oxford 100 yds record 1966); *m* 11 July 1966, Dame Mary Doreen Archer, DBE, *qv*, da of Harold Weeden (d 1971); 2 s (Hon William Harold b 1972, Hon James Howard b 1974); *Career* politician and author; Int Recognition Award Irish Book Awards 2014; memb GLC Havering 1966–70, MP (C) Louth 1969–74; dep chm Cons Pty 1985–86; tstee RWS 1989–; pres: Somerset AAA 1973, Somerset Wyverns 1983–98, World Snooker Assoc 1997–99; FRSA 1973; *Books* Not a Penny More, Not a Penny Less (1975, televised 1990), Shall We Tell The President? (1977), Kane and Abel (1979, televised 1986), A Quiver Full of Arrows (1980), The Prodigal Daughter (1982), First Among Equals (1984, televised 1986), A Matter of Honour (1986), Beyond Reasonable Doubt (play, 1987), A Twist in The Tale (short stories, 1989), Exclusive (play, 1989), As the Crow Flies (1991), Honour Among Thieves (1993), Twelve Red Herrings (1994), The Fourth Estate (1996), Collected Short Stories (1997), The Eleventh Commandment (1998), To Cut a Long Story Short (2000), The Accused (play, 2000), A Prison Diary (vol I, Hell) (2002), Sons of Fortune (2003), A Prison Diary (vol II, Purgatory) (2003), A Prison Diary (vol III, Heaven) (2004), Paths of Glory (screenplay, 2005), False Impression (2006, and screenplay 2006), Cat O'Nine Tales (short stories, 2006), The Gospel According to Judas by Benjamin Iscariot (with Prof Francis Moloney, 2007), A Prisoner of Birth (2008, Prix Polar Int Prix Cognac Awards 2009), Paths of Glory (2009, Prix Relay du Roman 'd'Évasion 2010), And Thereby Hangs A Tale (short stories, 2010), Only Time Will Tell (Vol 1 of The Clifton Chronicles, 2011), The Sins of the Father (Vol 2 of The Clifton Chronicles, 2012), Best Kept Secret (Vol 3 of The Clifton Chronicles, 2013), Be Careful What You Wish For (Vol 4 of The Clifton Chronicles, 2014), Mightier Than The Sword (Vol 5 of The Clifton Chronicles, 2015), Cometh The Hour (Vol 6 of The Clifton Chronicles, 2016), This Was a Man (Final vol of The Clifton Chronicles, 2016); *Recreations* theatre, auctioneering, watching Somerset play cricket; *Style*— The Lord Archer of Weston-super-Mare; ✉ c/o Jonathan Lloyd, Curtis Brown Ltd, Haymarket House, 28–29 Haymarket, London, SW1Y 4SP (e-mail questions@jeffreyarcher.co.uk, website www.jeffreyarcher.com)

ARCHER OF WESTON-SUPER-MARE, Lady; Dame Mary Doreen Archer; DBE (2012); *née* Weeden; da of Harold Norman Weeden (d 1971), and Doreen, *née* Cox (d 1994); *b* 22 December 1944; *Educ* Cheltenham Ladies' Coll, St Anne's Coll Oxford (MA), Imperial Coll London (PhD); *m* 11 July 1966, Baron Archer of Weston-super-Mare (Life Peer), *qv*; 2 s; *Career* jr res fell St Hilda's Coll Oxford 1968–71, temp lectr in chemistry Somerville Coll Oxford 1971–72, res fell Royal Instn of Great Britain 1972–76, fell and lectr Newnham Coll Cambridge and lectr in chemistry Trinity Coll Cambridge 1976–86; visitor Univ of Hertfordshire 1993–2005; pres: Nat Energy Fndn 1999– (chm 1989–99), UK Solar Energy Soc 1999–; chm Cambridge Univ Hosps NHS Fndn Tst (formerly Addenbrooke's Hosp NHS Tst) 2002–12 (non-exec dir 1993–99, vice-chm 1999–2002), chair E of England Stem Cell Network 2004–08, convenor UK Univ Hosps Chairs Gp 2008–12, chm Cambridge Healthcare 2012–14, chm Expert Advsy Bd Imperial Coll Health Partners 2013–, chm Expert Advsy Bd Centre for Personalised Medicine Oxford 2013–; pres Cambridge branch NHS Retirement Fellowship 2008–15; non-exec dir: Anglia Television Gp 1987–95, Mid Anglia Radio plc 1988–95, Cambridge and Newmarket FM Radio Ltd 1988–94, IPC plc 2002–10, CRAC 2007–11, icould 2012–, Hydrodec 2014–; memb Cncl: Lloyd's 1988–92, Cheltenham Ladies' Coll 1991–99; dir Fitzwilliam Museum Tst 1984–91, tstee Science Museum 1990–99 (chair 2015–), tstee and dep chm Addenbrooke's Charitable Tst 1997–2015, tstee Global eHealth Fndn 2015–, hon pres Addenbrooke's Abroad 2015–; pres Guild of Church Musicians 1989–, non-exec dir Britten Sinfonia 1998–; Melchett Medal Inst Energy 2002, Eva Philbin Award Int of Chemistry of Ireland 2007; hon fell St Anne's Coll Oxford 2013; Hon DSc Univ of Hertfordshire 1994; CChem, FRSC, FRSA; *Books* Rupert Brooke and the Old Vicarage, Grantchester (1989), Clean Electricity from Photovoltaics (2000), Molecular to Global Photosynthesis (2004), The 1702 Chair of Chemistry at Cambridge (2005), Nanostructured and Photoelectrochemical Systems for Solar Photon Conversion (2008), The Story of The Old Vicarage, Grantchester (2012); *Recreations* singing, theatre, cats; *Style*— Dame Mary Archer, DBE; ✉ The Old Vicarage, Grantchester, Cambridge CB3 9ND (☎ 01223 840213, fax 01223 842882); Peninsula Heights, 93 Albert Embankment, London SE1 7TY (☎ 020 7735 0077, fax 020 7582 2406)

ARCHIBALD, Ron; *Career* dir Tradeshow Access Prog and UKTI Enquiry Unit Sectors Gp UK Trade and Investment; *Style*— Ron Archibald, Esq; ✉ UK Trade and Investment, Tay House, 300 Bath Street, Glasgow G2 4DX (e-mail ron.archibald@ukti.gsi.gov.uk)

ARCULUS, Sir (Thomas) David Guy; kt (2005); s of Thomas Guy Arculus, and Mary, *née* Barton (d 1971); *b* 2 June 1946; *Educ* Bromsgrove Sch, Oriel Coll Oxford (MA), London Business Sch (MSc); *m* 11 Aug 1974, Anne Murdoch, da of Howard Leslie Sleeman; 1 da (Suzanne b 1 April 1976), 2 s (Thomas b 30 Jan 1978, Nicholas b 13 Nov 1979); *Career* VSO 1964–65, prodr BBC 1968–70; EMAP plc: joined 1972, gen mangr magazines 1974–81, md business magazines and exhbns 1981–84, gp dep md 1984–89, gp md 1989–97; chief operating offr United News and Media plc 1997–98; chm: IPC Magazines 1998–2001, Severn Trent plc 1998–2004 (non-exec dir 1996–2004), Earls Court and Olympia Exhibition Gp 2002–04, O2 2004–06 (non-exec dir 2003–07), ShortList Media 2007–13, Boat Int Gp 2007–10, Clarion Events 2007–13, Excel 2007–13, Numis Corp plc 2009–14, Aldermore Bank 2010–13, Energy UK 2015–; dir Nat Exhbn Centre 2016; non-exec dir: Norcros plc 1993–96, Barclays plc 1997–2006, Pearson 2006–15, Telefonica and Telefonica Europe 2006–15, Guiton Gp plc 2000–02; chm: PPA 1990, Better Regulation Task Force 2002–05; treas Fedn of Int Periodical Press 1992–94, dep pres CBI 2005 (memb President's Ctee 2003), memb Nat Consumer Cncl 1993–96; fell Industry and Parl Tst, memb Assoc of MBA 1972; Freeman City of London 1990, Liveryman Worshipful Co of Stationers and Newspaper Makers 1992; High Sheriff of Cambridgeshire 2016; Hon Dr Univ of Central England 2003; MInstD 1993; *Recreations* cricket, hill walking, reading; *Clubs* Oxford and Cambridge, MCC, Thirty, Groucho; *Style*— Sir David Arculus; ✉ Oxford & Cambridge Club, 71 Pall Mall, London SW1Y 5HD (☎ 07771 940343, e-mail darculus@gmail.com)

ARDALAN, Dr Ziba; da of Nosrat Ardalan (d 1989), and Kechvar, *née* Kamangar (d 2009); *b* Iran; *Educ* Univ of Geneva (MA, PhD), Whitney Museum of American Art NY (ISP), Columbia Univ (MA); *m* 1972, Pierre Jacques de Weck; 2 s (Philippe Thomas, Cyrus); *Career* res fell Univ of Geneva 1968–72, post doctoral MIT 1975–76, dir of res Univ of Zurich Med Sch 1977–80, res asst Whitney Museum of American Art NY 1982–83 (guest curator 1984), dir Swiss Inst NY 1986–90, lectr NY and Zurich 1990–99, dir Parasol unit Fndn for Contemporary Art London 2004–; dir Inst for Art Research Switzerland 1997–2000; memb RSA; *Recreations* skiing, walking, swimming; *Style*— Dr Ziba Ardalan; ✉ 15 Fitzroy Square, London W1T 6EF (☎ 020 7388 0738); Parasol unit, Foundation for Contemporary Art, 14 Wharf Road, London N1 7RW (☎ 020 7490 7373, e-mail ziba@parasol-unit.org)

ARDEN, Andrew Paul Russel; QC (1991); s of Sidney Russel Arden (d 2000), and Helen Anne, *née* Prevezer (d 1991); *b* 20 April 1948; *Educ* Stowe, Univ Coll Sch, UCL (LLB); *m* 19 Sept 1991, Joanne, da of Joseph Leahy, of Cramlington, Northumberland, and Sheila Leahy; 1 da (Emma b 1992); *Career* called to the Bar Gray's Inn 1974; dir Small Heath Community Law Centre Birmingham 1976–78, established Arden Chambers 1993; *Legal Publications* Manual of Housing Law (1978, 9 edn (jtly) 2012), Housing Act 1980 (1980), Quiet Enjoyment (jtly, 1980, 7 edn 2012), Rent Acts & Regulations, Amended and Annotated (jtly, 1981), Housing & Building Control Act 1984 (jtly, 1984), Homeless Persons: Part III, Housing Act 1985 (1982, 9 edn as Homelessness and Allocations, (jtly) 2012), Housing Law (jtly, 1983, looseleaf 2 edn 1994), Private Tenants Handbook (1985, 2 edn 1989), Public Tenants Handbook (1985, 2 edn 1989), Homeless Persons Handbook (1986, 2 edn 1988), Housing Act 1985 (1986), Landlord & Tenant Act 1985 (jtly, 1986), Housing Associations Act 1985 (jtly, 1986), Housing Act 1988 (jtly, 1989), Local

Government & Housing Act 1989 (jtly, 1990), Assured Tenancies (Vol 3 'The Rent Acts', jtly, 1989), Local Government Finance Law and Practice (jtly, 1994), Housing Act 1996 (jtly, 1996), Housing Grants, Construction and Regeneration Act 1996 (jtly, 1996), Local Government Constitutional and Administrative Law (jtly, 1999, 2 edn 2007); gen ed: Encyclopaedia of Housing Law (1978–), Housing Law Reports (1981–), Jl of Housing Law (1997–), Local Government Law Reports (1999–2001); *Fiction* The Motive Not The Deed (1975), No Certain Roof (1985), The Object Man (1986), The Programme (2001); also author series of 4 thrillers (written under pseudonym); *Recreations* Southern Comfort, Camels, Hill St Blues; *Clubs* Manzis Luncheon; *Style*— Andrew Arden, Esq, QC; ✉ Arden Chambers, 20 Bloomsbury Square, London WC1A 2NS (☎ 020 7242 4244, fax 020 7242 3224, e-mail andrew.arden@ardenchambers.com)

ARDEN, The Rt Hon Lady Justice; Rt Hon Dame Mary Howarth; DBE (1993), PC (2000); da of Lt-Col Eric Cuthbert Arden (d 1973); *Educ* Girton Coll Cambridge (MA, LLM), Harvard Univ (LLM); *m* 26 May 1973, Sir Jonathan Hugh Mance (Baron Mance, PC (Life Peer), *qv*); 2 da, 1 s; *Career* called to the Bar 1971, QC 1986, asst recorder of Crown and Co Courts 1990–93, dep High Court judge 1990–93, attorney-gen Duchy of Lancaster 1991–93, judge of the High Court of Justice (Chancery Div) 1993–2000, ad hoc judge European Court of Human Rights 2000, Lady Justice of Appeal 2000–, judge i/c int judicial rels (for Eng and Wales) 2005–, memb Permanent Ct of Arbitration The Hague 2011–; bencher of Lincoln's Inn 1994–; chm: Law Cmmn 1996–99, Judges' Cncl Working Pty on Constitutional Reform 2004–06; chm CAB Royal Courts of Justice Charitable Tst 1994–97; inspector Rotaprint plc under sections 432 and 444 of the Companies Act 1985 1988–91; pres: Assoc of Women Barristers 1994–98, Trinity Hall Law Soc 1996, Holdsworth Club Faculty of Law Univ of Birmingham 1999–2000; ed-in-chief Chancery Guide 1995–2000; chair Papers Ctee Cwlth Law Confs 2004–05; memb: Law Soc's Company Law Ctee (ldr Insolvency Working Pty) 1976–2007, Insolvency Sub-Ctee Consumer and Commercial Law Ctee of Law Soc (previously Jt Working Pty of the Bar and the Law Soc on Insolvency) 1979–97, Financial Law Panel 1993–2000, Bd Inst of Advanced Legal Studies 1996–99, Advsy Cncl for Socio-Legal Studies Univ of Oxford 1996–99, Steering Gp Company Law Review Project DTI 1998–2001, Ed Bd Practical Law for Cos (PLC magazine) 1998–, Common Law/Common Bond Project 1999–2000, Corporate and Commercial Law Advsy Ctee Faculty of Law Univ of Cambridge 1999–, Cncl Statute Law Soc 2001–07; The Times Woman of Achievement Lifetime Award 1997; elector: Herchel Smith Professorship in Intellectual Property Law Univ of Cambridge 1993–94, Downing Professorship of Laws of England 1996–2000, Professorship of English Law Univ of Oxford 1997, visitor Royal Holloway London 2008; memb Advsy Bd Centre of European Law King's Coll London 2008; hon memb: Soc of Public Teachers of Law 1993–, Soc Tst and Estate Practitioners (STEP) 1996–; academic tstee Kennedy Memorial Tst 1995–2005; hon fell Girton Coll Cambridge 1995–, hon fell Soc for Advanced Legal Studies 1997, memb Inst Advanced Legal Studies 1997–2000; Hon DUniv Essex 1997; Hon LLD: Univ of Liverpool 1998, Royal Holloway and Bedford New Coll London 1999, Univ of Warwick 1999, Univ of Nottingham 2002, Liverpool John Moores Univ 2006, UCL; *Publications* contrib to numerous legal reference works, author of numerous articles in legal jls; Buckley on the Companies Acts (jt gen ed, 2000), Human Rights and European Law: Building New Legal Orders (2015), Common Law and Modern Society: Keeping Pace with Change (2015); *Style*— The Rt Hon Lady Justice Arden, DBE, PC; ✉ c/o Royal Courts of Justice, Strand, London WC2A 2LL

ARESTIS, Prof Philip; *b* 24 October 1941, Famagusta, Cyprus; *Educ* Athens Grad Sch of Economics and Business Studies (BA), LSE (MSc), Univ of Surrey (PhD), Univ of Cambridge (MA); *Career* pt/t lectr: Kingston Poly 1968–69, Univ of Surrey 1969–80; Thames Poly: lectr in economics 1969–71, sr lectr in economics 1971–77, princ lectr in economics and head Economics Div 1977–88, memb Faculty Bd 1978–81, dep head Sch of Social Sciences 1987–88; prof of economics and head Dept of Applied Economics (later Dept of Economics) NE London Poly (later Poly of East London then Univ of E London) 1988–97 (numerous ctee appts incl chair Research Degrees Ctee 1991–95), research prof of economics Univ of E London 1997–2000, prof of economics and dir of research South Bank Univ Business Sch 2000–02, dir of research Centre of Economic and Public Policy Dept of Land Economy Univ of Cambridge 2004–, sr research fell Wolfson Coll Cambridge 2004–09 (memb Cncl 2005–, emeritus fell 2009–), prof of economics Univ of the Basque Country 2009–; hon research fell Dept of Economics UCL 1991, sr research fell Levy Economics Inst Bard Coll NY 1998–2012 (research prof of economics 2002–04, research assoc 2012–), visiting prof Dept of Economics Candido Mendes Univ Rio de Janeiro 2000–02, visiting prof of economics Leeds Business Sch Univ of Leeds 2003–, professorial research assoc Dept of Finance and Mgmnt Studies SOAS 2003–, adjunct prof Univ of Utah USA 2005–; academic conslt Macmillan Publishing Ltd 1997–, vice-chair Macroeconomics, Money and Finance Research Gp 1999–2012, chief academic (external) advsr to UK Govt Economic Serv on Professional Devpt in Economics 2005–13; jt ed Thames Papers in Political Economy 1979–93, ed Br Review of Economic Issues 1982–88 (memb Editorial Bd 1979–88), fndr and jt commissioning ed Int Papers in Political Economy 1993–, assoc ed and memb Editorial Bd Review of Social Economy 1995–, memb Editorial Advsy Bd EAST-WEST: Jl of Economics and Business 1997–, memb Managing Bd Jl of Post Keynesian Economics 1998–2014, Eastern Economic Jl 1999, assoc ed Applied Economics 2001– (memb Editorial Bd 1996–), assoc ed and memb Editorial Bd Greek Economic Review 2003–10, fndr Int Papers in Political Economy 2005–; memb Editorial Bd: Jl of Economic Issues 1988–91, Review of Political Economy 1988–93, Int Review of Applied Economics 1988–, Applied Economics Letters 1996–; author of numerous pubns in learned jls; memb: Cncl Royal Economic Soc 1994–99, Bd Eastern Economics Assoc USA 2004; Conference of Heads of Univ Dept in Economics: memb Panel HE Funding Cncl Research Assessment Exercise 1996, HE Funding Cncl Research Assessment Exercise 2001; memb various CNAA ctees and panels (incl: Economics Bd 1983–87, Social Sciences Research Degrees Sub-Ctee 1984–88), memb various ESRC and ESRC-funded research gps; advsr on economics-related degrees, staff appts and research to numerous univs, colls and polys, memb Hong Kong Cncl for Academic Accreditation 1990; numerous lectures, organiser and chair of confs; Br-Hispanic Queen Victoria Eugenia Fndn Award; awardfor contribution to the spreak of Keynesianism by the Brazilian Keynesian Assoc (AKB), AcSS award Academician of the Acad of Social Sciences for contributions to Social Sci (2012–14); Royal Economic Soc 1982–, Assoc for Evolutionary Economics 1982–, European Assoc for Evolutionary Economics 1988–93, Assoc for Social Economics 1995–, European Soc for the History of Economic Thought 1997–; *Books* most recent incl: Path Dependency and Macroeconomics (jtly, 2009), Housing Market Challenges in Europe and the United States (jtly, 2010), 21st Century Keynesianism (jtly, 2010), The Post 'Great Recession' US Economy: Implications for Financial Markets and the Economy (jtly, 2010), The Financial Crisis: Origins and Implications (jtly, 2011), An Assessment of the Global Impact of the Financial Crisis (jtly, 2011), New Economics as Mainstream Economics (jtly, 2011), Microeconomics, Macroeconomics and Economic Policy: Essays in Honour of Malcolm Sawyer (2011), The Euro Crisis (jtly, 2012), Economic Policies of the New Thinking in Economics (jtly, 2013), Financial Stability in the Aftermath of the 'Great Recesssion' (jtly, 2013), Economic Policies, Governance and the New Economics (jtly, 2013), Economic and Monetary Union Macroeconomic Policies, Current Practises and Alternatives (jtly, 2013), Fiscal and Debt Policies for the Future (jtly, 2014), Finance and the Macroeconomics of Environmental Policies (jtly, 2015), Emerging Economies During and After the Great Recession (jtly, 2015); *Style*— Philip Arestis, Esq; ✉ Cambridge Centre for Economic and Public Policy, Department of Land Economy, University of Cambridge, 19 Silver Street, Cambridge CB3 9EP (☎ 01223 766971, fax 01223 337130, e-mail pa267@cam.ac.uk)

ARGYLL, 13 Duke of (S 1701 and UK 1892); Sir Torquhil Ian Campbell; 15 Bt (NS 1627); also Lord Campbell (S 1445), Earl of Argyll (S 1457), Lord Lorne (S 1470), Marquess of Kintyre and Lorne, Earl of Campbell and Cowal, Viscount Lochow and Glenilla, and Lord Inveraray, Mull, Morvern and Tiry (all S 1701), Baron Sundridge (GB 1766), Baron Hamilton (GB 1776), Hereditary Master of HM's Household in Scotland, keeper of the Great Seal of Scotland, keeper of Dunoon, Carrick, Dunstaffnage and Tarbert Castles, Admiral of the Western Coasts and Isles, hereditary sheriff of Argyll, 27 Chief of Clan Campbell; only s of 12 Duke of Argyll (d 2001); *b* 29 May 1968; *Educ* Cargilfield Sch Edinburgh, Glenalmond Coll Perthshire, RAC Cirencester; *m* 8 June 2002, Eleanor Mary *née* Cadbury, da of Peter H G Cadbury; 2 s (Archie Frederick, Marquess of Lorne b 9 March 2004, Lord Rory James b 3 Feb 2006), 1 da (Lady Charlotte Mary b 29 Oct 2008); *Heir* s, Marquess of Lorne; *Career* page of honour to HM The Queen 1981–83; asst land agent Buccleuch Estates Ltd Selkirk 1991–93; sales mangr Grosvenor House (Trust House Forte plc) 1994–96; marketing mangr Casella Far East Ltd Hong Kong 1996–2001, Chivas Brothers (Pernod Ricard) London 2001– (currently global ambass); patron Keepers of the Quaich; Liveryman Worshipful Co of Distillers 2005; *Clubs* New (Edinburgh); *Style*— His Grace the Duke of Argyll; ✉ Inveraray Castle, Argyll PA32 8XF

ARIF QUADRI, Saleem; MBE (2008); s of Dr Syed A Quadri (d 2007), and Sayeedunisa Quadri; *b* 1949; *Educ* Birmingham Coll of Art, RCA (MA); *Career* artist; curator Kanu Gandhi's Mahatma: (touring exhbn) 1995–, co-curator An(other) Story (Folk & Tribal Arts from India New Art Exchange Gallery Nottingham) 2009; *Solo Exhibitions* incl: Art Heritage Gallery New Delhi 1984, Ipswich Museum 1986, Winchester Art Gallery 1987, Anderson O'Day Gallery London 1988, Laing Art Gallery Newcastle upon Tyne 1991, Birds of Breath (Midland Art Centre Birmingham) 1993, Arks Gallery London 1997, Open Studio London 1999, Drawing into Discovery (Scene Art Gallery NY) 2000, Sensual Songs (Art Exchange Gallery Nottingham) 2003, Shrishti Art Gallery Hyderabad 2006; *Group Exhibitions* incl: Serpentine Gallery Summer Show London 1981, Hayward Annual London and Edinburgh 1982, From Two Worlds (Whitechapel Gallery London and Fruitmarket Gallery Edinburgh) 1986, The Other Story (Hayward Gallery London and tours Wolverhampton Art Gallery and Cornerhouse Manchester) 1989–90, The Third World and Beyond (Art Int Confrontation of Contemporary Galleria Civica D'Arte Contemporánea Marsala Sicily) 1991, Cagnes-sur-Mer Int Exhibition (British Cncl) France; most important works: Itinerary 1972, Dante's Inferno (set of forty) 1980–81, Birds of Aspirations 1989, Birds of Breath 1991–93, Garden of Grace (The Central Library Birmingham) 1995–96, Essence of Oldham 1998, Landscape of Longing (Tate London) 1994–99, Sensual Songs of Sacred Space 2002–03, Invocations 2002–07, Geometry without Gravity (manuscript books) 2003–07; *Collections* incl: Govt Collection London, Ipswich Museum, Birmingham Museum and City Art Gallery, Manchester City Art Gallery, Preston Museum & Art Gallery, Tate London; *Video and Television* incl: Believing People (Tyne Tees TV) 1991, Islam in Britain 1999 (FO); *Awards* incl: prize winner Young Sculptor of the Year Sunday Telegraph Competition 1971, Italian Govt Bursary Florence 1982, Villers David Fndn travel award 1989; *Publications* The Spirit of Tomorrow: interview with the artist in Indian Express (1985), Seed of Celebrations and Moment of Grace in Arts and the Islamic World (text by Dr Sarah Wilson, 1994), Gardens of Grace (text by Mary Rose Beaumont, 1997), Geometry without Gravity (2006), Drawing into Discovery (2007); Artist's Statements on: Photography (2000), Painting (2000), Drawing into Discovery (2003), Geometry without Gravity (2003), Books without Boundaries (2010), Cusp within Creativity (2013); *Recreations* collecting Indian contemporary folk art, photography, travelling; *Style*— Saleem Arif Quadri, Esq, MBE; ✉ 1 Boadicea Street, Islington, London N1 0UA (e-mail saleemaquadri@hotmail.com, website www. saleem-arif-quadrie.co.uk)

ARIS, Brian; *Career* portrait and feature photographer; charity work incl: Save the Children Fund, Prince's Trust, Band Aid, Nordoff Robbins Music Therapy; estab stock library (incl: official portraits of HM The Queen, actors, musicians, pop stars and industrialists); *Recreations* music, reading, travel, walking; *Style*— Brian Aris, Esq; ✉ Queens Hall Studios, Forbes Road, Faversham, Kent ME13 8QE (☎ 01795 538805, mobile 07860 436600, e-mail info@brianaris.com, website www.brianaris.com)

ARKELL, James Rixon; TD, DL (Wiltshire 1996); s of Peter Arkell, and Anne, *née* Falcon; *b* 28 May 1951; *Educ* Milton Abbey; *m* 7 Sept 1974, Carolyn Jane, da of Charles Ralph Woosnam; 3 s (George b 9 Dec 1978, John b 17 April 1983, Alexander b 15 Aug 1985), 1 da (Emma 6 Feb 1976); *Career* Royal Wiltshire (Yeo) TA 1974, Sqdn-Ldr 1983, 2 i/c 1989, CO Royal Yeo Regt 1993–95; md Arkells Brewery Ltd Swindon; high sheriff of Wiltshire 2004–05; *Recreations* shooting, fishing, hunting, skiing; *Clubs* Cavalry; *Style*— James Arkell, Esq, TD, DL

ARKELL, Julian; OBE (1992); 2 s of William Joscelyn Arkell (d 1958), and Ruby Lilian, *née* Percival (d 1983); *b* 22 October 1934, Cumnor, Oxon; *Educ* Bryanston, King's Coll Cambridge (MA); *m* 1, 5 Sept 1964 (m dis 1976), Fiona Cox; 2 da (Claire b 25 Aug 1966, Katie b 8 July 1968); m 2, 29 April 1983, Elaine Wilson (d 2009); *Career* Shell-Mex and BP Ltd 1956–62, ptnr Robert Matthew Johnson-Marshall & Partners 1972–86 (partnership sec 1962–72), co sec RMJM Ltd 1986–91, dir Applied Service Economics Centre Geneva 1991–2012, ret; formerly in practice as conslt t/a International Trade and Services Policy (clients have incl: British Invisibles, RMJM Gp, Carana Corp (for US Agency for Int Devpt (USAID)), EC, FCO, Geneva Assoc, Hill & Knowlton, HTSPE (for DfID), Commonwealth Business Cncl, Cwlth Secretariat (for ACP Malaysia and Mauritius), ICC, Int Centre for Trade and Sustainable Devpt (ICTSD), Inst for Devpt Policy and Mgmnt (IDPM) Manchester, ITC, Maxwell Stamp, PricewaterhouseCoopers, Islamic Devpt Bd, OECD, The Services Gp (TSG) Inc (for USAID), UNCTAD, UNDP, DTI, UNICE, United Nations Inst for Trg and Research (UNITAR, for Tajikistan), US Dept of Commerce, UPS, World Bank, ACLI, Zurich); memb: Fees Ctee RIBA 1974–92, Lotis Ctee BI 1981–95, Export Fin Panel London Chamber for Commerce and Industry (LCCI) 1983–91, Exec Ctee British Conslts Bureau 1992, Bd Services World Forum Geneva 1992–2000; services rapporteur GATT Working Gp UNICE Brussels 1990–94; chm: Euro Community Servs Gp Working Pty Brussels 1986–93, Servs Gp WTO Ctee UNICE 1994–95; Hon RICS 1991; *Books* The Invisible Economy: a profile of Britain's invisible exports (contrib, 1988), BIEC Yearbook 1989–90 (contrib, 1989), Marketing Strategies for Services (contrib, 1994), Trading Services in the Global Economy (contrib, 2002), Doha Development Agenda: a global view (contrib, 2003), GATS An Introduction (contrib, 2007), International Trade in Services (contrib, 2010), The Future of Insurance Regulation and Supervision (contrib, 2010); numerous articles in learned jls; *Recreations* photography, bird watching; *Clubs* C G Jung Club London (hon treas), Cambridge Soc of Sussex (treas); *Style*— Julian Arkell, Esq, OBE; ✉ 17 Normandy House, 18 The Drive, Hove BN3 3JB (☎ 01273 911342, mobile 07896 353563, e-mail arkell@arkell.info, website www.arkell.info)

ARKWRIGHT, Johnnie; DL (2012); s of Pup Arkwright (d 1989), and Liz, *née* MacIlwaine, of Guilsborough, Northants; *b* 3 February 1953, Northampton; *Educ* Eton, Pembroke Coll Cambridge; *m* 1999, Arabella, *née* Robb; 2 s (Jack (twin) b 7 Sept 1989, Harry 16 Jan 2001), 2 da (Lucy (twin) b 7 Sept 1989, Violet b 4 Nov 2003); *Career* dir: Hatton Ltd 1983–, Pembroke plc 1986–89, Bibendum Wine Ltd 1988–2007, Mansford Hldgs Ltd

1995–2004, Bowmans Leisure Ltd 2001–; dir Countryside Alliance 2004–; fndr Warks Community Fund 2007–; High Sheriff Warks 2007–08; MRICS 1976; *Recreations* country sports, golf, tennis; *Clubs* White's, Annabel's; *Style—* Johnnie Arkwright, Esq, DL; ✉ Hatton House, Hatton, Warwick CV35 7LD (☎ 01926 843411, mobile 07721 411191, fax 01926 842023, e-mail jarkwright@hattonworld.com)

ARLIDGE, Anthony John; QC; s of John Maurice Arlidge, (d 1985) of Sidcup, and Doris Lilian, *née* Whitecross (d 1984); *b* 18 February 1937; *Educ* Chislehurst and Sidcup GS, Queen's Coll Cambridge; *m* 12 Aug 1964 (sep), Enid Beryl Townsend; 2 da (Catherine b 24 May 1966, Victoria b 1 May 1971), 2 s (John b 5 Nov 1968, Mathew 10 Oct 1974); *Career* barr; called to the Bar Middle Temple 1962, recorder of the Crown Court 1979–99, QC 1981; treas Middle Temple 2002; *Publications* Contempt of Court (with Eady and Smith), Fraud (with Parry), Shakespeare and the Prince of Love; *Recreations* sport, theatre, gardening; *Style—* Anthony Arlidge, Esq, QC

ARMAGH, Archbishop of and Primate of All Ireland 2013–; Most Rev Dr Richard Lionel Clarke; *b* 25 June 1949; *Educ* Wesley Coll Dublin, TCD (MA, PhD), KCL (BD); *m* 1975, Linda (d 2009); 1 s (Nicholas b 1977), 1 da (Lindsey b 1981); *Career* teacher Iran (Church Missionary Soc vol scheme) 1971–72; ordained: deacon 1975, priest 1976; curate: Holywood Co Down (Down Dio), St Bartholomew's with Christ Church Leeson Park (Dublin Dio) 1977–79; dean of residence (chaplain) TCD 1979–84, rector Bandon Union of Parishes (Cork Dio) 1984–93, dean St Fin Barre's Cathedral Cork (incl chaplaincies of UC Cork and the Univ Hosp) 1993–96, bishop of Meath and Kildare 1996–2013; *Publications* And Is It True? (2000), A Whisper of God (2006); *Recreations* walking, France, music (Mozart, jazz), cricket; *Style—* The Most Rev the Archbishop of Armagh; ✉ The See House, Cathedral Close, Co Armagh BT61 7EE

ARMAGH, Archbishop of (RC), and Primate of All Ireland 1996–; Cardinal Sean Baptist Brady; *b* 16 August 1939; *Educ* St Patrick's Coll Cavan, St Patrick's Coll Maynooth (BA, HDipEd), Pontifical Irish Coll Rome, Lateran Univ Rome (STL, DCL); *Career* ordained priest 1964; prof St Patrick's Coll Cavan 1967–80, vice-rector Irish Coll Rome 1980–87, rector 1987–93, parish priest Castletara Co Cavan 1993–95, co-adjutor archbishop of Armagh 1995–96, cardinal 2007–; chm Irish Episcopal Conf and Standing Ctee 1996–, chm of Episcopal Visitors to and tstees of St Patrick's Coll Maynooth 1996–2000; *Style—* His Eminence Cardinal Sean Brady, Archbishop of Armagh; ✉ Ara Coeli, Armagh BT61 7QY (☎ 028 3752 2045, fax 028 3752 6182, e-mail admin@aracoeli.com)

ARMATRADING, Joan Anita Barbara; MBE (2001); da of Amos Ezekiel Armatrading, and Beryl Madge, *née* Benjamin; *b* 9 December 1950; *Educ* Secdy Sch Birmingham, BA; *Career* singer and songwriter; first album Whatever's For Us 1972 (with Pam Nestor), stage debut Fairfield Hall Croydon 1972, first non-jazz act downstairs at Ronnie Scott's 1973, first major hit Love and Affection 1976, first gold album Joan Armatrading 1976, album Into the Blue debuted at number 1 on USA Billboard Blues Chart 2007 (first female UK artist to do so); numerous silver, gold and platinum discs; concerts: Blackbush with Bob Dylan (before 100,000 plus audience) 1978, Prince's Tst 1982 and 1986, Amnesty Int (Giant Stadium) 1986, Amnesty Int (Secret Policeman's Ball) 1987, Nelson Mandela's 70th Birthday 1988, First King's Tst Swaziland 1989 and 1990, series of concerts celebrating 20th anniversary of democracy in S Africa 2014 (only non-S African invited to take part); Ivor Novello Award for Best Contemporary Song Collection 1996; nominated: Grammy Best Female Vocal 1980 and 1983, Best Female Vocal UK 1976 and 1983, Best Female Artist Brit Awards 1995, Best Contemporary Blues Artist Grammy 2008; voted one of the top 100 influential women in rock VH1; Key to Sydney 1983, guest of honour St Kitt's Independence Celebration 1983; wrote special tribute song for Nelson Mandela, performed LSE April 2000; pres Women of the Year UK 2005–; hon fell Liverpool John Moores Univ, hon fell Univ of Northampton, Hon Dr Univ of Birmingham, Hon DLitt Aston Univ Birmingham 2006, Hon Dr Univ of Glasgow 2008, hon degree RSAMD 2008, Hon DLitt Univ of the West Indies 2013; *Recreations* reading British comics, owner of three vintage cars; *Style—* Miss Joan Armatrading, MBE; ✉ website www.joanarmatrading.com, Facebook www.facebook.com/joanarmatrading

ARME, Prof Christopher; s of Cyril Boddington Arme, of Smalley, Derbys, and Monica Henriette, *née* Hawkins; *b* 10 August 1939; *Educ* Heanor GS, Univ of Leeds (BSc, PhD), Keele Univ (DSc); *Children* 3 s (Patrick b 16 May 1965, Mark b 19 April 1967, Peter b 12 Aug 1969); *Career* SRC/NATO res fell Univ of Leeds 1964–66, res fell Rice Univ Houston 1966–68, lectr/reader in zoology Queen's Univ Belfast 1968–76, princ lectr in biology and head of biology N Staffs Poly 1976–79, prof of zoology Keele Univ 1979–, secondment as dir of terrestrial and freshwater sciences NERC 1993–95, dean of natural sciences Keele Univ 1998–2001; Br Soc of Parasitology: memb, Silver Jubilee lectr 1987, pres 1990–92, hon memb 1992; memb: American Soc of Parasitology, Linnean Soc, Inst of Biology (hon treas 1986–93); hon memb Czechoslovak Parasitological Soc 1990, hon memb All Russia Soc of Helminthologists 1992, hon treas Euro Fedn of Parasitologists 1992; K I Skryabin Medal 1995, Charter Award Inst of Biology 1995; Hon DSc Slovak Acad of Sciences 1995; *Publications* author of several books and over 100 scientific pubns incl: Parasitology (ed with R S Phillips), Parasites and Vectors (ed); *Style—* Prof Christopher Arme; ✉ School of Life Sciences, Keele University, Keele, Staffordshire ST5 5BG (☎ 01782 733028, e-mail c.arme@keele.ac.uk)

ARMFIELD, Diana Maxwell; da of (Joseph) Harold Armfield (d 1981), of Ty Newydd, Gwynedd, and Gertrude Mary, *née* Uttley (d 1983); *b* 11 June 1920, Ringwood, Hants; *Educ* Bedales, Bournemouth Art Sch, Slade Sch, Central Sch of Arts and Crafts; *m* 12 Feb 1949, (Andrew Harold) Bernard Dunstan, RA, *qv*, s of Dr Albert Ernest Dunstan (d 1960), of Cambridge; 3 s (Andrew Joseph b 1950, David James b 1952, Robert Maxwell b 1955 d 2007); *Career* painter; cultural activities organiser Miny of Supply 1942–46; tutor: Textile Dept Central Sch Art 1949–50, Byam Shaw Art Sch 1959–90; visiting tutor various art schs 1959–91, reg exhibitor Royal Acad 1966–; memb Cncl Royal Acad 1991–92; exhibitor: Festival of Britain 1951, Tonic for the Nation (V&A), Diana Armfield's Choice (Albany Gallery Cardiff) 1991, Albany Gallery Cardiff 1995, Glyn-Y-Weddw Llanbedrog N Wales 1995; artist in residence: Perth W Aust 1985, Jackson Wyoming USA 1989; NEAC Centenary Sothebys' 1986; one man show: Browse & Darby London 1979–2010, 90th Birthday show, RWS Featured Artist for 90th Birthday Year, Bala 1997, Gall Gérard Wassenaar Holland 1998, Art of the Garden (Lampeter Univ of Wales) 2000, Royal Cambrian Acad 2001, Albany Gallery Cardiff 2001 and 2006, etchings Curwen & New Acad Gallery 2005, prints Curwen & New Acad Gallery 50th anniversary show 2008, RA Now 2012; part retrospective (with Bernard Dunstan, RA, Belle Shenkeman Room RA) 2015–16; perm collections: V&A (textiles), cmmns Reuters 1986–87, Contemporary Art Soc Wales 1987, Nat Tst 1988–89, HRH Prince of Wales 1989, Farringdon Tst, Yale Center for British Art, Govt Picture Collection, Br Museum, Royal Watercolour Soc, Lancaster Co Museum, Royal W England Acad, Royal Acad Diploma Collection, Mercury Asset Mgmnt, HRH Queen's Diamond Jubilee Collection from Royal Acad Exhibition Buckingham Palace 2014; retrospective exhbn RA 1995; group exhibitions: Hollis Taggart Gallery Washington DC 1993, Barneys Greenwich Connecticut USA 1993 and 1995, Women Artists of Wales (Albany Gallery) 2002; guest artist S Wales Acad of Fine and Applied Art 2002; buyer for Contemporary Art Soc Wales 1990–91; memb: Cncl of the Protection of Rural Wales, Friends of the Earth; subject of book 'The Art of Diana Armfield' by Julian Halsby 1995; MCSD 1951, memb Royal Cambrian Acad (hon ret academician), memb NEAC 1970 (hon memb 2001), RWA 1975 (hon ret), RWS 1980 (hon ret), RA 1991 (ARA 1989); *Books* Painting In Oils (1982); *Recreations* musical appreciation, gardening; *Clubs* Arts; *Style—* Miss Diana Armfield, RA; ✉ 10 High Park Road, Kew, Richmond, Surrey TW9 4BH (☎ and fax 020 8876 6633); Llwyn Hir, Parc, Bala, Gwynedd (☎ 01678 540289)

ARMITAGE, Simon Robert; CBE (2010); s of Peter Armitage, and Audrey May Armitage, of Huddersfield, W Yorks; *b* 26 May 1963; *Educ* Colne Valley HS, Portsmouth Poly (BA), Univ of Manchester (CQSW, MA); *Career* poet; probation offr Greater Manchester Probation Serv, sr lectr Manchester Met Univ, prof of poetry Univ of Sheffield 2011–, prof of poetry Univ of Oxford 2015–; ed Poetry Chatto & Windus; wrote lyrics for Feltham Sings (film) 2002; singer and lyricist with band The Scaremongers; Eric Gregory Award, Forward Poetry Prize 1992, Sunday Times Young Writer of the Year 1993, Cholmondeley Award 2014, Hay Medal for Poetry 2014; for Feltham Sings: Ivor Novello Award, BAFTA; Hon DLitt: Univ of Huddersfield 1996, Univ of Portsmouth 1996, Sheffield Hallam Univ, Open Univ, Univ of Leeds; *Poetry Collections* Zoom! (1989, Poetry Book Soc Choice), Xanadu (1992), Kid (1992), Book of Matches (1993), The Dead Sea Poems (1995), CloudCuckooland (shortlisted Whitbread Poetry Award 1997), Killing Time (1999), Selected Poems (2001), The Universal Home Doctor (2002), Travelling Songs (2002), The Odyssey: A Retelling (2006), Tyrannosaurus Rex versus the Corduroy Kid (2006), Sir Gawain and the Green Knight (trans, 2007), Seeing Stars (2010), Paper Aeroplane (2014), Pearl (2016), Still (2016); *Prose* All Points North (1998), Little Green Man (2001), The White Stuff (2004), Gig: The Life and Times of a Rock-star Fantasist (2008), Walking Home (2015), Walking Away (2015); *Recreations* as expected; *Style—* Simon Armitage, CBE; ✉ c/o David Godwin Associates, 55 Monmouth Street, London WC2H 9DG (☎ 020 7240 9992)

ARMITSTEAD, Claire Louise; da of Charles Henry Wilfrid Armitstead (d 1996), of Haywards Heath, W Sussex, and Gillian Louise, *née* Bartley (d 1987); *b* 2 December 1958; *Educ* Bedales, St Hilda's Coll Oxford (BA); *m* 17 Sept 1983, John Christopher Yandell, s of Canon Owen James Yandell; 1 s (Arthur James Armitstead b 7 Sept 1990), 1 da (Rosa Louise Armitstead b 11 June 1993); *Career* journalist; sub-ed and theatre critic: South Wales Argus Newport 1983–84 (trainee reporter The News 1980–83), Hampstead & Highgate Express 1984–89; theatre critic The Financial Times 1986–92; The Guardian: theatre critic 1992–96, arts ed 1995–99, literary ed 1999–; memb: NUJ 1980, Critics' Circle 1990, Int Assoc of Theatre Critics 1988; *Recreations* finding time to read novels and keep fit; *Style—* Ms Claire Armitstead; ✉ The Guardian, 90 York Way, London N1 9GU (☎ 020 7278 2332, fax 020 7713 4366)

ARMITT, Sir John Alexander; kt (2012), CBE (1996); *Career* chm Laing Int and Civil Engrg Divs 1986–93 (joined as grad 1966); chief exec: Union Railways 1993–97, Costain 1997–2001, Railtrack plc 2001–02, Network Rail 2002–07; chm: Berkeley Gp, Nat Express 2013; chm: Olympic Delivery Authy 2007–14, City and Guilds 2012–; memb Bd Transport for London 2012, chm Airmitt Review 2012–15, memb Airports Cmmn 2012–15; pres Inst of Civil Engrs 2015–16; FREng, FICE; *Style—* Sir John Armitt, CBE; ✉ City & Guilds, 1 Giltspur Street, London EC1A 9DD

ARMOUR, Emeritus Prof Sir James; kt (1995), CBE (1989); s of James Angus Armour (d 1948), and Margaret Brown, *née* Roy (d 1959); *b* 17 September 1929, Basra, Iraq; *Educ* Marr Coll Troon, Univ of Glasgow (BVMS, MRCVS, PhD, Golf blue); *m* 1, 1953, Irene (d 1988), da of Arthur Brunton Morris (d 1971); 2 da (Linda Margaret 17 June 1954, Fiona Marion 22 Sept 1957), 2 s (Donald George b 10 Dec 1955, Malcolm Craig 30 Sept 1961); m 2, 1992, Christine McTavish Strickland; *Career* research offr Colonial Vet Serv Nigeria 1953–60, vet researcher Cooper McDougall & Robertson 1960–63; Univ of Glasgow: research fell 1963–67, lectr in vet parasitology 1967–71, sr lectr 1971–73, reader 1973–76, prof 1976–95, vice-princ 1990–95; chm: Vet Products Ctee 1987–95, Governing Body Inst for Animal Health 1990–95, Glasgow Dental Hosp and Sch NHS Tst 1995–99; vice-pres RSE 1997–2000; chm Moredun Fndn for Animal Health and Welfare 2000–05, chm St Andrews Clinics for Children in Africa 2000–11; RCVS: memb 1952, hon fell 1995, John Henry Steel Medal; BVA: memb 1952, Wooldridge Medal, Chiron Award; Bledisloe Award RASE, Pfizer Award for research World Assoc for Vet Parasitology, Bicentenary Medal RSE; Dr (hc) Univ of Utrecht 1981, DVMS (hc) Univ of Edinburgh 1995, Hon DUniv Glasgow 2001, Hon DUniv Stirling 2005; FRSE 1990; FMedSci 1998, Hon FIBiol 2001; *Books* Veterinary Parasitology (1988, 2 edn 1995); *Recreations* golf (Br Boys Champion 1947), watching football and rugby, travel; *Clubs* Royal Troon (Capt 1990–92, hon pres 2008–11); *Style—* Emeritus Prof Sir James Armour, CBE, FRSE, FMedSci; ✉ 4B Towans Court, Prestwick KA9 2AY (☎ 01292 470869, e-mail jamesarmour4b@btinternet.com)

ARMOUR, Robert Malcolm; OBE (2007), WS; *b* 25 September 1959, Edinburgh; *Educ* Edinburgh Univ (LLB, MBA); *m* 26 June 1987, Anne; *Career* admitted slr 1983, NP 1984; ptnr Wright Johnston & Mackenzie 1986–90, co sec Scottish Nuclear 1990–95 (dir of performance devpt 1993–95); British Energy Gp plc (formerly British Energy plc): co sec 1995–, dir of corp affrs 1997–2003, gen counsel 2000–; dir Nuclear Industries Assoc, dir Assoc of Electricity Prodrs, dir Foratom, former memb Civil Nuclear Police Authy; memb Bd Scottish Cncl for Devpt and Industry, memb CBI Cncl Scotland; In House Lawyer of the Year The Lawyer Awards 2005; memb Law Soc of Scotland; *Recreations* golf; *Clubs* New (Edinburgh); *Style—* Mr Robert Armour, OBE; ✉ British Energy Group plc, GSO Business Park, East Kilbride G74 5PG (e-mail robert.armour@british-energy.com)

ARMSON, (Frederick) Simon Arden; s of Frank Gerald Arden Armson (d 1982), and Margaret Fenella, *née* Newton (d 2002); *b* 11 September 1948, Yoxall, Staffs; *Educ* Denstone Coll, Univ of London (MSc), Dip Clinical Psychotherapy, Dip NLP; *m* 8 Feb 1975, Marion Albinia, da of David Hamilton-Russell (d 1988), and Pauline, *née* Slade (d 2009); 3 c (Meriel Albinia b 1979, Patrick David Arden b 1982, Katharine Geraldine b 1984); *Career* early trg in health serv mgmnt, various managerial and admin posts NHS 1970–84; pt/t lectr in NHS industrial rels Oxford Poly 1977–82; The Samaritans: asst gen sec 1984–89, gen sec 1989–90, chief exec 1990–2004; dir Samaritan Enterprises Ltd 1996–2004; clinical psychotherapist 2004–; assoc hosp mangr Apple Hill Independent Hosp 2016–; chm: Telephone Helpline Gp 1992–96, BBC Radio Helpline Advsy Cncl 1995–98, CancerBacup Service Devpt Advsy Ctee 1998–2001; memb: Exec Ctee ACENVO 1992–94, Steering Ctee for Structure Review of Br Red Cross Soc 1995–96, Suicide Prevention Sub-Gp Dept of Health Wider Health Working Gp 1995–97, RCN Men's Health Forum 1995–97, Steering Gp BT Forum for Better Communications Res Project into effective communication in young people 1995–98, Advsy Ctee Inst for Volunteer Research 1996–2001, Advsy Cncl Helplines Assoc 2010; Mental Health Act cmmr 2002–12, Mental Health Act mangr W London Mental Health NHS Tst 2012–, memb Bd Mental Health Act Cmmn 2004–09 (chm 2008–09), specialist lay memb First Tier Tbnl (Mental Health) 2006–; memb Market Reseach Soc Disciplinary Authy 2009–, memb Ind Advsy Panel Ministerial Bd on Deaths in Custody 2009–14; tstee: Yoxall Town Lands Charities 1974–, Yoxall United Charities 1982–, ChildLine 1999–2006, Broadcasting Support Servs 2003–09, Mental Health Media 2004–09, Nat Nightline 2005–06 (hon assoc 2006), Maytree Respite Centre 2005–14 (chm 2009–14, patron 2015–), Partnership for Children 2009– (vice-chm 2012–15); hon memb Telephone Helplines Assoc 1999; chm Panel of Judges: Guardian Jerwood Award 1995–99, Guardian Charity Award 2000–04; memb: Ringel Award Ctee 2001–03, Int Assoc for Suicide Prevention (IASP) 2001–03 (chair Nat Dels, memb Exec Ctee, UK nat rep 1996–2003), Suicide Prevention Advsy Gp 2001–04, Ind Ctee for the Supervision of Standards of Telephone Info Servs (ICSTIS) 2001–07, Nat Inst for Clinical Excellence (NICE) Self-Harm Guidelines Devpt Gp 2003–04; pres Mid-Thames branch CMI 2006–; memb UK Cncl for Psychotherapists (UKCP) 2003; FRSA 1993, CCMI (CIMgt 1995); *Publications* International Handbook of Suicide and Attempted Suicide (contrib, 2000), Every Family in the Land (contrib, 2004), Prevention and Treatment of Suicidal Behaviour (contrib, 2005); *Recreations* sailing, walking, music, cycling (cross country), mental health and emotional wellbeing, spending time with the family including two granddaughters and a grandson; *Clubs* Reform; *Style—* Simon Armson, Esq; ✉ Broad Oak, Old Honey Lane, Hurley, Maidenhead, Berkshire SL6 5LW (☎ 01628 824322, e-mail armson@btinternet.com); Bridge Psychotherapy and Counselling Service, website www.bridgepsych.com; Mind Garden Therapy, website www.reading-counselling.co.uk; Terapia Consultancy, website www.terapiaconsultancy.co.uk

ARMSTRONG, Alexander; *b* 2 March 1970, Rothbury, Northumberland; *Educ* Durham Sch, Trinity Coll Cambridge; *Career* comedian, actor and TV presenter; Edinburgh Fringe (with Ben Miller, *qv*) 1994 and 1996 (nominated Perrier Comedy Award); judge Costa Book Award 2008; *Television* Armstrong and Miller 1997–2001, Life Begins (ITV 1), Beast, The Trial of Tony Blair, Maggie Mae, The Armstrong and Miller Show 2007– (Best Comedy Prog BAFTA Television Award 2010), Mutual Friends (BBC) 2008, Reggie Perin (BBC) 2010, Hunderby (Sky) 2012, Danger Mouse (CBBC) 2015, Land of the Midnight Sun (ITV) 2015; presenter: Best of the Worst (Channel 4) 2006, Don't Call Me Stupid (ITV 1), Pointless (BBC); frequent guest host Have I Got News For You (BBC); *Radio* Weak at the Top (BBC Radio 4), Armstrong and Miller (BBC Radio 4) 1998, Alexander Armstrong (Classic FM); *Books* Land of the Midnight Sun (2015); *Style—* Mr Alexander Armstrong; ✉ c/o Public Eye Communications Ltd, Suite 313 The Plaza, 535 Kings Road, London SW10 0SZ

ARMSTRONG, Very Rev Christopher; s of John Armstrong, and Susan Elizabeth Armstrong; *b* 18 December 1947; *Educ* Dunstable GS, Bede Coll Durham (CertEd), Kelham Theol Coll, Univ of Nottingham (BTh); *m* 3 Jan 1976, Geraldine; 1 da (Sarah b 2 June 1978), 2 s (Jonathan b 1 Feb 1980, Simon b 23 July 1985); *Career* teacher Brewers Hill Sch Dunstable 1969–72; asst curate All Saints Maidstone 1975–79, chaplain St Hild and St Bede Coll Durham 1979–85, domestic chaplain to Archbishop of York and Diocesan Dir of Ordinands 1985–91, incumbent Scarborough St Martin Dio of York 1991–2001, dean of Blackburn 2001–; selector: ACCM, Advsy Bd of Miny (ABM); memb General Synod 2003–05, memb House of Bishops Inspectorate 2003–07; various chaplaincies to police, theatre and univ depts 1991–2001; chm Scarborough Christian Aid Ctee 1996–98, chm of govrs St Martin's Aided Deanery Jr Sch 1991–99, memb N Yorks LEA 1997–99, govr The Friends of the Anglican Centre Rome 1996–2010, chm Lancs Fairness Cmmn 2014–15; *Recreations* sport, mountaineering, theatre, music, gardening, travel; *Style—* The Very Rev The Dean of Blackburn; ✉ The Deanery, Preston New Road, Blackburn, Lancashire BB2 6PS (e-mail armstrong@deanery2001.fsnet.co.uk); Cathedral Office, Cathedral Close, Blackburn, Lancashire BB1 5AA (☎ 01254 503090, fax 01254 689666, e-mail dean@blackburncathedral.co.uk, website www.blackburncathedral.com)

ARMSTRONG, Christopher Paul (Kit); s of Robert Armstrong, of Preston, Lancs, and Pauline, *née* Moreland; *b* 19 October 1955; *Educ* Univ of Edinburgh (MB ChB, MD); *Children* 1 s (James Robert b 25 July 1986), 1 da (Charlotte Beth b 25 Dec 1988); *Career* trg in surgery various hosps (Edinburgh, Cape Town, Manchester, Bristol), conslt surgn Frenchay Hosp Bristol 1990–; specialist in laparoscopic surgery for gallstones, hiatus hernia and hernia; author of numerous pubns on the subject of surgery; FRCSEd 1982, FRCS 1984; *Style—* Kit Armstrong, Esq; ✉ Department of Surgery, Frenchay Hospital, Beckspool Road, Frenchay, Bristol BS16 1JE; Bupa Hospital, Bristol BS6 6UT

ARMSTRONG, Craig; OBE (2010); s of John Armstrong, and Barbara, *née* MacKenzie; *b* 29 April 1959; *Educ* Royal Acad of Music London (Charles Lucas Prize, Harvey Lohr Scholarship); *Career* composer and arranger; resident student composer London Contemporary Dance Theatre 1980, music and dance specialist Strathclyde Regnl Cncl 1982; cmmns incl: Arts Cncl 1985, Third Eye Centre 1988, Tron Theatre Co Glasgow 1988 and 1993, Scottish Chamber Orch 1989, RSC 1994, BT Ensemble 1999, Hebrides Ensemble 2000, Royal Scottish Nat Opera 2001; film scores incl: Romeo and Juliet 1996 (Anthony Asquith BAFTA Award 1996, Ivor Novello Award 1996), Orphans 1997, Plunkett & Macleane 1999, Best Laid Plans 1999, One Day in September 1999, The Bone Collector 1999 (ASCAP Award 1999), Moulin Rouge 2001 (World Soundtrack Award 2001, American Film Inst Award 2001, Australian IF Award 2001, Golden Globe 2002), Kiss Of The Dragon 2001 (Discovery of the Year Award 2001), The Quiet American 2002 (Ivor Novello Award 2002), The Magdalene Sisters 2003; solo albums: The Space Between Us 1998, As If To Nothing 2002, Piano Works 2004, Film Works 2005, Memory Takes My Hand 2008; GLAA Young Jazz Musician of the Year Award 1980; FTCL, FRAM; *Style—* Craig Armstrong, Esq, OBE; ✉ armstrongcraig@mac.com

ARMSTRONG, Prof David Millar; s of James Armstrong (d 1990), and Jean Alexandra, *née* Millar (d 1998); *b* 25 May 1941; *Educ* Workington GS, Univ of Oxford (BA, BSc), Australian Nat Univ (PhD); *m* 12 Aug 1964, Lucinda Russell, da of George Graham Kennedy (d 1955); 1 da (Katherine Anne b 1965), 1 s (James Graham b 1966); *Career* Univ of Bristol: lectr 1968–78, reader 1978–84, prof of physiology 1984–2004, head of dept 1990–95 and 2003–04, emeritus prof 2004–; memb: Neurosciences and Mental Health Bd MRC 1987–91, Trg Awards Ctee MRC 1989–93; memb: Marine Biological Assoc 1965, Physiological Soc 1968; *Recreations* walking, wildlife photography, reading, social and medical historical research; *Style—* Prof David Armstrong; ✉ School of Physiology and Pharmacology, School of Medical Sciences, University of Bristol, University Walk, Bristol BS8 1TD (☎ 0117 928 9101, fax 0117 928 8923, e-mail d.m.armstrong@bristol.ac.uk)

ARMSTRONG, Fiona Kathryn (Lady MacGregor of MacGregor); da of Robert Armstrong, of Cumbria, and Pauline, *née* Moreland; *b* 28 November 1956; *Educ* St Thomas Moore Sch Preston, Tuson Coll Preston, UCL; *m* 1, Sept 1987, Rodney Potts; m 2, 14 May 2005, Sir Malcolm MacGregor of MacGregor, Bt, *qv*; *Career* reporter Radio 210 Reading 1980–82, journalist BBC TV Manchester 1982–85, reporter Border TV Cumbria 1985–87, newscaster ITN 1987–92, presenter GMTV 1992–93, freelance 1993– (incl antiques, lifestyle, fishing and political progs for ITV and Sky), presenter Lookaround (ITV Border) 1993–2008, newscaster BBC News 2010–14, presenter/reporter Border Life (ITV); columnist: Scottish Field, Scotbanner and Courier (US); pres: Bookmark, Blairgowrie Book Festival; chm Clan Armstrong Tst, architect Border Reiver Trail; tstee: Second Chance Charity; patron Angling for Youth Devpt; memb: Salmon and Trout Assoc, Tyburn Angling Soc; memb Bd Univ of Central Lancs; HM Lord Lt of Dumfries; *Books* 'F' is for Flyfishing (1993), The Commuter's Cookbook (1995), Let's Start Flyfishing (1999), Big Food for Wee Macs (2004); *Recreations* fishing, cooking, clan history; *Clubs* New; *Style—* Ms Fiona Armstrong; ✉ e-mail fiona@borderheritage.co.uk; c/o Knight Ayton Management, 35 Great James Street, London WC1N 3HB (☎ 020 7831 4400, fax 020 7836 8333, e-mail info@knightayton.co.uk)

ARMSTRONG, Prof Isobel Mair; da of Richard Aneurin Jones (d 1953), and Marjorie, *née* Jackson (d 2004); *b* 25 March 1937, London; *Educ* Friends Sch Saffron Walden Essex, Univ of Leicester (BA, PhD); *m* 9 Aug 1961, (John) Michael Armstrong, s of Rev Charles Armstrong (d 1947); 2 s (Thomas b 5 Oct 1968, Stephen b 24 April 1975), 1 da (Ursula b 16 Aug 1971); *Career* post doctoral fell in English Westfield Coll London 1962–63, asst lectr then lectr in English UCL 1963–70, lectr then sr lectr in English Univ of Leicester 1970–79; prof of English: Univ of Southampton 1979–89, Birkbeck Coll London 1989–2002 (emeritus prof 2002–); Breadloaf Sch of English: visiting prof MA Prog Middlebury Coll Vermont, Robert Frost chair Sch of English 2002; visiting prof: Dept of English Princeton Univ, English Dept Harvard Univ, Hinkley prof English Dept Johns Hopkins Univ; sr research fell Inst of English Studies Univ of London 2003; gen ed British Council Writers and their Work (second series) 1990–2006; fndr ctee memb Ctee for Univ English, co-ed Women – A Cultural Review 1988, fndr ctee memb Br Assoc of Victorian Studies 2001; Br Acad Warton Lecture on English Poetry 2011; pres Br Assoc for Victorian Studies 2003–06 (memb 2000–); foreign hon memb American Acad of Arts and Sciences 2014; FBA 2003; *Books* critical books incl: Every Man Will Shout (with R Mansfield, 1964), The Major Victorian Poets – Reconsiderations (1969), Victorian Scrutinies (1972), A Sudden Line (1976), Language as Living Form in Nineteenth Century Poetry (1982), Jane Austen – Mansfield Park (1988), Victorian Poetry: Poetry, Poetics and Politics (1993), Jane Austen – Sense and Sensibility (1994), Nineteenth Century Women Poets: An Oxford Anthology (co-ed, 1996), The Radical Aesthetic (2000), Victorian Glassworlds: Glass Culture and the Imagination 1930–1980 (2008, John Russell Lowell Prize Modern Language Assoc 2009); contrib to various other books incl: Victorian Poetry (1968), Critical Essays on George Eliot (1970), Augustan Worlds (1978), The Oxford Literary Review (1981), Women Reading Women's Writing (1987), Dickens and Other Victorians (1988), Textuality and Sexuality (1993), Women's Poetry of the Enlightenment and Women's Poetry Late Romantic to Late Victorian (with Virginia Blain, 1999), Transactions & Encounters (2002), Multimedia Histories (2006), Meter Matters (2011), The Cambridge History of Victorian Literature (2012), The Cambridge Companion to the Pre-Raphaelites (2012), The Oxford Handbook of Victorian Poetry (2013), A Companion to George Eliot (2013), Anna Letitia Barbauld: New Perspectives (2014); poetry incl: Desert Collages (2007), Infinite Difference Other Poetries by UK Women Poets (2010), Harriet Martineau: Authorship, Society and Empire (2010); contrib reviews to various jls incl: Times Literary Supplements 1986–, Victorian Studies, Jl of Victorian Culture, Textual Practice; contrib and team memb NCSE online jls edn 2008; *Recreations* travel, drawing, writing; *Style—* Prof Isobel Armstrong, FBA; ✉ 15 Furzedown Road, Highfield, Southampton SO17 1PN; School of English and Humanities, Birkbeck College, Malet Street, London WC1E 7HX (☎ 020 7631 6000, fax 020 7631 6072, e-mail isobel.armstrong@logic-net.co.uk)

ARMSTRONG, Karen Andersen; OBE (2015); da of John Oliver Seymour Armstrong (d 1975), and Eileen Hastings, *née* McHale; *b* 14 November 1944; *Educ* Convent of the Holy Child Jesus Edgbaston Birmingham, St Anne's Coll Oxford (MA, MLitt, Violet Vaughan Morgan prize); *Career* writer and broadcaster; Soc of the Holy Child Jesus (RC teaching order of nuns) 1962–69, tutorial research fell Bedford Coll London 1973–76, head of English James Allen's Girls' Sch Dulwich 1976–82, freelance writer and broadcaster 1982–; *Awards* Calamus Fndn Annual Award 1991, Muslim Public Affrs Cncl Media Award 1999, Al-Azhar Univ Cairo Prize for Services to Islam 2007, Franklin D Roosevelt Four Freedoms Medal 2008, TED (Technology, Entertainment, Design) Prize 2008, Dr Leopold Lucas Prize Tubingen Univ 2009, Nayef Al-Rodhan Prize for Improving Transcultural Understanding British Acad 2013, ISESCO Prize for Educators 2015; *Television* work incl: The First Christian (six part documentary on St Paul) 1984, Varieties of Religious Experience (interview series) 1984, Tongues of Fire (interview series) 1985; *Books* Through the Narrow Gate (1981), Beginning the World (1983), The First Christian (1983), Tongues of Fire (1985), The Gospel According to Woman (1986), Holy War – The Crusades and their Impact on Today's World (1988), Muhammed – A Western Attempt to Understand Islam (1991), A History of God (1993), The End of Silence – Women and Priesthood (1993), A History of Jerusalem: One City, Three Faiths (1996), In the Beginning – A New Interpretation of Genesis (1996), The Battle for God – Fundamentalism in Judaism, Christianity and Islam (2000), Islam: A Short History (2000), Buddha (2001), The Spiral Staircase: My Climb Out of Darkness (2004), A Short History of Myth (2005), The Great Transformation: The Beginning of Our Religious Traditions (2006); *Recreations* music, theatre, fiction, having dinner with friends; *Style—* Ms Karen Armstrong, OBE

ARMSTRONG, Prof Peter; s of Alexander Armstrong, of London, and Ada, *née* Lapidas (d 1963); *b* 31 August 1940; *Educ* Marylebone GS, Middx Hosp Med Sch (MB BS); *m* Carole Jennifer Armstrong; 2 s (Damon Oliver b 17 Oct 1971 d 1972, Jethro Karl b 22 Feb 1974), 1 da (Natasha Janine b 23 Nov 1972),; *Career* house physician Middx Hosp 1963, house surgn Kettering General Hosp 1964; sr registrar in radiology: Middx Hosp 1965–68 (registrar 1964–65), Guy's Hosp 1968–70; conslt in radiology KCH 1970–77, prof and vice-chm of radiology Univ of Virginia Hosp 1981–89 (assoc prof 1977–81), prof of radiology and Mercer chair of diagnostic radiology Bart's 1989–2005; RCR: George Simon lectr 1993, warden clinical radiology 1994–98, pres 1998–2001; ed Clinical Radiology 1990–94; pres Euro Soc of Thoracic Imaging 1995–96; Robley Dunglison Prize Univ of Virginia Med Sch 1983 and 1984; memb: Br Inst of Radiology 1966, RSM 1984; FRCR 1968, FMedSci 1999, FRCP 2000; *Books* Diagnostic Imaging, Imaging of Diseases of the Chest, Diagnostic Radiology in Surgical Practice, Concise Textbook of Radiology; *Recreations* reading, theatre, art; *Clubs* Shadows Radiology; *Style—* Prof Peter Armstrong; ✉ 8 Westrow, Westleigh Avenue, London SW15 6RH (☎ 020 8789 2445, e-mail peterarmstrong@doctors.org.uk)

ARMSTRONG, His Hon Judge Peter John Bowden; s of William David Armstrong, MBE (d 1966), of Durham, and Kathleen Mary, *née* Wood (d 1997); *b* 19 December 1951; *Educ* Durham Johnston Grammar Tech Sch, Trinity Coll Cambridge (MA); *m* 1976, Joanna, da of late Brian Charles Arthur Cox; 2 da (Charlotte Kate b 8 Feb 1979, Helen Joanna b 1 Oct 1980); *Career* called to the Bar Middle Temple 1974; barr NE Circuit 1976–2000, head Fountain Chambers Middlesbrough 1992–2000, recorder 1994–2000 (asst recorder 1990–94), circuit judge (NE Circuit) 2000–; *Recreations* golf, cricket, rugby, music; *Clubs* Eaglescliffe Golf, Durham CCC; *Style—* His Hon Judge Armstrong; ✉ Teesside Combined Court Centre, Russell Street, Middlesbrough TS1 2AE (☎ 01642 340000, fax 01642 340002)

ARMSTRONG OF HILL TOP, Baroness (Life Peer UK 2010), of Crook in the County of Durham; Rt Hon Hilary Jane Armstrong; da of Rt Hon Ernest Armstrong (d 1996), and Hannah, *née* Lamb; *b* 30 November 1945; *Educ* Monkwearmouth Comp Sch Sunderland, West Ham Coll of Technol (BSc), Univ of Birmingham (Dip Social Work); *m* 17 Oct 1992, Paul Corrigan; *Career* VSO teacher Murray Girls' HS Kenya 1967–69, social worker Newcastle City Social Servs Dept 1970–73, community worker Southwick Neighbourhood Action Project Sunderland 1973–75, lectr in community and youth work Sunderland Poly 1975–86, sec/researcher to father Ernest Armstrong MP 1986–87, MP (Lab) Durham NW 1987–2010; oppn spokesman on educn 1988–93, PPS to John Smith, Leader of the Oppn 1992–94, Treasy Team 1994–95, shadow min for local govt 1995–97; min of state (local govt and housing 1997–99, local govt and English regions 1999–2001) DETR 1997–2001, Parly sec to the Treasy (Govt chief whip) 2001–06, min for the Cabinet Office and for social exclusion and Chllr of the Duchy of Lancaster 2006–07; memb Educn Select Ctee 1988, chm PLP Educn Ctee; memb Durham CC 1985–87; tstee VSO UK 2008–, chair VSO Fedn Cncl 2008–, chair Tony Blair Sports Fndn 2008–, chair Changing Lives 2010–, non-exec dir Durham and Darlington Fndn Tst 2010–14, tstee Lloyd's Bank Fndn; *Recreations* theatre, reading; *Style—* The Baroness Armstrong of Hill Top; ✉ House of Lords, London SW1A 0PW

ARMSTRONG OF ILMINSTER, Baron (Life Peer UK 1988), of Ashill in the County of Somerset; Sir Robert Temple Armstrong; GCB (1983, KCB 1978, CB 1974), CVO (1975); s of Sir Thomas (Henry Wait) Armstrong (d 1994), and Hester Muriel, *née* Draper (d 1982); *b* 30 March 1927; *Educ* Eton, ChCh Oxford; *m* 1953 (m dis 1985), Serena Mary Benedicta (d 1994), er da of Sir Roger James Ferguson Chance, 3 Bt, MC; 2 da (Hon Jane

Orlanda (Hon Mrs Joseph Whitlock Blundell) b 1954, Hon Teresa Brigid (Hon Mrs Simon Littlewood) b 1957); m 2, 1985, (Mary) Patricia, o da of Charles Cyril Carlow (d 1957); 1 step-da (Lt Polly Ann Charlotte McCowen RN b 1975); *Career* asst sec: Cabinet Office 1964–66, Treasury 1967–68; under sec Treasury 1968–70, princ private sec to PM 1970–75, dep under sec Home Office 1975–77, perm under sec 1977–79, sec of the Cabinet 1979–87, head Home Civil Service 1981–87; chm: Biotechnology Investments Ltd 1989–2000, Bristol and West Building Society 1993–97 (non-exec dir 1988–97), Forensic Investigative Associates (London) 1997–2003; non-exec dir: BAT Industries plc 1988–97, NM Rothschild and Sons Ltd 1988–97 (conslt 1997–2000), Rio Tinto plc (formerly RTZ Corporation plc) 1988–97 (non-exec dir CRA Ltd Dec 1995–97), Shell Transport and Trading plc 1988–97, Inchcape plc 1988–95, Lucas Industries plc 1989–92, Carlton Television Ltd 1991–95, IAMGOLD Corp Ltd (Canada) 1995–2003, Bank of Ireland 1997–2001, 3i Bioscience Investment Tst plc 2000–02; memb Advsy Panel E-Clear (UK) plc 2007–09; chm: Bd of Tstees V&A 1988–98, Hestercombe Gardens Tst Ltd 1996–2005, Bd of Govrs RNCM 2000–05, Leeds Castle Fndn 2001–07 (tstee 1987–2007), Sir Edward Heath Charitable Fndn 2005–13; tstee RVW Tst 1956–, memb Bd of Dirs Royal Opera House 1988–93 (sec 1968–87), tstee Derek Hill Fndn 2000–, memb Wells Cathedral Sch Fndn 2007–12; chllr Univ of Hull 1994–2006; Hon Liveryman Salters' Co 1983; fell Eton Coll 1979–94; hon student ChCh Oxford 1985, Rhodes tstee 1975–97, Hon FRAM 1985; hon bencher Inner Temple 1986; Hon LLD Univ of Hull 1994; *Recreations* music; *Clubs* Brooks's; *Style*— The Rt Hon the Lord Armstrong of Ilminster, GCB, CVO; ✉ House of Lords, London SW1A 0PW

ARMSTRONG-DAMPIER, Philip Donald; s of Donald Armstrong-Dampier, and Audrey Armstrong-Dampier; *b* St Asaph, Denbighshire; *m* Lynn, *née* Hoptrough; 2 s (Guy Yohji, Max Oliver Xan); *Career* TV prodr; early career with 20th Century Fox and CBS News, prodr and dir TVS 1988–93, freelance prodr and dir then md Outpost Films, head of factual, factual entertainment and corporate ITN Prodns 2002–11 (dep head and exec prodr 1999–2002), currently co-fndr and md 1212 Prodns; exec prodr of numerous documentaries and series for ITV, BBC TV, Channel 4, Five, Discovery Channel, Nat Geographic, Animal Planet, AETN, Travel Channel and AAN; exhbns: Oriel Theatr Clwyd, New Contemporaries ICA 1981, White Elephant Gallery Leeds; FRGS; *Recreations* swimming, travelling; *Clubs* Lansdowne; *Style*— Philip Armstrong-Dampier, Esq; ✉ e-mail philip@1212productions.co.uk

ARMSTRONG-JONES, Peregrine Thomas Owen Llewelyn; s of Ronald Owen Lloyd Armstrong-Jones, MBE, QC, DL (d 1966), and Jenifer, *née* Unite; yr half-bro of The Earl of Snowdon, GCVO, *qv*; *b* 15 November 1960, London; *Educ* Eton, Royal Agricultural Univ (Dip Ag); *m* 27 Oct 1987, Caroline Therese, *née* Bloy; 1 da (India Sophie b 22 Feb 1997), 1 s (Robert Owen Llewelyn b 13 Jan 2000); *Career* md Atlas Sound and Lighting Design 1981–84, fndr Bentley's Entertainments Ltd 1984– (events organiser to David and Victoria Beckham, Sir Elton John, Elizabeth Hurley, HRH The Princess Royal and Prince Albert II of Monaco); owner: Plas Dinas Estate North Wales, Plas Dinas Hotel; ambass: Holland and Holland, Backes and Strauss; *Style*— Peregrine Armstrong-Jones, Esq; ✉ Bentley's Entertainments Limited, 7 Square Rigger Row, Plantation Wharf, York Road, London SW11 3TZ; media enquiries: Fletcher Associates, Creative and Media Agency, 25 Parkway, London N20 0XN (✆ 020 8361 8061)

ARNAL, Mary Angela; da of William Francis Stapleton (d 1998), and Susan, *née* White (d 1999); *b* 21 April 1961, Newry, Co Down; *Educ* Univ of Manchester (BA), Univ of Edinburgh (MSc, PGCE); *m* 8 Sept 1988, Antonio Arnal, FRSA; 2 s (Martin Antonio b 27 March 1991, David Manuel b 2 Jan 1999); *Career* sr mistress St John's Sch 2004–13, headmistress St Teresa's Prep Sch Surrey until 2013, princ Sherborne Int Sch 2013–15, headmistress St Mary's Sch Shaftesbury UK 2016–; advsr Hillcrest HMC Sch Kenya; dir Piedmont Communication Consultancy Ireland, non-exec dir Piedmont Educn Madrid, dir Piedmont Global Education; govr: St John's Sch Leatherhead 2013–16, Hillcrest Sch Kenya 2013–16, Sherborne Prep Sch 2016–, St Mary's Hampstead 2016–; memb: IAPS ISA 2010, COBIS, ISA, 2010, Br Sociological Assoc, Br Cncl 2010, European Assoc for Language Testing and Assessment 2013; FRSA 2004; *Books* Alfonsus McCarthy's Journey to Salvation (novel), The Shore Road (1994), Bicycle Seeds (poetry anthology, ed 2015); *Recreations* music, reading, sailing, travel, walking; *Clubs* Univ Women's; *Style*— Mrs Mary Arnal; ✉ Bapthorpe House, St Mary's School, Shaftesbury, Dorset SP7 9LP (✆ 01747 854005, e-mail marnal@stmary.eu, website www.stmarys.eu)

ARNOLD, Bruce; OBE (2003); *b* 1936; *Educ* Kingham Hill Sch, TCD (MA), UCD (DLitt); *m*; 2 c; *Career* journalist 1960s: The Irish Times, The Irish Press, The Sunday Independent, Hibernia National Review; corr The Guardian 1962–68; Irish Independent: political commentator and parly corr 1972–86, London ed 1986–87, literary ed 1987–2000, chief critic 2000–14; hon fell Trinity Coll Dublin 2001, FRSL 1994; *Novels* A Singer at the Wedding, The Song of the Nightingale, The Muted Swan, Running to Paradise; *Non-Fiction* A Concise History of Irish Art, Orpen: Mirror to an Age, What Kind of Country, Margaret Thatcher: A Study in Power, An Art Atlas of Britain and Ireland (1991), William Orpen (1991), The Scandal of Ulysses (1991, revised edn 2004), Mainie Jellett and the Modern Movement in Ireland (1991), Haughey: His Life and Unlucky Deeds (1993), Jack Yeats (1998), Swift: An Illustrated Life (1999), Jack Lynch: Hero in Crisis (2001), The Spire and Other Essays in Irish Culture (2003), He That Is Down Need Fear No Fall (2008), The Fight for Democracy (2009), The Irish Gulag: How the State Betrayed Its Innocent Children (2009), Derek Hill (2010), The End of the Party (w Jason O'Toole, 2011); *Clubs* Athenaeum; *Style*— Bruce Arnold, Esq, OBE, FRSL; ✉ c/o Jonathan Williams Literary Agency, Rosney Mews, Upper Glengeary Road, Co Dublin, Ireland (✆ 00 353 1 280 3482)

ARNOLD, David; *b* 23 January 1962, Luton, Beds; *Career* film and television composer; television scores incl: Randall and Hopkirk (Deceased) 2000, Little Britain 2003–06, Little Britain USA 2008, Crooked House 2008, Free Agents 2009, Sherlock 2010, Come Fly With Me, Big School; film scores incl: Stargate 1994, Independence Day 1996 (Best Instrumental Composition Written for a Motion Picture or for Television Grammy Award), A Life Less Ordinary 1997, Godzilla 1998, six James Bond films (Tomorrow Never Dies 1997, The World Is Not Enough 1999, Die Another Day 2002, Casino Royale 2006, Quantum of Solace 2008, Skyfall 2012), Shaft 2000, Zoolander 2001, Changing Lanes 2002, 2 Fast 2 Furious 2003, The Stepford Wives 2004, Four Brothers 2005, Amazing Grace 2006, Hot Fuzz 2007, How to Lose Friends & Alienate People 2008, Made In Dagenham 2010, Morning Glory 2010, The Chronicles of Narnia: The Voyage of the Dawn Treader 2010, Paul 2011; music dir and writer Made In Dagenham The Musical; co-writer: The World Is Not Enough (Garbage), You Know My Name (Chris Cornell), Surrender (kd lang); collaborations with: Cast, The Cardigans, Kaiser Chiefs, Massive Attack, Pulp, Natasha Bedingfield, Melanie C, Björk, Chris Cornell, Shirley Manson, Mark Morriss; album prodr The Performance (Dame Shirley Bassey, DBE, *qv*); musical dir London Olympics 2012, music dir London 2012 Olympic and Paralympic closing ceremonies; ambass CARE Int; *Recreations* making Frankensteins; *Style*— David Arnold, Esq; ✉ Air Studios, Lyndhurst Road, London NW3 5NG

ARNOLD, Prof David John; s of Mansel John Arnold (d 1996), and May, *née* Dominey (d 1995); *b* 1 October 1946, London; *Educ* Univ of Exeter (BA), Univ of Sussex (DPhil); *m* 1988, Juliet, *née* Miller; *Career* former prof of the history of S Asia SOAS Univ of London, prof of Asian and global history Univ of Warwick 2006–; FBA 2004; *Books* The Problem of Nature: Environment, Culture and European Expansion (1996), Science, Technology and Medicine in Colonial India (2000), Gandhi (2001), The Age of Discovery 1400–1600 (2 edn, 2002), The Tropics and the Traveling Gaze: India, Landscape and Science 1800–1856 (2006); *Style*— Prof David J Arnold

ARNOLD, David Philip James; s of Philip Arthur Arnold (d 1988), and Christine May, *née* Rowe (d 2008); *b* 13 August 1955; *Educ* Merchant Taylors', Univ of Exeter; *m* 19 Aug 1978, Carol Alice, da of Arthur George Edward Williams (d 1973); 2 da (Kirsten b 7 Feb 1986, Lucy b 4 May 1993), 1 s (James b 7 July 1995); *Career* CA; ptnr Ernst & Young LLP 1988–2016; Freeman City of London 1976, Liveryman Worshipful Co of Fishmongers 1982; FCA 1979; *Style*— David Arnold, Esq; ✉ e-mail dpjarnold@gmail.com

ARNOLD, Jennette; AM; *Career* nurse 1973–81, health visitor 1981–86, pre-pregnancy project co-ordinator W Midlands Regnl HA 1986–87; RCN: industrial rels offr 1987–89, special advsr (on equalities) to Gen Sec 1989–91, sr offr NE Thames region 1991–94, sr advsr 1994–97; assoc Beacon Organisational Devpt and Trg Servs 1997–, dir JSA Consultancy 1997–; memb London Assembly GLA (Lab) London 2000– (chair 2008–); London Assembly: memb Mayor's Advsy Cabinet, memb Health and Public Service Ctee, memb Econ and Social Devpt Ctee, memb EU Ctee of the Regions; chair London Health Cmmn (LHC) 2004–, vice-chm London Cultural Consortium 2004; memb: Metropolitan Police Authy, Police Advsy Bd; memb Lab Pty Nat Policy Forum, memb Bd Lab Women's Network; memb London Regnl Cncl Arts Cncl, tstee Sadler's Wells Theatre Fndn; vice-chair Stephen Lawrence Charitable Tst, govr Coram Family Childcare Charity; *Style*— Mrs Jennette Arnold, AM; ✉ London Assembly, City Hall, Queens Walk, Southwark, London SE1 2AA (✆ 020 7983 4349, fax 020 7983 5874, e-mail jennette.arnold@london.gov.uk)

ARNOLD, Prof John André; s of Capt André Eugene Arnold (d 1974), and May, *née* Vickers (d 1977); *b* 30 April 1944, Preston, Lancs; *Educ* Haberdashers' Aske's, LSE (MSc); *Family* 2 da (Kate Lynne b 1976, Mandy Louise b 1978); m, 29 March 1997, Sylvia, *née* Bailey; *Career* teaching fell Mgmnt Studies LSE 1967–69, lectr in accounting Univ of Kent 1969–71; Univ of Manchester: lectr in accounting 1971–75, sr lectr 1975–77, prof of accounting 1977–86, KPMG Peat Marwick prof of accounting 1986–94, dean Faculty of Econ and Social Studies 1987–89, pro-vice-chllr 1990–94, dir Manchester Business Sch and KPMG prof of accounting and fin mgmnt 1994–2006; visiting prof Univ of Washington 1981–82; dir of research ICAEW 1987–94; non-exec dir PZ Cussons plc 2007–; pres Manchester Soc of CAs 1991–92 (vice-pres 1989–90, dep pres 1990–91), chm Pro Manchester 2007–08; Hon MA (Econ) Univ of Manchester; FCA 1967; *Books* Pricing and Output Decisions (1973), Topics in Management Accounting (1980), Accounting for Management Decisions (1983, 3 edn 1996), Management Accounting Research and Practice (1983), Financial Accounting (1985, 2 edn 1994), Management Accounting: British Case Studies (1987), Management Accounting: Expanding the Horizons (1987), Financial Reporting: The Way Forward (1990), The Future Shape of Financial Reports (1991); *Recreations* tennis, golf; *Clubs* Marple Golf; *Style*— Prof John Arnold; ✉ 3 Green Meadows, Marple, Cheshire SK6 6QF (✆ 0161 449 9432, e-mail john.arnold@manchester.ac.uk)

ARNOLD, Rt Rev John Stanley Kenneth; *see:* Salford, Bishop of

ARNOLD, Luqman; s of Claude Ian Morris Arnold (d 2003), and Muftiah, *née* Dutt (d 2011); *b* 16 April 1950, Calcutta; *Educ* Oundle, Univ of London (BSc (Econs)); *m* 14 April 1988, Chumsri Sawangpanit; 1 s (Jocelyn Sivakorn b 31 March 1994); *Career* First National Bank in Dallas 1972–76, Manufacturers Hanover Corporation 1976–82, head of investment banking origination Credit Suisse First Boston 1982–92, research sabbatical 1992–93, memb Exec Ctee and Bd Banque Paribas 1993–96, chm Gp Exec Bd and pres UBS AG 1996–2001, chief exec Abbey National plc 2002–04, sr advsr to chm Grupo Santander 2004–06, chm Olivant and Cartesius SA, co-fndr Cartesius Advsy Network (CAN); chm Design Museum 2005–; *Recreations* horse riding, tennis, skiing, photography; *Clubs* Royal Bangkok Sports, Tanglin; *Style*— Luqman Arnold, Esq; ✉ Cartesius Advisory Network (Thailand) Ltd, Unit 1605, 16th Floor, Park Ventures Ecoplex, 57 Wireless Road, Lumpini, Patumwan, Bangkok, 10330 Thailand (✆ 00 66 2108 2341)

ARNOLD, Malcolm; OBE (2012); s of Colin William Arnold (d 1988), and Jane, *née* Powell (d 2012); *b* 4 April 1940; *Educ* Verdin GS Winsford Cheshire, Loughborough Univ (BSc); *m* Madelyn, *née* Morrissey; 1 s (Andrew b 20 Jan 1966), 1 da (Helen b 27 Sept 1964); *Career* athletics coach; dir of coaching Uganda 1968–72, nat athletics coach Wales 1974–94, head of coaching and devpt British Athletic Federation 1994–97, exec dir Performance Athlete Services Ltd 1997–, head coach of track and field Univ of Bath 1998–99, performance mangr UK Athletics High Performance Centre Univ of Bath 1999–2009, nat coach (hurdles) UK Athletics 2009–; coach to Olympic teams: Uganda 1968 and 1972, GB and NI 1980, 1984, 1988, 1992, 2000, 2004, 2008 and 2012; head coach GB and NI Olympic Team 1996; coach to: late John Akii-Bua (Olympic 400m hurdles champion 1972, world record holder 1972–76), Colin Jackson (world champion 1993 and 1999, world record holder 60m and 110m hurdles), Kay Morley (Cwlth 100m hurdles champion 1990), Mark McKoy (Olympic 110m hurdles Gold medal 1992), Jason Gardener (World 60m Champion (indoors) 2004), Dai Greene (world champion 400m hurdles 2011), numerous Br int athletes; Hon EdD Univ of Bath 2013; *Books* author of ten athletics books; *Recreations* rally driver of enthusiasm but no distinction; *Style*— Malcolm Arnold, Esq, OBE; ✉ Froxfield House, 139 The Street, Broughton Gifford, Melksham, Wiltshire SN12 8PH (e-mail malarnold@aol.com)

ARNOLD, Michael; s of Dr Alan George Arnold (d 1990), and Kathleen, *née* McGuirk (d 1947); *b* 16 September 1947; *Educ* Royal Wolverhampton Sch, Univ of Reading (BSc); *m* 8 April 1972, Pauline Ann, da of Berwyn Elvet Pritchard (d 1995); 2 s (David Paul b 4 July 1975, Stuart Michael b 12 May 1978); *Career* actuarial trainee Prudential Assurance Co Ltd 1969–71; Hymans Robertson: joined as actuarial trainee 1971, ptnr 1974, sr ptnr 1995–2002; princ Milliman 2002–; Liveryman Worshipful Co of Actuaries 1985; FIA 1973; *Recreations* golf, travel; *Clubs* City Livery, Kingswood Golf, Walton Heath Golf; *Style*— Michael Arnold, Esq

ARNOLD, Michael John; s of Thomas Henry Arnold (d 1991), and Cecily May Arnold (d 1996); *b* 1 April 1935; *m* 21 Jan 1989, Jane, *née* Benson; *Career* Nat Serv Lt RA 1958–59; Hilton Sharpe & Clark 1951–57, qualified CA 1957, ptnr Arthur Young 1966–89 (joined 1960), chm AY Management Consultants 1973–83, nat dir Corporate Recovery and Insolvency 1975–89, sole practitioner (corp restructuring and recoveries) 1989–2015; dir: Roux Restaurants 1987–2000, Carlisle Group plc 1998–99, Jourdan 1998–2004, Behavioural Science Systems 2005–07; chm: Prelude Technology Holdings 1991–96, Luminar plc 1994–2001, Brooke Industrial Holdings plc 2000–03; court appointed receiver NUM 1984–86; hon treas: Youth Clubs UK 1984–92, Racehorse Owners' Assoc 1991–99; tstee Volunteer Reading Help 2001–07 (hon treas 2001–06); memb Fin Ctee Br Horseracing Bd 1993–2000; FCA, FIPA; *Recreations* horse racing, country; *Clubs* Turf; *Style*— Michael Arnold, Esq; ✉ Brockhill, Naunton, Cheltenham, Gloucestershire GL54 3BA (✆ 01451 850191, fax 01451 850199)

ARNOLD, Hon Mr Justice; Sir Richard David Arnold; kt (2008); s of late Francis Arnold, of London, and Ann, *née* Churchill; *b* 23 June 1961; *Educ* Highgate Sch, Magdalen Coll Oxford (MA), Westminster Univ (Dip Law); *m* 24 March 1990, Mary, da of Edwin Elford; 2 da (Judith Alice b 22 Oct 1996, Elizabeth Jean b 27 Oct 2000); *Career* called to the Bar 1985, QC 2000; chm Ctee on Code of Practice for Promotion of Animal Medicines 2001–08, appointed to hear trade mark appeals 2003–08, dep High Court judge 2004–08, judge of the High Court of Justice 2008–, judge i/c Patents Court 2013–; *Publications* Computer Software and Legal Protection in the UK (jtly, 1992), Entertainment and Media Law

Reports (ed, 1993–2004), Performers' Rights (2008, 5 edn 2015), Halsbury's Laws: Trade Marks (ed, 2014); *Recreations* music, cinema, theatre, opera, cooking, walking in Suffolk; *Clubs* MCC; *Style—* The Hon Mr Justice Arnold; ✉ Royal Courts of Justice, Rolls Building, Fetter Lane, London EC4A 1NL

ARNOLD, Sheila May; da of John Millar Arnold (d 1949), and Mabel, *née* Walker (d 1951); *b* 24 May 1930; *Educ* RCSI (LPCP, LPCS); *m* 4 April 1955, Thomas Matthew Maguire, s of Philip Francis Maguire (d 1932); 2 da (Ailsa Catherine b 1965, Kim Caroline b 1970); *Career* house surgn and physician Richmond Hosp Dublin 1954–55; sr house surgn: Kent and Sussex Hosp 1956, Derbys Royal Infirmary 1957, Newcastle Royal Infirmary 1959; personal physician and surgn to Pres Kwame Nkruma Ghana Med Serv investigating deafness in village children 1959–62, St Mary Abotts Hosp London 1963, sr registrar Guy's and Lewisham Hosps 1970–73, sr conslt ENT surgn Frimley Park Hosp 1973–; memb: Royal Soc of Med, Regnl Med Advsy Ctee Br Soc of Otolaryngologists; LRCP, LRCS 1954, DLO 1961, FRCS 1973; *Publications* The Vulnerability of the Chorda Tympani Nerve and Middle Ear Disease (paper, 1973); *Recreations* badminton, skiing, swimming, foreign travel, squash; *Style—* Miss Sheila Arnold; ✉ Robin Hill, 18 Murdoch Road, Wokingham, Berkshire RG40 2DE (☎ 0118 978 7027); Frimley Park Hospital, Portsmouth Road, Frimley, Surrey GU16 5UJ (☎ 01276 692777)

ARNOLD, Susan Hillary (Sue); da of Morny McHarg, and Marjorie James; *Educ* Elmhurst Ballet Sch Camberley, Trinity Coll Dublin (MA); *m* twice; 6 c; *Career* journalist: Lancashire Evening Telegraph Blackburn 1967–68, Evening Standard 1968–69, Tehran Jl 1969–70, The Observer 1970–; radio and audiobook reviewer The Observer and The Guardian 1970–, columnist The Independent 1998–; commended Magazine Writer Br Press awards 1982, Magazine Writer of the Year 1983; *Books* Little Princes (1981), Curiouser & Curiouser (1984), A Burmese Legacy (1996); *Recreations* housewifery; *Clubs* Chelsea Arts; *Style—* Ms Sue Arnold; ✉ c/o The Guardian, 90 York Way, London N1 9GU

ARNOLD, Tom; s of Arthur Arnold (d 1982), and Theresa, *née* Healy (d 1992); *b* 5 October 1948, Dublin; *Educ* Corduff National Sch, De La Salle Coll Skerries, Franciscian Coll Gormonston, UCD (BAgrSc), Catholic Univ Louvain (MBA), TCD (MSc); *m* 4 April 1986, Gillian Davidson; 1 s (Patrick b 19 Feb 1987), 1 da (Laura b 8 Feb 1989); *Career* EC 1973–83, sr economist Farm Advsy Serv (ACOT) Ireland 1983–88; Dept of Agriculture and Food: chief economist 1988–93, asst sec gen 1993–2001; ceo Concern Worldwide 2001–13 (special rep for hunger 2013–); DG Inst of Int and European Affrs 2013–; chm Ctee of Agriculture OECD 1993–98, vol UN Millennium Project Hunger Task Force 2003–05, memb Advsy Bd UN Central Emergency Response Fund 2006–, coordinator AI Scaling Up Nutrition (SUN) Movement 2014–, memb Global Panel on Agriculture and Food Systems for Nutrition 2014–; chm Irish Constitutional Convention 2012–14, chm Irish Times Tst 2013–; FRSA 2006; *Recreations* reading, tennis, travel; *Clubs* University Club Dublin; *Style—* Tom Arnold, Esq; ✉ Concern Worldwide, Camden Street, Dublin 2, Ireland (☎ 00 353 1 417 7775, e-mail tom.arnold@concern.net)

ARNOLD, Wallace; *see:* Brown, Craig Edward Moncrieff

ARNOLD, William; s of William Arnold (d 1963), and Ruth, *née* Hardwick (d 1990); *b* 13 May 1953, Rawtenstall, Lancs; *Educ* Bury GS, King's Coll Cambridge (scholar, sr scholar, MA); *m* 6 June 1992, Elizabeth Anne McLellan-Arnold; 2 s (William Matthew, Jason Bruce b 3 Nov 1998 (twins)); *Career* civil servant; Lord Chllr's Dept: joined 1974, asst private sec to Lord Chllr 1977–79, princ 1979; head Legal Servs Div 1987, dir of corp servs Nat Archives 1991, PM's Dept Canberra 1993, head Family Policy Div Lord Chllr's Dept 1994, dir of RDA sponsorship DETR (then DTI) 1999, head Criminal Justice Confidence Unit Home Office 2003, sec Cmmn for Judicial Appointments 2004, chief exec Family Justice Cncl 2006, chief exec Law Cmmn 2008–09, dir of corporate services UK Supreme Court 2009–; reader St Margaret's Church Putney 1989–2008, reader Mortlake with East Sheen 2009–; assoc memb CIPD 1980, FRSA 2000; *Recreations* family, walking, skiing; *Style—* William Arnold, Esq; ✉ The Supreme Court of the United Kingdom, Parliament Square, London SW1P 3BD (e-mail william.arnold@supremecourt.uk)

ARNOT, Richard James; s of Thomas Arnot, of Newcastle upon Tyne, and Judith, *née* Richardson; *b* 7 December 1966; *Educ* LLB; *Career* admitted slr 1992; trainee slr Mincoffs, head of licensing Dickinson Dees, ptnr and head of licensing Mincoffs 2005–; author of numerous articles on licensing law; owner of property business in NE; memb Law Soc 1992; *Recreations* running; *Style—* Richard Arnot, Esq; ✉ Mincoffs, 5 Osborne Terrace, Newcastle upon Tyne NE2 1SQ (☎ 0191 212 7703, fax 0191 281 8069, e-mail richard.arnot@mincoffs.co.uk)

ARON, HE Michael; s of late Maurice Aron, and Sheila, *née* Torrens; *b* 22 March 1959, Kuwait; *Educ* Exeter School, Univ of Leeds, Polytechnic of Central London; *m* (m dis) Rachel; 2 da (Rebecca, Natasha), 2 s (Joseph, Jonathan); *Career* diplomat; asst desk offr for Iran ME Dept FCO 1984–85, desk offr FCO 1986–88, first sec commercial and economic Brasilia 1988–91, desk offr ME Peace Process Near E and N Africa Dept FCO 1991–93, first sec ME and Cyprus UK Mission NY 1993–96, dep head ME Dept FCO 1996–97, head Comprehensive Spending Review Team FCO 1997–78, head Mgmnt Consultancy Servs FCO 1998–99, dep head of mission Amman 1999–2002, political counsellor UKRep Brussels 2002–06, Brussels EU dir and head Scottish Govt EU Office 2006–08, ambass to Kuwait 2008–09, head ME Dept FCO 2010–11, ambass to Iraq 2011–12, ambass to Libya 2012–15, ambass to Sudan 2015–; *Style—* HE Mr Michael Aron; ✉ c/o FCO (Khartoum), King Charles Street, London SW1A 2AH

ARONSON, Dr Jeffrey Kenneth; s of Samuel Aronson, and Sybil, *née* Solomon; *b* 1947, Glasgow; *Educ* Glasgow HS, Univ of Glasgow, Univ of Oxford; *m* Renée Elaine, *née* Wellins; 1s (Simon Mark b 21 July 1977), 1 da (Natalie Jane b 14 April 1980); *Career* hon conslt physician Oxford Univ Hosp NHS Tst; pres emeritus and hon fell Br Pharmacological Soc, chm Expert Advsy Gp on Nomenclature Br Pharmacopoeia Cmmn; memb: Advsy Bd Br Nat Formulary, Technol Appraisal Ctee NICE, Jls Library Bd Nat Inst for Health Research, Editorial Bd Drug Safety Case Reports; sr memb Assoc of Physicians of GB & I; emeritus fell Green-Templeton Coll Oxford; fell RCP 1985, hon FFPM 2007; *Publications* The Oxford Textbook of Clinical Pharmacology and Drug Therapy (jtly, 3 edn, 2002), The Oxford Handbook of Practical Drug Therapy (jtly, 2005, 2 edn 2011), Stephens' Detection and Evaluation of Adverse Drug Reactions (jt ed, 6 edn, 2011), Evidence-Based Monitoring: From Principles to Practice (jt ed, 2008); ed-in-chief Meyler's Side Effects of Drugs – The International Encyclopedia of Adverse Drug Reactions and Interactions (16 edn, 2015), author of over 400 original research papers, review articles, annotations and editorials in scientific jls, author or ed of over 50 books; *Recreations* reading, writing and arithmetic, skiing, cricket, crosswords; *Clubs* RSM; *Style—* Dr Jeffrey Aronson; ✉ Green-Templeton College, Oxford OX2 6HG (e-mail jeffrey.aronson@phc.ox.ac.uk, website www.phc.ox.ac.uk/team/researchers/jeffrey-aronson)

ARORA, Simon; *Educ* Manchester Grammar, Univ of Cambridge; *Career* md B&M Retail 2005–; *Style—* Simon Arora, Esq; ✉ B&M Retail Ltd, The Vault, Dakota Drive, Estuary Commerce Park, Speke, Liverpool L24 8RJ

ARRAN, 9 Earl of (I 1762); Sir Arthur Desmond Colquhoun Gore; 11 Bt (I 1662); also Viscount Sudley, Baron Saunders (both I 1758), and Baron Sudley (UK 1884); s of 8 Earl of Arran (d 1983), and Fiona, Countess of Arran; *b* 14 July 1938; *Educ* Eton, Balliol Coll Oxford; *m* 1974, Eleanor, er da of Bernard van Cutsem and Lady Margaret Fortescue, da of 5 Earl Fortescue; 2 da (Lady Laura Melissa b 1975, Lady Lucy Katherine b 1976); *Heir* kinsman, William Henry Gore; *Career* Nat Serv Grenadier Gds; asst mangr Daily Mail 1972–73, md Clark Nelson 1973–74, asst gen mangr Daily and Sunday Express 1974; dir Waterstone & Co Ltd 1984–87; a lord-in-waiting (Govt whip) 1987–89 and July 1994-Jan 1995; elected hereditary memb House of Lords; spokesman for: Home Office, DES and DHSS 1987–89, Dept of the Environment 1988–89; Parly under sec of state: for the Armed Forces MOD 1989–92, Northern Ireland Office 1992–94, Dept of the Environment 1994; dep chief whip (House of Lords) 1994–95; Parly consIt to Inst of Waste Mgmnt 1995–2000; chm Children's Country Holidays Fund, chm Waste Industry Nat Trg Orgn (WINTO); non-exec dir: HMV (Thorn/EMI) 1995–98, South West Enterprise Ltd 1996–98, Bonhams 1997–2000; tstee Chelsea Physic Garden 1998, dir Weather World 2005; *Recreations* tennis, golf, gardening; *Clubs* Turf, Beefsteak, Pratt's, White's, Annabel's; *Style—* The Rt Hon the Earl of Arran; ✉ The Garden House, Filleigh, Barnstaple, Devon EX32 0RG (☎ 01598 760227); House of Lords, London SW1A 0PW

ARTERTON, Gemma Christina; da of Barry Arterton, and Sally, *née* Heap; *b* 2 February 1986, Gravesend, Kent; *Educ* RADA (BA); *Career* actress; *Theatre* Love's Labour's Lost (Globe Theatre) 2007, The Little Dog Laughed (Garrick Theatre) 2010, The Master Builder (Almeida Theatre) 2010–11, The Duchess of Malfi (Sam Wannamaker Playhouse) 2013, Made In Dagenham 2014, Nell Gwynn (Apollo Theatre) 2016; *Film* incl: St Trinians 2007, Three and Out 2008, Quantum of Solace 2008, The Boat That Rocked 2009, The Disappearance of Alice Creed 2009, St Trinian's 2: The Legend of Fritton's Gold 2009, Prince of Persia: The Sands of Time 2010, Clash of the Titans 2010, Tamara Drewe 2010, Song for Marion 2012, Byzantium 2012, Hansel and Gretel: Witch Hunters 2013, Runner Runner 2013, Inside Number 9 2014, Gemma Bovery 2014, The Voices 2014, A Hundred Streets 2015, The History of Love 2016, The Girl with All the Gifts 2016, Orpheline 2016, We Happy Few 2016; *Television* incl: Capturing Mary 2007, Tess of the D'Urbervilles (BBC) 2008, Lost In Austen 2008, Inside Number 9 2014; *Style—* Ms Gemma Arterton; ✉ c/o Independent Talent Group, 40 Whitfield Street, London W1T 2RH

ARTHUR, Alan David; s of David Edward John Arthur, of Glamorgan, and Elizabeth Ann, *née* Howell; *b* 3 July 1949; *Educ* Bedwellty GS, UC of Wales Aberystwyth (BSc); *Career* chartered accountant; ptnr int practice Deloitte Haskins & Sells 1983–84 (previous posts in S Wales, W Yorks and Zambia), ptnr Booth & Co CAs 1986–89, former dir of corp fin WBS Corp Fin, currently chm and md Padarn Ltd; former treas Black Dyke Mills Band (Premier World's Best Brass Band); *Recreations* work, rugby, Rotary; *Clubs* Bradford, Bradford Blaize; *Style—* Alan Arthur, Esq; ✉ 76 Hallowes Park Road, Cullingworth, West Yorkshire BD13 5AR (☎ 01535 273074); Padarn Ltd (☎ 07877 269661, e-mail alan.arthur@talktalk.net)

ARTHUR, Christine; da of W J Arthur, of Hemel Hempstead, Herts, and R Arthur, *née* Campion; *b* 14 July 1966; *Educ* Parmiters Sch Watford, Univ of Birmingham (BA); *m* 1990, N J S Davies, s of Brian Davies; *Career* Rote PR 1988–92, assoc dir Haslimann Taylor 1992–93, md and main bd dir IAS Smarts (formerly Citigate Communications) Birmingham 1993–; author of various feature articles for nat, local and trade press; memb PRCA, MCIPR; *Recreations* tennis, foreign travel, piano, antiques; *Clubs* Moor Pool Tennis; *Style—* Ms Christine Arthur; ✉ IAS Smarts Ltd, 9 The Apex, 6 Embassy Drive, Edgbaston, Birmingham B15 1TP (☎ 0121 456 3199, fax 0121 456 3192, e-mail christine.arthur@iassmarts.com)

ARTHUR, Dr John Willins; s of Archibald Arthur (d 2003), and Mary Arthur (d 1998); *b* 1949, Edinburgh; *Educ* Boroughmuir Sr Secdy, Univ of Toronto (BSc), Univ of Edinburgh (PhD); *m* 1976, Norma; 1 da (Sarah Elizabeth), 1 s (Andrew John); *Career* engr; research fell Univ of Edinburgh: Dept of Physics 1974–76, Wolfson Microelectronics Liaison Unit 1976–79; Racal-MESL (now MESL Microwave Ltd): joined 1979, dir Signal Processing 1990–92, dir Electronic Products 1992–96, tech dir 1996–2003; ind conslt 2003–; awards for Racal-MESL: Queen's Award for Technol (jtly) 1989, Millennium Product Award Design Cncl 2000; memb Industrial Advsy Bd: Napier Univ 2000–04 (industrial advsr 1994–95, external examiner 1997–2000), Univ of Edinburgh 2000–01; Scot Optoelectronic Assoc: memb Cncl 1997–2001, memb Displays Subgroup Steering Ctee 1997–2001; memb Standing Ctee for Research and Secondment Schemes Royal Acad of Engrg 2003–07; tstee James Clerk Maxwell Fndn 2012–; hon fell Sch of Engrg Univ of Edinburgh 2006–12; Oliver Lodge premium IEE 1997, Donald G Fink Award IEEE 2010; CPhys 1976, CEng 1998, FIEE 1998, FRSE 2002, FREng 2002, FInstP 2002, SMIEEE 2003; *Publications* Understanding Geometric Algebra for Electromagnetic Theory (2011), Brilliant Lives: The Clerk Maxwells and the Scottish Enlightenment (2016); *Style—* Dr John Arthur, FREng, FRSE; ✉ e-mail john.arthur@tiscali.co.uk

ARTHUR, Prof Michael James Paul; s of Reginald Alfred John Arthur (d 1989), and Patricia Margaret, *née* Marsh (d 2010); *b* 3 August 1954, Purley, Surrey; *Educ* Burnt Mill Comp Sch Harlow, Univ of Southampton (BM, DM); *m* 17 March 1979, Elizabeth Susan, *née* McCaughey; 2 da (Rachel Susan b 11 Jan 1983, Sarah Elizabeth b 14 June 1985), 1 s (James William b 4 Oct 1987); *Career* SHO Nottingham 1978–80, med registrar Wessex rotation 1980–82; Univ of Southampton: lectr in med 1982–89, sr lectr in med 1989–92, prof of med 1992–2004, head Sch of Med 1998–2001, dean of med health and life sciences 2003–04; vice-chllr Univ of Leeds 2004–13, pres and provost UCL 2013–; Fogarty fell Univ of Calif San Francisco 1986–88, Fulbright distinguished scholar Mount Sinai Sch of Med NY 2002–; Fulbright cmmr US/UK Fulbright Cmmn 2008–; memb Cell and Molecular Panel Wellcome Tst 1998–2003 (chair 2003); chair Nat Steering Gp Nat Student Survey 2005–08, chair Worldwide Univs Network 2007–09 (memb Bd until 2013), memb Bd Qualifications and Curriculum Authy 2007–10, chair Advsy Gp Nat Specialist Services NHS 2010–13; pres Br Assoc Study of the Liver 2001–03, chair of tstees Br Liver Tst 2003–06 (vice-pres 2007–), memb Cncl Medical Research Cncl 2008–14; memb Bd Yorkshire Forward 2006–11, memb Bd Opera North 2007–13, chair Russell Gp of Univs 2009–12; Research Prize American Liver Fndn 1987, Linacre Medal RCP 1994, Gold Medal Amity Univ Delhi 2006; Hon DLett Univ of Southampton 2010; FRCP 1993, FMedSci 1998, FRSA 2006, princ FHEA 2016; *Publications* Wright's Liver and Biliary Disease (jt ed, 3 edn, 1993), author of numerous pubns in scientific jls on cell and molecular pathogenesis of liver disease and liver fibrosis; *Recreations* sailing; *Clubs* Royal Southern Yacht; *Style—* Prof Michael Arthur; ✉ Provost's Office, University College London, Gower Street, London WC1E 6BT

ARTHUR, Peter Alistair Kennedy; s of Jack Kennedy Arthur (d 1993), and Margaret Kerr, *née* Morisson (d 1999); *b* 16 June 1956; *Educ* Loretto, Univ of Edinburgh (LLB); *m* 5 June 1982, Dorothy, da of William Erskine; 3 s (Michael Kennedy b 22 Aug 1984, Graeme Erskine b 4 March 1987, Duncan Robert b 26 Oct 1989); *Career* trainee then asst slr Murray Beith & Murray 1977–80; co sec: Noble & Co 1980–83, ESCO Oil Management Ltd 1983–87; Edinburgh Fund Managers plc: asst co sec and compliance offr 1987–89, co sec 1989–90, admin dir 1990–95, jt md 1995–97; chief legal counsel for Europe Templeton Investment Management 1997–99, dir ISIS Asset Management plc (formerly Friends Ivory & Sime plc) 1999–2004; currently chm: R&A, Aberdeen Asian Income Fund Ltd; currently dir: AIC, Proven Health VCT plc, Longbow Growth & Income VCT plc; FCIS; *Recreations* golf, skiing, family; *Clubs* HCEG, Royal Troon, Royal Portrush; *Style—* Peter Arthur, Esq

ARTHUR, Terence Gordon (Terry); s of William Gordon Arthur (d 1971), of West Hartlepool, and Dorothy, *née* Baker; *b* 5 September 1940; *Educ* West Hartlepool GS, Univ of Manchester (BSc), Univ of Cambridge (Dip Statistics, Rugby blue); *m* 1, 15 May 1965 (m dis 1983), Valerie Ann Marie, da of Stephen Daniels; 2 da (Louise b 1966, Frances b 1968), 1 s (Richard b 1970); m 2, 25 Nov 1983, Mary Clare, *née* Austick; *Career* asst sec Equity & Law Life Assurance Soc 1967 (joined 1963), ptnr Duncan C Fraser & Co Actuaries 1969–76 (joined 1967), T G Arthur Hargrave Actuaries 1976–91 (fndr 1976) (merged with Bacon and Woodrow 1989); professional non-exec 1991–; dir: Financial Mathematics Ltd 1978, SVM Global Fund plc (formerly Warrants & Value Investment Tst plc) 1993–, WVT Dealing Ltd 1993–, Allianz Dresdner Second Endowment Policy Tst plc 1993–, TKM Gp Pensions Tst Ltd 1994–2006 (chm 1998–), Royal Mail Pensions Tstees Ltd (formerly Post Office Pensions Tstees Ltd) 1998–2004; former dir: Whittingdale Holdings Ltd, Whittingdale Ltd, Police Mutual Assurance Soc, Wesleyan Assurance Soc, Jupiter Extra Income Tst plc, Wiggins Teape Pensions Ltd, Scottish Provident Inst, AXA Rosenberg Investment Mgmnt; memb: Cncl Inst of Actuaries 1977–94 (treas 1985–86), Co of Actuaries; 2 caps England rugby football 1966; Freeman City of London; FIA 1966, FIS 1975, fell Inst of Pensions Mgmnt 1977; *Books* 95 per cent is Crap – A Plain Man's Guide to British Politics (1975), Crap: A Guide to Politics (2007); *Clubs* Royal Over-Seas League, Hawks' (Cambridge), Luffenham Heath Golf; *Style*— Terry Arthur, Esq; ✉ 17 Barnack Road, St Martin's Without, Stamford, Lincolnshire PE9 2NA (☎ 01780 753525, fax 01780 579073)

ARUNDEL AND BRIGHTON, Bishop of (RC) 2015–; Rt Rev Charles Phillip Richard Moth; s of Charles Ernest Moth, and Barbara Yvonne, *née* Hambly; *b* 8 July 1958, Chingola, Zambia; *Educ* Judd Sch Tonbridge, St John's Seminary Wonersh, St Paul Univ Ottawa (MA); *Career* ordained priest 1982, asst priest Clapham Park 1982–85, asst priest Lewisham 1987–92, private sec to the Archbishop of Southwark 1992–2001, RC Archdiocese of Southwark: vocations dir 1992–2001, vicar gen and chllr 2001–09, bishop of the Forces 2009–15; liaison bishop: for Catholic Scouting 2010–, for Prisons 2013–; memb Dept of Christian Responsibility and Citizenship Catholic Bishops' Conference 2009–, chair Mental Health Reference Gp Catholic Bishops' Conference 2009–; pres Southwark Metropolitan Appeal Tbnl 1994–2002, chair Mental Health Reference Gp 2009–; chair of govrs St Mary's UC (later St Mary's Twickenham) 2011–; memb Canon Law Soc of GB and I 1985; Freeman City of London, Freeman Skinners' Co 2013; *Recreations* horse riding, walking, music; *Clubs* Naval and Military; *Style*— The Rt Rev the Bishop of Arundel and Brighton; ✉ High Oaks, Old Brighton Road North, Pease Pottage, West Sussex RH11 9AJ (☎ 01293 526428, e-mail bishop@abdiocese.org.uk)

ASANTE-MENSAH, Evelyn Justina; OBE (2006); da of Kwaku Asante-Mensah (d 2004), of Ghana, and Beatrice Gyamfi, *née* Amoo-Mensah; *b* 11 October 1965, Ghana; *Educ* Nicholls Ardwick HS Manchester, South Manchester Coll, Manchester Met Univ (Dip Women's Studies, MA); *Partner* Yoni Ejo; 4 c (Leon Joseph b 23 June 1986, Sade Lydia b 4 May 1988, Esi b 3 June 2001, Afua b 31 Jan 2003); *Career* chief exec Black Health Agency 1992–; chair: Central Manchester PCT 2000–, Race for Health 2003–, Black and Minority Ethnic (BME) Advsy Gp NHS Appts Cmmn 2005–; cmmr Equal Opportunities Cmmn 2005–; strategic advsr Govt Office for the NW; memb ACEVO 2000–; Hon DLitt Manchester Met Univ 2002; FRSA 2003; *Recreations* reading, travel, gardening, time with family; *Style*— Ms Evelyn Asante-Mensah, OBE; ✉ Black Health Agency, 464 Chester Road, Old Trafford, Manchester M16 9HE (☎ 0161 875 2062, fax 0845 450 3247)

ASGHAR, Mohammad; AM; s of M Aslam Khan, and Zubada Aslam; *b* 30 September 1945, Peshawar, Pakistan; *Educ* Univ of Peshawar Pakistan (BA); *m* 1983, Firdaus; 1 da (Natasha); *Career* asst to Princ R Minty Chartered Accountants 1972–83, princ M A Assocs 1983–; memb Nat Assembly for Wales (Cons) South Wales East 2007–; Parly candidate (Plaid Cymru) Gen Election 2005; memb: AAT, IAF, CPA; *Recreations* cricket, athletics, badminton, flying (holds private pilot's licence); *Style*— Mohammad Asghar, Esq, AM; ✉ Constituency Office, Fairoak House, 15–17 Church Road, Newport NP19 7EJ (☎ and fax 01633 220022, website www.mohammadawgharam.co.uk); National Assembly for Wales, Cardiff Bay, Cardiff CF99 1NA (☎ 029 2089 8321, fax 029 2089 8726, e-mail mohammad.asghar@wales.gov.uk)

ASH, Douglas Terence (Doug); s of Sydney Alexander Ash (d 1993), and Doreen Victoria, *née* Gornall (d 2015); *b* 19 December 1947; *Educ* Wallington GS, Univ of Nottingham (BA), Harvard Business Sch (MBA); *m* 19 Aug 1972, Rhona Helen, da of Harold James Bennett (d 1978), former vice-pres Rotary Int; 3 da (Belinda 1975, Isobel b 1976, Amelia b 1981), 1 s (Laurence b 1981); *Career* formerly: exec dir Ocean Gp plc; chief exec: MSAS Cargo International, English First Division Rugby; dep chm Direct Wines Ltd, dir Refresh (UK) Ltd, dir Four Soft Ltd; *Recreations* Henley Rugby Football (pres); *Style*— Doug Ash, Esq; ☎ 07786 517380, e-mail dougtash@gmail.com

ASHBROOK, Kate Jessie; da of John Benjamin Ashbrook, of Denham Village, Bucks, and Margaret, *née* Balfour; *b* 1 February 1955; *Educ* High March Sch, Benenden, Univ of Exeter (BSc); *Career* sec Dartmoor Preservation Assoc 1981–84 (pres 1995–2011, tstee 1995–), gen sec Open Spaces Soc 1984– (memb Exec Ctee 1978–, Elinor Ostrom Award for Commons Practitioners 2013), ed Open Space 1984–; Ramblers: tstee 1982–2012 and 2016–, footpath sec and press offr Bucks, Milton Keynes and W Middx area 1986–, vice-chm 1993–95, chm 1995–98 and 2006–09, chm Access Ctee 1997–, pres 2012–16; chm Central Rights of Way Ctee 1991–98; sec Countryside Link Gp 1989–92; memb: Gen Cncl CPRE 1984–95, Exec Ctee Campaign for Nat Parks 1983– (vice-chm 1998–2003, chm 2003–09), Bd Countryside Agency 1999–2006, Nat Parks Review Advsy Panel DEFRA 2002, Common Land Stakeholder Working Gp DEFRA 2002–03, Nat England Rights of Way Stakeholder Working Gp 2008–; chm Turville Sch Tst 1994–95; memb Inst of Public Rights of Way and Access Management 1999; won landmark Appeal Court ruling (R (Ashbrook) v E Sussex CC); patron Walkers are Welcome towns network 2008–; Outdoor Personality of the Year Award Great Outdoors Magazine 2015; *Books* Severnside – A Guide to Family Walks (contrib The Southern Quantocks, 1977), The Walks of SE England (contrib A Walk Round Denham, 1975), Common Place No More, Common Land in the 1980s (1983), Make for the Hills (1983), Our Common Right (1987), Finding Common Ground (2010), Saving Open Spaces (2015), entry for Ronald Legg in Oxford Dictionary of National Biography (2015); *Recreations* walking, campaigning for access to countryside, music, learning birdsong; *Style*— Miss Kate Ashbrook; ✉ Telfer's Cottage, Turville, Henley-on-Thames, Oxfordshire RG9 6QL (☎ 01491 638396, website https://campaignerkate.wordpress.com); Open Spaces Society, 25A Bell Street, Henley-on-Thames, Oxfordshire RG9 2BA (☎ 01491 573535)

ASHBY, Prof the Hon Michael Farries; CBE (1997); er s of Baron Ashby, FRS (Life Peer; d 1992), and Elizabeth Helen Margaret, *née* Farries; *b* 20 November 1935; *Educ* Campbell Coll Belfast, Queens' Coll Cambridge (MA, PhD); *m* 1962, Maureen, da of James Stewart, of White House, Montgomery, Powys; 2 s, 1 da; *Career* asst Univ of Göttingen 1962–65, asst prof Harvard Univ 1965–69, prof of metallurgy Harvard Univ 1969–73, prof of engineering materials Univ of Cambridge 1973–89, Royal Society research prof Dept of Engineering Univ of Cambridge 1989–; visiting prof RCA 2001–; ed Acta Metallurgica 1974–94; memb Akademie der Wissenschaften zu Göttingen 1980–; Hon MA Harvard 1969; FRS 1979, FREng 1993; *Books* Engineering Materials (parts 1 and 2), Deformation-Mechanism Maps, The Structure and Properties of Cellular Solids, Materials Selection in Mechanical Design, Metal Foams: A Design Guide, Materials and Design: The Art and Science of Material Selection in Product Design, Materials, Processing, Science and Design, Materials and the Environment, Cellular Solids in Biology and Nature, Materials and Sustainability; *Recreations* music, design; *Style*— Prof the Hon Michael Ashby, CBE, FRS, FREng; ✉ 51 Maids Causeway, Cambridge CB5 8DE

ASHCROFT, Jane Rachel; CBE (2014); *b* 17 June 1966, Liverpool; *Educ* Univ of Stirling (BA); *m* 17 Nov 1990, (Andrew) Jonathan; *Career* formerly: asst sec Midlands Electricity plc, HR mangr and co sec Bromford Housing Gp, personnel dir BUPA; chief exec Anchor 2010– (joined 1999); non-exec dir Dignity plc 2012–, vice-chair Associated Retirement Community Operators 2015–; tstee The Silver Line 2012–; FCIS, MCIPD; *Style*— Ms Jane Ashcroft, CBE; ✉ Anchor Trust, 25 Bedford Street, London WC2E 9ES

ASHCROFT, Baron (Life Peer UK 2000), of Chichester in the County of West Sussex; Rt Hon Sir Michael Anthony Ashcroft; KCMG (2000), PC (2012); s of Frederic Parker Ashcroft, and Mary Lavinia Long; *b* 4 March 1946; *Educ* King Edward VI GS Norwich, Royal GS High Wycombe, Mid-Essex Tech Coll Chelmsford; *m* 1, 1972 (m dis 1984) Wendy Mahoney; 2 s, 1 da; m 2, 1986, Susi Anstey; *Career* int businessman, entrepreneur, author and philanthropist; chm BCB Hldgs 1987–2010; fndr and chm Crimestoppers Tst 1988–; former chm: Hawley Group, ADT Ltd; dir Tyco Int Ltd 1984–2002, varied business interests with investments and participation in public and private cos in UK, USA and Caribbean; Cons Pty: treas 1998–2001, dep chm 2005–10; sr independent advsr to Govt on sovereign base areas Cyprus 2011–, Govt's special rep for Veterans' Transition 2012–; treas Int Democratic Union 2007–; ambass of Belize to UN 1998–2000; chm Ashcroft Technol Acad 1991–, chllr Anglia Ruskin Univ (formerly Anglia Poly Univ) 2001–; tstee Cleveland Clinic 2004–, vice patron Intelligence Corps Museum 2009–, tstee Imperial War Museum and Museum Fndn 2012–, ambass SkillForce 2011–, pres and tstee West India Ctee 2011–; *Publications* Smell the Coffee: A Wake Up Call to the Conservative Party (2005), Dirty Politics, Dirty Times (2005), Victoria Cross Heroes (2006), Special Forces Heroes (2008), George Cross Heroes (2010), Minority Verdict: the Conservative Party, the voters and the 2010 election (2010), Armed Forces and Society (2012), It's Not You It's Them (2012), Degrees of Separation (2012), Heroes of the Skies (2012), Special Ops Heroes (2014); *Recreations* researching the Victoria Cross, entertaining friends, trying something new, messing about in boats; *Style*— The Lord Ashcroft, KCMG, PC; ✉ House of Lords, London SW1A 0PW (website www.lordashcroft.com, Twitter @lordashcroft)

ASHDOWN, David William; s of William Curtis Thomas, and Jean Vida Ashdown; *b* 11 December 1950; *Educ* Wandsworth Comp; *m* 12 Aug 1978, Carol, da of Andrew Allan Smith (d 1963); 2 s (Michael b 1974, Peter b 1979); 1 da (Elizabeth Rose b 22 Aug 1991); *Career* photographer: Keystone Press 1968–78, Daily Star 1978–86; chief sports photographer The Independent 1986–2011; FRPS; *Awards* Ilford Press Photographer of the Year 1974, runner-up Br Press Picture Awards 1979, Ilford Sports Picture of the Year 1985 and 1991, Nikon Press Sports Photographer of the Year 1987, Adidas Euro Sports Picture of the Year 1987, Sports Photographer of the Year 1987 and 1990, Euro Sports Photographer of the Year 1993, Photographer of the Year British Press Awards 1998; *Recreations* golf, old motorbikes; *Style*— David Ashdown, Esq; ✉ mobile 07710 613969

ASHDOWN OF NORTON-SUB-HAMDON, Baron (Life Peer UK 2001), of Norton-sub-Hamdon in the County of Somerset; Sir Jeremy John Durham (Paddy) Ashdown; GCMG (2006), CH (2015), KBE (2000), PC (1989); s of John W R D Ashdown, and Lois A Ashdown; *b* 27 February 1941; *Educ* Bedford Sch, Language Sch Hong Kong (qualified first class Chinese interpreter); *m* 1961, Jane Courtenay; 1 s (Hon Simon), 1 da (Hon Kate); *Career* RM 1959–72, served Borneo, Persian Gulf and Belfast, cmd Special Boat Section (SBS) in the Far East; first sec (FO) Br Mission to UN Geneva 1971–76, with Westland Helicopters 1976–78, sr mangr Morlands Ltd 1978–81, youth offr Dorset CC 1981–83, MP (Lib until 1988, Lib Dem 1988–2001) Yeovil 1983–2001 (Parly candidate (Lib) 1976); ldr Lib Dems 1988–99; Lib/Alliance/Lib Dem spokesman: on trade and industry 1983–86, on educn and sci 1987–88, on NI 1989–90; unpaid non-exec dir Time Gp 1999–2002; Peace Implementation Cncl's High Rep for Bosnia 2002–06, EU special rep for Bosnia and Herzegovina 2002–06; *Books* Citizen's Britain, Beyond Westminster, Ashdown Diaries Vols I and II, Swords and Ploughshares; *Clubs* National Liberal; *Style*— The Rt Hon the Lord Ashdown of Norton-sub-Hamdon, GCMG, CH, KBE, PC

ASHE, Geoffrey Thomas Leslie; MBE (2012); s of Arthur Ashe (d 1959), and Thelma Hoodless Ashe (d 1959); *b* 29 March 1923, Acton; *Educ* St Paul's, Univ of British Columbia (BA), Univ of Cambridge (MA); *m* 1, 1946, Dorothy Irene Train (d 1990); 4 s (Thomas b 1949, John b 1950, Michael b 1951, Brendan b 1958), 1 da (Sheila b 1953); m 2, 1998, Dr Patricia Chandler; *Career* admin asst Ford of Canada 1952–54, lectr in mgmnt studies The Polytechnic London 1956–62, co-fndr and sec Camelot Research Ctee 1965–74, full-time writer and lectr 1968–; visiting prof 1980–97: Univ of Southern Mississippi, Univ of Minnesota Duluth, Portland State Univ, Univ of Alabama Birmingham, Univ of New Mexico; memb: Medieval Acad of America, Int Arthurian Soc, Labour Party; Freeman of Glastonbury 2015; FRSL 1963; *Publications* incl: King Arthur's Avalon: The Story of Glastonbury (1957, new edn 1992, 50th Anniversary ed 2007), From Caesar to Arthur (1960), Land to the West: St Brendan's Voyage to America (1962), The Land and the Book: Israel, the Perennial Nation (1965), Gandhi: A Study in Revolution (1968, new edn 2000), The Quest for Arthur's Britain (ed and contrib, 1 edn 1968), Camelot and the Vision of Albion (1971, new edn 2015), The Quest for America (ed and contrib, 1971), Do What You Will: A History of Anti-Morality (1974, re-published as The Hell-Fire Clubs: A History of Anti-Morality 2000), The Finger and the Moon (novel, 1973, new edn 2004), The Virgin: Mary's Cult and the Re-Emergence of the Goddess (1976, new edn 1988), The Ancient Wisdom (1977), Miracles (1978), A Guidebook to Arthurian Britain (1980, re-published as A Traveller's Guide to Arthurian Britain 1997), A Certain Very Ancient Book: Traces of an Arthurian Source in Geoffrey of Monmouth's History (article in Speculum: The Journal of the Medieval Academy of America, 1981), Kings and Queens of Early Britain (1982, new edn 2000), Avalonian Quest (1982), The Discovery of King Arthur (1985, new edn 2003), The Arthurian Encyclopedia (ed and contrib, 1986), The Landscape of King Arthur (1987), The Arthurian Handbook (collaborator, 1990), Mythology of the British Isles (1990, new edn 2002), King Arthur: The Dream of a Golden Age (1990), The New Arthurian Encyclopedia (ed and contrib, 1991), Dawn Behind the Dawn (1992), Atlantis: Lost Lands, Ancient Wisdom (1992), The Book of Prophecy: From Ancient Greece to the Millennium (1999, new edn 2002), The Encyclopedia of Prophecy (2001), Merlin (2002), Labyrinths and Mazes (2003), Merlin: The Prophet and his History (2006), The Offbeat Radicals (2007); author of numerous articles in periodicals; *Style*— Geoffrey Ashe, Esq, MBE; ✉ Chalice Orchard, Well House Lane, Glastonbury, Somerset BA6 8BJ (☎ 01458 832485, e-mail ashemail@tinyworld.co.uk)

ASHE, (Thomas) Michael; QC (England and Wales 1994, Northern Ireland 1998); s of John Ashe (d 1977), and Nancy, *née* O'Connor (d 1992); *b* 10 March 1949; *Educ* Finchley Catholic GS, Inns of Court Sch of Law; *m* 23 April 1977 (m dis), Helen Morag, da of Lt Col Kenneth Wheeler Nicholson (d 1963); *Career* Estate Duty Office Inland Revenue 1967–70; called to the Bar: Middle Temple 1971 (bencher 1998), Ireland 1975, NI 1993; with Schroders and Arbuthnot Latham (merchant banks) 1971–76; in practice at Bar 1978–; memb Board Soc of Advanced Legal Studies 1997–2003, auditor and notary Diocese of Brentwood 1997–, recorder of the Crown Court 2000, sr counsel Irish Republic 2000; Knight of the Holy Sepulchre 2000; *Books* Money (4 edn, Halsbury's Laws of England, 1980), Injunctions (4 edn (reprint), Halsbury's Laws of England, 1991), Insider Trading (2 edn, 1993), Insider Crime (1993), International Tracing of Assets (ed, 1997), Guide to Financial Services Regulation (1997), Moneylaundering (2000, 2 edn 2007), Anti-Money Laundering Risks Compliance and Governance (2013); *Recreations* walking, railways, music; *Style*— Michael Ashe, Esq, QC; ✉ 9 Stone Buildings, Lincoln's Inn,

London WC2A 3NN (☎ 020 7404 5055, fax 020 7405 1551, e-mail masheqc@compuserve.com)

ASHE, Rosemary Elizabeth; da of late Philip Stephen Ashe, and Dorothy May, *née* Watts; *b* 28 March 1953, Lowestoft, Suffolk; *Educ* Lowestoft GS, Royal Acad of Music, London Opera Centre; *Career* soprano; LRAM, ARAM; *Theatre* roles incl: Lottie Grady in When We Are Married (Garrick), Lolly Tucker in The Bed Before Yesterday (Mill at Sonning), Mrs Fraser in Stepping Out (UK tour), Ruth in The Pirates of Penzance (UK and American tours), Madame Spritzer in 13 Rue De L'Amour (Northampton Theatre), Nunsense (Redgrave Theatre), Viv Nicholson in Spend, Spend, Spend! (West Yorkshire Playhouse), Miss Andrew in Mary Poppins (Prince Edward Theatre), Mrs Lovett in Sweeny Todd (Gothenburg Opera), Beggar Woman in Sweeney Todd (Royal Festival Hall), Mona Kent in Dames at Sea (The Union), Little Buttercup in HMS Pinafore (Raymond Gubbay), Call Me Merman (The Pheasantry), On the Sunny Side of the Street (Jermyn St Theatre), Grandma in The Secret Diary of Adrian Mole (Leicester Curve), Miss Bleacher in Crush (Belgrade Theatre Coventry), Sister Mary Lazarus in Sister Act (nat tour); *Opera* roles incl: The Queen of Night in The Magic Flute (Opera North), Marionette in The Cunning Widow (Wexford Festival), Fiakermilli in Arabella, Esmeralda in The Bartered Bride, Papagena in The Magic Flute, Venus in Orpheus in the Underworld (ENO), Lucy Lockitt in The Beggar's Opera and Despina in Cosi fan Tutte (dir Jonathan Miller for BBC TV), Musetta in La Bohème (Opera Northern Ireland), Frasquita in Carmen (Earls Court prodn repeated in Japan), Violetta in La Traviata (Holland Park), Dinah in Trouble in Tahiti (Music Theatre Transparant Belgium); roles in musicals incl: Janet in The Rocky Horror Show, Maria in West Side Story, Hortense in The Boy Friend, Yum Yum in The Mikado, created the role of Carlotta in The Phantom of the Opera, Manon and Sari in Bitter Sweet (Sadler's Wells Opera), title role in La Belle Hélène (New Sadler's Wells Opera), Cunegonde in Candide (Old Vic Theatre), Josephine in HMS Pinafore (City Center Opera NY), Julie in Showboat (RSC/Opera North), The Witch in Into the Woods (Wolsey Theatre Ipswich), Madame Thénardier in Les Misérables (Palace), Widow Corney in Oliver (Palladium); other performances incl: Masterpiece Theatre Anniversary Celebrations (New York Forbidden Broadway Company Los Angeles and Washington), The Killer Soprano (one-woman show), Annie in Annie Get Your Gun (Wolsey Theatre Ipswich), Hermia in A Midsummer Night's Dream (Barbados Festival), Orinthia in The Applecart (Wolsey Theatre Ipswich), Asphynxia in Salad Days (nat tour), Zou Zou in La Belle Vivette (ENO), Mrs Darling in Peter Pan (Theatre Royal Nottingham), Dottie Otley in Noises Off (Salisbury Playhouse), Felicia Gabriel in The Witches of Eastwick (Theatre Royal Drury Lane and Princess Theatre Melbourne, Olivier Award nomination); regular broadcaster on Friday Night is Music Night and Songs From The Shows (Radio 2); *Television* incl: The Music Game (Channel 4), Whale On (Channel 4), House of Eliott (BBC), An Audience With Ronnie Corbett (LWT), Monster TV (BBC); *Recordings* incl: The Phantom of the Opera, The Boyfriend, Bitter Sweet, Kismet, The Student Prince, The Song of Norway, Oliver, The Killer Soprano, The Witches of Eastwick, Serious Cabaret, Mary Poppins; *Recreations* badminton, swimming; *Clubs* Two Brydges; *Style*— Ms Rosemary Ashe; ✉ c/o Cole Kitchenn, Roar House, 46 Charlotte Street, London W1T 2GS (☎ 020 7427 5681, email info@colekitchenn.com, website www.rosemaryashe.com)

ASHENFORD, Marcus Frank; s of David Ashenford, of Minchinhampton, Glos, and Josephine, *née* Broomhall; *b* 5 December 1969; *Educ* Cheltenham Coll; *m* 24 Jan 1997, Kate, *née* Gregory; 1 da (Alicia b 5 Dec 1998); *Career* chef; worked at: Gloscat 1986–88, Calcot Manor Tetbury 1988–91 (1 Michelin Star), Waterside Inn Bray 1991–94 (3 Michelin Stars); head chef: Lovells Windrush Farm 1994–97 (1 Michelin Star, 1 Egon Ronay Star, Acorn Award, 3 AA Rosettes, 6/10 Good Food Guide), Chavignol Chipping Norton 1998–2001 (1 Michelin Star, 3 AA Rosettes, 7/10 Good Food Guide), Chavignol The Old Mill Shipston on Stour 2001–03 (1 Michelin Star, 7/10 Good Food Guide); chef and prop 5 North Street 2003– (1 Michelin Star 2004); *Recreations* golf; *Clubs* Bristol City FC; *Style*— Marcus Ashenford, Esq

ASHER, Bernard Harry; *Career* dir HSBC Holdings plc 1989–98, formerly exec dir investment banking HSBC Holdings plc, formerly chm HSBC Investment Banking plc (subsid); non-exec chm Lonrho Africa 1998–2004; non-exec dir: Rémy Cointreau SA 1992–2001, The China Fund Inc 1995–2000, Rangold Resources Ltd 1997–, Morgan Sindall plc 1998–, Seymour Pierce 2000–; vice-chm and sr ind dir Legal & General plc 2000–04 (non-exec dir 1998–2004), chm Lion Trust Asset Mgmnt plc 2004–; investment advsr and memb Advsy Panel RCP 1998–; tstee The Health Fndn 1998–, vice-chm of govrs LSE 1998–2004; *Style*— Bernard Asher, Esq

ASHER, Jane; da of Richard Alan John Asher (d 1969), and Margaret, *née* Eliot (d 2011); *b* 5 April 1946; *Educ* North Bridge House, Miss Lambert's PNEU; *m* Gerald Anthony Scarfe, *qv*, s of Reginald Thomas Scarfe (d 1972); 1 da (Katie b 1974), 2 s (Alexander b 1981, Rory b 1983); *Career* actress and novelist; proprietor Jane Asher Party Cakes and Sugarcraft Shop Chelsea; designer: Jane Asher range of bakeware and textiles, Jane Asher Home Baking Collection; contrib: TV and radio current affairs progs, newspaper and magazine articles; reg columns: Daily Telegraph, The Independent, The Express; patron numerous charities; pres: Nat Autistic Soc, Arthritis Care, Parkinson's UK; vice-pres: Child Accident Prevention Tst, Autistica; memb BAFTA, assoc RADA; Hon LLD Univ of Bristol; FRSA; *Theatre* incl: Housemaster 1957, Muriel Webster in Will You Walk A Little Faster (Duke of York's) 1960, Wendy in Peter Pan (Scala) 1961; Bristol Old Vic 1965–72: Cleo, Great Expectations, The Happiest Days of Your Life, Sixty Thousand Nights, Romeo and Juliet, Measure For Measure; Eliza Doolittle in Pygmalion (Watford), Juliet in Romeo and Juliet, Julietta in Measure for Measure (both City Centre NY) 1967, Look Back in Anger (Royal Court) 1969, Celia in The Philanthropist (Mayfair and Broadway) 1970, Sally in Old Flames (Bristol Old Vic) 1974, Ann in Treats (Royal Court and Mayfair) 1975, Charlotte in Strawberry Fields, To Those Born Later (NT) 1976, Dr Scott in Whose Life Is It Anyway? (Mermaid and Savoy), Peter in Peter Pan 1979, Before The Party (also prodr, Queens Theatre) 1981, Ruth in Blithe Spirit (Vaudeville) 1986, Robot/Wife in Hence forward.... (Vaudeville) 1989, Lady Sneerwell in The School for Scandal (RNT) 1990, Diana in Making It Better (Hampstead & Criterion) 1992/93, Laura in The Shallow End (Royal Court) 1997, Barbara in Things we do for Love (Gielgud) 1998, House and Garden (Royal Nat Theatre) 2000, What the Butler Saw (Theatre Royal Bath and tour) 2001, Festen (Almeida and Lyric) 2004, The World's Biggest Diamond (Royal Court) 2006, Bedroom Farce (Rose Theatre Kingston) 2009, Snow White (Richmond Theatre) 2009–10, Reluctant Debutante (nat tour) 2011, The Importance of Being Earnest (Rose Kingston) 2011, Farewell to the Theatre (Rose Kingston) 2011, Charley's Aunt (Menier Chocolate Factory) 2012, Pride and Prejudice (Regents Park Open Air Theatre) 2013, Claudia in Moon Tiger (Theatre Royal Bath and nat tour) 2014; *Television* incl: The Mill on The Floss, The Recruiting Officer, Hedda Gabler, Brideshead Revisited 1981, Love is Old Love is New, Voyage Round My Father, East Lynne, Bright Smiler, The Mistress 1986, Wish Me Luck 1987–89, Eats for Treats 1990, Closing Numbers 1993, The Choir 1995, Good Living 1997 & 1998, Crossroads 2003, Marple 2005, New Tricks 2005, A for Andromeda 2006, Holby City 2007–10, The Palace 2008, Maestro 2008, The Old Guys 2009–10, Dancing On The Edge 2011, posh lady in Pompidou (BBC) 2014, Mary Douglas in Eve (CBBC) 2014, Stella 2015, Pompidou 2015; *Radio* incl: Crown House, Winter Journey (Sony Award); *Films* incl: Mandy 1951, Greengage Summer 1961, Alfie 1966, Deep End 1970, Henry VIII and His Six Wives 1970, Runners 1984, Dream Child 1985, Paris By Night 1988, Tirant lo Blanc 2005, Death at a Funeral 2007, I Give It A Year 2012, Drunk on Love 2014, DAting Eliza 2014, The Gigolo 2014, Burn Burn Burn 2015; *Books* Jane Asher's Party Cakes (1982), Jane Asher's Quick Party Cakes (1983), Jane Asher's Fancy Dress (1983), Silent Nights for You and Your Baby (1984), Easy Entertaining (1987), Moppy Is Happy (with G Scarfe, 1987), Moppy Is Angry (with G Scarfe, 1987), Keep Your Baby Safe (1988), Jane Asher's Children's Parties (1988), Calendar of Cakes (1989), Eats for Treats (1990), Jane Asher's Complete Book of Cake Decorating Ideas (1993), Time to Play (1995), The Longing (1996), 101 Things I wish I'd Known (1996), The Question (1998), The Best of Good Living (1998), Good Living at Christmas (1998), Tricks of the Trade (1999), Losing It (2002), Cakes for Fun (2005), Moppy is Sad, Moppy is Calm (with G Scarfe, 2005), Beautiful Baking (2007), Classic Chefs (2010); *Recreations* Times crossword, reading, music; *Style*— Jane Asher; ✉ c/o Olivia Homan, United Agents, 12–26 Lexington Street, London W1F 0LE (☎ 020 3214 0800, fax 020 3214 0801, website www.unitedagents.co.uk); website www.janeasher.com

ASHER, Jeremy; s of Gerald Asher, of San Francisco, USA, and Judith Asher, of London; *b* 16 July 1958; *Educ* Winchester, LSE (BSc), Harvard Grad Sch of Business Admin (MBA); *m* 1, 30 May 1985 (m dis), Barrie, *née* Gilbert; 3 s (Alexander b 16 April 1988, John b 12 Jan 1991, Tamerlane b 26 Feb 1994); m 2, 9 Sept 2012, Tobsha Learner; *Career* conslt rising to mangr Oliver Wyman Washington DC 1980–84, co-head Global Oil Products Glencore AG 1985–89, md Beta Raffinerieges Wilhelmshaven mbH 1990–97 (memb Supervisory Bd), gp chief exec PA Consulting Gp 1998–2001, chm SkyVision Holdings Ltd 2002–04, chm Agile Energy Ltd 2005–, chm Tower Resources plc 2011– (dir 2007–), dep chm Gulf Keystone Petroleum Ltd 2008–10 and 2013–14; dir: Better Place LLC 2008–10, Better Place BV and AS 2009–13, Pacific Drilling SA 2011–, Oil Refineries Ltd 2014; *Recreations* tennis, soccer; *Clubs* Queen's, Monte Carlo Country; *Style*— Jeremy Asher, Esq; ✉ Agile Energy Limited, Rue de Rhône 60, Case Postale 3093, 1211 Genève 3, Switzerland (☎ 00 41 22 316 6620, fax 00 41 22 316 6625, e-mail jeremy.asher@agilenergy.co.uk)

ASHER, Michael John; s of Frederick William Asher (d 1992), of Stamford, Lincs, and Kathleen Frances Kew (d 1992); *b* 21 April 1953; *Educ* Stamford Sch, Univ of Leeds (BA), Leeds Poly (CertEd); *m* 1986, Mariantonietta, only da of Gen Pasquale Peru, of Rome, Italy, and Prof Italia Peru; 1 s (Burton Frederick Pascal b 1991), 1 da (Jade Isabelle b 2001); *Career* author and explorer; served 2 Bn Parachute Reg Europe, Malyasia, NI 1971–74 (awarded GSM NI 1972), 23 Special Air Serv Reg 1974–77, 2 Section Special Patrol Gp RUC Belfast 1978–79; vol teacher remote rural areas Sudan 1979–82, lived with Bedouin tribe (Kababish) Sudan 1982–85, conslt UNICEF 1985, made first west-east crossing of Sahara by camel (4,500 miles, with Mariantonietta Peru) 1986–87, project offr UNICEF Red Sea Hills Sudan 1988–89; travel incl: Papua New Guinea, Thar Desert of India/Pakistan 1989–90, journeys of Wilfred Thesiger and various expeditions 1990–94, crossing of Great Sand Sea Egypt by camel 1991, Jordan, Syria, Lebanon, Sinai, Palestine and Tibet 1994–; presenter: In Search of Lawrence (Channel 4) 1997, Death Deceit and the Nile (Channel 4) 2000, The Real Bravo Two Zero (Channel 4) 2002; dir Survivors (KTN) 2005; author of articles for: The Guardian, The Washington Post, Readers' Digest, Daily Telegraph, Geographical, World; dir Lost Oasis Expeditions – adventure camel treks in the Sahara; RGS Ness Award for exploration 1993, RSGS Mungo Park Medal for exploration 1996; FRGS 1984, FRSL 1996; *Books* In Search of the Forty Days Road (1984), A Desert Dies (1986), Impossible Journey (1988), Shoot to Kill – A Soldier's Journey Through Violence (1990), Thesiger – A Biography (1994), The Last of the Bedu – In Search of the Myth (1996), Sahara (with Kazoyoshi Nomachi, 1996), Phoenix Rising – The United Arab Emirates, Past, Present and Future (with Werner Forman, 1996), Lawrence: The Uncrowned King of Arabia (1998), The Eye of Ra (1999), Firebird (2000), Rare Earth (2002), The Real Bravo Two Zero (2002), Sandstorm (2003), Get Rommel (2004), Khartoum – The Ultimate Imperial Adventure (2005), The Great Saharan Railway (2006); *Recreations* travel, running; *Clubs* Geographical; *Style*— Michael Asher, Esq, FRSL; ✉ c/o David Higham Associates Ltd, 7th Floor, Waverley House, 712 Noel Street, London W1F 8GQ (☎ 020 7437 7888, fax 020 7437 1072, e-mail anthonygoff@davidhigham.co.uk); website www.lost-oasis.org

ASHKENAZY, Vladimir; s of David Ashkenazy (d 1997), of Gorky, and Evstolia Plotnova (d 1979); *b* 6 July 1937; *Educ* Moscow Central Sch of Music, Moscow Conservatory (second prize Chopin int piano competition 1955, first prize Brussels int piano competition 1956, first prize Tchaikovsky int piano competition 1962); *m* 25 Feb 1961, Thorunn Sofia, da of Johann Tryggvason, of Iceland; 2 s (Vladimir Stefan b 1961, Dimitri Thor b 1969), 3 da (Nadia Liza b 1963, Sonia Edda b 1974, Alexandra Inga b 1979); *Career* concert pianist and conductor; studied under Lev Oborin class Moscow Conservatory 1955, debut in the UK with London Symphony Orch 1963, debut solo recital London (Festival Hall) 1963; music dir: Royal Philharmonic Orch London 1987–95, Radio Symphony Orch (now Deutsches Sinfonie-Orchester) Berlin 1989–99, Czech Philharmonic Orch 1998–2003, NHK Symphony Orch Tokyo 2004–07, EU Youth Orchestra 2006–, Sydney Symphony Orch 2009–; Hon RAM 1972; Order of Falcon Iceland 1988; *Books* Beyond Frontiers (with Jasper Parrott, 1985); *Style*— Vladimir Ashkenazy, Esq

ASHLEY, Bernard John; s of Alfred Walter Ashley (d 1967), and Vera, *née* Powell (d 1978); *b* 2 April 1935, Woolwich, London; *Educ* Sir Joseph Williamson's Mathematical Sch Rochester, Trent Park Coll of Educn, Cambridge Inst of Educn (Advanced DipEd); *m* 1957, Iris Frances, da of Harold Edward Holbrook; 3 s (Christopher b 1 Jan 1961, David b 1 June 1963, Jonathan b 17 April 1965); *Career* writer; teacher in Kent until 1965; head teacher: Hertford Heath CP Sch 1965–71, Hartley Jr Sch Newham 1971–77, Charlton Manor Jr Sch London 1977–95; memb: Writers' Guild of GB, BAFTA; Hon DEd Univ of Greenwich, Hon DLitt Univ of Leicester; *Novels* The Trouble with Donovan Croft (1974, The Other Award 1975), Terry on the Fence (1975), All My Men (1977), A Kind of Wild Justice (1979), Break in the Sun (1981), Dodgem (1983), High Pavement Blues (1984), Janey (1985), Running Scared (1986), Bad Blood (1988), Johnnie's Blitz (1995), Tiger Without Teeth (1998), Little Soldier (1999), Revenge House (2002), Freedom Flight (2003), Ten Days to Zero (2005), Smokescreen (2006), Down to the Wire (2006), Flashpoint (2007), Angel Boy (2008), Solitaire (2008), No Way to Go (2009), Ronnie's War (2010), Aftershock (2011), Dive Bombing (2012), Jack and the German Spy (2013), Shadow of the Zeppelin (2014), Dead End Kids (2015); *Short Story Collections* Clipper Street (1988), Seeing Off Uncle Jack (1991), Dockside School (1992), The Puffin Book of School Stories (1993), City Limits (1997), Hero Girls (2013), The Way It Is (2015); *Picture Books* Cleversticks (with Derek Brazell, 1992), I Forgot, said Troy (with Derek Brazell, 1996), A Present for Paul (with David Mitchell, 1996), Growing Good (with Anne Wilson, 1999), Double the Love (with Carol Thompson, 2002), The Bush (with Lynne Willey, 2003); *Television* BBC TV serials: Break In the Sun (1981), Running Scared (1986), The Country Boy (1989), Dodgem (1991, winner Best Children's Entertainment Prog, RTS 1992); Three Seven Eleven (Granada TV series), Justin and the Demon Drop Kick (Carlton for EBU); *Plays* The Old Woman who lived in a Cola Can (tour, 1988/89), The Secret of Theodore Brown (Unicorn Theatre London, 1990), Little Soldier (2007); *Recreations* theatre, concerts; *Style*— Bernard Ashley, Esq; ✉ Events Agent, Speaking of Books Ltd, 46B Vanbrugh Park, Blackheath, London SE3 7JQ (☎ 020 8858 6616, e mail jan@speakingofbooks.co.uk, website www.bashley.com)

ASHLEY, Dr Cedric; CBE (1984); s of Ronald Bednall Ashley (d 1980), and Gladys Vera, *née* Fincher; *b* 11 November 1936, Birmingham; *Educ* King Edward's Sch Birmingham, Univ of Birmingham (BSc, PhD); *m* 1, 1960, Pamela Jane (decd), da of William Turner;

1 s (Paul); m 2, 1965 (m dis 1989), (Marjorie) Vivien, da of Arnold Joseph Gooch (d 1960); 1 da (Juliet b 1967), 1 s (William b 1971); m 3, 1991, Auriol Mary Keogh, da of John Kelly; *Career* with Rolls-Royce Ltd Derby 1955–60; lectr Univ of Birmingham 1965–73 (ICI research fell 1963), int tech dir Bostrom Div UOP Ltd 1973–77, dir Motor Industry Research Assoc 1977–87, md Lotus Engineering Ltd 1987–88, chm Cedric Ashley and Associates 1988–, chief exec British Internal Combustion Engine Research Inst 1989–91, md Steyr Power Technology Ltd 1992–; dir Euromotor 1992–2006, chm euromotor-autotrain LLP 2006–; chm: SEE 1970–72, RAC Tech Ctee 1980–87, Kingsgate Property (Mgmnt) Ltd 2008–; memb: SMMT Tech Bds 1977–87, Bd Assoc of Independent Contract Research Orgns 1977–86 (pres 1982–84), Coventry and District Engrg Employers' Assoc 1978–85, Court Cranfield Inst of Technol 1977–87, Engine and Vehicles Ctee DTI 1980–88, Three Dimensional Design Bd CNAA 1981–87; tstee Sir Henry Royce Meml Fndn 2006–13; Cementation Muffelite Award SEE 1968, Design Cncl Award 1974; Liveryman Worshipful Co of Carmen; FIMechE 1978 (chm Automobile Div 1990–91), FRSA 1983; *Recreations* dining, travel, motoring; *Clubs* Thursday; *Style—* Dr Cedric Ashley, CBE; ✉ 58 Jacoby Place, Priory Road, Birmingham B5 7UW (☎ 0121 472 2082, e-mail c.ashley@autotrain.org, website www.autotrain.org)

ASHLEY, Prof Christopher Charles; s of Charles Arthur Ashley, and Esther Lillian Ashley; *b* 29 August 1941; *Educ* King George V GS Southport, Univ of Bristol (BSc, PhD), Univ of Oxford (MA, DSc); *m* 1967, Catherine Helen Brown; 1 s, 2 da; *Career* Fulbright travel scholar 1965–68, NIH post-doctoral fell Univ of Oregon 1965–68, MRC post-doctoral fell Univ of Bristol 1968–70, lectr in physiology Univ of Bristol 1970–76, visiting prof Univ of Bochum Germany 1976–77; Univ of Oxford: lectr 1976–, fell and med tutor CCC Oxford 1976–2008 (Corange fell 1991–2008), prof of physiology emeritus 2008–, emeritus fell CCC 2008–; adjunct prof of molecular and cellular pharmacology Univ of Miami Med Sch 1991–; external examiner: Univ of Dundee 1980–83, Univ of Liverpool 1988–90; memb: MRC Grants Ctee A 1988–92, Muscular Dystrophy Scientific Ctee 1993–, MRC Advsy Bd 1997–, MRC Coll of Experts 2005–; ed Cell Calcium 1980–90, co-founding ed J Muscle Research & Cell Motility 1980–, special advsr HEFCE Res Assessment Exercise 2001, memb Sectional Ctee 3 Acad of Med Sci 2007–; co-founding ed Jl of Muscle Research and Cell Motility 1980–, contrib and ed of numerous reviews and chapters on biophysics, skeletal and cardiac muscle activation, calcium signalling and bioluminescience-aequorin; awarded: NIH Prog Grant (CoPI) 1986–90 and 1990–95, MRC Prog Grant (PI) 1990–95, Br Heart Fndn Prog Grant (CoPI) 1997–2003 and 2003–; EMBO Fellowship DESY Hamburg 1988 and 1990; memb: Biochemical Soc, Physiological Soc, American Physiological Soc (elected foreign memb), US Biophysical Soc; Hon MRCP 1998, FMedSci 2002; *Recreations* music, playing the piano, fell walking, natural history, collecting; *Style—* Prof Christopher Ashley; ✉ Corpus Christi College, Oxford OX1 4JF (☎ 01865 272115, e-mail ash@nexus.ox.ac.uk)

ASHLEY, (Hon) Jackie; da of Baron Ashley of Stoke (Life Peer), *qv*, and Pauline Kay, *née* Crispin (d 2003); *b* 10 September 1954; *Educ* Rosebery GS Epsom, St Anne's Coll Oxford (BA); *m* Aug 1987, Andrew Marr, *qv*, s of Donald Marr; 1 s (Harry Cameron b 5 July 1989), 2 da (Isabel Claire b 4 Oct 1991, Emily Catherine b 3 Nov 1994); *Career* news trainee BBC 1978–80, prodr Newsnight 1980–82, politics prodr C4 News 1982–86, presenter Their Lordships House and The Parliament Programme 1986–88, political corr ITN 1988–98, political ed New Statesman 2000–02; currently: columnist The Guardian, presenter The Week in Westminster (BBC Radio 4); *Recreations* running, swimming; *Style—* Ms Jackie Ashley

ASHLEY-SMITH, Prof Jonathan; s of Ewart Trist Ashley-Smith (d 1972), of Sutton Valence, Kent, and Marian Tanfield, *née* Smith (d 2006); *b* 25 August 1946; *Educ* Sutton Valence, Univ of Bristol (BSc, PhD), Univ of Cambridge; *m* 19 Aug 1967, Diane Louise, *née* Wagland; 1 s (Joseph Daniel b 1975), 1 da (Zoë Elizabeth b 1985); *Career* V&A: scientific offr 1973–77, head of Conservation Dept 1977–2002, sr res fell in conservation studies 2002–04; visiting prof RCA 2000–10; project ldr within EU research project Climate for Culture 2009–14; memb: Conservation Ctee Cncl for Care of Churches 1978–85, Crafts Cncl 1980–83 (memb Conservation Ctee 1978–83), Bd of Govrs London Coll of Furniture 1983–85, Bd Cultural Heritage National Training Organisation (formerly Museums Training Inst) 1997–2005; UK Inst for Conservation: memb 1974–, memb Exec Ctee 1978–84, vice-chm 1980–83, chm 1983–84; sec gen Int Inst for Conservation 2003–06, tstee Leather Conservation Centre 2009–13; Plowden Medal winner 2000; hon fell RCA 1992, Leverhulme fell 1994–95; Fell Int Inst for Conservation (FIIC) 1985, FRSC 1987, CChem 1987, FMA 1988; *Books* Science for Conservators (scientific ed, Vols 1–3, 1984), Risk Assessment for Object Conservation (1999); author of articles in learned jls; *Recreations* legal combinations of driving fast, getting drunk, and heavy rock music; *Clubs* Anglesea; *Style—* Prof Jonathan Ashley-Smith; ✉ e-mail jonathan.ashley.smith.1994@wolfsonemail.com

ASHMORE, Prof Jonathan Felix; s of Eric Peter Ashmore (d 1997), of Fermoy, Co Cork, and Rosalie Sylvia, *née* Crutchley (d 1997); *b* 16 April 1948; *Educ* Westminster (Queen's scholar), Univ of Sussex (BSc), Imperial Coll London (PhD), UCL (MSc); *m* 1974, Sonia Elizabeth Newby, da of George Eric Newby, CBE, MC, FRSL (d 2006); 1 s (Joseph Prospero b 14 Nov 1974), 1 da (Lucia b 30 May 1979); *Career* visiting scientist ICTP Trieste 1971–72, Nuffield biological scholar 1972–74, research asst Dept of Biophysics UCL 1974–77, visiting research physiologist Dept of Ophthalmology Univ of Calif San Francisco 1977–80; Univ of Sussex: temp lectr 1980–82, MRC research assoc 1982–83; Univ of Bristol: lectr 1983–88, reader in physiology 1988–93, prof of biophysics 1993–96; Bernard Katz prof of biophysics UCL 1996–, dir UCL Ear Inst 2005; chief scientific advsr Defeating Deafness 2002–07; Fulbright scholar 1977–80, G L Brown prize lectr Physiological Soc 1992–93, chaire Blaise Pascal Institut Pasteur Paris 2007–09, Croonian Medal and lectr Royal Soc 2017; author of various research reports in learned jls; memb Physiological Soc 1980 (vice-pres 2010–12, pres 2012–14); Hon DSc Univ of Sussex 2016; FRS 1996, FMedSci 2001, FRSB 2016; *Recreations* reading, travel (virtual and actual); *Style—* Prof Jonathan Ashmore, FRS FMedSci; ✉ Department of Neuroscience, Physiology and Pharmacology & UCL Ear Institute, University College London, Gower Street, London WC1E 6BT (☎ 020 7679 2141, fax 020 7813 0530, e-mail j.ashmore@ucl.ac.uk, website www.inner-ear.org)

ASHTIANY, Saphieh (Sue); da of Ali Asghar Nourredin Ashtiany (d 2004), and Amir Banou Faily (d 1993); *b* Iran; *Educ* Padworth Coll, Univ of Warwick (BA), Univ of Birmingham (MSocSci); *m* 1973, Prof Paul Lyndon Davies; 2 da (Megan b 1979, Tessa b 1981); *Career* ptnr: Cole & Cole Slrs (later Morgan Cole) 1989–2001, Nabarro LLP 2001–10 (also head Employment Gp, special counsel 2010–14), prop Ashtiany Assocs 2010–; special advsr Univ of Oxford 2010–14; vice-pres: Industrial Law Soc 1998–, Employment Lawyers Assoc (memb Policy Sub-Ctee); chair Oxfordshire Advsy Bd Common Purpose 2000–03, cmmr Equal Opportunities Cmmn 2000–07, tstee Equal Rights Tst 2008– (chair 2014–), ambass for diversity in public office 2010–, cmmr LSE Cmmn of Inquiry (Women, Power and Inequality) 2014–; visiting prof fell Queen Mary Univ 2014–; non-exec dir and vice-chair Oxfordshire Ambulance NHS Tst 1993–2003 (actg chair 2001–03), non-exec dir Channel 4 2003–09; tstee Charities Aid Fndn 2010– (vice-chair 2012), dir Oxford Playhouse 2011–, tstee Oxford Philharmonic 2011– (chair Advsy Cncl), memb Advsy Cncl WNO 2014–; Asian Woman of Achievement 2008; hon fell Harris Manchester Coll Oxford 2003; FRSA 2004; *Publications* Britain's Migrant Workers (1976), Tolley's Employment Law (contributing ed, chapter on Race Discrimination), FT Law and Tax Employment Precedents and Company Documents (contributing ed); author of articles in specialist publications incl Lawyer Jl, Solicitors Jl, Employment Lawyers Assoc and Personnel Today; *Recreations* music, opera, dance, theatre; *Style—* Ms Saphieh Ashtiany; ✉ Ashtiany Associates, 21 Warnborough Road, Oxford OX2 6JA

ASHTON, Andrew Keith Maxwell; s of Sqdn Ldr Hugh Alan Ashton, DFC (d 1989), and Joan Maxwell, *née* Mann (d 2004); *b* 18 September 1950; *Educ* Framlingham Coll, Wells Cathedral Sch, Trent Poly, Univ of London (LLB); *m* 20 April 1985, Dr Patricia Mary White, da of Norman Ernest White (d 1981); 1 s (Richard), 1 da (Catherine); *Career* admitted slr 1974; ptnr HMG-Law LLP 1976–2007 (conslt 2007–10); dir: Jennings Of Garsington Ltd 2010–, Beechwood 2011–; dir and sec Hinksey Sculling Sch Ltd 2013–; memb: Wallingford Rowing Club, Warborough and Shillingford Soc, Friends of Westonbirt Arboretum; memb Law Soc; *Recreations* watching children and their sporting endeavours, bar mgmnt, taming the garden, travel; *Clubs* Law Soc; *Style—* Andrew Ashton, Esq; ✉ Little Cranford, Moulsford, Oxfordshire OX10 9HU (☎ 01491 651305); Beechwood, The Old Post Office, 19 Banbury Road, Kidlington, Oxford OX5 1AQ (☎ 01865 893344, mobile 07814 122344, e-mail andrew@beechwoodsolicitors.com)

ASHTON, Christine H; *b* Liverpool; *Educ* Univ of Manchester (MSc), MIT; *Career* North West Water 1977–88, prog mangr business transformation United Utilities 1989–91, mktg mangr Tydac 1991–92, head of business systems United Utilities 1992–98, head of business systems Cable & Wireless Communications 1998, chief technol offr Octel 1998–2000, chief info offr Caudwell Gp Singlepoint 2000–01, commercial dir TransIT Lattice Gp 2001; BP: chief technol offr BP European Energy 2001–03, vice-pres Gas, Power and Renewables 2004–05, chief info offr refining and mktg digital and communications technol BP plc 2005–07; gp strategy and chief technol offr TfL 2008–10; BG Gp: regnl chief info offr 2010–12, chief info offr security and strategy 2012; sr vice-pres Technol Thomson Reuters 2013–; non-exec dir Home Office 2000–05; technol conslt in large-scale companies and data-driven industries, STEM ambass and advocate for women in technol; FBCS, CEng; *Publications* Design Structure Matrix – Methods and Applications; *Recreations* charity fundraising; *Style—* Ms Christine H Ashton; ✉ Thomson Reuters, 30 South Colonnade, Canary Wharf, London E14 5EP (e-mail christine.ashton@thomsonreuters.com)

ASHTON, David Julian; *b* 23 October 1948; *Educ* LSE (BSc); *m* April 1976, Marilyn Joy Ashton; 2 s (Richard b July 1977, Michael b March 1981); *Career* ptnr Arthur Andersen 1982–2002 (joined 1970), sr md LECG/FTI 2002–; memb Regulatory Decisions Ctee FCA 2006–; cncllr London Borough of Harrow 1998–2010 (ldr 2008–10); MEI (MInstPet), FCA; fell Acad of Experts (FAE), FIArb; *Recreations* politics, skiing, walking; *Style—* David Ashton, Esq; ✉ FTI Consulting LLP, 200 Aldersgate Aldersgate Street, London EC1A 4HD (☎ 020 3727 1027, fax 020 7632 5050, e-mail david.ashton@fticonsulting.com)

ASHTON, Prof John Richard; CBE (2000); s of Edward Ashton (d 1978), of Woolton, and Lena Irene Ashton, *née* Pettit (d 2005); *b* 27 May 1947, Woolton, Liverpool; *Educ* Quarry Bank HS Liverpool, Univ of Newcastle upon Tyne Med Sch (Nuffield Fndn scholar in tropical med Fiji Islands, Charlton scholar in med, MB BS), LSHTM (MSc, Sir Allen Daley meml prize in social med); *m* 1, 1968 (m dis 2001), Pamela Doreen, *née* Scott; 3 s (Keir Edward, Matthew James, Nicholas John); m 2, 2003, Catherine Benedicte Montague Ashton (aka Maggi Morris); 1 s (Fabian Ché Jed), 2 step s (Alesaunder James Wystan, Dylan Carey Michael); *Career* house physician and house surgn Newcastle upon Tyne Univ Hosp Gp 1970–71, gen practice locum Great Yarmouth and Mid Wales 1971, SHO in gen med and geriatrics 1971–72, SHO and registrar psychiatry 1972–74, princ in gen practice Newcastle upon Tyne and Northumberland 1974–75, lectr in primary med care (mental health) Univ of Southampton and princ in gen practice Hants Family Practitioner Ctee 1975–76, postgrad student in social med LSHTM 1976–78, sr registrar in community med Hants and lectr in community med Univ of Southampton 1978–79, sr lectr Dept of Community Med LSHTM 1980–82, sr lectr Dept of Public Health Univ of Liverpool 1983–93 (personal chair in public health policy and strategy 1993), dir Liverpool Public Health Observatory 1990–93; regnl dir of public health and regnl med offr: Mersey RHA 1993–94, NW Regnl Office NHS Exec 1994–2002, Govt Office NW 2002–06; dir of public health and county med offr Cumbria 2007–; pres Faculty of Public Health Royal Colleges of Physicians of London, Edinburgh and Glasgow 2013–, pres Epidemiology and Public Health Section RSM 2014–; external examiner Galway Coll, TCD, UCD and Cork Univ Coll; visiting prof Valencian Inst for Public Health Studies 1988, professorial fell Liverpool Sch of Tropical Med 1994, Oliver Tambo visiting prof Cape Town 1997, Wei Lun visiting prof Univ of Hong Kong 1998; visiting prof: Liverpool John Moores Univ 1998, Univ of Manchester 2001–, Univ of Central Lancs 2004, Univ of Lancaster 2006, Univ of Cumbria 2007; Chadwick lectr Chartered Inst of Environmental Health Officers 1990, Chadwick lectr Univ of Manchester 1997, Milroy lectr RCP London 2000, Audrey Wise lectr Univ of Central Lancashire 2005; Kings Fund Scholar N America 1974, Premio Nenufar Award for contributions to int public health Galicia 1997, Alwyn Smith Medal Faculty of Public Health Med for lifelong contribs to public health 2002; inaugural coordinator Euro WHO Healthy Cities Project 1986–88; advsr to WHO on the devpt of educn progs the devpt of city-based public health strategies (Europe, Eastern Mediterranean, The Americas, SE Asia); gen rapporteur 44th World Health Assembly Tech Discussions on urban health Geneva 1991; jt ed (with Prof Carlos Alvarez, Alicante) Jl of Epidemiology and Community Health 1998–2008; memb: Int Scientific Advsy Gp Inst of Public Health Valencia 1995, NW Regnl Assembly and NW RDA Health Partnership 1999–2001, Br Humanitarian Aid Delgn to Kosovo 1999; former memb Bd Faculty of Public Health Med and Exec RCP, tstee UK Public Health Assoc 2009–11, tstee Kendal Arts Int 2012–13; fndr memb The Duncan Soc Liverpool 1997; cncllr Hampshire CC 1981–82 (memb Educn and Police Ctees), chm of tstees Carston Cultural Village Liverpool 2006–09; tstee: Merseyside Fire Support Network 2007–10, Carlisle Youth Zone 2010–13, Nat Museums of Liverpool 2011–; govr Royal Liverpool Children's NHS Tst 2007–10, govr West Lakes Academy Cumbria 2008–10; life pres Duncan Soc 2010–; volunteer bus driver Western Dales Community Bus; hon fell Liverpool John Moores Univ 2003, fell Univ of Cumbria 2014; FFPHM 1986 (MFPHM 1979), MFFPRHC 1993, FRCPsych 1993 (MRCPsych 1975), FRCPEd 2003, FRCP 2004, FRSM 2007, FRSA 2012; *Books* Everyday Psychiatry (1980), Esmedune 2000 (A Healthy Liverpool) – Vision or Dream? (1986), The New Public Health – The Liverpool Experience (with H Seymour, 1988, Spanish edn 1990), Healthy Cities (ed, 1991), The Urban Health Crisis – Strategies for All in the Face of Rapid Urbanisation (ed, 1991), The Epidemiological Imagination – A Reader (ed, 1994), The Pool of Life – A Public Health Walk in Liverpool (with Maggi Morris, 1997, 2 edn 2008), The Gift Relationship (ed with Ann Oakley); also author of numerous book chapters, papers and editorials in learned jls; *Recreations* family, small holding, poultry keeping, walking and cycling, Liverpool FC, reading the papers; *Style—* John Ashton; ✉ 8 Church Road, Much Woolton, Liverpool L25 5JF (e-mail johnrashton@blueyonder.co.uk)

ASHTON, Prof Rosemary Doreen; OBE (1999); *b* 11 April 1947; *Educ* Univ of Aberdeen (MA, Seafield medal, Senatus prize), Newnham Coll Cambridge (Lucy fell, PhD); *Family* 3 c; *Career* temp lectr in English Univ of Birmingham 1973–74; UCL: lectr in English 1974–86, reader in English 1986–91, prof of English 1991–, Quain prof of English language and literature 2002–12, emeritus Quain prof and hon fell 2013–; Deutscher Akademischer Austauschdienst (DAAD) Stipendium Univ of Heidelberg 1966–67, Literary Review Award for The German Idea 1980, DAAD Travel Scholarship 1983, British Acad Thank-Offering to Britain fell 1984–85, British Acad Research Readership

1988–90, visiting fell Beinecke Library Yale Univ 1989, Leverhulme Res Fellowship 1995, sr research fell Inst of English Studies Sch of Advanced Study Univ of London 2012; memb Humanities Research Bd Br Acad; founding fell Eng Assoc 2000; FRSL 1999, FBA 2000, FRSA 2002; *Books* The German Idea: Four English Writers and the Reception of German Thought 1800–1860 (1980), George Eliot (1983), Little Germany: Exile and Asylum in Victorian England (1986), The Mill on the Floss: A Natural History (1990), G H Lewes: A Life (1991), The Life of Samuel Taylor Coleridge: A Critical Biography (1996), George Eliot: A Life (1996), Thomas and Jane Carlyle: Portrait of a Marriage (2002), 142 Strand: A Radical Address in Victorian London (2006), Victorian Bloomsbury (2012); author of numerous edition introductions and articles and reviews in jls; *Style*— Prof Rosemary Ashton, OBE, FBA; ✉ University College London, Gower Street, London WC1E 6BT (e-mail r.ashton@ucl.ac.uk)

ASHTON, William Michael Allingham; OBE (2010, MBE 1978); s of Eric Sandiford Ashton (d 1983), of Lytham St Annes, and Zilla Dorothea, *née* Miles (d 1944); *b* 6 December 1936; *Educ* Rossall Sch, St Peter's Coll Oxford (MA, DipEd); *m* 22 Oct 1966, Kay Carol, da of John Stallard Watkins (d 2000), of New Quay, Dyfed; 2 s (Grant b 1967, Miles b 1968), 1 da (Helen b 1983); *Career* Nat Serv RAF 1955–57; fndr and musical dir Nat Youth Jazz Orchestra (NYJO) 1965–; numerous appearances before royalty incl Royal Variety Performance 1978, toured many countries on behalf of Br Cncl (USA, USSR, Aust, Turkey); chm NYJO Ltd 1972– (pres and founding musical dir); composer of over 60 recorded songs; memb: Musicians' Union, Br Assoc of Jazz Musicians; owner Stanza Music; fell Leeds Coll of Music 1995; *Awards* for NYJO: Best Br Big Band Br Jazz Awards 1993, 1995, 1998 and 2002, Critics' Choice 1992, 1995 and 1997, BBC Radio 2 Award for Servs to Jazz 1995, Silver Jazz Medal Worshipful Co of Musicians 1996, All Party Parly Jazz Appreciation Gp Special Award 2007; *Recreations* reading, song writing, snorkelling; *Style*— William Ashton, Esq, OBE; ✉ 11 Victor Road, Harrow, Middlesex HA2 6PT (✆ 020 8863 2717, e-mail bill.ashton@virgin.net, website www.nyjo.org.uk)

ASHTON OF UPHOLLAND, Baroness (Life Peer UK 1999), of St Albans in the County of Hertfordshire; Catherine Margaret Ashton; PC (2006); da of late Harold Ashton, and late Clare Margaret Ashton; *b* 20 March 1956, Upholland, Lancs; *Educ* Upholland GS, Bedford Coll London (BSc); *m* 1988, Peter Jon Kellner, *qv*, s of late Michael Kellner; 1 s (Hon Robert Peter b 1989), 1 da (Hon Rebecca Clare b 1992), 2 step da (Tara b 1977, Katherine b 1979), 1 step s (Michael b 1981); *Career* administrative offr CND 1977–79, Coverdale Orgn 1979–81, Central Cncl for Educn and Trg in Social Work 1981–83, dir of community devpt and public affrs Business in the Community 1983–89, public policy advsr 1989–, dir Political Context 1996–98, seconded by London First to Home Office 1998–99; Parly under-sec of state: DfES 2001–04, DCA 2004–07, Miny of Justice 2007; ldr House of Lords and Lord Pres of the Cncl 2007–08, EU cmmr for external trade 2008–; chm Herts HA 1998–2001; advsr Lattice Fndn 2000–01, tstee Verulanium Museum, patron Grove Hospice St Albans, ambass Herts Guides; Min of the Year House Magazine 2005, Peer of the Year Channel 4 2005, Politician of the Year Stonewall 2006; *Clubs* Royal Cwlth Soc; *Style*— The Baroness Ashton of Upholland, PC; ✉ House of Lords, London SW1A 0PW (✆ 020 7210 8708, fax 020 7210 8620, e-mail catherine.ashton@cabinet-office.x.gsi.gov.uk)

ASHURST, Mark; *b* 10 May 1970, Bristol; *Educ* King Edward VI Sch Southampton, Itchen Sixth Form Coll Southampton, Ecole Nationale de la Musique Paris, Ecole Normale de la Musique Paris, UC Oxford (BA); *Career* writer and broadcaster; asst to Simon Hughes, MP, *qv*, 1992, copywriter Matla Tst (South African voter education gp) 1993–94 (also observer for Westminster Fndn for Democracy), political and media reporter Business Day South Africa 1994, conslt Strategic Planning Unit South African Broadcasting Corp 1995, South African corr FT 1995–98, business ed BBC Africa 1998–; prodr Fabulous (BBC Radio 5) 1993, presenter Crossing Continents (BBC Radio 4) 2002, contrib From Our Own Correspondent (BBC Radio 4); contrib: The Guardian, The Independent, Daily Telegraph, Newsweek, BBC Radio 5, BBC World, BBC News 24 TV; former columnist Independent Newspapers of South Africa; speechwriter Nelson Mandela's opening address to Union of African Radio and TV Broadcasters Congress Johannesburg 1995; one-man show Harare Int Festival of Arts Zimbabwe 2001; dir Africa Research Inst 2006–; Zanzibar Int Film Festival 2002; *Publications* The Day After Mugabe: Prospects for Change in Zimbabwe (jt ed), A Parliament with Teeth, for Tanzania (jtly); *Style*— Mark Ashurst, Esq; ✉ website www.africaresearchinstitute.org)

ASHWORTH, Prof Alan; s of Arthur Ashworth, and Dorothy Ashworth; *b* Bolton, Lancs; *Educ* Imperial Coll London (BSc), UCL (PhD); *m* 2011, Dr Amanda McGuigan; *Career* Inst of Cancer Research: joined 1986, dir Breakthrough Breast Cancer Research Centre 1999–2011, chief exec 2011–14; pres UCSF Helen Diller Family Comprehensive Cancer Centre; FRS 2008; *Style*— Prof Alan Ashworth, FRS; ✉ UCSF Helen Diller Family Comprehensive Cancer Centre, 1450 3rd Street, San Francisco, California, USA 94158

ASHWORTH, Prof Andrew John; CBE (2009), Hon QC (1997); s of Clifford Ashworth (d 1993), and Amy, *née* Ogden (d 2005); *b* 11 October 1947; *Educ* Rishworth Sch, LSE (LLB), New Coll Oxford (DCL), Univ of Manchester (PhD); *m* 1, 1971 (m dis), Gillian, *née* Frisby; 2 da (Susannah b 1974, Alison b 1976); m 2, Veronica, *née* Fellows; *Career* lectr then sr lectr in law Univ of Manchester 1970–78, fell and tutor in law Worcester Coll Oxford 1978–88, Edmund-Davies prof of criminal law and criminal justice KCL 1988–97, Vinerian prof of English law Univ of Oxford 1997–2013; ed Criminal Law Review 1975–99; memb Sentencing Advsy Panel 1999–2010 (chair 2007–10); bencher Inner Temple 1997; Hon LLD De Montfort Univ 1998, Hon JD Univ of Uppsala 2003, Hon LLD LSE 2014; FBA 1993; *Books* Principles of Criminal Law (1991, 8 edn 2016), Sentencing and Criminal Justice (1992, 6 edn 2015), The Criminal Process (1994, 4 edn 2010), Positive Obligations in Criminal Law (2013); *Recreations* travel, walking, bridge; *Style*— Prof Andrew Ashworth, CBE, QC, FBA; ✉ All Souls College, Oxford OX1 4AL (✆ 01865 279379, fax 01865 279299)

ASHWORTH, Anne Mary Catherine; s of Peter Ashworth (d 1997), of Wimbledon, and Joan, *née* Kay (d 1975); *b* 13 June 1954; *Educ* Ursuline Convent Wimbledon, King's Coll London (BA); *m* 1985, Tom Maddocks; 1 s (George b 1990); *Career* journalist; Accountancy magazine 1980–82, Sunday Express 1982–86, Today 1986, Daily Mail 1986–87, personal fin ed and assoc city ed Mail on Sunday 1987–94, personal fin ed then asst ed and property ed The Times 1994–; *Style*— Ms Anne Ashworth; ✉ The Times, 3 Thomas More Square, London E98 1XY

ASHWORTH, Jonathan; MP; *b* 14 October 1978, Salford, Lancs; *Educ* Univ of Durham; *m* Emilie Oldknow; 2 da (Grace, Annie); *Career* formerly: advsr to Rt Hon Gordon Brown, MP, head of party rels for Rt Hon Ed Miliband, MP, *qqv*; MP (Lab) Leicester S 2011–, shadow min without portfolio 2015–; *Recreations* cinema, fashion, music, reading, boxing, travel; *Clubs* Saffron Lane Working Men's; *Style*— Jonathan Ashworth, Esq, MP; ✉ House of Commons, London SW1A 0AA

ASHWORTH, Richard James; MEP; s of Maurice Ashworth, of Rye, E Sussex, and Eileen, *née* Simpson (d 1983); *b* 17 September 1947, Folkestone, Kent; *Educ* King's Sch Canterbury, Seale Hayne Coll Newton Abbott (NDA, Coll Dip in Agric (CDA), Coll Dip in Farm Mgmnt (CDFM)); *m* 6 Oct 1973, Sally, *née* Poulton; 3 da (Phillipa b 21 Jan 1976, Sarah b 13 May 1977, Joanna b 20 June 1979); *Career* farmer E Sussex 1970–2001; chm United Milk plc 1995–2003; MEP (Cons) SE England 2004– (UK Parly candidate N Devon 1997, European Parly candidate 1999), memb European Budget Ctee and European Agriculture Ctee, ldr Br Cons in the European Parl 2012–; chm Plumpton Coll 1992–2000; *Recreations* sport, music, country pursuits; *Clubs* Farmers'; *Style*— Richard Ashworth, Esq, MEP; ✉ Woodside, Brickhouse Lane, Newchapel, Lingfield, Surrey RH7 6HY (✆ 01342 604346); 5 Hazelgrove Road, Haywards Heath, West Sussex RH16 3PH (✆ 01444 474858, website www.richardashworth.com); WIB 6M 105, European Parliament, Rue Wiertz, B-1047 Brussels, Belgium (✆ 0032 228 45309, e-mail richardjames.ashworth@europarl.europa.eu)

ASKEW, Adrian William; *b* 21 May 1948, Guildford, Surrey; *Educ* St Michael's Coll Hitchin; *m* Jean; 1 s (Nathan), 2 da (Claudine, Katherine); *Career* trade unionist; engrg fitter Borg Warner Ltd 1968–71, memb and shop steward AEU 1968–71, engr British Aircraft Corp 1971–74; APEX: memb Assoc of Professional, Exec Clerical and Computer Staff (jtly APEX/GMB) 1971–, sr rep and branch sec 1972–74, area organiser 1974–77; EMA: negotiating offr Engrs and Mangrs Assoc 1977–80, gen sec Shipbuilding and Engrg Gp 1980–87; Soc of Telecom Execs (now Connect): asst sec 1987–96, dep gen sec 1996–2002, gen sec 2003– (gen sec designate 2002–03); pres Uni Europa Telecom 2007–; memb: Bd Shipbuilding Industry Trg Assoc 1982–87, Shipbuilding Negotiating Ctee Confedn of Shipbuilding and Engrg Unions 1984–87, EU Telecoms Social Dialogue Ctee 2002–, Bd e-Skills Sector Skills Cncl 2005–, Bd Union Modernisation Fund 2005–; memb Lab Pty 1972–; *Recreations* music, skiing; *Style*— Mr Adrian Askew; ✉ Connect, 30 St George's Road, Wimbledon, London SW19 4BD

ASKEW, Mark David; s of Nelson William Askew, of Rathmell, N Yorks, and Joan Margaret, *née* Taylor; *b* 24 July 1971, Lancaster; *Educ* Settle HS Yorks, Craven Coll Skipton; *m* 22 Oct 2005, Jane Frances, *née* Alexander; 1 s (Alife Nelson Jameson b 21 Jan 2009 (twin)), 1 da (Mabel Maud Mary b 21 Jan 2009 (twin)); *Career* chef; commis chef Savoy Hotel 1989–91; chef de partie: La Tante Claire 1991–92, Connaught Hotel 1992–94, Nico at 90 1994–95; chef de partie then sous chef Aubergine Restaurant 1995–97, commis chef Michel Bras Laguiole France 1997, chef de partie Les Maisons Bricourt Concale France 1998, head chef Aubergine Restaurant 1999, exec head chef Gordon Ramsay Holdings 1999–; co-fndr and operations dir Cirrus Inns 2012–, dir Jackson & Rye Restaurant 2013–, dir Grillshack Restaurant 2013–; *Clubs* Groucho; *Style*— Mark Askew, Esq; ✉ 106 Randolph Avenue, London W9 1PQ (✆ 07958 237322, e-mail markaskew1@yahoo.co.uk, Twitter @markaskew1)

ASLAM, Nadeem; *b* Pakistan; *Career* writer; *Books* Season of the Rainbirds (1993, Betty Trask Award, Best First Novel Author's Club Award, shortlisted Best First Novel Whitbread Award, shortlisted John Llewelyn Rhys Memorial Prize, longlist Booker Prize), Maps for Lost Lovers (2006, Kiriyama Prize 2005, shortlisted IMPAC 2006), The Wasted Vigil (2008), The Blind Man's Garden (2013); *Style*— Nadeem Aslam, Esq

ASLET, Clive William; s of Kenneth Charles Aslet, and Monica, *née* Humphreys; *b* 15 February 1955; *Educ* KCS Wimbledon, Peterhouse Cambridge (MA); *m* 27 Sept 1980, Naomi Selma, da of Prof Sir Martin Roth; 3 s (William Kenneth Samuel b 26 May 1995, John Francis Independence b 4 July 1997, Charles Emmanuel Martin b 21 Dec 2000); *Career* Country Life: architectural writer 1977–84, architectural ed 1984–88, dep ed 1988–92, ed 1993–2006, ed-at-large 2006–15; founding hon sec The Thirties Soc 1979–87, co-fndr Remember WW1 2013; *Books* The Last Country Houses (1982), The National Trust Book of the English House (with Alan Powers, 1985), Quinlan Terry, The Revival of Architecture (1986), The American Country House (1990), Countryblast (1991), Anyone for England? (1997), Inside The House of Lords (with Derry Moore, 1998), The Story of Greenwich (1999), Greenwich Millennium (2000), A Horse in the Country (2001), Landmarks of Britain (2005), The English House (2008), Villages of Britain (2010), The Edwardian Country House (2012), War Memorial (2012), An Exuberant Catalogue of Dreams (2013), The Birdcage (novel, 2014), The Age of Empire (2015); *Recreations* pleasures of the table, wool gathering; *Clubs* Garrick; *Style*— Clive Aslet, Esq; ✉ c/o Adrian Sington, Kruger Cowne Ltd, Unit 7c, 15 Lots Road, Chelsea Wharf, London SW10 0QJ (✆ 020 3124 1860, e-mail adrian@sington.co.uk)

ASLETT, Judy Jane; da of Michael Eric Aslett, and Gillian, *née* Kenyon; *b* 1 October 1962; *Educ* Culford Sch, Univ of St Andrews, Central London Poly (BA); *m* 1991, John Stephen, s of Stephen Parkin; 1 da (Emily Claire b 16 June 1992); *Career* editorial trainee ITN 1986–87, prodr Independent TV News 1987–90, corr South Africa Channel 4 News 1991–95 (Sky News 1990–91), foreign ed Channel 4 News 1995–97, diplomatic ed Channel 5 1997–2000, dir Streamline Productions 2000–; *Style*— Ms Judy Aslett; ✉ Streamline Productions, Hill Croft, Hartley Road, Cranbrook, Kent TN17 3QP

ASPDEN, Peter James; s of William James Aspden, and Aphrodite Aspden; *Educ* Latymer Upper Sch, St Edmund Hall Oxford, City Univ (Dip Journalism); *Career* journalist: Cambridge Evening News 1980–84, The Times Higher Education Supplement 1985–94, Financial Times 1994– (currently arts writer); *Recreations* watching Queens Park Rangers FC; *Style*— Peter Aspden, Esq; ✉ Financial Times, 1 Southwark Bridge, London SE1 9HL (✆ 020 7873 3450, e-mail peter.aspden@ft.com)

ASPEL, Michael Terence; OBE (1993); s of Edward Aspel, and Violet Aspel; *b* 12 January 1933; *Educ* Emanuel Sch; *m* 1, 1957 (m dis), Dian; 2 s (Gregory (decd), Richard); m 2, 1962 (m dis), Ann; 1 s (Edward), 1 da (Jane (twin)); m 3, 1977, Elizabeth Power; 2 s (Patrick, Daniel); *Career* writer and broadcaster; Nat Serv KRRC and Para Regt TA 1951–53; radio actor 1954–57, BBC TV news reader 1960–68 (announcer 1957–60), freelance 1968–; daily show Capital Radio 1974–84; presenter: The Six O'Clock Show (LWT), Aspel & Company (LWT) 1984–93, This Is Your Life (Thames TV until 1994 thereafter BBC TV) 1988–2003, BAFTA Awards, Strange... But True? (LWT), Antiques Roadshow (BBC TV) 2000–; Independent Radio Personality Variety Club Award 1983, ITV Personality Variety Club Award 1988, elected to RTS Hall of Fame 1996; vice-pres Baby Life Support Systems (BLISS) 1981–, hon vice-pres Assoc for Spina Bifida and Hydrocephalus (ASBAH) 1985–, patron Plan International 1986–; hon fell Cardiff Univ 2002; *Books* Polly Wants a Zebra (autobiography, 1974), Hang On! (for children, 1982); *Recreations* theatre, cinema, eating, travel, water sports; *Clubs* Lord's Taverners, RYA; *Style*— Michael Aspel, Esq, OBE; ✉ c/o Christina Shepherd, 4th Floor, 45 Maddox Street, London W1S 2PE (✆ 020 7495 7813, fax 020 7499 7535)

ASPINALL, Beverley Ann; da of David Thomas (d 1962), and Joyce Browning, *née* Ling; *b* 4 December 1958, Beds; *Educ* Univ of York (BA), Univ of Bedfordshire (DBA); *m* 15 June 2002, David Aspinall; 1 da (Eleanor Charlotte Bolton b 16 Jan 1989), 1 s (James Rhys Day Bolton b 19 Nov 1990); *Career* John Lewis Partnership: joined 1981, various roles in buying and selling, md John Lewis Peterborough 1995–97, md Peter Jones 1997–2005; md Fortnum & Mason 2005–12; non-exec dir Foyles 2014–; non-exec dir Univ of York Devpt Bd 2006–11; MInstD; *Recreations* classical music, gardening; *Style*— Mrs Beverley Aspinall

ASPINALL, Robin Michael; *b* 3 August 1949; *Educ* Cathedral Sch Bristol, Lancaster Univ (BA (Econ)), Univ of Manchester (MA (Econ)); *m*; 2 s; *Career* Barclays Bank plc 1966–69, univ 1969–73, mangr of forecasting Economic Models Ltd 1973–76, head of economics Imperial Group plc 1976–86, chief economist Schroder Securities Ltd 1986–89, dir of currency economics Security Pacific/Hoare Govett 1989–90, chief economist Schroders 1991–92, chief economist/strategist Panmure Gordon & Co 1992–96, chief economist Financial Mkts Europe National Australia Bank 1996–2000, co economist Teather & Greenwood Ltd 2000–02, currently with Rhombus Research Ltd; *Style*— Robin Aspinall, Esq

ASPINALL, Wilfred; *b* 14 September 1942; *Educ* Poynton Secdy Modern Sch, Stockport Coll for Further Educn; *m* 1973, Judith Mary (d 2005); 1 da (Isabel b 1980); *Career* memb European Econ and Social Consultative Assembly Brussels (MESC) 1986–98, princ Aspinall & Assocs and Aspinall Brussels Professionals in Europe 1990–; dir EU Public

Affairs Eversheds 1998–2000, EU Policy and Strategy advsr Eversheds Fin Serv Forum 2000–09, estab The Forum in the European Parliament for Construction (FOCOPE) European Parl 2003–; with National Provincial Bank Ltd 1960–69, asst gen sec Nat Westminster Staff Assoc 1969–75, memb Banking Staff Cncl 1970–77, gen sec Confedn of Bank Staff Assoc 1975–79, treas and conslt Managerial Professional and Staff Liaison Gp 1978–79; exec dir and conslt Fedn of Managerial Professional and General Assocs (MPG) 1979–94, vice-pres Confédération Européen des Cadres 1979–94, established The Strategy Centre Brussels 2004; memb: Hammersmith Special HA 1982–90, North Herts Dist HA 1982–86, North West Thames RHA 1986–88; *Publications* incl submission to House of Commons European Scrutiny Committee on the negotiations with the EU (2015); *Recreations* self-build house construction 2002–03 and 2015–; *Style—* Wilfred Aspinall, Esq; ✉ The Coach House, Shillington Road, Pirton, Hitchin, Hertfordshire SG5 3QJ (☎ 01462 712316, mobile 07872 953922, e-mail wilfredaspinall@me.com or wa@wilfredaspinall.eu)

ASPREY, William Rolls; s of John Rolls Asprey, of London, and Katrina Pauline Milnes Gaskell, *née* Culverwell; *b* 27 November 1965, London; *Educ* Monkton Combe Sr Sch, RMA Sandhurst; *m* 16 July 1994, Lucinda Jane, *née* Kinnell; 2 da (Emily Charlotte b 2 July 1996, Annabel Rachel b 16 Nov 1997), 1 s (Thomas John Rolls b 26 Sept 1999); *Career* Royal Green Jackets 3 Bn 1987–90; Asprey Bond Street 1990–99, William & Son 1999–; memb: Worshipful Co of Gunmakers, Worshipful Co of Goldsmiths; *Recreations* shooting, skiing, wine, food; *Clubs* Mark's, George, Walbrook, Annabel's; *Style—* William Asprey, Esq; ✉ William & Son, 34–36 Bruton Street, London W1J 6QX (☎ 020 7493 8385, fax 020 7493 8386, e-mail william.asprey@williamandson.com)

ASQUITH, The Hon Sir Dominic Anthony Gerard; KCMG (2012, CMG 2004); s of 2 Earl of Oxford and Asquith, KCMG, *qv*; *b* 7 February 1957, Zanzibar; *m* 12 May 1988, Louise E, only da of John E Cotton, of Wollaton, Nottingham; 2 da, 2 s; *Career* diplomat; Soviet Dept FCO 1983–84, Southern European Dept FCO 1984–85, 2 sec Damascus 1986–87, 1 sec (chancery) Muscat 1987–89, EC Dept (Internal) FCO 1989–90, private sec to Min of State FCO 1990–92, 1 sec Washington 1992–96, Drugs and Int Crime Dept FCO 1996, min and dep head of mission Buenos Aires 1997–2001, dep head of mission and consul-gen Riyadh 2001–04, dep special rep for Iraq and dep head of mission Baghdad 2004, dir Iraq FCO 2004–06, ambass to Iraq 2006–07, ambass to Egypt 2007–11, ambass to Libya 2011–13; *Style—* The Hon Sir Dominic Asquith, KCMG

ASTALL, (Amanda) Elisabeth (Lis); da of John W Iceton, of St Duen, Jersey, and Wendy Iceton; *b* 28 June 1960, St Helier, Jersey; *Educ* Jersey Ladies Coll St Helier, Université de Nice, LSE (BA); *m* 30 July 1988 (m dis 2011), Mark Astall; 1 da (Katie b 9 Nov 1989); *Career* Accenture (previously Arthur Andersen, then Andersen Consulting): joined as mgmnt info conslt 1984, ptnr 1994, global head of human servs industry 1997–98, global head of strategy in govt 1999–2001, chm UK and Ireland Cncl 2002–06, UK md 2003–06, Europe, Africa and Latin America md for govt 2006–09; non-exec dir: Defence Science and Technol Lab 2010–, Digital Jersey 2012–, Hyder plc 2013–14, UK Sport 2013–; memb: Nat Employment Panel 2003–07, E-skills Bd for Technol 2003–06, Cncl for Industry and HE 2003–06; vice-patron Working Families 2004–10, tstee Social Mobility Fndn 2007–, pres Br Show Jumping 2009–12, chm PPR Fndn (Brain Tumour Research); memb Cncl LSE 2008–; *Recreations* horse riding, sailing, skiing; *Style—* Mrs Lis Astall

ASTARITA, Mark; OBE (2015); *Career* dep chief exec Nat Deaf Children's Soc until 2003, dir of fundraising Br Red Cross 2003–; chair Inst of Fundraising 2011– (tstee 2008–); *Style—* Mark Astarita, Esq, OBE; ✉ British Red Cross, 44 Moorfields, London EC2Y 9AL

ASTBURY, Nicholas Paul (Nick); s of Nigel Astbury, and Yvonne, *née* Harburn; *b* 13 August 1971, Buenos Aires, Argentina; *Educ* Hills Road Sixth Form Coll Cambridge, UCL (BA, MA); *Career* entered HM Dip Serv 1994, desk offr EU Dept FCO 1994–95, second sec (Chancery) Colombo 1995–99, head of section EU Dept FCO 1999–2000, EU spokesman News Dept FCO 2001, private sec Parly Under Sec of State's Office FCO 2001–02, dep head of UK visas FCO 2002–04, dep head British Embassy Drugs Team Kabul 2005, ambass to Eritrea 2006–08, currently head Sudan Unit FCO; *Style—* Mr Nick Astbury

ASTLEY, Dr Neil Philip; s of Philip Thomas Astley, of Adelaide, Aust, and Margaret Ivy Astley (d 1976); *b* 12 May 1953; *Educ* Price's Sch Fareham, Univ of Newcastle upon Tyne (BA); *Career* md and ed Bloodaxe Books Ltd (fndr 1978); Hon DLitt Univ of Newcastle upon Tyne 1996; *Awards* Eric Gregory Award 1982, Poetry Book Soc Recommendation 1988, Dorothy Tutin Award for Servs to Poetry 1989; *Books* Ten North-East Poets (ed, 1980), Darwin Survivor (1988), Poetry with an Edge (ed, 1988 and 1993), Tony Harrison (ed, 1991), Biting My Tongue (1995), New Blood (ed, 1999), The End of My Tether (2002), Staying Alive (ed, 2002), Pleased to See Me (ed, 2002), Do Not Go Gentle (ed, 2003), Being Alive (ed, 2004), The Sheep who Changed the World (2005), Passionfood (ed, 2005), Bloodaxe Poetry Introductions (ed, vols 1 and 2, 2006, vol 3, 2007), Soul Food (jt ed, 2007), Earth Shattering (ed, 2007), In Person: 30 Poets filmed by Pamela Robertson-Pearce (ed, 2008), Being Human (ed, 2011), Essential Poems from the Staying Alive Trilogy (ed, 2012), Ten Poems About Sheep (ed, 2012), The World Record (jt ed, 2012), The Hundred Years' War (ed, 2014), Funny Ha-Ha, Funny Peculiar (ed, 2015); *Recreations* books, countryside, sheep, folklore; *Style—* Dr Neil Astley; ✉ Bloodaxe Books Ltd, Eastburn, South Park, Hexham, Northumberland NE46 1BS (*Tel* 01434 611581, fax 01434 611585, e-mail editor@bloodaxebooks.com

ASTLEY-COOPER, Sir Alexander Paston; 7 Bt (UK 1821), of Gadebridge, Herts; s of Sir Patrick Graham Astley-Cooper, 6 Bt (d 2002); *b* 1 February 1943; *Educ* Kelly Coll Tavistock; *m* 1974, Minnie Margeret, da of Charles Harrison (d 1959); *Career* engineering consultant and entrepreneur; *Recreations* cricket, badminton, rugby union, theatre, travel; *Clubs* Lions International; *Style—* Sir Alexander Astley-Cooper, Bt; ✉ Gadebridge, 8 Berkshire Close, Leigh-on-Sea, Essex SS9 4RT

ASTOR, David Waldorf; CBE (1994), DL (Oxon 2007); s of Hon Michael Langhorne Astor (MP for Surrey East 1945–51, d 1980, 3 s of 2 Viscount Astor), and his 1 w, Barbara Mary (d 1980), da of Capt Ronald McNeill; n of Hon Sir John Astor (d 2000); *b* 9 August 1943; *Educ* Eton, Harvard Univ (rusticated after failing Astronomy exam); *m* 19 Sept 1968, Clare Pamela, er da of Cdr Michael Beauchamp St John, DSC, RN; 2 s (Henry b 17 April 1969, Tom b 24 July 1972), 2 da (Joanna b 23 June 1970, Rose b 9 June 1979); *Career* short serv cmmn Royal Scots Greys 1962–65; farmer 1973–; dir: Jupiter Tarbutt Merlin 1985–91, Priory Investments Holdings 1990–2006; chm Classic FM 1986–91; chm: Cncl for the Protection of Rural England 1983–93, Southern Arts Bd 1998–2002, Action for Prisoners' Families 2003–10, Turn2Us 2007–10; Parly candidate (SDP) Plymouth Drake 1987; tstee: Glyndebourne Arts Tst 1995–2005, Elizabeth Finn Tst 2004–10; FRSA 1988; *Recreations* books, sport; *Clubs* Brooks's, Beefsteak, MCC; *Style—* David Astor, Esq, CBE, DL; ✉ Bruern Grange, Milton-under-Wychwood, Chipping Norton, Oxfordshire OX7 6HA (☎ 07968 721373, e-mail davidwastor@gmail.com)

ASTOR, 4 Viscount (UK 1917); William Waldorf Astor; also Baron Astor (UK 1916); only child of 3 Viscount Astor (d 1966), by his 1 w, Hon Sarah, *née* Norton, da of 6 Baron Grantley; *b* 27 December 1951; *Educ* Eton; *m* 1976, Annabel Lucy Veronica, da of Timothy Jones (himself s of Sir Roderick Jones, KBE, sometime chm of Reuters, and his w, better known as the writer Enid Bagnold) and Pandora, *née* Clifford (niece of 11 and 12 Barons Clifford of Chudleigh and sis of Lady Norwich); 1 da (Hon Flora Katherine b 7 June 1976), 2 s (Hon William Waldorf b 18 Jan 1979, Hon James Jacob b 4 March 1981); *Heir* s, Hon William Astor; *Career* a Lord in Waiting (Govt whip) 1990–93; Govt House of Lords spokesman: for DOE 1990–91, on home affrs 1991–92, on national heritage 1992–97; Parly under-sec of state: Dept of Social Security 1993–94, Dept of Nat Heritage 1994–95; oppn House of Lords spokesman: on home affrs 1997–, on transport 2001–03, DCMS 2004–06; chm Silvergatemedia; tstee Stanley Spencer Gallery Cookham; *Clubs* White's; *Style—* The Rt Hon The Viscount Astor; ✉ Ginge Manor, Wantage, Oxfordshire OX12 8QT (☎ 01235 833228)

ASTOR OF HEVER, 3 Baron (UK 1956); Rt Hon John Jacob Astor; PC (2015), DL; 3 Baron (UK 1956); s of 2 Baron Astor of Hever (d 1984), by his w, Lady Irene Violet Freesia Janet Augusta Haig (d 2001), da of FM 1 Earl Haig, KT, GCB, OM, GCVO, KCIE; *b* 16 June 1946; *Educ* Eton; *m* 1, 1970 (m dis 1990), Fiona Diana Lennox, da of Capt Roger Harvey, JP, DL, Scots Gds, and Diana (da of Sir Harry Mainwaring, 5 and last Bt, by his w Generis, eld da of Sir Richard Williams-Bulkeley, 12 Bt, KCB, VD, JP, and Lady Magdalen Yorke, da of 5 Earl of Hardwicke); 3 da (Hon Camilla Fiona b 1974, Hon Tania Jentie b 1978, Hon Violet Magdalene b 1980); m 2, 1990, Hon Elizabeth Constance, da of 2 Viscount Mackintosh of Halifax, OBE, BEM (d 1980), 1 s (Hon Charles Gavin John b 10 Nov 1990), 1 da (Hon Olivia Alexandra Elizabeth b 21 Aug 1992); *Heir* s, Hon Charles Astor; *Career* Lt LG 1966–70, served Malaysia, Hong Kong, NI; pres: Astor Enterprises Inc 1983–2010, Sevenoaks Westminster Patrons Club 1991–2010, Earl Haig Branch Royal Br Legion 1994–, Motorsport Industry Assoc 1995–2010, RoSPA 1996–99, Conservatives in Paris 2002–, Kent Branch Royal Br Legion 2003–; chm Cncl of St John Kent 1987–97; memb oppn whip's office House of Lords 1998–; Social Sec 1998–01; oppn front bench spokesman: Health 1998–2003, Foreign and Commonwealth Affairs 2001–, Int Devpt 2001–, Defence 2003–10; Parly under-sec of state MOD 2010–15; patron: Edenbridge Music and Arts Tst 1989–2010, Bridge Tst 1993–2010, Kent Youth Tst 1994–2010; govr Cobham Hall Sch 1992–96; tstee: Rochester Cathedral Tst 1988–2010, Canterbury Cathedral Tst 1992–2010, Astor of Hever Tst 1986–, Astor Fndn 1988–2010; Liveryman Worshipful Co of Goldsmiths; *Clubs* White's, Riviera Golf; *Style—* The Rt Hon the Lord Astor of Hever, PC, DL; ✉ House of Lords, London SW1A 0PW (☎ 020 7219 5475, e-mail astorjj@parliament.uk)

ATALLA, Ash; s of Albert Atalla, and Adele Atalla; *b* 18 June 1972, Cairo, Egypt; *Educ* Univ of Bath (BSc); *Career* former stockbroker; joined BBC features, former commissioning ed BBC Comedy, comedy ed Talkback Productions until 2007, founder Roughcut Television 2007; prodr: The Way It Is... (BBC Radio 4) 1998, Yes Sir I Can Boogie (BBC Radio 4 and BBC2 pilot) 1999 and 2000, Up Late With Ralph Little (BBC Choice) 2001, Come Together with Ricky Gervais (Play UK) 2001, The Office (2 series and Christmas Special, BBC2) 2001–03; script ed Comedy Nation (series 1, BBC2) 1998, presenter Freak Out (Channel 4) 2000; author of Last Word column Independent on Sunday 2000, author of articles on disability, sport and television Time Out, contrib The Guardian (columnist 2005); *Awards* for The Office: South Bank Show Award for Best Television Comedy 2001, Broadcast Award for Best Comedy 2002, Br Comedy Award for Best New Television Comedy 2002, BAFTA for Best Situation Comedy 2002 and 2003; for The Office Christmas Specials: Golden Globe for Best Musical or Comedy Series 2004, BAFTA for Best Situation Comedy 2004; *Recreations* messing around; *Style—* Ash Atalla, Esq

ATAMAN, Kutlug; *b* 1961, Istanbul; *Educ* UCLA (BA, MFA); *Career* film maker and artist; Carnegie Prize 2004, shortlisted Turner Prize 2004; *Solo Exhibitions* incl: Lux Gallery London 2000, Tensta Konsthal Sweden 2001, Long Streams (Serpentine Gallery London and Copenhagen Contemporary Art Centre) 2002, Lehmann Maupin NY 2002, Women Who Wear Wigs (Istanbul Contemporary Arts Museum) 2002, A Rose Blooms in the Garden of Sorrows (BAWAG Fndn Vienna) 2002, Long Streams (Serpantine Gallery London and Nikolaj Copenhagen Contemporary Art Centre) 2002, Stefan's Room (Lehmann Maupin NY) 2004, Kuba (Artangel and Museum of Contemporary Art Sydney) 2005, De-Regulation With the Work of Kutlug Ataman (MuHKA, Belgium) 2006, Paradise (Orange County Museum of Art) 2007, Art Basel Art Unlimited (Basel) 2007, Paradise (Vancouver and Harris Museum and Art Gallery Preston) 2008; *Group Exhibitions* incl: Istanbul Biennale 1997, Manifesta 2 Luxembourg 1998, 48th Venice Biennale 1999, Berlin Biennial 2001, Documenta 11 Kassel Germany 2002, Days Like These: Tate Triennial Exhibition of British Art (Tate Britain London) 2003, Witness (Barbican Art Gallery London) 2003, Testimonies: between Fiction and Reality (Nat Museum of Contemporary Art Athens) 2003, Istanbul Biennale 2003, Documentary Fictions (CaxiaForum Barcelona) 2004, Carnegie International Pittsburgh 2004, Without Boundary, Seventeen Ways of Looking (MOMA NY), Moscow Biennial 2007; *Style—* Kutlug Ataman; ✉ c/o Lehmann Maupin, 540 West 26 Street, NY, USA (☎ 00 1 212 255 2923, fax 00 1 212 255 2924)

ATHANAS, Christopher Nicholas (Chris); WS (1979); s of Nicholas Athanas (d 1947), and Elizabeth Christison, *née* Tasker (d 1972); *b* 26 August 1941, Aden; *Educ* Fettes, Univ of Aberdeen (MA, LLB); *m* 30 June 1963, Sheena Anne, *née* Stewart; 2 da (Gillian Elizabeth b 10 Oct 1964, Carol Anne b 11 Nov 1965), 1 s (Nicholas Murray b 14 Nov 1979); *Career* admitted slr Scotland 1966, NP 1969; slr specialising in corporate law and financial servs law; trainee then slr Paull & Williamsons 1964–68, ptnr Dundas & Wilson 1969–96 (slr 1968–69, memb Strategy Bd 1991–95), ptnr Tods Murray 1996–2006 (head Investment Funds and Financial Servs Gp 1997–2006), ret 2006; princ external legal advsr on oil-related deals Shetland Islands Cncl 1974–88; memb Law Soc of Scotland 1966; memb Soc of HM Writers to the Signet 1979; *Recreations* the arts, collecting, walking, golf, angling; *Clubs* Blairgowrie Golf, Royal Burgess Golfing Soc of Edinburgh, WS Golf, Square, Murrayfield/Cramond Probus; *Style—* Chris Athanas, Esq, WS; ☎ 0131 447 4315

ATHANASOU, Prof Nicholas Anthony; s of Anthony James Athanasou (d 1964), and Angela, *née* Pappas (d 1974); *b* 26 April 1953, Perth, Australia; *Educ* Sydney HS, Univ of Sydney (MB BS, MD), Univ of London (PhD); *m* 27 April 1985, Linda Joan, da of Anthony Hulls, of Chislehurst, Kent; *Career* conslt pathologist Nuffield Orthopaedic Centre 1991–; Univ of Oxford: prof of musculoskeletal pathology, fell Wadham Coll; MRCP 1981, FRCPath 1996 (MRCPath 1986); *Books* Hybrids (short stories, 1995), Atlas of Orthopaedic Pathology (1999), Pathological Basis of Orthopaedic and Rheumatic Disease (2001), The Greek Liar (novel, 2002), The Person of the Man (novel, 2012); *Recreations* cricket, reading, writing; *Clubs* Cook Soc; *Style—* Prof Nicholas Athanasou; ✉ Pathology Department, Nuffield Department of Orthopaedics, Rheumatology and Musculoskeletal Science, Nuffield Orthopaedic Centre, Headington, Oxford OX3 7HE (☎ 01865 738136, e-mail nick.athanasou@ndorms.ox.ac.uk)

ATHERTON, David; OBE; s of Robert Atherton, and Lavinia, *née* Burton; *b* 3 January 1944; *Educ* Univ of Cambridge (MA); *m* 1, 5 Sept 1970 (m dis 2012), Ann Gianetta, da of Cdr J F Drake (d 1978), of Ware, Herts; 2 da (Elizabeth b 13 Feb 1974, Susan b 10 June 1977 d 2014), 1 s (John b 14 May 1979); m 2, 24 Oct 2012, Eleanor Ann Roth, of San Diego, CA, USA; *Career* conductor and musical dir London Sinfonietta 1968–73 (co-fndr 1967) and 1989–91; Royal Opera House: repetiteur 1967–68, resident conductor 1968–80; Royal Liverpool Philharmonic Orch: princ conductor and artistic advsr 1980–83, princ guest conductor 1983–86; musical dir and princ conductor San Diego Symphony Orch 1980–87, princ guest conductor BBC Symphony Orch 1985–89, musical dir and princ conductor Hong Kong Philharmonic Orch 1989–2000; artistic dir and conductor: London Stravinsky Festival 1979–82, Ravel/Varèse Festival 1983–84; artistic dir and fndr Californian Mainly Mozart Festival 1988–2013, princ guest conductor BBC Nat Orch of Wales 1994–97, Conductor Laureate Hong Kong Philharmonic Orch 2000–09; co-fndr, pres and artistic dir Global Music Network 1998–2002; youngest conductor Henry Wood Promenade Concerts Royal Albert Hall and Royal Opera House 1968; Royal Festival Hall debut 1969;

concerts abroad incl: Europe, M East, Far East, Australasia, N America; major operas conducted incl over 150 performances at Royal Opera House 1968–80: Il Trovatore, Carmen, The Barber of Seville, Don Giovanni, Tosca, Eugene Onegin, We Come to the River (world premiere), King Priam, The Knot Garden, The Ice Break; other operas incl: Billy Budd (San Francisco Opera 1978, Met Opera NY 1985, ENO 1988 and 1991), Peter Grimes (Dallas Opera 1980, Met Opera 1985, 1997 and 1998, ENO 1991 and 1994), Stravinsky Le Rossignol and Ravel L'Enfant et les Sortileges (Royal Opera House 1987 and 1989), Berlioz Romeo and Juliet (Philharmonia Orch) 1989, The Love for Three Oranges (ENO) 1989, Wozzeck (Canadian Opera) 1990, Les Huguenots (Royal Opera House) 1991, Death in Venice (Metropolitan Opera) 1994, The Barber of Seville (Met Opera) 1995, Turandot (ENO) 1995, Midsummer Night's Dream (Met Opera 1996 and 2002, Glyndebourne 2001), Der Rosenkavalier (ENO) 1997, Salome (ENO) 1999 and (Canadian Opera) 2002, King Priam (Royal Albert Hall, BBC Nat Orch of Wales) 1999, The Makropulos Case (Glyndebourne in NYC) 2001, Carmen (ENO) 2004; awards incl: Composers' Guild of GB Conductor of the Year 1971, Edison Award 1973, Grand Prix du Disque 1977, Koussevitzky Award 1981, Int Record Critics' Award 1982, Prix Caecilia 1982; adapted and arranged Pandora by Roberto Gerhard for Royal Ballet 1975; *Books* The Complete Instrumental and Chamber Music of Arnold Schoenberg and Roberto Gerhard (ed, 1973), Pandora and Don Quixote Suites by Roberto Gerhard (ed, 1973), The Musical Companion (contrib, 1978), The New Grove Dictionary (1981); *Recreations* travel, computing, theatre; *Style—* David Atherton, Esq, OBE; ✉ c/o Askonas Holt, Lincoln House, 300 High Holborn, London WC1V 7JH

ATHERTON, Dr David John; s of Dr Desmond Joseph Atherton, of Coventry, and Hildegard, *née* Rowe, MBE; *b* 24 April 1949; *Educ* Ampleforth, Pembroke Coll Cambridge (MA, MB BChir); *m* 1971 (m dis); 3 s (James b 1976, Joseph b 1984, Jay b 1998); *Career* conslt in paediatric dermatology 1982–: Gt Ormond St Hosp for Children, St John's Inst of Dermatology; sr lectr in paediatric dermatology Inst of Child Health 1986–; FRCP; *Books* Eczema in Childhood (1994); *Recreations* tennis, gardening; *Style—* Dr David Atherton; ✉ Great Ormond Street Hospital for Children, London WC1N 3JH (☎ 020 7405 9200, fax 020 7829 8643)

ATHERTON, Howard William; s of William Atherton (d 1989), of Sudbury, Suffolk, and Rose Charlotte Atherton (d 1984); *b* 12 August 1947; *Educ* Sudbury GS, London Film Sch; *m* 12 Aug 1972, Janet Ruth, da of Ronald William Simpson, of Lavenham, Suffolk; 2 da (Rebecca Louise b 1977, Charlotte Letitia Rose b 1985), 1 s (Oliver Luke b 1979); *Career* director of photography; dir of photography in residence London Film Sch 2011–; memb: Br Soc of Cinematograpers, AMPAS; *Film* incl: Helen, Runners 1983, Keep Off the Grass, Fatal Attraction 1986, The Boost 1987, Mermaids 1989, Indecent Proposal 1992, Bad Boys 1994, Gulliver's Travels 1995, Lolita 1995, Deep Rising 1996, Hanging Up 1999, Abduction Club 2000, Colour Me Kubrick 2004, Lassie 2005, And When Did You Last See Your Father? 2006, All Things to All Men 2012; *Style—* Howard Atherton, Esq; ✉ Clarence House, 12 Clarence Drive, Englefield Green, Surrey TW20 0NL

ATHERTON, Jason; s of Sandra Bleakley, and step-s of David Keigthley; *Career* chef; commi chef La Tante Claire, chef de partie Chez Nico, chef de partie The Restaurant, chef de partie L'Auberge de I'Il (France), sous chef Coast, head chef Mash and Air, chef de partie El Bulli (Spain), head chef Frith Street Restaurant, exec chef Maze Ltd (partnership with Gordon Ramsay, *qv*, incl Maze London, Maze Grill and Maze Prague) until 2010; chef proprietor: Table no 1 by Jason Atherton 2010–, Pollen Street Social 2011–; *Awards* Egon Ronay Chef of the Year 1998, winner Daily Express Chef of the Year 1999, voted most likely to succeed in the new millennium, winner Michelin star at Maze London and Pollen Street Social; *Books* Maze The Cookbook; *Recreations* football, reading and collecting cookery books; *Style—* Jason Atherton, Esq

ATHERTON, Dr Kevin; s of late William Edward Atherton, and late Elizabeth, *née* Clague; *b* 25 November 1950; *Educ* Douglas HS for Boys IOM, IOM Coll of Art, Leeds Poly (BA), Nat Univ of Ireland (PhD); *m* 1977, Victoria (d 2005), da of Francis Sidney Thomas Robinson; *Career* sculptor, artist and lectr in art; pt/t teacher 1978–86: Slade Sch of Fine Art, RCA, Norwich Sch of Art, Winchester Sch of Art, Maidstone Coll of Art, Chelsea Sch of Art, Fine Art Dept Middx Poly, Fine Art Dept South Glamorgan Inst of Higher Educn Cardiff; artist in residence London Borough of Richmond upon Thames 1989; Kingston Poly: Picker lectr in public art Fine Art Dept 1989, Stanley Picker lectr in video performance and public art 1990; lecture tour of Australia 1990; princ lectr in media Fine Art Dept Chelsea Sch of Art 1990–99 (project ldr research project into Virtual Reality as a Fine Art Medium); head of postgrad fine art Nat Coll of Art and Design Dublin 2000–; organiser and speaker Virtual Reality and the Gallery conf (Tate Gallery) 1995; specialist advsr CNAA 1985–; awards incl ABSA Award for Best Cmmn in Any Media 1986; numerous exhbns in England and Europe incl: one-man exhbn Perth Inst of Contemporary Art 1990, Kevin Atherton, Three Decades, Three Works (mini retrospective, arthouse Dublin and Manx Museum Douglas IOM) 2001, In Two Minds – Past and Future Versions (video performance, Dundee Contemporary Arts) 2006, In Two Minds – Past Version (video performance, Tate Britain) 2006, In Two Minds – Past Version (video installation) and Time Embodied (Lewis Glucksman Gallery Cork) 2007; video installation incl in The Studio Sessions (San Francisco Museum of Modern Art) 2009, Changing Channels (Art and Television Mumuk Vienna) 2010, Remote Control (Inst of Contemporary Arts London) 2012; Virtual Reality Work selected for the 8th Biennial of the Moving Image Geneva 1999; *Work in Public Collections* Sheffield City Poly, Merseyside CC, Graves Art Gallery Sheffield; *Commissions* incl: A Body of Work (Tower Hamlets) 1982, Upon Reflection (Islington) 1985, Platforms Piece (BR Brixton) 1986, Cathedral (Forest of Dean, Glos) 1986, Iron Horses (BR) 1986–87, The Architect (Harlow New Town) 1990, Conversation Piece (Leicester CC) 1990, Art Within Reach (Hampshire Sculpture Tst) 1991, To The Top (New Civic Offices Twickenham) 1990, A Different Ball Game (Kingshill W Malling Kent) 1993, A Private View (Taff Viaduct Cardiff Bay) 1995, Virtual Reality Gallery Guide Museum of Contemporary Art Chicago 1997 and MOMA Stockholm 1998, Field of Vision (GlaxoSmithKline HQ Brentford) 2001, Handshake (HG Capital London) 2002, A Reflective Approach (Clarence Dock Leeds) 2007, Another Sphere (Ballymun Dublin) 2010, As Exciting As We Can Make It – Ikon in the 1980s (Ikon Gallery Birmingham) 2014; *Publications* Expanded Cinema – Art Performance Film (2011), Rewind – British Artists' Video in the 1970s and 1980s (ed by Cubbitt and Partridge, 2012), Kevin Atherton Auto-Interview (2012), Pillars, Tea Chests, Off-Cuts...Some Structures of Support An Interview with Kevin Atherton (Jamie Sutcliffe, Critical Wriitng in Art and Design, Royal Coll of Art and Design, 2013); *Recreations* the turf; *Style—* Dr Kevin Atherton; ✉ High Street, Inistioge, Co Kilkenny, Ireland (☎ 0035 356 775 8830, e-mail athertonk@ncad.ie)

ATHERTON, Michael Andrew (Mike); OBE (1997); s of Alan Atherton, and Wendy, *née* Fletcher; *b* 23 March 1968; *Educ* Manchester Grammar, Downing Coll Cambridge (MA, Cricket blue and capt); *Career* journalist and former professional cricketer; first class debut Cambridge Univ v Essex April 1987; Lancashire CCC: debut v Warwickshire July 1987, awarded county cap 1989, vice-capt 1992–2001, ret 2001; England: former English School's rep, capt Young England to Sri Lanka 1987 and Aust 1988, first team debut v Aust Aug 1989, first full tour Aust and NZ 1990–91, memb team touring India and Sri Lanka 1992–93, capt England July 1993–98 and 2001 (for two matches v Australia), capt team touring West Indies 1993–94, Aust 1994–95, South Africa 1995–96, Zimbabwe and NZ 1996–97 and West Indies 1998, memb winning team v South Africa 1998, memb squad Emirates Trophy 1998, memb team touring Aust 1998–99, memb team touring South Africa 1999–2000, memb team touring Pakistan and Sri Lanka 2000–01, highest test score 185 not out v South Africa 1995, 115 test matches, 54 one-day ints, ret 2001; Professional Cricketers' Assoc Young Cricketer of Year 1990, Cricket Writers' Young Cricketer of Year 1990, Wisden Cricketer of the Year 1991, Cornhill Player of the Year 1994; cricket commentator Channel 4 2002–05, subsequently cricket commentator Sky Sports; columnist Sunday Telegraph until 2008, sport corr The Times 2008–; Sports Journalist of the Year Br Press Award 2010; *Books* Opening Up (2002); *Recreations* reading, golf, squash, rugby, football (Manchester United supporter), good food; *Style—* Mike Atherton, Esq, OBE

ATHERTON, Peter; s of Joseph Ignatius Atherton (d 1984), of Wrightington, and Winifred, *née* Marsh; *b* 8 November 1952; *Educ* Mount St Mary's Coll Derby, Univ of Birmingham (LLB), Coll of Law; *m* 17 Oct 1981, Jennifer Marie, da of Charles Birch, of Ontario, Canada; 1 da (Hilary Anne b 4 Jan 1984), 1 s (Timothy Peter b 4 Sept 1985); *Career* called to the Bar Gray's Inn 1975; jr Northern Circuit 1978–79, recorder of the Crown Court 1999–; chm Young Barrs Ctee Senate of Inns of Ct and Bar Cncl for England and Wales 1982–83; *Recreations* tennis, golf, theatre; *Style—* Peter Atherton, Esq; ✉ Deans Court Chambers, 24 St John's Street, Manchester M3 4DF(☎ 0161 214 6000, e-mail atherton@deanscourt.co.uk)

ATHILL, Diana; OBE (2009); da of Col L F I Athill (d 1968), and Alice Katharine, *née* Carr (d 1990); *b* 21 December 1917, London; *Educ* Runton Hill Sch Norfolk, Lady Margaret Hall Oxford (BA); *Career* author; ed Allan Wingate publishers 1946–50, editorial dir André Deutsch Ltd 1951–92; FRSL; *Books* Instead of a Letter (1963), Don't Look at Me Like That (1967), After a Funeral (1986), Make Believe (1993), Stet (2000), Yesterday Morning (2002), Somewhere Towards the End (2008, Costa Biography Award 2009); *Recreations* reading, writing, gardening; *Style—* Ms Diana Athill, OBE; ✉ c/o The Royal Society of Literature, Somerset House, Strand, London WC2R 1LA

ATKIN, Edward; CBE (2011); s of David Atkin (d 1972), of London, and Klari, *née* Salpeter; *b* 30 August 1944, Bradford, Yorks; *Educ* Clifton Coll Bristol; *m* 1981, Celia; 1 s (Ross b 15 March 1982), 1 da (Lara b 11 Oct 1983); *Career* joined Cannon Rubber 1965 (suc f as md 1972); founded: Avent 1984, Avent America 1994, Cannon Avent Gp 1998 (sold Avent part of Gp 2005); md C A Hldgs plc; chm: ARCC Innovations Ltd, Motor Sport Magazine Ltd; memb Chllr's Court of Benefactors Univ of Oxford; 5 Queen's Awards, Civic Tst Award, various awards for architecture; *Recreations* golf, sailing, the arts, motor racing; *Clubs* Hampstead Golf, RAC, Arts; *Style—* Edward Atkin, Esq, CBE

ATKIN, Peter Richard (Pete); s of Cyril William Atkin (d 2004), and Elsie Rose Cowell (d 1980); *b* 22 August 1945; *Educ* Perse Sch Cambridge, St John's Coll Cambridge (BA); *m* 24 Nov 1973, Mary Louise, da of Lewis Lynch Lowance, of Manassas, VA; *Career* radio prodr; scriptwriter, critic, songwriter (with Clive James, *qv*) and recording artist of 6 albums 1970–75 (reissued See for Miles 1997 and 2001), former furniture maker and woodwork corr Vole magazine 1976–77; chief prodr BBC Radio Light Entertainment 1986–89 (prodr 1981, script ed 1983), head of network radio BBC South Bristol 1989–93, ind prodn co-ordinator BBC Radio 4 1993; ind radio prodr and conslt 1994–, script ed Hat Trick Productions 1994–2002; prodr: This Sceptred Isle (BBC Radio 4) 1995–99 (Best Non-Fiction Talkie of the Year Talkie Awards 1996), This Sceptred Isle: Empire (BBC Radio 4) 2006 (Best New Radio Prog Voice of the Viewer and Listener Awards 2006); voice dir: Bob the Builder (US version) 2004–07, Thomas the Tank Engine (US version) 2004–09 and (UK version) 2008–09, The Gruffalo 2009, Waybuloo 2010–11, The Gruffalo's Child 2011; voice actor Mr Crock in Wallace & Gromit: The Curse of the Were-Rabbit (film) 2006, asst voice dir Planet 51 2007–08; dir: The Glittering Prizes 2005, Fame and Fortune 2007, Kicking the Habit 2007–08, Final Demands 2010, A Thousand Kisses (BBC Radio 3) 2011, recordings of Just William stories read by Martin Jarvis; Together Again At Last (with Clive James, UK tour) 2002, The Lakeside Sessions (double CD) 2002, Words and Music (with Clive James, UK, Australia and Hong Kong tour) 2003, Winter Spring (CD, new songs with Clive James) 2003, At It Again (with Clive James, UK tour) 2005, Midnight Voices: The Clive James and Pete Atkin Songbook, Vol 1 (CD) 2007, The Colours of the Night: Songs by Clive James and Pete Atkins (CD) 2015; writer and dir The Mackinnon Extradition (BBC Radio 4) 2007; tstee St George's Music Tst Bristol 1990–2007; *Recreations* words, music, wood; *Style—* Pete Atkin, Esq; ✉ 19 Archfield Road, Bristol BS6 6BG (☎ 0117 942 1582, e-mail pete@peteatkin.com, website www.peteatkin.com)

ATKIN, Timothy John (Tim); s of Ronald George Atkin, and Brenda Irene, *née* Burton (d 1982); *b* 26 August 1961, Dartford, Kent; *Educ* St Dunstan's Coll London, Univ of Durham (BA), LSE (MSc); *m* 30 July 2009, Sue Wixley; *Career* with Haymarket Publishing 1985–89; wine corr: The Guardian 1989–93, The Observer 1993–2010; ed Harpers Wine & Spirit Weekly 2000–03; columnist The Times 2010–11; Glenfiddich Wine Writer of the Year 1989, 1991, 1993, 2004 and 2006, Lanson Wine Writer of the Year 1999, 2002, 2003 and 2004, Drink Writer of the Year World Food Media Awards 2008; memb: Greenpeace, Amnesty Int; MW 2001; *Publications* Chardonnay (1991), Vin de Pays D'Oc (1992), Grapevine (with Anthony Rose, 1993, 1994, 1995, 1996 and 1997); *Recreations* reading, tennis, golf, cinema, folk guitar, piano, collecting black and white photography; *Clubs* Groucho, Blacks, Royal Wimbledon Golf; *Style—* Tim Atkin, MW; ✉ c/o Vanessa Fogarty, PFD (e-mail vanessa@therightshouse.com)

ATKINS, Andy; *b* 9 October 1960, Eastleigh, Hants; *Educ* UCL, Open Univ; *m* Sarah; 3 c; *Career* gen sec Chile Ctee for Human Rights 1985–88, prog coordinator Working in Partnership Prog Catholic Agency for Overseas Devpt 1988–90, Latin American desk offr Catholic Inst for Int Rels 1990–97, policy and campaigns dir Tearfund 1997–2008, exec dir Friends of the Earth 2008; *Style—* Andy Atkins, Esq; ✉ Friends of the Earth, 26–28 Underwood Street, London N1 7JQ

ATKINS, Prof Anthony George; s of Walter George Atkins (d 1975), and Emily Irene, *née* Aldridge (d 1996); *b* 10 October 1939; *Educ* Canton HS Cardiff, UC Cardiff (BSc), Trinity Coll Cambridge (PhD, ScD), Exeter Coll Oxford (MA); *m* 4 March 1971, Margaret Ann, da of Lt-Col Richard Risely Proud, CVO, OBE (d 1976); 2 s (Philip George b 1973, Richard James b 1976), 1 da (Margaret Ruth b 1980); *Career* US Steel Corpn 1965–67, BSC fell Univ of Oxford 1967–70, assoc prof in mechanical engrg Univ of Michigan 1970–75, research mangr Delta Metal 1975–81, prof of mechanical engrg Univ of Reading 1981–2007 (now emeritus); visiting prof Imperial Coll London 2008–; tstee Nat Museum Wales; memb CPRE; FIMMM (FIM 1986), FIMechE 1987, CEng, FREng 2002, FLSW 2014; *Books* Strength and Fracture of Engineering Solids (jtly, 1984, 2 ed 1996), A History of GWR Goods Wagons (jtly, 1986, 3 edn 1999), Manufacturing Engineering (jtly, 1987), Elastic and Plastic Fracture (jtly, 2 edn, 1988), GWR Goods Services (jtly, Vol 1 2000, Vol 2 2008), The Cutting, Scratching and Puncturing of Materials (2009), GWR Docks & Marine (2014); *Recreations* music, skiing, woodwork; *Style—* Prof Tony Atkins, FREng; ✉ White House, Heads Lane, Inkpen Common, Hungerford, Berkshire RG17 9QS (☎ 01488 668253); Department of Engineering, Box 225, University of Reading, Whiteknights, Reading RG6 6AY (☎ 0118 931 8562, fax 0118 931 3327, e-mail a.g.atkins@reading.ac.uk)

ATKINS, Caroline Mary Ghislaine; da of Reginald Atkins, of Wedmore, Som, and Ghislaine, *née* Tullet; *b* 13 January 1981, Brighton, E Sussex; *Educ* Downlands Comp Sch, Burgess Hill Sch, Univ of Durham (BA, hon life memb Team Durham); *Career* cricketer; Sussex WCCC; England: Test debut v Aust 2001, memb Ashes-winning side 2008, memb touring squad Aust and NZ 2008, memb World Cup-winning side 2009; fitness instructor Univ of Durham 2002–04, mangr Elite Athlete Support Servs Univ of Bournemouth 2006–08, self-employed sports massage therapist and personal trainer and UKCCII cricket coach 2008–; coaching ambass Chance to Shine 2009–; accredited strength and conditioning coach The UK Strength and Conditioning Association (UKSCA) 2005; *Recreations* golf, tennis, travel; *Clubs* MCC; *Style*— Miss Caroline Atkins; ✉ e-mail carolineatkins@gmail.com; c/o The England and Wales Cricket Board, Lord's Cricket Ground, London NW8 8QZ

ATKINS, Dame Eileen June; DBE (2001, CBE 1990); da of late Arthur Thomas Atkins, and Annie Ellen, *née* Elkins (d 1984); *b* 16 June 1934; *Educ* Latymer GS, Guildhall Sch of Music and Drama (AGSM); *m* 1, 1957 (m dis 1966), Julian Glover, *qv*; m 2, 1978, William B Shepherd; *Career* actress; hon memb GSM; Hon DLitt Univ of Oxford 2011; *Theatre* incl: Twelfth Night, Richard III, The Tempest (Old Vic) 1962, The Killing of Sister George (Bristol Old Vic transfd Duke of York, Best Actress Standard Award) 1963, The Cocktail Party (Wyndham's transferred Haymarket) 1968, Vivat! Vivat! Regina! (Piccadilly, Variety Award) 1970, Suzanne Andler (Aldwych) 1973, As You Like It (Stratford) 1973, St Joan (Old Vic) 1977, Passion Play (Aldwych) 1981, Medea (Young Vic) 1986, Winter's Tale, Cymbeline (Olivier Award), Mountain Language (NT) 1988, A Room of One's Own (Hampstead, NY Critics' Special citation) 1989, Exclusive (Strand) 1989, Prin (NY) 1990, Hannah Jelkes in The Night of the Iguana (Critics' Circle Award) 1992, John Gabriel in Bork Man (NT) 1997, Agnes in A Delicate Balance (Haymarket Theatre Royal (Evening Standard Best Actress Award)) 1998, The Unexpected Man (RSC, The Pit and The Duchess) 1998, A Room of One's Own (Hampstead Theatre) 2001, Unexpected Man (Promenade Theatre NY) 2001, Honour (Cottesloe NT, Olivier Award), The Retreat from Moscow (Booth Theatre) 2003–04, The Birthday Party (The Duchess) 2005, Doubt (Walter Kerr Theatre NY) 2005–06, There Came a Gypsy Riding (Almeida) 2007, The Sea (Theatre Royal Haymarket) 2008, The Female of the Species (Vaudeville Theatre) 2008, All That Fall (Arts Theatre) 2012, Eileen Atkins is Ellen Terry (Sam Wannamaker Theatre) 2014; *Television* incl: The Duchess of Malfi, Sons and Lovers, Smiley's People, Nelly's Version, The Burston Rebellion, Breaking Up, The Vision, Mrs Pankhurst in In My Defence (series) 1990, A Room of One's Own 1990, Lost Language of Cranes 1992, The Maitlands 1993, A Dance to the Music of Time 1997, Talking Heads 1998, David Copperfield 1999, Madame Bovary 2000, Elizabeth and Bertie 2001, The Lives of Animals 2002, Waking the Dead 2006, Cranford 2007 (Best Actress BAFTA TV Awards and Press Awards 2008, Outstanding Supporting Actress Emmy Award 2008, Golden Glob Award), Psychoville 2008, Poitot: Murder on the Orient Express 2009, Upstairs Downstairs 2010, Doc Martin 2011 and 2013, The Scapegoat 2012; *Film* incl: Equus 1974, The Dresser 1984, Let Him Have It 1990, Wolf 1993, Cold Comfort Farm 1995, Jack and Sarah 1995, The Avengers 1998, Women Talking Dirty 1999, Gosford Park 2001, The Hours 2002, What a Girl Wants 2003, Vanity Fair 2003, Ask the Dust 2004, Evening 2007, Last Chance Harvey 2008, Robin Hood 2009, Suite Française 2014, Magic in the Moonlight 2014; also co-creator of Upstairs Downstairs and The House of Eliott, writer/adaptor Mrs Dalloway (1998); Best TV Actress Broadcasting Press Guild Awards 2008; *Style*— Dame Eileen Atkins, DBE; ✉ c/o Independent Talent, Oxford House, 76 Oxford Street, London W1D 1BS (☎ 020 7636 6565, fax 020 7323 0101)

ATKINS, Frances Elizabeth (Mrs Gerald Atkins); *née* Venning; da of Thomas Colyer Venning, MBE (decd), of Ilkley, W Yorks, and Hilary Susan, *née* Harris; *b* 8 September 1950, Maidstone, Kent; *m* 1, 1976 (m dis 1984), George Alfred Carman, QC (d 2001); m 2, 1984, Gerald Atkins, MA; *Career* chef and restaurateur; Atkins Restaurant: Great Missenden 1984–86, The Old Plow Inn Speen 1986–88, Farleyer House Aberfeldy 1988–92; chef prop Shaw's Restaurant 1993–96, prop The Yorke Arms 1996–; memb Bd of Scottish Chefs 1992; fell Master Chefs of GB 1993, memb Royal Soc of Culinary Arts 2015; César Country Inn of the Year 2000 Good Hotel Guide, Restaurant of the Year in Eng Which Good Food Guide 2001 (jtly), Chef of the Year Yorkshire Life Magazine 2002/03, Michelin Star 2003–13 (consecutive years), AA Top 200 Hotels 2004, Top 25 Restaurants in the UK Egon Ronay Guide 2005/06, UK Restaurant of the Year Good Food Guide 2008, number 3 in Top 100 Restaurants in the UK Sunday Times 2013/14; *Recreations* work, art appreciation, collecting furniture; *Style*— Mrs Gerald Atkins; ✉ Yew Bank House, Ramsgill-in-Nidderdale, Harrogate HG3 5RL

ATKINS, Prof Madeleine Julia; CBE (2012), DL (W Midlands); *Educ* Univ of Cambridge, Univ of Nottingham (PhD); *Career* head of dept, dean and pro-vice-chllr Newcastle Univ until 2004, vice-chllr Coventry Univ 2004–13, chief exec HE Funding Cncl for England; tstee NESTA Operating Co; CCMI, FRSA 2012; *Style*— Prof Madeleine Atkins, CBE, DL; ✉ Chief Executive's Office, Nicholson House, Lime Kiln Close, Stoke Gifford, Bristol BS34 8SR

ATKINS, Paul; *Educ* Univ of Sussex (BEd), Univ of Reading (MSc), Brunel Univ (Dip Business Mgmnt), CIM; *Career* field dir and team ldr Christian Outreach Thailand 1979–81, head of physics Robert Haining Sch Mytchett 1981–84, head of science, mathematics and computer studies St Andrew's Sch Kenya 1984–86; Br Cncl: asst dir Lesotho 1987–90, dep dir Malawi 1990–93, dep dir int seminars London 1993–95, dir (designate) Sierra Leone 1995–96, dir int seminars London and Oxford 1996–99, dir NZ 1999–2004; gp mangr Int Investments Fndn for Research Sci and Technol 2004–07, gp mangr communications and audience/market devpt Creative New Zealand 2007–08; md Boutiq Science Ltd 2013–; dir: Izon Science Ltd 2008–10, Paul Atkins Consulting Ltd 2008–, Arato Technologies Ltd 2011–14; ceo Nat Energy Research Inst NZ 2010–15, ceo Zealandia 2015–; co-chm for Br Cncl Hornby Tst 1996–97, chm Bd of Mgmnt Oxford Overseas Student Housing Assoc Ltd 1996–99, memb Mgmnt Bd Britain/NZ Link Fndn 1999–2004, chair Bd of Mgmnt Shakespeare's Globe Centre NZ 2004–, memb Bd of Tstees NZ String Quartet 2004–08, memb Catalyst UK Network, inaugural chair NZ Smart Grid Forum 2014; memb: Woodland Tst, RSPB, Wildfowl and Wetland Tst; CPhys, MInstP, FCMI, memb Royal Soc of NZ, CSci, MInstD; *Publications* Digital Developments in Higher Education – theory and practice (co-author, 2001); *Recreations* ornithology, conservation, photography, triathlon and multi-sport endurance events, squash, cycling; *Style*— Paul Atkins, Esq; ✉ e-mail consultpna@gmail.com

ATKINS, Prof Peter William; s of William Henry Atkins (d 1988), and Ellen Louise, *née* Edwards (d 1978); *b* 10 August 1940; *Educ* Dr Challoner's Amersham, Univ of Leicester (BSc, PhD), Univ of Oxford (MA), UCLA; *m* 1, 20 Aug 1964 (m dis 1983), Judith Ann Kearton; 1 da (Juliet b 1970); m 2, 30 March 1991 (m dis 2005), Baroness Greenfield, CBE (Life Peer), *qv*; m 3, 23 May 2008, Patricia-Jean Nobes, *née* Brand; *Career* Harkness fell 1964–65; Univ of Oxford: univ lectr in physical chemistry 1965–96, prof of chemistry 1996–2007, fell and tutor Lincoln Coll 1965–2007 (actg rector 2007); visiting prof: China, France, Israel, Japan, New Zealand; Dreyfus lectr California 1980, Firth visiting prof Univ of Sheffield 1984, Nyholm lectr and medal 1999; chm Ctee on Chemistry Educn IUPAC 2002–05, memb Cncl Royal Inst 1999–2005; memb Ct Univ of Leicester 2001; hon prof Mendeleyev Univ Moscow 2006; Hon DSc Univ of Utrecht 1992, Hon DSc Univ of Leicester 2002, Hon DSc Kazan State Technological Univ 2009; Meldola Medal 1969, Literaturpreis des Fonds der Chemischen Industrie 2003, Inst of Chemistry of Ireland Award 2008; hon assoc: Rationalist Assoc 1993, Nat Secular Soc 1998; patron Br Humanist Assoc 2005; FRSC 2002; *Books* The Structure of Inorganic Radicals (1967), Molecular Quantum Mechanics (1970, 5 edn 2010), Quanta: A Handbook of Concepts (1974, 2 edn 1991), Physical Chemistry (1978, 10 edn 2014), Solutions Manual for Physical Chemistry (1978, 7 edn 2002), The Creation (1981), Principles of Physical Chemistry (1982), Solutions Manual for MQM (1983, 4 edn 2005), The Second Law (1984), Molecules (1987, 2 edn 2003), Chemistry: Principles and Applications (1988), General Chemistry (1989, 2 edn 1992), Inorganic Chemistry (1990, 5 edn 2010), Atoms, Electrons and Change (1991), Elements of Physical Chemistry (1992, 6 edn 2013), Creation Revisited (1992), The Periodic Kingdom (1995), Concepts of Physical Chemistry (1995), Chemistry: Molecules, Matter and Change (1997, 6 edn 2013), Chemical Principles (1999, 7 edn 2016), Galileo's Finger (2003), Physical Chemistry for the Life Sciences (2006, 2 edn 2011), Four Laws That Drive the Universe (2007), Quanta, Molecules and Change (2009, 2 edn 2014), Laws of Thermodynamics, a very short introduction (2010), On Being (2011), Reactions (2011), What is Chemistry? (2013), Physical Chemistry, a very short introduction (2014), Chemistry, a very short introduction (2015); *Recreations* art; *Clubs* Athenaeum; *Style*— Prof Peter Atkins; ✉ Lincoln College, Oxford OX1 3DR (☎ 01865 279800, fax 01865 279802, e-mail peter.atkins001@btinternet.com)

ATKINS, Rachel; *Career* ptnr and head Legal Schillings; Woman of the Year Citywealth 2016; *Style*— Ms Rachel Atkins; ✉ Schillings, 41 Bedford Square, London WC1B 3HX

ATKINS, Rt Hon Sir Robert James; kt (1997), PC (1995); s of late Reginald Alfred Atkins, of Great Missenden, Bucks, and Winifred Margaret Atkins; *b* 5 February 1946; *Educ* Highgate Sch; *m* 1969, Dulcie Mary, da of Frederick Moon Chaplin, of Bexley, London; 1 da (Victoria Atkins, MP, *qv* b 1976), 1 s (James b 1979); *Career* MP (Cons): Preston N 1979–1983, South Ribble 1983–97; former jt sec Cons Parly Def Ctee and vice-chm Aviation Ctee, nat pres Cons Trade Unionists 1984–87; PPS to: Norman Lamont as Min of State for Industry 1982–84, Lord Young of Graffham as Min Without Portfolio and Sec of State for Employment 1984–87; Parly under sec of state DTI 1987–89, min for roads and traffic Dept of Tport 1989–90, Parly under sec of state Dept of the Environment and min for sport 1990, Parly under sec of state Dept of Educn and Science and min for sport 1990–92, min of state Northern Ireland Office 1992–94, min of state Dept of Environment 1994–95; MEP (Cons) NW England 1999–2014, dep ldr Br Cons MEPs 2004–08, chief whip 2008–10; pres: Wyre & Preston N Cons Assoc 2010–, Preston Cons Assoc 2014–; chm NW Conservatives 2015–; pres Lancs Assoc of Local Cncls 2015–; *Recreations* cricket, Holmesiana, ecclesiology, wine; *Clubs* MCC, Carlton, Middlesex CCC (hon memb), Lancashire CCC (vice-pres), Garstang CC (pres), Leyland CC (life vice-pres), Lord's Taverners, Preston Grasshoppers RFC (vice-pres), Garstang RUFC (vice-pres); *Style*— The Rt Hon Sir Robert Atkins

ATKINS, Rosie; da of Robert Vernon William Atkins, and Agnes Dunn Atkins; *Educ* St Michael's Girls Sch Limpsfield; *Career* journalist; Sunday Times 1968–82, columnist Today 1983–90, former ed Gardens Illustrated; gardening contrib various newspapers and magazines; Editor of the Year Br Soc of Magazine Editors 1996; curator Chelsea Physic Garden 2002–; bd memb: Thrive, Disabled Gardeners Assoc; *Recreations* gardening, travel, writing; *Clubs* Chelsea Arts; *Style*— Ms Rosie Atkins; ✉ Chelsea Physic Garden, 66 Royal Hospital Road, London SW3 4HS (☎ 020 7352 5646)

ATKINS, Victoria; MP; d of The Rt Hon Sir Robert Atkins, *qv*; *b* 1976, London; *m* Paul; 1 s; *Career* MP (Cons) Louth & Horncastle 2015–; *Style*— Ms Victoria Atkins, MP; ✉ House of Commons, London SW1A 0AA

ATKINSON, Prof Sir Anthony Barnes (Tony); kt (2000); s of Norman Joseph Atkinson (d 1988), and Esther Muriel, *née* Stonehouse (d 2004); *b* 4 September 1944; *Educ* Cranbrook Sch, Churchill Coll Cambridge (MA); *m* 11 Dec 1965, Judith Mary, da of Alexander Mandeville, of Swansea; 2 s (Richard b 1972, Charles b 1976), 1 da (Sarah b 1974); *Career* fell St John's Coll Cambridge 1967–71, prof of economics Univ of Essex 1971–76, prof Univ of London 1976–92 (Thomas Tooke prof of econ sci and statistics 1987–92), fell Churchill Coll and prof of political economy Univ of Cambridge 1992–94, warden Nuffield Coll Oxford 1994–2005, prof of economics Univ of Oxford 2007–09, Centennial prof LSE 2010–; ed Jl of Public Economics 1971–97; pres: Econometric Soc 1988, Euro Econ Assoc 1989, Int Econ Assoc 1989–92, Royal Econ Soc 1995–98, Section F BAAS; vice-pres Br Acad 1988–90; memb: Royal Cmmn on Distribution of Income and Wealth 1978–79, Retail Prices Advsy Ctee 1984–90, Conseil D'Analyse Economique 1997–2001, European Statistics Governance Advsy Bd 2009–12; chm World Bank Cmmn on Global Poverty 2015–16; UAP Sci prize 1986, Jerzy Neyman Medal 2012, Dan David Prize 2016; Freeman City of London 1983, Liveryman Worshipful Co of Barbers 1985; Hon Dr Rer Pol Univ of Frankfurt 1987; Hon DSc Econ Univ of Lausanne 1988; Hon DUniv: Liège 1989, Athens 1991, Stirling 1992, Edinburgh 1994, École Normale Supérieur Paris 1995, Essex 1995, Bologna 1996, South Bank 1996, Louvain 1996, Nottingham 2000, London Met 2002, European Univ Inst 2004, Antwerp 2004, Gent 2004, Molise 2005, Aix-Marseille 2010; hon fell Churchill Coll Cambridge 2015; hon memb American Econ Assoc 1985; FBA 1984, hon fell RSS 2016; Chevalier de la Légion d'Honneur 2001; *Books* Poverty in Britain and the Reform of Social Security (1969), Unequal Shares (1972), The Tax Credit Scheme (1973), Economics of Inequality (1975), Distribution of Personal Wealth in Britain (with A J Harrison, 1978), Lectures on Public Economics (with J E Stiglitz, 1980), Social Justice and Public Policy (1982), Parents and Children (jtly, 1983), Unemployment Benefits and Unemployment Duration (with J Micklewright, 1986), Poverty and Social Security (1989), Economic Transformation in Eastern Europe and the Distribution of Income (with J Micklewright, 1992), Public Economics in Action (1995), Incomes and the Welfare State (1996), Three Lectures on Poverty in Europe (1998), The Economic Consequences of Rolling Back the Welfare State (1999), Social Indicators: The EU and Social Inclusion (with B Cantillon, E Marlier and B Nolan, 2002), The Changing Distribution of Earnings in OECD Countries (2007), Public Economics in an Age of Austerity (2014), Inequality – What Can be Done? (2015); *Recreations* sailing; *Style*— Prof Sir Tony Atkinson; ✉ 93 Hamilton Road, Oxford OX2 7QA (☎ 01865 513373, e-mail tony.atkinson@nuffield.ox.ac.uk)

ATKINSON, Prof Helen Valerie; CBE (2014); *Educ* Univ of Cambridge (MA), Imperial Coll London (PhD); *m* Rt Rev Richard William Bryant Atkinson, OBE; *Career* Atomic Energy Authy 1981–87, lectr, sr lectr then reader in engrg materials Univ of Sheffield 1989–2002, chair in metals processing and head Dept of Engrg Univ of Leicester 2002–; former pres Engrg Profs' Cncl; FREng (tstee and former vice-pres), CEng, FIMMM, FIMechE; *Style*— Prof Helen Atkinson, CBE; ✉ Department of Engineering, University Road, Leicester LE1 7RH

ATKINSON, Jane Elizabeth; da of William Gledhill (d 1969), and Ethel, *née* Stopps (d 1978); *b* 20 July 1947; *Educ* Kesteven and Sleaford HS for Girls; *m* 1, 1967 (m dis 1973), David Hayward; 1 s (Anthony b 1967); m 2, 1975, George Ronald Atkinson; 1 s (Nicholas b 1980), 1 da (Caroline b 1984); *Career* sec until 1975, asst account exec Planned Public Relations International 1975–76, account exec Welbeck PR 1976–78, sr client conslt Bell Capper PR 1978–80, bd dir Eurocom PR 1980, jt md Granard Communications (after merger with Eurocom PR 1982) 1988, dep chm The Rowland Company (result of Granard merger with Kingsway PR) 1990–94, jt md Affinity Consulting Ltd (Countrywide Group) 1992–95, ptnr Atkinson Courage Communications 1995–97, dir Bell Pottinger Conslts (formerly Bell Pottinger Communications) 2000–02 (sr conslt 1997–2000), dir of global communications JCB 2002–03, dir Glenfern Communications Mgmnt Consultancy 2004–05, dir Surprisecharter 2004–, dir and co-fndr Atkinson Hardwick PR 2006–09, assoc Project Assocs Ltd 2010–; media advsr to Diana, Princess of Wales Jan-July 1996 (resigned); past pres Women in Public Relations; memb Bd Forum UK, memb Bd of Govrs Eastbourne Coll, chm Eastbourne Coll Fndn, memb Bd Women's Leadership Gp Prince's Tst, memb Advsy Bd Global Poverty Project; FRSA; *Recreations* cooking, reading, walking, amateur dramatics, boating; *Style*— Mrs Jane Atkinson; ✉ 77 Sutton Court Road, London W4 3EG (☎ 020 8994 7082)

ATKINSON, Prof John; s of John Jennings Atkinson (d 1974), and Cecil Priscilla, *née* Sully (d 1996); *b* 10 March 1942; *Educ* Norwich Sch, Imperial Coll London; *m* 17 July 1978, Josephine, da of John Thomas Kirby, of Brentford, Middx; 2 s (Robert b 1978, Nicholas b 1981); *Career* engr; Coffey & Ptnrs Brisbane 1967–69, Imperial Coll London 1969–73, Univ of Cambridge 1973–76, UC Cardiff 1976–80; currently prof of soil mechanics City Univ; CEng, CGeol, FICE, FGS; *Books* The Mechanics of Soils (1978), Foundations and Slopes (1981), The Mechanics of Soils and Foundations (1993); *Recreations* sailing, surfing, the countryside; *Clubs* Norfolk Punt; *Style*— Prof John Atkinson; ✉ Department of Civil Engineering, City University, Northampton Square, London EC1V 0HB (☎ 020 7040 5060, e-mail j.h.atkinson@city.ac.uk)

ATKINSON, Kate; MBE (2011); *b* York; *Educ* Univ of Dundee (MA); *Family* 2 da (Eve b 1975, Helen b 1984); *Career* writer; *Books* Behind the Scenes at the Museum (1995, Whitbread Book of the Year), Human Croquet (1997), Emotionally Weird (2000), Not the End of the World (2002), Case Histories (2004), One Good Turn (2006), When Will There Be Good News? (2008), Started Early, Took My Dog (2010), Life After Life (2013, winner Costa Novel Award 2013), A God In Ruins (2015); *Plays* Abandonment (2000); *Style*— Ms Kate Atkinson, MBE; ✉ c/o Doubleday, Transworld Publishers, 61–63 Uxbridge Road, London

ATKINSON, (Michael) Kent; s of Carl Kent Atkinson (d 1999), and Jill, *née* Gilbert (d 1980); *b* 19 May 1945, Recife, Brazil; *Educ* Blundell's; *m* 17 Oct 1970, Eufemia Alexandra, da of Enrique Alarcón; 2 s (Carl Kent b 15 March 1972, Michael Alexander b 24 March 1976); *Career* with Bank of London and S America (later acquired by Lloyds Bank) and various sr managerial positions in Latin America and the ME 1964–89; regnl exec dir S E Region Lloyds Bank 1990–94; Lloyds TSB Gp: fin dir 1994–2002, non-exec dir 2002–03; chm Link Plus Corp 2006–08; sr ind dir: Coca-Cola HBC SA 1998–2013 (also chm Audit Ctee), Telent plc (formerly Marconi Corp plc) 2002–07 (also chm Audit Ctee and memb Remuneration and Nomination Ctees), Cookson Gp plc 2002–04 (also chm Audit Ctee and memb Remuneration and Nominations Ctees), UK Asset Resolution Ltd (previously Northern Rock plc, which includes Northern Rock (Asset Mgmnt) plc and Bradford and Bingley plc) 2008– (also chm Audit Ctee and memb Risk Ctee); non-exec dir: Gemalto NV (previously Axalto NV) 2004–13 (also memb Audit, Strategy and M&A Ctees), Standard Life plc 2005–11 (also chm Gp Audit and Compliance Ctee and memb Investment and Risk and Capital Ctees), Millicom Int Cellular SA 2007–10 (also memb Audit Ctee), Bank of Ireland Gp 2012– (chm Gp Audit Ctee and memb Ct Risk Ctee); *Recreations* tennis and golf (active), Rugby Union, soccer, personal computers, theatre, travel; *Clubs* Effingham Golf, Horsley Sports; *Style*— M Kent Atkinson, Esq

ATKINSON, Prof Margaret Elizabeth (Maggie); *née* Cragg; da of Colin Cragg (d 2000), and Kathleen, *née* McLoughlin; *b* 16 September 1956, Barnsley, South Yorkshire; *Educ* Pope Pius X RC Comp Sch Wath-upon-Dearne, Mexborough VI Coll Yorkshire, Univ of Cambridge (BA), Univ of Sheffield (PGCE), Keele Univ (EdD); *m* 1999, Andrew; 2 step c; *Career* teacher Doncaster 1979–87, head of English Dewsbury 1987–89, Language In the National Curriculum (LINC) regional co-ordinator North and West Yorks 1989–91, educn advsr Birmingham 1991–92, inspector and curriculum advice mangr Kirklees 1992–98, asst dir of educn Warrington 1998–99, county mangr Inclusion and Sch Improvement Cheshire 1999–2003, dir of children's services Gateshead 2003–10, Children's Cmmr for England 2010–15, dir iMPOWER Consulting Ltd (public sector improvement, demand management, behaviour change, new service models) 2015–; memb DH Children and Young People's Health Outcomes Forum 2012–15, advsr to chief medical offr on annual reports 2012 and 2013, memb ministerial taskforce on children and young people's emotional and mental health 2014–15 leading to Future in Mind strategy published 2015, lead thinker Nat Educn Tst 2014–; hon prof Keele Univ 2013–, memb Univ Ct Grosseteste Univ Lincoln 2013–15; pres Assoc of Directors of Children's Services (ADCS) 2008–09 (vice-pres 2007–08, currently assoc memb); chair A New Direction (culture, arts and education charity) 2014–, tstee Michael Sieff Fndn 2015–, assoc memb Solace 2015–, memb Kidzania London think tank 2015–; regular columnist TES online 2015–, occasional author of blogs and other pieces for iMPOWER and others; President's Medal RCPsych 2014; DCL (hc) Northumbria Univ, DCL (hc) Keele Univ 2015; FInstAM, FInstLM, FRSA, MIFPA; *Books* CAMHS: Time to Transform (2015); *Publications* all pubns of the Office of the Children's Cmmr 2010–14, Disability and Economic Disadvantage: Facing the Facts (in BMJ Archive of Diseases in Childhood, 2015), chapter on the changes wrought by the participation of children and young people in decision making and service development (in Research in Practice, 2015); *Recreations* cinema, gardening, music, reading, travel, walking, theatre; *Clubs* Civil Service, Northumbrian Pipers Soc; *Style*— Prof Maggie Atkinson; ☎ 07832 719845, e-mail maggie.e.atkinson@gmail.com, Twitter @matkinson956

ATKINSON, Very Rev Peter Gordon; s of Thomas John Collins Atkinson (d 1986), of Maidstone, and Adèle Mary, *née* Cox (d 2000); *b* 26 August 1952; *Educ* Maidstone GS, St John's Coll Oxford (scholar, sr scholar, Denyer and Johnson student, Liddon student, MA), Westcott House Cambridge; *m* 1983, Lynne, da of Brian Wilcock (d 2010); 2 s (James David b 1985, Leo Francis b 1992), 1 da (Elizabeth Grace b 1987); *Career* ordained: deacon 1979, priest 1980; asst curate Clapham Old Town Team Miny 1979–83, priest-in-charge St Mary's Tatsfield 1983–90, rector of Holy Trinity Bath 1990–91, princ Chichester Theol Coll 1991–94, rector of Lavant 1994–97, residentiary canon Chichester Cathedral 1991–2007 (Bursalis preb 1991–94, chllr 1994–2007), proctor in convocation 2000–05, dean of Worcester 2007–; Hon DLitt Univ of Worcester 2014; FRSA 2006; *Publications* Friendship and the Body of Christ (2004), The Lion Encyclopedia of the Bible (2009); *Style*— The Very Rev the Dean of Worcester; ✉ The Deanery, 10 College Green, Worcester WR1 2LH (☎ 01905 732939, work tel 01905 732909, e-mail peteratkinson@worcestercathedral.org.uk)

ATKINSON, Rowan Sebastian; CBE (2013); s of Eric Atkinson (d 1984), and Ella May Atkinson (d 1998); *b* 6 January 1955; *Educ* Durham Cathedral Choristers' Sch, St Bees' Cumbria, Univ of Newcastle upon Tyne (BSc), The Queen's Coll Oxford (MSc); *m* 1990 (m dis 2015), Sunetra Sastry; *Career* actor and writer; *Theatre* West End performances incl: One Man Show 1981 and 1986 (SWET Award for Comedy Performance of the Year), The Nerd 1984, Chekhov's The Sneeze 1988, Oliver! 2009, Quartermaine's Terms 2013; one man show tours to Aust, Canada, USA, and Far East; *Television* for BBC incl: Not The Nine O'Clock News 1979–82, The Black Adder 1983, Blackadder II 1985, Blackadder the Third 1987, Blackadder Goes Forth 1989; other credits incl: Mr Bean (Tiger Aspect for ITV) 1990–95, The Thin Blue Line (Tiger Aspect for BBC) 1995 and 1996, Mr Bean (animated series) 2002–03 and 2014–15, Maigret 2016; *Films* The Tall Guy 1989, The Appointments of Dennis Jennings 1989, The Witches 1990, Hot Shots – Part Deux 1993, Four Weddings and a Funeral 1994, The Lion King (voiceover) 1994, Bean – The Ultimate Disaster Movie 1997, Blackadder Back and Forth (Millennium Dome) 1999, Maybe Baby 2000, Rat Race 2001, Scooby Doo 2002, Johnny English 2003, Love Actually 2003, Keeping Mum 2006, Mr Bean's Holiday 2007, Johnny English Reborn 2011; *Awards* BBC TV Personality of the Year 1980 and 1989, Br Acad Award 1980 and 1989; *Recreations* motor cars (regular columnist Car magazine 1992–94, columnist Octane magazine 2003–08), motor sport; *Style*— Rowan Atkinson, Esq, CBE; ✉ c/o PBJ and JBJ Management, 22 Rathbone Street, London W1T 1LA (☎ 020 7287 1112, fax 020 7287 1191, e-mail general@pbjmanagement.co.uk)

ATKINSON, Prof Sue; CBE (2002); *b* 10 August 1946; *Educ* Merchant Taylors' Sch for Girls, UCNW (BSc), Univ of Cambridge (MA, MB BChir), Middx Hosp Med Sch London; *m* 2004, Peter Coe; 1 da (Zoe), 3 step c (Toby, Luci, Jenny); *Career* paediatric, neonatal, paediatric oncology and paediatric research SHO, registrar and research posts Addenbrooke's Hosp Cambridge and Royal Hosp for Sick Children Bristol 1975–79, registrar then sr registrar in public health Avon AHA 1980 and 1982–85, res fell Nat Health and MRC Unit of Epidemiology and Preventative Med Univ of Western Australia 1980–81, GP 1981–82, conslt in public health med Bristol and Western HA 1985–87, sr lectr UMDS and conslt in public health Lewisham and N Southwark HA 1987, dir of public health and serv devpt Lewisham and N Southwark HA and sr lectr UMDS 1988–91, dir of public health SE London HA 1991–93 (actg chief exec 1993), dir of health strategy/regnl dir of public health Wessex then S and W RHA 1993–94, dir of public health/med dir S Thames RHA/RO 1994–98, dir of public health/med dir London RO 1999–2006, health advsr to Mayor and GLA and regnl dir of public health (London) Dept of Health 2000–06, Dept of Health lead for London Olympics and Paralympics bid 2005–; special advsr to House of Commons Select Ctee in its examination of NHS Reforms and NHS Tsts 1991–92; Faculty of Public Health Med: memb Bd 1990–93, memb Exec Ctee 1990–93; chair Gtr London Alcohol and Drug Alliance 2006–08, memb Bd Food Standards Agency 2008–14, chair Public Health Action Support Team (PHAST) 2008–; chair Ct LSHTM 2001–08 (also memb Bd), visiting prof Dept of Epidemiology and Public Health UCL 2002–, non-exec dir UCLH 2007–13; memb Bd Patients Assoc 1999–2001; Joan H Tisch distinguished fell in public health Hunter Coll NY 2012, res fell LSHTM 2014–15; FFPHM 1990 (MFPHM 1985); *Publications* author of numerous papers in professional jls, articles and chapters on vision screening, spastic diplegia, health impact assessment, public health issues, health and the GLA and mayor; *Recreations* theatre, cinema, music, art, furniture restoration; *Style*— Prof Sue Atkinson, CBE

ATKINSON, Sir William Samuel; kt (2008); s of William Benjamin Atkinson (d 2004), and Sara Jane Atkinson (d 1982); *b* 9 April 1950, St Ann, Jamaica; *Educ* KCL (MA); *m* 6 April 1974, Jacqueline Ann, *née* Burley; 3 s (Simon b 23 Dec 1975, Selwyn b 26 April 1980, Sheldon b 20 Feb 1985), 1 da (Lekisha b 17 Dec 1988); *Career* dep head: Henry Thornton London 1981–83, White Hart Lane Sch London 1983–86; headteacher: Copland Community Sch London 1986–87, Cranford Community Sch London 1987–95, Phoenix HS London 1995–; memb: Special Measures Action Recovery Team DfEE 1997, DfEE Standards Task Force 1997–2001, Home Office Justice Task Force 1999, Home Office London Youth Crime Reduction Task Force 2003–04, London BME Cracking Crime Partnership Bd until 2006, Br Board of Film Classification Advsy Panel on Children's Viewing; nat judge Teaching Awards 2002– (dep chair Nat Judging Panel 2006), chair London Teaching Awards Panel 2003; tstee: Inst for Citizenship, Shaftesbury Homes, Arethusa Charity; GG2 Teacher of the Year Leadership and Diversity Award 2002; television appearances incl: Just William (BBC 2) 1999, Crisis Command (BBC 2), The Unteachables (Channel 4); contrib to a range of TV and radio progs incl: Newsnight, Panorama, Any Questions, You and Yours, Today, Start the Week, Radio 5 Live, PM, BBC Question Time, Breakfast Television; memb Cncl Industrial Soc; hon doctorate Univ of North London 2002; FRSA 2002 (memb Cncl 2004); *Recreations* rugby, theatre, family; *Style*— Sir William Atkinson; ✉ Phoenix High School, The Curve, Shepherds Bush, London W12 0RQ (☎ 020 8735 1501, fax 020 8743 0913, e-mail william_atkinson@phoenix.llbhf.sch.uk, website www.phoenix.llbhf.sch.uk)

ATTA, Hatem Riad; s of Riad Gorgi Atta (d 1995), of Egypt, and Jozephine Matta, *née* Ebrahim (d 1989); *b* 12 August 1951, Tanta, Egypt; *Educ* Private Mission Sch Egypt, Tanta Univ Egypt (MB BCh), DO; *m* 26 June 1982, Janet Ann, da of Samuel John Saunders (d 1988); *Career* sr registrar in ophthalmology West Midlands RHA 1983–88, fell in ophthalmic ultrasonography Miami Sch of Med 1986–87, conslt ophthalmic surgn Aberdeen Royal Infirmary 1988–2012, currently conslt ophthalmic surgeon BMI Albyn Hosp Aberdeen; hon sr lectr Univ of Aberdeen 1988–12; author of papers in scientific jls; memb: Oxford Congress, Int Soc of Ophthalmic Ultrasound; FRCSEd 1982, FRCOphth 1988; *Books* Techniques and Application of Diagnostic Ultrasound (1990), Ophthalmic Ultrasound – a practical guide (1996), Ocular Echography in Multimodal Retinal Imaging (2014); *Recreations* racquet sports, golf, scuba diving; *Clubs* Aberdeen Petroleum, Royal Aberdeen Golf, Aberdeen Medical Golf Society, Royal Colleges' Golf (Edinburgh), Royal Northern and University (Aberdeen); *Style*— Hatem Atta, Esq; ✉ Sunningdale, Sunert Road, Milltimber, Aberdeen (☎ 01224 861849)

ATTALLAH, Naim Ibrahim; s of Ibrahim Attallah, and Genevieve Attallah; *b* 1 May 1931; *Educ* Battersea Poly; *m* 1957, Maria, da of Joseph Nykolyn; 1 s; *Career* foreign exchange dealer 1957, fin conslt 1966, dir of companies 1969–; book publisher and prop: Quartet Books 1976–, The Women's Press 1977–, Robin Clark 1980–; magazine prop: The Literary Review 1981–2001, The Wire 1984–2000, The Oldie 1991–2001; articles in The Literary Review, princ interviewer The Oldie; Asprey plc: fin dir and jt md 1979–92, chief exec 1992–95; md Mappin & Webb 1990–95, md Watches of Switzerland 1992–95, exec dir Garrard 1990–95; prop The Academy Club 1989–97; parfumier: launched Parfums Namara 1985 with Avant l'Amour and Aprés l'Amour, Naïdor in 1986, l'Amour de Namara 1990; theatrical prodr: Happy End (co-presenter, Lyric) 1975, The Beastly Beatitudes of Balthazar B (presenter and prodr, Duke of York's) 1981, Trafford Tanzi (co-prodr, Mermaid) 1982; film prodr: The Slipper and the Rose (co-prodr with David Frost) 1974–75, Brimstone and Treacle (exec prodr) 1982; also produced and presented TV documentaries; Retail Personality of the Year UK Jewellery Awards 1993; Hon MA Univ of Surrey 1993; FRSA; *Books* Women (1987), Singular Encounters (1990), Of a Certain Age (1992), More of a Certain Age (1993), Speaking for the Oldie (1994), A Timeless Passion (1995), Tara and Claire (1996), Asking Questions (1996), In Conversation with Naim Attallah (1998), A Woman a Week (1998), Insights (1999), Dialogues (2000), The Old Ladies of Nazareth (2004), The Boy In England (2005), In Touch with his Roots (2006), Fulfilment & Betrayal (2007); *Recreations* classical music, opera, theatre, cinema, photography; *Clubs* Arts, Beefsteak; *Style*— Naim Attallah, Esq; ✉ 25 Shepherd Market, London W1J 7PP (☎ 020 7499 2901, fax 020 7499 2914, e-mail nattallah@aol.com, website http://quartetbooks.wordpress.com)

ATTENBOROUGH, Sir David Frederick; OM (2005), CH (1996), kt (1985), CVO (1991), CBE (1974); s of Frederick Levi Attenborough (d 1973), and Mary, *née* Clegg (d 1961); bro of Baron Attenborough, CBE (Life Peer) (d 2014); *b* 8 May 1926; *Educ* Wyggeston GS for Boys Leicester, Clare Coll Cambridge (hon fell 1980); *m* 1950, Jane Elizabeth Ebsworth Oriel (d 1997); 1 s, 1 da; *Career* naturalist, traveller, broadcaster and writer; served RN 1947–49; editorial asst in an educational publishing house 1949–52, prodr talks and documentary progs BBC 1952, controller TV BBC2 1965–68, dir of Programmes TV and memb Bd of Management BBC 1969–72; zoological and ethnographic filming expeditions to: Sierra Leone 1954, Br Guiana 1955, Indonesia 1956, New Guinea 1957, Paraguay and Argentina 1958, South West Pacific 1959, Madagascar 1960, Northern Territory Australia 1962, Zambesi 1964, Bali 1969, Central New Guinea 1971, Celebes 1973, Borneo 1973, Peru 1973, Columbia 1973, Mali 1974, Br Columbia 1974, Iran 1974, Solomon Islands 1974, Nigeria 1975; writer and presenter BBC series: Zoo Quest 1954–64, Tribal Eye 1976, Life on Earth 1979, The Living Planet 1984, The First Eden 1987, Lost Worlds Vanished Lives 1989, The Trials of Life 1990, The Private Life of Plants 1995, The Life of Birds 1998, The Blue Planet 2001, Life In The Undergrowth 2005, Planet Earth 2006, Life in Cold Blood 2008 (Best Specialist Factual BAFTA 2009), Frozen Planet 2011, Africa 2012; tstee: World Wildlife Fund UK 1965–69, 1972–82 and 1984–90, World Wildlife Fund Int 1979–86, Br Museum 1980–, Science Museum 1984–87, Royal Botanic Gardens Kew 1986–92, Learning Through Landscapes 1990–; memb Nature Conservancy Cncl

1973–82, corresponding memb American Museum of Natural History 1985, Huw Wheldon Meml Lecture RTS 1987; fell BAFTA 1980; awards: Special Award SFTA 1961, Silver Medal Zoological Soc of London 1966, Silver Medal RTS 1966, Desmond Davis Award SFTA 1970, Cherry Kearton Medal RGS 1972, Kalinga Prize UNESCO 1981, Washburn Award Boston Museum of Science 1983, Hopper Day Medal Acad of Natural Sciences Philadelphia 1983, Founder's Gold Medal RGS 1985, Int Emmy Award 1985, Encyclopaedia Britannica Award 1987, Livingstone Medal RSGS 1990; Hon Freeman City of Leicester 1990; hon fell: Manchester Poly 1976, UMIST 1980; Hon DLitt: Univ of Leicester 1970, City Univ 1972, Univ of London 1980, Univ of Birmingham 1982; Hon LLD: Univ of Bristol 1977, Univ of Glasgow 1980; Hon DSc: Univ of Liverpool 1974, Heriot-Watt Univ 1978, Univ of Sussex 1979, Univ of Bath 1981, Ulster Univ 1982, Univ of Durham 1982, Keele Univ 1986, Univ of Oxford 1988; Hon DUniv: Open Univ 1980, Univ of Essex 1987; Hon ScD Univ of Cambridge 1984, Hon DSc Univ of Aberdeen 2008; Cdr of the Golden Ark (Netherlands) 1983; Hon FRCP 1991, FRS 1983, Hon FRSE 2005; *Books* Zoo Quest to Guiana (1956), Zoo Quest for a Dragon (1957), Zoo Quest in Paraguay (1959), Quest in Paradise (1960), Zoo Quest to Madagascar (1961), Quest under Capricorn (1963), The Tribal Eye (1976), Life on Earth (1979), The Living Planet (1984), The First Eden (1987), The Trials of Life (1990), The Private Life of Plants (1995), The Life of Birds (1998), The Blue Planet (2001), Life on Air (2002), Life of Mammals (2002), Life In The Undergrowth (2005); *Recreations* tribal art, natural history; *Style*— Sir David Attenborough, OM, CH, CVO, CBE, FRS; ✉ 5 Park Road, Richmond, Surrey TW10 6NS

ATTENBOROUGH, Hon Michael John; CBE (2013); s of Baron Attenborough, Kt CBE (Life Peer) (d 2014), and Sheila Beryl Grant, *née* Sim (d 2016); *b* 13 February 1950, London; *Educ* Westminster, Univ of Sussex (BA, pres Univ Drama Soc); *m* 1, 10 July 1971 (m dis 1976), Jane Seymour, *qv*; m 2, 14 April 1984, Karen Esther, yr da of Sydney Victor Lewis (d 1990), of London; 2 s (Thomas Frederick Richard b 13 Oct 1986, William Grant Oliver b 26 June 1991); *Career* theatre director; asst dir Gardner Centre Theatre 1972; assoc dir: Mercury Theatre Colchester 1972–74, Leeds Playhouse 1974–79, Young Vic Theatre 1979–80; artistic dir: Palace Theatre Watford 1980–84, Hampstead Theatre 1984–89, Turnstyle Group 1989–90; princ assoc dir RSC 1990–2002, artistic dir Almeida Theatre 2002–13; freelance work as dir incl prodns for: Open Space Theatre, Red Ladder, Newcastle Playhouse, Citadel Theatre Edmonton, Abbey Theatre Dublin, Tricycle Theatre, Royal Court Theatre London, National Theatre, Hampstead Theatre (Godchild, Luna Gale and Reasons to be Happy), The Queensland Theatre Co (Macbeth), Bill Kenwright Prodns (Dangerous Corner) and Washington Theatre Co (As You Like It), Queensland Theatre Company, Washington Shakespeare Company, Chichester Festival Theatre; dir of over 100 plays to date; hon prof of English Univ of Sussex 2011–; vice-chair Cncl RADA, dep chair Drama Panel Arts Cncl; former memb: Greater London Arts, Bubble Theatre Bd, Cncl Directors' Guild; dir Susan Smith Blackburn Prize; tstee Belarus Free Theatre; Time Out Theatre Award for Observe The Sons of Ulster Marching Towards The Somme 1986, nominated Best Dir London Theatre Critics Awards 1985, nominated Outstanding Achievement Award (as dir Hampstead Theatre) Olivier Awards 1986, Int Theatre Inst Award for Excellence in Int Theatre 2012; hon assoc artist RSC 2002; Hon DLitt: Univ of Sussex 2005, Univ of Leicester 2009; *Recreations* being with my family, football, music, theatre; *Style*— The Hon Michael Attenborough, CBE, DLitt; ✉ c/o United Agents, 12–26 Lexington Street, London W1F 0LE (☎ 020 3214 0800)

ATTLEE, 3 Earl (UK 1955); John Richard Attlee; TD; also Viscount Prestwood (UK 1955); o s of 2 Earl Attlee (d 1991), and his 1 w, Anne Barbara, eldest da of James Henderson, CBE; gs of 1 Earl Attlee, KG, OM, CH, PC (d 1967, Lab PM 1945–51); *b* 3 October 1956; *Educ* Stowe; *m* 27 Sept 2008, Teresa Ahern; *Career* with engrg and automotive industries until 1993; international aid with British Direct Aid in Bosnia 1993–94, in-country dir British Direct Aid in Rwanda 1995–96; oppn whip and spokesman for Trade and Industry House of Lords; oppn spokesman House of Lords: Energy and Defence 1998, NI 1998–2001, Tport and Defence, Trade and Industry until 2005, oppn whip and spokesman for maritime and shipping 2007–10, Govt whip, Lord in Waiting and Govt spokesman for tport, Dept for Communities and Local Govt, Home Office and NI House of Lords 2010–; pres Heavy Tport Assoc 1994–2009; TA Services Maj REME (V); *Recreations* restoration and repair of classic military and commercial vehicles; *Style*— The Earl Attlee, TD; ✉ House of Lords, London SW1A 0PW (☎ 020 7219 6071, fax 020 7219 5979, e-mail attleej@parliament.uk)

ATTWOOD, Brian Christopher; s of Raymond Attwood, and Eileen, *née* Power; *b* 29 February 1960, New Brighton, Wirral; *Educ* Watford Boys' GS, Univ of Stirling (BA), Centre for Journalism Cardiff (Dip Journalism); *m* 28 Sept 2002, Lisa, *née* Martland; 1 da (Eve Mary Chloe b 13 Sept 2001), 1 s (John Daniel b 19 April 2004); *Career* Chepstow Dist Reporter and News and Weekly Argus 1985, The Citizen Gloucester 1985–86, asst ed Stage and Television Today 1992–94 (reporter 1986–89, chief reporter 1989–92), ed The Stage 1994–; *Recreations* 20th century Irish history, entertainment, reading, the gym, family; *Style*— Brian Attwood, Esq; ✉ The Stage Newspaper Ltd, 47 Bermondsey Street, London SE1 3XT (☎ 020 7403 1818)

ATTWOOD, Frank Albert; s of late Eric George Attwood, of Broadstairs, Kent, and late Dorothy May, *née* Gifford; *b* 19 January 1943; *Educ* Simon Langton GS Canterbury, Leighton Park Sch Reading, Univ of Hull (BSc); *m* 10 July 1965, Pamela Ann Paget, da of late Samuel Kennedy Pickavor Hunter; 1 da (Rebecca b 1980); *Career* articled Sir Lawrence Robson 1965–68, CA 1968, chartered sec 1969, ptnr RSM Robson Rhodes LLP 1974–2004 (chm 1999–2004), ceo RSM International 1990–95 (conslt and non-exec dir 2004–), dir Medical Protection Soc 2004–13, dir Ridgeon Gp 2008–, dir Fortune Oil 2009–15, chm Urenco UK Pension Tstee Co 2009–; CCAB: former memb CAs Jt Int Cmmn, former memb Auditing Practices Ctee; ICAEW: former memb Insurance Sub-Ctee and Res Bd, jt auditor 1988–95; chm APC Lloyd's Working Pty 1982–90, dep chair Int Ethics Standards Bd for Accountants IFAC 2004–09; tstee East Malling Tst; Freeman City of London 1989, Liveryman Worshipful Co of Scriveners 1989; FCA, FRSA, MAE; *Books* De Paula's Auditing (jtly, 1976, 1982, 1986), Auditing Standards From Discussion Drafts to Practice (jtly, 1978); *Recreations* rambling, gardening, travel, modern novels, weight-training, watching cricket; *Style*— Frank Attwood, Esq; ✉ 30 Finsbury Square, London EC2P 2YU (☎ 020 7865 2512, fax 020 7865 2450, e-mail frank.attwood@uk.gt.com)

ATTWOOD, Keith; *b* 23 August 1960, Durban, SA; *Educ* Nottingham Trent Univ (MBA); *Career* dir and business mangr – overseas investments GPT Ltd 1994–97, ops dir GECMarconi Avionics Ltd 1997–98, ceo e2v Technologies plc 1998–; CBI: past chair and vice-chm East of England Regnl Cncl, chm Employment and Skills Bd; Hon DBA Anglia Ruskin Univ 2012; MCMI; *Style*— Keith Attwood, Esq; ✉ e2v Technologies plc, 106 Waterhouse Lane, Chelmsford, Essex CM1 2QU

ATWELL, Very Rev James Edgar; s of Joseph Norman Edgar Atwell (d 1965), of Rough Leaze Farm, Calne, Wilts, and Sybil Marion, *née* Burnett (d 1978); *b* 3 June 1946; *Educ* Dauntsey's Sch West Lavington, Exeter Coll Oxford (MA), The Divinity Sch Harvard Univ (ThM), Cuddesdon Theol Coll, Univ of Oxford (BD); *m* 1976, Lorna, da of Prof Geoffrey Goodwin (d 1995); 1 s (Luke Alexander Goodwin b 16 July 1978), 2 da (Elizabeth Anne Burnett b 8 Aug 1980, Mary Ellen Frances b 5 Nov 1982); *Career* ordained (Southwark Cathedral): deacon 1970, priest 1971; curate: of St John the Evangelist E Dulwich 1970–74, of Great St Mary's The Univ Church Cambridge 1974–77; chaplain of Jesus Coll Cambridge 1977–81, vicar of Towcester 1981–95 (rural dean 1983–91), dean of St Edmundsbury 1995–2006, dean of Winchester 2006–16 (dean emeritus 2016–); memb Cathedral Fabric Cmmn for England; hon prof Univ of Winchester 2011; Hon DD Univ of Winchester; *Publications* The Sources of the Old Testament (2004); *Recreations* driving a Land Rover, the countryside, travelling in the Middle East, fairground organs; *Style*— The Very Rev the Dean Emeritus of Winchester; ✉ 12 Ventress Farm Court, Cambridge, CB1 8HD

AUBREY, David John; QC (1996); s of Raymond John Morgan Aubrey (d 1976), and Dorothy Mary, *née* Griffiths (d 1990); *b* 6 January 1950; *Educ* Cathays HS Cardiff, Univ of Wales Cardiff (LLB), Inns of Court Sch of Law; *m* 4 Oct 1980, Julia Catherine, da of Melville John Drew; 1 da (Elinor Mary b 24 June 1991); *Career* called to the Bar Middle Temple 1976 (bencher 2002); head of chambers Temple Chambers Cardiff 1998–2011, head of chambers and door tenant Temple Court Chambers 2011–14 (door tenant), head of advocacy Public Defender Service Miny of Justice 2014–; recorder of the Crown Court 1998–; treas Wales & Chester Circuit 1999–2003; legal pres Mental Health Review Tbnl; memb: Personal Injuries Bar Assoc, Wales Medico-Legal Soc, Bar Cncl; pres The Boys' Bde in Wales, chm Boys' Bde Heritage Soc; *Recreations* gardening, cricket, music, collecting (chm Boys' Bde Heritage Soc), genealogy (memb Soc of Genealogists); *Clubs* Glamorgan CCC; *Style*— David Aubrey, Esq, QC; ✉ The Public Defender Service, Business Suite, 102 Petty France, London SW1H 9AJ (☎ 020 3334 4253, e-mail david.aubreyqc@legalaid.gsi.gov.uk); Temple Court Chambers Cardiff, Temple Court, 13a Cathedral Road, Cardiff CF11 9HA (☎ 029 2078 6509, mobile 01139 667886, e-mail david.aubrey1@virgin.net)

AUBREY, Juliet Emma; da of Roland Aubrey, of Llanelli, Dyfed, and Sylvia, *née* Sturgess, of Datchet, Berks; *Educ* Farnborough Hill Convent, Queen Anne's Sch Caversham, KCL (BA), Central Sch of Speech and Drama (Dip); *m* Steven James Dempster Ritchie; 2 da (Blythe, Lola-Blue); *Career* actress; *Theatre* incl: Anna Petrovna in Ivanov (RNT), Varvara in Summerfolk (RNT), Branwen in The Long Mirror (TheatrClwyd), Miranda in The Tempest (Oxford Stage Co), Pegeen in The Playboy of the Western World (King's Theatre), Irena in Three Sisters (Cry Havoc), Viola in Twelfth Night (Cry Havoc), Miss Nettles in Sammy's Magic Garden (Latchmere Theatre); *Television* incl: Madeleine in Ella and the Mothers, Elizabeth in Bertie and Elizabeth, Susan in The Mayor of Casterbridge, Esther in Cyclops, Annie in Extremely Dangerous, Sophia in The Unknown Soldier, Karen in Go Now, Dorothea in Middlemarch (BAFTA Award for Best Actress 1994, Broadcasting Press Guild Best Actress Award 1995), Sarah in The Moth, DI Chomsky in Supply and Demand, Isabella in Measure for Measure, Leah in Jacob, Kay in A Good Murder; *Radio* incl: Esther in Dirty Blonde, Marion in The Woman in White, Georgiana in Georgiana Duchess of Devonshire, Fanny Burney in Dear Little Burney, Portia in The Merchant of Venice, Desdemona in Othello, Eleanor in Chronicles of Barchester, Beatrice in Much Ado About Nothing; *Film* incl: Hannah in Jonah Who Lived in the Whale (Platea d'Oro Best Actress 1993), young Janet in Iris, Helen in Welcome to Sarajevo (official selection Cannes 1997), Martha in Time to Love, Madeleine in Food of Love (La Boule Best Actress 1997), Karen in Still Crazy (Golden Globe nomination 1999), Asya in The Lost Lover (Platea d'Oro Best Actress 2000), Lilian in For My Baby, Gloria in The Constant Gardener; *Style*— Ms Juliet Aubrey

AUBREY-FLETCHER, Sir Henry Egerton; 8 Bt (GB 1782), of Clea Hall, Cumberland; o s of Sir John Henry Lancelot Aubrey-Fletcher, 7 Bt (d 1992), and Diana Mary Fynvola, *née* Egerton (d 1996); *b* 27 November 1945; *Educ* Eton; *m* 1976, (Sara) Roberta, da of late Maj Robert Buchanan, of Blackpark Cottage, Evanton, Ross-shire; 3 s (John Robert b 1977, Thomas Egerton b 1980, Harry Buchanan b 1982); *Heir* s, John Aubrey-Fletcher; *Career* co dir; High Sheriff Bucks 1995–96, HM Lord-Lt Bucks 2006– (DL 1997, Vice Lord-Lt 1997–2006); *Style*— Sir Henry Aubrey-Fletcher, Bt; ✉ Estate Office, Chilton, Aylesbury, Buckinghamshire HP18 9LR (☎ 01844 265201, fax 01844 265203)

AUDLAND, William; QC (2015); s of Sir Christopher Audland, KCMG, and Lady Audland, *née* Sullivan; *b* 27 August 1966, Buenos Aires, Argentina; *Educ* Winchester, The Queen's Coll Oxford (BA), City Univ (DipLaw); *m* 2 July 1994, Maria Antonella, *née* Bonetti; 1 s (Edwin b 26 May 1997), 1 da (Esmé b 5 June 1999); *Career* called to the Bar 1992; memb: Professional Negligence Bar Assoc, Personal Injury Bar Assoc, European Circuit of the Bar; Chambers and Partners UK Bar Award for Personal Injury/Clinical Negligence Junior Barrister of the Year 2013; *Publications* Personal Injury Schedules: Calculating Damages (2010); *Recreations* cinema, opera, skiing, ski touring, theatre, diving, hockey, cycling; *Clubs* Richmond Hockey; *Style*— William Audland, Esq, QC; ✉ 12 King's Bench Walk, Temple, London EC4Y 7EL (☎ 020 7583 0811, e-mail audland@12kbw.co.uk, website www.12kbw.co.uk)

AUDLEY, Maxwell Charles (Max); s of Sir (George) Bernard Audley, *qv*, of London, and Barbara, *née* Heath; *b* 27 April 1954, London; *Educ* Highgate Sch London, Univ of Bradford (BA), Univ of Bonn, Coll of Law; *m* 18 June 1983, Rosamund, *née* Shore; 3 da (Laura b 4 June 1984, Alice b 15 Feb 1989, Claudia b 21 Oct 1992), 1 s (Charles b 24 Oct 1986); *Career* admitted slr 1980; founding ptnr and head of corp Hobson Audley 1983–2003, ptnr and London head of corp Faegre & Benson LLP 2003–08, ptnr then of counsel in corp gp Olswang 2008–; chm Trustis Ltd 1999–; dir GSS Energy Ltd 2011–; Brennan's Wig & Pen Law Prize 1980; Freeman City of London 1984, Liveryman Worshipful Co of Broderers, Liveryman Worshipful Co of Stationers and Newspaper Makers; memb Law Soc 1980; *Style*— Max Audley, Esq; ✉ Olswang, 90 High Holborn, London WC1V 6XX (☎ 020 7067 3484, fax 020 7067 3999, e-mail max.audley@olswang.com)

AUKIN, David; s of Charles Aukin (d 1981), and Regina, *née* Unger (d 2006); *b* 12 February 1942; *Educ* St Paul's, St Edmund Hall Oxford (BA); *m* 20 June 1969, Nancy Jane, da of Herman Meckler, of London and New York; 2 s (Daniel b 1970, Jethro b 1976); *Career* admitted slr 1965; literary advsr Traverse Theatre Club 1970–73, admin Oxford Playhouse Co 1974–75; dir: Hampstead Theatre 1978–83 (admin 1975–78), Leicester Haymarket Theatre 1983–86; exec dir RNT 1986–90, head of drama Channel 4 TV 1990–97, co-fndr of HAL Films 1998, ceo Daybreak Pictures Ltd; *Recreations* golf; *Clubs* RAC; *Style*— David Aukin, Esq; ✉ Elsinore House, 77 Fulham Palace Road, London W6 8JA

AULD, Prof (Alan) Graeme; s of Alan Talbert Auld, and Alice Jolly, *née* Coull; *b* 14 August 1941, Aberdeen; *Educ* Robert Gordon's Coll Aberdeen (Classical Dux, Mackenzie Shield), Univ of Aberdeen (MA, DLitt), Univ of Edinburgh (BD, PhD); *m* 23 Sept 1967, Dr Sylvia Joyce Auld, da of Maj Gen Stephen Lamplugh; 2 s (Alan Hamish b 20 Sept 1970, Fergus Stephen b 17 Feb 1973), 1 da (Caroline Mary b 28 April 1975); *Career* asst dir Br Sch of Archaeology Jerusalem 1969–72; Univ of Edinburgh: lectr 1972–85, sr lectr 1985–95, prof of Hebrew Bible 1995–2007, princ New Coll 2002–08; pres Soc for Old Testament Study 2005; FRSE, FSA Scot; *Books* Joshua, Moses and the Land (1980), Amos (1986), Kings without Privilege (1994), Jerusalem I: From the Bronze Age to the Maccabees (with Margreet Steiner, 1996), Joshua Retold: Synoptic Perspectives (1998), Samuel at the Threshold (2004), Joshua: Jesus Son of Naué in Codex Vaticanus (2005), I & II Samuel (2011); *Recreations* music, travel, walking; *Style*— Prof Graeme Auld; ✉ University of Edinburgh, New College, Mound Place, Edinburgh EH1 2LX (e-mail a.g.auld@ed.ac.uk)

AULD, Rosie; CBE (2011); *Career* head orthoptist Birmingham and Midland Eye Centre; memb Bd Br and Irish Orthoptic Soc 1990– (chm 2004–10); *Style*— Ms Rosie Auld, CBE; ✉ Birmingham Midland Eye Centre, City Hospital NHS Trust, Dudley Road, Birmingham B18 7QH

AUMONIER, John Martin; s of Lt Cdr Timothy Peppercorn Aumonier (d 1983), of Billingshurst, W Sussex, and Maureen, *née* Leonard (d 1985); *b* 5 January 1952; *Educ* John Fisher Sch Purley Surrey, Ledsham Ct Hastings, St Mary's Coll Guildford; *m* 17 Feb 1979, Sally Wallace, da of Maj John Wallace Goodwyn Kay (d 1972), of Cranleigh,

Surrey; 2 da (Jessica b 1985, Lucy b 1987); *Career* Advtg Dept London Evening News 1969–70, advtg exec Vogue 1970–72, media gp head Stewart & Jefferies Advertising 1972, sr exec Associated Independent Radio Services Ltd 1972–76, sales mangr Broadcast Marketing Services Ltd 1976–80; md: The Radio Business Ltd 1980–82, Radio Mercury plc 1982–92, Virgin Radio Ltd 1992–93, Talk Radio UK (third national independent station) 1993–95; chief exec Radio First plc; visiting examiner Crawley Coll of Technol; Ordre des Chevaliers du Bellay; *Recreations* radio, wine, food, travel; *Style*— John Aumonier, Esq; ✆ 01798 817414, e-mail johnaumonier@btopenworld.com

AUSSIGNAC, Pascal; s of Camille Aussignac, of La Rochelle, France, and Simone, *née* Robert; *b* 30 June 1967; *Educ* Lyceé Hotelier de Talence Bordeaux; *Career* chef; commis de cuisine Les Trois Marches Versailles 1984–85, commis de cuisine Le Divellec Paris 1985, chef de partie Le Potager du Roy Versailles 1985–87, chef de partie Jacques Cagna Paris 1987, chef de partie tournant Carré des Feuillants Paris 1988, private cook to the head of staff of the French Air Force (Nat Serv) 1988–89, chef de partie Wing Song (luxury cruise ship) 1990, chef de partie tournant Guy Savoy Paris 1990–91, pastry chef Stohrer Paris 1991–92, premier maître d'hôtel L'Escargot Montorgueil Paris 1992, head chef and event organiser Yvan Paris and Yes Receptions Paris 1993–96, fndr, mangr and chef de cuisine Les Restanques Grimaud 1997–98, fndr and co-prop Club Gascon (restaurant), Cellar Gascon (wine bar) and Comptoir Gascon (delicatessen, bakery and caterers) London 1998–, fndr Le Cercle 2004–; supporter Leuka; *Recreations* gardening, archery, diving; *Style*— Pascal Aussignac, Esq; ✉ Club Gascon, 57 West Smithfield, London EC1A 9DS (✆ 020 7796 0600, fax 020 7796 0601)

AUSTEN, David Lee; s of David Robert Austen, of Cambridge, and Joan Ellen, *née* Waters; *b* 11 April 1960; *Educ* Maidstone Coll of Art, RCA; *Partner* Mary Doyle; 1 da (Mia India b 19 Aug 1982), 1 s (Sam Joseph David b 21 Sept 1986); *Career* artist; solo exhibitions: Anthony Reynolds Gallery London 1986, 1988, 1991, 1992, 1994, 1995, 2000, 2001 and 2004, Serpentine Gallery 1987, Arnolfini Bristol 1988, Castle Museum and Art Gallery Nottingham 1989, Cirrus Los Angeles 1989, 1991, 1993 and 1994, Frith Street Gallery London 1990, Cornerhouse Manchester 1993, Mead Gallery Warwick Arts Centre 1997, Anthony Wilkinson London 1997, Inverleith House Edinburgh 1997, Galerie Holenbach Stuttgart 1997, Galerie Slewe Amsterdam 1998, Annandale Gallery Sydney 2001, Christchurch Mansion Ipswich 2001, Ingleby Gallery Edinburgh 2001, 2003 and 2006, Galleri Boumlou Bergen 2004, Peer London 2004, Milton Keynes Gallery 2007, Ingleby Gallery Edinburgh 2009, Stanley Picker Gallery Kingston Univ 2009, Modern Art Oxford 2010, Anthony Reynolds Gallery 2011, Edinburgh Film Festival 2012, The Gorgon's Dream, The Burns Monument (with Ingleby Gallery and Edinburgh Int Film Festival Edinburgh) 2012, The Gorgon's Dream, The Gorgon's Dream (ICA London) 2012, David Austen: Black Heart (Museo d'Arte Contemporanea di Cogliandrino (MACC) Contrada Timparossa Basilicata Italy) 2015, Basel Miami 2016; gp exhibitions incl: Between Identity & Politics (Gimpel Fils London/NY) 1986, Works on Paper (Anthony Reynolds Gallery London) 1986, Object and Image: Aspects of British Art in the 1980s (City Museum and Art Gallery Stoke-on-Trent) 1988, Poiesis (Graeme Murray Gallery Edinburgh 1990 and Fruitmarket Gallery Edinburgh 1992), New Voices (Centre de Conférences Albert Borschette Brussels) 1992, Twelve Stars (Belfast, Edinburgh and London) 1992–93, MOMA Oxford 1996, Whitechapel London 1997, Kettles Yard Cambridge 2003, Anthony Reynolds Gallery 2007, Watercolour (Tate Britain) 2012; Stanley Picker Fell in fine art Kingston Univ 2008–09, Working on the Inside (Tannery Arts @ The Drawing Room London) 2012, With An Apple I Will Astonish (Large Glass London) 2012, Language Games, an Introduction to the Art of Our Times (Centro de Artes Visuales Fundación Helgade Alvear Cáceres Spain) 2012, Drawing Biennial (Drawing Room London) 2013, Just what is it that makes today's homes so different, so appealing? (New Art Centre Salisbury) 2013, On Paper (Centro de Artes Visuales Fundación Helgade Alvear) 2013, Slow Learner (Timothy Taylor Gallery) 2014, The Nakeds (Drawing Room Tannery Arts London) 2014; *Style*— David Austen, Esq; ✉ c/o Ingleby Gallery, 6 Carlton Terrace, Edinburgh EH7 5DD (✆ 0131 556 4441, e-mail info@inglebygallery.com)

AUSTEN, Mark Edward; s of Capt George Ernest Austen (d 1987), of Ashtead, Surrey, and Eileen Gladys, *née* Thirkettle (d 1995); *b* 25 August 1949; *Educ* City of London Freemen's Sch, Harvard Business Sch (AMP); *m* 28 May 1977, Priscilla, da of Reginald Cyril Hart (d 1984), of Chiddingfold, Surrey; 1 s (Timothy b 1980), 1 da (Rachel b 1982); *Career* corp accounts trainee Reed International 1967–72, asst fin controller Henry Ansbacher 1972–75; PricewaterhouseCoopers Management Consultants (formerly Price Waterhouse before merger): conslt 1975–82, ptnr 1982–, ptnr in charge fin servs consltg UK 1985–90, Europe 1990–96 and worldwide 1996–2002, memb Global Consltg Mgmnt Bd 1996–2002, memb Global PwC Bd 2001–03; IBM Consulting Services 2003–04; dir: Smartstream Technologies 2004–07, Singer & Friedlander 2005–06, Standard Bank plc 2005–15, Temenos AG 2006–12, Liverpool Victoria Friendly Soc 2006 (chm 2013), IFB International 2006–09, Mott MacDonald Gp 2010–14, Home & Savings Bank; chm and fndr: Fair Food Fndn 2006–12, What's On Your Plate? (WOYP) 2006–12; tstee: Philharmonia Orch 2000–12, Arts & Business 2008 (chm 2011–12); Freeman City of London; FCMA 1976; *Recreations* music, squash, food, wine, golf; *Clubs* RAC, Colets, Royal St David's Golf; *Style*— Mark Austen, Esq; ✉ 18 Imber Park Road, Esher, Surrey KT10 8JB (e-mail mark.austen@gmail.com)

AUSTEN, Richard James; MBE (1996); s of late Capt George Albert Austen, MN, and late Joyce Margaret Austen; *b* 25 May 1955, Shoreham by Sea, W Sussex; *Educ* Steyning GS, Univ of Bristol (BA); *Career* diplomat; with Inland Revenue 1972–77, entered HM Dip Serv 1981, posted Dar es Salaam 1983, third sec (consular) Ottawa 1987–90, second sec FCO 1990–93, dep high cmmr Banjul 1993–96, first sec FCO 1996–2001, dep high cmmr Port Louis 2001–03, ambass to Mongolia 2004–06, ambass to Panama 2006–11; *Recreations* walking, reading, religion; *Style*— Mr Richard Austen, MBE; ✉ c/o Foreign & Commonwealth Office, King Charles Street, London SW1A 2AH

AUSTIN, Prof Brian; *b* 5 August 1951; *Educ* Mount Grace Comp Sch, Univ of Newcastle upon Tyne (BSc, PhD), Heriot-Watt Univ (DSc); *m* Dawn Amy, *née* Allen; 1 da (Aurelia Jean b 30 Sept 1987); *Career* res assoc Dept of Microbiology Univ of Maryland 1977–78 (postdoctoral fell 1975–77), sr scientific offr Fish Diseases Laboratory MAFF 1978–84; Dept of Biological Sciences Heriot-Watt Univ: lectr in aquatic microbiology 1984–89, reader 1989–92, head Div of Aquaculture 1990–93, prof 1992–, head of dept 1993–96; visiting prof: Central Univ of Venezuela 1985, 1992 and 1995, Univ of Kebangsaan 1989, Universidad del Zulia 1991; visiting scientist Ocean Univ of Qingdao 1990 and 1995 (guest prof 2000–); external examiner: Univ of Stirling 1982–83, Univ of Bombay 1984, Univ of Wales 1994, Univ of Rouen 1996, Robert Gordon Univ 1999, National Univ of Ireland 2000; non-exec dir Aquaculture Vaccines Ltd 1990–2002; memb: American Soc of Microbiology, Euro Assoc of Fish Pathologists, Soc of Applied Bacteriology, Soc for General Microbiology, UK Fedn of Culture Collections; author of numerous pubns and papers in learned jls; FRSA 1996, fell American Acad of Microbiology 1998, FHEA 2007; *Books* Modern Bacterial Taxonomy (with F G Priest, 1986, 2 edn 1993), Bacterial Fish Pathogens: disease in farmed and wild fish (with D A Austin, 1987, 4 edn 2007), Marine Microbiology (1988), Methods in Aquatic Bacteriology (ed, 1988), Methods for the Microbiological Examination of Fish and Shellfish (ed, 1989), Pathogens in the Environment (ed, 1991), The Genus *Aeromonas* (ed, 1996); *Recreations* gardening, literature, hiking, music, photography, theatre, travel, writing; *Style*— Prof Brian Austin; ✉ School of Life Sciences, John Muir Building, Heriot-Watt University, Riccarton, Edinburgh EH14 4AS (✆ 0131 451 3452, fax 0131 451 3009, e-mail b.austin@hw.ac.uk)

AUSTIN, David Charles Henshaw; OBE (2007); s of Charles Frederick Austin (d 1980), of Broad Oak, Shrewsbury, and Lilian, *née* Kidson (d 1981); *b* 16 February 1926; *Educ* Shrewsbury; *m* 24 March 1956, Patricia Josephine, da of Leonard Dudley Braithwaite (d 1970); 1 da (Claire Rose 1957), 2 s (David Julian Charles b 1958, James b 1959); *Career* farmer 1943–70; professional rose breeder 1970– (non-professional 1946–70), fndr David Austin Roses 1970 (introduced 200 new English roses, distributed worldwide); memb Br Assoc of Rose Breeders; Hon DSc Univ of East London 1997; *Awards* Gold Veitch Memorial Medal RHS 1995, Royal Nat Rose Soc Award for Innovation in Rose Breeding 1995, Dean Hole Medal Royal Nat Rose Soc 2000, James Mason Award Royal Nat Rose Soc 2000, Victoria Medal of Honour RHS 2002, Lifetime Achievement Award Garden Centre Association 2004, The Queen Mother's Int Rose Award Nat Rose Soc 2007; *Books* The Heritage of the Rose (1988), Old Roses and English Roses (1992), Shrub Roses and Climbing Roses (1993), David Austin's English Roses (1993), The English Rose (1998), The English Roses (2005), The Breathing Earth (poetry, 2014); *Recreations* reading and writing poetry, current affairs, swimming, looking at gardens and countryside, farming and walking with my Staffordshire Bull Terrier; *Style*— David Austin, Esq, OBE; ✉ David Austin Roses, Bowling Green Lane, Albrighton, Wolverhampton, West Midlands WV7 3HB (✆ 01902 376300, fax 01902 372142, e-mail retail@davidaustinroses.com, website www.davidaustinroses.com)

AUSTIN, Ian; MP; *b* 6 March 1965; *Educ* Dudley Sch; *m* 3 c; *Career* cncllr Dudley Cncl 1991–95; former political advsr to Rt Hon Gordon Brown MP, memb Lab Pty W Midlands election campaign team 1997; MP (Lab) Dudley N 2005–; Parly prive sec to the PM 2007–08, asst whip 2008–09, Parly under-sec of state Dept for Communities and Local Govt and min for the W Midlands 2009–10; *Style*— Ian Austin, MP; ✉ Turner House, 157–185 Wrens Nest Road, Dudley, West Midlands DY1 3RU (✆ 01384 342503); House of Commons, London SW1A 0AA (✆ 020 7219 801)

AUSTIN, Mark; *b* 1 November 1958, London; *m* 1991, Catherine; 1 s (Jack b 1992), 2 da (Madeleine b 1994, Beatrice b 1997); *Career* gen reporter Bournemouth Daily Echo 1976–80; BBC: joined as newsroom writer, gen news reporter 1982–85, sports reporter 1985–86; ITV: joined as sports corr 1986, Evening News 2003–06, ITV News 2006–09, News At Ten 2008–; reported on events incl: Iraqi invasion of Kuwait, handover of Hong Kong to China, Rwandan civil war, Bosnian crisis, war in Kosovo, Mozambique floods (Int Emmy Award), NY terrorist attacks, war in Afghanistan, Beijing Olympics, Haiti earthquake (Int Emmy Award 2011); presenter Real Crime (ITV) 2011; RTS Presenter of the Year 2014; *Clubs* MCC; *Style*— Mark Austin, Esq; ✉ ITV Network Centre, 200 Gray's Inn Road, London WC1X 8HF (Twitter @markaustinitv)

AUSTIN, Dr Wendy Elizabeth; MBE (2012); da of late Cecil William Stead Austin, of Londonderry and Belfast, and late Irene Elizabeth Austin, *née* Wilson; *b* 19 November 1951; *Educ* Victoria Coll Belfast, Queen's Univ Belfast; *m* 1, 1982 (m dis 1995), Peter Hutchinson; 1 s (Niall b 27 Sept 1983), 2 da (Kerry b 10 June 1985, Clare b 8 April 1988); m 2, 2003, Frank Hewitt; *Career* freelance broadcaster/presenter, conference moderator, awards MC; NI Radio Broadcaster of the Year CIPR Award 2006; Hon DLitt Univ of Ulster 2005; *Television* incl: Children in Need (BBC TV) 1980–, Inside Ulster (BBC NI TV) 1980–85, Breakfast Time (BBC NI TV) 1982–87, Open House (BBC NI TV) 1990–93, The DIY Show (BBC NI TV), Hillsborough Revisited 2007, In Your Corner 2010 and 2012; *Radio* incl: Woman's Hour (from NI and London, BBC Radio) 1981–99, PM (BBC Radio 4) 1992–, Good Morning Ulster (BBC Radio Ulster) 1992–2009, Talkback (BBC Radio Ulster) 2009–14, Inside Business (BBC Radio Ulster) 2014–; *Recreations* travel, music, walking, wine; *Style*— Dr Wendy Austin, MBE; ✉ BBC Broadcasting House, Ormeau Avenue, Belfast BT2 8HQ (✆ 028 9269 8356, e-mail wendy.austin@bbc.co.uk, website www.wendyaustin.com, Twitter @wendytalksbizz)

AUSTWICK, Dawn; OBE; da of Kenneth Austwick, of Bath, and Gillian, *née* Griffin; *Educ* Univ of London (BA), London Business Sch (MBA); *m* 1990, Henry Stewart; 2 da (Rebecca b 20 Nov 1992, Miriam b 15 June 1994), 1 s (Gabriel b 15 Aug 1997); *Career* formerly: dep dir Br Museum, project dir Tate Modern, princ conslt KPMG; chief exec Esmée Fairbairn Fndn until 2013, chief exec Big Lottery Fund 2013–; dir Big Society Capital; tstee Historic Royal Palaces, chair Fndns Forum; hon doctorate London Met Univ; CIMgt; *Style*— Mrs Dawn Austwick, OBE; ✉ Big Lottery Fund, 1 Plough Place, London EC4A 1DE

AVERILL, Michael Charles Edward; s of Charles Rochford Averill, of Harlaxton, Lincs, and Peggy Louise, *née* Cooke; *b* 14 May 1951, London; *Educ* Royal Sch of Mines Imperial Coll London (BSc), Cranfield Mgmnt Sch (MBA); *m* 15 March 1980, Janet Marjorie, *née* Phillips; 1 s (Thomas Rochford b 22 Dec 1981), 1 da (Lucy Jane b 21 Sept 1983); *Career* Henry Wiggin (Inco) Sales 1974–75, various positions (latterly bus devpt mangr) Plessey Co plc 1975–87, mktg dir Herga Electric Ltd 1987–89, md Environmental Servs Div Rechem/Shanks Gp 1989–94, gp chief exec Shanks Gp plc 1994–2007 (conslt 2007–08); non-exec dir: TDG plc 2003–08, Biffa Gp Hldgs Ltd 2013–; dir Environmental Services Assoc 1994–2007, pres European Federation of Waste Mgmnt (FEAD) 2006–08 (vice-pres 1995–2006), non-exec dir Waste and Resources Action Programme (WRAP) 2000–09; non-exec dir: Care UK plc 2006–10, Speedy Hire plc 2008–15; non-exec chm: Enviroco Ltd 2008–12, JBMI Ltd 2008–09, Rochford Gp Aust 2010–, Fishers Gp Ltd 2013–; dir Supervisory Bd Van Gansewinkel Groep Netherlands 2015–; ARSM, FCIWM 2004; *Recreations* golf, gastronomy, motor sport; *Clubs* Home House; *Style*— Michael Averill, Esq

AVERY, Dr Brice Johnson; s of William Johnson Avery, of Haultwick, Herts, and Margaret Norma, *née* Booth; *b* 31 December 1959; *Educ* Bishop's Stortford Coll, Univ of Reading (BSc), Univ of Southampton (BM BS), Univ of Edinburgh; *m* 10 Sept 1993, Tina Louise, da of Barry Stott; 1 s (b 20 June 2003); *Career* trained in psychology, med, psychiatry and psychoanalytic psychotherapy; child and family psychiatrist, adult psychotherapist, business conslt and writer; regular appearer on radio and TV in religious, psychological and science programmes; hon fell Univ of Edinburgh 2016; PPL 1989, MRCPsych 1991, memb Soc of Authors 1994; *Books* Churches and How to Survive Them (1994), The Pastoral Encounter – Hidden Depths in Human Contact (1996), Principles of Psychotherapy (1996), The Plug at the Bottom of the Sea (1997), The Switch on the Back of the Moon (1998), Goodnight, Sleep Tight (contrib, 2000); *Style*— Dr Brice Avery; ✉ 4 Millerfield Place, Edinburgh EH9 1LW (✆ 0131 667 0252, e-mail post@briceavery.com)

AVERY, Bryan Robert; MBE (2015); *b* 2 January 1944, Aston Tirrold, Berks; *Educ* De Monfort Univ (DipArch), Univ of Essex (MA); *Career* fndr and princ Avery Architects (London) Ltd 1978–; projects incl: Tomorrow's Habitat Tsukuba (UNESCO Bronze Medal 1985), Museum of the Moving Image South Bank 1988 (Civic Trust Award 1989, PA Award for Innovation in the Public Buildings category for innovation in building design and construction 1989), refurbishment to public areas of Plantation House City of London (City Heritage Award 1992), No 1 Neathouse Place 1997 (Westminster Soc's Award 1997, Glassex Award for Best Building 1997, High Commendation British Construction Industry Awards 1997, Commendation in Building Structure National Lighting Design Awards 1997/98, Shapemakers Award Aluminium Imagination Architectural Awards 1997, Best Urban Workplace Building British Council for Offices (BCO) Award 1998, Millennium Products Award 1999, designated landmark status Westminster City Cncl 2010), RADA (Camden Design Award Commendation 2001, ADAPT Tst Access Award 2001, RIBA Award 2001, Merit Award US Inst of Theatre Technicians 2003, Building

Quality Awards 2003), BFI London IMAX 1999 (High Commendation British Construction Industry Award 1999, Millennium Products Award 1999, Civic Trust Award 2000, The Independent Comedia Creative City Award for Urban Innovation 2000, National Drywall Awards 2001), The Princess Alexandra Hall Royal Overseas League 2006, The London Transport Museum 2007 (Museums and Heritage Award 2008), 7–10 Old Bailey offices 2009 (Chicago Athenaeum International Architecture Award 2010), Repton Sch Theatre 2011 (RICS East Midlands Award design and innovation category 2012, Chartered Inst of Architectural Technologists' Technical Excellence Award 2012, RIBA East Midlands Building of the Year Award 2013); memb for Oxford Design Panel 2012–14, memb Southwark Design Panel 2012–, memb RIBA Awards Nat Panel 2014, adjudicator for RIBA, WAN and Civic Tst awards schemes; Bene Merenti Medal 'Ad Majorem Architecturae' Ion Minco Univ Sch of Architecture Bucharest 2015; RIBA (memb Registration Bd); Bryan Avery (1996), Fragments of Wilderness City (2011); *Style*— Bryan Avery, MBE; ✉ Avery Associates Architects, 270 Vauxhall Bridge Road, London SW1V 1BB (☎ 020 7233 6262, e-mail enquiries@avery-architects.co.uk. website www.avery-architects.co.uk, Twitter @averyarchitects)

AVERY, Catherine Rosemary Reid (Kate); *b* 30 January 1960; *Educ* Cranfield Sch of Mgmnt (MBA); *m* 10 July 1999, Anthony Vine-Lott, *qv*; *Career* Barclays plc: joined 1978, project mangr then mktg mangr Barclaycard 1987–89, planning, research and budgeting mangr Personal Sector Mktg Dept 1989–91, md Barclays Stockbrokers Ltd 1995–96 (sales and mktg dir 1992–93, business planning dir 1993–95), md Barclays Bank Tst Co Ltd 1995–96; memb Conversion/Flotation Project Team Halifax plc 1996; Legal & General plc: gp mktg dir 1996, gp mktg and direct dir 1996–99, retail customer dir 1999–2001, gp dir partnerships and direct 2001–02, gp dir retail distribution 2002–06, gp exec dir wealth mgmnt 2006–09, chair Gp Equality and Diversity Ctee; chm Openwork; non-exec dir: Kelda Gp plc 2005–08, Newcastle Building Soc, Rathbone Brothers plc; memb Distribution and Regulatory Ctee ABI 2004–; FSI, FCIM, ACIB; *Recreations* sailing, golf, gardening; *Style*— Mrs Kate Avery

AVERY, Dr Charles Henry Francis; s of Richard Francis Avery, of Richmond, Surrey, and Dorothea Cecilia, *née* Wharton; *b* 26 December 1940; *Educ* KCS Wimbledon, St John's Coll Cambridge (MA, PhD), Courtauld Inst of Art London (Academic Dip); *m* 11 June 1966, (Kathleen) Mary, da of Charles Gwynne Jones (d 1969); 3 da (Charlotte Frances, Susanna Mary, Victoria Jane (triplets) b 24 Feb 1970); *Career* dep keeper of sculpture V&A 1965–79, dir Sculpture Dept Christie's 1979–90, currently ind fine art conslt; Leverhulme research fell 1997–99; Cavaliere Dell'ordine Al Merito della Repubblica Italiana 1979, Medal of Ministry of Culture Poland; *Books* Florentine Renaissance Sculpture (1970), Studies in European Sculpture (1981, 1987), Giambologna the Complete Sculpture (1987), Renaissance and Baroque Bronzes in the Frick Art Museum (1993), Donatello: An Introduction (1994), David Le Marchand (1674–1726), An Ingenious Man for Carving in Ivory (1996), Bernini, Genius of the Baroque (1997), Studies in Italian Sculpture (2001), Francesco Bertos, The Triumph of Motion (2008), School of Dolphins (2009), Joseph de Levis & Company, Renaissance Bronze-Founders in Verona (2016); *Recreations* writing, reading; *Clubs* Oxford and Cambridge; *Style*— Dr Charles Avery; ✉ North View, Huntingdon Road, Girton, Cambridge CB3 0LQ (☎ 01223 276633, e-mail charles-avery@btconnect.com)

AVERY, Thomas Tilstone (Tom); s of Julian Avery, and Quenelda, *née* Kinsey; *b* 17 December 1975; *Educ* Harrow, Univ of Bristol (BSc); *m* Mary, *née* Eckersley Hope; 3 da (Maud Elizabeth, Olive Hope b 23 Sept 2009 (twins), Nell Constance b 26 May 2012); *Career* explorer; ldr Br Inca Mountains expdn to S American Andes 1997, ldr Br Silk Mountains expdn to Kyrgyzstan (incl 9 virgin summits up to 20,000 feet) 2000, youngest Briton to walk to S Pole 2002, ldr fastest group to walk to N Pole (Barclays Capital Ultimate North team, retracing Robert Peary's 1909 expedition; world record time of 36 days 22 hours 11 minutes) 2005, ldr fastest group to cross Greenland (world record time of 9 days 19 hours 40 minutes) 2015, youngest Briton to walk to both N and S Pole; ldr and memb of numerous mountaineering expdns to Argentina, Chile, Morocco, Tanzania, NZ and the Himalayas; trainee accountant Arthur Andersen 1998–2000, fndr, co-owner and dir Ski Verbier Exclusive Ltd 2009–; currently motivational speaker and writer; ambass: Prince's Tst, London 2012 Olympic Games bid; FRGS; Pole Dance (2004), To the End of the Earth (2009); *Recreations* skiing, sailing, golf, cricket, mountaineering, foreign travel; *Clubs* MCC, RGS, Explorers, Cordon Rouge, Soho House; *Style*— Tom Avery, Esq; ✉ e-mail info@tomavery.net

AVERY JONES, Dr John Francis; CBE (1987); s of Sir Francis Avery Jones, CBE (d 1998), and Dorothea Bessie, *née* Pfirter (d 1983); *b* 5 April 1940, Bromley, Kent; *Educ* Rugby, Trinity Coll Cambridge (MA, PhD, LLM); *m* 5 April 1994, Catherine Susan, *née* Bobbett; *Career* admitted slr 1966, ptnr Bircham & Co 1970–85, sr ptnr Speechly Bircham 1985–2001; special cmmr of income tax 2002–09 (dep special cmmr 1991–2001), chm VAT and Duties Tbnls 2002–09 (pt/t chm 1991–2001); judge of the Upper Tbnl (Tax and Chancery Chamber) 2009–11; jt ed British Tax Review 1974–97, memb Editorial Bd Simon's Taxes 1977–2001, visiting prof of taxation LSE 1986–2009; pres Inst of Taxation 1980–82, chm Tax Law Review Ctee 1998–2005; memb: Keith Ctee 1980–84, Cncl Law Soc 1986–90, Cncl Inst of Fiscal Studies 1988–2011, Exec Ctee Int Fiscal Assoc 1988–94 (chm Br Branch 1989–91), Bd of Tstees Int Bureau of Fiscal Documentation 1989–2011 (chm 1991–2002), Bd of Govrs Voluntary Hosp of St Bartholomew 1984–2011, Court of Govrs LSE 1995–2011; memb Ct of Assts Worshipful Co of Barbers (Master 1985–86), memb Ct of Assts City of London Solicitors' Co (Master 1997–98); memb Law Soc; Hon FTII; *Books* Encyclopedia of VAT (1972), Tax Havens and Measures Against Tax Avoidance and Evasion in the EEC (1974); *Recreations* music (particularly opera); *Clubs* Athenaeum; *Style*— Dr John Avery Jones, CBE; ✉ e-mail j.averyjones@gmail.com

AVIS, Alice; MBE (2009); da of Anthony Charles Avis (d 2004), of Ilkley, W Yorks, and Helen Lela Kyriacopoulou Avis; *b* 31 May 1962, Bradford, W Yorks; *Educ* Univ of Cambridge (MA), INSEAD (MBA); *m* 6 March 1999, Martyn Ward; 2 da (Daisy b 6 June 1999, Lola b 15 Aug 2001); *Career* account exec BMP 1984–86, conslt Bain & Co 1986–90, head of strategy Still Price Lintas 1991–92, md Cutler & Gross 1992–93, conslt 1993–94, dep md Hartstone plc 1994–95, global brand dir Diageo 1995–99, mktg dir Flutter.com 2000–01, mktg and e-commerce dir Marks & Spencer plc 2003–04, ceo Sanctuary Spa Holdings Ltd 2005–08 (chair 2008–09), exec chair Lemene Oy 2012–; non-exec dir: Ignite Gp Ltd 2010–, Cyden Ltd 2011; *Style*— Ms Alice Avis, MBE; ✉ 26 Maida Avenue, Little Venice, London W2 1ST (e-mail alice.avis@btinternet.com)

AWDRY, William Richard (Will); s of Richard Charles Visger Awdry, of Penn, Bucks, and Jocelyn Genesta St George, *née* Poole (d 1990); *b* 11 February 1961; *Educ* Marlborough, BNC Oxford (BA); *m* 5 Dec 1992, Clare Julia, *née* Marshall; *Career* advtg exec; account mgmnt trainee rising to exec McCormick Intermarco Farmer 1983–85; Bartle Bogle Hegarty: copywriter 1986–94, bd dir 1992–94, gp creative head 1993–94; copywriter, head of copy and bd dir The Leagas Delaney Partnership 1994–96, rejoined Bartle Bogle Hegarty 1996, subsequently with Partners BDDH, creative dir int accounts DDB London 2003–; *Recreations* music (percussion drummer on various infrequent occasions), practical as opposed to theoretical oenology; *Style*— Will Awdry, Esq

AXWORTHY, HE Sally; *Career* desk offr Hungary and Czechoslovakia FCO 1987–88, Russian language trg 1988–89, third sec (Commercial) Moscow 1989–91, second sec (Economic) Kiev 1991–92, head Political Section UN Dept FCO 1993–94, secondment to the German Foreign Ministry 1994–96, first sec EU Bonn 1996–98, head Turkey, Cyprus and Malta Section EU Dept FCO 1998–2000, asst dir Devon and Cornwall Govt Office SW 2001–03, project ldr Vulnerable Adults Project Govt Office SW 2004–05, Sr Flexible Working Project Human Resources Directorate 2006, head Financial Skills FCO 2007–08, language trg 2008, dir Corporate Servs India 2009–11, head Great Lakes, E Africa and Somalia Dept FCO 2011, head Somalia Unit FCO 2011–13, jt head N Africa Dept FCO 2013–15, ambass to the Holy See 2016–; *Style*— HE Mrs Sally Axworthy, MBE

AYCKBOURN, Sir Alan; kt (1997), CBE (1987); s of Horace Ayckbourn, and Irene Maud, *née* Worley; *b* 12 April 1939; *Educ* Haileybury; *m* 1, 1959 (m dis 1997), Christine Helen, *née* Roland; 2 s (Steven, Philip); m 2, 1997, Heather Elizabeth, *née* Stoney; *Career* playwright and theatre director; worked in rep as stage mangr/actor Edinburgh, Worthing, Leatherhead, Oxford and with late Stephen Joseph's Theatre-in-the-Round Scarborough (artistic dir Stephen Joseph Theatre 1972–2009), fndr memb Victoria Theatre Stoke-on-Trent 1962, BBC Radio drama prodr Leeds 1964–70, co dir NT 1986–87, Cameron Mackintosh visiting prof of contemporary theatre Univ of Oxford 1992 (concurrently fell St Catherine's Coll Oxford); Lloyd's Private Banking Playwright of the Year Award 1998, Sunday Times Award for Literary Excellence 2001, Olivier Awards Soc Special Award 2009, Lifetime Achievement in Theatre Tony Award 2010, Critics Circle Award for Services to Arts 2010; Hon DLitt: Univ of Hull 1981, Keele Univ 1987, Univ of Leeds 1987, Univ of Bradford 1994, Univ of Cardiff 1995, Univ of Manchester 2003, York St John 2011; Hon DUniv: York 1992, Open Univ 1998; hon fell Bretton HAll 1982; FRSL, FRSA; *London Productions* Mr Whatnot (Arts) 1964, Relatively Speaking (Duke of York's) 1967 and (Greenwich) 1986 (televised 1969 and 1989), How the Other Half Loves (Lyric) 1970 and (Duke of York's) 1988, Time and Time Again (Comedy) 1972 (televised 1976), Absurd Person Singular (Criterion) 1973 and (Garrick) 2007 (Evening Standard Drama Award Best Comedy 1975, televised 1985), The Norman Conquests (trilogy, Globe) 1974 and (Old Vic) 2008 (Evening Standard Drama Award Best Play, Variety Club of GB Award, Plays and Players Award, televised 1977), Jeeves (musical with Andrew Lloyd Webber, Her Majesty's) 1975, Absent Friends (Garrick) 1975 (televised 1985), Confusions (Apollo) 1976, Bedroom Farce (NT) 1977 and (Duke of York) 2010 (televised 1980), Just Between Ourselves (Queen's) 1977 (televised 1978, Evening Standard Drama Award Best Play), Ten Times Table (Globe) 1978, Joking Apart (Globe) 1979 (Plays and Players Award), Sisterly Feelings (NT) 1980, Taking Steps (Lyric) 1980, Suburban Strains (musical with Paul Todd, Round House) 1981, Season's Greetings (Apollo) 1982 and (NT) 2010 (televised 1986), Way Upstream (NT) 1982 (televised 1987), Making Tracks (musical with Paul Todd, Greenwich) 1983, Intimate Exchanges (Ambassadors) 1984 (French films Smoking/NoSmoking 1994) A Chorus of Disapproval 1985 (also dir, Evening Standard Drama Award Best Comedy, Olivier Award Best Comedy, Drama Award Best Comedy 1985, transferred Lyric 1986, film 1989), Woman in Mind (Vaudeville) 1986 and 2009 (also dir), A Small Family Business (NT) 1987 (also dir, Evening Standard Drama Award Best Play), Henceforward... (Vaudeville) 1988 (also dir, Evening Standard Drama Award Best Comedy 1989), Man of the Moment (Globe) 1990 (also dir, Evening Standard Drama Award Best Comedy 1990), Invisible Friends (for children, NT) 1991 (also dir), The Revengers' Comedies (Strand) 1991 (also dir, televised 1999), Mr A's Amazing Maze Plays (for children, NT) 1993 (also dir, Best Show for Children and Young People TMA/Martini Regnl Theatre Awards), Time of my Life (Vaudeville) 1993 (also dir), Wildest Dreams (RSC) 1993 (also dir), Communicating Doors (Gielgud and Savoy) 1995 (also dir, Olivier Award nomination for Best Comedy 1996, Writers' Guild Award for Best West End Play 1996), Things We Do For Love (Savoy, Gielgud and Duchess) 1998 (also dir), adaptation of Ostrovsky's The Forest (RNT) 1999, Comic Potential (Lyric) 1999 (also dir), House & Garden (RNT (Olivier/Lyttleton)) 2000 (also dir), Damsels in Distress (trilogy (GamePlan, FlatSpin, RolePlay), Duchess) 2002 (also dir), Private Fears in Public Places (Orange Tree Theatre) 2005, Snake in the Grass (The Print Room) 2011, Drowning on Dry Land (Jermyn St Theatre) 2011, Neighbourhood Watch (Tricycle Theatre) 2012; *Scarborough Productions* Body Language 1990, This Is Where We Came In (for children) 1990, Callisto 5 (for children) 1990, My Very Own Story (for children) 1991, Dreams From A Summer House (a comedy with music by John Pattison) 1992, Haunting Julia 1994, The Musical Jigsaw Play (for children, with music by John Pattison) 1994, By Jeeves 1996 (music by Andrew Lloyd Webber; transferred to Duke of York's, Lyric Theatres (Br Regnl Theatre Awards 1996 Best Musical)), The Champion of Paribanou (for children) 1996, The Boy Who Fell Into A Book (for children) 1998, Callisto #7 1999, Whenever (children's play with music by Denis King) 2000, Snake in the Grass 2002, The Jollies (for children) 2002, Orvin – Champion of Champions (with music by Denis King) 2003, Sugar Daddies 2003, My Sister Sadie 2003, Drowning on Dry Land 2004, Private Fears in Public Places 2004, Miss Yesterday 2004, Improbable Fiction 2005, If I Were You 2006, Life and Beth 2008, Awaking Beauty (music by Denis King) 2008, My Wonderful Day 2008, Life of Riley 2010, Dear Uncle (adapt of Chekhov's Uncle Vanya) 2011, Neighbourhood Watch 2011, Surprises 2012, Arrivals & Departures 2013, Roundelay 2014, Hero's Welcome 2015, The Karaoke Theatre Company 2016; *Plays directed for National Theatre* Tons of Money 1986, A View from the Bridge 1987, A Small Family Business 1987, 'Tis Pity She's a Whore 1988; *Books* the majority of above plays are currently in print; The Crafty Art of Playmaking (2002); *Style*— Sir Alan Ayckbourn, CBE; ✉ c/o Casarotto Ramsay & Assoc Ltd, Waverley House, 7–12 Noel Street, London W1F 8GQ (☎ 020 7287 4450, fax 020 7287 9128); website www.alanayckbourn.net

AYERS, Kenneth Edwin (Ken); MBE (2010); s of John Arthur Ayers, and Lilian Maud, *née* Lugg; *b* 1 April 1938, Hatfield, Herts; *Educ* Sherrardswood Sch Welwyn Garden City; *m* 1, 1960 (m dis), Anne Elizabeth, *née* Zoller; 2 da; m 2, 1977, Vivienne Susan Mary, *née* Connolly (decd); 1 step s, 1 step da; m 3, 2006, remarried Anne Elizabeth McQueen Johnston; *Career* actuarial clerk Standard Life Assurance Co 1955–59, ptnr's asst Chase, Henderson & Tennant 1959–62, salesman and analyst Quilter & Co 1962–65, inspr then asst actuary Standard Life Assurance Co 1965–70; Laurie, Milbank & Co: gilt salesman 1970–72, gilt ptnr 1972–84, second sr ptnr and sr gilt ptnr 1984–86; Chase Manhattan Securities: head of sterling fixed interest 1986, gilts business mangr 1987, business devpt mangr bond distribution 1988; Frank Russell Int: client exec 1988–91, dep md 1991–93, md ME region 1993–96, PR 1996–2000, conslt 2000–06; advsr Allenbridge Gp plc 1996–2008; Nat Assoc of Pensions Funds (former chm Investment Cncl); former chm FTSE Actuaries Bond Index Ctee; author of numerous articles on pension fund investment; govr: Museum of London, Bridewell Royal Hosp; chm Speed Events Ctee RAC Motor Sports Assoc 1998–2009 (memb 1990–95 and 1996–2009); former vice-pres London District St John Ambulance; Order of St John (chm Investment Ctee 1999–2005); memb Common Cncl Ward of Bassishaw (chm Standards Ctee 2001–04, chm Community and Children's Servs Ctee 2006–09); Sheriff City of London 1995–96 (Chief Commoner 2012–13), fndr memb Worshipful Co of Actuaries 1979 (memb Ct of Assts 1986, Master 1991–92), memb Worshipful Co of Woodmen 2011– (memb Ct 2012–); FIA, FSS, FPMI; KStJ, Commandeur Ordre Nationale du Mérite (France); *Recreations* motorsport (Br sprint champion 1982); *Clubs* City Livery, Royal Soc of St George, Coleman St Ward, Bassishaw Ward, Cripplegate Ward, Guild of Freemen; *Style*— Ken Ayers, Esq, MBE; ✉ 8 The Postern, Barbican, London EC2Y 8BJ

AYLEN, Walter Stafford; QC (1983); s of Rt Rev Bishop Charles Arthur William Aylen (d 1972), and Elisabeth Margaret Anna, *née* Hills (d 1975); bro of Leo Aylen, *qv*; *b* 21 May 1937; *Educ* Winchester, New Coll Oxford (scholar, sr scholar, MA, BCL); *m* 1967, Peggy Elizabeth Lainé Woodford, *qv*, da of Ronald Curtis Woodford; 3 da (Alison b 1968, Frances b 1970, Imogen b 1974); *Career* Nat Serv cmmnd 2 Lt 1 Bn KRRC 1956–57; called to the Bar Middle Temple 1962 (Harmsworth entrance exhibitioner and scholar, bencher 1991); recorder of the Crown Court 1985–2003 (asst recorder 1982), head of

A

chambers 1991–2000, dep judge of the High Court 1993–2005; memb Gen Cncl of the Bar 1994–96, chm BSITC 1994 (vice-chm Fin Ctee 1995–96); ADR Chambers 2000–08, memb ADR Int Panel 2001–08; Northants CCC second XI 1955; FRSA 1989, MCIArb 1999–2009; *Recreations* music (especially lieder and opera), theatre, literature; *Style*— Walter Aylen, Esq, QC; ✉ 24 Fairmount Road, London SW2 2BL (☎ 020 8671 7301)

AYLETT, Dr Philip John; s of late Leonard Charles Aylett, and late Mair Marguerite Aylett; *b* 7 December 1951; *Educ* Wilmslow GS, Mansfield Coll Oxford (MA), Univ of Manchester (MPhil), Univ of London (PhD); *m* 1978, Anne Maria, da of late Alexander Rowles; 1 s (Christopher b 1983), 1 da (Sophie b 1987); *Career* various posts Nat Tst Tatton Park 1976–79, communications offr Univ of Manchester 1979–84, press offr Central Office of Information NW Region 1984–86; sr press offr: Dept of the Environment 1986–88, DTI 1988–89, Prime Minister's Office 1989–91; chief press offr Dept of Health 1991–93, press offr (Europe) FCO 1993–95, head of information ODA (later Dept for Int Devpt) 1995–98, head of news Dept of Health 1998–99, press sec Neill Ctee 1999–2001, clerk Public Admin Ctee House of Commons 2001–05; Office of the Party and Health Serv Ombudsman: dir of strategy and communications 2005–07, dir of policy, info and communications 2007–08; advsr House of Commons Speaker's Conference on Parly Representation 2009–10, clerk Public Accounts Ctee House of Commons 2010–12, sr clerk Scrutiny Unit House of Commons 2012–; chm Standards Ctee Herts CC 2004–12; memb Bd of Tstees POhWER charity 2009–15; FRSA; *Publications* several articles on the history of lawyers in 18th century England; *Recreations* reading about history and politics, listening to music, watching football; *Style*— Dr Philip Aylett

AYLING, John Vernon; OBE (2007); s of Stanley H Ayling (d 1990), and Phyllis E, *née* Jenkins (d 1994); *b* 18 April 1944, Fulmer, Bucks; *Educ* East Grinstead GS W Sussex, Univ of Exeter (BA); *m* 6 April 1982, Marilyn Whinray, *née* Lee-Hargreaves; 1 da (Caroline Jane b 18 Oct 1982); *Career* media asst Masius Wynne-Williams 1965–67, media planner buyer S H Benson 1967–68, media mangr Garland-Compton 1968–71, media dir Kirkwood Co 1971–78, exec chm John Ayling & Assocs 1978–; former dir and shareholder PHD, former chm and dir AMI and former Cncl IPA; *Recreations* cricket, golf, hockey, travel; *Clubs* MCC, Lord's Taverners (former chm), Solus (former pres), SWIGS Golf Soc (former pres), Oxted Hockey (hon life memb and pat capt), Wisley Golf, Tandridge Golf; *Style*— John Ayling, Esq, OBE; ✉ John Ayling & Associates, 27 Soho Square, London W1D 3QR (☎ 020 7439 6070, e-mail jaa@jaa-media.co.uk)

AYLING, Robert John; *b* 3 August 1946; *Educ* KCS Wimbledon; *m* 1972, Julia, *née* Crallan; 2 s, 1 da; *Career* admitted slr 1968; Elborne Mitchell & Co: joined 1969, ptnr 1971; DTI (formerly Dept of Trade): legal advsr 1974–79, asst slr and head of Aviation Law Branch 1979, UK delg UN Cmmn for International Trade Law 1979–83, under sec (legal) 1983–85; British Airways plc: legal dir 1985–91, co sec 1987–91, HR dir 1988–91, mktg and ops dir 1991–93, gp md 1993–96, chief exec 1996–2000; non-exec chm Holidaybreak plc 2003–09, chm Sanctuary Group plc 2006–07; non-exec dir: Royal & Sun Alliance Insurance Gp plc 1993–2004, Business in the Community 1995–2000, BTA 1996–99, New Millennium Experience Co 1996–2000, Qantas Airways Ltd 1996–2000, Dyson Ltd 2001–12 (chm 2010–12), Dwr Cymru (Welsh Water) 2008–16 (chm 2010–16); chm HM Courts and Tbnls Serv 2011–; govr KCS Wimbledon 1995–2006; Hon LLD Brunel Univ 1996; *Clubs* Brooks's, Royal Thames Yacht; *Style*— Robert Ayling, Esq

AYLWARD, Adrian John Francis; s of John James Aylward (d 1978), and Cynthia, *née* Minch (d 1966); *b* 12 November 1957; *Educ* Worth Sch Sussex, Exeter Coll Oxford (BA), King's Coll London (PGCE); *m* Aug 1990, Caroline Lesley, da of John Cramer; 2 da (Molly b Aug 1991, Freya b Aug 1996), 1 s (Joseph b Dec 1994); *Career* headmaster; former investment banker 1981–86, with Royal Sovereign Gp plc (latterly chief exec) 1986–91, dir Emess plc 1990–91, housemaster/head of religious studies Downside Sch 1992–96, headmaster Stonyhurst Coll 1996–2006; memb Irish Assoc, KM; *Recreations* fishing, philosophy, sport, travel; *Clubs* Brooks's; *Style*— Adrian Aylward, Esq

AYLWARD, Prof Sir Mansel; kt (2010), CB (2002); s of John Aylward (d 1991), and Cora Doreen, *née* Evans (d 2003); *b* 29 November 1942, Merthyr Tydfil; *Educ* Cyfarthfa Castle GS Merthyr Tydfil, Jesus Coll Oxford (BSc, Price open entrance scholar), London Hosp Med Coll Univ of London (MB BS, Buxton Prize, George Riddoch Prize); *m* 17 Aug 1963, Angela Bridget, *née* Besley; 1 s (Simon Mansel b 19 Jan 1965), 1 da (Rebecca Bridget b 24 July 1968); *Career* demonstrator in physiology London Hosp Med Coll 1963–66, house offr London Hosp 1967–68, MRC res fell (surgery) Experimental Surgery Dept London Hosp 1968–69, lectr in surgery London Hosp Med Coll 1969, GP Merthyr Tydfil and S Brecnockshire 1969–73, clinical asst minor surgery St Tydfil's Hosp Merthyr Tydfil 1970–76, research physician Singleton Hosp Swansea and Merthyr and Cynon Valleys 1973–76, chm and md Simbec Research Ltd Wales 1974–84 (BBC Company of the Year Award 1979, European Small Business Award 1980), pres Simbec Research (USA) Inc 1980–84, dir of clinical research Lyonaisse Industrielle Pharmaceutique France 1982–84, regnl med offr DHSS Cardiff 1985–88, SMO DSS London 1988–90, med sec Attendance Allowance Bd London 1990–91, princ med offr and dir of med policy Benefits Agency London 1991–95, CMO, med dir and chief scientist Dept for Work and Pensions (formerly DSS) 1995–2005, CMO and head Profession Agency MOD 1998–2005; specialist advsr on int engagement to Vice-Chllr Cardiff Univ 2013-' hon prof Univ of Wales Coll of Med 2002–, dir Centre for Psychosocial and Disability Research Sch of Psychology Sch of Medicine and prof Cardiff Univ 2004–, chair Academic Forum Faculty of Occupational Medicine 2007–, prof of public heath educn Sch of Medicine Cardiff Univ 2011–, hon prof Auckland Univ 2012–, vice-pres Coll of Occupational Therapists 2012–; chm Wales Centre for Health Welsh Assembly Govt Cardiff 2005–10, chm Royal Mail Attendance Acad 2006–11, chair Bevan Cmmn 2009–, chair Wales Occupational Health Review 2008–11, chair Public Health Wales NHS Tst 2009–, chair All Wales Mental Health Promotion Network 2009–; dir Women's Health Concern London 1976–86; chief med advsr Veterans Agency MOD 2001–05, med advsr States of Jersey, conslt Social Security Admin USA, civilian med advsr in disability medicine to Army 2004–; visiting prof: Harvard Univ, Leuven Univ Belgium, Karolinska Inst Sweden; Inaugural Ko Awatea visiting prof Counties Manukau Health Bd NZ 2012–; non-exec dir: Health Claims Bureau Ltd, AGIRX Ltd; memb Industrial Injuries Advsy Cncl 2005–, memb Health Honours Ctee 2006–12, memb Min for Health and Social Services Advsy Bd Wales 2009–12, memb Nat Advsy Bd (Health) 2009–12; judge Prince of Wales Integrated Health Awards 2009–; vice-pres Shaw Tst 2006–; patron Vocational Rehabilitation Assoc; life memb Imperial Soc of Knights Bachelor 2010; Tudor Hart lecture 2008, Edward Jones lecture 2010, RSM Spring lecture 2011; Expert Agrée Medicine Interne France 1982, Nat Innovation Award 2008; Freeman Merthyr Tydfil County Borough 2013; Hon DSc Univ of S Wales 2013; FRSM 1981 (academic dean and hon treas 2002–09), FFPM 1991, fell Assurance Med Soc 1997, FRCP 2001, DDAM 2001, FFOM 2003, hon memb Irish Soc of Occupational Med 2004, memb Soc of Occupational Med 2006, Hon FFPH 2008, fell Coll of Medicine 2011; *Publications* Management of the Menopause and Post-menopausal Years (1975), The Disability Handbook (jt ed, 1991, 2 edn 1998), Back Pain, Incapacity for Work and Social Security Benefits: An international review and analysis (jtly, 2005), The Scientific and Conceptual Basis of Incapacity Benefits (jtly, 2005), The Power of Belief (jt ed, 2006), Review of Health Commission Wales (2008), Review of Health and Social Care Provision in Merthyr Tydlfil and Environs (2008), Sickness and Disability in Britain Today (jtly, 2009), Models of Disability and Chronic Illness (jtly, 2010), Review: Child Protection and Safeguarding in NHS Wales (2011), NHS Wales, Forging a Better Future (2011); book chapters and papers; *Recreations* military history, travel, theatre, grandchildren, dining, reading everything, politics; *Clubs* Athenaeum; *Style*— Prof Sir Mansel Aylward, CB; ✉ Cefn Cottage, Cefn Coed-y-Cymer, Merthyr Tydfil CF48 2PH (☎ 01685 722324, fax 01685 375009); Centre for Psychosocial and Disability Research, Cardiff University, 53 Park Place, Cardiff CF10 3AT (☎ 029 2087 9311, fax 029 2087 0196, e-mail aylwardm@cardiff.ac.uk); Public Health Wales, 14 Cathedral Road, Cardiff CF11 9LJ (☎ 02920 348792, e-mail mansel.aylward@wales.nhs.uk, website www.publichealthwales.org)

AYOADE, Richard; *Career* comedian, actor, writer and dir; as actor: Garth Marenghi's Darkplace (Channel Four) 2004 (also writer and dir), Mighty Boosh (BBC) 2004–07, The IT Crowd (Channel Four) 2006–08, Noel Fielding's Luxury Comedy 2012, Neighbourhood Watch 2012 (film); as dir: My Mistakes Were Made For You (music video, The Last Shadow Puppets, Best Video NME Award 2009), Arctic Monkeys: At The Apollo DVD (Best DVD NME Award 2009), Submarine 2011 (film, also writer, Best Screenplay Br Ind Film Award 2011, Best Film NME Award 2012), The Double (2014); *Style*— Richard Ayoade, Esq; ✉ c/o Claire Nightingale, PBJ and JBJ Management, 22 Rathbone Street, London W1T 1LA (☎ 020 7287 1112, e-mail clairen@pbjmgt.co.uk, website www.pbjmgt.co.uk)

AYRE, HE Andrew; *m* Bettina; 1 s; *Career* diplomat; Economic Advsrs Dept FCO 1986–87, accountant Br Embassy Warsaw 1988–89, asst mgmnt offr Br Consulate-Gen Rio de Janeiro 1990–91, entry clearance offr/vice-consul Nicosia 1994–97, entry clearance offr/ entry clearance mangr Br Consulate-Gen Geneva 1997, third then second sec (political) Tel Aviv 1998–2001, second sec Vienna 2001–06, head Arabian Peninsula Team ME and N Africa Dept FCO 2006–08, head European Cncls and EU Budget Team Europe Directorate FCO 2009–11, high cmmr to Repub of Guyana 2011–15; *Style*— HE Mr Andrew Ayre; ✉ c/o British High Commission (Georgetown), BFPO 5540 HA4 6EP

AYRE, Richard; s of Thomas Henry (Harry) Ayre, and Beth Carson; *b* 1 August 1949, Newcastle-upon-Tyne; *Educ* Univ of Durham; *m* Guy Douglas Burch; *Career* BBC 1972–2000: news trainee working on Today prog Radio 4, Radio Solent and Belfast 1972–74, regnl journalist Belfast 1974, reporter Belfast 1975–76, dep news ed NI 1976–79, dep news ed Intake TV News rising to home news ed TV News 1979–82, six month fellowship in broadcast journalism Univ of Chicago 1984–85, ed Special Projects TV News 1985–87, chief asst to Dep Dir News and Current Affrs then to Dir News and Current Affrs 1987–88, head of editorial devpt News and Current Affrs 1988–89, head of BBC Westminster 1990–93, controller Editorial Policy 1993–96, dep chief exec BBC News 1996–2000; conslt in mgmnt and media ethics 2000–, Civil Service cmmr 2005–06; chm Asian and Afro-Caribbean Reporters' Tst 1997–2000, tstee and int bd memb Article 19 – The Global Campaign for Freedom of Expression 1999–2005 (chm 2002–05), memb Bd Food Standards Agency 2000–07, freedom of info adjudicator Law Soc 2001–15, bd memb for Eng Ofcom Content Bd 2006–10, govr Teachers' TV 2006–08, chm Dairy Partnership 2008–09, tstee BBC Tst 2010–; *Recreations* English and Welsh oak furniture of the 17th century; *Style*— Mr Richard Ayre; ✉ e-mail richardayre@whats2hide.com

AYRES, Andrew John William; QC (2015); *b* 18 March 1971, Bradford on Avon; *Educ* Eton, Univ Coll Oxford; *Career* called to the Bar 1996; in practice Commercial and Chancery Bar 1997–; accredited advocate Dubai Int Fin Centre; *Recreations* theatre, music, film, country pursuits; *Clubs* Ivy, Liver; ✉ Maitland Chambers, 7 Stone Buildings, Lincoln's Inn, London WC2A 3SZ

AYRES, Emeritus Prof Jonathan Geoffrey (Jon); OBE (2011); *b* 14 February 1950; *Educ* Woodhouse GS Finchley, Guy's Hosp (BSc, MB BS, MD); m; 1 s, 1 da; *Career* Guy's Hosp: house offr 1974–75, SHO 1976–78, res registrar 1979–81, registrar 1978–79 and 1981–82; SHO Brompton Hosp 1977–78, sr registrar E Birmingham Hosp 1982–84, conslt physician in respiratory and gen med Birmingham Heartlands Hosp 1984–2002, prof of respiratory med Univ of Birmingham 2000–02, prof of respiratory med Univ of Warwick 1996–2000, prof of environmental and occupational med Univ of Aberdeen 2002–08, prof of environmental and respiratory med Univ of Birmingham 2008–15 (currently emeritus prof); author of numerous scientific pubns on asthma, COPD and air pollution and health; chm: Ctee on Medical Effects of Air Pollution Dept of Health 2001–11 (memb 1992–2001), Advsy Ctee on Pesticides DEFRA 2006–11; memb: Br Thoracic Soc, American Thoracic Soc 1986, Int Epidemiology Assoc 1986, European Respiratory Soc 1988, Expert Panel on Air Quality Standards (DOE) 1994–2009, Soc of Occupational Medicine, Royal Cmmn on Environmental Pollution 2010–11; FRCP 1989, FRCP(Edin) 2003, FFOM 2005, fell RCPSGlas 2008; *Recreations* sketching in pencil and watercolours, singing; *Style*— Emeritus Prof Jon Ayres, OBE; ✉ Institute of Occupational and Environmental Medicine, School of Health and Population Sciences, Edgbaston, Birmingham B15 2TT (e-mail j.g.ayres@bham.ac.uk)

AYRES, Pam (Mrs Dudley Russell); MBE (2004); da of Stanley William Ayres (d 1981), of Stanford in the Vale, Oxon, and Phyllis Evelyn, *née* Loder (d 2001); *b* 14 March 1947; *Educ* Faringdon Secdy Modern Sch; *m* 1982, Dudley Russell, s of late Joe Russell; 2 s (William Stanley b 12 Dec 1982, James Joseph b 20 July 1984); *Career* poet, writer and entertainer 1974–; presenter: The Pam Ayres Radio Show (BBC Radio 2) 1996–99, Pam Ayres Open Road (BBC Radio 2) 2000–01, Ayres On The Air (BBC Radio 4) 2004, 2006, 2009 and 2012, Potting On (BBC Radio 4) 2008; *Books* incl: Pam Ayres: Some of Me Poetry, Some More of Me Poetry, Thoughts of a Late-Night Knitter, Will Anybody Marry Me?, The Works, With These Hands, Surgically Enhanced (2006), The Works – The Classic Collection (2008), The Necessary Aptitude (autobiography, 2011), You Made Me Late Again! (new poetry collection, 2013); *Recreations* beekeeping, gardening, painting; *Style*— Ms Pam Ayres, MBE; ✉ PO Box 64, Cirencester, Gloucestershire GL7 5YD (☎ 01285 644622, fax 01285 642291, website www.pamayres.com)

AYRES, Rosalind Mary (Mrs Martin Jarvis); da of Sam Johnson (d 1986), of Westbury, Wilts, and Daisy, *née* Hydon (d 1987); *b* 7 December 1946; *Educ* George Dixon GS for Girls Birmingham, Loughborough Coll of Educn (Dip Educn, BA); *m* 23 Nov 1974, Martin Jarvis, Esq, OBE, *qv*, s of Denys Jarvis, of Sanderstead, Surrey; *Career* actress, dir and prodr; Drama and Readings Producer of the Year Radio Academy 2012; *Theatre* incl: Hamlet, The Three Sisters, Uncle Vanya, The Perfect Party (Greenwich), Dracula (Shaftesbury), I Claudius (Queens's), A Dolis House (Thorndike), Exchange (Vaudeville), Just Between Ourselves (Greenwich), Now You Know (Hampstead); for LA Theatre Works: Make and Break, Exchange, Private Lives, The Third Man, The Norman Conquests, Thank You Jeeves (dir), The Doctor's Dilemma (dir), Another Time (dir), The Importance of Being Earnest; *Radio* Pack of Lies, A Small Family Business, A Room With A View, The Circle, Alphabetical Order, Modern Gal (dir), Black Pearls (dir), Spies (dir), On the Waterfront (dir), Glengarry Glen Ross (dir), You Never Can Tell; for NPR USA: The Doctor's Dilemma, Thank You Jeeves, Another Time, Cakewalk (Audie Award), Ten by Maugham (Audie Award), The Cherry Orchard, The Lion in Winter (dir), Orson's Shadow (dir), Breaking the Code (dir), Betrayal (dir), Enron (dir), Dracula (dir), School for Husbands (dir), Sorry, Wrong Number (dir); *Television* incl: The Mill, The House of Bernarda Alba, Juliet Bravo, The Bounder (series), Father's Day (series), Hindle Wakes, The Good Guys, Casualty, The Cinder Path (mini-series), A Face to Die For (mini-series, US), Heartbeat, Chicago Hope (US), Profiler (US), Just Shoot Me (series, US), Trevor's World of Sport, Outnumbered, Holby City, The Royal, Moving On, New Tricks, Poirot Dead Man's Folly; *Film* incl: The Lovers, Tales from Beyond the Grave, Mr Smith, Cry Wolf, That'll be the Day, Stardust, The Slipper and the Rose, Emily's Ghost, Black Beauty, Titanic, Gods and Monsters, Beautiful People, Christmas in the Clouds; *Recreations* interior design, illustration; *Style*— Ms Rosalind Ayres; ✉ c/o Lou

Coulson, 37 Berwick Street, London W1V 3RF (☎ 020 7734 9633, fax 020 7439 7569); c/o, CA&A, 1680 North Vine Street, #1016, Los Angeles, CA 90028, USA (☎ 00 1 323 463 8355)

AYRES-BENNETT, Prof Wendy Margaret; da of Charles Ernest Banks (d 2004), and Olive Margaret, *née* Heath (d 1996); *b* 18 February 1958, Farnborough, Hants; *Educ* Nonsuch HS for Girls Cheam, Girton Coll Cambridge (BA), Univ of Oxford (PhD); *m* 22 Sept 1983, Andrew Bennett; 2 s (Matthew James b 15 Dec 1985, Luke Richard b 24 June 1990); *Career* Julia Mann research fell St Hilda's Coll Oxford 1982–83; successively asst lectr, lectr, reader then prof Univ of Cambridge 1983– (head Dept of French 2001–05); fell Queens' Coll Cambridge 1987–2001, fell Murray Edwards Coll Cambridge 2001–; memb: Editorial Bd Legenda 1995–2005, Advsy Editorial Bd Jl of French Language Studies 2003–; pres Soc for French Studies 2000–02 (vice-pres 1999–2000 and 2002–03), pres Philological Soc 2013–; Prix d'Académie 1987, Prix Georges Dumézil 2013; Officier dans l'Ordre des Palmes Académiques; *Books* Vaugelas and the Development of the French Language (1987), A History of the French Language Through Texts (1996), Les Remarques de l'Académie Française sur le Quinte-Curce de Vaugelas (with P Caron, 1996), Problems and Perspectives: Studies in the Modern French Language (with J Carruthers, 2000), Sociolinguistic Variation in Seventeenth-Century France (2004), Remarques et Observations sur la Langue Française: histoire et évolution d'un genre (with M Seijido, 2011), Corpus des Remarques sur la Langue Française (XVIIe siècle) (2011); *Recreations* music; *Style*— Prof Wendy Ayres-Bennett; ✉ Department of Linguistics, University of Cambridge, Sidgwick Avenue, Cambridge CB3 9DA (☎ 01223 335010, fax 01223 335062, e-mail wmb1001@cam.ac.uk)

AYRTON, Pete; s of Alfred Ayrton (d 1988), and Kyra Gerard, *née* Diment (d 1971); *b* 17 July 1943; *Educ* Stowe Sch, ChCh Oxford (BA), Bedford Coll London (MPhil); *m* 30 June 1995, Sarah Martin; 1 da (Carla b 19 Feb 1986), 1 s (Oscar b 31 Dec 1988); *Career* translator for various publishers 1967–72, ed Pluto Press 1972–86, fndr Serpent's Tail 1986–2015, ret; memb PEN; Sunday Times Small Publisher of the Year 1988; Chevalier de l'Ordre des Arts et des Lettres France; *Books* No Man's Land, Writings from a World at War (2015), No Pasaran, Writings from the Spanish Civil War (2016); *Recreations* sampling N London gastropubs, listening to Chet Baker, walking the London Loop; *Clubs* PEN; *Style*— Pete Ayrton, Esq

AYTON, John; MBE (2012); *Educ* Univ of Oxford; *m* Annoushka Ducas, MBE; *Career* admitted slr (in England and Wales and Hong Kong) 1988; owner and chm Links of London 1990–2007; chm: Bremont Watch Co 2007–, Walpole Brands of Tomorrow 2007–; owner: Annoushka Ltd 2009–, Ski Floralie Ltd 2009–; *Recreations* skiing, horse riding; *Clubs* Brooks, MCC; *Style*— John Ayton, Esq, MBE; ✉ Bremont Watch Company, PO BOX 4741, Henley-on-Thames, Oxfordshire RG9 9BZ

AZAGURY-PARTRIDGE, Solange; da of Albert and Esther Azagury; *Career* jewellery designer; asst Butler & Wilson, asst Gordon Watson art dealer; set up own business 1990, opened London shop 1995 and now at 5 Carlos Place London, Madison Ave NY and Rue Saint-Honoré Paris, numerous jewellery and interior design commissions; creative dir Boucheron 2001–04, designed collection for H&M Christmas 2005; nominated Designer of the Year Design Museum 2003; *Exhibitions* Design Museum 2003, Musée des Arts Decoratifs du Louvre Paris 2004, V&A 2008, Unwearable Jewels (Sebastian Barquet) 2008; *Style*— Mrs Solange Azagury-Partridge; ✉ 27 Chilworth Street, London W2 3HA (☎ 020 7792 0197, e-mail london@solange.co.uk)

AZAM, Nasser; s of Khizr-e-Azam, of London, and Zohra Azam; *b* 15 September 1963, Jhelum, Pakistan; *Educ* Univ of Birmingham (BCom); *m* (m dis); 1 da (Zahra b 25 Aug 1992), 1 s (Tamoor b 27 Nov 1993); *Career* chief operating offr EMEA Merrill Lynch 1988–2008; artist 2008–; artist-in-residence County Hall Gallery London 2007–09; prop Maskerade Club Toyko 1996–98, fndr Zahra Modern Art Foundries 2010–13; memb Judging Panel Sovereign Arts Prize 2009; patron: Whitechapel Gallery London, Contemporary Art Soc, Inst of Contemporary Arts, Camden Arts Centre; *Selected Solo Exhibitions* Nasser Azam (Univ of Birmingham) 1982, Summer and Winter Exhbns Royal Birmingham Soc of Artists 1983, The View (Barber Inst of Fine Arts Birmingham) 1983, Recent Works (Univ of Aston) 1983, Azam Retrospective (County Hall Gallery London) 2007, Anatomica (County Hall Gallery London) 2008, Paintings and Bronzes (County Hall Gallery London) 2008, Azam Painting and Sculpture (Instanbul Contemporary Art) 2008, Life in Space (County Hall Gallery London) 2009, Colour over Form (County Hall Gallery London) 2009, Zabludowicz Collection (Inst of Contemporary Arts) 2011, Antarctica (London Underground and Tokyo Subway) 2011; *Performance Painting Projects* Zero Gravity Star City 2008, Antarctica 2010; *Sited Public Sculptures* Sepian Blue (Irish Nat Botanical Garden Dublin) 2008–, The Dance (Lambeth Cncl) 2008–10, Park Plaza Westminster 2010–, Athena (tallest bronze sculpture in UK, London City Airport) 2012–, Evolutionary Loop 517 (Univ of Aberdeen) 2013–; *Sited Public Painting Displays* Costata (SoHo NY) 2013/14, Marea (Manhattan NY) 2013/14; official portrait of Malala Yousafzai Barber Inst of Fine Arts Birmingham 2015; subject of Azam: A Short History of Sensation, Vol I (by John-Paul Stonard, 2008); *Style*— Nasser Azam, Esq; ☎ 020 7288 1951, e-mail info@azam.com

AZIM-KHAN, Rafi; *b* London; *Educ* Cranbrook Coll, Queen Mary Coll Univ of London (LLB), Coll of Law London; *m* Rebecca, *née* Bentley-Taylor; 2 da (Amélie b 27 March 2005, Ella Rose b 15 Feb 2012), 1 s (Sebastian b 10 July 2008); *Career* admitted slr 1993; slr: Lewis Silkin 1993–95, Cameron McKenna 1995–97, Theodore Goddard 1997–2000; ptnr and head of e-business and mktg law McDermott, Will & Emery LLP 2000–03, IP ptnr and head of mktg and e-commerce Wragge & Co LLP 2003–08, ptnr and head IP/ IT & Data Privacy Europe Pillsbury Winthrop Shaw Pittman LLP 2008–; chm Br American Business Law Forum, chm Advertising Lawyers Gp; memb Law Soc; *Publications* Regulation of the Internet (2001), E-Business: The Practical Guide (conslt ed, 2002, 2 edn 2008), International Marketing & Sales Promotion (2003), E-Commerce Cradle to Grave (2003), Encyclopaedia of E-Commerce Law (2005), Ad Law (co-author, 2005, 2 edn 2008); *Recreations* motor racing, travel, football, tennis, music; *Clubs* P1, Br American Business; *Style*— Rafi Azim-Khan, Esq; ✉ Pillsbury Winthrop Shaw Pitman LLP, Tower 42, Old Broad Street, London EC2N 1HQ (☎ 020 7847 9519, e-mail rafi@pillsburylaw.com)

AZIS, Jonathan Giles Ashley; s of Osman Azis, and Irene Elizabeth Winifred May, *née* Dean; *b* 14 April 1957; *Educ* Millfield, Pembroke Coll Oxford (MA); *m* 18 Aug 1984, Emily Susanna, da of Michael Fenwick Briggs, of Bath, and Isabel Colegate; 2 da (Matilda Winifred Katherine b 18 Dec 1986, Constance Irene Isabel b 28 Nov 1988), 1 s (Arthur Jonathan Osman b 25 March 1993); *Career* Barretts (slrs) 1979–82 and 1984–87, Walker Martineau (slrs) 1982–84, Nabarro Nathanson 1987, Kingston Smith (CAs) 1987–90, Beazer plc 1990–92; dir: Hanson plc 1997–98 (joined 1992, co sec 1995–97), Hanson Capital Ltd 1999–2009, Hanson Transport Gp 1999–2007; chief of staff Lord Hanson 1998–2004; chm Isotron plc 2003–07 (non-exec dir 2002), non-exec dir Victrex plc 2003–09, finance dir Hanson Westhouse 2006–12, gen counsel Westhouse Hldgs 2006–12, chm Molins plc 2009–10 (non-exec dir 2008), managing ptnr Parke Partnership LLP 2013–, non-exec dir Cadogan Tate 2013–; tstee: Prostate Cancer Charity 1998–2006, Lord Hanson Fndn 1999–2013, The Sanderson Fndn 2014–; memb Cncl Royal Albert Hall 2005– (treas 2011–); memb Law Soc; FRSA; *Recreations* books, music, ironing; *Clubs* Brooks's; *Style*— Jonathan Azis, Esq; ✉ Westwood Manor, Bradford on Avon, Wiltshire BA15 2AF (☎ 01225 863374, e-mail jonathan@azis.co.uk)

AZIZ, Prof Khalid; LVO (1997), DL (Hants 1998); s of Ahmad Aziz (d 1978), and Sheila Frances, *née* Light (d 2007); *b* 9 August 1953; *Educ* Westminster City Sch, Aitcheson Coll Lahore; *m* 1, 27 March 1974 (m dis), Barbara Elizabeth, da of Harry Etchells, of Sherburn in Elmet, N Yorks; 2 da (Nadira b 1977, Fleur b 1981); m 2, 16 June 1994, Kim Kemp, da of Muriel Haslam, of Bassett, Hants; *Career* broadcaster, journalist and dir; prodr/presenter: BBC Radio and TV 1970–81, TVS 1981–91; presenter: On Course (Channel 4) 1988–89, The Small Business Programme (BBC2/Channel 4) 1990, Starnet Business Programme 1990; TV Journalist of the Year 1987–88; chm: The Aziz Corporation (specialists in spoken communication) 1983–, The Safe Partnership 1997–2002, The Dever Soc 2000–03 (pres 2006–), Accipitor Ltd 2005–; visiting prof Sch of Mgmnt Univ of Southampton 2004–, hon prof Univ of Winchester 2006–; chm: Communication Ctee RAC Cirencester 1991–94, The Wessex Children's Hospice Tst 1992–97 and 1999–2013 (life pres 2013–), Prince's Tst Hants 1977–97, S Counties Bd Prince's Youth Business Tst 1977–97; chm Enham Tst 2012–; memb Advsy Ctee Office for Nat Statistics 1996–98; tstee: Winchester Med Tst, Winchester Med Fndn 1995–, Memorial Gates Tst 2000–; vice-pres Pestalozzi Int Children's Village; FRSA 2002; *Books* author of 11 books incl: The Barclays Guide to Small Business Computing (1990), Presenting to Win (2000); Managing in a Crisis (2004); *Recreations* aviation, fishing, shooting, computers; *Clubs* Naval and Military; *Style*— Prof Khalid Aziz, LVO, DL; ✉ No 1, Aziz Court, Parkhill, Winchester, Hampshire SO21 3QX (☎ 01962 774766, e-mail khalid@azizcorp.com, website www.azizcorp.com)

AZIZ, Mohammed Abdul; s of Moinul Islam, of Bangladesh, and Sundora Khatun; *b* 28 February 1971, Bangladesh; *Educ* St Paul's Way Sch Bow, Christ Church Coll Univ of Kent at Canterbury, UCL (LLB, LLM, PGCLE), Inns of Ct Sch of Law London; *m* 31 Oct 1998, Zayneb Duaa Izzidien; 2 s (Ihsan Karim b 30 Nov 2002, Adil Rahim b 27 April 2007), 1 da (Iman Sakinah b 30 Sept 2004); *Career* called to the Bar Gray's Inn 1997; home-sch liaison offr London Borough of Tower Hamlets 1992–94, co-ordinator religious studies prog Tower Hamlets Coll 1994–97, co-ordinator legal studies prog Islamic Fndn 1995–97, successively racial harrassment project offr, housing lawyer and princ racial harrassment policy offr London Borough of Tower Hamlets 1997–2000, founding ceo Forum Against Islamophobia and Racism 2000–02, founding ceo Br Muslim Research Centre 2002–04, co-dir FaithWise Ltd 2004–13; cmmr: Cmmn for Racial Equality 2004–07, Equal Opportunites Cmmn 2005–; memb: Nat Exec Ctee Young Muslim Orgn 1991–94, Nat Exec Ctee Fedn of Students Islamic Socs 1994–96, Nat Exec Ctee Assoc of Muslim Social Scientists 1998–2002 (sec 2000–02), Nat Exec Ctee Assoc of Muslim Lawyers 1998–2001, Nat Police-Community Consultative Panel Met Police Serv/ACPO 2001–02, Community Cohesion Faith Practitioners Panel Home Office 2002–03, Equality and Diversity Forum 2002–14 (vice chair 2011–14), Faith Princs' Chief Advsrs Gp 2002–06, Panel of Advsrs on Interface with Faith Communities Home Office 2003–04, Mgmnt Ctee UK Race & Europe Network 2003–14, Bd European Network Against Racism (ENAR) 2004–10 (chair 2007–10), Task Force then Steering Gp Cmmn for Equality and Human Rights DTI 2003–06, Advsy Gp on Social Housing ODPM 2004–06, Ind Advsy Gp London Criminal Justice Bd 2004–06, Cncl Liberty 2004–, Govt's Review of Treasy Counsel Appts 2004–06, Reference Gp Govt's Review of Equalities 2005–07, Honours Ctee (state and community, voluntary and local servs) 2005–11; chair Security Working Gp Preventing Extremism Taskforce Home Office 2005–06; tstee: E London Mosque and London Muslim Centre 1992–13, Book Fndn 2000–; dir Centre for Policy & Public Educn Woolf Inst Cambridge 2012; visiting fell Centre of Islamic Studies Univ of Cambridge 2010–12 (research assoc 2012–), Nohoudh Scholar SOAS Univ of London 2012–, assoc memb St Edmund's Coll Cambridge 2013–; *Publications* Religious Discrimination in the Community, Human Rights in the Community: Rights as Agents for Change by Colin Harvey (ed, 2005), Making Equality Simple: A plain English guide to the 2003 employment equality regulations on religion, belief and sexual orientation for voluntary and community organizations (jtly, 2005), Religion and Belief: respecting and accommodating faith and belief in the workplace (2006), Treasury Counsel Review Report on Treasury Counsel Appointments (jtly, 2006), Perceptions of Discrimination and Islamophobia: voices from members of Muslim communities in the European Union (jtly, 2006), Winning Hearts and Minds: Understanding and Engaging British Muslim Communities – an inter-departmental consultation paper for the Cabinet Office (jtly, 2009), Young, Muslim & Citizen – Identity, Empowerment and Change (co-ed, 2009), The Origins, History and Development of Multiculturalism in the UK, Debating Multiculturalism 1 by Max Farr (ed, 2012), Acknowledging a Shared Past to Build a Shared Future: Rethinking Multiculturalism & Muslim/ Non-Muslim Relations (e-book, 2012); *Recreations* swimming, gardening, reading; *Style*— Mohammed Aziz, Esq; ✉ CPPE, Woolf Institute, 12–14 Grange Road, Cambridge CB3 9DU (☎ 07739 848264, e-mail maa74@cam.ac.uk)

AZIZ, Suhail Ibne; s of Azizur Rahnan (d 1971), of Bangladesh, and Lutfunnessa Khatoon; *b* 3 October 1937; *Educ* RNC Dartmouth, Univ of London (BSc, MSc Econ); *m* 1960, Elizabeth Ann, da of Alfred Pyne, of Dartmouth; 2 da (Lisa, Rebecca); *Career* served Britannia RNC Dartmouth, RN Ships and Pakistan Navy 1954–61, served as RAF Offr 1968–70; East Pakistan Inland Water Transport Authy 1961–63, personnel mangr Lever Bros Pakistan Ltd 1963–66, clerical/exec offr Nat Bd for Prices and Income HM Factory Inspectorate/Health and Safety Cmmn 1967–68, industrial rels offr Royal Cmmn on Industrial Relations 1970–73, labour rels exec Ford Motor Co UK 1973–74, personnel offr Pedigree Petfoods Mars Gp 1974–78, dir Gen Servs Divs Cmmn for Racial Equality 1978–81, orgn devpt conslt PA Int Mgmnt Conslts 1981–83, head Employment and Econ Devpt Div and dep dir of econ devpt London Borough of Lewisham 1984–89, mgmnt conslt Fullemploy Consultancy 1989–90; chm and md The Brettonwood Partnership Ltd 1985–; estab Deptford Enterprise Agency; chm Lambeth Healthcare NHS Trust and Community Health South London NHS Tst 1997–2000, chair Gtr London Probation Bd (Home Office) 2001–07; memb: London Electricity Consumers Ctee, Race Relations Bd N Met Conciliation Ctee 1971–74, Exec Ctee Nottingham Community Relations Cncl 1975–78 (chm Employment Sub-Ctee), Labour, Econ, Finance, Taxation Assoc (LEFTA) 1975–79, Advsy Ctee on Community Support Progs and Initiatives Gulbenkian Fndn 1976–82 (memb Steering Ctee Black People in Britain – the Way Forward), Dept of Employment Min's Advsy Gp on Race Relations in Employment 1977–78, Home Sec's Advsy Cncl on Race Relations 1977–78, Advsy Ctee BBC Asian Unit 1977–82, Steering Ctee Int Devpt Forum 1997–99; cmmr Cwlth Scholarship Cmmn 1996–2002; estab (with Business in the Community) E London Small Business Assoc; chair: Jalalabad Overseas Orgn in the UK, E London Bangladeshi Enterprise Agency, London Boroughs Bangladeshi Assoc; conslt Plunkett Fndn for Co-operative Studies; memb: Exec Ctee Nat Orgn for African, Asian and Caribbean Orgns in the UK, Exec Ctee Tower Hamlets Community Relations Cncl; tstee: Community Devpt Fndn (Home Office) 1999–2009, Brixton Neighbourhood Community Assoc 1979–82; govr London Guildhall Univ 1995–2005 (memb Audit Ctee, memb Met Multi-Media Bd); author of articles and correspondence published in newspapers, professional journals, magazines, instnl pubns such as The Economist, The Times, The Guardian, Local Government Training Board magazine, ethnic minority newspapers/journals; written several professional research reports over the years; appearances on radio and television as commentator on current issues in the public domain; memb Cncl Int Consulting Economists Assoc; FCMI, FCMC, fell Inst of Consultancy; *Recreations* travel, reading political economy; *Clubs* RAF; *Style*— Suhail Aziz, Esq; ✉ e-mail brettonwood.partnership@btinternet.com; c/o The Royal Air Force Club, 128 Piccadilly, Mayfair, London W1J 7PY (☎ 020 7399 1000)

B

B

BABBIDGE, Adrian Vaughan; JP (1983); s of William Henry Vaughan Babbidge (d 2000), of Cwmbran, Gwent, and Violet, *née* Jenkins (d 1990); *b* 10 July 1949; *Educ* Jones' West Monmouth Sch Pontypool, UC Cardiff (BA), Univ of Leicester (postgrad museum studies cert, MA); *m* 24 Jan 2004, Rosemary Ewles; *Career* asst curator Thurrock Local History Museum Grays 1971–74, museum curator Borough of Torfaen Pontypool 1974–78, dir and sec Torfaen Museum Trust Pontypool 1978–89, dir E Midlands Museums Serv Nottingham 1989–2002 (sec 1992–2002), museum and heritage conslt co-fndr Egeria Heritage Consultancy 2002–; dir: Gwent Area Broadcasting Ltd 1981–89 (co sec 1981–85), Cardiff Broadcasting Co plc 1985–89, Museum Enterprises Ltd 1991–, Midlands Arts Marketing Ltd 1992–95 (vice-chair), Investors in People E Midlands Regnl Recognition Panel 1995–99; memb: Exec Ctee E Midlands Tourist Bd 1989–92, Kelmscott Ctee Soc of Antiquaries of London 2007–, London Cultural Reference Gp GLA 2009–13, Steering Gp Museum Standards Prog for Ireland 2010–, Cncl Shakespeare Globe Tst 2012–, Expert Panel Welsh Govt Review of Local Museum Provision 2014–15; hon lectr Inst of Archaeology UCL; external examiner (heritage studies) Nottingham Trent Univ 1995–99, Arts & Humanities Research Cncl Peer Review Coll 2006–14; tstee: Glamorgan-Gwent Archaeological Trust 1985–89, Museums Assoc Pension Fund 2008–12, Army Museums Ogilby Tst 2008–13; treas Royal Archaeological Inst 2008–10 (memb Cncl 2003–07); FMA 1982 (hon treas 1988–91, memb Ethics Ctee 1995–99); *Style*— Adrian Babbidge, Esq; ✉ 105 Greenway Avenue, London E17 3QL (☎ and fax 020 8926 0442, e-mail adrian.babbidge@egeria.org.uk)

BACK, Neil Antony; MBE (2004); *b* 16 January 1969, Coventry; *Educ* The Woodlands Sch Coventry; *m* 11 July 1998, Alison Margeret; 1 da (Olivia Grace b 27 Sept 1999, Finley Jude William b 25 Sept 2002); *Career* rugby union coach and former player; clubs: Barkers' Butts, Nottingham RFC until 1990, Leicester Tigers RFC 1990–2005 (338 appearances, 125 tries, sometime capt, winners 4 successive English league titles 1999–2002, winners Heineken Cup 2001 and 2002); England: 66 caps (4 as capt), 16 tries, 1 drop goal, debut v Scotland 1994, winners Six Nations Championship 2000, 2001 and 2003 (Grand Slam 2003), memb squad World Cup 1995 (4th place), 1999 and 2003 (champions), ranked no 1 team in the world 2003, ret 2004; memb Br Lions touring squad South Africa 1997, Aust 2001 and NZ 2005; RFU Player of the Year 1998, Players' Player of the Year Professional Players Assoc 1999, Premiership top try scorer 1999 (16 tries); tech (defence) coach Leicester Tigers 2005–08, head coach Leeds Carnegie 2008–; *Recreations* golf, tennis, squash; *Style*— Neil Back, Esq, MBE

BACKHOUSE, David John; s of Joseph Helme Backhouse (d 1989), and Jessie, *née* Chivers (d 2006); *b* 5 May 1941; *Educ* Lord Weymouth Sch Warminster, W of England Coll of Art; *m* (m dis); 2 da (Roma b 1977, Rosalind b 1984), 1 s (Theodore b 1980); partner, Jennifer Ann Weston; *Career* sculptor; many public sculptures in UK incl: The Animals in War Meml monument Park Lane London 2004, bronzes in collections worldwide; one man exhibitions in: London, NY, Washington DC; RWA, FRBS, FRSA; *Recreations* garden design, walking; *Style*— David Backhouse, Esq; ✉ Silenus, 8 Bishop Ken Close, Wells, Somerset BA5 3ND (☎ 01749 678046, e-mail jennieweston@yahoo.co.uk); La Chapelle Pommier, 24340 Mareuil, Dordogne, France

BACKHOUSE, James Anderson; s of John Anderson Backhouse (d 1998), and Anne-Heather, *née* Bolton; *b* 22 June 1967, Blackburn, Lancs; *Educ* Queen Elizabeth's GS Blackburn, Staffs Poly (LLB), Chester Coll of Law; *m* 28 May 1999, Wendy Louise, *née* Campbell; 2 da (Katie Louise b 22 Aug 2004, Charlotte b 7 Aug 2006); *Career* admitted slr 1992; slr specialising in regulatory tport law; slr Vaudreys Slrs 1993 (articled clerk 1990–92), Backhouse Jones Slrs (family firm, formerly Backhouses Slrs) 1994–; pres Blackburn Incorporated Law Assoc 2010–12; memb Law Soc 1992; author of numerous articles for professional pubns on road tport regulations incl Croners, Commercial Motor and Route One; *Recreations* shooting, sailing, horse riding, cycling; *Clubs* RAC, Dist and Union (Blackburn, pres); *Style*— James Backhouse, Esq; ✉ Backhouse Jones Solicitors, The Printworks, Hey Road, Clitheroe, Lancashire BB7 9WD (☎ 01254 828300, fax 01254 828301, e-mail james@backhouses.co.uk)

BACKHOUSE, Richard; s of T A Backhouse, of Polgooth, Cornwall, and Mrs R H Joel, *née* Mitchell; *b* 18 February 1968, Paignton, Devon; *Educ* Marlborough, Selwyn Coll Cambridge (MA); *m* 1993, Deborah; *Career* teacher Oundle Sch 1990–96; Bradfield Coll: head of economics and politics 1996–99, dir of pastoral and extra-curricular activities 1998–2000, housemaster 2000–05; princ Monkton Combe Sch 2005–15, princ Berkhamsted Schs Gp 2016–; *Recreations* rowing, skiing, reading, supporting Southampton FC; *Style*— Richard Backhouse, Esq; ✉ Monkton Combe School, Monkton Combe, Bath BA2 7HG (☎ 01442 358002, e-mail principal@berkhamstedschool.org, Twitter @rpbackhouse)

BACKLER, Dr Gary George; s of Robert Backler (d 1974), and Barbara, *née* Briers (d 2000); *b* 19 July 1955, Wirksworth, Derbys; *Educ* Merton Coll Oxford (MA), Univ of BC (MSc), Inst for Transport Studies Univ of Leeds (PhD); *m* 14 Oct 1990, Elizabeth Ann Edes; 2 da (Emily Victoria Elizabeth b 20 Aug 1992, Katherine Alexandra Lauren b 4 April 1994); *Career* research asst Centre for Transportation Studies Vancouver 1978–81, sr assoc Booz Allen & Hamilton 1985–90, supervising conslt Price Waterhouse Mgmnt Conslts 1990–94, asst dir of franchise mgmnt Office of Passenger Rail Franchising 1994–2000; Strategic Rail Authy: exec dir of regnl networks 2000–02, franchise dir north and west 2002–05; dir of rail contracts Dept for Transport 2005–10, md Backler Consulting Ltd 2011–; visiting research fell Inst for Transport Studies Univ of Leeds 2011–; tstee and planning dir Friends of the River Crane Environment (FORCE) 2011–, tstee Cncl Merton Soc 2012– (sec 2014–); FCMI 1982–2014; *Recreations* personal fitness, Brentford FC; *Style*— Dr Gary Backler; ✉ e-mail ggbackler@hotmail.co.uk

BACON, Prof Jean Margaret; *née* Goodram; da of Samuel Goodram (d 1994), and Annie, *née* Lee (d 2011); *b* 21 November 1942, Sheffield; *Educ* Royal Holloway Univ of London (BSc), Hatfield Poly (MSc, PhD, CNAA); *m* 1, 20 Dec 1964, Michael Bacon; 1 s (Thomas David b 3 March 1976); m 2, 30 Aug 2003, Ken Moody; *Career* Nat Physical Lab 1963, GEC Hirst Research Centre Wembley 1964, lectr Watford Coll of Technol 1968, sr and princ lectr Hatfield Poly 1973, successively lectr, reader and prof Univ of Cambridge Computer Lab 1985– (dir of studies in computer science 1997–), emeritus fell Jesus Coll Cambridge 2010 (fell 1997–2010), emeritus prof Univ of Cambridge 2014; visiting scientist: MIT 1994, ETH Zurich 1995, Victoria Univ Wellington NZ 2002, Tech Univ Darmstadt 2002; IEEE Computer Soc: Golden Core Award 2001, Distinguished Serv Award 2005; hon doctorate Open Univ 2013; memb Assoc for Computing Machinery 1980, CEng 1998, FBCS 2000 (MBCS 1987), FIEEE 2007 (MIEEE 1998, sr memb 2003); *Publications* Concurrent Systems (1993, 3 edn 2003), Operating Systems (co-author, 2003); numerous papers for jls and conferences; *Recreations* painting, wildlife, walking; *Style*— Prof Jean Bacon; ✉ University of Cambridge Computer Laboratory, J J Thomson Avenue, Cambridge CB3 0FD (☎ 01223 334604, fax 01223 334678, e-mail jean.bacon@cl.cam.ac.uk)

BACON, Dr Neil; *b* 8 April 1967; *Educ* Univ of Oxford, Harvard Univ; *m* Fiona Bacon; *Career* fndr IWantGreatCare 2008–; FRCP; *Recreations* extreme marathoning; *Style*— Dr Neil Bacon; ✉ IWantGreatCare, 4 Manor Farm Barns, Cornbury Park, Finstock OX7 3DG (☎ 01993 868428, e-mail neil@IWantGreatCare.org, info@IWantGreatCare.org, website www.IWantGreatCare.org)

BACON, Richard Michael; MP; s of Michael Bacon, and Mrs Sheila Campbell; step s of Prof John Campbell, OBE, *qv*; *b* 3 December 1962; *Educ* King's Sch Worcester, LSE (BSc), Goethe Institut Berlin; *m* 28 Jan 2006, Victoria Louise, da of Stephen Panton and Elizabeth Panton, of Market Drayton, Shropshire; 2 s; *Career* investment banker Barclays de Zoete Wedd 1986–89, financial journalist Euromoney Pubns 1993–94, dep dir Mgmnt Consultancies Assoc 1994–96, assoc ptnr Brunswick PR 1996–99, fndr English Word Factory 1999; MP (Cons) S Norfolk 2001– (Parly candidate Vauxhall (Cons) 1997); memb: Public Accounts Select Ctee 2001–, European Scrutiny Select Ctee 2003–07, Public Accounts Cmmn 2005–; held various posts in Cons Pty since 1978, co-fndr Cons Pty's Geneva project, chm and fndr All-Pty Parly Gp on Self-Build, Custom Build and Independent House Building; Parliamentarian of the Year The Spectator 2006, Backbencher of the Year House magazine 2006, Select Committee Member of the Year House magazine 2012, Conservative Backbencher of the Year Asian Voice Newspaper 2013; *Books* Why Every Government Gets Things Wrong – And What We Can Do About It (with Christopher Hope, 2013); *Recreations* words, music, playing the bongos; *Clubs* Ronnie Scott's; *Style*— Richard Bacon, Esq, MP; ✉ House of Commons, London SW1A 0AA (☎ 020 7219 3000); Constituency Office ☎ 01379 643728, fax 01379 642220

BACON, Stephen Francis Theodore; s of Frank David Bacon (d 1982), of Prestbury, Cheshire, and Cecilia Nancy, *née* Pursglove (d 2003); *b* 3 September 1945, Oldham, Lancs; *Educ* Perse Sch Cambridge, KCL (LLB, AKC), Inns of Court Sch of Law; *m* 1; 1 s (Nicholas Giles b 24 Sept 1977), 1 da (Hannah France b 15 March 1980 d 2009); m 2, 28 July 2001, Felicity Clare, *née* Quant; 1 da (Clio Francesca Grace b 25 Oct 2001); *Career* called to the Bar Gray's Inn 1969; practising barr Northern Circuit 1969–80, dep Northern legal mangr Daily Express 1980–87, head of legal Express Newspapers 1989–2011 (legal advsr 1987–89), currently media law conslt; chm Bar Assoc for Commerce, Finance and Industry (BACFI) 1998 and 2006–07 (currently vice-pres), memb Bar Cncl 1998–2008; regular contrib to legal jls; *Recreations* cricket, gardening, horse racing; *Style*— Stephen Bacon, Esq

BACON, Timothy Roger; s of Christopher Henry Bacon (d 1956), and Diana Sybil, *née* Richmond Brown (d 1995); *b* 4 December 1947; *Educ* Eton, Univ of Bristol (BSc); *m* 14 Sept 1985, Marylyn Rowan Ogilvie, da of William Arthur Grant; 2 da (Rosalind Sarah b 12 Jan 1987, Laura Charlotte b 11 July 1988); *Career* Brown Shipley & Co Ltd 1970–92 (dir 1988–92), md Colville Estate Ltd 1993– (dir 1976–), Columbus Asset Management Ltd 1992–2004; tstee Blind Veterans UK, patron Childhood First; *Recreations* opera, theatre, travel; *Clubs* City University, Pratt's; *Style*— Timothy Bacon, Esq; ✉ Ramsden Farm, Stone, Tenterden, Kent TN30 7JB (☎ 01797 270300)

BADAWI, Zeinab Mohammed-Khair; da of Mohammed-Khair El Badawi, of Southgate, London, and Asia Mohammed, *née* Malik; *b* 3 October 1959; *Educ* Hornsey Sch for Girls, St Hilda's Coll Oxford (BA), Univ of London (MA); *Partner* David Crook; 1 s (Joseph Badawi-Crook b 1994), 2 da (Sophia Badawi-Crook b 1996, Hannah Badawi-Crook b 1998); *Career* presenter and journalist in current affairs and documentaries Yorkshire TV 1982–86, current affairs reporter BBC TV 1987–88, newscaster and journalist ITN (Channel Four News) 1989–98, joined BBC 1998, BBC Live political programmer; presenter: The World Tonight (BBC Radio 4), Newshour (BBC World Serv), The World (BBC Four) 2005–07, World News Today (BBC Four) 2007–; vice-pres UN Int Assoc, chair Article 19 Int Organisation for Freedom of Speech; advsr Foreign Policy Centre; memb: Hansard Cmmn into Scrutiny Role of Parliament, Panel 2000; trustee: Nat Portrait Gallery, Br Cncl; *Recreations* yoga, opera, reading, languages; *Style*— Miss Zeinab Badawi

BADDELEY, Prof Alan David; CBE (1999); *b* 23 March 1934; *Educ* Cockburn HS Leeds, UCL (BA), Princeton Univ (MA), Univ of Cambridge (PhD); *m* 1964, Hilary Ann White; 3 s; *Career* memb scientific staff MRC Applied Psychology Unit Cambridge 1958–67, lectr then reader Univ of Sussex 1967–72, prof of psychology Univ of Stirling 1972–74, dir MRC Applied Psychology Unit Cambridge 1974–96, sr res fell Churchill Coll Cambridge 1987–95; prof of psychology Univ of Bristol 1995–; hon prof of cognitive psychology Univ of Cambridge 1991–95; memb: ESRC Psychology Ctee 1979–81; chm MRC Neurosciences Bd 1987–89 (memb 1981–85); memb Editorial Bds: Applied Cognitive Psychology (special editorial advsr), Cognition and Emotion, Consciousness and Cognition, Essays in Cognitive Psychology, European Jl of Cognitive Psychology, Learning and Individual Differences, Learning and Memory, Neuropsychological Rehabilitation; President's Award British Psychological Soc 1982 (Myers lectr 1980); pres: Experimental Psychology Soc 1984–86 (Bartlett lectr 1988), Euro Soc for Cognitive Psychology 1986–90; hon foreign memb American Acad of Arts and Scis 1996; Distinguished Scientific Contribution Award American Psychological Assoc 2001, Aristotle Prize 2001; Hon DPhil Umeå Univ Sweden 1991; Hon DUniv: Stirling 1996, Essex 1999, Plymouth 2001; Hon FBPsS 1995, FRS 1993, FMedSci 1998, FBA; *Books* The Psychology of Memory (1976), Your Memory: A User's Guide (1982, 2 edn 1993), Working Memory (1986), Human Memory: Theory and Practice (1990), Working Memory and Language (with S Gathercole, 1993); jt ed: Attention and Performance IX (1981), Research Directions in Cognitive Science: A European Perspective – Vol 1: Cognitive Psychology (1989), Human Factors in Hazardous Situations (1990), Attention: Selection, Awareness and Control – A Tribute to Donald Broadbent (1993), Handbook of Memory Disorders (1995, 2 edn 2002), Essentials of Human Memory (1999), Episodic Memory (2002), Working Memory: Thought and Action (2007), Memory (2009, 2 edn 2015); *Style*— Professor Alan Baddeley, CBE, FRS, FBA, FMedSci; ✉ Department of Psychology,

University of York, Heslington, York YO10 5DD (☎ 01904 432882, fax 01904 433181, e-mail ab50@york.ac.uk)

BADDELEY, Julie Margaret; da of Stuart Frank Weston, and Margaret Rose, *née* Burrows, of Cambridge; *Educ* St Felix Sch Southwold, Somerville Coll Oxford (MA); *m* 1972 (m dis 1995), Philip Stirling Baddeley; 1 s (John Philip b 13 Dec 1977), 1 da (Sarah Margaret b 28 April 1979); *Career* exec dir Woolwich plc 1998–2000; ptnr Andersen Consulting 1992–96; md: Baddeley Associates Ltd 1982–87, Sema Gp Consulting 1987–91; dir Chrysalis VCT plc; non-exec dir: Yorkshire Building Soc 2001–08, BOC Gp plc 2001–05, Computerland UK plc 2005–08, Greggs plc 2005–14, Sustain Ltd 2011– (chm 2011–), Harvey Nash plc 2011– (chm 2013–), Ebiquity plc 2014–; memb Audit Cmmn 1999–2003; non-exec dir: DWP Pensions Directorate 2000–06, Dept of Health 2005–10; dir Camelot Gp plc 2008–10; assoc fell Said Business Sch Oxford 1998–2010; Freeman City of London, Freeman Worshipful Co of Information Technologists 1990; *Books* Understanding Industry (1979); *Recreations* music; *Style*— Ms Julie Baddeley; ✉ 29 De Vere Gardens, London W8 5AW (e-mail juliebaddeley@gmail.com)

BADDELEY, Stephen John; s of William Baddeley, and Barbara Isabel; *b* 28 March 1961; *Educ* Chelsea Coll London (BSc); *m* 16 June 1984 (m dis 1997), Deirdre Ilene, *née* Sharman; 1 s (James Scott William b 25 Jan 1991), 1 da (Selene Sharman b 16 April 1993); partner Kirsten Irene Gwerder; 1 s (Karl Thomas Stephen b 13 Aug 2001), 1 da (Astrid-Marie Rose b 12 Sept 2005); *Career* former badminton player; Eng nat singles champion 1981, 1985 and 1987, Eng nat men's doubles champion 1985, 1987 and 1989; Euro singles champion 1990; Cwlth Games: Gold medal team event 1982, 1986 and 1990, Gold medal singles 1986; winner men's singles: Indian Open 1985, Scottish Open 1986; represented Europe v Asia 1983, 1984 and 1986; 143 caps for Eng; hon memb Badminton Writers' Assoc, memb and chair Eng Badminton Players' Assoc 1989–90, chm World Badminton Players' Fedn 1989–90, ret as player 1990; dir of coaching and devpt Scottish Badminton Union 1990–92, mangr Br Olympic Badminton Team 1990–92, coach Nat Centre de Badminton Lausanne (asst nat Swiss coach) 1992–96, dir of tournament World Badminton Championships Lausanne 1995, dir Elite Play and Nat Coaching Policy Badminton Assoc of England Ltd 1996–99, chief exec Badminton Assoc of England 1998–2004, dir of sport Sport England 2004–08 (interim chief exec 2005), dir of sport Univ of Bath 2010–; memb Mgmnt Bd Talented Athlete Scholarship Scheme (TASS) 2012–, chair Badminton GB Ltd 2016–, memb Cncl LTA 2016–; tstee: Bath Recreation Ground Tst 2013–, SkillsActive 2014–; *Books* Badminton In Action (1988), Go and Play Badminton (1992); *Recreations* swimming, tennis; *Style*— Stephen Baddeley, Esq

BADDIEL, David Lionel; s of Dr Colin B Baddiel, and Sarah Fabian-Baddiel; *b* 28 May 1964; *Educ* Haberdashers' Aske's, King's Coll Cambridge (MA), UCL; *Partner* Morwenna Banks; 1 da (Dolly Banks-Baddiel b 31 Aug 2001), 1 s (Ezra b 9 Nov 2004); *Career* comedian and writer; World Cup corr Evening Standard 2002, columnist The Guardian, The Times and FHM, occasional writer The Observer, The Times, The Independent, Daily Telegraph, Sunday Times, The Mirror and Esquire; judge Booker Prize 2002; supporter Holocaust Educnl Tst; FRSA; writer and singer (with Frank Skinner, *qv*, and Lightning Seeds): Three Lions (official song for Euro '96, UK no 1 (twice), Germany no 17, NME Brat Award 1996), Three Lions '98 (UK no 1); *Radio* writer and performer The Mary Whitehouse Experience (BBC Radio 1) 1988–90 (Sony Radio Award 1989); *Television* The Mary Whitehouse Experience (BBC2) 1990–92 (Radio Times Best Newcomer Award 1991), Stab in the Dark (Channel 4) 1992–93, Newman and Baddiel In Pieces (BBC2) 1993, Fantasy Football League (BBC2) 1994–96, Fantasy World Cup (ITV) 1998, Baddiel and Skinner Unplanned (ITV) 2000–, Baddiel's Syndrome (Sky TV) 2001; *Videos* From The Mary Whitehouse Experience 1991, History Today 1992, Newman and Baddiel at Wembley Arena 1993, Fantasy Football League Unseen 1996, The Too Much Information Tour 1997, Baddiel and Skinner Unplanned Live in the West End 2001; *Film* actor The Announcement 2002, writer/prodr The Infidel 2010; *One-Man Shows* Fame: Not the Musical 2013, My Family: Not the Sitcom 2016; *Publications* The Mary Whitehouse Experience Encyclopedia (1992), The Fantasy Football League Diary (1995); novels: Time For Bed (1996), Whatever Love Means (1999), The Secret Purposes (2004), The Death of Eli Gold (2011), The Parent Agency (2014), The Person Controller (2015), The Boy Who Could Do What He Liked (2016); *Recreations* football, tennis; *Clubs* Soho House, Camden Road; *Style*— David Baddiel, Esq; ✉ c/o Avalon Management Group Ltd, 4A Exmoor Street, London W10 6BD (☎ 020 7598 7321, fax 020 7598 7300); literary agent: c/o Rogers, Coleridge and White Ltd, 20 Powis Mews, London W11 1JN (☎ 020 7221 3717)

BADEN-POWELL, 3 Baron (UK 1929); Sir Robert Crause Baden-Powell; 3 Bt (UK 1922); s of 2 Baron Baden-Powell (d 1962); *b* 15 October 1936; *Educ* Bryanston; *m* 1963, Patience (d 2010), da of Maj Douglas Batty (d 1982); *Heir* bro, Hon Michael Baden-Powell; *Career* dir Bolton Building Soc 1972–88, md Fieldguard Ltd 1984–; vice-pres: World Scout Fndn 1978–88, Scout Assoc 1982– (chief scouts cmmr 1965–82); memb Cncl Scout Assoc 1965– (memb Ctee 1972–78), pres W Yorks Scout Cncl 1972–88, pres Surrey Youth Focus 2011–16; chm: Quarter Horse Racing UK 1985–88, Br Quarter Horse Assoc 1989–90 (memb Cncl 1984–90); vice-pres The Camping and Caravanning Club 2001– (pres 1992–2001); Liveryman Worshipful Co of Mercers; *Books* Diary of a Dog; *Recreations* breeding racing Quarter Horses, art collecting, music, greyhound rescue; *Style*— Lord Baden-Powell; ✉ Weston Farmhouse, The Street, Albury, Surrey GU5 9AY

BADENOCH, (Ian) James Forster; QC (1989); s of Sir John Badenoch (d 1996), and Anne Newnham, *née* Forster; *b* 24 July 1945; *Educ* Rugby, Magdalen Coll Oxford (open scholar, Demy, MA); *m* Marie-Thérèse Victoria, da of Martin Hammond Cabourn Smith; 1 da (Isabel Grace b 1 Jan 1980), 2 s (William James Cabourn b 30 Jan 1982, Rory Martin Cabourn b 3 Nov 1984); *Career* called to the Bar Lincoln's Inn 1968 (bencher 2000), admitted to Hong Kong Bar (ad eundem); memb Inner Temple, recorder of the Crown Court 1987–2012, dep judge of the High Court 1994–2012; a pres Mental Health Review Tbnl 2000–16, chm The Expert Witness Inst 2004–13 (now chm emeritus); memb: Harveian Soc of London, Medico-Legal Soc; FRSM; *Books* Medical Negligence (contrib, Butterworths 1990, 4 edn 2008), Urology and the Law (2006); *Recreations* fossil hunting, wildlife photography, the study of herons; *Style*— James Badenoch, Esq, QC; ✉ 1 Crown Office Row, Temple, London EC4Y 7HH (☎ 020 7797 7500, e-mail jb@jbadenoch.com)

BADGER, Prof Anthony John (Tony); s of Kenneth Badger (d 1979), and Iris Gwendoline, *née* Summerill (d 2010); *b* 6 March 1947; *Educ* Cotham GS, Sidney Sussex Coll Cambridge (MA), Univ of Hull (PhD); *m* 28 June 1979, Ruth Catherine, da of Ronald Davis; 2 s (Nicholas, Christopher (twins) b 22 Aug 1981); *Career* Dept of History Univ of Newcastle upon Tyne: lectr 1971–81, sr lectr 1981–91, head of dept 1988–91, prof 1991; Paul Mellon prof of American history Univ of Cambridge 1992–2014, fell Sidney Sussex Coll Cambridge 1992–2002 (vice-master 2000–02, hon fell 2003–), master Clare Coll Cambridge 2003–14, prof in American History Northumbria Univ 2014–; chair Kennedy Meml Tst 2009–16, ind reviewer Migrated Colonial Archive FCO 2011–; Hon DLitt Univ of Hull 1999, hon dr of Humane Letters North Carolina State Univ 2013; fell Soc of American Historians 2012, hon fell Br Assoc for American Studies 2013, Jubilee fell Historical Assoc 2014; *Books* Prosperity Road: The New Deal, North Carolina and Tobacco (1980), North Carolina and The New Deal (1981), The New Deal: The Depression Years 1933–1940 (1989), The Making of Martin Luther King and The Civil Rights Movement (ed with Brian Ward, 1996), Southern Landscapes (ed with Walter Edgar and Jan Nordby Gretland, 1997), Contesting Democracy: Substance and Structure in American Political History (ed with Byron Shafer, 2001), New Deal/New South: The Anthony J Badger Reader (2007), FDR: The First Hundred Days (2008); *Recreations* walking, supporting Bristol Rovers FC; *Style*— Prof Tony Badger; ✉ 1 Hunterscombe Court, Bingley, West Yorkshire BD16 3HG (☎ 01274 566349, e-mail ajb1001@cam.ac.uk)

BADRAWY, Dr Galal Akasha; s of Akasha Badrawy (d 1985), of Cairo, and Sanya Ahmed; *b* 4 June 1946; *m* 1974, Sylvia Anne, da of Edward Hatcher; 1 s (Adam b 1977), 1 da (Sarah b 1980); *Career* house surgn Mansoura Univ Hosp Egypt 1970–71, house physician Dar El Saha Hosp Beirut Lebanon 1971; SHO: Accident Emergency and Orthopaedics Princess Margaret Hosp Swindon 1972, Geriatric Med Stratton St Margaret's Hosp Swindon 1972–73, Orthopaedic Surgery Co Hosp York 1973–74; registrar: Naburn and Bootham Park Hosps York 1974–78 (SHO 1974), Child and Adolescent Psychiatry Southfield and Fairfield Units York 1978–79, York and Community Psychiatry St Andrew Day Hosp 1979–80; conslt psychiatrist and head Psychiatry Dept Abdulla Fouad Hosp Dammam Saudi Arabia, clinical asst Maudsley and The Bethlem Royal Hosp/Inst of Psychiatry 1982, registrar in psychiatry Horsham and Crawley Gen Hosp 1982–83; med dir Priory Psychiatric Clinic Lister Hosp 1984–89; locum conslt psychiatrist: Yorkshire RHA (with duties at St Mary's Hosp, Scarborough and Clifton Hosp, Scarborough Dist Hosp) 1983, Trent RHA (with duties at Rauceby Hosp Lincolnshire, Boston Gen Hosp, Skegness Gen Hosp) 1982–85, Ashford Gen Hosp Middx 1985–86; locum conslt: St Thomas' Hosp (based at Tooting, duties at Bec Hosp and Day Hosp Putney) 1986–87, Psychiatric Unit Basingstoke Hosp 1987, Abraham Cowley Unit St Peter's Hosp Chertsey 1987–88; locum conslt psychiatrist Wexham Park Hosp Slough 1988–90; in private practice Harley St 1983–, conslt psychiatrist Charter Nightingale Hosp Lisson Grove 1989– (med dir Arab Unit 1987–89), conslt psychiatrist The Ridgewood Centre, conslt psychiatrist Cardinal Clinic Windsor; subject of interviews by Harpers & Queen, several Arabic newspapers and by BBC Arabic stations; hon memb American Psychiatric Assoc; memb BMA; MRCPsych, FRSM; *Recreations* golf; *Clubs* Wentworth, Les Ambassadeurs; *Style*— Dr Galal Badrawy; ✉ 127 Harley Street, London W1N 1DH (☎ 020 7935 6875, mobile 07973 111426)

BADY, Jean-Baptiste; s of Edmond Bady, of Illiat, France, and Michèle, *née* Ray; *b* 13 July 1979, Rillieux la Pape, France; *Educ* College Eugène Dubois France, CFA Bernard Palissy France; *m* 18 Oct 2006, Elodie, *née* Calmettes; 1 da (Lisa b 1 Nov 2006), 1 s (Paul b 29 June 2008); *Career* chef; apprenti de cuisine L'Auberge des Bishonnières Amberieux en Dombes 1995–99, commis de cuisine then demi chef de partie Restaurant Georges Blanc France 1999–2000; chef de partie: L'Auberge du colombier Roquefort les Pins 2000, La C?te d'Or Bernard Loiseau Saulieu 2001–02, The Summer Lodge Evershot 2002–03; jr sous chef Kilworth House Hotel N Killworth 2003; Kinnaird Hotel Perthshire: sous chef 2004–07, head chef 2007– (3 AA Rosettes, 4 AA Red Stars), head chef Balfour Castle 2009–; Chef of the Year Scottish Hotel Award 2009; *Recreations* gardening, sport (gym, swimming, cycling), golf, cinema, fly fishing; *Style*— Jean-Baptiste Bady, Esq; ✉ Balfour Castle, Shapinsay, Orkney KW17 2DY (☎ 01856 711280, e-mail jean-baptistebady@balfourcastle.co.uk, website www.balfourcastle.co.uk)

BAGGALEY, Paul; *Career* mktg/bookshop mangr Waterstones 1985–98, Harvill Press 1998–2002, Random House 2002–05, publishing dir Harper Perennial 2004–08, publisher Picador 2008–; *Style*— Paul Baggaley, Esq; ✉ Picador, 20 New Wharf Road, London N1 9RR

BAGGALLAY, Roger; s of Merrik Baggallay (d 1988), and Valerie, *née* Thomas (d 1996); *b* 23 September 1954, Canterbury, Kent; *Educ* Marlborough (scholar), New Coll Oxford (MA); *m* 11 Sept 1982, Elizabeth Margaret, *née* Morcom; 2 s (Merrik David b 24 Oct 1984, Alexander Richard b 24 Aug 1987); *Career* admitted slr: England and Wales 1978, Hong Kong 1982; slr with Coward Chance London and Hong Kong 1978–87 (trainee slr 1976–78), ptnr Clifford Chance 1987–2007 (sometime head Finance, Corporate and Regulatory Litigation Gp and chm Int Litigation Gp, conslt 2007–14); memb Law Soc; *Publications* Aircraft Liens and Detention Rights (conslt ed Eng and Wales chapter, 1998), Butterworths International Litigation Handbook (conslt ed, 1999 and 2006); *Recreations* music, sport, gardening; *Style*— Roger Baggallay, Esq; ✉ 43 Lauder Road, Edinburgh EH9 1UE

BAGGE, (Alfred) James Stephen; 2 s of Sir John Alfred Picton Bagge, 6 Bt, ED, DL (d 1990); *b* 7 December 1952; *Educ* Eton; *m* 10 Oct 1981, Victoria I, er da of Michael A Lyndon Skeggs (d 2015); 1 da (Edwina Rose b 1985); *Career* Capt Blues and Royals, ADC to Govr S Australia 1975–77; barr 1979–93; ptnr Norton Rose Slrs 1993–2008; memb Hon Soc of Lincoln's Inn 1975–93; dir Bralco Ltd 2008–; *Clubs* Boodle's, Cavalry and Guards; *Style*— James Bagge, Esq

BAGGE, Sir (John) Jeremy Picton; 7 Bt (UK 1867), of Stradsett Hall, Norfolk; DL (Norfolk 1996); s of Sir John Alfred Picton Bagge, 6 Bt, ED, DL (d 1990), and Elizabeth Helena (Lena), *née* Davies (d 1996); *b* 21 June 1945; *Educ* Eton; *m* 1979, Sarah Margaret Phipps, da of late Maj James Shelley Phipps Armstrong, Agent-Gen for Ontario; 2 s (Alfred James John b 1 July 1980, Albert Daniel Bracewell b 1 April 1985), 1 da (Alexandra Mary Pleasance b 26 Dec 1982); *Heir* s, Alfred Bagge; *Career* farmer; fin advsr to HIH The Crown Prince of Ethiopia 1969–70; cncllr King's Lynn and West Norfolk Borough 1981–95 (chm Planning 1991–94, Hon Alderman 1995); chm: West Norfolk Enterprise Agency 1985–94, Norfolk Rural Devpt Cmmn 1989–99, Cambridge Rural Devpt Cmmn 1995–99, Norfolk Shaping the Future Agric Ctee 1998–2000, Norfolk Rural Strategy Ctee 1998–2002; pres Royal Norfolk Agricultural Assoc 2010–11; CLA: memb Norfolk Ctee CLA 1986–2006 (chm 1993–95), memb Exec 1997–2002, pres Norfolk 2008–13; High Sheriff Norfolk 2003–04; memb Bishop's Cncl (Ely Diocese) 1994–2005; dir and tstee Norfolk Hospice Tapping House 1999–2011; Freeman: City of London, Worshipful Co of Haberdashers; FCA 1968; *Recreations* shooting, stalking, skiing, water skiing; *Clubs* Boodle's, Air Squadron, Allsorts, Pratt's; *Style*— Sir Jeremy Bagge, Bt, DL; ✉ Marham House, Marham, King's Lynn, Norfolk PE33 9HS (☎ 01760 339559, e-mail office@stradsett.com or jeremybagge@stradsett.com, website www.stradsett.com)

BAGNALL, Air Chief Marshal Sir Anthony John Crowther; GBE (2003, OBE 1982), KCB (1998, CB 1994); *Educ* Stretford GS, RAF Coll Cranwell; *m* Pamela; 3 c; *Career* cmmnd RAF 1967, sqdn pilot then weapons instr (Lightnings) 1967–75, promoted Sqdn Ldr 1975, flt cdr 1975–78, attended RAF Staff Coll 1978, staff duties MOD 1978–80, promoted Wing Cdr 1980, Wing Cdr Air Defence HQ Strike Cmd 1980–83, CO 43 Sqdn then CO 23 Sqdn (Phantoms) Falkland Is 1983–85, promoted Gp Capt 1985, Dir of Air Staff Briefing and Co-ordination 1985–87, CO RAF Leuchars 1988–99, promoted Air Cdre 1990, RCDS 1990, Dir of Air Force Staff Duties MOD 1991–92, promoted Air Vice Marshal 1992, Asst Chief of Air Staff 1992–94, AOC No 11 Gp 1994–96, promoted Air Marshal 1996, Dep C-in-C Allied Forces Central Europe 1996–1998, Air Member for Personnel 1998–2000, promoted Air Chief Marshal 2000, C-in-C STC 2000–01, Vice Chief of Defence Staff 2001; FRAeS; *Recreations* fell walking, golf, bridge; *Style*— Air Chief Marshal Sir Anthony Bagnall, GBE, KCB, FRAeS; ✉ c/o Lloyds Bank plc, 55 King Street, Manchester M60 2ES

BAGNALL, John Keith; s of Alfred Studley Bagnall (d 1992), and Margaret Bagnall (d 1983); *b* 30 December 1941; *Educ* Oundle; *m* 10 Oct 1964, Valerie, da of Leslie Moxon (d 1985); 1 da (Caroline b 1966), 1 s (Stephen b 1968); *Career* Alfred Bagnall & Sons Ltd: dir 1962, gp md 1972–2004, chm 2004; treas Keighley and Dist Trg Assoc 1966–70; memb Standing Ctee: Safety Health and Welfare 1976–79, Fin 1976–98, Econ and Public Affrs Gp 1983–93; pres: Nat Fedn Painting and Decorating Contractors 1979–80, Fedn of Bldg Specialist Contractors 1983–84; chm Bldg Employers' Confedn 1992–93 (memb Nat Cncl 1978–85, vice-pres 1986–90, dep chm 1991–92); memb: Construction Industry Jt Taxation

Ctee 1990–2003, Good Practice of Construction Industry Bd 1996–99; FCA 1965, FIMgt 1972, CCMI 2008; *Recreations* travel, golf; *Style*— John Bagnall, Esq; ✉ Shackleton House Farm, North Walk, Harden, West Yorkshire BD16 1RY; Alfred Bagnall & Sons Ltd, 6 Manor Lane, Shipley, West Yorkshire BD18 3RD (✆ 01274 714800)

BAGRI, Hon Apurv; s of The Lord Bagri, CBE (Life Peer), *qv*, of London, and Usha, *née* Maheshwary; *b* 11 November 1959, Mumbai, India; *Educ* Cass Business Sch London; *m* 26 Feb 1982, Alka, *née* Rakyan; 2 da (Aditi b 29 Dec 1985, Amisha b 22 Sept 1988); *Career* pres and ceo Metdist Enterprises Ltd; past chm and current memb Bd Int Wrought Copper Cncl; memb Bd: Hong Kong Exchanges and Clearing Ltd, Dubai Financial Servs Authy; chm Governing Body London Business Sch, visiting prof Cass Business Sch, past pro-chllr and chm Governing Cncl City Univ (currently hon rector), memb Corporation UC Sch; chm Bd Royal Parks, cmmr Crown Estate Paving Cmmn; memb Bd HE Funding Cncl for Eng; tstee Asia House; hon fell London Business Sch; Hon DSc City Univ; *Style*— The Hon Apurv Bagri, Esq; ✉ Metdist Enterprises Limited, 80 Cannon Street, London EC4N 6EJ (✆ 020 7280 0000, fax 020 7606 6650)

BAGRI, Baron (Life Peer UK 1997), of Regent's Park in the City of Westminster; Raj Kumar; CBE (1995); s of Sohan Lal Bagri; *Career* fndr and chm Metdist Gp 1970, chm The London Metal Exchange Ltd 1993–2002 (dir 1983–2002, vice-chm 1990–93, hon pres 2003–06); memb Governing Body SOAS Univ of London 1997–2007, memb Ct City Univ; chm of tstees Rajiv Gandhi (UK) Fndn, tstee Sangam, chm Bagri Fndn; DSc (hc) City Univ 1999, DSc (hc) Univ of Nottingham 2000; hon fell London Business Sch 2004; *Recreations* fine art, classical music, antiques; *Clubs* MCC; *Style*— The Rt Hon the Lord Bagri, CBE; ✉ Metdist Group, 80 Cannon Street, London EC4N 6EJ (✆ 020 7280 0000, fax 020 7606 6650, e-mail vmanning@metdist.com)

BAGULEY, Joseph Brunel (Joe); *Educ* Imperial Coll London; *Career* sr conslt (support) Hewlett Packard UK Ltd 1993–96, technical conslt Morse 1996, sr systems conslt SHL Systemshouse 1996–98, infrastructure conslt Dimenica 1998–99, sr systems conslt Conchango 1999–2000, chief technol offr (Europe) Quest Software 2001–11, vice-pres and chief technol offr EMEA VMware 2011–; MBCS; *Recreations* shooting, climbing; *Style*— Joe Baguley, Esq; ✉ VMware UK Limited, Flow 1 & 2, River Park Avenue, Staines-upon-Thames TW18 3AP (e-mail jbaguley@vmware.com, Twitter @joebaguley)

BAGWELL, Air Marshal Gregory Jack (Greg); CB (2012), CBE (2007); *b* 6 October 1961, Dartford, Kent; *Educ* Tonbridge Sch, Univ of Madras (MSc); *m* 22 April 1989, Scarlett, *née* Van Gelder; 3 s (Scott b 21 Sept 1991, Glenn b 16 April 1993, Ross b 19 Nov 2000), 1 da (Alanah b 6 March 1996); *Career* cmmnd RAF 1981; pilot then flying offr then flight lt, sqdn ldr 1991, wing cdr 1997, CO No 9 Sqdn, Gp Capt 2001, Coalition Air Operations Chief Al Udeid Coalition Air Operations Centre 2004, Station Cdr RAF Marham 2004, Asst COS Crisis and Deliberate Planning Permanent Jt HQ, Air Offr Commanding No 1 Gp 2009, COS Jt Warfare Devpt Permanent Jt HQ, Dir Jt Warfare Jt Forces Command 2011, Dep Cdr (Operations) RAF Air Command 2013–16; currently dir L2 Network Ltd; assoc fell RUSI; *Style*— Air Marshal Greg Bagwell, CB, CBE; ✉ Twitter @gregbagwell

BAHL, Kamlesh; CBE (1997); da of Swinder Nath Bahl (d 1978), and Leela Wati, *née* Madan; *b* 28 May 1956; *Educ* Minchenden Sch Southgate, Univ of Birmingham (LLB); *m* 1986, Dr Nitin Nanji Lakhani; *Career* slr: GLC 1978–81, BSC 1981–84, Texaco Ltd 1984–87; Data Logic Ltd: legal and commercial mangr 1987–89, co sec and mangr Legal Servs 1989–93, legal conslt 1993–; chairwoman Equal Opportunities Cmmn 1993–98; Law Soc: memb Cncl 1990–2000 and 2002–, dep vice-pres 1998–99, chair Commerce and Industry Gp 1988–89, vice-pres 1999–2000; non-exec memb: Barnet HA 1989–90, Parkside HA 1990–93; memb: Ethnic Minorities Advsy Ctee 1991–94, Judicial Studies Bd 1991–93, Justice Sub-Ctee on Judiciary 1991–92, Cncl of Justice 1993–95, Cncl of Nat Assoc of HAs and Tsts 1993–94, EC Advsy Ctee on Equal Opportunities for Women and Men 1993–98 (vice-chair 1997–98), Cncl of Justice 1993–95; non-exec memb London Transport Bd 1999–2003; independent memb No 1 Diplomatic Service Appeal Bd of Foreign and Cwlth Office 1993–; EC Rep EC Consultative Cmmn on Racism & Xenophobia 1994–97; patron UN Year for Tolerance 1995; tstee Refuge 1998–; memb Cncl Scouts Assoc 1996–99; non-exec dir Univ of Westminster 1997, memb Cncl Open Univ 1999; FIPD 1997; *Books* Managing Legal Practice in Business (ed, 1989); *Recreations* swimming, singing, travelling, theatre; *Style*— Kamlesh Bahl, CBE

BAIER, Frederick John Watt; s of Francis Clair Wolfgang Baier, of Birkenhead, and Violet, *née* Wood; *b* 15 April 1949, Kingston-upon-Hull; *Educ* Bootham Sch York, Hull GS Kingston upon Hull, Canterbury Coll of Art, Birmingham Coll of Art (DipAD Furniture), RCA (MA, fell); *m* 1988, Lucy Elizabeth Strachan, the sculptor, da of David Rankin Strachan (d 1979); 2 da (Billie Anna b 26 Jan 1989, Rebecca b 4 Feb 1990); *Career* furniture designer; in partnership with Barry Joseph Leister and Keith Clarke in Empire Workshops (architectural reclamation, interior schemes and prototype furniture) 1977–79; teaching: pt/t at Brighton Poly 1979–82, Wendell Castle Sch USA 1986–88, pt/t at RCA and Wiltshire Studio 1989–; numerous exhbns worldwide; consultancy work incl: Design Cncl, Crafts Cncl, A B K Architects, Terry Farrell, *qv*, David Davies, also regnl arts assocs, interior designers, manufacturers and educnl instns; collections and cmmns incl: V&A Museum, Birmingham Museum and Art Gallery, Southern Arts, Crafts Cncl Gallery, Shipley Art Gallery, Templeton Coll Oxford, City of Leeds Museums, Carnegie Museum of Art Pittsburgh PA, Chiltern Sculpture Trail, Contemporary Art Soc, Kesler Lincoln's Inn, Lotherton Hall, US Ambass to Denmark, Steam Museum of GWR; FRCA; *Books* Fred Baier Furniture in Studio, Vision and Reality; *Style*— Frederick Baier, Esq; ✉ 45 High Street, Pewsey, Wiltshire SN9 5AF (✆ 01672 562974, fax 01672 563043, e-mail fredbaier@btopenworld.com); 5A High Street, Pewsey, Wiltshire SN9 5AE (e-mail fred@fredbaier.com, website www.fredbaier.com)

BAILEY, Adrian Edward; MP; s of Edward Arthur Bailey (d 1996), and Sylvia Alice Iles, *née* Bayliss; *b* 11 December 1945; *Educ* Cheltenham GS, Univ of Exeter (BA), Loughborough Coll of Librarianship (Dip Librarianship); *m* 3 April 1989, Jill Patricia, da of late William Hunscott; 1 step s (Daniel b 19 July 1983); *Career* librarian Cheshire County Cncl 1971–82, nat organiser Co-operative Pty 1982–2000, MP (Lab/Co-op) West Bromwich W 2000– (by-election); memb Labour Pty 1962–, memb Co-operative Pty 1974–; supporter and contrib: Action Aid, Friends of the Animals, Redwings Horse and Donkey Sanctuary; *Recreations* season ticket holder Cheltenham Town FC, dog walking, swimming; *Style*— Adrian Bailey, Esq, MP; ✉ House of Commons, London SW1A 0AA (✆ 020 7219 6060)

BAILEY, Anthony Cowper; s of Cowper Goldsmith Bailey, and Phyllis Bailey; *b* 5 January 1933; *Educ* Price's Sch Fareham, Churcher's Coll Petersfield, Merton Coll Oxford (MA); *m* 1957, Margot, *née* Speight; 4 da; *Career* Nat Serv 2 Lt 3 Bn Gold Coast Regt W Africa 1951–52; staff writer The New Yorker 1956–92; author of poems, short stories, essays, reportage, memoirs, fiction and biographies; speaker and visiting lectr at various univs; visiting fell Yale Center for Br Art 2002; US Overseas Press Club Award for Best Magazine Reporting from Abroad 1973, Lowell Thomas Award for Best Travel Book 1994; chm Burney Street Garden Project Greenwich 1981–90; memb Bd of Govrs Greenwich Theatre 1985–89; vice-pres The Turner Soc 1999–; hon Citizen Oakwood Ohio 1982; fell commoner Magdalene Coll Cambridge 1992; *Books* author of 23 books incl: Rembrandt's House (1978, paperback edn 2014) Acts of Union (1980), America, Lost and Found (1980), Major André (1987), Standing in the Sun – A Life of JMW Turner (1997, shortlisted James Tait Black Meml Biography Prize), A View of Delft – Vermeer Then and Now (2001, shortlisted Whitbread Biography Prize), John Constable: A Kingdom of his Own (2006), Velázquez and the Surrender of Breda (2011); work in various anthologies and trans into Dutch, German, Italian, Spanish, Hungarian and Japanese; *Style*— Mr Anthony Bailey; ✉ c/o Donadio & Olson, 121 West 27 Street, New York, NY 10001-6207 USA (✆ 00 1 212 691 8077, fax 00 1 212 633 2837); c/o Abnerstein, 10 Roland Gardens, London SW7 3PH (✆ 020 7373 0456, fax 020 7370 6316)

BAILEY, Charles Cooper; JP (N Yorks 1994); s of Gordon Nuttall Bailey, TD, FRCS (d 1990), and Isabel Ray, *née* Zossenheim, changed by Deed Poll to Leslie 1913 (d 1988); *b* 22 November 1947; *Educ* Harrow, RAC Cirencester (Dip Rural Estate Mgmnt); *m* 1, 20 Sept 1975 (m dis 2001), Camilla Margaret, da of John Kenneth Henderson (d 1990); 1 s ((Richard) Max Cooper b 3 Sept 1979, k in car crash 23 Oct 1998), 1 da (Zara Marcina b 8 May 1982); m 2, 26 June 2004 (m dis 2011), Elisabeth Susan (Libs) Going, er da of James Christy Brownlow; *Career* asst Agricultural & Country Depts Savills 1972–77, ptnr John German Ralph Pay 1977–85 (land agents), dir and regnl and functional md Hamptons Holdings plc until 1991 (previously ptnr Hampton & Sons), sr ptnr Charles C Bailey, FRICS, MRAC (chartered surveyors and land agents) 1991–; chm Harrogate Civic Soc 1995–97, memb Ripon Diocesan Bd for Social Responsibility 1994–97, memb Goldsborough & Flaxby PC 1995–2001, currently memb Harrogate Stray Defense Ctee; pt/t chm and lay memb NHS Independent Reviews 1995–2004, memb Health Care Cmmn 2005–06; vice-pres Kirkby Malzeard Playing Fields Assoc; MRAC 1971, FRICS 1981 (ARICS 1974); *Recreations* shooting, fishing, pictures, groundsman; *Style*— Charles C Bailey, Esq, JP, FRICS, MRAC; ✉ Beckley Cottage, Kirkby Malzeard, Nr Ripon, North Yorkshire HG4 3RS (✆ 01765 635555, fax 01765 650087, e-mail ccb@charlesbailey.co.uk)

BAILEY, Christopher; MBE (2009); s of Douglas Bailey, and Eliana Bailey; *b* 11 May 1971, Halifax, W Yorks; *Educ* Univ of Westminster (BA), RCA (Bill Gibb scholarship, MA); *Career* womenswear designer Donna Karan 1994–96, sr designer of womenswear Gucci 1996–2001; Burberry: creative dir 2001–09, chief creative offr 2009–14, chief creative offr and ceo 2014–; co-fndr Burberry Fndn 2008; hon patronage Dublin Trinity Coll Philosophical Soc 2009; British Fashion Awards: Designer of the Year 2005 and 2009, Menswear Designer of the Year 2007, 2008 and 2013; International Award Cncl of Fashion Designers of America 2010; hon doctorate Univ of Westminster 2006, Hon DSc Univ of Huddersfield 2007, hon doctorate Sheffield Hallam Univ 2011, hon doctorate RCA 2013; Hon FRCA 2003; *Style*— Christopher Bailey, Esq, MBE

BAILEY, Christopher Charles; *b* 23 December 1979, London; *Educ* Westminster Catering Coll; *Career* formerly with: Brown's Hotel London, Chez Bruce London, Zaranda Madrid; head chef Black Rat Restaurant Winchester (Michelin star 2011–); *Recreations* eating and drinking; *Style*— Christopher Bailey, Esq; ✉ The Black Rat, 88 Chesil Street, Winchester, Hampshire SO23 0HX (website www.theblackrat.co.uk and www.chefchrisbailey.com, Twitter @chefcbailey)

BAILEY, David; CBE (2001); s of William Bailey, and Agnes, *née* Green; *b* 2 January 1938; *m* 1, 1960, Rosemary Bramble; m 2, 1967 (m dis), Catherine Deneuve, the film actress; m 3, 1975 (m dis 1985), Marie Helvin; m 4, 1986, Catherine Dyer; 2 s, 1 da; *Career* photographer; photographer for Vogue (British, American, Italian and French) 1959–, dir of commercials (over 500) 1966–, dir and prodr of TV documentaries 1968– (subjects include Beaton, Warhol, Visconti, Catherine Bailey (The Lady is a Tramp) and Models Close Up), also feature film The Intruder; memb Arts Cncl 1983–; FRPS, FSIAD, FRSA, FCSD; *Exhibitions* Nat Portrait Gallery 1971, V&A Museum (one man retrospective) 1983, Int Centre of Photography NY 1984, Photographs from the Sudan for Live Aid (ICA and tour) 1985, Bailey Now! (Royal Photographic Soc, Bath) 1989, Hamiltons Gallery London 1989 and 1992–, Fahey Klein Gallery LA 1990, Camerawork Berlin and Carla Sozzni Milan 1997, A Gallery (New Orleans), Birth of the Cool (touring exhbn, Barbican Art Gallery) 1999, Nat Museum of Photography Film and Television Bradford 1999–2000, Modern Museet Stockholm 2000; *Awards* for commercials incl: The Golden Lion (Cannes), The Cleo (USA), American TV Award, D&AD Gold (London), D&AD Presidents Award, EMMY Award (USA); *Books* Box of Pin-Ups (1964), Goodbye Baby and Amen (1969), Warhol (1974), Beady Minces (1974), Papua New Guinea (1975), Mixed Moments (1976), Trouble and Strife (1980), David Bailey's London NW1 (1982), Black and White Memories (1983), Nudes 1981–84 (1984), Imagine (1985), If We Shadows (1991), The Lady is a Tramp (1995), David Bailey's Rock and Roll Heroes (1997), Models Close Up (1998), Archive One (1999), Chasing Rainbows (2001), Bailey's Democracy (2005); *Recreations* photography, aviculture, travel, painting; *Style*— David Bailey, Esq, CBE

BAILEY, His Hon Judge Edward Henry; s of Geoffrey Henry Bailey (d 1985), of London, and Ninette, *née* Adereth (d 1991); *b* 24 May 1949; *Educ* King's Sch Canterbury, Gonville & Caius Coll Cambridge (MA, LLB); *m* 30 July 1983, Claire Dorothy Ann, *née* From; 2 da (Cecilia Jane b 21 Oct 1985, Francesca Ann b 11 July 1993); *Career* called to the Bar Middle Temple 1970; circuit judge (SE Circuit) 2000–; lectr Inns of Court Sch of Law 1970–72; *Style*— His Hon Judge Bailey

BAILEY, George Henry Selborne; s of Dr Alison George Selborne Bailey (d 1997), of High Wycombe, Bucks, and Christine, *née* Delfosse (d 1982); *b* 13 August 1953; *Educ* Radley, Downing Coll Cambridge (BA); *m* 8 Nov 1986, Allison Gail; 2 s (Henry George Selborne b 15 Jan 1989, Matthew John Selborne b 15 March 1991); *Career* dir Sotheby's 1979–; ARICS 1978; *Clubs* Leander; *Style*— George Bailey, Esq; ✉ Sotheby's, 34–35 New Bond Street, London W1A 2AA (✆ 020 7293 5000)

BAILEY, Glenda Adrianne; OBE; da of John Ernest Bailey, and Constance, *née* Groome; *b* 16 November 1958; *Educ* Noel Baker Sch Derby, Kingston Univ (BA); *Career* fashion forecasting Design Direction 1983–84, prodr dummy magazine for IPC 1985; ed: Honey magazine 1986, Folio magazine 1987, marie claire magazine (UK) 1988–96, marie claire magazine (US) 1996–2001; ed-in-chief Harper's Bazaar 2001–; Hon MA 1995, Hon Dr Univ of Derby 2001; *Awards* Women's Magazine Ed of the Year BSME 1989, Best Magazine award PPA 1991, Consumer Magazine of the Year Media Week Press Awards and PPA 1991, Magazine of the Year Media Week Awards 1992, Editor's Editor of the Year and Women's Magazine Editor of the Year BSME 1992, Consumer Magazine of the Year PPA 1993, Consumer Magazine of the Year IPC Annual Editorial Awards 1993, Best International Magazine and Best International Consumer Magazine IDP International Press Awards 1994, Editor of the Year Adweek 2001, ASME Award for Best Cover 2006, 2007, 2008 and 2009, Lucie Award for Art Direction 2006, 2007, 2008 and 2009, Three Folio Ozzie Awards 2009; *Style*— Miss Glenda Bailey, OBE; ✉ c/o Harper's Bazaar, 300 West 57th Street, New York, 10019, USA (✆ 00 1 212 903 5000, fax 00 1 212 262 7101)

BAILEY, Julie Dawn; CBE (2014); *Career* campaigner; fndr Cure the NHS; *Style*— Julie Bailey, CBE; ✉ e-mail curethenhs@hotmail.co.uk, website www.curethenhs.co.uk, Twitter @CureTheNHS

BAILEY, Kim Charles; s of Kenneth Bailey (d 1996), and Bridgett Ann, *née* Courage (d 1987); *b* 25 May 1953; *Educ* Radley; *Family* 1 s (Harry), 1 da (Pandora); m, 3 March 2001, Clare Wills; 1 s (Archie); *Career* racehorse trainer 1979–; major races won: Seagram Grand National (Mr Frisk), Whitbread Gold Cup (twice, Mr Frisk and Docklands Express), SGB Chase (Man O Magic), Bollinger Chase (twice, Man O Magic and Kings Fountain), Golden Spurs Chase (Man O Magic), H & T Walker Chase (twice, Man O Magic and Kings Fountain), Scottish Champion Hurdle (Positive), BIC Razor Hurdle (Carnival Air), Anthony Mildway & Peter Cazalet Meml Handicap Chase (twice, Mr Frisk and Shifting Gold), Crown Paints Hurdle (Positive), Cheltenham Tote Gold Cup (Master Oats), Cheltenham Champion Hurdle (Alderbrook), Scottish Champion Hurdle (Alderbrook);

Recreations shooting, cricket, tennis, fishing; *Style*— Kim Bailey, Esq; ✉ website www.kimbaileyracing.com

BAILEY, (Robert) Malcolm; s of Brian Bailey, of Holmfirth, W Yorks, and Annie, *née* Hinchliffe; *b* 19 December 1950; *Educ* Holme Valley GS, Imperial Coll London (BSc); *m* 26 Aug 1972, Anne Elizabeth, da of late Thomas Edward Dawson; 2 da (Hannah Victoria, Ruth Mary), 1 s (Thomas Matthew); *Career* PricewaterhouseCoopers (formerly Price Waterhouse before merger): joined 1972, qualified CA 1975, ptnr 1984–, nat dir of human resources Nat Exec 1993–95, vice-chm World Petroleum Industry Gp 1995–97, sr client ptnr 1997–, global compliance offr 2006–; ARCS, FCA 1980; *Style*— Malcolm Bailey, Esq; ✉ PricewaterhouseCoopers, 1 Embankment Place, London WC2N 6RH (☎ 020 7583 5000, fax 020 7804 2655)

BAILEY, Prof Mark; *b* 21 November 1960, Castleford, W Yorks; *Educ* Ipswich Sch, Univ of Durham, Univ of Cambridge (PhD); *Career* fell Gonville and Caius Coll Cambridge 1986–96, fell CCC Cambridge 1996–99, headmaster Leeds GS 1999–2005, chief exec The Grammar Sch at Leeds 2005–10, prof of late medieval history UEA, high master St Paul's Sch 2011–; visiting fell All Souls Coll Oxford 2010, Ford lectr in Br history elect Univ of Oxford 2019; pres Univ of Cambridge RUFC, memb Professional Game Bd RFU; FRHistS 1990; *Books* Modelling the Middle Ages (2001), The English Manor 1200–1500 (2002), Decline of Serfdom in England (2014); *Clubs* Hawks, East India (hon memb); *Style*— Prof Mark Bailey; ✉ St Paul's School, Lonsdale Road, London SW13 9JT

BAILEY, (Christian) Martin; s of Dr Leslie Bailey, of Harpenden, Herts, and Marie Elisabeth, *née* Phillips; *b* 4 August 1949, London; *Educ* Aldwickbury Sch Harpenden, St Albans Sch, Royal Free Hosp Sch of Med (BSc, MB BS); *m* 24 April 1971, Dr Jane Nicola Rotha Bailey, da of John Stewart Barnfield; 1 s (Simon John Martin b 7 Aug 1975), 1 da (Laura Jane Susanna b 7 June 1978); *Career* past appts: Royal Free Hosp London (house surgn, house physician, SHO), SHO in otolaryngology Royal Nat Throat Nose & Ear Hosp London, SHO in gen surgery Royal Northern Hosp London, registrar then sr registrar in otolaryngology Royal Nat Throat Nose & Ear Hosp, sr registrar in otolaryngology Sussex Throat & Ear Hosp Brighton; TWJ Fndn clinical and research fell in otology and neuro-otology Univ of Michigan; conslt otolaryngologist: Great Ormond Street Hospital for Children London 1982–2009, Royal Nat Throat Nose & Ear Hosp London 1982–97; hon conslt otolaryngologist: St Luke's Hosp for the Clergy London 1984–2009, King Edward VII's Hosp Sister Agnes 1999–2001, St Luke's Healthcare for the Clergy 2009–, Great Ormond Street Hosp for Children London 2009–; hon sr lectr: Inst of Laryngology & Otology London 1982–2006, Inst of Child Health 1985–2010; exec chm TWJ Fndn 2008–; Gabriel F Tucker Award American Laryngological Assoc 2004, W J Harrison Prize Royal Soc of Med 2008, Bruce Benjamin Medal Australian & NZ Soc of Paediatric Otorhinolaryngology 2013; memb: BMA 1973, RSM 1976 (pres Section of Laryngology and Rhinology 2005–06, memb Soc Cncl and tstee 2011–15, hon sec 2014–18), ENT-UK 1982, European Soc of Pediatric Otorhinolaryngology 1998 (memb Cncl 2008–, memb Bd 2010–, sec-gen 2016–), Br Assoc for Paediatric Otorhinolaryngology 1990 (pres 2002–04); FRCS 1978, FRCSEd 2009; *Publications* over 135 peer-reviewed papers and textbook chapters on otolaryngology; *Recreations* fell walking, computers, cars; *Style*— Martin Bailey, Esq; ✉ 7 Heathgate, Hampstead Garden Suburb, London NW11 7AR (☎ 020 8455 8628, fax 020 8381 4292); 9 Harley Street, London W1G 9QY (☎ 020 7580 2426, fax 020 7436 1645, e-mail bailey@ent-london.co.uk, website www.ent-london.co.uk)

BAILEY, Simon; *Educ* Wymondham Coll, Norwich City Coll, Univ of Cambridge; *Career* Norfolk Constabulary: Dep Chief Constable 2010–13, Chief Constable 2013–; *Style*— Chief Constable Simon Bailey; ✉ Norfolk Constabulary, Operations and Communications Centre, Jubilee House, Falconers Chase, Wymondham, Norfolk NR18 0WW

BAILEY, Prof Dame Susan Mary (Sue); DBE (2013, OBE 2002); da of Frank Bailey, and Edith Mary Bailey; *b* 29 August 1950, Manchester; *Educ* Hulme GS for Girls, Watford GS for Girls, Univ of Manchester (MB ChB); *Children* 2 da; *Career* conslt child and adolescent forensic psychiatrist Gtr Manchester West Mental Health NHS Fndn Tst 1983, prof of child mental health UCLAN 2004; RCPsych: chair Child and Adolescent Faculty 2001–05, registrar 2005–10, pres 2012–14; section chair European Assoc of Child and Adolescent Psychiatry 2005–14, chair Children and Young People's Mental Health Coalition 2014, sr nat clinical lead for mental health Health Educn England; tstee Centre for Mental Health, tstee MAC-UK; chair Acad of Royal Med Colls 2015– (vice-chair 2012–14); FRCPsych 1996 (MRCPsych 1976), Hon FCPsych (SA), FRCPE; *Recreations* with children and grandchildren, walking, visual arts, music; *Style*— Prof Dame Sue Bailey, DBE; ✉ 10 Dallington Street, London EC1V 0DB

BAILEY, Sylvia (Sly); da of Thomas Lewis Grice, and Sylvia, *née* Bantick; *b* 24 January 1962; *Educ* St Saviour's and St Olave's GS for Girls; *m* 5 June 1998, Peter Bailey; *Career* IPC Magazines: joined 1989, advtg sales dir 1990–97, bd dir 1994–2002, md IPC tx 1997–99, chief exec IPC Media 1999–2002; chief exec Trinity Mirror 2003–12; non-exec dir: Press Assoc 2003–, EMI 2004–07, Ladbrokes plc 2009–; pres Newstraid Benevolent Soc 2003–, memb Women in Advtg and Communications London (WACL), govr English Nat Ballet Sch 2009–; Marcus Morris Award PPA 2002; *Recreations* family; *Style*— Mrs Sly Bailey

BAILEY, Terence Michael; s of Thomas Sturman Bailey, and Margaret Hilda, *née* Wright; *b* 22 October 1946, Northampton; *Educ* Kettering GS, Lanchester Poly Coventry (BA); *m* 1, 21 Oct 1972 (m dis), Penelope Ann, da of Geoffrey Lever Butler; 1 s (Tobin b 1976); m 2, 20 July 1985, Susan Jane, da of Frederick Peter Runacres; 3 s (Tim b 1986, Christopher b 1987, David b 1990); *Career* slr to Corby Devpt Corp 1972–73, ptnr Toller Hales & Collcutt (Northants) 1973–98 (conslt 1998–2000), sole practitioner 2001–08, sr ptnr Terence Bailey Slrs 2002–; chm Corby Industrial Gp (for promotion of industry in Corby area) 1991–94, Office Supervision of Solicitors Law Soc 1999–2001; tstee Lakelands Hospice Corby 2002–06; *Recreations* skiing, motor-cycling, gardening, keep-fit, reading; *Clubs* Northants Law Soc, Kettering Golf; *Style*— Terence M Bailey, Esq; ✉ Yew Tree Farm House, Little Oakley, Corby, Northamptonshire NN18 8HA (☎ 01536 742233)

BAILEY, Timothy Guy; s of William John Joseph Bailey, and Maureen Ann, *née* Neenan; *b* 9 September 1964; *Educ* English Martyrs Sch Hartlepool, Univ of Newcastle upon Tyne (BA, BArch); *m* 16 Jan 1999, Ruth Martina, da of Frank and Pauline Connorton; 1 s (Zachariah Stanley b 5 June 2001), 1 da (Thea Amy b 23 April 2005); *Career* Browne Smith Baker: joined 1990, assoc 1993–97, ptnr 1997–2000; princ xsite architecture 2000–08, ptnr Xsite Architecture LLP 2008–; chair Northern Architecture 1997–2006; dir Northern Stage (Theatrical Prodns) Ltd 1998– (chm 2006–12), dir Flo Culture Ltd 2012–; tstee Striding Edge Community Ltd 2009–11; RIBA: memb Cncl 1988–90, 1997–99 and 2012–, memb 1992–, chm Northumbria Branch 1994–96, chm Northern Region 1997–99; FRSA; *Publications* Design: A Practical Guide to RIBA Plan of Work 2013 Stages 2 and 3 (2015); *Recreations* reading, cooking; *Style*— Timothy Bailey, Esq; ✉ xsite architecture LLP, Foundry Lane Studios, Foundry Lane, Newcastle upon Tyne NE6 1LH (☎ 0191 287 2161, fax 0191 287 2166, website www.xsitearchitecture.co.uk)

BAILHACHE, Sir Philip Martin; kt (1996); s of Sqdn Ldr Lester Vivian Bailhache, RAF (d 2005), and Nanette Ross, *née* Ferguson (d 1997); *b* 28 February 1946; *Educ* Charterhouse, Pembroke Coll Oxford (MA); *m* 1, 1967 (m dis 1982); 2 s (Robert b 1968, John b 1974), 2 da (Rebecca b 1969, Catherine b 1972); m 2, 1984, Linda, da of late Martin Geoffrey Le Vavasseur dit Durell; 1 da (Alice b 1988), 1 s (Edward b 1990); *Career* called to the Bar Middle Temple 1968 (bencher 2003), called to the Jersey Bar 1969; advocate Jersey 1969–74 (dep for Grouville 1972–74), slr-gen Jersey 1975–86, attorney-gen Jersey 1986–93, QC 1989, bailiff of Jersey 1995–2009 (dep bailiff 1994–95), pres Jersey Court of Appeal 1995–2009, cmmr Royal Court 2009–11, asst chief min of Jersey 2011–13, min of external relations Jersey 2013–; chm Governing Body Inst of Law 2008–; ed: Jersey Law Review 1997–2006, Jersey and Guernsey Law Review 2007–; chm Jersey Arts Cncl 1987–89; hon fell Pembroke Coll Oxford 1995; *Recreations* music, the arts, gardening, wine; *Clubs* Reform, United (Jersey); *Style*— Sir Philip Bailhache; ✉ L'Anquetinerie, Grouville, Jersey (☎ 01534 852533); Ministry of External Relations, Cyril le Marquand House, St Helier, Jersey (☎ 01534 441102, fax 01534 441137)

BAILIE, Roy E; OBE; *Educ* Harvard Business Sch; *Career* currently chm W&G Baird Holdings Ltd (dir 1982–); dir: W&G Baird Ltd 1977–, Graphic Plates Ltd 1977–, MSO Clelland Ltd 1984–2014, Blackstaff Press Ltd 1995–, CDS Ltd 2000–; chm CBI (NI) 1992–94; non-exec dir: NI Cncl for HE 1985–90, Industrial Devpt Bd for NI 1990–95, Tacade 1990–99 (memb Advsy Cncl on Alcohol & Drug Educn), NI Tourist Bd 1996–2002 (chm), Ulster TV 1997–2013, Bank of England 1998–2003; chm: Nat Tst NI 2010–, NI Opera Co 2010–; memb Ct: Bank of England 1998–2004, Bank of Ireland 1999–2003; memb Exec Bd BPIF (vice-chm 1997–99, pres 1999–2001); *Recreations* sailing, golf, walking; *Style*— Roy Bailie, OBE; ✉ W&G Baird Holdings Ltd, Greystone Road, Antrim BT41 2RS (☎ 028 9446 6107, fax 028 9446 6266, e-mail roy.bailie@thebairdgroup.co.uk)

BAILIN, Alex; QC (2010); s of Prof David Bailin, and Dr Anjali Bailin; *b* 23 January 1969; *Educ* Emmanuel Coll Cambridge (MA); *m* Emma Saunders; 1 da, 1 s; *Career* called to the Bar Lincoln's Inn 1995; former derivatives trader, currently barr Matrix Chambers, recorder Crown Court, dep judge of the High Court; *Publications* contrib: Fraud: Criminal Law & Procedure, Blackstone's Criminal Practice, Human Rights and Criminal Justice; numerous articles in legal jls and the nat press; *Recreations* scuba diving, theatre, West African music, tennis, piano (classical); *Style*— Alex Bailin, QC; ✉ Matrix Chambers, Griffin Building, Gray's Inn, London WC1R 5LN (☎ 020 7404 3447, fax 020 7404 3448, e-mail alexbailin@matrixlaw.co.uk, website www.matrixlaw.co.uk)

BAILLIE, Andrew Bruce; QC (2001); s of Edward Oswald Baillie (d 1974), and (Molly Eva Lavers) Renée, *née* Andrews (d 1985); *b* 17 May 1948; *Educ* KCS Wimbledon, Université De Besancon, Univ of Kent (BA); *m* 11 Sept 1976, Mary Lou Meech (d 1988), da of Stanley Harold Palmer (d 1988), of Portsmouth, Hants; 2 da (Emma b 1979, Victoria b 1981), 1 s (Oliver b 1984); *Career* called to the Bar Inner Temple 1970, recorder of the Crown Court 1989–; memb Criminal Bar Assoc; *Recreations* numerous, from rugby football to flower arranging; *Style*— Andrew Baillie, Esq, QC; ✉ 9 Gough Square, London EC4 (☎ 020 7832 0500, e-mail abaillie@goughsquare.co.uk)

BAILLIE, Jackie; MSP; *b* 15 January 1964; *Career* Strathkelvin DC 1990–96, community devpt mangr East Dunbartonshire Cncl 1996–99, chair Scottish Labour Pty 1997–98; MSP (Lab) Dumbarton 1999–; min for social justice until 2001; memb Scottish Lab Pty Exec Ctee 1990–99; memb Bd of Volunteer Devpt Scotland; *Style*— Ms Jackie Baillie, MSP; ✉ Constituency Office, 11 Castle Street, Dumbarton G82 1QS (☎ 01389 734214, fax 01389 761498, e-mail jackie.baillie.msp@scottish.parliament.uk)

BAILLIE, Prof John; s of Arthur Baillie (d 1979), of Glasgow, and Agnes Baillie (d 1981); *Educ* Whitehill Sr Secdy Sch; *m* 1972, Annette; 1 da (Nicola), 1 s (Kenneth); *Career* CA 1967 (distinction and Gold Medal); ptnr: KPMG 1978–93, Scott-Moncrieff 1993–2001; currently runs own practice; author of various tech and professional papers to professional jls; ICAS: memb various ctees 1978–, convenor Research Ctee 1995–99; Johnstone Smith chair of accountancy Univ of Glasgow 1983–88, visiting prof of accountancy: Heriot-Watt Univ 1988–95, Univ of Glasgow 1998–2013, Univ of Edinburgh 2013–; memb Reporting Panel Competition Cmmn 2002–11, chair Accounts Cmmn 2008–13 (memb 2003–13), chair Audit Scotland 2008–10 (memb Bd 2004–13); Hon MA Univ of Glasgow 1983; *Books* Systems of Profit Measurement (1985), Consolidated Accounts and The Seventh Directive (1985); *Recreations* keeping fit, reading, golf, music, hill walking; *Clubs* Kilmacolm Golf; *Style*— Prof John Baillie; ✉ The Glen, Glencairn Road, Kilmacolm, Renfrewshire PA13 4PJ

BAILLIE, Timothy Mark (Tim); MBE (2013); s of Ken Baillie, and Christine, *née* Jones; *b* 11 May 1979, Aberdeen; *Educ* Westhill Acad, Univ of Nottingham (BEng); *m* 4 May 2013, Sarah Boudens; *Career* slalom canoeist; achievements incl: Bronze medal (team) World Championships 2009, Silver (team) and Bronze medals (individual) European Championships 2009, Bronze medal (team) European Championships 2010, Bronze medal (team) World Championships 2011, Gold medal (team) European Championships 2012, Gold medal (individual) Olympic Games 2012; *Style*— Mr Tim Baillie, MBE; ✉ c/o GB Canoeing, National Water Sports Centre, Adbolton Lane, Holme Pierrepont, Nottingham NG12 2LU (e-mail timbaillieuk@gmail.com, website www.bailliestottc2.co.uk, Twitter @timbaillie)

BAILLIEU, 3 Baron (UK 1953); James William Latham Baillieu; er s of 2 Baron Baillieu (d 1973), and his 1 w, Anne Bayliss, da of Leslie William Page; *b* 16 November 1950; *Educ* Radley, Monash Univ Melbourne (BEc); *m* 1, 1974 (m dis 1985), Cornelia, da of late William Ladd; 1 s (Hon Robert Latham b 2 Feb 1979); m 2, 1986 (m dis 1995), Clare, da of Peter Stephenson; *Heir* s, Hon Robert Baillieu; *Career* 2 Lt Coldstream Gds 1970–73; Banque Nationale de Paris (Melbourne) 1978–80, asst dir Rothschild Australia Ltd 1980–88, dir Manufacturers Hanover Australia Ltd 1988–90, dir Standard Chartered Asia Ltd 1990–92, asst dir Credit Lyonnais Asia Ltd 1992–94, asst dir Nomura Int (Hong Kong) Ltd 1995, gen dir Regent European Securities 1995–96, dir CentreInvest Gp Moscow 1996–99, dir Anthony Baillieu and Assocs (Hong Kong) Ltd 1992–, md Bank NIKoil 2000–; *Clubs* Boodle's, Australian (Melbourne), Hong Kong (Hong Kong); *Style*— The Rt Hon the Lord Baillieu

BAIN, Chris; s of Derek Bain, of Borden, Kent, and Mary, *née* Hill (d 1995); *b* 27 November 1953, London; *Educ* Univ of Leicester (BA), Middlesex Univ (MBA), Open Univ (MSC); *m* Philomena; *Career* head of campaigns Oxfam 1992–96, head of progs VSO 1996–2003, chief exec CAFOD 2003–; dir Disasters Emergency Ctee 2003–, chair British Overseas Aid Gp 2005–08 and 2013–; *Recreations* long distance pilgrimages, ale and whisky appreciation; *Style*— Chris Bain, Esq; ✉ CAFOD, Romero Close, 55 Westminster Bridge Road, London SE1 7JB (☎ 020 7326 5500, e-mail cdb@cafod.org.uk)

BAIN, Prof Sir George Sayers; kt (2001); s of George Alexander Bain (d 2006), of Winnipeg, Canada, and Margaret Ioleen, *née* Bamford (d 1988); *b* 24 February 1939; *Educ* Winnipeg State Sch System, Univ of Manitoba (BA, MA), Univ of Oxford (DPhil); *m* 1, 24 Aug 1962 (m dis 1987), Carol Lynne Ogden, da of Herbert Fyffe White (d 1986); 1 da (Katherine Anne b 1967), 1 s (David Thomas b 1969); m 2, 28 Dec 1988, (Frances) Gwynneth Rigby, *née* Vickers; *Career* Royal Canadian Naval Reserve, Midshipman 1957–60, Sub Lt 1960, Lt 1963, ret 1963; lectr in economics Univ of Manitoba 1962–63, res fell in industrial rels Nuffield Coll Oxford 1966–69, Frank Thomas prof of industrial rels UMIST 1969–70; Univ of Warwick: dir Industrial Rels Res Unit of SSRC 1974–81 (dep dir 1970–74), titular prof 1974–79, Pressed Steel Fisher prof of industrial rels 1979–89, chm Sch of Industrial and Business Studies 1983–89; princ London Business Sch 1989–97, pres and vice-chllr Queen's Univ Belfast 1998–2004 (currently prof emeritus); distinguished visiting prof Univ of Manitoba 1985, Cecil H and Ida Green visiting prof Univ of British Columbia 1987; memb res staff Royal Cmmn on Trade Unions and Employers' Assoc (The Donovan Cmmn) 1966–67, conslt to Nat Bd for Prices and Incomes 1967–69; chm: Cncl Univ Mgmnt Schs 1987–90 (exec memb 1984–90), Food Sector Working Gp NEDO 1991–92, Cmmn on Public Policy and Br Business Inst Public Policy Research 1995–97, Low Pay Cmmn 1997–2002 and 2008–09, NI Meml Fund 1998–2002, Conf of Univ Rectors in Ireland 2000–01, Work and Parents Task Force DTI 2001,

Pensions Policy Inst 2002–04, Ind Review of Fire Service ODPM 2002, ACU 2002–03, NI Legal Servs Review Gp 2005–06, NI Ind Strategic Review of Educn 2006, NI Review of Policy on the Location of Public Sector Jobs 2007–08, Cmmn on the Future of the Nat Minimum Wage and the Low Pay Cmmn Resolution Fndn 2013–14; memb: Exec Br Univs Industrial Rels Assoc 1971–80 (sec 1971–74), Mechanical Engrg Econ Devpt Ctee NEDO 1974–76 (conslt to NEDO 1982–85), Ctee of Inquiry on Industrial Democracy (Bullock Ctee) 1975–76, Cncl ESRC 1986–91, Cncl Nat Forum for Mgmnt Educn and Devpt 1987–90, Cncl Fndn for Mgmnt Educn 1991–97, American Assembly of Collegiate Schs of Business 1992–94, Int Cncl American Mgmnt Assoc 1993–96, Bd Fndn for Canadian Studies in the UK 1993–2001 and 2004–06, Sr Salaries Review Body 1993–96, Bd of Co-operation Ireland 1994–97, Cncl BESO 1995–97, Bd of Dirs Grad Mgmnt Admission Cncl 1996–97, GB Bd of Co-operation Ireland 1998–2004, Educn Honours Ctee 2005–10, McClay Fndn 2008–; dir: Blackwell Publishers Ltd 1990–97, The Economist Group 1992–2001, Canada Life Gp (UK) Ltd 1994–2014, Canada Life Assurance Company 1996–2003, Electra Private Equity plc 1998–2008, Bombardier Aerospace Short Brothers plc 1998–2007, NI Science Park Fndn 1999–2004, Canada Life Capital Corp 2003–14, Iain More Assocs 2004–07, Entertainment One 2007–10, Great West Lifeco Inc 2009–14; advsr on Royal Mail to Sec of State for Trade and Industry 2005–06; tstee: European Fndn for Mgmnt Devpt 1990–96 (memb Exec Ctee 1991–96, exec vice-pres 1991–95), Navan at Armagh 1999–2003, Scotch-Irish Tst 1999–2007, Cncl for Advancement and Support of Educn (CASE) 2004–08, CASE Europe 2004–07, (CASE chief-exec leadership award 2003); memb Ulster Orch Soc 2011– (chm 2011–); vice-chm Bd and chm Devpt Tst Lyric Theatre Belfast 2006–11, chm Keeper's Cncl Armagh Public Library 2014–16; patron Somme Assoc 2004–12; pres Involvement and Participation Assoc 2002–06; arbitrator/mediator for ACAS 1970–92; fell London Business Sch 1999, hon fell Nuffield Coll Oxford 2002; Hon DBA De Montfort Univ 1994; Hon LLD: NUI 1998, Univ of Guelph Canada 1999, UC of Cape Breton 1999, Univ of Manitoba 2003, Univ of Warwick 2003, Queen's Univ Canada 2004, Queen's Univ Belfast 2005; Hon DLitt: Univ of Ulster 2002, Univ of New Brunswick 2003; Hon DSc Cranfield Univ 2005; Canadian High Cmmr's Award (2003); BAM Lifetime Achievement Award 2014; FRSA 1987, AcSS 2000, CCMI (CIMgt 1991), FBAM 1994, companion Assoc of Business Schs 2007; *Books* Trade Union Growth and Recognition (1967), The Growth of White-Collar Unionism (1970), The Reform of Collective Bargaining at Plant and Company Levels (1971), Social Stratification and Trade Unionism (1973), Union Growth and the Business Cycle (1976), A Bibliography of British Industrial Relations (1979 and 1985), Profiles of Union Growth (1980), Industrial Relations in Britain (ed 1983); *Recreations* genealogy, family history, Western riding, piano playing, ice skating; *Clubs* Ulster Reform (Belfast); *Style—* Prof Sir George Bain; ✉ c/o The Queen's University of Belfast, University Road, Belfast BT7 1NN

BAIN, Dr Peter George; s of George Bain, and Hélène Marie Josephine; *b* 1957; *Educ* Worth Sch, The Queen's Coll Oxford (MA), Bart's Med Coll (MB BS, Christopher Frears Prize in Neurology), Univ of London (MD); *m* Jane Francesca; 1 da, 2 s; *Career* house physician Professorial Med Unit Bart's 1982–83, house surgn Royal Berks Hosp 1983, SHO (med) rotation Guy's 1983–84, SHO (A&E) St Mary's and St Charles Hosps 1985, SHO (neurology) SE Thames Regnl Neurological and Neurosurgical Centre Brook Hosp 1985–86 and 1987, med registrar Southmead Hosp Bristol 1986–87, neurology registrar Guy's 1987–89, visiting academic in neuropathology Dept of Neuropathology Inst of Psychiatry London 1989, tutor and demonstrator in physiology Dept of Physiology Univ of Bristol 1989–90, res registrar in neurology MRC Human Movement and Balance Unit Inst of Neurology London 1990–92, hon clinical asst in neurology Nat Hosp for Neurology and Neurosurgery London 1990–92, neurology registrar Radcliffe Infirmary Oxford 1992–94, neurology lectr and hon sr registrar Academic Unit of Neurosciences Charing Cross and Westminster Med Sch 1994–95, locum conslt neurologist Central Middx Hosp London 1995, conslt and sr lectr in neurology Imperial Coll Sch of Med London and W Middx Univ Hosp Tst 1995–99; Imperial Coll Sch of Med London: sr lectr in neurology 1999–2002, reader in neurology 2002–; GMC specialist register (neurology) 1996; clinical examiner Univ of London: MB BS med finals, MD thesis; Int Tremor Fndn: memb Advsy Panel ITF Tremor Investigation Gp (TRIG), fndr memb and hon sec Br Tremor Res Gp, memb Movement Disorder Soc Task Force on Tremor and Int Tremor Rating Scale Devpt Gp 2011–, memb European Fedn of Neurological Societies Guidelines on Essential Tremor Diagnosis and Mgmnt Gp 2012–; chm Tremor Section Map of Medicine RCP 2008; Assoc of Br Neurologists' advsr to NICE on deep brain stimulation 2006–; tstee Nat Tremor Fndn; memb: Movement Disorder Soc, European Neurological Soc, Assoc of Br Neurologists, European Coll of Sports Science; memb Int Congress Ctees Kiel 1997 and 2001; Int Congress lectr: Keil Germany 1997 and 2000, Barcelona 2000, Copenhagen 2000, London 2001, Kyoto 2006, Amsterdam 2007, Buenos Aires 2010, Stockholm 2012; memb Editorial Bd: Current Medical Literature: Neurology 1996–, Continuous Professional Development: Neurology 1998–2002, Movement Disorders Jl 1999–2004; Duke Elder Nat Prize for Ophthalmology Inst of Ophthalmology London 1982; memb RSM, FRCP 1998 (MRCP 1985); *Publications* Assessing Tremor Severity: a clinical handbook (jtly, 1993), Current Issues in Essential Tremor (jt monograph, 1999), Essential Tremor: The Facts (jtly, 2006), Deep Brain Stimulation (jtly, 2009); author of approx 300 editorials, reviews, papers for jls, letters, chapters, newsletters and conference work; *Recreations* surfing, rowing and sculling, karate (2nd dan), ju-jitsu (1st kyu), chess, zen koans, rock climbing, coaching football (UEFA B) and futsal (Nat U16s Champions 2013); *Clubs* London Rowing, Anglo-Japanese Karate Club Dojo, Worth Old Boys' Golf, Barnes Eagles FC, Surrey Football Coaches Assoc, FA Coaches; *Style—* Dr Peter Bain; ✉ Department of Neuroscience, Imperial College, Charing Cross Campus, Fulham Palace Road, London W6 8RF (☎ 020 3311 1182)

BAIN, William Thomas; s of William Bain, of Glasgow, and Catherine, *née* McCambridge; *b* 1972, Glasgow; *Educ* St. Roch's Secdy Sch Glasgow, Univ of Strathclyde (LLB, DipLP, LLM); *Career* sessional lectr and tutor Univ of Strathclyde 1998–2004, sr lectr in public law London South Bank Univ 2004–09; MP (Lab) Glasgow NE 2009–15; PPS to Rt Hon Sadiq Khan, MP *qv* (as Min of State Dept for Transport) 2010, shadow transport min 2010, shadow food, fisheries and agriculture min 2010–11, shadow min Scotland Office 2011–13, memb Business Innovation and Skills Select Ctee 2013–15; chair Sudan/ S Sudan All Pty Gp 2012–15; policy conslt and head Fin Servs and Fintech Policy Inline Policy 2016–; memb Fabian Soc, memb Amnesty Int; FRS 2011; *Publications* Where Next for Labour (contrib, 2011); *Recreations* tennis, reading, music, films; *Style—* William Bain, Esq; ✉ Twitter @william_bain

BAINBRIDGE, Guy Lawrence Tarn; s of David Tarn Bainbridge (d 1966), and Margaret, *née* Frost (d 2012); *b* 13 September 1960, Darlington, Co Durham; *Educ* Oundle, St Johns Coll Cambridge (MA); *m* 21 Sept 1991, Katherine, *née* Godber; 2 s (Oliver b 24 Dec 1993, Charlie 22 Oct 1998), 1 da (Emily b 7 Nov 1995); *Career* KPMG (formerly Peat Marwick Mitchell & Co) 1982– (memb UK Bd 2005–12); ACA 1985; *Recreations* tennis, golf, skiing; *Style—* Guy Bainbridge, Esq; ✉ KPMG, 15 Canada Square, London E14 (☎ 020 7311 1000, e-mail guy.bainbridge@kpmg.co.uk)

BAINBRIDGE, Richard Henry; s of Jill Bainbridge, *née* Bush; *b* 30 April 1982, Norwich; *Educ* Norwich City Coll Hotel Sch; *Career* station supervisor Norfolk Mead Hotel 1999, chef de partie Morston Hall Hotel Norfolk 1999–2001 and 2002, chef de partie/rounds chef Red Lion Inn Stockbridge MA USA 2001–02, jr sous chef Waterside Inn Bray 2003–06, sous chef Thronton's Dublin 2007–08, head chef Morston Hall Norfolk 2008–15 (Michelin Star 2008), chef-owner Benedicts 2015–; competitor Great British Menu (BBC2) 2010, 2011, 2013, 2015 (winner); *Style—* Richard Bainbridge, Esq; ✉ Benedicts, 9 St Benedicts Street Norwich, Norfolk, NR2 4PE (☎ 01603 926080, e-mail info@restaurantbenedicts.com)

BAINBRIDGE, Prof Simon; s of John Bainbridge (d 1978), and Nan, *née* Knowles (d 2010); *b* 30 August 1952, London; *Educ* RCM; *m* 21 Oct 1997, Lynda Richardson; 1 da (Rebecca b 17 Feb 1981); *Career* studied under John Lambert and Gunther Schuller (Tanglewood 1973 and 1974); Forman fell in composition Univ of Edinburgh 1976–78, US/UK Bicentennial Fellowship 1978–79, sometime Nat Theatre, composer in res Southern Arts 1983–85, head of composition Royal Acad of Music 1999–2007 (sr prof of composition 2007–), prof Univ of London 2001–; FRCM 1997, Hon RAM 2002; *Compositions* incl: Spirogyra (Aldeburgh Festival, 1971), Viola Concerto (cmmnd by Walter Trampler, 1978), Fantasia for Double Orch (1983–84), Double Concerto (cmmnd by Cheltenham Festival for Nicholas Daniel and Joy Farrell, 1990), Toccata (for orch, 1992), Ad Ora Incerta – Four Orchestral Songs from Primo Levi (1993), Clarinet Quintet (for Joy Farrall and Kreutzer String Quartet, 1993), For Miles (solo trumpet, 1994), Landscape and Memory (horn concerto for Michael Thompson and London Sinfonietta, 1995), Four Primo Levi Settings (cmmnd by Cheltenham Festival for Nash Ensemble and Susan Bickley, 1996), Éicha (Oxford Contemporary Music Festival, 1997), Scherzi (2000), Diptych (cmmnd by BBC Syphony Orch, 2007), Music Space Reflection (cmmnd by London Sinfonietta, Imperial War Museum North, Royal Ontario Museum, 2007), Concerti Grossi (cmmnd by Northern Sinfonietta, 2010); *Recordings* Fantasia for Double Orch, Viola Concerto, Concertante in Moto Perpetuo, Four Primo Levi Settings, Ad Ora Incerta; *Awards* Gemini Prize 1988, Univ of Louisville Grawemeyer Award for Music Composition (for Ad Ora Incerta) 1997; *Recreations* cinema, cricket, theatre, walking; *Style—* Prof Simon Bainbridge, Hon RAM, FRCM; ✉ Royal Academy of Music, Marylebone Road, London NW1 5HT

BAINES, Rt Rev Nicholas; *see:* Leeds, Bishop of

BAINES, Paul Martin; s of Cyril Baines, of Pershore, Worcs, and Marion, *née* Guy; *b* 28 January 1956, Gidea Park, Essex; *Educ* Brentwood Sch, Trinity Hall Cambridge (MA); *m* 16 June 1984, Rosemary, *née* Hanson; 2 s (Mark b 8 Oct 1986, Luke b 5 Dec 1988), 1 da (Lydia b 20 Aug 1990); *Career* admitted slr 1980; Freshfields 1978–80, Antony Gibbs & Sons Ltd 1980–84; Charterhouse: joined 1984, md 1989, head of corporate finance and chief exec 1996–2000; Hawkpoint Partners Ltd: md 2000–03, chief exec 2003–09, exec chm 2009–13; sr advsr Smith Square Ptnrs 2013–; memb Sr Advsy Bd Vermilion Ptnrs 2013–; dir Parayhouse Sch Ltd 2001–05, dir Collins Stewart Hawkpoint plc 2006–12, dir John Menzies plc 2016–; *Recreations* mountain walking, tennis, bridge; *Style—* Paul Baines, Esq; ✉ Smith Square Partners LLP, 21 St James's Square, London SW1Y 4SZ (☎ 020 3696 7260)

BAINES, Stephen Philip; s of Charles Philip Baines (d 1986), and Edna, *née* Millard; *b* 16 January 1947; *Educ* Neath GS, Avery Hill Coll of Educn London (CertEd), Univ of Oregon USA (BSc, MSc); *m* 14 Sept 1985, (Emilie) Micheline; 1 da (Katherine Sian b 27 April 1986), 1 s (David Alexander b 3 Oct 1988); *Career* sports administrator; physical educn teacher: Wandsworth Comp Sch 1969–71, Pendle Hill HS Sydney Aust (also sportsmaster) 1971–73; exec dir Canadian Rugby Union Ottawa 1975–81, md Pro-Motion International Toronto 1981–83, dir of mktg Nat Assoc of Boys' Clubs London 1983–86; chief exec: The Hockey Assoc 1986–97, English Hockey Assoc 1997–98, International Rugby Board 1998–2000; writer and advsr on sports matters 2002–, fndr and chief exec Sports Business Int 2004–; currently sr lectr in sports business mgmnt Univ of Lincoln; memb: Henley Royal Regatta Stewards Enclosure; fell Br Inst of Sports Administration (former vice-chm); MIMgt, FCIM; *Recreations* international sport, rugby, photography, travel, golf; *Clubs* London Welsh RFC, Neath RFC, International Sportsman's, East India, St Stephen's Green; *Style—* Stephen Baines, Esq

BAINS, Satwan Singh (Sat); s of Balbir Singh Bains, of Derby, and Tarsem Kaur Bains; *b* 28 February 1971, Derby; *m* May 1996, Amanda Jane, *née* Cooke; *Career* restaurateur; Le Petit Blanc Oxford 1996, head chef Martins Arms Colston Basset Notts, The Ashbourne Gallery Derbys, Restaurant Le Jardin des Sens France, head chef Hotel des Clos Nottingham (renamed Restaurant Sat Bains at Hotel des Clos 2002), currently chef and prop Restaurant Sat Bains with Rooms Nottingham; involved with Centre of Vocational Excellence New Coll Nottingham; *Awards* Roux Scholarship 1999; for Restaurant Sat Bains with Rooms: Michelin Star 2003–, AA Restaurant of the Year 2006, BMW Square Meal Best UK Restaurant of the Year 2007; *Style—* Sat Bains, Esq; ✉ c/o Monica Brown, Lotus, Studio 8, 39 Tadema Road, London SW10 0PZ (☎ 020 7751 5812, fax 020 7349 0059, e-mail monica@lotuspr.co.uk); Restaurant Sat Bains with Rooms, Lenton Lane, Nottingham NG7 2SA (Twitter @satbains1)

BAINSFAIR, Paul; s of Leslie John Bainsfair, and Doris, *née* Cressey; *m* Sophie; 2 s (Bruno, Teddy), 1 da (Phoebe); *Career* advtg exec JWT, joined Saatchi & Saatchi 1975 rising to md 1987; fndr Bainsfair Sharkey Trott 1990, sold to GGT plc 1997; chm TBWA UK Gp Ltd (part of Omnicom), pres (Europe) TBWA Worldwide 2004–; MIPA; *Recreations* golf, shooting, skiing; *Clubs* Salisbury and S Wiltshire Golf, Soho House, The Union, Harry's Bar, Mark's; *Style—* Paul Bainsfair, Esq; ✉ TBWA, 76–80 Whitfield Street, London W1T 4EZ (☎ 020 7573 6666, fax 020 7573 7119, mobile 0468 333666)

BAIRD, Andrew; s of John Henry Baird, and Sarah, *née* Pervis; *b* 12 July 1966, Sheffield, S Yorks; *Educ* Granville Coll Sheffield (Cert, Dip, Morewood Voccan Trophy); *m* 26 March 2001, Eilish, *née* Maguire; 2 s (Luke Ian b 29 July 2001, Charles Louis b 7 July 2003); *Career* second commis Caledonia Hotel Edinburgh 1984, first commis Ritz Hotel London 1985, first commis then jr chef de partie Ettington Park 1986–87, sr chef de partie Longueville Manor 1987–89, sous chef Hambleton Hall 1989–90; Longueville Manor: head chef 1990–2007, exec head chef 2007–; involved with introducing cooking into schs (Victoria Coll, De La Salle Coll, St Saviour Sch, Beaulieu Convent Sch); memb Acad of Culinary Arts 2000–; Young Chef of the Year 1985, St Lo Salon Culinaire Gold award (jtly, as part of the Jersey Culinary Team) 1992, 3 AA Rosettes 1993–, Michelin Star 1994–2003, Egon Ronay Star 1994, Light Bites and Snacks 1995, Ackerman Charles Heindsieck Guide Clover Leaf Award 1995; *Recreations* scuba diving (PADI divemaster), fishing, gardening, photography, golf, driving; *Clubs* Les Ormes Golf; *Style—* Andrew Baird, Esq; ✉ L'Avenir, La Cour Fountaine, St Saviour, Jersey, Channel Islands JE2 7RL (☎ 01534 878051, e-mail andrewbaird1@mac.com); Longueville Manor Hotel, St Saviour, Jersey, Channel Islands JE2 7WF (☎ 01534 725501, fax 01534 731613, e-mail abaird@longuevillemanor.com)

BAIRD, Nicholas Graham Faraday (Nick); CMG (2010), CVO; s of Colin Baird, of Reigate, Surrey, and Elizabeth, *née* Powell; *b* 15 May 1962, Redhill, Surrey; *Educ* Dulwich Coll, Emmanuel Coll Cambridge (MA); *m* 17 Aug 1985, Caroline Jane, *née* Ivett; 1 s (Dominic b 22 March 1989), 2 da (Eleanor b 14 Dec 1990, Antonia b 17 April 1992); *Career* former diplomat; joined FCO 1983, third sec Kuwait 1986–89, first sec UK Rep to the EU Brussels 1989–93, private sec to Parly Under-Sec of State FCO 1993–95, head EU Intergovernmental Conf Unit FCO 1995–97, dep head of mission Muscat 1997–98, cnsllr UK Rep to the EU Brussels 1998–2002, head EU Dept (Internal) FCO 2002–03, seconded as sr policy dir Immigration and Nationality Directorate Home Office 2003–06, ambass to Repub of Turkey 2006–09, DG Europe and Globalisation FCO 2009–11; chief exec UKTI, currently gp corp affrs dir Centrica; non-exec dir Nord Anglia Inc; tstee Royal Botanic Gardens Kew; *Recreations* reading, travel, jogging, tennis, music; *Style—* Mr Nick Baird, CMG, CVO; ✉ Centrica plc, Millstream, Maidenhead Road, Windsor, Berkshire SL4 5GD

BAIRD, Roger Neale; s of John Allan Baird (d 1992), of Edinburgh, and Margaret Edith, *née* Shand (d 1994), of London; *b* 24 December 1941; *Educ* Daniel Stewarts Coll Edinburgh, Univ of Edinburgh (BSc, MB ChB, ChM); *m* 12 Oct 1968, Affra Mary, da of Douglas Varcoe-Cocks (d 1964); 1 da (Susan b 1970), 1 s (Richard b 1972); *Career* SHO and registrar Royal Infirmary Edinburgh 1969–73 (house surgn 1966–67), res scholar in clinical surgery 1967–69, lectr and sr lectr Univ of Bristol 1973–81, Fulbright scholar Harvard Med Sch 1975–76, conslt surgn Royal Infirmary Bristol 1977–2006; med dir United Bristol Healthcare Tst 1996–99, chm Litfield House Medical Centre Ltd 1996–2000; Hunterian prof RCS 1980, Sir James Learmonth lectr RCSE 1980, Long Fox lectr Univ of Bristol 1981, John Kinmonth lectr RCS 1984, Justin Millar lectr Aust and NZ Chapter Int Soc for Cardiovascular Surgery 1997; pres: Bristol Medico-Chirurgical Soc 1994–95, Vascular Surgical Soc of GB and Ireland 2000–01, Cncl Bristol Clifton and W of England Zoological Soc 2000–05, Surgical Club of SW England 2003, Dolphin Soc 2008–09; chm Assoc of Int Vascular Surgns 2005–08; dir Clifton Club Co Ltd 2013–; charitable tstee: European Soc for Vascular Surgery 1987–2003, United Bristol Hosps 1997–99; hon memb: Australian and NZ Chapter Int Soc for Cardiovascular Surgery 1997, American Soc for Vascular Surgery 2002, European Soc for Vacular Surgery 2002; corresponding memb Vascular Soc of SA 1997; High Sheriff City of Bristol 2005–06; FRCS, FRCSEd; *Books* Diagnosis and Monitoring in Arterial Surgery (1980), Human Disease for Dental Students (1981); 150 pubns on vascular surgical topics; *Recreations* music, travel; *Clubs* Army and Navy, Clifton; *Style*— Roger Baird, Esq

BAIRD-SMITH, Robin Jameson; s of John Helenus Baird-Smith (d 1977), and Jean Marjorie Guthrie, *née* Priestman, OBE (d 1993); *b* 21 July 1946; *Educ* Winchester, Royal Acad of Music, Trinity Coll Cambridge (BA); *m* 17 Jan 1976, Sarah Mary-Ann (d 1994), da of Charles Stevens Hedley, MC (d 1976); 2 s (Max John b 1978, Archibald Victor b 1979 d 1994), 1 da (Leonora Frances b 1981); *Career* publisher; Darton Longman and Todd Ltd: ed 1968–71, editorial dir 1971–78; Collins Publishers: ed 1978–81, editorial dir 1981–85; Constable Publishers: editorial dir 1985–95, publishing dir 1992–95, jt md 1992–95; publisher and md Gerald Duckworth and Company Ltd 1995–99, publishing dir Bloomsbury/Continuum 1999–; dir Isis Medical Media Ltd (Oxford) 1997–99, dir The Tablet 1999–2015, tstee The Tablet Tst 2004–; opera critic Mail on Sunday Newspaper 1989–90; chm Guild of Catholic Writers 1984–85, memb Analytical Psychology Club 1985–; *Books* Living Water (1988), Winter's Tales Vols 2 – 11 (1986–95), God of the Impossible (1989), Death of a Child (contrib, 2011); *Recreations* idleness and religion; *Clubs* Travellers; *Style*— Robin Baird-Smith, Esq; ✉ 8 Lawn Road, London NW3 2XS (☎ 020 7722 0716, e-mail robin.baird-smith@bloomsbury.com)

BAKER; *see also:* Sherston-Baker

BAKER, Prof Alan; s of late Barnet, and Bessie, Baker; *b* 19 August 1939; *Educ* Stratford GS, UCL (BSc), Trinity Coll Cambridge (MA, PhD); *Career* Trinity Coll Cambridge: fell 1964–, res fell 1964–68, dir of studies in Mathematics 1968–74; prof of pure mathematics Univ of Cambridge 1974–2006 (prof emeritus 2006–); visiting prof Stanford Univ 1974 and other US univs, Royal Soc Kan Tong Po prof Univ of Hong Kong 1988, guest prof ETH Zürich 1989; MSRI Univ of Calif Berkeley 1993; Fields medal Int Congress of Mathematicians Nice 1970, Adams prize Univ of Cambridge 1972; Docteur (hc) Université Louis Pasteur Strasbourg 1998; hon fell UCL 1979, foreign fell Indian Nat Science Acad 1980, foreign fell Nat Acad of Sciences India 1993; memb Academia Europaea 1998, hon memb Hungarian Acad of Sciences 2001; FRS 1973; *Publications* Transcendental Number Theory (1975), A Concise Introduction to the Theory of Numbers (1984), New Advances in Transcendence Theory (ed, 1988), Logarithmic Forms and Diophantine Geometry (co-author, 2007), A Comprehensive Course in Number Theory (2012); numerous papers in scientific jls; *Style*— Professor Alan Baker, FRS; ✉ Department of Pure Mathematics and Mathematical Statistics, Centre for Mathematical Sciences, Wilberforce Road, Cambridge CB3 0WB; Trinity College, Cambridge CB2 1TQ (☎ 01223 338400, e-mail a.baker@dpmms.cam.ac.uk)

BAKER, Christopher James; MBE; s of late James Alfred Baker, and late Alice Marjorie Baker; *b* 5 November 1951; *Educ* Dulwich Coll, Christ's Coll Cambridge (MA); *m* 27 March 1978, Anne Elizabeth Sylvia, da of late Francis George James Morris; 2 s (James b 1981, Francis b 1985), 2 da (Amy b 1983, Hannah b 1988); *Career* principal HM Treasy 1973–80, banker Morgan Grenfell & Co Ltd 1981–83, dir Hill Samuel Bank Ltd 1987–89 (joined 1983), corp fin ptnr Coopers & Lybrand 1990–93, corp strategy dir The Littlewoods Organisation plc 1993–2000; non-exec chm Convergent Communications plc 2002–03 (dir 1998–); non-exec dep chm: Jacques Vert plc 2003–11 (dir 1999–), Blooms of Bressingham Holdings plc 2003–07 (dir 2001–); non-exec dir: Park Group plc 2001–13, AI Claims Solutions plc 2002–12, Teacher Training Agency (now Training and Devpt Agency for Schs) 2002–09 (chair 2009–12); chair Business Liverpool Ltd 2004–08, chair Aintree Univ Hosps NHS Fndn Tst 2008–14, chair Viapath LLP (formerly GSTS Pathology LLP) 2012–15, chair Nisa Retail Ltd 2013–; memb Governing Cncl Nat Coll of Sch Leadership 2008–09, memb Cncl Univ of Liverpool 2008–, external memb DfEAudit and Risk Ctee 2014–; *Recreations* hill walking, classic cars, theatre, family history; *Style*— Christopher J Baker, Esq, MBE; ✉ Woodlands, 18 Carrwood Road, Wilmslow, Cheshire SK9 5DL (☎ 01625 529663, e-mail christopherbaker@btconnect.com)

BAKER, David Leon; s of late Jack Charles Baker, of London, and Joan, *née* Grannard; *b* 14 May 1950; *Educ* St Marylebone GS London; *m* 23 June 1974, Helen Amanda (Mandy), da of Gerald Stone, and Joyce Stone, of London; *Career* Edward Erdman & Co, Erdman Lewis International Ltd (now Colliers Int) 1968–2003, md and jt chief exec Motcomb Estates 2003–06, currently md DLB Estates Ltd; dep res Brokerage Ctee Int Real Estate Fedn, fndr memb Steering Ctee Office Agents Soc; memb Ctee of Mgmnt Br Cncl for Offices, exec and govr Chartered Surveyors Trg Tst; memb Advsy Bd Jewish Museum 2011; memb Bd of Mgmnt Central Synagogue London W1 2011; tstee: Rheumatology Discretionary Fund UCL Charity, Critical Care, Lesley Margo Charitable Tst 2011; hon surveyor Thames Valley Univ 1992; Freeman City of London 1990; hon fell UCL 2003; int affiliate Soc of Industrial and Office Realtors (SIOR), FPCS, FFB, assoc memb Land Inst; *Recreations* theatre, cinema, the history of London architecture, tropical fish, watching most sport; *Style*— David L Baker, Esq; ✉ DLB Estates Ltd, 14 Nottingham Terrace, Regent's Park, London NW1 4QB (☎ 07768 500148, e-mail david@dlbestates.co.uk)

BAKER, HE Francis Raymond (Frank); OBE; s of late Raymond Albert Baker, and late Pamela Annis, *née* Morley; *b* 27 January 1961, Dartford, Kent; *Educ* Dartford GS; *m* Maria Pilar Fernandez; 1 da, 1 s; *Career* diplomat; Personnel Operations Dept FCO 1981–82, third sec Panama City 1983–86, third then second sec Buenos Aires 1986–91, desk offr Human Rights Policy Dept FCO 1991–93, first sec Ankara 1993–96, on secondment to US Govt Washington 1996–98, head Iraq Section ME Dept FCO 1998, private sec to Min of State FCO 1998–2000, head Africa Dept FCO 2000–03, political/military counsellor Washington 2003–07, dep dir ME FCO 2007–10, ambass to Kuwait 2010–14, ambass to Iraq 2014–; Special Class Order of Kuwait; *Style*— HE Mr Frank Baker, OBE; ✉ c/o FCO (Baghdad), King Charles Street, London SW1A 2AH

BAKER, Jeffrey; s of Peter Baker, of Norton-on-Tees, Cleveland, and Barbara Baker; *b* 22 October 1967; *Educ* Blakeston Comp Stockton-on-Tees; *m* Gosia; 1 da (Jessika b 23 Nov 2004), 1 s (Jay b 15 May 2010); by previous relationship, 1 s (Jack Bosco b 12 Oct 1994), 1 da (Jasmine b 31 Aug 1996); *Career* chef; commis chef de partie Greenhouse Mayfair, chef de partie Rue St Jacques London, chef de partie Waltons London, estagé Restaurant Riesbachli Zurich, estagé Chateau Montreuil France, sous chef Bishopstrow House Relais & Chateau Wilts, sous chef Sud Ouest Knightsbridge, sous chef Stephen Bull Restaurant London, head chef Brasserie Forty Four Ltd Leeds 1992–2005, head chef Pool Court at 42 1994–2005 (Michelin Star 1996), currently prop and chef J Bakers Bistro Moderne; *Recreations* eating out, following Middlesbrough FC; *Style*— Jeffrey Baker, Esq; ✉ J Bakers Bistro Moderne, 7 Fossgate, York YO1 9TA (☎ 01904 622688, website www.jbakers.co.uk)

BAKER, Hon Mr Justice; Sir Jeremy Russell Baker; kt (2013), QC (1999); *b* 9 February 1958; *Career* called to the Bar Middle Temple 1979; asst recorder 1996, recorder 2000, circuit judge (North Eastern Circuit) 2010–13, judge of the High Court 2013–; *Style*— The Hon Mr Justice Jeremy Baker; ✉ Royal Courts of Justice, Strand, London WC2A 2LL

BAKER, Prof Sir John Hamilton; kt (2003), Hon QC (1996); s of Kenneth Lee Vincent Baker, QPM, of Hintlesham, Suffolk, and Marjorie, *née* Bagshaw; *b* 10 April 1944; *Educ* King Edward VI GS Chelmsford, UCL (LLB, PhD), Univ of Cambridge (MA, LLD); *m* 1, 20 April 1968 (m dis 1997), Veronica Margaret, da of Rev William Stephen Lloyd, TD (d 1971); 2 da (Alys b 1973, Anstice b 1978); m 2, 13 Dec 2002, Fiona Rosalind Holdsworth, *née* Cantlay (d 2005); m 3, 18 June 2010, Prof Elisabeth Maria Cornelia van Houts, widow of Thomas Erle Faber; *Career* called to the Bar Inner Temple 1966 (hon bencher 1988), admitted Gray's Inn 1979 (hon bencher 2013); lectr in law UCL 1967–71 (asst lectr 1965–67, fell 1990); Univ of Cambridge: fell St Catharine's Coll 1971– (pres 2004–07, vice-master 2007), librarian Squire Law Library 1971–73, lectr in law 1973–83, jr proctor 1980–81, reader in English legal history 1983–88, prof of English legal history 1988–98, Downing prof of the laws of England 1998–2011, chm Faculty of Law 1990–92; lectr in legal history Inns of Court Sch of Law 1973–78; visiting prof: Euro Univ Inst Florence 1979, Harvard Law Sch 1982, Yale Law Sch 1987, NY Univ Sch of Law 1988–2010; literary dir Selden Soc 1992–2011 (jt literary dir 1981–91); Ames prize Harvard 1985; Hon LLD Univ of Chicago 1992; hon foreign memb American Acad of Arts and Sciences 2001; FRHistS 1980, FBA 1984; *Books* Introduction to English Legal History (1971, 4 edn 2002), English Legal Manuscripts (vol 1 1975, vol 2 1978), The Reports of Sir John Spelman (1977–78), Manual of Law French (1979, 2 edn 1990), The Order of Serjeants at Law (1984), English Legal Manuscripts in the USA (1985, 1990), The Legal Profession and the Common Law (1986), Sources of English Legal History: Private Law to 1750 (with S F C Milsom, 1986, 2 edn 2010), The Notebook of Sir John Port (1986), Readings and Moots in the Inns of Court, Part II: Moots (with S E Thorne, 1990), Reports from the Lost Notebooks of Sir James Dyer (1994), Catalogue of English Legal Manuscripts in Cambridge University Library (1996), Spelman's Reading on Quo Warranto (1997), Monuments of Endlesse Labours: English Canonists and their Work (1998), Caryll's Reports (1999), The Common Law Tradition (2000), The Law's Two Bodies (2001), Readers and Readings (2001), Year Books 12–14 Henry VIII (2002), Oxford History of the Laws of England, Vol VI (2003), Reports from the Time of Henry VIII (2004), Dalison's Reports (2007), English Legal MSS of Sir Thomas Phillipps (2008), The Men of Court (2012), Collected Papers (2013), Selected Readings and Commentaries on Magna Carta (2015); *Style*— Prof Sir John Baker, QC, FBA; ✉ St Catharine's College, Cambridge CB2 1RL

BAKER, Hon Mr Justice; Sir Jonathan Leslie Baker; kt (2009), QC (2001); s of Leslie Joseph Baker (d 1994), and Ethel Frances Isobel, *née* Walter (d 2003); *b* 6 August 1955; *Educ* St Albans Sch, St John's Coll Cambridge (open scholar, MA); *m* 1980, Helen Mary, da of Russell Sharrock, and Mary Sharrock; 1 s (James Jonathan b 26 Oct 1984), 1 da (Clare Rachel b 20 Nov 1987); *Career* called to the Bar Middle Temple 1978 (bencher 2010); memb Harcourt Chambers 1979–2009 (head of Chambers 2004–09), asst recorder 1998–2000, recorder 2000–09, dep judge of the High Court 2003–09, judge of the High Court 2009–, liaison judge Family Div Western Circuit 2011–; memb Ctee Family Law Bar Assoc 2005–09; chm Oxfordshire Relate 1997–2008; ed-in-chief Court of Protection Law Reports 2011–; govr Magdalen Coll Sch Oxford 2005–2014; *Publications* Contact: The New Deal (jtly, 2006), The Public Law Outline: The Court Companion (jtly, 2008); *Recreations* music, history, family life; *Style*— The Hon Mr Justice Baker; ✉ Royal Courts of Justice, Strand, London WC2A 2LL

BAKER, Dr Maureen; CBE (2004); da of William Murphy (d 1994), and Helen, *née* Nolan; *b* 20 September 1958, Motherwell; *Educ* Holy Cross HS Hamilton, Univ of Dundee (MB, ChB), Univ of Nottingham (DM); *m* 1984, Peter Lindsay Baker; 2 da (Carolyn Marie b 1988, Elena Louise b 1991); *Career* princ GP Lincoln 1985–2000, associate advsr in gen practice Univ of Nottingham 1992–, med advsr NHS Direct 2001–02, special clinical advsr Nat Patient Safety Agency 2002–07, nat clinical lead for safety NHS Connecting for Health 2007–; hon sec RCGP 1999–2009; author of numerous articles, chapters and books; MRCGP 1985; *Recreations* family, cinema; *Style*— Dr Maureen Baker, CBE; ✉ Royal College of General Practitioners, 14 Princes Gate, Hyde Park, London SW7 1PU

BAKER, Michael Verdun; s of Albert Ernest Thomas Baker (d 2008), and Eva Louisa Florence, *née* Phillips (d 2009); *b* 30 July 1942; *Educ* Caterham Sch; *m* 21 Sept 1963, Rita Ann, da of Walter James Marks (d 1998); 2 da (Carolyn b 1967, Louise b 1970); *Career* insurance official Alliance Assurance Co Ltd 1959–63, O & M systems analyst Plessey Co 1963–66, sr conslt Coopers & Lybrand 1967–72; The Stock Exchange: talisman project dir 1972–78, settlement dir 1978–82, admin dir 1982–84, divnl dir settlement servs 1984–87, exec dir markets 1987–90, chief exec Assoc of Private Client Investment Mangrs and Stockbrokers 1990–94, chm Consort Securities Systems Ltd 1994–96; *Recreations* walking, photography, travel, record collecting; *Style*— Michael Baker, Esq; ✉ 12 Bigbury Court, Bigbury, Kingsbridge, Devon TQ7 4AP (☎ 01548 810792)

BAKER, HE Nigel Marcus; OBE (2010), MVO (2003); s of Clive Baker (d 2007), and Mary Berg, *née* Appleyard (d 2008); *b* 9 September 1966, Birmingham; *Educ* Dulwich Coll, Gonville & Caius Coll Cambridge (sr scholar, MA); *m* 31 Dec 1997, Alexandra, *née* Cechova; 1 s (Benjamin James b 8 Sept 2008); *Career* diplomat; Cons Res Dept 1989, joined FCO 1989, desk offr for Libya and Tunisia Near East and North Africa Dept FCO 1990–91, third then second sec (econ) Br Embassy Prague 1992–93, dep head of mission Br Embassy Bratislava 1993–96, first sec FCO UK EU Presidency 1998, head of European defence Security Policy Dept FCO 1998–2000, asst private sec to HRH The Prince of Wales 2000–03, dep head of mission Br Embassy Havana 2003–06, ambass to Bolivia 2007–11, ambass to the Holy See 2011–16; tstee St Catherine's Fndn 2000–03, memb of Friends of ROH 2000–03; *Books* Britain and the Holy See: A Celebration of 1982 and the Wider Relationship (ed, 2013); *Clubs* Travellers, Crystal Palace FC; *Style*— HE Mr Nigel Baker, OBE, MVO; ✉ FCO, Holy See / PF43953, BFPO 5245 HA4 6EP (e-mail baker.sn@gmail.com); British Embassy, Holy See, Via XX Settembre 80a, 00187 Rome, Italy (☎ 0039 06 4220 4000, e-mail nigel.baker@fco.gov.uk)

BAKER, Norman; *Career* MP (Lib Dem) Lewes 1997–2015; Lib Dem shadow sec of state for transport 2007–10, Parly under-sec of state for tport 2010–13, min of state Home Office 2013–14; Inquisitor of the Year Zurich/Spectator Parly Awards 2001, Oppn Politician of the Year Channel 4 Awards 2002; pres Tibet Soc 2007–; *Style*— Norman Baker; ✉ House of Commons, London SW1A 0AA (☎ 020 7219 2864, e-mail bakern@parliament.uk)

BAKER, Richard James; MSP; s of Rev James Baker, and Rev Anne Baker, *née* Brown; *b* 29 May 1974, Edinburgh; *Educ* St Bees Sch Cumbria, Univ of Aberdeen (MA); *m* 16 Oct 2004, Dr Claire Baker, MSP, *née* Brennan; 1 da (Catherine b 23 Dec 2005); *Career* pres NUS Scotland 1998–2000, Scottish press offr Help the Aged 2000–02, MSP (Lab) NE Scotland 2003–; memb Amicus; *Recreations* choral singing, football, reading; *Style*—

B

Richard Baker, Esq, MSP; ✉ c/o Scottish Parliament Office, 68 Rosemount Place, Aberdeen AB25 2XJ (☎ 01224 641171, fax 01224 641104, e-mail richard.baker.msp@scottish.parliament.uk)

BAKER, Robert James; s of John Edward Baker (d 1990), and Margaret Elsie Mary, *née* Palmer (d 2003); *b* 9 December 1947; *Educ* UEA (BA); *m* 15 June 1973, Beverley Joan, da of Paul Archdale Langford (d 1976); 2 da (Hannah Alice b 1979, Amy Margaret b 1981); *Career* dir: Hobsons Publishing plc 1982–99, Harmsworth Publishing 1994–99, Harmsworth Information Publishing 1996–99; md: Hobsons Academic Relations 1996–, Communication Resources Ltd 1996–; dir: Educational Communications 2000–02, Care Choices Ltd 2000–; *Recreations* art, antique collecting, racing; *Clubs* Reform; *Style—* Robert Baker, Esq

BAKER, Prof Robin Richard Sebastian; OBE (2004); s of Walter Richard Baker (d 1975), and Victoria Rebecca, *née* Martin (d 1988); *b* 31 December 1942; *Educ* RCA (maj travelling scholar, Fulbright scholar, MA), Univ of Calif, Thames Poly; *m* 1, 1966 (m dis 1970), Teresa Osborne-Saul; m 2, 1971 (m dis 1975), Tamar Avital; m 3, 1981 (m dis 1990), Angela Mary Piers Dumas; m 4, 1991, Katherine Knowles; *Career* designer; designer with: Joseph Ezcherick Associates San Francisco 1964–65, Russell Hodgeson & Leigh (architects) 1965–66; fndr own design practice (maj exhibitions cmmns from Arts Cncl of GB, Br Airports Authy and Nat Tst) 1966–79, princ lectr (with responsibility for computer studies) Chelsea Sch of Art 1982–83, computer advsr Art & Design Inspectorate ILEA 1984–86, specialist advsr in computing Ctee for Arts & Design CNAA 1985–88, visitor in computing Art and Design Inspectorate and Poly of Hong Kong 1985, prof and dir of computing RCA 1987–94, dir Ravensbourne Coll of Design and Communication 1994–2015; design computing conslt to: Conran Fndn's Museum of Design 1987–, Comshare Ltd 1987–88, Arthur Young 1988–89, Burtons Ltd 1988–89, Marks & Spencer 1990–94, Centro Portugues 1992–93, National Tst 1994–97, Design Cncl 1996–; author of numerous articles in design technology jls; *Books* Designing the Future (1995); *Style—* Prof Robin Baker, OBE

BAKER, Professor Robin William; CMG (2005); s of William John David Baker (d 1971), and Brenda Olive, *née* Hodges (d 1978); *b* 4 October 1953; *Educ* Bishop Wordsworth's Sch, SSEES Univ of London (BA), UEA (scholar, PhD); *m* 1974 (m dis 1997), Miriam Joy, da of Bernard Frederick Turpin (d 1968); 2 s (Simeon Scott b 12 Nov 1979, Joel William b 3 Feb 1983); *Career* exec offr MOD 1976–80, doctoral research UEA 1981–84; British Council: trainee 1984–85, asst rep South Africa 1985–89, head of recruitment London 1989–90, asst dir Hungary 1990–93, dir Thessaloniki 1994–96, dep dir Russia 1996–99, dir West and South Europe 1999, dir Europe 1999–2002, dep DG 2002–2005; pro-vice-chllr Univ of Kent 2005–07, vice-chllr Univ of Chichester 2007–10, vice-chllr Canterbury Christ Church Univ 2010–12, ret; hon visiting fell SSEES Univ of London 1994–96, sr hon visiting fell Inst for Balkan Studies Greece 1995–, visiting prof Univ of Winchester 2015–, visiting scholar Sarum Coll 2015–; fell UCL 2005; memb: Société Finno-Ougrienne 1982, Inst Romance Studies Advsy Bd 1999–2002, SSEES Advsy Bd 1999–2009, Br Inst in Paris Governing Bd 1999–2002, Cncl for Assisting Refugee Academics 2002–13, Royal Soc Int Policy Ctee 2003–05, Cncl Univ of Kent 2003–05, Bd Chichester Festival Theatre 2007–10, Bd Creative Fndn 2010–12, Bd Canterbury Festival 2010–12; memb Bd/tstee: Finnish Inst 2008–15, Colleges and Universities of the Anglican Communion 2011–12; Kent ambass 2010–12; fell UCL 2004; FRSA 1998; *Books* The Development of the Komi Case System (1985), Hollow Men, Strange Women: Codes and Otherness in the Book of Judges (2016); *Recreations* opera, walking, jazz; *Clubs* Travellers; *Style—* Professor Robin Baker, CMG

BAKER, Roger; QPM (2008); s of William Ernest Baker (d 1982), and Norah Margaret, *née* Kay; *b* 15 November 1958, Bolsover, Derbys; *Educ* Shirebrook Comp Sch Mansfield, Univ of Manchester (MA), Univ of Derby (MBA); *m* 15 May 1999, Patricia Anne, *née* O'Callaghan; 2 da (Katie b 8 March 1989, Sophie b 1 June 1994); *Career* Chief Supt Derbys Constabulary 1999–2001 (joined 1977), Asst Chief Constable Staffs Police 2001–03, Dep Chief Constable N Yorks Police 2003–05, Chief Constable Essex Police 2005–09, HM inspector of constabulary 2009–; *Recreations* equestrian pursuits, golf, walking the dogs; *Style—* Roger Baker, Esq, QPM; ✉ HMIC, Unit 2, Wakefield Office Village, Fryers Way, Silkwood Park, Wakefield WF5 9TJ (☎ 01924 237722, fax 01924 237705)

BAKER, Sam; *Educ* Univ of Birmingham; *Career* journalist; successively practicals asst, dep practicals ed and features writer Chat 1989–92, sr features writer Take a Break 1992–93, dep ed New Woman 1995–96 (features ed 1993–95); ed: Just Seventeen 1996 (relaunched magazine as J-17), Minx 1997–98, Company 1998–2003, Cosmopolitan 2004–06; ed-in-chief Red 2006–; *Books* Fashion Victim (2005), This Year's Model (2008), The Stepmother's Support Group (2009); *Style—* Ms Sam Baker; ✉ Red, Hachette Filipacchi UK Ltd, 64 North Row, London W1K 7LL

BAKER, Simon; *Educ* Univ of Durham; *Career* European media analyst; co-head of UK Media Equity Research Team Societe Generale until 2006, dir Credit Suisse 2006–; *Style—* Simon Baker, Esq; ✉ Credit Suisse, One Cabot Square, London E14 4QJ

BAKER, Simon; *Educ* GSM; *Career* sound designer; assoc artist Kneehigh Theatre; theatre prodns incl: Don John (RSC and tour), Boeing Boeing (London and Broadway), The Lord of the Rings (Toronto and London), I Am Shakespeare (Chichester and UK tour), God of Carnage (London and Broadway), Our House (UK tour), Brief Encounter (Cinema Haymarket, UK tour, US tour and Broadway), The Norman Conquests (Old Vic and Broadway), Complicit The Real Thing (Old Vic), Arcadia (London), The Birds (Gate Theatre Dublin), As You Like It (Old Vic), The Tempest (Old Vic), Deathtrap (London), La Bête (London and Broadway), Wild Bride (tour), Umbrellas of Cherbourg (Gielgud), Batman Live (int arena tour), Matilda The Musical (Stratford, West End and Broadway) 2010– (Best Sound Design Olivier Award 2012), Amen Corner (NT), The Light Princess (NT) 2013 (Olivier nomination), Mojo (West End), Roaring Girl (RSC), Oliver (Sheffield), Shakespeare in Love (West End); *Style—* Mr Simon Baker; ✉ website www.simonbaker.co.uk; c/o The Agency, 24 Pottery Lane, Holland Park, London W11 4LZ

BAKER, Timothy (Tim); s of Maurice Baker, and Mary Baker; *b* 9 May 1953; *Educ* Abingdon Sch, Univ of York (BA), Univ of Leeds (MA); *Career* theatre dir; actor and teacher Action Projects in Educn 1976–78, actor Cardiff Laboratory Theatre 1977–80, dir Spectacle Theatre 1978–80 (writer in residence 1980–81), co memb and musician Theatr Bara Caws 1981–83, musical dir Cwmni Hwyl a Fflag 1982, artistic dir Theatre W Glamorgan 1982–97, assoc dir Clwyd Theatr Cymru (Nat Theatre of Wales) 1997–; assoc RNT 2000–, assoc dir Frec a Frec Theatre Co Barcelona; visiting lectr and dir Welsh Coll of Music and Drama, visiting dir Setagaya People's Theatre Tokyo; memb Dir's Guild of GB 1998; *Productions* for Spectacle Theatre: Do You Mind, Trouble; for Theatre W Glamorgan incl: When the Wind Blows (Welsh language version), Shirley Valentine (Welsh language version), Rape of the Fair Country, Combrogos (also writer), Sothach a Sglyfach; for Clwyd Theatr Cymru incl: Rape of the Fair Country (part 1 The Alexander Cordell Trilogy, Prodn of the Year Liverpool Daily Post 1997), Blue Remembered Hills, Art, Of Mice and Men, Hosts of Rebecca (part 2 The Alexander Cordell Trilogy), Song of the Earth (part 3 The Alexander Cordell Trilogy), Hard Times, Accidental Death of an Anarchist, To Kill a Mockingbird (Best Prodn Liverpool Daily Post 2001, Best Dir Liverpool Daily Post 2001, Best Prodn Wales Theatre Awards 2002), A View from the Bridge (Best Rgnl Prodn Liverpool Daily Post 2003); for Clwyd Theatr Cymru as writer incl: Flora's War, The Secret, Word for Word; for Frec a Frec Theatre Barcelona: Voler es Poder, FDV, Gabia; other prodns incl: Silas Marner (Theatr Clwyd), Canterbury Tales (Mappa Mundi Theatre), Threepenny Opera (RNT); *Recreations* music (guitar and piano); *Style—* Timothy Baker, Esq; ☎ 01352 758857, website www.tim-baker.com

BAKER OF DORKING, Baron (Life Peer UK 1997), of Iford in the County of East Sussex; Kenneth Wilfred Baker; CH (1992), PC (1984); s of late Wilfred M Baker, OBE, of Twickenham, Middx, and Mrs Baker, *née* Harries; *b* 3 November 1934; *Educ* St Paul's, Magdalen Coll Oxford; *m* 1963, Mary Elizabeth, da of William Gray Muir, of Edinburgh; 1 s, 2 da; *Career* Nat Serv Lt Gunners N Africa 1953–55, artillery instr to Libyan Army; industrial conslt; memb Twickenham BC 1960–62; contested (Cons): Poplar 1964, Acton 1966; MP (Cons): Acton 1968–70, St Marylebone 1970–83, Mole Valley 1983–97; memb Public Accounts Ctee 1969–70, Parly sec CSD 1972–74, PPS to Ldr of Oppn 1974–75, memb Exec 1922 Ctee 1975–81, min of state for industry (special responsibility for IT) 1981–84, min for local govt DOE 1984–85, sec of state for the environment 1985–86, sec of state for educn and science 1986–89, chm of the Cons Party and Chllr of the Duchy of Lancaster 1989–90, home sec 1990–92, chm Information Ctee House of Lords 2002–07, memb House Ctee 2007–12; chm Hansard Soc 1978–81, sec gen UN Conf of Parliamentarians on World Population and Devpt 1978; chm: The Belmont Press (London) Ltd 1999–2010, Business Serve plc 2000–06, Northern Edge Ltd 2000–05, Monstermob Ltd 2001–06, Teather & Greenwood 2004–07; dir: Hanson plc 1992–2005, Videotron Corporation Ltd 1992–97, Wavetek Corporation 1992–98, Bell Cablemedia plc 1994–97, Millennium Chemicals Inc 1996–2004, Genting UK plc 2001–, Graphite Resources Ltd 2008–12; advsr: Cross Border Enterprises LLC, Trilantic Capital Partners 2009–; pres Royal London Soc for the Blind 2000–10, chm Edge Educn Fndn, chm Baker Dearing Educnl Tst 2010–, vice-chm Cartoon Museum, tstee Booker Prize Fndn; *Books* I Have No Gun But I Can Spit (ed, 1980), London Lines (ed, 1982), The Faber Book of English History in Verse (ed, 1988), Unauthorised Versions: Poems and Their Parodies (ed, 1990), The Faber Anthology of Conservatism (ed, 1993), The Turbulent Years: my life in politics (1993), The Prime Ministers – An Irreverent Political History in Cartoons (1995), Kings and Queens – An Irreverent History of the British Monarchy (1996), The Faber Book of War Poetry (1996), A Children's English History in Verse (2000), The Faber Book of Landscape Poetry (2000), George IV: A Life in Caricature (2005), George III: A Life in Caricature (2007), G K Chesterton poems (2007), George Washington's War – in contemporary prints and cartoons (2009), 14–18: A New Vision for Secondary Education (2013), On the Burning of Books (2016); *Recreations* collecting books and caricatures; *Clubs* Athenaeum, Garrick; *Style—* The Rt Hon Lord Baker of Dorking, CH, PC; ✉ House of Lords, London SW1A 0PW (☎ 020 7219 3000)

BAKER-BATES, Rodney Pennington; s of Dr Eric Tom Baker-Bates (d 1986), and Nora Stuart, *née* Kirkham (d 1981); *b* 25 April 1944, Crosby, Liverpool; *Educ* Shrewsbury Sch, Hertford Coll Oxford (Open Scholar, MA); *m* 16 Sept 1972, Gail Elizabeth, *née* Roberts; 1 s (Piers b 22 Dec 1975); *Career* cadet Int Dept and Corp Fin Glyn Mills & Co 1966–68, articled clerk to Lead Mangr Consultancy Div Arthur Andersen & Co 1968–77, asst gen mangr and vice-pres to Mangr EMEA Shipping Div Chase Manhatten Bank NA 1977–84; Midland Bank: gen mangr Int Div 1984–85, gen mangr gp corp banking 1985–86, UK corp banking dir 1986–89, dep chief exec then md UK banking 1989–91, gp planning then gp fin control dir 1991–92; dir of fin and IT, memb Bd of Mgmnt and memb Exec Ctee BBC 1993–98; Prudential plc: md corp pensions 1998–99, chief exec gp pensions 1999–2000, chief exec Prudential Financial Servs 2000–01, conslt jt ventures 2001–02; chm Exec Managing Ptnrs C Hoare & Co (Bankers) 2002–06 (non-exec dir 2000–10), dep chm Co-Operative Financial Servs Ltd, Co-Operative Bank plc, Co-Operative Insurance Society Ltd and CIS Gen Insurance Ltd 2009–12; chm: Change Partnership Ltd 1997–2001, Hydra Assocs Ltd 1998–2001, CoralEurobet plc 1999–2002, Zenith Entertainment Ltd 2000–03, Burns e-commerce Hldgs Ltd 2002–04, FirstAssist Gp 2003–09, Cabot Financial (Europe) Ltd 2004–06, Helphire Gp plc 2006–09, Britannia Building Soc 2006–09 (also non-exec dir), Assura Gp plc 2008–10, Stobart Gp Ltd, Eg Consulting Ltd, XTAQ Ltd, G's Gp Hldgs Ltd, Willis Ltd, Ridgeons Gp 2012–; vice-chm AtlasFram Gp 2010–; non-exec dir: Aspen Gp plc 1997–99, Dexia Municipal Bank plc 1997–2001 (also chm Audit Ctee), Lloyds Register of Shipping 1998–2007 (chm Audit Ctee), Music Solution Ltd 2003–08, Bedlam Asset Mgmnt plc 2004–13, Strategic Investment Gp Ltd 2005–08, AtlasFram Gp Ltd; tstee: Life Fund Royal Nat Pension Fund for Nursing (memb Cncl and Audit Ctee 2000–01), Terra Consilia 1999–2003, Dolphin Square Tst Ltd 1999–2015, Burdett Tst for Nursing 2001–09; dir City Arts Tst 2001–04, memb Audit Ctee Wellcome Tst 2004–07, govr RSC 2003–08, govr and chm Fin and Gen Purpose Ctee Bedales Sch 1993–2002; FCA 1975, assoc Inst of Mgmnt Consultants 1976, FCIB 1988; *Clubs* Brooks's, Farmers; *Style—* Rodney Baker-Bates, Esq; ✉ Willis Ltd, 51 Lime Street, London EC3M 7DQ (☎ 07802 177284, e-mail rbb@bakerbates.co.uk)

BAKEWELL, Baroness (Life Peer UK 2011), of Stockport in the County of Greater Manchester; Dame Joan Dawson Bakewell; DBE (2008, CBE 1999); da of John Rowlands, and Rose, *née* Bland; *b* 16 April 1933; *Educ* Stockport HS for Girls, Newnham Coll Cambridge (BA); *m* 1, 1955 (m dis 1972), Michael Bakewell, 1 s, 1 da; m 2, 1975 (m dis 2001), Jack Emery (theatre and TV prodr); *Career* broadcaster and writer 1964–; TV critic The Times 1978–81, arts corr BBC 1981–87, columnist Sunday Times 1987–91; chm BFI 1999–2002 (vice-chm 1996–99), chair Nat Campaign for the Arts 2004–10, chair Shared Experience 2007–12; memb: Cncl Aldeburgh Productions 1987–99, Bd RNT 1997–2003, Cncl Members of the Tate Gallery; hon pres Soc of Arts Publicists 1988–92; pres Birkbeck Univ of London 2013; assoc fell Newnham Coll Cambridge 1990–91 (assoc 1984–87); FRCA; *Television* BBC incl: Meeting Point 1964, The Second Sex 1964, Late Night Line Up 1965–72, The Youthful Eye 1968, Moviemakers at the National Film Theatre 1971, Film '72 and Film '73, For the Sake of Appearance 1973, Where is Your God? 1973, Who Cares? 1973, The Affirmative Way (series) 1973, What's it all About? (2 series) 1974, Time Running Out (series) 1974, The Brontë Business 1974, The Shakespeare Business 1976, Generation to Generation (series) 1976, My Day with the Children 1977, The Moving Line 1979, Arts UK: OK? 1980, Arts corr 1982–87, The Heart of the Matter 1988–2000, My Generation 2000, One Foot in the Past 2000, Taboo 2001; ITV incl: Sunday Break 1962, Home at 4.30 1964, Thank You Ron (writer and prodr) 1974, Fairest Fortune 1974, Edinburgh Festival Report 1974, Reports Action (4 series) 1976–78, Pandora's Box (6 progs) 1977; also Memento (Channel 4) 1993, Portrait Artist of the Year (Sky Arts) 2013, 2014 and 2016, Landscape Artist of the Year 2015 and 2016; *Radio* Away from it All 1978–79, PM 1979–81, Artist of the Week (Radio 3) 1998–2000, The Brains Tst (Radio 3) 1998–2000, Belief (Radio 3) 2001–13, Inside the Ethics Committee (Radio 4) 2009–; radio plays: There and Back (Radio 4), Parish Magazine (3 episodes), Brought to Book (2005); *Books* The New Priesthood: British Television Today (with Nicholas Garnham, 1970), A Fine and Private Place (with John Drummond, 1977), The Complete Traveller (1977), The Heart of Heart of the Matter (1996), The Centre of the Bed (2003), Belief (2005), The View from Here (2006), All the Nice Girls (2009), She's Leaving Home (2010), Stop the Clocks (2016); *Recreations* cinema, theatre, travel, talk; *Style—* The Baroness Bakewell, DBE

BALDING, Andrew M A; s of Ian Anthony Balding, LVO, and Lady Emma Balding, *née* Hastings-Bass; bro of Clare Balding, *qv*; nephew of 16 Earl of Huntingdon, LVO; *b* 29 December 1972, London; *Educ* Radley, RAC Cirencester (BSc); *m* 15 July 2005, Anna Lisa, *née* Williams; 2 s (Jonno, Toby), 1 da (Florence b 2 Nov 2010); *Career* horse trainer; amateur jockey with 20 winners 1992–97, asst trainer to Mrs J R Ramsden 1996–98, asst trainer to Mr I A Balding 1999–2003, trainer Park House Stables Kingsclere 2003–

(notable wins: Vodafone Oaks, Canadian Int, Dubai Sheema Classic, Hong Kong Vase, Wonder Where SHRS, Imperial Cup, Kingwell Hurdle); IRB Int Trainer of the Year 2005; *Recreations* Southampton FC; *Clubs* Turf; *Style—* Andrew Balding, Esq; ✉ Park House Stables, Kingsclere, Newbury, Berkshire RG20 5PY (✆ 01635 298210, fax 01635 298305, e-mail admin@kingsclere.com)

BALDING, Clare Victoria; OBE (2013); da of Ian Balding, LVO, and Lady Emma Balding; sis of Andrew Balding, *qv*; niece of 16 Earl of Huntingdon, LVO; *b* 29 January 1971; *Educ* Downe House, Sorbonne, Univ of Cambridge (pres Cambridge Union); *Partner* Alice Arnold (civil partnership 2006); *Career* freelance broadcaster and journalist; TV work incl: racing presenter BBC 1998–, rugby league, swimming and equestrian presenter BBC coverage of Olympics, Paralympics and Winter Olympics from Atlanta, Sydney, Athens and Beijing, presenter Crufts, Housecall in the Country, Trooping the Colour, Lord Mayor's Show and Britain By Bike, presenter BBC coverage of London Olympics and Channel 4 coverage of London Paralympics 2012 (Best Presenter RTS Award 2013); radio work incl presenter Ramblings (BBC Radio 4), Wimbledon (BBC 5 Live), Saturday Live (Radio 4), Broadcasting House (Radio 4) and Weekend Breakfast (BBC 5 Live); columnist Evening Standard 1998–2003, columnist The Observer 2004–07; RTS Sports Presenter of the Year 2003, Horserace Writers and Photographers Racing Journalist of the Year 2003, Sir Peter O'Sullevan Broadcaster of the Year 2004, Special Award BAFTA 2013; *Books* My Family and Other Animals (2012); *Recreations* riding, tennis, skiing, theatre, cinema, travel, golf; *Style—* Miss Clare Balding, OBE; ✉ c/o James Grant Media Management, 94 Strand on the Green, London W4 3NN (✆ 020 8742 4950, e-mail david@jamesgrant.co.uk, website www.clarebalding.co.uk)

BALDRY, Rt Hon Sir Antony Brian (Tony); kt (2012), PC (2013), DL (Oxon 2016); eldest s of Peter Edward Baldry, and Oina, *née* Paterson; *b* 10 July 1950; *Educ* Leighton Park Sch Reading, Univ of Sussex (MA, LLB); *m* 1, 1979 (m dis 1996), Catherine Elizabeth, 2 da of Capt James Weir, RN (ret), of Chagford, Devon; 1 s, 1 da; m 2, 2001, Pippa Isbell, da of Lt-Col R Payne; *Career* barr and publisher; called to the Bar Lincoln's Inn 1975; currently head of chambers 1 Essex Court Temple; dir: New Opportunity Press 1975–90, Newpoint Publishing Group 1983–90; PA to Mrs Thatcher in Oct 1974 election, in ldr of oppn's office Mar-Oct 1975, memb Carlton Club Political Ctee, MP (Cons) Banbury 1983–2015 (Parly candidate (Cons) Thurrock 1979); memb Parly Select Ctee on Employment 1983–85, PPS to Min of State for Foreign and Cwlth Affrs 1985–87, PPS to Lord Privy Seal and Ldr of the House 1987–89, PPS to Sec of State for Energy 1989–90, Parly under sec of state Dept of Energy 1990, Parly under sec of state DOE 1990–94, Parly under sec of state FCO 1994–95, min of state MAFF 1995–97, memb Parly Select Ctee on Trade and Industry 1997–2000, memb Parly Select Ctee on Standards and Privileges 2001, chm Parly Select Ctee on Int Devpt 2001–05; chm Parly Mainstream Gp 1997–2000; Robert Schuman Silver medal (Stiftung FVS Hamburg) for contribs to Euro politics 1978; dep chm: Woburn Energy Resources plc, Westminster Gp plc 2016–; chm: Woburn Energy (formerly Black Rock Oil & Gas plc 2005–15), Blue Dragon Resources Ltd 2015–, Anglo-Kazakh TransAsian Pipeline Corporation plc 2015–; govr Cwlth Inst 1997–2005; ex-officio memb Gen Synod 2010–15, second church estates cmmr 2010–15, chm Church Bldgs Cncl 2015–, memb Gen Synod 2010–15, chair of tstees St Ethelburga's Centre for Peace and Reconciliation 2015–; lay canon Christ Church Cathedral Oxford; visiting fell St Antony's Coll Oxford 1998–99; Liveryman: Worshipful Co of Merchant Taylors, Worshipful Co of Stationers & Newspaper Makers; FCIOB, FCIPD, FCIArb, FInstD, FRSA; *Recreations* walking, beagling; *Clubs* Carlton, Farmers, Garrick, Brass Monkey, United and Cecil; *Style—* The Rt Hon Canon Sir Tony Baldry, DL

BALDRY, Lorraine Ingrid; OBE (2012); *Career* md Prudential Corp Pensions, chief operating offr Prudential Portfolio Mangrs (PPM), md PPM Property and dir info and business systems PPM Property Prudential Corp 1990–98, md Regus plc 1999–2000, sr advsr Investment Banking Div Property Gp Morgan Stanley 2000–02, chief exec Chesterton Int plc 2002–03; chm: Inventa Ptnrs Ltd 2002–, Tri-Air Devpt Ltd 2006–, London & Continental Railways Ltd 2011–, Schroder Real Estate Investment Tst (SREIT) 2014–; non-exec dir St Ives plc 2000–06, sr ind dir DTZ Hldgs plc 2010–11, sr ind dir and chm Remuneration Ctee Circle Hldgs plc 2011–, ind non-exec dir Thames Water Utilities 2014–; chm: Central London Partnership 2001–09, London Thames Gateway Devpt Corp 2004–08; memb Bd Olympic Delivery Authy 2006–14 (chm Planning Ctee); govr Univ of the Arts London 2008–; past pres Br Property Fedn; hon memb RICS; *Recreations* the arts, dog walking, good eating; *Style—* Mrs Lorraine Baldry, OBE; ✉ Inventa Partners Ltd, Golden Cross House, 8, Duncannon Street, Strand, London WC2N 4JF

BALDWIN, Clarissa Mary; CBE (2015, OBE 2005); da of Rev Basil Alderson Watson, OBE, RN (d 2004), of Greenwich, and Janet Isabel, *née* Roderick; *b* 9 February 1949; *Educ* St Agnes & St Michael's Sch E Grinstead, Dartmouth RN Coll; *m* 18 March 1977, Roger Douglas Baldwin, s of Douglas Baldwin; 1 s (James Douglas Alderson b 18 Dec 1980); *Career* fashion model 1968–70, positions with Cambridge Evening News and Evening Standard, chief exec Dogs Trust 1986–2014 (author slogan: A dog is for life....not just for Christmas); vice-pres Assoc of Dogs and Cats Homes, life vice-pres Hearing Dogs for Deaf People; chm: Greyhound Forum, Welfare Ctee Pet Plan Charitable Tst; Tstee: Dog Trust, Mission Rabies; *Recreations* tennis, travel, theatre, ballet; *Clubs* Kennel Club (hon memb); *Style—* Mrs Clarissa Baldwin, CBE; ✉ 4 Cloudesley Square, London N1 0HT (✆ 020 7278 2306, e-mail clarissabaldwin1@gmail.com)

BALDWIN, Dan Peter; s of Peter Baldwin (d 1986), and Sandra, *née* Santi; *b* 3 October 1975, Redbridge; *Educ* Trinity Catholic HS Woodford Green, Univ of the West of England; *m* 4 Aug 2007, Holly Willoughby, *qv*; 1 s (Harry James b 11 May 2009), 1 da (Belle b 14 April 2011); *Career* MTV UK & Ireland: series prodr (launched and exec prodr Total Request) 2002–03, head of prodn and planning 2003–04; series prodr Ministry of Mayhem (ITV) 2004–06, fndr Fused Prodns 2006–08; FremantleMedia UK: joined 2008, head of comedy entertainment then md Talkback 2010–; *Recreations* music, tennis, football; *Style—* Dan Baldwin, Esq; ✉ Talkback, 1 Stephen Street, London W1T 1AL (e-mail dan.baldwin@talkbalk.co.uk, Twitter @danpbaldwin)

BALDWIN, Harriett Mary Morison; MP; *née* Eggleston; da of Mr Anthony Eggleston, OBE, and Mrs Anthony Eggleston (d 2009); *b* 2 May 1960, Watford, Herts; *Educ* Marlborough, Univ of Oxford, McGill Univ Montreal (MBA); *m* 1; 1 s; m 2, Jim Baldwin; 2 step-da; *Career* MP (Cons) Worcs W 2010–; *Clubs* Carlton; *Style—* Mrs Harriett Baldwin, MP; ✉ House of Commons, London SW1A 0AA (e-mail harriett.baldwin.mp@parliament.uk, website www.harriettbaldwin.com, Twitter @hbaldwinmp)

BALDWIN, Prof Sir Jack Edward; kt (1997); *b* 8 August 1938; *Educ* Brighton GS, Lewes GS, Imperial Coll London (BSc, PhD); *Career* lectr Imperial Coll of Science and Technol London 1966–67 (asst lectr 1963–66), assoc prof of chemistry Pennsylvania State Univ 1969–70 (asst prof of chemistry 1967–69), prof of chemistry MIT 1971–78 (assoc prof of chemistry 1970–71), Daniell prof of chemistry King's Coll London 1972; Univ of Oxford 1978–: Waynflete prof of chemistry, fell Magdalen Coll Oxford, head Dyson Perrins Laboratory; memb BBSRC 1994–; author of numerous articles and papers in academic jls; corresponding memb Academia Scientiarum Gottingensis Göttingen 1988; Corday Morgan Medal and Prize Chemical Soc 1975, Medal and Prize for Synthetic Organic Chemistry RSC 1980, Paul Karrer Medal and Prize Univ of Zürich 1984, Medal and Prize for Natural Product Chemistry RSC 1984, Hugo Muller Medal RSC 1987, Max Tischler Award Harvard Univ 1987, Dr Paul Janssen Prize for Creativity in Organic Synthesis Belgium 1988, Davy Medal Royal Soc 1994; hon foreign memb American Acad of Arts and Sciences 1994; Hon DSc: Univ of Warwick 1988, Univ of Strathclyde 1989; FRS 1978; *Style—* Prof Sir Jack Baldwin, FRS; ✉ Chemistry Research Laboratory, University of Oxford, Mansfield Road, Oxford OX1 3TA (✆ 01865 275671)

BALDWIN, Dr John Paul; QC (1991); s of Frank Baldwin (d 2002), and Marjorie Baldwin (d 1966); *b* 15 August 1947; *Educ* Nelson GS, Univ of Leeds (BSc), St John's Coll Oxford (DPhil), Inns of Ct Sch of Law; *m* 19 Sept 1981, Julie, da of Merle Gowan, of N Adelaide, Aust; 2 da (Melissa Jay b 20 Sept 1982, Sarah Elizabeth b 21 March 1985); *Career* res fell Univ of Oxford 1972–75, barrister 1977, bencher Gray's Inn 2000, recorder 2004, dep judge of the High Court 2008, dep judge of Patent Court 2008; *Books* Patent Law of Europe and UK (jt ed, 1983), numerous scientific publications; *Recreations* tennis, gardening, theatre; *Clubs* Queen's, Campden Hill Lawn Tennis; *Style—* Mr John Baldwin, QC; ✉ 8 New Square, Lincoln's Inn, London WC2A 3QP (✆ 020 7405 4321, fax 020 7405 9955, e-mail clerks@newsquare.co.uk)

BALDWIN, Mark Phillip; OBE (2015); s of Ronald William Baldwin (d 2006), of New Zealand, and Rose Thersa Evans (d 1969), of Fiji; *b* 16 January 1954; *Educ* St Kentigerns Coll NZ, Pakuranga Coll NZ, Suva GS Fiji, Elam Sch of Fine Arts, Univ of Auckland NZ; *Career* choreographer; dancer with: Limbs Dance Co NZ (also fndr), NZ Ballet, Australian Dance Theatre, Rambert 1979 and 1982–92; major roles incl: Pierot in Glen Etley's Pierot Lunaire, Richard Alston's Sonda Lake; fndr The Mark Baldwin Dance Co 1993–2001; choreographer in res Sadlers Wells 1994–, res artist The Place 1995–96, choreographer in res Scottish Ballet 1996–, artistic dir Rambert 2002–; with Rambert: Island to Island 1991, Gone 1992, Spirit 1994, Banter Banter 1994, Constant Speed 2005, Eternal Light 2008, The Comedy of Change 2009, Seven for a Secret Never to be Told 2011, What Wild Ecstasy 2012, The Strange Charm of Mother Nature 2014, Dark Arteries 2015, The Creation 2016; Scottish Ballet: Hyden Pieces 1995, A Fond Kiss 1996, More Poulenc 1996; other works choreographed incl: Dance Umbrella (Mark Baldwin Dance Co) 1995–98, Labyrinth by Hans Werner Henze's (for Staatsoper Berlin) 1997, The Legend of Joseph by Richard Strauss (for Staatsoper Berlin) 1998, The Demon by Paul Hindemith (for Staatsoper Berlin) 1998, Towards Poetry (for the Royal Ballet) 1999, Ihi Frenzy (for Royal NZ Ballet) 2001, The Bird Sings with its Fingers 2001, The Wedding (for Royal NZ Ballet) 2006, M is for Man (for Dansgroep Amsterdam) 2007, The Rite of Spring (for Rambert Sch of Ballet and Contemporary Dance) 2013, Not a Cloud in the Sky (for Ballet des Saarlandischen Staatstheaters) 2014, Inala 2014; dance films: Echo 1996, Pointe Blank 2000, Frankenstein 2002; *Awards* incl: Time Out Dance Award, Special Judges' Prize for dance film Video Danse Grand Prix 1996, South Bank Show Award 2001, Theatrical Mgmnt Assoc (TMA) Award for Achievement in Dance 2006, Olivier Award for an Outstanding Year of New Work (awarded to Rambert) 2010; *Recreations* music, contemporary art, film, theatre; *Style—* Mark Baldwin, Esq, OBE

BALDWIN, Michael; s of Harold Jesse Baldwin (d 1990), of Meopham, Kent, and Elizabeth Amy Crittenden (d 1968); *b* 1930, Gravesend, Kent; *Educ* Gravesend GS for Boys, St Edmund Hall Oxford (open scholar); *m* 1, 1954 (m dis 1979), Jean Margaret Bruce; 2 s (Matthew James b 1959, Adam Richard b 1961); m 2, 1987, Gillian Beale; 1 s (Joel St John b 1988); *Career* author; Nat Serv Rifle Bde, Educn Corps and Airborne Forces 1949–50, cmmnd RA 1952, 415 Coast Regt RA (TA) 1950–55, 263 Light Regt RA (TA) 1955–60; lectr St Paul's Coll Cheltenham 1955–56, asst master St Clement Danes GS 1956–59, successively lectr, sr lectr, princ lectr, head of English and Drama Dept Whitelands Coll Putney 1959–78, head of English and drama elect Roehampton Inst 1978; Arvon Fndn: vice-chm 1972–90, chm Lumb Bank 1978–88; Rediffusion Prize 1970, honourable mention Japan Awards 1970, Cholmondeley Prize for Poetry 1983; FRSL 1984; *Publications* poetry: Death on a Live Wire (1962), How Chas Egget Lost his Way in a Creation Myth (1967), Hob (1972), The Buried God (1973), Snook (1980), King Horn (1983); autobiography: Grandad with Snails (1960), In Step with a Goat (1962); fiction: A World of Men (1962), Miraclejack (1963), Sebastian and Other Voices (short stories, 1966), The Great Cham (1967), Underneath and Other Situations (short stories, 1968), There's a War On (1970), The Cellar (1972), The Gamecock (1980), Exit Wounds (1988), Holofernes (1989), Ratgame (1991), The Rape of Oc (1993), The First Mrs Wordsworth (1996), Dark Lady (1998); pedagogic: Poems by Children, 1950–1961 (1962), Billy the Kid (anthology, 1963), The Way to Write Poetry (1982), The River and the Downs (topography, 1983), The Way to Write Short Stories (1986); *Recreations* hill walking on British mountains, motoring in Europe; *Clubs* Athenaeum; *Style—* Michael Baldwin; ✉ c/o PFD, Drury House, 34–43 Russell Street, London WC2B 5HA (✆ 020 7344 1000, fax 020 7836 9539)

BALDWIN, Nicholas Peter (Nick); s of Desmond Stanley Frederick Baldwin, of Guildford, and Beatrix Marie, *née* Walker; *b* 17 December 1952; *Educ* City Univ (BSc), Birkbeck Coll London (MSc); *m* Adrienne Plunkett; 1 da (Lauren b 1 Nov 1987), 1 s (Patrick b 15 Aug 1991); *Career* student apprentice Met Water Bd 1971–74, various positions Thames Water Authy 1974–80, various positions CEGB 1980–89; PowerGen: econ studies mangr 1989–90, business planning mangr 1990–92, head of strategic planning 1992–94, dir of strategy 1994–95, dir of generation 1995–96, md UK electricity prodn 1996–98, exec dir UK operations 1998–2001, chief exec 2001–02; non-exec dir: Nuclear Decommissioning Authy 2004–11, Scottish & Southern Energy plc 2006–11; chm Office for Nuclear Regulation 2011–; chair Public Weather Serv Customer Gp 2007–13; chm: Worcester Community Housing 2002–08, Ambitious About Autism (formerly Treehouse Tst) 2008–14; non-exec dir Sanctuary Housing 2008–09 (chm 2009–14); CEng 1979, MInstE 1982, FIMechE 1996 (MIMechE 1979), FRSA 1998, chartered dir (CDir) 2007; *Recreations* walking, cycling, jazz, long distance walking; *Clubs* Worcester CC; *Style—* Nick Baldwin, Esq

BALDWIN OF BEWDLEY, 4 Earl (UK 1937); Edward Alfred Alexander Baldwin; also Viscount Corvedale (UK 1937); s of 3 Earl (d 1976, 2 s of 1 Earl, otherwise Stanley Baldwin, thrice PM and 1 cous of Rudyard Kipling); *b* 3 January 1938; *Educ* Eton, Trinity Coll Cambridge (MA, PGCE); *m* 1970, Sarah MacMurray (d 2001), da of Evan James, of Upwood Park, Abingdon, Oxon (and sis of Countess of Selborne); 3 s (Benedict Alexander Stanley, Viscount Corvedale b 1973, Hon James Conrad b 1976, Hon Mark Thomas Maitland b 1980); *Heir* s, Viscount Corvedale; *Career* school teacher 1970–77, LEA educn offr 1978–87; sits as elected Peer in House of Lords; former memb Research Cncl for Complementary Med, chm Br Acupuncture Accreditation Bd 1990–98; jt chm Parly Gp for Integrated and Complementary Med 1992–2002, memb House of Lords Select Ctee Inquiry into Complementary and Alternative Med 1999–2000, sec Assoc Parly Food and Health Forum; *Recreations* mountains, tennis; *Clubs* MCC; *Style—* The Rt Hon The Earl Baldwin of Bewdley; ✉ 2 Scholar Place, Cumnor Hill, Oxford OX2 9RD (✆ 01865 865318)

BALE, Christian Morgan; *b* 30 January 1974, Pembrokeshire, Wales; *m* Sibi Blazic; 1 da; *Career* actor; hon memb bd of directors Ark Tst, memb bd of directors UKFilmLA; *Television* incl Heart of the Country 1986, Anastasia: The Mystery of Anna 1986, Treasure Island 1990, A Murder of Quality 1991, Mary, Mother of Jesus 1999; *Films* incl: Empire of the Sun 1987 (Best Juvenile Actor Nat Bd of Review 1988), Mio min Mio 1987, Henry V 1989, Newsies 1992, Swing Kids 1993, Little Women 1994, Prince of Jutland 1994, Pocahontas 1995, The Secret Agent 1996, The Portrait of a Lady 1996, Metroland 1997, Velvet Goldmine 1998, All the Little Animals 1998, A Midsummer Night's Dream 1999, American Psycho 2000, Shaft 2000, Captain Corelli's Mandolin 2001, Equilibrium 2001, Reign of Fire 2001, Laurel Canyon 2002, The Machinist 2004, Batman Begins 2005, The New World 2006, The Prestige 2006, 3:10 to Yuma 2007, I'm Not There 2007, The Dark Knight 2008, Terminator: Salvation 2009, Public Enemies 2009, The Fighter 2010 (Best Supporting Actor Golden Globe 2011, Outstanding Supporting Actor Screen Actors Guild Award 2011, Br Actor of the Year London Critics' Circle Award 2011, Best

Supporting Actor Acad Award 2011), The Flowers of War 2011, The Dark Knight Rises 2012, Out of the Furnace 2013, American Hustle 2013; *Style*— Christian Bale, Esq

BALE, Stephen William; s of Dennis Alfred Amer Bale (d 1981), and Ida, *née* George (d 1994); *b* 3 May 1952; *Educ* UC Cardiff (BA); *m* 14 July 1974, Fleur Elizabeth, da of late Richard John Gregory; 1 s (Owen John b 29 June 1980), 1 da (Lara Claire b 25 March 1985); *Career* Neath Guardian 1973–78 (NCTJ Proficiency Cert 1975), South Wales Evening Post Swansea 1978–80, South Wales Argus Newport 1980–83, Western Mail Cardiff 1983–86, rugby union corr The Independent 1988–96 (joined 1986), rugby corr Daily Express 1996–2014, Welsh rugby corr Sunday Times 2014–; memb: Welsh Rugby Writers' Assoc (chm 1996–97 and 2008–10), Sports Journalists' Assoc of GB, Rugby Union Writers' Club (chm 1998–2000, chm Welsh branch 2010–15); *Style*— Stephen Bale, Esq; ✉ 1 Orchard Barns, Broughton Lane, Shoreditch, Taunton, Somerset TA3 7BH (✆ 01823 251138, mobile 07768 446160, e-mail swbale951@btinternet.com)

BALEN, Paul; s of Henry Balen (d 2004), and Elswyth Balen (d 2013); *b* 25 February 1952, London; *Educ* Nottingham HS, Peterhouse Cambridge (MA); *m* 25 April 1981, Helen; 3 c; *Career* admitted slr 1977; slr specialising in medico legal cases, product liability, defamation and dispute resolution; Freeths LLP: joined as articled clerk 1975, ptnr 1980–2011, currently conslt; nat sec and memb Exec Ctee Assoc of Personal Injury Lawyers 1998–2000 (sr fell 2000), pres Nottinghamshire Law Soc 2005–06 (sec 1983–88), referral slr Action for Victims of Medical Accidents; past chief assessor Clinical Negligence Specialist Panel Law Soc, pres Notts Medico-Legal Soc 2007–08; memb: Assoc of Midlands Mediators, Trust Mediation; Nottingham Roosevelt scholar 1977, past chm of tstees Nottingham Roosevelt Scholarship Fund; past chm of govrs Nottingham HS, past pres Old Nottinghamians Soc; ADR accredited mediator; *Publications* Multi Party Actions (jtly, 1995), Clinical Negligence (2008 and 2013); contrib of several chapters to books and author of numerous articles; *Style*— Paul Balen, Esq; ✉ Freeths LLP, Cumberland Court, 80 Mount Street, Nottingham NG1 6HH (✆ 0845 050 3289, fax 0845 050 3249, e-mail paul.balen@freeths.co.uk, Twitter @paulbalen)

BALFOUR, Hon Charles George Yule; s of Eustace Arthur Goschen Balfour (d 2000), and (Dorothy Melicent) Anne, *née* Yule; bro of Earl of Balfour, *qv*; raised to the rank of an Earl's son 2004; *b* 23 April 1951; *Educ* Eton; *m* 1, 18 Sept 1978 (m dis 1985), Audrey Margaret, da of H P Hoare (d 1983), of Stourhead, Wilts; m 2, 1987, Svea Maria, da of Ernst-Friedrich Reichsgraf von Goess, of Carinthia, Austria; 1 da (Eleanor Cecilly Isabelle b 4 April 1989), 1 s (George Eustace Charles b 8 Dec 1990); *Career* Hoare Govett 1971–73, Hill Samuel 1973–76, Dillon Read 1976–79, exec dir Banque Paribas London 1979–91, dir Cragnotti and Partners Capital Investment (UK) Ltd 1991–92, md Nasdaq International 1993–2004, sr vice-pres: The Nasdaq Stock Market Inc 1993–2003, Fleming Family Ptnrs 2004–, chm Continental Petroleum Ltd 2005–; dir: Bound Oak Properties Ltd 2005–, Wharf Land Investments Ltd 2006–; memb Supervisory Bd MCC Global NV 2006–07; memb Queen's Body Guard for Scotland (Royal Co of Archers); *Recreations* gardening, shooting, fishing, bee-keeping; *Clubs* White's, Puffins; *Style*— The Hon Charles Balfour; ✉ 15 Oakley Street, London SW3;

BALFOUR, Doug John; s of Gwyn Balfour, of Bury St Edmunds, and Joy Balfour, of London; *b* 12 June 1958; *Educ* Univ of Southampton (MSc), Cranfield Sch of Mgmnt (MBA); *m* 1984, Anne Mary, da of Robin Watson; 1 da (Alexandra b 1988), 2 s (Jonathan b 1990, Ryan b 1993); *Career* sr exploration geologist De Beers (Kalahari desert) 1980–83, Lucas Industries (sr mgmnt conslt, materials mangr, sales and mktg mangr) 1984–89, support mangr Youth With A Mission Amsterdam 1989–92, relief dir MEDAIR Relief Agency (following Liberian Civil War) 1991–92, commercial mangr Lucas Engineering & Systems Ltd (internal mgmnt consultancy Lucas Gp) 1992–95, gen dir Tearfund (charity) 1995–2004, exec dir Integral (charity alliance) 2004–05; Geneva Global Inc (research co): int dir 2006–08, ceo and owner 2008–; *Recreations* travelling, history; *Style*— Doug Balfour; ✉ e-mail dbalfour@genevaglobal.com

BALFOUR, Dr (Elizabeth) Jean; CBE (1981), JP (Fife 1963); da of late Maj-Gen Sir James Syme Drew, KBE, CB, DSO, MC (d 1955), and late Victoria Maxwell of Munches; *b* 4 November 1927; *Educ* Univ of Edinburgh (BSc); *m* 1950, John Charles Balfour, OBE, MC, JP, DL (d 2009); 3 s; *Career* dir A J Bowen & Co Ltd, ptnr Balbirnie Home Farms and Balbirnie Dairy Farm; dir: Chieftain Industries 1983–85, Scot Dairy Trade Fedn 1983–86, Scot Agric Colls 1987–89, Loch Duart Ltd 1999–2008 (chm 1999–2006), Scottish Quality Salmon 2005–06; chm Crofling Gp SRPBA 2009–; pres Royal Scot Forestry Soc 1969–71, chm Countryside Cmmn for Scot 1972–83, A New Look at the Northern Ireland Countryside (report to govt) 1984, hon vice-pres Scot YHA 1983–, vice-pres E Scot Coll of Agric 1982–88 (govr 1958–88); memb: Fife CC 1958–70, Nature Conservancy Cncl 1973–80, Scot Economic Cncl 1978–83, Ct Univ of St Andrews 1983–87; vice-chm Scottish Wildlife Tst 1969–72 (hon vice-pres Fife and Kinross Membs Centre 1983–), memb Cncl Inst of Chartered Foresters 1984–87, chm Regnl Advsy Ctee Forestry Cmmn (E Scot) 1963–84 and (Mid Scot) 1987–2000, memb Ctee of Enquiry on Handling of Geographical Info 1987–89, memb RSE Foot and Mouth Enquiry 2001–02; chm W Sutherland Fisheries Tst 1996–99, dep chm Seafish Industry Authy 1987–90, dep chm Women's Sci Ctee Office of Sci and Technol (Cabinet Office) 1993–94; pres Scottish Arctic Club 1998–2001; memb: Forth River Purification Bd 1992–96, Scottish Office Task Force Trout Protection Orders 1998–; govr Duncan of Jordanstone Coll of Art 1992–94, tstee Royal Botanic Garden Edinburgh 1992–96, memb Cncl Scottish Landowners' Fedn 1992, chm Mid Scotland Branch and memb Cncl Timber Growers Assoc 2000–02; Order of the Falcon (Iceland) 1994; awarded Inst of Chartered Foresters Medal for services to Br forestry 1996; Hon DSc Univ of St Andrews 1977, Hon DUniv Stirling 1991; FRSA 1981, FRSE 1980, FICFor, FIBiol 1988, FRZS Scot 1983; *Recreations* hill walking, fishing, painting, exploring arctic vegetation, shooting; *Clubs* Farmers', New Edinburgh; *Style*— Dr Jean Balfour, CBE, FRSE; ✉ Kirkforthar House, Markinch, Glenrothes, Fife (✆ 01592 752233, fax 01592 610314, e-mail jean.balfour2014@btconnect.com); Scourie, by Lairg, Sutherland

BALFOUR, John Manning; s of James Richard Balfour, and Eunice Barbara, *née* Manning; *b* 2 October 1952; *Educ* Fettes, Worcester Coll Oxford (MA); *Career* ptnr: Frere Cholmeley Bischoff 1986–97 (slr 1979), Beaumont and Son 1997–2005, Clyde & Co 2005–; *Books* Air Law (contrib ed, 1988–96), European Community Air Law (1995); *Recreations* swimming, reading; *Clubs* Lansdowne; *Style*— John Balfour, Esq; ✉ Clyde & Co, The St Botolph Building, 138 Houndsditch, London EC3A 7AR (✆ 020 7876 5000, fax 020 7876 5111)

BALFOUR, Michael William (Mike); s of Alexander Balfour (d 1999), and Winifred, *née* Kerr; *b* 3 May 1949, London; *Educ* Brockenhurst GS; *m* 30 Sept 1978, Margaret; 1 da (Sarah b 28 March 1981), 1 s (James b 12 July 1983); *Career* dir Mannai Investment Co 1985–92; Fitness First Holdings Ltd: co-fndr 1992, ceo 1992–2004, opened first gym in Bournemouth 1993, co floated 1996, MBO 2003, dep chm 2004–; dir: Fitness Industry Assoc, Skills Active; Entrepreneur of the Year PLC Awards 1999, Nat Entrepreneur of the Year Award (leisure category) Ernst & Young 2000, Entrepreneur of the Year Int Health, Racquet and Sportsclub Assoc (IHRSA) 2001; Hon DBA Bournemouth Univ 2004; FCA 1972; *Recreations* golf, sailing; *Style*— Dr Mike Balfour; ✉ Fitness First, 58 Fleets Lane, Poole, Dorset BH15 3BT

BALFOUR, Robert Roxburgh; DL (Tweedale 1999); s of Alastair Norman Balfour (d 1996), and Elizabeth Eugenie, *née* Cowell (d 1997); *b* 29 June 1947; *Educ* Tabley House, Grenoble Univ (Dip), Madrid Univ (Dip); *m* 31 Jan 1973, (Camilla) Rose, da of Michael George Thomas Webster, of Hants; 1 s (Rupert Alastair b 23 April 1976), 2 da (Camilla Louise b 11 May 1979, Lara Selina b 1 June 1983); *Career* md Bell Lawrie White Financial Services Ltd 1984–93; dir: Bell Lawrie White & Co 1987–98, Stocktrade 1998–2009; chm Personal Equity Plan Managers Assoc 1995–98; PEP & ISA Managers Assoc: chm 1998–2000, non-exec dir 2000–02; memb: Red Deer Cmmn 1984–92, Firearms Consultative Ctee 1989–90, Queen's Body Guard for Scotland (Royal Co of Archers) 1977–; IBRC 1980–97; FInstD 1985; *Recreations* shooting, photography; *Clubs* New (Edinburgh); *Style*— Robert Balfour, Esq, DL; ✉ Wester Dawyck, Stobo, Peeblesshire EH45 9JU (✆ 01721 760226)

BALFOUR, 5 Earl of (UK 1922); Roderick Francis Arthur Balfour; s of Eustace Arthur Goschen Balfour (d 2000), and Anne, *née* Yule; suc kinsman, 4 Earl 2003; *b* 9 December 1948; *Educ* Eton, London Business Sch (Sr Exec Program); *m* 14 July 1971, Lady Tessa Fitzalan Howard, da of 17 Duke of Norfolk (d 2002); 4 da (Willa b 1973, Kinvara b 1975, Maria b 1977, Candida b 1984); *Career* ptnr Grieveson Grant and Co Stockbrokers 1972–81, investment dir Jessel Toynbee and Co 1981–83, dir UK investment Union Discount Co of London plc 1983–90, founder dir Winterflood Securities 1988–90, dir Rothschild Tst Gp 1990–2005, fndr/dir Virtus Tst Gp 2005–; dir: China Pathway Logistics NV, Agua Terra plc; past dir: Bateman Engrg NV, Nikanor plc; memb City of London Ctee STEP; Freeman City of London 1977, Liveryman Worshipful Co of Clothworkers 1986; *Recreations* gardening, music, painting, tennis, cricket, skiing, water skiing; *Clubs* White's, Eton Ramblers, Old Etonian Racquets and Tennis, I Zingari, Sussex; *Style*— The Rt Hon the Earl of Balfour; ✉ Burpham Lodge, Burpham, Arundel, W Sussex BN18 9RR; 1 Sloane Court East, London SW3 4TQ (e-mail eofbprivate@aol.com)

BALFOUR OF BURLEIGH, Lady; (Dr Janet Morgan); CBE (2008); da of Frank Morgan, and Shiela, *née* Sadler; *b* 5 December 1945; *Educ* Newbury Co Girls GS, St Hugh's Coll Oxford (MA), Nuffield Coll Oxford (DPhil), Univ of Sussex (MA), Harvard Univ (Kennedy Meml scholar); *m* 1993, 8 Lord Balfour of Burleigh, *qv*; *Career* res fell Wolfson Coll Oxford and res offr Univ of Essex 1971–72, res fell Nuffield Coll Oxford 1972–74, lectr in politics Exeter Coll Oxford 1974–76, dir of studies St Hugh's Coll Oxford 1975–76 and lectr in politics 1976–78, visiting fell All Souls Coll Oxford 1983; memb Central Policy Review Staff Cabinet Office 1978–81, dir Satellite Television Ltd 1981–83, special advsr to Dir-Gen BBC 1983–86, advsr to Bd Granada Group plc 1986–89, vice-pres Videotext Industry Assoc 1985–91; dir Hulton Deutsch Collection 1988–89; non-exec dir: Cable & Wireless plc 1988–2004, WH Smith Group plc 1989–95, Midlands Electricity plc 1990–96, Pitney Bowes plc 1991–92, Scottish American Investment Tst plc 1991–2008, Scottish Life plc 1995–2001, Scottish Oriental Smaller Companies Tst plc 1995–, Nuclear Liabilities Fund (formerly Nuclear Generation Decommissioning Fund Ltd) 1996–14 (chm 2004–14), NMT Gp plc 1997–2004, BPB plc 2000–05, Stagecoach plc 2000–10, Murray Int Investment Tst plc 2003–16, Close Enterprise VCT (now Albion Enterprise VCT) 2007–10; chm: Dorothy Burns Charity, Readiscovery (Scotland's Nat Book Campaign) 1994–96, Scottish Cultural Resources Access Network, Scottish Museum of the Year Award, Cable & Wireless Flexible Resource Ltd, Nuclear Liabilites Financing Assurance Bd 2008–15, Espirito Ltd 2012–14; tstee: American Sch in London 1985–88, Fairground Heritage Tst 1987–91, Cyclotron Tst 1988–89, Carnegie Trust for the Univs of Scotland 1994–2016, Nat Library of Scotland 2002–11, Trusthouse Charitable Fndn 2006–; memb: Lord Chllr's Advsy Cncl on Public Records 1982–86, Editorial Bd Political Quarterly, Bd Br Cncl 1989–99, Ancient Monuments Bd for Scotland 1990–97, Scottish Hosp Endowments Research Tst 1992–2000; Hon LLB Univ of Strathclyde, Hon DLitt Napier Univ; FSA Scot, FRSE, memb American Philosophical Soc; Chevalier de l'Ordre Grand-Ducal de la Couronne de Chêne (Luxembourg) 2014; *Books* The House of Lords and the Labour Government 1964–70 (1975), Reinforcing Parliament (1976), The Diaries of a Cabinet Minister 1964–70 by Richard Crossman 3 Vols (ed, 1975, 1976, 1977), Backbench Diaries 1951–63 by Richard Crossman (ed, 1980), The Future of Broadcasting (ed with Richard Hoggart, 1982), Agatha Christie: A Biography (1984), Edwina Mountbatten: A Life of her Own (1991), The Secrets of rue St Roch (2004); *Recreations* music of Handel and J S Bach, sea-bathing, ice skating out of doors, gardens, pruning; *Clubs* New, St Rule; *Style*— Lady Balfour of Burleigh, professionally known as Dr Janet Morgan, CBE

BALFOUR OF BURLEIGH, Jennifer, Lady; Jennifer Ellis; da of E S Manasseh (d 1962), of London, and Phyllis Annette, *née* Barnard (d 1970); *b* 27 October 1930; *Educ* St Paul's Girls' Sch, Lady Margaret Hall Oxford; *m* 1, 12 Dec 1951 (m dis 1968), John Edward Jocelyn Brittain-Catlin (d 1987), s of Sir George Edward Gordon Catlin (d 1979), and his 1 w, Vera Brittain; 3 s (Daniel b 1953, Timothy b 1961, William b 1966); m 2, 30 Oct 1971 (m dis 1993), 8 Lord Balfour of Burleigh, *qv*; 2 da (Hon Victoria b 1973, Hon Ishbel b 1976); *Career* PR exec: Butter Information Cncl 1953–55, Patrick Dolan & Assoc 1955–56; sr PR exec Erwin Wasey Ruthrauff & Ryan 1956–61; conslt PR advsr to various companies incl Acrilan, Hoover, Vono, Carnation Milk, Littlewoods Stores, Scottish Crafts Centre 1961–71; dir Jamaica Street Ltd property developers 1980–97, mangr London & Scottish Property Services 1985–2010; dir: Scottish Opera 1990–96, ECAT Ltd (Edinburgh Contemporary Arts Tst) 1989–97, Boxcar Films plc (non-exec) 1994–97; chm Deal Summer Music Festival 1999–2002; memb Bd Link Housing Assoc 1974–97 (former chm Central Region Ctee), life pres Ochil View Housing Assoc (founding chm 1988–93); memb: Visiting Ctee HM Instn Glenochil 1980–85, CAB Alloa 1988–92, Exec Ctee Clackmannan Social & Liberal Democrats until 1993, Cncl National Tst for Scotland 1991–96 (memb Fin Ctee 1995–97), Bd The Grassmarket Project 1994–2001 (patron 2001–), Bd Children's Music Fndn Scotland 1994–97; writer of numerous booklets, pamphlets, newspaper and magazine articles; *Recreations* music, theatre; *Style*—Jennifer, Lady Balfour of Burleigh; ✉ c/o 47 Grange Road, Broadstairs, Kent CT10 3ER

BALFOUR OF BURLEIGH, 8 (*de facto* and 12 but for the Attainder) Lord (S 1607); Robert Bruce; er s of 7 Lord Balfour of Burleigh (11 but for the Attainder, d 1967); *b* 6 January 1927; *Educ* Westminster; *m* 1, 30 Oct 1971 (m dis 1993), Jennifer, Lady Balfour of Burleigh, *qv*, da of E S Manasseh (d 1962), and former w of John Edward Jocelyn Brittain-Catlin; 2 da (Hon Victoria (Hon Mrs Bruce-Winkler) b 7 May 1973, Hon Ishbel b 28 Sept 1976); m 2, 29 Aug 1993, Dr Janet P Morgan, *qv*, da of Frank Morgan; *Heir* (hp) da, Hon Victoria Bruce-Winkler; *Career* served: 2 Herefords Bn Home Gd 1944–45, RN 1945–48; foreman and supt English Electric Co Ltd Stafford and Liverpool 1952–57; gen mangr: English Electric Co India Ltd 1957–64, English Electric Netherton Works 1964–66, D Napier & Son Ltd 1966–68; dir: Bank of Scotland 1968–91 (dep govr 1977–91), Scottish Investment Trust plc 1971–97, Tarmac plc 1981–90, William Lawson Distillers Ltd 1984–97, UAPT Infolink plc 1991–94; chm: Scottish Arts Cncl 1971–80, Viking Oil Ltd 1971–80, Fedn of Scottish Bank Employers 1977–86, Nat Book League Scotland 1981–86, Edinburgh Book Festival 1982–87 (dir 1982–97), The Turing Inst 1983–92, United Artists (Communications) Scotland Ltd (formerly Cablevision (Scotland) plc) 1983–96, Capella Nova 1988–2009, Advsy Bd Robert Gordon Univ Heritage Inst 1989–2002, Canongate Press plc 1991–93; memb: Forestry Cmmn 1971–74, Cncl ABSA 1976–94 (chm Scot Ctee 1990–94), BR (Scottish) Bd 1982–93; treas: Royal Scottish Corp 1967–2005, Royal Soc of Edinburgh 1989–94; tstee: Radcliffe Tst 1974–2014, John Muir Tst 1989–96, Bletchley Park Tst 1999–2009 (vice-pres 2009–); Vice Lord-Lt Clackmannan 1996–2001; chllr Univ of Stirling 1988–98; Hon DUniv Stirling 1988, Hon DLitt Robert Gordon Univ 1995; CEng, FIEE, Hon FRIAS 1982, FRSE 1986; Chevalier de l'Ordre Grand-Ducal de la Couronne de Chêne (Luxembourg) 2014, Officier Légion d'Honneur; *Recreations* music, climbing, woodwork; *Style*— The Rt Hon the Lord Balfour of Burleigh, CEng, FIEE, FRSE; ✉ Brucefield, Clackmannan FK10 3QF (✆ 01259 730228)

BALL, Anthony George (Tony); MBE (1986); s of Harry Clifford Ball, of Bridgwater, Somerset, and Mary Irene Ball; *b* 14 November 1934; *Educ* Bridgwater GS, Bromsgrove Coll of FE; *m* 1, 1957 (m dis 1997), Ruth, da of Ivor Parry Davies (d 1976), of Mountain

Ash, S Wales; 2 s (Kevin, Michael, *qv*), 1 da (Katherine); m 2, 2000, Jan Kennedy; *Career* indentured engrg apprentice Austin Motor Co 1951, responsible for launch of Mini 1959, UK sales mangr Austin Motor Co 1962–66, sales and mktg exec BMC 1966–67, chm Barlow Rand UK Motor Group 1967–78 (md Barlow Rand Ford South Africa 1971–73 and Barlow Rand Euro Ops 1973–78), chm and md British Leyland Int and Nuffield Press 1978–80, chm and md British Leyland Europe and Overseas 1979–82 (dir British Leyland Cars, British Leyland International, Rover Gp, Austin Morris, Jaguar Cars, Jaguar Rover Triumph Inc (USA) and BL overseas subsids), world sales chief BL Cars 1979–81 (responsible for BL Buy British campaign and launch of Austin Metro 1980), chief exec Henlys plc 1981–83, fndr Tony Ball Associates plc (mktg, product launch and event production agency) 1983–2013; dep chm: Lumley Insurance Ltd 1983–95, Lumley Warranty Services Ltd 1983–95; dir: Customer Concern Ltd 1986–92, Jetmaster Int 1989–97, Billy Marsh Associates Ltd (theatre agency) 1992–2015, Royal Carlton Hotel Blackpool 1998–2007 (Blackpool's Hotel of the Year 2002–03 and 2003–04); mktg advsr to: Sec of State for Agric and Food from Britain 1982, Sec of State for Energy 1983–87, Sec of State for Wales 1987–91; responsible for producing UK dealer launch of Vauxhall Astra for General Motors; launches and special events for: Br Motor Corp (BMC), Rover, Land Rover, Jaguar, MG, Mercedes-Benz, Fiat, Bedford Trucks, Mazda, Proton, Lada, Leyland DAF, LDV, Daihatsu, Optare Buses, AWD, GM Europe, Pioneer Electronics UK, Gillette Europe; responsible for prodn and promotion of SMMT Br International Motor Show 1986–96; mktg advsr to relaunch of London Zoo; creator and producer: Rugby World Cup opening and closing ceremonies 1991 (England) and 1999 (Wales), Lloyds Private Banking Playwright of the Year Award 1995–99, opening and closing ceremonies at Wembley Stadium of European Football Championships Euro '96, FA Cup Finals 1996–2000, RFU 125th Anniversary Twickenham 1996 and 6 Nations Championships 1996–99, Scottish Motor Show 1997, 1999 and 2001, special events Ferodo Centenary 1997, opening ceremony 6 Nations Rugby Championship for RFU Francais at Stade de France Paris 1998, opening ceremony Cricket World Cup 1999; responsible for production of British Motor Industry Centenary Year 1996 for SMMT; advance planning advsr Cwlth Games ceremonies 2002; contrib FA presentation for England's bid to host World Cup 2006; broadcaster, writer, lectr and after-dinner speaker, celebrity after dinner speaker P&O Cruises 2008–15; Meml Lecture Univ of Birmingham 1982, various TV and radio documentaries, prodr ITV documentary The Birth of Rugby 1991, panellist BBC Any Questions; pres Austin Ex-Apprentices Assoc 2006–15, chm Fellowship of the Motor Industry 2007–11 (pres 2011–15); patron Wordsworth Tst 2005–; winner Benedictine Awards Business After Dinner Speaker of the Year 1992–93; Freeman City of London 1980; govr Bromsgrove Coll of FE 1982–90; Liveryman: Worshipful Co of Coach Makers and Coach Harness Makers 1980, Worshipful Co of Carmen 1983; hon memb City & Guilds of London 1982, Prince Philip Medal for Mktg Achievement and Servs to Br Motor Industry 1984, IMI Lifetime Outstanding Personal Achievement Award for Services to the Motor Industry 2016; FIMI 1980, FCIM 1981, FCGI 1999; *Books* Metro – The Book of the Car (contrib), A Marketing Study of the Welsh Craft Industry (Govt report, 1988), Tales Out of School – Early Misdeeds of the Famous (contrib), Making Better Business Presentations (contrib), Men and Motors of The Austin (contrib); *Recreations* military history, theatre, after-dinner speaking, sharing good humour; *Clubs* Lord's Taverners; *Style*— Tony Ball, Esq, MBE; ✉ Roe Lodge, Sowerby Row, Carlisle, Cumbria CA4 0QH; 19 Grove End Gardens, Grove End Road, St John's Wood, London NW8 9LL (e-mail tonyball123@icloud.com, website www.tonyball.co.uk)

BALL, David Martin James; s of late Rev Thomas William Ball, of Perth, W Aust, and late Anne, *née* Rice; *b* 29 September 1943; *Educ* Annadale GS, Lisburn Inst of Technol, Belfast Metropolitan Univ (formerly Belfast Coll of Arts and Tech) (Dip Civil Engrg); *m* 1, 1969 (m dis 1985); 2 da (Heidi b 5 Oct 1974, Joanna b 14 Aug 1977); m 2, 1986, Jacqueline Bernadette Margaret Mary, da of late Maj Fredrick Jocelyn Clarke, and late Anne, *née* Mitchell Clarke, of Weybridge, Surrey; 1 da (Victoria Anne Helene b 20 Nov 1989); *Career* trainee civil engr Sir William Halcrow & Ptnrs 1959–1963, civil engr Middle Level Cmmrs March Cambridge 1963–66, technical mangr A L Curtis (ONX) Ltd Chatteris Cambridge 1966–70, chm David Ball Gp Ltd Cambridge 1970–, dir and chm David Ball Ireland Ltd Cork Ireland 1982–, chm David Ball Middle East Ltd 1998–; expert witness; chm: Cambridge Philharmonic Soc 1986, Q 103 FM (local commercial radio) 1988, Cambridge Structures Ltd 1995–, Concrete Bridge Devpt Gp 2007–; dir: Cambridge and Dist C of C Industry 1997– (pres 1981–83), Main Bd Gtr Cambridge Partnership Ltd 2005–; chm Cambridge Work Relations Gp; founding dir Cambridge Cleantech Ltd 2012–, memb Ctee Green Cements Accelerated Technol Implementation Team (GCAIT) 2013–; chm PCC, memb Synod, dir Ely Diocesan Bd of Fin Ltd 1991–, lay minister Diocese of St Edmundsbury and Ipswich and Ely 1994–; tstee Pye Fndn, founding govr Anglia Ruskin Univ 1990–, governing Cncl memb and fell Westcott House Coll Univ of Cambridge 2014–; pres Concrete Soc (dir and memb Cncl 2006–), memb of two technical ctees Br Standards Instn, memb American Concrete Inst (ACI); advsr: Royal Ct of Engrs Oman 2012, Bahrain Soc of Engrs 2012–; FCMI 1981, FRSA 1985, hon fell Chartered Inst of Concrete Technol 2015; *Publications* Ultra-low Permeability Concrete, Gypsum, Lime & Building Products (1998), Selecting Aggregates for Maximum Packing Density (in Concrete Journal, 1998), New Ultra-Low Permeable Concrete (2000), Nanocemology – The Key to the Future (2005), Inhibiting Corrosion Mechanisms in Concrete Structures (2006), Sustainable Concrete, The Designer's New Imperative (2007), The Beauty of No-Cement Concrete (2012); *Recreations* gardening, tennis, walking, arts, cinema, fashion, music, reading, travel; *Clubs* Lansdowne; *Style*— David Ball, Esq; ✉ Freckenham House, Freckenham, Suffolk IP28 8HX (☎ 01638 720975, e-mail dmjball@gmail.com); David Ball Group Ltd, Bourn Airfield, Cambridge CB23 3TQ (☎ 01954 780687, mobile 07801 416191, e-mail chairman@davidballgroup.com)

BALL, Prof Sir John Macleod; kt (2006); *b* 19 May 1948; *Educ* Mill Hill Sch, St John's Coll Cambridge (open exhibitioner, BA), Univ of Sussex (DPhil); *m* Sedhar; 3 c (Kesang, Tenzin, Palden); *Career* SRC postdoctoral res fell Brown Univ RI 1972–74; Heriot-Watt Univ: joined Dept of Mathematics 1972, lectr in mathematics 1974–78, reader in mathematics 1978–82, prof of applied analysis 1982–96; Sedleian prof of natural philosophy Mathematical Inst Univ of Oxford 1996–; visiting prof Dept of Mathematics Univ of Calif Berkeley 1979–80, sr fell SERC 1980–85, visiting prof Laboratoire d'Analyse Numérique Université Pierre et Marie Curie Paris 1987–88 and 1994, Ordway visiting prof Univ of Minnesota 1990, visiting prof Inst for Advanced Study Princeton 1993–94 and 2002–03, visiting prof Université Montpellier II 2003; pres: London Mathematical Soc 1996–98, Int Mathematical Union 2003–06; delg OUP 1998–2008; memb: EPSRC 1994–99, Conseil Scientifique CNRS 2010–14, Conseil Scientifique EDF 2010–14, Exec Bd ICSU 2011–; chair Scientific Steering Ctee Isaac Newton Inst 2006–14; memb editorial bds various mathematical and scientific jls and book series, author of numerous mathematical and scientific pubns; Whittaker Prize Edinburgh Mathematical Soc 1981, jr Whitehead Prize London Mathematical Soc 1982, Keith Prize RSE 1990, Naylor Prize London Mathematical Soc 1995, von Karman Prize 1999, Royal Medal RSE 2006, Sylvester Medal Royal Soc 2009, John von Neumann Lecture and Prize Soc for Industrial and Applied Mathematics 2012; foreign memb: French Acad of Sciences 2000, Istituto Lombardo 2005, Norwegian Acad of Science and Letters 2007; hon fell St John's Coll Cambridge 2005; Hon DSc: EPF Lausanne, Heriot-Watt Univ 1998, Univ of Sussex 2000, Montpellier II Univ 2003, Univ of Edinburgh 2004; hon memb Edinburgh Mathematical Soc 2008, memb Academia Europaea 2008; FRSE 1980, FRS 1989; *Recreations* chess, music, travel; *Style*— Prof Sir John Ball, FRS, FRSE; ✉ Mathematical Institute, University of Oxford, Andrew Wiles Building, Radcliffe Observatory Quarter, Woodstock Road, Oxford OX2 6GG (☎ 01865 615110)

BALL, Jonathan Macartney; MBE (1992); s of Christopher Edward Ball (d 1978), and Dorothy Ethel, *née* Macartney (d 2016); *b* 4 June 1947; *Educ* Truro Sch, AA (AADipl); *m* 29 June 1974, Victoria Mary Ogilvie, da of Dr Anthony Blood (d 2005), of Bude, Cornwall; 2 da (Jemima Veryan b 1976, Morwenna Victoria b 1979); *Career* co-fndr (with Tim Smit) The Eden Project Cornwall, fndr The Great Atlantic Way Cornwall; chartered architect and writer; princ The Jonathan Ball Practice Bude 1974–2001 (8 nat and 7 regnl design awards 1980–2000), fndr ptnr Triangle Estates; after dinner and conference speaker, assessor for architecture awards; RIBA: memb Cncl 1981–99, chm Parly Liaison Ctee 1981–87, vice-pres 1983–85 and 1991–93, hon sec 1988–91 and 1993–95, hon curator Spirit of Place Exhbn 2014, memb Nat Cncl 2015, memb Bd British Architectural Tst 2016–; tstee Br Architectural Library 1988–95; memb Editorial Bd: RIBA Handbook of Architectural Practice and Management, The Millennium Book for Cornwall; RNLI crew memb Bude lifeboat 1966–94 (sr helmsman 1986–94, dep launching authy 1994–2007), co-sponsor RNLI Beach Lifeguarding, memb RNLI Cncl 2007–; memb Bude Surf Life Saving Club 1959–, choir master Bude Lifeboat Singers 1967–93, pres Surf Life Saving GB (SLSGB) 2000–09, chm Rescue 2010 GB bid for World Life Saving Championships; SLSGB Long Service Award 1984 and 1989, Queen's Jubilee Medal 2002; Master Worshipful Co of Chartered Architects 2007–08 (Liveryman 1986, memb Ct of Assts 1991–); installed as Bard of the Cornish Gorseth 2002 for services to the RNLI and Surf Life Saving Cornwall (bardic name Tregarthen), Surf Life Saving Australia Certificate of Appreciation for Outstanding Contribution to SLSA 2011; ACIArb 1978, FRSA 1985; *Books* The Other Side of Eden (2014, nominated Holyer an Gof Literary Award 2015), The Winds Call No Man Sir (2015); *Recreations* enjoying Cornwall and the Isles of Scilly; *Clubs* Athenaeum; *Style*— Jonathan Ball, Esq, MBE; ✉ The Belvedere, 5 Belle Vue, Bude, Cornwall EX23 8JJ (☎ 01288 353898, e-mail jonathan@greatatlanticway.com, website www.jonathan-ball.com)

BALL, Michael Ashley; OBE (2015); s of Anthony George (Tony) Ball, MBE, *qv*, of Bidford-on-Avon, Warks, and Ruth Parry Davies; *b* 27 June 1962; *Educ* Plymouth Coll, Farnham Sixth Form Coll, Guildford Sch of Acting; *Career* actor and singer; patron Shooting Star/CHASE, patron Perfect Pitch, dir Royal Theatrical Fund; *Theatre* Surrey Youth Theatre 1980–81: The Boyfriend (1980), Under Milk Wood (1981); drama sch 1981–84, first professional role Judas/John the Baptist in Godspell 1984, first starring role Frederick in The Pirates of Penzance (Manchester Opera House) 1985, West End debut cr role of Marius in original prodn of Les Misérables (Barbican and Palace) 1985; other credits incl: Raoul in Phantom of the Opera (Her Majesty's) 1987, cr role of Alex in Aspects of Love (Prince of Wales 1989, Broadway debut 1990), Giorgio in Passion (Queen's) 1996, Alone Together (Donmar Warehouse) 2001, Caractacus Potts in Chitty Chitty Bang Bang (Palladium) 2002–03, Count Fosco in Woman In White (UK tour and Broadway) 2005, Reginald Bunthorne in Patience (NYC Opera) 2005, Hajj and The Poet in Kismet (ENO) 2007, Edna Turnblad in Hairspray 2007–09, title role in Sweeney Todd (Chichester Festival Theatre) 2011 and (Adelphi Theatre) 2012; numerous nat and int concert tours; *Television* incl: Coronation Street, Late Expectations, Save the Children Christmas Spectacular, Top of the Pops, Royal Variety Performance, GB rep Eurovision Song Contest 1992, two series of Michael Ball 1993 and 1994; Michael Ball in Concert (video) 1997, hosted National Lottery Live Show July 1997, An Evening with Michael Ball 1998, Lord Lloyd Webber's 50th Birthday 1998; judge Soapstar Superstar 2007, The Michael Ball Show (ITV) 2010; *Radio* incl: Michael Ball's Sunday Brunch (BBC Radio 2), Sunday Night With Michael Ball (BBC Radio 2); *Recordings* incl: Les Misérables (original London cast album 1986, int cast album 1987), Rage of the Heart 1987, London cast album Aspects of Love 1989, Michael Ball 1992, West Side Story 1993, Always 1993, One Careful Owner 1994, The Best of Michael Ball 1994, Michael Ball – The Musicals 1996, Michael Ball – The Movies 1998, Christmas 1999, Live at the Royal Albert Hall 1999, This Time it's Personal 2000, Centre Stage 2001, A Love Story 2003, Love Changes Everything: The Essential Michael Ball 2004, Music 2005, One Voice 2006, Bach to Bacharach 2007, The Very Best of Michael Ball – Past and Present 2009, Heroes 2011, Both Sides Now 2013; *Films* Henry Purcell in England My England, Tubby and Enid (BBC TV) 2014; *Awards* Most Promising Artiste Award Variety Club of GB 1989, The Variety Club Best Recording Artiste 1998, Theatregoers Club of GB Most Popular Musical Actor 1999, Best Actor in a Musical Olivier Award 2008 (for Hairspray), Best Actor in a Musical Whatsonstage Award 2013 (for Sweeney Todd), Best Actor in a Musical Olivier Award 2013 (for Sweeney Todd); *Recreations* music, theatre, cooking, wine, travel, reading; *Style*— Michael Ball, Esq, OBE; ✉ Management: c/o Live Nation (Music) UK Ltd, Regent Arcade House, 19–25 Argyll Street, London W1F 7TS (website www.michaelball.co.uk); Agent: c/o ARG Talent Agency, 4a Exmoor Street, London W10 6BD (website www.argtalent.com)

BALL, Sir Richard Bentley; 5 Bt (UK 1911), of Merrion Square, City of Dublin, and Killybegs, Co Donegal; s of Sir Charles Irwin Ball, 4 Bt (d 2002); *b* 29 January 1953; *Educ* Dragon Sch Oxford, Sherborne, Univ of Leicester; *m* 31 Aug 1991 (m dis 2015), Beverley Ann, da of late Bertram Joffre Wright; 1 da (Anna Frances b 20 Feb 1996); *Career* CA; Peat Marwick Mitchell 1975–82, International Computers Ltd 1982–99, interim fin mangr 2000–02, fin mangr Interserve Investments 2003, fin controller McAlpine Project Investments 2004–05, interim fin mangr Antler Homes & Pixology 2006–08, finance mangr Kajima Partnerships 2008–; *Recreations* hockey, travel, tennis; *Style*— Sir Richard Ball, Bt; ☎ 01372 464293, e-mail richardbball@btinternet.com

BALL, Simon Peter; s of Peter Ball, of Bexleyheath, Kent, and Maureen, *née* Bishop; *b* 2 May 1960, London; *Educ* Chislehurst and Sidcup GS, UCL; *m* 30 May 1992, Sandra Marie; 2 da (Hannah b 12 May 1993, Katie b 3 Jan 1995); *Career* CA 1984, qualified with Price Waterhouse & Co; with Kleinwort Benson Ltd (then Dresdner Kleinwort Benson) 1985–98 (latterly finance dir then chief operating offr), gp finance dir Robert Fleming Hldgs Ltd 1998–2000 (also md Chase Manhattan International Ltd after 2000), DG of finance Dept for Constitutional Affrs 2003–05, finance dir 3i Gp plc 2005–08; non-exec dir Cable & Wireless plc 2006–10, dep chm Cable & Wireless Communications plc 2010–; *Style*— Mr Simon Ball

BALL, Zoë; *b* 23 November 1970; *Educ* Holy Cross Sch Chalfont St Peter; *m* 1999, Norman Cook (aka Fatboy Slim); 1 s (Woody b 2000), 1 da (Nelly May Lois b 2010); *Career* runner Granada TV; researcher: BSkyB, Action Time; researcher and asst prodr Big Breakfast (Channel 4 TV Corp); TV presenter of progs incl: The Ozone (BBC TV, winner of Best Music Show Smash Hit Awards), The Big Breakfast 1996, Live & Kicking 1996–99 (BBC TV), The Priory 1999, Strictly Dance Fever (BBC) 2005 (contestant Strictly Come Dancing (BBC) 2005), Extinct (ITV) 2006, Soapstar Superstar (ITV) 2007, Grease is the Word (ITV) 2007, Strictly Come Dancing: It Takes Two (BBC 2) 2011–; radio presenter: Breakfast Show BBC Radio 1 1997–2000, XFM 2002–04, Saturday Breakfast Show BBC Radio 2 2009–; *Style*— Ms Zoë Ball

BALLAMY, Iain Mark; s of Mark Donald Ballamy, and Sylvia, *née* Thompson; *b* 20 February 1964; *Educ* Merton Tech Coll (City & Guilds, Musical Instrument Technol); *Partner* Alison Lorna Duffell; *Career* jazz saxophonist and composer; with Balloon Man 1983–93, Loose Tubes (fndr memb, 1984–90), Billy Jenkins V.O.G. 1985–, Bill Bruford's Earthworks (1986–92), Human Chain and Delightful Precipice (both with Django Bates, *qv*, 1992–), ACME (leader, 1996–), Food 1998–; fndr and co dir Feral Records with Dave

McKean; performed with numerous artists and bands incl: Hermeto Pascoal, George Coleman, Dewey Redman, Mike Gibbs, Gil Evans, Sankalpam (Indian dance gp), The Hungry Ants; performances in films incl: Legend, My Son the Fanatic, Joseph Losey – The Man with Four Names, Absolute Beginners, The Last Days of General Patten; numerous performances on radio and TV incl: The Tube, Bergerac, Right to Reply, Wogan, Signal to Noise (by Neil Gaiman, *qv*, and Dave McKean, BBC Radio 4); performed at numerous venues incl: Ronnie Scotts, Knitting Factory, FEZ and Bottom Line (all NY), New Morning (Paris), Royal Festival Hall, Royal Albert Hall, Barbican and most int jazz festivals; played Steve the prat in Out There (Simon Black's musical theatre prodn, 1995–96); Br Cncl concerts in Columbia, India, Lithuania, Senegal, Bosnia; memb: MU (Musicians' Union), PRS (Performing Rights Soc), MCPS (Mechanical Copyright Protection Soc), PAMRA (Performing Artists Media Rights Assoc); *Compositions* incl: Estuary English Apollo Saxophone Quartet 1995, Mirror Signal Manoeuvre Apollo Saxophone Quartet, ACME with Birmingham Jazz 1996, Oblique with Birmingham Jazz 1997, Four and a half minutes late (solo harpsichord, Jane Chapman, 1998), Walpurgis Night (duet for piano and tenor sax, Joanna MacGregor, 1998), cmmn work: Food Cheltenham Jazz Festival 1999, Bath Int Festival 2000 ; *Recordings* 45 CD appearances incl: Pepper Street Interludes (album), Food (album), ACME (album), All Men Amen (album), Balloon Man (album, 1989), Organic and GM Food (album, 2001); *Awards* Best Soloist John Dankworth Cup 1985, Best Ensemble BT British Jazz 1995, Special Award for Innovation BBC Jazz Awards 2001, Paul Hamlyn Fndn Composers Award 2007; *Recreations* black glass and early stoneware, metal detecting; *Style*— Iain Ballamy, Esq; ✉ website www.ballamy.com

BALLANTYNE, Prof Colin Kerr; s of Robert Morrison Ballantyne (d 1991), and Isabella Sturrock, *née* Kerr (d 1970); *b* 7 June 1951; *Educ* Hutchesons' GS Glasgow, Univ of Glasgow (MA), McMaster Univ (MSc), Univ of Edinburgh (PhD), Univ of St Andrews (DSc); *m* 1996, Rebecca Josephine, da of Graham Trengove; 1 s (Hamish Trengove b 16 July 1998), 1 da (Kate Iona b 19 June 2000); *Career* teaching asst McMaster Univ 1973–75, demonstrator Univ of Edinburgh 1977–79; Univ of St Andrews: lectr in geography 1980–89, sr lectr 1989–94, prof of physical geography 1994–, head Sch of Geography and Geosciences 1998–2001; hon life memb Quaternary Research Assoc 2014; Gordon Warwick Award Br Geomorphological Research Gp 1987, President's Medal Royal Scottish Geographical Soc 1991, Newbigin Prize Royal Scottish Geographical Soc 1992, Scottish Science Award Saltire Soc 1996, Wiley Award Br Geomorphological Research Gp 1999, Clough Medal Edinburgh Geological Soc 2010, Coppock Research Medal RSGS 2015, Lyell Medal Geological Soc of London 2015; FRSE 1996, FRSA 1996, FRSGS 2014; *Books* The Quaternary of the Isle of Skye (1991), The Periglaciation of Great Britain (1994), The Quaternary of Skye (2016); *Recreations* mountaineering, skiing, music, modern history, travel; *Style*— Prof Colin Ballantyne, FRSE; ✉ Birchwood, Blebo Craigs, Fife KY15 5UF; School of Geography and Geosciences, University of St Andrews, St Andrews, Fife KY16 9AL (☎ 07821 803829, e-mail ckb@st-and.ac.uk)

BALLARD, Beatrice Rosalind; da of James Graham Ballard, of Shepperton, Middx, and Mary, *née* Matthews (d 1964); *b* 29 May 1959; *Educ* St David's Sch Ashford Middx, UEA (BA), City Univ of London (Journalism Dip); *Career* reporter New Statesman 1981, writer and researcher Radio Times 1981–82, asst prodr and dir John Craven's Newsround BBC TV 1983–85, prodr special progs LWT 1986–88; series prodr: Saturday Night Clive, Fame in the Twentieth Century, Clive James Postcards From Miami, New York and Paris, Clive James Meets Ronald Reagan BBC TV 1988; exec prodr Entertainment BBC TV 1994–97, currently creative head Entertainment BBC TV; exec prodr incl: Any Dream Will Do, How Do You Solve a Problem Like Maria?, The Two Ronnies Sketchbook, Parkinson, One Night with Robbie Williams, Elton John at The Royal Opera House, Aunties All Time Greats BBC TV 60th Anniversary, Ruby Wax Meets Madonna, Carrie Fisher on Hollywood, Br Acad Awards, BAFTA Tribute to Billy Connolly, exec prodr Entertainment BBC TV; series prodr: Saturday Night Clive, Fame in the Twentieth Century, Clive James Postcards From Miami, NY and Paris, Clive James Meets Ronald Reagan BBC TV; prodr special progs LWT; asst prodr and dir John Craven's Newsround (BBC); memb Cncl BAFTA, chm Television Ctee; *Recreations* reading, cinema, travel, eating out; *Style*— Ms Beatrice Ballard; ✉ 225 Westbourne Grove, London W11 2SE (e-mail beaballard@tiscali.co.uk)

BALLARD, Jackie; *née* Mackenzie; da of late Alexander Mackenzie, and late Daisy, *née* Macdonald; *b* 4 January 1953; *Educ* Monmouth Sch for Girls, LSE (BSc), Yeovil Coll (FE Teacher's Cert); *m* 1975 (m dis 1989), Derek John Ballard; 1 da (Christina b 23 March 1979); *Career* formerly social worker London Borough of Waltham Forest then lectr in computing, psychology, communications and business studies, cncl support offr Assoc of Lib Dem Cncllrs 1993–97, MP (Lib Dem) Taunton 1997–2001 (Parly candidate 1992, memb Lib Dem Parly local govt team 1997–99, Lib Dem Parly spokesperson on women's issues 1997–99, dep home affrs spokesperson 1997–2001); DG RSPCA 2002–07, chief exec RNID 2007–12, chief exec Womankind Worldwide 2012–13, chief exec Alcohol Concern 2014–; computer mangr Paddy Ashdown's gen election team 1987, memb Lib Dems' Fed Policy Ctee 1990–95 and Fed Exec Ctee 1997–99; cncllr: South Somerset DC 1987–91 (dep ldr 1988–90, ldr 1990–91), Somerset CC 1993–97 (dep ldr 1993–95); memb Bd Newlon Housing Tst 2013–, currently chair Outward; *Recreations* swimming, Zumba, travel, reading; *Style*— Jackie Ballard; ✉ e-mail ballardjackie@hotmail.com

BALLARD, Richard Michael; s of Michael Agar Ballard, and Junella, *née* Ashton (d 1960); *b* 3 August 1953; *Educ* St Edmund's Coll Ware, Queens' Coll Cambridge (MA); *m* 28 Feb 1981, Penelope Ann, da of Dilwyn John Davies, DFC (d 1988), of Glamorgan; 3 s (Hayden b 1984, Thomas b 1985, James b 1992), 1 da (Sophie b 1987); *Career* admitted slr 1978; ptnr Freshfields 1984–; memb Law Soc; *Recreations* country pursuits; *Clubs* Oriental; *Style*— Richard Ballard, Esq; ✉ Freshfields Bruckhaus Deringer, 65 Fleet Street, London EC4Y 1HS (☎ 020 7936 4000, fax 020 7832 7001)

BALLIN, Robert Andrew; s of Harold Ballin (d 1976), and Mollie Ballin, *née* Dunn (d 1989); *b* 8 July 1943; *Educ* Highgate Sch, City of London Coll; *m* 27 Nov 1975, Serena Mary Ann, da of Richard Goode, OBE (d 1966); 1 s (Edward b 1980), 2 da (Annabel b 1981, Chloe b 1985); *Career* Shell-Mex and BP 1962–67, SH Benson 1967–69, Gallagher-Smail/Doyle Dane Bernbach 1969–73; Foote Cone & Belding: joined 1973, int dir Impact-FCB Belgium 1975–77, dir 1977–98, dep chm 1988–98; mktg and communications conslt 1999–; memb Epsom Race Ctee 1994–2015; *Recreations* music, theatre, sport; *Clubs* White's, MCC; *Style*— Robert Ballin, Esq; ✉ Church Farm, Upper Lambourn, Hungerford RG17 8RG (☎ 01488 670080)

BALLS, Alastair Gordon; CB (1995), DL (2010); s of Rev Ernest George Balls, of Stevenson, Ayrshire, and Elspeth Russell, *née* McMillan; *b* 18 March 1944; *Educ* Hamilton Acad, Univ of St Andrews (MA), Univ of Manchester (MA); *m* 26 Nov 1977, Beryl May, da of John Nichol, of Harlow, Essex; 1 s (Thomas b 1979), 1 da (Helen b 1982); *Career* asst sec Treasy Govt of Tanzania 1966–68, economist Dept of Tport UK Govt 1969–73, sec Cairncross Ctee on Channel Tunnel 1974–75, sr econ advsr HM Treasy 1976–79, under sec DOE 1983–87 (asst sec 1979–83), chief exec Tyne & Wear Urban Devpt Corp 1987–98; chm: NewcastleGateshead Initiative 2004–07, Northern Rock Fndn 2006–, The Int Centre for Life Newcastle upon Tyne (millennium project) 2007– (chief exec 1997–2007); non-exec dir Northumbrian Water Ltd 2002–11; memb ITC 1998–2003, memb HE Funding Cncl for England (HEFCE) 2006–13, chm Alzheimer's Soc 2007–13; CIMgt 1988; *Recreations* fishing, sailing, camping; *Clubs* Wylam Angling; *Style*— Alastair Balls, Esq, CB, DL; ✉ c/o The International Centre for Life Trust, Times Square, Scotswood Road, Newcastle upon Tyne NE1 4EP (e-mail alastair.balls@life.org.uk)

BALLS, Rt Hon Edward; PC (2007); s of Prof Michael Balls, and Carolyn Janet Balls; *b* 25 February 1967; *Educ* Nottingham HS, Keble Coll Oxford, Harvard Univ (Kennedy Scholar); *m* 10 Jan 1998, Yvette Cooper, MP, *qv*; 2 da (Meriel Eliza b 1 June 1999, Madelyn Beth b 26 July 2004), 1 s (Joel b 25 Aug 2001); *Career* teaching fell Dept of Economics Harvard Univ and Nat Bureau of Economic Research USA 1989–90, economics leader writer and columnist Financial Times 1990–94 (Young Financial Journalist of the Year Wincott Fndn 1992), economic advsr to Gordon Brown, MP 1994–99 (as shadow Chancellor of the Exchequer until 1997, then Chancellor of the Exchequer), chief economic advsr to HM Treasy 1999–2004, sr research fell Smith Inst 2004–05; MP (Lab) Normanton 2005–15; economic sec to HM Treasy 2006–07, sec of state for Children, Schs and Families 2007–10, shadow home sec 2010–11, shadow chllr of the Exchequer 2011–15; ed European Economic Policy 1994–97, princ ed World Bank Devpt Report 1995; sec Economic Policy Cmmn Lab Pty until 1997; Hon Dr of Laws Univ of Nottingham 2003; hon fell Keble Coll Oxford; *Publications* Reforming Britain's Economic and Financial Policy (with Gus O'Donnell, 2002), Microeconomic Reform in Britain (with Gus O'Donnell and Joe Grice, 2004); *Recreations* playing football, the violin and with children; *Style*— The Rt Hon Edward Balls; ✉ House of Commons, London SW1A 0AA

BALMOND, Dr Cecil; OBE (2015); s of Hugh Balmond (d 1986), and Ruth, *née* Herft (d 1991); *b* 26 February 1943, Colombo, Sri Lanka; *Educ* Univ of Southampton (BSc), Imperial College London (MSc, DIC); *m* 6 July 1968, Shirley, *née* Rogers; 2 s (John-Jehan b 1978, James b 1982), 1 da (Sarah b 1980); *Career* Ove Arup and Ptnrs Ltd: joined in 1968, dir 1990–, chm Europe 2000–04, dep chm 2004–, life-term tstee 2007, Arup fell and chm Arup Fells' Panel; numerous projects incl: Carlsberg Brewery Northampton 1970, Qatar Univ 1975, Royal London House 1983, Palazzo Citterio Milan 1987, Museo Thyssen-Bornemisza Madrid 1988, Portugese Pavilion for Expo '98 1995, Illinois Inst of Technol 1998, Serpentine Pavilion London (with Toyo Ito) 2002, Centre Pompidou (Metz) France 2004, Shenzhen Stock Exchange China 2006, Pedro and Ine? Bridge Coimbra Portugal; external examiner Architectural Assoc London, visiting prof Städelschüle Frankfurt-am-Main 1987–95, visiting Saarinen prof Sch of Architecture Yale Univ 1997–2002, visiting Kenzo Tange critic Harvard Grad Sch of Architecture 2000, visiting Graham prof Penn Design Univ of Pennsylvania 2003, prof Urban Cities Prog LSE 2003–04, Paul Phillipe Cret prof of architecture Penn Design Univ of Pennsylvania 2004–, dir Non-Linear Systems Organization (NSO) Penn Design 2005–; chm Yad Hanadiv Jerusalem Seminar in Architecture 2004; memb A+U Advsy Ctee 2006; Goldstein architecture, engrg and sci lectr MIT 2007; exhbns: Sports Stadion Chemnitz 2002 (Aedes Galerie Berlin) 1996, Informal (Arc en Reve Bordeaux) 2004, H_edge (Artists Space NY) 2006 and (Graham Fndn for Advanced Studies in Fine Arts Chicago) 2008, Frontiers of Architecture (Louisiana Museum of Art and Øresund Denmark) 2007, Forum 64 (Carnegie Museum of Art Pittsburg) 2009, Element (Tokyo Opera City Art Gallery Tokyo) 2010; *Public sculptures*: Caspar College Art (Wyoming) 2011, Net_work (Alberta) 2012, ArcelorMittal Orbit (London Olympic Park) 2012, Star of Caledonia (Gretna) 2014, H_Edge_ (London) 2014, Black Hawk Mini Park Art Project (Iowa City) 2016, Wilson Station (Chicago) 2016, Shade Sculpture (Mesa Arizona) 2016, Star of Caledonia (Scot/Eng border) 2016, Freedom: A Shared Dream (LA) 2016; Awards: FT Award 1980 and 2005, Nationale Staalprijs Telecommunicatiestand PTT (Eindhoven) 1988, recipient of several awards for Royal London House, Structural Steel Design Award (London) 1994, Gengo Matsui Prize 2002, Charles Jencks Award for Theory in Practice 2003, AA Dip 2003, Felix Candela Prize 2004, Arup Fellowship 2004, Sir Banister Fletcher Prize 2005, short-listed for Prince Philip Designers Prize 2005 and 2012, Mies van der Rohe Award 2007, nominated for EU Prize for contemporary architecture, Americans for the Arts Nat Pub Art Award 2012, Thomas Jefferson Foundation Medal in Architecture 2016; Hon DSc: Univ of London, Univ of Southampton; CEng, MiStructE, Hon FRIBA; Number 9: The Search for the Sigma Code: Nine Points Fixed in the Wind 1998, Informal: The Informal in Architecture and Engineering 2002 (Banister Fletcher Prize 2005), Element 2007, Crossover (2013); author of numerous articles, essays and interviews in learned jls; *Recreations* classical guitar; *Style*— Dr Cecil Balmond, OBE; ✉ Balmond Studio, Unit 9, 190A New North Road, London N1 7BJ (☎ 020 7043 0651, e-mail cb@balmondstudio.com, website www.balmondstudio.com)

BALNIEL, Lord; Anthony Robert Lindsay; DL (Fife 2013); s and h of 29 Earl of Crawford and (12 of) Balcarres, PC, *qv*; *b* 24 November 1958; *Educ* Eton, Univ of Edinburgh; *m* 12 Aug 1989, Nicola A, yst da of Antony Bicket, of Derwas, Dolwen, N Wales; 2 s (Alexander Thomas, Master of Lindsay b 1991, Hon James Antony b 10 Nov 1992), 2 da (Hon Katherine Ruth Vere b 4 Sept 1996, Hon Isabel Rosemary b 1 May 2001); *Heir* s, Hon Alexander Lindsay; *Career* md J O Hambro Investment Management Ltd 2004–09 (dir 1987–2009), ptnr James Hambro & Partners 2010–; *Clubs* New (Edinburgh), MCC; *Style*— Lord Balniel, DL; ✉ Balcarres, Colinsburgh, Fife; Holland Park, London W11 3RZ

BALSHAW, Iain; MBE (2004); *b* 18 April 1979, Blackburn, Lancs; *Educ* Stonyhurst; *Career* rugby union player (full back); clubs: Bath RUFC 1997–2004, Leeds Tykes 2004–06, Gloucester 2006–09, Biarritz 2009–; England: 35 caps, debut v Argentina 2000, winners Six Nations Championship 2001, ranked no 1 team in world 2003, winners World Cup Aust 2003; memb British and Irish Lions touring squad Aust 2001 (3 caps) and NZ 2005 (selected but missed tour following injury); *Recreations* golf; *Style*— Iain Balshaw, Esq, MBE; ✉ c/o Rugby Football Union, Rugby House, Rugby Road, Twickenham, Middlesex TW1 1DS

BAMBER, David James; s of late Ernest Bamber, of Walkden, Salford, and late Hilda, *née* Wolfendale; *b* 19 September 1954; *Educ* Walkden Co Secdy Modern Sch, Farnworth GS, Univ of Bristol, RADA; *m* July 1982, Julia Swift (the actress), da of David Swift; 2 s (Theo Elia b 27 Dec 1991, Ethan b 17 Dec 1998); *Career* actor; RADA William Peel Prize, Carol Brahams Musical Comedy Prize, Bancroft Gold Medal; *Theatre* for NT incl: Oresteia 1981, Charlie in The Strangeness of Others 1988, John Littlewit in Bartholomew Fair 1988, Horatio in Hamlet 1989, Streaky Bacon in Racing Demon 1990–91, Mole in Wind in the Willows 1990–91; others incl: Joseph and His Amazing Technicolor Dreamcoat (Palace Theatre Westcliff) 1979, Outskirts (RSC Warehouse) 1981, Masterclass (Leicester Haymarket, Old Vic, Wyndhams) 1983–84, Kissing God (Hampstead) 1984, Amadeus 1986, Three Birds Alighting on a Field (Royal Court) 1991, Hikatier in Schippel (Greenwich Theatre & Edinburgh Festival), Martin Mirkheim in Search and Destroy (Theatre Upstairs), Guy in My Night with Reg (Theatre Upstairs and Criterion (winner Olivier Award for Best Actor 1995)) 1994, The Cocktail Party (Edinburgh Festival) 1997, Black Comedy and The Real Inspector Hound (Comedy Theatre), On the Razzle (Chichester Festival Theatre); RNT: Pandarus in Troilus and Cressida, Antonio in Merchant of Venice, Honk!, The Glee Club (Bush Theatre and Duchess Theatre) 2002, Where There's a Will (dir by Sir Peter Hall, CBE, *qv*), The Lisbon Traviatam Otherwise Engaged (Criterion); *Television* incl: Call Me Mister (BBC) 1986, Cockles (BBC) 1983, Buddha of Suburbia (BBC) 1993, Stalag Luft (YTV) 1993, Wycliffe, Pride and Prejudice, Chalk, Neville's Island, My Dads a Boring Nerd, My Night with Reg, The Railway Children, Casualty, Lush in Daniel Deronda (BBC), Midsomer Murders, Rome (HBO), Collision, Psychoville, The Borgias; *Films* incl: Privates on Parade 1982, High Hopes 1988, Gangs of New York, Miss Potter 2006, Valkyrie 2008, The King's Speech 2010;

Recreations listening to music, playing the piano, trying to keep fit usually at a gym, being married to Julia; *Style*— David Bamber, Esq

BAMBER, Roger; s of Frederick William Bamber (d 1987), of Leicester, and Vera Lilian, *née* Stephenson; *b* 31 August 1944; *Educ* Beaumont Leys Secdy Modern Leicester, Leicester Coll of Art; *m* 1, 1970 (m dis 1973), Joan Bergquist; m 2, 2004, Shan Lancaster; *Career* news photographer; Fleetway Publications 1963–64, Leicester Coll of Art 1964–65, Daily Mail 1965–69, The Sun 1969–88, The Observer 1988–89, The Guardian 1989–; Hon MA Univ of Brighton 2005; FRPS; *Exhibitions* Royal Photographic Soc 1992, Brighton Museum and Art Gallery 1993, Tom Blau Gallery London 1994, Month of the Image Dieppe 1995, Worthing Museum and Art Gallery 1996; *Awards* Br News Photographer of the Year 1973, Photographer of the Year and News Photographer of the Year (Br Press Awards) 1983, Nikon Features Photographer of the Year 1991, Kodak Features Photographer of the Year 1991, Ilford Press Photographer of the Year 1992 (runner up 1991), UK Picture Editors' Guild Award for features photography 1996, UK Picture Editors' Guild Award (business and indust category) 1997 and 1999 (two awards), Nikon Arts and Entertainment Photographer of the Year 1997 (runner up 1996), Features Award UK Picture Editors Guild 2001, Business and Industry Award UK Picture Editors Award 2004; *Style*— Roger Bamber, Esq; ✉ c/o The Guardian, Kings Place, 90 York Way, London N1 9GU (☎ 020 7278 2332 and 01273 723689, mobile 078 6038 1255, e-mail pix@rogerbamber.co.uk, www.rogerbamber.co.uk)

BAMBERGER, Arnaud Marie; s of Jean Bamberger (d 1996), and Renée, *née* Trarieux-Lumiere; *b* 15 August 1945, Paris; *Educ* Lycée Janson de Sailly Paris; *m* 23 June 1989, Carla Jean, *née* Hubbard; 2 da (Clemence b 10 March 1979, Amelia b 16 Aug 1990), 1 s (Hugo b 25 June 1996); *Career* Lesieur Paris 1966–76; Cartier: export dir 1976–82, vice-pres Cartier Inc NY 1982–88, retail dir worldwide Cartier Int Paris 1988–92, md Cartier Ltd UK 1992–2010 (exec chm 2010–); tstee Le Dispensaire Français London; Conseiller du Commerce Exterieur de la France 1993–, pres Chambre de Commerce Franco-Britannique 2013– (vice-pres 1994–2013); Chevalier de l'Ordre National du Mérite 1997, Chevalier de la Legion d'Honneur 2009; *Recreations* golf, shooting, skiing; *Clubs* White's; *Style*— Arnaud Bamberger, Esq; ✉ 84 Eaton Terrace, London SW1W 8UG (☎ 020 7730 7786, fax 020 7730 7786); Cartier Ltd, 175–177 New Bond Street, London W1S 4RN (☎ 020 7408 5720, fax 020 7355 1799, e-mail arnaud.bamberger@cartier.com)

BAMBRIDGE, Ron; *b* 6 November 1953; *m* 15 Feb 1986, Rose Angela, *née* Nielsen; 1 da (Daisy b 10 Nov 1988); *Career* asst photographer Photographic Dept Foote Cone & Belding (advtg agency) 1973–77, freelance photographer 1977–; specialist in still life photography until 1985, landscape, people and special panoramic photography since 1985; work for various clients incl: BA, ICI, London Transport, Rothschilds, British Gas, National Power, British Airports Authy, Welsh Devpt Agency, Seacontainers, Peugeot; work included in English Landscape in Danger (exhbn and auction cmmnd by CPRE) 1987; cmmn Royal Mail London Landmark stamps 1996; memb Assoc of Photographers (formerly AFAEP); *Awards* incl: highly commended Advtg People Category Ilford Awards 1984, AFAEP Gold Award (for landscape series) 1986, AFAEP Merit Award (for people series) 1988, Best Photography Award (Nat Business Calendar Awards) 1988, AFAEP Merit Award (for landscape) 1993, AFAEP Bronze Award (Best of Book in Contact Photographers) 1993, London Photographic Awards (winner still life series, environmental series and environmental colour) 1997, Silver and Merit Awards (for landscape) XV Assoc of Photographers Awards 1998, Personal Portraits Series XVI Assoc of Photographers Awards 1999, Cmmnd Structure Category Assoc of Photographers Awards 2000; *Books* 100 Years of Brooklands, Motorsport and Aviation (2007); *Style*— Ron Bambridge, Esq; ✉ e-mail ronbambridge@btinternet.com, website www.ronbambridge.com

BAMFORD, Baron (Life Peer UK 2013), of Daylesford in the County of Gloucestershire and of Wootton in the County of Staffordshire; Sir Anthony Paul Bamford; kt (1990), DL (Staffs 1989); s of Joseph Cyril Bamford, CBE (d 2001); *b* 23 October 1945; *Educ* Ampleforth Coll; *m* 1974, Carole Gray Whitt; 2 s, 1 da; *Career* joined JCB 1964, chm and md J C Bamford Group 1975–; dir Tarmac plc 1988–94; memb: President's Ctee CBI 1986–88, Design Cncl 1987–89; pres: Staffs Agric Soc 1987–88, Burton on Trent Cons Assoc 1987–90; High Sheriff of Staffs 1985–86; Hon MEng Birmingham 1987, Hon DUniv Keele 1988, Hon DSc Cranfield 1994, Hon DBA Robert Gordon Univ Aberdeen 1996, Hon DTech Univ of Staffordshire 1998, Hon DTech Loughborough Univ 2002; Young Exporter of the Year 1972, Young Businessman of the Year 1979, Top Exporter of the Year 1995, Entrepreneurial Award Br American Business Inc (BABI) 2003; Hon FCGI 1993, Hon FCSD 1994, fell Inst of Agricultural Engrgs 2003, hon fell RAE 2014–, Hon FIMechE 2015; Chevalier de l'Ordre National du Mérite (France) 1989, Commendatore al merito della Republica Italiana 1995; *Recreations* farming and gardening; *Clubs* White's, British Racing Drivers', RYS; *Style*— The Lord Bamford, DL; ✉ c/o J C Bamford Excavators Ltd, Rocester, Staffordshire ST14 5JP

BAMFORD, Colin; s of Firth Bamford (d 1986), and Edna, *née* Cockshutt (d 2011); *b* 28 August 1950; *Educ* Queen Elizabeth's GS Blackburn, Trinity Hall Cambridge (scholar, MA); *m* 31 Jan 1975, Nirmala Rajah Bamford, da of Hon Mr Justice A P Rajah, of Singapore; 2 s (Rowan Firth Rajah b 13 March 1980, Daniel Chelva Rajah b 26 July 1986), 1 da (Roxanne Vijaya Rajah b 6 May 1990); *Career* Herbert Oppenheimer Nathan and Vandyk: articled clerk 1972–74, asst slr 1974–77, ptnr 1977–88; ptnr Richards Butler 1988–97, chief exec Financial Law Panel 1993–2002; called to the Bar Middle Temple 2002; dep chm Advsy Ctee Centre for Fin Regulation Cass Business Sch City Univ, memb Advsy Bd Centre for Corporate Law Studies Inst of Advanced Legal Studies Univ of London; visiting sr fell LSE 2009–12; hon fell Soc for Advanced Legal Studies (memb Advsy Cmmn); FRSA; *Publications* Principles of International Financial Law (2011, 2 edn 2015); *Style*— Colin Bamford, Esq; ✉ 3–4 South Square, Gray's Inn, London WC1R 5HP (☎ 020 7696 9900, fax 020 7696 9911, e-mail colinbamford@southsquare.com)

BAMFORD, Dr (Samuel Arnold) David; s of Samuel Arnold Brooks Bamford (d 2007), and Elsie, *née* Carew (d 1995); *b* 29 May 1946, Manchester; *Educ* Univ of Bristol (BSc), Univ of Birmingham (PhD); *m* 17 Jan 2004, Wendy Sheila, *née* Campbell; 2 da (Helen Elizabeth Brooks Hillard b 14 July 1976, Nicole Jennifer Bestford b 30 June 1984), 1 s (Matthew Bamford-Bowes b 2 Sept 1978); *Career* BP plc: joined 1980, chief geophysicist 1990–95, gen mangr W Africa 1995–98, gen mangr Norway 1998–99, head/vice-pres exploration 1999–2003; chm New Eyes Exploration Ltd 2005–; non-exec dir: Tullow Oil plc 2004–, Paras Ltd 2004–; FGS 1987; *Style*— Dr David Bamford

BAMFORD, David John; s of Samuel John Bamford, of Wellingborough, Northants, and Joan Sullivan, *née* Greenwood; *b* 28 June 1955; *Educ* Wellingborough GS, Univ of Aberdeen (MA), SOAS Univ of London (MSc); *m* 1, 19 July 1979 (m dis); 2 s (Thomas Rosh b 1981, Oliver Samuel b 1993); m 2, 4 Sept 2004, Maria Cecilia Caprari, da of Pasquale Caprari, of Collevecchio, Italy; *Career* BBC: political researcher Monitoring Serv 1980–83, journalist World Serv News 1983–, Ankara corr 1986–87, N Africa corr 1988–89, Nigeria corr 1991–93, W Africa corr 1994–97, sr broadcast journalist 1997–2000, N Africa corr 2001–02, Washington reporter 2003–04, Africa ed 2005–09, world news ed 2009–; contrib 1986–: The Guardian, Middle East Int, Middle East Economic Digest, Daily Telegraph, The Economist; *Style*— David Bamford, Esq; ✉ BBC World Service, Audience Relations Team, 1st Floor Brock House, 19 Langham Street, London, W1A 1AA (☎ 020 7240 3456, e-mail david.bamford@bbc.co.uk)

BAMJI, Dr Andrew Nariman; s of Dr Nariman Sorabji Bamji (d 1978), and Dr Joan Elizabeth Bamji, *née* Jermyn (d 2010); *b* 14 August 1950, London; *Educ* Highgate Sch, Middx Hosp Med Sch London (MB BS); *m* 10 June 1978, Elizabeth Mary, da of Raymond William Millard, of Wembdon, Somerset; 1 da (Alexandra b 1981), 1 s (Nicholas b 1985); *Career* conslt in rheumatology and rehabilitation: SE Thames RHA Brook Gen Hosp 1983–89, Queen Mary's Hosp Sidcup 1983–2009, Chelsfield Park Hosp Orpington 1985–2014, S London Healthcare Tst 2009–11; chm: SE Thames Region Specialty Sub-Ctee in Rheumatology 1992–97, Clinical Affairs Ctee Br Soc for Rheumatology 1998–2001; pres Br Soc for Rheumatology 2006–08, memb Cncl RCP 2006–08; Gillies archivist BAPRAS 2011–; Gillies gold medallist BAPRAS 2007 and 2015; memb: BMA, London Topographical Soc, Western Front Assoc, Royal Photographic Soc, Osler Club; hom memb BAPRAS; FRCP 1989 (Fitzpatrick lectr 2012); *Books* Atlas of Clinical Rheumatology (jt ed, 1986), Queen Mary's Hospital: A Commemoration 1974–94 (1994); articles on rheumatology topics and med aspects of Great War; *Recreations* antiques, travel, photography, comic verse; *Style*— Dr Andrew Bamji; ✉ Norman House, West Street, Rye, East Sussex TN31 7ES (e-mail bamji@btinternet.com, website www.gilliesarchive.org.uk)

BANBURY, Martin John; s of Raymond Francis Banbury, of Fareham, Hants, and Molly Louise Banbury; *b* 30 March 1957; *Educ* Chelsea Coll London (BSc); *m* 1 (m dis 1992), Sarah, da of Peter Andrew Campbell; 2 da (Amber Sarah Edna, Emma Lucie); m 2, Carol (d 2009), da of Colin White; 2 da (Jasmine, Rosie Kate), 1 s (Daniel Ray); *Career* mktg exec: Procter & Gamble 1979–82, Cussons 1982–84; jt chm Connect One plc 1985–1999; fndr/funder/ceo: Insure & Go 2000–10, The Mission Marketing Group plc 2004–06, MediaEquals 2007–, HomingPIN 2012–; *Recreations* flying, sailing; *Style*— Martin Banbury, Esq; ✉ Rookery Farm, Coles Oak Lane, Dedham, Essex CO7 6DN

BANBURY, (Nigel Graham Cedric) Peregrine; CVO (2010); s of Ralph Cecil Banbury (d 1951), of London, and Florence Leslie St Clair Keith; *b* 23 May 1948; *Educ* Gordonstoun; *m* 1, 17 Nov 1973, Rosemary Henrietta Dorothy, da of Capt Anthony Henry Heber Villiers, of Woodchester, Glos; m 2, 28 Sept 1978, Susan Margaret, da of Lt-Col Joseph Patrick Feeny (d 1970), of Estoril, Portugal; 2 s (Alexander b 1981, Ralph b 1987); m 3, 7 July 1992, Mrs Carol A Whistler, da of John Groves, CB, and former w of Laurence Whistler, CBE; *Career* Coutts & Co 1967–70, stockbroker 1971–81, Robert Fleming 1981–86, dir EBC Amro Asset Management Ltd 1986–87; Coutts & Co: head Asset Mgmnt 1987–96, ptnr Private Banking 1996–2000, dir Coutts & Co Investment Management 1996–2000, client gp head 2000–07, managing ptnr 2007–09; dir: Exeter Preferred Capital Investment Trust (latterly Exeter Selective Assets Tst) 1992–2005 (chm 2005), Schroder Income Growth Trust 1995–2010, Securities Inst 1995–2001, dir City Merchants Investment Tst 2005–06; non-exec dir: Henderson Global Property Cos Ltd 2006–11, Bankers Benevolent Fund 2006–09, Henderson Int Income Tst 2011–; currently sr advsr Bank and Clients (B&C) plc; tstee: Two Moors Festival 2010–14, Clive and Sylvia Richards Charity, Luke Somerfield Meml Tst; Freeman City of London; FSI; *Recreations* shooting, skiing, photography; *Clubs* White's, Pratt's; *Style*— Peregrine Banbury, Esq, CVO; ✉ Bank & Clients plc, 30 King Street, London EC2V 8EH (☎ 020 77042 9700)

BANCEWICZ, John; s of Dr Anthony Bancewicz (d 1997), of Airdrie, Lanarkshire, and Helen, *née* Ulinskas (d 1950); *b* 26 March 1945; *Educ* St Aloysius Coll Glasgow, Univ of Glasgow (BSc, MB ChB), Univ of Manchester (ChM); *m* 5 Jan 1972, Margaret Kathleen, da of Dr Charles Douglas Anderson, MC (d 1998); 1 s (Peter b 1973), 1 da (Ruth b 1976); *Career* res fell Harvard Med Sch 1974–75, lectr in surgery Univ of Glasgow 1976–79, reader in surgery and conslt surgn Univ of Manchester 1988–2005 (sr lectr 1979–88), ret; Salford Royal Hosps NHS Tst: clinical dir in general surgery 1994–96, med dir for surgical specialities 1996–2000; dir Hope Hosp Total Quality Mgmnt Prog 1989–92, chm Salford Dist Med Audit Ctee 1990–93, memb Cncl Int Soc for Diseases of the Esophagus 1989–2001, memb Cncl Br Soc of Gastroenterology 1991–94; examiner in surgery RCPSGlas 1988–2003; memb: MRC Working Party on Oesophageal Cancer 1991–97, MRC Working Party on Gastric Cancer 1993–97, Surgical Gastroenterology Gp Assoc of Surgns of GB and Ireland 1993–97, Cncl Assoc of Upper Gastrointestinal Surgns of GB and Ireland 1996–2000 (chm Educn and Research Ctee); chm: Upper Gastrointestinal Specialty Working Gp NHS Clinical Terms Project 1992–95, Surgical Section Br Soc of Gastroenterology 1994–97, NW Deanery Surgical Trg Ctee 1996–2002 (vice-chm 1993–96), MRC Working Party on Upper GI Cancer 1997–99, UKCCCR and NCRI Upper GI Cancer Gp 1999–2003; pres Surgical Section Manchester Med Soc 1999–2000; memb: Educn Ctee Assoc of Surgeons of GB and Ireland 1997–2000, Cncl, Editorial Ctee and Editorial Bd Br Jl of Surgery 1995–2003, Cncl RCPSGlas 2002–06, Steering Gp Nat Cancer Research Network 2003–05, MRC Independent Data Monitoring Ctee 2005–11; hon memb Romanian Soc of Surgery 1993, hon memb Senate Univ of Sibiu Romania; FRCSGlas 1973; *Recreations* sailing, hill walking; *Style*— John Bancewicz, Esq; ✉ Old Bank House, Lower Granco Street, Dunning, Perthshire PH2 0SQ (☎ 01764 684361)

BANCROFT, Craig John; s of John Haworth Bancroft (d 2001), of Portugal, and Susan, *née* Livsey; *b* 15 July 1961, Blackburn; *Educ* Denstone Coll; *m* 17 June 1990, Helen Elizabeth, *née* Grimshaw; 2 s (Christopher John b 20 Feb 1992, James Joseph b 31 March 1995); *Career* mgmnt trainee Trust House Forte 1979–83, gen mangr Northcote Manor 1983–86, md Northcote 1986–, co dir Sandshow Ltd 1989–2014, md Ribble Valley Inns 2004–, co dir Northcote Leisure Gp 2014–; memb Bd Pride of Britain 2011; memb Master Innholders 2010; Caterer and Hotelkeeper Acorn Award 1986; *Recreations* country sports, rugby, wine; *Clubs* Acad of Food and Wine Serv, Guild of Sommeliers, County Landowners Assoc; *Style*— Craig Bancroft, Esq; ✉ Northcote, Northcote Road, Langho, Blackburn, Lancashire (website www.northcote.com)

BANERJEE, Prof Arup Kumar; OBE (1996), JP; s of Ansumali Banerjee (d 1984), and Maya, *née* Chatterjee (d 2002); *b* 28 November 1935; *Educ* Univ of Calcutta Med Coll (MB BS); *m* 23 March 1959, Dr Aleya Banerjee, da of late Nakuleswar Banerjee; 3 s (Arpan b 14 Feb 1960, Anjan b 12 Sept 1962, Avijit b 2 Dec 1969); *Career* various jr hosp appts in India and UK 1958–67, sr registrar in med Southend Gen Hosp 1967–68, lectr in med Univ of Malaya Med Sch Kuala Lumpur 1968–71, sr registrar in elderly med Portsmouth and Southampton Univ Hosps 1971–73, conslt physician in elderly med Bolton Gen Hosp (now Royal Bolton Hosp) 1973–99 (med dir Bolton Hosp Tst 1994–98), hon clinical lectr in geriatric med Univ of Manchester 1975–, pt/t dir of Elderly Services and conslt physician in the elderly Univ of S Manchester 1998–2000, pt/t clinical dir of Elderly Services Wigan and Leigh NHS Tst 1999–2003; prof of health studies Univ of Bolton 2003–; conslt to Nat Health Advsy Serv, regnl specialist advsr in geriatric med RCP 1997–2002; memb NW RHA 1987–94 (vice-chm 1992–94); pres: Br Geriatrics Soc 1996–98, Manchester Med Soc 2002–03 (pres Med Section 1997–98), Over-50s Federation Bolton; county dir Research Into Aging N-W; memb: Geriatrics Ctee RCP London, Panel of Experts for Nat Registered Homes Tbnl; author of various pubns on med topics, regular feature writer Bolton News, ed Silver-surfers website Bolton News e-edn; govr Univ of Bolton 2010–; Hon DSc Univ of Bolton 2011; memb: Br Geriatrics Soc, BMA (memb Med Specialities Ctee 1986–94, memb CCSC 1986–94); FRCPGlas 1979 (MRCPGlas 1965), FRCPEd 1980 (MRCPEd 1967), FRCP 1982 (MRCP 1967), FRCPI 1997; *Books* Haematological Aspects of Systematic Disease (contrib, 1976), The Principles and Practice of Geriatric Medicine (contrib, 1985, 1991 and 1998), A Guide to the Care of the Elderly (1995); *Recreations* travel, music, literature; *Clubs* Rotary Club of Bolton; *Style*— Prof Arup Banerjee, OBE; ✉ 2 Pilling Field, Egerton, Bolton BL7 9UG (☎ 01204 305482, e-mail arupban28@btinternet.com)

BANGOR, Rt Hon Viscountess; *see:* Bradford, Sarah Mary Malet

BANGOR, 8 Viscount (I 1781); William Maxwell David Ward; also Baron Bangor (I 1770); s of 7 Viscount Bangor (d 1993), and his 3 w, Leila Mary, *née* Heaton (d 1959); *b* 9 August 1948; *Educ* UCL; *m* 1976, Sarah Bradford, *qv*, da of Brig Hilary Anthony Hayes, DSO, OBE, and formerly wife of Anthony Bradford; *Heir* half-bro, Hon Nicholas Ward; *Career* antiquarian bookseller; patron Bangor FC; *Recreations* history, music, antiquity, Bolton Wanderers; *Style*— The Rt Hon the Viscount Bangor; ✉ 31 Britannia Road, London SW6 2HJ

BANHAM, Sir John Michael Middlecott; kt (1992), DL (1999); s of Terence Middlecott Banham, FRCS (d 1995), and Belinda Joan Banham, CBE, *qv*; *b* 22 August 1940; *Educ* Charterhouse, Queens' Coll Cambridge (MA); *m* 30 Oct 1965, Frances Barbara Molyneux, MBE, da of Cdr Richard Molyneux Favell, DSC, RN (d 1995), of St Buryan, Cornwall; 1 s (Mark Richard Middlecott b 1968), 2 da (Serena Frances Tamsin b 1970, Morwenna Bridget Favell b 1972); *Career* temp asst princ HM Dip Serv 1962–64, mktg exec J Walter Thompson 1964–65, mktg dir Wallcoverings Div Reed International 1965–69; McKinsey & Co Inc: assoc 1969–75, princ 1975–80, dir 1980–83; first controller Audit Cmmn for Local Authorities 1983–87; DG CBI 1987–92; chm: Westcountry Television 1991–97, Local Govt Cmmn for England 1992–95, Labatt Breweries of Europe 1992–95, ECI Ventures (venture capital mangrs) 1992–2005, Tarmac plc 1994–2000, Kingfisher plc 1996–2001 (non-exec dir 1995), Whitbread plc 2000–05 (non-exec dir 1999), Geest plc 2002–05, Cyclacel Ltd 2002–06, Spacelabs Healthcare Inc 2006–08, Johnson Matthey plc 2006–11, Sultan Scientific Ltd 2010–14, Innoveas Int Ltd 2014–; dir: National Westminster Bank plc 1992–98, National Power plc 1992–98, Merchants Trust plc 1992–2005, Invesco Ltd 1999–2014, Cyclacel Pharmaceuticals Inc 2006–, Arthurian Life Sciences 2013–; chm RIBA Future Homes Cmmn 2012–14; managing tstee Nuffield Fndn 1988–97, hon treas Cancer Research Campaign 1991–2002; hon fell Queens' Coll Cambridge 1989; Hon LLD Univ of Bath 1987, Hon DSc Loughborough Univ 1989, Hon LLD Univ of Exeter 1993, Hon LLD Univ of Strathclyde 1995; Hon FCGI; *Books* Anatomy of Change (1994), A Plan for Growth for Cornwall and the Isles of Scilly (2011); author of numerous reports on mgmnt, health and local authy servs; *Recreations* gardening, cliff walking, sailing, ground clearing; *Clubs* Travellers; *Style*— Sir John Banham; ✉ Penberth, St Buryan, Cornwall TR19 6HJ

BANKS, (Arthur) David; s of Arthur Banks (d 1988), of Warrington, Cheshire, and Helen, *née* Renton (d 1997); *b* 13 February 1948; *Educ* Boteler GS Warrington; *m* Gemma, da of Francis Xavier Newton; 1 da (Natasha Kate b 12 Dec 1978), 1 s (Timothy James b 28 Sept 1982); *Career* jr reporter Warrington Guardian 1965–68, reporter/sub ed Newcastle Journal 1968–71, sub ed Daily Express 1971–72, asst night ed Daily Mirror 1972–79, asst managing ed New York Post 1979–81, night ed/asst ed The Sun 1981–86, dep managing ed New York Daily News 1986–87, dep ed The Australian 1987–89, ed Daily Telegraph Mirror Sydney 1989–92, ed Daily Mirror 1992–94; Mirror Group Newspapers Ltd: editorial dir 1994–96, new media advsr 1996–97; conslt ed Sunday Mirror 1997–98, dir of info Mirror Group 1998–99; presenter Breakfast Show Talk Radio 1999–2000; currently nat affrs corr and columnist Press Gazette; broadcaster: LBC BBC Radio Live TV, Channel 4; pres London Press Club Cncl 1995–2000; *Recreations* dining, dieting; *Style*— David Banks, Esq

BANKS, Elizabeth Christina; DL (Herefordshire 2004); da of Leslie Swain Saunders, and Elizabeth, *née* Culme Seymour; *b* 30 September 1941, Rockingham Castle, Leics; *Educ* NY Botanic Garden (Dip), Thames Poly (Dip); *m* 4 May 1963, Lawrence Banks, CBE, DL, *qv*; 2 s (Richard b 1965, Edward b 1967); *Career* landscape architect; mangr Hergest Croft Gardens; Land Use Consultants 1979–86, chair Elizabeth Banks Associates 1986–2005 (fndr 1986); pres RHS 2010–13; sec Int Dendrology's Conservation Ctee, memb Nat Arboreta Advsy Ctee; mayor Kington Town Cncl 2006–10; chm and tstee Queenswood Coronation Fund until 2010; memb: NCCPG, Nat Tst, Nat Tst for Scotland, Nat Art Collection Fund, Royal Sch of Needlework; winner of 4 Gold Medals and 1 Silver-gilt Medal Chelsea Flower Show; Liveryman Worshipful Co of Gardeners 2011; hon doctorate Greenwich Univ 2011, Hon DSc Univ of Worcester 2011; CMLI, FIHort 2011; *Publications* Creating Period Gardens (1991); articles published in Country Life, Landscape Design, The Garden and other magazines; *Recreations* gardening, fishing, walking; *Style*— Mrs Elizabeth Banks, DL; ✉ Ridgebourne, Kington, Herefordshire HR5 3EG (☎ 01544 230218, mobile 07860 530500, fax 01544 232031, e-mail elizabethb@hergest.co.uk, website www.hergest.co.uk)

BANKS, Emma; *Career* agent Creative Artists Agency; clients incl: Red Hot Chili Peppers, Jason Mraz, Kraftwerk, Arcade Fire, Lorde, Katy Perry, Stone Sour; *Style*— Ms Emma Banks; ✉ Creative Artists Agency, 5th Floor, 3 Shortlands, Hammersmith, London W6 8DA

BANKS, Gordon Raymond; s of William Banks (d 1968), and Patricia Marion, *née* MacKnight (d 1983); *b* 14 June 1955, Acomb, Northumberland; *Educ* Samuel Kings Sch Alston, Lornshill Acad Alloa, Glasgow Coll of Building and Printing, Univ of Stirling (BA); *m* 1981, Lynda, *née* Nicol; 1 da (Victoria Patricia Elizabeth b 1984), 1 s (Dominic Alexander William b 1986); *Career* Barratt: chief buyer Edinburgh 1976–84, chief buyer Falkirk 1984–86; dir Cartmore Building Supply Co Ltd 1986–; MP (Lab) Ochil & Perthshire S 2005–15, shadow min for busines, innovation and skills 2010–11, shadow min for Scotland 2012–15; memb Coeliac UK; *Recreations* songwriting, guitar, football, motorsport; *Style*— Gordon Banks, Esq; ☎ 01592 781800, e-mail gordon.banks@cartmore.com

BANKS, (Ernest) John; s of Ernest Frederick Banks (d 1995), and Marian Blanche, *née* Nuttall (d 1991); *b* 2 July 1945; *m* Rosemary Murray Banks; 1 da (Charlotte Frederique Marianne b 3 May 1983); *Career* formerly: gp int chm Young and Rubicam Int Advertising Agency, chm and managing ptnr Banks Hoggins O'Shea (formerly The Banks Partnership); gp chm and chief exec FCB London (formerly Banks Hoggins O'Shea) 1998–2005, chm Imagination 2008–10, Arden Telecom 2014–; hon sec IPA; FIPA; *Recreations* tennis, fishing, golf, shooting; *Clubs* Buck's, MCC, St Moritz Toboggan; *Style*— John Banks, Esq; ✉ The Banks Partnership, Upper Swell House, Upper Swell, Gloucestershire GL54 1EW (e-mail jb@thebankspartnership.com)

BANKS, (William) Lawrence; CBE (1998), DL (Co Hereford 2006); s of Richard Alford Banks, CBE (d 1997), and Lilian Jean, *née* Walker (d 1973); *b* 7 June 1938; *Educ* Rugby, ChCh Oxford (MA); *m* 1963, Elizabeth Christina, *qv*, da of Capt Leslie Swain Saunders, DSO, RN (d 1988), of Northants; 2 s (Richard b 1965, Edward b 1967); *Career* merchant banker; with Robert Fleming 1961–98, dep chm Robert Fleming Holdings Ltd 1996–98; chm: Caledonian Publishing 1993–96, Kington Connected Community Co Ltd 1993–2007, William Cook Holdings Ltd 1997–2002, Ambrian Ptnrs Ltd 2002–11, Ambrian Capital plc 2007–11 (dir 2005–07); dir: Roper Industries Inc 1994–2009, Blavod plc 2001–11; cmmr 1851 Exhbn 1996–2006 (chm Fin Ctee); non-exec dir Nat Blood Authy 1994–2000, chm Cncl Royal Postgrad Med Sch Hammersmith 1990–97 (former treas); hon treas: RHS 1981–92 (vice-pres 1993–, Victoria Medal of Honour), Imperial Coll London 1999–2001; chm Int Dendrology Soc 1998–2003, chm Herefordshire Community Fndn 2001–11; tstee: Chevening Estate 1978–2005 (chm Fin and GP Ctee 1998–2005), Hereford Mappa Mundi Tst, Hereford Cathedral Perpetual Tst (vice-chm 2008–13), Lister Inst 1998–2006, Sir Joseph Banks Archive Project (chm 2005–15); lay canon Hereford Cathedral 2007–10 (emeritus 2010–); hon fell Linnean Soc of London 2014; *Recreations* gardening, fishing, shooting, theatre; *Clubs* MCC, Pratt's, Flyfishers', Boodle's; *Style*— Lawrence Banks, Esq, CBE, DL; ✉ Ridgebourne, Kington, Herefordshire HR5 3EG (☎ 01544 230218, mobile 07967 390835, e-mail banks@hergest.co.uk)

BANKS, Roderick Charles I'Anson; s of Charles I'Anson Banks (d 1991), and Suzanne Mary Gwendoline, *née* Hall (d 2014); *b* 5 December 1951; *Educ* Westminster, UCL (LLB); *m* 11 Aug 1979, Susan Elizabeth Lavington, da of His Hon Albert William Clark (d 1998), of Worthing, W Sussex; 2 s (Oliver b 1982, Frederick b 1986); *Career* called to the Bar Lincoln's Inn 1974; head of chambers; legal author; CEDR accredited mediator 1993; conslt to Law Cmmn: Partnership Law Review 1998–2003, Limited Partnership Law Review 2001–03; fndr memb Assoc of Partnership Practitioners; memb CLA; *Books* Lindley on Partnership (co-ed, 14 edn 1979, 15 edn 1984), Lindley & Banks on Partnership (ed, 16 edn 1990, 17 edn 1995, 18 edn 2002, supplements 2005, 2007, 19 edn 2010, supplements 2011 and 2013, 20 edn in preparation), Encyclopedia of Professional Partnerships (ed, 1987–2010), Halsbury's Laws of England: Partnership Vol (conslt ed, 4 edn reissue 1994), Private Fund Dispute Resolution (contrib, 2014); *Recreations* reluctant gardener, TV/film addict; *Style*— Roderick I'Anson Banks, Esq; ✉ 9 King's Bench Walk, Temple, London EC4Y 7DX (☎ 020 7430 2005, fax 020 7831 1510)

BANN, Prof Stephen; CBE (2004); s of late Harry Bann, OBE, and Edna, *née* Pailin; *b* 1 August 1942, Manchester; *Educ* Winchester (scholar), King's Coll Cambridge (major scholar, state studentship, MA, PhD); *Career* University of Kent at Canterbury (now Univ of Kent): lectr in history 1967–75, sr lectr 1975–80, reader in modern cultural studies 1980–88, chair Bd of Studies in history and theory of art 1983–95, prof of modern cultural studies 1988–2000, dir Centre for Modern Cultural Studies 1990–2000, dir of grad studies Faculty of Humanities 1993–95, hon prof 2011–14; prof of history of art Univ of Bristol 2000–08 (emeritus prof and sr research fell 2008–); Mellon sr fell Canadian Centre for Architecture Montreal 2003, Edmond J Safra visiting prof Nat Gall of Art Washington DC 2005, Beatrix Farrand distinguished fell Dumbarton Oaks Research Library Washington DC 2009 (sr fell 2002–08), sr visiting fell Yale Center for Br Art 2011–14; chm Research Ctee Arts and Humanities Research Bd 1998–2000; pres Comité International d'Histoire de l'Art (CIHA) 2000–04; memb: Art Panel Arts Cncl of GB 1975–78, Art Panel South-East Arts 1976–79 and 1982–88, Int Assoc of Art Critics (AICA) 1984–, Cncl Friends of Canterbury Cathedral 1990–2000, Humanities Research Bd 1997–98, Leverhulme Research Awards Advsy Ctee 1998–2005, Museums and Galleries Ctee AHRC 2004–08, Mgmnt Bd Inst for Garden and Landscape History 2006–08; Leverhulme Emeritus Fellowship 2009; Hon DLitt Univ of Kent 2016; memb Academia Europaea 2014; FBA 1998, FSA 2009; *Books* Experimental Painting (1970), The Tradition of Constructivism (ed, 1974), The Clothing of Clio (1984), The True Vine (1989), The Inventions of History (1990), Under the Sign: John Bargrave as Collector, Traveller and Witness (1994), Romanticism and the Rise of History (1995), Paul Delaroche: History Painted (1997), Parallel Lines: Printmakers, Painters and Photographers in 19th Century France (2001, R H Gapper Prize for French Studies 2002), Jannis Kounellis (2003), The Reception of Walter Pater in Europe (ed, 2004), Ways around Modernism (2007), The Coral Mind: Adrian Stokes' Engagement with Architecture, Art History, Criticism and Psychoanalysis (ed, 2007), Painting History: Delaroche and Lady Jane Grey (with Linda Whiteley, 2010), Art and the Early Photographic Album (ed, 2011), Interlacing Words and Things: Bridging the Nature-Culture Opposition in Gardens and Landscape (2012), Distinguished Images: Prints in the Visual Economy of 19th Century France (2013), Midway: Letters from Ian Hamilton Finlay to Stephen Bann 1964–69 (ed, 2014), Bernard Lassus: The Landscape Approach (2014), Stonypath Days: Letters between Ian Hamilton Finlay and Stephen Bann 1970–72 (ed, 2016); *Recreations* travel, collecting; *Clubs* Savile; *Style*— Prof Stephen Bann, CBE, FBA; ✉ Department of History of Art, School of Humanities, University of Bristol, Bristol BS8 1TB

BANNATYNE, Duncan Walker; OBE; *b* 2 February 1949, Clydebank, Scotland; *m* 1, Gail; 4 c; m 2, 2006, Joanne McCue; 2 c; *Career* fndr: Quality Care Homes (sold 1996), Just Learning, Bannatyne Health Clubs; television appearances incl: Mind of a Millionaire (BBC 2) 2003, panel memb Dragon's Den (BBC 2) 2005–, presenter Mind Your Own Business (BBC), Fortune – Million Pound Giveaway (ITV), Rich List Give It Away (ITV), Bannatyne Takes On Tobacco (BBC 2) 2008, Beat the Bank 2008; fndr Bannatyne Charitable Fndn 2008, pres No Smoking Day 2008, tstee Comic Relief, UK ambass UNICEF 2009–; Hon DSc Glasgow Caledonian Univ 2006, Hon DBA Univ of Teesside 2009; *Style*— Duncan Bannatyne, Esq, OBE; ✉ Bannatyne Fitness Limited, Power House, Haughton Road, Darlington, Co Durham DL1 1ST

BANNER, Fiona; *b* 1966, Merseyside; *Educ* Kingston Poly (BA), Goldsmiths Coll London (MA); *Career* artist; *Solo Exhibitions* incl: 1301PE (Santa Monica) 2000, Soixante-Neuf (Charles H Scott Gallery Emily Carr Inst Vancouver) 2000, Rainbow (Hayward Gallery London) 2001, FIONA BANNER – ARSEWOMAN (Galerie Barbara Thumm Berlin and Murray Guy NY) 2001, (Wanker) (Frith Street Gallery London) 2002, My Plinth is your Lap (Dundee Contemporary Arts and Neuer Aachener Kunstverein) 2002, 130 IPE (Brian Butler LA) 2003, All the World's Fighter Planes (NY) 2006 and (Musée d'Art De Joliette) 2007, NUDE (Frith Street Gallery) 2006, Peace on Earth (Tate Britain) 2007, London the Bastard Word (Power Plant Toronto) 2007, The Naked Ear (Frith Street Gallery) 2010, The Duveen Galleries Commision: Harrier and Jaguar (Tate Britain) 2010, Snoopy Vs The Red Baron (Galerie Barbara Thumm) Berlin 2011, Unboxing: The Greatest Film Never Made (1301PE LA) 2012, A Room For London (with David Kohn Architects, one-bedroom installation on top of the Queen Elizabeth Hall in association with Artangel, Living Architecture and Southbank Centre London) 2012, The Vanity Press (Summerhall Edinburgh) 2013, Yorkshire Sculpture Park and Longside Gallery Leeds 2014, Mistah Kurtz – He Not Dead (PEER London) 2014; *Group Exhibitions* incl: To Infinity and Beyond: Editions for the Year 2000 (Brooke Alexander NY) 2000, The Living End (Boulder Museum of Contemporary Art) 2000, Murray Guy NY 2000, Summer Show (Frith Street Gallery London) 2000, Customized: Hot Rods, Low Riders and American Car Culture (ICA Boston) 2000, Eine Munition unter Anderen (Frankfurter Kunstverein) 2000, Ever get the feeling you've been...Cheated (A22 Projects London) 2000, All You Need is Love (Laznia Center of Contemporary Art Gdansk) 2000, CAB London 2001, A Pause for Breath (Frith Street Gallery London) 2001, American Tableaux (Walker Art Center Minneapolis) 2001, Total Object, Complete with Missing Parts (Tramway 2 Glasgow) 2001, Tatoo Show (Modern Art London) 2001, Dévoler (Institut d'art contemporain Villeurbanne) 2001, The Multiple Store (The New Art Centre Sculpture Park and Gallery Roche Court) 2001, Berlin Biennale 2001, Fiona Banner, Munro Galloway, Corey McCorkle (Murray Guy NY) 2001, Nothing: Exploring Invisibilities (Northern Gallery of Contemporary Art Sunderland, Rooseum Malmo and CAC Vilnius) 2001, definition (Murray Guy NY) 2001, Drawings (Frith Street Gallery London) 2001, Superman in Bed, Contemporary Art and Photography (The Collection Gaby and Wilhelm Schürmann Museum am Ostwald Dortmund) 2001, Featherweight (Susan Hobbs Gallery Toronto) 2001, City Racing (ICA London) 2001, The Green Room (Percy Miller Gallery London) 2001 and 2002, Remix: Contemporary Art and Pop (Tate Liverpool) 2002, Here, There and Elsewhere; Dialogues on Location and Mobility (London Print Studio Gallery) 2002, Turner Prize exhbn (Tate Britain London) 2002, Global Feminisms (Brooklyn Museum NY) 2007, That Was Then...This Is Now (MOMA NY) 2008, London Calling, Who Gets to Rule The World (Total Museum of Contemporary Art Seoul) 2009, Parade and Processions (Parasol Unit London) 2009, Sweep Me Off My Feet (Val de Marne Museum of Contemporary Art Paris) 2009, Just What Are They Saying (Jonathan Ferrara Gallery New Orleans) 2009, Let's Dance (MAC/VAL Paris) 2010, Musée Los

Angeles LA DLA 2010, Pipe Series: This is Sculpture (Tate Liverpool) 2010, Nothing Is Forever (S London Gallery) 2010, Echo... from the age I was able to see it (Koraalberg Gallery Antwerp) 2010, Alice In Wonderland (Tate Liverpool) 2011, Vis a Vis (Rossi Contemporary Brussels) 2011, Dance/Draw (ICA Boston) 2011, September 11 (MOMA PS1 NY) 2011, Friendship of the Peoples (Simon Oldfield London) 2011, Tracing the Century: Drawing As A Catalyst for Change (Tate Liverpool) 2012, Liverpool Graphology (The Drawing Room London) 2012, Text in Progress (RH Gallery NY) 2012, Neon, Who's Afraid of Red, Yellow and Blue? (La Maison Rouge Paris) 2012, So To Speak (BRIC Rotunda Gallery NY), Alice In Wonderland (Museo di Arte Moderna e Contemporanea di Trento e Rovereto) 2012, Postscript: Writing After Conceptual Art (The Power Plant Toronto) 2013, GLASSTRESS: White Light/ White Heat (Instituto Veneto di Scienze Lettere ed Arti, Venice Benniale) 2013, Postscript: Writing After Conceptual Art (Broad Art Museum Michigan) 2014, Building Site (Hardwick Hall Chesterfield) 2014, This Page Left Intentionally Blank (Akbank Art Center Istanbul) 2014; *Work in Public Collections* incl: Contemporary Art at Penguin London, Contemporary Arts Soc London, FSA London, Met Museum of Art NY, Neuberger & Berman NY, Philadelphia Museum, Sammlung Ringier Zurich, The Arts Cncl of England, Br Cncl London, Tate Gallery London, Van Abbe Museum Eindhoven, Walker Art Gallery Minneapolis, Worcester Museum MA, MOMA NYC; *Books* Performance Nude, Other Criteria (2009), Duveens Commission 2010: Harrier and Jaguar (Lizzie Carey-Thomas and Dave Hickey, 2010), Alice In Wonderland Through the Visual Arts (Gavin Delahunty and Benjamin Schulz, 2011), Snoopy Vs the Red Baron (catalogued Barbara Thumm, 2011), Against Expression, An Anthology of Conceptual Writing (ed by Craig Dworkin and Kenneth Goldsmith, 2011), The Vanity Press (2013); *Style—* Ms Fiona Banner; ✉ c/oAnn Marie Pena, Frith Street Gallery, 17–18 Golden Square, London W1F 9JJ

BANNER, Norman Leslie; DL (Cheshire 2009); s of Frank Leslie Banner (d 1986), of Warrington, and Clarice, *née* Rutter (d 1986); *b* 6 November 1947; *Educ* Lymm GS, Manchester Poly (BA); *m* 1, 1972 (m dis 1981), Andrea, *née* Atkinson; m 2, 1995 (m dis 2015), Louise, *née* Astley; 2 s (Mark William Astley b 22 Jan 1998, Edward James Astley b 20 June 2003); *Career* Robert Davies & Co slrs Warrington: articled clerk 1971, admitted slr 1973, ptnr 1978–95; ptnr Ridgway Greenall Warrington 1995–2003, sr ptnr Davies Ridgway Warrington 2003–08, memb Forshaws Davies Ridgway LLP 2008–13 (sr ptnr 2009–13, conslt 2013–); chm: Warrington Ctee for the Disabled 1978–91, Warrington Crossroads Care Attendant Scheme 1980–99, Birchwood Project (Warrington) Ltd 1984–, Warrington Hosp NHS Tst 1993–2001, N Cheshire Hosps Tst 2001–04; non-exec dir Mersey RHA 1991–93; pres Assoc of Crossroads Care Attendant Schemes 1992–96 (chm 1983–92); memb Bd St Rocco's Hospice Warrington 2008– (chm 2010–); dir Warrington Festival Tst 1982–93, dir Cheshire Community Fndn 2011–; memb Law Soc 1973, Rotary of Warrington 1984–2002 (past pres); *Clubs* Warrington; *Style—* Norman Banner, Esq, DL; ✉ 21 Palmyra Square, Warrington WA1 1BW (☎ 01925 230000, e-mail norman.banner@fdrlaw.co.uk)

BANNISTER, (Richard) Matthew; s of Richard Neville Bannister, of Sheffield, and Olga Margaret, *née* Bennett; *b* 16 March 1957; *Educ* King Edward VII Sch Sheffield, Univ of Nottingham (LLB); *m* 1, 23 June 1984, Amanda Gerrard Walker; 1 da (Jessica b 3 Dec 1984); m 2, 14 Jan 1989, Shelagh Margaret Macleod; 1 s (Joseph b 1 May 1990); m 3, 19 May 2007 (m dis 2013), Katherine Jane Hood; *Career* presenter and reporter BBC Radio Nottingham 1978–81, presenter and prodr Capital Radio 1981–83, presenter Radio One Newsbeat 1983–85, head of news Capital Radio 1987–88 (asst head of news 1985–87); BBC: rejoined as managing ed Greater London Radio 1988–91, chief asst to BBC's Dir of Corporate Affrs 1991–92, project co-ordinator BBC Charter Renewal 1992–93, controller Radio One 1993–98, dir BBC Radio 1996–98, chief exec BBC Prodn 1998–99, dir Marketing and Communication BBC 1999–2000, chm Wire Free Prodns Ltd 2012–, currently presenter BBC Radio 4 and BBC World Service; Hon DLitt Univ of Nottingham 2011; fell Radio Acad 1997; *Recreations* theatre, rock music, collecting P G Wodehouse first editions; *Style—* Matthew Bannister, Esq; ✉ c/o Sue Ayton, Knight Ayton Management, 35 Great James Street, London WC1N 3HB (☎ 020 7831 4400, e-mail info@knightayton.co.uk, website www.knightayton.co.uk)

BANNISTER, Sir Roger Gilbert; kt (1975), CBE (1955); s of late Ralph Bannister and Alice Bannister, of Harrow; *b* 23 March 1929; *Educ* Univ Coll Sch London, Exeter and Merton Colls Oxford (MA, MSc, BM BCh, DM), St Mary's Hosp Med Sch London; *m* 1955, Moyra, da of Per Jacobsson (chm IMF), of Sweden; 2 s, 2 da; *Career* Athletics: winner Oxford v Cambridge Mile 1947–50, pres OUAC 1948, capt Oxford and Cambridge Combined American Team 1949, finalist Olympic Games Helsinki 1952, Br mile champion 1951, 1953 and 1954, first man to run 4 minute mile 1954, Br Empire Mile title and record 1954, Euro 1500m title and record 1954; Medicine: jr med specialist RAMC 1958, Radcliffe travelling fell from Oxford Univ at Harvard 1962–63; hon conslt physician Nat Hosp for Nervous Diseases London (formerly conslt physician 1963–90); hon conslt neurologist: St Mary's Hosp London (formerly conslt neurologist 1963–85), Oxford Regnl and Dist Health Authy 1985–93; Master of Pembroke Coll Oxford 1985–93; chm Govt Working Pty on Univ Sports Scholarships 1996–97; memb: Cncl King George's Jubilee Tst 1961–67, Miny of Health Advsy Ctee on Drug Dependence 1967–70; chm: Sports Cncl 1971–74, Med Ctee St Mary's Hosp 1983–85; pres: Nat Fitness Panel NABC 1956–59, Sussex Assoc of Youth Clubs 1972–79, Int Cncl for Sport and Physical Recreation 1976–83, Alzheimer's Disease Soc 1982–84; tstee Leeds Castle Fndn 1981–2005, ed Leeds Castle Med Conf Health Challenge Beyond Year 2000; govr: Atlantic Coll 1985–92, Sherborne Sch 1989–93; Liveryman Worshipful Soc of Apothecaries; hon fell: UMIST 1974, Exeter Coll Oxford 1979, Merton Coll Oxford 1986, Harris Manchester Coll Oxford 2006; Hon LLD Univ of Liverpool 1972, Hon DLitt Univ of Sheffield 1978; Hon Dr: Jyvaskyla Univ Finland 1983, Univ of Bath 1984, Imperial Coll London 1984, Grinnell USA 1984, Univ of Rochester NY 1985, Univ of Pavia Italy 1986, Williams Coll USA 1987, Victoria Univ Canada 1994, Univ of Wales Cardiff 1995, Loughborough Univ 1996, UEA 1997, Cranfield Univ 2002, RCS(Ed) 2002; FRCP; *Books* First Four Minutes (1955, 50th anniversary edn 2004), Brain and Bannister's Clinical Neurology (ed, 3–7 edn 1966–92), Autonomic Failure (1983, 5 edn (with Christopher Mathias, *qv*) 2013); author of numerous papers on neurology and disorders of the autonomic nervous system; *Clubs* Athenaeum, Vincent's (Oxford); *Style—* Sir Roger Bannister, CBE; ✉ 21 Bardwell Road, Oxford OX2 6SU

BANSKI, Norman Alexander Fyfe Ritchie; s of Richard Carol Stanislaw Ba?ski, Lt 9 Polish Lancers (d 1970), of Kincardineshire, and late Marion Alexandra Watt Fyfe (later Mrs George A Ritchie); *b* 3 August 1955; *Educ* Laurencekirk Secdy Sch, Mackie Acad Stonehaven, Univ of Aberdeen (LLB); *m* 4 July 1997, Laura Ann Patricia, da of James George Emile Milton; 2 step da (Julia Dorothy Patricia Wardle, Alice Veronica Wardle); *Career* slr and NP; sr ptnr Banski & Co, registrar births deaths and marriages (ret), cemetery clerk (ret), census offr (S Kincardine) 1981 and 1991; tstee various local charitable tsts, dir Howe O'The Mearns Developments Ltd; sec and dir: Caledonian Railway (Brechin) Ltd, Kincardine and Mearns Area Partnership, Montrose Air Station Heritage Centre; sec: Villages in Control, Mearns Area Project, Mearns Challenge Project; hon vice-pres: Laurencekirk and Dist Angling Assoc, PM Lodge St Laurence 136; past princ Chapter Haran 8; memb: Cncl Law Soc of Scotland, Nat Tst for Scotland, Scottish Rural Property and Business Assoc, Esk Dist Fishery Bd 1991–2001, Laurencekirk and Dist Business Clu; treas Kincardine and Deeside Faculty of Slrs; *Recreations* golf, preserved railways, philately, rugby; *Clubs* Laurencekirk and Dist Angling Assoc, Laurencekirk and District Business, F P Rugby, Lodge St Laurence 136, Chapter Haran 8, Auchenblae Golf; *Style—* Norman Banski, Esq; ✉ Banski & Co, Royal Banks Buildings, Laurencekirk AB30 1AF

BANSZKY, Caroline Janet; da of Harold Arthur Armstrong While (d 1982), of East Molesey, Surrey, and Janet Bell Symington; *b* 1953; *Educ* Wycombe Abbey, Univ of Exeter (BA); *m* 31 March 1984 (m dis 1995), Baron Nicholas Laszlo Banszky von Ambroz, s of Baron Dr Laszlo Banszky von Ambroz; 2 da (Genevra b 1985, Antonella b 1987); *Career* formerly articled clerk rising to audit asst mangr KPMG Peat Marwick McLintock; N M Rothschild & Sons Ltd: Corp Fin Div 1981–84, Fin Div 1984–97, chief fin offr 1988–89, exec dir 1989–, fin dir 1995–97; dep chief exec SVB Syndicates Ltd 1997–98, chief operating offr SVB Holdings plc (now Novae plc) 1998–2001, md The Law Debenture Corp plc 2002–, dir 3i Gp plc; dir UK Cell Fndn, dir Br Neurological Research Tst 2002– (chm 2010–12), dir UK Stem Cell Fndn 2012–; Liveryman Worshipful Co of Farriers 1978, Liveryman Worshipful Co of Tinplate Workers alias Wireworkers' Co 1998; FCA 1991 (ACA 1978); *Recreations* children, walking, dogs, scottish dancing, beef cattle; *Clubs* Caledonian; *Style—* Caroline Banszky; ✉ The Law Debenture Corporation plc, Fifth Floor, 100 Wood Street, London EC2V 7EX (☎ 020 7696 5902, fax 020 7696 5243, e-mail caroline.banszky@lawdeb.com)

BANVILLE, John; *Educ* Christian Brothers' Schs, St Peter's Coll Wexford; *m* Janet Dunham; 2 s (Colm, Douglas); *Career* novelist and journalist 1969–; *Awards* incl: Allied Irish Banks Fiction Prize, American-Irish Fndn Award, James Tait Black Meml Prize, Guardian Prize for fiction, Guinness Peat Aviation Award, Premio Ennio Flaiano 1991, Premio Nonino 2003, Man Booker Prize 2005, Franz Kafka Prize 2011, Austria State Prize for Literature 2013, Prince of Asturias Award 2014; Chevalier de l'Ordre des Arts et des Lettres 2014; *Books* Long Lankin (short stories, 1970), Nightspawn (1971), Birchwood, Doctor Copernicus, Kepler, The Newton Letter, Mefisto, The Book of Evidence (shortlisted Booker Prize 1989), Ghosts (1993), Athena (1995), The Untouchable (shortlisted Whitbread Novel of the Year Award 1997), Eclipse (2000), Shroud (2002), Prague Pictures: Portraits of a City (non-fiction, 2003), The Sea (2005, Man Booker Prize 2005), The Infinities (2009), Ancient Light (2012), The Blue Guitar (2015); as Benjamin Black: Christine Falls (2006), The Silver Swan (2007), The Lemur (2008), Elegy for April (2010), A Death in Summer (2011), Vengeance (2012), Holy Orders (2013), The Black-eyed Blonde (2014), Even the Dead (2015); *Clubs* Kildare Street and University (Dublin); *Style—* John Banville, Esq; ✉ c/o Ed Victor Limited, 6 Bayley Street, Bedford Square, London WC1B 3HE

BARA?SKI, Prof Zygmunt Guido; s of Henryk Bara?ski (d 1984), and Sonia, *née* Mariotti (d 2011); *b* 13 April 1951, Nottingham; *Educ* St Bede's Coll Manchester, Univ of Hull (BA); *m* 7 April 1979, Margaret, *née* Watt; 1 da (Anna Matilde b 22 Oct 1986), 1 s (Edward Marek b 23 Sept 1989); *Career* lectr in Italian Univ of Aberdeen 1976–79; Univ of Reading: lectr in Italian studies 1979–89, sr lectr in Italian studies 1989–92, prof of Italian studies 1992–2002; Serena prof of Italian Univ of Cambridge 2002–11 (emeritus 2011–), fell New Hall Cambridge 2002–11; Notre Dame prof of Dante and Italian studies Univ of Notre Dame 2011–; visiting prof: McGill Univ 1988 and 1997, Univ of Virginia Charlottesville 1991, Univ of Connecticut 1993, Yale Univ 1995, Univ of Notre Dame 1996,1998, 2004, 2007 and 2010, Univ of Bari 2001, Univ of Calif Berkeley 2002, Univ of Reading 2002–, Univ of Calif LA 2008, Univ of Leeds 2012–, Monash Univ 2014, Univ of Basel 2016; Fondazione Il Campiello Medal for Italian literature 1990, Gold Medal of the City of Florence for Dante studies 1999, Valle dei Trulli Prize for literary criticism 2001; life memb Società Dantesca Italiana Florence 1997; Commendatore dell'Ordine della Stella della Solidarietà Italiana 2005; *Books* Libri Poetarum in Quattuor Species Dividuntur: Essays on Dante and Genre (1995), Luce Nuova, Sole Nuovo: Saggi sul Rinnovamento Culturale in Dante (1996), Pasolini Old and New (1999), Dante e i Segni (2000), Chiosar con Altro Testo: Leggere Dante nel Trecento (2001), Petrarch and Dante: Anti-Dantism, Metaphysics, Tradition (2009), Dante in Context (2015); *Recreations* following Manchester United FC, music, cycling; *Style—* Prof Zygmunt Bara?ski; ✉ Department of Romance Languages and Literatures, University of Notre Dame, 343 O'Shaughnessy Hall, Notre Dame, IN 46556, USA (☎ 001 574 631 6886, fax 001 574 631 3493)

BARBER, Antonia; *see:* Anthony, Barbara

BARBER, Sir Brendan Paul; kt (2013); s of John Barber (d 1996), of Southport, Merseyside, and Agnes Barber (d 2006); *b* 3 April 1951, Southport; *Educ* St Mary's Coll Crosby, City Univ (BSc, pres Students' Union); *m* 1981, Mary, *née* Gray; 2 da (Amy b 1985, Sarah b 1988); *Career* researcher Ceramic, Glass & Mineral Products ITB 1974–75; TUC: joined 1975, researcher Orgn Dept 1975–79, head Press and Information Dept 1979–87, head Orgn Dept 1987–93, dep gen sec 1993–2003, gen sec 2003–12; ACAS: memb Cncl 1995–2004, chair 2014–; memb Sport England 1999–2002; dir Ct Bank of England 2003–12, dir Transport for London 2013–, dir Banking Standards Bd 2015– (dep chm 2016–); memb Cncl City Univ London 2013–; visiting fell: Said Business Sch Oxford 2010–, Nuffield Coll Oxford 2013–; teacher VSO Ghana 1969–70; *Recreations* football (Everton FC and Barnet FC), golf, theatre, cinema; *Clubs* Muswell Hill Golf, Everton Supporters London Area; *Style—* Sir Brendan Barber

BARBER, Daniel Mark; s of David Barber, and Gillian Barber; *b* 21 September 1964; *Educ* JFS Comp Sch, St Martin's Sch of Art (BA); *m* 6 June 1992, Sandra, da of Lèo Rogg; 1 s (Moses b 1996); *Career* designer/dir Lambie Nairn & Co 1988–93; creator of title sequence for BBC Nine O'Clock News and station identities for BBC1, BBC2, Carlton TV and various Euro TV stations; Rose Hackney Barber Productions (formerly Rose Hackney): commercials dir 1993–2005, ptnr 1995–2005; co-fndr Knucklehead 2005–; creator of TV and cinema commercials for clients incl BMW, Sony, Orange, Ford, Adidas, Daewoo, Shell, Saab, and The RAF; dir Harry Brown 2009 (starring Sir Michael Caine); recipient of numerous awards/honours from industry bodies incl BAFTA, D&AD, BTA, RTS, Clio and Creative Circle, nominated Acad Award 2008 (for The Tonto Woman); subject of profile articles in many industry magazines in Europe and America, work published in major design and advtg pubns; memb D&AD; *Recreations* cinema, tennis, shopping, driving, dieting, travel; *Style—* Daniel Barber; ✉ Knucklehead, Unit 22–23, Archer Street Studios, 10–11 Archer Street, London W1D 7AZ

BARBER, Edward Simon Dominic; OBE (2013); s of Simon Barber, of London, and Penelope, *née* Baldock (d 1974); *b* 6 April 1969; *Educ* Leeds Poly (BA), RCA (MA); *Career* designer; fndr BarberOsgerby 1996–, co-owner Universal Design Studio Ltd 2001–, founding dir and co-owner MAP 2012; clients incl: Vitra, B&B Italia, Knoll, Louis Vuitton, Flos, Venini, Cappellini; commissioned to design furniture for De La Warr Pavilion Bexhill on Sea, RIBA, Portsmouth Cathedral; commissioned to design Olympic and Paralympic Torches for London Olympics 2012, commissioned to design £2 coin commemorating the London Underground's 150th anniversary; exhibited at: V&A, Haunch of Venison London, Sotheby's London, MoMA NY, Int Furniture Fair NY, Design Museum London, Crafts Cncl London, Design Miami/Basel; work in permanent collections: V&A London, Met Museum of Art NY, Design Museum London, Art Inst of Chicago, Indianapolis Museum of Art, Cooper-Hewitt, Smithsonian Design Museum NY; external examiner Royal Coll of Art; Hon DA Oxford Brookes Univ, Hon DArts Leeds Met Univ 2012; fell Ravensbourne Coll; MCSD 2003, FRSA 2005, RDI 2007; *Awards* incl: Best New Designer ICFF NY 1998, shortlisted for Compasso d'Oro 2004, Jerwood Prize for Applied Arts 2004, Furniture Designer of the Year Blueprint Magazine 2005, Best Product Red Dot Award 2006, Designer of Future (with Established & Sons) Basel 2006, Designers of the Year Elle Decoration 2007, Chicago Athenaeum Good Design Award 2011, D&AD

Yellow Pencil 2012, Icon Magazine Design Studio of the Year 2012, World Technology Award for Design 2012, Design Museum Design of the Year and Product Design of the Year 2012, German Design Cncl German Design Award 2012, Maison & Objet Designers of the Year 2013, shortlisted for Compasso d'Oro 2013; *Publications* The Design Work of Edward Barber and Jay Osgerby (2011), Ascent (2011); *Style*— Edward Barber, Esq, OBE; ✉ 37–42 Charlotte Road, London EC2A 3PG (✆ 020 7033 3884, fax 020 7033 3882, website www.barberosgerby.com)

BARBER, Frances Jennifer; da of S W Brookes, of Wolverhampton, and Gladys, *née* Simpson (d 1991); *b* 13 May 1958; *Educ* Municipal GS Wolverhampton, Univ of Bangor, Univ of Cardiff; *Career* actress; memb: Dr Barnardos, Terrence Higgins Tst, Cancer Research, The Labour Party; prodn bd memb BFI 1995–; *Theatre* incl: Ooh La La for Hull Truck (Plays and Players Award Most Promising Newcomer nomination 1980), Riff Raff Rules, Space Ache (Tricycle Theatre), La Guerra, Desperado Corner, Madam Louise (Glasgow Citizen's and Venice Festival), The Treat (ICA), The Mission (Soho Poly), Hard Feelings (Oxford Playhouse and Bush Theatre), Summer and Smoke (Leicester Haymarket), Viola in Twelfth Night, Lady Macbeth in Macbeth (Exchange Manchester), Eliza Doolittle in Pygmalion, Maxine Faulk in The Night of the Iguana (RNT), My Heart's A Suitcase (Royal Court), Over a Barrel (Palace Theatre Watford), Imagine Drowning (Hampstead), Insignificance (Donmar); for RSC credits incl: Camille (Olivier Award for Most Promising Newcomer 1985), Ophelia in Hamlet, Jacquetta in Love's Labour's Lost, Dolores in The Dead Donkey, Uncle Vanya (Regional Theatre Award for Best Supporting Actress, Olivier Award nomination Best Supporting Actress); *Television* incl: Home Sweet Home, A Flame to the Phoenix, Those Glory Days, Reilly Ace of Spies, Hard Feelings, Clem, Twelfth Night, Duck, Annie Besant, Behaving Badly, The Grasscutter, The Nightmare Years, The Storey Teller – The Greek Myths, Do Not Disturb, The Orchid House, Hancock, Inspector Morse, The Leaving of Liverpool, A Statement of Affairs, Inspector Alleyn, Spitting Image – Thatcherworld, Return to Blood River, In the Cold Light of Day, Dirty Old Town, Circle of Deceit, Rules of Engagement, Space Precinct, Rhodes, It Might be You, Royal Scandal, Real Women (3 part, BBC), Just In Time (Channel Four), Tea (MTV), Dalziel & Pascoe (BBC), The Ice House (BBC), Plastic Man, Love in a Cold Climate (BBC); *Films* incl: Rosie in Sammy and Rosie Get Laid, Megan in We Think the World of You, Leonie Orton in Prick up your Ears, A Zed and Two Noughts, Castaway, The Missionary, Acceptable Levels, White City, The Soul of the Machine, Young Soul Rebels, Secret Friends, The Lake, Soft Top, Hard Shoulder, The Fish Tale, Scarborough Ahoy! (Best Foreign Student American Academy Award), Three Steps to Heaven, Photographing Fairie, Still Crazy, Mauvaise passe, Esther Kahn, Shiner; also three french speaking films: Chambre a Part, Giorgino, Germaine et Benjamin; *Recreations* swimming, reading, walking the dog, poetry; *Style*— Ms Frances Barber

BARBER, Prof James; *b* 16 July 1940; *Educ* UC Swansea (tech state scholar, BSc), UEA (Nuffield biological fell, MSc, PhD); *m* 1 s (b 1969), 1 da (b 1971); *Career* Unilever Biochemical Soc European fell Biophysics Dept Univ of Leiden 1967; Imperial Coll London: lectr Dept of Botany 1968–74, reader in plant physiology 1974–79, prof of plant physiology 1979–90, dean Royal Coll of Science 1989–91, head Dept of Biochemistry 1989–99, dir Centre for Photomolecular Science 1990–, Ernst Chain prof of biochemistry 1990–; Selby lectr of the Aust Acad of Sci 1996; Miller visiting prof Univ of Calif Berkeley 1989 and 2001, Burrough-Wellcome prof Univ of Calif 2000, visiting prof Politecnico di Torino Italy 2007–, Lee Kuan Yew distinguished visitor and lectr Singapore 2008, visiting prof Nangang Technological Univ Singapore 2009–, G8 Univ Simmit Turin keynote speech 2009, Sir Ernst Chain distinguished lectr 2011; memb Cncl Weizmann Inst Fndn London 1991–2001 (memb Cncl 2001–); memb editorial bds of numerous scientific jls; memb Academia Europaea 1989; Flintoff Medal RSC 2002, Novartis Medal and Prize Biochemical Soc 2005, Italgas Prize for energy and the environment 2005, Wheland Medal and Prize Univ of Chicago 2007, Arnon Lecture and Prize Univ of California Berkeley 2008, Interdisciplinary Prize RSC 2013, Polar Medal European Photochemistry Assoc, Inter-American Photochemistry Soc and Asian and Oceanian Photochemistry Assoc 2016, Communication Award Int Soc of Photosynthesis Research 2016; Hon Dr Univ of Stockholm 1992, Hon DSc UEA 2010; CChem, FRSC 1980, FRS 2005; *Books* Topics in Photosynthesis Vol 1–12 (series ed, 1976–92), Techniques and New Developments in Photosynthesis Research (ed with R Malkin), Trends in Photosynthesis Research (ed with H Medrano and M G Guerrero), Advances in Molecular Biology Vol 11 (ed), Frontiers in Molecular Biology (ed with B Andersson); published over 600 papers; *Recreations* sailing, gardening, carpentry; *Clubs* Royal Soc; *Style*— Prof James Barber; ✉ Department of Life Sciences, Faculty of Natural Sciences, Sir Ernst Chain Building, Imperial College London, Exhibition Road, London SW7 2AZ (✆ 020 8747 1165, fax 020 7594 5267, e-mail j.barber@imperial.ac.uk)

BARBER, Prof Karin Judith; CBE (2012); da of Dr Charles Barber, and Barbara, *née* Best; *b* Gothenburg, Sweden; *Educ* Univ of Cambridge (BA, Eileen Alexander Prize), UCL (Dip Social Anthropology), Univ of Ife Nigeria (PhD); *Partner* Dr Paulo Fernando de Moraes Farias; *Career* teacher St Mary's Teacher Trg Coll Bukedea Uganda 1967–68, lectr Dept of African Languages and Literatures Univ of Ife Nigeria 1977–84, princ instr in Yorùbá language Dept of Linguistics/African Studies Center UCLA 1982, pt/t instr in Yorùbá language City Literature Inst London 1984–85; Centre of West African Studies Univ of Birmingham: lectr 1985–93, sr lectr 1993–97, reader in African cultural anthropology 1997–99, dir 1998–2001, prof of African cultural anthropology 1999–; Northwestern Univ Evanston: preceptor Inst for Advanced Study and Research in the African Humanities 1993–94, Melville J Herskovits chair in African Studies (visiting appt) 1999; Scholar for a Day Univ of Pennsylvania 2000, British Acad Research Readership 2001–03; pres African Studies Assoc of the UK (ASAUK) 2000–02 (memb Cncl 1987–90, vice-pres 1998–2000); FBA 2003 (memb Cncl 2007–10, vice-pres (humanities) 2008–10); *Publications* Yorùbá Dùn ún So: A Beginner's Course in Yorùbá (part 1, 1984), Discourse and its Disguises: The Interpretation of African Oral Texts (ed with P F de Moraes Farias, 1989), Self-assertion and Brokerage: Early Cultural Nationalism in West Africa (ed with P F de Moraes Farias, 1990), I Could Speak Until Tomorrow: Oríkì, Women and the Past in a Yorùbá Town (1991, Amaury Talbot Prize 1992), Yorùbá Popular Theatre: Three Plays by the Oyin Adéjobí Company (with Báyọ̀ Ògúndíjọ, 1994), West African Popular Theatre (with John Collins and Alain Ricard, 1997), Readings in African Popular Culture (ed, 1997), Yorùbá Wuyi (with Akin Oyetade, 1999), The Generation of Plays: Yorùbá Popular Life in Theater (2000, Herskovits Award 2001), Africa's Hidden Histories: Everyday Literacy and Making the Self (ed, 2006), The Anthropology of Texts, Persons and Publics: Oral and Written Cultures in Africa and Beyond (2007), Print Culture and the First Yoruba Novel: I B Thomas's Life Story of Me, Segilola and Other Texts (2012, Paul Hair Prize 2013); author of numerous research articles and contribs to books and jls; *Recreations* theatre; *Style*— Prof Karin Barber, CBE; ✉ Department of African Studies and Anthropology, School of History and Cultures, University of Birmingham, Edgbaston, Birmingham B15 2TT (✆ 0121 414 5125, e-mail k.j.barber@bham.ac.uk)

BARBER, (Franklin) Lionel; s of Frank Douglas Barber, and Joan, *née* Nolan; *b* 18 January 1955, London; *Educ* Dulwich Coll, St Edmund Hall Oxford (BA); *m* 13 Dec 1986, Victoria Greenwood; 1 da (Francesca b 5 May 1988), 1 s (Dashiell b 8 Aug 1990); *Career* reporter The Scotsman 1978–81, business corr Sunday Times 1981–85; FT: Washington corr then bureau chief Brussels 1985–98, news ed 1998–2000, ed Continental Europe edn 2000–02, managing ed US 2002–05, ed 2005–; tstee Tate 2011, tstee Carnegie Corp 2014; Laurence Stern fell Washington Post 1985, Woodrow Wilson Fndn fell, visiting fell European Univ Inst Florence 1996; Young Journalist of the Year Br Press Awards 1981, included in Le Nouvel Observateur's 101 most influential Europeans 1998, St George's Soc Medal of Honour 2009; *Publications* The Price of Truth: The story of Reuters' millions (co-author, 1985), Not with Honour: The inside story of the Westland scandal (co-author, 1986), Britain and the New Europe (1998); The Birth of the Euro (1998); *Recreations* opera, cycling, armchair rugby; *Style*— Lionel Barber, Esq; ✉ Financial Times, One Southwark Bridge, London SE1 9HL (✆ 020 7873 3000, fax 020 7873 3924, e-mail lionel.barber@ft.com)

BARBER, Lynn; da of Richard Barber, of Ebbesborne Wake, Wilts, and Beryl Barber; *b* 22 May 1944; *Educ* The Lady Eleanor Holles Sch, St Anne's Coll Oxford (BA); *m* 1971, David Maurice Cloudesley Cardiff (d 2003), s of Maj Maurice Cardiff, CBE, of Little Haseley, Oxford; 2 da (Rose b 1975, Theodora b 1978); *Career* asst ed Penthouse magazine 1967–72, staff writer Sunday Express Magazine 1984–89, feature writer Independent on Sunday 1990–93, contributing ed Vanity Fair 1992, feature writer The Observer 1996–2009, interviewer Sunday Times 2009–; Br Press Awards: Magazine Writer of the Year 1986 and 1987 (commended 1992), Feature Writer of the Year 1990, Interviewer of the Year 1997, 2002 and 2012; What the Papers Say Award Interviewer of the Year 1990; *Books* How to Improve Your Man in Bed (1973), The Single Woman's Sex Book (1975), The Heyday of Natural History (1980), Mostly Men (1991), Demon Barber (1998), An Education (2009), A Curious Career (2014); *Recreations* gossip; *Style*— Ms Lynn Barber; ✉ e-mail lynnbaba@aol.com

BARBER, Nicholas Charles Faithorn; CBE (2004); s of Bertram Harold Barber (d 1982), and Nancy Lorraine, *née* Belsham (d 1984); *b* 7 September 1940; *Educ* Shrewsbury, Wadham Coll Oxford (MA), Columbia Univ NY (MBA); *m* 8 Jan 1966, Sheena Macrae, da of Donald Graham (d 1984); 2 s (James Henry b 1969, George Belsham b 1974), 1 da (Fenella Macrae b 1972); *Career* lectr Marlboro Coll Vermont 1963–64; Ocean Group plc: joined 1964, dir 1980–94, gp md 1986–87, gp chief exec 1987–94; chm: Innovative Electronics Co 1996–99, Orion Publishing Group Ltd 1997–98, Bolero Int Ltd 1998–2016 (dir 1998–), Kappa IT Ventures (GP) Ltd 1999–2007; dir: Overseas Containers Ltd 1984–86, Costain Group plc 1990–93, Royal Insurance Holdings plc 1991–96 (dep chm 1994–96), Barings plc 1994–95, Bank of Ireland Financial Services UK plc 1994–2003 (dep chm 2001–03), Albright & Wilson plc 1995–99, Royal & Sun Alliance Insurance Group plc 1996–2003, Fidelity Japanese Values plc 2000–12, The Maersk Co 2004–08; tstee: Nat Museums and Galleries Merseyside 1986–94, British Museum 1993–2003 (chm British Museum Friends 1992–2003, chm British Museum Co 1996–2003), Country Houses Fndn 2004–; chm: Huron Univ USA in London Ltd 1998–2007, Ashmolean Museum Oxford 2003–10; vice-pres Liverpool Sch of Tropical Med 1988–2013; govr: NIESR 1991– (memb Exec Ctee 2001–), London Business Sch 1993–2001; dir Hult Int Business Sch Boston MA 2008–, dir Ashridge Business Sch 2015–; memb: Cncl Univ of Liverpool 1985–88, Advsy Ctee Tate Gallery Liverpool 1988–92, Supervisory Bd Columbia Business Sch NY 1991–2006, Cncl Industrial Soc 1993–99, Int Advsy Cncl Asia House 1996–; govr Shrewsbury Sch 1983–2003 (dep chm 1997–2003); tstee Shrewsbury Sch Fndn 1990–2006, chm Classics for All 2013–16 (tstee 2013–), tstee Strawberry Hill Tst 2013–, dir Int Dendrological Soc 2015–; dir Liverpool Playhouse 1982–87; hon fell Wadham Coll Oxford 2007, Distinguished Friend of Oxford 2010, fell Ashmolean Museum 2011; Hon Dr Marlboro Coll VT 2005; FRSA 1994; *Recreations* cricket, mountain walking, woodland gardening, museums, theatre, reading; *Clubs* Brooks's, Denham Golf, MCC (memb Arts and Library Ctee 2012–); *Style*— Nicholas Barber, Esq, CBE; ✉ 6 Lytton Court, 14 Barter Street, London WC1A 2AH

BARBER, Ralph Gordon; s of John Leslie Barber (d 2010), and Margaretta Primrose, *née* Sanders (d 2003); *b* 2 January 1951; *m* Elizabeth Anne Barber; *Career* advsr to Gp Chm HSBC Holdings plc; co sec: The Hongkong and Shanghai Banking Corporation 1986–92, HSBC Holdings plc 1990–2013, HSBC Bank plc 1994–96; FCIS, FRSA; *Clubs* The Hong Kong Golf; *Style*— Ralph Barber, Esq; ✉ HSBC Holdings plc, 8 Canada Square, London E14 5HQ (✆ 020 7991 0588, fax 020 7991 4639)

BARBER, Dr Richard William; s of Dr Geoffrey Osborn Barber (d 1988), of Dunmow, Essex, and Daphne, *née* Drew (d 1982); *b* 30 October 1941; *Educ* Felsted, Marlborough (sr scholarship), CCC Cambridge (MA, PhD, Trevelyan scholarship); *m* 1970, Helen Rosemary, *née* Tolson (d 2013); 1 s (Humphrey Thomas b 1974), 1 da (Elaine Mary b 1976); *Career* publisher and author; fndr md Boydell Press (now Boydell & Brewer Gp Ltd) 1969–2009, founding dir Boydell & Brewer Gp Ltd 2010–; founding dir Univ of Rochester Press NY 1989; hon fell Historical Assoc 2009; hon visiting prof Dept of History Univ of York 2012, Hon DLitt Univ of York 2014; FRSL 1970, FRHistS 1976, FSA 1978; *Books* Arthur of Albion (1961), Henry Plantagenet (1963), The Knight and Chivalry (1970, Somerset Maugham Award, new edn 1996), The Figure of Arthur (1974), Edward Prince of Wales and Aquitaine (1976), Companion Guide to Southwest France (1977, new edn 1998), A Companion to World Mythology (1979), The Arthurian Legends (1979), King Arthur (1986), Tournaments (with Juliet Barker, 1989), Pilgrimages (1991), The Holy Grail (2004), Edward III and the Triumph of England (2013); ed for Folio Soc: Aubrey's Brief Lives (1975), Life and Campaigns of the Black Prince (1979), The Pastons (1981), Fuller's Worthies (1987), The Worlds of John Aubrey (1988), Bestiary (1992), British Myths and Legends (1998), Legends of King Arthur (2000), Edward III's Round Table at Windsor (jtly, 2007), Legends of the Grail (2007), Edward III and the Triumph of England (2013), Henry II (2015), Medieval Court Festivals (2016); *Recreations* sailing, gardening, travel, music; *Style*— Dr Richard Barber, FSA, FRSL; ✉ Boydell & Brewer Ltd, PO Box 9, Suffolk IP12 3DF

BARBER, His Hon Trevor Wing; s of Robert Barber, and Margaret Barber; *b* 10 June 1943; *Educ* Worksop Coll, King's Coll Newcastle upon Tyne (LLB); *m* 1967, Judith Penelope, *née* Downey; 1 s, 1 da; *Career* called to the Bar Inner Temple 1967; in practice Sheffield 1967–92, circuit judge (NE Circuit) 1992–2014, ret; *Recreations* gardening, golf, reading; *Style*— His Hon Trevor Barber

BARBER OF TEWKESBURY, Baron (Life Peer UK 1992), of Gotherington in the County of Gloucestershire; Sir Derek Coates Barber; kt (1984); s of Thomas Smith-Barber (d 1967), and Elsie Agnes, *née* Coates (d 1967); descendant of John Coats whose three sons due to a disagreement swore not to bear his name 1870, instead they adopted Coates, Cotts and Coutts; *b* 17 June 1918; *Educ* RAC Cirencester; *m* 1 (m dis 1981); m 2, 1983, Rosemary Jennifer Brougham, da of Lt Cdr Randolph Brougham Pearson, RN (ka 1946); *Career* farmer and land conslt; fndr memb Farming & Wildlife Advsy Gp 1969, environment conslt Humberts Chartered Surveyors 1972–93, chm BBC's Central Agric Advsy Ctee 1974–80, conslt Humberts Landplan 1974–89, chm Countryside Cmmn 1981–91, chm Booker plc Countryside Advsy Bd 1990–96; pres: Glos Naturalists Soc 1982–2005, RSPB 1990–91 (chm 1976–81, vice-pres 1982–98), Royal Agric Soc of England 1991–92, The Hawk and Owl Tst 1992–96, Br Pig Assoc 1995–97; vice-pres Ornithology Soc of Middle East 1987–97, patron Pendle Heritage Tst 1990–, tstee Farming and Wildlife Tst 1984–91; chm New Nat Forest Advsy Bd 1991–95, dep chm The Groundwork Fndn 1985–91; memb: Bd Centre for Econ and Environmental Devpt 1983–99, Advsy Ctee Centre for Agric Strategy 1985–88, Cncl Br Tst for Ornithology 1987–89, Cncl Rare Breeds Survival Tst 1987–93 (pres 1991–95 and 1997–99); John Haygarth Gold Medal in Agric 1939, Bledisloe Gold Medal for Distinguished Servs to UK Agric 1969, RSPB Gold Medal for Servs to Wildlife Conservation 1983, Massey-Ferguson Agric Award 1989, RASE Gold Medal for Distinguished Service to Agric 1991; Queen's Silver Jubilee Medal 1977; Hon

DSc Univ of Bradford 1986; Hon FRASE 1986; *Books* Farming for Profits (with Keith Dexter, 1961), Farming in Britain Today (with Frances and J G S Donaldson, 1969), Farming and Wildlife: a Study in Compromise (1971), A History of Humberts (1980); *Recreations* birds, farming; *Style*— The Rt Hon Lord Barber of Tewkesbury; ✉ House of Lords, London SW1A 0PW

BARBIERI, Margaret Elizabeth; da of Ettore Barbieri, and Lea Barbieri; *b* 2 March 1947; *Educ* Durban, Royal Ballet Sr Sch; *m* 1982, Iain Webb, soloist with the Royal Ballet; 1 s (Jason Alexander b July 1987); *Career* Sadler's Wells Royal Ballet: joined 1965, princ 1970, sr princ 1974–90; guest artist with Birmingham Royal Ballet 1990 and 1991; prodr, freelance teacher and coach 1990–, dir Classical Graduates Course London Studio Centre, artistic dir Images of Dance Co 1990–, govr Royal Ballet 1992–2000; since 1990 has staged: Ashton's Façade, De Valois' Rake's Progress, Cranko's Pineapple Poll, Markova's Les Sylphides, Petipa's Raymonda Act III and Kingdom of the Shades Act from La Bayadère, Swan Lake Act II, Paquita Act II, La Corsaire Act III, Ashton's Façade (K Ballet Co Japan 2003, Oregon Ballet Theatre 2004), Nureyev's Raymonda Act III (K Ballet Co Japan 2003); appeared with Royal Ballet throughout Europe and in Canada, USA, South America, Australia, New Zealand, China, Japan, Yugoslavia, India, Egypt, Israel and elsewhere; made guest appearances in USA, Germany, South Africa, France, Norway and Czechoslovakia; *Performances* with Royal Ballet incl: Giselle (first performance in the role at Covent Garden 1968), Sleeping Beauty (first performance Leeds 1969), Swan Lake (first performance Frankfurt 1977), Romeo and Juliet (first performance Covent Garden 1979), Papillon, The Taming of the Shrew, Coppélia, Les Sylphides, Raymonda Act III, Le Spectre de la Rose, La Vivandière, Petrushka, Ashton's La Fille Mal Gardée, Two Pigeons, The Dream, Façade, Wedding Bouquet and Rendezvous, Cranko's Lady and the Fool, Card Game and Pineapple Poll, MacMillan's The Invitation and Solitaire, Elite Syncopation, Summer in The Four Seasons, de Valois' Checkmate and The Rake's Progress, van Manen's Grosse Fugue and Tilt, Tudor's The Lilac Garden, Howard's Fête Étrange, Layton's Grand Tour, Hynd's Summer Garden, both Killar's and Rodrigues' Cinderella; created roles in ballets incl: Tudor's Knight Errant, Drew's From Waking Sleep, Sacred Circles and The Sword, Cauley's Ante-Room, Layton's Oscar Wilde, Thorpe's Game Piano, Killar's The Entertainers, Hynd's Charlotte Brontë, Wright's Summertide, Bintley's Metamorphosis and Flowers of the Forest, Corder's The Wand of Youth; *Recreations* classical music, theatre, gardening; *Style*— Miss Margaret Barbieri; ✉ c/o London Studio Centre, 42–50 York Way, London N1 9AB

BARCLAY, Sir David Rowat; kt (2000); s of Frederick Hugh Barclay (d 1947), and Beatrice Cecilia, *née* Taylor (d 1989); er twin bro of Sir Frederick Barclay, *qv*; *b* 27 October 1934, Hammersmith, London; *Career* real estate agent and prop Hillgate Estate Agents (later became Barclays Hotels) in 1960s and 1970s (hotels owned since incl Londonderry, Lowndes, Grosvenor, Charing Cross and Great Western); jt prop (with bro, Frederick): Howard Hotel 1975–2000, Ellerman Gp 1983–, Gotaas-Larsen 1988–97, The European newspaper 1992–98, Automotive Financial Gp 1994–, Ritz Hotel 1995–, Scotsman Publications (pubns incl The Scotsman, Scotland on Sunday and Edinburgh Evening News) 1995–2006, The Business newspaper 1998–, Sears 1999–2000, Littlewoods 2002–, March UK (former GUS Gp catalogue business) 2003–, Telegraph Gp (pubns incl Daily Telegraph, Sunday Telegraph and The Spectator) 2004–, Hotel Mirabeau Monte Carlo, Maybourne Hotel Gp 2011–15; also investor in: Trigen Holdings, MonsterMob, SmartServ Online, Birdstep Technology; co-fndr and tstee The David and Frederick Barclay Fndn (formerly The Barclay Fndn) 1990–; co-owner Brecqhou (an island off Sark, CI) 1993–; Hon Dr Univ of Glasgow 1998; Papal Knight Order of St Gregory 2010, Commander Order of St Charles (Monaco) 2014 (Offr 2000); *Style*— Sir David Barclay; ✉ Le Montaigne, 7 avenue de Grande Bretagne, Monte Carlo 98000, Monaco

BARCLAY, HE Sir Frederick Hugh; kt (2000); s of Frederick Hugh Barclay (d 1947), and Beatrice Cecilia, *née* Taylor (d 1989); yr twin bro of Sir David Barclay, *qv*; *Career* real estate agent with bro David's co Hillgate Estate Agents (later became Barclays Hotels) in 1960s (appointed dir 1968, hotels co-owned since incl Londonderry, Lowndes, Grosvenor, Charing Cross and Great Western); jt prop (with bro, David): Howard Hotel 1975–2000, Ellerman Gp 1983–, Gotaas-Larsen 1988–97, The European newspaper 1992–98, Automotive Financial Gp 1994–, Ritz Hotel 1995–, Scotsman Publications (pubns incl The Scotsman, Scotland on Sunday and Edinburgh Evening News) 1995–2006, The Business newspaper 1998–, Sears 1999–2000, Littlewoods 2002–, March UK (former GUS Gp catalogue business) 2003–, Telegraph Gp (pubns incl Daily Telegraph, Sunday Telegraph and The Spectator) 2004–, Hotel Mirabeau Monte Carlo, Apollo antiques mag 2004–, Cavendish Hotel London 2006–, Maybourne Gp 2011–15; also investor in: Trigen Holdings, MonsterMob, SmartServ Online, Birdstep Technology; co-fndr and tstee The David and Frederick Barclay Fndn (formerly The Barclay Fndn) 1990–; co-owner Brecqhou (an island off Sark, CI) 1993–; HE ambass extraordinaire at large for the economic devpt of The Principality of Monaco 2010; Hon Dr Univ of Glasgow 1998; KSG 2010, Commander Order of St Charles (Monaco) 2014 (Offr 2000); *Style*— HE Sir Frederick Barclay; ✉ Le Montaigne, 7 avenue de Grande Bretagne, Monte Carlo 98000, Monaco

BARCLAY, Humphrey John; s of John Barclay, and Patricia Slade; cous of Julian Slade (d 2006); *b* 24 March 1941, Dorking, Surrey; *Educ* Harrow (head of sch), Trinity Coll Cambridge (BA); *Career* TV prodr; dir Cambridge Circus (Cambridge Footlights Revue starring John Cleese, *qv*, Graham Chapman, Tim Brooke-Taylor, *qv*, and Bill Oddie) West End, NZ and Broadway 1963; joined BBC Radio 1963 (prodr first 50 episodes I'm Sorry, I'll Read That Again), Rediffusion TV 1967–68 (invented Do Not Adjust Your Set (winner Prix Jeunesse 1968) starring Eric Idle, Terry Jones, Terry Gilliam and Michael Palin, Esq, CBE, *qqv*), LWT 1968–83 (head of comedy 1977–83), jtly estab ind prodn co Humphrey Barclay Prodns 1983, controller of comedy LWT 1996–99, head of comedy devpt Granada Media Int 1999–2000, devpt exec (comedy) Celador Prodns 2002–; assoc Limehouse Prodns 1983, sometime script ed Video Arts; progs produced for LWT incl: We Have Ways of Making You Laugh, The Complete and Utter History of Britain, No! No! No!, Doctor in the House, Hark at Barker (pairing Ronnie Barker, Esq, OBE and David Jason, Esq, OBE, *qv*), Six Dates with Barker, No – Honestly, Yes – Honestly, Pig in the Middle, The Pink Medicine Show, Two's Company, A Fine Romance, Bless Me Father, Now and Then, Agony (starring Maureen Lipman, CBE, *qv*, Best Situation Comedy Banff TV Festival), The Strange Case of the End of the World as We Know It, Metal Mickey, End of Part One (nominated Int Emmy Award), Whoops Apocalypse (Most Original Prog Award RTS), Maggie and Her, The Glums, Stanley Baxter's Christmas Box, Holding the Fort, The Top Secret Life of Edgar Briggs, Luck Feller, Mixed Blessings, Canned Laughter, Peter Cook and Co (Gold medal NY Film and TV Festival), No Problem!, Hale and Pace, Faith in the Future, Saturday Live, Blind Men, The People vs Jerry Sadowitz, Duck Patrol, Can We Still Be Friends?, Bostock's Cup, Jack and the Beanstalk, Cinderella, Spaced; progs produced for Humphrey Barclay Prodns: Party at the Palace, Relative Strangers (nominated Int Emmy Award, Silver Medal NY Film and TV Festival), Hot Metal, Thompson, Behaving Badly, Look Back in Anger, Surgical Spirit, Up The Garden Path, Conjugal Rites, What You Looking At?, Desmond's (Team Award and Silver Medal RTS, Br Comedy Best Sitcom Award), That's Love; progs produced for Limehouse Prodns: Short Vehicle, Up For Grabs, Celebration, Dream Stuffing; developed for Granada Media Int: Living Off Larry, Whetfish, Sit Down Shut Up; juror: BAFTA, Montreux Int Festival, RTS, Race in the Media Awards, Olivier Awards; ran comedy writing workshops in Johannesburg, Cape Town and Accra; adopted in the Ghanaian Royal family of Asona 2000, given the name Kwadwo Ameyaw Gyearbuor Yiadom I and appointed Nkosuohene (devpt chief) Kwahu Tafo 2001, fndr and chair Friends of Tafo 2002–; Freeman City of London, Liveryman Worshipful Co of Fishmongers; Br Empire Medal for Services to Kwahu Tafo (Birthday Honours 2014); *Recreations* watercolour painting, theatre, travelling; *Style*— Humphrey Barclay, Esq; ✉ website www.friendsoftafo.org

BARCLAY, James Christopher; OBE (2006); s of Theodore David Barclay (d 1981), and Anne Millard, *née* Bennett (d 1996); *b* 7 July 1945; *Educ* Harrow; *m* 1974, Rolleen Anne, da of Lt-Col Walter Arthur Hastings Forbes (d 1987); 2 c; *Career* served 15/19 King's Royal Hussars 1964–67; former bill broker; chm and jt md Cater Allen Ltd (bankers) 1981–98, chm Cater Allen Holdings plc 1985–98 (dep chm 1981–85); non-exec chm LTP Trade plc 2001–10; dir: M&G Equity Investment Trust plc 1996–2011 (chm 1998–2011), Abbey National Treasury Services plc 1997–98, Abbey National Offshore Holdings Ltd 1998–2001, Thos Agnew & Sons Ltd 1998–, New Fulcrum Investment Trust plc 1999–2005, UK Debt Management Office 2000–05, Rathbone Bros plc 2003–10; chm Liontrust Knowledge Economy Tst plc 2001–03; chm London Discount Market Assoc 1988–90; *Recreations* fishing, shooting, sailing; *Clubs* Pratt's, Boodle's; *Style*— James Barclay, Esq, OBE; ✉ Rivers Hall, Waldringfield, Woodbridge, Suffolk IP12 4QX

BARCLAY, John Adam; *b* 24 September 1986, Hong Kong; *Educ* Dollar Acad; *Career* rugby union player (flanker); with Glasgow Warriors 2004–; Scotland: 17 caps, debut 2008; *Style*— Mr John Barclay; ✉ c/o Glasgow Warriors, Firhil Stadium, Firhill Road, Glasgow G20 7AL

BARCLAY, Prof (Alan) Neil; s of Frank Rodney Barclay (d 2014), and Betty Cowie, *née* Watson (d 1987); *b* 12 March 1950, Wantage, Oxon; *Educ* Univ of Oxford (BA, DPhil); *m* 10 July 1975, Ella, *née* Quinn; 2 s (Mark Robert b 23 April 1977, Luke Stuart b 3 Jan 1984), 1 da (Alison Tanum b 18 Dec 1979); *Career* post doctoral research fell Univ of Goteborg Sweden 1976–78; Univ of Oxford: MRC scientific staff MRC Cellular Immunology Unit 1978–99, prof of molecular immunology 1998–, MRC external scientist 1999–2011, EPA Cephalosporin prof of chemical pathology 2011–15, fell Lincoln Coll Oxford 2011–15; fndr and chm Everest Biotech Ltd 1999–, fndr and chm Absolute Antibody Ltd 2012–; hon memb Scandinavian Soc for Immunology 1993, memb Br Soc for Immunology 1985; *Publications* The Leucocyte Antigens Factsbook (1992 and 1997); author of 150 pubns in scientific jls; *Recreations* running, music, writing children's stories (unpublished); *Style*— Prof Neil Barclay; ✉ Sir William Dunn School of Pathology, University of Oxford, South Parks Road, Oxford OX1 3RE (☎ 01865 275598, fax 01865 275591, e-mail neil.barclay@path.ox.ac.uk)

BARCLAY, Patrick; s of Patricia Barclay (d 1978), and Guy Deghy (d 1992); *b* 15 August 1947; *Educ* Dundee HS; *Children* 1 da (Jennifer b 29 Nov 1968), 1 s (Duncan b 9 Nov 1972); *Career* journalist; trainee Evening Telegraph Dundee 1963–64; sub-ed: Evening Express Aberdeen 1965, Scottish Daily Mail 1966, The Sun 1966–67; football reporter and columnist The Guardian 1976–86 (sub-ed 1967–76); football corr: Today 1986, The Independent 1986–90, The Observer 1990–96; football columnist The Sunday Telegraph 1996–2009, chief football corr The Times 2009–11, Evening Standard 2012–; Sports Journalist of the Year British Sports Journalism Awards 1993; *Style*— Patrick Barclay, Esq

BARCLAY, His Hon Paul Robert; s of John Alexander Barclay (d 1994), and Mabel Elizabeth, *née* McMullen; *b* 12 December 1948; *Educ* Nottingham HS, St John's Coll Cambridge (MA); *m* 29 July 1972, Sarah Louise, da of Philip Arthur Jones (d 2009), and Lois Mary Jones (d 1999); 4 c (Alice b 2 June 1975, Luke b 7 April 1977, Anna b 23 July 1979, Sam b 18 Feb 1982); *Career* barrister Albion Chambers Bristol 1972–98, recorder 1996–98 (asst recorder 1992–96), circuit judge (Western Circuit) 1998–2013, ret; *Recreations* real village cricket; *Style*— His Hon Paul Barclay

BARCLAY, Stephen Paul; MP; *b* 1972, Lancs; *Educ* King Edward VII Sch Lytham St Annes, Peterhouse Cambridge, Chester Coll of Law; *Career* slr Axa Insurance until 2001, FSA 2001–05, Barclays Bank 2005–10; MP (Cons) Cambs NE 2010–; *Style*— Stephen Barclay, Esq, MP; ✉ House of Commons, London SW1A 0AA

BARDELL, Hannah; MP; *b* 1 June 1983, West Lothian; *Educ* Univ of Stirling (BA); *Career* TV prodr GMTV 2005–07, office mangr to Rt Hon Alex Salmond, MSP, *qv* 2007–10, protocol and events mangr US Consulate Edinburgh 2010–12, communications mangr Subsea 7 2012–13, head of communications and mktg Storr Technical Servs 2013–14; MP (SNP) Livingston 2015–; *Style*— Ms Hannah Bardell, MP; ✉ House of Commons, London SW1A 0AA (e-mail Hannah.Bardell.MP@parliament.uk, Twitter @HannahB4LiviMP)

BARDEN-STYLIANOU, Dr Stephen; s of Eugene Stylianou (d 1983), and Constantia Stylianou, of Port Alfred, South Africa; *b* 26 June 1950, Arusha, Tanzania; *Educ* Paul Roos Gymnasium Stellenbosch, Centre for Applied Social Science Univ of Natal, Harvard Business Sch (PMD), Oxford Sch of Coaching and Mentoring, Univ of Middlesex (DProf); *m* 1, Aug 1970, Juliet; 1 c (Sascha b 27 July 1972); m 2, Feb 1979, Foszia; 2 c (Rishad b 1 Sept 1980, Nuria b 11 Feb 1983), m 3, May 2003, Sibylle; *Career* radio and TV broadcaster and journalist 1970–87; TV-AM: journalist 1982–87, managing ed 1988–91; chief operating offr BSkyB 1991–92, md and ceo News Datacom Ltd and News Digital Systems Ltd 1992–94; fndr and ceo tech start-ups 1995–98: Sigma Squared Ltd, Worldpipe Ltd, Millennium New Media Ltd; ceo Axel Springer TV GmbH 1998–2000, md Axel Springer TV Productions GmbH 1999–2000, ceo Quadriga Worldwide 2000–01, dir Stephen Barden Coaching Ltd 2001–; *Publications* Doctoral Thesis: Top Leaders' Experiences of Learning; *Clubs* Harvard Club of London, Maerkischer Golf (Potsdam Germany); *Style*— Dr Stephen Barden; ✉ Stephen Barden Coaching Ltd, 3 Hillcroft Avenue, Purley, Surrey CR8 3DJ (e-mail stephen@stephenbarden.org, website www.stephenbarden.org)

BARDHAN, Prof Karna Dev; OBE (2002); s of Maj-Gen Pramatha Nath Bardhan (d 1966), of Pune, India, and Anima, *née* Chaudhuri; *b* 16 August 1940; *Educ* Christian Med Coll of Vellore Univ of Madras (MB BS), Univ of Oxford (Rhodes scholar, DPhil); *m* 15 Dec 1972, Dr Gouri Bardhan, da of Maj-Gen P Ram Kumar, of Bangalore, India; 1 s (Satyajeet b 11 Nov 1977), 1 da (Suchitra Kaveri b 30 Sept 1980); *Career* house physician Oxford and Hammersmith Hosp London 1968–69, registrar Royal Hosp Sheffield 1969–70, conslt physician Dist Gen Hosp Rotherham 1973–, hon lectr in gastroenterology Sheffield Univ 1973– (lectr in med 1970–72); memb: Br Soc of Gastroenterology, Assoc of Physicians of GB and Ireland, American Gastroenterological Assoc, American Coll of Gastroenterology, American Coll of Physicians; FRCP, FACP; *Books* Perspectives in Duodenal Ulcer (1980), Topics in Peptic Ulcer Disease (ed, 1987), Non-Responders in Gastroenterology (ed 1991); *Recreations* photography; *Style*— Prof K D Bardhan, OBE; ✉ Rotherham General Hospital, Moorgate Road, Rotherham S60 2UD (☎ 01709 304570, fax 01709 304168)

BARFIELD, Julia Barbara; MBE (2000); da of Arnold Robert Barfield, and Iolanthe Mary Barfield; *b* 15 November 1952; *Educ* Godolphin & Latymer Sch, AA Sch of Architecture; *m* 17 July 1981, David Joseph Marks, MBE, RIBA, *qv*; 1 s, 2 da; *Career* architect; Tetra Ltd 1978–79, Richard Rogers Partnership 1979–81, Foster Associates 1981–88, Marks Barfield Architects 1989–, London Eye Co (formerly Millennium Wheel Co) 1994–2006, Spiral Cafe Lightbox Brighton i360; subject of and contrib to TV and radio progs incl: The Biggest Wheel in the World (BBC2) 1999, The Millennium Wheel (Discovery) 2000, Wheel (Channel 4) 2000 and 2001, Women in Architecture (Channel 4) 2001; delivered numerous lectures at instns worldwide; assessor: Civic Tst Awards, RIBA Awards;

memb Lambeth Democracy Cmmn 2000–01; memb: Cncl AA, Design Review Panel CABE, Thames Gateway Panel; memb ARCUK, RIBA; *Exhibitions* Tower Power Architecture Fndn, Royal Acad of Arts (annually) 1997–2001 and 2003–06, Sustainable London, RIBA, Materials Gallery Sci Museum (permanent exhbn); *Awards* Special Commendation Prince Philip Designers Prize 2000, American Inst of Architects Design Award 2000, Corus Construction Award 2000, Dupont Benedictus Award for Innovation 2000, London First Millennium Award 2000, People's Choice Award London Tourism Awards 2000, Tourism for Tomorrow Award 2000, Leisure Property Forum Award 2000, RIBA Award 2000, 2004 and 2006, RICS Award 2000, Walpole Award 2001, Euro Award for Steel Structures 2001, Silver and Gold D&AD Awards 2001, Design Week Special Award 2001, Blueprint Award 2001, Pride of Britain Award for Innovation 2001, Architectural Practice of the Year 2001, Queens Award for Enterprise 2003, CoolBrands (annually) 2003–06, Places and Genius overall winner BDI Awards 2005, Civic Tst Award 2006; *Recreations* family, travel, the Arts; *Style—* Ms Julia Barfield, MBE, RIBA; ✉ Marks Barfield Architects, 50 Bromells Road, London SW4 0BG (☎ 020 7501 0180, e-mail jbarfield@marksbarfield.com)

BARI, Dr Muhammad Abdul; MBE (2003); s of M Manikuddin (d 1999), and Karimun Nessa (d 1969); *b* 2 October 1953, Bangladesh; *Educ* Univ of Chittagong Bangladesh (BSc, MSc), KCL (PhD, PGCE), Open Univ (Cert); *m* 10 Oct 1981; 4 c; *Career* offr Bangladesh Air Force 1978–82, physics researcher Royal Holloway Coll 1987–90, science teacher Haringey 1991–96, specialist teacher Tower Hamlets 1997–2011; memb: Muslim Cncl of Britain, Islamic Forum Europe, East London Mosque, London Muslim Centre, Muslim Aid, LOCOG (London Organising Ctee Olympic Games 2012); hon fell Queen Mary Univ of London 2008; hon doctorate Univ of E London 2012; FRSA 2005; *Books* Building Muslim Families (2002), A Guide to Parenting (2003), Race, Religion and Muslim Identity in Britain (2005), Marriage and Family Building in Islam (2007), Addressing Adolescence (2011), British, Muslims, Citizens: Introspection and Renewal (2012), Meet the Challenge, Make the Change: A Call to Action for Muslim Civil Society in Britain (2013); *Recreations* reading, writing, gardening, community work, travelling; *Style—* Dr Muhammad Abdul Bari, MBE, FRSA; ✉ London Muslim Centre, 46–92 Whitechapel Road, London E1 1JX (☎ 020 7650 3000)

BARING, Sir John Francis; 3 Bt (UK 1911), of Nubia House, Northwood, Isle of Wight; s of Capt Raymond Alexander Baring (d 1967), and Margaret Fleetwood, OBE, JP, DL, *née* Cambell-Preston (who m 2, 6 Earl of Malmesbury and d 1994); suc unc Sir Charles Christian Baring, 2 Bt (d 1990); *b* 21 May 1947; *Educ* Eton, RAC Cirencester; *m* 1, 1971 (m dis 2005), Elizabeth Anne, yr da of late Robert David Henle Pillitz, of Buenos Aires, Argentina; 2 s (Julian Alexander David b 1975, James Francis b 1984), 1 da (Andrea Hermione b 1977); m 2, 2007, Penelope Ann, da of late Cdre John McGregor Doull, RCN; *Heir* s, Julian Baring; *Career* Citibank NA 1971–72, Chemical Bank (now JPMorgan) 1972–84, Kidder Peabody & Co 1984–89, GPA Group Ltd 1989, Hackman Baring & Co 1991–97, HB Communications Acquisition Corp (now Source Media Inc) 1993–95, Coopers & Lybrand Securities LLC (now PricewaterhouseCoopers Securities LLC) 1997–99, Mercator Capital LLC 1999–2004, Camphill Village USA Inc 2007–13, ret; *Recreations* fishing, gardening; *Style—* Sir John Baring, Bt; ✉ 500 Cathedral Drive, #2814, Aptos CA 95001

BARING, Louise Olivia; da of Aubrey George Adeane Baring (d 1987), and Marina, *née* Bessel; *m* 1997, Eric Franck, s of Louis Franck (d 1988), and Evelyn, *née* Aeby; 1 s (Misha Edward Franck b 1998); *Career* journalist; letters arts and home affrs writer Britain section The Economist 1983–89, commissioning ed You magazine The Mail on Sunday 1989–90, asst features ed The Independent on Sunday 1990–93, feature writer Condé Nast Publications 1994– (contrib ed 1997–2005), arts contrib Daily Telegraph 2005–; *Books* Martine Franck (2007), Norman Parkinson (2009), Emmy Andriesse (2013), Dora Maar (2017); *Style—* Ms Louise Baring; ✉ 7 Victoria Square, London SW1W 0QY (☎ 020 7630 5972, e-mail louisebaring@mail.com)

BARING, Nicholas Hugo; CBE (2003); s of Francis Anthony Baring (ka 1940), and Lady Rose Gwendolen Louisa McDonnell DCVO (d 1993); *Educ* Eton, Magdalene Coll Cambridge; *m* 1972, Elizabeth Diana, *née* Crawfurd; 3 s; *Career* late Lt Coldstream Gds; md Baring Brothers 1963–68, Barings plc 1968–89; dir Northern & Employers Assurance Co 1966, dir Commercial Union (following merger) 1968–98 (chm 1990–98); chm The Baring Fndn 1998–2004; chm Bd of Tstees Nat Gallery 1992–96; chm: Fitzwilliam Museum Tst 2004–11, Baring Archive Tst 2009–; memb Cncl Nat Tst 1978–2002; *Style—* N H Baring, Esq, CBE; ✉ The Old Rectory, Ham, Marlborough, Wiltshire SN8 3QR

BARKER, Hon Adam Campbell; s of William Alan Barker, of Sandwich, Kent (d 1988), and Rt Hon Baroness Trumpington, DCVO, PC (Life Peer), *qv*; *b* 31 August 1955; *Educ* King's Sch Canterbury, Queens' Coll Cambridge (MA); *m* 1985, Elizabeth Mary, da of Eric Marsden, OBE (d 1996); 1 da (Virginia Giverny b 1987), 1 s (Christopher Adam b 1989); *Career* solicitor and attorney; barr 12 King's Bench Walk 1978–80; assoc Webster & Sheffield NY 1980–90, ptnr Sedgwick Detert Moran & Arnold LLP (NY and London) 1990–2008, gen cnsl HCC Global Financial Products 2008–10, gen cnsl Ryan Specialty (Europe) Ltd 2010, dep chm ANV SL 2011–; *Recreations* golf, tennis, horse racing (steward: Lingfield Park Racecourse 1992–, Windsor 2007–, Kempton 2008–, Epsom 2011–), bridge; *Clubs* Turf, Royal St George's (Sandwich), Hurlingham, Pilgrims; *Style—* The Hon Adam Barker; ✉ October Cottage, Town Croft, Hartfield, East Sussex TN7 4AD (☎ 01892 770014); ANV, 4th Floor, 1 Minster Court, London EC3R 7AA (☎ 07850 706302)

BARKER, Bridget Caroline; da of Michael John Barker (d 2010), and Brenda, *née* Sawdon (d 1987); *b* 7 March 1958, UK; *Educ* Haberdashers' Monmouth Sch for Girls, Univ of Southampton (LLB); *m* Simon Herrtage; 1 da (Alexandra); *Career* admitted slr 1983; Macfarlanes: joined 1981, ptnr 1988, currently head investment mgmnt gp; Skadden Arps Slate Meagher & Flom NY 1986–87; memb: Law Soc, Int Bar Assoc, Assoc of Women Slrs, City of London Slrs Co; chm Gynaecological Cancer Fund (operated by Grace Belgravia); *Recreations* tennis, travel, gardening, swimming, bridge; *Clubs* Grace Belgravia, The Lansdowne; *Style—* Ms Bridget Barker

BARKER, David Edward; s of Edward Reginald Barker, of Radlett, Herts, and Frances Barker, *née* Solly; *b* 28 May 1946; *Educ* Bushey Sch, Watford Art Coll; *m* 9 Oct 1971, Jennifer Ann, da of Ernest Farnham (d 1960), of Morden, Surrey; 1 da (Cassia Eve b 1978), 1 s (Leo Farnham b 1979); *Career* art dir Leo Burnett Ltd London 1966–68, creative gp head J Walter Thompson London and NY 1970–75 (art dir 1968–70); creative dir: Rupert Chetwynd 1975–79, Benton & Bowles London 1979–80, Geers Gross 1980–84; fndr and creative dir Humphreys Bull & Barker 1984–86, fndr and exec creative dir KHBB 1986–90, dir The Reject Shop plc 1990–94, founding ptnr chm and creative dir Mountain View 1998 (formerly Barker and Ralston 1991–98), fndr Ebou Consulting 2003, marketing dir Votiva 2007, co-fndr dHelix Ltd Sales and Mktg 2010, creative and innovation conslt Fresh Tracks Canada and Fabris Lane UK; memb Ernest and Julio Gallo Global Strategy Bd 2003; *Recreations* motor racing, photography, music, SERV (Bloodrunner); *Clubs* FOC; *Style—* David Barker, Esq; ✉ Ebou Ltd, Dancers End Lodge, Dancers End, Tring, Hertfordshire HP23 6JY (☎ 01442 891660, website www.ebou.co.uk)

BARKER, Prof Eileen Vartan; OBE (2000); *née* MacLennan; da of Calman MacLennan (d 1943), and Mary Helen Muir (d 1972); *b* 21 April 1938, Edinburgh; *Educ* Cheltenham Ladies' Coll, Webber Douglas Sch of Singing & Dramatic Art (gold medal), LSE (BSc, PhD); *m* 1958, Peter Johnson Barker, MBE; 2 da (Judith Katherine b 1961 d 2005, Rachel Anna MacLennan b 1963); *Career* LSE: on staff 1970–, dean of undergraduate studies 1982–86, prof of sociology (with special reference to the study of religion) 1992–2003 (now emeritus); fndr and chm Info Network Focus on Religious Movements (INFORM) 1988–; Leverhulme Emeritus Fellowship 2004–07; Hobhouse Meml Prize 1970, SSSR Distinguished Book Award 1985, Martin Marty Award for the Promotion of the Understanding of Religion 2000, Lifetime Achievement Award Int Cultic Studies Assoc (ICSA) 2013; pres: Soc for the Scientific Study of Religion 1991–93, London Soc for the Study of Religion 1994–96, Assoc for the Sociology of Religion 2001–02; hon life pres ISORECEA 2006; hon research fell Inst of Philosphy Acad of Sci Kiev 2005, hon fell LSE 2011; Doctores Philosophiae (hc) Univ of Copenhagen 2000; FBA 1998, FAcSS 2016; *Books* New Religious Movements: A Perspective for Understanding Society (ed, 1982); Of Gods and Men (ed, 1983), The Making of a Moonie: Brainwashing or Choice? (1984), LSE on Freedom (ed, 1985), New Religious Movements: A Practical Introduction (1989), Secularization, Rationalism, and Sectarianism (co-ed, 1993), Twenty Years On: Changes in New Religious Movements (co-ed, 1995), New Religions and New Religiosity (co-ed, 1998), The Centrality of Religion in Social Life (ed, 2008), Religion and Diversification in New Religion Movements (ed, 2013); *Style—* Prof Eileen Barker, OBE, FBA; ✉ London School of Economics and Political Science, Houghton Street, London WC2A 2AE (☎ 020 7955 7289, e-mail e.barker@lse.ac.uk)

BARKER, Baroness (Life Peer UK 1999), of Anagach in Highland; Elizabeth Jean Barker; da of Horace Felstead Barker, of Hull, E Yorks; *b* 31 January 1961; *Educ* Dalziel HS Motherwell, Broadway Sch Oldham, Univ of Southampton (BSc); *Career* pres Union of Lib Students 1982–83, project co-ordinator Opportunities for Volunteering Prog 1983–88, grants offr Age Concern England 1988–92, field offr and mgmnt conslt to Age Concern orgns in ten London Boroughs 1992–2007, owner Third Sector Business consultancy 2007–; Lib Dem spokesperson on health 2004–11; patron Spare Tyre Theatre Co; *Style—* The Baroness Barker; ✉ c/o Liberal Democrat Whips Office, House of Lords, London SW1A 0PW

BARKER, Godfrey Raymond; s of Harold Lindsey Barker (d 1973), and Alys, *née* Singleton (d 1988); *b* 14 April 1945; *Educ* Dulwich Coll, Univ of Cambridge, Univ of Oxford and Cornell Univ (MA, DPhil); *m* 1974 (m dis 2004), Ann, da of Frederick Botsford Callender, of Pasadena, CA; 1 s (Frederick George Lindsey b 28 Oct 1983); *Career* Cons Res Dept 1966–67, second sec UN Dept FO 1972; The Daily Telegraph: joined 1972, parly sketchwriter and leader writer 1981–89, arts ed 1986, arts and political columnist 1989–97; arts columnist Evening Standard 1997–2000; articles in The Times, Daily Telegraph, Die Welt, Sunday Times, The Wall Street Journal, Forbes, The Economist, The Field, Art and Auction, Art Review and Artnews 2000–; lectr in history of the art market Sotheby's 2002–; broadcaster arts progs BBC Radio 3 and 4, World Service, BBC TV, BBC World TV and PBS America; memb Arts Minister's Advsy Ctee 1982–97 (chm (with Elizabeth Diaferia) 2013–); chm Young Masters Art Prize 2012–; *Books* Visions of Europe (with Margaret Thatcher and others, 1993), Sovereign Britain (with Norman Lamont, 1995), The International Art Markets (contrib, 2008), Vanity and Excess: The Art Market Since 1850 (2014), Vanity and Excess: The Rich and the Price of Art (Chinese edn, 2014, shortlisted Art Award of China 2015), Visions of Europe II (with John Redwood and others, 2016); *Recreations* campaigning for the National Heritage, opera, lieder, cricket; *Clubs* Beefsteak, Athenaeum; *Style—* Godfrey Barker, Esq; ✉ 26 Charles Street, Berkeley Square, London W1J 5DT (☎ 020 7499 8516, e-mail godfreybarker@aol.com)

BARKER, Prof Graeme William Walter; CBE (2015); s of Reginald Walter Barker (d 1987), and Kathleen, *née* Walton (d 1981); *b* 23 October 1946; *Educ* Alleyn's Sch Dulwich, St John's Coll Cambridge (Henry Arthur Thomas open scholar, BA, MA, PhD), Br Sch at Rome (Rome scholar in classical studies); *m* 1, 3 Jan 1976 (m dis 1991), Sarah Miranda Buchanan; 1 da (Rachel Jessica b 14 Feb 1980), 1 s (Lewis William b 26 May 1983 d 2005); m 2, 6 Sept 2008 (m dis 2016), Annie Grant; *Career* sr lectr in prehistoric archaeology Univ of Sheffield 1981–84 (lectr 1972–81), dir British Sch in Rome 1984–88; Univ of Leicester: prof and head Sch of Archaeological Studies 1988–2000, grad dean 2000–03, pro-vice-chllr 2003–04; Disney prof of archaeology and dir McDonald Inst for Archaeological Research Univ of Cambridge 2004–; professorial fell St John's Coll Cambridge 2004–; chm Soc for Libyan Studies 1988–94, pres Prehistoric Soc 2001–05, memb Arts and Humanities Research Cncl 2005–09; memb Ed Bds: CUP, Manuals in Archaeology, Jl of Mediterranean Archaeology, The Holocene, Antiquity; major field projects incl: Biferno Valley Survey 1974–80, UNESCO Libyan Valleys Survey 1979–89, Tuscania Survey 1986–91, Wadi Faynan Landscape Survey 1996–2000, Niah Caves Project 2000–05, Cultured Rainforest 2006–10, Cyrenaican Prehistory Project 2007–; Dan David Prize 2005; FSA 1979, FBA 1999, FSA; *Books* Landscape and Society: Prehistoric Central Italy (1981), Archaeology and Italian Society (co-ed with R Hodges, 1981), Prehistoric Farming in Europe (1985), Beyond Domestication in Prehistoric Europe (co-ed with C Gamble, 1985), Cyrenaica in Antiquity (co-ed with J Lloyd and J Reynolds, 1985), Roman Landscapes (co-ed with J Lloyd, 1991), A Mediterranean Valley: Landscape Archaeology and Annales History in the Biferno Valley (1995), The Biferno Valley Survey: the Archaeological and Geomorphological Record (1995), Farming the Desert: the UNESCO Libyan Valleys Archaeological Survey (with D Gilbertson, B Jones and D Mattingly, vol 1 1996, vol 2 1997), The Etruscans (with T Rasmussen, 1998), Companion Encyclopedia of Archaeology (ed, 1999), The Archaeology of Drylands: Living at the Margin (co-ed with D Gilbertson, 2000), The Archaeology of Mediterranean Landscapes (gen ed with D Mattingly, 5 vols, 2000), The Human Use of Caves in Peninsular and Island Southeast Asia (ed with D Gilbertson, 2005), The Agricultural Revolution in Prehistory: Why did foragers become farmers? (2006), Archaeology and Desertification: the Wadi Faynan Landscape Survey, Jordan (with D Gilbertson and D Mattingly, 2007), Why Cultivate? Anthropological and Archaeological Approaches to Foraging-Farming Transitions in Southeast Asia (with M Janowski, 2011), Rainforest Foraging and Farming in Island South-east Asia -The Archaeology of the Niah Caves Sarawak (2013), Cambridge World History Vol. II – A World with Agriculture (co-ed w C Goucher, 2015); *Recreations* walking, skiing, sailing; *Style—* Prof Graeme Barker, CBE, FBA; ✉ St John's College, Cambridge CB2 1JP (☎ 01223 338622); McDonald Institute for Archeological Research, University of Cambridge, Downing Street, Cambridge CB2 3ER (☎ 01223 333538, fax 01223 333536, e-mail gb314@cam.ac.uk)

BARKER, Graham Harold; TD (1985); s of Harold George Barker (d 1962), and Dorothy, *née* Speechley (d 1986); *b* 11 January 1949; *Educ* Cambridge GS, KCL, St George's Hosp Med Sch London (MB BS, AKC); *m* 1, 23 Sept 1978 (m dis 2003), Esther Louise, da of John Owen Farrow, of Norwich; 1 s (Douglas Graham b 23 June 1982), 1 da (Louise Elizabeth b 9 Jan 1987); m 2, 6 March 2010, Sophia Laureen Kellman; 1 s (Luke Graham James b 23 Jan 2014); *Career* Surgn 217 (L) Gen Hosp RAMC (V) 1973–91, Capt 1974, Maj 1980; lectr Inst of Cancer Res London 1977–79, registrar Queen Charlotte's and Chelsea Hosps London 1980, sr registrar in gynaecology and obstetrics Middx Hosp and UCH 1981–87, sr lectr in Obstetrics and Gynaecology St George's Hosp London 1987–2002, currently conslt gynaecologist and obstetrician Portland Hosp for Women London, Parkside Hosp London and London Bridge Hosp London; memb: Br Soc for Colposcopy and Cervical Pathology, Br Gynaecological Cancer Soc, Chelsea Clinical Soc; Astor fell Harvard Univ Hosps 1984; Freeman City of London, Liveryman Worshipful Soc of Apothecaries 1980; MD 1991; FRCSEd 1979, FRCOG 1993 (MRCOG 1978), FRSM; *Books* Family Health And Medicine Guide (1979), Your Search For Fertility (1981),

Chemotherapy of Gynaecological Malignancies (1983), The New Fertility (1986), Your Smear Test – A Guide To Screening, Colposcopy And The Prevention Of Cervical Cancer (1987), Overcoming Infertility (1990); founding ed Obstetrics and Gynaecology Today; *Recreations* classic cars, trumpet, piano; *Style—* Graham Barker, Esq, TD; ✉ 12 Wolsey Close, Kingston upon Thames, Surrey KT2 7ER (☎ 020 8942 2614); The Chimes, 11 The Suttons, Cambersands, Rye, East Sussex (e-mail grahambarker@colposcopy.org.uk, website www.colposcopy.org.uk)

BARKER, John Alfred; OBE (2006); s of Alfred Barker (d 1990), of Holborn, London, and Miriam Alice, *née* Kerley (d 1993); *b* 2 December 1929; *Educ* Neale's Mathematical Sch, City of London Coll; *m* 22 Sept 1962, Margaret Coutts (d 1999), da of Thomas Coutts Smith (d 1948), of Stonehouse, Lanark; *Career* Intelligence Corps TA & AVR 1959–69; Stock Exchange 1950–64, Inner London Probation Serv 1965–90, memb Local Review Ctee HMP Wandsworth 1986–90; common councilman City of London Corp: Cripplegate Without 1981–96, Cripplegate Within 1996– (dep 1993–); past master Cripplegate Ward Club; chm Port Health and Environmental Services Ctee 2002–05, chm Barbican Centre Ctee 2006–08; chm City Lands and Bridge House Estates Ctee 2008–09 (chief commoner), chm Establishment Ctee 2012–15, chm Guildhall Club Ctee 2015–; memb: Bd of Mgmnt Barbican YMCA 1986–2005 (chm 1990–2005), Ct City Univ 2001–11, Bd of Mgmnt City YMCA London 2005–14; govr: Bridewell Royal Hosp 1982–, King Edward's Sch Witley 1989–, Christ's Hosp 1991–; tstee: Soc for Relief of Homeless Poor 1982–2011, Neale's Educnl Fndn 1983–2011, Charity of John Land 1983–2011, Mitchell City of London Charity and Educnl Fndn 1991–, St Luke's Parochial Tst 1995–, Thames21 Ltd 2004–, Thames Festival Tst 2008–16, Tstees of the Charles Dickens Museum 2008–13; chm The Royal Soc of St George (City of London branch) 2012–13 (vice-pres 2014–); Freeman: City of London 1970, Worshipful Co of Basketmakers 1973 (Asst 2007, Prime Warden 2011); FRGS 1979, FZS 1980, FInstD 1984, MCMI (MIMgt 1985), FRSA 1992; *Recreations* travel, hill and mountain walking (until arthritis), club man, music, opera, theatre; *Clubs* Reform, Guildhall, City Livery, Royal Over-Seas League, Rotary (London), City Pickwick, Boisdale Jazz and Cigar; *Style—* John Barker, Esq, OBE; ✉ 319 Willoughby House, Barbican, London EC2Y 8BL (☎ 020 7628 5381 (callminder))

BARKER, Prof John Reginald; s of Thomas Reginald Barker (d 1965), of Bamford, Derbys, and Marjorie, *née* Cutler (d 1979); *b* 11 November 1942, Stockport, Cheshire; *Educ* New Mills GS, Univ of Edinburgh (BSc), Univ of Durham (MSc), Univ of Warwick (PhD); *m* 11 Aug 1966, Elizabeth Carol, da of George Patrick Maguire; 1 da (Emma Jane b 26 Aug 1970), 2 s (Tom Alexander Patrick b 31 July 1972, John Luke Patrick b 17 March 1974); *Career* SRC res student Dept of Applied Physics Univ of Durham 1966–67, jr res assoc Dept of Physics Univ of Warwick 1967–69, pt/t physics teacher Henry VIII GS Coventry 1968, pt/t lectr Canley Coll of FE; Univ of Warwick: SRC postdoctoral res fell Dept of Physics 1969–70, lectr 1970–84, sr lectr 1984–85; prof of electronics Dept of Electronics and Electrical Engrg Univ of Glasgow 1985–2008 (emeritus prof 2008); co-dir: NATO Advanced Study Inst 1979 and 1990, NATO Advanced Res Inst 1982; dir: 7th Int Workshop on Computational Electronics 2000, 4th Int Conference on Progress in Non-Equilibrium Green's Functions 2009; distinguished science lectr Yale Univ 1992; visiting prof: N Texas State Univ 1978, Colorado State Univ 1978–79 (affiliate prof 1979–83); visiting scientist: IBM T J Watson Res Centre NY 1978, NORDITA Neils Bohr Inst Copenhagen 1980, Bell Telephone Laboratories 1980–81, Electronics and Devices Laboratory US Army 1981; memb Cncl Royal Philosophical Soc Glasgow 2010–13, vice-pres Royal Philosophical Soc Glasgow 2014–; former memb of numerous SERC Ctees, presenter Venture series (Central) 1982, various appearances on Tomorrow's World and other science progs; FRSE 1990, FBIS 1992, FRAS 1999; *Publications* Physics of Non-Linear Transport in Semiconductors (1979), Physics of Granular Electronic Systems (1991); also author of over 360 scientific publications; *Recreations* hill walking, reading, photography, astronomy, Volvo driving; *Clubs* Nomads; *Style—* Prof John Barker, FRSE; ✉ 45 Hughenden Gardens, Glasgow G12 9YH (☎ 0141 338 6026, website www.johnreginaldbarker.co.uk); School of Engineering, University of Glasgow, Glasgow G12 8QQ (e-mail john.barker@glasgow.ac.uk)

BARKER, Jonathan David; MBE (2009); s of Thomas William Barker, and Dorothy Joan Barker; *b* 17 July 1949; *Educ* Victoria Boys' Sch Watford, Cassio Coll of Futher Educn Watford, Birkbeck Coll London (BA, Frank Newton Prize for English), Poly of N London (Dip Librarianship and Info Science); *m* 23 July 1983, Deirdre Mary, da of Cornelius Joseph Shanahan; *Career* arboriculturalist Whippendell Woods Watford 1969–70, library asst Kensington Central Reference Library 1970–72, poetry librarian Arts Cncl Poetry Library 1973–88, asst sec Poetry Book Soc Ltd 1973–83, dep dir of literature Br Cncl 1988–2006, sr literature conslt Br Cncl 2007–09; co-chair Cambridge Seminar on Contemporary Literature Downing Coll Cambridge 2005, 2007 and 2009, organiser Bernard Spencer: Mystery Poet seminar Inst of Eng Studies Univ of London 2012; literature assessor Arts Cncl England 2010–12; adjudicator numerous poetry competitions (incl: Arts Cncl Raymond Williams Prize for Community Publishing 1992 and 1993, Whitbread Book Awards 2002); memb Ctee Stephen Spender Tst 2009– (tstee 2015–), memb Bibliographical Soc Univ of London 2013–, memb Fulke Greville Soc 2015–; MCLIP (ALA 1985); *Publications* Arts Council Poetry Library Short-Title Catalogue (6 edn 1981), Selected Poems of W H Davies (ed, 1985, new edn 1992), Poetry Book Society Anthology (ed, 1986), The Art of Edward Thomas (ed, 1987), Thirty Years of The Poetry Book Society – 1956–1986 (ed, 1988), Norman Cameron Collected Poems and Selected Translations (jt ed, 1990, revised edn 2011), A Select Bibliography of Poetry in Britain and Ireland (1995), R W Dixon Poems (ed, 2012), D G Rossetti Sudden Light and Other Poems (ed, 2013); contrib various critical articles to reference books and jls; *Recreations* writing, music, gardening, travelling, book collecting; *Style—* Jonathan Barker, Esq, MBE; ✉ c/o Literature Department, British Council, 10 Spring Gardens, London SW1A 2BN

BARKER, Dr Juliet Rosemary Victoria; da of Richard Bateson, of Oxenhope, Yorks, and Judith, *née* Robinson; *b* 5 February 1958, Hull, Yorks; *Educ* Bradford Girls' GS, St Anne's Coll Oxford (MA, DPhil); *m* 4 Sept 1982, James Barker, DL; 1 s (John Edward b 17 Sept 1985), 1 da (Sophie Jane b 16 Feb 1993); *Career* curator and librarian Brontë Parsonage Museum 1983–89, author and broadcaster 1989–; regular contrib to TV and radio as expert on the Brontës, Wordsworth and medieval history (especially 15 century, chivalry, tournaments and warfare); winner Yorks Post Book of the Year 1995, shortlist AT&T Prize 1995, shortlist Marsh Biography Award 1995; hon lay canon Wakefield Cathedral, supporter Caring for Life; Hon DLitt Univ of Bradford 1999; memb Soc of Authors 1994, FRSL 2001; *Publications* incl: Tournaments in England 1100–1400 (1985), The Brontës (1994, new edn 2010), The Brontës: A Life in Letters (1998), Wordsworth: A Life (2000), Wordsworth: A Life in Letters (2001), Agincourt (2005), The Deafening Sound of Silent Tears: The Story of Caring For Life (2007), Conquest: The English Kingdom of France (2009), England Arise: The People, The King and the Great Revolt of 1381 (2014); *Recreations* hill walking, embroidery; *Style—* Dr Juliet Barker; ✉ Andrew Lownie Literary Agency Ltd, 36 Great Smith Street, London SW1P 3BU (☎ 020 7222 7574, fax 020 7222 7576, e-mail mail@andrewlownie.co.uk); e-mail juliet@julietbarker.co.uk

BARKER, Dame Katharine Mary (Kate); DBE (2014, CBE 2006); *b* 29 November 1957, Stoke-on-Trent, Staffs; *Educ* Stoke-on-Trent Sixth Form Coll, St Hilda's Coll Oxford; *m* 1982, Peter Donovan; 2 s (b 1988, b 1990); *Career* investment analyst Post Office Pension Fund 1979–81, res offr NIESR 1981–85, chief Euro economist Ford of Europe 1985–94, chief econ advsr CBI 1994–2001, memb Monetary Policy Ctee Bank of England 2001–10, sr advsr Credit Suisse 2010–16; non-exec dir: Yorkshire Building Society 1999–2001 and 2010–, Electra Private Equity plc 2010–, Taylor-Wimpey plc 2011–; commissioned by Govt to conduct ind review of UK Housing Supply 2003, ind review of Land Use Planning 2006, chair King's Fund Cmmn on Health and Social Care 2013–14; ldr Quality Review of UK Nat Accounts 2013–14; chm Br Coal Staff Superannuation Scheme 2014–; chair Soc of Business Economists 2013–; memb: HM Treasy independent panel of economic forecasting advsrs 1996–97, Bd of Govrs Anglia Ruskin Univ 1999–2010 (chair 2007–10), Bd Housing Corporation 2005–08, Bd Homes and Communities Agency 2008–11, Jersey Fiscal Policy Panel 2014–; non-exec memb Office for Budget Responsibility 2011–; chair FA Fin Advsy Ctee 2003–07, memb Football Regulatory Authy 2007–13; AcSS 2011; *Books* Housing – Where's the Plan? (2014); *Recreations* bell ringing; *Style—* Dame Kate Barker, DBE; ✉ e-mail kate.barker4@btinternet.com

BARKER, Meg-John; c of Dr Derek Barker, and Philippa, *née* Duffield; *b* 23 June 1974, Kingston-upon-Hull; *Educ* St Joseph's Coll Bradford, Univ of Nottingham (BSc, PhD), Univ of Sheffield (MA); *Partner* Edward Lord, OBE, JP, *qv*; *Career* author, psychotherapist and activist-academic; lectr: Univ of Glos 1998–2002, Univ of Worcester 2002–04, Middlesex Univ 2004; sr lectr London S Bank Univ 2004–08, trainee psychotherapist Guy's and St Thomas's NHS Tst 2006–10, sr lectr Open Univ 2008–; therapist: LGBT Fndn 2010–13, London Friend 2014–; clinical asoc Pink Therapy 2014–; visiting lectr City Univ of London 2015–, academic advsr Univ of Wisconsin-Stout 2015–; chair BiUK 2004–, memb Bd Nat LGB&T Partnership 2013–15; *Publications* Psychology & Sexuality (ed), Safe, Sane and Consensual (co-ed, 2007), Understanding Counselling and Psychotherapy (co-ed, 2010), Understanding Non-Monogamies (co-ed, 2010), Rewriting the Rules: An Integrative Guide to Love, Sex and Relationships (2012), The Bisexuality Report (lead author, 2012), Sexuality & Gender for Mental Health Professionals (co-author, 2013), Mindful Counselling & Psychotherapy (2013), Palgrave Handbook of the Psychology of Sexuality and Gender (co-ed, 2015), The Secrets of Enduring Love (co-author, 2016), Queer: A Graphic History (2016); *Recreations* cinema, comics and graphic novels, crime and horror fiction, food, mindfulness, music, walking, yoga; *Style—* Dr Meg-John Barker; ✉ The Open University, Walton Hall, Milton Keynes MK7 6AA (e-mail meg.john.barker@gmail.com, website www.rewriting-the-rules.com, Twitter @megjohnbarker)

BARKER, Nicolas John; OBE (2002); s of Sir Ernest Barker (d 1960), and Olivia Stuart, *née* Horner (d 1976); *b* 6 December 1932; *Educ* Westminster, New Coll Oxford (MA); *m* 11 Aug 1962, Joanna Mary Nyda Sophia, da of Col Henry Edward Mariano Cotton, OBE (d 1988); 2 s (Christian b 1964, Cosmo b 1973), 3 da (Emma b 1963, Olivia b 1967, Cecilia b 1969); *Career* with Bailliere Tindall & Cox and Rupert Hart-Davis 1959, asst keeper Nat Portrait Gallery 1964, with Macmillan & Co Ltd 1965, with OUP 1971, dep keeper British Library 1976–92, libraries advsr to Nat Tst 1992–2000; William Andrews Clark visiting prof UCLA 1986–87, Sandars reader in bibliography Univ of Cambridge 1999–2000; pres: Amici Thomae Mori 1978–89, Double Crown Club 1980–81, Bibliographical Soc 1981–85; chm: Laurence Sterne Tst 1984–2010, London Library 1994–2004 (memb Ctee 1971–, vice pres 2005–), Library Ctee RHS 1996–; ed The Book Collector 1965–; memb: Publication Bd of Dirs RNIB 1969–92, Appeals Advsy Ctee BBC and ITV 1977–86, Arts Panel Nat Tst 1979–92; tstee The Pilgrim Tst 1977–2007, feoffee Chetham's Hosp 2002–10; Panizzi Lectures Br Library 2001, Rosenbach Lectures Univ of PA 2002; hon fell New Coll Oxford 2011; Hon DUniv York 1994; FBA 1998; *Books* The Publications of the Roxburghe Club (1962), The Printer and the Poet (1970), Stanley Morison (1972), Essays and Papers of ANL Munby (ed, 1977), The Early Life of James McBey – An Autobiography 1883–1911 (ed, 1977), Bibliotheca Lindesiana (1977), The Oxford University Press and the Spread of Learning 1478–1978 (1978), A Sequel to an Enquiry (with John Collins, 1983), Aldus Manutius and the Development of Greek Script and Type (1985), The Butterfly Books (1987), Two East Anglian Picture Books (1988), Treasures of the British Library (compiler, 1989), S Morison: Early Italian Writing-Books (ed, 1990), Medieval Pageant (with A Wagner and A Payne, 1993), Hortus Eystettensis: The Bishop's Garden and Besler's Magnificent Book (1994), The Great Book of Thomas Trevilian (2000), Form and Meaning in the History of the Book (2002), The Calligraphic Work of Francesco Alunno (2009), Lady Anne Barnard's Watercolours and Sketches (2009), Horace Walpole's Description of the Villa at Strawberry Hill (2010), The Roxburghe Club: a Bicentenary History (2012), Esther Inglis's Les Proverbes de Salomon (2012), Visible Voices (2016); *Clubs* Garrick; *Style—* Nicolas Barker, Esq, OBE, FBA; ✉ 22 Clarendon Road, London W11 3AB (☎ 020 7727 4340)

BARKER, Patricia Margaret (Pat); CBE (2000); da of Moira Drake; *b* 8 May 1943; *Educ* Grangefield GS, LSE (BSc); *m* 29 Jan 1978, David Faubert Barker, s of Faubert Barker (d 1980); 1 s (John b 1970), 1 da (Annabel b 1974); *Career* novelist; jt winner Fawcett Prize 1983, elected one of twenty Best of British Young Novelists 1983, Guardian Fiction Prize 1993, Special Award Northern Electric Arts Awards 1993, Booksellers' Association Author of the Year Award 1996, Die Welt Literatur-Preis 2000; Hon MLitt Univ of Teesside 1993; Hon DLitt: Napier Univ 1996, Univ of Hertfordshire 1998, Univ of Durham 1998, Univ of London 2002, Univ of Leicester 2006; Hon Dr Open Univ 1997; memb: Soc of Authors 1983, PEN 1989; FRSL 1995; *Books* Union Street (1982, filmed as Stanley and Iris 1990 starring Robert de Niro and Jane Fonda), Blow Your House Down (1984), The Century's Daughter (1986, re-titled Liza's England 1996), The Man Who Wasn't There (1989), Regeneration (1991, filmed 1997, starring Jonathan Pryce, James Wilby and Jonny Lee Miller), The Eye in the Door (1993), The Ghost Road (1995, winner Booker Prize 1995), Another World (1998), Border Crossing (2001), Double Vision (2003), Life Class (2007); *Recreations* swimming, walking, reading; *Style—* Mrs Patricia Barker, CBE, FRSL; ✉ c/o Gillon Aitken Associates, 18–21 Cavaye Place, London SW10 9PT (☎ 020 7373 8672)

BARKER, Paul; s of Donald Barker (d 1981), and Marion, *née* Ashworth (d 1989); *b* 24 August 1935; *Educ* Hebden Bridge GS, Calder HS, BNC Oxford (MA); *m* 1960, Sally, da of James Huddleston (d 1965); 3 s (Nicholas b 1961, Tom b 1966, Daniel b 1973), 1 da (Kate b 1963); *Career* writer and editor; Nat Serv cmmnd Intelligence Corps 1953–55; lectr École Normale Supérieure Paris 1958–59; editorial staff: The Times 1959–63, Economist 1964–65; ed New Society 1968–86 (staff writer 1964, dep ed 1965–68), social policy ed Sunday Telegraph 1986–88, assoc ed The Independent Magazine 1988–90, social and political columnist Sunday Times 1990–91, social commentary London Evening Standard 1992–2007 (townscape and arts columnist 1987–92), townscape columnist New Statesman 1996–99; contrib essays and articles in many newspapers and magazines; visiting fell Centre for the Analysis of Social Policy Univ of Bath 1986–2000, Leverhulme research fell 1993–95, fell Built Environment 2000–02; BPG Award (jtly) for Outstanding Radio Programme (My Country, Right or Wrong) 1988; jt dir: The Fiction Magazine 1982–87, Pennine Heritage 1978–86; Inst of Community Studies: fell 1992–95, sr fell 1995–2000, sr research fell 2000–05, chm 2000–01 (tstee 1991–2001); sr research fell The Young Fndn 2005–; memb UK Advsy Ctee Harkness Fellowships 1995–97; FRSA 1990; *Books* Youth in New Society (contrib, 1966), Your Sunday Paper (contrib, 1967), A Sociological Portrait (ed, 1972), One for Sorrow, Two for Joy (ed and contrib, 1972), The Social Sciences Today (ed, 1975, Spanish edn 1979), Arts in Society (ed and contrib, 1977, revised edn 2006), The Other Britain (ed and contrib, 1982), Founders of the Welfare State (ed, 1985), Britain in the Eighties (contrib, 1989), Towards A New Landscape (contrib, 1993), Young at Eighty (contrib, 1995), Gulliver and Beyond (ed and contrib, 1996), Living as Equals (ed and contrib, 1996, Spanish edn 2000), A Critic Writes

B

(jt ed, 1997), Town and Country (contrib, 1998), Non-Plan (contrib, 2000), The Meaning of the Jubilee (contrib, 2002), William Turner: An English Expressionist (contrib, 2005), Porcupines in Winter (contrib, 2006), The Rise and Rise of Meritocracy (contrib, 2007), The Banham Lectures (contrib, 2009), The Freedoms of Suburbia (2009, Chinese edn 2012), Ordinariness (contrib, 2010), William Ralph Turner (contrib, 2010), David Hepher (2012), Hebden Bridge: A Sense of Belonging (2012), A Crooked Smile (2013), The Dead Don't Die (2014); *Recreations* architecture; *Style*— Paul Barker, Esq; ✉ 20 Leverton Street, London NW5 2PJ

BARKER, Timothy Gwynne; s of Lt-Col (Frank Richard) Peter Barker (d 1974), and Hon Olwen Gwynne, *née* Philipps (d 1998); *b* 8 April 1940; *Educ* Eton, Jesus Coll Cambridge (MA), McGill Univ Montreal; *m* 14 July 1964, Philippa Rachel Mary, da of Brig Mervyn Christopher Thursby-Pelham, OBE; 1 da (Camilla b 1968), 1 s (Christopher b 1970); *Career* DG: City Panel on Takeovers and Mergers 1984–85, Cncl for the Securities Indust 1984–85; vice-chm Kleinwort Benson Group plc 1993–98 (dir 1988–98), chm Kleinwort Benson Private Bank 1997–2004, vice-chm Dresdner Kleinwort Benson 1998–2000; chm Robert Walters plc 2000–07; sr ind dir: Electrocomponents plc 2000–, Drax Gp plc 2005–; memb Professional Oversight Bd Financial Reporting Cncl 2004–09; Liveryman Worshipful Co of Grocers; *Style*— Timothy Barker, Esq

BARKER OF BATTLE, Baron (UK Life Peer 2015) of Battle in the County of East Sussex; Rt Hon Gregory Barker; PC (2012); *b* 1967, Sussex; *Educ* Steyning GS, Lancing Coll, Royal Holloway Coll London; *Career* researcher Centre for Policy Studies 1987–89, equity analyst Gerrard Vivian Gray 1988–90, dir Int Pacific Securites 1990–97, assoc ptnr Brunswick Gp Ltd 1997–98, head int investor rels Siberian Oil Co 1998–2000, dir Bartlett Scott Edgar 1998–2001, MP (Cons) Bexhill and Battle 2001–15; memb Environmental Audit Select Ctee 2001–05, oppn whip 2003–05, shadow min for environment 2005–10, min of state Dept of Energy and Climate Change 2010–14, min for Business Engagement for India 2012–14; *Style*— The Rt Hon the Lord Barker; ✉ House of Commons, London SW1A 0AA

BARKLEM, His Hon Judge Martyn Stephen; s of Thomas Barklem (d 2007), and Edna Barklem; *Educ* Dauntseys Sch Wilts, Univ of London; *m* Naomi Ellenbogen, QC; 2 s (Jamie b 8 May 1989, Robbie b 19 May 1992); *Career* RN 1976–78; Royal Hong Kong Police 1979–88; called to the Bar Middle Temple (Harmsworth scholar) 1989; recorder 2002, circuit judge South Eastern Circuit 2012–; *Recreations* sailing, travel, cooking; *Clubs* Hong Kong Cricket, Bar Yacht, RNVR Yacht; *Style*— His Hon Judge Barklem; ✉ Harrow Crown Court, Hailsham Drive, off Headstone Drive, Harrow, London HA1 4TU

BARLEY, Dr Victor Laurence; s of George Alec Barley (d 1995), of Harrogate, N Yorks, and Evelyn Mary Barley (d 1971); *b* 16 June 1941; *Educ* Stamford Sch, Univ of Cambridge (MA, MB BChir), Univ of Oxford (MA, DPhil); *m* 1, 25 Jan 1969 (m dis 1989), Janet, da of Dr Stanley Devidson Purcell, of Clevedon, Avon; 1 s (Peter b 3 Dec 1969), 3 da (Elizabeth, Madeline (twins) b 6 Jan 1972, Christine b 16 July 1981); m 2, 3 Dec 1999, Anthea, da of Mr Sydney Sherlock Jones, of Cardiff; *Career* conslt clinical oncologist Bristol 1978–2003, clinical dir Bristol Oncology Centre 1988–96, Macmillan lead clinician Avon & Somerset Cancer Services 1997–99, clinical speciality advsr Nat Patient Safety Agency 2002–, consulting medical offr Reinsurance Gp of America 2007–; chm Hosp Med Ctee United Bristol Healthcare NHS Tst 1997–99; fell Br Inst of Radiology 2007; FRCSEd, FRCR; *Recreations* music; *Style*— Dr Victor Barley; ✉ Church Farm, Church Lane, Chew Stoke, Bristol BS40 8TU (☎ 01275 331086, e-mail victor.barley@tiscali.co.uk)

BARLING, Hon Mr Justice; Sir Gerald Edward Barling; kt (2007); s of Banks Hubert Barling (d 1983), and Barbara Margarita, *née* Myerscough (d 1991); *b* 18 September 1949, Preston; *Educ* St Mary's Coll Blackburn, New Coll Oxford (Peel fndn scholar, Thwaites travelling scholar (USA), Burnett open exhibitioner, MA), Inns of Court Sch of Law (Harmsworth entrance exhibitioner, Astbury law scholar); *m* Myriam Frances, *née* Ponsford; 3 da (Sophie, Bryony, Isobel); *Career* called to the Bar Middle Temple 1972 (bencher 2001); in practice: Manchester 1973–81, London 1981–2007; QC 1991, recorder of the Crown Court 1993–2007 (asst recorder 1989–93), actg deemster IOM Court of Appeal 1999–, dep high court judge 2007, judge of the High Court of Justice (Queen's Bench Div then Chancery Div) 2007–; pres Competition Appeal Tribunal 2007–13; memb: Bar Cncl Working Pty on Restrictive Practices 1988–90, Ctee Bar Euro Gp 1988–; chm: Western Euro Sub-Ctee Bar Cncl 1991–92, Bar Euro Gp 1994–96; lectr in law New Coll Oxford 1972–77, tutor in law UCL 1972–73; tstee Devpt Fund New Coll Oxford 2006–; *Publications* Butterworths European Court Practice (contrib, 1991), Butterworths European Law Service (conslt ed), Practitioners' Handbook of EC Law (joint ed, 1998); author of numerous professional papers on aspects of EC law and competition law; *Recreations* working up a thirst in the country; *Style*— The Hon Mr Justice Barling; ✉ Royal Courts of Justice, Strand, London WC2A 2LL

BARLOW, Gary; OBE (2012); s of Colin Barlow (d 2009), and Marjorie Barlow; *b* 20 January 1971, Frodsham, Cheshire; *m* 12 Jan 2000, Dawn, *née* Andrews; 1 s (Daniel b 16 Aug 2000), 2 da (Emily b 31 May 2002, Daisy b 14 Jan 2009); *Career* singer and songwriter; memb Take That 1990–96 and 2006–, solo 1996–99; judge X Factor (ITV) 2011–13; *Albums* with Take That: Take That and Party 1992, Everything Changes 1993, Nobody Else 1995, Greatest Hits 1996, Never Forget: The Ultimate Collection 2005, Beautiful World 2006, The Circus 2008, Progress 2010; solo: Open Road 1997, Twelve Months, Eleven Days 1999; *Singles* Do What You Like 1991, Promises 1991, Once You've Tasted Love 1992, It Only Takes a Minute 1992, I Found Heaven 1992, A Million Love Songs 1992, Could It Be Magic 1992, Why Can't I Wake Up With You 1993, Pray 1993 (UK no 1), Relight My Fire 1993 (with Lulu, UK no 1), Babe 1993 (UK no 1), Everything Changes 1994 (UK no 1), Love Ain't Here Anymore 1994, Sure 1994 (UK no 1), Back For Good 1995 (UK no 1), Never Forget 1995 (UK no 1), How Deep Is Your Love 1996 (UK no 1), Patience 2006 (UK no 1), Shine 2007 (UK no 1), I'd Wait For Life 2007, Rule The World 2007, Greatest Day 2008 (UK no 1), Up All Night 2009, Said It All 2009, The Flood 2010, Kidz 2011; solo: Forever Love 1996 (UK no 1), Love Won't Wait 1997 (UK no 1), So Help Me Girl 1997, Open Road 1997, Stronger 1999, For All That You Want 1999, Shame (with Robbie Williams, *qv*) 2010; *Awards* BRIT Awards: Best Br Single 1993 (for Could It Be Magic), 1994 (for Pray), 1996 (for Back For Good), 2007 (for Patience) and 2008 (for Shine), Best Br Video 1994 (for Pray), Best Br Live Act 2008, Best Br Band 2011; MTV Europe Music Awards: Best Group 1994, Best Live Act 1995; Ivor Novello Awards: Best Contemporary Song 1994 (for Pray), Songwriter of the Year 1994, Most Performed Work 1996 (for Back For Good) and 2008 (for Shine), Best Selling Song 1996 (for Back For Good); Outstanding Contribution Nat TV Award 2012, PRS For Music Outstanding Contribution to British Music Ivor Novello Award 2012, Music Industry Trust Award 2012; *Books* My Take (2006); *Style*— Mr Gary Barlow, OBE

BARLOW, James Mellodew; s of Capt Cecil Barlow (d 1988), of Oldham, Lancs, and Florence Patricia, *née* Mellodew (d 1997); *b* 23 December 1943; *Educ* Mill Hill Sch, Univ of Nottingham (LLB); *Career* admitted slr 1967; ptnr Clifford Chance LLP (formerly Coward Chance) 1980–; hon sec Cumberland LTC 1976–82 and 2004–; memb Worshipful Co of Slrs 1980; memb Law Soc 1967, ATII 1968; *Recreations* real tennis, tennis, skiing, fell walking, bridge; *Clubs* Old Millhillians, RAC; *Style*— James Barlow, Esq; ✉ 11 Edmunds Walk, London N2 0HU (☎ 020 8883 6972); Clifford Chance LLP, 10 Upper Bank Street, London E14 5JJ (☎ 020 7006 1000, fax 020 7006 5555, e-mail james.barlow@cliffordchance.com)

BARLOW, Prof Martin Thomas; s of Andrew Dalmahoy Barlow (d 2006), and Yvonne Rosalind Barlow; *b* 1953, London; *Educ* St Paul's, Trinity Coll Cambridge (entrance scholar, BA), Univ of Cambridge (Dip), Univ of Wales (PhD); *m* 6 Aug 1994, Colleen, *née* McLaughlin; *Career* research fell Univ of Liverpool 1978–80, fell Trinity Coll Cambridge 1979–92, Statistical Lab Univ of Cambridge 1981–85, Royal Soc univ research fell Univ of Cambridge 1985–92, prof Univ of BC 1992–; actg dir Pacific Inst for the Mathematical Science 2015–; author of papers in learned jls; winner Rollo Davidson Prize Univ of Cambridge 1984; FRSC, FRS 2005; *Style*— Prof Martin Barlow; ✉ Department of Mathematics, University of British Columbia, Vancouver, British Columbia, Canada V6T 1Z2 (☎ 001 604 822 6377)

BARLOW, Stephen William; s of George William Barlow, of Witham, Essex, and Irene Catherine, *née* Moretti; *b* 30 June 1954; *Educ* Canterbury Cathedral Choir Sch, King's Sch Canterbury, Trinity Coll Cambridge (organ scholar, MA); *m* Oct 1986, Joanna, da of Maj James Lumley; *Career* assoc conductor Glyndebourne Festival Opera 1980–81, resident conductor ENO 1980–83; music dir: Opera 80 1987–90, Queensland Philharmonic Orch 1996–99; artistic dir Opera Northern Ireland 1996–99; conducting debut The Rake's Progress Glyndebourne Touring Opera 1977; opera cos conducted incl: Scottish Opera, Dublin Grand Opera, Opera North, Royal Opera House, Vancouver Opera, Netherlands Opera, San Francisco Opera, Florida Grand Opera, Victoria State Opera Melbourne, Opera New Zealand, Deutsche Oper Berlin, Catania; orchs conducted incl: LPO, LSO, CBSO, LMP, RTE, ECO, BBC Scottish Symphony Orch, Orch of the Age of Enlightenment, Bournemouth Symphony Orch, Scottish Chamber Orch, Symphony Orch of Bilbao, City of London Sinfonia, Adelaide Symphony Orch, Canberra Symphony Orch, Melbourne Symphony Orch, Sydney Symphony Orch, New Zealand Symphony Orch, Detroit Symphony Orch, Belgrade Philharmonic Orch, Tafelmusik (Toronto); compositions incl: King (opera, premiered at Canterbury Cathedral) 2006, Pas de Deux (for flute and orch), Clarinet Concerto, string quartet and choral, orchestral and instrumental works; FRCO, FGSM 1986; *Recordings* incl: Joseph James' Requiem (Philharmonia), Graham Koehne Ballets (QPO), Peter and the Wolf (ENP), own composition Rainbow Bear (ENP); as pianist: The Complete Roger Quilter Songbook (with Mark Stone), English Love (with Mark Stone); *Recreations* cricket, wine, theatre, driving; *Style*— Stephen Barlow, Esq; ✉ c/o Peter Hall, Musichall, Vicarage Way, Ringmer, East Sussex BN8 5LA (☎ 01273 814240, fax 01273 813637)

BARNABY, Dr (Charles) Frank; s of Charles Hector Barnaby (d 1932), and Lilian, *née* Sainsbury; *b* 27 September 1927; *Educ* Andover GS, Univ of London (BSc, MSc, PhD); *m* 19 Dec 1972, Wendy Elizabeth, da of Francis Arthur Field, of Adelaide, Aust; 1 da (Sophie b 1975), 1 s (Benjamin b 1976); *Career* physicist: AWRE Aldermaston 1951–57, UCL 1957–67; exec sec Pugwash Conf on Sci and World Affrs 1967–71, dir Stockholm Int Peace Res Inst 1971–81, guest prof Free Univ of Amsterdam 1981–85, conslt Oxford Res Gp 1995–, ed Int Jl of Human Rights 1997–; Hon Doctorate: Free Univ of Amsterdam, Univ of Southampton, Univ of Bradford; *Books* Man and the Atom (1972), Nuclear Energy (1975), Prospects for Peace (1975), Verification Technologies (1986), Future Warfare (1986), Star Wars (1987), The Automated Battlefield (1987), The Gaia Peace Atlas (1989), The Invisible Bomb (1989), The Role and Control of Force in the 1990's (1992), How Nuclear Weapons Spread (1993), Instruments of Terror (1997), How To Build a Nuclear Bomb and Other Weapons of Mass Destruction (2003), The Future of Terror (2007); *Recreations* astronomy, bird watching; *Style*— Dr Frank Barnaby; ✉ Brandreth, Station Road, Chilbolton, Stockbridge, Hampshire SO20 6AW (☎ 01264 860423, fax 01264 860868, e-mail frank.barnaby1@btinternet.com)

BARNARD, Prof John Michael; s of John Claude Southard Barnard (d 1976), and Dora Grace, *née* Epps; *b* 13 February 1936; *Educ* King Alfred's GS Wantage, Wadham Coll Oxford (MA, BLitt); *m* 1 (m dis); 2 da (Josie b 1963, Clio b 1965), 1 s (Jason b 1966); m 2, 1991, Prof Hermione Lee, *qv*; *Career* Nat Serv sr radar technician RAF 1954–56; res asst Dept of English Yale Univ USA 1961–64, visiting lectr English Dept Univ of Calif Santa Barbara USA 1964–65; Sch of English Univ of Leeds: lectr then sr lectr 1965–78, prof 1978–2001; gen ed: Longman Annotated English Poets 1977–2010, The Cambridge History of the Book in Britain 2001–; Br Acad Warton lectr 1989, McKenzie lectr Univ of Oxford 2004; sr research fell Inst of English Studies Univ of London 2008–; pres Bibliographical Soc 2008–10 (memb Cncl 1990–94, vice-pres 1998–2008); foreign expert Miny of Educn and Science Netherlands 1992–93; memb Mid Wharfedale Parish Cncl 1974–84; fell English Assoc 1990; John Coffin Meml Lecture 2010; *Books* Congreve's The Way of the World (ed, 1972), Pope: The Critical Heritage (ed, 1973, reprinted 1995), John Keats: The Complete Poems (ed, 1973, 3 edn 1988), Etherege's The Man of Mode (ed, 1979, reprinted in Five Restoration Comedies, 1984, revised edn 2007), John Keats (1987), John Keats: Selected Poems (ed, 1988), The Early Seventeenth-Century Book Trade and John Foster's Inventory of 1616 (with Maureen Bell, 1994), Folio Society John Keats: The Complete Poems (ed, 2001), The Cambridge History of the Book in Britain, Volume IV 1557–1695 (gen ed with D F McKenzie (assisted by Maureen Bell), 2002), John Keats: Selected Poems (ed, 2007), John Keats: Selected Letters (ed, 2014); also of many articles on late 17th Century English literature, the Romantics, book history and bibliography in various learned jls; *Recreations* travel, walking; *Style*— Prof John Barnard; ✉ Lane End, Weeton Lane, Weeton, Nr Leeds LS17 0AN; Wolfson College, Oxford OX2 6UD

BARNARD, John Vianney; s of Arthur James Barnard, and Mary Agnes Isabella, *née* Loomes; *b* 25 February 1944; *Educ* City of Norwich GS, Norwich City Coll (I Eng AMI Prod E), Open Univ, RSA CLAIT; *m* 1970, Jacqueline, *née* Greig (d 2013); 2 s (James, Benjamin), 1 da (Joanna); *Career* furniture designer; prod mangr: Lawrence Scott Electromotors 1964–69, Duncan Tucker 1969–70, United Glass 1970–71; prop: The Design Workshop 1971–, John Barnard Furniture Ltd 1971–2015–; cmmns incl: Norfolk CC (incl wedding present for HRH the Prince of Wales and Lady Diana Spencer), UEA, SS Peter and Paul Church Wakefield, Reedham Church Norfolk (Craftsmanship Award Norfolk Assoc of Architects), Norwich City Cncl, Worshipful Co of Info Technologists, Victory project (Nelson's Flagship, Mike Hicks Cup for Merit Norfolk Furniture Makers), Arpana Tst; pres Norfolk Furniture Makers Assoc (fndr memb 1972); memb: Norfolk Contemporary Crafts Soc (past chair), Norfolk Contemporary Arts Soc, Furniture Liaison Panel Norwich City Coll, Fedn of Small Businesses (FSB, past chm Policy Ctee); Freeman City of London 1998, Liveryman Worshipful Co of Furniture Makers 1998 (chm Bespoke Guildmark Ctee 2009–12); MCSD 1997, IEng; *Recreations* design, reading, travel, squash, creativity; *Style*— John Barnard, Esq; ✉ 69 Nelson Street, Norwich NR2 4DW (☎ 07775 788131, e-mail johnvbarnard@gmail.com, website www.johnbarnardfurniture.co.uk)

BARNARD, Michael John; s of Cecil William Barnard, and Gladys Irene Mary, *née* Hedges; *b* 4 May 1944; *Educ* Licensed Victuallers Sch Slough; *m* 1 (m dis 1979), Jennifer, da of Charles Tyrrill; 1 s (Matthew b 15 Sept 1971); m 2, Charlotte Susan, da of Sir Kenneth Berrill; m 3, Jayne Ann (d 2007), da of Brian Jenkinson; *Career* journalist and publisher: Kent Web Offset Group 1962–66, Westminster Press 1966–67 and 1968–71; managing ed First Features Ltd 1967–68, prodn dir Macmillan Magazines 1971–79, chm and md Macmillan Production Ltd 1979–2007, non-exec dep chm Macmillan Ltd 2007–13, advsr on business responsibility Macmillan Science and Educn 2013–16; dir: Macmillan Publishers Ltd 1982–2007, Macmillan Ltd 1985–2007, Macmillan Publishers Group Administration Ltd 1988–2007; chm: Macmillan Distribution Ltd 1988–95 and 1997–2007, Macmillan Information Systems Ltd 1988–95; non-exec dir: Periodical Publishers' Association Ltd 1988–91, Gill & Macmillan Ltd 1990–94 and 1996–2002; chm New Media Investments Ltd 1994–2007; non-exec chm Macmillan Ltd 2007–15; chm Bd of Tstees

Printing Industries' Research Assoc 1995–2005; visiting prof London Inst (now Univ of the Arts London) 1998; Liveryman Worshipful Co of Stationers and Newspapermakers 1995 (Freeman 1993); MCB 1988, FRSA 1991, MILog 1993, FIOP 1999; *Books* Magazine and Journal Production (1986), Introduction to Print Buying (1987), Inside Magazines (1989), Introduction to Printing Processes (1990), The Print and Production Manual (1998), Transparent Imprint (2006), Business Etiquette in India (2009); *Recreations* music, gardening, reading, sailing; *Style*— Michael Barnard, Esq; ✉ Macmillan Ltd, Houndmills, Basingstoke, Hampshire RG21 6XS (☎ 01256 329242, fax 01256 331248)

BARNARD, Robert; s of Peter Barnard (d 2006), and Jeanne, *née* Meyers; *b* 29 July 1953, Dorking, Surrey; *Educ* Downsend Sch Leatherhead, St John's Coll Horsham, LAMDA; *m* 31 May 1980, Sarah, *née* Dorman; 2 s (William, Edward), 1 da (Holly); *Career* theatre sound, stage and lighting technician; Salisbury Playhouse 1971–72, sound technician Theatre Projects Ltd 1972–78; National Theatre: sound technician 1978–85, technical mangr 1990–2004, head of technical resources 2004–11, project mangr working on building devpt project 2011–15; Rayne Award National Theatre 2012; *Style*— Robert Barnard, Esq; ✉ e-mail robertbarnard@blueyonder.co.uk

BARNARD, Dr Robert; s of Leslie Barnard (d 1969), and Vera Doris, *née* Nethercoat (d 1998); *b* 23 November 1936; *Educ* Colchester Royal GS, Balliol Coll Oxford, Univ of Bergen Norway (DPhil); *m* 1963, Mary Louise Tabor, da of Geoffrey Tabor, of Armidale, Aust; *Career* author; lectr in English lit Univ of New England Armidale NSW 1961–66, lectr and sr lectr Univ of Bergen Norway 1966–76, prof of English lit Univ of Tromsø Norway 1976–83; memb: Soc of Authors, Crime Writers' Assoc (memb Ctee 1988–91); chm Brontë Soc 1996–99 and 2002–05 (memb Cncl and vice-chm 1991–95); Diamond Dagger for lifetime achievement in crime fiction 2003, Crime Writers' Assoc Award for Best Short Story 2006; *Books* incl: Death of An Old Goat (1974), Unruly Son (1978), Mother's Boys (1981), Sheer Torture (1981), A Corpse in a Gilded Cage (1984), A Short History of English Literature (1984), Out of the Blackout (1985), The Skeleton in the Grass (1987), City of Strangers (1990), Dead, Mr Mozart (as Bernard Bastable, 1995), A Scandal in Belgravia (1991), Masters of the House (1994), Unholy Dying (2000), Emily Brontë (2000), Cry from the Dark (2003), A Brontë Encyclopedia (2007), A Fall from Grace (2007), The Killings on Jubilee Terrace (2009), A Stranger in the Family (2010), A Charitable Body (2012, US only); *Recreations* walking, opera, Edwin Drood; *Style*— Dr Robert Barnard; ✉ Hazeldene, Houghley Lane, Leeds LS13 2DT (☎ and fax 0113 263 8955); c/o Gregory & Company, 3 Barb Mews, London W6 7PA (☎ 020 7610 4676, fax 020 7610 4686)

BARNARD, Stephen Geoffrey; s of Geoffrey Thomas Barnard, and Diana Pixie, *née* Rivron; *b* 4 May 1950; *Educ* Gresham's, Univ of Southampton (LLB); *m* 4 Oct 1980, Prof Jane Elizabeth Lisa *née* Maxim, da of Dr Oliver Vivian Maxim, of Gretton, Northants; *Career* admitted slr 1974; traveller 1974–75; Herbert Smith: joined 1976, NY 1980–82, ptnr 1983–2006; *Recreations* golf, bridge, walking, birds, skiing, reading, trying to paint, music, talking, wine; *Style*— Stephen Barnard, Esq

BARNES, Adrian Francis Patrick; CVO (1996), DL (Greater London 2002); s of Francis Walter Ibbetson Barnes (d 2000), and Heather Katherine, *née* Tamplin; *b* 25 January 1943; *Educ* St Paul's, Hague Acad of Int Law, Cncl of Legal Educn, City of London Poly (MA); *m* 31 May 1980, Sally Eve, da of Dr James Lawson Whatley (d 1986); 1 s (William b 1982), 1 da (Sophie b 1983); *Career* called to the Bar Gray's Inn 1973; Slr's Dept DTI 1975–82, dep remembrancer Corp of London 1982, City Remembrancer 1986–2003; doyen Gray's Inn Seniors in Hall 1992–2000, bencher 2000–; govr Music Therapy Charity 1995–2016 (chm 1997–2003, chm Research Ctee 2014–16); chm Exec Ctee Wimbledon Guild 2004–08 (memb 2003–, chm Centenary Ctee, Counselling Ctee and Mgmnt Ctee 2004–08); pres Merton Talking Newspaper 2015–; Freeman City of London 1982, Liveryman Worshipful Co of Merchant Taylors 1989–, Freeman Worshipful Co of Arts Scholars 2007–; *Recreations* music, cricket, rowing, biography, chess, City lore; *Clubs* Garrick, Guildhall, MCC; *Style*— Adrian Barnes, Esq, CVO, DL

BARNES, Benjamin (Ben); s of Thomas Barnes, and Tricia Barnes; *b* 20 August 1981, London; *Educ* Kings Coll Sch Wimbledon, Kingston Univ (BA, English Literature Award); *Career* actor; memb Nat Youth Music Theatre 1997–2001; *Theatre* incl: Sex, Chips and Rock 'n' Roll 2005, The History Boys 2006–07; *Films* incl: Stardust 2007, Bigga Than Ben 2008, The Chronicles of Narnia: Prince Caspian 2008, Easy Virtue 2008, Dorian Gray 2009, The Chronicles of Narnia: The Voyage of the Dawn Treader 2010, Locked In 2010, Killing Bono 2011; *Style*— Ben Barnes, Esq; ✉ c/o Creative Artists Management, First Floor, 55–59 Shaftesbury Avenue, London W1D 6LD

BARNES, Christian William; s of Oswald Edward Barnes (d 2002), of Great Houghton Hall, Northants, and Gillian, *née* Ralph; *b* 20 June 1959; *Educ* Uppingham, Univ of Durham (BA); *m* 1987, Melanie Joy, da of Kenneth Roy Eades (d 1996); 3 s (Elliot James Royston b 6 Feb 1991, Hamish William b 25 June 1993, Lewis Gabriel b 1 Jan 1996); *Career* advertisement sales mangr Dominion Press Ltd 1981–82, asst account mangr then account dir Leo Burnett Ltd 1982–87, fndr ptnr and co dir BV Gp plc 1987–2001, fndr ptnr and co dir The Blackbox Partnership Ltd 2001–13, strategic planning dir AML Gp Ltd 2013–, fndr ptnr and md MC Consulting Partnership Ltd 2014–; assoc The Rare Skills Set 2015–; *Recreations* music, skiing, sailing, travel; *Style*— Christian Barnes; ✉ christian@mcconsultingpartnership.com

BARNES, Geoffrey Frederick; s of Frederick Albert Barnes, of Hertford, and Iris Alice Maud, *née* Neslen (d 2002); *b* 14 April 1945; *Educ* Down Lane Central Sch; *m* 1, 29 Sept 1969 (m dis 1987), Sheila Emily Birtwhistle; 1 da (Alison Marguerite b 10 March 1974), 1 s (Andrew Geoffrey b 22 Jan 1976); m 2, 19 June 2004, Birgithe Edwards; *Career* joined Ogden Parsons (merged with Harmood Banner 1970 then with Deloitte Haskins Sells 1973) 1963, seconded to HM Treasy 1977–79; Casson Beckman (merged with Baker Tilly 1997): joined 1979, exec chm 1990–97, ceo and pres Baker Tilly International 2000–; chm Int Advsy Panel ICAEW (memb Cncl 2003–04); FCA; *Recreations* golf, walking, climbing, reading particularly the history of the American Civil War; *Clubs* Lord's Taverners, Ealing Golf; *Style*— Geoff Barnes, Esq; ✉ Baker Tilly International, 100 St Paul's Churchyard, London EC4M 8BU (☎ 020 3102 7600, e-mail geoff.barnes@bakertillyinternational.com)

BARNES, Prof Howard Anthony; OBE (1997); s of Elijah Barnes (d 1958), of Ystrad Mynach, Glamorgan, and Doris Mabel, *née* Liddy (d 1978); *b* 8 April 1944; *Educ* Bargoed GS, UC Wales Aberystwyth (BSc, PhD, DSc); *m* 1967, Pauline Sandra, *née* Brind; 3 s (Timothy b 7 March 1969, Andrew b 25 Sept 1971, Stephen b 3 Jan 1973); *Career* Unilever Research Port Sunlight Lab: scientist 1970–78, sr scientist 1978–2000, princ scientist 2000–04; research prof Univ of Wales Aberystwyth 2004–09; pres Br Soc of Rheology 1994–96 (chm of Founding Ctee of European Soc of Rheology 1996); chm: Applied Rheology Subject Gp Inst of Chem Engrg, European Federation of Chem Engrg; memb: Soft Solids Initiative EPSRC 1997– (chm 1994–97), Engrg and Physical Sciences Ctee BBSRC, Engrg Sciences Panel EC; external examiner: Univ of Wales Aberystwyth, Univ of Bangalore, Univ of Bradford, Univ of Bristol, Univ of Cambridge, Univ of Cardiff, Univ of Glamorgan, Univ of Leeds, Univ of Swansea, UCL, Univ of Birmingham, Univ of London, Univ Coll Dublin; memb Christian Brethren (lay preacher); Royal Soc of Chemistry Solids Processing Award 1984, Hanson Medal 1993, Br Soc of Rheology Annual Award 2001; FIChemE, FIM, FREng; *Books* Dispersion Rheology (1980), An Introduction to Rheology (with J Hutton & K Walters, 1989), A Handbook of Elementary Rheology (2000), Viscosity (2002); *Style*— Prof Howard Barnes, OBE, FREng; ✉ 55 Croft Avenue, Bromborough, Wirral L62 2BN (☎ 0151 334 2178, e-mail howard@rheology.co.uk)

BARNES, Jack Henry; s of James Barnes (d 1944), and Joan Ivy, *née* Sears; *b* 11 December 1943; *Educ* Hatfield Sch, Univ of Sussex (BA), LSE (MSc); *m* 1966, Nicola, *née* Pearse; 2 da (Sarah b 1969, Rachel b 1970); *Career* univ and private sector res conslt 1968–78; Dept of Health: Chief Scientist's Office 1978–83, Social Servs Inspectorate 1983–88, Res Mgmnt Div 1988–91, Primary Care Div NHS Exec 1991–95, head Int and Indust Div 1995–99; dir of res Nat Asthma Campaign 2000–03, dir of admin Br Soc for Allergy and Clinical Immunology 2003–; *Style*— Jack Barnes, Esq

BARNES, Jeremy (Jerry); s of John Woodley Barnes (d 2014), and Elizabeth Ann, *née* Polkinghorne (d 2013); *b* 11 February 1961; *Educ* Truro Sch, KCL (BA); *m* 1, 8 August 1987 (m dis 2005); 2 s (Matthew Robert b 1 March 1990, Henry Alexander b 6 Sept 1992); m 2, 27 Sept 2008, Delphine Peggy-Louise Solomon; 1 da (Peggy Ghislaine b 18 Feb 2006); *Career* trainee accountant Saffery Champness 1982–86, fin accountant S G Warburg 1986–87; Saffery Champness: rejoined 1987, ptnr 1990–2010; ptnr Smith & Williamson 2011–15, md Bristol Private Office Services Ltd 2015–, md Bristol Private Equity Ltd 2016–; chm Bristol Ctee Game and Wildlife Conservation Tst 2008–; FCA 1997 (ACA 1986); *Recreations* rugby, cricket, shooting and fishing; *Clubs* Farmers', Clifton (Bristol, dir 2008–13 and 2016–), MCC; *Style*— Jerry Barnes, Esq; ✉ Bpos Ltd, 6 The Avenue, Sneyd Park, Bristol BS9 1PA (☎ 07831 308143, e-mail jerry.barnes@bpos.uk.com)

BARNES, Prof Jonathan; s of Albert Leonard Barnes (d 1992), and Kathleen Mabel, *née* Scoltock (d 1997); *b* 26 December 1942; *Educ* City of London Sch, Balliol Coll Oxford; *m* Jennifer Mary, da of Ormond Postgate; 2 da (Catherine, Camilla); *Career* Univ of Oxford: fell Oriel Coll 1968–78, lectr in philosophy 1968, fell Balliol Coll 1978–94, prof of ancient philosophy 1989–94; prof of ancient philosophy: Univ of Geneva 1994–2002, Univ of Paris IV-Sorbonne 2002–06; visiting appointments at: Univ of Chicago, Inst for Advanced Study Princeton, Univ of Massachusetts Amherst, Univ of Texas Austin, Wissenschaftskolleg zu Berlin, Univ of Edmonton, Univ of Zürich, Istituto Italiano per gli Studi Filosofici Naples, École Normale Supérieure de Paris, Scuola Normale di Pisa; hon fell Oriel Coll Oxford 2007; Dr (hc): Univ of Geneva 2010, Univ of Berlin 2012; Condorcet Medal 1996; FBA 1987, Hon FAAAS 1999; hon citizenship of Velia 2010; *Books* The Ontological Argument (1972), Aristotle's Posterior Analytics (1975), The Presocratic Philosophers (1979), Aristotle (1982), Early Greek Philosophy (1987), The Toils of Scepticism (1990), Logic and the Imperial Stoa (1997), Porphyry: Introduction (2003), Truth, etc (2006), Coffee with Aristotle (2008), Method and Metaphysics (2011), Zenone e l'infinito (2011), Logical Matters (2012), Proof, Knowledge and Scepticism (2013), Mantissa (2015); *Style*— Prof Jonathan Barnes, FBA; ✉ Les Charmilles, L'Auvergne, 36200 Ceaulmont, France

BARNES, Matthew; *Career* Aldi: grad area mangr 1997–2000, operations dir SW UK 2000–02, regnl md NW 2002–06, md Corp Buying Aust 2007–09, jt md UK & I 2010–15, ceo UK & I 2015–; *Style*— Matthew Barnes, Esq; ✉ Aldi Stores, Holly Lane, Atherstone, Warwickshire CV9 2SQ

BARNES, Prof Michael Patrick; s of Capt William Edward Clement Barnes (d 1999), and Gladys Constance, *née* Hooper (d 2012); *b* 28 June 1940, Finchley, London; *Educ* High Canons Sch, Wynstones Sch Gloucester, Freie Waldorfschule Stuttgart, UCL (BA, MA, Rosa Morrison prize), Nansenskolen Lillehammer, Univ of Oslo; *m* 8 Aug 1970, Kirsten Heiberg, da of Trygve Ole Mathias Røer (d 1980); 3 da (Catherine b 1971, Anne Helen b 1973, Kirsten Emily b 1980), 1 s (William Michael b 1978); *Career* Dept of Scandinavian Studies UCL: asst lectr 1964–67, lectr 1967–75, reader 1975–83, prof of Scandinavian philology 1983–94, prof of Scandinavian studies 1994–2005 (prof emeritus 2005–); Viking Soc for Northern Research: memb 1963–, ed Saga Book 1970–83, jt hon sec 1983–2006; ed NOWELE 1989–; memb: UCU (formerly AUT) 1964–, Royal Gustavus Adolphus Acad Uppsala 1984 (corresponding memb 1977–84), Norwegian Acad of Science and Letters 1997; Swedish Acad Award 2009; Hon Dr Univ of Uppsala 2002; fell Soc of Antiquaries of Scotland 2009; Knight Icelandic Order of the Falcon 1992, Knight First Class The Royal Norwegian Order of Merit 2008; *Books* Old Scandinavian Texts (1968), Draumkvæde: an edition and study (1974), The Runic Inscriptions of Maeshowe, Orkney (1994), The Runic Inscriptions of Viking Age Dublin (jtly, 1997), The Norn Language of Orkney and Shetland (1998), A New Introduction to Old Norse I: Grammar (1999), Faroese Language Studies (2001), Introduction to Scandinavian Phonetics: Danish, Norwegian and Swedish (jtly, 2005), The Scandinavian Runic Inscriptions of Britain (jtly, 2006), Runes: A Handbook (2012); *Recreations* badminton, drinking real ale, walking disused railways; *Style*— Prof Michael Barnes; ✉ 93 Longland Drive, Totteridge, London N20 8HN (☎ 020 8445 4697, e-mail michael@runes.demon.co.uk); Department of Scandinavian Studies, University College London, Gower Street, London WC1E 6BT (☎ 020 7679 7175, fax 020 7679 7750)

BARNES, (David) Michael William; QC (1981); s of David Charles Barnes (d 1954), and Florence Maud, *née* Matthews (d 1967); *b* 16 July 1943; *Educ* Monmouth, Wadham Coll Oxford (BA); *m* 5 Sept 1970, Susan Dorothy, da of William Turner; 3 s (Andrew b 1972, Edmund b 1974, Peter b 1979); *Career* called to the Bar Middle Temple 1965 (bencher 1989); recorder of the Crown Court 1984–; hon res fell LMH Oxford 1979; chm Hinckley Point 'C' Public Inquiry 1988; visiting fell Univ of Auckland NZ 1996; *Publications* Leasehold Reform Act 1967 (1967), Hill and Redman's Law of Landlord and Tenant (ed 15–18 edns, 1970–88), Hill and Redman's Guide to Rent Review (2001), Law of Compulsory Purchase and Compensation (2014); *Recreations* crime fiction, walking; *Clubs* Beefsteak; *Style*— Michael Barnes, Esq, QC; ✉ Wilberforce Chambers, 8 New Square, Lincoln's Inn, London WC2A 3QP (☎ 020 7306 0102, fax 020 7306 0095)

BARNES, Prof Neil Christopher; s of Douglas Barnes (d 1988), and June, *née* Deacon; *b* 24 June 1954; *Educ* Vyners GS Ickenham, Trinity Hall Cambridge (MA), Westminster Med Sch (MB BS); *m* 1983, Mari; 3 s (Christopher b 20 July 1985, Andrew b 25 Dec 1987, Oliver b 14 Feb 1995); *Career* research fell KCH until 1987, sr registrar London Chest Hosp 1987–88, conslt Royal London Hosp and London Chest Hosp 1988–2013, prof of respiratory medicine Queen Mary Univ of London 2002–, jt dir of R&D Barts and the London NHS Tst and Barts and the London Med Coll 2005–09, medical head Global Respiratory Franchise GlaxoSmithKline London 2013–; assoc ed Thorax 1990–2002; author of more than 130 peer-reviewed pubns and 120 invited articles on the subject of asthma and other lung disorders; former tstee Educn for Health Charity; work with: Nat Asthma Campaign, Br Lung Fndn; memb Sci Ctee Global Initiative for Asthma (GINA) Guidelines 2010–13; memb: Br Thoracic Soc (chair Pharmacology Section UK Asthma Guidelines 1998–2013), listed in The Sunday Times Top 100 UK Doctors list; BMA; FRCP 1995, hon fell Ceylon Coll of Physicians 2014; *Recreations* skiing, reading; *Style*— Prof Neil Barnes; ✉ GSK House, 980 Great West Road, Brentford Middlesex, TW8 9GS (☎ 020 8990 4539, e-mail neil.c.barnes@gsk.com)

BARNES, Dr Nicholas Martin Limer; CBE (2009); s of Geoffrey Lambe Barnes (d 1984), and Emily *née* Dicken (d 1976); *b* 18 January 1939; *Educ* King Edward's Sch Birmingham, Imperial Coll London (BScEng), UMIST (PhD); *m* 23 Feb 1963, Diana Marion, da of Barrie Campbell (d 1968); 1 da (Kate b 1964), 1 s (Matthew b 1966); *Career* res fell Univ of Manchester 1968–71, ptnr Martin Barnes and Partners 1971–85, ptnr Coopers and Lybrand Associates mgmnt conslt 1985–96; exec dir The Major Projects Assoc 1997–2006; visiting prof Univ of Birmingham 1998–2003; assoc fell: Templeton Coll Oxford 2001–07, Saïd Business Sch Univ of Oxford 2007–10; Churchill Fellowship 1971; ACGI,

FREng, FICE, FAPM (chm 1986–91, pres 2003–12), FCInstCES (pres 1978–86); *Books* Measurement in Contract Control (1977), The CESMM2 Handbook (1986), Engineering Management: Financial Control (ed, 1990), The CESMM3 Handbook (1992); *Recreations* railway and canal history, victorian paintings, choral singing; *Style*— Dr Martin Barnes, CBE, FREng; ✉ Cornbrash House, Kirtlington, Oxfordshire OX5 3HF (☎ 01869 350828, e-mail cornbrash@aol.com)

BARNES, Paul Alastair; s of William Barnes, and Rosemary Elizabeth, *née* Williamson; *b* 25 August 1970, Harlow, Essex; *Educ* Univ of Reading (BA); *m* 9 May 1998, Sheila Margaret Jack; 1 da (Isabel Emily b 2 May 1999), 1 s (George Robert b 9 Jan 2001); *Career* art dir Roger Black Inc 1992–95 (redesigned Nesweek, Esquire and Foreign Affairs), typographic conslt and graphic designer 1995–, art dir Spin magazine 1997–98, ptnr (with Christian Schwartz) Commercial Type 2009–; advsr and conslt on numerous publications incl The Sunday Times Magazine, The Guardian (co-designed Guardian Egyptian typeface), The Observer, GQ, Wallpaper*, Harper's Bazaar and frieze; designed books for publishers incl Schirmer Mosel, OUP and Tate; worked on identities for Givenchy, Gianvito Rossi and Schirmer Graf; D&AD Black Pencil (for Guardian redesign), nominated Design Museum Designer of the Year 2005; featured in: Wallpaper's 40 Most Influential Designers Under 40 and The Guardian's 50 Best Designers in Britain; FRSA 2000; *Style*— Paul Barnes, Esq; ✉ 45 Benbow Road, London W6 0AU (e-mail paul@moderntypography.com, website www.moderntypography.com)

BARNES, Prof Peter John; s of John Barnes (d 1989), and Eileen, *née* Thurman (d 1998); *b* 29 October 1946; *Educ* Leamington Coll, St Catharine's Coll Cambridge (scholar, MA, numerous prizes), Worcester Coll Oxford (BM BCh, DM, DSc); *m* 1976, Olivia Mary, *née* Harvard-Watts; 3 s (Adam b 2 Jan 1978, Toby b 20 Feb 1981, Julian b 14 Nov 1988); *Career* med registrar UCH London 1975–78, MRC research fell Royal Postgrad Med Sch 1978–81, MRC travelling fell Cardiovascular Res Inst San Francisco 1981–82, sr registrar Hammersmith Hosp 1979–82, sr lectr/conslt physician Royal Postgrad Med Sch and Hammersmith Hosp London 1982–85, prof of clinical pharmacology Cardiothoracic Inst London 1985–87; currently: prof of thoracic med, dir Dept of Thoracic Med and head of respiratory med Imperial Coll Sch of Med, hon conslt physician Royal Brompton Hosp London; author of over 1000 peer-reviewed papers, numerous invited review papers and chapters, ed over 50 books on asthma, COPD, lung pharmacology and related topics; former ed: Pulmonary Pharmacology, Respiratory Res; assoc ed Chest; hon degrees from Univs of Ferrara, Athens, Tanpere, Leuven and Maastricht; hon fell St Catharine's Coll Cambridge; memberships incl: Physiological Soc, Br Pharmacology Soc, Br Thoracic Soc, American Thoratic Soc, European Respiratory Soc (pres 2013–14, fell 2014), Academia Europaea 2012, American Assoc of Physicians; FRCP 1988, FMedSci 1999, FRS 2007, master fell American Coll of Chest Physicians 2012; *Recreations* travel, gardening; *Style*— Prof Peter Barnes; ✉ National Heart and Lung Institute, Dovehouse Street, London SW3 6LY (☎ 020 7351 8174, fax 020 7351 5675, e-mail p.j.barnes@imperial.ac.uk)

BARNES, Richard Hugh; *b* 10 June 1962, London; *Educ* Harrow, N E London Poly (BSc, MSc); *m* 1994; 3 c; *Career* Hillier Parker 1984–86, Vigers 1986–88, Bernard Thorpe 1988–92, Mourant Gp 1995–2001, Barnes and Partners 2001–07, currently chm Invesco Property Income Tst; dir of a number of listed and private property cos; RICS (former chm Jersey branch); *Style*— Richard Barnes, Esq; ✉ Vinchelez de Bas Manor, La Route de Vinchelez, St Ouen, Jersey JE3 2DB (☎ 01534 484434, mobile 07700 700252, e-mail rhbarnes@me.com)

BARNES, Richard Michael; AM; s of John William Barnes (d 1977), and Kate (Kitty), *née* Harper; *b* 1 December 1947; *Educ* Trinity HS Northampton, Wolverhampton Grammar Tech Sch (head boy), Univ of Wales Inst of Sci and Technol (BSc); *Career* ldr London Borough of Hillingdon 1991–1993 and 1998–2000 (ldr Cons Gp 1991–2000); GLA: memb London Assembly (Cons) Ealing and Hillingdon 2000–, dep mayor 2008–, chair 7 July Review Ctee, memb Health Ctee, memb Audit Panel Ctee; memb Met Police Authy 2000–08; dep chair Hillingdon HA 1998–2002, non-exec dir NW London SHA 2006–; patron Hillingdon AIDS Response Tst, tstee NW London Community Tst 2002–; fndn advsr The Book Tst; Freeman City of London; FRSA 2007; *Recreations* field sports, opera, music, literature, chelonia; *Style*— Councillor Richard Barnes, AM; ✉ Greater London Assembly, City Hall, Queens Walk, Southwark, London SE1 2AA (☎ 020 7983 4414, fax 020 7983 4419, e-mail richard.barnes@london.gov.uk, website www.richard.barnes.info)

BARNES, Prof Robert Harrison; s of Robert H Barnes (d 1985), and Edna, *née* Farrier (d 2002); *b* 11 October 1944, Jacksonville, TX; *Educ* Reed Coll USA (BA), Univ of Oxford (BLitt, DPhil); *m* 29 June 1968, Ruth, *née* Weinlich; 1 da (Ina Florence b 11 Sept 1974), 1 s (Jan Lawrence b 14 Feb 1979); *Career* visiting asst prof Univ of Southern Calif 1972–74, lectr Univ of Edinburgh 1974–77, lectr Univ of Oxford 1978–96, faculty fell St Antony's Coll Oxford 1987–, prof of social anthropology Univ of Oxford 1996–; memb: Royal Anthropological Soc 1969, Assoc of SE Asianists UK 1977, Assoc of Social Anthropologists of the Cwlth 1980; *Books* Kédang: A Study of the Collective Thought of an Eastern Indonesian People (1974), Two Crows Denies It: A History of Controversy in Omaha Sociology (1984, 2 edn 2005), Sea Hunters of Indonesia (1996); *Recreations* walking; *Style*— Prof R H Barnes; ✉ Institute of Social and Cultural Anthropology, 51 Banbury Road, Oxford OX2 6PE (☎ 01865 274676, fax 01865 274630, e-mail robert.barnes@anthro.ox.ac.uk); St Antony's College, Woodstock Road, Oxford OX2 6PF (☎ 01865 284701)

BARNES, Scott; s of late Ronald Barnes, of Leeds, and Sheila; *b* 3 December 1955, Morley, Leeds; *Educ* Univ of Oxford; *m* Irene nee Evans, 1 s (Adam), 1 da (Laura); *Career* Grant Thornton LLP: joined 1984, ptnr 1987–, head of London and South East recovery 1994–95, UK head of recovery and reorganisation 1995–2001, managing ptnr for specialist financial services 2001–07, global head of advsy services 2007–08, ceo UK 2008–15 (chair Global Bd 2015–); FCA; *Recreations* Watching cricket, Football, and Rugby, swimming, theatre, cinema; *Clubs* RAC, Pall Mall, Keble Assoc (pres); *Style*— Scott Barnes, Esq; ✉ Grant Thornton International, Grant Thornton House, Melton Street, Euston Square, London NW1 2EP

BARNES, Simon Seton; s of Edward Walter Taylor Barnes (d 2001), of Chelsea, London, and Joan Constance Barnes (d 1985); *b* 26 January 1958; *Educ* Shiplake Coll, INSEAD (Advanced Mgmnt Prog); *m* 19 Aug 1983, Wendy Clare; 2 s (Oliver b 13 June 1986, Edward b 19 Jan 1988), 1 da (Phoebe b 9 July 1990); *Career* Alexander Howden Reinsurance Brokers Ltd: joined as trainee 1976, dir 1983, md 1986–90, chief exec 1990–95; md and chief operating offr Alexander Howden Non-Marine 1995–97, md Aon Group Ltd Non-Marine Reinsurance 1997–2001, ptnr Jardine Lloyd Thompson Risk Solutions Ltd 2001–06, dir Reinsurance Div Miller Insurance Services Ltd 2006–09, dir FIB Ltd 2009–13 (md 2012–13), dir Alsford Page and Gems Ltd 2013–; *Recreations* golf, rugby, tennis; *Clubs* Roayl Ashdown Forest Golf, City of London; *Style*— Simon Barnes, Esq; ✉ Alsford Page and Gems Ltd, Minories House, 2–5 Minories, London EC3N 1BJ (☎ 020 7 456 0513, e-mail simon.barnes@apg.net)

BARNES, Timothy Paul; QC (1986); s of late Arthur Morley Barnes, of Seal, Kent, and Valerie Enid Mary, *née* Wilks; *b* 23 April 1944; *Educ* Bradfield, Christ's Coll Cambridge (MA); *m* Aug 1969, Patricia Margaret, da of Leslie Ralph Gale (d 1974); 1 s (Christopher b 1973), 3 da (Olivia b 1975, Jessica b 1978, Natasha b 1986); *Career* called to the Bar Gray's Inn 1968 (bencher); asst recorder 1983–87, recorder of the Crown Court 1987–; memb Midland & Oxford Circuit; chm Greenwich Soc 1999–; *Recreations* hockey,

gardening, music; *Clubs* MCC; *Style*— Timothy P Barnes, Esq, QC; ✉ 7 Bedford Row, London WC1R 4BU (☎ 020 7242 3555)

BARNETT, Prof Anthony Howard (Tony); s of Geoffrey Barnett, and Beulah, *née* Statman; *b* 29 May 1951; *Educ* Roundhay GS Leeds, KCH London (BSc, MB BS, MD); *m* 11 Nov 1975, Catherine Elizabeth Mary, da of John O'Donnell (d 1977); 3 s (James John, Jonathan Andrew, Robert David), 3 da (Clare Joanne, Sarah Suzanne, Anna Lucy); *Career* sr fell MRC 1979–81, sr registrar in med diabetes and endocrinology Christchurch NZ and Southampton 1981–83; Univ of Birmingham: sr lectr and conslt physician 1983, reader in med 1989, prof of med 1992–; sec NZ Diabetes Assoc 1981–82; ed med educn jls: Hypertension Management, Modern Diabetes Management, Obesity in Practice, Practical Cardiovascular Risk Mgmnt; author of research papers in Nature, Nature Genetics, Lancet, New England Jl of Medicine, Brit Med 3, Diabetes and other learned jls; Banting Meml Lecture Diabetes UK 2011, Lifetime Achievement Award South Asian Health Fndn UK 2012; memb: Assoc of Physicians of GB and Ireland, Br Diabetic Assoc, Euro Assoc for the Study of Diabetes; FRCP 1989 (MRCP 1978); *Books* Immunogenetics of Insulin Dependent Diabetes (1987), Hypertension and Diabetes (1990, 3 edn 2006), Lipids, Diabetes and Vascular Disease (1992, 2 edn 1997), Shared Care in Diabetes (1998), Insulin Made Easy (2001, 2 edn 2004), Clinical Management of Hypertension in Diabetes (2002), Diabetes Annual (2002), Current Diabetes (2003), Diabetes and the Heart (2004), Obesity and Diabetes (ed, 2004, 2 edn 2009), Diabetes and Cardiovascular Disease (2004), Diabetes, Obesity and Cardiovascular Disease (2005), Diabetes and Renal Disease (2005), Applying the Evidence: Clinical Trials in Diabetes (2005), Diabetes: Best Practice and Research Compendium (2006), Patient Compliance in Diabetes (2007), New Therapies for Diabetes (2007), Type 2 Diabetes (2007, 2 edn 2012), Complications and Costs of Diabetes (2 edn 2012); *Recreations* reading, sport and family; *Style*— Prof Tony Barnett; ✉ Birmingham Heartlands Hospital, Diabetes Centre, Birmingham B9 5SS (☎ 0121 424 3587, fax 0121 424 0593, e-mail anthony.barnett@heartofengland.nhs.uk)

BARNETT, Anthony Peter John; *Educ* Univ of Essex (MA), Univ of Sussex; *Career* writer and publisher; editorial dir Allardyce, Barnett, Publishers 1981–, ed Fable Bulletin – Violin Improvisation Studies 1993–, prodr AB Fable Recording 2002–, ed Snow Lit Rev 2013–; visiting scholar Meiji Univ Japan 2002; *Poetry and Prose* incl: Poem About Music (1974), Blood Flow (1975), Fear and Misadventure/Mud Settles (1977), A White Mess (1981), North North, I Said, No, Wait a Minute, South, Oh, I Don't Know (148 Political Poems) (1985), The Resting Bell (collected, 1987), Little Stars and Straw Breasts (1993), The Poetry of Anthony Barnett – Essays, Interview and Letters (1993), Carp and Rubato (1995), Anti-Beauty (1999), Lisa Lisa (2000); collaborations with artists: Forest Poems Forest Drawings (with David Nash, 1987), Would You Tread on a Quadruped? An Animal Alphabet of Questionable Rhymes (with Natalie Cohen, 1992), Etiquette in the City (with Yolski, 2001), Miscanthus: Selected and New Poems (2005), Citations Followed On (2010), Antonyms and Others (2012), Poems & (2012), Translations (2012), Antonyms Anew: Barbs & Lores (2016); covered in anthologies incl: A Various Art (1987 and 1990), Poets On Writing – Britain, 1970–1991 (1992), Other: British and Irish Poetry since 1970 (1999), Contemporary Poetry: Poets and Poetry since 1990 (2009); collected poetry to 1999 included in Chadwyck-Healey Twentieth-Century English Poetry online database; translations from Italian, French, Norwegian, Swedish and Japanese; *Music Books* Desert Sands: The Recordings and Performances of Stuff Smith, An Annotated Discography and Biographical Source Book (1995), Up Jumped the Devil (1998), Black Gypsy: The Recordings of Eddie South, An Annotated Discography and Itinerary (1999), Listening for Henry Crowder (2007), UnNatural Music: John Lennon & Yoko Ono in Cambridge (2016); contrib: New Grove Dictionary of Jazz, New Grove Dictionary of Music and Musicians; *Recreations* music, mountains; *Style*— Anthony Barnett; ✉ Allardyce, Barnett, Publishers, 14 Mount Street, Lewes, East Sussex BN7 1HL (website www.abar.net)

BARNETT, Dr Christopher Andrew; s of Peter Alan Barnett (d 2006), and Gwladys Joan, *née* Cullis (d 1977); *b* 1 February 1953, Brentwood, Essex; *Educ* Cedars Sch Leighton Buzzard, Oriel Coll Oxford (exhibitioner, MA), Univ of Oxford (DPhil); *m* 1976 (m dis 2015), The Hon Laura, da of Lord Weidenfeld (Life Baron), *qv*; 3 s (Benjamin Lawrence Maximilian b 23 Feb 1979, Rowan Alexander b 16 April 1981, Nathaniel Peter Edward b 18 June 1984), 1 da (Clara Auriana b 23 Nov 1986); *Career* lectr in economics Brunel Univ 1975–77, head History Dept Bradfield Coll Berks 1978–87, second master Dauntsey's Sch Wilts 1987–91, headmaster Whitgift Sch Croydon 1991–; exhibition dir Hidden Treasures from the Mary Rose 2009, exhibition dir Remembering 1916 2016; schoolmaster fell Downing Coll Cambridge 1987, Evelyn Wrench scholar ESU 1990; pres Croydon Music Festival 1992–2013, dir Surrey CCC Whitgift Festival 2000–11; memb HMC 1991–; Chevalier des Palmes Académiques 2013; *Books* John Whitgift, Elizabeth I's last Archbishop of Canterbury (2015); *Recreations* opera, political Victoriana, horse racing, hill-walking, travel; *Clubs* Athenaeum; *Style*— Dr Christopher Barnett; ✉ c/o Miss Tates Shuldham, Whitgift School, Haling Park, South Croydon CR2 6YE (☎ 020 8680 7485)

BARNETT, Correlli Douglas; CBE (1997); s of D A Barnett; *b* 28 June 1927; *Educ* Trinity Sch Croydon, Exeter Coll Oxford (MA); *m* 1950, Ruth Murby; 2 da; *Career* writer and historian; Intelligence Corps 1945–48; N Thames Gas Bd 1952–57, public rels 1957–63; Churchill Coll Cambridge: fell 1977–, keeper of the Churchill Archives Centre 1977–95; lectr in def studies Univ of Cambridge 1980–83; memb: Cncl RUSI 1973–85, Ctee London Library 1977–79 and 1982–84; chm Lit Panel and memb Exec Ctee E Arts Assoc 1972–78, pres E Anglian Writers 1969–88; historical conslt/writer to BBC TV series: The Great War 1963–64 (Screenwriters' Guild Award 1964), The Lost Peace 1965–66, The Commanders 1972–73; Chesney Gold medal RUSI 1991; hon nat pres Western Front Assoc 1992–, Hon DSc Cranfield Univ 1993; FRHistS, FRSL, FRSA, Hon FCGI 2003; *Books* The Hump Organisation (1957), The Channel Tunnel (with Humphrey Slater, 1958), The Desert Generals (1960, 2 edn 1983), The Swordbearers (1963), Britain and Her Army (1970, RSL award 1971), The Collapse of British Power (1972), Marlborough (1974), Bonaparte (1978), The Great War (1979), The Audit of War (1986), Hitler's Generals (ed, 1989), Engage the Enemy More Closely: The Royal Navy in the Second World War (1991, Yorkshire Post Book of the Year 1991), The Lost Victory: British Dreams, British Realities 1945–1950 (1996), The Verdict of Peace: Britain Between her Yesterday and the Future (2001), Leadership in War: From Lincoln to Churchill (2012); contrib to: The Promise of Greatness (1968), Governing Elites (1969), Decisive Battles of the Twentieth Century (1976), The War Lords (1976), The Economic System in the UK (1985), Education for Capability (1986); *Style*— Mr Correlli Barnett, CBE, FRSL

BARNETT, Prof David Braham; CBE (2007); s of Joseph Barnett (d 1998), and Jeanne Barnett (d 1995); *b* 17 July 1944; *Educ* Sheffield Univ Med Sch (MB, Hon ChB, MD); *Career* Merck Int travelling fell 1975–76, sr lectr Univ of Leicester 1976–84, prof of clinical pharmacology Univ of Leicester and hon conslt physician Leicester Royal Infirmary 1984–; non-exec dir Leicester Royal Infirmary NHS Tst 1993–2000, chm Specialist Advsy Ctee for Gen (Internal) Med RCP 1995–99, chm Appraisals Ctee Nat Inst for Clinical Excellence 1999; FRCP 1981; *Publications* over 150 res publications in the fields of molecular pharmacology and gen cardiovascular clinical pharmacology with special interest in ischaemic heart disease; *Recreations* travel, reading, theatre; *Style*— Professor David Barnett, CBE; ✉ Department of Cardiovascular Sciences, Clinical Pharmacology Group, Level 4, Robert Kilpatrick Clinical Sciences Building, Leicester Royal Infirmary, Leicester LE2 7LX (☎ 0116 252 3126, fax 0116 252 3108)

BARNETT, Emma; *b* 5 February 1985, Manchester; *Educ* Manchester HS for Girls, Univ of Nottingham, Cardiff Univ (postgrad); *Career* reporter Media Week 2007–09; The Telegraph: technol and digital media ed 2009–12, women's ed (founded women's section) 2012–16; presenter Sunday Drive (LBC 97.3 FM) 2011–14, presenter Sunday Evening 5 Live Hit List (BBC 5 Live) 2014–, guest presenter Woman's Hour (BBC Radio 4) 2013–, documentary maker BBC Radio 4, presenter morning programme (10 am to 1 pm Wednesday to Friday) BBC 5 Live 2016– (only solo female presenter on network), columnist Sunday Times (Tough Love column) 2016–; works regularly for BBC News, ITV News and Sky News, presented TED talk 2015; Digital Journalist of the Year AOP 2011, Best New Radio Presenter Arqiva 2012, 30 Under 30 Radio Acad 2012 and 2013; memb Steering Ctee Women's Equality Pty; fndr Smartworks; FRSA 2011; *Recreations* cinema, music, reading, tennis, travel, walking, art, theatre; *Clubs* Soho House; *Style—* Ms Emma Barnett; ✉ e-mail emma.barnett@bbc.co.uk, website www.emmabarnett.org, Twitter @EmmaBarnett

BARNETT, Jonathan Ian; *s* of Louis and Frances Barnett; *Educ* St Marylebone GS; *m* Nava, 3 *s* (James, Joshua, Edward); *Career* sports agent; with: Curzon House Casino 1970–78, Coral Leisure 1978–82; self-employed conslt 1982–91, dir Stellar Promotions & Management 1991–; responsible for some of the most important transfers in Br football; prodr Come On You Reds by Manchester United (single, highest chart position no 1); memb Bd of various charities; represented England schoolboys at swimming and rugby; *Recreations* collecting wine and art; *Style—* Jonathan Barnett, Esq; ✉ The Stellar Group Ltd, 16 Stanhope Place, London W2 2HH (✆ 020 7298 0080, fax 020 7298 0099, e-mail jonathan.barnett@stellargroup.co.uk)

BARNETT, His Hon Kevin Edward; *s* of Arthur Barnett (d 1987), of Solihull, W Midlands, and Winifred, *née* Jones; *b* 2 January 1948; *Educ* Wellesbourne Sch, Tudor Grange GS, City of Birmingham Coll (LLB, London); *m* 6 May 1972, Patricia Margaret, da of Dr Charles Hanby Smith; 1 da (Elizabeth Clare *b* 6 Aug 1981); *Career* called to the Bar Gray's Inn 1971; in practice Wales & Chester Circuit, recorder 1994–96 (asst recorder 1991), head of chambers 1995–96, circuit judge (Wales & Chester Circuit) 1996–2014, ret; *Recreations* photography, painting, cooking; *Clubs* Lansdowne; *Style—* His Hon Kevin Barnett; ✉ c/o Wales and Chester Circuit Office, Churchill House, Churchill Way, Cardiff CF1 4HH

BARNETT, Rosemary; *da* of Leslie Wilson Barnett (d 1976), of Kingston Hill, Surrey, and Ella, *née* Renwick; *b* 12 August 1940; *Educ* Kingston Sch of Art, Royal Acad Schs (Landseer Prize, Edward Stott Scholarship and Silver Medal); *m* 1963, Nigel John Burfield Holmes; 2 *s* (Mark Burfield *b* 1968, Robert Murton *b* 1970), 2 da (Sasha Renwick *b* 1971, Tanya Renwick *b* 1973); *Career* sculptor; princ Sir Henry Doulton Sch of Sculpture, dir and fndr Frink Sch of Figurative Sculpture 1996–2005, curator Jerwood Sculpture Park at Witley Court 1999–2003, fndr Glass House Studios Staffs Moorlands 2006, studio Hartington Derbs 2008–; designed Quaker Service Memorial for the Nat Memorial Arboretum 2013; dir Ceramic and Allied Trade Union (CATU) Commemorative Project 2000–05; Br Inst Award 1959; memb Bd Lichfield Int Music Festival 1993–98, memb Lichfield Cathedral Artreach 2002–04; memb Soc for the Study of Normal Psychology 1970; FRBS 1998 (memb RBS 1966, memb Cncl 1992–95); *Recreations* walking, gardening; *Clubs* Reynolds (memb Cncl 1989–91); *Style—* Rosemary Barnett; ✉ 25 Brookfield's Road, Ipstones, Staffordshire ST10 2LY (e-mail info@rosemarybarnett.co.uk)

BARNETT, Sam; *s* of Grant Teasdale, of Herts, and Circe, *née* Barnett; *b* 9 June 1983, Beckenham, London; *Educ* Univ of Leicester (LLB), Coll of Law London (LPC); *m* 14 Aug 2009, Aaron, *née* Bushby; *Career* fndr and ceo Struq 2008–; personal awards: Rising Star Mktg Week Award 2011, Technol and Design Award and 30 under 30 in 2011 Square Mile Awards, Digital Hall of Fame BIMA, BIMA Hot 100 People with the Biggest Impact on Digital, Courvoisier Future 500 Rising Stars, finalist Ernst and Young Entrepreneur of the Year, finalist Young Entrepreneur of the Year Growing Business Award, Sunday Times Rich List Under 30 (ranked 7 2011, ranked 9 2012, ranked 11 2013); company awards: Best Advertising and Mktg Co in Europe Telegraph Start Up Awards, Most Innovative Co in Europe Entrepreneur Country Award 2011, Smarta Most Exciting and Disruptive New Business, Wall Street Jl Top 10 Start Ups and Innovators; *Style—* Sam Barnett, Esq; ✉ Struq Ltd, 5th Floor, Waverley House, 7–11 Noel Street, London W1F 8GQ (✆ 020 7121 9750, e-mail sam@struq.com, website www.struq.com, Twitter @barnettsam)

BARNICOAT, Thomas Humphry (Tom); *s* of John Barnicoat, and Jane Wright; *b* 21 October 1952; *Educ* Lycée Français de Londres, St John's Coll Oxford; *m* 1980, Katrina Chalmers; 3 da (Rebecca Jane *b* 29 Sept 1981, Laura Veronica *b* 22 Oct 1983, Phoebe Emmeline *b* 2 July 1991), 1 dog (Tug *b* 7 March 2000); *Career* BBC: grad trainee 1977, scriptwriter TV news 1979, prodr and dir TV current affrs 1981–86; prodr Crown Television 1986, dir of public affrs Sotheby's 1986–87, prodr Business Television 1987–89; Endemol UK plc (Broadcast Communications plc until 2000): dir of corp devpt 1990–93, dep chief exec 1993–95, chief exec 1995–2004; chief operating offr Endemol Group 2005–07; chm Somethin' Else 2008–; *Clubs* Reform, Hurlingham; *Style—* Tom Barnicoat, Esq; ✉ e-mail tbarnicoat@mac.com

BARNSLEY, Victoria (The Hon Mrs Nicholas Howard); OBE (2009); da of late T E Barnsley, OBE, and Margaret Gwyneth, née Llewellin; *b* 4 March 1954; *Educ* UCL (BA), Univ of York (MA); *m* Feb 1992, Hon Nicholas Paul Geoffrey Howard, 2 *s* of Baron Howard of Henderskelfe (d 1984); 1 da (Blanche Mary *b* 5 Oct 1994); *Career* fndr and publisher Fourth Estate Publishers 1984–2000, chief exec Harper Collins Publishers 2000–; dir Tate Enterprises Ltd; memb Cncl Publishers Assoc 2001– (pres 2010–11); hon fell UCL 2005; *Style—* Ms Victoria Barnsley, OBE; ✉ Elsinore House/77 Fulham Palace Rd, London W6 8JB (✆ 020 8741 7070)

BARON, Frank; *b* 5 May 1947, London; *Educ* Tulse Hill Sch; *m* 1983, Lorna Margaret, da of Brian Dearnaley; 2 *s* (Christopher *b* 1983, Alexander *b* 1986); *Career* asst photographer Keystone Press Agency 1963–67, photographer Daily Sketch 1967–72, fndr and photographer Sporting Pictures 1972–85, sports photographer The Guardian 1985–2013, ret; winner Sports Picture of the Year 1974, winner News Photographer of the Year 1999; fndr memb Professional Sports Photographers' Assoc, fndr Int Tennis Photographers' Assoc; *Recreations* tennis; *Clubs* Norbury Lawn Tennis, Woldingham Lawn Tennis; *Style—* Frank Baron, Esq; ✉ 30 Hilltop Walk, Woldingham, Surrey CR3 7LG (✆ 07836 500993)

BARON, John Charles; MP; *s* of Raymond Arthur Ernest Baron, and Kathleen Ruby Baron; *b* 21 June 1959; *Educ* 8 state and grammar schs by age 16 then Queen's Coll Taunton, Jesus Coll Cambridge; *m* 29 Aug 1992, Thalia Anne Mayson, da of Barrie Laird; 2 da; *Career* Capt RRF 1984–88; dir Henderson Private Investors 1988–99, dir Rothschild Asset Mgmnt 1999–2001; MP (Cons) Billericay 2001–; NI Medal, UN Medal; MCSI; *Books* The Future of Conservatism (2011), Financial Times Guide to Investment Trusts: Unlocking the City's Best Kept Secret (2013), monthly investment column in Investors Chronicle magazine and other pubns; *Recreations* financial journalism, gardening, website (johnbaronportfolios.co.uk); *Clubs* One Nation; *Style—* John Baron, Esq, MP; ✉ House of Commons, London SW1A 0AA (tel 020 7219 8138 or 01268 520765)

BARON-COHEN, Prof Simon; *b* 15 August 1958; *Educ* New Coll Oxford (BA), UCL (MRC studentship, PhD), Inst of Psychiatry Univ of London (Univ of London scholarship, MPhil); *Career* lectr Dept of Psychology UCL 1987–88 (jt with Dept of Psychiatry St Mary's Hosp Med Sch London), sr lectr in developmental psychology Depts of Psychology and Child Psychiatry Inst of Psychiatry Univ of London 1991–94 (New Blood lectr 1988–91); Depts of Experimental Psychology and Psychiatry Univ of Cambridge: lectr in psychopathology 1994–99, reader in developmental psychopathology 1999–2001, prof of developmental psychopathology 2001–; fell Trinity Coll Cambridge 1995–, dir Cambridge Autism Research Centre (ARC) 1997–; conslt clinical psychologist Developmental Psychiatry Section NHS Lifespan Healthcare Tst Cambridge 1999–, dir CLASS (Cambridge Lifespan Asperger Syndrome Services) 1999–; Br Psychological Soc Spearman Medal 1990, American Psychological Assoc (Div 7) McCandless Award 1990, Br Psychological Soc (Clinical Psychology Section) May Davison Award 1993, BAAS Joseph Lister lectr 1998, nominated BAFTA Award Best DVD in off-line learning 2001; FBPsS 1996; *Publications* Autism: The Facts (jtly, 1993), Understanding Other Minds: Perspectives from Autism (jt ed, 1993), Mindblindness: An Essay on Autism and Theory of Mind (1995), Synaesthesia: Classic and Contemporary Readings (jt ed, 1997), The Maladapted Mind: Essays in Evolutionary Psychopathology (ed, 1997), Tourette Syndrome: The Facts (jtly, 1998), Teaching Children with Autism to Mind-read (jtly, 1999), Understanding Other Minds: Perspectives from Developmental Cognitive Neuroscience (jt ed, 2000), Mindreading: The Interactive Guide to Emotions (DVD-ROM, 2002), The Essential Difference: Men, Women and the Extreme Male Brain (2003), The Exact Mind (jt ed, 2003), Prenatal Testosterone in Mind (jtly, 2003); *Style—* Prof Simon Baron-Cohen; ✉ Autism Research Centre, Departments of Experimental Psychology and Psychiatry, University of Cambridge, Douglas House, 18B Trumpington Road, Cambridge CB2 2AH (✆ 01223 746057, fax 01223 746033, e-mail s.baron-cohen@psychol.cam.ac.uk)

BAROUGH, Nina; CBE (2006); *Career* fndr and chief exec Walk the Walk; Fundraiser of the Year and Woman of the Year Pride of Britain Award 2008; Hon DUniv Napier Univ Edinburgh 2016; *Style—* Ms Nina Barough, CBE; ✉ Walk the Walk Worldwide, Unit 6 Genesis Business Park, Albert Drive, Woking, Surrey GU21 5RW

BARR, Alison Harvey; *da* of George Kidd Barr, and Muriel Margaret, *née* Harvey; *Educ* Uddingston GS Glasgow, Univ of Glasgow (MA); *Career* ed Routledge 1990–92 (assoc ed 1988–90), ed Scripture Union 1993–97; SPCK: ed 1997, sr ed 1998–2014, publisher 2014–; *Books* Christmas According to St Luke: A Cantata (1983), Time for Christmas: Six Songs for Children (1985); *Recreations* music, walking, photography; *Style—* Ms Alison Barr; ✉ SPCK, 36 Causton Street, London SW1P 4ST (✆ 020 7592 3958, fax 020 7592 3939, e-mail abarr@spck.org.uk)

BARR, Felicity Jane; *da* of Alan Marshall Barr, and Mary Elizabeth, *née* Snell; *Educ* Chiltern Edge Sch, Henley Coll; *Career* reporter, newsreader and presenter 2TenFM radio station Reading 1990–95, sports reporter and presenter Meridian TV 1996–99 (also presenter A406), news and sports presenter and reporter London Tonight, presenter Goals Extra 1999–2001, sports corr and presenter ITV News 2001–06 (ITN's first female sports corr), London co-anchor Al Jazeera Int 2006–; *Recreations* theatre, ice skating, skiing, eating; *Clubs* Cats Protection; *Style—* Ms Felicity Barr

BARR, Ian; *b* 29 April 1950; *Educ* Salford Univ (BSc, pres Students' Union); *m*; *Career* grad recruitment offr rising to personnel mangr BL plc 1976–82, manpower resourcing mangr Watney Mann and Truman Brewers Ltd 1983, co-owner and dir Berry Wilson Associates Ltd 1983–86, gp personnel dir Chloride Gp plc 1987–89, HR dir NFC plc 1989–95, gp human resources dir Scholl plc 1995–98, co-fndr and jt md Ionann Management Consultants Ltd 1998–99, md Astar Managment Consultants Ltd 1999–; non-exec dir RTITBS Ltd 1991–95; memb CBI Equal Opportunities Panel 1992–95, memb CBI Equality Forum 2001–, cmmr Cmmn for Racial Equality 2002–06, chm Employment Tbnls System Steering Bd 2006–, fndr memb Leadership Gp Race for Opportunity Campaign; tstee and treas Windsor Fellowship 2000–; *Style—* Ian Barr, Esq; ✉ Astar Management Consultants Ltd, PO Box 6927, London W1A 6FB (✆ 020 7224 0771, e-mail ianbarr@astarltd.co.uk)

BARRACLOUGH, Rachael Querida Maria; *da* of Dr Michael Barraclough, and Jenny, *née* Isard; *b* 16 January 1968; *Educ* Camden Sch for Girls, Univ of Bristol (BA); *Career* fndr Book Aid (charity sending books to Russia, collected over 2 million books) 1991–92; opening co-ordinator Eurotunnel; politics researcher Rory Bremner Who Else 1994–97, fndr Modern Ground contemporary design co 1998–, curator Sotheby's Contemporary Decorative Arts 1999–, co-fndr and creative dir LOSA 2001–, working with Haunch of Venison 2007–; *Recreations* dancing, being a hostess, cooking, collecting contemporary decorative arts; *Style—* Miss Rachael Barraclough; ✉ Modern Ground, 56 Ferry Street, London E14 3DT (e-mail modernground@hotmail.com)

BARRAN, Petra; *da* of Tristram Barran (d 1992), and Miranda Mitchell Cotts, of Suffolk; *b* 29 December 1975, Ipswich; *Educ* King Edward VI Sch Suffolk, Gr Cornard Upper Sch Suffolk, Univ of Manchester, UCL (postgrad); *Career* fndr: Choc Star 2005–11, Eat Street, 2009–12; fndr and dir KERB 2012–; *Recreations* cinema, music, travel, walking; *Style—* Ms Petra Barran; ✉ website www.kerbfood.com, Instagram @PetraBarran

BARRATT, Jeffery Vernon Courtney Lewis; *s* of Arnold Douglas Courtney Lewis, and Edith Joyce, *née* Terry; *b* 31 October 1950; *Educ* Scots Coll Wellington NZ, Univ of Adelaide (LLB), Univ of Sydney (LLB, LLM); *Career* articled clerk Giovanell and Burges 1971–73, slr Stephen Jaques and Stephen 1973–75; Norton Rose: ptnr 1979–2014 (estab Bahrain Office 1979–82, trg ptnr 1987–91), head SE Asian Project Fin Gp Hong Kong 1993–95, head Project Finance Worldwide 1995–2011, chm Partnership Ctee 1997–2002, global head of banking 2002–06, memb Exec Ctee 2002–06, sr banking ptnr 2006–14, conslt 2014–; memb: Editorial Bd Butterworths Jl of Int Banking and Fin Law, Banking Law Sub-Ctee Law Soc 1991–93; author of numerous articles on selling loan assets, sterling commercial paper, securitisation and project fin in learned jls; chm MENA Ctee IPFA 2010–; memb: London Legal Educn Ctee 1987–91, TheCityUK (formerly Int Financial Services London and Br Invisibles) 1999– (chm Infrastructure and Energy Exec Bd 2013–), Law Soc, IBA, Summer Sch Faculty QMC London Regnl Cncl CBI 2011– (memb Int Ctee 2014–); non-exec dir Int Project Finance Assoc; memb Advsy Bd Beanstalk, patron Dyspraxia Fndn; visiting prof London Met Univ 2013–; Freeman City of London 2014–; chm Cook Soc 2015–; *Recreations* cricket, squash, skiing, tennis, opera; *Clubs* Hampstead Cricket (capt 1987), Blackheath CC (Surrey, chm 2002–06), RAC, MCC; *Style—* Jeffery Barratt, Esq

BARRATT-CAMPBELL, Fiona Dawn; *da* of Peter Barratt, and Angela, *née* Dobson; *b* 14 May 1980, Hexham; *Educ* Central Newcastle HS, Chelsea Coll of Art and Design (BA), Parsons Sch of Design NY (BA, Dean's List); *m* 17 July 2010, Sulzeer Campbell; 2 da (Isabella *b* 3 June 2011, Georgiana *b* 10 Sept 2015), 1 *s* (Ethan *b* 1 May 2013); *Career* interior designer and furniture designer; Kelly Hoppen Interiors 2003–06, fndr Fiona Barratt Interiors 2006–, fndr FBC London 2013–; Homes & Gardens Bathroom Designer of the Year 2015; memb BIID 2015; *Recreations* cinema , fashion, music, travel; *Clubs* Walpole; *Style—* Ms Fiona Barratt-Campbell; ✉ Fiona Barratt Interiors, 12 Francis Street, London SW1P 1QN (✆ 020 3262 0320, website www.fionabarrattinteriors.com)

BARRELL, Prof John; *s* of John Ellis Barrell, CBE (d 1982), and Beatrice Mary Barrell (d 1988); *b* 3 February 1943; *Educ* Dulwich Coll, Trinity Coll Cambridge (open exhbn, scholar, MA), Univ of Essex (PhD); *m* 1, 1965 (m dis 1975), Audrey Jones; 2 *s* ((John) Matthew *b* 1965, Joseph Ezra David *b* 1967); *m* 2, 1975 (m dis 1978), Jania Miller; *m* 3, 1992, Prof Harriet Guest; 1 da (Helena Frances *b* 1992); *Career* asst master Raine's Fndn GS London 1964–65, lectr Dept of Literature Univ of Essex 1968–72, coll lectr Newnham Coll Cambridge 1972–84, lectr Univ of Cambridge 1972–85 (fell King's Coll), prof of English Univ of Sussex 1986–93, prof of English Univ of York 1993– (hon res fell 1992–

93), prof of English Queen Mary Univ of London 2012; American Soc for Eighteenth-Century Studies fellowship Houghton Library Harvard 1993, Schaffner visiting prof Univ of Chicago 2002, visiting fell Inst of Advanced Study Univ of Indiana 2002, distinguished visiting prof Carleton Univ Ottawa 2009, visiting prof EU Modern Univ Project Univ of Warsaw, hon prof Univ of York 2013; Leverhulme res award 1990, Br Acad readership 1991–93, Leverhulme major res fell 2002–04; James Clifford Prize American Soc for Eighteenth-Century Studies 1986; memb Editorial Bd History Workshop Jl 1989–94, assoc ed Trent Editions 1998–, advsy ed Nineteenth-Century Contexts 1993–, editorial advsr Cambridge Studies in Romanticism 1989–; memb Editorial Bd: Rural History 1988–, Literature in History 1991–, Textual Practice 1995–, Visual Culture in Britain 1998–; Hon DHL Chicago Univ 2008, Hon DLitt Courtauld Inst of Art Univ of London 2010, Hon Dip Univ of Warsaw 2012, hon fell King's Coll Cambridge 2014; fell English Assoc 2001; FBA 2001; *Books* The Idea of Landscape and the Sense of Place 1730–1840: An Approach to the Poetry of John Clare (1972), Samuel Taylor Coleridge: On the Constitution of the Church and State According to the Idea of Each (ed, 1972), The Penguin Book of Pastoral Verse (ed with John Bull, 1974), The Dark Side of the Landscape: the Rural Poor in English Painting 1730–1840 (1980), English Literature in History 1730–1780 (1983), The Political Theory of Painting from Reynolds to Hazlitt: The Body of the Public (1986), Poetry, Language and Politics (1988), The Infection of Thomas De Quincey: A Psychopathology of Imperialism (1991), The Birth of Pandora and the Division of Knowledge (1992), Painting and the Politics of Culture: New Essays on British Art 1700–1850 (ed, 1992), Imagining the King's Death: Figurative Treason, Fantasies of Regicide 1793–1796 (2000), Exhibition Extraordinary!! Radical Broadsides of the Mid 1790s (ed, 2001), The Spirit of Despotism (2006), Trials for Treason and Sedition 1792–1794 (ed with Jon Mee, 8 vols, 2006–07), The Complete Writings of William Fox (ed with Timothy Whelan, 2011), Edward Pugh of Ruthin 1763–1813: A Native Artist (2013); *Recreations* gardening, book collection, hill-walking; *Style*— Prof John Barrell; ✉ The Old Hall, Brilley, Herefordshire HR3 6JF

BARRELL, Prof Raymond John; s of Herbert Harry Barrell (d 1981), of London, and Eva, *née* Parr (d 1996); *b* 25 May 1950; *Educ* Ambrose Fleming Sch Enfield, LSE (BSc, MSc); *Partner* Ursula van Almsick; 1 step s (Dominic van Almsick b 9 April 1992); *Career* lectr: Univ of Stirling until 1979, Brunel Univ until 1984; econ advsr HM Treasy 1984–87, sr res fell NIESR 1990– (sr res offr 1988–90); visiting prof of economics Imperial Coll London 1997–2004, pt/t prof Euro Univ Inst Florence 1998–99; memb Editorial Bd: Jl of Common Market Studies, Economic Modelling; *Publications* incl: Economic Convergence and Monetary Union (ed, 1992), Macroeconomic Policy Coordination in Europe: the ERM and Monetary Union (ed with J Whitley, 1992), The UK Labour Market (ed, 1994), Modern Budgeting in the Public Sector (ed with F Hubert, 1999), Investment, Innovation and the Diffusion of Technology in Europe (ed with N Pain, 1999), Productivity, Innovation and Economic Performance (ed with G Mason and M O'Mahony, 2000); reg contrib to NIESR Review; *Recreations* skiing, mountaineering; *Style*— Prof Raymond Barrell

BARRELL, Dr Samantha (Sam) Ruth; CBE (2014); da of Anthony Barrell, and Jean, *née* Hawkes; *b* 22 February 1968, Taplow, Bucks; *Educ* MB BS, BSc; *m* 26 Jan 1963; 1 da (Samantha Ruth), 1 s (Andrew Mark); *Career* formerly anaesthetist then GP, chief clinical offr S Devon and Torbay Clinical Commissioning Gp until 2015, chief exec Taunton and Somerset NHS Fndn Tst 2015–; memb: Gen Advsy Cncl King's Fund, Innovation Health and Wealth Implementation Bd NHS Eng, Health Advsy Bd IPPR; MRCGP 2000; *Recreations* sailing, skiing, walking, swimming, cycling; *Style*— Dr Sam Barrell, CBE; ✉ Taunton and Somerset NHS Foundation Trust, Musgrove Park Hospital, Taunton, Somerset TA1 5DA (Twitter @SamBarrell1)

BARRETT; *see also:* Scott-Barrett

BARRETT, Prof Ann; OBE (2010); *née* Brown; da of R D Brown, of Suffolk; *b* 27 February 1943; *Educ* Queen Elizabeth's Girls' GS Barnet, Bart's Hosp Med Sch (LRCP, MRCS, MB BS, MD); *m*; 3 c; *Career* sr house offr in general med Whipps Cross Hosp 1969–70 (house surgn and physician 1968–69), sr house offr in radiotherapy Bart's 1969–70, registrar in radiotherapy UCH and Middx Hosp 1971–72, sr registrar Dept of Radiotherapy Middx Hosp and Mount Vernon Hosp 1972–74, seconded to Fndn Curie and Institut Gustav-Roussy 1974, locum conslt radiotherapist Westminster Hosp 1975–76 (lectr in oncology 1974–75), chef de clinique Hôpital Tenon and Institut Gustav-Roussy 1976–77; Royal Marsden Hosp: sr lectr and hon conslt Inst of Cancer Res 1977–83, conslt in radiotherapy and oncology 1983–86; dir Beatson Oncology Centre Western Infirmary Glasgow 1986–91, prof of radiation oncology Univ of Glasgow 1986–2002, registrar RCR 2000–02, prof of oncology UEA 2002–08, dean Faculty of Oncology RCR 2002–04; pres: Scottish Radiological Soc 1995–97, Euro Soc for Therapeutic Radiotherapy and Oncology 1997–99; tstee: Assoc for Cultural Exchange Cambridge, Readeasy UK, Cobalt 2016–; FRCR 1974, FRCPGlas 1989, FRCP 1990, FMedSci; *Publications* author of 5 books and over 150 medical pubns; *Style*— Prof Ann Barrett, OBE

BARRETT, Prof Anthony Gerard Martin; s of Claude Edward Valentine Barrett, and Margaret Teresa, *née* Bannon; *b* 2 March 1952; *Educ* Imperial Coll of Sci and Technol London (BSc, PhD, DIC, Hofmann Prize, Edmund White Prize for Organic Chem, Frank Hatton Prize, RSA Silver Medal); *m* 1, 15 Aug 1983 (m dis 2011), Jennifer Mary, da of Charles Madge; 1 s (Edward Michael b 14 Nov 1980), 1 da (Roxanne Eloise b 30 Oct 1982); m 2, 13 Sept 2011, Cristiniana, *née* de Jesus Oliveira; 1 s (Bryan de Jesus Oliveira Barrett b 20 April 2011); *Career* Imperial Coll of Sci and Technol: lectr 1975–82, sr lectr 1982–83, dir Wolfson Centre for Organic Chem in Med Sci 1993–, Glaxo prof of organic chem 1993–, Sir Derek Barton prof of synthetic chem 1999–; prof of chem: Northwestern Univ 1983–90, Colorado State Univ 1990–93; conslt: W R Grace & Co 1981–90, Pfizer Central Research 1982–84, G D Searle & Co (now Pfizer) 1983–2003, B F Goodrich 1986–88, Amoco Technol 1987–91, Parke Davis (now Pfizer) 1992–2006, Roche Products Ltd 1993–2001, Quest International 1994, AECI 1994–2000, Celltech 1995–98, Unilever 1996–2003, Ligand Pharmaceuticals Inc 1996–98, Jouveinal (now Pfizer) 1997–2003, Eastman Chemical Co 1998–, Cooper Conslt Inc 1998–99, Teva Pharmaceutical Industries Ltd (formerly Ratiopharm GmbH) 2006–12, Eli Lilly 2007–, Sanofi Aventis 2008–, Bristol-Myers Squibb 2010–, Actavis Gp 2010–; chm Scientific Advsy Bd Diversomer Technologies 1996–97, dir of science and non-exec dir ChemMedICa (now Argenta Discovery Ltd) 1998–2010, non-exec dir iThemba Pharaceuticals 2008–13; memb: Scientific Advsy Bd Myco Pharmaceuticals 1993–96, Exec Scientific Advsy bd ChemGenics Pharmaceuticals Inc 1996–97, Scientific Advsy Bd NSC Technologies 1996–99, Bd of Scientific Advisors in Medicinal Chem Rhône-Poulenc Rorer Recherche-Développement 1996–98, Sci Advsy Bd New Chemical Entities Inc 1998–2000, NIH Medicinal Chemical A Study Section 1986–89, Chemicals Panel Technol Foresight Prog Office of Sci and Technol 1994, Perkin Div Cncl RSC 1996–98, Bd Fondation de la Maison de la Chimie (France) 2012–; RSC Meldola Medal 1980, Imperial Coll Armstrong Medal 1981, RSC Harrison Medal 1982, ACS Arthur C Cope Scholar Award 1986, RSC Corday-Morgan Medal 1986, Camille and Henry Dreyfus Teacher-Scholar Award 1987, Japan Soc for the Promotion of Sci Fellowship 1989, RSC Award in Synthetic Organic Chem sponsored by CIBA Specialty Chemicals 1997, Glaxo Wellcome Award for Innovative Chem 2000, RSC Award in Natural Products Chem 2001, Royal Soc Wolfson Research Merit Award 2002, RSC Pedler Lectr 2004, RSC Simonsen Lectr, RSC Charles Rees Award 2010; MACS, MRSC, FRS 1999, FMedSci 2003; *Publications* author of over 400 scientific papers and articles; *Style*— Prof Anthony Barrett, FRS, FMedSci; ✉ Department of Chemistry, Imperial College London, London SW7 2AZ (☎ 020 7594 5766, fax 020 7594 5805, e-mail agm.barrett@imperial.ac.uk)

BARRETT, Felix; MBE (2016); *Educ* Univ of Exeter; *Career* fndr and artistic dir Punchdrunk 2000– (designer and/or dir: The Cherry Orchard 2000, The House of Oedipus 2000, The Moonslave 2000, Johnny Formidable: Mystery at the Pink Flamingo 2001, Midsummer Night's Dream 2002, Chair 2002, The Tempest 2003, Sleep No More 2003 and 2009, Woyzeck 2004, The Firebird Ball 2005, Marat/Sade 2005, Faust 2006–07 (Best Design Critics' Circle Drama Award 2006), The Masque of the Red Death 2007–08, Tunnel 228 2009, It Felt Like A Kiss 2009; *Style*— Felix Barrett, Esq, MBE

BARRETT, John Edward; MBE (2007); s of Alfred Edward Barrett, and Margaret Helen, *née* Walker; *b* 17 April 1931, Mill Hill, London; *Educ* UCS Hampstead, St John's Coll Cambridge (MA); *m* 1967, (Florence) Angela Margaret, *née* Mortimer; 1 s, 1 da; *Career* former tennis player, tennis promoter and sports conslt; currently journalist, broadcaster and author; Nat Serv RAF 1950–52; Dunlop Slazenger International Ltd (formerly Slazengers Ltd): mgmnt trainee 1957–59, asst home sales mangr 1959–65, asst mangr Tournament Dept 1965–74, mangr Tournament Dept 1974–75, tournament dir 1975, dir 1978–81, conslt 1981–94; tennis player: Middx jr doubles champion 1947 and 1948, nat schs singles and doubles champion 1949, rep Cambridge Univ v Oxford Univ 1952–54 (capt 1954), rep Oxford and Cambridge Univs v Harvard and Yale Univs (Prentice Cup) 1952 and 1954, RAF champion 1950 and 1951, nat indoor doubles champion (with D Black) 1953, competed at Wimbledon 1950–70, GB rep Davis Cup 1956–57 (non-playing capt 1959–62), ranked nationally 1952–70 (highest position 5); tennis admin: dir LTA Training Squad (Barrett Boys) 1965–68, qualified LTA coach 1969 (memb Trg Ctee), fndr and dir BP Int Tennis Fellowship 1968–80, fndr BP Cup (int under 21 team event) 1973–80, fndr and organiser Pepsi-Cola Jr Int Series 1975–79, fndr bd memb Assoc of Tennis Professionals 1972–73; tennis commentator: BBC TV 1971–2006, Channel 9 Aust 1981–86, Channel 10 Aust 1987, Channel 7 Aust 1988–2008, various cable networks USA 1977–95, Hong Kong Championships for ATV and TVB 1981–97, Canadian Open for CTV 1989–97; lawn tennis corr Financial Times 1963–2007 (crossword contrib 1986–), editorial conslt and contrib LTA's magazine Serve and Volley (renamed ACE 1996) 1988–97; pres Dan Maskell Tennis Tst 1997–2011; inducted (as contrib) into Int Tennis Hall of Fame Newport RI 2014; *Books* World of Tennis (fndr ed and contrib, annually 1969–2001), Tennis and Racket Games (1975), Play Tennis With Rosewall (1975), 100 Wimbledon Championships: a celebration (1986), From Where I Sit (with Dan Maskell, 1988), Oh, I Say! (with Dan Maskell, 1989), Wimbledon: The Official History of the Championships (2001), Centre Court – the Jewel in Wimbledon's Crown (co-ed with Ian Hewitt, 2009), Wimbledon: The Official History (4 edn 2014), Wimbledon: The Singles Draws 1877–2012 (ed); *Recreations* music, theatre, reading; *Clubs* All England Lawn Tennis (memb 1955–, memb Ctee 1989–2004, vice-pres 2004), Queen's, International Lawn Tennis Club of GB (memb 1953–, memb Ctee 1957–, chm 1983–94, pres 2004–08, vice-pres 2008–); *Style*— John Barrett, Esq, MBE; ✉ All England Lawn Tennis Club, Church Road, Wimbledon, London SW19 5AE (e-mail jbcourtier@aol.com)

BARRETT, Patrick William Austin; s of William Barrett, of Bletchingly, Surrey, and Sylvia, *née* Austin; *b* 16 March 1970; *Educ* St Bede's Redhill, Lancaster Univ (BA), Journalists Trg Centre Mitcham (NVQ); *m* 15 May 1999, Rosamunde, da of Dr Brian Snowdon; 1 s (Samuel Christopher Snowdon Barrett, b 20 July 2001); *Career* reporter then dep news ed Supermarketing Magazine 1994–96, reporter then dep news ed Marketing Magazine 1996–98, news ed then ed Media Week 1998–2002, freelance media journalist The Guardian 2002–04, dir The Media Foundry 2004–08, business devpt dir Limelight PR 2008–09, fndr Simpatico PR 2010–; *Recreations* mountain hiking, guitar, travel, film; *Style*— Patrick Barrett, Esq

BARRETT, Prof Spencer Charles Hilton; *Educ* Univ of Reading (BSc), Univ of Calif Berkeley (PhD); *Career* weed biologist Cwlth Devpt Corp Swaziland Irrigation Scheme 1969–70, aquatic weed conslt Int Research Inst Jari Lower Amazon Brazil 1974, prof Univ of Toronto 1986–2008 (tenure granted 1982, univ prof 2008–); visiting research scientist Genetic Resources Prog Div of Plant Industry CSIRO Canberra 1983–84, research assoc Dept of Botany Royal Ontario Museum 1992–, visiting prof Dept of Botany Univ of Hong Kong 1994, visiting Mellon scholar Rancho Santa Ana Botanic Garden Calif 1997, distinguished guest prof Wuhan Univ 2001–03, adjunct prof Xishuangbanna Tropical Botanical Garden Chinese Acad of Sciences Menglun 2004–06; memb: Ctee on the Scientific Basis for Predicting the Invasive Potential of Non-indigenous Plants and Plant Pests in the USA Nat Acad of Sciences and Nat Research Cncl USA 1999–2001, Expert Panel on the Future of Food Biotechnology Royal Soc of Canada 2000–01; ed Proceedings of the Royal Soc Series B, memb Editorial Bd Trends in Ecology and Evolution, ed-in-chief Proceedings of the Royal Soc of London (Biological Sciences) 2015; E W Steacie Meml Fellowship Natural Sciences and Engrg Research Cncl of Canada 1988–90, Outstanding Teaching Award Faculty of Arts and Sciences Univ of Toronto 1992–93, Canada Research Chair 2001, Merit Award Botanical Soc of America 2003, Lawson Medal Canadian Botanical Assoc 2006, Premier's Discovery Award in Life Sciences Medicine 2007, Sewall Wright Award 2008, Queen Elizabeth II Diamond Jubilee Medal, Flavelle Medal Royal Soc of Canada 2014; foreign hon memb American Acad of Arts and Sciences 2009, hon fell Sociedad Cientifica Mexicana de Ecologia; FRSC 1998, FRS 2004; *Publications* Evolution and Function of Heterostyly (ed, 1992), Floral Biology: Studies on Floral Evolution in Animal-Pollinated Plants (jt ed, 1996), Ecology and Evolution of Flowers (jt ed, 2006), Major Evolutionary Transitions in Flowering Plant Reproduction (ed, 2008), Invasion Genetics: The Baker and Stebbins Legacy (jt ed, 2016); 300 scientific articles in jls and book chapters; *Style*— Prof Spencer Barrett; ✉ Department of Ecology & Evolutionary Biology, University of Toronto, 25 Willocks Street, Toronto, Ontario, M5S 3B2, Canada

BARRETT, (Nicholas) Vincent John; s of Sidney Gordon Barrett (d 1999), and Francine Constance Alice, *née* Collins (d 2014); *b* 9 June 1956; *Educ* Haileybury and ISC, Guy's Hosp (BDS), Univ of Texas San Antonio (MS), M D Anderson Cancer Hosp (Cert Maxillofacial Prosthodontics); *m* (m dis); 3 s (James Frederick b 12 Nov 1993, Daniel John b 26 July 1995, Peter Nicholas b 16 Nov 1998), 1 da (Naomi Francine b 28 July 2003); *Career* Guy's Hosp: house surgn Dept of Oral and Maxillofacial Surgery 1980, house offr Dept of Prosthetic Dentistry 1980–81; assoc in gen dental practice Feb-June 1981, dental practice London 1985–; conslt King Edward VII Hosp; appts also held: Westminster Hosp 1985–90, King's Coll Dental Sch 1986–87, Guy's Hosp Dental Sch 1986–97; Newland Pedley travelling scholar 1981, American Dental Soc award 1981; memb: American Dental Soc of London (pres 2011–12), American Dental Soc of Europe, BDA, Int Coll of Dentists 2011; *Books* Colour Atlas of Occlusion and Malocclusion (jtly, 1991); *Recreations* tennis; *Clubs* Paddington Sports; *Style*— Vincent Barrett, Esq; ✉ 152 Harley Street, London W1G 7LH (☎ 020 7935 8621, e-mail info@vincentbarrettdental.co.uk, website www.vincentbarrettdental.co.uk)

BARRIE, Carol Hazel; da of Harry Batson, of Rowley Regis, W Midlands, and Prudence, *née* Crompton; *b* 23 December 1945; *Educ* Rowley Regis GS; *m* 30 Sept 1967, Robert Barrie, s of Robert Barrie; *Career* CA; with Charlton & Co (now part of Deloitte & Touche) Birmingham 1964–72 (articled clerk 1964–70); Peat Marwick Mitchell & Co (now KPMG): joined 1972, chm Nat Tax Gp for Partnerships 1988–95, head of tax Midlands Region 1995–97; Robson Rhodes: head of tax Midlands Region 1998–2001, nat head of private client servs 2001–04; tax ptnr Bentley Jennison (now RSM Tenon) 2004–11 (head of tax Midlands, chm Nat Gp for Property and Construction); lectr for a variety of

Professional Bodies, past memb Inst of Bankers' Approved Panel of Speakers, regular radio broadcasts for local radio, contrib to newspapers and technical jls; non-exec memb N Birmingham HA 1988–96; FCA 1971; *Recreations* reading, embroidery, theatre, classical music; *Style—* Mrs Carol Barrie; ✉ 7 Carnoustie Close, Sutton Coldfield, West Midlands B75 6UW (✆ 0121 378 2465, mobile 07836 761455)

BARRIE, Christopher (Chris); s of Alexander Barrie, and Anne, *née* Pitt; *b* 7 November 1958; *Educ* St Dunstan's Coll Catford, Univ of Exeter (BA); *m* 7 April 1990, Elspeth Jane, da of Dr Craig Sinclair; 3 s (Thomas Alexander Sinclair b 9 Nov 1993, Gabriel Henry Sinclair, William Felix Sinclair (twins) b 3 May 1996); *Career* Municipal Group London 1983–85, Autotrade (Morgan-Grampian publishers) 1985–86; The Engineer: asst ed 1986–89, news ed 1989–91, ed 1991–94; freelance journalist with The Guardian, Evening Standard and BBC 1994–95, fin writer The Guardian 1995–2000, columnist Evening Standard 1995–2000; dir Citigate Dewe Rogerson 2000–; Industrial Magazine Journalist of the Year 1990 (Industrial Journalism Awards), Business Journalist Award British Press Awards 1997; tstee Wandsworth Museum 2009–16; *Recreations* hill walking, reading; *Style—* Chris Barrie, Esq; ✉ 3 London Wall Buildings, London Wall, London EC2M 5SY (✆ 020 7638 9571)

BARRIE, (Charles) David Ogilvy; CBE (2010); s of Alexander Ogilvy Barrie (d 1969), and Patricia Mary, *née* Tucker; *b* 9 November 1953; *Educ* Bryanston, BNC Oxford (MA); *m* 1978, Mary Emily, da of Rt Hon Sir Ralph Gibson, PC (d 2003); 2 da (Eleanor Ann Ogilvy b 11 Feb 1983, Miranda Jane Ogilvy b 30 June 1985); *Career* HM Diplomatic Serv: FCO 1975–76, Dublin 1976–80, seconded to Cabinet Office 1980–81, first sec and later asst head of dept FCO 1981–87; transferred to Home Civil Serv Cabinet Office 1988–92 (resigned); exec dir Japan Festival 1989–92, dir The Art Fund (formerly Nat Art Collections Fund) 1992–2009, fndr and chair Ruskin Today 1995–2016, chair Make Justice Work 2010–13; project advsr Two Temple Place Gallery 2009–13, advsr William Morris Gallery 2009–10; dir Guild of St George 1992–2004 (companion 1991); memb Bd Museums, Libraries and Archives Cncl 2000–06, memb Acceptance in Lieu Panel 2000–06; tstee: Civitella Ranieri Fndn 1995–99, Ruskin Fndn 1996–, Butterfly Conservation 2003–07, Campaign for Museums 2004–09, BALTIC Centre for Contemporary Art 2015, Pilgrim Tst 2016–; hon research fell Univ of Leicester 2010; Good Guide to Britain Heritage Man of the Year 1999; FRIN 2015; *Books* Modern Painters (ed, by John Ruskin, 1987, 2 edn 2000), Sextant: A Voyage Guided by the Stars and the Men Who Mapped the World's Oceans (2014); *Recreations* sailing, drawing, scuba diving, entomology, celestial navigation; *Clubs* Royal Cruising, Arts, Emsworth Sailing; *Style—* David Barrie, Esq, CBE, FRIN; ✉ 13 Wingate Road, London W6 0UR (e-mail cdobarrie@gmail.com)

BARRIE, Dr Herbert; *b* 9 October 1927; *Educ* Wallington Co GS, UCL and Med Sch London (MB BS, MD, McGrath scholarship); *m* 1963, Dr Dinah Barrie; 1 s (Michael), 1 da (Caroline); *Career* registrar Hosp for Sick Children Gt Ormond St 1955–57, research fell Harvard Univ Children's Med Center 1957, sr registrar and sr lectr Dept of Paediatrics St Thomas' Hosp 1959–65; conslt paediatrician Charing Cross Hosp (paediatrician 1966–84, physician in charge 1984–86); examiner Univ of London and RCP; former memb Vaccine Damage Tbnl; memb Editorial Bd: Midwife and Health Visitor, Maternity and Mothercraft; hon memb Br Assoc for Perinatal Medicine; FRCP 1972, FRCPCH; *Publications* Resuscitation of Newborns (1963); numerous contributions on neonatal special care; *Recreations* tennis, writing; *Style—* Dr Herbert Barrie; ✉ 3 Burghley Avenue, New Malden, Surrey KT3 4SW (✆ 020 8942 2836, e-mail herbert.barrie@virgin.net)

BARRIE, Jane Elizabeth; OBE (2004), DL (Somerset 2007); *née* Pearson; da of William Pearson, of Somerset, and Bessie, *née* Knowles; *b* 11 September 1946; *Educ* Bishop Fox GS for Girls, Imperial Coll of Sci and Technol London (BSc); *m* 12 Dec 1970, Dr William Robert Ian Barrie, s of Dr Robert Barrie, of Somerset; *Career* stockbroker; regnl dir NatWest Stockbrokers 1990–93; chm: Taunton Deane and W Somerset Div Avon and Somerset Constabulary Crime Prevention Panel 1987–91, Somerset Trg and Enterprise Cncl 1999–2001, Somerset Learning and Skills Cncl 2001–07; non-exec dir Taunton and Somerset NHS Tst 1991–94, chm Somerset HA 1994–2002, chm Dorset and Somerset SHA 2002–06, chm Somerset Primary Care Tst 2006–13, chm Health Educn SW 2013–; pres Soroptimist Int of GB and I 1990–91, dir Number 63 (Soroptimist) Ltd 2015–; memb Bd: Fairplay South West 2001–10, Connexions Somerset 2002–07, NHS Commercial Advsy Bd 2003–07; pres Care Focus Somerset 2006–; chm Bishop Fox's Educnl Fndn 2011–; patron St Margaret's (Somerset) Hospice 2005–; chm of govrs: Bishop Fox's Sch Taunton 1984–2002, Taunton Sch 2001–15; tstee Somerset Community Fndn 2014 (chm of tstees 2015–); ARCS, FRSA, FRSM; *Recreations* sailing, bridge, wine appreciation; *Clubs* Royal Dart Yacht, RSM; *Style—* Mrs Jane E Barrie, OBE, DL; ✉ Hollydene, Kingston St Mary, Taunton, Somerset TA2 8HW (✆ 01823 451388, e-mail jbarrie@btinternet.com)

BARRISON, Dr Ian Graeme; s of Joseph Barrison (d 1991), and Zelda, *née* Sherr (d 2008); *b* 16 July 1950, Salford, Lancs; *Educ* Manchester Grammar, Medical Sch of St Bartholomew's Hosp Univ of London (BSc, MB BS); *m* 27 May 1974, Penelope, *née* Norbrook; 1 da (Anna b 25 May 1977), 1 s (Ben b 24 Oct 1979); *Career* registrar West Middx Hosp 1977, registrar and tstees research fell Charing Cross Hosp 1978–81, sr registrar St Mary's Hosp, Central Middx Hosp, West Middx Hosp 1981–88, conslt physician and gastroenterologist St Albans City and Hemel Hempstead Hosps 1988–2010; assoc dean Univ of Herts Postgrad Medical Sch 2010–; chair Specialist Trg Ctee on Gen Internal Med London Deanery 2003–08, chm Clinical Servs and Standards Ctee Br Soc of Gastroenterology 2006–09, chair Specialist Advsy Ctee in Acute and Internal Medicine 2008–12 (sec 2007–08), pres European Bd of Gastroenterology 2014– (memb 2007–14); censor RCP 2005–07; contrib to med jls incl Br Jl of Haematology and Br Med Jl; Brackenbury Prize BMA 1980, President's Medal Br Soc of Gastroenterology 2008; FRCP 1993 (MRCP 1977); *Recreations* cricket, walking, antiquarian books; *Style—* Dr Ian Barrison; ✉ School of Postgraduate Medicine, University of Hertfordshire, Hatfield AL10 9AB (e-mail i.g.barrison@herts.ac.uk)

BARRIT, Desmond; s of Samuel Islwyn Brown (d 1998), and Gwyneth, *née* West (d 1970); *b* 19 October 1944; *Educ* Garw GS; *Career* actor; pres Friends of Theatre, vice-pres Friends of RSC; assoc actor RSC, dir Ohyesitiz Prodns; ambass for Prince's Tst; organiser of charity events incl: Samaritans, The Lighthouse, Children in Need, Children North East, Richard Haines Charitable Tst; *Theatre* Brogard in Scarlet Pimpernel (Chichester and Her Majesty's), Cliton in The Liar (Old Vic), Then Again (Lyric Hammersmith), Birdboot and Harold in The Real Inspector Hound and Black Comedy (Comedy Theatre), Eddie Carbonne in A View from the Bridge (Greenwich Theatre), Monsieur Henri in Euridice (Whitehall Theatre), Bertozzo in Accidental Death of an Anarchist (Donmar Warehouse), Shylock in The Merchant of Venice (Chichester Festival Theatre), Sorin in The Seagull (Chichester Festival Theatre), Midsummer Night's Dream (Broadway); RNT incl: Archille Blond in The Magistrate, chauffeur in Jacobowsky, Charlie in 3 Men on a Horse (also at Vaudeville), Toad in Wind in the Willows, Brazen in The Recruiting Officer, Cotrone in The Mountain Giants, Pseudolus in A Funny Thing Happened on the Way to the Forum, Dick Cheney in Stuff Happens, The History Boys (also Broadway and Wyndhams Theatre London), Bottom in Fairy Queen (Glyndebourne), The Habit of Art (RNT), Die Federmaus (Welsh Nat Opera), The Birthday Party (Royal Exchange Manchester), Thérèse Raquin, Harvey (Birmingham Rep), A Damsel in Distress (Chichester Festival Theatre); RSC incl: Trinculo in Tempest, Gloucester in King Lear, Porter/Ross in Macbeth, Tom Errand in Constant Couple, Banjo in The Man Who Came to Dinner 1990–91, Antipholus in Comedy of Errors, Bottom in A Midsummer Night's Dream, Malvolio in Twelfth Night, Falstaff in Henry IV Parts 1 and 2 (nomination Olivier Award for Best Actor in a Supporting Role 2002), Comedy of Errors (dir, Chicago), Toby Belch in Twelfth Night, Sir Joseph Porter in HMS Pinafore, Wizard of Oz in Wicked, Falstaff in The Merry Wives of Windsor, Cat on a Hot Tin Roof, Before I Leave; *Television* incl: Boon, The Bill, Homer and his Pigeons, Poirot, True Tilda, Le Show, Dalziel and Pascoe, Oliver Twist, Madame Bovary, Midsomer Murders, Endeavour, Holby City; *Film* incl: Lassiter, Rebecca's Daughters, A Midsummer Night's Dream, All for Love, Alice Through the Looking Glass, Christmas Carol, Northanger Abbey, Endeavour; *Concerts* My Fair Lady (LA), 3 Musketeers (6 concerts, Denmark); *Awards* Clarence Derwent Award for Trinculo, Olivier Award for Best Comedy Performance in Comedy of Errors 1988; for A Midsummer Night's Dream: Helen Hayes Award for Best Actor, Critics' Circle Award nomination, Fany Award nomination; Olivier Award nomination for Falstaff in Henry IV Part I and II; *Recreations* antiques, cooking, travel; *Style—* Desmond Barrit, Esq; ✉ c/o Lou Coulson, 37 Berwick Street, London W1F 8RS (✆ 020 7734 9633)

BARRON, John Raymond (Christopher); OBE (2015); s of Arthur William John Barron (d 1981), and Enid Caroline, *née* Brooks; *b* 17 November 1949; *Educ* Cheltenham GS, Central Sch of Speech and Drama, Univ of Wales (BA); *m* 29 Sept 1984, Julia, *née* Tompsett; *Career* stage mangr Glyndebourne, '69 Theatre Co, Wexford and Batignano Festivals 1967–74, gen mangr Watford Palace Theatre 1978–81, gen mangr Buxton Festival and Opera House 1981–84, gen mangr and assoc dir Edinburgh Int Festival 1984–92, dir Manchester City of Drama 1992–94, chief exec and artistic dir Brighton Festival and Dome 1995–2000, chief exec Scottish Ballet/Scottish Opera 2000–05, chief exec Birmingham Royal Ballet 2005–; bd dir: Dance Umbrella, Dance4 Dance Agency, Elmhurst Sch of Dance; chm SE Dance Agency 1996–2000 (also fndr); Manchester Evening News Horniman Award for outstanding services to theatre 1994; *Recreations* hill walking, cabinet making; *Style—* Christopher Barron, OBE

BARRON, Rt Hon Sir Kevin John; kt (2014), PC (2001), MP; s of Richard Barron and Edna Barron; *b* 26 October 1946; *Educ* Ruskin Coll; *m* 1969; 1 s, 2 da; *Career* NCB 1962–83 (NUM exec for Maltby Colliery), pres Rotherham and District TUC; MP (Lab) Rother Valley 1983–; shadow min for: energy 1988–92, employment 1992–93, health 1995–96, public health 1996–97; PPS to Neil Kinnock 1985–88 as Leader of the Opposition; memb: Energy Select Ctee 1983–85, Environment Select Ctee 1992–93, Intelligence and Security Ctee 1997–2005; chair: Yorkshire Gp of Lab MPs 1987–, PLP Health Ctee 1997–, All-Pty Gp on Pharmaceutical Industry 1997–2005, All-Pty Gp on Smoking & Health 1997–, Food Standards Agency Ctee, Health Select Ctee 2005–10, Standards and Privilages Ctee 2010–; vice-pres Royal Soc of Health 2007–; lay memb GMC 1999–2008; *Style—* The Rt Hon Sir Kevin Barron, MP; ✉ House of Commons, London SW1A 0AA (✆ 020 7219 6306, fax 020 7219 5952, barronk@parliament.uk, website www.kevinbarronmp.com)

BARRON, Prof Laurence David; s of Gerald Landon Barron, of Southampton, and Stella, *née* Gertz; *b* 12 February 1944; *Educ* King Edward VI GS, Northern Poly (BSc), Lincoln Coll Oxford (DPhil); *m* 10 Aug 1969, Sharon Aviva, da of Denis Harris Wolf; 1 da (Susannah Mira b 23 Sept 1971), 1 s (Daniel Morris 17 May 1973); *Career* Ramsay meml fell Univ of Cambridge 1974–75 (research asst 1969–74); Univ of Glasgow: lectr 1975–80, reader 1980–84, prof of chemistry 1984–99, Gardiner prof of chemistry 1999–2008, emeritus Gardiner prof of chemistry 2008–; G M J Schmidt meml lectr Weizmann Inst of Sci Israel 1984, F L Conover meml lectr Vanderbilt Univ USA 1987, visiting Miller research prof Univ of Calif Berkeley 1995, sr fell EPSRC 1995–2000, Tetelmen visiting fell Jonathan Edwards Coll Yale Univ 2008, J Schechter meml lectr Bar Ilan Univ Israel 2012, Zhang Dayu meml lectr Dalian Inst of Chemical Physics China 2012; Corday-Morgan Medal and Prize Chemical Soc 1979, Sir Harold Thompson Award for Spectroscopy 1993, Chirality Medal Societa Chimica Italiana 2011; memb: RSC, APS, ACS; FInstP, FRSC, FRSE 1992, FRS 2005; *Books* Molecular Light Scattering and Optical Activity (2004); *Recreations* music, walking, watercolour painting, radio controlled model aircraft; *Style—* Prof Laurence Barron, FRS, FRSE; ✉ 84 Erskine Hill, London NW11 6HG

BARRON, Steve; *Career* film and video dir/prodr; chm Limelight (London) Ltd 1996–; early career experience as camera asst on films incl Superman 1 and 2, A Bridge Too Far (dir Richard Attenborough, *qv*) and Duellists (dir Ridley Scott), concurrently experimented in early music video (The Jam and Sham 69) 1977, conceived and directed multi award winning promo Billy Jean (Michael Jackson) 1982, other promos incl Take on Me (A-HA, over 40 awards) 1985 and Money for Nothing (Dire Straits, MTV Video of Year) 1986, subsequently dir of various commercials incl Motorcycle Chains (D&AD Award) and others in UK and USA for clients incl Pepsi, Coca-Cola, Ford and Renault, dir Electric Dreams (first feature film, Best Dir Madrid Film Festival and Best Film Award Avoriaz Fantastique Film Festival) 1984, dir Hans my Hedgehog (Emmy Award), Fearnot and Sapsorrow (Storyteller episodes for NBC TV) 1987, dir Teenage Mutant Ninja Turtles (highest grossing ind film, CBS TV Award for Best Family Entertainment Film of Year) 1990, subsequently dir of music promos Calling Elvis (Dire Straits, Grammy nomination) 1991, Unforgettable (Natalie Cole, Billboard Best Dir Award) 1991 and Let's Get Rocked (Def Leppard, MTV nomination) 1992, dir feature film Coneheads 1993, exec prodr The Specialist (feature with Sylvester Stallone and Sharon Stone) 1994, exec prodr ReBoot (animated TV show, ABC TV 1994, UK 1995), exec prodr While You Were Sleeping 1995; dir: The Adventures of Pinocchio 1996, Merlin (NBC) 1998 (nominated for 15 Emmys and 4 Golden Globes), Arabian Nights (ABC) 1999 (5 Emmy nominations), Rat, Mike Bassett: England Manager 2001, Dreamkeeper 2003, Choking Man 2006, Treasure Island 2012; *Style—* Steve Barron, Esq; ✉ c/o Michael Sheresky, United Talent Agency (✆ 001 310 776 8174)

BARRON, Tanya; OBE (2016); da of Donald Barron (d 2000), and Edna, *née* Hulley (d 2001); *b* 18 March 1954, London; *Educ* Dartington Hall Sch Devon, Central London Poly (BA), Roehampton Inst (PGCE); *m* 8 July 2000, Gregory Knowles; 1 da (Ella (Mrs Camplin) b 16 June 1982), 1 s (Gabriel Knowles Barron b 26 Sept 1986); *Career* sr assoc memb St Anthony's Coll Oxford; formerly: head of progs for Eastern Europe and former Soviet Union VSO, ceo Home-Start Int, int dir Leonard Cheshire Disability; chief exec Plan UK 2013–; chair UNICEF NGO Ctee Geneva 1993–98; tstee: Topsham Edcn Tst, LEF Pillon Tst; European Woman of Achievement (Humanitarian) 2003; hon doctorate York St John Univ; *Clubs* Farmers; *Style—* Ms Tanya Barron, OBE; ✉ Plan UK, Finsgate, 5–7 Cranwood Street, London EC1V 9LH

BARRONS, Gen Sir Richard; KCB (2013), CBE (2003, OBE 1999, MBE 1993); *b* 17 May 1959; *Educ* Queen's Coll Oxford; *m* Cherry; 2 da; *Career* cmmnd RR of Artillery 1977, various posts UK, Europe and Far East, tours of duty NI, Bosnia, Kosovo, Iraq and Afghanistan; Cdr: 3 Regt RHA, 39 Infantry Brigade; Dep Commanding Gen Multi-National Corps Iraq; COS Allied Rapid Reaction Corps 2009, dir Force Reintegration Int Security Assistance Force, Asst Chief of the Gen Staff 2010, Dep Chief of Defence Staff (Military Strategic Operations) 2011, Cdr Jt Forces Cmd 2013–; Col Cmdt and pres Hon Artillery Co, Hon Col 3 Regt RHA; DSc (hc) Cranfield Univ 2014; *Books* The Business General: Transform your business using seven secrets of military success (2006); *Style—* Gen Sir Richard Barrons, KCB, CBE, ADC Gen; ✉ Joint Forces Command, The Permanent Joint Headquarters, Northwood, Middlesex, HA6 3HP

BARROS D'SA, Prof Abilio Anacleto Joseph (Leo); s of Inaçio Francisco Purificação Saúde D'Sa (d 1978), of London, and Maria Eslinda Inês, *née* Barros (d 1998); *b* 28 April 1933;

Educ Westminster Coll (Arbour E Day Award), Coll of Law London, Hon Soc of the Inner Temple (Inns of Court Sch of Law), Univ of Manchester (Arch, Kendal exhbn, PhD Law), PNL (DipArch), UCL (MSc), UCL Law Teachers Trg, Univ of Leicester (LLM), Univ of Middx (MA), King's Coll and Inst of Advanced Legal Studies Univ of London (postdoctoral), Wolfson Coll Cambridge (MSt), Kenwar MS National Prize, MKG Prize; *m* 12 Sept 1969, Erika, da of Friedrich Völkl, of Fürth, Bavaria; *Career* formerly asst architectural practices incl: WS Atkins, Farmer & Dark 1957–67; dir Professional Design Servs; md Greathead Ltd 1967–76; DOE architect, PSA design team ldr, superintending offr, conslt liaison and project mangr 1976–79, innovator of audit systems 1979, focal point for Conservation of Central London Bldgs of Special and Historical Interest 1982–87, PSA liaison Parliamentary House Jl and Ironbridge Museum 1983, conslt liaison Party Wall Awards 1984, area auditor and reviewer 1985, head of bldg advsy section, PSA rep on HSE and BSI Ag?ment Cert Ctees, HQ advsr Cardington Consultative Ctee on govt contracts 1985–87, visiting lectr PhD law supervisor and examiner Univ of London, Univ of Oxford and Univ of Cambridge 1987– (visiting prof 1991 and 2000–), seconded from PSA to assist chm of DOE/DTI ministerial review on professional liability 1987–88, promotion bd panellist for sr professionals, acad advsr to postgrads, UCL law res postgrad 1989–91, HQ princ lectr in law and advsr on negotiation and pursuit of negligence claims for MOD and Civil Dept projects in UK regns home and abroad incl Gibraltar 1989–95, first govt appointed head of PSA Directorate Specialist Legal Services 1991 (md post privatisation 1995–), asst dir PSA Projects Bd 1992–95, law research into reform concurrent tortfeasors in solidum liability 1991–96, assoc dir head of TBV Legal Claims 1992–95, referee professional jls, Human Rights 2000 conf 1996, res into Latham-Egan reforms 1998–2001; sr ptnr: Leo Barros D'Sa Associates 1995–2003, Erika Barros D'Sa Ferneyhough Brown 2003–; jt chm Ethics and Transparency 2002–07; distinction award for res into Euro Court of Justice Acquired Rights Directive infractions and ambiguities 1992; memb: RIBA, Judicial Div Int Assoc of the American Bar Assoc, IPMS 1976–, CIArb 1976–97, Soc of Construction Law 1990–, Socio-Legal Studies Assoc 1996–, IOD, Soc Public Teachers of Law, Acad of Construction Adjudicators, Assoc of Univ Teachers, Euro Assoc of Psychology and Law, Int Soc of Criminologists, UK Assoc Legal & Social Philosophy, American Psychology-Law Soc, American Soc of Criminology, Amnesty Int, Legal Action Gp, Justice 1999, Bd CIDU 2003–, Liberty; fndr memb The Adjudication Soc 2000–; Freeman City of London 1988, memb Worshipful Co of Chartered Architects; FRSA, FFB, FIMgt; *Publications* books incl: Professional Liability and Construction (1987 edn), PSA Tech Digests (co-author, 1988), Tech Feedback (PSA ed, 1988–89), Bishop Report (contrib Analysis 2 chapters, 1989); author and presenter of numerous papers on professional negligence and employment law, corporate crime, recidivism, femicide and other criminological issues; *Recreations* chess, opera, cine-soc, literature, scribbling, doodling, Tyrolean walks; *Clubs* Oxford and Cambridge, Royal Over-Seas League; *Style*— Prof Leo Barros D'Sa; ✉ 52 Elm Park Road, Winchmore Hill, London N21 2HS (☎ 020 8360 0074, fax 020 8360 8700); Erika Barros D'Sa Ferneyhough Brown (☎ 020 8245 9840); University of Cambridge CB3 9BB

BARROTT, Michael Anthony Cooper; s of Brian Robert James Barrott (d 1963), and Betty Doreen, *née* Berryman (d 1998); *b* 9 December 1954; *Educ* Reading Sch, St John's Coll Oxford (scholar, MA), Open Univ (MBA); *m* 29 May 1982, Elizabeth Jelisaveta, da of Stojan Stosic (d 1994); 1 s (William b 12 Aug 1996); *Career* Price Waterhouse 1976–87, Scandinavian Bank plc 1987–90 (div dir 1989–90), fin dir Mortgage Trust Ltd 1990–95, chief exec Strategy, Finance & Governance 1995–; hon vice-pres Thames Valley Housing Assoc 2005–15 (non-exec dir 1992–2004, chm 1998–2004); memb Nat Cncl Nat Housing Fedn 1999–2004; chm Centenary Meml Sunday Sch Tst 2016–, vice-pres Old Redingensians 2016–; FCA 1990 (ACA 1979); *Recreations* music, skiing, golf, history, restoring Georgian houses; *Style*— Michael Barrott, Esq; ✉ Strategy, Finance & Governance, 126 Kennington Road, London SE11 6RE (☎ 020 7582 2453, e-mail michael.barrott@btinternet.com)

BARROW, Andrew James; s of Gerald Ernest Barrow, MBE, of Gustard Wood, Herts, and Angela Eileen, *née* Frank; *b* 17 May 1954; *Educ* King's Sch Canterbury, Univ of Nottingham (LLB); *m* 16 April 1983, Helen Elizabeth, da of Brian Carter; 3 s (Charles Andrew b 24 May 1984, Frederick Nicholas b 26 May 1986, Joshua Barnaby b 9 April 1993), 1 da (Clementine Elizabeth b 17 March 1988); *Career* slr; Travers Smith LLP: articled clerk 1976–78, asst slr 1978–83, ptnr 1983–2009, conslt 2009–10, princ Andrew Barrow Assocs LLP 2010–; *Recreations* family, golf, powerboating, motorbikes, allotment holding; *Clubs* Brooks's, City of London, Royal Wimbledon, Royal St George's, Royal County Down; *Style*— Andrew Barrow, Esq; ☎ 020 8546 1225 (home) or 020 8549 2061 (office), mobile 07831 386119, e-mail info@andrewbarrowassociates.co.uk

BARROW, Colin; CBE (2004); s of Reginald Barrow (d 1981), of Gosport, Hants, and Margaret, *née* Jones (d 1994); *b* 18 June 1952, Fareham, Hants; *Educ* Dulwich Coll, Clare Coll Cambridge (MA); *m* 1, 25 June 1994 (m dis 2007), Angelica, da of Hermann Bortis; 2 s (Simon b 26 Feb 1997, James b 29 Nov 1998); m 2, 5 Jan 2009, Ana Smaldon; *Career* commercial mangr John Brown Gp 1974–83, md Funds Div E D & F Man Gp 1983–96, chm Sabre Fund Mgmnt Gp 1996–2005, chm Alpha Strategic plc 2005–14; qualified mediator CEDR 2014–; chm IDeA 2000–04; chm Nat Autistic Soc 2005–11 (treas 2004); dir: Rambert Dance Co 1997–2003, Policy Exchange 2002–05; memb: Suffolk CC 1997–2002, Westminster City Cncl 2002–12 (dep ldr 2005–08, ldr 2008–12), Mayor of London's Cmmn on Health 2013–14, Expert Advsy Bd Imperial Coll Health Partners 2013–, Cncl Univ of Southern California Sol Price Sch of Public Policy (vice-chm Bd of Cncllrs 2016–); *Recreations* inexpert skier, scuba diver, bridge player; *Style*— Colin Barrow, Esq, CBE; ✉ e-mail colin.barrow1@gmail.com

BARROW, Gregory Jonathan; s of Graham Barrow (d 2004), and Patricia, *née* Dixon; *b* 22 April 1966, London; *Educ* Wilson's Sch Wallington, Magdalene Coll Cambridge (MA); *m* 2000, Jane Standley; 1 da (Malaika May), 1 s (Nelson Roscoe John); *Career* BBC 1989–2004, Southern Africa corr BBC Johannesburg 1998–2001, UN corr BBC NY 2001–04, sr public affairs offr UN World Food Prog UK 2004–08, global media coordinator UN World Food Prog Italy 2008–10, dep dir of communications UN World Food Prog Italy 2010–12, dir London Office UK World Food Prog 2012–; *Recreations* travel, reading; *Style*— Gregory Barrow, Esq; ✉ c/o World Food Programme, 10 Furnival Street, London EC4A 1AB (☎ 020 7240 9001, website www.wfp.org)

BARROW, Dame Jocelyn; DBE (1992, OBE 1972); *b* 15 April 1929; *Educ* Univ of London (BA); *m* Henderson Downer; *Career* dep chm Broadcasting Standards Cncl (and chm of its Complaints Ctee) 1985–92; govr: BBC 1981–88, Farnham Castle (centre for training Third World workers), Cwlth Inst (and chair of its Educn Ctee), Cwlth of Learning; gen sec Campaign Against Racial Discrimination 1964–69, vice-chm International Human Rights Year Ctee 1968, memb Community Relations Cmmn 1968–72, national vice-pres Nat Union of Townswomen's Guilds 1978–80 and 1987–, memb EC Econ and Social Ctee 1990–, devpt dir Focus Consultancy Ltd 1996–; fndr (now pres) Community Housing Assoc Camden, vice-chm E London Housing Assoc; govr and patron Goldsmiths Coll London (memb Equal Opportunities Ctee), patron Caribbean Centre (and its Caribbean Int Studies network); former sr lectr in educn Furzedown Teachers Coll, seconded to Inst of Educn Univ of London; chair Mayor's Cmmn on African & Asian Heritage 2003–05; Hon DLitt Univ of E London 1992; FRSA; *Style*— Dame Jocelyn Barrow, DBE

BARROW, John Anthony; s of Jack Farmer Barrow, and Nancy Elwyn Jones; *b* 1948, Australia; *Educ* C of E Boys' GS Brisbane, Queensland Univ of Technol, Royal Aust Inst of Architecture; *m* 1988, Frances Thomson; *Career* architect; ptnr Marshall Haines Barrow 1979–87; dir: Lister Drew Haines Barrow 1987–1991, Atkins Architects 1991–93, Marshall Haines Barrow Ltd 1994–2000; sr princ HOK Sport Ltd 2001–08, sr princ Populous (formerly HOK Sport) 2009–12 (sr advsr 2013–); current and recent projects incl: Dubai Expo 2020, Rubin Kazam Stadium, Sochi Olympic Stadium Russia, Olympic Lyonnais Stadium France, Glasgow 2014 Cwlth Games bid, Leeds Arena, masterplanning, overlay and venue planning London 2012 Olympic Games, O2 Arena Greenwich London, Formula 1 racetrack redevelopment Silverstone, Formula 1 autodrome Dubai, stadium Milton Keynes, Palasport Speed Skating Arena Turin 2006 Winter Olympic Games, O2 Arena Dublin, Benfica stadium Lisbon, Algarve stadium Faro, Odyssey Arena Belfast, Dubai World Expo 2020; adjunct prof Queensland Univ of Technol; RIBA 1976; *Recreations* motor sports, antique car restoration, golf; *Clubs* RAC; *Style*— John Barrow, Esq; ✉ Populous, 14 Blades Court, Deodar Road, London SW15 2NU (☎ 020 8874 7666, fax 020 8874 7470)

BARROW, Prof John David; s of Walter Henry Barrow (d 1979), of London, and Lois Miriam, *née* Tucker (d 1998); *b* 29 November 1952; *Educ* Ealing GS, Van Mildert Coll Durham (BSc), Magdalen Coll Oxford (DPhil); *m* 13 Sept 1975, Elizabeth Mary, da of James William East (d 1978), of London; 2 s (David Lloyd b 1978, Roger James b 1981), 1 da (Louise Elizabeth b 1984); *Career* jr res lectr ChCh Oxford 1977–80; Univ of Sussex: lectr 1981–89, prof of astronomy 1989–99, dir Astronomy Centre 1995–99; currently prof of mathematical sciences Univ of Cambridge (dir Millennium Math Project 1999–), fell Clare Hall Cambridge 1999– (vice-pres 2004–07); Gordon Godfrey visiting prof Univ of NSW 1999, 2000 and 2003, concurrent prof Univ of Nanjing 2005–, Gresham prof of astronomy 2003–07; emeritus Gresham prof of astronomy 2007–, Gresham prof of geometry 2008–12; Br Assoc: pres Physics Section 2009–10, pres Mathematics Section 2011–12; Lindemann fell English Speaking Union Cwlth 1977–78, Miller fell Univ of Calif Berkley 1980–81, Nuffield fell 1986–87, Gifford lectr Univ of Glasgow 1988, Scott meml lectr Leuven 1989, Collingwood meml lectr Univ of Durham 1990, Sigma-Tau-Laterza lectures Milan Univ 1991, Leverhulme fell Royal Soc 1992, George Darwin lecture RAS 1992, Kelvin lecture 1999, Flamsteed lecture 2000, Tyndall lecture 2001, Darwin lecture 2001, Whitrow lecture RAS 2002, Brasher lecture 2002, Newton Lecture 2004, Hubert James lecture 2004, Von Weizsäcker lectures 2004, McCrea lecture 2004, Wood lecture 2005, Hamilton lecture 2005, Knight lecture Monkton Coll Bath 2006, Borderlands lecture Univ of Durham 2007, Boyle lecture St Mary-le-Bow London 2007, Roscoe lecture John Moore Univ Liverpool 2007, Gunnar and Gunnel Källén lecture Lund 2007, Si-Wei lectures Chengchi Univ Taiwan 2008, Dennis Sciama Memorial Lecture Univ of Oxford and Univ of Trieste 2008, David Phillips Memorial Lecture Univ of Cardiff 2008, Tizard Lecture 2010, William Herschel lecture 2010, Van Mildert Tst lecture 2010, Marcelo Anile meml lecture 2011, Gregynog lecture 2011, Real Soc Matemática Española centenary lecture 2011, Winsten lecture Univ of Essex 2012, Zeeman lecture 2012, presidential lecture Br Science Assoc Maths Section Univ of Aberdeen 2012, McCrea astronomy lecture Royal Irish Acad Cork Univ 2013, Correspondents Day lecture Isaac Newton Inst Cambridge 2014, IMO celebrity lecture Int Mathematics Olympiad Univ of Cape Town 2014, Enriques lecture Dipartimento Matematico Univ of Milan 2014; Samuel Locker Award 1989, Templeton Award 1995, Kelvin Medal 1999, Premi Ubu Theatre Prize 2002, Italgas Prize 2004, Lacchini Medal 2005, Queen's Anniversary Prize 2006, Templeton Prize 2006, Faraday Medal 2008, IOP Kelvin Medal 2009, Gresham Prize 2009, Premio Oriente Science Prize 2010, Merck-Serono Prize 2011, LMS and IMA Zeeman Medal 2012, Antico Pignolo Literary Prize 2012, Dirac Gold Medal Inst of Physics 2015, Gold Medal Royal Astronomical Soc 2016; external examiner Open Univ; PPARC sr fell 1994–99, memb Cncl RAS 1999–, memb various ctees SERC; Hon DSc: Univ of Herts 1999, Univ of Szczecin 2007, Univ of Durham 2008, Univ of Sussex 2010, Univ of S Wales 2014; hon fell Van Mildert Coll Durham Univ 2015; memb: Int Astronomical Union, ISSR, Academia Europaea; titular memb L'Acad Int de Philosophie Sciences 2009; FRS, FRAS, FInstP, FRSA; *Books* The Left Hand of Creation (1983), The Anthropic Cosmological Principle (1986), L'Homme et Le Cosmos (1984), The World Within the World (1988), Theories of Everything (1991), Perché il mondo è matematico? (1992), Pi in the Sky (1992), The Origin of the Universe (1994), The Artful Universe (1995), Impossibility (1998), Between Inner Space and Outer Space (1999), The Universe That Discovered Itself (2000), The Book of Nothing (2000), The Constants of Nature (2002), The Infinite Book (2005), The Artful Universe Expanded (2005), New Theories of Everything (2007), Cosmic Imagery (2008), One Hundred Essential Things You Didn't Know You Didn't Know (2008), The Book of Universes (2011), One Hundred Essential Things You Didn't Know You Didn't Know About Sport (2012), Mathletics (2013), One Hundred Essential Things You Didn't Know About Maths and the Arts (2014); *Recreations* athletics, books, theatre (play Infinities performed in Milan and Valencia 2002–03); *Clubs* RAS Dining; *Style*— Prof John D Barrow, FRS; ✉ DAMTP, University of Cambridge, Wilberforce Road, Cambridge CB3 0WA (fax 01223 765900, e-mail j.d.barrow@damtp.cam.ac.uk)

BARROW, Simon Hoare; s of G Erskine Barrow (d 1979), of IOM, and Margaret Armine MacInnes (d 1977); *b* 4 November 1937; *Educ* Harrow, ChCh Oxford, Hill Sch Pennsylvania (ESU exchange); *m* 1, 1964 (m dis 1977), Caroline Peto Bennett; 1 s (Thomas), 3 da (Sasha, Emmeline, Rebecca); m 2, 1983, Sheena Margaret, da of Maj-Gen Sir John Anderson, KBE; 2 da (Kate, Florence); *Career* 2 Lt Scots Gds 1956–58; brand mgmnt for Best Foods and Colgate-Palmolive 1967–78, dir Charles Barker Gp 1978–92; chief exec: Ayer Barker 1978–86, Barkers Human Resources 1987–92; chm: People in Business mgmnt communication conslts 1992–12, Human Resource Interest Group Market Research Soc 1995–2000; dir Beyond the Deal M&A Conslts 2012–14, people dir Westbourne Communications 2012–, Simon Barrow Assocs employer brand and M&A conslts 2014–; memb Advsy Cncl European Movement 1992–; tstee Alde & Ore Assoc 2002–, tstee Teachers Award Tst 2011, memb Ethics Ctee Cwlth War Graves 2012–; church warden All Saints Sudbourne; *Books* The Employer Brand: Bringing the best of brand management to people at work (2005), Employee Communications During Mergers and Acquisitions (2009); *Recreations* sailing, tennis; *Clubs* Brooks's, Beefsteak; *Style*— Simon Barrow, Esq; ✉ 16 Chelsea Embankment, London SW3 4LA (☎ 020 7352 7531, e-mail simon@simonbarrow.org.uk, website www.sbaemployerbrand.com); Cowton House, Sudbourne, Suffolk IP12 2HB (☎ 01394 450737)

BARRY, Helen; da of Bernard Barry (d 2001), and Patricia Barry (d 1986); *b* 18 August 1961, Liverpool; *Educ* Convent of Mercy GS Liverpool, Victoria Univ of Manchester (LLB), Chester Coll of Law; *Children* 1 da (Rachel b 3 Feb 1997); *Career* admitted slr 1986; articles Maxwell Cooke & Co 1984–86, Aneurin, Rees & Davis 1986–87, Anthony Landes Slrs 1987–88, equity ptnr Yaffe, Jackson Ostrin 1988–96, head of clinical negligence and equity ptnr EAD Solicitors LLP (formerly Edwards, Abrams, Doherty) 1996–; memb Specialist Clinical Negligence Panel Law Soc, memb Negligence Panel Action Against Medical Accidents; memb: Encephalitis Soc, Assoc of Personal Injury Lawyers (also sr litigator), Law Soc; *Recreations* theatre, swimming, reading; *Style*— Miss Helen Barry; ✉ EAD Solicitors LLP, Prospect House, Columbus Quay, Liverpool L3 4DB (☎ 0151 735 1000, fax 0151 291 2555, e-mail helen.barry@eadsolicitors.co.uk, website www.eadsolicitors.co.uk and ask.eadsolicitors.co.uk)

BARRY, Michael; *see:* Bukht, Michael John

BARRY, Mike; *Educ* Univ of Sheffield (BSc); *Career* head of sustainable business Marks & Spencer; *Style*— Mike Barry, Esq; ✉ Marks and Spencer Group plc, Waterside House, 35 North Wharf Road, London W2 1NW

BARRY, Sebastian; s of Francis Barry, and Joan O'Hara; *b* 5 July 1955, Dublin; *Educ* Catholic Univ Sch, TCD; *m* Alison; 3 c (Merlin, Coral, Tobias); *Career* playwright and novelist; writer in assoc Abbey Theatre 1989, writer fell TCD 1996, Heimbold visiting chair in Irish studies Villanova Univ PA 2006; Dublin Lord Mayor's Award 2009; Hon DLitt: Univ of E Anglia 2010, NUI (Nat Univ Ireland) Galway 2011, Open Univ 2014; memb Aosdana (Ireland), FRSL 2009; *Plays* Boss Grady's Boys (1988, BBC/Stewart Parker Award), The Steward of Christendom (1995, Christopher-Ewart Biggs Memorial Prize, American Ireland Fund Literary Prize, Best New Play London's Critics' Circle, Best Fringe Play Writer's Guild, Playwright of the Year Award), Our Lady of Sligo (1998, Peggy Ramsay Play Award), Hinterland (2002), Whistling Psyche (2004), The Pride of Parnell Street (2007), Dallas Sweetman (2008); *Novels* Elsewhere: The Adventures of Belemus (children's book, 1985), The Whereabouts of Eneas McNulty (1998), Annie Dunne (2002), A Long Long Way (2005, Kerry Group Irish Fiction Award, shortlisted Man Booker Prize), The Secret Scripture (2008, shortlisted Man Booker Prize 2008, shortlisted LA Times Book Award 2009, Costa Novel Award 2009, Costa Book of the Year Award 2009, Hughes and Hughes Irish Novel Award 2009, Tubridy Listener's Choice Award 2009, James Tait Black Meml Prize 2010), On Canaan's Side (2011, longlisted Man Booker Prize 2011, winner Walter Scott Prize for Historical Fiction 2012), The Temporary Gentleman (2014); *Poetry* The Water Colourist (1983), Fanny Hawke Goes to the Mainland Forever (1989), The Pinkening Boy (2004); *Recreations* building, fly fishing; *Style*— Sebastian Barry, Esq; ✉ c/o Derek Johns, United Agents, 12–26 Lexington Street, London W1F 0LE

BARRY-WALSH, Paul Frederick; s of Michael Henry Barry-Walsh (d 1993), and Hazel Lillian, *née* Kerr (d 1999); *b* 18 August 1955, London; *Educ* Rossall Sch Fleetwood (scholar), Univ of Liverpool; *m* 18 May 1984, Jane, *née* McIlvenny; 1 da (Olivia b 6 Aug 1985), 1 s (Edward b 11 May 1988); *Career* joined IBM 1977, fndr and ceo SafetyNet 1986–2000, fndr and chm NetStore 1996– (ceo 2001–04), founding ptnr Frank Investments 2014–; chm Frederick's Fndn 2001–; runner-up IT Entrepreneur of the Year 2002, Queen's Award for Enterprise Promotion, Beacon Award for Creative Giving, CNBC European Philanthropist of the Year 2009; FRSA 2002; *Recreations* golf, skiing, motor sport, cycling; *Clubs* Queenwood Golf; *Style*— Paul Barry-Walsh, Esq; ✉ Derrydown House, Derrydown, St Mary Bourne, Andover, Hampshire SP11 6BS

BARSTOW, Dame Josephine Clare; DBE (1995, CBE 1985); da of Harold Barstow, of Sussex, and Clara Edith, *née* Shaw; *b* 27 September 1940, Sheffield, S Yorks; *Educ* Univ of Birmingham (BA), London Opera Centre; *m* 1, 1964 (m dis 1967), Terry Hands, *qv*; m 2, 1969, Ande Anderson (d 1996); *Career* soprano; debut with Opera for All 1964, studied at London Opera Centre 1965–66, Opera for All 1966, Glyndebourne Chorus 1967; contract principal: Sadler's Wells 1967–68, WNO 1968–70; freelance 1971–; US debut as Lady Macbeth in Miami 1977; has appeared with ENO, SNO, WNO, Glyndebourne, Opera North; has appeared at numerous international venues incl: Covent Garden, Vienna Staatsoper, Aix-en-Provence Festival, Bayreuth Festival, Salzburg, Munich, Zurich, Toulouse, San Francisco, Met Opera NY, Houston, Chicago, Adelaide, Bolshoi Moscow, Riga and Tbilisi; Hon DMus: Univ of Birmingham, Kingston Univ 1999, Sheffield Hallam Univ 1999, Univ of Hull 2000, Univ of Leeds 2006; *Roles* with WNO incl: Violetta in La Traviata, Fiordiligi in Cosi fan Tutte, Amelia in Simon Boccanegra, Elisabeth de Valois in Don Carlos 1973, Jenufa 1975, Ellen Orford in Peter Grimes 1978 and 1983, Tatyana in Eugene Onegin 1980, title role in Tosca 1985, Amelia in Un Ballo in Maschera 1986; at Covent Garden incl: Alice Ford in Falstaff 1975, title role in Salome 1982, Santuzza in Cavalleria Rusticana 1982, Ellen Orford in Peter Grimes 1988, Attila 1990, Fidelio 1993; with Glyndebourne Festival Opera incl: Lady Macbeth in Macbeth (for TV) 1972, Elektra in Idomeneo 1974, Leonore in Fidelio 1981; with ENO incl: various in The Tales of Hoffman, Emilia Marty in The Makropulos Case, Natasha in War and Peace, Violetta in La Traviata, Octavian and The Marschallin in Der Rosenkavalier 1975 and 1984, title role in Salome 1975, Elisabeth in Don Carlos 1976 and 1986, Tosca 1976 and 1987, Leonora in La Forza del Destino 1978 and 1992, title role in Aida 1979, Leonore in Fidelio 1980, Senta in Der Fliegende Holländer 1982, Mimi in La Boheme 1982, Sieglinde in Die Walküre 1983, Donna Anna in Don Giovanni 1986, Lady Macbeth of Mtsensk 1987 and 1991; appearances in world première performances incl: Denise in Tippett's The Knot Garden 1970, Marguerite in Crosse's The Story of Vasco 1974, Gayle in Tippett's The Ice Break 1977, Benigna in Penderecki's Die Schwarze Maske (Salzburg) 1986; other performances incl: Gudrun in Götterdämmerung (Bayreuth) 1983, title role in Katya Kabanova, Elizabeth I in Britten's Gloriana (Opera North Leeds and Covent Garden) 1994, Kostelnicka in Jenufa (Opera North) 1995, Medea and Marie in Wozzeck (Opera North) 1996, Aida (Opera North) 1997, Mother Marie in Carmelites (ENO) 1999, Kostelnicka (Antwerp) 1999, Alice (Opera North) 2000, Kabanicha (Amsterdam and ROH) 2000, Countess in Queen of Spades (ROH) 2001, Lady Billows (Opera North) 2002; *Films* Owen Wingrave 2001, Gloriana: A Film; *Recordings* incl: Un Ballo in Maschera, Kiss me Kate, Albert Herring, Gloriana: A Film, Jenufa, The Knot Garden, Wozzeck, Gloriana, Street Scene, Carmelites; *Recreations* breeding Arabian horses (stud farm in Devon); *Style*— Dame Josephine Barstow, DBE; ✉ c/o Musichall, Vicarage Way, Ringmer, East Sussex BN8 5LA

BARTFELD, Jason; QC (2015); *Educ* Westminster, Durham Univ (BA); *m* Annabel, *née* Nahon; *Career* called to the Bar Middle Temple (Jules Thorn Scholar) 1995; memb Criminal Bar Assoc; *Recreations* cricket, motorsport, sailing, skiing, travel, polo; *Clubs* Sussex Polo; *Style*— Jason Bartfeld, Esq, QC; ✉ 187 Fleet Street, London EC4A 2AT

BARTLAM, Thomas Hugh; s of Howard Bennett Bartlam (d 1970), and Mary Isobel Bartlam, *née* Lambert (d 2002), of Arkholme, Lancs; *b* 4 December 1947; *Educ* Repton, Selwyn Coll Cambridge (MA); *m* 4 June 1977, Elizabeth Gabriel, da of Andrew David Arthur Balfour, of Shalford, Surrey; 2 s (Edward b 1979, Henry b 1985), 1 da (Harriet b 1981); *Career* merchant banker; dir: Charterhouse Bank 1984–89, Charterhouse Venture Capital Fund, Charterhouse Buy-Out Fund, Charterhouse Business Expansion Fund; md Intermediate Capital Group plc 1989–2005 (non-exec dir 2005–09); non-exec chm: Pantheon International Participations plc, Polar Capital Hldgs plc 2007–, Jupiter UK Growth Tst plc; non-exec dir Diverse Income Tst plc; memb Governing Cncl Univ of Reading, FCA; *Recreations* opera, gardening, farming; *Clubs* Boodle's, MCC; *Style*— Thomas H Bartlam, Esq; ✉ Polar Capital plc, 16 Palace Street, London SW1E 5JD

BARTLE, His Hon Judge Philip Martyn; QC (2003); *Career* called to the Bar 1976; recorder 2004, circuit judge (South Eastern Circuit) 2012–; *Style*— His Hon Judge Bartle, QC; ✉ Luton Crown Court, 7 George Street, Luton LU1 2AA

BARTLETT, Adrian; s of Alan Baskerville Bartlett (d 1981), and Marjorie Jesse, *née* Launder; *b* 31 March 1939; *Educ* Bedales, Camberwell Sch of Art, Univ of Durham; *m* 17 July 1962, Victoria Anne Bartlett, *qv*, *née* Howitt; 2 da (Zoë b 27 March 1965, Eve b 9 Feb 1967); *Career* artist; head of printmaking Morley Coll 1963–99; visiting lectr Univ of Oxford; UK rep Florence Biennale 1976; featured in Culture Show (BBC) 2009; finalist Hunting/Observer Prize 1992, Sir Peter Blake Award for Most Original Work 2009; pres London Gp 1993 (memb 1979); *Solo Exhibitions* incl: British Cncl Athens 1985, Oxford Gallery 1987, Blenheim Gallery 1988, Tsikalioti Museum Greece 1989, Morley Gallery 1996, Walk Gallery 1999, Piers Feetham Gallery 2007; *Group Exhibitions* numerous RA Summer Exhbns, 6th Int Art Fair London 1991; *Public Collections* Ashmolean Museum Oxford, British Museum, British Cncl, Berlin Graphothek, Dept for Educn, Herbert Art Gallery Coventry, McNay Inst Texas, Oldham City Art Gallery, St Thomas' Hosp, Surrey Educn Authy; *Books* Drawing and Painting the Landscape (1982), British Art in the Eighties (1983); *Clubs* Chelsea Arts; *Style*— Adrian Bartlett, Esq; ✉ 132 Kennington Park Road, London SE11 4DJ (☎ 020 7735 0272)

BARTLETT, Andrew Vincent Bramwell; QC (1993); *Educ* Whitgift Sch, Jesus Coll Oxford (BA); *Career* called to the Bar Middle Temple 1974 (bencher); dep High Court judge, judge Upper Tbnl; chartered arbitrator; FCIArb; *Style*— Andrew Bartlett, Esq, QC; ✉ Crown Office Chambers, 2 Crown Office Row, Temple, London EC4Y 7HJ (☎ 020 7797 8100, fax 020 7797 8101)

BARTLETT, Anthony David (Tony); s of Clifford Sydney McDonald Bartlett, of Church Stretton, Salop, and late Sylvia Patricia, *née* Samson; *b* 21 February 1951; *Educ* Stamford Sch; *m* 1; 1 da (Melissa b 1982), 1 s (Joshua b 1984); m 2, 19 Aug 1993, Alison McNeill Kerr, da of late William Kerr; *Career* CA; Neville Russell & Co (now Mazars Neville Russell) 1971–74, ptnr Coopers & Lybrand 1984–95 (joined 1975), md Beeson Gregory 2002 (dir and head of corp fin 1995–2002); Arden Partners plc: chm of corp fin 2003–06, ceo 2006–08, non-exec dir 2008–10; *Recreations* golf, fishing; *Clubs* Royal Dornoch Golf, Royal Cape Golf, Metropolitan Cape Town; *Style*— Tony Bartlett, Esq; ✉ Skelbo House, Dornoch IV25 3QE (☎ 07802 302401, e-mail bartletts@btinternet.com)

BARTLETT, George Robert; QC (1986); s of Cdr Howard Volins Bartlett, RN (d 1988), of Putney, London, and Angela Margaret, *née* Webster (d 2004); *b* 22 October 1944; *Educ* Tonbridge, Trinity Coll Oxford (MA); *m* 6 May 1972, Dr Clare Virginia, da of Gordon Chalmers Fortin (d 1995), of Castle Hedingham, Essex; 3 s (William b 1973, Frederick b 1979, Charles b 1982); *Career* called to the Bar Middle Temple 1966 (bencher 1995); recorder of the Crown Court 1990–2000, dep judge of the High Court 1994–; asst parly boundary cmmr 1992–98, pres Lands Tbnl 1998–2009, pres Lands Chamber Upper Tbnl 2009–12; *Books* Ryde on Rating (ed); *Style*— George R Bartlett, Esq, QC

BARTLETT, James Michael Gilbert; s of Maj Michael George Bartlett, TD (d 2002), and Elizabeth Marjorie, *née* Grieve (d 1997); *b* 21 March 1947; *Educ* Bromsgrove Sch; *m* 20 Sept 1975, (Patricia) Anne, da of Ronald Dean Cranfield (d 1976); 1 da (Catherine Anne b 1978), 1 s ((James) Michael Ronald b 1981); *Career* princ Bartlett & Co Chartered Accountants 1983–89, sr ptnr Bartlett Hall Chartered Accountants 1989–96, managing ptnr Bartlett Kershaw Trott Chartered Accountants 1996–; dir: BKT Consltg Ltd, Tax Mangr Ltd; formerly: chm Winchcombe Deanery Synod, memb Glos Diocesan Synod, dir Glos Diocesan Bd of Fin; treas Glos Branch Cncl for Preservation of Rural England 1987–93, vice-chm UK Nat Cadet Class Assoc 1996–97 (treas 1992–96); Freeman City of London 1979, Liveryman Worshipful Co of Builders Merchants; FCA 1971, FIMgt 1988; *Recreations* sailing; *Clubs* Royal Ocean Racing, Royal Northumberland Yacht, South Cerney Sailing (Cdre 1991–94), Mylor Yacht; *Style*— James Bartlett, Esq; ✉ Cleeve House, West Approach Drive, Cheltenham, Gloucestershire GL52 3AD; Bartlett Kershaw Trott, 4 Pullman Court, Great Western Road, Gloucester GL1 3ND (☎ 01452 527000, fax 01452 304585)

BARTLETT, Jeanne Elizabeth; da of Peter Anthony Bartlett, of Northam, E Sussex, and Joan, *née* Proctor; *Educ* Alleyne's GS Uttoxeter, UCW Aberystwyth (LLB); *Career* asst slr Slaughter & May 1984–90, sr assoc Linklaters and Pains Hong Kong 1990–93, vice-pres Bankers Tst 1993–96, gen counsel (capital markets) Bank of America 1996–99, co-managing ptnr Orrick, Herrington & Sutcliffe 2000–01, head of capital markets and securitisation DLA 2001–07, ptnr and global head of Islamic and structured finance Appleby 2008–12, ceo and specialist advsr AB 2012–; *Recreations* art, literature, tennis, travel; *Style*— Ms Jeanne Bartlett; ☎ 020 7349 9339, e-mail jeannebartlett613@btinternet.com

BARTLETT, Matthew; s of Clive Bartlett (d 2007), and Joan, *née* Perry, of Stourbridge; *b* 17 March 1967, Stourbridge; *Educ* Jesus Coll Cambridge (BA, MA), Durham Univ (PGCE), Univ of Manchester (NPQH); *Career* asst history master Manchester GS 1991–97, head of history Nottingham HS 1997–2002, dep headmaster St Bede's Coll Manchester 2002–10, headteacher Dover GS for Girls 2011–16, headmaster St Aloysius Coll Glasgow 2016–; nat ldr of educn 2015–; memb HMC; *Recreations* travel, food and wine; *Clubs* Caledonian, Lansdowne; *Style*— Matthew Bartlett, Esq; ✉ St Aloysius College, 45 Hill Street, Glasgow G3 6RJ (☎ 0141 331 9274, e-mail MDBartlett@staloysius.org)

BARTLETT, Michael (Mike); *Career* playwright; *Plays* incl: My Child (Royal Court) 2007, Cock (Royal Court) 2009, Love, Love, Love (Plymouth Theatre Royal) 2010 and (Royal Court) 2012, Earthquakes in London (NT) 2010, 13 (NT) 2011–12, Chariots of Fire (Hampstead Theatre) 2012 and (Gielgud Theatre) 2012–13, Bull (Crucible Studio Theatre Sheffield) 2013 and (Young Vic) 2015, (59E59 NY) 2013 and (Young Vic) 2014, King Charles III (Almeida and Wyndham's) 2014–15, (Broadway) 2015–16 and (UK tour) 2015–, Game (Almeida 2015), Wild (Hampstead) 2016; *Radio* incl: Love Contract (BBC Radio 4) 2007, Liam (BBC Radio 4) 2009, Heart (BBC Radio 4) 2011, The Core (BBC Radio 4) 2011, The Right Honourable 2013; *Television* incl: The Town (ITV) 2012, Doctor Foster (BBC 1) 2015; *Style*— Mike Bartlett, Esq

BARTLETT, Neil; OBE (2000); *b* 23 August 1958; *Educ* Magdalen Coll Oxford; *Partner* James Gardiner; *Career* author, director, translator and performer; artistic dir Lyric Theatre Hammersmith 1994–2004; prodns incl: A Vision of Love Revealed in Sleep 1987–90, The School for Wives 1990, A Judgement in Stone 1992, The Game of Love and Chance 1992, Night After Night 1993, The Picture of Dorian Gray 1994, Splendid's 1995, The Letter 1995, Romeo and Juliet 1995, Mrs Warren's Profession 1996, Sarrasine 1996, A Christmas Carol 1996, The Seven Sacraments of Nicholas Poussin 1997, Then Again 1997, Cause Célèbre 1998, Seven Sonnets of Michaelangelo 1998, Cinderella 1998, The Dispute 1999, The Servant 2001, The Prince of Homburg 2002, The Island of Slaves 2002, A Christmas Carol 2002, Pericles 2003, Oliver Twist 2004 and 2007, Don Juan 2004, Dido, Queen of Carthage 2005, The Rake's Progress 2006, The Maids 2007, The Pianist 2007, Twelfth Night 2007, An Ideal Husband 2008, Romeo and Juliet 2008, Everybody Loves A Winner 2009, The Turn of The Screw 2009, The Girl I Left Behind Me 2010, Or You Could Kiss Me 2010, The Queen of Spades 2011, The Picture of Dorian Gray 2012, The Britten Canticles 2013, Great Expectations 2013, Owen Wingrave 2014; fndr memb Gloria; *Stage Plays* incl: A Vision of Love Revealed in Sleep (1989), Sarrasine (1990), A Judgement in Stone (1992), Night After Night (1993), The Picture of Dorian Gray (1994), Lady into Fox (1996), The Seven Sacraments of Nicolas Poussin (1997), In Extremis (2000), A Christmas Carol (2002), Oliver Twist (2004), Solo Voices (2005), Great Expectations (2007), The Girl I Left Behind Me (2010), Or You Could Kiss Me (2010), For Alfonso (2011), Queer Voices (2012), The Picture of Dorian Gray (2012); *Translations* The Misanthrope (Molière), The School for Wives (Molière), Bérénice (Racine), The Game of Love and Chance (Marivaux), The Dispute (Marivaux), Splendid's (Genet), The Threesome (Labiche), The Prince of Homburg (Kleist), The Island of Slaves (Marivaux), Camille (Dumas), La Casa Azul (Faucher), Don Juan (Molière), The Maids (Genet); *Films and Television* That's What Friends Are For (1988), Where is Love? (1988), That's How Strong My Love Is (1989), Pedagogue (with Stuart Marshall, 1988), Now That It's Morning (1992); *Biography* Who Was that Man – A Present for Mr Oscar Wilde (1988); *Novels* Ready To Catch Him Should He Fall (1990), Mr Clive & Mr Page (1996), Skin Lane (2007), The Disappearance Boy (2014); *Style*— Neil Bartlett; ✉ c/o The Agency, 24 Pottery Lane, London W11 4LZ (☎ 020 7727 1346, fax 020 7727 9037, e-mail fdavies@theagency.co.uk); website www.neil-bartlett.com

BARTLETT, Robert Hardington; s of Maj Derek Bartlett (d 2016), and Joan, *née* Breyfogle (d 2004); *b* 3 April 1965, Windsor, Berks; *Educ* Eton, George Washington Univ (BSc); *m* 5 Sept 1992, Susannah, *née* Maclean; 3 da (Catriona b 31 Oct 1993, Albany b 5 Nov 1997, Talullah b 26 Oct 2000); *Career* ptnr Cluttons 1993–2006, ceo Chesterton Global

Ltd 2006–, fndr and ptnr Hardington Capital Mgmnt LLP; non-exec dir: REAP Ltd 2012–, Springtide Capital Ltd 2012–, Agents Mutual Ltd 2013–; MRICS 1995, FAAV 1996; *Recreations* country sports, MFH 2006–09, skiing, rowing (represented GB between 1985–92, Olympic Games 1992); *Clubs* Leander, Annabels; *Style*— Robert Bartlett, Esq; ✉ Chesterton Global Limited, 1–3 Mount Street, London W1K 3NB (☎ 020 3040 8240, e-mail robert.bartlett@chestertons.com)

BARTLETT, Victoria Anne; da of Edgar Howitt; *b* 25 March 1940; *Educ* Camberwell Sch of Art, Univ of Reading; *m* 17 July 1962, Adrian Bartlett, *qv*; 2 da (Zoë b 27 March 1965, Eve b 9 Feb 1967); *Career* artist; visiting lectr: Morley Coll London 1975–99, Ruskin Sch of Drawing and Fine Art Univ of Oxford 1980–94, Goldsmiths Coll London 1982–2002; work in various public and private collections in UK and abroad; *Solo Exhibitions* The Egg & The Eye Gallery LA 1974, Van Doren Gallery San Francisco 1975, Morley Gallery London 1976, Edward Totah Gallery London 1981, Camden Arts Centre 1981, Galerie Simoncini Luxembourg 1985, Benjamin Rhodes Gallery London 1987 and 1991, Peralta Pictures 1994, Piers Feetham Gallery 2007, Piers Feetham Gallery 2012; *Group Exhibitions* incl: RA Summer Exhbn 1973, 1979, 1989 and 1993, Flowers Gallery London 1977, The London Group Open and membs exhbns 1978–2016, Galerie Etienne de Causans Paris 1980, Central Museum of Textiles Lódz 1986, Ikon Gallery Birmingham touring exhbn 1987 and 1988, Browse and Darby London 1994–2005, Chicago International Art Fair 1995; *Style*— Ms Victoria Bartlett; ✉ 132 Kennington Park Road, London SE11 4DJ

BARTLETT, Warwick Winston; s of Leslie Winston Bartlett (d 1994), and Elizabeth Mary, *née* Kensett; *b* 13 March 1947, Paignton, Devon; *Educ* Tividale Comp Sch; *m* Jennifer Anne; 1 s (Richard Leslie), 1 da (Sarah Jane); *Career* dir Bartletts Investments Ltd 1966–84, chm Cashline Ltd 1984–, chm Racing Data plc 1993–98, owner Global Betting & Gaming Conslts 1999–, dir Satellite Information Services Ltd 2005–11; chm: British Betting Office Assoc 1992–2002, Assoc of Br Bookmakers 2002–12; memb Horserace Betting Levy Bd 2002–07 (chm Bookmakers Ctee 2002–07); memb Cons Pty; *Publications* The Global Gambling Report, The Smoking Ban: Casinos and Bingo; *Recreations* swimming, reading, music, golf; *Style*— Warwick Bartlett, Esq; ✉ Rose Cottage, 28 Bowling Green Road, Castletown, Isle of Man IM9 1EB (e-mail warwick@gbgc.com, website www.gbgc.com)

BARTLEY, Christopher Roger (Chris); *b* 2 February 1984, Wrexham, Clwyd; *Educ* Kings Sch Chester, Univ of Nottingham; *Career* rower; achievements incl: Bronze medal (lightweight quadruple scull) World Championships 2007, Gold medal (lightweight four) World Championships 2010, Bronze medal (lightweight four) World Championships 2011, Silver medal (lightweight four) Olympic Games 2012; *Clubs* Leander; *Style*— Mr Chris Bartley

BARTLEY, Luella Dayrell; MBE (2010); da of Michael Francis Dayrell Bartley, of Salcombe, Devon, and Pamela Higgins, of Shipston on Stour, Warks; *b* 4 May 1973, Stratford-upon-Avon; *Educ* Trinity Sch Leamington Spa, St Martins Sch of Art (BA); *Partner* David Sims; 1 s (Kip Dustin b 25 June 2003), 1 da (Stevie Willow Frances b 9 April 2005); *Career* fashion designer; journalist: Evening Standard newspaper 1993–96, Evening Standard magazine 1996–97, Vogue UK 1997–99; prop Luella Bartley Ltd 1999–; Luella (own label): debut London Fashion Week 2000, regular exhibitor at seasonal shows worldwide, numerous stockists worldwide incl Harvey Nichols and Saks Fifth Avenue; created collection for New Look 2002; Elle Designer of the Year 2001; *Style*— Miss Luella Bartley, MBE; ✉ Luella Bartley Limited, Rochelle School, Arnold Circus, London E2 7ES (☎ 020 7739 7566, fax 020 7739 9172)

BARTOLO, David Charles Craig; s of Albert Edward Bartolo (d 1993), of Malta, and (Evelyne Valerie) Jean, *née* Callie; *b* 21 July 1949; *Educ* Queen Elizabeth GS Carmarthen, St Mary's Hosp Med Sch Univ of London (MB BS, MS); *Children* 2 da (Victoria b 1979, Rebecca b 1980), 1 s (James b 1985); *Career* sr registrar SW RHA 1982–86, sr registrar St Mark's Hosp London 1985, hon conslt surgn Bristol Royal Infirmary 1987–90, conslt sr lectr Univ of Bristol 1987–90, conslt surgn Royal Infirmary of Edinburgh Lothian Health Bd 1990–, currently prof of surgery Univ of Western Australia and conslt colorectal surgn Fiona Stanley Hosp Murdoch Perth Western Australia; Hunterian prof RCS 1984–85, Moynihan travelling fell Assoc of Surgns of GB and Ireland 1987, jt winner Patey Prize SRS 1988, jt winner New England surgical prize American Soc of Colon and Rectal Surgns 1988; past memb Cncl Assoc of Coloproctology UK and Ireland, past memb Cncl Surgical Res Soc, memb Br Soc of Gastroenterology; hon life fell South African Assoc of Gastroenterology 1997, hon memb Section of Colon and rectal Surgery Royal Australasian Coll of Surgeons 2001, hon memb Chilean Assoc of Coloproctology 2001, hon memb Spanish Assoc of Coloproctology 2009; FRCS 1976, FRACS 2015; *Publications* over 250 peer-reviewed papers, two books and numerous book chapters in surgical texts; *Recreations* music, travel, good food and wine; *Clubs* New (Edinburgh); *Style*— David Bartolo, Esq; ✉ 2/52 Rollinson Road, North Coogee, Western Australia 6163 (☎ 00 61 451 764 862, e-mail dccb2107@gmail.com)

BARTON, Dominic Stephen; *Educ* Univ of Br Columbia (BA), BNC Oxford (MPhil); *Career* McKinsey & Co: joined 1986, head Korea Office 2000–04, chm Asia 2004–09, global md 2009–; memb: Singapore Economic Devpt Advsy Bd 2011–, Bd Asia Pacific Fndn 2011–, Canadian PM's Advsy Bd on Public Sector 2013–16; chm: US Pres's Advsy Cncl on Doing Business in Africa 2014–, Economic Advsy Cncl Canadian Govt 2016–; tstee Brookings 2009–, tstee Rhodes 2009–; Shanghai Govt Gold Magnolia Award, INSEAD Business Ldr of the Year Award 2011, Acad of Int Business Exec of the Year 2014; hon fell BNC Oxford, adjunct prof Tsinghua University; Order of Civil Merit (Peony Medal) South Korea; *Books* Dangerous Markets: Managing in Financial Crises (2002), China Vignettes: An Inside Look at China (2007), Capitalism for the Long Term (2011), Focusing Capital on the Long Term (2014), People Before Strategy: a New Role for the CHRO (2015), Where the Boards Fall Short (2015); *Recreations* rowing; *Style*— Dominic Barton, Esq; ✉ McKinsey & Co, No 1 Jermyn Street, London SW1Y 4UH

BARTON, Geoff; s of Sidney Barton (d 1989), and Amy, *née* Hartman (d 1995); *b* 27 October 1962, Stafford; *Educ* Walton HS Stafford, Univ of Lancaster (BA), Univ of Leicester (PGCE); *m* 5 Aug 1989, Philippa, *née* Nettleton; 2 s (Nicholas b 22 March 1993, Matthew b 5 Sept 1995); *Career* teacher Garforth Comprehensive Sch Leeds 1985–90, head English then asst head Sixth Form Huntington Sch York 1990–97, dep head Thurston Community Coll Suffolk 1997–2002, headteacher King Edward VI Sch Suffolk 2002–; founding fell English Assoc 2000; *Books* Don't Call it Literacy! (2013), Teach Now (2015); *Recreations* cinema, reading, collecting American radio jingles; *Style*— Geoffrey Barton, Esq; ✉ King Edward VI School, Grove Road, Bury St Edmunds, Suffolk IP33 3BH (☎ 01284 761393, e-mail head@king-ed.sufolk.sch.uk, website www.king-ed.suffolk.sch.uk, Twitter @RealGeoffBarton)

BARTON, Glenys; da of Alexander James Barton, and Gertrude Elizabeth, *née* Farmer; *b* 24 January 1944, Stoke-on-Trent; *Educ* RCA (MA); *m* Martin Hunt; 1 s (Felix b 1982); *Career* artist; pt/t lectr: Portsmouth Poly 1971–74, Camberwell Sch of Arts and Crafts 1971–87; *Solo Exhibitions* Museum of Decorative Art Copenhagen 1973, Sculpture and Drawings (Angela Flowers Gallery) 1974, Galerie Het Kapelhuis 1976, Germeenttelijk Museum Het Princessehof 1976), Sculpture and Reliefs (Angela Flowers Gallery) 1981 and 1983, Glenys Barton at Wedgwood (Crafts Cncl Gallery) 1977, Heads: Sculpture and Drawings (Angela Flowers Gallery) 1986, Artists and Green Warriors (Flowers East) 1990, Northern Centre for Contemporary Art 1991, New Sculpture (Flowers East) 1993, Portraits (Angela Flowers Gallery) 1994, New Sculpture (Flowers East at London Fields) 1996, Glenys Barton Portraits (Nat Portrait Gallery) 1997, Dreaming Edge (Manchester City Art Gallery and Stoke-on-Trent) 1997 and 1998, In Profile (Flowers West Gallery Santa Monica CA) 2000, Children of Silence and Slow Time (Flowers Central) 2003, Enduring Love (Flowers East London) 2004, Flowers NY 2007, Dancers and Angels (Flowers Central) 2009, Glenys Barton Sculpture (One Canada Square) 2010, Glenys Barton (Cartwright Hall Bradford) 2010–11; *Group Exhibitions* Images of Man (ICA) 1980, Sculptures in Clay (Yorkshire Sculpture Park) 1980, Nudes (Angela Flowers Gallery) 1980–81, Art into the Eighties (Walker Art Gallery and The Fruitmarket) 1981, A Taste of British Art Today (Contemporary Art Soc Brussels) 1982, South Bank Show (Arts Cncl) 1982, Small Is Beautiful – Part 3 (Angela Flowers Gallery) 1983, Black and White (Angela Flowers Gallery) 1985, Small Is Beautiful – Part 4 (Angela Flowers Gallery) 1985, Sixteen Years Sixteen Artists (Angela Flowers Gallery) 1986, Multiplemedia (Nicholson Gallery) 1986, Sixteen Artists – Process and Product (Turnpike Gallery) 1987, Contemporary Portraits (Flowers East) 1988 and 1990, Figure 11 Naked (Aberystwyth Arts Centre and tour) 1988, The Face (Arkansas Arts Center) 1988, Out of Clay (Manchester City Art Gallery) 1988, Small Is Beautiful – Part 6 (Flowers East) 1988, Angela Flowers Gallery 1990 (Barbican Centre) 1989, Badge Art 11 (Flowers East) 1989, Colours of the Earth (Arts Cncl tour) 1990, Small Is Beautiful – Part 8 The Figure (Flowers East) 1990, Angela Flowers Gallery 1991 (Flowers East) 1991, Nudes (Watermans Arts Centre) 1991, Artist's Choice (Flowers East) 1992, Small Is Beautiful – Part 10 Animals (Flowers East) 1992, Portrait of the Artist's Mother Done From Memory (Flowers East) 1992, Decouvertes (Grand Palais Paris) 1993, The Portrait Now (National Portrait Gallery) 1993, The Contemporary Print Show (Barbican) 1995, Contemporary Sculpture (Collyer Bristow) 1995, The Twenty Fifth Anniversary Exhibition (Flowers East) 1995, Flowers at Koplin (Koplin Gallery LA) 1995, Methods and Materials of Sculpture (Nat Portrait Gallery) 1995, Angela Flowers Gallery (Ireland) 1996, Hot off the Press (Carlisle and tour) 1996, Gwenda Jay Gallery (Chicago) 1997, British Figurative Art Part Two Sculpture Flowers East, Angela Flowers Gallery 30th Anniversary Exhibition (Flowers East London and Flowers West Santa Monica CA) 2000, Flowers One (Flowers Central) 2000, Small is Beautiful – Self Portraits (Nat Portrait Gallery) 2000, Royal Acad Summer Exhbn 2000, 2001 and 2002, Mirror Mirror (Nat Portrait Gallery) 2001, Glenys Barton and Carole Hodgson – Multiples and Monoprints (Flowers Graphics) 2001, Small is Beautiful – Still Life (Flowers East) 2001, Mirror Mirror (Nat Portrait Gallery) 2001, Aboutface (Croydon Clocktower) 2002, Small is Beautiful – Voyage (Flowers East) 2002, Stirling Stuff (Gallery Pangolin Chalford) 2002 (also at Royal Acad and Sigurjon Olafsson Sculpture Museum Reykjavik 2003), Thinking Big (Guggenheim Venice) 2002, Relative Values (PM Gallery and House London) 2003, Small is Beautiful XXII (Flowers Central) 2004, Sculptures and Drawings (Flowers East) 2005, 35th Anniversary Exhbn (Flowers East London) 2005, Five Figurative Sculptors (Flowers Central, Francis Burrows Fine Art, Arts Creative Chesterfield) 2005, Discerning Eye (Mall Galleries London) 2005 and 2006, Small is Beautiful (Flowers Central) 2005, Sculpture in Paradise (Chichester Cathedral) 2006–07, New Works by Gallery Sculptors (Flowers Central) 2006, Heads (Flowers East and Catmose Gallery Rutland) 2006, Small is Beautiful (Flowers Central) 2007, 2010, 2013 and 2015, (Flowers NY) 2007, 2014 and 2015 and (Flowers East) 2009 and 2012, Royal Acad Summer Exhbn 2008, Summer Selections (Flowers NY) 2008, Best of Silver: Selected Sculptures in Silver (Pangolin London) 2011, Art (Lloyd's Club London) 2012, Sculptor's Drawings and Works on Paper (Pangolin London) 2012, British Design 1948–2012: Innovation in the Modern Age (V&A) 2012, Selected Artists (Flowers Central) 2013, Angela Flowers at 80 (Flowers East) 2013, Blue and White: British Printed Ceramics (V&A) 2015, FiveSixSevenEight (Here Arts Centre NY) 2015, The British Figure (Flowers East) 2015; *Work in Public Collections* incl: Birmingham Museum and Art Gallery, Contemporary Art Soc, Crafts Cncl, Leeds Museum and Art Gallery, National Gallery of Victoria, Princessehoff Museum, Royal Scottish Museum (now Nat Museums Scotland), Manchester Museum and Art Gallery, Stockholm Museum, Pennsylvania State Univ MOMA, V&A, National Portrait Gallery, Scottish National Portrait Gallery, Ashmolean Museum, Br Museum, Museum Van Bonijams Beuningen, The Hepworth Wakefield, Wedgewood Museum, Norwich Castle Museum and Art Gallery, Southampton City Art Gallery; *Projects* Landmark East (East of Eng Devpt Agency competition) 2004, Somewhere We Meet (wall sculpture) for Hextable Dance 2006 (shortlisted Rowse Kent Public Art Awards), collaboration with film dir Roger Michell on Enduring Love 2003 (practice, studio and sculptures inform and feature in the film, incl portrait commissions of Bill Nighy and Daniel Craig), medal for British Art Medal Soc Dept for Coins and Medals Br Museum 2012; *Style*— Ms Glenys Barton; ✉ c/o Flowers East, 82 Kingsland Road, London E2 8DP

BARTON, Jonathan Edmund (Jon); s of Edmund Barton (d 1985), and Marjorie, *née* Pitt-Watson (d 2007); *b* 7 September 1950; *Educ* King James's GS Huddersfield, The Lakes Comp Sch Windermere, Emmanuel Coll Cambridge (sr scholar, MA), Dept of Educn Univ of Oxford (CertEd); *m* 1972, Margaret, *née* Course; 2 da (Sarah b 1975, Hannah b 1985), 1 s (Joseph b 1977); *Career* schoolteacher 1971–78, head of languages International School Moshi Tanzania 1978–80; freelance local radio reporter 1980–81, prodr Radio Derby 1981–84 (progs incl Barbed Wireless); BBC TV: prodr of current affrs (progs incl Sixty Minutes, The Money Programme, Breakfast Time) 1985, sometime asst ed Six O'Clock News, asst ed then dep ed and acting ed Newsnight 1988–94, ed One O'Clock News and Six O'Clock News 1994–96; ed Today Radio 4 BBC Radio 1996–98, exec ed of current affrs BBC TV 1998–2000; Reuters fell Green Coll Oxford 2000, conslt Trinity Communications Brunswick Gp 2000–01, head of media Christian Aid 2001–02, dir of communications Nat Tst 2002–04, fndr Clarify Communications 2004; *Recreations* music, literature, mountains, politics, cross-country running, making things work, cycling, canoeing; *Style*— Jon Barton, Esq; ✉ 38B Brook Street, Watlington, Oxfordshire OX9 5JH (☎ 01491 612519, e-mail jon.barton@btinternet.com)

BARTON, (Malcolm) Peter Speight; DL (Gtr London); s of Michael Hugh Barton (d 1996), and Diana Blanche, *née* Taylor (d 2007); *b* 26 March 1937; *Educ* St Edward's Sch Oxford, Magdalen Coll Oxford (MA); *m* 7 Sept 1963, Julia Margaret, da of Hon James Louis Lindsay (d 1997); 1 da (Fenella (Mrs Nicholas Clements) b 1965), 2 s (Henry (Harry) b 1967, Christopher b 1970); *Career* Nat Serv 2 Lt Oxford and Bucks LI (later 1 Greenjackets) 1955–56, Capt London Rifle Bde Rangers TA 1960–63; admitted slr 1964; ptnr Travers Smith Braithwaite 1967–86; md corp fin Lehman Bros 1986–95; dir: Robert Fleming & Co Ltd 1995–99, Lambert Fenchurch Group plc 1998–99, Alliance & Leicester plc 1998–2007 (dep chm 2000–07), Jupiter (formerly F&C) US Smaller Companies plc 1998–, The Guinness Partnership 1999–2011 (chm 2007–11), Bramdean Alternatives Ltd 2007–09, easyGroup Hldgs Ltd 2008–, Howard de Walden Estates Ltd (chm 1998–), Bramdean Asset Mgmnt LLP (chm 2008–12), Chelsminster Gp Ltd (chm 2009–13), G Martin Construction Ltd (chm 2012–14), Winmark Ltd (chm 2014–); chm of tstees Alliance & Leicester Pension Fund 2007–09; advsr Armstrong Bonham Carter LLP; chm Leonard Ingrams Fndn 2007–16; memb: Gloucester Diocesan Finance Ctee 2005–15, Audit and Scrutiny Ctee Univ of Oxford 2007–14, Finance Ctee Royal Cmmn for the Exhibition of 1851 2009–14, Law Soc, Cncl Stelios Philanthropic Fndn; MSI (memb Stock Exchange 1986); High Sheriff Gtr London 2000–01; *Recreations* walking, shooting; *Clubs* Brooks's, City of London, City Law, Rifle Brigade; *Style*— Peter Barton, Esq, DL; ✉ Sydenhams, Bisley, Gloucestershire GL6 7BU (☎ 01452 770837, e-mail peter.barton@sydenhams.net)

BARTON, HE Philip; CMG, OBE; *m* Amanda; 2 c; *Career* diplomat; asst desk offr Economic Relations Dept FCO 1987, third then second sec (chancery) Caracas 1987–91, head Instns

Section EU (Internal) Dept FCO 1993–94, first sec (external) New Delhi 1994–96, private sec to the PM 1997–2000, dep high cmmr Nicosia 2000–04, dep govr Gibraltar 2005–08, additional dir S Asia FCO 2008–09, dir foreign policy and Afghanistan/Pakistan coordinator Cabinet Office 2009–11, dep head of mission Washington DC 2011–13, high cmmr to Pakistan 2014–16; *Style—* HE Mr Philip Barton, CMG, OBE; ✉ c/o FCO (Islamabad), King Charles Street, London SW1A 2AH

BARTON-BRECK, Jules; *née* Breck; da of Verdun Breck, of Rothes, Scotland, and Jilly, *née* Harding (d 2000); *b* 15 December 1965, London; *Educ* Newstead Wood GS for Girls, Orpington Coll of FE; *m* 30 Aug 2000, Dr Andrew Barton-Breck; *Career* assoc ed Prima 1995–99; ed: Safeway Magazine 1999–2002, Family Circle 2002–04, Essentials 2004–13; freelance ed/ lifestyle and interiors journalist 2013–; memb BSME 1999–; BSME Ed of the Year 2011; *Recreations* holidaying in France, dinner parties, reading, online shopping, American TV, pottering in the garden, The Telegraph crosswords, walking my Dachshunds, relaxing in Isles of Scilly, 500 card game, renovating 400-year-old cottage; *Style—* Jules Barton-Breck; ✉ e-mail julessaysso@icloud.com

BARWELL, Gavin Laurence; MP; s of David Barwell (d 2005), and Jennifer, *née* Maeer; *b* 23 January 1972, Cuckfield, W Sussex; *Educ* Trinity Sch of John Whitgift Croydon, Trinity Coll Cambridge; *m* 2001, Karen; 3 s; *Career* memb Croydon Cncl 1998–2010, ops dir Cons Pty until 2006, MP (Cons) Croydon Central 2010–; memb Court of Govrs Whitgift Fndn, chm Trinity Sch of John Whitgift Croydon; *Recreations* football, tennis, reading, gardening; *Style—* Gavin Barwell, Esq, MP; ✉ House of Commons, London SW1A 0AA (☎ 020 7219 7044)

BARYLSKI, Patricia Ann; da of Theodore Barylski, and Teresa Sporcic Barylski; *Educ* Univ of Illinois (Phi Beta Kappa academic honours, BA), SOAS Univ of London (MA); *m* Geoffrey Newman, OBE; *Career* Business International Geneva 1977–81, Time-Life Books 1981–82; freelance publishing and teaching 1982–87: British Museum, Cncl of Europe, SOAS External Services, SOAS Intermediate Certificate Course; dep ed The Dictionary of Art 1987–94, series ed Art & Ideas Phaidon Press 1994–2002, managing ed teaching and learning materials City & Guilds 2002–; awarded: Fulbright grant to India 1965–66, SOAS External Studies Fellowship 1981–82; memb: Friends of British Library, Friends of British Museum, Royal Asiatic Soc, Soc for S Asian Studies; *Books* The Hindu World (1982), India, Pakistan and Bangladesh: A Handbook for Teachers (1982), Hinduism (1984); *Style—* Ms Patricia Barylski; ✉ City & Guilds, 1 Giltspur Street, London EC1A 9DD (☎ 020 7294 8191, e-mail pat.barylski@cityandguilds.com)

BASELEY, Stewart; *Career* Crest Homes Weybridge: land and sales mangr 1982–93, land and sales dir 1983–85, dep md 1985–87; Charles Church plc: exec dir 1987–90, ceo 1990–96; Beazer Gp plc (following takeover): chm and ceo Charles Church 1996–98, memb Bd 1996–98, chm Beazer Strategic Land 1996–98; chm and ceo Centex UK 1998–2005, exec chm Home Builder's Fedn 2005– (memb Bd 2002–, chm 2004–05); chm: Habitat for Humanity 2012–, Housebuilder Media Ltd; memb Bd: Nat House Building Cncl, Banner Homes Gp plc 2007–15, H&H Int A/S Denmark, Medi System sp zoo, Akomex, Pro Service sp zoo, UEPC, Druk-Pak SA (Poland), Zrew Transformatory SA (Poland); patron Children with Special Needs Fndn; *Clubs* Harlequins Rugby, West Hill Golf, Royal Berks Racquet, Mosimann's, Wentworth, RAC Pall Mall, Quinto Do Lago Laranjal; *Style—* Stewart Baseley, Esq; ✉ Home Builders Federation, HBF House, 27 Broadwall, London SE1 9PL

BASS, Stephen Michael John; s of late John Charles Bass, CBE, of Weston Favell, Northants, and late Jean Edith Angel, *née* Stark; *b* 6 May 1958; *Educ* Northampton Sch for Boys, Oriel Coll Oxford (MA), Univ of Manchester (BLD), St Cross Coll Oxford (Osmaston scholarship, MSc); *m* 4 Sept 1982 Christine Anne, da of Lt-Col Kenneth Sydney Gittens; 2 da (Maria Hannah Danai b 7 Jan 1989, Sophie Anne Rose b 13 April 1991); *Career* World Conservation Union 1984–89: social forestry advsr to Aga Khan Fndn Pakistan, res advsr to Nat Conservation Strategies (Nepal and Zambia), set up seven-country prog in Southern Africa; Warren Weaver Fellowship Rockefeller Fndn 1989–90 developing grant progs in forestry and biodiversity; Int Inst for Environment and Devpt: dir of forestry and land use 1990–, dir of progs responsible for 25-country prog of research and training 1999–2003; chief environment advsr DfID 2003–05; chair Ecosystem Services for Poverty Alleviation DFID/NERC/ESRC; sr assoc Int Inst for Environment and Devpt 2005–, fell Worldwide Fund for Nature, hon sr fell World Conservation Monitoring Centre; Coopers Hill War Meml Prize 1984, Queen's Award for Forestry (for services to int forest initiatives) 2001; MSB 2010 (MIBiol 1986); *Books* co-author of several books incl: Plantation Politics (1992), Strategies for National Sustainable Development (1994), The Forest Certification Handbook (1995), The Sustainable Forestry Handbook (1999), Policy That Works for Forests and People (1999), Sustainable Development Strategies (2002), Reducing Poverty and Sustaining the Environment (2005), The Challenges of Environmental Mainstreaming (2009), Scoping a Green Economy (2013); author of numerous scientific papers and articles; *Recreations* jazz (play drums), drawing, gardening, kitsch ephemera; *Style—* Stephen Bass, Esq; ✉ International Institute for Environment and Development, 80–86 Gray's Inn Road, London WC1X 8NH (☎ 020 3463 7399, e-mail stephen.bass@iied.org)

BASSAM OF BRIGHTON, Baron (Life Peer UK 1997), of Brighton in the County of East Sussex; John Steven (Steve) Bassam; s of late Sydney Steven and Enid Bassam, of Colchester, Essex; *b* 11 June 1953; *Educ* Clacton Secdy Sch, NE Essex Tech Coll, Univ of Sussex (BA), Univ of Kent (MA); *Partner* Jill; 2 s (Thomas Harry b 1988, Gregory John b Sept 1994, d Oct 1994), 2 da (Lauren Stephanie b 1990, Ellen Rose b 1995); *Career* social worker E Sussex CC 1976–77, legal advsr N Lewisham Law Centre 1979–83; policy advsr: London Borough of Camden 1983–84, GLC Policy Ctee 1984–86, London Strategic Policy Unit 1986–87; asst sec Police Fire Environmental Health and Consumer Affairs AMA 1988–97, head of environment health and consumer affairs Local Govt Assoc 1997–98; occasional journalist for local govt publications; memb (Lab) Brighton BC 1983–97 (ldr 1987–97), memb Brighton and Hove Unitary Cncl 1996–99 (ldr 1996–); min Home Office 1999–2001, Govt min Whips Office and spokesman for Home Offfice, Dept for Tport and Dept for Communities and Local Govt, chief whip 2008–15, Chief Whip House of Lords 2015–; patron Brighton Festival; memb: Labour Pty, Co-op Pty, Fabian Soc; hon fell Univ of Sussex, fell Brighton Coll; *Recreations* cricket, football fan (Brighton & Hove Albion), running; *Clubs* Preston Village CC; *Style—* The Rt Hon the Lord Bassam of Brighton; ✉ House of Lords, London SW1A 0PW (e-mail bassams@parliament.uk)

BASSET, Gerard Francis Claude; OBE (2011); s of Pierre René Basset (d 1976), and Marguerite, *née* Conorton; *b* 7 March 1957; *Educ* Lycee Albert Camus Firminy France, Ecole Hoteliere de Dardilly Lyon France; *m* 1997, Nina, *née* Howe; 1 s (Romané b 17 May 1999); *Career* sommelier; commis de cuisine Frantel Hotel Marseille 1981–83, head waiter The Crown Hotel Lyndhurst Hants 1984–85 (chef de rang 1983–84), head waiter Morel's Haslemere 1985–86, Manley's Storrington W Sussex 1986–87, head waiter The Crown Hotel Lyndhurst 1987–88, chef sommelier Chewton Glen Hotel New Milton Hants 1988–94; co-fndr and dir Hotel du Vin Hotel Gp 1994–2004, co-prop Hotel du Vin & Bistro Winchester 1994–2004, gp hotels in Tunbridge Wells, Bristol and Birmingham; prop Hotel TerraVina Hants 2007–; dir GB Wine Consultancy Ltd; fell Acad of Food and Wine Service (tech dir 1997), vice-chm Ct of Master Sommeliers; memb: Commendeur of French Gastronomy 1988, 3 Ceps St Bris 1989, Acad of Wine Service 1989, Cava and Penedes Inst 1993, Verre Galant (Cognac Camus) 1993, Coll du Cognac 1993, Cognac Inst 1994, Sommeliers Club of GB 1994, Acad of Culinary Arts 1995, Inst Masters of Wine 1998; assoc memb UK Bartenders Guild; *Awards* Best Sommelier for french wines and spirits in UK 1988 and 1992, Wine Waiter of the Year 1989 and 1992, winner Southern Sommelier Competition 1989, Calvet Cup of Acad of Wine Service (for overall outstanding achievement in wine knowledge and service) 1989, 1990 and 1992, Bronze Medal Best Sommelier in Euro Competition Reims 1990 and 1992, Champagne Travel Bursary 1990, winner Ruinart UK Selection for Euro 1990, winner Int Sommelier Competition Paris 1992, Silver Medal World Championship Rio de Janeiro 1992, Courvoisier Best of the Best Sommelier 1992, Marques de Caceres Food & Wine Person of the Year 1993, Rame d'Honneur (for servs given to wine) 1993, winner Euro Trophee Ruinart Reims 1996, World's Best Sommelier Association de la Sommellerie 2010, Int Wine Challenge Personality of the Year 2010, Harpers Wine and Spirit Personality of the Year 2011, Imbibe Industry Legend 2011, UK Restaurateurs Hall of Fame 2013, Best Ambassador and Communicator for French Wines Harpers 2013, Inaugural Catey for The Wine & Spirit Ambassador 2014; for Hotel du Vin: Egon Ronay Cellnet Guide Newcomer of the Year 1996, Catey Award Newcomer of the Year 1996, Caesar Good Hotel Guide Best Hotel with Wine Theme 1998; Cesar Best Small Hotel Good Hotel Guide (for Hotel TerraVina) 2009, Decanter Man of the Year 2013; *Books* The Wine Experience (2000); *Recreations* chess, ice-skating; *Style—* Gerard Basset, Esq, OBE; ✉ Hotel TerraVina, 174 Woodlands Road, Woodlands, Southampton SO40 7GL (☎ 02380 293784, e-mail g.basset@btinternet.com, website www.hotelterravina.co.uk, Twitter @GerardBassetOBE)

BASSEY, Dame Shirley; DBE (2000); *b* 1937, Cardiff; *Career* singer; early career as worker in local factory, perfomer Al Read Christmas Show (Adelphi Theatre London) 1955, performer Such Is Life 1956, live show NY and Las Vegas 1962, released numerous hit singles 1960s-; theme tunes for James Bond films Goldfinger 1964, Diamonds are Forever 1971 and Moonraker 1979; *Albums* incl: The Fabulous 1959, Shirley Bassey 1961, Shirley 1962, Lets Face the Music 1965, Shirley Bassey at the Pigalle 1965, Shirley Stops The Shows 1966, I've Got a Song For You 1967, And We Were Lovers 1968, This Is My Life 1969, Does Anybody Miss Me? 1970, Something 1970, Live at Talk of the Town 1970, Shirley Bassey Is Really Something 1971, Something Else 1972, I Capricorn 1972, And I Love You So 1973, Live at Carnegie Hall 1973, Never, Never, Never 1974, Nobody Does It Like Me 1974, Shirley Means Bassey 1975, Good, Bad But Beautiful 1976, Love, Life and Feelings 1978, Magic Is You 1982, All by Myself 1985, Sassy Bassey 1989, La Mujer 1991, New York, New York 1991, Keep the Music Playing 1995, Sings the Songs of Andrew Lloyd Webber 1998, Birthday Concert 1998, 'S Wonderful, Nobody Does It Like Me 1998, Let Me Sing and I'm Happy 1998, Sings the Movies 1998, Power of Love 1999, Something 2002, That's What Friends Are For 2003, Old Friends and Lovers 2003, Thank You for the Years 2003; *Style—* Dame Shirley Bassey, DBE

BASSI, Avinash; *b* 16 April 1960, Punjab, India; *m* 19 Aug 1980, Nina; 2 da (Tina b 30 Oct 1982, Natasha b 29 Jan 1986), 1 s (Rahul b 26 Feb 1992); *Career* entrepreneur; market trader 1978, prop Talk of the Town (8 shops) 1982–88, estab distribution centre 1983, fndr and owner Duke Clothing Co and Bassi Fashions Ltd 2000–, prop Rockford, fndr and owner Bassi Properties Ltd (a div of Bassi Gp (Nottingham)); memb Nottingham C of C; London Thames Today magazine Best Co of the Year 2003; runner-up Asian Jewels Awards 2006; *Recreations* badminton, exercise, travelling; *Clubs* David Lloyd, Global Punjabi Soc; *Style—* Avinash Bassi, Esq; ✉ Duke Clothing Company, Duke House, Northern Court, Vernon Road, Basford, Nottingham NG6 0BJ

BASSI, (Paramjit) Paul Singh; CBE (2010), DL (W Midlands 2009); s of Santokh Singh Bassi, of Birmingham, and Avtar Kaur, *née* Chaudry; *b* 21 March 1962, Birmingham; *Educ* Harlington Comp Sch Hayes, Sandwell Coll; *m* Priya Paula, *née* Narang; 2 da (Terri Kaur b 6 July 1988, Nikita b 1 Sept 1991), 1 s (Bobby Singh b 11 June 1990); *Career* fndr chm Bond Wolfe 1985–, regnl chm Coutts Bank 2000– (memb Executive Steering Bd 2006–), non-exec dir Real Estate Investors plc, vice-chm Bigwood Chartered Surveyors 2006, chief exec Real Estate Investors plc 2007, non-exec chm CP Bigwood Chartered Surveyors; former dir Birmingham Hippodrome; dir EFG IFA 2011; West Midlands ambass, former vice-pres C of C, pres Birmingham C of C 2009; Entrepreneur of the Year Asian Jewel Awards 2003, Lifetime Achievement Award Lloyds TSB 2005, Entrepreneur of the Year Midlands Finance Insider Award 2010; High Sheriff W Midlands 2009; hon doctorate: Birmingham City Univ 2010, Aston Univ 2011; *Recreations* tennis, racquetball, keep-fit, sport, reading, travel, prestige cars; *Style—* Paul Bassi, Esq, CBE, DL

BASU, Dr Dijendra (Dijen); QC (2015); s of Dr Dipendra Bhushan Basu, and late Dr Shashi Kanta Basu; *b* 10 August 1968, Solihull, W Midlands; *Educ* Guy's Hosp (MB BS); *Children* 1 da (Alyana b 20 July 2004); *Career* called to the Bar 1994; recorder of the Crown Ct 2009; memb AGs Panel of Special Advocates 2010; *Recreations* flying; *Style—* Dr Dijen Basu, QC; ✉ 5 Essex Court, Temple, London EC4Y 9AH (☎ 020 7410 2000, e-mail basu@5essexcourt.co.uk)

BASU, Dr Himansu Kumar; s of Sudhangsu Kumar Basu (d 1992), and Rajlaxmi, *née* Ghosh (d 1950); *b* 10 April 1934; *Educ* Gopalpur Acad and Calcutta Med Coll Univ of Calcutta (MB BS), Univ of Liverpool (PhD); *m* Lynda Ann, da of late Ronald Sanders, of Rochester, Kent; 1 da (Maya Louise b 1979), 1 s (Christopher Kumar b 1984); *Career* lectr in obstetrics and gynaecology Univ of Liverpool 1965–72, conslt obstetrician and gynaecologist Dartford and Gravesham NHS Tst 1972–98, med dir Multicare Int London 1998–2000; medical dir Rotarian Action Gp on Population Devpt 2012–, co-ordinator on maternal and child health Rotary Int 2013–; SE Gynaecological Soc: sec 1976–82, vice-pres 1984–86, treas 1987–91, pres 1991–96; RCOG: memb Cncl 1977–83, 1988–91 and 1993–99, memb Fin and Exec Ctee 1980–83 and 1998–99, memb Examination Ctee 1981–84; Overseas Doctors Training offr 1996–1999, convenor MRCOG courses 1999–2002, prog dir Calmed Maternal Mortality Reduction Prog; Section of Obstetrics and Gynaecology RSM: memb Cncl 1979–88 and 1994–2006, hon sec 1983–84, vice-pres 1985–88, pres 1995–96; chm Osprey's Gynaecological Soc 1981–84; examiner for MB ChB, DRCOG, MRCOG and FRCS; Ethel Boyce fell Univ of Liverpool 1967, William Blair Bell lectr RCOG 1969, Catherine Bishop Harman prize BMA 1969, Eden fell RCOG 1970, Rotary Champions of Change Award 2016, Time Sternberg Award 2016; memb: Br Fertility Soc, Br Soc of Gynaecological Endoscopy, American Assoc of Gynaecological Laparoscopists (int advsr 1998–2001); chm Int Fellowship of Rotarian Physicians 1999–, district govr Kent and E Sussex Rotary Int 2004–05; FRCSEd, FRCOG; *Recreations* travel, photography, radio broadcasting; *Clubs* Royal Over-Seas League; *Style—* Dr Himansu Basu; ✉ Glengarry, Woodlands Lane, Shorne, Gravesend, Kent DA12 3HH (☎ and fax 01474 822294, e-mail drhbasumd@gmail.com)

BATCHELOR, Andrew Goolden Grant; s of Lt-Col Hugh Thomas Nicolas Batchelor (d 1976), and Margaret Irene, *née* Grant; *b* 28 August 1951; *Educ* Whitchurch HS, St Mary's Hosp Med Sch Univ of London (BSc, MB BS); *m* 3 Nov 1973, Rosemary Marion, da of Horace William Gibson, of Melksham, Wilts; 1 s (Thomas b 18 April 1980), 1 da (Elizabeth b 6 Oct 1982); *Career* surgical res King Edward VII Hosp Paget Bermuda 1978–79, sr house offr in gen surgery St Mary's Hosp London 1979–80, registrar in gen surgery Queen Elizabeth II Hosp Welwyn Gdn City 1980–81, sr house offr in plastic surgery Wexham Park Hosp Slough 1981–82, registrar in plastic surgery Nottingham City 1982–84, sr registrar W of Scotland Regnl Plastic Surgery Unit 1984–86, sr clinical lectr in surgery Univ of Leeds 1986–; conslt plastic surgn: St James's Hosp Gen Infirmary Leeds 1986–, S York Dist Hosp 1988– (clinical dir plastic surgery 1993–); memb Cncl British Assoc of Plastic Surgns 1993– (memb 1986); memb: Br Microsurgical Soc 1982, Br Soc of Head and Neck Oncologists 1986, Br Assoc of Aesthetic Plastic Surgns 1988; FRCS, FRCS (Plastic Surgns); *Books* contrib: Essential Surgical Practice (1988), Tissue Expansion

(1989), Excision and Reconstruction in Head and Neck Cancer (1993); *Recreations* sailing, shooting; *Style*— Andrew Batchelor, Esq; ✉ Field House, 10 Sicklinghall Road, Wetherby, West Yorkshire LS22 6AA (☎ 01937 583654); Department of Plastic Surgery, St James's University Hospital, Beckett Street, Leeds LS8 1DF (☎ 0113 243 3144)

BATCHELOR, Lance; s of David Batchelor, and Sarah, *née* Glasson; *b* 9 January 1964, London; *Educ* Cranleigh Sch, Univ of Wales Aberystwyth (BSc), Harvard Business Sch (MBA); *m* Wendy, *née* Doran; 4 s; *Career* Lt Royal Navy 1985–91; mktg dir Procter & Gamble 1991–2000, gen mangr Amazon.com 2000–02, Vodafone 2002–06, mktg dir Tesco 2007–08, chief exec Tesco Telecoms 2008–11, ceo Domino's Pizza Gp plc 2011–14, ceo Saga plc 2014–; tstee Nat Gall 2011–; *Recreations* sailing, fine art; *Clubs* 67, Royal Naval Sailing Assoc; *Style*— Lance Batchelor, Esq; ✉ Saga plc, Enbrook Park, Sandgate, Kent CT20 3SE

BATCHELOR, Paul Anthony; s of Joseph John Batchelor (d 1963), and Irene Margaret, *née* Shoobridge (d 2011); *b* 4 July 1946; *Educ* Ashford GS, St John's Coll Cambridge (coll scholar, MA, Dip Devpt Econs, Philip Lake Prize, Hughes and Wright Prizes, Larmor Award, David Richards travelling scholar); *m* 5 July 1969, Janet, da of Jack Rowden King; 1 da (Emma Jane b 16 May 1972), 1 s (Jonathan Mark b 12 Feb 1976); *Career* vol teacher Miny of Educn Zambia 1965, supervisor of studies in geography St John's Coll Cambridge 1968–69, govt economist Swaziland 1969–72, acting chief economist Office of the President & Cabinet Malawi 1973–74 (sr economist 1972–73); PricewaterhouseCoopers (formerly Coopers & Lybrand before merger): joined as econ conslt 1974, ptnr 1982–2004, chm Int Mgmnt Consulting Servs Exec 1989–95, ptnr i/c Mgmnt Consulting Servs Europe 1990–94, exec ptnr i/c Coopers & Lybrand Europe 1994–98, memb Global Mgmnt Team 1998–2004, global geography and strategy ldr 2002–04; dir: PricewaterhouseCoopers Development Associates Ltd 2004–06, EBE Ltd 2004–13, Langham Partnership UKI 2005–14, Abacus Consulting (Pvt) Ltd Pakistan 2008–; chm: Oxford Policy Mgmnt Ltd 2006–13, Crown Agents Ltd 2007–15, Crown Agents Bank 2008–, Stour Music Festival 2012–; memb Int Advsy Cncl Transparency Int until 2015, memb Int Steering Gp AIESEC 2003–10, currently memb UK Advsy Cncl Transparency Int; churchwarden St Nicholas Sevenoaks 2001–07; tstee WaterAid 2009–15; Liveryman Worshipful Co of Mgmnt Conslts 1994; FIBC 1980, FIMC 1980–; *Recreations* classical music, gardening, golf, mountain walking; *Clubs* Hever Golf, Royal Overseas League; *Style*— Paul Batchelor, Esq; ✉ 3 Burntwood Grove, Sevenoaks, Kent TN13 1PZ (e-mail pauljanetbatchelor@yahoo.co.uk); 172 Route de la Corne, La Beunaz, St Paul en Chablais 74500, France; Crown Agents, St Nicholas House, St Nicholas Road, Sutton, Surrey SM1 1EL (☎ 020 8643 3311)

BATE, David Christopher; QC (1994); s of Robert Leslie Bate (d 1954), of Mill Hill, London, and Brenda Mabel, *née* Price; *b* 2 May 1945; *Educ* Hendon Co GS, Univ of Manchester (LLB); *m* 1; 3 s (Tristan David Leslie b 1 June 1976, Simeon James Jonathan b 13 Nov 1978, Diccon Mark Julian b 30 March 1983), 1 da (Wendy Jeanne Alison b 3 Feb 1981); m 2, 20 Oct 2003, Fiona Adele, da of Samuel Graham; *Career* called to the Bar Gray's Inn 1969, VSO 1969–71, crown counsel Protectorate British Solomon Islands 1971, asst recorder 1989, recorder of the Crown Court 1992–; memb Criminal Bar Assoc; *Recreations* trying to sing in tune, with Counterpoint and Cantemus, swimming; *Style*— David Bate, Esq, QC; ✉ QEB Hollis Whiteman Chambers, 2 Laurence Pountney Hill, London EC4R 0EU (☎ 020 7933 8855, e-mail barristers@qebhw.co.uk)

BATE, Dr Jennifer Lucy; OBE (2008); da of Horace Alfred Bate, and Dorothy Marjorie, *née* Hunt; *b* 11 November 1944; *Educ* Tollington GS, Univ of Bristol (BA); *Career* asst organist St James Muswell Hill 1955–78; superintendent Shaw Library LSE 1966–69; full time musician 1969–, int organist performing in over 40 countries including most major festivals and BBC Promenade concerts, specialist in eighteenth century Eng organ music, appeared frequently with Dolmetsch Ensemble at Haslemere Festival of Early Music, interpreter of romantic and modern music; world authy on works of the composer Olivier Messiaen, soloist at Br Première of Messiaen's Livre du Saint Sacrement at Westminster Cathedral, opened a series on the complete organ works of Messiaen on Radio France in the presence of the composer; designer (with Mander Organs) portable pipe organ and (with Wyvern Organs) a new type of digital electronic organ; collaborator with many contemporary composers; teacher: Master Classes, lectures and talks (for all ages in 5 languages), lead tutor annual Jennifer Bate Organ Acad St Catherine's Sch Bramley 2004; works written for her incl: Paraphrase on 'Salve Regina' (by Flor Peeters), Blue Rose Variations (by Peter Dickinson), Fenestra (by William Mathias); memb: Royal Soc of Musicians, Royal Philharmonic Soc, Br Music Soc (vice-pres), Incorporated Soc of Musicians; Hon Dr Univ of Bristol 2007; FRCO, LRAM (organ performer), ARCM (organ performer); FRSA 2002; Officier de l'ordre des Arts et des Lettres 2011, Chevalier de la Légion d'Honneur 2011; *Awards* GLAA Young Musician 1972, Personnalité de l'Année (France) 1990; Silver plaque for services to music: Alassio (Italy), Garbagna (Italy) and hon citizenship for servs to music 1996; *Recordings* over 30 incl: From Stanley to Wesley (6 Vols, winner Retailers' Assoc Award for Early Music 1991), Liszt & Schumann, Elgar and his English Contemporaries, complete organ works of Franck and Messiaen (awarded Grand Prix du Disque for Livre du Saint Sacrement), Organ Music by Samuel Wesley, The Wesleys and their Contemporaries, The Complete Organ Works of Felix Mendelssohn, The Complete Solo Organ Works of Peter Dickinson, Messiaen – La Nativité du Seigneur (DVD); *Music Published* Introduction and Variations on an Old French Carol, Four Reflections, Hommage to 1685, Toccata on a Theme of Martin Shaw, Canone Inglese, Lament: Variations on a Gregorian Theme, Grove's Dictionary of Music and Musicians (contrib); *Recreations* gardening, cooking; *Style*— Dr Jennifer Bate, OBE; ✉ 35 Collingwood Avenue, Muswell Hill, London N10 3EH (☎ 020 8883 3811, fax 020 8444 3695, e-mail jenniferbate@classical-artists.com, website www.classical-artists.com/jbate)

BATE, Prof Sir (Andrew) Jonathan; kt (2015), CBE (2006); s of Ronald Montagu Bate (d 1978), and Sylvia Helen, *née* Tait (d 2003); *b* 26 June 1958; *Educ* Sevenoaks Sch, St Catharine's Coll Cambridge (T R Henn English scholar, Charles Oldham Shakespeare scholar, MA, PhD); *m* 1, 1984 (m dis 1995), Hilary Lorna, da of Prof Maxwell Gaskin; m 2, 1996, Paula Jayne, da of Timothy Byrne; 2 s (Thomas Montague b 1998, Harry Sebastian b 2006), 1 da (Elinor Clare b 2000); *Career* Harkness fell Harvard Univ 1980–81; research fell St Catharine's Coll Cambridge 1983–85, fell Trinity Hall and lectr Girton Coll Cambridge 1985–90; King Alfred prof of English literature Univ of Liverpool 1991–2003, prof of Shakespeare and Renaissance literature Univ of Warwick 2003–11; provost Worcester Coll Oxford 2011–, prof of English literature Univ of Oxford 2011–; Br Acad research reader 1994–96, Leverhulme personal research prof 1999–2004, vice-pres (humanities) Br Acad 2011–14; memb Cncl AHRC 2007–11; memb Bd Royal Shakepeare Co 2003–12 (govr 2002–); hon fell St Catharine's Coll Cambridge 2000; FBA 1999, FRSL 2004; *Books* Shakespeare and the English Romantic Imagination (1986), Lamb's Essays (ed, 1987), Shakespearean Constitutions (1989), Romantic Ecology (1991), The Romantics on Shakespeare (ed, 1992), Shakespeare and Ovid (1993), The Arden Shakespeare: Titus Andronicus (ed, 1995), Shakespeare: An Illustrated Stage History (ed, 1996), The Genius of Shakespeare (1997), The Cure for Love (1998), The Song of the Earth (2000), John Clare: A Biography (2003, NAMI Book Award USA, Hawthornden Prize for Literature, James Tait Black Meml Prize for Biography), I Am: The Selected Poetry of John Clare (ed, 2004), The RSC Shakespeare: Complete Works (ed, 2007), Soul of the Age (2008, runner-up American PEN Biography Prize), The RSC Shakespeare: Individual Works (34 vols, 2008–12), English Literature: A Very Short Introduction (2010), The Public Value of the Humanities (ed, 2011), Shakespeare Staging the World (jtly, 2012), Shakespeare's Britain (jtly, 2012), Collaborative Plays by Shakespeare and Others (ed, 2013), Ted Hughes: The Unauthorised Life (2015, shortlisted Samuel Johnson Prize); *Plays* Being Shakespeare/The Man from Stratford (one man play for Simon Callow, 2010–14); *Recreations* tennis, walking, music; *Clubs* Oxford and Cambridge, Garrick; *Style*— Prof Sir Jonathan Bate, CBE; ✉ The Provost's Lodgings, Worcester College, Oxford OX1 2HB

BATEMAN, Prof Ian J; OBE (2013); *b* 14 September 1961, Birmingham; *Educ* Univ of Birmingham (BSocSci), Univ of Manchester (MA, Dehn Prize in Economics), Univ of Nottingham (PhD); *m* Fiona; 1 s (Ben), 2 da (Freya, Natasha); *Career* lectr in economics and agric economics Dept of Economics Univ of Exeter 1987–89, economist The Boots Co plc 1989; Sch of Environmental Sciences UEA: lectr 1989–96, appointed reader 1996, currently prof; dir Centre for Social and Economic Research on the Global Environment (CSERGE) UEA/UCL 1991–, head of economics UK Nat Ecosystem Assessment 2009–11; assoc prof: Univ of Western Australia, Univ of Waikato NZ, Lincoln Univ NZ; memb UK Nat Forum for Environmental Economics, memb Science Advsy Cncl DEFRA 2011–, memb UK Govt Natural Capital Ctee 2012–, memb Jt Nature Conservation Ctee 2015; chief ed Environmental and Resource Economics, memb Editorial Bd Int Jl of Agricultural Resources, Governance and Ecology, memb Editorial Bd Int Jl of Global Warming, series ed The Economics of Non-Market Goods and Resources; FRSA 2013, FSB 2014; *Books* incl: Environmental Economics: An Elementary Introduction (jtly, 1994), Valuing Environmental Preferences: Theory and Practice of the Contingent Valuation Method in the US, EU and Developing Countries (jt ed, 1999), Environmental Risk Planning and Management (jt ed, 2001), Waste Management and Planning (jt ed, 2001), Economics of Coastal and Water Resources: Valuing Environmental Functions (jt ed, 2001), Water Resources and Coastal Management (jt ed, 2001), Urban Planning and Management (jt ed, 2001), Environmental Ethics and Philosophy (jt ed, 2002), Economic Valuation with Stated Preference Techniques: A Manual (jtly, 2002), Applied Environmental Economics: A GIS Approach to Cost-Benefit Analysis (jtly, 2003), Environmental Decision Making and Risk Management: Selected Essays (jt ed, 2004); *Style*— Prof Ian J Bateman, OBE, FRSA, FSB; ✉ Land, Environment, Economics and Policy Institute, Lazenby Building, Prince of Wales Road, University of Exeter, Exeter EX4 4PJ

BATEMAN, Paul Terence; s of Nelson John Bateman (d 1983), and Frances Ellen, *née* Johnston (d 2003); *b* 28 April 1946; *Educ* Westcliff HS for Boys, Univ of Leicester (BSc); *m* 18 Jan 1969, Moira; 2 s (Michael b 1973, Timothy b 1977); *Career* Save and Prosper Group Ltd: graduate in secretarial dept 1967–68, asst to gp actuary 1968–73, mktg mangr 1973–75, gp mktg mangr 1975–80, gp mktg and devpt mangr 1980–81, exec dir mktg and devpt 1981–88, chief exec 1988–95; exec dir Robert Fleming Holdings Ltd (parent co of Save & Prosper) 1988–, exec chm Robert Fleming Asset Management (subsequently merged with Chase Manhattan) 1995–2000, global head Chase Fleming Asset Management (subsequently merged with JPMorgan) 2000, global head (outside America) JPMorgan Fleming Asset Management 2000–02, global ceo JPMorgan Fleming Asset Management 2002–07, chm JPMorgan Asset Mgmnt 2007–; dir: Lautro Ltd 1988–94, Personal Investment Authy 1993–94; chm Bd of Govrs Westcliff HS for Boys 1988–95, chm Barts City Lifesavers 1995–2011; pro-chllr Univ of Leicester 2009–; *Recreations* yachting, squash, golf, skiing; *Style*— Paul Bateman, Esq; ✉ 95 Thorpe Bay Gardens, Thorpe Bay, Essex SS1 3NW (☎ 01702 587152); JPMorgan Asset Management, Finsbury Dials, 20 Finsbury Street, London EC2Y 9AQ (☎ 020 7742 8475, fax 020 7751 8024, e-mail paul.t.bateman@jpmorgan.com)

BATES, Dan; *Career* W Yorks Playhouse 1987–2004 (joined as stage mangr, rising to exec dir), chief exec York Theatre Royal 2004–09, chief exec Sheffield Theatres 2009–; *Style*— Dan Bates, Esq; ✉ Sheffield Theatres Trust, 55 Norfolk Street, Sheffield S1 1DA

BATES, Prof David Richard; s of Jack Bates (d 1977), of Nuneaton, Warks, and Violet Anne Bates (d 1996); *b* 30 April 1945; *Educ* King Edward VI GS Nuneaton, Univ of Exeter (BA, PhD); *m* 4 Sept 1971, Helen Mary, *née* Fryer; 1 s (Jonathan Edward b 19 Nov 1975), 1 da (Rachel Emily b 23 Aug 1977); *Career* research asst Documents Section Imperial War Museum 1969–71 (head of section 1971); UC Cardiff (later Univ of Wales Cardiff): fell Univ of Wales Dept of History 1971–73, lectr 1973–87, memb Senate 1980–83 and 1986–92, sr lectr 1987–90, reader 1991–94, head of history and Welsh history 1988–92; Univ of Glasgow: Edwards prof of medieval history 1994–2003, head Dept of Medieval History 1995–97, head Sch of History and Archaeology 1995–97, dir Centre for Medieval and Renaissance Studies 1996–98, head Dept of History 1997–2001, memb Senate; dir Inst of Historical Research Univ of London 2003–08, prof of medieval history UEA 2008–10 (professorial fell 2010–), prof Université de Caen Basse-Normandie 2009–12; A level examiner 1973–84 and 1986, examiner (admin grade admissions) Civil Service 1978–84; Wolfson fellowship 1983, Huntington Library fell Henry E Huntington Library Pasadena 1984, professeur invité Ecole Nationale des Chartes Paris 1999, Br Acad Marc Fitch research reader 2001–03, visiting fell commoner Trinity Coll Cambridge 2002–03, directeur d'etudes invité Ecole Pratique des Hautes Etudes Paris 2003, James Ford lectr in Br history Univ of Oxford 2009–10, dir Battle Conf on Anglo-Norman Studies 2010–13; delivered numerous lectures and conferences and symposia worldwide; gen ed The Medieval World (Longman/Pearson series) 1987–2001; Dr (hc) Univ of Caen 2000; centenary fell Historical Assoc 2006, life memb Clare Hall Cambridge 2009–, memb Acad of Europe 2009–, Leverhulme emeritus fell 2013–15; FRHistS 1985 (memb Cncl 1995–99, vice-pres 2003–06), FSA 1993, FFCS 2001, FRSA 2007; *Books* Normandy before 1066 (1982), A Bibliography of Domesday Book (1986), William the Conqueror (1989, reissued 2001), Bishop Remigius of Lincoln 1067–1092 (1992), England and Normandy in the Middle Ages (jt ed, 1994), Conflict and Coexistence: Nationalism and Democracy in Modern Europe (jt ed, 1997), Regesta Regum Anglo-Normannorum: The Acta of William I, 1066–1087 (1998), Reordering the Past and Negotiating the Present in Stenton's First Century (2000), Domesday Book (jt ed, 2001), Writing Medieval Biography 750–1250: Essays in honour of Frank Barlow (jt ed, 2006), East Anglia and its North Sea World in the Middle Ages (jt ed, 2013), The Normans and Empire (2013); also author of numerous articles in learned jls; *Recreations* walking, music, reading, watching sport; *Style*— Prof David Bates; ✉ School of History, University of East Anglia, Norwich, Norfolk NR4 7TJ (☎ 01603 592070, e-mail david.bates@uea.ac.uk)

BATES, Django Leon; s of Ralf Bates, and Frances Sinker, *née* Roseveare; *b* 2 October 1960; *Educ* Ilea Centre for Young Musicians, Morley Coll; *m* 2015, Sophie Schudel; 1 da (Florence Edith b 22 June 2015); 2 da (Lulu Holiday b 7 May 1989, Amélie Waterhouse b 13 Feb 2003), 1 s (Archy Woodrow 29 Oct 1992) from a previous relationship; *Career* jazz keyboard player, E-flat hornist and composer; fndr memb Loose Tubes 1983; band leader: Human Chain (originally Humans) 1980–, Delightful Precipice 1991–, Stormchaser 2005–, Belovèd 2010; resident composer: Copenhagen 1996, Harrogate Int Festival 1997; prof in Rhythmic Music Rhythmic Music Conservatory (RMC) Copenhagen 2005–11, prof in Jazz Bern Univ of the Arts Switzerland 2011–; performed in numerous countries incl: Japan, China, USA, India; artistic dir Fuse Festival Leeds 2004; assoc in music London Coll of Music, Hon RAM 2000, fell Leeds Coll of Music (FLCM) 2005; *Compositions* incl: Out There (music theatre prodn) 1993, What it's like to be alive (piano concerto for Joanna MacGregor) 1996, Interval Song 1996, Umpteenth Violin Concerto 2004, The Study of Touch 2013, commissions for Köln WDR Orch, London Sinfonietta; *Recordings* incl: Music for the third policeman 1990, Summer Fruits (and unrest) 1993, Autumn Fires (and green shoots) 1994, Winter Truce (and homes blaze) 1995, Good Evening...here is the news 1996, Like Life 1998, Quiet Nights 1998, You Live and Learn...(apparently) 2004, Spring Is Here (shall we dance?) 2008, Belovèd Bird 2010, Confirmation 2012; *Awards* Young Professional Musician of the Year Wavendon All Music 1987, Best UK Composer Wire Magazine 1987 and 1990, Best Band Wire Magazine 1989 (for Loose Tubes), Bobby Jaspar Prize French Academie du Jazz 1994, Danish Jazzpar Prize 1997; *Recreations* cooking, reading, real ale; *Style*— Django Bates, Esq; ✉ c/o Jeremy Farnell, 21 St Johns Church Road, London E9 6EJ (📞 020 8985 8754, e-mail management@djangobates.co.uk)

BATES, Prof (Alexander) John; *b* 18 August 1950, Buxton, Derbys; *Educ* Univ of Nottingham (BSc), Harvard Grad Sch of Business Admin (Baker scholar, MBA); *Career* devpt chemist Co-operative Wholesale Soc 1972, area sales mangr Eli Lilly & Co 1972–74, gen sales mangr Baird & Tatlock Zambia 1974–77, gp mktg mangr International Paint plc 1979–83, fndr, chm and md Datapaq Ltd 1984–92, fndr and dir Cambridge Mgmnt Gp 1984–, fndr and md Newmarket DataSystems Ltd 1993–97, exec dir Fndn for Entrepreneurial Mgmnt 1998–2005, fndr and non-exec dir Sussex Place Ventures Ltd 1998–, non-exec chm Multimedia Mapping Ltd (Multimap.com) 1998–2007, non-exec chm London Technology Network Ltd 2001–, non-exec dir and prog dir Centre for Creative Business Ltd 2004–; instr Harvard Grad Sch of Business Admin 1983–84, teaching fell London Business Sch 1984–2002; visiting lectr: Templeton Coll Oxford 1985–93, Institut Theseus (France Telecom) 1990–94, Cable & Wireless Coll 1994–96; visiting prof Univ of the Arts London 2002–, adjunct prof London Business Sch 2002–; chm London Region Judging Panel Ernst & Young Entrepreneur of the Year Award 2000–04, memb Invention and Innovation Awards Ctee NESTA 2002–06; *Style*— Prof John Bates, Esq; ✉ London Business School, Regent's Park, London NW1 4SA (📞 020 7000 8166, e-mail jbates@london.edu)

BATES, Laura; BEM (2015); *b* 27 August 1986; *Educ* St John's Coll Cambridge (MA); *Career* feminist activist and writer; fndr Everyday Sexism Project 2012–; contrib to Women Under Siege Project, writer Guardian, TIME and Telegraph; patron Somerset and Avon Rape and Sexual Abuse Support (SARSAS); Woman of the Year Award Cosmopolitan 2013, Woman of the Year Award Red Magazine 2014, Georgina Henry Award British Press Awards 2015; *Books* Everyday Sexism (2014), Girl Up (2016); *Style*— Ms Laura Bates, BEM; ✉ c/o Georgia Garrett, Rogers, Coleridge & White, 20 Powis Mews, London W11 1JN (website www.rcwlitagency.com)

BATES, Matthew Oldham; *s* of David Oldham Bates, and Gillian, *née* Miles; *Educ* Downside, Univ of Reading (BA), Coll of Law London; *Career* articled clerk Boodle Hatfield Slrs 1989–91, asst to literary agent Sheil Land Associates 1992–95, literary agent The Sayle Agency 1995–; *Style*— Matthew Bates, Esq; ✉ Sayle Screen Ltd, 11 Jubilee Place, London SW3 3TE (📞 020 7823 3883, fax 020 7823 3363)

BATES, Baron (Life Peer 2008), of Langbaurgh in the County of Yorkshire; Michael Bates; *s* of John Bates, and Ruth Bates; *b* 26 May 1961; *Educ* Heathfield Sr HS Gateshead, Gateshead Technical Coll, Wadham Coll Oxford (MBA); *m* 1, 25 June 1983 (m dis 2008), Carole, *née* Whitfield; 2 s; *m* 2, 20 July 2012, Xuelin, *née* Li; *Career* jr ptnr J M Bates & Co 1979–83, inspr Clerical Medical Investment Group 1983–86, conslt Hogg Robinson (benefit conslts) 1986–88, investment advsr Joseph Nelson (fund mangrs) 1988–91, asst dir Godwins Ltd (pensions conslts and actuaries) 1991–; MP (Cons) Langbaurgh 1992–97 (Parly candidate (Cons): Tyne Bridge 1987, Langbaurgh (by-election) 1991); PPS to: Rt Hon Nicholas Scott, MBE, MP as min of state DSS 1992–93, Rt Hon Sir John Wheeler, MP as min of state NI Office 1994: asst Govt whip 1994–95, Lord Cmmr HM's Treasy (sr Govt whip) 1995–96, Paymaster-Gen 1996–97, NE Sponsor Min 1996–97, shadow min Cabinet Office 2008–, dep speaker House of Lords 2013–14, Lord in Waiting (Govt whip) 2013–; Shell fell Industry and Parl Tst 1997–; dir of consultancy and research Oxford Analytica Inc 1998–2006 (sr advsr 2006); dir: Financial Standards Foundation (Bermuda) Ltd 2001–03, estandardsforum Inc (NY) 2001–03, Congregational & General plc 2001–06, Walton Bates Assocs 2006–11; non-exec dir Vardy Gp of Companies 2006–10; memb: RIIA 1998–2003, Caux Roundtable 2001– (tstee 2006–), European Ideas Network 2002–06, Business Advsy Forum Saïd Business Sch Univ of Oxford; chm Northern Area Young Conservatives 1985–87, memb YC Nat Advsy Ctee 1984–89; memb SCR Wadham Coll Oxford 1998, chm Int Property Awards 2013–, memb HE Cmmn 2013–; *Style*— The Lord Bates; ✉ House of Lords, London SW1A 0PW (📞 020 7219 6528, e-mail batesm@parliament.uk)

BATESON, Lynne; *b* 16 August 1952; *Educ* Univ of London (external BSc); *Career* gen reporter Pudsey News 1973–77, feature writer Yorkshire Evening Post 1978–81; city writer: United Newspapers 1981–84, Thomson Regnl Newspapers 1984–86; personal fin writer Daily Express 1986–87, features ed Money Magazine 1987–88; Sunday Express: personal fin ed 1988–94, fin ed 1994–95, asst ed 1995–96; dep gp managing ed Express Newspapers 1996–97, freelance journalist writing for Sunday Express (Battling Bateson consumer column), Daily Mail, Mail on Sunday, The Guardian, London Evening Standard, The Times and Sunday Times, also corporate brainstorming and media trg 1997–2001, ldr writer and features writer Daily Express and Sunday Express 2002–06, freelance writer for British nat newspapers, US corr Northern Soul webzine, blogger for The Spectator Online, editorial conslt, media and presentation trg, copywriter, screenwriter, writer and performer of stand-up comedy 2007–; special commendation Bradford & Bingley's Personal Fin Journalist of the Year Award 1990, Br Insurance and Investment Brokers' Assoc Consumer Journalist of the Year (tabloid) 1993, Best General Insurance National Newspaper Writer 1999; *Recreations* mystery, history, the psychic world, Wagner, Puccini, Debussy and soul, experiencing the USA, vegan Asian food, hot baths; *Style*— Ms Lynne Bateson; ✉ e-mail lynne.bateson@gmail.com

BATESON, Prof Sir (Paul) Patrick Gordon; kt (2003); *s* of Capt Richard Gordon Bateson (d 1956), and Solvi Helene, *née* Berg (d 1987); *b* 31 March 1938; *Educ* Westminster, King's Coll Cambridge (BA, PhD, ScD); *m* 20 July 1963, Dusha, da of Kenneth Matthews, of Halesworth, Suffolk; 2 da (Melissa b 1968, Anna b 1972); *Career* Harkness fell Stanford Univ Med Center California 1963–65; Univ of Cambridge: sr asst in res Sub-Dept of Animal Behaviour 1965–69, lectr in zoology 1969–78, dir Sub-Dept of Animal Behaviour 1976–88, reader in animal behaviour 1978–84, prof of ethology 1984–2005, provost King's Coll 1988–2003 (professorial fell 1984–88); pres: Assoc for the Study of Animal Behaviour 1977–80, Cncl Zoological Soc of London 1989–92; tstee Inst for Public Policy Studies 1988–95, biological sec and vice-pres Royal Soc 1998–2003; memb Museum & Galleries Cmmn 1995–2000; foreign memb American Philosophical Soc 2006; Scientific Medal ZSL 1976, Assoc for the Study of Animal Behaviour Medal 2001, Frink Medal ZSL 2014; Hon Dr Univ of St Andrews 2001; hon fell: Queen Mary Univ of London 2001, ZSL 2002 (pres 2004–14); FRS 1983; *Books* Growing Points of Ethology (ed with R A Hinde, 1976), Perspectives in Ethology Vols 1–9 (ed with P H Klopfer, 1972–91), Mate Choice (ed, 1983), Defended to Death (with G Prins & Others, 1984), Measuring Behaviour (with P Martin, 1986, 3 edn 2007), The Domestic Cat: The Biology of its Behaviour (ed with D Turner, 1988, 3 edn 2014), The Development and Integration of Behaviour (ed, 1991), The Behavioural and Physiological Effects of Culling Red Deer (1997), Design for a Life: How Behaviour Develops (with P Martin, 1999), Inquiry into Dog Breeding (2010), Review of Research Using Non-Human Primates (2011), Plasticity, Robustness, Development and Evolution (with P Gluckman, 2011) Play, Playfulness, Creativity and Innovation (with P Martin, 2013); *Recreations* gardening, opera; *Style*— Prof Sir Patrick Bateson, FRS; ✉ The Old Rectory, Rectory Street, Halesworth, Suffolk IP19 8BL (📞 01986 873182)

BATEY, Prof Peter William James; *s* of Rev George Thomas Batey (d 1994), and Ruth, *née* Garstang (d 1998); *b* 17 August 1948; *Educ* Bury GS, Univ of Sheffield (BSc), Univ of Liverpool (MCD, PhD); *m* 1975, Joyce, da of Reginald Dover (d 1989); 1 da (Rachel Alexandra b 1979), 1 s (James Richard b 1981); *Career* planning offr Lancs CC 1969–73, sr planning offr Gtr Manchester CC 1973–75; Univ of Liverpool: lectr 1975–84, sr lectr 1984–87, reader 1987–89, Lever prof of town and regnl planning 1989–2015 (emeritus prof 2015–), head Dept of Civic Design 1989–97, dean Faculty of Social and Environmental Studies 1997–2003; Fulbright sr research scholar regnl sci program Univ of Illinois at Urbana-Champaign 1981–82; chm Conf of Heads of Planning Schs 1990–96; co-ed Town Planning Review 1992–; dir Mersey Estuary Management Plan Study 1992–96, chm Mersey Basin Campaign 2004–10, dir ESRC NW Doctoral Trg Centre 2011–15, chm Healthy Waterways Tst; world pres Regnl Sci Assoc Int 1997–98; Silver Jubilee Medal Hungarian Economic Assoc 1985, Kingfisher Award Mersey Basin Campaign 1996; foreign memb Russian Acad of Architecture and Construction Sciences 1994; FRGS 1969, FRSA 1988, FRTPI 1988 (MRTPI 1975), FAcSS 2000, CGeog 2003, fell Regnl Science Assoc Int 2006; *Publications* contrib to various planning jls and pubns incl: Town Planning Review, Jl of Regnl Sci, Economic Systems Research, Jl of Geographical Systems, Socio-Economic Planning Sciences, Regnl Studies, Environment and Planning A: Applied Spatial Analysis and Policy; *Recreations* hill walking, travelling; *Style*— Prof Peter Batey; ✉ 11 Blundell Road, Hightown, Liverpool L38 9EE; Civic Design Department of Geography and Planning, University of Liverpool, Liverpool L69 7ZQ (📞 0151 794 3811, fax 0151 794 3125, e-mail pwjbatey@liv.ac.uk)

BATH, 7 Marquess of (GB 1789); Sir Alexander George Thynn (sic, reverted to this spelling); 10 Bt (E 1641); also Viscount Weymouth and Baron Thynne of Warminster (E 1682); *s* of 6 Marquess of Bath, ED (d 1992), and his 1 w, Hon Daphne Winifred Louise (Hon Mrs Fielding) (d 1997), da of 4 Baron Vivian; *b* 6 May 1932; *Educ* Eton, ChCh Oxford (MA); *m* 1969, Anna (Anna Gael, former actress, currently journalist and novelist), da of Laszlo Izsak Gyarmathy (d 2004), originally of Budapest but latterly of Los Angeles; 1 da (Lady Lenka Abigail b 1969), 1 s (Ceawlin Henry Laszlo, Viscount Weymouth b 1974); *Heir* s, Viscount Weymouth; *Career* late Lt Life Gds & Royal Wilts Yeo; contested: Westbury (Feb 1974) and Wells (1979) in Wessex Regionalist Pty's interest, Wessex (Euro elections 1979) Wessex Regionalist and European Fed Pty; on Lib Dem benches House of Lords 1993–99; painter; opened perm exhibition of murals in private apartments of Longleat 1973; planted first of the mazes within 'the Labyrinths of Longleat' 1975, Center Parcs Village Longleat Forest opened 1994; *Books* (as Alexander Thynne before 1976, Thynn thereafter); The Carry Cot (1972), Lord Weymouth's Murals (1974), A Regionalist Manifesto (1975), The King is Dead (1976), Pillars of the Establishment (1980), The New World Order of Alexander Thynn (2000); Strictly Private to Public Exposure (autobiography, 4 vols): The Early Years (2002), Top Hat and Tails (2003), Two Bites of the Apple (2003), A Degree of Instability: The Oxford Years (2005), Some Sonnets (2011), Cocoons Fantasies Therapies (2011); *Record* I Play the Host (1974, singing own compositions); *Style*— The Most Hon the Marquess of Bath; ✉ Longleat, Warminster, Wiltshire BA12 7NN (home 📞 01985 844300, fax 01985 844888, business 📞 01985 844400, fax 01985 844885)

BATH AND WELLS, Bishop of 2014–; Rt Rev Peter Hancock; *s* of Kenneth Albert Hancock, of Hampshire, and Jean Margaret, *née* Crump; *b* 26 July 1955; *Educ* Price's Sch Fareham, Selwyn Coll Cambridge (MA), Oak Hill Coll Southgate (BA), Univ of Nottingham (MA); *m* 1979, Elizabeth Jane, da of Cyril John Sindall; 2 da (Claire Jane b 26 March 1982, Charlotte Emma b 1 Dec 1987), 2 s (Richard Andrew b 4 Aug 1984, William Peter b 18 Dec 1989); *Career* ordained: deacon 1980, priest 1981; curate Christ Church Portsdown 1980–83, curate Radipole and Melcombe Regis Team Miny Emmanuel Church 1983–87, vicar St Wilfrid Cowplain 1987–99, rural dean of Havant 1993–98, archdeacon of Meon Dio of Portsmouth 1999–2010, bishop of Basingstoke 2010–14, bishop of Bath and Wells 2014–; hon canon of Portsmouth Cathedral 1997 (dir of Mission 2003–06); *Recreations* walking, skiing, environmental and third world issues; *Style*— The Rt Rev the Bishop of Bath and Wells

BATISTE, Spencer Lee; *s* of late Samuel Batiste, and late Lottie Batiste; *b* 5 June 1945, London; *Educ* Carmel Coll, Sorbonne, Univ of Cambridge; *m* 1969, Susan Elizabeth, da of late Ronald William Atkin; 1 s, 1 da; *Career* slr in private practice 1970–2000; Euro Parly candidate (Cons) Sheffield, Chesterfield and NE Derbyshire 1979, MP (Cons) Elmet 1983–97; PPS to min of state for: Indust and Info Technol 1985–87, Def Procurement 1987–89; PPS to Sir Leon Brittan as Vice-Pres of EC Cmmn 1989–97; memb Select Ctees: on Energy 1985, on Sci and Technol 1992–97, on Info 1992–97; vice-chm: Cons Space Ctee 1986–97 (sec 1983–85), Cons Trade and Indust Ctee 1989–97, Small Business Bureau 1983–92; pres Cons Trades Unionists 1987–90 (chm Yorks Area 1984–87), chm Cons Academic Liaison Prog 1988–97; adjudicator Immigration Appellate Authy 1997–2002, vice-pres Immigration Appeal Tbnl 2002–05, sr immigration judge 2005–10, judge Upper Tbnl 2010–13; Guardian of the Sheffield Assay Office 1974–2015 (law clerk 1973–2000); memb: Cncl Univ of Sheffield 1982–92, British Hallmarking Cncl 1988–2000; *Recreations* gardening, reading, photography, travel; *Style*— Spencer Batiste, Esq; ✉ c/o Guardians Hall, Sheffield Assay Office, Beulah Road, Sheffield S2 2AN

BATSON, Brendon Martin; OBE (2015, MBE 2001); *b* 6 February 1953, Grenada, West Indies; *Career* professional footballer (over 400 Football League appearances): Arsenal FC 1969–74, Cambridge United FC 1974–78, West Bromwich Albion FC 1978–84; dep chief exec PFA 1984–2002 (PFA rep to Kick It Out professional football anti-racism campaign), md West Bromwich Albion FC 2002–03, appointed head of internal review of the FA's disciplinary procedure 2003, chm Professional Players Fedn 2006–; memb Bd: Sports Ground Safety Authority (SGSA) (formerly Football Licensing Authy) 2007–15, Sporting Equals 2008–15 (chm 2010–15), EU Athletes 2011–, Sport and Recreation Alliance 2015–; *Recreations* cycling, golf, swimming, reading, theatre; *Style*— Brendon Batson, Esq, OBE; ✉ The FA Group, St George's Park, Burton-Upon-Trent, Staffordshire DE13 9PD

BATSON, HE Philip David; *m* Joanna; 1 s; *Career* diplomat; joined FCO 1987; entry clearance offr Mumbai 1991–94, third sec political Paris 1995–97; FCO: desk offr Overseas Territories Dept 1997–99, EU Africa summit/Pan-Africa coordinator Africa Directorate 1999–2000, head Horn of Africa Section Africa Directorate 2000–02, head France/Benelux Section 2002–04; dep head of mission Tunis 2004–08, FCO: dep head Corp Services Prog 2008–11, games-time coordinator and crisis planner 2011–13; ambass to Repub of Moldova 2013–; *Style*— HE Mr Philip Batson; ✉ c/o Foreign and Commonwealth Office (Chisinau), King Charles Street, London SW1A 2AH

BATTEN, Stephen Duval; QC (1989); *s* of Brig Stephen Alexander Holgate Batten, CBE (d 1957), and Alice Joan, *née* Royden, MBE (d 1990); *b* 2 April 1945; *Educ* Uppingham, Pembroke Coll Oxford (BA); *m* 5 June 1976, Valerie Jean, da of George Ronald Trim (d 1982); 1 s (Henry b 1978), 1 da (Sarah b 1980); *Career* called to the Bar Middle Temple 1968 (bencher), recorder of Crown Court 1988–; *Recreations* golf, gardening, and the pursuit of private peace; *Style*— Stephen Batten, Esq, QC; ✉ 3 Raymond Buildings, Gray's Inn, London WC1R 5BH (📞 020 7400 6400, fax 020 7242 4221)

BATTERSBY, Prof Sir Alan Rushton; kt (1992); *s* of William Battersby (d 1967), and Hilda, *née* Rushton (d 1972); *b* 4 March 1925; *Educ* Leigh GS, Univ of Manchester (BSc, MSc), Univ of St Andrews (PhD), Univ of Bristol (DSc), Univ of Cambridge (ScD); *m* 18 June 1949, Margaret Ruth (d 1997), da of Thomas Hart (d 1965); 2 s (Martin b 29 July 1953, Stephen b 24 April 1956); *Career* asst lectr in chemistry Univ of St Andrews 1948–53,

Cwlth Fund fell at Rockefeller Inst NY 1950–51 and Univ of Illinois 1951–52, lectr in chemistry Univ of Bristol 1954–62; second chair of organic chemistry Univ of Liverpool 1962, elected to chair of organic chemistry Univ of Cambridge 1969–92 (elected to 1702 chair 1988), hon fell St Catharine's Coll Cambridge; memb Cncl Royal Soc 1973–75, pres Bürgenstock Conf 1976, chm Exec Cncl Novartis Fndn 1983–90 (tstee 1992–2000); Chemical Soc: Corday-Morgan Medal 1959, Tilden Medal and lectr 1963, Hügo Müller Medal and lectr 1972, Flintoff Medal 1975, Award in Natural Product Chemistry 1978, Longstaff Medal 1984, Robert Robinson lectr and Medal 1986; Royal Soc: Paul Karrer Medal and lectr Zürich Univ 1977, Davy Medal 1977, Royal Medal 1984, Copley Medal 2000; Roger Adams Award in Organic Chemistry ACS 1983, Havinga Medal Holland 1984, Antoni Feltrinelli Int Prize for Chemistry Rome 1986, Varro Tyler lectr and Award Purdue 1987, Adolf Windaus Medal Göttingen 1987, Wolf Prize Israel 1989, Arun Guthikonda Meml Award Univ of Columbia 1991, August Wilhelm von Hofmann Meml Medal Gesellschaft Deutscher Chemiker 1992, Tetrahedron Prize 1995, Hans-Herloff Inhoffen Medal Braunschweig Germany 1997, Robert A Welch Award for Chemistry 2000, Robert B Woodward Award for Porphyrin Chemistry 2004; Hon DSc: Rockefeller Univ NY 1977, Univ of Sheffield 1986, Heriot-Watt Univ 1987, Univ of Bristol 1994, Univ of Liverpool 1996; Hon LLD Univ of St Andrews 1977; FRS 1966; memb: Deutsche Akademie der Naturforscher Leopoldina (Germany) 1967, Soc Royal de Chimie (Belgium) 1987; hon memb American Acad of Arts and Sci (USA) 1988, foreign fell Nat Acad of Scis India 1990, memb Academia Europaea 1990, foreign fell Indian Nat Sci Acad 1993; *Recreations* music, camping, hiking, sailing, gardening, fly fishing; *Style*— Prof Sir Alan Battersby, FRS; ✉ 20 Barrow Road, Cambridge CB2 8AS (☎ 01223 363799); University Chemical Laboratory, Lensfield Road, Cambridge CB2 1EW (☎ 01223 336400, fax 01223 336362)

BATTIE, David Anthony; s of Donald Charles Battie (d 1988), and Peggy Joan Battie; *b* 22 October 1942; *Educ* King James I Sch; *m* 1 Jan 1972, Sarah, da of Philip James Francis (d 1987); 2 da (Henrietta Victoria b 17 Aug 1977, Eleanor Harriet b 4 June 1980); *Career* dir Sotheby's 1976–99; expert BBC TV Antiques Roadshow 1977–, conslt Sworders Auctioneers;, lectures, writes and broadcasts widely; FRSA; *Books* Price Guide to 19th Century British Pottery (1975), Sotheby's Encyclopedia of Porcelain (ed, 1990), Sotheby's Encyclopedia of Glass (co-ed, 1991), Readers' Digest Treasures in Your Home (conslt ed, 1992), Understanding 19th Century British Porcelain (1994); *Recreations* book binding, building Gothic folly; *Style*— David Battie, Esq; ☎ 01342 715244, e-mail battie@wildgoose.fsbusiness.co.uk

BATTISCOMBE, Christopher Charles Richard; CMG (1992), JP (2001); s of Lt-Col Christopher Robert Battiscombe (d 1989), and Karin Sigrid, *née* Timberg (d 1983); *b* 27 April 1940; *Educ* Wellington, New Coll Oxford (BA); *m* 1972, Brigid Melita Theresa, da of Peter Northcote Lunn; 1 da (Antonia b 1975), 1 s (Max b 1977); *Career* HM Dip Serv: MECAS 1963, second sec FO (later FCO) 1963, third sec Kuwait 1965, asst private sec to Chllr of Duchy of Lancaster 1969, UK delg OECD Paris 1971, first sec UK mission to UN New York 1974, asst head Eastern Euro and Soviet Dept FCO 1978, cnsllr (commercial) Cairo 1981, cnsllr (commercial) Paris 1984, cnsllr FCO 1986–90, ambass to Algeria 1990–94, asst under sec (public depts) FCO 1994–97, ambass to Jordan 1997–2000; DG Soc of London Art Dealers 2001–, sec Br Art Market Fedn 2001–; chm Anglo Jordanian Soc 2001–09; *Recreations* golf, tennis, skiing; *Clubs* Kandahar, Temple; *Style*— Christopher Battiscombe, Esq, CMG

fy198,3,6.4,7.4BATTY, Andrew James; s of Francis Leslie Batty (d 1971), and Pamela, *née* Ball (d 2005); *b* 12 April 1956; *Educ* Roundhay GS, Jacob Kramer Coll Leeds, Leeds Coll of Art; *m* 24 Oct 1992, Rachel Jane, *née* Sharman; 2 s (James Mark b 1995, Joseph Andrew b 1999), 1 da (Kathryn Ellen b 1997); *Career* copywriter Charles Walls Advertising 1975–79, creative dir Severn Advertising 1979–81, dir MCS Robertson Scott Yorks 1981–82, chm and md Creative Marketing Services 1982–; chm: Publicity Assoc of Bradford, Yorks Advertising and Communications Training, Nat CAM Graduates Assoc; chm East Keswick PC; MSIAD 1978, MIMgt 1984, FInstSMM 1987, Registered Marketer 1996, Chartered Marketer 1998, FCIM 1998 (MInstM 1981, chm Leeds Branch), MInstD 1999, FIPA 2001, FCAM 2003 (MCAM 1979), FIDM 2004 (MIDM 1996); *Publications* East Keswick Millennium Book (compiler, 2000); *Recreations* voluntary activities in advertising training, local history, vice chm East Keswick PC; *Style*— Andrew Batty, Esq; ✉ Larks Rise, Keswick Grange, East Keswick, West Yorkshire LS17 9BX (☎ 01937 574692); Creative Marketing Services, Hollinthorpe Hall, Swillington Lane, Leeds LS26 8BZ (☎ 0113 287 7973, fax 0113 287 5074, e-mail andrew.batty@cmsadvertising.co.uk, websites www. cmsadvertising.co.uk, www.creativemarketingservices.co.uk and www.cmsrecruitment.co.uk)

BATTY, His Hon Judge Christopher Michael; s of Michael Batty, and Joyce Batty; *b* 13 October 1966, Leeds; *Educ* Liverpool Poly; *m* Kate; 1 s (Samuel), 1 da (Millie); *Career* called to the Bar 1989; St Paul's Chambers Leeds 1989–2009, circuit judge (North Eastern Circuit) 2009–; *Recreations* called to the Bar 1989; St Paul's Chambers Leeds 1989–2009, circuit judge (North Eastern Circuit) 2009–; memb Operational Rules Tbnl Rugby Football League; *Style*— His Hon Judge Christopher Batty; ✉ The Court House, 1 Oxford Row, Leeds LS1 3BG (☎ 0113 306 2800)

BATTY, Prof (John) Michael; CBE (2004); s of Jack Batty (d 1970), of Cheltenham, Glos, and Nell, *née* Marsden (d 1995); *b* 11 January 1945; *Educ* Quarry Bank HS Liverpool, Univ of Manchester (BA, Clifford Holliday Prize), Univ of Wales (PhD); *m* 4 Jan 1969, Susan Elizabeth, da of Horace Howell; 1 s (Daniel Jack b 28 Sept 1976); *Career* asst lectr Dept of Town and Country Planning Univ of Manchester 1966–69, res asst Urban Systems Res Unit Dept of Geography Univ of Reading 1969–72, lectr in geography Univ of Reading 1972–74 and 1975–76 (reader 1976–79), asst prof (visiting) Dept of Civil Engrg Univ of Waterloo Ontario 1974–75 (adjunct prof of civil engrg 1976, 1977 and 1978); Univ of Wales Cardiff: prof of city and regnl planning 1979–90, dean Sch of Environmental Design 1983–86, head of dept 1985–89; dir Nat Center for Geographic Information and Analysis (NCGIA) and prof of geography State Univ of NY Buffalo 1990–95, chm Centre for Advanced Spatial Analysis (CASA) and prof of spatial analysis and planning UCL 1995–2004, Bartlett prof of planning UCL 2004–; memb: Scientific Computing Advsy Panel SERC 1989–90, Advsy Panel on Public Sector Information 2003–10; Wesley Dougill Prize 1992, Back Award RGS 1999, Alonso Meml Prize RSA 2011, UCGIS Research Prize 2012, Laureat Prix Int de Geographie Vautrin Lud 2013, Founders Medal RGS 2015; Hon DLH State Univ of NY Buffalo 2008, Hon LLD Univ of Leicester 2015; AcSS 2001; FRSA 1982, FRTPI 1983 (MRTPI 1971), FCILT 1990 (MCILT 1984), FBA 2001, FRS 2009; *Books* Urban Modelling (1976), Microcomputer Graphics (1987), Fractal Cities (1994), Cities and Complexity (2005), The New Science of Cities (2013); *Recreations* Indian Food, discovering America, China, reading, travel; *Style*— Prof Michael Batty, CBE; ✉ 9 White Horse House, 1 Little Britain, London EC1A 7BX (☎ 020 7600 8186); University College London, Centre for Advanced Spatial Analysis, 90 Tottenham Court Road, London W1T 4TJ (☎ 020 3108 3877, fax 020 3108 3258, e-mail m.batty@ucl.ac.uk)

BATTY, His Hon Judge Paul Daniel; QC (1995); s of Vincent Batty (d 1973), of Seaham Harbour, and Catherine, *née* Kane; *b* 13 June 1953; *Educ* St Aidan's GS, Univ of Newcastle upon Tyne (LLB); *m* 30 Sept 1986, Angela Jane; 1 da (Sarah Georgina b 2 Nov 1987); *Career* called to the Bar Lincoln's Inn 1974 (bencher 2003); mess jr Newcastle Bar 1980–83, jr North Eastern Circuit 1984, recorder of the Crown Court 1994–2003 (asst recorder 1989–94), circuit judge (Northern Circuit) 2003–; *Recreations* swimming, boating, angling; *Clubs* Northern Counties; *Style*— His Hon Judge Batty, QC; ✉ Carlisle Crown Court, Earl Street, Carlisle, Cumbria CA1 1DJ (☎ 01228 882120)

BATTY, Dr Vincent Bernard; s of Henry Joseph Batty, of London, and Ena Violet, *née* Cavenagh; *b* 8 June 1951, London; *Educ* St Aloysius Coll Highgate, Middx Hosp Med Sch (BSc, MB BS, DMRD, MSc, FRCR); *m* 21 Feb 1987, Dr Wilma Westensee, da of Rolf Westensee, of Grahamstown, South Africa; 1 s (Adam b 1980), 2 da (Louise b 1980, Anke b 1989); *Career* house physician Watford Gen Hosp 1977, house and casualty surgn Middx Hosp 1978, GP Hythe Hants 1979, conslt in radiology and nuclear med Southampton Gen Hosp 1984– (registrar in radiology 1979, sr registrar in radiology 1982), sr registrar in ultrasound and nuclear med Royal Marsden Hosp 1984; memb: Br Inst of Radiology, Br Nuclear Med Soc, Br Soc of Head and Neck Radiology, European Assoc of Musculo-Skeletal Radiology, European Soc of Radiology; memb Br Medical Pilots Assoc; memb Worshipful Soc of Apothecaries; FRCR; *Publications* Nuclear Medicine In Oncology (ed, 1986); author of papers on general and musculo-skeletal radiology and on nuclear med; *Recreations* general aviation, gardening, music, photography; *Style*— Dr Vincent Batty; ✉ Department of Nuclear Medicine, Southampton General Hospital, Tremona Road, Southampton SO16 6YD (☎ 023 8120 6203, fax 023 8120 6927, e-mail vince.batty@uhs.nhs.uk)

BATY, Robert John (Bob); OBE (2002); s of Robert George Baty (d 1986), and Sarah, *née* Hall (d 2007); *b* 1 June 1944, Timperley, Cheshire; *Educ* Calday Grange GS West Kirby Wirral, Liverpool Coll of Building; *m* Oct 1975, Patricia, *née* Fagan; 2 da (Claire Louise, Philippa Jane); *Career* NW Water: princ/resident engr 1974–83, dist mangr 1983–85, regnl mangr 1985–88; SW Water: engrg and scientific dir 1988–96, chief exec 1996–2006; non-exec dir Royal Devon & Exeter NHS Fndn Tst; registered cmmr Infrastructure Planning Cmmn 2010–12; Herbert Lapworth Medal IWEM 1981, Gold Medal for Environmental Work ICE 1995; CEng 1970, FCIWEM 1981, FIWO 1990, CCMI 1990, FICE 1992, FREng 2000; *Recreations* sport (especially rugby), recreational flying, car restoration; *Style*— Bob Baty, Esq, OBE; ✉ Hillcot, 78 Oldfield Drive, Heswall, Wirral CH60 9HA (☎ and fax 0151 348 4921, e-mail rjbaty@tiscali.co.uk)

BAUCHER, Her Hon Judge Heather Anne; *née* Robertson; da of Keith Robertson, of Formby, Merseyside, and Margaret Patricia, *née* Kenny (d 2009); *Educ* Univ of Sheffield (Jacqueline Falconer Prize, LLB), Chester Law Coll; *m* 16 May 1987, Gerald Marsh Baucher (d 2012); 1 da (Grace Naomi b 21 Nov 1991), 1 s (Abraham Edward b 21 Feb 1995); *Career* admitted slr 1986; articled clerk Davis Campbell 1984–86, slr 1986–89, salaried ptnr 1989–91, equity ptnr/memb 1991–2008, recorder 2004–, circuit judge (South Eastern Circuit) 2009–; memb Slrs Disciplinary Tbnl 2002–09; memb Law Soc Roll of Slrs 1986; *Recreations* walking, Liverpool FC, St Nicholas Church, swimming, gardening, theatre; *Style*— Her Hon Judge Baucher; ✉ c/o The South Eastern Circuit, 289–293 High Holborn, London WC1V 7HZ

BAUDINO, Dr Catherine Anne; da of Jean Rene Baudino, and Anne-Marie, *née* Camus; *b* 26 October 1952; *Educ* Lycee Français de Londres, UCL (BA, PhD); *Career* dir Institutional Investor 1980–87; chief exec: Maxwell Satellite Communications Ltd 1987–89, Baudino Enterprises Ltd 1989–; non-exec dir VideoLink Business Communications Ltd 1992–94; cncllr to the French C of C 1991–95, pres The Franco-Br Construction Indust Gp 1992–94, business devpt dir The NASDAQ Stock Market 1994–95; md: BRIDGE Telecom Ltd 1999–2002, ID-360 Ltd 2002–08, Baudino & Co Ltd 2015–; *Recreations* opera, theatre, wine and food; *Style*— Dr Catherine A Baudino; ✉ cab@baudino.net

BAUER, Eran Nicodemus; s of Dr Jacob Bauer (d 1961), and Gitta, *née* Gaal; *b* 25 February 1954, Lincoln; *Educ* King's GS Grantham; *m* 1, 27 Aug 1994 (m dis 2001), Penelope Jane, *née* Griffiths; 2 da (Florence Eloise and Charlotte Amelia (twins) b 10 April 1995), 1 s (Max Jacob b 14 Nov 1996); m 2, 14 Feb 2009, Linda Margaret Houston Bowser, da of John Wilson, of Tealby, Lincs; *Career* Parachute Regt 16 Ind Co (V) 1973–78; dir: Universal Cleaning Services (historic bldgs restoration conslt), Civil Defence Supply 1980–, MASC Exec Ltd (security conslts) 2012–, Phazzer Inc USA 2015–; chm: PGI Br Standards Ctee PH/3/12 Police Protective Equipment, Br Standards BS 7971 Ctee; co-designer, patentee and inventor of military and police special ops equipment, patented first interlocking riot shield, introduced new side-handled batons and trg to UK police, chemical warfare civil def advsr to Saudi Arabian Govt during Gulf War, contrib pubns on police technol, security conslt to UK Govt depts, tech advsr to TV and films; county cncllr Ruskington and Cranwell Div Lincs 2009–14, Lincs CC rep on Regnl Emergency Mgmnt Bd, bd dr Regnl Control Centre Castle Donnington; dir Business Link Lincolnshire and Rutland 2001–08, dir Mercian Matrix Enterprises 2001–08; National DTI & ISI Interforum e-Commerce Award 1999; chm Weirfield Wildlife Hosp 2000–10, memb RUSI for Def Studies, MRAeS, tstee HILT Disability Fndn (HDFL) Lincs 2014–16, patron-mentor Templar Scholars Singers 2014–; Knight Cdr Order of the Temple of Jerusalem Grand Priory of Knights Templar in England and Wales 2007 (Chevalier Knight 2005, Preceptor East of England 2006–14), fndr memb Knights Templar Priory of the Poor Knights of Christ 2013 (commander E of Eng commandery 2014–); *Publications* Policing UK (2013); *Recreations* architecture, architectural drawing and rendering, flying, sports sponsorship, writing; *Clubs* Special Forces; *Style*— Eran Bauer, Esq; ✉ Ashby Hall, Ashby de la Launde, Lincoln LN4 3JG (e-mail bauer@civil-defence.org)

BAUER, Willy Benedikt (ne Gegen-Bauer); OBE (2012); s of Willy Gegen-Bauer (d 1990), of Stuttgart, Germany, and Maria, Elizabeth, *née* Schuhbauer (d 1965); *b* 8 November 1937; *Educ* GS and HS Biberachy, Hotel Sch Heidelburg (Dip); *Career* hotelier; mgmnt trg Hotel Rad Biberach Germany 1957–60; hotel trg: Lausanne and Geneva Switzerland 1961–62, Grand Hotel Eastbourne 1962–63, Grand Metropolitan Hotel London 1963–65; banqueting mgmnt trg Hilton International London 1965; various mgmnt positions Trust Houses 1965–69; gen mangr Trust House Forte: Red Lion Colchester 1969–71, Cairn Hotel Harrogate 1971–72, St George's Hotel Liverpool 1972–75, Hyde Park Hotel 1975–80; exec dir and gen mangr Grosvenor House Park Lane 1980–81, gen mangr The Savoy London 1982–83, md The Savoy Management Ltd (The Savoy, The Lygon Arms, Wiltons, St Quintous Restaurants) 1983–89, chief exec The Wentworth Group 1989–; dir: The Westbury Hotels (London and NY), Molton Brown; chm A B Hotels; memb The Walpole Ctee; European Hotelier of the Year 1985, Hotel of the Year Award 1988; Freeman City of London 1987; memb: Master Innholders 1987, Chaîne des Rotisseurs, Reunion des Gastronomes, Savoy Gastronomes (pres 2000), Univ of Surrey Food & Wine Soc 1986, RAGB 1990, IoD; hon memb Acad of Culinary Arts; FHCIMA 1987, FRSA 1993; *Recreations* music, theatre, sport, gardening, architecture, design, antiques; *Clubs* The Duke's 100–1990, Wentworth, Home House, RAC, Groucho (hon memb); *Style*— Willy B G Bauer, Esq, OBE, FHCIMA; ✉ A B Hotels, 50–60 Great Cumberland Place, London W1H 8DD

BAUGH, (John William) Matthew (Matt); OBE (2013); Dr David Baugh, and Nicola Baugh; *b* 24 July 1973, Ndola, Zambia; *Educ* Oratory Sch Reading, Univ of Bristol (BA, MSc), Jt Services Command and Staff Coll UK Defence Acad; *m* Dr Caroline Baugh; 3 c; *Career* diplomat; DFID: head Kosovo Crisis Unit 1999–2000, head Humanitarian Policy and Global Response Team 2000–01, head Afghanistan Crisis Team 2001–02; first sec Khartoum 2002–04, head UK Post-Conflict Reconstruction Unit 2005–06, head Iraq Dept DFID 2006–07, PPS to Sec of State for Int Devpt 2008–09, UK sr rep for Somalia Br Office for Somalia 2010–12, non-resident ambass to the Somali Repub 2012–13, head Central and Southern Africa Dept FCO 2013–14, head East and West Africa Dept FCO

2014–; *Recreations* rugby, skiing, mountaineering; *Style—* Mr Matt Baugh, OBE; ✉ c/o FCO, King Charles Street, London SW1A 2AH

BAUGHAN, Michael Christopher; s of Prof Edward Christopher Baughan, CBE (d 1995), and Jacqueline Fors, *née* Hodge (d 1986); bro of Julian Baughan, QC, *qv*; *b* 25 April 1942; *Educ* Westminster Sch; *m* 1975, Moira Elizabeth, da of Percy Reginald Levy, MBE; 2 s (James b 1977, Nicholas b 1979); *Career* N M Rothschild & Sons 1959–66; Lazard Brothers & Co Ltd: joined 1966, dir 1979–86, md 1986–99, dir 2000–02, sr advsr 2002–03; memb Bd of Govrs Westminster Sch and Cncl Westminster Sch Soc 1980–, memb Slrs Disciplinary Tbnl 1990–; tstee The Pilgrim Tst 2011–; *Clubs* Brooks's, Garrick; *Style—* Michael C Baughan, Esq

BAUM, Louis Clarence; s of Rudolf Josef Baum (d 1984), and Heather, *née* Shulman; *b* 15 March 1948; *Educ* SA Coll Sch, Univ of Cape Town (BA); *m* 1971 (m dis 1982), Stephanie, *née* Goodman; 1 s (Simon b 1979); *Career* author of children's books; journalist Cape Times 1969–74; The Bookseller: journalist 1976–79, ed 1980–99, ed rights report 1999–; *Books* JuJu and the Pirate (1983), I Want to see the Moon (1984), After Dark (1984), Are We Nearly There? (1986), Joey's Coming Home Today (1989), Tea with Bea (2006); *Recreations* writing; *Clubs* The Groucho (dir 1984–98); *Style—* Louis Baum, Esq

BAUMAN, Irena; da of Zygmunt Bauman, and Janina, *née* Levinson; *b* 19 December 1955; *Educ* Poland, Israel, Lawnswood HS Leeds, Univ of Liverpool Sch of Architecture (BA, BArch); *m* 30 April 1983, Maurice Patrick Lyons; 1 s (Alexander b 26 July 1985), 1 da (Hannah b 21 March 1989); *Career* architect; estab: Bauman Pickles Assocs 1989, Bauman Lyons Architects 1992; projects incl: regeneration of the South Promenade Bridlington (commendation Nat Civic Tst Awards 1999, RIBA Award for Architecture 2000, RICS Pro Yorks Award for Tourism 2001), office conversion 31 The Calls Leeds (Leeds Architecture Award 1999), conversion of agriculture barns for Yorkshire Sculpture Park, Host Media Centre Leeds (Leeds Architecture Commendation 2001, commendation Civic Tst 2002, shortlisted RIBA Award 2002), bus shelters Bradford (shortlisted White Rose Award 2002, shortlisted Int Transport Award 2002, BBDA Award 2002, shortlisted RIBA Award 2003); cmmr CABE, advsr Architecture and Built Environment Panel Arts Cncl, memb Leeds Architecture and Design Initiative; delivers lectures throughout UK, external examiner Sheffield Sch of Architecture 2002–; featured in several books and jls on contemporary Br architecture; Corus Colourcoat Sustainable Devpt Award 2002, runner-up Eurocity Awards 2002, winner Designs on Democracy 2003; RIBA 1981, ARB 1981; *Exhibitions* incl: Imminent & Eminent Practices (Site Gallery Leeds) 1997, Interventions (Site Gallery Leeds) 1998, Quality in Urban Spaces (Design Centre Barnsley) 1999, New Architects 2 (Architecture Fndn) 2001, Designs on Democracy (RIBA Gallery) 2003, Do IT Better (RIBA Gallery) 2003; *Style—* Ms Irena Bauman; ✉ Bauman Lyons Architects Ltd, Regent House, 15 Hawthorn Road, Leeds, West Yorkshire LS7 4PH (☎ 0113 294 4200, fax 0113 294 1234, e-mail irena@baumanlyons.co.uk)

BAUME, Jonathan Edward; s of George Frederick Baume (d 1998), and Mary Louisa, *née* Hardwick (d 1990); *b* 14 July 1953; *Educ* Queen Elizabeth GS Wakefield, Keble Coll Oxford (MA); *Career* with Oxfordshire CC 1974–77, Dept of Employment Gp 1977–87, TUC 1987–89 (memb Gen Cncl 2001–); FDA (formerly Assoc of First Division Civil Servants): asst gen sec 1989–94, dep gen sec 1994–97, gen sec 1997–2012; memb: Ministerial Advsy Gp on Openness in the Public Sector 1998–99, Ministerial Advsy Gp on Implementation of the Freedom of Information Act 2001–, Age Advsy Gp DTI 2004–; memb: CPRE, Nat Tst; FRSA; *Recreations* yoga, jazz, world music, rambling; *Clubs* Athenaeum; *Style—* Jonathan Baume, Esq

BAVIDGE, Elizabeth Mary (Liz); OBE (1997), JP (1979); da of Walter Robert Ashton (d 1972), and Mary Newton, *née* Donaldson (d 1986); *b* 24 August 1945; *Educ* Carlisle and Co HS for Girls, Univ of Newcastle upon Tyne (BA); *m* 1972, Nigel Patrick Bavidge (d 2010), s of Dr Kenneth George Scott Bavidge (d 1972); 2 c (Gabrielle Mary b 1972, Fintan Nicholas Ashton b 1975); *Career* graduate trainee Shell-Mex and BP Ltd 1967–72, pt/t lectr in English language and literature Percival Whitley Coll 1980–87, asst princ Airedale and Wharfedale Coll Leeds 1992 (lectr in flexible learning opportunities 1987–92); nat pres Nat Cncl of Women 1990–92 (nat vice-pres 1988–90), co-chair Women's Nat Cmmn 1995–97, cmmr Cmmn on Women and the Criminal Justice System 2003–09; dir EM Associates (orgn devpt conslts), dir Bavidge Consulting Ltd; chair: Yorks and The Humber Fair Play Consortium 2002–, Fair Play Partnership 2002–09, Yorkshire Youth and Music; chair Bd Together Women 2012–, dir Women Returners' Network 1998–99, tstee Austin Friars St Monica's Sch 2013–, tstee Community Fndn for Calderdale 2015–; Hon Freeman Borough of Calderdale 2000; FRSA (memb Working Gp on Early Educn); *Books* Let's Talk to God (1980); *Recreations* playing the piano, making bread, speaking French, eating; *Style—* Mrs E M Bavidge, OBE; ✉ 22 Savile Park, Halifax, West Yorkshire HX1 3EW (☎ 01422 353955, e-mail lizbavidge@aol.com)

BAXENDALE, Helen; *Career* actress; *Theatre* After Miss Julie (Donmar Warehouse) 2004, Swimming with Sharks (Vaudeville) 2007; *Television* Cardiac Arrest 1994, Dangerfield 1994, In Suspicious Circumstances 1994, Friends 1998–99, An Unsuitable Job for a Woman 1998, Cold Feet 1998–2003, Tales From The Mad House 2000, Adrian Mole – The Cappuccino Years 2001, The Only Boy for Me 2006, Dead Clever: The Life and Crimes of Julie Bottomley 2007, Marple: A Pocket Full of Rye 2008, Kidnap and Ransom 2010; *Films* The Marshall 1993, Truth or Dare 1996, Crossing the Floor 1996, Bolse Vita 1996, Macbeth 1997, The Investigator 1997, Respect 1998, Ordinary Decent Criminal 1999, Dead by Monday 2001, Flyfishing 2002, Skagerrak 2003; *Style—* Ms Helen Baxendale

BAXENDALE, Presiley Lamorna; QC (1992); da of Geoffrey Arthur Baxendale, and Elizabeth, *née* Stevenson (decd); *b* 31 January 1951; *Educ* St Mary's Sch Wantage, St Anne's Coll Oxford (BA); *m* 1978, Richard Kieran Fitzgerald; 1 da (Felicity b 3 Dec 1981), 1 s (Charles b 9 April 1986); *Career* called to the Bar Lincoln's Inn 1974, jr counsel to Crown 1991; memb: ICSSTIS 1986–90, Cncl Justice 1994–2003 (vice chm Exec Ctee 1994–96); counsel to Scott Inquiry 1992–95; memb Ct of Govrs LSE 1988–; memb Administrative Law Bar Assoc; *Clubs* CWIL; *Style—* Miss Presiley Baxendale, QC; ✉ Blackstone Chambers, Temple, London EC4Y 9BW

BAXI, Vibhaker Kishore; s of Kishore Jayantilal Baxi (d 1967), and Indira Kishore Baxi; *b* 25 December 1947, Jamnagar, India; *Educ* Brooklands Co Tech Coll, Univ of Surrey Guildford (BSc), Brunel Univ (PGCE), Manchester Business Sch (MBA); *m* 12 Nov 1978, Hina, da of Indulal Vaikunthrai Vaidya (d 2007), and Devi Indulal Vaidya (d 2012); 1 da (Dr Mamta Ruparel b 1982); *Career* fin inst account offr Citibank Dubai 1975–76, asst treas Citibank NA Dubai 1976–78; treas: Citibank NA Bahrain 1979–80, Chemical Bank Hong Kong 1981–85; head and md Money Market & Securities Trading Chemical Bank London 1985–89, sr risk mangr (interest rates) Hongkong & Shanghai Banking Corp London 1989–92, jt md James Capel Gilts Ltd (HSBC subsid) 1991–92, global mangr money markets HSBC/Midland Global Markets 1992–94; chm and md Navras Records Ltd 1992–, risk mgmnt conslt and investment mangr 1994–, trading advsr Emeritus Fund SA (formerly Opus Fund SA) 1995–, advsr/mangr Amas Hinduja AAA Bond Fund Banque Amas SA 1996–98; UK Hindi Ctee Award for Services to (Indian) Culture 2005, Music Forum Media Award for Contib to Indian Classical Music (on behalf of Int Fndn for Fine Arts) 2006; MInstD; *Recreations* travel, music, current affairs, reading, fine wines, sports, fine art; *Clubs* Middlesex CCC; *Style—* Vibhaker Baxi, Esq; ✉ 22 Sherwood Road, London NW4 1AD (☎ 020 8203 2553, fax 020 8203 2542, e-mail vibbaxi@gmail.com)

BAXTER, Alan James; CBE (2011); *Career* fndr Alan Baxter & Associates LLP 1974; projects incl: Paddington Station, Tate Britain, Oxford Castle, LSE, London Bridge Station, St Martin-in-the-Fields, Hampton Court, Nat Gallery; *Style—* Alan Baxter, Esq, CBE; ✉ Alan Baxter & Associates LLP, 75 Cowcross Street, London EC1M 6EL

BAXTER, Canon Dr Christina Ann; CBE (2005); da of Leslie John David Baxter (d 2011), and Madge Adeline, *née* Law; *b* 8 March 1947; *Educ* Walthamstow Hall Sch Sevenoaks, Univ of Durham (BA), Univ of Bristol (CertEd), Univ of Durham (PhD); *Career* head of religious educn John Leggott Sixth Form Coll Scunthorpe 1973–76 (asst teacher 1969–73), pt/t tutor St John's Coll Durham and univ research student 1976–79; St John's Coll Nottingham: lectr in Christian doctrine 1979–, dean 1988–97, princ 1997–2012, ret; guest prof of theol Princeton Theol Seminary 1990, Warfield lectr Princeton 1996; chm House of Laity Gen Synod C of E 1995–2010 (vice-chm 1990–95); memb Archbishops' Cncl C of E 1999–2010; DTh Univ of Chester (hc) 2013; *Recreations* swimming, gardening, all things creative; *Style—* Canon Dr Christina Baxter, CBE; ✉ 18 St Michael's Square, Bramcote, Nottingham NG9 3HG (☎ 0115 922 4087, e-mail drchristinabaxter@btinternet.com)

BAXTER, (Charles) Duncan; s of James Leslie Baxter, of Kingston upon Thames, and Doris, *née* Watson; *b* 20 February 1953, Malton, Yorks; *Educ* Trinty Coll Oxford (scholar, MA); *m* July 1977, Neredah, *née* Coupland; 2 s (Alexander b 13 April 1981, Sebastian b 11 Nov 1983); *Career* asst master Gresham's 1975–84, head of Eng and drama and academic dir Wycliffe Coll Stonehouse 1984–91, headmaster Kingston GS 1991–2009; FRSA, HMC 1991; *Publications* various articles on the poetry of John Milton 1988–, articles on educn in nat press 1992–; *Recreations* choral music, church architecture, hill walking, cricket, writing; *Clubs* East India; *Style—* Duncan Baxter, Esq

BAXTER, Glen; s of Charles Bertie Baxter (d 1993), and Florence Mary, *née* Wood (d 1988); *b* 4 March 1944; *Educ* Cockburn HS Leeds, Leeds Coll of Art (NDD); *m* Carole Agis; 1 da (Zoë b 1975), 1 s (Harry b 1978); *Career* artist; pt/t lectr Goldsmiths Coll London 1974–87; regular contrib to Le Monde; Chevalier Ordre des Arts et des Lettres 2013; exhibitions: Gotham Book Mart Gallery NY 1974, 1976 and 1979, ICA London 1981, MOMA Oxford 1981, Nigel Greenwood 1981, 1983, 1987 and 1990, Galleria Del Cavallino Venice 1984, Royal Festival Hall 1984, Holly Solomon Gallery NY 1985 and 1988, Sydney Biennale 1986, Fuller Goldeen San Francisco 1986, Saouma Gallery Paris 1987, 1989 and 1993, Musée de L'Abbaye Sainte-Croix Les Sables D'Olonne 1987, MUHKA Antwerp 1988, DC Art Sydney 1990, Adelaide Festival 1992, Michael Nagy Gallery Sydney 1992 and 1996, Anthony Wilkinson Fine Art London 1994 and 1996, Ginza Art Space Tokyo 1994, Artothèque de Caen France 1995, Le Salon d'Art Brussels 1996, Galerie de la Châtre Paris 1997, 2001 and 2004–05, Modernism Gallery San Francisco 1997, 1998, 2002 and 2006, Galerie de la Châtre Paris 1998, Angoulême France and Chatou Paris 1999, Palais de Congrès Paris 1999, Château Châlus 1999, Chris Beetles Gallery London 1999, La Louvière 1999, St Malo 2000, Lombard Freid Gallery NY 2001, Galerie Daniel Blau Munich 2001, Wetering Galerie Amsterdam 2004, Flowers Central London 2004 and 2006, Flowers Gallery NY 2005, Martine & Thibault de la Châthe Paris 2006, 2010 and 2012, Sens Dessus Dessous, Le Monde à l'Envers (Centre Regnl d'Art Contemporain Sete) 2008, Flowers Central London 2009, Fondation Espace Ecureuil Toulouse 2009, Galerie Daniel Blau Munich 2009, Poitiers Museum 2010, Meymac Contemporary Art Centre France 2010, Flowers Gallery London 2011, 2012 and 2014, Museé de Cognac 2011, Comedie du Livre Montpellier 2012, Visual Humour in Art Fitzwilliam Museum Cambridge 2015, Foire au Jambon City of Bayonne France 2016, Galerie Isabelle Gounod Paris 2016; Glen Baxter Tableware launched by Richard Dennis Kensington London 1999; Glen Baxter Tapestry Commande Publique manufactured in Limousin and exhibited at Château Chalus Chabrol; *Books* The Impending Gleam (1981), Atlas (1982), His Life (1983), Jodhpurs in the Quantocks (1987), Charles Malarkey and the Belly Button Machine (with William and Bren Kennedy), Welcome to the Weird World of Glen Baxter (1989), The Billiard Table Murders – A Gladys Babbington Morton Mystery (1990), Glen Baxter Returns to Normal (1992), The Collected Blurtings of Baxter (1993), The Wonder Book of Sex (1995), Glen Baxter's Gourmet Guide (1997), Blizzards of Tweed (1999), Podium (album of woodblock prints, 1999), The Unhinged World of Glen Baxter (2001), Trundling Grunts (2002), Loomings over the Suet (2004), Haro sur le Suif (2005), Speech with Humans (jtly, 2007), Ominous Stains (2010), Le Safari Historico – Gastronomique en Poitou Charentes (2010), Colonel Baxter's Dutch Safari (2012), New and Selected Blurtings (2016); *Recreations* croquet, marquetry and stump work; *Clubs* Chelsea Arts, Ale and Quail, Academy (London); *Style—* Glen Baxter, Esq; ✉ website www.glenbaxter.com

BAXTER, Margaret Eleanor (Maggie); OBE (2010); da of Charles Frank Alexander Baxter, of Shaftesbury, Dorset, and Eleanor Frances Mary, *née* Bloomer; *b* 7 July 1947; *Educ* Godolphin Sch, Open Univ (BA); *m* 1 (m dis); m 2, George Sean Baine, s of Roney Baine (d 1988), of Belfast; 1 s (Alex b 13 May 1981), 1 da (Holly b 30 Jan 1985), 2 step s (Jack b 10 Feb 1972, Kieran b 25 May 1974); *Career* project dir Action Res Centre 1972–75, dir Dame Colet House Settlement Stepney 1975–80, vol orgns offr London Borough of Camden 1982–89, advsr Baring Fndn 1989–91; Comic Relief/Charity Projects: grants dir (UK) 1991–94, grants dir (UK & Africa) 1994–, grants dir and dep chief exec 1997–99, acting chief exec (secondment) Diana Princess of Wales Fund 1997–98, exec dir WOMANKIND Worldwide 1999–2007; ind conslt 2007–; advsr True Colours Tst 2009; project mangr Two Little Girls campaign 2009; tstee: Tst for London, City Parochial Fndn 1989–2010, Hilden Charitable Fund 1997, Dance United 2001–09 (chair), Women at Risk 2003–07, Green Belt Movement Int 2005 (chair Europe), Women for Refugee Women 2007–13 (chair), Rosa – UK Women's Fund 2008 (chair 2008–15), Tst for London Fleet Grants Ctee 2011; assoc memb Oxfam 2001–06; ex-govr Beckford Sch (former chm); *Recreations* family, theatre, cinema, tennis; *Style—* Ms Maggie Baxter, OBE; ✉ 14 Ebbsfleet Road, London NW2 3NA (e-mail maggiebaxter100@gmail.com)

BAXTER, Prof Murdoch Scott; s of John Sawyer Napier Baxter (d 1977), and Margaret Hastie, *née* Murdoch (d 2011); *b* 12 March 1944, Glasgow; *Educ* Hutchesons' Boys' GS, Univ of Glasgow (BSc, PhD); *m* 3 Aug 1968, Janice, da of James Henderson (d 1990), of Shawlands, Glasgow; *Career* visiting res fell (Apollo 11 Lunar Res) NY State Univ 1969–70, sabbatical res conslt IAEA International Laboratory of Marine Radioactivity Monaco (radioactive waste disposal) 1981–82; Univ of Glasgow: lectr in environmental radiochemistry Dept of Chemistry 1970–85, prof 1985–95, dir Scottish Univ Res and Reactor Centre 1985–90; dir IAEA Marine Environment Laboratory Monaco 1990–97; environmental conslt 1997–; advsr to Inst of Nuclear Technol (ITN) Portugal 2000–03; memb: Challenger Soc, Scottish Assoc for Marine Science, various IAEA expert gps, Editorial Bd Journal of Radioanalytical and Nuclear Chemistry 1985–2000; hon invited memb Int Union of Radioecology (memb advsy panel) 1999–; Fell Int Union of Eco-Ethics 1999–; CChem, FRSC 1984, FRSE 1989; Chevalier Order of St Charles 1997; *Publications* fndr ed Journal of Environmental Radioactivity, series ed Radioactivity in the Environment 1999–2012; author of more than 180 res papers in scientific lit; *Recreations* sports, walking, good food, volunteering; *Clubs* Queens Park FC, Balvicar Golf, Scotch Malt Whisky Soc; *Style—* Prof Murdoch Baxter, FRSE; ✉ Ampfield House, Clachan Seil, By Oban, Argyll PA34 4TL (☎ 01852 300351, e-mail baxter@isleofseil.demon.co.uk)

BAYES, Rt Rev Paul; *see:* Liverpool, Bishop of

BAYFIELD, Rabbi Dr Anthony Michael (Tony); CBE (2011); s of Ronald David Bayfield, of Redbridge, Essex, and Sheila Queenie, *née* Mann; *b* 4 July 1946; *Educ* Royal Liberty Sch

Gidea Park, Magdalene Coll Cambridge (MA), Leo Baeck Coll London (Rabbinic ordination), Lambeth (DD); *m* 3 Aug 1969, Linda Gavinia, da of Hyman Rose (d 1976); 2 da (Lucy b 1972, Miriam b 1979), 1 s (Daniel b 1975); *Career* rabbi NW Surrey Synagogue 1972–82; chief exec Reform Synagogues of Great Britain and head The Movement for Reform Judaism 1994–2011 (pres 2011–); lectr Leo Baeck Coll 1973–; dir: The Sternberg Centre for Judaism 1983–2011, Manor House Tst 1983–2011, Centre for Jewish Education Tst 1986–; cnsllr Spelthorne MGC 1973–82; chm: Assembly of Rabbis Reform Synagogues of GB 1980–81, Cncl of Reform and Lib Rabbis 1983–85; pres Cncl of Christians and Jews 2004–; tstee Michael Goulston Educnl Fndn; fndr ed Manna (quarterly jl) 1983–2011; *Books* Prejudice (1974), Churban – The Murder of the Jews of Europe (1982), Dialogue with a Difference (ed with Marcus Braybrooke, 1992), Sinai, Law and Responsible Autonomy: Reform Judaism and the Halakhic Tradition (1993), He Kissed Him and They Wept (ed with Brichto and Fisher, 2002); *Recreations* family, reading, walking, watching football; *Style*— Rabbi Dr Tony Bayfield, CBE; ✉ The Sternberg Centre for Judaism, The Manor House, 80 East End Road, Finchley, London N3 2SY (☎ 020 8349 5645, fax 020 8349 5699, e-mail president@reformjudaism.org.uk)

BAYLEY, Sir Hugh; kt (2015); s of Michael Bayley (d 2013), and Pauline Bayley (d 2006); *b* 9 January 1952, Oxford; *Educ* Haileybury, Univ of Bristol (BSc), Univ of York (BPhil); *m* 1984, Fenella, *née* Jeffers; 1 s, 1 da; *Career* nat offr NALGO 1977–82 (dist offr 1975–77), gen sec International Broadcasting Tst 1982–86, res fell in health economics Univ of York 1987–92 (lectr in social policy 1986–87); MP (Lab): York 1992–97 (also contested 1987), City of York 1997–2010, York Central 2010–15; PPS to sec of state for Health 1997–99, min DSS 1999–2001, dep speaker 2010; memb House of Commons Select Ctees: Health 1992–97, Int Devpt 2001–15; memb Chairmen's Panel, chm Public Bill Ctees 2005–15; memb NATO Parly Assembly 1997–99 and 2001–15 (chm Ctee on Economics and Security 2008–11, vice-pres 2010–12, pres 2012–14); chair Africa All-Pty Parly Gp 2003–13 (vice-chair 2013–15); cncllr London Borough of Camden 1980–86 (chm Lab Gp 1982–85); memb York DHA 1988–90; *Publications* The Nation's Health (1995), Health Crisis – What Crisis? (ed, 1996), Why NATO Matters (2014), A Citizen's Guide to NATO's Priorities After the Wales Summit (2014); *Recreations* photography, hill-walking; *Style*— Sir Hugh Bayley; ✉ 9 Holly Terrace, York YO10 4DS

BAYLEY, Prof Peter James; s of late John Henry Bayley, of Portreath, Cornwall, and Margaret, *née* Burness; *b* 20 November 1944; *Educ* Redruth GS, Emmanuel Coll Cambridge (MA, PhD), Ecole Normale Supérieure Paris; *Career* Univ of Cambridge: fell Emmanuel Coll 1969–71, fell Gonville & Caius Coll 1971–, lectr in French 1978–85, Drapers prof of French 1985–2010, chm Sch of Arts and Humanities 2001–03; hon sr res fell Inst of Romance Studies Univ of London 1990; vice-pres Assoc of Univ Profs of French 1989–97; pres Soc for French Studies 1990–92; Chevalier du Tastevin (Burgundy) 1997, Commandeur des Palmes Académiques (France) 2006 (Officier 1988); *Books* French Pulpit Oratory 1598–1650 (1980), The Equilibrium of Wit: essays for Odette de Mourgues (ed with D Coleman, 1982), Selected Sermons of the French Baroque (1983), Présences du Moyen Âge et de la Renaissance en France Classique (2003); contrib: Critique et création littéraires en France (ed Fumaroli, 1977), Bossuet: la Prédication au XVIIe siècle (ed Collinet and Goyet, 1980), Catholicism in Early Modern History: a guide to research (ed O'Malley, 1988), Convergences: rhetoric and poetic in seventeenth-century France (ed Rubin and McKinley, 1989), Dictionnaire des littératures (ed Didier, 1994), Oxford Companion to Literature in French (ed France, 1995); contrib: Cambridge Review, Dix-Septième Siècle, French Studies, Modern Language Review, Seventeenth-Century French Studies, Acts of the North American Soc for Seventeenth-Century French Literature; *Recreations* Spain, wine and food, gardening; *Style*— Prof Peter Bayley; ✉ Gonville & Caius College, Cambridge CB2 1TA (☎ 01223 332439, e-mail pb47@cam.ac.uk)

BAYLEY, Stephen Paul; s of late Donald Sydney Staines Bayley, of Staffs, and late Anne, *née* Wood; *b* 13 October 1951; *Educ* Quarry Bank Sch Liverpool, Univ of Manchester (BA), Univ of Liverpool (MA); *m* 29 Sept 1981, Flo, da of Richard Ernest Fothergill, of London; 1 s (Bruno b 3 June 1985), 1 da (Coco b 9 March 1987); *Career* history and theory of art lectr: Open Univ 1974–76, Univ of Kent 1976–80; chief exec Design Museum 1981–90, dir Boilerhouse Project 1981–86; princ Eye-Q Ltd 1990–; creative dir New Millennium Experience 1997–98; contributing ed: GQ 1991–, Esquire 1997–, Management Today 1999–, Car magazine; former memb Design Policy Ctee LRT, govr History of Advertising Tst 1985–96; Columnist of the Year PPA 1995; fell Liverpool Inst of Performing Arts 2002, hon fell Univ of Wales Inst 2007, hon fell RIBA 2009; Chevalier de l'Ordre des Arts et des Lettres (France) 1989; *Books* In Good Shape (1979), Albert Memorial (1981), Harley Earl (1983), Conran Directory of Design (1985), Sex, Drink and Fast Cars (1986), Commerce and Culture (1989), Taste: The Secret Meaning of Things (1991), The Beefeater Two-Day Guide to London (1993), The Paris Style Guide (1994), The Lucky Strike Packet (1998), Labour Camp (1998), General Knowledge (2000), Sex (2001), The Dictionary of Idiocy (2003), Life's a Pitch (2007), Intelligence Made Visible (2007), Work: The building of the Channel Tunnel rail link (2008), Cars: Freedom style sex power motion colour everything (2008), Woman as Design (2009), Liverpool: Shaping the City (2010), La Dolce Vita (2011), Ugly: The Aesthetics of Everything (2012); *Recreations* words, pictures, food, drink, travel, sport; *Clubs* Hurlingham, Chelsea Arts; *Style*— Stephen Bayley; ✉ 23 Ganton Street, London W1F 9BW

BAYLEY, Trevor John; OBE (2007); *b* 22 September 1951; *Educ* Newcastle-under-Lyme HS; *m*; 5 c; *Career* articled clerk Alex G Duncan & Co 1970–74, PA to ptnr L George Fetzer & Co 1974–76, gp accountant Alfred Clough Ltd 1976–79; Britannia Building Society: fin accountant 1979–85, chief accountant 1985, dep gen mangr 1986, gen mangr (fin) 1987–88, fin dir 1988–94, gp fin dir 1994–98, corp devpt dir 1998–2000; also dir various subsid companies; fin dir and dep ceo Nat Savings and Investment 2001–06 (acting ceo 2006); dir: Saffron Building Soc 2007–14, A B Publishing Ltd 2007–12, Waterloo Mills Ltd 2011–; FCA (ACA 1974); *Recreations* clay pigeon shooting, sport, music; *Style*— Trevor Bayley, Esq, OBE; ✉ Woodside, Clay Lake, Endon, Stoke-on-Trent, Staffordshire, ST9 9DD

BAYLIS, Prof Peter H; s of Derek Howard Baylis (d 1995), and Lore Bertha, *née* Ahrens; *b* 9 August 1943; *Educ* Wallington GS, Univ of Bristol (BSc, MB ChB), Univ of Birmingham (Fulbright-Hays scholar, MD); *m* 1968, Susan Mary Baylis; 1 s (Mark Richard b 2 June 1973), 2 da (Katherine Louise b 6 May 1975, Vanessa Ruth 23 April 1983); *Career* registrar and research fell Professorial Unit Birmingham 1974–77, clinical research fell in endocrinology Indiana Univ Sch of Med Indianapolis 1977–78, lectr in med Univ of Birmingham 1978–80; conslt physician Royal Victoria Infirmary 1980–; Med Sch Univ of Newcastle upon Tyne: sr lectr in med and endocrinology 1980–90, prof of experimental med 1990–2005, dean of med 1997–2005, provost Faculty of Med Sci 2002–05; non-exec dir Newcastle Hosps NHS Tst 2003–10 (sr ind non-exec dir 2011–); major research projects incl successful devpt of laboratory ways to measure small peptides, vasopressin and oxytocin with application to resolve clinical problems; vice-pres Age Concern Newcastle 2001–; memb Assoc of Physicians of GB and I 1984; FRCP 1983, FMedSci 1998; *Books* Endocrinology (contrib, 2001), Oxford Textbook of Med (contrib, 2003); *Recreations* theatre, music, gardening, road running (jogging now); *Style*— Prof Peter H Baylis; ✉ 53 The Rise, Darras Hall, Ponteland, Newcastle upon Tyne NE20 9LQ (☎ 01661 823244, e-mail phbaylis@hotmail.com); The Medical School, University of Newcastle upon Tyne, Framlington Place, Newcastle upon Tyne NE2 4HH (☎ 0191 222 7003, fax 0191 222 6621, e-mail dean-of-medicine@ncl.ac.uk)

BAYLIS, Trevor Graham; CBE (2015, OBE 1997); s of late Cecil Archibald Walter Baylis, and late Gladys Jane Baylis; *b* 13 May 1937; *Career* inventor; *early career* GB swimmer (aged 15) 1952, staff Soil Mechanics Lab Southall 1953–57 (pt/t day release to study mech and structural engrg at local tech coll), Nat Serv PT instr 1957–61 (rep Army and Imperial Services at swimming), salesman Purley Pools 1961, turned professional swimmer, stuntman and entertainer (incl performances as underwater escape artiste in Berlin circus), fndr Shotline Displays (aquatic display co) and Shotline Steel Swimming Pools (pool mfrs); *latter career* inventor: Orange Aids (for the disabled) 1985, wind up radio 1991 (manufactured as the Freeplay Radio from 1997); chm Trevor Baylis Brands plc; recipient: BBC Design for Best Product and Best Design 1996, Presidential Gold Medal IMechE 1998, Walpole Medal of Excellence 2001, Export Times Exporter of the Year Award, Rotary Club Paul Harris Fellowship; numerous appearances on TV incl: Tomorrow's World, QED, This is Your Life; visiting prof Univ of Buckinghamshire; lectr and demonstrator British Council Africa and Australia 1998; vice-pres: European Women of Achievement Awards, Techknowlogy; after dinner speaker; hon memb: CBI, Radio Soc; patron: Heathrow Special Needs Farm (formerly Spelthorne Farm Project for the Handicapped), POPAN (Prevention of Professional Abuse Network), Motor Sport Endeavour; DTech (hc): Nottingham Trent Univ, Southampton Inst, Univ of Brighton; Hon MSc: UEA, Univ of Teesside; Hon DUniv Open Univ, Hon Dr Middx Univ, Hon MBA Univ of Luton, Hon Degree Brunel Univ, Hon DUniv Oxford Brookes Univ, Hon DSci Heriot Watt Univ 2003, Hon DEng Leeds Met Univ 2005; hon res fell Sch of Journalism Univ of Wales Cardiff, hon fell Univ of Wolverhampton, hon fell Univ of Wales Inst; *Publications* Clock This (1999); *Style*— Trevor Baylis, Esq, CBE; ✉ Haven Studio, Eel Pie Island, Twickenham, Middlesex TW1 3DY (☎ 020 8891 1151, fax 020 8891 0673, e-mail trevor@trevorbaylis.com)

BAYLISS, Hon Mrs (Mary Selina); CVO (2015), DL (Berks 2007), JP (1978); *née* Bridgeman; da of 2 Viscount Bridgeman, KBE, CB, DSO, MC (d 1982), and Hon Mary Kathleen, *née* Lane-Fox, JP (Viscountess Bridgeman, d 1981); *b* 14 January 1940, Bramham, Yorks; *Educ* St Mary's Sch Wantage; *m* 1962, Jeremy David Bagot Bayliss, *qv*; 3 s (Jonathan Andrew Bagot b 2 Jan 1964, Richard Charles b 11 Dec 1965 d 2015, Patrick Thomas Clive b 6 March 1968); *Career* chm Family Panel 1994–97, chm Reading Bench 1998–2001; Lord Lt Royal Co of Berks 2008–15; pres Swallowfield Horticultural Soc, hon life pres Berks Community Fndn; patron Reading Mencap, county vice-pres Royal Br Legion, pres Wokingham and District Cancer Care Tst; memb Order of St Frideswide; *Recreations* music, gardening, travel; *Style*— The Hon Mrs Bayliss, CVO, DL, JP

BAYLISS, Jeremy David Bagot; s of Edmund Bayliss (d 1990), of Guernsey, and Marjorie Clare Thompson (d 1983); *b* 27 March 1937; *Educ* Harrow, Sidney Sussex Coll Cambridge (MA); *m* 1962, Hon Mary Selina, *qv*, 3 da of 2 Viscount Bridgeman, KBE, CB, DSO, MC (d 1982); 3 s (Jonathan Andrew Bagot b 2 Jan 1964, Richard Charles b 11 Dec 1965, Patrick Thomas Clive b 6 March 1968); *Career* Nat Serv 2 Lt Coldstream Gds 1956–57; Gerald Eve 1960–97: ptnr 1967, jt sr ptnr 1988, sr ptnr 1990–97; chm Gerald Eve Financial Services Ltd 1989–96; RICS: memb Gen Cncl 1987–97, pres Planning and Devpt Div 1989–90, pres 1996–97; chief exec Royal Botanic Gardens Kew Fndn 1997–2002; Hon Co Organiser (Berks) NGS 2001–07; govr Bearwood Coll 2000–08 (chm 2003), tstee The Royal Merchant Navy Sch Fndn 2003–07, tstee Soc for Horticulture Therapy (Thrive) 2004–09; FRICS 1971 (ARICS 1962); *Recreations* gardening, country pursuits, reading; *Clubs* Boodle's; *Style*— Jeremy Bayliss, Esq; ✉ Loddon Lower Farm, Swallowfield, Berks RG7 1JE (☎ 0118 988 3218, e-mail jeremy@baylissnet.com)

BAYLISS, His Hon Judge Thomas William Maxwell; QC (2003); s of Thomas Maxwell Bayliss (d 1975), and Dorothy Vera Bayliss (d 2007); *b* 24 June 1954, Gloucester; *Educ* Univ of Leeds (LLB); *m* 3 Sept 1977, Caroline Jane, *née* Allpress; 1 da (Alice Caroline (Mrs Langley) b 16 Aug 1979), 1 s (Nicholas b 10 Aug 1982); *Career* called to the Bar 1977; standing cnsl to Inland Revenue (crime) North Eastern Circuit 1993–2003, asst recorder 1993, recorder 2000, governing bencher Inner Temple 2010–, fee-paid judge First-Tier Tbnl (Health, Educn and Social Care Chamber) 2011, circuit judge (North Eastern Circuit) 2012–; *Style*— His Hon Judge Bayliss, QC; ✉ Leeds Combined Court Centre, The Courthouse, 1 Oxford Row, Leeds, West Yorkshire LS1 3BG

BAZALGETTE, Sir Peter Lytton; kt (2012); s of Paul Bazalgette(d 1999), and Diana, *née* Coffin (d 1995); *b* 22 May 1953; *Educ* Dulwich Coll, Fitzwilliam Coll Cambridge (MA, pres Cambridge Union); *m* 1985, Hilary Jane, *née* Newiss; 1 da (b 1986), 1 s (b 1990); *Career* BBC News trainee 1977; TV formats created: Ready Steady Cook (BBC2), Can't Cook Won't Cook (BBC1), Changing Rooms (BBC2), Ground Force (BBC1); formats sold to 30 countries; md Bazal Productions 1987–98, Endemol: UK prodr Big Brother (Channel 4), chm Endemol UK plc 2002–07, gp chief creative offr 2005–07, chm UK Holocaust Memorial Fndn 2015–; non-exec dir: Victoria Real, Zeppotron, Channel 4 2001–04, YouGov.com 2005–15, ITV 2013–; dep chm Nat Film and TV Sch 2002–09, chm Arts Cncl England 2013–, chm ITV 2016–; pres RTS 2010–; Ind Prodr of the Year Broadcast Prodn Awards 1997, McTaggart lectr Edinburgh Int TV Festival 1998, Hat Trick Pioneer Award Indies 1998, Indie-vidual Award for Outstanding Personal Contribution to the Ind Sector 2000, RTS Weldon Lecture 2001, Judges' Award RTS 2003; chm Crossness Engines Tst, vice-chm Br Acad of Gastronomes 1993–, tstee ENO 2004–; fell BAFTA 2000, FRTS (pres 2010–); *Books* BBC Food Check (jtly, 1989), The Food Revolution (jtly, 1991), You Don't Have to Diet (jtly, 1993), The Big Food and Drink Book (jtly, 1994), Billion Dollar Game (2005), Egon Ronay – A Memoir of A Man Who Taught Britain How To Eat (2011); *Recreations* arts; *Clubs* BAFTA; *Style*— Sir Peter Bazalgette; ✉ c/o Vikki Stewart (e-mail vikki@newbaz.com)

BEACHAM, Stephanie; *b* 28 February 1947; *Educ* Convent of the Sacred Heart Whetstone, QEGGS, RADA, Mime Sch Paris; *m* 2 da (Phoebe b 1974, Chloe b 1977); *Career* actress; spokesperson American Speech Language and Hearing Assoc; *Theatre* incl: Tea Party and The Basement (Duchess) 1969, London Cuckolds (Royal Court) 1977, Venice Preserved (NT) 1985, The Rover (RSC) 1988, An Ideal Husband (Broadway and Australia) 1997, Funny About Love 1999, A Busy Day (Lyric Theatre) 2000, Nobody's Perfect 2001, Elizabeth Rex 2002; *Television* incl: Tenko 1982, Connie 1984, The Colbys and Dynasty (ABC USA) 1985–87 and 1988–89, Sister Kate (NBC USA) 1989, The Picnic (BBC), The Silent Preacher (BBC), All The World's A Stage (BBC), French and Saunders (series II), To Be The Best, Riders (Anglia), Seaquest (Amblin/NBC), Dorothea Grant in No Bananas (BBC), Bad Girls (ITV), Coronation Street (ITV) 2009, Trollied 2012, Death in Paradise 2012; *Films* incl: The Games, Tam Lyn, The Nightcomers, The Wolves of Willoughby Chase, The Lilac Bus, Foreign Affairs, Unconditional Love, Would I Lie to You, Love and Other Disasters; *Style*— Ms Stephanie Beacham; ✉ c/o United Agents Ltd, 12–26 Lexington Street, London W1F 0LE (☎ 020 3214 0800, fax 020 3214 0801, website www.unitedagents.co.uk)

BEAL, Clifford Franklin; s of Clifford F Beal, and Lorraine F Beal; *b* 3 May 1958; *Educ* East Providence HS RI (Pell Medal in US History), Univ of Vermont (BA), Univ of Sussex (MA); *Career* asst ed Jl of Defence and Diplomacy 1984–86, public info offr American Inst of Aeronautics and Astronautics Washington DC 1986–89, managing ed Defense World 1989–90, freelance defence and aerospace journalist 1990–91, aerospace ed rising to ed-in-chief Jane's International Defense Review 1991–98, ed-in-chief Jane's Defence Weekly 1998–2003, dir The Strix Consultancy Ltd 2003–; guest lectr Ashridge Mgmnt Coll and Univ of Cardiff; broadcast commentator on defence issues; shortlisted BT Technol Journalist of the Year 1996 and 1997, shortlisted RAeS Journalist Awards 1998, BSME Ed of the Year 2000; memb Soc of Authors; memb RUSI, FRAeS; *Publications*

Quelch's Gold (2007), Gideon's Angel (2013), The Raven's Banquet (2014), The Guns of Ivrea (2016), The Witch of Torinia (2017); numerous articles in publications incl: Jane's Defence Weekly, Jane's IDR, Sunday Times, Military History Quarterly, New Scientist, Focus, Frontiers, World Monitor, International Herald Tribune, Daily Mail; *Recreations* museums and galleries, boating, shooting, cinema, reading, motoring; *Clubs* Whitefriars, Savile, RAF, Devonshire Soc of St James's; *Style*— Clifford Beal, Esq, FRAeS; ✉ c/o The Savile Club, 69 Brook Street, London W1K 4ER (e-mail clifford@cliffordbeal.com, website www.cliffordbeal.com, Twitter @clifford_beal)

BEAL, Dr Peter George; s of William George Beal, and Marjorie Ena, *née* Owen; *b* 16 April 1944, Coventry, Warks; *Educ* King Henry VIII GS Coventry, Univ of Leeds (BA, PhD); *m* 1, 1974 (m dis 1980), Gwyneth Morgan; m 2, 1982 (m dis 1994), Sally Josephine Taylor; 1 step s; m 3, 1998, Grace Janette Ioppolo; *Career* research ed Bowker Publishing and Mansell Publishing Ltd 1974–79; Sotheby's London: English manuscript expert 1980–2005, dir in Dept of Printed Books and Manuscripts 1996–2005 (dep dir 1990–96); J P R Lyell reader in bibliography Univ of Oxford 1995–96, visiting prof English Dept Univ of Reading 2000–02, sr research fell Inst of English Studies Univ of London 2002–, building on-line Catalogue of English Literary Manuscripts 1450–1700 (CELM) 2005–; memb Editorial Bd: English Literary Renaissance 2001–, Renaissance English Text Soc 2002–; advsr and conslt to various presses and projects incl OUP, Scolar Press, CUP and the Oxford DNB; numerous invited lectures in the UK, USA and Canada; memb: Cncl Br Acad 2000–01, Mgmnt Ctee Centre for Editing Lives and Letters QMC London 2001–07; FBA 1993, FSA 2007; *Publications* incl: Index of English Literary Manuscripts (Vol I Parts 1 and 2, 1980, Vol II Part 1 1987, Vol II Part 2 1993), English Verse Miscellanies of the Seventeenth Century (gen ed , 5 vols 1990), In Praise of Scribes: Manuscripts and their Makers in Seventeenth-Century England (1998), A Dictionary of English Manuscript Terminology 1450–2000 (2008); co-fndr and co-ed English Manuscript Studies 1100–1700 (Vol 1 1989, Vol 2 1990, Vol 3 1992, Vol 4 1993, Vol 5 1995, Vol 6 1997, Vol 7 1998, Vol 8 2000, Vol 9 2000, Vol 10 2002, Vol 11 2002, Vol 12 2005, Vol 13 2007, Vol 14 2008, Vol 15 2009, Vol 16 2011, Vol 17 2012, Vol 18 2013), Queen Elizabeth I and the Culture of Writing (co-ed, 2007); author of numerous articles in learned jls; *Style*— Dr Peter Beal, FBA, FSA; ✉ Institute of English Studies, Senate House, Malet Street, London WC1E 7HU (e-mail peter.beal@sas.ac.uk)

BEALBY, Walter; s of Harry Bealby, of Nottingham, and Heulwen, *née* Morris; *b* 8 January 1953; *Educ* Henry Mellish GS Nottingham, Univ of Bristol (BA); *m* 22 Nov 1980 (m dis 2012), Finnula Leonora Patricia, da of Daniel O'Leary, of Abingdon, Oxon; 1 s (Thomas Henry b 21 Jan 1985), 1 da (Polly Megan b 5 July 1988); *Career* called to the Bar Middle Temple 1976; Blackstone scholarship 1977; *Recreations* motor cycling, opera; *Style*— Walter Bealby, Esq; ✉ 5 Fountain Court, Steelhouse Lane, Birmingham B4 6DR (☎ 0121 606 0500, fax 0121 606 1501)

BEALE, Claire Elizabeth; da of Brian Beale, of Tamworth, Staffs, and Valerie, *née* Bingham; *b* 26 November 1966, Staffs; *Educ* Wilnecote HS, Univ of Manchester (BA); *Children* 1 s (Emerson b 28 Oct 2001), 1 da (Cordelia b 21 Dec 2005); *Career* media ed Marketing Magazine 1992; Campaign: media ed 1995, dep ed 2000, ed 2004–; columnist The Independent; memb Women in Advtg and Communications London (WACL); *Recreations* film, literature, walking; *Style*— Miss Claire Beale; ✉ Campaign, Haymarket Business Publications Ltd, 174 Hammersmith Road, London W6 7JP (☎ 020 8267 4683, e-mail claire.beale@haymarket.com)

BEALE, Prof Hugh Gurney; Hon QC (2002); s of Charles Beale, TD (d 1989), and Anne Freeland, *née* Gurney-Dixon (d 1953); *b* 4 May 1948; *Educ* The Leys Sch Cambridge, Exeter Coll Oxford (BA); *m* 18 July 1970, Jane Wilson, da of Nathan Cox (d 1980), of Clarkton, N Carolina; 2 s (Ned b 1977, Thomas b 1979), 1 da (Martha b 1981); *Career* lectr Univ of Connecticut 1969–71, called to the Bar Lincoln's Inn 1971 (hon bencher 1999–), lectr UCW Aberystwyth 1971–73, reader Univ of Bristol 1986–87 (lectr 1973–86), prof of law Univ of Warwick 1987–; law cmmr 2000–07; memb Commission for Euro Contract Law 1987–99; sr research fell Harris Manchester Coll Oxford 2014–17; FBA 2004; *Books* Remedies for Breach of Contract (1980), Contract Cases and Materials (with W D Bishop and M P Furmston, 1985, 1990, 1995, 2001 and 2007), Principles of European Contract Law, Part 1 and Part 2 (1995 and 1999), Chitty on Contracts (31 edn 2012 and 32 edn 2015), Casebooks on the Common Law of Europe: Contract (2 edn with B Fauvarque-Cosson, J Rutgers, D Tallon and S Vogenauer, 2010); *Recreations* fishing, music, walking; *Style*— Prof Hugh Beale, QC; ✉ School of Law, University of Warwick, Coventry CV4 7AL (e-mail hugh.beale@warwick.ac.uk)

BEALE, Inga; da of Raymond John Beale (d 2014), and Astri, *née* Gisholt (d 2009); *m* March 2014, Philippe Pfeiffer; *Career* with GE Insurance 1992–2006, gp ceo Converium Switzerland 2006–08, memb Gp Mgmnt Bd Zurich Insurance Gp 2008–11, gp ceo Canopius 2012–13, ceo Lloyd's 2014–; *Style*— Ms Inga Beale; ✉ Lloyd's, One Lime Street, London EC3M 7HA (website www.lloyds.com)

BEALE, Nicholas Clive Lansdowne; s of Prof Evelyn Martin Lansdowne Beale, FRS (d 1985), and Violette Elizabeth Anne, *née* Lewis; *b* 22 February 1955; *Educ* Winchester (scholar), Trinity Coll Cambridge (scholar, MA); *m* 16 July 1977, Christine Anne, da of Peter McPoland, of Bedford; 1 s (Rupert Christopher Lansdowne b 1977), 2 da (Rebecca Merryn Elizabeth b 1980, Rose Theodora Elizabeth b 1991); *Career* social philosopher and mgmnt conslt; md Beale Electronic Systems 1977–85, vice-chm Beale International Technology 1985–88, conslt McKinsey & Co 1988–89; chm: Beale Holdings 1988–95, Sciteb 1989–; dir: First Film Fndn 1991–95, Sector Dialogue Process 1992–; Oblate Alton Abbey 1994–; Freeman City of London 1996, Liveryman Worshipful Co of Information Technologists 1997 (dep chm Ethical & Spiritual Devpt Panel); FRSA 1991, FIMA 2012; *Books* R&D Short-Termism? (1991), Sciteb/Sunday Times Poll of R&D Effectiveness (1992), Industry/City Dialogue Guide (1994), City Science and Technology Dialogue (with Sir Brian Jenkins, *qv*, 1995), Addressing IMT in NHS Organisations (co-author), Cybernauts Awake! (co-author, 1999), Rational Values in the New Economy (ed and co-author), Constructive Engagement (2005), Oil and Troubled Waters (2005), Questions of Truth (co-author with John Polkinghorne, *qv*, 2009), Individual versus Systemic Risk and the Regulator's Dilemma (with Robert May, *qv*, and others, 2011), In Business and Battle (co-ed with Charles Style and David Ellery, 2012), The Fall of Richard Fausto – a Play (with Prof Marcus Miller, 2013), Volpone, or the Biter Bitten (with Prof Marcus Miller, 2013); articles in HBR China including Why is the UK such a great place for Innovation? (with David Willetts and Greg Clark, *qqv*) and in Tsinghua Financial Review; *Recreations* piano, music, running marathons, sailing; *Clubs* Royal Inst, IOD, City Livery, Soc of Authors, London Corinthian Sailing, Shoreham Sailing, Serpentine Running, RSA; *Style*— Nicholas Beale, Esq; ✉ Sciteb, 1 Heddon Street, Mayfair, London W1B 4BD (☎ 020 7381 1481, fax 020 7385 7979, e-mail nicholas.beale@sciteb.com)

BEALE, Lt-Gen Sir Peter John; KBE (1992); s of Basil Hewett Beale (d 1987), of Romford, Essex, and Eileen Beryl, *née* Heffer; *b* 18 March 1934; *Educ* St Paul's Cathedral Choir Sch, Felsted, Gonville & Caius Coll Cambridge (BA), Westminster Hosp (MB BChir, DTM&H); *m* 1, 22 Aug 1959, Julia Mary (d 2000), da of John Clifton Winter; 4 s (Simon Russell b 12 Jan 1961, Timothy John, Andrew Mark (twins) b 17 Jan 1962, Matthew James Robert b 25 Jan 1974), 2 da (Katie Louise b 28 June 1964, Lucy Ann b 10 Dec 1967 d 1971); m 2, 2 Dec 2001, Mary Elisabeth, da of Charles James Stanley Lucas; *Career* RMO 34 LAA Regt RA 1960–63, trainee and specialist physician 1963–71, conslt physician 1971–, cmd Med 2 Div 1981–83, Col AMD 3 1983–84, cmd Med 1 Br Corps 1984–87, cmd Med UKLF 1987–90, Surgn-Gen and DG Army Med Servs 1991–94; chief med advsr British Red Cross 1994–2000; vice-pres Wilts SSAFA; former govr Yehudi Menuhin Sch; pres: Tidworth Golf Club 1989–2003, Army Offrs Golf Soc 2001–05; author of various articles in med jls on mil med matters, jt author First Aid Manual; QHP 1988–94; memb: BMA, RIPHH, RSTM&H; FRCP, FFCM, FFOM; *Recreations* golf, squash, tennis, music (conducting and singing); *Style*— Lt-Gen Sir Peter Beale, KBE; ✉ The Old Bakery, Avebury, Marlborough, Wiltshire SN8 1RF

BEALES, Prof Derek Edward Dawson; s of Edward Beales (d 1984), and Dorothy Kathleen, *née* Dawson (d 1993); *b* 12 June 1931, Felixstowe; *Educ* Bishop's Stortford Coll, Sidney Sussex Coll Cambridge (MA, PhD, LittD); *m* 14 Aug 1964, Sara Jean (Sally), da of Francis Harris Ledbury (d 1971); 1 da (Christina Margaret (Kitty) b 1965), 1 s (Richard Derek b 1967); *Career* Nat Serv Sgt RA 1949–50; Univ of Cambridge: asst lectr 1962–65, lectr 1965–80, prof of modern history 1980–97 (emeritus 1997–), chm Bd of History 1979–81; Sidney Sussex Coll Cambridge: res fell 1955–58, fell 1958–, vice-master 1973–75; visiting lectr Harvard Univ 1965, visiting prof Central European Univ Budapest 1995–97; fndr's meml lectr St Deiniol's Library Hawarden 1990, Stenton lectr Univ of Reading 1992, Birkbeck lectr Trinity Coll Cambridge 1993; chm Editorial Bd Historical Jl 1990–97 (ed 1971–75), chm Mgmnt Ctee Centre of Int Studies 1993–95; memb: Univ Library Syndicate Cambridge 1981–89, Gen Bd of the Faculties 1987–89, Standing Ctee for Humanities Euro Science Fndn 1994–99; Leverhulme emeritus fell 2000; author articles in learned jls; Paolucci/Bagehot Book Award Intercollegiate Studies Inst Wilmington DE 2004; FRHistS (memb Cncl 1984–88), FBA (memb 1989); *Books* England and Italy 1859–60 (1961), From Castlereagh to Gladstone (1969), The Risorgimento and the Unification of Italy (1971, new edn with E F Biagini 2002), History and Biography (1981), History Society and the Churches (ed with Geoffrey Best, 1985), Joseph II – in the Shadow of Maria Theresa 1741–80 (1987), Mozart and the Habsburgs (1993), Sidney Sussex College Cambridge: Historical Essays in Commemoration of the Quatercentary (ed with H B Nisbet, 1996), Prosperity and Plunder: European Catholic Monasteries in the Age of Revolution, 1650–1815 (2003), Enlightenment and Reform in Eighteenth-Century Europe (2005), Joseph II: Against the World 1780–1790 (2009), St John's College Cambridge: A History (contrib, 2011), Pietro Leopoldo d'Asburgo Lorena, Relazione sullo Stato della Monarchia (1784) (co-ed with Renato Pasta, 2013), I-bok on Mozart (contrib, ed Cliff Eisen 2014); *Recreations* music, walking, bridge; *Clubs* Athenaeum; *Style*— Prof Derek Beales, FBA; ✉ Sidney Sussex College, Cambridge CB2 3HU (☎ 01223 338833, e-mail derek@beales.ws)

BEAMISH, David Richard; s of Richard Ludlow Beamish (d 2008), and Heather Margaret Ensor, *née* Lock (d 2001); *b* 20 August 1952, Carlisle, Cumbria; *Educ* Marlborough, St John's Coll Cambridge (MA, LLM); *m* 30 Sept 1989, Dr (Fiona) Philippa Tudor, *qv*, da of (James) Brian Tudor; 1 da (Amelia May Tudor b 31 May 1994); *Career* House of Lords: clerk 1974, sr clerk 1979, seconded to Cabinet Office as private sec to Leader of the House of Lords and Govt Chief Whip 1983–86, chief clerk 1987–93, princ clerk 1993, clerk of the jls 1993–95, clerk of ctees and clerk of the overseas office 1995–2002, clerk of the jls 2002–05, reading clerk 2003–07, clerk asst 2007–11, clerk of the Parliaments 2011–; winner Mastermind BBC TV 1988; *Publications* The House of Lords at Work (jt ed with Donald Shell, 1993); *Style*— David Beamish, Esq; ✉ david@davidbeamish.uk; Clerk of the Parliaments, House of Lords, London SW1A 0PW (☎ 020 7219 3000, e-mail beamishdr@parliament.uk)

BEAMISH, Sally; da of William Anthony Alten Beamish, of Sussex, and Ursula Mary, *née* Snow; *b* 26 August 1956; *Educ* Camden Sch for Girls, Trinity Coll of Music (jr), RNCM; *m* 1988, Robert Irvine, s of Joseph Irvine; 2 s (Laurence George b 3 Jan 1989, Thomas Stuart b 2 June 1990), 1 da (Stephanie Rose b 1 Oct 1995); *Career* composer; viola: Raphael Ensemble, London Sinfonietta, Lontano; artistic dir and co-fndr Chamber Group of Scotland 1991–98; co-host composers' course: Scottish Chamber Orch Hoy (with Sir Peter Maxwell Davies) 1994 & 1995, St Magnus Composers' Course (with Alasdair Nicholson) 2007–; composer in residence Swedish and Scottish Chamber Orchs 1998–2002; appearances on: BBC Radio 3, BBC TV, Scottish TV, Channel 4; works incl: Symphony no 1 1992, Tam Lin for oboe and orch 1993, Concerto for violin and orch 1994, Concerto no 1 for Viola and Orchestra (premiered BBC Proms) 1995, Concerto River for cello and orchestra 1997, Symphony No 2 1998, recordings 971, 1161, 1171, 1511 (BIS label), BBC Proms cmmn Knotgrass Elegy 2001, Viola Concerto no 2 2001 various film and TV scores; opera: Monster 2002; stage musical: Shenachie 2006; Arts Cncl Composer's Bursary 1989, Paul Hamlyn Award 1993, Scottish Arts Cncl Bursary 1999, Creative Scotland Award 2000, Royal Philharmonic Soc Award 2011; Hon Doctorate Univ of Glasgow 2001; memb: Performing Rights Soc, APC, RSM, MCPS, Classical Exec Ctee BASCA 2015; *Recreations* painting, writing; *Style*— Dr Sally Beamish; ✉ c/o Scottish Music Centre (e-mail info@scottishmusiccentre.com, www.sallybeamish.com, Twitter @sfbeamish)

BEAN, Prof Sir Charles Richard; kt (2014); s of Charles Ernest Bean, of Wilmslow, Cheshire, and Mary, *née* Welsh; *b* 16 September 1953; *Educ* Brentwood Sch, Emmanuel Coll Cambridge (MA), MIT (PhD); *m* Elizabeth Nan Callender; *Career* HM Treasy: economic asst 1975–79, economic advsr 1981–82; LSE: lectr 1982–86, reader 1986–90, prof 1990–2000 and 2014–; Bank of England: chief economist and exec dir 2000–08, memb Monetary Policy Ctee 2000–14, dep govr 2008–14; advsr: HM Treasy 1992–2000, Treasy Select Ctee House of Commons 1997–2000; pres Royal Economic Soc 2013–15; author of numerous pubns in learned jls; *Publications* Independent Review of UK Economic Statistics (2016); *Recreations* cricket, opera; *Style*— Prof Sir Charles Bean; ✉ Department of Economics, London School of Economics, Houghton Street, London WC2A 2AE (☎ 020 7955 6907)

BEAN, Rt Hon Lord Justice; Rt Hon Sir David Michael Bean; PC (2015), kt (2004); s of George Joseph Bean (d 1973), and Zdenka, *née* White; *b* 25 March 1954; *Educ* St Paul's, Trinity Hall Cambridge; *m* 2004, Dr Ruth Thompson; *Career* called to the Bar Middle Temple 1976 (bencher 2001); recorder of the Crown Court 1996–2004, QC 1997, judge of the High Court of Justice (Queen's Bench Div) 2004–14, presiding judge South Eastern Circuit 2007–10, Lord Justice of Appeal 2014–; chm Gen Cncl of the Bar 2002; chm Employment Law Bar Assoc 1999–2001, chm Immigration Servs Tbnl 2001–04; memb: GMC 2003–04, Civil Justice Cncl 2003–05, Judicial Appointments Cmmn 2010–14; chm Law Cmmn of England and Wales 2015–; *Publications* Law Reform for All (ed, 1996), Injunctions (12 edn, 2015); Enforcement of Injunctions and Undertakings (with His Hon Judge Fricker, QC, 1991); *Recreations* opera, hill walking, books; *Clubs* Reform; *Style*— The Rt Hon Lord Justice Bean

BEAN, Richard; *b* 1956, East Hull; *Educ* Loughborough Univ; *Career* playwright; work incl: Toast (Royal Court) 1999, Mr England (Crucible Sheffield) 2000, The Mentalists (Nat Theatre) 2002, Le Pub! (Nat Theatre) 2002, The God Botherers (Bush Theatre) 2003 and (Synapse Theatre Newcastle) 2004, Under the Whaleback (Royal Court) 2003 (George Devine Award 2002), Smack Family Robinson (Live Theatre Newcastle) 2003, Honeymoon Suite (Royal Court) 2004 and (Hull Truck Theatre) 2008 (Pearson Award for Best New Play 2002), Harvest (Royal Court) 2005 (Best Play Evening Standard Award 2005, Best Play Critics' Circle Award 2006, Best Play Olivier Award 2006), The Hypochondriac (Almeida) 2005, Up On Roof (Hull Truck Theatre) 2006, The English Game (tour) 2008, England People Very Nice (Nat Theatre) 2009, The Big Fellah (Lyric Hammersmith) 2010, House of Games (Almeida) 2010 (adapted from screenplay by David Mamet), The Heretic (Royal Court) 2011 (Best Play Evening Standard Award 2011), One Man, Two Guvnors (Nat Theatre and Adelphi Theatre) 2011 and (Music Box Theatre and Haymarket Theatre) 2012 (Best Play Evening Standard Award 2011); *Style*—

Richard Bean, Esq; ✉ c/o Rose Cobbe, United Agents, 12–26 Lexington Street, London W1F 0LE

BEAN, Sean; *Career* actor; *Theatre* Romeo in Romeo and Juliet (RSC Stratford/Barbican), Spencer in Fair Maid of the West (RSC Stratford/Mermaid), Starvling in A Midsummer Night's Dream, Who Knew Mackenzie & Gone (Royal Court), Lederer in Deathwatch (Young Vic Studio), Last Days of Mankind (Citizens' Theatre Glasgow); *Television* BBC incl: Mellors in Lady Chatterley's Lover 1993, Fools Gold, Clarissa, Prince, Tell Me That You Love Me, Wedded, Small Zones, My Kingdom For A Horse, Accused; Central incl: title role in Sharpe's: Rifles, Gold, Company, Eagle, Enemy, Honour, Battle, Sword, Regiment, Seige, Mission, Revenge, Challenge, Peril (separate progs 1993–2008); Channel 4 incl: The Loser, The Border Country, Red Riding: 1974, Red Riding: 1983; other credits incl: A Woman's Guide to Adultery (ITV) 1993, Inspector Morse (Thames), Troubles (LWT), 15 Streets (World Wide/Tyne Tees), War Requiem (Anglo-Int Films), Winter Flight (Enigma), Samson & Delilah (Flamingo Films), The True Bride (TVS Films), Fenton in Scarlett, Esav in Jacob, Neal Byrne in Extremely Dangerous, Robert Aske in Henry VIII 2003, Crusoe, Game of Thrones, Accused (Best Actor (Male) RTS Award 2013); *Radio* title role in The True Story of Martin Guerre (Radio 4) 1992; *Audio* Sharpe's Devil; *Film* Sean Miller in Patriot Games, Rannucio in Caravaggio 1986, Carver Doone in Lorna Doone, Tadgh in The Field 1990, Brendan in Stormy Monday (Channel 4) 1987, Windprints 1989, Black Beauty, Shopping, Jimmy Muir in When Saturday Comes 1995, 006 in Goldeneye 1995, Spence in Ronin 1998, Jason Locke in Essex Boys 1999, Partridge in Equilibrium 2000, Koster in Don't Say a Word 2000, Paul in Tom and Thomas 2001, Boromir in Lord of the Rings: The Fellowship of the Ring 2001, The Two Towers 2002 and The Return of the King 2003, The Big Empty 2003, Odysseus in Troy 2004, National Treasure 2005, The Island 2005, Percy Jackson & the Lightning Thief 2010, Ca$h 2010, Black Death 2010, Age of Heroes 2011, Soldiers of Fortune 2012, Cleanskin 2012, Mirror Mirror: The Untold Adventures of Snow White 2012; *Style—* Sean Bean, Esq; ✉ c/o Independent Talent Group Ltd, 40 Whitfield Street, London W1T 2RH (☎ 020 7636 6565, fax 020 7323 0101)

BEANEY, Linda Margaret; da of Kenneth Ashley Beaney, of Gidea Park, Essex, and Kathleen Margaret, *née* Stainforth; *b* 1 December 1952; *Educ* Coborn Sch for Girls London; *Career* trainee property sales negotiator Edward Erdman & Co Mayfair London 1969; Hampton & Sons: joined 1976, ptnr 1981, md London 1989–91; dir Hornchurch Theatre Trust Ltd 1985–90, dir P H Gillingham Investments 1986–2000, jt chief exec Hamptons Residential Developments 1989–91, sr ptnr Beaney Pearce 1992–; memb Devpt Cncl The Globe Theatre 1998–2006, tstee Vitalise 2008–; Freeman City of London 1984; memb Land Inst 1988, FInstD 1991, FNAEA 1992; *Recreations* theatre, tennis and golf; *Clubs* Queen's; *Style—* Ms Linda Beaney; ✉ Beaney Pearce, 14 Culford Gardens, Sloane Square, London SW3 2ST (☎ 020 7590 9500, fax 020 7589 1171, e-mail lbeaney@beaneypearce.co.uk)

BEAR, Carolyn Ann; da of Richard E L Salter (d 1983), and Marjorie, *née* Rix; *b* 10 April 1944; *Educ* Univ of Newcastle upon Tyne (BA); *m* 1968, Peter Julian Bear, s of late Leslie W Bear, CBE; 2 da (Claudia b 1970, Leonora b 1974); *Career* writer; also multimedia and film scriptwriter; vol BESO; *Books* as Chloë Rayban: Under Different Stars (1988), Wild Child (1991), Virtual Sexual Reality (1994, shortlisted for Guardian Children's Fiction Prize 1995, feature film 1999), Love in Cyberia (1996, shortlisted for Guardian Children's Fiction Prize 1996, shortlisted for Carnegie Medal 1996), Models Series (1997), Models Move On (1998), Back 2 Back (1999), Terminal Chic (2000), Drama Queen (2004), Wrong Number (2004), My Life Starring Mum (2006), Hollywood Bliss: My life so far (2007), Mwah Mwah (2008); as Carolyn Bear: The Last Loneliest Dodo (1974), No Time for Dinosaurs (1975), Johnny Tomorrow (1978), The Tangled Spell (1986), Scrapman (1996); for adults: Lost & Found (2015), How to Knit an Opera (2015); *Recreations* painting, collage, drawing; *Clubs* Hurlingham; *Style—* Mrs Carolyn Bear; ✉ c/o Laura Cecil (Literary Agent), 17 Alwyne Villas, London N1 2HG

BEAR, Sir Michael David; kt (2012), JP; *b* 21 January 1953; *Educ* Clifton Coll Bristol, Univ of Witwatersrand SA (BSc), Cranfield Univ (MBA); *m* 22 July 1979, Barbara Anne, *née* Sandler; 1 da (b 22 Jan 1987), 1 s (b 29 March 1990); *Career* project engr Hawkins Hawkins and Osborne 1974–78, project engr Sir Frederick Snow 1978–81, business analyst Taylor Woodrow 1981–82, int business devpt mangr Balfour Beatty Engrg Ltd 1982–88, md Iberia Devpts 1988–89, European property devpt dir London and Edinburgh Tst plc 1989–93, chief exec Spitalfields Devpt Gp 1991–2010, md Balfour Beatty Property Ltd 1993–2012; regeneration dir Hammerson UK Ltd 2006–12 (special projects dir 2003–06); UKTI: co-chair CEO Forum for UK/China Infrastructure, chm High Value Opportunities Supervisory Bd 2012–14, chm Regeneration Investment Orgn 2013–, UK special envoy for sustainable urbanisation China 2014–; non-exec dir Arup Gp 2009; past memb Lord Green's Ministerial Strategic Advsy Gp; govr Thomas Coram Fndn 2008– (pres 2012–15), tstee Museum of London Archaeology 2013–; common councilman (Portsoken Ward) City of London Corp 2003, alderman (Portsoken Ward) City of London 2005, sheriff City of London 2007–08, Lord Mayor City of London 2010–11; magistrate Worshipful Co of Paviors 2002– (ct asst 2006, master 2012), Worshipful Co of Chartered Surveyors 2006 (memb Ct of Assts 2007), Worshipful Co of Engrs 2009 (memb Ct of Assts 2010); memb Guild of Freemen 2008, Hon Freeman Worshipful Co of Environmental Cleaners 2010, Hon Liveryman Co of Security Professionals 2010; CEng, FICE 2008 (MICE 1979), MBIM, MInstD, FRICS 2009, Hon FREng 2010, Hon FICE 2011; KStJ 2011; *Recreations* small business ventures, scuba diving, tennis, opera, theatre, international travel, supporting the England rugby team; *Clubs* The Walbrook, Athenaeum, East India; *Style—* Alderman Sir Michael Bear; ✉ c/o City of London Corporation, Guildhall, PO Box 270, London EC2P 2EJ (☎ 01993 881563, e-mail michael@thebearsinc.com)

BEARD, Alex; CBE (2013); s of Charles Henry Beard (d 1980), and Patricia Ann Beard; *b* 14 October 1963, London; *Educ* Manchester GS, Westminster Sch, KCL; *m* 1993, Katharine Betty, *née* Warde-Aldam; 1 da (Betty b 6 Feb 1996), 1 s (Alfred b 14 April 1998); *Career* dep dir Tate 2002–13 (joined 1994), chief exec ROH 2013–; chm High House Prodn Park Ltd; memb Bd: Glyndebourne 2008–13, Global Giving UK 2007–13, memb Bd: 14–18 NOW 2013–, West End Partnership; *Recreations* cricket, music, opera, tennis, visual arts; *Style—* Alex Beard, Esq, CBE; ✉ Royal Opera House, Covent Garden, London WC2E 9DD

BEARD, Prof (Winifred) Mary; OBE (2013); da of Roy Whitbread Beard (d 1978), and Joyce Emily, *née* Taylor (d 1995); *b* 1 January 1955, Much Wenlock, Salop; *Educ* Newnham Coll Cambridge (MA), Univ of Cambridge (PhD); *m* 1985, Robin Sinclair Cormack; 1 da (Zoe Troy b 26 Oct 1985), 1 s (Raphael Christian b 24 July 1987); *Career* lectr in classics KCL 1979–83; Univ of Cambridge: fell Newnham Coll 1984–, lectr in classics 1984–99, reader in classics 1999–2004, prof of classics 2004–; prof of ancient literature Royal Acad of Arts 2013–; classics ed TLS 1992–; chair Faculty of Archaeology, History and Letters British Sch at Rome 2002–06 (memb 1994–98); *Publications* Rome in the Late Republic (jtly 1985, 2 edn 1999), The Good Working Mother's Guide (1989), Pagan Priests (co-ed, 1990), Classics: A Very Short Introduction (jtly, 1995, 2 edn 1999), Religions of Rome I (co-author, 1998), Religions of Rome II: A Sourcebook (co-author, 1998), The Invention of Jane Harrison (2000), Classical Art: From Greece to Rome (jtly, 2001), The Parthenon (2002), The Colosseum (jtly, 2004), The Triumph (2007), Pompeii: The life of a Roman town (2008), Confront the Classics (2013), Laughter in Ancient Rome: on joking, tickling and cracking up (2014); numerous scholarly articles, reviews and journalism; *Style—* Prof Mary Beard, OBE; ✉ Newnham College, Cambridge CB3 9DF (☎ 01223 335162, fax 01223 335409, e-mail mb127@cam.ac.uk)

BEARDER, Catherine Zena; MEP; s of Ernest James Bailey (d 1979), and Joan Irene Clare, *née* Lane (d 2004); *b* 14 January 1949, Broxbourne, Herts; *Educ* Hawthorn Sch Frinton on Sea, St Christophers Sch Letchworth; *m* 14 Jan 1974, Prof Simon Kenneth Bearder; 3 s (Timothy Martin b 1976, Ian Corthan b 1978, Peter Ernest b 1981); *Career* mangr Bicester Citizens Advice Bureau 1990–94, devpt offr Nat Fedn of Women's Insts 1994–98, devpt offr Victim Support Oxon 1998–2000, dir SE England Britain in Europe 2001–09; MEP (Lib Dem) South East 2009–; FRSA; *Style—* Mrs Catherine Bearder, MEP; ✉ 27 Park End Street, Oxford OX1 1HU (☎ 01865 249838, e-mail admin@bearder.eu or catherine@bearder.eu)

BEARDSELL, Matthew Robert; s of Geoffrey James Beardsell, of Handforth, Cheshire, and Pauline, *née* Griffiths (d 2012); *b* 2 August 1974, Uckfield, Sussex; *Educ* Falmouth Sch of Art and Design (HND), De Montfort Univ (BA); *m* 25 Jan 2003, Tracy, *née* Yates; 1 s (Benjamin Arthur b 14 Aug 2006), 1 da (Ruthie Kate b 11 July 2011); *Career* prodn mangr Tucker Clarke-Williams 2000–01, prodn dir Love Creative 2001–06, freelance prodn conslt 2006–07, founding ptnr and md Music 2007–; memb D&AD 2001–; *Recreations* music, walking, Lego with son and reading with daughter; *Style—* Matthew Beardsell, Esq; ✉ Music, Third Floor, 24 Lever Street, Manchester M1 1DZ (☎ 0161 237 5600, e-mail matthew.beardsell@ideasbymusic.com, website www.ideasbymusic.com, Twitter @mattbeardsell)

BEARSTED, 5 Viscount (UK 1925); Sir Nicholas Alan Samuel; 5 Bt (UK 1903); er s of 4 Viscount Bearsted, MC, TD (d 1996), and his 2 w, Hon Elizabeth Adelaide (d 1983), da of Baron Cohen, PC (Life Peer, d 1973); *b* 22 January 1950; *Educ* Eton, New Coll Oxford (BA); *m* 1975, Caroline Jane, da of Dr David Sacks; 4 da (Hon Eugenie Sharon b 1977, Hon Natalie Naomi b 1979, Hon Zöe Elizabeth b 1982, Hon Juliet Samantha b 1986), 1 s (Hon Harry Richard b 23 May 1988); *Heir* s, Hon Harry Samuel; *Career* owner N A Samuel Consultancy 1980–, sr ptnr Farley Farms 1976–; ceo Hulton Deutsch Collection Ltd 1994–96; chm: Insignia Solutions plc 1988–2006, Powerstax plc 1997–; dir: Samuel Properties plc 1975–85, Mayborn Gp plc 1978–2006, St James's Venture Capital Fund 1983–92, Alliance Imaging Inc 1984–87, Alliance Medical Ltd 1990–2006, Affinity Solutions Inc 2002–, ExactTrak Ltd 2012–; Case Communications plc 1977–80; Royal Free Medical Sch 1992–98, memb Cncl UCL 1998–2004; *Recreations* bridge, puzzles; *Clubs* Whites, Portland; *Style—* The Rt Hon the Viscount Bearsted

BEASLEY, Prof Dame Christine Joan; DBE (2008, CBE 2002); da of Mr De'Ath (d 1986), and Mrs De'Ath, *née* Harris (d 1974); *b* 13 June 1944, London; *Educ* DipN, DMS; *m* 1, 1967; 3 s (Simon b 29 Aug 1969, Timothy b 5 July 1971, Matthew b 18 July 1976); m 2, 1982; m 3, 1989, Jack Beasley; *Career* registered gen nurse, registered dist nurse; chief nurse advsr Riverside Health NHS 1989–91, acting chief exec Riverside Health NHS 1991–92, chief nurse advsr Riverside Hosps 1992–94, regnl dir of nursing London NHS 1995–2003, partnership devpt dir Modernisation Agency 2003–04, chief nursing offr for England Dept of Health 2004–; tstee Marie Curie Cancer Care; pro-vice chllr Thames Valley Univ; Hon MD Univ of Nottingham; Hon DSc: Univ of Wolverhampton, Univ of Keele, City Univ London; Hon DUniv Sheffield Hallam, Hon DCL Univ of Northumbria; fell Queen's Nursing Inst, memb RCN 1965; *Recreations* theatre, travelling, entertaining; *Style—* Prof Dame Christine Beasley, DBE; ✉ Department of Health, Richmond House, 79 Whitehall, London SW1A 2NS (☎ 020 7210 5598, e-mail christine.beasley@dh.gsi.gov.uk)

BEASLEY-MURRAY, Caroline Wynne; da of Arthur Maelor Griffiths (d 2001), and Mavis Gwyneth, *née* Baker (d 2001); *b* 25 January 1946, Porthcawl, Glamorganshire; *Educ* Grove Park Girls' GS Wrexham, Girton Coll Cambridge (MA), Univ of Manchester (PGCE), Manchester Poly (CPE), Inns of Court Sch of Law; *m* 26 Aug 1967, Rev Dr Paul Beasley-Murray, *qv*; 3 s (Jonathan Paul b 6 Aug 1969, Timothy Mark b 19 Nov 1971, Benjamin James b 6 March 1976), 1 da (Susannah Caroline Louise b 21 Sept 1973); *Career* called to the Bar Inner Temple; barr: 5 Pump Court 1990–93, Tindal Chambers Chelmsford 1993–97, Fenners Chambers Cambridge 1997–2000; HM senior coroner for Essex 2000–; pres Mental Health Review Tbnls 1996–; JP: Trafford Bench 1980–86, Croydon Bench 1986–92; history mistress Bury GS for Girls 1968–69, home tutor Trafford Educn Authy 1980–86; past pres E Anglia Coroners Soc, past pres SE England Coroner Soc; memb: Coroners' Soc of England and Wales, Magistrates' Assoc, Br Acad of Forensic Sci; *Recreations* theatre, concerts, family, friends, church, entertaining, travel, tapestry work; *Clubs* Cambridge Soc; *Style—* Mrs Caroline Beasley-Murray; ✉ The Old Manse, 3 Roxwell Road, Chelmsford, Essex CM1 2LY (☎ 01245 347016, fax 01245 267203, e-mail carolinebeasleymurray@gmail.com); HM Coroner's Office, Seax House, Victoria Road South, Chelmsford CM1 1QH (☎ 01245 506763, e-mail caroline.beasley-murray@essex.gov.uk)

BEATH, Prof John; OBE (2015); s of James Beath, and Marion Spence; *b* 15 June 1944, Thurso, Caithness; *Educ* Univ of St Andrews (MA), Univ of Cambridge (MA), Univ of London (MPhil), Univ of Pennsylvania (Thouron scholar); *m* Dr Monika Schroder; *Career* research offr Univ of Cambridge 1972–79, lectr Univ of Bristol 1979–91, prof Univ of St Andrews 1991–2009 (prof emeritus 2009–); sec-gen Royal Econ Soc 2008–, memb Cncl ESRC 2009–14, memb Competition Appeal Tbnl 2009–, memb Prison Service Pay Review Body 2010–16; FRSA, FRSE, FAcSS 2015; *Recreations* gardening, golf; *Clubs* Penn (NY), Leven Golfing Soc; *Style—* Prof John Beath, OBE; ✉ School of Economics and Finance, University of St Andrews, St Andrews, Fife, KY16 9AL (e-mail jab@st-and.ac.uk)

BEATON, Alistair; s of John Beaton, and Grace Whitfield; *b* 1946, Glasgow; *Educ* Univ of Edinburgh, Univ of Bochum, Univ of Moscow; *Career* writer; *Theatre* (book and lyrics): The Metropolitan Mikado, The Rateplayers' Iolanthe (Olivier Award), Small Expectations (all with Ned Sherrin, *qv*); other credits incl: The Nose (Nottingham Playhouse, Berlin, Bucharest), Die Fledermaus (English version for D'Oyly Carte Co), La Vie Parisienne (adaptation), Feelgood (Garrick Theatre, Evening Standard Theatre Award Best Comedy, What'sOnTheatre.com Award Best New Comedy, nominated Olivier Award Best New Comedy), Follow My Leader (Birmingham Rep, Hampstead Theatre), King of Hearts (Hampstead Theatre and Theater am Schlosspark Berlin), Caledonia (Edinburgh Int Festival King's Theatre); *Television* Not the Nine O'clock News (BBC), It'll be all Over in Half an Hour (with Jonathan Dimbleby, *qv*), A Question of Fact (BBC 2), Spitting Image (ITV), Minder (ITV), The Way, The Truth, The Video (Channel 4), Incident on the Line (Channel 4), Dunrulin' (BBC), Downwardly Mobile (co-author, ITV), Russian Language and People (BBC), Children of Icarus (ZDF), Mit Fünfzig Küssen Männer Anders (Regina Ziegler Filmproduktion), A Very Social Secretary (Channel 4), The Trial of Tony Blair (Channel 4), script conslt NDF Entertainment; *Radio* writer: Something Appealing, Something Appalling, Week Ending, Electric Ink (co-written with Tom Mitchelson); writer/presenter: The World Tonight, Dome Alone; presenter Fourth Column; contrib: The News Huddlines, The Jason Explanation, Loose Ends; devised/presenter: Little England, Big World, The Beaton Generation; guested on: Quote Unquote, The News Quiz; *Books* The Thatcher Papers (with Andy Hamilton), Drop the Dead Donkey, The Little Book of Complete Bollocks, The Little Book of New Labour Bollocks, The Little Book of Management Bollocks, A Planet for the President; *Clubs* Two Brydges; *Style—* Mr Alistair Beaton; ☎ 020 7253 6226, e-mail abr@alanbrodie.com, website www.alistairbeaton.com

BEATSON, Rt Hon the Lord Justice; Sir Jack Beatson; kt (2003), PC (2013); s of John James Beatson (d 1961), and Miriam, *née* White (d 1991); *b* 3 November 1948; *Educ*

Whittingehame Coll Brighton, BNC Oxford (MA, BCL), Univ of Oxford (DCL), Univ of Cambridge (LLD); *m* 1973, Charlotte, da of Lt-Col John Aylmer Christie-Miller, CBE, of Bourton-on-the-Hill, Glos; 1 s (Samuel J b 1976 d 2004), 1 da (Hannah A b 1979); *Career* called to the Bar Inner Temple 1972 (hon bencher 1993, bencher 2003); law cmmr England and Wales 1989–94, recorder 1994, QC 1998, judge of the High Court of Justice (Queen's Bench Div) 2003–13, Lord Justice of the Court of Appeal 2013–; law lectr Univ of Bristol 1972–73, fell and tutor Merton Coll Oxford 1973–94 (hon fell 1995–); Univ of Cambridge: Rouse Ball prof of English law 1993–2003, fell St John's Coll 1994–2003 (hon fell 2005–), dir Centre for Public Law 1997–2001, chm Faculty of Law 2001–03; visiting prof: Osgoode Hall Law Sch Toronto 1979, Univ of Virginia 1980 and 1983; pres Br Acad of Forensic Sci 2007–09; memb: Civil Ctee Judicial Studies Bd 1994–98, Competition Cmmn 1996–2001; memb Editorial Bd Law Quarterly Review; hon fell BNC Oxford 2009–; *Books* Administrative Law – Cases and Materials (jtly 1983, 2 edn 1989), The Use and Abuse of Unjust Enrichment (1991), Chitty on Contracts (jt ed, 1982–94), Good Faith and Fault in Contract Law (jt ed, 1995), European Public Law (jt ed, 1997), Anson's Law of Contract (27 edn, 1998, 28 edn 2002, 29 edn 2010, 30 edn 2016), Human Rights: The 1998 Act and the European Convention (jtly, 1999), Unjustified Enrichment: Cases and Materials (jt ed, 2003), Jurists Uprooted: German-Speaking Émigré Lawyers in Twentieth Century Britain (jt ed, 2004), Human Rights: Judicial Protection in the UK; *Recreations* trying to relax; *Style—* The Rt Hon the Lord Justice Beatson; ✉ Royal Courts of Justice, Strand, London WC2A 2LL

BEATTIE, Dr Alistair Duncan; s of Alexander Nicoll Beattie (d 1965), of Paisley, and Elizabeth McCrorie, *née* Nisbet (d 1961); *b* 4 April 1942; *Educ* Paisley GS, Univ of Glasgow (MB ChB, MD); *m* 29 Oct 1966, Gillian Margaret, da of Dr James Thomson McCutcheon (d 1964); 2 da (Charlotte b 23 May 1968, Deirdre b 25 May 1972), 3 s (Duncan b 16 Feb 1970, Douglas b 30 April 1975, Neil b 26 Aug 1979); *Career* res fell Scottish Home and Health Dept 1969–73, lectr materia medica Univ of Glasgow 1973–76, res fell MRC Royal Free Hosp 1974–75, conslt physician S Gen Hosp Glasgow 1976–2002, pt/t conslt advsr MOD 2002–; vice-pres (med) RCPSGlas 1999–2001; chm Med and Dental Def Union of Scotland 2002–12; FRCPGlas 1983, FRCP 1985 (MRCP 1973), FFPM 1989, FRCPEd 1997; *Books* Emergencies in Medicine (jt ed, 1984), Diagnostic Tests in Gastroenterology (1989); *Recreations* golf, music; *Clubs* Douglas Park Golf; *Style—* Dr Alistair Beattie; ✉ Flat 3/2, 47 Novar Drive, Glasgow G12 9UB (☎ 0141 334 0101)

BEATTIE, Basil; *b* 1935; *Educ* Royal Acad Schs; *Career* artist, lectr and reader; lectr Goldsmiths Coll London until 1998; RA 2006; *Solo Exhibitions* Greenwich Theatre Gallery London 1968, Mayfair Gallery London 1971, Consort Gallery London 1973, Hoya Gallery London 1974, New 57 Gallery Edinburgh 1978, Newcastle Poly 1979, Goldsmiths' Gallery London 1982, Minories Gallery Colchester 1982, Bede Gallery Jarrow 1984, Gray's Art Gallery Hartlepool 1986, Curwen Gallery London 1987 and 1990, Drawing on the Interior (installation at The Eagle Gallery London) 1991, Castlefield Gallery Manchester 1993, MAAK Gallery London 1993, Todd Gallery London 1994, 1995 and 1996, Ikon Gallery 1994, Newtown Gall Johannesburg 1994, Angel Row Gallery Nottingham 1995, Path Gallery Aalst Belgium 1996, Reg Vardy Gallery Sunderland 1997, Renate Bender Gallery Munich 1997, Todd Gallery London 1998, Storey Gallery Lancaster 2000, Works on Paper 1980–90 (Curwen Gallery London) 2001, That Irresistible Climb (paintings and prints, Advanced Graphics Gallery London) 2001, Above and Below (Sadler's Wells London) 2002, Making a Year (studio show) 2005, Drawings – Two Rooms (NZ) 2006, Basil Beattie – BP New Displays (Tate Britain) 2007, Basil Beattie – Two Rooms (NZ) 2008, Paintings from the Janus Series (Purdy Hicks Gallery London) 2009, Drawn In Drawn Out (Eagle Gallery London) 2009, Paintings from the Janus Series II (Abbot Hall Cumbria) 2010, Onward and Upward (James Hyman Gallery London) 2011, Basil Beattie (Hilton Fine Art Gallery Bath) 2013, Jerwood Gallery Hastings 2013, Basil Beattie (Hales Gallery London) 2014; *Group Exhibitions* incl: John Moores Exhbn 4 (Liverpool) 1965, Large Paintings (Hayward Gallery) 1970, London Now in Berlin (Germany) 1970, Four Painters (MOMA Oxford) 1971, British Painting (Hayward Gallery) 1974, Hayward Annual (Hayward Gallery) 1980, Hayward Annual – British Drawing (Hayward Gallery) 1982, European Painting (Trier Germany) 1984, British Art Show (Arts Cncl travelling exhbn) 1984, John Moores Exhbn 15 (Liverpool) 1987, Presence of Painting (Mappin Gallery Sheffield) 1988, Three British Painters (Northern Centre for Contemporary Art Sunderland) 1988, John Moores Exhbn 16 (Liverpool) 1989, The Abstract Connection (Flowers East Gallery London) 1989, John Moores Exhbn 17 (Liverpool) 1991, Painting and Sculpture at the MAAK Gallery 1992, (Pomeroy Purdy Gallery London) 1992, Moving into View (Royal Festival Hall London) 1993, Summer Exhibition (Royal Academy London) 1993, (Morgan Stanley Bank) 1994, Painters and Prints (Curwen Gallery London) 1994, Lead and Follow (Bede Gallery Jarrow and Atlantis Gallery London) 1994, Summer Exhibition (Royal Academy London) 1994, Paintmarks (Kettles Yard Cambridge) 1994, British Abstract Art Part 1 (Flowers East Gallery London) 1994, Monotypes (Art Space Gallery London) 1995, Green on Red Gallery Dublin 1995, Ace! Arts Cncl Collection (travelling exhbn) 1996–97, Yellow (Todd Gallery London) 1997, John Moores Exhbn 20 (Liverpool) 1997, Jerwood Painting Prize Exhbn 1998, Four Artists (Eagle Gallery London) 1999, Thinking Aloud (Camden Art Centre London) 1999, Open Studio (Brooklyn New York) 1999, Summer Exhibition (Royal Academy London) 1999, Works on paper (West Beth Gallery NY) 1999, Regrouping (The Nunnery London) 1999, British Airways Terminal (JFK Airport NY) 2000, London Contemporary Art Fair 2000, 5 Br Abstract Painters (Flowers West Gallery LA) 2000, Contemporary Art Fair Islington 2001, Master Class (Alain de Gailiard Gallery Paris) 2001, Retrospective I (Eagle Gallery London) 2001, Master Class (Stephen Lacey Gallery London) 2001, Tradition and Innovation (York City Art Gallery) 2001, Monoprints (Art Space Gallery London) 2001, Jerwood Prize Shortlist Exhbn (Jerwood Gallery London) 2001, Royal Acad Summer Exhbn London 2001, Br Abstract Painting (Flowers East Gallery London) 2001, Made in Hartlepool (Art Gallery Hartlepool) 2001, Three Painters (Sarah Myerscough Gallery London) 2001, Drawing (ecArt London) 2001, Contemporary Art Fair (Islington London) 2002, Square Root (Sarah Myerscough Gallery London) 2002, Contemporary Drawing Exhibition (Prospect Gallery London) 2002, Drawings (Sarah Myerscough Gallery London) 2002, Summer Exhibition (RA London) 2002, Prospects (National Contemporary Drawing Exhbn London) 2003, Art 2003 (Advanced Graphics Contemporary Art Fair London) 2003, Contemporary Art Soc London 2003, Summer Exhbn (Royal Acad) 2003, Drawn to be Alive (Hales Gallery London) 2003, 20 x 5 Drawings (Eagle Gallery London) 2003, Eagle Gallery London 2004, The Spiral of Time (OHOS Gallery Reading) 2005, Basil Beattie & Ian Tyson (Eagle Gallery London) 2006, Painting – Two Rooms (NZ) 2007, Rabley Drawing Centre UK 2007, Exchange Dublin/London Paul Kane Gallery Dublin 2008, In Drawing (Purdy Hicks Gallery London) 2008, Invisible Cities (Jerwood Space London) 2009, The Justice and its Symbols (Palace of Justice Milan)2009, Purdy Hicks Gallery London 2010, Spoilt for Choice (prints, Kings Place Gallery London) 2010; *Collections* incl: Tate Gallery, Arts Cncl Collection London, Contemporary Arts Soc, Saatchi Collection, Govt Art Collection, Birmingham Museum and Art Gall, BUPA Collection London, Natwest Gp Collection London, The Creasy Collection of Contemporary Art and other public and private collections in the UK and overseas; *Commissions* incl: mural for Manors Station Newcastle Metro for Northern Arts; *Awards* major Arts Cncl Award 1976, Athena Awards winner 1986, John Moores second prize winner 1989, Nordstern Print Prize 1999; *Books* Basil Beattie Taking Steps – Large Works 1986–2009 (2011); *Style—* Basil Beattie, Esq; ✉ c/o Paul Hedge, Hales Gallery, Tea Building, 7 Bethnal Green Road, London E1 6LA (☎ 020 7033 1938)

BEATTIE, Colin; MSP; *b* 17 October 1951; *Career* MSP (SNP) Midlothian N & Musselburgh 2011–; *Style—* Colin Beattie, Esq, MSP; ✉ The Scottish Parliament, Edinburgh EH99 1SP

BEATTIE, Jennifer Jane Belissa (Mrs Geoffrey Luckyn-Malone); da of Maj Ian Dunbar Beattie (d 1987), of Brighton, E Sussex, and Belissa Mary Hunter Graves, *née* Stanley (d 2014); *b* 20 July 1947; *Educ* Queen Anne's Sch Caversham; *m* 11 July 1992, Maj William Geoffrey Luckyn-Malone, late Argyll and Sutherland Highlanders; *Career* slr; ptnr: Blacket Gill & Langhams 1973–77 (joined 1971), Blacket Gill & Swain 1977–85, Beattie & Co 1985–2005; conslt Wedlake Bell 2005–; Women's Nat Cancer Control Campaign: dep chm 1983–86, vice-pres 1986–92, dir 1992–2001; memb Law Soc 1972; *Recreations* racing, tennis, reading, cooking; *Clubs* Naval and Military; *Style—* Mrs Geoffrey Luckyn-Malone; ✉ 41 Great Percy Street, London WC1X 9RA (☎ 020 7278 5203); Miss Jennifer Beattie, Wedlake Bell, 70 Queen Victoria Street, London EC4V 4AY (☎ 020 7395 3051, fax 020 7406 1601, e-mail jbeattie@wedlakebell.com)

BEATTIE, Trevor Stephen; s of John Vincent Beattie (d 1980), and Ada Alice, *née* Page; *b* 24 December 1958; *Educ* Moseley Art Sch Birmingham (BA), Wolverhampton Poly; *Career* copywriter Allen Brady & Marsh advtg agency 1981–83, dep creative dir Ayer Barker 1983–87, gp head Boase Massimi Pollitt 1987–90; creative dir TBWA (formerly TBWA Holmes Knight Ritchie) 1993–97 (joined 1990), creative dir BDDP GGT (merger of BST-BDDP and GGT Advertising) 1997–98; TBWA GGT Simons Palmer (following merger of TBWA International and BDDP Worldwide): creative dir 1998–2005, chairman 2001–2005; co-fndr Beattie McGuinness Bungay (BMB) 2005–; media columnist The Guardian 1997–, prodr Immodesty Blaize and Walter's Burlesque (Arts Theatre West End) 2005; *Recreations* film making, flying, tourism; *Style—* Trevor Beattie, Esq

BEATTY, Malcolm; *b* Belfast; *Educ* Univ of Aberdeen (BSc, MSc), Univ of Warwick (MSc); *m* 1978, Dr Helen, *née* Taylor; *Career* civil servant; chief exec Forest Serv of NI 1998–2006; Dept of Agriculture and Rural Devpt NI: dir of logistics Veterinary Serv Gp 2006–09, dir Rural Payments and Inspections Serv Delivery Gp 2009–11; chief exec Forest Serv of NI 2011–; FICFor 2000, CPFA 2008; *Clubs* E Down Yacht, Civil Service; *Style—* Malcolm Beatty, Esq; ✉ Forest Service, Department of Agriculture and Rural Development, Dundonald House, Upper Newtownards Road, Belfast BT4 3SB (☎ 028 9052 4463)

BEATY, Dr Robert Thompson (Bob); OBE (2003); s of Laurence Beaty, of Ayrshire, and Elizabeth Todd, *née* Beattie; *b* 13 October 1943; *Educ* Hamilton Acad, Univ of Glasgow (Hoover scholar, BSc); *m* Anne Veronica, da of George Gray Gillies (d 1990); 2 s (Kenneth Robert b 23 Dec 1968, Steven Gillies b 5 Oct 1971); *Career* trainee then test engr Hoover Cambuslang 1966–68; IBM: quality engr Greenock Plant 1968–69, Uithoorn Devpt Lab Holland 1969–71, World Trade HQ White Plains NY 1973–74, second level mgmnt 1974 (mgmnt 1971), functional mangr quality assurance 1976–78, mangr PCB Business Unit 1978–80, various sr mgmnt positions 1980–87, asst plant mangr 1987–89, dir of ops European HQ Paris 1989–92, dir technol prod ops 1992, dir of manufacturing ops and location exec 1993, dir IBM Greenock 1994–96; chief exec Scottish Electronics Forum (SEF) 1996–97; md: RTB Professional Services 1996–98, GlenCon Ltd 1998–2006; non-exec dir: Semple Cochrane plc 1996–99, Turnkey Holdings Ltd 1996–2002, Calluna plc 1996–2003, MetFab Engrg Ltd 1998–99; visiting prof of product design Univ of Glasgow 1996–; dir: Renfrewshire Enterprise Co 1994–2003 (chm 1999–2003), Greenock Tall Ships 1999 Ltd 1996–98, Eng Educn Scheme Scotland 1997–; memb Bd: Engrg Educn Scheme for Scotland (EESS) 1999–, Scottish Inst for Enterprise 2002–05; memb Ct Univ of Paisley (now Univ of the West of Scotland) 1999–2010 (vice-chair 2002–05, chair 2005–10), memb Mgmnt Ctee James Watt Coll 2000–07 (vice-chair 2005–07), Scottish Industrial Devpt Advsy Bd (SIDAB) 2003–10; hon doctorate Univ of W Scotland 2010; FIEE 1985, FIProdE 1987, FREng 1989; *Recreations* golf, hill walking, cycling, France; *Clubs* Largs Golf; *Style—* Dr R T Beaty, OBE, FREng; ✉ Glenside, 89 Newton Street, Greenock, Renfrewshire PA16 8SG (☎ 01475 722027, mobile 07961 068614, e-mail bob.beaty@btopenworld.com); ☎ 0033 4 67 443703

BEAUCHAMP; *see also:* Proctor-Beauchamp

BEAUCLERK-DEWAR, Peter de Vere; RD (1980, bar 1990), JP (Inner London 1983); s of James Dewar, MBE, GM, AE (d 1983), and Hermione de Vere (d 1969), yr da and co-heir of Maj Aubrey Nelthorpe Beauclerk, of Little Grimsby Hall, Lincs (d 1916, heir-in-line to Dukedom of St Albans); recognised by Lord Lyon King of Arms 1965 in additional surname and arms of Beauclerk; *b* 19 February 1943, Tenterden, Kent; *Educ* Ampleforth; *m* 4 Feb 1967, Sarah Ann Sweet Verge, elder da of Maj Lionel John Verge Rudder, DCLI (d 2012); 1 s (James William Aubrey de Vere b 30 Sept 1970), 3 da (Alexandra Hermione Sarah (Mrs Gideon Palmer) b 1 Aug 1972, Emma Diana Peta (Mme Amaury Amblard-Ladurantie) b 6 Sept 1973, Philippa Caroline Frances b 8 Aug 1982); *Career* Lt Cdr RNR 1977 (cmmnd London Div 1966), Intelligence Branch 1979–92, ret 1992; currently chm HMS President Reserve Officers Assoc (vice-chm 2011–14); genealogist; Falkland Pursuivant Extraordinary 1975, 1982, 1984, 1986, 1987, 1991, 1994, 1996, 1997, 1999, 2001, 2003, 2006, 2008, 2010, 2012 and 2014; usher: (Silver Stick) Silver Jubilee Thanksgiving Serv 1977, (Liaison) HM Queen Elizabeth The Queen Mother's 80th Birthday Thanksgiving Serv 1980; heraldry conslt to Christie's Fine Art Auctioneers 1979–, hon fell Assoc of Genealogists and Record Agents 2012– (chm 1982–83), vice-pres Royal Stuart Soc 1995 (hon treas 1985–94), tstee Inst of Heraldic and Genealogical Studies 1992– (hon treas 1979–94, chm of tstees 2009–); chief accountant Archdiocese of Westminster 1982–85; dir: Mgmnt Search International Ltd 1985–87, Five Arrows Gp 1986–87, Clifton Nurseries (Holdings) Ltd 1986–88, Room Twelve Ltd 1987–88; underwriting memb Lloyd's 1987–97; princ and fndr Peter Dewar Associates 1988–, sr conslt Sanders and Sidney plc 1990–99; court chm Family Proceedings Court (Inner London) 1991–2013, chm Inner London Magistrates' Assoc 2000–04 (vice-chm 1994–95), dep chm East Central Petty Sessional Div 1994–2000; govr: More House Sch SW1 1986–95 (dep chm 1991–95), Good Shepherd Sch W12 (vice-chm) 1993–2003; hon treas Br Red Cross Queen Mother's Meml Fund 2002–06, chm and tstee Oregon Historical Soc (UK) 2003–10; emeritus dir Royal Caledonian Educnl Tst 2011– (dir 1988–2011); pres London Membs' Centre Nat Tst for Scotland 2015– (chm 2005–11, vice-pres 2011–15); NADFAS lectr 1998–2015; memb Queen's Body Guard for Scotland (Royal Co of Archers) 1981–; Queen's Golden Jubilee Medal 2002, Queen's Diamond Jubliee Medal 2012; Liveryman Worshipful Co of Haberdashers 1968; FSA Scot 1968, FFA 1979, FMAAT 1982, Hon FHG 1982, FCMI (FIMgt 1988); Knight of Honour and Devotion SMOM 1971 (Dir of Ceremonies Br Assoc 1989–95, vice-chllr Br Assoc 2012–), Knight of Justice Sacred Mil Order of Constantine St George 1981, OStJ 1987, Cdr of Merit with Swords 'Pro Merito Melitensi' 1989; *Books* The House of Nell Gwyn 1670–1974 (co-author), The House of Dewar 1296–1991, The Family History Record Book (1991), Burke's Landed Gentry of Scotland (ed, 2001), Right Royal Bastards (co-author, 2006), Historian of Clan Dewar, contributor to many pubns; *Clubs* Puffin's, New (Edinburgh); *Style—* Peter Beauclerk-Dewar, Esq, RD, JP; ✉ 22 Faroe Road, Brook Green, London W14 0EP (☎ and fax 020 7610 4163, mobile 078 6061 4817, e-mail peterbdewar@icloud.com, website www.peterdewar.com)

BEAUMAN, Christopher Bentley; s of Wing Cdr Eric Bentley Beauman (d 1989), of London, and Katharine Burgoyne, *née* Jones (d 1998); *b* 12 October 1944; *Educ* Winchester, Trinity Coll Cambridge, Johns Hopkins Sch of Advanced Int Studies and Columbia Univ

(Harkness fell); *m* 1, 1966 (m dis 1976), Sally, *née* Kinsey-Miles; m 2, 1976, Nicola Beauman, *qv*, da of Dr Francis Mann (d 1991), of London; 1 s, 1 da, 3 step c; *Career* corp fin exec Hill Samuel 1968–72; dir: Guinness Mahon 1973–76, FMC Ltd 1975–81; advsr to chm: BSC 1976–81, Central Policy Review Staff 1981–83, Morgan Grenfell Group 1983–91 (planning dir 1989–91); sr advsr European Bank for Reconstruction and Development 1995– (sr banker 1991–95); memb Advsy Bd LSE Centre for Climate Change Economics and Policy (CCCEP) 2014–; *Publications* incl: Privatizzazione E Nuove Strategie D'Impresa: Il Caso Della British Steel (2000); *Recreations* family, London, climate change; *Style*— Christopher Beauman, Esq; ✉ 35 Christchurch Hill, London NW3 (☎ 020 7435 1975)

BEAUMAN, Nicola Catherine; da of Dr F A Mann, CBE (d 1991), and Lore, *née* Ehrlich (d 1980); *b* 20 June 1944; *Educ* St Paul's Girls' Sch, Newnham Coll Cambridge; *m* 1, 1965 (m dis 1976), Nicholas Lacey, s of John Lacey; 2 s (Josh b 1968, William b 1973), 1 da (Olivia b 1970); m 2, 1976, Christopher Beauman, *qv*, s of Wing Cdr Eric Bentley Beauman (d 1989); 1 da (Francesca b 1977), 1 s (Ned b 1985); *Career* freelance reviewer, ed and journalist 1967–; freelance writer; fndr Persephone Books 1998; memb Mgmnt Ctee Soc of Authors; assoc Newnham Coll Cambridge; winner Women in Publishing Pandora Award 2002; *Books* A Very Great Profession: The Women's Novel 1914–39 (1983), Cynthia Asquith: A Life (1987), Morgan: A Life of E M Forster (1993), The Other Elizabeth Taylor (2009); *Recreations* urban conservation, walking on Hampstead Heath, rediscovering twentieth century women writers; *Style*— Mrs Nicola Beauman; ✉ 35 Christchurch Hill, London NW3 1LA (☎ 020 7435 1975); Persephone Books, 59 Lamb's Conduit Street, London WC1N 3NB (☎ 020 7242 9292, e-mail nicola@persephonebooks.co.uk)

BEAUMONT, Mark Ian Macleod; s of Kevin Beaumont, of Edinburgh, and Una, *née* MacLeod; *b* 1 January 1983, Swindon, Wilts; *Educ* HS of Dundee, Univ of Glasgow (MSc, Graduate of the Year 2009); *m* Nicola, *née* Kitchin; 1 da (Harriet); *Career* Guinness World Record holder for cycling from Cairo to Cape Town (6750 miles in 41 days, 10 hours and 22 minutes), former Guinness World Record holder for the Fastest True Circumnavigation of the World by Bicycle (18,297 miles in 194 days and 17 hours); cycled across Scotland aged 12; hon pres Scottish Student Sport; BBC documentaries: The Man Who Cycled the World, The Man Who Cycled the Americas, Rowing the Arctic, The Queen's Baton Relay; patron: Orkidstudio, Saltire Fndn, Archie Fndn; Glenfiddich Spirit of Scotland Top Scot Award 2010; hon doctorate Dundee Univ 2013; *Publications* The Man Who Cycled the World (2009), The Man Who Cycled the Americas (2011); *Recreations* skiing, cycling, fell running, adventuring, music (cellist), art; *Style*— Mark Beaumont, Esq; ✉ e-mail mark@markbeaumontonline.com, website www.markbeaumontonline.com, Twitter @mrmarkbeaumont

BEAUMONT, Martin Dudley; s of Patrick Beaumont, DL, and late Lindesay, *née* Howard; *b* 6 August 1949; *Educ* Stowe, Magdalene Coll Cambridge (MA); *m* 12 June 1976, Andrea Evelyn, *née* Wilberforce; 3 da (Alice b 11 July 1980, Jessica b 22 Dec 1981, Flora b 4 Oct 1989); *Career* ptnr KPMG (formerly Thomson McLintock) 1983–87 (dir 1980–83), gp fin dir Egmont Publishing Group 1987–90; chief exec Children's Best Sellers Ltd 1989–90; United Cooperatives: chief financial offr 1990–92, chief exec 1992–2002; dir Cooperative Bank plc 1996–2000 (dep chair 2000–07), gp chief exec The Cooperative Gp 2002–07, dep chair Cooperative Fin Servs Ltd 2002–07, dir Cooperative Insurance Soc 2002–07, chm Skillsmart Retail Ltd 2007–12, chm Kind Consumer Ltd 2009–; dir Chester Race Co Ltd 2007– (chair 2011–); dep chm NW Business Leadership Team 2006–07; memb Cncl Duchy of Lancaster 2007–; High Sheriff Cheshire 2013–14; FCA 1977, FIGD 2002; *Recreations* family, fishing, tennis, horse racing; *Style*— Martin Beaumont, Esq

BEAUMONT, Lady Mary Rose; *née* Wauchope; da of Charles Edward Wauchope (d 1969), and Elaine Margaret, *née* Armstrong-Jones (d 1965); *b* 6 June 1932, Petersfield, Hants; *Educ* Prior's Field Godalming, Courtauld Inst Univ of London (BA); *m* 1955, Timothy Wentworth Beaumont (The Lord Beaumont, d 2008), s of Michael Wentworth Beaumont; 2 s (Hon Hubert Wentworth b 1956, Hon Alaric Charles Blackett b 1958 d 1980), 2 da (Hon Atalanta Armstrong b 1961, Hon Ariadne Grace b 1963); *Career* fndr Centre for the Study of Modern Art at ICA 1972; teacher at art schs and polys, lectr at Tate Gallery and National Gallery, lectr at Modern Art Studies Christie's Educn 1990–2001, lectr in humanities City & Guilds of London Art Sch 1996–2008; writer and art critic for newspapers and periodicals incl: FT, Sunday Telegraph, Art International, Arts Review, Art and Design; author of numerous catalogue introductions for individual artists; exhbn curator: for Br Cncl in E Europe and Far East 1983–87, The Human Touch (Fischer Fine Art) 1986, The Dark Side of The Moon (Benjamin Rhodes Gallery) 1990, Three Scottish Artists (Pamela Auchincloss Gallery NY) 1990; Picker Fellowship at Kingston Poly; exec and memb Cncl Contemporary Arts Soc 1980–90, memb Advsy Ctee Govt Art Collection 1994–2000; memb AICA, hon fell RBS 2008; *Publications* Jean Macalpine: Intervals in Light (1998), Carole Hodgson (1999), George Kyriacou (1999), Jock McFadyen (contrib, 2000), New European Artists (contrib, 2001), Albert Irvin: The Complete Prints (2010); *Recreations* listening to opera and reading novels; *Clubs* Chelsea Arts, Royal Overseas League; *Style*— Mary Rose, Lady Beaumont; ✉ 40 Elms Road, London SW4 9EX (☎ 020 7498 8664)

BEAVEN, Richard James; s of John Edwin Beaven, of Bath, Somerset, and Patricia Anne Merrifield, of Exeter, Devon; *b* 5 May 1966; *Educ* Hele's Sch Exeter, Exeter Coll, Bristol Poly (HND Business Studies); *m* Marie-Regine Elisabeth, da of Jacques Astic; 1 da (Martha Beaven b 15 Dec 1997); *Career* media planner/buyer Geers Gross Advertising 1988–89, media mangr StarCom (formerly Leo Burnett Advertising) 1989–93, gp media dir Saatchi & Saatchi Advertising 1993–95, jt exec media dir/bd dir Leo Burnett Advertising 1996 (gp media dir 1995–96), former exec vice-pres and md MediaVest NY, ceo North America Initiative 2006–08, ceo Worldwide Initiative 2008–; *Recreations* photography, Chelsea FC, hill walking (first completed 3 Peaks Challenge in 1992); *Style*— Richard Beaven, Esq

BEAVERBROOK, 3 Baron (UK 1917); Sir Maxwell William Humphrey Aitken; 3 Bt (UK 1916); s of Sir Max Aitken, 2 Bt, DSO, DFC (d 1985; suc as 2 Baron Beaverbrook 1964, which he disclaimed for life 1964) by his 3 w, Violet (*see* Lady Aitken); *b* 29 December 1951; *Educ* Charterhouse, Pembroke Coll Cambridge, Royal Coll of Defence Studies; *m* 1974, Susan Angela (Susie), da of Francis More O'Ferrall and Angela (niece of Sir George Mather-Jackson, 5 Bt, and da of Sir Anthony Mather-Jackson 6 Bt, JP, DL, by his w, Evelyn, da of Lt-Col Sir Henry Stephenson, 1 Bt, DSO); 2 s (Hon Maxwell Francis b 1977, Hon Alexander Rory b 1978), 2 da (Hon Charlotte 1982, Hon Sophia b 1985); *Heir* s, Hon Maxwell Aitken; *Career* dir Ventech Ltd 1983–86, chm and pres Ventech Healthcare Corporation Inc 1988–92 (chm 1986); govt whip House of Lords 1986–88; treas: Cons Party 1990–92 (dep treas 1988–90), European Democratic Union 1990–92; chm Highway One Corporation Ltd 1996–99, chm Pine Ventures plc 2006–, dir British Racing Drivers Club Ltd 2006–08 and 2015–; tstee Beaverbrook Fndn 1974– (chm 1985–); memb Cncl Homeopathic Tst 1989–92, chm Nat Assoc of Boys' Clubs 1989–92; European Grand Touring Car Champion 1998, Harmsworth Trophy 2004; dir British Powerboat Racing Club 2004–; RAuxAF: Air Cdre 2004–09, Air Vice-Marshal 2009–, hon Inspector-Gen 2009–16, Commandant Gen 2016–; churchwarden St James Denchworth 1988–2006; *Clubs* White's, Royal Yacht Squadron, Br Racing Drivers, RAF, Br Powerboat Racing; *Style*— The Rt Hon the Lord Beaverbrook

BEAZLEY, Thomas Alan George; QC (2001); s of late Derek Beazley, of Newport, and Rosemary Beazley; *b* 2 March 1951; *Educ* Emmanuel Coll Cambridge (BA, LLB); *m* 1980, Ingrid, da of late Ian Marrable; 2 da (Kim b 8 Sept 1980, Beatrice 14 Jan 1984); *Career* called to the Bar Middle Temple 1979; *Publications* Holding the Balance – Effective Enforcement, Procedural Fairness and Human Rights in Regulating Financial Services and Markets in the 21st Century (ed Ferran and Goodheart, 2001); articles on private international law and financial services; *Style*— Thomas Beazley, Esq, QC; ✉ Blackstone Chambers, Temple, London EC4Y 8BW (☎ 020 7583 1770, e-mail thomasbeazley@blackstonechambers.com)

BEBB, Guto; MP; *b* 9 October 1968; *Educ* Univ of Aberystwyth; *m* Esyllt; 5 c; *Career* formerly self-employed economic and business conslt; MP (Cons) Aberconwy 2010–; Parly under-sec of state for Wales 2016–; *Style*— Guto Bebb, Esq, MP; ✉ House of Commons, London SW1A 0AA

BEBE, Dawn; *b* 17 April 1966; *Educ* Dip Journalism; *Career* feature writer: South Wales Echo, Just 17; ed: Big!, Bliss, New Woman; publishing dir Red 1999–2000, publishing dir New Woman 1999–2000, md Emap Elan Women's Media 2000–02, md Emap Elan 2002–; memb Ctee BSME; winner: Magazine of the Year PPA Awards 1998, Most Improved Publication EMAP Awards 1998; *Style*— Miss Dawn Bebe

BECHER, Sir John William Michael (WRIXON-); 6 Bt (UK 1831), of Ballygiblin, Cork; s of late Sir William Wrixon-Becher, 5 Bt, MC, by his 1 w, Hon Vanda Vivian, later Countess of Glasgow (d 1984); *b* 29 September 1950; *Educ* Harrow, Neuchâtel Univ Switzerland; *Career* Lloyd's underwriter G N Rouse 1971–74, Lloyd's Brokers 1974–87, dir Wise Speke Financial Services 1987–93, fin conslt HSBC Gibbs Ltd 1993–99, ptnr Ford Reynolds and Associates Ltd 2000–05, princ Becher Ford Reynolds 2006–10, conslt Weatherbys Private Bank and Weatherbys Hamilton Insurance Brokers 2014–; dir: Old Street Productions Ltd 2001–03, Wind Energy Ltd 2003–05; chm Future Electric Ltd 2010–; *Recreations* shooting, fishing, golf; *Clubs* White's, MCC, I Zingari, Royal Overseas League; *Style*— Sir John Wrixon-Becher, Bt

BECHTLER, Hildegard Maria; da of Richard Bechtler (d 1973), and Klara, *née* Simon (d 1993); *b* 14 November 1951; *Educ* Camberwell Sch of Art, Central St Martins Sch of Art and Design; *m* Nov 1984, Bill Paterson, *qv*; 1 s (Jack b 10 April 1985), 1 da (Anna b 28 Sept 1989); *Career* set, costume and production designer; memb London Inst (LIMA) 2001; FRSA 2001; *Theatre and Opera* numerous credits incl: Electra (RSC) 1989, King Lear (RNT and world tour) 1990, La Wally (Bregenz Festival and Amsterdam Muziktheater) 1990, Electra (Riverside Studios and Bobigny Paris) 1991, Heddar Gabler (Abbey Dublin and Playhouse London) 1991, Peter Grimes (ENO and Munich Staatsoper) 1991, Don Carlos (Opera North) 1992, Wozzeck (Opera North) 1992, Coriolanus (Salzburg Festival) 1993, Lohengrin (ENO) 1993, Footfalls (Garrick) 1994, Don Giovanni (Glyndebourne) 1994–95, St Pancras Project 1995, Richard II (RNT) 1995, Simon Boccanegra (Munich Staatsoper) 1995, The Changing Room (Royal Court Classic Season and Duke of York's) 1996, The Doll's House (Odean Theatre de l'Europe Paris) 1997, Paul Bunyan (ROH)1997, Boris Godunov (ENO) 1998, Dialogue Des Carmélites (Seito Kinen Festival Japan and Palais Garnier Paris Opèra) 1998–99, The Merchant of Venice (RNT) 1999, Kátà Kabanova (Opera North) 1999, Der Ring Der Nibelungen, Rheingold (Scottish Opera and Edinburgh Festival) 2000 (also Walküre 2001, Siegfried 2002, Götterdämmerung 2003, The Ring Cycle 2003), War and Peace (ENO) 2000 and 2001, Blasted (by Sarah Kane, Royal Court Theatre) 2001, Lady Macbeth of Mjinsk (Sydney Opera) 2002, Terrorism (Royal Court Theatre Upstairs) 2003, The Masterbuilder (Albery Theatre) 2003, Blood (Royal Court Theatre) 2003, The Goat (Almeida and Apollo Theatre) 2004, The Sweetest Swing in Baseball (Royal Court Theatre) 2004, Iphigenia at Aulis (RNT) 2004, Primo (RNT) 2004, Forty Winks (Royal Court Theatre) 2004, By the Bog of Cats (Wyndham's Theatre) 2004, Dialogue des Carmélites (Bastille Paris Opera) 2004, My Name is Rachel Corrie (Royal Court Theatre Upstairs) 2005, La Cenerentola (Glyndebourne Festival Opera) 2005, Primo (Musicbox Theatre Broadway NY) 2005, Richard II (Old Vic Theatre) 2005, The Crucible (RSC) 2006, Dido and Aeneas (La Scala Milan) 2006, My Name is Rachel Corrie (Playhouse London and Minetta Lane Theatre NY) 2006, Exiles (NT) 2006, Krapp's Last Tape (Royal Court) 2006, Thérèse Racquin (NT) 2006, The Crucible (Apollo Theatre) 2006, The Seagull (Royal Court) 2007, The Lady from Dubuque (Haymarket) 2007, The Jewish Wife (Young Vic) 2007, The Hothouse (Nat Theatre) 2007, All About My Mother (Old Vic) 2007, Kátà Kabanova (Opera North) 2007, Madame Butterfly (Opera North) 2007, The Hour We Knew Nothing of Each Other (RNT) 2008, Harper Reagan (RNT) 2008, Roshersholme (Almeida Theatre) 2008, Now or Later (Royal Court Theatre) 2008, The Seagull (Broadway) 2008, Hedda Gabler (Broadway) 2009, La Cenerentola (Deutsche Oper Berlin) 2009, The Letter (Santa Fe Opera) 2009, Dido and Aeneas, Acis and Galatea (ROH) 2009, Werther (Opera North) 2009, The Misanthrope (West End) 2009, Arcadia (West End) 2009 and (Broadway) 2011, After the Dance (RNT) 2010, Aida (Canadian Opera Co) 2010, Blithe Spirit (Theatre Royal Bath and Apollo Theatre) 2011, The Damnation of Faust (ENO) 2011 and (Palermo, Antwerp and Gent) 2012 (also filmed for BBC4 2011), Cause Célèbre (Old Vic) 2011, Tophat (West End) 2012, Farewell to the Theatre (Hampstead Theatre) 2012, The Makropulos Case (Edinburgh Festival Theatre and Opera North) 2012; *Television and Film* numerous credits incl: Coming up Roses (feature) 1985, Hedda Gabler (BBC) 1993, The Waste Land (BBC) 1995, Richard II (BBC) 1996, The Merchant of Venice (RNT 1999) 2000, Krapp's Last Tape (BBC 4) 2007, Primo (HBO/BBC) 2007; *Awards* Olivier Award for Best Prodn (for Hedda Gabler) 1991, French Critics' Best Foreign Prodns Award (for Richard II) 1996, Olivier Award for Best Prodn (for Paul Bunyan) 1997, Evening Standard Award for Outstanding Achievement in Opera 1997, Japanese Critics Award for Best Production of the Year (for Dialogue Des Carmélites) 1999, Barclays TMA Award for Outstanding Achievement in Opera (for Walküre and Siegfried) 2002, South Bank Award for Best Opera Production (for The Ring Cycle) 2004, nominated Best Designer Evening Standard Awards (for Iphigenia at Aulis) 2004, Olivier Award for Best Revival (for The Crucible) 2007, Green Room Award for Set Design (for Lady Macbeth of Mtsenk) 2010, Best Production and Best Costume Design Olivier Award (for After the Dance) 2011; *Style*— Ms Hildegard Bechtler; ✉ Cruickshank Cazenove Limited, 97 Old South Lambeth Road, London SW8 1XU (☎ 020 7735 2933, fax 020 7582 6405, e-mail office@cruickshankcazenove.com)

BECK, Andrew; s of James Albert Beck (d 1997), and Kathleen May, *née* Ellis (d 2001); *b* 9 April 1958, Leeds; *Educ* Temple Moor HS Leeds, Huddersfield Poly (BA); *m* 19 July 1980, Diane Lesley, *née* Clough; 1 da (Samantha Victoria b 26 June 1984), 1 s (Richard Andrew b 13 June 1989); *Career* Walker Morris: slr 1989–96, ptnr 1996–; memb: Assoc of Northern Mediators, Property Litigation Assoc, Law Soc; *Style*— Andrew Beck, Esq; ✉ Walker Morris, Kings Court, Leeds LS1 2HL (☎ 0113 283 2520, fax 0113 245 9412, e-mail ayb@walkermorris.co.uk)

BECK, Charles Theodore Heathfield; s of Richard Theodore Beck, and Margaret Beryl, *née* Page; *b* 3 April 1954; *Educ* Winchester, Jesus Coll Cambridge (MA); *m* 19 Sept 1992, Nathakan Piyawannahong, da of Wan Saklor; 1 s; *Career* Bank of England 1975–79; J M Finn & Co: joined 1979, ptnr 1984, fin ptnr 1988–91 and 1993–98, compliance and systems partner 1998–2006, dir of compliance 2006–; Freeman City of London 1980, Liveryman Worshipful Co of Broderers 1981; FCSI, ASIP; *Recreations* fencing, Japanese fencing; *Style*— Charles Beck, Esq; ✉ J M Finn & Co, 4 Coleman Street, London EC2R 5TA (☎ 020 7600 1660, fax 020 7600 1661, e-mail charles.beck@jmfinn.com)

BECK, Clive; s of Sir Edgar Charles Beck, CBE (d 2000), and his 1 wife, Mary Agnes, *née* Sorapure (d 2000); *b* 12 April 1937; *Educ* Ampleforth; *m* 28 April 1960, Philippa Mary, da of Dr Philip Flood (d 1968), of Wimbledon; 3 da (Nicola b 17 Feb 1961, Emma b 19

Dec 1967, Sarah b 16 July 1971), 3 s (David b 28 July 1962, Andrew b 22 Sept 1964, Simon b 30 Dec 1965); *Career* 2 Lt The Life Guards 1955–57; John Mowlem & Co 1957, joined SGB Gp plc 1967 (dir 1968, chm 1985), rejoined John Mowlem & Co plc as dep chm and jt md; chm London Management Ltd; Freeman of City of London 1960, Liveryman Worshipful Co of Plaisterers; *Recreations* golf, travel; *Clubs* Royal Wimbledon Golf, Swinley Forest Golf; *Style—* Clive Beck, Esq; ✉ 8 Atherton Drive, Wimbledon, London SW19 5LB (☎ 020 8946 5076)

BECK, David Clive; s of Clive Beck, and Philippa, *née* Flood; *b* 28 July 1962; *Educ* Ampleforth, Univ of Kent at Canterbury (BA); *m* 18 July 1992, Katherine, *née* Millar; 2 da, 1 s; *Career* Bell Pottinger Financial Ltd (formerly Lowe Bell Financial): joined 1986, dir 1992–2002, dep md 1995–97, md 1997–2002; dir of communications Marconi Corp plc 2002–06, dir Bell Pottinger Gp 2009–; *Recreations* golf, fishing, tennis; *Clubs* Swinley Forest Golf; *Style—* David Beck, Esq; ✉ 69 Burbage Road, London SE24 9HB

BECK, Dr Michael Hawley; s of William Hawley Beck (d 2005), and June Aldersey Beck (d 2004); *b* Stoke-on-Trent, Staffs; *Educ* Sandbach Sch, Univ of Liverpool (MB ChB); *m* 18 March 1978, Gerralynn (Lynn), da of John Harrop (d 1986), of Worsley, Manchester; 2 s (Jamie b 1979, Robin b 1981); *Career* SHO: Clatterbridge Hosp Wirral 1972–74, neurosurgery Walton Hosp 1974; registrar in med Trafford HA 1976–77, registrar and sr registrar in dermatology Salford HA 1977–81 (SHO (gen med) 1974–76), conslt dermatologist Salford and Bolton NHS Tsts 1981–2008, dir Contact Dermatitis Investigation Unit Hope Hosp Salford 1981–2008; Univ of Manchester: hon assoc lectr in dermatology 1981–92, hon clinical lectr in dermatology and occupational health 1992–2008, hon clinical lectr Occupational and Environmental Health Gp 2009–; dermatological advsr to the Ileostomy Assoc of UK and Ireland 1982–2001; chm NW Regnl Sub-Ctee on Dermatology 1985–88; memb: Ctee Br Contact Dermatitis Gp 1981–2008 (chm 1992–95), Med Advsy Panel Nat Eczema Soc 1991–96, Steering Gp Epi-Derm 1994–2008, Scientific Ctee Jadassohn Centenary Congress 1996, Scientific Ctee Int Symposium on Contact Dermatitis (ISCD) Seoul 2003; memb Cncl: Euro Contact Dermatitis Soc 1992–95, N of England Dermatological Soc 1993–95, Manchester Med Soc 1995–98; memb Organising Ctee Euro Contact Dermatitis Soc Symposium 2016, memb Editorial Bd: Exogenous Dermatology 2001–06, Jl of Dermatological Treatment, Contact Dermatitis; author of over 160 articles and chapters in med jls and books relating to clinical dermatology and contact dermatitis; Schering-Plough orator Clinical Assts Meeting Manchester 2002, Prosser White orator Br Assoc of Dermatologists meeting Brighton 2003; memb: Euro Contact Dermatitis Soc, Br Assoc of Dermatologists; hon memb Br Soc of Occupational Medicine 2006–, hon memb Br Soc for Cutaneous Allergy; FRCP 1991 (MRCP 1977); *Recreations* genealogy, Bolton Wanderers FC, walking; *Clubs* Dowling (pres 2010–11), Lion of Vienna; *Style—* Dr Michael Beck

BECK, Paul William; *b* 19 June 1962, Northallerton, Yorks; *Educ* Nunthorpe GS York, Univ of Newcastle (HND); *m* 15 June 1996, Rachael, *née* Young; 1 da (Olivia b 12 March 1997), 1 s (James b 18 April 1999); *Career* Dunn & Bradstreet 1983–86, fndr PBA 1986–2001, fndr and chief exec LBM 1996–2006, fndr Bek Helicopters 2005–; managed and ran Andrew Flintoff Benefit Year 2006; *Recreations* owner of 30 racehorses, Lancs CCC (sponsor); *Style—* Paul Beck, Esq; ✉ Wrenshot House, Wrenshot Lane, Cheshire WA16 6PG

BECK, Dr Peter; CVO (2016); s of Frank Beck (d 1981), and Kitty Eileen, *née* Clark (d 1959); *b* 4 July 1941, Leicester; *Educ* Wyggeston Boys' Sch Leicester, St Mary's Hosp Med Sch London (MB BS, MD), Univ of Wales (MA); *m* 9 Sept 1964, Lyn, *née* Davies; 1 s (Jonathan Rhys b 19 Dec 1967), 1 da (Rhiannon Lyn b 31 Aug 1969); *Career* SHO St Mary's Hosp and Hammersmith Hosp 1965–67, SHO then registrar Cardiff Royal Infirmary 1967–70, lectr in med WNSM Cardiff 1970–71, MRC clinical research fell Cardiff 1971–73, Wellcome travelling fell Harvard Med Sch 1974–75, conslt physician Cardiff Teaching Hosps 1974–2003; published 40 papers on haemophilia, angio-oedema, immuno-assay, diabetes and medical ethics; chm St John Cncl for Cardiff 2006–08, pres St John Cncls for Cardiff and Vale of Glamorgan 2008–, pres S Glamorgan Boy Scouts 2008–, pres Wales Festival of Rememberance 2008–, vice-pres RFCA 2008–, memb Devpt Ctee Prince's Tst Cymru 2009–, pres SAAFA 2011–; Surgeon Cdr RNR 1975–91; VSO Jordan 1961–62; DL 1994–2008, HM Lord-Lt S Glamorgan 2008–16; FRCP; KStJ 2016 (CStJ 2008, OStJ 2006); *Recreations* family, golf, rugby, art; *Clubs* Army and Navy, Cardiff and County, Royal Porthcawl Golf; *Style—* Dr Peter Beck, CVO; ✉ Tyla Teg, 46 Ty Gwyn Road, Penylan, Cardiff, South Glamorgan CF23 5JG (☎ 029 2048 5982, e-mail pandlbeck@tiscali.co.uk)

BECK-COULTER, (Eva Maria) Barbara; da of Wilhelm Beck (d 1979), of Hameln/Weser, Germany, and Clara Herta Edith Ursula Kothe (d 1989); *b* 14 October 1941, Berlin; *Educ* Victoria-Luise Gymnasium Hameln, Munich Univ, Univ of London (BSc); *m* 1971, Ian Coulter (d 2008), s of William Coulter; 2 s (William Angus b 29 Sept 1974, Benjamin Ian b 19 June 1976), 1 da (Catherine Barbara b 10 Sept 1978); *Career* The Economist: researcher 1965–69, writer on business affairs 1969–74, ed Euro Community Section 1974–78, Euro ed 1978–81, asst ed 1980–81, special reports ed 1995–; sec gen Anglo-German Fndn for the Study of Industrial Soc 1981–91, ed International Management Magazine (part of Reed Elsevier) 1991–94, head of public affairs (Europe) Andersen Consulting 1994; memb Cncl RIIA 1984–90 (memb Exec Ctee 1989–90), memb Academic Cncl Wilton Park (FCO Conf Centre) 1984–91, memb Steering Ctee Königswinter Conf 1982–91, memb Int Cncl Sci Centre Berlin (Social Sci Res) 1990–94, memb Cncl Federal Tst 1993–94; broadcaster, writer and lectr on current affairs in English and German; FRSA 1990; family and friends, classical music, walking, gardening, food, horse riding; *Recreations* family, classical music, walking, gardening, food; *Clubs* Reform (chm 1992–93, tstee 1995–); *Style—* Mrs Barbara Beck-Coulter; ✉ c/o The Economist, 25 St James's Street, London SW1A 1HG (☎ 020 7830 7168, mobile 07894 521491, fax 020 7839 2968, e-mail barbarabeck@economist.com)

BECKET, Michael Ivan H; *b* 11 September 1938; *Educ* Wynyard Sch Ascot, Sloane Sch Chelsea, Open Univ; *Career* Nat Serv 1957–59; lathe operator Elliot Bros (London) Ltd 1956–57, exhibition organiser Shell International Petroleum 1959–61, journalist Electrical & Radio Trading 1961, market res Young & Rubicam 1962; civil serv 1962–68 (Bd of Trade, Nat Bd for Prices and Incomes, Nat Econ Devpt Office); Daily Telegraph 1968–2003, freelance writer and journalist 2003–; wedding and portrait photographer 2011–; tstee and ed annual Kensington Soc 2013–; *Books* Computer by the Tail (1972), Economic Alphabet (1976, 2 edn 1981), Bluff Your Way in Finance (1990), Office Warfare: An Executive Survival Guide (1993), An A-Z of Finance (1999), Stakeholder Pensions (2001), How the Stock Market Works (2002, 5 edn 2014), Starting Your Own Business (2003); *Style—* Michael Ivan H Becket, Esq; ✉ 9 Kensington Park Gardens, London W11 3HB (☎ 020 7727 6941, e-mail becket@photobecket.co.uk)

BECKETT, Frances Mary (Fran); OBE (2006); da of Josephine Godwin, *née* Beckett; *b* 20 November 1951; *Educ* CSQW, Cert in Biblical Studies, MSc Vol Sector Orgn; *Career* trainee mental welfare offr Somerset CC 1969–71, professional social work trg Trent Poly Nottingham 1971–73, rejoined Somerset CC as social worker 1973–75, religious educn studies ANCC Herts 1975–77, student counselling 1977–81, community worker and advice centre mangr 1981–86; Shaftesbury Society: social work advsr 1986–90, community care coordinator 1990–92, urban action dir 1992–95, chief exec 1995–2002; chief exec Church Urban Fund 2002–08, dir Fran Beckett Consultancy Ltd 2008–14; chair: ACEVO 2002–05, Home Office Voluntary and Community Sector Advsy Gp 2003–06, Restore (Peckham) 2004–13, XLP/Soul in the City 2005–07, Rebuilding Community Tst 2005–14, Vol and Community Sector Cabinet Office Advsy Gp 2006–08, Orbit South and East Housing Assoc 2011–; memb Bd and dir FBRN 2005–11, memb Bd NCVO 2005–07, memb Bd London Devpt Agency 2008–12, Bd Southwark CAB 2010–, memb Bd and dir Orbit Housing 2011–, chair of tstees Urban Expression 2014–, chair of friends of Brimmington Park 2014–16, memb Bd Action Tutoring 2014–; memb: Cncl of Reference, Social Workers Christian Fellowship, Links Int; FRSA 2002; *Books* Called to Action (1989), Love in Action (1993), Rebuild (2001); also author of various articles in religious and professional jls; *Recreations* local church involvement, jazz, cinema, theatre; *Style—* Ms Fran Beckett, OBE; ✉ Fran Beckett Consultancy, 108 Meeting House Lane, London SE15 2TT (☎ 020 7732 0923)

BECKETT, Rt Hon Dame Margaret Mary; DBE (2013), PC (1993), MP; da of Cyril Jackson, and Winifred Jackson; *b* 15 January 1943, Ashton-under-Lyne, Lancs; *Educ* Notre Dame HS, Manchester Coll of Sci and Technol, John Dalton Poly; *m* 1979, Leo Beckett; *Career* formerly: engrg apprentice (metallurgy) AEI Manchester, experimental offr Univ of Manchester; researcher (industrial policy) Lab Pty HQ 1970–74; MP (Lab, TGWU supported): Lincoln Oct 1974–79 (also contested Feb 1974), Derby South 1983–; PPS to min of Overseas Devpt 1974–75 (political advsr 1974), asst Govt whip 1975–76, min DES 1976–79; princ researcher Granada TV 1979–83; oppn front bench spokesman on social security 1984–89, shadow chief sec to the Treasy 1989–92, dep ldr of the opposition 1992–94 (ldr May-July 1994), shadow ldr of the House of Commons and Lab campaign co-ordinator 1992–94, candidate Lab Pty leadership and dep leadership elections 1994, shadow sec of state for health 1994–95, shadow sec of state for trade and industry 1995–97, Pres Bd of Trade (sec of state for Trade and Industry) 1997–98, Pres of the Cncl and Ldr of the House of Commons 1998–2001, sec of state for environment, food and rural affrs 2001–06, sec of state FCO 2006–07, min of state for housing 2008–09, chair Intelligence and Security Ctee 2008–; memb: TGWU 1964–, Lab Pty NEC 1980–81, 1985–86 and 1988–98, Fabian Soc, NUJ, Anti-Apartheid Movement, BECTU, Socialist Educn Ctee, Derby Co-op Pty, Socialist Environment and Resources Assoc, Amnesty Int; memb Cncl St George's Coll Windsor 1976–82; hon pres Lab Friends of India; *Publications* Renewing the NHS (1995), Vision for Growth – A New Industrial Strategy for Britain (1996); *Recreations* cooking, reading, caravanning; *Style—* The Rt Hon Dame Margaret Beckett, DBE, MP; ✉ House of Commons, London SW1A 0AA

BECKETT, Martin; s of Vernon Beckett, of New Milton, Hants, and Dorothy Evelyn, *née* Heywood (d 1993); *b* 5 May 1954; *Educ* Ludlow GS, Manchester Poly; *Partner* Janet Ibbotson; *Career* photographer; formerly asst to many photographers incl David Swan, Alan Dunn and Chris Holland; Silver Award 1989 and Merit Award 1995 Assoc of Photographers; work exhibited in exhbns throughout Europe and featured in Art Dirs' Awards NY; chm Assoc of Photographers 1994–95 (vice-chm 1993–94), pres Pyramide Europe 2001–; ed Image Magazine, Fuji Times columnist Br Jl of Photography and Amateur Photographer; *Recreations* cuisine; *Style—* Martin Beckett, Esq; ✉ c/o Alex Vaughan, 59 Lambeth Walk, London SE11 6DX (☎ 020 7735 6623, website www.martinbeckett.co.uk)

BECKFORD, Prof James Arthur (Jim); *b* 1 December 1942; *Educ* Univ of Reading (BA, PhD, DLitt); *m*; 1 s, 2 da (twins); *Career* lectr in sociology Univ of Reading 1966–73, lectr rising to sr lectr in sociology Univ of Durham 1973–88, prof of sociology Loyola Univ of Chicago 1988–89, prof of sociology Univ of Warwick 1989– (emeritus prof 2008–); visiting assoc prof Carleton Univ Ottawa 1974, visiting scholar Tsukuba Univ 1978, Fulbright sr visiting fell Univ of Calif Berkeley and Grad Theological Union Berkeley 1982–83; directeur d'études invité: Ecole des Hautes Etudes en Sciences Sociales Paris 2001, Ecole Pratique des Hautes Etudes Paris 2004; pres: Assoc for the Sociology of Religion 1988–89 (memb Cncl 1985–89 and 2003–06), Int Soc for the Sociology of Religion 1999–2003 (vice-pres 1995–99, chair Editorial Ctee 2003–07), Soc for the Scientific Study of Religion 2010–11; vice-pres Int Sociological Assoc 1994–98 (chair Pubns Ctee 1994–98), govr Information Network Focus on Religious Movements (INFORM) 1991– (actg chm 1993–94); ed Current Sociology 1980–87, editorial assoc History of Sociology 1984–2008; assoc ed: Sociological Analysis 1983–86, International Sociology 1984–90 and 1998–2004, Review of Religious Research 1991–; memb Editorial Bd: Sage Studies in Int Sociology 1980–87, Religion 1989–99, Identity and Culture 1993–2006, Jl of Contemporary Religion 1994–2004, Encyclopedia of Politics and Religion 1996–99, Arxius 1996–, British Jl of Sociology 1998–2008, New Critical Thinking in Religious Studies 1999–, Religion-Staat-Gesellschaft 1999–; memb Comité de Rédaction Social Compass 1983–, memb Council of Reference Implicit Religion 1998–, memb Steering Ctee Dictionnaire des Faits religieux 2004–; dr Univ of Lausanne (hc); fell Soc for the Scientific Study of Religion, FBA 2004; *Publications* incl: The Trumpet of Prophecy: A Sociological Study of Jehovah's Witnesses (1975), Religious Organization: A Trend Report and Bibliography (1975), Cult Controversies: Societal Responses to New Religious Movements (1985), Religion and Advanced Industrial Society (1989), The Changing Face of Religion (ed with T Luckmann, 1989), Secularization, Rationalism and Sectarianism (ed with E Barker and K Dobbelaere, 1993), Religion in Prison: Equal Rites in a Multi-Faith Society (with S Gilliat, 1998), Social Theory and Religion (2003), Challenging Religion: Essays in Honour of Eileen Barker (ed with J T Richardson, 2003), Muslims in Prison: Challenge and Change in Britain and France (with D Joly and F Khostokhavar, 2005), Theorising Religion: Classical and Contemporary Debates (ed with John Walliss, 2006), The Sage Handbook of the Sociology of Religion (ed with N J Demerath III, 2007), Migration and Religion (ed, 2 vols, 2015); also author of numerous articles, book chapters and reports; *Style—* Prof Jim Beckford; ✉ Department of Sociology, University of Warwick, Coventry CV4 7AL

BECKHAM, David Robert Joseph; OBE (2003); s of Ted Beckham, of Chingford, London, and Sandra Beckham; *b* 2 May 1975, Leytonstone, London; *Educ* Chingford HS; *m* 4 July 1999, Victoria Beckham, *qv*, *née* Adams; 3 s (Brooklyn Joseph b 4 March 1999, Romeo James b 1 Sept 2002, Cruz b 20 Feb 2005), 1 da (Harper Seven b 10 July 2011); *Career* former professional footballer; clubs: Manchester United FC until 2003 (first team debut Coca-Cola Cup v Brighton & Hove Albion 1992, League debut v Leeds United 1995, over 300 appearances, 64 goals, Premier League champions 1996, 1997, 1999, 2000, 2001 and 2003, winners FA Cup 1996 and 1999 (runners-up 1995), winners Charity Shield 1996 and 1997, winners European Champions League 1999), Real Madrid 2003–07, LA Galaxy 2007–12, AC Milan (on loan) 2009 and 2010, Paris St-Germain 2013, ret; England: 115 caps and 17 goals, capt 2000–06, debut v Moldova 1996, memb squad World Cup 1998, 2002 and 2006, memb squad European Championships 2000 and 2004; Young Player of the Year 1996/97, Sky Football Personality of the Year 1997, runner-up FIFA World Footballer of the Year 1999 and 2001, BBC Sports Personality of the Year 2001 (runner-up 1999), BBC Sports Personality of the Year Lifetime Achievement Award 2010; *Books* My World (2000), My Side (2003); *Recreations* family, dining and winetasting; *Style—* David Beckham, Esq, OBE

BECKHAM, Victoria; *née* Adams; da of Tony and Jackie Adams, of Goff's Oak, Herts; *b* 17 April 1974; *m* 4 July 1999, David Beckham, OBE, *qv*; 3 s (Brooklyn Joseph b 4 March 1999, Romeo James b 1 Sept 2002, Cruz b 20 Feb 2005), 1 da (Harper Seven b 10 July 2011); *Career* fashion designer and former pop singer; fndr memb (with Emma Bunton, Melanie Brown (Mel B), Melanie Chisholm (Mel C), *qv*, and Geri Halliwell) Spice Girls 1993, signed to Virgin Records 1995; creative dir dvb Style 2006–, launched dvb Denim 2007, launched dress collection 2008 and 2010; *Albums* (in excess of 40m albums sold worldwide): Spice 1996 (UK no 1), Spiceworld 1997 (UK no 1, platinum UK, double platinum US, no 1 in Holland, Norway, Denmark, New Zealand, Finland and Austria), Forever 2000; solo album Victoria Beckham 2001; *Singles* from album Spice Girls incl: Wannabe 1996 (debut single, UK no 1, first all-girl group to attain position since the Supremes 1964, 4m copies sold worldwide, no 1 in 31 territories incl American Billboard (first UK act to attain position on debut single) 1997), Say You'll Be There 1996 (UK no 1), 2 Become 1 1996 (UK Christmas no 1), Mama/Who Do You Think You Are (double A-side) 1997 (UK no 1, thus first ever band to go to no 1 in the UK with first 4 singles); from album Spiceworld: Spice Up Your Life 1997 (UK no 1), Too Much 1997 (UK Christmas no 1), Stop 1998 (UK no 2), Viva Forever 1998 (UK no 1), Goodbye 1998 (UK Christmas no 1); from album Forever: Holler/Let Love Lead The Way (double A-side) 2000 (UK no 1); solo singles: Out Of Your Mind (with Dane Bowers and Truesteppers) 2000 (UK no 2), Not Such an Innocent Girl 2001, A Mind of its Own 2002, Let Your Head Go/This Groove 2003; *Performances* incl: The Prince's Tst Gala Manchester 1997, Royal Variety Performance 1997 and 1998, Spiceworld world tour 1998, Spice Girls Reunion Tour (UK, Europe and N America) 2007–08; *Film* Spiceworld The Movie 1997; *Awards* Best Video (for Say You'll Be There) and Best Single (for Wannabe) Brit Awards 1997, two Ivor Novello song writing awards 1997, Best Br Band Smash Hits Show 1997, three American Music Awards 1998, Special Award for International Sales Brit Awards 1998, Outstanding Contribution to Music Brit Awards 2000, Brits Performance of 30 Years Brit Award 2010, Designer Brand Br Fashion Award 2011, Woman of the Decade Glamour Award 2013; *Books* Learning to Fly (2001), That Extra Half an Inch (2006); *Style*— Victoria Beckham; ✉ c/o 19 Entertainment Ltd, Unit 33 Ransomes Dock, 35–37 Parkgate Road, London SW11 4NP (☎ 020 7801 1919, fax 020 7801 1920)

BECKINGHAM, Peter; *b* 16 March 1949; *Educ* Chigwell Sch, Selwyn Coll Cambridge; *m* 1975, Jill Mary, *née* Trotman; 2 da; *Career* Decca Record Co 1970–74, Br Overseas Trade Bd 1974–79, entered HM Dip Serv 1979, consul (info) NY 1979–83; FCO: News Dept 1984, Science, Energy and Nuclear Dept 1984–86, East African Dept 1986–88; first sec Stockholm 1988–92, first sec and head Political Section Canberra 1992–96, dir Jt Export Promotion Directorate FCO 1996–99, consul-gen and DG (trade and investment) Sydney 1999–2004, ambass to the Philippines 2005–09, dep high cmmr Mumbai 2010–13, govr Turks and Caicos Islands 2013–16; *Recreations* golf, tennis, cricket, music; *Style*— Mr Peter Beckingham; ✉ e-mail peter.beckingham@hotmail.com

BECKINSALE, Kate; da of Richard Beckinsale (d 1979), and Judy Loe; *b* 26 July 1973, London; *Educ* Godolphin & Latymer Sch; *m* (m dis) 2004, Len Wiseman; 1 da by previous relationship (Lily Sheen *b* 1999); *Career* actress; *Theatre* The Seagull (nat tour), Sweetheart (Royal Court), Closer (NT Studio); *Television* incl: One Against the Wind 1991, Rachel's Dream 1992, Anna Lee 1993, Cold Comfort Farm 1995, Emma 1997, Alice Through the Looking Glass 1999; *Films* incl: Much Ado About Nothing 1993, The Prince of Jutland 1994, Uncovered 1994, Haunted 1995, Shooting Fish 1997, The Last Days of Disco 1998, Brokedown Palace 1999, The Golden Bowl 2000, Pearl Harbour 2001, Serendipity 2001, Laurel Canyon 2002, Underworld 2003, Tiptoes 2003, Van Helsing 2004, The Aviator 2005, Underworld: Evolution 2006, Click 2006, Snow Angels 2007, Vacancy 2007, Winged Creatures 2008, Nothing But the Truth 2008, Whiteout 2009, Everybody's Fine 2009, Contraband 2012, Underworld: Awakening 2012, Total Recall 2012, The Trials of Cate McCall 2013, Stonehearst Asylum 2014, The Face of an Angel 2015, Absolutely Anything 2015, Love and Friendship 2016; *Style*— Kate Beckinsale

BECKLAKE, Dr (Ernest) John Stephen; s of Ernest Becklake, of Weare Gifford, Devon, and Evelyn Beatrice, *née* Stevens; *b* 24 June 1943; *Educ* Bideford GS, Univ of Exeter (BSc, PhD, Rugby colours); *m* 21 Aug 1965, Susan Elizabeth, da of Norman Buckle; 2 s (Peter Julian *b* 23 Nov 1972, Robin Edward *b* 22 April 1977); *Career* sr scientist EMI Electronics Wells 1967–69, postdoctoral fell Univ of Victoria BC 1969–70, sr engr Marconi Space and Def Systems Frimley 1970–72; Science Museum London: asst keeper (curator of space technol collection) 1972–80, head of engrg 1980–90, head of technol (dir of curatorial activities of all technol collections) 1990–94, sr res fell in astronautics 1994–, managing ed DERA History Project 1995–99; dir of numerous exhbn projects at Science Museum incl: Exploration 1977, Telecommunications 1982, Exploration of Space 1986, Robotics Japan 1991; conslt rocket history Aerospace Museum Cosford 1997–, head of astronautics Observatory Science Centre 1997–; memb and tstee Int Acad of Astronautics 1989–; FRAeS 1996; *Books* incl: Man and the Moon (1980), The Population Explosion (1990), Pollution (1991); author of over twenty papers on history of rocketry and spaceflight; *Recreations* sport (particularly rugby and golf), gardening, reading; *Clubs* Puttenham Golf, Farnborough RFC; *Style*— Dr John Becklake

BECKWITH, Peter Michael; OBE (2007); s of Col Harold Andrew Beckwith (d 1966), of Hong Kong, and Agnes Camilla McMichael, *née* Duncan (d 1980); *b* 20 January 1945; *Educ* Harrow, Emmanuel Coll Cambridge (MA); *m* 19 Oct 1968, late Paula, da of late Robin Stuart Bateman, of Cliftonville, Kent; 2 da (Tamara Jane *b* 1970, Clare Tamsin *b* 1972); *Career* admitted slr 1970; chm: London & Edinburgh Trust plc 1992, PMB Holdings Ltd 1992–, Aspria Holdings BV 2000–; Hon LLD Univ of Cambridge; *Recreations* association football, tennis, skiing, theatre, opera, gardening, dogs; *Clubs* Riverside Racquets (chm 1989–95), Old Harrovian AFC, Chelsea FC, Downhill Only (Wengen), Harbour (London and Milano), Austria Haus, Vail USA, The World of Residensea; *Style*— Peter Beckwith, Esq, OBE; ✉ PMB Holdings Ltd, Hill Place House, 55A High Street, Wimbledon, London SW19 5BA (☎ 020 8944 1288, fax 020 8944 1054)

BEDDINGTON, Prof Sir John; kt (2010), CMG (2004); s of Henry John Beddington, and Mildred, *née* Weale; *Educ* Monmouth, LSE (BSc, MSc), Univ of Edinburgh (PhD); *Career* lectr in population biology Univ of York 1970–80, sr fell Int Inst of Environmental Devpt 1980–83; Imperial Coll London: lectr rising to reader 1984–91, prof 1991–, dir Centre for Environmental Technol 1994–98, dir T H Huxley Sch 1998–2001, head Dept of Environmental Sci and Technol 2001–04; chief scientific advsr to UK Govt and head Govt Office of Sci 2008–13, sr advsr Oxford Martin Sch Oxford Univ 2013–; chm Science Advsy Cncl DEFRA 2005–07; chm Rothamsted Research 2013–, non-exec dir Met Office 2013–; memb NERC 2000–06; City of Heidelberg Prize for Environmental Excellence 1997; pres ZSL 2014–; FRS 2001; Order of the Rising Sun Japan 2014; *Publications* various articles in learned jls and professional literature; *Recreations* hill walking, bird watching, amateur astronomy, paintings and sculpture; *Clubs* Travellers; *Style*— Prof Sir John Beddington, CMG, FRS; ✉ Oxford Martin School, University of Oxford, 34 Broad Street, Oxford OX1 3BD (e-mail john.beddington@oxfordmartin.ox.ac.uk)

BEDELIAN, Haro Moushegh; OBE (1986); s of Moushegh Haroutune Bedelian (d 1974), and Annig, *née* Nigogosian (d 2000); *b* 6 March 1943; *Educ* English Sch Nicosia Cyprus, St Catharine's Coll Cambridge (MA); *m* 1970, Yvonne Mildred, da of Stephen Gregory Arratoon (d 1993); 1 s (Stepan *b* 1973), 2 da (Lisa *b* 1975, Claire *b* 1978); *Career* dir Balfour Beatty Ltd 1988–98; chief exec: Transmanche Link (TML) 1993–97, Connect 1997–98; pres Export Gp for Constructional Industries (EGCI) 1995–98, visiting prof of civil engrg Univ of Portsmouth 1993–, ind conslt 1998–; vice-pres: ICE 2001–04 (memb Cncl 1987–90), World Fedn of Engrg Organisations 2011–; memb Cncl: Fedn of Civil Engrg Contractors 1989–93, Royal Acad of Engrg 1991–94; hon fell St Catharines Coll Cambridge 2010–; FREng 1989; *Recreations* tennis, golf; *Clubs* RAC; *Style*— Haro Bedelian, OBE, FREng; ✉ e-mail hbedelian@aol.com

BEDELL-PEARCE, Keith Leonard; CBE (2009); s of Leonard Bedell-Pearce, of Sanderstead, Surrey, and Irene, *née* Bedell; *b* 11 March 1946; *Educ* Trinity Sch of John Whitgift, Univ of Exeter (LLB), Univ of Warwick Business Sch (MSc); *m* 2 Oct 1971, Gaynor Mary, da of Frederick Charles Pemberthy Trevelyan, of Exeter, Devon; 2 da (Olivia *b* 1976, Harriet

b 1988), 1 s (Jack *b* 1980); *Career* systems analyst: Plessey 1969–70, Wiggins Teape 1970–72; Prudential Assurance Co Ltd: computer projects mangr 1972–75, Legal Dept 1975, slr 1978, gen mangr field operations 1986 (additional responsibility for mktg 1987), dir 1988–2001; chief exec and dir Prudential Financial Services Ltd 1991–95; dir: Prudential Portfolio Managers Ltd 1985, Prudential Unit Trust Managers Ltd 1986, various Prudential subsid cos, Staple Nominees Ltd 1991–, Prudential plc 1992–2001 (md UK Div 1995–96, dir Int Devpt 1996–2001), e-Commerce 2000–01; chm: Prudential Corporation Australia Ltd 1996–98, Prudential Europe 1999–2001, Norwich & Peterborough Building Soc 2001–09; dir F&C Asset Mgmnt plc 2002–14; chm: The Student Loans Co Ltd 2001–08, Directgov 2004–09, 4D Data Centres Ltd 2007–; Warwick Business Sch: memb Bd 1995–, hon prof 2001–; chm Croydon HS for Girls Scholarship Tst 2003–08; govr Trinity School of John Whitgift 2015–; memb Royal Soc Investment Advsy Ctee 2006–; memb Cncl Univ of Warwick 2009– (hon treas 2011–); memb Law Soc, fell Mktg Soc; *Books* Checklists for Data Processing Contracts (1978), Computers and Information Technology (1979, 2 edn 1982); *Recreations* shooting, modern British art; *Style*— Keith Bedell-Pearce, Esq, CBE, ✉ 4D Data Centres Ltd, Sirius II, 122 Oyster Lane, Byfleet, Surrey KT14 7JU (☎ 020 8660 0819, fax 020 8660 2099, e-mail kbp3@btinternet.com)

BEDFORD, 15 Duke of (E 1694); Andrew Ian Henry Russell; s of 14 Duke (d 2003); *b* 30 March 1962; *Educ* Harrow, Harvard Univ (BA); *m* 16 Oct 2000, Louise Rona, da of late Donald Ian Crammond, of Champignolles, France, and The Dowager Lady Delves Broughton; 1 da (Lady Alexandra Louisa Clare *b* 9 July 2001), 1 s (Marquess of Tavistock *b* 7 June 2005); *Heir* s, Marquess of Tavistock; *Career* dir: Tattersalls Ltd, Woburn Enterprises Ltd; *Recreations* country sports; *Clubs* Jockey, A D (Boston); *Style*— His Grace the Duke of Bedford; ✉ Woburn Abbey, Woburn, Bedfordshire MK17 9WA (☎ 01525 290333)

BEDFORD, Anthony Peter; s of Philip Derek Bedford (d 1962), and Jean Rachel, *née* Whyman; *b* 30 September 1951; *Educ* King's Sch Canterbury, St Catherine's Coll Oxford (MA), Univ of London (MPhil); *m* 1, 14 March 1974, Anita Susan (d 1992), da of Charles Hamilton-Matthews, of Cornwall; 1 s (Tobias *b* 1974), 1 da (Anouska *b* 1977); *m* 2, 16 Jan 2003, Sandra Anne, da of Raymond Osborne Goodrich, of Essex; *Career* chartered clinical psychologist; head of Psychology Dept St Andrew's Hosp Northampton 1974–84; dir: Psychiatric and Psychological Consultant Services Ltd 1981–, PPCS Properties Ltd 1988–; dir of psychological servs AMI Psychiatric Div 1984–87; dir: Centre for Occupational Res 1984–94, The Rehabilitation Group 1989–92; AFBPsS; *Recreations* riding, aviation; *Style*— Anthony P Bedford, Esq; ✉ Flat 1, 14 Devonshire Place, London W1G 6HX (e-mail info@ppsltd.co.uk)

BEDFORD, His Hon Judge Robin Steven; *Career* admitted slr 1988; district judge 2007 (dep district judge 2002), circuit judge (South Eastern Circuit) 2013–; *Style*— His Hon Judge Bedford; ✉ Hastings County Court, The Law Courts, Bohemia Road, Hastings, East Sussex TN34 1QX

BEDFORD, Dr (John Leslie) William; s of late Walter Bedford, and late Florence Winifred Bedford; *b* 9 December 1943; *Educ* Univ of Sheffield (BA, Moore Smith prize, Gibbons prize, PhD); *m* 13 Jan 1978, Fiona Mary, da of Rev Frederick William Hartland White, MBE, QHC; 1 da (Rachael Mary *b* 27 Jan 1987), 1 s (Thomas William *b* 3 Feb 1989); *Career* writer and poet; claims and new business broker with various Lloyds brokers 1963–71, founding ed Enigma 1966–67, postgrad tutor Univ of Sheffield 1977–79, ed Delta 1978–79, lectr Middlesex Poly 1980–81, tutor Open Univ 1981–82, contrib to Agenda (also occasional ed 1980, 1988 and 1989), Catholic Herald, Daily Telegraph, Encounter, Essays in Criticism, Harpers, The Independent, International Literary Quarterly, London Review of Books, London Magazine, The Nation (NY), Poetry Review, Punch, The Southern Review, Temenos Review, The Tribune, Warwick Review, The Manchester Review, Washington Times, Poetry Library website, The Tablet, The New Statesman and others 1978–, The John Clare Society Jl, The New Statesman, The Ted Hughes Society Jl; memb Editorial Bd Poetry Salzburg Review (also contrib); Arts Cncl Major Bursary 1978, runner-up Guardian Fiction Prize 1990, Soc of Authors Award 1993, Yorkshire and Humberside Arts Award 1993, Yorkshire Arts Award 2000, Royal Literary Fund Award 2007, Royal Literary Fund fell Oxford Brookes Univ, winner Roundel Poetry Prize 2014, winner London Magazine Int Poetry Prize 2014, shortlisted London Magazine Int Short Story Prize 2014; *Books* Annual Bibliography of English Language and Literature (contrib, 1974, 1975 and 1976); *Poetry* Whatever There is of Light (1975), The Hollow Landscapes (1977), Journeys (1988), Imaginary Republics (1993), The Redlit Boys (2000), The Fen Dancing (2014), The Bread Horse (2015); *Anthologies* incl: New Poetry (1975), Ten English Poets (1976), Go and open the door (1987), God gives nuts to those who have no teeth (1990), Wild and Wonderful (2002), Collecting Bottle Tops: Selected Poems 1960–2008, None of the Cadillacs Was Pink: Selected Short Stories and Non-Fiction 1984–2008, Something Happens, Sometimes Here (2015), Born Into Loss (2016); *Fiction* Happiland (1990), Golden Gallopers (1991), All Shook Up (1992), Nightworld (1992), Catwalking (1993), The Lost Mariner (1995), Jacob's Ladder (1996), The Freedom Tree (1997), The Joy Riders (1998), Esme's Owl (1999), The Stowaway (2001), Great Expectations: a retelling (2002), Whitemen (2003), Nicholas Nickleby: a dramatisation (2004), Theseus and the Minotaur: a retelling (2004), The Glow-worm Who Lost Her Glow (2004), The Coral Island: a retelling (2004); *Drama* The Man Who Invented Words (BBC Radio Sheffield 1979), The Piano Player (BBC Radio 4, 2003); *Recreations* music, walking, theatre; *Style*— Dr William Bedford; ✉ c/o Rogers Coleridge & White Ltd, 20 Powis Mews, London W11 1JN (☎ 020 7221 3717, website www.williambedford.co.uk)

BEDI, Prof Raman; s of Satya-Paul Bedi, and Raj, *née* Kaur; *b* 20 May 1953, India; *Educ* Headlands Sch, Univ of Bristol (BDS, DDS, DSc), Trinity Coll Bristol (DipTh), Univ of Manchester (MSc), AT Still Univ AZ (DHL); *m* 1986, Kathryn Jane, *née* Walter; 3 s; *Career* lectr in paediatric dentistry: Univ of Manchester 1979–82, Univ of Hong Kong 1983–86, Univ of Edinburgh 1988–91; sr lectr in paediatric dentistry Univ of Birmingham 1991–96, prof and head Dept of Transcultural Oral Health Eastman Dental Inst UCL 1996–2002, chief dental offr for England Dept of Health 2002–05, head Centre for Int Child Oral Health KCL 2005–; co-dir WHO Collaborating Centre for Disability, Culture and Oral Health 1998–2008, dir Global Child Dental Health Taskforce 2005–, chair Global Child Dental Fund 2008–; non-exec dir Dental Defence Agency 2002–05; chair Oral Health Working Gp World Fedn of Public Health Assoc 2012–; memb Bd HE Funding Cncl Wider Participation 2003–09, memb Bd HE Funding Cncl Leadership Fndn until 2006; int advsr RCPSGlas 2013; chair Dieco Ltd 2006–10; memb Gen Synod C of E 1995–2005; tstee Children's Soc 2006–09; chm Br Assoc of Physicians of Indian Origin (BAPIO) 2006–09, sec gen Global Assoc of Physicians of Indian Origin 2008–10; Asian Jewel Award 2004, Asian Guild Award for Community Serv 2004, US Public Health Servs Medal 2005, Annual Award for Outstanding Serv BAPIO 2005; Hon DDS Univ of Brisol 1992, Hon DSc Univ of Brisol 2003, Hon DHL AT Still Univ 2007; FDSRCSE 1982, FDSRCS 2002, FFPH 2003, FGDP 2004, FDSRCS Glas 2012; *Publications* Betel-quid and Tobacco Chewing among the Bangladeshi Community in the United Kingdom: Usage and Health Issues (ed with P Jones, 1995), Embracing Goodwill: Establishing Healthy Alliances with Black Organisations (with P Jones, 1996), Dentist, Patients and Ethnic Minorities Towards the New Millennium (jt ed, 1996), Best Practice in Primary Healthcare: Oral Healthcare Delivery in a Multi-Ethnic Society (with P A Lowe, 1997), The Root Cause: Oral Healthcare in Disadvantaged Communities (with J Sardo Infirri,

1999), Indian Health Professionals Worldwide – a common agenda (with E Davidson and J J Liu, 2012); contribs to scientific jls; *Recreations* chess, tennis, travelling; *Clubs* Athenaeum; *Style*— Prof Raman Bedi; ✉ 12 Manor Way, Potters Bar, Hertfordshire EN6 1EL; Centre for International Child Oral Health, Rooms 329–331, 26–29 Drury Lane, London WC2B 5RL (website www.gcdfund.org)

BEDINGFELD, Sir Henry Edgar (PASTON-); 10 Bt (E 1661), of Oxburgh, Norfolk; s of Sir Edmund Bedingfeld, 9 Bt (d 2011), and his 1 w, Joan Lynette, *née* Rees (d 1965); *b* 7 December 1943; *Educ* Ampleforth; *m* 7 Sept 1968, Mary Kathleen, da of Brig Robert Denis Ambrose, CIE, OBE, MC (d 1974); 2 da (Katherine Mary b 4 Oct 1969, Charlotte Alexandra b 6 May 1971), 2 s (Richard Edmund Ambrose (Father Benedict) b 8 Feb 1975, Thomas Henry b 6 Sept 1976); *Career* chartered surveyor 1968; Rouge Croix Pursuivant of Arms 1983–93, York Herald of Arms 1993–2010, Norroy and Ulster King of Arms 2010–14; sec Standing Cncl of the Baronetage 1984–88 (memb Exec Ctee 2012–); pres Norfolk Heraldry Soc 2006– (fndr chm 1975–80, vice-pres 1980–2006); vice-pres: Cambridge Univ Heraldic and Genealogical Soc; vice-pres Royal Soc of St George; rep of the Duke of Norfolk 1994–97, Cmmn d'Information et de Liaison des Associations Nobles d'Europe 1997–; delg of the Assoc of Armigerous Families of GB to the Cmmn; patron Breckland Soc 2003–, memb The Pilgrims, hon sec West India Ctee 2012–; Freeman City of London 1985, Liveryman Worshipful Co of Scriveners (Master 2012); memb Académie Internationale d'Héraldique; Knight of Sov Mil Order of Malta 1975 (genealogist Br Assoc 1995–2000); *Books* Oxburgh Hall – The First 500 years (1982), Heraldry (jtly, 1993); *Clubs* Beefsteak; *Style*— Sir Henry Bedingfeld, Bt; ✉ Oxburgh Hall, Norfolk PE33 9PS (☎ 01366 328269)

BEECH, Her Hon Judge Jacqueline Elaine; *Career* called to the Bar 1981; chm Transport Tbnl (now Upper Tbnl (Administrative Appeals Transport)) 2001, recorder 2002, legal memb London Bus Permits Appeals Tbnl 2002 (chm 2005); circuit judge: South Eastern Circuit 2007–12, Northern Circuit 2012–; *Clubs* Reform; *Style*— Her Hon Judge Beech; ✉ Preston Combined Court Centre, The Law Courts, Openshaw Place, Ring Way, Preston, Lancashire PR1 2LL

BEECH, Sydney John; s of Sydney Beech, of Stoke-on-Trent, Staffs, and Ruth, *née* Baskeyfield; *b* 6 February 1945; *Educ* Hanley HS, Univ of Sheffield (BA); *m* 6 Sept 1969, Jean Ann, da of Bertram Gibson, of Gillow Heath, Staffs; *Career* grad trainee Peat Marwick Mitchell & Co 1966–69, lectr in accounting taxation and quantitative techniques 1969–72; Lyon Griffiths: PA to ptnr 1972–74, ptnr 1974–86, sr ptnr 1986–2003, conslt 2003–; counsellor CBI NW Region CBI 2003–09; gp fin dir Fayrefield Gp Ltd; dir: Fayrefield Foods Ltd, Lacto Foods A/S, Promovita Ltd, Fayrefield Foodtec A/S, Dairy Solutions Ltd, Fayrefield Int BV, Nutriceut Ltd, Fayrefield Ingredients Ltd, Promovita Ingredients Ltd, Good Carb Food Co Ltd (also chm); CTA, FCA; *Recreations* golf, weightlifting, music; *Clubs* Reaseheath Golf; *Style*— S J Beech, Esq; ✉ 8 Woodland Avenue, Nantwich, Cheshire CW5 6JE; Fayrefield Foods Ltd, Englesea House, Barthomley Road, Crewe, Cheshire CW1 5UF (☎ 01270 589311, fax 01270 582269)

BEECHAM, Alan; *b* 12 June 1935; *Educ* Boston GS, Open Univ (BA); *m* (m dis); 2 s (Jonathan b 1967, Christopher b 1969); *Career* Nat Serv Royal Lincolnshire Regt Malaya 1955–57; journalist 1951–62; newspapers: Lincolnshire Standard Series, Southern Times, Southern Journal, Surrey Comet, News Chronicle, Daily Express; external news serv BBC 1961–62; radio news and current affrs BBC 1962–89: chief sub ed 1967–69, duty ed 1969–70, sr duty ed 1970–78, asst ed radio news 1978–87, news output ed 1987–89; for radio: general election, Euro election, referenda, budget, local and by-election news progs, Falklands War coverage, Royal Weddings 1964–89; created modern BBC internal news agency and news serv between London and local radio; writer and journalist; film historian and lectr 2000–; Jack Cardiff in Conversation with Alan Beecham CD released 2004; FRSA (Silver Medal, advanced English); *Recreations* media, theatre, cinema, writing, Italy and France; *Clubs* The Arts (elected distinguished memb 2008), Groucho, RA Academicians, RSA; *Style*— Alan Beecham, Esq; ✉ 7 Thalia Close, Greenwich, London SE10 9NA (☎ 020 8858 7887)

BEECHAM, Baron (Life Peer UK 2010), of Benwell and Newcastle upon Tyne in the County of Tyne and Wear; Sir Jeremy Hugh Beecham; kt (1994), DL (Tyne & Wear 1994); s of Laurence Beecham (d 1975), of Newcastle upon Tyne, and Florence, *née* Fishkin (d 1986); *b* 17 November 1944; *Educ* Royal GS Newcastle upon Tyne, UC Oxford (MA); *m* 7 July 1968, Brenda Elizabeth (d 2010), da of Dr Sidney Woolf; 1 da (Sara b 1972), 1 s (Richard b 1973); *Career* admitted slr 1968; ptnr Beecham Peacock 1968–2002 (conslt 2002–10); memb Lab Pty: NEC Local & Regnl Govt Sub-Ctee 1971–83, Jt Policy Ctee 1992–, Domestic and Int Policy Ctee 1992–98, NEC 1998–2010 (vice-chm 2004–05, chm 2005–06), dir N Devpt Co Ltd 1986–91; memb: Theatre Royal Tst 1985–, Cncl Neighbourhood Energy Assoc 1987–89, President's Ctee Business in the Community 1988–; Newcastle upon Tyne City Cncl: cncllr 1967–, chm Social Serv Ctee 1973–77, chm Policy and Resources Ctee 1977–94, leader 1977–94, chm Fin Ctee 1979–84, Devpt Ctee 1995–97; oppn spokesman on local govt and health House of Lords 2010–12, shadow justice min House of Lords 2012–; AMA: dep chm 1984–86, vice-chm 1986–91, chm 1991–; cmmr English Heritage 1983–87; Parly candidate (Lab) Tynemouth 1970; vice-chm Northern Regnl Cncls Assoc 1985–91, vice-chm Local Govt Assoc 2004–10 (chm 1995–2004), memb Cncl Common Purpose 1989–; memb NHS Modernisation Bd 2000–; memb Int Advsy Bd Harold Hartog Sch of Govt Tel Aviv Univ 2006–, memb Bd New Israel Fund 2007– (vice-chm 2009–); pres: Age Concern Newcastle 1995–, BURA 1996–2010, Newcastle Choral Soc 1997–; tstee Tyneside Cinema 1999–2010; Hon Freeman Newcastle upon Tyne 1995; hon fell Newcastle upon Tyne Poly 1989, Hon DCL Univ of Newcastle upon Tyne 1992; *Recreations* reading (esp novels and history), music; *Style*— The Lord Beecham, DL; ✉ 39 The Drive, Gosforth, Newcastle upon Tyne NE3 4AJ (☎ 01912 851 888)

BEECROFT, (Paul) Adrian Barlow; s of Thomas Ford Beecroft (d 1989), of E Yorks, and Jean Margaret, *née* Barlow; *b* 20 May 1947; *Educ* Hymers Coll Hull, The Queen's Coll Oxford (Hastings exhibitioner, MA), Harvard Business Sch (Harkness Fellow, Baker scholar, MBA); *m* 13 May 1972, Jacqueline Ann, *née* Watson; 2 da (Claire Damaris Watson Beecroft b 14 June 1977, Imogen May Watson Beecroft b 8 Feb 1991), 1 s (James Nicholas Watson Beecroft b 4 March 1980); *Career* account exec ICL 1968–73, project exec Ocean Transport and Trading 1973–74, vice-pres Boston Consulting Group 1976–84, sr managing ptnr Apax Partners Worldwide LLP 1984–2008, chm Dawn Capital 2010–; non-exec dir various cos incl: Alkane plc until 2003, Healthcare at Home Ltd until 2007, Brait SA until 2010; chm Br Venture Capital Assoc 1991–92; memb BVCA Hall of Fame 2009; tstee: MCC, Nat Science Museum Fndn; memb Chllr's Ct of Benefactors Univ of Oxford, sponsor Beecroft Inst for Particle Astrophysics and Cosmology Univ of Oxford, jt sponsor Oxford Acad; hon fell Queen's Coll Oxford; FCSI 1993, FInstP; *Recreations* cricket, physics, steam railways, classic cars, travel; *Clubs* MCC (tstee), CCC, Incogniti CC, Brooks's; *Style*— Adrian Beecroft, Esq; ✉ Apax Partners, 33 Jermyn Street, London SW1Y 6DN (☎ 020 7872 6330 e-mail adrian.beecroft@apax.com)

BEEDHAM, Prof Trevor; *b* 1942, Nottingham; *Educ* Univ of London (BDS, MB BS); *m* Anne; 2 s, 1 da; *Career* Barts and the London NHS Tst: conslt obstetrician and gynaecologist 1981–2009, clinical dir Women and Children's Directorate 2003–08, dep medical dir 2006–; assoc dean Barts and the London Sch of Med and Dentistry 2006– (prof 2008–); examiner: MB BS London, Aberdeen and Birmingham, DRCOG and MRCOG; RCOG: NE Thames regnl advsr 1991–94, careers offr 1994–98, chm CME Ctee 1998–2001; chair Ctee of Mgmnt Diploma in the Forensic and Clinical Aspects of Sexual Assault of the Soc of Apothecaries (DFCASA) 2008–12; memb United Examining Bd 1993–2003, Medical Forensics Specialist Gp 2013; GMC: Part 1 Panel PLAB 2000–08, visitor Medical Sch 2001–13, memb Appeals Panel 2005–; pres Friends of the Royal London Hosp 2015–; Freeman City of London 1984, Asst Worshipful Soc of Apothecaries 1996 (Sr Warden 2008, Master 2009–10, Dean 2012–); Hon DSc Univ of Buckingham 2011; FRSM, MIBiol 1979, FRCOG 1989 (MRCOG 1977); *Books and Publications* Treatment and Prognosis in Obstetrics and Gynaecology (1988), The Examination of Women (2001), Consultant Appraisal (2002), The Examination of Women (2007), Medical Education and the Apothecaries (2012); *Recreations* swimming; *Clubs* Athenaeum, City Livery; *Style*— Prof Trevor Beedham

BEER, Prof Dame Gillian Patricia Kempster; DBE (1998); *née* Thomas; da of Owen Thomas, and Ruth Winifred Bell, *née* Burley; *b* 27 January 1935; *Educ* Bruton Sch for Girls, St Anne's Coll Oxford (Charles Oldham scholar, MA, BLitt), Univ of Cambridge (LittD); *m* 7 July 1962, Prof John Bernard Beer, FBA, *qv*, s of Jack Beer; 3 s (Daniel b 1965, Rufus b 1968, Zachary b 1971); *Career* asst lectr Bedford Coll London 1959–62, pt/t lectr Univ of Liverpool 1962–64; Univ of Cambridge: fell Girton Coll 1965–94, asst lectr 1966–71, lectr then reader in literature and narrative 1971–89, Grace I prof of English 1989–94, pres Clare Hall 1994–2001, King Edward VII prof 1994–2002; vice-pres Br Acad 1994–96 (res reader 1987–89); chair Poetry Book Soc 1993–96, pres Br Assoc of Comparative Literature 2003–10, pres Br Soc of Literature and Science 2004–, pres Modern Humanities Research Assoc 2011; memb: Cwlth Scholarship Cmmn 1987–94, Bd of Tstees of British Museum 1992–2002; Andrew W Mellon sr fell Yale Center for Br Art 2009–11; Gold medallist MIT 2001; Hon LittD: Univ of Liverpool 1996, Anglia Poly Univ 1998, Univ of Leicester 1999, Univ of London 2001, Université de Paris Sorbonne 2001, Univ of Oxford 2005, Queen's Univ Belfast 2005, Harvard Univ 2012, Univ of St Andrews 2013; hon fell: Clare Hall Coll Cambridge, St Anne's Coll Oxford, Girton Coll Cambridge, Univ of Wales Cardiff; hon foreign memb American Acad of Arts and Scis 2002, int memb American Philosophical Soc 2010; FBA 1991, FRSL 2006; *Books* Meredith: A Change of Masks (1970), The Romance (1970), Darwin's Plots (1983, 3 edn 2009), George Eliot (1986), Arguing with the Past (1989), Forging the Missing Link (1992), Open Fields (1996), Virginia Woolf: the Common Ground (1996), Jabberwocky: Collected Poems of Lewis Carroll (2012), Alice in Space: the sideways Victorian world of Lewis Carroll (2016); *Recreations* music, travel, conversation; *Style*— Prof Dame Gillian Beer, DBE, FBA; ✉ Clare Hall, Herschel Road, Cambridge CB3 9AL (☎ 01223 332360, fax 01223 332333, e-mail gpb1000@cam.ac.uk)

BEER, Prof Janet Patricia; da of Derek Stanley John Beer, of Bath, Somerset, and Jean Patricia, *née* Bovey (d 1996); *b* 1 August 1956, Bath, Somerset; *Educ* City of Bath Girls' Sch, Univ of Reading (BA), Univ of Warwick (MA, PhD); *m* 1, 1978, Andrew Goodwyn; 1 s (Thomas Andrew b 1986), 1 da (Helena Patricia b 1988); m 2, 1996, David Roy Woodman; *Career* Univ of Warwick 1979–80 and 1981–83, Inner London Educn Authy 1983–89, Roehampton Univ 1989–97, Manchester Met Univ 1998–2007, vice-chllr Oxford Brookes Univ 2007–15, vice chllr Univ of Liverpool 2015–; chair: HE Public Info Steering Gp 2008–, Univ Alliance 2009–12; memb: Br Assoc for American Studies 1998–, Advsy Bd Higher Educn Policy Inst (HEPI) 2007–, Bd Nat Centre for Univs and Business (NCUB) 2013–; vice-pres England and NI UUK 2013–; memb Int Women's Forum, chair Equality Challenge Unit 2011–; tstee: UCAS 2012–, Br Cncl 2014–; visiting fell Nuffield Coll Oxford 2011–15; *Books* Edith Wharton: Traveller in the Land of Letters (1990, 2 edn 1995), Kate Chopin, Edith Wharton and Charlotte Perkins Gilman: Studies in Short Fiction (1997, 2 edn 2005), Edith Wharton (2002), Edith Wharton: Sex, Satire and the Older Woman (jtly, 2011); *Recreations* swimming, theatre, walking, literature; *Clubs* Athenaeum; *Style*— Prof Janet Beer; ✉ The Foundation Building, 765 Brownlow Hill, Liverpool L69 7ZX

BEER, Prof John Bernard; s of late John Bateman Beer, and late Eva, *née* Chilton; *b* 31 March 1926; *Educ* Watford GS, St John's Coll Cambridge (MA, PhD, LittD); *m* 7 July 1962, Prof Dame Gillian Beer, DBE, FBA, *qv*, *née* Thomas; 3 s (Daniel, Rufus, Zachary); *Career* RAF 1946–48; lectr Univ of Manchester 1958–64; Univ of Cambridge: res fell St John's Coll 1955–58, fell Peterhouse 1964–93 (emeritus fell 1993), univ lectr 1964–78, reader 1978–87, prof of English literature 1987–93 (emeritus prof 1993), Leverhulme emeritus fell 1995–96, Stanton lectureship in philosophy of religion 2006–07; pres Charles Lamb Soc 1989–2002; FBA 1994; *Books* Coleridge the Visionary (1959), The Achievement of E M Forster (1962), Coleridge's Poems (ed, 1963 and 1993), Milton Lost and Regained (1964), Blake's Humanism (1968, electronic version 2006), Blake's Visionary Universe (1969), Coleridge's Variety: Bicentenary Studies (ed, 1974), Coleridge's Poetic Intelligence (1977), Wordsworth and the Human Heart (1978), Wordsworth in Time (1979), E M Forster – A Human Exploration (ed with G K Das, 1979), A Passage to India – Essays in Interpretation (ed, 1985), Coleridge's Writings (general ed, 1990–), Aids to Reflection – Collected Coleridge (ed, 1993), Romantic Influences: Contemporary – Victorian – Modern (1993), Against Finality (1993), Questioning Romanticism (ed, 1995), Selected Poems of A H Clough (ed, 1998), Providence and Love: Studies in Wordsworth, Channing, Myers, George Eliot and Ruskin (1998), Coleridge's Writings on Religion and Psychology (ed, 2002), Romantic Consciousness: Blake to Mary Shelley (2003), Post-Romantic Consciousness: Dickens to Plath (2003), William Blake: A Literary Life (2005), Romanticism, Revolution and Language: the fate of the word from Samuel Johnson to George Eliot (2009), Coleridge's Play of Mind (2010), D H Lawrence: Nature, Narrative, Art, Identity (2014); *Recreations* walking in town and country, listening to music; *Style*— Prof John Beer, FBA; ✉ Peterhouse, Cambridge CB2 1RD (☎ 01223 356384, fax 01223 337578)

BEESE, Darcus; OBE (2014); s of Darcus Howe, and Barbara Beese; *b* 15 December 1969; *Educ* Henry Compton Boys' Sch Fulham; *m* 5 July 2003, Alison, *née* Lawrence; 2 s (Chad, Darcus b 10 Oct 2005), 1 da (Darcey b 7 Apr 1999); *Career* jr asst Promotions Dept Island Records 1988–91, jr A&R 4th & Broadway Big Life 1991–94, A&R 4th & Broadway 1994–2003; Island Records: sr A&R 2003–06, dir of A&R 2006–08, co-pres 2008–13, pres 2013–; *Recreations* music, running; *Style*— Darcus Beese, Esq, OBE; ✉ Island Records UK, Universal, 364–366 Kensington High Street, London W14 8NS, (Twitter @darcus)

BEESLEY, Mark; s of Nigel Patrick Beesley, of Steyning, West Sussex, and Mary Josephine; *b* 14 May 1961; *Educ* Univ of Essex (MA), Univ of Sussex (MSc); *m* 14 April 1990, Jan, *née* Collins; 1 da (Natasha b 14 Sept 1990), 1 s (Gregory b 1 Dec 1993); *Career* researcher Univ of Sussex 1984–87; opera singer; bass: studied under Elisabeth Abercrombie and Dennis Wicks, sung with various regnl opera cos incl City of Birmingham Touring, Opera 80 and Opera North 1987–89, princ bass Royal Opera 1989–96, freelance 1996–, princ bass ENO 1998–; *Roles* incl: Colline in La Bohème, Timur in Turandot, Sprecher in Die Zauberflöte, Ancient Hebrew in Samson and Delilah, Lodovico in Othello, Angelotti in Tosca, Sam in A Masked Ball; other roles incl: Fiesco in Simon Boccanegra with WNO, Pistol in Falstaff, Colline in La Bohème and Daland in The Flying Dutchman all with the ENO; int appearances incl: Midsummer Nights Dream at Aix-en-Provence, Peter Grimes at Palermo, First Nazarine in Salome at the Théâtre du Châtelet, Traviata at the Royal Opera Baden-Baden; *Recordings* incl: Pietro in Simon Boccanegra and Lodovico in Otello under Sir Georg Solti, First Nazarine in Salome under Sir Edward Downes, L'Incoronazione di Poppea under Richard Hickox, Pulcinella under Robert Craft, title role in Mendelssohn's Paulus; *Style*— Mark Beesley, Esq; ✉ c/o Athole Still

International, Foresters Hall, 25–27 Westow Street, London SE19 3RY (☎ 020 8771 5271, fax 020 8771 8172); website www.markbeesley.com

BEESLEY, Peter Frederick Barton; s of Ronald Fitzgerald Barton Beesley, and Mary Kurczyn, *née* Parker; *b* 30 April 1943; *Educ* King's Sch Worcester, Univ of Exeter (LLB), Coll of Law Guildford; *m* 1974, Elizabeth Jane, *née* Grahame; 1 s, 2 da; *Career* articled clerk and asst slr Windeatt & Windeatt 1965–68; Lee Bolton & Lee: asst slr 1968–69, ptnr 1969–2013, sr ptnr 2000–08, conslt 2013–; jt registrar: Dio of St Albans 1969–78, Dio of Ely 1978–2013, Dio of Hereford 1983–2013; registrar: Faculty Office of the Archbishop of Canterbury 1981–2016, Dio of Guildford 1981–2013, Woodard Corp 1987–2011; pres City of Westminster Law Soc 1991–92; sec: Ecclesiastical Law Assoc 1978–98 (vice-chm 1998–2000, chm 2000–02), Ecclesiastical Law Soc 1987–2010; legal advsr Nat Soc (C of E) for Promoting Religious Educn 1975–2013, memb Legal Advice Cmmn Gen Synod of C of E 1992–; tstee Arbory Tst 2000–14, Bishopsland Educational Tst 2002–; govr: Hampstead Parochial Sch 1983–2003 (chm of govrs 1986–95), Sarum Hall Sch 1997–; chm Glaziers' Tst 2000–03 (memb 1996–, vice-chm 1998–2000), chm London Stained Glass Repository 2009–12, vice-chm Glaziers Fndn 2012–; Master Worshipful Co Glaziers and Painters of Glass 2005 (Liveryman 1981, memb Ct of Assts 1995–); *Books* Encyclopaedia of Forms and Precedents (jt contrib vol 13 Ecclesiastical Law, 1987), Anglican Marriage in England and Wales, a Guide to the Law for Clergy (1992); *Clubs* Athenaeum, MCC; *Style—* Peter Beesley, Esq; ✉ Lee Bolton Monier-Williams, 1 The Sanctuary, Westminster, London SW1P 3JT (☎ 020 7222 5381, fax 020 7799 2781)

BEESON, Andrew Nigel Wendover; s of Capt Nigel Wendover Beeson (d 1944), and Anne Margaret, *née* Sutherland; *b* 30 March 1944; *Educ* Eton; *m* 1, 1971 (m dis 1983), Susan Roberta Caroline, da of Guy Standish Gerard (d 1981); 1 da (Susanna Caroline b 27 June 1973), 1 s (James Gerard b 26 March 1976) m 2, 17 July 1986, Carrie Joy, da of Norman Joseph Martin (decd); 1 da (Christabel Alexandra Robina Martin b 4 Sept 1989); *Career* stockbroker; ptnr Capel-Cure-Carden 1972–85; dir: ANZ Merchant Bank 1985–87, ANZ McCaughan 1987–89; chm Evolution Gp plc 2001–02, chm Beeson Gregory Ltd 2001 (chief exec 1989–2001); non-exec dir: IP Gp 2000–04, Schroders 2004– (chm 2012–), Queen's Club Hldgs Ltd 2007–11, Datawind Gp plc 2007–13, Westhouse Hldgs plc 2009–12; *Recreations* real tennis, shooting, collecting; *Clubs* White's, Pratt's, MCC, Swinley; *Style—* Andrew N W Beeson, Esq; ✉ 21 Warwick Square, London SW1V 2AB (☎ 020 7834 2903, e-mail andrew@thebeesons.com)

BEESON, Headley Thomas; s of Thomas Benjamin Beeson (d 1942), and Elizabeth, *née* Brezovits (d 2000); *b* 20 August 1942; *Educ* Clark's GS Surbiton; *m* 7 Sept 1968, Lesley Ann, da of Roland Conrad Wontner (d 1993); 1 s (Miles b 1973), 1 da (Caroline b 1975); *Career* Fenn & Crosthwaite stockbrokers 1962–67, investment mgmnt and mktg Barclays Bank Group 1967–81; dir: N M Schroder Unit Trust Managers Ltd 1981–88, Schroder Investment Management Ltd 1988–99, Brewin Dolphin Securities Ltd 1999–2001, founding dir Beeson Maisey Ltd 2006–; tstee Anglo-Austrian Soc 2009–; ASIP 1972; *Recreations* rowing, motor sports; *Style—* Headley Beeson, Esq; ✉ Courtlands, 14 The Ridings, Cobham, Surrey KT11 2PU; Beeson Maisey Limited, PO Box 577, Walton on Thames KT12 9DX (☎ 01932 242253, e-mail headleybeeson@beesonmaisey.co.uk, website www.beesonmaisey.co.uk)

BEESTON, Kevin Stanley; s of Denis Beeston (d 2002), and Patricia, *née* Hurle; *b* 18 September 1962, Ipswich, Suffolk; *Educ* Gorleston GS Great Yarmouth; *m* 12 April 1991, Jayne Anne, *née* Knowles; 2 s (Oliver b 9 April 1992, Lloyd b 25 Nov 1993), 1 da (Kathryn b 29 Sept 1995); *Career* Serco Gp plc: joined 1985, finance mangr Serco Services Ltd 1986–88, finance dir Serco Education Ltd 1988–89, finance dir then commercial dir Serco Space Ltd 1990–92, finance dir then md International Aeradio Ltd 1992–94, dir Serco Ltd 1992–94, chm and chief exec Serco International Ltd 1994–95, gp finance dir 1996–99, gp chief exec 1999–2002, gp exec chm 2002–07, non-exec chm 2007–; non-exec dir: IMI plc 2005–, Infinitas Learning 2007–; non-exec chm Domestic & General Gp Ltd; chm Public Services Strategy Bd and memb President's Ctee CBI; non-exec chm Partnerships in Care Ltd 2007–; dir Ipswich Town Football Club plc 2003–; FCMA 1990; *Recreations* soccer and rugby (spectating); *Style—* Kevin Beeston, Esq; ✉ Serco Group plc, Palm Court, 4 Heron Square, Richmond, Surrey TW9 1EW (☎ 020 8334 4331, fax 020 8334 4301, e-mail kevin.beeston@serco.com)

BEEVERS, Prof (David) Gareth; s of Rev Charles Edward Beevers, CBE (d 1973), sometime rector of The Lophams, Norfolk, and Mabel, *née* Charlton (d 1991); *b* 4 June 1942, Pontypridd, S Wales; *Educ* Dulwich Coll, The London Hosp Med Coll (MB BS, MD); *m* 2005, Surjit Kaur, *née* Powar; *Career* clinical scientist MRC Blood Pressure Unit Western Infirmary Glasgow 1972–77, prof of med Univ of Birmingham 1977–2007 (prof emeritus 2010), hon conslt physician City Hosp Birmingham 1977–2011; founding ed Jl of Human Hypertension, past pres Br Hypertension Soc; memb: BMA, Int Soc of Hypertension, Euro Soc of Hypertension, Int Soc for the Study of Hypertension in Pregnancy, American Soc for Hypertension; FRCP 1981 (MRCP); *Books* ABC of Hypertension (with G Y H Lip and E O'Brien, 1982, 6 edn 2014); *Recreations* collecting medical postage stamps and old toy soldiers; *Style—* Prof D G Beevers; ✉ Department of Medicine, City Hospital, Birmingham B18 7QH (☎ 0121 554 3801)

BEEVOR, Antony James; s of John Grosvenor Beevor (d 1986), and Carinthia Jane, *née* Waterfield; *b* 14 December 1946, London; *Educ* Winchester, RMA Sandhurst; *m* 1 Feb 1986, Artemis Cooper, *qv*, da of 2 Viscount Norwich, CVO, *qv*; 1 da (Eleanor Allegra Lucy), 1 s (Adam John Cosmo); *Career* historian; Lt 11 Hussars (PAO) 1967, served BAOR and UK 1967–70; freelance journalist 1970, various mktg and advtg positions 1971–75, first novel published 1975, occasional journalist and literary critic; Lees-Knowles lectr Univ of Cambridge 2002–03, visiting prof Birbeck Coll London 2003–, visiting prof Univ of Kent; participant Armed Forces into the 21st Century seminars KCL 1993–95, memb Exec Cncl French Theatre Season London 1996–97, tstee London Library 2002–04, chm Soc of Authors 2003–05 (memb Cncl 2002–), memb Waterloo 200 Ctee; judge Shiva Naipaul Meml Prize 2000, judge Br Acad Book Prize 2004–05, judge David Cohen Prize 2005, memb Steering Ctee Samuel Johnson Prize 2004–; Pritzker Lit Award for Lifetime Achievement in Military Writing 2014, Norton Medlicott Medal for Services to History 2016; Hon DLitt: Univ of Kent 2004, Univ of Bath 2010, UEA 2014, Univ of York 2015; FRSL 1999; Chevalier de l'Ordre des Arts et des Lettres (France) 1997, Order of the Cross of Terra Mariana (Estonia) 2008, Hon FKC 2016; *Publications* four novels; The Spanish Civil War (1982), Inside the British Army (1990), Crete: The Battle and the Resistance (1991, Runciman Prize), Paris After the Liberation (with Artemis Cooper, 1994), Stalingrad (1998, Samuel Johnson Prize, Wolfson History Prize, Hawthornden Prize), Berlin: The Downfall (2002, Longman-History Today Award), The Mystery of Olga Chekhova (2004), A Writer at War: Vasily Grossman with the Red Army 1941–1945 (2005), The Battle for Spain: The Spanish Civil War 1936–1939 (2006, La Vanguardia Prize), D-Day: The Battle for Normandy (2009, Prix Henry Malherbe, RUSI Duke of Westminster Medal for Military Literature), The Second World War (2012), Ardennes 1944 – Hitler's Last Gamble (2015, shortlisted Prix Medicis France); *Recreations* reading, gardening; *Clubs* Brooks's; *Style—* Antony Beevor, Esq; ✉ c/o Andrew Nurnberg Associates, 20–23 Greville Street, London EC1N 8SS (website antonybeevor.com)

BEEVOR, Antony Romer; MBE (2010); s of Miles Beevor (d 1994), of Welwyn, Herts, and Sybil, *née* Gilliat (d 1991); *b* 18 May 1940; *Educ* Winchester, New Coll Oxford; *m* 1970, Cecilia, da of John Hopton (d 1969); 1 s, 1 da; *Career* slr Ashurst Morris Crisp 1962–72, Hambros Bank Ltd 1972–98 (exec dir 1982, on secondment DG Panel on Takeovers and Mergers 1987–89), dir Hambros plc 1990–98, md SG Hambros (a div of Société Générale) 1998–2000, chm Fairbridge 1999–2009, dep chm Panel on Takeovers and Mergers 1999–2013; non-exec dir: Rugby plc 1993–2000, Gerrard Gp plc 1995–2000, Croda International plc 1996–2005 (chm 2002–05), Helical Bar plc 2000–12, Nestor Healthcare Gp plc 2000–03 (chm 2002–03); govr Francis Holland Schools Tst 2013–; *Style—* Antony Beevor, Esq, MBE

BEGBIE, David John; s of Donald Begbie, of Edinburgh, and Gwendoline Mary, *née* Potter; *b* 30 April 1955, Edinburgh; *Educ* Hereson Co Secdy Sch for Boys, Thanet Tech Coll, Winchester Sch of Art, Gloucestershire Coll of Art and Design (BA), Slade Sch of Fine Art (HDFA); *m* 1, 1980 (m dis 1994), Katherine Frances, da of Maj Michael Everitt; 1 da (Rosalind Ruth b 1987); m 2, 2007, Eva Angela, da of Richard Selker; 1 da from a previous relationship (Danya Long b 1987); *Career* sculptor; Gane Travel Scholarship 1979, Elizabeth Greenshields Award 1980; ARBS 1993; *Solo Exhibitions* Aleria Il Ponte Rome 1986, Forum Zurich 1986, Navy Pier Chicago 1986, Savacou Fine Art Toronto 1986, Simpsons of Piccadilly of London – Special Collaborative One Man Exhibition 1986, Brompton Gallery London 1984, 1985 and 1986, Salama-Caro Gallery London 1987, 1989, 1990 and 1991, ICAF Olympia London 1987, Crucifix (Winchester Cathedral) 1988, Henley 88 Festival 1988, Wates City Tower London 1990, Gallery Different and Differentiate London 1992–2012, Fire Station Gallery Sydney Australia 1994 (Powerhouse Museum Sydney), Emporio Armani Brompton Road London 1994, Special Collaboration (Joel Kessler Gallery Miami FL) 1994, Magidson Fine Art Aspen Colorado 1995, Posner Fine Art Santa Monica CA 1995, Artopia NY 1996, Hannah Peschar Gallery and Sculpture Garden Surrey 1996, The Festival of Erotica (Olympia London) 1997, Begbie Selected Retrospective early Work 1983–1991 and 1998 (London), Inauguration of Stirling Square St James London 1999, Sir James Stirlings Final Building 1999, Plus One Plus Two Galleries London 2002 and 2003, Online – Platform for Art (Gloucester Road London) 2002, Buschlen Mowatt Galleries Vancouver 2002, Galerie Bernd Duerr Munich 2002, Camino Real Gallery Boca Raton Florida 2003, Magidson Fine Art Aspen Colorado 2003, Int Art Consultants Spectrum London 2003, Number Nin Birmingham 2003, Festival Gallery Henley Festival 2003 and 2004, Hotel Linde Maria Wörth Austria 2004 and 2012, Herman Miller Int Art Consultants London 2004, Nuduu (Catto Gallery London and Etienne & Van Loon Netherlands) 2005, Number Nine Birmingham 2006, Il Ponte Contemporanea Rome 2007, Galerie Van Loon en Simmons Netherlands 2007, Form 2007 (Olympia London) 2007, Antebodies (Buschlen Mowatt Galleries Vancouver) 2007, Genii (Albemarle Gallery London) 2008, Grandslam 2008 Maquette (ALTEC Wimbledon and Albemarle Gallery London) 2008, Nudus (Number Nine Birmingham) 2009, Biennale (Galerie Van Loon en Simons Vught Netherlands) 2009 (incl Rhythmic Ties violin concert), Unud (Somerville Gallery Plymouth) 2009 and (AM Gallery Almeria Spain) 2010, Queens Elm Gallery Chelsea 2009 (incl Rhythmic Ties concert), Thin Air (Air Gallery London) 2010, Aria Sottile (Vecchiato Arte Padua) 2010, Iconii (Chapter House Canterbury Cathedral) 2010, Archetypes (Moorhouse London) 2010 and 2011, Skindeep (Ode to Art Singapore) 2010 and 2011 and (Van Loon en Simons Vught Netherlands) 2011, Genus (Australian Galleries Sydney and Melbourne) 2011, David Begbie (Albemarle Gallery London) 2011, Cork Street Open Exhibition, Plateaux Gallery, HUS Gallery, Gallery Tanner and Lawson 2012 and 2013, Albemarle Gallery, Marriott Burns Night Ball, Byard Art Cambridge, Sculpt Gallery Essex, Hannah Peschar Sculpture Garden Surrey, Artparks Int Guernsey, Number Nine the Gallery Birmingham and Edinburgh Art Fair, Somerville Gallery Plymouth, The Berkeley Gallery Berkhamstead, Opiom Gallery Cannes, Rarity Gallery Mykonos, Van Loon Galleries Netherlands, Bloom Cologne and Leipzig Galerie Irrgang, HUS Gallery Gstaad Switzerland, Hotel Linde Austria, nyb12 Hauset Belgium, Vecchiato Art Galleries Padua, Pietrasanta and Milan Italy, AM Gallery Almeria and Madrid Spain, Hooke Sculpture Gallery Sag Harbour NY, Global Art Miami, Toronto Int Art Fair and Vancouver Elliott-Louis Gallery, Affordable Art-fair Hong Kong and Singapore Ode to Art, Shanghai Art Fair Van Loon Galleries; *Museum Collections and Permanent Public Installations* Galleria Nazionali de Arte Moderna Rome, National Gallery Canberra, Museum Beelden aan Zee Netherlands, National Gallery of Canada, Citibank London, Southwark Bridge London, Figure & Fountain 1989, City Place House London, Back to Front Diptych and Venus 1991, Hyatt Carlton London, Peak Health Series 1993, Cannons City Gym London, Archetypes 1994, Royal Caribbean Cruise Lines 1996, Swimmingtrunсs 1997, Hyatt Hamburg, Composure 1998, Ladbroke Sporting Casino London, Chance 1999, Jam House Birmingham, Anangel and Manangel 1999, 60 Queen Victoria Street, Humantouch 1999, Dyptich, Faith Zone Millennium Dome London, Faith 1999, Millennium Sculpture St Mary the Less, Chilbolton, Winchester, Cruciform 1999, Fleet Place House, Holborn Viaduct, Fishnet 2000, Bedes World Museum Jarrow, Worldsapart 2000, Ten Covent Garden Connaught Rooms London, Heavenlybodies 2001, Lowry Hotel Manchester, Suspense 2001, Milan Bar Grants of Croydon, Anangel 2002, Hotel Linde Maria Wörth Austria, Nuda 2004, Radisson Edwardian Hotel London, Genus Series 2007, 62 Threadneedle Street, Totu 2006, Way of Therapy London, Otuu 2007, All England Lawn Tennis and Croquet Club Centre Court Wimbledon, Grandslam 2008, Coloplast Ltd Peterborough, Olso 2008, Hanover Grange Montego Bay Jamaica, Statu I and Statu II 2010, Nuwdstill 2008, Transcend and Transpose (Buddha-Bar Knightsbridge) 2012, An Eye for the Buoys – Fine Art Sails (London Excel) 2013, ANTU (Hotel Linde Mariawörth Austria) 2013, SOLA (Mews of Mayfair Knightsbridge) 2013; *Recreations* primat art, music, travel; *Clubs* Soho House; *Style—* David Begbie, ARBS; ✉ 289c Rotherhithe Street, Silverhouse, London SE16 5EY (☎ 020 7232 1023, e-mail info@davidbegbie.com, website www.davidbegbie.com)

BEGBIE, Hannah; da of Nigel Begbie, and Jenifer Begbie; *b* 22 December 1976, London; *Educ* City of London Sch for Girls, Univ of Cambridge (BA); *m* 27 Sept 2008, Tom Edge; *Career* with Outline Productions 1999–2000, agent representing comedians and writers for film and TV PFD 2003–07 (joined 2000), agent United Agents 2007–14; tstee Cystic Fibrosis Tst; memb BAFTA; *Publications* Catalogue Rasionee of Paul Rego's prints (compiler), articles for London Review of Breakfasts, Mumsnet and The Guardian; *Style—* Miss Hannah Begbie

BEGENT, Prof Richard Henry John; s of Harry Begent (d 2003), of Devon, and Doris, *née* Burton; *b* 14 February 1945, London; *Educ* Haileybury and ISC, St Bartholomew's Hosp Med Sch London (MB BS, MD); *m* Dr Nicola Begent; 3 c; *Career* emeritus prof of oncology UCL; author of pubns on med oncology, targeted cancer therapy and medical informatics; FRCP, FRCR, FMedSci; *Recreations* ancient woodland; *Style—* Prof Richard Begent; ✉ UCL Cancer Institute, Paul O'Gorman Building, 72 Huntley Street, London WC1E 6BT (☎ 020 7679 0759, e-mail r.begent@ucl.ac.uk)

BEGG, Dr Alan Robert; s of Robert William Begg (d 2001), and Sheena Margaret, *née* Boyd; *b* 27 June 1954; *Educ* Kelvinside Acad Glasgow, St John's Coll Cambridge (MA, PhD, pres Grad Common Room); *m* 5 August 1978, Sara Margaret, *née* Stewart; 2 s (Jonathan Peter b 8 May 1983, Henry Stewart b 15 Sept 1986); *Career* engineer; research scientist TI Research Labs 1979–81, project ldr BP Research Centre 1985–88 (sr research scientist 1981–85), head of mgmnt team BP Metal Composites 1988–93, md T&N Technology 1993–98, vice-pres of technol Technol Federal-Mogul 1998–2000, tech dir Morgan Crucible 2001–04, chief exec Automotive Acad 2004–07, gp sr vice-pres of technol devpt and quality SKF 2007–; chm Tstee Bd T&N Pensions 1999–2000, non-exec dir Bekaert NV 2008–; memb: Advsy Bd Materials Dept Univ of Nottingham 1994–98, IRC Steering Ctee Materials Dept Univ of Birmingham 1994–98, External Advsy Ctee Materials Dept

Univ of Cambridge 1996–, Advsy Ctee Materials Dept Univ of Oxford 1997–, External Advsy Ctee Materials Dept Univ of Leeds 2001–, Industrial Advsy Bd Materials Dept Imperial Coll London 2003–, Technology Strategy Bd DTI 2004–; DSAC: memb Materials Ctee 1989–94, memb Aerospace Technol Bd 1992–93, chm Technol Bd 2004–07; Technol Foresight Office of Sci and Technol: memb Materials Panel 1994–96 and 2000– (vice-chm 1997–98), chm EPSRC Foresight Challenge 1996, memb Steering Gp Foresight Vehicle 1996–98, chm Engine and Powertrain Foresight Vehicle 1997–98, fndr and chm Materials Media Advsy Gp 1997–98; Inst of Materials, Minerals and Mining: memb Editorial Panel 1988–93, memb MMC Ctee 1991–93, memb Cncl 1998–2002, chm Materials Strategy Cmmn 1999– (memb 1997–98); memb: Engrg Ctee Soc of Motor Manufacturers 1994–98, R&D Ctee European Automotive Component Prodrs Assoc (CLEPA) 1995–98, Cncl TWI 1995–98, Industrial Liaison Serv MIT 1999–2000 and 2002–, Materials Centre Advsy Bd Nat Physical Lab 2002–; CEng 1981, FIM 1992, FREng 2002; *Style*— Dr Alan Begg; ✉ Claremont House, Grovehurst Park, Stoneleigh Abbey, Kenilworth, Warwickshire CV8 2XR (☎ and fax 024 7684 9300, e-mail alanrbegg@hotmail.com)

BEGG, Dame Anne; DBE (2011); da of David Begg, and Margaret Catherine, *née* Ross; *b* 6 December 1955; *Educ* Brechin HS, Univ of Aberdeen (MA), Aberdeen Coll of Educn (Secdy Teaching Cert); *Career* teacher of English and history Webster's HS Kirriemuir 1978–88, princ teacher of English Arbroath Acad 1991–97 (asst princ teacher of English 1988–91), MP (Lab) Aberdeen S 1997–2015; memb Work and Pensions Select Ctee (chair 2010–), memb House of Commons Chm's Panel 2002–10, vice-chair Speaker's Conference on Political Participation 2008–10; memb: Educn Inst of Scotland, Gen Teaching Cncl for Scotland; patron: Scottish Motor Neurone Disease Assoc, Access to Employment and Trg; memb GMB; Disabled Scot of the Year 1988; *Recreations* reading, theatre, cinema, TV drama; *Style*— Dame Anne Begg, DBE; ✉ House of Commons, London SW1A 0AA (☎ 020 7219 2140, Twitter @annebegg)

BEGG, Prof David; *Educ* BA, DSc; *Career* chm Tube Lines 2006–; non-exec dir FirstGroup plc; *Style*— Prof David Begg; ✉ Tube Lines, 15 Westferry Circus, Canary Wharf, London E14 4HD

BEGG, Prof David Knox Houston; s of Robert William Begg, of Glasgow, and Sheena Margaret, *née* Boyd; *b* 25 June 1950; *Educ* Kelvinside Acad Glasgow, Univ of Cambridge, Univ of Oxford (MPhil), MIT (PhD); *m* 2002, Jennifer Holland; *Career* Lloyd's fell in econs Worcester Coll Oxford 1977–86, visiting prof Princeton Univ 1979, research dir Centre Econ Forecasting London Business Sch 1981–83, research fell Centre Econ Policy Research 1983–2012, founding managing ed of Economic Policy 1984–2000, advsr econ policy research Bank of England 1986, prof of economics Birkbeck Coll London 1987–2003 (actg vice-master 1997), princ Business Sch Imperial Coll London 2003–12; chair Begg Cmmn on the UK and the Euro 2003; non-exec dir: Trace Gp 2006–07, Imperial Innovations 2012–; memb: Academic Panel HM Treasy 1981–95, Research Awards Advsy Ctee Leverhulme Tst 1987–93; specialist advsr: Treasy and Civil Serv Ctee House of Commons 1983, House of Lords Euro Communities Ctee 1988–89, Commission of the Euro Cmmn 1989–90, Federal Govt of Czechoslovakia 1990–91, IMF 1995–97; FRSE 2004, FCGI 2006; *Books* The Rational Expectations Revolution in Macroeconomics (1982), Economics (with S Fischer and R Dornbusch, 1984, 11 edn 2014), Foundations of Economics (with S Fischer and R Dornbusch 2001, 5 edn 2013), Monitoring European Integration: The Impact of Eastern Europe (1990), Monitoring European Integration: The Making of Monetary Union (1991), Monitoring European Integration: The Economics of EC Enlargement (1992), Monitoring European Integration: Making Sense of Subsidiarity (1993), EMU: Getting the End Game Right (1997); *Recreations* gardening, sport, food; *Style*— Prof David Begg, FRSE, FCGI; ✉ Camberlot Place, Camberlot Road, Upper Dicker, Hailsham BN27 3RQ (e-mail d.begg@imperial.ac.uk)

BEGG, Prof Hugh MacKemmie; s of Hugh Alexander Begg (d 1978), of Glasgow, and Margaret Neil, *née* MacKemmie (d 1994); *b* 25 October 1941; *Educ* HS of Glasgow, Univ of St Andrews, Univ of British Columbia, Univ of Dundee; *m* 20 July 1968, Jane Elizabeth, da of Charles Wilfred Harrison (d 1995), of Salt Spring Island, BC; 2 da (Mary Margaret b 26 April 1970, Susan Morven b 28 Sept 1973); *Career* asst lectr Univ of St Andrews 1966–67, res fell Tayside Study 1967–69, lectr Univ of Dundee 1969–76, asst dir Tayside Regnl Cncl 1976–79, head Sch of Town and Regnl Planning Univ of Dundee 1981–93 (sr lectr 1979–81), visiting prof of economic devpt Univ of Abertay Dundee 2000–; conslt UN Devpt Project 1986–2003, conslt economist and chartered town planner in private practice 1993–; self employed reporter Scottish Exec Directorate of Planning and Environmental Appeals 1994–2014; external complaints adjudicator Scottish Enterprise 1997–2002, convener RTPI Scotland 1991, convenor Standards Cmmn for Scotland 2002–03; memb Local Govt Boundary Cmmn for Scotland 1999–2008; author of numerous pubns in professional and learned jls; FRTPI 1989; *Recreations* hill walking, puppy walking guide dogs, watching rugby; *Clubs* Monifieth and Dist Rotary, Bonnetmaker Craft of Dundee; *Style*— Prof Hugh M Begg; ✉ 4 Esplanade, Broughty Ferry, Dundee DD5 2EL (☎ and fax 01382 779642, e-mail hughbegg@blueyonder.co.uk)

BEGGS, Roy; MLA; s of John Robert (Roy) Beggs, *qv*, and Elizabeth Wilhemina Beggs; *b* 3 July 1962, Larne; *Educ* Larne GS, Queen's Univ Belfast (BEng); *m* 1989, Sandra Maureen, *née* Gillespie; 2 s, 1 da; *Career* former prodn mangr and technical mangr; MLA (UUP) E Antrim 1998–; NI Assembly: memb Employment and Learning Ctee 1999–2002, memb Ctee of the Centre 2000–03, vice-chair Public Accounts Ctee 2007–11 (memb 1999–2003 & 2015–), chm All Pty Children and Young People's Gp 2007–09, memb Fin and Personnel Ctee 2007–08 (vice-chm 2002–03), chm All Pty Gp for Community and Voluntary Sector 2009–, dep speaker NI Assembly 2011–, memb Assembly and Exec Review Ctee 2011–, memb Ctee for Health, Social Services and Public Safety 2012–14; memb Carrickfergus BC 2001–11; memb social delopment ctee 2014–; former vice-chair Carrickfergus Local Strategic Partnership and Community Safety Partnership, chair Carrickfergus District Policing Partnership Bd 2006; hon sec Ulster Young Unionist Cncl 1986–87, hon sec Larne Div 1991–98, hon sec E Antrim Ulster Unionist Assoc 1992–2002; offr 1 Raloo Boys' Bde; memb Ctee Raloo Presbyterian Church 1999–, govr Glynn Primary Sch; *Recreations* cycling, walking, assisting on family farm; *Clubs* Larne RFC; *Style*— Roy Beggs, MLA; ✉ East Antrim UUP Advice Centre, 3 St Brides Street, Carrickfergus, Co Antrim BT38 8AF (☎ 028 9336 2995, e-mail roy.beggs@mla.niassembly.gov.uk, website www.roybeggs.co.uk); Northern Ireland Assembly, Parliament Buildings, Stormont, Belfast BT4 3XX (☎ 028 9052 1546, fax 028 9052 1556)

BEGGS, Roy J; MBE (2015); *b* 20 February 1936, Belfast; *Educ* Ballyclare HS, Stranmillis Training Coll; *m* Wilma; 2 s (1 of whom Roy Beggs, MLA, *qv*), 2 da; *Career* teacher/vice-princ Larne HS 1957–82; MP (UUP) Antrim E 1983–2005; memb House of Commons Public Accounts Cmmn 1984–2005, memb NI Affrs Select Ctee 1997–2005; chief whip UUP 2000–05; memb Larne BC 1973–2015, Mayor of Larne 1978–83; elected to NI Assembly at Stormont 1982–86, chm Economic Devpt Ctee 1982–84; memb NE Educn and Library Bd 1973–2015 (chm 1985–87 and 2007–09), pres Assoc Educn and Library Bds NI 1984–85; memb NI Drainage Cncl 2006–15, chm Mid and E Antrim Local Action Gp; dir Larne Economic Devpt Co; farmer and landowner; vice-pres Gleno Valley Young Farmers' Club, vice-pres Mounthill Fair Soc; memb Ulster Farmers' Union; *Recreations* fishing, agriculture; *Style*— John Robert Beggs, MBE; ✉ 171 Carrickfergus Road, Larne, Co Antrim BT40 3JZ (☎ 07711 842550, e-mail jroybeggs@gmail.com)

BEGLEY, Kim Sean Robert; s of William Begley (d 1989), of Birkenhead, and Elizabeth, *née* Cooke; *b* 23 June 1952; *Educ* Rock Ferry HS Birkenhead, Wimbledon Sch of Art, Guildhall Sch of Music and Drama, National Opera Studio; *m* 20 Oct 1986, Elizabeth Mary, da of Charles Collier; 2 s (Edward Charles William b 29 Jan 1988, William George b 17 May 1991); *Career* tenor; princ tenor Royal Opera House Covent Garden 1983–89, has also performed with numerous other opera cos and all major Br orchs; former actor, with Liverpool Playhouse and Watermill Theatre Newbury (also West End and tours of England and Canada), with RSC in Stratford and London 1977–78; fndr Broomhill Tst; *Performances* over thirty roles with Royal Opera incl: Lysander in A Midsummer Night's Dream, Achilles in King Priam, Prince in Zemlinsky's Florentine Tragedy, Cassio in Otello, Froh in Das Rheingold, Walther von der Vogelweide in Tannhäuser, Tichon in Katya Kabanova; others incl: Don Ottavio in Don Giovanni (Glyndebourne Touring Opera 1986, Opera Northern Ireland 1988, ENO 1991), Boris in Katya Kabanova (Glyndebourne Touring Opera 1989, Glyndebourne Festival Opera 1990), Graf Elemer in Arabella (Glyndebourne Festival) 1989, High Priest in Idomeneo (Glyndebourne Festival) 1991, Pellegrin in Tippett's New Year (Glyndebourne Festival and Touring) 1991, Laca in Jenufa (Glyndebourne Festival and Touring) 1992, Tanzmeister in Ariadne auf Naxos (Frankfurt Opera), title role in Lohengrin (Frankfurt Opera), Alfred in Die Fledermaus (Frankfurt Opera), Nadir in The Pearl Fishers (Scottish Opera), Prince Shuisky in Boris Godunov (Opera North), Fritz in Der Ferne Klang (Opera North), Satavyan in Savitri (Rome Opera), Vaudemont in Yolanta (Opera North), Dr Caius in Falstaff (Salzburg Easter Festival) 1993, Narraboth in Salome (Salzburg Summer Festival) 1993, Grigori in Boris Godunov (under Edo de Wart, Geneva) 1993, Male Chorus in Rape of Lucretia (ENO) 1993, Golitsin in Khovanshchina (ENO) 1994, Albert Gregor in The Makropulos Case (WNO 1994, Glyndebourne 1995 and 1997, Chicago Lyric Opera 1995/96), Jimmy Mahoney in the Rise and Fall of the City of Mahagonny (Opéra de la Bastille Paris) 1995, Skuratov in From the House of the Dead (Opéra de Nice) 1995, Loge in Das Rheingold (under James Conlon, Cologne) 1995, Florestan in Leonore (Salzburg and BBC Proms under John Eliot Gardiner) 1996, Regista in Un re in Ascolta (Chicago Lyric Opera) 1996, Loge in Das Rheingold (La Scala under Riccardo Muti) 1996, Novagerio in Palastrina (Royal Opera Covent Garden) 1997, Tambour Major Wozzeck (La Scala under Giuseppi Sinopli) 1997, Max in Der Freischutz (Deutsches Staatsoper Berlin under Zubin Mehta) 1997; concert engagements incl: Don Basilio in The Marriage of Figaro (with LPO under Sir Georg Solti in London, Paris, Frankfurt and Cologne), Alfred in Die Fledermaus (with RPO under Andre Previn), Dream of Gerontius (with the Philharmonia under Vernon Handley), Tippett's New Year (with LPO), Beethoven Ninth Symphony and Haydn Nelson Mass (with BBC Symphony Orch), Verdi Requiem (with Bournemouth Symphony Orch), Beethoven Ninth (with Cleveland Symphony Orch under Dohnányi), Janácek Glagolitic Mass (with London Philharmonic), Tambour Major in Wozzeck (with Cleveland Orch under Dohnányi, Carnegie Hall NY) 1995, Mahler 8th Symphony (with Cleveland Orch under Dohnányi) 1995, Mahler 8th Symphony (with LPO under Andrew Davis at BBC Proms) 1995, Britten War Requiem (Zürich Opera) 1995, Mahler 8th Symphony (with Halle Orchestra under Kent Nagano) 1996, Bruckner's Te Deum (Salzburg Festival under Claudio Abbado) 1997, title role in Stravinsky's Oedipus Rex (Cleveland Orchestra under Christoph von Dohnányi) 1997, Captain Vere in Billy Budd (Bastille) 1998, Max in Der Freischültz (La Scala) 1998, Jimmy Mahoney in Mahagonny (Chicago) 1998, Parsifal (ENO) 1998; *Recordings* audio incl: Turandot, Der Rosenkavalier, Falstaff (under Solti, Decca), Das Rheingold (under Dohnányi, Decca), Salome (under Dohnányi, Decca), Florestan in Leonore (under John Eliot Gardiner, Deutsche Grammophon) 1996; video incl: Norma (with Dame Joan Sutherland and Richard Bonynge), La Traviata (with Carlo Rizzi); *Style*— Kim Begley, Esq

BEHAN, David; CBE (2003); *b* Blackburn, Lancs; *Educ* Univ of Bradford; *m* ; 2 s; *Career* social worker then team mangr Children's Servs Social Servs Dept Wakefield Met Dist Cncl, various posts (incl area mangr N Bristol) Avon CC 1984–89; Cleveland CC (subsequently Middlesbrough Cncl): sr asst dir, dep dir, dir of social servs 1989–96; dir of social servs London Borough of Greenwich 1996–2003, chief inspector Cmmn for Social Care Inspection 2003–06, DG of social care, local govt and care ptnrships Dept of Health 2006–; memb: Bd Greenwich PCT 1996–2003, Professional Exec Ctee 1996–2003; pres Assoc of Dirs and Social Servs 2003; Hon LLD Univ of Greenwich 2004; *Style*— David Behan, Esq, CBE; ✉ Department of Health, 79 Whitehall, London SW1A 2NS

BEHAN, Prof Peter Oliver; s of Patrick Behan (d 1985), and Mary Ellen, *née* Ryan; *b* 8 July 1935; *Educ* Christian Brothers Schs Athy, Univ of Leeds (MB ChB, MD), Nat Univ of Ireland (DSc); *m* 23 Aug 1968, Dr Wilhelmina Behan, da of Dr William Hughes (d 1981); 1 da (Charlotte b 1969), 2 s (Miles b 1973, Edmund b 1977); *Career* demonstrator in pathology Univ of Cambridge, res fell in psychiatry and special res fell neurology Harvard Univ, special res fell in neurology Univ of Oxford, asst prof of neurology Univ of Boston; Univ of Glasgow: lectr, sr lectr, reader, prof of neurology; med patron Scot Motor Neurone Disease Assoc; visiting prof Sch of Life Sciences Glasgow Caledonian Univ 2008–; memb: Neuroimmunology Res Gp World Fedn of Neurology, Rodin Acad for Dyslexia Res; pres Ramsay Soc, patron ME Assoc; Pattison Medal for Research, Dutch Int Award for Study of Fatigue States 1994; FRCP, FRCPG, FRCPI, FACP, FLS, fell American Neurological Assoc, hon fell Norwegian Neurological Assoc; *Books* Clinical Neuroimmunology (with S Curie, 1978), Clinical Neuroimmunology (with W Behan and J Aarli, 1987); *Recreations* salmon fishing, gardening; *Clubs* Savile, Flyfishers'; *Style*— Prof Peter Behan; ✉ 17 South Erskine Park, Bearsden, Glasgow G61 4NA (☎ 0141 942 0018, website www.researchgate.net/profile/peter_behan, Twitter @peterobehan); Division of Clinical Neuroscience, Faculty of Medicine, University of Glasgow, Southern General Hospital, Glasgow G51 4TF (e-mail peter.behan@glasgow.ac.uk); School of Life Sciences, Glasgow Caledonian University, Govan Mbeki Health Building, Cowcaddens Road, Glasgow G4 0BA

BEHRENS, Robert Fredrick; CBE (2016); s of L A Behrens (d 1992), and Joan, *née* Lazarus (d 2016); *b* 19 January 1952, Manchester; *Educ* Univ of Nottingham (BA), Univ of Exeter (MA); *m* 21 July 1985, Deborah, *née* Sandler; 2 s (Benjamin b 14 June 1991, Samuel b 22 Dec 1994); *Career* dir Southern Africa Devpt Gp Civil Service Coll 1992–97, dir Int Consultancy Gp Civil Service Coll Cabinet Office 1997–2001, dir Int Public Service Gp Cabinet Office 2001–03, sec Ctee on Standards in Public Life 2003–06, complaints cmmr Bar Standards Bd 2006–08, chief exec and ind adjudicator Office of the Ind Adjudicator for HE (OIA) 2008–16; memb Bd and chair Qualifications Ctee Bar Standards Bd, memb European Network of Ombudsmen in HE (ENOHE) 2008–; *Recreations* 19th and 20th Century history and art; *Clubs* RSA, MCFC; *Style*— Robert Behrens, Esq, CBE; ✉ Twitter @RobBehrens1884

BEITH, Baron (Life Peer UK 2015) of Berwick upon Tweed in the County of Northumberland; Rt Hon Sir Alan James Beith; kt (2008), PC (1992); o s of James Beith (d 1962), of Poynton, Cheshire, and Joan Beith (d 1998); *b* 20 April 1943; *Educ* King's Sch Macclesfield, Balliol Coll and Nuffield Coll Oxford; *m* 1, 1965, Barbara Jean Ward (d 1998); 1 s (d 2000), 1 da; m 2, 2001, Baroness Maddock (Life Peer), *qv*; *Career* lectr Dept of Politics Univ of Newcastle upon Tyne 1966–73; MP (Lib, now Lib Dem) Berwick-upon-Tweed 1973–2015 (also contested 1970), Lib chief whip 1976–85, Lib dep ldr and foreign affrs spokesman 1985–87, Treasy spokesman Lib Democrats 1988–94, home affairs spokesman Lib Democrats 1994–97, Lib Dem spokesman on home and legal affairs 1997–2001, dep ldr of Liberal Democrats 1992–2003, memb Intelligence and Security Ctee 1994–2008, chm Justice Ctee (formerly Lord Chllr's Dept Select Ctee then Constitutional Affrs Ctee) 2003–15, chair Liaison Ctee 2010–15; hon bencher Middle Temple 2014; memb House of Commons Cmmn 1979–97; chm Historic Chapels Tst 2002–

14 (tstee 1993–2014); Hon DCL Univ of Newcastle upon Tyne 1998, Hon DCL Northumbria Univ 2010, Hon Dr of Humane Letters Earlham Coll Indiana 2014; *Recreations* walking, music; *Clubs* Nat Liberal, Athenaeum, Northern Counties (Newcastle-upon-Tyne); *Style*— The Rt Hon the Lord Beith; ✉ 28 Castle Terrace, Berwick-upon-Tweed, Northumberland TD15 1NZ

BEITH, Ian Mark; s of Sir John Greville Stanley Beith, KCMG (d 2000), of Winchester, Hants, and Diana, *née* Gilmour (d 1987); *b* 2 December 1950; *Educ* Univ of Cambridge (MA), Harvard Univ; *m* 18 Oct 1975, Mary Jane, da of late Harry Selwyn Spicer Few; 2 s (Mark b 9 Jan 1983, Nick b 29 Jan 1985); *Career* Citibank: Energy Dept UK Corp Bank 1972–75, Metals and Mining Dept NY 1975–80, team head Oil and Mining Dept London 1980–82, dir Euro Training Centre London 1982–84, head N Euro Shipping Gp 1984–86, head of UK corp banking 1986–88; Charterhouse Bank Ltd: dir of mktg debt related servs 1988, md and head of debt servs 1988–99; head Fin Dept Berwin Leighton until 1999; exec chm INSYS Ltd 2001–05, conslt Wyvern Partners 2009–11; *Recreations* shooting, films, theatre; *Style*— Ian Beith, Esq; ✉ 26 Sutherland Street, London SW1V 4LA (☎ 020 7834 4111)

BELBEN, Michael (Mike); s of John Belben (d 1994), and Rosemary Belben (d 2006); *b* 20 May 1952, Swindon, Wilts; *Educ* Marlborough GS, Coll for the Distributive Trades (HND); *m* (m dis); 1 s (Jeremy b 20 Nov 1994); *Career* restaurateur; early career as grad trainee rising to asst account exec Young & Rubicam, subsequently gen mangr Peppermint Park and mangr Smiths of Covent Garden and Melange, co-owner The Eagle pub London 1991–; ptnr: Anchor and Hope Southwark, Great Queen St Holborn; Pub Chef Special Achievement Award Morning Advertiser 2007, Restaurateur of the Year London Restaurant Awards 2008; *Style*— Mike Belben, Esq; ✉ The Eagle, 159 Farringdon Road, Farringdon, London EC1R 3AL

BELBEN, Rosalind Loveday; da of Capt G D Belben, DSO, DSC, AM, RN (d 1944), and Joyce Belben (d 1972); *b* 1 February 1941, Dorset; *Educ* Stover, Henley Lodge; *Career* author; DAAD Berliner Künstlerprogramm fell 1987, FRSL 1999; *Books* The Limit (1974), Dreaming of Dead People (1979), Is Beauty Good (1989), Choosing Spectacles (1995), Hound Music (2001), Our Horses in Egypt (2007, James Tait Black Meml Prize for Fiction 2007); *Style*— Miss Rosalind Belben; ✉ c/o Anthony Sheil, Aitken Alexander Associates Ltd, 18–21 Cavaye Place, London SW10 9PT (☎ 020 7373 8672, e-mail reception@aitkenalexander.co.uk)

BELCHAMBERS, Anthony Murray; s of Lyonel Eustace Belchambers (d 1981), of Ashburton, Devon, and Dorothy Joan, *née* Wylie; *b* 14 April 1947; *Educ* Christ Coll Brecon; *m* Joanna Anthonia Vestbirk; *Career* called to the Bar Inner Temple; in practice Western Circuit 1972–75; lawyer: DTI 1975–82, Dir of Public Prosecutions 1982–84, Treasy 1984–86; co sec and gen counsel Assoc of Futures Brokers and Dealers 1986–89, gen counsel Jt Exchanges Ctee 1989–93, chief exec The Futures and Options Assoc 1993–13; chm: Saxo Capital Markets, Jt Trade Assoc Gp; dep chm Cross-Border Regulation Forum; memb various City ctees concerning financial services; chm London Capital Club; *Publications* incl: Soviet Financial Services: The Need for Technical Assistance and Training (1991), Poems from the Square Mile (1992), The British Derivatives Markets Handbook (1993); *Recreations* tennis, riding, bridge; *Clubs* HAC, London Capital; *Style*— Anthony Belchambers, Esq; ✉ The Futures and Options Association, 2nd Floor, 36–38 Botolph Lane, London EC3R 8DE

BELCHER, Antonia Denise (Toni); da of Dennis Frederick Belcher, of Chertsey, Surrey, and Kathleen Patricia, *née* Backhouse; *b* 26 February 1957; *Educ* Salesian Coll Chertsey, Poly of the South Bank (BSc); *m* 16 May 1981, Andrea Margaret, da of Victor Ernest Whatley; 2 s (Nicholas Anthony b 8 July 1983, Shaun Anthony b 21 Feb 1987), 1 da (Justine Emma b 22 Oct 1991); *Career* Mellersh & Harding: trainee surveyor 1975, salaried ptnr 1985, equity ptnr 1990, currently fndg memb Mellersh & Harding Building Consultancy LLP; FRICS 1981, DipArb 1994, FCIArb, MAPM, FBEng; *Recreations* skiing, badminton, gardening, fishing, restoration of French house, travel; *Clubs* Porsche; *Style*— Ms Toni Belcher; ✉ MHBC (Mellersh & Harding Building Consultancy LLP), 4 St Paul's Churchyard, London EC4M 8AY (☎ 020 7029 3888, fax 020 7029 3889, mobile 07780 740 501, e-mail abelcher@thisismhbc.com)

BELCHER, Her Hon Judge Penelope Mary (Penny); da of Arthur John Lucas, of Gloucester, and Margaret Elizabeth, *née* Attwood; *b* 27 August 1957, Beaconsfield, Bucks; *Educ* King Edward VI HS for Girls Birmingham, St Hugh's Coll Oxford (MA); *m* 13 April 1985, Simon James Belcher; 1 s (Timothy James b 24 Dec 1987), 1 da (Fiona Jane b 18 July 1991); *Career* called to the Bar Middle Temple 1980, admitted State Bar of California 1988, admitted slr 1993; practising barr and memb of chambers 4 Paper Buildings 1980–90, attorney Irvine & Cooper Palo Alto 1988–89; slr: Eversheds 1993–99 (ptnr 1995), Hammonds 2000–06 (asst dir for advocacy); recorder 2003–06, circuit judge 2006–; memb Law Soc 1993; *Recreations* sailing, racket sports, flute playing, classical music, theatre, reading; *Style*— Her Hon Judge Belcher; ✉ Leeds Combined Court Centre, The Court House, 1 Oxford Row, Leeds LS1 3BG (☎ 0113 306 2800, e-mail hhjudgepenelope.belcher@judiciary.gsi.gov.uk)

BELL, Alan Scott; *b* 8 May 1942, Sunderland; *Educ* Ashville Coll, Selwyn Coll Cambridge (MA), Univ of Oxford (MA); *m* 1966, Olivia, da of late Prof J E Butt, FBA; 1 s, 1 da; *Career* asst registrar Royal Cmmn on Historical Manuscripts 1963–66, asst keeper Nat Library of Scotland 1966–81, visiting fell All Souls Coll Oxford 1980, librarian Rhodes House Library Univ of Oxford 1981–93, librarian The London Library 1993–2001; advsy ed Oxford DNB 1993–, memb Advsy Bd Oxford Edn Writings of Evelyn Waugh 2011–; chm Marc Fitch Fund 2001–11; FSA 1995; *Books* Sydney Smith (1980), Leslie Stephen's Mausoleum Book (ed, 1976), Lord Cockburn (ed, 1979), Henry Cockburn: Selected Letters (2005), John Kay's Original Portraits (ed, 2007), Oxford Companion to the Book (contrib, 2010), History of Oxford University Press Vol 3 (2013); *Clubs* Brooks's; *Style*— Alan Bell, Esq, FSA; ✉ 38 Danube Street, Edinburgh EH4 1NT

BELL, Anne Margaret; *see:* Jobson, Anne Margaret

BELL, Dr Catherine; CB (2003); da of late Frank Douglas Howe, and Phyllis, née Walsh; *Educ* Balshaw's GS, Girton Coll Cambridge (BA), Univ of Kent (PhD); *m* 1993, Richard John Weber; 1 s; *Career* DTI: joined 1975, princ 1981–84, asst sec 1984–89, under sec 1989–91, head Competition Policy Div 1991–93, maternity leave 1993–94, on secondment to Cabinet Office as resident chm Civil Serv Selection Bd 1994–95, head DTI Central Policy Unit 1995–97, head inter-departmental review of utilities regulation 1997–99, DG Competition and Markets Gp 1999–2002, DG Services Gp 2002–05, actg permanent sec 2005; non-exec memb Bd Dept of Health 2011–16; non-exec dir: Swiss Re GB plc 1999–2008, CAA 2006–14, Ensus Ltd 2006–11, United Utilities plc 2007–, Nat Grid Gas plc 2014–, Nat Grid Electricity Transmission plc 2014–; govr London Sch of Economics 2008–, tstee Charity for Civil Servants 2010–; *Style*— Dr Catherine Bell, CB

BELL, Christopher; s of Shirley Aurelia, *née* Copping; *b* 18 November 1957; *Educ* Mexborough GS, Wolverhampton Poly (BA); *m*; 2 da; *Career* commercial trainee 1980–82, mktg mangr Ind Coope & Allsopp 1982–87, mktg, planning and co-ordination mangr Ind Coope Burton Brewery 1987–1988, mktg dir Allied Beer Brands 1988–89, mktg and buying dir Victoria Wine Co 1989–91; Hilton Gp plc: md Ladbroke Racing 1995–2000 (mktg dir 1991–93, dep md 1993–95), chief exec Ladbrokes Worldwide 2000–, exec dir Hilton Gp plc 2000–; non-exec dir Game Gp plc 2003–, dir Satellite Information Services; chm Betting Office Licensees Assoc 1998–, vice-chm Assoc of British Bookmakers; memb: Bookmakers Ctee, Horserace Betting Levy Bd, Horserace and Betting Ctee, Animal Health Tst, Princess Royal Industry Ctee; memb Fundraising Bd NSPCC; *Recreations* travel, wine, food, flying, reading; *Clubs* Mark's; *Style*— Christopher Bell, Esq; ✉ Ladbroke Worldwide, Imperial House, Imperial Drive, Rayners Lane, Harrow, Middlesex HA2 7JW (☎ 020 8868 8899, fax 020 8866 1980)

BELL, Sir David Charles Maurice; kt (2004); s of R M Bell (d 1992), and M F Bell (d 1973); *b* 30 September 1946; *Educ* Worth Sch, Trinity Hall Cambridge (BA), Univ of Pennsylvania (MA); *m* 30 Dec 1972, Primrose Frances, da of E S Moran (d 1973); 1 da (Emma Theodora b 1975), 2 s (Charles Alexander b 1977, Thomas George b 1981); *Career* Oxford Mail and Times 1970–72; Financial Times: news ed, int ed 1978–80, asst ed features 1980–85, managing ed 1985–89, advertisement and mktg dir 1989–93, chief exec 1993–96, chm 1996–2009; dir: Pearson plc (parent co of FT) 1996–2009, Economist 1996–, Vitec plc 1997–2007, Zen Research plc 2000–02; chm: Islington SDP 1981–86, Int Youth Fndn 1998–2007 (memb Bd 1996–2011), Crisis 2002–12, Sadlers Wells 2005–, IWPR 2005–, London Transport Museum 2007–, Cncl Univ of Roehampton 2008–, Common Purpose Charitable Tst 2010–11, Millennium Bridge Tst; tstee Common Purpose 1994–, chm Common Purpose Int 1996–2011; Civil Serv cmmr 2001–07; assessor Leveson Inquiry into Press 2011–; dir Ambache Chamber Orch 1987–2007, chm Bath Mozartfest 2010–, memb Finance Ctee Cambridge Univ Press 2010–, tstee Esmee Fairbairn Fndn 2011–; *Recreations* theatre, cycling, family, Victorian social history, Italy, Arsenal FC; *Clubs* Garrick; *Style*— Sir David Bell; ✉ 35 Belitha Villas, London N1 1PE (☎ 020 7609 4000)

BELL, Dr David John; s of John Bell (d 1991), and Eileen, *née* McMaster (d 2013); *b* 13 July 1961, Downpatrick, Co Down; *Educ* Methodist Coll Belfast, Univ of Edinburgh (MA, PhD (also Deutsche Sporthochschule), Horslie Hill-Scott Bursary, C S Edgar Prize, 2 DAAD scholarships, Full Blue Table Tennis); *Partner* Joanna Davies; 2 s (Rafe John b 17 April 1995, Gabriel John Campo Davies b 5 April 2006); *Career* product mangr ICI Colours and Fine Chemicals 1987–89, account mangr BJL Advtng 1989–92, md Cheetham Bell 1992–2001, chief exec Cheetham Bell 2001–; jt prop Black White Denim; patron and memb Cncl Tate Liverpool; silver medal Salford World Cup Triathlon Sprint Relay 2005 and 2007; MIPA; *Recreations* cycling; *Style*— Dr David Bell; ✉ 9 South Road, Bowdon, Cheshire WA14 2JZ (☎ 0161 941 4208); Cheetham Bell, Astley House, Commercial Wharf, 6 Commercial Street, Manchester M15 4PZ (☎ 0161 832 8884, e-mail david.bell@jwt.com)

BELL, Sir David Robert; KCB (2011); *Educ* Univ of Glasgow (MEd), Jordanhill Coll of Educn (PGCE); *Career* civil servant; former primary sch teacher (incl dep head then headteacher Kingston Primary Sch Essex), asst dir of educn Newcastle City Cncl 1990–95, dir of educn and libraries Newcastle City Cncl 1995–2000, chief exec Beds CC 2000–02, HM chief inspector of schs Office for Standards in Educn 2002–06; perm sec: Dept for Educn and Skills 2006–07, Dept for Children, Schs and Families 2007–10, Dept for Educn 2010–12; vice-chllr Univ of Reading 2012–; *Style*— Sir David Bell, KCB; ✉ University of Reading, Whiteknights, PO Box 217, Reading, Berkshire RG6 6AH

BELL, Prof (Geoffrey) Duncan; s of Sqdn Ldr Robert Charles Bell (d 2002), of Gosforth, Newcastle upon Tyne, and Phyllis Pearl Hunter Codling (d 1992); *b* 19 June 1945; *Educ* Royal GS Newcastle upon Tyne, St Bartholomew's Hosp Med Coll, Univ of London (MB BS, LRCP, MSc, MD)); *m* 21 June 1969, Joanna Victoria (d 2016), da of Capt Joseph Henry Patterson (d 1981); 2 s (Jonathan b 8 March 1970 d 1994, Robert b 13 Oct 1977), 2 da (Anne Hélène b 30 Oct 1973 d 1975, Karen b 7 May 1980); *Career* lectr in med St Bartholomew's Hosp Med Sch 1973–76, sr lectr in therapeutics Univ of Nottingham 1976–83, conslt gastroenterologist Ipswich Hosp 1983–97, conslt gastroenterologist and prof of gastroenterology Sunderland Royal Hosp 1997–2002, hon conslt gastroenterologist Norfolk and Norwich Univ Hosp 2002–07, dir Regnl Endoscopy Trg Centre Norwich 2004–09; chm and medical dir Disect Systems Ltd 2007–11; dir Fisher's Ideas Ltd 2010–; hon prof Sch of Computing Sciences UEA 2002–; visiting prof Sch of Computing and Technol Sunderland Univ 2002–08, visiting prof Sch of Electrical, Electronic and Computer Engrg Univ of Newcastle upon Tyne 2003–09, visiting prof of medicine Sch of Science, Technol and Health Univ Campus Suffolk 2011–; developer (with BT) of virtual reality remote endoscopy; memb Assoc of Physicians 1979, chm working party on endoscopic safety and monitoring Br Soc of Gastroenterology, fndr memb Suffolk Branch Br Digestive Fndn, Hunterian prof RCS 1990; Dr (hc) Univ Campus Sussex 2014; MRCS, FRCP 1985 (MRCP), FRCPEd 1998; *Recreations* canoeing, microscopy, 3-D printing; *Style*— Prof Duncan Bell; ✉ Fishers Cottage, Falkenham, Ipswich IP10 0QY (☎ 01394 448251)

BELL, (Edward) Eddie; s of Edward and Jean Bell; *b* 2 August 1949; *Educ* Airdrie HS, Cert Business Studies; *m* 1969, Junette, da of Malcolm Bannatyne; 2 da (Catherine b 22 Oct 1969, Joanne b 24 May 1973), 1 s (Edward b 19 June 1984); *Career* Hodder & Stoughton 1970–85 (latterly dep md), md Collins Gen Div 1985–89 (dep md Fontana William Collins 1985), fndr Harper Paperbacks USA 1989–90; HarperCollins UK: dep chief exec and publisher 1990–91, chief exec and publisher 1991–92, exec chm and publisher 1992–2000, chm Bell Lomax Moreton 2001–11; dir beCogent 2001–10; non-exec dir: Haynes Publishing Gp plc 2000–16 (chm 2016), Mgmnt Diagnostics (Boardex) 2000–12, New Century Media Ltd 2010–; non-exec chm OAG Worldwide Ltd 2001–06; *Recreations* reading, golf, collecting old books; *Clubs* RAC, Addington Golf; *Style*— Eddie Bell, Esq

BELL, Eileen Helen Marie; CBE (2008); da of Joseph and Mary Neeson; *b* 15 August 1943; *Educ* Dominican Coll Belfast, Univ of Ulster (BA); *m* 1968, Derek Bell; *Career* Alliance Pty: gen sec 1986–90, chair 1997–99, pres 2000–01, dep ldr 2001–, memb Pty Strategy Ctee, spokesperson Equality and Community Relations, former spokesperson Educn and Women's Issues; cncllr (representing Bangor W) N Down BC 1993–2000; memb: Policy and Resources Ctee, Leisure Tourism and Community Devpt Ctee (chair sub-ctees: Community Rels, Leisure Centres), Planning and Econ Devpt Ctee, Environmental and Tech Amenities Ctee, Corp Strategy Ctee, Health Ctee, Advsy Bd on Grant Applications for vol bodies; MLA (Alliance) N Down 1998–2007; presiding offr (speaker) NI Assembly 2006–07; memb: Assembly Cmmn, Educn Ctee, Ctee for the Central Dept; delg: Brooke-Mayhew Talks 1991–92, Dublin Forum for Peace and Reconciliation 1994–96 (memb: Fundamental Rights Ctee, Co-ordinating Ctee), NI Forum for Political Dialogue 1996 (memb Educn Ctee), Castle Building Talks (Good Friday Agreement) 1996–98; memb: N Down District Partnership 1996–2000, NI Probation Bd 1997–2003, NI Assoc for Care and Resettlement of Offenders; former memb: SE Educn and Library Bd, Local Govt Staff Cmmn; participated in Local Govt Research Consortium Univ of Warwick; *Recreations* reading, theatre, music; *Style*— Mrs Eileen Bell, CBE; ✉ 27 Maryville Road, Bangor BT20 3RH (☎ 028 9145 2321, fax 028 9145 5995)

BELL, Emily Jane; da of Peter Bell, and Bridget Bell; *b* 14 September 1965, King's Lynn, Norfolk; *Educ* ChCh Oxford (MA); *m* 1994, Edmund Hugh Crooks; 3 s; *Career* reporter Big Farm Weekly 1987–88, reporter Campaign 1988–90; The Observer: reporter 1990–96, dep business ed 1996–98, business ed 1998–2000; fndr and ed mediaguardian.co.uk 2000, ed-in-chief Guardian Unlimited 2001–06, dir of digital content Guardian News and Media 2006–; columnist Broadcast; visiting prof Sch of Media UC Falmouth 2009–; *Publications* The Media Directory (jtly, 2004); *Recreations* child management, cooking, opera and theatre going, reading, Arsenal FC season ticket holder; *Style*— Ms Emily Bell; ✉ Guardian News and Media, 90 York Way, London N1 9GU (☎ 020 3353 3500, e-mail emily.bell@guardian.co.uk, website www.guardian.co.uk)

BELL, Dr Gary Thomas; s of Thomas George Bell, of Brisbane, Aust, and Constance Beth *née* Goodman; *b* 1 October 1953; *Educ* Brisbane GS, Univ of Qld (BA, MB BS); *m* 5 Oct 1991 Marcia Rosalind, da of Desmond Laurence Hall; 2 da (Ghillian Naomi Cavell b 24

Dec 1992, Elizabeth Richenda Cavell b 10 Aug 1999), 1 s (Christian Thomas Cavell b 24 Nov 1995); *Career* lectr and hon sr registrar Middx Hosp and UCH 1985–89, sr lectr and hon conslt Bart's 1989–93, conslt psychiatrist Royal Nat Orthopaedic Hosp Stanmore 1994–97, conslt psychiatrist Cancer Treament Centre Mount Vernon Hosp Northwood 1997–; hon conslt St Luke's Healthcare for the Clergy 2008–; visiting conslt psychiatrist: Cardinal Clinic Windsor 1992–, Spire Thames Valley Hosp Wexham 1997–, The London Clinic 2007–, Wellington Hosp 2007–, Hosp of St John and St Elizabeth 2007–; staff conslt psychiatrist and clinical tutor Priory Hosp Roehampton 2004–05, medical dir Cwlth Healthcare 2005–08, founding ptnr LLP Consulting 2007–, medical dir Invictus Health 2011–; examiner: RCPsych 1998–2005, United Examining Bd 1998–2005; various chapters and original articles on med educn and liaison psychiatry; Historic Houses Assoc: memb Nat Exec Ctee, hon treas Thames and Chiltern region 1996–2005; chm Windsor Golden Jubilee Parade Ctee 2001–02, corporate companion Coll of St George Windsor Castle 2006–, lay steward St George's Chapel Windsor Castle 2007–; Liveryman Worshipful Soc of Apothecaries 1992 (memb Ct of Assts 2001), Fndr Liveryman Co of Arts Scholars 2014 (memb 2008); FRCPsych 2000 (MRCPsych 1985); CStJ 2004 (OStJ 1999, memb Cncl 1997–, chm Cncl Order of St John Berks 1999–2008); *Recreations* opera, period house and garden restoration, British pictures; *Style*— Dr Gary Bell, FRCPsych; ✉ Hall Place, Beaconsfield, Buckinghamshire HP9 1NB (☎ 01628 760066, fax 01494 676710, e-mail gary.bell@lppconsulting.org)

BELL, Ian Ronald; MBE (2006); *b* 11 April 1982, Coventry; *Educ* Princethorpe Coll; *Career* cricketer; Warwickshire CCC 1999– (winners Benson and Hedges Cup 2002 and County Championship 2004); England: 46 Test caps, 79 one day appearances, 2 Twenty20 appearances, Test debut v WI The Oval 2004, one day debut v Zimbabwe Harare 2004, memb Ashes-winning team 2005, memb squad World Cup WI 2007; NBC Denis Compton Award 1999, 2000 and 2001, Professional Cricketers Assoc Young Player of the Year 2004, ICC Emerging Player of the Year 2006; columnist The Guardian; *Style*— Mr Ian Bell, MBE; ✉ c/o England and Wales Cricket Board, Lord's Cricket Ground, St Johns Wood Road, London NW8 8QZ

BELL, Jason; s of Peter Alexander Bell, of London, and Susan Margaret St. Claire Laws, *née* Carruthers; *b* 1969, Camden, London; *Educ* Univ of Oxford; *Partner* Guy Harrington (civil partnership 2007); *Career* portrait photographer; subjects incl: Scarlett Johansson, Johnny Depp, Emily Blunt, Claire Danes, David Beckham, Nicole Kidman, John Malkovich, Kate Winslet, Daniel Craig; film posters incl: Love Actually, Billy Elliot, About A Boy, Bridget Jones 2, Golden Compass, Inkheart; official photographer for the christening of HRH Prince George; hon fell RPS 2011; *Style*— Jason Bell, Esq; ✉ c/o Soho Management, 21 Queen Elizabeth Street, London SE21 2PD (e-mail mail@sohomanagement.co.uk, website www.jasonbellphoto.com, Twitter @jasonbellphoto, Instagram @jasonbellphoto)

BELL, Prof Sir John Irving; kt (2008), GBE (2015); *b* 1 July 1952; *Educ* Ridley Coll Canada, Univ of Alberta (Province of Alberta scholar, BMedSci), Magdalen Coll Oxford (Rhodes scholar, Cwlth scholar, BA, BM BCh, DM, Radcliffe Infirmary prize in surgery, Spray prize in clinical biochemistry); *Career* house offr John Radcliffe Hosp Oxford (Nuffield Dept of Clinical Med and Regnl Paediatric Surgery Serv) 1979–80; SHO: to Dept of Clinical Cardiology Hammersmith Hosp London 1980–81, to Renal Unit Guy's Hosp London 1981, in neurology Nat Hosp for Neurological Diseases Queen Square London 1981–82; res fell Nuffield Dept of Clinical Med Univ of Oxford 1982, clinical fell Dept of Med and postdoctoral fell Dept of Med Microbiology Stanford Univ 1982–87, Wellcome sr clinical fell and hon conslt physician Nuffield Dept of Clinical Med and Surgery John Radcliffe Hosp Oxford 1987–89; regius prof of med Univ of Oxford 2001– (univ lectr 1989–92, Nuffield prof of clinical med 1992–2001), emeritus fell Magdalen Coll Oxford, student CCC Oxford; chm Office for Strategic Co-ordination of Health Research (OSCHR), chm Oxford Health Alliance, fndr Wellcome Tst Centre for Human Genetics; pres and fndr fell Acad of Med Scis; memb Bd UK Biobank Ltd; tstee: Rhodes Tst, Nuffield Med Tst, Ewelme Almshouse Charity; FRCP 1992, FRS 2008; *Style*— Prof Sir John Bell, GBE

BELL, Sir John Lowthian; 5 Bt (UK 1885), of Rounton Grange, Co York; s of Sir Hugh Francis Bell, 4 Bt (d 1970), and his 2 w, Mary, *née* Howson (d 2000); *b* 14 June 1960; *Educ* Glenalmond, RAC Cirencester; *m* 22 June 1985, Venetia Mary Frances, 2 da of J A Perry, of Taunton, Somerset; 1 s (John Hugh b 1988), 1 da (Sophia Amelia Bridget b 10 April 1990); *Heir* s, John Bell; *Career* farmer; *Recreations* fishing, shooting; *Style*— Sir John Bell, Bt; ✉ Arncliffe Hall, Ingleby Cross, Northallerton, North Yorkshire (☎ 01609 882202)

BELL, Joshua; *b* 1967, Indiana; *Career* violinist; studied with Josef Gingold, int debut with the Philadelphia Orch under Riccardo Muti 1981; appeared with orchs incl: London Philharmonic, Royal Philharmonic, BBC Symphony, The Philharmonia, Chicago Symphony, Boston Symphony, Cleveland Orch, NY Philharmonic, LA Philharmonic, Orchestre de la Suisse Romande, Orchestre Philharmonique, Acad of St Martin in the Fields, Czech Philharmonic, City of Birmingham Symphony, Berlin Philharmonic, Santa Cecilia Rome; worked with conductors incl: Vladimir Ashkenazy, Paavo Berglund, Riccardo Chailly, Charles Dutoit, John Eliot Gardiner, James Levine, Andrew Litton, Seiji Otawa, André Previn, Esa-Pekka Salonen, Leonard Slatkin, Yuri Temirkanov, Michael Tilson Thomas, Lorin Maazel, Sir Neville Marriner, Roger Norrington; gave premiere of Nicholas Maw violin concerto written specially for him 1993; regular guest at summer festivals incl: Salzburg, Tanglewood, Mostly Mozart, Edinburgh, BBC Proms, Ravinia; *Recordings* Mendelssohn and Bruch violin concertos, Tchaikovsky Violin Concerto and Wieniawski D Minor Violin Concerto, Lalo Symphonie Espagnole and Saint-Saëns Violin Concerto No 3, two recital and chamber music albums of French repertoire, Poeme (album of virtuoso classics, with RPO under Andrew Litton), Mozart Concertos Nos 3 and 5 (with Eng Chamber Orch under Peter Maag), Prokofiev Violin Concertos (with Montreal Symphony Orch under Charles Dutoit), Prokofiev Recital Disc (with Olli Mustonen), Kreisler Pieces (with Paul Coker), Brahms and Schumann Concertos (with Cleveland Orch under Dohnányi), Walton & Barber Concerti (with Baltimore Symphony under Zinman); formerly under exclusive contract to Decca, currently with Sony, new recordings with Sony: Goldmark/Sibelius Concertos, Nicholas Maw Concerto (Mercury Music Prize 2000, Grammy Award 2001), Gershwin Porgy and Bess Fantasy, Short Trip Home, The Red Violin (Music Soundtrack, Academy Award), Beethoven Conceto, Mendelssohn Concerto, Bernstein Serenade, West Side Story Suite, Romance of the Violin; *Recreations* chess, computers, golf, tennis, baseball; *Style*— Joshua Bell, Esq; ✉ c/o Kathryn Enticott, IMG Artists, London, The Light Box, 111 Power Road, London W4 5PY (☎ 020 8233 5800, e-mail kenticott@imgworld.com, website www.joshuabell.com)

BELL, Kevin; s of Ronald Bell, of Durham, and Sylvia, *née* Hampton; *b* 24 September 1957; *Educ* Washington GS, Univ of Reading (BA); *Career* public affrs/PR conslt; advsr to MPs and PA to Cons Pty candidates 1979, 1983, 1987, 1992 and 1997 gen elections; account exec K H Publicity 1979–80, dir Michael Forsyth Associates 1980–84; The Grayling Company: dir 1984–86 and 1990–94, md 1991–93; Westminster Strategy: dir 1986–94, dep md 1990–93, md 1993–94; dir: St James's Corporate Communications 1991–94, Pagette Communications 1991–94; md Lowe Bell Political 1994–, md and vice-chm GPC 2000–, md Fleishman-Hillard UK, dep chm Bell PottingerPublic Affairs (formerly Lowe Bell Consultants) 1994–99; tstee IEA; *Recreations* keeping fit, gardening, opera, eating and drinking well, teasing my friends; *Clubs* Paris Gym, Reform; *Style*— Kevin Bell, Esq; ✉ GPC, 40 Longacre, London WC2E 9LG (☎ 020 7395 7171, fax 020 7395 7194, e-mail kevin.bell@gpcinternational.com)

BELL, Laurence Bonamy Simon; s of Denys Le Merchant Bell, and Susan Hart Collier, *née* Abbott; *b* 22 October 1965, St John's Wood, London; *Educ* St Alban's Secdy Sch Ipswich; *partner* Jacqueline Marie Rice; *Career* buyer Tower Records 1988–90, A&R Fire Records 1990–93, fndr and md Domino Recording Co 1993–; *Style*— Laurence Bell, Esq; ✉ Domino Recording Co Ltd, Unit 3, Delta Business Park, Smugglers Way, London SW18 1EG (☎ 020 8875 1390, fax 020 8875 1391)

BELL, Marian Patricia; CBE (2005); da of (Joseph) Denis Milburn Bell (d 1997), and Wilhelmina Maxwell, *née* Miller; *b* 28 October 1957, London; *Educ* Hertford Coll Oxford (BA), Birkbeck Coll London (MSc); *m* 1988, Richard Adkin; 2 da; *Career* London Enterprise Agency 1980–82, economist Royal Bank of Scotland 1982–89, economic advsr HM Treasury 1989–91, Royal Bank of Scotland 1991–2000 (latterly head of research, treasury and capital markets), dir Alpha Economics 2000–02 and 2005–, memb Monetary Policy Ctee Bank of England 2002–05; memb: Fiscal Policy Panel States of Jersey 2007–14, Int Advsy Cncl Zurich Financial Servs 2007–14, Fiscal Policy Panel States of Guernsey 2010–11; govr Nat Inst of Economic and Social Research 2014–; non-exec dir Emerging Health Threats Forum 2006–12; govr Contemporary Dance Tst 2007–14 (vice-chair 2008–14); FRSA; *Recreations* contemporary dance, art; *Style*— Ms Marian Bell, CBE

BELL, Michael John Vincent; CB (1992); s of Christopher Richard Vincent, OBE (d 2006), and Violet Irene Edith Lorna (Jane) Bell, MBE (d 1989); *b* 9 September 1941, Nakuru, Kenya; *Educ* Winchester, Magdalen Coll Oxford (MA); *m* 3 Sept 1983, Mary, da of John William Shippen (d 1957); 1 s (John b 1985), 2 da (Julia b 1987, Jane b 1989); *Career* res assoc Inst for Strategic Studies 1964–65, asst princ MOD 1965, asst private sec to Sec of State for Def 1968–69, princ MOD 1969, private sec to Perm Under Sec MOD 1973–75, asst sec MOD 1975, on loan to HM Treasy 1977–79, asst under sec MOD 1982, asst sec gen def planning and policy NATO 1986–88, dep under sec of state (Fin) MOD 1988–92, dep under sec of state (Defence Procurement) 1992–95 (post re-titled dep chief of def procurement (Support) 1995–96), on secondment as project dir European Consolidation BAE Systems plc (formerly British Aerospace plc) 1996–99, gp head of strategic analysis BAE Systems plc 1999–2003, conslt export controls BAE Systems plc 2003–12, sr advsr MK Technology 2012–; *Recreations* military history; *Style*— Michael Bell, Esq, CB; ☎ 07921 023250, e-mail mjvbell@inweb.co.uk

BELL, Nicholas Julian; s of Malcom Graham Bell, and Rose Ellen Bell; *b* 15 January 1961; *Educ* Lancing (1st XI football colours, 1st XI cricket colours); *m* 1991, Angela Joanne, *née* Herbert; 2 da (Tiffany b 1993, Elly-May b 1996), 1 s (Charles b 2000); *Career* writer Abbot Mead Vickers 1987–95; Leo Burnett: writer 1995–97, dep exec creative dir 1998–99, exec creative dir 1999–2003; exec creative dir J Walter Thompson (latterly JWT) 2003–07, int creative dir DDB Europe 2008–; memb Bd of Dirs Br TV Advt Awards, pres D&DA 2004; MIPA; *Awards* Cannes Advertising Festival Grand Prix, 4 Cannes Gold Lions, 2 Design and Art Direction Silver Awards, 10 Campaign Press Silver Awards, 2 NY Clio Gold Awards, US Andy Award of Excellence; *Recreations* football (1st XI Lancing Old Boys FC 1982–97, Arthurian League Premier Div champions 6 times, Arthur Dunn cup winner 4 times incl league and cup double 1983–1985), cricket; *Style*— Nicholas Bell, Esq

BELL, Prof Patrick Michael; s of Benjamin Jonathan Bell (d 1982), and Jane, *née* McIllveen; *b* 9 March 1953; *Educ* Friends' Sch Lisburn, Queen's Univ Belfast (MB BCh, BAO, MD, MSc); *m* 28 June 1979, (Dorothy Lavina) Patricia, da of Canon Leslie Walker, of Ballylesson, Co Down; 2 da (Jane b 1980, Katie b 1982), 1 s (Jonathan b 1987); *Career* DHSS res fell Royal Victoria Hosp and Belfast City Hosp 1981–82, sr registrar Royal Victoria Hosp 1982–84, Mayo Fndn fell in endocrinology (as Fulbright scholar) Mayo Clinic USA 1984–85, sr registrar Belfast City Hosp 1985–86, conslt physician Royal Victoria Hosp 1986–2016, ret, hon prof Queen's Univ Belfast 2002–; Central Exec Ctee Alliance Pty of NI 1987–94, chm NI Ctee Br Diabetic Assoc 1992–98; numerous articles in learned jls on glucose metabolism; memb Assoc of Physicians of GB and Ireland 1994; FRCPGlas 1988, FRCPEd 1992, FRCPI 1992 (MRCPI 1989), FRCP 1995; *Books* Multiple Choice Questions in Medicine (1981); *Style*— Prof Patrick Bell; ✉ 14 Clonevin Park, Lisburn, Co Antrim BT28 3BL (☎ 028 9267 4703)

BELL, Prof Sir Peter Robert Frank; kt (2002); s of late Frank Bell, of Sheffield, S Yorks, and late Ruby, *née* Corks; *b* 12 June 1938; *Educ* Marcliffe Secdy Sch Sheffield, High Storrs GS Sheffield, Univ of Sheffield (MB ChB, MD); *m* 26 Aug 1961, Anne, da of Oliver Jennings (d 1981), of Dewsbury, W Yorks; 2 da (Jane Marie b 1962, Louise b 1963), 1 s (Mark b 1967); *Career* registrar in surgery Sheffield Health Bd 1963–65, Sir Henry Wellcome travelling fell Wellcome Fndn Denver Coll 1968–69, sr lectr in surgery Univ of Glasgow 1969–74 (lectr 1963–68), fndn prof of surgery Univ of Leicester 1974–2003; formerly memb: Cell Bd MRC, Transplant Mgmnt Ctee DHSS, Advsy Panel Br Cwlth Fellowship, Bd of Govrs De Montfort Univ; past ed Euro Jl of Vascular Surgery, past cncl memb and hon treas British Jl of Surgery Society Ltd; past pres: Int Soc for Vascular Surgery, Vascular Society of GB & Ireland, Leicester Med Soc; vice-pres Cncl RCS (chm Research Bd); memb: Int Transplantation Soc (past sec), Surgical Research Soc (past hon sec and pres), American Soc of Transplant Surgns, Br Soc of Immunology and Transplantation (past Ctee memb), Royal Med Chirurgical Soc of Glasgow, Vascular Surgical Soc (past Ctee memb and chm Vascular Advsy Ctee), Collegium Internationale Chirurgiae, Br Transplantation Soc, European Soc for Vascular Surgery (past pres), Soc for Academic Surgns (past chm), Acad of Med Sciences; treas Euro Surgical Assoc; pres Hope Fndn Charity for Cancer Research, chm Circulation Fndn Charity for Vascular Research; FRCS 1965 (past memb Surgical Advsy Ctee), FRCSGlas 1969; *Books* Operative Arterial Surgery (1983), Surgical Aspects of Haemodialysis (1985), Vascular Surgery (ed and contrib, 1985), Arterial Surgery of the Lower Limb (1991), Surgical Management of Vascular Disease (ed jtly and contrib, 1991), Minimal Access Therapy for Vascular Disease (ed and contrib, 2002); author of numerous articles in academic jls; *Recreations* painting, gardening, woodwork; *Style*— Prof Sir Peter Bell; ✉ 22 Powys Avenue, Oadby, Leicester LE2 2DP (☎ 0116 270 9579, fax 0116 210 7361, e-mail peterrfbell@googlemail.com)

BELL, Rachel Anne; da of Stuart Bell (d 1997), and Sylvia, *née* Walker; *b* 25 February 1968; *Educ* Sandy Upper Sch; *m* 2 March 2000, Peter Hayward, s of Norman Hayward; 1 da (Isobel Stuart b 17 Aug 2000); *Career* with Hyatt Hotels 1985–89, account exec rising to account dir Freishman Hillard Int 1989–97, fndr and chm Shine Communications 1998– (winner of numerous industry awards); Media Boss of the Year 2000; memb: Consultancy Mgmnt Standard (CMS), PRCA, Mktg Soc; MIPR; *Style*— Ms Rachel Bell

BELL, Richard; s of John Reed Bell (d 2003), and Audrey Holt Bell; *b* 4 March 1966; *Educ* Bury GS, Univ of Birmingham (BComm); *m* Vicky; 2 da (Charlotte, Beatrix); *Career* head of transaction servs UK regions Deloitte; ACA 1990; *Recreations* football, golf, skiing, music; *Style*— Richard Bell, Esq; ✉ Deloitte & Touche LLP, PO Box 500, 2 Hardman Street, Manchester M60 2AT

BELL, Stuart; *Career* co-fndr (with Richard Dawes) DawBell Ltd 2009– (clients incl: Sir Paul McCartney, *qv*, James Corden, *qv*, Harry Styles, Rihanna, Take That, Leona Lewis, The BRIT Awards, Mercury Prize Awards, Queens Of The Stone Age, The Kills, Beck, Iggy Pop, Isle of Wight Festival, Google Play, Lionel Richie, Pharrell); Best Ind PR Co of the Year Record of the Day Award, Best PR Campaign Music Week Awards 2004 and 2008; *Style*— Stuart Bell, Esq; ✉ DawBell Ltd, First Floor, 1–11 Carteret Street, London SW1H 9DJ

BELL, Baron (Life Peer UK 1998), of Belgravia in the City of Westminster; Sir Timothy John Leigh (Tim) Bell; kt (1990); s of Arthur Leigh Bell (d 1963), of SA, and Greta Mary, *née*

Findlay; *b* 18 October 1941; *Educ* Queen Elizabeth's GS Barnet; *m* 11 July 1988, Virginia Wallis, da of Dr John Wallis Hornbrook, of Sydney, Aust; 1 da (Hon Daisy Alicia Wallis b 1988), 1 s (Hon Harry Leigh b 22 April 1991); *Career* ABC TV 1959–61, Colman Prentis & Varley 1961–63, Hobson Bates 1963–66, Geers Gross 1966–70, chm and md Saatchi & Saatchi Compton 1975–85 (md 1970–75), gp chief exec Lowe Howard-Spink Campbell Ewald 1985–87, dep chm Lowe Howard-Spink & Bell 1987–89; currently chm Chime Communications plc; special advsr to chm NCB 1984–86; former dir Centre for Policy Studies; memb: PR Ctee Gtr London Fund for the Blind 1979–86, Public Affrs Ctee WWF 1985–88, Indust Ctee Save the Children Fund; pres Charity Projects 1993– (chm 1984–93); memb: Cncl Royal Opera House 1982–85, S Bank Bd 1985–86; govr BFI 1983–86; FIPA; *Books* Right and Wrong (2014); *Recreations* golf, politics; *Clubs* RAC, Royal Prince Edward Yacht (Sydney); *Style—* The Rt Hon the Lord Bell; ✉ Bell Pottinger, 49 Charles Street, London W1J 5EN

BELL BURNELL, Prof Dame (Susan) Jocelyn; DBE (2007, CBE 1999); *née* Bell; da of George Philip Bell (d 1982), of Solitude, Lurgan, NI, and Margaret Allison Bell, MBE, JP, *née* Kennedy (d 2009); *b* 15 July 1943, Belfast; *Educ* The Mount Sch York, Univ of Glasgow (BSc), New Hall Cambridge (PhD); *m* 21 Dec 1968 (m dis 1989), Martin Burnell, s of Arnold Burnell, of London; 1 s (Gavin b 1973); *Career* Univ of Southampton: SRC fell 1968–70, jr teaching fell 1970–73; Mullard Space Sci Laboratory UCL: pt/t grad programmer 1974–76, pt/t assoc research fell 1976–82; Royal Observatory Edinburgh: pt/t sr research fell 1982–86, astronomer i/c Visitor Centre 1985–86, pt/t sr sci offr and head of James Clerk Maxwell Telescope Section 1986–89, pt/t grade 7 and head of James Clerk Maxwell Telescope Section 1989–91; prof of physics Open Univ 1991–2001 (tutor, conslt, guest lectr 1973–88), dean of sci Univ of Bath 2001–2004, professorial fell Mansfield Coll Oxford 2004–; pro-chllr Univ of Dublin 2013–; visiting prof: Princeton Univ 1999–2000, Univ of Oxford 2004–; ed The Observatory 1973–76; pres: RAS 2002–04 (memb Cncl 1978–81 and 1992–97, vice-pres 1995–97), Inst of Physics 2008–10 (first female pres); memb various bds, ctees and panels PPARC and SERC 1978– (incl: vice-chm Astronomy 1 Ctee 1983–84, chair Public Understanding of Sci Advsy Panel 2001–05, chair Advanced LIGO Oversight Ctee 2003–), chair EC Physics TMR-TTR Panel 1996–98 (vice-chair 1995); hon memb Royal Irish Acad 2012; hon fell: Univ of Edinburgh 1988–91, New Hall Cambridge 1996–, Glyndwr Univ 2011; hon assoc Nat Cncl of Women 1995–; hon memb Sigma Pi Sigma 2000–, memb Bd Edinburgh Int Sci Festival 1991–96, foreign memb Onsala Observatory Bd Sweden 1996–2002, memb Scientific Ctee for Physics Int Solvay Insts 2004–; Michelson medal Franklin Inst Philadelphia 1973, J Robert Oppenheimer meml prize Center for Theoretical Studies Miami 1978, Beatrice Tinsley prize American Astronomical Soc (first recipient) 1987, Herschel medal RAS London 1989, Edinburgh Medal (City of Edinburgh and Science Festival) 1999, Magellanic Premium (American Philosophical Soc) 2000, Robinson Medal Armagh Observatory 2004, Kelvin Medal Royal Philosophical Soc Glasgow 2007, Grote Reber Medal Australia 2011, Helen Sawyer Hogg Prize Canada 2012, Sven Berggren Prize Sweden 2012, Medalla de Oro Consejo Superior de Investigaciones Spain 2016, Royal Medal Royal Soc London 2015; memb: Br Cncl of Churches Assembly 1978–90, Scottish Churches Cncl 1982–90 (Exec Ctee 1984–88), Open Univ Cncl 1997–99; tstee Nat Maritime Museum Greenwich 2000–09; Hon DSc: Heriot-Watt Univ 1993, Univ of Warwick 1995, Univ of Newcastle upon Tyne 1995, Univ of Cambridge 1996, Univ of Glasgow 1997, Univ of Sussex 1997, Univ of St Andrews 1999, Univ of London 1999, Haverford Coll (USA) 2000, Univ of Leeds 2000, Williams Coll (USA) 2000, Univ of Portsmouth 2002, Queen's Univ Belfast 2002, Univ of Edinburgh 2003, Univ of Keele 2005, Univ of Durham 2007, Univ of Michigan 2008, Univ of Southampton 2008, Trinity Coll Dublin 2008, Univ of Leicester 2009, Loughborough Univ 2009, Univ of Lancaster 2009, Nat Univ of Ireland 2009, Univ of Aberdeen 2013, UCL 2013, Univ of Manchester 2014, McGill Univ 2015, Edinburgh Napier Univ 2015, Strathclyde Univ 2015, Univ of Hull 2015, Rutgers Univ 2016, Univ of Alberta 2016; Hon DUniv York 1994, Hon SD Harvard Univ 2007, Hon DUniv Open Univ 2009, Hon DPhil Dublin City Univ 2015; hon fell: Science Museum 2010, European Physical Soc 2010; memb: Int Astronomical Union 1979, American Astronomical Soc 1992 (hon memb 2015); foreign assoc US Nat Acad of Sciences 2005, hon memb Science Acad Istanbul 2016, foreign memb American Philosophical Soc 2016, hon pres Soko Fund 2016–2020; FRAS 1969, FInstP 1992 (Hon FInstP 2012), FRS 2003 (memb Cncl 2004–06), FRSE 2004 (pres-elect (first female pres) 2014); *Recreations* swimming, learning languages, knitting and sewing, Quaker activities; *Clubs* Athenaeum; *Style—* Prof Dame Jocelyn Bell Burnell, DBE

BELLAMY, Sir Christopher William; kt (2000); s of Dr William Albert Bellamy, TD (d 1960), of Waddesdon, Bucks, and Vyvienne Hilda, *née* Meyrick (d 2001); *b* 25 April 1946; *Educ* Tonbridge, BNC Oxford; *m* Deirdre Patricia, da of Alexander Turner (d 1961); 1 s (Edward Alexander William), 2 da (Charlotte Elizabeth, Alexandra Anne); *Career* called to the Bar Middle Temple 1968, bencher 1994; in practice specialising in EC, public law and related matters 1970–92; QC 1986; asst recorder Crown Ct 1989–92, judge of the Ct of First Instance of European Communities 1992–99, pres Competition Cmmn Appeal Tribunals 1999–2003, pres Competition Appeal Tribunal 2003–07, dep High Ct judge 2000–16, judge of Employment Appeal Tbnl 2000–07, recorder Crown Ct 2001–07, sr conslt and chm Global Competition Practice Linklaters 2007–; pres: Assoc of European Competition Law Judges 2002–06 (hon pres 2008–), UK Assoc of European Law 2003–09; memb Cncl of Mgmnt Br Inst of Int and Corp Law 2002–06 (memb Advsy Bd 2006–); govr Ravensbourne Coll of Design and Communication 1988–92; Memb Ct of Assts Worshipful Co of Broderers; Commandeur de l'Ordre Grand-Ducal de la Couronne de Chêne (Luxembourg) 2014; *Books* Common Market Law of Competition (with G Child, 1 edn 1973 and 7 edn (as European Community Law of Competition), 2013, ed V Rose and D Bailey); *Recreations* history, walking, family life; *Clubs* Athenaeum, Garrick; *Style—* Sir Christopher Bellamy, QC; ✉ Linklaters, 1 Silk Street, London EC2Y 8HQ (☏ 020 7456 3457)

BELLAMY, David; *Educ* Sutton High GS Plymouth; *Career* St James's Place plc: joined 1991, previous roles incl gp ops dir and md, memb Bd 1997, ceo 2007–; tstee St James's Place Fndn; memb Practitioner's Panel FCA; *Style—* David Bellamy, Esq; ✉ St James's Place plc, 1 Tetbury Road, Cirencester, Gloucestershire GL7 1FP (☏ 01285 640302)

BELLAMY, Prof David James; OBE (1994); s of Thomas James Bellamy (d 1988), and Winifred May, *née* Green (d 1979); *b* 18 January 1933; *Educ* Sutton County GS, Chelsea Coll of Sci and Technol (BSc), Bedford Coll London (PhD); *m* 3 Jan 1959, (Shirley) Rosemary, da of Frederick Herbert Froy (d 1959); 2 s (Rufus b 8 June 1966, Eoghain b 9 May 1975), 3 da (Henrietta b 14 Feb 1970, Brighid b 7 March 1972, Hannah b 24 June 1978); *Career* Univ of Durham: lectr in botany 1960–68, sr lectr in botany 1968–82, hon prof of adult educn 1982–; Univ of Nottingham: special prof of botany 1987–99, special prof of geography 2000–; visiting prof of natural heritage studies Massey Univ NZ 1989; dir: Botanical Enterprises Ltd, (fndr) Natural Heritage Conservation Fndn NZ, Conservation Fndn London; memb various professional ctees, recipient of many awards incl UNEP Global 500 1990; memb Cncl Zoological Soc of London 2003; Parly candidate (Referendum Party) Huntingdon 1997; hon prof Univ of Central Queensland 1998–; Hon DUniv Open Univ, Hon DSc CNAA; Hon FLS, FIBiol, FRGS, fell Inst of Environmental Sci, FRIN; Order of the Golden Ark (Netherlands) 1988, Commemoration medal (NZ) 1990, Busk medal RGS 2001; *Television* for BBC incl: Life in Our Sea 1970, Bellamy on Botany 1973, Bellamy's Britain 1975, Bellamy's Europe 1977, Up a Gum Tree 1980, Backyard Safari 1981, The Great Seasons 1982, Bellamy's New World 1983, You Can't See The Wood 1984, Seaside Safari 1985, Bellamy Rides Again 1992, Blooming Bellamy 1993; for ITV incl: Botanic Man 1979, The End of the Rainbow Show 1986, Bellamy's Bugle 1986, Turning the Tide 1986, Bellamy's Birds Eye View 1988, Don't Ask Me, It's Life, It's More Life, The Gene Machine, Swallow, Bellamy on Top of the World, Paradise Ploughed, The Owl and the Woodsman, England's Lost Wilderness 1991, England's Last Wilderness 1992, Routes of Wisdom 1993; other television incl: Moa's Ark (TVNZ) 1990, Westwatch 1996, A Welsh Herbal 1998, Buzz of Biodiversity 1999, Salt Solutions 1999, Can of Worms 2006; *Books* Bellamy on Botany (1972), Peatlands (jtly, 1973), Bellamy's Britain (1974), Life Giving Sea (1975), Green Worlds (jtly, 1975), The World of Plants (1975), It's Life (1976), Bellamy's Europe (1976), Botanic Action (1978), Botanic Man (1978), Half of Paradise (1979), Forces of Life (1979), Bellamy's Backyard Safari (1981), The Great Seasons (jtly, 1981), Il Libro Verde (1981), Discovering the Countryside (1982 and 1983), The Mouse Book (jtly, 1983), Bellamy's New World (1983), The Queen's Hidden Garden (jtly, 1984), Bellamy's Ireland (1986), Turning the Tide (jtly, 1986), Bellamy's Changing Countryside (1987), England's Last Wilderness (jtly, 1989), England's Lost Wilderness (jtly, 1990), Wetlands (jtly, 1990), Wilderness Britain (jtly, 1990), How Green are You (jtly, 1991), Tomorrow's Earth (jtly, 1991), World Medicine: Plants Patients and People (jtly, 1992), Blooming Bellamy (1993), Trees of the World (jtly, 1993), Poo You and the Potoroo's Loo (1997), Jolly Green Giant (autobiography, 2002), The Glorious Trees of Britain (jtly, 2002), A Natural Life (autobiography, 2003), The Bellamy Herbal (2003), Conflicts in the Countryside (2005); *Clubs* Farmers; *Style—* Prof David Bellamy; ✉ Mill House, Bedburn, Bishop Auckland, Durham DL13 3NN

BELLAMY, Martin; *b* 4 May 1969, Birmingham; *Educ* Univ of Reading (MBA); *Career* formerly: offr Br Army, assoc dir WPP, exec dir Williams Lea; co-fndr, chm and ceo Salamanca Gp 2002–; FRGS; *Style—* Martin Bellamy, Esq; ✉ Salamanca Group, Nash House, St George Street, London W1S 2FQ (☏ 020 7495 7070, e-mail m.bellamy@salamanca-group.com)

BELLAMY, Matthew James (Matt); *b* 9 June 1978, Cambridge; *Children* 1 s (Bingham Hawn b July 2011); *Career* singer, songwriter and musician; memb Muse (with Dominic Howard and Chris Wolstenholme); albums: Showbiz 1999, Origin of Symmetry 2001, Absolution 2003 (UK no 1), Black Holes and Revelations 2006 (UK no 1), The Resistance 2009 (UK no 1); singles incl: Sunburn 2000, Unintended 2000, Plug In Baby 2001, New Born 2001, Bliss 2001, Hyper Music/Feeling Good 2001 (double A-side), Dead Star/In Your World 2002 (double A-side), Time Is Running Out 2003, Hysteria 2003, Sing for Absolution 2004, Butterflies and Hurricanes 2004, Supermassive Black Hole 2006, Starlight 2006, Knights of Cydonia 2006, Invincible 2007, May of the Problematique 2007, Uprising 2009, Undisclosed Desires 2009, Resistance 2010, Survival 2012 (official song of the London 2012 Olympic Games); hon DA Univ of Plymouth 2008; *Awards* NME Awards: Best New Artist 2000, Best Live Act 2005, Best British Band 2007, 2010 and 2011, Best Live Band 2008 and 2009; Kerrang! Awards: Best British Band 2001, Best British Live Act 2002, Best Album 2004 (for Absolution), Best Live Act 2006; Q Awards: Innovation Award 2004, Best Live Act 2004, 2006 and 2007; Best Live Act BRIT Award 2005 and 2006, Best Rock Album Grammy Award 2011 (for The Resistance); *Style—* Mr Matt Bellamy; ✉ c/o Anthony Addis, Elphian House, New Bailey Street, Salford M3 5FS

BELLAMY-JAMES, Stephen Howard George Thompson; QC (1996); s of George Bellamy (d 1976), and Clarice, *née* Thompson (d 1997); *b* 27 September 1950; *Educ* The GS Heckmondwike, Trinity Hall Cambridge (MA); *m* 15 Oct 1988, Rita Mary James; 1 da (Nina Claudia Carla b 6 Nov 1991); *Career* called to the Bar Lincoln's Inn 1974 (bencher 2006); in practice SE Circuit, specialist in family law, recorder of the Crown Court 2000– (asst recorder 1997–2000), dep judge of the High Court 2000–; asst boundary cmmr 2000–10; family mediator; memb Ctee Family Law Bar Assoc 1989–96, memb Gen Cncl of the Bar 1993–96, chm Bar Cncl Scholarship Tst 2000–12, pres Nat Safeguarding Panel Sport Resolutions UK 2012; tstee Wooden Spoon Charity 2011; memb Br Inst of Int and Comparative Law; Master Worshipful Co of Fruiterers 2016; fell Inst of Advanced Legal Studies; *Recreations* music, opera, gardening, tennis, skiing, sailing; *Clubs* Oxford and Cambridge; *Style—* Stephen Bellamy-James, Esq, QC; ✉ 1 King's Bench Walk, Temple, London EC4Y 7DB (☏ 020 7936 1500, fax 020 7936 1590, e-mail clerks@lkbw.co.uk)

BELLANY, Prof Ian; s of James Bellany (d 1984), of Sheffield and Bristol, and Jemima, *née* Emlay; *b* 21 February 1941; *Educ* Preston Lodge, Prestonpans, Firth Park Sheffield, Balliol Coll Oxford (state scholar, MA, DPhil); *m* 7 Aug 1965, Wendy Ivey, da of Glyndwr Thomas (d 1978), of Gilwern, Abergavenny; 1 s (Alastair b 1968), 1 da (Alison b 1971); *Career* asst princ FCO 1965–68, res fell ANU 1968–70; Lancaster Univ: lectr in politics 1970–74, sr lectr 1974–79, prof of politics 1979–2006, dir of the Centre for the Study of Arms Control and Int Security 1979–90, emeritus prof 2006–; founding ed Arms Control; external examiner in: Int Rels LSE 1985–88 and 1999–2002, Int Studies Univ of Birmingham 1989–92, Int Rels Univ of Aberdeen 1996–99; First Prize Trench Gascoigne Essay 2002, Leverhulme res fell 2003–04; *Books* Australia in the Nuclear Age (1972), Anti-Ballistic Missile Defence in the 1980s (ed 1983), The Verification of Arms Control Agreements (ed 1983), The Nuclear Non Proliferation Treaty (ed 1985), New Conventional Weapons and Western Defence (ed 1987), A Basis for Arms Control (1991), Reviewing Britain's Defence (1994), The Environment in World Politics (1997), Curbing the Spread of Nuclear Weapons (2005), Terrorism and Weapons of Mass Destruction (ed, 2007); *Recreations* broadcasting, carpentry and computing; *Style—* Prof Ian Bellany

BELLANY, Dr John; CBE (1994); s of Richard Weatherhead Bellany (d 1985), of Port Seton, E Lothian, and Agnes Craig Maltman Bellany; *b* 18 June 1942; *Educ* Cockenzie Sch, Preston Lodge Prestonpans, Edinburgh Coll of Art (DA), RCA (MA); *m* 1, 1964 (m dis 1974), Helen Margaret, da of late Harold Percy, of Golspie, Sutherland; 2 s (Jonathan b 22 Dec 1965, Paul b 21 Aug 1968), 1 da (Anya b 30 Sept 1970); m 2, 1980, Juliet Gray, *née* Lister (d 1985); m 3, 1986, his first wife Helen Margaret; *Career* lectr in fine art Winchester Sch of Art 1969–73, head Faculty of Painting Croydon Coll of Art 1973–78, visiting lectr in painting RCA 1975–84, lectr in fine art Goldsmiths Coll London 1978–84; artist in residence Victorian Coll of the Arts Melbourne 1983, fell commoner Trinity Hall Cambridge 1988; subject of: Bellany – Life, Death and Resurrection (film), A Day With John Bellany (book); Major Arts Cncl Award 1981, jt first prize Athena Int Award 1985, Korn Ferry Int Award Royal Acad of Arts 1993; elected sr fell RCA; Hon Dr: Univ of Edinburgh, Heriot-Watt Univ; Hon RSA 1987, RA 1991 (elected ARA 1986); *Exhibitions* major solo exhbns: Drian Gallery London 1970, 1971, 1972, 1973 and 1974, Aberdeen City Art Gallery 1975, Acme Gallery London 1977 and 1980, Scottish Arts Cncl Gallery 1978, 3rd Eye Centre Glasgow 1979, Southampton Art Gallery, Rosa Esman Gallery NY 1982, 1983 and 1984, Beaux Arts Gallery Bath 1989 and 1990, Fischer Fine Art London 1986, 1987, 1989 and 1991, Scot Nat Gallery of Modern Art 1986 and 1989, Raab Gallery Berlin 1989, Fitzwilliam Museum Cambridge 1991, Terry Dintenfass Gallery NY 1995, Gallerio Kin Mexico 1997, Beaux Arts Gallery London 1997, 1998, 1999 and 2003, Solomon Gallery Dublin 1999 and 2002, Irish Gallery of Modern Art Dublin 2000, Flowers West LA 2002, Open Eye Gallery Edinburgh 2002; Arts Cncl touring exhibition 1983: Ikon Gallery Birmingham, Walker Art Gallery Liverpool, Graves Art Gallery Sheffield; Arts Cncl touring exhibition 1984: Christine Abrahams Gallery Melbourne, Düsseldorf Gallery Perth, Roslyn Oxley Gallery Sydney, Nat Portrait Gallery 1986, Galerie Kirkhaar Amsterdam; one man exhibition (Beaux-Arts Gallery London) 2000, one man exhibition (Solomon Gallery Dublin) 2000; retrospective exhbns: Scot Nat Gallery of Modern Art 1986, Serpentine Gallery London, RCA Gallery 1987, Kunsthalle Hamburg 1989, Roslyn Oxley Gallery Sydney, Butler Gallery Kilkenny Castle, Hendrix

Gallery Dublin, 3rd Eye Centre Glasgow (prints) 1988, Ruth Siegel Gallery NY 1988 and 1990, The Renaissance of John Bellany (Nat Gallery of Modern Art) 1988, Fisher Fine Art London 1988 and 1991, Raab Gallery Berlin 1990, Fitzwilliam Museum Cambridge 1991, A Long Night's Journey into Day: The Art of John Bellany (Kelvingrove Art Gallery and Museum, Glasgow) 1992, Berkeley Square Gallery London 1993, Recent Acquisitions: John Bellany (Nat Gallery of Modern Art Dublin) 2000; 60th birthday exhbn: Scottish Gallery of Modern Art, Beaux Arts Gallery London, Solomon Gallery Dublin, Flowers East LA, Open Eye Gallery Edinburgh, Ricci Museum Barga Italy; major gp exhbns: British Romantic Painting (Madrid), El Greco – Mystery and Illumination (Nat Gallery), Every Picture tells a Story (Br Cncl touring exhibition Singapore and Hong Kong), Eros in Albion (House of Messaccio Italy), Scottish Art since 1990 (Nat Gallery of Scotland and Barbican London), Scotland Creates 1990, The Great British Art Show 1990, Bellany and MacTaggart the Elder (Edinburgh Art Centre Festival Exhibition) 2000, Sea Change: John Bellany and Sir William MacTaggart (Edinburgh City Art Centre) 2000, Bourne Fine Art Festival exhibition 2000, John Bellany at Sixty (Scottish Nat Gallery of Modern Art) 2002, John Bellany in Italy (Ricci Fndn Tuscany) 2002; *Work in Public Collections* Aberdeen Art Gallery, Arts Cncl of GB, Br Cncl, Br Govt Collection Whitehall, Contemporary Arts Soc, Hatton Art Gallery, Kelvingrove Art Gallery, Leeds Art Gallery, Leicester Art Gallery, Middlesbrough Art Gallery, Nat Gallery of Poland Warsaw, Nat Library of Congress Washington DC, MOMA NY, Met Museum NY, Nat Portrait Gallery, Nat Gallery of Modern Art Scotland, Gulbenkian Museum Lisbon, J F Kennedy Library Boston, V&A, Br Museum, Tate; *Clubs* Chelsea Arts, Scottish Arts (Edinburgh); *Style—* Dr John Bellany, CBE, RA; ✉ The Clockhouse, Shortgrove Hall, Saffron Walden, Essex CB11 3TX (website www.bellany.com); 19 Great Stuart Street, Edinburgh EH3 7TP; c/o Berkley Square Gallery, 23A Bruton Street, London W1X 7DA (☎ 020 7493 7939); represented by Beaux Arts Gallery, Cork Street, London W1S 3NA (☎ 020 7437 5799)

BELLAS, Moira Aileen; da of Norman Spencer Bellas, of Worthing, and Catherine Winifred, *née* Whysall (d 1986); *b* 21 March 1950; *Educ* Woodfield Secdy Modern Sch Hounslow; *m* Dec 1974, Clive Alan Banks; 1 da (Kelly May b May 1987); *Career* jr clerk Pye Records 1965–67, press office asst Paragon Publicity 1967–68, press offr EMI Records 1968–70, press offr Three's Company (PR co) 1970–71; WEA Records (formerly Kinney Records): sec/PA 1971–73, press offr 1973–86, dir Artistic Devpt and Mktg 1986–92, md 1992–2000; co-founder MBC (PR co) 2000– (clients incl Rod Stewart, David Walliams, Mark Ronson, *qqv*, Kasabian, Madonna, Russell Brand and Melanie C); Leslie Perrin Publicity Award, Woman of the Year Women of the Year Awards (music industry) 2001; *Style—* Ms Moira Bellas; ✉ Warm Seas House, 23 Wellington Road, London NW8 9SL (☎ 020 449 4333)

BELLENGER, Rt Rev Dom (Dominic) Aidan; s of Gerald Bellenger, of London, and Kathleen Patricia, *née* O'Donnell; *b* 21 July 1950; *Educ* Finchley GS, Jesus Coll Cambridge (Lightfoot scholar, MA, PhD), Angelicum Univ Rome; *Career* asst master St Mary's Sch Cambridge 1975–78; Downside Abbey: Benedictine monk 1982, priest 1988, parish priest 1995–2015, prior 2001–06, abbot 2006–14; Downside Sch: asst master 1978–82, housemaster 1989–91, head master 1991–95, govr 1999–2015, chm of govrs 2006–15; titular abbot of St Albans 2014–; English Benedictine Congregation: delg Gen Chapter 2001–06, annalist 2009–; p/t lectr: Univ of Bristol 1996–2006, Bath Spa Univ (formerly Bath Spa UC) 1997–2007 (hon fell 2014), Univ of Birmingham 1998–2000, UC Worcester 1999–2000; assoc lectr Open Univ 1997–2004; pres English Catholic History Assoc 1991–; memb: Ctee Ecclesiastical History Soc 1982–85, Ctee English Benedictine Historical Cmmn 1987–, Cncl Catholic Record Soc 1990–99 and 2005–11, Cncl Somerset Record Soc 1998–; tstee: Catholic Family History Soc 1990–99, Friends of Somerset Churches 1996–2011, Glastonbury Abbey 2009–; English corr Revue d'Histoire de l'Eglise de France 1982–85, ed South Western Catholic History 1982–2012, memb Editorial Ctee Somerset Notes and Queries 2005–, ed The Downside Review 2011–15; govr: Moor Park Sch Ludlow 1991–99, St Anthony's Leweston 1991–93, St Mary's Sch Shaftesbury 1992–96, Moreton Hall Sch 1994–2000, St Joseph's Malvern 1997–2000, St Gregory's Bath 2001–05; Leverhulme Research Award 1986, first York Minster lectr 2001, visiting scholar Sarum Coll 2004–14, visiting scholar St Edmund's Coll 2014–; FRHistS, FRSA, FSA, FHEA; chaplain Knights of Malta 2004–; *Books* English and Welsh Priests 1558–1800 (1984), The French Exiled Clergy (1986), Opening the Scrolls (ed, 1987), Les Archives du Nord, Calendar of 20 H (jt ed, 1987), St Cuthbert (1987), Letters of Bede Jarrett (jt ed, 1989), Fathers in Faith (ed, 1991), The Great Return (ed, 1994), Downside, A Pictorial History (ed, 1998), Princes of the Church: The English Cardinals (2001), William Bernard Ullathorne (2001), Medieval Worlds (2003), The Mitre and the Crown: The Archbishops of Canterbury (2005), Medieval Religion (2006), Downside Abbey: an architectural history (2011), St Wulstan's Little Malvern (2013), Time and Place (2013), 200 Downside Monks (2014), St Benedict's Stratton on the Fosse (2014), Monks with a Mission (2014), Monastic Identities (2014), Keeping the Rule (2013), Fearless Resting Place (2015), Here and There (2015); author of articles in jls, newspapers and periodicals; *Recreations* books, church architecture, travel, the visual arts, writing; *Clubs* Stratton-on-the-Fosse CC (pres 1991–95), Oxford and Cambridge; *Style—* The Rt Rev Dom Aidan Bellenger, FSA; ✉ Downside Abbey, Stratton-on-the-Fosse, Bath BA3 4RJ (☎ 01761 235119, e-mail abbot@downside.co.uk)

BELLEW, Patrick John; s of James Kevin Bellew (d 1972), and Judith Anne Bellew, *née* Peckston; *b* 12 June 1959, Osmotherley, N Yorks; *Educ* Stonyhurst Coll, Univ of Bath; *m* 9 Feb 1985, Lois Jane, *née* Clay; 2 da (Zoe Diana b 17 Dec 1986, Freya Judith b 23 Dec 1991), 1 s (Ruaraidh Alexander James b 12 May 1988); *Career* with Buro Happold Bath 1981–97, dir Synergy Consltg Engrs 1987–90; projects incl Greenpeace UK HQ; princ Atelier Ten Consltg Engrs 1990–, also dir Atelier Ten NY LLC and L'Atelier; projects incl: Charities Aid Fndn HQ West Malling, sustainable primary sch Notley Green, The Earth Centre, Forestry and Sculpture Sch, BioMed Lab Yale Univ, Herbarium, Alpine House and Jodrell Lab Kew Gardens, Baltic Centre for Contemporary Arts Gateshead, Federation Sq Melbourne, Virginia Museum of Fine Art, Grand Rapids Art Museum, The Ashmolean Museum Oxford, The Esplanade Theatre Singapore, Gardens by the Bay Singapore, British Pavilion Expo Shanghai 2010, WWF UK HQ Woking; visiting lectr and tutor: Bartlett Sch of Architecture UCL 1991–93, Sch of Construction Univ of Reading 1991–2004, Grad Sch of Architecture Yale Univ 2001–; Saarinen prof of architecture Yale Univ 2010–; govr Building Centre Tst 1996–2010, memb Design Review Ctee Cmmn for Architecture and the Built Environment (CABE) 1999–2004, founding memb UK Green Building Cncl 2006; memb: Eco-Towns Panel Cmmn for Architecture and the Built Environment 2009–, RIBA Nat Awards Panel 2012–, RIBA Int Awards Panel 2016–; external examiner Architectural Assoc 2015–; tstee UK-GBC 2010; Happold Medal 2008; FRSA 1997, Hon FRIBA 2000, FEI 2001 (memb 1987), FCIBSE 2001 (MCIBSE 1985), FREng 2004, RDI 2010; *Books* Green House: Green Engineering (2012), Invisible Architecture (2015); *Recreations* guitar, music, reading; *Style—* Patrick Bellew, RDI, FREng; ✉ Atelier Ten, 19 Perseverance Works, 38 Kingsland Road, London E2 8DD (☎ 020 7749 5950, e-mail patrick.bellew@atelierten.com, website www.atelierten.com)

BELLI, Prof Anna-Maria; da of Bartolomeo Antonio Luigi Belli, of Cwmgyn, Swansea, West Glam, and Carmen, *née* Lombardelli; *b* 5 August 1957; *Educ* Glanmôr Sch for Girls, Univ of London, Middx Hosp Med Sch (MB BS); *Career* sr registrar in radiology St George's Hosp 1985–87 (registrar 1982–85); sr lectr and hon conslt in radiodiagnosis: Univ of Sheffield 1987–90, Royal Postgrad Med Sch Hammersmith Hosp 1990–92; currently

conslt St George's Hosp London and prof of interventional radiology St George's Hosp Med Sch; memb Cncl BSIR 1993 (pres 2001–03); fell CIRSE 1994 (pres 2013–15), FRCR 1985; *Books* An Imaging Atlas of Human Anatomy (contrib 1 edn, 1992), Vascular Diseases in the Limbs (contrib 1 edn, 1993), Practical Interventional Radiology of the Peripheral Vascular System (contrib and ed, 1993); *Style—* Prof Anna-Maria Belli; ✉ Department of Radiology, St George's Hospital, Blackshaw Road, London SW17 0QT (☎ 020 8725 1481, fax 020 8725 2936)

BELLI, Lorella; *Educ* Univ of Venice (MA); *Career* literary agent; early career with several large publishers and literary agencies; estab Lorella Belli Literary Agency (LBLA) 2002 (representing award-winning, debut and bestselling authors and clients worldwide incl fiction, non-fiction and young adult, both commercial and literary); memb: Assoc of Authors' Agents, Romantic Novelists Assoc, Crime Writers' Assoc, Women In Publishing, Byte the Book, The Book Soc; *Style—* Ms Lorella Belli; ✉ Lorella Belli Literary Agency, 54 Hartford House, 35 Tavistock Crescent, Notting Hill, London W11 1AY (☎ 020 7727 8547, fax 0870 787 4194, e-mail info@lorellabelliagency.com, website www.lorellabelliagency.com, Facebook Lorella Belli Literary Agency, Twitter @lblaUK)

BELLINGER, Christopher Henry; s of Clifford Bellinger (d 1992), of Cardiff, and Margaret Joy, *née* Boddington (d 2013); *b* 20 February 1943; *Educ* Abingdon Sch; *m* 24 June 1972, Diana Penelope Margaret, da of Maj Frank Albert Bowater (d 1982), of London; *Career* BBC TV: Film Dept Wales 1964–70, TV presentation 1971–78, prodr Multi-Coloured Swap Shop, ed Saturday Superstore 1982, ed Going Live! 1986–93, ed Live and Kicking 1993–98; head of Children's Entertainment BBC Production 1998–2003, ed Xchange 2003–04, exec prodr ITV 2004–06, freelance exec prodr 2006–; *Recreations* photography, motorcycling; *Style—* Christopher Bellinger, Esq; ✉ e-mail mr.bellinger@ntlworld.com

BELLINGHAM, Sir Henry Campbell; kt (2016), MP; s of (Arthur) Henry Bellingham (d 1959), and June Marion, *née* Cloudesley Smith; *b* 29 March 1955; *Educ* Eton, Magdalene Coll Cambridge, Cncl of Legal Educn; *m* 1993, Emma Whiteley; 1 s (Jamie); *Career* called to the Bar Middle Temple 1978; MP (Cons) Norfolk NW 1983–97 and 2001–; vice-chm Cons Backbench Smaller Business Ctee 1987–90 (jt sec 1983–87), vice-chm Cons Backbench NI Ctee 1987–90 (jt sec 1983–87), memb Environment Select Ctee 1987–90, chm Cons Cncl on Eastern Europe 1989–93, PPS to Rt Hon Malcolm Rifkind 1990–97, memb British-Irish Parly Body 1992–97 and 2001–08, memb NI Affrs Select Ctee 2001–02, memb DTI Select Ctee 2002–03, shadow min for trade and industry and for small businesses 2002–05, oppn whip 2005–06, shadow min for legal services 2006–10, Parly under-sec of state FCO and min for Africa, UN, overseas territories, conflict issues and Caribbean 2010–12; chm Westminster Fndn for Democracy 2013–, co-chm 2015 Global Law Summit, chm Policy Research Unit; *Style—* Sir Henry Bellingham, MP; ✉ House of Commons, London SW1A 0AA

BELLINGHAM, Kate; da of Roger Bellingham, of Pocklington, E Yorks, and Barbara, *née* Stapleton; *b* 7 July 1963; *Educ* Mount Sch York, The Queen's Coll Oxford (BA), Univ of Hertfordshire (MSc); *m* 10 June 1995; 2 c; *Career* science and technology broadcaster; computer programmer CAP Alderley Edge 1984–87, trainee electronic engr BBC Radio (London) 1987–90; presenter: BBC/IEE Faraday lecture tour 1988–89, Techno (BBC Schs TV) 1989, Tomorrow's World (BBC TV) 1990–94, The Acid Test (BBC Radio 5 Live) 1994–97, Showcase (BBC Schs TV) 1995–97, The Big Bang (ITV) 1996–97, Open Saturday (BBC) 1998, Science for Today (Channel 4) 1998, Troubleshooting (BBC TV) 1999, Testing Times (BBC Radio 4) 1999, Engineering Your Environment (BBC TV) 2002; pres Young Engineers 1997– (media advisor 1995–97); memb: EPSRC Coll, Pubns Advsy Bd IEE; BBC Engrg qualification 1990; Hon DTec Staffordshire Univ 1997; memb Women's Engrg Soc, MIEE; *Recreations* music, crosswords, choral singing, crosswords, school classroom helper; *Style—* Ms Kate Bellingham; ✉ c/o Dave Winslett, 6 Kenwood Ridge, Kenley, Surrey CR8 5JW (☎ 020 8668 0531, fax 020 8668 9216, e-mail info@davewinslett.com)

BELLIS, Michael John; s of Herbert Henry Bellis (d 1976), of Sherborne, Dorset, and Marjorie Dudley, *née* Charlton (d 2006); *b* 28 April 1937; *Educ* Bancroft's Sch Woodford Green, Coll of Law; *Partner* Anthony Richard Baron (civil partnership 21 Dec 2005); *Career* Nat Serv RCS 1956–58; admitted slr 1968, cmmr for oaths 1973; Edward Oliver and Bellis: sr ptnr 1975–90, conslt 1991–96; conslt Lucas Baron Jacobs 1997–2000; md Heritage Heirlooms (UK) Ltd 1990–2003; chm Med Serv Ctee FPC London Boroughs of Redbridge and Waltham Forest 1978–89, lay serv ctee memb Norfolk Family Health Serv Authy 1991–96, memb Mgmnt Ctee The Intaglio Fndn Norwich 1996–98, chm Discipline Panel Norfolk HA 1996–2002, chm Norfolk Dental Contracts Disputes Panel 2006–; former vice-pres W Essex Law Soc; hon slr and hon memb Rotary Club Ilford (former pres), Rotary Int Paul Harris fell; tstee, fundraising chm and memb Exec Ctee Redbridge Community Tst 1992–95, tstee London NE Community Fndn 1996–97; memb Law Soc 1968; Freeman City of London, Liveryman Worshipful Co of Bakers (memb Ct of Assts 1994, Master 2004–05, Dep Master 2005–06, Hon Ct of Assts 2014); *Recreations* collecting rare books, travel, eating asparagus; *Clubs* Norfolk (Norwich), Law Society; *Style—* Michael John Bellis, Esq; ✉ Baron Art, 17 Chapel Yard, Albert Street, Holt, Norfolk NR25 6HG (☎ 01263 588435, e-mail michaelbellis1@gmail.com)

BELLOS, Prof David Michael; s of Nathaniel Bellos, of London, and Katharine Mabel, *née* Shapiro; *b* 25 June 1945; *Educ* Westcliff HS, Univ of Oxford (MA, DPhil); *m* 1, 31 Dec 1966 (m dis 1985), Ilona, da of Sandor Roth (d 1945); 1 s (Alexander b 1969), 2 da (Amanda b 1971, Olivia b 1974); *m* 2, 1 July 1989 (m dis 1995), Susan Esther Currie, da of Prof A C Lendrum; *m* 3, 25 June 1996, Pascale Voilley, da of Jean Voilley; *Career* fell Magdalen Coll Oxford 1969, lectr in French Univ of Edinburgh 1972, prof of French Univ of Southampton 1982, prof and head Dept of French Studies Univ of Manchester 1985–96, prof of French and comparative literature Princeton Univ 1997–, dir Program in Translation and Intercultural Communication Princeton Univ 2007–; Man Booker Int Translator's Award 2005; Chevalier de l'Ordre des Palmes Académiques France 1988, Prix Goncourt de la biographie France 1994; *Books* Balzac Criticism in France, 1850–1900 (1976), Georges Perec – Life A User's Manual (trans, 1987), Georges Perec – A Life in Words (1993), Ismail Kadare – The Pyramid (trans, 1996), Jacques Tati – His Life and Art (1999), Ismail Kadare – The Siege (trans, 2008), Romain Gary: A Tall Story (2010), Is That a Fish in Your Ear? (2011); *Recreations* cycling; *Style—* Prof David Bellos; ✉ Department of French and Italian, Princeton University, Princeton, NJ 08544–5264, USA (☎ 00 1 609 258 4500, fax 00 1 609 258 4535, e-mail dbellos@princeton.edu)

BELMAHI, (HE) Mohammed; *b* 18 August 1948, Rabat, Morocco; *Educ* Moulay Youssef HS Rabat, Nat Sch of Architecture Toulouse, Grad Sch of Public Admin NYU, Harvard Univ, Inst for Int Devpt, London Business Sch; *m* 2 Nov 1973, Åse Ask; 1 da; *Career* Moroccan diplomat; staff memb and conslt UN Centre for Housing, Bldg and Planning NY 1974–76, conslt Grad Sch of Social Work Columbia Univ NY 1976; head Urban Planning Div Miny of Housing and Land Use Planning 1977, dir of nat land use planning Miny of Housing and Land Use Planning 1978–79, memb task force for state owned enterprise reform PM's Office 1979–82, dir of tourism Miny of Tourism 1982–87, DG Moroccan Nat Tourist Office (ONMT) 1987–88, gen mangr (tourism and real estate sector) and advsr to chm and ceo ONA Gp Casablanca 1988–96 (also memb Exec Ctee and md Casablanca World Trade Centre), ambass to India and Nepal 1996–99, ambass to the Ct of St James's 1999–2009; rep of Moroccan govt at experts gp meetings; responsible for creation of Moroccan Pavilion Disney World EPCOT Centre Florida 1982–84, memb Organising Ctee for Promotion of Moroccan Pavilion Seville World Expo

1992; memb Bd Moroccan American Cmmn for Educn and Cultural Exchange (Fulbright Cmmn) 1992–96; memb Bureau Int Union of Urbanists 1984, memb Steering Ctee Euro-Mediterranean Conf of Tourism Ministers 1993–96; prof of urban and regnl planning and admin orgn Nat Inst of Statistics and Applied Economics (INSEA) Rabat 1978–81, conslt for estab Inst of Strategic Studies Al Alkhawayn Univ Ifrane 1994; World Trade Centres Assoc NY (WTCA): bd dir WTCA Hldgs Ltd 1994, bd dir and chm Ctee on Trade Policy and Facilitation 1994–96, rep Exec Secretariat ME and N Africa Econ Summit Casablanca 1994 and Amman 1995; bd dir: Royal Air Maroc 1982–93, Hospitality Hldg Co 1988–96, Moussafir Hotels Co 1988–96, Societe Africaine de Tourisme 1988–96, Full Service Trade Card Ltd 1995–99; memb Admin Cmmn Ribat Al Fath Assoc 1988–, memb Delhi Rotary Club 1997–98, pres Br-Moroccan Soc 1999–2009; Indira Gandhi Meml Award 1997–98; Freeman City of London 2006; Offr Order of Merit (Portugal) 1990, Knight Cdr Royal Order of Francis I (KCFO) 2003; *Publications* Slums and Squatter Settlements in Urban Areas of the Third World (1975), Global Review of Human Settlements (1976), Les Relations Etat-Entreprises Publiques (1981), Ambassadors and Envoys of the Kingdom of Morocco to the United Kingdom 1588–2000 (2001), Islam and Secularism (2004), The Other in the Making of National Identity: The Case of Britain and Morocco (2006), The First Diplomatic Contact Between the Kingdom of Morocco and the United Kingdom in the Year 1213: Its Genesis and Impact (2013), Introducing the Debate on Morocco's New Geopolitics (2013), The Position of the Moroccan Jewish Community within Anglo-Moroccan Diplomatic Relations from 1840–1886 (2015); also author of various articles; *Recreations* golf, swimming, travel, portrait drawing, art history; *Clubs* Dar Es Salam Golf (Rabat); *Style*— Ambassador Mohammed Belmahi, KCFO; ✉ 23H Nevern Square, London SW5 9PD (e-mail mbelmahi@hotmail.com)

BELMORE, 8 Earl of (I 1797); John Armar Lowry Corry; also Baron Belmore (I 1781) and Viscount Belmore (I 1789); s of 7 Earl of Belmore, JP, DL (d 1960), and Gloria Anthea Harker (d 2005); *b* 4 September 1951; *Educ* Lancing; *m* 1984, Lady Mary Jane Meade, 2 da of 6 Earl of Clanwilliam (d 1989); 2 s (John Armar Galbraith, Viscount Corry b 1985, Hon Montagu Gilford George b 1989), 1 da (Lady Martha Catherine b 27 May 1992); *Heir* s, Viscount Corry; *Career* farmer; memb Bd of Govrs and Guardians Nat Gallery of Ireland 1998–2003; *Recreations* art; *Clubs* Kildare St, Univ Club Dublin; *Style*— The Rt Hon the Earl of Belmore; ✉ The Garden House, Castle Coole, Enniskillen BT74 6JY

BELSHAW, Prof Deryke Gerald Rosten; s of Leonard Gerald Belshaw (d 1987), of Ash Vale, Hants, and Phyllis Guiver, *née* Rosten (d 2003); *b* 9 September 1932; *Educ* Hampton GS, Selwyn Coll Cambridge (MA), Hertford Coll Oxford (Dip Agric Econ); *m* 15 Aug 1959, Audrey Gladys, da of John Newell, MBE, VMH (d 1984), of Ringwood, Hants; 1 s (Jeremy b 1960), 2 da (Sarah b 1962, Anna b 1963); *Career* Nat Serv RA seconded to RWAFF Nigeria, gunner 1954, 2 Lt 1955, Lt 1956; res offr Sch of Agric Univ of Cambridge 1958–60, sr lectr then reader in agric economics Makerere Coll Univ of E Africa 1964–70 (lectr 1960–64); UEA: sr lectr then reader in agric economics 1970–85, dean 1981–84, prof of rural devpt 1985–97, prof emeritus 1997–; UK Govt economic advsr Govt of Kenya 1970–72, UNDP and FAO regnl devpt advsr Govt of Tanzania 1974–77 and 1980–82, FAO food strategy advsr Govt of Ethiopia (on secondment from Overseas Development Group Ltd UEA) 1986–89, World Bank UNDP visiting prof of economics Makerere Univ Uganda 1992–94, conslt UN Regnl Devpt Centre (Sri Lanka, Kenya, Zimbabwe, Malawi) 1993–99; dir Belshaw Consulting and Research Ltd 1999–2007, dir Christians Against Poverty in Tropical Africa and Asia Ltd (CAPITAA) 1999–; pres Agric Econ Soc 2001–04; memb: Advsy Bd Oxford Devpt Studies, Advsy Bd Concordis Int Cambridge 1999–; dean of devpt studies Oxford Centre for Mission Studies 1999–2005 (fell 1992–99), dir Inst for Devpt Res Oxford 2001–06; visiting scholar Wolfson Coll Oxford 1998–2000; conslt on biofuels and developing countries Advsy Bd Irish Aid 2007–08; awarded Jerusalem Tst research grant for post-disaster recovery projects in Ethiopia and Uganda 2005; *Books* Towards a Food and Nutrition Strategy for Ethiopia (1989), Regional Development Policy Analysis (1996), Faith in Development: The World Bank and the Church in Africa Partnership (2001), Renewing Development in Sub-Saharan Africa (2002), Development Economics and Social Jsutice (contrib, 2005); *Recreations* vinous evaluation; *Style*— Prof Deryke Belshaw; ✉ Oxford Centre for Development Research, 38 Arlington Drive, Old Marston, Oxford OX3 0ST

BELSHAW, Kenneth John Thomas; s of John Everton Belshaw (d 2002), and Lilian Elizabeth, *née* Stewart (d 2001); *b* 14 May 1952; *Educ* Orangefield Sch for Boys Belfast; *m* 24 Nov 1979, Iris Elizabeth, da of Sydney Miller McKeown (d 1998), of Stewartstown, Co Tyrone, NI; 3 da (Maeve Elizabeth b 1983, Barbara Ruth and Jennifer Mary (twins) b 1 Aug 1992), 1 s (Stephen John Doran b 1987); *Career* recruitment conslt; co-fndr and dir: Grafton Recruitment Ltd (Ireland's largest employment agency), Grafton Recruitment UK Ltd 1982–; visiting prof Dept of Mgmnt and Leadership Univ of Ulster Business Sch 2011–; hon consul of Hungary in NI 2012–; chm Player Services Bd Irish Rugby Football Union/Irish Rugby Players Assoc 2013–; Queen's Award for Enterprise 2002 and 2006, Gratias Agit Award (for significant contribution to promotion of the Czech Republic) Czech Govt 2006; hon fell Nat Recruitment Fedn of Ireland 2013; *Recreations* fine wines, reading; *Clubs* Kildare St and Univ (Dublin), Holywood Golf, Castlerock Golf (NI); *Style*— Kenneth Belshaw, Esq; ✉ Grafton Recruitment, 35–37 Queens Square, Belfast BT1 3FG (☎ 028 9024 2824, fax 028 9024 2897)

BELTRAMI, Joseph; s of Egidio Beltrami (d 1971), and Isabel, *née* Battison; *b* 15 May 1932; *Educ* St Aloysius Coll Glasgow, Univ of Glasgow (BL); *m* 18 Jan 1958, Brigid, da of Edward Fallon; 3 s (Edwin Joseph b 23 Sept 1962, Adrian Joseph Beltrami, QC b 8 Nov 1964, Jason Joseph b 23 Sept 1967); *Career* Intelligence Corps 1954–56: attached to Br Mil Delgn to Euro Def Community at Br Embassy Paris, Detachment Cdr Field security SW Dist Taunton; admitted slr 1956, ptnr Beltrami & Co (slr in cases of only two Royal pardons in Scotland last century: Maurice Swanson 1975, Patrick Meehan 1976), advocate; instructed in more than 350 murder trials; first slr-advocate to address Scottish Criminal Ct of Appeal; hon memb Scottish Law Soc 2009– (first memb to be appointed slr-advocate with High Ct appearance entitlement 1993); formerly: pres Bothwell Bowling Club, mangr and coach Bothwell AFC; *Books* The Defender (1980), A Celebration (contrib, 1984), Tales of the Suspected (1988), A Deadly Innocence (1989). A Scottish Childhood (contrib, 1998); *Style*— Joseph Beltrami, Esq; ✉ 12 Valance Tower, Regents Gate, Bothwell G71 (☎ 01698 817841)

BEN-DAVID, Zadok; s of Moshe Ben-David, of Israel, and Hana Ben-David; *b* 1949, Yemen; *Educ* Bezalel Acad of Art and Design Israel, Univ of Reading, St Martin's Sch of Art; *Career* asst to N H Azaz 1974, sculpture teacher St Martin's Sch of Art 1977–82, teacher Ravensbourne Coll of Art and Design 1982–85, visiting artist Stoke-on-Trent Museum 1987; sculptor; public cmmns: Runcorn Shopping City 1977, Tel-Hai Museum Israel 1983, Harlow Essex 1984, Villa Nova de Cerviera Portugal 1986, Forest of Dean Sculpture Project Glos 1988, Tel Aviv Promenade Israel 1989, Keren Karev Jerusalem 1990, ORS Building Tel Aviv 1990, Heaven and Earth (public sculpture) Tel Aviv 1995, sculpture for Beijing Olympics 2008; solo exhibitions incl: AIR Gallery London 1980, Woodlands Art Gallery London 1982, 121 Gallery Antwerp 1984, Benjamin Rhodes Gallery London 1985, 1987, 1990 and 1992, Art and Project Amsterdam 1986, Albert Totah Gallery NY 1987, Newcastle Poly Gallery 1988, Luba Bilu Gallery Melbourne 1989, Collins Gallery Glasgow 1990, Annandale Gallery Sydney 1991, Albrecht Gallery Munich Germany 1991, Galerie im Happacher Esslingen 1993, Ecke Galerie Augsburg, Castlefield Gallery Manchester 1994, Jason Rhodes Gallery London 1995, Evolution and Theory (Israel, Germany, Australia) 1997, (USA and Holland) 1998, (Germany and Singapore) 1999, (Germany) 2000 and (Portugal) 2003, Refusalon (San Francisco Art Inst USA) 2000, Leuchter & Peltzer Dusseldorf 2000, Magica Realta (Place Arte Conteporanea Torino) 2001 and (Galleria Civica d'arte Moderna e Conteporanea Aosta) 2003, Esplanade Culture Centre Singapore 2003, Magica Realta Innerscapes (Annandale Galleries Sydney) 2004, Innerscapes (Cass Sculpture Fndn London) 2004, 1918 Artspace Shanghai 2006, Janet Oh Gallery Seoul 2006, Guangdong Art Museum Guangzhou 2007, Oroom Fndn Sch Korea 2007, Blackfield (Hales Gallery London and Janet Oh Gallery Seoul) 2007, (Annandale Galleries Sydney) 2008, (Shoshana Wayne Gallery LA) 2009, (Verso Arte Contemporanea Turin Italy and Galerie Albrecht Berlin) 2010 and (Artclub 1563 Seoul Korea) 2011, Invisible Reality (Guangdong Art Museum China) 2007, (Annandale Galleries Sydney) 2008, (Galerie Albrecht Berlin and Shoshana Wayne Gallery LA) 2009 and (Verso Arte Contemporanea Turin) 2010, Four Seasons (Sotheby's) 2008, Human Nature (Tel Aviv Museum Israel) 2009, 1918 (Art Space Shanghai) 2010, The Story I Am About To Tell You (Magic Box Cerveira Portugal) 2011, solo show presented by Sotheby's (Singapore Botanic Gardens) 2012, Simple Line (Mysteski Arsenal Kiev Ukraine) 2012, The Other Side of Midnight (Shoshana Wayne Gallery LA and Annandale Galleries Sydney) 2013, gp exhibitions incl: Atlantis Gallery London 1983, 80 Years of Sculpture (Israel Museum Jerusalem) 1984, Who's Afraid of Red Yellow & Blue? (Arnolfini Gallery Bristol) 1985, From Two Worlds (Whitechapel Art Gallery) 1986, IV Int Biennale Portugal 1986, Ek'ymose Art Contemporain Bordeaux 1987, Fresh Paint (Israel Museum Jerusalem) 1987, Museum of Israeli Art Ramat Gan Israel 1987, Israeli Artists (Brooklyn Museum NY) 1988, Galerie Albrecht Munich (with Joel Fisher and Franz Bernhard) 1989, Gimmel Gallery Jerusalem 1990, Kunst Europa Germany 1991, Places and Mainstream (Museum Hara Tokyo) 1991, The New Metaphysics (Ivan Dougherty Gallery Sydney) 1992, Nat Museum of Contemporary Art Seoul 1992, A Collaboration of Music and Art (with Peter Gabriel, Land Mark Tower Yokahama Japan) 1993, Anti Patos (Israel Museum Jerusalem) 1993, Locus (Fisher Gallery Los Angeles) 1993, Public Art (Annadale Gallery Sydney Australia) 1994, VIII Bienal Portugal 1995, 100 Park Lane London 1996, IX International Bienal Portugual 1997, Fantasia (Herzliya Museum Israel) 1997, Eight by Eight (Chichester) 1997, BUPA House London 1998, MOMA Croatia 1998, British Figurative Art Part 2 – Sculpture (Flowers East Gallery London) 1998, Israeli Sculpture 1948–1998 (Israel) 1998, The Shape of the Century (Salisbury Cathedral and Canary Wharf London) 1999, ANIMAL (Musee Bourdelle Paris) 1999, BRONZE (Holland Park London) 2000, Looking ahead – vision of Israel (ICA San Jose) 2000, L'Homme qui Marche (Palais Royal Paris) 2000, Narcisse Blesse (Passage de Retz Paris) 2000, Den Haag Sculpture 2000 and 2001, Tempo (Kunst im Schloss Untergroningen) 2001, Galerie en Lijstenmakerij The Hague 2001, The Train Ride (video installation, Herzliya Museum of Art Israel) 2001 and (Ambrosino Gallery Miamai) 2002, Blue (Place arte Conteporanea Cavgnolo) 2002, Sculptura Internazionale a la Mandria (Torino) 2002, Salto Naturale (Kunst im Schloss Untergroningen) 2002, Paper art Bienale (Leopold-Hoesch Museum Duren) 2002, Thinking Big (Peggy Guggenheim collection Venice) 2002, About Face (Croydon Clock Tower) 2002, Landscape (Pump Gallery Battersea) 2003, Science Fiction (Singapore Museum of Art) 2003, Telltale (Ewha Art Centre Seoul) 2005, Fatamorgana (Haifa Museum of Contemporary Art) 2006, Sequences & Repetition (Brunel Arts Centre Brunel Univ and Jerwood Space London) 2007, Rummage: Sculptors' Drawings (Winchester Gallery Univ of Southampton) 2007, Animal (Kunst im Schloss Untergroningen) 2007, Sculptuur Biennale The Hague 2007, XIV Biennal de Cerveira (Municipal Museum Caminha) 2007, Animal (Kunst im Schloss Germany) 2007, Sculptuur Biennale (Den Haag) 2007, Sequences & Repetition (Jerwood Space London) 2007, Blackfield (XIV Biennal de Cerveira Municipal Museum Caminha Portugal) 2007, Animal and Nature (Chateau des Bousval Belgium) 2007, Beyond Limits (Sotheby's Chatsworth) 2008, Wonder (Singapore Biennale) 2008, Of The Outer World (I-Myu Projects London) 2008, Dreams (Passage de Retz Paris) 2008, OK Bienale Cuvee (Linz Austria) 2009, Vivid Fantasy KiSS (Kunst in Schloss Untergreningen Germany) 2009, IV Int Biennal Vila nova de Cerveira Portugal 2009, Animals Contemporary Vision (Nave Gallery Parco Culturale Le Serre Turin) 2009, Present and experience of the Past (Int Sculpture in Racconigi Turin) 2010, Living in Evolution (Busan Biennale S Korea) 2010, Beyond Limits (Sotheby's at Chatsworth Derbys) 2010; various collections in: UK, Europe, Israel, USA, Aust; jointly represented Israel Venice Biennale 1988 (with Moti Mizrachi), Nat Museum of the Republic of Kazakhstan Astana 2014, Art Gallery of Uzbekistan Tashkent 2015, Israel Museum Jerusalem 2015; commissioned to make sculpture for Beijing Olympic Games 2008; Tel Aviv Museum Prize for Sculpture 2005, Grande Prémio Biennial Internacional de Arte de Vila Nova de Cerveira Portugal 2007; *Publications* features in and is subject of numerous publications; *Style*— Zadok Ben-David, Esq; ✉ 11 Blackburn Road, London NW6 1RZ (☎ 020 7328 6857, website www.zadokbendavid.com)

BENBOW, Michael; s of Arthur Benbow, of Cowbridge, Mid Glamorgan, and Sylvia, *née* Bailey; *b* 22 February 1957; *Educ* Trinity Secdy Modern Sch Bradford-on-Avon, Trowbridge Tech Coll, Salisbury Coll of Art, Cardiff Coll of Art (Dip Industrial Design Engrg); *m* 19 Sept 1981, Christine, da of Peter Collier; 1 da (Annette b 14 Oct 1994); *Career* design consultant; staff designer Gnome Photographic Products Ltd 1978–80, design mangr Bissell Appliances Ltd 1980–88, sr designer and business devpt mangr Ogle Design Ltd 1988–90, business devpt mangr Grey Matter Design Consultants plc 1990, design conslt 1990–; to date cmmnd to design attractive products for high volume manufacture; injection moulded plastics expertise; projects incl electronic consumer products, nursery equipment and housewares; first prize industrial design Eisteddfod Festival 1978; SIAD: working pty leader Diploma Members' Gp 1983, memb Product Gp 1986–90; corp MCSD 1985, CSD membership assessor (product) 1996–2000; appointed LEA govr Staples Rd Jr Sch 1999–2007; press offr Loughton Residents Assoc 2002; govr Roding Valley HS 2006–11; *Recreations* cycling, hill walking, lawn tennis, Loughton improvement; *Clubs* Woodford Wells, Election Agent Independent Loughton Residents Assoc; *Style*— Michael Benbow, Esq; ✉ 28 Brook Road, Loughton, Essex IG10 1BP

BENDER, Sir Brian Geoffrey; KCB (2003, CB 1998); s of Arnold Eric Bender, of Leatherhead, Surrey, and Deborah, *née* Swift; *b* 25 February 1949; *Educ* Greenford GS, Imperial Coll London (BSc, PhD); *m* 1974, Penelope Gay, *née* Clark; 1 da (Laura Ann b 1979), 1 s (Russell Paul b 1983); *Career* DTI: admin trainee 1973–77, private sec to Sec of State for Trade (The Rt Hon Edmund Dell) 1976–77, first sec (Trade Policy) Office of UK Perm Rep to the EC 1977–82, princ Minerals and Metals Div 1982–84, cnsllr (Indust and Energy) Office of UK Perm Rep to the EC 1985–89, asst sec Mgmnt Servs and Manpower Div 1989–90, under sec and dep head of European Secretariat Cabinet Office 1990–93, head of Regnl Devpt Div DTI 1993–94, dep sec and head Euro Secretariat Cabinet Office 1994–98, head of public service delivery Cabinet Office 1998–99, perm sec: Cabinet Office 1999–2000, MAFF 2000–01, DEFRA 2001–05, DTI 2005–07, Dept for Business, Enterprise and Regulatory Reform 2007–09, ret; chm London Metal Exchange 2010–, dir Financial Reporting Cncl 2014–, dir Pool Reinsurance Co 2014–; chm Water UK 2015–; *Style*— Sir Brian Bender, KCB

BENDRE, Rajiv Ratnakar; OBE (2004); s of Ratnakar Bendre, of Poona, India, and Nalini Bendre (d 1995); *b* 9 November 1955, Bombay, India; *Educ* Cathedral Sch Bombay, Stowe, Keble Coll Oxford; *m* 1984, Katherine, *née* Staniforth; 2 da (Rebecca b 1988, Radhika b 1990); *Career* Price Waterhouse 1979–83, First Chicago 1984–85; Br Cncl: London 1985, Baghdad 1986–88, Amman 1989–91, Nigeria 1991–2000, Sierra Leone 2000–05, Baghdad

2005–06, Zimbabwe 2006–10, New Zealand 2010–; annual public lecture series in Sierra Leone; tstee Prince's Sch of Traditional Arts London; memb ICAEW; *Books* Den Ol Bod Ose: Creole Architecture in Sierra Leone; *Recreations* dogs, reading; *Clubs* Royal Over-Seas League; *Style—* Rajiv Bendre, Esq, OBE; ✉ 337 Avonhead, Christchurch 8042, New Zealand

BENJAMIN, Baroness (Life Peer UK 2010), of Beckenham in the County of Kent; Floella Karen Yunies Benjamin; OBE (2001), DL (Gtr London 2008); *b* 23 September 1949, Pointe-à-Pierre, Trinidad; *Career* actress, television presenter and businesswoman; chief exec Floella Benjamin Prodns 1987–2012; former chm BAFTA Television, vice-pres Royal Cwlth Soc, vice-pres RTS; chllr Univ of Exeter 2006–16; Educn Award RTS 2003, Special Lifetime Award BAFTA 2004, J M Barrie Award 2012; Hon DLitt Univ of Exeter 2005; *Television* as presenter incl: Playschool (BBC), What's Inside (BBC), Fast Forward (BBC), Playaway (BBC), Switch on to English (BBC), How Dare You, About Books, Lay on Five (BBC), Flo's Frolics (BBC), Daytime Live (BBC), A Houseful of Plants (Channel 4), Tree House (Channel 4), Playabout (Sky), Hullaballoo (Channel 4), Jamboree (ITV), Mamma Mirabelle's Home Movies (CBeebies); as actress incl: Within These Walls, Crown Court, Doctor on the Go, Send in the Girls, Anansi, Angels, Mixed Blessings, Kids, Waterloo Sunset, The Ladies, Hole in Babylon, The Gentle Touch, Strangers, Coming to England, Line of Beauty, Sarah Jane Adventures, Chuggington (BBC), Bedtime Stories (CBeebies); *Style—* The Baroness Benjamin, OBE, DL; ✉ c/o Benjamin-Taylor Associates, 73 Palace Road, London SW2 3LB; House of Lords, London SW1A 0PW

BENJAMIN, George; CBE (2010); s of William Benjamin, and Susan, *née* Bendon; *b* 31 January 1960; *Educ* Westminster, Paris Conservatoire, King's Coll Cambridge; *Career* composer, conductor, pianist; prof of composition Royal Coll of Music 1985–2001, Henry Purcell prof of musical composition KCL 2002–; princ works incl: Ringed by the Flat Horizon 1980, A Mind of Winter for soprano and orch 1981, At First Light (cmmnd by London Sinfonietta) 1982, Antara for computerised keyboards and ensemble (cmmnd for 10 anniversary of Pompidou Centre Paris) 1987, Upon Silence for mezzo-soprano and 5 viols (written for Fretwork) 1990, Sudden Time (written for London Philharmonic Orch) 1989–93, Three Inventions for Chamber Orch (cmmnd for 75 Salzburg Festival) 1995, Sometime Voices for baritone, chorus and orch (cmmnd for the opening of the Bridgewater Hall Manchester) 1996, Viola Viola (cmmnd by Tokyo Opera City) 1997, Palimpsests for orch (cmmnd by LSO) 2002, Shadowlines for piano 2001, Dance Figures for orch (premièred by Chicago Symphony Orch) 2004, Into the Little Hill (Paris Opera) 2006, Duet for Piano and orchestra (cmmnd by Roche) 2008, Written on Skin (Aix-en-Provence Festival) 2012, Dream of the Song (premièred by the Concertgebouw Orchestra) 2015; conductor of major int orchs and ensembles incl: Concertgebouw, Berlin Philharmonic, Cleveland, LSO, Ensemble Modern, London Sinfonietta; ROH debut 2013; artistic dir Meltdown Festival South Bank 1993; dir Tanglewood Festival of Contemporary Music 2000; artistic conslt Sounding the Century (BBC Radio 3) 1996–99; By George (LSO, Barbican) 2002–03; retrospectives: Brussels 2003, Berlin 2004–05, Strasbourg 2005, Madrid 2005, Paris 2006, Lucerne 2008, San Francisco 2010, Frankfurt 2011, London (Olympic Festival) 2012, Milan/Turin 2013, Toronto 2015, New York 2015; hon fell King's Coll Cambridge 2014; awards incl: Lili Boulanger Award (Boston) 1985, Grand Prix du Disque (Paris) 1987, Gramophone Contemporary Music Award 1990 and 2014, Edison Award (Amsterdam) 1998, Schönberg Prize Berlin 2002, RPS Awards 2003, 2004, 2009 and 2014, World Premiere of the Year Opera Award 2013, Grand Prix of French Critics 2013, Composer of the Year Musical America 2014, Musician of the Year UK Critics Circle 2015, Prince Pierre Composition Prize Monaco 2015; FRCM 1994, Hon RAM 2003, Hon GSM 2009, hon memb RPS 2011; Commandeur de l'Ordre des Arts et des Lettres (France) 2015 (Chevalier 1996), memb Bavarian Acad of Arts 2000; *Style—* George Benjamin, Esq, CBE; ✉ c/o Faber Music, Bloomsbury House, 74–77 Great Russell Street, London WC1B 3DA (☎ 020 7908 5310, fax 020 7908 5339)

BENJAMIN, John Circus; s of Bernard Benjamin, and Doris, *née* Mindel; *b* 15 January 1955; *Educ* John Lyon Sch Middx; *m* 27 June 1986, Patricia Adele Ruane, da of Sqdn Ldr Michael Joseph Francis Burgess, of Hale, Cheshire; *Career* ind jewellery conslt; broadcaster, author and lectr on history of jewellery; formerly int dir of Jewellery Phillips Auctioneers 1990–99; expert Antiques Roadshow (BBC) 1991–; admitted memb Worshipful Co of Goldsmiths 2000, fndr liveryman Worshipful Co of Arts Scholars 2014; memb Nat Assoc of Goldsmiths, assoc memb Art Workers' Guild 2015; FGA 1975, DGA 1976, fell Inst of Registered Valuers (FIRV); *Books* Starting to Collect Antique Jewellery, The Jewellery and Silver of H G Murphy (co-author); *Style—* John Benjamin, Esq; ✉ PO Box 7, Aylesbury, Buckinghamshire HP22 5WB (☎ 01296 615522, e-mail johncbenjamin@btopenworld.com, website www.johnbenjamin.co.uk)

BENJAMIN, HE Jon; *b* 19 January 1963, London; *Educ* Univ of Surrey (BSc); *m* 25 April 2014, Carolina Vasquez; 1 s (Louis b 17 Aug 2012); *Career* diplomat; policy offr for Br aid prog to Pakistan FCO 1986, policy offr Burma and Laos SE Asian Dept FCO 1986–87, second sec Political Section Jakarta 1988–91, head of section Central Asia and Caucasus FCO 1992–93, COS to Min responsible for EU and Latin America FCO 1993–95, head Political and Public Affrs Section Ankara 1996–99, head Zimbabwe Emergency Unit FCO 2000, dep head Drugs and Int Crime Dept FCO 2000–02, head Human Rights Policy Dept FCO 2002–05, counter terrorism counsellor to the Ambass Washington 2005, dep Br consul gen/dep head of mission then acting consul gen NY 2005–08, secondment as global risk advsr American Int Gp NY 2008, secondment as advsr to CEO Eurasia Gp NY 2009, ambass to Chile 2009–14, Br high cmmr to Ghana and non-resident ambass to Togo, Benin and Burkina Faso 2014–; ed FCO Annual Human Rights Report 2002–04; dir Alexander Selkirk Fndn; *Style—* Mr Jon Benjamin; ✉ c/o FCO, King Charles Street, London SW1A 2AH (e-mail jon.benjamin@fco.gov.uk)

BENJAMIN, Leanne; OBE (2005); *b* 13 July 1964, Rockhampton, Australia; *Educ* Royal Ballet Upper Sch (Adeline Genée Gold Medal, Prix de Lausanne); *m* 30 June 2001, Tobias Round; 1 s (Thomas Evan b 2003); *Career* ballet dancer; Sadler's Wells Royal Ballet: joined 1983, soloist 1985–87, princ 1987–88; princ dancerLondon Festival Ballet 1988–90, Deutsche Oper Ballet Berlin 1990–92, princ Royal Ballet 1993– (first soloist 1992–93); *Roles* princ roles with Birmingham Royal Ballet: Swan Lake, Giselle, La Fille mal gardée, The Sleeping Beauty, Balanchine's Tchaikovsky Pas de deux, Kenneth MacMillan's Las Hermanas, Quartet, Concerto and Elite Syncopations, Hans Van Manen's Five Tangos, cr role of Greta in Metamorphosis, cr role of Gerda in The Snow Queen, Flowers of the Forest; London Festival Ballet: Juliet and Livia in Romeo and Juliet, lead in The Nutcracker, Olga in Onegin, Sphinx, Third Movement in Symphony in C, Swanhilda in Coppélia, lead girl in Études, cr role in Symphony in Three Movements, Odette/Odile in Swan Lake; Deutsche Oper Ballet incl: A Folktale, Apollo, First and Fourth Movement Symphony in C, Carmen, Giselle, Who Cares?, Twilight, Paquita, pas de trois, Different Drummer, Cinderella, Brunhilda in The Ring; Royal Ballet incl: Odette/Odile in Swan Lake (debut) 1993, title role in Romeo and Juliet, Manon, Anastasia, Irina in Winter Dreams, Girl in The Invitation, First Sister in My Brothers, My Sisters, Danses Concertantes, La Fin du Jour, Requiem, Triad, Herman Schmerman, Caught Dance, Sugar Plum Fairy in The Nutcracker, Thaïs pas de deux, Voices of Spring, Rhapsody, title role in Cinderella, Ballet Imperial, Marie in Different Drummer, Macmillan's Concerto, Swanhilda in Coppélia, title role in The Firebird, title role in Dance Variations, Song of the Earth, The Leaves are Fading, Beyond Bach, Polyphonia, Spectre de la Rose, Girl in Blue in Les Biches, Stravinsky Violin Concerto, Jewels, Dances at a Gathering, L'Invitation au voyage, Rushes, Voluntaries, Mr Worldy Wise, Amores, Two Part Invention, When We Stop Talking 1998, Purple Girl in Masquerade 1999, Qualia 2003, Spring Rites 2004, Tanglewood 2005, Despite 2006, Queen of the Earth in Homage to The Queen 2006, DGV: Danse à grande vitesse 2006, The Girl in Children of Adam 2007, cr role in Sensorium, cr role in Infra, cr role in Limen; guest appearances: Peter Wright's Mirrors Walkers pas de deux in honour of Sir Frederick Ashton Royal Opera House 1988, Madrid 1989, Le Corsaire pas de deux with Peter Schaufuss Saville 1990, Swan Lake (Dresden Ballet) 1991, Kirov Theatre 1991, Spain 1991; gala appearances: World Festival Tokyo 1985, pas de deux from La Fille mal gardée with Australian Ballet Bicentennial celebrations 1988, CRUSAID charity gala 1991, Tchaikovsky Gala Royal Opera House 1994; *Television* appearances incl: The Snow Queen (Birmingham Royal Ballet), BBC Masterclass, BBC documentary about David Bintley and making of Metamorphosis, Swan Lake (London Festival Ballet); with Royal Ballet: The Judas Tree, Symphony in C, The Nutcracker, The Dream, Don Quixote, Gloria 1999, Coppélia 2000, The Firebird 2001, Voices of Spring 2004; *Style—* Ms Leanne Benjamin, OBE; ✉ c/o The Royal Ballet, Royal Opera House, Covent Garden, London WC2E 9DD

BENN, Hilary James Wedgwood; PC (2003), MP; s of Rt Hon Tony Benn (disclaimed Viscountcy of Stansgate for life 1963); *b* 26 November 1953; *Educ* Holland Park Sch, Univ of Sussex; *m* 1, Rosalind Retey (d 1979); m 2, Sally Clark; 3 s, 1 da; *Career* Labour memb Ealing Cncl 1979–99, chair of educn and dep leader of Ealing Cncl 1986–90; chm Acton Labour Party, former head of Policy and Communications MSF; special advsr to sec of state for Educn and Employment 1997–99; MP (Lab) Leeds Central 1999–; Parly under-sec of state: Dept for Int Devpt 2001–02, Home Office 2002–03; min of state Dept for Int Devpt June-Oct 2003, sec of state Int Devpt 2003–07, sec of state for environment, food and rural affrs 2007–11, shadow ldr of the House of Commons 2010–11, shadow sec of state for communities and local govt 2011–15, shadow sec of state for foreign and Cwlth affrs 2015–16; *Style—* The Rt Hon Hilary Benn, Esq, MP; ✉ House of Commons, London SW1A 0AA

BENN, Timothy John; s of Sir John Andrews Benn, 3 Bt (d 1984), and Hon Ursula Lady Benn, *née* Hankey (d 2006); *b* 27 October 1936; *Educ* Harrow, Clare Coll Cambridge (MA), Princeton, Harvard Business Sch USA; *m* 1982, Christina Grace Townsend; *Career* served HM Forces 2 Lt Scots Gds 1956–57; Benn Brothers Ltd: memb Bd 1961–82, md 1972–82, dep chm 1976–81; chm Benn Brothers plc 1981–82; Ernest Benn: memb Bd 1967–82, md 1973–82, chm and md 1974–82; chm: What-A-Mess Ltd 1978–82, Timothy Benn Publishing 1983–97, Bouverie Publishing Co 1983–97, Buckley Press 1984–97, Henry Greenwood and Co 1987–97, Dalesman Publishing Co 1989–2004, Countryman Publishing Co 2000–04, Huveaux plc 2001–06; prop Creel Press 1990–2008; chm: Benn Publishing Ltd 2008–, Benn Brothers Ltd 2008–;memb Bd Country Publications Ltd 2016–; memb Cncl Advtg Assoc 1962, chm Periodocal Publishing Assoc 1970–72, chm Nat Advtg Benevolent Soc 1970–71, memb Special Projects Ctee Crafts Cncl 1979–82; pres Tonbridge Civic Soc 1982–87; chm Kennel Appeal Bd Battersea Cats and Dogs Home 2010–14; pres Thirty Club of London 1983–84; Liveryman Worshipful Co of Stationers & Newspaper Makers; FCIM; *Books* The (Almost) Compleat Angler (1985); *Recreations* gardening, toymaking, flyfishing, opera, skiing; *Style—* Timothy Benn, Esq; ✉ Chase Cottage, Chase Lane, Haslemere, Surrey GU27 3AG

BENN, Rt Rev Wallace Parke; *see:* Lewes, Bishop of

BENNER, Mike; s of Peter Benner, of Notts, and Anita, *née* James; *b* 6 July 1966, Rotherham, S Yorks; *Educ* The McAlley Sch Doncaster, Univ of Middlesex (BA); *m* 6 June 1997, Helen Lomax; 1 da (Victoria), 3 s (Christian, Elliot, Rafael); *Career* CAMRA: press mangr 1995–97, head of campaigns and communications 1997–2004, chief exec 2004–; sr press offr Ernst & Young 1997; chm Campaign for Sustainable Harlington; memb ACEVO 2004; *Recreations* guitar, running, pubs; *Style—* Mike Benner, Esq; ✉ Campaign for Real Ale Headquarters, 230 Hatfield Road, St Albans AL1 4LW (☎ 01727 798441, e-mail mike.benner@camra.org.uk)

BENNET, George Charters; s of George Charters Bennet (d 1968), and Euphemia, *née* Igoe; *b* 8 August 1946; *Educ* Holy Cross Acad, Univ of Edinburgh Med Sch (BSc, MB ChB); *m* 17 June 1978, (Kathryn) Louise, da of Dr Bernard Gwillam Spilbury; 3 s (George b 1979, Simon b 1982, Matthew b 1987); *Career* former med appts London, Oxford, Southampton and Toronto; currently: conslt surgn Royal Hosp for Sick Children Glasgow, hon clinical sr lectr Univ of Glasgow, hon conslt to the Army Children's Orthopaedic Surgery and Trauma, memb Bd Medical and Dental Defence Union of Scotland; past pres Br Soc for Children's Orthopaedic Surgery; FRCS, FBOA; *Books* Paediatric Hip Disorders (1987); chapters and research papers on children's orthopaedic surgery; *Recreations* game fishing, golf; *Style—* George C Bennet, Esq; ✉ Tamarack House, Moor Road, Strathblane, Stirlingshire G63 9HA (☎ 01360 771249, e-mail georgecbennet@aol.com); Royal Hospital For Sick Children, Yorkhill, Glasgow G3 8SJ (☎ and fax 0141 201 0275)

BENNETT, Alan; *b* 9 May 1934; *Educ* Leeds Modern Sch, Exeter Coll Oxford (MA); *Career* dramatist and actor; tstee Nat Gallery 1993–98; Hon DLitt Univ of Leeds 1990; hon fell Exeter Coll Oxford 1987; hon fell Royal Acad; Freeman City of Leeds 2006; *Theatre* incl: Beyond the Fringe (Royal Lyceum Edinburgh 1960, Fortune London 1961, NYC 1962); Forty Years On (Apollo) 1968, Getting On (Queen's) 1971, Habeas Corpus (Lyric) 1973, The Old Country (Queen's) 1977, Enjoy (Vaudeville) 1980, Kafka's Dick (Royal Court) 1986, Single Spies (NT, double bill of A Question of Attribution (BPG TV & Radio Writer's Award 1992)), An Englishman Abroad (also dir, NT) 1988, Wind in the Willows (adaptation, RNT) 1990, The Madness of George III (RNT) 1991–93, The Lady in the Van 1999, The History Boys (RNT) 2004, The Habit of Art (RNT) 2009, People (RNT) 2012; *Television* incl: On the Margin (series) 1966, A Day Out 1972, Sunset Across the Bay 1975, A Little Outing, A Visit from Miss Prothero 1977, Doris and Doreen 1978, The Old Crowd 1978, Me! I'm Afraid of Virginia Woolf 1978, All Day on the Sands 1979, Afternoon Off 1979, One Fine Day 1979, Intensive Care, Say Something Happened, Our Winnie, Marks, A Woman of No Importance, Rolling Home, An Englishman Abroad 1983, The Insurance Man 1986, Talking Heads (series) 1988 (Hawthornden Prize), 102 Boulevard Haussmann 1991, A Question of Attribution 1992, Talking Heads II 1998; TV documentaries: Dinner at Noon 1988, Portrait or Bust 1994, The Abbey 1995, Heavenly Stories 1997, Telling Tales 2000; *Films* A Private Function 1984, Prick Up Your Ears 1987, The Madness of King George (Evening Standard Award for Best Screenplay) 1995, The History Boys 2006; *Books* Beyond the Fringe (with Peter Cook, Jonathan Miller and Dudley Moore, 1962), Forty Years On (1969), Getting On (1972), Habeas Corpus (1973), The Old Country (1978), Enjoy (1980), Office Suite (1981), Objects of Affection (1982), A Private Function (1984), The Writer in Disguise (1985), Prick Up Your Ears (screenplay, 1987), Two Kafka Plays (1987), Talking Heads (1988, Hawthornden Prize), Single Spies (1989), The Lady in the Van (1990), The Wind in the Willows (adaptation, 1991), The Madness of George III (1991), Writing Home (1994, Bowater Book of the Year British Book Awards 1995), The Clothes They Stood Up In (1998), The Complete Talking Heads (1998), Father! Father! Burning Bright (2000), Telling Tales (2000), The Laying on of Hands (2001), The History Boys (2004), Untold Stories (2005), The Uncommon Reader (2007), Smut (2011); *Style—* Alan Bennett, Esq; ✉ c/o United Agents Ltd, 12–26 Lexington Street, London W1F 0LE (☎ 020 3214 0800, fax 020 3214 0801, website www.unitedagents.co.uk)

BENNETT, Andrew John; CMG (1998); s of Leonard Charles Bennett (d 1994), and Edna Mary, *née* Harding (d 1984); *b* 25 April 1942, Henley-on-Thames, Oxon; *Educ* St Edward's Sch Oxford, UCNW Bangor (BSc), Univ of W Indies Trinidad (Dip in Tropical

Agriculture (DTA)), Univ of Reading (MSc), Univ of Cranfield (DSc); *m* 1996, Yin Yin May , *née* Yonemo; 1 da; *Career* Lt 6/7 Bn Royal Welch Fus TA 1961–66; VSO Kenya 1965–66, agric res offr Govt of St Vincent W Indies 1967–69, maize agronomist Govt Republic of Malawi 1971–74, chief research offr (agric) Regnl Miny of Agric Southern Sudan 1976–80; DfID (formerly ODA): agric advsr 1980–83, nat resources advsr SE Asia Devpt Div Bangkok 1983–85, head Br Devpt Div in the Pacific Fiji 1985–87, chief nat research advsr 1987–2002, strategic dir Physical and Natural Environment 1998–99, dir Rural Livelihoods and Environment 1999–2002; dir Syngenta Fndn for Sustainable Agric 2002–16, non-exec dir CABI 2009–15; memb: Cncl RASE 1988–2004, Cncl ODI 2003–08, Tropical Agric Assoc (pres 2003–); dir Doyle Fndn 2002–; chair of tstees: Centre of Int Forestry Research 2002–10, SciDev.net 2007–14, GCP/CGIAR 2012–16, tstee African Fellowship tst 2015–; dir Eynesbury Estates Ltd 1989–2008; tstee: Int Baccelaureate Orgn (UK) 2009–, Int Network for Bamboo and Rattan 2011– (chair 2015–), Crop Innovations 2012–; FRSA 1998; *Recreations* walking, gardening; *Style*— Andrew Bennett, Esq, CMG; ✉ Chroyle, Gloucester Road, Bath BA1 8BH (☎ 01225 851489, e-mail andrewj.bennett@btinternet.com)

BENNETT, Dr Anna Teresa Natalie; da of Sydney Bennett (d 1974), and Ardene Hilton, of Devon; *b* 20 May 1959; *Educ* Lycée Français de Londres, Inst of Archaeology Univ of London (BSc), Inst of Archaeology UCL (PhD, Br Acad scholar); *Children* 2 s (Maximilian b 1996, Theodore b 1998); *Career* asst conservator English Heritage London 1978–79, antiquities conservator J Paul Getty Museum Los Angeles 1982–84, post-doctoral res fell Univ of London 1988–89, commercial art conservation and analytical practice at Univ of London 1989–; project admin for conservation of Uppark contents on behalf of Nat Tst; conservation advsr Apulum Project in Romania, organiser of seminars on disaster mgmnt in the field of cultural heritage, author of numerous papers and lectrs on archaeology and conservation (incl The Sevso Treasure 1994); dir Centre for the scientific investigation of works of art Univ of London; television presenter BBC2 series on architectural history 2001–03; provider of conservation and analytical services to numerous musuems and cultural institutions throughout the world as well as for commercial auction houses, dealers in antiquities and collectors incl: Barbier Mueller Museum Geneva, Br Museum, Denver Museum, Dar al-Athar al-Islamiyyah Museum Kuwait, Nat Tst, English Heritage, Sotheby's, Christie's, Bonhams, corporate clients and private collectors; frequent expert witness in legal claims in Br High Courts and the US Federal Court; memb Vetting Ctee Antiquities Masterpiece Art Fair London; hon fell Univ of London 1989–; memb: Int Inst for Conservation of Works of Art (IIC), Int Cncl of Museums (ICOM); FRS 2001; *Publications* The Environmental Management of a Collection (2002), Fonte á la Cire Perdu (2006), Bulletin de l'Ecole Française d'Extrême-Orient (contrib, 2006), Archaeology in Southeast Asia (contrib, 2008), Trading Gold in Early Asia (2010), Gold in Early Southeast Asia (2010), The Importance of Iron – Its Development and Complexity in the Southeast Asian Iron Age (contrib, 2013), The High Tin Bronzes of Thailand (contrib, 2013); *Style*— Dr Anna Bennett; ✉ Conservation and Technical Services Ltd, PO Box 26157, London SW8 1FT (☎ 00 32 479 658 110, e-mail atnbennett@analyzeark.com, website www.analyzeart.com)

BENNETT, Clive Ronald Reath; CBE (2007); s of Ron Bennett, of Mayals, Swansea, and Betty Bennett; *b* 20 December 1947; *Educ* Hatfield Poly (BSc(Eng)); *m* 1970, Pauline, *née* Weeks; 2 da (Rochelle Clair (Mrs Elwood) b 1 Aug 1973, Leah Colette (Mrs Page) b 13 Dec 1976); *Career* held various sr exec positions: Rank Xerox, Polycell Products, Sara Lee Household & Personal Care; gp ops and business excellence dir Norton Healthcare 1995–2000, chief exec Driver and Vehicle Licensing Agency 2000–; CEng; MILT, MIEE, MInstD; *Style*— Clive Bennett, Esq, CBE; ✉ Driver and Vehicle Licensing Agency, Longview Road, Morriston, Swansea SA6 7JL (☎ 01792 782363, fax 01792 783003)

BENNETT, David Anthony; s of late Albert Henry Bennett, of Solihull, W Midlands, and Doris May Bennett (d 2007); *b* 4 October 1948; *Educ* Harold Malley GS Solihull, Univ of Portsmouth, Johns Hopkins Univ, Sch of Advanced Int Studies (scholar, BSc Econ, Dip Int Affrs); *m* Douska Krish; 1 s (Julius Oliver b 20 July 2002), 1 da (Freya Rose b 7 Aug 2005); *Career* stagiaire and admin Euro Cmmn 1973–74, Econ Planning Div Br Gas 1976–84, dir public affairs Eurofi 1984–87, md Powerhouse Europe 1987–92, chm and md Beaumark Ltd 1993–2001, dir Citigate Public Affairs 2001–04, head City of London Office to EU Instns 2004–06, chief exec Assoc of Private Client Investment Managers and Stockbrokers (APCIMS) 2007–10, conslt and memb Advsy Bd Convention of Ind Financial Advsrs Geneva; princ DB Assocs 1984–; fndr and dep chm Europe Analytica Ltd 1999–2014, chm Nat Assoc of Mutual Guarantee Socs 1993–2002; dir: Euro Assoc of Mutual Guarantee Schemes 1997–2002, Assoc of Professional Political Consultants 1997–2001; conslt speaker for Euro Cmmn, alternate memb Econ and Social Ctee of Euro Communities 1982–84 (expert 1990–91); sec Labour Econ Fin and Taxation Assoc (LEFTA) 1979–81; Parly candidate (SDP/Alliance) 1983 and 1987, Euro Parly candidate 1984, chm Lib Democrats Euro Gp 1991–97; MCIPR; *Books* The European Economy in 1975 (1975); *Recreations* tennis, skiing, walking, travel, theatre; *Style*— David Bennett, Esq; ✉ 20 Regent's Bridge Gardens, London SW8 1JR (☎ 020 7735 0241, e-mail david.awbennett@btopenworld.com)

BENNETT, David Jonathan; s of Peter Bennett, and Brenda Bennett; *b* 26 March 1962; *Educ* KCS Wimbledon, Queens' Coll Cambridge; *m* Susan Elizabeth, da of George Moss; 2 s (Sam b 17 Oct 1994, Rory b 23 Sept 1996); *Career* fin dir Cheltenham & Gloucester plc 1995–96, dir of risk mgmnt Nat Bank of NZ 1996–98, chief exec Countrywide Bank 1998; Alliance & Leicester plc: gp treas 1999–2000, gp exec dir 2000–01, gp fin dir 2001–07, gp chief exec 2007–08; exec dir Abbey 2008–09; non-exec dir: easyJet 2005–, Paypal Europe, Bank of Ireland UK plc; chm Homeserve Membership Ltd; memb: Assoc of Corp Treasurers, Guild of Int Bankers; *Recreations* watching Gloucester RFC, hiking; *Style*— David Bennett, Esq

BENNETT, Dr David William; s of William Edwin Bennett, of Halesowen, W Midlands, and Irene Joan, *née* Davis; *b* 3 August 1955, Wolverhampton, Staffs; *Educ* Halesowen GS, Univ of Birmingham (BSc, SWJ Smith Prize), Trinity Coll Oxford (DPhil), London Business Sch (Cert in Corporate Finance); *Career* mangr Shell Research Ltd 1979–82, mangr Shell Int Petroleum Co 1982–86, dir McKinsey & Co Inc 1986–2004 (latterly sr ptnr), head PM's Policy Directorate and PM's Strategy Unit 2005–07, chm The 10 Partnership Ltd 2007–11; chief exec Monitor Ind Regulator NHS Fndn Tsts 2010–15 (chm Monitor 2011–14); non-exec dir GHK Hldgs Ltd 2008–12, chair Viapath LLP 2016–; contrib research papers to Nuclear Physics 1977–1980; visiting prof Institute of Global Health Innovation Imperial Coll London 2016–; FRSA; *Recreations* motor sports, cycling, squash; *Style*— Dr David Bennett; ✉ e-mail david@bennetts-online.net

BENNETT, His Hon Judge Dudley Paul; s of late Patrick James Bennett, of Bognor Regis, W Sussex, and Mary, *née* Edmondson; *b* 4 August 1948; *Educ* Bradfield Coll, Univ of London (LLB); *Children* 2 da (Olivia Mary b 4 Feb 1988, Emma-Jayne b 5 Oct 1989); *Career* called to the Bar Inner Temple 1972; recorder of the Crown Court 1988–93, circuit judge (Midland & Oxford Circuit) 1993–; *Recreations* gardening, travel; *Style*— His Hon Judge Bennett; ✉ Nottingham Crown Court, Canal Street, Nottingham NG1 7EJ

BENNETT, Guy Patrick de Courcy; s of Patrick John de Courcy Bennett (d 2001), of Thames Ditton, and Pamela Mary Ray, *née* Kirchner (d 2003); *b* 27 October 1958; *Educ* Wimbledon Coll, Univ of Manchester (BSc); *m* 5 Nov 1988, Monica Beatrice, da of Alfred Cecil Francis Brodermann (d 1974); 3 da (Emily b 1990, Olivia b 1991, Beatrice b 1994); *Career* investment analyst Equity & Law Life 1980–83; dir: Marketable Securities Div CIN Management 1984–96, EFM Japan Trust 1992–97, Genesis Malaysia Maju Fund 1992–96, Taiwan Capital Fund 1994–96; sr portfolio mangr Goldman Sachs Asset Management 1996–2001, Batterymarch 2001–; *Recreations* golf, tennis, squash; *Style*— Guy Bennett, Esq

BENNETT, Linda Kristin; OBE (2007); da of Peter Bennett, of London, and Hafdis, *née* Herbertsdottir; *b* 8 September 1962; *Educ* Haberdashers' Aske's Sch for Girls, Univ of Reading (BSc); *m* 29 July 2000, Philip W Harley, s of late Christopher Harley; 1 da (Isabel Kristin b 29 Jan 2001); *Career* shoe design asst Robert Clegerie France 1986, opened first L K Bennett shop Wimbledon Village 1990 (currently 35 shops incl flagship store Brook Street London and Rue de Grenelle Paris); Hon LLD Univ of Reading, hon fell Univ of the Arts London; *Awards* winner Consumer Product category Nat Ernst & Young Entrpreneur of the Year Awards 2002, winner Smaller Multiple category Drapers Record Awards 2002, Best Combined Clothing and Footwear Retailer UK Footwear Awards 2002, Best Women's Footwear Retailer UK Footwear Awards 2003, Veuve Clicquot Business Woman of the Year 2004 (finalist 1999); *Recreations* architectural history, British 20th century art, walking, travel, cinema; *Style*— Ms Linda Bennett, OBE; ✉ e-mail linda.bennett@lkbennett.com

BENNETT, Prof Michael David; OBE (1996); s of Stanley Roland Bennett, and Marion, *née* Woods; *b* 6 October 1943; *Educ* Gravesend Boys' GS, UC Wales Aberystwyth (BSc, PhD); *m* 28 Aug 1971, Anita Lucy, da of Harry Ring, of Northfleet, Kent; 2 da (Michelle b 1976, Danielle b 1977), 1 s (Nathan b 1980); *Career* res scientist (cytogeneticist) Plant Breeding Inst Cambridge 1968–87, BP Venture res fell 1986–92; Royal Botanic Gardens Kew: keeper of Jodrell Laboratory 1987–2006, hon research fell 2006–; visiting prof Univ of Reading 1988–2007, hon prof Sch of Pure and Applied Biology Univ of Wales Cardiff 1989–98, Cardiff Sch of Biosciences Cardiff Univ 1999–2003, visitor of the Botanic Gardens Univ of Oxford 2004–08; fell Univ of Wales Aberystwyth 1999–; pres British Israel Bible Truth Fellowship 1987–; memb Annals of Botany Co 1988–2014 (vice-chm 2000–04, chm 2004–08); memb Editorial Bd: Jl Cell Science Cambridge 1984–90, Canadian Jl Genetics & Cytology (renamed Genome 1987) 1983–90; FLS 1988; *Publications* The Principles of Prophecy Vol 1 (1969) and Vol 2 (1972), The Exodus (2010); author or ed of numerous scientific papers and int conference presentations, also of biblical studies and numerous articles and pamphlets; *Recreations* gardening, reading, bible study; *Style*— Prof Michael Bennett, OBE; ✉ La Jolla, 26 Wilbraham Road, Cambridge CB21 5GT (☎ 01223 881053, e-mail michaelbennett26@btinternet.com)

BENNETT, Natalie Louise; *b* Sydney, Australia; *Educ* MLC Sch for Girls Burwood NSW, Univ of Sydney, Univ of New England, Univ of Leicester; *Career* Green Pty: memb 2006–, internal communications co-ordinator 2007–11, ldr 2012–16; *Style*— Ms Natalie Bennett; ✉ Green Party, The Biscuit Factory, A Block, Second Floor, 100 Clements Road, London SE16 4DG

BENNETT, Neil Edward Francis; s of Dr (Albert) Edward Bennett, of Liston, Long Melford, Suffolk, and Jean Louise, *née* Dickinson; *b* 15 May 1965; *Educ* Westminster, UCL (BA), City Univ London (PGDip Journalism); *m* 19 Sept 1992, Carole, da of William Kenyon, of Allestree, Derby; 2 da (Violet Xanthe b 30 Oct 1995, Clementine Elizabeth b 13 March 1998); *Career* feature writer Investors' Chronicle 1987–89; The Times 1989–95: City reporter 1989–90, banking corr 1990–93, ed Tempus column 1993, dep ed Business News until 1995, City ed Sunday Telegraph 1995–2002, chief exec Gavin Anderson & Co UK 2002–04; Maitland: managing ptnr 2004–10, ceo 2010–; financial columnist: jagnotes-euro.com 1999–2000, Hemscott.net 2001–02; Wincott Jr Financial Journalist of the Year 1992, Business Journalist of the Year British Press Awards 1998 and 1999; tstee John Schofield Tst 2012–; *Recreations* antiquarian book collecting, long-distance running; *Clubs* Reform; *Style*— Neil Bennett, Esq; ✉ Maitland, Orion House, 5 Upper St. Martin's Lane, London WC2H 9EA

BENNETT, Dr Peter John; s of Thomas Ronald Bennett (d 1992), and Ivy, *née* Wakelam (d 2007); *b* 13 September 1952, Wolverhampton; *Educ* High Arcal GS Dudley, SOAS (BA, PhD); *Career* fieldworker among Vaishnavas of the Pushti Marg tradition in Ujjain India 1977–78, pt/t teacher and youth worker 1978–83, asst govr HM Young Offenders Instn Everthorpe 1983–88, head Hull Special Unit for dangerous and disruptive prisoners 1988–90, staff offr HM Prison Service HQ 1990–92, head of inmate activities HM Young Offenders Instn Moorland 1992–93, govr HMP Nottingham 1993–98, ops mangr Prison Serv Contracts and Competitions Gp 1998–2000, govr HMP Wellingborough 2000–02, govr HMP Springhill and HMP Grendon Therapeutic Community Prison Bucks 2002–11, dir Int Centre for Prison Studies 2012–14, ind cnslt on Global Prison reform 2014–; tstee: Koestler Tst 2006–12, New Bridge Fndn 2008; FRAI 1985; *Books* The Path of Grace: Social Organization and Temple Worship in a Vaishnava Sect (1993); *Recreations* poetry, South Asian cultures and religions; *Style*— Dr Peter Bennett

BENNETT, Dr Peter Norman; s of Norman Bennett (d 1989), and Elizabeth Jane, *née* Ogston (d 1997); *b* 25 November 1939; *Educ* Nairn Acad, Univ of Aberdeen (MB ChB, MD((Hons)), Cash Prize); *m* 31 Aug 1963, Jennifer Mary, da of Eric Arthur Brocklehurst, of Hull, Yorks; 2 s (Michael John b 1965, Neil Robert b 1968), 1 da (Sally-Ann Elizabeth b 1972); *Career* lectr in med Univ of Aberdeen 1967–71, Wellcome res fell UCH London 1971–73, lectr Royal Postgrad Med Sch 1973–76, conslt physician in clinical pharmacology and dir Clinical Pharmacology Unit Royal United Hosp Bath 1976–2004 (hon conslt physician 2004–); School of Postgrad Med Univ of Bath: sr lectr in clinical pharmacology 1976–90, dir Centre for Med Studies 1978–89, assoc dean 1989, reader in clinical pharmacology 1990–2004 (hon reader 2004–07); memb Br Pharmacological Soc (treas Clinical Section 1982–87), chm WHO (Euro) Working Gp on Drugs and Breast Feeding 1983–90, memb Bd Euro Ethical Review Ctee 1990–2004 (co-chm 1997); FRCP 1981, FRCPGlas 1981, FRCPEd 1999; *Books* Clinical Pharmacology (with D R Laurence, 5 edn 1980, 6 edn 1987, 7 edn 1992; with D R Lawrence and M J Brown, 8 edn 1997; with M J Brown, 9 edn 2003, 10 edn 2008; with M J Brown and P Sharma, 11 edn 2012), Multiple Choice Questions on Clinical Pharmacology (with D R Laurence and F Stokes, 1 edn 1983, 2 edn 1988), Drugs and Human Lactation (ed, 1988, 2 edn 1996), Ethical Responsibilities in European Drug Research (ed, 1991), Good Clinical Practice and Ethics in European Drug Research (ed, 1994), Self Assessment in Clinical Pharmacology (with D R Lawrence and M J Brown, 1999), The Practice of Physick by Alexander Gordon (ed, 2012); *Publications* Alexander Gordon (1752–99 and his writing (J R Coll Physicians Edinb 2012: 42); *Recreations* fly fishing, theatre; *Clubs* RSM; *Style*— Dr Peter Bennett; ✉ Denmede, Southstoke Road, Combe Down, Bath BA2 5SL (☎ 01225 832371, e-mail mpspnb@bath.ac.uk)

BENNETT, Dr Philip Anthony; s of George Joseph Bennett (d 1997), of Welling, Kent, and Rita, *née* Skelton (d 1984), of Brigg, of Lincs; *b* 1 September 1947, Brigg, Lincs; *Educ* Univ of York/Open Univ (PhD); *m* 1, 20 Sept 1969 (m dis 1996), Kathryn Margaret, da of Sidney French (d 1977); 2 s (Lance Andrew b 3 Jan 1972, Robin Michael b 3 Jan 1980); m 2, 1 Sept 2000, Eleanor Kathleen, da of Wilfred Allen Dolan (d 1975); *Career* apprenticeship Richard Thomas & Baldwin (later part of British Steel) 1963–69, sr engrg positions British Steel 1969–81, chm CSE International Ltd 1984–2008, chm York Software Engineering Ltd 1995–2006, systems int and technol dir Crossrail Ltd 2007–09, currently princ Phil Bennett Consulting; sr professional positions on major projects incl: Channel Tunnel, Hong Kong Airport, Heathrow Terminal 5; prof of safety critical systems Dept of Computer Science Univ of York 1993–2006, visiting prof Dept of Computer Science Univ of York 2010–; chm The Hazards Forum 1993–99; scouting 1977–91 (Cmmr); Freeman City of London 1990, Liveryman Worshipful Co of Engrs 1991 (memb Ct of Assts 1998–2012, asst emeritus 2012); FIEE 1989, CEng 1989, FREng 1991,

FICE 1995; *Books* Software Engineers Reference Book (contrib, 1991), Safety Aspects of Computer Control (ed, 1992), Transmission and Distribution Electrical Engineering (contrib, 1995), Loss Prevention in the Process Industries (contrib, 1996); *Recreations* fly fishing, travel, reading; *Clubs* Royal Over-Seas League; *Style—* Dr P A Bennett, FREng; ✉ The Old Manor House, Riverside, Scotter, Lincolnshire DN21 3UG (☎ 01724 764745, mobile 07850 740263, e-mail pabennett@iee.org)

BENNETT, Prof Richard Mark; s of Edward Bennett (d 1991), and Barbara, *née* Lack; *b* 4 June 1957, Chiswick; *Educ* St Paul's, Univ of Reading (BSc, PhD), Univ of Oxford (MSc); *m* 20 March 1981, Fiona, *née* Horne; 2 da (Alice b 20 June 1992, Constance b 2 June 1995); *Career* research fell, lectr, sr lectr then prof of agric economics Univ of Reading 1985–; memb Cncl and tstee Universities Fedn for Animal Welfare 1998–, tstee Humane Slaughter Assoc 1998–, memb Farm Animal Welfare Cncl 2005–, memb England Implementation Gp Animal Health and Welfare Strategy for GB 2005–, tstee Farm Animal Welfare Tst 2008–; *Recreations* keen tennis player; *Style—* Prof Richard Bennett; ✉ Department of Agricultural and Food Economics, University of Reading, 4 Earley Gate, PO Box 237, Reading RG6 6AR (☎ 0118 378 6478, fax 0118 935 6467, e-mail r.m.bennett@rdg.ac.uk)

BENNETT, Prof Robert John; s of Thomas Edward Bennett, of Southampton, and Kathleen Elizabeth, *née* Robson; *b* 23 March 1948; *Educ* Taunton's Sch Southampton, St Catharine's Coll Cambridge (MA, PhD); *m* 5 Sept 1971, Elizabeth Anne, da of William Allen, of Ormskirk, Lancs; 2 s (Phillip Stewart Edward b 1982, Richard John Charles b 1986); *Career* lectr UCL 1973–78, visiting prof Univ of Calif Berkeley 1978, lectr Univ of Cambridge 1978–85 (fell, tutor and dir of studies Fitzwilliam Coll 1978–85); LSE: prof of geography 1985–96, Leverhulme prof 1996–2000; prof of geography Univ of Cambridge 1996–2011 (emeritus prof 2011–), fell St Catharine's Coll Cambridge 1996–2011 (emeritus fell 2011–); gen ed Government and Policy 1982–2010; memb: Govt and Law Ctee ESRC 1982–87, Cncl Inst of Br Geographers 1985–87 (treas 1990–94); chm Election Studies Advsy Ctee ESRC 1987–88; conslt to House of Commons: Employment Ctee 1988–89, Scottish Affrs Ctee 1994–95, Educn and Employment Ctee 1997–2000; memb: Cncl Royal Geographic Soc 1995–2001 (vice-pres 1993–95 and 1998–2001), Research Awards Advsy Ctee Levenhulme Tst 2001–07; chm Postgraduate Review Ctee Br Acad 2000–01, vice-pres and chm Research Ctee Br Acad 2001–08; MInstD; FRGS 1982, FBA 1991; *Books* incl: Environmental Systems – Philosophy, Analysis and Control (with R J Chorley, 1978), Local Business Taxes in Britain and Germany (with G Krebs, 1988), Enterprise and Human Resource Development: local capacity building (with A McCoshan, 1993), Local and Regional Economic Development (with D Payne, 2000), Local Business Voice: The History of Chambers of Commerce 1760–2011 (2011), Entrepreneurship, Small Business and Public Policy (2014); *Recreations* genealogy, the family; *Style—* Prof Robert Bennett, FBA; ✉ Department of Geography, University of Cambridge, Downing Place, Cambridge CB2 3EN

BENNETT, Prof Viv; *Career* dep chief nursing offr then dir Nursing Dept of Health, chief nurse Public Health England 2013–; *Style—* Prof Viv Bennett, CBE

BENNETT-JONES, Peter; CBE (2014); s of Dr N Bennett-Jones (d 2007), and Ruth H Bennett-Jones; *b* 11 March 1955; *Educ* Winchester, Magdalene Coll Cambridge (MA); *m* 29 June 1990, Alison, *née* Watts; 2 s (Ludovic Robin Devereux b 1991, Albert George (Bertie) b 1994), 1 da (Matilda Emma b 1992); *Career* dir OCSC Ltd 1977–79, freelance prodn mangr 1979–81 (projects incl Bubble Theatre UK, Chung Ying Theatre Hong Kong, course dir City Univ London), dir Pola Jones Associates 1982–, md Talkback Productions 1983–86, md Corporate Communication Group Ltd 1986–88; chm: Tiger Television 1988–2011, PBJ Management 1988– (clients incl Rowan Atkinson, Lenny Henry, Barry Humphries, Harry Enfield, Eddie Izzard, Armando Iannucci, Reeves and Mortimer, Howard Goodall and Chris Morris), Tiger Aspect Productions 1993–2011; co-chair United Artists 2007–08; dir TEAM plc 1993–98; Tiger Aspect prodns incl: Mr Bean (ITV, winner numerous awards incl Int Emmy and Golden Rose of Montreux), The Vicar of Dibley (BBC 1), Robin Hood (BBC 1), Harry Enfield and Chums (BBC1), Murphy's Law (BBC 1), Teachers (Channel 4), The Catherine Tate Show (BBC 2), Billy Elliot (Universal), Blackadder Back and Forth (NMEC and BSkyB), Our House (winner Olivier Award for Best New Musical 2003); chair of tstees Comic Relief 1997–2013, tstee RNT 2010–, chair Save the Children UK 2015–; sch govr and chair Arnold Fndn for Rugby Sch 2009–; RTS Lifetime Achievement Award 2011, BAFTA Special Award 2011; hon fell Univ of Bangor 2008; FRTS 2009; *Recreations* numerous; *Clubs* Oxford and Cambridge, Groucho; *Style—* Peter Bennett-Jones, Esq, CBE; ✉ PBJ Management, 22 Rathbone Street, London W1T 1LG (☎ 020 7054 5975, e-mail pbj@pbjmgt.co.uk)

BENNETTS, Denise Mary Margaret; da of James Smith, of Edinburgh, and Agnes Smith; *b* 26 January 1953, Edinburgh; *Educ* Heriot Watt Univ (BArch, DipArch), Edinburgh Coll of Art; *m* 23 Aug 1974, Robert (Rab) Bennetts; 1 s (Julian b 15 March 1984), 1 da (Louise b 31 Dec 1989); *Career* architect Casson Conder Partnership 1978–88, fndr and dir Bennetts Assocs 1987–; maj projects incl: Sophos HQ, Wessex Water Ops Centre, Basinghall Avenue, John Menzies, Powergen HQ, World Business Centre Heathrow; awards assessor Civic Tst 1997–, award assessor RIBA 2005, sometime examiner; RIBA 1978; *Recreations* travel, supporting Arsenal FC; *Style—* Ms Denise Bennetts; ✉ Bennetts Associates Architects, 1 Rawstorne Place, London EC1V 7NL (☎ 020 7520 3300, fax 020 7520 3333, e-mail denise.bennetts@bennettsassociates.com)

BENNETTS, Rab; OBE (2003); s of Frank Vivian Bennetts, of Edinburgh, and Frances Bennetts; *b* 14 April 1953; *Educ* Heriot-Watt Univ (BArch), Edinburgh Coll of Art (DipArch); *m* 23 Aug 1974, Denise Margaret Mary, da of James Smith; 1 s (Julian b 15 March 1984), 1 da (Louise b 31 Dec 1989); *Career* architect; with Arup Assocs 1977–87; fndr ptnr Bennetts Assocs 1987–, maj projects incl Powergen HQ, John Menzies bldg Edinburgh, Heathrow Vistors' Centre, Gateway Centre Loch Lomond, Wessex Water Ops Centre, Hampstead Theatre, Brighton & Hove Central Library and Royal Shakespeare Theatre; special advsr to Govt on environmental sustainability and architecture; memb: Competition Ctee RIBA, Bd UK Green Buildings Cncl; sometime lectr; author of numerous articles and pubns; dir Sadler's Wells Theatre; RIBA, FRSA; *Style—* Rab Bennetts, Esq, OBE; ✉ Bennetts Associates, 1 Rawstorne Place, London EC1V 7NL

BENNEWITH, Anthony John (Tony); s of Frank Bennewith (d 1999), and Elsie, *née* Poll (d 1997); *b* 14 January 1946; *Educ* Catford Secdy Boys' Sch; *m* 8 June 1968, Babs, da of Jack Connolly; 4 da (Christine b 9 Jan 1971, Ruth b 4 June 1972, Heather b 8 Sept 1974, Antonia b 12 May 1988), 1 s (Graham b 15 Jan 1979); *Career* articled clerk 1962–67, internal audit Castrol Oil 1968–69; mangr Griffin Stone Mosscrop 1969–72; Neville Russell (latterly Mazars): mangr London 1972–73, ptnr Guildford 1974–86; own practice 1986–; memb Cncl ICAEW 1996–; treas Guildford Hospice, treas Guildford Sch of Acting, govr Rodborough Technol Coll, pres Guildford Opera Co, pres South Eastern Soc of Chartered Accountants; memb Worshipful Co of Chartered Accountants, Freeman City of London; FCA 1978 (ACA 1968, Dip 2012), FRSA 2005, FFA 2006, FCPA 2008, FFTA 2011; *Recreations* opera, walking, skiing, philately; *Clubs* County; *Style—* Tony Bennewith, Esq; ✉ Elmfield, Tuesley Lane, Godalming, Surrey GU7 1SJ (☎ 01483 415107); A J Bennewith & Co, Ynot House, 3 Wey Court, Mary Road, Guildford, Surrey GU1 4QU (☎ 01483 539777, fax 01483 576235, mobile 07808 093806, e-mail tony@bennewith.co.uk, website www.bennewith.co.uk)

BENNINGTON, Prof Geoffrey Peter; s of Jonathan Bennington, of Embsay, N Yorkshire, and Lilian, *née* Lowther; *b* 24 July 1956; *Educ* Chesterfield Sch, St Catherine's Coll Oxford (jr and sr Heath Harrison travelling scholar, MA, DPhil); m 1, 1987 (m dis 1991), Rachel, *née* Bowlby; 1 step s (Louis Collard b 8 July 1986), 1 da (Alice b 15 Aug 1992); m 2, 2007, Elissa Marder; *Career* Laming fell Queen's Coll Oxford 1980–82, former prof of French Univ of Sussex (lectr 1983–89, sr lectr 1989–92), dir Centre for Modern French Thought Univ of Sussex 1997; currently Asa Griggs Candler prof of modern French thought Emory Univ; *Books* Sententiousness and the Novel (1985), Lyotard: Writing the Event (1988), Jacques Derrida (1991), Dudding: des noms de Rousseau (1991), Legislations (1994), Interrupting Derrida (2000), Frontières Kantiennes (2000), Frontiers (2003), Other Analyses (2005), Open Book/Livre ouvert (2005), Deconstruction is not what you think (2006), Late Lyotard (2006); *Recreations* chess, computing, cricket, music (violin); *Style—* Prof Geoffrey Bennington; ✉ e-mail gbennin@emory.edu

BENNISON, Richard; s of Douglas Bennison (d 2000), and Vera, *née* Weaver; *b* 17 April 1958, Windsor, Berks; *Educ* Maidenhead GS; *m* Francesca Short; 1 s (Timothy b 11 April 1986), 2 da (Clare (twin) b 11 April 1986, Lucy b 9 Sept 1990); *Career* KPMG: trainee chartered accountant 1977, pntr 1991, head of financial servs audit 1997, head Financial Servs Advsy Practice 2003, head of UK audit and memb Bd 2006, chief operating offr KPMG Europe LLP and KPMG UK LLP 2009–13 (ret); chm: Tokio Marine Kiln Syndicates, Tokio Marine Kiln Insurance, Taylor Clark; govr Motability; ICAEW1981; *Recreations* skiing, sailing, walking; *Style—* Richard Bennison, Esq; ✉ 4 Nottingham Mansions, Nottingham Street, London W1U 5EN (e-mail richrdbennison@mac.com)

BENSBERG, HE Mark; *m* Jacqueline Margaret; 1 da (Katherine Emma); *Career* diplomat; Western European Dept 1980–82, attaché Paris 1982–85, Africa and ME floater 1985–87, vice-consul Vienna 1988–91, Drugs and Int Crime Dept FCO 1991–94, 2 sec political, press and public affrs Accra 1994–97, head Press and Public Affrs Section Brussels 1997–2000, Corporate Performance Unit UK Trade and Investment 2000–02, Afghanistan Emergency Unit FCO 2001–02, dep head Passports and Documentary Servs Gp and mangr iCon Consular Modernisation Prog FCO 2002–04, dep head of mission and consul Kinshasa 2004–06, high cmmr to Namibia 2007–11, dep dir Estates and Security Directorate FCO 2011–14, ambass to Côte d'Ivoire 2014–16; *Style—* HE Mr Mark Bensberg; ✉ c/o FCO, King Charles Street, London SW1A 2AH

BENSON, Sir Christopher John; JP, DL; s of late Charles Woodburn Benson and Catherine Clara, *née* Bishton; *b* 20 July 1933; *Educ* Worcester Cathedral Kings Sch, The Incorporated Thames Nautical Training Coll HMS Worcester; *m* 1960, Margaret Josephine (Jo) (Lady Benson, OBE, JP, DL), da of Ernest Jefferis Bundy; 2 s; *Career* Sub Lt RNVR; chartered surveyor and agricultural auctioneer Worcs, Herefords, Wilts, Dorset and Hants 1953–64; dir Arndale Developments Ltd 1965–69; fndr chm: Dolphin Developments 1969–71, Dolphin Property Ltd 1969–72, Dolphin Farms Ltd 1973; MEPC plc: dir 1974–93, md 1976–88, chm 1988–93; Royal & Sun Alliance Insurance Group plc (formerly Sun Alliance Group plc): dir 1988–98, dep chm 1992–93 and 1997–98, chm 1993–97; chm: London Docklands Devpt Corp 1984–88, Reedpack Ltd 1989–90, The Boots Co plc 1990–94, The Housing Corp 1990–94, Costain plc 1993–96, Albright and Wilson 1995–99, Bradford Particle Design plc 1999–2002, Cross London Rail Links Ltd (Crossrail) 2001–04; dep chm Thorn Lighting Group plc 1994–98; dir: House of Fraser plc 1982–86, Royal Opera House Covent Garden Ltd 1984–92, Eredene Capital Ltd 2006–13; pres Br Property Fedn 1981–83, pres London C of C 2000–02 (hon vice-pres 2002–); chm: Civic Tst 1985–90, Property Advsy Gp to Dept of the Environment 1988–90, Steering Ctee British Red Cross Soc 1994–95, Funding Agency for Schools 1994–97, Coram Family 2005–09, Stratford (E London) Renaissance Partnership 2005–09, Salisbury Vision 2009–13; memb: Cncl Marlborough Coll 1982–90, Advsy Bd RA 1987–90, Cncl Inns of Court Disciplinary Tbnl 2009–13, Bd Swindon and Wiltshire Local Economic Partnership 2012–14, Bd Swindon and Wiltshire Local Enterprise Tst 2012–14; lay memb The Take Over Panel 1994–2003; sponsor: Middle Temple and Southampton Univ Scholarships, William Pye Font, Salisbury Cathedral (with Jerusalem Tst), Benson Suite Salisbury District Hosp; tstee: Metropolitan Police Museum 1986–2011, Wessex Medical Research; pres Nat Deaf Children's Soc 1994–, chm Br-Australia Soc Educn Tst 2010–; vice-pres: Royal Soc of Arts 1992–, Macmillan Cancer Relief 1992–; patron: Changing Faces 1993–, Friends of Erlestoke Prison 2012–, River Bourne Community Farm; lay govr Royal London Hosp Med Coll 1993–95, govr Inns of Court Sch of Law 1996–2001 (princ 2000); lay canon Salisbury Cathedral 2000–11; Past Master Co of Watermen and Lightermen; Liveryman: Honourable Co of Air Pilots, Worshipful Co of Gold and Silver Wyre Drawers, Worshipful Co of Chartered Surveyors; assoc Hon Co of Master Mariners; hon bencher Middle Temple 1984; hon fell Wolfson Coll Cambridge 1990, hon fell Univ of Southampton 2014–; Hon DSc: City Univ 2000, Univ of Bradford 2001; FRICS, FRSA 1987, Hon FRCPath 1992, Hon FCIOB 1992; *Books* Send for Benson! A Life of Sir Christopher Benson (biography by His Hon Eric Stockdale, 2015); *Recreations* farming, aviation, opera, swimming; *Clubs* Garrick, Oxford and Cambridge; *Style—* Sir Christopher Benson; ✉ Pauls Dene House, Castle Road, Salisbury SP1 3RY; Flat 2, 50 South Audley Street, London W1K 2QE (e-mail sircjbenson@me.com)

BENSON, David Holford; s of Lt-Col Sir Reginald (Rex) Lindsay Benson, DSO, MVO, MC (d 1968), of Singleton, W Sussex, and Leslie, *née* Foster (d 1981); *b* 26 February 1938; *Educ* Eton, Madrid; *m* 1964, Lady Elizabeth Mary, *née* Charteris, da of 12 Earl of Wemyss and (8 of) March, KT, JP; 1 s, 2 da; *Career* merchant banker; with Shell International 1957–63; Kleinwort Benson Group plc (latterly Dresdner Kleinwort): joined 1963, vice-chm 1989–92, non-exec dir 1992–98; sr advsr Fleming Family & Partners 2001–, chm Charter European Tst plc 1992–2003; non-exec dir: BG plc 1988–2004, Wemyss and March Estate Co, Daniel Thwaites plc 1998–2006, Murray Int Investment Tst plc until 2009, The Rouse Co (NYSE listed co) until 2004, Dover Corporation (NYSE listed co) until 2014; chm Charities Official Investment Fund (COIF) 1985–2005, tstee Fleming Wyfold Fndn; tstee The Phoenix Tst 1996–2001; *Recreations* painting; *Clubs* White's, ESU; *Style—* David Benson, Esq; ✉ Stonehage Fleming Family & Partners, 15 Suffolk Street, London SW1Y 4HG

BENSON, (John) Graham; s of late Marshall Benson, and Beatrice, *née* Stein; *b* 29 April 1946; *Educ* Central Foundation Boys' GS London; *m* 13 May 1978, Christine Margaret, *née* Fox; 1 da (Fay Cecily (Mrs Christopher Flavin) b 1 Nov 1983); *Career* stage mangr in theatre 1965–68, TV prodn mangr and assoc prodr Drama Plays Dept BBC 1968–76; prodr: Premiere Films, BBC and other TV drama 1976–78; Fox for Euston Films 1979; Euro prodn exec The Robert Stigwood Group 1980–82, freelance/independent prodr 1982–86, md Consolidated Productions 1986, controller of drama for TVS and dir Telso Communications 1987–92, chm and chief exec Blue Heaven Productions Ltd (prodrs of The Ruth Rendell Mysteries) 1992–97; dir: Clivia Ltd (film financiers) 1998–2001, PrimeEnt plc 2001–02; freelance prodr many films incl: Thank You Comrades (BBC1) 1978, A Hole in Babylon (BBC1) 1978, Outside Edge (LWT) 1982, Red Monarch (theatrical feature, Channel 4) 1982, Meantime (Central/Channel 4) 1983, Charlie (Central) 1983, Honest Decent and True (BBC2) 1984, Coast to Coast (BBC1) 1984; chm: BAFTA 1985–87 (memb Cncl 1980–93), PACT 1996–98 (memb Cncl 1991–2005, patron 2009, hon memb 2012), TV12 IOW 1998–2002, Media Circus Gp plc 1999–2001, Headwater Cross Media plc 2000–01, Screen South 2002–, Trinorth Ltd 2004–, Directors' Cut Ltd 2006–07, All Out Cricket Ltd 2009–, Cornhill and Harvest Ltd 2009–, Arcola Theatre Devpt Bd 2014–, Tstees Continuum Ensemble 2015–; memb: American Advisory Gp DTI 1996–2003, Markets Gp Br Trade Int 1998–2001, Marshall Aid Commemoration Cmmn 1998–2004 (chm ARM Ctee 2004–15), UKTI Creative Export Gp 2000–10; exec conslt and dep chm FT Weekend Oxford Literary Festival 2005–, UK advsr Banff World TV Festival

1996–2003 and 2006–07, consl t/advsr Drama Content Hub South African Broadcasting Corp 2009–10; Hon DLitt Southampton Solent Univ 2003; FRSA 1987, FRTS 2000; *Recreations* food, drink, literature, jazz, opera, cricket, football, contemporary art; *Clubs* Savile, Surrey CCC, Ventnor CC, Ventnor Yacht, Ventnor Arts (chm Fndrs' Ctee); *Style—* Graham Benson, Esq; ✉ mobile 07786 448854, e-mail fcgbenson@aol.com

BENSON, John Trevor; QC (2001); s of Trevor Benson (d 1985), and Ruth, *née* Oliver (d 2004); *b* 22 January 1955, Oxford; *Educ* Helsby County GS, Univ of Liverpool (LLB); *m* (m dis) Sheila, *née* Riordan; 3 c (Kate b 17 Jan 1988, Jack, Lily (twins) b 22 Nov 1991); *Career* barr; recorder 1998–, head of chambers Atlantic Chambers 2005–09 (also practising from Chambers of Lord Gifford QC), currently head 1MCB Chambers (also practising from Atlantic Chambers); *Recreations* Liverpool FC, Italy, wine, gardening, walking; *Style—* John Benson, Esq, QC; ✉ The Common Cottage, Grafton, Oxfordshire OX18 2RY (☎ 01367 810460); 1MCB Chambers, 15 New Bridge Street, London EC4V 6AV (☎ 020 7452 8900); Atlantic Chambers, 4–6 Cook Street, Liverpool L2 9QU (☎ 0151 236 4421)

BENSON, Hon Michael D'Arcy; yr s of Baron Benson, GBE (Life Peer; d 1995), and Anne Virginia, *née* Macleod; *b* 23 May 1943; *Educ* Eton; *m* 1969, Rachel Candia Woods; 2 da (Catherine Rachel b 1971, Harriet Anne b 1974), 1 s (Charles D'Arcy b 1976); *Career* memb Research Dept L Messel & Co (Stockbrokers) 1965–67 (clerk on dealing floor 1963–65); Lazard Brothers & Co Ltd: joined 1967, dir Lazard Securities Ltd 1978 (head Private Client Dept and admin dir 1980), dir Lazard Brothers 1980–85, jt md Lazard Securities Ltd 1980, dir Lazard Securities (Jersey) Ltd 1981–85, dir Lazard Bros & Co (Jersey) Ltd 1981–85, dir Lazard Securities (Hong Kong) Ltd 1984–85, dir Lazard Bros & Co (Guernsey) Ltd 1984–85; md Scimitar Asset Management Ltd (London) 1985–92; dir: Standard Chartered Merchant Bank Ltd 1985, Gracechurch Nominees Ltd 1985–92, Scimitar Asset Management (CI) Ltd 1986, Scimitar Global Asset Management Ltd 1986–92, Scimitar Asset Management Asia Ltd 1986–92, Scimitar Worldwide Selection Fund Ltd 1986–92, Scimitar Asset Management (Singapore) Ltd 1988–92; chm: Scimitar Asset Management Ltd 1985–91, Scimitar Unit Trust Managers Ltd 1989–92; dir: Chartered Financial Holdings Ltd 1990, Capital House Investment Management 1992–93, Capital House Asia 1992–93, Capital House (Singapore) Ltd 1992–93; chief exec: Asia Pacific Region Invesco Group 1994–96, Invesco Global Asset Management 1996–2001; vice-chm Amvescap plc 2001–05 (dir 1994–); currently non-exec chm Ashmore Gp plc; non-exec dir Morse plc 2007–09; dir: Border Asset Mgmnt Ltd 2006–11, Badanloch Estates Ltd, Trinity Street Asset Mgmnt 2011–; dir York Minster Fund 2006–; *Style—* The Hon Michael Benson; ✉ Grange Farm, Westow, York YO60 7NJ (☎ 01653 658296)

BENSON, Neil; s of Eric Benson (d 2000), and Vera, *née* Mower (d 1976); *b* 22 October 1954; *Educ* City GS Sheffield; *m* Joan Philippa; 2 s (Joseph Samuel b 29 Oct 1992, Rory Christopher b 15 March 1994), 1 da (Meredith Hope b 12 May 1995); *Career* The Star Sheffield 1974–79 (trainee reporter, sr reporter, news desk asst, news sub ed), Daily Express Manchester 1979–85 (features sub ed, sr news sub ed), Telegraph & Argus Bradford 1985–88 (features ed, asst ed), dep ed Chronicle & Echo Northampton Jan-June 1989, dep ed Telegraph & Argus Bradford 1989–91, ed and dir Coventry Evening Telegraph 1991–93, ed Newcastle Evening Chronicle 1993–96, new business devpt dir Newcastle Chronicle & Journal Ltd 1998–99 (exec ed daily newspapers 1996–98), md Gazette Media Co 1999–2001, editorial dir Trinity Mirror Regionals 2001–, interim business devpt dir BPM Media 2007–08; chm Guild of Eds Northern Region 1996–97, chm Hold the Front Page 2005–11 (memb Bd 2014–), memb Bd Soc of Eds 2002–14 (vice- pres 2002–03, pres 2003–04), memb Editors' Code Ctee; ind lay memb Standards Ctee Wrexham CBC; *Recreations* cricket, gym, supporting Leeds RLFC and Newcastle United; *Clubs* Gresford Cricket; *Style—* Neil Benson, Esq; ✉ Trinity Mirror plc, Maple House, Sealand Road, Chester CH1 4RN (e-mail neil.benson@trinitymirror.com)

BENSON, His Hon Judge Peter Charles; s of Robert Benson (d 1970), of Baildon, W Yorks, and Dorothy, *née* Cartman; *b* 16 June 1949; *Educ* Bradford GS, Univ of Birmingham (BSocSc); *Career* called to the Bar Middle Temple 1975, in practice NE Circuit 1975–, junior of NE Circuit 1979–80, recorder of the Crown Court 1995–2001 (asst recorder 1991–95), circuit judge 2001–, liaison judge to the Calderdale magistrates 2003–; memb Parole Bd 2003–09; *Recreations* golf, reading, conversation; *Clubs* Ilkley Golf, Ilkley Bowling, Ganton Golf, Bradford, East India; *Style—* His Hon Judge Peter Benson; ✉ Bradford Crown Court, Exchange Square, Bradford BD1 1JA

BENSON, Hon Peter Macleod; LVO (2001); er s of Baron Benson, GBE (Life Peer; d 1995), and Anne Virginia, *née* Macleod (d 1998); *b* 1940; *Educ* Eton, Univ of Edinburgh (MA); *m* 1, 1970 (m dis 1987), Hermione Jane Boulton; 2 da (Candida Jane b 1972, Hermione Emily b 1980), 1 s (Edward Henry b 1975); m 2, 3 Aug 1989 (m dis 2003), Señora Maria de los Angeles Martin, da of Don Victoriano Martinez Latasa; *Career* qualified CA 1965; ptnr PricewaterhouseCoopers (formerly Coopers & Lybrand before merger) 1971–2000; chm: Sense Worldwide Gp 2003–16, UK Biocentre 2011–13; dir: Pixology plc 2003–07, UK Biobank Ltd 2004–13, Spectrum Interactive plc 2005–10; memb Bd of Mgmnt RNT 1991–2003 (chm RNT Fndn 2003–13), vice-chm English Nat Ballet Sch 1996–2010, dir Chichester Festival Theatre 2002–12; chm: Edward James Fndn 2009–, Nat Campaign for the Arts 2007–13; memb Cncl RADA 2007–, dir Nuffield Theatre 2013–; *Recreations* shooting, golf, theatre; *Clubs* Brooks's, Hurlingham, MCC, Tandridge Golf, Itchenor Sailing Club; *Style—* The Hon Peter M Benson, LVO; ✉ 2 King's Quay, Chelsea Harbour, London SW10 0UX

BENSON, Richard Anthony; QC (1995); s of Douglas Arthur Benson (d 1983), and Muriel Alice, *née* Fairfield (d 1984); *b* 20 February 1946; *Educ* Wrekin Coll, Inns of Court Sch of Law; *m* 1, 15 Sept 1967 (m dis 1996), Katherine Anne, da of Tom Anderson Smith, of Highfield, Glos; 1 s (Jake Alexander Fairfield b 22 Feb 1970), 2 da (Amy Rebecca b 26 April 1972, Chloe Kate b 25 Aug 1981); m 2, 29 May 2000 (m dis 2004), Sarah, da of Roger and Jenette Gaunt, of Montpon-Menesterol, France; 3 s (Max Jean-Luc b 1 Feb 1997, Oscar Morgan b 12 Jan 1999, Archie Richard b 6 Dec 2001), 1 da (Elysia Naomi b 23 Nov 2000); m 3, 23 Sept 2006, Dr Alison Jane Simmons, da of Michael and Barbara Simmons, of Roxburghshire, Scotland; 2 s (Hugo Frederick William, Theo Howard Angus b 20 Oct 2008 (twins)); *Career* called to the Bar Inner Temple 1974; in practice Midland Circuit, asst recorder 1990, recorder 1995–; *Recreations* flying, offshore cruising, drama, after dinner speaking; *Clubs* British Airways Flying, Bar Yacht, HTC; *Style—* Richard Benson, Esq, QC; ✉ e-mail rabqc@btopenworld.com, Twitter @dickyqc; Cornwall Street Chambers, 85–87 Cornwall Street, Birmingham B3 3BY (☎ 0121 233 7500, e-mail richard.benson@cornwallstreet.co.uk, website www.cornwallstreet.co.uk)

BENSON, Prof Roger Smith; s of Joseph Benson, and Hilda Benson; *b* 10 July 1944, Morecambe, Lancs; *Educ* Haslingden GS, Univ of Swansea, UMIST (MSc, PhD); *m* Kathlyn; 2 s (Richard, Martyn), 1 da (Louise); *Career* ICI 1971–2001 (positions incl control and electrical gp mangr and chief engr technol), ABB Engrg Servs 2001–05; chm: Perceptive Engrg Ltd, Tuneable Diodes Ltd; visiting prof: Dept of Chem Engrg Univ of Newcastle upon Tyne 1995–, Dept of Engrg Univ of Teesside 1996–2008, Dept of Chem Engrg Imperial Coll London 1996–2009; hon pres Centre for Process Analytics and Control Techol (CPACT); judge Britain's Best Factory Award 1993–; memb Fédération Européenne d'Associations Nationales d'Ingénieurs (FEANI) 1991; CEng 1982, FIChemE 1982, FIEE 1991, FREng 1999; *Publications* Bench Marking in the Process Industries (jtly, 1999); also author of five reports and 85 papers; *Recreations* golf, cycling, fly fishing; *Style—* Prof Roger Benson, FREng; ✉ Benson Consulting Ltd, 8 Church Garth, Great Smeaton, Northallerton, North Yorkshire DL6 2HW (☎ 01609 881366, mobile 07813 148081, e-mail rrsbensonfreng@gmail.com)

BENSON, Stephen John; s of John Benson, and Elizabeth Benson; *b* 5 November 1955, Burnley, Lancs; *Educ* Bishop Vesey GS Sutton Coldfield, Univ of Manchester, Chester Coll of Law; *m* Gillian; 2 da (Helen Louise b 25 Sept 1988, Emma Clare b 3 Aug 1990), 1 s (Nicholas Edward b 6 Oct 1995); *Career* slr; sr ptnr Cobbetts LLP 2005–2013 (ptnr 1985–2013), client strategy ptnr DWF LLP 2013–; dir Artreach Tst Ltd, dir City Co (Manchester) Ltd; memb Law Soc; FRSA; *Recreations* keeping fit, outdoor pursuits, motor cars, contemporary art, photography; *Style—* Stephen Benson, Esq; ✉ DWF LLP, 1 Scott Place, 2 Hardman Street, Manchester M3 3AA (☎ 0161 838 0496, e-mail stephen.benson@dwf.co.uk)

BENTATA, (Morris) David Albert; s of Robert Victor Bentata (d 1961), of Didsbury, Manchester, and Joyce Ethel, *née* Weinberg; *b* 21 July 1938; *Educ* Blundell's, ChCh Oxford (MA); *m* 20 Feb 1964 (m dis 1991), Alison Jessica, da of Christopher Henley Boyle Gilroy, of Boundstone, Surrey; 1 da (Victoria b 10 Feb 1966), 1 s (Robert b 5 Nov 1968); *Partner* Linda Joan Smith; *Career* Nat Serv: enlisted N Staffs Regt 1957, OCS Eaton Hall and Mons 1957–58, cmmnd 2 Lt Intelligence Corps 1958, serv BAOR 1958–59, cmmnd Lt Intelligence Corps (TA) 1959, RARO 1963; md M Bentata & Son Ltd 1962–67, fndr int mangr Hill Samuel & Co Ltd 1969–72 (investment analyst 1968–69), int investment mangr Charterhouse Japhet Ltd 1972–79, dir Charterhouse Investment Management Ltd 1986–88 (int dir 1979–86), md Charterhouse Portfolio Managers Ltd 1986–88, fndr chm Bentata Associates Ltd 1988–; dir: Pegasus Financial Holdings Ltd 1989–92, INVESCO Perpetual European Investment Trust plc (formerly Murray European Investment Trust plc and European Project Investment Trust plc) 1990–2009 (dep chm 2004–09), Liberty Funds Europe (formerly Newport Capital Ltd) 1991–2003, Marcher Diagnostics plc 1996–98, DLSN Ltd 1997, Optimay Corporation Inc 1997–98, Camlab Ltd 1998–2005 (chm 2000–02), Lexicon Data Ltd 2004–, Lemdex Ltd 2006–08; chm: Sage Partners Ltd 1991–95, MMS Petroleum Services Ltd (formerly Gandalf Explorers International Ltd) 1996–98 (fndr fin dir 1989), Marine & Mercantile Securities plc 1996– (dir 1994–), VI Group plc 1998–99, Knowledge Mgmnt Software plc 1999–2001, Popkin Software & Systems Inc 2000–01, K M Ventures plc 2000–01, Composite Metal Technologies plc 2006; dep chm Composite Metal Technology Ltd 2002– (dir 1998–); elected Lloyd's underwriter 1976; vice-chm and chm Stoke d'Abernon Residents' Assoc 1969–77, memb Ctee Oxshott Cons Assoc 1969–72, vice-pres Oxford Univ Rifle Club 2002 (pres 2012–), co-chm N Herts Inter-Faith Forum 2008–13; memb The Sherlock Holmes Soc of London (memb Cncl 1992); tstee: N London Rifle Club Bisley 2009–, Intelligence Corps Assoc 2010–, Feltmakers Co Charitable Fndn 2011–; Freeman City of London 1984, Liveryman Worshipful Co of Feltmakers 1983 (Steward 1989–91, memb Ct of Assts 1993, Fourth Warden 1998, Third Warden 1999, Renter Warden 2000, Upper Warden 2001, Master 2002), Liveryman Worshipful Co of Gunmakers 2004; ASIP 1969 (formerly AIIMR), FInstD 1988, FRGS 1988, FRSA 1995; *Recreations* full-bore rifle shooting, travel, dancing the minuet (Covent Garden Minuet Co); *Clubs* City of London, Athenaeum, Oxford and Cambridge Rifle Assoc (pres 2012); *Style—* David Bentata, Esq

BENTHALL, Jonathan Charles Mackenzie; s of Sir (Arthur) Paul Benthall, KBE (d 1992), and Mary Lucy, *née* Pringle (d 1988); *b* 12 September 1941; *Educ* Eton (King's scholar), King's Coll Cambridge (MA); *m* 23 Oct 1975, Hon Zamira, da of Baron Menuhin, OM, KBE (Life Peer, d 1999); 2 s (Dominic b 1976, William b 1981), 1 step s (Lin-Siao Fou-Menuhin b 1964); *Career* sec ICA 1971–73, dir RAI 1974–2000 (dir emeritus 2015–); ed Anthropology Today 1985–2000 (RAIN 1974–84), hon research fell Dept of Anthropology UCL 1994–; advsr on projects relating to Islamic charities to Swiss Federal Dept of Foreign Affrs 2005–12, expert advice and testimony in legal cases 2006–14; chair Int NGO Trg & Research Centre 1998–2003, co-dir Gulf Charities Workshop Univ of Cambridge 2012; tstee Alliance of Religions & Conservation 1997–2004; Save the Children Fund: former memb UK Child Care Ctee, memb Cncl, memb Overseas Advsy Ctee, memb Assembly 1990–98; Anthropology in Media Award American Anthropological Assoc 1993, Patron's Medal RAI 2001; memb Assoc of Social Anthropologists 1983, assoc fell Humanitarian and Conflict Research Inst Univ of Manchester 2009–; Chevalier de l'Ordre des Arts et des Lettres (France) 1973; *Books* Science and Technology in Art Today (1972), The Body Electric – Patterns of Western Industrial Culture (1976), Disasters, Relief and the Media (1993, 2 edn 2010), The Best of Anthropology Today (ed, 2002), The Charitable Crescent: Politics of Aid in the Muslim World (jtly, 2003, 2 edn 2009), Returning to Religion: Why a Secular Age is Haunted by Faith (2008), Gulf Charities and Islamic Philanthropy in the 'Age of Terror' and Beyond (co-ed 2014), Islamic Charities and Islamic Humanism in Troubled Times (2016); *Recreations* listening to music, swimming, mountain walking, books, writing light verse; *Clubs* Athenaeum; *Style—* Mr Jonathan Benthall; ✉ Downingbury Farmhouse, Pembury, Tunbridge Wells, Kent TN2 4AD (website www.ucl.ac.uk/anthropology/people/honorary/j_benthall)

BENTHAM, Howard Lownds; QC (1996); s of William Foster Bentham (d 1982), and Elsie, *née* Lownds (d 1982); *b* 26 February 1948; *Educ* Malvern Coll, Univ of Liverpool (LLB); *m* Elizabeth, da of Robert Pickering Owen; 1 s (Robert b 29 Dec 1982); *Career* called to the Bar Gray's Inn 1970; recorder 1996– (asst recorder 1985); *Recreations* watching wildlife, rebuilding, driving, racing Lotus cars; *Style—* Howard Bentham, Esq, QC

BENTINCK, Timothy; *see:* Portland, 12 Earl of

BENTLEY, Alexander Rufus; s of William Herbert Bentley, of London, and Carole-Ann Butler-Howe; *b* 2 February 1966; *Educ* Woolverstone Hall Sch Ipswich, Westminster Hotel Sch (Dip Professional Cooking); *Career* chef; Connaught Hotel London (under Michel Bourdin) 1986–89, Capital Hotel London (under Philip Britten, *qv*) 1989–91, St James Restaurant Johannesburg Sun and Towers 1991–93, Villa del Palazzo Palace Hotel Sun City (under Gaetano Ascione) 1993–94, Bill Bentley's London 1993–97, Monsieur Max Hampton 1997–2004 (Best French Restaurant London Carlton Awards 1999, one Michelin Star 1999, Gault Millau 2000, 7 out of 10 Good Food Guide 2003, 3 AA Rosettes 2003), Petersham Hotel Richmond 2004–; *Style—* Alexander Bentley, Esq; ✉ The Petersham, Nightingale Lane, Richmond, Surrey TW10 6UZ

BENTLEY, Dan; s of Malcolm Bentley, and Sandra Bentley; *Career* Paralympic boccia player; mixed team achievements with David Smith, Zoe Robinson and Nigel Murray, MBE, *qqv*, incl: Gold medal Paralympics Beijing 2008, Bronze medal Paralympic Games 2012; *Style—* Dan Bentley, Esq

BENTLEY, Keven Arthur; s of Royden Eccles Bentley (d 1992), of London, and Kaye, *née* Crichton Young; *b* 16 June 1958, Bangkok, Thailand; *Educ* Bradfield Coll Reading; *m* 1, 1987 (m dis 1992), Nicola Jane Rivière; m 2, 1992, Katherine Anne, *née* Palmer; 4 da (Kinvara b 24 Nov 1992, Olivia b 26 Aug 1994, Cordelia b 10 Oct 1995, Athena b 11 Mar 1998), 1 s (Edward b 22 Nov 2004); *Career* Lloyds broker C E Heath & Co 1979–84, Lloyds broker and dir Byas Mosley & Co 1984–96, fndr and chm Lonsdale Insurance Brokers 1996–; fndr and tstee Ackroyd Tst 1995–; Freeman City of London, Liveryman Worshipful Co of Carpenters 1998; memb Inst Registered Insurance Brokers; *Recreations* tennis, gardening; *Clubs* City of London Club, Hurlingham; *Style—* Keven Bentley, Esq; ✉ Burrow Farm Cottages, Hambleden, Henley on Thames RG9 6LX; Lindsay House, 7 Gloucester Road, London SW7 4PP (☎ 07768 195068, fax 020 7816 0029); Lonsdale Insurance Brokers, 24 Creechurch Lane, London EC3A 5JX (☎ 020 7816 0028, e-mail keven.bentley@lonsdaleib.com)

BENTLEY, Phillip (Phil); s of Alan William Bentley, of Leeds, and Betty Bentley; b 14 January 1959, Bradford, W Yorks; *Educ* Woodhouse Grove Sch Bradford, Univ of Oxford (MA), INSEAD (MBA); m 25 June 1988, Mhairi McEwan, qv; 1 s, 1 da; *Career* finance and accountancy with BP 1980–95 (UK, China, US and Egypt), gp treas Grand Metropolitan 1995–97, gp treas and dir of risk mgmnt Diageo 1997–99, finance dir Guinness-UDV 1999–2000; Centrica plc: gp finance dir 2000–07, md British Gas 2007–13; ceo Cable & Wireless 2013–; non-exec dir Kingfisher plc 2002–; MCT, fell Chartered Inst of Mgmnt Accountants; *Recreations* rugby, golf, wine, riding, skiing; *Style*— Phil Bentley, Esq; ✉ Cable and Wireless plc, 3rd Floor, 26 Red Lion Square, London WC1R 4HQ

BENTLEY, Rosemary (Rose); da of Donald Bruce Cameron (d 1987), of London, and Ruth Margaret, *née* Watson; b 16 February 1961; *Educ* Lady Margaret GS, Wadham Coll Oxford (MA); m 27 March 1999, Adam Bentley; 1 da (Leonora b 1993); *Career* news reporter and feature writer City of London Recorder 1982–84, PR conslt Communications Arc Ltd (subsid of General Advertising Ltd) 1984–85; Chambers Cox PR Ltd: sr PR conslt 1985–86, account dir 1986–89, dir 1989–93, md 1993–; memb Br Guild of Beer Writers 2001; Daily Express Young Sportswriter of the Year 1978; Freeman City of London 2000, Liveryman Worshipful Co of Tin Plate Workers alias Wireworkers 2000; MIPR, MInstD; *Recreations* theatre, cinema, music, drama, short story writing, cookery (finalist BBC Masterchef 1992), wine, literature, travel; *Style*— Ms Rose Bentley; ✉ Chambers Cox PR Ltd, 192–198 Vauxhall Bridge Road, London SW1V 1DX (✆ 020 7592 3100)

BENTLEY, Simon Anthony; s of Walter Bentley (d 2006), and Edith Bentley (d 2012); b 11 June 1955, London; m Esther, *née* Garbacz; 2 da (Debbie b 18 April 1980, Tanya b 2 June 1991), 2 s (Josh b 28 July 1982, Paul b 15 Nov 1985); *Career* trainee BDO Stoy Hayward 1974–79, sr ptnr Landau Morley until 1991, chm and chief exec Blacks Leisure Gp plc 1989–2002; chm: Sports Direct, Umberto Giannini, Mischon de Reya 2002–09, Cash on the Move; dir: Powerleague, Global Brands SA; dir Supervisory Bd Global Home; dep chm Leadership Tst, tstee Kisharon; FCA 1979; *Recreations* triathlons, skiing; *Clubs* RAC; *Style*— Simon Bentley, Esq; ✉ 32 Moreland Court, Finchley Road, London NW2 2PL (✆ 020 7726 7010)

BENTLEY, Tom; s of Richard Bentley, and Penelope, *née* Cheetham; b 7 July 1973, London; *Educ* Raine's Fndn Sch London, Haverstock Sch, Wadham Coll Oxford (BA); m 12 Feb 2000, Kylie Kilgour; 2 da (Esther b 5 Dec 2000, Iris b 24 Sept 2004); *Career* researcher Demos 1995–98, special advsr to Rt Hon David Blunkett, MP (as Sec of State for Educn and Employment) 1998–99, dir Demos 1999–2006, assoc dir Aust and NZ Sch of Govt 2006–, exec dir Victorian Premiers' Dept Aust 2006–07, policy dir Office of the Dep PM (Hon Julia Gillard) Aust 2007–; tstee: NESTA 2003–06, Community Action Network 1999–2006, Eidos Inst 2006, State Library of Victoria 2006–, Per Capita think tank 2007–; *Publications* Learning beyond the Classroom (1998), The Adaptive State (2003), Everyday Democracy (2005); *Style*— Tom Bentley, Esq; ✉ c/o DPMO, 4 Treasury Place, Melbourne, VIC 3002, Australia (✆ +61 9639 7877, e-mail tom.bentley@dpm.gov.au)

BENTLIFF, Georgina Mary; da of D G R Bentliff, and A B Bentliff; b 1960; *Educ* James Allen's GS London, Clare Coll Cambridge (MA), Birkbeck Coll London (BSc); m Sept 1997, Teige O'Donovan; 2 da, 1 s; *Career* publisher medical books and journals Churchill Livingstone 1986–92, manager medical books publishing Saunders UK 1992–94, dir of medical and health science publishing Hodder Arnold 1994–2004, md Hammersmith Press Limited 2004–, strategic devpt dir Copyright Licensing Agency 2006–11, project lead NIHR Jls Library 2011–13, md Hammersmith Books 2012–; memb and Main Ctee Guild of Health Writers; Freeman City of London, memb Worshipful Co of Merchant Taylors; FRSM; *Recreations* illustration; *Clubs* RSM; *Style*— Ms Georgina Bentliff; ✉ Hammersmith Books Limited, 14 Greville Street, London EC1N 8SB (website www.hammersmithpress.co.uk)

BENTON, Joseph Edward (Joe); JP; s of Thomas Benton, and Agnes Benton; b 28 September 1933; *Educ* St Monica's Secdy Sch, Bootle Tech Coll; m Doris; 4 da; *Career* apprentice fitter 1949, Nat Serv RAF 1955; sometime personnel mangr Pacific Steam Navigation Co, with Girobank 1982–90; MP (Lab) Bootle 1990–2015; memb: Select Ctee on Energy 1991–92, House of Commons Privileges Ctee 1997–, Educn Sub-Ctee 1997–, Speaker's Panel of Chm 1997–, Br-Irish, Br-Spanish and Br-IOM All-Pty Gps; sometime NW regional Lab whip; cncllr Derby Ward Sefton Borough Cncl 1970–90 (ldr Lab Gp 1985–90), chm Bd of Govrs Hugh Baird Coll of Technol; memb Inst of Linguists, affiliate memb Inst of Personnel Mgmnt; *Recreations* reading, listening to classical music, squash, swimming; *Style*— Joe Benton, Esq; ✉ House of Commons, London SW1A 0AA

BENTOVIM, Dr Arnon; s of Zvi Harry Bentovim (d 1989), and Gladys Rachel, *née* Carengold (d 1985); b 24 July 1936; *Educ* St Thomas' Hosp London (MB BS, DPM); m 1, 2 April 1958 (m dis 1987), Cecily Anne; 1 da (Ayalah b 1970); m 2, 1989, Marianne; *Career* psychoanalyst, family and child psychiatrist; registrar Maudsley Hosp 1962–66, sr registrar and conslt child psychiatrist Hosps for Sick Children Gt Ormond St 1966–94, hon sr lectr Inst of Child Health 1966–; conslt Tavistock Clinic 1975–94, conslt specialist advsr to House of Commons Select Ctee 1978–79, conslt Huntercombe Manor Hosp 1994–98; fndr: CIBA Fndn Study Gp, Trg Advsy Gp for the Sexual Abuse of Children, first sexual treatment prog in UK at Hosps for Sick Children 1981–94; pubns on: child psychiatry, family therapy, aspects of child abuse; fndr memb: Assoc for Family Therapy, Br Assoc for the Prevention of Child Abuse and Neglect, Inst of Family Therapy; pres Relate 1997, pres Int Family Therapy Assoc 2003; chm Faithful Fndn, tstee Michael Sieff Fndn 1994; FRCPsych 1966; *Books* Family Therapy, Complimentary Frameworks of Theory and Practice (1984–89), Child Sexual Abuse within the Family – Assessment & Treatment (ed, 1988), Trauma Organised Systems – Physical & Sexual Abuse in the Family (1996), The Family Assessment: Assessment of Family Competance, Strengths and Difficulties (2001), Assessing Support Needs for Adopted Children and Their Families (2006); *Recreations* music (particularly jazz), theatre, opera, travel; *Style*— Dr Arnon Bentovim

BENYON, Richard; MP; *Educ* Bradfield Coll, RAC Cirencester (Dip Real Estate Mgmnt); *Career* cmmnd Royal Green Jackets 1980–85; chartered surveyor 1987–, farmer 1990–; cncllr (Cons) Newbury DC 1991–95; Parly candidate (Cons) 1997 and 2001, MP (Cons) Newbury 2005–; min for natural environment and fisheries DEFRA 2010–13; *Style*— Richard Benyon, Esq, MP; ✉ House of Commons, London SW1A 0AA (e-mail richard.benyon.mp@parliament.uk, website www.richardbenyon.com)

BENYON, Thomas Yates; OBE (2010); s of Capt Thomas Yates Benyon (d 1958, s of Capt Thomas Yates Benyon (d 1893) and Hon Christina Philippa Agnes, OBE, da of 11 Baron North, JP), and his 2 wife, Joan Ida Walters (d 1982); b 13 August 1942; *Educ* Wellington Sch, RMA Sandhurst, Wycliffe Hall Oxford (dip Bible and Theology); m 1968, (Olivia) Jane, da of Humphrey Scott Plummer by his w, Hon Pamela, *née* Balfour, da of 2 Baron Kinross, KC; 2 s (Rev Thomas Yates Benyon, Rev Oliver William Yates Benyon), 2 da (Rev Clare Hayns (chaplain ChCh Oxford), Camilla Sinclair); *Career* Lt Scots Gds 1963–67, served Kenya, Muscat; MP (Cons) Abingdon 1979–83; chm Milton Keynes HA 1990–94, dir Bucks Purchasing Authy 1994–96; fndr Insurance Insider Publishing plc 1997–; fndr and dir Zane – Zimbabwe, a National Emergency 2000–; chm Assoc of Lloyd's Membs 1982–86, fndr Soc of Names 1990–; *Publications* London Insurance Insider, As Easy as ABC (study on electoral reform); *Recreations* music; *Clubs* Pratt's, Third Guards; *Style*— Thomas Benyon, Esq, OBE

BENZIE, Alan Athol Emslie; s of Athol Emslie Benzie (d 1976), of Aberdeen, and Helen Margaret, *née* Ritchie (d 1980); b 5 May 1947; *Educ* Lindisfarne Coll N Wales; m 3 June 1971, Penny Jane, da of Albert Victor Maynard; 1 da (Annie b 13 April 1973), 2 s (Toby b 11 Aug 1976, Ollie b 22 Sept 1984); *Career* articled clerk Thornton Baker 1964–69; Peat Marwick Mitchell: Manchester, Johannesburg and London 1969–75; KPMG 1975–: ptnr 1977, head NW region corp fin 1984–95, managing ptnr Manchester 1989–95, UK gen ptnr 1995–, sr regnl ptnr 1996–97, chm Northern Business Area 1997–, memb UK Bd 1999–; chm: Corp Appeals Ctee Christies, K Ventures; memb Educational Leadership Team Business in the Community; FCA (ACA 1970); *Recreations* fishing, shooting, golf, gardening; *Clubs* Wilmslow Golf, Birdsgrove Fly Fishing; *Style*— Alan Benzie, Esq; ✉ KPMG, St James' Square, Manchester M2 6DS (✆ 0161 838 4000)

BERCOW, Rt Hon John Simon; PC (2009), MP; s of late Charles Bercow, and of Brenda Bercow; b 19 January 1963; *Educ* Finchley Manorhill Sch, Univ of Essex (BA); m Sally Illman; 2 s (Oliver b Dec 2003, Freddie b Nov 2005), 1 da (Jemima b April 2008); *Career* credit analyst Hambros Bank 1987–88, public affrs conslt Rowland Sallingbury Casey 1988–95 (board dir 1994–95); special advsr to: chief sec to the Treasy 1995, sec of state for Nat Heritage 1995–96; MP (Cons) Buckingham 1997–2009, (Parly candidate Motherwell S 1987 and Bristol S 1992), MP (Speaker) 2009–; oppn spokesman educn and employment 1999–2000, shadow Home Office min 2000–01, shadow chief sec to the Treasy 2001–02, shadow min for work and pensions 2002, shadow sec of state for int devpt 2003–04, speaker House of Commons 2009–; memb Select Ctees: Welsh Affrs 1997–98, Trade and Industry 1998–99, Office of the Dep PM 2002–04, Home Affrs 2003, Office of the Dep PM (Urban Affrs Sub-Ctee) 2003–04, Int Devpt 2004–09, Procedure 2004–05, Chm's Panel 2005–09, Jt Ctee on Consolidation, Etc, Bills 2005–09, Quadripartite (Ctees on Strategic Export Controls)/ Arms Export Controls 2006–09; ex-officio chair House of Commons Cmmn 2009–; ex-officio chair Boundary Cmmns for England, NI, Scotland and Wales 2009–; chair: Speaker's Ctee on the Electoral Cmmn 2009–, Speaker's Ctee for the Independent Parly Standards Authy 2009–; cncllr Lambeth BC 1986–90 (dep leader Cons oppn gp 1987–89), nat chm Cons students 1986–87; chllr Univ of Bedfordshire 2014–; Freeman City of London 2016; hon doctorate: Univ of Essex 2010, Buckingham Univ 2013, De Montfort Univ 2014, City Univ 2014; *Books* Tennis Maestros (2014); *Recreations* tennis (trying to play and watching Roger Federer), swimming, reading, cinema, music, Arsenal season ticket holder; *Style*— The Rt Hon John Bercow, MP; ✉ House of Commons, London SW1A 0AA (✆ 020 7219 6346)

BERDAL, Prof Mats; s of Eivind and Ester Berdal, of Oslo, Norway; b 5 October 1965; *Educ* LSE (BSc), St Antony's Coll Oxford (DPhil); m Dr Dominique Jacquin-Berdal (d 2006), da of Paul Jacquin; 1 da (Ingrid b 29 Sept 2001); *Career* res assoc IISS 1992–97 (res fell 1994–97), res fell St Antony's Coll Oxford 1997–2000, dir of studies IISS 2000–03, prof Dept of War Studies Sch of Social Sci and Public Policy KCL 2003–; visiting prof Norwegian Defence UC Oslo 2007–14; consulting sr fell IISS 2009–10; *Publications* Whither UN Peacekeeping? (1993), Disarmament and Demobilisation after Civil Wars (1996), Greed and Grievance: Economic Agendas in Civil Wars (co-ed with David Malone, 2000), United Nations Inverventionism 1991–2004 (contrib and co-ed with Spyros Economides, 2007), Reintegrating Armed Groups After Conflict – politics, violence and transition (co-ed with David H Ucko, 2009), Building Peace After War (2009), Political Economy of Statebuilding (contrib and co-ed with Dominik Zaum, 2013); *Style*— Prof Mats Berdal; ✉ Department of War Studies, School of Social Science and Public Policy, King's College London, Strand, London WC2R 2LS

BERESFORD, Elisabeth; MBE (1998); da of J D Beresford (the novelist), and Beatrice, *née* Roskams; b Paris; *Educ* St Mary's Hall Brighton, Brighton & Hove HS; m; 1 da (b 1951), 1 s (b 1956); *Career* author; formerly: shorthand typist CCO, ghost writer, reporter/ interviewer Today and Woman's Hour (BBC Radio 4); creator: The Wombles (books and BBC TV series) 1973, The Adventures of Dawdle (ITV series) 1996; numerous other children's books published; Tokyo video award (for film Rosebud), Puffin award (for selling a million copies); dir Craigie Robertson Ltd; chm Aurignoco Ltd Media Services; fndr The Alderney Youth Tst 1982; *Recreations* gardening, entertaining, filming; *Style*— Ms Elisabeth Beresford, MBE; ✉ c/o Juvenilia, Avington, Winchester, Hampshire SO21 1DB (✆ 01962 78656)

BERESFORD, Marcus de la Poer; CBE (2003); s of late Anthony de la Poer Beresford, TD, of Harrow-on-the-Hill, Middx, and Mary, *née* Canning; b 15 May 1942; *Educ* Harrow, St John's Coll Cambridge (MA); m 25 Sept 1965, Jean, da of late H T Kitchener, of Shepreth, Cambs; 2 s (Thomas, William); *Career* Smiths Industries 1960–83 (operating gp md 1979–83), dir and gen mangr Lucas Electronics & Systems 1983–85, md Siemens Plessey Controls Ltd 1985–92, dir Siemens plc 1991–92, dir GKN plc and md GKN Industrial Servs 1992–2001, chief exec GKN plc 2001–02; chm Ricardo plc 2003–; non-exec dir: Spirent plc (formerly Bowthorpe plc) 1999–2006, Cobham plc 2004–; Freeman City of London 1963, Liveryman Worshipful Co of Skinners; FIEE; *Recreations* golf; *Style*— Marcus Beresford, Esq, CBE

BERESFORD, Sir (Alexander) Paul; kt (1990), MP; b 6 April 1946; *Educ* Waimea Coll Richmond NZ, Univ of Otago NZ; m Julie Haynes; 3 s, 1 da; *Career* dental surgeon; London Borough of Wandsworth: cncllr 1978–94, former chm various ctees, ldr 1983–92; MP (Cons): Croydon Central 1992–97, Mole Valley 1997–; House of Commons: Parly under-sec of state Dept of Environment 1994–97; memb: Procedure Select Ctee 1997–2001, Tport Local Govt and the Regions Select Ctee 2001– (memb Urban Select Sub-Ctee 2001–), Security Joint Ctee 2010–, Finance and Services Ctee 2010–, Standards and Privileges Ctee 2010–13, House of Commons Commission of Mgmnt 2010–, Standards Ctee 2013–, Privileges Ctee 2013–; chair: All-Pty Gp for SE Tranport Integration, All-Pty Parliamentary Gp (APPG) Skin 2010–, APPG Dentistry 2010–; co-chair APPG Police; *Recreations* DIY, reading; *Style*— Sir Paul Beresford, MP; ✉ House of Commons, London SW1A 0AA (✆ 020 7219 3000)

BERESFORD, Dr Richard Charles; s of Eric Beresford, of Whichford, Warks, and Barbara, *née* Gatenby (d 1989); b 25 February 1958; *Educ* Uppingham, Courtauld Inst of Art (BA, PhD), London Business Sch (MBA); *Career* research asst rising to curator of paintings pre 1800 The Wallace Collection 1982–94, curator Dulwich Picture Gallery 1995–97, sr curator (European Art, pre 1900) Art Gallery of New South Wales 1997–; *Publications* A Dance to the Music of Time by Nicolas Poussin (1995), Dulwich Picture Gallery Complete Illustrated Catalogue (1998), The James Fairfax Collection of Old Master Paintings, Drawings and Prints (2003), Victorian Visions: nineteenth-century art from the John Schaeffer collection (2010); *Style*— Dr Richard Beresford; ✉ Art Gallery of New South Wales, Art Gallery Road, Sydney 2000, NSW, Australia (✆ 00 61 29 225 1700, fax 00 61 29 225 1874, e-mail richard.beresford@ag.nsw.gov.au)

BERGENDAHL, (Carl) Anders; s of Carl Johan Bergendahl (d 1995), of Djursholm, Sweden, and Ingrid Bergendahl (d 1964); b 20 March 1952; *Educ* Djursholm's Samskola, Stockholm Sch of Econs; m 18 March 1984, Maria, da of Stephen Heineman (d 1967); 2 s (David b 11 Sept 1985, Alexander b 18 June 1987); *Career* assoc Merrill Lynch 1977–, md Merrill Lynch & Co 1985, head of EMEA investment banking relationship mgmnt and business orgination Merrill Lynch 1994, co-head Global Debt Capital Markets Merrill Lynch & Co Inc 1996–99, ceo Benelux & Nordic Regions and head of investment banking Switzerland Merrill Lynch 1999–2001, global co-head of global industries Merrill Lynch & Co 2001–04, vice-chm Investment Banking Merrill Lynch Int 2004–; pres Minna-James-Heineman Stifung 1993; memb Bd of Dirs: Heineman Medical Research Inc 1992, Heineman Fndn for Research, Educational, Charitable and Scientific Purposes Inc 1994; *Recreations* sailing, tennis, squash, skiing; *Clubs* Sallskapet, RAC; *Style*— Anders

Bergendahl, Esq; ✉ Merrill Lynch International Ltd, Merrill Lynch Financial Centre, 2 King Edward Street, London EC1A 1HQ (☎ 020 7995 2800, fax 020 7995 0901)

BERGER, Herbert; s of Herbert Berger, and Hedwig; *b* 19 April 1953; *Educ* Catering Coll Salzburg; *m* 16 Feb 1989 (m dis 2010), Jane, *née* Crawford; 1 da (Annie b 2 April 1990); *Career* apprentice Grand Hotel Zell/See Austria 1968–71, seasonal work various hotels Switzerland 1971–75, chef de partie then sous chef Fredericks Restaurant 1975–76, head chef Le Connoisseur Restaurant London (Michelin Star) 1977–79, various positions rising to sous chef Connaught Hotel 1980–85, premier sous chef Claridges Hotel 1985–86, head chef Mirabelle Restaurant Curzon Street 1986–88, owner Keats Restaurant Hampstead (Michelin Red M within 6 months of opening) 1988–91, ptnr Berger & Sawyer Restaurant Ltd 1988–91, ptnr Restaurant Partnership 1991–, exec chef Café Royal 1992–97, head chef, gen mangr and shareholder 1 Lombard St Restaurant 1997–2011 (Michelin Star 2000–11), fndr Berger Restaurants Ltd 2012–; subject of various magazine articles; guest appearances: Ascot Racecourse, The Good Food Show (BBC), The Restaurant Show, Telegraph House & Garden Food Show, Masterchef, Nat Museums & Galleries of Wales, Nat Gallery Washington DC, Trimbach Food and Wine Masterclass, Marco Polo Cruise Liner, The Big Breakfast, After Five Dilly Dines Out; guest chef: The Restaurauteurs Dinner, Assoc Culinaire de France Dinner, SOS Charity Dinner, Fundraising Acad Dinners, Action Against Hunger Charity Dinner 2007; memb: Académie Culinaire de France UK 1986–, Euro Togue 1995, Assoc Culinaire de France, World Master Chef Soc 2012; *Awards* mention d'honneur Prix Pierre Taittinger 1983, AA 3 Rosettes, Egon Ronay Star, Michelin Star (Grill Room Café Royal), Eros Award 1995, Mumm Stars of Gastronomy, Best New Restaurant Carlton Awards, Maitrisse Escoffier 2003, Cordon Rouge Assoc Culinaire the France 2008, Commendation IFWS 2015; Freeman Worshipful Co of Cooks 2015; *Books* Off Duty (contrib); contrib to various other books; *Recreations* travel, gastronomic tours, eating out, music, the arts, skiing, shooting; *Clubs* The Tabasco, Ordre de Coteaux de Champagne, Reunion des Gastronomes, Club des Amis Connaught Hotel; *Style*— Herbert Berger, Esq; ✉ e-mail berbertberger@btinternet.com; Berger Restaurants Ltd @ The Worshipful Company of Innholders, 30 College Street, London EC4R 2RH

BERGER, Luciana Clare; MP; *b* 1981; *Educ* Haberdashers' Aske's Sch for Girls, Univ of Birmingham, Birkbeck Coll London; *Career* MP (Lab/Co-op) Liverpool Wavertree 2010–, shadow min for mental health 2015–; FRSA; *Style*— Luciana Berger, MP; ✉ House of Commons, London SW1A 0AA (e-mail luciana.berger.mp@parliament.uk, website www.lucianaberger.com, Twitter @lucianaberger)

BERGIN, Prof Joseph; s of late Cornelius Bergin, and late Brigid, *née* Phelan; *b* 11 February 1948; *Educ* Rockwell Coll Co Tipperary Eire, UCD (BA, MA), Peterhouse Cambridge (PhD); *m* 1978, Sylvia Papazian; 1 s (Edward b 1981), 1 da (Olivia b 1985); *Career* lectr in history Maynooth Coll Eire 1976–78; Univ of Manchester: lectr in history 1978–88, sr lectr 1988–92, reader 1992–96, prof 1996–11, prof emeritus 2011–; winner Prix Richelieu 1995; LittD Univ of Manchester 2004; FRHistS 1988, FBA 1996; Officier de l'Ordre des Palmes Academiques 2010, Médaille des Antiquités de France Académie des Inscriptions et Belles-Lettres Paris 2010 (correspondant étranger 2011), Medaille Richelieu Sorbonne 2010, Correspondant étranger Institut de France 2011; *Books* Cardinal Richelieu: Power and the Pursuit of Wealth (1985), The Rise of Richelieu (1991), The Making of the French Episcopate 1589–1661 (1996), Crown, Church and Episcopate under Louis XIV (2004), Church, Society and Religious Change in France 1580–1730 (2009), The Politics of Religion in Early Modern France (2014), History of France (2015); *Recreations* sports, book hunting; *Style*— Prof Joseph Bergin, FBA; ✉ Department of History, University of Manchester, Oxford Road, Manchester M13 9PL (☎ 0161 275 3084, e-mail j.bergin@man.ac.uk)

BERINGER, Guy; CBE (2016), QC (2006); *b* 12 August 1955; *Educ* Campbell Coll Belfast, St Catharine's Coll Cambridge (MA); *m* 1979, Margaret Catherine, *née* Powell; 3 da; *Career* Allen & Overy: asst 1980–85, ptnr 1985–2000, sr ptnr 2000–08; non-exec chm and chair Mgmnt Bd Export Credits Guarantee Dept (ECGD) 2010–; memb Law Soc; *Style*— Guy Beringer, Esq, CBE, QC

BERKELEY, Andrew Wilson Atkins; s of Andrew Berkeley, JP (d 1952), of Cookstown, Co Tyrone, and Mabel Berkeley; *b* 15 July 1936; *Educ* Rainey Sch Co Derry, Queen's Univ Belfast (BSc), Harvard Business Sch (AMP), KCL (MSc), Birkbeck (MA); *m* 30 Nov 1968, Carolyn Blyth Hinshaw Ross, of Milngavie, Glasgow; 2 da (Kirsten b 16 Nov 1972, Iona b 27 April 1978); *Career* called to the Bar Gray's Inn 1965; Legal Dept ICI Ltd 1966–78, gen counsel The British Nat Oil Corp 1981–84, legal dir STC plc 1984–87, gen counsel Laporte plc 1987–92; conslt Int Chamber of Commerce 1995–2007; int commercial arbitrator; FCIArb; *Clubs* Athenaeum; *Style*— Andrew Berkeley, Esq; ✉ 49 Arden Road, London N3 3AD (☎ 020 8343 4050, fax 020 8343 1762, e-mail aberkeley@virginmedia.com)

BERKELEY, 18 Baron (E 1421); Anthony FitzHardinge Gueterbock; OBE (1989); sits as Baron Geuterbock (Life Peer UK 2000), of Cranford, London Borough of Hillingdon; o s of Brig Ernest Adolphus Leopold Gueterbock, late RE (d 1984), and Hon Cynthia Ella Foley (d 1991); suc aunt Mary Lallé Foley Berkeley, Baroness Berkeley (d 1992); *b* 20 September 1939; *Educ* Eton, Trinity Coll Cambridge (MA); *m* 1, 10 July 1965 (m dis 1998), Diana Christine, er da of Eric William John Townsend, MRCS, LRCP; 2 s (Hon Thomas FitzHardinge b 1969, Hon Robert William b 1970), 1 da (Hon Philippa Louise b 1975); m 2, 8 May 1999 (m dis 2011), Julia, o da of Michael Clarke; *Heir* s, Hon Thomas Gueterbock; *Career* engrg, construction and planning Sir Alexander Gibb and Partners 1961–67, construction, planning and business devpt George Wimpey plc 1967–85, public affrs mangr Eurotunnel plc 1985–95; chm: The Piggyback Consortium 1993–99, Rail Freight Group 1996–; advsr ADtranz 1995–2001; pres European Rail Freight Assoc 2009–11 (memb Bd 2007–); Lab whip and spokesman on tport House of Lords 1996–97, memb European Select Ctee 1998–99; harbour cmmr Port of Fowey 2007–14; Hon DSc Univ of Brighton 1996; CEng, MICE, FRSA, FCIT, Hon FIMechE; *Recreations* sailing, skiing; *Style*— The Rt Hon the Lord Berkeley, OBE; ✉ House of Lords, London SW1A 0PW

BERKELEY, (Robert) John Grantley; TD (1967), JP (Glos 1960), DL (Glos 1982, Hereford and Worcester 1983); s of Capt Robert George Wilmot Berkeley (d 1969, himself 13 in descent from Hon Thomas Berkeley (4 s of 1 Baron Berkeley cr 1421, gs of 4 Baron Berkeley cr 1295, and descended in direct male line from Eadnoth the Staller, pre-Conquest Anglo-Saxon nobleman at Court of King Edward the Confessor) by his 2 w Isabel, da and co-heir of Thomas Mowbray, 1 Duke of Norfolk and Hon Myrtle, da of 14 Baron Dormer; *b* 24 July 1931; *Educ* The Oratory, Magdalen Coll Oxford; *m* 25 Jan 1967, Georgina Bridget, eld da of Maj Andrew Charles Stirling Home Drummond Moray (d 1971), of Easter Ross, Comrie, Perthshire; 2 s (Robert Charles b 1968, Henry John Mowbray b 1969); *Career* Maj Queen's Own Warks Yeo 1963; jt master Berkeley Hunt 1960–84; High Sheriff: Worcs 1967, Glos 1982–83; *Clubs* Cavalry and Guards'; *Style*— R J Berkeley, Esq, TD, DL; ✉ Berkeley Castle, Gloucestershire (☎ 01453 810202, e-mail email@berkeleyestate.co.uk); Spetchley Park, Worcestershire (☎ 01905 345224)

BERKELEY OF KNIGHTON, Baron (UK Life Peer 2013), Knighton in the County of Powys; Michael Fitzhardinge Berkeley; CBE (2012); s of Sir Lennox Randal Francis Berkeley, CBE (d 1989), of 8 Warwick Ave, London, and Elizabeth Freda, *née* Bernstein; *b* 29 May 1948; *Educ* Westminster Cathedral Choir Sch, The Oratory, Royal Acad of Music (ARAM), postgrad work with Sir Richard Rodney Bennett, CBE, *qv*; *m* 19 Nov 1979, Deborah Jane, da of Guy Coltman Rogers (d 1976), of Stanage Park, Knighton, Powys; 1 da (Jessica Rose b 28 June 1986); *Career* composer and broadcaster; phlebotomist St Bartholomew's Hosp 1969–71, announcer BBC Radio 3 1974–79, regular broadcaster on music and the arts BBC radio and TV 1974–; music panel advsr Arts Cncl of GB 1986–90, artistic dir Cheltenham Int Festival of Music 1995–2004; memb: Central Music Advsy Ctee BBC 1986–89, Gen Advsy Cncl BBC 1990–95, Bd of Dirs ROH 1996–2003 (chm Opera Bd 1998–99); co-artistic dir Spitalfields Festival 1995–97; assoc composer Scottish Chamber Orch 1979, composer-in-assoc BBC Nat Orch of Wales and Welsh Coll of Music and Drama 2001–; visiting prof Univ of Huddersfield 1991–94; govr National Youth Orch of GB 1994–96, chm Bd of Govrs Royal Ballet 2003–; tstee Britten-Pears Fndn 1997–; compositions incl: Meditations (Guinness prize for composition) 1977, Primavera 1979, Uprising 1980, Wessex Graves 1981, Or Shall We Die? (oratorio) 1982, Music from Chaucer 1983, Fierce Tears 1984, Pas de Deux 1985, Songs of Awakening Love 1986, Organ Concerto 1987, The Red Macula 1989, Gethsemane Fragment 1990, Clarinet Concerto 1991, Baa Baa Black Sheep (opera) 1993, Viola Concerto 1994, Magnetic Field 1995, Winter Fragments 1996, Torque and Velocity 1997, Secret Garden 1997, The Garden of Earthly Delights 1998, Tristessa (orchestra) 2003, Jane Eyre (opera) 2000, Concerto for Orchestra 2005, For You (opera) 2008, Show Down (ochestra) 2008, Gabriel's Lament (orchestra) 2009; FRAM 1996, fell Royal Welsh Coll of Music and Drama (FRWCMD) 2003, FRNCM 2004; *Publications* The Music Pack (1994); author of various articles in The Observer, The Guardian, The Listener, The Sunday Telegraph and Vogue; *Recreations* looking at paintings, reading, walking, skiing, tennis, hill farming in Mid Wales; *Style*— The Lord Berkeley of Knighton, CBE

BERKOFF, Steven; *b* 3 August 1937; *Career* writer, actor and dir; fndr London Theatre Group 1968 (first professional prodn In The Penal Colony); Hon DLitt Brunel Univ 2010; *Theatre* adapted/dir/toured: The Trial, Metamorphosis, Agamemnon, Salome, The Fall of the House of Usher; dir/toured: Hamlet, Macbeth, own one man show (GB, USA, Aust); dir: Coriolanus (NY, Aust, UK and world tour also title role), Kvetch, Richard II (NY); Shakespeare's Villains (West End and world tour), Messiah (Edinburgh and Old Vic), The Secret Love Life of Ophelia, Sip and Shiver ((LA), Richard II (Ludlow Festival), On the Waterfront (Theatre Royal Haymarket) 2009, Oedipus (Liverpool Everyman and Nottingham Playhouse) 2011; *Television* appearances incl: Sins, War and Remembrance, Michaelangelo – Season of Giants; TV prodns incl: West (Channel Four) 1984, Metamorphosis (BBC 2) 1989, Harry's Christmas, Silent Night (Channel Four) 1991, Tell Tale Heart (Channel Four) 1991; *Radio* title role in Macbeth (Radio 4) 1995, the MC in Cabaret (musical debut, Radio 2) 1996, An Actor's Tale (Radio 4) 1997; *Film* appearances incl: The Tourist, A Clockwork Orange, Barry Lyndon, The Passenger, McVicar, Outlands, Octopussy, Beverly Hills Cop, Rambo, Underworld, Revolution, Under the Cherry Moon, Absolute Beginners, Prisoner of Rio, The Krays, Fair Game, Decadence, Flynn, Another 9 1/2 Weeks, Legionnaire, Rancid Aluminium, The Henchman; *Publications* original plays: East (first original play presented at Edinburgh Festival 1975), Decadence (1982), Greek (1982), West (1985), Harry's Christmas (1985), Lunch (1985), Sink The Belgrano! (1987), Massage (1987), Kvetch (1987), Acapulco (1987), Sturm und Drang, Brighton Beach Scumbags, Ritual in Blood, Messiah, The Secret Love Life of Ophelia (2001); other publications incl: The Trial (play adaptation, 1978), Gross Intrusion (1979), America (poetry and prose, 1988), A Prisoner in Rio (film journal, 1989), I am Hamlet (prodn diary, 1989), Coriolanus in Deutschland (1992), The Theatre of Steven Berkoff (photographic history), Meditations on Metamorphosis (1995), Free Association (autobiography, 1996), Graft: Tales of An Actor (1998), Shopping in the Santa Monica Mall (2002), Tough Acts! (2003), My Life in Food (2007), Richard II in New York (2008), You Remind Me of Marilyn Monroe (2009), Diary of a Juvenile Delinquent (2010), Tales from an Actor's Life (2011), One Act Plays (2012); *Style*— Steven Berkoff, Esq

BERKSHIRE, Archdeacon of; *see:* Russell, Ven Norman Atkinson

BERLIN, Barry; *Educ* Brunel Univ (BSc); *Career* called to the Bar Gray's Inn 1981; currently memb St Philips Chambers; provincial Treasy counsel 1995–, memb Attorney Gen's A List (Crime) 2003, recorder Midland Circuit; hon lectr Univ of Birmingham; *Recreations* current affairs, British history, theatre, football, cricket; *Style*— Barry Berlin, Esq; ✉ St Philips Chambers, 55 Temple Row, Birmingham B2 5LS

BERMAN, Sir Franklin Delow; KCMG (1994, CMG 1987); s of Joshua Zelic Berman, of Cape Town, and Gertrude, *née* Levin; *b* 23 December 1939; *Educ* Rondebosch Boys' HS, Univ of Cape Town (BA, BSc), Wadham and Nuffield Colls Oxford (MA); *m* 24 July 1964, Christine Mary, da of Edward Francis Lawler (d 1978); 2 s (Jonathan b 1966, Stefan b 1968), 3 da (Katharine b 1972, Judith b 1972, Victoria b 1972); *Career* called to the Bar Middle Temple 1966 (bencher 1997); joined HM Dip Serv 1965, asst legal advsr FCO 1965–71, legal advsr Br Mil Govt Berlin 1971–72, legal advsr Br Embassy Bonn 1972–74, legal cnsllr FCO 1974–82, cnsllr UK Mission UN NY 1982–85, legal advsr FCO 1991–99 (dep legal advsr 1988–91); judge ad hoc Int Court of Justice 2003–05, memb Perm Court of Arbitration 2010–; J C Smith visiting fell Univ of Nottingham 1993; chm: Dip Serv Assoc 1979–82, Appeals Bd Int Oil Pollution Compensation Fund 1985–2004, Austrian Nat Fund for Compensation of Victims of Nazi Persecution 2001–, Diplomatic Serv Appeals Bd 2002–06; memb: Bd Inst of Advanced Legal Studies Univ of London 1991–99, Governing Cncl Br Inst of Int and Comp Law 1992–2005, Cncl Br Branch Int Law Assoc 1992–, Appeals Bd Western EU 1994–96 and 2002–05, Editorial Bd Br Yearbook of Int Law 1994–, Advsy Cncl Centre for Euro and Comparative Law Univ of Oxford 1995–, Advsy Cncl Univ of Oxford Law Fndn 1998–2004; tstee: Edward Fry Memorial Library 1991–99, The Whittuck Tst 1992–, Greenwich Fndn Royal Naval Coll 1997–2005, Univ of Cape Town Tst 1999– (chm 2010–), Australian SAS Resources Tst 2005–09, Br Inst of Int and Comp Law 2007– (chm 2011–); patron The Pimpernel Tst; visiting prof of international law Univ of Oxford and Univ of Cape Town; hon QC 1992; hon fell: Wadham Coll 1995, Soc of Advanced Legal Studies 1997–; Grand Decoration of Honour in Gold with Star (Austria) 2007, Grand Croix de l'Ordre Royal (Cambodia) 2015; *Publications* articles and chapters in learned jls and Oxford Dictionary of National Biography; *Recreations* reading, walking, choral singing, gardening; *Style*— Sir Franklin Berman, KCMG, QC; ✉ Essex Court Chambers, 24 Lincoln's Inn Fields, London WC2A 3EG (☎ 020 7813 8000, fax 020 7813 8080, e-mail fberman@essexcourt.net)

BERNARD, Daniel Camille; s of Paul Bernard, and Simone, *née* Doise; *b* 18 February 1946; *Educ* Lycee Camille Desmoulins Cateau, Lycee Faidherbe Lille, HEC Business Sch, Univ of Paris; *m* 1968, Chantal Leduc; 1 s, 2 da; *Career* divnl mangr Mammouth 1976–81, ceo Metro France 1981–89, memb Bd and chief operating offr Metro Int 1989–92; Carrefour Gp: ceo 1992–98, chm and ceo 1998–2005; Kingfisher plc: jt dep chm 2006–07, dep chm 2007–09, chm 2009–; pres Provestis, chm Majid Al Futtaim Retail Gp 2010–; non-exec dir: Alcatel-Lucent (formerly Alcatel) 1997–, Cap Gemini 2005–; sr advsr Towerbrook Capital Ptnrs 2010–; chm HEC Fndn 2008–; *Recreations* mountains, skiing, opera; *Style*— Daniel Bernard, Esq; ✉ Kingfisher plc, 3 Sheldon Square, London W2 6PX

BERNAYS, Richard Oliver; s of Robert Hamilton Bernays, MP (MP for Bristol North 1931–45, ka 1945), and Nancy, *née* Britton (d 1987); *b* 22 February 1943; *Educ* Eton, Trinity Coll Oxford (MA); *m* 1, 12 Feb 1972 (m dis 1993), Karen Forney, of New Castle, PA; 3 da (Lucy b 1975, Mary b 1977 d 1993, Amy b 1979); m 2, 22 Feb 1996, Rosamund Horwood-Smart, QC, *qv*; *Career* vice-chm Mercury Asset Management plc, dir Mercury Fund Managers Ltd 1971–92; chief exec: Hill Samuel Investment Management Group 1992–96, Old Mutual International, Capel-Cure Sharp 1998–2001; chm: Gartmore Global Tst 2002–12, Impax Environmental Markets Tst 2002–14, Throgmorton Tst 2005–12, Hermes Pensions Management 2005–08, Quantum Gp Management 2010–; tstee N M Rothschild Pension Scheme; dir: Singer & Friedlander Gp 2003–05, WNS Gp 2006–13,

Cossack Bond Fund; chm Cncl Cheltenham Ladies' Coll 1999–2004, tstee American Museum in Britain 2010–; *Recreations* golf, fishing, gardening, music; *Clubs* Brooks's, Beefsteak, Swinley Forest, Sunningdale Golf; *Style*— Richard Bernays, Esq; ✉ E72 Montevetro, 100 Battersea Church Road, London SW11 3YL

BERNEY, Sir Julian Reedham Stuart; 11 Bt (E 1620), of Parkehall in Reedham, Norfolk; s of Lt John Berney (ka Korea 1952), and Hon Jean Davina Stuart (d 2003, who m 2, Percy William Jesson; and 3, Michael D Ritchie), da of 1 Viscount Stuart of Findhorn, CH, MVO, MC, PC; suc gf 1975; *b* 26 September 1952; *Educ* Wellington, N E London Poly; *m* 1976, Sheena Mary, da of Ralph Day, of Maldon, Essex; 2 s (William Reedham John b 1980, Hugo Reedham Ralph b 1987), 1 da (Jessica Mary Reedham b 1982); *Heir* s, William Berney; *Career* chartered surveyor; Freeman Worshipful Co of Fishmongers; FRICS; *Recreations* sailing, travel, reading, photography; *Clubs* Royal Yacht Sqdn, Royal Ocean Racing, Royal Cruising; *Style*— Sir Julian Berney, Bt; ✉ Reeds House, 40 London Road, Maldon, Essex CM9 6HE (☎ 01621 853420)

BERNS, Richard Michael; s of Leonard Berns (d 1978), and Elizabeth Grace, *née* Turner (d 2005); *b* 16 August 1947; *Educ* Dulwich Coll; *Children* 1 s (Ashley b 1969), 1 da (Antonia b 1974); *Career* slr; owner Berns Legal Consultancy Ltd (BLCL); memb Law Soc; *Recreations* cinema, music, reading, sailing, skiing, travel, walking, motorcycling; *Style*— Richard M Berns, Esq; ✉ BLCL at Leigh Hill Place, 31 Leigh Hill Road, Cobham, Surrey KT11 2HU (☎ 07836 227653, e-mail rb@psbberns.fsbusiness.co.uk); Sherrards LLP, 7 Swallow Place, London W1B 2AG (e-mail richard.berns@sherrards.com)

BERNSTEIN, David Alan; CBE (2014); s of Henry Bernstein (d 2001), and Anne Bernstein (d 1998); *b* 22 May 1943; *Educ* Christ's Coll Finchley; *m* Gillian; 4 s (Lawrence, Peter, Richard, Nicholas); *Career* chartered accountant Bright Grahame Murray (subsequently jt sr ptnr) 1968–88, jt md Pentland Group plc 1988–94, non-exec chm Blacks Leisure Gp plc 1995–2011; chm: Manchester City FC 1998–2003, Frank Thomas Ltd 2003–11; non-exec dir French Connection Gp plc 1995–2001, Ted Baker plc 2003–, Wembley Nat Stadium Ltd 2003–11, Carluccio's 2005–11; chm FA 2010–13, chm Chandos Tennis Club; FCA 1996; *Recreations* sport (especially golf, running), theatre, opera, politics; *Style*— David Bernstein, Esq, CBE; ✉ 48 Fitzalan Road, Finchley, London N3 3PE (☎ 020 8346 2345, fax 020 8343 0625)

BERNSTEIN, Dr Robert Michael; s of Dr Fred Julian Bernstein (d 1986), and Dr Emilie Ellen Bernstein, *née* Guthmann (d 1995); *b* 31 December 1947; *Educ* Highgate Sch, King's Coll Cambridge (MA, MD, BChir), UCH Med Sch; *m* 29 Sept 1978, Frances Jane Northcroft, da of Dr Christopher Tibbits Brown, of Wareham, Dorset; 3 s (Jonathan b 1979, Nicholas b 1983, Jeremy b 1993), 3 da (Laura b 1981, Alice b 1986, Clare b 1991); *Career* sr registrar Royal Postgrad Med Sch Hammersmith Hosp 1981–85, visiting scientist Cold Spring Harbor Laboratory USA 1983–84, conslt rheumatologist and hon clinical lectr Univ of Manchester and Manchester Royal Infirmary 1985–2007; currently conslt rheumatologist in private and medicolegal practice; late memb Res Advsy Panel Lupus UK; late memb Specialty Advsy Ctee in Rheumatology, former chm Fibromyalgia Assoc UK; late members' columnist RCP, late memb Editorial Bd Clinical and Experimental Immunology; late memb Nat Ctee Lupus UK, late bd memb Br Assoc for Performing Arts Med; late memb Cncl Reform Synagogues of GB; FRCP 1990 (MRCP 1975); *Recreations* mountains, music; *Style*— Dr Robert Bernstein; ✉ BMI Alexandra Hospital, Mill Lane, Cheadle, Cheshire SK8 2PX (☎ 0161 295 7702, fax 0161 495 7703)

BERRIDGE, Baroness (Life Peer UK 2011), of The Vale of Catmose in the County of Rutland; Elizabeth Rose Berridge; *Educ* Catmose Coll Oakham, Emmanuel Coll Cambridge (BA); *Career* called to the Bar 1996; barr Kings Chambers 36 Young St Manchester 1996–2005, exec dir Conservative Christian Fellowship 2005–10; co-chair All Pty Parly Gp on Int Religious Freedom, project dir Cwlth Initiative for Freedom of Religion or Belief; memb: London Policing Ethics Panel 2014–, Select Ctee for Social Mobility, Steering Ctee Int Panel of Parliamentarians for Freedom of Religion or Belief; *Recreations* tennis, lifelong interest in Ghana, Central African Republic; *Style*— The Baroness Berridge; ✉ House of Lords, London SW1A 0PW (☎ 020 7219 8943, website www.baronessberridge.com, Twitter @baronesseb)

BERRIDGE, Prof Sir Michael John; kt (1998); s of George Kirton Berridge and Stella Elaine, *née* Hards; *b* 22 October 1938; *Educ* UC of Rhodesia and Nyasaland (BSc), Univ of Cambridge (PhD); *m* 5 March 1965, Susan Graham, *née* Winter; 1 da (Rozanne b 4 June 1967), 1 s (Paul b 19 March 1969); *Career* post doctoral fell Univ of Virginia 1965–66, res assoc Case Western Res Univ 1967 (post doctoral fell 1966–69); Univ of Cambridge: sr scientific offr Unit of Invertebrate Chemistry and Physiology 1969, chief sci offr Unit of Insect Neurophysiology and Pharmacology 1987–90; Agric Food Res Cncl Laboratory of Molecular Signalling 1990–94, The Babraham Inst Laboratory of Molecular Signalling 1994–2003 (emeritus Babraham fell 2003–); hon prof of cell signalling Univ of Cambridge 1994–; fell Trinity Coll Cambridge 1972; awards incl: Feldberg Prize 1984, The King Faisal Int Prize in Sci 1986, Louis Jeantet Prize in Med 1986, William Bate Hardy Prize (Cambridge Philosophical Soc) 1987, Abraham White Scientific Achievement Award (George Washington Univ Sch of Med) 1987, Gairdner Fndn Int Award 1988, Baly Medal (RCP) 1989, Albert Lasker Basic Med Res Award 1989, Heineken Prize Royal Netherlands Acad of Arts and Sciences 1994, The Wolf Fndn Prize in Med 1995, Shaw Prize in Med 2005; foreign assoc Nat Acad of Science Washington DC 1999, foreign hon memb American Acad of Arts and Science 1999, memb American Philosophical Soc 2007, hon memb Hungarian Acad of Sciences 2014; FRS 1984 (Royal Medal); *Recreations* golf, gardening; *Style*— Prof Sir Michael Berridge, FRS; ✉ Laboratory of Molecular Signalling, Babraham Institute, Babraham, Cambridge CB22 3AT (☎ 01223 496621, e-mail michael.berridge@babraham.ac.uk)

BERRIGAN, Frances (Mrs Berrigan-Taplin); *b* 1943; *Educ* Santa Maria Ladies' Coll WA, Univ of Western Aust (BA, DipEd); *m*; 2 c; *Career* television prodr/dir; teacher Aust 1964–65, prodr educnl progs Australian Broadcasting Cmmn 1965–66, researcher children's and higher educn progs BBC TV 1969–70, prodr educn and community progs BBC Radio London 1970–72, freelance broadcaster and journalist Paris 1973–75 (features contrib BBC Radio 4 progs incl The World Tonight, World at One and Today, contrib TES and THES, media conslt and writer for UNESCO), research fell Middx Poly 1976–77, lectr in media research methods Open Univ 1976–78, prodr/dir and co-ordinating ed BBC Open Univ Prodn Centre 1979–84; Cicada Films: joined 1984 (after producing Nature in Focus series), md and prodr/dir 1987–, latterly md and sole proprietor; Cicada prodns incl: Blue Eye of Siberia (for Channel 4 Fragile Earth strand, NY Film Festival Silver Medal, Channel 4 entry in Prix D'Italia), Birds as Prey (for Fragile Earth), Unnatural Disasters, China: An Environment in Crisis, Making the Grade (for BBC Forty Minutes strand) and Soviet co-prodns Philby and The Krogers, Cutting Edge (Channel 4), The Club (Channel 4, finalist BAFTA Awards, 1995), Hidden Scrolls of Herculaneum (Channel 4), To the Ends of the Earth (Channel 4), In Search of Eden (Channel 4), The Volcano that Blew a World Away (Channel 4), Veerapan – The Last Bandit (Channel 4), various other wildlife and environmental films for Channel 4, BBC and others; *Style*— Ms Frances Berrigan

BERRY, Amanda; OBE (2009); da of Thomas Berry, and Anita, *née* Booth; *b* 20 August 1961, Darlington, Co Durham; *Educ* York Coll of Art, Newcastle Poly; *Career* co-dir Duncan Heath Assoc (now ICM) 1982–88, res light entertainment and current affairs LWT 1989–90, prodr and devpt exec Scottish Television Enterprises 1990–98, dir of devpt and events BAFTA 1998–2000, chief exec BAFTA 2000–; Woman of the Year 1999, Media Boss of the Year 1999, The Times British Film Power 100, Women in Film and TV Power List, Women: Inspiration and Enterprise Power 50; *Recreations* cinema, travel, art, music; *Clubs* Groucho, Soho House; *Style*— Ms Amanda Berry, OBE; ✉ The British Academy of Film & Television Arts, 195 Piccadilly, London W1J 9LN (☎ 020 7734 0022, e-mail amandab@bafta.org)

BERRY, Andrew John; s of late John Frederick Berry, and Avril Jean, *née* Leicester; *b* 16 April 1958; *Educ* Hurstpierpoint Coll, King's Sch Canterbury; *m* 1, 24 April 1982 (m dis 1998), Gail Louise, da of late Peter Newmark; 1 s (Alexander Andrew John b 15 Feb 1987), 1 da (Georgia Louise b 19 June 1988); m 2, Emily Sarah, da of late Dr Alastair Gordon Aitchison; *Career* vice-pres Merrill Lynch 1985–88, dir Chase Manhattan Bank 1988–1991, md Fimat Int Banque 1992–2000, chm Bawag-Refclear (Worldwide Gp) 2000–03, md ICAP plc 2004–06, ptnr Zodiac Partnership 2007–; Freeman Worshipful Co of Horners; *Recreations* shooting, gardening, driving; *Style*— Andrew Berry, Esq; ✉ Little Fishfolds, Mayes Green, Ockley, Surrey RH5 5PN (☎ 01306 621231, fax 01306 621271, e-mail andrewjohnberry@aol.com)

BERRY, Anthony Charles; QC (1994); s of Geoffrey Vernon Berry (d 1983), and Audrey Millicent, *née* Farrar (d 2001); *b* 4 October 1950; *Educ* Downside, Lincoln Coll Oxford (BA); *m* Susan Carmen, da of Derek Traversi, CBE; 3 s (Edward Paul b 8 Jan 1983, James Andrew b 15 Aug 1985, Richard John b 15 Aug 1985), 1 da (Tessa Jane b 17 March 1990); *Career* called to the Bar 1976, bencher Gray's Inn 2002; sec Criminal Bar Assoc 1991–93, memb Bar Cncl 1994–97, memb Panel of Int Advocates 2012; *Recreations* golf, tennis, real tennis; *Clubs* Royal Mid Surrey Golf; *Style*— Anthony Berry, Esq, QC; ✉ 9 Bedford Row, London WC1R 4AZ (☎ 020 7489 2727, fax 020 7489 2928)

BERRY, Prof Christopher Jon (Chris); s of Joseph Berry (d 1988), and Audrey, *née* Barnes (d 1989); *b* 19 June 1946, St Helens, Lancs; *Educ* Upholland GS, Univ of Nottingham (BA), LSE (PhD); *m* 3 Aug 1968, Christine Emma, *née* Claxton; 2 s (Craig Adrian b 11 Nov 1976, Paul Duncan b 20 May 1979); *Career* Univ of Glasgow: successively asst lectr, lectr, sr lectr and reader Dept of Politics 1970–95, prof of political theory 1995–2011 (emeritus prof 2011–, hon professorial research fell 2011–), head Dept of Politics 1998–2002, head Grad Sch and dep dean Faculty of Law, Business and Social Sciences 2005–10; visiting prof: Univ of Pittsburgh 1973–74, Coll of William and Mary Williamsburg USA 1980–81; FRSA 2001, FRSE 2005; *Publications* Hume, Hegel and Human Nature (1982), Human Nature (1986), The Idea of Democratic Community (1989), The Idea of Luxury: A Conceptual and Historical Investigation (1994, Chinese translation 2005), Social Theory of the Scottish Enlightenment (1997, Chinese translation 2013), Hume (2009), Idea of Commercial Society in Scottish Enlightenment (2013, Japanese translation 2015), Oxford Handbook of Adam Smith (jt ed, 2013); over 50 academic articles and book chapters; *Recreations* contemporary fiction; *Style*— Prof Chris Berry; ✉ School of Social and Political Sciences, Adam Smith Building, University of Glasgow, Glasgow G12 8RT (☎ 0141 330 5064, e-mail christopher.berry@glasgow.ac.uk)

BERRY, Dave; s of Robert Berry, of London, and Marian, *née* Flynn; *b* 14 September 1978, London; *Educ* John Roan Secdy Sch, Greenwich; *Career* television and radio presenter; *Television* Nickelodeon 2001–2, MTV 2002–5, T4 and Channel 4 2204–, TRL 2003–05, CD UK 2005, Vodafone TBA 2006–08, Real Stories (Channel 4) 2009–12, Surprise Surprise (ITV) 2013–, Through the Keyhole (ITV) 2013–; *Radio* XFM 2008–11, Capital Radio 2011–, Capital Breakfast 2012–; vice pres Demelza Children's Hospice, youth ambass Charlton Athletic Community Tst, ambass Balls to Cancer; TRIC Award 2013, Radio Academy Gold Award 2014; *Recreations* cinema, music, tennis, walking, football; *Clubs* Ivy, Century, Hospital; *Style*— Mr Dave Berry; ✉ c/o TROIKA, 10a Christina Street, London EC2A 4PA

BERRY, David Stuart; s of George Arthur Berry (d 1970), and Margaret Stuart, *née* Brown (d 1984); *b* 13 April 1948, London; *Educ* North Berwick HS, Univ of Edinburgh (BSc); *Career* computer engr Honeywell London 1971–73, devpt engr Siemens AG Munich 1973–77, hardware mangr Applied Computer Systems CA 1977–82, product planning mangr AMD CA 1982–87, mktg mangr Adaptec CA 1987–91, conslt on databases Loch Moy Ltd 1991–; cncllr (North Berwick Ward) E Lothian Cncl 1999– (ldr 2007–10); memb: Bd SEPA 2002–12, Nat Exec SNP 2003–13; convener Assoc of Nationalist Cncllrs 2005–10; *Publications* Standardising Upper Level Network Protocols – Computer Design (1984), Protocol Standardisation on the OSI Model – Electronics (1984); *Recreations* marine wildlife, creative writing; *Style*— Councillor David Berry; ✉ East Lothian Council, John Muir House, Haddington, East Lothian EH41 3HA

BERRY, (Michael) James Ellwood; MP; s of Dr Michael Berry, TD (d 2013), and Mrs Margaret Berry *née* Harvey; *b* Canterbury, Kent; *Educ* UCL (LLB, Wolfson scholarship, Sweet & Maxwell Prize), Harvard Law Sch (LLM); *m* 31 Aug 2013 Nehali Shah; *Career* called to the Bar (Lincoln's Inn, Hardwicke scholarship) 2006; MP (Cons) Kingston and Surbiton 2015–; *Style*— James Berry, Esq, MP; ✉ House of Commons, London SW1A 0AA

BERRY, James Jacob Gilchrist (Jake); MP; s of John David Gilchrist Berry, and Ann Elizabeth, *née* Curtis; *b* 29 December 1978, Liverpool; *Educ* Liverpool Coll, Univ of Sheffield (BA), Coll of Law Chester; *Career* slr; Bremner Sons and Corlett 2001–02, City Law Partnership 2002–04, DWF Slrs 2004–07, Halliwells LLP 2007–10, conslt (tourism/leisure) Squire Patton Boggs (UK) LLP 2011–; MP (Cons) Rossendale & Darwen 2010–; *Recreations* sailing, skiing, fishing; *Clubs* Cons (Rawtenstall), St James's (Manchester), Carlton; *Style*— Jake Berry, Esq, MP; ✉ House of Commons, London SW1A 0AA (e-mail jake.berry.mp@parliament.uk)

BERRY, Jamie Alistair Jagoe; s of Raymond Berry, of Stonor, Oxon, and Phyllis, *née* Pegg; *b* 22 December 1955; *Educ* Harrow; *m* 2, 25 June 1992, Oonagh Mary Dode Patricia, da of U Alen-Buckley; 1 da (Venetia Marina Patricia b 22 April 1993), 1 s (George Michael Jagoe b 3 Aug 1995), 3 step c (Orlaith, Cian, Sorcha); *Career* GT Management plc 1973–81, md Berry Asset Management plc 1981–, dir T&G AIM VCT plc 2001–09; FIMBRA (memb Cncl 1984–87); *Recreations* sailing, shooting; *Clubs* City of London, Royal Thames Yacht, Sea View Yacht; *Style*— Jamie Berry, Esq; ✉ 23 King Street, London SW1Y 6QY (☎ 020 7667 6600)

BERRY, John; CBE (2014); s of John Berry, of Cheshire, and Celia, *née* Hughes; *b* 22 July 1961, Bolton, Lancs; *Educ* Sandbach Secdy Sch, Huddersfield Tech Coll, RNCM, Mannes Coll Music NYC (scholar); *m* 2000, Philippa Dames-Longworth; *Career* early career studied clarinet with Janet Hilton and Gervase de Peyer, fndr and dir Brereton Symposium 1990–97, subsequently freelance artistic conslt and advsr (incl BBC TV, Channel Four, Panel Met Opera Cncl Awards); ENO: casting dir and dir of opera 1994–2005, artistic dir 2005–; advsr Royal Coll of Music 1999–2005; conslt on many opera films incl: Death of Klighoffer (Channel 4, Vienna TV Award and Prix Italia), Trouble in Tahiti (BBC2, Vienna TV Award), The Turn of the Screw (Best Fiction Award Vienna TV Festival); *Recreations* horse riding, watching films; *Style*— John Berry, Esq, CBE; ✉ 36 St Anne's Crescent, Lewes, East Sussex BN7 1SB (☎ 07880717946, e-mail jberry@eno.org); ENO, London Coliseum, St Martin's Lane, London WC2N 4ES (☎ 020 7845 9325)

BERRY, John Richard; s of Richard William Berry, and Margaret Berry; *b* 5 August 1948, Kent; *Educ* Berkhamsted Sch, Univ of Glasgow, IMEDE, INSEAD, Harvard Univ; *m* Anne Sarah; 1 s (Paul Mark), 1 da (Rachel Kathryn); *Career* various dir roles incl ceo Retail Abbey National 1969–2003, ceo Customer Buyology Ltd 2009–; int banking conslt 2004–, dir Hermes Pacific 2012; *Publications* Franchising in Retail Financial Services (Making a Difference on the High Street), Retail Banking Services and Conduct (Chartered Insurance Institute); *Recreations* gardening, sport (spectator!), classic cars; *Clubs* IoD;

Style— John R. Berry, Esq; ☎ 07785 330043, e-mail john_berry@btinternet.com and john@customerbuyology.com

BERRY, (Gwenda) Lynne; OBE (2006); *b* 27 January 1953, Wrexham, N Wales; *Educ* Cambridge Coll of Arts and Technol (BA), UC Cardiff (Postgrad Dip); *Career* social worker 1976–79, community worker Camden 1979–82, lectr in social sciences Poly of Central London 1983–85, head of mgmnt Nat Inst for Social Work 1985–89, Dept of Health 1989–91, chief exec Family Welfare Assoc 1991–96, exec dir Charity Cmmn 1996–99; chief exec: Equal Opportunities Cmmn 1999–2001, Gen Social Care Cncl 2001–07, WRVS 2007–11; chair Child Poverty Action Gp 2005–09, vice-chair Ann Frank Tst 2010–13, dep chair Canal and River Tst (formerly Br Waterways) 2011–, chair Bwrdd Gland?r Cymru 2015–, chair Cmmn on Ageing and the Voluntary Sector 2013–, chair Breast Cancer Now 2015–; non-exec dir/tstee: Better Regulation Taskforce/Cmmn 2005–11, Office of Third Sector/Civil Soc Cabinet Office 2007–11; sr ind dir Cambridge Univ Hosp Fndn Tst 2012–15; tstee Cumberland Lodge 2009–, tstee Addenbrooke's Charitable Tst 2013–15; assoc Civil Exchange 2011; sr fell Cass Business Sch 2011 (visiting prof Cass Business Sch, City Univ 2014–), hon fell Cardiff Univ 2012; Social Care Assoc Award of Merit 2006; hon doctorate Anglia Ruskin Univ 2010, Hon DSc Univ of Beds 2011; Fellow Commoner, Lucy Cavendish Coll, Univ of Cambridge 2015–; Freeman of the Company of the Watermen and Lightermen of the River Thames; *Recreations* messing about on rivers, opera; *Clubs* The Gardener's Club; *Style—* Ms Lynne Berry, OBE; ✉ 62 Hungerford Road, Islington, London N7 9LS (☎ 07411 447431, e-mail lynne@lynneberry.co.uk, Linkedin lynneberry1)

BERRY, Mary; CBE (2012); *b* 24 March 1935; *m* Paul Hunnings; *Career* food writer; cookery ed: Housewife magazine 1966–70, Ideal Home magazine 1970–73; lauched own product range (with da Annabel) 1994; judge The Great British Bake Off (BBC 2) 2010– (Features Prog BAFTA 2012), presenter Mary Berry Cooks (BBC 2) 2014; radio appearances incl: Woman's Hour (BBC Radio 4), Chris Evans Breakfast Show (BBC Radio 2) 2011 and 2012, Desert Island Discs 2012; patron: Nat Osteoporosis Soc 2009, Child Bereavement Charity 2009; *Books* over 80 books incl: Cook Book (1970), Good Afternoon Cookbook (1976), Television Cook Book (1979), The Perfect Sunday Lunch (1982), Crockery Cookery (1983), Cooking at Home (1983), Complete Television Cook Book (1983), Fast Desserts (1983), Family Cooking (1984), Kitchen Wisdom (1985), New Freezer Cook Book (1985), Cooking for Celebrations (1986), Chocolate Delights (1987), Mary Berry's Favourite Recipes (1990), Mary Berry's Food Processor Cookbook (1992), Fast Cakes (1992), Mary Berry's Cookery Course (1993), Mary Berry's Quick and Easy Cakes (1993), Mary Berry's Freezer Cookbook (1994), More Fast Cakes (1994), Fast Suppers (1994), Favourite French Recipes (1995), Classic Home Cooking (1995), Mary Berry's Perfect Sunday (1996), The Aga Book (1996), Mary Berry Cooks Puddings & Desserts (1997), Favourite Cakes (1997), Mary Berry Cooks Cakes (1998), Mary Berry at Home (2001), Mary Berry's Cakes, Pudding & Breads (2001), Mary Berry's Classic Meat Dishes (2001), Cook Now, Eat Later (2002), Mary Berry's New Aga Cookbook (2003), Mary Berry's Simple Cakes (2006), Mary Berry's Christmas Collection: Over 100 Fabulous Recipes for Your Favourite Festive Food (2006), How to Cook (2007), Kitchen Favourites (2007), Real Food Fast (2007), Stress-free Kitchen (2008), Mary Berry's Christmas Collection: Over 100 Fabulous Recipes and Tips for a Trouble-free Festive Season (2008), Mary Berry's Baking Bible (2009), Mary Berry & Lucy Young Cook Up A Feast (2010), My Kitchen Table: 100 Cakes and Bakes (2011), Mary Berry's Family Sunday Lunches (2011), My Kitchen Table: 100 Sweet Treats and Puds (2011), Mary Berry Cookery Course (2012), Mary Berry Cooks (2014), Mary Berry Cooks The Perfect (2014); *Style—* Mrs Mary Berry, CBE; ✉ c/o Lucy Young, Watercroft, Church Road, Penn, Buckinghamshire HP10 8NX

BERRY, Peter Fremantle; CMG (1998); s of Dr John Berry of Tayfield, CBE, DL, FRSE (d 2002), of Tayfield, Newport-on-Tay, Fife, and Hon Bride Faith Louisa, *née* Fremantle (d 2003); bro of William Berry, WS, *qv*; *b* 17 May 1944, St Andrews, Fife; *Educ* Eton, Lincoln Coll Oxford (MA); *m* 1972, Paola, da of Giovanni Padovani (d 1951); 2 da (Sara b 1974, Anna b 1977), 1 s (Richard b 1979); *Career* mgmnt appts Harrisons & Crosfield plc SE Asia 1967–73, dir Anglo-Indonesian Corp plc 1974–82; dir assocs and subsids notably: Anglo-Asian Investments Ltd, Ampat Sumatra Rubber Estate Ltd, Central Province Ceylon Tea Holdings Ltd, Colman & Co (Agric) Ltd, Walker Sons & Co Ltd; Crown Agents For Overseas Governments and Administrations Ltd: dir Asia and Pacific (res Singapore) 1982–84, dir Middle East, Asia and Pacific 1984, md and Crown Agent 1988, dir various subsids and assocs, exec chm 1998–2002, chm 2002–07; pres The Crown Agents Fndn 2003–11; dir: Thomas Tapling & Co Ltd 1987– (chm 2006–), Anglo-Eastern Plantations plc 1990–93, The Scottish Eastern Investment Tst 1994–99, Henderson T R Pacific Investment Tst plc 1994–2008, Keir Group plc 1997–2007, Martin Currie Capital Return Tst plc 1999–2000, Martin Currie Global Portfolio Tst plc 1999–2012 (chm 2000–12); advsr on int and econ devpt Corp of London 2003–14; memb: Indonesia Assoc 1974–93 (chm 1986–89), Cncl Malaysia, Singapore and Brunei Assoc 1982–87, Whitehall Export Promotion Ctee 1992–98, Transparency Int (Berlin) Int Cncl 1993–, CBI Int Ctee 1997–2002, Br Trade Int Business Advsy Gp 1998–2003, UK Trade and Investment Int Sectors Advsy Panel 2003–04; pres Transparency Int (UK) 2003–, dir UK-Japan 21st Century Gp 2000–03, dep chm Charities Aid Fndn 2004–09 (tstee 2000–09, chm Int Ctee 2000–09), dir Charity Bank 2003–09, dir and tstee Scottish Crop Research Inst 2007–11 (chm 2008–11), dir Mylnfield Research Servs Ltd 2007–14 (chm 2008–11); Liveryman Worshipful Co of Musicians 2008; FRSA; Order of the Rising Sun (gold rays and neck ribbon, Japan) 2008; *Recreations* international development, wildlife, country pursuits, Italy; *Clubs* RAC; *Style—* Peter Berry, Esq, CMG; ✉ Crown Agents, St Nicholas House, Sutton, Surrey SM1 1EL (☎ 020 8643 3311, fax 020 8643 6518)

BERRY, (Anthony) Scyld Ivens; s of Prof Francis Berry (d 2006), of Winchester, Hants, and Nancy Melloney, *née* Graham (d 1967); *b* 28 April 1954; *Educ* Westbourne Sch Sheffield, Ampleforth, Christ's Coll Cambridge (MA); *m* 2 April 1984, Sunita, da of Brig M K Ghosh; 2 s (Sceaf b 17 April 1993, Ankush b 10 Jan 1997), 1 da (Freya b 3 July 1991); *Career* cricket corr: The Observer 1978–89, Sunday Correspondent 1989–90, Independent on Sunday 1991–93, Sunday Telegraph 1993–; ed Wisden Cricketers' Almanack 2008–11; *Books* Cricket Wallah (1982), Train to Julia Creek (1984), The Observer on Cricket (ed, 1988), Cricket Odyssey (1988), Cricket's Burning Passion (jtly, 2006); *Recreations* village cricket; *Clubs* Hinton Charterhouse CC; *Style—* Scyld Berry, Esq; ✉ The Daily Telegraph, 111 Buckingham Palace Road, London SW1W 0DT

BERRY, (Roger) Simon; QC (1990); s of Kingsland Jutsum Berry, of Bristol, and Kathleen Margaret, *née* Parker; *b* 9 September 1948; *Educ* St Brendan's Coll Bristol, Univ of Manchester (LLB); *m* 1974, Jennifer Jane, da of Jonas Birtwistle Hall; 3 s (Richard James b 27 Nov 1979, Nicholas Peter b 25 June 1981, William Patrick b 17 Aug 1986); *Career* admitted slr 1973, ptnr Stanley Wasbrough (now Veale Wasbrough) 1975–77; called to the Bar Middle Temple 1977 (ad eundum Lincoln's Inn), (bencher of Lincoln's Inn 1996), recorder 2000, dep High Ct judge 2001–; memb: Middle Temple, Lincoln's Inn, Western Circuit, Chancery Bar Assoc, Ctee Chancery Bar Assoc 1984 and 1985, Professional Negligence Bar Assoc, Property Bar Assoc, Bar Cncl 1996–99; memb Theatre Panel of Judges for the Olivier awards 2000; *Recreations* family, the performing arts, cycling, skiing, keeping fit; *Clubs* Ski Club of GB, Riverside; *Style—* Mr Simon Berry, QC

BERRY, William; DL, WS; er s of Dr John Berry of Tayfield, CBE, DL, FRSE (d 2002), of Tayfield, Newport-on-Tay, Fife, and Hon Bride Faith Louisa, *née* Fremantle (d 2003); bro of Peter Fremantle Berry, CMG, *qv*; *b* 26 September 1939; *Educ* Eton, Univ of St Andrews (MA), Univ of Edinburgh (LLB); *m* 1973, Elizabeth, da of Sir Edward Warner, KCMG, OBE (d 2002), of Blockley, Glos; 2 s (John b 1976, Robert b 1978); *Career* Murray Beith Murray WS Edinburgh: ptnr 1967–2000, sr ptnr 1991–2000, chm 2000–04; former dir: Scottish American Investment Co, Fleming Continental European Investment Trust, Alliance Trust, Second Alliance Trust, Scottish Life Assurance Co (chm 1993–99), Dawnfresh Hldgs Ltd, Inchcape Family Investments Ltd (chm 2000–03); memb Queen's Body Guard for Scotland (Royal Co of Archers); dep chm Edinburgh Int Festival 1985–89; chm: New Town Concerts Soc Edinburgh, Edinburgh Family Service Unit, Scottish Fiddle Soc; mangr New Club; tstee: Royal Botanic Garden Edinburgh 1986–94, Hopetoun House Preservation Tst, Cockburn Assoc, Edinburgh Civic Tst, Scottish Ctee Marie Curie Tst, Patrons Exec Ctee National Museums of Scotland, Exec Ctee Thistle Fndn; sr govr Univ of St Andrews 2002–07 (Cllr's assessor 2007–10); FRSA; *Recreations* music, shooting, forestry, urban and rural conservation; *Clubs* New (Edinburgh); *Style—* William Berry, Esq, DL, WS; ✉ Tayfield, Newport-on-Tay, Fife DD6 8HA

B

BERRY OTTAWAY, Peter; s of Cecil Berry Ottaway (d 1986), of Sutton St Nicholas, Hereford, and Myfanwy, *née* Thomas (d 1999); *b* 17 February 1942; *Educ* Steyning GS, Univ of London (BSc), UC of Rhodesia and Nyasaland; *m* 1, 21 Dec 1963 (m dis 2006), Andrea, da of Richard Sampson, ED, of Palm Springs, CA; 2 s (Gareth b 10 July 1965 (decd), Charles b 9 Oct 1986), 2 da (Samantha b 30 April 1969, Georgina b 17 Jan 1981); m 2, 9 July 2011, Susan Mary France, da of A E J Mayne, of Bartestree, Herefordshire; *Career* cmmnd Trg Branch RAFVR 1968–95 (Sqdn Ldr); res scientist Zambian Govt WHO 1963–65; res mgmnt: Unilever Ltd 1965–67, General Foods Ltd 1967–74; int consultancy in food technol, food science and nutrition 1974–81, dir of science and technol (Europe) Shaklee Corporation Calif 1981, md Berry Ottaway & Associates Ltd, dir Mercia Testing Laboratories Ltd, consulting scientist 1987–; chair Food Standards Agency Working Gp on Food Irradiation 2007–12; visiting lectr: Univ of Surrey, Bath Spa Univ; memb: Duke of Edinburgh's Award Ctee Herefordshire 1978–99, Ctee Sports Nutrition Fndn 1986–99, Exec Ctee SSAFA Herefordshire 2008–; CSci, CBiol, FRSH 1974, MSB 1978, FIFST 1981, FRIPH; *Books* Food for Sport (1985), Nutrition in Sport (ed with Dr D H Shrimpton, 1986), Preservatives in Food (1988), Nutritional Enhancement of Food (jtly, 1989), The Technology of Vitamins in Food (ed, 1992), The Harmonisation of European Union Food Legislation (1995), The Sanyati Survival Expedition (1996), The Addition of Micronutrients to Foods (ed, 1997), Food Labelling (jtly, 1999), Forever Aircrew (ed, 1999), Prebiotics – New Developments in Functional Foods (jtly, 2000), Functional Foods (jtly, 2000), European Food Law (jtly, 2001), Gum and Stabilisers for the Food Industry (contrib, 2002), The Nutrition Handbook for Food Processors (contrib, 2002), International Review of Food Science and Technology (ed, 2002–09), Natural Antimicrobials for the Minimal Processing of Foods (contrib, 2003), Functional Foods, Ageing and Degenerative Disease (contrib, 2004), Regulation of Functional Foods and Nutraceuticals (contrib, 2005, 2 edn 2013), Long-Chain Omega-3 Specialty Oils (contrib, 2007); assoc ed and contrib Encyclopaedia of Food Science and Nutrition (2003), Food Fortification and Supplementation (2008, Russian and Chinese edns 2011), Functional and Speciality Beverage Technology (contrib, 2009), Chemical Deterioration of Food (contrib, 2010), Fermentation, Effects on Food (contrib, 2012), A Sapper In Flanders (2014), International Food Law and Policy (contrib, 2016); *Recreations* light aviation, hill walking, art; *Clubs* RAF; *Style—* Peter Berry Ottaway, Esq; ✉ Kivernoll Cottage, Kivernoll, Much Dewchurch, Herefordshire HR2 8DS

BERTIN, Baroness (Life Peer UK 2016), of Battersea in the London Borough of Wandsworth; Gabrielle Louise (Gabby) Bertin; da of Claude Bertin, and Lynne Dawson; *b* 14 March 1978, Croydon; *Educ* Croydon HS; *Career* equity trader BNP Paribas 2000–02, press sec to Rt Hon David Cameron, MP, *qv*, 2010–; *Style—* The Baroness Bertin; ✉ 10 Downing Street, London SW1A 2AA

BERTRAM, Dr Brian Colin Ricardo; s of Dr George Colin Lawder Bertram (d 2001), and Dr Cicely Kate Ricardo Bertram (d 1999); *b* 14 April 1944, Cairo; *Educ* Perse Sch Cambridge, St John's Coll Cambridge (BA, PhD, TH Huxley Award Certificate of Commendation); *m* 3 May 1975, Katharine Jean, da of Francis Blaise Gillie, CBE (d 1981); 2 da (Joanna Mary Ricardo b 1981, Felicity Kate Ricardo b 1983), 1 s (Nicholas Blaise Ricardo (twin) b 1983); *Career* res fell Serengeti Res Inst Tanzania 1969–73, sr res fell King's Coll Cambridge 1976–79, curator of mammals Zoological Soc of London 1980–87, DG The Wildfowl & Wetlands Tst 1987–92; freelance zoological advsr 1993–99; co-ordinator overseas conservation prog Federation of Zoological Gardens 1994–96, special projects co-ordinator Bristol Zoo Gardens 1995–2003, zoological conslt Wildscreen Bristol (later Wildwalk @t Bristol) 1997–2000; on Sec of State's list of zoo inspectors since 1983; memb Cncl: Zoological Soc of London 1993–97, 1999–2002, 2004–07, 2010–14 and 2015– (vice-pres 2011–12), World Pheasant Assoc 2010– (vice-pres 1990–98); memb Zoos Expert Ctee (formerly Zoos Forum) 2005–15; FIBiol 1979; *Books* Pride of Lions (1978), The Ostrich Communal Nesting System (1992), Lions (1998); *Recreations* family, animals, garden, friends, reading, sailing, skiing, travel, walking, zoos; *Clubs* Zoological; *Style—* Dr Brian Bertram; ✉ Fieldhead, Amberley, Stroud, Gloucestershire GL5 5AG (☎ 01453 872796, e-mail bbertram@btopenworld.com)

BERTRAM, (Charles) William; s of Lt-Col Richard Bertram (d 1995), and Elizabeth Florence Oriana, *née* Bedwell (d 1991); *Educ* Sherborne, Architectural Assoc (AADipl); *m* 16 Nov 1963, Victoria Harriette, da of Reginald Addington Ingle, of Priston, nr Bath; 2 da (Clare Victoria Harriette b 1965, Josephine Alice b 1967), 1 s (Robert William b 1970); *Career* fndr architectural practice William Bertram and Fell of Bath 1969, fndr William Bertram Consulting Architect 1996; personal architect to HRH the Prince of Wales at Highgrove Glos 1987–98, conslt to Eastern Region Duchy of Cornwall 1989–2014, architectural advsr to RNLI 2002–08; converted Nos 15 and 16 Royal Crescent Bath into 5 star hotel, converted Cliveden into hotel 1986–89, designer of Cavendish Lodge Bath, redesigned Sir Winston Churchill's and Churchill family graves at Bladon 1998, restoration of Dinmore Manor and Gardens 2000–04, substantial reordering of Rockley Manor and creation of new out buildings 2001–04, reordering of Parnham House 2003, Encombe House Dorset 2005 (Georgian Gp Award 2006), Old Rectory Combe Hay Somerset 2009 (B&NES Design Quality Award); received: UK Cncl Euro Architectural Heritage Year Award 1975, Civic Tst Award for conservation of Abbotsbury Village Dorset, Civic Tst award for Dower House Bath 1986, Bath Conservation Area Advsy Ctee Environmental Award 1987, award for environmental design St Ann's Place and Environs; tstee Bath Preservation Tst 1966–68, listed in Architects Registration Cncl of UK; memb Br Soc of Architects, RIBA; *Books* The Origins of Queen Square Bath (1962), An Appreciation of Abbotsbury (1973), The Architect's Tale (2009); *Recreations* tennis, walking, garden design, sketching; *Style—* William Bertram, Esq; ✉ The Studio, Woodrising, Loves Hill, Timsbury, Bath BA2 0EU (☎ 01761 470718, e-mail williambertramofbath@gmail.com)

BERTRAM-BROWN, Harvey; s of Dennis H Brown, of London, and Sandra M, *née* Finklestein; *b* 9 January 1966; *Educ* Haberdashers' Aske's, St Martin's Sch of Art, Ravensbourne Coll of Art & Design (BA), RCA (MA); *Career* fndr memb The New Renaissance 1991– (multi media co formerly specialising in fashion and accessory design, display, styling and art direction, currently directing TV commercials and music promos through The Pink Film Co); exhbns incl: Fouts and Fowler Gallery London 1991, Liberty London 1991, Premiere Classe Paris 1991, The World of The New RenaisCAnce (Royal Festival Hall and Parco Gallery Tokyo) 1992, Crafts in Performance (Crafts Cncl touring exhbn) 1993, In the Swim (Bremerhaven Germany) 1993; window design for Liberty and Harvey Nichols London; commercial and music promos incl: PowerGen 'Weathergens',

Gordon's Gin, Diamond White Cider, George Michael, Elton John, LeAnn Rimes; *Style*— Harvey Bertram-Brown, Esq; ✉ website www.thenewrenaissance.co.uk

BESLEY, Crispian George; s of Christopher Besley (d 2004), of Wimbledon, London, and Pamela Geraldine Margaret Edgeworth, *née* David (d 2014); *b* 21 November 1958; *Educ* Wellington Coll; *m* 1, 1988 (m dis 1992), Elizabeth, da of Thomas Bridger; m 2, 1994, Sarah (Sally) Helen Catherine, da of Stanley Morris; 2 s (Hugo Alexander Edgeworth b 14 Nov 1996, Charlie George b 25 Jan 1999); *Career* formerly dir Prudential Bache Securities Japan 1986–87; dir Smith New Court Int 1987–95, main bd dir Schroder Securities 1996–2000, dir Schroder Japan 1996–2000, dir Credit Suisse First Boston (Europe) 2000–06, md Credit Suisse 2007–; *Recreations* amateur racing driver, skiing, Cresta run, shooting, all motorsports, classic cars; *Clubs* Brooks's, Annabel's, St Moritz Toboggan; *Style*— Crispian Besley, Esq; ✉ c/o Credit Suisse, One Cabot Square, London E14 4QS (☎ 020 7888 8888, mobile 07860 209241, e-mail cgbesley@aol.com)

BESLEY, Prof Timothy John; CBE (2010); s of John Besley, of Oxford, and June, *née* Turton; *b* 14 September 1960; *Educ* Univ of Oxford (BA, MPhil, DPhil); *m* Aug 1993, Gillian, *née* Paull; 2 s (Thomas Arthur b 31 July 1995, Oliver John b 21 Oct 1997); *Career* fell All Souls Coll Oxford 1984–89, asst prof Princeton Univ 1989–95; LSE: prof of economics 1995–2002, prof of economics and political science 2002–, Kuwait prof of economics and political sciences 2007–12, sch prof of economics and political sciences 2012–, W Arthur Lewis prof of devpt economics 2015–; memb Cncl Econometric Soc 2002–08, memb Monetary Policy Ctee Bank of England 2006–09; pres European Economic Assoc 2010, pres Int Economic Assoc 2014–17; co-ed American Economic Review 1998–2005, author of numerous contribs to scholarly jls; Richard Musgrave Prize 1999, Yrjö Jahnsson Prize 2005; fell Econometric Soc 2000, FBA 2001, foreign hon memb American Acad of Arts and Sciences 2013; *Recreations* squash, playing violin, watching cricket, Fulham FC; *Style*— Prof Timothy Besley, CBE; ✉ London School of Economics and Political Science, Houghton Street, London WC2A 2AE (☎ 020 7955 6702, e-mail t.besley@lse.ac.uk)

BESSBOROUGH, Madeleine, Countess of; Madeleine Lola Margaret Bessborough; OBE (2010); *née* Grand; da of Maj-Gen Laurence Douglas Grand, CB, CIE, CBE (d 1975), of Delaford Manor, Iver, Bucks, and Irene, *née* Mathew, MBE (d 1971); *b* 8 November 1935, Aldershot, Hants; *Educ* St Mary's Sch St Leonards-on-Sea, Priors Field Godalming; *m* 1963, as his 3 w, 11 Earl of Bessborough (d 2002); 2 s (Hon Matthew Douglas Longfield b 1965, Hon Charles Arthur Longfield b 1967); *Career* fndr: The New Art Centre London 1957–, Roche Court Sculpture Park 1998, Roche Court Educnl Tst 2005; lay canon Salisbury Cathedral 2008; patron Salisbury Hospice 1999–2007, vice-pres Wilts Historic Churches Tst; memb Cncl Royal Coll of Art 1963–72 (hon fell 1973); *Recreations* gardening; *Style*— Madeleine, Countess of Bessborough, OBE; ✉ Roche Court, East Winterslow, Salisbury, Wiltshire SP5 1BG (☎ 01980 862244, fax 01980 862447, e-mail mb@sculpture.uk.com)

BESSELL, Dr Eric Michael; s of William Henry Bessell (d 2005), and Doris Mabel, *née* Willson (d 1992); *b* 17 December 1946; *Educ* Radcliffe Sch Wolverton, Univ of Bristol (BSc), Inst of Cancer Research London (PhD), St Mary's Hosp Med Sch London (MB BS); *m* 31 July 1971, Deborah Jane; 1 da (Laura Elizabeth b 29 Dec 1976), 1 s (Andrew Thomas b 29 Sept 1979); *Career* registrar in clinical oncology Royal Postgrad Med Sch Hammersmith Hosp London 1980–83, sr registrar in clinical oncology Royal Marsden Hosp London 1983–85, conslt in clinical oncology Nottingham HA 1985–2011, conslt oncologist The Park Hospital Nottingham 1985–, clinical dir Dept of Clinical Oncology Nottingham 1986–96 and 2003–07; chm Nottingham Div BMA 1990; examiner RCR 1994–2000, memb Lymphoma Clincal Studies Gp Nat Cancer Research Inst 2003–05; author of numerous papers on malignant lymphomas in learned jls; FRCR 1984, FRCP 1993 (MRCP); *Recreations* mountain walking, piano playing, opera; *Style*— Dr Eric Bessell; ✉ The Park Hospital, Sherwood Lodge Drive, Nottingham NG5 8RX (☎ 0115 966 2120, fax 0115 966 2191, e-mail ebessell@hotmail.co.uk)

BESSEY, Peter John Harvey; s of Cyril Leonard Bessey, of Twickenham, Middx, and Catherine Elizabeth, *née* Drury; *b* 17 May 1944, Norwich; *Educ* Gunnersbury GS, Ealing Sch of Art, Central Sch of Art & Design (RSA bursary, industrial and furniture design DipAD); *Children* 1 s (Matthew John Harvey b 1991); *Career* res and analytical chemistry BP Sunbury 1961–66; assoc: Keith Townend Associates 1970–78, Satherley Design Associates 1978–85; sr product engr PA Design (later Brand New Product Development Ltd) 1985–89, fndr ptnr Hothouse Product Development Partners 1989–2011, ind design and devpt conslt 2011–; projects incl: Xenotron XVC3 Graphic Workstation/Terminal 1985 (COID Design Award), Esselte Meto System 2500 retail anti-theft system 1989–90 and System 2600 1994, Gerry Baby Products Co nursery monitor 1994, Kimberley-Clark Handy Pack wipes dispenser 1995 (DBA Design Effectiveness Finalist 1996), Kimberley-Clark Roll Control wipes dispenser 1997 (DBA Design Effectiveness Award 1998, Millennium Product Selection 1998), ERA Security Products Codemaster digital door lock 1997, Klippan Prima and Futura Child Safety Seats 1999 (Mother and Baby Gold Awards 2000), PUR Ultimate Water Filtration Pitcher 2001 (PRW Plastics Industry Award Finalist 2002), Spinlock Bullseye BE Range 2002 (MAME Award Commendation 2002), Burgopak CD/DVD Cases 2002–03, Elekta Synergy Radiotherapy Machine 2003 (DBA Design Effectiveness Award 2003), Quin Systems SRV400 Motion Controller Range 2003, Elekta Oncology KVS X-Ray Imaging System 2004, Spinlock PXR Cleat Range 2006, TBS CX1 and CX4 Plug Charger Range 2010, TBS Smart Li-PowerPak Range 2011, ECM Systems Bingo Tablet 2012, TBS CX2 Smart Charger 2012, Scarlett Innovations Safesip Anti-Spill Drinks Cover 2012, TBS 5000 Series Hi-Cap Powerpack 2013, Smarterkey Cellphone/ cloud Electronic Door Entry Controller 2013, ISIS Flare pan devpt 2013, Univ of Ulster 'SolaCatcher' solar-thermal pre-heater 2013, TBS Rugged Powerpack 2013, TBS Wireless Charger 2014, Smarterkey GSM Electronic Door Lock 2014, TBS CX5 Hi-rate Charger 2014; fndr memb and treas SIAD Alternative Design Gp 1974, chm CSD Product Gp 1986–88, CSD rep Cncl Camberwell Sch of Art 1987–89, visiting tutor Central St Martin's Sch of Art 1988–95, memb IT Task Gp DBA 1996–98, student mentor MAID Central St Martin's London Univ of Arts 1996–; hon res fell London Inst Central St Martin's Sch of Art 2000–; FCSD (1985, MSIAD 1977), FRSA 2005; *Publications* contrib Rapid Prototyping Casebook 2001; *Recreations* dinghy racing, board sailing, photography, archaeology, travel; *Clubs* Upper Thames Sailing; *Style*— Peter Bessey, Esq; ✉ 6 Temple Sheen Road, London SW14 7PX

BEST, Andrew Roger Riddell; s of John Riddell Best (d 1992), and Stella Mary, *née* Whitley (d 2003); *Educ* Charterhouse, Worcester Coll Oxford (MA); *m* 1984, Virginia, da of Angus and Wanda Lloyd; 1 da (Amanda b 1987), 3 s (James b 1989, John b 1991, Angus b 1995); *Career* Union Bank of Switzerland (UBS) 1986–88, NatWest Markets 1988–92, Shandwick Consultants 1992–99 (dir), managing ptnr Shared Value Ltd 2000–; memb Investor Rels Soc; *Clubs* Royal Ashdown Forest Golf; *Style*— Andrew Best, Esq; ✉ Shared Value Ltd, 7–10 Adam Street, London WC2N 6AA (☎ 020 7321 5020, fax 020 7321 5010, e-mail abest@sharedvalue.net)

BEST, Eve; *b* 31 July 1971, London; *Educ* Wycombe Abbey Girls' Sch, Lincoln Coll Oxford, RADA; *Career* actress and director; *Theatre* incl: 'Tis Pity She's a Whore (Young Vic) 1999 (Best Newcomer Evening Standard Award, Best Newcomer Critics' Circle Award), Hedda Gabler 2005 (Best Actress Olivier Award, Best Actress Critics' Circle Award), A Moon For The Misbegotten (Old Vic and Broadway) 2006 (Best Actress New York Critics' Circle Award, Best Actress New York Drama Desk Award), As You Like It (Sheffield Crucible) 2007, The Homecoming (Broadway) 2008, Much Ado About Nothing (Shakespeare's Globe) 2011, The Duchess of Malfi (Old Vic) 2012, Macbeth (dir, Shakespeare's Globe) 2013, Anthony and Cleopatra (Shakespeare's Globe) 2014, Old Times (Broadway) 2015; *Television* incl: Shackleton 2002, Lie with Me 2004, Prime Suspect 2006, Nurse Jackie 2009–14, The Shadow Line 2011, The Honourable Woman 2013, Life in Squares 2014, Lucky Man 2015; *Film* incl The King's Speech 2010; *Style*— Ms Eve Best; ✉ c/o Independent Talent Group Ltd, 40 Whitfield Street, London W1T 2RH

BEST, Gary Martin; s of Charles William Best, of South Shields, and Doreen, *née* Wright; *b* 6 October 1951; *Educ* South Shields Grammar Tech Sch, Exeter Coll Oxford (MA), Oxford Dept of Educn (PGCE); *m* 9 Aug 1975, Frances Elizabeth, da of Edward Albert Rolling, of Redruth; 1 da (Claire Frances b 1981); *Career* asst history teacher King Edward's Sch Bath 1974–80, head of Sixth Form Newcastle under Lyme Sch 1983–87 (head of history 1980–83), headmaster Kingswood Sch 1987–2008, research fell Wesley Coll Bristol 2008–10; Methodist local preacher; Warden New Room Bristol 2009–; *Books* Seventeenth-Century Europe (1980), Wesley and Kingswood (1988), Continuity and Change (1998), John Wesley (2003), Charles Wesley (2007), Transforming Lives (2008), Oliver Twist Investigates (2010), Wuthering Heights Revisited (2011), The Seven Sisters (2012), Susanna Wesley (2013), The Jacobite Murders (2013); *Recreations* painting, music, reading, walking; *Style*— Gary Best, Esq; ✉ Cherwell, 77A Englishcombe Lane, Bath BA2 2EH (☎ 01225 310302, e-mail g_best@sky.com)

BEST, Keith Lander; TD; s of Peter Edwin Wilson Best (d 1984), of Hurstpierpoint, W Sussex, and Margaret Louisa, *née* Ambrose (d 1991); *b* 10 June 1949; *Educ* Brighton Coll, Keble Coll Oxford (MA); *m* 28 July 1990, Elizabeth Margaret Gibson; 2 da (Phoebe b 22 Oct 1991, Ophelia b 2 Aug 1993); *Career* Maj 289 Parachute Battery RHA (V) and Commando Forces, served on HMS Bulwark 1976, naval gunfire liaison offr; called to the Bar Inner Temple 1971, barr in Old Steine Brighton 1971–87; borough cncllr Brighton 1976–80, MP (Cons) Anglesey Ynys Môn 1979–87 (PPS to Sec of State for Wales 1981–84); direct mail conslt Nat Children's Home 1987, dir Prisoners Abroad 1989–93; chief exec: Immigration Advsy Serv 1993–2009, Medical Fndn for the Care of Victims of Torture (Freedom from Torture) 2010–14, SurvivorsUK 2015–; chm: Assoc of Regulated Immigration Advsrs 2003–09, Electoral Reform Soc, Cons Action for Electoral Reform, World Federalist Movement, Assoc of World Federalists, Electronic Immigration Network Charity, Electoral Reform Int Servs 2007–14; vice-chair European Cncl on Refugees and Exiles 2011–14, memb Foreign Sec's Advsy Panel on Torture Prevention 2010–14; chair Wyndham Place Charlemagne Tst 2014–, pres The Holyhead Festival Ltd, chm Charity 2020 2015–, tstee and sec Parly Outreach Tst 2015–, sec and vice-chair London for Europe (European Movement) 2015–, sec European Movement 2015–; tstee Cranstoun Drug Servs 2003–09; Freeman City of London, Liveryman Worshipful Co of Loriners; FRSA; *Books* Write Your Own Will (1978), The Right Way to Prove a Will (1980); *Recreations* walking, skiing, photography, being useful; *Clubs* New Cavendish; *Style*— Keith Best, Esq, TD; ✉ 15 St Stephen's Terrace, London SW8 1DJ (☎ 020 7735 7699, mobile 07785 323200, e-mail keithbest@hotmail.com); 7 Alderley Terrace, Holyhead, Anglesey, Gwynedd LL65 1NL

BEST, Baron (Life Peer UK 2001), of Godmanstone in the County of Dorset; Richard Stuart Best; OBE (1988), DL (N Yorks 2012); s of Walter Stuart Best, JP, DL (d 1984), and Frances Mary, *née* Chignell (d 1967); *b* 22 June 1945; *Educ* Shrewsbury, Univ of Nottingham (BA); *m* 1, 1970 (m dis 1976), Ima Akpan; 1 s (Peter b 1971), 1 da (Lucy b 1974); m 2, 1978, Belinda Janie Tremayne, da of Geoffrey Eustace Stemp, DFC, of Lamberhurst, Kent; 1 da (Jessica b 1981), 1 s (William b 1985); *Career* dir: Br Churches Housing Tst 1970–73, Nat Fedn of Housing Assocs 1973–88, Joseph Rowntree Fndn 1988–2006; sec Duke of Edinburgh's Inquiry into Br Housing 1984–91, cmmr Rural Devpt Cmmn 1989–98; chm: RDC Social Advsy Panel 1990–98, UK Nat Cncl UN City Summit 1995–96, Hull Partnership Liaison Bd 2003–04, The Giving Forum 2005–12, House of Lords Audit Ctee 2005–10, Hanover Housing Assoc 2006–14, Cmmn on the Future of Housing in NI 2009–10, Cncl of the Property Ombudsman 2009–, All Pty Parly Gp on Housing and Care 2009–, Housing for an Ageing Population Panel for Innovation 2009–10, Local Govt Assoc/Dept for Communities and Local Govt Housing Cmmn 2010, House of Lords Select Ctee on Communications 2014–; vice-chm: Westminster City Cncl Standards Ctee 2008–12, All Party Parly Urban Devpt Gp 2007–; pres Local Govt Assoc 2005–, vice-pres Town and Country Planning Assoc 2007–; memb: Social Policy Ctee of C of E Bd for Social Responsibility 1986–91, BBC/IBA Central Appeals Advsy Ctee 1988–91, Exec Ctee Assoc Charitable Fndns 1989–92, Community Advsy Panel IBM UK Ltd 1990–93, Cncl for Charitable Support 1995–2005, NCVO Advsy Cncl 2001–15, House of Lords Economic Affrs Ctee 2007–12, House of Lords Information Ctee 2013–14, Select Ctee on Olympic and Paralympic Legacy 2013–; advsr: Environment Ctee House of Commons 1993, Min of Housing's Sounding Bd 1999–2001, DTI Foresight Built Environment Panel 1999–2001, Min of Local Govt's Sounding Bd 2001–05; hon treas RSA 2009–12; tstee: Tree Cncl 2006–14, Zimbabwe Phoenix Fund 2007–15; pres Continuing Care Conf 2003–12; CAB Parliamentarian of the Year 2010; Hon Dr: Univ of Sheffield, Univ of York; hon life memb Chartered Inst of Housing; Hon FRIBA 2001, FAcSS; *Clubs* Travellers, Farmers; *Style*— The Rt Hon the Lord Best, OBE, DL; ✉ House of Lords, London SW1A 0PW

BESTERMAN, Tristram Paul; s of Prof Edwin Melville Mack Besterman, of Stony Hill, Jamaica, and Audrey, *née* Heald; *b* 19 September 1949; *Educ* Stowe (music scholar), Univ of Cambridge (MA); *m* 1977, Peregrine Mary Louise, da of Gilbert Garceau; 2 s (Julius b 12 July 1979, Hugo b 9 Oct 1980), 1 da (Anna b 21 April 1983); *Career* BBC Radio 1971–73, res and design Geological & Mining Mus Sydney 1974, jackaroo on cattle station Queensland 1974, educn offr Sheffield City Mus 1974–78, dep curator and keeper of geology Warwickshire Museums 1978–85, city curator Plymouth City Museums & Art Gall 1985–93, dir Manchester Museum 1994–2006; convenor Ethics Ctee UK Museums Assoc 1995–2001; memb: Coll Collections Advsy Bd UCL 1997–, Bd Sainsbury Centre for Visual Arts UEA 1998–, Ministerial Working Gp on Human Remains 2001–03; numerous articles in scientific and museological jls; FGS 1979, FMA 1985 (AMA 1979), FRSA 2001; *Recreations* music, cellist in chamber orchestras and quartets; *Style*— Tristram Besterman, Esq

BESWICK, David; s of Donald Beswick, of Shenstone, Staffs, and Eileen, *née* Thomas (d 2013); *b* 18 February 1963, Liverpool; *Educ* John Wilmot Sch Sutton Coldfield, Univ of Newcastle upon Tyne (LLB), Coll of Law Chester; *m* 15 July 1989, Sally, *née* Webb; 2 da (Lois, Kirsty (twins) b 17 March 1998); *Career* admitted slr 1987; Eversheds 1985–2002 and 2009– (sr ptnr Birmingham 2011–), Hammonds 2002–09; memb Employment Lawyers Assoc; memb Birmingham Forward; *Recreations* badminton, gym, theatre; *Style*— David Beswick, Esq; ✉ Eversheds LLP, 115 Colmore Row, Birmingham B3 3AL (☎ 0121 232 1495 or 0845 497 1495, e-mail davidbeswick@eversheds.com)

BESWICK, Rt Rev Esme Christiana; MBE (2001); da of Nathan Coleman (d 1973), of Jamaica, and Ambroline Coleman (d 1980); *b* 9 April 1938; *Educ* Wyma Nursing HS Kingston Jamaica, West Ham Coll, Central Bible Inst (DipTh), Univ of London (extra mural studies); *m* 2 Nov 1962, Herbert George Beswick; 2 s (Derick Paul b 14 Feb 1964, Mark Anthony b 21 July 1965), 2 da (Michelle Marcia b 15 Oct 1969, Sharon Deborah b 24 May 1971); *Career* student nurse Queen Mary Hosp Sidcup and St Leonard's Hosp Bromley 1961–63; ordained Pentecostal Church Jamaica 1961; pastor of The New Testament Assembly Brixton 1975, hosp chaplain Whipps Cross Hosp 1986–91, gen sec Jt Cncl for Anglo Caribbean Churches 1989, fndr Jt Cncl of Anglo Caribbean Churches Bible Sch, bishop Jt Cncl of Anglo Caribbean Churches 2015–, fndr Nebaioth Ministries

2016–; pres Churches Together in England 2002–06, pres Christian and Muslim Forum 2005–10 (hon pres 2011–); memb: British Cncl of Churches 1980–89, Cncl of Churches for Britain and Ireland 1989–; former memb Inner City Religious Cncl; current pres: Jt Cncl for Anglo Caribbean Churches, Christian and Muslim Forum, Esme Beswick Educn Fndn Tst; former ecumenical borough dean of Lambeth; patron: Christian Cncl on Ageing, Race Equality in Employment Programme (REEP); sitter Nat Portrait Gallery 2005–; *Recreations* reading, swimming, cricket; *Style*— The Rt Rev Bishop Esme Beswick, MBE; ✉ 6 Leasowes Road, Leyton, London E10 7BE (☎ 020 8539 2310, mobile 07903 672097, e-mail esmebeswick7@aol.com, website www.jcacc.co.uk)

BETHEL, Martin; QC (1983); s of Rev Ralph Arnold Bethel (d 1946), and Enid Ambery, *née* Smith (d 1996); *b* 12 March 1943; *Educ* Kingswood Sch Bath, Fitzwilliam Coll Cambridge (MA, LLM); *m* 14 Sept 1974, Kathryn Jane, da of Isaac Allan Denby, of Riddlesden, W Yorks; 1 da (Sarah b 1976), 2 s (Thomas b 1980, William b 1981); *Career* called to the Bar Inner Temple 1965; recorder of the Crown Court (NE Circuit) 1979–, dep judge of the High Ct 1995–; memb: Criminal Injuries Compensation Bd 1999–2000, Criminal Injuries Compensation Appeals Panel 2000–10; pres Runswick Bay Rescue Boat 2001–04; *Recreations* golf, skiing, boating; *Style*— Martin Bethel, Esq, QC; ✉ St Pauls Chambers, Trafalgar House, 29 Park Place, Leeds LS1 2SP

BETHEL, Dr Robert George Hankin; s of Horace Hankin Bethel (d 1961), of London and Eastbourne, and Eileen Maude (Mollie), *née* Motyer (d 1996); *b* 7 June 1948; *Educ* Eastbourne GS, Pembroke Coll Cambridge (BA, MA, MB BChir), St Mary's Hosp Med Sch; *Career* med practitioner; house physician Queen Elizabeth II Hosp London 1972, house surgn Nottingham Gen Hosp 1973, SHO Northwick Park Hosp and Clinical Res Centre Harrow 1974, registrar W Middx Univ Hosp 1974–76, gen med practitioner Englefield Green and Old Windsor 1976–2005, sr ptnr Runnymede Med Practice 1997–2005; course tutor Open Univ 1979–80, hosp practitioner in geriatrics 1980–91, pt/t rheumatologist Heatherwood Hosp Ascot 1976–92, trainer for GP (Oxford region) 1984–2005, assoc teacher Imperial Coll of Sci, Technol and Med (formerly St Mary's Hosp Med Sch) 1989–2004; med memb Ind Tbnl Serv (Disability) 1991–99, med offr Brunel Univ 1993–98; author of various scientific papers in med jls with particular interest in rheumatological and gen practice topics; advsy ed Horizons 1988–91; performance assessor and PLAB examiner GMC 2002–; memb Exec Ctee E Berks BMA 1977–93 (divnl sec 1983–85), SW Thames Faculty Bd memb RCGP 1983–92, vice-pres Section of Gen Practice RSM 1995–97 (hon sec 1993–95); The Cambridge Soc: memb Cncl 1991–2007, vice-pres Surrey Branch 1995– (sec 1982–85, chm 1988–95); wandsman St Paul's Cathedral 1988–, vice-chm Old Windsor Day Centre 1989–94, tstee Worshipful Co of Curriers Millennium Tst 2002–; govr Sons of the Clergy 2011, life govr Royal Humane Soc 2014– (govr 2011); life govr Sheriffs' and Recorder's Fund City of London; memb Soc of Genealogists; Freeman City of London 1977, memb Guild of Freemen City of London 1979, memb Ct of Assts Worshipful Soc of Apothecaries 1998– (Freeman 1977, Liveryman 1981, Warden 2008–10, Master 2010–11, Hon Treas 2014–), Liveryman Worshipful Co of Curriers 2011; fell Med Soc of London 1995; FRSM 1975, MRCGP 1979, FRSH 1989; *Recreations* genealogy, books, gardening; *Clubs* Oxford and Cambridge, MCC, Sussex Archaeological Soc, Manchester and Lancs Family History Soc; *Style*— Dr Robert Bethel; ✉ The Worshipful Society of Apothecaries, Apothecaries' Hall, Blackfriars Lane, London EC4V 6EJ (☎ 020 7236 1189, e-mail robert.bethel@cantab.net)

BETHELL, Dr Hugh James Newton; MBE (1995); s of Brig Richard Brian Wyndham Bethell, DSO (d 1990), and Jackomina Alice, *née* Barton (d 1979); *b* 31 March 1942; *Educ* Tonbridge, St John's Coll Cambridge (BA), Guy's Hosp (MB BChir, DObstRCOG, MD); *m* 1, 1968, Astrid Jill, *née* Short (d 1979); 2 da (Katharine Emma b 25 Dec 1969, Christina Louise b 12 April 1973); m 2, 1984, Lesley, *née* Harris; *Career* cardiac registrar Charing Cross Hosp 1969–72, dermatology registrar Guy's Hosp 1972–74, princ in gen practice 1974–2002; dir Basingstoke and Alton Cardiac Rehabilitation Unit 1976–2002; chm Advsy Ctee on Coronary Rehabilitation to the Coronary Prevention Gp 1987–, founding pres British Assoc for Cardiac Rehabilitation, memb Br Cardiac Soc; fndr chm Alton Joggers; FRCGP 1991 (MRCGP), FRCP 1995 (MRCP); *Publications* Exercise Based Cardiac Rehabilitation (1996); author of numerous scientific papers, review articles, and book chapters; *Recreations* running, cinema; *Clubs* Hawks' (Cambridge); *Style*— Dr Hugh Bethell, MBE; ✉ Timbers, Boyneswood Road, Medstead, Alton, Hampshire GU34 5DY (☎ 01420 563932, e-mail hugh@boyneswood.fsnet.co.uk)

BETHELL, 5 Baron (UK 1922); James Nicholas Bethell; 5 Bt (UK 1911); s of 4 Baron Bethell (d 2007), and Cecilia Mary Lothian, *née* Honeyman (d 1977); *b* 1 October 1967; *Educ* Harrow, Univ of Edinburgh (MA); *m* 2004, Melissa, da of Douglas Wong, of Newport Coast, CA; 2 s (Hon Jacob Nicholas Douglas b 17 Oct 2006, Hon Gabriel Barlow b 1 Oct 2014), 2 da (Hon Elizabeth Cecilia Maria b 12 Oct 2009, Hon Rosalie Cinnamon Honeyman Wong b 8 July 2011); *Heir* s, Hon Jacob Bethell; *Career* intern US Senate 1985, stagiere European Cmmn 1990, reporter Sunday Times 1991–93, md Miny of Sound 1993–2001, managing ptnr Portland 2005–08, dir PoliticsHome 2009–10, dir Westbourne 2010–; Cons candidate for Tooting 2005; *Recreations* mountaineering, backgammon; *Clubs* Soho House, Pratts; *Style*— The Lord Bethell; ✉ Lockeridge Down, Lockeridge, Marlborough, Wiltshire SN8 4EL (☎ 01672 861192, e-mail james@jbethell.com)

BETTERIDGE, Neil John; s of George Henry Betteridge, and Eileen Eva, *née* Swift (d 2005); *b* 23 September 1960, Nuneaton, Warks; *Educ* King Edward VI GS, King Edward VI Coll, Univ of Liverpool (prize for Eng Lit, BA, MPhil); *Partner* Kate Llewelyn; *Career* devpt offr Young Arthritis Care 1991–93, head of memb services Royal Assoc of Disability and Rehabilitation (RADAR) 1993–95, head of projects and campaigns RADAR 1995–2000; Arthritis Care: head of public policy and campaigning 2000–04, dir of public affairs 2004–05, chief exec 2005–; memb Cmmn for Integrated Transport 2003–09; chair Disabled Persons Transport Advsy Ctee 2003–09, chair Arthritis and Muskuloskeletal Alliance (ARMA) 2005–09; patient and public champion of 18 weeks prog Dept of Health 2007–09, patient and public advsr on elective care Dept of Health 2009–; vice-pres European League Against Rheumatism (EULAR) 2009–; *Recreations* writing (published in several magazines), physical activity (good self-management for joints affected by juvenile arthritis); *Style*— Neil Betteridge, Esq; ✉ Arthritis Care, 18 Stephenson Way, London, NW1 2HD (☎ 020 7380 6558, fax 020 7380 6505, e-mail neilb@arthritiscare.org.uk)

BETTISON, Paul David; OBE (2016); s of Kenneth Henry David Bettison (d 2005), of Worcester Park, Surrey, and Ona Patricia, *née* Ratcliffe (d 2008); *b* 18 April 1953; *Educ* Tiffin Boys' Sch Kingston upon Thames; *m* 15 May 1976, Jean Margaret, da of Kenneth Charles Bradshaw (d 2004), of Ewell, Surrey; 2 da (Clare Louise b 1983, Emily Margaret b 1985); *Career* memb mgmnt Rockwell Graphic Systems Ltd 1978–87; md: Graphic Systems International Ltd 1987–2003, Caxton House (UK) Ltd 2001–03; chm iESE Ltd 2012–; dir: Factistel Ltd 1988–2003, Tolerans Ingol (UK) Ltd 1990–93, Topefa Limited 1990–95, Pizza De Action Ltd 1995–2003, Pizza Cake Ltd 1995–2003, Tolerans Ingol Ltd 1999–2002, The Code Corporation (UK) Ltd 2001–03, Localis Research Ltd 2001–, Caxton International Ltd 2002–03, Bettison Associates Ltd 2003–, Gangmasters' Licensing Authy 2012–15, Public Fundraising Regulatory Assoc 2013–14, Tribune Digital Ltd 2015–, Purple Homes Ltd 2015–; memb (Cons) Sandhurst Town Cncl 1991– (dep mayor 1992–93, mayor 1993–95), memb Bracknell Forest Cncl 1992– (chm Health and Safety Ctee 1993–95, vice-chm Personnel Ctee 1993–95, ldr Cons Gp 1996–, ldr Cncl 1997–, chm Strategy and Policy Ctee 1997–2001, chm Fin and Property Ctee 1997–2000, chm Electoral Review Ctee 1997–2001, chm Town Centre Ctee 1997–2012); chm: Local Govt Assoc Housing Exec 2000–02, Rural Cmmn 2002–04, Local Govt Assoc Environment Bd 2006–09, Improvement and Efficiency SE 2008–12, Local Govt Regulation 2009–12; e-govt champion 2003–, Cons nat lead peer 2003–; memb: Local Govt Assoc Cons Gp Exec 1999–2003 and 2005–13 (Gp Whip 2000–03), Bd Cons Cncllr's Assoc 2000– (dep chm 2008–11), Directgov 2004–08, Local Govt Assoc Exec 2006–12; cmmr Cmmn on Local Governance 2001–04; Cons nat local govt spokesman on ICT issues 2000–; memb Ct and Cncl Univ of Reading 1999–; govr: New Scotland Hill Primary Sch 1991–2008, Uplands County Primary Sch 1992–2008, RNLI 1994–; tstee Keep Britain Tidy Gp 2010–; CInstSMM 1996 (FInstSMM 1979); Hon FCIWM 2007, FRSA 2010; *Recreations* politics, flying light aircraft, travel, cars, wine; *Style*— Paul Bettison, Esq, OBE; ✉ Longdown House, Mickle Hill, Little Sandhurst, Berkshire GU47 8QL (☎ 01344 352041, mobile 07836 287050, e-mail paul.bettison@bracknell-forest.gov.uk)

BETTON, David John William; s of John Clifford Betton (d 1993), of Taunton, Somerset, and Evelyn Naomi, *née* Byatt; *b* 30 December 1947, Hammersmith, London; *Educ* Dulwich Coll, Emmanuel Coll Cambridge (MA); *m* 1, 6 Jan 1970 (m dis 1975), Christine Judith Patey, da of Very Rev Edward Patey, Dean of Liverpool, Merseyside (d 2007); m 2, 5 Sept 1980 (m dis 1994), Nicola Mary Mallen, da of John McGregor Carter (d 1983); 1 s (Jack David McGregor), 3 da (Victoria Christine Naomi, Polly Nicola, Nancy Evelyn Mary); m 3, 19 Jan 1996, Baroness Gillian van Overstraeten, da of Rylance John Taylor; *Career* called to the Bar 1972; sr legal advsr HM Customs and Excise 1976–86, nat dir of VAT Clark Whitehill CAs 1986–91, senior VAT conslt KPMG 1991–; Freeman City of London, Liveryman Worshipful Co of Plumbers; *Publications* VAT on Printing, VAT Factbook; *Recreations* cricket, theatre, walking, golf; *Clubs* MCC; *Style*— David Betton, Esq

BETTS, Charles Valentine; CB (1998); s of Harold Blair Betts (d 2010), and Mary Ellis, *née* France (d 1990); *b* 10 January 1942, Hove, Sussex; *Educ* Seaford Coll Worthing, Lysses Sch Fareham, Ryde Sch Isle of Wight, Merchant Taylors' Crosby, St Catharine's Coll Cambridge (MA, capt of boats), RNC Greenwich (Cert Naval Architecture), UCL (MPhil); *m* 20 April 1965, Rev Patricia Joyce Betts (ordained priest 1997), er da of William Gordon Bennett, of Great Crosby, Liverpool; 2 s (Christopher Jeremy b 3 April 1968, Richard Anthony b 25 March 1970); *Career* postgrad trg for RCNC: RNEC Manadon Plymouth 1963–64, RNC Greenwich 1964–66; asst constructor FE Fleet 1966–67, constructor MOD Foxhill Bath 1971 (asst constructor 1967–70), seconded as lectr in naval architecture UCL 1971–74, constructor HM Dockyard Portsmouth 1974–77; chief constructor: MOD Foxhill Bath 1979–83 (constructor 1977–79), MOD London 1983–85; seconded as prof of naval architecture UCL 1985–89; MOD Foxhill Bath: dir Surface Ships B 1989–92, DG Surface Ships 1992–94, DG Submarines 1994–98; dep controller RN 1994–98, head RCNC 1992–98; ret from MOD 1998; non-exec dir: BMT Group 1999–2001, BMT Reliability Consits Ltd 2000–01, British Maritime Technology Ltd 2001–05, BMT Gp Ltd 2005–12; tstee BMT Gp Employee Benefit Tst 2006–12 (chm of tstees 2010–12), chm of tstees BMT Pension and Life Assurance Scheme 2006–12; tstee and vice-chm The Coverdale Tst (formerly Alpha International Ministries) 1996–2004; vice-pres RINA 2003–09 (memb Cncl 1985–2002 and 2003–09), memb Nat Historic Ships Ctee 2000–06; memb Ct Univ of Bath 2006–15; CEng 1968, FRINA 1981 (MRINA 1968), FREng 1991, FRSA 1992; *Books* The Marine Technology Reference Book (contrib, 1990), The Royal Corps of Naval Constructors, 130th Anniversary, Our Modern History: 1983 to 2013 (2014); *Recreations* sailing, music, Christian activities; *Clubs* RNSA, Royal Victoria Yacht; *Style*— Charles Betts, Esq, CB, FREng; ✉ c/o BMT Group Limited, Goodrich House, 1 Waldegrave Road, Teddington, Middlesex TW11 8LZ

BETTS, Clive James Charles; MP; s of Harold Betts (d 1992), of Sheffield, and Nellie, *née* Ellis (d 1991); *b* 13 January 1950; *Educ* King Edward VII Sch Sheffield, Pembroke Coll Cambridge (BA); *Career* economist TUC 1971–72; local govt offr: Derbyshire 1973–74, South Yorks 1974–86, Rotherham 1986–91; Parly candidate: Sheffield Hallam 1974, Louth 1979; MP (Lab) Sheffield Attercliffe 1992–; former chm Treasy Departmental Ctee Lab Pty, former memb Treasy Select Ctee, memb Lab Ldr's Campaign Team with responsibility for Environment and Local Govt, appointed Lab Pty oppn whip 1996–97, asst govt whip 1997–98, a Lord Cmmr (Govt whip) 1998–2001, memb Select Ctee Office of the dep PM 2001–; Lab Pty Sheffield City Cncl: cncllr (Lab) 1976–92, chm Housing Ctee 1980–86, chm Fin Ctee 1986–88, dep ldr 1986–87, ldr 1987–92; vice-pres Assoc of Met Authorities 1988–91 (chm Housing Ctee 1985–89); pres: Organising Ctee XVI Universiade 1990–91, SE Sheffield CAB; patron: Br Deaf Sports Cncl, Mosborough Township Youth Project; former patron Nat Assoc for Therapeutic Educn, former vice-pres Energy from Waste Assoc; memb Lab Pty 1969–; *Recreations* Sheffield Wednesday FC, squash, cricket, walking, real ale; *Style*— Clive Betts, Esq, MP; ✉ Barkers Pool House, Burgess Street, Sheffield S1 2HF (☎ 0114 275 7788); House of Commons, London SW1A 0AA (☎ 020 7219 5114, e-mail clive.betts.mp@parliament.uk)

BETTS, Thomas Matthew (Tom); s of Christopher Betts, of Charlbury, Oxon, and Ann, *née* Blyton; *b* 21 November 1964; *Educ* Warwick Sch, UCL (LLB), Coll of Law London; *m* 1, 1991 (m dis 1997), Janet Morrison; 1 s (Jack Alexander b 4 Feb 1993), 1 da (Katherine Alice b 15 Oct 1994); m 2, 1998, Karen, da of John Meek; 2 da (Eva Tallulah b 9 Jan 1998, Ruby Rose b 2 Sept 1999); *Career* legal asst United International Pictures 1987–88, articled clerk Denton Hall 1988–90, slr entertainment and media dept Denton Hall 1990–91, legal advsr Central Productions Ltd 1991–93; controller of commissioning and network business affairs Carlton TV 1994–97, commercial dir Carlton TV 1997–2001, dir of business devpt Granada Media 2002–04, acting md ITV Broadcasting 2005, chief operating offr ITV Consumer 2005–07, commercial and acquisitions dir ITV plc 2007–; dir: HTV Gp Ltd 2000–01, Arsenal Broadcasting Ltd 2002–07, MUTV Ltd 2002–08, liverpoolfc.tv Ltd 2004–07; bd observer Arsenal Hldgs plc 2002–07; chm: Digital 3 & 4 Ltd 1999–2001, ITV2 Ltd 2000–01, Digital TV Services Ltd (Freeview) 2007 (dir 2003–); memb Law Soc 1990; *Recreations* football, cinema, modern British literature, my four children; *Clubs* Bentham, Tottenham Hotspur FC; *Style*— Tom Betts, Esq; ✉ Granada Media, London Television Centre, Upper Ground, London SE1 9LT

BETTS, Torben Anthony; s of Martin Frankland Betts, and Jennifer Ann Betts; *b* 10 February 1968; *Educ* Stamford Sch, Univ of Liverpool (BA); *m* 1997, Victoria, *née* Witcomb; 2 s (Stanley b 24 Sept 2001, Leo b 14 May 2005), 1 da (Lara b 13 July 2008); *Career* dramatist and screenwriter; plays incl: The National Joke, Get Carter, What Falls Apart, Invincible, Muswell Hill, A Listening Heaven (nominated TMA Best New Play 2001), Incarcerator, Mummies and Daddies, Five Visions of the Faithful, Clockwatching, The Biggleswades, The Last Days of Desire, The Optimist, The Lunatic Queen, The Unconquered (Best New Play Critics Awards for Theatre in Scotland 2007), The Error of Their Ways, The Swing of Things, The Company Man, Lie of the Land, The Seagull; screenplay Downhill; *Publications* Invincible, Plays One, Plays Two, Plays Three, The Lunatic Queen, The Error of their Ways, The Unconquered, Lie of the Land, Muswell Hill, What Falls Apart, The Seagull, The National Joke; *Style*— Torben Betts, Esq; ✉ c/o Cathy King, Independent Talent, 40 Whitfield Street, London W1T 2RH

BETZ, Charles John Paul; s of Col Francis Betz (d 1949), of Calif, and Martha Abusdal Flannery (d 1988); *b* 8 September 1946; *Educ* American Grad Sch of Int Management (MBA), Stanford Univ (Cert), Calif State Univ (BS), Univ of Uppsala (Cert); *m* 6 Dec 1969, Birgitta, da of Erik Gideon Thorell, of Solleron, Sweden; 2 da (Anika Ingrid (Mrs Nicholas A Keynes) b 1975, Martina Mary b 1980), 2 s (Christian Michael b 1977, Clark Paul Erik b 1982); *Career* dir customer serv Transworld Airlines NY 1970–72, regnl vice-pres Bank of America London 1979–86 (various appts San Francisco 1973–76, vice-pres NY 1976–

79), md Carré Orban and Ptnrs 1986–91, European Bank for Reconstruction and Devpt 1991–92, chm Int Acad for Educn and Devpt 1993–94; md: Bridge Information Systems/ Bridge Int Brokering 1995–97, Saracen Partners 1997–2002, Betz & Co Int 2003–; chm and organizer Champion Polo Benefit; *Recreations* polo, real tennis; *Clubs* Buck's, Pilgrims, West Wycombe Polo, Schs and Univs Polo Assoc (chm), SAPA Ltd (chm), Holyport Real Tennis; *Style*— Charles Betz, Esq; ✉ c/o Atkins Farm, Great Missenden, Buckinghamshire (☎ 01494 863762); 12129 Bayview Edison Road, Mount Vernon, Washington, USA 98273–8228 (☎ 00 1 831 233 4956)

BEVAN; *see also:* Evans-Bevan

BEVAN, Anthony Richard Van (Tony); s of Adrian Van Cruiskerken Bevan, of Harbury, Warks, and Margaret Betty, *née* Pemberton; *b* 22 July 1951; *Educ* Bradford Sch of Art, Goldsmiths Coll of Art and Design London, Slade Sch of Fine Art London; *Partner* Glenys Johnson; 1 da (Rosa Elizabeth Donna Johnson Glen Bevan b 25 Jan 1991); *Career* artist; RA 2007; *Solo Exhibitions* incl: Matt's Gallery London 1981, 1982, 1986 and 1996, Portraits and Emblems (Galeria Akumulatory 2 Poznan Poland) 1983, The Honest Portrait (Nat Portrait Gallery London) 1985, Paintings 1980–87 (ICA London touring Orchard Gallery Derry, Kettles Yard Cambridge and Cartwright Hall Bradford) 1987–88, Neue Bilder (Kunsthalle Kiel) 1988, Staatsgalerie Moderner Kunst Haus der Kunst Munich 1989, Kunstverein Lingen Germany 1990, Whitechapel Art Gallery 1993, Paintings from the 80's and 90's (Cottbus Germany) 1997, Abbot Hall Art Gallery Kendal 1999, Milton Keynes Gallery 2003, Works From Deptford (Abbot Hall Art Gallery Kendal) 2003, retrospective Institut Valencia d'Art Modern (IVAM) 2005–06, Tony Bevan: Self Portraits (Nat Portrait Gallery London) 2011; *Style*— Tony Bevan, Esq; ✉ c/o Ben Brown Gallery, 21 Cork Street, London W1S 3LZ (☎ 020 7734 8888, fax 020 7734 8892)

BEVAN, HE Sir James David; KCMG (2012); *Career* diplomat; Western European Dept FCO 1982–83, Nr East and North Africa Dept FCO 1983–84, second sec Kinshasa 1984–86, first sec UK Delgn to NATO Brussels 1986–90, EU Dept FCO 1991–92, first sec Paris 1992–93, first sec Washington 1994–98, head Africa Dept (Equatorial) FCO 1998–2000, head EU Dept FCO 2000–01, dir Balkans FCO 2002–03, dir Africa FCO 2003–06, visiting fell Centre for Int Affrs Harvard Univ 2006–07, chief operating offr and DG for corporate affrs FCO 2007–11, high cmmr to India 2011–; *Style*— HE Sir James Bevan, KCMG; ✉ c/o Foreign & Commonwealth Office (New Delhi), King Charles Street, London SW1A 2AH

BEVAN, His Hon Judge John Penry Vaughan; QC (1997); s of Llewelyn Vaughan Bevan (d 1987), and Hilda Molly, *née* Yates (d 2009); *b* 7 September 1947; *Educ* Radley, Magdalene Coll Cambridge (BA); *m* 1, 1971 (m dis 1976), Dinah, *née* Nicholson; 2 da (Amelia b 1972, Lucinda b 1975); m 2, 1978, Veronica, *née* Aliaga-Kelly; 1 s (Henry b 1981), 1 da (Charlotte b 1985); *Career* called to the Bar Middle Temple 1970 (bencher 2001); recorder of the Crown Court 1987–2004 (asst recorder 1983–87), sr prosecuting counsel to the Crown at Central Criminal Court 1991–97, circuit judge (South Eastern Circuit) 2004–11, sr circuit judge Central Criminal Court 2011–; *Recreations* sailing, tennis; *Clubs* Leander, Aldeburgh Yacht, Orford Sailing; *Style*— His Hon Judge Bevan, QC

BEVAN, (Edward) Julian; QC (1991); s of Capt Geoffrey Bevan (d 1994), and Barbara, *née* Locke (d 1991); *b* 23 October 1940; *Educ* Eton; *m* 17 Sept 1966, Bronwen Mary, da of Brig James Windsor Lewis, DSO, MC; 2 s (David, Dickon), 2 da (Anna, Henrietta); *Career* called to the Bar Gray's Inn 1962 (bencher 1989); standing counsel Inland Revenue 1973–77, first sr treasy counsel Central Criminal Court 1989 (jr treasy counsel 1977–84, sr treasy counsel 1984); *Style*— Julian Bevan, Esq, QC; ✉ 11 Cheyne Place, London SW3 4HH

BEVAN, Simon; s of David Howard Bevan (d 1994), and Margaret Mary Bevan (d 2009); *b* 17 September 1959, London; *Educ* Desborough Sch Maidenhead, Univ of York; *Career* BDO LLP: joined 1981, ptnr 1988–, managing ptnr 2000–01, sr ptnr 2010–; chm Assoc of Partnership Practitioners; FCA (memb ICA 1984–); *Publications* Audit and Accounts of Property Companies (1994), Evolving Business Structures for Law Firms (2010); *Recreations* music, travel, skiing, most sports; *Clubs* Home House; *Style*— Simon Bevan, Esq; ✉ BDO LLP, 55 Baker Street, London W1U 7EU (e-mail simon.bevan@bdo.co.uk, website www.bdo.co.uk)

BEVAN, Tim; CBE (2005); *b* 1957; *Educ* Sidcot Sch; *m* 1 (m dis), Joely Richardson; 1 da (Daisy b 1992); m 2, Amy Gadney; 1 da (Nell b 2001), 1 s (Jago b 2003); *Career* film prodr; Working Title Films: co-fndr (with Sarah Radclyffe, *qv*) 1984, co-chm (with Eric Fellner, *qv*) 1992–, launched Working Title 2 (with Eric Fellner); films produced by Working Title: My Beautiful Laundrette 1985, Caravaggio 1985, Personal Services 1986, Wish You Were Here 1986 Sammy and Rosie Get Laid 1987, A World Apart 1987, Paperhouse 1987, For Queen and Country 1987, The Tall Guy 1988, Diamond Skulls 1988, Chicago Joe and the Showgirl 1989, Fools of Fortune 1989, Dakota Road 1990, Drop Dead Fred 1990, Rubin and Ed 1990, Edward II 1991, Robin Hood 1991, London Kills Me 1991, Bob Roberts 1992, Map of the Human Heart 1993, The Young Americans 1993, Romeo is Bleeding 1993, Posse 1993, The Hudsucker Proxy 1994, Four Weddings and a Funeral 1994, The Eye the Sky 1994, Panther 1995, French Kiss 1995, Moonlight and Valentino 1995, Loch Ness 1995, Dead Man Walking 1995, Fargo 1996, Matchmaker 1996, Bean 1997, The Borrowers 1997, The Big Lebowski 1998, What Rats Won't Do 1998, Elizabeth 1998, The Hi-Lo Country 1998, Plunkett & Macleane 1999, Notting Hill 1999, Oh Brother, Where Art Thou? 2000, Billy Elliot 2000, The Man Who Cried 2000, High Fidelity 2000, Captain Corelli's Mandolin 2001, Bridget Jones's Diary 2001, The Man Who Wasn't There 2001, Long Time Dead 2002, My Little Eye 2002, 40 Days and 40 Nights 2002, Ali G Inda House 2002, About a Boy 2002, The Guru 2002, Johnny English 2003, Ned Kelly 2003, Love Actually 2003, The Calcium Kid 2003, The Shape of Things 2003, Thirteen 2003, Shaun of the Dead 2004, Gettin' Square 2004, Thunderbirds 2004, Wimbledon 2004, Bridget Jones: The Edge of Reason 2004, The Interpreter 2005, Pride and Prejudice 2005, Nanny McPhee 2005, Mickybo and Me 2005, United 93 2006, Gone 2006, Sixty Six 2006, Smokin' Aces 2007, Catch a Fire 2007, Hot Fuzz 2007, Mr Bean's Holiday 2007, Golden Age 2007, Atonement 2007, Definitely Maybe 2008, Wild Child 2008, Burn After Reading 2009, Frost/Nixon 2009, The Boat That Rocked 2009, State of Play 2009, The Soloist 2009, Green Zone 2009, Nanny McPhee and the Big Bang 2010, Johnny English Reborn 2011, Tinker Tailor Soldier Spy 2011, Senna 2011, Anna Karenina 2012, Les Misérables 2012, Big Miracle 2012, Contraband 2012; govr Nat Film and TV Sch; 6 Oscars, 30 BAFTA Awards, GQ Entrepreneur of the Year 2003, Michael Balcon Award for outstanding contribution to Br cinema 2004, Alexander Walker Film Award 2005; *Style*— Tim Bevan, Esq, CBE; ✉ Working Title Films, 26 Aybrook Street, London W1U 4AN (☎ 020 7307 3000)

BEVERIDGE, Crawford William; CBE (1995); s of William Wilson Beveridge, and Catherine Crawford Beveridge; *b* 3 November 1945; *Educ* Univ of Edinburgh (BSc), Univ of Bradford (MSc); *Career* various appts Hewlett Packard 1968–77, Digital Equipment Corp 1977–81, vice-pres corp resources Sun Microsystems 1985–90, chief exec Scottish Enterprise 1991–2000, exec vice-pres and chief HR offr Sun Microsystems Inc 2000–; non-exec dir: Memec Inc 2002–, Autodesk, Scottish Equity Partners; *Style*— Crawford W Beveridge, Esq, CBE

BEVERIDGE, David J; *Educ* Washington and Jefferson Coll (BA), Univ of Texas at Austin (JD); *m* Diane; 1 s (Michael), 1 da (Josephine); *Career* admitted to the NY Bar; slr specialising in int capital markets and banking and finance; ptnr Shearman & Sterling LLP (London office Capital Markets Gp 1998–); *Style*— David J Beveridge, Esq; ✉ Shearman & Sterling LLP, Broadgate West, 9 Appold Street, London EC2A 2AP (☎ 020 7655 5005, fax 020 7655 5500, e-mail dbeveridge@shearman.com)

BEVERIDGE, John Caldwell; QC (1979); s of Prof William Ian Beardmore Beveridge (d 2006), and Patricia Dorothy Nina, *née* Thomson (d 1996); *b* 26 September 1937, Sydney, Aust; *Educ* Jesus Coll Cambridge (MA, LLB); *m* 1, 2 Aug 1973 (m dis 1989), Frances Ann Clunes Grant, da of Dr John Sutherland, of Edinburgh; m 2, 7 July 1989 (m dis 2003), Lilian, da of John Weston Adamson (d 1977); m 3, 22 April 2005, Rebecca Rosemary Amara, da of Peter Boulos-Hanna (d 2009); *Career* called to the Bar Inner Temple 1963 (bencher 1985); recorder of the Crown Court (Western Circuit) 1975–96; QC NSW Australia 1980; dir Barker Poland Financial Mgmnt Ltd 2000–06, ptnr Perfect Pitch 2008–; tstee Dogs Tst 1998, Cons memb Westminster City Cncl 1968–72; vice-pres Manchester Dogs Home 1999–2013; chm St James's Conservation Tst 1999 (patron 2014–); jt master Westmeath Foxhounds 1976–79; Freeman City of London 1965, Liveryman Worshipful Co of Goldsmiths; Cdr Star of Honour (Ethiopia) 1992; *Recreations* wine, art; *Clubs* Beefsteak, Pratt's, Turf, Brook (NY); *Style*— John Beveridge, Esq, QC; ✉ Tilden Farm, Hawkhurst, Kent TN18 5AY (☎ 01760 444444, e-mail beveridge1@me.com)

BEVERLEY, Nigel; s of Jack Beverley, of Salhouse, Norfolk, and Amelia, *née* Hartley; *b* 22 June 1952; *Educ* High Storrs GS Sheffield, Univ of Nottingham (BSc); *m* Mary Elizabeth; 1 da (Katherine b 7 Dec 1983), 1 s (James b 25 May 1987); *Career* nat mgmnt trainee NE Thames RHA 1973–75, asst sector admin UCH 1975–77, sector admin Hammersmith Hosp 1977–80, asst dist admin Havering Dist Barking and Havering AHA 1980–82, unit gen mangr Colchester Gen Hosp 1985–88 (unit admin 1982–85), dist gen mangr Southend HA 1988–90, chief exec Southend Healthcare NHS Tst 1990–91, head Reforms Gp and head NHS Tst Unit NHS Mgmnt Exec 1991–92, tst unit dir NHS Exec (N Thames) 1992–96, chief exec Wellhouse NHS Tst 1996–98, chief exec North Essex Health Authority 1998, actg chief exec Cambridge City PCT 2006; currently business dept dir Atos Origin Medical Services; bd dir: Synovia Ltd, Get Well UK; MHSM (DipHSM), MInstD; *Recreations* squash, golf, skiing; *Style*— Nigel Beverley, Esq

BEWES, Michael Keith; s of Rev Canon Thomas Francis Cecil Bewes (d 1993), and (Nellie) Sylvia Cohu, *née* De Berry; bro of Rev Prebendary Richard Thomas Bewes, OBE, *qv*; *b* 4 March 1936; *Educ* Marlborough, Emmanuel Coll Cambridge (MA); *m* 10 Oct 1964, (Patricia) Anrôs, *née* Neill; 3 s (Jonathan b 1965, Nicholas b 1967, Anthony b 1971), 1 da (Rebecca b 1973); *Career* Nat Serv 2 Lt RA 1954–56; BR 1959–66, Royal Exchange Assurance 1966–68, Guardian Royal Exchange plc 1968–96, chm The Willis Partnership 1996–2011; Chartered Insurance Inst: treas 1985–87, dep pres 1987–88, pres 1988–89; chm Insurance Industry Trg Cncl 1982–88; memb Governing Cncl Business in the Community 1983–96; chm of govrs Coll of Insurance 1992–99, pres Insurance Benevolent Fund 1995–96; chm Cncl Scripture Union 1988–94, tstee Dio of Central Tanganyika; govr Stowe Sch 1971–2005, dir Allied Schs; Freeman City of London 1990, Master Worshipful Co of Insurers 2003–04, Liveryman Worshipful Co of Fan Makers; FCIPD (FIPD 1983), FRSA 1989; *Recreations* fly fishing, heraldic painting, photography, music, Napoleon commemorative medals, various sports – lawn tennis and hockey; *Clubs* RAC, National, Hawks' (Cambridge); *Style*— Michael Bewes, Esq; ✉ Clifton House, Church Lane, Lexden, Colchester, Essex CO3 4AE (☎ 01206 542710, e-mail michael@bewes.com); The Willis Partnership, 6 Vigo Street, Mayfair, London W1S 3HF

BEWES, Rev Prebendary Richard Thomas; OBE (2005); s of Rev Canon Thomas Francis Cecil Bewes (d 1993), and (Nellie) Sylvia Cohu, *née* De Berry; bro of Michael Keith Bewes, *qv*; *b* 1 December 1934; *Educ* Marlborough, Emmanuel Coll Cambridge (MA), Ridley Hall Theol Coll Cambridge; *m* 1, 18 April 1964, Elisabeth Ingrid, da of Lionel Jaques (d 2006); 2 s (Timothy b 1966, Stephen b 1971), 1 da (Wendy b 1968); m 2, 21 July 2012, Pamela Joy, wid of Michael Wright (d 2011); *Career* vicar: St Peter's Harold Wood 1965–74, Emmanuel Northwood 1974–83; rector All Souls Langham Place London 1983–2004, prebendary St Paul's Cathedral 1988–; chm: C of E Evangelical Cncl 1992–2001, Anglican Evangelical Assembly 1992–2001; host Open Home Open Bible and Book by Book (TV and DVD) 2000–; memb Guild of Br Songwriters 1975; Freedom of the City of Charlotte NC 1984; *Books* God in Ward 12 (1973), Advantage Mr Christian (1975), Talking About Prayer (1979, revised edn 2013), The Pocket Handbook of Christian Truth (1981), John Wesley's England (1981, revised edn 2003), The Church Reaches Out (1981), The Church Overcomes (1983), On The Way (1984), Quest For Life (1985), Quest For Truth (1985), The Church Marches On (1986), When God Surprises (1986), The Resurrection (1989), A New Beginning (1989), Does God Reign? (1995), Speaking in Public – Effectively (1998), Great Quotes of the 20th Century (1999, revised edn (as Words that Circled the World) 2002), The Lamb Wins (2000), The Bible Truth Treasury (2000), The Stone That Became a Mountain (2001), The Top 100 Questions (2002), Beginning the Christian Life (2004), 150 Pocket Bible Thoughts (2004), The Goodnight Book (2009), Equipped to Serve (2013); *Recreations* tennis, photography, broadcasting, reading, writing; *Style*— The Rev Prebendary Richard Bewes, OBE; ✉ Montreat, 2 Home Close, Virginia Water, Surrey GU25 4DH (e-mail richardandpambewes@gmail.com, website www.richardbewes.com)

BEWICK, Tom; *b* 4 February 1971, Coventry; *Educ* Univ of Bath (BSc, MSc (jtly with Lljubljana Univ)); *Career* policy advsr TEC Nat Cncl 1994–96, policy advsr (educn and employment) Lab Party 1997–99, dir NTO Nat Cncl 1999–2001, ministerial advsr DfES 2001–03, dir LSC Thames Gateway 2003–04, chief exec Creative and Cultural Skills 2004–10, chief exec Enterprise UK 2010–11, dir Tom Bewick Consultancy 2011–; co-fndr Centre for Social Inclusion 1996, chm Int Network of Sector Skills Organisations 2011–; non-exec dir TLMH Ltd 2005–2007; FRSA 1999, MInstD 2006; *Publications* Learning and Earning in the 21st Century (1996); *Recreations* travel, cricket, reading, social history; *Clubs* England Cricket Supporters; *Style*— Tom Bewick, Esq

BEYFUS, Drusilla Norman (Mrs Milton Shulman); da of late Norman Beyfus, and late Florence Noël Barker; *Educ* RN Sch, Channing Sch; *m* 1956, Milton Shulman (d 2004); 1 s (Jason), 2 da (Alexandra Shulman, *qv*, Nicola (The Most Hon the Marchioness of Normanby)); *Career* assoc ed Queen Magazine 1958–63, home ed The Observer 1963–64, assoc ed Daily Telegraph colour supplement 1964–70, ed Brides Magazine 1971–79, assoc ed British Vogue Magazine Condé Nast 1979–86, ed Harrods Magazine 1987–88, columnist Daily Mail magazine 1988–89, contributing ed Telegraph Magazine 1990–2009, weekly columnist You magazine (Mail on Sunday) 1994–2001; visiting tutor Central St Martin's Coll of Art 1989–2007; author and broadcaster; Hon MA London Inst 2002; *Books* Lady Behave (co-author), The English Marriage, The Bride's Book, The Art of Giving, Modern Manners (1992); The Done Thing: Courtship, Parties (1992), Business, Sex (1993), The You Guide to Modern Dilemmas (1996), Vogue on Hubert de Givenchy (2013), Vogue on Valentino Garavani (2015); *Style*— Miss Drusilla Beyfus; ✉ 51G Eaton Square, London SW1W 9BE (☎ 020 7235 7162)

BHATIA, Vineet; s of Ved Prakash Bhatia, of Mumbai, India, and Sheila Bhatia; *b* 9 December 1967; *Educ* Inst of Hotel Mgmnt, Catering Technol and Applied Nutrition Bombay (Dip Hotel Mgmnt and Catering Technol), Univ of Bombay (BA), Alliance Française New Delhi (Cert), Oberoi Sch of Hotel Mgmnt New Delhi (Dip Food Prodn), Westminster Coll (Dip); *m* 18 June 1997, Rashima, da of Capt Brij Dev Madhok; 2 c (Varaul b 27 June 1998, Ronit b 24 Jan 2000); *Career* chef; exec chef Star of India London 1993–98, chef patron Vineet Bhatia Indian Restaurant London 1998–99, chef and patron Zaika and Bar Zaika Bazaar London 1999–2004, chef and patron Rasoi Restaurant 2004–, chef patron Urban Turban Restuarant 2008–10; conslt: Tantra LA, Safran Le Touessrok

Hotel Mauritius, BA (first class and business class in-flight food), Indego Grosvenor House Hotel Dubai, Indus Moscow, Rasoi by Vineet Mandarin Oriental Hotel du Rhone Geneva 2008, Maharaja by Vineet Movenpick Hotel Al-Khobar 2008, Bird by Vineet Alea Casino Leeds 2008, Saffron Lounge Doha Qatar 2010, Ziya The Oberoi Mumbai India 2010, Azok by Vineet Oakwood Premier Juhu Mumbai India 2010, F-Mumbai Lounge Mumbai 2012, Qatar Airways In-flight 2012; fell Guild of Master Craftsmen 1996; *Awards* Cert of Ingenuity Assoc of Italian Chefs 1994, Evening Standard Eros Award 1995, 1996 and 1997, 3 AA Rosettes 1999, 2000, 2001, 2002, 2003 and 2005, Indian Restaurant of the Year Moët & Chandon London Awards 2000 (nominee Best Chef and Best Newcomer), Restaurant Personality of the Year Best in Britain Awards 2001, Restaurateur's Restaurant of the Year 2001, Most Innovative Chef Cobra Awards 2001, Michelin Star 2001– (first Indian chef to be awarded a Michelin Star for 102 years), nominee Best Kitchen Tatler Restaurant Awards 2003; Best Indian Restaurant: The Times 1997 and 2000/01, Hardens 2000/01, Zagat 2000/01, Good Food Guide 2000/01, Best in Britain Awards 2001, Restaurant Magazines Restaurateur Awards 2002, Best Newcomer Tatler Restaurant Awards 2005, Best Indian Restaurant Tio Pepe ITV Carlton Restaurant Awards 2005; *Books* Rasoi: New Indian Kitchen (2009); *Recreations* travelling, writing; *Style*— Vineet Bhatia, Esq; ✉ Rasoi Restaurant, 10 Lincoln Street, London SW3 2TS (website www.rasoi-uk.com and www.vineetbhatia.com)

BHATTACHARYYA, Baron (Life Peer UK 2004), of Moseley in the County of West Midlands; Sir (Sushantha) Kumar Bhattacharyya; kt (2003), CBE (1997); s of late Sudir Bhattacharyya, of Calcutta, India, and late Hemanalini, *née* Chakraborty; *b* 6 June 1940, Dacca, India; *Educ* IIT Kharagpur (BTech), Univ of Birmingham (MSc, PhD); *m* 1981, Brigid Carmel, da of Charles Rabbitt; 3 da (Anita b 16 April 1984, Tina b 9 March 1986, Malini b 17 Feb 1988); *Career* various positions in prodn and industrial mgmnt Lucas Industries Ltd 1961–67, head of mfrg systems Univ of Birmingham 1967–80, prof of mfrg Univ of Warwick 1980–, chm WMG (formerly Warwick Mfrg Gp); non-exec dir Technol Rover Group 1986–92; tstee: IPPR, Coventry 2020; memb: Nat Consumer Cncl Agency 1990–93, Cncl for Science and Technol 1993–2003, W Midlands Devpt Agency 1999–2004, Nurse Review Advsy Panel; advsr to various int cos and govts on matters of competitive industrial policy; Mensforth Int Gold Medal IEE 1998, Sir Robert Lawrence Award ILT 1999; hon prof: Hong Kong Poly Univ 1992, Univ of Technol Malaysia 1993, Min of Machinery Beijing 1994; hon dean Harbin Inst of Technol 2003; Hon DSc: Univ of Surrey 1992, Univ of Technol Malaysia 1993, Univ of Birmingham 2004; Hon Dr Hong Kong Poly Univ 2003, Hon LLD Monash Univ Australia 2015; FIMechE, FIEE 1975, FREng 1991, FILT 1996, CCMI 1996, FRS 2014; Padma Bhusan (India) 2002; *Recreations* family, flying, cricket; *Clubs* Athenaeum; *Style*— The Rt Hon the Lord Bhattacharyya, CBE; ✉ International Manufacturing Centre, University of Warwick, Coventry CV4 7AL (☎ 024 7652 3155, fax 024 7652 4827, mobile 07798 906166, e-mail s.k.bhattacharyya@warwick.ac.uk)

BHOGAL, Rev Dr Inderjit; OBE (2005); s of Gian Singh Bhogal (d 1984), of India, and Rajinder Kaur; *b* 17 January 1953; *Educ* Dudley Tech Coll, Cliff Coll, Univ of Manchester (BA), Westminster Coll Oxford (MA); *m* 1 Nov 1986, Kathryn Anne, da of Henry Robinson (decd); 2 c (Liamarjit b 8 Aug 1989, Anjuli b 14 Jan 1991); *Career* labourer Dudley Brass Foundry 1974–75; min Wolverhampton 1979–84, min Wolverhampton and co-ordinator Wolverhampton Inter Faith Gp 1984–87, min Sheffield W chaplaincy in higher educn Sheffield 1987–94, dir of studies Urban Theology Unit and min in Sheffield Inner City Ecumenical Mission 1994–97, dir Urban Theology Unit Sheffield 1997–2004, theological conslt Christian Aid 2004–05, dir Yorks and Humber Faiths Forum 2005–11, ldr Corrymeela Community NI 2011–14, learning and devpt offr Methodist Church 2014–; pres Methodist Conf 2000–01; convener Br Black Theology Forum Sheffield; fndr memb Sheffield Homeless and Rootless Gp, fndr City of Sanctuary Sheffield; Hon DUniv: Oxford Brookes 2001, Sheffield Hallam 2002; *Publications* A Table for All (2000), Theology on the Hoof (2001), Unlocking the Doors (2002), Pluralism and Mission in Today's World (2007), Building a City of Sanctuary (jtly, 2009), Understanding Sikhism (jtly, 2010), West Highland Way - Diary of a Walker (2009); author of various articles on theology; *Recreations* walking, cooking, photography; *Style*— Rev Dr Inderjit S Bhogal, OBE; ✉ c/o Methodist Church House, 25 Marylebone Road, London NW1 5JR (☎ 020 7486 5502)

BHOPAL, Prof Rajinder Singh (Raj); CBE (2001); s of late Jhanda S Bhopal, and late Bhagwanti K Bhopal; *b* 10 April 1953; *Educ* Shawlands Acad Glasgow, Univ of Edinburgh (BSc, MB ChB, MD), Univ of Glasgow (MPH, MacKinlay prize 1985); *m*; 4 c; *Career* surgical/house offr 1978–79, med house offr 1979, SHO in accident and emergency 1979–80, trainee GP 1980–81, SHO in general med 1981–82, SHO in infectious and tropical diseases 1982, sr registrar in community med 1985 (registrar 1983–85), lectr and hon sr registrar in community med Univ of Glasgow 1985–88; Univ of Newcastle upon Tyne: sr lectr 1988–91, hon conslt in public health med 1988–99, prof of epidemiology and public health 1991–99, head Dept of Epidemiology and Public Health 1991–98; Bruce and John Usher chair of public health Univ of Edinburgh 1999–, head Div of Community Health Sci 2000–03; visiting prof Dept of Epidemiology Sch of Public Health Univ of North Carolina 1996–97; hon conslt in public health medicine Lothian Health Bd 1999–; non-exec dir Newcastle HA 1992–94, vice-chm and non-exec dir Newcastle and N Tyneside HA 1994–96, non-exec dir Health Educn Authy England 1996–99; visiting worker MRC Med Sociology Unit Glasgow 1986–94, memb Advsy Bd Int Respiratory Infection Taskforce Schering Plough 1993–96; assoc ed Jl of Public Health Med 1989–90, memb Editorial Bd Jl of Epidemiology and Community Health 1993–98; memb: MRC Health Services Research and Public Health Bd 1999–2003, GMC 1978–, MRC Advsy Bd 1997–99, MRC Cross Bd Gp 2000–02, Sci Ctee Biobank UK 2003–04, Steering Ctee Nat Resource Centre for Ethnic Minority Health Scot (chair 2002–08); chair World Congress of Epidemiology 2011; Soc of Public Health: Maddison Research Prize 1992, J T Neech Prize 1994; Royal Soc for the Promotion of Health JW Starkey Silver Medal 2000, Cert of Recognition Sikh Heritage in Scotland 2007, Nat Award Br Assoc of Physicians of Indian Origin 2008, S Asian Health Fndn Award 2008, Sam Ramaiah Award Faculty of Public Health 2011; author of numerous pubns, papers and book chapters on the health and health care of ethnic minorities, infectious diseases and environmental health, epidemiology and public health; Hon DSc Queen Margeret Univ Coll 2005; MRCP 1982, FRCPEd 2000, FFPHM 1995 (Littlejohn Gairdner prize 1986, MFPHM 1987); *Books* Concepts of Epidemiology (2002, winner Public Health Category BMA Book Awards 2003, 2 edn 2008, highly commended Public Health Category BMA Book Awards 2008), The Epidemic of Coronary Heart Disease in South Asian Populations (ed with K C R Patel, 2003), Public Health: Past, Present and Future (ed with J Last, 2004), Ethnicity, Race and Health in Multicultural Societies (2007, Specialist Book Award Medical Journalists' Assoc 2008, 2 edn retitled Migration, Ethnicity, Race and Health 2014); *Recreations* chess, hill climbing, photography, travel, golf, cycling and walking; *Style*— Prof Raj Bhopal, CBE; ✉ Centre for Population Health Sciences, Institute of Population Health Sciences and Medical Infomatics, University of Edinburgh, Medical School, Teviot Place, Edinburgh EH8 9AG (☎ 0131 650 3216, fax 0131 650 6909, e-mail raj.bhopal@ed.ac.uk)

BHUGRA, Prof Dinesh Kumar; CBE (2012); s of Makhan Lal Bhugra (d 1989), and Shanta, *née* Chugh; *b* 8 July 1952, Yamuna Nagar, India; *Educ* MB BS, MSc, MPhil, MA, PhD; *Career* SHO (orthopaedics) Cork 1979–80, SHO (med) Northampton 1980, SHO then registrar (psychiatry) Leicester 1981–86, sr registrar (psychiatry) Maudsley Hosp 1986–89, researcher/lectr in psychiatry MRC Social and Community Psychiatry Unit 1989–92; Inst of Psychiatry London: sr lectr in psychiatry 1992–2000, reader in cultural psychiatry 2001–02, prof of mental health and cultural diversity 2002–14; RCPsych: chm Faculty of Gen and Community Psychiatry 1997–2001, sub-dean 2001–03, dean 2003–08, pres 2008–11, convenor working parties on homelessness and mental health 1992 and 1996 and on caring for a community 1995; pres World Psychiatry Assoc 2014–17 (pres-elect 2011–14), past pres Section of Psychiatry Steering Gp RSM; Mental Health Fndn (MHF): chair 2011–14, pres 2014–17, co-chair Enquiry on Psychiatric Services in the 21st Century; crafted policy satements for World Psychiatry Assoc on: discrimination 2016, LGBT mental health 2016, refugee and migrant mental health and recruiting students into psychiatry (all 2016), developed bill of rights for individuals with mental illness 2016; non-exec dir Tavistock & Portman Fndn NHS Tst; tstee Centre for Applied Research and Evaluation International Foundation (careif); Presidential Commendation American Psychiatric Association 2015; FRCP, FRCPE FRCPsych, Hon FACP, FFPH, fell Acad of Medicine of Singapore; *Books* SAQs in Psychiatry (1990), Case Presentations in Psychiatry (1992), Management for Psychiatrists (1992, 3 edn 2007), Principles of Social Psychiatry (1993, 2 edn 2010), Religion and Psychiatry (1996), Homelessness and Mental Health (1996), Troublesome Disguises (1997, 2 edn 2015), Ethnicity: An Agenda for Mental Health (1999), Mental Health of Ethnic Minorities: an annotated bibliography (1999), Cultural Psychiatry: A practical guide (2000), Psychiatry in Multicultural Britain (2001), Colonialism and Psychiatry (2001), Culture and Self-Harm (2004), Handbook of Psychiatry (2005), Mad Tales from Bollywood: Portrayal of Mental Illness in Conventional Hindi Cinema (2006), Culture and Mental Health (2007), Work Place Based Assessments in Psychiatry (2007), Handbook for Psychiatric Trainees (2007), Textbook of Cultural Psychiatry (2007), Management for Psychiatrists (2007), Clinical Topics in Cultural Psychiatry (2010), Mental Health of Refugees and Asylum Seekers (2010), Professionalism in Mental Healthcare (2010), Psychiatry's Contract with Society (2010), Migration and Mental Health (2010), Workplace Based Assessments in Psychiatric Training (2011), Leadership in Psychiatry (2013), Psychiatry in Practice (2016), Routledge Handbook of Psychiatry in Asia (2016), Pluralism in Psychiatry (2016); *Recreations* reading, theatre, cinema; *Clubs* Reform; *Style*— Prof Dinesh Bhugra, CBE; ✉ HSPRD, PO 25 Institute of Psychiatry, King's College London, De Crespigny Park, London SE5 8AF (☎ 020 7848 0500, fax 020 7848 0333, website www.dineshbhugra.net, Twitter @dineshbhugra)

BIAGI, Marco; MSP; *b* 31 July 1982; *Educ* Univ of St Andrews, Univ of Glasgow; *Career* MSP (SNP) Edinburgh Central 2011–; *Style*— Marco Biagi, Esq, MSP; ✉ The Scottish Parliament, Edinburgh EH99 1SP

BIBBY, Neil; MSP; *b* 6 September 1983, Paisley, Renfrewshire; *Educ* Gryffe HS Renfrewshire, Univ of Glasgow (MA); *Career* MSP (Scot Lab) W of Scotland 2011–; *Style*— Neil Bibby, Esq, MSP; ✉ The Scottish Parliament, Edinburgh EH99 1SP (☎ 0131 348 6385, e-mail neil.bibby.msp@scottishparliament.uk);Regional Office: 1st Floor, 4 St Mirren Street, Paisley PA1 1UA (☎ 0141 889 0457, website www.neilbibby.com)

BICHAN, Dr (Herbert) Roy; *b* 5 November 1941; *Educ* Univ of Aberdeen (BSc), Univ of Leeds (PhD); *m* Fiona Keay; 2 da (Inga Jane b 16 Feb 1967, Susan Elizabeth b 1 Aug 1971), 1 s (Michael Roy b 8 May 1969); *Career* chm: The Robertson Group plc 1988–91, Force Petroleum Ltd 1998–2004, The Welsh Distillery Co Ltd 1999–2005, Beer and Partners Ltd 2010–; formerly dep chm Simon-Robertson, dir HSBC Enterprise Fund for Wales 1998–, dir and chm Clinical Diagnostic Chemicals Ltd 2000–, gp chm KMC Int 2004–08; memb Cncl CBI 1991– (chm Wales 1993–95), chm Welsh Industrial Devpt Advsy Bd, dep chm Welsh Development Agency 1993–95, chm N Wales Economic Forum 2008–; Adrian fell Univ of Leicester 1988–90; vice-chm of govrs Llandrillo Coll 2003–12, chm of govrs Gp Llandrillo Memai 2012–; FIMM (pres 1988–89), FREng 1989; *Recreations* golf; *Style*— Dr Roy Bichan, FREng

BICHARD, Baron (Life Peer UK 2010), of Nailsworth in the County of Gloucestershire; Sir Michael George Bichard; KCB (1999); s of George Bichard (d 1981), and Nora, *née* Reeves (d 1971); *b* 31 January 1947, Southampton; *Educ* King Edward VI GS Southampton, Univ of Manchester (LLB), Univ of Birmingham (MSocSci); *m* Gillian; 1 s (Philip Michael), 2 da (Charlotte Emma Christine, Emma-Louise Christine); *Career* articled clerk, slr then sr slr Reading BC 1969–73, county liaison officer Berkshire CC 1973–77, head of Chief Exec's Office Lambeth BC 1977–80; chief exec: Brent BC 1980–86, Glos CC 1986–90, Benefits Agency 1990–95; perm sec: Dept of Employment 1995, Dept for Education and Employment 1995–2001; rector Univ of the Arts London (formerly London Inst) 2001–; chair: Soham/Bichard Inquiry 2004, Legal Services Cmmn 2005–08; chair: Design Cncl 2008–11, Social Care Inst for Excellence 2013–; founding dir Inst for Govt 2008–10, chair Nat Audit Office 2015–; chair Rathbone Trg Ltd 2001–08; non-exec chm RSE Consulting 2003–08, non-exec dir The Key (education support co); govr Henley Mgmnt Coll 2002–08; dir River and Rowing Museum Fndn 2002–, chair Film Club 2007–13, tstee Globe Fndn 2009–, chair Shakespeare's Globe; Hon Dr: Leeds Metropolitan Univ, Univ of Birmingham, Middx Univ, Southampton Inst 2002, Bradford Univ, Cranfield Univ, Univ of Glos; FIPD, FRSA; *Recreations* food, wine, music, walking, Manchester United; *Clubs* Groucho; *Style*— The Lord Bichard, KCB

BICK, David Robert; s of Roy Leslie Samuel Bick (d 2005), and Vera Grace, *née* Collis; *b* 9 April 1957; *Educ* Glyn GS Epsom, Univ of Essex; *m* 21 July 1984, Susan Christine, da of Joseph Esmond Stobbs (d 1979); 2 s (Charles b 1991, Henry b 1994), 2 da (Antonia b 1987, Harriet b 1989); *Career* PA to David Atkinson MP 1979–80; exec: KH Publicity Ltd 1980–81, Shandwick Conslts Ltd 1981–83; account dir Good Relations City Ltd 1984–85, dir and jt fndr Lombard Communications plc 1985–93; dir: Buchanan Communications Ltd 1993–95, Financial Dynamics Feb 1995–98, fndr Squarel Consulting (formerly Holborn PR) 1998–; cncllr London Borough of Lambeth 1980–86 (chm Amenity Servs 1982); *Recreations* English cricket, football, sleep; *Style*— David R Bick, Esq

BICKELL, Brian; *Career* Shaftesbury plc: joined 1986, dir 1987, fin dir until 2011, chief exec 2011–; *Style*— Brian Bickell, Esq; ✉ Shaftesbury plc, Pegasus House, 37–43 Sackville Street, London W1S 3DL

BICKERS, Patricia Evelyn; da of Norman Sefton Reece Bickers, and N Evelyn, *née* Hill; *b* 26 December 1950; *Educ* Sch of Saints Helen & Katharine Abingdon, Univ of Sussex (BA); *Career* lectr in art history: Harrow Sch of Art 1978–89 (lectr 1974–78), Univ of Westminster (formerly Poly of Central London) 1989–; external assessor: Glasgow Sch of Art 1997–, St Martin's Sch of Art 2000–03; Art Monthly: assoc ed 1989–91, dep ed 1991–92, ed 1992–; curator Print the Legend: Contemporary Art and the Myth of the West (Fruitmarket Gallery) 2008; co-selector BT New Contemporaries 1993–94, judge Turner Prize Tate Britain 2001, judge Northern Art Prize 2009; TV and radio broadcaster: Kaleidoscope (BBC Radio 4) 1994–, World at One, Today Prog, BBC 24, Newsnight; buyer Contemporary Arts Soc 2003–04; memb Mgmnt Ctee Matt's Gallery 1992–2003, tstee Serpentine Gallery 1995–; memb: Assoc of Art Historians 1978, Int Assoc of Art Critics 1999; FRSA 2002 (memb Cncl 2004–08); *Books* The Brit Pack: Contemporary British Art, the view from abroad (1995), Talking Art: Art Monthly Interviews Since 1976 (2007), Print the Legend: The Myth of the West (2008); *Clubs* Lansdowne; *Style*— Miss Patricia Bickers; ✉ Art Monthly, 4th Floor, 28 Charing Cross Road, London WC2H 0DB (☎ 020 7240 0389, fax 020 7497 0726, e-mail editorial@artmonthly.co.uk)

BICKFORD, (James) David Prydeaux; CB (1995); s of William Alfred John Prydeaux Bickford, of London, and Muriel Adelyn, *née* Smythe (d 1973); *b* 28 July 1940; *Educ* Downside; *m* 24 April 1965, Carolyn Jane, da of Maj William Arthur Richard Sumner (d 1943); 3 s (Nicholas b 1966, James b 1967, Peter John b 1972); *Career* slr of the Supreme Ct 1963, in practice with J J Newcombe & Co Devon 1963–69, crown counsel and legal advsr to Turks and Caicos Island Govt 1969–71, asst legal advsr then counsellor to the FCO 1971–87, legal advsr Br Military Govt Berlin 1979–82, under sec of state and legal advsr to the Security and Intelligence Agencies 1987–95, visiting prof of law Cleveland-Marshall Coll of Law Cleveland State Univ USA 1995–96, currently chm Bickford Associates; memb Panel of Legal Experts Int Telecommunications Satellite Orgn, chm Assembly Maritime Satellite Orgn 1985–87; Judge Ben C Green lectr in nat security law Case Western Univ Ohio USA; hon memb Nat Security Ctee American Bar Assoc; memb Law Soc; author and scriptwriter (Silver IVCA Award for Best Drama 2008 and Best Drama Finalist Certificate NY Film Festival 2008 for Was Any of This Your Fault? (jtly, with wife Carolyn)); *Publications* Land Dealings Simplified in the Turks and Caicos Islands (1971), The Face of Tomorrow (novel, 2004); articles, lectures and web contributions on intelligence, money laundering and organised crime; *Recreations* the family, fishing, sailing; *Style*— David Bickford, Esq, CB; ✉ c/o National Westminster Bank, Torrington, Devon

BICKHAM, Edward Sidney Côver; s of Eric Edward Bickham (d 1987), of Ringwood, Hants, and Frances Agnes, *née* Potter (d 2000), of Reading, Berks; *b* 10 August 1956; *Educ* Brockenhurst GS, St John's Coll Oxford (MA); *m* 1997, Elizabeth, *née* Ballard; 2 s (Rupert Francis Côver, Lysander Edmund Oliver); *Career* asst to Chairman Macmillan Publishers Ltd 1977–80, European offr Cons Research Dept 1980–83, special advsr to sec of state for NI 1983–85, special advsr to Home Sec 1985–88, exec dir Corp Communications British Satellite Broadcasting 1988–90, special advsr to Foreign Sec 1991–93, md corp and public affrs Hill & Knowlton (UK) Ltd 1993–2000 (dep chm and dir of strategy 1998–2000), exec vice-pres external affrs Anglo American plc 2000–09; chair Int Investment Panel CBI 2005–09, memb Bd Extractive Industries Transparency Initiative 2006–13; sr advsr: World Gold Cncl 2010–14, Critical Resource Ltd 2010–; strategic advsr Int Cncl on Mining and Metal 2010–15, memb Steering Bd UK Nat Contact Point for OECD Guidelines for Multinational Enterprises 2014–; contested (Cons) Vauxhall ILEA seat 1986, dep chm Cons Gp for Europe 2003–06 and 2016–; chm Inst Business Ethics 2014– (tstee 2010–14), tstee Hansard Soc 2011–14; tstee Care Int UK 2014–; visiting fell Cranfield Sch of Mgmnt 2011–; Robert Schuman Silver Medal for Servs to European Unity 1983; MIPR 1995, FRSA 2001; *Publications* incl: Raising Kane? Preserving Diversity in Media Ownership (1990); *Recreations* cinema, theatre, tennis, current affrs; *Style*— Mr Edward Bickham; ✉ 109 Black Lion Lane, London W6 (☎ 020 8563 1614, e-mail edward@ebickham.co.uk)

BICKMORE, Peter Christopher; s of Lt-Col Lawrence Hyde Neild Bickmore, OBE (d 1997), of Kensington, London, and Anne Windsor Lewis, *née* Drummond (d 1985); *b* 4 April 1943; *Educ* Charterhouse; *m* 22 July 1975, Isabel Margaret, da of Maj-Gen Lord Michael Fitzalan Howard, KCVO, MC, of Fovant, Wilts; 2 s (Andrew Ralph b 1979, Rupert Nicholas b 1985), 1 da (Fiona Clare b 1981); *Career* Lt short serv cmmn Life Gds 1962–68; md: Pegasus Insurance Services Ltd 1979–89, BBA Insurance Services Ltd 1989–96, British Bloodstock Agency plc 1992–95; bloodstock insurance conslt Alexander Forbes Risk Servs Ltd 1999–2004, chm Bloodlines Thoroughbred Insurance Agency Ltd 2004–11; dir Stuart Canvas Products 2006–10 (sports conslt 1995–2006); memb Insurance Brokers' Registration Cncl 1986; Freeman City of London 1964, Liveryman Worshipful Co of Skinners 1969; High Sheriff Oxfordshire 2006–07; *Recreations* golf, shooting; *Clubs* White's, Pratt's; *Style*— Peter Bickmore, Esq; ✉ The Old Rectory, Incomb, Cheltenham, Gloucestershire GL54 1JB (☎ 01451 831301, mobile 07860 964545, e-mail peter@icombrectory.co.uk)

BICKNELL, Julian; s of Wing Cdr Nigel Bicknell, DSO, DFC (d 1990), and Sarah Greenaway, *née* Leith (d 2010); *b* 23 February 1945; *Educ* Winchester, King's Coll Cambridge (MA, DipArch); *m* 18 Nov 1967, Treld, da of Arthur K O Pelkey (d 1979), of West Hartford, CT; 1 s (Titus P b 1971), 1 da (Poppaea E b 1982); *Career* architect and teacher; asst later ptnr Edward Cullinan 1966–72; tutor and dir of Project Office RCA 1973–80: The Old Gaol Abingdon (RIBA Award 1976), The Garden Hall and Library, Castle Howard (Carpenters' Award 1984); staff architect Arup Assocs 1981–84 (reconstruction of Bedford Sch); in private practice 1984–; projects incl: Henbury Rotonda, Upton Viva, Nagara Country Club Japan, High Corner, The Georgian Club Tokyo, Shakespeare Country Park Maruyama Japan, Forbes House, Jubilee Sun Dial for Palace of Westminster, Hunterian Museum RCS, Royal Crest House Takasaki, Carden Hall; external examiner Leeds Metropolitan Univ Sch of Architecture 1990–94, memb Advsy and Academic Bd and tutor Prince of Wales Inst of Architecture 1991–98; chm Judges' Panel York Design Awards 2014; RIBA 1971, memb AA 1987, FRSA 1988, elected to Art Workers' Guild 1995 (Master 2013); *Books* The Design for Need Papers (1979), Hiroshige in Tokyo (1994), Julian Bicknell: Designs and Buildings 1980–2000 (2000); *Recreations* architecture, music, the countryside; *Style*— Julian Bicknell, Esq; ✉ The Annexe Studio, 32A Larkfield Road, Richmond, Surrey TW9 2PF (☎ 020 3274 1070, fax 020 3274 1080, e-mail info@julianbicknell.co.uk)

BIDDER, His Hon Judge Neil; QC (1998); s of Glyn Turner Bidder (d 1997), and Constance Mabel Longman; *b* 22 July 1953; *Educ* Ogmore GS, Queens' Coll Cambridge (MA), Dalhousie Univ Canada (LLM); *m* 1978, Madeleine, da of Dewi Thomas; 2 s (Rhys Michael b 13 October 1982, Patrick Thomas b 8 November 1985); *Career* called to the Bar 1976, recorder 1994–2004 (asst recorder 1991–94), circuit judge (Wales and Chester Region) 2004–; fndr chm Welsh Personal Injury Lawyers Assoc, hon sec Cncl of HM's Circuit Judges 2011–; memb: Lincoln's Inn, Personal Injury Bar Assoc; *Recreations* choral singing, gardening, sport; *Style*— His Hon Judge Bidder, QC

BIDDISS, Prof Michael Denis; s of Daniel Biddiss (d 1984), of Orpington, and Eileen Louisa, *née* Jones (d 1984); *b* 15 April 1942; *Educ* St Joseph's Acad Blackheath, Queens' Coll Cambridge (MA, PhD), Centre des Hautes Études Européennes Univ of Strasbourg; *m* 8 April 1967, Ruth Margaret, da of late Dr Frederick Fox Cartwright, of Swallowfield, Berks; 4 da (Clare b 1969, Kate b 1972, Sarah b 1974, Beth b 1977); *Career* fell and dir of studies in history and social and political sciences Downing Coll Cambridge 1966–73, lectr and reader in history Univ of Leicester 1973–79; Univ of Reading: prof of history 1979–2004, dean Faculty of Letters and Social Science 1982–85, emeritus prof 2004–; visiting professorships: Univ of Victoria BC 1973, Univ of Cape Town 1976 and 1978, Monash Univ 1989, Nanjing Univ 1997; chm History at the Univs Defence Gp 1984–87; memb Cncl: Historical Association 1985– (pres 1991–94, fell 2006–), Royal Historical Soc 1988–92 (jt vice-pres 1995–99); chm Bd of Dirs Government and Opposition Ltd 1996–2003; hon fell Faculty of History of Med Worshipful Soc of Apothecaries 1986– (pres 1994–98, Osler medal 1989, Locke medal 1996, Sydenham medal 2001, Master's medal 2009); FRHistS 1974; *Books* Father of Racist Ideology (1970), Gobineau – Selected Political Writings (ed, 1970), Disease and History (jtly, 1972, new edn 2014), The Age of the Masses – Ideas and Society in Europe since 1870 (1977), Images of Race (ed, 1979), Thatcherism – Personality and Politics (jt ed, 1987), The Nuremberg Trial and the Third Reich (1992), The Uses and Abuses of Antiquity (jt ed, 1999), The Humanities in the New Millennium (jt ed, 2000), Themes in Modern European History 1890–1945 (jt ed, 2008), The Wiley-Blackwell Dictionary of Modern European History since 1789 (jtly, 2011); *Recreations* cricket, mountain walking, music and opera, theatrical adaptations; *Style*— Prof Michael Biddiss; ✉ e-mail m.d.biddiss@reading.ac.uk

BIDDLE, Donald Frank; s of Kenneth Barrington Biddle, of Poole, Dorset, and Judy Hill, *née* Downie (d 1964); *b* 6 March 1933; *Educ* Uppingham; *m* 3 Oct 1963, Anne Muriel, da of Maj Charles Deane Cowper; 2 s (Justin b 1968, Mark b 1971), 2 da (Georgina, Anne-Marie (twins) b 1973); *Career* chartered accountant; 2 Lt RA Germany 1956–57, HAC 1957–63; Price Waterhouse 1957–62, ptnr Smith and Williamson 1962–93, gen cmmr of taxation 1970–87 and 1989–2008; tstee: English Language Servs Int (Int House) 1963–99, Ada Lewis Housing Tst 1967–82 (chm 1978–80), Samuel Lewis Housing Tst 1978–94, Southern Housing Gp 1993–94, Titsey Fndn 1995–2016, Bembridge Harbour Tst 2005–15 (chm 2005–11); sec Int Dragon Assoc 1982–89; memb Olympic Yachting Ctee 1964–74; Yr Bro Trinity House; FCA; OStJ (treas Cncl Order of St John of Jerusalem Dorset 1993–2003); *Recreations* yachting, wine; *Clubs* Carlton, Royal Yacht Sqdn, Bembridge Sailing; *Style*— Donald F Biddle, Esq; ✉ Vernon House, St Helens, Isle of Wight PO33 1XY (☎ 01983 875593)

BIDDLE, Prof Martin; CBE (2014, OBE 1997); s of Reginald Samuel Biddle (d 1971), and Gwladys Florence, *née* Baker (d 1986); *b* 4 June 1937; *Educ* Merchant Taylors', Pembroke Coll Cambridge (MA), Univ of Oxford (MA); *m* 1, 9 Sept 1961 (m dis 1966), Hannelore Bäcker; 2 da (Joanna b 1962, Barbara b 1965); m 2, 19 Nov 1966, Birthe (d 2010), da of Landsretssagfører Axel Th Kjølbye (d 1972), of Sønderborg, Denmark; 2 da (Signe b 1969, Solvej b 1971); *Career* 2 Lt 4 RTR 1956, Ind Sqdn RTR Berlin 1956–57; asst inspr of ancient monuments Miny of Public Bldg and Works 1961–63, lectr in medieval archaeology Univ of Exeter 1963–67, visiting fell All Souls Coll Oxford 1967–68, dir Winchester Research Unit 1968–, dir Univ Museum and prof of anthropology and history of art Univ of Pennsylvania 1977–81, lectr of the house ChCh Oxford 1983–86, Astor sr research fell in medieval archaeology and tutor in archaeology Hertford Coll Oxford 1989–2002, prof of medieval archaeology Univ of Oxford 1997–2002, emeritus fell Hertford Coll Oxford 2002–, emeritus prof of medieval archaeology Univ of Oxford 2002–, Leverhulme Emeritus Fell 2005–06; author of numerous books and articles; excavations with: Sir Mortimer Wheeler St Albans and Stanwick 1949 and 1952, Dame Kathleen Kenyon Jericho 1957–58; fieldwork: Nonsuch Palace 1959–60, Winchester 1961–71, St Albans 1978, 1982–84, 1991, 1994–95, 2003 and 2006 (with Birthe Kjølbye-Biddle), Repton 1974–88 and 1993 (with Birthe Kjølbye-Biddle), Holy Sepulchre Jerusalem 1989–93 and 1998 (with Birthe Kjølbye-Biddle), Qasr Ibrim Nubia Egypt 1989–90, 1992, 1995, 2000 (with Birthe Kjølbye-Biddle); ptnr Biddle & Biddle archaeological consltts, clients incl: Canterbury Cathedral, St Albans Abbey and Cathedral Church, Eurotunnel, British Telecom, etc; chm: Rescue The Trust for Br Archaeology 1971–75, Winchester in Europe (Nat Referendum 1975), Fabric Advsy Ctee Winchester Cathedral 2013–; served Cons Pty Ctees in: Winchester 1973–77, Oxford 1982–97; cmmr Royal Cmmn on the Historical Monuments of England 1984–95; pres Soc for Medieval Archaeology 1995–98, vice-pres Soc of Antiquaries 2006–09 (sr vice-pres 2008–09); Hon Knight of the Hon Soc of Knights of the Round Table 1971; Freeman: City of London 1963, Worshipful Co of Merchant Taylors 1963, City of Winchester 2010; Univ of Pennsylvania: Hon MA 1977, Hon Phi Beta Kappa 1978; Hon DLitt King Alfred's Coll/Univ of Southampton 2003; hon fell Pembroke Coll Cambridge 2006, hon memb Br Numismatic Soc 2008; FSA 1964, FRHistS 1970, FBA 1985; *Publications* Future of London's Past (1973), Winchester in the Early Middle Ages (ed, 1976), Object and Economy in Medieval Winchester (1990), Das Grab Christi (1998), The Tomb of Christ (1999), King Arthur's Round Table (2000), The Church of the Holy Sepulchre (2000), Henry VIII's Artillery Fort at Camber Castle (2001), Nonsuch Palace: The Material Culture of a Restoration Household (2005), The Winchester Mint (ed, 2012), XPICTIANA RELIGIO and the Tomb of Christ (in Early Medieval Monetary History, Studies in Memory of Mark Blackburn, ed Rory Naismith et al, 2014), Danish Royal Burials in Winchester: Cnut and his Family (in Danes in Wessex, eds Ryan Lavelle and Simon Roffey, 2016); gen ed and ed Winchester Studies (8 vols 1976–2016 and continuing); *Recreations* travel, especially Hellenic, Middle East and S Asia, reading; *Style*— Prof Martin Biddle, CBE, FBA; ✉ Hertford College, Oxford OX1 3BW (e-mail martin.biddle@hertford.ox.ac.uk, mobile 0788 716915); research office (☎ 01865 559017)

BIDDLE, Neville Leslie; s of Walter Alan Biddle, of Nannerch, N Wales, and Beryl Mary, *née* Meadows; *b* 24 April 1951, W Kirby; *Educ* Wrekin Coll, UCW Aberystwyth (BSc(Econ)); *m* 1; 4 da (Caroline b 22 Nov 1980, Josephine b 27 July 1982, Rebecca b 2 June 1986, Charlotte b 15 July 1991); m 2, 7 June 2012, Maureen Bernadette, *née* Redmond; *Career* called to the Bar Gray's Inn 1974; recorder 1996; memb Criminal Bar Assoc; non-exec dir R S Clare & Co; *Recreations* gardening, music, sailing, theatre, travel; *Clubs* West Kirby Sailing; *Style*— Neville Biddle, Esq; ✉ 7 Harrington Street, Liverpool L2 9YH

BIDDULPH, 5 Baron (UK 1903); (Anthony) Nicholas Colin Maitland Biddulph; er s of 4 Baron Biddulph (d 1988), and Lady Mary Maitland, da of Viscount Maitland, s of 15 Earl of Lauderdale; *b* 8 April 1959; *Educ* Cheltenham, RAC Cirencester; *m* 28 Aug 1993, Hon Sian Diana Gibson-Watt (m dis 2001), yr da of Baron Gibson-Watt, MC, PC (d 2002); 2 s (Hon Robert Julian Watt b 1994, Hon David Michael William b 1997); *Heir* s, Hon Robert Maitland Biddulph; *Career* interior designer, farmer and sporting mangr; Liveryman Worshipful Co of Armourers and Brasiers; *Recreations* shooting, fishing, racing, skiing, painting; *Clubs* Cavalry and Guards, White's; *Style*— The Rt Hon Lord Biddulph; ✉ Makerstoun, Kelso, Roxburghshire TD5 7PA (☎ 01573 460234); 8 Orbel Street, London SW11 3NZ (☎ 020 7228 9865)

BIDWELL, James Richard Philip; s of Sir Hugh Bidwell, GBE, and Jenifer Celia, *née* Webb (d 2001); *b* 19 January 1965, London; *Educ* Eton, Univ of Bristol (BA); *m* 28 Jan 1995, Rebecca, *née* Mathiesen; 3 da (Lili Sarah b 29 April 1997, Willow Anna b 10 Oct 1999, Sage Jenifer b 8 June 2006); *Career* grad trainee Lowe Howard-Spink Advtg 1989–92, mktg mangr Walt Disney Attractions 1992–97, mktg dir Europe eToys Inc 1999–2001, mktg dir Selfridges plc 2001–05, ceo Visit London 2005–08, md Anthropologie Europe 2009–10, fndr Bidwell and Co 2010–; non-exec dir: Goodwood Estate 2011–, Cass Arts 2011–; tstee Cass Sculpture Fndn 2008; memb Mktg Gp of GB 2001 (memb Cncl 2008); fell Mktg Soc 2007 (memb 1994); Liveryman Worshipful Co of Grocers; *Recreations* skiing, mountain biking, flyfishing; *Clubs* Frensham Flyfishers, Home House; *Style*— James Bidwell, Esq; ✉ e-mail james@bidwellandco.com

BIDWELL, Dr Robin O'Neill; CBE (1999); s of Philip John Bidwell (d 1993), and Ellen O'Neill, *née* Gibbons (d 1995); *b* 15 September 1944, Simla, India; *Educ* Charterhouse, ChCh Oxford (MA), Bradford Mgmnt Centre (PhD); *m* 1, 1970; 1 da (Charlotte b 1972), 1 s (Matthew b 1974); m 2, 1995, Veronica Rosemary Lucia, *née* Verey; *Career* ERL (now ERM): joined 1973, dir 1974–, md 1977–93, exec chm 1993–2008, gp pres 2008–11, chm ERM Fndn Low Carbon Enterprise Fund 2008–, chm Insitor Social Impact Fund; non-exec memb Ofgem 2003–10; advsr Int Business Ldrs Forum 1993–2008; tstee Heritage Tst 1987–96; memb: Exec Ctee Green Alliance 1995–2008 (chm 2008–14), Sustainability Challenge Fndn Netherlands 1993–2003, NERC 1996–2002, UK Roundtable of Sustainable Devpt 1998–2000, Advsy Ctee on Business and the Environment 1999–2003; chm Field Conservation Advsy Ctee ZSL; *Recreations* conservation, gardening, skiing, reading; *Style*— Dr Robin Bidwell, CBE; ✉ Woodchester Park House, Nympsfield, Gloucester GL10 3UN (e-mail robin.bidwell@erm.com)

BIELCKUS, Colin David; s of Louis Reginald Bielckus, of Thornhill, Southampton, and Lorna Elizabeth Mary Bielckus; *b* 17 June 1956; *Educ* King Edward VI Sch Southampton, UEA (BSc); *m* 11 Oct 1981, Lorraine, da of Reginald Alexander, of Southampton; 1 da

(Penelope Louise b 18 May 1995); *Career* chartered accountant; audit mangr Alliott Wingham (formerly Alliott Millar) Fareham 1985–90, audit ptnr Alliott Wingham Fareham 1990–2002, prop Avenue Business Services 2002–, pres and chm Central Southern England Div Nat Deposit Friendly Soc 2002–09 (chm 1990–2002), non-exec dir Nat Deposit Friendly Soc 2003–09, chm Audit Ctee 2003–09, finance dir Davis World Travel Ltd 2006–10; memb Rotary Club of Fareham Meon 2000–; chm Community and Vocational Serv Ctee 2002–03 (chm entertainments 2003–04, vice-pres 2005–06, pres 2006–07); cncllr Whiteley Parish Cncl 2009– (chm Finance Ctee 2009–); chm Rotary District 1110 Community Service 2012–; treas: Abbeyfield Winchester Soc Ltd 2010–, Fareham Music Festival 2011–; *Recreations* music, railways, collecting books, collecting beermats, collecting cacti and other succulent plants; *Style*— Colin Bielckus, Esq; ✉ 1 Silvertrees, Lady Bettys Drive, Titchfield, Hampshire PO15 6RJ; Avenue Business Services, 72 The Avenue, Fareham, Hampshire PO14 1PB (☎ 01489 580433, fax 01489 885555, e-mail cb@avenue-bs.com)

BIENZ, Dr Mariann; da of Jürg Bienz, and Lilly Bienz-Gubler; *b* 21 December 1953; *Educ* Gymnasium Winterthur Switzerland, Univ of Zürich (Dip Zoology, PhD); *m* 25 May 1996, Sir Hugh Pelham, FRS, *qv*; 1 da (Maya Joanne b 24 July 1990), 1 s (Benjamin Peter b 23 May 1993); *Career* postdoctoral research MRC Lab of Molecular Biology Cambridge 1981–86, asst prof Univ of Zürich 1986–90 (assoc prof 1990), sr staff scientist MRC Lab of Molecular Biology Cambridge 1991– (jt head Cell Biology Div 2007–08, jt head Protein Nucleic Acid Chemistry Div 2008–); author of articles on cell and molecular biology in int jls; memb EMBO 1989–; Friedrich Miescher Prize 1990; FRS 2003, FMedSci 2006; *Recreations* music, mountain walking; *Style*— Dr Mariann Bienz; ✉ MRC Laboratory of Molecular Biology, Francis Crick Avenue, Cambridge Biomedical Campus, Cambridge CB2 0QH (☎ 01223 267093, fax 01223 268305)

BIERMAN, James; *m* Kate Bierman, *née* Mitchell; 2 da (Leah, Clara), 1 s (Max); *Career* exec prod Donmar Warehouse 2006–11, co-fndr and producer (with Michael Grandage, CBE, *qv*) Michael Grandage Co 2011–; memb BAFTA; *Style*— James Bierman, Esq; ✉ Michael Grandage Company, Fourth Floor, Gielgud Theatre, Shaftesbury Avenue, London W1D 6AR

BIGGAR, Allan Ramsay; s of Allan Ramsay Biggar, and Betty, *née* Tyson, of Galashiels, Scotland; *b* 27 January 1963; *Educ* Queen Elizabeth HS Hexham; *m* 11 May 2002, Bridget Susan, *née* Lucking; 1 da (Isobel Gillian Seddon b 27 May 1988), 2 s (Charles Arthur John Seddon b 18 Sept 1992, Jack Ramsay Biggar b 25 July 2002); *Career* Liberal Pty: vice-chm National League of Young Liberals 1980–83, memb Nat Exec 1981–84; area agent E Anglia 1984–87; Burson-Marsteller: md ME 1994–97, chm Public Affairs Europe 1997–2000, pres and chief exec UK 2000–04, jt chief exec Europe 2001–04, memb Worldwide Exec Bd 2001–05, global chm Corp and Fin Practice 2004–05, chm UK 2004–05; chm: I-SYT Ltd 2001–05, Brand Faith Ltd 2005–, InMotion Sport Ltd 2008–, Ideal Interface Ltd 2009–, Freshly Made Content 2012–; chair International Insights Ltd 2005–, chm and ceo All About Brands plc 2006–, non-exec chm Open Soho Ltd 2007–; non-exec dir: Corp Television Networks 2001–05, Smartcells Ltd 2005–06, Brandsmiths Ltd 2007–; chm Business Advsy Gp UMIST Corp Communications MSc course 2002–, co-fndr European Communications Acad Univ of Brussels; previous owner/dir various PR and publishing ventures, reg writer on current affairs and political issues, currently chief commercial offr Electric Juke Box Co and Magic Works Media Ltd; memb Jericho Chambers LLP 2014–; *Publications* Effective Politics (1983); *Recreations* travel, antiques, cooking; *Clubs* RAC, National Liberal, Soho House, IVy; *Style*— Allan R Biggar, Esq; ✉ Bluebell House, Newlands Drive, Maidenhead, Berkshire SL6 4LL (☎ 01628 770481); Jericho Chambers LLP, 12A Charterhouse Square, London EC1M 6AX (e-mail allan.biggar@jerichochambers.com)

BIGGLESTONE, John George; s of John Bigglestone (d 1992), and Lillian Bigglestone (d 1978); *b* 10 August 1934; *Educ* Bablake Sch Coventry, Coventry Coll of Art, Univ of Birmingham, Wiltshire Coll Salisbury, Arts Univ Bournemouth; *m* 1, 17 March 1956 (m dis 1982), Erica Gillian, da of Hamlet Hopkins, and Winifred Hopkins, of Newport, Monmouthshire; m 2, 22 Dec 1984 (m dis 2005), Annette Vivian, da of Kenneth Bull, and Audrey Bull, of Devizes, Wilts; m 3, 13 April 2014, Susan Brown, da of Marga Andersen, of Düsseldorf, Germany; *Career* professional photographer (prop Wharf Studios Devizes), journalist and lectr; sr lectr in photography: Salisbury Coll of Art 1966–93, Guildford Coll, Croydon Coll and City of Bristol Coll 1993–98; dir of studies, princ and sr tutor PPTutor-Online (online learning, professional photography) 1999–; formerly nat examiner photographic courses City & Guilds of London Inst and Further Educn Funding Cncl (FEFC) inspr; currently chief examiner higher level photography courses City & Guilds Europe; contrib to photographic magazines; photographic clients incl many leading industrial and advtg cos; sponsored seminar presenter to professional photographers and colls; exhibitions of work in Aberdeen, London and Devizes 2009; associateship BIPP 1969; memb Assoc of Photographers, memb Frame W Midlands Photographers; FRSA; *Recreations* learning; *Style*— John Bigglestone, FRSA; ✉ The Wharf Studio, Glenmore Business Centre, Devizes, Wiltshire SN10 2EQ (☎ 01380 729527, mobile 07850 819219, e-mail johnbigglestone@me.com, website www.thewharfstudio.com, www.pptutor-online.com, www.upstartsimagebank.com)

BIGGS, John Robert; AM; s of Robert Edmund Biggs (d 1974), and Mary Jeanette, *née* Phillips; *b* 19 November 1957; *Educ* Queen Elizabeth's Boys Sch Barnet, Univ of Bristol (BSc), Univ of London (Dip Com Sci), Univ of Westminster (Dip Law, LPC); *m* 1993 (m dis 2015), Christine Ann, da of Brian Sibley; 1 da (Helen b 3 Nov 1990); *Career* various positions Health Service and the City 1979–91, oppn and Cncl ldr 1991–95, dir and vice-chm Tower Hamlets Housing Action Tst 1996–2004, dir Socialist Health Assoc (affiliate of Lab Pty) 1998–2000; GLA: memb London Assembly (Lab) City & East 2000–, chair Budget Ctee, lead memb Lab Gp on Olympics and Thames Gateway, memb Met Police Authy 2000–03 and 2009–12, memb London Fire and Emergency Planning Authy 2003–04; mayor of Tower Hamlets 2015–; vice-chair London Devpt Agency 2004–08, dep chm London Thames Gateway Urban Devpt Corp 2004–08, memb London Health Cmmn 2008–11; ind govr Birkbeck Coll London 2009–, hon fell Queen Mary London 2009; *Recreations* reading, walking; *Style*— The Worshipful the Mayor of Tower Hamlets, John Biggs, AM; ✉ 30 Stepney City Apartments, 49 Clark Street, London E1 3HS (mobile 07974 918322); London Assembly, City Hall, Queens Walk, Southwark, London SE1 2AA (☎ 020 7983 4350, fax 020 7983 4418, e-mail john.biggs@london.gov.uk)

BIGGS, Prof Lewis; OBE (2011); s of Ian Biggs, of Culachy, Fort Augustus, Inverness-shire, and Penelope, *née* Torr; *Educ* Wellington, New Coll Oxford (scholar, BA), Courtauld Inst Univ of London (MA); *m* 1, 1983 (m dis 2002), Ann, da of Michael Compton; 1 da (Alison b 1987), 1 s (Nicholas b 1989); m 2, 2011, Lisa Katherine Milroy, RA; *Career* gallery co-ordinator Arnolfini Bristol 1979–84, exhibition offr Fine Art Dept Br Cncl 1984–87, curator of exhibitions Tate Gallery Liverpool 1987–90 (dir 1990–2000), chief exec Liverpool Biennial of Contemporary Art 2000–11; co-curator Aichi Triennale 2013, curator Folkestone Triennial 2014 and 2017; visiting prof Sch of Art and Design Liverpool John Moores Univ 2001–, visiting prof of contemporary art Univ of Glasgow 2011–14, hon prof Glasgow Sch of Art 2011, advsr Coll of Fine Arts Univ of Shanghai 2011–15, prof of public art Coll of Art Shanghai Univ 2015–18; dir: Oriel Mostyn Llandudno 1991–97, Art Transpennine Ltd 1996–2002, NW Arts Bd 1998–2002, Culture Campus Ltd 2006–11, Another Place Ltd 2006–11, Inst for Public Art HK 2013–, Int Awards for Art Criticism (IAAC) Ltd 2014–; tstee: Liverpool Architecture and Design Tst 1997–99, Liverpool Biennial Tst 1998–2000, Cass Sculpture Fndn Goodwood 2010–11, Situations Bristol 2011–13, FACT (Fndn for Art and Creative Technol) 2011–14, John Moores Liverpool Exhibition Tst 2011–, Centre for Chinese Contemporary Art Manchester 2011–15; memb: Visual Arts Advsy Ctee Br Cncl 1992–2002, Fabric Advsy Ctee Liverpool Cathedral 1995–98, Visual Arts Panel Arts Cncl of England 1996–99, Int Ctee Rockbund Art Musuem Shanghai 2011–13; Citizen of Honour City of Liverpool 2011; assoc fell Univ of Liverpool 1992–95; hon fell Liverpool John Moores Univ 1998, Hon MA Univ for the Creative Arts (UCA) 2014; memb ICOM 1983–, CIMAM, memb AICA UK; FRSA; *Publications* Tate Modern Artists (series ed, 2000–14); *Style*— Prof Lewis Biggs, OBE; ✉ website www.folkestonetriennial.org.uk, www.ljmu.ac.uk, www.cfcca.org.uk, www.ipa.org, www.iaac-m21.com/english/index.html; c/o Creative Foundation, The Quarterhouse, Mill Bay, Folkestone, Kent CT20 1JR

BIGGS, Prof Norman Linstead; s of Joseph John Biggs (d 1965), and Dorothy Linstead (d 1982); *b* 2 January 1941; *Educ* Harrow Co GS, Selwyn Coll Cambridge (MA), Univ of London (DSc); *m* 1, 1968 (m dis 1975), Rita Elizabeth, *née* Kelly; m 2, 20 March 1975, Christine Mary, da of Eric Richard Farmer, of Bromley, Kent; 1 da (Juliet b 1980); *Career* lectr Univ of Southampton 1963–70, reader in pure mathematics Royal Holloway Coll London 1976–88 (lectr 1970–76); LSE: prof of mathematics 1988–2006 (emeritus prof 2006–), govr 1995–99, dir Centre for Discrete and Applicable Mathematics 1995–2006, vice-chm Appts Ctee 1993–96; London Mathematical Soc: memb Cncl 1979–85 and 1999–2006, librarian 1999–2002, gen sec 2002–06, chm Computer Science Ctee 1985–89; chm Royal Soc Mathematical Instruction Ctee 1991–94, vice-pres Br Soc for the History of Mathematics 2014; memb Br Numismatic Soc (memb Cncl 2001–03 and 2009–11); *Books* Finite Groups of Automorphisms (1971), Algebraic Graph Theory (1974, 2 edn 1993), Graph Theory 1736–1936 (jtly, 1976), Interaction Models (1977), Permutation Groups and Combinatorial Structures (jtly, 1979), Introduction to Computing With Pascal (1989), Computational Learning Theory (jtly, 1992), English Weights (1993), Mathematics for Economics and Finance (jtly, 1996), Antique Weights (1998), Discrete Mathematics (2 edn 2002), Codes: An Introduction to Information, Communication and Cryptography (2008), Quite Right: The Story of Mathematics, Measurement, and Money (2016); *Recreations* metrology and numismatics; *Style*— Prof Norman Biggs; ✉ London School of Economics and Political Science, Houghton Street, London WC2A 2AE (☎ 020 7955 7640, e-mail nlbiggs@gmail.com)

BIGNELL, Janet; QC (2015); *Educ* Hertford Coll Oxford (BCL), Downing Coll Cambridge (MA); *Career* called to the Bar Lincoln's Inn 1992; recorder of the Crown Ct and Chancery 2009, bencher Lincoln's Inn 2015; FCIArb; *Publications* Registered Land Law and Practice (2004), Lewison's Drafting Business Leases (2007 and 2013); *Style*— Miss Janet Bignell, QC; ✉ Falcon Chambers, London EC4Y 1AA

BIGNELL, Marc Richard; s of Derek Roy Bignell, and Beryl Patricia, *née* Butler; *b* 22 July 1967, Edgware, Middlx; *Educ* Keele Univ (BA), Harvard Business Sch; *m* 9 Sept 2000, Claire Catherine, *née* Aherne; 2 da (Florence Lily b 24 April 2001, Dorothy Lily b 22 March 2006); *Career* grad buyer Zenith Media 1987–90, head of broadcast media and dir OMD UK 1990–2004, Camelot 2002, jt md Opera Media 2004–10, trading dir Omnicom Media Gp EMEA 2010–12, chief investment offr Worldwide Omnicom Media Gp 2012–14, head of trading EMEA Yahoo 2014–; *Recreations* tennis, running, music, family; *Clubs* Luton Town FC, Soho House, Harpenden Collective; *Style*— Marc Bignell, Esq; ✉ Yahoo, 125 Shaftesbury Avenue, London WC2H 8AD (e-mail bignellm@yahoo-inc.com)

BIGNON, Arnaud; *b* France; *Career* former sous chef The Bristol, Spondi Athens until 2012, exec chef The Greenhouse 2012– (Michelin star); *Style*— Mr Arnaud Bignon; ✉ The Greenhouse, 27a Hayâs Mews, Mayfair, London W1J 5NY

BIGSBY, Prof Christopher William Edgar; s of Maj Edgar Edward Leo Bigsby (d 1968), and Ivy May, *née* Hopkins; *b* 27 June 1941; *Educ* Sutton GS, Univ of Sheffield (BA, MA), Univ of Nottingham (PhD); *m* 9 Oct 1965, Pamela Joan, da of Stephen Joseph Lovelady; 2 s (Gareth Christopher b 1968, Ewan James b 1976), 2 da (Kirsten Rebecca b 1972, Bella Juliet Natasha b 1974); *Career* prof of American studies UEA; writer and broadcaster; TV with Malcolm Bradbury: The After Dinner Game 1975, Stones 1976; BBC radio: Patterson 1983 (with Malcolm Bradbury), Fictions 1984, Long Day's Journey 1988, Kaleidoscope, Third Ear, Meridian; Fulbright Scholar 1963, Makitterick Prize for Best First Novel 1994, Bernard Hewitt Award in Theatre History 1999, American Library Assoc Notable Book 2002, Betty Jean Jones Award for Outstanding Teacher of American Theatre and Drama 2006, American Studies Network Prize 2008, Education Abroad Leadership Award 2015; FRSL 2000, FRSA 2006; *Books* Confrontation and Commitment (1967), Albee (1969), Three Negro Plays (ed, 1969), The Black American Writer (2 vols, 1971), Dada and Surrealism (1972), Edward Albee (ed, 1975), Superculture (ed, 1975), Approaches to Popular Culture (ed, 1976), Tom Stoppard (1980), The Second Black Renaissance (1980), Contemporary English Drama (ed, 1981), A Critical Introduction to 20th Century American Drama (3 vols, 1982, 1984 and 1985), Joe Orton (1982), The Radical Imagination and the Liberal Tradition (ed, 1982), David Mamet (1985), Cultural Change in the United States since World War II (ed, 1986), Plays by Susan Glaspell (1987), File on Miller (1987), Arthur Miller and Company (1990), Modern American Drama 1945–1990 (1992), Nineteenth Century American Short Stories (ed, 1995), The Portable Arthur Miller (ed, 1995), The Cambridge Companion to Arthur Miller (ed, 1997), The Cambridge History of American Theatre (3 vols, ed with Don B Wilmeth, 1998, 1999, 2000), Jack London: The Call of the Wild and Other Stories (ed, 1998), Contemporary American Playwrights (1999), Edgar Allen Poe: The Pit and the Pendulum and Other Stories (ed, 1999), The Cambridge History of American Literature Vol 7 (with Morris Dickstein, John Bort, Wendy Steiner and Cyrus Patell, 1999), Modern American Drama 1945–2000 (2000), Writers in Conversation (2 vols, ed, 2000–01, vols 3, 4 and 5, ed, 2011–13), The Cambridge Companion to David Mamet (ed, 2004), Arthur Miller: A Critical Study (2004), Remembering Arthur Miller (ed, 2005), A New Introduction to American Studies (ed, 2005), Remembering and Imagining the Holocaust: The Chain of Memory (2006), The Cambridge Companion to Modern American Culture (ed, 2006), Neil La Bute (2007), The Cambridge Companions to August Wilson (ed, 2007), Arthur Miller: the Biography 1915–1962 (2008), Arthur Miller: the Biography 1962–2005 (2011), Viewing America: Twenty-First Century Television Drama (2013); *Novels* Hester (1994), Pearl (1995), Still Lives (1996), Beautiful Dreamer (2002), One Hundred Days: One Hundred Nights (2007), Poe, or the Revenant (2012), Ballygoren (2014), Flint (2015); *Recreations* so far undiscovered; *Style*— Prof Christopher Bigsby; ✉ 3 Church Farm, Colney, Norwich NR4 7TX, (☎ 01603 456048); School of American Studies, University of East Anglia, Norwich NR4 7TJ (☎ 01603 592789)

BILES, John Anthony; TD; s of Kenneth Robert William Biles, of Pinner, Middx, and Sheila Colville, *née* Stones; *b* 29 June 1947, Norwich; *Educ* John Lyon Sch Harrow, Univ of Exeter (BSc); *m* 11 Sep 1976, Francoise Marie Doris, *née* Phillips; 2 da (Caroline Sarah Louise b 26 May 1979, Nicola Clare Victoria b 12 March 1982); *Career* Price Waterhouse & Co 1968–76, EMI Ltd 1976–78, AFA-Minerva (EMI) Ltd 1978–81, fin dir of various subsids Racal Electronics plc 1981–91; gp fin dir: Chubb Security plc 1991–97, FKI plc 1998–2004, dir: Amey plc 2001–03, Armorgroup Int plc 2004–08, Chapelthorpe plc 2005–07, Charter Int plc 2005–12, Northern Ireland Electricity plc 2005–11, Hermes Fund Managers Ltd 2005–11, Sutton and E Surrey Water plc 2006–, Bodycote plc 2007–15, HellermannTyton Gp plc 2013–, Skyepharma plc 2014–; capt and memb HAC; memb Ct

Worshipful Co of Ironmongers; FCA 1971; *Recreations* gardening, walking, travel, shooting, antiques; *Style—* Mr John Biles

BILES, Dr Michael Edwin; s of Ronald James Biles (d 1993), of Winchester, Hants, and Rhoda Jessie, *née* Knight; *b* 9 December 1951; *Educ* Peter Symonds' GS Winchester (head boy, Hockey colours), Kingston Univ (BA), Univ of Southampton (PhD), Inns of Court Sch of Law; *m* 15 July 1978, Tina Margaret, da of Roy Bernard Phillips; 2 s (Mark Edwin b 7 June 1982, Craig Alexander b 15 Feb 1986), 1 da (Sally Kim Christina b 4 Nov 1993); *Career* called to the Bar Middle Temple 1983; head Sch of Law Southampton Inst 2001–, visiting prof of law Southampton Business Sch; housing ombudsman; MCIArb 1999, Hon MCIH; *Publications* author of numerous papers and articles in legal jls; *Recreations* hockey, cycling, gardening, DIY, reading, listening to music, spending time with family and friends; *Clubs* Winchester Hockey; *Style—* Dr Michael Biles; ✉ 81 Aldwych, London WC2B 4HN (☎ 020 7421 3800, fax 020 7831 1942, e-mail ombudsman@housing-ombudsman.org.uk)

BILIMORIA, Baron (Life Peer UK 2006), of Chelsea in the Royal Borough of Kensington and Chelsea; Karan Faridoon Bilimoria; CBE (2004), DL (Hounslow, 2005); *b* 26 November 1961; *Educ* Hebron Sch Ooty India, Indian Inst of Mgmnt and Commerce Osmania Univ (BCom), London Met Univ (Dip), Sidney Sussex Coll Cambridge (MA, Polo half blue, vice-pres Cambridge Union), Cranfield Univ Sch of Mgmnt; *m* Heather, *née* Walker; 2 s (Kai, Josh), 2 da (Zara, Lily); *Career* trainee then CA Ernst & Young 1982–87, consulting accountant Cresvale Ltd 1988, sales and mktg dir European Accounting Focus magazine 1989, fndr Cobra Beer Ltd 1989 (chief exec 1989–2007, chm 2007–), fndr General Bilimoria Wines 1999, fndr and chm Cobrabyte Technologies 2000–; non-exec dir: Brake Bros Ltd 2004–07, Booker Gp plc 2007–; memb Advsy Bd Boston Analytics 2005–; fndr and publishing dir Tandoori Magazine and tandoorimagazine.com 1994–2003; memb: London Business Sch Fndn for Entrepreneurial Mgmnt 1999–, New Deal Taskforce DfEE 1999–2001, Young Presidents' Orgn London 2000– (chm 2004–05, memb Int Educn Ctee 2003–05), Nat Employment Panel Dept for Work and Pensions 2001–07 (chm Small and Medium Size Enterprise Bd 2001–05), The Indus Entrepreneurs (TiE) UK 2002– (memb Bd 2003–06), Tyson Taskforce on the Recruitment and Devpt of Non-Exec Dirs 2003, Neighbourhood Renewal Private Sector Panel ODPM 2003–05, Advsy Bd Birmingham Business Sch 2005–, HRH the Duke of York's Business Advsy Cncl 2006–, Advsy Bd Judge Business Sch Univ of Cambridge 2008–, Cmmn on the Future of Mgmnt 2014–; visiting entrepreneur Centre for Entrepreneurial Learning Univ of Cambridge 2004–, founding patron Oxford Entrepreneurs 2004–, nat champion Nat Cncl for Grad Entrepreneurship 2004–, hon pres Training for Life 2004–, champion Make Your Mark campaign Enterprise Insight 2005–, enterprise ldr Prince's Tst 2008–; memb UK-India Consultative Gp FCO 2002–03, UK chm Indo-British Partnership 2003–, vice-chm Asian Business Assoc London C of C and Industry 2003–08, chm UK India Business Cncl (formerly Indo-British Partnership Network) 2007–09, memb UK-India Round Table 2005–; founding chair Zoroastrian All-Pty Parly Gp (APPG) 2013–, treas APPG on Br Curry and Catering Industry 2014–, vice-chair APPG on Beer 2015–; memb APPGs on: Maldives 2015–, Mgmnt 2015–, SA 2015–, Armed Forces 2015–, Students 2015–; patron: Thare Mache Starfish Initiative 2001–, Rethink 2003–, RSA India 2005–, Thames Community Fndn 2005–, India Int Fndn 2006–, Children in Need Inst UK 2008–, Global Forum for Indian Leadership 2014–, Indian Assoc 2014–; vice-patron Meml Gates Tst 1999–2004 (chm Ctee 2003–); memb Advsy Bd: Shrimati Pushpa Wati Loomba Meml Tst 2001– (chm), Abad Tst 2007–, Roundhouse Tst 2008–; champion Roko Cancer Appeal 2005–; tstee Br Cardiac Research Tst 2006–; cmmr Royal Hosp Chelsea 2006–11; memb Pres's Ctee London First 2002–06, int envoy for London 2005–, ambass London 2012 Olympic Bid 2005; chllr Thames Valley Univ 2005– (govr 2001–04), ambass Interactive Univ UK 2005–, chllr Univ of Birmingham 2014; govr Ditchley Fndn 2004–; hon memb Cranfield Mgmnt Assoc 2005, hon fell Sidney Sussex Coll Cambridge 2007; Liveryman Worshipful Co of Drapers 2008 (Freeman 2005), Liveryman The Brewers' Co of the City of London 2008; Hon DBA Brunel Univ 2005, Hon DLitt Heriot-Watt Univ 2005, Hon DBA London Met Univ 2008; hon doctorate: Staffs Univ 2006, Cranfield Univ 2009, Univ of West London 2012, Univ of Birmingham 2014, Univ of Exeter 2014; FCA 2002 (ACA 1987), Hon Life FRSA 2004 (memb Cncl 2004–07, memb Devpt Bd 2005–07), FInstD 2005, CCMI 2005; *Awards* Non-Resident Indian Millennium Honour India 2001, Outstanding Achievement Award Execs Assoc of GB 2002, Asian of the Year 2002, London Entrepreneur of the Year 2003, Entrepreneur of the Year Asian Achievers Awards 2003, Business of the Year (Cobra Beer Ltd) Asian Business Awards 2003, Entrepreneur of the Year London C of C and Industry 2003, Excellence Award Non-Resident Indian Inst 2003, Entrepreneur of the Year Nat Business Awards (London and SE) 2004, Pride of India Award Non-Resident Indian Inst 2004, Outstanding Achievement Award ICAEW 2005, Hon Award Bangladesh Caterer's Assoc 2007, Pravasi Bharti Samman 2008, Entrepreneur Alumnus of the Year Cranfield Sch of Mgmnt 2008, Director Magazine Good Director Award for Leadership IOD 2008, Int Indian of the Year Award India Link Int 2015; numerous Monde Selection awards for Cobra Beer Ltd 2001–14; *Books* Bottled For Business (with Steve Coomber, 2007), Against the Grain (with Steve Coomber, 2009); *Recreations* reading, current affairs, travel, art, music, theatre, tennis, riding, golf, scuba diving, sailing; *Clubs* Carlton, Guards Polo, Delhi Gymkhana, Secunderabad, Hawks' (Cambridge), Royal Cwlth Soc, Univ Pitt (Cambridge), Delhi Golf, FRIMA Golf (Dehra Dun), Kelvin Grove (Cape Town); *Style—* The Lord Bilimoria, CBE, DL; ✉ www.lordbilimoria.co.uk

BILL, Simon Jonathan Robert; *b* 1958, Kingston; *Educ* St Martins Sch of Art, RCA; *Career* artist; *Solo Exhibitions* From Hell (Cabinet Gallery London) 1992, I've Got Demons in My Stomach (Cabinet Gallery London) 1994, Blind Idiot God (Bloom Gallery Amsterdam) 1996, Simon Bill (Crown Gallery Brussels) 1997, 1500 to the Present Day (Crown Gallery Brussels) 1998, Corn Hole (Modern Art London) 1999, Bio Pop (Modern Art London) 2001, (The Cornerhouse Manchester) 2002; *Group Exhibitions* incl: Pet Show (Union Street London) 1993, Pop Maudite (Cabinet Gallery London) 1993, Unfair 93 (Koln Germany) 1993, MPD multiple personality disorder (Cabinet Gallery London) 1993, Please Don't Hurt Me (Gallerie Snoie Rotterdam) 1994, Painter's Opinion (Bloom Gallery Amsterdam) 1995, Please Don't Hurt Me (Cabinet Gallery London) 1995, White Hysteria (Contemporary Art Center Adelaide) 1996, The Death of the Death of Painting (NY) 1995, Yerselfesteem (Words and Pictures London) 1996, Popocultural (S London Gallery London) 1996, Popocultural II (Southampton City Art Gallery) 1997, Dissolution (Laurent De Laye Gallery London) 1997, Multislot (London) 1997, There's Something Odd about Painting (Konig Gallery Vienna) 1998, Show Me the Money (Dukes Mews London) 1998, Exit Art (NY) 1999, Papermake (Modern Art London) 1999, Animal Magic (Kunsthaus Karstruhe Germany) 1999, Abstract Art (Delfina Gallery London) 2000, Beck's Futures 2 (ICA London) 2001, Tattoo Show (Modern Art London) 2001; *Publications* Kindred Spirits (1991), 'Gavin, What's Your Work About?' (1993), Some Things Which Fell to Earth (1994), Rabbit Droppings (essay, 1996), Essay on Gary Hume (1996); *Recreations* gardening, collecting antique edged weapons; *Style—* Simon Bill, Esq; ✉ 22 Tyers Estate, Bermondsey Street, London SE1 3JG (☎ 020 7967 9037)

BILLINGHAM, Baroness (Life Peer UK 2000), of Banbury in the County of Oxfordshire; Angela Theodora; da of Theodore Vincent Case (d 1941), and Eva, *née* Saxby (d 1964); *b* 31 July 1939; *Educ* Aylesbury GS, Univ of London, Dept of Educn Oxford; *m* 1962, Anthony Peter Billingham (d 1992), s of late Cyril Billingham; 2 da (Zoë Ann b 31 Dec 1964, Caroline Lucy b 12 July 1967); *Career* numerous teaching posts most recently at Banbury Sch, former examiner for an examinations bd; cncllr: Banbury BC 1970–74, Cherwell DC 1974–84, Oxfordshire CC 1993–94; mayor of Banbury 1976; magistrate 1976–; contested gen election (Lab) Banbury 1992, MEP (Lab) Northants and Blaby 1994–99; chief whip Party of European Socialists (PES), shadow spokesman for sport and the Olympic Games House of Lords; memb: European Sub-Ctee F, Information Ctee; chair Lighter Evenings All Pty Gp; pres Oxon Lawn Tennis Assoc, memb House of Lords Bridge Team; patron and/or supporter: CAARE charity, Nat Osteoporosis Gp, Save the Children, Every Child, Earl Educn; *sporting achievements* tournament and county tennis player for 25 years and co tennis tea chairm, co hockey and badminton player; *Recreations* tennis, gardening, cinema, bridge; *Clubs* Lords and Commons Tennis (chair), All-England Lawn Tennis; *Style—* The Rt Hon the Baroness Billingham; ✉ 6 Crediton Hill, London NW6 1HP (☎ 020 7431 5570); House of Lords, London SW1A 0PW

BILLINGHAM, Prof John; s of Charles Noel Billingham, of Dudley, W Midlands, and Florence May, *née* Dennison; *b* 10 October 1939; *Educ* Dudley GS, Univ of Birmingham (BSc), Univ of Warwick (PhD); *m* 1962, Heather Doreen, da of Frederick Homer; 2 da (Jane Elizabeth b 1963, Carolyn Leslie 1966), 1 s (David John b 1977); *Career* Gillette Res Lab 1962–65, BSA Res Labs 1965–67, Fulmer Res Labs 1970–73; Cranfield Univ 1973–2004: dir Marine Technol Centre 1981–84, head Marine Technol Dept 1984–98, prof 1984– (emeritus 2004–), head Sch of Industrial and Mfrg Sci 1998–2004; David Partridge Marine Technol Award 1994; FIM, FSUT, FREng 2000; *Publications* Steel – A Versatile Material in Marine Environments, Performance of High Strength Steels in Offshore Structures; *Recreations* golf, gardening, music; *Clubs* St Neots Golf; *Style—* Prof John Billingham; ✉ 104C Green End Road, Great Barford, Bedford MK44 3HD (☎ 01234 870203)

BILLINGHAM, Richard; *b* 1970, Birmingham; *Educ* Univ of Sunderland (BA); *Career* photographer; artist in residence Irish MOMA 2001 (artists' work prog), Sargeant fellowship Br Sch at Rome 2002, Prince of Wales bursary for the Arts Athens 2003, Wonders of the Black Country Jubilee Arts West Midlands 2003, Art Sway residency New Forest Hampshire 2003, artist in residence VIVID Birmingham 2004; multimedia work incl Fishtank (film) 1998; patron Project Ethiopia; *Solo Exhibitions* Anthony Reynolds Gallery London 1996 and 1998, Nat Museum of Film and Photography Bradford 1996, Portfolio Gallery Edinburgh 1996, Luhring Augustine NY 1997, Regen Projects LA 1997, Galerie Jennifer Flay Paris 1997, Galeria Massimo De Carlo Milan 1997, Galerie Monika Reitz Frankfurt am Main 1999, Galerie Mot & Van de Boogaard Brussels 1999, Br Sch at Rome 1999, Contemporary Art Museum Nuoro 2000, Ikon Gallery Birmingham 2000 (and tour), Douglas Hyde Gallery Dublin, Nikolaj Contemporary Art Centre Copenhagen, Brno House of Arts Czech republic, Hasselblad Centre Gothenburg, Kunsthalle Willhelmshaven, New Pictures (Anthony Reynolds Gallery London) 2003, Trafo House of Contemporary Arts Budapest 2003, Sint Lukas Brussels 2004, New Forest (Art Sawy Galleries Hampshire) 2004, Black Country (New Art Gallery Walsall, La Fabrica Madrid, Galleria Marabini Bologna, Galway Arts Festival, Anthony Reynolds Gallery London) 2005, Zoo (Compton Verney Warks) 2006, Zoo (La Fabrica Madrid, Wolverhampton Art Gallery Wolverhampton, Anthony Reynolds Gallery London, Glynn Vivian Gallery Swansea) 2007, Constable (Town Hall Galleries Ipswich) 2007, People, Places, Animals (ACCA Melbourne Australia) 2007; *Books* Ray's A Laugh (1996), Richard Billingham (catalogue, 2000), Black Country, Richard Billingham (2004), Zoo, Richard Billingham (2007), Landscapes, 2001–03 (2008); *Style—* Richard Billingham, Esq; ✉ c/o Anthony Reynolds, 60 Great Marlborough Street, London W1F 2BA (☎ 020 7439 2201, fax 020 7439 1869, e-mail info@anthonyreynolds.com)

BILLINGTON, Guy; s of Reginald Arthur Billington (d 1960), of 1 Arterberry Rd, London, and Constance May, *née* Riches; *b* 12 November 1946; *Educ* KCS Wimbledon, St John's Coll Cambridge (MA); *m* 5 July 1966, Christine Ellen, da of Rev Frederick Charles Bonner, of Upton upon Severn, Worcs; 2 da (Nicole b 13 Dec 1966, Suzanne b 21 Jan 1971); *Career* articled clerk Lovell White & King 1969–72, ptnr McKenna & Co 1977–97 (asst slr 1972–77), ptnr CMS Cameron McKenna 1997–2007; non-exec dir Royal Nat Orthopaedic Hosp Tst; *Recreations* rugby, music, cricket; *Clubs* Rosslyn Park Football, Surrey CCC; *Style—* Guy Billington, Esq; ✉ 16 Belvedere Grove, London SW19 7RL (☎ 020 8946 4889, e-mail guy.billington@btinternet.com)

BILLINGTON, (Edward) John; CBE (1996), RD, DL; s of Edward Billington, and Nesta, *née* Boxwell; *b* 21 December 1934; *Educ* Uppingham; *m* 5 Dec 1964, Fenella, da of Dr Hamilton-Turner; 2 s (Edward b 1966, Richard b 1970), 1 da (Suzetta b 1968); *Career* RNR 1953–86 (hon cdr 1986–); commodity broker; chm Edward Billington & Son Ltd; memb: NW Bd DTI 1988–96, Cncl Univ of Liverpool 1986–97; chm Mersey Partnership 1991–92, tstee: Nat Museums and Galleries on Merseyside 1986–96, Liverpool Sch of Tropical Med; dir Royal Liverpool Philharmonic Orch, dir Park Foods plc; High Sheriff Merseyside 1990–91; CIMgt; *Style—* John Billington, Esq, CBE, RD, DL; ✉ Edward Billington & Son Ltd, Cunard Building, Liverpool L3 1EL (☎ 0151 243 9000)

BILLINGTON, Lady Rachel Mary; OBE (2012); *née* Pakenham; da of 7 Earl of Longford, KG, PC (d 2001), and Elizabeth, Countess of Longford, CBE (d 2002); *b* 11 May 1942; *Educ* Univ of London; *m* 16 Dec 1967, Kevin Billington, *qv*; 2 s (Nathaniel b 1970, Caspar b 1979), 2 da (Catherine Rose b 1973, Chloe b 1976); *Career* author of 21 novels and 8 children's books; pres English PEN 1997–2000, memb Soc of Authors; *Novels* incl: A Women's Age, Occasion of Sin, Loving Attitudes, Theo and Matilda, Bodily Harm, Magic and Fate, Perfect Happiness, Tiger Sky, A Woman's Life, Far-Out! (for children), The Space Between, One Summer, Lies and Loyalties, There's More to Life (for children), The Missing Boy, Poppy's Hero (for children, 2012), Maria and the Admiral (2012), Poppy's Angel (for children, 2013), Glory – A Story of Gallipoli (2015); *Non-Fiction* incl: The Family Year, The Great Umbilical – Mother Daughter Mother, The Unbreakable Bond, The Life of Jesus (for children), The Life of St Francis (for children); *Style—* Lady Rachel Billington, OBE; ✉ The Court House, Poyntington, Sherborne, Dorset DT9 4LF

BILMES, Alexander Ernest (Alex); *b* 19 January 1973, Essex; *Career* journalist; features ed GQ 2000–10, contributing ed Vogue 2006–10, ed Esquire 2010– (currently ed-in-chief), ed-in-chief The Big Black Book; contrib to numerous newspapers and magazines; PPA Magazine Writer of the Year 2006, PPA Highly Commended 2007, MJA Interviewer of the Year 2007; *Clubs* Groucho, London Library; *Style—* Alex Bilmes, Esq; ✉ Esquire, Hearst Magazines UK, 72 Broadwick Street, London W1F 9EP

BILSTON, Baron (Life Peer UK 2005), of Bilston in the County of West Midlands; Dennis Turner; s of Thomas Herbert Turner (d 1981), and Mary Elizabeth, *née* Peasley (d 1974); *b* 26 August 1942; *Educ* Stonefield Secdy Sch Bilston, Bilston Coll of Further Educn; *m* 19 June 1976, Patricia Mary, da of Joseph Henry Narroway (d 1984), of Bilston; 1 s (Hon Brendon Robert b 1977), 1 da (Hon Jenny Mary b 1980); *Career* chm Springvale Enterprises Ltd Bilston; dep ldr Wolverhampton MDC 1979–86 (sometime chm Social Servs, Housing Further Educn and Econ Devpt Ctees), cncllr W Midlands CC 1975–86; MP (Lab/Co-op) Wolverhampton SE 1987–2005; Lab whip for Health, Educn and Defence W Midlands 1987–97, PPS to Clare Short as Sec of State Int Devpt 1999–2003; chm House of Commons Catering Ctee 1997–2005, memb Exec Ctee Br Branch Cwlth Parly Assoc, memb Exec Ctee Inter-Parly Union, chm All Pty Parly FE Colls Gp, chm W Midlands Parly Gp of Labour MPs, pres All Pty Parly Save Our Pubs Gp, jt chm All Pty Parly Gp for Greyhounds, sec All Pty Parly Gp for Non-Profit Making Clubs; vice-pres Local Govt Assoc; pres: Bilston Community Assoc, Bradley Community Assoc; sec and tstee Bradley and Dist Sr Citizens' Centre; Hon DLitt Univ of Wolverhampton 2006, Freeman City of Wolverhampton 2007; *Recreations* compereing, beer tasting, all card games; *Clubs* New Springvale Sports & Social (Bilston); *Style*— The Rt Hon the Lord Bilston; ✉ Aubyn, King Street, Bradley, Bilston, West Midlands (☎ 01902 491822)

BINDER, Alan Naismith; OBE (1974); s of Frederick John Binder (d 1961), and Kathleen Mary, *née* Darker (d 1967); *b* 4 August 1931; *Educ* Bedford Sch, Magdalen Coll Oxford (MA); *m* 1958, Gillian Patricia (d 2014), da of George Francis Wilson, of Sussex; 2 da (Jennifer b 1959, Stephanie b 1960), 1 s (Jonathan b 1962); *Career* dir Shell International Petroleum Co Ltd 1984, pres Shell International Trading Co 1987–91; chm: United Communications Ltd 1991–99, Expro International Group 1992–99; dir: The Housing Finance Corporation 1993–2001, RJB Mining plc 1995–2000; *Recreations* tennis, reading, music; *Clubs* Leander, MCC, Mosimann's, Carlton; *Style*— Alan Binder, Esq, OBE; ✉ Old Place, Speldhurst, Kent TN3 0PA (☎ 01892 863227, fax 01892 861478, e-mail alan.binder@talktalk.net)

BINDING, Paul; s of Leonard Hubert Binding (d 1972), of Devon, and Muriel Hope, *née* Middleton (d 1965); *b* 7 January 1943; *Educ* Berkhamsted Sch, New Coll Oxford (open scholar, BA, BLitt); *Career* lectr in Eng literature Umeå Sweden 1970–72, a managing ed Oxford Univ Press 1974–77, dep literary and arts ed New Statesman 1979–81, writer in residence (Arts Cncl fellowship) St John's Sch Epping 1984, Eudora Welty visiting prof of Southern studies Millsaps Coll Jackson Mississippi 1985–86, lectr in Eng literature Univ of Macerata Italy 1987–89; lectr on works of Lorca, American Southern literature, animal issues, Scandinavian cultures, and other literary and cultural matters in US, UK, Sweden, Norway, Denmark, Finland, Belgium and Netherlands; contribs literary reviews to various pubns and articles on animal rights and Scandinavian and Dutch matters to Independent on Sunday, Independent, Times Literary Supplement, Guardian Literary Review, etc, author of various introductions to works published by Virago Modern Classics, Gay Modern Classics and Antipelago Books US; sr assoc memb St Antony's Coll Oxford 1999–2001; bicentennial lecture on Hans Christian Andersen Br Library 2005, Br delg to Ibsen Centenary Conf Oslo 2006; juror Vondel Prize for best translation from Dutch 2007 and 2009; memb: League Against Cruel Sports, Animal Aid, WWF (adopter of rhinocerus and orang-utan), Green Party, Br Union Against Vivisection, WSPA, PEN; awarded prize by Sveriges Författarfond for promotion of Swedish literature; *Books* Separate Country (1979, revised edn 1988), Harmonica's Bridegroom (novel, 1984), Lorca – The Gay Imagination (1985), Dreams and Speculations (poems, with John Horder, 1986), Kingfisher Weather (novel, 1989), St Martin's Ride (autobiography, 1990, J R Ackerley prize), Eudora Welty: Portrait of a Writer (1994), An Endless Quiet Valley: A Reappraisal of John Masefield (1998), Babel Guide to Scandinavian and Baltic Fiction (1999), My Cousin the Writer (novel, 2002), Imagined Corners: Exploring the World's First Atlas (2003), Tom, Dick and Harry (poems, 2003), With Vine-Leaves in His Hair: The Role of the Artist in Ibsen's Plays (2006), The Sailor's Revenge (novel, 2010); *Recreations* listening to music, exploring Britain and Scandinavia, the Shropshire countryside, herbs and houseplants, the company of animals; *Style*— Paul Binding, Esq; ✉ The House, Bull Street, Bishop's Castle, Shropshire (☎ 01588 638117, e-mail paulbinding@yahoo.co.uk)

BINDMAN, Sir Geoffrey Lionel; kt (2007), Hon QC (2011); s of Dr Gerald Bindman (d 1974), and Lena Bindman (d 1989); *b* 3 January 1933; *Educ* Royal GS Newcastle upon Tyne, Oriel Coll Oxford; *m* 1961, Lynn Janice; 2 s, 1 da; *Career* slr; sr ptnr then conslt Bindman LLP (formerly Bindman & Partners); chm Legal Action Gp 1976–78, legal advsr Cmmn for Racial Equality 1977–83, pres Discrimination Law Assoc 1999–, chm Soc of Labour Lawyers 1999–2001, chm Br Inst of Human Rights 2005–13; hon visiting prof of law UCL 1990–, hon visiting fell in civil legal process Univ of Kent 1991–, hon visiting prof of law London South Bank Univ 2003–; tstee: Wordsworth Tst 1993–2003, Helen Bamber Fndn 2006–13; Gazette Centenary Award for Human Rights Achievement Law Soc 2003; Hon LLD De Montfort Univ 2000, Hon DLaw Kingston Univ 2006; hon fell Soc of Advanced Legal Studies 1998–; *Books* Race and Law (co-author, 1972), South Africa: Human Rights and the Rule of Law (ed, 1988); *Recreations* book collecting, music, walking; *Clubs* Law Soc; *Style*— Sir Geoffrey Bindman, QC; ✉ 236 Gray's Inn Road, London WC1X 8HB (☎ 020 7833 4433, fax 020 7837 9792, e-mail g.bindman@ucl.ac.uk)

BINFIELD, Prof (John) Clyde Goodfellow; OBE (1991); s of Edward John Binfield, DSC (d 1976), and Margaret Florence, *née* Goodfellow (d 1976); *b* 5 December 1940; *Educ* Dover GS, Emmanuel Coll Cambridge (minor scholar, exhibitioner, Bachelor scholar, MA, PhD); *m* 1969, Noreen Helen, da of late William George Maycock; 2 da (Emma Victoria (Mrs James Stone) b 1970, Anna Alexandra b 1972); *Career* Univ of Sheffield: asst lectr in modern history 1964–67, lectr 1967–74, sr lectr 1974–84, reader 1984–98, head Dept of History 1988–91, assoc prof 1999–2004, emeritus prof 2004–; memb Exec Ctee World Alliance of YMCAs 1981–91 (chm of two ctees), chm Nat Cncl of YMCAs 1992–97 (vice-chm 1982–90), vice-pres YMCA England 1999–; pres: Ecclesiastical History Soc 1990–91, Chapels Soc 1992–98, Friends of Dr Williams's Library 1993–, United Reformed Church History Soc 2002–08; chm Voluntary Action Sheffield 1990–93; govr: Stocksbridge Coll of Further Educn 1975–88, Northern Coll Manchester 1976–2005 (memb Educn Ctee, pres Bd of Govrs 2000–05), Silcoates Sch Wakefield 1977–2011 (vice-chm 1982–83, chm of govrs 1983–93), Dunford (YMCA) Coll Sussex 1981–87, Loxley Tertiary Coll 1988–90; memb Cncl: YMCA George Williams Coll 1991–2001, Governing Bodies Assoc (GBA) 2000–03; tstee: Yorkshire Historic Churches Tst 1993–, South Yorkshire Historic Buildings Tst 1994– (chm 2004–06), Firth's Homes 1995– (chm 2013–14), Dr Williams's Library 2005–, Historic Chapels Tst 2006–, Sheffield GS Fndn; chm Fabric Advsy Ctee Wakefield Cathedral 2006–, memb Cncl Friends of Sheffield Cathedral 2006–12; FRHistS 1983 (memb Cncl 1997–2002), FSA 1987; *Publications* George Williams and the YMCA: A Study in Victorian Social Attitudes (1973), So Down to Prayers: Studies in English Nonconformity 1780–1920 (1977), Pastors and People: The Biography of a Baptist Church: Queen's Road Coventry (1984), This Has Been Tomorrow: The World Alliance of YMCAs since 1955 (1991), The Contexting of a Chapel Architect: James Cubitt 1836–1912 (2001); ed of various books and jls and author of numerous articles, book chapters and reviews; *Recreations* travel, architecture, opera; *Clubs* Royal Over-Seas League; *Style*— Prof Clyde Binfield, OBE; ✉ 604 Royal Plaza, 2 Westfield Terrace, Sheffield S1 4GG (☎ 0114 272 2554)

BING, His Hon Inigo Geoffrey; s of Geoffrey Bing, QC, and Crystal Bing; *b* 1 April 1944; *Educ* St Olave's GS Southwark, Univ of Birmingham (LLB); *m* 1, Shirley-Anne Holmes (d 2003); m 2, 31 March 2004, Her Hon Judge Judith Hughes, QC, *qv*; *Career* called to the Bar Inner Temple 1967 (bencher 2012); district judge (formerly met stipendiary magistrate) 1989–2000, recorder 1996–2000, circuit judge (South Eastern Circuit) 2000–12; *Publications* Criminal Procedure and Sentencing in the Magistrates' Court 1990 (5 ed 1999); *Recreations* music, travel, studying history and philosophy; *Clubs* Reform; *Style*— His Hon Inigo Bing

BINGHAM, Andrew Russell; MP; s of Tony Bingham (d 2009), and Mary, *née* Blackwell; *b* 23 June 1962, Buxton, Derbys; *Educ* Long Lane Sch Chapel-en-le-Frith, High Peak Coll of FE Buxton; *Career* co dir ARB Sales Ltd 1983–2003; cncllr High Peak Borough Cncl 1999–2011, MP (Cons) High Peak 2010–; *Recreations* football, cricket, badminton, cooking; *Style*— Andrew Bingham, Esq, MP; ✉ House of Commons, London SW1A 0AA

BINGHAM, Charlotte; *see:* Brady, Hon Mrs (C M T)

BINGHAM, Lord; George Charles Bingham; s of 7 Earl of Lucan (decd), and Countess of Lucan; *b* 21 September 1967; *Educ* Eton, Trinity Hall Cambridge; *Career* investment banker; formerly with Kleinwort Benson Ltd then head of UK and European structured fin Dresdner Kleinwort Benson, currently dir of research Bailey Coates Asset Mgmnt; *Clubs* Turf, White's, Pratt's; *Style*— Lord Bingham

BINGHAM, Dr James Stewart; TD (1982); s of Dr William Bingham, of Cultra, Co Down, and Nora Mary, *née* Beckett; *b* 31 July 1945; *Educ* Campbell Coll Belfast, Queen's Univ Belfast (MB BCh, BAO); *m* 21 Sept 1974, Elizabeth Eleanor, da of Charles Arnold Stewart; 1 s (Stewart Mark b 20 Jan 1983); *Career* Univ Offrs' Trg Corp 1963–69, 253 (NI) Field Ambulance and 217 (L) Gen Hosp RAMC(V) 1969–83, resigned as Lt-Col; house physician and surgn The Royal Victoria Hosp Belfast 1969–70; training posts in obstetrics and gynaecology in Belfast, Salisbury (Rhodesia) and Vancouver (Canada) 1970–75; The Middlesex Hosp London: sr registrar in genitourinary med 1975–77, conslt 1977–92, dir of serv 1983–91; conslt in genitourinary med Guy's and St Thomas' Hosps London 1992– (clinical dir 1997–2000); hon conslt in genitourinary med to Br Army 2000–09; Med Soc for Study of Venereal Diseases: hon treas 1986–93, pres 1993–95, hon life fell 2007; chm Assoc for Genitourinary Med 1999–2001; pres Int Union Against Sexually Transmitted Infections 2001–03 (hon treas 1995–99), hon treas Br HIV Assoc 1996–2000 (scrutineer 2008–10), memb Specialist Advsy Ctee in Genitourinary Med 1988–95 and 2003– (chm 1993–95); UK rep Dermatovenereology Monospecialty Ctee Union of European Monospecialties 2003– (treas 2004–09); examiner European Bd Examination in Dermato-venereology 2007–09; memb Bd of Examiners for Dip Genitourinary Med: Soc of Apothecaries of London 1982–2007 (convenor of examiners 1992–95), Univ of Liverpool 1996–98; memb Bd of Examiners for Dip HIV Med 2005–07; external examiner Dip HIV Med Univ of Liverpool 1996–98, external examiner for MSc in Sexually Transmitted Infection UCL 2005–07; Harrison lectr Br Assoc for Sexual Health and HIV 2010; memb: Genitourinary Sub-Ctee CCSC BMA 1986–92 (rep Sub-Ctee on CCSC 1989–91), Dermatology and Venereology Sub-Ctee CCSC BMA 1992–2007 (chm 1998–2000), European Mgmnt Guidelines for STIs 2007–09, European Dermatology Forum Mgmnt Guidelines Ctee 2008–10; Specialist Advsy Ctee in Genitourinary Med RCP 1988–95 (sec 1990–93, chm 1993–95); conslt for Br Cncl to Botswana 1984, WHO conslt to Bulgaria 1993 and Uzbekistan and Turkmenistan 2008; memb Editorial Bd: International Journal of STD and AIDS 1990– (ed Continuing Med Educn 1995–2000, asst ed 2003–), Genitourinary Med 1993–95; Yeoman Worshipful Soc of Apothecaries of London 2012–, Freeman City of London 2013–; memb: BMA, RSM, Br Assoc for Sexual Health and HIV (Harrison lectr 2010), Soc for the Study of Sexually Transmitted Diseases in Ireland, Euro Acad of Dermatology and Venereology, Achievers' Club Family Planning Assoc 2010–; life memb Br HIV Assoc (BHIVA); FRCOG, FRCP, FRCPE; *Books* Sexually Transmitted Diseases (1984, 2 edn 1990); *CD-ROMs* co-author Sexually Transmitted Infections and Genital Dermatoses – diagnosis and therapy (1998); *Recreations* British military history with particular emphasis on the Anglo-Irish contrib, reading military and political biographies, gardening; *Clubs* Army and Navy, City Volunteer Officers', RAC; *Style*— Dr James Bingham, TD; ✉ The Thatched House, The Downs, Givons Grove, Leatherhead KT22 8LH (☎ 01372 362584, e-mail james.bingham@btinternet.com)

BINGHAM, Judith Caroline; da of Jack Bingham (d 1993), and Peggy, *née* MacGowan (d 1997); *b* 21 June 1952; *Educ* High Storrs GS for Girls Sheffield, Royal Acad of Music; *m* 1985, Andrew Petrow; *Career* composer; studied under Hans Keller; singer BBC Singers 1983–95; works incl: The Divine Image 1976, Cocaine Lil 1977, A Hymn Before Sunrise in the Vale of Chamouni 1982, Into the Wilderness 1982, Cradle Song of the Blessed Virgin 1983, Scenes from Nature 1983, Just Before Dawn 1985, Brazil 1985, A Cold Spell 1987, Christmas Past, Christmas Present 1988, Chartres 1988, Dove Cottage by Moonlight 1989, I Have a Secret to Tell 1990, Unpredictable but Providential 1991, Four Minute Mile 1991, The Stars Above: The Earth Below 1991, The Uttermost 1992–93, Irish Tenebrae 1992, The Ghost of Combermere Abbey 1993, O Magnum Mysterium 1994, Santa Casa 1994, Beyond Redemption 1994–95, Evening Canticles 1995, Epiphany 1995, Salt in the Blood 1995 (premiered BBC Proms 1995), The Red Hot Nail (educn project for LSO, 1995), The Temple At Karnak 1996, The Mysteries of Adad 1996, No Discord 1996, The Waning Moon 1997, Gleams of a Remoter World 1997, Below the Surface Stream 1997, Chapman's Pool 1997, Passagio 1998, Missa Brevis 1998, The Clouded Heaven 1998, Shelley Dreams 1998, Unheimlich 1998, Vorarlberg 1998, Walzerspiele 1999, The Cathedral of Trees 1999, Water Lilies 1999, The Shooting Star 1999, Otherworld 2000, Starry Snowy Night 2000, Annunciation 2000, The Shepherd's Gift 2000, The Necklace of Light 2000, St Bride, Assisted by Angels 2000, These are OUR Footsteps 2000, 50 Shades of Green 2001, The Shadow Side of Joy Finzi 2001, The Island of Patmos 2001, First Light 2001, Der Spuk 2001, Bright Spirit 2001, My Father's Arms 2002, Ave Verum Corpus 2002, Enter GHOST 2002, Aquileia 2002, Uppon First Sight of New-England 2002, Incarnation with Shepherds Dancing 2002, Missa Brevis 2003, The Road to Emmaeus 2003, Ancient Sunlight 2003, The Moon over Westminster Cathedral 2003, The Christmas Truce 2003, Bach's Tomb, O Clap Your Hands 2003, The Ivory Tree 2004, The Secret Garden 2004, The Yearning Strong 2004, Limehouse Nocturne 2004, Lo in the Silent Night 2004, Our Faith is a Light 2004, Margaret Forsaken 2004, Down and Out 2004, Touch'd by Heavenly Fire 2004, In Nomine 2004, Hidden City 2006; BBC Young Composer 1977, Barlow Prize for Choral Music 2004, British Composer Award for Liturgical Music and for Choral Music 2004; ARAM; *Recreations* reading, friends, art; *Style*— Miss Judith Bingham

BINGHAM, Liz; da of Anthony Palmer Bingham, of E Preston, W Sussex, and Pauline Anne, *née* King (d 2010); *b* 22 March 1962, Bucks; *Educ* English Sch of Paris, Worthing Sixth Form Coll; *Partner* Linda Mary Clark (civil partnership 9 Sept 2006); *Career* qualified and licensed insolvency practitioner; Ernst & Young: joined 1986, head of UK restructuring 2007–10, managing ptnr for people and talent 2010–; memb: Insolvency Practitioner Assoc, Assoc of Business Recovery Professionals (pres 2013–14); Women in Banking and Finance Award for Achievement 2012, Cranfield 100 Women to Achieve Board Positions 2013, BBC Radio 4 Woman's Hour 100 Power Women in the UK 2013; ambass Stonewall, supporter MS Soc, co-fndr The Why Factor; *Recreations* cinema, gardening, horse racing, music, opera, travel, walking; *Style*— Ms Liz Bingham; ✉ Ernst & Young, 1 More London Place, London SE1 2AF (☎ 020 7951 9970, e-mail lbingham@uk.ey.com, website www.ey.com, Twitter @lbinghamey)

BINGHAM, Prof Nicholas Hugh; s of Robert Llewelyn Bingham (d 1972), of Dolgellau, and Blanche Louise, *née* Corbitt (d 2008); *b* 19 March 1945; *Educ* Tadcaster GS, Trinity Coll Oxford (MA), Churchill Coll Cambridge (PhD, ScD); *m* 13 Sept 1980, Cecilie Ann, da of Ralph William Gabriel (d 1973), of Leigh-on-Sea; 2 s (James b 1982, Thomas b 1993), 1 da (Ruth b 1985); *Career* Univ of London: lectr then reader Westfield Coll 1969–84, reader 1984–85, prof of mathematics Royal Holloway and Bedford New Coll 1985–95, prof of statistics Birkbeck Coll 1995–99; prof of statistics Brunel Univ 2000–03, prof of probability Univ of Sheffield 2003–06, prof of math Imperial Coll London 2006–; ed book reviews 1981–90; memb London Mathematical Soc, Inst of Mathematical Statistics; RSS; *Books* Regular Variation (1987), Risk-Neutral Valuation (1998), Regression (2010); *Recreations* running, gardening; *Style*— Prof Nicholas Bingham; ✉ 13 Woodside Grange Road, London N12 8SJ (☎ 020 8445 5779, e-mail nick.bingham@btinternet.com); Department of Mathematics, Imperial College, London SW7 2AZ (☎ 020 7594 2085, e-mail n.bingham@ic.ac.uk)

BINLEY, Brian; *b* 1942; *Educ* Finedon Mulso Secdy Modern; *m* Jacquie; 2 s (James b 1970, Matthew b 1984); *Career* fndr and chm BCC Marketing Services 1988–, co-fndr Beechwood House Publishing Co Ltd 1993; joined Cons Pty 1959, cncllr (Cons)

Northamptonshire CC 1997– (finance spokesman, chm Finance and Resources Security Ctee 2001–05, finance portfolio holder 2005–), MP (Cons) Northampton S 2005–15; FRSA; *Style*— Brian Binley, Esq; ✉ House of Commons, London SW1A 0AA; Constituency Office ☎ 01604 633414, e-mail brian.binley@brianbinley.com, website www.brianbinley.com

BINNEY, Prof James Jeffrey; s of Harry Augustus Roy Binney (d 1999), and Barbara, *née* Poole (d 1975); *b* 12 April 1950; *Educ* Univ of Cambridge (BA), Univ of Oxford (DPhil); *m* 1993, Lucy Elliot, da of A D Buckingham; 1 da (Carola Barbara b 1995), 1 s (Peter Amyand Jeffrey b 1998); *Career* Univ of Oxford: fell Magdalen Coll 1975–79, fell and tutor in physics Merton Coll 1981–2007 (professorial fell 2007–), univ lectr 1981–90, ad hominem reader in theoretical physics 1990–96, prof of physics 1996–; Princeton Univ: Lindemann fell 1976, visiting asst prof in astrophysical sciences 1979–81, sometime visiting fell; Fairchild distinguished scholar Caltech 1983, visitor Inst of Advanced Study; IAU: pres Cmmn 33 1994–97, pres Div VII 1994–97; memb: Theory Panel SERC 1986–88, Theoretical Research Panel PPARC 1997–99 and 2005–06, Jt Infrastructure Bd PPARC 1999–2000; Maxwell Prize and Medal Inst of Physics 1986, Brouwer Award American Astronomical Soc 2003, Dirac Medal Inst of Physics 2010, Eddington Medal Royal Astronomical Soc 2013, Medal of the Inst Astrophysique de Paris 2013; memb American Astronomical Soc 1976; FRAS 1973, FRS 2000, FInstP 2000; *Books* Galactic Astronomy (jtly, 1981), Galactic Dynamics (jtly, 1987 and 2008), Pick for Humans (jtly, 1990), The Theory of Critical Phenomena (jtly, 1992), Galactic Astronomy (jtly, 1998), The Physics of Quantum Mechanics (jtly, 2008); *Recreations* wood, metal and stone work, walking; *Style*— Prof James Binney; ✉ Rudolf Peierls Centre for Theoretical Physics, University of Oxford, 1 Keble Road, Oxford OX1 3NP (☎ 01865 273979, fax 01865 273947, e-mail binney@thphys.ox.ac.uk)

BINNIE, Ann; da of late Jeffery Wyatt, of Brackley, Northants, and late Doreen Eugenie, *née* Manly; *b* 10 March 1953; *Educ* Brentwood Co HS for Girls, Univ of Bradford (BSc, MSc); *m* 8 Sept 1973, late David John Binnie, s of late Harold F Binnie; 1 da (Isla Jane b 28 Sept 1987), 1 s (Jamie Joe b 24 July 1990); *Career* staff: Br Inst of Mgmnt 1975–77, Rex Stewart Group 1977–79, W S Crawford 1979–80; various positions rising to bd planning dir DMB&B (formerly DMM) 1980–87, bd planning dir/head of planning KHBB 1987–90, planning conslt 1990–92, bd planning dir/head of planning Arc Advertising 1992–94; planning conslt to ad hoc clients and retained by: Group X (for Royal Mail and Budgens), Arc Advertising (for BBC Network Radio and Reckitt & Colman) 1994–; fndr: Ann Binnie Brand Planning 1996 (planning conslt to clients incl: ARCOM, Ogilvy, The Communications Unit, The Children's Society, Landor, JWTSC, Mongrel Worlds Ltd, Grey Advertising), Enneagram Facilitators 1998 (conslt to clients incl: Young & Rubicam, Henley Centre, Grey Advertising, Lloyds TSB), Amethist 2000 (mktg conslt to clients incl: Pedigree Masterfoods, AT Cross, Norwich Union, JWT, Landor, Ogilvy & Mather, More, Freestone, Charities Aid Fndn, BP, Reputation Inst), Brand Architects 2000 (brand strategy and design conslt to clients incl: Tradelink, Hummingbird Bakery, Corio); fndr Tovera Consulting (corporate brand and reputation strategy conslt) 2015; tutor European Communications Sch 2012–, certified teacher of Enneagram in Narrative Tradition with Helen Palmer, Enneagram self-awareness and leadership devpt Mercedes-Benz UK and Reputation Inst 2013, special adviser, brand and qualitative research, coaching, training Reputation Inst 2013–; special advsr Reputation Inst 2012–15; memb Judging Panel APA ICM Awards 2000–12; memb Judging Panel DBA Effectiveness Awards 1990 and 1992, memb Judging Panel APA ICM Awards 2000–; memb: MRS, Mktg Soc, Ind Conslts Gp (ICG); FRSA; *Recreations* reading, theatre, life drawing, yoga, singing, local community activity; *Style*— Mrs Ann Binnie; ✉ Amethist (mobile 07778 675987, e-mail ann@amethist.co.uk, website www.tovera.consulting and http://uk.linkedin.com/in.annbinnie, Twitter @AnnBinnie)

BINNIE, Prof Colin David; s of Horace David Binnie, of Leigh-on-Sea, Essex, and Doris Amy, *née* Read (d 1966); *Educ* Felsted, Univ of Cambridge (MD, MA, BCh), Guy's Hosp Med Sch; *m* 1, 31 Oct 1964, (Florence) Margaret, da of George Shields (d 1980); 1 da (Caroline b 1965), 1 s (Nicholas b 1968); m 2, 11 April 2006, Alexandra Vivien MacKay, widow of Geoffery Eldin-Taylor; *Career* physician i/c Dept of Clinical Neurophysiology Bart's and Southend Hosp 1972–76, head of clinical neurophysiology serv Inst Voor Epilepsie Bestrjding Heemstede Netherlands 1976–86, conslt clinical neurophysiologist Bethlem Royal Hosp and Maudsley Hosp 1986–, clinical dir of neurosciences 1991–95, prof of clinical neurophysiology GKT 1995–2003, emeritus prof of clinical neuroscience GKT 2003–; visiting prof of physiology UCL; pres British Soc for Clinical Neurophysiology, chm Neurosurgical Cmmn of International League against Epilepsy; memb: Int League Against Epilepsy, chm Electroencephalography and Clinical Neurophysiology Educnl Bd, Electrophysiological Tech Assoc, RSM 1965, Assoc Br Clinical Neurophysiologists 1970, Br Assoc for Neuropsychiatry 1988, Assoc of British Neurologists; MRCS, FRCPGlas, FRCP; *Publications* A Manual of Electroencephalographic Technology (1982), Biorhythms and Epilepsy (1986), Clinical Neurophysiology (vol 1 2003, vol 2 2005), numerous pubns on Electroencephalography and Epilepsy; *Recreations* opera, languages; *Style*— Prof Colin Binnie; ✉ Department of Clinical Neurophysiology, King's College Hospital, Denmark Hill, London SE5 9RS (☎ 020 7346 4342, fax 020 7346 3725, e-mail colin.binnie@kcl.ac.uk)

BINNS, Malcolm; s of Douglas Priestley Binns (d 1988), of Keighley, W Yorks, and May, *née* Walker; *b* 29 January 1936; *Educ* Bradford GS, RCM; *Career* prof RCM 1961–65; concert pianist: London debut 1959, debut Promenade Concerts 1960, regular performances at Proms 1962–, Royal Festival Hall debut 1961, has appeared in London Philharmonic seasons 1962–; soloist with all major Br orchs, over 30 recordings, first complete recording of Beethoven Piano Sonatas on original instruments, played Far E and toured with Scot Nat Orch and Limbourg Orch 1987–88; ARCM; *Recreations* gardening; *Style*— Malcolm Binns, Esq; ✉ c/o Michael Harrold Artist Management, 13 Clinton Road, Leatherhead, Surrey KT22 8NU (☎ 01372 375728)

BINTLEY, David Julian; CBE (2001); s of David Bintley, of Honley, W Yorks, and Glenys, *née* Ellinthorpe; *b* 17 September 1957; *Educ* Holme Valley GS, Royal Ballet Upper Sch; *m* 12 Dec 1981, Jennifer Catherine Ursula, da of Bernard Mills, of San Diego, CA; 2 s (Michael b 21 March 1985, Gabriel b 7 Sept 1995); *Career* Sadler's Wells Royal Ballet 1976–86: debut The Outsider 1978, resident choreographer and princ dancer 1983–86; resident choreographer and princ dancer Royal Ballet 1986–93, freelance 1993–95, artistic dir Birmingham Royal Ballet 1995–, artistic dir Nat Ballet of Japan 2010–14; other works incl: Galanteries 1986, Allegri Diversi 1987, Hobson's Choice 1989, Edward II 1995, Carmina Burana 1995; Evening Standard Award for Choros and Consort Lessons 1983, Olivier Award for performance in Petrushka (title role) 1984, Manchester Evening News Award for Still Life at the Penguin Café 1988, De Valois Award for Outstanding Achievement 2000, Lifetime Achievement Award Whats On Magazine 2016; Hon DUniv Univ of Central England 1999, Hon DLett Univ of Birmingham 2001; *Style*— David Bintley, Esq, CBE; ✉ Birmingham Royal Ballet, Hippodrome Theatre, Thorp Street, Birmingham B5 4AU (☎ 0121 622 2555, fax 0121 689 3070, e-mail davidbintley@brb.org.uk)

BION, Dr Julian Fleetwood; s of Dr Wilfred Ruprecht Bion, DSO (d 1979), and Francesca, *née* Purnell; *b* 30 July 1952; *Educ* Harrow, Charing Cross Hosp, Univ of London (MB BS); *m* 15 June 1985, Nitaya, da of Sanit Tangchurat (d 1979), of Bangkok, Thailand; 2 c (Alexander, Victoria (twins) b 14 April 1992); *Career* previous appts in anaesthesia, gen med and cardiology, sr anaesthetist Red Cross surgical team Thai-Cambodian border 1983; Univ of Birmingham: sr lectr in intensive care 1989–97, reader in intensive care med 1997–; former memb Editorial Bds: British Jl of Hosp Med, Clinical Intensive Care, Intensive Care Med, Intensive and Critical Care Nursing; author of numerous publications on aspects of intensive care med, audit, infection-prevention, outcome prediction and scoring systems; BUPA Med Fndn Dr of the Year award 1985; pres European Soc of Intensive Care Med (memb Cncl) 2004–06; memb: Intensive Care Soc UK (memb Cncl 1993–99), Assoc of Anaesthetists, BMA, Intercollegiate Bd for Trg in Intensive Care Med (chair competency-based trg working gp) 1998–2004; advsr Commonwealth Scholarships Cmmn; FFARCS 1982, FRCA 1988, MD 1991, FRCP 1996 (MRCP 1980); *Style*— Dr Julian Bion; ✉ University of Birmingham, N5, Queen Elizabeth Hospital, Birmingham B15 2TH (☎ 0121 627 2060, fax 0121 627 2062)

BIRCH, Carol; da of Frederick Fidler (d 1981), and Nancy, *née* Rowe (d 1989); *b* 3 January 1951; *Educ* Manchester Central GS for Girls, Keele Univ (BA); *m* 1, 1981 (m dis 1990), Leonard William Birch; m 2, 1990, Martin Lucas Butler, s of Arthur Butler; 2 s (Joseph Lucas b 1989, Richard Lyman b 1991); *Career* author; memb Soc of Authors 1988; *Books* Life in the Palace (1988, David Higham Prize for Best First Novel), The Fog Line (1989, Geoffrey Faber Meml Award 1991), The Unmaking (1992), Songs of the West (1994), Little Sister (1998), Come Back, Paddy Riley (1999), Turn Again Home (2003), In a Certain Light (2004), The Naming of Eliza Quinn (2005), Scapegallows (2007), Jamrach's Menagerie (2011, nominated Booker Prize 2011); *Recreations* reading, research, drawing, music, theatre; *Style*— Ms Carol Birch; ✉ c/o Mic Cheetham Agency, 50 Albemarle Street, London W1S 4BD

BIRCH, Clive Francis William; MBE (2001); s of Raymond William Birch, CBE (d 1980), and (Olive Edith Charlton) Valerie, *née* Fry (d 2000); *b* 22 December 1931; *Educ* Uppingham; *m* 1, 1957 (m dis 1961), Gillian May, *née* Coulson; m 2, 1961 (m dis 1978), Penelope Helen, *née* Harman; 1 s (James b 1962), 1 da (Emma b 1964), 1 adopted s (Richard b 1957), 1 adopted da (Cally b 1959); m 3, 16 April 1983, Carolyn Rose, da of Thomas Desborough (d 1978); 1 step da (Katie b 1970), 1 step s (Jamie b 1974); *Career* Nat Serv radar RAF 1950–52; office jr Stretford Telegraph 1952, reporter Stockport Express 1952, dist reporter Kent and Sussex Courier 1953, chief reporter Herts Newspapers 1954, ed Bucks Examiner 1956, press offr Frigidaire Div General Motors Ltd 1958, product devpt Metro-Cammell Weyman Ltd 1959, gp advertisement mangr Modern Transport Publishing Co Ltd 1965, mangr Electrical Press Ltd 1966; dir: Birch Bros Ltd 1966–2011, Illustrated Newspapers Ltd 1969; ed Illustrated London News 1970, dir Northwood Publications Ltd 1971, md designate Textile Trade Pubns Ltd 1972, publishing dir Mercury House Ltd 1973, fndr chm Barracuda Books Ltd 1974–92, dir Quotes Ltd 1985–97, princ Radmore Birch Associates 1991–, dir TLC Pharmacies Ltd 1995–98, fndr Baron Books 1997–, publishing conslt Boltneck Publications Ltd 2005–06, publishing dir Boltneck Publications Ltd and Medavia Publishing 2006–10; RCA: fndr Carmen Research Fellowship 2001, visiting lectr 2002–, Carman visiting tutor 2003–, memb Ct 2007–, pathway ldr (urban flow) 2007–10, fndr Carmen Research Readership 2008, RCA managing ptnr London Tport Museum 2010– (memb Futures Bd 2012–, memb Acad Advsy panel 2015–); visiting lectr Boston Univ (London Sch) 2006–; fndr chm Buckingham and Dist Chamber of Trade Commerce and Industry 1983; pres Buckingham Heritage Tst 1997–2001 (founder chm 1985), tstee Camberwell Housing Soc 2002–16; hon life memb: Chiltern Car Club 1956, Inst of the Royal Corps of Tport 1985; govr Royal Latin Sch Buckingham 1989–93, former memb Cncl Chesham Round Table; Freeman City of London 1960; Worshipful Co of Carmen: Freeman and Liveryman 1960, memb Ct of Assts 1969–, Master 1984–85, Dep Master 1988–89, hon ed 2002–, memb Awards Ctee 1969–2008 (chm 1999–2008, advsr 2010–), fndr chm Charity Ball 1985, chm RSA Carmen Lectures 1991–2011, chm Media and Mktg Ctee 1994–2007, chm Past Masters 2004–08, sr past master 2005–, chm Livery Ctee 2008–10, chm Tport Ctee 2008–09, memb Membership Ctee 2008–10; HRH The Princess Royal Gold Medal 2008; FRSA 1980, FSA 1981; Chevalier Confrérie des Chevaliers du Trou Normand 1991; *Books* incl: The Book of Chesham (1974, 4 edn 1997), The Book of Aylesbury (1975, 3 edn 1993), The Freedom-History and Guilds of the City of London (jtly, 1982), Buckingham in Camera (1987), Chiltern Thames in Camera (1990), Yesterday's Town: Amersham (jtly, 1991), Old Milton Keynes in Camera (1992), On the Move – The Road Haulage Association 1945–94 (jtly, 1995), Wish You Were Here: Buckingham (1997), Wish You Were Here: Chesham (1997), Carr & Carman (1999), Royal College of Art Vehicle Design (ed, annually 2006–15), A Decent Man (novel, 2006), Moving Forward (assoc author, 2006), What's in it for You? (ed, 2012), Gold to Gulag (e-novel, 2013), Visicon: Light the Car (2015); *Style*— Clive Birch, MBE; ✉ Radmore Birch Associates, King's Cote, Valley Road, Finmere, Buckingham MK18 4AL (☎ 01280 848847, e-mail clive.birch@booksbybaron.co.uk)

BIRCH, Prof David; s of late James William Birch, and late Hilda Mary, *née* Gibbons; *b* 19 December 1949, Southport, Lancs; *Educ* Victoria Univ of Manchester (BSc, PhD); *m* 1976, Gilly Bonny; 1 s (Samuel b 1988); *Career* temp lectr in physics Victoria Univ of Manchester 1974–75, mass spectrometry physicist VG Micromass Ltd 1976–78; Univ of Strathclyde: lectr in applied physics 1978, sr lectr in physics and applied physics 1987, reader in physics and applied physics 1990, prof of photophysics 1993–, dir Femtosecond Research Centre 1994–, head Dept of Physics 2004–10, co-dir Centre for Molecular Nanometrology 2005–; visiting scientist Univ of Perugia 1975, Sir C V Raman Endowment visiting chair Univ of Madras 1999, visiting prof Kyoto Inst of Technol 2000, visiting prof of applied physics Czech Tech Univ Prague 2002–; Royal Soc industrial research fell 1987 and 1989, Nuffield Fndn science research fell 1988, Japanese Soc for the Promotion of Science visiting research fell 2000; memb: Scientific Advsy Bd Kalibrant Ltd 1997–2002, Physics and Astronomy Sectional Ctee RSE 2003–06, Enterprise Fellowships Ctee RSE 2003–06, Scottish Univs Physics Alliance Exec Ctee 2004–10, EPSRC and BBSRC Colls 2005–, Research Fellowships Ctee RSE 2007–10, Int Exchanges Ctee RS 2010–; ed-in-chief Measurement Science and Technology 2012–, co-ed-in-chief Methods App Fluorescence 2012–; memb Editorial Bd: Jl of Fluorescence 1990–2002, Jl of Biomedical Optics 1995–, Measurement Science and Technology 2000–, Research on Chemical Intermediates 2002–03; author of over 200 jl pubns on molecular fluorescence, sensors, optical techniques and bionanotechnology; fndr co-dir IBH Ltd 1977–2003, dir Horiba Jobin Yvon IBH Ltd 2004–; FInstP, CPhys 1986, FRSC, CChem 2001, FRSE 2003; *Recreations* orinthology; *Style*— Prof David Birch; ✉ University of Strathclyde, Glasgow G4 0NG (☎ 0141 548 3377, e-mail djs.birch@strath.ac.uk)

BIRCH, Paul; s of Ronald Arthur Birch (d 1997), and Dorothy, *née* Channer; *b* 22 March 1952; *Educ* Dr Challoner's GS, AA Sch of Architecture (AADipl); *m* 1988, Janet, *née* Simpson; 1 s (James b 1989); *Career* architect; with GMW Partnership 1976–82 (projects incl Univ of Riyadh Saudi Arabia, Mobil HQ Strand London and office building Monument London), assoc Covell Matthews Wheatley Partnership 1982–88 (projects incl offices in Ropemaker St London, Appold St London and Swindon), dir Hamilton Architects Ltd 1988–2010 (projects incl offices in Bow Churchyard London and 40 Berkeley Square London, Plough Place London (Commerical Bldg of the Year 2001), and HQs for Burmah Castrol, AIT and Perpetual), conslt Grid Architects Ltd 2010–11, md HKR Architects Ltd 2011–12 (projects incl offices Moorgate Exchange Fore Street City of London), ptnr Starc Architects LLP 2012–; sometime contrib of articles on commercial office buildings Property Week magazine; RIBA 1982, ARB 1982, FRSA 2006; *Recreations* motor racing, football, theatre, cinema, travel; *Style*— Paul Birch; ✉ Starc

Architects LLP, 39 Bear Lane, London SE1 0UH (☎ 07831 212443, e-mail paul.birch@starc-architects.com, website www.starc-architects.com)

BIRCH, Paul John; JP (West Midlands 1999); s of Harrold James Birch, and Beryl, *née* Saul (d 1994); *b* 12 November 1954, Croydon; *Educ* Aston Univ, J L Kellogg Business Sch Northwestern Univ Chicago, Richard Ivey Business Sch Univ of Western Ontario (ATCO Calgary RD Southern scholar), Univ of Wolverhampton Business Sch (MBA); *m* 12 Sept 1992, Olivia, *née* Darling; 1 s (Joshua Harrison b 22 Sept 1991), 2 da (Hannah Rachael b 20 Jan 1995, Eleanor Louise b 17 Sept 2003); *Career* cr cr Heavy Metal Records 1979, cr Revolver Records 1980 (acts incl Stone Roses, Jayne's Addiction, Diamond Head, UFO, Misfits, Scorpions, UK Subs and Vibrators, catalogue of 4000 copyrights), developed Revolver Recording studios 1990, awarded more than 20 gold discs; cr MIDEM venture and trade show, launched Br Midlands Music 2007, launched Revolver World 2009 (not-for-profit prodr of Fairtrade organic cotton, with surplus to eleviate childhood poverty in the developing world); visiting lectr in business strategy Brimingham Univ Business Sch; memb Bd: BPI 1990– (former chair Educn Ctee and Int Ctee, former memb Copyright Strategy Ctee), Phonographic Performance Ltd 1998 (co-chair Int Ctee until 2005, memb New Business Ctee), IFPI (memb European Exec Ctee and Main Bd); sec: UK Trade Investment North American Alumni Assoc DTI, Music West Midlands, North American Scholarship Assoc; memb Bd Birmingham-Chicago Sister City Ctee; former chair Victim Support charity; govr Wolverhampton GS, helped launch Birmingham Univ Business Sch's Innovation Exchange; hon fell Univ of Wolverhampton 2015; MBPI 1981, FCIM 1995, AIM 1996 (fndr memb); *Publications* The Record Industry and the Community, Creating Competitive Advantage Through Knowledge, Music UK – Music and the Regions; *Recreations* family, church, business, music; *Style*— Paul John Birch, JP; ✉ Revolver Music Ltd, 152 Goldthorn Hill, Penn, Wolverhampton WV2 3JA (☎ 01902 345345, fax 01902 345155, e-mail paul.birch@revolverrecords.com, website www.revolverworld.com, Twitter @RevolverWorld)

BIRD, Baron (Life Peer UK 2015), of Notting Hill in the Royal Borough of Kensington and Chelsea; A John Bird; MBE (1995); s of Alfred Ernest Bird (d 1983), and Eileen Mary, *née* Dunne (d 1973); *b* 30 January 1946; *Educ* St Thomas More's Secdy Modern, Chelsea Sch of Art, Ealing Coll of HE (BA); *m* 1, 30 August 1965 (m dis 1971), Linda, *née* Haston; 1 da (Emily Jane b 3 April 1966); m 2, 10 March 1973 (m dis 2004), Isobel Theresa, *née* Ricketts; 1 s (Patrick Jack b 12 August 1975), 1 da (Eileen Diana b 15 November 1977); m 3, Parveen Kaur Sodhi; 1 s (Sonny John b 2005), 1 da (Ishpriya Maria b 2006); *Career* currently prop and ed-in-chief The Big Issue; pres Oxford Univ Homeless Action Gp; advsr Sch for Social Entrepreneurs; visiting prof Lincoln Univ; pres Friends of 18th Century Soc; Eds' Ed of the Year Award 1994; Hon Dr Oxford Brookes Univ 2001; fell Liverpool John Moores Univ; MInstD 1998; *Publications* The Necessity of Poverty (2012), Why Drawing Naked Women is Good for the Soul (2013); *Recreations* cycling, reading, writing, dancing, walking; *Style*— The Lord Bird, MBE; ✉ The Big Issue, 113–115 Fonthill Road, London N4 3HH (☎ 020 7526 3200, fax 020 7526 3261, e-mail john.bird@bigissue.com, website www.bigissue.com)

BIRD, Prof Colin Carmichael; CBE (2000); s of John G C Bird (ka Italy 1943), and Sarah, *née* Carmichael (d 2007); *b* 5 March 1938; *Educ* Lenzie Acad, Univ of Glasgow (MB ChB, PhD); *m* 20 March 1964, Ailsa Mary, *née* Ross; 1 da (Elayne b 10 Jan 1965), 2 s (Scott b 4 May 1966, Alan b 7 Dec 1971); *Career* lectr in pathology: Univ of Glasgow 1965–67 (McGhie cancer research fell 1963–65), Univ of Aberdeen 1967–72; MRC (Goldsmith's) travelling fell Univ of Chicago 1970–71; sr lectr in pathology Univ of Edinburgh 1972–75, prof and head Dept of Pathology Univ of Leeds 1975–86; Univ of Edinburgh: prof and head Dept of Pathology 1986–95, provost Faculty of Med and Veterinary Med 1995–2002, dean Faculty of Med 1995–2002, emeritus prof 2002; author of approx 200 pubns in various scientific jls on cancer and cancer genetics; memb: Pathological Soc of GB and I 1964 (hon fell 2006), Assoc of Clinical Pathologists 1976 (hon fell 2001); Dr (hc) Univ of Edinburgh 2004; FRCPath 1978, FRCPEd 1989, FRSE 1992, FRCSEd 1995, FAMS 1998; Knight's Cross of Merit (Poland) 2006; *Recreations* golf, walking, reading and music; *Clubs* New (Edinburgh), HCEG, R&A; *Style*— Prof Colin C Bird, CBE, FRSE; ✉ 45 Ann Street, Edinburgh EH4 1PL (☎ 0131 332 5568, e-mail colin@colinailsa.com)

BIRD, Michael George; OBE (2000); s of George Bird, and Margaret, *née* Stephens; *b* 5 January 1960; *Educ* Bedales (scholar), Emmanuel Coll Cambridge (senior scholar, MA), Voronezh Univ (British Cncl scholar), Harvard Univ (Kennedy scholar); *m* 12 April 2003, Simone Lees; *Career* British Council: London 1985–87, Moscow 1987–91, UK Research and HE Liaison Office Brussels 1991–93, regnl dir St Petersburg and North-West Russia 1993–97, dir Ukraine 1997–2001, dir Scotland 2001–05, dir Germany 2005–09, regnl dir SE Europe 2009–10, regnl dir wider Europe 2011–15, dir Russia 2015–; *Style*— Michael Bird, Esq, OBE; ✉ British Council, Ulitsa Nikoloyamskaya 1, Moscow 109189, Russia (e-mail michael.bird@britishcouncil.org)

BIRD, Stephen; *Educ* St John's Coll Cambridge (MA); *Career* divnl md Weir Oil & Gas 2005–09, chief exec Vitec Gp plc 2009–; non-exec dir Umeco plc; *Style*— Stephen Bird, Esq; ✉ Vitec Group plc, Bridge House, Heron Square, Richmond TW9 1EN

BIRD, (Irene) Veronica; OBE (2002); da of late George Bird, and late Ethel, *née* Goodlad; *Educ* Ackworth Sch Pontefract; *Career* prison offr HMP Holloway and HMP Pucklechurch 1968–73, princ offr HMP Styal 1973–78, chief offr HMP Risley 1978–82; dep govr: HMP Styal 1982–87, HMP Thorn Cross 1987–91, HMP Armley 1991–94; controller HMP Buckley Hall 1994–98; govr: HMP Brock Hill 1998–2000, HMP New Hall 2000–; winner Butler Tst Award 2000; tstee Shannon Tst; memb Prison Govrs Assoc 1982; *Recreations* gardening, swimming, interior design, photography, travel, after dinner speaking; *Clubs* Harrogate Luncheon (chm); *Style*— Miss Veronica Bird, OBE; ✉ 100 Cornwall Road, Harrogate, North Yorkshire HG1 2NG (☎ 01423 569316)

BIRDWOOD, 3 Baron (UK 1938), of Anzac and of Totnes, Devon; Sir Mark William Ogilvie Birdwood; 3 Bt (UK 1919); s of 2 Baron, MVO (d 1962), and (Elizabeth) Vere Drummond, CVO (d 1997), da of Lt-Col Sir George Drummond Ogilvie, KCIE, CSI; *b* 23 November 1938; *Educ* Radley, Trinity Coll Cambridge; *m* 27 April 1963, Judith Helen, er da of Reginald Gordon Seymour Roberts; 1 da (Sophie); *Career* former 2 Lt RHG; chm: Martlet Ltd 1986–, Fiortho Ltd 1992–2002, Steeltower Ltd; dir: IMS plc 1997–2000, The Character Group plc 1997–, Jasmin plc 1998–2000; memb House of Lords Select Ctee on Sci and Technol 1999–2000; head of fundraising Centre for Philosophy of Natural and Social Sci LSE; memb Terra Consilia (Terra Firma Capital Partners strategy cncl); Liveryman Worshipful Co of Glaziers & Painters of Glass 1975–2009; *Clubs* Brooks's, Pratt's; *Style*— The Rt Hon the Lord Birdwood; ✉ Russell House, Broadway, Worcestershire WR12 7BU; 5 Holbein Mews, London SW1W 8NW (e-mail mbirdwood@gmail.com)

BIRKENHEAD, Bishop of 2007–; Rt Rev (Gordon) Keith Sinclair; s of Donald Sinclair (d 1975), and Joyce, *née* Ellis; *b* 3 December 1952, Westminster; *Educ* ChCh Oxford (MA), St John's Coll and Cranmer Hall Univ of Durham (BA); *m* 6 May 1989, Rosemary, *née* Jones; 2 s (Peter b 10 June 1992, David b 6 Sept 1996), 1 da (Anna b 14 Sept 1993); *Career* admitted slr 1979; ordained church min 1984; formerly vicar: Birmingham, Coventry; chair Govt Interim Partnership Bd New Deal for Communities Aston; *Style*— The Rt Rev the Bishop of Birkenhead; ✉ Bishop's Lodge, 67 Bidston Road, Prenton, Wirral, Merseyside CH43 6TR (☎ 0151 652 2741, e-mail bpbirkenhead@chester.anglican.org)

BIRKETT, Aidan; *b* 22 February 1953; *Educ* St Cuthbert's GS Newcastle upon Tyne; *m* Maureen; 2 c (Alex, Thomas); *Career* global head of business recovery servs PricewaterhouseCoopers until 2001, currently managing ptnr corporate finance and memb Exec Ctee Deloitte; Professional of the Year Soc of Turnaround Professionals 2002; ACA 1977, ACT 1980; *Recreations* food, drink, music, opera, travel, motor cars; *Style*— Aidan Birkett, Esq; ✉ Deloitte & Touche LLP, Athene Place, 66 Shoe Lane, London EC4A 3BQ

BIRKETT, 2 Baron (UK 1958); Michael Birkett; s of 1 Baron Birkett (d 1962); *b* 22 October 1929; *Educ* Stowe, Trinity Coll Cambridge; *m* 1978, Gloria (d 2001), da of Thomas Taylor, of Queen's Gate, London; 1 s (Hon Thomas b 25 July 1982); *Heir* s, Hon Thomas Birkett; *Career* film prodr 1961–; prodns incl: The Caretaker, Marat/Sade, A Midsummer Night's Dream, King Lear; dep dir Nat Theatre 1975–77, conslt to Nat Theatre on films, TV and sponsorship 1977–79, dir Recreation and the Arts GLC 1979–86; govr BRIT Sch for Performing Arts and Technol Croydon 1980–; chm Donatella Flick Conducting Competition 1990–2008; Master Worshipful Co of Curriers' 1975–76; *Recreations* the arts; *Style*— The Rt Hon the Lord Birkett; ✉ Great Allfields, Balls Cross, Petworth, West Sussex GU28 9JU (☎ 01403 820226)

BIRKETT, Peter Vidler; QC (1989); s of Neville Lawn Birkett, JP, of Kendal, Cumbria, and Marjorie Joy, *née* Vidler; *b* 13 July 1948; *Educ* Sedbergh, Univ of Leicester (LLB); *m* 11 Dec 1976, Jane Elizabeth, da of Robert Hall Fell, MBE (d 1981); 2 s (Nicholas Robert b 12 Dec 1984, Michael Peter Vidler b 20 Dec 1986); *Career* called to the Bar Inner Temple 1972 (bencher 1996); barr N Circuit 1972–, recorder of the Crown Court 1989–, leader N Circuit 1999–2001; actg deemster IOM; memb Gen Cncl of the Bar; *Recreations* golf, music, travel, conversation, Manchester United FC; *Clubs* Wilmslow Golf; *Style*— Peter Birkett, Esq, QC; ✉ 18 St John Street, Manchester M3 4EA (☎ 0161 278 1800)

BIRKHEAD, Prof Timothy Robert; s of Robert Harold Birkhead, and Nancy Olga, *née* Thomson; *b* 20 February 1950, Leeds; *Educ* Univ of Newcastle upon Tyne (BSc), Wolfson Coll Oxford (DPhil); *m* 25 Sept 1976, Miriam Enid, *née* Appleton; 3 c; *Career* Dept of Animal and Plant Sciences Univ of Sheffield: lectr 1976–86, sr lectr 1986–89, reader 1989–92, prof of behavioral ecology 1992–; pres Int Soc for Behavioral Ecology 1996–98; co-fndr New Networks for Nature; Consul Cremer Prize 2003, Senate Award for Sustained Excellence in Teaching Univ of Sheffield 2007, Teacher of the Year Award Dept of Animal & Plant Sciences Univ of Sheffield 2009, Elliot Coues Medal American Ornithologists' Union 2011, Assoc for the Study of Animal Behaviour Medal 2012, Best Bird Book of 2012 (for Bird Sense), UK Bioscience Teacher of the Year 2013, Silver Medal ZSL 2014, Eisenmann Medal Linnean Soc of NY 2016, Godman-Salvin Medal Br Ornithologists' Union 2016; Nuffield research fell 1990–91, Leverhulme research fell 1995–96; Hon DSc Univ of Newcastle upon Tyne 1989; FRS 2004; *Books* Avian Ecology (with C M Perrins, 1983), The Atlantic Alcidae (ed with D N Nettleship, 1985), The Survival Factor (with M E Birkhead, 1989), The Magpies (1991), The Cambridge Encyclopedia of Ornithology (1991, McColvin Medal), Sperm Competition in Birds (1992), Great Auk Islands (1993), Sperm Competition and Sexual Selection (1998), Promiscuity (2000), The Red Canary (2003, Consul Cremer Prize), The Wisdom of Birds (2008), Bird Sense (2012), Ten Thousand Birds: Ornithology Since Darwin (co-author, 2014), The Most Perfect Thing: the Inside (and Outside) of a Bird's Egg (2016); author of articles in pubns incl Nature and Science; *Recreations* art, music, walking; *Style*— Prof Timothy Birkhead; ✉ Department of Animal and Plant Sciences, University of Sheffield, Western Bank, Sheffield S10 2TN (☎ 0114 222 4622, fax 0114 222 0002, e-mail t.r.birkhead@sheffield.ac.uk)

BIRKIN, Sir John Christian William; 6 Bt (UK 1905), of Ruddington Grange, Ruddington, Notts; o s of Sir Charles Lloyd Birkin, 5 Bt (d 1985), and Janet Ramsay, *née* Johnson (d 1983); *b* 2 July 1953, Dublin, Ireland; *Educ* Eton, TCD, London Film Sch; *m* 25 June 1994, Emma Louise, da of Roger Leonard Gage, of Aveton Gifford, S Devon; 1 s (Benjamin Charles b 4 Nov 1995), 1 da (Daisy Burda b 17 Dec 2000); *Heir* s, Benjamin Birkin; *Career* TV dir 1978–2001, commercials dir 2001–; dir The Great Barn Devon; *Style*— Sir John Birkin, Bt; ✉ c/o The Great Barn, Higher Ashton, Exeter EX6 7QP

BIRLEY, Prof Susan Joyce (Sue); *Educ* UCL (BSc), Harvard Univ (Int Teachers Prog scholar), Univ of London (PhD); *Career* advanced and scholarship mathematics teacher Dunsmore Sch 1964–66, lectr in quantitative aspects Dept of Economics and Mgmnt Lanchester Poly 1966–68, sr lectr in business policy Mgmnt Sch Poly of Central London 1970–72 (lectr in quantitative methods 1968–70), sr research fell City Univ 1972–74; London Business Sch: lectr in small business 1974–79, sr research fell Inst of Small Business 1979–82, dir New Enterprise Prog 1979–82; assoc prof of strategy and entrepreneurship Coll of Business Univ of Notre Dame USA 1982–85 (adjunct assoc prof 1978–82), Philip & Pauline Harris prof of entrepreneurship Cranfield Sch of Mgmnt Cranfield Inst of Technology 1985–90 (also dir of research and dir Cranfield Entrepreneurship Research Centre), dir of research and prof of mgmnt in the field of entrepreneurship Mgmnt Sch ICSTM 1990–2003; visiting prof INSEAD 1991 (visiting lectr 1978); fndr dir: The Guidehouse Group plc 1980–85, Greyfriars Ltd 1982–85, Newchurch & Co (chm) 1986–97; non-exec dir: National Westminster Bank plc 1996–2000, PSE Ltd 1997–2003, BAE Systems plc 2000–; advsr Dept of Econ Devpt NI 1985–88, academic dir Euro Fndn for Entrepreneurship Research 1988–90, vice-chm Exec Ctee Br Acad of Mgmnt 1988–89, govr Harris City Technol Coll 1990–92, bd memb Local Enterprise Devpt Unit (LEDU) N Ireland 1991–93 (advsr 1988–89), currently conslt advsr Grant Thornton; memb: Postgrad Bd CNAA 1979–82, Steering Ctee UK Nat Small Firms Policy and Research Conf 1985–90, Adjudication Ctee Prince of Wales' Award for Innovation 1986–, Bd of Dirs Strategic Mgmnt Soc 1987–90, Cncl NI Econ Cncl 1988–94, Deregulation Advsy Bd DTI 1988–90, Polytechnics and Colls Funding Cncl 1988–93, E European Links Advsy Bd British Cncl 1990–91, Advsy Cncl Sheffield Business Sch 1990–93, Growing Business Target Team Business in the Community 1990–91, Enterprise and Econ Devpt Leadership Team Business in the Community 1992–93, Technology Foresight Steering Gp 1998–; Conf of Teachers of Mgmnt 1986 (also chm), Tenth UK Nat Small Firms Policy and Res Conf 1987, Annual Global Conf on Entrepreneurship Research (jtly) 1990–; author of numerous jl articles, conf papers, reports, case studies and books; Freeman City of London; *Books* The Small Business Casebook (1979), New Enterprises (1982), The British Entrepreneur (jtly, 1990), Building European Ventures (ed, 1990), Mastering Enterprise (1997), Franchising: Pathway to Wealth Creation (2003); *Style*— Prof Sue Birley; ✉ Beech House, Forest Grange, Horsham RH13 6HX

BIRMINGHAM, Archdeacon of; *see:* Osborne, Ven Hayward

BIRRELL, Christopher Ros Stewart; *b* 11 March 1954; *Educ* Radley, Mansfield Coll Oxford (MA); *m* 1984, Georgie; 2 s (Edward b 31 January 1987, Henry b 23 January 1989), 1 da (Claudia b 13 September 1991); *Career* with: Price Waterhouse 1977–82, Matheson & Co Ltd 1982–83, Henderson Admin Ltd 1983–85; gp fin dir SBJ Gp Ltd 1993–2008 (joined 1985), Centrix Insurance Hldgs Ltd 2009–; memb: ICAEW 1981–, ACT 1993–; *Recreations* sailing, shooting, fishing, golf, opera; *Clubs* Flyfishers, Buck's; *Style*— Christopher Birrell; ✉ 25 Turret Grove, London SW4 0ES; Centrix Insurance Holdings Limited, Duke's House, 32–38 Duke's Place, London EC3A 7LP (☎ 020 7280 0130, e-mail christopher.birrell@lonmar.com)

BIRRELL, Ian; s of Norman Alistair Birrell, of Sussex, and Patricia Ann, *née* Foll; *b* 30 January 1962; *Educ* Ampleforth, Univ of Aberdeen (MA), City Univ (Dip Journalism); *m* 1990, Linnet, *née* MacIntyre; 1 s (Hamish b 10 Sept 1991), 1 da (Iona b 16 Oct 1993); *Career* Wolverhampton Express & Star 1985–86, Hampstead & Highgate Express 1987–88; Sunday Times 1988–95: news ed, managing ed News Review; dep ed Sunday Express 1996, exec ed Daily Mail 1996–98, dep ed The Independent 1998–2010, currently contrib ed Daily Mail and Mail on Sunday; co-fndr Africa Express; *Recreations* Everton FC, diving, munro-bagging, guitar, music; *Style*— Ian Birrell, Esq

BIRSS, Hon Mr Justice; Sir Colin Ian Birss; kt (2013), QC (2008); s of Dr Ian Birss, and Davina, *née* Carson; *b* 28 December 1964, Thurso, Caithness; *Educ* Largs Acad, Lancaster Royal GS, Downing Coll Cambridge (MA, exhibitioner), City Univ London (Dip); *m* 1 Aug 1987, Kate, *née* Squibbs; 2 s (Arnot b 27 March 1993, Ned b 27 Dec 1994), 1 da (Dorothea b 31 May 2001); *Career* called to the Bar Middle Temple 1990 (Stanley Levy Prize 1990); UKAEA 1983, Arthur Andersen & Co 1986–88, memb Chambers of Simon Thorley, QC 1990–2010, standing counsel to the Comptroller Gen for Patents Designs and Trade Marks 2004–08, chm Copyright Tbnl 2010– (dep chm 2009–10), judge Patents County Court 2010–13, judge of the High Court of Justice (Chancery Div) 2013–; *Books* Terrell on the Law of Patents (15 edn 2000, 16 edn 2006, 17 edn 2011); *Recreations* beekeeping; *Style*— The Hon Mr Justice Birss; ✉ Royal Courts of Justice, Strand, London WC2A 2LL

BIRT, Baron (Life Peer UK 2000), of Liverpool in the County of Merseyside; Sir John Birt; kt (1998); s of Leo Vincent Birt (d 2009), and Ida Birt (d 2005); *b* 10 December 1944; *Educ* St Mary's Coll Liverpool, St Catherine's Coll Oxford (MA); *m* 1, 14 Sept 1965 (m dis 2006), Jane Frances, da of James Harris Lake (d 1982, 2 Lt US Navy), of Chevy Chase, Maryland, USA; 1 s (Jonathan b 1968), 1 da (Eliza b 1971); m 2, 2006, Eithne Victoria Wallis, CB; *Career* prodr Nice Time 1968–69, jt ed World in Action 1969–70, prodr The Frost Programme 1971–72, exec prodr Weekend World 1972–74, head of current affairs LWT 1974–77, co-prodr The Nixon Interviews 1977, controller of features and current affairs LWT 1977–81, dir of programmes LWT 1982–87; BBC: dep DG 1987–92, DG 1992–2000; advsr to the PM on Criminal Justice 2000–01, strategy advsr to the PM 2001–05; memb Cabinet Office Strategy Bd 2003–05; advsr: McKinsey & Co 2000–05, Terra Firma 2005–, Capgemini 2006–10; chm: Lynx New Media (subsequently Lynx Capital Ventures) 2000–04, Waste Recycling Gp 2006, Infinis 2006–07, Host Europe Gp 2013–, CPA Global 2015–; non-exec dir: PayPal (Europe) Ltd 2004–10 (chm 2010–14), Eutelsat 2006– (vice-chm 2012–), Maltby Capital Ltd 2007–10, Infinis 2007–13, Shopcade 2011–; memb: Wilton Park Academic Cncl 1980–83, Media Law Gp 1983–94, Working Pty on the New Technols Broadcasting Research Unit 1981–83 (memb Exec Ctee 1983–87), Opportunity 2000 (formerly Women's Economic) Target Team BITC 1991–98, Int Cncl Museum of TV and Radio NY 1994–2000; visiting fell Nuffield Coll Oxford 1991–99; hon fell St Catherine's Coll Oxford 1992; Hon DLitt: Liverpool John Moores Univ 1992, City Univ 1998, Univ of Bradford 1999, Univ of Westminster 2010; winner Emmy (for outstanding contrib to int TV) 1995; FRTS (vice-pres 1994–2000); *Publications* The Harder Path (autobiography, 2002); various articles in newspapers and jls; *Recreations* football, walking, cinema; *Style*— The Rt Hon the Lord Birt; ✉ House of Lords, London SW1A 0PW

BIRTS, His Hon Peter William; QC (1990), QC (NI 1996); s of John Claude Birts (d 1969), of Sussex, and Audrey Lavinia, *née* McIntyre (d 2015); *b* 9 February 1946, Brighton; *Educ* Lancing, St John's Coll Cambridge (choral scholar, MA); *m* 1, 24 April 1971 (m dis), Penelope Ann, da of Wing Cdr Anthony Eyre, DFC (d 1946); 2 da (Melanie b 1972, Charlotte b 1975), 1 s (William b 1979); m 2, 3 Oct 1997, Angela Forcer-Evans, *née* Sivell; *Career* called to the Bar Gray's Inn 1968 (bencher 1998); recorder of the Crown Court 1989–2005, dep High Court judge 2000–05, circuit judge (SE Circuit) 2005–16, ret; memb: Bar Cncl 1990–95, Judicial Studies Bd 1991–96, County Court Rule Ctee 1991–98; chm Bar Cncl Legal Aid and Fees Ctee 1994–95; asst cmmr Parly Boundary Cmmn for England 1992–2005, legal memb Mental Health Review Tbnls 1994–, legal memb Parole Bd 2006–; govr Benenden Sch 1990–93; Freeman of City of London 1967, Liveryman Worshipful Co of Carpenters 1967 (Jr Warden 2015–16); *Books* Trespass: Summary Procedure for Possession of Land (with Alan Willis, 1987), Remedies for Trespass (1990); author of articles on trespass and countryside law; contrib and ed Butterworths Costs Service (2000–09); *Recreations* music, tennis, skiing, country pursuits; *Clubs* Hurlingham; *Style*— His Hon Peter Birts, QC; ✉ e-mail pbirts@gmail.com

BIRTWISTLE, Adam; s of Sir Harrison Birtwistle, CH, *qv*, and Sheila Margaret Wilhelmina, *née* Duff; *b* 1 April 1959; *Educ* Chelsea Coll of Art; *Career* artist; first one-man show Piano Nobile Galleries London 1986; portrait cmmns incl: Sir Harrison Birtwistle, Sir Peter Blake, Richard Borchard, Alfred Brendel, Elvis Costello, Sir George and Lady Christie, Sir Peter Hall, Peter Harper, David Hockney, Sir Michael Hopkins, Jeremy Irons, Sir Patrick Moore, Paul Myners, Dame Marjorie Scardino, David Sylvester, Sir Michael Tippett, Very Rev Archbishop Desmond Tutu; work displayed: Nat Portrait Gallery, Royal Acad of Music, Sadler's Wells, Glyndebourne, Denver Museum and Art Gallery USA; exhibitions: Admirable Twist: Ten Race Reversal Portraits 2008, Retrospective Exhibition (Atkinson Gall Millfield Sch) 2010; *Publications* Cocks and Faces: recent paintings by Adam Birtwistle (1994), Glyndebourne Programme Book (contrib, 2001), Birtwistle's Beasts: 20 Years of Painting (2006); *Style*— Adam Birtwistle, Esq; ✉ c/o Dr Robert Travers, Piano Nobile Fine Paintings, 129 Portland Road, London W11 4LW (☎ and fax 020 7229 1099, e-mail art@paino-nobile.com)

BIRTWISTLE, Sir Harrison; CH (2001), kt (1988); s of Frederick Birtwistle (d 1985), and Margaret, *née* Harrison (d 1970); *b* 15 July 1934; *Educ* Royal Manchester Coll of Music, Royal Acad of Music London (LRAM); *m* 4 Jan 1958, Sheila Margaret Wilhelmina (d 2012), da of George Duff (d 1986); 3 s (Adam Birtwistle, *qv*, b 1959, Silas b 1963, Thomas b 1965); *Career* composer; associate dir music Nat Theatre London 1976–88, Henry Purcell prof of composition King's Coll London 1995–2001, composer-in-residence LPO, visiting prof of composition Royal Acad of Music; visiting fell Princeton Univ USA 1968, visiting prof of music Swarthmore Coll Pennsylvania USA 1975, Slee visiting prof NY State Univ at Buffalo USA 1977, Harkness fell Univ of Colorado Boulder USA 1969; retrospective Secret Theatres South Bank Centre 1996; Hon FRMCM and ARMCM 1986, Hon FRAM, hon fell Akademie der Kunst Berlin; Chevalier de l'Ordre des Arts et des Lettres (France) 1986; *Works* incl: Tragoedia (1965), Punch and Judy (first staged Aldeburgh Festival 1967), Meridian (1971), The Mask of Orpheus, Ritual Fragment, The Triumph of Time (1972), Secret Theatre (1984), Earth Dances (1986), Gawain (1991), Antiphonies, Nomos, An Imaginary Landscape, The Second Mrs Kong (premiered Glyndebourne 1994), Panic (saxophone concerto premiered BBC Proms 1995), Slow Frieze (1996), Pulse Shadows (1997), Exody (1998), The Woman and the Hare (1999), The Axe Manual (2001), The Shadow of Night (2002), Thesus Game (2003), The Io Passion (2004), Night's Black Bird (2004), Orpheus Elegies (2005), Neruda Madrigales (2006), The Minotaur (2008), The Corridor (2008), Angel Fighter (2009), Trio (2010), Concerto for Violin and Orchestra (2011), In Broken Images (2011), The Moth Requiem (2012), Songs from the Same Earth (2013), Responses (2014), The Silk House Sequences (2015), Fire Lessons in a Frame (2016); *Awards* Evening Standard Award for Opera 1986, Grawemeyer Award Univ Louisville Kentucky USA 1986, Royal Philharmonic Soc Award for large scale composition 1992 (for Gawain), Siemens Prize 1995; *Recreations* fishing, walking; *Style*— Sir Harrison Birtwistle, CH; ✉ c/o Rayfield Allied, Southbank House, Black Prince Road, London SE1 7SJ

BIRTWISTLE, Sue Elizabeth; da of Frank Edgar Birtwistle (d 1987), and Brenda Mary, *née* Higham (d 1998); *m* 14 July 1973, Sir Richard Charles Hastings Eyre, CBE, *qv*, s of Cdr Richard Galfredus Hastings Giles Eyre; 1 da (Lucy b 25 Sept 1974); *Career* theatre dir: Royal Lyceum Theatre in Educn Co 1970–72, Nottingham Playhouse Roundabout Co 1973–78, freelance 1978–80; freelance TV prodr 1980–; work incl: Hotel du Lac (BBC, BAFTA Award 1987, ACE Award 1988), Scoop (LWT), 'v' (Channel 4, RTS Award), Or Shall We Die? (Channel 4), Dutch Girls (LWT), Ball-Trap on the Côte Sauvage (BBC), Anna Lee (LWT) 1993, Pride and Prejudice (BBC) 1995 (4 BAFTA nominations, 4 Emmy nominations, 2 ACE Award nominations, TRIC Award, VVL Award 1995/96, Peabody Award 1996, 2 BANFF Awards incl Victor Laudorum Prize, TV Critics of America Award, BVA Award, English Heritage Award), Emma (ITV) 1996, King Lear (BBC) 1998 (Peabody Award 1999), Wives and Daughters (BBC) 1999 (3 British Press Guild Awards, 5 BAFTA Awards), Armadillo (BBC) 2001, Cranford (BBC) 2007 (4 Broadcasting Press Guild Awards, RTS Award); memb Drama Panel Arts Cncl 1975–77; *Books* The Making of Pride and Prejudice (1995), The Making of Jane Austen's Emma (1996); *Recreations* the countryside, books, theatre, music, croquet; *Style*— Miss Sue Birtwistle; ✉ c/o Nick Marston, Curtis Brown, 4th Floor, Haymarket House, 28–29 Haymarket, London SW1Y 4SP (☎ 020 7396 6600)

BISCHOFF, Sir Winfried Franz Wilhelm (Win); kt (2000); s of late Paul Helmut Bischoff, and Hildegard, *née* Kühne; *b* 10 May 1941; *Educ* Marist Bros Inanda Johannesburg, Univ of the Witwatersrand (BCom); *m* 1972, Rosemary Elizabeth, da of Hon Leslie Leathers; 2 s; *Career* md Schroders Asia Ltd Hong Kong 1971–82; J Henry Schroder & Co Ltd: dir 1978–2000, chm 1983–94; Schroders plc: dir 1983–2000, gp chief exec 1984–95, chm 1995–2000; chm Citigroup Europe 2000–09, acting ceo Citigroup Inc 2007; chm: Citigroup Inc 2007–09, Lloyds Banking Gp plc 2009–14, JP Morgan Securities plc 2015–; non-exec dir: Cable and Wireless plc 1991–2003 (dep chm 1995–2003), McGraw-Hill USA 1999–, Land Securities plc 1999–2007, IFIL Finanziaria di Partecipazioni SpA Italy 1999–2003, Eli Lilly and Co USA 2000–14, Siemens Holdings plc 2001–04, Prudential plc 2007–09; chm Financial Reporting Cncl 2014–; chm Career Academies UK 2000–10; DSc (hc) City Univ 2000; *Publications* UK International Financial Services – The Future (report, co-chm); *Recreations* opera, music, golf; *Clubs* Frilford Heath Golf, Swinley Forest Golf, Loch Lomond Golf, Blind Brook Golf (USA); *Style*— Sir Win Bischoff; ✉ 125 London Wall, London EC2Y 5AS (☎ 020 7492 2401)

BISH-JONES, Trevor Charles; *b* 23 April 1960; *Educ* Varndean GS Brighton, Portsmouth Sch of Pharmacy (BSc); *m* 8 Sept 1990, Amanda Jane, *née* Zeil; 2 da (Alexa Rose b 12 June 1995, Florence Rose b 8 May 1998); *Career* research chemist The Tosco Corp CO 1980–81, Boots plc 1981–87, various sr commercial, mktg and operational roles 1987–94; Dixons Stores Gp: md Currys, Dixons and The Link, commercial dir PCWorld 1997–2002; ceo Woolworths Gp plc 2002–08, co-fndr Mypeoplebiz.com 2009–11, chief operating offr Extra Saudi Arabia 2010–14; non-exec dir Royal London Gp 2005–11, chm Alfaisaliah Gp 2014–; patron Macmillan Milton Keynes Appeal; govr Ashridge Mgmnt Coll; fell Mktg Soc 1997, CCMI 2002; *Recreations* riding, golf, travel, football; *Style*— Trevor Bish-Jones, Esq

BISHOP, Alan; *Educ* Univ of Oxford (MA History); *Career* Hobson Bates 1974–78, fndr ptnr Milton Sharam Gottlieb 1978–81, Foote Cone & Belding 1981–83, bd account dir and new business dir Ted Bates 1983–85; Saatchi & Saatchi: joined as bd dir 1985, gp account dir 1988–90, chief operating offr 1990–91, vice-chm 1991–94, regnl account dir Procter & Gamble Health & Beauty Care Europe and ME 1992–94, chief operating offr Saatchi & Saatchi North America Inc NY 1994–95, pres, chm and ceo Saatchi & Saatchi North America Inc NY 1995–97; chm: Saatchi & Saatchi London 1997–98, Saatchi & Saatchi International 1998–2002; chief exec COI 2002–09, chief exec Southbank Centre 2009–; *Style*— Alan Bishop, Esq; ✉ Southbank Centre, Belvedere Road, London SE1 8XX

BISHOP, Andrew Lawrence; s of Lawrence Bishop, of Bristol, and Maureen, *née* Williams; *b* 28 November 1965, Bristol; *Educ* St Brendan's Coll Bristol, Univ of Exeter (LLB); *m* 16 April 1994, Sarah, *née* Hellier; 3 da (Hannah, Megan, Lily); *Career* admitted slr 1989, slr advocate 1999; ptnr Bishop & Light Slrs 1995–; vice-chm Criminal Law Slrs Assoc 2005–; memb Law Soc 1989– (memb Mental Health Review Tbnl Panel 1996); *Recreations* sailing, football, running; *Style*— Andrew Bishop, Esq; ✉ 56 Bramble Gardens, Burgess Hill RH15 8UQ; Bishop & Light, Cambridge House, Cambridge Grove, Hove BN3 3ED (e-mail andrewbishop@bishopandlight.co.uk)

BISHOP, (Dr) Catherine Jane (Cath); da of Brian Reynold Bishop, and Jean Muriel, *née* Kellie; *b* 22 November 1971; *Educ* Westcliff HS for Girls, Pembroke Coll Cambridge (MA, Rowing blue), Univ of Wales Aberystwyth (MPhil), Univ of Reading (PhD); *m* Matthew Tillett; 1 s (Jonathan Luke Kellie Tillett b 16 July 2011), 1 da (Lucy Jennifer Tillett b 12 March 2013); *Career* amateur rower; memb: Cambridge Univ Boat Club 1991–93 (incl varsity boat races 1991 and 1993), Marlow Rowing Club (hon life memb), GB squad 1995–2004; achievements incl: Bronze medal England eights Cwlth Games Canada 1994, Silver medal coxless pairs World Championships 1998, winner coxless pairs World Cup 1998, 1999 and 2003, Gold medal coxless pairs World Championships 2003, Silver medal coxless pairs Olympic Games Athens 2004; Olympian 1996, 2000 and 2004; indoor rowing: world champion 1999, world record holder 2000–02; after-dinner speaker at rowing clubs and univs; diplomat FCO 2001–14; leadership speaker and conslt 2013–; *Recreations* running, fitness training, travel abroad, reading contemporary literature, writing fiction, learning languages, pianist and accompanist; *Clubs* Leander, Marlow, Henley Royal Regatta; *Style*— Cath Bishop; ✉ mobile 07905 054263, e-mail cjbishop@btinternet.com

BISHOP, Christopher Charles Rigby; s of Michael Rigby Bishop (d 1996), and Beatrice, *née* Villemer; *b* 17 November 1952; *Educ* Stonyhurst, Magdalene Coll Cambridge (MA), St Thomas' Hosp Med Sch (MB BChir, MChir); *m* 17 Sept 1977, Anthea Jane, *née* Tilzey; 4 s (Charles Alexander Rigby b 17 May 1983, Hugo Guy Pierre b 8 July 1984, Thomas Christopher b 22 Oct 1993, Alexander Michael Pierre b 17 Nov 2010), 2 da (Lucie Marie Henrietta, Gabrielle Marie Susanna (twins) b 11 Sept 1986); *Career* surgical registrar Southampton Univ Hosps 1980–82, sr surgical registrar St Thomas' Hosp 1987–90 (surgical registrar 1982–84, lectr in surgery 1984–87), conslt surgn UCL Hosps 1991–; vascular fell Scripps Clinic and Research Fndn Calif 1989, Hunterian prof RCS 1991; *Recreations* yachting, skiing; *Style*— Christopher Bishop, Esq; ✉ 5 Devonshire Place, London W1G 6HL (☎ 020 7034 6202, mobile 078 3163 1007)

BISHOP, Prof Dorothy Vera Margaret; da of Aubrey Francis Horace Bishop, and Annemarie Sofia Eucken; *b* 14 February 1952; *Educ* St Hugh's Coll Oxford (MA), Inst of Psychiatry Univ of London (MPhil), Univ of Oxford (DPhil); *m* 1976, Patrick Michael Anthony Rabbitt; *Career* probationer grade clinical psychologist Maudsley and Bexley Hosps 1973–75; res offr Neuropsychology Unit Univ of Oxford 1975–82, Fulford jr res fell St Anne's Coll Oxford 1976–78, Bowra res fell Wadham Coll Oxford 1980–81, visiting scientist Montreal Neurological Inst 1981, MRC sr res fell Univ of Newcastle upon Tyne 1982–86, MRC sr res fell Univ of Manchester 1986–91, MRC sr res scientist Cognition and Brain Sciences Unit Cambridge 1991–98 (special appt 1998–), sr res fell Churchill Coll Cambridge 1993–98, Wellcome princ res fell Univ of Oxford 1998–, prof of developmental neuropsychology Univ of Oxford 1999–, supernumerary fell St John's Coll Oxford 2006–; adjunct prof Dept of Psychiatry Univ of WA 1999–2002 and 2005–; memb Ctee Experimental Psychology Soc 1986–88, memb Med Educn and Info Unit Spastics Soc 1988–91, memb ctee Assoc for Child Psychology and Psychiatry 1989–92, hon sec Br Neuropsychological Soc 1990–93, bd memb and chair Research Evaluation Ctee ESRC 1996–; assoc ed: Quarterly Jl of Experimental Psychology 1985–89, Br Jl of Disorders of Communication 1987–90, Br Jl of Developmental Psychology 1988–91; memb editorial bd: Developmental Medicine and Child Neurology 1987–97, European Jl of Disorders of Communication 1991–, Laterality 1995–, Autism: Int Jl of Research and Practice 1996–, Developmental Review 1996–, Applied Psycholinguistics 1997–; chief ed Jl of Child

Psychology and Psychiatry 1994–97 (co-ed 1990–94); memb: Experimental Psychology Soc, Multiple Births Fndn, Nat Autistic Soc, Br Neuropsychological Soc, BAAS (pres Psychology Section 1999); hon memb Assoc for Child Psychology and Psychiatry, hon fell Coll of Speech and Language Therapists 1992, pres Experimental Psychology Soc 2000; MD (hc) Univ of Lund 2004, Hon DSc Univ of Western Australia 2012, Hon DSc Newcastle Univ 2013; FMedSci 2000, FBA 2006, Hon FRCPCH 2008, FRS 2013, Hon FBPsS 2013; *Books* Language Development in Exceptional Circumstances (jt ed, 1988), Handedness and Developmental Disorders (1990), Uncommon Understanding: development and disorders of language comprehension in children (1997, Br Psychological Soc Annual Book Prize 1999), Speech and Language Impairments in Children: causes, characteristics, intervention and outcome (jt ed, 2000); author of numerous articles and research papers in learned journals; *Recreations* Victorian novels, pre-1945 films, novel-writing under pen-name Deevy Bishop; *Style*— Prof Dorothy Bishop, FRS, FBA, FMedSci; ✉ website deevybee.blogspot.com, Twitter @deevybee; Department of Experimental Psychology, South Parks Road, Oxford OX1 3UD (☎ 01865 271369, fax 01865 281255)

BISHOP, John Anthony Fremantle; s of Evan Winfrid Bishop, OBE, of Lymington, Hants, and Mary, née Godwin-Smith (d 1983); b 17 February 1949; *Educ* Warminster Sch, LAMDA; *Career* BBC TV: floor asst 1971, asst floor mangr, then prodn mangr 1974, dir light entertainment 1980, prodr light entertainment 1984, exec prodr 1988, asst head of variety and light entertainment 1988–91; controller of entertainment and comedy Carlton Television 1991–99, TV exec ITV and BBC 2000–; *Recreations* theatre and swimming; *Style*— John Bishop, Esq; ✉ Calle Victoria 21, Portals Nous, 07181 Calvia, Mallorca, Spain

BISHOP, John Joseph; b 30 November 1966, Runcorn, Cheshire; *m* Melanie; 3 s; *Career* comedian; stand-up incl: Elvis Has Left the Building 2009, The Sunshine Tour 2010, Rollercoaster 2012; television appearances incl: Michael McIntyre's Comedy Roadshow, 8 Out of 10 Cats, Live at the Apollo, Mock the Week, Have I Got News for You, Would I Lie to You?, QI, regular panelist A League of Their Own, host John Bishop's Britain; Best Male Comedy Breakthrough Artist Br Comedy Award 2010; *DVDs* Elvis Has Left The Building (2010), John Bishop Live: The Sunshine Tour (2011); *Style*— Mr John Bishop

BISHOP, John Maurice; s of Edwin Maurice Bishop, of Paignton, Devon, and Joyce Emily, née Edmonds; b 6 May 1947; *Educ* Sherborne, QMC London (LLB); *m* 1, 30 March 1970 (m dis 1985), Maureen, née Maloney; 1 s (Edward b 19 Dec 1973), 4 da (Laura b 6 March 1976, Sophie b 10 Nov 1979, Alice, Chloe (twins) b 26 July 1982); *m* 2, 18 April 1986 (m dis 1998), Virginia, née Welsh; 1 step da (Sophie b 22 April 1980); *m* 3, 18 April 2002, Pauline, née Crogan; *Career* slr; Masons (now Pinsent Masons LLP): articled clerk 1969–71, asst slr 1971, salaried ptnr 1972, equity ptnr 1973, managing ptnr 1987–90, sr ptnr 1991–2003, resident sr ptnr Asia Pacific 2003–, chief rep Beijing office 2007–; life pres Technol and Construction Slrs' Assoc (chm 1990–94); memb Law Soc 1969, admitted slr Hong Kong 1983; FFB 1975, ACIArb 1980; *Recreations* golf; *Clubs* Rye Golf, Foreign Correspondents (Hong Kong), China (Hong Kong and Beijing); *Style*— John Bishop, Esq; ✉ Pinsent Masons, 10th Floor, China Resources Building, no 8 Jianguo Menbei Avenue, Beijing 100005, China

BISHOP, John Michael; s of Lt Wilfred Charles John Michael Bishop (d 1988), and Margery Bains, née Emmerson (d 1990); b 1 March 1947; *Educ* Kent Coll Canterbury, LSE (LLB), Inns of Court Sch of Law; *m* 12 Aug 1982 (m dos 2004), Laurie Marie, da of Lyman Charles Harris (d 1980), of Virginia Beach, Virginia, USA; 2 da (Heather Virginia, Lucy Cecilia); *Career* Kent and Co of London Yeomanry (TA) 1965–67; practising barrister, head of chambers at 7 Stone Buildings 1986–99; memb: Hon Soc Middle Temple, Hon Soc Lincoln's Inn; *Recreations* photography, antiquarian books; *Style*— John Bishop, Esq; ✉ Invictus Chambers, 1 Mitre Court Buildings, Temple, London EC4Y 7BS (☎ 020 7583 9170, e-mail j.bishop@invictuschambers.org, website www.barristerbishop.co.uk)

BISHOP, His Hon Judge Mark Andrew; s of Francis Robin Bishop (d 2005), and Joyce Bishop; b 12 July 1958, Cambridge; *Educ* Leys Sch Cambridge, Downing Coll Cambridge (MA); *m* 12 July 1986, Christine, née Smart; 3 da (Alexandra b 4 July 1988, Theodora b 29 July 1990, Christiana b 8 March 1993); *Career* called to the Bar 1981; recorder 2001, legal memb Mental Health Review Tbnl 2007, circuit judge (South Eastern Circuit) 2009–; ordained 2002; chllr Dio of Lincoln 2007, assoc priest Dio of Ely; pres Cambridge Union 1980; *Recreations* family, holidays, music; *Style*— His Hon Judge Bishop; ✉ c/o The South Eastern Circuit, 289–293 High Holborn, London WC1V 7HZ

BISHOP, Patrick Joseph; s of Ernest Bishop, of Wimbledon, London, and Kathleen, née Kelly; b 17 October 1952; *Educ* Wimbledon Coll, CCC Oxford (exhibitioner, BA); *m* 1, 1989 (m dis), Marie, da of William Colvin, of Oyster Bay, NY; *m* 2, 12 June 2008, Henrietta Miers, da of Col Douglas, and Mrs Richenda Miers, of Lettoch, N Kessock, Inverness; 1 da (Honor Bridget b 3 Dec 2006); *Career* journalist; training scheme Mirror Group Newspapers 1974–76, freelance 1976–78, news reporter Evening Standard 1978–79, The Observer 1979–84 (news reporter, NI corr, corr with Br Forces in Falklands War), reporter ITN Channel Four News 1984–85, reporter and diplomatic corr The Sunday Times 1985–87, sr corr The Sunday Telegraph 1987–88; The Daily Telegraph: Middle East corr 1988–92, sr foreign corr 1992–95, foreign ed 1995–97, assoc ed (foreign) 1997–99, Paris corr 1999–2002, special corr 2002–07; dir Medécins sans Frontières (UK) 1992–2002 (chm 1995–2000); *Books* The Winter War (with John Witherow, 1982), The Provisional IRA (with Eamonn Mallie, 1987), Famous Victory (1992), The Irish Empire (1999), Fighter Boys (2003), Bomber Boys: Fighting Back 1940–45 (2007), 3 Para (2007), A Good War (novel, 2008), Ground Truth (2009), The Battle of Britain (2009), Follow Me Home (novel, 2011), Target Tirpitz (2012), Wings (2012), The Reckoning (2014), The Cooler King (2015); *Recreations* fishing; *Clubs* Savile; *Style*— Patrick Bishop, Esq; ✉ e-mail patrickbishop2001@hotmail.com

BISHOP, Prof Paul; b 17 November 1949, Gosford, NSW, Aust; *Educ* Macquarie Univ Sydney (PhD, DSc); *Career* Univ of Sydney until 1989, Monash Univ Melbourne 1989–97 (latterly dir Grad Sch of Environmental Science), prof of geography Univ of Glasgow 1998–; memb NERC Science and Innovation Strategy Bd 2007–10; Br Soc for Geomorphology Wiley Award for best paper in society's jl 2007; FRSE 2004, fell Geological Soc of America 2011; *Style*— Prof Paul Bishop; ✉ School of Geographical and Earth Sciences, University of Glasgow, University Avenue, Glasgow G12 8QQ (☎ 0141 330 6654, e-mail paul.bishop.3@glasgow.ac.uk)

BISHOP, Prof Peter Antony; s of Jack Lionel Thomas Bishop (d 2001), of Eastbourne, and Audrey Florence, née Barker; b 15 September 1953, London; *Educ* Trinity Sch of John Whitgift, Univ of Manchester (BA, schs open scholar, RTPI Prize, Heywood Medal); *m* 7 Feb 1998, Lesley Williams; 1 da (Freya Clare b 13 Aug 1996), 1 s (Adam Stirling b 24 Aug 1998); *Career* devpt planner: Westminster 1976–78, Newham 1978–80; head of res London Borough of Islington 1980–83, head of planning Tower Hamlets 1984–87 (schemes incl Spitalfields and Canary Wharf), dir of property and planning Haringey 1987–97; dir of environment: London Borough of Hammersmith and Fulham 1997–2001 (i/c White City and Imperial Wharf devpts), London Borough of Camden 2001–06 (devpts incl Kings Cross); dir Design for London 2007–11, dep chief exec London Devpt Agency 2009–11, dir Allies and Morrison architects 2011–; prof of urban design Bartlett Sch of Architecture and Planning UCL 2012–; visiting prof Nottingham Trent Univ 2008–; memb London Advsy Ctee English Heritage 2007–12, chair Nat Assoc of Architecture Centres 2010; hon doctorate Univ of Kingston 2011; hon fell UCL 2008; FRSA 2007–12,

hon fell RIBA 2009; *Publications* The Bishop Review: the future of design in the built environment (2011), The Temporary City (jtly, 2012), Planning and politics – King's Cross a case study (2016); *Recreations* rock climbing, European cinema; *Style*— Prof Peter Bishop; ✉ Allies and Morrison, 85 Southwark Street, London SE1 0HX (☎ 020 7921 0100, e-mail pbishop@alliesandmorrison.co.uk)

BISS, Adele; b 18 October 1944; *m* Roger Davies; *Career* grad trainee Consumer Product Mktg Unilever 1968–70, Thomson Holidays 1970–78, dir Biss Lancaster until 1990 (fndr 1978, sold to WCRS, now Aegis Gp Plc); chm BTA and English Tourist Bd 1993–96, fndr chm A S Biss & Co (political and public affrs) 1996–; non-exec dir Eurostar (UK) Ltd, dir Engine 2006–; govr Univ of Middlesex until 2006, memb Cncl UCL until 2006; *Style*— Ms Adele Biss; ✉ A S Biss & Co, 5th Floor, 36 Broadway, Westminster, London SW1H 0BH (☎ 020 7340 6200, fax 020 7340 6250)

BISSELL, Frances Mary; da of Robert Maloney, and Mary, née Kelly; b 19 August 1946; *Educ* Goyt Bank HS, Cape Town HS, Allerton HS Leeds, Univ of Leeds (BA); *m* 12 Dec 1970, Thomas Emery Bissell, s of Thomas Wilson Bissell (d 1975), of Pittsburgh, USA; 1 step da (b 1958); *Career* VSO Nigeria 1965–66, asst École Normale 1968–69, British Cncl 1970–97 (leave of absence 1987–97), freelance writer, author, broadcaster and conslt on cookery and food 1983–, The Times Cook 1987–2000; guest cook: Mandarin Oriental Hong Kong 1987 and 1990, Intercontinental Hotel London 1987 and 1988, Manila Peninsula 1989, Dusit Thani Bangkok 1992, Café Royal 1994–95, George V Paris 1995, The Mark New York 1997, 1999 and 2000; conslt: Ta' Frenc Restaurant Gozo Malta 2005–, Sloane Club 2006–13; TV: Frances Bissell's Westcountry Kitchen 1995, Frances Bissell's Westcountry Christmas; guest speaker: Swan Hellenic 2000–, Hebridean Spirit 2005–09, Hebridean Princess 2010–12, Hebridean River Cruises 2016; fndr memb Guild of Food Writers 1985, Glenfiddich Cookery Writer of the Year 1994, James Beard Fndn Award 1995, Shackleton Ctee Fellowship 2001; fell Royal Academy of Culinary Arts; *Books* A Cook's Calendar (1985), The Pleasures of Cookery (1986), Ten Dinner Parties for Two (1988), The Sainsbury's Book of Food (1989), Oriental Flavours (1990), The Real Meat Cookbook (1992), The Times Cookbook (1993), Frances Bissell's Westcountry Kitchen (1996), An A-Z of Food and Wine in Plain English (with Tom Bissell, 1999), Modern Classics (2000), The Organic Meat Cookbook (2000), Entertaining (2002), Frances Bissell's Country Kitchen (2002), Preserving Nature's Bounty (2006), The Scented Kitchen (2007, 2 edn 2012), The Floral Baker (2014), The Fragrant Pantry (2016); *Recreations* travelling, writing and cooking; *Clubs* Groucho, Sloane; *Style*— Mrs Thomas Bissell; ✉ 2 Carlingford Road, London NW3 1RX

BITEL, Nicholas Andrew (Nick); s of Max Bitel (d 2007), of London, and Cecilia, née Singer (d 1980); b 1959, London; *Educ* St Paul's, Davidson Coll NC (Dean Rusk scholar), Univ of Manchester (LLB); *m* 1982, Sharon, née Levan; 3 s (Daniel b 1985, Adam b 1987, Jonathan b 1992); *Career* ptnr Max Bitel Greene 1983–; ceo London Marathon 1995–, memb Cncl UK Sport 2002–08, dir Olympic Park Legacy Co 2009–, chair Sport England 2013–; memb Law Soc 1983–; *Recreations* sport, theatre; *Clubs* MCC; *Style*— Nick Bitel, Esq; ✉ Kerman & Co LLP, 200 Strand, London WC2R 1DJ

BJORGOLFSSON, Thor; s of Bjorgolfur Gudmundsson, and Thora Hallgrimsson; b 19 March 1967, Reykjavik, Iceland; *Educ* Iceland Coll of Commerce Reykjavik, NY Univ; *partner* Kristin Olafsdottir; 1 s; *Career* mktg dir in brewing industry Iceland and Russia 1992, co-fndr and chm Bravo International Ltd St Petersburg 1996 (sold to Heineken International 2002), chm Pharmaco (latterly Actaris) 2002, co-fndr and chm of the Bd Samson 2002 (also chm Straurmur Burdanas), fndr Novator Partners LLP 2004, private investor in telecommunication cos in countries incl Finland, Poland, Bulgaria and Greece 2004–; elected to Young Global Leaders World Econ Forum 2005 and 2006, memb Bd of East West Inst 2006; Man of the Year in Business Vidskiptabladid newspaper 2003, IMARK Award Icelandic Mktg Assoc 2005, Investor of the Year Bulgarian Radio 2006, Business Man of the Year Frettabladid newspaper 2006; *Recreations* skiing, sailing, mountain biking, motorbiking; *Style*— Thor Bjorgolfsson, Esq; ✉ Novator Partners LLP, 25 Park Lane, London W1K 1RA (☎ 020 7647 1500, fax 020 7491 1148, e-mail helene@novator.co.uk)

BLACK, Prof Dame Carol Mary; DBE (2005, CBE 2002); da of Edgar Herbert, and Annie Herbert; b 26 December 1939; *Educ* Univ of Bristol (BA, PGDip, pathology travelling scholar, Martin Memorial Pathology Prize, Surgery Prize, Obstetrics Prize, MB ChB, MD); *m* 1, 1973 (m dis 1983), James Black; *m* 2, 2002, Dr Chris Morley; *Career* consult rheumatologist W Middx Univ Hosp 1981–89; Royal Free and UC Medical Sch Univ of London: conslt rheumatlogist 1989–94, prof of rheumatology 1994–2006, currently emeritus prof of rheumatology; nat dir for health and work 2006–; medical dir Royal Free Hosp 2000–02; chair Nuffield Tst for Research and Policy Studies in Health Services 2006–; non-exec dir NHS Inst for Innovation and Improvement 2006–, memb CBRC Scientific Advsy Bd Guy's and St Thomas' Medical Sch 2007–, vice-chm Bd and chm Research Ctee Imperial Coll Healthcare Charity 2008–, founding memb Ctee for the Queen's Awards for Voluntary Service 2009–, public appointments ambass Govt Equalities Office Cabinet Office 2009–, chm Governance Bd Centre for Workforce Intelligence 2010–, memb Life Sciences Strategy Bd Cogent 2011–, memb Employee Engagement Task Force Dept for Business, Innovation and Skills 2011–; pres: Scleroderma Soc 2006–, Br Lung Fndn 2007–, Raynaud's and Scleroderma Assoc 2007–; patron Treat Tst Wales 2009–; hon physician Royal Soc of Musicians of GB 2008–; pro-chllr Univ of Bristol 2007–; tstee Nat Portrait Gallery 2010–; hon degrees of 12 UK univs and fellowships of 22 Royal Colls, Faculties and similar instns worldwide; hon fell: Lucy Cavendish Coll Cambridge 2004, UCL 2004; FRCP 1988 (MRCP 1974), FMedSci 1996, CCMI 2004, master American Coll of Physicians 2005, foreign assoc memb Inst of Medicine USA 2006, master American Coll of Rheumatology 2006; *Publications* Systemic Sclerosis (jtly, 1985), Scleroderma (jtly, 1988); author of numerous articles, reviews and chapters in books; *Recreations* hill walking, running, opera, reading, travel; *Clubs* Athenaeum; *Style*— Prof Dame Carol Black, DBE, PRCP; ✉ 28 Cornwall Terrace Mews, London NW1 5LL (☎ 020 7487 3067, mobile 07989 384739, e-mail profblack@btinternet.com)

BLACK, Don; OBE (1999); s of Morris Blackstone (d 1979), of Hackney, London, and Betsy, née Kersh (d 1966); b 21 June 1938; *Educ* Cassland Rd Sch Hackney; *m* 7 Dec 1958, Shirley Kitty, da of James Berg; 2 s (Grant Howard b 28 Jan 1961, Clive Darren b 24 Aug 1963); *Career* lyricist; office jr New Musical Express 1955, music publisher, professional comedian, agent and mangr for Brian Epstein's NEMS co; chm Br Acad of Songwriters Composers and Authors 1986–, frequent broadcaster and chm of the Vivien Ellis prize held at the Guildhall Sch of Music; worked with well known composers incl: Andrew Lloyd Webber, John Barry, Henry Mancini, Elmer Bernstein, Charles Aznavour, Quincy Jones, Jule Styne, Charles Strouse; Hon Dr of Arts City Univ 2005; *Musicals* incl: Tell Me on Sunday, Billy, Aspects of Love, Song and Dance, Sunset Boulevard, Bombay Dreams, Dracula, Bonnie and Clyde, Stephen Ward, Mrs Henderson Presents; *Films* incl: Born Free, To Sir With Love, Diamonds are Forever, Ben, The Man With The Golden Gun, Thunderball, True Grit, Tomorrow Never Dies, The World Is Not Enough; *Awards* Oscar Award (for Born Free 1966), 5 Oscar nominations, Golden Globe Award, 6 Ivor Novello Awards, 4 Tony Nominations, 2 Tony Awards, numerous Platinum, Gold and Silver discs, inducted into Songwriters Hall of Fame 2007; *Publications* subject of Wrestling with Elephants (2003); *Recreations* swimming, snooker; *Clubs* RAC, Groucho, St James's; *Style*— Don Black, Esq, OBE; ✉ c/o John Cohen, Clintons Solicitors, 55

Drury Lane, London WC2B 5SQ (☎ 020 7379 6080, fax 020 7240 9310, e-mail donlyric@aol.com)

BLACK, Air Vice-Marshal George Philip; CB (1987), OBE (1967), AFC (1962, and bar 1971); s of William Black, and Elizabeth Edward, *née* Philip; *b* 10 July 1932; *Educ* Aberdeen Acad, Jt Servs Staff Coll, RCDS; *m* 1954, Ella Ruddiman, da of Edwin Stanley Walker (d 1961); 2 s (Stuart Douglas b 1955, Ian Craig b 1959); *Career* joined RAF 1950, flying trg Canada 1951, serv fighter pilot, carrier pilot (on exchange to FAA), flying instr, HQ Fighter Command, Cdr No 111 (Fighter) Sqdn 1964–66, ldr Lightning Aerobatic Team 1965, Cdr Lightning Operational Conversion Unit 1967–69, Cdr No 5 (Fighter) Sqdn 1969–70, jssc 1970, air plans MOD 1971–72, Station Cdr RAF Wildenrath 1972–74, Cdr Harrier Field Force RAF Germany 1972–74, Gp Capt Ops HQ 38 Gp 1974–76, RCDS 1977, Gp Capt Ops HQ 11 (Fighter) Gp 1978–80, Cdr Allied Air Defence Sector One 1980–83, Commandant ROC 1983–84, DCS (Ops), HQ AAFCE 1984–87, Air ADC to HM The Queen 1981–83; sr def advsr Ferranti Defence Systems Edinburgh 1987–92, dir of mil business Marconi Electronic Systems Ltd 1993–99, def advsr BAE Sensor Systems Division 1999–2000, def conslt BAE Systems (Avionics) 2000–, defence conslt Selex Ltd 2005–11; FIMgt 1977, FRAeS 2000; *Recreations* military aviation, model railways; *Clubs* RAF; *Style—* Air Vice-Marshal George Black, CB, OBE, AFC, FIMgt, FRAeS, RAF (ret); ✉ RAF Halton House Officers' Mess, Wendover, Buckinghamshire

BLACK, Her Hon Judge Helen Mary; da of Denis Clifford, and Carole Clifford; *Educ* Ashburton HS, Coll of Law Chester; *Career* articled clerk Stafford Clark & Co 1978–82, admitted slr 1982, slr and ptnr Addison Madden 1982–2000, dep district judge Princ Registry of the Family Div 1995–2000, district judge Princ Registry of the Family Div 2000–07, recorder Western Circuit 2005–07, circuit judge (South Eastern Circuit) 2007–08 and (Western Circuit) 2008–; memb: Law Soc 1982–, Slr Family Law Assoc (SFLA) 1990–2000; *Publications* Atkins Court Forms: Husband and Wife/Co-habitation (ed, 2002), Atkins Court Forms: Marriage, Civil Partnership and Cohabitation (ed, 2006), Butterworths Family Law Service (ed), Atkins Court Forms: Family: Relationships and their Breakdowns (2012); *Recreations* skiing, marathon running, scuba diving, golf, walking, having fun; *Style—* Her Hon Judge Black; ✉ Portsmouth County Court, Winston Churchill Avenue, Portsmouth, Hampshire PO1 2DQ

BLACK, Prof Jeremy; MBE; s of Cyril Black, and Doreen, *née* Ellis; *b* 30 October 1955; *Educ* Queens' Coll Cambridge; *m* 9 July 1981, Sarah Elizabeth, *née* Hollis; 1 s (Timothy James b 1987), 1 da (Phillipa Rosemary b 1989); *Career* lectr, sr lectr, reader and prof Durham Univ 1980–95, prof Univ of Exeter 1996–; memb Cncl: Br Records Assoc 1989–2005, Royal Historical Soc 1993–96 and 1997–2000, List and Index Soc 1997–; memb Editorial Bd: History Today, Int History Review, Jl of Military History, Media History, RUSI Jl; *Books* author of over 120 books, incl: A Military Revolution? Military Change and European Society 1550–1800 (1991), Eighteenth-Century Britain 1688–1783 (2001), The English Press 1621–1861 (2001), British Diplomats and Diplomacy 1688–1800 (2001), The Politics of James Bond: from Fleming's Novels to the Big Screen (2001), Walpole in Power: Britain's First Prime Minister (2001), Western Warfare 1775–1882 (2001), War in the New Century (2001), Europe and the World 1650–1830 (2002), European International Relations 1648–1815 (2002), America as a Military Power 1775–1882 (2002), The World in the Twentieth Century (2002), Warfare in the Eighteenth Century (2002), War: An Illustrated World History (2003), George III: America's Last King (2008), London: a history (2009), The War of 1812 in the Age of Napoleon (2010); *Recreations* cinema, reading, travel, walking; *Clubs* Athenaeum; *Style—* Prof Jeremy Black, MBE; ✉ Department of History, University of Exeter, Amory Building, Rennes Drive, Exeter EX4 4RJ

BLACK, Rt Hon Lady Justice; Rt Hon Dame Jill Margaret Black; DBE (1999), PC (2010); da of Dr James Irvine Currie, of Leeds, and late Margaret Yvonne, *née* Rogers; *b* 1 June 1954; *Educ* Penrhos Coll Colwyn Bay, Trevelyan Coll Durham (BA); *m* 1, 10 June 1978, David Charles Black, s of Norman John Black; 1 da (b 14 Sept 1982), 1 s (b 14 June 1986); m 2, 28 March 2013, Rt Hon Lord Justice McCombe, *qv*; *Career* called to the Bar Inner Temple 1976, QC 1994, recorder NE Circuit 1999, judge of the High Court of Justice 1999–2010, judge of the Court of Appeal 2010–; fell Br-American Project; FRSA; *Books* A Practical Approach to Family Law (jtly, latest edition 2015), The Family Court Practice (jtly); *Style—* The Rt Hon Lady Justice Black, DBE; ✉ Royal Courts of Justice, Strand, London WC2A 2LL

BLACK, John Alexander; QC (1998); s of John Alexander Black (d 2000), and Grace, *née* Cornock (d 1994); *b* 23 April 1951; *Educ* St James Choir Sch Grimsby, Univ of Hull (LLB); *m* 1, 4 June 1977 (m dis 2007), Penelope Anne Willdig; 3 c (Katherine b 1987, Alistair b 1992, Harriet b 1992); m 2, 20 Sept 2008, Fiona Rosalind Jackson; *Career* called to the Bar Inner Temple 1975, in practice Criminal Bar 1976–; *Recreations* classical music, motor cars, political history; *Style—* John Black, Esq, QC; ✉ 33 Chancery Lane, London WC2A 1EN (☎ 020 7430 9950, fax 020 7430 2818)

BLACK, Michael Jonathan; QC (1995); s of Samuel Black (d 1971), and Lillian, *née* Ruben (d 1988); *Educ* Stand GS, UCL (LLB); *m* 1984, Ann, da of late Keith Pentol; 2 s (Samuel Simon Joshua b 25 July 1985, Benjamin David Louis b 30 Jan 1989); *Career* pupillage 1977–79, called to the Bar: Middle Temple 1978 (bencher 2006), Dubai Int Financial Centre 2006, Eastern Caribbean Supreme Ct 2007; in practice Deans Court Chambers Manchester 1979–95, trained as mediator Harvard Law Sch 1992, barr, arbitrator and mediator (commercial disputes especially in construction indust) Byrom Chambers Manchester and London 1995–2000, recorder of the Crown Court 1999–2013 (asst recorder 1995–99), dep judge Technol and Construction Court 2000–13, barr 2 Temple Gardens 2001–08, barr 24 Old Buildings 2008–, dep judge of the High Court 2008; memb: Civil Procedure Rule Ctee 2000–04, Court of Appeal Panel of Mediators 2001–03, Civil Justice Cncl 2005–08; asst cmmr Parly Boundary Cmmn for England; visiting research fell Univ of Manchester Inst of Sci and Technol 1996–2002, visiting prof of construction and engrg law Univ of Manchester 2002–; memb: American Bar Assoc, Forum on Construction Indust (USA), Technol and Construction Bar Assoc, Northern Circuit Commercial Bar Assoc, London Court of International Arbitration, Professional Negligence Bar Assoc, Int Bar Assoc; Freeman City of London, Liveryman Worshipful Co of Arbitrators; FCIArb 1991, FInstCES 2000; *Books* The Sanctuary House Case: an Arbitration Workbook (contrib, 1996), New Horizons in Construction Law (contrib, 1998), The Law and Practice of Compromise (contrib, 5 edn 2002, 6 edn 2005, 7 edn 2010), Discovery Deskbook (contrib, 2005), International Construction Law (contrib, 2009); *Clubs* Athenaeum, Capital (Dubai); *Style—* Michael Black, Esq, QC; ✉ 24 Old Buildings, Lincoln's Inn, London WC2A 3UP (☎ 020 7691 2424, fax 0845 280 1950, e-mail mbqc@xxiv.co.uk)

BLACK, (Francis) Peter; s of Francis Raymond Black (d 1985), and Rosina Mary, *née* De Burgh; *b* 20 August 1932; *Educ* Gunnersbury GS, Hammersmith Coll of Art; *m* 15 March 1958, Jillian Elsie; 2 da (Susan b 1961, Caroline b 1964); *Career* architect with Norman and Dawbarn for 4 years designing Imperial Coll building; joined Scott Brownrigg and Turner 1961 (ptnr 1970–); buildings include Sport City Dubai and three airports in Iraq, also responsible for biothermal waste to energy plants in Redhill and Cambridge; dir: Building Design Services (BDS) Ltd 1992–, Consolidated Development Group 1992–; conslt Internation Banking Group responsible for devpt of infrastructure in Myanmar, Laos and CIS; pres Chertsey Agric Assoc 1990; govr St Paul's Sch (grant maintained); RIBA, FSIAD, FCSD, FRSA, MBIM, MaPS; Ecclesia et Pontifici (Vatican) 1990; *Recreations* runs a small farm at Englefield Green specialising in breeding and showing Dexters, short-legged rare breed of British cattle; *Style—* Peter Black, Esq; ✉ Peter Black Associates, Woodside, Broomfield Park, Sunningdale SL5 0JS (☎ 01344 628285, e-mail peter_black@btopenworld.com)

BLACK, Cncllr Peter Malcolm; s of John Malcolm Black, and Joan Arlene, *née* Phillps, of Saughall Massie, Wirral; *b* 30 January 1960, Clatterbridge, Wirral; *Educ* Wirral GS for Boys, UC Swansea (BA); *m* Angela; *Career* exec offr Land Registry for Wales 1983–99; memb Nat Assembly for Wales (Lib Dem) South Wales West 1999–2016; memb City and County of Swansea for Cwmbwrla Ward 1984–; *Recreations* theatre, poetry, films; *Style—* Councillor Peter Black; ✉ 115 Cecil Street, Manselton, Swansea, SA5 8QL (☎ 01792 473743, website peterblack.blogspot.com and www.peterblack.wales)

BLACK, Prof Robert; QC (Scot 1987); s of James Little Black, of Lockerbie, Scot, and Jeannie Findlay, *née* Lyon; *b* 12 June 1947; *Educ* Lockerbie Acad, Dumfries Acad, Univ of Edinburgh (LLB), McGill Univ Montreal (LLM); *Career* advocate of the Scot Bar 1972, sr legal offr Scot Law Cmmn 1975–78, in practice Scot Bar 1978–81, prof of Scots law Univ of Edinburgh 1981–2004, now emeritus (lectr 1972–75); Temp Sheriff 1981–94; gen ed The Laws of Scotland: Stair Meml Encyclopaedia 1988–96 (dep then jt gen ed 1981–88); dir Gannaga Lodge CC S Africa 2005–; FRSA 1991, FRSE 1992, FFCS (founding fell Inst of Contemporary Scot) 2001; *Books* An Introduction to Written Pleading (1982), Civil Jurisdiction: The New Rules (1983); many articles on Lockerbie Disaster; *Recreations* beer, wine, tea (not always in that order); *Style—* Prof Robert Black, QC, FRSE; ✉ 6/4 Glenogle Road, Edinburgh EH3 5HW (☎ 0131 557 3571, e-mail rblackqc@gmail.com); Nov-April: 4 Vygie Street, Middelpos 8193, Northern Cape, South Africa (☎ 0027 87 802 6467); website http://lockerbiecase.blogspot.co.uk

BLACK, Prof Dame Susan Margaret (Sue); DBE (2016, OBE 2001); *née* Gunn; da of Alasdair Gunn, of Inverness, and Isabel, *née* Bailey; *b* 7 May 1961, Inverness; *Educ* Univ of Aberdeen (BSc, PhD); *m* 26 March 1993, Thomas Black; 3 da (Elizabeth Margaret b 5 March 1984, Grace Alexandra b 7 Feb 1995, Anna Louise b 28 Dec 1996); *Career* lectr in human anatomy St Thomas' Hospital 1987–92, conslt forensic anthropologist Univ of Glasgow 1992–2003, head of profession Br Forensic Team Kosovo 1999–2000, dir Centre for Anatomy and Human Indentification Univ of Dundee 2003–, dir Leverhulme Research Centre for Forensic Science Univ of Dundee; fndr Br Assoc for Human Identification 2002 (pres 2009), advsr Disaster Victim Identification Ctee Home Office (police communication 2008); pres Assoc of Science Educn (Scot) 2011–; hon prof Royal Scottish Acad 2014; Lucy Mair Medal 2008, Police Commendations 2009 and 2016, Fletcher of Saltoun Award 2014, Wolfson Research Merit Award 2014, Jephcott Gold Medal 2016; Hon DSc Robert Gordon Univ 2003, Hon DSc Abertay Univ 2009; FRSE 2005, hon fell RCPSGlas 2007, fell Royal Anthr Inst 2009, Hon FRCPEd 2012, FRSB; *Publications* Developmental Juvenile Osteology (2000), The Juvenile Skeleton (2004), An Introduction to Forensic Human Identification (2006), Juvenile Osteology (2009), Disaster Victim Indentification (2009); *Style—* Prof Dame Sue Black, DBE; ✉ Centre for Anatomy and Human Identification, College of Life Sciences, University of Dundee, Dundee DD1 5EH (☎ 01382 385776, fax 01382 386817, e-mail s.m.black@dundee.ac.uk)

BLACK OF BRENTWOOD, Baron (Life Peer UK 2010), of Brentwood in the County of Essex; Guy Vaughan Black; s of late Thomas Black, and late Monica, *née* Drew; *b* 6 August 1964, Chelmsford, Essex; *Educ* Brentwood Sch, Peterhouse, Cambridge (John Cosin scholar, MA, Sir Herbert Butterfield prize); *m* 2006, Mark William Bolland, *qv* (civil partnership converted); *Career* with Corp Banking Div BZW 1985–86, with Cons Res Dept 1986–89, special advsr to sec of state for Energy 1989–92, account dir Westminster Strategy 1992–94, assoc dir Lowe Bell Good Relations 1994–96, dir PCC 1996–2003, press sec to Rt Hon Michael Howard, MP (ldr Cons Pty) 2004–05, dir of media Cons Central Office 2004–05, exec dir Telegraph Media Group 2005–; chm Cwlth Press Union Media Tst 2009–; dir Advtg Standards Bd of Finance, chm Press Standards Bd of Finance 2009–, dir European Newspaper Publishers' Assoc 2014–, pres Inst of Promotional Marketing 2015–; tstee: Sir Edward Heath's Charitable Fndn 2006–10, Imperial War Museum 2007–15, RCM, Mayor of London's Fund for Young Musicians 2011–12; life vice-pres NI Schs Debating Competition, hon pres London Press Club 2012–, pres Printing Charity 2013–14, govr Brentwood Sch 2013–, patron Rory Peck Tst 2014–, chm Hanover Band 2014–, pres Journalists' Charity 2014–; memb (Cons) Brentwood BC 1988–92; patron Peterhouse Politics Soc; FRSA 1997, MCIPR 2007; *Recreations* music (playing and listening), reading (mainly historical biography), enjoying fine wine, getting to Umbria as much as possible; *Clubs* Athenaeum; *Style—* The Lord Black of Brentwood

BLACKADDER, Dame Elizabeth Violet; DBE (2003, OBE 1982); da of Thomas Blackadder (d 1941), and Violet Isabella, *née* Scott (d 1984); *b* 24 September 1931, Falkirk; *Educ* Falkirk HS, Univ of Edinburgh, Edinburgh Coll of Art; *m* 1956, John Houston, OBE (d 2008), s of Alexander Anderson Houston (d 1947); *Career* artist; lectr Sch of Drawing and Painting Edinburgh Coll of Art 1962–86; numerous solo exhibitions since 1960 (Mercury Gallery 1965–), shows regularly at Royal Scottish Acad and Royal Acad, Browse Darby London, Tapestry designs (woven by Dovecot Studios) in private collections Robert Fleming Holdings Ltd, Reckitt & Colman plc; solo exhibitions incl: Retrospective (Scottish Arts Cncl & touring) 1981–82, Retrospective (Aberystwyth Arts Centre & touring) 1989; works in the collections of: Scottish Arts Cncl, Scottish Nat Gallery of Modern Art, Scottish Nat Portrait Gallery, Nat Portrait Gallery, Govt Art Collection, Kettle's Yard Univ of Cambridge, Univ of Edinburgh, Hunterian Art Gallery Univ of Glasgow, Univ of St Andrews, Univ of Stirling, Nat Museum of Women in the Arts Washington DC, McNay Art Museum San Antonio Texas, Heriot-Watt Univ, Robert Fleming Holdings Ltd; Guthrie award Royal Scottish Acad 1963, Pimms award Royal Acad 1983, Watercolour Fndn Royal Acad 1988; HM Painter and Limner in Scotland 2001; memb: Soc of Scottish Artists, Royal Glasgow Inst of the Fine Arts, Royal Scottish Soc of Painters in Watercolours; hon memb: Royal W of Eng Acad, RWS, Royal Soc of Painter-Printmakers; hon fell RIAS; Hon DLitt: Heriot-Watt Univ 1989, Univ of Aberdeen, Univ of Strathclyde 1998, Univ of London 2004; Hon Dr Univ of Edinburgh 1990; Hon LLD: Univ of Glasgow 2001, Univ of St Andrews 2003; Hon DUniv Stirling 2002, DLit (hc) Univ of London 2004; hon fell Edinburgh Coll of Art 2004; Hon FRSE, RSA 1972, RA 1976; *Recreations* gardening and golf; *Style—* Dame Elizabeth Blackadder, DBE, RA, RSA

BLACKBEARD, HE Roy; *b* 16 April 1953, Johannesburg; *Career* Botswana diplomat; MP 1989–95, asst min of agriculture 1992–94, min of agriculture 1994–97; high cmmr to the Ct of St James and ambass to Spain, Israel, Portugal and the Czech Republic 1998–; Botswana Award for Meritorious Service; *Style—* HE Mr Roy Blackbeard; ✉ Botswana High Commission, 6 Stratford Place, London W1C 1AY

BLACKBURN, Dr Bonnie Jean; da of John Hall Blackburn (d 1990), and Ruth Gwendolyn, *née* Moore (d 1992); *b* 15 July 1939, Albany, NY; *Educ* Wellesley Coll Mass (BA), Univ of Chicago (MA, PhD); *m* 1, 10 Sept 1971, Edward E Lowinsky (d 1985); m 2, 6 Jan 1990, Leofranc Holford-Strevens; 1 da (Paula Garner b 17 July 1967); *Career* visiting assoc prof Dept of Music Univ of Chicago 1986, lectr Sch of Music Northwestern Univ 1987, visiting assoc prof State Univ of NY at Buffalo 1989–90, freelance ed of scholarly books Oxford 1990–, gen ed Monuments of Renaissance Music 1993–; memb Editorial Bd: Early Music History, Early Music, Saggiatore Musicale, Alamire Jl, Analysis in Context, Music & Letters; John Simon Guggenheim Memorial Fndn Fellowship 1989–90; corresponding memb American Musicological Soc 2006; FBA 2005; *Books* author: Music for Treviso Cathedral in the Late Sixteenth Century: A Reconstruction of the Lost Manuscripts 29 and 30 (1987), The Oxford Companion to the Year (jtly, 1999), Composition, Printing and

Performance: Studies in Renaissance Music (2000), The Oxford Book of Days (jtly, 2000), The Josquin Companion (contrib, 2000), The New Oxford History of Music (contrib, 2001); ed: Johannis Lupi Opera omnia (3 vols, 1980–89), A Correspondence of Renaissance Musicians (jtly, 1991), The Perfect Musician (jtly, 1995), Théorie et analyse musicales 1450–1650/Music Theory and Analysis: Actes du colloque international Louvain-la-Neuve 23–25 septembre 1999 (jtly, 2001), Music as Concept and Practice in the Late Middle Ages (jtly, 2001), New Josquin Edition Vols 21–22 (2003–07), Canons and Canonic Techniques 14th -16th Centuries: Theory, Practice, Reception History (jtly, 2007), Florentius de Faxolis: Book on Music (jtly, 2010), Eroticism in Early Music (jtly, 2015); *Recreations* travel; *Style*— Dr Bonnie Blackburn, FBA; ✉ 67 St Bernard's Road, Oxford OX2 6EJ (☎ 01865 552808, fax 01865 512237, e-mail bonnie.blackburn@wolfson.ox.ac.uk)

BLACKBURN, Dean of; *see:* Armstrong, The Very Rev Christopher

BLACKBURN, Elizabeth; QC (1998); da of late Robert Arnold Parker, and late Edna, *née* Baines; *b* 5 October 1954; *Educ* City of London Sch for Girls, Univ of Manchester (BA); *m* 1979, John Blackburn, QC; 2 s (David John b 11 May 1986, Jack Alexander b 20 July 1989); *Career* called to the Bar Middle Temple 1978 (Harmsworth scholar, bencher 2008), memb Specialist Commercial and Admiralty Chambers 1980–, examiner of the High Court 1987–90; Lloyd's Form arbitrator 2009; memb: Exec Ctee Br Maritime Law Assoc, Advsy Ctee on Historic Wreck Sites DCMS, UK Delgn 2003 IOPC Supplementary Fund Diplomatic Conf, ICC UK Arbitration and ADR Gp 2010, Baltic Exchange 2016; *Recreations* gardening, family life, France; *Style*— Mrs Elizabeth Blackburn, QC; ✉ Stone Chambers, 4 Field Court, Gray's Inn, London WC1R 5EA (☎ 020 7440 6900, fax 020 7242 0197, e-mail mrseblackburn@aol.com)

BLACKBURN, Julia Karen Eugénie; da of Thomas Blackburn (d 1977), of London and N Wales, and Rosalie, *née* De Meric (d 1999); *b* 12 August 1948; *Educ* Putney HS, Univ of York (BA); *m* 1, (m dis 1996), Hein Bonger; 1 da (Natasha b Aug 1978), 1 s (Martin Thomas b Nov 1983); m 2, Herman Makkink; *Career* writer; JR Ackerley Award 2009, Costa biography shortlist 2012; FRSL 2002; *Books* The White Men (1978), Charles Waterton – Traveller and Conservationist (1989), The Emperor's Last Island (1991), Daisy Bates in the Desert (1994), The Book of Colour (1995), The Leper's Companions (1999), Thomas Blackburn: Selected Poems (ed, 2001), Old Man Goya (2002), With Billie (2005), My Animals and Other Family (2007), The Three of Us (2008), Thin Paths (2011), Threads – The Delicate Life of John Craske (2015); plays and stories for BBC Radio 4: A Good Death (2001), Betsy and Napoleon (2004), My Animals and Other Family (5 stories, 2006), An Italian Bestiary (5 stories, 2008), The Need for Nonsense (2009), The Spellbound Horses (2012); stories in PN Review 1990–91 and Granta 1998; *Style*— Ms Julia Blackburn; ✉ c/o Victoria Hobbs, A M Heath, 6 Warwick Court, London WC1R 5DJ (☎ 020 7242 2811, website www.juliablackburn.com)

BLACKBURN, Bishop of 2013–; Rt Rev Julian Tudor Henderson; *b* 23 July 1954, London; *Educ* Radley Coll, Keble Coll Oxford (MA); *m* May 1984, Heather Henderson; 1 da (Susannah b 6 July 1985), 1 s (James b 17 March 1987); *Career* ordained: deacon 1979, priest 1980; curate Islington St Mary London 1979–83, vicar Emmanuel and St Mary in the Castle Hastings 1983–92, vicar Holy Trinity Church Claygate 1992–2005, archdeacon of Dorking 2005–13; chair Business Ctee C of E General Synod 2011–13; *Style*— The Rt Rev the Bishop of Blackburn; ✉ Bishop's House, Ribchester Road, Blackburn BB1 9EF (☎ 01254 248234, e-mail bishop@bishopofblackburn.org.uk)

BLACKBURN, Richard Finn; *see:* Warrington, Bishop of

BLACKBURN, Prof Simon Walter; s of Cuthbert Blackburn (d 1984), and Edna, *née* Walton (d 1986); *b* 12 July 1944, Bristol; *Educ* Clifton, Trinity Coll Cambridge (sr scholar); *m* 1968, Angela, *née* Bowles; 1 da (Gwendolen b 1973), 1 s (James b 1975); *Career* jr research fell Churchill Coll Cambridge 1967–69, tutorial fell in philosophy Pembroke Coll Oxford 1969–90, Edna J Koury distinguished prof of philosophy Univ of N Carolina Chapel Hill 1990–2001, prof of philosophy Univ of Cambridge 2001–11; vice-pres Br Humanists Assoc; FBA 2001, hon foreign memb AAAS 2008, memb AAH (Australian Acad of the Humanities) 2015; *Books* Reason and Prediction (1973), Spreading the Word (1984), Essays in Quasi-Realism (1993), The Oxford Dictionary of Philosophy (1994), Ruling Passions (1998), Think (1999), Being Good (2001), Lust (2004), Truth: A Guide for the Perplexed (2005), Plato's Republic (2006), How to Read Hume (2008), Practical Tortoise Raising (2010), Mirror, Mirror (2014); *Recreations* walking, talking; *Style*— Prof Simon Blackburn; ✉ 141 Thornton Road, Girton, Cambridge CB3 0NE (☎ 01223 528278); Trinity College, Cambridge CB2 1TQ

BLACKBURN, Stuart Andrew; s of John Blackburn, and Joyce, *née* Hudson; *b* 9 June 1965, Blackpool, Lancashire; *Educ* Univ of Birmingham; *m* 17 June 2009, Naomi Parker; *Career* former theatre prodr; writer: The Bill, Doctors, Casualty, Ballykissangel; prodr: Emmerdale 2011–13 (story ed until 2011), Coronation Street 2013–; Best Ongoing Drama BAFTA (as producer) 2014; Hon Dlitt Leeds Beckett Univ; *Recreations* gardening, music, reading, shooting, travel; *Style*— Stuart Blackburn, Esq; ✉ Coronation Street Studios, Trafford Wharf Road, Manchester M17 1FZ

BLACKETT, His Hon Judge Jeff; s of Lt Cdr William Blackett, RN (d 2013), and Gwen V M, *née* Angell; *Educ* Portsmouth GS, Britannia RNC Dartmouth, UC London, St Antony's Coll Oxford; *m* 25 July 1981, Sally Fulford; 1 s (William b 30 Dec 1982), 1 da (Sophie b 18 March 1985); *Career* Royal Navy 1973–2004 (ret as Cdre); called to the Bar Gray's Inn (bencher 2008); recorder 2000–04, circuit judge (South Eastern Circuit) 2004–, judge advocate gen of HM Forces 2004–, dep High Court judge 2013–; RFU: hon discipline offr 2003–13, chm of governance 2014–, dir on Bd of Dirs 2014; tstee Help for Heroes; *Books* Rant on the Court Martial and Service Law (2009); *Recreations* rugby, golf, squash; *Clubs* RAC; *Style*— His Hon Judge Blackett; ✉ Office of the Judge Advocate General, 9th Floor, Thomas More Building, Royal Courts of Justice, Strand, London WC2A 2LL

BLACKETT, Karen; OBE (2014); *Career* MediaCom UK: chief operations dir EMEA 2008–10, ceo 2011–15, chairwoman 2015–; *Style*— Ms Karen Blackett, OBE; ✉ MediaCom, 124 Theobalds Road, London WC1X 8RX

BLACKETT, Thomas Richard (Tom); s of Thomas Blackett (d 1983), of Worthing, W Sussex, and Phyllis Sutcliffe (d 1984); *b* 25 January 1947; *m* Bridget Jane, da of Nick and Barbara Arlidge; 2 s (William b 7 Oct b 1974, Freddie b 10 Dec 1987); *Career* labourer 1968–69, Attwood Statistics 1969–72, Research Bureau Ltd 1972–77, MAS Survey Research 1977–78, Inbucon Management Consultants 1978–83, Interbrand Group Ltd 1983–2008, Siegel + Gale 2009–10; *Books* Trademarks (1997), Co-Branding (jtly, 1999), Brand Medicine (jtly, 2001); *Recreations* family, garden, rugby, cricket, rowing, wine, theatre, good food; *Clubs* Naval and Military, Windsor Rugby (pres 1993–95), London Rowing; *Style*— Tom Blackett, Esq; ✉ Coutts & Co, 440 Strand, London WC2R 0QS

BLACKFORD, Richard; *b* 13 January 1954; *Educ* Royal Coll of Music (Tagore Gold Medal); *Career* composer for theatre, television and film; publishing contracts with Schott, OUP and Novello; composer in residence Balliol Coll Oxford 1982, dir of music Royal Ballet Sch 1990–96, guest prof of film music composition Royal Acad of Music 1995–; *Theatre* credits incl: The Prince's Play (RNT), The Labourers of Herakles (Delphi Int Festival), The Kaisers of Carnuntum (Carnuntum Festival Vienna), The Rose Tattoo (Theatr Clywd), Macbeth (Theatr Clywd), The Devils (Theatr Clywd), Full Moon (Theatr Clywd and Young Vic), King (Piccadilly), Plea to Autumn (ROH), Medea (Lyric Hammersmith); *Opera* incl: The Pig Organ (Royal Opera cmmn for The Round House), Gawain and Ragnall (Radio 3), Metamorphoses (Royal Coll of Music Centenary Cmmn), Sir Gawain and The Green Knight (42 prodns, Argo Records); *Television* Millennium (CNN/BBC, Emmy nomination for Outstanding Achievement in Music), Preston Front (BBC), Degrees of Error (BBC), Pigeon Summer (Channel 4), A Little Bit of Lippy (Edinburgh Film Festival/Screen Two), Ruth Rendell Mysteries (TVS feature), Profound Scoundrels (TVS), Family (Channel 4), Buddy Breathing (TVS), Finding Sarah (Channel 4), Columbus (BBC), The Vanishing Man (ITV), Space Island One (Sky One); 53 television films for German TV; documentary credits for BBC incl: Secrets of Calcutta, Scharansky, St Luke's Gospel, St Mark's Gospel, Richard Strauss Remembered (prodr, 1st prize Huston Int Film Festival), When I Get to Heaven, Shout, Opinions (RTS Award), Great Women of Our Century; for Channel 4 incl: The Shadow of Hiroshima, A Maybe Day in Kazakhstan (with Tony Harrison, *qv*), A Walk Up Fifth Avenue, To The End of The Rhine (with Bernard Levin, CBE); commercials incl: Hilton Hotels Two Little Boys (Saatchi & Saatchi); *Film* City of Joy (Indian compositions, dir Roland Joffe), Prometheus (also with Tony Harrison), Song for a Raggy Boy; *Compositions* Mirror of Perfection (Sony Classical), Sinfonie Poliziane, Music for Carlow; String Quartet Canticles of Light, Concerto for Seven, A Portrait of Hans Sachs, Zodiac Dances, Postumous Leonatus, Carol: Lullay my Liking, Dragon Songs of Granny Chang, Three Cornish Pieces, Voices of Exile; *Style*— Richard Blackford, Esq; ✉ Novello, Promotion Department, 8/9 Frith Street, London W1D 3JB (☎ 020 7432 4209, fax 020 7287 6329)

B

BLACKHURST, Christopher Charles (Chris); s of Donald Blackhurst, of Barrow-in-Furness, Cumbria, and Rose Bestwick, *née* Wood; *b* 24 December 1959; *Educ* Barrow-in-Furness GS, Trinity Hall Cambridge (MA); *m* 1, 1986 (m dis 2003), Lynette Dorothy Wood, da of Philip Grice, and Mollie Grice; 2 s (Harry Max Thomas b 20 Sept 1987, Barnaby Samuel b 15 April 1992), 1 da (Daisy Natasha b 25 Dec 1988); m 2, 2004, Annabelle Sara, da of Norman Fisher, and Mary Fisher; 1 s (Archie Norman Donald b 6 March 2005), 1 da (Grace Rose Frances b 15 Feb 2007); *Career* articled clerk Cameron Markby 1982–84, asst ed International Financial Law Review (Euromoney Publications) 1985–86, sr writer Business Magazine 1987–88 (staff writer 1986–87), dep ed Insight The Sunday Times 1990 (business reporter 1989–90), city ed Sunday Express 1990–92, sr business writer The Independent on Sunday 1992–93, Westminster corr The Independent 1993–94, sr journalist The Observer 1994–95, Westminster corr The Independent 1995–96, asst ed The Independent on Sunday 1996–98; dep ed: The Independent 1998, The Express 1998–2001; city ed Evening Standard 2002–11; The Independent: ed 2011–13, gp editorial dir 2013–14, gp head of business 2014–15; exec dir CTF Ptnrs 2016–; dir and tstee Rose Theatre Kingston-upon-Thames 2004–11; TSB/PIMS Fin Journalist of the Year 1988, highly commended British Press Awards 1993 and 2007, Feature Writer of the Year Business Journalist Awards 2005, highly commended London Press Club Awards 2006; *Recreations* golf, tennis, watching sport, opera, music, theatre; *Clubs* Roehampton (chm), Soho House, George; *Style*— Chris Blackhurst; ✉ website www.chrisblackhurst.media

BLACKIE, Prof John Walter Graham; s of Walter Graham Blackie (d 1972); *b* 2 October 1946; *Educ* Uppingham, Peterhouse Cambridge, Harvard Univ, Merton Coll Oxford, Univ of Edinburgh; *m* 1972, Jane; *Career* advocate 1974, lectr in Scots law Univ of Edinburgh 1975 (sr lectr 1988–91), visiting lectr Univ of Göttingen 1981 and 1990, prof of law Univ of Strathclyde 1991–2009 (emeritus 2009–); dir Blackie & Son Ltd (Publishers) 1970–93; *Publications* Personal Bar (with E Reid), articles and essays on Scottish private law, especially the Law of Obligations, aspects of medical law, comparative law and doctrinal legal history; *Recreations* sailing (especially classic boats), playing the horn; *Clubs* Royal Northern and Clyde Yacht, Clyde Corinthian Yacht; *Style*— Prof John Blackie; ✉ 23 Russell Place, Edinburgh EH5 3HW (☎ 0131 202 6481); University of Strathclyde, The Law School, Graham Hills Building, Level 7, 50 George Street, Glasgow G1 1BA (fax 0141 548 3639, e-mail john.blackie@strath.ac.uk)

BLACKISTON, Galton Benjamin; s of B L J Blackiston, of Morston Hall Hotel, Norfolk, and Anne, *née* Skerrett-Rogers; *b* 13 August 1962; *Educ* Homewood Sch Tenterden Kent; *m* 12 Dec 1987, Tracy Jane Rowe; 2 s (Harry Galton, Sam Henry); *Career* restaurateur and hotelier; weekly Galtons Goodies stall on Rye Market 1979, trained under John Tovey of Miller Howe 1980–86, head chef Miller Howe 1986–90 (involved with public demonstrations for TV and radio and work in USA, SA and Canada), prop Morston Hall Hotel Holt 1991–, prop No 1 Cromer Fish and Chip Restaurant and Takeaway (Top 5 Fish and Chip Restaurant 2016); finalist The Great British Menu (BBC TV); television appearances incl: Saturday Kitchen (BBC 1), Market Kitchen (BBC 1), Put Your Money Where Your Mouth Is (BBC 2); memb RAGB, memb Guild of Food Writers, Master Chef GB; patron Macmillan; *Awards* AA Best Newcomer Award 1992, Independent Newspaper Country Hotel of the Year, Catey Award for Best Newcomer, 3 Red AA Stars and 3 Rosettes, Michelin Star, Tourist Bd Hotel of the Year (Gold Rated) EATB, Hotel and Restaurant of the Year Craft Guild of Chefs 2001, EDP Norfolk Chef and Restaurant of the Year Awards 2003; Morston Hall Cook Book (2002), More from Morston (2005), A Return to Real Cooking (2006), Summertime (2009), Fish Cook Book (2016); *Recreations* cricket, eating out, wine, reading cookery books old and new, golf; *Clubs* MCC; *Style*— Galton Blackiston, Esq; ✉ Morston Hall, Morston, Holt, Norfolk NR25 7AA (☎ 01263 741041, fax 01263 740419, e-mail galton@blackiston.com, website www.morstonhall.com)

BLACKLEDGE, Michael Glyn; s of Edward John Blackledge (d 1981), of Bromley, Kent, and Winifred May, *née* Hemsley (d 2015); *b* 24 October 1954; *Educ* Colfe's GS London, South Bank Poly (Dip Estate Mgmnt), Garnett Coll (Cert Ed), Coll of Estate Management (Dip Arbitration, David Lawrence Prize), Univ of Surrey (PGDip); *m* 21 Aug 1976, Janet May, da of Edward Arthur Connell, of Seaview, Isle of Wight; 2 s (Jonathan b 1984, Alexander b 1990); *Career* surveyor Thames Water Authy 1974–78; valuer: City of Westminster 1978–79, London Borough of Croydon 1979–81; sr lectr: Vauxhall Coll of Bldg and Further Educn 1981–88, Thames Poly 1988–89; sr surveyor King & Co 1989–91; sr lectr: Portsmouth Poly 1991–92, Univ of Portsmouth 1992–; sole princ conslt 1992–2015; tutor Coll of Estate Mgmnt 1989–2012; Freeman City of London, memb Worshipful Co of Feltmakers; FRICS 1990 (ARICS 1978); *Publications* Introducing Property Valuation (2009, 2 edn 2016); *Recreations* writing, golf, soccer, athletics, military history; *Style*— Michael Blackledge, Esq; ✉ e-mail michael.blackledge@sky.com

BLACKLEY, Emma Clare; da of John Barney Blackley (d 1988), and Cecily Clare Coales, *née* Stuart-Prince; *b* 11 June 1956; *Educ* Berkhamsted Sch for Girls, Lady Margaret Hall Oxford (BA); *m* 10 Dec 1988, Dr (Alan) Nicholas Spoliar, s of Stanislas Vjekoslav Spoliar; 1 s (Frederick Francis Blackley b 21 Dec 1992), 1 da (Anna Lucy Faithful b 18 Jan 1995); *Career* sec to dir Old Master Drawings Dept P & D Colnaghi & Co Ltd 1979–80, PA to editorial dir Cassell Ltd 1980–81; Octopus Books Ltd: asst ed Fiction Dept 1981–82, ed Children's and Fiction Depts 1982–84, publishing mangr Children's and Fiction Depts 1984–86, dep publisher Children's and Fiction Depts 1986–87, dep publisher New Edns Div 1987–89, publisher New Edns Div 1989–90; publishing dir Octopus Illustrated Publishing (div of Reed Consumer Books Ltd) 1990–92, divnl md Reed Illustrated Books 1992–93, gp publishing devpt dir Reed Consumer Books 1993–95; publishing conslt 1995–97 (clients incl Ryland Peters & Small Ltd and Phaidon Press Ltd); princ conslt KPMG Consulting 1997–2002, ind conslt 2002–03, commercial devpt mangr KPMG People Services 2003–05, chief operating offr CIM/ICE Advsy KPMG LLP 2005–11, assoc dir Joint Ventures Practice KPMG LLP 2011–; *Recreations* walking, tennis, squash, opera, cinema, literature, wine, travel; *Style*— Ms Emma Blackley; ✉ 47 Malvern Road, London E8 3LP (☎ 020 7275 8566)

BLACKLEY, Neil Ramsay; s of (Samuel) Ramsay Blackley, OBE, and Deirdre, *née* Wilson; *b* 30 August 1955; *Educ* Malvern Coll, Imperial Coll London (BSc), London Business Sch (MBA); *m* Fiona, *née* Andrews; 3 da (Emily, Natasha (twins) b 1996, Arianne b 2002); *Career* shipping analyst Lindsay Blee (chartering) Ltd 1979–82; investment/media analyst: Esso Pension Fund 1982–83, James Capel 1983–93, Goldman Sachs 1993–96, Merrill Lynch 1996–2003; chm Media Advsy Bd APAX 2003–09; non-exec dir: Freud Communications 2001–05, Stage Three Music 2005–10, Ingenious Media, IMAC 2005–14, Simplestream, Supadu, iSat, Infinity Creative Media; ambass Scope; ACGI 1977; *Publications* incl: The Design Consultancy Marketplace, The Global Advertising Marketplace, Electronic Retailing, Broadband Interactive Services, European Pay TV & Cable, Blueprint for Media Investment; *Recreations* squash; *Clubs* Groucho; *Style*— Neil Blackley, Esq

BLACKLOCK, Telfer George; s of Telfer Blacklock, of Edinburgh, and Mary, *née* Miller (d 2006); *b* 3 March 1958, Edinburgh; *Educ* St Mark's Swaziland, George Heriots Edinburgh, Univ of Edinburgh (MA, LLB, DipLP); *m* 4 June 1988, Mairead Catriona, *née* Black; 4 s (Calum Telfer William b 14 Oct 1990, Angus Telfer b 8 Oct 1992, Struan Miller Macphail b 23 May 1996, Ross Donald b 9 June 1999); *Career* admitted slr 1983; Balfour & Manson: trainee 1982–84, asst 1984–88, ptnr 1988–91; co-fndr Blacklock Thorley (now Blacklocks) 1992–; *Recreations* golf, bridge, cinema; *Clubs* Murrayfield Golf; *Style*— Telfer Blacklock, Esq; ✉ Blacklocks, 89 Constitution Street, Edinburgh EH6 7AS (☎ 0131 555 7500, fax 0131 555 5535, e-mail tgb@blacklocks.co.uk)

BLACKMAN, Malorie; OBE (2008); *b* 8 February 1962, London; *Educ* Thames Poly (HNC), Nat Film and Television Sch; *Career* writer; Children's Laureate 2013–15; ambass Reading Agency, ambass Nat Literacy Tst, govr RSC; FCBG Children's Book Award 2002, Smarties Silver Book Award 2004, Eleanor Farjeon Award 2005; FRSL 2009; *Books* incl: Trust Me (1992), Hacker (1992), Operation Gadgetman! (1993), Jack Sweettooth the 73rd (1995), The Space Stowaway (1995), Whizziwig (1995), Thief! (1996), A.N.T.I.D.O.T.E (1997), Pig Heart Boy (1997), Animal Avengers (1999), Dangerous Reality (1999), Hostage (1999), Tell Me No Lies (1999), Whizziwig Returns (1999), Noughts & Crosses series (Noughts & Crosses (2001), An Eye for an Eye (2003), Knife Edge (2004), Checkmate (2005), Double Cross (2008)), Dead Gorgeous (2002), Cloud Busting (2004), The Deadly Dare Mysteries (2005), The Stuff of Nightmares (2007), Boys Don't Cry (2010), Noble Conflict (2013), The Ripple Effect (2013), Contact (2015), Robot Girl (2015), Peacemaker (2016), Chasing The Stars (2016); *Recreations* cinema, music, reading, computer games; *Style*— Ms Malorie Blackman, OBE; ✉ c/o The Agency (London) Ltd, 24 Pottery Lane, Holland Park, London W11 4LZ (☎ 020 7727 1346, e-mail hd-office@theagency.co.uk, website www.theagency.co.uk, Twitter @malorieblackman)

BLACKMAN, Robert John (Bob); MP; s of Robert Benjamin Blackman (d 1979), and Winifred, *née* French; *b* 26 April 1956, Hammersmith, London; *Educ* Preston Manor HS (head boy), Univ of Liverpool (BSc); *m* 29 July 1988, Nicola, *née* Jennings; *Career* pres Guild of Undergrads Univ of Liverpool 1978–79, Burroughs Machines/Unisys 1979–90, BT 1991–2010; cncllr Brent Borough Cncl 1986–2010 (ldr 1991–96, dep ldr 2006–10), memb London Assembly (Cons) Brent and Harrow 2004–08, MP (Cons) Harrow E 2010–; memb Connect; *Recreations* football (Tottenham Hotspur FC season ticket holder), cricket, bridge, reading; *Clubs* Carlton; *Style*— Bob Blackman, Esq, MP; ✉ Room 92, Upper Committee Corridor South, House of Commons, London SW1A 0AA (☎ 020 7219 7082, fax 020 7219 0257, e-mail bob.blackman.mp@parliament.uk)

BLACKMAN-WOODS, Dr Roberta; MP; *b* 16 August 1957, Belfast; *Educ* Univ of Ulster (BSc, PhD); *m* Tim Blackman; 1 da (b 1987); *Career* prof of social policy and assoc dean Univ of Northumbria; MP (Lab) City of Durham 2005–; former chair Newcastle E and Wallsend CLP, chair City of Durham CLP; vol Save the Children, Child Poverty Action Gp; chair of govrs Durham Johnston Sch; memb: GMB, AUT; *Style*— Dr Roberta Blackman-Woods, MP; ✉ House of Commons, London SW1A 0AA

BLACKMORE, Prof Stephen; CBE (2011); s of Edwin Arthur Blackmore, and Josephine, *née* Henwood; *b* 30 July 1952; *Educ* Cheltenham GS, St George's Sch Hong Kong, Univ of Reading (BSc, PhD); *m* 7 July 1973, Patricia Jane Melrose, *née* Hawley; 1 da (Elizabeth Jane b 27 Oct 1979), 1 s (Roger Arthur b 20 June 1982); *Career* botanist Royal Soc Aldabra Res Station Seychelles 1976–77, lectr in botany and head Nat Herbarium Univ of Malawi 1978–80; Natural History Museum: head of palynology Dept of Botany 1980–90, keeper of botany 1990–99, assoc dir of life sciences 1992–95; regius keeper Royal Botanic Garden Edinburgh 1999–13 (hon fell 2014–), HM Botanist in Scotland 2010; pres Systematics Assoc 1994–97, chm UK Systematics Forum 1993; Linnean Soc: Trail Crisp medal 1987, Bicentenary medal 1992, Linnean Medal for Botany 2012; author of over 130 scientific papers and 9 botanical books; chm Darwin Expert Ctee 2013–; memb Bd Seychelles Islands Fndn 1998, chm Bd of Dirs Botanic Gardens Conservation Int 1999 (chair 2014–), memb Bd of Dirs Edinburgh Coll of Art 2004–10; FLS 1976, FSB 1993, FRSE 2001, FRGS 2009–13; *Recreations* photography, blues guitar music, hill walking; *Style*— Prof Stephen Blackmore, CBE; ✉ Royal Botanic Garden Edinburgh, 20A Inverleith Row, Edinburgh EH3 5LR (☎ 0131 248 2826, fax 0131 248 2903, e-mail s.blackmore@rbge.org.uk)

BLACKMORE, Tim; MBE (1999); s of Rev Harry J Blackmore (d 1964), and Marjorie, *née* Walker; *b* 3 July 1944, Hull; *Educ* King's Sch Pontefract, Blyth GS; *m* 6 May 1967, Margaret, *née* Hughes; 1 da (Joanna b 26 July 1968), 1 s (Simon b 29 Nov 1970); *Career* prodr BBC Radio 1962–77, head of programmes Capital Radio 1977–83, first dir Radio Acad 1987–88, prog dir Unique Broadcasting 1989–2001, editorial dir UBC Media Gp 2001–14; chm Sony Radio Acad Awards 1998–2011; chm Charles Parker Tst 2009–15, chm Lydiard Millicent Parish Cncl 2013–14; fell Radio Acad 1994; *Recreations* DIY, dining, music, grandchildren; *Style*— Tim Blackmore, Esq, MBE; ✉ Bayshill View, 21 St George's Road, Cheltenham, Gloucestershire GL50 3DT (☎ 01242 521829, e-mail tim@timblackmore.com, website www.timblackmore.com)

BLACKSHAW, Prof Dr Ian Stewart; s of late William Parkington Blackshaw, of Derbys; *b* 18 December 1943; *Educ* King Edward VII Sch Lytham St Anne's, Coll of Law London, Madrid Univ, Anglia Ruskin Univ (LLM, LLD); *m* 1970, Christine, da of late Thomas Haworth, of Lytham St Anne's; 2 s (Rupert b 1976, Daniel b 1978); *Career* admitted slr 1967, private practice in NW England, London and Madrid and corp practice with Coca-Cola and GKN 1967–80, sec of Bd and legal advsr Monsanto plc 1980–81, counsel for int affrs Gomez-Acebo & Pombo Madrid 1981–86; legal advsr: Br Embassy Madrid 1981–86, Br C of C Spain 1981–86; legal counsel EMEA Div RJR Nabisco Geneva 1986–90, vice-pres (legal affrs) ISL Sports Marketing Group AG Lucerne 1990–91; in int practice London and Spain 1991–96, int sports mktg conslt and academic 1996–; visiting prof of int business law Inst of Int Legal Studies Salzburg, visiting prof Int Sports Studies Centre Neuchatel Univ 2001–, visiting prof and memb Int Law Unit Anglia Ruskin Univ 2006–, visiting prof Sports Law Centre Univ of Johannesburg 2008–, visiting prof Int Sports Law Centre Univ of Staffs 2010–, visiting prof Int Acad of Sport Science and Technol (AISTS) Lausanne Switzerland 2013–, visiting fell Adams & Adams Intellectual Property Law Centre Univ of Pretoria 2013–; fell: Int Sports Law Centre TMC Asser Instituut The Hague 2000–, UK Sports Dispute Resolution Panel 2001–, Int Court of Arbitration for Sport Lausanne 2002–; memb WIPO Arbitration and Mediation Center Geneva 2004–, memb WIPO Expert Determination Panel 2008–, memb Isapele Consulting Legal and Business Trg Gp Johannesburg 2009–, memb TCA Trg and Consulting Gp Nairobi 2009–, memb EQUESTES ADR Panel Netherlands 2010–; contributing ed The Int Sports Law Jl, contrib New Oxford Companion of Law 2008–, consulting ed Global Sports Law and Taxation Reports 2010–, author of several books and articles on sports law and other legal subjects; memb: Int Bar Assoc, LES Int; *Recreations* music, travel, sport, family pursuits; *Clubs* Travellers, Baur au Lac (Zurich); *Style*— Prof Dr Ian S Blackshaw; ✉ e-mail ian.blackshaw@orange.fr

BLACKSTONE, Baroness (Life Peer UK 1987), of Stoke Newington in Greater London; Tessa Ann Vosper Blackstone; PC (2001); er da of late Geoffrey Vaughan Blackstone, CBE, GM (d 1989), and Joanna, *née* Vosper (d 2010); *b* 27 September 1942; *Educ* Ware GS for Girls, London Sch of Economics and Political Science (BSc, PhD); *m* 1963 (m dis), Thomas Charles Evans (d 1985); 1 s (Hon Benedict), 1 da (Hon Liesel); *Career* assoc lectr in sociology Enfield Coll of Technol 1965–66, asst lectr then lectr in social admin LSE 1966–75, fell Centre for Studies in Social Policy 1972–74, advsr Central Policy Review Staff Cabinet Office 1975–78, prof of educnl admin Inst of Educn Univ of London 1978–83, dep educn offr (resources) ILEA 1983–86, clerk to the Authy and dir of educn ILEA 1986, Rowntree special research fell Policy Studies Inst 1986–87, master Birkbeck Coll London 1987–97, min of state Dept for Educn and Employment 1997–2001, min of state for the Arts 2001–03; vice-chllr Univ of Greenwich 2004–11; chm: Fabian Soc 1984–85, General Advsy Cncl BBC 1987–91, IPPR 1988–97, RIBA Tst 2004–10, Gt Ormand St Hosp Tst 2009–, Br Library 2010–, Bd Orbit Gp 2013–; co-chair Franco-British Cncl 2013–; dir: Fullemploy Group 1984–91, Br Assoc for Central and Eastern Europe 1987–96, Thames Television 1991–92, Granada Learning 2003–06; non-exec dir: VT Gp 2004–10, Mott-McDonald 2005–08; memb: Arts Cncl Planning Bd 1986–90, Bd Royal Opera House 1987–97 (chm Ballet Bd 1991–97), Mgmnt Ctee King Edward's Hosp Fund for London 1990–95, Panel 2000; tstee Natural History Museum 1992–97, tstee ROH 2009–14; hon degrees and fellowships from 15 univs; Legion d'Honneur 2016; *Books* Students in Conflict: The LSE in 1967 (co-author, 1970), A Fair Start: The Provision of Pre-School Education (1971), The Academic Labour Market: Economic and Social Aspects of a Profession (co-author, 1974), Disadvantage and Education (co-author, 1982), Testing Children: Standardised Testing in Local Education Authorities and Schools (co-author, 1983), Response to Adversity (co-author, 1983), Inside the Think Tank: Advising the Cabinet 1971–83 (co-author, 1988), Prisons and Penal Reform (1990), Race Relations in Britain (co-ed, 1997); *Recreations* opera, ballet, tennis, walking; *Style*— The Rt Hon the Baroness Blackstone, PC; ✉ House of Lords, London SW1A 0PW (☎ 020 7219 5409, e-mail blackstonet@parliament.uk)

BLACKWELL, Nigel Stirling; s of Richard Blackwell, DSC (d 1980), and Marguerite, *née* Holliday (d 2015); *b* 18 March 1947; *Educ* Winchester, St Edmund Hall Oxford (MA); *m* 1, 22 Sept 1984, Eliza Pumpelly (d 1995), da of Frank Mauran III, of Rhode Island; 1 da (Georgina Stirling b 27 July 1986), 1 s (Richard Raphael Holliday b 17 June 1989); m 2, 5 Sept 2005, Christina Jane Lowry, da of Rolf Pasold of Geneva, Switzerland; *Career* dep chm and ceo Blackwell N America 1979–86, jt md BH Blackwell 1980–83 (dir 1974), md The Blackwell Gp 1983–89, chm and md Blackwell Retail Gp 1983–89; chm: Blackwell Publishers Ltd (formerly Basil Blackwell Ltd) 1985–2001, Blackwell Science (formerly Blackwell Scientific) 1990–2001 (dir 1980–2001), Munksgaard Publishers Copenhagen 1992–2001 (dir 1987–2001), Blackwell Publishing Ltd 2001–07; vice-pres Western Provident Assoc 2004– (dir 1992–2004); memb York Harbor Vol Veteran Firemans' Assoc; *Recreations* country pursuits, boating, collecting; *Clubs* Leander, Dunes (Narragansett RI), Vincent's (Oxford), White's, York Harbor Reading Room (Maine); *Style*— Nigel Blackwell, Esq; ✉ e-mail trudyoffice@googlemail.com

BLACKWELL, Baron (Life Peer UK 1997), of Woodcote in the County of Surrey; Dr Norman Roy Blackwell; s of Albert Edward Blackwell (d 1972), and Frances Evelyn, *née* Lutman; *b* 29 July 1952; *Educ* Latymer Upper Sch Hammersmith, Royal Acad of Music (jr exhibitioner), Trinity Coll Cambridge (MA), Wharton Business Sch Univ of Pennsylvania (Thouron Scholar, MBA, PhD); *m* 1974, Brenda, da of Thomas Clucas; 2 da (Hon Jane b 1979, Hon Sarah b 1983), 3 s (Hon Simon b 1981, Hon Richard b 1987, Hon William b 1989); *Career* strategic planning Plessey Co 1976–78, with McKinsey & Co 1978–86, special advsr PM's Policy Unit 1986–87, ptnr McKinsey & Co 1988–95, head PM's Policy Unit 1995–97, dir gp devpt NatWest Group plc 1997–2000; special advsr KPMG Corp Fin 2000–08; chm: Centre for Policy Studies 2000–09; non-exec chm: Smartstream Technologies Ltd 2001–05, Interserve plc 2005–16; non-exec dir: Dixons Gp plc 2000–03, Corporate Services Gp 2000–06, SEGRO plc (formerly Slough Estates plc) 2001–10, Standard Life plc 2003–12, Office of Fair Trading 2003–10, Ofcom 2009–14, Halma plc 2010–14; chm: Scottish Widows Gp Ltd 2012–14, Lloyds Banking Gp plc 2014– (non-exec dir 2012–); *Recreations* classical music, walking, gardening; *Clubs* Carlton, RAC; *Style*— The Rt Hon Lord Blackwell; ✉ House of Lords, London SW1A 0PW

BLACKWOOD, Nicola Claire; MP; *b* 1979, Johannesburg; *Educ* Trinity Coll of Music, St Anne's Coll Oxford (BA), Emmanuel Coll Cambridge (MPhil); *Career* MP (Cons) Oxford W and Abingdon 2010–; PPS to Matthew Hancock, MP, *qv*, 2013–; memb Home Affrs Select Ctee 2010, chair All Pty Parly Gp Women, Peace and Security; vice-chair Cons Pty Social Action 2010–13; *Style*— Ms Nicola Blackwood, MP; ✉ House of Commons, London SW1A 0AA (☎ 020 7219 7126, e-mail nicola.blackwood.mp@parliament.uk, website www.nicolablackwood.com)

BLAHNÍK, Manolo; Hon CBE (2007); s of E Blahník (d 1986), and Manuela, *née* Rodrigo-Acosta (d 2009); *b* 27 November 1942; *Educ* Univ of Geneva, Louvre Art Sch Paris; *Career* designer of shoes and furniture; co-proprietor 1973–; subject of Manolo Blahnik exhbn at Design Museum London 2003; Hon Dr Arts RCA 2001, Hon RDI (RSBA) 2001; La Medalla de Oro en Merito en las Bellas Artes (Spain) 2002; *Awards* CFDA Special Award 1987, Fashion Cncl of America Award 1987, 1990 and 1998, Hispanic Inst Washington Antonio Lopez Award 1990, Br Fashion Cncl Award 1990 and 1999, American Leather New York Award 1991, Houston Museum of Fine Art Silver Slipper Award 1999 (first shoe designer to receive this award), Neiman Marcus Award 2000, La Aguja de Oro (The Golden Needle) Madrid 2001, La Medalla de Oro en Merito en las Bellas Artes Spain 2002, La Medalla de Oro de Canarias Spain 2003, Shoe Designer of the Year Footwear News 2003, Accessory Designer of the Year Lycra British Style Awards 2003, Pinnacle in Art & Design Award Pratt Inst NY 2005, Rodeo Drive Walk of Style Award Beverley Hills 2008, Best International Professional Aim Prix Marie Claire Prix de la Mode Spain 2008, Felicidad Duce Fashion Prize Spain 2010; *Publications* subject of: Manolo Blahník (by Colin McDowell, 2000), Manolo Blahnik Drawings (2003), Blahník by Boman (by Eric Boman, 2005), Manolo's New Drawings (2010); *Recreations* travel and painting; *Style*— Manolo Blahník, Esq, CBE; ✉ 49–51 Old Church Street, London SW3 5BS (☎ 020 7352 8622 and 020 7352 3863, website www.manoloblahnik.com)

BLAIN, Harry Christian Peter; s of Peter Blain, and Sharon-Anne Blain; *b* 12 September 1967; *Educ* De Burgh Sch Epsom; *m* 23 June 2001, Bodil Bjerkvik; 1 s (August Peter b 30 Oct 2006), 1 da (Milla Sophia b 20 Oct 2008), 1 da from previous m (Chyna Emma b 27 Aug 1995); *Career* gallery owner; estab Blain's Fine Art 1992, estab (with Graham Southern, *qv*) Haunch of Venison 2002; memb Cncl Serpentine Gallery; *Recreations* skiing, sailing, diving, art; *Style*— Harry Blain, Esq; ✉ Haunch of Venison, 6 Haunch of Venison Yard, London W1K 5ES (☎ 020 7495 5050, fax 020 7495 4050, mobile 07973 347744, e-mail harry@haunchofvenison.com)

BLAIR, Rt Hon Anthony Charles Lynton (Tony); PC (1994); s of Leo Charles Lynton Blair, and late Hazel Blair; *b* 6 May 1953; *Educ* Durham Choristers Sch, Fettes, St John's Coll Oxford; *m* 1980, Cherie Booth, QC, *qv*, da of Tony Booth, the actor; 3 s (Euan Anthony b 19 Jan 1984, Nicholas John b 6 Dec 1985, Leo George b 20 May 2000), 1 da (Kathryn

Hazel b 2 March 1988); *Career* called to the Bar Lincoln's Inn 1976; Parly candidate Beaconsfield by-election 1982, MP (Lab) Sedgefield 1983–2007; memb Shadow Cabinet 1988–97, chief oppn spokesman on energy 1988–89, chief oppn spokesman on employment 1989–92, chief oppn spokesman on home affrs 1992–94, ldr Lab Pty 1994–2007, ldr of HM Oppn 1994–97, Prime Minister, First Lord of the Treasury and Minister for the Civil Service 1997–2007; Middle East envoy on behalf of US, Russia, UN and EU 2007–; pt/t sr advsr JP Morgan 2008–; *Books* A Journey (autobiography, 2010); *Style*— The Rt Hon Tony Blair

BLAIR, Bruce Graeme Donald; QC (1989); *b* 12 April 1946; *Educ* Harrow, Magdalene Coll Cambridge; *m*; 3 da; *Career* called to the Bar 1969; barr specialising in family law, currently head of chambers 1 Hare Court; recorder 1994–, dep judge of the High Court (Family Div) 1990–; memb Family Law Bar Assoc; *Publications* Practical Matrimonial Precedents (co-author, 1989, 27 edn 2004); *Recreations* bridge, tennis, turf; *Style*— Bruce Blair, Esq, QC; ✉ 1 Hare Court, Temple, London EC4Y 7BE

BLAIR, Isla Jean; da of Ian Baxter (d 1981), of Horsham, W Sussex, and Violet Barbara Skeoch (d 2005); *Educ* St Marays Dunblane, West Preston Manor Rustington, RADA; *m* 1968, Julian Glover, *qv*; 1 s (Jamie Blair Glover b 1969); *Career* actress; narrator for numerous audio books; Voice of the Year Spoken Word Award 2002; *Theatre* Prospect Theatre Co: The Padlock, Geraldine in What the Butler Saw, Miss in Her Teens, title role in Miss Julie, Regan in King Lear, Lydia Languish in The Rivals, Viola in Twelfth Night, Fanny Burney in Boswell's Life of Johnson, Thieves Carnival; Yvonne Arnaud Theatre Guildford: Amanda in Private Lives (and tour), Nora in A Doll's House (and tour); Bristol Old Vic: Kate in Kiss Me Kate, Heloise in Abelard and Heloise, Maggie in Hobson's Choice, Varya in The Cherry Orchard, Mary in Vivat Regina, Dotty in Jumpers, Desdemona in Othello, Clea in Black Comedy, Millie in The Browning Version; Triumph Prodns: Sarah in Say Who Your Are, Myra in Hay Fever; Palace Theatre Watford: Ruth in So Long on Lonely Street, Linda/Maud in Suite in Two Keys, Mrs Erlynne in Lady Windermere's Fan; RSC: Aglaya in Subject Fits, Emilia in The Man of Mode; other credits incl: Mad, Bad and Dangerous to Know (Ambassadors and Doolittle Theater USA), Belise in The Sisterhood (Minerva Chichester), Marchesa Matilde Spina in Henry IV (Wyndham), Jenny in The Health Farm (King's Head), Regan in King Lear (Compass), Gilda in Design for Living (Nottingham Playhouse), Lydia Languish in The Rivals (American tour), Lady Teazle in The School for Scandal (Thorndike Leatherhead), Philia in A Funny Thing Happened on the Way to the Forum (Strand), Nora in A Doll's House (Thorndike Leatherhead), Rhoda in Popkiss (Globe), Irene Molloy in The Matchmaker (Chichester Theatre), Keyboard Skills (Southampton), Mrs Prentice in What the Butler Saw (RNT), The Verge (Orange Tree), Dotty in Noises Off (Picadilly Theatre), Lydia in In Praise of Love (nat tour), Gertrude in Hamlet, Elmire in Tartuffe, Nurse Ratched in One Flew Over the Cuckoo's Nest, Louisa Kitteridge in Six Degrees of Separation, Mrs Kitty Warren in Mrs Warren's Profession, Helen Lancaster in Waters of the Moon (Salisbury Playhouse), Domina in A Funny Thing Happened on the way to the Forum (RNT), Stuff Happens (RNT), Mrs Patrick Campbell in Mrs Pat (Theatre Royal York), Mrs Lintott in The History Boys (Wyndhams Theatre), Raisa Gorbachev in The President's Holiday (Hampstead Theatre) 2008, Pauline Strauss in Collaboration (Chichester Festival Theatre) 2008; *Television* roles for BBC incl: Caroline in A Legacy, Lady Caroline in When the Boat Comes In, title role in Jean Brodie (Open Univ), title role in 'Alexa' Love Story, Flora in The History Man, Jenny in The Beggars' Opera, Ruth in Mother Love (series), In Your Dreams, True Tilda, A Touch of Frost, Heaven on Earth, Claire Carlsen The Final Cut – House of Cards; other credits incl: Sarah in The Liars, Daphne in Present Laughter,Linda in The Doctors, Elizabeth in Off Peak, Laura in The Bounder (series), Caroline in Boon VI, Maggie in The Good Guys, Jenny in 'Cherubim and Seraphim' Inspector Morse VI, Katherine Dunbar in The Advocates (series), Dr Jane Moore in Midsomer Murders; BBC appearances incl: Blake's Seven, An Englishman's Castle, Forgotten Love Songs, Doctor Who, Holby City, New Tricks, Casualty; other appearances incl: The Avengers, Space 1999, Only When I Laugh, Six Centuries of Verse, C.A.T.S. Eyes, Taggart, Bookie (series), Haggard, The Darling Buds of May, Medics, Dr Finlay, Hellfire, In Suspicious Circumstances, Mrs Bradley Mysteries, The House of Angelo, Heaven on Earth, Dalziel and Pascoe, The Office, Heartbeat, Blakee the home secretary in Quartermas; *Radio* incl: Mary Bannister in The House (series), Titania in A Midsummer Night's Dream, Lady Windermere's Fan; *Film* incl: The Tennis Court, Real Life, Lucy in Taste the Blood of Dracula, Battle of Britain, Mrs Donovan in Indiana Jones and The Last Crusade, Mrs Hawkins in Treasure Island, The Baroness in Valmont, Mother Agatha in The Monk, Sheila in The Match, Matron in Mrs Caldicot's Cabbage War, Dr Jackson in After Life; *Style*— Ms Isla Blair; ✉ c/o Sarah MacCormick, Curtis Brown, Haymarket House, 28–29 Haymarket, London SW1Y 4SP

BLAIR, Jon; CBE (2015), JP; *b* 30 October 1950, Cape Town; *Educ* St Stithian's Coll SA, St Paul's Sch London, LSE (BSc); *m* 7 Feb 2004, Yvonne, *née* Sellins; 1 da (Tanya b 27 March 1973), 3 s (Ben b 25 Nov 1979, Arthur b 17 Aug 2000, Louis b 17 Aug 2000 (twins)); *Career* journalist and film and television producer, director and writer; co-fndr and dir Spitting Image Prodns 1983–86, fndr Jon Blair Film Co 1984–; memb Acad of Motion Picture Arts and Sciences 1996– (dep chair London Ctee); Hon PhD Stockton Univ USA; *Films* incl: Schindler 1984 (Best Documentary BAFTA), Spalding Gray's Monster in a Box 1992, Anne Frank Remembered 1995 (Best Documentary Feature Academy Award 1996, Int Emmy, Int Documentary Assoc Distinguished Achievement Award, CableACE Award and others), Dancing with the Devil 2009; *Television* incl: This Week South Africa There is No Crisis 1976 (prodr), Spitting Image 1984–86 (co-fndr, co-creator, prodr and exec prodr), Do You Mean There Are Still Real Cowboys? (narrated by Robert Redford and Glenn Close) 1985, The Kimberley Carlile Inquiry 1986, The Age of Terror 2002 (series, Best Multi Channel Programme Broadcast Award), Reporters at War 2004 (series, Outstanding Historical Documentary News and Documentary Emmy, Gold Award NY Festival and others), Ochberg's Orphans 2007 (shortlisted Academy Award for short documentary), Bahrain Shouting in the Dark 2011 (Grand Prize, Robert F Kennedy Journalism Award, Feature Story of the Year Award UK Foreign Press Assoc, Best Int TV & Radio Award Amnesty Int, Golden Nymph Monte Carlo TV Festival and others); *Theatre* incl: The Biko Inquest; *Recreations* cinema, reading, skiing; *Style*— Jon Blair, Esq, CBE, JP

BLAIR, Michael Campbell; Hon QC (1996); s of Sir Alastair Campbell Blair, KCVO, TD, WS (d 1999); bro of Robin Blair, Esq, CVO, WS, *qv*; *b* 26 August 1941; *Educ* Cargilfield Sch Edinburgh, Rugby, Clare Coll Cambridge (MA, LLM), Yale Univ (MA); *m* 1966, Halldóra Isabel, da of late Richard Anthony Conolly Tunnard, DL, of Lincs; 1 s (Alastair Magnus b 1974); *Career* called to the Bar Middle Temple 1965 (bencher 1995, treas 2008); circuit admin Midland & Oxford Circuit 1982–86, under sec Lord Chllr's Dept 1982–87 (joined 1966, private sec to Lord Chllr and dep Serjeant at Arms House of Lords 1968–71); FSA: dir legal servs 1987–91, gen counsel 1991–93, head Policy and Legal Affrs 1993–95, dep chief exec 1996–98, gen counsel to Bd 1998–2000; in ind practice at the Bar and memb of chambers 3 Verulam Buildings 2000–; chm: Personal Investment Authy 2000–02, Investment Mgmnt Regulatory Orgn 2000–02, Securities and Futures Authy 2001–02, Review Body on Doctors' and Dentists' Remuneration 2001–07; pres Guernsey Fin Servs Tbnl 2002–08, memb Competition Appeal Tbnl 2000–15, memb Bd Dubai Financial Servs Authy 2004–13; dir Financial Services Compensation Scheme Ltd 2000–05, dir Chicago Mercantile Exchange (Europe) Ltd 2013–; memb Gen Cncl of the Bar 1989–99 (chm Professional Standards Ctee 1994, treas 1995–98), chm Bar Assoc for Commerce Fin and Indust 1990–91, memb Cncl of Legal Educn 1992–97; chm SWX Europe Ltd 2008–09; FRSA 1993; *Books* Sale of Goods Act 1979 (1980), Financial Services: the New Core Rules (1991), Butterworths' European Law Service (vol on Banking and Financial Services, conslt ed 1992), Blackstone's Guide to the Bank of England Act 1998 (1998), Blackstone's Guide to the Financial Services and Markets Act 2000 (2001, 2 edn 2009), Butterworths' Financial Regulation Service (gen ed, 2002), Halsbury's Laws of England Financial Services Title (consulting ed, 2003), Financial Services Law (jt ed, 2006, 3 edn, consulting ed, 2014), Financial Markets and Exchanges Law (jt ed, 2007, 2 edn 2012); *Recreations* family life, cross-country skiing; *Clubs* Athenaeum; *Style*— Michael Blair, Esq, QC; ✉ 3 Verulam Buildings, Gray's Inn, London WC1R 5NT (☎ 020 7831 8441, fax 020 7831 8479, e-mail mblair@3vb.com)

BLAIR OF BOUGHTON, Baron (Life Peer UK 2010), of Boughton in the County of Cheshire; Sir Ian Warwick Blair; kt (2003), QPM (1999); *Educ* Wrekin Coll, Harvard HS LA, ChCh Oxford (MA); *m* Felicity; 1 s, 1 da; *Career* police constable (grad entry) rising to Inspr Met Police 1974–85, DCI CID N London and mangr Met Police Crime Investigation Project 1988–89, Supt Kensington Div 1989–91, Chief Supt and staff offr to HM's Chief Inspr Constabulary Home Office 1991–93, offr i/c Operation Gallery 1993–96, Asst Chief Constable then Dep Chief Constable Thames Valley Police 1994–97, Chief Constable Surrey Police 1998–2000, Metropolitan Police Cmmr 2005–08 (Dep Cmmr 2000–05); tstee Shakespeare's Globe Theatre 2009–; chair Woolf Inst for the Study of the Abrahamic Faiths 2016–; visiting scholar Int Centre for Advanced Studies NYU, visiting fell Nuffield Coll Oxford, visiting prof John Jay Coll NY 2010; hon student ChCh Oxford; hon doctorate of laws Univ of Lincoln 2013; *Publications* Investigating Rape: A New Approach for Police (1985), Policing Controversy (2009); *Recreations* skiing, tennis, theatre; *Clubs* Atheneaum; *Style*— The Lord Blair of Boughton, kt, QPM

BLAKE, HE Alison; *Educ* Merton Coll Oxford (MA); *m* Col P A Henry; *Career* diplomat; MOD 1989–95 (including asst private sec to Sec of State for Defence), joined FCO 1996, first sec UK Delgn to NATO Brussels 1996–99, dep head Eastern Adriatic Dept FCO 1999–2000, first sec Washington DC 2001–05, dep dir Defence and Overseas Secretariat Cabinet Office 2006–07, head Conflict Gp FCO 2007–10, dep high cmmr Islamabad 2011–14, high cmmr Dhaka Bangladesh 2016–; *Style*— HE Ms Alison Blake

BLAKE, His Hon Judge Andrew Nicholas Hubert; s of John Berchmans Blake, of Clitheroe, Lancs, and Beryl Mary, *née* Murphy; *b* 18 August 1946; *Educ* Ampleforth, Hertford Coll Oxford (MA); *m* 7 July 1978, Joy Ruth, da of Ronald Shevloff (d 1986), of Southport; 1 s (Ben b 4 June 1980); *Career* called to the Bar Inner Temple 1971, recorder of the Crown Court 1988–99, circuit judge (Northern Circuit) 1999–; *Recreations* skiing, the Turf, fishing; *Style*— His Hon Judge Andrew Blake; ✉ Manchester Crown Court, Crown Square, Manchester M3 3FL

BLAKE, Carole Rae; da of Maisie Lock, *née* Pitt, and step da of Gilbert Lock; *b* 29 September 1946, London; *Educ* Pollards Hill Co Secdy Sch; *m* 1, 1970 (m dis 1982), David Urbani; m 2, 1983 (m dis 2012), Julian Friedmann; *Career* rights mangr George Rainbird 1963–70, rights and contracts mangr Michael Joseph 1970–74, rights and contracts mangr W H Allen 1974–75, mktg dir Sphere 1975–76, fndr literary agency 1977, merged with Julian Friedmann Agency forming Blake Friedmann 1983, currently head Book Div and jt md Blake Friedmann; pres Assoc of Authors' Agents 1992–95; chm Bd of Dirs Book Trade Benevolent Soc 2004–08 (pres 2010–13, lifelong patron), memb Soc of Bookmen 1991– (chair 1997–98), hon vice-pres Romantic Novelists' Assoc, patron Chipipng Norton Literary Festival; Advsy Bd: City Univ postgrad publishing course, UCL Centre for Publishing; life story recordings form part of oral history project Book Trade Lives (British Library); Pandora Award for significant and sustained services to publishing 2013; *Books* From Pitch to Publication (1999); *Recreations* reading, classical music, dollshouse miniatures, African wildlife, art, medieval history; *Style*— Ms Carole Blake; ✉ c/o Blake Friedmann Literary Agency Ltd, First Floor, Selous House, 5–12 Mandela Street, London NW1 0DU (☎ 020 7387 0842, fax 020 7691 9626, e-mail carole@blakefriedmann.co.uk, website www.blakefriedmann.co.uk, Twitter @caroleagent)

BLAKE, David William John; s of William Morley Blake (d 1985), and Winifred Juliet, *née* Virgo (d 1975); *b* 19 October 1946; *Educ* King Henry VIII GS Abergavenny, Univ of Sussex (BSc); *m* 1972 (m dis 1992), Marianne Neville-Rolfe, *qv*; *Career* journalist; roving European economic reporter Sunday Times 1970–72; The Times: joined 1973, foreign ed Business News, economics corr 1977–78, economics ed 1978–82, home ed 1982–86, managing ed Business News 1986–87; fndr then dep ed Sunday Correspondent 1987–91, assoc ed The European 1991–94, exec dir Goldman Sachs 1994–; parly candidate (Lab) East Grinstead 1974, local cncllr 1974–78; *Books* The Economics of Prosperity (ed with P Ormerod, 1980); *Recreations* Arsenal FC, music, travel; *Clubs* Reform; *Style*— David Blake, Esq; ✉ 42 Wilmington Square, London WC1X 0ET (☎ 020 7837 4320)

BLAKE, Howard David; OBE (1994); s of Horace Claude Blake (d 1985), and Grace, *née* Benson (d 1990); *b* 28 October 1938; *Educ* Brighton GS, Royal Acad of Music (LRAM); *Career* composer; dir Performing Right Soc 1978–87, fndr memb Assoc of Professional Composers 1980, visiting prof of composition Royal Acad of Music 1992; FRAM 1989; *Film and Theatre* film scores incl: The Avengers (final series scores), The Duellists 1977, The Riddle of the Sands 1978, The Snowman 1982, The Lords of Discipline 1983, A Month in the Country 1986, Granpa 1989, A Midsummer Night's Dream 1996, The Bear 1998, My Life So Far 1998, The Snowman Stage Show 1998; theatre: Henry V (RSC) 1984, As You Like It (RSC) 1985; stage works: The Annunciation 1979, The Station 1987; ballet: The Annunciation, Reflections, Diversions, Court of Love, The Snowman 1993, Eva (Gothenburg Opera House) 1996; *Instrumental works* orchestral works: Symphony in One Movement 1967, Toccata 1976, The Snowman 1982, Concerto for Clarinet and Orchestra 1984, Nursery Rhyme Overture 1984, The Conquest of Space 1988, Granpa 1988, Diversions 1989, The Bells 1991, Piano Concerto (cmmnd by The Philharmonia for the birthday of HRH The Princess of Wales) 1991, Violin Concerto (cmmnd by City of Leeds) 1993, The Land of Counterpane 1994, La Belle Dame Sans Merci 1994, Agatha Suite 1994, All God's Creatures 1995, Sleepwalking 1998, The Rise of the House of Usher 2003, Enchantment of Venus 2006; chamber music: Reflections 1974, The Up and Down Man 1974, Concert Dances (wind band) 1988, Serenade for Wind Octet 1991; piano and instrumental music: Penillion 1975, Dances for Two Pianos 1976, Prelude for Solo Viola 1979, Lifecycle 1996, Speech After Long Silence 2010; brass ensemble and brass band: Sinfonietta 1981, Fusions 1986; *Vocal works* Three Sussex Songs 1973, A Toccata of Gallupi's 1978, Walking in the Air, Shakespeare Songs 1987, Make Believe 1985; choral music: The Song of St Francis 1976, The New National Songbook 1976, Benedictus 1979, Festival Mass 1987, Four Songs of the Nativity 1991, Charter for Peace (cmmnd for UN fiftieth anniversary celebrations) 1995, Still Falls The Rain 1996, Songs of Truth and Glory (The Elgar Cmmn) 2005, Winterdream 2006, The Passion of Mary 2008, Spieltrieb (string quartet) 2010; *Recordings* The Snowman 1982, Clarinet Concerto 1986, Benedictus 1988, Granpa 1988, Violin Concerto 1993, A Midsummer Night's Dream 1996, Lifecycle (24 piano pieces) 2003, Chamber Music 2006, The Land of Counterpane 2007, Piano Concerto/Diversions/Toccata 2008, Violin Sonata/Piano Quartet 2008, The Passion of Mary/Four Songs of the Nativity 2009, Spieltrieb (Edinburgh String Quartet) 2010, Woodwind Concertos Marriner 2012, Piano Music Ashkenazy 2013; *Recreations* reading, walking, swimming; *Clubs* Groucho, Chelsea Arts, Ivy; *Style*— Howard Blake, Esq, OBE; ✉ Highbridge Music Ltd, Studio 6, 18 Kensington Court Place, London W8 5BJ (e-mail howard@howardblake.com); c/o Anna Menzies (mobile 07711 617718, e-mail anna@annamenzies.com)

BLAKE, Jeremy Michael; s of Norman Edward Blake (d 1994), and Betty Mary, *née* Whiting (d 2011); *b* 10 April 1953, Faversham, Kent; *Educ* Sir Roger Manwood's GS Sandwich, Univ of Newcastle upon Tyne (H B Saint scholarship, BA, BArch), British Sch at Rome (Rome scholar in architecture); *m* 1 Sept 1984, (Eleanor) Katharine Margaret, da of Rev (Francis) John Bacon; 3 s (Matthew David b 8 Feb 1986, Jonathan Paul b 22 April 1989, Timothy Stephen b 4 June 1992); *Career* architect; L J Couves & Partners Newcastle upon Tyne 1972–77, APP Horsham 1978–80, EPR London 1980, own practice Sussex 1980–84, Erith & Terry Dedham 1984–87, Fitzroy Robinson Ltd Cambridge 1987–2000, Fitzroy Robinson Ltd London 2000–05, Aukett Fitzroy Robinson 2005–07, princ Purcell Miller Tritton LLP 2007–12, princ Purcell 2012–; hon sec RIBA Traditional Architecture Gp 2003–07, memb Lime Forum Ctee 2007–16 (vice-chm 2009–11, chm New Buildings Sub Ctee 2009–16, chm 2011–15), chm European Hotel Awards Judging Panel 2008–10, chm Hemp Lime Construction Products Assoc 2008–12; memb: RIBA 1980, Faculty of Architecture Br Sch at Rome 1980, Soc of Architectural Historians of GB, RIAS 2009; AABC 2003 (memb Bd 2007–); *Books* La Falsa Prospettiva in Italian Renaissance Architecture (1982), Ss Vincenzo e Anastasio at Tre Fontane Near Rome (with Dr Joan E Barclay Lloyd, 2006); *Recreations* classical music, painting, surfing, swimming, gardening, reading; *Clubs* Goodwood Road and Racing Club (GRRC), Aston Martin Owners Club (AMOC); *Style*— Jeremy Blake, Esq; ✉ Purcell, 15 Bermondsey Square, London SE1 3UN (☎ 020 7397 7171, e-mail jeremy.blake@purcelluk.com)

BLAKE, John Michael; s of Maj Edwin Francis Blake, MBE (d 1972), of London, and (Evelyn) Joyce, *née* Meadows; *b* 6 November 1948; *Educ* Westminster City GS, NW London Poly; *m* 29 June 1968, Diane Sutherland, da of Peter John Campbell (d 1973), of London; 2 da (Emma b 1969, Charlotte b 1971), 1 s (Adam b 1985); *Career* reporter: Hackney Gazette 1965–68, Evening Post Luton 1968–69, Fleet Street News Agency 1969–71; columnist: London Evening News 1971–80, London Evening Standard 1980–82, The Sun 1982–84; asst ed Daily Mirror 1984–88, ed The People 1988–90, prodr Sky Television 1990; md: Blake Publishing 1991–, John Blake Publishing 2000–, Metro Publishing 2001–; Small Publisher of the Year Br Book Award 2005, Nielsen Gold Book Award 2006, Bookseller Ind Publisher of the Year 2010, Trade Publisher of the Year Ind Publishing Award 2010; *Books* Up And Down With The Rolling Stones (1979), All You Needed Was Love (1981); *Recreations* messing about in boats; *Clubs* Groucho, Chelsea Arts; *Style*— John Blake, Esq; ✉ John Blake Publishing, 3 Bramber Court, 2 Bramber Road, London W14 9PB (e-mail john@blake.co.uk)

BLAKE, Jonathan Elazar; s of Asher Blake, of London, and Naomi, *née* Düm; *b* 7 July 1954; *Educ* Haberdashers' Aske's, Queens' Coll Cambridge (MA, LLM); *m* 3 Aug 1980, (Marion) Isabel, da of Joseph Horovitz, of London; 1 da (Lucy Esther b 1984), 3 s (David Edward b 1987, Simon Andrew b 1989, Michael Alexander b 1993); *Career* slr; Stephenson Harwood 1977–82, ptnr King & Wood Mallesons (formerly SJ Berwin) 1982– (sr ptnr 2006–12, currently head Int Funds Dept); memb: Law Soc, Chartered Inst of Taxation, Corporate Financier (ICAEW), Br Venture Capital Assoc, Euro Venture Capital Assoc; *Books* Venture Capital Fund Structures in Europe, Venture Capital in Europe (contrib), AIM and EASDAQ: the New Enterprise Markets; *Recreations* family, theatre, walking, skiing; *Style*— Jonathan Blake, Esq; ✉ King and Wood Mallesons LLP, 10 Queen Street Place, London EC4R 1BE (☎ 020 7111 2317, fax 020 7111 2000, e-mail jonathan.blake@sjberwin.com)

BLAKE, Hon Mr Justice; Sir Nicholas John Gorrod Blake; kt (2007); s of Leslie Gorrod Blake (d 1960), and Jean Margaret, *née* Ballinger; *b* 21 June 1949; *Educ* Cranleigh, Magdalene Coll Cambridge (exhibitioner, MA), Inns of Court Sch of Law; *m* 5 July 1986, Clio, da of Chris Whittaker; 4 c (Lydia Beatrice b May 1986, Harrison b and d May 1987, Sophia Isobel b Oct 1988, Sebastian Patrick b June 1991); *Career* called to the Bar Middle Temple 1974 (bencher 2002); practising barr specialising in immigration law and human rights until 2007, fndr memb Matrix Chambers (chair 2000–02), QC 1994, recorder 2000–07, judge of the High Court of Justice (Queen's Bench Division) 2007– (dep High Court judge 2003–07), pres Upper Tbnl Immigration and Asylum Chamber 2010–13; memb Bd National Portrait Gallery 2005–13; FRSA; *Publications* Police, the Law and the People (1978), Wigs and Workers (1980), Policing the Miners' Strike (contrib, 1983), Jury Trial Under Attack (contrib, 1985), The New Nationality Law (with Ian Macdonald, 1983), Immigration Law and Practice (with Ian Macdonald, 1990 and 1995), Immigration Law (contrib, 2002), Human Rights and Immigration Law (co-author, 2002); *Style*— The Hon Mr Justice Blake; ✉ Royal Courts of Justice, Strand, London WC2A 2LL

BLAKE, Sir Peter; kt (2002), CBE (1983); s of Kenneth Blake, and Betty Blake; *b* 25 June 1932, Dartford, Kent; *Educ* Gravesend Sch of Art, RCA; *m* 27 April 1987, Chrissy; 3 da (Liberty, Daisy, Rose); *Career* artist; teacher: St Martin's Sch of Art 1960–62, Harrow Sch of Art 1960–63, Walthamstow Sch of Art 1961–64, RCA 1964–76; fndr memb Brotherhood of Ruralists 1975; album cover designer: Sgt Pepper's Lonely Hearts Club Band by The Beatles 1967, New Boots and Panties by Ian Dury and the Blockheads 1977, Stanley Road by Paul Weller 1995, Gettin' in Over my Head by Brian Wilson 2004, Me and Mr Johnston by Eric Clapton 2004; designer: Live Aid poster 1985, Live 8 poster 2005; assoc artist Nat Gallery London 1994, sr hanger Summer Exhibition (Royal Acad of Arts London) 2001, prof of drawing Royal Acad Schs 2002; Hon Dr RCA London 1998; RA 1981–2005 (ARA 1974), RDI 1981; *Solo Exhibitions* incl: Portal Gallery London 1962, Robert Fraser Gallery London 1965, Leslie Waddington Prints London 1969, Stedelijk Museum (and European tour) 1973–74, Galerie Claude Bernard Paris 1984 and 1995, Nishimura Gallery Tokyo 1988, Govinda Gallery Washington DC 1992, Tabernacle Cultural Centre Machynlleth 1993, Nat Gallery London and Whitworth Art Gallery Manchester 1996–97, Morley Gallery London 1999, Tate Gallery Liverpool 2000, One to Ten (Waddington Gallery London) 2005, Peter Blake: A Retrospective (Tate Liverpool touring to Museo de Bellas Artes de Bilbao) 2008, Galerie Thomas Levy Hamburg touring to Lorenzelli Arte Milan 2008–09; *Selected Group Exhibitions* with Brotherhood of Ruralists incl: Summer Exhibition (Royal Acad of Arts London) 1976, Arnolfini Gallery Bristol (and tour) 1981; *Work in Public Collections* incl: Arts Cncl of GB London, Baltimore Museum of Art, Bristol City Art Gallery, Br Cncl London, Leeds City Art Gallery, Museum Ludwig Cologne, Museum Moderner Kunst Vienna, MOMA NY, RCA London, Tate Gallery London, V&A London, Whitworth Art Gallery Manchester; *Clubs* Groucho, Gerry's, Max Miller Appreciation Soc; *Style*— Sir Peter Blake, CBE, RDI; ✉ c/o Waddington Gallery, 11 Cork Street, London W1X 1PD

BLAKE, Sir Quentin Saxby; kt (2013), CBE (2005, OBE 1988); s of William Blake, and Evelyn Blake; *b* 16 December 1932; *Educ* Downing Coll Cambridge (MA); *Career* freelance artist and illustrator; head of Dept of Illustration RCA 1978–86 (visiting prof 1989–); hon fell: Univ of Brighton 1992, Downing Coll Cambridge 2000, Royal Acad of Art 2001; Hon Dr: London Inst 2000, RCA 2001, Univ of Northumbria 2001; Hon DLitt Cantab 2004; first Children's Laureate 1999–2001; RDI, FCSD, sr fell RCA 1988; Chevalier de l'Ordre des Arts et des Lettres (France) 2002 (Officier 2007), Legion D'Honneur 2014; *Books* over 250 books; subject of: Words and Pictures, Laureate's Progress, Beyond the Page; *Style*— Sir Quentin Blake, CBE, RDI; ✉ 30 Bramham Gardens, London SW5 0HF (website www.quentinblake.com)

BLAKEMORE, Prof Sir Colin Brian; s of Cedric Norman Blakemore (d 1987), of Kidlington, Oxford, and Beryl Ann, *née* Smith; *b* 1 June 1944; *Educ* King Henry VIII Sch Coventry, CCC Cambridge (MA), Univ of Calif Berkeley (PhD), Univ of Oxford (MA, DSc), Univ of Cambridge (ScD); *m* 28 Aug 1965, Andrée Elizabeth, da of Ronald George Washbourne (d 1995), of Coventry, Warks; 3 da (Sarah Jayne b 1974, Sophie Ann b 1976, Jessica Katy b 1979); *Career* Univ of Calif Berkeley Harkness fell of the Cwlth Fund 1965–67; Univ of Cambridge: demonstrator in physiology 1967–72, official fell and dir of med studies Downing Coll 1971–79, lectr in physiology 1972–79, Royal Soc Locke res fell 1976–79; Waynflete prof of physiology Univ of Oxford and professorial fellow Magdalen Coll Oxford 1979–; dir: McDonnell-Pew Centre for Cognitive Neuroscience 1990–, MRC Interdisciplinary Research Centre for Cognitive Neuroscience 1996–; visiting prof: Dept of Psychology NY Univ 1970, Dept of Psychology MIT 1971; visiting scientist Salk Inst San Diego 1982, 1983 and 1992, McLaughlin visiting prof McMaster Univ Hamilton Ontario 1992, Regents' prof Univ of Calif Davis 1995–96; memb: BBC Sci Consultative Gp 1975–79, Scientific Advsy Bd Cognitive Neuroscience Inst NY 1981–, Sci Ctee Bristol Exploratory 1983–, Professional Advsy Ctee Schizophrenia: A National Emergency (SANE) 1989– (tstee 2001–), Exec Ctee Dana Alliance for Brain Initiatives NY and Washington DC 1996–, Nat Ctee for the 2000 Forum of Euro Neuroscience Brighton 1998–, UK Forum for Genetics and Insurance 1998–, Sci Advsy Ctee of the Volkswagen Stiftung Germany 1999–, Ind Expert Gp on Mobile Phones established by the Dept of Health 1999–, prog mgmnt ctee of the UK Mobile Telecommunications and Health Res Prog 2000–, strategic advsy ctee of Proseed Capital Holdings 2000–, Royal Soc Sci in Soc Ctee 2001–, cncl COPUS (formerly ctee on the Public Understanding of Sci) 2001–, Royal Soc Michael Faraday Award Ctee 2001–, joint Royal Soc/Acad of Med Sci Working Gp on the Sci of Transmissible Spongiform Encephalopathies (BSE, CJD etc) 2001–; chm Exec Ctee and chief exec Euro Dana Alliance for the Brain 1997–; chm: Royal Soc Public Prog Working Gp 2001–, Royal Soc Partnership Grants Ctee 2001–, Br Assoc for Advancement of Sci 2001–; pres Biosciences Fedn 2002–; patron CORPAL (support gp for families affected by ageneis of the corpus callosum and Aicardi's Syndrome) 1989–, patron and sr advsr at Bristol 1996–, patron Assoc for Art, Sci, Engrg and Technol (ASCENT) 1997–, patron and memb Professional Advsy Panel Headway (Nat Head Injuries Assoc) 1997–, patron Clifton Scientific Tst Bristol 1999–, patron Oxford Univ Scientific Soc 2000–, tstee Brain Child (charity supporting research into the developmental neuropsychology of cognitive disorders 1991–; conslt to Home Office and Police Fedn on TETRA (police communication) 2001–; memb Home Office/Defence Sci and Technol Lab TETRA Health and Safety Mgmnt Ctee 2001–; chm Weak Electric Field Effects Gp Nat Radiological Protection Bd 2001–; conslt: Wellcome Tst exhbn Head On: Art with the Brain in Mind 2001–, Thriving Child Project JABADAO (Centre for the Study of Movement, Learning and Health) 2002–, Electromagnetic Fields and Neurological Disease WHO 2002–03; participant 'Bright Sparks' Festival of Br Science India 1999; presenter The Next Big Thing (10 debates on current issues in sci, BBC) 2000; advsr Y Touring Theatre of Science project (sci drama for inner city schs) 2000–; memb Advsy Gp Dana Centre at the Wellcome Wolfson Building Science Museum 2002; memb Exec Cncl Novartis Fndn 2002–; fell World Innovation Fndn 2002–; conslt Wellcome Tst Exhbn Head On – Art with the Brain in Mind 2001–02; numerous named lectures, hon appointments and awards incl: BBC Reith lectr 1976, Lethaby prof RCA 1978–79, Royal Soc Michael Faraday Award and Medal 1989, Osler Medal (RCP) 1993, Ellison-Cliffe Medal (RSM) 1993, Royal Soc lectr (Assoc for Sci Educn) 1995, Physiological Soc Prize Review Lecture 1995, Leverhulme Research Grant 1995–96, Alcon Prize Alcon Research Inst 1996, Memorial Medal Charles Univ Prague 1998, Alfred Meyer Award (Br Neuropathological Soc) 2001, Inst of Biology Charter Award and Medal 2001, Baly Medal RCP (Dyster Tst) for distinction in the sci of physiology 2001, Outstanding Contribution to Neuroscience Award (Br Neuroscience Assoc) 2001, Menzies Medal Menzies Fndn Aust 2001; Liveryman Worshipful Co of Spectacle Makers 1998–; memb: Br Neuroscience Assoc 1968 (memb Nat Ctee 1973–77 and 1997–, pres 1997–), Physiological Soc 1968 (hon memb 1998–, pres 2001–), Experimental Psychological Soc 1968, Euro Brain and Behaviour Soc 1972 (memb Ctee 1974–76), Int Brain Res Orgn 1973 (memb Governing Cncl 1973–, memb Exec Ctee 1979–91), Cambridge Philosophical Soc 1975–79, Euro Neuroscience Assoc 1977 (memb Nominating Ctee 1988), Soc for Neuroscience 1981, Oxford Med Soc 1986, Child Vision Res Soc 1986 (memb Organising Ctee 1986–), Nat Conf of Univ Profs 1989, Br Assoc for the Advancement of Science 1990 (vice-pres 1990–, treas 1993, pres 1997–98, hon memb 2001–), Euro Biomedical Research Assoc (fndr memb) 1994, Academia Europaea 1995, Cncl of Fedn of European Neuroscience Socs 1998–, Int Soc on Infant Studies 2001–, Interim Exec Ctee for UK Fedn of Life Sciences 2002–, Advsy Gp Sense about Science 2002–, Med Panel (Seriously Ill for Medical Research) SIMR 2002–, Sci, Engrg and Environment Advsy Ctee Br Cncl 2003–; hon patron Wrexham Sci Festival 2002–; foreign memb Royal Netherlands Acad of Arts and Sciences 1993, hon memb Maverick Club 1999–, hon assoc Rationalist Int 2000–, hon assoc Cheltenham Festival of Sci 2001–; Hon DSc: Aston Univ 1992, Univ of Salford 1994; hon fell: CCC Coll Cambridge 1994, Cardiff Univ of Wales 1998, Downing Coll Cambridge 1999; fell World Economic Forum 1994–98; fndr FMedSci 1998; FRS 1992, FIBiol, CBiol; *Books* Handbook of Psychobiology (1975), Mechanics of the Mind (1977), Mindwaves (1987), The Mind Machine (1988), Images and Understanding (1990), Vision: Coding and Efficiency (1990), Gender & Society (1999), The Oxford Companion to the Body (2001); *Publications* varied editorial work incl: memb Editorial Bds Vision Research and Int Review of Neurobiology, assoc ed NeuroReport 1989–, ed-in-chief Oxford Companion to the Body (OUP) 1996–; *Recreations* running, the arts; *Clubs* Chelsea Arts; *Style*— Prof Sir Colin Blakemore, FRS; ✉ University Laboratory of Physiology, Parks Road, Oxford OX1 3PT (☎ 01865 272470, fax 01865 272488, e-mail colin.blakemore@clneuro.ox.ac.uk)

BLAKEMORE, Michael Howell; AO (2003), OBE (2003); s of Dr Conrad Howell Blakemore (d 1976), and Una Mary, *née* Litchfield (later Mrs Heyworth, d 1982); *b* 18 June 1928, Sydney, NSW; *Educ* Cranbrook Sch, The King's Sch, Univ of Sydney, RADA; *m* 1, 1960 (m dis 1986), Shirley Mary Bush; 1 s (Conrad); m 2, 1986, Tanya McCallin, *qv*, da of Clement McCallin (actor, d 1978); 2 da (Beatrice b 1981, Clementine b 1984); *Career* stage and film director (occasional writer and actor); co-artistic dir Glasgow Citizen's Theatre 1966–68, assoc dir NT 1971–76, resident dir Lyric Theatre Hammersmith 1980; freelance dir of prize winning prodns: A Day in the Death of Joe Egg 1968, Arturo Ui 1969, Forget-Me-Not-Lane 1971; also dir of: The National Health 1969, Plunder 1975, Long Day's Journey Into Night 1971, The Front Page 1972 (Plays and Players Best Dir Award for the latter two prodns), The Wild Duck, Make and Break, Noises Off, Design for Living, Knuckle, Candida, Separate Tables, Privates on Parade (also the film), Deathtrap, All My Sons, Benefactors (London and Broadway), Made in Bangkok, Lettice and Lovage (London and Broadway), Uncle Vanya, After The Fall, City of Angels (Broadway and London), Noises Off (London and Broadway, received Drama Desk Award 1984), The Sisters Rosensweig (Old Vic), Death Defying Acts (off-Broadway 1995), The Life (Broadway 1997), Alarms and Excursions (London) 1998, Kiss Me Kate (Broadway) 1999 (Tony and Drama Desk Awards 2000) and 2001 (Victoria Palace Theatre London), Copenhagen (RNT 1998, London 1999, Paris 1999 (Moliere Award) and Broadway 2000 (Tony and Drama Desk Awards)), Three Sisters (London) 2003, Democracy (NT) 2003, Embers (Duke of York's) 2006, Deuce (Broadway) 2007, Is He Dead? (Broadway) 2007, Afterlife (NT) 2008, Blithe Spirit (Broadway) 2008 and (Gielgud Theatre) 2014; film A Personal History of the Australian Surf (also wrote and acted, Peter Sellers' Award for Comedy in the Standard Film Awards); actor The Last Bastion for Channel 10 television in Australia 1984; film actor/writer/dir Country Life (Aust) 1994; inducted into the American Theatre Hall of Fame 2011; *Books* Next Season (1969), Arguments with

England (2004), Stage Blood (2013); *Clubs* RAC; *Style*— Michael Blakemore, AO, OBE; ✉ 47 Ridgmount Gardens, London WC1E 7AT (☎ 020 7209 0608, fax 020 7209 0141)

BLAKENHAM, 2 Viscount (UK 1963); Michael John Hare; s of 1 Viscount Blakenham, OBE, PC, VMH (d 1982, 3 s of 4 Earl of Listowel), and (Beryl) Nancy, *née* Pearson, da of 2 Viscount Cowdray; *b* 25 January 1938; *Educ* Eton, Harvard Univ (AB Econ); *m* 12 Jan 1965, his 1 cous, Marcia Persephone, da of Maj Hon Alan Victor Hare, MC (d 1995); 1 s, 2 da; *Career* 2 Lt The Life Gds 1956–57; English Electric 1958, Lazard Bros 1961–63, Standard Industrial Group 1963–71, Royal Doulton 1972–77, CE Pearson plc 1978–83; chm: Pearson plc 1983–97, Financial Times Group Ltd 1983–93, MEPC plc 1993–98 (dir 1990–98), Japan 2001 1999–2002; ptnr Lazard Ptnrs 1984–97 (dir 1975–97); dir: Sotheby's Inc 1987–2013, UK-Japan 21st Century Gp 1990–, Lafarge 1997–2007; memb: Int Advsy Bd Lafarge 1979–97, Int Advsy Gp Toshiba Corporation 1997–2002; memb House of Lords Select Ctee on: Sci and Technol 1985–88, Sustainable Development 1994–95; memb Nature Conservancy Cncl 1986–90, pres Sussex Wildlife Tst 1983–2008, chm Royal Soc for the Protection of Birds 1981–86, chm Royal Botanic Gardens Kew and Wakehurst Place 1997–2003; *Style*— The Rt Hon Viscount Blakenham; ✉ Cottage Farm, Little Blakenham, Ipswich IP8 4LZ

BLAKER, Gary; QC (2015); s of Marshall Blaker, and Philippa, *née* Ross; *b* 20 June 1970, London; *Educ* Haberdashers Aske's, Christ's Coll Cambridge (MA); *m* 23 Aug 1998, Sharon Horwitz; 1 da (Isabella Blaker b 17 Dec 2009); *Career* called to the Bar Middle Temple 1993, bencher 2015; chm Middle Temple Hall Ctee 2012–13, Middle Temple rep Bar Cncl 2014–; memb: Chancery Bar Assoc, Property Bar Assoc, Professional Negligence Bar Assoc; Liveryman Worshipful Co of Fanmakers 1992 (memb Ct of Assts 2014–); *Recreations* cinema, cricket, opera, travel, theatre, watching Arsenal FC; *Style*— Gary Blaker, Esq, QC; ✉ Selborne Chambers, 10 Essex Street, London WC2R 3AA (☎ 020 7420 9500, e-mail gary.blaker@selbornechambers.co.uk)

BLAKER, Lt-Col (Guy) Peter; s of Guy Stewart Blaker (d 1969), of Rotherfield Greys, Henley-on-Thames, and Dawn Laetitia Prudence, *née* Watson (d 1997), gda of Gen Sir John Watson, VC, GCB (d 1919); *b* 10 November 1936, London; *Educ* Boxgrove Sch, Lancing, Jesus Coll Cambridge (MA, LLB); *m* 18 Jan 1969, Hiltegund Maria, da of Dr Hermann Bastian (d 1945), of Freiburg-im-Breisgau; 1 da (Alexandra Maud b 14 March 1970), 2 s (Guy Dominic Mansel b 16 Sept 1971, Nicholas William Hermann b 21 Feb 1975); *Career* Nat Serv, cmmnd W Yorks Regt 1957, Royal Green Jackets 1961–84, served Malaya, Borneo, Singapore, Cyprus, UK, Germany, Belgium (SHAPE); Army Aviation Pilot 1964–67, Staff Coll 1968, cmd Cambridge Univ Offrs Trg Corps 1979–82; Queen's Messenger 1984–85; gen mangr Newdata Publishing 1985–86; sec Gen Cncl and Register of Osteopaths 1987–95, sec Blackie Fndn Tst 1996–98; co-ordinator Br Southern Slav Soc 1998–99; regnl dir Ormonde Advsy Service 1998–2011; lay chm Rotherfield Greys PCC 1985–97; chm Berkshire Automobile Club 1990–2009 (pres 2009–); *Recreations* classical music, history, languages, ornithology, fly fishing, rowing; *Clubs* Naval and Military, Army and Navy, MCC, Leander (assoc), Phyllis Court; *Style*— Lt-Col Peter Blaker; ✉ Greys Piece, Rotherfield Greys, Henley-on-Thames, Oxfordshire RG9 4QG (☎ 01491 628308, e-mail pblaker@globalnet.co.uk)

BLAKEWAY, Richard Anthony; *b* 14 October 1978; *Educ* BA; *Career* advsr on housing GLA 2008–12, dep mayor of London for housing, land and property 2012–; tstee Chartered Inst of Housing; young ambass Samaritans; FRSA; *Style*— Richard Blakeway, Esq; ✉ Greater London Authority, City Hall, The Queen's Walk, More London, London SE1 2AA (☎ 020 7983 4000, e-mail richard.blakeway@london.gov.uk, website www.london.gov.uk)

BLAKISTON, Sir Ferguson Arthur James; 9 Bt (GB 1763), of the City of London; s of Sir (Arthur) Norman Hunter Blakiston, 8 Bt (d 1977); *b* 19 February 1963; *Educ* Lincoln Coll NZ (DipAg), Auckland Inst of Technology (Cert Marketing), NZ Inst of Business Studies (Dip Travel Writing and Photography); *m* 3 April 1993, Linda Jane, da of late Robert John Key, of Queenstown, NZ; 2 da (Lydia Mary Ann b 28 Nov 1996, Emma Charlotte Helen b 21 Oct 1999); *Heir* bro, John Blakiston; *Career* builder, farmer, freelance writer and photographer; *Style*— Sir Ferguson Blakiston, Bt; ✉ 7 Hewlings Street, Geraldine, South Canterbury, New Zealand

BLANC, Raymond René Alfred; Hon OBE (2008); s of Maurice Blanc, and Anne-Marie, *née* Tournier; *b* 19 November 1949; *Educ* Besançon Coll France (Dip BEPC); *m* 1, 14 Jan 1974 (m dis 1986), Jennifer Colbeck; 2 s (Olivier b 18 Oct 1974, Sebastien b 15 April 1981); m 2, 18 Dec 1990 (sep), Katalin Szoke; *Career* chef; chef patron: Les Quat' Saisons Oxford 1977, Maison Blanc 1978–88 (conslt 2009), Le Manoir Aux Quat' Saisons 1984–, Le Petit Blanc (relaunched as Brasserie Blanc 2006) Oxford 1996 (Michelin star), Cheltenham 1998, Birmingham 1999, Manchester 2000, Tunbridge Wells 2004, Leeds 2007, Milton Keynes 2007, Winchester 2008, Bristol 2008, Portsmouth 2009, Chichester 2010, Berkhamsted, St Paul's, Opera Terrace, Tower of London, Threadneedle St, Chancery Lane, Charlotte St and Southbank all 2012, Farnham 2013, Beaconsfield 2014; chef patron and chm Blanc Restaurants Ltd 1984–, vice-pres Orient-Express Hotels Ltd 2010, culinary dir Business Premier Class Eurostar 2012–; TV appearances incl: Food and Drink 1987, In At the Deep End 1989, Chef's Apprentice 1989; own TV series: Blanc Mange (BBC 2) 1994, The Restaurant (BBC 2) 2007–09, Kitchen Secrets (BBC 2) 2010, The Very Hungry Frenchman (BBC 2) 2012, Hot to Cook Well (BBC 2) 2013; memb: Academy of Culinary Arts, Syndicat de l'Haute Cuisine Française, Relais Et Chateaux Tradition Et Qualité; Personalité de l'année 1990; 2 Michelin stars 1999, Hotelympia Lifetime Achievement Award 2012; Hon DBA Oxford Brookes Univ 1999; Cdr de l'Assoc Int des Maîtres Conseils en Gastronomie Française; *Books* Le Manoir Aux Quat'Saisons (1988), Cooking for Friends (1991), Blanc Mange (1994), A Blanc Christmas (1996), Blanc Vite (1998), Foolproof French Cookery (2002), A Taste of My Life (2008). Kitchen Secrets (2011), My Kitchen Table: 100 Recipes for Entertaining (2012); *Recreations* reading, music, tennis, swimming; *Style*— Raymond Blanc, Esq, OBE; ✉ Le Manoir aux Quat' Saisons, Church Road, Great Milton, Oxfordshire OX44 7PD (☎ 01844 278881, fax 01844 278847)

BLAND, Sir (Francis) Christopher Buchan; kt (1993); eldest s of James Franklin MacMahon Bland, of Co Down, and Jess Buchan, *née* Brodie; *b* 29 May 1938; *Educ* Sedbergh, The Queen's Coll Oxford; *m* 1981, Jennifer Mary, elder da of late Rt Hon William Morrison May, MP, of Co Down, and formerly w of Viscount Enfield (now 8 Earl of Strafford); 1 s; *Career* chm: Sir Joseph Causton & Sons 1977–85, LWT Holdings plc 1984–94, Life Sciences International, NFC plc 1995–, Bd of Govrs BBC 1996–2001, British Telecom plc 2001–07; dep chm Independent Broadcasting Authy (IBA) 1972–79; *Recreations* fishing, skiing; *Clubs* Beefsteak; *Style*— Sir Christopher Bland

BLAND, Prof David Edward; OBE (1998); s of Rev Albert Edward Bland, of Blackburn, and Lily, *née* Simmons; *b* 9 December 1940; *Educ* Queen Elizabeth GS Blackburn, UC Durham (BA, MLitt), Univ of Sheffield (PhD); *Career* warden of Sorby Hall and pro-vice-chllr Univ of Sheffield 1964–89, DG Chartered Insurance Inst 1989–2000, head E London Business Sch Univ of E London 2000–02; visiting prof City Univ 1994–; chm: Postwatch SE England 2002–07, Thames Region CCWater 2005; CII Gold Medal 2000; Master: Worshipful Co of Insurers 2006–07, Worshipful Co of Firefighters 1999–2000 and 2010–11; fell Inst of Co Accountants 1970 (pres 1990–91), FSCA, FCIPD 1991, FCII 1994, FIRM (memb 2000); *Books* Can Britain Survive? (with KW Watkins, 1971), Managing Higher Education (1990), Principles and Practice of Insurance (1994), Treasury Risk (2000), Sinking Britain (2013), Rottenomics: Replacing Economics (2015); *Recreations* walking, music; *Clubs* Athenaeum; *Style*— Prof David Bland, OBE; ✉ 23 Orient Wharf, 74 Wapping High Street, London E1W 2YG (☎ 020 7533 0086)

BLAND, Jeff; s of Albert Bland, and Marjory Bland; *b* 17 August 1953; *Educ* Carlton GS Bradford, Bradford Tech Coll (City & Guilds, Student of the Year); *m* Jill, *née* Hepburn; *Career* various positions rising to sous chef Gleneagles Hotel 1973–77, relief chef Br Transport Hotels 1978–80, chef Station Hotel Inverness 1980–82; exec chef: Gosforth Park Newcastle 1982–87, Caledonian Edinburgh 1987–90, Cameron House Hotel Alexandria 1990–97 (Scottish Hotel of the Year 1991, 3 AA Rosettes, Egon Ronay Award, Macallan Decanter Restaurant of the Year 1992, RAC Blue Ribbon 1994, Michelin Star 1995 and 1996, AA Hotel of the Year 1995), Balmoral Hotel Edinburgh 1997– (Michelin Star 2003, 2004, 2005, 2006, 2007 and 2008); demonstrator Good Food Show 1995; guest appearances: Square Meals, Junior Masterchef; guest chef fundraising dinner Michigan USA (raised 1 million dollars); memb: Craft Guild of Chefs 1974, Académie Culinaire de France 1988 (mentor, chm Scottish branch); Craft Guild Chef of the Year 1995, Chefs of GB Chef of the Year 1995, Scottish Chef of the Year Scottish Chef Awards 2003, Icon of Scotland Award 2004, four RAC Dining Awards 2005, Fine Dining Experience Scottish Restaurant Award 2008; *Recreations* eating out, wine, entertaining friends, running (completed various half marathons and London marathon); *Style*— Jeff Bland, Esq; ✉ Balmoral Hotel, Princes Street, Edinburgh EH2 2EQ (☎ 0131 556 2414)

BLANDFORD, Mark Robert; s of Roy Blandford, of Brobury, Herefordshire, and June, *née* Farr; *b* 25 November 1957, Hereford; *Educ* Hereford Cathedral Sch, Wolverhampton Poly (HND, DipM); *m* 16 May 1981, Patricia, *née* Bowen; 2 da (Lucy b 22 Nov 1987, Sophie b 27 March 1989); *Career* Star Aluminium 1979–80, Sun Valley Poultry 1980–82, Radio Wyvern 1982–84, fndr Blandford Betting 1984–97, fndr Sportingbet plc 1997–2007; nat finalist Entrepreneur of the Year 2000, AIM Entrepreneur of the Year 2002; memb Inst of Mktg 1979; *Recreations* football (Hereford United), horse racing (owner); *Clubs* Home House, Annabel's; *Style*— Mark Blandford, Esq

BLANDFORD, Prof Roger David; s of Jack George Blandford, and late Janet Margaret Blandford; *b* 28 August 1949; *Educ* King Edward's Sch Birmingham, Magdalene Coll Cambridge (BA, Charles Kingsley Bye Fell, MA, PhD), Univ of Chicago (ScD); *m* 1972, Elizabeth Denise Kellett; 2 s; *Career* res fell St John's Coll Cambridge 1973–76; California Inst of Technol: asst prof 1976–79, prof 1979–89, Richard Chace Tolman prof of theoretical astrophysics 1989–2003, exec offr for astronomy 1992–95; Luke Blossom prof of physics, prof Stanford Linear Accelerator Centre and dir and Pehong & Adele Chen prof Kavli Inst for Particle Astrophysics and Cosmology Stanford Univ 2003–13; memb Inst for Advanced Study Princeton 1974–75 and 1998, Alfred P Sloan res fell 1980–84, Guggenheim fell 1988–90; Helen B Warner Prize American Astronomical Soc 1982, Dannie Heineman Prize American Astronomical Soc 1998, Eddington Medal Royal Astronomical Soc 1999, Gold Medal Royal Astronomical Soc 2013; FRS 1989, FRAS, FAAAS 1993, memb American Astronomical Soc, memb Nat Acads of Sci; *Style*— Prof Roger Blandford, FRS; ✉ Stanford University, Kavli Institute for Particle Astrophysics & Cosmology (e-mail rdb3@stanford.edu)

BLANDFORD, Prof Sonia; da of Terence Blandford, and Pauline, *née* Byrnes, of Swindon; *b* 11 March 1958; *Educ* Longford Comp Sch Feltham, Bretton Hall Coll of HE (CertEd), Univ of Leeds (BEd), Univ of Reading (MA), Univ of Bath (MPhil), Univ of Bristol (EdD); *m* 3 Aug 1991, Charles Henry Eldridge; 2 da (Bethany b 29 Jan 1998, Mia b 16 April 2002); *Career* educn leader; music teacher The Corsham Sch Wilts 1980–85, head of music St Gregory's RC Sch 1985–86, dir of music King Edward's Sch Bath 1986–89, head of faculty Brentford Sch for Girls 1989–92, head of year/ transition/ pastoral Hengrove Sch Bristol 1992–94, doctorate programme lead Oxford Brookes Univ 1995–99, dep dean Oxford Brookes Univ 1999–2002, prof, dean and pro-vice chllr Canterbury Christ Church Univ 2002–05, dir Research and Leadership Prog Teach First 2008–10, prof of educnl leadership and innovation Univ of Warwick 2010–12, prof of social enterprise and educn UCL Inst of Educn 2013–; fndr and ceo Achievement for All 3As 2011–; advsr to exec Teach First 2008–, founding tstee Children United Fndn 2012–, founding tstee Coll of Teaching; hon prof Univ of Warwick; *Publications* Don't Like Mondays, Make School Better, Love to Teach, Take the Lead, Developing Professional Practice 0–7; over 150 articles, columns and books on educnl leadership, special educnl needs, teaching and learning, professional devpt and music educn; *Recreations* gardening, music, travel, walking; *Style*— Prof Sonia Blandford; ✉ Achievement for All 3As, St Annes House, Oxford Square, Oxford Street, Newbury, Berkshire RG14 1JQ (01635 279470, e-mail sonia.blandford@afaeducation.org, website www.afa3as.org.uk, Twitter @SoniaAFA3As)

BLANK, Sir (Maurice) Victor; kt (1999); s of Joseph Blank, and Ruth, *née* Levey; *b* 9 November 1942; *Educ* Stockport GS, St Catherine's Coll Oxford (MA); *m* 29 June 1977, Sylvia Helen, *née* Richford; 2 s (Simon b 1 May 1978, Robert b 23 June 1984), 1 da (Anna b 16 Sept 1979); *Career* ptnr Clifford-Turner (slrs) 1969–81; Charterhouse plc: head of corporate finance and md Charterhouse Bank Ltd 1981–85, chief exec 1985–96, chm 1991–97, chm Charterhouse Bank Ltd 1985–97; chm Mirror Gp 1998–99, chm Trinity Mirror plc 1999–2006, dep chm Coats plc (formerly Coats Viyella plc) 1999–2003 (non-exec dir 1989–2003); GUS plc (formerly The Great Universal Stores plc): non-exec dir 1993, dep chm 1996–2000, chm 2000–06; chm Lloyds TSB Gp plc 2006–09; non-exec dir: Williams plc 1995–2000, Chubb plc 2000–04; Br business ambass 2008–12; chm: WellBeing of Women (formerly Birthright) 1993–, Union of Jewish Students 1998–, Industrial and Devpt Advsy Bd 1999–2004, Rothschild Foundation (Hanadiv) Europe 2010–, Social Mobility Foundation 2013–; memb: Cncl Univ of Oxford 2000–07, Fin Reporting Cncl 2003–09, Advsy Cncl Orch of the Age of Enlightenment, Advsy Bd GLF Fndn 2009–; tstee Oxford Univ Law Fndn 1998–2001; advsr: Oxford Environmental Change Unit, RSA; vice-pres Oxford Philomusica; chm of govrs UCS 1998–2010, chm Advsy Bd Cheung Kong Grad Sch of Business 2011–; Freeman City of London; hon fell St Catherine's Coll Oxford 2003–; memb: City of London Slrs' Co, Law Soc; CIMgt, Hon FRCOG 1998; *Books* Weinberg and Blank on Takeovers and Mergers; *Recreations* family, cricket, tennis, theatre; *Clubs* IOD; *Style*— Sir Victor Blank; ✉ PO Box 57793, London NW11 1HJ

BLANKSTONE, Michael David; s of Solomon Julius Blankstone (d 1981), and Isabel, *née* Franklin (d 1979); *b* 20 November 1936; *Educ* Quarry Bank HS Liverpool; *m* 17 June 1963, Anne, *née* Harrison; 2 s (Mark Lewis b 13 April 1964, Neil Simon b 6 Jan 1968); *Career* with family furniture mfrg business 1953–59, trainee then stockbroker Hornby Tobin & Ockleston 1959–66, ptnr Neilson Hornby Crichton 1966–75, sr ptnr Blankstone Sington & Co 1975–89 (co-fndr), chm Blankstone Sington Ltd 1989–; chm Blankstone Investments Ltd; chm The Stock Exchange Liverpool 1988–90 (vice-chm 1986–88), former memb Stock Exchange NW Advsy Gp, former chm Liverpool Stock Exchange Benevolent Fund, memb London Stock Exchange Benevolent Fund 1999; former memb: Cncl Liverpool Sch of Tropical Med, Nat Museums and Galleries on Merseyside Devpt Tst; tstee Liverpool Jewish Youth & Community Centre; past tstee: Hillsborough Disaster Appeal, Royal Liverpool Philharmonic Soc Jubilee Fndn Tst; MSI (memb Stock Exchange 1964); *Recreations* travel, reading, charity work; *Style*— Michael D Blankstone, Esq; ✉ Blankstone Sington Ltd, Walker House, Exchange Flags, Liverpool L2 3YL (☎ 0151 236 8200, fax 0151 243 3535)

BLANNING, Prof Timothy Charles William (Tim); s of Thomas Walter Blanning, and Gwendolyn Marchant, *née* Jones; *b* 21 April 1942; *Educ* King's Sch Bruton, Sidney Sussex Coll Cambridge (MA, PhD, LittD); *m* 1988, Nicky Jones; 1 s (b 2001), 1 da (b 2004); *Career* Univ of Cambridge: asst lectr in history 1972–76, lectr in history 1976–87, reader in modern European history 1987–92, prof of modern European history 1992–2009 (emeritus prof 2009–); fell Sidney Sussex Coll Cambridge 1968– (res fell 1965–68); FBA 1990; *Books* Joseph II and Enlightened Despotism (1970), Reform and Revolution in Mainz 1740–1803 (1974), The French Revolution in Germany (1983), The Origins of the French Revolutionary Wars (1986), The French Revolution: Aristocrats versus Bourgeois? (1987), Joseph II (1994), The Oxford Illustrated History of Modern Europe (ed, 1996), The French Revolutionary Wars 1787–1802 (1996), The Rise and Fall of the French Revolution (ed, 1996), History and Biography: Essays in Honour of Derek Beales (ed, 1996), The French Revolution: Class War or Culture Clash? (1998), The Short Oxford History of Europe: The Eighteenth Century (ed, 2000), The Short Oxford History of Europe: The Nineteenth Century (ed, 2000), The Oxford History of Modern Europe (ed, 2000), The Culture of Power and the Power of Culture: Old Regime Europe 1660–1789 (2002), Unity and Diversity in European Culture c 1800 (ed, 2006), The Pursuit of Glory: Europe 1648–1815 (2007), The Triumph of Music: Composers, Musicians and Audiences 1700 to the present (2008), The Romantic Revolution (2010), Frederick the Great King of Prussia (2015); *Recreations* music, football (Tottenham Hotspur FC); *Clubs* Athenaeum; *Style*— Prof Tim Blanning, FBA; ✉ Sidney Sussex College, Cambridge CB2 3HU (☎ 01223 338854, e-mail tcb1000@cam.ac.uk)

BLASONE, Massimiliano; s of Giovanna, *née* Ricciardi; *b* Frosinone, Italy; *Educ* Hotellerie Sch Rieti Italy; *Career* formerly: sous chef La Pergola Waldorf Astoria Hilton Rome, exec chef Onice Recais Chateaux Villa la Vedetta (Michelin star), exec chef Il Ristorante Castello Banfi (Michelin star); exec chef Apsleys Lanesborough Hotel London 2009– (Michelin star 2010–); Chef of the Year Inst of Advanced Study Trieste Italy 2007; *Style*— Mr Massimiliano Blasone; ✉ Apsleys, Lanesborough Hotel, Hyde Park Corner, London SW1X 7TA; c/o Thomas Proxta, UNITAS (UK), 3rd Floor, 137–139 City Road, London EC1V 1JN (☎ 07831 591438)

BLATCHFORD, Ian; *b* 17 August 1965; *Educ* Mansfield Coll Oxford (MA), Birkbeck Coll London (MA); *Career* grad trainee Bank of England 1986–88, corp finance exec Barclays de Zoete Wedd 1988, financial controller and deputy finance dir Arts Cncl of GB 1989–94, financial controller Cricket Communications 1994–96, dir of finance and projects Royal Acad of Arts 1996–2002, dir of finance and resources V&A 2002–04, dep dir V&A 2004–10, dir and chief exec Science Museum Gp 2010–; chm Bd of Govrs De Montfort Univ; Pushkin Medal 2015; FCMA 2002 (ACMA 1994), FSA 2011; *Clubs* Athenaeum; *Style*— Ian Blatchford, Esq

BLATHERWICK, Sir David Elliott Spiby; KCMG (1997, CMG 1990), OBE (1973); s of late Edward S Blatherwick; *b* 13 July 1941; *Educ* Lincoln Sch, Wadham Coll Oxford; *m* 1964, (Margaret) Clare, *née* Crompton; 1 da (b 1969), 1 s (b 1972); *Career* HM Dip Serv (ret); MECAS 1964, third later second sec Foreign Office 1966–68, second sec Kuwait 1968–70, first sec Dublin 1970–73, first sec FCO 1973–77, first sec and head of Chancery Cairo 1977–81, cnsllr and head of Political Affrs Div Northern Ireland Office 1981–83, head of Energy, Sci and Space Dept 1983–85, on leave to Stanford Univ California 1985–86, cnsllr and head of Chancery UK Mission to UN NY 1986–89, princ fin offr and chief inspector FCO 1989–91: HM ambass: Dublin 1991–95, Cairo 1995–99; chm Egyptian Br Chamber of Commerce 1999–2015, tstee Br Univ in Egypt 2005–; jt chm Anglo-Irish Encounter 2003–08; *Publications* The International Politics of Telecommunications (1987); *Clubs* Athenaeum; *Style*— Sir David Blatherwick, KCMG, OBE; ✉ c/o The Athenaeum, 107 Pall Mall, London SW1Y 5ER

BLATTLER, Daniel; s of Bruno Blattler, of Switzerland, and Adelheid Blattler; *m* 7 Dec 1990, Norma, da of Clifford Wint; 1 s (Louis), 1 da (Gemma); *Career* apprenticeship as reproduction specialist Switzerland; fndr memb Lith-Work Switzerland 1988–92, diploma lectr in pre-press prodn Switzerland 1990, md e-fact London 1997–2003 (prodn mangr 1996–97), fndr blattler ltd (brand and mktg consultancy and print mgmnt) 2003; recipient: numerous awards annually for best poster and fine art reproduction 1988–92, various awards for best catalogue prodn 1996–2003; e-fact recipient of numerous awards for design and photography 1996–2003; MInstD, memb Mktg Soc; *Style*— Daniel Blattler, Esq; ✉ 7a Acacia Gardens, West Wickham, Kent, BR4 9LD (☎ 020 8663 3261, fax 020 8663 1842, e-mail daniel@blattler.com)

BLAZWICK, Iwona; OBE (2008); *Educ* Univ of Exeter; *Career* dir AIR Gallery 1984–86, dir of exhibitions ICA 1986–93, independent curator 1993–97, head of exhibitions and displays Tate Modern until 2001, dir Whitechapel Art Gallery 2001–; memb: Jury Turner Prize 1993, Jury Jerwood Painting Prize 1997, Int Arts Advsy Cncl Wexner Prize Wexner Center 2002, Jury Max Mara Art Prize, Advsy Ctee Government Art Collection, London Cultural Strategy Gp, Jury Film London Jarman Award, Fourth Plinth Commissioning Gp, Paul Mellon Advsy Bd; tstee Harewood House; offr Order of Arts and Letters 2013; *Style*— Ms Iwona Blazwick, OBE; ✉ Whitechapel Art Gallery, 77–82 Whitechapel High Street, London E1 7QX

BLEAKLEY, Christine Louise; *b* 2 February 1979, Newry, Co Down, NI; *Educ* Bloomfield Collegiate Sch Ballyhackamore Belfast; *Career* television presenter; co-presenter The One Show (BBC 1) 2007–10, co-presenter Daybreak (ITV) 2010–11, presenter Duran Duran: For One Night Only (ITV) 2011, presenter Guess The Star (ITV) 2012, co-presenter Dancing on Ice (ITV) 2012–; *Style*— Ms Christine Bleakley; ✉ c/o Avalon, 4a Exmoor Street, London W10 6BD; Twitter @clbleakley

BLEARS, Rt Hon Hazel; PC (2005); *Career* MP (Lab) Salford 1997–2015; Parly under-sec of state: for Health 2001–02, for Public Health 2002–03, min of state Home Office 2003–06, chair Lab Party and min without portfolio 2006–07; sec of state for the community and local govt 2007–09; *Style*— The Rt Hon Hazel Blears

BLEASDALE, Cyril; OBE (1988); s of Frederick Bleasdale (d 2001), and Alice Bleasdale (d 1976); *b* 8 July 1934; *Educ* Stanford Business Sch; *m* 1970, Catherine Valerie; 2 da (Jane b 1970, Emma b 1972); *Career* md Freightliner 1975–82, dir BR Intercity 1982–86, gen mangr BR LM 1986–89, dir Scotrail 1990–94; md Railnews Ltd 1997–, DG Chartered Inst of Logistics and Tport 1999–2009; chm Hertford Business Incubation Centre 2002–09; FCILT 1956, FIMgt; *Recreations* global travel, keep fit; *Clubs* RAC; *Style*— Cyril Bleasdale, Esq, OBE, FCILT; ✉ 22 Trafalgar Street, Cheltenham GL50 1UH (☎ 01242 210163)

BLEASDALE, Paul; QC (2001); *Educ* LLB; *Career* called to the Bar Inner Temple 1978 (bencher); head of chambers No5 Chambers, recorder Crown and County Court; dep chm Agricultural Lands Tbnl; *Style*— Paul Bleasdale, Esq, QC; ✉ No5 Chambers, 5 Fountain Court, Steelhouse Lane, Birmingham B4 6DR

BLENCATHRA, Baron (Life Peer UK 2011), of Penrith in the County of Cumbria; David John Maclean; PC (1995); *b* 16 May 1953; *Career* MP (Cons) Penrith and the Border July 1983–2010 (by-election); *Style*— The Rt Hon the Lord Blencathra; ✉ House of Lords, London SW1A 0PW

BLENKINSOP, Thomas Francis (Tom); MP; s of William Blenkinsop, and Barbara, *née* Shields; *b* 14 August 1980, Middlesbrough, Teesside; *Educ* Newlands Sch FCJ Saltersgill, St Marys Sixth Form Coll Saltersgill, Univ of Teesside (BSc), Univ of Warwick (MA); *m* Victoria, *née* Emtage; *Career* constituency researcher to Dr Ashok Kumar MP 2002–08, full time official Community Trade Union 2008–10; MP (Lab) Middlesbrough S & E Cleveland 2010–; oppn whip (House of Commons) 2011–; *Recreations* football (Middlesbrough FC, Guisborough Town FC); *Style*— Tom Blenkinsop, Esq, MP; ✉ Harry Tout House, 8 Wilson Street, Guisborough TS14 6NA (☎ 01287 610878, e-mail info@tomblenkinsop.com, website www.tomblenkinsop.com, Twitter @tomblenkinsop); House of Commons, London SW1A 0AA

BLENNERHASSETT, Sir (Marmaduke) Adrian Francis William; 7 Bt (UK 1809), of Blennerville, Co Kerry; s of Lt Sir Marmaduke Charles Henry Joseph Casimir Blennerhassett, 6 Bt, RNVR (d 1940), and Gwenfra Mary, *née* Harrington-Morgan; *b* 25 May 1940; *Educ* Michael Hall, McGill Univ Montreal (BSc), Imperial Coll London (MSc), Cranfield Business Sch (MBA); *m* 1972, Carolyn Margaret, da of late Gilbert Brown; 1 da (Celina Mary Charlotte b 1973), 1 s (Charles Henry Marmaduke b 1975); *Heir* s, Charles Blennerhassett; *Career* previous positions in corporate finance, formerly gen mangr Claremount Oil & Gas Ltd and tech dir Peninsula Petroleum Ltd, currently non-exec chm Nostra Terra Oil & Gas; *Clubs* Travellers; *Style*— Sir Adrian Blennerhassett, Bt

BLESSED, Brian; OBE (2016); s of William Blessed, of Bolton-on-Dearne, S Yorks, and Hilda, *née* Wall; *b* 9 October 1936; *Educ* Bolton-on-Dearne Secondary Modern; *m* 28 Dec 1978, Hildegard Neil *née* Zimmermann; 1 da (Rosalind Josephine b 16 April 1975); *Career* actor; pres: Cncl for Nat Parks, Yorkshire Wildlife Tst; tstee Bowles Rocks Tst; patron: Freshfields, Kinder Mountain Rescue, The Nepal Tst, Scope; *Theatre* RSC: Claudius in Hamlet, Hastings in Richard III, Exeter in Henry V; other roles incl: Maxim Gorky in State of Revolution, John Freeman in Metropolis, Old Deuteronomy in Cats, Henry II in The Lion in Winter; An Evening with Brian Blessed (one man show) 1992–93 & 1995–96, Hard Times (West End), Sir Tunbelly Clumsey in The Relapse (RNT), Baron Bomburst in Chitty, Chitty, Bang, Bang (London Palladium) 2002–03; *Television* PC Fancy Smith in Z Cars, Augustus Caesar in I Claudius, Albert in George's Sand, King Guthram in Churchill's People, Porthos in The Three Musketeers, Pepone in The Little World of Don Camillo, Spiro in My Family and Other Animals, King Richard in Blackadder (first series), The Boy Dominic, Prof Atticus in Magyver – Lost Treasure of Atlantis, Squire Western in Tom Jones; *Films* Prince Vultan in Flash Gordon, Long John Silver in Return to Treasure Island, Talthybius in Trojan Women, Pedro in Man of La Mancha, Exeter in Henry V, General Zukov in War and Remembrance, Lord Locksley in Robin Hood Prince of Thieves, General Gonse in Prisoners of Honour, Antonio in Much Ado About Nothing, The Ghost in Hamlet, Lear (also dir), Clayton in Walt Disney's Tarzan, Boss Nass in Star Wars – The Phantom Menace, Leonidas in Alexander The Great, both Duke Sr and Duke Friedrich in As You Like It (dir Kenneth Branagh), Pope Piccolomini in The Conclave, Back in Business, Re-Evolution, The Pirates! In an Adventure with Scientists!; *Books* The Turquoise Mountain, The Dynamite Kid, Nothing's Impossible, Blessed Everest, Quest for the Lost World; *Style*— Brian Blessed, Esq, OBE; ✉ c/o Derek Webster, Associated International Management, 1 Blythe Road, London W14 0HG (☎ 020 7348 4850, fax 020 7348 4851, e-mail info@aimagent.com, website www.aimagents.com)

BLETHYN, Brenda; OBE (2003); *Educ* Guildford Sch of Dance and Drama; *Career* actress; Hon DLitt Univ of Kent at Canterbury 1999, Hon DLitt Univ of Surrey 2009; *Theatre* NT incl: Beaux Stratagem (Best Actress nomination), Troilus and Cressida, Tambourlaine, Tales From the Vienna Woods, Madras House, The Passion, Bedroom Farce, The Double Dealer, Fruits of Enlightenment, Strife, A Midsummer Night's Dream, The Guardsman, The Provoked Wife, Dalliance; other roles incl: Steaming (Comedy Theatre, Best Supporting Actress Award), Benefactors (Vaudeville, Best Actress nomination), Crimes of the Heart (Bush), A Doll's House (Royal Exchange), Born Yesterday (Royal Exchange Manchester), An Ideal Husband (Royal Exchange Manchester), Glass Menagier (Best Actress Award), Haunted (Manchester, NY and Sydney), The Dramatic Attitudes of Miss Fanny Kemble (Southampton), Absent Friends (Manhattan Theater NY, Theater World Award for Outstanding Performance), Wildest Dreams (RSC), The Bed Before Yesterday (Almeida), Habeas Corpus (Donmar), Mrs Warren's Profession (Strand), Haunted (Manchester Royal Exchange, NY and Sydney Opera House); *Television* incl: The Labours of Erica (2 series), Death of An Expert Witness, A Chance in a Million (3 series, Comedy Award), Alas Smith and Jones, Tales of the Unexpected, The Shawl, All Good Things, Bedroom Farce, Play for Today (Grown Ups), The Richest Woman In The World, Yes Minister, King Lear, Henry VI, The Story Teller, The Bullion Boys, The Buddha of Suburbia, Sleeping with Mickey, Outside Edge (3 series, Best TV Comedy Actress Award), Between the Sheets, Belonging, War and Peace, Vera, King of the Teds, Law and Order (Best Actress Emmy nomination), Vera (4 series); *Film* incl: The Witches, A River Runs Through It 1992, Secrets and Lies 1996 (Best Actress Award Cannes 1996, Golden Globe Award for Best Actress 1997, London Film Critics' Circle Award for Best British Actress 1997, Oscar nomination for Best Actress 1997, BAFTA Award for Best Actress 1997), Remember Me 1996, Girl's Night 1997, Music From Another Room 1997, In the Winter Dark 1997, Little Voice 1997 (Oscar, Golden Globe, Screen Actors Guild, and BAFTA nominations for Best Supporting Actress 1999), Night Train 1998, Daddy and Them 1998, RKO 281 1999, Saving Grace 1999 (Golden Globe nomination for Best Actress 2001, Variety Club (GB) Best Actress Award 2001), On the Nose 2000, The Sleeping Dictionary 2000, Anne Frank 2001 (Emmy nomination for Best Supporting Actress 2001), Lovely and Amazing 2002, Pumpkin 2002, Plots with a View 2002, Sonny 2002, Blizzard 2002, The Sleeping Dictionary 2003, Beyond the Sea 2004, A Way of Life 2004, Pride & Prejudice 2005, Atonement 2007, Dead Man Running, The Calling, London River Clubland, Enemy Way 2013; *Publications* Mixed Fancies; *Style*— Miss Brenda Blethyn, OBE; ✉ c/o Independent Talent, Oxford House, 76 Oxford Street, London W1N 0AX (☎ 020 7636 6565, fax 020 7323 0101, e-mail b.blethyn@btinternet.com)

BLEWITT, Maj Sir Shane Gabriel Basil; GCVO (1996, KCVO 1989, CVO 1987, LVO 1981); s of late Col Basil Blewitt; *b* 25 March 1935; *Educ* Ampleforth, ChCh Oxford (MA); *m* 1969, Julia, da of late Robert Henry Calvert, and wid of Maj John Morrogh-Bernard, Irish Gds; 1 s, 1 da, 1 step s, 1 step da; *Career* Army Service Irish Gds 1956–74 (BAOR, Germany, NI, Aden, Hong Kong); Antony Gibbs & Sons Ltd 1974; Keeper of the Privy Purse and Treas to HM The Queen 1988–96 (Asst Keeper 1975–85, Dep Keeper 1985–87), Extra Equerry to HM The Queen 1996–; memb: Kings Fund Gen Cncl 1989–2010, Cncl King Edward VII Hosp 1989–2010; *Style*— Maj Sir Shane Blewitt, GCVO; ☎ 01798 342143, e-mail blewittshane@aol.com

BLISS, Andrew (Andy); QPM (2010); s of George William Bliss (d 1979), and Phyllis Emily Bliss (d 2011); *b* 1960, London; *Educ* Durham Univ (BA), Univ of Cambridge (Dip); *m* 1985, Hazel, *née* Hammond; 1 s (Alexander b 1994); *Career* joined Sussex Police 1982; Essex Police: Asst Chief Constable 2004–06, Dep Chief Constable 2007–11 (temp Chief Constable 2009); Chief Constable Herts Police 2011–; chm Drugs Ctee ACPO, chm Heritage Crime Ctee; *Recreations* opera, skiing, cycling, fly fishing; *Style*— Andy Bliss, Esq, QPM; ✉ Hertfordshire Constabulary Headquarters, Stanborough Road, Welwyn Garden City, Hertfordshire AL8 6XF

BLISS, Prof Christopher John Emile; s of John Llwelyn Bliss of London (d 1978), a founder of the BBC TV service from 1936, working as a 'boffin' designer, etc, and Patricia Paula, *née* Dubern; *b* 17 February 1940, London; *Educ* Finchley Catholic GS, King's Coll Cambridge (BA, PhD); *m* 1, 1964, Heather, da of Cyril Midmer, of Dublin; 1 s (John Benet b 1966), 2 da (Anna Katharine b 1968, Madeline Frances b 1974); m 2, 1983, Ghada, da of Adel Saqf El Hait, of Jordan; 1 s (Larry Kareem b 1996); *Career* fell Christ's College Cambridge 1965–71, lecturer in economics Univ of Cambridge 1967–71 (asst lecturer 1965–67), prof of economics Univ of Essex 1971–77; fell Nuffield Coll Oxford 1977–, Nuffield prof of economics Univ of Oxford 1992– (Nuffield reader in economics 1977–92); ed: Review of Economic Studies 1967–71, Oxford Economic Papers 1989–96, Economic Jl 1996–2004; fell Econometric Soc 1978, FBA 1988; *Books* Capital Theory of the Distribution of Income (1975), Palanpur: the Economy of an Indian Village (with N

H Stern), Trade, Growth and Inequalit (2007); *Recreations* music; *Style*— Prof Christopher Bliss, FBA; ✉ 11 Heyford Road, Steeple Aston, Oxfordshire OX25 4SU; Nuffield College, Oxford OX1 1NF (☎ 01865 278573, e-mail christopher.bliss@nuffield.ox.ac.uk)

BLISS, Dr Timothy Vivian Pelham; s of late Cdr Pelham Marryat Bliss, RN, and Elizabeth Cotton, *née* Sproule; *b* 27 July 1940; *Educ* Dean Close Sch Cheltenham, McGill Univ Montreal (BSc, PhD), Imperial Coll London, Hatfield Poly (BSc); *m* 1, 1975 (m dis 1994), Virginia Catherine Morton-Evans; 2 step da (Clara, Catherine), 1 step s (James); m 2, 1994, Isabel Frances Vasseur; 2 step s (Roman, Blaise); 1 da by Katherine Sarah Clough (Linnea Ann Susan b 5 Feb 1981); *Career* memb scientific staff MRC 1967–2006, head Div of Neurophysiology Nat Inst for Medical Research 1988–2006, visiting scientist Nat Inst for Medical Research 2006–; visiting prof: Dept of Physiology UCL 1993–, Univ of Paris Sud Orsay 1996; memb: Scientific Advsy Ctee Louis Jeantet Fndn 2005–12, Lister Inst 2006–12, Feldberg Fndn 2007–13; tstee Sir John Soane's Museum 2004–09; Bristol Myers Squibb Award for Neuroscience (with E R Kandel) 1991, Feldberg Prize 1994, Br Neuroscience Assoc Award 2003, Royal Soc Croonian Lecture 2012, Ipsen Prize for Neuronal Plasticity 2013, Greta Lundbeck Brain Prize 2016 (with R G M Morris and G L Collingridge); hon degree: Dalhousie Univ 2011, Univ of Hertforshire 2014; FRS 1994, FMedSci 1998; *Books* Long-term Potentiation (co-ed, 2004), The Hippocampus Book (co-ed, 2006); *Recreations* Shakespeare, wine, travelling; *Clubs* Academy; *Style*— Dr T V P Bliss, FRS; ✉ 18 Market Place, Aylsham, Norwich NR11 6EH

BLITZ, James Simon; s of John Blitz (d 1970), and Claudia Newnham, *née* Cohen; *b* 3 May 1961, London; *Educ* City of London Sch, St Andrews Univ (MA), St Antony's Coll Oxford (MPhil); *m* 10 Feb 1995, Fiona Slomovic; 1 s (Sam b 30 Nov 1995), 2 da (Lara b 19 Feb 1997, Sophie b 12 Jan 1999); *Career* news trainee BBC 1985–88, Moscow corr Sunday Times 1989–92; Financial Times: economics reporter 1993, political corr 1994–97, Rome bureau chief 1997–2002, political ed 2002–07, defence and diplomatic ed 2007–12, leader writer 2012–16, Whitehall ed 2016–; David Watt Prize 2004; *Recreations* opera; *Style*— James Blitz, Esq; ✉ Financial Times, 1 Southwark Bridge, London SE1 9HL (☎ 020 7873 4192, mobile 07767 301226, e-mail james.blitz@ft.com)

BLOCH, (Andrew Charles) Danby; s of late Prof Moishe Rudolf Bloch, and Mary Hall Bloch; *b* 19 December 1945; *Educ* Tonbridge, Wadham Coll Oxford (MA); *m* 1968, Sandra, da of late William Wilkinson; 1 s (Adam b 1972), 1 da (Hester b 1974); *Career* researcher Oxford Centre for Mgmnt Studies (now Templeton Coll) 1968–70; dir: Grosvenor Advisory Services Ltd 1971–74, Oxford Fine Arts Ltd 1975–85, Raymond Godfrey & Partners Ltd 1974–, Taxbriefs Ltd (acquired by Centaur Media plc) 1975–2010 (editorial dir 2010–), Nucleus Financial Gp Ltd 2010–16; conslt Centaur Financial 2014–; chm Rivington Street Hldgs Ltd (formerly T1PS.com) 2000–07, chm Helm Godfrey Ptnrs Ltd 2000–; memb: Investment Ctee Wadham Coll Oxford 1992–2011, Steering Ctee for Investment Advice Cert of Securities Inst 1994–2006; regular weekly column on taxation (and related topics): The Times 1979–82 and 1986–88, Sunday Times 1988–91; regular fin column in Daily Telegraph 1982–86; chm Bd of Govrs Oxford Brookes Univ (formerly Oxford Poly) 1998–2004 (memb 1990–, dep chm 1993–98), pro-chllr Oxford Brookes Univ 2004–11; tstee Oxford Inst of Legal Practice 1993–98 (chm 1994–95 and 1996–97), patron Friends of the Pitt Rivers Museum Oxford 2000–, chm Oxfordshire Visual Arts Devpt Assoc (OVADA) 2004–09, memb Advsy Bd Modern Art Oxford (formerly MOMA Oxford) 2006–10 (memb Cncl 1990–2006), chm Bd Oxford Playhouse 2009–, tstee Equal Rights Tst 2012–; memb Personal Fin Soc (conslt on member events 2008–14); Hon DUniv Oxford Brookes 2004; FRSA 2004; *Books* Providing Financial Advice, Financial Advice, Planning for School and College Fees (co-author), Financial Planning Practice (2009), Process of Financial Planning (co-author); ed CII dip in financial planning learning texts: Taxation, Trusts, Tax and the Legal Aspects of Business, Pension Income Options, Pension Funding Options, Investments; *Style*— Danby Bloch, Esq; ✉ The Stone House, 47 Mill Street, Kidlington, Oxfordshire OX5 2EE (☎ 01865 512661); Taxbriefs Financial Publishing, Wells Point, 79 Wells Street, London W1T 3QN (e-mail danby@bloch.com)

BLOCH, Prof Maurice E F; *b* 21 October 1939, Caen, France; *Educ* sch in Paris, LSE (BA), Univ of Cambridge (PhD); *m*; 2 c; *Career* lectr Univ of Wales Swansea 1967–68, lectr LSE 1968–76, reader Univ of London 1976–83, prof of anthropology Univ of London 1983–; convenor Anthropology Dept LSE 1985–88 and 1990–; visiting prof: Univ of Calif Berkeley 1974–75, Univ of Paris Nanterre 1979, Univ of Stockholm 1980–81, Nat Ethnology Museum of Japan 1984; dir d'études associé École des Hautes Études en Sciences Sociales France 1982–83; Rivers Medal Royal Anthropological Inst 1983; fell Danish Centre for the Humanities Copenhagen 1988; FBA 1990; *Books* Placing the Dead: Tombs, Ancestral Villages and Kinship Organization in Madagascar (1971), Political Laguage, Oratory and Traditional Society (ed, 1975), Marxist Analyses and Social Anthropology (ed, 1975), Death and the Regeneration of Life (ed, 1982), Marxism and Anthropology: The History of a Relationship (1983), From Blessing to Violence: History and Ideology in the Circumcision Ritual of the Merina of Madagascar (1986), Ritual, History and Power – Selected Papers in Anthropology (1989), Money and the Morality of Exchange (ed, 1989), Prey into Hunter: The Politics of Religious Experience (1991); author of numerous articles in publications and jls; *Style*— Prof Maurice Bloch, FBA; ✉ Department of Anthropology, London School of Economics and Political Science, Houghton Street, London WC2A 2AE (☎ 020 7405 7686, fax 020 7242 0392)

BLOCH, Michael Anthony; s of Richard Bloch, and Ruth, *née* Grant; *b* 24 September 1953; *Educ* Portadown Coll, St John's Coll Cambridge (MA, LLB); *Career* called to the Bar Inner Temple 1978; assisted Maître Suzanne Blum of Paris with affairs of the Duchess of Windsor and her Estate 1979–88; literary executor of James Lees-Milne (d 1997), cr website www.jamesleesmilne.com; author; *Books* The Duke of Windsor's War (1982), Operation Willi (1984), Wallis and Edward (1986), The Secret File of the Duke of Windsor (1988), The Reign and Abdication of Edward VIII (1990), Ribbentrop (1992, new edn 2003), The Duchess of Windsor (1996), FM: The Life of Frederick Matthias Alexander (2004), James Lees-Milne: The Life (2009); ed later diaries of James Lees-Milne: Deep Romantic Chasm 1979–81 (2000), Holy Dread 1982–84 (2001), Beneath a Waning Moon 1985–87 (2003), Ceaseless Turmoil 1988–92 (2004), The Milk of Paradise 1993–97 (2005); also abridged James Lees-Milne's complete diaries in three vols: 1942–54 (2006), 1971–83 (2007), 1984–97 (2008), Jeremy Thorpe (2014), Closet Queens: Some 20th Century British Politicians (2015); *Recreations* eating, bridge, playing Chopin; *Clubs* Savile, Cambridge Union Soc, Oxford & Cambridge; *Style*— Michael Bloch, Esq; ✉ 2 Strathearn Place, London W2 2NQ (☎ 020 7723 2220, e-mail mab@michaelbloch.co.uk); c/o Ed Wilson, 45 Camberwell Green, London EC1R 0HT (☎ 020 7251 0125, e-mail ed@johnsonandalcock.co.uk)

BLOCH, Michael Gordon; QC (1998); s of John Bloch, of Hants, and Thelma Bloch; *b* 18 October 1951; *Educ* Bedales, Univ of Cambridge (MA), UEA (MPhil); *m* 1, (m dis), Caroline, da of Sir Leonard Williams; 2 da (Susannah, Claudia); m 2, 12 Sept 1998, Lady Camilla Bingham, da of 7 Earl of Lucan; 2 s (Cameron Charles b 28 Feb 2002, Angus John Patrick b 31 July 2003); *Career* called to the Bar 1979; tstee Childline; govr Bedales; *Clubs* RAC; *Style*— Michael Bloch, Esq, QC; ✉ Wilberforce Chambers, 8 New Square, Lincolns Inn, London WC2A 3QP (☎ 020 7306 0102, fax 020 7306 0095, e-mail chambers@wilberforce.co.uk)

BLOCH, Selwyn; QC (2000); *Educ* Univ of Stellenbosch SA (BA, LLB); *Career* called to the Bar 1982; practising barr specialising in employment and commercial law; int banking Allen & Overy, slr Webber Wentzel, memb Littleton Chambers 1982–; *Publications* Restrictive Covenants and Confidential Information (co-author, 3 edn 2009); *Style*— Selwyn Bloch, Esq, QC; ✉ Littleton Chambers, 3 King's Bench Walk North, Temple, London EC4Y 7HR

BLOCK, Simon Jonathan; s of Abraham Hyman (Michael) Block (d 1999), and Winifred Joy Harris; *b* 13 February 1950, London; *Educ* Sunbury GS, East Grinstead GS, Crawley Coll of FE; *m* 27 June 1998, Annette Mary Dunphy; 1 s (Robin Timothy b 14 Dec 1977), 1 step da (Cheryl Ann Sexton b 10 May 1972); *Career* boxer Crawley Amateur Boxing Club 1965–68; Br Boxing Bd of Control: joined 1979, sec Southern Area Cncl 1981–96, gen sec 2000–08, sec charitable tst 2000–08; hon sec Cwlth Boxing Cncl 1980–; co-sec European Boxing Union 2000–08; vice-pres: Sussex Ex-Boxers' Assoc, Kent Ex-Boxers' Assoc, Hastings Ex-Boxers' Assoc; hon memb London Ex-Boxers' Assoc; memb Soc of Friends Ashdown Forest; *Recreations* walking, riding, music, food; *Clubs* St George's Day, Royal Commonwealth Soc; *Style*— Simon Block, Esq; ✉ Commonwealth Boxing Council, 22 Bis, Rue du Charme, Ricarville du Val, 76510 Normandie, France (☎ 0033 961 052534, e-mail sblock@commboxing.com, website www.commboxing.com)

BLOCKLEY, Prof David Ian; s of Harold Gwynne Blockley (d 1972), and Olive Lydia Blockley (d 1979); *b* 18 September 1941; *Educ* Bemrose Sch Derby, Univ of Sheffield (BEng, PhD), Univ of Bristol (DSc); *m* 6 Aug 1966, Karen Elisabeth Blockley; 1 s (Andrew David b 1968), 1 da (Alison Mary b 1973); *Career* devpt engr BCSA Ltd London 1967–69; Univ of Bristol: lectr 1969–82, reader 1982–89, prof 1989–, head Dept of Civil Engrg 1989–95 and 2002–, dean of engrg 1994–98; pres Inst of Structural Engrs 2001–02; corresponding memb: Argentinian Acad of Engrs, Argentinian Acad of Science; Telford Gold Medal Inst of Civil Engrs 1978, George Stephenson Medal Inst of Civil Engrs 1981, Oscar Faber Dip Inst of Structural Engrs 1986; FREng 1992, FICE, FIStructE, FRSA; *Books* The Nature of Structural Design and Safety (1980), Engineering Safety (1992), Doing it Differently (2000), Penguin Dictionary of Civil Engineering (2005), Bridges (2010), Very Short Introduction to Engineering (2012), Very Short Introduction to Structural Engineering (2014); *Recreations* reading, gardening, watching sport (esp soccer and cricket); *Style*— Professor D I Blockley, FREng; ✉ Department of Civil Engineering, University of Bristol, Bristol BS8 1TR (fax 0117 928 7783)

BLOMEFIELD, Sir (Thomas) Charles Peregrine; 6 Bt (UK 1807), of Attleborough, Co Norfolk; s of Sir Thomas Edward Peregrine Blomefield, 5 Bt (d 1984), and Ginette, *née* Massart; *b* 24 July 1948; *Educ* Wellington, Mansfield Coll Oxford; *m* 1975, Georgina Geraldine, da of late Cdr Charles Over, RN, of Lugger End, Portscatho, Cornwall; 2 da (Emma Georgina b 1980, Harriet Elizabeth b 1986), 1 s ((Thomas) William Peregrine b 1983); *Heir* s, William Blomefield; *Career* fine art and philatelic conslt; Christies 1970–75, Wildenstein and Co 1975–76; dir: Lidchi Art Gallery Johannesburg 1976–78, Thomas Heneage and Co 1981–87, Fleetwood-Hesketh Ltd 1982–, Direct Import Ltd 1985–; md Charles Blomefield and Co 1980–; *Recreations* travel; *Clubs* English Speaking Union; *Style*— Sir Charles Blomefield, Bt; ✉ 42 Simpson Street, London SW11 3HW

BLOND, Oliver; *Career* formerly headmaster Henrietta Barnett Sch, headmaster Roedean 2013–; founding memb and academic dir Prince's Teaching Inst (PTI); *Style*— Oliver Blond, Esq; ✉ Roedean School, Roedean Way, Brighton, BN2 5RQ

BLOOD, Baroness (Life Peer UK 1999), of Blackwatertown in the County of Armagh; May Blood; MBE (1995); da of William Blood (d 1978), of Belfast, and Mary, *née* McKeen (d 1978); *b* 26 May 1938, Belfast, NI; *Educ* Linfield Secdy Sch; *Career* community worker; memb: NI Women's Coalition, GI Shankill Partnership; involved with: Integrated Educn Fund, Ulster Historical Fndn; memb Senate Queen's Univ Belfast; Catherine Dunfey Peace Award (USA) 1997; Hon DUniv: Ulster 1998, Queen's Belfast 2000, Open Univ 2001; *Books* Watch My Lips, I'm Speaking (2007); *Recreations* gardening, reading, DIY; *Style*— The Rt Hon the Baroness Blood, MBE; ✉ 7 Blackmountain Place, Belfast BT13 3TT (☎ 028 9032 6514); Alessie Centre, 60 Shankill Road, Belfast BT13 3BB (☎ 028 9087 4000, fax 028 9087 4009, mobile 07752 475883)

BLOOM, Alan; s of Ronnie Bloom, of Spain, and Anne, *née* Needleman (d 2004); *b* 9 November 1955, London; *Educ* Haberdashers' Aske's; *m* 18 April 1982, Gillian, *née* Galler; 2 s (Mark b 27 Nov 1983, Richard b 28 Jan 1987); *Career* CA 1980; Ernst & Young: joined 1981, ptnr 1988–, global head of restructuring 2006–; pres Soc of Practitioners of Insolvency; author of many articles and presentations on corporate restructuring and insolvency; fundraiser for Aspire; FCA; *Recreations* golf, watching football, theatre; *Style*— Alan Bloom, Esq; ✉ Ernst & Young, 1 More London Place, London SE1 2AF (☎ 020 7951 9898, e-mail abloom@uk.ey.com)

BLOOM, Anthony Herbert; s of Joseph Bloom, and Margaret Roslyn Bloom; *b* 15 February 1939; *Educ* King Edward VII HS, Univ of the Witwatersrand (BCom, LLB), Harvard Law Sch (LLM), Stanford Univ Graduate Sch of Business (Sloan fell); *m* 10 Jan 1973, Gisela; 2 da (Rosemary Claire b 24 Jan 1963, Alexis Monica b 27 May 1975), 2 s (Andrew Martin b 7 Sept 1965, Nicholas Peter b 10 Dec 1973); *Career* with Hayman Godfrey & Sanderson 1960–64; Premier Group Ltd: joined 1966, dir 1969, dep chm 1975, chm 1979–87; dir: Barclays Nat Bank and First Nat Bank of Southern Africa Ltd 1980–88, Liberty Life Association 1982–88, The South African Breweries Ltd 1983–89, CNA Gallo Ltd 1983–89; former non-exec dir Sketchley plc, former dir RIT Capital Partners plc; currently chm Cineworld Gp plc; dir: LSO Live, Technoserve; LLD (hc) Harvard Law Sch; *Recreations* karate, opera, ballet, theatre, music; *Style*— Anthony Bloom, Esq; ✉ 8 Hanover Terrace, London NW1 4RJ (☎ 020 7723 3422); c/o Allen & Co, 103 Mount Street, London W1K 2TJ (☎ 020 7016 1200)

BLOOM, Claire; CBE (2013); da of late Edward Bloom and Elizabeth Bloom; *b* 15 February 1931; *Educ* Badminton, USA and privately; *m* 1, 1959 (m dis 1969), Rod Steiger; 1 da (Anna Steiger b 1960); m 2, 1969 (m dis 1976); m3, 1990 (m dis 1995), Philip Roth; *Career* actress; *Theatre* The Condemned of Altona (Royal Court), Duel of Angels (Globe), The Lady's Not For Burning (Globe), Ring Around the Moon (Globe), various Shakespeare, Ivanov, A Doll's House (NY and London), The Cherry Orchard (Chichester Festival Theatre), A Streetcar Named Desire, Hedda Gabler, Vivat! Vivat Regina!, The Turn of the Screw (NY), Till We Awaken the Dead (Almeida), King John, Hamlet and A Winter's Tale (Stratford), The Cherry Orchard 1993, A Long Day's Journey into Night 1996, Electra 1998, Conversations After a Burial (Almeida) 2000, A Little Night Music (NYC) 2003; *Television* Henry VIII, Hamlet, Cymbeline and King John (BBC Shakespeare series), Brideshead Revisited, Time and the Conways, Shadowlands (BAFTA Best Actress Award), Oedipus the King, The Ghost Writer, Anne & Debbie, The Belle of Amhurst (Int Emmy Award), Intimate Contact, Queenie, Anastasia, Liberty, The Camomile Law (Channel 4), Miss Marple – The Mirror Cracked (BBC), Family Money (Channel 4), The Lady in Question, Love and Murder, Yesterday's Children; *Films* Limelight, The Man Between, Alexander the Great, Richard III, Look Back in Anger, The Spy Who Came in From the Cold, The Outrage, The Brother Karamazov, The Buccaneer, Charly, The Brothers Grimm, A Doll's House, Islands in the Stream, Clash of the Titans, Sammie & Rosie Get Laid, Crimes and Misdemeanours, Shakespeare's Women and Claire Bloom, The Book of Eve, Imagining Argentina; *Books* Limelight and After, Leaving A Doll's House; *Style*— Miss Claire Bloom, CBE

BLOOM, Prof Margaret Janet; CBE (2003); da of John Sturrock (d 1992), and Jean Elizabeth, *née* Ranken (d 1997); *b* 28 July 1943; *Educ* Sherborne, Girton Coll Cambridge (MA); *m* 1965, Prof Sir Stephen Bloom, s of Dr Arnold Bloom (d 1992); 2 da (Sarah Elizabeth b 1970, Chloë Isabel b 1976), 2 s (Nicholas Alexander b 1973, James Duncan b 1978); *Career* economist rising to dep gp economist John Laing & Son plc 1965–69, gp economist Tarmac plc 1969–70, Nat Econ Devpt Office 1970–86, Sci & Technol Secretariat Cabinet Office 1986–89, grade 5 DTI 1989–95, grade 4 rising to grade 3 Agencies Gp Cabinet

Office 1995–96, dir of competition enforcement OFT 1997–2003; sr conslt Freshfields Bruckhaus Deringer 2003–; pt/t lectr UCL 1977–80, external examiner UCL 1985–88, visiting prof KCL 2002–15 (hon prof 2015–); tstee Money Advice Tst 2004–15 (dep chair 2007–15), ind memb Link Consumer Cncl (formerly Link Standing Ctee on Consumer Issues) 2006–, , ind dir Lending Standards Bd 2012–, vice chair Professional Standards Cncl for Asset Based Finance Assoc 2013–; *Recreations* family, foreign travel, eating out, rambling; *Style*— Prof Margaret Bloom, CBE; ✉ Dickson Poon School of Law, King's College London, Strand, London WC2R 2LS (☎ 020 7435 0912, e-mail margaret.bloom@kcl.ac.uk)

BLOOM, Prof Sir Stephen Robert (Steve); kt (2012); s of Arnold Bloom, and Edith Nancy Page Bloom, *née* Fox; *b* 24 October 1942, Maidstone, Kent; *Educ* Mill Hill Sch London, Univ of Cambridge (Science Prize, Walter Knox Chemistry Prize, Bacteriology Prize, Histology Cert, Ophthalmology Prize, Radiotherapy and Radiology Prize, MB BChir, MA, MD), Middx Hosp Med Sch London (DSc); *m* 1965, Margaret Janet, *née* Sturrock; 2 da (Sarah Elizabeth b 1970, Chloe Isabel b 1976), 2 s (Nicholas Alexander b 1973, James Duncan b 1978); *Career* Middx Hosp London: gastroenterology house physician 1967–68, cardiology house physician 1968; house surgn Mount Vernon Hosp London 1968–69, casualty MO Middx Hosp London 1969, endocrinology house physician Hammersmith Hosp London 1969–70; Middx Hosp London: Leverhulme research scholar Inst of Clinical Research 1970, registrar Med Unit 1970–72, MRC clinical research fell Inst of Clinical Research 1972–74; Hammersmith Hosp London: sr lectr and conslt physician Royal Postgrad Med Sch (RPMS) 1974–78, reader in med RPMS 1978–82, prof of med and conslt physician Faculty of Med Imperial Coll 1982–, dir of endocrinology 1982–, dep dir Dept of Med RPMS 1984–97, dir of chemical pathology 1994–, clinical dir Pathology and Therapy Servs 1996–; chm Div of Investigative Science Imperial Coll London 1997–; chm Higher Degrees Ctee RPMS 1991–96, chm Academic Bd RPMS 1995–97; Hammersmith Hosps Tst: chm Jr Doctors Hours Ctee 1995–2000, chm Hosp Med Ctee 1995–, memb Tst Bd 1996–; chm Local Negotiating Ctee BMA 1995–, memb Mgmnt Planning Gp Imperial Coll London 1997–2001, memb Princs Advsy Gp Faculty of Med Imperial Coll London 1997–; RCP: sr examiner MRCP 1987–, memb Ethics Ctee 1991–96, pro-censor 1993–95, second censor 1994–97, academic vice-pres 1999–2001; referee Queen's Univ Belfast 1994–; memb: Int Steering Ctee GI Hormones 1980–87, Nat Inst Biological Standards Bd 1985–99 (memb Reorganisation Ctee 1991, chm Scientific Ctee 1993–99), Research Corp Tst Med Sciences Bd 1986–88, Scientific Steering Ctee Int Endocrine Soc 1986–89, WHO Expert Advsy Ctee on Biological Standardization 1989–, Global Assessment Ctee Inst of Child Health 1990, Clinical Specialities Liaison Ctee 1991–93, Regional Med Advsy Ctee 1991–95, Sub-Ctee on Biologicals Ctee on Safety of Meds 1992–95, Fin and Gen Purposes Ctee Nat Inst for Biological Standards and Control (NIBSC) 1992–99, Subject Panel in Gen Med Univ of London 1993–96; chm Bioscientifica 2005, dir Thiakis Ltd 2006–08; selected summaries corr Gastroenterology 1979–83, fndr and ed-in-chief Regulatory Peptides 1979–84, ed Endocrinology 1995–98; memb Editorial Bd: Jl of Developmental Physiology 1980–85, Excerpta Medica Endocrinolgy 1981–86, Gut 1982–86, European Jl of Clinical Pharmacology 1982–86, Jl of Endocrinology 1983–87, Diabetes Research and Clinical Practice 1986–90, Archives Internationale de Pharmacodynamie et de Therapie 1987–, Biomedical Research 1988–91, Clinical Autonomic Research 1989–92, Jl of Neuroendocrinology 1990–92; author of numerous articles in learned jls incl: Nature, Science, Diabetes, Neuroscience, Lancet, BMJ; Lawrence lectr Br Diabetic Assoc 1976, Copp lectr American Diabetic Assoc 1978, Goulstonian lectr RCP 1979, Bengt Ihre lectr Swedish Acad of Science 1979, Prossor White oration 1981, Transatlantic lectr American Soc for Endocrinology 1985, Arnold Bloom lectr Br Diabetic Assoc 1995; Br Soc of Gastroenterology Research Medal 1977, Eric-Sharpe Prize for Oncology, Dale Medal Soc for Endocrinology 2003; memb: American Diabetic Assoc, Assoc of Physicians, Bayliss & Starling Soc (chm 1980–92), Br Diabetic Assoc (memb Scientific Ctee 1991–95, chm Research Ctee 1996–99), Endocrine Soc (American), European Assoc for the Study of Diabetes, European Neuroscience Assoc, Med Research Soc (memb Ctee 1992–95, chm 1995–99), Physiological Soc, RSM, Soc for Endocrinology (memb Ctee 1983–87 and 1994–99, sec-gen 1999–2002, chm 2002–), Soc of Gastroenterology (Br and American); FRCP 1978, FRCPath 1993, FMedSci 1997, FRS 2013; *Books* Gut Hormones (ed, 1978, 2 edn (jtly) 1981), Gastrointestinal and Related Hormones (jt ed, 1979), Radioimmunoassay of Gut Regulatory Peptides (jt ed, 1981), Basic Science in Gastroenterology (jt ed, 1982), Systemic Role of Regulatory Peptides (jt ed, 1982), Gastrointestinal and Hepatobiliary Cancer (jt ed, 1983), Endocrine Tumours (jt ed, 1985), Toohey's Medicine for Nurses (14 edn (jtly) 1986, 15 edn 1995), Somatostatin (jt ed, 1986), Therapeutic Applications of LHRH (jt ed, 1986), Peptides: A Target for New Drug Development (jt ed, 1991), Surgical Endocrinology (jt ed, 1993); *Style*— Professor Sir Stephen Bloom; ✉ Department of Investigative Medicine, Division of Investigative Science, Imperial College Faculty of Medicine, Hammersmith Hospital Campus, Du Cane Road, London W12 0NN (☎ 020 8383 3242, fax 020 8383 8320)

BLOOMER, Dr (Robert John) Giles; OBE (1998), DL (1999); s of Robert Bloomer (d 1984), and Aileen Edith, *née* Morris (d 1986); *b* 1943; *Educ* Rotherham GS, Univ of Birmingham (BSc, PhD); *m* 1967, Elizabeth, *née* Broughton; 1 da (Katherine b 1970), 2 s (Robert b 1972, Jonathan b 1976); *Career* water engr/hydrologist Cornwall River Authy and Water Resources Bd 1967–72, dir Bramall Construction and Keepmoat plc 1972–85, chm Aizlewoods Bldg Materials 1985–2002; pres Rotherham C of C 1990, chair Rotherham TEC 1992–97; govr Thomas Rotherham Coll 1990–2015, tstee and dir Magna Tst 1998–2013, non-exec dir Rotherham Hosp NHS Fndn Tst 2005–11, tstee S Yorks Community Fndn 2006–16; High Sheriff S Yorks 2008–09, Vice Lord-Lt S Yorks; Liveryman Worshipful Co of Builders Merchants, Freeman City of London; MICE 1969; *Recreations* family; *Clubs* Rotary (Rotherham); *Style*— Dr Giles Bloomer, OBE, DL

BLOOMER, Jonathan William; *b* 23 March 1954; *Educ* Imperial Coll London (BSc, ARCS); *m* Sept 1977, Judy; 3 c; *Career* Arthur Andersen: joined 1974, ptnr Fin Mkts Div Audit and Business Advsy Practice 1987–91, managing ptnr Euro Insurance Practice 1991–94; Prudential plc: gp fin dir 1995–99, dep gp chief exec 1999–2000, chief exec 2000–05, md Cerberus UK Advsrs LLP 2005–; chief exec Lucida 2006–; non-exec dir: Hargreaves Lansdown plc 2007–, Autonomy plc 2009–11; memb: Urgent Issues Task Force 1995–99, Bd Assoc of Br Insurers 2001–05; former memb Financial Services Practitioner Panel (chm 2003–05); FCA; *Recreations* sailing, rugby; *Style*— Jonathan Bloomer, Esq

BLOSSE; *see:* Lynch-Blosse

BLOW, Bridget Penelope; CBE (2014); *Career* chief exec ITNET plc 1994–2005; non-exec dir Bank of England 2000–05, non-exec dir Alba/Harvard Int 2005–07, non-exec chm Trustmarque Gp Ltd 2006–13, non-exec dir Coventry Building Soc 2007–10, chm Alba/Harvard Int 2007–12, chm Coventry Building Soc 2010–16; non-exec dir Birmingham Hippodrome 2006–12, pres Birmingham Chamber of Commerce 2008–09, non-exec chm Greater Birmingham and Solihull LEP Devpt Bd 2010–11, non-exec chm City of Birmingham Symphony Orchestra 2012–; non-exec dir England Netball 2015–; *Style*— Ms Bridget Blow, CBE; ✉ 18 Symphony Court, Birmingham B16 8AD

BLOW, Selina (Mrs Levinson); da of Jonathan Blow (d 1977), and Helga, *née* de Silva; *b* 19 September 1966; *Educ* Hatherop Castle Sch, Queen's Coll London; *m* 1998, Charles Levinson; 1 s (Augustus b Dec 1998), 1 da (Violet b July 2002); *Career* fashion designer: ready-to-wear collection 1992, new generation 1992, opened Selina Blow shop 1993, menswear and childrenswear launched 2000; *Recreations* film, painting, gardens, cooking, Sri Lanka; *Style*— Ms Selina Blow

BLOXHAM, Tom; MBE (1999); *b* 20 December 1963, Fleet, Lincs; *Educ* Manchester Univ; *m*;; *Career* chm and co-fndr (with Jonathan Falkingham) Urban Splash 1993–; chllr Univ of Manchester 2008–15; chair: Manchester Int Arts Festival, IPPR Centre for Cities Think Tank; memb: Arts Cncl England (chair NW), Urban Sounding Bd ODPM, Property Advsy Gp ODPM, Govt's Urban Task Force Working Gps; dir Liverpool Capital of Culture; tstee: Tate Gallery 2009, Manchester United Fndn Charity, Bloxham Charitable Tst; govr and fndr New Islington Free Sch; UK Property Entrepreneur of the Year Property Week 1998 and 2002, Ernst & Young Young Entrepreneur of the Year 1999, Young Entrepreneur of the Year IOD NW 1999, Manchester Evening News Business of the Year 2002, RIBA Client of the Year 2002, Property Entrepreneur of the Year Building Magazine 2003, Property Personality of the Year Insider Awards 2004, Property Entrepreneur of the Year EN magazine 2004, Royal Soc of Arts Bicentenary Medal 2008, Coll of Estate Management Property Award 2008; hon fell: John Moores Univ Liverpool 2001, Univ of Central Lancashire 2003; Hon DDes Oxford Brookes Univ 2004, hon degree Univ of Manchester 2007, hon degree Univ of Plymouth 2009, hon degree Univ of Cumbria 2010, hon doctorate Univ of Plymouth 2011; Hon FRIBA 2000, hon fell Royal Soc of Architects; *Books* Transformation by Urban Splash (2011); *Style*— Tom Bloxham, Esq, MBE; ✉ Urban Splash, Timber Wharf, 16–22 Worsley Street, Manchester M15 4LD (☎ 0161 839 2999, fax 0161 839 8999, e-mail tombloxham@urbansplash.co.uk)

BLUE, Rabbi Lionel; OBE (1994); s of Harry Blue (d 1965), and Hetty Blue; *b* 6 February 1930; *Educ* Westminster City Sch, Hendon Co Sch, Balliol Coll Oxford (MA), UCL (BA), Leo Baeck Coll (Rabbinical Dip, fell); *Career* minister Settlement Synagogue 1957, rabbi Middx New Synagogue 1959, religious dir for Euro Bd World Union for Progressive Judaism 1963–66, lectr Leo Baeck Coll 1963–, convener Ecclesiastical Ct Reformed Synagogues of GB 1969–89; broadcaster: Prayer for the Day, Thought for the Day, Pause for Thought, In Search of Holy England; writer, columnist The Tablet, co-ed Forms of Prayer 1969–, retreat leader; memb Rabbinical Assembly Reformed Synagogues of GB (hon vice-pres), vice-chm Standing Conf of Jews, Christians and Moslems in Europe; Hon DUniv Open Univ 1998, Hon DD Univ of Durham 2006; FRSA; *Books* To Heaven with Scribes and Pharisees (1975), Forms of Prayer Vols 1 and 2 (1977), A Backdoor to Heaven (1978), Kitchen Blues (1985), Bright Blue (1985), Blue Heaven (1987), Guide to Here and Hereafter (jtly, 1988), Blue Horizons (1989), How to get up when life gets you down (jtly, 1992), The Little Blue Book of Prayer (jtly, 1993), Tales of Body and Soul (1994), Kindred Spirits (jtly, 1995), My Affair with Christianity (1998), Sun, Sand and Soul (jtly, 1999), Little Book of Blue Thoughts (2001), Blue's Jokes (2001), Hitchhiking to Heaven (2004), The Best of Blue (2006), The Godseeker's Guide (2010); *Recreations* monasteries, charity shops, painting, travelling; *Style*— Rabbi Lionel Blue, OBE; ✉ Leo Baeck College, 80 East End Road, London N3 2SY (☎ 020 8349 4525)

BLUME, Dame Hilary Sharon Braverman; DBE (2008); da of Henry Braverman (d 1986), of London, and Muriel, *née* Millin (d 2005); *b* 9 January 1945; *Educ* LSE, Univ of Sussex; *m* 1, 5 Sept 1965 (m dis 1977), Prof Stuart Blume; 2 s (Toby b 22 Aug 1972, Joby b 12 July 1975); m 2, 25 July 1977, Prof Michael Aslan Norton, OBE, s of Richard Michael Norton (d 1985); 1 da (Poppy b 15 June 1978); *Career* dir Charities Advsy Tst 1982–, dir Greenway Hotels India; chm Finnart House Tst; cmmr National Lottery Cmmn 1999–2000; patron Trees for London, hon patron UK Jewish Film; FRSA 2002–08 (memb Cncl 2004–07); memb Vol Advsy Bd Canal and River Tst; *Books* Fund-raising: A Comprehensive Handbook, The Charity Trading Handbook, The Museum Trading Handbook, Charity Christmas Cards, Charity Shop Handbook; *Style*— Dame Hilary Blume, DBE (or Mrs Michael Norton); ✉ Charities Advisory Trust, Radius Works, Back Lane, London NW3 1HL (☎ 020 7794 9835)

BLUMENTHAL, Heston Marc; OBE (2006); s of Stephen Jeffrey Blumenthal, and Celia Blumenthal; *b* 27 May 1966; *Educ* Latymer Upper Sch, John Hampden GS; *m* 10 Aug 1991, Susanna Clare; 1 s (Jack Stephen b 18 Jan 1993), 2 da (Jessica Ella b 19 Dec 1994, Joy Mae b 6 Oct 1997); *Career* credit controller Team Leasing (family equipment leasing co) for nine years; self taught chef; chef/prop The Fat Duck 1995–, prop The Hinds Head 2004–; *Awards* Michelin Star 1999, 2 Michelin Stars 2002, 3 Michelin Stars 2004; Good Food Guide: Restaurant of the Year 1997, 9 out of 10 1999, Chef of the Year 2001, 8 out of 10 2002, 10 out of 10 2008; AA Restaurant Guide: 4 Rosettes 1997, Restaurant of the Year 2001, Chefs' Chef of the Year 2002, Wine Award (nat winner and winner for England) 2002, 5 Rosettes 2002, 2003, 2004 and 2006; Time Out Eating and Drinking Guide (one of best restaurants in London area) 1997, Egon Ronay Guide 1997, Decanter Magazine Restaurant of the Year 1997–98, Evening Standard London Restaurant Guide, Harpers & Queen Premier Crew Award for Service 2001, Chef of the Year Catey Awards 2004, Best Out of Town Restaurant Tatler Magazine Awards 2004, Best Out of Town Restaurant Square Meal/BMW Awards 2004, Best Restaurant Observer Food Monthly Awards 2004, Restaurant Magazine World's Best Restaurant 2005 (Second Best 2004), 19/20 Gault Millau Guide 2005; *Books* Family Food (2002); *Recreations* food, wine, sport, family; *Style*— Heston Blumenthal, Esq, OBE; ✉ The Fat Duck, High Street, Bray, Berkshire SL6 2AQ (☎ 01628 580333, fax 01628 776188)

BLUNDELL, Prof Derek John; s of Frank Herbert Blundell (d 1978), and Irene Mary, *née* Davie (d 1963); *b* 30 June 1933; *Educ* East Grinstead GS, Univ of Birmingham (BSc), Imperial Coll London (PhD, DIC); *m* 15 Sept 1960, Mary Patricia, da of Archibald James Leonard (d 1968); *Career* lectr in geology Univ of Birmingham 1959–70, reader in geophysics Lancaster Univ 1971–75 (sr lectr 1970–71), prof of environmental geology Univ of London 1975–98 (emeritus prof of geophysics 1998–); head Dept of Geology: Chelsea Coll London 1975–85, Royal Holloway Coll London 1992–97 (dean of Research and Enterprise 1995–98); Leverhulme emeritus fell 1998–2000; pres Geological Soc 1988–90; Coke Medal Geological Soc 1993; hon fell Royal Holloway Coll London 2005; memb Academia Europaea 1990–; FGS 1956, CGeol 1990–98; *Publications* A Continent Revealed – The European Geotraverse (1992), Tectonic Evolution of Southeast Asia (Geological Soc Special Pubn 106, 1996), Lyell: The Past is the Key to the Present (Geological Soc Special Pubn 143, 1998), The Timing and Location of Major Ore Desposits in an Evolving Orogen (Geological Soc Special Pubn 204, 2002); Geodynamics and Ore Deposit Evolution in Europe (2005); contrib to various jls on seismic exploration, earthquake hazards, mountain building and mineral deposits; *Clubs* Athenaeum; *Style*— Prof Derek Blundell; ✉ Department of Earth Sciences, Royal Holloway, University of London, Egham, Surrey TW20 0EX (☎ 01784 443811, fax 01784 471780, e-mail d.blundell@es.rhul.ac.uk)

BLUNDELL, John; s of James Blundell (d 2000), and Alice Margaret, *née* Taylor (d 1996); *b* 9 October 1952, Congleton, Cheshire; *Educ* King's Sch Macclesfied, LSE (BSc (Econ)); *m* 1977, Christine Violet, da of Charles Henry Lowry; 2 s (Miles John b 1982, James Lowry b 1989); *Career* head Parly Press Office Fedn of Small Business 1976–82; pres: Inst for Humane Studies 1982–91, Atlas Economic Research Fndn 1987–91, CG Koch Fndn 1991–93; DG IEA 1993–; memb of various economic research orgns in UK, USA, India and Peru; memb: Fairbridge Cncl 1998–, John Templeton Fndn Radnor PA 2001–, Selection Ctee Milton Friedman Prize 2002–; Nat Free Enterprise Award 2000; *Publications* Beyond Left and Right (1998), Regulation without the State (1999), Regulation without the State: The Debate Continues (2000), Waging the War of Ideas (2001, expanded 3 edn 2007), A Tribute to Peter Bauer (2002), Friend or Foe? What Americans should know about the European Union (2004); *Recreations* golf, cricket, American football, genealogy, writing; *Clubs* Marin Cricket; *Style*— John Blundell, Esq; ✉ 43 Ponsonby Place, Wesminster, London SW1P 4PS (☎ 020 7828 8431); Institute of Economic Affairs, 2 Lord North Street,

Westminster, London SW1P 3LB (☎ 020 7799 8900, fax 020 7799 2137, e-mail jblundell@iea.org.uk)

BLUNDELL, Prof Sir Richard William; kt (2014), CBE (2006); *b* 1 May 1952; *Educ* Univ of Bristol (BSc), LSE (MSc); *Career* lectr in econometrics Univ of Manchester 1975–84, prof of economics UCL 1984–; dir of research Inst for Fiscal Studies 1986–; dir: Society for Economic Analysis Ltd 1988–93, ESRC Centre for Micro-Economic Analysis of Fiscal Policy 1991–; visiting assoc prof Univ of Br Columbia 1980; visiting prof: MIT 1993, Univ of Calif Berkeley 1994 and 1999; elected Leverhulme personal research prof 1999; memb Cncl: Royal Economic Soc 1990–94 (pres 2010), European Economic Assoc 1997–, Econometric Soc 1998; ed Jl of Econometrics 1991–97, co-ed Econometrica 1997–2001; memb Editorial Bd: Jl of Applied Econometrics 1985–89, Fiscal Studies 1986–, Ricerche Economiche 1993–, Int Jl of Taxation 1993–; Jrjö Jahnsson Prize 1995, Frisch Prize 2000, Jean-Jacques Laffont Prize Toulouse 2008, CES Prize Munich 2010, IZA Prize Bonn Germany 2012, BBVA Frontiers of Knowledge Prize Madrid 2015, Nemmers Prize in Economics Chicago 2016; hon doctorate: Univ of St Gallen, NHH Norwegian Sch of Economics Bergen 2011, Univ of Mannheim Germany 2011, Università della Svizzera Italiana Lugano Switzerland 2016; pres: Euro Economics Assoc 2004 (vice-pres 2002), Soc for Labour Economics 2010, Royal Economic Soc 2010–13; hon memb American Economic Assoc 2001; fell Econometric Soc 1991 (memb Cncl 1999, pres 2006), FBA 1997, FAAAS 2002, Hon FIA 2003; *Books* Unemployment, Search and Labour Supply (with I Walker, 1986), The Measurement of Household Welfare (with I Preston and I Walker, 1994), Seeking a Premier Economy: The Economic Effects of British Economic Reforms 1980–2000 (2004), Advances in Economics and Econometrics: Theory and Applications Econometric Society Ninth World Congress Vols I, II and III (co-ed, 2006), The Mirrlees Review (co-ed, 2011); author of numerous articles in books and jls; *Recreations* music; *Style*— Prof Sir Richard Blundell, CBE, FBA; ✉ Department of Economics, University College London, Gower Street, London WC1E 6BT (website www.ucl.ac.uk/~uctp39a)

BLUNDELL, Prof Stephen; *b* 1967; *Educ* Univ of Cambridge (MA, PhD); *Career* prof of physics Univ of Oxford 2004–, professorial fell Mansfield Coll Oxford, lectr CCC Oxford; CPhys, MInstP; *Books* Magnetism in Condensed Matter (2001), Concepts in Thermal Physics (with K Blundell, 2006), Superconductivity, A Very Short Introduction (2009), Magnetism, A Very Short Introduction (2012), Quantum Field Theory for the Gifted Amateur (with T Lancaster, 2014); *Style*— Prof Stephen Blundell; ✉ Oxford University Department of Physics, Clarendon Laboratory, Parks Road, Oxford OX1 3PU

BLUNDELL, Prof Sir Thomas Leon (Tom); kt (1997); s of Horace Leon Blundell, of Sussex, and Marjorie, *née* Davis; *b* 7 July 1942; *Educ* Steyning GS, BNC Oxford (BA, DPhil); *m* 1, 1964 (m dis 1973), Lesley; 1 s (Ricky b 19 Nov 1969); m 2, 1973 (m dis 1983), Reiko; m 3, 22 May 1987, Lynn Bancinyane, da of Phineas Sibanda, of Zimbabwe; 2 da (Sichelesile 5 Jan 1988, Samkeliso b 25 June 1989); *Career* postdoctoral res fell Molecular Biophysics Laboratory Univ of Oxford 1967–72 (jr res fell Linacre Coll 1968–70), lectr in biological sci Univ of Sussex 1973–76, prof of crystallography Birkbeck Coll London 1976–90 (govr 1985–89), DG Agric and Food Research Cncl 1991–94, chief exec BBSRC 1994–96, Sir William Dunn prof of biochemistry and head of Dept Univ of Cambridge 1996–2009, chair Sch of Biological Sciences Univ of Cambridge 2003–09, emeritus prof and dir of research Dept of Biochemistry Univ of Cambridge 2009–; professorial fell Sidney Sussex Coll Cambridge 1995–2009 (emeritus fell 2009–); chm Royal Cmmn on Environmental Pollution 1998–2005; chm Biofabrica 1989–91; industrial conslt: CellTech 1981–86, Pfizer Central Research 1984–90, Abingworth Management Ltd 1988–90 and 1997–; scientific advsr Oxford Molecular Ltd 1996–99; memb Research Bd: SmithKline Beecham plc 1997–2000, Bioprocessing Ltd 1997–99; memb Scientific Advsy Bd: Protein Mechanics Calif 2001–04, Teraview 2002–06; non-exec dir Celltech plc 1997–2004 (chm Scientific Advsy Bd 1998–2004), co-fndr and non-exec dir Astex Therapeutics Cambridge 1999–2010 (also chm Sci Advsy Bd), chair SAB Astex Pharma 2011– (purchased by Otsuka Hldgs Japan, currently memb Bd Astex Therapeutics Ltd); hon dir ICRF Structural Molecular Biology Unit 1989–96, dir Int Sch of Crystallography Erice Italy 1982–, chm Biological Sci Ctee SERC 1983–87 (memb Cncl 1989–90), chair Biotechnology and Biological Sciences Research Cncl 2009–15; memb: Cncl AFRC 1985–90, Advsy Cncl on Science and Technol 1988–90, Advsy Bd Research Cncls 1991–94, European Sci and Technol Assembly (ESTA) 1995–97, Bd Babraham Inst 1997–2003; memb Editorial Advsy Bd: Biochemistry 1986–89, Protein Science 1992–98; jt ed Progress in Biophysics and Molecular Biology 1979–; pres UK Biosciences Fedn 2004–08, pres UK Science Cncl 2011–; cncllr Oxford CBC 1970–73 (chm Planning Ctee 1972–73); tstee Lawes Tst 1998–2009; Hon DSc: Univ of Edinburgh 1993, UEA 1993, Univ of Sheffield 1994, Univ of Strathclyde 1994, Univ of Warwick 1995, Univ of Antwerp 1995, Univ of Nottingham 1996, Univ of South West England 1997, Univ of Stirling 2000, Univ of Sussex 2001, Univ of St Andrews 2002, Univ of Pavia 2002, Univ of London 2003, Univ of Dundee 2007, Univ of Chile 2011; Alcon Award 1985, Gold Medal Inst of Biotechnological Studies 1987, Sir Hans Krebs Medal Fedn of Euro Biochemical Socs 1987, Ciba Medal UK Biochemical Soc 1988, Feldberg Prize in biology and medicine 1988, Gold Medal Soc for Chem Indust 1995, Bernal Medal Royal Soc 1998, European Prize for Innovative Science 1998; hon fell: Birkbeck Coll London 1989, BNC Oxford, Linacre Coll Oxford 1991; fell Indian Nat Acad 1994; memb: EMBO 1984, Academia Europaea 1993; pres Biochemical Soc 2009–11; FRS 1984 (memb Cncl 1997–98), Hon FRASE 1993, FMedSci 1998, hon fell RSC 2006, hon memb Br Biophysical Soc 2008, foreign memb Third World Acad of Sciences 2008, foreign memb Chilean Acad of Sciences 2011, FSB 2012; *Books* Protein Crystallography (1976); *Recreations* playing jazz, listening to opera, walking; *Style*— Prof Sir Tom Blundell, FRS; ✉ Department of Biochemistry, University of Cambridge, Tennis Court Road, Cambridge CB2 1GA (☎ 01223 333628, e-mail tlb20@cam.ac.uk)

BLUNDEN, George Patrick; s of Sir George Blunden (d 2012), and Anne, *née* Bulford; *b* 21 February 1952; *Educ* St Edward's Sch Oxford, UC Oxford (BA); *m* 8 July 1978, Jane Rosemary, da of Gp Capt Charles Eric Hunter (d 1986); 2 da (Victoria Jane b 10 Sept 1980, Eleanor Louise b 18 Sept 1985), 1 s (George Edward Paul b 4 Aug 1982); *Career* dir: Seccombe Marshall & Campion 1983–86, S G Warburg Securities 1986–92, S G Warburg Discount 1989–92; chief exec Union plc 1992–97, dir Alliance Capital Whittingdale Ltd 1997–2004; non-exec dir: Beazley Furlonge Ltd 1994–, Beazley plc 2010–, Meridian Ltd 2010–11; chm: Raglan Housing Assoc 2010–15, Charity Bank 2010–, Stonewater 2015–; chm and tstee Southern Housing Group 1990–2004; Freeman City of London 1988; Liveryman Worshipful Co of Goldsmiths; *Clubs* MCC, Hurlingham; *Style*— George Blunden, Esq; ✉ 46 Hurlingham Court, Ranelagh Gardens, London SW6 35Q (☎ 07867 548248, e-mail gpblunden@gmail.com)

BLUNKETT, Baron (Life Peer UK 2015), of Brightside and Hillsborough in the City of Sheffield; Rt Hon David Blunkett; PC (1997); s of Arthur Blunkett (d 1960), and Doris Matilda Elizabeth, *née* Williams (d 1983); *b* 6 June 1947; *Educ* Univ of Sheffield (BA), Huddersfield Holly Bank Coll of Educn (PGCE); *Children* 4 s; *Career* clerk typist 1967–69, lectr and tutor in industrial rels and political admin Barnsley Coll of Technol 1973–87, on secondment as ldr Sheffield City Cncl 1981–87, dep chm AMA 1984–87; Sheffield City Cncl: memb 1970–88, chm Family and Community Servs Ctee 1976–80, ldr 1980–87; memb S Yorks Metropolitan CC 1973–77; memb Lab Pty NEC 1983–98, chm Lab Pty Ctee on Local Govt 1984–92, MP (Lab) Sheffield Brightside 1987–2015, oppn front bench spokesman on the environment 1988–92, memb Shadow Cabinet 1992–97; chief oppn spokesman on: health 1992–94, educn 1994–95, educn and employment 1995–97; sec of state for educn and employment 1997–2001, sec of state Home Office 2001–04, sec of state for work and pensions 2005; chm Labour Party 1993–94 (vice-chm 1992–93); prof of politics in practice and chair Bd Crick Centre Univ of Sheffield 2015–; *Books* Local Enterprise and Worker's Plans (1981), Building from the Bottom: the Sheffield Experience (1983), Democracy in Crisis: the town halls respond (1987), On a Clear Day (1995, revised edn 2002), Politics and Progress (2001), The Blunkett Tapes – My Life in the Bear Pit (2006); *Recreations* walking, music, sailing, being with friends; *Style*— The Rt Hon the Lord Blunkett; ✉ House of Lords, London SW1A 0PW (☎ 020 7219 6926)

BLUNT, Crispin Jeremy Rupert; MP; s of late Maj Gen Peter Blunt, CB, MBE, GM, and late Adrienne, *née* Richardson; bro of Oliver Blunt, QC, *qv*; *b* 15 July 1960; *Educ* Wellington, RMA Sandhurst, UC Durham (BA), Cranfield Inst of Technol (MBA); *m* 15 Sept 1990 (sep), Victoria Ainsley, *née* Jenkins; 1 da (Claudia b 22 Feb 1992), 1 s (Frederick b 22 Aug 1994); *Career* cmmnd 13/18 Royal Hussars 1980; troop ldr: UK and Cyprus 1980–81, BAOR 1984–86; regimental signals offr/ops offr BAOR/UK 1985–87, sqdn ldr, 2 i/c UK 1987–89, resigned cmmn 1990, representative Forum of Private Business 1991–92, conslt Politics International 1993; special advsr to: sec of state for Defence 1993–95, foreign sec 1995–97: MP (Cons) Reigate 1997–; oppn frontbench spokesman on NI 2001–02, shadow min for trade and industry 2002–03, oppn whip 2004–09, shadow min for home affrs and counter-terrorism 2009–10, Parly under-sec of state for justice 2010–12; memb House of Commons Select Ctee on: Def 1997–2000 and 2003–04, Environment Tport and Regions 2000–01; chm Cons ME Cncl 2003–08, chm Foreign Affrs Select Ctee 2015–; *Publications* Britain's Place in the World – Time to Decide (1998); *Recreations* cricket, skiing; *Clubs* Reigate Priory Cricket, MCC; *Style*— Crispin Blunt, Esq, MP; ✉ House of Commons, London SW1A 0AA (☎ 020 7219 2254, website www.blunt4reigate.com)

BLUNT, David Graeme; CVO; *m* Geirid Bakkeli Blunt; 3 s; *Career* diplomat; Repub of Ireland Dept FCO 1978–79, second then first sec Vienna 1979–83, first sec Beijing 1983–87, FCO 1987–89, first sec and head Political Section Canberra 1989–94, dir BBC Monitoring Serv Review 1994, Mgmnt Consultancy Serv FCO 1995–97, dep head of mission Oslo 1997–2001, dep govr Gibraltar 2002–05, FCO 2005, head Br Office then ambass Pristina 2006–08, ambass to Croatia 2008–12; Gamesa: dir of public policy UK and EU instns 2012–13, md UK 2013–; *Style*— Mr David Blunt, CVO; ✉ 16 Palace Street, London SW1E 5JD

BLUNT, David John; QC (1991); s of Vernon Egerton Rowland Blunt (d 1990), of Staunton-on-Wye, Hereford, and Catherine Vera, *née* Jones; *b* 25 October 1944; *Educ* Farnham GS, Trinity Hall Cambridge (MA), Inns of Court Sch of Law (Colombos Prize for Public Int Law); *m* 28 Feb 1976, Zaibonisa, da of Isaak Ebrahim (d 1962), of Cape Town, South Africa; 1 da (Dr Nadia Shaida b 1980), 1 s (Joseph Isaac b 1987); *Career* called to the Bar Middle Temple 1967 (bencher 2000, master of the bench 2001, Michaelmas reader 2016); asst recorder 1985–90, recorder of the Crown Court 1990–, dep judge of Tech and Construction Court 1993, dep High Court judge 2003; chm Bonhams Gp Ltd 1990–2000; memb Lib Dem Pty; Parly candidate (Lib): Lambeth Central 1978 and 1979, Cornwall SE 1983; *Recreations* reading, writing, running, cycling, gardening, old cars; *Clubs* Thames Hare and Hounds; *Style*— David Blunt, Esq, QC; ✉ 4 Pump Court, Temple, London EC4Y 7AN (☎ 020 7842 5555)

BLUNT, James; né James Hillier Blount; s of Col Charles Blount, and Jane Ann Farran Blount; *b* 22 February 1974, Tidworth, Wilts; *Educ* Harrow, Univ of Bristol (BEng), RMA Sandhurst; *Career* Capt Life Guards (HCR and HCMR) 1996–2002, armoured reconnaissance offr NATO Peacekeeping Force Kosovo 1999; singer and songwriter 2004–; albums: Back to Bedlam 2004, All the Lost Souls 2007, Some Kind of Trouble 2010, Moon Landing 2013; singles: High 2004, Wisemen 2005, You're Beautiful 2005, Goodbye My Lover 2005, No Bravery 2006, 1973 2007, Carry You Home 2008, Stay The Night 2011, Bonfire Heart 2013; *Awards* incl: Best New Act MTV Europe Music Awards 2005, Best New Act Q Awards 2005, Best Pop Act Digital Music Awards 2005, Best Int Newcomer NRJ Music Awards (France) 2006, Best Pop Act and Best Male Brit Awards 2006, Best Int Newcomer ECHO Awards (Germany) 2006, Song of the Year MTV Australia Video Music Awards 2006, Most Performed Work and Int Hit of the Year Ivor Novello Awards 2006, Best Male Video and Best Cinematography MTV Awards (US) 2006, Best New Artist in the World and Biggest Selling Br Artist in the World World Music Awards 2006, Choice Music Male Artist Teen Choice Award (US) 2006, Best Int Male Artist ECHO Award (Germany) 2008, Best Int Male Artist Regenbogen Award (Germany) 2010; 5 Grammy Award nominations 2006; *Style*— James Blunt; ✉ c/o Rocket Music, 1 Blythe Road, London W14 0HG

BLUNT, Oliver Simon Peter; QC (1994); s of late Maj-Gen Peter John Blunt, CB, MBE, GM, of Ramsbury, Wilts, and Adrienne, *née* Richardson; bro of Crispin Blunt, MP, *qv*; *b* 8 March 1951; *Educ* Bedford Sch, Univ of Southampton (LLB); *m* 29 Sept 1979, Joanna Margaret, da of Robert Dixon (d 1985); 3 da (Felicity b 1981, Emily b 1983, Susannah b 1991), 1 s (Sebastian b 1989); *Career* called to the Bar Middle Temple 1974 (bencher 2008); asst recorder 1991, recorder 1995; *Recreations* cricket, golf; *Clubs* Roehampton, Barnes Sports, Rosslyn Park; *Style*— Oliver Blunt, Esq, QC; ✉ 106 Priory Lane, Roehampton, London SW15 5JL (☎ 020 8876 3369); Furnival Chambers, 32 Furnival Street, London EC4A 1JQ (☎ 020 7405 3232)

BLUNT, Dr Stavia Brigitte; da of Harry Blunt (d 2007), of Kenya, and Elly, *née* Sfalagacos (d 1981); *Educ* Malvern Girls' Coll (head girl), Univ of Oxford (BA, John Llewellyn scholarship, John Cooney scholarship, Martin Wronker Prize), Westminster Med Sch, Inst of Neurology (PhD); *m* 12 Sept 1987, George Leggatt, QC, *qv*, s of Rt Hon Sir Andrew Leggatt, *qv*; 1 s (Peter b 4 April 1990), 1 da (Elly b 25 Feb 1993); *Career* jr dr at various London teaching hosps; neurology specialist trg: Hammersmith Hosp, Nat Hosp for Neurology, Charing Cross Hosp, Atkinson Morley's Hosp; conslt and sr lectr in neurology Hammersmith Hosp 1994–98; conslt: Charing Cross Hosp 1998–2004 (hon sr lectr 1998–), Parkside Hosp 1998–2011, 27 Harley St 2008–2011; former sec Neurology Section RSM; memb Bd Research Advsy Ctee Royal Hosp for Neurodisability; dir Liquid Gold Products Cretan Gourmet Health Foods 2012–; MRC Trg fell 1988–91, Vera Down Res Award BMA 1993, Royal Soc Res Award 1994; FRCP 2000 (MRCP 1987); *Publications* Having a Baby (1997), Shaping Up During and After Pregnancy (1998), Working Mother (1999); author of numerous book chapters and over 50 medical papers in peer-reviewed jls; *Recreations* songwriting, swimming; *Style*— Dr Stavia Blunt; ✉ e-mail staviablunt@gmail.com

BLYTH, Sir Charles (Chay); kt (1997), CBE (1972), BEM (1967); s of Robert Blyth (d 1971), and Jessie Pat, *née* Patterson (d 1965); *b* 14 May 1940; *Educ* Hawick HS; *m* 1, 1962 (m dis 1992), Maureen Margaret, da of Albert Morris (d 1956); 1 da (Samantha b 1967); m 2, 1995, Felicity Rayson; *Career* served 3 Bn Para Regt 1958–67, Sgt; Cadbury Schweppes 1968–69, dir Sailing Ventures (Hampshire) Ltd 1969–73; md: Rainbow Charters Ltd 1974–, South West Properties Ltd 1978–94, The Challenge Business Ltd 1989–2006; conslt Hill & Knowlton Ltd 1983–92; rowed N Atlantic with Capt John Ridgeway 1966, circumnavigated world westwards solo in yacht British Steel 1970–71, circumnavigated world eastwards with crew of paratroopers in yacht Great Britain II Whitbread Round the World Yacht Race 1973–74 (winner Elapsed Time prize), Atlantic sailing record Cape Verde to Antigua 1977, winner Round Britain Race in yacht Great Britain IV (crew Robert James) 1978, winner Observer/Europe 1 Doublehanded Transatlantic Race in record time (crew Robert James) 1981, captained yacht United Friendly (first British yacht home) Whitbread Round the World Race 1981/82, in yacht Brittany Ferries GB came

2nd overall and first in Class I Round Britain and Ireland Race 1982 and first in Class Plymouth Vilamoura Plymouth Race 1983, in trimaran Beefeater II (with Eric Blunn) capsized off Cape Horn during NY-San Francisco record attempt and spent 19 hours in water before rescue 1984, co-skipper Virgin Atlantic Challenger I 1985, co-skipper Virgin Atlantic Challenge II on the successful Blue Riband 1986; chm: Silk Cut Awards Ctee 1983–92, British Steel Challenge Round the World Yacht Race 1992–93, BT Global Challenge Round the World Yacht Race 1996/97; Man of the Year 1966; Yachting Journalists' Assoc: Yachtsman of the Year 1971, Special Award for Outstanding Servs to Yachting 1994; Chichester Trophy RYS 1971; pres Inst of Professional Sales 1999, pres CIM (Wessex Branch) 1999; Hon DTech Univ of Plymouth 1994, Hon LLD Univ of Portsmouth 1999; *Books* A Fighting Chance (1966), Innocent Aboard (1968), The Impossible Voyage (1971), Theirs is the Glory (1974), Challenge (1993); *Recreations* horse riding, skiing; *Clubs* Royal Southern Yacht, Royal Ocean Racing; *Style*— Sir Chay Blyth, CBE, BEM

BLYTH, Mark Terence; s of Terence Blyth, of Esher, Surrey, and Patricia, *née* Vincent; *b* 2 September 1965, Woking; *Educ* Poole GS, Univ of Warwick (LLB), Guildford Coll of Law; *m* 20 Aug 1989, Melanie, da of Frank Russell; 2 da (Alexandra Charlotte b 22 May 1998, Helena Catherine b 27 Aug 1999); *Career* articled clerk Allen & Overy 1988–90; Linklaters: slr 1990–2001, ptnr 2001–, currently head of pensions litigation; author of numerous articles relating to pensions litigation; memb: Assoc of Pension Lawyers, Assoc of Contentious Tst and Probate Specialists, Law Soc; *Recreations* jogging, gardening, cars, photography; *Style*— Mark Blyth, Esq; ✉ Linklaters, One Silk Street, London EC2Y 8HQ (☎ 020 7456 2000, fax 020 7456 2222, e-mail mark.blyth@linklaters.com)

BLYTHMAN, Joanna; *Career* food journalist and author; weekly columnist Sunday Herald Glasgow; contrib to numerous newspapers and magazines incl: Observer, Daily Mail, The Guardian, Daily Telegraph, The Independent, The Grocer; appearances on: Tonight, BBC Breakfast, GMTV, The Money Prog, Dispatches, Time Shift, The Food Prog, Woman's Hour; Derek Cooper Award BBC Radio 4 Food and Farming Awards 2004, Outstanding Contribution to Food Good Housekeeping Award 2007; *Books* The Food We Eat: The Book You Cannot Afford to Ignore (2 edn, 1998, Glenfiddich Special Award, Guild of Food Writers Award), The Food Our Children Eat: How to Get Children to Like Good Food (1999), How to Avoid GM Food: Hundreds of Brands, Products and Ingredients to Avoid (1999), Shopped: The Shocking Power of British Supermarkets (2004, Glenfiddich Food Book of the Year Award 2005), Bad Food Britain: How a Nation Ruined Its Appetite (2006), What to Eat: Food That's Good for Your Health, Pocket and Plate (2012), Swallow This: Serving Up the Food Industry's Darkest Secrets (2015); *Style*— Ms Joanna Blythman; ✉ c/o Curtis Brown Group, Haymarket House, 28–29 Haymarket, London SW1Y 4SP

BOADEN, Helen; da of William John Boaden, and Barbara Mary Boaden; *b* 1 March 1956; *Educ* Univ of Sussex (BA); *m* 1994, Stephen Burley; *Career* care asst Hackney Social Servs 1978, reporter Radio WBAI NY 1979, reporter Radio Tees and Radio Aire 1980–83, prodr BBC Radio Leeds 1983–85, reporter File on 4 (BBC Radio 4) and Brass Tacks (BBC2) and presenter Woman's Hour (BBC Radio 4) 1985–91, presenter Verdict (Channel 4) 1991–, ed File on 4 (BBC Radio 4) 1991–94, head of network current affrs BBC Manchester 1994–97, head of business progs BBC News 1997, head of current affrs and business progs BBC 1998–2000, controller BBC Radio 4 2000–04, controller BBC7 2002–04, dir BBC News Gp 2004–12, dir BBC Radio 2013–; visiting prof Univ of the Arts London 2009; chair Radio Acad 2003– (fell 2002), memb Bd BBC 2011–; hon pres HF Holidays 2014; tstee: Stephen Joseph Theatre 2014, Alcohol Research UK 2014; Sony Gold Awards for: investigation into AIDS in Africa (File on 4) 1987, investigation into bullying in Feltham Young Offenders Inst (File on 4) 1993, Radio Station of the Year (BBC Radio 4) 2003 and 2004; Hon Dr: UEA, Univ of Sussex, Univ of York; Hon DUniv: Open Univ 2011, Brighton 2012; hon fell Univ of the Arts London 2011; *Recreations* walking; *Style*— Ms Helen Boaden

BOAITEY, Charlotte; da of Kwaku Yentumi Boaitey (d 1944), and Lydia, *née* Sarpong (d 1989); *b* 21 March 1944; *Educ* Aburi Girls' Sch Ghana, Univ of London (LLB), Lady Margaret Hall Oxford (MPhil Social Anthropology); *m* 19 Oct 1972, Alfred Kwasi Kwarteng, s of Kodua Kwarteng; 1 s (Kwasi Addob b 26 May 1975); *Career* barrister; fndr memb Legal Dept of Community Relations Cmmn (now Cmmn for Racial Equality) 1972–75, called to the Bar Middle Temple 1976, currently head of chambers 12 Old Square; asst boundary cmmr, chm Review Cncllr Renumeration, pt/t legal chm Mental Health Review Tbnl; conslt anthropologist Granada TV series Disappearing World 1982; chm Queensbury Methodist Home and Overseas Mission; tstee of various charities; *Recreations* gardening, house keeping; *Style*— Miss Charlotte Boaitey; ✉ 12 Old Square, 1st Floor, Lincoln's Inn, London WC2A 3TX (☎ 020 7404 0875)

BOARD, Prof Kenneth; s of George Herbert Board, of Llanelli, and Beryl, *née* Roberts; *b* 15 April 1941; *Educ* Llanelli Boys' GS, Univ of Wales Swansea (BSc, MSc, DSc), Univ of Bangor (PhD); *m* 30 July 1966, Meriel, da of Gwilym Leonard Jones, of Bynea, Llanelli, Dyfed; 2 s (Meirion b 1973, Alun b 1976); *Career* research scientist: GEC Hirst Research Centre, Philips Research Lab 1969–75; Dept of Electrical Engrg Univ of Wales Swansea: lectr 1975–82, sr lectr 1982–84, reader 1984–86, prof 1986–, head of dept 1992–99, chm of faculty 1996–97, Technium chair of entrepreneurship 1998–2003, dir Knowledge Exploitation Centre; co-fndr and dir Enfis Ltd 2001–; MIEEE 1982, FIEE 1997, FREng 2001; *Books* Introduction to Semiconductor Microtechnology (1983); *Recreations* squash, running, music; *Clubs* Clyne Golf; *Style*— Prof Kenneth Board; ✉ Knowledge Exploitation Centre, Department of Electrical Engineering, University of Wales Swansea, Singleton Park, Swansea SA2 8PP (☎ 01792 295415, fax 01792 513398, e-mail k.board@swansea.ac.uk)

BOARDMAN, Sir John; kt (1989); s of Frederick Archibald Boardman (d 1938), and Clare, *née* Wells (d 1975); *b* 20 August 1927; *Educ* Chigwell Sch, Magdalene Coll Cambridge (MA, Walston student); *m* 26 Oct 1952, Sheila Joan Lyndon Stanford (d 2005); 2 c (Julia b 1955, Mark b 1957); *Career* Mil Serv 2 Lt Intelligence Corps 1950–52; asst dir Br Sch of Athens 1952–55 (vice-pres), asst keeper Ashmolean Museum Oxford 1955–59, reader in classical archaeology Univ of Oxford 1959–78, Lincoln prof of classical archaeology and art Univ of Oxford 1978–94; Merton Coll Oxford: fell 1963–78, subwarden 1975–78, hon fell 1978; Geddes-Harrower prof Univ of Aberdeen 1974; visiting prof: Columbia Univ 1965, Aust Inst of Archaeology 1987; prof of ancient history Royal Acad of Arts 1990–; ed: Jl of Hellenic Studies 1958–65, Lexicon Iconographicum 1972–; conducted excavations on: Chios 1953–55, Crete, Tocra in Libya 1964–65; vice-pres Archaeological Soc of Athens 1998; delg OUP 1979–89; Cromer Greek prize Br Acad 1959, Kenyon Medal British Acad 1995, Onassis Prize 2010; corr fell: Bavarian Acad of Sciences 1969, Athens Acad 1997; fell: Inst of Etruscan Studies Florence 1983, Austrian and German Archaeological Insts; hon fell: Magdalene Coll Cambridge 1984, Lincoln Coll Oxford 1995; Hon Dr: Univ of Athens 1991, Univ of Paris (Sorbonne) 1994; foreign memb: Royal Danish Acad 1979, American Philosophical Soc 1999, Acad dei Lincei Rome 1999, Russian Acad of Sciences 2003; membre associé Académie des Inscriptions et Belles Lettres Institut de France 1991; Hon MRIA 1986; FSA 1957, FBA 1969; Hon RA; *Publications* incl: Cretan Collection in Oxford (1961), Island Gems (1963), Archaic Greek Gems (1968), Athenian Black Figure Vases (1974), Harari Collection of Finger Rings (with D Scarisbrick, 1978), The Greeks Overseas (1980), Escarabeos de Piedra de Ibiza (1984), The Oxford History of the Classical World (jtly 1986), Athenian Red Figure Vases, Classical Period (1989), The Oxford History of Classical Art (jtly 1993), The Diffusion of Classical Art in Antiquity (1994), Greek Art (1996), The Great God Pan (1997), Early Greek Vase Painting (1998), Persia and the West (2000), The History of Greek Vases (2001), The Archaeology of Nostalgia (2002), The World of Ancient Art (2006), The Marlborough Gems (2009), Pure Gold (2012), The Triumph of Dionysos (2014), The Greeks in Asia (2015); articles in various learned jls; *Clubs* Athenaeum; *Style*— Sir John Boardman, FBA; ✉ 11 Park Street, Woodstock, Oxfordshire OX20 1SJ (☎ 01993 811259, fax 01865 278067)

BOARDMAN, Hon Nigel Patrick Gray; s of Baron Boardman, MC, TD, DL (Life Peer, d 2003); *b* 1950; *Educ* Ampleforth, Univ of Bristol; *Family* 5 da (Tamsin b 1980, Charlotte b 1981, Rebecca b 1984, Cordelia b 1987, Elizabeth b 1992), 1 s (Hugo b 1990); *Career* admitted slr 1975; ptnr Slaughter and May; *Style*— The Hon Nigel Boardman; ✉ Slaughter and May, 1 Bunhill Row, London EC1Y 8YY (☎ 020 7090 3418, fax 020 7090 5000)

BOAS, (John) Robert Sotheby; s of Edgar Henry Boas, of Teddington, Middx, and Mary Katherine, *née* Beattie; *b* 28 February 1937; *Educ* Clifton, CCC Cambridge; *m* 25 Sept 1965, (Karen) Elisabeth, da of Gunnar Gersted, of Copenhagen, Denmark; 1 da (Helena b 1970), 2 s (Christopher b 1972, Nicholas b 1975 d 1998); *Career* 2 Lt Royal Signals 1955–57; merchant banker; Price Waterhouse 1960–64, ICI 1964–65, S G Warburg & Co Ltd 1965–95, md SBC Warburg Dillon Read 1995–98, advsr UBS Warburg 1998–2002; non-exec dir: Chesterfield Properties 1978–99, Norwich Union 1998–2000, Trident Safeguards 1998–2002, Invesco Smaller Continental Companies Tst 1998–2004, Prospect Publishing 2000–16, Telecom Italia 2004–07; memb Bd Securities Assoc 1988–96; dir: ENO 1990–99, Donmar Warehouse 1997–2001; memb Bd Cncl The English Stage Co 1978–83; chm Fedn of Br Artists 2001–07; tstee: Nat Heritage Meml Fund and Heritage Lottery Fund 1998–2002, Paintings in Hosp 1998–2007, Nat Life Stories Fndn 1998–, Guildhall Sch Tst 2000–09, Classical Opera Co 2001–13, Gabrieli Tst 2001–13, Paul Hamlyn Fndn 2002–09; chm London String Quartet Fndn 2006–10; FCA; *Recreations* music, painting, theatre, reading; *Style*— Robert Boas, Esq; ✉ 22 Mansfield Street, London W1G 9NR

BOATENG, Ozwald; OBE (2006); s of Kwasi Domfeh, of London, and Mary Domfeh; *b* 22 February 1967; *Educ* Southgate Coll (Dip Fashion); *m* 1 Sept 1999 (m dis 2010), Gyunel; 1 da (Emilia), 1 s (Oscar); *Career* fashion designer; fndr Bespoke Couture; produces two ready-to-wear collections each year, designer Givenchy men's collections 2003–07; memb Mayor of London Skills and Employment Bd 2007; *Awards* Best Male Designer Trophées de la Mode Paris 1996, Br Fashion Award Best Menswear Designer 2000, Cologne Fashion Award for Menswear 2002, nominated Best Dressed Man GQ Magazine Awards 2002, Best Dressed Male Vanity Fair 2006; *Recreations* film, tailoring and fashion; *Style*— Ozwald Boateng, Esq, OBE; ✉ 30 Savile Row, London W1S 3PT (☎ 020 7440 5242, fax 087 0777 1477)

BOATENG, Baron (Life Peer UK 2010), of Akyem in the Republic of Ghana and of Wembley in the London Borough of Brent; Rt Hon Paul Yaw Boateng; PC (1999); s of Kwaku Boateng, of Ghana and England, and Eleanor, *née* McCombie; *b* 14 June 1951; *Educ* Accra Acad, Apsley GS, Univ of Bristol (LLB); *m* 1980, Janet, da of Leonard Alleyne; 3 da (Mirabelle b 1980, Beth b 1982, Charlotte b 1983), 2 s (Benjamin b 1984, Seth b 1987); *Career* admitted slr 1976, sr slr Paddington Law Centre 1976–79, slr and ptnr BM Birnberg & Co 1979–87; called to the Bar Gray's Inn 1989; legal advsr Scrap Sus Campaign 1977–81, memb (Lab) for Walthamstow GLC 1981–85 (chm Police Ctee 1981–85, vice-chm Ethnic Minorities Ctee 1981–85); Parly candidate (Lab) Herts W 1983, MP (Lab) Brent S 1987–2005; memb House of Commons Environment Ctee 1987–89, oppn spokesman on Treasy and Economic Affairs 1989–92, oppn spokesman on Legal Affairs (Lord Chllr's Dept) 1992–97; Parly under sec of state Dept of Health 1997–98, min of state Home Office 1998–2001, fin sec to the Treasy 2001–02, chief sec to the Treasy 2002–05; high cmmr to South Africa 2005–09; broadcaster; presenter: Looking Forward to the Past (BBC Radio 4), Nothing But The Truth (Channel 4), Behind the Headlines (BBC2); chm Afro-Caribbean Educn Resource Project 1978–86; memb Bd: ENO 1984–97, English Touring Opera 1993–97; memb: Exec NCCL 1980–86, World Cncl of Churches Cmmn Prog to Combat Racism 1984–91; chm of govrs Priory Park Sch 1978–84; govr: Police Staff Coll Bramshill 1981–84, English Speaking Union 2010–, LSE 2011–; Hon DL Univ of Lincoln USA, Hon LLD Univ of Bristol; *Books* Reclaiming the Ground (contrib with Rt Hon John Smith, QC, MP), contrib foreword to Sense and Sensibility (in Complete Works of Jane Austen, HarperCollins); *Style*— The Lord Boateng, PC

BOBROW, Dr Lynda Geraldine; *née* Strauss; da of Jakobus Gideon Nel Strauss, QC (d 1990), of South Africa, and Joy, *née* Carpenter; *b* 23 October 1939; *Educ* Barnato Park Johannesburg, Univ of the Witwatersrand Med Sch (MB BCh); *m* 1963, Prof Martin Bobrow, CBE, *qv*; 3 da (Catherine Sue (Mrs Nicholls) b 1969, Gina (Mrs Creaton) b 1971, Jennifer Loren b 1975); *Career* patholgy trg Churchill, Radcliffe and John Radcliffe Hosps Oxford 1965–75; conslt histopathologist: Leiden 1981–83, UCL and ICRF London 1983–91, Guy's Hosp London 1991–95, Addenbrooke's Hosp Cambridge 1995–2006; memb Br Breast Gp 1993–; FRCPath 1989 (MRCPath 1977); *Recreations* walking, reading, theatre, scuba diving; *Style*— Dr Lynda Bobrow; ✉ The Old School, Balsham, Cambridge CB21 4DJ (e-mail lgb21@cam.ac.uk)

BOBROW, Prof Martin; CBE (1995); s of late Joe Bobrow, of Ontario, Canada, and Bessie, *née* Rosin; *b* 6 February 1938; *Educ* Johannesburg, Univ of the Witwatersrand (BSc, MB BCh, DSc); *m* 1963, Dr Lynda Geraldine Bobrow, *qv*, da of Jakobus Strauss, QC, of South Africa; 3 da (Catherine, Gina, Jennifer); *Career* MRC Population Genetics Res Unit 1965–72, Genetics Lab Univ of Oxford 1972–74, prof of human genetics Univ of Amsterdam 1981–82, Prince Philip prof of paediatric res Guy's Hosp 1982–95, prof of med genetics Univ of Cambridge 1995–2005 (emeritus prof 2005–); memb Editorial Bd Jl of Med Genetics 1976–89 and 1995–98 (ed 1995–98); series ed: Monographs in Med Genetics 1984–2005; author of numerous articles on clinical and molecular genetics; memb: Cncl MRC 1988–92 and 1993–94, Ctee to Examine the Ethical Implications of Gene Therapy and Gene Therapy Advsy Ctee Dept of Health 1989–95, Central Res and Devpt Ctee Dept of Health 1991–96, Acad of Med Sci 1998–2002; non-exec memb: Lewisham NHS Tst Bd 1993–95, Human Genetics Advsy Cmmn 1996–99, Nuffield Cncl on Bioethics 1998–2003 (dep chm 2001–03), Bd Cambridge Univ Hosp NHS Fndn Tst 2004–14; vice-chair Global Alliance for Genomics and Health 2014–16; chm: Ctee on the Med Aspects of Radiation in the Environment Dept of Health 1985–92, Unrelated Living Transplant Regulatory Authy 1990–99, Molecular and Cellular Med Bd MRC 1992–94, Muscular Dystrophy Gp 1995–2010, Expert Advsy Gp on Data Access (EAGDA) 2011–; pres Clinical Genetics Soc 1993–94 (vice-pres 1992–93 and 1995–96); govr Wellcome Tst 1996–2007 (dep chm 2004–07); FRCPath 1990 (MRCPath 1978), FRCP, FRCPH, FMedSci (founding fell), FRS; *Style*— Prof Martin Bobrow, CBE, FRS

BODDY, Su-Anna Margaret; da of late Bernard Henry Peter Boddy, and late Audrey May, *née* Murphy; *b* 7 September 1952; *Educ* Brighton and Hove HS, St Bartholomew's Hosp London (BSc, MB, BS); *m* 11 Sept 1982, Nicholas Paul Madden, *qv*; 1 s (Christopher Paul b 6 Feb 1987), 1 da (Katherine Anna b 15 Sept 1988); *Career* house physician gastroenterology & nephrology St Bartholomew's Hosp London 1977, house surgn general surgery Luton & Dunstable Hosp 1977–78, temporary lectr in anatomy St Bartholomew's Hosp London 1978; SHO: accident service & Orthopaedics Luton & Dunstable Hosp 1978–79, paediatric surgery & urology Great Ormond Street Hosp for Sick Children 1979, general & oncological surgery Royal Marsden Hosp London 1979–

80, neurosurgery National Hosp for Nervous Diseases London 1980; jr registrar St Bartholomew's Hosp 1980–81; registrar: Luton & Dunstable Hosp 1981–83, Birmingham Children's Hosp 1983–85; research registrar in urology St Bartholomew's Hosp London 1985–88 (MS 1992); sr registrar in paediatric surgery: Leeds General Infirmary and St James's Univ Hosp Leeds 1988–91, St George's Hosp London and Queen Mary's Hosp Carshalton 1992; locum conslt paediatric surgn 1992–93, conslt paediatric surgn and paediatric urologist St George's Hosp London 1993–2004 (conslt paediatric urologist 2004–); flexible trg advsr RCS 1998–2005; treas Br Assoc of Paediatric Urology 2004–07, elected memb Cncl RCS 2007–; memb: Br Assoc of Paediatric Surgns, Br Assoc of Paediatric Urologists, Br Assoc of Urologists, Euro Soc of Paediatric Urologists, Medical Womens' Fedn, Women in Surgical Trg; FRCS 1983; author of several articles in various learned jls; *Recreations* swimming, skiing, cooking; *Style*— Miss Su-Anna Boddy; ✉ 15 Bridgefield Road, Cheam, Surrey SM1 2DG; Department of Paediatric Surgery, St George's Hospital, Blackshaw Road, London SW17 0QT (☎ 020 8725 2456, fax 020 8725 0711)

BODEN, John Peter (Johnnie); s of Lt Col Patrick Anthony Drummond Boden (d 2000), of Twyford, Hants, and Rosemary Jane, *née* Huttenbach (d 2003); *b* 1 June 1961; *Educ* Eton, Oriel Coll Oxford; *m* 1992, Sophia Henrietta, da of Martin Lampard; 3 da (Anna Edith b 1994, Katherine Nathalie b 1996, Stella Lucinda b 2000); *Career* with Barclays Merchant Bank (later BZW) 1983–86, with SG Warburg Securities 1986–88, fndr and exec chm JP Boden & Co 1991–; Best Overall Consumer Catalogue and Best Internet Site for Consumer Business ECMOD 2001, Rising Star Award Retail Week 2002, Best E-Business Application European Retail Solutions 2002; incl in: Virgin Top 100 Fastest Growing Companies in UK 1998, 1999 and 2000, Deloitte & Touche/Independent on Sunday Top 100 Fastest Growing Companies in the UK 2001 and 2002; *Recreations* family, riding, walking; *Style*— Johnnie Boden, Esq; ✉ JP Boden & Co, Boden House, 114–120 Victoria Road, London NW10 6NY (☎ 020 8453 4377, fax 020 8453 1445, e-mail jboden@boden.co.uk)

BODEN, Prof Margaret Ann; OBE (2002); da of Leonard Forbes Boden, OBE (d 1986), and Violet Dorothy, *née* Dawson (d 1967); *b* 26 November 1936, London; *Educ* City of London Sch for Girls, Newnham Coll Cambridge (MA), Harvard Graduate Sch for Arts and Scis (AM, PhD), Univ of Cambridge (ScD); *m* 24 June 1967 (m dis 1981), John Raymond Spiers, *qv*; 1 s (Ruskin b 1968), 1 da (Jehane b 1972); *Career* lectr in philosophy Univ of Birmingham 1959–65, res prof of cognitive science Univ of Sussex 2002– (lectr and reader 1959–65, prof of philosophy and psychology 1980–2002), founding dean Sch of Cognitive and Computing Science Univ of Sussex 1987–; visiting scientist Yale Univ 1979, external advsr Centre for the Study of Existential Risk Univ of Cambridge 2013–; Duijker Lecture Amsterdam 1985, Royal Instn Friday Discourses 1990 and 2002, Templeton Lecture Sydney 1994, Dacre Lecture Peterhouse Cambridge 1994, Science Prestige Lecture Univ of Canterbury NZ 1997, Hagerstrom lectr Univ of Uppsala 1999, Gramlich lectr Dartmouth Coll 2002, Royal Inst of Philosophy Millennial Lecture 2000, Pufendorf lectr Univ of Lund 2003, Turing Meml Lecture 2009, Symbolic Systems distinguished speaker Stanford 2009; co-fndr and dir Harvester Press Ltd 1968–85 (sec 1968–79); chm Cncl and vice-pres Royal Inst of GB 1993–95 (memb Cncl 1992–95), pres General Section BAAS 1992–93; memb: Advsy Bd Res Cncls 1989–91, Animal Procedures Ctee (Home Office) 1994–98, Royal Soc Gp on Machine Learning 2015–; tstee Cncl for Science and Society (chm Working Pty on Benefits and Dangers of Knowledge-Based Systems 1987–88); Covey Prize (Int Assoc Computing and Philosophy) 2013; Gold Medal Univ of Sussex (50th Anniv) 2013; memb: Mind Assoc, Aristotelian Soc, Royal Inst of Philosophy (memb Cncl 1988–), Br Soc for Philosophy of Science; Hon DSc: Univ of Sussex 2001, Univ of Bristol 2002, Open Univ 2004; FBA 1983 (memb Cncl 1988–, vice-pres 1989–91), FRSA 1992, fell American Assoc for Artificial Intelligence 1993, memb Academia Europaea 1993; *Books* Purposive Explanation in Psychology (1972), Artificial Intelligence and Natural Man (1977/1987), Piaget (1979), Minds and Mechanisms (1981), Computer Models of Mind (1988), Artificial Intelligence in Psychology (1989), The Philosophy of Artificial Intelligence (ed, 1990), The Creative Mind (1990/2004), Dimensions of Creativity (ed, 1994), The Philosophy of Artificial Life (ed, 1996), Artificial Intelligence (ed, 1996), Mind as Machine (2006), Creativity and Art (2010), AI, Its Nature and Future (2016); *Recreations* dressmaking, travel; *Clubs* Reform; *Style*— Prof Margaret Boden, OBE; ✉ Centre for Research in Cognitive Science, University of Sussex, Falmer, Brighton, East Sussex BN1 9QJ (☎ 01273 678386, fax 01273 671320, e-mail m.a.boden@sussex.ac.uk, website www.ruskin.tv/margaretboden)

BODEN, Richard; s of Leslie Boden, and Katherine, *née* Hurst; *b* 4 January 1953; *Educ* St Philip's GS Birmingham, Bournville Coll of FE, Univ of Exeter (BA); *m* 16 April 1983, Sylvie, da of William McRoberts; 2 s (James b 8 Jan 1987, Edward b 3 March 1989); *Career* BBC TV: floor asst 1974–76, asst floor mangr 1976–79, light entertainment prodn mangr 1979–83, dir of light entertainment 1983–89, prodr of light entertainment 1989–95; head of comedy Carlton TV and Central TV 1995–, dir Columbia TriStar Carlton UK Prodns 1995–99, freelance prodr and dir 1999–, dir of progs Delightful Industries/Boom Pictures; prodr and dir: Best of British Comedy (BBC TV, 1983), No Place Like Home (BBC TV, 1983–84), I Woke Up One Morning (BBC TV, 1984), Birds of a Feather (BBC TV, 1985), In Sickness and in Health (BBC TV, 1986–90), Cabaret at Jongleurs (BBC TV, 1987), You Must be the Husband (BBC TV, 1987–88), Blackadder (BBC TV, 1988–89, BAFTA 1989), Allo Allo (BBC TV, 1988), 2 Point 4 Children (BBC TV, 1991–95), Health and Efficiency (BBC TV, 1993–94), Every Silver Lining (BBC TV, 1993), Loved By You (Carlton TV, 1996–97), Paul Merton in Galton & Simpson's..... (Carlton TV, 1996–97), Time Gentlemen Please (Sky TV, 2000 and 2001–02), Just Shoot Me (Universal Studios, 2001), The Sketch Show (ITV, 2001, BAFTA 2001), The IT Crowd (BAFTA 2010), Count Arthur Strong; memb: Comedy Jury Golden Rose of Montreux 1996, SitCom Jury Golden Rose of Montreux 1998; *Recreations* sports; *Clubs* BAFTA, RTS, Mensa, Hurlingham; *Style*— Richard Boden, Esq; ✉ c/o Nick Marston, Curtis Brown, Haymarket House, 28–29 Haymarket, London SW1Y 4SP (☎ 020 7393 4400)

BODEY, Hon Mr Justice; Sir David Roderick Lessiter Bodey; kt (1999); s of Reginald Augustus Bodey (d 1987), and Betty Frances Ada, *née* Lessiter (d 1987); *b* 14 October 1947; *Educ* King's Sch Canterbury, Univ of Bristol (LLB); *m* 28 Feb 1976, Ruth, da of Dr Denis MacAdorey, of Healing, Lincs; 1 s (Simon Christopher b 13 Jan 1980), 1 da (Katherine Sarah b 29 April 1982); *Career* called to the Bar Middle Temple (Harmsworth scholar) 1970; legal assessor to UK Central Cncl for Nursing Midwifery and Health Visiting 1983; QC 1991, recorder of the Crown Court 1993–98 (asst recorder 1989–93), dep judge of the High Court (Family Div) 1995, judge of the High Court of Justice (Family Div) 1999–, liaison judge for London (Family Div) 1999–2001, liaison judge for NE Circuit (Family Div) 2001–07, memb Family Justice Cncl 2007–08; chm Family Law Bar Assoc 1997 (sec 1995), dir of family trg Judicial Studies Bd 1998–; fell Int Acad of Matrimonial Lawyers 1995, memb Family Ctee of Justice 1995–98, memb Supreme Court Procedure Ctee 1995–97; *Recreations* music,sometime marathon running, attempting to keep Triumph TR3 on the road; *Style*— The Hon Mr Justice Bodey; ✉ Royal Courts of Justice, Strand, London WC2A 2LL

BODIWALA, Gautam Govindlal; CBE (2000), JP, DL (2001); s of Dr Govindlal R Bodiwala (d 1983), and Sumanben, *née* Parikh; *b* 11 October 1943; *Educ* Univ of Gujarat (MS); *m* 28 Dec 1969, Gita, da of Prabhulal G Thanawala, of Thana, India; 1 s (Dhaval b 1973), 1 da (Janki b 1977); *Career* conslt and head A&E Serv Leicester 1977–2003; pro-chllr De Montfort Univ; chm Jt Ctee on Higher Trg in A&E Med; sr examiner: Royal Coll of Emergency Med, Fellowship of RCSEd; int co-ordinator Br Assoc for A&E Med; lectr: Europe, Israel, India, Australia, USA, Canada, Africa, Hong Kong, Singapore, Korea, China, Mexico etc; world pres Int Fedn for Emergency Medicine 2006–10; hon treas British Assoc for A&E Med, memb Rotary Int, fndr pres Leics Medico-Legal Soc; Lifetime Achievement Award: Int Fedn for Emergency Med, Soc for Emergency Med India, Global Assoc for Physicians of Indian Origin; name given to Gautam Bodiwala Lifetime Leadership Award Int Fedn for Emergency Med; memb: BMA, American Coll of Emergency Physicians; founding fell and treas Faculty of A&E Med; fell: Int Coll of Surgns, Int Coll of Angiology; Hon DSc Univ of Leicester 2000, Hon DSc De Montfort Univ 2012; FRCEM, FRCS, FRCP, FRSM, FICS, FICA, FRSA, FESEM, FIFEM (fell Int Fedn for Emergency Medicine); *Publications* author of over 70 scientific papers and one book; *Recreations* music and reading; *Clubs* Rotary (Oadby); *Style*— Gautam Bodiwala, Esq, CBE, DL; ✉ Lykkebo, 7 Blackthorn Lane, Oadby, Leicester LE2 4FA (☎ 0116 271 8899)

BODMER, Sir Walter Fred; kt (1986); s of Dr Ernest Julius Bodmer (d 1968), and Sylvia Emily, *née* Bodmer; *b* 10 January 1936; *Educ* Manchester Grammar, Univ of Cambridge (BA, PhD); *m* 1956, Julia Gwynaeth (d 2001), da of William Gwyn Pilkington (d 1976); 2 s (Mark, Charles), 1 da (Helen); partner Dr Ann Ganesan; *Career* Univ of Cambridge: research fell Clare Coll 1958–60, official fell 1961, demonstrator Dept of Genetics 1960–61; prof Dept of Genetics Stanford Univ Sch of Med 1968–70 (asst prof 1962–66, assoc prof 1966–68), prof of genetics Univ of Oxford 1970–79; ICRF: dir of research 1979–91, DG 1991–96; princ Hertford Coll Oxford 1996–2005, head Cancer Research UK (formerly ICRF) Cancer and Immunogenetics Lab Weatherall Inst of Molecular Medicine Oxford 1996–; consltg prof Stanford Univ 2007–13; chm: Ctee on Public Understanding of Science 1990–93, Science Consultative Gp BBC 1981–87, Nat Radiological Protection Bd 1998–2003, Orgn of Euro Cancer Insts 1990–93; pres: Royal Statistical Soc 1984–85, BAAS 1987–88 (chm Cncl 1996–2001), Assoc for Science Educn 1989, Br Soc for Histocompatibility and Immunogenetics 1990–91, Human Genome Orgn 1990–92, Int Fedn of Assocs for the Advancement of Science and Technol 1992 (first pres), Br Assoc for Cancer Research 1998–2002, Galton Inst 2008–14; tstee: Natural History Museum (formerly Br Museum (Natural History)) 1983–93 (chm 1988–93), Sir John Soane's Museum 1982–2003, Gtr Manchester Museum of Science and Industry 1989–90; vice-pres Royal Instn 1981–82, memb Advsy Bd for the Research Cncls 1983–88, memb Bd of Patrons St Mark's Hosp and Academic Inst London 1996; chllr Univ of Salford 1995–2005; non-exec dir Fisons plc 1990–96; chm Bd of Dirs Laban London 2000–05, memb Bd Trinity Laban 2005–08; chm Leukaemia Research Fund Medical and Scientific Advsy Panel 2003–09, tstee Porter Fndn 2006–; William Allan Meml Award 1980, Conway Evans Prize 1982, Rabbi Shai Shacknai Meml Prize Lectureship in Immunology and Cancer Research 1983, John Alexander Meml Prize Lectureship 1984, Rose Payne Distinguished Scientist Lectureship 1985, Michael Faraday Award Royal Soc 1994, Romanes Lecture Univ of Oxford 1995, Harveian Orator Royal Coll of Physicians 1996, Dalton Medal Manchester Literary and Philosophical Soc 2002, D K Ludwig Award 2002, Seroussi Award 2003, Royal Soc Royal Medal 2013; hon memb: American Assoc of Immunologists, St Mark's Assoc London 1995; Liveryman Worshipful Co of Scientific Instrument Makers, Hon Liveryman Drapers' Co; hon fell: Keble Coll Oxford 1981, Clare Coll Cambridge 1989, Green Coll Oxford 1993, Hertford Coll Oxford 2005; Laurea (hc) in Med and Surgery Univ of Bologna 1987; Hon DSc: Univ of Bath 1988, Univ of Oxford 1988, Univ of Edinburgh 1990, Univ of Hull 1990, Univ of Bristol 1991, Loughborough Univ of Technol 1993, Lancaster Univ 1994, Univ of Aberdeen 1994, Univ of Plymouth 1995, Univ of Salford 1996, Univ of London 1996, UMIST (now Univ of Manchester) 1997, Univ of the Witwatersrand 1998; Hon MD Univ of Birmingham 1992, Dr (hc) Univ of Leuven 1992, Hon LLD Univ of Dundee 1993, Dr (hc) Masaryk Univ Brno 1994, Dr (hc) Univ of Haifa 1998; Companion Trinity Laban 2008; foreign memb American Philosophical Soc USA 1989; foreign hon memb American Acad of Arts and Scis 1972, foreign assoc US Nat Acad Scis 1981; fell: Br Soc for Histocompatibility and Immunogenetics, Br Transplantation Soc (hon memb 2002), Royal Statistical Soc, Pathology Soc, Br Soc of Immunology; CBiol, FIBiol, FRCPath, FRS 1974, Hon FRCP, Hon FRCS, Hon FRSE 1992, Hon FRSM 1994, FMedSci 1998, hon fell BAAS 2006; *Books* The Genetics of Human Populations (with L Cavalli-Sforza, 1971, 2 edn 1999), Our Future Inheritance: Choice or Chance? (with A Jones, 1974), Genetics, Evolution and Man (with L Cavalli-Sforza, 1976), The Book of Man (with Robin McKie, 1994); *Recreations* playing the piano, riding, swimming, scuba diving; *Clubs* Athenaeum, Oxford and Cambridge; *Style*— Sir Walter Bodmer, FRS, FRCPath; ✉ University of Oxford, Cancer and Immunogenetics Laboratory, Weatherall Institute of Molecular Medicine, John Radcliffe Hospital, Oxford OX3 9DS (☎ 01865 222356, fax 01865 222431, e-mail walter.bodmer@hertford.ox.ac.uk)

BODMIN, Archdeacon of; *see:* Cohen, Ven Clive Ronald Franklin

BOE, Alfred Giovanni Roncalli (Alfie); *b* 29 September 1973, Blackburn, Lancs; *Educ* Royal Coll of Music; *Career* tenor; performances in prodns incl: La bohème (Broadway and ENO), Kismet (ENO), Les Misérables (Queen's Theatre London), The Mikado (ENO); other performances incl: Canterbury Cathedral, Festival of Remembrance (Royal Albert Hall), Pleasure Beach Arena Blackpool, St George's Day celebration concert (Trafalgar Square), Hampton Court Palace Festival, Last Night of the Proms, Diamond Jubilee Concert; *Albums* Onward 2007, La Passione 2007, Bring Him Home 2010, Alfie 2011; *Style*— Mr Alfie Boe; ✉ c/o Heulwen Keyte, The Agency Group Ltd, 361–373 City Road, London EC1V 1PQ

BOEVEY; *see:* Crawley-Boevey

BOGDANOR, Prof Vernon; CBE (1998); s of Harry Bogdanor (d 1971), and Rosa, *née* Weinger (d 1987); *b* 16 July 1943; *Educ* The Queen's Coll Oxford (MA); *m* 1, 23 July 1972 (m dis 2000), Judith Evelyn, da of Frederick Beckett (d 1985); 2 s; m 2, 1 Aug 2009, Sonia Margaret, da of William Preston; *Career* fell Brasenose Coll Oxford 1966– (sr tutor 1979–85 and 1996–97), reader in govt Univ of Oxford 1990–96, prof of govt and politics Univ of Oxford 1996–; prof of law Gresham Coll London, research prof KCL 2010–; special advsr: House of Lords Select Ctee on Euro Communities 1982–83, House of Commons Public Service Ctee; memb: Political Studies Assoc 1966–, Cncl Hansard Soc for Parly Govt, Nat Ctee for Electoral Reform 1981–, Court Univ of Essex 1982–84, UK delgn CSCE Conf Oslo 1991, Cncl Inst of Jewish Affairs 1991–, Cncl Euro Movement 1994–; hon bencher Middle Temple 2010; Sir Isaiah Berlin Prize for Lifetime Contribution to Political Studies 2008; Hon DLitt Univ of Kent 2010; hon fell Soc for Advanced Legal Studies 1997, hon fell Queen's Coll Oxford 2009; FRSA 1992, FBA 1997; Chevalier de la Legion d'Honneur 2009; *Books* incl: The Age of Affluence 1951–64 (jt ed, 1970), Devolution (1979), The People and the Party System (1981), Liberal Party Politics (ed, 1983), Multi-Party Politics and the Constitution (1983), Science and Politics (ed, 1984), The Blackwell Encyclopaedia of Political Institutions (ed, 1987), Comparing Constitutions (jtly, 1994), The Monarchy and the Constitution (1995), Essays on Politics and the Constitution (1996), Power and the People: A Guide to Constitutional Reform (1997), Devolution in the United Kingdom (1999), The British Constitution in the Twentieth Century (ed, 2003), Joined-Up Government (ed, 2005), The New British Constitution (2009), From the New Jerusalem to New Labour: British Prime Ministers from Attlee to Blair (2010), The Coalition and the Constitution (2011); *Recreations* music, walking, talking; *Style*— Prof Vernon Bogdanor, CBE, FBA; ✉ 21 Edmunds Walk, London N2 0HU

BOGDANOV, Dr Michael; s of Francis Benzion Bogdin (d 1962), and Rhoda, *née* Rees (d 1988); *b* 15 December 1938; *Educ* Lower Sch of John Lyon, Harrow, Trinity Coll Dublin (MA), Univ of Munich, Sorbonne; *m* 1, 17 Dec 1966 (sep 2000), Patricia Ann, da of Walter Stanley Warwick (d 1985); 2 s (Jethro Rhys Warwick b 1968, Malachi Taplin b 1969), 1 da (Ffion b 1971); m 2, 22 Sept 2000, Ulrike Engelbrecht; 1 da (Pia Caitlin b 1997), 1 s (Cai Johann b 1999); *Career* director and producer; dir and prodr Radio Telifís Éireann (RTE) 1966–69; artistic dir: Phoenix Theatre Leicester 1973–77, Young Vic 1978–80; assoc dir RNT 1980–88, fndr and artistic dir English Shakespeare Co 1986–98, artistic dir and exec prodr Deutsches Schauspielhaus Hamburg 1989–92; fndr and artistic dir Wales Theatre Co 2003–; hon prof Glamorgan Univ 2008; awarded Sr Academic Fellowship by Leicester Poly (now De Montfort Univ) 1992 and Univ of Wales Cardiff 1993; fell: Welsh Coll for Music and Drama, Univ Sunderland; hon fell TCD, Hon DLitt TCD 2005, hon fell Univ of Swansea 2008, hon fell Shakespeare Birthplace Tst 2011; *Awards* SWET Award (for dir of the year) 1979 (for The Taming of the Shrew (RSC)), Olivier Award (for dir of the year) 1989 (for The Wars of the Roses (English Shakespeare Co)), Drama Award (for outstanding achievement) 1987, Melbourne Spoleto Golden Pegasus Award 1988, BAFTA nomination and RTS Award 1994 (for Shakespeare on the Estate (BBC documentary)), Best Drama Documentary Banff Film Festival 1995 (for Shakespeare on the Estate), Best Director/Best Production nomination 1997 (Timon of Athens (Chicago Shakespeare Rep Theatre)), RTS Award for Best Regional Film 1999 (A Light in the Valley (BBC TV)), Best Prodn Wales Theatre Award 2005 (for Hamlet), Rolph Mares Preis Best Dir Warten Auf Godot (Hamburg) 2006, Intega Preis Best Touring Prodn German Speaking Countries 2010 (for Frost/Nixon), Best Ten Prodns German Speaking Countries (Hamburg) 2012 (for The King's Speech), Pegasus Preis 2013 (for The King's Speech); *Books* The English Shakespeare Company – The Wars of the Roses (jtly), Hiawatha, The Ancient Mariner, Shakespeare – The Director's Cut Vols 1, 2 and 3, The Director's Cue; *Recreations* sport, music, Celtic languages, wine, Georgian glass, Dylan Thomas; *Clubs* Lord's Taverners, MCC, BAFTA; *Style*— Dr Michael Bogdanov; ✉ e-mail mbogdin@hotmail.com or walestheatreco@hotmail.co.uk, website www.walestheatrecompany.co.uk or www.michaelbogdanov.com

BOGGIS, Andrew Gurdon; s of Edmund Allan Theodore Boggis (d 1974), of Devizes, Wilts, and Myrtle Eirene, *née* Donald (d 2008); *b* 1 April 1954; *Educ* Marlborough, New Coll Oxford (MA), King's Coll Cambridge (PGCE); *m* 23 July 1983, Fiona Mary, da of Rev James Edmund Cocke; 2 da (Rosie b 14 March 1987, Lucy b 10 Oct 1988), 1 s (Edmund b 27 April 1991); *Career* teacher; Eng language asst Salzburg 1975–76, asst master Hitchin Boys' Sch 1978–79, asst master Eton Coll 1979–92, master-in-coll Eton Coll 1984–92, warden Forest Sch 1992–2009; HMC: memb Ctee 2001–07, chm N London Div 2002–03, chm 2006; inspr HMC/Independent Sch's Inspectorate 1998–2009, dir HMC Projects in Eastern and Central Europe 2012–; memb Independent Schs Examination Bd (ISEB) (chm Languages Sub-Ctee 1995–2001), memb Educn Ctee ESU 2004–09; dir Common Entrance Publications Ltd 1993–2001; govr: King's Coll Sch Cambridge 1994–99, Skinner's Sch for Girls 1997–2009, Purcell Sch 2007–11, Canford Sch 2012–, West Buckland Sch 2013–; chm of govrs Skinners' Kent Acad 2009–13; memb Ct Univ of Essex 1997–2002; tstee Dorset Historic Churches Tst 2012–; Liveryman Worshipful Co of Skinners 1990 (extra memb Ct of Assts 2004–06, memb Ct of Assts 2009–, Master 2011); memb HMC 1992–2009 (hon memb 2009–), memb ASCL 1992–2009; *Publications* contrib to educational publications incl Conference & Common Room; *Recreations* Austria, Scotland, music (particularly opera), playing the organ, poetry, philosophy, cookery, skiing, pigs; *Clubs* East India; *Style*— Andrew Boggis, Esq; ✉ Church Cottages, Hooke, Beaminster, Dorset DT8 3PA (☎ 01308 861176)

BOGGIS-ROLFE, Richard; s of Paul Boggis-Rolfe (d 1988), of Paris, France, and (Anne) Verena, *née* Collins; *b* 5 April 1950; *Educ* Eton, Trinity Coll Cambridge (MA), London Business Sch; *m* 7 March 1987, Lucy Elisabeth, da of Lt-Col Stephen Jenkins, MC, DL, of Hampnett, Glos; 2 da (Elisabeth Verena b 30 Aug 1988, Alice Catherine b 8 Jan 1990), 1 s (James Edward b 22 Jan 1994); *Career* cmmnd Coldstream Gds 1970, ADC to Lt Gen Sir Richard Worsley (GOC 1 (Br) Corps) 1975–77, Co Cdr 1977–79, Staff Capt QMG MOD 1979–80, ret Hon Maj 1980; dir: Russell Reynolds Associates 1983, Norman Broadbent International Ltd 1984–97; md Norman Broadbent (Hong Kong) 1986; chm Barkers Human Resource Advertising Ltd 1992–97, chm NB Selection Ltd 1995–97 (chief exec 1987–95), gp md BNB Resources plc 1995–97, chm Odgers Berndtson 1998–, dir OPD plc 2005–09; chm: Nat Employers Advsy Bd 2010–, Holfords of Weestonbirt Tst 2010–; tstee Poppy Factory; Freeman City of London, past Master Worshipful Co of Pewterers; *Recreations* hunting, gardening, travel; *Clubs* Brooks's, Beefsteak, Pratt's; *Style*— Richard Boggis-Rolfe, Esq; ✉ The Glebe House, Shipton Moyne, Tetbury, Gloucestershire (☎ 01666 880441, e-mail richard.boggis-rolfe@odgers.com); L'Hermitage, Basse Nouailette, Hautefort, Dordogne, France

BOGLE, Prof (Ian) David Lockhart; s of Brig Bruce Lockhart Bogle, of Porlock, Somerset, and Susan Gowan, *née* Christie; *b* 22 December 1957, Sydney, Aust; *Educ* Peninsula Sch Mt Eliza Aust, Imperial Coll London (BSc, MSc, PhD); *m* 6 Sept 1996, Jenny Elizabeth, *née* Brown; 1 da (Eleanor May Lockhart b 15 Jan 1999); *Career* sr scientist Br Gas Corp 1983–86, lectr Univ of Adelaide 1986–90; UCL: lectr 1990–94, sr lectr 1994–97, reader 1997–2000, prof 2000–, head Grad Sch 2005–; UK rep Working Pty on Computer Aided Process Engrg European Fedn of Chem Engrs 1997–, memb Cncl IChemE 2004–08, memb Natural Sciences Ctee UK Nat Cmmn for UNESCO 2004–11, memb Bd Engrg Cncl 2007–; chair Steering Ctee League of European Research Univs Doctoral Studies Community 2008–; author of over 100 pubns; memb Bd New London Orch; Cncl Medal IChemE 2005; Liveryman Worshipful Co of Engrs 2003; CEng 1993, FIChemE 1997, FREng 2005, memb European Acad of Sci and Arts 2007; *Recreations* playing the violin; *Style*— Prof David Bogle; ✉ The Graduate School, North Cloisters, University College London, Gower Street, London WC1E 6BT (☎ 020 7679 7844, fax 020 7679 7043, e-mail gradschoolhead@ucl.ac.uk)

BOHUON, Olivier Jean; s of Claude Bohuon, and Odile Guinnebault; *b* 3 January 1959, Paris; *Educ* Univ of Paris (Doctorate), HEC Paris (MBA); *m* 26 Sept 1981, Alexandra, *née* Polliot; *Career* mktg dir then ops dir Glaxo France 1991–95, ceo then pres SmithKline Beecham France 1995–2001, sr vice pres and dir European Commercial Ops GlaxoSmithKline 2001–03, with Abbott Laboratories rising to exec vice pres Pharmaceutical Products 2003–10, chief exec Laboratoires Pierre Fabre 2010–11, chief exec Smith & Nephew plc 2011–; non-exec dir: Shire plc, Virbac plc; Légion D'Honneur; *Recreations* golf, sailing; *Clubs* St James's (Paris), St Cloud Golf (France), Dinard Golf (France), RAC; *Style*— Olivier Bohuon, Esq; ✉ Smith & Nephew plc, 15 Adam Street, London WC2N 6LA

BOISSIER, Vice Adm (Robin) Paul; CB; *b* 14 October 1953; *Educ* Univ of Cambridge (MA), London Business Sch (MSc); *Career* RN: joined 1974, DG logistics (fleet) and chief of fleet support 2004, chief naval warfare offr 2007, ret 2009; chief exec RNLI 2009–; *Style*— Vice Adm Paul Boissier, CB; ✉ RNLI, West Quay Road, Poole BH15 1HZ

BOIZOT, Peter James; MBE (1986), DL (Cambridgeshire 1998); s of Gaston Charles Boizot, and Susannah, *née* Culshaw; *b* 16 November 1929; *Educ* King's Sch Peterborough (chorister Peterborough Cathedral 1940–44), St Catharine's Coll Cambridge (MA, fell commoner 1996); *Career* Nat Serv 1948–50, cmmnd RASC; capt MV YARVIC 1959; various sales jobs 1953–64; owner and admin Great Northern Hotel 1959–2009; PizzaExpress: fndr 1965, chm and md 1965–93, chm PizzaExpress plc (following flotation) 1993–96, pres 1996–; proprietor: Pizza on the Park 1976–2012, The Broadway 2000– (Peterborough), Miss Pears 2001– (Peterborough); dir Connoisseur Casino 1970–82; former owner and chm Peterborough United FC; former publisher: Jazz Express magazine, Boz magazine, Hockey Sport, World Hockey; pres Hampstead & Westminster Hockey Club 1986, vice-pres Hockey Assoc 1990, hon vice-pres English Hockey Assoc; fndr memb Soho Soc, fndr chm Soho Restaurateurs' Assoc 1980, former dir Soho Jazz Festival; chm Westminster Chamber of Commerce 1992–94, memb Cncl London Chamber of Commerce 1992–; Parliamentary candidate (Lib) Peterborough Gen Elections Feb and Oct 1974, former pres Eastern Region Liberal Party; Bolla Award 1983, Hotel and Caterer Food Service Award 1989, Hon LLD Westminster Univ 1995, Hon DLitt Loughborough Univ; Commendatore dell'Ordine al Merito della Repubblica Italiana 1996; *Books* Pizza Express Cook Book (1976, new edn 1991), Mr Pizza and All That Jazz (autobiography, 2014); *Recreations* hockey; *Clubs* National Liberal, Hawks' (Cambridge); *Style*— Peter Boizot, Esq, MBE, DL; ☎ 01733 343910

BOLAM, Simon; MBE (2009); s of Alexander Crossman Bolam (d 1963), of Berwick-upon-Tweed, and Elizabeth Mary, *née* Drybrough (d 1990); *b* 5 September 1942; *Educ* St Mary's Sch Melrose, Glenalmond Coll; *m* 6 July 1968, Sylvia Forsyth, da of Sidney Dawson Ranson; 2 da (Caroline b 5 March 1970, Valerie b 5 May 1971); *Career* with Royal Insurance Edinburgh then Liverpool 1961–70; E H Ranson & Co Insurance Brokers: joined 1970, ptnr 1971, owner 1972–2010; Insurance Soc of Edinburgh: sec 1986, dep pres 1988, pres 1989, a vice-pres 1990–; Chartered Insurance Inst: memb Cncl 1988–99, chm Mktg and Pubns Ctee and hon ed CII Jl 1989, chm Educn Ctee and a govr CII's Coll of Insurance 1992, dep pres 1993, pres 1994–95, chm CII Audit Ctee 2000–04; Br Insurance Brokers' Assoc: chm Scottish Ctee 1986, chm Motor Ctee 1986, chm Educn and Employment Policy Ctee 1996–98, memb Nat Bd 1996–2000, chm Gen Insurance Broking Ctee 1997–98 (dep chm 1996–97), nat dep chm 1997–98, chm 1998–2000; chm Smaller Businesses Practitioner Panel Financial Servs Authy 2008–10; memb: Nat Exec Round Table 1981–83, Cncl Insurance Brokers Registration Cncl 1997–2001, Bd Gen Insurance Standards Cncl 1999–2005 (chm Smaller Practitioners' Ctee 2001–04), Bd Fin Servs NTO 2000–02; underwriting memb Lloyd's 1989–99; Liveryman Worshipful Co of Insurers 1990–2011; Moderator of High Constable City of Edinburgh 1997–99; FCII 1971 (ACII 1961); *Recreations* hill walking, cycling; *Style*— Mr Simon Bolam, MBE, FCII; ✉ 14/3 Ramsay Garden, Edinburgh EH1 2NA (☎ 0131 225 1849)

BOLD, Dr (Richard) Andrew; s of Rev W E and Mrs K M Bold; *Educ* Monmouth, Howardian HS Cardiff, ChCh Oxford (BA), Univ of Wales Cardiff (MSc), Centre for Euro Industrial Studies Univ of Bath (PhD); *Career* res offr Greater London Trade Union Resource Unit 1985–87, researcher to Barry Jones, MP (shadow sec of state for Wales) 1987, sr researcher to Lab Peers House of Lords 1987–89, res offr Wales Lab Pty 1989–94, asst gen sec (policy) Wales Lab Pty 1994–99; special advsr to: Rt Hon Alun Michael, MP 1999–2000, Rt Hon Paul Murphy, MP 2000–02, Rt Hon Peter Hain, MP 2002–; *Style*— Dr Andrew Bold; ✉ Office of the Secretary of State for Wales, National Assembly Building, Cardiff Bay, Cardiff CF99 1NA (☎ 029 2089 8549, fax 029 2089 8138)

BOLDY, Dr Steven; *Career* fell Emmanuel Coll Cambridge, univ sr lectr and head Dept of Spanish and Portuguese Univ of Cambridge; *Books* The Novels of Julio Cortázar (1980), Before the Boom: Four Essays on Latin-American Literature before 1940 (ed, 1991), Memoria Mexicana (1998), The Narrative of Carlos Fuentes: Family, Text, Nation (2002); *Style*— Dr Steven Boldy; ✉ Department of Spanish and Portuguese, Faculty of Modern and Medieval Languages, University of Cambridge, Sidgwick Avenue, Cambridge CB3 9DA

BOLÉAT, Mark John; s of Paul John Boléat, and Edith Maud, *née* Still; *b* 21 January 1949, Jersey; *Educ* Victoria Coll Jersey, Lanchester Poly (BA), Univ of Reading (MA); *m* 13 May 1991, Elizabeth Ann, *née* Barker; *Career* teacher Dulwich Coll 1972, economist Industry Policy Gp 1973; Building Societies Assoc: asst sec 1974–76, under sec 1976–79, dep sec 1979–81, dep sec gen 1981–86, sec gen 1986–87, DG 1987–93; sec gen Int Union of Housing Finance Instns 1986–89; DG: Cncl of Mortgage Lenders 1989–93, Assoc of Br Insurers 1993–99; prop Boleat Consulting 1999–; chm The Green Corridor 2008–11; dir: Scottish Mutual and Abbey National Life 1999–2004, Comino Gp 2000–05, Countryside Properties 2001–05, Travelers Insurance Co 2005–10; chm: Assoc of Labour Providers 2004–12, Jersey Competition Regulatory Authy 2010–, State of Jersey Devpt Co 2011–15, Guernsey Competition and Regulatory Authy 2012–; memb: Nat Consumer Cncl 2000–05, Gibraltar Finance Services Cmmn 2000–09, Regulatory Parly Ctee 2010–12; chm Hillingdon Community Tst 2003–08; memb Ct of Common Cncl City of London 2002– (chm Policy and Resources Ctee); FCIB; *Books* The Building Society Industry (1982, 2 edn 1986), National Housing Finance Systems – A Comparative Study (1985), The Mortgage Market (with Adrian Coles, 1987), Building Societies – The Regulatory Framework (1992), Housing in Britain (1993), Trade Association Strategy and Management (1996), Models of Trade Association Co-operation (2000), Good Practice in Trade Association Governance (2001), Trade Association Mgmnt (2003), An Agenda for Better Regulation (2009), Jersey's Population – A History (2015); *Recreations* golf, reading; *Clubs* Moor Park Golf; *Style*— Mark Boléat, Esq

BOLES, Mike James; s of Leonard Boles, of Exeter, Devon, and Ann Louise, *née* Elliott; *b* 29 July 1965, Exeter, Devon; *Educ* Teign Sch Kingsteignton, S Devon Tech Coll Torquay, Maidstone Coll of Art (BA, D&AD student awards winner); *m* 4 June 1994, Patricia, *née* Doherty; 2 s (Elliot Louis Charles b 5 April 1998, Truman Ethan James b 17 April 2000); *Career* Saatchi & Saatchi 1986–94 (Saatchi & Saatchi NY 1990–91), BMP DDB 1994–98, Rainey Kelly Campbell Roalfe 1998–99, RKCR/Y&R 1999–2014, Mike Boles Ltd 2014–; memb jury: D&AD Awards, Campaign Press & Creative Circle Awards; tutor D&AD student workshops, contrib Aerial Fndn; memb: D&AD, IPA; *Awards* Silver D&AD 1992 and 2010 (nominated 1996, 2002 and 2003), Gold Campaign Press and Poster Awards 1992 and 2002 (Silver 1992, 1995, 1998, 2001, 2002, 2003, 2005 and 2006), Silver Cannes Lions 2002, 2003, 2004 and 2010, Gold Clio 2000, Gold Creative Circle 2008 and 2010, Gold BTAA 2010, Marketing Soc winner 2012 and 2013, Thinkbox Awards 2016; work incl in Greatest 100 TV Ads Channel Four 2000; *Books* D&AD The Copy Book (2011); *Recreations* clarinet, photography, painting, poetry, badminton; *Style*— Mike Boles, Esq; ✉ 153 Chevening Road, London NW6 6DZ (☎ 07901 587554, e-mail mikeboles33@gmail.com, website http://uk.linkedin.com/pub/mike_boles/35/b73/1b0)

BOLES, Nicholas Edward Coleridge (Nick); MP; *b* 1965; *Educ* Winchester, Magdalen Coll Oxford, John F Kennedy Sch of Govt Harvard Univ; *Career* fndr and non-exec chm Longwall Hldgs Ltd (chief exec until 2000); fndr and dir Policy Exchange 2002–07, COS to Boris Johnson, *qv*, 2008, MP (Cons) Grantham & Stamford 2010– (Parly candidate Hove 2005), PPS to Nick Gibb, MP, *qv* (as min of state for schs) 2010–12, parly under sec of state for planning Dept for Communities and Local Govt 2012–14, min of state for skills and equalities BIS (jtly with DFE) 2014–15, min of state for skills BIS (jtly with DFE) 2015–; political fell Inst for Govt 2010–12; *Style*— Nick Boles, Esq, MP; ✉ House of Commons, London SW1A 0AA (☎ 020 7219 7079, e-mail nick.boles.mp@parliament.uk, website www.nickboles.co.uk, Twitter @NickBolesMP)

BOLGER, Dermot; s of Roger Bolger, of Dublin, and Bridie, *née* Flanagan (d 1969); *b* 6 February 1959; *Educ* St Canice's Boys' Sch, Nat Sch Finglas, Beneavin Coll Finglas; *m* 17 Dec 1988, Bernadette (d 2010), da of Vincent Clifton; 2 s (Donnacha b 30 Nov 1990, Diarmuid b 1 May 1992); *Career* writer; factory hand 1978–79, library asst 1979–84, ed and fndr Raven Arts Press 1979–92, exec ed New Island Books 1992–, playwright in assoc Abbey Theatre Dublin 1997; memb: Arts Cncl of Ireland 1989–93, Aosdána 1991–; ed of numerous poetry and prose anthologies incl The Picador Book of Contemporary

Irish Fiction (1993, revised edn 2000); *Novels* Night Shift (1985, A E Meml prize 1986), The Woman's Daughter (1987, extended version 1991, Macaulay fell 1987, shortlisted Hughes Fiction prize 1988), The Journey Home (1990, shortlisted Irish Times/Aer Lingus prize 1992, shortlisted Hughes Fiction prize 1990), Emily's Shoes (1992), A Second Life (1994), Father's Music (1997), Finbar's Hotel (ed and co-author, 1997), Ladies Night at Finbar's Hotel (ed, 1999), Temptation (2000), The Valparaiso Voyage (2001), The Family on Paradise Pier (2005), New Town Soul (2010), The Fall of Ireland (2012), Tanglewood (2015); *Poetry* The Habit of Flesh (1979), Finglas Lilies (1980), No Waiting America (1981), Internal Exile (1986), Leinster Street Ghosts (1989), Taking My Letters Back: New and Selected Poems (1998), The Chosen Moment (2004), External Affairs (2009), The Venice Suite (2012), That Which is Suddenly Precious (2015); *Plays* The Lament for Arthur Cleary (first staged Dublin Theatre Festival 1989, Samuel Beckett award, Stewart Parker BBC award, Edinburgh Fringe First), Blinded by the Light (Abbey Theatre Dublin 1990, A Z Whitehead prize), In High Germany (Dublin Theatre Festival 1990, filmed for RTE TV) 1993, The Holy Ground (Gate Theatre Dublin) 1990, One Last White Horse (Dublin Theatre Festival and Abbey Theatre) 1992, April Bright (Abbey Theatre) 1995, The Passion of Jerome (Abbey Theatre) 1999, Consulting Adults (Fishamble) 2000, These Green Heights (Axis) 2004, The Townlands of Brazil (Axis) 2006, Walking the Road (Axis) 2007, The Consequences of Lightning (Axis) 2008, The Parting Glass (Axis) 2010, Tea Chests and Dreams (Axis) 2012; *Films* The Disappearance of Finbar (C4) 1996; *Recreations* soccer, golf; *Clubs* Donabate Golf (Dublin); *Style—* Dermot Bolger, Esq; ✉ c/o New Island Books, 16 Priory Office Park, Stillorgan County, Dublin (☎ 00353 1 2784225, website www.dermotbolger.com)

BOLLAND, Alexander; QC (1992); s of James Bolland, of Kilmarnock, and Agnes Elizabeth, *née* Anderson; *b* 21 November 1950; *Educ* Kilmarnock Acad, Univ of St Andrews (BD), Univ of Glasgow (LLB); *m* 4 July 1973, Agnes Hunter Pate, da of George Pate Moffat; 2 da (Hilary Louise b 11 Sept 1980, Sophia Francesca b 1 Sept 1984), 1 s (Miles Louis James b 6 Aug 1991); *Career* apprentice Maclay, Murray & Spens 1976–77, pupil advocate 1977–78, admitted Scottish Bar 1978, capt Army Legal Services (later Army Legal Corps) BAOR and UKLF 1978–80, procurator fiscal depute 1980–82, in private practice Scottish Bar 1982–, standing jr counsel to Dept of Employment 1988–92, temp sheriff 1989–99; pt/t chm Employment Tbnls 1992–, pt/t chm Pensions Appeal Tbnl (Scotland) 2008–, chm Dental Vocational Ctee 2011–; *Recreations* reading, hellenistics; *Clubs* New (Edinburgh); *Style—* Alexander Bolland, Esq, QC; ✉ 60 North Street, St Andrews, Fife KY16 9AH (☎ 01334 474599); Advocates' Library, Parliament House, Edinburgh EH1 1RF

BOLLAND, Mark William; s of Robert Arthur Bolland (d 1993), and Joan, *née* Barker; *b* 10 April 1966; *Educ* King's Manor Sch Middlesbrough, Univ of York (BSc); *m* 2006, Guy Vaughan Black (The Lord Black of Brentwood), *qv* (civil partnership converted June 2015); *Career* mktg exec IBM (UK) Ltd 1987–88, advsr to DG Advtg Standards Authy 1988–91; Press Complaints Cmmn: exec asst to Chm 1991–92, dir 1992–96; dep private sec to HRH The Prince of Wales 1997–2002 (asst private sec 1996–97); communications conslt 2002–; columnist Evening Standard 2006–09; vice-pres Journalists' Charity 2007–; tstee: The Helen Hamlyn Tst 2008–14, The Open Futures Tst 2010–14, The David Ross Fndn 2011–, The David Ross Educn Tst 2012–15, Middlesbrough and Teesside Philanthropic Fndn 2012–14; dir Bertarelli Fndn 2013–; *Recreations* reading, Italy, music, walking; *Clubs* Garrick; *Style—* Mark Bolland, Esq; ✉ 34 Cannon Court, 5 Brewhouse Yard, London EC1V 4JQ (e-mail mark@markbolland.com)

BOLT, Christopher Wesley; CB (2010); s of Kenneth Bolt (d 1989), and Mary, *née* Sawtell (d 2005); *b* 4 October 1953, Plymouth; *Educ* Plymouth Coll Plymouth, Gonville and Caius Coll Cambridge (MA), UCL (MSc Econ); *m* 29 Oct 1981 Gillian; 1 s (Tom b 8 Aug 1982), 1 d (Rose b 24 June 1984); *Career* joined civil service 1975, with Department of the Environment 1988–89, head of economic regulation Ofwat 1989–94, rail regulator Office of the Rail Regulator 1998–99 (joined 1994), regulation and corp affrs dir Transco plc 1999–2001, gp dir Regulation and Public Policy Lattice Gp 2001–02, arbiter London Underground PPP Agreements 2002–11, chm Office of Rail Regulation 2004–09, regulation advsr Berwin Leighton Paisner 2011–, fin dir West Somerset Railway plc 2014–; chm Expert Advsr Panel UK Regulation Network 2015– (memb 2014–); non-exec dir Affinity Water Ltd 2015–; *Recreations* gardening, reading, heritage railways; *Style—* Chris Bolt, CB; ✉ e-mail cwbolt@gmail.com

BOLT-ORR, Annabelle Elizabeth; da of Harry Collett Bolt (d 1995), and Eileen Nellie, *née* Ellicott (d 2003); *Educ* Oakdene Sch, Univ of York; *m* 16 Sept 1978, George William Michael Orr; 2 s (Alexander Dundas b 8 Nov 1979, James Harry b 3 Feb 1981), 2 da (Lucinda Emily b 19 Oct 1982, Sophie Olivia b 14 July 1984); *Career* called to the Bar Gray's Inn 1970; in practice Commercial Bar 1970–72; HM Customs and Excise: advsr VAT 1972–81, head Int Criminal Div 1990–, advsr prosecuted customs crime (involving drugs and arms trafficking); conslt on maritime priacy and maritime domain crime IMO; memb: Int Assoc of Prosecutors, UN ODC, Bar Cncl; author of papers on transnational co-operation in crime and maritime drug trafficking; *Recreations* travel, skiing, gardening; *Style—* Mrs Annabelle Bolt-Orr; ✉ Manor House, Charwelton, Northamptonshire NN11 3YY

BOLTON, Ivor; *b* 17 May 1958; *Educ* Clare Coll Cambridge, RCM, Nat Opera Studio; *m* Dr T Knighton (musicologist, journalist and broadcaster); 1 s (Sam b 26 June 1991); *Career* conductor Schola Cantorum Oxford, fndr St James's Baroque Players 1984; music dir: Eng Touring Opera 1991–93, Glyndebourne Touring Opera 1992–97 (joined 1982); chief conductor Scottish Chamber Orch 1994–96; reg conductor: Bayerische Staatsoper Munich, Teatro Comunale Florence; chief conductor Mozarteum Orch Salzburg 2004; conducting debut ENO 1992 (Handel's Xerxes), BBC Proms debut 1993 (with St James's Baroque Players), ROH debut 1995, returned to Proms 1996, 2000 and 2006; *Opera* Glyndebourne Festival incl: Gluck's Orfeo 1989, Don Giovanni 1994, Le Nozze di Figaro 1994, Owen Wingrove 1997, Iphigenie en Aulide 2002; with Glyndebourne Touring Opera: Il Barbiere di Siviglia, The Magic Flute, The Rake's Progress, La Clemenza di Tito, Eugene Onegin, Owen Wingrave; work for other cos incl: La Cenerentola and Carmen (English Touring Opera), Rossini's La Gazza Ladra (Opera North), Mozart's La Finta Giardinera (WNO), Ariadne (Garsington), Giulio Cesare, Cosi Fan Tutte, Serse, Poppea, Marriage of Figaro, Ariodante, Don Giovanni, Orfeo, Ulisse, Clemenza di Tito, Rinaldo and The Rake's Progress (Bayerische Staatsoper), Poppea (Teatro Communale Bologna with Graham Vick), Iphigenie en Tauride (Teatro Colon Buenos Aires), Il Barbiere di Siviglia (Australian Opera), Ariadne (Opera Zuid Netherlands), Goehr's Arianna, Don Giovanni, Ipheigenie en Tauride, La Calisto, Tamerlano (all Royal Opera House), Paisiello's La Molinara (Bologna), Ariodante (ENO, televised by BBC), Giulio Cesare, Poppaea and Iphigenie en Tauride (all Paris Opera) 1997, Iphigenie en Tauride, Haydn's Armida, Theodora (Salzberg Festival); *Concert performances* with LSO, BBC Scottish Symphony Orch, London Mozart Players, English Chamber Orch, English Northern Philharmonia, Bournemouth Sinfonietta, Ulster Orch, BBC Symphony Orch (recording), Montreal Symphony, Nat Arts Centre Orch Ottawa, Netherlands Chamber Orch (series Concertgebouw Amsterdam), Mozarteum Orch Salzberg, Munich Orch; *Recordings* with St James's Baroque Players: all Bach Harpsichord Concertos, Purcell's Dido and Aeneas, Baroque Music from Bologna; Brahms and Mendelssohn violin concertos (with London Philharmonic and Xue Wei), Popular Operatic Arias (with Lesley Garrett), Saxophone Concerti (with John Harle), Vivaldi's Stabat Mater (for Thames TV), Poppea and Ariodante (Munich Opera), Bruckner Symphonies 3, 5, 7, 8 and 9, L'Enfance du Christ, The Creation and The Seasons (all with Mozarten Orch Salzberg), Orphée; *DVDs* Mozart Die Entführung (Salzburg Festival), Zaide (Salzburg Festival), La Finta Giardiniera (Salzburg Festival) *Awards* Bayerischer Theaterpreis (awarded by Prime Minister of Bavaria) 1998; *Clubs* Garrick; *Style—* Ivor Bolton, Esq; ✉ c/o Ingpen & Williams Ltd, 7 St George's Court, 131 Putney Bridge Road, London SW15 2PA

BOLTON, Roger John; s of Harold Bolton, and Olive Yarker, *née* Buck; *b* 13 November 1945; *Educ* Carlisle GS, Univ of Liverpool (BA); *m* 1 (m dis); 2 s (Alexander b 1970, Giles b 1973); m 2, 1987, Julia Helene McLaren; 2 da (Olivia b 1988, Jessica b 1989); *Career* BBC TV: gen trainee 1967, ed Tonight Prog 1977–79, ed Panorama 1979–81, ed Nationwide 1981–83, head Manchester Network Prodn Centre 1983–86; Thames TV: ed This Week 1986–89, controller of network factual progs 1989–92; fndr Roger Bolton Productions Ltd 1993–, currently chm Flame Group; ind prodr BBC's Heart of the Matter series 1992–; former presenter Right to Reply (Channel 4), currently presenter Sunday and Feedback (BBC Radio 4); former chair Edinburgh TV Festival, memb Cncl PACT; FRTS; *Books* Death on the Rock and Other Stories (1990); *Recreations* reading history, visiting churches, walking, five-a-side football; *Style—* Roger Bolton, Esq

BOLTON, Prof Thomas Bruce; *b* 14 November 1941; *Educ* Woodhouse Grove Sch (State scholar), RVC Univ of London (BSc, BVetMed, biology, physiology, biochemistry and pharmacology medals, 2 Centenary prizes, Thomson prize, Cecil Aldin prize), Univ of London (PhD), Univ of Oxford (MA), MRCVS; *m*; 3 c; *Career* veterinary surgn; lectr RVC 1965–66, Royal Soc Locke research fell Brasenose Coll and Dept of Pharmacology Oxford 1969–76; St George's Hosp Med Sch: sr lectr 1976–80, prof 1980–, head Dept of Pharmacology and Clinical Pharmacology 1985–2003, dean of R&D 1997–2001, chm and memb Cncl Academic Bd 1989–91 and 1995–2001; memb Int Interest Gp Wellcome Tst 1992–94 (Physiology and Pharmacology Panel 1985–90), memb Physiological Sciences Funding Ctee 2004–06, memb and vice-chm Horserace Scientific Advsy Ctee for British Racing 1971–85, chm Basic Med and Dental Sciences Assessment Panel Research Assessment Exercise 1992 and 1996, memb UFC and HEFCE Jt Medical Advsy Ctee 1993–95; memb: EC Biomed Panel 1995, Chairs and Programme Grants Ctee British Heart Fndn 1995–98; ed: British Jl of Pharmacology 1975–81, Jl of Physiology 1985–92; Hon DSc Kingston Univ 2010, Hon DSc St George's Univ of London 2014; memb: British Pharmacological Soc 1970, Research Defence Soc 1971, Univ Fedn of Animal Welfare 1971, Physiological Soc 1971, Biochemical Soc 1987, American Biophysical Soc 1988, Academia Europaea 1998; FMedSci 1998; *Books* Biography of Edith Bülbring (with A F Brading, 1992), Smooth Muscle Excitation (with T Tomita, 1996); *Recreations* sport and building; *Style—* Prof Thomas B Bolton; ✉ Division of Biomedical Sciences, St George's University of London, Cranmer Terrace, London SW17 0RE (☎ 020 8725 5570, e-mail sgkl180@sgul.ac.uk)

BOMPAS, (Anthony) George; QC (1994); s of Donald George Bompas, and Freda Vice, *née* Smithyman; *b* 6 November 1951; *Educ* Merchant Taylors', Oriel Coll Oxford (scholar, MA); *m* 16 Jan 1981, Donna Linda, da of John Oscar Schmidt; 2 s (Samuel Henry b 13 July 1983, Caleb George b 6 Aug 1989), 1 da (Abra Mae b 8 Aug 1985); *Career* called to the Bar Middle Temple 1975, jr counsel to DTI (Chancery) 1989–94, ordinary judge Cts of Appeal of Guernsey and Jersey 2014; Liveryman Worshipful Co of Merchant Taylors 1982; *Style—* George Bompas, Esq, QC; ✉ 4 Stone Buildings, Ground Floor, Lincoln's Inn, London WC2A 3XT (☎ 020 7242 5524, fax 020 7834 7907)

BOND, Andy; *Educ* Kings GS Grantham, Salford Univ, Cranfield Sch of Mgmnt (MBA); *m* 2 c; *Career* early career with British Gas (joined 1987) and Hopkinsons Ltd; Asda: joined as mktg mangr 1994, corp mktg dir 1998–99, European private label dir 1999–2000, md George 2000–04, chief operating offr 2004–05, chief exec 2005–11; Republic: chairman 2011–13; *Style—* Mr Andy Bond; ✉ Asda Group Limited, Asda House, South Bank, Great Wilson Street, Leeds LS11 5AD

BOND, Annabelle Sarah; OBE (2006); da of Sir John Bond, *qv*, and Elizabeth Caroline, *née* Parker; *b* 12 July 1969, Singapore; *Educ* Riddlesworth Hall, Cobham Hall, Inst Alpin Vidamanette Switzerland; *Career* mountaineer; fastest woman and fourth fastest person to climb seven summits (highest mountains on seven continents) 2004–05, N Pole with Prince Albert of Monaco 2006; FPD Savills Hong Kong 1991–2000; fundraiser: Eve Appeal, Laureus Sports Awards; award from the Chilean Army for Everest Expedition 2004; *Style—* Ms Annabelle Bond, OBE; ✉ c/o IMG (☎ 020 8233 5065, e-mail clacy@imgworld.com)

BOND, Christopher Michael; s of Lt-Col James Hugh Bond, MC (d 1983), and Winifred Dodman, *née* Goodall (d 1989); *b* 28 June 1943; *Educ* Wellington, Trinity Hall Cambridge (BA); *m* 19 Feb 1966, Lindsay, da of late Arthur Lewis Cruickshank; 1 s (Neil Alexander), 1 da (Lara Marianne); *Career* admitted slr 1969, gen counsel and asst co sec Reuters plc 1972–76, ptnr Field Fisher Waterhouse 1979–2005; sr advsr Chartered Inst for Securities & Investment 2005–, conslt Raymond James Investment Services Ltd 2005–, conslt Mitsubishi UFJ Tst Int 2005–, conslt Europa Partners Ltd 2006–; non-exec dir Westpac Europe Ltd 2006–, non-exec dir Triland Metals Ltd; chm Exec Ctee European Legal Alliance 2002–05, memb Cncl Compliance Inst 2001–05 (chm Professional Educn Bd 2003–05); lectr int confs in: America, Europe, Japan, Korea, Taiwan, UK; hon advsr Taipei Representative Office 2002–12; author of articles in: Chartered Inst for Securities & Investment Review, Compliance Inst Gazette, Compliance Monitor, Complinet; ed Change, ed International Banker; ed Somerset Gardens Tst magazine, speaker to Somerset Gardens Clubs, memb Cncl Somerset Gardens Tst, chm Festival Run Glastonbury; memb: Ct, Communications Ctee; Worshipful Co of Int Bankers 2013–; memb Law Soc 1969–2005; *Books* Investing in the United Kingdom (1986), Investing in the United Kingdom: The Basic Issues (1987); *Recreations* music, reading, poetry, gardening, woodlands, jogging; *Style—* Christopher Bond, Esq

BOND, Edward; *b* 18 July 1934, London; *m* 1971, Elisabeth Pablé; *Career* playwright and director; Northern Arts literary fell 1977–79, George Devine award 1968, John Whiting award 1968, Obie 1976; Hon DLitt Yale 1977, Hon DLitt Newman Univ Birmingham 2013; City of Lyon Medal 2007; *Plays* The Pope's Wedding (1962), Saved (1965), Narrow Road to the Deep North (1968), Early Morning (1968), Passion (1971), Black Mass (1971), Lear (1972), The Sea: A Comedy (1973), Bingo (1974), The Fool (1976), A-A-America! (Grandma Faust and The Swing) (1976), Stone (1976), Collected Plays (9 vols, 1977–2011), The Bundle (1978), The Woman (1979), The Worlds with The Activist Papers (1980), Restoration (1981), Summer: a play for Europe, and Fables (short stories) (1982), Derek (1983), Human Cannon (1984), The War Plays (part 1 Red Black and Ignorant, part 2 The Tin Can People, part 3 Great Peace, 1985), Jackets (1989), In the Company of Men (1990), September (1990), Olly's Prison (1993), Tuesday (1993), Coffee: A Tragedy (1995), At the Inland Sea (a play for young people, 1996), Eleven Vests (1997), The Crime of the Twenty-first Century (1998), The Children (a play for two adults and sixteen children, 2000), Chair (2000), Have I None (2000), Existence (2002), The Balancing Act (2003), The Short Electra (2004), The Under Room (2005), My Day: A Song Cycle for young people (2005), Arcade (2006), Born, (2006), Tune (2007), People (2008), Innocence (2009), A Window (2009), The Edge (2011), The Broken Bowl (2012), The Chair Plays (2012), The Testament of This Day (2013), The Angry Roads (2014), The Price of One (2015), Dea (2016); *Opera Libretti* We Come to the River (1976), The English Cat (1983), Early Morning (music by Laura Brewer, 2016); *Ballet Libretto* Orpheus (1982), the latter three: music by Hans Werner Henze; *Translations* Chekhov's The Three Sisters (1967), Wedekind's Spring Awakening (1974), L?I? (with Elisabeth Bond-Pablé, 1992); *Other Publications* Theatre Poems and Songs (1978), Collected Poems 1978–85 (1987), Notes on

Post-Modernism (1990), Letters (5 Vols, 1994–2001), Notes on Imagination (1995), The Hidden Plot: Notes on Theatre and the State (2000), Selected Notebooks (Vol 1, 2000, Vol II, 2001), Edward Bond and the Dramatic Child (2005), Edward Bond: The Playwright Speaks (2015); *Style*— Edward Bond, Esq; ✉ c/o Casarotto Ramsay Ltd, Waverley House, 7–12 Noel Street, London W1F 8GQ; website www.edwardbond.org

BOND, Graham; s of Thomas Carlile (d 1980), of Blackburn, Lancs, and Mary, *née* Dixon (d 1999); *Educ* Queen Elizabeth's GS Blackburn, Royal Coll of Music (exhibition scholar, various prizes); *Career* repetiteur London Opera Centre 1970; London Festival Ballet/English Nat Ballet: conductor 1970–76, princ conductor 1976–94, music dir 1983–94; chief conductor Royal Danish Ballet 1994–; tours incl: Australia, France, Spain, Italy, Germany, Yugoslavia, Greece, Denmark, Venezuela, Turkey, China, USA, Japan; orchs worked with incl: Monte Carlo Philharmonic, Tivoli Symphony Copenhagen, Stanislavsky Theatre Moscow, Opera House Turin, Hong Kong Philharmonic, Danish Radio, Royal Opera Copenhagen, Opera Teatro Massimo Sicily, Cairo Symphony; guest conductor: Stuttgart Ballet, San Carlo Opera Orch Naples, Metropolitan Opera NY 1989, Deutsche Oper Berlin 1990–93, Bolshoi Ballet tour of England 1990, Opera House Budapest 1992, Palacio de Bella Artes Mexico 1993, Sofia Opera Orch 1993, Bergen Festival 1996, Royal Opera House 1995, Dutch Nat Ballet 1996 and 1997, Teatro Real Madrid 1997, Royal Ballet in China 1999, Paris Opera 1999, Royal Opera House 2000–2004, Bolshoi and Maryinsky Russia 2003, Royal Opera Stockholm 2003–05; chief guest conductor Royal Swedish Ballet 2007–; memb conducting staff Royal Coll of Music 1985–94; awards incl: Worshipful Co of Musicians medal for a Distinguished Student Royal Coll of Music, Adrian Boult scholarship for study at the Accademia Chigiana Siena; Hon RCM 1994; *Recreations* theatre, walking; *Style*— Graham Bond, Esq; ✉ 8 Calverley Park Crescent, Tunbridge Wells, Kent TN1 2NB (☎ and fax 01892 536994); c/o Royal Theatre, Copenhagen, Denmark (☎ 00 45 33 69 69 33)

BOND, Jennie; da of Kenneth Bond, and Pamela, *née* Collins; *b* 19 August 1950; *Educ* St Francis' Coll Letchworth, Univ of Warwick (BA); *m* 1982, Jim Keltz; 1 da (Emma b 17 Feb 1990); 2 step c (Stephen, Danielle); *Career* broadcaster, news presenter and royal correspondent; reporter: Richmond Herald 1972–75, Evening Mail (Slough & Hounslow) 1975–77; BBC Radio 1977–88 (incl Woman's Hour, Today), BBC TV News 1988–2003; Reporting Royalty (2001), Elizabeth: Fifty Glorious Years (2002), Elizabeth: 80 Glorious Years (2006), Elizabeth, A Diamond Jubilee Portrait (2012); *Recreations* dancing, laughing, enjoying fine wine and great company; *Style*— Ms Jennie Bond; ✉ c/o Knight Ayton Management, 29 Gloucester Place, London W1U 8HX

BOND, Sir John Reginald Hartnell; kt (1999); s of Cdre Reginald Harold Arthur Bond, OBE (d 1978), of Hampshire, and Edith Christine Alice, *née* Powell; *b* 24 July 1941; *Educ* Tonbridge, Cate Sch Calif (ESU scholar); *m* 27 April 1968, Elizabeth Caroline, da of John Anthony Parker; 2 da (Annabelle Sarah b 12 July 1969, Lucy Candida b 18 Dec 1972), 1 s (Jonathan Simon b 13 Nov 1976); *Career* Hongkong and Shanghai Banking Corporation: joined Hongkong Bank 1961, chief exec Wardley Ltd (HSBC subsid) Hong Kong 1983–87 (dep md 1982–83), exec dir and chief exec Americas Regnl Office USA 1988–90 (gen mangr and chief exec 1987–88), exec dir banking Gp Head Office Hong Kong 1990–91, pres and chief exec Marine Midland Banks Inc Buffalo 1991–92, gp chief exec HSBC Holdings plc London 1993–98, gp chm HSBC Holdings 1998–2006, chm HSBC Bank USA 1997–2006, chm HSBC Americas Inc 1997–2006, chm HSBC Bank plc 1998–2006; non-exec chm Vodafone 2006–11 (non-exec dir 2005–11), chm KKR Asia 2009–(advsr 2006–), chm Xstrata plc 2011–; non-exec dir: Ford Motor Co 2000–08, Bank of England 2001–04; chm Inst of Int Fin Washington DC 1998–2003, pres Int Monetary Conf 2001–02; hon fell London Business Sch 2003; Hon DEc Richmond American Int Univ in London 1998, Hon DLitt Loughborough Univ 2000; Hon LLD: South Bank Univ 2000, Univ of Bristol 2005, Univ of Nottingham 2005; Hon DLitt Univ of Sheffield 2002, Hon DSc City Univ London 2004, Hon Dr London Met Univ 2004; FCIB 1983, CIMgt 1993; Magnolia Gold Award Shanghai Municipal People's Govt 2003, Foreign Policy Assoc Medal NY 2003; *Recreations* skiing, golf and reading biography; *Clubs* MCC, Hong Kong, Royal Ashdown Forest Golf, John's Island (Florida); *Style*— Sir John Bond

BOND, (Thomas) Michael; CBE (2015, OBE 1997); s of Norman Robert Bond, and Frances Mary Bond; *Educ* Presentation Coll Reading; *Career* served: RAF 1943–44, Middx Regt 1944–47; with BBC 1941–43, BBC Monitoring Serv 1947–54, TV cameraman BBC 1954–65, full-time writer 1965–; patron Action Medical Research; Hon DLitt Univ of Reading 2007; *Books* Paddington novels: A Bear Called Paddington (1958), More about Paddington (1959), Paddington Helps Out (1960), Paddington Abroad (1961), Paddington at Large (1962), Paddington Marches On (1964), Paddington at Work (1966), Paddington Goes to Town (1968), Paddington Takes the Air (1970), Paddington's Blue Peter Story Book (1973), Paddington on Top (1974), Paddington Takes the Test (1979), Paddington on Screen (1981), Paddington – A Classic Collection (1998), Paddington Treasury (2001), Paddington Here and Now (2008), Paddington Races Ahead (2012), Love from Paddington (2014); Paddington picture books: Paddington and the Christmas Surprise (1997), Paddington Bear (1998), Paddington at the Zoo (1998), Paddington the Artist (1998), Paddington and the Tutti Frutti Rainbow (1998), Paddington at the Fair (1998), Paddington at the Carnival (1998), Paddington – My Scrapbook (1999), Paddington Minds the House (1999), Paddington at the Palace (1999), Paddington and the Marmalade Maze (1999), Paddington's Busy Day (1999), Paddington's Party Tricks (2000), Paddington in Hot Water (2000), Paddington at the Circus (2000), Paddington Goes to Hospital (2001), Paddington's Garden (2002), Paddington and the Grand Tour (2003), Paddington Rules the Waves (2008), Paddington: My Book of Marmalade (2008), Paddington at the Rainbow's End (2009), Paddington King of the Castle (2009), Paddington and the Disappearing Sandwich (2009), The Paddington Treasur for the Very Young (2010), Paddington's London Treasury (2011), Paddington's Guide to London (2011), Paddington's Cookery Book (2011), Paddington Goes for Gold (2012); other children's books: Here Comes Thursday! (1966), Thursday Rides Again (1968), Thursday Ahoy! (1969), Parsley's Tail (1969), Parsley's Good Deed (1969), Parsley's Last Stand (1970), Parsley's Problem Present (1970), Thursday in Paris (1971), The Tales of Olga Da Polga (1971, 2 edn 2001), Parsley's Parade (1972), The Day the Animals Went on Strike (1972), Parsley the Lion (1972), Olga Meets Her Match (1973, 2 edn 2001), Windmill (1975), Mr Cram's Magic Bubbles (1975), Parsley and Herbs (1976), Olga Carries On (1976, 2 edn 2001), J D Polson and the Liberty Head Dime (1980), J D Polson and the Dillogate Affair (1981), Olga Takes Charge (1982, 2 edn 2001), The Caravan Puppets (1983), Olga Moves House (2001), Olga Follows her Nose (2002); adult novels: Monsieur Pamplemousse (1983), Monsieur Pamplemousse and the Secret Mission (1984), Monsieur Pamplemousse on the Spot (1986), Monsieur Pamplemousse Takes the Cure (1987), Monsieur Pamplemousse Aloft (1989), Monsieur Pamplemousse Investigates (1990), Monsieur Pamplemousse Rests His Case (1991), Monsieur Pamplemousse Stands Firm (1992), Monsieur Pamplemousse on Location (1992), Monsieur Pamplemousse Takes the Train (1993), Monsieur Pamplemousse Afloat (1998), Monsieur Pamplemousse on Probation (2000), Monsieur Pamplemousse on Vacation (2002), Monsieur Pamplemousse Hits the Headlines (2003), Monsieur Pamplemousse and the Militant Midwives (2006), Monsieur Pamplemousse and the French Solution (2007), Monsieur Pamplemousse and the Carbon Footprint (2010), Monsieur Pamplemousse and the Tangled Web (2014); non-fiction: The Pleasures of Paris (1987), Bears and Forebears: A Life So Far (1996); *Television* Paddington animated series (56 episodes), The Herbs (13 episodes), The Adventures of Parsley (32 episodes); *Style*— Michael Bond, Esq, CBE; ✉ The Agency, 24 Pottery Lane, Holland Park, London W11 4LZ (☎ 020 7727 1346, fax 020 7727 9037)

BOND, His Hon Richard Henry; s of Lt-Col Ashley Raymond Bond, MBE, DL, JP (d 1975), of Creech Grange, Wareham, Dorset, and Mary, *née* Bowles (d 1952); *b* 15 April 1947; *Educ* Sherborne; *m* 25 April 1987, (Annabel) Susan, da of Brig John Henry Peter Curtis, MC (d 1999); 1 s (Henry b 30 Oct 1988), 1 da (Annabel b 27 Feb 1990); *Career* called to the Bar Inner Temple 1970; recorder of the Crown Court 1995–97, circuit judge (Western Circuit) 1997–2016, ret; *Recreations* gardening, walking; *Clubs* Travellers; *Style*— His Hon Richard Bond; ✉ The Courts of Justice, Deansleigh Road, Bournemouth BH7 7DS (☎ 01202 502800)

BOND, His Hon Judge Richard Ian Winsor; *Career* called to the Bar 1988; recorder 2009, circuit judge (Midland Circuit) 2013–; *Style*— His Hon Judge Richard I W Bond; ✉ Queen Elizabeth II Law Courts, 1 Newton Street, Birmingham B4 7NA

BOND, Samantha; da of Philip Bond, of Abergwynfi, and Pat Sandys, *née* Trotter (d 2000); *b* 27 November 1961; *Educ* Godolphin & Latymer Sch, Bristol Old Vic Theatre Sch; *m* 1989, Alexander Hanson; 1 da (Molly b 22 Oct 1991), 1 s (Arthur (Tom) b 12 Jan 1993); *Career* actor; patron Shooting Star CHASE, ambass Prince's Tst, ambass Macmillan Cancer Support, vice-chair Royal Theatrical Fund; *Theatre* repertory incl: Coventry, Southampton, Edinburgh, Derby, Bristol; credits incl: Juliet in Romeo and Juliet (Lyric Hammersmith) 1986, Beatrice in Much Ado About Nothing (Phoenix and tour) 1988, Infanta in Le Cid (RNT) 1994 (nomination Olivier Award), C in Three Tall Women (Wyndham's) 1995, Amy in Amy's View (RNT and Broadway) 1997 (nomination Tony Award), Mary in Memory of Water (Vaudeville) 1998, Lady Macbeth in Macbeth (Albery) 2002, Karen in Dinner with Friends (Hampstead) 2001, title role in A Woman of No Importance (Theatre Royal Haymarket) 2003, Esther Rubenstein in The Rubenstein Kiss (Hampstead) 2005, Lady Driver in Donkeys' Years (Comedy) 2006 (nomination Olivier Award), Hannah Jarvis in Arcadia (Duke of York's) 2009, Mrs Cheveley in An Ideal Husband (Vaudeville) 2010, What the Butler Saw (Vaudeville) 2012, Nell in Passion Play (Duke of York's) 2013, Muriel in Dirty Rotten Scoundrels (Savoy) 2014; RSC 1992–93 incl: Hermione in The Winter's Tale, Rosalind in As You Like It; *Television* incl: The Ginger Tree, Emma, Family Money, Tears Before Bedtime, Morse, NCS Manhunt, The Hunt, Donovan (2 series), Distant Shores (2 series), The Murder Room, Wolfenden, Clapham Junction, Outnumbered (5 series), Fanny Hill, Marple: Why Didn't They Ask Evans?, Downton Abbey (5 series); *Film* Eric The Viking 1989, What Rats Won't Do 1998, Blinded 2003, Yes 2003, A Bunch of Amateurs 2008; Moneypenny in: GoldenEye 1995, Tomorrow Never Dies 1997, The World is Not Enough 1999, Die Another Day 2002; *Recreations* playing with children, watching cricket, Scrabble; *Style*— Miss Samantha Bond; ✉ c/o Conway van Gelder Ltd, 18–21 Jermyn Street, London SW1Y 6HP (☎ 020 7287 0077, fax 020 7287 1940)

BONE, Charles William Henry; s of William Stanley Bone (d 1966), and Elizabeth, *née* Burfoot; *b* 15 September 1926; *Educ* Farnham Coll of Art, RCA; *m* 1950, Sheila Mary (d 2006), da of Lionel Mitchell (d 1956); 2 s (Richard, Sebastian); *Career* artist; lectr Brighton Coll of Art 1950–86, conslt COSIRA 1952–70; craft advsr Malta Industries Assoc 1952–78, designer Stourhead Ball 1959–69, dir RI Galleries Piccadilly 1965–70; critic for Arts Review; memb Cncl RI 1964 (vice-pres 1974), govr Fedn of Br Artists 1976–81 and 1983–(memb Exec Cncl 1983–84 and 1986–88), pres Royal Inst of Painters in Water Colours 1979–89 (vice-pres 1974–79); Hunting Gp Prize for the Most Outstanding Watercolour by a Br Artist 1984; hon memb: Botanical Artists, Medical Art Soc, Fedn of Canadian Artists; ARCA; *Exhibitions* oils and water colours in exhibitions: Medici Gallery 1950–, London Gp, NEAC, RBA 1950–, RA 1950–; 50 one-man exhibitions 1950– (most recently Spain 2007); *Works in Private Collections* France, Italy, Malta, America, Canada, Japan, Aust, Norway, Sweden, Germany; *Other Work* incl: ceramic mural on the history of aerial photography, other murals in Italy and Spain, film on painting for Castle Communications plc 1990, book on Waverley Surrey 1991; *Books* The Author's Circle (1998), Anglican Cathedrals (2000); *Clubs* Chelsea Arts; *Style*— Charles Bone, Esq; ✉ Winters Farm, Puttenham, Guildford, Surrey GU3 1AR (☎ 01483 810226, website www.charlesbone.com); 17 Carlton House Terrace, London SW1

BONE, Prof Sir (James) Drummond; kt (2008); s of William Drummond Bone (d 1979), and Helen, *née* Yuill (d 1973); *b* 11 July 1947; *Educ* Ayr Acad, Univ of Glasgow, Balliol Coll Oxford (Snell exhibitioner); *m* 1970, Vivian Clare Bone, *née* Kindon; *Career* lectr Dept of English and Comparative Literary Studies Univ of Warwick 1972–80; Univ of Glasgow: lectr then sr lectr Dept of English 1980–95, prof of English literature 1995–2000, dean Faculty of Arts 1992–95, vice-princ 1995–99; princ Royal Holloway Univ of London 2000–02, vice-chllr Univ of Liverpool 2002–08, master Balliol Coll Oxford 2011–, pro vice-chllr Univ of Oxford 2016–; pres Univ UK 2005–07; academic ed The Byron Jl 1978–88, co-ed Romanticism 1995–, author of many articles on Romanticism and also the occasional short story; chm Liverpool Culture Co 2005–07; chm: FACT (Fndn for Art and Creative Technol) 2004–10, Graduate Prospects 2005–08, Northern Way Innovation and Industry Strategy Gp 2007–09, UK Research Reserve 2007–16, Observatory of Borderless Educn 2008–, Int Advsy Bd Laureate Inc 2008–11, Int Grad Insight Gp 2009–, Arts and Humanities Research Cncl 2014–; hon fell Royal Holloway and Bedford New Coll 2004; Hon DLitt: Univ of Liverpool 2008, Chester Univ 2008, Univ of Lancaster 2009; Hon DUniv Glasgow 2010, Hon DEd Univ of Edinburgh 2014, Dr (hc) Bucharest Univ 2016, Dr (hc) Xi'an Jiaotong-Liverpool Univ (XJTLU) 2016; Freeman Worshipful Co of Coachmakers and Coach Harness Makers; FRSA 1995, FRSE 2008; *Publications* Writers and their Work: Byron (2000), Cambridge Companion to Byron (ed, 2004); *Recreations* music, skiing, Maseratis (chm Maserati Club 2002–07); *Clubs* Athenaeum; *Style*— Prof Sir Drummond Bone

BONE, Peter; MP; *b* 19 October 1952, Billericay, Essex; *Educ* Westcliff-on-Sea GS; *Career* chartered accountant 1977, finance dir Essex Electronics and Precision Engrg Gp 1977–83, chief exec High Tech Electronic Co 1983–90; cncllr (Cons) Southend-on-Sea BC 1977–86; Parly candidate (Cons): Islwyn 1992, Pudsey 1997, Wellingborough 2001; MP (Cons) Wellingborough 2005–; *Style*— Peter Bone, Esq, MP; ✉ House of Commons, London SW1A 0AA

BONE, Dr Quentin; s of Stephen Bone (d 1958), and Sylvia Mary, *née* Adshead (d 1995); *b* 17 August 1931; *Educ* Warwick Sch, St John's Coll and Magdalen Coll Oxford (DPhil); *m* 9 Aug 1958, Susan Elizabeth, da of Sidney Smith (d 1963), of Witney, Oxon; 4 s (Matthew b 5 June 1959, Oliver b 2 Jan 1961, Alexander b 13 Aug 1963, Daniel b 21 Nov 1965); *Career* Plymouth Lab of the Marine Biological Assoc UK: zoologist 1959–, dep chief scientific offr 1987–91, emeritus res fell 1992–; ed Philosophical Transactions of the Royal Soc – Biological Sciences 1988–94; Gold Medal for Zoology Linnean Soc 1999, Frick Medal Zoological Soc of London 2004; FRS 1984; *Books* Biology of Fishes (with N B Marshall and J S Blaxter, 1994, 3 edn with R Moore, 2007), Biology of Pelagic Tunicates (1998); *Recreations* botany, travel, repairing machines; *Style*— Dr Quentin Bone, FRS; ✉ Marchant House, Church Road, Plymstock, Plymouth PL9 9BG; The Marine Laboratory, Citadel Hill, Plymouth PL1 2PB (☎ 01752 633100, e-mail qb@mba.ac.uk)

BONE, Sir Roger Bridgland; KCMG (2002, CMG 1996); s of Horace Bridgland Bone (d 1979), and Dora Rose, *née* Tring (d 1997); *b* 29 July 1944; *Educ* Palmer's Sch Grays Essex, St Peter's Coll Oxford (MA); *m* 3 July 1970, Lena Marianne, da of Georg Bergman (d 1975); 1 s (Christopher b 1977), 1 da (Marianne b 1980); *Career* HM Dip Serv: UK Mission to UN 1966, FCO 1967, third sec Stockholm 1968–70, first sec Moscow 1973–

75, first sec UK Representation to the Euro Communities Brussels 1978–82, private sec to Sec of State for Foreign and Cwlth Affrs 1982–84, visiting fell Harvard Center for Int Affrs 1984–85, cnsllr Washington 1985–89 (head of Chancery 1987–89), cnsllr FCO 1989–91, asst under sec of state FCO 1991–95, ambass Sweden 1995–99, ambass Brazil 1999–2004; chm Anglo Latin American Fndn 2005–10, memb Cncl Brazil Chamber of Commerce 2005–10; pres Boeing UK 2005–14, dir Foreign and Colonial Investment Tst plc 2008– (sr ind dir 2015–); dir Continental Data Graphics Ltd 2010–14, dir ITM Power plc 2014–, non-exec dir Over Ltd; ambass for Br business UK Trade and Industry 2009–15; memb Exec Cncl RUSI 2007–12 (tstee 2013–), memb Cncl Air League 2008– (pres 2015–), memb Cncl Industry and HE (CIHE) 2011–13, dir and tstee Nat Centre for Univs and Business (NCUB) 2013–; Hon FIED 2013, Hon DEng 2015, Hon CRAeS 2015; *Recreations* wine, music; *Style*— Sir Roger Bone, KCMG

BONELLI, Federico; *b* Italy; *Educ* Turin Dance Acad; *Career* ballet dancer; soloist Zürich Ballet 1997–99 (joined 1996), princ Dutch Nat Ballet 2002–04 (joined 1999), princ Royal Ballet 2004–; second prize Concour Int de Havana Cuba, first prize Reiti Int Ballet Competition, Prix de Lausanne scholarship 1996; *Performances* incl: Cinderella, Romeo and Juliet, La Sylphide, Onegin; roles with the Royal Ballet incl: Romeo, the Prince in Cinderella, Albrecht, Daphnis, Lensky, Polyphonia, Agon; danced in works by: Balanchine, Forsythe, Van Manen, Massine, Robbins, Tetley; *Style*— Federico Bonelli, Esq; ✉ c/o The Royal Ballet, Royal Opera House, Covent Garden, London WC2E 9DD

BONEY, His Hon Guy Thomas Knowles; QC (1990); s of Lt-Col Thomas Knowles Boney (d 1975), of Llandudno, and Muriel Hilary Eileen, *née* Long (d 1984); *b* 28 December 1944; *Educ* Winchester, New Coll Oxford (MA); *m* 4 Dec 1976, Jean Ritchie, QC, *qv*, da of Walter Ritchie (d 1979), of Solihull; 2 s (R Oliver b 21 Jan 1979, Christian V K b 29 March 1981); *Career* called to the Bar Middle Temple 1968 (bencher 1997); in practice Western Circuit 1969–2003, recorder of the Crown Court 1985–2003, head Pump Court Chambers 1992–2001, dep judge of the High Court 1994–2003, circuit judge (Western Circuit) 2003–14; chm Friends of Winchester Coll 2001–; contrib to horological jls; Lord of the Manor of Stockbridge (Nat Tst appt) 2003–; *Books* The Road Safety Act 1967 (1971), Halsbury's Laws of England vol 40 (contrib); *Recreations* horology, music, amateur drama; *Clubs* Reform, Garrick; *Style*— His Hon Guy Boney, QC; ✉ 31 Southgate Street, Winchester, Hampshire SO23 9EB (☎ 01962 868161, fax 01264 811180)

BONFIELD, Andrew Robert John; s of Terence Bonfield, and Roberta Alexandra, *née* Stackhouse; *b* 17 August 1962; *Educ* Univ of Natal (BCom, Postgrad Dip Accountancy); *m* Sandra; 2 s (Cameron, Scott); *Career* Price Waterhouse: South Africa 1984–87, London 1987–90; SmithKline Beecham plc: exec Corporate Planning 1990–91, dir and vice-pres Corporate Accounts 1991–95, corp controller 1995–97, dep fin dir and sr vice-pres 1997–99, chief fin offr 1999–2000; exec dir BG Gp plc 2001–02, sr vice-pres and chief fin offr Bristol-Myers Squibb 2002–09, chief fin offr Cadbury plc 2009–10, fin dir National Grid 2010–; memb South African ICA, memb ICAEW; *Recreations* golf; *Style*— Andrew Bonfield, Esq

BONFIELD, Dr Astrid Elizabeth; CBE (2014); *b* 21 May 1969, Welwyn Garden City, Herts; *Educ* Univ of Southampton (BA), Univ of Manchester (MA, PhD); *Partner* David Godwin; 1 da (Elizabeth b 23 Feb 2009), 1 s (Rupert b 1 April 2011); *Career* dir Inter-Country People's Aid Zimbabwe 1997–2001, prog devpt specialist Bernard van Leer Fndn 2001–04, dir of policy Aga Khan Fndn 2004–05, chief exec Diana, Princess of Wales Meml Fund 2005–12, chief exec Queen Elizabeth Diamond Jubilee Tst 2012–; tstee: Assoc of Charitable Fndns 2005–10, Int Agency for the Prevention of Blindness 2014–; chair European Funders Gp for HIV/AIDS 2005–11, memb Bd Big Lottery Fund 2012–; *Recreations* gardening, contemporary dance; *Clubs* Athenaeum; *Style*— Dr Astrid Bonfield, CBE; ✉ The Queen Elizabeth Diamond Jubilee Trust, 128 Buckingham Palace Road, London SW1W 9SA

BONFIELD, Sir Peter Leahy; kt (1996), CBE (1989); s of George Bonfield, and Patricia Bonfield; *b* 3 June 1944; *Educ* Hitchin Boys' GS, Loughborough Univ (BTech); *m* 1968, Josephine Houghton; *Career* Texas Instruments Inc Dallas USA 1966–81, dep chief exec STC plc 1987–90, chief exec British Telecommunications plc 1996–2002; dir: BICC plc 1992–96, MCI Inc 1996–98, LM Ericsson Sweden 2002–15, Mentor Graphics Corp Inc USA 2002–, TSMC Taiwan 2002–; dep chm ICL plc 1997–2000 (chm and chief exec 1985–96), memb Advsy Bd Sony Corp 2004–14, memb Supervisory Bd Actis LLP 2005–13, non-exec dir Corporate Bd DCA 2005–08, chm Supervisory Bd NXP 2006–, non-exec dir Dubai Int LLP 2006–10; vice-pres Br Quality Fndn 1993–2011; memb Int Advsy Bd Citi; former memb: Euro Round Table, EU-Japan Business Dialogue Round Table; ambass for Br business; Nat Electronics Cncl Mountbatten Medal 1995, Inst of Mgmnt Gold Medal 1996; Freeman City of London 1990, Liveryman Worshipful Co of Information Technologists 1992; hon citizen of Dallas; hon doctorates from Univs of: Loughborough, Surrey, Mid Glamorgan, Nottingham Trent, Brunel, Open Univ, Northumbria at Newcastle, London (Royal Holloway), Kingston, Cranfield, Essex; FIEE 1990, FBCS 1990, FCIM 1990, FRSA 1992, FREng; Cdr of the Order of the Lion of Finland 1995; *Recreations* music, sailing, skiing; *Clubs* RAC, Royal Thames Yacht; *Style*— Sir Peter Bonfield, CBE, FREng; ✉ PO Box 129, Shepperton, Middlesex TW17 9WL

BONFIELD, Prof William; CBE (1998); s of Cecil William Bonfield (d 2001), of Baldock, Herts, and Ellen Gertrude, *née* Hawkes (d 1981); *b* 6 March 1937; *Educ* Letchworth GS, Imperial Coll London (Perry Meml medal, Bessemer Medal, Ernest Edward Glorney Prize, BSc(Eng), PhD, ARSM, DIC); *m* 18 June 1960, Gillian Winifred Edith, da of John Hamilton Cross; 1 s (Peter William b 25 June 1963), 2 da (Stephanie Jane b 10 Sept 1965, Astrid Elizabeth b 21 May 1969); *Career* Honeywell Res Center Minnesota 1961–68; Queen Mary Univ of London 1968–99: head Dept of Materials 1980–90, chm Sch of Engrg 1981–88, govr 1984–87, dean of engrg 1985–89, prof of materials 1974–99 and dir Interdisciplinary Res Centre in Biomedical Materials 1990–99; Univ of Cambridge: prof of med materials 2000–05, dir Pfizer Inst for Pharmaceutical Materials Science 2002–05, emeritus prof 2005–; distinguished visiting prof Univ of Toronto 1990, visiting prof Henry Ford Hosp Detroit 1992, hon prof Univ of Sichuan China 1992–, adjunct prof Univ of Naples 1993–, visiting prof Nat Univ of Singapore 2007–; hon professorship UCL 2007–; dir: Apatech Ltd 2001–10, OrthoMimetics Ltd 2007–09, AtoCap Ltd 2011–; ed: Jl of Materials Science 1973–2002, Jl of Materials Science Letters 1981–2002, Materials in Medicine 1990–2006, Jl of the Royal Soc of London: Interface 2004–10; A A Griffith Silver Medal Inst of Medals 1991, Royal Soc Armourers and Brasiers' Co Medal 1991, George Winter Award Euro Soc for Biomaterials 1994, Kelvin Medal Instn of Civil Engrs 1995, Acta Metallurgica J Herbert Holloman Award 2000, Chapman Medal IMMM 2003, Japanese Soc for Biomaterials Medal 2003, Prince Philip Gold Medal Royal Acad of Engrg 2004, President's Prize UK Soc for Biomaterials 2004, Int Union of Physical and Engrg Sciences in Medicine (IUPSEM) Award of Merit 2009; Freeman City of London 1998, Liveryman Worshipful Co of Armourers and Brasiers 1999 (Freeman 1994, memb Ct of Assts 2001, Renter Warden 2005, Upper Warden 2006, Master 2007–08); hon memb: Canadian Orthopaedic Res Soc 1984, Indian Materials Res Soc 1993; memb Euro Soc for Biomaterials 2005; Hon DSc Univ of Aberdeen 2002, Hon DSc Univ of Turku Finland 2011; hon fell Queen Mary Univ of London 2007; CEng 1972, FIMMM (FIM 1972), FREng 1993, founding fell in biomaterials, sci and engrg (FBSE) Euro Soc for Biomaterials 1995, FRS 2003, CPhys 2003, FIPEM 2003, FInstP, FRSC 2005, FMedSci 2010, FCGI 2012; *Publications* Bioceramics (with G W Hastings and K E Tanner, 1991); author of over 500 scientific papers and 80 patents; *Recreations* cycling; *Clubs* Athenaeum, North Road Cycling; *Style*— Prof William Bonfield, CBE, FRS, FREng, FMedSci; ✉ Department of Materials Science and Metallurgy, University of Cambridge, 27 Charles Babbage Road, Cambridge CB3 0FS (e-mail wb210@cam.ac.uk)

BONHAM, Nicholas; s of late Leonard Charles Bonham, and late Diana Maureen, *née* Magwood (d 1995); *b* 7 September 1948; *Educ* Trent Coll; *m* 7 April 1977 (m dis), Kaye Eleanor Ivett; 2 da (Katie b 1981, Jessica b 1982); m 2, 25 Sept 2003, Susan Angela Chester; *Career* dir Bonhams Group Ltd 1970–2004, md 1975–87, dep chm Bonhams 1987–2004, owner Nicholas Bonham Consultancy 2004–; chm: Noble Investments plc 2004–08, Corporate Communications 2005–08, Sugar Collection Inc 2006–; dir Hodie Ltd 2001–; Freeman City of London 1970, Master Worshipful Co of Pewterers 2009–10; *Recreations* sailing, tobogganing, skiing, scuba diving; *Clubs* South West Shingles Yacht, Acton Turville Bobsleigh, St Moritz Toboggan, Royal Thames Yacht, Royal Corinthian Yacht, Seaview Yacht, Kennel, Royal Yacht Squadron; *Style*— Nicholas Bonham, Esq; ✉ Prospect Quay, Point Pleasant, London SW18 1PS

BONHAM CARTER, Edward Henry; s of Hon Raymond Bonham Carter (d 2004), and Elena, *née* Propper de Callejon; bro of Helena Bonham Carter, CBE, *qv*; *b* 24 May 1960, London; *Educ* Harrow, Univ of Manchester; *m* Victoria; 2 s (Harry b 1996, Tobias b 2004), 1 da (Maud b 1999); *Career* fund mangr and analyst Schroders 1982–86, fund mangr and dir Electra Investment Tst 1986–94; Jupiter Asset Management: dir 1994–, chief investment offr 1999–2010, chief exec 2000–14, vice chm 2014–; non-exec dir Land Securities Gp plc 2014–, sr ind dir Land Securities Gp plc 2016–; memb Bd Investor Forum; *Recreations* ping pong, yoga; *Clubs* Brooks's; *Style*— Edward Bonham Carter, Esq; ✉ Jupiter Fund Management plc, The Zig Zag Building, 70 Victoria Street, London SW1E 6SQ (☎ 020 3817 1000)

BONHAM CARTER, Helena; CBE (2012); da of Hon Raymond Bonham Carter (d 2004), and Elena, *née* Propper de Callejon; sis of Edward Bonham Carter, *qv*; *b* 26 May 1966; *Educ* S Hampstead HS, Westminster; *Career* actress; Richard Harris Award (for outstanding contribution by an actor to Br film) Br Independent Film Award 2010; *Theatre* incl: Woman in White (Greenwich), The Chalk Garden (Windsor), The House of Bernarda Alba (Nottingham Playhouse), Barber of Seville (Palace Theatre Watford) 1992, Trelawney of the Wells (Triumph, Guildford, Brighton and West End); *Television* incl: The Vision (BBC) 1987, Arms and the Man (BBC) 1988, Beatrix Potter 1989, Dancing Queen (Granada) 1993, A Dark Adapted Eye (BBC) 1993, Absolutely Fabulous (BBC), Jo Brand Through the Cakehole (Noel Gay TV), Enid (Best Performance By An Actress Int Emmy Award 2010); *Radio* incl: The Reluctant Debutant, Marie Antoinette, The Seagull; *Film* incl: Lady Jane (Paramount) 1985, A Room with a View (Merchant Ivory) 1986, A Hazard of Hearts 1987, Francesco 1988, Hamlet (Nelson Ent) 1990, Where Angels Fear to Tread (Merchant Ivory) 1990, Howard's End (Merchant Ivory) 1990, Fatal Deception (Eliott Friedgen & Co) 1992, Frankenstein 1993, Butter (Sundial Pictures), The Gallery (Talking Pictures), Margaret's Museum (Glace Bay Pics Inc) 1994, Mighty Aphrodite (Sweetheart Prodn) 1995, Chinese Portraits (IMA Prodn) 1995, Twelfth Night 1996, The Wings of the Dove (Renaissance Films/Miramax, Oscar nomination for Best Actress 1998) 1996, The Revenger's Comedies (Artisan Films) 1996, The Theory of Flight 1997, Keep the Aspidistra Flying 1997, Fight Club 1998, Women Talking Dirty 1999, Carnivale 1999, Novocaine 2000, Planet of the Apes 2001, Till Human Voices Wake Us 2001, The Heart of Me 2001, Big Fish 2003, Wallace and Gromit: The Curse of the Were-Rabbit 2005, Corpse Bride 2005, Sweeney Todd: The Demon Barber of Fleet Street 2007, Terminator Salvation 2009, Harry Potter and the Half-Blood Prince 2009, Alice in Wonderland 2010, The King's Speech 2010 (Best Supporting Actress Br Independent Film Award 2010, Best Supporting Actress BAFTA 2011), Harry Potter and the Deathly Hallows: Part 1 2010, Harry Potter and the Deathly Hallows: Part 2 2011; *Style*— Miss Helena Bonham Carter, CBE

BONHAM-CARTER OF YARNBURY, Baroness (Life Peer UK 2004), of Yarnbury in the County of Wiltshire; Jane Mary Bonham Carter; da of Baron Bonham-Carter (Life Peer, d 1994), and Leslie Adrienne, da of late Condé Nast; *b* 20 October 1957, London; *Educ* St Paul's Girls' Sch, UCL (BA); *Partner* Baron Razzall, *qv*; *Career* prodr Panorama and Newsnight (both BBC) 1988–93, prog ed A Week in Politics (Channel 4) 1993–96, dir of communications Lib Dem Pty 1996–98 (memb Lib Dem Communications and Campaigns Ctee 1998–2006), ind prodr Brook Lapping Prodns (latterly part of Ten Alps plc) 1998–2010); sits as Lib Dem in House of Lords 2004–, memb Sub-Ctee on Home Affrs 2004–07, memb Select Ctee on the BBC Charter Review 2005–06, memb Select Ctee on Communications 2007–10; memb Cncl Britain in Europe 1998–2005 (memb Referendum Campaign Team 2004–05); memb Advsy Ctee Centre Forum (formerly Centre for Reform) 1998–; involvement with RAPt (Rehabilitation for Addicted Prisoners Trust) 1999–, memb Bd Nat Campaign for the Arts 2010–, tstee The Lowry 2011–; *Clubs* Groucho, Electric; *Style*— The Rt Hon the Lady Bonham-Carter of Yarnbury; ✉ House of Lords, London SW1A 1PW (e-mail bonhamcarterj@parliament.uk)

BONINGTON, Sir Christian John Storey (Chris); kt (1996), CVO (2010), CBE (1976), DL (Cumbria 2004); s of Charles Bonington (d 1983), and Helen Anne, *née* Storey (d 1999); *b* 6 August 1934; *Educ* UCS London, RMA Sandhurst; *m* 1962, (Muriel) Wendy, da of Leslie Marchant; 2 s (and 1 s decd); *Career* cmmnd RTR 1956, served in N Germany, Army Outward Bound Sch (mountaineering instr); mgmnt trainee Unilever 1961–62; freelance writer, photographer and mountaineer 1962–; non-exec dir Berghaus Ltd 1997– (chm 1998–); pres: LEPRA 1983–, Br Orienteering Fedn 1985–, Br Mountaineering Cncl 1988–91 (vice-pres 1976–79 and 1985–88), Nat Tst Lake Dist Appeal, Cncl for National Parks 1992–99, The Alpine Club 1996–98; chm Cncl of Mgmnt Mount Everest Fndn 1999–2001, chm Mountain Heritage Trust 2000–05; chllr Lancaster Univ 2005–; vice-pres: Army Mountaineering Assoc 1980–, Young Explorers' Trust, Youth Hostels Assoc, Br Lung Fndn; tstee: Outward Bound Tst, Himalayan Adventure Tst; hon fell UMIST 1976; Hon MA Univ of Salford 1973, Hon DSc Univ of Sheffield 1976, Hon DSc Lancaster Univ 1983, Hon Dr of Common Law Univ of Northumbria 1996, Hon DUniv Sheffield Hallam 1998, Hon DLitt Univ of Bradford 2002; Lawrence of Arabia Medal RSAA 1986, David Livingstone Medal RSGS 1991; FRGS (Founder's Medal 1974); *Ascents and Expeditions* first ascent: Annapurna II (26,041 feet) Nepal with Dick Grant 1960, Nuptse (25,850 feet), third peak of Everest with Sherpa Ang Pemba 1961, Central Pillar of Freney Mont Blanc with Whillans, Clough and Djuclosz 1961; first Br ascent North Wall of the Eiger with Clough 1962; first ascent: Central Tower of Paine Patagonia with Whillans 1963, Old Man of Hoy with Patey and Bailey 1966; ascent Sangay in Ecuador (highest active volcano in the world) 1966; ldr: Annapurna South Face Expdn 1970, Br Everest Expdn 1972; first ascent: Brammah (21,036 feet) Kashmir with Estcourt 1973, Changabang Garhwal Himalayas with Boysen, Haston, Scott and Sandhu 1974; ldr Br K2 Expdn 1978, climbing ldr Br Mount Kongur Expdn 1981 (first ascent with Boardman, Rouse and Tasker 1981), ldr Br Everest Expdn NE Ridge 1982, first ascent W Summit of Shivling (21,330 feet) Gangotri with Fotheringham 1983, first Br ascent (solo) Mount Vinson (highest in Antarctica) 1983, ascent of Mount Everest (29,028 feet) as a memb of 1985 Norwegian Everest Expdn, ldr Norwegian-Br Menlungtse Expdn 1987, ldr Tibet Expdn 1988 which made first ascent West Summit Menlungtse, first ascent W Ridge Panch Chuli II Kumoan Himalayas 1992, first ascent Meslin in Lemon Mountains 1993, first ascent Rangrik Rang Kinnaur Himalayas 1994, first ascent Drangnag-Ri 1995, ldr Sepu Kangri Expdn to Tibet 1997 and 1998, first ascent Danga II (6,194 metres) 2000, first ascent Jaraun Peak Kullu (5,205 metres) 2003; *Books* I Chose to Climb (autobiography, 1966), Annapurna South Face (1971), The Next Horizon (autobiography,

1973), Everest South West Face (1973), Changabang (jt author), Everest the Hard Way (1976), Quest for Adventure (1981), Kongur – China's Elusive Summit (1982), Everest – The Unclimbed Ridge (with Dr Charles Clarke, *qv*, 1983), The Everest Years (1986), Mountaineer – Thirty Years of Climbing on the World's Great Peaks (autobiography, 1989), The Climbers (1992), Sea, Ice and Rock (with Sir Robin Knox-Johnston, CBE, RD, *qv*, 1992), Great Climbs (gen ed, 1994), Tibet's Secret Mountain (with Dr Charles Clarke, 1999), Boundless Horizons (compendium of earlier autobiographies, 2000), Chris Bonington's Everest (2002), Everest Expeditions (2003); *Recreations* mountaineering, skiing, orienteering; *Clubs* Alpine (pres 1996–99), Climbers', Fell and Rock Climbing, Army and Navy, Travellers; *Style*— Sir Christian Bonington, CVO, CBE, DL; ✉ Badger Hill, Hesket Newmarket, Wigton, Cumbria CA7 8LA (☎ 01697 478286, e-mail chris@bonington.com, website www.bonington.com)

BONNEFOY, Olivier; s of Maurice Bonnefoy, and Elizabeth Durand; *b* 25 April 1973, Paris; *Educ* UN International School NY, St Andrews Univ; *m* 20 Oct 2010, Miriam, *née* Doering; 1 s (Louis-Balthazar b 21 Feb 2016); *Career* sr broker Fimat, Newedge and Société Générale 1994–2004, dir Gentlemen's Tonic 2004–, dir EvoShave Ltd 2013–; *Recreations* music, reading, skiing, travel, rugby; *Clubs* 12 Hay Hill, Eight Club; *Style*— Olivier Bonnefoy, Esq; ✉ 24 Cottesmore Gardens, London W8 5PR; Gentlemen's Tonic, 31a Bruton Place, London W1J 6NN (e-mail olivier@gentlemenstonic.com or o.bonnefoy@evoshave.com, websites www.gentlemenstonic.com and www.evoshave.com)

BONNET, Robert (Rob); s of Harold Geoffrey Bonnet (d 1990), of Beckenham, Kent, and Margaret Mary, *née* Beevers; *b* 27 September 1952; *Educ* Dulwich Coll, Univ of Sussex (BA); *m* 1980, Margaret Suzanne, *née* Harvey; 2 da (Clare Louise b 1981, Eleanor Jane b 1983); *Career* media buyer Benton and Bowles advtg agency 1976–77, disc jockey Evian-les-Bains 1977; BBC: station asst BBC Radio Brighton 1978–80, prodr BBC Radio Norfolk 1980–82, prodr BBC Radio Sport 1982–85, sports reporter BBC East (Norwich) 1985–87, sports corr BBC TV News 1989–95 (sports reporter 1987–89), sports presenter/reporter BBC TV News and Radio Sport 1995–; RTS Sports Report of the Year (for 9 O'Clock News coverage of Sydney winning Olympic Games for 2000) 1993; *Recreations* golf, travel; *Clubs* Studley Wood Golf; *Style*— Rob Bonnet, Esq; ✉ BBC TV News and Current Affairs, BBC Broadcasting House, Portland Place, W1A 1AA

BONNET, Tim; s of Maj-Gen Peter Bonnet, CB, MBE, of East Anstey, Devon, and Sylvia Mary, *née* Coy; *b* 6 June 1964; *Educ* Monkton Combe Sch, Kingston Business Sch (BA); *Career* with Aer Lingus gp of cos 1989–91; md then ceo TEQUILALondon, subsequently md of global clients BEING, chm Communications Div Creston plc 2011–; memb Business Advsy Gp Comic Relief; memb Bd Mktg Communications Consulting Assoc (MCCA) 2000; fndr and tstee Tusk Force; *Recreations* skiing, sailing, waterskiing, travel, tennis; *Style*— Tim Bonnet, Esq; ✉ Creston plc, 16 Charles II Street, London SW1Y 4QU

BONNEVILLE, Hugh Richard (ne Williams); s of John Pritchard Williams, FRCS, of W Sussex, and Patricia Adèle, *née* Freeman; *b* 10 November 1963; *Educ* Sherborne, CCC, Webber Douglas Acad; *m* 1998, Lulu Evans, *née* Conner; 1 s; *Career* actor; theatrical prodr: Beautiful Thing (Duke of York's Theatre), Half Time (Donmar Warehouse), Enemy of The People (Chichester); *Theatre* RNT roles incl: The Devil's Disciple, School for Scandal, Juno and the Paycock, School for Wives, Entertaining Strangers, Yerma; RSC (nominee Ian Charleson Award) incl: Hamlet, Amphibians, The Alchemist, 'Tis Pity She's a Whore, Two Gentlemen of Verona, The Virtuoso; other credits incl: Us and Them (Hampstead), Habeas Corpus (Donmar), My Night With Reg (Criterion), The Handyman (Chichester), Cloaca (Old Vic); rep work at Leicester Haymarket and Colchester Mercury; *Television* incl: Mosley, Madame Bovary, Take a Girl Like You, The Cazalets, Armadillo, Impact, Tipping the Velvet, Dr Zhivago, Daniel Deronda, The Commander, Love Again, Hear the Silence, The Robinsons, Courting Alex, Beau Brummell, Tsunami: The Aftermath, Five Days, Freezing, Diary of a Nobody, Filth: the Mary Whitehouse Story, Miss Austen Regrets, Lost in Austen, Bonekickers, Hunter, Ben Hur, Downton Abbey (nomination Best Actor in a Mini Series Golden Globe Award), Rev, Dr Who, Twenty Twelve (nomination Best Comedy Actor BAFTA), Getting On, Da Vinci's Demons, W1A; *Radio* incl: People Like Us, Married, Romantic Friction; *Film* incl: Frankenstein, Mansfield Park, Notting Hill, Tomorrow Never Dies, Blow Dry, Iris (BAFTA nomination Best Supporting Actor, Berlin Film Festival Award Best Young Talent), Conspiracy of Silence, Stage Beauty, Asylum, Underclassman, Piccadilly Jim, Man to Man, Four Last Songs, Scenes of a Sexual Nature, French Film, Knife Edge, Shanghai, From Time To Time, Glorious 39, Burke & Hare, Third Star, The Muppets...Again, The Monuments Men, Paddington, Hollow Crown, Viceroy's House; *Clubs* Garrick, Soho House; *Style*— Hugh Bonneville, Esq; ✉ c/o Gordon and French, 12–13 Poland Street, London W1F 8QB (☎ 020 7734 4818, fax 020 7734 4832, website www.hughbonneville.co.uk)

BONO, (Paul Hewson); Hon KBE (2007); s of Robert (Bob) Hewson, and Iris Hewson; *b* 10 May 1960; *Educ* Mount Temple Sch; *m* Alison (Ali); 2 da, 2 s; *Career* lead singer and fndr memb U2 1978– (with The Edge, Adam Clayton, and Larry Mullen, Jr, *qqv*); first U2 release U23 (EP) 1979; *Albums* Boy 1980, October 1981, War 1983 (entered UK chart at no 1), Under A Blood Red Sky 1983 (live album), The Unforgettable Fire 1984 (entered UK charts at no 1), Wide Awake in America 1985, The Joshua Tree 1987 (entered UK charts at no 1, fastest selling album ever in UK, Album of the Year Grammy Awards 1987), The Joshua Tree Singles 1988, Rattle & Hum 1988 (entered UK charts at no 1), Achtung Baby 1991, Zooropa 1993 (no 1 in 18 countries, Best Alternative Album Grammy Awards 1993), Pop 1997 (no 1), The Best of 1980–1990 1998, All That You Can't Leave Behind 2000 (no 1, Best Rock Album Grammy Awards 2002), The Best of 1990–2000 2002, How To Dismantle An Atomic Bomb 2004 (Album of the Year and Best Rock Album Grammy Awards 2006), U218 Singles 2006, No Line on the Horizon 2009; *Singles* incl: Fire 1981, New Year's Day (first UK Top Ten hit) 1983, Pride (In the Name of Love) 1984, Unforgettable Fire 1985, With or Without You 1987, I Still Haven't Found What I'm Looking For 1987, Where The Streets Have No Name 1987 (Best Video Grammy Awards 1989), Desire (first UK no 1 single) 1988 (Best Rock Performance Grammy Awards 1989), Angel of Harlem 1988, When Love Comes to Town 1989, All I Want Is You 1989, Night & Day (for AIDS benefit LP Red Hot & Blue) 1990, The Fly (UK no 1) 1991, Stay 1993, Discotheque (UK no 1) 1997, Staring at the Sun 1997, Sweetest Thing 1998, Beautiful Day (UK no 1) 2000 (Record of the Year, Song of the Year and Best Rock Performance by a Duo or Group with Vocal Grammy Awards 2001), Stuck in a Moment You Can't Get Out Of 2001 (Best Song by a Pop Duo or Group Grammy Awards 2002), Elevation 2001 (Best Rock Performance by a Duo or Group with Vocal Grammy Awards 2002), Walk On 2001 (Record of the Year Grammy Awards 2002), Electrical Storm 2002, Vertigo (UK no 1) 2004 (Best Rock Performance by a Duo or Group with Vocal, Best Rock Song and Best Short Form Music Video Grammy Awards 2004), Sometimes You Can't Make It On Your Own (UK no 1) 2005 (Song of the Year, Best Rock Duo or Group Vocal and Best Rock Song Grammy Awards 2006), City of Blinding Lights 2005 (Best Rock Song Grammy Awards 2006), All Because of You 2005, the Saints are Coming 2006, Window in the Skies 2007, Get on Your Boots 2009, Magnificent 2009, I'll Go Crazy If I Don't Go Crazy Tonight 2009, Ordinary Love 2013 (Best Original Song – Motion Picture Golden Globe Award 2014); also duet with Frank Sinatra I've Got You Under My Skin 1993; *Film* Rattle & Hum 1988; *Tours* incl: UK, US, Belgium and Holland 1980, UK, US, Ireland and Europe 1981–83, Aust, NZ and Europe 1984, A Conspiracy of Hope (Amnesty International Tour) 1986, Joshua Tree tour 1987 (Best Rock Performance Grammy Awards 1987), Rattle & Hum tour 1988, Zoo TV tour (played to 5 million people) 1992–93, Popmart tour 1997–98, Elevation tour 2001, Vertigo tour 2005; also appeared at: Live Aid 1985 (Best Live Aid Performance Rolling Stone Readers' Poll 1986), Self Aid Dublin, Smile Jamaica (Dominion Theatre, in aid of hurricane disaster relief) 1988, New Year's Eve concert Dublin (broadcast live to Europe and USSR) 1989; performed at venues incl: Wembley Stadium, Madison Square Garden NY, Longest Day Festival Milton Keynes Bowl, Croke Park Dublin, Sun Devil Stadium AZ; *Awards* Best Band Rolling Stone Readers' Poll 1986 (also jt winner Critics' Poll), Band of the Year Rolling Stone Writers' Poll 1984, Best International Act BPI Awards 1989 and 1990, Best Live Act BPI Awards 1993, Best International Group Brit Awards 2001, Outstanding Contribution to the Music Industry Brit Awards 2001, Outstanding Song Collection Ivor Novello Awards 2003, Golden Globe Award (for Hands that Built America) 2003, Oscar nomination (for Hands that Built America) 2003; *Publications* U2 by U2 (2006); *Style*— Bono; ✉ c/o Regine Moylett Publicity, 2C Woodstock Studios, Woodstock Grove, London W12 8LE (☎ 020 8749 7999)

BONSALL, David Charles; s of Leonard Dale Bonsall (d 1984), and Nellie Bonsall; *b* 26 July 1956; *Educ* Winchester, St John's Coll Cambridge (MA, LLM); *m* 11 Oct 1980, Margaret Ruth, da of Arthur George Shaw, OBE (d 2003), of St Albans, Herts; 2 da (Philippa Ruth b 25 Sept 1989, Kathryn Penelope b 20 June 1992); *Career* admitted slr 1981; ptnr Freshfields 1987–93 (articled clerk 1979–81), global head Asset Backed Fin UBS Ltd 1993–98, int head of asset securitisation CIBC World Markets 1998–2000, Bonsall Ptnrs 2001–; Trade Receivables Mgmnt Servs, dir AIG Trade Finance Ltd; Freeman Worshipful Co of Slrs; *Books* Securitisation (1990); *Recreations* golf, skiing, music; *Clubs* The Royal St George's Golf (capt 2003–04), R&A, Rye Golf, Sunningdale Golf, Royal Worlington and Newmarket Golf, Pine Valley Golf; *Style*— David Bonsall, Esq; ✉ 25 Margaretta Terrace, London SW3 5NU (☎ 020 7352 4902, e-mail dcbonsall@btinternet.com)

BONSOR, Anthony Miles; s of late David Victor Bonsor, and late Sheila Valerie, *née* Graham; *b* 3 May 1948; *Educ* Eton, Univ of Southampton (LLB); *m* 1980, Frances Elizabeth, da of David Bankes; 2 da (Sophie Elizabeth b 27 Aug 1982, Laura Frances b 17 June 1988), 1 s (Miles David b 12 Sept 1984); *Career* articled clerk Farrer & Co 1971–73, admitted slr 1974, Richards Butler & Co 1975–76; Denton Hall 1976–79, ptnr Hong Kong Office 1979–83, ptnr Denton Wilde Sapte (formerly Denton Hall) 1983–; memb Law Soc; *Style*— Anthony Bonsor, Esq; ✉ Denton Wilde Sapte, 1 Fleet Place, London EC4M 7WS (☎ 020 7242 1212, fax 020 7246 7777)

BONSOR, Michael John Kinsley; s of David Bonsor (d 2014), and Marion Bonsor, of Inverness; *Educ* Univ of Strathclyde (BA); *m* 14 Sept 2014, Andrew Pike; *Career* Bristol Lounge Four Seasons Boston 2000–02, dir of restaurants and bars Pierre Hotel New York 2005, private events dir Four Seasons Hotel Toronto 2005–06, asst dir of food and beverage Four Seasons Hotel New York 2006–09, food and beverage mangr Claridge's 2009–11, hotel operations mangr 2011–13, hotel mangr Rosewood London 2013–; *Recreations* fashion, gardening, music, opera, skiing, tennis, travel; *Style*— Michael Bonsor, Esq; ✉ Twitter @MichaelBonsor

BONSOR, Sir Nicholas Cosmo; 4 Bt (UK 1925), of Kingswood, Epsom, Surrey; DL (Bucks 2007); s of Sir Bryan Cosmo Bonsor, 3 Bt, MC, TD (d 1977), and Elizabeth, *née* Hambro (d 1995); *b* 9 December 1942; *Educ* Eton, Keble Coll Oxford (MA); *m* 4 Sept 1969, Hon Nadine Marisa Lampson, da of 2 Baron Killearn (d 1996); 3 da (Sacha Henrietta b 1975, Elizabeth Nadine, Mary Catherine (twins) b 1987), 2 s (Alexander Cosmo b 1976, James Charles b 1983); *Heir* s, Alexander Bonsor; *Career* served The Royal Bucks Yeo (RA TA) 1964–69; called to the Bar Inner Temple 1967; in practice 1967–75 and 2003–11, jt head of chambers 2004–; MP (Cons): Nantwich 1979–83, Upminster 1983–97; min of state FCO 1995–97; vice-chm Tourism Sub-Ctee 1980–83, vice-chm Cons Parly Foreign Affrs Ctee 1981–83, vice-chm Cons Parly Defence Ctee 1987–90, chm Commons Select Ctee on Defence 1992–95, memb Select Ctee on Broadcasting 1992–95, memb Liaison Ctee 1992–95, vice-chm Cons Parly Constitutional Ctee 1992–95; chm: Verdin Tst for the Mentally Handicapped 1982–91, Cyclotron Tst for Cancer Treatment 1984–92 (pres 1992–), Food Hygiene Bureau Ltd 1986–95, Br Field Sports Soc 1988–94, Baronets' Tst 1993–95, Leadership (UK) Ltd 2000–05, You to Coach plc 2000–03; dir Govt Rels Crosby MTM 1998–2003; memb Cncl: Lloyd's 1987–92, RUSI 1992–95 and 1997–99, China Br Business Cncl 2000–03; chm Standing Cncl of the Baronetage 1990–93 (vice-chm 1987–89); dir: Blue Note Mining.ca 2007–09, London Mining plc 2008–, Tomco plc 2009–, Clinical Metallon Corporation plc 2011–; Hon Col 60 Signals Sqdn (V) 2000–10; chm Bucks RFCA 2001–10; Freeman City of London 1988; FRSA 1970; *Recreations* sailing, military history, shooting; *Clubs* White's, Royal Yacht Sqdn, House of Commons Yacht (Cdre 1985–86), Pratt's; *Style*— Sir Nicholas Bonsor, Bt; ✉ c/o White's Club, St James's, London SW1A 1JG (e-mail bonsors@yahoo.co.uk)

BONSOR, (Angus) Richard; s of Sir Bryan Cosmo Bonsor, 3 Bt, MC, TD (d 1977), of Leighton Buzzard, Beds, and Elizabeth, *née* Hambro (d 1995); *b* 3 February 1947; *Educ* Eton, Keble Coll Oxford (BA); *m* 14 Jan 1971, Susan Anne, da of David Henry Lewis Wigan, of Diss, Norfolk; 2 s (Rupert James b 26 Sept 1974, Edward Richard b 16 July 1976), 1 da (Clare Lucinda b 3 Sept 1981); *Career* ptnr Rowe & Pitman 1978 (joined 1968); dir: S G Warburg Securities 1986, associated to Matheson Securities 1989–92, UBS Ltd 1992–95, J O Hambro Investment Management 1995–; MSI; *Recreations* golf, racquets; *Clubs* White's, Turf, Pratt's, Sunningdale, Royal West Norfolk Golf; *Style*— Richard Bonsor, Esq; ✉ J O Hambro Investment Management, 21 St James's Square, London SW1Y 4HB

BONYNGE, Richard; AC (2012, AO 1983), CBE (1977); s of C A Bonynge, of Epping, NSW; *b* 29 September 1930; *Educ* Sydney HS, Sydney Conservatorium, Royal Coll of Music; *m* 1954, Dame Joan Sutherland (d 2010); 1 s; *Career* opera conductor; official debut as conductor Santa Cecilia Orch Rome 1962; artistic dir: Sutherland/Williamson Int Grand Opera Co Aust 1965, Vancouver Opera 1974–77; musical dir Aust Opera 1976–86; conducted many operas in: Metropolitan Opera, San Francisco, Chicago Lyric Opera, Teatro Liceo, Barcelona, Royal Opera House Covent Garden, San Diego Opera, Sydney Opera, Teatro Colòn Buenos Aires, Teatro Real Madrid, Teatro San Carlo Naples, San Carlos Lisbon, Vienna; has made numerous recordings of opera and ballet; Socio d'onore Royal Accademia Filarmonica di Bologna 2007; Commandeur L'Ordre National des Arts et des Lettres France 1989; *Style*— Richard Bonynge, Esq, AC, CBE; ✉ c/o Ingpen & Williams Ltd, 7 St Georges Court, 131 Putney Bridge Road, London SW15 2PA

BOOBIER, Nigel John; s of Derek James Boobier, of Exeter, Devon, and Ruth Mary, *née* Gresswell; *b* Okehampton, Devon; *Educ* Exeter Coll, Univ of Birmingham (LLB); *m* 28 Dec 1991, Michelle Maria-Theresa, *née* Gore; 1 da (Chloe Victoria), 3 s (Joseph Michael, Laurence Daniel, Edward James); *Career* slr; trainee slr Anstey Sargent and Probert 1992–95, slr Dibb Lupton Broomhead 1995–97; Osborne Clarke LLP: slr and assoc 1997–2002, ptnr 2002–; licensed insolvency practitioner 1998, regular speaker at conferences on restructuring and insolvency, contrib to jls on restructuring and insolvency; memb Law Soc; fell Assoc of Business Recovery Professionals (former chm S Wales and SW branch); *Recreations* family, cricket, rugby, food and drink; *Style*— Nigel Boobier, Esq; ✉ Osborne Clarke LLP, 2 Temple Back East, Temple Quay, Bristol BS1 6EG (☎ 0117 917 4164, fax 0117 917 4165, e-mail nigel.boobier@osborneclarke.com)

BOOKBINDER, Alan Peter; s of Geoffrey Ellis Bookbinder (d 1990), and Bridget Mary, *née* Doran (d 2006); *b* 16 March 1956; *Educ* Manchester Grammar, St Catherine's Coll Oxford (BA), Voronezh Univ (Br Cncl scholar), Harvard Univ (MA); *m* Victoria, *née* Ambery-Smith; 1 s (Joe Ambery b 9 June 1993), 1 da (Holly Ambery b 7 June 1996); *Career* BBC:

joined as trainee asst prodr 1980, asst prodr (current affrs) 1982–85, prodr (documentaries) 1985–86, series prodr (documentaries) 1986–92, series ed Under the Sun 1992–96, exec prodr (science) 1997–2001, head of religion and ethics 2001–06; dir Sainsbury Family Charitable Tsts 2006–; memb Advertising Standards Authy Cncl 2012–; cmmr Marshall Aid Commemoration Cmmn 2016–; contrib to newspapers and magazines; *Books* Comrades (1985); *Style—* Alan Bookbinder, Esq; ✉ Sainsbury Family Charitable Trusts, The Peak, 5 Wilton Road, London SW1V 1AP (☎ 020 7410 7035, e-mail alan.bookbinder@sfct.org.uk)

BOOKER, Christopher John Penrice; s of late John Mackarness Booker, of Shillingstone, Dorset, and Margaret Booker (d 1991); *b* 7 October 1937; *Educ* Shrewsbury, CCC Cambridge; *m* 1, 1963 (m dis), Hon Mrs Emma C Tennant, *qv*; m 2, 1972 (m dis), Christine Verity; m 3, 1979, Valerie, da of late Dr M S Patrick, OBE; 2 s; *Career* author, journalist and broadcaster; Liberal News 1960, jazz critic Sunday Telegraph 1961, ed Private Eye 1961–63 (contrib 1965–); resident scriptwriter: That Was The Week That Was 1962–63, Not So Much A Programme 1963–64; contrib Daily Mail 1969–, columnist Sunday Telegraph 1990–; former contrib: Spectator, Daily Telegraph (Way of the World column as Peter Simple II 1987–90); wrote extensively on property devpt, planning and housing 1972–77, TV prog City of Towers: the Rise and Fall of a Twentieth Century Dream (1979); memb Cowgill Enquiry into post-war repatriations from Austria 1986–90; *Books* The Neophiliacs: A Study of the Revolution in English Life in the 50's and 60's (1969), Goodbye London (with Candida Lycett-Green, 1973), The Booker Quiz (1976), The Seventies (1980), The Games War: A Moscow Journal (1981), Repatriations from Austria in 1945 (jtly, 1990), The Mad Officials (with Richard North, 1994), The Castle of Lies: Why Britain Must Get Out of Europe (1996), A Looking Glass Tragedy (1997), The Great Deception: A Secret History of the European Union (with Richard North, 2003), The Seven Basic Plots: Why Do We Tell Stories? (2004), The Great Deception: Can the European Union Survive? (2005), Scared to Death: From BSE to Global Warming, How Scares Are Costing Us The Earth (2007); contrib to Private Eye anthologies incl John Major Diaries and St Albion's Parish News; *Recreations* the psychology of storytelling, nature, music, playing village cricket, teasing global warmists; *Style—* Christopher Booker, Esq; ✉ The Old Rectory, Litton, Bath, Somerset (☎ 01761 241263)

BOOKER, Michael William; s of Donald Booker, of Great Longstone, Derbys, and Mary Elizabeth, *née* Trickett; *b* 5 October 1955; *Educ* King Edward VII Sch Sheffield, Univ of Liverpool Med Sch (BM BCh); *m* 1, 1979 (m dis 1991), Judith Anne, da of Donald Ryder; 2 da (Laurie Anne b 15 Sept 1982, Chloe Maxine b 5 June 1985); m 2, 1994, Elizabeth Mary, da of Gordon Ball; 2 s (James Michael b 14 April 1996, Thomas William b 3 Nov 1998); *Career* research fell then lectr in obstetrics and gynaecology King's Coll Sch of Med and Dentistry 1984–89; conslt in obstetrics and gynaecology: Singapore Gen Hosp 1989–90, Croydon Univ Hosp Croydon 1990– (estab centre for reproductive med and in-vitro fertilization and embryo transfer clinic (transport IVF prog) 1992); district tutor (Croydon Health Dist) RCOG; author of numerous contribs to med jls; memb: BMA 1978, RSM 1988, AFS 1988, BFS 1991, ESHRE 1994, FRCOG; *Recreations* windsurfing, scuba diving, jazz; *Style—* Michael Booker, Esq; ✉ Croydon University Hospital, London Road, Croydon, Surrey CR7 7YE (☎ 020 8655 5550, fax 020 8655 5599, e-mail mbooker@uk-consultants.co.uk)

BOON, Dr Nicholas Antony; s of Capt John Nicholas Boon, MC, of Loudwater, nr Rickmansworth, Herts, and Doreen Myrtle, *née* Francke; *b* 31 December 1950; *Educ* Canford, Gonville & Caius Coll Cambridge (MA, MB BChir), Middx Hosp Med Sch (MD); *m* 19 May 1979, (Grace) Anne, da of Prof W B Robertson, of Wimbledon; 2 da (Victoria b 11 Aug 1982, Sarah Jane b 15 March 1984); *Career* clinical lectr and sr registrar John Radcliffe Hosp Oxford 1983–86, conslt cardiologist Royal Infirmary of Edinburgh 1986–2010, hon reader Univ of Edinburgh 2005–15 (hon sr lectr 1986–2005); pres Br Cardiac Soc 2007–09; FRCP 1988, FESC 1996, FACC 2009; *Publications* author of numerous scientific pubns and contrib to various med textbooks incl Oxford Textbook of Medicine and Davidson's Principles and Practice of Medicine (co-ed); *Recreations* golf, skiing; *Clubs* Hon Co of Edinburgh Golfers; *Style—* Dr Nicholas Boon; ✉ 4 Latimer Chase, Chorleywood, Hertfordshire WD3 6FA (☎ 01923 593641, e-mail boons79@gmail.com)

BOONHAM, Nigel Francis; *b* 30 May 1953, Aldershot, Herts; *Educ* Kent Coll Canterbury, Brighton Tech Coll, Woolwich Adult Educn Inst; *m* Mayuri; 1 da (Athena Akhilandeshwari b 2012); *Career* sculptor; early career as asst to Oscar Nemon; commissions incl: portrait sculptures and monuments to John Hunter 1979, Lord Runcie 1981, Dr Joseph Needham 1985, Diana Princess of Wales 1991, Archbishop Daniel Mannix and Boadicea 1999, Dame Cicely Saunders OM 2001, The Basil Hume Memorial Garden and Statue (unveiled by HM The Queen) 2002; work features in collections incl: Nat Portrait Gall, Manchester Free Trade Hall, Int Courts of Justice The Hague, Worshipful Co of Goldsmiths, Entombed Christ Altar, Cathedra and Sanctuary Screens St Mary's Cathedral Sydney (consecrated by HH Pope Benedict XVI 2008), Risen Christ and Mary Magdalene statues Carrara marble St Mary's Cathedral Sydney 2010, Lectern of the Apostles (polished brass) and Risen Christ (bronze) (Chapel of Domus Australia Rome) 2011, Sir Leo Schultz exterior niche of the Guildhall (Kingston upon Hull) 2011, Ginger McCain (Aintree Racecourse) 2012, John Donne Meml (St Pauls Churchyard) 2012, monument to the First World Cup winners (bronze) (West Auckland Co Durham); pres Soc of Portrait Sculptors 2004–09 (memb 1996–, vice-pres 1999–2004); Jean Masson Davidson Medal Soc of Portrait Sculptors 2012; FRBS 1983 (ARBS 1980); *Exhibitions* Royal Acad Summer Exhbn 1975 and 1976, Soc of Portrait Sculptors 1976, 1977 and annually 1996–2013, Portraits of Today (Nat Portrait Gall London) 1981, Phoenix Gall Lavenham 1982, Royal Soc of Br Sculptors (Scone Palace Scotland) 1983, Vauxhall Studio London 1984, Notting Hill London 1989 and 1990, 20th Century Portraits (Nat Portrait Gall) 1995, Markovitch Gall London 1996 and 1997, Addison-Ross Gall London 1998, In This Sacred Place (SPS Winchester Cathedral Exhbn) 2012; *Recreations* books, music, sculpture, dance; *Style—* Nigel Boonham, FRBS; ✉ 5 Havelock Walk, Forest Hill, London SE23 3HG (☎ 020 8291 3604, e-mail nigelboonham@hotmail.com, website www.boonham.com)

BOORMAN, John; CBE (1994); s of George Boorman, and Ivy, *née* Chapman; *b* 18 January 1933; *Educ* Salesian Coll Chertsey; *Career* film director; contrib articles to Manchester Guardian and various magazines 1950–54, successively broadcaster, critic BBC radio, film ed ITN London 1955–58, dir/prodr Southern TV 1958–60, head of documentaries BBC TV Bristol (dir The Citizens series and The Newcomers documentaries) 1960–64, Lee Marvin: A Personal Portrait by John Boorman 1998; fell BAFTA 2004; *Films* Catch us if you can 1965, Point Blank 1967, Hell in the Pacific 1968, Leo the Last 1969, Deliverance 1970, Zardoz 1973, The Heretic 1976, Excalibur 1981, The Emerald Forest 1985, Hope and Glory 1987, Where the Heart is 1989, I Dreamt I Woke Up 1991, Beyond Rangoon 1994, Two Nudes Bathing 1995, The General 1997 (Best Film Evening Standard British Film Awards 1999, Best Dir Cannes), The Tailor of Panama 2000, Country of my Skull 2003, The Tiger's Tail 2007, Queen and Country 2014; *Books* The Legend of Zardoz (1973), Money into Light (1985), Hope and Glory (1987), Projections 1–7 (1992), Projections 1–13 (1992–1999), Adventures of a Suburban Boy (2003); *Style—* John Boorman, Esq, CBE

BOOTH; *see also:* Gore-Booth

BOOTH, His Hon Judge Alan James; s of His Hon James Booth (d 2000), and Joyce Doreen, *née* Mather; *b* 18 January 1955, Stockport, Gtr Manchester; *Educ* Bolton Sch, Selwyn Coll Cambridge; *m* 4 April 1983, Anne Lesley, *née* Binns; 1 da (Jane Katherine b 29 March 1987), 1 s (Charles Edmund b 13 Nov 1988); *Career* called to the Bar 1978; barr Deans Court Chambers Manchester 1979–2009, asst recorder 1996, recorder 2000, circuit judge (Northern Circuit) 2009– (memb 1978, jr 1981); memb Family Law Bar Assoc 1983– (chm Manchester 2006–09); memb Water Polo Ctee Br Swimming 2008–13, former chm Technical Water Polo Ctee and memb Bd NW Region Amateur Swimming Assoc, chm GB Men's Water Polo Mgmnt Gp 2013–14; *Recreations* sport; *Clubs* Hawks' (Cambridge), Sale Harriers, City of Manchester Water Polo; *Style—* His Hon Judge Booth; ✉ Blackburn County Court, 64 Victoria Street, Blackburn BB1 6DJ (e-mail hhjudge.booth@judiciary.gsi.gov.uk)

BOOTH, Anthony John; CBE (1993); s of Benjamin Booth, and Una Lavinia, *née* Cumberpatch; *b* 18 March 1939; *Educ* Bungay GS, Univ of London (BSc (Eng)), Ealing Coll (DMS); *m* 4 Sept 1965, Elspeth Marjorie, da of Rev Francis Stewart Gordon Fraser, MBE, TD (d 1962); 1 da (Caroline Ruth b 1968), 1 s (Richard Mark b 1970); *Career* British Telecom (formerly GPO): scientific asst Res Dept PO 1957, exec engr then sr exec engr Telecom HQ 1965–71, asst staff engr Central HQ Appts 1971–74, head of section and div External Telecom Exec 1974–78, head of div Telecommunications HQ 1978–79, dir of int networks 1979–80, regnl dir London Region 1980–83, md British Telecom International 1983–91, corp dir British Telecommunications plc 1984–94, md BT Business Communications 1991–92, md BT Special Businesses and International Affairs 1992–94; chm Ericsson Ltd 1994–2002; dir RB Phusion Ltd 2001–; dir and tstee AQA (Assessment and Qualifications Alliance Ltd) 2000–06 (vice-chm 2003–06); memb: Regnl Affairs Ctee C of C and Industry 1980–84, London Regnl Ctee CBI 1982–84, Overseas Ctee CBI 1984–94; tstee AQA Pension Scheme 2006–11; govr Ealing Coll 1989–91, chm Bd of Govrs Thames Valley Univ 1992–96; memb: Bd HEFCE 1996–2001, Cncl Univ of Surrey 1998–2004, Bd of Companions CMI 1999–2006; chm: SE Regn RLSS UK 1997–2001, IOD W Surrey 1999–2002 (pres 2002–11); memb Guild of Freemen of the City of London 1982; Hon DPhil Thames Valley Univ 1995; CEng 1985, FIEE 1985, CCMI (CIMgt 1986), FRSA 1991, FInstD 1997; *Recreations* opera, golf; *Clubs* Caledonian, Camberley Heath Golf; *Style—* Anthony Booth, Esq, CBE; ✉ 63 Hillsborough Park, Camberley, Surrey GU15 1HG

BOOTH, Cherie; CBE (2013), QC (1995); da of Anthony George Booth, of Co Cavan, Ireland, and Gale, *née* Smith; *b* 23 September 1954, Bury; *Educ* Seafield Convent GS Liverpool, LSE (LLB); *m* 29 March 1980, Rt Hon Tony Blair, *qv*, s of Leo Charles Lynton Blair; 3 s (Euan Anthony b 19 Jan 1984, Nicholas John b 6 Dec 1985, Leo George b 20 May 2000), 1 da (Kathryn Hazel b 2 March 1988); *Career* called to the Bar Lincoln's Inn 1976 (Hardwicke and Kennedy scholar, Ede & Ravenscroft Prize for highest bar finals results, bencher); in practice: Alexander Irvine (now Baron Irvine of Lairg, PC (Life Peer), *qv*) 1976–77, New Court Chambers 1977–91, Gray's Inn Square Chambers 1991–2000, Matrix Chambers 2000–14, Chambers of Miss C Booth, QC 2014–; recorder 1999–2015 (asst recorder 1996–99); chair Omnia Strategy LLP; chair IT Ctee Bar Cncl 1991, vice-chair (IT) Bar Services and Information Technology Ctee 1995–96, chair Bar Conf 1997; Parly candidate (Lab) Thanet North Gen Election 1983; hon chair World Justice Project; memb Advsy Bd Citizenship Fndn; pres Loomba Fndn, vice-pres 4Children, St Joseph's Hospice and Family Mediators Assoc, tstee Citizenship Fndn, ambass London 2012, hon vice-pres Barnardo's, fndr Cherie Blair Fndn for Women, patron of numerous charities; Legal Personality of the Year (The Lawyer magazine) 1997, Cwlth Award for Distinguished Service 2011; chllr emeritus and hon fell Liverpool John Moores Univ, chllr Asian Univ for Women Chittagong Bangladesh 2011, visiting prof of law Open Univ 2011, visiting prof of law St Mary Univ 2015; hon fell LSE, govr and hon fell Open Univ; Hon LLD: Univ of Westminster, Univ of Liverpool 2003, Western Univ Canada 2013; Hon DLitt UMIST 2003, hon doctorate Ben Gurion Univ of the Negev 2013; Freeman City of London 2006; hon bencher King's Inn Dublin 2002; hon fell Inst of Advanced Legal Studies, FRSA; *Books* The Goldfish Bowl (jtly, 2004), Speaking for Myself (2008); *Recreations* reading, keeping fit, the arts, spending as much time as possible with my children; *Style—* Ms Cherie Booth, CBE, QC; ✉ PO Box 60519, London W2 7JU

BOOTH, Prof Sir Clive; kt (2003); s of Henry Booth and Freda Frankland; *b* 18 April 1943; *Educ* King's Sch Macclesfield, Trinity Coll Cambridge (MA), Univ of Calif Berkeley (Harkness fell, MA, PhD); *m* 1969, Margaret Sardeson; *Career* joined DES 1965, princ private sec to Sec of State for Educn and Sci 1975–77, asst sec 1977–81; dep dir Plymouth Poly 1981–84, memb HM Inspectorate DES 1984–86, vice-chllr Oxford Brookes Univ (formerly Oxford Poly) 1986–97; asst cmmr Nat Cmmn on Educn 1992–94, chm Teacher Trg Agency 1997–2003, sr advsr to Br Cncl 1997–2003; chm Review Body for Nurses and Professions Allied to Med 1998–2004, dep chm SE England Devpt Agency (SEEDA) 1999–2004, chm Central Police Trg and Devpt Authy (CENTREX) 2002–, interim chm (overseeing merger) New Opportunities Fund and Community Fund 2004–, chm Big Lottery Fund 2004–; memb: Governing Cncl SRHE 1981–90, Advsy Ctee Brunel Univ Educn Policy Centre 1986–90, Computer Bd for Univs and Res Cncls 1987–92, CNAA Ctee for Info and Devpt Servs 1987–91, Fulbright Academic Administrators Selection Ctee 1988–97, Br Cncl Ctee for Int Cooperation in Higher Educn 1988–97, Cncl for Indust and Higher Educn 1990, Fulbright Cmmn 1992–97, Oxford Inst of Nursing Bd 1991–96, Cwlth Scholarships Cmmn 1992–97, UK ERASMUS Cncl 1992–97, Br Cncl Bd 1995–97, LSC for Milton Keynes, Oxon and Bucks 2001–05; dir: Thames Action Resource Gp for Educn and Trg 1986–97, Thames Valley Technol Centre 1989–97, Oxfordshire Business Link 1995–2003; chm: Oxfordshire Learning Partnership Ltd 1999–, Oxfordshire Connexions Mgmnt Ctee 2000–03, The PhD Consortium 2000–04, The Big Lottery Fund Bd 2004–10; vice-chm Ctee of Vice-Chllrs and Princs 1992–94; govr Headington and Wheatley Park Schs, jt ed Higher Educn Quarterly 1986, memb Ed Bd Oxford Review of Educn 1990–2015; tstee Lloyds TSB Fndn for England and Wales 2011–, chm Berks Bucks and Oxon Wildlife Tst 2011–, vice chm Oxford Civic Soc 2012–; Leverhulme res fell 1983; *Recreations* cycling, walking, bridge, opera, gardening; *Clubs* RSA; *Style—* Prof Sir Clive Booth; ✉ 43 St John Street, Oxford OX1 2LH (☎ 01865 557762, mobile 07979 590820, e-mail boothclive99@gmail.com)

BOOTH, Dr (Vernon Edward) Hartley; OBE (2010); s of Vernon William Hartley Booth, and Eilish, *née* Morrow; *b* 17 July 1946; *Educ* Queens Coll Taunton, Univ of Bristol (LLB), Downing Coll Cambridge (LLM, Dip Int Law, PhD); *m* 30 July 1977, Adrianne Claire Cranefield, da of Knivett Garton Cranefield, DFC; 1 da (Emily Claire Hartley b 1982), 2 s (Peter Toby Hartley b 1985, Thomas Edward Hartley b 1988); *Career* called to the Bar Inner Temple; practising 1970–84, special advsr to PM and memb 10 Downing St Policy Unit 1984–88, chief exec and md Br Urban Devpt Ltd 1988–90, co-fndr and first chm British Urban Regeneration Assoc 1990–92; Parly candidate (Cons) Hackney and Stoke Newington 1983, MP (Cons) Finchley 1992–97; PPS to: Rt Hon Douglas Hogg, QC, MP 1992–94, Eric Forth, MP 1996–97; memb: Select Ctee on European Legislation 1992, Select Ctee on Home Affairs 1992, Euro Standing Ctee 1995–97; chm: Urban Affrs Ctee 1994–97, All-Pty Central Asia Ctee 1995–97; dir Canford Gp plc 1978–; conslt: Berwin Leighton 1991–2000, Fenners Solicitors 2001–03, Maclay Murray Spens 2003–, Dentons 2007–; fndr dir Sustainable Village Ltd 2004 (currently dep chm); external dir Edexcel Fndn 1999–2002; co-chm Uzbek br Trade Cncl 1998–2012; former leader writer Daily Telegraph; vice-pres RLSS; pres Resources for Autism 2004– (co-fndr and first chm 1997–2003); chm Br Uzbek Soc 2001–; *Books* British Extradition Law and Procedure (volume I 1980, volume II 1981), Victims of Crime (1992), Into the Voids (1993), There Goes the Neighbourhood (1994), Return Ticket (1994); *Style—* Dr Hartley

Booth, OBE; ✉ c/o Gregg Latchams, Milner House, 14 Manchester Square, London W1U 3PP

BOOTH, John David Sebastian; s of D Booth, of Clayton-le-Moors, Lancs; b 25 July 1958, Lancs; *Educ* Merton Coll Oxford (MA); *Career* ptnr Hutton Int Assocs 1986, sr vice-pres Prudential Securities 1988, md Bankers Tst Int plc 1992; chair: Integrated Asset Mgmnt plc, Maintel Hldgs plc, London Theatre Co, Natilik Ltd; chm and co-fndr Link Gp plc; various non-exec directorships; memb: Chllr's Ct of Benefactors Univ of Oxford, Chllr's Forum Univ of the Arts London, Archbishops' Cncl Finance Ctee 1999–2011, Gen Synod of Church of England 1999–, Crown Appointments Cmmn 2004, Crown Nominations Cmmn 2013; chm Chichester Diocesan Bd of Finance; govr Pusey House Oxford, chm of govrs Byam Shaw Sch of Art 1996–2006, tstee Pallant House Gallery (currently chm of tstees), tstee of various charities incl Chatsworth House Tst; Guardian of Shrine of Our Lady of Walsingham 2000–; hon fell: St Stephen's House Oxford, Merton Coll Oxford; FRSA 2010; Knight of the Order of St Lazarus of Jerusalem (KLJ) 2010; *Recreations* collecting modern British art, opera; *Clubs* Buck's; *Style*— John Booth, Esq; ✉ 8 St Paul's Court, 56 Manchester Street, London W1U 3AF (☎ 07767 474343, e-mail j@johnbooth.com)

BOOTH, Michael John; QC (1999); s of Eric Charles Booth of Hale, and Iris, *née* Race; b 24 May 1958; *Educ* Manchester Grammar (scholarship), Trinity Coll Cambridge (open scholarship, MA); *Family* 1 da (Abigail b 22 July 1992), 2 s (Henry b 31 Oct 1994, Freddie b 27 Oct 1997); partner, Geraldine Riley; *Career* called to the Bar Lincoln's Inn 1981 (bencher), memb Bar Cayman Islands; *Recreations* walking, reading, swimming, football, wine, history in general, Alexander the Great in particular; *Style*— Michael J Booth, Esq, QC; ✉ 13 Old Square Chambers, 13–14 Lincoln's Inn, London WC2A 3UE (☎ 020 7831 4445, fax 020 7841 5825, e-mail boothqc@leadingcounsel.co.uk)

BOOTH, Peter John Richard; s of Eric Albert Booth, and Edith, *née* Brown; b 27 March 1949; *Educ* Benton Park Secdy Modern Sch; m 27 July 1970, Edwina Ivy; 3 s (Peter Tristan b 24 Jan 1971, Jonathen Richard b 11 Sept 1972, James Lee b 19 Sept 1978); *Career* Dyers Operative 1964; Nat Union of Dyers Bleachers and Textile Workers: dist offr 1973, nat res offr 1975, nat organiser 1980; TGWU: joined 1982, nat trade gp organiser 1982, textile nat gp sec 1986–93, nat organiser (mfrg) 1999–; pres Int Textile Garment & Leather Workers' Fedn 1996–2004 (memb Exec Ctee); vice-pres Br Textile Confedn 1989–97, vice-pres European Trade Union Ctee of Textiles Clothing and Leather; dir: Apparel Knitting and Textiles Alliance 1989–, Man-Made Fibres Industry Trg Advsy Bd 1986–, Nat Textile Trg Gp 1988–; chm Carpet Industry Trg Cncl 1986–; memb: Presidium 1982–96, Textiles Clothing and Footwear Industries Ctee TUC 1976–, Confedn of Br Wool Textiles Trg Bd 1986–, Health and Safety Ctee Cotton and Allied Textiles Industries Advsy Ctee, Health and Safety Cmmn Texile Industry Advsy Ctee, Textiles Industry Advsy Cmmn (TEXIAC), Skillfast UK, Textile Clothing and Strategy Gp, DTI Manufacturing Forum, TUC Manufacturing Task Gp, Exec Ctee Gen Fedn of Trade Unions 2003–, delg EU Consultative Cmmn on Industrial Change 2006–; tstee Cotton War Meml Tst; Gold Medal TGWU 2007, Gold Badge Int Textile Garment and Leather Workers Fedn 2008 FRSA; *Books* The Old Dog Strike (1985); *Recreations* walking, gardening, dominoes, chess; *Clubs* Yeadon Trades Hall; *Style*— Peter Booth, Esq

BOOTH, Robin Godfrey; s of Frank Booth (d 1990), of York, and Dorothy, *née* Johnson; b 11 August 1942; *Educ* Winchester, King's Coll Cambridge (DipArch, MA), Univ of Edinburgh (MSc); m 10 July 1971, Katherine, da of Arthur Middleton, of Lynchburg, VA; 1 da (Emily b 1974), 1 s (Richard b 1977); *Career* architect and town planner; master planner and job architect Devpt Dept of Architecture and Civic Design GLC 1965–71, architect planner for South West Area Traffic and Devpt Branch GLC 1971–72, project architect for New County HQ for Hereford-Worcester (RIBA commendation 1978) Robert Matthew Johnson-Marshall & Partners 1972–76, sr architect concerned with design of various projects overseas and in London John S Bonnington Partnership 1976–80, project architect then ptnr for Standard Chartered Bank's HQ (special award Marble Architectural Awards West Europe 1987), Fitzroy Robinson Ltd 1980–2001 (formerly ptnr then dir Thames Exchange and Scottish Widows London Wall projects and dir i/c of works on the Union Bank of Switzerland in London and Barclaycard HQ Northampton), architect dir Building Design Partnership London Corp Gp 2001–; author of various articles in Architects Jl and RIBA Jl; Plasterers' trophy for fibrous plasterwork 1985, Br Assoc of Landscape Industries principal award for interior landscaping 1986; RIBA 1970 (memb Eastern Regions Competitions Ctee 1979–80), MRTPI 1978; *Books* Neufert: Architectural Data (contrib 1980 edn); *Recreations* music, theatre, travel, photography; *Clubs* Baconian Society (St Albans); *Style*— Robin Booth; ✉ Robin Booth Architect and Planning Consultant, 23 Hill Street, St Albans, Hertfordshire AL3 4QS (☎ and fax 01727 856504)

BOOTH-JONES, Christopher Charles; s of Lt Col C E Booth-Jones; b 4 October 1943, Castle Cary, Somerset; *Educ* Dover Coll, RAM (ARAM); m 15 April 1995, Leonora Lane, da of late Frank Colin Bagnall; 2 s from previous m (Benedict b 1 Jan 1982, Luke b 20 Sept 1984), 4 step c (Hannah, Emily, Polly, William); *Career* baritone; joined WNO 1971, ENO 1983– (princ baritone for 18 years); worked with: Glyndebourne Festival and Touring Opera, English Music Theatre, Kent Opera, Opera North, Royal Opera House, Monteverdi Choir; worked in many countries and festivals incl: Russia, Hong Kong, USA, Brazil, Italy, Festival Estival Paris; *Roles* with ENO: Papageno in The Magic Flute, Guglielmo in Cosi fan Tutte, Dr Falke in Die Fledermaus, Schaunard in La Bohème, Grosvenor in Patience, Silvio in Pagliacci, Novice's Friend in Billy Budd, Elviro in Xerxes, Music Master in Ariadne, Yeletsky in Queen of Spades, Herald in Lohengrin, Faninal in Rosenkavalier, Demetrius in Midsummer Night's Dream, Count in The Marriage of Figaro, Germont in La Traviata, Sharpless in Madam Butterfly; also Narrator in Caucasian Chalk Circle (Newcastle Festival) and Morales in Carmen (Royal Opera House), Melot in Tristan and Isolde (Royal Opera House), Spirit Messenger in Die Frau ohne Schatten (Royal Opera House); *Concerts* appearances incl: Carmina Burana, Messiah, Bach's Mass in B minor, St John's Passion, St Matthew Passion, Handel's Samson, Faure's Requiem, Brahms' Requiem, Vaughan Williams' Sea Symphony; *Recordings* Julius Caesar and Pacific Overtures, Tosca, Great Things (album of English song), Bright is the Ring of Words (2nd vol of English song, 20th Century English song cycles), World premiere of requiem Even Such is Time (by Andrew Mildinhall); videos of The Gondoliers, Rusalka, Xerxes, Billy Budd, Carmen; *Recreations* mountain and hill walking, gadgets, wines, reading, exploring above and below ground!; *Style*— Christopher Booth-Jones, Esq; ✉ c/o Helen Sykes Artists' Management, 100 Felsham Road, London SW15 1DQ (☎ 020 8780 0060, fax 020 8780 8772)

BOOTHBY, Sir Brooke Charles; 16 Bt (1660), of Broadlow Ash; DL (S Glamorgan 2008–); s of Sir Hugo Boothby, 15 Bt (d 1986); b 6 April 1949; *Educ* Eton, Trinity Coll Cambridge (BA); m 1976, Georgiana Alexandra, da of Sir John Wriothesley Russell, GCVO, CMG (d 1984), and Lady (Aliki) Russell (d 2002); 2 da; *Heir* kinsman, George Boothby; *Career* Fontygary Parks Ltd: md 1979–95, vice-chm 1995–2003, chm 2004–; chm: Tourism Quality Services Ltd 1990–, Associated Quality Services Ltd 1994–2007, TQS (1994) Ltd 1994–2002, TQS (Ireland) Ltd 1995–2002, AQS Ltd 1998–2007; dir: Wales Tourism Alliance Ltd 2001–09, Bradford Rural Estates Ltd 2001–, Bradford Industrial Ownership Ltd 2014–, Bradford Investments and Securities Ltd 2016–; chm: Nat Caravan Cncl Parks Div 1987–90, Adventure Activities Licensing Authy 1996–2007, Capital Region Tourism Ltd 2002–03, Historic Houses Assoc Wales 2009–, AAL Service 2007–; pres: Glamorgan Branch Country Landowners Assoc 1991–94, Vale of Glamorgan Nat Tst 1998–; treas

Consular Assoc in Wales 2010–14; govr United World Coll of the Atlantic 2003–06 (dir UWC Ltd, tstee of fndn); High Sheriff S Glamorgan 1986–87, Vice Lord Lt 2011–; hon consul of Malta for Wales 2008–; *Recreations* gardening; *Style*— Sir Brooke Boothby, Bt, DL; ✉ Penllyn, Cowbridge, Vale of Glamorgan CF71 7RQ (☎ 01446 775666, e-mail fonmon_castle@msn.com)

BOOTHBY, Chris; s of Guy Keable Boothby (d 1995), and Edna Constance, *née* Goss; b 10 February 1960, Worthing, W Sussex; *Educ* Chancellors Sch, Univ of Hull (BSc); m 15 June 1991, Caroline, *née* Cronin; 2 s (Sam Jonathan b 10 Oct 1992, Christian Guy b 15 May 1997), 1 da (Chloe Elizabeth b 11 April 1994); *Career* sales Guardian Newspapers 1981–82; TV advtg buying: Colman RSGG 1982–83, Allen Brady Marsh 1983–85, WCRS Advtg 1985–89; broadcast dir BBJ Media 1989–99, commercial dir Vzeum UK 1999–2005, global head of investment mgmnt Aegis Media 2005–; MIPA 1995; *Recreations* cricket, football, golf; *Clubs* Brocket Hall; *Style*— Chris Boothby, Esq; ✉ Aegis Media, Parker Tower, 43–49 Parker Street, London WC2B 5PS (☎ 020 7550 3216, e-mail chris.boothby@aemedia.com)

BOOTHBY, Richard Charles Brooke; s of George William Bernard Boothby (d 1972), and Avril Alice (d 1993), *née* Innell; b 16 December 1955; *Educ* Barry Boys' Comp Sch, Univ of Manchester (MusB, study with David Fallows), Salzburg Mozarteum (with Nikolaus Harnoncourt); m 1, 23 May 1992 (m dis 2001), Fiona Clare, da of Peter Padfield; 1 s (Maximillian Brooke b 31 Jan 1995), 1 da (Megan Miranda b 3 Feb 1998); m 2, 9 April 2005, Giovanna del Perugia; 1 s (Cosimo William b 13 Feb 2006); *Career* viola da gamba player and 'cellist; fndr and memb Purcell Quartet 1984–; fndr memb Fretwork 1985–; regularly tours world with these ensembles, and as soloist; prof of viola da gamba RCM; *Recordings* 50 recordings with Purcell Quartet and nearly 30 with Fretwork; prime mover in commissioning new works for the viol incl music by George Benjamin, Michael Nyman, Sir John Tavener, Elvis Costello, Orlando Gough, Alexander Goehr, Tan Dun, Sally Beamish, Duncan Druce, Barry Guy, etc; *Recreations* cooking, walking; *Style*— Richard Boothby, Esq; ✉ e-mail forqueray1@mac.com, website www.fretwork.co.uk

BOOTHMAN, Clive Nicholas; s of Thomas Hague Boothman (d 1996), and Margaret, *née* Knox; b 28 May 1955; *Educ* Charterhouse, Trinity Coll Oxford (BA); m 28 May 1983, Anne, da of Wace Philo; 2 s (Alexander b 4 July 1986, Harry b 9 July 1988), 1 da (Georgina b 1 Aug 1990); *Career* Arthur Young McClelland Moores Jersey CI 1976–81, accountant Moore Stephens & Butterfield Bermuda 1982–83; Schroder Gp: joined 1983, asst dir J Henry Schroder Wagg & Co Ltd 1986–87 (mangr 1985–86, investment res 1983–85), md Schroder Unit Tsts Ltd 1988–98, md Schroder Private Client Gp 1998–2000, dir Schroder Investment Mgmnt Ltd 1992–2000; ceo Gerrard Ltd 2000–01, ceo Cofunds Ltd 2002–03; chm Fundsdirect 2005–; chm Assoc of Unit Tsts and Investment Funds until 1997; ACA 1980, AIIMR 1984; *Recreations* sailing, windsurfing, tennis, vintage cars; *Style*— Clive Boothman, Esq; ✉ 331 Riverside Walk, Smugglers Way, London SW18 1ED (☎ 020 8871 9048, e-mail cliveboothman@hotmail.com)

BOOTHROYD, Baroness (Life Peer UK 2001), of Sandwell in the County of West Midlands; Betty Boothroyd; OM (2005), PC (1992); da of Archibald Boothroyd (d 1948), of Dewsbury, W Yorks, and Mary Boothroyd (d 1982); b 8 October 1929; *Educ* Dewsbury Coll of Commerce and Art; *Career* MP (Lab): West Bromwich 1973–74, West Bromwich West 1974–2000 (Parly candidate (Lab): Leicester SE (by-election) 1957, Peterborough 1959, Nelson and Colne (by-election) 1968, Rossendale 1970); asst Govt whip 1974–76, UK memb European Parl 1975–77, former memb Select Ctee on Foreign Affrs, memb Speaker's Panel of Chairmen 1979–87, Lab Pty Nat Exec Ctee 1981–87, House of Commons Cmmn 1983–87, second dep chm Ways and Means and dep speaker 1987–92; Speaker House of Commons 1992–2000; memb Hammersmith Borough Cncl 1965–68; memb Ct Univ of Birmingham 1982–, chllr Open Univ 1994–2006; hon master of the bench Middle Temple 2011; The Spectator Parliamentarian of the Year Award 1992; Liveryman Worshipful Co of Feltmakers; Hon Liveryman Worshipful Co of Grocers 2005; Hon LLD: Univ of Birmingham, Leeds Metropolitan Univ, Leicester South Bank Univ, Univ of Cambridge, North London Univ, Univ of Oxford, Univ of St Andrews 2003; Hon FCGI; *Publications* Betty Boothroyd – The Autobiography (2001); *Recreations* reading, theatre, travel; *Style*— The Rt Hon the Baroness Boothroyd, OM, PC; ✉ House of Lords, London SW1A 0PW (☎ 020 7219 3000)

BOOTLE, Roger Paul; s of David Bootle, MBE (d 1972), and Florence Ethel, *née* Denman (d 1982); b 22 June 1952; *Educ* Downer GS, Merton Coll Oxford (BA), Nuffield Coll Oxford (BPhil); *Career* lectr in economics St Anne's Coll Oxford 1976–78, with Citibank 1978–79, dep head economic policy CBI 1979–81; chief economist: Capel Cure Myers 1982–86, Lloyds Merchant Bank 1986–87 (dir 1986–87); conslt 1987–89; chief economist and dir of research HSBC Greenwell (formerly Greenwell Montagu Gilt Edged) 1989–96, gp chief economist HSBC Holdings plc 1996–98; md Capital Economics Ltd 1999–; specialist advsr House of Commons Treasy Select Ctee 1997–; econ advsr Deloitte & Touche 1999–2011; visiting prof Manchester Business Sch 1995–2003; memb HM Treasy ind panel of economic forecasting advsrs 1996–97; columnist Sunday Telegraph 2000–06, columnist Daily Telegraph 2006–; contrib: Financial Times, Times, numerous pubns; various TV and radio appearances as commentator on economic affairs; *Books* Theory of Money (jtly, 1978), Index-Linked Gilts (1986, 2 edn 1991), The Death of Inflation (1996), Money for Nothing (2003), The Trouble with Markets (2009), The Trouble with Europe (2014); *Recreations* bridge, squash, horseracing, classical music, theatre; *Style*— Roger Bootle, Esq; ✉ Capital Economics, 150 Buckingham Palace Road, London SW1W 9TR (☎ 020 7823 5000, fax 020 7823 6666, e-mail roger.bootle@capitaleconomics.com)

BOOTON, Prof Paul; s of Arthur Terence Booton, and Jean Brunhilde Mary, *née* Price; b 11 May 1955; *Educ* Hornchurch GS, The London Hosp Med Coll (BSc, MB BS); *Children* 1 da (Caitlin Margaret b 1998), 1 s (Keir Thomas b 2000); *Career* physician to Prof J M Ledingham London Hosp 1980, MO to Kaitak and Sham Shui Po refugee camps UN High Cmmn on Refugees 1981, SHO and registrar med Oldchurch Hosp Romford 1982–86, lectr gen practice UMDS 1988–90; King's Coll Sch of Med and Dentistry: lectr Dept of Gen Practice 1990–94, curriculum sub-dean 1991–94, sr lectr in med educn 1994–2004, undergrad sub-dean 1994–98, head of Dept of Med & Dental Educn and asst clinical dean 1998–2002; currently: dep head Sch of Public Health, dir of undergrad educn in primary care and chair Finals Bd of Examiners (Year 5) Imperial Coll London, prof of general practice and primary care St George's Univ of London 2012–; memb Lab Pty; FRCP 2008 (MRCP 1984), MRCGP 1988; *Books* A Textbook of General Practice (jtly); *Recreations* walking, skiing, cycling, theatre, music; *Style*— Prof Paul Booton; ✉ St George's, University of London, Cranmer Terrace, London SW17 0RE (☎ 020 8725 5508, e-mail pbooton@sgul.ac.uk)

BORDEN, Prof Iain Michael; s of Anthony Ian Borden, of Oxford, and Shelagh Mary, *née* Birks; b 9 November 1962; *Educ* Univ of Newcastle upon Tyne (BA), UCL (MSc), UCLA (MA), Univ of London (PhD); m Claire, *née* Haywood; 1 s (Samuel Anthony Alan b 11 Aug 2006); *Career* UCL: sub-dean Faculty of the Built Environment 1996–99, dir architectural history and theory 1999–2014, reader in architecture and urban culture 1999–2002, head Bartlett Sch of Architecture 2001–09, prof of architecture and urban culture 2002–, vice-dean Faculty of the Built Environment 2010–; Freeman City of Oxford; Hon FRIBA; *Books* Architecture & the Sites of History (co-ed, 1995), Strangely Familiar (co-ed, 1996), City Culture Reader (co-ed, 2000), Gender Space Architecture (co-ed, 2000), The Dissertation (co-author, 2000), Intersections (co-ed, 2000), Skateboarding, Space and the City (2001), The Unknown City (co-ed, 2001), Manual: The Architecture and Office of Allford Hall Monaghan Morris (2003), Bartlett Works (co-ed, 2004),

Transculturation (co-ed, 2005), Bartlett Design (co-ed, 2009), Drive: Journeys through Film, Cities and Landscapes (2012), Forty Ways of Thinking About Architecture (co-ed, 2014), The Dissertation (co-author, 2014); *Recreations* skateboarding, car driving, cycling, film, photography; *Style*— Prof Iain Borden; ✉ Bartlett School of Architecture, University College London, 22 Gordon Street, London WC1H 0QB (e-mail i.borden@ucl.ac.uk)

BORDISS, Andrew Raymond; s of Raymond George Bordiss (d 2008), of Brockworth, Glos, and Joyce, *née* Edwards; *b* 12 February 1957; *Educ* Brockworth Sch; *m* 17 Sept 1983, Deborah Anne, da of Robert Ellis; 2 s (Samuel Andrew b 1984, John George b 1988), 1 da (Isabelle Megan b 1990); *Career* journalist; night ed Today 1986–89, ed Auto Express 1989–93, assoc night ed Daily Telegraph 1993–98, dep ed Evening Standard 1998–; memb Cncl IAM 1992–2001; *Recreations* golf, cycling, rugby; *Clubs* Press Golfing Soc, Surrey RFC, Rosslyn Park RFC, Hampton Court Palace Golf; *Style*— Andrew Bordiss, Esq; ✉ Evening Standard, 2 Derry Street, London W8 5EE

BORE, Sir Albert; kt (2002); *Career* Birmingham City Cncl: cncllr 1980–, ldr 1999–2004 and 2012–; chair Univ Hospitals Birmingham NHS Fndn Tst 2006–13; *Style*— Sir Albert Bore; ✉ Council House, Victoria Square, Birmingham B1 1BB

BORG, Dr Alan Charles Nelson; CBE (1991); s of Charles John Nelson Borg (d 1986), and Frances Mary Olive, *née* Hughes (d 1985); *b* 21 January 1942; *Educ* Westminster, BNC Oxford (MA, Fencing blue), Courtauld Inst of Art London (MA, PhD); *m* 1, 1964; 1 s (Giles b 1965), 1 da (Emma b 1970); m 2, 1976, Lady Caroline Sylvia Hill (raised to the rank of a Marquess's da 1992), da of Lord Francis Hill and sis of late 8 Marquess of Downshire; 2 da (Leonora b 1980, Helen b 1982); *Career* lectr in English Univ d'Aix-Marseille 1964–65, lectr in history of art Univ of Indiana 1967–69, asst prof of history of art Princeton Univ 1969–70, asst keeper Royal Armouries HM Tower of London 1970–78, keeper Sainsbury Centre for Visual Arts UEA 1978–82, DG Imperial War Museum 1982–95, dir V&A 1995–2001, librarian St John's Gate 2007– (dep librarian 2004–07); visiting prof Dept of History Univ of Reading 2011–; chm Conf of Dirs of Nat Museums and Galleries 1998–2001; pres: Meyrick Soc 1994–, Elizabethan Club 1995–2000; govr: Coram Family 1995–2006, Westminster Sch 1998–; tstee: The Foundling Museum 1998– (chm 2006–09, vice-pres 2010–), St Paul's Cathedral Fndn 2001–06, Handel House Museum 2002–; memb Bd of Dirs Musée du Louvre 1999–2001; Freeman City of London 1997, Liveryman Worshipful Co of Painter-Stainers 1997; Hon Dr Sheffield Hallam Univ 2000; Hon FRCA 1991, Hon FRIBA 2001, FSA; KStJ 2012 (OStJ 1998); *Books* Architectural Sculpture in Romanesque Provence (1972), European Swords and Daggers in the Tower of London (1974), Torture and Punishment (1975), Heads and Horses (1976), Arms and Armour in Britain (1979), War Memorials (1991), The History of the Painters' Company (2005), A History of the Worshipful Company of Cooks (2010), Vauxhall Gardens, A History (with David Coke, 2011); *Recreations* music, travel; *Clubs* Special Forces, Beefsteak, MCC; *Style*— Dr A C N Borg, CBE, FSA; ✉ Telegraph House, 36 West Square, London SE11 4SP (☎ 020 7582 8122, e-mail acnborg@gmail.com)

BORIE, Stéphane; *b* France; *Career* chef and proprietor The Checkers (Michelin star 2012–); *Style*— Mr Stéphane Borie; ✉ The Checkers, Broad Street, Montgomery, Powys SY15 6PN

BORMAN, Dr Edwin Miles; s of David Bevil Borman (b 1936), and Sophia, *née* Miller; *b* 9 September 1961; *Educ* Theodor Herzl HS Port Elizabeth, Univ of Cape Town Med Sch (MB ChB); *Career* house offr Groote Schuur Hosp Cape Town 1985; Plymouth HA 1986–91 (SHO posts in surgical and med specialities 1986–90), S Birmingham HA 1991–94 (registrar posts in anaesthetics and intensive care), Coventry and Birmingham rotation 1995–97 (sr registrar posts in anaesthetics and intensive care), conslt anaesthetist Walsgrave Hosp Coventry 1997–2013, medical dir Shrewsbury and Telford Hosp NHS Tst 2013–; chm LNC Walsgrave Hosp 1998–2007, clinical dir Anaesthetics and Pain Services 2007–13; BMA: chm Jr Doctors Ctee 1991–94, memb Cncl 1991–2012, memb Jt Conslts Ctee 1991–94 and 1999–2010, chm Int Ctee 1999–2007; GMC: memb Cncl 1994–2008, chm Ctee for Diversity and Equality 2003–08, chm Working Gp on Consent 2006–08; memb: Ministerial Gps on 'Achieving a Balance' and 'The New Deal' 1991–94, CMO's Working Gps on Specialist Med Trg 1992–93 and on Overseas Doctors in the UK 1994, Perm Working Gp of Euro Jr Hosp Doctors 1993–96, Euro Bd of Anaesthesiology and Reanimation 1995–97, Dept of Health Steering Gp on Refugee Health Professionals 2001–06, Dept of Health Steering Gp Working Time Directive 2001–03; European Union of Med Specialists (UEMS): UK memb 1998–2011, vice-pres 2006–08, chm Working Gp on Continuing Professional Devpt 2000–12, chm EACCME Taskforce 2009–13, sec gen 2012–15; dep chm Central Conslts and Specialists Ctee 2002–04, ldr UK delgn Comité Permanent des Médicins Européens 2001–07; memb Bd Global Alliance for Medical Educn 2004–07; invited lectr Canada, USA, India and Europe; memb BMA 1986, FFARCSI 1993, FRCA 1994; *Publications* book chapters on the integration of refugee doctors, and on medical professionalism; policy papers on medical educn and quality in healthcare; *Recreations* classical music, Eastern art, African art; *Style*— Dr Edwin Borman; ✉ 30 Clover Drive, Bartley Green, Birmingham B32 3DJ (☎ 0121 426 5760); Royal Shrewsbury Hospital, Shrewsbury SY3 8XQ (☎ 01743 261262, e-mail edwin.borman@sath.nhs.uk)

BORN, Gary Brian; s of Clyde R Born, of Camden, SC, and Eleanor Born; *b* 14 September 1955, NY; *Educ* Haverford Coll (BA), Univ of Pennsylvania (JD); *m* 1988, Beatrix von Wedel-Goedens; 1 da (Natascha b 1988), 1 s (Henrik b 1990); *Career* memb DC Bar 1984; law clerk to Henry J Friendly (circuit judge Second Circuit Court of Appeal) 1981–82, law clerk to William H Rehnquist (assoc justice US Supreme Court) 1982–83, assoc Wilmer Cutler & Pickering 1984–88, ptnr Wilmer Cutler & Pickering Washington DC 1988–91, sr ptnr Wilmer Cutler Pickering Hale and Dorr LLP London 1991–; adjunct prof of law: Univ of Arizona Coll of Law 1987–90, Georgetown Law Sch 1987–91, Pepperdine Univ Law Sch London 1994–98; visiting lectr UCL 1991–94; memb: Exec Cncl American Soc of Int Law 1991–94, Bd Inst for US Studies 1996–; memb American Law Inst 1999–; *Books* The Extraterritorial Application of National Laws (co-author, 1987), International Civil Litigation in United States Courts (3 edn 1996, 4 edn 2007), International Arbitration and Forum Selection Agreements: Drafting and Enforcing (1999, 2 edn 2006), International Commercial Arbitration: Commentary and Materials (2 edn, 2000); *Recreations* scuba diving, hiking; *Clubs* Athenaeum; *Style*— Gary Born, Esq; ✉ Wilmer Cutler Pickering Hale and Dorr LLP, 4 Carlton Gardens, London SW1Y 5AA (☎ 020 7872 1000, fax 020 7389 3537, e-mail gary.born@wilmerhale.com)

BORRIE, Baron (Life Peer UK 1995), of Abbots Morton in the County of Hereford and Worcester; Sir Gordon Johnson Borrie; kt (1982), QC (1986); s of Stanley Borrie, of Croydon, Surrey; *b* 13 March 1931; *Educ* John Bright GS Llandudno, Univ of Manchester (LLB, LLM); *m* 1960, Dorene, da of Herbert Toland (d 2010); *Career* Nat Serv Army Legal Servs, HQ Br Cwlth Forces Korea 1952–54; called to the Bar Middle Temple 1952, bencher 1980, in practice 1954–57, lectr then sr lectr Coll of Law 1957–64; Univ of Birmingham: sr lectr 1965–68, prof of Eng law and dir Inst of Judicial Admin 1969–76, dean Law Faculty 1974–76; DG Office of Fair Trading 1976–92, chm Commission on Social Justice 1992–94, pres Inst of Trading Standards Admin 1992–97, chm Direct Mktg Authy 1997–2000; dir: Woolwich Building Society (now Woolwich plc) 1992–2000, Three Valleys Water Services plc 1992–2003, Mirror Group Newspapers plc 1993–99, Telewest plc 1994–2001, General Utilities plc 1998–2003; chm: Accountancy Fndn 2000–03, Advtg Standards Authy 2001–07, Cncl Ombudsman for Estate Agents 2007–09; govr Birmingham Coll of Commerce 1966–70; former memb Law Cmmn Advsy Panel for Contract Law; memb: Parole Bd 1971–74, Cncl Consumers' Assoc 1972–75, Equal Opportunities Cmmn 1975–76; contested: (Lab) Croydon NE 1955, Ilford South 1959; Hon LLD: City of London Poly (now City of London Univ) 1989, Univ of Manchester 1990, Univ of Hull 1991, Univ of Dundee 1993, UWE 1997, Univ of Nottingham 2005; hon dr Nottingham Trent Univ 1996; hon memb SPTL 1989, FRSA 1982; *Books* Commercial Law (1962, 6 edn 1988), The Development of Consumer Law and Policy (1984), others in joint authorship; *Recreations* gastronomy, piano playing, travel; *Clubs* Reform, Garrick, Pratt's; *Style*— The Rt Hon Lord Borrie, QC; ✉ Manor Farm, Abbots Morton, Worcestershire (☎ 01386 792330); 4 Brick Court, Temple, London EC4 (☎ 020 7353 4434)

BORROW, David Stanley; s of James Borrow, and Nancy, *née* Crawshaw; *b* 2 August 1952; *Educ* Mirfield GS, Coventry Univ (BA); *Career* grad trainee Yorkshire Bank 1973–75, Valuation Tbnl Service 1975–97 (clerk to Merseyside Valuation Tbnl 1983–97); MP (Lab) S Ribble 1997–2010; PPS: to Tport Min 2003–04, to Higher Educn Min 2004–05; chair Back Bench Ctee on: Trade & Industry, Defence, Agric; vice-chair All-Pty Gp on: Aids and HIV, Penal Affrs; sec PLP Regnl Govt Gp; cncllr Preston BC 1987 (leader 1992–94 and 1995–97), elected to Preston City Cncl 2011, elected to Lancashire CC 2013 (appointed dep ldr); memb: Inst of Rating, Revenues & Valuation, Soc of Clerks of Valuation Tbnls (pres 1990–92 and 1996–97), All-Pty Aerospace Gp 1999– (chair 1999–), Agric Select Ctee 1999; memb Labour Campaign for Electoral Reform; *Style*— David Borrow, Esq

BORROWS, Simon Alexander; s of Kenneth Ambrose Borrows (d 2004), and Ailsa Nancy, *née* McLeod; *b* 24 January 1959, Taplow, Bucks; *Educ* Rossall Sch, Univ of London (LLB), London Business Sch (MBA); *m* 31 Oct 1987, Sally Ann, *née* Weston; 2 da (Polly Louise b 2 Jan 1990, Maisie Ellen b 13 March 1992), 1 s (George Henry b 1 Oct 1993); *Career* dir Baring Bros & Co Ltd 1988–98 (head of M&A 1995–98), ptnr Greenhill & Co 1998– (founding ptnr London office), co-pres Greenhill & Co Inc 2004–07, co-chief exec Greenhill & Co Inc 2007–; memb Advsy Bd London Business Sch 2000–03; *Recreations* family, golf, skiing, shooting, theatre; *Clubs* Hankley Common Golf, Queenwood Golf, Rye Golf; *Style*— Simon Borrows, Esq; ✉ Greenhill & Co, Lansdowne House, 57 Berkeley Square, London W1J 6ER (☎ 020 7198 7400, fax 020 7198 7500, e-mail sborrows@greenhill.com)

BORSUK, Teresa; da of Jan Bosuk (d 2012), and Agnieszka, *née* Lichwa d 2009); *b* 1956; *Educ* Bartlett Sch of Architecture UCL (BSc, DipArch), Univ of Kansas; *Career* architect; Pollard Thomas Edwards: joined 1984, dir 1987–99, exec dir 1999–2014, sr equity ptnr 2014–; Woman Architect of the Year Architects' Jl 2015; RIBA 1981, ARB, CDA; *Style*— Ms Teresa Borsuk; ✉ Pollard Thomas Edwards, Diespeker Wharf, 38 Graham Street, London N1 8JX

BORTHWICK, 24 Lord (S 1450); John Hugh Borthwick of that Ilk; Baron (territorial) of Heriotmuir; er (twin) s of 23 Lord Borthwick, TD, JP, DL (d 1996), and Margaret, *née* Cormack (d 1976); *b* 14 November 1940; *Educ* Gordonstoun, Edinburgh Sch of Agric (SDA, NDA); *m* 1974, Adelaide, o da of Archy Birkmyre, of Comrie, Perthshire; 2 da (Hon Georgina b 18 Dec 1975, Hon Alexandra b 25 Aug 1977); *Heir* twin bro, Hon James Borthwick of Glengelt; *Career* landowner and former farmer; *Recreations* trout fishing, stalking, cigarette card collecting; *Clubs* New (Edinburgh); *Style*— The Rt Hon the Lord Borthwick

BORTHWICK, Stephen William (Steve); *b* 12 October 1979, Carlisle, Cumbria; *Educ* Hutton GS, Univ of Bath, Univ of Herts; *Career* rugby union player (lock); clubs: Bath 1998–2008, Saracens 2008–14; England: 57 caps, capt 2008–10; rugby union coach Japan Nat Rugby Team 2014–15; hon fell Univ of Cumbria; *Style*— Mr Steve Borthwick; ✉ c/o Saracens, Allianz Park Stadium, Greenlands Lane, London NW4 1RL

BORWICK, 5 Baron (UK 1922); Sir Geoffrey Robert James (Jamie) Borwick; 5 Bt (UK 1916); s of Hon Robin Sandbach Borwick (d 2003), of Wells, Somerset, and Hon Patricia Borwick, *née* McAlpine (d 2009); suc half-unc 4 Baron Borwick (d 2007); *b* 7 March 1955, London; *Educ* Eton; *m* 1981, Victoria Lorne Peta Borwick, MP, *qv*, da of R Dennis Poore (d 1987), of London; 3 s (Edwin b 1984, Thomas b 1987, William b 1997), 1 da (Alex b 1990); *Heir* s, Edwin Borwick; *Career* chm: Federated Trust Corporation Ltd 1981–, London Taxis International Ltd 1984–2003, Hansa Trust plc 1985–2012, Manganese Bronze Holdings plc 2001–03 (chief exec 1984–2001), Modec Ltd 2004–10; md Love Lane Investments Ltd 1984–; memb FSA Listing Authy Advsy Ctee 1997–2003; tstee Br Lung Fndn 2003–09 and 2011–; memb House of Lords 2013–; memb EU Select Ctee House of Lords 2015–16, memb Science and Technol Ctee House of Lords 2016–; *Recreations* travel; *Clubs* Garrick; *Style*— The Lord Borwick; ✉ e-mail borwickgr@parliament.uk

BORWICK, Lady; Victoria Lorne Peta; MP; *née* Poore; da of R Dennis Poore (d 1987), of London, and M S Peta, *née* Coast; *b* 26 April 1956, London; *Educ* Wispers Sch Haslemere; *m* 20 March 1981, 5 Baron Borwick, *qv*; 3 s (Edwin b 14 April 1984, Thomas b 1 Aug 1987, William b 9 April 1997), 1 da (Alexandra b 12 May 1990); *Career* dir Clarion Events (part of P&O Gp) 1976–2002, dir Treasrs Dept Cons Central Office 2002–04, commercial dir ACI 2004–06, Open Europe 2007–15; MP (Cons) Kensington 2015–; cncllr Royal Borough of Kensington and Chelsea 2002–16, memb London Assembly (Cons) 2008–15, memb Met Police Authy 2008–12, chm Civil Liberties Panel, chair Health and Public Services Ctee 2010–12, Royal Borough of Kensington and Chelsea appointee to Governing Body Royal Brompton and Harefield NHS Fndn Tst 2010–; Dep Mayor of London 2012–15; MP (Cons) Kensington 2015–; govr Golborne Children's Centre (formerly Ainsworth Sch) 1990–, tstee Federated Fndn; Freeman City of London 1999, Liveryman Worshipful Co of Clockmakers; FRSA 1989; The Cost of the London Mayor (2007), Streets Ahead: Relieving Congestion on Oxford Street, Regent Street and Bond Street (2010), Responding to G20 (2010), Protecting the Innocent, the London Experience of DNA (2011), In from the Cold, tackling fuel poverty in London (2012), Tackling Childcare Affordability in London (2012); *Recreations* making fudge, skiing, tennis, boating; *Style*— Mrs Victoria Borwick, MP; ✉ House of Commons, London, SW1A 0AA (☎ 020 7219 6100, e-mail kensington@parliament.uk)

BORYSIEWICZ, Prof Sir Leszek Krzysztof; kt (2001), DL (Cambs); s of Jan Borysiewicz, and Zofia Helena, *née* Woloszyn; *b* 13 April 1951, Cardiff; *Educ* Welsh Nat Sch of Medicine (MB ChB), Royal Postgrad Medical Sch (PhD); *Career* chief exec MRC 2007–10; vice-chllr Univ of Cambridge 2010–; hon prof Shanghai Jiao Tong Univ 2011; memb Review Panel Research Excellence Framework 2016–; memb Siemens Corporation Bd 2015–; memb Cancer Research UK (chm 2016–); Moxon Tst Medal RCP 2002, Galen Medal in Therapeutics 2011, Bene Merito Medal 2011; Hon DSc: Univ of Southampton 2008, Univ of Hull 2008, Univ of London, Queen Mary's Westfield 2009, Univ of Glasgow 2011, Hong Kong Univ 2012, Peking Univ 2012; Hon MD Univ of Sheffield 2010; fell Univ of Cardiff 2006, fell Imperial Coll London 2008, hon fell Univ of Wales Inst Cardiff (now Cardiff Met Univ) 2011; founding FLSW, FRS, FRCP, FRCPath, FMedSci, FCGI; *Style*— Prof Sir Leszek Borysiewicz, DL; ✉ Office of the Vice-Chancellor, The Old Schools, Trinity Lane, Cambridge CB2 1TN

BOSANQUET, Prof Nicholas Francis Gustavus; s of Lt-Col Neville Richard Gustavus Bosanquet (d 2003), of Wilts, and Nancy Bosanquet, *née* Mason (d 2003); *b* 17 January 1942; *Educ* Winchester, Clare Coll Cambridge, Yale Univ, LSE; *m* 31 Aug 1974 (m dis 1993), Anne Connolly; 2 da (Kate b 1978, Helen b 1981); m 2, 9 Nov 1996, Anna Zarzecka; *Career* sr res fell Centre for Health Econ Univ of York, lectr in economics LSE and City Univ, prof of health policy Royal Holloway and Bedford New Coll London 1988–93, prof of health policy Imperial Coll London 1993–; special advsr to Health Ctee House of Commons; econ advsr: Nat Bd for Prices and Incomes, Royal Cmmn on Distribution of Income and Wealth; conslt: World Bank, OECD, health authorities and cos in Britain;

arbitrator ACAS; dir: Reform, TBS GB; contrib to Economic Jl, BMJ; *Books* Industrial Relations in the NHS: The Search for a System (1980), After the New Right (1983), Family Doctors and Economic Incentives (1989), The Economics of Cancer Care (2006); *Recreations* collecting books on WWI; *Style*— Prof Nick F G Bosanquet; ✉ Department of Bioengineering, Imperial College, Bagrit Centre, Exhibition Road, London SW7 2AZ (☎ 020 7594 3355, fax 020 7584 4297)

BOSCAWEN, Hon Evelyn Arthur Hugh; DL (2009); s and h of 9 Viscount Falmouth; *b* 13 May 1955; *Educ* Eton, RAC Cirencester, Harvard Business Sch; *m* 1977 (m dis 1995), Lucia Caroline, da of Ralph Vivian-Neal, of Poundisford Park, Somerset; 1 s ((Evelyn George) William b 1979), 1 da (Laura Frances b 1982); m 2, 1995, Katharine Helen, eldest da of Mark Maley, of Nayland, Suffolk; 2 s (Frederick Mark b 1996, Archard Hugh b 1998), 1 da (Cecilia Rose b 2001); *Career* Goonvean: dep chm 1979–2000, chm 2000–; Liveryman Worshipful Co of Clockmakers; High Sheriff Cornwall 2007–08; *Style*— The Hon Evelyn Boscawen, DL; ✉ c/o Tregothnan Estate Office, Truro, Cornwall

BOSE, Mihir; s of Kiran Chandra Bose, and Sova Rani Bose; *b* 12 January 1947, Kolkata, India; *Educ* BSc; *m* 1, 1986 (m dis 1999), Kalpana; 1 da (Indira); m 2, 2002, Caroline Alison Gascoyne-Cecil; *Career* journalist, writer and broadcaster; corr LBC 1974–75, foreign corr Sunday Times 1975–78, reporter Accountancy 1978–80, ed Property Guide 1980–81, ed Pensions 1981–83, city ed and dep ed Financial Weekly 1983–86, city features ed London Daily News 1987, sports news reporter Sunday Times 1987–95, sports columnist Daily Telegraph 1995–2006, sports ed BBC News 2007–09; Business Columnist of the Year 1990, Sports Story of the Year 1997, Sports News Reporter of the Year 1999, jt winner (with Daily Telegraph) Team Award Sports Journalists' Assoc Sports Writer and Photographer Awards; tstee Sporting Equals 2009–16; hon doctorate Loughborough Univ; FCA 1974; *Books* cricket titles: Keith Miller: A Cricketing Biography, All in a Day: Great Moments in Cup Cricket, A Maiden View: The Magic of Indian Cricket, Cricket Voices, A History of Indian Cricket (Cricket Soc Literary Award 1990); football titles: Behind Closed Doors: Dreams and Nightmares at Spurs, Manchester Unlimited, The Rise and Rise of World's Premier Football Club, Manchester DisUnited: Trouble and Takeover at the World's Richest Football Club, The World Cup: All You Need To Know, Game Changer: How the Premier League Came to Dominate the World, The Game Changer; general sporting titles: Sporting Colours: Sport and Politics in South Africa (runner-up William Hill Sports Book of the Year 1994), Sporting Babylon, The Spirit of the Game; history and biography titles: The Lost Hero: A Biography of Subhas Bose, The Aga Khans, Michael Grade: Screening the Image, Memons, False Messiah: The Life and Times of Terry Venables, Raj, Spies, Rebellion, Bollywood: A History, From Midnight to Glorious Morning? (2016); business titles: The Crash: The 1987–88 World Market Slump, A New Money Crisis: A Children's Guide to Money, Are You Covered? An Insurance Guide, Fraud – The Growth Industry of the 1980s (jtly), How to Invest in a Bear Market, William Hill: The Man and the Business (jtly, 2014); autobiography: The Sporting Alien; *Recreations* organising my own cricket team, cinema, walking, travel; *Clubs* Reform, MCC; *Style*— Mihir Bose, Esq; ✉ 30 Poplar Grove, London W6 7RE (☎ 020 7371 3976, fax 020 7610 4111, e-mail mihir@mihirbose.com, website www.mihirbose.com)

BOSSOM, Bruce Charles; s and h of Hon Sir Clive Bossom, 2 Bt, *qv*, and Lady Barbara, *née* North, of London; *b* 22 August 1952; *Educ* Eton, Coll of Estate Mgmnt, Harvard Business Sch (PMD); *m* 1985, Penelope Jane, da of Edward Holland-Martin (d 1981), of Overbury Court, Glos; 2 da (Rosanna Emily b 1986, Amanda Lucy b 1988), 1 s (George Edward Martin b 1992); *Career* Jones Lang Wootton 1972–86 (ptnr 1981); dir: Phoenix Properties & Finance plc 1986–89, Mountleigh Group plc 1989–93, LaSalle Partners 1993–99; fndr Orion Capital Managers; Liveryman Worshipful Co of Grocers; FRICS, FRSA; *Clubs* White's; *Style*— Bruce Bossom, Esq; ✉ Overbury Court, Tewkesbury, Gloucestershire GL20 7NP (☎ 01386 725312, fax 01386 725528); 21 Queensdale Place, London W11 4SQ (☎ 020 7348 0865, fax 020 7348 0659); Orion Capital Managers, 2 Cavendish Square, London W1G 0PU (☎ 020 7199 2003, fax 020 7199 2023, e-mail bbossom@orioncapman.com)

BOSTELMANN, Michael John; s of Martin Horst Bostelmann; *b* 16 November 1947; *Educ* Bradfield; *m* 1973, Gillian, da of Allan Vickery; 2 s (Richard b 1979, David b 1981); *Career* Arnold Hill & Co CAs London: ptnr 1972–2011, sr ptnr 1985–2011; dir: British Paper Co 1974–2003, Quadrem Hope Ltd 1977–2003; gp md Fandstan Electric Gp 1998–2014; treas Royal Commonwealth Soc, pres Thames Hare and Hounds 2005–10; FCA, TEP; *Recreations* long distance running (fastest marathon 2 hrs 37 mins 1983), music, gardening, golf; *Clubs* Thames Hare and Hounds, Hurlingham; *Style*— Michael Bostelmann, Esq; ✉ 33 West Temple Sheen, East Sheen, London SW14 7AP (☎ 020 8878 2316)

BOSTOCK, Kate; *Educ* De Montfort Univ (BA); *Career* product dir for childrenswear Next 1994–2001, product dir Asda 2001–04, exec DG merchandise Marks & Spencer 2008– (joined as dir of womenswear 2004, memb Bd 2008–); hon doctorate: De Montfort Univ 2008, Manchester Met Univ 2008; *Style*— Ms Kate Bostock; ✉ Marks & Spencer Group plc, Waterside House, 35 North Wharf Road, London W2 1NW

BOSTOCK, Martin James; s of Alfred William Bostock, and Muriel Mary, *née* Alder; *b* 1953, Sussex; *Educ* Churcher's Coll Petersfield, Univ of Hull (BA); *m* 1988, Sue Batcheler; 1 da (Poppy b 1990), 1 s (Charlie b 1993); *Career* VSO teacher Thailand 1971–72, asst mangr El Vino Wine Bar London 1975–76; account dir: Extel Advertising and PR 1977–82, Abel Hadden Assoc 1982–83; gp account dir Good Relations 1983–84, head of press and publicity London Borough of Hackney 1984–86, chm Nelson Bostock Communications 1987–; dir Comms Div Creston plc; non-exec dir Tavistock & Portman NHS Fndn Tst; tstee Citizenship Fndn 2007–; memb PRCA 1989; *Recreations* collecting vintage guitars and playing the blues, tennis; *Style*— Martin Bostock; ✉ Nelson Bostock Communications, Compass House, 22 Redan Place, London W2 4SA (☎ 020 7229 4400, website www.nelsonbostock.com)

BOSTOCK, Thomas Geoffrey (Tom); *b* 14 December 1949; *Educ* St Lawrence Coll Ramsgate, Univ of Edinburgh (BArch); *Career* architect; architectural asst Oxford Architects Partnership 1971–72; Reiach and Hall Ltd (formerly Alan Reiach Eric Hall & Partners): architectural asst 1974–75, architect 1975–80, assoc 1980–83, ptnr 1983–93 (i/c opening Glasgow office 1986), dir and co sec 1993–; RIBA Regnl Awards (for British Steel Corporation office bldg Airdrie 1978 and Strathclyde Graduate Business Sch 1992); memb: Cncl Edinburgh Architectural Assoc 1982–85, Awards Ctee RIAS 1985–90; various lectures on practice mgmnt Univ of Edinburgh and Edinburgh Coll of Art 1986–, examiner RIBA Part III 1989–2000; RIBA, ARIAS; *Style*— Tom Bostock, Esq; ✉ Reiach and Hall Architects, 6 Darnaway Street, Edinburgh EH3 6BG (☎ 0131 225 8444, fax 0131 225 5079, e-mail tom.bostock@reiachandhall.co.uk)

BOSTRIDGE, Dr Ian Charles; CBE (2004); s of late Leslie John Bostridge, and Lilian Winifred, *née* Clark; *b* 25 December 1964; *Educ* Westminster (Queen's scholar), St John's Coll Oxford (scholar, MA, DPhil), St John's Coll Cambridge (MPhil); *m* 1992, Lucasta Frances Elizabeth, da of late Tim Miller; 1 s (Oliver Timothy b 28 July 2000), 1 da (Ottilie Allegra Amelia b 14 Dec 2006); *Career* tenor; débuts: Royal Festival Hall (young sailor in Tristan und Isolde) 1993, Barbican (Hylas in Les Troyens) 1994, Wigmore Hall (recital) 1995, Royal Opera House (Third Jew in Salome) 1995, ENO (Tamino in The Magic Flute) 1996, Bavarian State Opera (Nerone in L'Incoronazione di Poppea) 1998, Carnegie Hall (Les Nuits d'Été and Serenade for tenor, horn and strings) 1999, La Scala (recital) 2007; roles incl: Tom Rakewell, Peter Quint, Belmonte, Tamino, Young Man in Janá?ek's Diary of One Who Vanished, Idomeneo, Monteverdi's Orfeo, Aschenbach in Death in Venice, Madwoman in Curlew River (UK, US and Europe) 2013–; numerous recitals and concerts in Berlin, Paris, Sydney, NY, Brussels, Amsterdam, Edinburgh, Vienna, San Francisco, Salzburg, Florence and Milan; exclusive contract with EMI 1997–2014; humanities prof of classical music Univ of Oxford 2014–15; lectr Music and Magic Univ of Edinburgh Festival Lecture 2000; dedicatee Hans Werner Henze's Sechs Gesänge aus dem Arabischen; hon fell CCC Oxford 2001, hon fell St John's Coll Oxford 2010; Hon DMus Univ of St Andrews 2004; Hon RAM 2002; *Awards* NFMS Award 1991, Young Concert Artists' Tst Award 1992, Royal Philharmonic Soc Debut Award 1995, Gramophone Solo Vocal Award 1996 and 1998, South Bank Show Classical Music Award 1996, Echo Award 1997 and 1999, Munich Festival Prize 1998, Le Monde de la Musique Prize 1998, Opernwelt Male Singer of the Year 1998, Edison Award 1998 and 2001, Grammy 1999 and 2009 (12 time nominee), Time Out Award 1999, Brit Award 2000, Prix Caecilia 2001 and 2014, Preis der Deutscher Schallplattenkritik 2001, Japanese Recording Acad Award 2001, Gramophone Opera Award 2003 and 2010; *Books* Witchcraft and its Transformations c1650-c1750 (1997), A Singer's Notebook (2011), Schubert's Winter Journey: Anatomy of an Obsession (2014); *Recreations* reading, cooking, looking at pictures; *Style*— Dr Ian Bostridge, CBE; ✉ c/o Askonas Holt, Lincoln House, 300 High Holborn, London WC1V 7JH

BOSVILLE MACDONALD OF SLEAT, Sir Ian Godfrey; 17 Bt (NS 1625), of Sleat, Isle of Skye; also 25 Chief of Sleat; DL (East Riding of Yorkshire 1997); s of Sir (Alexander) Somerled Angus Bosville Macdonald of Sleat, 16 Bt, MC (24 Chief of Sleat, d 1958), and Mary Elizabeth, *née* Gibbs (d 2004); *b* 18 July 1947; *Educ* Pinewood Sch, Eton, RAC Cirencester; *m* 1970, Juliet Fleury, o da of late Maj-Gen John Ward-Harrison, OBE, MC; 2 da (Deborah Fleury b 1973, Isabel Mary b 1983), 1 s (Somerled Alexander b 1976); *Heir* s, Somerled Alexander Bosville Macdonald, yr of Sleat; *Career* chartered surveyor; memb: Royal Soc of Health 1972, Economic Research Cncl 1979–; memb (for Bridlington S) Humberside CC 1981–85; pres: Humberside Branch Br Red Cross 1988–96, Br Food and Farming Humberside 1989, Hull and East Riding Branch Br Red Cross 1996–2003, Humber and Wolds Rural Community Cncl 1997–2013, Humberside Young Farmers; chm: Rural Devpt Cmmn Humberside 1988–95, East Riding of Yorkshire Cncl Rural Partnership 1999–, Northern Region Br Red Cross 2000–03, Clan Donald Land & Tst 2008–; memb Bd of Tstees Br Red Cross 2001–06; High Sheriff Humberside 1988–89; FRICS 1986 (ARICS 1972), MRSH 1972–2008, RSPH 2009; *Recreations* ornithology; *Clubs* White's, New, Puffins, Lansdowne; *Style*— Sir Ian Bosville Macdonald of Sleat, Bt, DL; ✉ Hazel Bush House, York YO32 9TR (☎ 01904 468239, e-mail anauldman@gmail.com)

BOSWALL; *see:* Houstoun-Boswall

BOSWELL, Lindsay; *Educ* Merchiston Castle Sch Edinburgh; *m*; 2 da; *Career* offr rising to maj Argyll and Sutherland Highlanders Inf Regt 1978–89; Raleigh Int: co dir for Zimbabwe, Botswana, Chile and Malaysia 1990–94, prog dir 1994–98; London dir Prince's Tst Volunteers 2000, chief exec Inst of Fundraising 2000–10, chief exec FareShare; tstee SOFII Fndn, memb Bd Fedn of European Foodbanks; *Recreations* gardening; *Style*— Lindsay Boswell, Esq; ✉ FareShare, Unit 7 Deptford Trading Estate, Blackhorse Road, London SE8 5HY (☎ 020 7394 2465)

BOSWELL, Lindsay Alice; QC (1997); da of Graham Leonard William Boswell, OBE (d 1988), and Erica Margaret Boswell (d 1996); *b* Nov 1958, Kenya; *Educ* St Mary's Ascot, Brooke Hse Market Harborough, UCL (BSc), City Univ London (Dip Law); *m* 28 March 1987, Jonathan Acton Davis, QC, *qv*; 1 s; *Career* called to the Bar Gray's Inn 1982 (bencher); legal memb Proscribed Orgns Appeal Cmmn; *Recreations* bees, sheep, cool water swimming; *Clubs* RAF, Dolphin Club San Francisco; *Style*— Miss Lindsay Boswell, QC; ✉ Quadrant Chambers, 10 Fleet Street, London EC4Y 1AU (☎ 020 7583 4444, fax 020 7583 4455, e-mail lindsay.boswell@quadrantchambers.com)

BOSWELL OF AYNHO, Baron (Life Peer UK 2010), of Aynho in the County of Northamptonshire; Timothy Eric Boswell; DL (Northants 2010); s of Eric New Boswell (d 1974), of Banbury, and Joan Winifred Caroline, *née* Jones (d 2003); *b* 2 December 1942; *Educ* Marlborough, New Coll Oxford (MA, post grad dip); *m* 2 Aug 1969, Helen Delahay, da of Rev Arthur Delahay Rees (d 1954), of Swansea; 3 da (Hon Victoria Prentis, MP, *qv*, b 1971, Hon Emily b 1975, Hon Caroline b 1978); *Career* head of Econ Section Cons Res Dept 1970–73 (agric and economics advsr 1966–73); managed family farm from father's death in 1974; MP (Cons) Daventry 1987–2010; memb Commons Select Ctee on Agriculture 1987–89, PPS to fin sec to the Treasy 1989–90, asst Govt whip 1990–92, a Lord Cmmr of the Treasury (sr whip) 1992, Parly under sec of state Dept for Education 1992–95, Parly under sec of state MAFF 1995–97; oppn frontbench spokesman on: Treasy 1997, DTI matters 1997–99, educn and employment 1999–2001, people with disabilities 1999–2003, work and pensions 2001–02; shadow min: for educn and skills 2002–03, for legal, constitutional and home affrs 2003–04, for work 2004–06; PPS to Party Chm 2005–07; memb Commons Select Ctee on Innovation, Univs, Sci and Skills 2007–10, princ dep chm of ctees and chair EU Select Ctee House of Lords 2012–; memb UK Delgn Parly Assembly Cncl of Europe 2007–12; chm Parly Charity Law Reform Panel 1988–90; chm Daventry Constituency Cons Assoc 1979–83 (treas 1976–79); chm Northants Leics and Rutland Counties branch NFU 1983; memb: Cncl Perry Fndn for Agric Research 1966–90 (pres 1984–90), AFRC 1988–90; govr: Univ of Wales Inst Cardiff 2007–12, Univ of Northampton 2010–12; FSA 2016; *Recreations* shooting, countryside, snooker, poetry; *Clubs* Farmers'; *Style*— The Lord Boswell of Aynho, DL; ✉ Lower Aynho Grounds, Banbury, Oxfordshire OX17 3BW

BOSWOOD, Anthony Richard; QC (1986); s of late Noel Gordon Paul Boswood, of Radnage, Bucks, and Cicily Ann, *née* Watson; *b* 1 October 1947; *Educ* St Paul's, New Coll Oxford (BCL, MA); *m* 4 Jan 1973, Sarah Bridget, da of Sir John Lindsay Alexander; 3 da (Eleanor b 1976, Louise b 1978, Grace b 1983); *Career* called to the Bar Middle Temple 1970; *Recreations* opera, riding, racing; *Clubs* Athenaeum; *Style*— Anthony Boswood, Esq, QC; ✉ Fountain Court, Temple, London EC4Y 9DH (☎ 020 7583 3335, fax 020 7353 0329/1794, mobile 07713 106918, e-mail aboswood@fountaincourt.co.uk); Podere Casanuova, Pieveasciata, Castelnuovo Berardenga (SI), Italy; South Hay House, Kingsley, Bordon, Hampshire GU35 9NR

BOSWORTH, Simon Charles Neville; s of Sir Neville Bruce Alfred Bosworth, CBE (d 2012), and Lady Charlotte Marian Bosworth (d 2003); *b* 6 August 1946; *Educ* Stouts Hill Gloucester, Bradfield; *m* 2 Feb 1979, Evelyn Fay, da of William Leslie Wallace (d 1984); 1 da (Claudia b 1984); *Career* dir: W H Cutler (Midlands) Ltd 1968–70, Sutton (Wine Bars) Ltd 1972–74, Hill Alveston & Co Ltd 1973–98, Luttrell Park Investments Ltd 1974–2009, Berkswell Properties Ltd 1983–, Berkswell Investments Ltd 1984–; *Recreations* football, gardening; *Style*— Simon C N Bosworth, Esq; ✉ Chance, Banbury Hill, Shutford, Banbury, Oxfordshire OX15 6PE

BOTHAM, Sir Ian Terence; kt (2007), OBE (1992); s of Les Botham, and Marie Botham; *b* 24 November 1955; *Educ* Buckler's Mead Secdy Sch Yeovil; *m* 31 Jan 1976, Kathryn; 1 s (Liam James b 26 Aug 1977), 2 da (Sarah Lianne b 3 Feb 1979, Rebecca Kate b 13 Nov 1985); *Career* former professional cricketer; Somerset CCC: second XI 1971, first class debut 1974, awarded county cap 1976, capt 1984–85, benefit 1984; Worcestershire CCC 1987–91 (capped 1987), Queensland Aust off-season 1987–88, Durham CCC 1992–93 (capped 1992); England: 116 one day ints, 102 test matches 1977–92, capt 12 tests 1980–81, highest score 208 v India Oval 1982, best bowling 8 for 34 v Pakistan Lord's 1978; tours: Pakistan/NZ 1977–78, Aust 1978–79, Aust and India 1979–80, W Indies 1980–81, India 1981–82, Aust/NZ 1982–83, W Indies 1985–86, Aust 1986–87, NZ/Aust

1991–92; pt/t technical advsr England squad Zimbabwe and New Zealand 1996–97; test records incl: scored 1000 runs and took 100 wickets in fewest matches, first player to score a century and take 8 wickets in an innings (v Pakistan Lord's 1978), scored third fastest double century by Englishman (200 in 272 minutes v India Oval 1982); BBC TV Sporting Personality of the Year 1981; team capt Question of Sport (BBC 1) until 1996, currently cricket commentator Sky TV; various appearances in pantomime, raised over £6m for Leukaemia Research through long-distance walks; *Books* incl: Botham Down Under, High, Wide and Handsome, It Sort of Clicks (with Peter Roebuck), Cricket My Way (with Jack Bannister), The Incredible Tests (with late Peter Smith), Botham: My Autobiography (with Peter Hayter, 1994), The Botham Report (1997), Botham's Century (2001), Head On: The Autobiography (2007), Ian Botham on Fishing (2008), My Sporting Heroes (2009); *Recreations* golf, shooting, salmon and trout fishing, flying; *Style*— Sir Ian Botham, OBE; ✉ Essentially, 3rd Floor, 62 Buckingham Gate, London SW1E 6AJ (e-mail ross.connolly@essentiallygroup.com)

BOTT, Alan John; OBE (1995); s of Albert Henry John Bott, and Eileen Mary, *née* Spiers; *b* 30 March 1935; *Educ* KCS Wimbledon, Merton Coll Oxford (MA, postmaster); *m* 10 Sept 1966, Caroline Gaenor, da of Frank Leslie Williams (d 1943); 2 s (Jonathan b 3 April 1968, Simon b 26 June 1970), 1 da (Alison b 24 March 1972); *Career* dir: The NZ Shipping Co 1971 (joined 1956), P&O Containers Ltd (formerly Overseas Containers Ltd) 1976–96; chm: The Aust and NZ Shipping Confs 1978–94, The Europe Southern Africa Shipping Conf 1990–96, NZ/UK C of C and Indust 1990–96; dir and vice-pres ECSA, dir and vice-chm CENSA until 1996; extra mural lectr in architecture London and Surrey Univs 1962–, NADFAS lectr 1997–, memb Guildford Diocesan Advsy Ctee 2001–, memb Surrey Archaeological Soc Cncl 2000–03 and 2005–09; Swan Hellenic lectr 2000–; churchwarden Godalming Parish Church 1979–2000 and 2001–02 (dep churchwarden 1979 and 2002–10, emeritus churchwarden 2011), tstee Godalming Museum 1986– (chm 1994–); Bodley fell Merton Coll Oxford 2001 (memb SCR 1993–); FSA 1965; FCIT 1990; *Books* Monuments in Merton College Chapel (1964), Sailing Ships of The NZSCO (1973), Godalming Parish Church (1978, 4 edn 2012), Baptisms and Marriages at Merton College Oxford (1981), Rake Manor, Godalming (1990), Merton College, A Short History of the Buildings (1993), Wall Paintings in Godalming Church (1996), The Ancient Roofs and Heraldic Bosses in Godalming Church (1999), Compton Parish Church (2000), The Heraldry in Merton College Oxford (2001), Witley and Thursley Parish Churches (2003), Beddgelert Parish Church (2004), Dunsfold and Hascombe Parish Churches (2005), Peper Harow and Shackleford Parish Churches (2007, addendum 2014), British Box Business: A History of OCL (Overseas Containers Ltd) (ed, 2009), Chiddingfold Parish Church (2009), Treasures of Merton College (contrib, 2013), Merton College, a Longer History of the Buildings and Furnishings (2016); *Recreations* tennis, golf, gardening, writing and lecturing on the history of European architecture; *Clubs* Travellers; *Style*— Alan Bott, Esq, OBE; ✉ Rake Court, Milford, Godalming, Surrey GU8 5AD (☎ 01483 416546)

BOTT, Valerie; MBE (2014); da of Rowland Bott (d 1993), and Joan Evelyn, *née* Lydeard (d 2003); *b* 16 December 1948; *Educ* Thistley Hough Sch for Girls Stoke-on-Trent, UCL (BA), Univ of Leicester (Dip Museum Studies, MA); *Partner* 1967–, James Wisdom; *Career* sr asst Vestry House Museum Waltham Forest 1971–75, keeper Grange Museum Brent 1975–86, museum devpt offr Wandsworth 1986–88, head Newham Museum Service 1988–93, conslt curator to Fairground Heritage Tst 1994–96 (also freelance cmmns), dep dir Museums & Galleries Commission 1996–2000, Museum Consultancy 2000–; chair Museum Professionals Gp 1979–80, pres London Fedn of Museums & Galleries 1988–91, chair London Museums Consultative Ctee 1990–93, hon treas, tstee and hon sec Thames Explorer Tst, memb London Regnl Ctee Heritage Lottery Fund 2001–07, chair William Hogarth Tst 2001–08 and 2011–, tstee The Cartoon Museum; FMA 1980 (AMA 1974); *Recreations* keeping ducks, gardening, museums, local history/garden history research; *Style*— Ms Valerie Bott, MBE; ✉ 25 Hartington Road, Chiswick, London W4 3TL (fax 020 8994 4231, e-mail valbott@museums.freeserve.co.uk, websites www.valbott.co.uk, http://nurserygardeners.com and http://williamhogarthtrust.org.uk)

BOTTING, (Elizabeth) Louise; CBE (1993); da of Robert Young (d 1956), and Edith, *née* Roberts (d 1981); sis of John R C Young, CBE, *qv*; *b* 19 September 1939; *Educ* Sutton Coldfield HS, LSE (BSc Econ); *m* 1, 1964 (m dis 1986), Douglas Botting; 2 da (Catherine b 1966, Anna b 1967); *m* 2, 23 May 1989, Leslie Carpenter, *qv*; *Career* broadcaster and financial journalist; investment analyst Kleinwort Benson 1961–65, columnist Daily Mail 1970–75, Br Forces Broadcasting 1971–83; Douglas Deakin Young fin consultancy: joined 1975, md 1982–88, chm 1988–95; presenter Money Box (BBC Radio 4) 1977–92; chm New 102 Ltd 1996–2001; non-exec dir: Trinity Mirror (formerly Trinity plc) 1991–99, London Weekend Television (Holdings) plc 1992–94, General Accident 1992–98, CGU plc 1998–2000 (following merger with Commercial Union); memb Bd Camelot 1999–2010; memb Senior Salaries Review Body 1987–94; *Style*— Louise Botting, CBE

BOTTOLI, Marcello Vittorio; *b* 5 January 1962; *Educ* Bocconi Univ Milan (MBA); *m*; 4 c; *Career* chm and ceo Louis Vuitton Malletier 2001–02, pres and ceo Samsonite Corp 2004–09, interim ceo then chm Pandora A/S 2010–14, operating ptnr Advent Int Corp 2010–14, ceo My Azzurra Ltd 2016–; *Style*— Marcello Bottoli, Esq

BOTTOMLEY, Sir Peter James; kt (2011), MP; s of Sir James Bottomley, KCMG; bro of Susan Whitfield, *qv*; *b* 30 July 1944; *Educ* Westminster, Trinity Coll Cambridge (MA); *m* 1967, Virginia Hilda Brunette Maxwell (Baroness Bottomley of Nettlestone, PC (Life Peer)), *qv*, da of John Garnett, CBE (d 1997); 1 s, 2 da; *Career* MP (Cons): Greenwich, Woolwich W June 1975–83 (also contested both 1974 gen elections), Eltham 1983–97, Worthing West 1997–; PPS to: Min of State FCO 1982–83, Sec of State for Social Servs 1983–84, Sec of State for NI 1990; Parly under sec of state: Dept of Employment 1984–86, Dept of Transport (min for roads) 1986–89, NI Office (min for agriculture and for environment) 1989–90; chm: Br Union of Family Orgns 1973–80, Family Forum 1980–82, C of E Children's Soc 1983–84; tstee Christian Aid 1978–84; memb Ct of Assts Worshipful Co of Drapers; *Recreations* family time, sailing; *Style*— Sir Peter Bottomley, MP; ✉ House of Commons, London SW1A 0AA

BOTTOMLEY, Stephen John; s of Frederick John Bottomley, of Norwich, and Jean Mary, *née* Moore; *b* 23 October 1954; *Educ* Sutton Valence, UEA (BA), IOD (Cert); *Family* 2 da (Clare b 1987, Emma b 1989), 1 s (Charles b 1991); *Career* admitted slr: Eng and Wales 1980, Hong Kong 2008; ptnr Bartletts De Reya 1984–88, dir Johnson Fry Corporate Finance Ltd 1988, ptnr Mayer Brown (formerly Rowe & Maw) 1988–; Freeman Worshipful Co of Slrs; memb Law Socs of Eng & Wales and of Hong Kong; *Recreations* golf, cycling, skiing; *Style*— Stephen Bottomley, Esq; ✉ 22B Taggart House, 109 Repulse Bay, Hong Kong (☎ 00 852 2812 2063); Mayer Brown JSM, 16th-19th Floors, Prince's Building, 10 Chater Road, Central, Hong Kong (☎ 00 852 2843 2201)

BOTTOMLEY OF NETTLESTONE, Baroness (Life Peer UK 2005), of St Helens in the County of Isle of Wight; Virginia Hilda Brunette Maxwell Bottomley; PC (1992), DL (Surrey 2006); *née* Garnett; da of John Garnett, CBE (d 1997); *b* 12 March 1948; *Educ* LSE (MSc); *m* 1967, Peter James Bottomley, MP, *qv*; 1 s, 2 da; *Career* social scientist 1971–84, chm Lambeth Juvenile Court 1981–84; Parly candidate (Cons) IOW 1983, MP (Cons) Surrey SW 1984–2005; PPS to: Min of State for Educn and Sci 1985–86, Min for Overseas Devpt 1986–87, Sec of State for Foreign and Cwlth Affrs 1987–88; Parly under sec of state DOE 1988–89, min of state Dept of Health 1989–92, sec of state for health 1992–95, sec of state for nat heritage 1995–97; chm Millennium Cmmn 1995–97, vice-chair Br Cncl (memb Bd 1997–2000); pro-chllr Univ of Surrey 2005–15, chllr Univ of Hull 2006–; memb: Ct of Govrs LSE 1985–2016, MRC 1987–88, Governing Body ICC UK, Int Cncl Chugai Pharmaceutical Co, Int Bd of Overseeers Sabanci Univ Istanbul; govr: London Univ of the Arts 2000–06, Ditchley Fndn 1991–; chair bd practice Odgers Berndtson, dir Mid Southern Water Co 1987–88, memb Supervisory Bd AkzoNobel NV 2000–12, non-exec dir BUPA 2007–13, non-exec dir Smith & Nephew 2012–; ind tstee The Economist 2006–; JP Inner London 1975–84; pres Abbeyfield Soc 2003–09; lay canon Guildford Cathedral 2004–13; fell Industry and Parliament Tst 1987; Freeman City of London 1989, Sheriff Kingston upon Hull 2013–; *Recreations* family; *Clubs* Athenaeum; *Style*— The Rt Hon the Baroness Bottomley of Nettlestone, DL; ✉ House of Lords, London SW1A 0PW

BOTTOMS, Prof Sir Anthony Edward; kt (2001); s of Dr James William Bottoms (d 1980), and Dorothy Ethel, *née* Barnes (d 1983); *b* 29 August 1939, Shillong, India; *Educ* Eltham Coll, Corpus Christi Coll Oxford (MA), Corpus Christi Coll Cambridge (Dip Crim, MA), Univ of Sheffield (PhD); *m* 1962, Janet Freda, da of Rev E L Wenger; 2 da (Catharine b 1966, Erica b 1970), 1 s (Stephen b 1968); *Career* probation officer 1962–64, research officer Inst of Criminology Univ of Cambridge 1964–68; Univ of Sheffield: lectr 1968–72, sr lectr 1972–76, prof of criminology 1976–84, dean of Faculty of Law 1981–84; dir Inst of Criminology Univ of Cambridge 1984–98, Wolfson prof of criminology Univ of Cambridge 1984–2006 (emeritus prof 2006–), professorial fell Univ of Sheffield 2002–07 (hon prof 2008–); visiting fell Simon Fraser Univ BC Canada 1982, visiting prof Queen's Univ Belfast 1999–2000, life fell Fitzwilliam Coll Cambridge 2006– (pres 1994–98, fell 1984–2006); ed Howard Journal of Penology and Crime Prevention 1975–81; memb: Parole Bd for England and Wales 1974–76, Home Office Research and Advsy Gp on Long-term Prison System 1984–90; specialist advsr House of Commons NI Ctee 1998, 2003–04 and 2007; author of numerous books and articles on criminological topics; chm of tstees Westminster Coll Cambridge 2008–14; Sellin-Glueck Award American Soc of Criminology 1996, European Criminology Award European Soc of Criminology 2007; Hon LLD: Queen's Univ Belfast 2003, Univ of Sheffield 2009, Univ of Edinburgh 2015; hedersdoktor Malmö Univ 2014; hon fell Corpus Christi Coll Oxford 2012–; FBA 1997; *Style*— Prof Sir Anthony Bottoms, FBA; ✉ Institute of Criminology, Sidgwick Avenue, Cambridge CB3 9DA (☎ 01223 335360, fax 01223 335356, e-mail aeb11@cam.ac.uk)

BOTTONE, Bonaventura; s of Bonaventura Bottone, of Harrow, and Kathleen, *née* Barnes; *b* 19 September 1950; *Educ* Lascelles Secdy Modern Sch Harrow, Royal Acad of Music London; *m* 28 April 1973, Jennifer, da of Ralph Dakin (d 1973); 2 s (Benjamin Nicholas b 13 Jan 1978, Jonathan Samuel b 16 March 1984), 2 da (Francesca Louise, Rebecca Charlotte (twins) b 23 Nov 1979); *Career* tenor; appeared at numerous international venues incl: Royal Opera House Covent Garden, London Coliseum, Glyndebourne Festival, Nice Opera, Batignano Festival Opera, Houston Opera, Met Opera NY, Munich Bavarian State Opera, Cleveland Symphony Orch Blossom Festival 1997, Santiago Chile 1998; has sung with numerous prominent int conductors incl: Richard Bonynge, Sir Andrew Davis, Jacques Delacote, Sir Edward Downes, Sir Mark Elder, Rafael Fruhbeck de Burgos, Bernard Haitink, KBE, CH, Richard Hickox, Vladimir Jurowski, James Levine, Sir Charles Mackerras, Sir Neville Marriner, Carlo Rizzi, Jeffrey Tate; frequent BBC broadcaster, concert artist worldwide; FRAM 1998 (ARAM 1984); *Roles* with ENO incl: David in Die Meistersinger, The Duke of Mantua in Rigoletto, Alfred in La Traviata, Beppe in I Pagliacci, Nanki-Poo in The Mikado, Sam Kaplan in Street Scene, Truffaldino in The Love for Three Oranges, Lenski in Eugene Onegin 1994, Rodolfo in La Boheme, title role in Dr Ox by Gavin Bryars (premier) 1998; with Royal Opera Co incl: the Italian Tenor in Der Rosenkavalier (Covent Garden debut), Cassio in Otello, Alfredo in Die Fledermaus, the Italian Tenor in Capriccio, Raoul de Nangis in Les Hugenots, Torquemada in L'Neure Espagnole, Comte Liebenskof in Viaggio a Reims; with Scottish Opera incl: Governor General in Candide, Loge in Das Rheingold, Narraboth in Salome; others incl: Italian Tenor in Capriccio (Glyndebourne Festival Opera) 1990, Alfredo in La Traviata (Opera North) 1990, title role in Le Comte Ory (WNO) 1992, Pedrillo in Die Entführung aus dem Serail (Houston Opera, US debut), Fernando in La Favorita (WNO) 1993, Dream of Gerontius (Royal Festival Hall) 1994, the Italian Tenor in Capriccio (Chicago Lyric Opera debut) 1994, Governor General in Candide (Lisbon debut) 1994, BBC Proms 1996, Turiddu in Cavelleria Rusticana (WNO) 1996, Faust in Damnation of Faust 1997, Pinkerton in Madama Butterfly (Florentine Opera Milwaukee) 2000, Alfred in Die Fledermaus (Opéra National de Paris Bastille) 2000, Riccardo in Un Ballo in Maschera (Atlanta Opera debut, 2001), Damnation de Faust (Brisbane Symphony Orchestra) 2002, Troilus in Troilus and Cressida (Philharmonia Orchestra) 2002, Faust in Faust et Hélèn (Deutsches Symphonic Orchestra Berlin) 2002, Nanki Poo Mikado (La Fenice Venice) 2003, Loge in Das Rheingold (Lyric Opera Chicago) 2005, Rodolfo in La Bohèmè (Opera Queensland) 2005, Ménélaus in La Belle Hélène (ENO) 2006, Alfred in Die Fledermaus (Glyndebourne Festival and Chicago Lyric Opera) 2006, Govr in Candide (La Scala Milan debut) 2007, Torquemada in L'Heure Espagnole (ROH) 2007, Licht in Der Zerbrochene Krug (LA debut) 2008, Nick in Puccini's La Fanciulla Del West (ROH) 2008, Britten Serenade for Tenor Horn and Strings (Edmonton Symphony Orchestra) 2009, The Duke of Dunstable in Patience (BBC Prom) 2009, Govr in Candide (Kobe and Tokyo) 2010, L'Abate in Cilea's Adriana Lecouvreur (ROH) 2010, Les Illumination (Edmonton Symphony Orch) 2011, Basilio in Le Nozze de Figaro (ROH) 2012, Fanciulla del West 2014, Der Rosenkavalier (City of Birmingham Symphony Orchestra) 2014, Grand Messe de Mort (Cambridge Philharmonic Orchestra) 2014, Jacobin (Buxton Festival) 2014, On Wenlock Edge (Edmonton Symphony Orchestra) 2014, Tribute to Mario Lanza (Edmonton Symphony Orchestra) 2014, Lucia di Lammermoor (Buxton Festival) 2015; *Recordings* incl: Cassio in Otello, Arturo in Lucia di Lammermoor, Nanki-Poo in The Mikado (with ENO (highlights), also with D'Oyly Carte), The Student Prince, Orpheus In The Underworld (with ENO), Sondheim's A Little Night Music, Weill's Street Scene, Tippett's The Ice Break, Vaughan Williams' Hugh the Drover (Hyperion), Lily Boulanger's Faust et Hélène (Chandos), Golden Operetta Highlights, Verdi Otello, All-Star Tenors Salute The World 1990, Bernstein Candide 1993, Kismet 1995, Italian Tenor Der Rosenkavalier (ROH) 1995, L'Abate in Cilea's Adriana Lecouvreur (ROH) 2010, Der Zerbrochene Krug (LA Opera) 2012; *Recreations* gardening, cycling, boating; *Style*— Bonaventura Bottone, Esq; ✉ c/o Rayfield Allied, Southbank House, Black Prince Road, London SE1 7SJ (☎ 020 3176 5500, fax 07006 024143, e-mail info@rayfieldallied.com); website www.bonaventurabottone.com

BOUCH, Dr (Dennis) Clive; s of Tom Bouch (d 1967), and Elizabeth Anderson, *née* Errington (d 2011); *b* 12 September 1939; *Educ* Nelson Thomlinson GS Wigton, Univ of Edinburgh (BSc, MB ChB); *m* 12 Sept 1968, (Valerie Alexander) Sandra, da of Alexander Lamb (d 1983), of Edinburgh; 2 s (David Christopher b 1972, Jeremy Clive b 1973), 2 da (Caroline Anne b 1975, Katharine Mary b 1978); *Career* lectr in pathology Univ of Edinburgh 1966–75, conslt pathologist to Leics HA 1976–2004, head of dist pathology serv 1985–94, Home Office pathologist 1984–2010, dir of forensic pathology Univ of Leicester 1990–2010; chm: Dist Hosps Med Staff Ctee Leics HA 1984–88, Dist Med Advsy Ctee Leics HA 1990–94; conslt memb Policy Advsy Gp Leics HA 1990–94; memb Home Office Policy Advsy Bd for Forensic Pathology 2000–07; FRCPath 1985; *Style*— Dr Clive Bouch; ✉ 21 Ashfield Road, Leicester LE2 1LB

BOULDING, Philip Vincent; QC (1996); s of Vincent Fergusson Boulding, of Cambridge, and Sylvia Boulding; *b* 1 February 1954, Cambridge; *Educ* Downing Coll Cambridge (scholar, MA, LLM, Rugby blue, pres CU Amateur Boxing Club); *m* Helen Elizabeth, da of Joseph William Richardson; 1 s (Joseph William b 1993), 1 da (Harriet Helen b 1995); *Career* called to the Bar: Gray's Inn 1979 (Holker Entrance Award 1978, Sr Holker Award

1979, bencher 2004), Hong Kong Bar 1997; specialist in construction, engrg and technol law worldwide, regularly sits as an arbitrator, adjudicator and mediator in construction and engrg disputes; practising in Hong Kong and the Far East on, amongst others, large commercial developments and infrastructure projects since 1997 in addition to practising in the UK; conslt ed Construction Law Reports; former memb Ctee Official Referees' Bar Assoc; memb: London Common Law and Commercial Bar Assoc, London Court of Int Arbitration (LCIA), TECBAR Ctee; arbitration panellist: Hong Kong Int Arbitration Centre (HKIAC), KLRC; appointed govr Hills Road VI Form Coll Cambridge 1997–2000; played rugby for England (at under 23 level) 1977 and Bedford RUFC; sr pres Downing Coll Griffins Club 2003–; *Publications* Keating on Construction Contracts (contrib), Construction Law Reports (gen ed); *Recreations* sport generally, fine wine, cutting grass; *Clubs* Hawks' (Cambridge), RAC; *Style*— Philip Boulding, Esq, QC; ✉ Keating Chambers, 15 Essex Street, Outer Temple, London WC2R 3AA (☎ 020 7544 2600, fax 020 7240 7722, e-mail pboulding@keatingchambers.com)

BOULOS, Prof Paul Bernard; s of Bernard Boulos (d 1964), of Khartoum, Sudan, and Evelyn, *née* Haggar; *b* 10 March 1944; *Educ* Comboni Coll Khartoum, Univ of Khartoum (MB BS); *m* 1 March 1979, Marilyn Lesley, da of Ronald Robert Went (d 1994), of Highgate, London; 1 s (Mark Ronald b 22 Aug 1980), 2 da (Sarah-Jane b 15 Sept 1981, Paula Louise b 28 Dec 1984); *Career* surgical registrar UCH 1970–73; lectr in surgery Faculty of Med Univ of Khartoum 1973–76, res fell Dept of Surgical Studies Middx Hosp 1976–77, sr surgical registrar UCH 1977–80 and St Mark's Hosp 1980–81; UCL: sr lectr in surgery 1981–92, reader in surgery 1992–97, prof of surgery 1997–; conslt surgn: UCH 1981–, The Middlesex Hosp 1993–; memb: RSM (memb Cncl Coloproctology Section), Assoc of Surgns of GB and I, Br Soc of Gastroenterology, Assoc of Coloproctology of GB and I, Surgical Res Soc, BMA, American Soc of Colon Rectal Surgns, Soc of Expert Witnesses; RCSEng surgical tutor; RCSEd examiner; NE Thames coll rep, coll tutor Hong Kong, Univ of London examiner; MS, FRCS, FRCSEd, Hon FCS (Hong Kong); *Style*— Prof Paul Boulos; ✉ St Anne, 15 Richmond Road, New Barnet, Hertfordshire EN5 1SA (☎ 020 8449 6552, fax 020 8449 6252); Academic Division of Surgery and Interventional Science, University College London Medical School, The Medical School Building, 74 Huntley Street, London WC1E 6AU (☎ 020 7679 6490, fax 020 7679 6470, e-mail p.boulos@ucl.ac.uk)

BOULT, Geoffrey Pattisson; *b* 6 June 1957; *Educ* St Edward's Sch Oxford, Hatfield Coll Durham (BA), Univ of Durham (PGCE); *m* 27 July 1984, Katie, *née* Goddard; 4 da (Alice b 2 March 1986, Tessa b 30 April 1988, Zoë b 28 Aug 1991, Matilda b 2 Aug 1997); *Career* geography teacher Canford Sch 1980–87, teacher Geelong GS Australia 1984–85, head of geography Cranleigh Sch 1987–92, housemaster Field House St Edward's Sch Oxford 1994–2001, headmaster Giggleswick Sch 2001–; sec Oxford Conf in Educn 1986–88; chm Boarding Schs Assoc 2007–08; *Recreations* golf, walking, hockey, reading, music; *Clubs* Pedagogues, Cryptics, Tallow Chandler; *Style*— Geoffrey Boult, Esq; ✉ Giggleswick School, Settle, North Yorkshire BD24 0DE (☎ 01729 893005, fax 01729 893150, e-mail headmaster@giggleswick.org.uk)

BOULTON, Prof Andrew James Michael; s of Prof James Thompson Boulton, and Margaret Helen, *née* Leary; *b* 21 February 1953; *Educ* Nottingham HS, Univ of Newcastle upon Tyne (MB BS, MD); *m* 1, 3 July 1976 (m dis 1996), Helen Frances; 1 s (Jonathan David b 1 July 1978), 2 da (Caroline Helen b 14 Sept 1979, Sarah Elizabeth b 24 July 1985); m 2, 18 Aug 1997, Dr Loretta Vileikyte; *Career* sr med registrar Royal Hallamshire Hosp 1981–86 (diabetes res fell 1979–81), visiting asst prof of med Univ of Miami Florida 1983–84, conslt and prof in med Manchester Royal Infirmary 1995– (conslt and sr lectr 1986–91, reader and conslt 1991–95); R D Lawrence lectr Br Diabetic Assoc 1990, Pecoraro lectr American Diabetes Assoc 1996, Camillo Gogli lectr European Diabetes Assoc 2003; ed Diabetic Medicine 1991–95 (formerly dep ed); chm: Postgrad Educn Euro Diabetes Assoc 1995–2001, Diabetic Foot Study Gp Europe 1998–2001; pres Euro Diabetes Assoc 2011– (hon sec 2001–04, vice-pres 2008–11), chair Foot Cncl American Diabetes Assoc 2005–07; author numerous papers on diabetic complications; Hon DSc Univ of Cluj-Napoca Romania 2003; FRCP 1992 (MRCP 1979); *Books* The Foot In Diabetes (jtly, 1987, 4 edn 2006), Diabetes In Practice (jtly, 1989), Diabetic Neuropathy (1997); *Recreations* campanology, classical music; *Style*— Prof Andrew Boulton; ✉ Department of Medicine, Manchester Royal Infirmary, Oxford Road, Manchester M13 9WL (☎ 0161 276 4452, fax 0161 274 4740, e-mail andrew.j.boulton@man.ac.uk)

BOULTON, Fiona Jane; da of Michael Harry Lockton, and (Elizabeth) Iona, *née* Williams; *b* 11 April 1964, Sutton Coldfield, W Midlands; *Educ* UC Cardiff (BSc), Exeter Coll Oxford (PGCE), Inst of Educn Univ of London (MA, NPQH); *m* 23 July 1994, Richard Edward Stanley Boulton, *qv*, s of Sir Clifford Boulton, GCB, DL; 2 da (Honor Olivia Anne b 26 April 1998, Katia Jane Imogen b 23 Sept 2001), 1 s (Fraser William James b 22 Jan 2000); *Career* housemistress: Stowe Sch 1989–91, Marlborough Coll 1991–95; headmistress Guildford HS 2002– (dep head 1996–2002); *Recreations* family, cooking, walking, reading, art; *Style*— Mrs Fiona Boulton; ✉ Guildford High School, London Road, Guildford, Surrey GU1 1SJ (☎ 01483 561440, mobile 07769 705010, e-mail fiona.boulton@church-schools.co.uk)

BOULTON, Prof Geoffrey Stewart; OBE (2000); s of George Stewart Boulton (d 2000), of Forsbrook, Staffs, and Rose Boulton (d 1990); *b* 28 November 1940; *Educ* Longton HS, Univ of Birmingham (BSc, PhD, DSc); *m* Denise Bryers, da of Joseph Lawns; 2 da (Katherine Elisabeth b 7 March 1973, Olivia Frances b 28 April 1976); *Career* Br Geological Survey 1962–64, Keele Univ 1964–65, Univ of Birmingham 1965–67, Water Dept Nairobi 1968, lectr then reader Sch of Environmental Science UEA 1968–86, prof Univ of Amsterdam 1980–86; Univ of Edinburgh: regius prof of geology and mineralogy 1986–2008, provost and dean Faculty of Science 1994–99 (vice-princ 1999–2008); chm: NERC Polar Science Bd until 1994, NERC Earth Science and Technol Bd, Royal Soc Section Ctee for Earth Science and Astronomy, Academic Advsy Cncl Univ of Heidelberg 2009–, Royal Soc Science Policy Advsy Gp 2012–; memb: Natural Environment Research Cncl, Nature Conservancy Cncl for Scotland Science Bd until 1992, Royal Cmmn on Environmental Pollution 1994–2000, Cncl Royal Soc 1997–2000 and 2012–, Scottish Higher Educn Funding Cncl 1997–2003, Scottish Science Advsy Ctee 2002–08, Cncl for Science and Technol 2004–10, Strategic Cncl Univ of Geneva; gen sec RSE 2007–11, pres Scottish Assoc of Marine Science 2013–, pres Ctee on Data for Science and Technol (CODATA) Int Cncl for Science (ICSU); contrib to numerous books and papers in glaciology, Polar science and global environmental change; Kirk Bryan Medal Geological Soc of America, Seligman Crystal Int Glaciological Soc, Lyell Medal Geological Soc of London 2006, Tedford Medal for Science Inst for Contemporary Scotland 2006, James Croll Medal Quaternery Research Assoc 2011, Founder's Royal Medal RGS 2014, Polar Medal 2015; Hon DTech Chalmers Univ, Hon DSc Univ of Birmingham, Hon DSc Univ of Keele, Hon DSc Univ of Heidelberg; FRS 1991, FRSE 1989, FGS; Commandeur de l'Ordre des Palmes Accademiques 2009; *Recreations* climbing, violin, sailing; *Clubs* New (Edinburgh); *Style*— Prof Geoffrey Boulton; ✉ 19 Lygon Road, Edinburgh EH16 5QD (☎ 0131 667 2531); Department of Geology and Geophysics, Grant Institute, Kings Buildings, University of Edinburgh, Edinburgh EH9 3JW (☎ 0131 650 4844, fax 0131 668 3184, e-mail g.boulton@ed.ac.uk)

BOULTON, Richard Edward Stanley; QC (2011); s of Sir Clifford Boulton, GCB, DL, and Anne, *née* Raven; *b* 3 May 1959; *Educ* Marlborough (Wedgwood scholar), Oriel Coll Oxford (MA, half blue), Guildford Coll of Law (Dip Law), BPP Law Sch (Bar vocational course); *m* 23 July 1994, Fiona Jane Boulton, *qv*, da of Michael Harry Lockton; 2 da (Honor Olivia Anne b 26 April 1998, Katia Jane Imogen b 23 Sept 2001), 1 s (Fraser William James b 22 Jan 2000); *Career* Arthur Andersen: joined 1981, ptnr 1990, head of Econ and Fin Consulting 1994–97, head of Business Consulting 1995–97, global managing ptnr strategy and planning 1997–2000, global managing ptnr Business Consulting 2000–01, chief info offr 2000–01; dir LECG 2002–11 (sr md and global head of finance and accounting servs 2007–11); barr One Essex Court 2003–; advsr to Office of Rail Regulator 1994, conslt to Scott Inquiry 1995; treas Tate members 1993–2006; FAE 1994, FCA 1996 (ACA 1984); *Publications* co-author Cracking the Value Code: How Successful Businesses are Creating Wealth in the New Economy (2000); *Recreations* golf, running, travel, wine, modern art; *Clubs* MCC, Wisley Golf; *Style*— Richard Boulton, Esq, QC; ✉ Waterton, Cleardown, Woking, Surrey GU22 7HH (☎ 01483 760258, e-mail rboulton@oeclaw.co.uk)

BOURCHIER-O'FERRALL, Philip Justin; s of Anthony Bourchier-O'Ferrall; *b* Berks; *Educ* Univ of Reading; *Career* formerly: gen mangr Chyron Corporation, vice-pres Nokia Ventures, exec dir Twofour Television Gp; currently sr vice-pres: MTV, Nickelodeon, Comedy Central; listed as one of Evening Standard's 1000 most influential people in London 2009; memb: BAFTA, RTS; *Recreations* boating, motor racing, polo; *Clubs* Century, Groucho, BAFTA, RTS, IOD, Soho House; *Style*— Philip Bourchier-O'Ferrall, Esq; ✉ MTV Networks UK & Ireland, 17–29 Hawley Crescent, London NW1 8TT (e-mail philip@mtv.co.uk, website www.mtvnetworks.co.uk); 1540 Broadway, New York, NY, USA

BOURKE, Dr Brian Eamonn; s of Edmund Egan Bourke (d 1961), and Joan Eileen, *née* Kiernan; *b* 29 April 1948; *Educ* Beaumont Coll, King's Coll and King's Coll Hosp Univ of London (MB BS); *m* 25 March 1972, Elisabeth Janie, da of Brig Christopher Percy Sibthorpe Bright, CBE (d 1988), of Henley-on-Thames, Oxon; 2 da (Serena Katherine b 15 March 1974, Imogen Elisabeth b 6 July 1984), 2 s (Henry Edmund b 12 April 1976, Piers Christopher b 18 Aug 1978); *Career* house surgn KCH London 1972, house physician Royal Berks Hosp Reading 1972, sr house offr in med The London Hosp 1972–74, med registrar St Stephen's Hosp London 1974–76, registrar and sr registrar Charing Cross Hosp London 1976–81, conslt physician and hon sr lectr St George's Hosp and Med Sch London 1981–; hon sec Br Soc for Rheumatology 1990–94, memb BR Soc for Immunology; pres Section of Rheumatology Royal Soc of Med, MRCP 1974, FRCP 1989; *Recreations* tennis, golf, shooting, skiing, travel; *Clubs* Hurlingham, Queen's, Huntercombe; *Style*— Dr Brian Bourke; ✉ 136 Harley Street, London W1G 7JZ (☎ 020 7371 7448)

BOURNE, Debra Lysette; da of Brian Neville Bourne, and Leila Ruby Simcovitch; *b* 12 February 1964; *Educ* Ilford Co HS for Girls, E Ham Tech Coll, NE London Poly; *m* 9 Sept 2001, David Henry Rosen; 1 s (Johnny Curtis Bourne Rosen b June 1999); *Career* co dir Lynne Franks PR 1990–92 (joined 1984), PR conslt 1993–; specialist in consumer public relations focusing on youth market, brand positioning, image creation and promotion, clients incl: Katharine Hamnett, Jean Paul Gaultier, Pepe Jeans, Knickerbox, Coca Cola Clothes, Ghost, Swatch, Fiorucci; creative conslt 1997–, clients incl: The Beatles, Donna Karan, Frank Magazine; co-fndr All Walks and Beyond the Catwalk 2009–; exec fashion ed Arena and Arena Homme Plus magazines 1995–99, contrib ed GQ magazine 2000–; *Style*— Ms Debra Bourne; ✉ 12a Clifton Gardens, London W9 1DT (☎ 020 7289 6588, fax 020 7289 6230, e-mail debra.bourne@mailbox.co.uk)

BOURNE, Henry; s of Prof Kenneth Bourne (d 1992), and Eleanor Anne, *née* Wells (d 1996); *b* 10 May 1963; *Educ* City of London Sch, Crown Woods Sch; *m* 2002, Harriet Anstruther; *Career* photographer; photographic asst to Michael Joseph 1982–84, freelance photographic asst 1984–86, freelance photographer of portraits, fashion, architecture, still life and landscapes; cmmns incl contribs to: Vogue UK, USA, Japan, Germany, Australia, France, Russia, China, India and Korea, Arena Homme Plus, Bloom, Vanity Fair, Condé Nast Traveler UK and US, Elle UK, Harper's Bazaar (US), ID, New York Times Magazine, T, Saturday Telegraph Magazine, Numero, Vogue Living, World of Interiors, Wonderland, W Magazine, Wall Street Jl Magazine, Wallpaper*; exhbns: Fashion Acts 1996, 1997 and 1998, Condé Nast Traveller 1999 and 2002, DIFFA NY 2000–01, British Folklore Portraits Exhibition (Central State Exhibition Hall) Manege St Petersburg 2010, Now and Then (Harris Lindsay London) 2011, Folklore & Photography (Towner Gallery for Contemporary Art) 2012, Vogue 100: A Century of Style (Nat Portrait Gall London) 2016; work part of Nat Portrait Gall's permanent collection of portrait photography; visiting lectr St Martins Coll of Art 2008; Gold Medal Photography Award Soc of Pubn Designers USA 1997, St Petersburg Photo Vernissage Best Photograph Award 2010, American Photography AP26 Award 2011; *Books* The Ivy: The Restaurant and its Recipes, Le Caprice, Arcadia Britannica, a Modern British Folklore Portrait (2015); *Style*— Henry Bourne, Esq; ✉ 43 Thurloe Square, London SW7 2SR (☎ 020 7584 4601, e-mail info@henrybourne.com, website www.henrybourne.com)

BOURNE, Prof (Frederick) John; CBE; s of Sydney John Bourne (d 1960), of Evesham, Worcs, and Florence Beatrice, *née* Craven (d 1988); *b* 3 January 1937; *Educ* Prince Henry's GS Evesham, RVC (BVetMed, MRCVS), Univ of Bristol (PhD); *m* 12 Sept 1959, Mary Angela, da of William Reginald Minter (d 1990); 2 s (Stephen b 1962, Nigel b 1964); *Career* asst in gen vet practice Cornwall 1961–62, jr ptnr in 2-man vet practice Glos 1962–66; Univ of Bristol: lectr in animal husbandry 1966–74, reader in animal husbandry 1974–80, prof and head Dept of Vet Med 1980–88, BBSRC prof of animal health 1988–97; visiting prof Univ of Reading 1988–97; dir BBSRC Inst for Animal Health 1988–97; chm Govt Ind Scientific Gp on Control of Cattle TB 1998–2007; memb: Technol Interaction Bd BBSRC 1992–97, Agric and Veterinary Ctee Br Cncl 1994–98; hon fell Edward Jenner Inst for Vaccine Res 2001–, hon fell The Pirbright Inst 2015–; foreign memb Polish Acad of Scis; *Publications* Advances in Veterinary Immunology (1984 and 1985); over 250 scientific papers and chapters in over 20 books; *Recreations* golf, fishing; *Style*— Prof John Bourne, CBE; ✉ Westlands, Jubilee Lane, Langford, Bristol BS40 5EJ (☎ and fax 01934 852464, e-mail johnbourne26@gmail.com)

BOURNE, Sir Matthew Christopher; kt (2016), OBE (2001); s of Harold Jeffrey (Jim) Bourne, of London, and June Lillian, *née* Handley; *b* 13 January 1960; *Educ* Sir George Monoux Sch London, The Laban Centre (BA); *Career* dancer Transitions Dance Co 1986, fndr, artistic dir, resident choreographer and performer Adventures In Motion Pictures (AMP) 1987, artistic dir New Adventures 2001–; hon fell Laban Centre 1997 (memb bd of dirs 2000–); *Choreography* for AMP incl: Overlap Lovers 1987, Buck and Wing 1988, Spitfire 1988, The Infernal Galop 1989 (revived 1992), Green Fingers 1990, Town and Country 1991, Deadly Serious 1992, Nutcracker (co-prodn with Opera North 1992, revived 1993), The Percys of Fitzrovia 1992, Highland Fling 1994, Swan Lake 1995 (TV 1996, revised for LA 1997 and NY 1998–99), Cinderella 1997 (revised for LA 1999), The Car Man (2000/01); performed with choreographers incl: Jacob Marley, Brigitte Farges, Ashley Page; fndr memb Lea Anderson's Featherstonehaughs 1988; choreography for theatre incl: As You Like It (RSC, Stratford and Barbican) 1989, Singer (RSC, Stratford and Barbican) 1989, Leonce and Lena (Crucible Sheffield) 1989, Children of Eden (Prince Edward Theatre) 1991, A Midsummer Night's Dream (Aix-en-Provence Opera Festival) 1991, The Tempest (Nat Youth Theatre 1991, revived 1993), Show Boat (Malmö Stadsteater Sweden) 1991, Peer Gynt (Ninagawa Co Oslo, Barbican and World Tour) 1994, Watch with Mother (Nat Youth Dance Co) 1994, Cameron Mackintosh's revival of Oliver! (London Palladium) 1994, Boutique (Images of Dance) 1995, Watch Your Step (Irving Berlin Gala) 1995, Franch and Saunders Live 2000, My Fair Lady (RNT and Drury Lane) 2001, South Pacific (RNT) 2002, Dearest Love (George Piper Dances) 2003;

with New Adventures: Play without Words (RNT) 2002, Nutcracker! (Sadlers Wells) 2002; *Television* incl: Late Flowering Lust (BBC/Ecosse Films) 1993, Drip: A Self-Love Story (BBC) 1993, Roald Dahl's Little Red Riding Hood (BBC) 1995, Swan Lake (BBC) 1996, subject of South Bank Show 1997, presenter Channel 4 Dance 1999, The Car Man (Channel 4), Bourne to Dance (Channel 4) 2002, Nutcracker! (BBC 1) 2003; *Awards* incl: Place Portfolio Award 1989, Bonnie Bird Choreography Award 1989, Barclays New Stages Award 1990, nominated for Most Outstanding Achievement in Dance Olivier Award 1992, nominated for Best New Dance Prodn (The Nutcracker) Olivier Awards 1994; over 25 awards for Swan Lake incl: Olivier Award for Swan Lake 1996, Los Angeles Drama Critics Circle and Dramalogue Awards for Swan Lake 1997, Time Out Special Award 1997, SouthBank Show Award 1998, 2 Drama Desk Awards 1999, 2 Outer Critics Circle Awards 1999, 2 Tony Awards (dir and choreographer) 1999, Astaire Award 1999, Olivier Award for Outstanding Choreography 2002, Hamburg Shakespeare Prize 2003, Olivier Awards for Outstanding Choreography and Best Entertainment for Play Without Words 2003; *Publications* Matthew Bourne & His Adventures in Motion Pictures (ed Alastair Macauley, 1999); *Recreations* theatre, cinema, the choreography of Frederick Ashton and Fred Astaire, the music of Percy Grainger, Ella Fitzgerald and most pre-1950 singers; *Clubs* Soho House; *Style—* Sir Matthew Bourne, OBE; ✉ 21 Stamford Road, London N1 4JP (e-mail mattbourneathome@aol.com); c/o Jessica Sykes, ICM, Oxford House, 76 Oxford Street, London W1 2SH (☎ 020 7636 6565, fax 020 7323 0701)

BOURNE, Stephen Robert Richard; s of Colyn Morton Bourne, and Kathleen, *née* Turner; *b* 20 March 1952, Kampala; *Educ* Berkhamsted Sch, Univ of Edinburgh (MA), Univ of Cambridge (MA); *m* 1978, Stephanie Ann Bickford; 1 da (Jessica b 1985), 1 s (Robert b 1987); *Career* Lycée d'Etat Mixte à Saumur 1972–73, Deloitte Haskins & Sells 1974–80, Exxon Chemical Asia-Pacific Ltd 1980–86, Dow Jones Telerate 1986–94; md Burrups Ltd and Westerham Press Ltd 1994–96, Cambridge Univ Press 1997–2013 (chief exec and univ printer 2002–12, pres 2012–13), chapter clerk and administrator Ely Cathedral 2013–; chm Britten Sinfonia Ltd 2000–15 (dir 2003–15); dir Wine Soc 2004–15; chm: Hong Kong Water Ski Assoc 1980–85, Nat Offender Mgmnt Service Employer Gp E Anglia 2008–09, CBI Cncl E of England 2010–12; vice-chm and treas RSPCA Hong Kong 1981–86; memb Br Library Advsy Cncl 2011–16; former memb: UKTI China Business Working Pty, Advsy Bd China Book Int, Publishing Studies Advsy Bds City Univ, UCL and Univ of the Arts; Prince of Wales' ambass E of England for Business in the Community 2009; China Book Int Award 2011; chm Theatre Royal Bury St Edmunds 2012–; govr: Perse Sch for Girls 1998–2004, Berkhamsted Sch 2008–13; pres The Old Berkhamstedians 2011–13; Liveryman Worshipful Co of Stationers and Newspaper Makers, Freeman Worshipful Co of Educators; official fell Clare Hall Cambridge 2001– (vice-pres 2015–); fell Inst of Paper, Printing and Publishing (IP3); FCA 1977 (ACA 1974), FRSA; *Publications* Ten Chapters on Publishing (2012); monthly columns in: China Book International 2011, China Today 2012, China Business Focus 2013; *Recreations* performing arts, cricket, skiing, fine wines; *Clubs* Athenaeum, The Arcades, Royal Scots, Wynkyn de Worde Soc, Hong Kong, Hong Kong Soc, Aberdeen BC (Hong Kong), Kent CCC, Surrey CC, Exning CC (hon vice-pres), Cambridge Univ Lawn Tennis (hon vice-pres), Order of St Etheldreda, Farmers' (Bury St Edmunds); *Style—* Stephen Bourne, Esq; ✉ Falmouth Lodge, Snailwell Road, Newmarket, Suffolk CB8 7DN (☎ 01638 667006, e-mail stephenrrbourne@gmail.com); Chapter House, Ely Cathedral, Ely, Cambridgeshire CB7 4DL (☎ 01353 660308, e-mail s.bourne@elycathedral.org)

BOURNE OF ABERYSTWYTH, Baron (Life Peer UK 2013), of Aberystwyth in the County of Ceredigion and of Wethersfield in the County of Essex; Nicholas Bourne; *b* 1 January 1952; *Educ* King Edward VI GS Chelmsford, UCW Aberystwyth (LLB), Univ of Cambridge (LLM), Univ of Wales (LLM); *Career* called to the Bar Grays Inn 1976 (Bacon Holt and Uthwatt entrance scholar, Lee essay prize, Holker sr scholar, Arden Atken and Reid prize); formerly dean of Swansea Law Sch, asst princ Swansea Inst of HE; supervisor in law: Corpus Christi Coll Cambridge 1974–80, St Catharine's Coll Cambridge 1974–82, LSE 1975–79; princ Chart University Tutors Ltd 1979–88, co sec and dir Chart Foulks Lynch plc 1984–88, dir Holborn Gp Ltd 1988–91, dir of studies Holborn Law Tutors Ltd 1988–91, sr lectr in law South Bank Univ 1991–92, lectr in company law UCL 1991–96; lecture tours in Singapore and Malaysia 1980–1992, visiting lectr Univ of Hong Kong 1996–2008; consultancies incl: external examiner Univ of London LLB 1991–2000, editorial bd Malaysian Law News 1991–2004, editorial advsy bd Business Law Review 1991–, West Wales TEC for the provision of legal advice 1992–96; memb Nat Assembly for Wales (Cons) Wales Mid & West (regnl list) 1999–2011, ldr Cons Pty Nat Assembly for Wales 1999–2011 (ldr of the Oppn 2007–11), parly under-sec of state Dept of Energy and Climate Change and Wales Office 2015–; a Lord in Waiting 2014–; memb: NE Thames RHA 1990–92, W Glamorgan HA 1994–97; *Publications* Duties and Responsiblities of British Company Directors (1982), British Company Law and Practice (1983), Business British Law for Accountants (1987), Scottish Company Law (with Brian Pillans, 1996, 2nd edn, 1999), Essential Company Law (2nd edn, 1997), Business Law and Practice (1994), Bourne on Company Law (6 edn, 2013); regular contrib to business and company law journals; *Recreations* walking, tennis, badminton, squash, cricket, theatre, rugby, travel, cinema, Nat Tst, NSPCC, The British Heart Fndn; *Clubs* Oxford and Cambridge; *Style—* The Lord Bourne of Aberystwyth; ✉ House of Lords, London SW1A 0PW

BOURNE-ARTON, His Hon Judge Simon Nicholas; QC (1994); yr s of Maj Anthony Temple Bourne-Arton, MBE (d 1996), of West Tanfield, N Yorks, and (Margaret) Elaine (d 2001), da of W Denby Arton, of Sleningford Park, N Yorks; *b* 5 September 1949; *Educ* Harrow, Teesside Poly (HND), Univ of Leeds (LLB); *m* 1974, Diana Carr-Walker; 2 s (James b 3 Aug 1977, Tom b 19 March 1980), 1 da (Isabel b 15 Aug 1983); *Career* called to the Bar Inner Temple 1975 (bencher 2003); in practice NE Circuit, recorder of the Crown Court 1993–, sr circuit judge (North Eastern Circuit) 2012–; *Recreations* golf, tennis, walking, wine, family and friends; *Style—* His Hon Judge Bourne-Arton, QC; ✉ Park Court Chambers, 16 Park Place, Leeds LS1 2SJ (☎ 0113 243 3277, fax 0113 242 1285)

BOURNEMOUTH, Archdeacon of; *see:* Harbidge, Ven Adrian Guy

BOURSNELL, Clive; s of Raymond Robert Morgan, of Sunningdale, Berks, and Vera, *née* Kossick; *b* 2 June 1942; *Educ* Corona Stage Sch; *Career* professional photographer (initially working in fashion, currently specialising in portraits and feature work); child actor appearing on TV and in films: Hunted (with Dirk Bogarde) 1952, The Beggar's Opera (with Laurence Olivier) 1952; woodman Windsor Great Park Berks 1958–60; extensive travelling throughout Canada 1960–64: successively dairy farmer, pit labourer in uranium and gold mines, door-to-door magazines salesman, prospector for natural gas and oil, asst glaciologist Geography Dept McGill Univ Montreal, mountaineer High Arctic 1964–67; fashion photographer's asst London, staff photographer Ambassador Magazine 1968–69, freelance photographer 1969–; work featured in various pubns incl: The Observer, Vogue and Honey magazines, Sunday Times and Telegraph magazines, Independent on Sunday, Illustrated London News, Country Living, Country Life; nat and int lectures and slide shows on English gardens and photographing gardens; fndr memb Photographers Assoc 1968 (variously memb Cncl), memb The Garden Media Guild, memb Professional Garden Photographer (former memb Cncl and chair); *Books* Covent Garden Market (1977), The Royal Opera House (1982), English Herb Gardens (1986), English Water Gardens (1987), Making of the English Garden (1989), The Curious Gardener (2001 and 2002), Covent Garden Fruit, Vegetable & Flower Market (2008), Houses of the Lake District (2011), Covent Garden Then & Now (2013), Remaking A Garden: The Laskett Transformed (jtly, with Sir Roy Strong, 2014); *Recreations* photography, opera, dance, walking, climbing (lone attempt of Mt McKinley Alaska, mountaineer on Arctic expedition to Alex Hieberg), being me; *Style—* Clive Boursnell, Esq; ✉ 5A Borneo Street, London SW15 1QQ (☎ 020 8789 8956, mobile 078 3164 7244); The Old Chapel, Bucks Mill, Bideford, Devon EX39 5DY

BOUSTED, Dr Mary; *Career* head Sch of Educn Univ of Kingston, gen sec Assoc of Teachers and Lectrs; *Style—* Dr Mary Bousted; ✉ Association of Teachers and Lecturers, 7 Northumberland Street, London WC2N 5RD

BOUTWOOD, Nigel Peter Ralph; *b* 12 May 1951; *Educ* Lancing; *m* 2 April 1977, Jeanette Elsma; 2 da (Emma Jane Elsma b 1980, Tiffany Roberta b 1982), 1 s (Charles Peter Warner b 1991); *Career* J Walter Thompson 1970, Thames TV 1971–78, Southern TV 1978–82, TVS 1982–85, chm and md Boutwood Advertising Ltd 1985–; chm of tstees Charlie's Challenge Charity (raising funds for research into children's brain tumours) 1995–; *Recreations* sailing, skiing, tennis; *Clubs* Itchenor Sailing, Cowes Corinthian Yacht; *Style—* Nigel Boutwood, Esq; ✉ Boutwood Advertising Ltd, PO Box 225, Heathfield, East Sussex TN21 1DR (☎ 01825 873014, e-mail info@boutwood.com)

BOVEY, Philip Henry; s of Cdr Norman Henry Bovey, OBE, DSC, VRD (d 2005), and Dorothy Yvonne, *née* Kent Williams (d 2003); *b* 11 July 1948; *Educ* Rugby, Peterhouse Cambridge (scholar, MA); *m* 14 Sept 1974, Jenet Alison, da of Canon James Mitchell McTear (d 1973); 2 c (Katherine b 1976, Stephen b 1978); *Career* FCO 1970–71; admitted slr 1974; Slaughter & May 1972–75, DTI 1976–77, Cabinet Office 1977–78; DTI 1978–2007: under sec 1985–, dir of legal servs 1996–2004, dir Co Law Reform Bill Project 2005–07; inspr Companies Act 1984–88; assoc Royal Photographic Soc 2008; *Publications* Buckley on the Companies Acts (contrib); *Recreations* photography; *Style—* Philip Bovey, Esq; ✉ 102 Cleveland Gardens, Barnes, London SW13 0AH (☎ 020 8876 3710)

BOVILL, Chris; *Career* creative ptnr Fallon until 2012, head 4Creative Channel 4 2012–; *Style—* Chris Bovill, Esq; ✉ 4Creative, Channel 4, 124 Horseferry Road, Westminster, London SW1P 2TX

BOWDEN, Sir Andrew; kt (1994) MBE (1961); s of William Victor Bowden, of Brighton, E Sussex, and Francesa Wilson; *b* 8 April 1930; *Educ* Ardingly; *m* 1970, Benita, da of B A Napier, of Brighton, E Sussex; 1 s, 1 da; *Career* worked in paint industry 1955–68, personnel conslt 1967–; memb Wandsworth BC 1956–62, nat chm Young Cons 1960–61; Parly candidate (Cons): N Hammersmith 1955, N Kensington 1964, Kemptown Brighton 1966; MP (Cons) Brighton Kemptown 1970–97; memb Select Ctees on: Expenditure 1973–74, Abortion 1975, Employment 1979–97; jt chm All-Pty Parly Gp for Pensioners 1971–97, int chm People to People 1981–83, memb Cncl of Europe 1987–97; int conslt to Global Equities Corp NY 2004–09; nat pres Captive Animals Protection Soc 1975–97; *Books* Dare We Trust Them – A New Vision for Europe (jtly, 2005); *Recreations* chess, golf, poker; *Clubs* Carlton; *Style—* Sir Andrew Bowden, MBE; ✉ 35 Wanderdown Road, Ovingdean, Brighton BN2 7BT (☎ 01273 552136)

BOWDEN, (HE) James Nicholas Geoffrey (Jamie); CMG (2012), OBE (2002); *b* 27 May 1960; *Educ* Eton; *m* Sarah, *née* Peaslee; 5 c; *Career* Royal Green Jackets 1980–86; desk offr Repub of Ireland Dep FCO 1987–88, dep then acting consul gen Aden 1990–91, 2 sec political and information Khartoum 1991–93, head Political Section UN Dept FCO 1993–96, 1 sec (ME affairs and counter terrorism) Washington 1996–99, 1 sec economic and commercial Riyadh 1999–2000, seconded to Cabinet Office 2000–03, dep head of mission Baghdad 2004–05, dep head of mission Kuwait 2005–06, ambass to Bahrain 2006–11, ambass to Oman 2011–14; dep private sec responsible for foreign and Cwlth affrs to the Prince of Wales and the Duchess of Cornwall 2014–; *Style—* Mr Jamie Bowden, CMG, OBE

BOWDERY, Philip (Phil); *Career* concert promoter; formerly roadie, prodn mangr and tour mangr, currently exec pres Touring Live Nation; clients incl: Tom Jones, Madonna, U2, Coldplay, Cirque du Soleil, Fleetwood Mac, Barbara Streisand; *Style—* Phil Bowdery, Esq

BOWDLER, Timothy John (Tim); CBE (2006); s of Henry Neville Bowdler (d 2003), and Barbara Mary, *née* Richardson; *b* 16 May 1947, Wolverhampton; *Educ* Wrekin Coll, Univ of Birmingham (BSc), London Business Sch (MBA); *m* 1976, Brita Margaretha, *née* Eklund; 2 da (Emma b 27 May 1978, Anna b 17 July 1980); *Career* grad mgmnt trainee rising to branch admin mangr GKN Stanley Ltd 1969–73; RHP Bearings Ltd: commercial mangr 1975–77, gen mangr Business Ops 1977–81; Sandvik Ltd: dir and gen mangr Sandvik Steel 1981–84, md Spooner Industries Ltd 1984–87; md Chloride Motive Power Chloride Gp plc 1987–88, dir Northern Div Tyzack & Partners Ltd 1989–90; Cape plc: divnl md Cape Architectural Products 1990–92, divnl md Cape Building and Architectural Products 1992–94; Johnston Press plc: gp md 1994–97, chief exec 1997–2009; non-exec chm: PA Gp 2009–10, Laidlaw Interiors Gp Ltd 2012–16; chm Press Standards Bd of Finance Ltd 2000–09; non-exec dir: Assoc Br Ports Holdings plc 2001–06, Press Assoc 2001–10, Miller Gp 2004–12, Tullis Russell Gp Ltd 2010–14; Newspaper Soc: pres 2002–03, memb Cncl, chm Political, Editorial and Regulatory Affrs (PERA) Ctee; FRSA 2003; *Recreations* golf, skiing, Swedish summerhouse, sailing, fishing; *Clubs* Bruntsfield Links Golfing Soc, Honorable Co of Edinburgh Golfers; *Style—* Tim Bowdler, Esq, CBE

BOWE, Prof Michael; *Educ* Keble Coll Oxford, Univ of Manchester, Carleton Univ Ottawa (Cwlth scholar); *m* Julie Anne Carr; 3 da (Alexandra b 27 Jan 1991, Madeleine b 27 April 1994, Rebecca b 14 Feb 1996); *Career* asst prof of economics Simon Fraser Univ 1984–93, joined Manchester Sch of Mgmnt 1993, currently prof of int finance Univ of Manchester and head Manchester Accounting and Finance Div Alliance Manchester Business Sch; Bank of Valletta prof of int banking and finance Univ of Malta 1993–2015; visiting prof: Helsinki Sch of Economics and Business Admin 1988–2000, Univ of Vienna 1996, Emory Univ 1999, Nat Univ of the Ukraine Kyiv-Mohyla Inst 2003, Univ of Vaasa 2012–16; research assoc Columbia Univ NY 1986–89, fell Nat Univ of Singapore 1992–93; conslt to various instns incl: World Bank, Canadian Int Dept Agency, Govt of BC, Den Danske Bank, Bank of Valletta, Singapore Stock Exchange, Finnish Options Market; memb: Royal Economic Soc, American Economics Assoc, Acad of Int Business, European Finance Assoc, European International Business Acad, Eastern Finance Assoc; FCIB; *Books* incl: Eurobonds (1988), Has the Market Solved the Sovereign-Debt Crisis? (jtly, 1997), Banking and Finance in Islands and Small States (jt ed, 1998); *Recreations* cricket coaching; *Clubs* Marple Cricket; *Style—* Prof Michael Bowe; ✉ Manchester Business School, The University of Manchester, Booth Street West, Manchester M15 6PB

BOWEN, Christopher Richard Croasdaile (Kit); s of Christopher James Croasdaile Bowen (ka 1944), and Helen Florence Anderton, *née* Lyons; *b* 7 October 1944; *Educ* Rugby; *m* 22 April 1972, Janet Margaret Bowen, *qv*, da of Capt Alexander Francis Matheson, RN; 1 da (Nicola Frances b 26 March 1976), 1 s (Robert James Croasdaile b 28 April 1978); *Career* Royal Tank Regt 1963–68; IBM (UK) 1969–79; chartered accountant 1983; Saffery Champness: joined 1980, ptnr 1983–2008, dep chm 1993–95, chm 1995–97; FCCA 1979; *Recreations* the countryside; *Style—* Christopher Bowen, Esq; ✉ Kinellan House, Strathpeffer, Ross-shire IV14 9ET (☎ 01997 421476, e-mail kit@kinellan.org)

BOWEN, Prof Emeritus David Quentin; s of William Esmond Bowen (d 1984), of Heddlys, Glasfryn, Llanelli, and Jane, *née* Williams (d 1992); *b* 14 February 1938, Llanelly, Carmarthenshire; *Educ* Llanelli GS, UCL (BSc, PhD); *m* 18 Sept 1965, Elizabeth, da of David Islwyn Williams (d 1989); 2 s (Huw b 1966, Wyn b 1969); *Career* prof of physical geography UCW Aberystwyth 1983–85, prof of geography Royal Holloway Coll London 1985–88; prof and dir Inst of Earth Studies UCW 1988–93; Univ of Wales Cardiff: prof of quaternary geology 1994–2004, emeritus prof 2005–, Leverhulme emeritus fell 2005–

07; fndr ed-in-chief Quaternary Sci Review 1982–94, pres Quaternary Res Assoc (UK) 1979–81, pres INQUA Stratigraphy Cmmn (Int Union for Quaternary Res) 1991–93; memb and chm: NERC Ctees 1978–96, UGC Earth Sci Review 1988, Nature Conservancy Cncl 1986–91, Jt Nature Conservation Ctee (GB) 1990–97, Dutch Univs Earth Sci Review 1996, American Geophysical Union; chm Llanelli Millennium Coastal Park Forum 1996–2001, dep chm Countryside Cncl for Wales 1990–2000; BBC Wales Annual Lecture 1996; hon fell Int Union for Quaternary Research (INQUA) 1999; FGS 1963; *Books* Quaternary Geology (1978, Russian edn 1982), The Llanelli Landscape (1980), Glaciations in the Northern Hemisphere (1986); *Recreations* music, rugby, cricket; *Style—* Prof Emeritus David Bowen; ✉ School of Earth, and Ocean Sciences, Cardiff University, Cardiff CF10 3YE (☎ 029 2087 4337, fax 029 2087 4326, e-mail bowendq@cardiff.ac.uk)

BOWEN, Sheriff Principal Edward Farquharson; CBE (2010), TD (1977), QC (Scot 1992); s of Stanley Bowen, CBE; *b* 1 May 1945; *Educ* Melville Coll Edinburgh, Univ of Edinburgh (LLB); *m* 1975, Patricia Margaret, da of Rev Robert Russell Brown, of Perth; 2 s (James, David), 2 da (Helen, Alexandra); *Career* admitted slr 1968, passed advocate 1970; advocate depute 1979–83, Sheriff of Tayside Central and Fife at Dundee 1983–90, ptnr Thorntons WS 1990–91, resumed practice at Scottish Bar 1991; Sheriff Princ of: Glasgow and Strathkelvin 1997–2005, Lothian and Borders 2005–11; temp judge Court of Session 2000–15; memb Criminal Injuries Compensation Bd 1996, chm Ind Review of Sheriff and Jury Procedure 2009–10; chm Northern Lighthouse Bd 2003–05; chllr's assessor Univ of Edinburgh 2011–; *Recreations* golf; *Clubs* New (Edinburgh), Hon Co of Edinburgh Golfers, Panmure Golf, R&A; *Style—* Sheriff Principal Edward Bowen, CBE, TD, QC; ✉ The Old Manse, Lundie, Angus DD2 5NW

BOWEN, Janet Margaret; da of Capt Alexander Francis Matheson, RN; *m* 22 April 1972, Kit Bowen, *qv*; 1 da (Nicola Frances b 26 March 1976), 1 s (Robert James Croasdaile b 28 April 1978); *Career* Lord-Lt Ross and Cromarty 2007–; *Style—* Mrs Janet Bowen; ✉ Kinellan House, Strathpeffer IV14 9ET (website www.lordlieutenant-rossandcromarty.org.uk)

BOWEN, Jeremy; s of Gareth Bowen, of Cardiff, and Jennifer, *née* Delany; *b* 6 February 1960; *Educ* Cardiff HS, UCL (BA), Johns Hopkins Sch of Advanced International Studies Washington DC and Bologna (MA); *m* Julia Williams; 1 da (Mattie b 11 Jan 2001), 1 s (Jack b 18 July 2003); *Career* BBC News: news trainee 1984–86, fin reporter 1986, corr Geneva 1987, sometime presenter Breakfast News, foreign affrs corr 1988–95, corr Middle East 1995–2000, presenter Breakfast from BBC News 2000–02, Rome corr 2004–05, Middle East ed 2005– (Int Emmy (jtly with BBC team) for reporting of Israel-Lebanon war 2006); special corr BBC News pubns Six Days 2003; presenter documentaries incl: Son of God (BBC 1) 2000, Moses (BBC 1) 2002, Booze (BBC 1) 2002, Noah (BBC 1) 2003, Jeremy Bowen on the Frontline (BBC 1) 2005, The Birth of Israel (BBC 2); winner: Silver Nymph Monte Carlo TV Festival 1994, Gold Medal NY TV Festival, RTS Award 1996, Sony Gold Award 2004, Bayeux War Corr First Prize TV Grand Format 2009, Charles Wheeler Prize 2010, Bayeux War Corr First Prize for radio reporting from Syria 2012, Peace Through Media Award 2012, RTS Specialist Journalist of the Year 2013, RTS Journalist of the Year 2014, Peabody Award 2014 (as part of BBC team for coverage of Syria), Emmy Award 2014 (also for Syria coverage), RTS Interview of the Year (Assad) 2015, James Cameron Award for contribution to journalism 2015, Frontline Award for Yemen coverage; fell UCL 2005, hon fell Cardiff Univ 2009, hon fell Univ of S Wales 2013, fell Aberystwyth Univ 2014, hon dr Nottingham Trent Univ 2014, hon fell Cardiff Met Univ 2015, hon fell Univ of Wales Trinity St David 2016; *Publications* Six Days: How the 1967 War Shaped the Middle East (2004), War Stories (2006), The Arab Uprisings: The People Want The Fall of the Regime (2012); *Recreations* cooking, drinking, wine, skiing; *Clubs* Frontline; *Style—* Jeremy Bowen, Esq

BOWEN, Kenneth John; s of Hector John Bowen (d 1980), of Llanelli, Carmarthenshire, and Sarah Ann (Sally), *née* Davies (d 1939); *b* 3 August 1932; *Educ* Llanelli GS, UC Wales Aberystwyth (BA), St John's Coll Cambridge (MA, MusB), Inst of Educn Univ of London; *m* 31 March 1959, Angela Mary, da of George Stanley Evenden, of Morecambe, Lancs; 2 s (Geraint, Meurig); *Career* Flying Offr Educn Branch RAF 1958–60; prof of singing Royal Acad of Music 1967–98 (head of vocal studies 1987–91); conductor: London Welsh Chorale 1983–2008, London Welsh Festival Chorus 1987–90; former concert and operatic tenor (ret 1988); debut Tom Rakewell New Opera Co Sadler's Wells 1957; appeared: Promenade concerts, Three Choirs Festival, Aldeburgh and other maj festivals; performed at: Royal Opera House, ENO, WNO, Glyndebourne Touring Opera, English Opera Gp, English Music Theatre, Kent Opera, Handel Opera Soc; numerous recordings and int appearances (Europe, USA, Canada, Israel, Far East), winner first prize Munich Int Competition and Queen's prize; adjudicator Royal Nat Eisteddfod of Wales and Llangollen Int Eisteddfod; dir Br Youth Opera; patron Welsh Music Guild, vice-pres Hon Soc of Cymmrodorion, vice-pres London Welsh Tst, former chm Assoc of Teachers of Singing, former pres RAM Club; memb Gorsedd of Bards; Hon DMus Univ of Wales 2003; Hon RAM, FRSA; *Recreations* golf, walking, theatre, wine; *Style—* Dr Kenneth Bowen; ✉ 61 Queens Crescent, London NW5 3QG

BOWEN, William George (Will); s of Humphry John Moule Bowen, and Ursula Hill; *b* 30 October 1957; *Educ* Marlborough (jr scholarship), Balliol Coll Oxford (BA, DPhil); *Career* stage designer; res chemist Borax Consolidation Ltd 1975–79; fndr Almeida Theatre Islington (with Pierre Audi and Chris Naylor 1979); set builder Oxford Playhouse Co 1979–82; memb: SBTD 2000, Royal Inst 2004; tstee The Story Museum; *Theatre* as prodn carpenter: Camelot (Apollo Victoria Theatre London) 1982, The Boyfriend (Old Vic and UK tour) 1984, Guys & Dolls (NT UK tour) 1985; as prodn mangr: Charley's Aunt (Aldwych Theatre) 1983, Trumpets & Raspberries (The Phoenix Theatre) 1984, The Nerd (Aldwych Theatre) 1984, Torch Song Trilogy (Albery Theatre) 1985, Kiss Me Kate (Old Vic and UK tour) 1987, Henry IV (nat tour) 1990, The Rehearsal (Garrick Theatre) 1990; as design co-ordinator: Phantom of the Opera (Her Majesty's Theatre) 1986, Aspects of Love (Prince of Wales Theatre) 1989, The Hunting of the Snark (Prince Edward Theatre) 1991, Oliver! (Palladium Theatre) 1994; as tech designer: The Wind in the Willows (NT) 1990, Sunset Boulevard (Adelphi Theatre) 1993, Jesus Christ Superstar (Lyceum Theatre) 1996, Chitty Chitty Bang Bang (Palladium Theatre) 2002, His Dark Mateials (NT) 2003; as theatre designer: Waking Hours (Lyric Hammersmith) 1984, Born in the Gardens (Questors Theatre) 1988, Under Milk Wood 1992, Julius Caesar (NYT) 1992, Helping Harry 2001; as musical designer: Days of Hope (Oxford Playhouse and Hampstead Theatre) 1991, Girlfriends (Arts Theatre) 1992, Romance/Romance (Gielgud Theatre) 1997, The Canterville Ghost (Northcott Theatre Exeter) 1998, Peter Pan (Royal Festival Hall) 2002; as comedy designer: Rowan Atkinson (also designer and prodn mangr, West End, Broadway and world tours) 1980–92, Mel Smith & Griff Rhys Jones (Cabaret) 1983, Eddie Izzard (West End and UK tour) 1996, One Word Improv (Albery Theatre) 1997, Derren Brown (Palace Theatre) 2004, (Cambridge Theatre) 2005, (UK tour) 2007, (Garrick Theatre) 2008, (Adelphi Theatre) 2009 and (Shaftesbury Theatre) 2011; as concert designer: Fairuz (Royal Festival Hall) 1986, John Harle (Queen Elizabeth Hall) 1987, The Music of Andrew Lloyd Webber (Seville) 1992; as lighting designer: Rowan Atkinson (UK tour) 1983–88, John Harle's Berliner Band (London and Aldeburgh) 1986–90, Ute Lemper (Barbican Concert Hall) 1990; as theatre conslt: Royal Albert Hall (stage extension project) 1992, Soho Theatre London 1996–98, Olivier Environment (NT) 1999, Abbey Theatre Dublin 2007; as theatre building designer: Combe Barns 1987, Sydmonton Court 1991, Great Offley Barns 1995, Lyttelton Theatre Transformation (NT) 2002; *Opera* Evenings at Combe 1987–2006, Don Pasquale (Holland Park 1997), La Fedelta Premiata (Guidhall) 1997, La Traviata (Stowe Opera) 1997, Lucia di Lammermoor (Stowe Opera) 1998, Carmen (Clonter Opera 1998), Il Tabarro (Clonter Opera) 1999, Falstaff (British Youth Opera (BYO)) 1999, The Barber of Seville (BYO) 1999, May We Borrow Your Husband (Lichfield Festival) 1999, Don Pasquale (Clonter Opera) 1999, Seraglio (BYO) 2000, Xerxes (BYO) 2000, The Rape of Lucretia (BYO) 2000, Carmen (Holland Park Opera) 2001, Bevenuto Cellini (Bloomsbury Theatre) 2002, Suor Anjelica (Holland Park) 2002, I Pagliacci (Holland Park) 2002, Macbeth (Icelandic Opera) 2003, Norma (Holland Park) 2004, La Fanciulla del West (Holland Park) 2004, Tosca (Icelandic Opera) 2005, La Bohème (Icelandic Opera) 2012, Carmen (Icelandic Opera) 2013; *Television* Comic Relief 1986, Hysteria 1989, Rowan Atkinson HBO Special 1991, Derren Brown – Something Wicked This Way Comes 2006, The Story of Music (BBC) 2011; *Film* The Girl in the Red Dress 2002; *Recreations* mathematics, landscape, natural history, photography, travel; *Style—* Will Bowen, Esq; ✉ c/o Noel Gay Artists, 19 Denmark Street, London WC2H 8NA (☎ 020 7836 3941, fax 020 7287 1816)

BOWEN-SIMPKINS, Dr Peter; s of Horace John Bowen-Simpkins (d 1969), and Christine Dulce, *née* Clarke; *b* 28 October 1941, Hitchin, Herts; *Educ* Malvern Coll, Selwyn Coll Cambridge (MA, MB, BChir), Guy's Hosp; *m* 19 Aug 1967, Kathrin, da of Karl Otto Ganguin (d 1987), of Chelmsford, Essex; 2 da (Emma Jane b 6 Nov 1969, Philippa b 28 Dec 1971); *Career* resident MO Queen Charlotte's Maternity Hosp London 1971, resident surgical offr Samaritan Hosp for Women London 1972, sr registrar and lectr in obstetrics and gynaecology Middx Hosp and Hosp for Women 1972–78, conslt gynaecologist Singleton Hosp Swansea 1979–2005, medical dir London Women's Clinic London, Swansea and Cardiff 2005–, exec medical dir J D Healthcare; inspr of nullity for Wales, past lectr in family planning Margaret Pyke Centre London; contrib chapters in various books on obstetrics and gynaecology, and author of papers and pubns in med jls incl: Br Med Jl, Br Jl of Obstetrics and Gynaecology (BJOG); examiner: Royal Coll of Obstetricians and Gynaecologists, Univ of Wales, Univ of Hong Kong, Univ of Kartoum Sudan, Coll of Physicians and Surgeons of Pakistan, GMC; RCOG: memb Cncl 1993–2005, memb Fndn Bd Faculty of Family Planning 1994–97, hon treas 1998–2005, press offr 2000–05; tstee Wellbeing of Women; past exec chm BJOG; hon treas Royal Medical Benevolent Fund 2008–14, currently medical liaison offr and patron Royal Medical Benevolent Fund; Handcock Prize for Surgery RCS 1966; co-fndr and past pres Victor Bonney Soc, ldr Cambridge Expedition to Eritrea 1963; currently vice-chm Reynoldston Community Cncl; Freeman City of London, Liveryman Worshipful Soc of Apothecaries 1976, Liveryman Welsh Livery Guild (Urdd Lifrai Cymru) 1995; LRCP 1966, MRCS 1966, MRCOG 1973, FRCOG 1985, MFFP 1993, fell Faculty of Sexual and Reproductive Healthcare 2005; *Books* Pocket Examiner in Obstetrics & Gynaecology (1983), A Practice of Obstetrics and Gynaecology (2000); *Recreations* fly fishing, golf, skiing, walking; *Clubs* Athenaeum; *Style—* Dr P Bowen-Simpkins; ✉ London Women's Clinic (☎ 020 7563 4301, e-mail pbs@reynoldston.com)

BOWERMAN, David William; CBE (2004), JP (1970), DL (W Sussex 1992); s of Alfred Hosegood Bowerman (d 1982), of Champs Hill, Coldwaltham, and Margaret, *née* Vellacott; *b* 9 January 1936; *Educ* Monkton Combe Sch, Univ of Reading (BSc); *m* 9 Sept 1961, (Clarice) Mary, da of Prof William Melville Capper (d 1975), of Clifton, Bristol; 3 da (Janet Mary (Mrs William Taylor) b 28 June 1962, Katharine Emma b 9 July 1964, Anna Margaret (Mrs Simon Downham) b 28 May 1966); *Career* farmer; chm: Arundel Bench 1985–89 (memb 1970–96), Arundel Juvenile Bench 1980–85 (memb 1972–86), Bd of Visitors HM Prison Ford 1979–82 (memb 1970–85), W Sussex Probation Ctee 1988–94 (memb 1975–94), W Sussex Forum for Offender Accommodation 1979–94, Exec Bd Sussex Crime Reduction Initiative (CRI) 1995–2001 (memb and vice-chm 1979–2001), Music at Boxgrove 1991–2003, Chichester Cathedral Millennium Endowment Tst 1997–2005, Bowerman Charitable Tst 1982–, Elgar Fndn and Birthplace Tst 1998–2005; memb: Local Review Ctee 1966–69, Central Cncl of Magistrates' Courts 1981–84, Central Cncl of Probation 1988–94; tstee: Mary How Tst, Chichester Cathedral Tst, Chichester Cathedral Cncl, Royal Coll of Organists, English Chamber Orchestra and Music Soc, Cncl Royal Philharmonic Soc, King Edward VII Hosp Midhurst (memb Instn); High Sheriff W Sussex 1990–91; Hon RCM 2006; *Recreations* music, fly fishing, art; *Clubs* Mosimann's; *Style—* David Bowerman, Esq, CBE, JP, DL, Hon RCM; ✉ Champs Hill, Coldwaltham, Pulborough, West Sussex RH20 1LY (e-mail david@thebct.org.uk)

BOWERMAN, John Ernest; s of Ernest James Bowerman (d 1973), and Irene May, *née* Partridge (d 1993); *b* 13 March 1931; *Educ* Torquay GS, Dental and Med Schs Univ of Bristol (scholar, BDS, MB ChB, numerous prizes and awards, Badminton colours); *m* 20 March 1955, Hilary Winifred, da of Charles Frederick Hazlewood; 1 s (Martin John b 15 Aug 1959), 1 da (Sarah Jane b 2 May 1962); *Career* Lt RADC 1954–55, ret Capt 1956; house surgn Univ of Bristol Dental Sch 1954, in gen dental practice 1955–60, dental surgn Marlpitts Geriatric Hosp Honiton Devon 1958–59, registrar in dental surgery Univ of Bristol Dental Sch and Maxillofacial Unit Frenchay Hosp Bristol 1960–61, house physician in gen med Professorial Med Unit United Bristol Hosps 1965–66, house surgn in gen and ENT surgery Frenchay Hosp Bristol 1966; sr registrar in oral surgery 1967–69: Westminster Hosp and Queen Mary's Univ Hosp Roehampton (registrar in oral surgery 1966–67), UCH Dental Sch; hon conslt in oral and maxillofacial surgery Royal Dental Hosp of London and St George's Hosp Tooting London 1974–81; conslt in maxillofacial surgery: Westminster Hosp 1969–91, Queen Mary's Univ Hosp 1969–94, Epsom Dist Hosp 1978–94; currently: hon consulting surgeon in maxillofacial surgery Chelsea and Westminster Hosp & Queen Mary's Univ Hosp; visiting prof: Univ of Cairo and Egyptian Air Force Hosp 1984, Univ of Alexandria and Maadi Armed Forces Hosp 1985, Univ Dental Sch Kenyatta Nat Hosp 1988; dental clinical tutor Roehampton Postgrad Med Centre 1977–93, examiner RCS 1983–89; memb: Euro Assoc for Cranio-Maxillofacial Surgery (memb Cncl 1986–92), Regional Hosp Dental Surgery Ctee SW Thames RHA (chm 1975–83); memb BMA; FDS RCS 1964, FRCSEd 1985, fell BAOMS (memb Cncl 1983–84); *Publications* Dental Manifestations of Systemic Disease (Radiology in Clinical Diagnosis Series, with D H Trapnell, 1973); contrib chapters to numerous med and dental textbooks, author of numerous published articles in learned jls; *Recreations* salmon fishing, DIY; *Style—* John Bowerman, Esq; ✉ Pond Cottage, Whitmore Vale, Grayshott, Hampshire GU26 6JB (☎ and fax 01428 713314, e-mail johnbowerman.maxtac@btinternet.com)

BOWERS, Daniel Selwyn (Danny); s of Philip Louis Bowers, and Iris, *née* Pash; *b* 13 October 1958; *Educ* Manchester Poly (BA), London Coll of Printing (Dip Radio Journalism); *m* 12 March 1989, Elizabeth, da of Lawrence Abramson; 1 s (Adam Benjamin b 4 March 1992), 1 da (Emma Sarah b 19 Sept 1994); *Career* news reporter and prodr (Midlands) BBC Radio 1980–83, dep news ed and sports ed (Staffs and Cheshire) Signal Radio 1983–85, news/business reporter LBC/IRN 1985–86, fin corr LBC Radio 1986–90; freelance: Pink Section London Evening Standard 1990–91, Business Daily (C4) 1990–91; fin ed Independent Radio News (ITN Radio) 1991–95; co-fndr Electronic Media Relations 1989–91 (resigned as dir 1991), md MoneyWorld UK (formerly Lizdan Ltd) 1995– (dir 1991–); *Recreations* playing tennis, running and playing with the children, pony trekking; *Style—* Danny Bowers, Esq

BOWERS, John Simon; QC (1998); s of Alf Bowers, and Irene Bowers, of Cleethorpes, Humberside; *b* 2 January 1956; *Educ* Matthew Humberstone Comp Sch Cleethorpes, Lincoln Coll Oxford (open scholar, BA, BCL); *m* Suzanne Franks; 3 c (Emma, Hannah, Benjamin); *Career* called to the Bar 1978; recorder Midland Circuit 2003–, dep judge High Ct 2010–; chair Employer Law Bar Assoc; memb: Home Office Task Force on Human

Rights, Bar Cncl Race Relations Ctee, Employer Law Assoc 1990, Standards Bd for Eng 2001–; hon legal advisor Public Concern at Work; hon prof Univ of Hull 2002–; *Publications* Bowers on Employment Law (1980), Atkins Court Forms Volume 38 (1986), Modern Law of Strikes (1987), Employment Tribunal Procedure (1987), The Employment Act 1988, Termination of Employment (1988), Basic Procedure in Courts and Tribunals (1990), Textbook on Employment Law (1990), Employment Law Updates (1991), Transfer of Undertakings: the Legal Pitfalls (1996); *Style—* John Bowers, Esq, QC; ✉ Littleton Chambers, 3 King's Bench Walk North, Temple, London EC4Y 7HR (☎ 020 7797 8600, fax 020 7797 8600)

BOWERS, Dr Peter John; s of Dr Arthur Clifford Bowers (d 1947), and Doris Bowers (d 2005); *b* 2 June 1946; *Educ* Queen Elizabeth GS, Univ of London (BSc, AKC), Univ of Manchester (MB ChB, MSc); *m* 1 Aug 1970, (Patricia) Lesley, da of Philip Bethell, of Darlington, Co Durham; 1 da (Juliet b 1974), 2 s (Jonathan b 1975, Anthony b 1982); *Career* house physician and surgn Central Manchester Hosps 1973–74, sr house offr in paediatrics Booth Hall Hosp 1974–75, sr registrar in child psychiatry S Manchester Hosp 1978–81 (registrar in psychiatry 1975–78), tutor Dept of Child Psychiatry Univ of Manchester 1981–82, conslt in child and adolescent psychiatry NW RHA 1983–94, conslt in child and adolescent psychiatry and med dir Tameside and Glossop Community and Priority Servs NHS Tst 1994–2002, conslt in child and asolescent psychiatry Pennine Care Fndn Tst 2002–08 (lead conslt Child and Adolescent Mental Health Services 2005–08); expert witness for official slr and guardian-ad-litems 1984–2014; memb: Manchester Med Soc, Assoc for Child and Adolescent Mental Health; FRCPsych; *Recreations* amateur dramatics and operatics, theatre, jogging, travel; *Style—* Dr Peter Bowers; ✉ 6 Clifton Avenue, Fallowfield, Manchester M14 6UB (☎ 0161 224 9508, e-mail peterjohnbowers@doctors.org.uk)

BOWERS, Rupert; QC (2015); s of late Dr John Robert Bowers, and Patricia Ann Maureen Bowers; *b* 29 January 1971, New York; *Educ* Oundle, Univ of Newcastle-upon-Tyne, Coll of Law, Inns of Court Law Sch; *m* Olivia Charlotte Elliot-Lockhart; 3 da (Hannah Maisie b 2002, Amber Queenie b 2006, Iona Isabella b 2008); *Career* called to the Bar 1995, now specialising in judicial review with an emphasis on challenging search and seizure, arrest and detention, and in white collar criminal work as well as sports law; *Publications* Blackstone's Guide to the Terrorism Act (co-author, 2006); regular contrib to legal pubns; *Recreations* skiing, climbing, mountaineering; *Style—* Rupert Bowers, Esq, QC; ✉ Doughty Street Chambers, 54 Doughty Street, London WC1N 2LS (e-mail r.bowers@doughtystreet.co.uk)

BOWERY, Prof Norman George; s of George Bowery (d 1971), and Olga, *née* Beevers (d 1991); *b* 23 June 1944; *Educ* Christ's Coll Finchley, Univ of London (PhD, DSc); *m* 14 Feb 1970, Barbara Joyce, da of Eric Norman Westcott, of Goring-by-Sea, W Sussex; 2 da (Nicole Louise b 1973, Annette Jane b 1977), 1 s (Andrew James b 1975); *Career* sr lectr St Thomas' Hosp London 1982–84 (lectr 1975–82), section ldr Neuroscience Res Centre MSD Harlow 1984–87, Wellcome prof of pharmacology Univ of London 1987–95, prof of pharmacology The Med Sch Univ of Birmingham 1995–2004 (now emeritus); vice pres and head of biology GlaxoSmithKline Psychiatric CEDD Verona 2004–06; memb and vice-chm Biological Cncl 1988–91; ed-in-chief Current Opinion in Pharmacology 2000–13; memb: MRC Neuroscience Ctee 1983–87 and 1995–97, SERC Link Ctee 1988–90; Gaddum Meml Award 2004; memb: American Neuroscience Assoc, Br Neuroscience Assoc; Laurea (hc) Univ of Florence; hon fell Br Pharmacological Soc 2007 (hon gen sec 1995–97, pres 1999–2000); *Books* Actions and Interactions of GABA and Benzodiazepines (1984), GABAergic Mechanisms on the Periphery (1986), GABA Basic Research and Clinical Applications (1989), GABAB Receptors in Mammalian Function (1990), The GABA Receptors (1996), GABA: Receptors, Transporters and Metabolism (1996), Allosteric Receptor Modulation in Drug Targeting (2006); *Recreations* gardening, socialising; *Style—* Prof Norman Bowery; ✉ e-mail n.g.bowery@bham.ac.uk

BOWES LYON, Sir Simon Alexander; KCVO (2005); s of Hon Sir David Bowes Lyon, KCVO (d 1961), and Rachel Pauline, *née* Spender Clay (d 1996); *b* 17 June 1932; *Educ* Eton, Magdalen Coll Oxford; *m* 11 April 1966, Caroline Mary Victoria, er da of Rt Rev Victor Joseph Pike, CB, CBE, MA, DD, Bishop of Sherborne 1959–76; 1 da (Rosie (Mrs David Glazebrook) b 1968), 3 s (Fergus b 1970, David b 1973, Andrew b 1979); *Career* dir SPW Securities Ltd and other cos; farmer; HM Lord-Lt Herts 1986–2007; Hon LLD Univ of Herts; FCA 1959; KStJ 1996; *Recreations* shooting, gardening, walking, music; *Clubs* Brooks's, Whites; *Style—* Sir Simon Bowes Lyon, KCVO; ✉ 12 Morpeth Mansions, London SW1 1ER (☎ 020 7828 8057, e-mail spw@boweslyon.demon.co.uk)

BOWES-LYON, David James; DL (Midlothian, 1992); s of Maj-Gen Sir James Bowes-Lyon, KCVO, CB, OBE, MC (d 1977), and Mary, *née* De Trafford; *b* 21 July 1947; *Educ* Ampleforth; *m* 1976, Elizabeth Harriet Bowes-Lyon (Lady-in-Waiting to HRH The Princess Royal), da of Sir John Colville, CB, CVO, of Broughton, Hants; 2 da (Georgina b 1977, Alexandra b 1986), 2 s (James b 1979 (Page of Honour to HM The Queen), Charles b 1989); *Career* Capt 14/20 Kings Hussars 1970–78 NI, W Germany, Cyprus, Zaïre; The Union Discount Co of London 1979–92 (dir various subsid cos); dir: Scottish Business Achievement Tst 1981–, Aitken Campbell and Co Ltd 1987–96, Lothian Racecourse Ltd (Edinburgh) 1987–, Independent Pension Trustees plc 1993–2003, Christies International UK Ltd 1994–; chm Queen Mother's Meml Fund for Scotland 2003–; offr Queen's Body Guard for Scotland (Royal Co of Archers); *Recreations* shooting, fishing, racing; *Clubs* White's, New (Edinburgh, chm 2004); *Style—* David Bowes-Lyon, Esq, DL; ✉ Heriot Water, Heriot, Midlothian EH38 5YE

BOWIS, John Crocket; OBE (1981); s of Thomas Palin Bowis (d 1957), of Brighton, and Georgiana Joyce Bowis, *née* Crocket (d 2008); *b* 2 August 1945; *Educ* Tonbridge, BNC Oxford (MA); *m* 1968, Caroline Taylor, of Oxon; 1 da (Imogen b 1970), 2 s (Duncan b 1972, Alistair b 1978); *Career* Cons Central Office 1972–80, public affrs dir Br Insurance Brokers' Assoc 1981–86, cncllr Royal Borough of Kingston upon Thames 1982–86 (chm of educn 1984–86); MP (Cons) Battersea 1987–97, memb Select Ctee on Membs Interests 1987–90; PPS to: Min for Inner Cities and Local Govt 1989–90, Sec of State for Wales 1990–93; Parly under-sec of state Dept of Health 1993–96, min for Road Safety and Transport in London Dept of Transport 1996–97; MEP (Cons) London 1999–2009, spokesman Environment Health and Consumer Ctee of Euro Parl, dep ldr Cons MEPs 2002–03; chm Cons Europe Gp 2011–; int policy advsr to WHO on mental health 1997–99; pres: Br Youth Cncl 1987–92, Cons Trade Unionists 1990–94, Torche 1999–2009, Health First Europe 2009–; vice-pres: Br Epilepsy Assoc, Battersea Soc, Apex, Wandsworth Symphony Orch, Friends of Battersea Parish Church, Battersea Army Cadet League, European Health Forum Gastein 2009–, Diabetes UK; chm: Nat Cncl for Civil Protection 1990–93, Health Advsy Bd GSK 2009–, European Alliance for Personalised Medicine 2012–, European Partnership for Alcohol Health Promotion 2014–16; vice-chm Int Soc for Human Rights 1989–92; memb Bd: RNT 1990–93, South Bank 1990–93, Royal Acad of Dancing 1992–98, CARA 1995–2009, International Social Services 1997–99, European Men's Health Forum 2004–, TBVI 2009–16, Global Initiative on Psychiatry 2009–, Gamian Europe 2009–; advsr: FIPRA 2009–, Instinctif (formerly Policy Action) 2010–, Hanover 2010–; patron Fund for Epilepsy; ambass: Nat Aids Tst 1997–, Epilepsy Research Fndn 1997–, Share Community 1997–, Mosaic Clubhouse 1997–99, Int Inst of Special Needs Offenders 1998–99, Alzheimer's Soc 2010–; European Public Health Alliance Award for Service to Public Health 2009; Hon FRCPsych 2003, Hon FRCP 2009; *Recreations* theatre, music, art, sport; *Style—* John Bowis, OBE; ✉ 44 Howard Road, New Malden, Surrey KT3 4EA (☎ 020 8949 2555, e-mail johnbowis@aol.com)

BOWKER, (Steven) Richard; CBE (2005); s of Roger William Bowker, and Dr Sylvia Grace Bowker, *née* Walker; *b* 23 April 1966, Oldham, Lancs; *Educ* Queen Elizabeth's GS Blackburn, Univ of Leicester (BA); *m* 8 June 2002, Madeline Victoria, da of Alan Ivemy; 2 s (William Alexander b 30 Aug 2004, Charles Anthony b 14 Aug 2007), 1 da (Lucy Arabella b 27 Jan 2011); *Career* head of PFI London Underground Ltd to 1996, princ Babcock & Brown 1996–99, founding dir Quasar Associates Ltd 1999–2000, co-chm Virgin Rail Gp Ltd 2000–01 (non-exec dir 1999–2000), gp commercial dir Virgin Gp of Companies 2000–01, chm and chief exec Strategic Rail Authy 2001–04, chief exec Partnership for Schools 2005–06, chief exec National Express Gp plc 2006–09, chief exec Etihad Rail Co PJSC Abu Dhabi 2009–12; sr advsr EC Harris LLP 2013–, dir Criterium Cycle Co Ltd 2013– (chm 2016–); ind non-exec dir Football League Ltd 2012–, memb Cncl FA 2012–, cmmr Football Regulatory Authy 2014–, memb Int Ctee FA 2014–15, ind dir Super League (Europe) Ltd 2014–16, dir London Marathon Events Ltd 2015–; memb Bd: British Waterways 2004–09 (vice-chm Bd 2008–09), Countryside Alliance 2005–09; dep pres Heritage Railway Assoc, memb Advsy Bd Greengauge 21 2006–09, vice-pres Settle and Carlisle Railway Tst 2009– (former tstee); vice-pres Friends of the Nat Railway Museum York; FILT, FCIT 2002 (MCIT 1996), FCMA 2003 (ACMA 1993), CGMA 2012; *Recreations* Blackburn Rovers FC, music, hill walking, canal boating and inland waterways, wine, reading, running; *Clubs* Reform; *Style—* Richard Bowker, Esq, CBE

BOWKETT, Alan John; s of John Bowkett, and Margaret, *née* Nicholson; *b* 6 January 1951, Bilsthorpe, Notts; *Educ* King Charles I GS, UCL (BSc), London Business Sch (MSc); *m* 1 Aug 1975, Joy Dianne, *née* Neale; 2 da (Alexandra b 22 Sept 1980, Camilla b 24 July 1982); 3 s (Rupert b 15 March 1984, Hugo b 2 Feb 1986, Charlie b 2 May 1996); *Career* md Boulton & Paul plc 1985–87; ceo: RHP Bearings Ltd 1987–91, Berisford plc 1992–99; chm: Metzeller APS SA 2000–05, Acordis BV 2000–04, Doncaster Gp 2003–06, Seton House (formerly Britax plc) 2005–07, Redrow plc 2007–10, Strix Ltd 2008–, Norwich City FC 2009–15, Avio SpA 2009–, McCarthy & Stone 2010–13, Euromedic BV 2012–14, Diaverum BV 2016–; non-exec dir Greene King plc 1994–2006; chm London Borough of Ealing Social Servs 1978–82; chm Univ of Law 2013–15; fell UEA 1993 (treas 1988–93); *Recreations* shooting, salmon fishing, opera, everything Italian, growing vegetables; *Clubs* Carlton, RAC, Farmers; *Style—* Alan Bowkett, Esq; ✉ Croxton Park, Croxton, Cambridgeshire PE19 6SY (☎ 01480 880058, fax 01480 880345); University of Law, 2 Bunhill Row, Moorgate, London EC1Y 8HQ

BOWLER, Dr John Vaughan; *b* 1959; *Educ* King George V Sch Hong Kong, Worksop Coll, St Thomas' Hosp Med Sch (BSc, MB BS, MD, Cochrane prize, MRC scholarship, Third Beaney prize, Mead medal, Perkins prize); *Career* house surgn St Helier Hosp Carshalton 1984–85, house physician Dept of Med St Thomas' Hosp London 1985; SHO: intensive therapy St Thomas' Hosp London 1985–86, neurology Hammersmith Hosp 1986, cardiology Nat Heart Hosp 1986–87; registrar: gen med Queen Mary's Hosp Sidcup 1987, neurology Atkinson Morley's Hosp 1987–88; Chest, Heart and Stroke Assoc res fell in neurology Dept of Clinical Neuroscience Charing Cross and Westminster Med Sch 1988–90, registrar in neurology Regnl Neurosciences Centre Charing Cross Hosp 1991–92, clinical fell in neurology Dept of Clinical Neurological Sciences Univ of Western Ontario 1992–95, lectr (hon sr registrar) in clincal neurology Dept of Clinical Neurosciences Charing Cross and Westminster Med Sch 1995–98, conslt neurologist Royal Free Hosp and N Middx Hosp, conslt neurologist Nat Hosp for Neurology and Neurosurgery 2010–; , Royal Free and UC Med Sch and 1998–; memb Assoc of Br Neurologists, fndr memb Int Soc for Vascular Behavioural and Cognitive Disorders; FRCP (MRCP 1987); *Publications* ed one book on vascular dementia; author of numerous refereed papers, reports, review articles, editorials, abstracts and book chapters; *Recreations* current affairs, classical music, wine, computers; *Style—* Dr J V Bowler; ✉ Royal Free Hospital, Pond Street, London NW3 2QG (☎ 020 7830 2865, e-mail john.bowler@nhs.net)

BOWLER, Prof Peter J; *Educ* Univ of Toronto (PhD); *Career* MRIA, fell AAAS, FBA; *Books* The Fontana History of Environmental Sciences (1992), Making Modern Science: A Historical Survey (2005), Evolution: The History of an Idea (25th anniversary edn 2009); *Style—* Prof Peter Bowler; ✉ School of History and Anthropology, The Queen's University, Belfast BT7 1NN

BOWLES, Andrew Graham; s of John Russell Bowles (decd), and Anne Bowles; *b* 28 June 1960; *Educ* Uppingham, Oxford Poly Sch of Architecture (BA, DipArch); *m* Claire Etienne, *née* Brown; 3 s (Henry Worthington b 1992, Charles Andrew John b 1995, Maxwell Alexander b 1998); *Career* architect; Wyn Jones Paul Andrews Associates 1983–84; Sheppard Robson (architects, planners and interior designers) London: joined 1986, assoc 1997–98, ptnr 1998–, currently head of science; projects incl: Swan Theatre High Wycombe 1991–92, 55 King William St London for Skansa AB 1992, The Helicon EC2 for London & Manchester 1992–95 (RIBA Regnl Award for Architecture and Civic Tst Award commendation 1998), The BAA Project Process 1995, office devpt Chiswell St for City Univ 1996, office devpt 59–67 Gresham St EC2 for Legal & General and Stanhope 1998; chm London Constructing Excellence Club; RIBA; *Recreations* mountains, cricket, music, wine; *Style—* Andrew Bowles, Esq; ✉ Sheppard Robson, 77 Parkway, London NW1 7PU

BOWLES, Hamish Philip; s of David Victor Bowles, of London, and Anne, *née* Burmester; *b* 23 July 1963; *Educ* Simon Langton Boys' GS Canterbury, William Ellis Sch Highgate, St Martin's Sch of Art; *Career* guest fashion ed Teenage Issue Harpers & Queen 1983, London and Paris ed Harpers' Bazaar Australia 1983–84, contributing ed 1983–84 (Harpers & Queen, The Face, Arena, GQ, Vanity Fair); Harpers & Queen: jr fashion ed 1985, fashion dir 1987, style dir 1989–92; style ed American Vogue 1992–; creative conslt Met Museum of Art; memb The Costume Soc 1976; *Recreations* collecting vintage couture, travel, theatre; *Style—* Hamish Bowles, Esq

BOWLES, Peter John; s of Herbert Reginald Bowles, and Sarah Jane, *née* Harrison; *b* 16 October 1936; *Educ* High Pavement GS Nottingham, RADA (scholar, Kendal prize); *m* 8 April 1961, Susan Alexandra, da of David Cyril Bennett; 2 s (Guy Rupert b 24 Sept 1962, Adam Peter b 26 Jan 1964); 1 da (Sasha Jane b 12 Oct 1966); *Career* actor; Comedy Actor of the Year Pye Awards 1984, ITV Personality of the Year Variety Club 1984; Hon DLitt Nottingham Trent Univ 2002; *Theatre* London debut in Romeo and Juliet (Old Vic) 1956; other work incl: Happy Haven and Platonov (Royal Court) 1960, J.B. (Phoenix) 1961, Bonne Soupe (Comedy/Wyndhams) 1962, Afternoon Men (Arts Theatre) 1961, Absent Friends (Garrick) 1975, Dirty Linen (Arts Theatre) 1976, Born In the Gardens (Globe) 1980, Some of My Best Friends are Husbands (Haymarket Leicester and nat tour) 1985, The Entertainer (Shaftesbury) 1986, Canaries Sometimes Sing (Albery) 1987, Man of The Moment (Globe) 1990, Otherwise Engaged (nat tour) 1992, Separate Tables (Albery) 1993, Pygmalion (Chichester) 1994, In Praise of Love (Apollo) 1995, Gangster No1 (Almeida) 1995, Present Laughter (Wyndhams) 1996, The School for Wives (Piccadilly) 1997, The Misanthrope, Major Barbara (Piccadilly) 1998, Sleuth (Mobile UK tour) 1999, Hedda Gabler (UK Tour) 1999, The Beau (Theatre Royal Haymarket) 2001, The Royal Family (Haymarket) 2001, Sleuth (Apollo) 2002, Our Song (UK tour) 2003, Wait Until Dark (Garrick) 2003, The Old Masters (Comedy) 2004, The Unexpected Man (nat tour) 2005, Joe & I (Kings Head) 2005, Hay Fever (Haymarket) 2006, Waltz of the Toreadors (Chichester) 2007, Relatively Speaking (UK tour) 2008, Love's Labour Lost (Rose Kingston) 2008, Swan Song: The Browning Version (Sir Peter Hall Season Bath) 2009,

The Rivals (Bath) 2010 and (Theatre Royal Haymarket) 2011, The Governess (UK tour) 2013; *Television* incl: The Avengers, The Prisoner, The Persuaders, The Protectors, Danger Man, Rumpole of The Bailey, To The Manor Born, Only When I Laugh, The Bounder, The Irish RM, Lytton's Diary (devised series), Executive Stress, Perfect Scoundrels (co-devised series), Running Late (TV film, also co-prodr, winner The Golden Gate Award San Francisco), Little White Lies, Ballet Shoes, Poirot, Murder, Murder (2015); *Film* incl: Blow Up, The Charge of the Light Brigade, Laughter In The Dark, A Day in the Death of Joe Egg, The Hollywood Ten, Love and War in the Appennines, Colour Me Kubrick, Freebird, The Bank Job 2008, Love's Kitchen 2011, Lilting 2014, Peterman (forthcoming), We Are Tourists (2015); exec prodr Gangster No1; *Books* Ask Me If I'm Happy (autobiography, 2010), Behind the Curtain, The Job of Acting (2012); *Recreations* motoring and physical jerks; *Clubs* Ivy, Chelsea Arts; *Style*— Peter Bowles, Esq; ✉ c/o Conway van Gelder Ltd, 8–12 Broadwick Street, London W1F 8HW (✆ 020 7287 0077, fax 020 7287 1940)

BOWLES OF BERKHAMSTED, Baroness (Life Peer UK 2015), of Berkhamsted, of Bourne End in the County of Hertfordshire Sharon Margaret Bowles; da of Percy Bowles (d 2010), and Florence, *née* Sutcliffe (d 2009); *b* 12 June 1953, Oxford; *Educ* Our Lady's Convent Abingdon, Univ of Reading (BSc), Lady Margaret Hall Oxford (postgrad research); *m* 25 Sept 1981, Andrew Horton; 2 s (Remy Andrew Horton b 10 July 1981, Damian Andrew Horton b 15 June 1982); *Career* chartered patent attorney 1981–2014, European patent attorney 1981–2014, ptnr Bowles Horton Partnership 1981–2014; MEP (Lib Dem) SE England 2005–14 (chair Economic and Monetary Affairs Ctee 2009–14); non-exec dir The London Stock Exchange Gp plc and The London Stock Exchange plc 2014–; memb Advsy Bd Centre for Progressive Capitalisms; memb Chartered Inst of Patent Attorneys 1981–2014; *Recreations* music, travel; *Clubs* Nat Liberal; *Style*— The Baroness Bowles of Berkhamsted

BOWMAN, Angela Dawn; *b* 17 March 1971; *Educ* Chiltern Edge Secdy Sch, Henley Coll, Univ of Southampton (LLB), Guildford Coll of Law (DipLP); *Career* slr specialising in trust and probate disputes for nat and local charities; trainee slr Kidd Rapinet 1995–97, ptnr and head Charities Probate Litigation Team Henmans Freeth Slrs (joined 1997); memb Assoc of Contentious Tst and Probate Specialists (ACTAPS); memb: Charity Law Assoc, Inst of Legacy Mgmnt; Contentious Slr of the Year ACTAPS 2013; *Recreations* tennis, golf, piano, walking; *Clubs* Greyfriars Church (Reading), David Lloyd (Oxford); *Style*— Ms Angela Bowman; ✉ Henmans Freeth, 5000 Oxford Business Park South, Oxford OX4 2BH (✆ 01865 781000, fax 01865 778504, e-mail angela.bowman@henmansllp.co.uk)

BOWMAN, Alderman Charles Edward Beck; *b* 8 December 1961, London; *Educ* Uppingham Sch, Univ of Bristol; *m* 28 Sept 1999, Samantha Jane, *née* Kemball; 2 da (Grace b 3 Sept 1999, Charlotte b 11 March 2001); *Career* PricewaterhouseCoopers: joined 1983, ptnr 1995– (currently a sr ptnr), set up Audit and Assurance Practice, non-exec dir Tax Practice, ptnr responsible for Building Public Trust Prog, ldr Sr Networking Prog; ICAEW: former chm Audit and Assurance Faculty, chm Audit Quality Forum, memb Advsy Cncl Prince of Wales's Accounting for Sustainability Project; past memb City of London Corporation Ctees: Policy and Resources, Finance, Audit and Risk, Markets; govr Park Side Primary Sch Acad Hackney, tstee Lord Mayor's Appeal Ctee, advsr Mansion House Scholarship Scheme; alderman Lime Street Ward City of London 2013–, Aldermanic Sheriff City of London 2015–; memb Ct Worshipful Co of Grocers, Liveryman Worshipful Co of Chartered Accountants of England and Wales; *Recreations* golf, art, architecture, the countryside (helping shepherd a small flock of sheep); *Clubs* Royal Worlington and Newmarket Golf, Roy St George's Golf, R&A, MCC, In & Out; *Style*— Alderman Charles Bowman, JP; ✉ The Park House, Tostock, Bury St Edmunds, Suffolk IP30 9PR (✆ 01359 271633); PwC LLP, 1 Embankment Place, London WC2N 6RH (e-mail charles.bowman@uk.pwc.com, Twitter @CharlieBowman)

BOWMAN, Edith Eleanor; *see:* Smith, Edith Eleanor

BOWMAN, James Thomas; CBE (1997); s of Benjamin and Cecilia Bowman, *née* Coote; *b* 6 November 1941; *Educ* Ely Cathedral Choir Sch, King's Sch Ely, New Coll Oxford; *Partner* Terry Winwood (civil partnership Feb 2006); *Career* counter-tenor; operatic debuts incl: Glyndebourne Festival 1970, Scottish Opera 1971, Royal Opera House Covent Garden 1972, Sydney Opera 1978, Opéra Comique Paris 1979, Theatre du Châtelet Paris 1983, Badisches Staatstheater Karlsruhe 1984, ENO 1985, La Scala Milan 1987; Gentleman-in-Ordinary HM Chapels Royal St James's Palace 2000; pres: Dorking Halls Concertgoers Soc 1994–, The Holst Singers 1995–; vice-pres Bach Choir 2006–; patron New Chamber Opera Oxford 1995–; Hon Gentleman Epiphany Usher HM Chapels Royal St James's Palace 2010; Hon DMus Univ of Newcastle upon Tyne 1996; hon fell New Coll Oxford 1998, fell Royal Sch of Church Music 2012; RSM 2004; Medal of Honour City of Paris 1992, Officier de l'Ordre des Arts et des Lettres (France) 1995 (Chevalier 1992); *Clubs* Athenaeum; *Style*— James Bowman, Esq, CBE; ✉ 4 Brownlow Road, Redhill, Surrey RH1 6AW (e-mail jamestbowman@hotmail.com)

BOWMAN, Philip; s of Thomas Patrick Bowman (d 1987), and Norma Elizabeth, *née* Deravin; *b* 14 December 1952; *Educ* Westminster, Pembroke Coll Cambridge (MA); *Career* Price Waterhouse London 1974–78, Gibbs Bright & Co Pty Ltd Melbourne 1978–83; Bass plc: joined 1985, fin dir Bass plc 1991–94, chief exec Retail Div 1994–95; fin dir Coles Myer Ltd Melbourne 1995–96; Allied Domecq plc: fin dir 1998–99, chief exec 1999–2005; chief exec Scottish Power plc 2006–07, chief exec Smiths Gp 2007–; chm: Chateau Lascombes 1994–95, Liberty plc 1998–2000, Coral Eurobet 2004–05; non-exec dir: British Sky Broadcasting Gp 1994–2003, Burberry Gp plc 2002–, Scottish & Newcastle 2006–07; memb Advsy Bd Alchemy Partners 2000–; FCA 1983; *Recreations* opera, entomology, scuba diving, computers and electronics; *Clubs* Victoria Racing, Royal Automobile of Victoria (Melbourne), National Golf (Victoria); *Style*— Philip Bowman, Esq

BOWMAN, Victoria Jane (Vicky); *née* Robinson; *b* 12 June 1966; *Educ* Pembroke Coll Cambridge (BA); *m* 1, 1991 (m dis 1998), Mark Bowman; m 2, 2006, Htein Lin; *Career* diplomat; entered HM Dip Serv 1988, third then second sec Rangoon 1990–93, first sec FCO 1993, first sec (info and press) UKREP Brussels 1996–99, Cabinet of European Cmmr (Rt Hon Chris Patten, now Baron Patten of Barnes, CH, PC (Life Peer), *qv*) 1999–2002, ambass to Burma 2002–06, dir global and economic issues FCO 2008–11, global practice ldr external affrs Rio Tinto 2011–13, dir Myanmar Centre for Responsible Business 2013–; hon fell Pembroke Coll Cambridge 2016; *Style*— Ms Vicky Bowman; ✉ 15 Shan Yeiktha Street, Sanchaung, Yangon, Myanmar, Burma (website www.mcrb.org.mm)

BOWN, Christopher Michael; s of Michael John David Bown, of Le Touquet, France, and Dora Winifred, *née* Horsfall; *b* 25 August 1956; *Educ* Haileybury, Queens' Coll Cambridge (exhibitioner), Coll of Law; *m* 17 Oct 1987, Lorna Mary, da of Arthur Southcombe Parker; 2 s (Alexander b 27 April 1989, Dominic b 24 June 1995), 2 da (Sophia b 25 March 1991, Florence b 19 April 1993); *Career* Baker & McKenzie: articled clerk 1979, assoc London 1981–82 and 1984–87, seconded to Frankfurt 1983, ptnr 1987–98; ptnr Freshfields Bruckhaus Deringer 1998–; *Recreations* sailing, rowing, cycling, skiing; *Style*— Christopher Bown, Esq; ✉ Freshfields Bruckhaus Deringer, 65 Fleet Street, London EC4Y 1HS (✆ 020 7936 4000, e-mail christopher.bown@freshfields.com)

BOWN, Prof Stephen Glendening; s of Eric Inston Bown (d 1988), of Bexhill-on-Sea, and Olive Mary Kirkman, *née* Payne; *b* 13 December 1944, Beckenham, Kent; *Educ* St Dunstan's Coll Catford, Univ of Cambridge (MA, MB BChir, MD), Harvard Univ (AM); *m* 3 April 1982, Sheila Alyson, da of Peter Taylor (d 1991), of Bexhill-on-Sea; 2 da (Philippa Lucy b 1989, Sophie Elizabeth b 1991); *Career* Nat Med Laser Centre UCL Med Sch: dir 1986–2013, prof of laser med and surgery 1990–; conslt physician UCL Hosps NHS Tst 1987–; currently working with CHASE Africa to develop family planning progs in Kenya; memb Bd Int Photodynamic Assoc 1992–, past pres Br Med Laser Assoc; over 300 sci pubns on med applications of lasers, past ed Lasers in Medical Science, lectures in 45 countries; tstee Population Matters; Hon DSc King George's Medical Univ Lucknow India; Freeman City of London 1982; memb: Br Soc of Gastroenterology 1977, BMA 1974; MRCP 1974, FRCP 1991; *Recreations* squash, travel, tennis; *Clubs* Radlett Lawn Tennis and Squash; *Style*— Prof Stephen Bown; ✉ 10 Watling Street, St Albans, Hertfordshire AL1 2PX (✆ 01727 833701); Research Department of Tissue & Energy, Division of Surgery & Interventional Science, Wing 2.4 Cruciform Building, University College London, Gower Street, London WC1E 6BT (✆ 020 7679 9060, e-mail s.bown@ucl.ac.uk)

BOWNE, Prof Anthony; s of Tony Alfred Bowne, and Kathleen, *née* Doran; *b* 23 April 1956, Leicester; *Educ* Univ of Southampton (BSc), Laban Centre for Movement and Dance (Dip), Bartlett Sch of Architecture UCL (MSc); *m* Dr Emma Redding; 1 s (Ben Redding-Bowne), 1 da (Florence Emily Bowne); *Career* sr financial analyst Rover Cars 1978–81; Laban: lectr in lighting design 1983–86, sr lectr 1987–94, dep chief exec 1994–2003, chief exec 2003–, chief exec Trinity Laban 2003–, princ Trinity Laban Conservatoire of Music and Dance 2010– (formerly jt princ); tech/admin dir Transitions Dance Co 1983–94, tech dir GB tour Nat Youth Dance Co 1986–87, sr lectr in theatre lighting design Hong Kong Acad for Performing Arts 1996–98, prof of dance Lasalle Coll Singapore 2004–, prof City Univ 2010–; lighting designer 1993–, prodns in UK, Taiwan, Hong Kong, Singapore and Shanghai; London Dance and Performance Award for Lighting Design of No Respite 1992; one of ten lighting designers chosen as 'ones to watch' in the next decade Designer for the 90's 1990; guest teacher: Social Hall of Education Taipei 1988, Keene State Coll NH 1991, 1993 and 1995, Univ of the Arts Philadelphia 1991 and 1993, Poly Univ Hong Kong 1997, Arts Cncl England/CABE 2004; memb: Scholarship Review Panel Western Australia Acad for Performing Arts, Govt Dance Forum; chair Cholmondeleys and Featherstonehaughs Dance Co 2000–08; memb Bd: Bonnie Bird Choreography Fund, Granada/Univ of California Davis Artists-in-Residence program, Bird Coll Sidcup, Creative Process 2008–13, London Higher 2008, London Cultural Strategy Gp 2013–; memb Ctee Student Experience Strategic Ctee 2013–; govr Finnish Inst London; FRSA 2002; *Recreations* skiing; *Style*— Prof Anthony Bowne; ✉ Trinity Laban Conservatoire of Music and Dance, King Charles Court, Old Royal Naval College, Greenwich, London SE10 9JF (✆ 020 8305 4391, fax 020 8305 9444, e-mail a.bowne@trinitylaban.ac.uk)

BOWNES, Prof Mary; OBE (2006); *b* 14 November 1948, Drewsteignton, Devon; *Educ* Univ of Sussex (BSc, DPhil); *Career* postdoctoral assoc Univ of Freiburg and Univ of Calif Irvine 1973–76, lectr in genetics and developmental biology Univ of Essex 1976–79; Univ of Edinburgh: lectr in molecular biology 1979–89, sr lectr 1989–91, reader 1991–94, personal chair in developmental biology 1994–, assoc dean for postgrads Faculty of Science and Engrg 1997–98, head Inst of Cell and Molecular Biology 1998–2001, vice-princ 2003–12, sr vice princ 2012–14, memb numerous univ ctees and gps; dir Scottish Initiative for Biotechnology Educn 2002–; memb Editorial Advsy Bd Jl of Embryology and Experimental Morphology/Development 1982–88, memb Editorial Bd Insect Molecular Biology 1990–, assoc ed Developmental Biology 1992–95, memb Editorial Bd Jl of Endocrinology 2000–; author of numerous papers in jls, book chapters and review articles; external examiner: Univ of Sussex 1996–2000, Univ of Oxford 2001–03, Univ of York 2004–06, Univ of Glasgow 2005–09, Univ of Leicester 2007–09, Educn Cmmn; chair: Steering Ctee Science and Plants for Schs (SAPS) Biotechnology Scotland Project 2000–09 (memb 1998–2000), Bd then chair Edinburgh Centre for Rural Research 2003–11 (memb 1999, memb Exec Ctee 2000–03), Strategy Bd BBSRC 2004–07, Studentships and Fellowships Strategy Panel BBSRC 2004–08, Young People's Ctee RSE 2003–11; memb: Bd Genetics Soc 1980–83, Ctee Br Soc for Developmental Biology 1982–87 (treas 1984–89), Advsy Bd Inst for Science Educn Scotland 2002–03, Advsy Bd MRC 2002–03, Cell and Molecular Biology Section Ctee RSE 2004–06, Public Engrg on Educn Ctee RSE 2009–, Meetings Ctee RSE 2005–09, Skills Ctee 2011 SFC 2006–09, Bd Highlands and Islands Enterprise 2008–14, Bd Exec Ctee RSE 2008–, Bd Scot Assoc of Marine Sciences 2008–14, Bd Royal Zoological Soc Scotland 2014–; CBiol, FIBiol, FRES, FRSE, FRSA 2009–16; *Books* Metamorphosis (jt ed, 1985), Ecdysone from Metabolism to Regulation of Gene Expression (ed, 1986), Private Giving: Public Good – The Impact of Philanthropy at the University of Edinburgh (2014); *Style*— Prof Mary Bownes, OBE; ✉ University of Edinburgh, Charles Stewart House, 9–16 Chambers Street, Edinburgh EH1 1HT

BOWNESS, Baron (Life Peer UK 1995), of Warlingham in the County of Surrey and of Croydon in the London Borough of Croydon; Sir Peter Spencer Bowness; kt (1987), CBE (1981), DL (Greater London 1982); s of Hubert Spencer Bowness (d 1981), of Cardiff, and Doreen (Peggy) Blundell, *née* Davies; *b* 19 May 1943; *Educ* Whitgift Sch Croydon; *m* 1, 27 July 1969 (m dis 1983), Marianne, da of Robert Hall, of Croydon; 1 da (Hon Caroline b 1977); m 2, 6 June 1984, Mrs Patricia Jane Cook, da of John Cullis, of Abergavenny; *Career* slr and Notary Public; ptnr Weightman Sadler Solicitors Purley 1970–2002, conslt Streeter Marshall Solicitors Croydon, Purley and Warlingham 2002–11; ldr Croydon Cncl 1976–79 and 1980–94, ldr Opposition Croydon Cncl 1994–96, chm London Boroughs Assoc 1978–94, dep chm Assoc of Metropolitan Authorities 1978–80; memb: Audit Cmmn England & Wales 1983–95, London Residuary Body 1985–93, Nat Trg Task Force 1989–92, Congress (formerly Standing Conf) of Local and Regnl Authorities of Europe (Cncl of Europe) 1990–98, UK Delgn Ctee of Regions Euro Union 1993–98, Bureau COR 1993–98; memb Bd London First/London Forum 1993–94; sits as Cons House of Lords, oppn spokesman on local govt 1997–98, House of Lords rep UK Delgn to EU Charter of Fundamental Rights Drafting Convention 1999–2000; chm of Sub-Ctee House of Lords Foreign Policy Defence and Developmental Aid of the EU Select Ctee 2003–06, memb House of Lords EU Select Ctee 2003–07 and 2009–14, memb Jt Ctee on Human Rights 2004–08 and 2009–12, chm Justice and Instns Sub-Ctee of House of Lords EU Select Ctee 2009–13, memb Secondary Legislation Scrutiny Ctee, memb EU Energy and Environment Sub-Ctee 2014–16; OSCE Parly Assembly: memb 2007–, ldr UK Delgn 2014–, vice-pres 2015–; former govr Whitgift Fndn; Freeman City of London 1987, Hon Freeman London Borough of Croydon 2002; Hon Col 151 (Greater London) Tport Regt (V) 1988–93; *Recreations* travel, gardening; *Style*— The Rt Hon Lord Bowness, CBE, DL; ✉ House of Lords, London SW1A 0PW (e-mail bownessp@parliament.uk)

BOWRAN, Peter Anthony Graham (Tony); s of James Eric Bowran (d 2008), and Charlotte, *née* Peacock (d 1981); *b* 23 August 1953, Middlesburgh; *Educ* Calday Grange GS, London Coll of Printing, Inst of Contemporary Music Performance; *m* Linda Rosena Peryer; *Career* photographer; commissioned by London and worldwide advertising agencies; personal work published in several books on photography and exhibited in London and Cornwall; photography awards incl: Assoc of Photographers (AFAEP) Gold, Silver and Merit, D&AD, Creative Circle, Clio Communication Arts, One Show and London Photographic; fencer (fenced for GB in several Fedn Int Escrime World Cup events); *Clubs* Lansdowne, Épée, Soho House; *Style*— Tony Bowran, Esq; ✉ 5 Wandon Road, London SW6 2JF (✆ 020 7731 2689, e-mail ltb.studio1@talktalk.net, website www.tonybowran.com)

BOWRING, Clive John; s of George Edward Bowring (d 1997), of Guernsey, and Kathleen Elma (Jane), *née* Tyte (d 1993); *b* 1 September 1937; *Educ* Rugby Sch; *Career* Nat Serv 1956–58, Lt RNR; C T Bowring & Co Ltd 1958–80 (dir C T Bowring (Insurance Holdings

Ltd) 1976); Robert Fleming Insurance Brokers Ltd: dir 1980–96, chm 1996–2007; dir Forest North Holdings Ltd; pres New Forest and Hants Agricultural Show Soc 2011, tstee New Forest 9th Centenary Tst, govr Queen Elizabeth's Fndn 1984; Freeman City of London 1984, Liveryman Worshipful Co of Insurers 1984; *Recreations* sailing, travel, the countryside; *Clubs* City of London, Royal Ocean Racing, Hurlingham, Lloyds Yacht, Pilgrims; *Style*— Clive Bowring, Esq; ✉ RFIB Group Limited, 20 Gracechurch Street, London EC3V 0AF (☎ 020 7621 1263, fax 020 7626 5692)

BOWRING, Rev Lyndon; s of Arthur Bowing, of Caerphilly, Mid Glam, and Ellen May, *née* Gardner; *b* 15 February 1948; *Educ* Caerphilly GS, London Bible Coll; *m* 25 May 1974, Celia Joan, da of Capt Edward Ernest Bartholomew (d 1983), of Shoreham-by-Sea; 2 s (Daniel Alexander, Andrew Gareth), 1 da (Emma Charlotte); *Career* Elim pentecostal minister Kensington Temple 1972–80, chm NFOL 1981–83, exec chm CARE 1983–; vice-chm: Luis Palau's Mission 1984, Billy Graham's Mission 1989; chm Maranatha Christian Tst, dir London and Nationwide Missions; public speaker; *Recreations* family, reading, walking, gardening, exploring London; *Style*— The Rev Lyndon Bowring; ✉ 22 Thornton Avenue, Chiswick, London W4 (☎ 020 8747 3796); CARE, 53 Romney Street, London SW1 (☎ 020 7233 0455, fax 017 233 0983)

BOWRING, Prof Richard John; s of Richard Arthur Bowring (d 1987), and Mabel, *née* Eddy; *b* 6 February 1947; *Educ* Blundell's, Downing Coll Cambridge (BA, PhD, LittD); *m* 30 Jan 1970, Susan, da of Wilfred Raymond Povey, of Stoke-on-Trent, Staffs; 1 da (Imogen Clare b 17 May 1977); *Career* mgmnt trainee Cathay Pacific Airways 1968–70, lectr in Japanese Monash Univ Melbourne 1976–78, asst prof of Japanese Columbia Univ NY 1978–79, assoc prof of Japanese Princeton Univ 1979–84, prof of Japanese studies Univ of Cambridge 1985–2012 (lectr in Japanese 1984), fell Downing Coll Cambridge 1985–2000 (hon fell 2000–), Master Selwyn Coll Cambridge 2000–2013, ret; readership British Acad 1995–97; memb Review Ctee for Oriental Studies Univ of Oxford 2000; tstee Cambridge Fndn 1989–98, advsr to UFC 1991–92, Crown rep Governing Body SOAS Univ of London 1994–99, chm HEFCE Working Pty on Funding of SOAS 2000; tstee Daiwa Anglo-Japanese Fndn 2013–; Order of the Rising Sun (Third Class, Japanese Govt); *Books* Mori Ogai and the Modernisation of Japanese Culture (1979), Murasaki Shikibu: Her Diary and Poetic Memoirs (1982), Murasaki Shikibu: The Tale of Genji (1988), Introduction to Modern Japanese (1992), Cambridge Encyclopedia of Japan (1993), The Diary of Lady Murasaki (1996), Fifty Years of Japanese at Cambridge (1998), Cambridge Intermediate Japanese (2002), The Religious Traditions of Japan, 500–1600 (2005), The Myotei Dialogues: a Japanese Christian Critique of Native Traditions (2015); *Style*— Prof Richard Bowring

BOX, Stephen John; s of Ronald Tully Box (d 1981), and Mollie Rita, *née* Clarke (d 2000); *b* 13 September 1950; *Educ* Ardingly; *m* 25 April 1992, Christine Elisabeth, da of Robert Beevers (d 1989), of Rockhampton, Qld, Aust; *Career* CA; articled clerk Hilton Sharp & Clarke 1967–71; Coopers & Lybrand: sr 1971–73, mangr 1973–82, ptnr 1982–97; fin dir National Grid Gp plc 1997–2002; non-exec dir: Michael Page International plc 2001–, South East Water Ltd, Wales and West Utilities Ltd; memb Financial Reporting Review Panel; FCA 1971; *Recreations* opera, theatre, travel, gardening, bridge, reading, swimming; *Style*— Stephen Box, Esq

BOX, Stephen Thomas; s of Thomas George, of Nuneaton, Warks, and Edith Helen, *née* Reid; *b* 13 January 1951, Baxterley, Warks; *Educ* Queen Elizabeth GS Atherstone, Univ of Salford (BSc), Physical Electronics City Business Sch (DipBA); *m* 8 Jan 1988 (m dis 1995), Sarah, da of Dennis Grimwood Roscow; 2 da (Daisy Philippa b 24 Aug 1988, Imogen Poppy b 9 Aug 1990); *Career* sci offr AERE Harwell 1968–74, computer conslt CSI Ltd 1974–76, systems analyst Chase Manhattan Bank 1976–78, head int systems devpt Citicorp 1978–80, freelance mgmnt conslt 1980–86, dir debt securities ops Kleinwort Benson Ltd 1987–89, mgmnt conslt and corp financier Stephen Box & Co 1989–90, co-fndr and dir Blue Skies Corporation plc 1990–94, dir UNIVEST Corporation Ltd 1995–2007; contrib to Manuale del Project Finance 1999; Liveryman Worshipful Co of Gunmakers 2003; *Recreations* shooting, tennis, golf, music, opera; *Style*— Stephen Box, Esq; ✉ Farthing Lodge, 20 Stamford Road, Weldon, Northamptonshire NN17 3JL (☎ 01536 402960, e-mail stephen.box@btinternet.com)

BOXER, Prof David Howell; s of William H S Boxer, of Aberdare, and Sarah, *née* Davies; *b* 11 June 1947; *Educ* Aberdare Boys' GS, Univ of Bristol (univ scholar, Lord Kitchener Nat Meml Fund scholar, BSc, PhD, CertEd); *m* Dr Maureen Boxer, da of Matthew McGuckin; 1 s (Iain b 6 Oct 1983); *Career* Univ of Dundee: Nuffield Fndn sci res fell 1982–83, head Dept of Biochemistry 1988–93, personal chair 1991, prof of microbial biochemistry 1991–2002, dean Science and Engrg Faculty 1994–99, dep princ 2000–02, vice-princ (research and enterprise) 2002–09; dir Inst of Food Research 2009–; SERC: memb Molecular Recognition Initiative Ctee 1989–93, chm Biochemistry and Biophysics Sub Ctee 1991–93; external examiner: Univ of Stirling 1992–, Univ of Edinburgh 1992–, Univ of Newcastle upon Tyne 1993–, Univ of Sheffield 1994–; ed: Molecular Microbiology 1986–91, Biochemical Jl 1989–90, Methods in Microbiology 1991–; author of numerous pubns in scientific jls, regular invited speaker at Univs and int meetings; memb: Biochemical Soc 1974–, Soc for General Microbiology 1980–, Br Biophysical Soc 1980–, American Soc for Microbiology 1981–, Inorganic Biochemistry Discussion Gp 1983–, American Chemical Soc 1990–; *Recreations* walking, cycling, skiing; *Style*— Prof David Boxer

BOYACK, Sarah; MSP; da of James Boyack (d 1989), and Alma Boyack, *née* Graham; *b* 16 May 1961; *Educ* Royal HS Edinburgh, Univ of Glasgow (MA), Heriot-Watt Univ (Dip Town & Country Planning); *Career* planning asst London Borough of Brent 1986–88, sr planning offr Central Regional Cncl 1988–92, lectr in planning Edinburgh Coll of Art Heriot-Watt Univ 1992–99; MSP (Lab): Edinburgh Central 1999–2011, Lothians 2011–; min for tport and environment 1999–2001, min for tport and planning 2001, memb European Ctee, convenor Environment and Rural Devpt Ctee 2003–07, dep min for environment 2007, shadow cabinet spokesperson for environment, climate change and rural affrs 2007–; *Style*— Ms Sarah Boyack, MSP

BOYCE, Sir Graham Hugh; KCMG (2001, CMG 1991); s of Cdr Hugh Boyce, DSC, RN, and Madeline Millicent, *née* Manley; *b* 6 October 1945; *Educ* Hurstpierpoint Coll, Jesus Coll Cambridge (MA); *m* 11 April 1970, Janet Elizabeth (Lady Boyce), da of Rev Gordon Charles Craig Spencer, of Bath; 1 s (James b 1971), 3 da (Rachel b 1974, Sara b 1980, Josephine b 1984); *Career* VSO Antigua 1967; FCO: HM Dip Serv 1968, third then second sec Ottawa 1971, MECAS Shemlan 1972–74, first sec Tripoli 1974–77, FCO 1977–81, first sec Kuwait 1981–85, asst head ME Dept 1985–86, cnsllr and consul-gen Stockholm 1987–90, ambass and consul-gen Doha 1990–93, head Environment Science and Energy Dept 1993–96, ambass to Kuwait 1996–99, ambass to Egypt 1999–2001; vice-chm VT Int Servs 2002–06, jt chm Windsor Energy Gp 2005–09, chm MEC Int 2011–13; chm Middle East Advsy Bd: Lehman Bros 2005–08, Invensys 2005–10; chm Common Purpose Int 2013– (chm ME Advsy Gp 2011–), chm NYA Int 2016–; sr advsr Nomura Int 2009–13, sr advsr Bank of America Merrill Lynch 2013–; memb: Int Advsy Cncl Kuwait Investment Office 2004–; advsr: Shell 2001–06, Air Products 2005–14, DLA Piper 2009–14; vice-chm Middle East Assoc 2004–11; *Recreations* tennis, reading, golf; *Clubs* Oxford and Cambridge; *Style*— Sir Graham Boyce, KCMG; ✉ e-mail ghbhc@aol.com

BOYCE, Baron (Life Peer UK 2003), of Pimlico in the City of Westminster; Adm of the Fleet (Sir) Michael Cecil Boyce; KG (2011), GCB (1999), OBE (1982), DL (Gtr London 2003); *b* 2 April 1943; *Career* joined RN 1961, submariner 1965, served HM Submarines Anchorite, Valiant and Conqueror 1965–72; cmd HM Submarines: Oberon 1973–74, Opossum 1974–75, Superb 1979–81; cmd HMS Brilliant 1983–84, Capt (SM) Submarine Sea Trg 1984–86, RCDS 1988, Cdre 1988, Sr Naval Offr Middle East 1989, Dir Naval Staff Duties 1989–91; Rear Adm 1991; Flag Offr: Sea Trg 1991–92, Surface Flotilla 1992–94; Cdr Anti-Submarine Warfare Striking Force 1992–94, Vice Adm 1994, Adm 1995, Second Sea Lord and C-in-C Naval Home Cmd 1995–97, C-in-C Fleet, C-in-C Eastern Atlantic, Cdr Allied Naval Forces North Western Europe 1997–98, First Sea Lord, Chief of the Naval Staff and First and Principal Naval ADC to HM Queen 1998–2001, Chief of the Defence Staff 2001–03, ADC to HM Queen 2001–03, Col Cmdt SBS 2003–; Lord Warden of the Cinque Ports and Constable Dover Castle 2004–; pres: Officers Assoc 2003–12, RN Submarine Museum 2005–; vice pres: White Ensign Assoc 2013– (memb Cncl 2003–, chm 2007–10), vice-pres RNLI 2013– (memb Cncl 2004–13, chm 2008–13); govr Alleyn's Sch 1995–2005, patron Submariners Assoc 2003–, dir Naval and Military Club 2003–10 (vice-pres 2014–), patron Sail 4 Cancer 2003–, tstee Nat Maritime Museum 2005–13, patron Forces in Mind Tst 2012–, chm HMS Victory Preservation Co 2012–; non-exec dir: WS Atkins 2004–13, VT Group plc 2004–10; pres London Dist St John Ambulance 2003–11; hon bencher Middle Temple 2012; Freeman City of London 1999, elder bro Trinity House 2006– (younger bro 1999–2006), Master Drapers' Co 2013–14; Hon LLD Univ of Portsmouth 2005, hon doctorate Canterbury Christ Church Univ 2011, Hon DCL Univ of Kent 2013; King of Arms Order of Bath 2009–, KStJ 2002, Cdr Legion of Merit (USA) 2009; *Style*— Admiral of the Fleet the Rt Hon the Lord Boyce, KG, GCB, OBE, DL; ✉ House of Lords, London SW1A 0PW

BOYCE, Sir Robert Charles Leslie; 3 Bt (UK 1952), of Badgeworth, Co Gloucester; s of Sir Richard (Leslie) Boyce, 2 Bt (d 1968), and Jacqueline Anne Boyce-Dennis, *née* Hill; *b* 2 May 1962; *Educ* Cheltenham Coll, Univ of Salford (BSc), Univ of Nottingham (BMedSci, BM BS); *m* 1985, Fiona Margaret, 2 da of John Savage, of Coventry, Warks; 1 s (Thomas Leslie b 3 Sept 1993), 1 da (Amelia Moira b 23 March 1996); *Heir* s, Thomas Boyce; *Career* conslt ophthalmic and oculoplastic surgn; md Minor Ops Ltd; FRCSEd; *Clubs* BMA; *Style*— Sir Robert Boyce, Bt

BOYCE, William; QC (2001); *b* 29 July 1951; *Educ* St Joseph's Acad GS Blackheath, Univ of Kent (BA); *Career* called to the Bar Gray's Inn 1976, recorder 1997–, bencher 2007; sr Treasy counsel Central Criminal Court 1997–2001 (jr Treasy counsel 1991–97); *Style*— William Boyce, Esq, QC; ✉ QEB Hollis Whiteman, 1–2 Laurence Pountney Hill, London EC4R 0EU (☎ 02079 338855)

BOYCOTT, Geoffrey (Geoff); OBE (1981); s of late Thomas Wilfred Boycott, and Jane, *née* Speight; *b* 21 October 1940; *Educ* Kinsley Secdy Modern, Hemsworth GS; *m* 26 Feb 2003, Rachael, *née* Swinglehurst; 1 da (Emma Jane); *Career* former cricketer; played for: Yorks CCC 1962–86 (co cap 1963, capt 1971–78), England 1964–74 and 1977–82 (capt 1977–78, 4 tests); scored one hundredth first class century 1977 (England v Australia), scored one hundred and fiftieth century 1986, exceeded world record no of runs scored in Test Matches Delhi 1982; hon life memb Yorks CCC (memb Bd 2004–10, pres 2012–13); sometime commentator: BBC, TW1, World Tel, Espn/Star Sports, Talk Radio, SABC, Channel 4, BBC Radio, Channel 9 (Aust), Channel 10 TV (Aust), NZTV, Channel Five, Ten Sports; cricket writer Daily Telegraph; patron Yorkshire Air Ambulance 2015–; *Books* Geoff Boycott's Book for Young Cricketers (1976), Put to the Test: England in Australia 1978–79 (1979), Geoff Boycott's Cricket Quiz (1979), Boycott On Batting (1980), Opening Up (1980), In the Fast Lane: England in the West Indies (1981), Master Class (1982), Boycott, The Autobiography (1987), Boycott on Cricket (1990), Geoffrey Boycott The Best XI (2008), Learn Cricket the Right Way (2010); *Videos* Boycott on Batting (1990), Geoff Boycott's Greatest England Team (1991), Geoffrey Boycott on Cricket (1999); *Recreations* golf; *Clubs* Pearl Valley Golf Estate (SA), Moor Allerton Golf (Leeds); *Style*— Geoff Boycott, Esq, OBE; ✉ Yorkshire County Cricket Club, Headingley Cricket Ground, Leeds LS6 3DP

BOYCOTT, Rosel Marie (Rosie); da of Maj Charles Boycott, and Betty, *née* Le Sueur (d 1981); *b* 13 May 1951; *Educ* Cheltenham Ladies' Coll, Univ of Kent; *m* 1, (m dis 1998), David Leitch; 1 da (Daisy Anna b 9 Aug 1983); *m* 2, 1999, Charles Howard, QC, *qv*; *Career* journalist and author; fndr: Spare Rib magazine 1972, Virago Press 1973; ed Osrati (Kuwaiti women's magazine) 1976–79, freelance contrib to various nat newspapers, full-time appts at Daily Mail, Daily Telegraph and Harpers & Queen, ed British Esquire 1992–96; ed: Independent on Sunday 1996–98, The Independent 1998, The Daily Express 1998–2001; currently chm London Food Bd and food advsr to Mayor of London; contrib to progs on TV and radio and to Daily Mail and The Observer, regular guest Newsnight Review; memb NESTA Lab; tstee: Wye Literary Festival, Hay Colombia; *Books* Loka: The Buddhist Journal of Naropa (ed, 1975), Batty, Bloomers and Boycott (1981), A Nice Girl Like Me (autobiography, 1983), All For Love (novel, 1985), Spotted Pigs and Green Tomatoes: A Year in the life of a small-holding (autobiography, 2007); *Recreations* sailing, tennis, riding, gardening; *Clubs* Globe, Groucho, Academy; *Style*— Ms Rosie Boycott

BOYD, Alan Robb; s of Alexander Boyd (d 1963), and Mary Herd, *née* Robb (d 1998); *b* 30 July 1953; *Educ* Irvine Royal Acad, Univ of Dundee (LLB), Open Univ (BA); *m* 1973, Frances Helen, da of Joseph Donaldson; 2 da (Carol Jane b 10 Sept 1975, Fiona Anne b 22 March 1979); *Career* admitted slr 1976, princ legal asst Shetland Islands Cncl 1979–81, princ slr Glenrothes Development Corporation 1981–84, legal advsr Irvine Development Corporation 1984–97, dir of Public Law McGrigors LLP Slrs 1997–2010, dir McGrigors Public Policy 1999–2010, conslt McGrigors LLP Slrs 2010–12, conslt Pinsent Masons LLP Slrs 2012–15; pres Euro Co Lawyers' Assoc 1992–94, pres Law Soc of Scotland 1995–96 (vice-pres 1994–95, memb Cncl 1985–97); NP 1982; *Recreations* golf, music, gardening; *Clubs* Turnberry Golf; *Style*— Alan Boyd, Esq; ✉ 26 Hannah Wynd, St Quivox, Ayr KA6 5HB (☎ 01292 521936, e-mail a-boyd2@sky.com); Pinsent Masons LLP, 141 Bothwell Street, Glasgow G2 7EQ (☎ 0141 567 8400, fax 0141 567 8401)

BOYD, (Morgan) Alistair; CMG (1990); s of Preb Norman Robert Boyd (d 1945), and Muriel Katherine, *née* Humby (d 1984); *b* 1 May 1934; *Educ* Marlborough, Wadham Coll Oxford (MA); *m* 26 May 1959, Judith Mary, da of Preb Henry Wilfred Lawrence Martin, of Christ Church, Jerusalem; *Career* Commonwealth Devpt Corp: mgmnt trainee 1957, investigations exec Malaysia and rep Economist Intelligence Unit Liaison Office for the Fedn of Br Industry 1961, mangr E Caribbean Housing and related mortgage fin cos in the Caribbean 1967, attached to FO for mission to Turks and Caicos Islands 1970, gen mangr Tanganyika Development Finance Co Tanzania 1970–74, seconded as advsr on establishing Industrial Devpt Bank to Kenya Govt 1975, regnl controller Central Africa Lusaka 1976–80, regional controller E Africa Nairobi 1980–83, head of new business worldwide London 1983, dir of operations in Africa London 1985, dep chief exec 1991–94, advsr 1994–2000; memb Cncl Africa Centre 1995–2004, chm UK Southern Africa Business Assoc 1995–2006, vice-chm Royal African Soc 1996–; dir AMREF UK 1999–2007 (chm 2001), chm Gateway to Growth 2005–08; memb Bd: Hub River Power Co Pakistan 1994–96, EDESA Management AG Switzerland 1994–97, Laxey Investment Tst (formerly Tea Plantations Investment Trust plc) 1998–2012; memb: Ctee on South African Trade 1995–2001, Steering Ctee World Congress (1998) Land Ownership and Resource Mgmnt 1996–2000, Directorate of Tropical Africa Advsy Gp 1997–2000; tstee CDC Pension Fund 1995–2001; lectr for Maurice Frost Lecture Agency and ESU 1956–62 (USA tour 1961), Malaysia corr Far Eastern Economic Review 1963–66; fndr memb Youth Resource Centre Kabale Uganda 2004–, tstee Amref Tst Fund 2004–, dir African Fellowship Tst 2008–; memb English Speaking Union, memb Royal Inst of Int Affrs; FRGS 1959, FRSA (memb 1990); *Books* Royal Challenge Accepted (1961), Get Up and

Go (2009); *Recreations* sailing, music; *Clubs* Naval, ESU; *Style*— Alistair Boyd, Esq, CMG; ✉ 7 South Hill Mansions, South Hill Park, London NW3 2SL (e-mail morgaliboyd@yahoo.com)

BOYD, Darren; s of John Boyd, and Maureen, *née* Lade; *b* 30 January 1971, Hastings, E Sussex; *Educ* William Parker Secdy Sch for Boys Hastings, E Sussex Coll of Art and Design (Dip); *m* 24 June 2004, Amanda, *née* Ashy; 1 da (Eliza Jane Ashy Boyd b 31 Aug 2012); *Career* actor; *Television* incl: Kiss Me, Kate 1998–2001, Hippies 1999, Smack the Pony 1999–2003, Los Dos Bros 2001, The Jury 2002, Watching Ellie 2002–03, Little Robots 2003, The Legend of the Tamworth Two 2004, Broken News 2005, Green Wing 2006, ReGenesis 2006, The Jane Show 2006–07, Saxondale 2007, Ladies and Gentlemen 2007, Christmas at the Riviera 2007, Bike Squad 2008, Little Dorrit 2008, May Contain Nuts 2009, Personal Affairs 2009, Royal Wedding 2010, Whites 2010, Holy Flying Circus 2011, Dirk Gently 2010–12, Spy 2011– (Best TV Comedy Actor Br Comedy Award 2011, Best Male Performance in a Comedy Prog BAFTA Award 2012), Case Sensitive 2011–12, The Guilty 2013; *Film* incl: High Heels and Low Lifes 2001, Imagine Me and You 2005, Magicians 2007, Four Lions 2010, Alan Partridge: Alpha Papa 2013, The World's End 2013; *Style*— Mr Darren Boyd; ✉ c/o Independent Talent Group, 40 Whitfield Street, London W1T 2RH (☎ 020 7636 6565, Twitter @darrenjboyd)

BOYD, Douglas; s of Marcus Alexander Boyd (d 1985), and Agnes (Nan), *née* Hollis (d 2001); *b* 1 March 1959; *Educ* RAM under Janet Craxton, studied with Maurice Bourgue in Paris; *m* 1, 1986 (m dis 1990), Gabielle Lester; 1 s (Samuel Marcus b 1988); m 2, 1994, Sally Pendlebury, cellist; 1 da (Iona Elizabeth b 1999), 1 s (Sebastian Alexander b 15 May 2003); *Career* former professional oboist, currently conductor; *As Oboist* debut Salzburg Festival 1990; soloist in important musical centres of Europe, Far East and America; co-fndr Chamber Orch of Europe (princ oboist, leading memb Wind Soloists); prof RAM (Hon ARAM 1990); concerto appearances incl: Chamber Orch of Europe, Scottish Chamber Orch, Vienna Symphony Orch, BBC Scottish Symphony, Bournemouth Sinfonietta, Orch of St Johns Smith Square, Acad of St Martin in the Fields, Moscow Virtuosi, Hong Kong Philarmonic, Basle Radio Symphony, Nat Arts Centre Orch Ottawa, Royal Scot Nat Orch, Northern Sinfonia of England, Winterthur Orch, Orchestre National de Lyon (debut), Cincinnati Symphony Orch (debut), Budapest Festival Orch; work with conductors incl: Claudio Abbado, Paavo Berglund, Sir Yehudi Menuhin, Alexander Schneider, Michael Tilson Thomas; int festivals incl: Berlin, City of London, Edinburgh, Korsholm, Vancouver, Charleston, Spoleto; *Recordings* Bach Oboe Concerto (dir and soloist, Deutsche Grammophon) 1990, Vivaldi Oboe Concerti (dir and soloist, Deutsche Grammophon) 1992, Schumann Recital (with Joao Maria Pires, Deutsche Grammophon) 1995; Strauss Oboe Concerto (ASV) 1990, Zelenka Trio Sonatas (claves) 1998, Ligeti Double Concerto (Jaques Zoon and Claudio Abbado, Deutsche Grammophon) 1998; as conductor: Beethoven Symphonies Cycle (with Manchester Camerata, Avie Records), Mahler Symphony No 4 and Das Lied von der Erde (with Manchester Camerata, Avie Records), Schubert Symphonies with Musikkollegium Winterthur, Vaughan Williams Symphony 5 with Musikkollegium Winterthur, Schumann Violin Concerto with Anthony Marwood; *As Conductor* princ conductor Manchester Camerate 2001–11 (also music dir), princ guest conductor City of London Sinfonia 2002–08, artistic ptnr St Paul Chamber Orch Minnesota, princ guest conductor Colorado Symphony 2008–11; music dir Musikkollegium Winterthur 2009, artistic dir Garsington Opera 2013–, music dir L'Orchestre de Chambre de Paris 2015–; appears with major orchestras throughout the world, incl: Royal Scottish Nat Orch, BBC Symphony Orch, City of Birmingham Symphony Orch, Gürzenich Orch of Cologne, Tonhalle Orchester and the Sydney and Melbourne Symphony Orchs (where he conducted the complete cycle of Beethoven Symphonies); in North America he has also led such prominent orchestras as: Toronto Symphony Orch, Detroit Symphony Orch, Baltimore Symphony Orch, Seattle Symphony Orch; *Style*— Douglas Boyd, Esq; ✉ c/o Ingpen & Williams Ltd, 7 St George's Court, 131 Putney Bridge Road, London SW15 2PA (☎ 020 8874 3222, e-mail dougieboyd@dsl.pipex.com)

BOYD, Douglas Turner; OBE (2006); s of David Findlay Boyd (d 1979), and Edith May, *née* Turner (d 1981); *b* 7 April 1939; *Educ* Hutchesons' GS; *m* 2 Sept 1968, Sheena Lynam Park, da of John Lynam Henderson (d 1970); 2 da (Catriona Henderson b 8 April 1970, Aileen Elizabeth b 30 Aug 1971); *Career* qualified CA (ICAS); KPMG 1956–98; dir: Hanover (Scotland) Housing Association Ltd 1998–2010 (chm 2004–10), Scottish Food Quality Certification Ltd 1998–2005, Taylor Clark Ltd 2000–13, Checkmate International plc 2001–07, Cairnstar Ltd 2001–11; memb: Doctors and Dentists' Pay Review Body 1987–92, Scottish Milk Mktg Bd 1994–2002; lay memb General Optical Cncl 1986–2001; govr: Macaulay Land Use Research Inst 1997–2003, Royal Scottish Acad of Music and Drama 1998–2007 (vice-chm 2003–07); chm of tstees RCS Tsts 2008–16; preceptor Hutchesons' Hospital 2014–; dir Scottish Int Piano Competition Ltd 2011–; memb: Incorporation of Gardeners (Glasgow) 1986, The Weavers' Soc of Anderston 1987 (pres 2015 and 2016), Merchants' House of Glasgow 1990 (Lord Dean of Guild 2011–13); FRSAMD 2006; *Recreations* keep fit, golf; *Clubs* Western (Glasgow, chm 2013–14), Lenzie, Lenzie Golf; *Style*— Douglas T Boyd, Esq, OBE, FRSAMD; ✉ e-mail douglas.boyd2@ntlworld.com

BOYD, Fionnuala; da of Joseph Douglas Allen Boyd (d 1990), and Doreen, *née* Wilson; *b* 13 April 1944; *Educ* The Grammar Sch Welwyn Garden City, St Albans Art Sch, Univ of Leeds (BA); *m* 1965, Leslie Douglas Evans, *qv*, s of Leslie Edward Evans; 1 s (Jack Luis b 1969), 1 da (Ruby Rose b 1971); *Career* artist; began working with Leslie Evans 1968, Bi-Centennial fellow USA 1977–78; artist in residence: Milton Keynes Devpt Corp 1982–84, RGS 1991, Brunei Rainforest Project 1991–92; *Exhibitions* with Leslie Evans: Angela Flowers Gallery 1972, 1974, 1977, 1979, 1980, 1982, 1984, 1986, 1988, 1990, 1992, 1994, 1996, 1998, 2000, 2002 and 2003, Park Square Gallery Leeds 1972, Boyd and Evans 1970–75 (Turnpike Gallery Leigh) 1976, Fendrick Gallery Washington DC 1978, Graves Art Gallery Sheffield 1978, Spectro Arts Workshop Newcastle 1980, Ton Peek Utrecht 1981, A Decade of Paintings (Milton Keynes Exhibition Gallery) 1982–83, Drumcroon Art Centre Wigan 1985, Bird (Flowers East, London) 1990, English Paintings (Brendan Walter Gallery Santa Monica) 1990, Angela Flowers (Ireland) Inc Rosscarberry Ireland 1990, Flowers East London 1991, Brunei Rainforest (Milton Keynes, Brunei, Malaysia & Singapore) 1993, New Rain Forest Paintings (Flowers East) 1994, Portrayal (Flowers East) 1996, Western Photographs (Flowers East) 1999, Natural Wonder (Flowers West Santa Monica) 1999, solo show (Flowers West Santa Monica) 1999 and 2001, solo show (Flowers East London) 2000, Colour in Black & White (Flowers Graphics London and Keller & Greene LA) 2003, Landmarks (Milton Keynes Gallery and Flowers Central London) 2005, Color in Black & White (Flowers NY) 2006, Boyd & Evans (Galerie d'Art Int Solana Beach CA) 2006, Looking Differently (Flowers East London) 2007, Black and White (Flowers East London) 2009, Portrait of a Landscape (LewAllen Gallery Santa Fe) 2011, Views (Ikon Gallery Birmingham) 2012, New Photographs (Flowers Central London) 2012, Collecting (Flowers Central London) 2012, Paintings (Flowers Central London) 2013, Photographs (Leeds Coll of Art) 2013, A Big Tree and Other Photographs (Milton Keynes Coll) 2014; *Group Exhibitions* incl: Postcards (Angela Flowers Gallery) 1970, British Drawing 1952–72 (Angela Flowers Gallery) 1972, Imagini Come Strumenta di Realta (Studio la Citta Verona) 1973, New Image Painting (First Tokyo Int Biennale of Figurative Art) 1974, Body and Soul (Peter Moores, Liverpool) 1975, British Realist Show (Ikon Gallery) 1976, Aspects of Realism (Rothmans of Pall Mall, Canada) 1976–78, The Real British (Fischer Fine Art) 1981, Black and White Show (Angela Flowers Gallery) 1985, Sixteen (Angela Flowers Gallery) 1986, State of the Nation (Herbert Gallery, Coventry) 1987, Contemporary Portraits (Flowers East) 1988, The Thatcher Years (Flowers East) 1989, Picturing People: British Figurative Art since 1945 (touring exhibition Far East) 1989–90, Art '90 London (Business Design Centre) 1990, 25th Anniversary Exhibition (Flowers East) 1995, Wheels on Fire (Wolverhampton Stoke-on-Trent) 1996, Sight Lines (Honiton Festival) 1996, Contemporary British Landscape (Flowers East) 1999, Double Signature (Fermyn Woods Northants) 2009, This Could Happen to You (Ikon Gallery Birmingham) 2010; work in public collections of: Arts Cncl of GB, Br Cncl, MOMA NY, Metropolitan Museum NY, Sheffield City Art Gallery, Wolverhampton City Art Gallery, Leeds City Art Gallery, Contemporary Art Soc, Leicester Educn Authy, Manchester City Art Gallery, Unilever plc, Tate Gallery, Williamson Art Gallery, Borough of Milton Keynes; *Awards* prizewinner Bradford Print Biennale, first prize 6th Festival Int de la Peinture Cagnes-sur-Mer, Visitors Choice Prize Threadneedle 2010; *Recreations* books, films, hills, friends, exercise, music; *Style*— Fionnuala Boyd; ✉ website www.boydandevans.com

BOYD, Prof Ian Lamont; s of J Morton Boyd (d 1998), and Winifred, *née* Rome (d 2011); *b* 9 February 1957; *Educ* George Heriot's Sch Edinburgh, Univ of Aberdeen (BSc, DSc), Univ of Cambridge (PhD); *m* 4 Sept 1982, Sheila, *née* Aitken; 1 s (Euan b 6 April 1985), 2 da (Helen b 1 Dec 1986, Lauren b 6 April 1989); *Career* res scientist NERC Inst of Terrestrial Ecology 1982–87, memb Br Antarctic Survey 1987–2001, prof of biology Univ of St Andrews 2001–, dir NERC Sea Mammal Res Unit 2001–12, chief exec SMRU Ltd 2006–09, dir Scottish Oceans Inst 2009–12, actg dir Marine Alliance for Sci and Technol for Scotland (MASTS) 2009–10, memb Scottish Science Advsy Cncl 2010–15, chief scientific advsr Dept for Environment, Food and Rural Affrs 2012–; advsr to Princ Univ of St Andrews 2012–; memb Bd Fera Science Ltd 2015–; memb Cncl: Natural Environment Research Cncl 2013–, Biotechnology and Biological Sciences Research Cncl 2013–; ed-in-chief Jl of Zoology until 2008, memb Bd of Reviewing Eds Science 2011–; memb Cncl of Mgmnt Hebridean Tst 1992–2012; Bruce Medal Royal Soc of Edinburgh 1995, Scientific Medal ZSL 1996, Marshall Award ZSL 2006; hon prof Univ of Birmingham 1997; FRSE 2002, FSB 2011; *Publications* author or ed of 8 books and over 180 scientific pubns; *Recreations* walking, sailing; *Style*— Prof Ian Boyd; ✉ College Gate, University of St Andrews, St Andrews KY16 9AJ (☎ 01334 476161, e-mail ilb@st-andrews.ac.uk)

BOYD, Prof (Thomas) James Morrow; s of Thomas James Boyd (d 1979), and Isobel Cameron, *née* Morrow (d 1998); *b* 21 June 1932, Larne, Co Antrim; *Educ* Larne GS, Queen's Univ Belfast (BSc, PhD); *m* 5 Sept 1959, Marguerite Bridget, da of William Snelson (d 1980), of Drayton Manor, Stafford; 2 da (Rebecca b 1964, Marguerite b 1968); *Career* res fell Univ of Birmingham 1957–59, conslt engr Gen Dynamics Corp San Diego California 1959–60, asst res prof Univ of Maryland 1959–61, Ford fndn fell Princeton Univ 1962, sr res assoc UKAEA Culham Lab 1962–65, sr lectr Univ of St Andrews 1965–68, conslt physicist UKAEA Culham Lab 1966–77, conslt Central Laser Facility Rutherford Appleton Lab 1977–87; Univ of Wales Bangor: prof of applied mathematics and computation 1968–82, prof of theoretical physics 1982–90, dean Faculty of Science 1981–85; prof of physics Univ of Essex 1990–99 (res prof of physics 1999–2009, prof emeritus 2010–); visiting prof of physics Univ of Br Columbia 1975, Fulbright sr fell and visiting prof of physics Dartmouth Coll 1987–88, visiting scientist Theory Div Los Alamos Nat Lab New Mexico 1988 and 1989, visiting research prof Instituto Nacional de Investigaciones Nucleares Mexico 2002–; Ballard-Mathews lectr Univ of Wales Bangor 2011; memb UK-Austrian Mixed Cmmn 1977–87; memb NY Acad of Sciences 1987; CPhys, FInstP 1974 (chm Plasma Physics Gp 1975–77); *Books* Plasma Dynamics (with J J Sanderson, 1969, Chinese edn 1977), Electricity (with C A Coulson, 1979), The Physics of Plasmas (with J J Sanderson, 2002, Chinese edn 2005), George Hartley Bryan, Prophet without Honour (2015); *Recreations* skiing, climbing, travel, choral music; *Style*— Prof James Boyd; ✉ 6 Frog Meadow, Brook Street, Dedham, Colchester CO7 6AD (☎ 01206 323170, mobile 07796 140239); Mullion Cottage, Meirion Lane, Bangor, Gwynedd LL57 2BU (☎ 01248 364108); Centre for Physics, University of Essex, Wivenhoe Park, Colchester, Essex CO4 3SQ (☎ 01206 874439, e-mail tjmb@essex.ac.uk)

BOYD, (David) John; QC (1982); s of David Boyd (d 1964), and Ellen Jane, *née* Gruer (d 1953); *b* 11 February 1935; *Educ* Eastbourne Coll, St George's Sch Newport RI, Gonville & Caius Coll Cambridge (MA); *m* 1960, Raija Sinikka (d 2011), da of Onni Lindholm (d 1952), 1 da (Karin b 1969), 1 s (Roderick b 1972 d 2012); *Career* called to the Bar Gray's Inn 1963 (bencher 1988); sec asst ICI 1957–62, legal asst Pfizer 1962–66, legal offr Henry Wiggin and Co 1966–68; joined Inco Europe Ltd 1968, sec and chief legal offr Inco Europe Ltd 1972–86 (dir 1984–86); in private practice at Bar 1986; Digital Equipment Co: dir of legal servs 1986–93, dir of public affrs and communications 1993–95; dir Digital Equipment Scotland Ltd 1987–95, chm AXXIA Systems Ltd 1995–2008; immigration adjudicator 1995–2005, immigration judge 2005–08; commercial arbitrator 2000–; chm Competition Panel CBI 1988–93, dir Impala Platinum 1972–78, gen cmmr of Income Tax 1978–81, memb Senate of Inns of Court and Bar 1978–81, chm Bar Assoc for Commerce Finance and Industry 1980–81, sec-gen Assoc des Juristes d'Enterprise Européens 1983–84, legal advsr Review Bd for Govt Contracts 1984–91, memb Monopolies and Mergers Cmmn Electricity Panel 1991–98, dir Centre for Euro Dispute Resolution 1991–94; vice-pres Cncl of Immigration Judges 1998–99; memb: Cncl Centre for Commercial Law Studies Queen Mary & Westfield Coll London 1989–93, Exec Ctee Royal Acad of Dance 1991–99; chm Contemporary Dance Tst and The Place theatre London 1995–98, dir Oxford Orchestra da Camera 1996–2001; treas Upton Bishop PCC 2004–; accredited mediator 2006; FCIArb; *Recreations* viticulture, France; *Style*— John Boyd, Esq, QC; ✉ Beeches, Upton Bishop, Ross-on-Wye, Herefordshire HR9 7UD (☎ 01989 780214)

BOYD, Sir John Dixon Iklé; KCMG (1992, CMG 1985); s of Prof James Dixon Boyd (d 1968), of Cambridge, and Amélie, *née* Lowenthal (d 1998); *b* 17 January 1936; *Educ* Westminster, Clare Coll Cambridge (BA), Yale Univ (MA); *m* 1, 28 Jan 1968 (m dis 1977), Gunilla Kristina Ingegerd, da of Gösta Rönngren, of Västerås, Sweden; 1 s (Jonathan b 1969), 1 da (Emily b 1971); m 2, 11 Nov 1977, Julia Daphne, da of Capt Antony Edward Montague Raynsford, DL, RN (d 1993), of Milton Malsor Manor, Northampton; 3 da (Jessica b 1978, Alice b 1979, Olivia b 1981); *Career* HM Dip Serv: Hong Kong 1962–64, Peking 1965–67, FCO 1967–69, Washington 1969–73, Peking 1973–75, HM Treasy (on loan) 1976, Bonn 1977–81, UK Mission to UN 1981–84, political advsr Hong Kong 1985–87, dep under-sec of state FCO 1987–89, chief clerk 1989–92, ambass to Japan 1992–96; master Churchill Coll Cambridge 1996–2006 (fell 2006–), advsr East Asia Inst Univ of Cambridge 1998–2006; hon fell Inst of Linguistics 1998–, memb UK-Japan 21st Century Gp 2006–, emeritus fell Br Assoc for Japanese Studies 2007–; non-exec dir BNFL 1997–2000, memb ASEM Vision Group 1998–2000; vice-chm Menuhin Prize 1996–, chm David Davies Memorial Inst 1997–2000, co-chm Nuffield Languages Inquiry 1998–2000, memb ANA Advsy Panel 2003–10; govr RSC 1996–2006; fell 48 Gp 2008; memb Bd Winston Churchill Fndn of the US 1966–; chm of tstees Cambridge Union Soc 1997–2006; tstee: Br Museum 1996–2006 (chm 2002–06, tstee emeritus 2007–), Wordsworth Tst 1997–2013, RAND (Europe) UK 2001–, GB Sasakawa Fndn 2001–, Dr Busby's Tst 2004–, Joseph Needham Research Inst 2005– (chm 2008–); advsr Iran Heritage Fndn 2009–, memb Advsy Ctee LSO 2009–; chm of govrs Bedales Sch 1996–2001, chm Asia House 2010–; hon fell Clare Coll Cambridge 1994; Grand Cordon Order of the Rising Sun (Japan) 2007; *Recreations* music, fly fishing; *Clubs* Hawks' (Cambridge), Hong Kong, Athenaeum, Beefsteak; *Style*—

Sir John Boyd, KCMG; ✉ Churchill College, Cambridge CB3 0DS; Asia House, 63 New Cavendish Street, London W1G 7LP

BOYD, Michael Neil Murray; s of late Lt Cdr Neil Kenneth Boyd, DSC*, and late Felicity Victoria, *née* Weston; *b* 17 August 1946; *Educ* Bryanston; *m* 30 May 1970, Belinda Rachel Elizabeth, da of Capt Basil Harry Lawrence (d 1973); 1 da (Zara b 18 Sept 1975), 1 s (Ashleigh b 21 June 1980); *Career* Ernst & Young (formerly Ernst & Whinney): ptnr London 1975, NY 1979–82, ptnr i/c London Audit Dept 1984–86, memb Exec and Firm's Cncl 1986–89 and 1992–2000, fin ptnr 1987–89, chm Int Extractive Industries Ctee 1988–92, chm Ernst & Young Eastern Europe 1988–90, nat audit ptnr 1989–92, managing ptnr London Office 1992–95, vice-chm (global accounts) Ernst & Young Global 1999–2003, global managing ptnr (quality and risk mgmnt) 2003–05, chm and area managing ptnr Ernst & Young Far East 2005–07, managing ptnr strategic accounts and sectors London 2007–09; UKTI: md strategic relations 2011–12, md investment 2012–; vice-chm Auditing Practices Bd 1991–94; memb: Cncl Corp of Cranleigh Sch and St Catherine's Bramley 1975–99, Oil Industry Accounting Ctee 1988–94, Cncl E Euro Trade Cncl 1989–92; govr Cranleigh Sch 1975–79 and 1985–99; MInstPet 1983, FCA 1975 (memb 1969); *Recreations* tennis, skiing, sailing, opera; *Clubs* City of London, Salcombe Yacht, China, Hong Kong, Hong Kong Jockey, Leander; *Style*— Michael Boyd, Esq; ✉ e-mail mboyd@btinternet.com

BOYD, Prof Sir Robert David Hugh; kt (2004); s of Prof James Dixon Boyd (d 1968), of Cambridge, and Dr Amélie Boyd (d 1998); *b* 14 May 1938; *Educ* Univ of Cambridge, UCH London; *m* 1 April 1966, Meriel Cornelia, da of T G Talbot, CB, QC, of Edenbridge, Kent; 1 s (Thomas b 1967), 2 da (Diana b 1969, Lucy b 1974); *Career* med posts: UCH, Brompton Hosp, Gt Ormond St Hosp; res fell and sr lectr UCH 1967–80; Faculty of Med Univ of Manchester: prof of child health and paediatrics 1981–96, dean 1989–93; princ St George's Hosp Med Sch London 1996–2003; pro-vice chllr Univ of London 2000–03; chair: Manchester HA 1994–96, Nat Centre for Research and Development in Primary Care 1994–96, Cncl of Heads of UK Med Schs 2001–03, Lloyds TSB Fndn England and Wales 2003–09, Cncl for At Risk Academics 2004–10; non-exec chair NuovoPROBE 2007–15; pt/t dir Gtr Manchester Research Alliance 2004–08; govr Univ of Manchester 2004–09; Hon DSc: Kingston Univ, Keele Univ; FRCP, FRCPCH, FMedSci, FFPH; *Publications* Placental Transfer-Methods and Interpretations (co-ed, 1981), Perinatal Medicine (co-ed, 1983), Paediatric Problems in General Practice (jtly, 1989, 3 edn 1997), Placenta (ed, 1989–95); pubns on healthcare systems, child health, gen practice, and foetal and placental physiology; *Recreations* flute playing; *Style*— Prof Sir Robert Boyd; ✉ Stone House, Adlington, Cheshire SK10 4NU (☎ 01625 872400, e-mail r.boyd@manchester.ac.uk)

BOYD, Stewart Craufurd; CBE (2005), QC (1981); s of late Leslie Balfour Boyd, CBE, and Wendy, *née* Blake; *b* 25 October 1943; *Educ* Winchester, Trinity Coll Cambridge (MA); *m* 1970, Catherine (Hon Mrs Boyd), da of late Baron Jay, PC (Life Peer); 1 s (Matthew b 1975), 3 da (Rachel b 1972, Emily b 1973, Hannah b 1987); *Career* called to the Bar Middle Temple 1967 (bencher 1990); non-exec dep chm and dir FSA 1999–2005; *Books* Scrutton on Charterparties and Bills of Lading (ed), Commercial Arbitration (jtly with The Rt Hon Lord Mustill); *Recreations* sailing, gardening, music; *Style*— Stewart Boyd, Esq, CBE, QC; ✉ 1 Gayton Crescent, London NW3 1TT (☎ 020 7431 1581); Wraxall Manor, Higher Wraxall, Dorchester, Dorset DT2 0HP (☎ 01935 83283); Essex Court Chambers, 24 Lincoln's Inn Fields, London WC2A 3ED (☎ 020 7813 8000, fax 020 7813 8080)

BOYD, William Andrew Murray; CBE (2005); s of Alexander Murray Boyd (d 1979), and Evelyn, *née* Smith; *b* 7 March 1952; *Educ* Gordonstoun, Univ of Nice (Dip), Univ of Glasgow (MA), Jesus Coll Oxford; *m* Susan Anne, da of David Leslie Wilson (d 2003), of Maxwell Park, Glasgow; *Career* lectr in English literature St Hilda's Coll Oxford 1980–83, TV critic New Statesman 1981–83; author; Hon DLitt: Univ of St Andrews 1997, Univ of Stirling 1997, Univ of Glasgow 2000, Univ of Dundee 2008; hon fell Jesus Coll Oxford 2007; FRSL 1985; Officier de l'Ordre des Arts et des Lettres (France) 2005; *Films* Good and Bad at Games (1983), Dutch Girls (1985), Scoop (adaptation from Evelyn Waugh novel, 1986), Stars and Bars (1988), Aunt Julia and the Scriptwriter (adaptation from Mario Vargas Llosa novel, 1990), Mister Johnson (adaptation from Joyce Cary novel, 1990), Chaplin (1992), A Good Man in Africa (1994), The Trench (dir,1999), Sword of Honour (adaptation from the novels of Evelyn Waugh, 2001), Armadillo (2001), Man to Man (2005), A Waste of Shame (2005), Any Human Heart (2010), Restless (2012); *Novels* A Good Man in Africa (1981, Somerset Maugham Award, Whitbread Prize first novel 1981), On the Yankee Station (1981), An Ice-Cream War (1982, John Llewelyn Rhys Prize 1982), Stars and Bars (1984), School Ties (1985), The New Confessions (1987), Brazzaville Beach (1990, James Tait Black Meml Prize 1991, McVitie's Prize 1991, Scottish Writer of the Year 1991), The Blue Afternoon (1993, Sunday Express Book of the Year 1993, Los Angeles Times Award for Fiction 1995), The Destiny of Nathalie 'X' (1995), Armadillo (1998), Nat Tate: an American Artist (1998), Any Human Heart (2002, Prix Jean Monnet 2003), Fascination (2004), Bamboo (2005), Restless (2006, Costa Novel of the Year), Ordinary Thunderstorms (2009), Waiting for Sunrise (2012), Solo (2013), Sweet Caress (2015); *Recreations* strolling; *Clubs* Chelsea Arts, Two Brydges Place, Groucho, Soho House; *Style*— William Boyd, Esq, CBE, FRSL; ✉ c/o The Agency, 24 Pottery Lane, Holland Park, London W11 4LZ

BOYD OF DUNCANSBY, Baron (Life Peer UK 2006), of Duncansby in Caithness Colin David Boyd; PC (2000), QC (Scot 1995), WS (2008); s of Dr David Hugh Aird Boyd, of Edinburgh, and Betty Meldrum, *née* Mutch; *b* 7 June 1953; *Educ* Wick HS Caithness, George Watson's Coll Edinburgh, Univ of Manchester (BA), Univ of Edinburgh (LLB); *m* 1979, Fiona Margaret, da of Archibald MacLeod; 1 da, 2 s; *Career* slr 1978–82 and 2007–, admitted Faculty of Advocates 1983, advocate depute 1993–95, slr-gen for Scotland 1997–2000, Lord Advocate of Scotland 2000–06, conslt and head of public law Dundas & Wilson LLP 2007–12; memb Cmmn on Scottish Devolution 2008; legal assoc RTPI 1991; senator Coll of Justice Scotland 2012–; hon prof of law Univ of Glasgow 2008–13; memb House of Lords Select Ctee on Delegated Powers and Regulatory Reform 2007–10, memb House of Lords European Ctee Sub-Ctee E (Justice and Instns) 2010–12; FRSA 2000, memb Law Soc of Scotland 2007; *Books* The Legal Aspects of Devolution (contrib, 1997); *Recreations* reading, hill walking, watching rugby; *Style*— The Rt Hon the Lord Boyd of Duncansby, PC; ✉ Court of Session, Parliament House, Parliament Square, Edinburgh EH1 1RF (☎ 0131 225 2595)

BOYD-CARPENTER, Sir (Marsom) Henry; KCVO (2002, CVO 1994); s of Francis Henry Boyd-Carpenter (d 1984), of East Lambrook Manor, Somerset, and Nina, *née* Townshend (d 1982); *b* 11 October 1939; *Educ* Charterhouse, Balliol Coll Oxford (MA); *m* 18 Sept 1971, Lesley Ann, da of William Henry Davies (d 1986), of Billericay, Essex; 1 s (William Henry Francis b 28 July 1975), 1 da (Alexandra Mary b 28 June 1979); *Career* admitted slr 1966; ptnr Farrer & Co 1968–2002 (sr ptnr 2000–02), slr Duchy of Cornwall 1976–94, private slr to The Prince of Wales 1994–96, private slr to HM The Queen, HM Queen Elizabeth The Queen Mother, The Duke of York and The Earl of Wessex 1995–2002; govr St Mary's Sch Gerrards Cross 1967–70, hon auditor Law Soc 1979–81, hon steward Westminster Abbey 1980–, memb Governing Body Charterhouse Sch 1981–2004 (chm 2000–04), memb Cncl Chelsea Physic Garden 1983–2002, memb Bd of Govrs Sutton's Hosp 1994–2004, hon legal advsr Canterbury Cathedral Tst 1994–2001, memb Cncl Prince of Wales Inst of Architecture 1995–99, memb Bd Br Library 1999–2007 (dep chm 2003–2007), memb Cncl Inst of Cancer Research 2001–06; tstee and dep chm Duchy of Cornwall Staff Pension Fund 1994–; tstee: Nat Gardens Scheme 1998–2003, The Merlin Tst 1998–2004, UK Flagship Project 2012–13; memb RHS Governance Working Pty 2000–01; pres Wood Green: The Animals Charity 2001–, tstee Br Library Tst 2012–16; memb Law Soc 1966; Ritterkreuz des Herzoglich Sachsen-Coburg und Gotha'schen Hausordens 2010; *Recreations* reading, listening to music, gardening; *Style*— Sir Henry Boyd-Carpenter, KCVO; ✉ Georgian Wing, Williamscot House, Williamscot, Oxfordshire OX17 1AE (☎ 01295 758992)

BOYES, Roger F; *Career* fin dir Linpac Containers International Ltd until 1986, gp fin dir Fenner plc 1986–90; Leeds Permanent Building Society: fin dir 1990–93, actg chief exec 1993–94, chief exec 1994–95; gp fin dir Halifax plc 1995–2001; Heywood Williams Gp plc: non-exec dir 2002–03, exec chm 2003–04, non-exec chm 2004–; non-exec dir: Expro International Gp plc 2002–, British Vita plc; chm British Vita Pension Trust Ltd; CIMgt; FCMA, MInstD; *Style*— Roger Boyes, Esq

BOYLAN, Brian; *Educ* Glasgow Sch of Art; *Career* Wolff Olins: joined as designer 1970, dep chm until 1997, chm (following MBO) 1997–; former/current clients incl: ICI, National Power, Citibank, Coopers and Lybrand, General Motors, Halifax, NatWest, Vauxhall, Credit Suisse Group, Heathrow Express, Inland Revenue, Allied Irish Bank; int speaker on corp identity; FRSA; *Style*— Brian Boylan, Esq; ✉ Wolff Olins, 10 Regents Wharf, All Saints Street, London N1 9RL (☎ 020 7713 7733, fax 020 7713 0217)

BOYLE, Alan Gordon; QC (1991); s of Dr M M Boyle, and Mrs H I Boyle, *née* Hallworth, of Keswick, Cumbria; *b* 31 March 1949; *Educ* Shrewsbury, St Catherine's Coll Oxford (open exhbn, MA), Inns of Court Sch of Law; *m* 1981, Claudine-Aimée, *née* Minne-Vercruysse; 2 da (Julia b 17 July 1981, Zoe b 26 May 1984); *Career* called to the Bar Lincoln's Inn 1972 (Hardwicke scholar); memb: Chancery Bar Assoc, Assoc of Trusts and Probate Specialists, Insolvency Lawyers' Assoc; *Publications* The Practice and Procedure of the Companies Court (1997); *Recreations* music, hill walking, photography; *Style*— Alan Boyle, Esq, QC; ✉ Serle Court, 6 New Square, Lincoln's Inn, London WC2A 3QS (☎ 020 7242 6105, fax 020 7405 4004, e-mail aboyle@serlecourt.co.uk)

BOYLE, Francis Martin Patrick (Frankie); *b* 16 August 1972, Glasgow; *Educ* Holyrood RC Secdy Sch Glasgow, Univ of Sussex (BA); *Children* 1 s, 1 da; *Career* stand-up comedian; stand-up incl: The Voice of Black America (Edinburgh Fringe Festival) 2006, Morons I Can Heal You (Edinburgh Fringe Festival) 2007, Frankie Boyle Live (nat tour) 2008; Daily Telegraph Open Mic Award 1996; *Television* incl: The Stand Up Show 1995, The Live Floor Show (BBC Scotland) 2002, regular panelist Mock The Week (BBC 2) 2005–09, Live At The Apollo 2007 (BBC 1), When Were We Funniest? (UKTV Gold) 2008, Frankie Boyle's Tramadol Nights (Channel 4) 2010; *Style*— Frankie Boyle, Esq; ✉ c/o Chambers Management, 39–41 Parker Street, London WC2B 5PQ

BOYLE, Gerard Paul; s of Edward Boyle, of Glasgow; *b* 29 June 1971; *Educ* Univ of Strathclyde (BA); *m* 21 Oct 2001, Caroline; *Career* media manager Leo Burnett Advtg 1994–97, strategist Michaelides & Bednash 1997–99; ZenithOptimedia: managing ptnr Zenith Media 1999, md 2003–07, UK chief exec 2007–; *Recreations* golf, cooking, wine appreciation, travel; *Style*— Gerard Boyle, Esq; ✉ ZenithOptimedia, 24 Percy Street, London W1T 2BS (e-mail gerry.boyle@zenithmedia.co.uk)

BOYLE, Prof Nicholas; s of Hugh Boyle (d 1955), and Margaret Mary Faith, *née* Hopkins (latterly Mrs Boothroyd, d 2003); *b* 18 June 1946, London; *Educ* King's Sch Worcester, Magdalene Coll Cambridge (open scholar, MA), Univ of Cambridge (PhD, LittD); *m* 1983, Rosemary Angela, *née* Devlin; 3 da (Mary Rose b 1986, Elisabeth Doran b 1992, Angela Margaret b 1996), 1 s (Michael Hugh b 1989); *Career* Magdalene Coll Cambridge: research fell 1968–72, official fell 1972–2000, coll lectr in German (also Girton Coll) 1972–74, dir of studies in modern languages 1972–90, dean 1979–82, tutor 1984–93, garden steward 1987–2012, professorial fell 2000–13 (emeritus fell 2014–), pres 2006–11; Univ of Cambridge: lectr 1979–93 (asst lectr 1974–79), reader in German literary and intellectual history 1993–2000, prof of German literary and intellectual history 2000–06, memb Faculty Bd Modern and Medieval Languages 1982–90 and 1996–2001 (sec 1982–85), head Dept of German 1996–2001, Schröder prof of German 2006–13; scholar Alexander von Humboldt Fndn Göttingen Univ 1978 and 1980–81, Br Acad research reader in the humanities 1990–92, research fell John Rylands Research Inst Univ of Manchester 1993, fell Wissenschaftskolleg zu Berlin 1994–95, third Erasmus lectr Univ of Notre Dame 2002–03, corresponding fell Göttingen Acad of Sciences 2010; memb Cncl English Goethe Soc 1993–; pres Cambridge Modern Language Soc 1987–90, chm Cambridge Cyrenians 1970–71; Goethe Medal Goethe-Institut 2000, Friedrich Gundolf Prize German Acad of Language and Literature 2009, Gold Medal Goethe Soc of Weimar 2017; Hon DHL Univ of Georgetown 2004; FBA 2001 (memb Cncl 2008–11); *Books* Realism in European Literature: Essays in honour of J P Stern (jt ed, 1986), Goethe: Faust, Part One (1987), Goethe: The Poet and the Age, Vol One The Poetry of Desire (1749–1790) (1991, W Heinemann Prize RSL, J G Robertson Meml Prize Univ of London), Goethes Werke auf CD-ROM (editorial conslt, 1995), Who Are We Now? Christian Humanism and the Global Market from Hegel to Heaney (1998), J W von Goethe: Selected Works (ed, 1999), Goethe: The Poet and the Age, Vol Two Revolution and Renunciation (1790–1803) (2000, Annibel Jenkins Prize American Soc of Eighteenth Century Studies), Goethe and the English-Speaking World (jt ed, 2002), Sacred and Secular Scriptures: A Catholic Approach to Literature (2004), German Literature: A very short introduction (2008), 2014 – How to Survive the Next World Crisis (2010), The Impact of Idealism: The Legacy of Post-Kantian German Thought Vols 1–4 (jt gen ed, 2013); author of numerous articles in learned jls; *Recreations* visiting gardens; *Style*— Prof Nicholas Boyle, FBA; ✉ Magdalene College, Cambridge CB3 0AG (☎ 01223 332100, e-mail nb215@cam.ac.uk)

BOYLE, Patrick; *Career* chief exec and accounting offr Rent Service until 2008, chief exec Independent Living Fund 2008–; *Style*— Patrick Boyle, Esq; ✉ Independent Living Fund, Equinox House, Island Business Quarter, City Link, Nottingham NG2 4LA

BOYLE, Prof Paul; CBE (2016); *Educ* Lancaster Univ (BA, PhD); *Career* lectr: Univ of Wales Swansea, Univ of Leeds, Univ of Canterbury NZ; chair Human Geography and head Sch of Geography and Geosciences Univ of St Andrews, chief exec ESRC until 2014, pres and vice-chllr Univ of Leicester 2014–; pres Science Europe 2011–14, chair Scottish Science Advsy Cncl 2016–; FBA, FRSE; *Style*— Prof Paul Boyle, CBE; ✉ The University of Leicester, University Road, Leicester LE1 7RH

BOYLE, Dr Philip David; s of David Boyle, and Valerie Olive, *née* Woodvine; *b* 7 May 1976, Birkenhead, Wirral; *Educ* UMIST (BSc, PhD); *Career* diplomat: postdoctoral researcher Inorganic Chemistry Lab and tutor Jesus Coll Univ of Oxford 2001–02; desk offr Falkland Islands Overseas Territories Dept FCO 2002–03, Arabic language training 2004–05, second sec political Sana'a Yemen 2005–08, French language training 2008, consul-gen Lille 2008–11, first sec political Islamabad 2011–12, ambass to Repub of Mali and Repub of Niger 2012–14, dep head Intelligence Policy Dept FCO 2014–; MRSC 2001, CChem 2001; nine articles in peer-reviewed chemistry jls; *Style*— Dr Philip Boyle; ✉ c/o Foreign & Commonwealth Office, King Charles Street, London SW1A 2AH

BOYLE, (Hon) Robert William; s of 14 Earl of Cork and Orrery (d 2003), and Mary, *née* Gordon Finlayson; bro of 15 Earl of Cork and Orrery, *qv*; *b* 5 March 1948, Perth; *Educ* Harrow, ChCh Oxford (MA); *m* 9 May 1987, Fiona Mary, *née* St Aubyn; 1 s (Richard Piers b 8 Aug 1988); *Career* articled clerk rising to chm European entertainment and media industry practice PricewaterhouseCoopers LLP (formerly Coopers & Lybrand) 1969–2006 (ptnr 1982–2006); dir: Maxis Berhad 2006–16, Witan Investment Tst plc 2007–, Prosperity Voskhod Fund Ltd 2008–15, Schroder AsiaPacific Fund plc 2009–14,

Centaur Media plc 2009–; ind memb Audit Ctee Nat Tst 2006–12, ind memb Audit Ctee English Heritage 2015–; dir Hants NHS Fndn Tst 2008–12, dir Hants Cultural Tst 2015–; FCA (memb ICA 1972); *Recreations* sailing, skiing, tennis, reading, theatre, opera, travel; *Clubs* Brooks's, Sea View Yacht; *Style—* Robert Boyle, Esq; ✉ St Andrews House, Kilmeston, Alresford, Hampshire S024 0NL (☎ 01962 771941, e-mail rb@rboyle.eu)

BOYLE, Prof Sir Roger Michael; kt (2011), CBE (2004); Dr Michael Boyle (d 2001), and Hazel, *née* Hallworth; *b* 27 January 1948; *Educ* Shrewsbury, London Hosp Med Coll (MB BS); *m* Margo, da of F Gardner Cox, of Philadelphia, USA; 3 s (Peter b 1 Nov 1977, Thomas b 2 April 1979, Edward b 20 Oct 1981), 1 da (Amy b 13 October 2002); *Career* The London Hosp: house physician Cardiac and Haematology Depts 1972–73, house surgn Dept of Surgery 1973, SHO Dept of Med 1973–75, SHO in cardiology 1975; Chelmsford and Essex Hosp: registrar in gen med and neurology 1975–77, research registrar 1977–78; research registrar (Br Heart Fndn) Regional Cardiac Centre Wythenshawe Hosp Manchester 1978–80, lectr in cardiology Dept of Cardiovascular Studies Univ of Leeds and hon sr registrar in cardiology Leeds Gen Infirmary, Univ Hosp of St James and Killingbeck Hosp Leeds 1980–83, conslt cardiologist York District Hosp; York Health Servs NHS Tst: chm Med Servs Div of Med York Dist Hosp 1988–96, pt/t gen mangr Med Servs York Health Servs Tsts 1996–98, memb Exec Bd 1996–99, memb Med Advsy Gp 1991–98, memb Computer Systems Programme Bd 1994–98, memb Tst Strategy Gp 1995–99, currently conslt cardiologist and physician; nat dir for heart disease and stroke Dept of Health 2000–11; hon conslt cardiologist St Mary's Hosp NHS Tst London 2003–, hon chair UCL 2006–; conslt med advsr General Accident Life Assurance 1985–96, chief med offr Leeds Life 1994–96; advsr: W Cumbria HA 1992–93, W Surrey HA 1996, S Essex HA 1997, Havering Hosps Tst 1999; memb Med Advsy Ctee Purey Cust Nuffield Hosp York 1995–2000; memb Advsy Panel: Pfizer UK 1994–2000, BUPA 1995, Schering Plough 1996–97, Roche Products Ltd 1997–98; visiting prof Dept of Cardiology Cornell Med Center NY 1987; external examiner Univ of Newcastle upon Tyne 1996; Dept of Health: advsr Nat Casemix Office 1993–96, chm Nat Coronary Heart Disease Task Force 2000–, memb Expert Design Panel Primary Care Collaborative 2000–, memb NHS Top Team, memb Cross Taskforce Prevention Gp, memb Clinical Priorities Gp, memb Cardiovascular Research Funders Gp, memb Coronary Heart Disease Collaborative Core Gp, memb Coronary Heart Disease Beacons Selection Panel; memb Editorial Bd and regular reviewer of papers Br Heart Jl (now Heart) 1991–, reviewer European Heart Jl 1994–; RCP: co-opted memb Specialty Advsy Ctee in Cardiology Calman Report 1993, memb Jt Cardiology Ctee RCP/Br Cardiac Soc 1993–, sec Specialty Advsy Ctee 1994–97 (chm 1997–2000), memb Jt Ctee on Higher Med Trg 1994–2000; Br Cardiac Soc: memb 1984–, memb Cncl 1991–96 (ex officio memb 1998–), memb Sub-Ctee on Radiation Hazards Protection for Cardiologists 1992, sec Sub-Ctee on Cardiology in Dist Gen Hosps 1992–94, memb Advsy Ctee to Tomlinson Report 1993, memb Abstract Selection Panel AGM 1994–2000, memb Trg and Manpower Ctee 1995– (chm 1997–98), rep to Specialty Workforce Advsy Gp NHSE 1995–; advsr on trg issues Irish Cardiology Bd 1998–2000; author of numerous presentations to learned socs and of articles in jls incl Br Heart Jl, BMJ, Jl of the RCP, European Heart Jl and Int Jl of Cardiology; memb: Yorks Thoracic Soc 1982–, York Med Soc 1983– (sec 1983–90), Med Research Soc, RSM; FRCP 1991 (MRCP 1976), FESC 1994, FRCPEd 2002; *Recreations* piano, walking, sailing; *Clubs* Corinthian Yacht (Philadelphia), Percuil Sailing (Portscatho), Mantoloking Yacht (New Jersey), St Mawes Sailing; *Style—* Prof Sir Roger Boyle, CBE; ✉ Lanhoose Barn, Portscatho, Truro, Cornwall TR2 5EP (e-mail roger.boyle5@btinternet.com)

BOYLSTON, Prof Arthur William; s of George Arthur Boylston, and Marie, *née* Showers; *b* 16 November 1942; *Educ* Phillips Exeter Acad, Yale Univ (BA), Harvard Univ (MD); *m* 1 July 1978, Anthea, da of John Murray Phelps; 2 s (Thomas Arthur b 1980, Nicholas John b 1984); *Career* sr asst surgn US Public Health Serv 1970–72, lectr, sr lectr then reader St Mary's Hosp Med Sch London 1972–88, prof of pathology Univ of Leeds 1988–; FRCPath 1988; *Recreations* gardening, walking; *Clubs* Athenaeum; *Style—* Prof Arthur Boylston; ✉ Molecular Medicine Unit, Clinical Sciences Building, St James's Hospital, Leeds LS9 7TH (☎ 0113 206 5681, fax 0113 244 4475)

BOYNE, 11 Viscount (I 1717); Gustavus Michael Stucley (Tavie) Hamilton-Russell; DL (Salop); also Baron Hamilton of Stackallen (I 1715) and Baron Brancepeth (UK 1866); sits as Baron Brancepeth; s of 10 Viscount Boyne, KCVO, JP (d 1995), and Rosemary Anne, *née* Stucley; *b* 27 May 1965; *Educ* Harrow, RAC Cirencester (Dip Rural Estate Mgmnt); *m* 1, 1 June 1991, Lucy, *née* Potter; 1 da (Hon Emelia Rose b 25 Jan 1994), 3 s (Frederick Gustavus George b 23 March 1997, Hon (Gustavus) Archie Edward b 30 June 1999, Hon Jack Gustavus Michael b 30 June 1999); m 2, 20 April 2013, Julia, da of Sir John Howard-Lawson, Bt; *Heir* s, Hon Archie Hamilton-Russell; *Career* conslt Carter Jonas Chartered Surveyors; dir Ludlow Race Club; MRICS; *Recreations* cricket, skiing, travel; *Clubs* Turf; *Style—* The Rt Hon the Viscount Boyne; ✉ Burwarton House, Bridgnorth, Shropshire WV16 6QH (☎ 01746 787221)

BRABAZON OF TARA, 3 Baron (UK 1942); Rt Hon Ivon Anthony Moore-Brabazon; PC (2013), DL (IOW 1993); s of 2 Baron Brabazon of Tara, CBE (d 1974, whose f, 1 Baron, was Min of Aircraft Production after Beaverbrook; the Bristol-Brabazon airliner was named after him); *b* 20 December 1946; *Educ* Harrow; *m* 8 Sept 1979, Harriet, da of Mervyn de Courcy Hamilton, of Harare, Zimbabwe, by his w, Lovell Ann, da of Rowland Cullinan, of Olifantsfontein, Transvaal; 1 s (Hon Benjamin Ralph b 1983), 1 da (Hon Anabel Mary b 1985); *Heir* s, Hon Benjamin Moore-Brabazon; *Career* memb London Stock Exchange 1972–84; a Lord in Waiting (government whip) 1984–86; spokesman for Dept of Transport 1984–85, and for Treasy, Dept of Trade and Industry, Energy 1985–86; Parly under-sec of state for Transport and min for Aviation and Shipping 1986–89, min of state Foreign and Commonwealth Office 1989–90, min of state Dept of Tport 1990–92, oppn spokesman environment, tport and the regions 1998–2001, chm of ctees House of Lords 2003–12 (princ dep chm 2001–03); pres UK Warehousing Assoc 1992–, dep chm Fndn for Sport and the Arts 1992–2015, memb RAC Public Policy Ctee 1992–99, memb Cncl Shipwrecked Mariners Soc 1993–, tstee Medical Cmmn on Accident Prevention 1994–99; pres: Br Int Freight Assoc 1997–99, Inst of the Motor Indust 1998–2004 (dep pres 1997–98); *Recreations* sailing, Cresta Run, golf; *Clubs* Royal Yacht Sqdn; *Style—* The Rt Hon the Lord Brabazon, DL; ✉ House of Lords, London SW1A 0PW (e-mail brabazoni@parliament.uk)

BRABBINS, Martyn Charles; s of Herbert Henry Brabbins (d 1985), and Enid Caroline, *née* Pope (d 1985); *b* 13 August 1959; *Educ* Sponne Sch Towcester, Goldsmiths Coll London, Leningrad State Conservatoire; *m* 31 August 1985, Karen Maria, da of John Christopher Evans; 2 s (Alexander John b 17 June 1989, Leo John b 30 June 1992), 1 da (Nina Pamela b 13 Sept 1994); *Career* conductor; winner Leeds Conductors Competition 1988; professional debut Scottish Chamber Orch 1988; assoc princ conductor BBC Scottish Symphony Orch 1992–, princ conductor Sinfonia 21 1994–, princ conductor Huddersfield Choral Soc; artistic dir Cheltenham Int Festival of Music 2005–; conductor: RPO, LPO, Philharmonia Orch, BBC Symphony Orch, Royal Liverpool Philharmonic Orch, BBC Nat Orch of Wales, Ulster Orch, North German Radio Orch, St Petersburg Philharmonic, Australian Youth Orch, English Chamber Orch, Northern Sinfonia, ENO, Opera North, Scottish Opera, English Touring Opera, Kirov Opera, Nash Ensemble, Bavarian Radio Symphony Orch, Lahti Symphony; princ guest conductor Royal Flemish Philharmonic Orchestre 2009–; *Recordings* Henselt Piano Concerto, Hindemith Viola Concertos, Britten War Requiem, Parry Piano Concerto, Stanford Piano Concerto, orchestral works by Mackenzie, Wallace and Maccunn, Korngold Die Katrin (winner of the Opera Section Cannes Music Awards, Birtwistle, Woolrich, Crosse, Keal, Finissy, Bedford, Bainbridge); *Publications* Cambridge University Press Handbook of Conducting (contrib, 2003); *Recreations* cooking, running, travelling, reading, being with my family; *Style—* Martyn Brabbins, Esq; ✉ c/o Susie Mcleod, Intermusica, Crystal Wharf, 33 Graham Street, London N1 8GJ

BRACEWELL-SMITH, Sir Charles; 4 Bt (UK 1947), of Keighley, Co York; s of Sir George Bracewell Smith, 2 Bt, MBE (d 1976); suc bro, Sir Guy Bracewell Smith, 3 Bt 1983; *b* 13 October 1955; *Educ* Harrow; *m* 1; m 2, 25 July 1996, Nina, *qv*, da of K C Kakkar, of New Delhi, India; *Heir* none; *Career* former dir Park Lane Hotel; fndr The Homestead Charitable Tst, composer The Death of Shubert and The Maiden Quartet; *Books* as Francis O'Donovan: The Song of Saints, The Eternal Triangle, The Thought Police, Bottom and Other Stories, Philosophy is Minimalism; *Recreations* comparative religion, mystical theology, philosophy, psychology, Arsenal FC, music, reading poetry; *Clubs* RAC; *Style—* Sir Charles Bracewell-Smith, Bt

BRACEWELL-SMITH, Lady; Nina Bracewell-Smith; da of K C Kakkar, and Swadesh, *née* Kumar; *b* 14 November 1965, Bonn, Germany; *Educ* DAV Inst of Mgmnt New Delhi (BBA); *m* 25 July 1996, Sir Charles Bracewell-Smith, Bt, *qv*; *Career* dir: Tymals Investment Co 1994–2001, Sheraton Park Lane 1996–97, Arsenal FC 2005–; tstee Homestead Charitable Tst; *Recreations* bridge, tennis, travelling; *Clubs* RAC; *Style—* Lady Bracewell-Smith

BRACKENBURY, (Frederick Edwin) John Gedge; CBE (2000); s of Claude Russell Brackenbury (d 1978), and Florence Edna, *née* Gedge (d 1976); *b* 9 February 1936; *Educ* Mercers Sch London; *m* 1, 1958 (m dis 1977), Pauline Hinchliffe; 2 da (Amanda (Mrs Fry) b 22 March 1961, Sara Ann (Mrs Rao) b 21 Feb 1963), 1 s (Jonathon b 30 Aug 1964); m 2, 4 Nov 1979, Desiree Sally, *née* Taylor; 1 s (James b 8 June 1979); *Career* Justerini & Brooks Ltd 1954–62 (local dir 1957, Bd dir 1958), md City Cellars 1962–65, chm Morgan Furze 1965–67, IDV Ltd 1967–72 (md Leisure Finance 1968, chief exec Marriott Watney Int 1971, gp md Leisure Int Ltd), fndr own consultancy firm 1972–75, exec dir G & W Walker 1975–83 (gp operational dir Brent Walker 1976–83), md All Weather Sports Activities Ltd 1983–88, exec dir Brent Walker Gp plc 1988–96; chm: Pubmaster Ltd 1996–2002 (exec chm 1988–96, conslt 1996), Brackenbury Leisure Ltd 1996–, Active Media Capital Gp Ltd 2000–07, Avanti Screenmedia Gp 2003–07, Avanti Communications Gp plc 2007–14 (dep chm 2014–, also fndr chm); non-exec dir: Happy Eater Ltd 1972–75, Aspen Gp plc 1997–99, Western Wines Ltd 1997–2002, Hotel & Catering Trg Co 1998–2002, SFI Gp plc 1998–2005, Holsten (UK) Ltd 2000–04, Isle of Capri Casinos Inc 2004–10; dir: Isle of Capri Casinos Ltd 2004–09, Blue Chip Casinos plc 2006–09; life pres Business in Sport & Leisure 2005–13 (chm 1985–2005, also fndr memb), chm People 1st (previously Hospitality Trg Fndn) 1997–2005, dir Brewing Research Fndn 2002–04, tstee and vice-pres GamCare 2009–; dir and tstee: Springboard Educnl Tst 1999–, Bradfield Coll Fndn; memb Worshipful Co of Distillers; *Recreations* golf, tennis, study of wine and olives, shooting; *Clubs* Carlton, Hurlingham; *Style—* John Brackenbury, Esq, CBE; ✉ c/o Amanda Fry, 46 Fieldsend Road, Cheam, Surrey SM3 8NR (☎ 07973 658295, fax 020 8644 5505, e-mail johnbrackenbury@btconnect.com)

BRACKLEY, Rt Rev Ian James; s of Frederick Arthur James Brackley (d 1987), of Westcliff-on-Sea, Essex, and Ivy Sarah Catherine, *née* Bush (d 1980); *b* 13 December 1947; *Educ* Keble Coll Oxford (MA), Cuddesdon Theol Coll; *m* 12 June 1971, Penelope (Penny) Ann, da of Arthur William Saunders; 2 s (Christopher James b 7 April 1973, Alexander Jonathan b 1 Aug 1975); *Career* ordained deacon 1971, priest 1972; asst curate St Mary Magdalene with St Francis Lockleaze Bristol 1971–74; Bryanston Sch: asst chaplain 1974–76, chaplain 1976–80, master i/c cricket 1975–80; vicar St Mary's E Preston with Kingston 1980–88, rural dean Arundel and Bognor 1982–87; team rector St Wilfrid's Haywards Heath 1988–96, rural dean Cuckfield 1989–95; bishop of Dorking 1996–2015; commissary bishop: Guildford 2003–04, Portsmouth 2009–10, Guildford 2013–14; proctor in convocation and memb Gen Synod 1990–95, memb House of Bishops 2001–10; *Recreations* cricket, golf, pipe organs, theatre, reading; *Style—* The Rt Rev Ian Brackley; ✉ 1 Bepton Down, Petersfield, Hants GU31 4PR (☎ 01730 266465, e-mail ijbrackley@gmail.com)

BRADBEER, Harry James; s of Thomas Linthorn Bradbeer, of Devon, and Vivyen Elise, *née* Atterbury; *b* 21 September 1966; *Educ* Marlborough, UCL (BA), Univ of Michigan; *m* 1998, Hon Nino Natalia O'Hagan Strachey, da of 4 Baron O'Hagan , *qv*, and Princess Tamara Imeretinsky; 1 s (Caspian Thomas Charles b 20 July 2001); *Career* TV and film dir; script reader to John Schlesinger 1991–93; TV Serials/Single Drama BAFTA judge 2008–09; *Television* credits incl: The Bill 1996, This Life 1997, The Cops 1998–99 (Best Drama Series BAFTA Awards 1998–99, Best Drama Series RTS Awards 1999), Attachments 2000, A is for Acid 2002, The Brides in the Bath 2003, Outlaws 2004 (nominee Best Drama Serial BAFTA Awards 2004), No Angels 2004–05, Sugar Rush 2005–06 (Int Emmy 2006, nominee Best Drama Series BAFTA Awards 2006), Perfect Day 2006 (nominee Best Comedy Prog Rose d'Or Montreux Festival 2007), Messiah 2007, Lip Service 2009, The Hour 2010 (nominee Best Mini-Series Golden Globe 2011, nominee Best Serial Broadcast Award 2011, Reflet d'Or Cinema tous Ecrans 2011), Prisoners' Wives 2011–12 (winner RTS North Best Drama Series 2012), Grantchester 2014, No Offence 2015 (Best Drama Series RTS 2016, nominee Best Drama Series BAFTA 2016), Dickensian 2015, Fleabag 2016; *Films* A Night with a Woman. A Day with Charlie 1994, As The Beast Sleeps 2001 (Best Single Drama Belfast Arts Awards 2002, nominee Best Single Drama IFTA Awards 2002); *Theatre* dir and acting coach The Collective; *Recreations* skiing, sailing, cooking; *Clubs* Soho House, BAFTA; *Style—* Harry Bradbeer, Esq; ✉ c/o St John Donald, United Agents, 12–26 Lexington Street, London W1F 0LE (☎ 020 3214 0800, fax 020 3214 0801, website www.unitedagents.co.uk)

BRADBOURN, Philip Charles; OBE (1994), MEP; s of Horace Bradbourn (d 1978), and Elizabeth, *née* Cox (d 1992); *b* 9 August 1951, Tipton, Staffordshire; *Educ* Tipton GS, Wulfrun Coll, Worcester Coll (Dip); *Career* local govt offr 1967–87, political advsr Wolverhampton City Cncl 1987–99, MEP (Cons) W Midlands 1999–, Cons chief whip European Parl 2003–07 and 2009–, Cons spokesman on justice and home affairs 2007–09; nat chm Cons Political Centre 1990–93, regnl chm W Midlands Cons Pty 1997–99, 1 vice chm Civil Liberties, Justice and Home Affairs Ctee 2007–09, chm Inter-parliamentary Delegation for Relations with Canada 2009–; *Recreations* gardening; *Style—* Philip Bradbourn, Esq, OBE, MEP; ✉ 1st Floor, Temple House, Greenhough Road, Lichfield, Staffordshire WS8 7AU(☎ 01543 251975); European Parliament, ASP 3F370, Rue Wiertz, 1047 Brussels, Belgium (☎ 00 322 283 1636, fax 00 322 284 7407, e-mail philip.bradbourn@europarl.europa.eu)

BRADBURY, Michael Raymond; s of Arnold Needham Bradbury, of Wetherby, W Yorks, and Rita Ann, *née* Fenwick; *b* 26 April 1952; *Educ* Leeds GS, Liverpool Univ Sch of Architecture (BA, BArch); *m* 1, (m dis); 1 s (Augustus William b 16 Oct 1978), 2 da (Sally Elizabeth Rose b 21 April 1983, Laura Jane b 26 Feb 1986); m 2, July 2005, Janet White; *Career* Poynton Bradbury Wynter Cole (formerly Poynton Bradbury Wynter): joined Robert A Poynton, RIBA as architectural asst 1976, qualified 1977, assoc 1979, equal ptnr 1983–2012, fndr Mike Bradbury Design Architects (with Janet White) 2012; chm Poynton Bradbury Wynter Cole Ltd (new co) 2008–12; RIBA: chm Cornwall Branch 1989–91 (sec 1995–98), chm South Western Region 1993–95 (vice-chm 1991–93), elected to Nat Cncl 1999–2002; memb Exec Ctee Cornwall Branch CPRE 1991–; chm of tstees Island Centre St Ives 2000–12; winner various CPRE and RIBA awards; ARCUK 1977, RIBA 1977, MFB 1995; *Recreations* sailing, cycling, walking; *Clubs* Mounts Bay Sailing;

Style— Michael R Bradbury, Esq; ✉ Bellair, School Lane, Truro TR1 2HT (☎ 01872 272713, e-mail mikebdesign@btinternet.com)

BRADES; *see:* Ferleger Brades

BRADFORD, Barbara Taylor; OBE (2007); *née* Taylor; da of Winston Taylor (d 1981), and Freda Walker Taylor (d 1981); *b* Leeds, Yorks; *Educ* Northcote Sch for Girls; *m* 24 Dec 1963, Robert Bradford; *Career* author and journalist; women's ed Yorkshire Evening Post 1951–53 (reporter 1949–51), fashion ed Woman's Own 1953–54, columnist London Evening News 1955–57, exec ed The London American 1959–62, ed National Design Center Magazine USA 1965–69; nationally syndicated columnist: Newsday (New York) 1968–70, Chicago Tribune/New York Daily News Syndicate 1970–75, Los Angeles Times Syndicate (New York) 1975–81; memb: Cncl The Authors' Guild Inc USA 1989, PEN USA; Northwood Univ Distinguished Women's Award, inductee literary legend Writers Hall of Fame of America 2003; Hon DLitt Univ of Leeds 1992, Hon DLitt Univ of Bradford 1995, Hon DLit Sienna Coll NY 2006, Hon DLitt Mount Saint Mary Coll 2009; *Novels* A Woman of Substance (1980, Matrix Award for books from New York Women in Communications 1985, Prix Litteraire Deauville Film Festival 1994, screen adaptation (miniseries) 1984), Voice of the Heart (1983, screen adaptation (CBS) 1990), Hold the Dream (1985, screen adaptation (miniseries) 1986), Act of Will (1986, screen adaptation 1989), To Be The Best (1988, screen adaptation (miniseries) 1992), The Women in his Life (1990), Remember (1991, screen adaptation (NBC) 1993), Angel (1993), Everything to Gain (1994, screen adaptation (CBS) 1996), Dangerous to Know (1995), Love In Another Town (1995, screen adaptation (CBS) 1997), Her Own Rules (1996, screen adaptation (CBS) 1998), Power of a Woman (1997), A Secret Affair (1998, screen adaptation (CBS) 1999), A Sudden Change of Heart (1999), Where You Belong (2000), The Triumph of Katie Byrne (2001), Three Weeks in Paris (2002), Emma's Secret (2003), Unexpected Blessings (2004), Just Rewards (2005), The Ravenscar Dynasty (2006), The Ravenscar Heir (2007), Being Elizabeth (2008), Breaking the Rules (2009), Playing the Game (2010), Letter From A Stranger (2012), Secrets From The Past (2013), Hidden (2013), Cavendon Hall (2014); *Non-fiction* published in USA incl: Complete Encyclopedia of Homemaking Ideas (1968), How To Be The Perfect Wife (1969), How to Solve Your Decorating Problems (1976), Luxury Designs for Apartment Living (1981); *Style—* Mrs Barbara Taylor Bradford, OBE

BRADFORD, Prof Henry Francis; s of Henry Bradford (d 1996), and Rose Bradford (d 2003); *b* 9 March 1938; *Educ* Dartford GS, UCL (MB BS), Univ of Birmingham (BSc), Inst of Psychiatry Univ of London (PhD, DSc); *m* 1, 28 March 1964, Helen (d 1999), da of Benjamin Caplan (d 1985); 1 da (Sonya Helen b 25 Jan 1968), 1 s (Daniel Benjamin Alexander b 24 Aug 1969); m 2, 4 Sept 1999, Mary-Thérèse, da of Harold Nazareth (d 1987), and Isabel Nazareth (d 2002); *Career* MRC research fell in neuroscience Instn of Psychiatry Univ of London 1964–65; Imperial Coll London: lectr in biochemistry 1965–, reader in biochemistry 1975–, prof of neurochemistry 1979–2003 (emeritus prof and sr res fell 2003–), dir of undergraduate studies 1988–; visiting prof Dept of Anatomy Nat Univ of Singapore 2005–; ed: Jl of Neurochemistry 1973–81, The Biochemist 1989–95 (chief ed 1988–95), Jl of Brain Science 1995–; Silver Jubilee lectr Indian Inst of Chemical Biology Calcutta 1982, Sandoz lectr Inst of Neurology London 1976 and 1985, guest lectr Int Soc for Neurochemistry Japan 1985, 1995 and 1997, visiting prof of neurochemistry Univ of California at Irvine 1986, Harold Chaffer Meml lectr Univ of Otago NZ 1987; plenary lectr: Japanese Brain Science and Neurosurgery Congress Okinawa 1997, Annual American Parkinson's Disease Assoc Patients' Symposium Seattle USA 2005, (on epilepsy) St John's Hosp Medical Sch Bangalore India 2007; author of about 490 scientific papers (incl 10 scientific reviews), ed and contrib 3 vols of scientific reviews 1981–88; awarded £10 million in neuroscience/med res grants 1971–2003; chm MRC Epilepsy Res Co-ordinating Ctee 1978–88 (memb Neuroscience Ctee and Bd 1973–82), scientific advsr Brain Res Tst 1985–95, hon archivist UK Biochemical Soc 1988–98 (hon sec 1973–81), memb Wellcome Tst Ctee for the History of Med 1985–, memb Brain Tumour Bd Eisenhower Medical Centre UCLA 2009–; Bronze medal for contrib to neurochemistry Univ of Okayama Japan 1985; memb: UK Biochemical Soc, Int Soc Neurochemistry, Brain Res Assoc, London Natural History Soc; FRCPath 1988 (MRCPath 1976); *Books* Chemical Neurobiology (1985); *Recreations* history of science, natural history, music; *Style—* Prof Henry Bradford; ✉ Division of Cell and Molecular Biology, Department of Life Sciences, Faculty of Natural Sciences, Imperial College, South Kensington, London SW7 2AZ (☎ 020 8464 4615, e-mail h.bradford@imperial.ac.uk)

BRADFORD, Katie; da of Frank Bradford, and Thelma, *née* Jones (d 1999); *b* Coventry; *Educ* Barrs Hill GS Coventry, UCL (LLB, LLM), Coll of Law; *m* 13 Sept 1986, Paul Matthews; *Career* solicitor; Linklaters: ptnr, head of property and fin litigation; arbitrator, accredited mediator, fndr Commercial Mediation Gp; fndr and former chair Property Litigation Assoc, vice-chair Civil Mediation Cncl; memb: Law Soc 1982, Law Soc and RICS panels for third party appts; Property Litigation Assoc Woman of the Year 1999, Blundell lectr 2001; Liveryman City of London Slrs Co; FRSA, FCIArb; *Publications* Butterworths Business Landlord and Tenant Handbook; articles in legal and property press; *Recreations* theatre, opera, choral singing, cricket; *Clubs* MCC, Middlesex CCC, Surrey CCC, RSA; *Style—* Ms Katie Bradford; ✉ Linklaters, One Silk Street, London EC2Y 8HQ (☎ 020 7456 4234, fax 020 7456 2222, e-mail katie.bradford@linklaters.com)

BRADFORD, 7 Earl of (UK 1815); The Rt Hon Richard Thomas Orlando Bridgeman; 12 Bt (E 1660); also Baron Bradford (GB 1794) and Viscount Newport (UK 1815); s of 6 Earl of Bradford, TD (d 1981); *b* 3 October 1947; *Educ* Harrow, Trinity Coll Cambridge (MA); *m* 1, 1979 (m dis), Joanne Elizabeth, da of Benjamin Miller, of London; 3 s (Alexander Michael Orlando, Viscount Newport b 6 Sept 1980, Hon Henry Gerald Orlando b 18 April 1982, Hon Benjamin Thomas Orlando b 7 Feb 1987), 1 da (Lady Alicia Rose b 27 Dec 1990); m 2, 2008, Dr Penelope Law; *Heir* s, Viscount Newport; *Career* proprietor Porters English Restaurant Covent Garden 1979–, proprieter Covent Garden Grill 2003–; chm Weston Park Enterprises Ltd 1986–99 (tstee The Weston Park Fndn 1988–99); IOD: memb Midlands Ctee 1989–97, memb Cncl 1997–99; Tidy Britain Gp (now EnCams): chm W Midlands Advsy Ctee 1990–2001, chm Policy and Advsy Ctee 1998–2000 (memb 1994–98), vice-chm 1998–2002, memb Cncl 2002–05; chm: Wrekin Heritage Assoc 1987–2000, Westminster Considerate Restaurateurs Assoc 1992–98; chm Restaurant Assoc 2010– (memb Ctee 1977–82 and 1992–); pres: Wrekin Tourism Assoc (now Telford and Shropshire Marketing Partnership) 1980–2006, Newport Branch RNLI 1981–98, Wolverhampton Friends of the Samaritans 1982–98, Telford Victim Support 1986–99, Master Chefs of GB 1990–2003, Assoc of Conf Execs 1990–95, Stepping Stones Appeal for the Fndn for Conductive Educn 1991–94; vice-pres Re-Solv (The Campaign Against Solvent Abuse) 1989– (pres 1984–89); memb GB Great Food Working Pty 1990–95, memb Bd Nat Restaurant Assoc (USA) 2005–13; tstee Castle Bromwich Hall Gardens Tst; patron: Rodbaston Agric Coll 1998–2007, Miracles 1998–; pres Shropshire Victim Support 1999–2005; *Publications* My Private Parts and The Stuffed Parrot (compilation, 1984), The Eccentric Cookbook (1985), Stately Secrets (1994), Porters English Cookery Bible – Ancient and Modern (with Carol Wilson, 2004), Porters Seasonal Celebrations Cookbook (with Carol Wilson, 2007); online publications: Fake Titles (www.faketitles.com); *Recreations* cooking, gardening; *Style—* The Rt Hon the Earl of Bradford; ✉ 46 Sutton Court Road, Chiswick, London W4 4NL (☎ 020 8994 4846, e-mail bradfordr@porters.uk.com)

BRADFORD, Sarah Mary Malet (Viscountess Bangor); da of Brig Hilary Anthony Hayes, DSO, OBE (d 1984), and Mary Beatrice de Carteret Malet (who m 2, Keith Murray, and d 1995); *b* 3 September 1938; *Educ* St Mary's Convent Shaftesbury, Lady Margaret Hall Oxford (state scholarship, coll history scholarship); *m* 1, 1959 (m dis), Anthony John Bradford, s of John Frank Bradford; 1 da (Annabella Mary b 1964), 1 s (Edward John Alexander b 1966); m 2, 1976, 8 Viscount Bangor, *qv*; *Career* author, reviewer and broadcaster; *Books* The Story of Port (1978, new edn 1983, first published as The Englishman's Wine 1969), Portugal and Madeira (1969), Portugal (1973), Cesare Borgia (1976), Disraeli (1982), Princess Grace (1984), King George VI (1989), Sacheverell Sitwell (1993), Elizabeth, A Biography of Her Majesty The Queen (1996), America's Queen: The Life of Jacqueline Kennedy Onassis (2000), Lucrezia Borgia, Life, Love and Death in Renaissance Italy (2004), Diana (2006), Queen Elizabeth II: Her Life in Our Times (2012); *Recreations* reading biographies, diaries and letters, gardening, travelling, watching Liverpool FC; *Style—* Sarah Bradford; ✉ c/o Aitken Alexander Associates, 18–21 Cavaye Place, London SW10 9PT (☎ 020 7373 8672, fax 020 7373 6002, e-mail recep@gillonaitken.co.uk)

BRADLEY, Prof (John) Andrew; s of Colin Bradley, and Christine Bradley, of Cape Town, SA; *b* 24 October 1950; *Educ* Univ of Leeds (MB ChB), Univ of Glasgow (PhD); *m* 31 May 1987, Eleanor Mary, *née* Bolton; *Career* conslt surgn Western Infirmary Glasgow 1984–97, prof of surgery and immunology Univ of Glasgow 1994–97 (formerly surgical research fell then lectr in surgery), prof of surgery Univ of Cambridge and hon conslt surgn Addenbrooke's Hosp Cambridge 1997–; author of numerous pubns mainly concerned with organ transplantation; FRCSGlas, FRCSEng, FMedSci; *Recreations* skiing, hill walking; *Style—* Prof Andrew Bradley; ✉ University Department of Surgery, Box 202, Level 9, Addenbrooke's Hospital, Cambridge CB2 2QQ (☎ 01223 336976, fax 01223 762523, e-mail jab52@cam.ac.uk)

BRADLEY, Anna Louise; da of Donald Ernest Bradley, of London, and Angela Lucy, *née* Bradley; *b* 29 July 1957, London; *Educ* Univ of Warwick (BA, MBA); *Partner* Norman Howard Jones; 1 da (Natasha Storm b 11 March 1988), 1 s (Nathan Blaze b 12 Oct 1990); *Career* sr sub ed Marshall Cavendish Partworks Ltd 1978–82; Consumers' Assoc: sr project ldr 1982–87, project mangr 1987–88, head of food and health 1988–91, dep res dir 1991–93; exec dir and co sec Inst for the Study of Drug Dependence 1993–98, dir Nat Consumer Cncl 1999–2002, dir of retail themes FSA 2002–05; consumer and communications conslt Frontfoot Consultancy 2006–, advsy conslt Fishburn Hedges 2006–09, chair Gen Optical Cncl 2010–12, chair Healthwatch England 2012–; non-exec dir/cmmr Care Quality Cmmn 2012–; chm: DEFRA Horizon Scanning Advsy Panel 2002–04, Ofcom Consumer Panel 2008–11, Southern Water Customer Challenge Gp 2012; chm Organic Standards Bd Soil Assoc 2006–10, non-exec dir Soil Assoc Certification Ltd 2006–09 (chair 2010–13), chair Cncl for Licensed Conveyancers 2010–15, chm Rail Safetry Standards Bd 2015–, memb Zurich Financial Ind Governance Ctee; jt asst sec All-Pty Parly Gp on Drug Misuse 1994–98; memb: The Patients' Assoc 1985–88, Advsy Cncl on the Misuse of Drugs 1996–98, Consumer Policy Review Advsy Bd 1999–2002, Camelot Ind Advsy Panel on Social Responsibility 2000–02, Agric Economics and Biotechnology Cmmn 2000–2005, DEFRA Chief Scientist's Science Advsy Gp 2002–03, Public Debate on GM Bd 2002–03, Sustainable Farming and Food Implementation Gp 2002–03, Royal Soc Science in Society Ctee 2003–05, Science Advsy Cncl 2004–05; tstee Addaction 2006–12, non-exec dir Life Tst Fndn 2007–09, memb Bd Colchester Univ Fndn Tst 2010–12; *Books* Healthy Living (co-author, 1985), Understanding Additives (ed, 1988), Healthy Eating (1989), Caring for Someone with AIDS (contrib, 1990); author of numerous articles in jls and research papers; *Style—* Ms Anna Bradley

BRADLEY, Prof Anthony Wilfred; Hon QC (2011); s of David Bradley (d 1970), of Dover, Kent, and Olive Margaret, *née* Bonsey (d 1964); *b* 6 February 1934; *Educ* Dover GS, Emmanuel Coll Cambridge (MA, LLM); *m* 5 Sept 1959, Kathleen, *née* Bryce; 1 s, 3 da; *Career* slr of the Supreme Ct 1960–89, fell Trinity Hall Cambridge 1960–68; Univ of Edinburgh: prof of constitutional law 1968–89, dean Faculty of Law 1979–82, emeritus prof 1990; research fell Inst of European and Comparative Law Univ of Oxford 2003–; ed Public Law 1986–92; called to the Bar Inner Temple 1989, in practice 1989–2009; memb: Ctee of Inquiry into Local Govt in Scotland 1980, Ctee to Review Local Govt in the Islands of Scotland 1983–84; legal advsr House of Lords Ctee on the Constitution 2002–05; vice-pres Int Assoc of Constitutional Law 2004–07; chm Edinburgh Cncl for Single Homeless 1984–88; Hon LLD: Staffs Univ 1993, Univ of Edinburgh 1998; *Books* Justice Discretion and Poverty (with M Adler, 1976), Governmental Liability (with J Bell, 1991), Constitutional and Administrative Law (with K Ewing and C Knight, 16 edn 2014), European Human Rights Law (with M Janis and R Kay, 3 edn 2008); *Recreations* making and listening to music; *Style—* Prof Anthony Bradley; ✉ 20 Abingdon Road, Cumnor, Oxford OX2 9QN

BRADLEY, Christopher; s of Hugh Bradley (d 1968), of Glasgow, and Jean McQueen, *née* Dunn (d 1987); *b* 29 May 1950; *Educ* St Aloysius Coll, Blackpool and Fylde Coll (HND Hotel Mgmnt); *m* 3 May 1979, Judy Patricia, *qv*, da of Robin Cousins; *Career* asst mangr Trust House Forte 1971–72, sales mangr Grand Metropolitan & Centre Hotels 1972–75, internal auditor Lord Chllr's Office 1975–78, systems conslt ICL and NCR 1978–80, chef/patron Mr Underhill's 1981– (Michelin star 1994, Etoiles Mondials de la Gastronomie 1994, 4/5 Good Food Guide 1996 and 1997, 8 out of 10 Good Food Guide 1999, Michelin star 1999–); MHCIMA; *Recreations* motor racing, gardening, not cooking; *Style—* Christopher Bradley, Esq; ✉ Mr Underhill's at Dinham Weir, Dinham, Ludlow, Shropshire SY8 1EH (☎ 01584 874431)

BRADLEY, Clive; CBE (1996); s of Alfred Bradley (d 1970), and Annie Kathleen, *née* Turner (d 1990); *b* 25 July 1934; *Educ* Felsted, Clare Coll Cambridge (MA), Yale Univ; *Career* PO RAF 1953–55; called to the Bar Middle Temple 1961; BBC 1961–63 and 1965, broadcasting offr Lab Party 1963–64, political ed The Statist and broadcaster 1965–67, gp lab advsr IPC 1967–69, dep gen mangr Daily and Sunday Mirror and controller of admin IPC Newspapers 1969–71, project dir IPC 1971–73, dir The Observer 1973–76, chief exec Publishers Assoc 1976–97; convenor Confederation of Information Communication Industries 1984–2014; chm Book Power Ltd 2009–11; author of various pubns on politics, econs, media, industrial rels and law; dep chm Central London Valuation Panel 1973–2007; govr Felsted Sch 1971–2008; chair Richmond upon Thames Arts Cncl 2004–09, former chair Age Concern Richmond, pres U3A Richmond 2011–; Mellon fell Yale Univ; *Style—* Clive Bradley, Esq, CBE; ✉ 8 Northumberland Place, Richmond upon Thames, Surrey TW10 6TS (☎ 020 8940 7172, e-mail bradley_clive@btopenworld.com)

BRADLEY, Prof David John; s of late Harold Robert Bradley, and Mona Bradley; *b* 12 January 1937; *Educ* Wyggeston Sch Leicester, Selwyn Coll Cambridge, UCH Med Sch (Atchison scholar, Magrath scholar, MB BChir, MA, Trotter medal in surgery, Liston gold medal in surgery, Frank Smart prize), Univ of Oxford (DM); *m* 1961, Lorne Natalie, da of late Maj L G Farquhar; 2 s, 2 da; *Career* med res offr Bilharzia Res Unit Tanzania 1961–64, sr lectr Makerere Univ of East Africa Uganda 1966–69 (lectr 1964–66), Royal Soc tropical res fell Sir William Dunn Sch of Pathology Oxford 1969–73, sr res fell and Staines med fell Exeter Coll Oxford 1971–74, clinical reader in pathology Oxford Clinical Med Sch 1973–74, prof of tropical hygiene London Sch of Hygiene and Tropical Med 1974–2000 (Ross prof emeritus 2000–); dir Malaria Reference Laboratory 1974–, hon conslt public health medicine HPA 1974–, hon conslt in tropical and communicable diseases Camden and Islington DHA 1983, Westminster PCT 2002–; memb: WHO Expert Advsy Panel on Parasitic Diseases 1972–, Panel of Experts on Environmental Mgmnt 1981–; chm Div of Communicable and Tropical Diseases LSHTM 1982–88; ed: Jl of

Tropical Med and Hygiene 1981–95, Tropical Med and Int Health 1995–98; RSTM&H: Chalmers Medal 1980, Macdonald Medal 1996, pres 1999–2001; foreign corresponding memb Royal Belgian Acad of Med 1984, corresponding memb German Tropenmedizingingesellschaft 1980; Harben Gold Medal RIPHH 2002; FIBiol 1974, FFPHM 1979, Hon FCIWEM 1981, FRCPath 1981, FRCP 1985, FMedSci 1999; *Books* Drawers of Water (with G F and A U White, 1972), Health in Tropical Africa During the Colonial Period (with E E Sabben-Clare and B Kirkwood, 1980), Sanitation and Disease (jtly, 1983), Travel Medicine (jtly, 1992), The Malaria Challenge (with M.Coluzzi, 1999); *Recreations* landscape gardens, natural history, travel; *Style*— Prof David Bradley; ✉ Flat 3, 1 Taviton Street, London WC1H 0BT (☎ 020 7383 0228); Department of Infectious and Tropical Diseases, London School of Hygiene and Tropical Medicine, Keppel Street, London WC1E 7HT (☎ 020 7927 2233, fax 020 7580 9075)

BRADLEY, Dominic; MLA; *b* 29 August 1960; *Educ* Queen's Univ Belfast (BA, PGCE), Univ of Ulster (MA); *m* Mary; 1 s (Christopher); *Career* teacher of English, Irish, religion and drama St Paul's HS Bessbrook 1978–2004; MLA (SDLP) Newry and Armagh 2003–, SDLP spokesperson for educn and the Irish language; *Style*— Dominic Bradley, Esq, MLA; ✉ Northern Ireland Assembly, Parliament Buildings, Belfast BT4 3XX (website www.dominicbradley.com)

BRADLEY, Judy; da of Robin Cousins (d 1989), of Flowton, Suffolk, and Ruby, *née* Gant (d 2002); *b* 5 May 1950, Washbrook, Suffolk; *Educ* Amberfield Sch Nacton; *m* 3 May 1979, Christopher Bradley, *qv*; *Career* restaurateur; various hotels whilst travelling 1967–70, Trust House Forte Hotels 1970–74, fin administrator Arnolfini Bristol 1975–77, PA to Owner and fin administrator Pomegranates Restaurant London 1977–80, prop with husband Christopher Bradley) Mr Underhill's Suffolk and Ludlow Salops 1980–; *Recreations* all virtual – holidays, travelling, relaxing; *Style*— Mrs Judy Bradley; ✉ Mr Underhill's, Dinham Weir, Ludlow, Shropshire SY8 1EH (☎ 01584 874431)

BRADLEY, Rt Hon Karen Anne; PC (2016), MP; *née* Howarth; *b* 12 March 1970; *Educ* Buxton Girls Sch, Imperial Coll London (BSc); *m* Neil Austin; 2 s; *Career* CA; tax mangr Deloitte & Touche 1991–98, KPMG 1998–2004 and 2007–10; MP (Cons) Staffs Moorlands 2010–, asst Govt whip 2012–3, Lord Cmmr (whip) 2013–14, Parly under sec of state Home Office 2014–16, sec of state for culture, media and sport 2016–; *Style*— The Rt Hon Karen Bradley, MP; ✉ House of Commons, London SW1A 0AA (e-mail karen.bradley.mp@parliament.uk, website www.karenbradley.co.uk)

BRADLEY, Baron (Life Peer UK 2006), of Withington in the County of Greater Manchester; Keith John Charles Bradley; PC (2001); s of John Bradley, and Beatrice Bradley; *b* 17 May 1950, Birmingham; *Educ* Bishop Vesey's GS, Manchester Poly (BA), York Univ (MPhil); *m* 16 May 1987, Rhona, *née* Graham; 2 s (Jonathan b 23 Dec 1987, Matthew b 12 April 1996), 1 da (Rebecca b 18 Oct 1990); *Career* MP (Lab) Manchester Withington 1987–2005; shadow min: for social security 1991–96, for tport 1996–97; Parly under-sec of state DSS 1997–98, dep chief whip and treas HM Household 1998–2001, min of state for Criminal Justice, Sentencing and Law Reform Home Office 2001–02, memb Health Select Ctee 2003–05; Manchester City Cncl: cncllr 1983–88, chm Environmental Servs Ctee 1984–88; dir: Manchester Ship Canal Co 1984–87, Manchester Airport plc 1984–87; chair Manchester Salford and Trafford Liftco, chair Bury Tameside Glossop Liftco, non-exec dir Pennine Care NHS Fndn Tst 2015–; tstee: Prison Reform Tst, Centre for Mental Health; hon special advsr Univ of Manchester; *Publications* The Bradley Report on People with Mental Health Problems or Learning Difficulties in the Criminal Justice System (2009); *Recreations* football, cricket, rugby, theatre, food and drink; *Clubs* Lloyds Bowling; *Style*— The Rt Hon the Lord Bradley; ✉ House of Lords, London SW1A 0PW (e-mail bradleykj@parliament.uk)

BRADLEY, Michael John; CMG (1990), QC (Cayman Islands) 1983; *b* 1933; *Educ* Queen's Univ Belfast (LLB); *m*; 1 s; *Career* attorney gen: British Virgin Islands 1977–78, Turks and Caicos Islands 1980, Montserrat 1981, Cayman Islands 1982–87; govr Turks and Caicos Islands WI 1987–93, law revision cmmr Cayman Islands 1994–2009, constitutional advsr Overseas Territories Dept FCO 2001–09; memb Law Soc NI; *Style*— Mr Michael Bradley, CMG, QC

BRADLEY, Prof Patrick James; s of Gerard Bradley (d 1967), of Dublin, and Nan, *née* O'Leary (d 1990); *b* 10 May 1949, Thurles, Co Tipperary, Ireland; *Educ* Glenstal Abbey Sch Murroe Co Limerick, UCD Med Sch (MB BCh, BAO, DCH); *m* 17 May 1974, Sheena, da of Frank Kelly (d 1954), of Draperstown, Co Derry; 2 da (Paula b 19 Nov 1975, Caitriona b 5 June 1984), 3 s (Darragh Francis b 19 Nov 1976, Cormac b 12 Dec 1978, Eoin Patrick b 16 Oct 1980); *Career* Nottingham HA: conslt otolaryngologist and head and neck oncologist 1982–2009, clinical dir Dept of Otolaryngology 1991–96, clinical dir of audit, risk and effectiveness 1996–2000, memb Theatre Users (former chm); nat clinical lead Head and Neck Cancer NHS 2003–08; Hunterian prof RCS 2007–08, prof of head and neck oncologic surgery Univ of Nottingham 2008–13; hon visiting prof Sch of Health and Educn Middlesex Univ 2007–, emeritus visiting prof Sch of Medicine Univ of Nottingham 2013; vice-chm: Trent Regnl Advsy Ctee (Otolaryngology), ACCEA East Midlands 2003–06; chm: Nottingham Section BMA 1994–95, Clinical Practice Br Assoc of Otorhinolaryngologists Head and Neck Surgns 1995–98, Educn and Trg Ctee BAO-HNS 1999–2002; memb Cncl: Otorhinolaryngological Res Soc (treas 1993–96, hon memb 2010), RSM (memb Section of Laryngology/Rhinology 1991–2000, pres 1998–99); pres: Young Otolaryngologist Head and Neck Surgeons 1993–94 (hon memb 1997), Assoc of Head and Neck Oncologists GB 2003–05 (hon memb 2010, also Cncl memb and tstee), European Laryngological Soc 2004–06, Midlands Inst Otolaryngology 2005–07 (hon memb 2010); memb Bd: European Head and Neck Soc 2005–, European Acad of Otolaryngology 2006–09, Head and Neck Surgery 2006– (also vice-pres), European Salivary Gland Soc 2006– (pres 2007–09); memb: Br Assoc of Surgical Oncologists (memb Cncl 1998–2001, pres 2007–, hon fell 2010), Br Assoc of Head and Neck Oncologists (pres 2003–05, hon memb 2010),Br Assoc of Otorhinolaryngologists (hon memb 2010); corresponding memb: American Laryngological Assoc, Triological Soc, Assoc of Head and Neck Surgns; FACS, DCH, FRCSI, FRCSEd, FRCS, Hon FRSSLT, Hon FRACS, FHKCORL, Hon FRCS; *Books* Ear, Nose and Throat Disease (1989), Robb and Smith (contrib, 1992), Scott-Brown's ORL (contrib, 1994, 1995 and 2006 edns), Mawson's Head and Neck (contrib, 1997), ABC of Ear, Nose and Throat (jt ed, 6 edn 2012), Salivary Gland Diseases and Disorders: Diagnosis and Management (jt ed, 2013), Current Opinions Otolarygology, Head and Neck Surgery (co-ed), Advances in Otorhinolaryngology (series ed); also author of various pubns on head and neck cancer diagnosis and mgmnt; *Recreations* travel, skiing, good food, archeology; *Clubs* RAC, RSM, Notts Golf, Dooks Golf; *Style*— Prof Patrick J Bradley, MBA, FRCS; ✉ 10 Chartwell Grove, Mapperley Plains, Nottingham NG3 5RD (☎ 0115 920 1611, e-mail pjbradley@zoo.co.uk)

BRADLEY, Rev Peter; s of David Noel Bradley, and Doris, *née* Howarth; *b* 4 June 1949, Liverpool; *Educ* Old Swan Tech Coll, Ian Ramsey Coll, Lincoln Theol Coll and Univ of Nottingham (BTh); *m* 1970, Pat; 3 s; *Career* ordained: deacon 1979, priest 1980; asst curate UpHolland Team Miny 1979–83, vicar Holy Spirit Dovecot 1983–94, team rector UpHolland Team Miny 1994–2011, hon canon Liverpool Cathedral 2000–, archdeacon of Warrington 2001–15, ret; dir Continuing Ministerial Educn 1989–2001, dep dir In-Service Trg 1988–89; sec: Diocesan Bd of Miny 1983–88, Gp for Urban Miny and Leadership 1984–88; memb: Gen Synod 1990–2010, Evangelism and Renewal at Home Ctee Central Bd for Mission and Unity 1992–95 (contrib A Time for Sharing report); pt/t memb of staff: Aston Trg Scheme 1988–97, Diocesan OLM Scheme 1995–2001; *Recreations* walking, reading, music; *Style*— The Rev Peter Bradley; ✉ 30 Sandbrook Road, Orrell, Wigan WN58 7UD (e-mail archdeacon@peterbradley.fsnet.co.uk)

BRADLEY, Peter Richard; CBE (2005); s of Patrick John Bradley, of NZ, and Mary, *née* China; *b* 28 December 1957; *Educ* Temple Moor GS Leeds, Univ of Otago NZ (MBA); *m* 14 Jan 1978 (sep), Mary Elisabeth, *née* Verhoeff; 1 s (Luke Paul b 12 Oct 1979), 2 da (Kathryn Marie b 10 Dec 1980, Allanah Louise b 25 Sept 1984); *Career* Commercial Bank of Aust 1973–76; St John Ambulance Serv Auckland: joined 1976, qualified paramedic 1986, chief ambulance offr 1993–95; London Ambulance Serv: joined 1996, dir of ops 1998–2000, chief exec 2000–; nat ambulance advsr 2004–; pres Ambulance Serv Assoc 2003–04; Queen's Golden Jubilee Medal 2002; MIMgt 1996, fell NZ Inst of Mgmnt (FNZIM) 1999, fell Ambulance Serv Inst (FASI) 2001; OBStJ 1994 (SBStJ 1992); *Recreations* personal fitness, reading, sports; *Style*— Peter Bradley, Esq, CBE; ✉ London Ambulance Service NHS Trust, 220 Waterloo Road London SE1 8SD (☎ 020 7463 2567, fax 020 7921 5127, e-mail peter.bradley@lond-amb.nhs.uk)

BRADLEY, Philip Herbert Gilbert; s of Herbert Bradley (d 1981), of S Ireland, and Phyllis Eleanor Josephine, *née* Marshall (d 2003); *b* 11 November 1949; *Educ* Charterhouse, Trinity Coll Dublin (BA, BAI (engrg)); *m* 3 Sept 1977, Charlotte Knollys Olivia, da of Lt-Col John Clairmont Wood, of Coombe Down, Beaminster, Dorset; 3 s (William b 6 Oct 1980, Piers b 9 Dec 1982, Timothy b 14 March 1985); *Career* Coopers & Lybrand chartered accountants 1974–78, Robert Fleming & Co Ltd bankers 1978–79, Jardine Fleming & Co Ltd bankers Hong Kong 1979–81; dir: Robert Fleming & Co bankers London 1984–97, Chaffeigh Ltd 1998–, London & Lochside Investments Ltd; govr Milton Abbey; ACA; *Recreations* travel, music, opera, fishing, farming, skiing; *Clubs* Kildare Street (Dublin), Flyfishers; *Style*— Philip Bradley, Esq; ✉ 30 Smith Terrace, Chelsea, London SW3 4DH (☎ 07785 733106, e-mail philiphgbradley@gmail.com)

BRADLEY, (Philip) Stephen; s of Robert Bradley, of St Annes on Sea, and Hilda, *née* Whalley; *b* 22 August 1949; *Educ* Queen Elizabeth's GS Blackburn; *m* 1, 4 April 1976 (m dis 1985), Janet Elizabeth, da of Eric Hollingworth; 2 s (Richard b 26 Oct 1980, Alexander b 2 Sept 1982); m 2, 21 May 1993, Anne, da of Diana May Hill; *Career* chartered accountant; articled clerk Waterworth Rudd & Hare Blackburn 1967–71; PricewaterhouseCoopers (formerly Price Waterhouse before merger): audit sr Manchester 1972–75, mgmnt conslt Manchester 1975–77, mgmnt conslt Nairobi 1978–84, ptnr 1980, mgmnt conslt ptnr London 1987–2002; ptnr IBM Business Consulting Services 2002–; FCA 1971, FIMC 1980, MILDM 1987; *Style*— Stephen Bradley, Esq

BRADMAN, Godfrey Michael; s of William Isadore Bradman (d 1973), and Anne Brenda, *née* Goldsweig; *b* 9 September 1936; *m* 2, 1975, Susan, da of George Bennett; 1 s (Daniel b 1977), 2 da (Camilla b 1976, Katherine b 1976), 1 step s (Christian), 1 step da (Sophie); *Career* CA 1961; sr ptnr Godfrey Bradman and Co 1961–69, chm and chief exec London Mercantile Corporation 1969, chm Rosehaugh plc 1979–91; chm and jt chief exec European Land & Property Corporation 1992–; chm: European Land and Property Investments Co 1993–, Ashpost Finance 1993–, Pondbridge Europe Ltd 1994–; jt chm Victoria Quay Ltd 1993–; fndr and dir AIDS Policy Unit 1987–90; established: Parents Against Tobacco Campaign (jt chm), Opren Victims Campaign (pres), CLEAR Campaign for Lead Free Air 1981–91, Campaign for Freedom of Information 1983–, Citizen Action and European Citizen Action 1983–91; pres Soc for the Protection of Unborn Children Educnl Research Tst 1987–, chm Friends of the Earth Tst 1983–91; memb: Cncl UN Int Year of Shelter for the Homeless 1987, Governing Body LSHTM 1988–91; Wilkins fell Cambridge; hon fell: KCL, Downing Coll Cambridge 1997; Hon DSc Univ of Salford; FCA; *Recreations* riding, family, reading; *Style*— Godfrey Bradman, Esq

BRADSHAW, Adrian; s of Sydney Bradshaw, of Wilmslow, Cheshire, and Nina, *née* Gerrand; *b* 24 February 1957; *Educ* Urmston GS, Univ of Central England (BA); *m* 12 Sept 1984, Valerie Joy, da of Dr Ivor Citron; 1 da (Charlotte b 16 Jan 1986), 1 s (Benjamin b 11 Oct 1989); *Career* Citicorp Scrimgeour Vickers 1978–81, Bell Lawrie White 1981–82, corp fin Nat West Markets 1982–83, dir Guidehouse Ltd 1983–89, md Corp Fin Div and memb Bd Arbuthnot Latham Bank 1989–91, chm and chief exec Incepta Gp plc 1991–93, dir Bradmount Investments Ltd 1994–2010, chief exec Hamilton Bradshaw Capital Partners 2010–; non-exec dir Atlantic Global plc 2007–12; MInstD; *Recreations* tennis, golf, skiing, theatre, cuisine, travel; *Clubs* Groucho, Annabel's, George; *Style*— Adrian Bradshaw, Esq; ✉ Hamilton Bradshaw Capital Partners, 60 Grosvenor Street, Mayfair, London W1K 3HZ (☎ 020 7399 6745, e-mail ab@hbcp.co.uk)

BRADSHAW, Rt Hon Benjamin (Ben); MP, PC (2009); s of Canon Peter Bradshaw, and Daphne, *née* Murphy; *b* 30 August 1960; *Educ* Thorpe St Andrew Sch Norwich, Univ of Sussex (BA); *m* Neal Thomas Dalgleish; *Career* reporter: Express and Echo Exeter 1984–85, Eastern Daily Press Norwich 1985–86, BBC Radio Devon Exeter 1986–89; BBC correspondent Berlin 1989–91, reporter World at One and World This Weekend (BBC Radio 4) 1991–97; MP (Lab) Exeter 1997–; PPS to John Denham MP 2000–01, Parly under sec of state FCO 2001–02, Parly sec Privy Cncl Office 2002–03, Parly under sec of state DEFRA 2003–06, min of state DEFRA 2006–07, min for the SW and min of state for health 2007–09, sec of state for culture, media and sport 2009–10, memb DCMS Select Ctee 2012–; Consumer Journalist of the Year 1988, Anglo-German Fndn Journalist of the Year 1990, Sony News Reporter Award 1993; memb: NUJ, GMB, USDAW; *Recreations* cycling, walking in Devon, cooking, gardening; *Clubs* Whipton Labour (Exeter); *Style*— The Rt Hon Ben Bradshaw, Esq, MP; ✉ House of Commons, London SW1A 0AA (☎ 020 7219 6597, fax 020 7219 0950, e-mail bradshawb@parliament.uk)

BRADSHAW, Stephen Paul; s of Eric Douglas Bradshaw, and Victoria, *née* Gibbons; *b* 26 November 1948; *Educ* Nottingham HS, Queens' Coll Cambridge (MA); *m* 27 May 1972, Jenny, da of Michael Richards; 2 s (Nicholas b 4 Oct 1973, Rusty b 2 May 1977), 1 da (Melissa b 17 Aug 1980); *Career* prodr BBC Radio London 1970–73, columnist New Society, The Listener and Crawdaddy 1972–78; reporter and presenter: File on 4 (BBC Radio Four) 1977–80, Newsweek (BBC2) 1980–83, People and Power (BBC1) 1983, Newsnight (BBC2) 1984–87; corr Panorama (BBC1) 1987–2007, documentary writer and dir BBC1 and BBC4 2007–08; series ed: Life on the Edge (TVE/BBC World TV) 2007–11, Future Food (TVE) 2012, Life Apps (TVE/Al Jazeera) 2012–13; memb Int Consortium of Investigative Journalists; Amnesty Int Media Award, Outstanding Int Investigative Journalism Award, DuPont Columbia Award, Peabody Award, One World Int Documentary Award, Emmy Award for Investigative Journalism, other reporting and directing awards; *Books* Cafe Society (1978); *Recreations* grandchildren, gardening; *Style*— Stephen Bradshaw, Esq; ✉ e-mail sbflaxmoor@aol.com, website www.steve-bradshaw.com

BRADSHAW, William Martin (Bill); s of Leslie Charles Bradshaw (d 1971), of Lobley Hill, Gateshead, and Vera, *née* Beadle; *b* 12 December 1955; *Educ* Gateshead GS and Saltwell HS, Darlington NCTJ Journalism Sch; *m* 1, 13 June 1981 (m dis 2005), Fiona Judith, da of William MacBeth (d 1974); 1 s (Kit Leslie b 12 Nov 1990), 1 da (Holly b 15 Feb 1993); m 2, 4 Sept 2006, Jill Theresa Mitchell; *Career* jr then sr reporter Halifax Courier 1975–77, news reporter Newcastle Evening Chronicle 1977–79, sports reporter (covering soccer and athletics) Newcastle Journal 1979–83, sports ed The People London 1990–94 (sports reporter Manchester 1983–85 and London 1985–89), ed The Journal Newcastle 1994–96, former asst ed Sunday Mirror, currently asst ed and head of sport Daily Express; memb: Football Writers' Assoc 1981, SWA 1985; Sports Journalist of the Year 1990, Sports Reporter of the Year 1990; *Recreations* cricket, soccer, water skiing, reading, golf; *Style*— Bill Bradshaw, Esq

BRADSHAW, Baron (Life Peer UK 1999), of Wallingford in the County of Oxfordshire; Prof William Peter Bradshaw; s of Leonard Charles Bradshaw (d 1978), and Ivy Doris, *née* Steele (d 1980); *b* 9 September 1936; *Educ* Slough GS, Univ of Reading (BA, MA); *m* 30 Nov 1957, Jill Elsie (d 2002), da of James Francis Hayward, of Plastow Green, Hants; 1 s (Robert William b 1966), 1 da (Joanna b 1968); m 2, 30 Aug 2003, Diana Mary, da of Leslie Norman Whatley, of Oxford; *Career* Nat Serv 1957–59; BR: mgmnt trainee 1959, div movements mangr Bristol 1967, div mangr Liverpool 1973, chief ops mangr London Midland Region 1976, dep gen mangr London Midland Region 1977, dir of ops BR HQ 1978, dir Policy Unit BR HQ 1980, gen mangr W Region 1983–85; prof of tport mgmnt Univ of Salford 1986–92 (visiting prof Sch of Mgmnt 1992–2000); chm Ulsterbus 1987–93; dir: Northern Ireland Transport Holding Co 1988–93, Lothian Regional Transport 1997–99; special advsr Tport Select Ctee House of Commons 1992–97; memb: Oxfordshire CC 1993–2008, Thames Valley Police Authy 1997–2008 (vice-chm 1997–2003), Strategic Rail Authy 1999–2001, Cmmn for Integrated Transport 1999–2001; chm Bus Appeals Body 1998–2000; Lib Dem spokesman on transport House of Lords 2003–15; hon fell Wolfson Coll Oxford 2004– (supernumerary fell 1988–2003); *Recreations* growing hardy perennial plants; *Clubs* Nat Lib; *Style—* The Rt Hon the Lord Bradshaw; ✉ House of Lords, London SW1A 0PW

BRADY, Hon Mrs (Charlotte Mary Thérèse); *née* Bingham; da of 7 Baron Clanmorris (d 1988); *b* 29 June 1942; *Educ* The Priory Haywards Heath, Sorbonne; *m* 1964, Terence Joseph Brady, s of Frederick Arthur Noel Brady (d 1985), of Montacute, Somerset; 1 da (Candida b 1965), 1 s (Matthew b 1972); *Career* playwright, novelist; writes as Charlotte Bingham; *Books* Coronet Among the Weeds (1963), Lucinda (1965), Coronet Among the Grass (1972), Rose's Story (with husb Terence Brady 1973), Yes Honestly (1977), Belgravia (1983), Country Life (1984), At Home (1985), To Hear A Nightingale (1988), The Business (1989), In Sunshine or in Shadow (1991), Stardust (1992), By Invitation (1993), Nanny (1993), Change of Heart (1994), Debutantes (1995), The Nightingale Sings (1996), Country Wedding (1996), Grand Affair (1997), Love Song (1998), The Kissing Garden (1999), The Love Knot (2000), The Blue Note (2000), The Season (2001), Summertime (2001), Distant Music (2002), The Chestnut Tree (2002), The Wind off the Sea (2003), The Moon at Midnight (2003), Daughters of Eden (2004), The House of Flowers (2004), The Magic Hour (2004), Friday's Girl (2004), Out of the Blue (2005), In Distant Fields (2006), The White Marriage (2007), Goodnight Sweetheart (2007), The Enchanted (2008), The Land of Summer (2008), The Daisy Club (2009), Mums on the Run (2010), A Dip Before Breakfast – Mums on the Run 2 (2012), The Light on the Swan (2014), Coronet Among the Spooks (2016); *Plays* with Terence Brady: I Wish I Wish, Coming of Age, The Shell Seekers (adaptation), Below Stairs, Four Hearts (2013); *TV Series* (with Terence Brady): Take Three Girls, Upstairs Downstairs, No Honestly, Yes Honestly, Play for Today, Thomas and Sarah, Nanny, Pig in the Middle, Forever Green, Oh Madeline! (USA), Father Matthew's Daughter; *TV Films* Love With A Perfect Stranger, This Magic Moment; *Ballets* with Terence Brady: Les Copines (Ballet under the Stars) 2016, Les Columbes 2016; *Recreations* horse breeding, riding, gardening, racing, swimming; *Style—* The Hon Mrs Brady; ✉ c/o United Authors Ltd (✆ 07970 614754) or Hardway Publications (✆ 01749 813890)

BRADY, Adrian; *Educ* Trinity Coll Dublin (BSc), UCD (MSc); *Career* chief exec Eulogy 1996–; Agency of the Year and Best B2B Campaign PRCA Awards 2009, Best PR Campaign B2B Marketing Award 2009, PR Week Top 20 Ind Agency 2013, Medium Consultancy of the Year PRCA Awards 2013 PR Week Top 25 Ind Agency 2015; *Style—* Adrian Brady, Esq; ✉ Eulogy, 10 Bakers Yard, Bakers Row, London EC1R 3DD (✆ 020 3077 2000, e-mail adrian@eulogy.co.uk, website www.eulogy.co.uk)

BRADY, Angela; OBE (2015); da of late Peter Gerard Brady, FRCSI, and Deirdre Rowan Brady; *b* Dublin; *Educ* Holy Child Dublin Secdy Girls Sch, Bolton St Sch of Architecture Dublin, Kunstacademie Copenhagen, Westminster Sch of Architecture; *m* 1986, Robin Mallalieu, *qv*; 2 c; *Career* architect and TV broadcaster; experience in London, Toronto, Copenhagen and Dublin; dir Brady Mallalieu Architects Ltd 1987–; pres RIBA 2011–13; architectural advsr: Civic Tst Nat and Int Panel, English Heritage/CABE Urban Panel; RIAI: memb Cncl 2014, chm London Forum; memb: Ctee RIBA Women in Architecture (chair 2000–05), Bd London Devpt Agency as Design Champion, Panel Design for London GLA, Ctee Women's Irish Network 2014; tstee dir Building Exploratory Hackney (BEH); ambass STEMnet; Br Cncl ambass to Vietnam for Innovation and Design 2013–14; judge: Tamayouz first Iraq Women in Architecture Award 2014, RIAS Student Awards 2014, Curragh Race Course Stadium 2014, RIAI Schs Competition 2014; dir/author of: Hot Property (Channel 5), BBC 1 London Radio architectural debate, BBC Radio 3, BBC Radio 4, Building The Dream (65 part TV series, ITV), The Home Show (6 part series of designs around Europe, Channel Four) 2008; co-writer/presenter Designing Ireland (4 part series, RTE) 2015 and 2016; creator 'Why Study Architecture – The Role of the Architect' video on RIBA website 2014; contrib: London Biennale, Architecture Week; overseas correspondent Architecture Ireland, correspondent First Woman online magazine; curator Diversecity Global Snowball (exhbn promoting women and ethnic minorities in architecture, visited cities incl LA, Chicago, Boston, Brussels, Luxembourg, Paris, Istanbul, Beijing, Zhengzhou, Sydney, Auckland, Dublin, Athens and UK tour, website www.women-in-architecture.com), curator 7 Hands (travelling exhbn of Irish crafts) 2015, art/sculpture cmmn of steel and glass panels for Murphy Gp HQ, currently exhibiting in 4 art shows with glassworks incl The Garden (with Holger Lonze) West Cork Creates Skibbereen 2016; assist RIBA Architects in Schools Initiative; gives talks and writes articles on sustainable eco-friendly design and runs sch design workshops, numerous interviews on video and radio; built environment expert (BEE) for design review Design Cncl CABE, pres Architects Benevolent Soc 2015–18; memb: Int Irish Business Network (IIBN), London Irish Construction Network (LICN); Hon Dr DIT Dublin Sch of Architecture 2011, Hon Dip Russian Architects Assoc 2012; hon memb Br Inst of Interior Designers 2013, hon fell Soc for the Environment 2014; hon fell and President's Medal AIA USA 2013, hon fell and President's Medal RIAC Canada 2013; ARB, RIBA, Hon FRIAI 1999, FRSA 2004, Hon FRIAS 2013, hon fell Inst of Structural Engineers; *Awards* RIAI Award for house renovation in Islington London 1991, Irish Post/AIB Bank Personal Achievement Award 1993, RIAI Award for office fitout for Groundwork Hackney London 1995, RIAI Award for Sch of Architecture London Met Univ 1997, RIAI Award for house in Knightsbridge London, Brick Awards for Dublin Foyer Housing and Sports Centre 2003, RIAI Award Barra Park Open Air Theatre 2005, highly commended finalist Women in Construction Atkins Awards Women of Outstanding Achievement 2007, Business Partnership Award Greenwich Educn Business Partnership 2007, RIAI Award for Mastmaker Road (200 new homes in London) 2010, Best New Homes Evening Standard 2010, Lifetime Achievement Award – Women In Construction 2012, WISE Award – Women of Outstanding Achievement for Leadership 2013; *Publications* Dublin: a guide to contemporary architecture (with Robin Mallalieu, 1997), The China Papers (2013 and 2014), series of 20 essays from leading UK architects, engineers and leaders in sustainable design and city making, The British Papers (ed and publisher, 2015); *Recreations* painting unique art works for hospitals and doctors' surgeries, glass art works and jewellery, Making videos on architecture and design; *Clubs* Chelsea Arts, Women's Irish Network; *Style—* Ms Angela Brady, OBE; ✉ Brady Mallalieu Architects Ltd, 90 Queens Drive, London N4 2HW (✆ 020 8880 1544, e-mail bma@bradymallalieu.com, website www.bradymallalieu.com and http://angelabradyriba.tumblr.com, Twitter @AngelaBradyRIBA, @BradyMallalieu, @7HandsCrafts and @DesignEire)

BRADY, Graham; MP; s of John Brady, and Maureen Brady; *b* 20 May 1967; *Educ* Altrincham GS, Univ of Durham (BA); *m* 1992, Victoria Anne Lowther; 1 da (Catherine b 1993), 1 s (William b 1998); *Career* trainee Shandwick plc, with Centre for Policy Studies 1990–92, public affrs dir Waterfront Partnership (business consultancy) 1992–97; MP (Cons) Altrincham and Sale West 1997–; PPS to chm Cons Pty 1999–2000; oppn whip 2000, oppn spokesman on educn and employment 2000–01, PPS to Rt Hon Michael Howard, QC, MP 2003–14; memb Select Ctee on Educn and Employment 1997–2001 and 2007–10, memb Treasy Select Ctee 2007–10; 1922 Exec Ctee: memb 1998–2000 and 2007–10, chm 2010–; sec Cons Backbench Educn and Employment Ctee 1997–2000; memb Advsy Cncl Centre for Policy Studies, memb Cncl Alliance of European Conservatives and Reformists 2015–; vice-patron Friends of Rosie; Spectator Backbencher of the Year 2010; *Recreations* family, garden; *Clubs* Carlton; *Style—* Graham Brady, Esq, MP; ✉ House of Commons, London SW1A 0AA (✆ 020 7219 4604, fax 020 7219 1649)

BRADY, Janet Mary (Jan); *née* Hicks; da of Allan Frederick Mount, MBE (d 2006), of Oxford, and Doreen Margaret, *née* Hicks; *b* 26 February 1956; *Educ* Rochester GS, Medway and Maidstone Coll of Technol; *m* 2014, Philip John Cartwright; *Career* legal asst Mobil Oil 1974–77, tax asst Marathon Oil 1977–81, account dir Sterling PR 1982–85, dir PR American Express (UK and Ireland) 1985–87, fndr dir Kinnear PR 1988–89, chief exec Cadogan Management Ltd 1994–95 (md 1989–94), chm Specialtours Ltd 1990–95, md The Albermarle Connection 1995–99; co sec Oxford Sch of Osteopathy 1999–2001; co sec and chief exec SportsAid Southern Region 2001–04; chm Women in Mgmnt 1991–94, pres Soc of Consumer Affrs Professionals UK 1993; gen mangr Mill Court Clinical Centre Oxford Brookes Univ 1999–2001; advsr Independent Public Relations 1999–2012, sr exec coach and mangr of reputations (people, products and plcs); advsr: Br Sports Assoc for the Disabled (now DSE) 1990–99, East London Partnership 1991–98, Spencer House 1990–2012, Groundwork UK 1997–2000; dir: Bulgarian Period Properties 2005–, Pest Properties Kft 2006–12; ind memb Heathrow Airport Conslt Ctee 1998–2005; *Recreations* stonemasonry, landscape gardening, writing, healing, interior design, tree house design; *Clubs* Bluebird; *Style—* Ms Jan Brady; ✉ 23 Lyne Road, Kidlington, Oxford OX5 1AE (e-mail janbrady56@gmail.com)

BRADY, Joan; da of Robert Alexander Brady (d 1963), and Mildred Alice, *née* Edie (d 1965); *b* 4 December 1939; *Educ* Columbia Univ (Phi Beta Kappa); *m* 23 Sept 1963, Dexter Wright Masters, s of Thomas Davis Masters; 1 s (Alexander Wright b 12 Oct 1965); *Career* author; formerly dancer: San Francisco Ballet 1955–57, NYC Ballet 1960; awarded Nat Endowment for the Arts (Washington) 1986; *Books* The Impostor (1979), The Unmaking of a Dancer (1982), Theory of War (1993, Whitbread Novel of the Year 1993, Whitbread Book of the Year 1994, Prix de Meilleur Livre Etranger 1995), Prologue (1994), Death Comes For Peter Pan (1996), The Emigre (1999), Bleedout (2005), Venom (2010), The Blue Death (2012), America's Dreyfus: The Case Nixon Rigged (2015); *Clubs* Soc of Authors, Authors' Guild; *Style—* Joan Brady; ✉ e-mail joan@joanbrady.co.uk, website www.joanbrady.co.uk; c/o George Lucas, Inkwell Management, 521 5th Avenue, 26th Floor, New York NY 1017 (e-mail george@inkwellmanagement.com)

BRADY, Baroness (Life Peer UK 2014), of Knightsbridge in the City of Westminster; Karren Brady; CBE (2014); da of Terry Brady, of Enfield, and Rita, *née* Chambers; *b* 4 April 1969; *Educ* Poles Convent Sch, Alderham Sch; *m* 1995, Paolo (Paul) Peschisolido; *Career* jr exec Saatchi & Saatchi 1987–88, sales exec London Broadcasting Company (LBC) 1988–89, mktg and sales dir Sport Newspapers Ltd 1989–93, md Birmingham City FC plc 1993–2009, vice-chm West Ham United FC 2010–; non-exec dir: Mothercare 2003–, Channel 4 2004–, Kerrang! Radio 2004– (chm); memb Bd Sport England 2005–; appearances as memb of the bd The Apprentice (BBC2) 2010–; *Style—* The Baroness Brady, CBE; ✉ West Ham United FC, Boleyn Ground, Green Street, Upton Park, London E13 9AZ

BRADY, Prof Sir (John) Michael; kt (2004); s of John Brady, OBE, and Priscilla Mansfield, *née* Clark; *b* 30 April 1945; *Educ* Prescot GS, Univ of Manchester (BSc, MSc), ANU (PhD); *m* 2 Oct 1967, Naomi, *née* Friedlander; 2 da (Sharon b 1971, Carol b 1973); *Career* sr lectr Univ of Essex 1978–80 (lectr 1970–78), sr res scientist MIT 1980–85, prof Univ of Oxford 1985–; memb Bd of Dirs: GCS, Miranda Solutions, Oxford Instruments, AEA Technology; dep chm Oxford Instruments plc 2000–; founding ed International Journal of Robotics Research 1981–99, ed Artificial Intelligence; Hon DUniv: Essex 1996, Manchester 1998, Liverpool 1999, Southampton 1999, Paul Sabatier Toulouse 2000; MIEEE, FRSA, FIEE, FREng 1992, FRS 1997; *Books* Theory of Computer Science (1975), Computer Vision (1981), Robot Motion (1983), Computational Models of Discourse (1983), Robotics (1985), Robotics Science (1989), Mammographic Image Analysis (1999); *Recreations* Dickens, wine, Everton FC; *Style—* Prof Sir Michael Brady, FRS, FREng; ✉ Department of Engineering Science, University of Oxford, Ewert House, Ewert Place, Summertown, Oxford OX2 7BZ (✆ 01865 280930, fax 01865 280922, e-mail jmb@robots.ox.ac.uk)

BRADY, Cardinal Sean Baptist; *see:* Armagh, Archbishop of (RC)

BRADY, Terence Joseph; s of (Frederick Arthur) Noel Brady (d 1985), of Montacute, Somerset, and Elizabeth Mary Moore (d 1986); *b* 13 March 1939, London; *Educ* Merchant Taylors', TCD (BA, MA); *m* 1964, Hon Charlotte Mary Thérèse Bingham, *qv*, da of Lord Clanmorris, of London; 1 s (Matthew), 1 da (Candida); *Career* playwright, novelist, actor and painter; contrib: Daily Mail, Daily Express, Sunday Express, Mail on Sunday, Country Homes and Interiors, Punch, The Field; theatre credits as actor incl: Glory Be!, The Dumb Waiter, Would Anyone Who Saw The Accident, Beyond The Fringe, A Quick One 'Ere (co-writer with Michael Bogdanov), In The Picture, A Present From The Corporation, Clope; as playwright with Charlotte Bingham: I Wish, I Wish, Coming of Age, The Shell Seekers (adaptation), Below Stairs, Four Hearts 2013; as sole playwright: Anyone for Tennis?, Change of Heart, Adam and Eve (adaptation), Noel and Cole 2010, Crossing the Line 2012; TV series and plays with Charlotte Bingham incl: Take Three Girls, Upstairs Downstairs (shared BAFTA for series 1 and 2), Play for Today, 6 Plays of Marriage, No Honestly, Yes Honestly, Thomas and Sarah, Nanny, Pig in the Middle, Take Three Women, Father Matthew's Daughter, Oh Madeleine (US); films with Charlotte Bingham: Love with A Perfect Stranger, This Magic Moment, Riders, Polo,All That Glitters; TV as actor incl: Dig This Rhubarb, Broad and Narrow, First Impressions, Z Cars, My Name is Dora, Cribbins, A Man For Today, N F Simpson Series, Time For The Funny Walk, Boy Meets Girl, Life and Law; radio as writer and performer incl: Hear Hear!, Thank Goodness It's Saturday, The Victoria Line (with Charlotte Bingham), Lines From My Grandfather's Forehead (Writers Guild Award for Best comedy; films as actor incl: Baby Love, Foreign Exchange; exhbns incl NT, Wykeham Gall, Teddy House Gall; co-creator (with Charlotte Bingham) No Honestly (musical, music by Peter Skellern) 2015; *Books* Rehearsal (1972), The Fight against Slavery (with Evan Jones, 1976), McCann's Dog (2010), The White Horse (2013); with Charlotte Bingham: Roses Story (1973), Victoria – Victoria and Company, Yes Honestly (1977), A History of Point-to-Pointing (1991), A View of Meadows Green (2013); *Recreations* racing, horse breeding, riding, music, painting; *Clubs* PEN; *Style—* Terence Brady, Esq; ✉ c/o Marsha Hackett Management (✆ 01749 813017, e-mail marshahackett@aol.com)

BRAGG, (Henry) John; OBE (2008); s of Henry Bragg, of Torquay, Devon; *b* 28 November 1929; *Educ* Torquay GS, Chelsea Poly, Univ of London; *m* 1, 1954, Jean, *née* Harris (d

1969); 1 s, 2 da; m 2, 1972, Anthea, da of Kew Shelley, QC (d 2010); 1 step s, 1 step da; *Career* Nat Serv RAMC 1951–53; Glaxo Laboratories 1953–55, Pfizer Ltd 1955–70, md Calor Gas Ltd 1970–80, dir Imperial Continental Gas Assoc 1978–85, md Calor Group 1980–85, dir Advanced Petroleum Technology Ltd 1985–89; chm: Canterbury and Thanet HA 1986–94, E Kent HA 1994–96; memb Professions Allied to Med Whitley Cncl 1990–96; Canterbury Christ Church Univ: govr 1991–2005, chm Bd of Govrs 1999–2005; tstee: Kent Community Housing Tst 1992–2011, Sandwich United Charities 1992–; mayor of Sandwich 1989–92; memb: Sandwich Town Cncl 1985–, Dover DC 1989–2003; Hon Freeman Town and Port of Sandwich 2010; Hon DCL Univ of Kent 1996; hon fell Canterbury Christ Church Univ; FCILT, FRPharmS, DBA; *Recreations* golf, books, maps; *Clubs* Royal St George's Golf; *Style*— John Bragg, Esq, OBE; ✉ Hideway House, St George's Road, Sandwich, Kent CT13 9LE

BRAGG, Baron (Life Peer UK 1998), of Wigton in the County of Cumbria; **Melvyn Bragg;** s of Stanley Bragg, of Wigton, Cumbria, and Mary Ethel, *née* Parks; *b* 6 October 1939; *Educ* Nelson Thomlinson GS Wigton, Wadham Coll Oxford (open scholar, MA); *m* 1, 1961, Marie-Elisabeth Roche (decd); 1 da; *m* 2, 1973, Catherine Mary (see Cate Haste, *qv*), da of Eric Haste, of Crantock, Almondsbury, Avon; 1 da (Hon Alice b 1977), 1 s (Hon Tom b 1980); *Career* writer and broadcaster; general traineeship BBC 1961, prodr on Monitor (BBC) 1963; ed BBC 2 1964: New Release (arts magazine latterly called Review, then Arena), Writers World (documentary), Take It or Leave It (literary programme); presenter: In The Picture (Tyne Tees) 1971, 2nd House (BBC) 1973–77, Start the Week (BBC Radio 4, TRIC Award 1990 and 1994) 1988–98, In Our Time (BBC Radio 4) 1998–, Routes of English (BBC Radio 4) 1999–; presenter and ed: Read All About It (BBC) 1976–77, South Bank Show (ITV) 1978– (BAFTA Prix Italia 5 times, TV Music ad Arts Programme of the Year TV and Radio Industry Awards 2000), Adventure of English (also writer, ITV); dir LWT Productions 1992, controller Arts Dept LWT 1990– (head of arts 1982–90), chm Border Television 1990–96 (dep chm 1985–90); govr LSE 1997–, chllr Univ of Leeds 1999–; pres MIND 2002–; occasional contrib Observer, Sunday Times and Guardian, weekly column Times 1996–98; memb RSL 1977–80, pres Nat Campaign for the Arts; Hon DUniv Open Univ 1988, Hon LLD Univ of St Andrews 1993; Hon DLitt: Liverpool 1986, Lancaster 1990, CNAA 1990, South Bank Univ 1997, Univ of Leeds 2000, Univ of Bradford 2000, Queen's Univ Belfast 2005; Hon DCL Univ of Northumbria 1994; Hon DSc: UMIST 1998, Brunel Univ 2000; Hon DA Univ of Sunderland 2001; hon fell Lancashire Poly; Domus fell St Catherine's Coll Oxford 1990, hon fell Library Assoc 1994, hon fell Wadham Coll Oxford 1995, hon fell Univ of Wales Cardiff 1996; FRSL, FRTS, fell BAFTA 2010; *Awards* John Llewelyn Rhys Award and PEN Awards for Fiction, BAFTA Richard Dimbleby Award for Outstanding Contribution to TV 1987, RTS Gold Medal 1989, winner BAFTA Huw Wheldon Award for Best Arts Programme or Series (for An Interview with Dennis Potter) 1994, winner BAFTA for Debussy film (with Ken Rusell), Radio Broadcaster of the Year (for In Our Time and Routes of English) Broadcasting Press Guild Radio Awards 1999, VLV Award – Best Individual Contributor to Radio (for In Our Time and Routes of English) 2000, VLV Award – Best New Radio Series (for Routes of English) 2000; *Novels* For Want of a Nail (1965), The Second Inheritance (1966), Without a City Wall (1968), The Hired Man (1969), A Place in England (1970), The Nerve (1971), Josh Lawton (1972), The Silken Net (1974), A Christmas Child (1977), Autumn Manoeuvres (1978), Kingdom Come (1980), Love and Glory (1983), The Cumbrian Trilogy (1984, comprising The Hired Man, A Place in England and Kingdom Come), The Maid of Buttermere (1987), A Time to Dance (1991, BBC TV series 1992), Crystal Rooms (1992), Credo: An Epic Tale of Dark Age Britain (1996), The Soldier's Return (1999, W H Smith Literary Award 2000), A Son of War (2001), Crossing the Lines (2003), Remember Me (2008); *Non fiction* Land of the Lakes (1983), Laurence Olivier (1984), Rich (1988, biog of Richard Burton), Speak for England – oral history of England since 1900 (1976), Ingmar Bergman: The Seventh Seal (1996), On Giant's Shoulders (1998), The Adventure of English (2004), 12 Books That Changed the World (2006), The Book of Books: The Radical Impact of the King James Bible 1611–2011 (2011); *Musicals* Mardi Gras, Orion (TV, 1976), The Hired Man (W End 1985, Ivor Novello Award 1985); *Screenplays* Isadora, Jesus Christ Superstar, The Music Lovers, Clouds of Glory, Play Dirty; *Stage Play* King Lear in New York 1992; *Recreations* walking, books; *Clubs* Garrick; *Style*— The Rt Hon the Lord Bragg; ✉ 12 Hampstead Hill Gardens, London NW3 2PL; The South Bank Show, The London Television Centre, Upper Ground, London SE1 9LT (✆ 020 7157 3170, e-mail melvyn.bragg@itv.com)

BRAGGE, Master; Nicolas William; s of Norman Hugh Bragge (d 2001), and Nicolette Hilda, *née* Simms (d 1989); *b* 13 December 1948, Ashford, Kent; *Educ* S Kent Coll of Technol Ashford, Holborn Coll of Law London (LLB), Inns of Court Sch of Law; *m* 22 Dec 1973, Pamela Elizabeth Brett; 3 s (Thomas Hereward b 1976, Christopher Joseph b 1980, Alasdair Charles b 1986); *Career* visiting lectr in law Poly of Central London 1970–73; called to the Bar Inner Temple (Gray's Inn) 1972; in practice at Intellectual Property and Chancery Bars 1973–97; a dep master High Court (Chancery Div) 1993–97, master of the Sr Court (Chancery Div) 1997– (formerly the Supreme Court, acting chief master 2013–14); pt/t chm: Social Security Appeal Tbnls 1990–97, Disability Appeal Tbnls 1992–97; a dep social security cmmr 1996–2000; an ed Civil Procedure 2000–; author of various articles on legal and historical subjects; Freeman City of London 1970, Master Worshipful Co of Cutlers 2003–04, memb Court of Assts Guild of Freemen of the City of London 2005–14, memb Cncl City of London Branch Royal Soc of St George 2008–12; *Style*— Master Bragge; ✉ Rolls Building, Royal Courts of Justice, London EC4A 1NL

BRAHAM, Philip John Cofty; s of Ronald Marcus Braham, of Innellan, Argyll, and Dorothy May, *née* Cofty; *b* 8 April 1959; *Educ* Bearsden Acad, Duncan of Jordanstone Coll of Art Dundee (Br Cncl scholar, Dip Fine Art), Royal Acad of Fine Art The Hague (Greenshields Award, special commendation for postgrad studies); *m* 1, (m dis), Barbara, *née* Campbell; 1 da (Robyn b 13 March 1987); *m* 2, 2 Aug 2007, Katherine, *née* Ayres; 1 s (Ben b 3 April 2009), 1 da (Emma b 27 April 2013); *Career* artist; visiting artist UCLA 1981–82; subject of various exhibition catalogues; lectr in fine art Duncan of Jordanstone College of Art Univ of Dundee 2000– (course dir Art, Philosophy and Contemporary Practices); *Solo Exhibitions* Main Fine Art Glasgow 1984, The Scottish Gallery Edinburgh 1985, 1988, 2005 and 2014, Glasgow Art Centre 1987, The Raab Gallery London 1989, 1992, 1994 and 1995, Compass Gallery Glasgow 1993 and 1999, Galerie Christian Dam Copenhagen 1994, Galerie Christian Dam Oslo 1997, Boukamel Contemporary Art London 1997, 2000 and 2003, Talbot Rice Gallery Edinburgh 2000, Osborne Samuel Gallery London 2006, Royal Scottish Acad 2010, Union Gallery Edinburgh 2011, Raab Gallery Berlin 2011; *Group Exhibitions* incl: The Human Touch (Fischer Fine Art London) 1985, Artists at Work (Edinburgh Festival Event) 1986, The Vigorous Imagination (Nat Gallery of Modern Art Edinburgh) 1987, Metamorphosis (Raab Gallery London and Berlin) 1989, Landscape and Cityscape (Raab Gallery London) 1990, Cimal (Lucas Gallery Valencia) 1990, Galerie Bureaux et Magasins Ostend 1991, Scottish Art in the 20th Century (Royal W of England Acad Bristol) 1991, Scottish Painters (Flowers East London) 1993, Visions of Albion – Aspects of British Landscape I, II and III (Collyer-Bristow Gallery London) 1992, 1993 and 1994, The Power of the Image (Martin Gropius Bau Berlin) 1995, Aspects of Landscape (Scottish Gallery) 1996, Love and Poetry (Tobias Hirschmann Frankfurt) 1996, Aspects of Landscape (The Scottish Gallery) 1996, The Vigorous Imagination Ten Years on (The Scottish Gallery) 1997, International Kunst (Galerie Christian Dam Copenhagen) 1997, Artaid 98 (City Art Centre Edinburgh) 1998, Art from Scotland (Forbes Building NY) 1998, Art and Nature (Botanic Gardens Cagliari)

1998, Mountain (Wolverhampton Art Gallery and Museum) 1999, New European Artists (Sotheby's Amsterdam) 2001, Artaid (London) 2002, Demarco 40th Anniversary Exhibition (City Arts Centre Edinburgh) 2003, The Call of the Sea (Open Eye Gallery Edinburgh) 2005, Scottish Landscape (Park Gallery Falkirk) 2008, Inspired (Mitchell Library Glasgow) 2009, Six Artists at Albany Lane (Albany Lane Gallery Edinburgh) 2009, Public Image (Cooper Gallery Univ of Dundee) 2010, Me, Myself, I (Raab Gallerie Berlin) 2010, DIY: Photographers and Books (Cleveland Museum of Art Ohio) 2011, Surrealism vs The Sublime (Raab Gallery Berlin) 2011, Savage and Tender (Robert Burns Birthplace Museum Alloway) 2013; *Collections* incl: Scottish Arts Cncl, Scottish Nat Gallery of Modern Art, Aberdeen Art Gallery, BBC, The Contemporary Arts Soc, RCP (Edinburgh), Life Assoc of Scotland, Educnl Inst of Scotland, Fleming Holdings, Texaco Holdings, Rainbow GmbH, Dundee Art Gallery, The City Arts Centre Edinburgh, Pallant House Gallery, Scottish Exec Edinburgh, Royal Scottish Acad; *Awards* incl: EIS Award 1985, SAC Award 1989, RSA Guthrie Award 1995, Bursary for Research Friends of the Royal Scottish Acad 2003, Royal Scottish Acad Morton Award for Lens-based Work 2009; *Recreations* fitness, walking, music; *Clubs* Scottish Malt Whisky Soc; *Style*— Philip Braham, Esq; ✉ e-mail philbraham@virginmedia.com, website www.philipbraham.com

BRAIDWOOD, Keith Donald; s of Donald Braidwood, of The Gauldry, Fife, and Jane, *née* Griffiths; *b* 7 April 1966, St Andrews, Fife; *Educ* Madras Coll St Andrews; *m* 5 Oct 1991, Nicola Braidwood, *qv*, *née* Robinson; *Career* restaurateur; commis chef Peat Inn Fife 1983–85, commis chef Inverlochy Castle Fort William 1985–87, chef de parti Mallory Court Hotel Leamington Spa 1988, chef de parti Royal Oak Yattendon 1988–89, sous chef Murrayshall Hotel Perth 1990–92, co-head chef Shieldhill Hotel Biggar 1993, chef and prop (with Nicola Braidwood) Braidwoods Restaurant 1994– (AA Restaurant of the Year 2000, Taste of Scotland Restaurant of the Year 2000, Michelin Star 2000–); memb Master Chefs of GB (fell 2007); Scottish Chef of the Year 2000; The Flavour of Scotland (contrib), Scotland on a Plate (contrib); *Recreations* golf; *Clubs* West Kilbride Golf, Royal Troon Golf; *Style*— Keith Braidwood, Esq; ✉ Drumastle Mill, Dalry, North Ayrshire KA24 4LN (✆ 01294 833544, fax 01294 833533, e-mail keithbraidwood@btconnect.com); Braidwoods Restaurant, Dalry, North Ayrshire KA24 4LN

BRAIDWOOD, Nicola; da of Robert Nicholas Robinson, of Lancs, and Joyce, *née* Armstrong; *b* 13 February 1968, Bolton, Lancs; *Educ* Carnforth HS Lancs, Lancaster and Morecambe Coll; *m* 5 Oct 1991, Keith Donald Braidwood, *qv*; *Career* restaurateur; commis chef Royal Oak Yattendon Berks 1982–89, chef de partie Murrayshall Hotel Perth 1989–92, sous chef Shieldhill Hotel Biggar 1993, chef and prop (with Keith Braidwood) Braidwoods Restaurant 1994– (AA Guide Restaurant of the Year 2000, Taste of Scot Restaurant of the Year 2000, Michelin Star 2000–); Young Scottish Chef of the Year 1991; *Recreations* golf; *Clubs* West Kilbride Golf; *Style*— Mrs Nicola Braidwood; ✉ Drumastle Mill Cottage, Dalry, North Ayrshire KA24 4LN (✆ 01294 833544, fax 01294 833533); Braidwoods Restaurant, Dalry, North Ayrshire KA24 4LN

BRAILSFORD, Sir David John (Dave); kt (2013), CBE (2009, MBE 2005); *b* 29 February 1964, Derby; *Educ* Sheffield Business Sch (MBA); *Career* progs dir then performance dir Br Cycling 2003–, mangr Team Sky 2010–; BBC Sports Personality of the Year Coach Award 2008 and 2012; *Style*— Sir Dave Brailsford, CBE; ✉ Team Sky, National Cycling Centre, Stuart Street, Manchester M11 4DQ

BRAILSFORD, Hon Lord; (Sidney) Neil Brailsford; s of Sidney James Brailsford, of Edinburgh, and Jean Thelma More, *née* Leishman; *b* 15 August 1954; *Educ* Daniel Stewart's Coll Edinburgh, Univ of Stirling (BA), Univ of Edinburgh (LLB); *m* 7 Sept 1984, Elaine Nicola, yr da of late John Mausie Robbie; 3 s (Sidney Joshua Lawrence b 25 Jan 1995, Nathaniel Oliver Robbie b 29 July 1996, Samuel James Liberty b 11 July 1999); *Career* apprentice Messrs Biggart Baillie & Gifford, WS Edinburgh and Glasgow 1979–80, admitted to Faculty of Advocates 1981 (treas 2000–), standing jr counsel Dept of Agric and Fisheries in Scot 1987–92, called to the English Bar Lincoln's Inn 1990, QC (Scot) 1994, advocate depute 1999–2000, senator Coll of Justice 2006–; sec Advocates' Business Law Gp 1988–; chm Discipline Ctee ICAS 2003–; memb Ct Univ of Stirling 2001–06; *Recreations* swimming, travel, food and wine, history (particularly American history and politics); *Clubs* New (Edinburgh); *Style*— The Hon Lord Brailsford; ✉ 29 Warriston Crescent, Edinburgh EH3 (✆ 0131 556 8320); c/o Advocates' Library, Parliament House, Edinburgh EH1 1RF (✆ 0131 226 5071, fax 0131 225 3642, e-mail lord.brailsford@scotcourts.gov.uk); 135 Kidder Hill Road, Grafton, Vermont 05146, USA (✆ 00 1 802 843 2120, fax 00 1 802 843 2118)

BRAIN, Rt Rev Terence John; s of Reginald John Brain, of Coventry, Warks, and Mary, *née* Cooney; *b* 19 December 1938; *Educ* King Henry VIII GS Coventry, Cotton Coll, Oscott Coll Birmingham; *Career* ordained RC priest (Birmingham) 1964; asst priest St Gregory's Longton Stoke-on-Trent 1964–65, on staff Cotton Coll 1965–69, hosp chaplain Birmingham 1969–71, private sec to Archbishop of Birmingham 1971–82; parish priest: Bentilee Stoke-on-Trent 1982–88 (memb Staffordshire LEA Ctee 1982–91), St Austin's Stafford 1988–91; aux bishop of Birmingham and titular bishop of Amudarsa 1991–97, bishop of Salford 1997–2014, ret; bishop for prisons 1994–2013; chm Bishop's Social Welfare Ctee 1992–2003; episcopal advsr: Union of Catholic Mothers 1993–2013, Nat Cncl of Lay Assocs 1993–2005; *Recreations* watercolour painting, crossword puzzles; *Style*— The Rt Rev Terence Brain; ✉ 106 Crow Hill South, Alkrington, Manchester M24 1JU

BRAITHWAITE, Althea; da of Air Vice-Marshal Francis Joseph St George Braithwaite (d 1956), and Rosemary, *née* Harris (Lady Earle (d 1978)); *b* 20 June 1940; *Educ* Felixstowe Coll; *m* 1, 1966 (m dis 1974), Malcolm Gordon Graham-Cameron (d 2010); 1 s (Duncan Charles b 1968); *m* 2, 1979, Edward James Parker; *Career* artist, writer and illustrator of about 230 books for children 1968–; specialises in information books covering numerous topics; fndr and managing ed Dinosaur Publications Ltd (sold to Collins 1984); glass artist; solo exhbn Painted Glass 2002 and 2011, Kiln Fused Glass 2005, 2007, 2009, 2011 and 2014, now specialising in fused glass exhibited from own studio and in galleries in London, Lincoln, Stamford and East Anglia; *Style*— Ms Althea Braithwaite; ✉ The Studio at Beechcroft House, Over, Cambridge CB24 5NE (e-mail althea@altheabraithwaite.net, website www.altheabraithwaite.net)

BRAITHWAITE, Andrew; s of Norman Braithwaite (d 2005), and Dorina Cox, *née* Soleri; *b* 23 October 1959, Bromley, Kent; *Educ* St Olave's GS, Univ of Southampton (LLB), Nottingham Trent Univ; *m* July 2006, Nicola Webb; *Career* admitted slr 1985; articled clerk Ingledew Brown Bennison & Garrett 1983, slr Stein, Swede, Jay & Bibring (now Finers) 1985 (ptnr 1986), ptnr Wansbroughs (now Beachcrofts) 1989 (head of company commercial 1993), ptnr and head of commercial Osborne Clarke 1997–; chair Bristol Interactive Cluster 2000–04; memb Law Soc 1985, affiliate Br Franchise Assoc 1995; *Recreations* travelling, walking, good food (cooking and eating); *Style*— Andrew Braithwaite, Esq; ✉ Osborne Clarke, 2 Temple Back, Temple Quay, Bristol BS1 6EG (✆ 0117 917 4178, fax 0117 917 4179)

BRAITHWAITE, HE Julian; *Career* diplomat; FCO: joined 1994, desk offr Bosnia and NATO issues 1994–95, special advsr to the UN Special Rep of the Sec Gen Zagreb 1995, first sec Political Belgrade 1996–98; press offr No 10 Downing Street 1998–2000, special advsr to the Supreme Allied Commander NATO Military HQ 1999, speech writer No 10 Downing St 2000–02, dir of communications Office of the High Rep Bosnia 2002–04, cnsllr for global issues Washington 2004–08, dir Consular Servs FCO 2008–11, head Libya Communications Team No 10 Downing St 2011, permanent rep Political and

Security Ctee EU UKREP Brussels 2011–15, ambass and permanent rep UK Mission Geneva 2015–; *Style*— HE Mr Julian Braithwaite

BRAITHWAITE, Michael; *b* 10 December 1937; *Educ* City Univ (BSc); *m* 4 Feb 1967, (Pamela) Margaret; 1 da (Sally b 4 Oct 1969), 1 s (James b 7 Jan 1971); *Career* UKAEA 1958–69; ptnr: Deloitte (formerly Touche Ross) 1969–97, Braithwaite Associates 1997–2012; Liveryman Worshipful Co of Info Technologists 1988; CEng, MBCS, FInstMC; *Recreations* skiing, scuba diving, gardening; *Style*— Michael Braithwaite, Esq; ✉ (*E-mail* michael-braithwaite@msn.com)

BRAITHWAITE, William Thomas Scatchard (Bill); QC (1992); s of John Vernon Braithwaite (d 1975), and Nancy Phyllis Scatchard (d 1995); *b* 20 January 1948; *Educ* Gordonstoun, Univ of Liverpool (LLB); *m* Sheila, *née* Young; 1 da (Dawn Plint), 1 s (Ross Thomas Vernon); *Career* called to the Bar Gray's Inn 1970, pupil to His Hon Judge Arthur, currently in personal injury litigation practice; memb: Euro Brain Injury Soc, Spinal Injuries Assoc, Headway, Assoc of Personal Injury Lawyers; conslt ed The Quantum of Damages 1995–2004, jt ed Medical Aspects of Personal Injury Litigation; author of articles and lectures on brain and spine litigation in England, Europe and America; *Books* Brain and Spine Injuries – The Fight for Justice; *Recreations* cars and wine; *Style*— Bill Braithwaite, QC; ✉ Exchange Chambers, Pearl Assurance House, Derby Square, Liverpool L2 9XX (✆ 0151 236 7747, fax 0151 236 3433, e-mail braithwaiteqc@exchangechambers.co.uk)

BRAKA, Ivor Isaac; s of Joseph Braka, and Margaret Elizabeth, *née* Dodds; *b* 19 December 1954; *Educ* Oundle, Pembroke Coll Oxford (BA); *m* 1991 (m dis 1999), Camilla Mary, da of Duncan Henry Davidson; 1 s (Joseph Duncan b 10 Nov 1996); *Career* art dealer; *Style*— Ivor Braka, Esq; ✉ 63 Cadogan Square, London SW1X 0DY (✆ 020 7235 0266)

BRAKE, Rt Hon Thomas (Tom); PC (2011), MP; s of Mike and Judy Brake; *b* 6 May 1962; *Educ* Lycée International Paris, Imperial Coll London (BSc); *m* Candida; 1 da, 1 s; *Career* trainee computer programmer Hoskyns (now Cap Gemini) rising to princ conslt 1983–97, MP (Lib Dem) Carshalton and Wallington 1997– (contested seat 1992); environment spokesman 1997–2001; Lib Dem shadow tport min 2001–03, Lib Dem shadow int devpt sec of state 2003–05, Lib Dem shadow transport sec of state 2005–06, Lib Dem shadow min for Dept of Communities and Local Govt 2006–, Lib Dem London spokesman 2007–, co-chair Lib Dem Home Affrs, Justice and Equalities 2010–12, dep ldr House of Commons 2013–15, Lib Dem chief whip 2015–, Lib Dem foreign affrs spokesman 2015–; memb: Tport Select Ctee 2002–03, Accommodation and Works Ctee, Franco-Br Parly Relations Gp; cncllr (Lib Dem): London Borough of Hackney (sometime jt lead memb on environment) 1988–90, Sutton (sometime memb Policy and Resources Ctee and vice-chm Policy Sub-Ctee) 1994–98; *Style*— The Rt Hon Tom Brake, MP; ✉ Constituency Office, Kennedy House, 5 Nightingale Road, Carshalton, Surrey SM5 2DN (✆ 020 8255 8155); House of Commons, London SW1A 0AA (✆ 020 7219 0924, e-mail info@tombrake.co.uk, website www.tombrake.co.uk)

BRAKEWELL, Jeanette; da of James Joseph Brakewell, of Brindle, Lancs, and Clara May, *née* Scambler; *b* 4 February 1974; *Educ* St Michael's C of E HS Chorley; *Career* three day eventer; achievements (all on Over to You) incl: team Gold medal European Championships 1999, 2001, 2003 and 2005, team Silver medal Olympic Games Sydney 2000, team Bronze medal and individual Silver medal World Equestrian Games 2002, team Silver medal Olympic Games Athens 2004; Horse Trials Support Gp Scholarship 1997, Raymond Brooks-Ward Meml Trophy 1997, British Equestrian Fedn Medal of Honour 2003; *Recreations* skiing, swimming; *Style*— Miss Jeanette Brakewell

BRAMALL, Field Marshal Baron (Life Peer UK 1987), of Bushfield in the County of Hampshire; Edwin Noel Westby; KG (1990), GCB (1979, KCB 1974), OBE (1965), MC (1945) JP (1986); yr s of Maj Edmund Haselden Bramall, RA (d 1964), and Katharine Bridget, *née* Westby (d 1985); bro of Sir Ashley Bramall (d 1999); *b* 18 December 1923; *Educ* Eton; *m* 1949, Dorothy Avril Wentworth, only da of Brig-Gen Henry Albemarle Vernon, DSO, JP (ggggs of Henry Vernon by his w Lady Henrietta Wentworth, yst da of 1 Earl of Strafford, Henry Vernon being himself 2 cous of 1 Baron Vernon); 1 s, 1 da; *Career* 2 Lt KRRC 1943, served NW Europe WWII, Japan 1946–47, Middle East 1953–58, Instr Army Staff Coll 1958–61, staff offr to Lord Mountbatten for re-organising MOD 1963–64, served Malaysia during Indonesian confrontation 1965–66 (CO 2 Greenjackets KRRC), cmd 5 Airportable Bde 1967–69, IDC 1970, GOC 1 Div BAOR 1971–73, Lt-Gen 1973, Cdr Br Forces Hong Kong 1973–76, Gen 1976, Col Cmdt 3 Bn Roy Green Jackets 1973–84, Col 2 Gurkhas 1976–86, C-in-C UKLF 1976–78, Vice-Chief Defence Staff (Personnel and Logistics) 1978–79, Chief General Staff 1979–82, ADC Gen to HM The Queen 1979–82, Field Marshal 1982, Chief of the Defence Staff 1982–85; pres Gurkha Bde Assoc 1987–, pres (Army) Not Forgotten Assoc; tstee Imperial War Museum 1983–98 (chm 1989–98); HM Lord-Lt Greater London 1986–98; pres: MCC 1988–89 (hon life vice-pres 1989), Greater London Playing Fields Assoc 1990–, London Age Concern; OStJ; *Books* The Chiefs: The Story of the UK Chiefs of Staff (co-author); *Clubs* MCC, Travellers' (chm 1998–2003), Pratt's; *Style*— Field Marshal the Lord Bramall, KG, GCB, OBE, MC; ✉ House of Lords, London SW1A 0PW

BRAMBLE, Roger John Lawrence; DL (Greater London 1986); s of Courtenay Parker Bramble, CIE (d 1987), of Childer Thornton, Cheshire, and Margaret Louise Bramble, MBE (d 1989), da of Sir Henry Lawrence, KCSI; *b* 3 April 1932, Bombay; *Educ* Eton, King's Coll Cambridge (MA); *Career* cmmnd Coldstream Gds 1951; chm: Lloyd's Brokers, BDB Ltd, Mithras Underwriting Ltd 2011; memb Lloyd's 1960–2003; dir ENO 1986–98, dir Eng Nat Ballet 1986–2002 (dep chm 1990–99), memb Cncl Nat Opera Studio 2000–, chm Cncl for Dance Educn and Trg 2000–, chm Young Musicians Symphony Orch 2001–; chm Benesh Inst 1986–97; tstee: Serpentine Gallery 1990–, Albert Meml 1996–2000, Paddington Devpt Tst 1998; Parly candidate (Cons) Shoreditch and Finsbury 1964, cncllr City of Westminster 1968–98, Lord Mayor of Westminster 1985–86; High Sheriff of Gtr London 1999, chm Assoc of High Sheriffs 2001–04, chm DebtCred (High Sheriffs' Financial Educn Charity) 2001–; FRSA 1989; Order of the Aztec Eagle Mexico 1985, Order of Merit Qatar 1985, Order of Southern Cross Brazil 1993, Order of the Stella Italiana 2003; *Recreations* music, farming, languages; *Clubs* Turf, Mark's; *Style*— Roger Bramble, Esq, DL; ✉ 2 Sutherland Street, London SW1V 4LB (✆ and fax 020 7828 2439); Sutton Hosey Manor, Long Sutton, Langport, Somerset TA10 9NA

BRAMLEY, Andrew; s of Peter Bramley (d 1989), of Ridgeway, Derbys, and Tessa Bramley, *qv*, *née* Hardwick; *b* 18 January 1966; *Educ* Henry Fanshawe Sch Derbys, Warwick Business Sch (PhD), Bradford Mgmnt Sch (MBA), Harvard Business Sch, Ecole Superieure de Commerce Toulouse; *m* 27 Sept 1998, Carole Rena, da of Colin Mills, of Derby; *Career* mangr family business until 1985, converted Old Vicarage (family home) into restaurant 1985–87, owner and mangr Old Vicarage 1987– (Good Food Guide Newcomer of Year 1988, Derbyshire Restaurant of the Year 1988–90, Egon Ronay star 1988–94 (2 stars 1995–99), Clover Leaf in Ackerman Guide 1990–95, Northern Restaurant of the Year award Chef Magazine 1991, Egon Ronay Dessert of the Year 1998, Michelin star 1999); dir Vicarage Wine Cellars 2002; featured in major Food and Wine Guides; TV and radio appearances; memb: Restaurant Assoc of GB, Sheffield C of C; *Books* Women Chefs of Great Britain (with Tessa Bramley, 1990); *Recreations* cooking, writing, painting; *Style*— Andrew Bramley, Esq; ✉ The Old Vicarage, Ridgeway Moor, Ridgeway, Derbyshire S12 3XW (✆ 0114 247 5814, fax 0114 247 7079, e-mail andrew@theoldvicarage.co.uk)

BRAMLEY, Robin Thomas Todhunter; s of E A Bramley (d 1991), and Mary, *née* Todhunter (d 2001); *b* 16 June 1950; *Educ* Ampleforth, Univ of Exeter (LLB); *m* 20 Oct 1973, Patricia Anne, da of Maj E S L Mason (d 1996), of Bungay, Suffolk; 1 da (Henrietta b 1979), 1 s (George b 1982); *Career* chartered surveyor and mediator; landowner and farmer Gillingham Estate, sr ptnr Francis Hornor & Son chartered surveyors Norwich 1992–97 (ptnr 1976–92), ptnr Francis Hornor Brown & Co 1997–2000, ptnr Brown & Co 2000–; dir Consensus Mediation Ltd 2002–; CEDR accredited mediator 1998; memb of Lord Chllr's Panel of Arbitrators 1992; memb: The Broads Authy 1989–99, Norfolk Police Authy 1994–2001; chm: Broads Soc 1986–87, Waveney Harriers 1995–; JP; FRICS 1978, QDR 1996, MCIArb 1999; *Recreations* shooting, riding, fishing, history, conservation; *Clubs* Norfolk, MCC; *Style*— R T T Bramley, Esq; ✉ Hill Farm, Gillingham, Norfolk NR34 0EE (✆ 01502 677325, fax 01502 679050, e-mail rttbramley@hfgn.co.uk)

BRANAGH, Sir Kenneth Charles; kt (2012); s of William Branagh, and Frances Branagh; *b* 10 December 1960, Belfast, NI; *Educ* Meadway Comp Sch Reading, RADA; *Career* actor and dir; assoc memb RADA; Gielgud Golden Quill 2000 (yst ever winner), Variety Award Br Ind Film Awards 2011; *Theatre* with RSC 1984–85 (plays incl: Henry V (yst Henry V in RSC history), Hamlet, Love's Labour's Lost), co-fndr (with David Parfitt, *qv*) Renaissance Theatre Co (RTC) 1987 (plays incl: Public Enemy (also writer) 1987, Hamlet 1988, Look Back In Anger 1989, King Lear (also dir) 1990, A Midsummer Night's Dream (also dir) 1990, Uncle Vanya (dir) 1991, Coriolanus 1992); other credits incl: Another Country (Queen's Theatre) London 1982 (SWET Award and Most Promising Newcomer Plays and Players Award), Hamlet (RSC) 1992–93, The Play What I Wrote (dir, West End) 2001, Richard III (Crucible Theatre) 2002, Edmond (Nat Theatre) 2003, Ducktastic (dir, Albery Theatre) 2005, The Painkiller (Belfast Lyric Theatre) 2011, Macbeth (Manchester Int Festival) 2013, The Winter's Tale, Harlequinade, The Painkiller, Romeo and Juliet (dir) and The Entertainer (all Garrick Theatre) 2015–16; *Television* incl: The Billy Plays 1981–86, Boy in the Bush 1984, Fortunes of War 1987, Look Back in Anger 1989, Conspiracy 2001, Shackleton 2002, Warm Springs 2005, Wallander 2008–12 (Best Actor Broadcasting Press Guild Awards 2009, Best Actor BAFTA Television Awards 2010); *Film* incl: Coming Through 1985, A Month in the Country 1987, Henry V (also dir and author screenplay) 1989, Dead Again (also dir) 1991, Peter's Friends (also dir and prodr) 1992, Much Ado About Nothing (also dir, prodr and author screenplay) 1993, Frankenstein (also dir and prodr) 1994, Othello 1995, Hamlet (also dir and author screenplay) 1996, The Theory of Flight 1998, The Dance of Shiva 1998, Celebrity 1999, Wild Wild West 1999, Love's Labour's Lost (also dir, prodr and author screenplay) 2000, Rabbit-Proof Fence 2002, Harry Potter and the Chamber of Secrets 2002, Five Children and It 2004, Sleuth 2007 (also prodr and dir), Valkyrie 2008, The Boat That Rocked 2009, My Week With Marilyn 2011, Jack Ryan 2013 (also dir), Cinderella 2014 (also dir); as dir and author screenplay: In the Bleak Midwinter 1995, Listening 2003, The Magic Flute 2006, As You Like It (also prodr); dir Thor 2011; *Publications* Public Enemy (1988), Beginning (1989); *Recreations* reading, playing the guitar; *Style*— Sir Kenneth Branagh; ✉ The Kenneth Branagh Company, c/o Pinewood Studios, Pinewood Road, Iver Heath, Buckinghamshire SL0 0NH

BRANCH, Prof Michael Arthur; CMG (2000); s of Arthur Frederick Branch (d 1986), and Mahala, *née* Parker; *b* 24 March 1940; *Educ* Shene London, SSEES Univ of London (BA, PhD), Univ of Helsinki; *m* 11 Aug 1963, (Ritva-Riitta) Hannele, da of Erkki Lauri Kari (d 1982), of Heinola, Finland; 3 da (Jane, Jean, Ann); *Career* Univ of London: lectr Finno-Ugrian Studies 1971–73 (asst lectr 1967–71), dir Sch of Slavonic and E Euro Studies 1980–2001, prof of Finnish 1986–2001 (lectr 1973–77, reader 1977–86), fell UCL 2001–, Leverhulme emeritus fell 2004–06; Hon DPhil Univ of Oulu Finland 1983; Commander of the Finnish Lion Finland 1980, Commander of the Order of Merit Poland 1993, St Mary's Land Cross of Estonia 2000, Grand Duke Gedeminas Cross Lithuania 2002; *Books* A J Sjögren: Travels in the North (1973), Finnish Folk Poetry – Epic (jtly, 1977), Student's Glossary of Finnish (jtly, 1981), Kalevala – translated by W F Kirby (ed, 1985), Edith Södergran (jt ed, 1992), The Great Bear (jtly, 1993), Uses of Tradition (jt ed, 1994), Finland and Poland in the Russian Empire (jt ed, 1995), The Writing of National History and Identity (ed, 1999), Defining Self: Essays on emergent identities in Russia Seventeenth to Nineteenth Centuries; *Recreations* walking; *Style*— Prof Michael Branch, CMG; ✉ 33 St Donatt's Road, New Cross, London SE14 6NU

BRAND, Charles David William; s of Michael Brand (d 2012), and Laura, *née* Smith (d 1999); *b* 1 July 1954, London; *Educ* Bryanston, Univ of Reading (BA); *m* 20 Jan 1992, Virginia, da of Baron Bonham-Carter (Life Peer, d 1994); 1 s (Henry), 1 da (Violet); *Career* researcher and prodr LWT 1977–87 (progs incl: Sunday Sunday, James Bond – The First 21 Years, An Audience with Mel Brooks, The World According to Smith and Jones), freelance prodr Free Nelson Mandela Concert 1987, prodr Tiger Television 1988–93 (progs incl: The Movie Life of George, Clive James Meets Jane Fonda, The Driven Man, Life of Python, Funny Business); Tiger Aspect Prodns: md and memb Bd 1993– (exec prodr: Kid in the Corner, Births Marriages and Deaths, Playing the Field, Country House, Streetmate), dir Specialist Factual and US dir Documentary & Factual Programming 2002–12 (progs incl: Human Mutants, Virtual History, Pinochet in Suburbia, Boris Johnson and the Dream of Rome, The Monastery, The Islamic Retreat); exec prodr: Billy Elliott 2000, Lib Dem Party political broadcasts; currently freelance film prodr; chair Int Edinburgh Television Festival 2002, memb Exec Ctee MediaGuardian Edinburgh Int Television Festival (MGEITF) 2002–10, chair Channel of the Year Awards; tstee Centre Forum 2010–; BAFTA 1990; FRTS 2004 (memb 1991); *Publications* Broadcasting by Consent, The BBC, PSB and Charter Renewal in 2017 (ed, 2015); *Recreations* cinema, reading, travel, walking; *Clubs* Groucho; *Style*— Charles Brand, Esq; ✉ 1 Kingswood Avenue, London NW6 6LA (mobile 07785 770509, e-mail charles@brandbc.co.uk)

BRAND, Harriett; da of Sam Brand (d 1969), and Ann Weisberg Brand; *b* Brooklyn, NY; *Educ* Brooklyn Coll, City Univ of NY (BA), INSEAD (MBA); *Career* early career in int marketing and promotion EMI Music; sr vice-pres Music MTV Networks Europe & Int (joined 1993), sr vice-pres Business Devpt Universal Music; UK Music Industry Woman of the Year 2003; supporter Thrangu Tst (involved with Tibetan Buddhist community in Nepal, Tibet and India), patron Bottletop.org, rainmaker Rainmaker Fndn; FRGS, FRSA; *Style*— Ms Harriett Brand; ✉ mobile 07785 353879, e-mail h@harriettbrand.com

BRAND, Jo; *b* 23 July 1957, Clapham, London; *m* ; 2 c; *Career* psychiatric nurse until 1988, stand-up comedienne 1988–; Best Female TV Comic Br Comedy Award 2011 and 2012; *Television* incl: Through the Cakehole 1993, Jo Brand Goes Back to Bedlam 1994, All the Way to Worcester 1996, A Big Slice of Jo Brand 1996, Jo Brand Burns Rubber 1997, Commercial Breakdown 1999, Jo Brand's Hot Potatoes 2002, Getting On 2009 (also co-writer; Best Writer – Comedy RTS Award 2011, Best Female Performance in a Comedy Prog BAFTA 2011), host Have I Got News For You 2009, 2010 and 2011; appearances incl: Question Time 2000, What Not to Wear on the Red Carpet 2003, Comic Relief does Fame Academy 2003, Star Spell 2004, Parkinson 2006, QI; *Film* incl: Human Traffic, Horrid Henry 2011; *Radio* regular panellist on Windbags (BBC Radio 1) 1993–94; *Books* A Load of Old Balls (1995), A Load of Old Ball Crunchers (1997), Sorting Out Billy (2004), It's Different for Girls (2005), The More You Ignore Me (2007), Look Back In Hunger (autobiography part 1, 2009), Can't Stand Up For Sitting Down (autobiography part 2, 2010); *Style*— Ms Jo Brand; ✉ c/o The Richard Stone Partnership, Suite 3, De Walden Court, 85 New Cavendish Street, London W1W 6XD (✆ 020 7497 0849, fax 020 7497 0869)

BRAND, Prof Paul Anthony; s of Thomas Joseph Brand (d 1994), and Marjorie Jean, *née* Smith (d 1999); *b* 25 December 1946, Whitechapel, London; *Educ* Hampton GS, Magdalen

Coll Oxford (MA, DPhil); *m* 1970, Vanessa Carolyn Alexandra, da of J L Rodrigues (d 2009); *Career* asst keeper Public Record Office London 1970–76, lectr in law Univ Coll Dublin 1976–83, research fell Inst of Historical Research London 1993–99; visiting prof Columbia Univ Law Sch 1995 and 2003, sr research fell All Souls Coll Oxford 1999–2014 (fell 1997–99, visiting fell 1995, academic sec 2004–09, emeritus fell 2014–); Donald W Sutherland prize American Soc for Legal History 1988; treas Pipe Roll Soc, memb Cncl and vice-pres (UK) Selden Soc; memb American Law Inst 2000, hon bencher Middle Temple 2014; Gold medal Irish Legal History Soc 2006; FRHistS 1980, FBA 1998; *Books* The Origins of the English Legal Profession (1992), The Making of the Common Law (1992), The Earliest English Law Reports vols I and II (1996), vol III (2005) and vol IV (2007), Kings, Barons and Justices: The Making and Enforcement of Thirteenth Century Legislation (2003), Plea Rolls of the Exchequer of the Jews vol VI (2006); *Recreations* theatre, looking at buildings; *Style*— Prof Paul Brand, FBA; ✉ 155 Kennington Road, London SE11 6SF (☎ 020 7582 4051); The Old Rectory, Church Street, Fenny Compton, Southam CV47 2YE (☎ 01295 770457); All Souls College, Oxford OX1 4AL (e-mail paul.brand@all-souls.oxford.ac.uk)

BRANDON, (David) Stephen; QC (1996); s of James Osbaldeston Brandon (d 1992), and Dorothy, *née* Wright; *b* 18 December 1950; *Educ* Univ of Nottingham (BA), Keele Univ (LLM); *m* 1987, Helen Beatrice, da of Frank Lee; 1 da (Arabella Beatrice May b 1989); *Career* lectr in law Keele Univ 1975–85, called to the Bar Gray's Inn 1978, in practice at Revenue Bar 1981; *Books* Taxation of Migrant and Non-Resident Companies (1989), Taxation of Non-UK Resident Companies and their Shareholders (2002); *Recreations* art (especially collecting early woodcuts), opera, nurturing woodlands; *Style*— Stephen Brandon, Esq, QC; ✉ Clopton Manor, Clopton, Northamptonshire; 24 Old Buildings, 1st Floor, Tax Chambers, Lincoln's Inn, London WC2A 3UU (☎ 020 7242 2744, fax 020 7831 8095)

BRANDRETH, Gyles Daubeney; s of Charles Daubeney Brandreth (d 1982), and Alice, *née* Addison (d 2010); *b* 8 March 1948; *Educ* Bedales, New Coll Oxford (MA); *m* 8 June 1973, Michele, da of Alec Brown; 1 s (Benet Xan b 1975), 2 da (Saethryd Charity b 1976, Aphra Kendal Alice b 1978); *Career* author, broadcaster, producer and publisher; MP (Cons) City of Chester 1992–97; PPS: to Fin Sec to the Treasy 1993–94, to Sec of State for Nat Heritage 1994–95, to Sec of State for Health 1995, govt whip 1995–96, a Lord Cmmr of HM's Treasy (govt whip) 1996–97; journalist, TV and radio presenter 1969–, ed-at-large Sunday Telegraph Review; writer/performer Zipp! The Musical (Edinburgh Festival Most Popular Show Award 2002, Duchess Theatre London 2003, UK tour 2004), Malvolio in Twelfth Night The Musical 2005, one-man show (Edinburgh) 2010 and (UK tour) 2011, Lady Bracknell in The Importance of Being Earnest 2012, Looking for Happiness (Edinburgh and UK tour) 2013, Word Power! (Edinburgh and UK tour) 2015–16; fndr: Nat Teddy Bear Museum, Nat Scrabble Championships; vice-pres National Playing Fields Assoc 1993– (appeals chm 1984–88, chm 1989–93); co-curator exhbn of children's writers Nat Portrait Gallery 2002; *Books* various incl: Created in Captivity (1972), Under the Jumper (autobiography, 1993), Who is Nick Saint? (novel, 1996), Venice Midnight (novel, 1998), Breaking the Code: Westminster Diaries 1990–97 (1999), John Gielgud: An Actor's Life (2000), Brief Encounters: Meetings with Remarkable People (2001), Philip and Elizabeth: Portrait of a Marriage (2004), Charles and Camilla: Portrait of a Love Affair (2005), Oscar Wilde and the Candlelight Murders (novel, 2007), Oscar Wilde and the Ring of Death (novel, 2008), Oscar Wilde and the Dead Man's Smile (novel, 2009), Something Sensational to Read on the Train (diaries, 2009), Oscar Wilde and the Nest of Vipers (novel, 2010), Oscar Wilde and the Vatican Murders (novel, 2011), Oscar Wilde and the Murders at Reading Gaol (novel, 2012), Oxford Dictionary of Humorous Quotations (ed, 2013), The Seven Secrets of Happiness (2013), The Lost Art of Having Fun (with Saethryd Brandreth, 2013), Novelty Knits (with Saethryd Brandeth, 2014), Word Play 2015; *Recreations* sometime holder of world record for longest-ever after-dinner speech (12 1/2 hours); *Style*— Gyles Brandreth, Esq; ✉ e-mail contact@gylesbrandreth.net, website www.gylesbrandreth.net

BRANNAN, Tom; s of James Brannan (d 2010), and Rebecca Brannan (d 1994); *b* 21 August 1951; *Educ* St Patrick's Secdy Sch Coatbridge, Univ of Strathclyde (BA); *m* 1, (m dis); 2 da (Kirsty b 14 Dec 1976, Sarah b 11 Aug 1979); m 2, 23 Oct 1999 (re-married), Jacqueline Blenkinsop; *Career* export exec Black & Decker 1971–75, sales dir Hestair Group 1975–81, sales and mktg dir Shelvoke & Drewry 1981–82, mktg dir Lancer Boss 1982–84, client servs dir Primary Contact Advertising (Ogilvy Group) 1984–95; currently dir YesCity Ltd; mktg advsr and speaker for various charities, business gps and other bodies; nat chm CIM 1996; FCIM 1990 (MCIM 1983), FRSA 1996, Chartered Marketer 1998; *Books* The Effective Advertiser (1993), A Practical Guide to Integrated Marketing Communications (1995, 2 edn 1998), Gower Handbook of Marketing (contrib), Profit from Strategic Marketing (contrib), Aye-Aye to Zorilla, an alphabet of rare and curious creatures (2013); *Recreations* fly fishing, reading, antiquities, antiques; *Clubs* Flyfishers; *Style*— Tom Brannan, Esq; ✉ Staddlestones, Station Road, Great Wishford, Wiltshire SP2 0PA (e-mail tom.brannan@yescity.biz)

BRANSON, Nigel Anthony Chimmo; s of Anthony Hugh Chimmo (Tony) Branson (d 1989), and Isobel Mary Mearns (d 2000); *b* 1 July 1942; *Educ* Tonbridge; *m* 10 July 1971, Nancy Jane, da of George Sexton Mooney III (d 1980), of Boston, MA; 1 da (Jessica b 1973), 1 s (Douglas b 1974); *Career* Sedgwick Group plc: joined London 1960, Johannesburg 1964–65, Lusaka 1966–68, Edinburgh 1973–79, jt md Sedgwick UK Risk Services Ltd 1996–97, Lark Insurance Broking Group 1997–2000; underwriter Lloyd's 1983–97; vice-chm Haberdashers' Aske's Hatcham City Tech Coll 1995–2002 (govr 1991–2002, responsible offr 1996–2000); chm: Audit Ctee Grant Maintained Schs Fndn 1997–98 (also tstee), Red Cross City Christmas Fayre 1999, SW Kent PCT 2004–06; vice-chm Kent and Medway Strategic HA 2002–04, dir Cathedral Enterprises Ltd 2001–04; tstee: REMAP 1997–2004, English Schs Orch 1998–, League of Mercy 1999–, Royal Humane Soc 2003–05, Reeve Fndn 2004–06, Maritime Heritage Fndn 2011–; govr Bow Boys' Sch 2002–04; accredited appropriate adult and ind visitor Young Lives Fndn 2015–; Sheriff City of London 2000; memb Ct of Common Cncl: Bassishaw Ward 1996–99, Langbourn Ward 2002–06; Freeman: City of London 1969, Worshipful Co of Haberdashers 1970 (memb Ct of Assts 1990, Master 2006–07), Worshipful Co of Broderers 2000 (memb Ct of Assts 2004–08, Warden 2008); JP 1996–2012; *Recreations* Lake District, walking, reading, trout fishing, golf; *Clubs* Wildernesse, Pickwick, Langbourn Ward (chm 2000); *Style*— Nigel Branson, Esq; ✉ Thornhill, Oak Lane, Sevenoaks, Kent TN13 1UF (mobile 07850 332680)

BRANSON, Sir Richard Charles Nicholas; kt (2000); s of Edward James Branson, and Evette Huntley, *née* Flindt; bro of Vanessa Branson, *qv*; *b* 18 July 1950; *Educ* Stowe; *m* 1, 1969 (m dis), Kristen Tomassi; m 2, 20 Dec 1989, Joan Sarah Drummond, da of John Templeman (d 1988), of Glasgow, Scotland; 1 s (Sam Edward Charles b 12 Aug 1985), 1 da (Holly Katy b 20 Nov 1981); *Career* ed Student magazine 1968–69; fndr: Student Advsy Centre (now Help) 1970, Virgin Mail-Order Co 1969, Virgin Retail 1970, Virgin Records 1973, Virgin Atlantic Airways 1984, Voyager Group Ltd 1986; chm and chief exec: Virgin Management, Virgin Retail Group, Virgin Communications, Virgin Holdings, Virgin Radio 1993–97, Virgin Direct 1995–, V2 Music 1996–, Virgin Rail 1996–; life pres Virgin Music 1992–; tstee: Healthcare Fndn (fndr 1987), Charity Projects; patron: Nat Holiday Fund, Paul O'Gorman Fndn, Trevor Jones Tst, London Sch for Performing Arts & Technol; pres Br Disabled Water Ski Assoc, hon vice-pres Operation Raleigh, hon memb Ctee The Friends of the Earth; capt Atlantic Challenger II, winner Blue Riband for fastest crossing of the Atlantic by boat 1986, world record crossings of Atlantic and Pacific by hot air balloon with Per Lindstrand 1987 and 1991; Excellent Hon Prof of Economics Miyazaki Sangyo Keiei Univ Japan, Key to the City of NY, hon Japanese citizen (City of Miyakanojo); Hon DTech Loughborough 1993; *Books* Losing my Virginity: The Autobiography (1998); *Recreations* tennis, skiing, swimming, ballooning; *Clubs* Roof Garden (proprietor), British Balloon and Airship; *Style*— Sir Richard Branson; ✉ The Battleship Building, 179 Harrow Road, London W2 6NB

BRANSON, Vanessa Gay; da of Edward James Branson, of Shamley Green, Surrey, and Evette Huntley, *née* Flindt; sis of Sir Richard Branson, *qv*; *b* 3 June 1959; *Educ* Box Hill Sch, New Acad of Art Studies; *m* 1983 (m dis), Robert Devereux, s of Humphrey Devereux; 3 s (Noah Edward b 1987, Louis-Robert de Lacey b 1991, Ivo Edmund Bouchier b 9 March 1995), 1 da (Florence b 1989); *Career* with: Posterbrokers 1981–83, Picturebrokers 1983–86; prop: Vanessa Devereux Gallery 1986–91, Riad el Fenn Marrakech, Eilean Shona, Argyll; fndr: Portobello Contemporary Art Festival, The Marrakech Biennale; curator Wonderful Fund Collection; *Recreations* theatre, cinema, sport, food; *Style*— Vanessa Branson; ✉ 55 St James's Gardens, London W11 4RA (☎ 020 7229 6485, fax 020 7727 7582, websites www.el-fenn.com, www.eileanshona.com and www.marrakechbiennale.org)

BRASLAVSKY, Dr Nicholas Justin; QC (1999); s of Rev Cyril Braslavsky (d 1980), and Stella, *née* Fisher; *b* 9 February 1959; *Educ* Blackpool GS, High Pavement GS Nottingham, Univ of Birmingham (LLB, MJur, PhD), Inns of Court Sch of Law; *m* 1990, Jane, *née* Margolis; 2 s (Max b 28 April 1992, Miles b 22 July 1996), 1 da (Millie b 7 Feb 1994); *Career* called to the Bar 1983 (Social Sci Research Cncl scholar 1979–82, Inner Temple scholar 1982); recorder 2001–; memb Kings Chambers (formerly 40 King Street); memb: Professional Negligence Bar Assoc 1990, Personal Injuries Bar Assoc 1990, Ctee Northern Circuit Med Law Assoc; *Style*— Dr Nicholas Braslavsky, QC; ✉ Kings Chambers, 36 Young Street, Manchester M3 3FT (☎ 0161 832 9082, fax 0161 835 2139)

BRASON, Paul; s of John Ainsley Brason, and Audrey, *née* Wheldon; *b* 17 June 1952; *Educ* King James I GS Newport IOW, Camberwell Coll of Art; *Family* 2 s (Oliver Louis b 11 April 1983, Simon Nicholas b 9 June 1987), 1 da (Anne Louise b 9 June 1987); *Career* artist, portrait painter; has exhibited regularly at Nat Portrait Gall, Royal Acad and Royal Soc of Portrait Painters; work in many private and public collections incl: Royal Collection Windsor Castle, Nat Portrait Gall, The Duke of Westminster, The Duke of Buccleuch, The Duke of Richmond, The Bodleian Library Oxford, Balliol Coll Oxford, Trinity Coll Oxford, CCC Oxford, Merton Coll Oxford, Eton Coll, Museums and Galleries Cmmn, HSBC Bank, and others; Ondaatje Prize for Portraiture 1998; memb Royal Soc of Portrait Painters 1994, pres RP 2001, elected memb Royal W of Eng Acad (RWA) 2002; *Clubs* Arts, Chelsea Arts; *Style*— Paul Brason, Esq, PPRP, RWA

BRASSE, His Hon Glenn Clifford; s of Robert Brasse (d 2000), and Iris, *née* Bendel (d 1968); *m* Dr Valerie, *née* Hauser; 3 s (Simon b 25 Feb 1977, Jonathan b 9 Nov 1980, Joseph b 11 Aug 1985); *Career* barr 1971–95, former memb 14 Gray's Inn Square; district judge Principal Registry of the Family Div 1995–2006, circuit judge (South Eastern Circuit) 2006–16, ret; *Style*— His Hon Glenn Brasse; ✉ c/o The South Eastern Circuit, 289–293 High Holborn, London WC1V 7HZ

BRATHWAITE, James Everett; CBE (2001); s of James Brathwaite (d 2004), and Louise Brathwaite; *b* 31 March 1953, St Lucy, Barbados; *Educ* Univ of Sheffield (BSc), Open Univ (Dip); *m* Barbara; 4 da (Catherine b 14 Nov 1973, Camilla b 9 June 1986, Charlotte b 26 Sept 1988, Cressida b 28 April 1991), 1 s (James b 4 April 1995); *Career* grad trainee accountant then salesman and sales trainer Beecham Pharmaceuticals UK Ltd 1975–79, product mangr then mktg mangr Bayer Pharmaceuticals UK Ltd 1979–82, fndr and ceo Epic Multimedia Gp plc (previously VPS) 1982–97, fndr dir and chief exec XL Entertainment plc 1997–; chm: SEAL Ltd 2000–10, Community Alerts Ltd 2002–12, Splash FM 2002–, Brighton & Hove Radio Ltd 2003–12, Morgan Everett Ltd 2003–10; dir: Exam on Demand 1998–2014, Nat Business Angels Network Ltd 2003–04, Organisational Technol Res 2005–, Regional Satellite TV Ltd 2005–; non-exec chm SEEDA 2002–10 (memb Bd 2001–10); exec chm Drenl 2011–; memb: Caribbean Advsy Gp FCO 1998–2002, Small Business Cncl 2000–04, Americas Advsrs Gp Trade Partners UK 2001–03, Int Trade Devpt Advsy Panel UK Trade and Investment 2002–05, Investment Ctee DTI 2002–06, Public Serv Agreements Sounding Bd ODPM 2003–05, Manufacturing Forum DTI 2004–, London 2012 Forum 2004–, Bd Environment Agency 2005–12, Sustainable Procurement Taskforce DEFRA 2005–06; non-exec dir Sussex Enterprise Ltd 1994–2002, founding chm Business Link Sussex Ltd 1995–2003 (memb Nat Business Link Accreditation A Advsy Bd 1999–2000), fndr dir Wired Sussex 1996–2002, memb Bd Arundel Festival Ltd 1998–2002 (chm 2001), dir Farnham Castle Tstees and Farnham Castle Briefings Ltd 2004–13; patron Asian Business Cncl; business rep Bd Brighton & Hove Sixth Form Coll, memb Ct Univ of Sussex 2002–07 (memb Cncl 1995–2001), dir Univ of Greenwich 2002–12; memb Bd Rockinghorse charity 1994–96, fundraiser Alexandra Hosp for Sick Children Brighton; chm: Pathway to Zero Waste, European Pathway to Zero Waste 2008–13, Work this Way Charity 2009–14; memb BAFTA; hon fell UC Chichester, hon doctorate of business Univ of Solent; MInstD, Hon FCGI 2005, FRSA; *Recreations* music, skiing, watching all sport especially football and Manchester United, coaching rugby; *Clubs* Reform, Cwlth, RSA; *Style*— James Brathwaite, Esq, CBE

BRATZA, Sir Nicolas Duan; kt (1998); s of Milan Bratza (concert violinist, d 1964), and Hon Margaret Bratza, *née* Russell (d 1981); *b* 3 March 1945; *Educ* Wimbledon Coll, Brasenose Coll Oxford (MA); *Career* instr Univ of Pennsylvania Law Sch 1967–68; called to the Bar Lincoln's Inn 1969 (bencher 1993); jr counsel to the Crown (common law) 1978–88, QC 1988, recorder of the Crown Court 1993–98, UK memb European Cmmn of Human Rights 1993–98, judge of the High Court of Justice (Queen's Bench Div) 1998–2012, judge of the European Court of Human Rights 1998–2012 (section pres 1998–2000 and 2001–07, vice-pres Ct 2007–11, pres Ct 2011–12); chm Br Inst of Int and Comparative Law 2014– (memb Advsy Cncl 2004–13, pres 2013–14); memb: Cncl of Legal Educn 1988–92, Advsy Cncl Br Inst of Human Rights 2004– (vice-chm 1989–98, govr 1985–2004), Int Cmmn of Jurists 2013, Bd Int Service for Human Rights 2013–; memb Editorial Bd European Human Rights Law Review 1996–, memb Editorial Bd European Law Review 2004–; chm Int Advsy Panel on Ukraine 2013–15; memb: Helen Bamber Fndn 2015–, Bd Surrey Hills Int Music Festival 2013–; ambass Toynbee Hall 2012–; hon fell BNC 2011, hon bencher King's Inns Dublin 2012, hon prof Univ of Nottingham Law Sch 2013–16; Hon DUniv Essex, Hon LLD Univ of Glasgow 2007; *Books* Halsbury's Laws of England (4 edn, jt contrib of titles Contempt of Court and Crown Proceedings); *Recreations* music, cricket; *Clubs* Garrick, MCC; *Style*— Sir Nicolas Bratza

BRAUDE, Prof Peter Riven; OBE (2015); s of Barnett Braude (d 1988), and Sylvia Carmen, *née* Grumberg (d 2001); *b* 29 May 1948; *Educ* King Edward VII Sch Johannesburg, Univ of the Witwatersrand (BSc, MB BCh), Univ of Cambridge (MA, PhD), Soc of Apothecaries (Dip Philosophy of Med (DPMSA)); *m* 1973, Beatrice Louise, *née* Roselaar; 2 s (Philip Roselaar b 1983, Richard Roselaar b 1986); *Career* demonstrator in anatomy Univ of Cambridge 1974–79, SHO St Mary's Hosp London and Addenbrooke's Hosp Cambridge 1979–81, sr research assoc Dept of Obstetrics and Gynaecology Univ of Cambridge 1981–83, registrar in obstetrics and gynaecology Rosie Maternity Hosp Cambridge 1983–85; Univ of Cambridge: MRC clinical research conslt in obstetrics and gynaecology 1986–89, conslt sr lectr in obstetrics and gynaecology 1989–91; prof of obstetrics and gynaecology UMDS 1991–2011, head Dept of Women's Health Sch of Med KCL 1991–

B

2011; Guy's and St Thomas' Hosp: clinical dir Women's Servs 1993–94, dir Assisted Conception Unit and Fertility Serv 1993–99, dir Centre for Pre-implantation Genetic Diagnosis Guy's and St Thomas' Fndn Tst 1999–2011; currently emeritus prof of obstetrics and gynaecology KCL; memb: HFEA 1999–2004, HFEA expert panel to review mitochondrial diseases 2011–14, Ct Safety of Blood Tissues and Organs 2008–12, Nuffield Cncl of Bioethics Working Gp on Novel Techniques for the Prevention of Mitochondrial DNA Disorders 2012; chair: Scientific Advsy Ctee RCOG 2004–06, Expert Ctee on Umbilical Stem Cell Banking RCOG 2005–06, Expert Gp on Multiple Pregnancy After IVF HFEA 2005–06; external advsr to Singapore Bioethics Advsy Ctee 2014–; 75th Jubilee Gold Medal for achievement in sci Univ of the Witwatersrand 1997, Hosp Dr Innovation Award 2006, Academic Award RCOG 2016; FRCOG 1993 (MRCOG 1982), FMedSci 2006, FSB 2011; *Publications* ABC of Superfertility (jtly), Preimplantation Genetics Diagnosis in Clinical Practice (jtly); author of various publications on human developmental embryology, male and female infertility and preimplantation genetics; *Recreations* narrowboating, gardening, skiing; *Style—* Prof Peter Braude, OBE; ✉ Division of Women's Health, King's College London, 10th Floor, North Wing, St Thomas' Hospital, London SE1 7EH (☎ 020 7188 4138, fax 020 7620 1227)

BRAUER, Irving; s of Jack Brauer (d 1972), of Hackney, London, and Lily, *née* Croll (d 1978); *b* 8 August 1939, London; *Educ* Davenant Fndn, Northern Poly (DipArch); *m* 21 April 1964, Stephanie Margaret, da of Edwin Sherwood, of Florida, USA; 1 da (Amelia b 1965), 1s (Marlow b 1975); *Career* architect and designer, worked in London and NY 1960–63, partnership Beryl Gollins 1963–76, ptnr Brauer Associates 1976–; chm PIA (Product Innovation in Archtecture) 2002–08, chartered memb Network Gp for Composites in Construction (NGCC) (memb Steering Gp 2010–15); visiting tutor: Canterbury Sch of Architecture 1967–70, Central London Poly 1968–71; elected memb CSD 1967 (elected fell 1976–2005); RIBA; *Recreations* house renovation, theatre, reading, travel; *Style—* Irving Brauer, Esq; ✉ 1 Veronica Close, Manor Road, East Preston, West Sussex BN16 1PZ; Brauer Associates, 1–5 Vyner Street, London E2 9DG (e-mail irving@brauerassociates.com)

BRAWER, Rabbi Dr Naftali; *b* 5 February 1970; *Educ* Rabbinical Coll of America Morristown NJ (BRS), Yeshiva Tomchei Tmimim Brooklyn NY, London Sch of Jewish Studies Univ of London (Dip, MA), UCL (PhD); *m* Dina, *née* Elmaleh; 4 c; *Career* ordained rabbi 1992; rabbi and educnl dir Friends of Lubavitch of Bergen Co NJ 1992–96 (also assoc chaplain Bergen Co Prison Annex), rabbi Northwood United Synagogue London 1996– (also chaplain Mt Vernon Hosp), sr rabbi Borehamwood & Elstree United Synagogue 2007–11 (also tstee Yavneh Coll), dir Spiritual Capital Fndn 2011–; lectr London Sch of Jewish Studies 2005–; memb Advsy Bd: Consultative Cncl of Jewish Orgns René Cassin, Children of Abraham, Home Office Steering Ctee on Muslim-Jewish Dialogue Conf; fndr orgns incl Jewish Business Network (New Jersey); speaker at int confs; contrib to progs on BBC Radio 4, World Serv and BBC 2; contrib: The Jewish Standard 1994–96, The Jewish Chronicle 1998– (monthly columnist 2003–); memb: Rabbinical Cncl of America, Rabbinical Cncl of the United Synagogue (UK), Chief Rabbi's Cabinet UK (Social Ethics Portfolio 1999–2004, Jewish-Muslim Rels Portfolio 2004–); *Publications* Faith Based Radicalism: Between Constructive Activism and Destructive Fantacism (contrib, 2007), A Brief Guide Judaism: Theology, History and Practice (2008); *Style—* Rabbi Dr Naftali Brawer; ✉ 91 Furzehill Road, Borehamwood, Hertfordshire WD6 2DN

BRAY, Angie; da of Benedict G C T Bray (d 1987), of the Isle of Man, and Patricia, *née* Measures; *b* 13 October 1953; *Educ* Downe House, Fairlawn Sch Cambridge, Univ of St Andrews (MA); *Partner* Nigel Hugh-Smith; *Career* radio presenter and reporter: Br Forces Broadcasting Gibraltar, LBC Radio 1981–88; head of broadcasting Cons Pty and press sec to Pty Chm 1989–92, sr conslt in public affrs 1992–2000; GLA: memb London Assembly (Cons) W Central 2000–08, Cons spokesman for the congestion charge, memb Tport, Environment and Business Mgmnt and Appts Ctees; MP (Cons) Ealing Central 2010–15 (Parly candidate (Cons) East Ham 1996–97), PPS to Rt Hon Francis Maude, MP, *qv* (as Cabinet Office min and Paymaster Gen) 2010–12, memb House of Commons Culture, Media and Sport Select Ctee 2012–; *Recreations* tennis, history, music, walking my dogs; *Style—* Angie Bray; ✉ House of Commons, London SW1A 0AA

BRAY, Julian Charles; s of Flt Lt Reginald Charles Julian Bray, and Irene Audrey, *née* Stewart; *b* 23 May 1945; *Educ* Ayr Acad; *m* 1, 1965 (m dis 1970), Julie; 1 da (Amanda Caroline); m 2, 1971 (m dis 1981), Judith Marina; 2 s (Dominic Julian b 13 Oct 1977, Oliver William b 13 June 1980); m 3, 1985 (m dis 2001), Vivienne Margaret Carlton; 1 s (William Charles b 18 Aug 1989); *Career* independent TV prodr and presenter, broadcaster, writer and journalist; prodr/dir ASM Productions; md: Leadenhall Associates Ltd 1986–90, Alpha Strategy Management Ltd 1991–92; non-exec dir CNS (City News Service) 1986–90 (ed 1990–); dir: NTN TV News Ltd 1988, DTI Eureka Information Bureau 1990, Marketmetro Ltd 2002–; business devpt dir Extel PR, head of media relations Welbeck PR Ltd; sr ptnr Carlton Consulting 1993–2001, ceo Media Assocs, exec prodr Rascal TV & Film Prodns Inc 2007–; int lectr and writer on econ and European affrs 1994–; currently TV and radio broadcaster and analyst (referred to as an aviation security and airline operations expert); memb: Equity, NUJ, The Magic Circle, Int Brotherhood of Magicians USA (sec Eng Ring 1999, memb Br Ring No 25); MCIPR; *Books* Information Technology in the Corporate Environment (1980); blog: Julian Bray Aviation Security News; *Recreations* theatre, microbreweries and fine wine, travel, magic; *Clubs* The Magic Castle (Hollywood), Peterborough City, DPiP Digital People (Peterborough); *Style—* Julian Bray, MCIPR, MMC; ✉ 17 Kedleston, Heritage Park, Peterborough PE2 8XL (☎ 01733 345581, mobile 07944 217476, ISDN 01733 345020, e-mail julianbray@aol.com, Twitter @julianbray, Skype Julian.Bray.UK)

BRAY, Michael Peter; s of Sqdn Ldr William Charles Thomas Bray, DFC (d 1985), and Ivy Isobel, *née* Ellison (d 1986); *b* 27 March 1947; *Educ* Caterham Sch, Univ of Liverpool (LLB); *m* 1, 25 July 1970 (m dis 2007), Elizabeth-Ann, da of Hubert John Harrington (d 1981); 2 da (Natasha Jane b 13 April 1977, Samantha Louise b 13 April 1984); m 2, 18 April 2010, Gabrielle Taylor; *Career* slr; ptnr Clifford Chance 1976– (formerly Coward Chance, joined 1970), chief exec Clifford Chance 2000–03; memb Jt Working Pty on Banking Law of the Law Reform Ctees of the Law Soc and Bar Cncl; Freeman City of London Slrs' Co 1976; memb Law Soc; *Recreations* theatre, reading, skiing, photography, golf; *Style—* Michael Bray, Esq; ✉ Clifford Chance, 10 Upper Bank Street, London E14 5JJ (☎ 020 7600 1000, fax 020 7600 5555)

BRAY, Noreen; OBE (1996); *Educ* Heathfield House RC HS, Univ of Wales (BA); *Children* 2 s; *Career* PR conslt; grad trainee BBC 1971–73, TV and radio news and current affairs journalist BBC Wales 1976–89, bd dir Good Relations Ltd (part of Chime Communications) 1989– (currently chair Cardiff Office); cmmr for Wales Equal Opportunities Cmmn 1990–95, pres SCOPE (formerly Spastics Soc) Wales 1996–2000; dir Bank of Wales 1999–2001, dir Real Radio 2000–02, govr Univ of Wales Inst Cardiff (UWIC) 1994–2007, Privy Cncl nominee Ct Univ of Cardiff, memb Bd Br Chambers of Commerce 2006–08, dep chair Cardiff & Co 2008–; memb NUJ; MIPR, FRSA; *Recreations* reading, music, exercise; *Style—* Mrs Noreen Bray, OBE; ✉ Sophia House, 28 Cathedral Road, Cardiff CF11 9LJ

BRAY, His Hon Richard Winston Atherton; s of Winston Bray, CBE (d 2003), and Betty Atherton, *née* Miller; *b* 10 April 1945; *Educ* Rugby, CCC Oxford; *m* 6 Jan 1978, Judith Elizabeth Margaret, da of Maj C B Ferguson (d 1980); 1 s (Edward b 2 Oct 1984), 3 da (Hester b 24 May 1981, Miranda b 12 Sept 1986, Rosalind b 23 Aug 1989); *Career* called to the Bar Middle Temple 1970; recorder Midland & Oxford circuit 1987–93; circuit judge (Midland & Oxford Circuit) 1993–2014, ret; *Recreations* cricket, real tennis, gardening; *Clubs* MCC, Frogs; *Style—* His Hon Richard Bray

BRAYFIELD, Celia Frances; da of Felix Francis Brayfield (d 1975), and Ada Ellen, *née* Jakeman (d 1995); *b* 21 August 1945, London; *Educ* St Paul's Girls' Sch, Universitaire de Grenoble; *Children* 1 da (Chloe Elizabeth b 8 Oct 1980); *Career* writer and broadcaster; trainee Nova IPC Magazines 1968–69, asst to women's ed The Observer 1969, feature writer Daily Mail 1969–71, TV critic Evening Standard 1974–82, TV critic The Times 1983–88, columnist Sunday Telegraph 1989–90; dir Nat Acad of Writing 2000–03; reader in creative writing Brunel Univ 2007– (sr lectr 2005–07), vice-pres One Parent Families 2007–; tstee One Parent Families 1990–2007, memb Mgmnt Ctee Soc of Authors 1995–98; *Books* The Body Show Book (co-author, 1982), Pineapple Dance Book (co-author, 1984), Glitter – The Truth About Fame (1985), Pearls (1987), The Prince (1990), White Ice (1993), Harvest (1995), Bestseller (1996), Getting Home (1998), Sunset (1999), Heartswap (2000), Mister Fabulous and Friends (2003), Wild Weekend (2004), Deep France (2004), Arts Reviews (2008), New Writing (2010); *Recreations* family life; *Clubs* Chelsea Arts; *Style—* Ms Celia Brayfield; ✉ c/o Curtis Brown Ltd, 28/29 Haymarket, London SW1Y 4SP (☎ 020 7396 6600, e-mail celia.brayfield@brunel.ac.uk)

BRAYNE, Mark Lugard; s of Thomas Lugard Brayne (d 2009), and Audrey Diana, *née* Thompson; *b* 17 April 1950, London; *Educ* Gresham's, Wymondham Coll, Univ of Leeds (BA), De Montfort Univ (MA); *m* 1, 25 March 1977 (m dis, remarried 1 Nov 2013), Jutta, da of Fritz Hartung (d 1992); 2 s (Christopher b 1980, Alastair b 1982), 1 da (Katharine b 1987); m 2, 20 Sept 2002 (m dis 2013), Sue, da of John Bowes (d 2008); *Career* Moscow and E Berlin Reuters News Agency 1973–78; BBC: German service corr Berlin 1979–81, Central Euro corr Vienna 1981–84, Beijing corr China 1984–87; BBC World Service: dip corr 1988–92, dep head Central European Serv 1992–93, dep head Russian Serv 1993–94, regnl ed Europe 1994–2002, dir Braynework Ltd 2002–, dir EMDR Focus Ltd 2015–; dir: BBC project for journalism and trauma 2002–03, Europe Dart Centre for Journalism and Trauma 2002–08; UK Cncl for Psychotherapy (UKCP) reg psychotherapist, EMDR reg conslt, writer and lectr on journalism, trauma and ethics, contrib to many learned books and jls; memb Bd Euro Soc for Traumatic Stress Studies (ESTSS) 2005–08, tstee and memb Bd EMDR UK and Ireland Assoc 2014–15; *Recreations* cycling, singing; *Clubs* Frontline; *Style—* Mark Brayne, Esq; ✉ mobile 07711 888682, e-mail mark@braynework.com, website www.braynetwork.com, blog www.psychlotherapist.com

BRAZIER, Julian William Hendy; TD, MP; s of Lt-Col Peter Hendy Brazier, and Patricia Audrey Helen, *née* Stubbs, ggda of Bishop Stubbs of Oxford noted lectr and author of the Stubbs Charters (Constitutional History of England); *b* 24 July 1953; *Educ* Dragon Sch Oxford, Wellington, BNC Oxford (scholar, MA), London Business Sch; *m* 21 July 1984, Katharine Elizabeth, da of Brig Patrick Blagden, CBE; 3 s (William, Alexander (twin), John b 3 Dec 1992); *Career* SSLC with RE and Capt TA in SAS Reserves; with Charter Consolidated Ltd (now plc) 1975–84 (sec to Exec Ctee of the Bd of Dirs 1981–84), H B Maynard Int Mgmnt Conslts 1984–87; MP (Cons) Canterbury 1987–; PPS to Rt Hon Gillian Shephard, MP, *qv*, 1990–93; oppn whip 2001–02, shadow min for home affrs 2002, shadow min for work and pensions 2002–03, shadow min for trade and int devpt 2003–04, shadow min for transport (aviation and shipping) 2004–09; memb House of Commons Defence Select Ctee 1997–2001 and 2009–14, memb Cmmn on Reserve Forces 2010–11, min for Reserve Forces 2014–; *Recreations* bicycling, history, science, philosophy; *Style—* Julian Brazier, Esq, TD, MP; ✉ House of Commons, London SW1A 0AA

BRAZIER, Paul; *b* 29 July 1962; *Career* advtg exec; art dir Cogent Elliott 1984–87, WCRS 1987–91; Abbott Mead Vickers BBDO: joined 1991, now chief creative offr and chm; pres D&AD 2009–10; 200 awards incl 8 D&AD Pencils, 11 Cannes Lions and The Big Won; AMV most creatively awarded agency in the UK for six consecutive years; Hon Degree in Visual Arts (Graphics) Wolverhampton; *Style—* Paul Brazier; ✉ Abbott Mead Vickers BBDO Ltd, Bankside 3, 90 Southwark Street, London SE1 0SW (☎ 020 3787 0100)

BREACH, Peter John Freeman; s of Andrew Breach, CBE, LLD (d 1992), and Christine Ruth, *née* Watson (d 1973); *b* 12 January 1942; *Educ* Clifton, Univ of Bristol (BA); *m* 17 Dec 1966, Joan, da of (William) Raymond Livesey, of Clitheroe, Lancs; 3 s (Harry William Freeman b 1972, Christopher Andrew Talbot (Kit) b 1974, Alexander Robin Livesey b 1989); *Career* Coopers & Lybrand 1963–68, Hoare Govett 1968–69, County Bank Ltd 1969–70, JH Vavasseur & Co Ltd 1970–73, pres and ceo Major Holdings & Devpts Ltd 1972–73, divnl md Bath & Portland Gp Ltd 1974–78, md James Dixon/Viners Ltd 1978–82, fin dir Bristol & West Building Soc 1988–91 (dir 1976–91, exec dir 1983–91); chm 1992–: Hawksworth Securities plc (dir 1988), Principality Holdings Gp (dir 1972), Farthingford Properties Ltd (dir 1972), Surthurst Ltd (dir 1983); govr and chm Redland HS for Girls 1987–2012; Freeman: City of London, City of Bristol; Liveryman Worshipful Co of Basketmakers; FCA, CTA, FCT; *Recreations* sailing, skiing, gardens, historic houses; *Clubs* Royal Thames Yacht, Royal Dart Yacht, City Livery Yacht; *Style—* Peter Breach, Esq; ✉ 7 Park Street, Bristol BS1 5NF (☎ 0117 925 9494, fax 0117 927 2462, mobile 07779 330706, e-mail peter.breach@hawksworthplc.com)

BREADY, Robert; *b* 19 May 1968, Newport; *Educ* City Univ; *Career* merchandiser River Island 1990–95, head of merchandising Arcadia 1995–2005, product and trading dir ASOS plc 2005–; *Style—* Robert Bready, Esq; ✉ ASOS plc, Greater London House, Hampstead Road, London NW1 7FB

BREAKWELL, Prof Dame Glynis Marie; DBE (2012), DL (2010); da of Harold Breakwell, of Tipton, and Vera, *née* Woodhall (d 1993); *b* 26 July 1952; *Educ* Univ of Leicester (BA), Univ of Strathclyde (MSc), Univ of Bristol (PhD), Univ of Oxford (MA, DSc); *Career* prize fell in social psychology Nuffield Coll Oxford 1978–82; Univ of Surrey: lectr in social psychology 1981–87, sr lectr in psychology 1987–88, reader 1988–91, prof of psychology 1991–2001, head Dept of Psychology 1990–95, pro-vice-chllr 1994–2001, head Sch of Human Sciences 1997–2001; vice-chllr Univ of Bath 2001–, hon prof Shandong Univ China; dir UUK 2005– (chair Funding and Mgmnt Policy Network 2008–, chair HE Funding Task Gp 2010); chair: HERDA-SW 2006–08, Nat Cataloguing Unit Archives of Contemporary Scientists 2001–09, HEFCE Widening Participation Review Gp 2004–06, Advsy Bd Univ of Lisbon Inst of Social Sciences 2010–14; memb: CVCP/HEFCE Steering Gp on Costing and Pricing 1997–2001, 1994 Gp Bd 2001–12, Int Policy Ctee Royal Soc 2002–05, HEFCE Leadership Governance & Mgmnt Ctee 2004–13, Social Sciences Panel Finnish Research Assessment Exercise 2005, Royal Soc/Acad of Medical Sciences Ctee on Pandemic Influenza 2006, Financial Sustainability Strategy Gp HEFCE 2008–, HEFCE Accountability Burden Project Steering Gp 2008–10, Research Cncls UK Panel of Public Engagement in Science 2009–, Science and Industry Cncl SW 2006–10, HE Task Force CBI 2009, Fruits of Curiosity Report Royal Soc 2009–10, Ctee World Culture Cncl Mexico 2010–, Cncl ESRC 2011 (memb Coll of Postgrad Trg Assessors 1996–2001, chair Resarch Ctee 2011), HEFCE TRAC Strategy Gp; research advsr to MAFF and Food Standards Agency 1991–2001, advsr Royal Soc Research on Public Communication of Science 2005, dir HE Career Services Unit 2007–10, dir Leadership Fndn for HE 2013; dir Student Loans Co Ltd 2011–, dir West of England Local Economic Partnership 2011–14 (chair Research Advsy Ctee); pres Psychology Section BAAS 1994–95 (vice-pres 1995–96); Br Psychological Soc: Young Social Psychologist Award 1978, assoc fell 1984, fell 1987, Myers Award 1993, memb Social Psychology Section Ctee 1995–99 (chair 1997–99); dir New Swindon Co 2002–07, dir Theatre Royal Bath 2001–06, chair Bath Festivals Ltd 2006–09, chair Daphne Jackson Tst 2009–14, dir Univs Superannuation Scheme 2009;

tstee Holburne Museum Bath 2001–04; memb Cncl Cheltenham Ladies Coll 2009; Top 100 Leading UK Practising Scientists 2014; MA (by special resolution) Univ of Oxford 1978; Hon LLD Univ of Bristol 2004; CPsychol 1988; FRSA 1997, FAcSS 2002, Hon FBPsS 2009; *Books* Social Psychology: A Practical Manual (jt ed, 1982), Social Work: The Social Psychological Approach (with C Rowett, 1982), Threatened Identities (ed, 1983), The Quiet Rebel (1985), Doing Social Psychology (jt ed, 1988), Human Behaviour: Encyclopedia of Personal Relationships Vol 17: Shaping Your Life and Vol 18: Coping with Change (ed, 1990), Coping with Threatened Identities (1986), Facing Physical Violence (1989), Interviewing (1990), Social Psychology of Political and Economic Cognition (ed, 1991), Careers and Identities (jtly, 1992), Social Psychology of Identity and the Self Concept (ed, 1992), Empirical Approaches to Social Representations (with D V Canter, 1993), Basic Evaluation Methods (with L Millward, 1995), Research Methods in Psychology (with S Hammond and C Fife-Schaw, 1995, 4 edn 2012), Changing European Identities: Social Psychological Analyses of Change (jtly ed with E Lyons, 1996), Coping with Aggressive Behaviour (1997), Doing Social Psychology Research (ed, 2004), The Psychology of Risk (2007, 2 edn 2013), Identity Process Theory: Identity, Social Action and Social Change (jt ed, 2014); also author of numerous journal articles, monographs and book chapters; *Recreations* painting, racket sports; *Clubs* Athenaeum; *Style—* Prof Dame Glynis Breakwell, DBE, DL; ✉ University of Bath, Claverton Down, Bath BA2 7AY (☎ 01225 386262, fax 01225 386626)

BREALEY, Prof Richard Arthur; s of Albert Brealey (d 1974), and Irene Brealey (d 1994); *b* 9 June 1936; *Educ* Queen Elizabeth's Sch Barnet, Exeter Coll Oxford (MA); *m* 10 Feb 1967, Diana Cecily, da of Derek Brown-Kelly (d 2003); 2 s (David Andrew b 1970, Charles Richard b 1972); *Career* Investment Dept Sun Life Assurance Co of Canada 1959–66, mangr computer applications Keystone Custodian Funds of Boston 1966–68; London Business Sch: prof of fin 1973–98, dir Inst of Fin and Accounting 1974–84, memb Body of Govrs, dep princ and academic dean 1984–88, visiting prof 1998–2001, emeritus prof 2001–; visiting prof: Univ of Calif Berkeley, Univ of Br Colombia, Univ of Hawaii, Aust Grad Sch of Mgmnt; special advsr to Govr Bank of England 1998–2001; dir Swiss Helvetia Fund 1987–96 and 2009–; former dir: Sun Life Assurance Co of Canada UK Holdings plc, Tokai Derivative Products, HSBC Investor Funds; dep chm Balancing and Settlement Code Panel 1998–2015; former: pres European Fin Assoc, dir American Fin Assoc; FBA; *Books* incl: Introduction to Risk and Return from Common Stocks (2 edn, 1983), Fundamentals of Corporate Finance (jtly, 1994, 8 edn 2015), Principles of Corporate Finance (with S C Myers and F Allen, 12 edn, 2016); *Recreations* trekking, skiing, horse riding; *Style—* Prof Richard Brealey, FBA; ✉ Haydens Cottage, The Pound, Cookham, Berkshire SL6 9QE (☎ 01628 520143); London Business School, Sussex Place, Regent's Park, London NW1 4SA (☎ 020 7262 5050, fax 020 7724 3317)

BREARLEY, Christopher John Scott; CB (1994), DL (Herts 2007); s of Geoffrey William Brearley (d 1968), and Winifred Marion, *née* Scott (d 1995); *b* 25 May 1943; *Educ* King Edward VII Sch Sheffield, Trinity Coll Oxford (MA, BPhil); *m* 1971, Rosemary Nanette, da of Lt-Col Wilfrid Sydney Stockbridge (d 1993), and Dorothea Stockbridge (d 2001); 2 s (Thomas b 1973, William b 1976); *Career* civil servant; former dir: Scottish Servs, Property Servs Agency 1981–83; under sec Cabinet Office 1983–85; DOE: dir Local Govt Fin 1985–88, dir Planning and Devpt Control 1988–89, dep sec Local Govt 1990–93, Local Govt and Planning 1994–95, Local Devpt Gp 1996–97, DG Planning, Roads and Local Transport Gp DETR 1997–2000; chair Nat Retail Planning Forum 2005–13; cncllr Three Rivers DC 2003–07 (chm Licensing Ctee 2004–07, memb Chiltern Conservation Bd 2004–07); non-exec dir John Maclean & Son 1986–88; govr Watford GS for Boys 1988–2004 (chm of govrs 1998–2004), tstee Watford Grammar Schs Fndn 1992–2004 and 2010– (chm 2015–), govr Oxon and Bucks Mental Health NHS Tst 2008–11, govr Herts Partnership NHS Tst 2011– (lead govr 2013–16); tstee Motability Tenth Anniversary Tst 2001–, memb Policy Ctee CPRE 2001–07; chm: CPRE – The Hertfordshire Soc 2004–09, SW Herts Lib Dems 2004–07 and 2008–11; Freeman City of London; *Recreations* family history, sudoku, seeing friends; *Style—* Christopher Brearley, Esq, CB, DL; ✉ Middlemount, 35 South Road, Chorleywood, Hertfordshire WD3 5AS (☎ 01923 283848, e-mail c.brearley461@btinternet.com)

BREARLEY, Stephen; s of Roger Brearley, of Mossley Hill, Liverpool, and Joyce Mary, *née* Hewitt; *b* 17 March 1953, Liverpool; *Educ* Liverpool Coll, Gonville & Caius Coll Cambridge (MA), Middx Hosp Med Sch (MB BChir, MChir (Cantab)); *m* 1980, Margaret Faith, da of Edward Collier; 2 s (Jonathan Joshua b 5 March 1982 d 2002, Samuel Sebastian James b 1 Dec 1985); *Career* research fell Birmingham Gen Hosp 1983–84, surgical sr registrar W Midlands Region 1988–91; conslt gen and vascular surgn: Whipps Cross Univ Hosp London 1992– (chm Med Staff Assoc 1998–2006), Royal London Hosp 2011–, BUPA Roding Hosp Ilford, Holly House Hosp Buckhurst Hill; hon sr lectr Bart's and the Royal London Sch of Medicine and Dentistry (Queen Mary London), RCS surgical tutor Whipps Cross Hosp 1992–98, dir Whipps Cross Higher Surgery Course 1992–2015, memb Redbridge and Waltham Forest Research Ethics Ctee 1993–99; external examiner Univ of Oxford 2008–13; memb: Jr Doctors' Ctee BMA 1979–91 (chm 1983–84), GMC 1984–2008 (chm Registration Ctee 1998–2008), Permanent Working Gp of Euro Jr Hosp Doctors 1985–91 (chm Educn Sub-Ctee), Standing Ctee on Postgraduate Med Educn 1989–92 (fndr memb), Assoc of Surgns of GB and I, Vascular Soc, RSM; fndr memb Expert Witness Inst; FRCS 1981; *Publications* author of articles on GI and vascular surgery, med educn and medicine in Europe; *Recreations* playing, conducting and listening to music; *Style—* Stephen Brearley, Esq; ✉ Whipps Cross University Hospital, London E11 1NR (☎ 020 8535 6670, fax 020 8535 6670, mobile 077 7098 1609, e-mail vascusurg@btconnect.com)

BREARS, Peter Charles David; s of Charles Henry, and Mary Theresa Margaret, Brears; *b* 30 August 1944; *Educ* Castleford Tech HS, Leeds Coll of Art (DipAD); *Career* keeper of folk life Hampshire Co Cncl 1967–69; curator: Shibden Hall Halifax 1969–72, Clarke Hall Wakefield 1972–75, Castle Museum York 1975–79; dir Leeds City Museums 1979–94, museum conslt and writer 1994–; pres Soc for Folk Life Studies 1992; FMA 1980, FSA 1980; *Books* The English Country Pottery (1971), Yorkshire Probate Inventories (1972), The Collectors' Book of English Country Pottery (1974), Horse Brasses (1981), The Gentlewoman's Kitchen (1984), Traditional Food in Yorkshire (1987), North Country Folk Art (1989), Of Curiosities and Rare Things (1989), Treasures for the People (1989), Images of Leeds (1992), Leeds Described (1993), Leeds Waterfront Heritage (1993), The Country House Kitchen (1996), The Old Devon Farmhouse (1998), Ryedale Recipes (1998), A Taste of Leeds (1998), All the King's Cooks (1999), The Compleat Housekeeper (2000), The Boke of Keruynge (2003), A New and Easy Method of Cookery (ed, 2005), Cooking and Dining in Medieval England (2008, André Simon Food Book for 2008), Traditional Food in Shropshire (2009), Jellies and their Moulds (2010), Cooking and Dining with the Wordsworths (2011), A Leeds Life (2013), Traditional Food in Northumbria (2013), Traditional Food in Yorkshire (2014), Cookery and Dining in Tudor and Early Stuart England (2015), The Real Wuthering Heights (with S Wood, 2016); numerous articles in Folk Life, Post-Medieval Archaeology and others; *Recreations* hill walking, drawing, cooking; *Style—* Peter Brears, Esq, FSA; ✉ 4 Woodbine Terrace, Headingley, Leeds LS6 4AF (☎ 0113 275 6537)

BRECHIN, Bishop of 2011–; Rt Rev Dr Nigel Peyton; JP (Notts 1987); s of late Hubert Peyton, and Irene Louise, *née* Ellis; *b* 5 February 1951; *Educ* Latymer Upper Sch, Univ of Edinburgh (MA, BD), Edinburgh Theological Coll, Union Theological Seminary NY (Scottish fellowship, STM), Univ of Lancaster (PhD); *m* 1981, Anne Marie Therese Campbell, *née* McQuillan, wid of Colin Campbell; 3 c (Emily Anne b 1972, Jennifer Rose b 1977 d 1995, Mark Niall b 1982); *Career* ordained: deacon 1976, priest 1977; chaplain St Paul's Cathedral Dundee 1976–82, diocesan youth chaplain 1976–85, priest-in-charge All Souls Invergowrie 1979–85, chaplain Univ Hosp Dundee 1982–85, vicar All Saints Nottingham 1985–91, chaplain Nottingham Bluecoat Sch 1990–92, priest-in-charge Lambley 1991–99, diocesan miny devpt advsr 1991–99, archdeacon of Newark 1999–2011; bishops' selector 1992–2000, proctor in Convocation 1995–2010, sr selector 2001–11; hon canon Des Moines Iowa 2012–, bishop Mission to Seafarers Scotland 2013–; hon teaching fell Univ of Lancaster 2010–; dir Ecclesiastical Insurance Gp 2005–12; columnist Dundee Courier 2012–; govr Abertay Univ Dundee 2013–; *Publications* Dual Role Ministry (1998), Managing Clergy Lives (2013); *Recreations* grandparenting, music, reading, gardening, walking, real ale; *Clubs* Nottingham Forest FC, Royal Scots (Edinburgh); *Style—* The Rt Rev the Bishop of Brechin; ✉ Bishops House, 5 Glamis Drive, Dundee DD2 1QG (☎ 01382 641586 or 459569, e-mail bishop@brechin.anglican.org, website www.brechin.anglican.org)

BRECKENRIDGE, Prof Sir Alasdair Muir; kt (2004), CBE (1995); s of Thomas Breckenridge (d 1973), of Arbroath, and Jane, *née* Mackay (d 1986); *b* 7 May 1937; *Educ* Bell Baxter Sch, Univ of St Andrews (MB ChB, MD); *m* 28 Feb 1967, Jean Margaret, da of Trevor Charles William Boyle, of East London, South Africa; 2 s (Ross Alexander b 1969, Bruce Gordon b 1971); *Career* Dundee Royal Infirmary 1961–62 (house physician); Hammersmith Hosp and Royal Postgrad Med Sch London 1962–74: house physician, res fell, registrar, sr registrar, lectr, sr lectr; prof of clinical pharmacology Univ of Liverpool 1974–2002; chm: Jt Med Advsy Ctee HEFCE 1997–2002, Ctee on Safety of Medicines 1999–2003, Medicines and Healthcare Products Regulatory Agency 2003–12; FRCP 1974, FRSE 1991, FMedSci 1999; *Recreations* golf; *Clubs* Athenaeum; *Style—* Prof Sir Alasdair Breckenridge, CBE, FRSE; ✉ Cree Cottage, Feather Lane, Heswall, Wirral L60 4RL

BREEDON, Timothy James (Tim); CBE (2013); s of Peter Breedon (d 2003), and Ruth, *née* Davis; *b* 14 February 1958; *Educ* Calthorpe Park Comp Sch Fleet, Farnborough Sixth Form Coll, Worcester Coll Oxford (MA), London Business Sch (MSc); *m* 1982, Susan Margaret, *née* Hopkins; 3 s (Alexander b 1988, Matthew b 1990, William b 1996); *Career* Legal & General Investment Mgmnt Ltd: joined 1987, dir 1994–2012; Legal & General Gp plc: gp dir (investments) 2002–05, dep chief exec 2005, chief exec 2006–12; non-exec dir Barclays 2012–, chm APAX Global Alpha 2015–; lead non-exec dir Miny of Justice 2012–15; dir Financial Reporting Cncl (FRC) 2004–07, chm Assoc of Br Insurers 2010–12; *Style—* Tim Breedon, Esq, CBE; ✉ e-mail tim.breedon@gmail.com; Barclays, 1 Churchill Place, London E14 5HP

BREEN, Mary; *Career* Eton Coll 1991–98 (head of physics 1996–98), headmistress St Mary's Sch Ascot 1999– (first lay headmistress); *Style—* Mrs Mary Breen; ✉ St Mary's School, St Mary's Road, Ascot, Berkshire SL5 9JF

BREEZE, Prof David John; OBE (2009); s of Reginald Coulson Breeze, of Blackpool, and Marian, *née* Lawson; *b* 25 July 1944; *Educ* Blackpool GS, Univ of Durham (BA, PhD); *m* 22 July 1972, Pamela Diane, da of Victor James William Silvester; 2 s (Simon David b 10 March 1976, Christopher John b 16 Jan 1979); *Career* pt/t lectr Dept of Archaeology Univ of Durham 1968–69, successively asst inspr of ancient monuments, inspr then princ inspr Scottish Office (formerly DOE) 1969–89, chief inspr ancient monuments Historic Scotland 1989–2005, head of special heritage projects Historic Scotland 2005–09; visiting prof Dept of Archaeology Univ of Durham 1994–, hon prof Univ of Edinburgh 1996–, hon prof Univ of Newcastle upon Tyne 2003–; pres: South Shields Archaeological and Historical Soc 1983–85, Soc of Antiquaries of Scotland 1987–90 (vice-pres 1984–87), Soc of Antiquaries of Newcastle upon Tyne 2008–11, Royal Archaeological Inst 2009–12 (vice-pres 2002–07), Cumberland and Westmorland Antiquarian and Archaeological Soc 2011–14 (vice-pres 2002–11); tstee Senhouse Museum Trust 1985–; chm: Hadrian's Wall Pilgrimages 1989, 1999 and 2009, British Archaeological Awards 1993–2009, Int Ctee of the Congress of Roman Frontier Studies 2000– (memb 1983–), Senhouse Museum Tst Maryport 2013–; memb Hadrian's Wall Advsy Ctee 1977–97; author of many articles in British and foreign jls; Archaeologist of the Year 2009, The European Archaeological Heritage Prize 2010; Hon DLitt Univ of Glasgow 2008; corresponding memb German Archaeological Inst 1979; FSA 1975, FRSE 1991, Hon FSA Scot 2005 (FSA Scot 1970), Hon MIFA 2006 (MIFA 1990); *Books* incl: Hadrian's Wall (with B Dobson, 1976, 4 edn 2000), The Romans in Scotland – An Introduction to the Collections of The National Museum of Scotland (with D V Clarke and G MacKay, 1980), The Northern Frontiers of Roman Britain (1982), Roman Forts in Britain (1983), Hadrian's Wall – A Souvenir Guide to the Roman Wall (1987), A Queen's Progress (1987), Invaders of Scotland (with Anna Ritchie, 1991), Roman Officers and Frontiers (with B Dobson, 1993), Roman Scotland: Frontier Country (1996, 2 edn 2006), The Stone of Destiny (with G Munro, 1997), Historic Scotland (1998), Historic Scotland, People and Places (2002), The Stone of Destiny: Artefact and Icon (with R Welander and T Clancy, 2003), Frontiers of the Roman Empire (with S Jilek and A Thiel, 2005), J Collingwood Bruce's Handbook to the Roman Wall (14 edn, 2006), The Antonine Wall (2006), Roman Frontiers in Britain (2007), Edge of Empire: Rome's Scottish Frontier – The Antonine Wall (2008), Frontiers of the Roman Empire: The European Dimension of a World Heritage Site (jt ed, 2008), Frontiers of the Roman Empire, the Antonine Wall (2009), Excavation and Survey at Roman Burgh-by-Sands (jt ed, 2009), First Contact: Rome and Northern Britain (jt ed, 2009), Frontiers of the Roman Empire, Hadrian's Wall (2011), The Frontiers of Imperial Rome (2011), The First Souvenirs, Enamelled Vessels from Hadrian's Wall (2012), 200 Years, The Society of Antiquaries of Newcastle upon Tyne 1813–2013 (2013), Hadrian's Wall, A History of Archaeological Thought (2014); *Recreations* reading, travel; *Style—* Prof David Breeze, OBE, FSA, FRSE; ✉ 36 Granby Road, Edinburgh EH16 5NL (☎ 0131 667 8876)

BREMNER, Charles John Fraser; s of John Fraser Bremner, and Rosemary, *née* Ives; *b* 16 June 1951; *Educ* Blairmore Sch, St Peter's Coll S Aust, New Coll Oxford (BA), UC Cardiff (Dip Journalism Studies); *m* 1, 1973 (m dis 1982), Valeria, *née* Gaidukowski; 1 da (Anna Lucy b 1977); m 2, 1987 (m dis 2006), Fariba, da of Abbas Shirdel; 1 s (James Charles Farhad b 1991), 1 da (Leila Jenny b 1993); *Career* Reuters: trainee 1975–77, Moscow corr 1977–79, Mexico City corr 1979–80, Paris corr 1981–83, bureau chief Moscow 1983–86; The Times: New York corr 1987–92, Paris corr 1992–95 and 1999–, Europe corr 1995–99; *Recreations* flying, sailing, music; *Style—* Charles Bremner, Esq; ✉ c/o The Times, 1 Pennington Street, Wapping, London E1 9XN (e-mail charles.bremner@thetimes.co.uk)

BREMNER, Eric; s of Hamish Bremner, of Edinburgh, and Mary Wotherspoon Thomson, *née* Ross; *b* 9 July 1958; *Educ* Trinity Acad Edinburgh, Grays Sch of Art Aberdeen, Harrow Coll of Further Educn (Dip Fashion Design), RCA (MA); *m* 1 Sept 1979, Jane Catherine Mary, da of Donald Bruce Scott; 2 s (Hamish Scott b 10 May 1986, Fergus Ross b 1 Sept 1996), 1 da (Grace Francine b 5 March 1991); *Career* design asst Margaret Howell 1984; design dir Laura Ashley 1993–94, sr designer Sportmax/Max Mara Italy 1994– (designer 1984–94); design conslt: Marina Rinaldi Italy 1986–93, Prisma Commerciale Abbigliamento Italy 1987–93; pt/t tutor Fashion Sch RCA 1987–; external assessor: fashion (MDes) Edinburgh Coll of Art 1989–94, fashion (BA) Nat Coll of Art and Design Dublin 1989–94; *Recreations* cooking, music; *Style—* Eric Bremner, Esq; ✉ 9 High Street, Sutton Courtenay, Oxfordshire OX14 4AW (☎ 01235 848620)

BREMNER, Rory Keith Ogilvy; s of Maj Donald Stuart Ogilvy Bremner (d 1979), and Anne Ulithorne, *née* Simpson (d 2000); *b* 6 April 1961; *Educ* Wellington, KCL (BA); *m* 1, 8 Jan 1987 (m dis 1996), Susan Catherine, *née* Shackleton; m 2, 11 Sept 1999, Tessa Elizabeth, *née* Campbell Fraser; 2 da (Ava b 9 June 2001, Lila b 4 Aug 2003); *Career* satirical impressionist, actor, writer and performer 1984–; series BBC TV 1986–92, series Channel 4 1992–2010, Between Iraq and a Hard Place 2003; translations: Der Silbersee 1999, Carmen 2001, Brecht's A Respectable Wedding (Young Vic) 2007, Orpheus in the Underworld (Scottish Opera) 2011, Weill's Seven Deadly Sins 2014; columnist New Statesman and FT; Press Prize (Montreux) 1987, Top Male Comedy Performer (BCA) 1992, BAFTA 1994, 1995 and 1996, RTS Award 1995, 1998 and 1999; hon doctorate Heriot-Watt Univ, Hon DUniv Queen Mary's Coll; FKC 2005; *Recreations* cricket, travel, tennis, opera, golf; *Clubs* Lord's Taverners; *Style—* Rory Bremner, Esq; ✉ c/o PBJ Management, 22 Rathbone Street, London W1T 1LG (☎ 020 7287 1112)

BRENDEL, Alfred; Hon KBE (1989); s of Albert Brendel, and Ida, *née* Wieltschnig; *b* 5 January 1931, Kocianau, Czech Republic; *Educ* High Sch Graz Austria, Conservatory Graz, masterclasses Edwin Fisher Lucerne; *m* 1, 1960 (m dis 1972), Iris Heymann-Gonzala; 1 da (Doris); m 2, 1975 (m dis 2012), Irene, da of Dr Johannes Semler; 1 s (Adrian), 2 da (Anna-Sophie, Katharina); *Career* pianist and writer; concert career since 1948; recordings for Vox, Turnabout, Vanguard, Philips, Decca; Evening Standard Outstanding Artistic Achievement Award 1995, Léonie Sonning Music Prize 2002, Ernst von Siemens Prize 2004, Prix Venezia 2007, Herbert von Karajan Music Prize 2008, South Bank Show Award 2009, Praemium Imperiale Japan Arts Assoc 2009, Musikpreis Duisburg 2010, Franz Liszt Ehrenpreis Weimar 2011, Gramophone Award 2012; Hon DMus: Univ of London 1978, Univ of Sussex 1981, Univ of Oxford 1983, Univ of Warwick 1991, Yale Univ 1992, Univ of Cologne 1995, Dublin Univ Coll 1997, Univ of Exeter 1998, London Royal Coll of Music 1999, Univ of Southampton 2002, UCD 2007, Boston New England 2009, New England Conservatory, Bukarest Musik Univ 2011, Montreal McGill Univ 2011, Univ of Cambridge 2012, Juilliard Sch NY 2013, Univ of Bristol 2016; fell Exeter Coll Oxford; memb Acad of Arts and Sciences USA 1989, memb Deutsche Akademie für Sprache und Dichtung 2010; Hon RAM, FRNCM 1990; Ordre pour le Mérite (Germany) 1991, Commandeur de l'Ordre des Arts et des Lettres (France) 2003 (Chevalier 1985); *Books* Musical Thoughts and Afterthoughts (essays, 1976), Music Sounded Out (essays, 1990), Fingerzeig (45 texts, German, 1996), Störendes Lachen Während des Jaworts (44 texts, German, 1997), One Finger Too Many (poetry, London 1998, New York 1999), Kleine Teufel (poems, German, 1999), Collected Essays on Music (a cappella, 2000), Ausgerechnet Ich (2001), The Veil of Order (2002), Spiegelbild und schwarzer Spuk (collected poems, German, 2003), Über Musik (2005), Friedrich Hebbel, Weltgericht mit Pausen (2008), Nach dem Schlussakkord (2010), Playing the Human Game (collected poems, 2010), A bis Z eines Pianisten (2012), A Pianist's A to Z (2013), Wunderglaube und Misstonleiter (2014), Music, Sense and Nonsense: collected essays and lectures (2016); *Recreations* reading, theatre, films, arts, unintentional humour, kitsch; *Style—* Alfred Brendel; ✉ c/o Ingpen & Williams Ltd, 7 St George's Court, 131 Putney Bridge Road, London SW15 2PA (☎ 020 8874 3222, fax 020 8877 3113)

BRENDON, John Patrick; *b* 27 March 1947; *Educ* Tonbridge, Univ of Manchester (BA); *Children* 1 da (Camilla b 4 Oct 1985), 1 s (Richard b 2 May 1987); *Career* PricewaterhouseCoopers (formerly Price Waterhouse): joined London office 1968, ptnr 1980–2007, NY office 1984–87, memb UK firm Supervisory Bd 1998–2007, memb Global Oversight Bd 2000–01, UK ethics ptnr 2004–06, global chief accountant 2004–07, conslt Hong Kong 2007–; memb Appeal Ctee ICAEW 2007–13; tstee Glastonbury Abbey 2009– (chm 2010–), tstee Brandon Tst 2013–15; FCA (ACA 1972); *Clubs* MCC, Sherborne Golf; *Style—* John Brendon, Esq; ✉ 91 Princes House, Kensington Park Road, London W11 3BW (☎ 07976 691895)

BRENMAN, Greg; *Career* co-chm Tiger Aspect Pictures, head of drama and memb Bd of Dirs Tiger Aspect Prodns; *Television* prodr: Jane Eyre (ITV), Deacon Brodie (BBC1), Births Marriages and Deaths, (BBC2, Best Drama Broadcast Awards, nominee BAFTA Award and Indie Award), Kid in the Corner (Channel 4, three Golden Nymph Awards, Mental Health Award, nominee BAFTA Award), Playing The Field (BBC1, Best Indie Drama, nominee RTS Award and BAFTA Award), Shockers (Channel 4), Hound of The Baskervilles (BBC1), Rescue Me (BBC1), Murphy's Law (BBC1), Fat Friends (ITV), My Fragile Heart, (ITV, nominee RTS Award and Broadcast Award), Bodily Harm, (Channel 4, RTS nomination), Murder, (BBC2, BAFTA Award), Omagh (Channel 4), Family Business (BBC1); *Film* prodr: Billy Elliott 2000 (Best Newcomer Prodr Award Producers Guild of America, nominee Best Picture Golden Globe Award, Best Independent Film Br Independent Film Awards), The Martins 2001, The League of Gentlemen's Apocalypse 2005; *Style—* Greg Brenman, Esq; ✉ Tiger Aspect Productions, 4th Floor, Shepherds Building Central, Charecroft Way, London W14 0EE

BRENNAN, Baron (Life Peer UK 2000), of Bibury in the County of Gloucestershire; Daniel Joseph; QC (1985); s of Daniel Brennan (d 1969), of Bradford, and Mary, *née* Ahearne (d 1966); *b* 19 March 1942; *Educ* St Bede's GS Bradford, Univ of Manchester (LLB); *m* 21 Aug 1968, Pilar, da of Luis Sanchez Hernandez, of Madrid (d 1980), and Nieves Moya Dominguez; 4 s (Daniel b 1971, Patrick b 1972, Michael b 1977, Alexander b 1980); *Career* called to the Bar: Gray's Inn 1967, King's Inn Dublin 1990, NI 2001; recorder of the Crown Court 1982–; memb Criminal Injuries Compensation Bd 1989–97; bencher Gray's Inn 1993; chm Personal Injury Bar Assoc 1995–97; chm Gen Cncl of the Bar 1999 (vice-chm 1998); ind advsr to Home Sec and Min of Def on compensation for miscarriages of justice; pres Catholic Union of GB; Hon LLD: Nottingham Trent 1999, Univ of Manchester 2000, Univ of Bradford 2007; FRSA 2000; *Publications* Bullen & Leake on Pleadings (gen ed, 16 edn, 2007); *Style—* Lord Brennan, QC; ✉ Matrix Chambers, Griffin Building, Gray's Inn Road, London WC1R 5LN (☎ 020 7611 9359, fax 020 7404 3448)

BRENNAN, Kevin Denis; MP; s of Michael Brennan (d 2006), of Cwmbran, and Beryl, *née* Evans; *b* 16 October 1959; *Educ* St Alban's RC Comp Sch Pontypool, Pembroke Coll Oxford (BA), UC Cardiff (PGCE), Univ of Glamorgan (MSc); *m* 1988, Amy Lynn, da of Charles Wack; 1 da (Siobhán Lynn b 15 March 1994); *Career* head of econ Radyr Comp Sch 1985–94; researcher for Rt Hon Rhodri Morgan, MP 1995–2000, special advsr Nat Assembly for Wales 2000; MP (Lab) Cardiff W 2001–; a Lord Cmmr of HM Treasy (Govt whip) 2005–07, Parly under sec of state Dept of Children, Schs and Families 2007–08, Parly sec Cabinet Office 2008–09, min of state Dept for Business Innovation and Skills 2009–10; memb Select Ctee for Public Admin 2001–05; memb Cardiff City Cncl 1991–2001 (chair Finance, chair Econ Scruntiny); memb Lab Campaign for Electoral Reform; memb: Fabian Soc, Bevan Fndn, Socialist Health Assoc; memb Parly rock band MP4; *Recreations* sport (particularly watching rugby), music; *Clubs* Canton Labour; *Style—* Kevin Brennan, MP; ✉ House of Commons, London SW1A 0AA (☎ 029 2022 3207, e-mail brennank@parliament.uk)

BRENNAN, Dame Ursula; DCB (2013); *b* 28 October 1952; *Educ* Putney HS, Univ of Kent at Canterbury (BA); *m* 28 June 1975, Denis Brennan; *Career* ILEA 1973–75, various posts rising to DG DWP 1999–2004, DG DEFRA 2004–06; Miny of Justice: DG Office for Criminal Justice Reform 2006–07, head Organisational Review Team 2007, DG corporate performance 2008; MOD: second perm under sec 2008–10, perm sec 2010–; *Style—* Dame Ursula Brennan, DCB

BRENNAND-ROPER, Dr David Andrew; s of Dr John Hanson Brennand-Roper (d 1974), of Guernsey, CI, and Joyce Brennand-Roper, *née* Deans; *b* 22 August 1946; *Educ* Bryanston, BNC Oxford (MA), Guy's Hosp Med Sch (BM BCh); *m* Sheila Jane, *née* Boswell; 4 c (Tanya Alexandra b 8 June 1982, Anneka Louise b 18 June 1984, Alexander James Boswell b 4 Aug 1992, Giles William John b 24 Aug 1995); *Career* Sir Phillip Oppenheimer res fell in nuclear cardiology 1979–81, sr registrar in cardiology Guy's Hosp 1981–82, conslt cardiologist Guy's and St Thomas' Tst and Dartford Hosps 1982–2002, emeritus conslt cardiologist Guy's and St Thomas' Hosps 2002–; lectr of the Br Heart Fndn; memb European Soc of Cardiology; Freeman City of London 1977, former Freeman Worshipful Co of Tobacco Pipe Makers 1977–82; memb BMA; FRCP; *Recreations* golf, photography, oenology; *Style—* Dr David Brennand-Roper; ✉ Suite 401, St Olaf House, London Bridge Hospital, 27 Tooley Street, London SE1 2PR (☎ 020 7357 8467, fax 020 7357 0994, e-mail londoncardiologypractice@gmail.com)

BRENT, Michael Hamilton; s of Allan Henry David George Brent (d 1978), and Irene Dorothy, *née* Jameson; *b* 18 March 1943; *Educ* Charterhouse; *m* 1973, Janet, da of Irvine McBeath; 1 s, 2 da; *Career* chm and md Trimite Ltd 1975–; FCA; *Recreations* bridge, chess, golf, sailing, skiing, tennis; *Clubs* Wentworth Golf; *Style—* Michael Brent, Esq, FCA; ✉ Trimite Ltd, Arundel Road, Uxbridge, Middlesex UB8 2SD (☎ 01895 251234, fax 01895 256789); c/o HSBC, PO Box 41, High Street, Uxbridge, Middlesex

BRENTON, Howard John; s of Donald Henry Brenton, and Rose Lilian, *née* Lewis; *b* 13 December 1942; *Educ* Chichester HS for Boys, St Catharine's Coll Cambridge (BA); *m* 31 Jan 1970, Jane Margaret, da of William Alfred Fry; 2 s (Samuel John b 23 Sept 1974, Harry William Donald b 6 Sept 1976); *Career* playwright; plays incl: Christie in Love (Portable Theatre) 1969, Revenge (Royal Court Theatre Upstairs) 1969, Hitler Dances (Traverse Theatre Workshop Edinburgh) 1972, Measure for Measure, after Shakespeare (Northcott Theatre Exeter) 1972, Magnificence (Royal Court Theatre) 1973, Brassneck (with David Hare, Nottingham Playhouse) 1973, The Churchill Play (Nottingham Playhouse) 1974 and twice revived by the RSC in 1978 and 1988, Government Property (Aarhus Theatre Denmark) 1975, Weapons of Happiness (NT) 1976 (winner of the Evening Standard Best Play of the Year award), Epsom Downs (Jt Stock Theatre Co) 1977, Sore Throats (RSC) 1979, The Romans in Britain (NT) 1980, Thirteenth Night (RSC) 1981, The Genius (Royal Court Theatre) 1983, Bloody Poetry (Foco Novo Theatre) 1984 and revived by the Royal Court Theatre 1988, Pravda (with David Hare, NT) 1985 (winner of the Evening Standard Best Play of the Year award), Greenland (Royal Court Theatre) 1988, Iranian Nights (with Tariq Ali, Royal Court Theatre) 1989, HID – Hess is Dead (RSC and Mickery Theatre Amsterdam) 1989, Moscow Gold (with Tariq Ali, RSC) 1990, Berlin Bertie (Royal Court) 1992, Playing Away (opera libretto, Opera North) 1994, Faust (RSC) 1995, In Extremis (Univ of Calif) 1997, Ugly Rumours (with Tariq Ali, Tricycle Theatre) 1998, Nasser's Eden (BBC Radio) 1998, Collateral Damage (with Tariq Ali and Andy de la Tour, Tricycle Theatre) 1999, Snogging Ken (with Tariq Ali and Andy de la Tour, Almeida Theatre) 2000, Kit's Play (RADA Jerwood Theatre) 2001, Paul (RNT) 2005, In Extremis (Shakespeare's Globe) 2006, Never So Good (RNT) 2008, The Ragged Trousered Philosophers (Liverpool Everyman and Chichester Festival) 2010, Danton's Death (RNT) 2010, Anne Boleyn (Shakespeare's Globe) 2010–11; TV plays incl: A Saliva Milkshake (BBC) 1975, The Paradise Run (Thames) 1976, Desert of Lies (BBC) 1984, the four part series Dead Head (BBC) 1986, Spooks (writer of several episodes, BBC) 2002, 2003, 2004 and 2005 (Best Drama Series BAFTA Awards); Arts and Humanities Research Bd Fellowship Univ of Birmingham 2000–03; Freeman City of Buffalo NY; Hon Dr Univ of North London, Hon DLitt Univ of Westminster; *Books* Diving for Pearls (1989), Hot Irons (1995, 2 edn 1998); *Recreations* painting; *Style—* Howard Brenton, Esq; ✉ c/o Casarotto Ramsey, Waverley House, 7–12 Noel Street, London W1F 8GQ (☎ 020 7287 4450, fax 020 7287 9128, website www.casarotto.co.uk)

BRENTON, Jonathan Andrew; *b* 24 December 1965, Kampala, Uganda; *Educ* Univ of Bristol (MA), Boston Univ Mass (MA), Girton Coll Cambridge (PhD); *m* Sayana Yakovlena; 2 da (Aleksandra, Diana), 1 s (Jakob); *Career* diplomat; FCO: joined 1994, desk offr EU Dept 1994–96, second sec (commercial) then first sec (economic) Moscow 1996–2000, head Wider Europe Section EU Dept 2000–02, first sec (media) Berlin 2003–06, dep head Africa Dept (Equatorial) 2006–08, head Jt Mgmnt Office 2008–10, ambass to Belgium 2010–14, acting head Campaigns and Engagement FCO 2014–15, min-cnsllr Br Embassy Moscow 2015–; *Style—* Mr Jonathan Brenton; ✉ British Embassy Moscow, British Forces Post Office (BFPO) 5203, Foreign and Commonwealth Office, West End Road, Ruislip, Middlesex HA4 6EP (e-mail jonathan.brenton@fco.gov.uk)

BRENTON, Timothy Deane; QC 1998; s of Cdr Ronald William Brenton, MBE (d 1982), and Peggy Cecilia Deane, *née* Biggs; *b* 4 November 1957; *Educ* King's Sch Rochester, BRNC Dartmouth, Univ of Bristol (LLB); *m* 29 Aug 1981, Annabel Louisa, da of Alan Harry Robson, of Sharrington, Norfolk; 1 da (Louisa Elizabeth b 8 April 1990), 1 s (Benjamin Alexander b 27 April 1993); *Career* RN 1975–79; lectr in law KCL 1980, called to the Bar Middle Temple 1981, standing counsel to Treas Slr in Admiralty matters 1991–98, hon counsel to King George's Fund for Sailors 2000–09; memb Panel Lloyds Arbitrators; memb Commercial Bar Assoc, supporting memb London Marine Arbitrators Assoc; *Recreations* golf, fishing, country pursuits, music; *Style—* Timothy Brenton, Esq, QC; ✉ 7 King's Bench Walk, Temple, London EC4Y 7DS (☎ 020 7910 8300, fax 020 7583 0950, e-mail tbrenton@7kbw.co.uk)

BRENTON, Will; s of John Kenneth Williamson (d 1997), and Doreen Mary Brenton (d 2006); *b* 11 November 1962, Leeds; *Educ* Old Hall HS Maghull Liverpool, Welsh Coll of Music and Drama (Dip Dramatic Arts); *Children* 2 da (Ella b 1996, Boo b 2008); *Career* actor, dir and prodr; co-fndr Tell Tale Prodns 1994–, fndr Wish Films Ltd 2005 (producing Jim Jam & Sunny for ITV); actor: Godspell 1987, Flying Lady 1988, Playdays 1988–90, Inspector Morse 1989, Blood Brothers 1990–91; actor and writer of pantomimes in Coventry 1990–2000; dir: Playdays 1990–94 (and writer), Coronation Street 1996–97, Emmerdale 1997–98, Bitsa 1996; creator, dir and prodr Fun Song Factory 1994–2004; writer, creator and prodr: Tweenies 1998–2004, Tweenies Live 2000–04, Boo! 2001–04, Sprogs 2002–04, Ella 2004; writer and prodr Wibbly Pig (BBC) 2007–09, writer, dir and prodr Florries Dragons 2008–10; writer and dir: Doctor Who Live 2010, Cbeebies Live 2012, Hairy Bikers Live! 2012, CBeebies Live – Big Band 2014; creator and dir The Great Big Gig London Southbank Centre 2014; BAFTA (for Tweenies) 2000, nominee BAFTA Award 1999, 2000, 2001, 2002 and 2003; FRTS 2000; *Books* Elephant White (2012); *Style—* Will Brenton, Esq; ✉ Wish Films Limited, Elstree Film Studios, Shenley Road, Borehamwood, Hertfordshire WD6 1JG (☎ 020 8324 2308, e-mail will@wishfilms.com, website www.willbrenton.com)

BRERETON, Donald; CB (2001); s of Clarence Vivian Brereton (d 1965), and Alice Gwendolin, *née* Galpin; *b* 18 July 1945; *Educ* Plymouth Coll, Univ of Newcastle upon Tyne (BA); *m* 12 April 1969, Mary Frances, da of William Turley (d 1967); 2 da (Kathryn Vivian b 15 Nov 1972, Sally Clare b 21 Dec 1974), 1 s (Samuel Edward b 21 Feb 1977); *Career* VSO Malaysia 1963–64, asst princ Miny of Health 1968–71, asst private sec to sec of state for Social Servs 1971–72, private sec to Permanent Sec DHSS 1972–73, princ Health Servs Planning 1973–79, princ private sec to Sec of State for Social Servs 1979–82; asst sec: DHSS Policy Strategy Unit 1982–84, Housing Benefit 1984–89; under-sec and head PM's Efficiency Unit 1989–93, policy dir DSS 1993–2001, dir Disability and Carers Gp DWP 2001–03; dir Motability 2004–08 (chair Pension Fund Tstees 2010–); vice-chair Standing Cmmn on Carers 2007–14; selector VSO, vice-pres Carers UK 2013–; memb Nat Quality Bd 2008–14; *Recreations* tennis, holidays, books, bridge; *Clubs* Civil Service, Walthamstow Cricket and Tennis (treas); *Style—* Donald Brereton, Esq, CB; ✉ e-mail don.brereton@live.co.uk

BRETT, Nicholas Richard John; s of Reginald Sydney Brett (d 1993), and Urania Rhoda, *née* Morris; *b* 6 February 1950, Newcastle upon Tyne; *Educ* Abingdon Sch, Bedford Coll London (BA, pres Students' Union), Pennsylvania State Univ (MA), Kellogg Business Sch Northwestern Univ (Exec Prog); *m* 1 (m dis); m 2, 3 Dec 1981, Judith Anne, da of

Norman Armitage Miller; 2 da (Camilla Beatrice Brett-Miller b 31 May 1980, Harriet Lucy Brett-Miller b 3 July 1983); *Career* news reporter then news ed East Ender (Stratford Express series) 1977, chief reporter Camden Journal 1978–81, prodn ed Times Health Supplement 1981; The Times: sports sub-ed 1982, chief sub-ed Saturday section 1982, dep ed Saturday section 1983, ed Saturday section 1984, asst features ed 1985, dep features ed 1986, features ed 1986–88; ed Radio Times and editorial dir BBC Magazines 1988–96, publishing dir Radio Times 1996–97, dir Radio Times Arts and Factual Gp 1997–2001, dep md BBC Magazines 2001–11, gp editorial dir BBC Magazines 2006–11, md magazines BBC Worlwide 2011–13, dir UK Publishing BBC Worldwide 2013–15, dir of editorial governance BBC Worldwide 2015–; memb Code of Practice Ctee Press Standards Bd of Fin 1992–94; pres European Assoc of TV Magazines 1993–95 (vice-pres 1992–93), chm BSME 1992, chm Periodicals Trg Cncl 2003–13; dir Bristol Magazines Ltd 2004–11, dir Worldwide Media (Mumbai) 2004–11; visiting prof of journalism Cardiff Univ 2006–; Radio Times winner Magazine of the Year Magazine Publishing Awards 1991, Ed of the Year BSME Awards 1993, Ed of the Year PPA Magazines Awards 1996, BSME Mark Boxer Award 2006, PPA Chm's Award 2007; *Recreations* Arsenal, birdwatching, carpentry, walking, growing Dahlias; *Clubs* Groucho; *Style—* Nicholas Brett, Esq; ✉ BBC Worldwide, Television Centre, 2C 04, 101 Wood Lane, London W12 7FA (e-mail nicholas.brett@bbc.com); nrjbrett@gmail.com

BRETT, Simon Anthony Lee; OBE (2016); s of Alan John Brett (d 1979), and Margaret, *née* Lee (d 2001); *b* 28 October 1945; *Educ* Dulwich Coll, Wadham Coll Oxford (maj scholar, BA, pres OUDS); *m* 27 Nov 1971, Lucy Victoria, da of late Alastair Dixon McLaren; 1 da (Sophie b 9 Oct 1974), 2 s (Alastair b 22 July 1977, Jack b 11 March 1981); *Career* writer; Father Christmas Toy Dept Shinners of Sutton 1967; prodr light entertainment: BBC Radio 1968–77 (worked on progs incl: Week Ending, Frank Muir Goes Into..., The News Huddlines, Lord Peter Wimsey, The Hitch-Hikers Guide to the Galaxy), LWT 1977–79 (worked on progs incl: End of Part One, Maggie and Her, The Glums); full time writer 1979–; writing for TV incl After Henry (nominated for 1988 and 1989 BAFTA Awards), How to be a Little Sod; writing for radio incl: Afternoon Theatre, Frank Muir Goes Into..., Semicircles, Molesworth, After Henry (BPG Award for Outstanding Radio Programme 1987), Dear Diary, No Commitments, Foul Play, Smelling of Roses; Writers' Guild Award for Best Radio Feature Script (with Frank Muir) 1973; pres Detection Club 2001–; chm: Crime Writers' Assoc 1986–87, Soc of Authors 1995–97; chair PLR Advsy Ctee 2003–08; *Publications* crime novels featuring actor-detective Charles Paris: Cast, In Order of Disappearance, So Much Blood, Star Trap, An Amateur Corpse, A Comedian Dies, The Dead Side of The Mike, Situation Tragedy, Murder Unprompted, Murder in the Title, Not Dead Only Resting, Dead Giveaway, What Bloody Man is That?, A Series of Murders, Corporate Bodies, A Reconstructed Corpse, Sicken and so Die, Dead Room Farce; other crime novels: A Shock to the System (Best Novel Award nomination by Mystery Writers of America, filmed starring Michael Caine), Dead Romantic, A Nice Class of Corpse, Mrs Presumed Dead, Mrs Pargeter's Package, The Christmas Crimes at Puzzel Manor, Mrs Pargeter's Pound of Flesh, Singled Out, Mrs Pargeter's Plot, Mrs Pargeter's Point of Honour, The Body on the Beach, Death on the Downs, The Torso in the Town, Murder in the Museum, The Hanging in the Hotel, The Witness at the Wedding, The Stabbing in the Stables, Death Under the Dryer, Blood at the Bookie's, The Poisoning at the Pub; crime short stories: A Box of Tricks, Crime Writers and Other Animals; others, incl various humorous books; *Recreations* real tennis; *Clubs* Groucho, Garrick; *Style—* Simon Brett, Esq, OBE; ✉ c/o Michael Motley, The Old Vicarage, Tredington, Tewkesbury, Gloucestershire GL20 7BP (☎ 01684 276390, website www.simonbrett.com)

BRETT, District Judge Trevor Graham; s of Joseph Brett (d 1986), and Nellie Kathleen, *née* Dean (d 1994); *b* 26 January 1950; *Educ* Borden GS Sittingbourne, Birmingham Poly (LLB London); *m* 5 April 1975, Gillian Margaret, da of Ernest Charles Fluck; 3 s (Mark Graham b 7 July 1978, Andrew Graham b 5 Dec 1980, Oliver Graham b 4 Nov 1985); *Career* articled 1972–74, admitted slr 1974; in private practice: Bradbury & Co Camberwell 1974–75, Basset & Boucher Rochester 1975–85, Dakers Green Brett Chatham 1985–92; district judge Uxbridge, Slough and Reigate Co Cts Apr 1992–93; district judge Bromley Co Cts 1993–; memb Law Soc 1974– (sec Rochester, Chatham and Gillingham Law Soc 1982–92); *Recreations* sport, especially golf, soccer and badminton, reading; *Style—* District Judge Brett

BREWER, David; s of William Watson Brewer (d 1968), and Eileen, *née* Hall (d 2002); *b* 24 July 1946; *Educ* Brigg GS, Emmanuel Coll Cambridge (BA), Regent St Poly (DMS); *m* 26 May 1973, Elizabeth Margaret, da of John William Ferguson (d 1986); 1 da (Jane b 1975); *Career* British Coal: area chief accountant South Midlands 1979–85, chief accountant 1985–87, head of fin servs 1987–91, fin controller 1991–93, head of fin 1993–95; fin and operations dir Scottish Coal 1995–97, business conslt 1997–98, dir and UK gen mangr Miller Mining The Miller Gp Ltd 1998–2000, commercial and financial conslt to the mining industry 2000–03, DG Confedn of UK Coal Prodrs 2003–14; chair Yorkshire Miners' Welfare Convalescent Homes Tst 2016–; assoc MIMM 1990, ACMA 1978; *Style—* David Brewer, Esq; ✉ 161 Chelsea Road, Sheffield S11 9BQ (☎ 0114 255 8392, e-mail davidbreweris@hotmail.com)

BREWER, Sir David William; KG (2016), kt (2007), CMG (1999), CVO (2015), JP (1979); s of Dr H F Brewer, and Elizabeth, *née* Nickell-Lean; *b* 28 May 1940, Luton, Beds; *Educ* St Paul's, Univ of Grenoble; *m* 1985, Tessa Suzanne Mary, OBE, *née* Jordá; 2 da (Olivia b 1988, Gabriella b 1990); *Career* joined Sedgwick Gp 1959, rep Sedgwick Gp Japan 1976–78; dir: Sedgwick Gp Devpt Cos 1982–98, Sedgwick Far East Ltd 1982–99 (chm 1993–97), Sumitomo Marine & Fire Insurance Co (Europe) Ltd 1985–98, Sedgwick Int Risk Mgmnt Inc 1990–99; chm: Sedgwick Insurance and Risk Mgmnt Consits (China) Ltd 1993–97, Sedgwick Japan Ltd 1994–97; non-exec dir Tullett Prebon SITICO (China) Ltd 2007–15, non-exec dir Nat Bank of Kuwait (Int) plc 2008–; sr advsr: DealGlobe 2014–, ECO Capacity Exchange 2015–; vice-pres GB-China Centre 2004– (chm 1997–2004), chm China-Britain Business Cncl 2007–13 (hon treas 1991–2007), chm Financial Servs Ctee China-Br Business Cncl/The City UK 2010–13; vice-pres City of London Sector Br Red Cross Soc 1986–, pres Insurance Inst of London 2006–07 (vice-pres 2005–06); pres City of London Branch RNLI 2007– (memb 1989–, chm 1997–2006); pres London Cornish Assoc 2005–13; tstee Daiwa Anglo-Japanese Fndn 2007–13; memb Advsy Cncl LSO 1999–2016; govr Sons and Friends of the Clergy 1993–2015 (sr treas 2010–12); chm St Paul's Cathedral Cncl 2015–; Hon Master of the Bench Gray's Inn 2004–; HM Cmmr of Lieutenancy for City of London 2005–09, HM Lord Lt of Gtr London 2008–15; Alderman Bassishaw Ward City of London 1996–2010 (memb Ct of Common Cncl 1992–96, Sheriff City of London 2002–03, Lord Mayor of London 2005–06; pres Camel Valley and Bodmin Moor Protection Soc 2015–; Liveryman Worshipful Co of Merchant Taylors 1968 (memb Ct of Assts 1985–, Master 2001–02), Hon Liveryman Worshipful Co of Insurers 2010, Warden Ct of Assts Worshipful Co of Blacksmiths 2007– (Prime Warden 2009–10), Hon Liveryman Worshipful Co of Security Professionals 2008; Hon DSc City Univ, Hon DPhil London Met Univ, Hon LLD Univ of Exeter, Hon DSc(Econ) London, Hon LLD Univ of Nottingham; FCII 1966, Hon FCSI 2006, Hon FIoD 2010 (life fell); Order of the Rising Sun (Japan) 2006, Magnolia Gold Award Mayor of Shanghai 2006; *Recreations* music (especially opera and choral music), golf, mechanical gardening, chocolate, paronomasia; *Clubs* Garrick, MCC, St Enodoc Golf, New Zealand Golf; *Style—* Sir David Brewer, CMG, CVO; ✉ Orchard Cottage, Hellandbridge, Bodmin, Cornwall PL30 4QR (☎ 01208 841268, e-mail david.brewer@dwbrewer.com)

BREWER, HE Dame Nicola; DCMG (2011, CMG 2003); da of Trevor Brewer; *Educ* Belfast Royal Acad, Univ of Leeds (PhD); *m* Geoff Gillham; 1 s, 1 da; *Career* diplomat; joined FCO 1983, 2 sec chancery Mexico City 1984–87, 1 sec FCO 1987–91, 1 sec economic Paris 1991–94, dep head then head Common Foreign and Security Policy Dept FCO 1995–97, asst dir personnel policy FCO 1997–98, political counsellor New Delhi 1998–2001, dir global issues FCO 2001–02, DG regional progs Dept for Int Devpt 2002–04, DG Europe FCO 2004–07, chief exec Equality and Human Rights Cmmn 2007–09, high cmmr to South Africa 2009–13; memb Justice Sec's Advsy Panel on Judicial Diversity 2009–10, hon bencher Middle Temple 2011; tstee Pilgrim Tst 2008; Hon LLD Univ of Leeds 2009; *Clubs* Athenaeum; *Style—* HE Dame Nicola Brewer, DCMG; ✉ FCO (Pretoria), King Charles Street, London SW1A 2AH

BREWSTER, Martyn Robert; s of Robert Richard Frederick Brewster of Watford, Herts, and Doreen Violet, *née* Lilburn; *b* 24 January 1952, Oxford; *Educ* Watford Boys GS, Herts Coll of Art, Brighton Poly (BA, Postgrad Dip Painting and Printmaking, Art Teachers Cert); *m* 1988 (m dis 1997), Hilary Joy, da of Peter John Carter; 1 da (Sophie Roberta b 19 Aug 1988); partner, Susie Louise James; 1 da (Isabelle Emily Teresia b 7 Oct 2004); *Career* painter and printmaker; lectr in art East Herts Coll 1980–89; sr lectr in fine art Bournemouth Coll of Art and Design 1988–2004; visiting lectr various arts schs 1980–89 incl: Winchester, Bournemouth, London Coll of Furniture; Space Studio in London 1983–90, Jill George Gallery 1986–2011, Park Studios London 1990–, studio in Dorset 1990, joined Waterhouse and Dodd Fine Art 2011; Eastern Arts Award 1977, awarded various Regnl Arts Association grants 1979–86, Br Cncl travel award 1991, Arts Cncl devpt grant 1994; memb Brighton Open Studios 1975–79; *Two-man Exhibition* Thumb Gallery Soho 1987–; *Solo Exhibitions* incl: Peterborough City Museum and Art Gallery 1983, London Coll of Furniture 1984, Warwick Arts Tst London 1986, Winchester Gallery 1986, Minories Essex 1986, Woodlands Gallery London 1987, Thumb Gallery (Shadows and Light 1987, Light Falls 1990), Atlanta 1991, Jill George Gallery 1992 (Nature Paintings 1994, Lowick Prints 1995, Beauty and Sadness 1996), Paintings, Prints & Drawings 1969–1997 Russell-Cotes Art Gallery Bournemouth 1997 and tour, Night Music (Jill George Gallery) 1998, Royal West of England Acad 2001, King Alfred's Coll Winchester 2001, Nature Paintings Jill George Gallery 2000 and 2002, Study Gallery of Modern Art Poole 2004, The George Gallery 2005, 2006 and 2008, Coastal Light (Waterhouse & Dodd London) 2012, Night Poetry (Waterhouse & Dodd London) 2014, Recent Paintings and Drawings (Waterhouse & Dodd) 2016; *Group Exhibitions* incl: Spirit of London (Festival Hall) 1983, English Expression (Warwick Arts Tst) 1984, Int Art Fair London 1985, Angela Flowers Gallery 1985–86, Int Art Fairs LA 1987–90, London Group (RCA) 1988, Art London (Thumb Gallery) 1989–90, Critics Choice (Air Gallery London and Ianetti Lanzone Gallery San Francisco) 1989; *Works in Collection* of: Warwick Arts Tst, The Open Univ, Wiltshire Educn Authy, Russell-Cotes Art Gallery and Museum, Pallant House Chichester, Study Gallery Poole, Arts Inst Bournemouth, British Museum, Ashmolean Museum Oxford, various hosps, Peterborough Museum, V&A, Tate Gallery Library London, Univ of Bournemouth, The Hepworth Wakefield, various private collections worldwide; *Books* Monograph on Artist (text by Simon Olding and Mel Gooding, 1997), Re-Inventing The Landscape – Contemporary Painters and Dorset (by Vivienne Light, 2002), Martyn Brester Prints 1975–2007 (by Vivienne Light and Simon Olding, 2008); *Recreations* reading, walking, gardening, music, tennis; *Style—* Martyn Brewster, Esq; ✉ 15 West Road, Boscombe, Bournemouth, Dorset BH5 2AN; (studio 01202 423300, mobile 07966 259463, website www.martynbrewster.org); c/o Waterhouse and Dodd, 47 Albermarle Street, London W1S 4JW (website www.waterhousedodd.com)

BREWSTER, Thomas (Tom); s of Thomas Brewster, and Catherine, *née* Craig; *b* 10 April 1974, St Andrews, Scotland; *m* 2 Sep 2005, Kimberly, *née* Morris; 1 s (Ethan b 16 Dec 2007), 1 da (Charlotte b 29 June 2012); *Career* curler; mangr Curl Aberdeen 2004–; achievements incl: Bronze medal World Championships 2002, Silver medals World Championships 2011 and 2012, Bronze medal European Championships 2013, Bronze medal World Championships 2013, Silver medal Winter Olympic Games 2014; *Recreations* cinema, golf, travel; *Clubs* Curl Aberdeen, Laurencekirk Curling; *Style—* Tom Brewster, Esq; ✉ c/o Curl Aberdeen, Eday Walk, Aberdeen AB15 6LN (☎ 01224 810369, e-mail tom.brewster@curl-aberdeen.co.uk, website www.curl-aberdeen.co.uk)

BRIANCE, Richard Henry; o s of John Albert Perceval Briance, CMG (d 1989), and Prunella Mary, *née* Chapman; *b* 23 August 1953; *Educ* Eton, Jesus Coll Cambridge (BA); *m* 13 Oct 1979, Lucille, *née* de Zalduondo; 2 da (Zoe b 1982, Clementine b 1987), 2 s (Henry b 1984, Frederick b 1989); *Career* merchant banker; md Credit Suisse First Boston Ltd until 1991, vice-chm UBS Ltd 1991–97, chief exec West Merchant Bank Ltd 1997–99; Hawkpoint Partners Ltd: chief exec 1999–2003, dep chm 2004–10; chief exec Edmond de Rothschild Ltd 2010–15, chm PMB Capital Ltd 2015–; non-exec dir: Oxford Analytica 1999–2010, Mint Hotels plc; memb Fin Law Panel 2000–02; tstee: London Children's Ballet, Legatum Inst, Floreat Educn; *Clubs* Brooks's, Hawks' (Cambridge), Hurlingham, Pilgrims, Queenwood; *Style—* Richard Briance, Esq; ✉ The Old House, Holland Street, London W8 4NA (☎ 020 7937 2113)

BRICKWOOD, Prof Alan John; s of Robert James Brickwood (d 1988), of Hants, and Kathleen Agnes Brickwood (d 1978); *b* 16 October 1945; *Educ* Clapham Coll London, RCA (MDes); *Family* 2 s (Benjamin James b 21 Nov 1971, Thomas Alan David b 4 July 1999); *Career* research asst HUSAT (Human Scis and Advanced Technol) Research Gp Loughborough Univ 1970–74, fndr and dir Molehurst Ltd 1974–76, head of tport design Coventry Univ 1976–84, pro-vice-chllr Staffordshire Univ 1984–95, prof Dept of Design Brunel Univ 1996–98, industrial advsr Innovation Unit DTI 1996–98, fndr and princ Alan Brickwood & Associates Ltd 1999–; CNAA: memb Cncl and Gen Ctee 1984–87, chm Ctee for Art and Design 1984–90; auditor HEQC 1992–96; memb Advsy Gps HEFCE 1993–95; chm Conf for HE in Art and Design (CHEAD) 1992–95; memb: Design Ctee RSA 1988–91, Cncl Polytechnics and Colls Funding Cncl (PCFC) 1988–93, Prince of Wales 'Partners in Innovation' Highgrove 1991, Industry 96 1994–97, DTI Task Gp 'Action for Engrg' 1995–96; tstee CNAA Art Collection Tst 2003; CIMechE 1997; FRSA 1980, FCSD 1981; *Style—* Prof Alan Brickwood; ✉ 40 St Nicholas Church Street, Warwick CV34 4JD (☎ 07940 536526, e-mail alan@alanbrickwood.co.uk)

BRIDGE, Andrew; s of Peter Bridge, and Roslyn Bridge; *b* 21 July 1952; *Educ* Port Regis Sch, Bryanston, LAMDA, Theatre Projects London; *m* Susan Bridge; 2 s (Oliver b 1988, Alex b 1994), 1 da (Tessa (twin) b 1994); *Career* lighting designer; numerous projects incl: Siegfried and Roy spectacular (Mirage Hotel Las Vegas), Disneyland's Buffalo Bill's Wild West Show (France), Torvill and Dean, flood lighting Lloyds of London, designer to Shirley Bassey in Concert (for ten years); conslt Imagination (industrial and architectural lighting); memb: Assoc of Lighting Designers (Brit), United Scenic Artist (local 829, USA); *Theatre* UK credits incl: Carte Blanche, The Card, An Evening with Tommy Steele, Bing Crosby and Friends, Time, Oliver (also Broadway), The Boyfriend, Billy Bishop goes to War, Tomfoolery, Little Me, Blondel, The Hunting of the Snark, Five Guys Named Moe (also USA, Aust), Sunset Boulevard, Phantom of the Opera (also USA, Japan, Austria, Canada, Sweden, Germany, Aust, Switzerland, Holland), Joseph and the Amazing Technicolor Dreamcoat (also USA, Canada, Aust, Germany), Heathcliff, Doctor Dolittle; *Awards* for Phantom of the Opera incl: Tony Award, Drama Desk Award (NY), Outer Circle Critics' Award (NY), Dora Mavor Award (Canada), Los Angeles Critics' Award; for Sunset Boulevard incl: Tony Award, Los Angeles Critics' Award and Ovation Award; for Lloyds of London Nat Lighting Award; *Style—* Andrew Bridge, Esq; ✉ c/o

Performing Arts Management, 6 Windmill Street, London W1P 1HF (☎ 020 7255 1362, fax 020 7631 4631)

BRIDGE, Wayne Michael; *b* 5 August 1980, Southampton; *Partner* Francesca (Frankie) Sandford; 1 s (Parker b 2013); *Career* professional footballer; clubs: Southampton FC 1997–2003 (finalists FA Cup 2003), Chelsea FC 2003–09 (winners FA Premiership 2005 (runners-up 2004 and 2007), League Cup 2005 and 2007, FA Cup 2007), Fulham FC (on loan) 2006, Manchester City FC 2009–13, West Ham (on loan) 2011, Sunderland (on loan) 2012, Brighton (on loan) 2012–13, Reading FC 2013–; England: 36 caps, 1 goal, debut v Holland 2002, memb squad World Cup 2002 and 2006, memb squad European Championship 2004; *Style*— Mr Wayne Bridge; ✉ c/o Reading Football Club, Madejski Stadium, Junction 11, M4, Reading RG2 0FL

BRIDGEMAN, Viscountess; (Victoria) Harriet Lucy; CBE (2014); *née* Turton; da of Ralph Meredyth Turton, TD (d 1988), of Kildale Hall, Whitby, N Yorks, and Mary Blanche, *née* Chetwynd-Stapylton (d 2009); *b* 30 March 1942, Low Middleton Hall, Co Durham; *Educ* privately, St Mary's Sch Wantage, TCD (MA); *m* 10 Dec 1966, 3 Viscount Bridgeman, *qv*; 4 s (1 decd); *Career* exec ed The Masters 1966–68; ed: Discovering Antiques 1968–70, Going, Going, Gone series (Sunday Times Colour Magazine) 1973; fndr and chief exec The Bridgeman Art Library Ltd 1972–; fndr memb and memb Ctee Br Assoc of Picture Libraries and Agencies, memb Br Copyrght Cncl (rep for Artists' Collecting Soc CIC), fndr Artists' Collecting Soc CIC 2006, tstee Br Sporting Art Tst, tstee Chichester Art Tst; European Woman of the Year Award (Arts Section) 1997, Int Business Woman of the Year 2005, Trinity Alumni Award 2010; FRSA; *Books* author and ed of numerous books incl: The Encyclopaedia of Victoriana, The Illustrated Encyclopaedia of Needlework, The Last Word, Society Scandals, Guide to Gardens of Europe; *Recreations* reading, family, travelling; *Clubs* Chelsea Arts, RSA; *Style*— The Rt Hon the Viscountess Bridgeman, CBE, FRSA; ✉ 19 Chepstow Road, London W2 5BP (☎ 020 7727 5400); Watley House, Sparsholt, Winchester, Hampshire SO21 2LU (☎ 01962 776297); Bridgeman Images, 17–19 Garway Road, London W2 4PH (☎ 020 7727 4065, e-mail harriet@bridgemanimages.com, website www.bridgemanimages.com and www.artistscollectingsociety.org.uk)

BRIDGEMAN, John Stuart; CBE (2001), TD (1994), DL (Oxon 1989); s of James Alfred George Bridgeman (d 1961), and Edith Celia, *née* Watkins (d 1994); *b* 5 October 1944; *Educ* Whitchurch Sch Cardiff, UC Swansea (BSc); *m* 1967, Lindy Jane, da of Sidney Fillmore, of Gidea Park, Essex; 3 da (Victoria b 1972, Philippa b 1974, Annabel b 1980); *Career* previously with: Alcan Industries 1966, Aluminium Co of Canada 1969, Alcan Australia 1970; commercial dir Alcan (UK) Ltd 1977–80, vice-pres (Europe) Alcan Basic Raw Materials 1978–82, divnl md British Alcan Aluminium plc 1983–91 (divnl md Alcan Aluminium (UK) Ltd 1981–83), dir of corp planning Alcan Aluminium Ltd (Montreal) 1992–93, md British Alcan Aluminium plc 1993–95; DG Office of Fair Trading 1995–2000, vice-pres Trading Standards Inst 2001–; chm Novares Consortium 2000–01, advsr to Norton Rose 2000–02, dir Cardew Chancery 2001–03, memb Bd Br Waterways 2006–12 (chm Fair Trading Ctee 2007–12, chm Wales Advsy Bd 2008–12, vice-chm 2009–12); chm: Audit and Standards Ctee Warwickshire CC 2000–, howtocomplain.com 2000–12, Warwickshire Police Authy 2001–08, Direct Marketing Authy 2001–07 (currently ind appeals cmmr), Regulatory Ctee Br Horseracing Authy 2007–08 (formerly chm Jockey Club Regulatory Bd), Recovery Career Services 2014–15; ind complaints adjudiator Assoc for TV on Demand 2007–10, regulatory dir Br Horse Racing Authy 2009–12; memb Monopolies and Mergers Cmmn 1990–95; visiting prof of mgmnt: Keele Univ 1992–2010, Imperial Coll London 2001–04, Univ of Surrey 2004–07; chm Aluminium Extruders' Assoc 1987–88 (memb Cncl 1982–91), vice-pres Aluminium Fedn 1995 (memb Bauxite Advsy Gp 1977–81); US Aluminium Assoc prize winner 1988; dir Oxford Psychologists Press 2001–06; chm: North Oxon Business Gp 1984–92, Enterprise Cherwell Ltd 1985–91, Oxfordshire Economic Partnership 2000–07; govr North Oxon Coll 1985–98 (chm 1989), memb Bd Heart of England TEC 1990–2002 (chm 2000–02), dir Oxford Orchestra da Camera 1996–2000; chm of tstees Banbury Sunshine Centre 2003–; tstee: Fndn for Canadian Studies 1995–2010 (vice-chm 2005–10), Oxon Community Fndn 1996–2002, Oxfordshire Yeomanry Tst 1997–, Canal and River Tst 2011–14, Br Horseracing Pension Fund 2008–; pres: Canada-UK C of C 1997–98 (vice-pres 1995–96), Oxford Gliding Club 1998–2006; memb: Cncl Canada-UK Colloquia 1993–1998 and 2003– (treas 2005), Ctee Canada Club 1994–2010; TA and Reserve Forces: cmmnd 1978, QOY 1981–84, Maj REME (V) 1985–94, Staff Coll 1986, memb Oxon and E Wessex TAVRA 1985–2000, memb Nat Employer Liaison Ctee for Reserve Forces 1992–2002 (chm 1997–2002), Hon Col 5 (Queen's Own Oxfordshire Hussars) Sqdn 31 (City of London) Signal Regt 1996–2012, memb South Eastern Reserve Forces and Cadets Assoc (SERFCA) 2001–09; memb Def Sci Advsy Cncl 1991–94; High Sheriff Oxon 1995; memb Ct of Assts Worshipful Co of Turners 2004– (Master Steward 2011, Master 2014–15); Hon Dr Sheffield Hallam Univ 1996; hon fell Univ of Wales Swansea 1997; hon memb Inst of Consumer Affairs 1999; CIMgt, FRGS, FRSA, FInstD, Hon FICM 1998; *Recreations* horses, Oxfordshire affairs, Territorial Army, gardening, shooting, skiing, turning; *Clubs* MCC, Reform; *Style*— John S Bridgeman, CBE, TD, DL; ✉ Recovery Career Services, Alhambra House, Charing Cross Road, London

BRIDGEMAN, 3 Viscount (UK 1929); Robin John Orlando Bridgeman; s of Brigadier Hon Geoffrey John Orlando Bridgeman, MC, FRCS (d 1974, 2 s of 1 Viscount Bridgeman, sometime Home Sec and First Lord of the Admiralty), and Mary Meriel Gertrude (d 1974), da of Rt Hon Sir George Talbot, a High Court Judge; suc unc, 2 Viscount, 1982; *b* 5 December 1930; *Educ* Eton; *m* 10 Dec 1966, (Victoria) Harriet Lucy (Viscountess Bridgeman, CBE, *qv*); 3 da of Ralph Meredyth Turton, TD (d 1988), of Kildale Hall, Whitby; 3 s (and 1 s decd); *Heir* s, Hon Luke Bridgeman; *Career* 2 Lt Rifle Bde 1950–51; CA 1958; ptnr stockbrokers Henderson & Crosthwaite 1973–76, Henderson Crosthwaite & Co Stockbrokers 1976–86; dir: Guinness Mahon & Co Ltd 1988–90, Nestor-BNA plc 1989–94, SPLIT plc 1996–97; dir The Bridgeman Art Library Ltd 1972–; chm Asset Management Investment Co plc 1994–2001; oppn whip House of Lords 1998–2010; Reed's Sch: pres Fndn Appeal 1992–93, chm 1995–2002, jt life pres 2002–; special tstee Hammersmith Hospitals NHS Tst 1986–99, chm Friends of Lambeth Palace Library 1992–2008; treas: Florence Nightingale Aid in Sickness Tst 1995–2006, New England Co 1996–2006; tstee: Winchester Theatre Fund 1985–2001, Friends of Music at Winchester 1998–2006; chm: Hosp of St John and St Elizabeth 1999–2007, CORESS 2006–12; Knight SMOM; *Recreations* gardening, travel, music; *Clubs* MCC, Beefsteak; *Style*— Viscount Bridgeman; ✉ 19 Chepstow Road, London W2 5BP (☎ 020 7727 5400); Watley House, Sparsholt, Winchester SO21 2LU (☎ 01962 776297, e-mail contactholmember@parliament.uk)

BRIDGEN, Andrew James; MP; *b* 1964, Burton upon Trent, Staffs; *Educ* Pingle Sch Swadlincote, Univ of Nottingham; *m* (m diss 2014) Jacqueline; 2 s (Alexander, Benjamin); *Career* co-fndr AB Produce 1988; MP (Cons) Leics NW 2010–; chair Regulatory Reform Select Ctee 2015–; *Clubs* Carlton; *Style*— Andrew Bridgen, Esq, MP; ✉ House of Commons, London SW1A 0AA

BRIDGES, Prof James Wilfrid (Jim); s of Wilfrid Edward Seymour Bridges (d 1994), of Cuxton, Kent, and Mary Winifred, *née* Cameron (d 1987); *b* 9 August 1938; *Educ* Bromley GS, KCL (BSc), St Mary's Hosp Med Sch London (PhD), Univ of London (DSc); *m* Dr Olga Bridges; *Career* lectr St Mary's Hosp Med Sch London 1962–68; Univ of Surrey: reader in biochemistry 1968–78, dir Robens Inst of Industrial and Environmental Health and Safety 1978–95, prof of toxicology and environmental health 1979–2003 (emeritus prof 2003–), dean Faculty of Sci 1988–92, head Euro Inst of Health and Scis 1995–2000, dean for int strategy 2000–03; visiting prof: Univ of Texas 1973 and 1979, Univ of Rochester NY 1974, Centro de Investigacion y de Estudios Avanzados Mexico 1991; visiting sr scientist Nat Inst of Environmental Health Sciences USA 1976; chm Br Toxicology Soc 1980–81, first pres Fedn of Euro Socs of Toxicology 1985–88, memb Exec Ctee Euro Soc of Biochemical Pharmacology 1983–89, fndr Euro Drug Metabolisms Workshops, chm Veterinary Residue Ctee 2000–04; memb: Veterinary Products Ctee MAFF 1982–98, Advsy Ctee on Toxic Substances HSE 1986–89, Air Soil and Water Contaminants Ctee DHSS/DOE 1984–90, UK Shadow Gp on Toxicology DHSS 1984–2000, Watch Ctee HSE 1987–2004, Food Safety and Applied Res Consultative Ctee 1989–90, Advsy Ctee on Irradiated and Novel Foods MAFF 1982–88, Maj Hazards Ctee Working Party (HSE) 1982–84, Corporation of Farnborough Coll of Technology 1992–2000; EEC: memb Scientific Ctee on Animal Nutrition 1990–97, memb Scientific Steering Gp on Consumer Health 1997–2003, chm Scientific Ctee on Toxicity, Ecotoxicity and the Environment 1997–2004, chm Harmonisation of Risk Assesment Task Force 1998–2003, chm Scientific Ctee on Emerging and Newly Identified Health Risks 2004–, memb European Parl/EU Mirror Gp 2006–; expert advsr: European Food Safety Authy 2003–, DG Research 2005–; Inst of Biology: chm Food Policy Gp 1990–93, memb Policy Ctee 1993–97; memb Bd of Dirs Int Life Scis Inst (Europe) 2000–04; chm Environmental Advsy Bd Shanks plc 2004–; hon memb Soc of Occupational Med 1989, fell Collegium Ramazzini 1990, hon memb Royal Acad of Vet Scis Spain 2008; Hon DSc Baptist Univ Hong Kong; CChem, CBiol 1981, FRSC, FIBiol, MInstEnvSci 1980, MRCPath 1984, FRSA 1989, FIOSH 1990; *Publications* incl: Progress in Drug Metabolism (ed with Dr L Chasseaud, Vols 1–10), Watershed 89 The Future for Water Quality in Europe Vols I and II (ed with M L Richardson and D Wheeler), Animals and Alternatives in Toxicology (ed with M Balls and J Southee), Losing Hope: The Environment and Health in Russia (with Dr Olga Bridges, 1996); jt ed of 17 books and over 370 res pubns and reviews in scientific jls; *Recreations* theatre, concerts, travel; *Style*— Prof Jim Bridges; ✉ Research for Sustainability, Liddington Hall Drive, Guildford, Surrey GU3 3AE (mobile 07768 004595, e-mail j.bridges@surrey.ac.uk)

BRIDGES, Hon Mark Thomas; CVO (2012); er s and h of 2 Baron Bridges, GCMG; *b* 25 July 1954; *Educ* Eton, CCC Cambridge; *m* 1978, Angela Margaret, da of J L Collinson (d 1997); 3 da (Venetia Rachel Lucy b 21 Feb 1982, Camilla Frances Iona b 22 June 1985, Drusilla Katharine Anne b 12 July 1988), 1 s (Miles Edmund Farrer b 1 July 1992); *Career* slr; dir The Abinger Hall Estate Co 1984–92, ptnr Farrer & Co 1985–; slr to the Duchy of Lancaster 1998–2012, private slr to HM The Queen 2002–; memb Cncl Royal Sch of Church Music 1989–97, treas The Bach Choir 1992–97, chm Music in Country Churches 2006; tstee: UCLH Charities 1992–2010, Leeds Castle Fndn 2007–; govr: Purcell Sch 2000–12, Sherborne Sch for Girls 2001–11, Hanford Sch 2004–13; academician Int Acad of Estate and Tst Law; memb Ct of Assts Worshipful Co of Goldsmiths; *Recreations* sailing (yacht 'Makai of Orford', 'Powder Monkey'), reading, music; *Clubs* Brooks's, House of Lords' Yacht, Noblemen and Gentlemen's Catch; *Style*— The Hon Mark Bridges, CVO; ✉ 66 Lincoln's Inn Fields, London WC2A 3LH

BRIDGES, Stephen John; LVO (1998); s of Gordon Alfred Richard Bridges, of Wembury, Devon, and Audrey Middleton Bridges; *b* 19 June 1960; *Educ* Devonport HS, Plymouth Poly (Dip Law and Accounting), LSE, Leeds (MA); *m* 30 June 1990, Kyung Mi, da of Chan Young Yoon; *Career* joined FCO 1980, third sec Luanda 1984–87, third then second sec Seoul 1987–91, second then first sec UN and SE Asia Depts 1991–96, first sec and head of political section Kuala Lumpar 1996–2000, ambass to Cambodia 2000–05, dep high cmmr Bangladesh until 2007, consul gen Chicago 2013–; md Gtr Mekong Resources Ltd 2007–11, corp advsr Elemental Energy Technologies Ltd 2007–; *Recreations* golf, food and wine, Coco and Montague the dogs; *Style*— Stephen Bridges, Esq, LVO

BRIDGES, Stuart John; s of Frederick Francis Bridges (d 2012), and Gladys Mary, *née* Hayhoe (d 2004); *b* 16 September 1960; *Educ* Dalriada Sch, Gonville & Caius Coll Cambridge (nat engrg scholar, MA); *m* 14 Sept 1996, Diane Leonie, *née* Forrester; 2 s (Sebastian Charles Henry b 18 April 1997, Alexander George Richard b 29 April 2000); *Career* Arthur Andersen & Co 1983–89, Richard Ellis 1989–91, Henderson Investors 1991–94, exec dir Jacobs Holdings plc 1995–97, chief fin offr Hiscox Ltd 1999–2015, gp fin dir ICAP plc 2015–; non-exec dir Caledonia Investments plc 2013; memb Finance Ctee The Royal Inst 2016–; ACA 1987 (memb ICAEW Audit Ctee); *Recreations* golf, sailing; *Clubs* MCC; *Style*— Stuart Bridges, Esq; ✉ ICAP plc, 2 Broadgate, London, EC2M 7UR (☎ 020 7000 5000, e-mail stuart.bridges@icap.com)

BRIDGEWATER, Adrian Alexander; s of Maj Philip Alexander Clement Bridgewater (d 1980), and Hon Ursula Vanda Maud Vivian (d 1984); *b* 24 July 1936; *Educ* Eton, Magdalene Coll Cambridge (MA); *m* 1, 11 April 1958 (m dis 1968), Charlotte, da of Rev Michael Ernest Christopher Pumphrey (d 1982); 2 da (Emma Mary b 23 Dec 1960, Sophy Charlotte b 31 July 1962), 1 s (Thomas Michael George b 12 Nov 1963); m 2, 7 Nov 1969, Lucy Le Breton (d 2006), da of Sir Basil Bartlett, 2 Bt (d 1986); 2 da (Nancy le Breton b 10 Aug 1971, Daisy Maud b 27 Jan 1973), 1 s (Benjamin Hardington b 20 March 1979); m 3, 25 March 2014, Annabel Gooch, da of Dr Charles Raymond Greene (d 1982); *Career* founder and dir CRAC 1963–74, founder and chm Hobsons Press Ltd 1974–87; chm: Hobsons Publishing plc 1987–92, Johansens Ltd 1987–92, Care Choices Ltd 1993–, Connect Publishing Ltd 1993–, ECCTIS Ltd 1991–2009, Elephant Design Ltd 2004–14; dep chm Papworth Tst 1989–2012; fndr memb Cncl: Inst for Manpower Studies 1966–67, Open Univ 1974–80, RCA 1979–81, Nat Inst Careers Education and Counselling 1966–92, VSO 1980–82, Br Sch Osteopathy 1989–91; tstee Careers Res and Advsy Centre (CRAC) 1993–2006, Ind Schs Careers Orgn 1994–2003; govr King's Coll Choir Sch Cambridge 1988–92; *Books* Wasted Opportunity: The Rise and Fall of a Family Business (with Stan Jewson, 2012); *Recreations* walking, surfing, racing; *Clubs* Garrick; *Style*— Adrian Bridgewater, Esq; ✉ Manor Farm, Great Eversden, Cambridgeshire CB23 1HW (☎ 01223 263229, e-mail adrianbridgewater@gmail.com)

BRIDGWATER, Prof John; s of Eric Bridgwater, of Birmingham, and Mabel Mary, *née* Thornley; *b* 10 January 1938; *Educ* Solihull Sch, Univ of Cambridge (MA, PhD, ScD), Princeton Univ (MSE); *m* 29 Dec 1962, Diane, da of Arthur Edgarton Tucker (d 1965); 1 s (Eric Arthur b 1966), 1 da (Caroline Mary b 1967); *Career* chemical engr Courtaulds Ltd 1961–64; Univ of Cambridge 1964–71: demonstrator and lectr in chemical engrg, emeritus fell St Catharine's Coll 2004–; visiting assoc prof Univ of British Columbia 1970–71; Univ of Oxford 1971–80: fell Balliol Coll (former fell Hertford Coll), lectr in engrg sci; dean Faculty of Engrg Univ of Birmingham 1989–92 (prof 1980–93, head Sch of Chemical Engrg 1983–89); Univ of Cambridge: head Dept of Chemical Engrg 1993–98, sr tutor St Catharine's Coll 2004, currently emeritus prof of chemical engrg; visiting prof Univ of Calif Berkeley 1992–93, visiting Erskine fell Univ of Canterbury 2002, sr academic visitor Dept of Materials Science and Engrg UNSW 2004–; pres Instn of Chemical Engrs 1997–98; chm Bd Chemical Engrg Sci 1983–2003; memb Engrg Bd SERC 1986–89; pres World Cncl for Particle Technol 1999–2002; dir Tunku Abdul Rahman Centenary Fund 2004–06, govr Gordano Sch 2010–14; FIChemE 1974, FREng 1987; *Recreations* travel, gardening, mountain walking; *Style*— Prof John Bridgwater, FREng; ✉ Department of Chemical Engineering, University of Cambridge, Pembroke Street, Cambridge CB2 3RA (☎ 01223 334777, fax 01223 334796, e-mail jb231@cam.ac.uk)

BRIDPORT, 4 Viscount (UK 1868); Alexander Nelson Hood; also Baron Bridport (I 1794) and 7 Duke of Bronte in Sicily (cr 1799 by Ferdinand IV, the 'Lazzarone' King of the Two Sicilies, largely for Nelson's role in exterminating the Parthenopean Republic). In

1801 a Br Royal Licence was issued to Admiral Lord Nelson allowing him to accept for himself and his heirs the Dukedom of Bronte; s of 3 Viscount (d 1969, fourth in descent from the union of 2 Baron Bridport (2 s of 2 Viscount Hood) and Lady Charlotte Nelson, da of 1 Earl and niece of the great Admiral), and Sheila Jeanne Agatha, *née* van Meurs (d 1996); *b* 17 March 1948; *Educ* Eton, Sorbonne; *m* 1, 1972 (m dis 1979), Linda Jacqueline, da of Lt-Col Vincent Rudolph Paravicini; 1 s (Hon Peregrine Alexander Nelson b 30 Aug 1974); m 2, 1979 (m dis 1999), Mrs Nina Rindt, da of Curt Lincoln; 1 s (Hon Anthony Nelson b 7 Jan 1983); *Heir* s, Hon Peregrine Hood; *Career* with Kleinwort Benson Ltd 1967–80, Robert Fraser & Ptnrs 1980–83, exec dir Chase Manhattan Ltd 1983–85, gen mangr Chase Manhattan Bank (Suisse) 1985–86, md Shearson Lehman Hutton Finance (Switzerland) 1986–90, managing ptnr Bridport & Cie SA 1991–; *Recreations* skiing, diving, bridge; *Clubs* Brooks's; *Style*— The Rt Hon the Viscount Bridport; ✉ 1 Place Longemalle, 1204 Geneva, Switzerland (☎ 00 41 22 817 7000, fax 00 41 22 817 7050, e-mail bridport@bridport.ch)

BRIEN, Nicolas Frederich (Nick); s of Hubert Barrie Brien, of London, and Ursula, *née* Pfaller; *b* 18 January 1962; *Educ* King's Coll Wimbledon, Coll for Distributive Trades London; *m* Anastasia; 1 s (Lucas Barrie); *Career* Lerner & Grey June-Dec 1982, Grey Advertising 1983–84, Benton & Bowles 1984–85, WCRS 1985–89, BBJ Media Services 1989–92; Leo Burnett: exec media dir 1992–96, dep md 1994–96, md 1996–98, appointed chief exec 1997; subsequently pres of corp business devpt Starcom MediaVest Gp, ceo Arc Worldwide 2004–05, worldwide ceo Universal McCann 2005–; memb Media Res Gp IPA; MInstD; *Recreations* polo, skiing, tennis, golf, squash, tae kwon do (former UK nat champion), theatre, ballet, opera, reading; *Clubs* RAC; *Style*— Nick Brien, Esq

BRIER, Norma; OBE (2013), JP (2009); *b* 23 December 1949; *Educ* Henrietta Barnet Sch, Goldsmiths Coll London (BA), LSE (MSc, CQSW); *m* Sam Brier; 2 c; *Career* social worker and supervisor Student Unit London Borough of Camden 1971–76 (LSE 1973–74), pt/t lectr in social work and sociology and course organiser Counselling Skills for Teachers London Borough of Harrow 1976–83, charity work for learning-disabled children 1983–85; Ravenswood Fndn (now Norwood Ravenswood): joined as dir of community and social servs 1985, exec dir 1989–96, jt exec dir (following merger with Norwood) 1996–99, chief exec 1999–2011; dir Cross-Sector Consultancy Ltd 2011–, interim exec dir Scope 2012; conslt Aid for Belarussian Children Project, chair Voluntary Organisations Disability Gp 1998–2001; tstee Karten CTec 1997; memb: Panel of Ind Inquiry into Royal Brompton and Harefield Cardiology Services 1999–2001, Learning Disability Advsy Gp Dept of Health 1999–2001; co-chair Women in Jewish Leadership 2013–; Office for Public Mgmnt Prize for Leadership 1994; *Recreations* gardening, theatre, cinema; *Style*— Mrs Norma Brier, OBE, JP; ✉ Norwood, Broadway House, 80–82 Broadway, Stanmore, Middlesex HA7 4HB (☎ 020 8954 4555, fax 020 8420 6800)

BRIERLEY, Anthony William Wallace (Tony); s of William Derrik Brierley (d 1993), and Rose Mary, *née* Woodford (d 2013); *b* 1 October 1949, Nottingham; *Educ* Forest Fields GS Nottingham, Trent Poly Nottingham (BA), Inns of Court Sch of Law London; *Career* called to the Bar Inner Temple 1981; admitted slr 1990; W E Brierley & Sons Ltd 1968–77, legal advsr Notts Magistrates Courts 1981–83; 3i Gp plc: legal advsr 1983–90, head of legal 1990–94, dep co sec 1994–95, gen counsel, co sec, dir legal and regulatory and memb Exec Ctee 1996–2007; dir: Ship Mortgage Finance Co plc 1995–2007, 3i Europe plc 1995–2007, Baronsmead Investment Tst 1998–2007, 3i Asia Pacific plc 2000–07; non-exec dir: Gardens Pension Tstees Ltd 2008–, The Pensions Regulator 2008–; memb Leadership Team Business in the Environment 2002–07; memb Commerce and Industry Gp Law Soc 2002–07 (memb Corp Governance Ctee 2002–05, chm Trg Ctee 2004–07); memb Ct and Cncl Royal Coll of Art 2007–16, memb Bd of Govrs Nottingham Trent Univ 2009–15; *Recreations* the arts, collecting; *Style*— Tony Brierley, Esq

BRIGGS, Prof (George) Andrew Davidson; s of John Davidson Briggs, of Cambridge, and Catherine Mary, *née* Lormer; *b* 3 June 1950, Dorchester, Dorset; *Educ* The Leys Sch Cambridge (scholar), St Catherine's Coll Oxford (Clothworkers' scholar, MA), Queens' Coll Cambridge (PhD, Chase Prize for Greek), Ridley Hall Cambridge; *m* 1981, Diana Margaret Ashley, *née* Johnson; 2 da (Felicity Claire Davidson b 22 June 1983, Elizabeth Catherine Davidson b 29 July 1985); *Career* Royal Soc research fell in the physical sciences 1982–84; Univ of Oxford: lectr in metallurgy and science of materials 1984–96, reader in materials 1996–99, prof of materials 1999–2002, prof of nanomaterials 2002–; fell Wolfson Coll Oxford 1984–2002 (emeritus fell 2003), professorial fell St Anne's Coll Oxford 2003–; dir Quantum Info Processing Interdisciplinary Research Collaboration and professorial research fell EPSRC 2002–09; professeur invité Ecole polytechnique fédérale de Lausanne 1992–2002, visiting prof Univ of NSW 2002; memb: Bd of Mgmnt Ian Ramsey Centre 2001–15, EPSRC Peer Review Coll 2006–09, Sci and Engrg Fellowships Ctee Royal Cmmn for the Exhbn of 1851 2006–, Int Bd of Advsrs John Templeton Fndn 2007–09 and 2011–13, Engrg Panel Newton Int Fellowships 2008–; memb Editorial Bd: Science and Christian Belief 2001, Current Opinion in Solid State and Materials Science 2002–09, Nanotechnology 2005–06, Jl of Physics D: Applied Physics 2009–12; Holliday Prize Inst of Metals 1986, Buehler Tech Paper Merit Award for Excellence 1994, Metrology for World Class Mfrg Award 1999; involved with: St Andrew's Church Oxford, Christians in Science; memb Lambeth Partnership 2011, memb Int Soc for Science and Religion 2013; Liveryman Worshipful Co of Clothworkers; Hon FRMS 1999, FInstP 2004, memb Academia Europaea 2011; *Publications* An Introduction to Scanning Acoustic Microscopy (1985), Acoustic Microscopy (1992, 2 edn 2010), The Science of New Materials (ed, 1992), Advances in Acoustic Microscopy 1 (1995), Advances in Acoustic Microscopy 2 (1996), The Penultimate Curiosity (2016); also author of numerous contribs to learned jls; *Recreations* Christian theology, opera, skiing, sailing, flying; *Style*— Professor Andrew Briggs; ✉ University of Oxford, Department of Materials, Parks Road, Oxford OX1 3PH (☎ 01865 273725, fax 01865 273730, e-mail andrew.briggs@materials.ox.ac.uk, website www.andrewbriggs.org)

BRIGGS, Prof Anthony David Peach; s of Horace Briggs (d 1972), and Doris Lily, *née* Peach; *b* 4 March 1938; *Educ* King Edward VII Sch Sheffield, Trinity Hall Cambridge (MA), Univ of London (PhD); *m* 28 July 1962, Pamela Anne, da of Harry Metcalfe; 2 da (Fiona b 4 Nov 1966, Antonia 15 Aug 1970), 1 s (Julian b 2 Jan 1974); *Career* Nat Serv 1956–58, trained as Russian interpreter CSC interpretership 1958; Univ of Bristol 1968–87: lectr in Russian, sr lectr, reader, head Russian Dept; prof of Russian language and lit Univ of Birmingham 1987–99; memb Br Assoc for Slavonic and E Euro Studies; *Books* Mayakovsky, A Tragedy (1979), Alexander Pushkin: A Critical Study (1983), A Wicked Irony (Lermontov's A Hero of Our Time) (with Andrew Barratt, 1989), The Wild World (Pushkin, Nekrasov, Blok) (1990), Eugene Onegin (1992), Mikhail Lermontov: Commemorative Essays (1992), Alexander Pushkin (1997), Omar Khayyam (1998), English Sonnets (1999), Shakespeare's Love Poetry (1999), Alexander Pushkin: a Celebration (1999), Love, Please! (2001), Tolstoy's War and Peace (trans, 2005), Remember: Poems of Childhood (2005), Tolstoy's The Death of Ivan Ilyich and Other Stories (trans, 2008), Tolstoy's Resurrection (trans, 2009), Tolstoy's A Confession, and What is Religion? (trans, 2009), Leo Tolstoy, a Biography (2009), Dostoevsky, a Biography (2011), Five Russian Dog Stories (2012), Alexander Pushkin, The Queen of Spades and Selected Works (trans, 2013), Alexander Pushkin, Yevgeny Onegin (verse trans, 2016), Leonid Andreyev, Seven Hanged (trans, 2016); *Recreations* Mozart, Shakespeare, classical music, Russian culture, travel; *Style*— Prof Anthony Briggs; ✉ Custard Mead, Stoppers Hill, Brinkworth, Wiltshire SN15 5AW (☎ 01666 510075, e-mail adpbriggs@aol.com)

BRIGGS, Rt Hon the Lord Justice; Sir Michael Townley Featherstone Briggs; kt (2006), PC (2013); s of Capt James William Featherstone Briggs, and late Barbara Nadine, *née* Pelham Groom; *b* 23 December 1954; *Educ* Charterhouse, Magdalen Coll Oxford (MB); *m* 1981, Beverly Ann, da of late Gerald Alan Rogers; 3 s (Nicholas b 1984, James b 1986, Richard b 1988), 1 da (Jessica Molly b 1992); *Career* called to the Bar Lincoln's Inn 1978; jr counsel to the Crown in Chancery 1990–94, QC 1994, attorney gen to Duchy of Lancaster 2001–, judge of the High Court of Justice (Chancery Div) 2006–13, a Lord Justice of Appeal 2013–; *Recreations* sailing, singing, garden steam railways, cooking; *Clubs* Royal Yacht Sqdn, Bar Yacht, Goodwood Road Racing; *Style*— The Rt Hon the Lord Justice Briggs; ✉ Royal Courts of Justice, Strand, London WC2A 2LL

BRIGGS, Dr (Michael) Peter; OBE (2010); s of Hewieson Briggs (d 1992), and Doris, *née* Habberley (d 1999); *b* 3 December 1944, Sheffield; *Educ* Abbeydale Boys' GS Sheffield, Univ of Sussex (BSc, DPhil); *m* 1969, Jennifer Elizabeth, da of late Donald Watts; 1 da (Alison Mary b 26 Jan 1976), 1 s (Andrew Peter b 30 July 1981); *Career* jr research fell Dept of Chemistry Univ of Sheffield 1969–71, research asst Dept of Architecture Univ of Bristol 1971–73, deputation sec Methodist Church Overseas Div 1973–77, area sec (Herts and Essex) Christian Aid Br Cncl of Churches 1977–80; BAAS: educn mangr 1980–86, public affrs mangr 1986–88, dep sec 1988–90, exec sec 1990–97, chief exec 1997–2002; princ Southlands Coll and pro-rector Univ of Surrey Roehampton 2002–04, pro-vice-chllr and princ Southlands Coll Roehampton Univ 2004–07, special advsr to the Vice-Chllr and Princ Southlands Coll Roehampton Univ 2007–09; educnl conslt 2009–; chm Mgmnt Ctee Methodist Church Div of Social Responsibility 1983–86, exec memb Ctee on the Public Understanding of Science 1986–2002; memb Bd Int Assoc of Methodist Schs, Colls and Univs 2008–11; tstee: Central Fndn Schs of London 2009–15, Fernley Hartley Lecture 2010–, Wesley House Cambridge 2012–, The Dulwich Estate 2013–15; Master Co of Educators 2011–12; Hon DSc Univ of Leicester 2002; FRSA 1990, hon fell Br Assoc for the Advancement of Science (FBAASc) 2002; *Recreations* walking; *Style*— Dr Peter Briggs, OBE; ✉ 42 The Lawns, Hatch End, Pinner, Middlesex HA5 4BL (e-mail m_p_briggs@hotmail.com)

BRIGGS, Rachel Anne; OBE (2014); *b* 14 December 1976; *Educ* Girton Coll Cambridge (BA); *m* da of Howard Briggs, and Mary *née*Halden; *Career* head: Risk and Security Programme Foreign Policy Centre 1999–2003, Int Strategy Demos 2003–08; dir Hostage UK 2007–; memb: Editorial Bd Renewal, Advsy Bd Wilton Park 2005–15; co-chair Radicalisation Awareness Network (RAN) Working Gp on Internet and Social Media EC 2012–14; hon research fell Univ of Warwick 2011–14; assoc fell RUSI 2010–; *Books* The Kidnapping Business (2001); *Recreations* music, travel; *Style*— Miss Rachel Briggs, OBE; ✉ website www.rachelbriggs.wordpress.com

BRIGGS, Raymond Redvers; s of Ernest Redvers Briggs, and Ethel, *née* Bowyer; *b* 18 January 1934; *Educ* Rutlish Sch Merton, Wimbledon Sch of Art, Slade Sch of Fine Art (DFA); *m* 1963, Jean Patricia (d 1973), da of Arthur Taprell Clark; *Career* author, book illustrator and designer; hon fell Univ of the Arts London; FRSL; *Books* Father Christmas (1973), Fungus the Bogeyman (1977), The Snowman (1978), When the Wind Blows (book, radio play and stage play, 1982–83), The Man (1992), The Bear (1994), Ethel and Ernest (1998), Ug, Boy Genius of the Stone Age (2001), Blooming Books (2003), The Puddleman (2004); *Style*— Raymond Briggs, Esq; ✉ e-mail raymondbriggs@hotmail.com

BRIGHT, His Hon Judge Andrew John; QC (2000); s of Joseph Henry Bright (d 1970), of Wells, Somerset, and Freda Madeleine Phyllis, *née* Cotton; *b* 12 April 1951; *Educ* Wells Cathedral Sch, UCL (LLB); *m* 3 Jan 1976, Sally Elizabeth, da of Charles Carter, of Rochester, Kent; 3 s (Daniel b 1980, Charles b 1981, Christopher b 1990), 1 da (Emily b 1993); *Career* called to the Bar Middle Temple 1973, practised from the chambers of Louis Blom-Cooper QC 1974–86, joined chambers of H Michael Self QC 1986, asst recorder 1999, recorder 2000, circuit judge (South Eastern Circuit) 2007–, resident judge St Albans Crown Court 2010; *Recreations* singing in a male voice choir, foreign travel; *Clubs* Old Wellensians; *Style*— His Hon Judge Bright, QC; ✉ St Albans Crown Court, Bricket Road, St Albans AL1 3JW (☎ 07768 414610, e-mail andrew.bright@judiciary.gsi.gov.uk)

BRIGHT, Christopher Reuben; s of Eric Bright, OBE (d 1988), and Anne Bright (d 1985); *b* 12 April 1959; *Educ* Univ of Wales (BSc), Dalhousie Law Sch (LLM), Jesus Coll Oxford (BCL); *m* 1985, Susan; 3 s (Samuel b 1987, Thomas b 1989, Jacob b 2000); *Career* teaching asst Dalhousie Law Sch 1980–81, lectr in law Jesus Coll Oxford 1984–86; admitted slr 1985; Linklaters & Paines: slr 1992–99, ptnr 1992–2001, head of EU competition and regulation 1999–2001; conslt Shearman & Sterling LLP 2001–; memb Advsy Cncl: Oxford Inst of Euro and Comparative Law 1996–, Oxford Law Fndn; non-exec dir Jersey Competition Regulators Assoc 2004–; memb: Disciplinary Tbnl Accountancy Investigation and Discipline Bd 2004–, Competition Cmmn 2006–; sr visiting research fell in law Univ of Oxford 2004–; memb City of London Slrs' Co; *Books* Public Procurement Handbook (1994), Understanding the Brussels Process (1995); *Recreations* daydreaming and gardening; *Style*— Christopher Bright, Esq; ✉ 27 Lathbury Road, Oxford OX2 7AT (☎ 01865 451199); Shearman & Sterling LLP, 9 Appold Street, London EC2A 2AP (☎ 020 7655 5000, fax 020 7655 5500, e-mail cbright@shearman.com)

BRIGHT, Sir Graham Frank James; kt (1994); s of late Robert Frank Bright, and Agnes Mary, *née* Graham; *b* 2 April 1942; *Educ* Hassenbrook Comp Sch, Thurrock Tech Coll; *m* 16 Dec 1972, Valerie, da of late Ernest Henry Woolliams; 1 s (Rupert b 1984); *Career* chm and md Dietary Foods Ltd 1977–2013; chm Int Sweetness Assoc Brussels 1997–2004 (dir and treas 2014–); Parly candidate (Cons): Thurrock 1970 and 1973, Dartford 1974; MP (Cons): Luton E 1979–83, Luton S 1983–97; PPS to: David Waddington QC MP and Patrick Mayhew QC MP as Mins of State Home Office March-June 1983, David Waddington and Douglas Hurd MP as Mins of State Home Office June-July 1983, David Waddington and Giles Shaw MP 1984–86, Earl of Caithness at DOE 1988–89 and as Paymaster Gen 1989–90, John Major as Chllr of the Exchequer and as PM 1990–94; vice-chm Cons Pty 1994–97; sec Backbench Cons Smaller Business Ctee 1979–80 (vice-chm 1980–83), sec Backbench Aviation Ctee 1980–83, memb Select Ctee on House of Commons Servs 1982–84, chm Cons Smaller Businesses Ctee 1983–84 and 1987–88, vice-chm Cons Aviation Ctee 1983–85, sec Backbench Food and Drink Sub-Ctee 1983–85; introduced Private Members Bills: Video Recordings Act 1984, Entertainments (Increased Penalties) Act 1990; jt sec Parly Aviation Gp 1984, vice-chm Aviation Ctee 1987–88; candidate Euro Parly elections eastern region 1999; memb: Thurrock BC 1966–79, Essex CC 1967–70; Cons Pty: chm Eastern Region 2006–10 (dep regnl chm 2002–06), area chm Cambs and Beds 2003–07; former nat vice-chm Young Cons; police and crime cmmr Cambridgeshire & Peterborough 2012–16; former dir Small Business Bureau Ltd 1989, dir and treas Mainstream Tst 2001–07, treas Former Membs of Parliament Assoc 2004–10 and 2015– (chm 2010–15), tstee Parly Pension Fund 2007–; chm Hassenbrook Technol Coll 2005–11, chm Hassenbrook Acad 2011–13; hon fell Univ of Luton 1993–; *Recreations* gardening and golf; *Clubs* Carlton; *Style*— Sir Graham Bright; ✉ e-mail graham@grahambright.com

BRIGHTMAN, Dr David Kenneth; s of Brian George Brightman (d 2004), and Dorothy Brightman (d 1969); *b* 12 August 1954, Luton, Beds; *Educ* Univ of Nottingham (PhD); *m* 1982 (m dis 1991); 2 s (Samuel Theodore b 15 April 1983, Oliver William b 6 March 1985); *Partner* Gillian Theresa Bolton; *Career* early career as lectr in crop prodn 1980–82, ptnr in family farm business 1982–; dir and co sec Arable Crop Storage Ltd 1995–, co sec Arable Crop Services Ltd 1995–2012, dir and tstee Rothamsted Research 2005–13, dir Centaur Producers Ltd, dir Centaur Grain Marketing Ltd 2006–08; BBSRC: memb

Cncl 2003–09, memb Audit Bd 2009–12, memb SSC Project Audit Ctee 2009–11; memb Research and Knowledge Transfer Ctee AHDB Cereals & Oilseeds 2014–; current and former memb several bds, ctees and consultation panels NFU, local farming interest gps and MAFF, DEFRA and DETR projects; CBiol, FSB 2005, FRAgS 2011 (ARAgS 2005); *Publications* contrib articles in various scientific and trade jls; *Recreations* playing golf, watching other sports; *Style*— Dr David Brightman

BRIGNALL, Rt Rev Peter Malcolm; *see:* Wrexham, Bishop of

BRIGSTOCKE, Dr Hugh; s of Canon G E Brigstocke (d 1971), and Mollie, *née* Sandford (d 2002); *b* 7 May 1943; *Educ* Marlborough, Magdalene Coll Cambridge (MA), Univ of Edinburgh (PhD); *m* 1969, Anthea, née White; 1 s (Julian), 1 da (Sophie); *Career* curator of Italian, French and Spanish pictures National Gallery of Scotland 1968–83; ed-in-chief Grove Dictionary of Art 1983–87 (consulting ed 1987–89, hon consulting ed 1989–96); Dept of Old Master Paintings Sothebys: conslt 1989, dir 1990, head of dept 1993–94, sr expert 1994–95; freelance writer, ed and art historian 1995–, ed The Oxford Companion to Western Art 1995–2001, ed The Walpole Soc 2000–12; guest scholar Getty Museum CA 1983–84, hon visiting fell in history of art Univ of York 1996, Paul Mellon fell Br Sch Rome 2001; *Publications* A Critical Catalogue of the Italian and Spanish Paintings in the National Gallery of Scotland (1978, 2 edn 1993), Poussin Bacchanals and Sacraments (exhbn catalogue National Gallery of Scotland, 1981), William Buchanan and the 19th Century Art Trade: 100 letters to his agents in London and Italy (1982), A Loan Exhibition of Drawings by Nicolas Poussin from British Collections (exhbn catalogue Ashmolean Museum, 1990), Masterpieces from Yorkshire Houses – Yorkshire Families at Home and Abroad 1700–1850 (jtly, exhbn catalogue York City Art Gallery, 1994), Italian Paintings from Burghley House (jtly, exhbn catalogue Frick Art Museum Pittsburgh and five other museums in USA 1995–96), En torno a Velázquez (jtly, exhbn catalogue Museo de Bellas Artes de Asturias Oviedo, 1999), A Poet in Paradise: Lord Lindsay and Christian Art (jtly, exhbn catalogue Nat Gall of Scotland Edinburgh, 2000), Oxford Companion to Western Art (2001), Procaccini in America (exhbn catalogue, NY, 2002), John Flaxman and William Young Ottley in Italy (jtly, Walpole Soc vol, 2010), British Travellers in Spain 1760–1849 (Walpole Soc vol, 2015); author of numerous articles on Italian and French painting in various jls incl Burlington Magazine, Apollo, British Art Jl, Revue de l'Art, Revue du Louvre and Paragone; *Recreations* opera, theatre, wine, horse racing; *Style*— Dr Hugh Brigstocke; ✉ 118 Micklegate, York YO1 6JX (e-mail hugh.brigstocke@zen.co.uk)

BRIGSTOCKE, Nicholas Owen; s of Mervyn Owen Brigstocke (d 1996), and Janet Mary, *née* Singleton (d 2011); *b* 25 June 1942; *Educ* Epsom Coll; *m* 17 May 1969, Carol Barbara, da of Air Marshal Sir Walter Philip George Pretty, CB, KBE (d 1975); 1 da (Lucinda b 1971), 2 s (Marcus b 1973, Henry b 1981); *Career* Shell Mex and BP Ltd 1961–69, de Zoete and Bevan Ltd 1969–78, ptnr de Zoete and Bevan Ltd 1978–86; Barclays de Zoete Wedd Securities Ltd: dir and head of UK equity sales 1986–89, md corporate broking 1989; chm: de Zoete and Bevan Ltd 1994–97 (dep chm 1991–94), Credit Suisse First Boston de Zoete and Bevan Ltd 1997–2001, DDDGroup plc; non-exec dir PetroMaroc Corp plc; MInstD; MSI Dip; *Recreations* tennis, cricket, golf; *Clubs* MCC, Turf; *Style*— Nicholas Brigstocke, Esq; ✉ St Ann's, Sheep Lane, Midhurst, West Sussex GU29 9NT (fax 020 7376 7099, mobile 07860 834485, e-mail nick@shawfieldst.com)

BRIMACOMBE, Michael William; s of Lt-Col Winston Brimacombe, OBE (d 1995), of Torquay, Devon, and Marjorie Gertrude, *née* Ling (d 1998); *b* 6 March 1944; *Educ* Kelly Coll London (LLB); *m* 8 April 1968, Pamela Jean, da of Charles Mark Stone (d 2005); 1 s (John Mark b 1969), 2 da (Ruth Michelle b 1972, Helen Marie-Anne b 1976); *Career* sr ptnr Norman Allport & Co 1972–2006, ptnr Price Waterhouse (UK and Jersey) 1975–85; md Legal Tstees (Jersey) Ltd 1985–2000, chm Jobstream Group plc 1993–2015, chm nGame Ltd 1998–2002, dir MForma Group Inc 2002–04; FCA 1968, FRSA 1987; *Recreations* reading, travelling, walking; *Style*— Michael Brimacombe, Esq; ✉ Temple View, Rue des Marettes, Faldouet, St Martin, Jersey JE3 6DS (☎ 01534 851087); L T Group Ltd, PO Box 779, Jersey JE4 0SE (☎ 01534 856442, fax 01534 856442)

BRIMBLECOMBE, Prof Peter; s of Arthur Brimblecombe, of Kaitaia, NZ, and Betty Brimblecombe; *b* 23 January 1949, Australia; *Educ* Univ of Auckland (BSc, MSc, PhD); *m* 16 Dec 1995, Caroline; *Career* prof of atmospheric chemistry Sch of Environmental Sciences UEA, prof of environmental chemistry Sch of Energy and Environment City Univ of Hong Kong; sr ed Atmospheric Environment 1990–; *Books* incl: Air Composition and Chemistry (1986), The Big Smoke (1987), Evolution of the Global Biogeochemical Sulphur Cycle (co-ed, 1989), The Silent Countdown: Essays in European Environmental History (co-ed, 1990), The Science, Responsibility, and Cost of Sustaining Cultural Heritage (jtly, 1994), The Urban Atmosphere and its Effects (co-ed, 2001), The Effects of Air Pollution on the Built Environment (ed, 2003), An Introduction to Environmental Chemistry (jtly, 2003), The Atlas of Climate Change Impact on European Cultural Heritage (co-ed, 2010), Urban Pollution and Changes to Materials and Building Surfaces (2015); *Recreations* cycling, running, photography; *Style*— Prof Peter Brimblecombe; ✉ School of Energy and Environment, City University of Hong Kong, Hong Kong (☎ 00 852 3442 4676, e-mail p.brimblecombe@uea.ac.uk)

BRIMS, Charles David; DL (Berks 2013); s of David Vaughan Brims (d 1993), and Eve Georgina Mary, *née* Barrett; *b* 5 May 1950; *Educ* Winchester, BNC Oxford; *m* 1973, Patricia Catherine, da of John Desmond Henderson, of Brimpton; 2 s (David b 1980, Edward b 1982); *Career* dir: Courage (Western) Ltd 1980–83, Imperial Inns and Taverns Ltd 1983–86, Imperial Leisure and Retailing Ltd 1985–86; chief exec Portsmouth and Sunderland Newspapers plc 1986–99; chm: Balfour 2000 Ltd 2000–03, George Gale & Co Ltd 2003–06, McMullen & Sons Ltd 2003–; non-exec dir: Claverley Hldgs Ltd 1999–, Midland News Assoc Ltd 1999–, CN Gp Ltd 1999–, Newbury News Ltd 1999–, Kent Messenger Ltd 2008–; pres Newspaper Soc 1998–99; tstee Stable Family Home Tst 2002–11, dir tstee Greenham Common Community Tst Ltd 2011–; High Sheriff Royal County of Berks 2012–13; Liveryman Worshipful Co of Brewers; *Recreations* sport; *Clubs* MCC, Vincent's (Oxford), Swinley Forest Golf; *Style*— Charles Brims, Esq, DL; ✉ Brimpton Lodge, Brimpton, Berkshire RG7 4TG

BRIMSON LEWIS, Stephen John; s of David Raymond Lewis (d 1969), and Doris Agnes, *née* West; *b* 15 February 1963; *Educ* The Barclay Sch, Herts Coll of Art and Design, Central Sch of Art and Design (BA); *Career* set and costume designer; assoc artist RSC 2013–, dir of design RSC 2014–; memb United Scenic Artists; *Theatre* credits as designer incl: Once In A While The Odd Thing Happens (RNT), Uncle Vanya (RNT), Design for Living (Donmar Warehouse and Gielgud, winner Olivier Award 1995), Les Parents Terribles (RNT (Indiscretions on Broadway, winner Olivier Award 1995, Tony and Drama Desk nominations for set and costume)), A Little Night Music (RNT) 1995, Private Lives (RNT) 1999, Timon of Athens (RSC) 1999, Macbeth (RSC) 2000, Rose (Broadway) 2000, King John (RSC) 2001, Much Ado About Nothing (RSC, Evening Standard Award nomination) 2002, The Taming of the Shrew (RSC) 2003, The Tamer Tamed (RSC) 2003, Arsenic and Old Lace (West End) 2003, All's Well That Ends Well (RSC, West End) 2004, Othello (RSC) 2004, A Midsummer Night's Dream (RSC) 2005, Antony and Cleopatra (RSC) 2006, Julius Caesar (RSC) 2006, Merry Wives of Windsor (RSC) 2006, No Man's Land and Waiting for Godot (Broadway) 2013, Relative Values (West End) 2014, Henry IV Parts I and II (RSC) 2014, Richard II (RSC) 2014, Death of a Salesman (RSC and West End) 2015, Volpone (RSC) 2015, Henry V (RSC) 2015, King and Country (RSC London, China and New York) 2016, The Tempest (RSC) 2016; sets for: Otello (Vienna State Opera), Turn of the Screw (Aust Opera), Tales of Hoffman (Aust Opera), Dorian Gray (Monte Carlo Opera), Dirty Dancing (worldwide) 2008, Waiting for Godot (West End) 2009; costumes for: Acorn Antiques (West End), Mrs Klein (RNT), American Clock (RNT), Jeffrey Bernard Is Unwell (West End), Vanilla (West End), L'Elisir D'Amore (Dallas Opera), The Barber of Seville (ROH), Separate Tables (Chichester Festival Theatre) 2009, Ghosts (West End) 2010, Master Builder (Chichester Festival Theatre) 2010, An Ideal Husband (West End) 2010, Flare Path (West End) 2011, The Tempest (West End) 2011, La Boheme (WNO) 2012; *Television* incls costumes for The Nightmare Years (TTN Cable USA); *Exhibitions* work incl Making Their Mark, Shakespeare in Art (Compton Verney Art Gall) 2016; *Film* Bent (Film Four Int) 1996, Macbeth (Channel 4/RSC/Illuminations) 2001; *Style*— Stephen Brimson Lewis, Esq; ✉ e-mail clarevidalhall@email.com, website www.clarevidalhall.com

BRINDLE, Ian; *b* 17 August 1943; *Educ* Rossall Sch, Blundell's, Univ of Manchester (BA); *m* Elisabeth; 2 s (Michael, Andrew), 1 da (Jennie); *Career* chartered accountant; PricewaterhouseCoopers (formerly Price Waterhouse before merger): articled in London 1965 (Toronto 1971), ptnr 1976–2001, memb Supervisory Ctee 1988–2001, dir Audit & Business Advsy Servs 1990–91, memb UK Exec 1990–2001, sr ptnr UK 1991–2001, chm UK 1997–2001, dep chm Europe; non-exec dir: 4Imprint Group plc 2003–, Elementis plc 2005–, Spirent Communications plc 2006–; dep chm Financial Reporting Review Panel 2001–; memb: Auditing Practices Ctee 1986–90 (chm 1990), Urgent Issues Task Force Accounting Standards Bd 1991–93, Accounting Standards Bd 1993–, Cncl ICAEW; FCA; *Recreations* tennis and golf; *Style*— Ian Brindle, Esq

BRINDLE, Michael John; QC (1992); s of John Arthur Brindle, and Muriel, *née* Jones (d 1975); *b* 23 June 1952; *Educ* Westminster, New Coll Oxford (BA, Ella Stephen scholar); *Career* called to the Bar Lincoln's Inn (Hardwicke scholar) 1975, pupillage with Denis Henry (now Lord Justice Henry) at 2 Crown Office Row Temple 1975–76, tenancy Fountain Court 1976–, asst recorder 1999, recorder 2000; chm of tstees Public Concern at Work 1997–2001, memb Fin Reporting Review Panel 1998–, chm Commercial Bar Assoc 2001 (treas 1999–2000), memb Financial Markets Law Ctee 2002–; *Recreations* classical music, travel, bridge; *Style*— Michael Brindle, Esq, QC; ✉ Fountain Court, Temple, London EC4 9DH (☎ 020 7583 3335, e-mail mbrindle@fountaincourt.co.uk)

BRINDLEY, Lewis Alan; *b* 22 October 1983; *Educ* King Edward VI GS Chelmsford, Univ of Manchester; *Career* fndr and md Yogscast Ltd 2008–; *Style*— Lewis Brindley, Esq; ✉ The Yogscast, PO Box 3125, Bristol BS2 2DG

BRINDLEY, Dame Lynne Janie; DBE (2008); adopted da of Ronald Williams, and Elaine, *née* Chapman; *b* 2 July 1950; *Educ* Truro HS, Univ of Reading (BA), UCL (MA); *m* 1972, Timothy Stuart Brindley; *Career* head of mktg and chief exec's office British Library 1979–85, dir of library and info services and pro-vice-chllr Aston Univ 1985–90, princ conslt KPMG 1990–92, librarian and dir of info services LSE 1992–97; Univ of Leeds: librarian 1997–2000, pro-vice-chllr 1997–2000, visiting prof of knowledge mgmnt 2000–10; chief exec British Library 2000–12; master Pembroke Coll Oxford 2013–; memb: Lord Chancellor's Advsy Ctee on Public Records 1992–98, Jt Info Systems Ctee HEFCE 1992–98, Int Ctee on Soc Sci Info UNESCO 1992–97, Research Resources Bd ESRC 1997–2003, Library and Info Cmmn DCMS 1999–2000, Stanford Univ Advsy Cncl for Libraries and Info Resources 1999–, Bd Museums, Libraries and Archives Cncl 2003–08, Strategic Advsy Bd for Intellectual Property 2008–11, AHRC 2008–14, Bd Strategic Advsy Bd for Intellectual Property 2008–, Arts and Humanities Research Cncl 2008–, Bd Ofcom 2011–; chair Electronic Libraries Prog HEFCE Review of HE Libraries 1992–93; tstee Thackray Med Museum Leeds 1999–2001; memb Arts and Humanities Panel Wolfson Tst 2012–; Freeman City of London 1989, Liveryman Worshipful Co of Goldsmiths and Silversmiths 1993 (Court Memb 2006–); hon fell: UCL 2002, Univ of Wales Aberystwyth 2007, LSE 2008; Hon DLitt: Nottingham Trent Univ 2001, Univ of Leicester 2002, Univ of Oxford 2002, Univ of Sheffield 2004, Univ of Reading 2004, Univ of Leeds 2006, Open Univ 2006, Aston Univ 2008; Hon DPhil London Guildhall Univ 2002, Hon DSc City Univ 2005, hon degree De Montfort Univ, hon degree Univ of Manchester, hon degree Univ of Loughborough, hon doctorate De Montfort Univ 2011, Hon DLitt Univ of Manchester 2011, hon doctorate Univ of Loughborough 2011, Hon DLitt Trinity Coll Dublin 2012, Hon DLit Sch of Advanced Studies Univ of London 2012, Hon DCL Durham Univ 2013; fell Inst of Info Sci 1990, FLA 1990, FRSA 1993, Hon FBA 2015; *Recreations* classical music, theatre, modern art, hill walking; *Clubs* Reform; *Style*— Dame Lynne Brindley, DBE; ✉ Pembroke College, Oxford OX1 1DW (☎ 01865 276401, e-mail lynne.brindley@pmb.ox.ac.uk)

BRINDLEY, Richard Graham; s of John G Brindley (d 1990), and Dorothy Jean, *née* Smith; *b* 31 July 1954; *Educ* Jamaica Coll Kingston Jamaica, Denstone Coll, UCL (BSc, DipArch); *m* 20 June 1980, Prof Nicola Brindley, da of Hallimond Robinson; 2 s (James (Hal) b 25 April 1985, Jack W b 17 May 1987); *Career* chartered architect; Eric Cole & Partners 1980–84, co architect Prowting Homes 1984–88, ops dir Boyer Design Gp 1988–89, dir Llewelyn-Davies 1990–99, dir Broadway Malyan 1999–2001, dir Clague 2001–03, exec dir Professional Services RIBA 2003–16, chm R Brindley Conslt 2015–; memb Exec Bd Architects Cncl of Europe 2016–; Master Worshipful Co of Chartered Architects 2016–17; RIBA 1979, MIMgt 1989; *Recreations* theatre, swimming; *Style*— Richard Brindley, Esq; ✉ 27 Milman Road, Queens Park, London NW6 6EG (☎ 020 8969 4943, e-mail rbrindley.architect@gmail.com)

BRINE, Stephen Charles (Steve); MP; *b* 28 January 1974, Guildford, Surrey; *Educ* Bohunt Comp Sch Hants, Highbury Coll Portsmouth, Liverpool Hope Univ; *m* Susie; 1 da (Emily b 2007), 1 s (William b 2010); *Career* MP (Cons) Winchester 2010–; *Style*— Steve Brine, Esq, MP; ✉ House of Commons, London SW1A 0AA

BRINING, James; s of Colin Brining, of Leeds, and Christine, *née* Wells; *b* 10 June 1968, Leeds; *Educ* Leeds GS, Girton Coll Cambridge (BA); *m* 9 July 2004, Beverley, *née* Meason; 1 s (Cameron), 1 da (Ellie); *Career* theatre dir; artistic dir Rendezvous Theatre Co 1989–90, artistic dir Proteus Theatre Co 1991–95 (administrative dir 1990–91), community dir Orange Tree Theatre 1995–97, artistic dir Tag Theatre Co 1997–2003, artistic dir and chief exec Dundee Rep Theatre 2003–; vice-chair Fedn of Scottish Theatre; memb Bd: Playwright's Studio Scotland, Ek Theatre, East Glasgow Youth Theatre; memb Dir's Guild of GB; *Recreations* football (playing and watching); *Style*— James Brining, Esq; ✉ West Yorkshire Playhouse, Playhouse Square, Quarry Hill, Leeds, LS2 7UP

BRINK, Adrian Charles; s of Charles Oscar Brink (*né* Karl Oskar Levy), and Daphne Hope, *née* Harvey; *Educ* Gordonstoun, Trinity Coll Cambridge (BA, MA); *Career* journalist Time and Tide 1967–69, sub ed Country Life 1969–71, ed Weidenfeld & Nicolson 1971–73, md James Clarke & Co 1973–; *Recreations* flying; *Style*— Adrian Brink, Esq; ✉ James Clarke & Co, PO Box 60, Cambridge CB1 2NT (☎ 01223 350865, fax 01223 366951, e-mail adrian@lutterworth.com)

BRINK, Prof Chris; *b* 31 January 1951, Upington, SA; *Educ* Univ of Cambridge (PhD), Univ of Johannesburg (DPhil); *m* Tobea; 2 da (Carmen, Hestia), 1 s (Peter); *Career* prof and head Dept of Mathematics and Applied Mathematics Univ of Cape Town 1995–99 (co-ordinator of strategic planning 1997), pro-vice chllr Univ of Wollongong Aust 1999–2002, vice-chllr Stellenbosch Univ SA 2002–07, vice-chllr Univ of Newcastle 2007–16; fell Royal Soc of SA, fndr memb Acad of Sci of SA; Relational Methods In Computer Science (jt ed, 1997), A Paradigm for Program Semantics: Power Structures and Duality (jtly, 2001), No Lesser Place – The Taaldebat at Stellenbosch (2006); *Style*— Prof Chris Brink; ✉ Newcastle University, King's Gate, Newcastle Upon Tyne NE1 7RU (e-mail chris.brink@ncl.ac.uk)

BRINTON, Baroness (Life Peer UK 2011), of Kenardington in the County of Kent; Sarah Virginia (Sal) Brinton; da of Timothy Denis Brinton (d 2009), and Jane-Mari, *née* Coningham; *b* 1 April 1955; *Educ* Benenden Sch Kent, Churchill Coll Cambridge, Central Sch of Speech and Drama; *m* Feb 1983, Tim Whittaker; 2 s (Christopher b 24 Aug 1983, Joseph b 20 Dec 1988), 1 da (Helen b 5 March 1987); *Career* elected cncllr Cambs CC 1993; fndr memb Bd East of England Devpt Agency 1998–2004 (dep chair 2001–04); currently non-exec dir Univ of Industry (Learndirect); bursar: Lucy Cavendish Coll Cambridge 1992–97, Selywn Coll Cambridge 1997–2002; East Anglian Entrepreneurial Businesswoman of the Year Award 1997; Hon PhD Anglia Ruskin Univ 2003; *Style*— The Baroness Brinton; ✉ House of Lords, London SW1A 0PW

BRISAC, Cécile; *b* 20 June 1969, Firminy, France; *Educ* Baccalauréat série C Paris, Mathématiques Supérieures Saint-Maur-dès-Fossés Paris, Architectural Assoc Sch of Architecture (AA Dip); *m* Edgar Gonzalez; *Career* asst architect various offices in Paris 1990–92; project architect: Ian Ritchie Architects 1995–96, Estudio de Arquitectura Miami 1996–98; design architect Kohn Pederson Fox Int 1998–99, co-fndr Brisac Gonzalez 1999–; projects incl: Scheller Areal Dietikon 1996, Museum of World Culture Gothenburg 2004, Peacock Visual Arts Centre Aberdeen 2005–, Bergen Nat Academy of the Arts Norway 2005, Halle polyvalente Aurillac 2007, Pajol Sports Centre Paris 2012, Lot O4A, ZAC Clichy-Batignolles Paris 2012–, Condorcet Campus Great Library and Learning Centre Aubervilliers 2014; regular visiting critic at schs incl Univ of E London and Architectural Assoc 1995–; external examiner Central St Martins 2011–15; memb Cncl Architectural Assoc 2006–08, Unit master Architectural Assoc 2008–09, memb Ordre Des Architects 1996, memb Southwark Design Review Panel 2008–; memb: ARB 1999, RIBA 2002, Academie Royale de Belgique 2014–; *Awards* AIA Design commendation 2000, Young Architects of the Year France 2003/04, Kasper Salins Prize 2004, AIA/UK Chapter Excellence in Design Award 2005, selected work Mies van der Rohe Award 2005, Premio Internazionale Dedalo Minossa 2006, nominated ARHVA French Prize for Women in Architecture 2013, Prix Georges de Hens 2014; Young Architects of the Year France 2003/04, 40 under 40 2008; numerous lectures and articles in jls, magazines and newspapers; *Style*— Mrs Cécile Brisac; ✉ Brisac Gonzalez Architects, 7 Bermondsey Exchange, 179–181 Bermondsey Street, London SE1 3UW (☎ 020 7378 7787, fax 020 7378 7796, e-mail admin@brisacgonzalez.com)

BRISBY, John Constant Shannon McBurney; QC (1996); s of Michael Douglas James McBurney Brisby (d 1965), of London, and Liliana, *née* Daneva (d 1998); *b* 8 May 1956; *Educ* Westminster, ChCh Oxford (MA); *m* 20 April 1985, Claire Alexandra Anne, da of Sir Donald Arthur Logan, KCMG, of London; *Career* 2 Lt 5 Royal Inniskilling Dragoon Gds 1974, transferred Reserve 1975–77; called to the Bar Lincoln's Inn 1978 (bencher 2005), dep high ct judge 2004; chm Friends of Bulgaria (Charitable Orgn); *Clubs* Travellers, Beefsteak; *Style*— John Brisby, Esq, QC; ✉ 4 Stone Buildings, Lincoln's Inn, London WC2A 3XT

BRISCOE, Penny; MBE; da of Donald Briscoe, and Joan, *née* Whitehead, of Telford, Shropshire; *b* 17 September 1965, Telford, Shropshire; *Educ* Univ of Birmingham (BA), Loughborough (PGCE); *m* 12 July 2002, Alan Edge; 1 s (Lewis Briscoe Edge b 20 Sept 2002), 1 da (Lizzy Briscoe Edge b 16 Nov 2003); *Career* teacher Wheldon Sch Nottingham 1988–94, lectr Stafford Coll 1995, sr nat coach British Canoe Union 1996–2001, performance mangr Br Paralympic Assoc 2001–02, dir of sport Br Paralympic Assoc 2002– (chef de mission ParalympicsGB Sochi Winter Paralympic Games 2014 and Rio Paralympic Games 2016); memb UK Sport Mission Panel 2009–; *Recreations* cycling, running, watersports; *Clubs* 4Life Triathlon, Nottingham Clarion Cycling, Rushcliffe Athletics; *Style*— Ms Penny Briscoe, MBE; ✉ British Paralympic Association, 60 Charlotte Street, London W1T 2NU

BRISE; *see:* Ruggles-Brise

BRISTER, Graeme Roy; s of Royston George Brister, of Cambridge, and Eileen Gladys Brister; *b* 5 May 1955; *Educ* Forest Sch, Phillips Exeter Acad New Hampshire, BNC Oxford (MA); *m* 1, 26 July 1986 (m dis 1999), Ashley Fiona; 1 da (Leander b 1988), 1 s (Hugo b 1992); m 2, 28 May 2001, Anita Maria; 1 da (Caitlin b 2003); *Career* admitted slr 1979, ptnr Linklaters and Paines 1985–96, managing ptnr (London) Pinsent Curtis 1997–2000, ptnr Legal First 2001–, ptnr Blaqwell 2001–12; dir: First Tracks Ltd 2003–04, Mistral Elan Ltd 2014–, Innchurn Ltd 2014–; tstee The Inst for Citizenship 1997–2012 (chm 2000–12), vice-chm Chedworth Parish Cncl 2010–; memb: Law Soc 1979, City of London Slr's Co 1981, American Bar Assoc; MCIArb; *Recreations* country, sport, travel, food and wine; *Clubs* Lord's Taverners, Travellers; *Style*— Graeme R Brister, Esq

BRISTOL, 8 Marquess of (UK 1826); Frederick William Augustus Hervey; also Baron Hervey of Ickworth (E 1703), Earl of Bristol (GB 1714) and Earl Jermyn (UK 1826); Hereditary High Steward of the Liberty of St Edmund; s of 6 Marquess of Bristol (d 1985); suc half-bro, 7 Marquess of Bristol (d 1999); *b* 19 October 1979; *Educ* Eton, Univ of Edinburgh; *Career* dir: Bristol & Stone Baltic Real Estate 2003–10, Bristol Estates Ltd 2010–; patron: Gwrych Castle Preservation Tst 2002–, The Athenaeum Bury St Edmunds 2005–, The Friends of West Suffolk Hosp; tstee Gen The Hon William Hervey Charitable Tst 1999–, chm and tstee Ickworth Church Conservation Tst 2006–; *Recreations* shooting, travel, reading, emerging markets; *Clubs* Whites, Turf; *Style*— The Most Hon the Marquess of Bristol; ✉ Bristol Estates Ltd, 2 Eaton Gate, London SW1W 9BJ (e-mail fb@bristolestates.co.uk)

BRISTOL, Bishop of 2003–; Rt Rev Michael Arthur Hill; s of Arthur Hill, of Congleton, Cheshire, and Hilda, *née* Fisher; *b* 17 April 1949; *Educ* Wilmslow Co GS, N Cheshire Coll of FE (Dip Business Studies), Ridley Hall Cambridge, Fitzwilliam Coll Cambridge (CertTheol); *m* Anthea Jean, da of Michael Longridge (d 1958); 4 da (Naomi Annabel, Charis Rebeccah, Alexa Helen, Eleanor Fay), 1 s (Nicholas Michael); *Career* mgmnt trainee/jr exec in printing industry 1969–72, memb Scargill House Community 1972–73; theol educn 1973–77 (ordained 1977); asst curate St Mary Magdalene Croydon (then Dio of Canterbury) 1977–80, curate-in-charge Christ Church Slough (Dio of Oxford) 1980–83, priest-in-charge St Leonard Chesham Bois (Dio of Oxford) 1983–90, rector of Chesham Bois 1990–92, archdeacon of Berkshire 1992–98, bishop of Buckingham 1998–2003; *Recreations* sport, reading, civil aircraft; *Style*— The Rt Rev the Lord Bishop of Bristol; ✉ The Bishop's House, 58 High Street, Winterbourne, Bristol BS36 1JQ (☎ 01454 777728, e-mail bishop@bristoldiocese.org)

BRISTOL, Timothy Arnold Neil; s of Arnold Charles Verity Bristol (d 1984), of Wotton, Surrey, and Lillias Nina Maud, *née* Francis-Hawkins (d 1990); *b* 21 February 1941; *Educ* Cranleigh Sch, Guildford Art Sch, RMA Sandhurst; *m* 7 Sept 1968, Elizabeth Olivia, da of late John Gurney, of Walsingham Abbey, Norfolk; 1 da (Arabella Fredericka Ann (Mrs Jack Trinity) b 19 Aug 1970), 2 s (Benjamin Timothy Fitzroy b 7 Nov 1972, Biggles Samuel Frederick John b 3 Sept 1983); *Career* 1 Bn KOSB 1960–67, served in the Radfan, Borneo, S Arabia and Dhofar campaigns, seconded to the Sultan of Muscat's Forces 1966–67, ret as Capt; diamond valuer De Beers 1967–70, seconded to the Sierra Leone Govt Diamond Office 1969–70; publishing mangr Medici Society Ltd 1970–72, chm and chief exec Eastern Counties Printers and Publishing Gp 1972–85, publisher and managing ed Insight Magazine 1982–84, dir Marlar International Ltd 1986–90; chm and ceo Sheffield International (Hldgs) Ltd 1990–2005, md: Sheffield International Selection Ltd 1995–2004, Sheffield International Ltd 2004–11; dir Meroncroft Ltd 1992–, chm Meroncroft Investments Ltd 1994–2005; memb Ely Cathedral Finance Ctee 2000–12; *Recreations* gardening, reading, writing, travel; *Clubs* Army & Navy; *Style*— Timothy Bristol, Esq; ✉ The Chantry, Ely, Cambridgeshire CB7 4EW

BRISTOW, Mark; MBE (2009); *b* 8 July 1962, Nazeing, Essex; *Career* Paralympic cyclist; achievements incl: 2 Bronze medals (road race and kilo time trial) World Disability Championships 2006, Gold medal team sprint World Disability Championships 2007, 2 Gold medals (men's kilo time trial and men's team sprint (with Darren Kenny and Jody Cundy, *qv*)) Paralympics Beijing 2008, 2 Gold medals (men's kilo time trial and men's sprint (with Darren Kenny and Jody Cundy)) World Disability Championship 2009; *Style*— Mark Bristow, Esq, MBE; ✉ c/o British Cycling, Stuart Street, Manchester M11 4DQ

BRITNELL, Dr Mark Douglas; s of Robert Douglas Britnell (d 1991), and Veronica Leigh, *née* Higgins; *b* 5 January 1966, Chester; *Educ* Queens Park HS Chester, Univ of Warwick (BA); *m* 30 July 2005, Stephanie, *née* Joy; 1 da (Beatrix Ella b 19 Feb 2005), 1 s (Reuben Hubert Guy b 20 Jan 2010); *Career* NHS mgmnt trg scheme 1989–91, gen mangr St Mary's Hosp 1991–95, dir Central Middx Hosp 1995–98; Univ Hosp Birmingham: dir 1998–2000, chief exec 2000–06; chief exec South Central SHA 2006–07, DG commissioning and system mgmnt Dept of Health 2007–09, ptnr and head of health for Europe KPMG 2009–; sr assoc Kings Fund; columnist for Health Serv Jl; hon sr fell Health Serv Mgmnt Centre Univ of Birmingham; *Recreations* sport, politics, history, family; *Clubs* Reform; *Style*— Dr Mark Britnell

BRITNELL, Prof Richard Hugh; s of Ronald Frank Britnell (d 1987), and Edith, *née* Manson; *b* 21 April 1944, Wrexham; *Educ* Sir William Borlase GS Marlow, Bedford Modern Sch, Clare Coll Cambridge (BA, PhD); *m* 24 March 1973, Jennifer Joan, *née* Beard (d 2011); 2 s (John Richard b 12 Sept 1976, David James b 16 Sept 1978); *Career* Univ of Durham: lectr in economic history 1966–85, lectr in history 1985–86, sr lectr in history 1986–94, reader in history 1994–97, prof of history 1997–2003, emeritus prof 2003–; FRHistS 1988, FBA 2005; *Books* Growth and Decline in Colchester 1300–1525 (1986), The Commercialisation of English Society 1000–1500 (1993, 2 edn 1996), The Closing of the Middle Ages? England 1471–1529 (1997), Britain and Ireland, 1050–1530: Economy and Society (2004), Records of the Borough of Crossgate Durham 1312–1531 (ed, 2008), Markets, Trade and Economic Development in England and Europe 1050–1550 (2009); *Recreations* amateur dramatics, keyboard playing (clavichord, piano, organ), cooking, swimming, walking; *Clubs* Durham Bede Rotary; *Style*— Prof Richard Britnell; ✉ 25 Orchard House, New Elvet, Durham DH1 3DB (☎ 0191 383 0409, e-mail r.h.britnell@durham.ac.uk)

BRITTAIN, Alison; *b* 1965; *Educ* Univ of Stirling, Cambridge Judge Business Sch; *Career* Barclays 1988–2007, exec dir Retail Banking Santander UK 2007–11, gp dir Retail Banking Lloyds Banking Gp 2011–16, ceo Whitbread 2016–; non-exec dir Marks and Spencer plc 2014–; memb PM's Business Advsy Gp 2015–; *Style*— Mrs Alison Brittain; ✉ Whitbread plc, 120 Holborn, London EC1N 2TD

BRITTAIN, Clive Edward; s of Edward John Brittain (d 1948), of Calne, Wilts, and Priscilla Rosalind, *née* Winzer (d 1990); *b* 15 December 1933; *Educ* Calne Secdy Modern Sch; *m* 23 Feb 1957, Maureen Helen, *née* Robinson; *Career* Nat Serv 1954–56; racehorse trainer 1972–; major races won incl: 1000 Guineas 1984, Eclipse Stakes, Dubai Champion Stakes and Breeders Cup Turf USA 1985 (Pebbles), Japan Cup Tokyo 1986 (Jupiter Island), St Léger 1978 (Julio Mariner), 2000 Guineas 1991 (Mystiko), Oaks Stakes Epsom, Irish Oaks, The Curragh, St Leger Doncaster 1992 (User Friendly), 1000 Guineas 1993 (Sayyedati), Hong Kong International Vase 1996 and 1997 (Luso), Queen Elizabeth Stakes Ascot 1997 (Air Express), Coronation Stakes Ascot 2000 (Crimpelene), Coronation Cup Epsom 2003 and 2004 (Warrsan); *Recreations* shooting; *Clubs* Jockey Club Rooms; *Style*— Clive Brittain, Esq; ✉ Carlburg, 49 Bury Road, Newmarket, Suffolk CB8 7BY (☎ 01638 663739); Carlburg Stables, 49 Bury Road, Newmarket, Suffolk CB8 7BY (☎ 01638 664347, fax 01638 661744, mobile 077 8530 2121, e-mail carlburgst@aol.com)

BRITTAIN, Nicholas John; s of Denis Jack Brittain, MBE (d 1977), of Hungerford, Berks, and Irene Jane, *née* Williams (d 1945); *b* 8 September 1938; *Educ* Lord Wandsworth Coll, Jesus Coll Oxford (MA); *m* 1964, Patricia Mary, da of Alan Francis John Hopewell (d 1957); 1 s (James b 1969), 2 da (Charlotte b 1971, Rebecca b 1973); *Career* Unilever plc 1960–82, head of gp fin Legal and General plc 1982–86, chief accountant Barclays plc, Barclays Bank plc and dir of various subsid cos 1986–96; with London First 1997–98; Cncl The Bow Gp 1973–75; govr Alexandra Tst 1980–2016; chm Accounting Ctee BBA 1987–96; ACCA: Cncl 1988–97, Small Business Ctee 1992–2001 (chm 1992–96), Fin Servs Network Panel 1997–2003 (vice-chm 2000–03); dir: Providence Row Housing Assoc 1981–2010 (chm Fin Ctee 1986–2010), Cncl Project Fullemploy 1990–91; memb: Accounting Standards Bd FSOSIC 1994–96, Cncl Speakability (Action for Dysphasic Adults) 1998–2015; pres Witley branch Cons Assoc 2000–15 (chm 1978–80 and 1995–96), Cncl SW Surrey Cons Assoc 1987–93 (CPC chm 1987–90, pres 1990–93); Freeman City of London 1993, Liveryman Worshipful Co of Painter-Stainers 1995; FCCA, FRSA; *Recreations* learning to speak and write, watching cricket and rugby, gardening, cooking, church, politics, charitable work, painting; *Clubs* MCC, Surrey CCC, Brook CC, Privateers CC, Hungerford CC, 59, Walbrook Ward (chm 1993–95), Royal Soc of St George, National; *Style*— Nicholas J Brittain, Esq; ✉ Churchfields, Church Lane, Witley, Godalming, Surrey GU8 5PP (☎ 01428 682509)

BRITTAN, Lady; Diana Brittan; DBE (2004, CBE 1995); da of Leslie Howell Clemetson (d 1964), and Elizabeth Agnes, *née* Leonard (d 1996); *b* 14 October 1940; *Educ* Westonbirt Sch, Univ of Grenoble, Hartwell House; *m* 1, 1965 (m dis 1980), Dr Richard Peterson; 2 da (Katharine b 10 Sept 1966, Victoria b 12 Sept 1968); m 2, 1980, Baron Brittan of Spennithorne, PC, QC, DL (Life Peer), *qv*; *Career* managing ed EIBIS International (int tech press agency) 1977–88; Equal Opportunities Commission (EOC): cmmr 1988–96, chair Legal Ctee 1994–96 (memb 1988–96), dep chair EOC 1994–96; magistrate City of London Magistrates' Court 1984–2010 (chair of Bench 1990–2010), dep chair Human Fertilisation and Embryology Authy (HFEA) 1990–97 (also chair Licensing and Fees Ctee), memb Lord Chancellor's Advsy Ctee on Legal Educn and Conduct 1997–99, chair Community Fund 1999–2004; pres Nat Assoc for Connexions Partnerships 2005–08, chair The Connexion at St Martins 2005–, chair Carnegie Cmmn for Rural Community Devpt 2005–07, chair The Wensleydale Partnership (The Dales Festival of Food and Drink) 2006–, tstee Carnegie UK Tst 2009–, chair Independent Age 2009–; memb Bd of Mgmnt Br Sch of Brussels 1990–99; tstee: Action on Addiction 1993–98, Open Univ Fndn 1995–2000, Rathbone Training 1992–2004 (non exec chair 1992–2001), Runnymede Tst until 2007, Carnegie UK Tst 2009; pres Townwomen's Guilds 1995–, chair Nat Family Mediation 2001–07; distinguished assoc Darwin Coll Cambridge 1998; *Recreations* arts, botany, travel; *Style*— Lady Brittan, DBE; ✉ 79 Alderney Street, London SW1V 4HF

BRITTAN, Sir Samuel; kt (1993); s of Dr Joseph Brittan and Rebecca, *née* Lipetz; er bro of Baron Brittan of Spennithorne, PC, QC, DL (Life Peer), *qv*; *b* 29 December 1933; *Educ* Kilburn GS, Jesus Coll Cambridge; *Career* with Financial Times 1955–61, economics ed Observer 1961–64, advsr Dept of Econ Affairs 1965, econ commentator Financial Times 1966–, asst ed Financial Times 1978–96, visiting fell Nuffield Coll 1974–82, visiting prof Chicago Law Sch 1978; hon prof of politics Univ of Warwick 1987–92, hon fell Jesus Coll Cambridge 1988–; memb: Peacock Ctee on the Finance of the BBC 1985–86; Sr Wincott Prize for Financial Journalism 1971, George Orwell Prize 1980, Ludwig Erhard Prize for Econ Writing 1988; Hon DLitt Heriot-Watt Univ 1985, Hon DUniv Essex 1994; *Books* Left or Right – The Bogus Dilemma (1968), The Price of Economic Freedom – A Guide to Flexible Rates (1970), Steering the Economy (1971), Is There an Economic Consensus? (1973), Capitalism and the Permissive Society (1973, revised edn entitled A Restatement of Economic Liberalism, 1988), The Delusion of Incomes Policy (with Peter

Lilley, 1977), The Economic Consequences of Democracy (1977), The Role and Limits of Government – Essays in Political Economy (1983), Capitalism with a Human Face (1995), Essays, Moral, Political and Economic (1998), Against the Flow (2005); *Style*— Sir Samuel Brittan; ✉ The Financial Times, Number One, Southwark Bridge, London SE1 9HL (☎ 020 7873 3000, fax 020 7873 4343)

BRITTEN, Alan Edward Marsh; CBE (2003); s of Robert Harry Marsh Britten (d 1987), and Helen Marjorie, *née* Goldson; *b* 26 February 1938; *Educ* Radley, Emmanuel Coll Cambridge (MA), Williams Coll Massachusetts, Princeton Univ NJ; *m* 23 Sept 1967, Judith Clare, da of Cdr Anthony Charles Akerman, OBE, DSC, RN, of Edinburgh; 2 da (Tamara b 22 July 1970, Sophie b 29 Feb 1972); *Career* Northamptonshire Regt 1956–57, 2 Lt Cheshire Regt 1957–58, served Malaya; md Mobil Oil Co Ltd UK 1987–89 (joined 1961), vice-pres Mobil Europe Ltd 1990–96 (co assignments USA and Italy); md: Mobil Oil Kenya Group, Mobil Oil A/S Denmark, Mobil Oil Portuguesa SARL, Mobil Oil BV Group Rotterdam, Mobil Oil Co Ltd; dir Br Tourist Authy 1997–2003; chm English Tourism Cncl 1999–2003; chair: Tourism Quality Review Gp 2002–08, Tourism Attractions Review 2006–07, Tourism Sustainability Review 2007–08; memb Cncl Royal Warrant Holders Assoc (pres 1997–98), commissioning ed A Peerage for Trade 2002, chair Royal Warrant Holders Charity Fund 2012–; tstee Queen Elizabeth Scholarship Tst 1997–2002 (chm 1998–2002); UEA: memb Cncl 1996–2005 (vice-chm 2003–05), tstee dir Overseas Devpt Gp 1997–2007, chm Learning Through Earning Steering Ctee 1998–2000, chm Careers Centre Advsy Bd 1997–99; memb Cncl Aldeburgh Fndn 1989–99, pres Friends of Aldeburgh Music 2000–; memb Advsy Bd 10 Days At Princeton; govr Trinity Coll of Music 2001–04, memb Bd Trinity Coll London 2003–15, govr Trinity Laban 2004–10, chm Leeds Castle Enterprises 2010–15; tstee: Leeds Castle Fndn 2004–15 (vice-chm 2012–), Integrated Neurological Services 2006– (dep chm 2008–), Transglobe Expedition Tst 2006–, TCM Tst 2008–; hon fell Trinity Laban Conservatoire 2010, hon fell Trinity Coll London 2015; Hon DCL UEA 2010; *Recreations* music, travel, gardening; *Clubs* Garrick, Noblemen and Gentlemen's Catch and Glee, Aldeburgh Golf; *Style*— Alan Britten, Esq, CBE

BRITTEN, Philip Stanley; s of late Keith Stanley Britten, and Kathleen Josephine, *née* Burton; *b* 29 August 1957; *Educ* Queen Elizabeth GS Faversham, Ealing Tech Coll London (City & Guilds); *Career* chef; Dorchester Hotel London 1973–78, Kulm Hotel St Moritz and Victoria Jungfrau Interlaken 1978–80; sous chef Hambleton Hall Leics 1980–82, head chef Dans Restaurant London 1982–83; Chez Nico London: sous chef 1983–85 (2 Michelin stars), chef patron 1985–87 (1 Michelin star); head chef Capital Hotel London 1988–99 (1 Michelin star, 4 out of 5 Good Food Guide 1999); The Carlton London Restaurant Awards Outstanding London Chef 1999–; md Oscar Samuel Ltd 1993–, dir Solstice Ltd 1996–; *Recreations* driving/motor sports; *Clubs* RAC, Freedom of Poulters, Classic Sports Car; *Style*— Philip Britten, Esq

BRITTIN, Matthew (Matt); s of Sid Brittin, and Shirley, *née* Fryer; *b* 1 September 1968; *Educ* Univ of Cambridge (MA), London Business Sch (MBA); *m* 1995, Kate, *née* Betts; 2 s (Fred b 1999, Nick b 2001); *Career* Connell Wilson 1989–95, McKinsey & Co 1997–2004, dir of strategy and digital Trinity Mirror 2004–06; Google: joined 2007, md Google UK 2009–11, vice-pres for Northern and Central Europe Google 2011–14; vice-pres for EMEA 2014–; non-exec dir J Sainsbury plc 2011–; tstee: Climate Gp 2010–, Media Tst 2010–; memb Br Rowing Team 1985–89; *Recreations* cycling to work in the rain; *Style*— Matt Brittin, Esq; ✉ c/o Vicki Gostling, Google, Central St Giles, 1–13 St Giles High Street, London WC2H 8AG

BRITTON, Prof Celia Margaret; da of James Nimmo Britton (d 1994), of London, and Jessie Muriel, *née* Robertson (d 1991); *b* 20 March 1946; *Educ* N London Collegiate Sch, New Hall Cambridge (MA, Dip Linguistics), Univ of Essex (PhD); *m* 2003, Lyle Conquest; *Career* lectr: KCL 1972–74, Univ of Reading 1974–91; Carnegie chair of French Univ of Aberdeen 1991–2002, pt/t chair of French UCL 2003–11; pres Soc for French Studies 1996–98, chair French Panel HEFCE Res Assessment Exercise 2001, memb Scottish Academic Awards Scheme Panel 1992–2001; FBA 2001; Chevalier dans l'Ordre des Palmes Académiques 2003; *Books* Claude Simon: Writing the Visible (1987), The Nouveau Roman: Fiction, Theory and Politics (1992), Claude Simon (ed, 1993), Edouard Glissant and Postcolonial Theory (1999), Race and the Unconscious: Freudianism in French Caribbean Thought (2002), The Sense of Community in French Caribbean Fiction (2008), Language and Literary Form in French Caribbean Writing (2014); *Recreations* travel, cinema, cookery, photography; *Style*— Prof Celia Britton; ✉ e-mail brittoncelia@gmail.com

BRITTON, Fern Mary Philomena; da of Tony Britton, of London, and Ruth Aves, *née* Hawkins; *b* 17 July 1957; *Educ* Dr Challoner's HS, Central Sch of Speech and Drama; *m* 24 May 2000, Phil Vickery, *qv*; 2 s (Jack, Harry (twins) b 1993), 2 da (Grace b 1997, Winifred b 2001); *Career* television presenter; stage mangr Cambridge Theatre Co 1977–80; presenter: Spotlight (BBC Plymouth) 1981–83, BBC News 1983, BBC Breakfast Time 1983, Coast to Coast (TVS) 1985–92, London Tonight 1992–93, GMTV 1993, Ready Steady Cook 1993, This Morning 1998–2009 (nominated Best Factual Presenter RTS 2003, Best Factual Prog NTA 2005), Fern (Channel 4) 2011, Fern Britton Meets 2009–; patron Genesis Tst; *Publications* Fern's Family Food (1997), Winter Treats and Summer Delights (1999), Phil and Fern's Family Food (2003), Fern – My Story (autobiography); five novels, all Sunday Times bestsellers; *Recreations* gardening, motorcycling, golf, reading, cycling, motorsport; *Clubs* Mensa; *Style*— Ms Fern Britton; ✉ c/o Troika, 10a Christina Street, London EC2 (☎ 020 7336 7868)

BRITTON, (Berry) Julian; s of Capt Gordon Berry Cowley Britton, CBE, RN (d 1979), of Southampton, and Vera, *née* Hyman (d 1988); *b* 9 November 1941; *Educ* Taunton Sch Southampton, Bart's Med Sch (MB BS, MS, MA); *m* 20 April 1968, (Edith) Mona, da of Robert Cowans (d 1967), of Gateshead; 1 da (Rachel b 1970), 1 s (Jonathan b 1972); *Career* lectr in surgery Bart's 1972–74, reader in surgery Univ of Oxford 1976–80, conslt surgn Oxford Radcliffe Hosp 1980–2004; Green Templeton Coll Oxford: fell 1979–2004 (emeritus fell 2005–), sr tutor 1979–83, vice-warden 1989–92; dir clinical studies Univ of Oxford 1985–88; author of chapters and scientific papers on hernia and hepato-biliary and pancreatic surgery; memb: BMA, RSM; FRCS; *Recreations* fly fishing, music, woodwork, stick dressing; *Style*— Julian Britton, Esq; ✉ Humphries House, Scaleby Hill, Carlisle CA6 4NB (☎ 01228 675987, e-mail bj.britton@btinternet.com)

BRITTON, Moira Jean; OBE (2003); da of Douglas Barker, and Jeannie, *née* Thomson; *b* 20 February 1953; *Educ* Roundhay HS, Univ of Leeds (MBA); *m* 2 Sept 1972, Stephen Britton; 2 da (Heather b 1981, Stephanie b 1987), 1 s (Christopher b 1989); *Career* sr admin asst Leeds AHA 1975–79, unit administrator then unit gen mangr S Tees DHA 1979–83, chief exec S Tees Community and Mental Health NHS Tst 1993–99, chief exec Tees and NE Yorks NHS Tst 1999–2006; memb Bd Erimus Housing Ltd; dep registrar of wedding ceremonies N Yorks CC; memb Inst of Health Serv Admin 1977; govr Middlesborough Coll; Hon Dr Univ of Teesside 2006; *Recreations* aerobics, travel, wining and dining, gardening, reading; *Style*— Mrs Moira Britton, OBE; ☎ 01642 701445

BRIXWORTH, Bishop of 2011–; Rt Rev John Edward Holbrook; s of Edward George Holbrook, and Elizabeth Anne, *née* Bond; *b* 14 June 1962, Bristol; *Educ* Bristol Cathedral Sch, St Peter's Coll Oxford (MA), Ridley Hall Cambridge; *m* 13 July 1985, Elizabeth Anne, *née* Mighall; 1 s (Thomas Robert b 13 May 1992), 1 da (Anna Mary Elizabeth b 8 March 1995); *Career* ordained: deacon 1986, priest 1987; curate St Mary the Virgin Barnes 1986–89, sr curate St Mary's Church Bletchley and curate-in-charge Whaddon Way Ecumenical Church 1989–93, vicar Adderbury 1993–2002, rural dean of Deddington 2000–02, rector Wimborne Min and priest-in-charge Witchampton, Stanbridge and Long Crichel 2002–11, rural dean of Wimborne 2004–11, canon and prebend of Salisbury Cathedral 2006–11, canon of Peterborough Cathedral 2011–, acting bishop of Leicester 2015–16; *Style*— The Rt Rev the Bishop of Brixworth; ✉ Orchard Acre, 11 North Street, Mears Ashby, Northampton NN6 0DW (☎ 01733 562492, e-mail bishop.brixworth@peterborough-diocese.org.uk)

BROACKES, Simon Nigel; s of Sir Nigel Broackes (d 1999), and late Joyce Edith, *née* Horne; *b* 31 July 1966; *Educ* Eton; *m* 2008, Claire, *née* Nicolson; 1 da from a previous relationship (Nigella Elizabeth b 29 Dec 2004); *Career* quantity surveyor Trollope and Colls Ltd (awarded BEC mgmnt trg prize 1985), sr conslt to Sir Robert McAlpine Ltd (previous roles incl mgmnt of special projects div 1987–95), co-fndr and chm Neptune Land Ltd 2004–; exec dir SQ Group of Cos; dir: London International Exhibition Centre Ltd (ExCel), Greycoat Victoria plc, Madisons Coffee plc, Lanica plc, Newultra Ltd, BHW Investments Ltd, Q.ton Ltd, Carwardines of Bristol Ltd, Expovenue Ltd, Richoux Restaurants Ltd; memb: Gen Cncl Westminster Property Owners' Assoc 1987–92, Lime St Ward Club 1986, Land Inst 1988, Met Special Constabulary 1986–91; *Recreations* classic cars, tennis; *Clubs* Lansdowne, Bluebird, Harrington; *Style*— Simon Broackes, Esq; ✉ Neptune Land Ltd, 102 Sydney Street, London SW3 6NJ (e-mail simon.broackes@neptuneland.co.uk)

BROADBENT, Jim; *b* 24 May 1949; *Career* actor; *Theatre* incl Theatre of Blood (RNT) 2005; *Television* incl: Bird of Prey 1982, Birth of a Nation 1982, Black Adder 1983, Only Fools and Horses 1983–91, Happy Families 1985, The Insurance Man 1985, Tales of the Unexpected 1988, Blackadder's Christmas Carol 1988, Work! 1990, Murder Most Horrid 1991, A Sense of History 1992 (also writer), Gone to Seed 1992, Inspector Morse 1992, The Last Englishman 1995, The Peter Principle 1997, The Gathering Storm 2002, The Young Visiters 2003, Pride 2004, Longford 2006 (Best Actor in a Mini-series or Movie Golden Globe 2008), Einstein and Eddington 2008, Any Human Heart 2010 (Best Actor RTS Award 2011); *Film* incl: The Shout 1978, The Passage 1979, The Dogs of War 1980, Breaking Glass 1980, Time Bandits 1981, The Hit 1984, Brazil 1985, Superman IV: The Quest for Peace 1987, The Good Father 1987, Vroom 1988, Erik the Viking 1989, Life is Sweet 1990, Enchanted April 1992, The Crying Game 1992, Bullets Over Broadway 1994, Princess Caraboo 1994, Widow's Peak 1994, Wide-Eyed and Legless 1994, Richard III 1995, Rough Magic 1995, Smilla's Feeling for Snow 1997, The Borrowers 1997, The Avengers 1997, Little Voice 1998, Topsy-Turvy 1999 (BAFTA nomination), Bridget Jones's Diary 2001, Moulin Rouge 2001 (BAFTA Award for Best Supporting Actor 2002), Gangs of New York 2001, Iris 2001 (Oscar for Best Supporting Actor 2002, Golden Globe for Best Supporting Actor 2002), Nicholas Nickelby 2002, Bright Young Things 2003, Tooth 2004, Around the World in 80 Days 2004, Vanity Fair 2004, Vera Drake 2004, Bridget Jones: The Edge of Reason 2004, The Magic Roundabout 2005, Robots 2005, Valiant 2005, The Chronicles of Narnia: The Lion, the Witch and the Wardrobe 2005, Art School Confidential 2006, Hot Fuzz 2007, And When Did You Last See Your Father? 2007, Indiana Jones and the Kingdom of the Crystal Skull 2008, Inkheart 2008, The Young Victoria 2009, The Damned United 2009, Harry Potter and the Half-Blood Prince 2009, Perrier's Bounty 2009, Another Year 2010, The Iron Lady 2011; *Style*— Jim Broadbent, Esq; ✉ c/o Harriet Robinson, Independent Talent Group, 40 Whitfield Street, London W1T 2RH

BROADBENT, John Michael (Mike); s of Ronald William Percy Broadbent (d 1979), and Marion, *née* White (d 1963); *b* 24 November 1933; *Educ* Manchester Grammar; *m* 29 July 1961, Sandra Elizabeth, da of Lewis Phillips (d 1966), of Runcorn, Cheshire; 3 da (Maryan b 1965, Jane b 1969, Philippa b 1971 d 1972), 2 s (Adam b 1971, Simon b and d 1967); *Career* Nat Serv Bombardier RA 1953–55; journalist: Kemsley Newspapers 1950–57, Star Newspaper 1957–59; BBC 1959–91: scriptwriter TV News, prodr (later ed) Westminster 1968–72, ed Nine O'Clock News, ed (news) Sixty Minutes, founding ed One O'Clock News, ed Commons TV, asst head BBC Westminster; freelance journalist, broadcasting consl and lectr 1991–; accompanying offr FCO (OVIS) 1991–95; memb Luton Town Supporters Club; *Recreations* supporting Luton Town FC, cinema, hospice volunteer; *Style*— Mike Broadbent, Esq; ✉ 382 Icknield Way, Luton, Bedfordshire LU3 2JX (☎ 01582 527470, e-mail mike.broadbent@yahoo.co.uk)

BROADBENT, (John) Michael; s of John Fred Broadbent (d 1973), and Hilary Louise, *née* Batty (d 1998); *b* 2 May 1927; *Educ* Rishworth Sch, Bartlett Sch of Architecture, UCL (Certificate in Architecture); *m* 19 June 1954, Mary Daphne (d 2015), da of Edgar Lionel Joste (d 1985); 1 da (Emma b 9 Jan 1959), 1 s (Bartholomew b 11 Jan 1962); *Career* Nat Serv RA 1945–48 (2 Lt and asst adj Dover Castle 1947–48); trainee Laytons Wine Merchants London 1952–53, Saccone and Speed London 1953–55, John Harvey and Sons Ltd 1955–66 (dir 1963–66); Christie Manson and Woods Ltd: head of Wine Dept 1966–92, dir 1967–97, chm Christie's South Kensington 1978–82, dir Christie's Wine Course 1982–2012; non-exec dir Christie's Fine Art Ltd 1998–2001, dir Wineworld plc 1998–2000, dir Christie's Int (UK) Ltd 2001–07 (sr consl 2007–); chm Wine Trade Art Soc 1972–2007, pres Int Wine and Food Soc 1985–92, chm Wine & Spirit Trades' Benevolent Soc 1991–92, hon pres Wine and Spirit Educn Tst 2007–09; princ wine columnist Decanter magazine 1978–2013; Lifetime Achievement Award Bacchus Soc of America 1992, Lifetime Achievement Award Int Wine Challenge 2008, Wine Media Guild of New York's Hall of Fame 2010; Master Worshipful Company of Distillers 1990–91 (Liveryman 1964, memb Ct of Assts 1969), Liveryman Worshipful Co of Vintners 2006 (Freeman (hc) 2001); Master of Wine 1960, memb Inst Masters of Wine (chm 1971–72); Membre d'Honneur l'Académie du Vin de Bordeaux 1973, Chevalier dans l'Ordre National du Mérite 1979, La Medaille de la Ville de Paris Echelon Vermeil 1989, Membre d'Honneur L'Académie International du Vin 1994, and 30 other honours and awards; *Books* Wine Tasting (1968–90), The Great Vintage Wine Book (1980, II 1991), Pocketbook of Vintages (1992–2006), Vintage Wine (2002, The James Beard Fndn Best Book on Wine 2003, The Best Wine Book in the World Gourmand World Awards 2003, Golden Laurel Historia Gastronomica Helvetica (Best Wine Book of the Year) 2004, Goldener Feder Gastronomische Akademie Deutschlands 2005, Gourmand World Award Best out of 12 Years of Awards 2008), Michael Broadbent's Pocket Vintage Wine Companion (2007); *Recreations* drawing, piano playing, music, travel; *Clubs* Brooks's, Saintsbury; *Style*— Michael Broadbent, Esq; ✉ 87 Rosebank, London SW6 6LJ (☎ 020 3632 9412); Foudry House Cottage, Stratfield Mortimer RG7 3NR

BROADBENT, Rt Rev Peter Alan (Pete); *see:* Willesden, Bishop of

BROADBENT, (Sir) Richard; KCB (2003); s of John Barclay Broadbent, of Norwich, and Faith Joan Laurie, *née* Fisher; *b* 22 April 1953; *Educ* Univ of London (BSc), Univ of Manchester (MA), Stanford Business Sch (Harkness fell); *Children* 1 s (Alexander Brooke b 25 Jan 1980), 1 da (Louise Rosalind b 19 Oct 1981); *Career* HM Treasy 1975–86, Schroders plc 1986–99, chm HM Customs and Excise 2000–03, chm Arriva plc 2003–10, chm Tesco plc 2011–, sr ind dir Barclays plc 2003–; chm The GSB Tst; MSI; *Clubs* 2 Brydges Place, The Walbrook; *Style*— Richard Broadbent

BROADFOOT, Prof Patricia Mary; CBE (2006); *née* Cole; da of Norman John Cole (d 1977), and Margaret Grace, *née* Potter (d 1997); *b* 13 July 1949, London; *Educ* Queen Elizabeth's Girls' GS Barnet, Univ of Leeds (BA), Garnett Coll London (PGCE), Univ of Edinburgh (MEd), Open Univ (PhD), Univ of Bristol (DSc); *m* 9 Aug 1980, David Charles Rockey, s of Prof Kenneth Rockey; 2 s (James Charles b 1981, Aurin Laurence b 1983), 1 da (Elanwy Grace b 1987); *Career* teacher Wolmer's Boys' HS Kingston Jamaica 1971–73, research offr Scottish Cncl for Research in Educn 1973–77, pt/t tutor Open Univ 1976–77, sr lectr Westhill Coll Birmingham 1977–81; Univ of Bristol: lectr in educn 1981–90, reader in educn 1990–91, prof of educn 1991–2006, head Grad Sch of Educn 1993–97, dean of social sciences 1998–2002, pro-vice-chllr (educn and widening participation) 2002–06, visiting prof of educn 2006–10, prof of educn 2010–14, prof of educn emeritus 2014–; vice-chllr Univ of Glos 2006–10; visiting prof Macquarie Univ Sydney 1986, visiting prof Univ of Western Sydney 1991; BERA: memb 1977–2007, pres 1987–88; Br Assoc for Int and Comparative Educn: memb 1977–2007, pres 1997; ESRC: memb Cncl 2001–06, chair Int Advsy Ctee 2001–03, chair Research Resources Bd 2003–06, chair Governing Bd UK Longitudinal Household Study 2008–15; chair HERDA-SW Strategy Bd 2009–10, chair Advsy Bd Paul Hamlyn Fndn: 'What Works: Student Retention and Success Change Programme' 2009–; memb: Burgess Ctee on Assessment in HE 2005–10, HEFCE Teaching Quality and Student Experience Ctee 2005–10, Educn Advsy Ctee Nuffield Fndn 2006–10, Research Advsy Bd Educnl Testing Serv Princeton 2007–09, Bd Univs and Colls Employers Assoc 2007–10, Bd HE Acad 2007–09, Bd Univs UK 2008–10, Advsy Bd Cabot Inst Univ of Bristol 2010–15, Expert Advsy Panel Edexcel 2011–, Social Science Expert Panel DEFRA/DECC 2012–15, Leverhulme Advsy Panel 2013–, Bd Univ of St Mark and St John Plymouth; cmmr Marmot Review of Strategies to Reduce Health Inequalities Beyond 2010 2009–10; chair Vital Partnerships Professional Services Ltd; tstee St Monica Tst Bristol 2005–09, tstee and vice-chair Lloyds TSB Fndn 2011–; govr Royal Agricultural Coll 2010–; canon emeritus Gloucester Cathedral, licensed reader Gloucestershire Dio, memb Bishop's Cncl 2015–; memb Cncl AcSS 2015–; Standing Conf for Studies in Educn Annual Book Prize 1979, Samuel J Messick Meml Lecture Award Educnl Testing Serv (ETS) Princeton 2003; Hon LLD Univ of Bristol 2010; FRSA 1992, AcSS 1999; *Books* incl: Assessment, Schools and Society (1979), The Impact of Research on Policy and Practice in Education (jtly, 1980), Politics and Educational Change: An International Survey (jt ed, 1981), Keeping Track of Teaching: Assessment in the Modern Classroom (jtly, 1982), Selection, Certification and Control: Social Issues in Educational Assessment (ed, 1984), Profiles and Records of Achievement: A Review of Issues and Practice (ed, 1986), Introducing Profiling: A Practical Manual (1987), Profiling in TVEI: A Research Report (jtly, 1989), Changing Educational Assessment: International Perspectives and Trends (jt ed, 1990), Policy Issues in National Assessment (jt ed, 1993), Perceptions of Teaching: Primary School Teachers in England and France (jtly, 1993), Education, Assessment, and Society: A Sociological Analysis (1996), Promoting Quality in Learning: Does England Have the Answer? (jtly, 2000), What Teachers Do: Changing Policy and Practice in Primary Education (jtly, 2000), What Pupils Say (jtly, 2000), Culture Learning and Comparison: Lawrence Stenhouse's Vision of Education for Empowerment (2000), Assessment: What's in it for Schools? (jtly, 2002), A World of Difference: Comparing Learners Across Europe (jtly, 2003), An Introduction to Assessment (2007), 50 Years of Comparitive Education (jntly, 2007); *Recreations* riding, gardening, swimming, walking; *Style—* Prof Patricia Broadfoot, CBE; ✉ e-mail edpmb@bris.ac.uk

BROADHURST, Norman Neill; s of Samuel Herbert Broadhurst, and Ruth Broadhurst; *b* 19 September 1941, Stockport, Cheshire; *Educ* Cheadle Hulme Sch; *m* 1964, Kathleen Muriel Joyce; 2 da; *Career* Platt Saco Lowell 1970–81 (latterly finance dir), financial controller then divnl mangr (finance and admin) China Light and Power 1981–86, finance dir United Engineering Steels 1986–90, finance dir then jt dep chief executive (finance/commercial) VSEL plc 1990–94, finance dir Railtrack 1994–2000; non-exec chm: Chloride Gp plc 2001–10 (non-exec dir 1998–), Freightliner Gp Ltd 2001–08, Cattles plc 2006–09 (non-exec dir 2001–); non-exec dir: Clubhaus 1997–2000, Taylor Woodrow plc 2000–03 (dep chm 2003), Old Mutual plc 1999–2008, United Utilities plc 1999–2008, Tomkins plc 2000–06; FCA 1975, FCT 1995; *Clubs* Ulverston Golf, Grange-over-Sands Golf; *Style—* Mr Norman Broadhurst; ✉ Hobroyde, Penny Bridge, Ulverston, Cumbria LA12 7TD

BROADIE, Prof Alexander; *Educ* Royal HS Edinburgh, Univ of Edinburgh (MA), Balliol Coll Oxford (BLitt), Univ of Glasgow (PhD, DLitt); *Career* prof of logic and rhetoric Univ of Glasgow 1991–2009, hon professorial research fell Univ of Glasgow 2009–; RSE Henry Duncan prize lectr in Scottish studies 1990–93; Gifford lectr in natural theology Univ of Aberdeen 1994; Hon DUniv Blaise Pascal Univ 2007; FRSE 1991; *Books* A Samaritan Philosophy (1981), George Lokert: Late Scholastic Logician (1983), The Circle of John Mair (1985), Notion and Object: Aspects of Late Medieval Epistemology (1989), The Tradition of Scottish Philosophy (1990), Paul of Venice: Logica Magna (1990), Robert Kilwardby OP: On Time and Imagination (1993), Introduction to Medieval Logic (2 edn, 1993), The Shadow of Scotus (1995), The Scottish Enlightenment: An Anthology (1997), Why Scottish Philosophy Matters (2000), The Scottish Enlightenment: The Historical Age of the Historical Nation (2001), The Cambridge Companion to the Scottish Enlightenment (2003), Thomas Reid on Logic, Rhetoric and the Fine Arts (2005), George Turnbull: Principles of Moral and Christian Philosophy (2005), A History of Scottish Philosophy (2009), Agreeable Connexions: Scottish Enlightenment Links with France (2012); *Style—* Prof Alexander Broadie, FRSE; ✉ University of Glasgow, Glasgow G12 8QQ (☎ 0141 339 8855 ext 4509, e-mail alexander.broadie@glasgow.ac.uk)

BROADIE, Prof Sarah Jean; da of J C Waterlow, and A P C Waterlow, *née* Gray; *Educ* Univ of Oxford (MA, BPhil), Univ of Edinburgh (PhD); *m* 2 March 1984, Frederick Broadie, s of I Broadie; *Career* lectr Univ of Edinburgh 1967–84; prof of philosophy: Univ of Texas at Austin 1984–86, Yale Univ 1987–91, Rutgers Univ 1991–93, Princeton Univ 1993–2001, Univ of St Andrews 2001–; John Simon Guggenheim Meml Fellowship 1986–87; FAAAS 1991, FRSE 2002, FBA 2003; *Books* as Sarah Waterlow: Nature, Change, and Agency in Aristotle's Physics (1982), Passage and Possibility (1982); as Sarah Broadie: Ethics with Aristotle (1991), Aristotle: the Nicomachean Ethics (with Christopher Rowe, 2001); *Style—* Prof Sarah Broadie; ✉ Department of Moral Philosophy, University of St Andrews, Edgecliffe, The Scores, St Andrews, Fife KY16 9AL (☎ 01334 462486, fax 01334 462485, e-mail sjb15@st-andrews.ac.uk)

BROADLEY, Philip Arthur John; s of Jack Broadley (d 2015), and Daphne Broadley (d 2012); *b* 31 January 1961; *Educ* Eastbourne Coll, St Edmund Hall Oxford (MA), LSE (MSc), Warwick Univ Business Sch (Dip BA); *m* 1989, Gillian, *née* Barlow; 1 da, 1 s; *Career* Arthur Andersen 1983–2000 (ptnr 1993–2000), gp finance dir Prudential plc 2000–08, gp finance dir Old Mutual plc 2008–14, membr Code Cmtee The Takeover Panel 2007–; non-exec dir Egg plc 2005–07; chm Hundred Gp of Finance Dirs 2005–07; vice-chm of govrs Eastbourne Coll, memb Oxford Univ Audit and Scrutiny Ctee; FCA, FRSA; *Recreations* skiing, flying, music; *Clubs* Naval and Military; *Style—* Philip Broadley, Esq

BROCK, Prof George Laurence; s of Michael Brock, of Oxford, and Eleanor, *née* Morrison; *b* 7 November 1951, Oxford; *Educ* Winchester, CCC Oxford (MA); *m* 1 July 1978, Kay, *née* Sandeman; 2 s (Patrick b 6 April 1983, Oliver b 8 May 1985); *Career* grad trainee reporter Yorkshire Evening Press 1973–76, reporter The Observer 1976–81; The Times: feature writer 1981–84, opinion page ed 1984–87, foreign ed 1987–90, bureau chief Brussels 1991–95, European ed 1995–97, managing ed 1997–2004, Saturday ed 2004–08, int ed 2008–09; prof of journalism City Univ London 2009–, head of journalism City Univ London 2009–14; pres World Eds Forum 2004–08 (memb Bd 2001–14), memb Defence, Press and Broadcasting Advsy Ctee 1998–2004, memb Bd Int Press Inst 2000–15 (chair Br Exec 2011–15), memb Editorial Bd The Conversation UK 2013–; theatre panel judge Olivier Awards 2004; govr The Ditchley Fndn 2003–12; tstee: Nat Acad of Writing 2008–16, Bureau of Investigative Journalism 2010–, Int News Safety Inst (UK) 2011–13; memb Cncl Gresham Coll 2012–; *Publications* Siege: Seven Days at the Iranian Embassy (co-author, 1980), Thatcher (co-author, 1983), Out of Print: Newspapers, Journalism and the Business of News in the Digital Age (2013); *Recreations* music, walking, theatre, travel; *Style—* Prof George Brock; ✉ Department of Journalism, City University, Northampton Square, London EC1V 0HB

BROCK, Kay; CBE (2016), LVO (2002), DL; *née* Stewart Sandeman; da of George Roland Stewart Sandeman (d 1992), and Helen, *née* McLaren (d 2004); *b* 23 May 1953, Fordingbridge, Hants; *Educ* Sherborne Sch for Girls, Somerville Coll Oxford (MA), London Business Sch (MBA); *m* 1 July 1978, George Laurence Brock; 2 s (Patrick Michael b 6 April 1983, Oliver Roland b 8 May 1985); *Career* MAFF 1975–85 (private sec to the Perm Sec 1980–81), conslt in int trade 1985–88, Spicers Consulting Gp 1988–89, dir PDN Ltd 1990–91, European Cmmn 1992–95, advsr UK Knowhow Fund and EBRD 1995–99, asst private sec to HM The Queen 1999–2002, COS to Lord Mayor of London 2004–09, dir Ashridge Strategic Mgmnt Centre 2010, Archbishop of Canterbury's sec for public affrs 2012–13, Archbishop of Canterbury's COS 2013–16; memb Ind Monitoring Bd HMP Wandsworth 2003–04; pres Somerville Coll Alumni Assoc 2004–08; tstee Dance United 2008–13 (chm 2008–12), tstee Acad of Ancient Music 2009–13, memb Advsy Cncl London Symphony Orch 2009–16, govr Sherborne Girls Sch 2011–; Liveryman Worshipful Co of Founders 2005–, Freeman Worshipful Co of Merchant Taylors 2009; *Recreations* music, Italy, cycling; *Clubs* Farmers; *Style—* Mrs Kay Brock, CBE, LVO, DL

BROCK-DOYLE, Jacqueline; OBE; *b* Sittingbourne; *Career* dir of communications and public affrs London 2012 Olympic and Paralympic Games until 2013, gp chief exec Good Relations Gp 2013–; chair Good Relations 2015–; memb Int Olympic Ctee's Coordination Cmmn for Rio 2016 Olympic Games; PR Week PR Professional of the Year and Campaign of the Year 2012, Debrett's 500 Most Influential 2014; *Style—* Ms Jacqueline Brock-Doyle, OBE; ✉ The Good Relations Group, Holborn Gate, 26 Southampton Buildings, London WC2A 1PQ

BROCKBANK, Anthony Lionel; s of Maj-Gen Robin Brockbank (d 2006), and Gillian, *née* Findlay; *b* 17 December 1960, London; *Educ* Eton, ChCh Oxford (BA), Coll of Law; *m* 17 May 1997, Caroline, *née* Walford; 2 da (Eleanor b 15 Sept 2000, Rosanna b 23 Feb 2002), 1 s (Robin b 8 July 2008); *Career* slr; Linklaters 1984–89, Hobson Audley 1989–2000 (ptnr 1993), ptnr Field Fisher Waterhouse 2000–; *Style—* Anthony Brockbank, Esq; ✉ Field Fisher Waterhouse LLP, Riverbank House, 2 Swan Lane, Londno EC4R 3TT (☎ 020 7861 4000, fax 020 7488 0084, e-mail anthony.brockbank@fieldfisher.com)

BROCKBANK, Thomas Frederick; s of John Bowman Brockbank (d 1990), of Hilton, and Alice Margaret, *née* Parker (d 1987); *b* 6 March 1938; *Educ* Bootham Sch York, Loughborough Coll (DLC Mech Engrg); *m* 16 Dec 1967 (m dis 1992), Joan Emma, da of Martin Israelski, of Leamington; 3 da (Eleanor Clare b 1970, Laura Katherine b 1973, Harriet Elisabeth b 1975); *Career* merchant banker; Courtaulds Ltd 1960–65, mgmnt conslt Arthur Andersen & Co London 1965–68, RTZ Conslts (part of RTZ Corp) 1968–73, Hill Samuel Bank Ltd 1973–93 (dir of corp fin 1985–93); currently: company dir and mgmnt conslt, chm Nightingale Square Properties plc, tstee Buskaid; author of numerous lectures and articles, particularly on finance for growing companies, flotation and general strategy; MIMC, MSI, FRSA; *Recreations* music, theatre, art, photography, travel; *Style—* Thomas Brockbank, Esq; ✉ Nightingale Square Properties plc, 30A Edgarley Terrace, London SW6 6QD (☎ 020 7731 7343, fax 020 7731 7420)

BROCKES, Prof Jeremy Patrick; s of Bernard Arthur Brockes, of Stonor, Henley-on-Thames, and Edna, *née* Heaney (d 1959); *b* 29 February 1948, Haslemere, Surrey; *Educ* Winchester, St John's Coll Cambridge (BA), Univ of Edinburgh (PhD); *Career* postdoctoral fell Harvard Medical Sch 1972–75, research assoc UCL 1975–78, assoc prof of biology California Inst of Tech 1981–83 (asst prof of biology 1978–81); memb MRC Biophysics Unit KCL 1983–88, memb Ludwig Inst for Cancer Research 1988–97, prof UCL 1991–97, MRC research prof UCL 1997–; scientific medals: Zoological Soc of London 1985, Biological Cncl 1990; Newcomb Cleveland Prize AAAS 2008; memb: EMBO 1988, Academia Europaea 1989; FRS 1994; *Publications* Comparative aspects of animal regeneration (Annual Review of Cell and Developmental Biology, 2008); *Recreations* soprano saxophone, chess; *Style—* Prof Jeremy Brockes, FRS; ✉ Institute of Structural and Molecular Biology, UCL, Gower Street, London WC1E 6BT (☎ 020 7679 4483, e-mail j.brockes@ucl.ac.uk)

BROCKINGTON, Prof John Leonard; s of Rev Leonard Herbert Brockington (d 1978), and Florence Edith, *née* Woodward (d 2009); *b* 5 December 1940; *Educ* Mill Hill Sch, CCC Oxford (MA, DPhil); *m* 2 Aug 1966, Mary, da of Joseph Gascoigne Fairweather (d 1988); 1 da (Anne b 1967), 1 s (Michael b 1971); *Career* Univ of Edinburgh: lectr in Sanskrit 1965–82, head of dept 1975–99, sr lectr 1982–89, reader 1989–98, prof of Sanskrit 1998–2005; vice-pres Int Assoc of Sanskrit Studies 2012– (sec gen 2000–12), interim academic dir Oxford Centre for Hindu Studies 2016–17; Hon DLitt Sipakorn Univ Bangkok 2015; FRSE 2001; *Books* The Sacred Thread – Hinduism in its Continuity and Diversity (1981), Righteous Rama: The Evolution of an Epic (1985), Hinduism and Christianity (1992), The Sanskrit Epics (1998), Epic Threads: John Brockington on the Sanskrit Epics (with Greg Bailey and Mary Brockington, 2000), Rama the Steadfast: An early form of the Ramayana (with Mary Brockington, 2006), Battle, Bards and Brahmins (ed, 2012), The Other Ramayana Women (ed, with Mary Brockington, 2016); *Style—* Prof John Brockington; ✉ 113 Rutten Lane, Yarnton, Oxfordshire OX5 1LT (e-mail j.l.brockington@ed.ac.uk)

BROCKLEBANK, Sir Aubrey Thomas; 6 Bt (UK 1885), of Greenlands, Co Cumberland and Springwood, Co Lancaster; s of Sir John Montague Brocklebank, 5 Bt, TD (d 1974), and Pamela Sue, *née* Pierce (d 2005); *b* 29 January 1952; *Educ* Eton, UC Durham (BSc); *m* 1979 (m dis 1990), Dr Anna-Marie, da of Dr William Dunnet; 2 s (Aubrey William Thomas b 1980, Hamish John b 1987); m 2 (m dis 2012), Hazel, da of Brian Roden; 1 s (Archie Thomas b 1999); *Heir* s, Aubrey Brocklebank; *Career* financial conslt; chm: Hargreave Hale AIM VCT plc, Puma 8 VCT plc; dir Downing 4 plc and various other cos; *Clubs* Brooks's; *Style—* Sir Aubrey Brocklebank, Bt

BROCKLEBANK-FOWLER, Simon Edward; *b* 29 September 1961; *Educ* Westminster, Jesus Coll Cambridge (exhibitioner, MA); *m* 24 April 1993 (m dis 2011), Alexandra Robson, *qv*, da of Sir John Robson, KCMG; 1 da; *Career* FCO 1982–86, investment banker 1986–92, dir Shandwick Consultants Ltd 1992–94, md Citigate Communications Ltd 1995–98, fndr and chm Cubitt Consulting 1998–; memb Advsy Bd Cass Business Sch 2004–08 (hon visiting fell 2008–); tstee Policy Exchange 2010–; fell Investor Rels Soc 1998–; FRSA 2004–10; *Recreations* shooting, tennis; *Clubs* Brooks's, Leander, Queen's; *Style—* Simon Brocklebank-Fowler, Esq; ✉ Cubitt Consulting Ltd, The West Wing, Somerset House, Strand, London WC2R 1LA (☎ 020 7367 5100, e-mail simon.brocklebank-fowler@cubitt.com)

BRODE, Andrew S; *b* 2 September 1940, Birmingham; *Educ* King Edwar's Sch Birmingham, Victoria Univ of Manchester (BA); *Career* Arthur Andersen & Co 1965–71, Rothschild Intercontinental Bank 1971–76, Croner Pubns Ltd 1976–77, Wolters Kluwer plc 1977–90, Eclipse Pubns Ltd 1990–2000, dir RWS Hldgs plc 2000– (exec chm); chm: Electric World plc, Learning Technologies Gp (LTG) plc 2013–; non-exec dir: Vitesse Media plc, Hotbed Ltd, Epic Gp plc, IT Governance Ltd; FCA 1965; *Recreations* golf, tennis; *Clubs* RAC, Moor park Golf; *Style—* Andrew Brode, Esq; ✉ RWS Holdings plc, Europa House, Chiltern Park, Chiltern Hill, Chalfont St Peter, Buckinghamshire SL9 9FG

BRODIE, Alan; s of Maxwell Brodie (d 1998), of Glasgow, Scotland, and Judy, *née* Jacobson; *b* 11 January 1955; *Educ* HS of Glasgow, Univ of Edinburgh (BA, LLB); *m* 1, 15 Nov 1982 (m dis 1994), Rosemary Anne Squire; 1 s (Daniel Henry b 1987), 1 da (Jennifer b 1986); m 2, 20 Oct 1996 (m dis 2000), Caroline Louise Diprose; m 3, 1 June 2009, Alison Mary Havell; *Career* dir Michael Imison Playwrights Ltd (Literary Agents) 1981–89, fndr

Alan Brodie Representation 1989–93 and 1996–, dir International Creative Management Ltd 1993–96; former co-chair Personal Managers Assoc; chair of tstees Noël Coward Fndn, patron Chicken Shed Theatre Co, memb Down's Syndrome Assoc; *Style*— Alan Brodie, Esq; ✉ Paddock Suite, The Courtyard, 55 Charterhouse Street, London EC1M 6HA

BRODIE, (James) Bruce; s of John Hobson Brodie (d 1979), of Graaff-Reinet, South Africa, and Edith Florence, *née* Murray (d 2001); *b* 19 March 1937; *Educ* Union HS, Univ of Natal (BA), Fitzwilliam Coll Cambridge (MA); *m* 15 Dec 1962, (Amie) Louise, da of Kenneth Turner James, MBE (d 1964), of Fetcham, Surrey; 2 da (Sarah b 1964, Nicola b 1966); *Career* former slr and ptnr Frere Cholmeley (chm 1990–92), barr and arbitrator 1993–2014; *Recreations* cricket, fishing; *Clubs* Hawks' (Cambridge), MCC, Groucho, Western Province Cricket, Kelvin Grove; *Style*— Bruce Brodie, Esq; ✉ Penthouse E, St John's Wood Court, London NW8 8QT (☎ 020 7289 0657, e-mail bruce.brodie@hotmail.co.uk)

BRODIE, Charles (Chic); MSP; s of Charles Gilchrist (d 1989), and Eileen Isobel, *née* Robertson (d 2009); *b* Dundee; *Educ* Univ of St Andrews (BSc); *m* Mary Ann Mann; *Career* fin dir Tandem Computers Ltd, dir/gen mangr Twinsoft Europe; MSP (SNP) S of Scotland 2011–; *Style*— Chic Brodie, Esq, MSP; ✉ 23 Maybole Road, Ayr KA7 2PZ (☎ 01292 294603, e-mail cbrodie@calstiat.freeserve.co.uk); The Scottish Parliament, Edinburgh EH99 1SP

BRODIE, Prof David Alan; s of William Brodie, and Margaret, *née* Blackwell; *b* 24 June 1946; *Educ* King's Sch Worcester, Univ of Nottingham (BEd), Loughborough Univ (MSc, PhD), Univ of Coventry (DSc); *m* 1971, Megan Elizabeth, da of Elvet Plummer; 1 da (Jo-Anne Beth b 1973), 1 s (Tom David b 1977); *Career* dir of physical welfare Abingdon Sch 1969–72, lectr in physical educn Saltley Coll 1972–74, sr res fell Carnegie Sch Leeds Poly 1974–81, prof and head Dept of Movement Sci and Physical Educn Univ of Liverpool 1990–2001 (dir of physical educn and recreation 1981–90); head Research Centre for Society and Health Buckinghamshire New Univ 2001–; memb: Int Soc for the Advancement of Kinanthropometry 1991, Br Cardiac Soc 2002, Physiological Soc 2003, RSM 2007; *Books* Fitness Training for Rugby (jtly, 1978), Get Fit for Badminton (with J Downey, 1980), Microcomputing in Sport and Physical Education (with J J Thornhill, 1983), Citysport Challenge (jtly, 1992), Inner City Sport: who plays, what are the benefits? (with K Roberts, 1992), HE Departmental Leadership/Management – An Exploration of Roles and Responsibilities (with P Partington, 1992), Research Methods in Health Sciences (jtly, 1994), Health Matters at Work (1995), Treacherous Games (2012); *Recreations* exercise, gardening, travel; *Clubs* Pensby Runners; *Style*— Prof David Brodie; ✉ e-mail profbrodie@hotmail.co.uk, website www.davidbrodie.org

BRODIE, Rt Hon Lord; Philip Hope; PC (2013); s of Very Rev Dr Peter Philip Brodie (d 1990), of Stirling, and Constance Lindsay, *née* Hope; *b* 14 July 1950; *Educ* Dollar Acad, Univ of Edinburgh (LLB), Univ of Virginia (LLM); *m* 16 April 1983, Carol Dora, da of Dr Ian Stanley McLeish, of Bearsden, Glasgow; 2 s (Alexander b 1984, Peter b 1986), 1 da (Alice b 1988); *Career* admitted Faculty of Advocates 1976; called to the Bar Lincoln's Inn 1991 (bencher 2013); standing jr counsel (Scot) MOD (Procurement) Health and Safety at Work Exec 1983–87, QC (Scot) 1987, pt/t chm Industrial Tbnls 1987–91, pt/t chm Med Appeal Tbnls 1991–96, memb Mental Welfare Cmmn for Scot 1985–96, advocate depute 1997–99, senator Coll of Justice 2002–, chm Judicial Studies Ctee 2006–12; chm Cockburn Assoc 2008–16; pres Franco-Scottish Soc; *Style*— The Rt Hon Lord Brodie; ✉ 2 Cobden Crescent, Edinburgh EH9 2BG (☎ 0131 667 2651); The Court of Session, Parliament House, Edinburgh EH1 1RQ (☎ 0131 225 2595)

BRODIE, Stanley Eric; QC (1975); s of Dr Abraham Brodie (d 1978), of Allerton, Bradford, and Cissie Rachel Garstein (d 1998); uncle Sir Israel Brodie, former chief rabbi of GB and The Cwlth; *b* 2 July 1930, Bradford, Yorks; *Educ* Bradford GS, Balliol Coll Oxford (MA); *m* 1, 31 July 1956, Gillian Rosemary, da of Sir Maxwell Joseph; 2 da (Henrietta b 1957, Charlotte b 1960); m 2, 29 Oct 1973, Elizabeth (Rt Hon the Lady Justice Gloster, DBE), *qv*, da of Peter Gloster; 1 da (Sophie b 1978), 1 s (Samuel b 1981); *Career* called to the Bar Inner Temple 1954, recorder Crown Court 1975, bencher Inner Temple 1984 (reader 1999, treas 2000), memb Bar Cncl 1987; *Publications* English Legal System in the 21st Century (contrib, 2001), The Cost to Justice (2011); *Recreations* fishing, boating, opera, holidays; *Clubs* Flyfishers', Athenaeum, Beefsteak; *Style*— Stanley Brodie, Esq, QC; ✉ Balgreen Lodge, Hollybush, Ayr KA6 7EB; Blackstone Chambers, Blackstone House, Temple, London EC4Y 9BW (☎ 020 7583 1770)

BRODIE OF LETHEN, Ewen John; CVO (2015); s of David James Brodie of Lethen (d 1966), and Diana Davidson (d 1991); *b* 16 December 1942; *Educ* Harrow; *m* 4 Aug 1967, Mariota, yr da of Lt Col Ronald Steuart Menzies, of Culdares; 3 da (Sarah b 30 Dec 1967, Jane b 5 May 1970, Katherine b 21 Jan 1972); *Career* Lt Grenadier Guards 1961–64; mktg mangr IBM (UK) Ltd 1965–74; estate mgmnt 1975–; memb Regnl Advsy Ctee (N Scotland) Forestry Cmmn 1977–89, vice-chm Timber Growers Scotland 1979–82; dir John Gordon & Son Ltd 1992–2011; HM Lord-Lt Nairnshire 1999– (DL 1980–99); *Recreations* countryside sports; *Clubs* New (Edinburgh); *Style*— Ewen Brodie of Lethen, CVO; ✉ The Dower House, Lethen, Nairn IV12 5PR (☎ 01667 452123, e-mail ejbrodie@btinternet.com)

BROERS, Baron (Life Peer UK 2004), of Cambridge in the County of Cambridgeshire; Prof Sir Alec Nigel Broers; kt (1998), DL (Cambs 2000); s of Alec William Broers (d 1987), of Melbourne, Aust, and Constance Amy, *née* Cox (d 2001); *b* 17 September 1938; *Educ* Geelong GS, Univ of Melbourne (BSc), Gonville & Caius Coll Cambridge (BA, PhD); *m* 1964, Mary Therese, da of Michael Phelan (d 1944); 2 s (Hon Mark b 1965, Hon Christopher b 1967); *Career* numerous managerial positions incl mangr Photon and Electron Optics IBM T J Watson Res Lab 1965–81; mangr: Lithography and Technology Tools 1981–82, Advanced Devpt IBM E Fishkill Lab 1983–84; prof of electrical engrg and head Electrical Div Engrg Dept Univ of Cambridge 1984–92 (head of dept 1992–96), master Churchill Coll Cambridge 1990–96, vice-chllr Univ of Cambridge 1996–2003; pres Royal Acad of Engrg 2001–06 (memb Cncl 1993–), memb IBM Corp Tech Ctee 1984; memb Cncl: EPSRC 1994–2000, Univ of Melbourne 2000–02; chm Plastic Logic Ltd 2004–06; non-exec dir: Lucas Industries 1995–96, Vodafone 1998–2007, R J Mears LLC 2003–11; sr advsr to Warburg Pincus 2004–08; chm House of Lords Select Ctee for Science and Technol 2004–07; chm Bd Diamond Light Source 2008–, chm Bio Nano Consulting Ltd 2010–; chm of judges Queen Elizabeth Prize for Engrg 2012–; IEEE Cledo Brunetti Award 1985, American Inst of Physics Prize for Industrial Applications of Physics 1982, Prince Philip Medal Royal Acad of Engrg 2000, Australian of the Year in the UK 2006; memb American Philosophical Soc; tstee Br Museum 2004–; IBM fell 1977; fell: Trinity Coll Cambridge 1985–90, Churchill Coll Cambridge, Imperial Coll London 2004; hon fell: Gonville & Caius Coll Cambridge, Trinity Coll Cambridge, St Edmund's Coll Cambridge, Aust Acad of Technological Sciences and Engrg, Cardiff Univ 2001; ScD Univ of Cambridge 1991; Hon DEng Univ of Glasgow 1996, Hon DSc Univ of Warwick 1997, Hon DUniv Anglia Poly, Hon DTech Univ of Greenwich 2000, Hon PhD Univ of Peking 2002, Hon DEng UMIST 2002, Hon LLD Univ of Melbourne 2002, Hon LLD Univ of Cambridge 2004, Hon DEng Univ of Durham 2007, Hon DEng Univ of Sheffield 2007, Hon DSc Tufts Univ 2007, Hon Doctorate Sheffield Hallam Univ 2008, Hon LLD Monash Univ 2009; foreign assoc Nat Acad of Engrg USA; Hon FMedSci, Hon FIEE, FInstP, FRS, FREng 1985, Hon FIMechE 2004; *Publications* author of BBC Reith Lectures 2005, also numerous papers, book chapters and patents on integrated circuit microfabrication and related subjects; *Recreations* music, sailing, skiing, tennis; *Style*— The Rt Hon the Lord Broers, DL, FRS, FREng; ✉ House of Lords, London SW1A 0PW

BROKE, Adam Vere Balfour; OBE (2010); s of Charles Vere Broke (d 1944), and Violet Rosemary, *née* Balfour; *b* 16 April 1941; *Educ* Eton; *m* 27 March 1965, Sarah Penelope, da of Norman Lanyon, DSC (d 1981); 3 da; *Career* chartered accountant; conslt Mercer & Hole; former pres Inst of Taxation; Past Master Worshipful Co of Tax Advsrs; FCA 1964, fell CTA 1971; *Recreations* music, gardening, shooting; *Clubs* Boodle's; *Style*— Adam Broke, Esq, OBE; ✉ Mercer & Hole, 2 Fleet Place, London EC4M 7RF (☎ 020 7236 2601)

BROKENSHIRE, Rt Hon James; PC (2015), MP; s of Peter Brokenshire (d 2015), and Joan, *née* Pavey; *b* 1968, Southend-on-Sea, Essex; *Educ* Davenant Fndn GS Loughton, Cambridge Centre for Sixth Form Studies, Univ of Exeter (LLB); *m* 1999, Cathrine, *née* Mamelok; 2 da (Sophie b 2002, Jemma b 2005), 1 s (Benjamin b 2006); *Career* slr; ptnr Jones Day Gouldens 1999–2005; MP (Cons): Hornchurch 2005–10, Old Bexley & Sidcup 2010–; memb Constitutional Select Affrs Ctee 2005–06, shadow home affrs min 2006–10, Parly under-sec of state Home Office 2010–14, min of state for immigration and security Home Office 2014–15, min of state for immigration 2015–16, sec of state for NI 2016–; former nat vice-chm Young Conservatives; *Style*— The Rt Hon James Brokenshire, MP; ✉ House of Commons, London SW1A 0AA (☎ 020 7219 8400, e-mail brokenshirej@parliament.uk, website www.jamesbrokenshire.com, Twitter @JBrokenshire)

BROMLEY-DAVENPORT, Sir William Arthur; KCVO (2010), JP (Cheshire 1975); only s of Lt-Col Sir Walter Bromley-Davenport, TD, DL (d 1989), of Capesthorne Hall, and Lenette, *née* Jeanes (d 1989); *b* 7 March 1935; *Educ* Eton, Cornell Univ; *m* 29 Dec 1962, Elizabeth Boies, da of John Watts, of Oldwick, NJ; 1 s (Nicholas Walter b 11 June 1964), 1 da (Liberty Charlotte b 25 Dec 1970); *Career* Nat Serv 2 Bn Grenadier Guards 1953–54, Hon Col 3 (Vol) Bn 22 Cheshire Regt 1985–99, Hon Col (Cheshire) The King's and Cheshire Regt 1999–2005; pres TAVRA NW of England and IOM 1998–2003; landowner (UK and Norway); county pres: Cheshire Magistrates' Assoc 1990–2010, Youth Fedn for Cheshire, Halton, Warrington and Wirral 1990–2008, Cheshire Branch SSAFA – Forces Help 1992–2010, Cheshire Branch RBL 1998–2016, Reaseheath Coll Tst 1991–2010; pres: Cheshire Scout Cncl 1990– (chm 1981–90), Cheshire Agricultural Soc 1993–96 (patron 2001–), Cheshire Cncl Order of St John 1998–2010; chm of govrs King's Sch Macclesfield 1986–2005; Hon DLitt Univ of Chester 2006; High Sheriff Cheshire 1983–84, HM Lord-Lt Cheshire 1990–2010 (DL 1982); ACA 1966; *Style*— Sir William A Bromley-Davenport, KCVO; ✉ The Kennels, Capesthorne, Macclesfield, Cheshire SK11 9LB; Fiva, 6300 Aandalsnes, Norway

BROMLEY-MARTIN, Michael Granville; QC (2002); s of Capt David Eliot Bromley-Martin, RN (d 2002), and Angela Felicity, *née* Hampden-Ross (d 2013); *b* Bosham, Sussex; *Educ* Eton Coll, Univ of Southampton (BSc); *m* 26 Nov 1983, Anna Frances, *née* Birley; 1 s (Charles b 28 May 1988), 2 da (Alexandra b 22 May 1990, Olivia b 10 July 1994); *Career* called to the Bar 1979; memb of chambers 3 Raymond Buildings 1980–; inspr DTI 1989 and 1990; recorder of the Crown Court 2003; *Recreations* sailing, shooting, fishing, tennis; *Clubs* Royal Ocean Racing, Garrick, Itchenor Sailing; *Style*— Michael Bromley-Martin, Esq, QC; ✉ 3 Raymond Buildings, Gray's Inn, London WC1R 5BH (☎ 020 7400 6400, fax 020 7400 6464, e-mail chambers@3rblaw.com)

BROMWICH, Prof Michael; s of William James Bromwich (d 1982), and Margery, *née* Townley (d 1977); *b* 29 January 1941; *Educ* Wentworth Secdy Modern Southend, LSE (BSc); *m* 10 Aug 1972, Prof Christine Margaret Elizabeth Whitehead, OBE, da of Edward Daniel Whitehead, MBE, of Tunbridge Wells, Kent; *Career* mangr Ford Motor Co Ltd 1965–66 (accountant 1958–62); lectr LSE 1966–70, prof UWIST 1970–77, prof Univ of Reading 1977–85, CIMA prof LSE 1985–2006 (emeritus 2006–); chm Bd of Accreditation of Educnl Courses 1987–89, pres CIMA 1987–88; Distinguished Academic of the Year 1999; memb: Industry and Employment Ctee SSRC/ESRC 1980–84, Accounting Standards Ctee 1981–84, Research Grants Bd ESRC 1992–96, Academic Panel OFT 2002–10; additional memb Monopolies and Mergers Cmmn 1992–2000; hon treas Disability Alliance 2007–11, hon treas Disability Rights UK 2011–; Gold Medal CIMA 2009; Hon DSc Lund Univ; assoc memb CIPFA 1977, FCMA (ACMA 1963); *Books* Economics of Capital Budgeting (1976), Economics of Accounting Standards (1985), Financial Reporting Information and Capital Markets (1992), Management Accounting: Pathways to Progress (1994), Accounting for Overheads: Critique and Reforms (1997), Following the Money: The Economic Failure and the State of Corporate Disclosure (jtly, 2003), Worldwide Financial Reporting: The Development and Future of Accounting Standards (2006), Management Accounting: Retrospect and Prospect (2009); *Recreations* work, eating in restaurants; *Style*— Prof Michael Bromwich; ✉ 14 Thornhill Road, London N1 1HW (☎ 0207 607 9323)

BRON, Eleanor; da of Sydney Bron (d 1995), and Fagah Bron (d 1990); *b* 14 March 1938; *Educ* N London Collegiate Sch, Newnham Coll Cambridge (BA); *Career* actress and writer; with De La Rue Co 1961, subsequent revue work and appearances at Establishment Nightclub Soho 1962 and in NY 1963; dir: Actor's Centre Bd 1982–93, Soho Theatre Co Bd 1993–2000; *Theatre* incl: Jennifer Dubedat in The Doctor's Dilemma, 1966, title role in The Prime of Miss Jean Brodie 1967 and 1984, title role in Hedda Gabler 1969, Portia in The Merchant of Venice 1975, Amanda in Private Lives 1976, Elena in Uncle Vanya 1977, Charlotte in The Cherry Orchard 1978 (also Varya 1985), Margaret in A Family 1978, On Her Own 1980, Goody Biddy Bean in The Amusing Spectacle of Cinderella and her Naughty, Naughty Sisters 1980, Betrayal 1981, Heartbreak House 1981, Duet for One 1982, The Duchess of Malfi 1985, The Real Inspector Hound and The Critic (double bill) 1985, Jocasta/Ismene in Oedipus and Oedipus at Colonus 1987, Infidelities 1987, The Madwoman of Chaillot 1988, The Chalk Garden 1989, Frosine in The Miser 1991, Isabella in The White Devil 1991, Gertrude in Hamlet 1993, Agnes in A Delicate Balance 1996, Katherine in A Perfect Ganesh 1996, Dona Rosita (Almeida) 1997, Be My Baby 1998, Making Noise Quietly 1999, Tuppence to Cross the Mersey 2005, The Clean House 2006, In Extremis 2007, All About My Mother 2007, The Clean House (tour) 2008, The Late Middle Classes 2010; other performances incl: Façade by Walton, Oral Treason by Kagel (Almeida Festival of Contemporary Music) 1987, Die Glückliche Hand by Schönberg (Nederlandse Opera) 1990, Desdemona – If You Had Only Spoken (one-woman show, Almeida 1991, Edinburgh Festival 1992); *Music* author of song-cycle with John Dankworth 1973 and verses for Saint-Saens' Carnival of the Animals 1975; *Television* appearances in Not So Much a Programme More a Way of Life (BBC) 1964 and several TV series written with John Fortune; other TV progs and series incl: Making Faces (by Michael Frayn) 1976, Pinkerton's Progress 1983, Inspector Alleyn 1992, Absolutely Fabulous 1992 and 1993, Fat Friends 2000 and 2002, Gypsy Girl 2000, Randall and Hopkirk 2001, Ted and Alice 2002; TV plays incl: Nina 1978, My Dear Palestrina 1980, A Month in the Country 1985, Quartermaine's Terms 1987, Changing Step 1989, The Hour of the Lynx 1990, The Strawberry Tree 1993, The Blue Boy 1994, The Saint Exupéry Story 1994, Wycliffe 1995, Vanity Fair 1998, Foyle's War 2009, Midsomer Murders 2011; *Film* Help! 1965, Alfie 1966, Two for the Road 1967, Bedazzled 1967, Women in Love 1969, The National Health 1973, The Day That Christ Died 1980, Turtle Diary 1985, Little Dorrit 1988, Black Beauty 1993, Deadly Advice 1994, A Little Princess 1994, The House of Mirth 2000, Iris 2001, The Heart of Me 2002, Wimbledon 2003, Streetdance 2010, Hyde Park on Hudson 2012; *Radio* Carol Tregorran in The Archers 2012–; *Books* Is Your Marriage Really Necessary (with John Fortune, 1972), My Cambridge (contrib, 1976), More Words (contrib, 1977),

Life and Other Punctures (1978), The Pillow Book of Eleanor Bron (1985), Desdemona – If You Had Only Spoken (by Christine Brückner, trans 1992), Double Take (novel, 1996), Cedric Price Retriever (co-ed, 2006); *Style*— Miss Eleanor Bron; ✉ c/o Rebecca Blond Associates, 69A King's Road, London SW3 4NX (☎ 020 7351 4100, fax 020 7451 4600)

BRONDER, Peter; s of Johann Bronder, and Gertrude, *née* Kastl; *b* 22 October 1953; *Educ* Letchworth GS, RAM; *Career* tenor; Bayreuth Festival Chorus 1983, Glyndebourne Festival Chorus 1985, princ tenor WNO 1986–90 (performances for WNO in NY and Milan 1989, Tokyo 1990), freelance 1991–, regular guest appearances with major UK Opera cos; debut: Royal Opera Covent Garden 1986, ENO 1989, Glyndebourne Festival 1990, Theâtre Champs Elysées Paris 1991, Bavarian State Opera 1995, Int Festival Istanbul 1995, Brussels La Mounaie 1999; live on BBC Radio 3: Snape Maltings Concert 1987, Richard Strauss' Salome 1988, Bellini's Somnambula 1989, Gluck's Iphigenie en Tauride 1992, Donizetti's Maria Stuarda 1994, Strauss' Der Rosenkavalier 1994, Beethoven's Choral Symphony 1995, Tchaikovsky's Enchantress 1998, Wagner's Parsifal 1998, Berg's Wozzeck 1998, Love Cries (Birtwistle and Berkeley, World Premiere) 1999, Clemenza di Tito (Glyndebourne) 1999; recordings: Kiri Te Kanawa recital 1988, Adriana Lecouvreur Cilea 1988, Osud Janácek 1989, Weill's Street Scene 1991, Beethoven's Choral Symphony 1991, Rossini's Turco in Italia 1992, Stravinsky's Rake's Progress 1997, Leoncavallo's I Pagliacci 1997, Verdi's Falstaff 1998; many appearances on TV and radio incl: BBC TV Laurence Olivier Awards 1985, Verdi's Falstaff (with WNO) 1989, Berg's Wozzeck (with ENO) 1990, Salome (ROH) 1997; ARAM, LRAM, LGSM; *Recreations* sports, photography, electronics, motorcycling; *Style*— Peter Bronder, Esq; ✉ c/o Rayfield Allied, Southbank House, Black Prince Road, London SE1 7SJ

BRONNERT, Deborah Jane; CMG (2012); da of Preb Rev Dr D L E Bronnert, and Mrs B Bronnert; *Educ* Univ of Bristol, UCL (MA); *m* Alfonso Torrents; 1 s; *Career* diplomat; memb Secretariat Royal Cmmn on Environmental Pollution 1990–91, second sec (environment) UK Representation Brussels 1991–93, secretariat Sir Michael Latham's Review on the Construction Industry 1993–94, team ldr EU Dept (Internal) FCO 1994–95, memb Neil Kinnock's Cabinet European Cmmn 1995–99, dep head Southern European Dept FCO 1999–2001, counsellor (economic) Moscow 2002–05, head Future of Europe Dept FCO 2006–08, dir Prosperity (formerly Global and Economic Issues) FCO 2008–11, ambass to Zimbabwe 2011–14, chief operating offr FCO 2014–15, DG Economic & Consular FCO 2016–; non-exec dir Merlin (charity) 2010–13, tstee British Cncl 2015–; *Publications* Making Government Policy: The G8 and G20 in 2010 (chapter 5 in The New Economic Diplomacy, ed Nicholas Bayne and Stephen Woolcock, 3 edn 2011); *Style*— Ms Deborah Bronnert, CMG; ✉ c/o Foreign and Commonwealth Office (Harare), King Charles Street, London SW1A 2AH

BROOK, Michael; s of John Brook (d 1981), and Mary, *née* Gilpin (d 2001); *b* 1 September 1949, Dewsbury, W Yorks; *Educ* Batley GS, Leeds Poly (BA); *m* 21 April 1973, Lynn, da of Leonard Sargeant Allan; 2 da (Alison Judith b 7 Feb 1976, Joanne Elizabeth b 25 May 1977); *Career* asst sales mangr British Jeffrey Diamond Wakefield 1972–73, asst mktg controller Yorkshire Electricity Bd 1974–76, brands mangr Thomas Eastham & Sons 1976–79; Graham Poulter Partnership: account mangr 1979–80, account dir 1980–82, assoc dir 1982–83, dir and ptnr 1983–91; md Ken Geddes Associates Ltd 1991–92, dir Lumley Warranty Services 1992–93; Creative Communications: account dir 1993–2014, md 1994–96; project dir On Demand Information: Internet 2 1996–97, mktg dir New Media Publishing Div 1997–98; md Whitaker's Advertising 1998–99, product devpt dir IQ Business Ltd 1999–2014 ret; MCIM 1976; *Recreations* golf, cricket, photography, music, travelling, Heritage Steam Railways; *Clubs* Howley Hall Golf, Keighley and Worth Valley Railway, N Yorks Moors Railway, Middleton Railway, Great Central Railway; *Style*— Michael Brook, Esq; ✉ 3 Woodkirk Gardens, Leeds Road, Dewsbury, West Yorkshire WF12 7HZ (☎ 01924 475544, e-mail mike.brook49@sky.com)

BROOK, Prof Peter; s of Ernest John Brook (d 1986), and Jenny, *née* Waters; *b* 17 January 1947; *Educ* Barry GS, Univ of Swansea (BSc), Univ of London (MSc); *m* 1978, Deirdre Teresa, da of Terence Handley; 2 da (Jessica Frances b 3 Dec 1982, Elizabeth Mary b 2 April 1987); *Career* head Computer Networks Div RSRE 1981–85, head Air Defence & ATC Gp RSRE 1985–87, dir of sci (Land) MOD 1987–89, head Battlefield Systems Gp DRA 1989–94, chief scientist CIS DERA 1994–96, chief scientist Land Systems DERA 1996–98, dir Int Cncl on Systems Engrg (INCOSE) 1997–, dir Systems Engrg DERA 1998–2000, head Integration Authy DPA 2000–05, strategic conslt QinetiQ Ltd 2005–10, Dashwood Consulting 2010–; visiting prof Cranfield Univ (Defence Acad Shrivenham); FIET, FREng 1999, FBCS 2004, FINCOSE 2015; *Publications* Systems Engineering – Coping with Complexity (1998); numerous technical publications: microwave systems, military command and control and systems engrg; *Recreations* choral singing, photography, walking, theatre, concerts; *Style*— Prof Peter Brook, FREng; ✉ Dashwood House, Manby Road, Malvern, Worcestershire WR14 3BB (☎ 01684 893472, e-mail peterbrook47@gmail.com)

BROOK, Prof Sir Richard John; kt (2002), OBE (1988); s of late Frank Brook, and late Emily Sarah, *née* Lytle; *b* 12 March 1938; *Educ* Univ of Leeds (BSc), MIT (ScD); *m* 3 March 1961, Elizabeth Christine, da of Thomas Aldred; 1 da (Madeline Sarah b 13 June 1965), 1 s (Jonathan Henry b 21 Dec 1967); *Career* res asst MIT 1962–66, asst prof Univ of Southern California 1966–70, gp ldr AERE Harwell 1970–74, prof and head Dept of Ceramics Univ of Leeds 1974–88, dir Max Planck Institut for Metals Research Stuttgart 1988–91, fell St Cross Coll Oxford 1991–, prof of materials Univ of Oxford 1991–, chief exec EPSRC 1994–2001, dir Leverhulme Tst 2001–11; Cmmr fo the Exhibition of 1851 2009–; non-exec dir and memb Bd: Carbon Tst 2002–11, ERA Fndn 2002–11 (chm 2012–15); hon prof Univ of Stuttgart 1988–, memb Senate Max Planck Soc 1999–2011; author of res pubns (on ceramic sci and engrg), 11 patents; ed Jl of the European Ceramic Soc 1989–2011; Dr (hc) Univ of Aveiro Portugal; DSc (hc): Univ of Bradford, Loughborough Univ, Nottingham Trent Univ, Brunel Univ, Univ of Strathclyde, Limoges Univ France; membre d'honneur Société Française de la Métallurgie et des Matériaux 1995, distinguished life fell American Ceramic Soc 1995, memb Deutsche Akademie der Naturforscher Leopoldina 2002; CEng; FIM 1986, FREng 1998, Hon FRAM 2008, Hon FBA 2011; *Style*— Prof Sir Richard Brook, OBE, FREng; ✉ University of Oxford, Department of Materials, Parks Road, Oxford OX1 3PH

BROOK, Rosemary Helen (Mrs Dickie Arbiter); da of Charles Rex Brook (d 1971), and Nellie Beatrice, *née* Yare (d 1998); *b* 7 February 1946; *Educ* Gravesend Sch for Girls, Newnham Coll Cambridge (MA); *m* 1, 1970 (m dis 1979), Roger John Gross; m 2, 1984, Dickie Arbiter, LVO; 1 step da (Victoria b 1974); *Career* account mangr McCann Erickson Ltd 1975–77, head of public affrs Wiggins Teape Gp Ltd 1977–82 (Euro mktg co-ordinator 1968–75), Euro gen mangr Edelman Public Relations Worldwide 1992–94, UK chm and chief exec Edelman (UK) 1982–94, chm Brook Wilkinson Ltd 1994–2001, exec chm Argyll Consultancies plc 2005–11 (dir 2001–), dir and shareholder Kaizo Ltd 2011–; Industry and Parly Tst: memb 1998–, tstee 2006–14, chm Mgmnt Bd (formerly Exec Ctee) 2007–14, vice-pres 2014–; tstee Royal Voluntary Service 2013–; Freeman City of London 1985, Master Guild of PR Practitioners 2003–04; assoc fell Newnham Coll Cambridge 1999–2003; FCIPR (FIPR 1977, pres 1996); *Recreations* opera, ballet, reading, music; *Clubs* Reform; *Style*— Miss Rosemary Brook; ✉ Kaizo Ltd, 1 Quality Court, Chancery Lane, London WC2A 1HR (☎ 020 3176 4700, e-mail rosemary.brook@kaizo.co.uk, website www.kaizo.co.uk, LinkedIn RosemaryBrook)

BROOK-PARTRIDGE, Bernard; s of Leslie Brook-Partridge (d 1933), and Gladys Vere, *née* Brooks, later Mrs Burchell (d 1989); *Educ* Selsdon Co GS, Cambs Tech Coll, Univ of Cambridge, Univ of London; *m* 1, 3 Nov 1951 (m dis 1965), (Enid) Elizabeth, da of Frederick Edmund Hatfield (d 1951); 2 da (Eva Katharine Helen (Mrs New) b 6 Dec 1952 d 2001, Katrina Elizabeth Jane b 18 Aug 1954); m 2, 14 Oct 1967, Carol Devonald, da of Arnold Devonald Francis Lewis (d 1989); 2 s (Charles Gareth Devonald b 21 Dec 1969, James Edward Devonald b 4 June 1974); *Career* Nat Serv 1944–49; memb Gray's Inn 1950, cashier and accountant Dominion Rubber Co Ltd 1950–51, asst export mangr British & General Tube Co Ltd 1951–52, asst sec Assoc of Int Accountants 1952–59, sec-gen Inst of Linguists 1959–62, various teaching posts FRG 1962–66, special asst to md M G Scott Ltd 1966–68, business conslt (incl various directorships) 1968–72, memb Peterborough Devpt Corp 1972–88, ptnr Carsons, Brook-Partridge & Co 1972–2004, dir and sec Roban Engineering Ltd 1975–96, chm Queensgate Management Services Ltd 1981–87; dir: Brompton Troika Ltd 1985–, Edmund Nuttall Ltd 1986–92, PEG Management Consultants plc 1988–92, Kyle Stewart Ltd 1989–92, Lucknam Park Hotels Ltd 1994–95, Wilding Properties Ltd 1995–2003, UK Immigration Services Ltd 1999–2004, Ethical Developments Ltd 1999–2002; chm: Daldorch Estates Ltd 1995–98, Dick Robson plc 1996–97, Robson Dunk Ltd 1996–98, Simplify-your development Ltd 2008–10; dep chm World Trade Centre Ltd 1997–2001; conslt Paul Whitley Architects 1998–2002; memb Cncl ICSA 1982–97 (pres 1986); local govt and political advsr Transmanche-Link 1988 and 1989; contested (Cons) St Pancras N LCC 1958, memb (Cons) St Pancras MBC 1959–62, prospective parly candidate (Cons) Shoreditch and Finsbury 1960–62, contested (Cons) Nottingham Central 1970; GLC: memb for Havering 1967–73, memb for Havering (Romford) 1973–85, chm of Cncl 1980–81; chm: Environmental Planning (NE) Area Ctee 1967–71, Town Devpt Ctee 1971–73, Arts Ctee 1977–79, Public Servs and Safety Ctee 1978–79; oppn spokesman: on arts and recreation 1973–74, on police matters 1983–85; memb: Exec Ctee Gtr London Arts Assoc 1973–78, Exec Cncl Area Museums Serv for SE England 1977–78, Cncl and Exec Gtr London and SE Cncl for Sport and Recreation 1977–78, GLC Ldrs Ctee with special responsibility for law and order and police liaison matters 1977–79; dep ldr Recreation and Community Servs Policy Ctee 1977–79; memb: Exec Ctee Exmoor Soc 1974–79, BBC Radio London Advsy Cncl 1974–79, Gen Cncl Poetry Soc 1977–86 (treas 1982–86), London Orchestral Concert Bd Ltd 1977–78, LCDT 1979–84; dir ENO 1977–79; tstee: London Festival Ballet 1977–79, Sadler's Wells Fndn 1977–79; chm: London Symphony Chorus Devpt Ctee 1981–88, The Young Vic Theatre 1983–87 (dir 1977–88), London Music Hall Tst Ltd 1983–90, Royal Philharmonic Soc 1991–95; vice-chm London Music Hall Protection Soc Ltd (Wilton's Music Hall) 1983–97 (memb Bd 1978–, chm 1981–83); chm: Samuel Lewis Housing Tst Ltd 1985–92 (tstee 1976–94), City & Coastal Housing Association Ltd 1991–94, St George's Housing Association Ltd 1985–92, Shipworkers Jubilee Housing Tst 1985–92 (both now part of Samuel Lewis Housing Tst Ltd), Spearhead Housing Tst 1986–92; govr and tstee SPCK 1976–95 (vice-pres 1995–); pres: Br Sch of Osteopathy Appeal Fund 1980–84, Witan Rifle Club 1979–92, City of London Rifle League 1980–2004, Gtr London Horse Show 1982–86, GLA City Hall branch (formerly Gtr London Co Hall branch) Royal Br Legion 1988–2005; hon sec The Henley Soc 1998–2000; dir Central London Masonic Centre Ltd 1999–2009 (dep chm 2000–09); Freemason 1973–; hon fell and Hon PhD Columbia Pacific Univ USA 1984; FCIS 1970, FCPU 1984, MCMI 1978, hon fell Inst of Incorporated Engrgs; Order of Gorkha Dakshina Bahu (second class, Nepal) 1981; *Books* Europe – Power and Responsibility – Direct Elections to the European Parliament (with David Baker, 1972), author of numerous contribs to learned jls and periodicals on various subjects; *Recreations* conversation, opera, classical music, being difficult; *Clubs* Athenaeum; *Style*— Bernard Brook-Partridge, Esq; ✉ 28 Elizabeth Road, Henley-on-Thames, Oxfordshire RG9 1RG (☎ 01491 412080, e-mail bbrookpartridge@gmail.com)

BROOKE, Rt Hon Dame Annette; DBE (2015, OBE 2013), PC (2014); da of Ernest Henry Kelley, and Edna Mabel Kelley; *b* 7 June 1947; *Educ* Romford Tech Coll, LSE (BSc), Hughes Hall Cambridge (CEd); *m* Mike Brooke; 2 da; *Career* lectr and teacher of economics and social sciences Open Univ and various local schs incl Talbot Heath Sch until 1994; cncllr Broadstone Poole BC 1986–2003, dep ldr Lib Dem Gp 1995–97 and 1998–2000, chair of planning 1991–96, chair Environment Strategy Working Pty 1995–97, chair of educn 1996–2000, sheriff 1996–97, mayor 1997–98, dep mayor 1998–99; MP (Lib Dem) Dorset Mid and N Poole 2001–15; memb Lib Dem Home Affrs team 2001–03, spokesperson for Children in Educn team 2004–10; chair All-Pty Parly Gp on ME, co-chair All-Pty Parly Gp on Breast Cancer, vice-chair All-Pty Parly Gp on Microfinance, memb Panel of Chairs; chair Lib Dem Parly Pty House of Commons 2013–15; jt owner of small family business (rocks, minerals and gemstones); *Style*— The Rt Hon Dame Annette Brooke, DBE

BROOKE, Sir Francis George Windham; 4 Bt (UK 1903), of Summerton, Castleknock, Co Dublin; s of Sir George Cecil Francis Brooke, 3 Bt, MBE (d 1982), and Lady Melissa Eva Caroline Brooke; *b* 15 October 1963, Dublin; *Educ* Eton, Univ of Edinburgh (MA); *m* 8 April 1989, Hon Katharine Elizabeth Hussey, o da of Baron Hussey of North Bradley (d 2006), and Lady Susan Hussey, DCVO, *qv*; 1 s (George Francis Geoffrey b 10 Sept 1991), 2 da (Olivia Nancy b 12 Jan 1994, Sarah Mary b 20 March 1996); *Heir* s, George Brooke; *Career* Foreign and Colonial Management 1989–97, Merrill Lynch Investment Managers 1997–2004, Troy Asset Management 2004–; tstee Ascot Authy 2011–; *Clubs* Turf, White's, Royal St George's, Pratt's, Swinley Forest, Jockey; *Style*— Sir Francis Brooke, Bt; ✉ Flat 8, 34 Elm Park Gardens, London SW10 9NZ; Glenbevan, Croom, Co Limerick, Ireland

BROOKE, Rt Hon Sir Henry; kt (1988), CMG (2012); yr s of Baron Brooke of Cumnor, CH, PC (Life Peer, d 1984), and Baroness Brooke of Ystradfellte, DBE (Life Peer, d 2000); bro of Baron Brooke of Sutton Mandeville, CH, PC (Life Peer), *qv*; *b* 19 July 1936; *Educ* Marlborough, Balliol Coll Oxford (MA); *m* 16 April 1966, Bridget Mary, da of Wilfrid George Kalaugher (d 1999), of Jesmond, Newcastle upon Tyne; 3 s (Michael John b 1967, Nicholas George b 1968, Christopher Robert b 1973), 1 da (Caroline Mary b 1973); *Career* Nat Serv 2 Lt RE 1955–57; called to the Bar Inner Temple 1963 (bencher 1987); jr counsel to the Crown (Common Law) 1978–81, QC 1981, counsel to Sizewell B Nuclear Reactor Inquiry 1983–85, recorder SE Circuit 1983–88, a judge of the High Court of Justice (Queen's Bench Div) 1988–96, a Lord Justice of Appeal 1996–2006, judge in charge of modernisation 2001–04; vice-pres Court of Appeal (Civil Div) 2003–06; DTI inspr into the affairs of House of Fraser Holdings plc 1987–88; chm: Professional Standards Ctee Bar Cncl 1987–88, Ethnic Minorities Advsy Ctee Judicial Studies Bd 1991–94, Law Commission 1993–95, Cncl Centre for Crime and Justice Studies 1997–2001, Judges' Standing Ctee on IT 1997–2001, Civil Mediation Cncl 2007–11; pres Soc for Computers and Law 1992–2001, exec vice-pres Cwlth Magistrates and Judges Assoc 2006–09, tstee Prisoners of Conscience Appeal Tst 2007–16 (chm 2009–16), patron Public Law Project 2007–; pres Slynn Fndn 1998–2015; patron Peace Brigade Int (UK) Ltd 2007–; tstee Wordsworth Tst 1995–2001 (fell 2003–), chm of tstees Br and Irish Legal Info Inst 2001–11; gen ed The White Book (Sweet & Maxwell's Civil Procedure) 2004–09; hon fell Balliol Coll Oxford 2014–; *Clubs* Brooks's; *Style*— The Rt Hon Sir Henry Brooke, CMG; ✉ Fountain Court, Temple, London EC4Y 9DH

BROOKE, Prof John Hedley; s of Hedley Joseph Brooke, and Margaret, *née* Brown; *b* 20 May 1944, Retford, Nottinghamshire; *Educ* King Edward VI GS Retford, Fitzwilliam Coll Cambridge (Wallerstein exhbn, sr scholarship, BA, MA, PhD); *m* 30 Aug 1972, Janice Marian, da of Albert Heffer; *Career* res fell Fitzwilliam Coll Cambridge 1967–68, tutorial fell Univ of Sussex 1968–69; Lancaster Univ: lectr 1969–80, sr lectr 1980–91, reader 1991–

92, prof of history of science 1992–99; Gifford lectr Univ of Glasgow 1995–96; Univ of Oxford: Andreas Idreos prof of science and religion 1999–2006, dir Ian Ramsey Centre, fell Harris Manchester Coll; Inst of Advanced Study distinguished fell Univ of Durham 2007; visiting prof Univ of Leeds 2013–, hon research assoc UCL 2016–; ed Br Jl for the History of Science 1989–93, corresponding memb Int Acad of History of Science 1993; pres Science and Religion Forum 2006–; consltt Open Univ; memb: Center for Theological Inquiry Princeton, Center for Theology and the Natural Sciences Berkeley; coordinator European Science Fndn Network: Science and Human Values 2001–04; Templeton Prize for Outstanding Books in Science and Religion 1992; memb: BAAS (pres historical section 1996–97), Br Soc for the History of Science (pres 1996–98), Br Soc for the History of Philosophy, History of Science Soc (Watson Davis Prize 1992), Soc for the History of Alchemy and Chemistry, Int Soc for Science and Religion (pres 2008–11); *Books* Science and Religion: Some Historical Perspectives (1991, new edn 2014), Thinking About Matter (1995), Reconstructing Nature: The Engagement of Science and Religion (jtly, 1998), Science in Theistic Contexts (ed, 2001), Heterodoxy in Early Modern Science and Religion (ed, 2005), Religious Values and the Rise of Science in Europe (ed, 2005), The Cambridge Companion to Darwin (contrib, 2 edn 2009), The Cambridge Companion to the Origin of Species (contrib, 2009), Science and Religion Around the World (ed, 2011), Oxford Handbook of Natural Theology (consltt ed, 2013); *Recreations* music (opera), foreign travel, walking in the Lake District, chess, rhododendrons; *Style*— Prof John Brooke; ✉ Harris Manchester College, Oxford OX1 3TD (☎ 01865 271006, fax 01865 271012, e-mail john.brooke@theology.ox.ac.uk)

BROOKE, Patrick Thomas Joseph; s of Robert Samuel Brooke (d 1974), and Mary Agnes, *née* Coleman (d 1987); *b* 4 February 1947, Ross on Wye, Herefordshire; *Educ* Ross GS; *m* Rosemary Elizabeth Joyce; 2 s (Daniel Patrick Coleman b 31 Oct 1983, Lewis Samuel Joseph b 9 Oct 1985); *Career* qualified CA 1970; ptnr Waugh Haines Rigby 1974 (merged Cheltenham office with Grant Thornton 1986), managing ptnr 1986–92 and 1998–2003, nat ptnr responsible for Single Euro Market Servs 1989–2001, regnl sales and mktg ptnr 1992–2004; chm Local Support Gp for Cotswold Nuffield Hosp 1992–2005; non-exec dir: Glos TEC 1991–2001 (resigned), Glos Devpt Agency 1998–2000 (resigned); Cheltenham Arts Festivals: memb Devpt Ctee 1996–2000, memb Fin Advsy Gp 2000–07; Univ of Glos: memb Devpt Advsy Bd 2001–02, ind memb Cncl 2003–07; Cheltenham Coll: memb Cncl, memb Finance and Gen Purposes Ctee and chair Campaign Gp 2008–10; govr All Saints' Acad Cheltenham 2013–; memb Cheltenham Art Gallery & Museum Devpt Tst 2008–15; ATII 1972, FCA 1979 (ACA 1970); *Recreations* golf, tennis, music, reading; *Clubs* The New Cheltenham, Cotswold Hills Golf (capt 2005), Hon Co of Glos (fndr memb); *Style*— Patrick Brooke, Esq; ✉ 130 Albert Road, Cheltenham, Gloucestershire GL52 3JF (☎ 01242 574730, mobile 07973 252823)

BROOKE, Sir Rodney George; kt (2007), CBE (1996), DL (1989); s of George Sidney Brooke (d 1967), of Morley, W Yorks, and Amy, *née* Grant; *b* 22 October 1939; *Educ* Queen Elizabeth GS Wakefield; *m* 2 Sept 1967, Dr Clare Margaret Brooke, da of William Martin Cox (d 1985), of Moseley, Birmingham; 1 s (Magnus b 1971), 1 da (Antonia b 1973); *Career* asst slr: Rochdale CBC 1962–63, Leicester City Cncl 1963–65; dir of admin Stockport CBC 1971–73 (sr asst slr 1965–67, asst town clerk 1967–69, dep town clerk 1969–71), chief exec and clerk W Yorks CC 1981–84 (dir of admin 1973–81), clerk to W Yorks Lieutenancy 1981–84, chief exec Westminster City Cncl 1984–89, hon sec London Boroughs Assoc 1984–90, clerk to Gtr London Lieutenancy 1987–89, chm Bradford HA 1989–90, assoc Ernst and Young 1989–90, advsr Longman Group 1989–90, sec Assoc of Metropolitan Authorities 1990–97, chm Electricity Consumers' Ctee (Yorks) 1997–2001, chm Cmmn on Accessible Transport in London 1998–2003, chm National Electricity Consumers Cncl 1999–2001, chm Quality Assurance Agency for HE 2009–; visiting res fell: Royal Inst of Public Admin 1989–91, Nuffield Inst for Health Service Studies Univ of Leeds 1989–96; sr visiting res fell Univ of Birmingham 1997–2013; chm: Durham Univ Public Serv Devpt Fndn 1994–98, Dolphin Square Tst 2002–11 (dir 1987–2011), Gen Social Care Cncl 2002–08, W Yorks Playhouse 2011–, Leeds Theatres Tst 2011–; dir: Fndn for IT in Local Govt 1988–91, Riverside Community Health Tst 2000–02, Westminster Primary Care Tst 2002–06, Capacitybuilders 2008–11; memb: Ethics Standards Bd for Accountants 2001–04, Nat Info Governance Bd for Health and Social Care Records 2007–13, GMC 2009; tstee: Community Devpt Fndn 1996–99, Dolphin Square Charitable Fndn 2006–11, Internet Watch Fndn 2007–14, RNID (Action on Hearing Loss) 2008–14; assoc Local Govt Mgmnt Bd 1997–99; chm Pimlico Sch (govr 2000–07), memb Cncl Tavistock Inst 2006–12; Freeman City of London 1993; hon fell Inst of Local Govt Univ of Birmingham 1987; FRSA; OM (France) 1984, Order of Aztec Eagle (Mexico) 1985, Medal of Merit (Qatar) 1985, Order of Merit (Germany) 1986, Order of Merit (Senegal) 1988; *Books* Managing the Enabling Authority (1989), The Environmental Role of Local Government (1990), City Futures in Britain and Canada (jtly, 1991), The Handbook of Public Services Management (jtly, 1992), A Fresh Start for Local Government (jtly, 1997), The Utilities: A Consumers Eye View (2000), Councillors (2005); *Recreations* skiing, opera, theatre, Byzantium; *Clubs* Athenaeum, Ski of GB; *Style*— Sir Rodney Brooke, CBE, DL; ✉ Stubham Lodge, Middleton, Ilkley, West Yorkshire LS29 0AX (☎ 01943 601869, fax 01943 816731); 706 Grenville House, Dolphin Square, London SW1V 3LR (☎ and fax 020 7798 8086, e-mail brooke2@tiscali.co.uk)

BROOKE, (Christopher) Roger Ettrick; OBE (2005); s of Maj Ralph Brooke, RAMC; *b* 2 February 1931; *Educ* Tonbridge, Trinity Coll Oxford; *m* 1958, Nancy; 3 s, 1 da; *Career* HM Dip Serv 1955–66; dep md IRC 1966–69, dir Pearson Group Ltd 1971–79, gp md EMI Ltd 1979–80; Candover Investments plc: chief exec 1981–91, chm 1991–99; chm: The Audit Cmmn 1995–98, Innisfree Ltd 1998–2006, Advent 2VCT plc 1998–2005, Accord plc 1999–2005, Foresight4VCT plc 2005–; dep chm Carillion plc 1999–2001; dir: Slough Estates plc 1980–2001, Beeson Gregory Gp plc 2000–02, IP Group plc (formerly IP2IPO plc) 2002–11, dir Royal Soc Enterprise Fund 2008–; *Recreations* theatre, golf; *Style*— Roger Brooke, Esq, OBE; ✉ Watermeadow, Swarraton, Alresford, Hampshire SO24 9TQ

BROOKE OF SUTTON MANDEVILLE, Baron (Life Peer UK 2001), of Sutton Mandeville in the County of Wiltshire; Peter Leonard Brooke; CH (1992), PC (1988); s of Baron Brooke of Cumnor, CH, PC (Life Peer, d 1984), and Baroness Brooke of Ystradfellte, DBE (Life Peer, d 2000); bro of Rt Hon Lord Justice Brooke, *qv*; *b* 3 March 1934; *Educ* Marlborough, Balliol Coll Oxford (MA), Harvard Business Sch (MBA); *m* 1, 1964, Joan (d 1985), da of Frederick Smith, of São Paulo, Brazil; 4 s (Jonathan b 8 May 1965, Daniel b 1 June 1967, Sebastian b 6 Sept 1968, Patrick b 17 Oct 1970 (decd)); m 2, 1991, Mrs Lindsay Allinson; *Career* Royal Engineers 1952–53 (invalided out); res assoc IMEDE Lausanne and Swiss corr Financial Times 1960–61, with Spencer Stuart Management Consultants 1961–79 (chm 1974–79); MP (Cons): City of London and Westminster S 1977–97, Cities of London and Westminster 1997–2001; asst Govt whip 1979–81, Lord Cmmr of the Treasy (Govt whip) 1981–83, under sec of state for educn and sci 1983–85, min of state Treasy 1985–87, Paymaster Gen Treasy 1987–89, chm Cons Pty 1987–89, sec of state for NI 1989–92, sec of state for nat heritage 1992–94; chm: Cusichaca Project 1978–98, Churches Conservation Tst 1995–98, Conf on Trg for Architectural Conservation 1995–98, Building Socs Ombudsman Cncl 1996–2001, Select Ctee on NI Affairs 1997–2001, Assoc of Cons Peers 2004–06; pres: Br Antique Dealers Assoc 1995–2005, Br Art Market Fedn 1996–2014, Friends of Wilts Churches 2009–14; vice-pres Friends of Friendless Churches 2009; chm and pro-chllr Univ of London 2002–06 (memb Cncl 1994–, dep chm 2001–02); sr fell RCA 1987, presentation fell KCL 1989; Liveryman Worshipful Co of Drapers, founding Master Livery Co of Art Scholars (formerly Guild of Art Scholars, Dealers and Collectors) 2006; hon fell Queen Mary & Westfield Coll London 1996; Hon DLitt Univ of Westminster 1999, Hon DLitt London Guildhall Univ 2001, Hon LLB Univ of London 2006; FSA 1998; *Recreations* cricket, reading, walking, visual arts; *Clubs* Beefsteak, Brooks's, City Livery, Grillions, I Zingari, MCC; *Style*— The Rt Hon the Lord Brooke of Sutton Mandeville, CH, PC, FSA; ✉ House of Lords, London SW1A 0PW

B

BROOKEBOROUGH, 3 Viscount (UK 1952); Sir Alan Henry Brooke; 7 Bt (UK 1822), DL (Co Fermanagh 1987); er s of 2 Viscount Brookeborough, PC, DL (d 1987), and Rosemary, Viscountess Brookeborough; *b* 30 June 1952; *Educ* Harrow, Millfield; *m* 12 April 1980, Janet Elizabeth, o da of John Cooke, of Doagh, Co Antrim; *Heir* bro, Hon Christopher Brooke; *Career* cmmnd 17/21 Lancers 1972, transferred to UDR pt/t 1977, Co Cdr 4 Bn UDR 1980–83, transfer UDR pt/t 1983, Maj-Co Cdr UDR 1988–93, Lt Col Royal Irish Regt 1993–, Hon Col 4/5 Bn The Royal Irish Rangers TAVR 1997–2008; non-exec dir Basel International (Jersey) 2000– (chm 1996–2001); non-exec dir Green Park Healthcare Tst 1992–2001; farmer; memb: EEC Agric Sub-Ctee House of Lords 1988–97, Select Ctee on European Communities 1998–2002, Sub-Ctee Br Energy Industry and Transport 1998–2002, Sub-Ctee D 2007–, EU Ctee Sub-Ctee A Economic and Fin Affrs 2012–; memb NI Policing Bd 2001–06, memb Nat Employer Advsy Bd (NEAB) 2005–10; pres Army Benevolent Fund NI 1995–; High Sheriff Co Fermanagh 1995; Lord in Waiting to HM The Queen 1997–, HM Lord Lieutenant for Co Fermanagh 2012; *Recreations* riding, fishing, shooting, skiing; *Clubs* Cavalry and Guards'; *Style*— The Rt Hon the Viscount Brookeborough, DL; ✉ Colebrooke, Brookeborough, Co Fermanagh (☎ 028 895 31402)

BROOKES, John A; MBE (2004); s of Edward Percy Brookes (d 1982), and Margaret Alexandra, *née* Reid; *b* 11 October 1933; *Educ* Durham Sch, Durham Co Sch of Horticulture, UCL (DipLD); *Career* landscape designer; formerly apprentice with/to: Parks Dept Nottingham Corp, Brenda Colvin, Dame Sylvia Crowe; in private practice 1964–; work currently in progress incl private gardens in USA, GB, Japan and Argentina; formerly: lectr in landscape design Inst of Park Admin, asst lectr in landscape design Regent Street Poly, dir Inchbald Sch of Garden Design; lectr in landscape design Royal Botanic Gardens Kew; fndr: Inchbald Sch of Interior Design Teheran Iran 1978, Clock House Sch of Garden Design (within estab garden of Denmans W Sussex) 1980; regular lectr on garden design worldwide; past chm Soc of Garden Designers; Hon DUniv Essex; hon fell Kew Guild 2008; FSGD; *Books* Room Outside (1969, reprint 1979), Gardens for Small Spaces (1970), Garden Design and Layout (1970), Living in the Garden (1971), Financial Times Book of Garden Design (1975), Improve Your Lot (1977), The Small Garden (1977, reprint 1984), The Garden Book (1984), A Place in the Country (1984), The Indoor Garden Book (1986), Gardens of Paradise (1987), The Country Garden (1987), The New Small Garden Book (1989), John Brookes' Garden Design Book (1991), Planting the Country Way (1994), John Brookes' Garden Design Workbook (1994), The New Garden (1998), John Brookes Garden Masterclass (2002), John Brookes' Garden Design Course (2007); *Style*— John Brookes, Esq, MBE; ✉ Clock House, Denmans Lane, Fontwell, Arundel, West Sussex BN18 0SU (☎ 01243 542808, fax 01243 544064, e-mail denmans@denmans-garden.co.uk)

BROOKES, Nicholas Kelvin; s of Stanley Brookes (d 2004), and Jean, *née* Wigley; *b* 19 May 1947, London; *Educ* Harrow; *m* 22 Aug 1968, Maria, *née* Crespo; 1 da (Katrina b 8 Aug 1969), 2 s (David b 14 Jan 1971, Miguel b 3 Sept 1973); *Career* Texas Instruments Inc: fin dir Spain 1974–80, md Canada 1980–84, European md and gp vice-pres 1985–91, vice-pres and gp pres 1991–95; ceo Spirent plc 1995–2004, chm De La Rue plc 2004–; non-exec dir: Axel Johnson Inc Corporacion Financiera Alba SA; memb Cncl IOD 2006–, CCMI, FCA 1973, FInstD 1998; *Recreations* tennis, golf, chess; *Clubs* Reform; *Style*— Nicholas Brookes, Esq; ✉ Wolvers Hall, Ironsbottom Lane, Reigate, Surrey RH2 8PU (☎ 01293 862335, fax 01293 862384); De La Rue plc, Jays Close, Viables, Basingstoke, Hants RG22 4BS (☎ 01256 605326, fax 01256 605347, e-mail nicholas.brookes@uk.delarue.com)

BROOKES, Peter; s of late G H Brookes, and late J E Brookes, *née* Owen; *b* 28 September 1943; *Educ* Heversham GS, RAF Coll Cranwell (BA), Central Sch of Art & Design (BA); *m* 1971, Angela, *née* Harrison; 2 s (Ben, Will); *Career* freelance illustrator and cartoonist 1969–; tutor: Central Sch of Art & Design 1977–79, RCA 1979–89; cover artist The Spectator 1986–, political cartoonist The Times 1995–, contrib to numerous pubns incl The Listener, Radio Times and TLS; stamp designs for Royal Mail 1995, 1999 and 2003; Political Cartoonist of the Year Cartoon Art Tst Awards 1996, 1998 and 2006, Cartoonist of the Year Br Press Awards 2002, 2007, 2010, 2011 and 2012, Cartoonist of the Year Political Cartoon Soc 2006 and 2009, Caricaturist of the Year Cartoon Art Tst Award 2010; memb Alliance Graphique Internationale (AGI) 1988, FRSA 2000, RDI 2002; *Publications* Nature Notes (1997), Nature Notes: The New Collection (1999), Nature Notes III (2001), Peter Brookes of The Times (2002), Nature Notes: The Natural Selection (2004), The Best of Times (2009), Hard Times (2011), Sign of the Times (2013); *Recreations* music, arguing; *Clubs* Queens Park Rangers FC; *Style*— Peter Brookes, Esq, RDI; ✉ The Times, 1 Pennington Street, London E98 1TT (☎ 020 7782 5074, fax 020 7782 5639, e-mail peter.brookes@the-times.co.uk)

BROOKING, Sir Trevor David; kt (2004), CBE (1999, MBE 1981); *b* 2 October 1948; *m* 1970, Hilkka Helakorpi; 2 c; *Career* former professional footballer; with West Ham United 1965–84, over 500 appearances, FA Cup winners' medal 1975 and 1980; England: debut 1974, 47 caps, scored 5 goals, ret 1982; football commentator, analyst and presenter BBC TV and Radio 1988–2004; Sport England (formerly Sports Cncl): memb 1989–, chm 1999–2002 (actg chm 1998–99); co-chm Lottery Sports Panel; non-exec dir West Ham United FC until 2004 (sometime actg coach 2003), dir of football devpt FA 2004–14; *Books* My Life In Football (2014); *Style*— Sir Trevor Brooking, CBE; ✉ c/o Jane Morgan Management Ltd, Argentum, 2 Queen Caroline Street, London W6 9DX (☎ 020 3178 8071, e-mail enquiries@janemorganmgt.com)

BROOKMAN, Baron (Life Peer UK 1998), of Ebbw Vale in the County of Gwent; (David) Keith Brookman; *b* 3 January 1937; *Educ* Nantyglo GS Gwent; *Career* Nat Serv RAF; steel worker Richard Thomas & Baldwin Ltd Ebbw Vale 1953–73; Iron and Steel Trades Confedn: divnl organiser 1973, asst gen sec 1985–93, gen sec 1993–99; memb Exec Cncl Confedn of Shipbuilding and Engrg Unions 1989–95; chm Nat Steel Co-ordinating Ctee 1993–99 (memb 1991–93); TUC: memb Educn Advsy Ctee for Wales 1976–82, memb Steel Ctee 1985–90, memb Gen Cncl 1992–99; British Steel: memb Jt Accident Prevention Advsy Ctee (JAPAC) 1985–93, memb Advsy Ctee on Educn and Trg (ACET) 1986–93, operatives' sec Long Products General Steels Jt Standing Ctee 1993–98, operatives' sec Strip Trade Bd 1993–98, memb Bd UK Steel Enterprise 1993–2015; Labour Pty: memb Exec Ctee Wales 1982–85, memb Nat Constitutional Ctee 1987–91, memb NEC 1991–92; International Metalworkers' Fedn: hon sec IMF British Section 1993–99, pres IMF Iron and Steel and Non-Ferrous Metals Dept 1993–99; operatives' sec Jt Industrial Cncl for the Slag Industry 1985–93; memb: Exec Cncl European Metalworkers' Fedn 1985–95, Euro Coal and Steel Community Consultative Ctee 1993–2002; employees' sec Euro Works Cncl British Steel 1996–98; govr Gwent Coll of HE 1980–84, tstee Julian Melchett Tst 1985–95; *Style*— The Lord Brookman; ✉ House of Lords, London SW1A 0PW (☎ 020 7219 8633)

BROOKS, Prof David James; s of Prof James Leslie Brooks, and Doris Margaret Adeline Brooks; *b* 4 December 1949, Sheffield; *Educ* ChCh Oxford (open scholar, BA), UCH Med Sch London (MB BS), Univ of London (MD, DSc); *m* Prof Gillian Patricia Rowlands; *Career* jr res fell Wolfson Coll Oxford 1973–74; house surgn rising to consltt and sr lectr at various hosps, hon conslt and Hartnett prof of neurology Imperial Coll Sch of Med London, Hammersmith Hosps and Inst of Neurology 1993–, head of neurology MRC Clinical Sciences Centre Hammersmith Hosp 1993–2011, hon sr lectr Inst of Psychiatry 1993–; dep head Div of Brain Science Imperial Coll London 2011–12; prof of neurology Aarhus Univ Denmark 2013–; visiting prof Univ of Innsbruck; clinical dir Hammersmith Imanet Ltd Hammersmith Hosp 2001–11; head of neurology medical diagnostics and CMO Imanet GE Healthcare plc 2002–12; chm: Cncl of Mgmnt UK Parkinson's Disease Assoc 1997–98 (tstee 1996–99), Scientific Issues Ctee Movement Disorder Soc 1998–2002; memb: Grants Ctee MRC Neurosciences and Mental Health Bd 1995–97, Med Advsy Panel UK Parkinson's Disease Soc 1995– (chm 1996–97), Med Advsy Panel UK Huntington's Disease Assoc 1996–, MRC Med Advsy Bd 1997–2000, Neuroscience Panel Wellcome Tst 2000–03, Int Advsy Bd German Parkinson Network 2000–06, Int Advsy Bd Dementia Network 2007–, Advsy Bd European Soc for Clinical Neuropharmacology, European Multiple Systems Atrophy Steering Gp, Int Advsy Bd Michael J Fox Fndn 2002–, EC Concerted Actions on Neural Transplantation (NECTAR/NEST), Bd MRC Neuroscience 2004–, Austrian Clinical Research (Neuroscience) Advsy Panel (KLIF) 2011–14, Bioscience Advsy Bd Alzheimer's Soc UK 2013–; memb industrial advsy bds: Glaxo SmithKline, Orion-Pharma, Aventis, Astra-Zeneca, Novartis, Solvay, TEVA; conslt: Shire, Motac Neuroscience, Lundbeck; assoc ed Brain 2012–; memb Editorial Bd: Jl of Neural Transmission, Jl of Neurology, Neurosurgery and Psychiatry, Synapse, Movement Disorders; patron Alzheimer's Soc 2007–; Stanley Fahn lectr 2002, Cotzias lectr 2003, Charles Wilson lectr 2004, Kuhl-Lassen lectr 2005, Sprague lectr 2006; memb: Assoc of Br Neurologists, BMA, European Neurological Soc, American Assoc of Neurology, Movement Disorder Soc, American Neurological Assoc, Assoc of Physicians (UK), Int Soc of Cerebral Blood Flow and Metabolism (a dir 1993–97), Soc for Neuroscience, Int Basal Ganglia Soc, Australian and NZ Assoc of Neurologists, Atlanto-Euro-Mediterranean Acad of Med Scis; FRCP 1993 (MRCP 1982), FMedSci 2001; *Publications* author of over 350 papers in peer-reviewed jls, symposia proceedings, reviews and abstracts; *Recreations* music; *Clubs* Athenaeum; *Style—* Prof David J Brooks; ✉ 186 Jersey Road, Osterley, Middlesex TW7 4QN (e-mail david.brooks@imperial.ac.uk)

BROOKS, Jason; s of Michael David Brooks, and Patricia, *née* Morgan; *b* 1968; *Educ* Oakwood Comp Sch Rotherham, Thomas Rotherham Coll, Rotherham Coll of Arts and Technol, Cheltenham and Gloucester Coll of Art and Design, Chelsea Coll of Art and Design; *Career* artist; *Solo Exhibitions* Entwistle London 1997–98, 2000 and 2003, Harewood House Leeds 2001, Archimede Staffolini Gallery Nicosia 2002, Auto (Max Wigram Gallery London) 2005, Stellan Holm Gallery NY 2006; *Selected Group Exhibitions* Get Real (Riverside Studios London) 1992, Abstractions from the Domestic Suburb Scene (SIN) (Benjamin Rhodes Gallery London) 1992, SS Excess (Factual Nonsense London) 1993, To Boldly Go... (Cubitt Street Gallery London) 1993, BT New Contemporaries (Serpentine Gallery London and tour) 1993, Likeness: Representing Sexualities (Manchester City Art Galleries) 1997, John Moores 20 Liverpool Exhibition (Walker Art Gallery Liverpool) 1997, The Whitechapel Open (Whitechapel Art Gallery London) 1998, Postcards on Photography (Cambridge Darkroom and tour) 1998, Near (Sharjah Art Museum UAE), Painting Lab (Entwistle London) 1999, The Flower Show (Harewood House) 1999, John Moores 21 Liverpool Exhibition (Walker Art Gallery Liverpool) 1999, Fresh Paint (Scottish Gallery of Modern Art Glasgow) 1999, Natural Dependency (Jerwood Gallery London) 1999, Psycho Soma (Lombard Freid NY) 2000, I Am A Camera (Saatchi Gallery London) 2001, Besides, It Is Always Others Who Die (291 London) 2001, Open Plan (Alphadelta Gallery and Artio Gallery Athens) 2001, Babel (Nat Museum of Contemporary Art Korea) 2002, Yes I Am a Long Way from Home (Wolverhampton Museum and Art Gallery, The Nunnery London, and Northern Centre for Contemporary Art Sunderland) 2003, The Flower Show (Rhodes & Mann London) 2003, Pale Fire (Galerie Nordenhake Berlin) 2003, Blow Up: New Painting and Photoreality (St Paul's Gallery Birmingham) 2004, John Moores 23 Liverpool Exhibition (Walker Art Gallery Liverpool) 2004, Appearance (Whitewall Waterfront Leeds) 2005, Darkness Visible (Ferens Art Gallery Hull and Southampton City Art Gallery) 2006, Heads (Flowers East London) 2006, Harewood House 2006, Museum of Art Donna Regina Naples 2006, Timer (Triennale Bovisa Milan) 2007; *Work in Collections* The Berardo Collection MOMA Sintra, British Telecom London, Cheltenham & Gloucester Building Soc Cheltenham, Coopers & Lybrand London, James Moores Collection Liverpool, William Morris Agency LA, Saatchi Collection London, Speyer Collection NY, Unilever London, ABN AMRO London, Neuberger Berman NY, Ferens Art Gallery Hull, Harewood House Tst, Dakis Collection; *Awards* Rome Travel Bursary Br Sch in Rome 1990, British Telecom artist-in-residence 1994, co-prizewinner John Moores Exhbn 1997, winner NatWest Art Prize 1999; *Recreations* golf, tennis, sports cars; *Style—* Jason Brooks, Esq

BROOKS, Prof John Stuart; s of Ernest Brooks (d 2005), and Maude, *née* Langford (d 1981); *b* 8 March 1949, Holloway, London; *Educ* Cheshunt GS, Univ of Sheffield (BSc, PhD, DSc); *m* 14 Aug 1971, Jill, *née* Pusey; 2 s (Thomas David b 3 Jan 1998, Christopher John b 12 Nov 1999); *Career* Sheffield City Poly: lectr 1973–84, head Applied Physics Dept 1984–90, dir Materials Research Inst 1990–92; asst princ Sheffield Hallam Univ 1992–98, vice-chllr Univ of Wolverhampton 1998–2005, vice-chllr Manchester Met Univ 2005–15, ret; author of 75 papers on materials, spectroscopy and surface engrg; CPhys 1985, FInstP 1985, CEng 1992, Hon FRIBA; *Recreations* travel, walking, music, bridge; *Style—* Prof John Brooks; ✉ Manchester Metropolitan University, All Saints Building, All Saints, Manchester M15 6BH (☎ 0161 247 1560, e-mail john.brooks@mmu.ac.uk)

BROOKS, Dr Nicholas Hugh; s of Lt-Col A Brooks, of Great Missenden, Bucks, and Mary, *née* Gerrard; *b* 6 July 1947; *Educ* Perse Sch Cambridge, Bart's Med Coll and Univ of London (MB BS, MD); *m* 16 March 1974, Barbara Mary, da of Dr Robert Boal, of Southampton, Hants; 1 s (Alexander James b 1977), 1 da (Victoria Jane b 1979); *Career* Bart's: house surgn Surgical Professional Unit 1971, house surgn in cardiothoracic surgery then SHO in gen med 1972, registrar in cardiology 1973–74; house physician Southampton Gen Hosp 1971, Br Heart Fndn res fell St George's Hosp 1976–77 (registrar in med 1975), clinical lectr and hon sr registrar London Chest Hosp and London Hosp 1977, conslt cardiologist Univ Hosp of S Manchester (formerly Wythenshawe Hosp) 1984–; chm Specialist Advsy Ctee JCHMT 2000–03 (sec 1998–2000), ldr Taskforce on Clinical Standards and MCQs European Soc of Cardiology; hon sec Cardiology Ctee RCP 1988–93, hon sec Br Cardiac Soc 1996–98 (hon asst sec 1994–96); pres Br Cardiac Soc 2005–07 (pres-elect 2003–05); FRCP 1990 (MRCP), FESC 1996; *Books* Diseases of the Heart (contrib, 1989 and 1996); *Recreations* tennis, skiing, music; *Style—* Dr Nicholas Brooks; ✉ Oldcroft House, Elm Grove, Alderley Edge, Cheshire SK9 7PD (☎ 01625 582853, e-mail nhbrooks@talk21.com)

BROOKS, Rebekah; *née* Wade; da of late Robert Wade, and Deborah Wade; *b* 27 May 1968; *Educ* Appleton Hall, Sorbonne; *Career* features ed, then assoc ed rising to dep ed News of the World 1989–98, dep ed The Sun 1998–2000, ed News of the World 2000–02, ed The Sun 2003–09, chief exec News International 2009–11 and 2015–; fndr memb and pres Women in Journalism; *Style—* Mrs Rebekah Brooks

BROOKS, Richard John; s of Peter John Brooks (d 2000), and Joan, *née* Maxwell (d 1965); *b* 5 February 1946; *Educ* Univ of Bristol (BA); *m* Jane Elizabeth; 2 da (Kate b 13 July 1981, Anna b 5 Dec 1984); *Career* journalist; Bristol Evening Post 1968–71, Daily Mail 1971, BBC 1971–79, The Economist 1979–80, Sunday Times 1980–85, media ed The Observer 1985–99, arts ed Sunday Times 1999–; *Recreations* watching films, playing sport; *Style—* Richard Brooks, Esq; ✉ Sunday Times, 1 Pennington Street, London E1 (☎ 020 7782 5735)

BROOKS, Richard William; s of Roger William Brooks, of Lancs, and Jennifer Ann, *née* Hawkard; *b* 18 February 1969, Malta; *Educ* Arnold Sch Blackpool, Univ of Warwick (LLB), Chester Sch of Law; *m* 1 May 2004, Victoria Jane, *née* Hopwell; *Career* slr; ptnr: Chalk Smith Brooks 1999, Withy King Slrs 2004–; memb Law Soc; *Recreations* rugby, horseracing; *Style—* Richard Brooks, Esq; ✉ 27 Newbury Street, Lambourn, Berkshire RG17 8PB (☎ 07775 918757); Withy King, Ailesbury Court, High Street, Marlborough SN8 1AA (e-mail richard.brooks@withyking.co.uk)

BROOKS, Robert; s of late William Frederick Brooks, of Enton, Surrey, and Joan Patricia, *née* Marshall; *b* 1 October 1956; *Educ* St Benedict's Sch Ealing; *Career* dir: Christie's S Kensington Ltd 1984–87 (joined 1975), Christie Manson and Woods Ltd 1987–89; estab Brooks (Auctioneers) Ltd 1989; chm Bonhams 2000–08; FIA (Gp N) Euro Touring Car champion 1999; *Recreations* golf, cricket; *Clubs* British Racing Drivers (chm 2007–11); *Style—* Robert Brooks, Esq

BROOKS, Thomas Alan Kieran (Thom); *b* 14 October 1973; *Educ* Xavier HS Middletown Connecticut, William Paterson Univ NJ (BA, distinguished student award), Arizona State Univ (MA), UCD (MA, Professor Magennis Meml Prize Dept of Philosophy), Univ of Sheffield (PhD), Newcastle Univ (Postgrad Certificate in Academic Practice); *m* Claire Brooks; *Career* tutor Univ of Sheffield 2002–03; Newcastle Univ: lectr in political thought 2004–07, reader in political and legal philosophy 2007–12; Durham Univ: reader in law 2012–14, prof of law and govt 2014–, dir Centre for Criminal Law and Criminal Justice 2014–16, dean and head of sch Durham Law Sch 2016–; memb SCR Durham Univ: Collingwood Coll, Grey Coll, Univ Coll; visiting fell: Univ of St Andrews 2004–05, Univ of Oxford 2010–11, Uppsala Univ 2011, St John's Coll Oxford 2012, Yale Univ 2015; founding ed Jl of Moral Philosophy 2003; chair Ctee on Philosophy and Law American Philosophical Assoc 2009–12, assoc memb Scottish Centre for Crime and Justice Research 2012–, memb Exec Ctee Soc of Legal Scholars 2013–; Community Involvement Panel CPS NE 2015–; Grad Essay Prize Hegel Soc of GB 2004, Outstanding Contributions to Media Award Faculty of Social Scis and Health Durham Univ 2013, Lecturer of the Year Faculty of Social Scis and Health Durham Students' Union 2014, Law Teacher of the Year Durham Law Sch 2015; columnist Newcastle Journal; digital communications lead Phil Wilson, MP and Sedgefield Constituency Lab Pty 2015–; FAcSS 2009, FRHistS 2010, FRSA 2012, FHEA 2014; *Publications* incl: Rousseau and Law (2005), The Legacy of John Rawls (2005), Hegel's Political Philosophy: A Systematic Reading of the Philosophy of the Right (2007, 2 edn 2013), Locke and Law (2007), The Global Justice Reader (2008), The Right to a Fair Trial (2009), Ethics and Moral Philosophy (2011), New Waves in Ethics (2011), Global Justice and International Affairs (2012), Hegel's Philosophy of Right (2012), Justice and the Capabilities Approach (2012), Punishment (2012), Rawls and Law (2012), Just War Theory (2013), The 'Life in the United Kingdom' Citizenship Test: Is It Unfit for Purpose? (2013), Ethical Citizenship (2014), Law and Legal Theory (2014), Deterrence (2014), Juvenile Offending (2014), New Waves in Global Justice (2014), Retribution (2014), Sentencing (2014), Shame Punishment (2014), Alcohol and Public Policy (2015), Rawls's Political Liberalism (with Martha C Nussbaum, 2015), Current Controversies in Political Philosophy (2015), Becoming British: UK Citizenship Examined (2016); *Recreations* music, reading, travel; *Style—* Prof Thom Brooks; ✉ Durham Law School, Durham University, Palatine Centre, Stockton Road, Durham DH1 3LE (☎ 0191 3344365, e-mail thom.brooks@durham.ac.uk, website www.thombrooks.info, Twitter @thom_brooks)

BROOM, Prof Donald Maurice; s of Donald Edward Broom (d 1971), and Mavis Edith Rose, *née* Thompson (d 2002); *b* 14 July 1942; *Educ* Whitgift Sch, St Catharine's Coll Cambridge (MA, PhD, ScD); *m* 31 May 1971, Sally Elizabeth Mary, da of Thomas Edward Fisher (d 1969), of Ufton Nervet, Berks; 3 s (Oliver b 1973, Tom b 1976, Giles b 1981); *Career* lectr (later reader) Dept of Pure and Applied Zoology Univ of Reading 1967–86, Colleen Macleod prof of animal welfare Dept of Veterinary Med Univ of Cambridge 1986–2009 (emeritus 2009–), fell St Catharine's Coll Cambridge 1987–2009 (pres 2001–04, emeritus fell 2009–); visiting asst prof Dept of Zoology Univ of Calif 1969, visiting lectr Dept of Biology Univ of WI Trinidad 1972, visiting scientist Div of Animal Prodn Cwlth Sci and Industrial Res Orgn Perth 1983, memb NERC Ctee on Seals 1986–97, invited advsr Cncl of Euro Standing Ctee on Welfare of Animals Kept for Farming Purposes 1987–2000, chm Euro Union Scientific Veterinary Ctee (Animal Welfare) 1990–97, memb Euro Union Sci Ctee on Animal Health and Animal Welfare 1997–2003, vice-chm Euro Food Safety Authy Panel on Animal Health and Welfare 2003–09 (memb 2009–12), Euro Union rep on Quadripartite Working Gp on Humane Trapping Standard 1995–96; chm World Orgn for Animal Health (OIE) Gp on Animal Welfare During Land Tport 2003–07; memb: UK Miny of Agric Farm Animal Welfare Cncl 1991–99, UK Home Office Animal Procedures Ctee 1998–2006; hon res assoc Inst of Grassland and Environmental Res 1985–, tstee Farm Animal Care Tst 1986–2009 (chm 1999–2009), hon treas Assoc for the Study of Animal Behaviour 1971–80 (memb Cncl 1971–83); pres Int Soc for Applied Ethology 1987–89 (memb Cncl 1981–84, vice-pres 1986–87 and 1989–91); memb: Int Ethological Ctee 1976–79, Br Tst for Ornithology, Br Soc of Animal Sci, Assoc of Veterinary Teachers and Res Workers, Int Soc of Anthrozoology, BBC Rural Affrs Ctee 2007–, Veterinary, Agriculture, Food Panel for assessing research in univs HE Funding Cncl 2013–14; UK NC3Rs memb Fellowship and Grant Selection Panels MRC 2012–14; pres St Catharine's Soc 2005–06 (vice-pres 2004–05 and 2006–07), vice-pres Old Whitgiftian Assoc 2000–; scientific advsr EU Delgn to WTO (measures prohibiting the importation and marketing of seal products) 2013, gave evidence on the welfare of animals in relation to cloning Euro Parl 2015; lectr: on OIE standards courses (Thailand, Vietnam, China, Malaysia) World Orgn for Animal Health 2015, on technical barriers to trade (TBT) World Trade Orgn 2015; George Fleming Prize for best paper in Br Veterinary Jl 1990, Br Soc of Animal Sci/RSPCA Award for innovative devpts in animal welfare 2001, Eurogroup Medal for work to improve the welfare of animals 2001, RSPCA Michael Kay Award for servs to animal welfare in Europe 2007, RSPCA Sir Patrick Moore Award 2014, Univs Fedn for Animal Welfare (UFAW) Medal for outstanding contributions to animal welfare science 2016; hon coll fell Myerscough Coll Univ of Central Lancs 1999, Hon DSc De Montfort Univ 2000; prof (hc) Univ of Salvador Argentina 2004, Hon Dr Norwegian Univ of Life Sciences 2005, Hon DSc Univ of Buenos Aires Argentina 2016; hon socio corrispondanti Accademia Peloritana di Pericolanti Messina 2005; FIBiol 1986, FZS (memb Animal Welfare Ctee 1986–95), hon fell Int Soc for Applied Ethology 2009; *Books* Birds and their Behaviour (1977), Biology of Behaviour (1981), Encyclopaedia of Domestic Animals (ed, with P A Messent, 1986), Farmed Animals (ed, 1986), Farm Animal Behaviour and Welfare (with A F Fraser, 1990), Stress and Animal Welfare (with K G Johnson, 1993), Coping with Challenge: Welfare in Animals Including Humans (ed, 2001), The Evolution of Morality and Religion (2003), Sentience and Animal Welfare (2014), Domestic Animal Behaviour and Welfare (with A F Fraser, 5 edn 2015); *Recreations* squash, modern pentathlon, ornithology; *Clubs* Hawks' (Cambridge); *Style—* Prof Donald Broom; ✉ Department of Veterinary Medicine, University of Cambridge, Madingley Road, Cambridge CB3 0ES; St Catharine's College, Cambridge CB2 1RL (☎ 01223 337697, fax 01223 337610, e-mail dmb16@cam.ac.uk, website http://www.neuroscience.cam.ac.uk/directory/profile.php?dmb16)

BROOM, Douglas Philip; s of late George Edward Shirley Broom, of Haxey, Lincs, and late Joyce Elizabeth, *née* Williams; *b* 27 December 1956, London; *Educ* Holy Trinity Sch

Crawley, Highbury Coll Portsmouth (NCTJ course); *m* 20 Oct 1979, Susan Mary, da of late Kenneth Dudley, of Harrold, Beds; 1 s (Thomas Edward b 16 Feb 1989), 1 da (Sophia Elizabeth b 22 July 1991); *Career* The News Portsmouth 1976–79 (joined as trainee, later dist chief reporter), dep news ed Bury Free Press Bury St Edmunds 1979–80, chief law courts reporter Cambridge Evening News 1980–82, law courts reporter Press Assoc 1982–86 (educn correspondent 1986–88); The Times: educn reporter 1988–90, local govt correspondent 1990–92, contrib 1992–; ed Public Finance magazine 1993–97 (asst ed 1992); VNU Business Pubns: ed Accountancy Age 1997–99, ed dir Business and Finance 1999–2000, gen mangr Learned Information (Europe) Ltd 2000–01, publisher Business and Finance 2001–02; dir CCH Magazines 2002–, head of magazines and professional devpt Wolter Kluwers UK 2005– (head of CCH info 2009–10, head of CCH content 2010–, head of training and communications 2015–, head of communications UK and Global Legal Software 2016–); memb: High Court Journalists' Assoc 1982–86 (chm 1985–86), Educn Correspondents' Gp 1986–90, Ctee Br Soc of Magazine Eds 1997–2000; FRSA 1995; *Recreations* reading, walking, opera; *Style*— Douglas Broom, Esq; ✉ Wolters Kluwer (UK) Ltd, 145 London Road, Kingston upon Thames, Surrey KT2 6SR (☎ 020 8247 1372, e-mail douglas.broom@wolterskluwer.co.uk)

BROOME, Prof John; s of Richard Broome (d 1986), of Corfe Castle, Dorset, and Tamsin, *née* Luckham (d 1994); *b* 17 May 1947, Kuala Lumpur; *Educ* Trinity Hall Cambridge (BA), MIT (PhD), Bedford Coll London (MA); *m* 1970, Ann, da of Herbert Rowland; 1 da (Kitty b 1975), 1 s (Richard b 1978); *Career* lectr in economics Birkbeck Coll London 1972–78; Univ of Bristol: reader 1979–91, prof of economics 1991–95; prof of philosophy Univ of St Andrews 1996–2000, White's prof of moral philosophy Univ of Oxford 2000–14, visiting prof of philosophy Stanford Univ 2014–; adjunct prof Australian National Univ 2010–; foreign memb Royal Swedish Acad of Sciences 2007, foreign hon memb American Acad of Arts and Sciences 2014; Hon PhD Lund Univ 2013; FRSE 1999, FBA 2000; *Books* The Microeconomics of Capitalism (1983), Weighing Goods: Equality, Uncertainty and Time (1991), Counting the Cost of Global Warming (1992), Ethics out of Economics (1999), Weighing Lives (2004), Climate Matters: Ethics in a Warming World (2012), Rationality Through Reasoning (2013); *Recreations* sailing; *Style*— Prof John Broome; ✉ Corpus Christi College, Oxford OX1 4JF (e-mail john.broome@philosophy.ox.ac.uk, website http://users.ox.ac.uk/~sfop0060/)

BROOMFIELD, Graham Martin; s of Herbert Broomfield (d 1989), of W Sussex, and Muriel Joyce, *née* Robinson (d 1994); *b* 12 February 1945; *Educ* Dorking County GS, Chelsea Coll London (BSc); *m* 5 Oct 1974, Wai Yu (Miranda), da of Leung Fu Ping (d 1972); 1 s (Lee b 1978), 1 da (Amy b 1981); *Career* CA; Charles Comins & Co (now Baker Tilly) 1967–72, Peat Marwick Mitchell & Co (now KPMG) 1972–76, Warner Communications Inc (now AOL Time Warner) 1977–81, Prager & Fenton 1981–87, GM Broomfield & Co Ltd 1983–; govr St Clements & St James Sch until 2009; *Recreations* politics, history; *Style*— Graham M Broomfield, Esq; ✉ 17 Cromwell Grove, London W6 7RQ (☎ 020 7603 4487, fax 020 7371 4908, e-mail info@almg.co.uk)

BROOMFIELD, Nicholas (Nick); *b* 30 January 1948, London; *Educ* Univ of Cardiff, Univ of Essex, Nat Film Sch; *Partner* Joan Churchill; 1 s; *Career* documentary filmmaker; *Films* Who Cares 1970, Proud to Be British 1973, Behind the Rent Strike 1974, Whittingham 1975, Juvenile Liaison 1976, Fort Augustus 1976, Marriage Guidance 1977, Tattoed Tears 1978, Soldier Girls 1980, Chicken Ranch 1982, Lily Tomlin 1986, Driving Me Crazy 1988, Diamond Skulls 1989, Juvenile Liaison 2 1990, The Leader, His Driver, The Driver's Wife 1990, Monster in a Box 1991, Too White For Me 1992, Aileen Wuornos: The Selling of a Serial Killer 1993, Tracking Down Maggie 1994, Heidi Fleiss: Hollywood Madam 1995, Fetishes 1996, Kurt & Courtney 1997, Biggie and Tupac 2002, Aileen: Life and Death of a Serial Killer 2003, His Big White Self 2006, Ghosts 2007, Battle for Haditha 2008, Sarah Palin: You Betcha 2011; *Awards* Robert Flaherty Award BAFTA, Prix Italia, Dupont Columbia Award For Outstanding Journalism, Peabody Award, RTS Award, John Grierson Award, The Hague Peace Prize, Chris Award, Amnesty Int Award DOEN, Special Jury Award Melbourne Film Festival, BAFTA Tribute Evening 2005, Best Dir Silver Shell Award San Sebastian Film Festival 2007, Best Drama Documentary John Grierson Award 2008; First Prize: Sundance Film Festival, US Film Festival, Chicago Film Festival, Festival of Mannheim, Fesitval di Popoli; *Style*— Nick Broomfield, Esq; ✉ Lafayette Films, PO Box 5048, Santa Monica, CA 90409, USA (e-mail nick@nickbroomfield.com); Deans Mill, Lindfield, West Sussex RH16 2QY

BROTHERHOOD, James; s of Frederick Arthur Brotherhood (d 1974), and Isabel, *née* Bradley (d 1991); *b* 5 June 1946; *Educ* King's Sch Chester; *m* 1, 2 Aug 1969, Susan Elizabeth, da of Thomas Ian Jodrell Toler, of Cheshire; 3 s (Jonathan Alexander Jodrell b 1973, Philip Richard Thomas b 1975, Michael Rupert Benjamin b 1981), 2 da (Katherine Mary b 1978, Eleanor Elizabeth b 1984); *m* 2, 11 March 1989, Rosalind Ann, da of late Dr Robert Alan Blyth, of Cheshire; 1 da (Emily Victoria b 1991); *Career* architect; fndr James Brotherhood & Associates; pres Cheshire Soc of Architects 1978–80, chm NW Region RIBA 1983; RIBA: memb ctee 1982, prof practice external examiner; pres Chester Assoc of Old King's Scholars 1998; fndr Chester Heritage Trust 1997; Dip Arch (Hons) 1973, RIBA 1974, AABC 1999, memb IHBC 2013; *Recreations* shooting, fishing; *Clubs* City (Chester); *Style*— James Brotherhood, Esq; ✉ James Brotherhood & Associates, Golly Farm, Golly, Burton, Rossett, Wrexham LL12 0AL (☎ 01244 579000, e-mail james@jba-architects.co.uk)

BROTHERSTON, Lez; s of Leslie Brotherston, of Liverpool, and Irene, *née* Richardson; *b* 6 October 1961; *Educ* Prescot GS, St Helens Sch of Art, Central Sch of Art and Design (BA); *Career* set and costume designer; artistic assoc New Adventures Theatre, artistic assoc Mathew Bournes New Adventures; *Theatre* for Greenwich Theatre: Northanger Abbey, The Last Romantics, Handling Bach, The Sisters Rosensweig (also Old Vic), Falling over England, Under the Stars, The Prisoner of Zenda, Schippel the Plumber (also Edinburgh Festival), The Government Inspector, Side by Side by Sondheim; for Actors' Touring Co: No Way Out, The Maids, The Triumph of Love, Hamlet, Princess Ivona, Dr Faustus, Heaven Bent Hellbound; for Oldham Coliseum: Wuthering Heights, Love on the Dole; other prodns incl: Hindle Wakes (Manchester Royal Exchange), Rosencrantz and Guildenstern are Dead (RNT), Enjoy (Nottingham Playhouse), Neville's Island (Apollo West End), The Schoolmistress (Chichester Festival Theatre), Jane Eyre (Playhouse West End), Comedians (West Yorkshire Playhouse and Lyric Hammersmith), Jane Eyre (Theatr Clwyd and Thorndike), Mystery Plays (Coventry Belgrade), The School for Wives (Belfast Arts), Jane Eyre (Derby Playhouse), A Midsummer Night's Dream (Royal Exchange), Speedking (Liverpool Playhouse), The Daughter-In-Law (Bristol Old Vic), The Little Foxes (Leeds Playhouse), The Beaux Stratagem (Stephen Joseph Theatre), The Man of Mode (Swan Theatre Worcester), Pinocchio Boys (Paines Plough), The Eleventh Commandment (Hampstead), Alarms & Excursions (Gielgud Theatre), Hindle Wakes (Royal Exchange), Nude With Violin (Royal Exchange), A Midsummer Night's Dream (Albery), French & Saunders Live (UK tour), Little Foxes (Donmar Warehouse), Victoria Wood At It Again (Royal Albert Hall), Bedroom Farce (Aldwych), Design for Living (Manchester Royal Exchange), Text Without Words (RNT), The Crucible (Sheffield Crucible), The Miracle Worker (Charlotte Rep Theatre), The Dark (Donmar Warehouse), Tonight's the Night (Victoria Palace Theatre), The Crucible (Sheffield Crucible), Play Without Words (RNT), Playing With Fire (RNT), Rise and Fall of Little Voice (Vaudevelle Theatre), Women Beware Women (NT), The Real Thing (Old Vic), Duet For One (Vaudeville, Almeida and tour); *Musicals* incl: Camelot (BOC Covent Garden Festival), Face (Queen's Theatre Hornchurch and tour), Maria Friedman by

Special Arrangement (Donmar Warehouse), Annie (Liverpool Playhouse), Cabaret (Sheffield Crucible), Closer than Ever (Manchester Library Theatre), High Society (West Yorkshire Playhouse), Songbook (Watermill Newbury), Spend Spend Spend (Picadilly Theatre West End and UK tour), My One and Only (UK premiere Chichester Festival Theatre, also at Piccadilly Theatre), Tonight's the Night (Phil McIntyre Prodns), Acorn Antiques (Haymarket London), Far Pavillions (Shaftesbury Theatre London), The Pirate Queen (The Point Dublin), Sister Act (Paladium London); *Dance* for Northern Ballet Theatre: Dracula, The Brontës, A Christmas Carol (also BBC), Swan Lake, Romeo and Juliet (also BBC), Strange Meeting, Giselle, Hunchback of Notre Dame, Carmen; for Adventures in Motion Pictures: Swan Lake (Olivier Award Best New Dance Prodn, London, LA and Broadway), Highland Fling, Cinderella (Piccadilly and LA), The Car Man (Old Vic and UK tour), Dorian Gray (Edinburgh Festival and Sadler's Wells); other credits incl: Grey Matter (Ballet Rambert), Just Scratchin the Surface and Night Life (Scottish Ballet), Bounce (Stockholm, Sweden and The Roundhouse, London), 6 Faces (K Ballet Japan), Edqard Scissorhands (New Adventures Theatre), Soldiers Tale (ROH), wroter, dir and designer Les Liasons Dangereuses (Tokyo and Sadlers Wells), Seven Deadly Sins (Royal Ballet); *Opera* for Opera North: Le Roi Malgre Lui, Madam Butterfly (set only), Masquerade, The Flying Dutchman; for Buxton Festival Opera: The Impresario, Il Sogno Di Scipione, David and Goliath, Sir Gawain and the Green Knight, Maria Padilla; for Opera Zuid: Hänsel and Gretel, A Cunning Little Vixon, Ariadne Auf Naxos, Werther; for Hong Kong Arts Festival: Der Rosenkavalier, The Marriage of Figaro; for Camden Festival: Silver Lake, The Tsar has his Photograph Taken, The Protagonists; other prodns incl: Falstaff (Teatro Bellini, Sicily and Copenhagan), Dido and Aeneas/Venus and Adonis (Festwochen der Alten Musik, Innsbruck & De Vlaamse Opera, Antwerp), Cornet Christoph Rilke's Song of Love and Death (Glyndebourne Touring Opera), L'Italiana in Algeri (Dublin Grand Opera), Rigoletto (Opera Northern Ireland), Don Giovanni (Opera 80), Hänsel and Gretel (set only, WNO), Die Fledermaus (Opera East), La Traviata (Phoenix Opera), Don Giovanni (Surrey Opera), Hänsel and Gretel (Opera Northern Ireland), La Somnambula (Teatro Municipale, Rio de Janeiro), L'Esior Damour (Glyndebourne); *Film* Swan Lake (AMP/BBC/NVC), Letter to Brezhnev (Palace Pictures), The Car Man (AMP/Channel 4); *Costume and Props* for BBC: Dr Who, The Cleopatras, Richard III, Henry VI (parts I, II and III), King Lear, Antony and Cleopatra, The Merchant of Venice; for ITV: Deceptions (mini-series), The Far Pavilions; other prodns incl: Highlander, Bullshot Drummond, Brazil, Young Sherlock and the Pyramid of Fear, The Last Emperor; *Awards* winner Outstanding Achievement in Dance Olivier Award for Cinderella (Piccadilly Theatre) 1998; Olivier Award nominations incl: Outstanding Achievement in Dance (for Northern Ballet Theatre Season at the Royalty Theatre), Best Set Design (for Neville's Island), Best Set Design (for Spend Spend Spend), Best Design (for Play Without Words); Manchester Evening News and Br Regional Theatre nomination for Best Designer (for Hindle Wakes), Outstanding Set and Costume Design (for Little Foxes); for Swan Lake on Broadway: Drama Desk Award for Best Costume Design, Drama Desk Award for Best Set Design for a Musical, Outer Critic Circle Award for Best Costume Design, Tony Award for Best Costume Design; Drama Critics Circle Award for Outstanding Costume Design (for Cinderella, LA), Critics Circle Dance Award for Achievement in Design, Drama Desk Nomination for Best Set and Costumes (for Play Without Words NY); *Style*— Lez Brotherston, Esq; ✉ c/o Judy Daish Associates, 2 St Charles Place, London W10 6EG

BROUCHER, David Stuart; s of late Clifford Broucher,and late Betty Elma, *née* Jordan; *b* 5 October 1944; *Educ* Manchester Grammar, Trinity Hall Cambridge (BA); *m* 1, 25 Nov 1971 (m dis 2014), Marion Monika, da of late Mr Wilkinson Gill, of Stagshaw, Northumberland; 1 s (Nicholas David b 1972); *m* 2, Lorela Viorica, *née* Corbeanu; *Career* Foreign Office 1966–68, Br Mil Govt Berlin 1968–72, Cabinet Office 1972–75, Br Embassy Prague 1975–78, FCO 1978–83, UK perm rep to the EC 1983–85, cnsllr Jakarta 1985–89, cnsllr (economic) Bonn 1989–93, FCO 1994–97, ambass to Czech Republic 1997–2001, ambass to Conf on Disarmament 2001–04, personal advsr to pres of Romania 2005, visiting fell Univ of Southampton 2006–09, conslt advsr on foreign policy 2007–; FCO Assoc: vice-chm 2008–15, chm 2015–; *Recreations* golf, music, sailing; *Style*— David Broucher, Esq

BROUGH, Paul; s of Douglas Brough of London, and Liese Cattle, *née* Banks; *b* 15 July 1963, London; *Educ* Dulwich Coll, RCM, St Michael's Coll Tenbury, Magdalen Coll Oxford (MA, Mackinnon scholar), Royal Acad of Music (Henry Wood scholar); *Career* freelance conductor 1986–, conductor The Hanover Band 2004– (princ conductor 2007–10), conducting tutor and acad studies lectr Royal Acad of Music 2004–; guest conductor: BBC Singers 2007– (princ guest conductor 2011–16), many BBC broadcasts and recordings), BBC Philharmonic, BBC Concert Orchestra, Royal Philharmonic Orchestra, Ulster Orchestra, Britten Sinfonia, Manchester Camerata, St James's Baroque 2011–, BBC Symphony Orchestra 2013–; Boult Mem Prize 1986, Ernest Read Prize 1997; ARAM 2007; *Recreations* friends, solitude; *Clubs* Savage; *Style*— Paul Brough, Esq; ✉ website www.paulbrough.com

BROUGHAM, Hon David Peter; s of 4 Baron Brougham and Vaux (d 1967); *b* 22 August 1940; *Educ* Sedbergh; *m* 1, 1969, Moussie Christina Margareta Hallström, da of Sven Hörnblad, of Stockholm, Sweden; 1 s (Henry b 1971); *m* 2, 1977, Caroline Susan, only da of Lt-Col James Michael Heigham Royce Tomkin, MC, of Wissett, Suffolk, by his w Margaret Elinor, da of Sir Charles Henry Napier Bunbury, 11 B, and former w of Julian Dixon; 1 s (Oliver b 1978); *Career* dir Standard Chartered plc 1993–98 (joined as head of credit 1989), responsible for banking activities in Europe, America, Africa, ME and S Asia; non-exec dir: Asia Pacific Debt Recovery Co Hong Kong, Alliance and Leicester plc, Hamden Holdings plc, Matrix e-ventures Fund VCT plc; *Style*— The Hon David Brougham; ✉ 3 Chancellor House, Hyde Park Gate, London SW7 5DQ (☎ and fax 020 7589 1634)

BROUGHAM AND VAUX, 5 Baron (UK 1860); Michael John Brougham; CBE (1995); s of 4 Baron (d 1967) by his 2 w, Jean (d 1992), da of late Brig-Gen Gilbert Follett, DSO, MVO, and Lady Mildred, *née* Murray (d 1972), da of 7 Earl of Dunmore, DL; *b* 2 August 1938; *Educ* Lycée Jaccard Lausanne, Millfield, Northampton Inst of Agric; *m* 1, 1963 (m dis 1968), Olivia Susan (d 1986), da of Rear Adm Gordon Thomas Seccombe Gray, DSC (d 1997); 1 da; *m* 2, 1969 (m dis 1981), Catherine (who m 1981 Rupert Edward Odo Russell, gs- of Sir Odo Russell, KCMG, KCVO, CB, himself 2 s of 1 Baron Ampthill), da of William Gulliver (d 1967); 1 s; *Heir* s, Hon Charles Brougham; *Career* Parly conslt and co dir; pres RoSPA 1986–89 (vice-pres 1989–); former chm Tax Payers' Soc; a dep chm House of Lords 1993–, a dep speaker House of Lords 1995–, memb Select Ctee on House of Lords Officers 1997, memb Refreshment Ctee House of Lords 2008–12, memb Admin and Work Ctee House of Lords 2009/2014; memb Exec Gp Assoc of Cons Peers 1991–98 and 2008–10 (dep chm 1998–2007); chm European Secure Vehicle Alliance (ESVA) 1993–2006; pres: Nat Health and Safety Gps Cncl 1994–, London Health and Safety Gp 2000 (hon vice-pres 2008); *Recreations* rugger, tennis, photography; *Style*— The Rt Hon the Lord Brougham and Vaux, CBE; ✉ 11 Westminster Gardens, Marsham Street, London SW1P 4JA

BROUGHTON, Hon James Henry Ailwyn; s and h of 3 Baron Fairhaven, JP; *b* 25 May 1963; *Educ* Harrow; *m* 22 March 1990, Sarah Olivia, da of Harold Digby Fitzgerald Creighton; 2 da (Sophie Rose b 30 April 1992, Emily Patricia b 15 May 1995), 1 s (George Ailwyn James b 17 March 1997); *Career* Capt Blues and Royals 1984–94; Baring Asset Management Ltd 1994–97, currently owner and mangr Barton Stud; *Recreations* racing, gardening, shooting; *Style*— The Hon James Broughton; ✉ Barton Stud, Great Barton, Bury St Edmunds, Suffolk IP31 2SH (☎ 01284 787226, fax 01284 787231)

BROUGHTON, Sir Martin Faulkner; kt (2011); *b* 1947; *Educ* Westminster City GS; *m* 1974, Jocelyn Mary, *née* Rodgers; 1 s, 1 da; *Career* British American Tobacco plc: joined 1971, fin dir BAT Industries plc 1988–92, chm Wiggins Teape Gp 1989–90, chm Eagle Star 1992–93, gp chief exec and dep chm 1993–98, chm 1998–2004; chm British Airways plc 2004–13 (non-exec dir 2000–13); co-chm TransAtlantic Business Dialogue 2006–09, dep chm Int Airlines Gp 2010–16; non-exec dir Whitbread plc 1993–2000; pres CBI 2007–09; memb: Takeover Panel 1996–2000, Fin Reporting Cncl 1998–2004; chm: British Horseracing Bd 2004–07 (ind dir 2000–07), Liverpool FC 2010, Sports Investment Partners 2010–; FCA; *Recreations* theatre, golf, horseracing; *Clubs* Tandridge Golf; *Style*— Sir Martin Broughton; ✉ Sports Investment Partners, 1 Heddon Street, London W1B 4BD

BROUGHTON, Dr Peter; s of Thomas Frederick Broughton (d 1983), of Skipton, and Mary Theodosia, *née* Bracewell (d 1993); *b* 8 September 1944; *Educ* Univ of Manchester (BSc, PhD); *m* Aug 1968, Janet Mary, da of Ronald George Silveston (d 1996); 2 s (Jonathan b 3 May 1971, Nicholas b 8 Jan 1974); *Career* research student then research asst in structural engrg Univ of Manchester 1966–71, structural engrg surveyor Lloyds Register of Shipping 1971–74, ptnr subsid of Campbell Reith and Partners (chartered engrs) 1974–75, soils/structural engr Burmah Oil Trading Ltd 1975–76, sr soils/structural engr rising to supervising structural engr British National Oil Corporation 1977–79; Phillips Petroleum Co: sr structural engr UK Div 1979–82, civil engrg supervisor UK Div 1982–86, princ project engr and co rep (for Ekofisk Protective Barrier Project) Norway Div 1986–90, princ project engr and co rep then engrg and procurement mangr UK Div 1990–93, engrg and construction project mangr for sub-structures Norway Div 1994–98, Maureen Platform refloat and decommissioning project mangr UK Div 1998–2003; conslt to Peter Fraenkel and Ptnrs Ltd 2003–, assoc to Gaffney Cline and Assocs Ltd 2007–08; dir of marine engrg Energy Solutions Ltd 2013–; visiting prof Dept of Civil Engrg Imperial Coll London 1991–2005, Royal Acad of Engrg visiting prof Dept of Engrg Sci Univ of Oxford 2004–07; CEng, FICE, FIMarEST, FIStructE, FRINA, FREng 1996; *Awards* Special Award Instn of Structural Engrs 1990, Stanley Gray Award Inst of Marine Engrg, Sci and Technol 1992, George Stephenson Medal ICE 1993, Bill Curtin Medal ICE 1997, Overseas Premium ICE 1998, David Hislop Award ICE 1999, Contribution to Institution Activity Award ICE 2002; *Publications* The Ekofisk Protective Barrier (1992), The Analysis of Cable and Catenary Structures (1994), The Effects of Subsidence on the Steel Jacket and Piled Foundation Design for the Ekofisk 2/4X and 2/4J Platforms (1996), Challenges of Subsidence at the Norwegian Ekofisk Oil Field (Royal Soc of Edinburgh/Royal Acad of Engrg lectr, 1998), Steel Jacket Structures for the New Ekofisk Complex in the North Sea (1998), The Removal of the Maureen Steel Gravity Platform (1999), Decommissioning of the Maureen Oil Platform (2000), Foundation Design for the Refloat of the Maureen Steel Gravity Platform (2002), Refloating the Maureen Platform (2002); also author of numerous other pubns; *Recreations* gardening, walking, swimming, trout fishing; *Style*— Dr Peter Broughton, FREng; ✉ Peter Fraenkel and Partners Ltd, South House, 21–37 South Street, Dorking, Surrey RH4 2JZ

BROWN; *see also:* Holden-Brown

BROWN, Adam; *Career* photographer; fndr Orlebar Brown 2007–; *Style*— Adam Brown, Esq; ✉ Orlebar Brown, Great Western Studios, Studio 101, 65 Alfred Road, London W2 5EU

BROWN, Alan; *b* 8 November 1956; *Career* chief fin offr ICI plc 2005–08, ceo Rentokil plc 2008–; *Style*— Alan Brown, Esq; ✉ Rentokil Initial plc, Riverbank, Meadows Business Park, Blackwater, Camberley, Surrey, GU17 9AB

BROWN, Andrew Charles; s of Gordon Charles Brown (d 1965), and Joan, *née* Tomlin (d 1985); *b* 30 October 1957, Barnet, London; *Educ* Ashmole Sch London, Southbank Poly (BSc); *m* 30 July 1983, Marion Denise, *née* Chamberlain; 1 da (Joanna Charlotte b 5 March 1990), 1 s (James Peter b 26 August 1994); *Career* chartered surveyor; property negotiator Healey and Baker 1981–84; St Quintin: investment surveyor 1984–87, assoc ptnr 1987–91, ptnr 1991–94; Church Commissioners: chief surveyor 1994–2003, sec/chief exec 2003–; CEDR accredited mediator 2012–; chair CMS Pensions Tst 2013–; dir: William Leech Fndn 2007–, William Leech (Investments) Ltd 2007–; church warden St Paul's Church St Albans 1987–93, memb Investment Ctee Lionheart 2006–, chair of tstees The 2:67 Project 2007–10, memb Allchurches Tst 2008–, tstee Mediation Hertfordshire 2015–; memb PCC St Paul's Church St Albans; FRICS 1994 (ARICS 1982); *Recreations* sport, family, local church; *Style*— Andrew Brown, Esq; ✉ Church House, Great Smith Street, London SW1P 3AZ (☎ 020 7898 1785, e-mail andrew.brown@churchofengland.org)

BROWN, Anthony Nigel; s of Sydney Brown, of Birmingham, and Gene, *née* Laitner; *b* 12 June 1955; *Educ* Clifton, Univ of Manchester (LLB); *m* 16 April 1989, Gail Denise, da of Dr Nathaniel Rifkind, of Glasgow; 2 s (Joshua Jack b 10 April 1991, Nathan Avi b 15 Jan 2000), 1 da (Sasha Jade b 14 Oct 1993); *Career* admitted slr 1980; voluntary asst Artlaw 1978–81, asst slr Janners 1980–84; fndr and md: Connaught Brown 1984–, The Affordable Art Company Ltd 1991–99; fndr Lenson Twelve 2012; exhibitions: Northern Spirit 1986, The Year of the Horse 2002, Miro Sculptures 2007, Albert Marquet Retrospective 2010, The Games – Inspiring Images 2012, British Sculpture: Post War 2014, Ben Nicholson: Landscape into Abstraction 2015; organised Artlaw auction Royal Acad 1981 and Dulwich Art '90; memb: Educn Advsy Ctee Dulwich Art Gallery, Soc of London Art Dealers; memb Ctee Br Friends of the Art Museums Israel (former chm); FRSA; *Recreations* looking at art, reading, swimming; *Clubs* RAC; *Style*— Anthony Brown, Esq; ✉ Connaught Brown, 2 Albemarle Street, London W1X 3HF (☎ 020 7408 0362, fax 020 7495 3137, e-mail art@connaughtbrown.co.uk)

BROWN, Prof Archibald Haworth (Archie); CMG (2005); s of Rev Alexander Douglas Brown (d 1979), of Darvel, Ayrshire, and Mary, *née* Yates (d 2006); *b* 10 May 1938; *Educ* Annan Acad, Dumfries Acad, City of Westminster Coll, LSE (BSc(Econ)), Univ of Oxford (MA); *m* 23 March 1963, Patricia Susan, da of Percival Walter Leslie Cornwell (d 1970); 1 da (Susan Woolford b 19 Jan 1969), 1 s (Alexander Douglas b 19 Oct 1971); *Career* Nat Serv 1956–58; reporter Annandale Herald and Annandale Observer 1954–56; lectr in politics Univ of Glasgow 1964–71 (Br Cncl exchange scholar Moscow Univ 1967–68); Univ of Oxford: lectr in Soviet institutions 1971–89, prof of politics 1989–2005, emeritus prof 2005; St Antony's Coll Oxford: faculty fell 1971–89, professorial fell 1989–2005 (emeritus fell 2005–), dir Russian and East Euro Centre, sub-warden 1995–97; distinguished visiting fell Kellog Inst for Int Studies Univ of Notre Dame 1998; visiting prof of political science: Yale Univ and Univ of Connecticut 1980, Columbia Univ NY 1985; visiting prof (Frank C Erwin Jr centennial chair of govt) Univ of Texas at Austin 1990–91; Henry L Stimson Lectures Yale Univ 1980, Arnold Wolfers Visiting Fell Lecture Yale Univ 1989, Lothian Euro Lecture Edinburgh 1999, Alexander Dallin Meml Lecture Stanford 2006, City of Aberdeen Gorbuchev Lecture 2007, James Chace Meml Lecture NY 2010, BEARR Tst Annual Lecture 2014, Winston Churchill Meml Lecture Presidential Summer Palace Cascais Portugal 2015; Political Studies Assoc (PSA) Diamond Jubilee Lifetime Achievement in Political Studies Award 2010, Distinguished Contributions to Slavic, East European and Eurasian Studies Award Assoc for Slavic, East European and Eurasian Studies (ASEEES) Philadelphia 2015; memb Cncl SSEES 1992–98; memb: Political Studies Assoc (PSA), American Political Science Assoc, British Assoc of Slavonic and E Euro Studies, Assoc for Slavic, E European and Eurasian Studies (USA), Cncl Br Acad 2014–; foreign hon memb American Acad of Arts and Sciences 2003; elected founding AcSS 1999; FBA 1991; *Books* Soviet Politics and Political Science (1974), The Soviet Union Since the Fall of Khrushchev (co-ed and contrib, 1975, 2 edn 1978), Political Culture and Political Change in Communist States (co-ed and contrib, 1977, 2 edn 1979), Authority, Power and Policy in the USSR: Essays dedicated to Leonard Schapiro (co-ed and contrib, 1980), The Cambridge Encyclopedia of Russia and the Former Soviet Union (co-ed and contrib, 1982, 2 edn 1994), Soviet Policy for the 1980s (co-ed and contrib, 1982), Political Culture and Communist Studies (ed and contrib, 1984), Political Leadership in the Soviet Union (ed and contrib, 1989), The Soviet Union: A Biographical Dictionary (ed and contrib, 1990), New Thinking in Soviet Politics (ed and contrib, 1992), The Gorbachev Factor (1996, W J M Mackenzie Prize, Alec Nove Prize), The British Study of Politics in the Twentieth Century (co-ed and contrib, 1999), Contemporary Russian Politics: A Reader (ed and contrib, 2001), Gorbachev, Yeltsin, and Putin: Political Leadership in Russia's Transition (co-ed and contrib, 2001), The Demise of Marxism-Leninism in Russia (ed and contrib, 2004), Seven Years that Changed the World: Perestroika in Perspective (2007), The Rise and Fall of Communism (2009, W J M Mackenzie Prize, Alec Nove Prize), The Myth of the Strong Leader: Political Leadership in the Modern Age (2014); *Recreations* novels and political memoirs, opera, ballet, watching cricket, football and tennis; *Style*— Prof Archie Brown, CMG, FBA; ✉ St Antony's College, Oxford OX2 6JF

BROWN, Ben Robert; s of Antony Victor Brown, of Smarden, Kent, and Sheila Mary, *née* McCormack; *b* 26 May 1960; *Educ* Sutton Valence, Keble Coll Oxford (open scholar, BA), UC Cardiff (Dip Journalism); *m* Geraldine Anne, *née* Ryan; 1 da (Ella Olivia b 31 Oct 1992); *Career* journalist; reporter: Radio Clyde Glasgow 1982–83, Radio City Liverpool 1983–85, Radio London 1985–86, Independent Radio News 1986–88; BBC TV News: gen reporter 1988–90, foreign affrs corr 1990–91, Moscow corr 1991–94, gen corr then foreign affrs corr 1994–; major assignments incl: fall of the Berlin Wall, Gulf War (from Riyadh and Kuwait), collapse of the Soviet Union; *Books* All Necessary Means – Inside the Gulf War (with David Shukman, 1991); *Recreations* theatre, cinema, soccer, reading novels and biographies; *Style*— Ben Brown, Esq; ✉ c/o BBC TV News, BBC Broadcasting House, Portland Place, London W1A 1AA (☎ 020 8743 8000)

BROWN, Brian Michael John; s of Arthur John Frederick Brown (d 1978), and Ethel Louise, *née* Redsull (d 1982); *b* 11 February 1937; *Educ* Sir Roger Manwoods GS Kent; *m* 1, 22 Feb 1960 (m dis 1989), Maureen Ivy Ticehurst (d 1994); 1 da (Rachel Suzanne b 17 March 1961), 2 s (Mark Stephen John b 12 March 1964, Timothy John Michael b 18 Jan 1967); m 2, 20 April 1989 (m dis 2008), Elizabeth Charlotte, da of Maj Thomas John Saywell; m 3, 16 July 2011, Lesley Mary Boswell, da of William Frederick Whittaker (d 1994); *Career* serv Royal Hampshire Regt 1955–57, Intelligence Corps 1957–58; Trustee Savings Bank: London 1959–60, South Eastern 1960–67; TSB Trust Company Ltd: mktg mangr 1967–71, gen mangr 1971–83, dir 1976, md 1983–88, chief exec 1988–91; conslt and lectr in bancassurance Zebu Consultants 1991–2007; chm: Protection & Investment Ltd 1999–2005 (dir 1999–2012), Conker Financial Servs Ltd 2004–; memb: Unit Trust Assoc Exec Ctee 1980–88, Lautro Selling Practices Ctee 1989–91, SIB Trg and Competence Panel 1992–94, Chartered Insurance Inst Accreditation Bd 1995–97; chm Andover Dist Community Health Care NHS Tst 1992–97; govr: Cricklade Coll Andover 1989–94 (chm 1991), Wherwell Primary Sch 1998–2003, King Alfred's Coll Winchester 1999–2004, UC Winchester 2004–05, Univ of Winchester 2005–09; vice-pres: Deal Wanderers RFC 1972–2005, Deal and Betteshanger Rugby Club 2005–, Winchester and Dist Macmillan Servs Appeal 1986–98, Countess of Brecknock House Charitable Tst 1998–; FIMgt 1976, FCIB 1977; Allfinanz Without Limits (1991); *Recreations* railways, coin and stamp collecting, walking, reading, concerts and theatre, eating out; *Style*— Brian Brown, Esq; ✉ Cranmore, 13 Durnford Close, Chilbolton, Stockbridge, Hampshire SO20 6AP (☎ 01264 860127)

BROWN, Catherine; *Career* formerly: fin dir and dep chief exec Newham Community Health Services NHS Tst, md BUPA Wellness, chief exec Animal Health and Veterinary Laboratories Agency DEFRA; chief exec Food Standards Agency 2012–; *Style*— Ms Catherine Brown; ✉ Food Standards Agency, Aviation House, 125 Kingsway, London WC2B 6NH

BROWN, Cedric Harold; s of late William Herbert Brown, and Constance Dorothy, *née* Frances; *b* 7 March 1935; *Educ* Sheffield, Rotherham and Derby Coll of Technol; *m* 1956, Joan Hendry; 1 s, 3 da (1 da decd); *Career* East Midlands Gas Bd: pupil gas distribution engr 1953–58, various engrg posts 1958–75; engr asst Tunbridge Wells Borough Cncl 1959–60, dir of engr E Midlands Gas 1975–78; British Gas Corporation: asst dir ops and dir construction 1978–79, dir Morecambe Bay Project 1980–87, regnl chm British Gas West Midlands 1987–89; British Gas plc: dir of exploration and prodn 1989–90, memb Bd and md 1989–91, sr md 1991–92, chief exec 1992–96; prop C B Consultants Ltd 1996–, chm Atlantic Caspian Resources plc 1999–2006, chm Intellipower 2003–06; Freeman City of London 1989, Liveryman Worshipful Co of Engrs 1988; FREng 1990, CEng, FIGasE (pres 1996–), FICE; *Publications* author of various tech papers to professional bodies; *Recreations* sport, countryside, places of historic interest; *Style*— Cedric Brown, Esq, FREng

BROWN, Christina Hambley (Tina) (Lady Evans); CBE (2000); da of George Hambley Brown, and Bettina Iris Mary, *née* Kohr (d 1998); *b* 21 November 1953; *Educ* Univ of Oxford (MA); *m* 20 Aug 1981, Sir Harold Matthew Evans, s of Frederick Albert Evans (d 1982); 1 s (George Frederick Evans b 26 Jan 1986), 1 da (Isabel Harriet Evans b 22 Oct 1990); *Career* columnist Punch 1978, ed Tatler 1979–83; ed-in-chief: Vanity Fair 1984–92, The New Yorker 1992–98, Talk magazine 1998–2002; fndr The Daily Beast 2008–13; chm Talk Media 1998–, presenter ...with Tina Brown (CNBC) 2003–05; columnist: The Times 2002, Washington Post 2003–; Catherine Pakenham Prize Most Promising Female Journalist (Sunday Times) 1973, Young Journalist of the Year 1978, Advertising Age Magazine Editor of the Year Award 1988, USC Journalism Alumni Assoc Distinguished Achievement in Journalism Award 1994; Hon Dr London Inst 2001; *Books* Loose Talk (1979), Life as a Party (1983), The Diana Chronicles (2007); *Style*— Ms Tina Brown, CBE

BROWN, Dr Christopher Paul Hadley; CBE (2011); *b* 15 April 1948; *Educ* Merchant Taylors' Sch, St Catherine's Coll Oxford (MA, Dip Art History), Courtauld Inst (PhD); *m*; 2 c; *Career* National Gallery London: asst keeper 1971–79, dep keeper 1979, curator Dutch and Flemish 17th c paintings, chief curator 1989–98; undergraduate and postgrad teaching and external examiner Courtauld Inst and UCL; fell Netherlands Inst for Advanced Study in the Humanities and Social Scis Wassenaar 1993–94; lectures at: Univ of London, Univ of Cambridge, Univ of Oxford, Univ of Utrecht, Harvard Univ, Yale Univ, Princeton Univ, NY Inst of Fine Art; memb Ctee: Assoc of Art Historians 1978–81, Art Galls Assoc 1978–80; memb British Ctee of Comité Int d'Histoire de l'Art; chm: Art History Seminar Centre for Low Countries Studies; tstee Dulwich Picture Gall; dir Ashmolean Museum Oxford 1998–; *Books* Bruegel (1975), Dutch Painting (1976), Burgundy (co-author, 1977), Rembrandt – The Complete Paintings (2 vols, 1980), Carel Fabritius – Complete Edition with a Catalogue Raisonne (1981), A Chatelet – Early Dutch Painting (co-trans, 1981), Van Dyck (1982), Scenes of Everyday Life – Seventeenth-Century Dutch Genre Painting (1984), Anthony Van Dyck: Drawings (1991), Rubens's Landscapes (1996), Van Dyck 1599–1641 (with Hans Vlieghe, 1999); author of numerous exhbn catalogues and articles in The Times, TLS, Burlington Magazine, Apollo, Nat

Gall Technical Bulletin and other jls; *Style—* Dr Christopher Brown, CBE; ✉ Ashmolean Museum, Beaumont Street, Oxford OX1 2PH (☎ 01865 278005)

BROWN, Colin; s of George Wilfred Brown (d 1970), and Gladys Lilian, *née* Carter (d 1963); *b* 8 April 1950; *Educ* Burscough Secdy Sch, Wigan Tech Coll; *m* Dorothy Amanda Golding; *Career* municipal corr: Southport Visiter 1968–73, Sheffield Star 1973–78; political corr: Yorkshire Post 1978–79, The Guardian 1978–86, The Independent 1986–; political ed: Independent on Sunday 2000–02, Sunday Telegraph 2002–04; dep political ed The Independent 2004–; chm Parly Lobby Journalists 1999–2000; *Books* Fighting Talk: The Biography of John Prescott (1997); *Recreations* skiing, windsurfing; *Clubs* Ski Club of GB, Whitstable Yacht, RYA, Soho House; *Style—* Colin Brown, Esq; ✉ The Independent, 2 Derry Street, London W8 5TT

BROWN, Prof Colin Bertram; s of Prof Leslie Julius Brown (d 1981), of South Africa, and Adolfinna Anna, *née* Rose (d 1985); *b* 24 May 1942; *Educ* King David HS South Africa, Guy's Hosp Med Sch London (BSc, MB BS, MRCS, LRCP); *m* 1, Barbara Alice, *née* Fink; 2 s (Nicholas Daniel b 1966, Jason Peter b 1971); m 2, 22 Sept 1975, Jacquelynne Anne, *née* Baldwin; 2 da (Kate Victoria b 1978, Hannah Camilla Lester b 1982); *Career* res fell Harvard Med Sch 1974–75, sr registrar Guy's Hosp 1973–78, conslt renal physician Sheffield Kidney Inst and hon prof Univ of Sheffield 1979–2007, dir ML Laboratories plc 1997–2005; chm Public Cmmn of Peritoneal Dialysis; memb: Ctee on Renal Diseases RCP, Section on Renal Disease MRC, Int Soc of Nephrology, Euro Dialysis and Transplant Assoc, Int Soc of Peritoneal Dialysis, Registry Ctee Renal Assoc of GB (sec); inventor of Adept (for abdominal adhesion prevention); FRCP 1985; *Publications* incl Manual of Renal Disease (1984); contrib incl: Guy's Hospital Reports (1965), Lancet (1970), British Journal of Urology (1972), American Journal of Physiology (1977), Cornell Seminars in Nephrology (1978), Journal of Infection (1983), British Medical Journal (1984), Transplantation (1986), Bone (1981), Clinica Chimica Acta (1988), Nephron (1989), Kidney International (1990), Nephrology Dialysis and Transplantation (1995), American Journal of Kidney Disease (1999), Harrison's Textbook of Medicine On-Line (2000), Human Reproduction (2002), Nephron (2003), Transplantation (2004), Clinical Nephrology (2006), Fertility and Sterility (2007); over 200 pubns; *Recreations* sailing, golf; *Style—* Prof C B Brown; ✉ Platts Farm, Ughill, Bradfield, Sheffield S6 6HU (☎ 01142 851334, e-mail cbbrown1@btinternet.com)

BROWN, Craig Edward Moncrieff; s of Edward Peter Moncrieff Brown (d 2001), of Duncton, W Sussex, and Hon Jennifer Mary, *née* Bethell, da of 2 Baron Bethell; *b* 23 May 1957; *Educ* Eton, Univ of Bristol; *m* 1987, Frances J M, da of (James) Colin Ross Welch (d 1997), of Aldbourne, Wilts; 1 da (Tallulah b 1988), 1 s (Silas b 1990); *Career* freelance journalist and columnist; articles for numerous newspapers and magazines incl: New Statesman, The Observer, TLS, Mail on Sunday, New York, Stern, Corrière della Serra; columnist The Times 1988– (Parly sketch writer 1987–88), restaurant critic Sunday Times 1988–93, columnist Daily Mail (Columnist of the Year – Popular, Critic of the Year and Best of Humour Press Awards 2012); columnist (as Wallace Arnold): The Spectator 1987–, Private Eye 1989–, The Independent on Sunday 1991–; columnist: Evening Standard (as Craig Brown) 1993–, The Guardian (as Bel Littlejohn) 1995–; *Books* The Marsh Marlowe Letters (1983), A Year Inside (1988), The Agreeable World of Wallace Arnold (1990), Rear Columns (1992), Welcome to My Worlds (1993), Craig Brown's Greatest Hits (1993), The Hounding of John Thenos (1994), The Private Eye Book of Craig Brown Parodies (1995), The Marsh-Marlowe Letters (2001), This is Craig Brown (2003), Craig Brown's Imaginary Friends: The Collected Parodies 2000–2004 (2004), 1966 and All That (2005), This is Tony's Britain: Craig Brown's Blair Years (2005); *Recreations* flower arrangement, needlework, tidying, deportment, macramé; *Clubs* The Academy; *Style—* Craig Brown, Esq

BROWN, Daniel; s of Paul Graham Brown, and Christine Malvern; *b* 30 May 1977, 1977, Liverpool; *Career* creative technologist; Liverpool John Moores Univ's Learning Methods Unit 1993–95, Amaze Ltd 1996, multimedia dir SHOWstudio (with Nick Knight, *qv*) 2002–, fndr Play/Create Ltd 2002–; conslt technologist Amaze plc 2011–; projects completed for: Mulberry, RSA, V&A Museum, Conran Architects, W Hotels, Park Hotels, Swarovski, Design4Science, Wellcome Fndn, Nick Knight, SHOWstudio, BBC, MagneticNorth, Sony Playstation, Visionaire, onedotzero, Amaze, Warp Records, Saatchi and Saatchi, IDEO, Vodafone, MTV, POP Magazine, Dazed and Confused, Private Commission, D'Arcy Thompson Museum Dundee, Selfridges & Co, Lady Gaga, Le Printemps Paris; works incl in perm collection: San Francisco Museum of Modern Art, V&A; *Awards* incl: Creative Futures: Stars of the New Millennium Creative Review 1999, Top Ten Web Designers Internet Business Magazine 2001, Webby Award (for SHOWstudio) 2003, Designer of Year Design Museum London 2004; *Publications* work featured in: 21st Century Design (by Marcus Fairs), Creative Island II: Inspired Design from Great Britain (by John Sorrell), The Fundamentals of Digital Art (by Richard Colson), Nick Knight (by Nick Knight), and others; *Style—* Daniel Brown, Esq; ☎ 020 7490 1608, mobile 07801 704143, e-mail daniel@danielbrowns.com, website www.danielbrowns.com

BROWN, Danielle; MBE (2013); da of Duncan Brown; *Career* Paralympic archer; achievements incl: world champion 2007, Gold medal women's compound open Paralympic Games 2008, Gold medal women's compound team (with Nicky Hunt and Nichola Simpson) Cwlth Games 2010, Gold medal women's individual compound Paralympic Games 2012; *Style—* Ms Danielle Brown, MBE

BROWN, Darren; *b* 23 April 1973; *Career* head chef: West Stoke House Chichester 2003–10 (1 Michelin Star 2008–10), Restaurant Angélique Dartmouth 2010–11, private chef in the Costwolds 2013–14, gp devpt chef The Lucky Onion Gp Cheltenham 2015–; *Style—* Darren Brown, Esq; ✉ c/o The Lucky Onion, Unit 1.5, Andoversford Industrial Estate, Cheltenham, Gloucestershire GL54 4LB

BROWN, Sir David Martin; kt (2001); s of Alan Brown (d 2012), and Laura Marjorie, *née* Richardson; *b* 14 May 1950, Wolverhampton; *Educ* Portsmouth Polytechnic (BSc); *m* 1975, Denise Frances Brown, da of Edward John Bowers; 2 s (Matthew David b 1982, Andrew James b 1986); *Career* chm Motorola Ltd 1997–2008; non-exec dir: Peninsular and Oriental Steam Navigation Co 2002–06, Domino Printing Sciences plc 2008–15; chm DRS Data & Research Services plc 2008–15, sr ind dir Ceres Power Hldgs plc 2008–12, non-exec dir TTG Global Gp Ltd (formerly Siatel Hldgs Ltd) 2010–; pres: Assoc for Sci Educn 1998, Fedn of the Electronics Industry 1999–2000, IEE 2003–04, Chartered Quality Inst 2007–08; Faraday lectr IEE 1982–83 and 1994–95; chm Br Standards Instn 2012– (non-exec dir 2010–12); visiting fell Kellogg Coll Univ of Oxford, memb Ct Cranfield Univ 2011–; fell St George's House Windsor Castle 2008–; IEE Mountbatten Medal 2005; Hon Dr: Univ of Bath, Univ of Kingston, Univ of Portsmouth, Univ of Surrey; CIMgt, CEng, Hon FIET, FREng 1999, hon fell Chartered Quality Inst (Hon FCQI); *Recreations* literature, art, theatre; *Clubs* Athenaeum; *Style—* Sir David Brown, FREng; ✉ Bridleway Cottage, Stanmore, Newbury, Berkshire RG20 8SR (☎ 01635 281825, mobile 07802 350136, e-mail sir.david.brown@googlemail.com)

BROWN, Prof David William; s of David William Brown, and Catherine, *née* Smith; *b* 1 July 1948; *Educ* Keil Sch Dunbarton, Univ of Edinburgh (MA), Oriel Coll Oxford (MA), Clare Coll Cambridge (PhD), Univ of Edinburgh (DLitt); *Career* fell, chaplain and tutor in theology and philosophy Oriel Coll Oxford 1976–90, lectr in ethics and philosophical theology Univ of Oxford 1984–90, Van Mildert prof of divinity Univ of Durham 1990–2007, canon residentiary Durham Cathedral 1990–2007, prof of theology, aesthetics and culture Univ of St Andrews 2007–15 (Wardlaw prof 2008–15); C of E: memb Doctrine Cmmn 1985–95, memb Gen Synod 1991–95; tstee Scott Holland Tst 1983–2009, govr St Stephen's House Oxford 1984–2008; FBA 2002, FRSE 2012; *Books* Choices: Ethics and the Christian (1983), The Divine Trinity (1985), Continental Philosophy and Modern Theology (1987), Signs of Grace (with D Fuller, 1995), Tradition and Imagination (1999), Discipleship and Imagination (2000), God and Enchantment of Place (2004), Through the Eyes of the Saints (2005), God and Grace of Body (2007), God and Mystery in Words (2008), Divine Humanity (2011), Durham Cathedral: History, Fabric and Culture (2015); *Recreations* listening to music, gardening; *Style—* Prof David Brown; ✉ School of Divinity, St Mary's College, St Andrews, Fife KY16 9JU

BROWN, Derren; *b* 27 February 1971, Croydon, Surrey; *Educ* Whitgift Sch, Univ of Bristol; *Career* psychological illusionist; *Theatre* incl: Derren Brown Live 2003 and 2004, Something Wicked This Way Comes (UK tour) 2005 and 2006 (Olivier Award 2005), Svengali (UK tour) 2011– (Best Entertainment and Family Olivier Award 2012); *Television* incl: Mind Control 2000–01, Derren Brown Plays Russian Roulette Live 2003, Trick of the Mind 2004–06, Séance 2004, Messiah 2005, The Gathering 2005, The Heist 2006, Trick or Treat 2007–08, The System 2008, An Evening of Wonders 2009, The Events 2009, Derren Brown Investigates 2010, The Experiments 2011 (Best Entertainment Prog RTS Award 2012, Best Entertainment Prog BAFTA 2012); *Books* Pure Effect (2000), Absolute Magic (2003), Tricks of the Mind (2006); *Recreations* taxidermy, parrots, single malts; *Style—* Derren Brown; ✉ c/o Michael Vine, Michael Vine Associates, 1 Stormont Road, London N6 4NS

BROWN, Edward Forrest (Ted); s of George J Brown (d 1971), of Aberdeen, and Margaret, *née* Forrest (d 1996); *b* 14 August 1951; *Educ* Warwick Sch, Lanchester Poly Coventry (BA); *m* 1980, Frances Mary, da of Brian Houlden; 2 da (Catherine b 17 Oct 1983, Lyndsay b 26 Sept 1986), 1 s (Douglas b 24 Aug 1988); *Career* commercial trainee British Steel 1970–74; mktg mangr: Kwikform Ltd 1974–79, Bland Payne UK/Segwick Gp 1979–81; successively trainee exec, branch mangr, mktg mangr, divisional mangr, divisional md, area md, regnl md, chief operating offr and sector md Rentokil Ltd/Rentokil Initial plc 1981–2006; ceo: Morgan Everett plc 2006–09, Morgan Everett Ltd; chm Cophall Associates Ltd 2006–; non-exec dir: Morrison Facility Servs 2008–13, Moat Housing Gp 2008–14, Norland Managed Services 2009–14; chm Energy Saving Tst 2012–; non-exec dir Anticimex 2013–; Freeman Worshipful Co of World Traders 2007; MInstD 1999; *Recreations* music, tennis, riding, sailing, skiing; *Clubs* RAC, Cwlth, Royal Scots; *Style—* Edward F Brown; ✉ Cophall Associates, Cophall, Fairwarp, East Sussex TN22 3BU (☎ 01825 713472, e-mail edward.brown@cophall.com)

BROWN, Gavin Lindberg; s of William Lindberg Brown, of Edinburgh, and Jacqueline, *née* Currie; *b* 4 June 1975, Kirkcaldy, Fife; *Educ* Fettes (Wallace meml scholar, head boy), Univ of Strathclyde (LLB, Dip LP); *m* 7 July 2006, Hilary Jane, *née* Fergus; 1 da (Ava Catherine b 10 April 2007), 2 s (Gregor Lindberg b 30 June 2009, Callan John Fergus b 24 Sept 2011); *Career* slr McGrigor Donald 1998–2002, dir Speak with Impact Ltd 2002–; MSP (Cons) Lothians 2007–16, shadow min for enterprise, energy and tourism 2007–11, shadow min for finance, employment and sustainable growth 2011–15; memb Jr Chamber Int (JCI World Debating Champion 1999 and 2002, JCI Most Outstanding Trainer in the World 2004); memb Law Soc of Scot; *Recreations* Tae Kwon Do (black belt, 1st degree); *Style—* Gavin Brown, Esq; ✉ e-mail gavin@speakwithimpact.com, website www.speakwithimpact.com

BROWN, Geoffrey Howard; s of John Howard Brown (d 1983), and Nancy, *née* Fardoe (d 1996); *b* 1 March 1949; *Educ* King Henry VIII GS Coventry, Pembroke Coll Cambridge (BA), Sch of Film and TV RCA (MA); *m* 16 Sept 1985, Catherine Ann, da of Adolf Surowiec; *Career* contrib to Time Out 1974–81, contrib to Monthly Film Bulletin 1974–91, dep film critic Financial Times 1977–81, film critic Radio Times 1981–89, music critic The Times 1999– (dep film critic 1981–90, film critic 1990–98); *Books* Walter Forde (1977), Launder and Gilliat (1977), Der Produzent – Michael Balcon und der Englische Film (1981), Michael Balcon – The Pursuit of British Cinema (lead essay, 1984), The Common Touch – The Films of John Baxter (1989), Directors in British and Irish Cinema (assoc ed, 2006), Alistair Cooke at the Movies (ed, 2009); *Recreations* art exhibitions, children's books; *Style—* Geoffrey Brown, Esq

BROWN, Rt Hon (James) Gordon; PC (1996); s of Rev Dr John Brown (d 1998), and J Elizabeth Brown (d 2004); *b* 20 February 1951; *Educ* Kirkcaldy HS, Univ of Edinburgh (MA, PhD); *m* 3 Aug 2000, Sarah Jane, da of Ian Macauley; *Career* rector Univ of Edinburgh 1972–75 (temp lectr 1975–76), lectr in politics Glasgow Coll of Technol 1976–80, journalist then ed Current Affairs Dept Scottish TV 1980–83; memb Scottish Exec Lab Party 1977–83, Parly candidate (Lab) S Edinburgh 1979, MP (Lab) Dunfermline E 1983–2005, Kirkcaldy & Cowdenbeath 2005–15, chm Lab Party in Scotland 1983–2010, oppn front bench spokesman on trade and industry 1985–87, memb Shadow Cabinet 1987–97, shadow chief sec to the Treasy 1987–89, chief oppn spokesman on trade and industry 1989–92, chief oppn spokesman on Treasy and econ affrs (shadow chllr) 1992–97, chllr of the Exchequer 1997–2007, Prime Minister, First Lord of the Treasury and Minister for the Civil Service 2007–10; memb TGWU; Hon DCL Univ of Newcastle upon Tyne 2007; *Books* Maxton (1986), Where There Is Greed (1989), John Smith: Life and Soul of the Party (1994), Values Visions and Voices: An Anthology of Socialism (1995); *Recreations* tennis, films, reading; *Style—* The Rt Hon Gordon Brown

BROWN, Graham Stephen; s of Frank George John Brown, and Gwen, *née* Thompson; *b* 28 November 1944; *Educ* Farnborough Sch, Univ of Bristol (LLB), KCL (LLM), Catholic Univ of Louvain (Dip); *m* 1972, Jacqueline, da of John Purtill, of Dublin; *Career* Payne Hicks Beach Solicitors: admitted slr 1969, ptnr 1972, sr ptnr 1994–2008, conslt 2009–14; sometime memb: Capital Taxes Sub-Ctee and Fin Servs Act Working Party of Law Soc, Ctee Holborn Law Soc; hon bencher Lincoln's Inn 2009–; tstee: Arthritis Research Campaign until 2008, Nat Churches Tst until 2011, St John's Smith Square until 2012; presentation govr Christ's Hosp; Liveryman Worshipful Co of Clockmakers; FRSA; *Books* A Lincoln's Inn Commonplace Book (2016); *Recreations* music, theatre, fine arts and architecture; *Clubs* Clifton, Athenaeum; *Style—* Graham S Brown; ✉ Payne Hicks Beach, 10 New Square, Lincoln's Inn, London WC2A 3QG (☎ 020 7465 4300, fax 020 7465 4400, e-mail gbrown@phb.co.uk)

BROWN, Hamish Macmillan; MBE (2001); s of William Dick Brown (d 1968), of Dollar and Kinghorn, and Effie Grace, *née* Swanson (d 1988); *b* 13 August 1934; *Educ* Dollar Acad; *Career* Nat Serv RAF Egypt and E Africa; asst Martyrs Meml Church Paisley 1958–59, outdoor educn Braehead Sch 1960–71, outdoor activities adviser Fife 1972–73; freelance author, photographer, lectr, poet, mountaineer, traveller and authority on Morocco 1974–; served SMLTB, dir SROW, creator TGO Challenge event; expeditions to: Morocco, Andes, Himalayas, Arctic, Africa, etc; contribs in over 100 pubns; Hon DLitt Univ of St Andrews 1997, DUniv Open 2007; FRSGS 1990; *Books* Hamish's Mountain Walk (1978, SAC Award, 2 edn 2010), Hamish's Groats End Walk (1981, shortlist for W H Smith Travel Prize), Poems of the Scottish Hills (1982), Speak to the Hills (1985), The Great Walking Adventure (1986), Travels (1986), Hamish Brown's Scotland (1988), The Island of Rhum (1988), Climbing the Corbetts (1988), Scotland Coast to Coast (1990), Walking the Summits of Somerset and Avon (1991), From the Pennines to the Highlands (1992), Fort William and Glen Coe Walks (1992), The Bothy Brew (short stories, 1993), The Last Hundred (1994), 25 Walks Skye & Kintail (2000), Along the Fife Coast Path (2004), 25 Walks Fife (2005), Seton Gordon's Scotland (2005), Exploring the Edinburgh to Glasgow Canal (2006), The Mountains Look on Marrakech (2007), A Scottish Graveyard Miscellany (2008), Achnashellach (poems, 2008), Seton Gordon's Cairngorms

(2010), Hamish's Mountain Walk, Hamish's Groat End Walk, Climbing the Corbetts (series, 2010–12), Walking the Mull Hills (2011), The Oldest Post Office in the World and Other Scottish Oddities (2012), The High Atlas (2012), Tom Weir, An Anthology (2013), Fantasies, Fables, Fibs and Frolics (stories, 2014); *Recreations* canoeing, alpine flowers, gardening, music, books; *Clubs* Alpine, Scottish Mountaineering; *Style*— Dr Hamish M Brown, MBE; ✉ 3 Links Place, Burntisland, Fife KY3 9DY (☎ 01592 873546)

BROWN, Heath Garydd Albert Edward; s of Frederick Brown, and Marina May, *née* Ward; *b* Radcliffe Hall, Radcliffe, Lancs; *Educ* The Derby GS Radcliffe, Rochdale Coll of Art, St Martin's Sch of Art (BA), Cambridge Sch of Art Anglia Ruskin Univ Cambridge (MA); *Career* concurrently freelance journalist London Evening Standard, You magazine, German Vogue and British W 1991–92, dep ed-in-chief International Collections Magazine (menswear lifestyle quarterly) 1992–94, contributing fashion ed Financial Times and The Times Saturday magazine 1994–95, fashion news ed FHM magazine 1995–96, fashion dir The Times Magazine 1996–2004, contrib style writer Daily Telegraph 2004–06, sr reporter The Daily London and freelance ed 2009–, conslt ed Matches Magazine and Matchesfashion.com 2011–13; fine art photographer with exhibitions in London, Cambridge and the Netherlands; visiting lectr Univ of the Arts London 2016–; memb Press Ctee Br Fashion Cncl, memb Chartered Inst of Journalists; memb Lab Pty; MRPS; *Recreations* hill walking, travel, sculpture, photography; *Clubs* Met Bar, Soho House; *Style*— Heath Brown, Esq; ✉ www.heathbrown.net

BROWN, Dr Iain Gordon; s of Reginald Sydney Brown (d 1982), of Durban, South Africa and Edinburgh, and Irene, *née* Young; *b* 10 October 1950; *Educ* George Watson's Coll, Univ of Edinburgh (MA), St John's Coll Cambridge (PhD); *m* 2006, Dr Patricia Rosalind Andrew, da of late Prof E Raymond Andrew, FRS; *Career* pt/t lectr Dept of Extra-Mural Studies Univ of Edinburgh 1975–76, asst keeper Dept of Manuscripts Nat Library of Scotland 1977–99; curator of seven major and many smaller exhbns 1978–2011, princ curator Manuscripts Division 1999–2011, hon fell Nat Library of Scotland 2012; author of approx 250 articles in learned jls, essays, reviews, exhbn catalogues and book chapters, contrib to several major standard works of reference; Scottish rep Friends of the Nat Libraries 1985–, memb Advsy Ctee Yale Edns of the Private Papers of James Boswell 1987–, vice-pres Edinburgh Decorative and Fine Arts Soc (NADFAS) 1990–; Old Edinburgh Club: memb Cncl 1989–93 and 1995–2010, memb Editorial Bd 1991–, vice-pres 1996–2003 and 2005–07, pres 2007–10; memb Robert Adam Bicentenary Co-ordinating Ctee 1990–92, chm James Craig Bicentenary Publications Ctee 1994–95; memb David Hume Commemoration Ctee Saltire Soc 1993–98, memb D O Hill Bicentenary Ctee 2000–02; memb Editorial Advsy Bd The History of the Book in Scotland 1998–, memb Editorial Bd Scottish Archives 2005–; memb Cncl Scottish Records Assoc 1998–2004 and 2006–09; tstee Penicuik House Preservation Tst 1985–, pres Edinburgh Sir Walter Scott Club 2009–10, tstee Edinburgh World Heritage Tst 2011–14, memb Curatorial Expert Advsy Panel Abbotsford Tst 2011–, memb Jt Abbotsford Advsy Ctee Faculty of Advocates 2012–; conslt to Adam Drawings Project Sir John Soane's Museum 2014–; memb Incorporation of Hammermen of Edinburgh 1995–; Burgess and Free Citizen of Edinburgh 2007; FSA Scot (memb Cncl 1989–92, memb Editorial Bd of Soc's Proceedings 1992–2002), FRSA 1980, FSA 1985 (memb Cncl 2000–03), FRSE 1997 (curator RSE, memb Exec Bd and tstee RSE Scotland Fndn 2012–); *Books* Scottish Architects at Home and Abroad (with T A Cherry, 1978), The Hobby-Horsical Antiquary (1980), Poet and Painter: Allan Ramsay, Father and Son 1684–1784 (1984), The Clerks of Penicuik: Portraits of Taste and Talent (1987), History of Scottish Literature, vol II: 1660–1800 (contrib, 1987), Scott's Interleaved Waverley Novels: An Introduction and Commentary (ed and princ contrb, 1987), Building for Books: The Architectural Evolution of the Advocates' Library 1689–1925 (1989), For the Encouragement of Learning: Scotland's National Library (contrib, 1989), Monumental Reputation: Robert Adam and the Emperor's Palace (1992), The Role of the Amateur Architect (contrib, 1994), The Todholes Aisle (ed, 1994), Scottish Country Houses (contrib, 1995), James Craig 1744–1795 (contrib, 1995), Elegance and Entertainment in the New Town of Edinburgh (1995, reprinted 1997 and 2002), Antonio Canova: The Three Graces (contrib, 1995), Witness to Rebellion (with H Cheape, 1996, reprinted 2010), The Tiger and the Thistle (contrib, 1999), Allan Ramsay and the Search for Horace's Villa (ed and contrib, 2001), International Dictionary of Library Histories (contrib, 2001), Egypt through the Eyes of Travellers (contrib, 2002), Abbotsford and Sir Walter Scott: The Image and the Influence (ed and contrib, 2003), Archives and Excavations (contrib, 2004), The Grand Tour and its Influence (contrib, 2008), Scots in London in the Eighteenth Century (contrib, 2010), Rax Me That Buik (2010), History of the Book in Scotland (contrib, 2012), James Hall: Diario Siciliano (introduction, 2013), Scotland's Cultural Identity and Standing (contrib, 2013), David Hume: My Own Life (ed, 2014); *Recreations* travel, the Mediterranean world, looking at buildings, military history, books, antiquarian pursuits, buying ties, raking in skips; *Clubs* New (Edinburgh); *Style*— Dr Iain Gordon Brown, FSA, FRSE; ✉ 4 Abercromby Place, Edinburgh EH3 6JX (☎ 0131 556 6929, e-mail voleforceone@btinternet.com

BROWN, Ian; s of George Brown, and Jean Brown; *b* 20 February 1963, Warrington, Cheshire; *m* Fabiola; 1 s (Emilio), 2 other s (Frankie, Casey); *Career* musician; lead vocalist Stone Roses 1984–96, solo artist 1996–; top 20 singles incl: My Star 1998, Corpses in Their Mouths 1998, Be There (UNKLE featuring Ian Brown) 1999, Dolphins Were Monkeys 2000, F.E.A.R 2001, Keep What Ya Got 2004, Time is My Everything 2005, All Ablaze 2005; albums: Unfinished Monkey Business 1998, Golden Greats 1999, Music of the Spheres 2001, Remixes of the Spheres 2002, Solarized 2004, The Greatest (compilation) 2005; Godlike Genius NME Award 2006; *Style*— Ian Brown, Esq; ✉ c/o Natalie Nissim, Fiction Records (Polydor), 364–366 Kensington High Street, London W14 8NS

BROWN, Ian; s of Ronald Brown (d 1983), and Jessie, *née* Bowtell (d 2002); *b* 8 March 1951, Sawbridgeworth, Herts; *Educ* King's Sch Ely, Central Sch of Speech and Drama (Dip Dramatic Art); *Career* artistic dir Tag Theatre Co Glasgow 1984–88, artistic dir Traverse Theatre Edinburgh 1988–96, artistic dir and chief exec West Yorkshire Playhouse 2002–12, ind theatre maker Ian Brown Prodns 2012–; freelance teacher of acting; *Recreations* travel, architecture, design, film, theatre, opera, art; *Style*— Ian Brown, Esq; ✉ e-mail ianbrownlondon@hotmail.com

BROWN, Prof Ian James Morris; s of Bruce Beveridge Brown (d 1957), of Alloa, Scotland, and Eileen Frances, *née* Carnegie (d 1986); *b* 28 February 1945; *Educ* Dollar Acad, Univ of Edinburgh and Crewe and Alsager Coll (MA, DipEd, MLitt, PhD); *m* 8 June 1968 (m dis 1997), Judith Ellen, da of George Woodall Sidaway, of Adelaide; 1 da (Emily b 1972), 1 s (Joshua b 1977); m 2, 7 June 1997, Nicola Dawn, da of Donald Robert Axford; *Career* playwright 1967–, poet 1977–; sch teacher 1967–69 and 1970–71; lectr in drama: Dunfermline Coll Edinburgh 1971–76, Br Cncl Edinburgh and Istanbul 1976–78; princ lectr Crewe and Alsager Coll 1978–86 (seconded as sec Cork Enq into Professional Theatre 1985–86); drama dir Arts Cncl of GB 1986–94; prof and dean Faculty of Arts Queen Margaret UC Edinburgh 1999–2002 (reader in drama 1994–95, head Drama Dept 1995–99); dir Scottish Centre for Cultural Management and Policy 1996–2002; int arts and educn conslt 2002–09; freelance scholar 2007–10, prof in drama Kingston Univ 2010–14 (emeritus prof 2014–); visiting prof in Scottish lit Glasgow Univ 2006–, external prof Centre for the Study of Media and Culture in Small Nations Univ of Glamorgan 2006–13; prog dir Alsager Arts Centre 1980–86; chm Scot Soc of Playwrights 1973–75, 1984–87, 1997–99 and 2010–13, convenor NW Playwrights' Workshop 1982–85, pres Assoc for Scottish Literary Studies 2010–15 (publications convenor 2012–), vice-chair Standing Conference of Univ Drama Depts 2013–16; memb Cncl Saltire Soc 2010– (memb Exec Bd 2011–, nat convenor 2014–16); chm: British Theatre Inst 1985–87 (vice-chm 1983–85), Dionysia Chianti World Festival of Theatre 1991–93; chm: Highlands and Islands Theatre Network 2005–09, Dràma Na h-Alba theatre festival 2005–08; FRSA 1991, FHEA 2010; *Books* Antolоija Auvremene kotske Drame (An Anthology of Contemporary Scottish Drama, ed, 1999), Kulturnig Turizm: Konvergentsiga Kultury Turizmana Poroge XXI veka (Cultural Tourism: the convergence of culture and tourism at the start of the 21st Century) (ed, 2001), Poems for Joan (2001), Journey's Beginning: The Gateway Theatre Building and Company, 1884–1965 (ed, 2004), The Edinburgh History of Scottish Literature (3 vols, gen ed, 2007), Changing Identities: Ancient Roots (ed, 2006), The Edinburgh Companions to Scottish Literature (series ed, 2007–13), The Edinburgh Companion to Twentieth-Century Scottish Literature (jt ed, 2009), From Tartan to Tartanry: Scottish Culture, History and Myth (ed, 2010), The Edinburgh Companion to Scottish Drama (ed, 2011), Literary Tourism, The Trossachs and Walter Scott (ed, 2012), Lion's Milk: Poems by Scottish Poets on Turkish Topics (jtly, 2012), Scottish Theatre: Diversity, Language, Continuity (2013), The International Companions to Scottish Literature (series ed, 2013–), Roots and Fruits: Scottish Identities, History and Contemproary Literature (jt ed, 2014), Collyshangles Among the Canopy (poems, 2015), History as Theatrical Metaphor: History, Myth and National Identities in Modern Scottish Drama (2016); *Plays* incl: Antigone 1969, Mother Earth 1970, The Bacchae 1972, Positively the Last Final Farewell Performance (ballet scenario) 1972, Carnegie 1973, Rune (choral work) 1973, The Knife 1973, Rabelais 1973, The Fork 1976, New Reekie 1977, Mary 1977, Runners 1978, Mary Queen and the Loch Tower 1979, Pottersville 1982, Joker in the Pack 1983, Beatrice 1989, First Strike 1990, The Scotch Play 1991, Bacchai 1991, Wasting Reality 1992, Margaret 2000, A Great Reckonin 2000, An Act o Love 2011; *Recreations* theatre, cooking, sport, travel; *Style*— Prof Ian Brown; ✉ 15/3 Bells Brae, Edinburgh EH4 3BJ

BROWN, Jeremy Ronald Coventry; s of Kenneth Coventry Brown, MBE (d 1987), of Durban, South Africa, and Mavis Kathleen, *née* Keal; *b* 2 May 1948; *Educ* Westville Boys HS, Univ of Natal (MSc), Univ of South Africa (B Iuris); *m* 23 Nov 1996, Stephanie, *née* Pollak; *Career* Spoor and Fisher (patent attorneys) South Africa 1971–78, Linklaters London 1978–; pres Licensing Execs Soc Int 1995–96; memb: Licensing Execs Soc Br and Ireland (pres 1991–92), Cncl AIPPI UK; *Recreations* tennis, travel, the Arts; *Clubs* Roehampton, Kelvin Grove (Cape Town), Durban Country; *Style*— Jeremy Brown, Esq; ✉ Linklaters, One Silk Street, London EC2Y 8HQ (☎ 020 7456 2000)

BROWN, Dr John; CBE (2011); *Educ* Univ of Edinburgh (BSc, PhD) Middlesex Business Sch (MBA); *Career* Acambis plc: fin dir 1995–97, ceo 1997–2003; chm: BTG plc 2008–12, Axis-Shield plc 2010–12 (memb Bd 2009–), Cell Therapy Catapult Ltd, CXR Biosciences Ltd, ProStrakan Gp, Touch Bionics Ltd; non-exec dir: Vectura Gp plc, BioCity Nottingham Ltd, Electrical Geodesics Inc; non-exec dir Technol Strategy Bd 2004–13; chm Scottish Life Sciences Assoc 2008–14, co-chair LISAB (Life Sciences Advsy Bd), chm Roslin Fndn; hon prof Univ of Edinburgh; FRSE; *Recreations* golf, skiing; *Style*— Dr John Brown, CBE, FRSE; ✉ ProStrakan Group, Galabank Business Park, Galashiels TD1 1QH (e-mail john@brown-net.com)

BROWN, Prof John Campbell; OBE (2016); s of John Brown, of Dumbarton, and Jane Livingstone Stewart, *née* Campbell; *b* 4 February 1947; *Educ* Dumbarton Acad, Univ of Glasgow (numerous undergraduate prizes and bursaries, Denny Medal, Kelvin Prize and Medal, BSc, PhD, DSc); *m* 18 Aug 1972, Dr Margaret Isobel Logan, da of Dr James Cameron Purse Logan; 1 s (Stuart John Logan b 30 June 1976), 1 da (Lorna Margaret b 9 May 1979); *Career* Univ of Glasgow: lectr in astronomy 1968–78, sr lectr 1978–80, reader 1980–84, prof of astrophysics 1984–96, regius prof of astronomy 1996–2010, emeritus prof 2010–; hon prof: Univ of Edinburgh 1996–, Univ of Aberdeen 1997–; Astronomer Royal for Scotland 1995–; visitorships: Harvard-Smithsonian Observatory Massachusetts 1967 and 1969, Univ of Tübingen 1971–72, Univ of Utrecht 1973–74, Australian Nat Univ 1975, NCAR High Altitude Observatory Colorado 1977 and 2010, Univ of Maryland 1980, Nuffield science research fell Univ of Amsterdam and Univ of Calif San Diego 1984, Brittingham prof Univ of Wisconsin Madison 1987, Univ of Sydney 1993, Spinoza visiting fell Univ of Amsterdam 1999, Trinity Coll Dublin 2011; visiting fell: Eigenodische Technische Hochschule (ETH) Zürich 1999, Centre Nationale de Recherche Spatial (CNRS) Paris Observatory 1999, Universities Space Research Assoc (USRA) NASA Goddard 1999; visiting prof Univ of Alabama Huntsville 2003–, visiting scientist Univ of California Berkeley 2005, emeritus fell Leverhulme 2012–16; memb Cncl: RSE 1997–2000, RAS 2013–; Marlar lectr Rice Univ TX 2006; Inst of Physics Award for Promoting Public Understanding of Physics 2003, Royal Astronomical Soc Gold Medal (Geophysics) 2012; FRAS 1973, FRSE 1984, FInstP 1996; *Books* Inverse Problems in Astronomy (with I J D Craig, 1986), The Sun: A Laboratory for Astrophysics (ed with J T Schmelz, 1993); *Recreations* oil painting, jewellery making, woodwork, magic, cycling, walking, photography, reading; *Style*— Prof John C Brown, OBE, FRSE; ✉ 21 Bradfield Avenue, Glasgow G12 0QH (☎ 0141 581 6789); Astronomy and Astrophysics Group, School of Physics and Astronomy, University of Glasgow, Glasgow G12 8QQ (☎ 07976 270904, e-mail john.brown@glasgow.ac.uk)

BROWN, John Davies; *b* 1964; *Career* formerly: finance dir Paladin Resources, dir Br Linen Advsrs, gp finance dir Thistle Mining Inc; currently finance dir BowLeven plc; *Recreations* golf, shooting, arts; *Clubs* Bruntsfield Links Golfing Soc, Scottish Arts; *Style*— John Brown, Esq; ✉ Gulf Marine Services plc, 40 Dukes Place, London EC3A 7NH

BROWN, John Domenic Weare; s of Sir John Gilbert Newton Brown, CBE (d 2003), and Virginia, *née* Braddell (d 2009); *b* 29 May 1953, London; *Educ* Westminster, London Coll of Printing (HND); *m* 14 Dec 1987, Claudia Frances, *née* Zeff; 1 da (Lily Rebecca Zeff b 17 Sept 1989), 1 s (Jack Samuel Darcy b 6 April 1993); *Career* book publishing various companies 1975–82, md Virgin Books 1982–87, fndr and chm John Brown Publishing 1987–2004, fndr and chm John Brown Enterprises 2004–, chm: Bob Books Ltd 2006–, Wild Frontiers Ltd 2008–, Pippa Small Ltd 2013–; dir: John Wisden & Co 2003–08, Wanderlust Publications 2004–13, Punk Publishing, Songlines Ltd 2013–; tstee Keiskamma Tst, tstee Sch of Social Entrepreneurs 2009–, chm Camara UK 2010–; memb PPA 1998–2004; hon fell Univ of the Arts 2011; Marcus Morris Award 1997; *Recreations* music, cars, travel, sport; *Clubs* Soho House; *Style*— John Brown, Esq; ✉ c/o John Brown, 241A Portobello Road, London W11 1LT (☎ 020 7243 7400, fax 020 7243 7433, e-mail john@johnbrown.co.uk)

BROWN, John Neville; CBE (1995); s of Alfred Herbert Brown (d 1978), of Tutbury, Staffs, and Jessie Wright (d 1991); *b* 18 November 1935; *Educ* Denstone Coll, Selwyn Coll Cambridge (MA); *m* 3 April 1965, Ann Hilliar (d 2002), da of George William Hubert Edmonds; 1 da (Sara Elizabeth Hilliar b 2 July 1966), 1 s (Hamish John Benedict b 19 Dec 1968); *Career* articled clerk Shipley Blackburn Sutton & Co (Chartered Accountants) 1960–63; Ernst & Young (and predecessors): sr 1965, mangr 1968, ptnr 1986–94; princ VAT conslt Binder Hamlyn 1994–95; pres VAT Practitioners' Gp 1992–96; pt/t memb VAT and Duties Tbnls until 2010; pres Old Denstonian Club 1997–98, vice-pres World Pheasant Assoc; fin advsr and memb Cncl Staffordshire Regt until 2007, chm Bucks Army Cadet League 1995–2001, memb Staffordshire Regtl Charity 2007–10; chm Friends of the Vale of Aylesbury 2003–09; hon treas and chm Leonard Cheshire Thames Valley Care at Home Service until 2005, hon treas and memb Cncl The Calvert Tst 2000–03, tstee Hindu Kush Conservation Assoc, churchwarden St Margaret Lothbury until 2008, chm Friends of St Mary's Haddenham, pres Haddenham and District Rotary Club 2013–14; hon treas: The Old Berkeley Beagles until 2013, Aylesbury Vale Prostate Cancer Support Gp, Haddenham Cons Assoc, After Eights Past Masters' Assoc; Liveryman Worshipful Co of Tax Advsrs, Liveryman Worshipful Co of Plaisterers, Master Worshipful Co of Glovers 2007–08; FCA 1964, AInsT 1966, FRGS 1988; *Recreations* photography, travel, fishing, reading, ornithology, conservation; *Clubs* Royal Over-Seas League; *Style*— John Brown, Esq, CBE; ✉ 22 Wykeham Way, Haddenham, Aylesbury, Buckinghamshire HP17 8BX (☎ and fax 01844 290430, e-mail john.n.brown@btinternet.com)

BROWN, Rev Prof Judith Margaret (Mrs P J Diggle); da of Rev W G Brown (d 1968), of London, and Joan Margaret, *née* Adams (d 1998); sis of Peter Brown, CBE, *qv*; *b* 9 July 1944, India; *Educ* Sherborne Sch for Girls, Girton Coll Cambridge (exhibitioner, MA, PhD, research studentship); *m* 21 July 1984, Peter James Diggle (d 2015), s of late J Diggle; 1 s (James Wilfred Lachlan b 9 Nov 1986); *Career* Girton Coll Cambridge: research fell 1968–70, official fell 1970–71, dir of studies in history 1969–71; Univ of Manchester: lectr in history 1971–82, sr lectr 1982–90, reader-elect 1990; Beit prof of cwlth history Univ of Oxford and fell Balliol Coll 1990–2011, emeritus fell Balliol Coll Oxford 2011–; tstee Charles Wallace Tst 1996–2008, memb Scholars' Cncl Library of Congress Washington DC 2001–09; govr: Bath Spa Univ (formerly Bath Coll of HE) 1997–2011, SOAS Univ of London 1999–2007, Sherborne Sch for Girls 2003–14; ordained deacon C of E 2009, ordained priest C of E 2010; Hon DSSc Univ of Natal 2001; memb Academia Europaea 2011; FRHistS 1972; *Books* Gandhi's Rise to Power: Indian Politics 1915–22 (1972), Gandhi and Civil Disobedience. The Mahatma in Indian Politics 1928–34 (1977), Men and Gods in a Changing World (1980), Modern India: The Origins of an Asian Democracy (1984, 2 edn 1994), Gandhi. Prisoner of Hope (1989, Italian trans 1995), Migration. The Asian Experience (ed with Prof Rosemary Foot, *qv*, 1994), Gandhi and South Africa. Principles and Politics (ed with Prof Martin Prozesky, 1996), Hong Kong's Transitions, 1842–1997 (ed with Prof Rosemary Foot, 1997), Nehru (1999), The Oxford History of the British Empire Vol IV: 20th Century (ed with WR Louis, 1999), Christians, Culture and India's Religious Traditions (ed with R E Frykenberg, 2002), Nehru: A Political Life (2003), Global South Asians: Introducing the Modern Diaspora (2006), Mahatma Gandhi The Essential Writings (2008), Windows into the Past: Life Histories and the Historian of South Asia (2009), The Cambridge Companion to Gandhi (ed with A Parel, 2011); *Recreations* gardening, classical music; *Style*— Rev Prof Judith M Brown; ✉ Balliol College, Oxford OX1 3BJ

BROWN, June Muriel; MBE (2008); da of Henry William Brown (d 1960), and Louisa Ann, *née* Butler (d 1961); *b* 16 February 1927, Suffolk; *Educ* Ipswich HS, Old Vic Drama Sch London; *m* 1, John Garley (d 1957); m 2, Robert Arnold (d 2003); 5 da (Louise b 1959, Chloe b 1960 d 1960, Sophie b 1961, Chloe b 1964, Naomi b 1966), 1 s (William b 1962); *Career* actress; Hon MA Univ of E London, hon doctorate Univ Campus Suffolk; *Television* incl: Nora 1969, Doctor Who 1973–74, South Riding 1974, The Prince and the Pauper 1976, The Duchess of Duke Street 1976–77, Now and Then 1984, LACE 1984, EastEnders 1985–93, 1997–2012 and 2013–, Performance Bed 1995, Gormenghast 2000, Margery and Gladys 2003; *Film* incl: It Started in Paradise 1952, Inadmissable Evidence 1969, Sunday Bloody Sunday 1971, Straw Dogs 1971, Psychomania 1972, The Fourteen 1973, Murder by Decree 1979, Nijinsky 1980, Misunderstood 1984, Bean: The Movie 1997; *Theatre* incl: Provok'd Wife (Vaudeville Theatre) 1963, seasons at Royal Court Theatre 1970s, Letters Home (New End Theatre) 1980, Double D (Edinburgh Festival and King's Head London) 1993, Absolute Hell (NT) 1994, Calendar Girls (Noel Coward Theatre) 2009; *Style*— Ms June Brown, MBE; ✉ c/o A I M, Fairfax House, Fulwood Place, London WC1V 6HU

BROWN, Karen Veronica; *née* Jennings; da of John David Jennings, and Katharine Veronica Mary, *née* Pollok (d 1996); *b* 13 July 1952; *Educ* Benenden Sch, Univ of Bristol (LLB), Camberwell Sch of Arts, Univ of the Arts London (BA); *m* 1, 1978, (m dis 1988), Mark Brown; m 2, 1999, John Blake; *Career* with Granada TV 1979–87; Channel Four TV: Dispatches 1987–92, commissioning ed for educn 1992–96, controller of factual progs 1996–97, dep dir of progs 1997–2001, md 4Learning 2000–01; non-exec dir The Television Corp 2002–06; accredited mediator; assoc PMDU; memb Gen Teaching Cncl for England 2002–05, Learning Champion Royal Botanical Gardens Kew 2006–07, chair Action Aid, tstee Action Aid Int until 2010, tstee Mary Ward Settlement and Space to Create until 2013, chair Oxfam GB and tstee Oxfam Int 2011–, chair Booktrust 2014–, tstee Ravensbourne Coll 2014–; FRSA 1998; *Recreations* making and looking at art, walking; *Clubs* BAFTA; *Style*— Ms Karen Brown

BROWN, Keith; MSP; *b* 20 December 1961, Edinburgh; *Educ* Tynecastle HS Edinburgh, Univ of Dundee; *Career* served with Royal Marines; MSP (SNP): Ochil 2007–11, Clackmannanshire and Dunblane 2011–; minister for schs and skills 2009–10, min for housing and tport 2010–14, cabinet sec for infrastructure, investment and cities 2014–16, cabinet sec for economy, jobs and work 2016; *Style*— Keith Brown, Esq, MSP; ✉ The Scottish Parliament, Edinburgh EH99 1SP

BROWN, Keith Clark; OBE (2015); s of George Harold Brown (d 1970), and Sophie Eleanor, *née* Clark; *b* 14 January 1943; *Educ* Forest Sch, City of London Coll; *m* Rita Hildegard, da of Jack Stanley Rolfe (d 1977); 1 da (Lucy b 1976), 1 s (Timothy b 1979); *Career* stockbroker and investment banker; ptnr W Greenwell & Co 1978–86, md Greenwell Montagu Securities 1987, md Morgan Stanley Dean Witter 1987–99; chm Int Advsy Bd Bipop-Carire 2000–02; memb Bd London Regional Transport 1984–94, dir British Aerospace plc 1989–2003; cncllr Brentwood DC 1976–86 (chm 1983–84, hon alderman); chm Racecourse Assoc 2001–04; memb: Br Horseracing Bd 2001–04, Betting Levy Bd 2001–04; treas Essex CCC 2003–13; chm Beyond Youth 2011–14, tstee Fryerning Fndn; Liveryman and memb Ct of Assts Worshipful Co of Coopers (Master 2002–03), memb Master Court Incorporation of Coopers of Glasgow (deacon 2008–09), Collector of the Trades House of Glasgow 2014–15; FSI, ASIP; *Recreations* cricket, racing and charitable affairs; *Clubs* Carlton, Royal Ascot Racing, Western (Glasgow); *Style*— Keith Brown, Esq, OBE; ✉ Fryerning House, Ingatestone, Essex CM4 0PF (☎ 01277 352959, fax 01277 355051, e-mail keith@fryerning.com, website www.fryerning.com)

BROWN, Kenneth Edward Lindsay; s of Col Thomas Pyne Brown, OBE (d 1957); *b* 17 October 1940, Port of Spain, Trinidad and Tobago; *Educ* Sherborne; *m* 1968, Mary Ruth, da of Thomas Forrester (d 1969); 3 s; *Career* dir A R Brown McFarlane & Co Ltd 1967– (chm 1972–2004); memb ICAEW 1965; FCA; *Recreations* antiques; *Style*— Kenneth Brown Esq; ✉ 65 St Andrews Drive, Glasgow G41 4HP (☎ 0141 423 8381, e-mail pbrown@aol.com); A R Brown McFarlane & Co Ltd, Unit 7, Lonmay Place, Panorama Business Village, Glasgow G33 4ER (☎ 0141 771 9045)

BROWN, Prof Lawrence Michael (Mick); s of Bertson Waterworth Brown, and Edith, *née* Waghorne (d 1989); *b* 18 March 1936; *Educ* Univ of Toronto (BASc), Univ of Cambridge (MA, DSc), Univ of Birmingham (PhD); *m* Dr Susan Drucker Brown, da of David Drucker, of Oronoque Village, Connecticut, USA; 2 da (Sarah May b 1969, Isabel b 1971), 1 s (Toby Solomon b 1974); *Career* Univ of Cambridge: W M Tapp fellowship Gonville & Caius Coll 1963, demonstrator 1965, lectr 1970, fndr fell Robinson Coll 1977–, reader 1982–90, prof 1990–2001, prof emeritus 2001–; Rosenhain Medal (Inst of Metals), R F Mehl Medal (Metals Soc and Inst of Metals), Guthrie Medal and Prize (Inst of Physics); FRS 1981, FInstP, FIM; *Style*— Prof Mick Brown, FRS; ✉ Robinson College, Cambridge CB3 9AN

BROWN, Lyn Carol; MP; da of Joseph Brown, of London, and Iris Brown; *b* 13 April 1960, London; *Educ* Plashet Comp, Whitelands Coll Roehampton Inst (BA); *m* 24 June 2008, John Cullen; *Career* residential social work: London Borough of Ealing 1984, Newham Vol Agencies Cncl 1984–8, London Borough of Waltham Forest 1987–2005; MP (Lab) West Ham 2005–; chair: London Library Devpt Agency 1999–2007, Cultural Servs Exec Local Govt Assoc (LGA) 2000–03, Culture and Tourism Panel Assoc of London Govt (ALG) 2002–05; memb: London Region Sports Bd until 2007, London Arts Bd until 2007, Museums, Libraries and Archives Cncl London until 2007, Co-op Pty, Fabian Soc, Unison; *Recreations* reading crime fiction (judge Golden Dagger Award 2005, 2006 and 2007), walking, relaxing with friends; *Style*— Ms Lyn Brown, MP; ✉ House of Commons, London SW1A 0AA (☎ 020 7219 6999, fax 020 7219 0889, e-mail brownl@parliament.uk or lyn@lynbrown.org.uk)

BROWN, Maggie; da of Cecil Walter Brown and Marian, *née* Evans; *b* 7 September 1950; *Educ* Colston's Girls' Sch, Univ of Sussex, Univ of Bristol (BA), Univ of Cardiff (Dip Journalism); *m* 22 June 1979, Charles John Giuseppe Harvey (3 Baron Harvey of Tasburgh), s of Hon John Wynn Harvey, of Coed-y-Maen, Meifod, Powys (s of 1 Baron Harvey of Tasburgh); 3 da (Hon Elena b 27 Dec 1982, Hon Nina b 11 Aug 1985, Hon Stephanie b 8 May 1989), 1 s (Hon John b 1 May 1993); *Career* trainee journalist Birmingham Post & Mail 1972–74; staff writer: Birmingham Post 1974–77, Reuters 1977–78; news editor: Financial Weekly 1979–80, Guardian 1980–86; media editor The Independent 1986; media commentator Guardian Media section, reg contrib BBC radio; contrib Evening Standard Media section; *Books* A Licence to be Different – The Story of Channel 4 (2007); *Recreations* reading, gardening, being a mother, horse riding; *Style*— Ms Maggie Brown; ✉ c/o The Guardian, 90 York Way, London N1 9GU

BROWN, Malcolm Ronald; s of Ronald Ernest Charles Brown, MBE (d 1988), of Orpington, Kent, and Peggy Elizabeth, *née* Mitchener; *b* 2 August 1946; *Educ* Quintin GS, Univ of London (BSc); *m* 3 Oct 1970, Lyntina Sydnie, da of Clinton Sydney Squire; 1 da (Samantha Anne b 13 Feb 1972), 1 s (Philip Clinton b 18 May 1975); *Career* construction analyst: de Zoete & Gorton 1968–72, James Capel & Co 1972– (ptnr 1981, sr exec 1984); dir HSBC Investment Bank 1997–2006, chm Steppe Cement Ltd 2008–; AIIMR; *Recreations* ocean racing, chess, gardening; *Style*— Malcolm Brown, Esq; ✉ Carbery House, Carbery Lane, Ascot, Berkshire (☎ 01344 622620)

BROWN, Prof Malcolm Watson; s of Denis Brown (d 2001), and Vivian Irene, *née* Watson (d 2001); *b* 24 February 1946, Sheffield; *Educ* St John's Coll Cambridge (open scholarship, Wright Prize, Hockin Prize, research scholarship, MA), Univ of Cambridge (PhD); *m* 6 April 1974, Geraldine Ruth, *née* Hassall; 1 s (Roger Hassall b 7 July 1982), 1 da (Andrea Francesca b 4 May 1985); *Career* asst in research Dept of Anatomy Univ of Cambridge 1972–74, visiting research scientist NIH 1973, research fell Downing Coll Cambridge 1973–74; Dept of Anatomy Univ of Bristol: research asst 1974–75, lectr in anatomy 1975–91, sr lectr in anatomy 1991–94, reader in anatomy and cognitive neuroscience 1994–98, prof of anatomy and cognitive neuroscience 1998–2010 (emeritus 2010–), head of dept 1998–2004 (dep head 1996–98), exec memb MRC Centre for Synaptic Plasticity 1999–2010; research dir Faculty of Med and Vet Sciences Univ of Bristol 2003–10; BBSRC: memb Animal Sciences and Psychology Grants Ctee 1994–97, memb Network Panel 1997–2000; MRC: panel referee for the allocation of research studentships 1991–94, panel referee for clincal research fellowships 1997–99, memb MRC Advsy Bd (MAB) 2000–10; delivered numerous lectures at univ depts and int scientific meetings worldwide; author of numerous academic jl papers and research chapters in books; memb: Br Neuroscience Assoc 1973–, European Brain and Behaviour Soc 1984–2010, Anatomical Soc of GB and I 1998–2010; Univ of Bristol Merit Awards 1989, 1990 and 1997, AFRC Special Research Fellowship 1991–92; memb and elder Christ Church Nailsworth; FRS 2004; *Recreations* travel; *Style*— Prof Malcolm Brown; ✉ University of Bristol, School of Physiology, Pharmacology and Neuroscience, Medical Sciences Building, University Walk, Bristol BS8 1TD (☎ 0117 331 1909, fax 0117 331 2288, e-mail m.w.brown@bris.ac.uk)

BROWN, Prof Margaret Louise; OBE (2015); *née* Seed; da of (Frederick) Harold Seed (d 1960), and Louisa, *née* Shearer (d 1991); *b* 30 September 1943, Liverpool; *Educ* Merchant Taylors' Sch for Girls Crosby, Newnham Coll Cambridge (MA), Inst of Educn Univ of London (PGCE), Chelsea Coll Univ of London (PhD); *m* 1970, Hugh Palmer Brown; 3 s (Richard Christopher b 24 Oct 1977, Michael Philip b 13 Nov 1979, Peter Nicholas b 16 March 1983); *Career* mathematics teacher Cavendish Sch Hemel Hempstead 1966–69, lectr then sr lectr Chelsea Coll Univ of London 1969–86; KCL: reader 1986–90, prof of mathematics educn 1990–2012 (emeritus 2012–), head Sch of Educn 1992–96; chair: Jt Mathematical Cncl of the UK 1991–95, of tstees Sch Mathematics Project 1996–2006, Educn Panel Research Assessment Exercise 2008; pres: Mathematical Assoc 1990–91, Br Educnl Research Assoc 1997–98; memb: Nat Curriculum Mathematics Working Gp 1987–88, Numeracy Task Force 1997–98, Advsy Ctee on Mathematics Educn 2005–08; expert advsr Rose Primary Curriculum Review 2008–09; Royal Soc Kavli Medal 2013; Hon EdD Kingston Univ 2002, Hon DSc Loughborough Univ 2010; FKC 1996, AcSS 2000; *Publications* Statistics and Probability (jtly, 1972), Low Attainers in Mathematics 5–16 (jtly, 1982), Children Learning Mathematics (jtly, 1984), Graded Assessment in Mathematics (1992), Intuition or Evidence? (jtly, 1995), Effective Teachers of Numeracy (jtly, 1997); author of numerous jl articles and chapters in books; *Recreations* walking, music; *Style*— Prof Margaret Brown, OBE; ✉ 34 Girdwood Road, Southfields, London SW18 5QS (☎ and fax 020 8789 4344); Department of Education and Professional Studies, King's College London, Franklin-Wilkins Building, Waterloo Bridge, London SE1 9NN (e-mail margaret.brown@kcl.ac.uk)

BROWN, His Hon Judge (Laurence Frederick) Mark; s of Rt Rev Ronald Brown, and Joyce, *née* Hymers (d 1987); *b* 16 March 1953; *Educ* Bolton Sch, Univ of Durham (BA, Adam Smith Prize for Economics); *m* 5 Aug 1978, Jane Margaret, da of Rev Dr F H Boardman; 1 s (Nicholas Edward b 29 April 1984); *Career* called to the Bar Inner Temple 1975, bencher 2009; pt/t tutor in law Univ of Liverpool 1976–83, in practice Northern Circuit 1976–2000, recorder 1997–2000 (asst recorder 1993–97), asst boundary cmmr 2000, circuit judge (Northern Circuit) 2000–15, ethnic minority liaison judge for Liverpool 2002–05, liaison judge for Knowsley Beach 2002–11, liaison judge for Wirral Bench 2012–15, sr circuit judge and resident judge Lancashire Crown Courts 2015–; hon recorder of Preston 2016–; memb Parole Bd for Eng and Wales 2003–10, lectr and tutor judge Judicial Coll 2008–16; *Recreations* golf, gardening; *Clubs* Royal Liverpool Golf; *Style*— His Hon Judge Mark Brown; ✉ The Law Courts, Openshaw Place, Ringway, Preston PR1 2LL

BROWN, Mark Finlay; *b* 16 March 1963; *Educ* Loughborough Univ of Technol (BScEcon); *Career* economist; equity market strategist and investment banker: CBI 1984, HM Treasy 1985–87, Phillips & Drew 1987–89; strategist UBS 1990–93; ABN AMRO Hoare Govett: head of strategy and economics 1994–96, head of research 1996–98, chief exec ABN AMRO Equities (UK) Ltd 1998–2000; global head of research HSBC plc 2000–02, global head of research ABN AMRO 2002–04, chief exec Arbuthnot Securities 2004–08, chief exec Collins Stewart plc 2008–; *Recreations* rugby, mountaineering; *Style*— Mark Brown, Esq; ✉ Collins Stewart Europe Limited, 88 Wood Street, London EC2V 7QR (☎ 020 7523 8008, fax 020 7523 8133, e-mail mark.brown@collinsstewart.com)

BROWN, Martin Ernest; TD (1999); *b* 9 June 1966; *Educ* Whitgift Sch Croydon; *m* 6 June 1998, Helen, *née* O'Connor; *Career* private sec to the Sec of State for Transport 1987–89, with Westminster Strategy (govt and media conslts) 1989–95; Design Cncl: head of corp affrs 1995–98, dir Govt & Communication 1998–2002; dir Fishburn Hedges (cmmn conslts) 2002–; FRSA; *Style*— Martin Brown, Esq, TD

BROWN, Michael Russell; s of Frederick Alfred Brown, and Greta Mary Brown, OBE, *née* Russell; *b* 3 July 1951; *Educ* Littlehampton, Univ of York; *Career* memb Middle Temple; mgmnt trainee Barclays Bank 1972–74; lectr Swinton Cons Coll 1974–76, res asst to Michael Marshall MP 1975–77, Parly research asst to Nicholas Winterton MP 1977–79; MP (Cons): Brigg and Scunthorpe 1979–83, Brigg and Cleethorpes 1983–97; sec Parly NI Ctee 1981–87 (vice-chm 1987), PPS to Hon Douglas Hogg MP as min of state DTI 1989–90, min of state FCO 1990–92, PPS to Sir Patrick Mayhew as sec of state for NI 1992–93, asst Govt whip 1993–94; political columnist The Independent 1998–; *Style*— Michael Brown, Esq

BROWN, Prof Morris Jonathan; s of Arnold Aaron Brown (d 1970), and Irene Joyce, *née* Goodman; *b* 18 January 1951; *Educ* Edinburgh Acad, Harrow, Trinity Coll Cambridge (scholar, MA, MD), UCH Med Sch (scholar, MSc); *m* 31 July 1977, Diana Costa, da of Kostas Phylactou, of Cyprus; 3 da (Emily Irene Annie b 1981, Chrysothemis Celia Margaret b 1982, Ophelia Wendy Elizabeth b 1986); *Career* MRC sr fell Royal Postgrad Med Sch 1982–85, conslt physician Addenbrooke's Hosp Cambridge 1985–; Univ of Cambridge: prof of clinical pharmacology 1985–, fell Gonville & Caius Coll 1989–, dir of translational medicine 2008–; chm MRS 1990–96; pres Br Hypertension Soc 2005–07 (vice-pres 2003–05); author of papers on treatment and genetics of hypertension and adrenal disorders; Lilly Gold Medal Br Pharmacological Soc 2001, Walter Somerville Medal Br Card Soc 2006, Hospital Doctor of the Year 2003; FRCP 1986, FMedSci 1999, FAHA 2003, fell Br Pharmacological Soc 2013; *Books* Advanced Medicine (1986), Clinical Pharmacology (jtly, 1997, 2003, 2008 and 2012); *Recreations* violin and oboe; *Clubs* RSM, Athenaeum; *Style*— Prof Morris Brown; ✉ Clinical Pharmacology Unit, University of Cambridge, Level 6, ACCI, Addenbrooke's Hospital, Box 110, Cambridge CB2 2QQ (✆ 01223 762577, fax 01223 762576, e-mail mjb14@medschl.cam.ac.uk)

BROWN, Rt Hon Nicholas Hugh; PC (1997), MP; s of late R C Brown, and late G K Brown, *née* Tester; *b* 13 June 1950; *Educ* Tunbridge Wells Tech HS, Univ of Manchester (BA); *Career* memb Newcastle upon Tyne City Cncl 1980–84; MP (Lab): Newcastle upon Tyne E 1983–97 and 2010–, Newcastle upon Tyne E and Wallsend 1997–2010; oppn frontbench dep spokesman on legal affrs 1985–87, oppn frontbench Treasy spokesman 1987–94, dep to Margaret Beckett, MP as Shadow Ldr of the Commons 1992–94, oppn spokesman on health 1994–95, oppn dep chief whip 1995–97, Parly sec to the Treasy (Govt chief whip) 1997–98, sec of state for Agriculture, Fisheries and Food 1998–2001, min of state for Work 2001–03, dep chief whip 2007–08, Govt chief whip 2008–10; memb Select Ctee on Broadcasting 1994–95; *Style*— The Rt Hon Nicholas Brown, MP; ✉ House of Commons, London SW1A 0AA; ✆ 0191 261 1408

BROWN, Prof Nigel Leslie; OBE (2014); s of Leslie Charles Brown (d 1983), and Beryl Brown (d 2004); *b* 19 December 1948; *Educ* Beverley GS, Univ of Leeds (BSc, PhD); *m* 7 Aug 1971, Gayle Lynnette, da of John Wallace Blackah (d 2001), of Beverley, E Yorks; 3 da (Sally b 1975, Louise b 1976, Katie b 1977); *Career* ICI fell MRC Lab of Molecular Biology 1974–76, lectr in biochemistry Univ of Bristol 1976–81, Royal Soc sr research fell 1981–88, visiting fell in genetics Univ of Melbourne 1987–88; Univ of Birmingham: prof of molecular genetics and microbiology 1988–2008, head of biology 1994–99, dep head of biosciences 1999–2000, Leverhulme Tst research fell 2000–01, head of chemistry 2003–04; dir of science and technol BBSRC 2004–08 (memb Strategy Bd 1997–2004); Univ of Edinburgh: prof of molecular microbiology 2008–12, vice-princ and head Coll of Sci and Engrg 2008–11, sr vice-princ and vice-princ planning, resources and research policy 2011–12, emeritus prof of molecular microbiology 2012–; hon prof: Univ of Nottingham 2011–, Swansea Univ 2012–; chm and tstee dir Genome Analysis Centre 2013–, conslt Blackah-Brown Consulting 2013–; chief ed Fedn of European Microbiology Socs (FEMS) Microbiology Reviews 2000–04; memb: Governing Cncl John Innes Centre 1999–2004, Scottish Sci Advsy Cncl 2010–15; chm: Deans Science and Egrg Scotland 2010–12, Scottish Consortium on Rural Research 2011–12, NERC Training Advsy Gp 2014–; hon pres: W Midlands Assoc for Science Educn 1997–98, Soc of Gen Microbiology 2012–15; hon memb Microbiology Soc (formerly Soc of Gen Microbiology) 2016; Hon DSc Univ of Edinburgh 2014; CBiol, FRSB 1989, CChem, FRSC 1990, FRSE 2011; *Publications* various pubns in scientific jls, books and magazines; *Recreations* travel, science, public engagement on science; *Style*— Prof Nigel Brown, OBE, FRSE; ✉ Saddlestone Barn, Huntenhull Lane, Chapmanslade BA13 4AS (e-mail profnigelbrown@gmail.com)

BROWN, Sir (Austen) Patrick; KCB (1995); *b* 14 April 1940, Newcastle upon Tyne; *Educ* Royal GS Newcastle upon Tyne, SSEES Univ of London; *m* 1966, Mary; 1 da; *Career* Carreras Ltd until 1969: joined 1961, Cyprus office 1965–66, Belgium office 1967–68; mgmnt conslt Urwick Orr & Partners 1969–72, DOE 1972–76, asst sec Property Services Agency (PSA) 1976–80; Dept of Tport: asst sec 1980–83, under sec (fin and ports & buses privatisation) 1983–88; dep sec (privatisation of water industry) DOE 1988–90, chief exec PSA 1990–91, perm sec Dept of Tport 1991–97; dep chm: Kvaerner Corp Devpt Ltd 1998–99, Review of Ex-Service Charities 2000; non-exec chm: Go-Ahead Group plc 2002–13 (non-exec dir 1999–), Amey plc 2004–08; non-exec dir: Hunting plc 1998–2001, Arlington Securities plc 1999–2004, Northumbrian Water Gp plc 2003–11, Camelot plc 2010–; chair Oil and Gas Authy 2015–; chm: Mobility Choice 1998–2008, Ind Tport Cmmn 1999–2008, Advsy Bd Alexander Proudfoot 2010–12; tstee Charities Aid Fndn 1998–2006; *Style*— Sir Patrick Brown, KCB

BROWN, Paul; s of Alan Tertius Brown, of Wales, and Enfys Ann, *née* Jones; *b* 13 May 1960; *Educ* Univ of St Andrews; *Career* theatre designer; trained under Margaret Harris; Diploma of Honour Praque Quadrennial 1999; *Theatre* designs for: Almeida, Royal Court, Traverse, Bush, Lincoln Centre NY; prodns 1985–87: A Lie of the Mind, Ourselves Alone, Road; Almeida (at the Gainsborough Studios), Richard II, Coriolanus, The Tempest (Critic Circle Award for Best Designer 2000), Platanov (Critic Circle Award for Best Designer 2001, Evening Standard Award for Best Designer 2001), King Lear, Man of La Mancha (Broadway), Hamlet (Setagua Theatre Tokyo, Sadlers Wells London), False Servant (RNT), As You Desire Me (West End), Country Wife (Haymarket) 2007, The Sea (Haymarket) 2007, Marguerite (Haymarket) 2008, Oedipus (NT), Emeror and Galilean (NT) 2011; *Opera* prodns incl: Mitridate (Covent Garden) 1991, Hamlet (Monte Carlo) 1993, L'Incoronazione di Poppea (Bologna) 1993, Zemire et Azor 1993 (Drottningholm Court Theatre Sweden), King Arthur (Paris Châtalet and Covent Garden) 1995, Lady Macbeth of Mtsensk (Met NY) 1995, Tom Jones (Drottningholm Court Theatre Sweden) 1995, The Midsummer Marriage (ROH) 1996, Fidelio (ENO) 1996, Lulu (Glyndebourne) 1996, Parsifal (Bastille Paris) 1997, I Masnadieri (Covent Garden) 1999, Moses und Aron (Metropolitan NY) 1999, Pelléas et Mélislande (Glyndebourne) 1999, Don Carlos (Sydney Opera House) 1999, Falstaff (re-opening Covent Garden) 1999, Peter Grimes (Bastille Paris) 2001, Vanessa (Monte Carlo) 2001, Rigoletto (Madrid) 2001, Thias (Lyric Opera Chicago), Katya Kabanova (Santa Fe), La Traviata (Verona Arena), Mefistofele (Amsterdam) 2004, Die Zauberflöte (Festspielhaus Saltzburg) 2005, The Magic Flute (Bolshoi Moscow) 2005, Lucio Silla (Santa Fe) 2005, Tosca (ROH) 2006, The Tempest (Santa Fe) 2006, Turn of the Screw (Glyndebourne) 2006, Electra (Kirov St Petersburg) 2007, Anna Bolena (Verona) 2007, Tannhäuser (San Francisco) 2007, Marriage of Figaro (Santa Fe) 2008, Aida (Bregenz), Fairy Queen (Glyndebourne) 2009, Don Giovanni (Glyndebourne), Die Gezeichneten (Palermo) 2010, Die Frau Ohne Schatten (Mariinsky St Petersburg) 2011, Tristan und Isolde (Deutsche Oper) 2011, Otello (Zurich) 2011, Flying Dutchman (ENO) 2012, Mittwoch Aus Licht (Birmingham) 2012, Nabucco (Tokyo) 2013, Hippolyte et Aricie (Glyndebourne) 2013, Guillaume Tell (Pesaro) 2013, Curro Vargas (Madrid) 2014, Manon Lescaut (Covent Garden and Shanghai) 2014, War and Peace (Mariinsky St Petersburg) 2014, Le Rois Arthus (Paris) 2015; *Ballet* Giselle (La Scala Milan) 2001; *Films* Angels and Insects (Oscar nomination 1997), Up At the Villa; *Style*— Paul Brown, Esq; ✉ c/o Simon Ash, Loesje Sanders Ltd, Pound Square, North Hill, Woodbridge, Suffolk IP12 1HH

BROWN, Paul Ray Beck; s of Sqdn Ldr Frederick Beck Brown (d 1997), of Linslade, Beds, and Kathleen, *née* May; *b* 20 July 1944; *Educ* Churcher's Coll Petersfield; *m* 1964, Maureen Ellen Ann, da of Joseph Archibald McMillan (d 1982); 2 da (Lucy Elizabeth Beck b 10 Feb 1965 d 2001, Clara Louise Beck b 20 Jan 1968); *Career* indentured: East Grinstead Courier 1963–65, Lincolnshire Standard 1965–66, Leicester Mercury 1966–68; investigative reporter Birmingham Post 1968–74, news ed Evening Post-Echo Hemel Hempstead 1980–81 (joined 1974), The Sun 1981–82, environment correspondent The Guardian 1989–2005 (joined 1982), currently columnist The Guardian and co-ed Climate News Network; tutor Guardian Fndn and UN Environment Prog (UNEP) courses in journalism; Midlands Journalist of the Year 1974; press fell Wolfson Coll Cambridge 2007–08; memb The Geologists' Assoc; FRGS, FRSA; *Books* The Last Wilderness, 80 Days in Antarctica (1991), Greenpeace (1993), Global Warming, Can Civilisation Survive (1996), Anita Roddick and the Body Shop (1996), Energy and Resources (1998), Just the Facts, Pollution (2002), North South East West (2005), Global Warning: Last Chance for Change (2006), Voodoo Economics and the Doomed Nuclear Renaissance (2008), Leighton Buzzard and Linslade: A History (2008), All Sorts of Bassetts from Rags to Riches (2012), The Secrets of Q Central, How Leighton Buzzard Shortened the Second World War (2014); *Recreations* badminton, travel, geology, bowls; *Style*— Paul Brown, Esq; ✉ 54 Mentmore Road, Linslade, Leighton Buzzard, Bedfordshire LU7 2NZ (✆ 01525 374050, e-mail paulbrown5@mac.com)

BROWN, Prof Peter; s of John Brown, of Sutton, Surrey, and Eugenie, *née* Karazeri; *b* 3 August 1960; *Educ* KCS Wimbledon, Trinity Coll Cambridge, Middlesex Hosp Med Sch; *m* 10 Jan 1987, Pauline Lilian, da of Harold Buchanan; 2 da (Alexzandra Eugenie b 8 Dec 1993, Alisha Helen b 20 July 1995); *Career* sr clinical scientist MRC 1995–2001, conslt neurologist Nat Hosp for Neurology and Neurosurgery 1995–2010; dir Medical Res Cncl Brain Network Dynamics Unit Univ of Oxford 2015–; UCL: reader 2001–04, prof of neurology 2004–10; Nicholas Kurti sr Res Fellowship Brasenose Coll Oxon; FRCP 1999; *Publications* over 300 publications on clinical neuroscience in learned jls; *Style*— Prof Peter Brown; ✉ Nuffield Department of Clinical Neurosciences, University of Oxford, Oxford OX3 9DU

BROWN, Peter David; s of David Phillip Brown, of Kirkcaldy, Fife, and Christina Ross, *née* Coventry (d 2001); *b* 22 April 1962, Musselburgh, E Lothian; *Educ* Dunfermline HS, Univ of St Andrews (MA), RSA (Dip), Heriot-Watt Univ (MBA); *m* 20 July 1995, Carmen Rosa (Vicky) Hernández Garcia; 1 s (Alexander Peter b 23 Sept 1998), 1 da (Carmen Christina b 22 April 2001); *Career* early career with Royal Bank of Scotland then English teacher Int House Istanbul; Br Cncl: teacher of English Bilbao Spain 1989–92, asst dir of studies Las Palmas de Gran Canaria 1993–95, teaching centre mangr Venezuela 1995, asst dir Venezuela 1996–98, asst dir Hungary 1998–2002, dir Abuja and head of educn Nigeria 2002–04, dep dir Nigeria 2004–05, dir Mozambique 2005–; *Style*— Peter Brown, Esq

BROWN, Peter Michael; s of Michael George Harold Brown (d 1969), of Sussex, and Dorothy Margaret, *née* Douty; *b* 11 July 1934; *Educ* Rugby; *m* 1963, Rosemary Anne Brown, OBE, da of Hubert Simon (d 1979), of Geneva and Baden-Baden; 2 s (Hugo Michael Hubert b 1964, Dominic Peter b 1965); *Career* Nat Serv 2 Lt Somerset Light Infantry; chm: Enterprise Dynamics Ltd, Synergy Holdings Ltd, Charity and Fundraising Appointments Ltd, Gabbitas Educational Consultants Ltd, IPPlus plc; pres Coram Fndn, chm Fountain Soc; tstee: Tomorrow's Achievers, Young Enterprise; Liveryman Worshipful Co of Skinners; FInstD, FRSA, FCA, FIDL, FCIM; *Recreations* charity work, bridge, opera; *Clubs* Hurlingham, Lansdowne; *Style*— Peter Michael Brown, Esq; ✉ 12 Hyde Park Place, London W2 2LH; 9 Savoy Street, London WC2R 0BA (✆ 020 7402 6050, fax 020 7706 7666, e-mail peter@synergyholdings.co.uk)

BROWN, Peter Wilfred Henry; CBE (1996); s of Rev Wilfred George Brown (d 1968), and Joan Margaret, *née* Adams (d 1998); bro of Prof Judith M Brown, *qv*; *b* 4 June 1941; *Educ* Marlborough, Jesus Coll Cambridge (MA); *m* 29 March 1969 (m dis), Kathleen (d 2010), da of Hugh Clarke (d 1982); 1 da (Sonya b 1971); *Career* asst master in classics Birkenhead Sch 1963–66, lectr in classics Fourah Bay Coll Univ of Sierra Leone 1966–68, asst sec SOAS Univ of London 1968–75, sec Br Acad 1983–2006 (dep sec 1975–83, acting sec 1976–77); memb Cncl Br Inst in Eastern Africa 1983–2013 (treas 2011–13, hon life vice-pres 2014); fell Nat Humanities Center NC 1978, hon fell Br Sch at Rome 2007; Hon DLitt: Univ of Birmingham, Univ of Sheffield; Knight Cross Order of Merit of the Republic of Poland; *Recreations* sedentary pursuits, musical, bookish; *Clubs* Athenaeum; *Style*— P W H Brown, Esq, CBE; ✉ 34 Victoria Road, London NW6 6PX (e-mail pwhbrown398f@btinternet.com)

BROWN, Ralph William John; s of John F W Brown, and Heather R Laming; *b* 18 June 1957; *Educ* LSE (LLB); *m* 25 July 1992, Jennifer Jules; *Career* actor, writer, director and producer; musician with Brighton Beach Boys (live shows incl Pet Sounds v Sgt Pepper); *Theatre* incl: West 1985, Deadlines 1986, Panic 1987, Macbeth 1987, Earwig 1990, The Dysfunkshonalz 2007; *Television* incl: West 1986, Christabel 1988, Rules of Engagement 1989, The Black & Blue Lamp 1989, Say Hello to the Real Dr Snide 1990, Requiem Apache 1993, Devil's Advocate 1994, Karaoke 1995, Place of the Dead 1995, Ivanhoe 1996, A Respectable Trade 1997, The Last Train 1998, Cleopatra 1998, Extremely Dangerous 1999, Lock, Stock and Four Stolen Hooves etc 1999–2000, NCS Manhunt 2001, Lenny Blue 2001, Julius Caesar 2002, The Agency 2003, Footballer's Lives 2004, Lawless 2004, Big Dippers 2004, Nighty Night 2005, Rich Hall's Cattle Drive 2005, Spooks 2005, Coronation Street 2005, The Flood 2006, Cold Blood 2006, Cape Wrath 2006–07, Life on Mars 2007, Nearly Famous 2008, Jack Taylor: The Guards 2009, Him & Her 2010–13 (Best Sitcom BAFTA), George Gently 2012, Poison Tree 2012, Law and Order 2012, The Mimic 2012, New Tricks 2013, Law & Order 2013, The Assets 2014, Pramface 2014, Babylon 2014, Turn 2014, Elementary 2014, Agent Carter 2015, Blacklist 2015, Legends 2015, Turn 2016; *Film* incl: Withnail and I 1986, Buster 1987, Diamond Skulls 1988, Impromptu 1989, Alien III 1991, The Crying Game 1991, Undercover Blues 1992, Psychotherapy 1992, Wayne's World II 1993, Up N Under 1997, Amistad 1997, Star Wars: Episode 1 – The Phantom Menace 1997, New Year's Day 1999, The Final Curtain 2000, The Man Outside 2000, Mean Machine 2001, I'll Be There 2002, Exorcist Dominion – The Beginning 2003, Puritan 2004, Stoned 2004, Straightheads 2005, The Contractor 2006, Caught in the Act 2007, The Boat that Rocked 2008, The Kid 2009, Huge 2009, Sus 2009, Mission:London 2009, Killing Bono 2010, Dark Tide 2010, I, Anna 2011, Jack the Giant Slayer 2011, Tower Block 2011, Stoker 2011, Sexual Healing 2013, The 17th Kind 2014, My Hero 2014, Jackie 2016; as writer: Sanctuary (Samuel Beckett Award for Best First Play) 1987, Drive Away the Darkness 1988, Sanctuary DC 1988 (Helen Hayes Nomination Best Musical 1989), Zone 1991, The Passion 1992–94, New Year's Day 1995–98 (also assoc prodr 1999; award winner Raindance Film Festival 2001, award winner Sapporo Film Festival 2001), Black Madonna 2001, High Times 2003, Red Light Runners 2003, In God's Footsteps 2004, Willing and Able 2004; dir: Danny and the Deep Blue Sea 1995, Host (The Crocketts) Pop Promo, The Murmuration 2001, The Last of the Toothpaste 2002; *Recreations* blog (https://magicmenagerie.wordpress.com/about/); *Clubs* Groucho; *Style*— Ralph Brown, Esq; ✉ Oriana Elia, Curtis Brown Group, Haymarket

House 28–29 Haymarket, London SW1Y 4SP (☎ Office 02073 934312 Mobile 07891 623 361, website www.curtisbrown.co.uk/actors); Michael Lazo (US agent), Untitled Entertainment, 350 South Beverly Drive, Beverly Hills, CA (☎ 001 90212 310 601 2362)

BROWN, Richard Howard; CBE (2007), DL; *b* 23 February 1953; *Educ* Marlborough, Trinity Hall Cambridge (MA), UCL (MPhil), Harvard Business Sch; *m*; 3 c; *Career* grad trainee British Railways Bd 1977–79, corp planning asst rising to nat account sales mangr Freightliners Ltd 1979–84; British Railways Bd 1984–96: PA, business planning mangr InterCity HQ, mangr InterCity West Coast and Midland Main Lines, dir InterCity Midland Cross Country, md Midland Mainline Ltd; National Express Gp plc 1996–2002: chief exec Trains Div, gp commercial dir and memb Bd; ceo Eurostar Gp Ltd 2002–10, chm Eurostar Int Ltd 2010–13, chm Catalyst Housing Gp 2011–; chm Assoc of Train Operating Cos 2000–02, chm Railway Forum 2008, pres CILT 2008; memb: Derby City Partnership 1995–99, Bd Derby and Derbys Economic Partnership, Bd Dept of Transport 2013–; fndr memb Derby Rail Forum; dep pres French C of C in GB; FRSA, FCILT; *Recreations* sailing, skiing, walking, gardening; *Style*— Richard Brown, Esq, CBE, DL; ✉ Eurostar International Ltd, Times House, Regent Quarter, 5 Bravington's Walk, London N1 9AW (e-mail richard.brown@eurostar.com)

BROWN, Roy Drysdale; s of William Andrew Brown (d 1975), of Cambridge, and Isabelle Drysdale, *née* Davidson (d 1987); *b* 4 December 1946; *Educ* Tonbridge, UCL (BSc), Harvard Business Sch (MBA); *m* 1978, Carol Jane, da of Dr Keene Manning Wallace, of Charleston, S Carolina; 2 s (Alexander b 1980, Cameron b 1984); *Career* Univ Scholarship course GEC 1965–69, commercial gen mangr Vosper Thornycroft Ltd 1972–74; Unilever plc: industrial conslt 1975–77, mktg mangr Uracem Div 1978–80, commercial dir Food Industries Ltd 1981–82, chm Pamol Plantations Sdn Bhd 1982–86, chm PBI Cambridge Ltd 1987–88, tech dir Birds Eye Walls Ltd 1988–90, chm Lever Brothers Ltd 1991–92; Unilever plc/NV: regnl dir Africa, Middle E and Agribusiness 1992–96 (with additional responsibilty for Central and Eastern Europe 1994 and Turkey 1995), pres for Food and Beverages Europe 1996–2001, main bd dir 1992–2001, ret 2001; non-exec dir: GKN plc 1996–2012 (non-exec chm 2004–12), Brambles Industries plc 2001–07, BUPA 2001–07, Lloyd's Franchise Bd 2003–08, Alliance & Leicester plc 2007–12, Abbey National plc/ Santander 2008–15; CEng 1983, FIMechE 1983, FIEE 1990; *Recreations* classical music, opera, carpentry, photography, military history; *Style*— Roy Brown, Esq; ✉ GKN plc, 2nd Floor, 50 Pall Mall, London SW1Y 5JH

BROWN, Russell Leslie; s of Howard Russell Brown (d 1987), and Muriel, *née* Anderson (d 2002); *b* 17 September 1951; *Educ* Annan Acad; *m* 3 March 1973, Christine Margaret Calvert; 2 da (Sarah Ann b 12 Aug 1977, Gillian b 8 April 1979); *Career* cncllr: Dumfries & Galloway Regnl Cncl 1986–96 (chm Public Protection Cmmn 1990–94), Annandale & Eskdale DC 1988–96, Dumfries & Galloway Unitary Cncl 1995–97; MP (Lab): Dumfries 1997–2005, Dumfries & Galloway 2005–15; PPS to: Rt Hon Lord Williams of Mostyn, PC, QC 2002–03, Rt Hon Baroness Amos, PC 2003–05; memb House of Commons Select Ctee on: Euro Legislation 1997–99, Deregulation and Regulatory Reform 1999–2001, Scottish Affairs 2000–01, Standards and Privileges 2001–03, Regulatory Reform 2001–05; memb Scottish Lab Pty; *Recreations* walking, sport (as a spectator); *Style*— Russell Brown, Esq; ✉ House of Commons, London SW1A 0AA (☎ 020 7219 4429, fax 020 7219 0922, e-mail brownr@parliament.uk)

BROWN, Russell William; s of Derek Brown (d 1983), and Suzanne Sadie, *née* Mundy (d 2010); *b* 9 May 1967, W Sussex; *Educ* Richard Lander Sch Truro, Truro Sixth Form Centre, Cornwall Coll; *m* 16 Sept 2000, Eléna Marie, *née* Clark; *Career* restaurateur; head chef Yalbury Cottage Hotel Lower Bockhampton 1998–2001, sous chef then head chef Horn of Plenty Gulworthy 2001–2002, chef and prop Sienna Restaurant Dorchester 2003– (3 AA Rosettes 2006–, Michelin star 2010–); consultancy role with various food producers, restaurants and Dorset CC; Chefs Forum Ctee memb for Dorset; fell Master Chefs of GB 2008 (memb 1999); *Recreations* reading, music, food and wine; *Style*— Russell Brown, Esq; ✉ Sienna Restaurant, 36 High West Street, Dorchester, Dorset DT1 1UP (☎ 01305 250022, e-mail browns@siennarestaurant.co.uk)

BROWN, Prof (James) Scott; *b* 28 November 1954, Glasgow; *Educ* Queen's Univ Belfast (MB BCh, BAO, MD); *m* Anne; 2 da (Susan, Alison), 1 s (Finlay); *Career* SHO: in gen med Royal Victoria Hosp Belfast 1980–81 (jr house offr 1979–80), in paediatrics Royal Belfast Hosp for Sick Children 1981–82, in obstetrics and gynaecology Waveney Hosp Ballymena 1982–83; GP registrar Portglenone Health Centre 1983–84, princ in gen practice Coleraine and MO to Univ of Ulster at Coleraine 1984–; GP trainer 1989–98, GP postgrad tutor 1992–98; chair of Gen Practice Studies Inst of Postgraduate Med and Health Services Univ of Ulster; Royal Coll of Gen Practitioners: NI Faculty rep on London Cncl 1989–, memb Clinical Research Div 1990–93, memb AIDS/HIV Working Pty 1991–93, chm Servs to Membs and Faculties Div 1992–93, chm Publishing Mgmnt Gp 1992–, chm PR Gp 1993–94, chm Services Network 1993–, memb Central Exec Ctee 1993–, memb RCGP/DOH Stress Fellowship Steering Gp 1995–97, memb RCGP Reaccreditation Fellowship Steering Gp 1995–, vice-chm RCGP 1996–99, memb RCGP Int Ctee 1997–; Astra/Shell Research Trg Fellowship (RCGP) 1988–90, Campbell Young Prize (NI Faculty RCGP) 1988 and 1990, hon research fell Dept of Gen Practice Queen's Univ Belfast 1988–94; author of various articles in peer-reviewed jls; DRCOG, DCH (RCPSI), FRCGP; *Recreations* golf, choral music singing, theatre; *Style*— Prof Scott Brown; ✉ Mountsandel Surgery, 4 Mountsandel Road, Coleraine, Co Londonderry BT52 1JB (☎ 02870 342650, fax 02870 321000, e-mail jsbdoc@btopenworld.com)

BROWN, Simon John Saville; s of Ven Robert Saville Brown, and Charlotte, *née* Furber; *b* 6 July 1950; *Educ* Berkhamsted Sch, Selwyn Coll Cambridge (MA); *m*; 2 c; *Career* with Slaughter and May 1972–77 (admitted slr 1974), ptnr Denton Wilde Sapte (formerly Denton Hall) 1980– (joined 1977); *Recreations* jogging, music; *Style*— Simon Brown, Esq; ✉ Denton Wilde Sapte, 1 Fleet Place, London EC4M 7WS

BROWN, Dr Stewart; *Educ* Falmouth Sch of Art (BA), Univ of Sussex (MA), Univ of Wales (PhD), Univ of Nottingham (CertEd); *Career* teacher: Bayero Univ Kano Nigeria, Univ of the WI Barbados; currently dir Centre of West African Studies Univ of Birmingham; exhibition BABEL: beautiful, unsayable, meaningless, profound (Errol Barrow Centre for Creative Imagination Univ of the West Indies Care Hill Barbados) 2007, (Tanzania Publishing House Dar es Salaam) 2009, (The Drum Arts Centre Birmingham) 2010, (Castellani House Nat Gallery of Guyana) 2011 and (Rotunda Gallery Univ of Birmingham) 2013, Six Eight Kaffé (Birmingham) 2016; *Books* incl: Beasts (1975), Room Service: Poems and Photographs (with Barry Hesson, 1977), Specimens (1979), Caribbean Poetry Now (ed, 1984, 2 edn 1992), Perfume of Decay (1985), Zinder (1986), Voiceprint: An Anthology of Oral and Related Poetry from the Caribbean (jt ed, 1989), Writers from Africa (1989), Lugard's Bridge (1989), Caribbean New Wave: Contemporary Short Stories (ed, 1990), James Berry (1991), The Art of Derek Walcott (ed, 1991), The Pressures of the Text: Orality, Texts and the Telling of Tales (ed, 1995), The Art of Kamau Brathwaite (ed, 1995), African New Voices (ed, 1997), Elsewhere: New and Selected Poems (1999), Kiss and Quarrel: Yorùbá/English Strategies of Mediation (2000), All Are Involved: The Art of Martin Carter (2000), The Oxford Book of Caribbean Short Stories (ed with John Wickham, 2000), The Oxford Book of Caribbean Verse (ed with Mark McWatt, 2005), Poems: Martin Carter (ed with Ian McDonald, 2006), Tourist, Traveller, Troublemaker: Essays on Poetry (2007), The Bowling was Superfine: West Indian Writers on West Indian Cricket (ed with Ian McDonald, 2012); *Style*— Dr Stewart Brown; ✉ Centre of West African Studies, School of Historical Studies, The University of Birmingham, Edgbaston, Birmingham B15 2TT (website www.catalystpress.co.uk)

BROWN, Prof Stewart Jay; s of Vernon George Brown, of St Charles, Illinois, and Marion Eleanor, *née* Little; *b* 8 July 1951; *Educ* Glenbard West HS, Univ of Illinois (BA), Univ of Chicago (MA, PhD); *m* 2 Sept 1972, Teri Beth, da of Thomas Dorsey Hopkins (d 1981); 1 s (Adam b 1977), 1 da (Elizabeth b 1980); *Career* Whiting fell in humanities Univ of Chicago 1979–80, asst to dean and lectr in history Northwestern Univ 1980–82, assoc prof and asst head Dept of History Univ of Georgia 1982–88; Univ of Edinburgh: prof of ecclesiastical history 1988–, dean Faculty of Divinity 2000–04, head Sch of Divinity 2010–13; ed Scottish Historical Review 1993–99; memb Cncl: Scot Church History Soc (hon pres 2006–); vice-pres Ecclesiastical History Soc 2015–; Dr of Theology (hc) Reformed Univ of Debrecen Hungary 2013; FRHistS, FRSE; *Books* Thomas Chalmers and the Godly Commonwealth in Scotland (1982), Scotland in the Age of the Disruption (jtly, 1993), William Robertson and the Expansion of Empire (1997), Piety and Power in Ireland 1760–1960 (jtly, 2000), Scottish Christianity in the Modern World (jtly, 2000), The National Churches of England, Ireland and Scotland 1801–1846 (2001), Cambridge History of Christianity vol VII: Enlightenment, Reawakening and Revolution 1660–1815 (jtly, 2006), Providence and Empire: Religion, Politics and Society in the United Kingdom, 1815–1914 (2007), The Union of 1707: New Dimensions (jtly, 2008), The Oxford Movement: Europe and the Wider World 1830–1930 (jtly, 2012), Religion, Identity and Conflict in Britain: From the Restoration to the Twentieth Century (jtly, 2013); *Recreations* swimming, hill walking; *Style*— Prof Stewart J Brown; ✉ 160 Craigleith Hill Avenue, Edinburgh EH4 2NB (☎ 0131 539 2863); Department of Ecclesiastical History, University of Edinburgh, New College, Mound Place, Edinburgh EH1 2LU (☎ 0131 650 8951, e-mail s.j.brown@ed.ac.uk)

BROWN, Stuart Christopher; QC (1991); s of Geoffrey Howard Brown (d 1960), and Olive Lilian Baum, *née* Ford (d 2007); *b* 4 September 1950; *Educ* Acklam HS Middlesbrough, Worcester Coll Oxford (BA, BCL); *m* 7 July 1973, Dr Imogen Brown, da of Edward Arthur Luca (d 2008), of London; 2 da (Sophie b 1976, Katherine b 1979); *Career* called to the Bar Inner Temple 1974, in practice N Eastern Circuit, recorder of the Crown Court 1992–, dep judge of the High Ct 1994–, ldr N Eastern Circuit 2009–11; memb Leeds & W Riding Medico-Legal Soc (pres 1988–90); *Recreations* theatre, travel; *Style*— Stuart C Brown, Esq, QC; ✉ Parklane Plowden, 19 Park Lane, Leeds LS1 2RD (☎ 0113 228 5049, fax 0113 228 1500)

BROWN, Terence Gibbin; s of Rex Brown (d 1990), and Mary Kathleen, *née* Gibbin (d 1971); *b* 14 September 1943, Peterborough, Cambs; *Educ* All Souls Roman Catholic Sch Peterborough, King's Sch Peterborough, Sch of Architecture Architectural Assoc (Mastic Asphalt Assoc scholar, AA Dipl, RIBA pt III); *m* 1, 10 June 1972 (m dis 1991), Jacqueline Lesley Chinnery; 1 da (Sophie Madelaine b 26 June 1975), 1 s (Edric Samuel b 29 Sept 1977); m 2, 29 Aug 1992, Lucille Julia Cooper, da of Thomas Higgins; *Career* worked for Howard V Lobb & Partners (before completion of AA course); GMW Partnership: joined 1969, assoc 1979, design ptnr 1984, a sr ptnr 1991–2009, conslt 2009–12; Terence Brown Consultancy 2012–, princ tgb-design 2014–; work incl: Zurich Insurance Portsmouth 1977, Minster Ct London 1991, Barclays Bank HQ London 1993, Midsummer Place Milton Keynes 2000, CIPD HQ Wimbledon 2002, Tower 42 London, 41 Lothbury London 2005, 50 Grosvenor Hill Mayfair; chair and coordinator Friends of the Earth Wandsworth; highly commended Br Construction Industry Awards 1990, MIPIM Euro Shopping Centre of the Year (St Enoch Centre Glasgow) 1991, Br Cncl for Offices Award 2013 (for 50 Grosvenor Hill); memb: ARB (formerly ARCUK) 1971, RIBA 1971, AA 1969, Assoc of Conslt Architects 1989 (memb Cncl 2005, hon treas 2009–11, vice-pres 2010–11, pres 2011–14), Twentieth Century Soc 1993, Town & Country Planning Assoc 1993, Urban Design Gp 1998, Catenians Assoc (pres Balham Circle 350) 2014–15; MInstD 1990, FRSA 1995; *Style*— Terence Brown, Esq; ✉ 24 West Hill Road, London SW18 1LN (☎ and fax 020 8874 3805, e-mail terry@tgb-uk.com, website www.tgb-uk.com)

BROWN, Tim; *Career* qualified accountant Nat Audit Office; formerly: business strategy dir Royal Mail, sales and mktg dir Parcelforce Worldwide, sales and mktg dir DHL Express; ceo Postal Servs Cmmn 2008–; *Style*— Tim Brown, Esq; ✉ Jersey Post, Postal Headquarters, Jersey JE1 1AA

BROWN, Timothy Colin; s of Peter Brindley Brown (d 2005), and Margaret Jean, *née* McIntosh (d 2011); *b* 20 September 1957; *Educ* Eton, RMA Sandhurst; *m* 1, 24 Jan 1987 (m dis 1995), Lady Vanessa Petronel Pelham, yst da of 7 Earl of Yarborough; m 2, 19 March 2004, Melissa Stimpson, *née* Currie; 2 da (Annabel Georgina b 16 Dec 2004, Alexandra Siena b 8 July 2006); *Career* 4/7 Royal Dragoon Gds 1976–82 (A/Capt 1980); City & Commercial Communications plc 1983–91 (dir 1987–91), jt chief exec Tavistock Communications Ltd 1992–99 (dir 1991–99), investor relations dir Vodafone AirTouch 1999–2000, gp corp affrs dir Vodafone Gp 2000–04, Mere Consultancy 2004–07, COS Nyland 2007–; *Recreations* equestrian sports, skiing, shooting, backgammon; *Clubs* Cavalry and Guards'; *Style*— Timothy Brown, Esq

BROWN, Prof Tom; s of Tom Brown, of Barnsley, S Yorks, and Catherine, *née* Beardshall; *b* 10 November 1952; *Educ* Broadway GS Barnsley, Univ of Bradford (BTech, PhD); *m* Dorcas Jemema Selverani, da of Jacob Samuel; 1 s (Tom b 23 Sept 1982), 1 da (Asha b 20 April 1984); *Career* postdoctoral research: Dept of Chemistry Univ of Nottingham 1978–79, Dyson Perrins Laboratory Univ of Oxford 1979–82, Chemical Laboratory Univ of Cambridge 1982–85; prof of nucleic acid chemistry Univ of Edinburgh 1985–95, prof of chemical biology Univ of Southampton 1995–2013; Univ of Oxford: prof of nucleic acid chemistry 2013–, assoc head Dept for Research 2016–; dir Oligonucleotide Service Wellcome Trust (OSWEL) 1986–2001; fndr: Oswel Ltd 1989–, ATDBio Ltd 2005–, Primer Design Ltd 2005–; Griffin and George Prize Univ of Bradford 1975, MakDougall-Brisbane Prize RSE 1992, Josef Loschmidt Award RSC 1992, Caledonian research fell RSE 1993, Royal Soc sr research fell 2005, RSC Award for Nucleic Acids Chemistry 2007, RSC Prize for interdisciplinary research 2009, Chemistry World Entrepreneur of the Year 2014; author of 350 research papers and patents; CChem, FRSC (pres Chemistry and Biology Interface Div 2015–18), FRSE; *Recreations* gardening, jogging; *Style*— Prof Tom Brown, CChem, FRSE; ✉ Professor of Nucleic Acid Chemistry, Department of Chemistry, University of Oxford, Chemistry Research Laboratory, 12 Mansfield Road, Oxford OX1 3TA

BROWN, Tony; *Career* joined Asda 1979 (rising to regnl md South and South West), operations dir Somerfield 1998, retail dir British Home Stores 2000–08, chief exec Beale plc 2008–; *Style*— Tony Brown, Esq; ✉ 99p Stores Ltd, Swan Valley, Northampton NN4 9EX

BROWN, Prof William Arthur; CBE (2002); s of Prof Arthur Joseph Brown, of Leeds, and Joan Hannah Margaret Brown; *b* 22 April 1945; *Educ* Leeds GS, Wadham Coll Oxford (BA); *m* 1993 (m dis 2013), Kim Barbara, *née* Saunders; *Career* economic asst NBPI 1966–68, res assoc Univ of Warwick 1968–70; SSRC's Industrial Res Unit Univ of Warwick: res fell 1970–79, dep dir 1979–81, dir 1981–85; Univ of Cambridge: Montague Burton prof of industrial relations 1985–2012, fell Wolfson Coll 1985–2000, chm Faculty of Economics and Politics 1992–96, chm Sch of Humanities and Social Sciences 1993–96, chm Bd of Graduate Studies 2000–, master Darwin Coll 2000–12, chm Faculty of Social and Political Science 2003–08, head Sch of Humanities and Social Sciences 2009–12; memb: Low Pay Cmmn 1997–2007, ACAS 1998–2004; Hon DSc Univ of Sydney; *Books* Piecework Bargaining (1973), The Changing Contours of British Industrial Relations (1981), The Individualisation of Employment Contracts in Britain (jtly, 1999), The Evolution of the Modern Workplace (jtly, 2009); *Recreations* gardening, walking; *Style*— Prof William A Brown, CBE; ✉ Darwin College, Silver Street, Cambridge

CB3 9EU (☎ 01223 335668); Faculty of Economics and Politics, Cambridge CB3 9DD (e-mail wab10@econ.cam.ac.uk)

BROWN OF CAMBRIDGE, Baroness (Life Peer 2015), of Cambridge in the County of Cambridgeshire; Julia Elizabeth King; DBE (2012, CBE 1999); da of Derrick King (d 1997), and Jane, *née* Brewer (d 2006); *b* 11 July 1954; *Educ* Godolphin & Latymer Sch, Murray Edwards Coll Cambridge (MA, Posener scholar, PhD); *m* 4 Aug 1984, Dr Colin William Brown; *Career* Rolls-Royce research fell Girton Coll Cambridge 1978–80, lectr Univ of Nottingham 1980–87; Univ of Cambridge: British Gas/Fellowship of Engrg sr research fell 1987–92, teaching fell Churchill Coll 1987–94 and 2002–, lectr 1992–94, asst dir Technol Centre for Ni-Base Superalloys 1993–94; head of materials Rolls-Royce Aerospace Group 1994–96, dir of advanced engrg Rolls-Royce Industrial Power Group 1997–98, md Fan Systems Rolls-Royce plc 1998–2000, dir of engrg and technol Marine Rolls-Royce plc 2000–02; chief exec Inst of Physics 2002–04, princ Faculty of Engrg Imperial Coll London 2004–06, vice-chllr Aston Univ 2006–; chair MOD DSAC 2003–07; hon sec for educn and trg Royal Acad of Engrg 2003–06; memb: Foresight Panel for Defence & Aerospace 1994–97, Foresight Panel for Materials 1994–96, Materials Bd DSAC 1996–98, Tech Opportunities Panel EPSRC 1997–99, Link/TCS Bd 1998–2001, EPSRC Cncl 2000–03 and 2012–, Cncl Royal Acad of Engrg 2002–06, Engrg and Technol Bd 2003–08, Technol Strategy Bd DTI 2004–09, Dept of Business, Enterprise and Regulatory Reform Advsy Gp on Manufacturing 2007–09, HE Statistics Agency Bd 2007–12 (chair 2011–12), Dept of Innovation, Univs and Skils Strategic Bd 2008–09, UK Govt Ctee on Climate Change 2008–, Governing Bd of European Inst of Innovation and Technol 2008–12, World Economic Forum Automotive Cncl (formerly World Economic Forum's Global Agenda Cncl on the Future of Transportation then Agenda Cncl on Automotive) 2008–12, Nat Security Forum 2009–10, Browne Review of Univ Funding and Student Fees 2009–10, Univs UK Bd 2011–15, Science and Technol Honours Ctee 2012–, UK Airports Cmmn 2012–, UAE-UK Business Cncl 2013–2014, Bd Gtr Birmingham and Solihull Local Enterprise Partnership 2013–15, Bd of Tstees Cumberland Lodge 2013–15, Cncl and Bd of Dirs Nat Centre for Univs and Businesses (NCUB); non-exec memb Mgmnt Bd Dept of Business, Innovation and Skills 2009–13, chair UK Innovation & Growth Policy Network 2011–15; UK low carbon business ambass 2009–; chair King Review of Low Carbon Cars HM Treasy Part 1 2007 and Part 2 2008; memb Editorial Bd: Int Jl of Fatigue 1989–96, Fatigue and Fracture of Engrg Materials and Structures 1990–97; author of numerous papers on fatigue and fracture in structural materials; memb Women's Engrg Soc; non-exec dir: Angel Trains 2012–15, Green Investment Bank 2012–; Grunfeld Medal Inst of Materials 1992, Japan Soc for Promotion of Sci Fellowship 1993, Bengough Medal (jtly) Inst of Materials 1995, Kelvin Medal 2001, John Collier Medal IChemE 2010, Lunar Soc Medal 2011, President's Medal Engrg Professors' Cncl 2012, Erna Hamburger Prize Swiss Federal Inst of Technol, Constance Tipper Medal Int Congress on Fracture/World Acad of Structural Integrity, Leonardo Da Vince Medal European Soc for Engrg Educn 2014; hon fell: Murray Edwards Coll Cambridge 2003, Univ of Cardiff 2003, Soc for the Environment 2011, Br Science Assoc 2011, Polymer Processing Acad India 2012; Hon DSc: Queen Mary Univ of London 2008, Univ of Manchester 2014, Univ of Exeter 2015; Liveryman Co of Goldsmiths 1998, Freeman City of London 1998; FREng 1997, FIMMM, FRAeS, FIMarEST, FInstP, FCGI, FEI; *Publications* Educating Engineers for the 21st Century (lead author and ed, 2007; King Review reports: Part 1: the potential for CO2 reduction (2007), Part 2: recommendations for action (2008); *Recreations* collecting modern prints (particularly of plants and places), photography, walking; *Style*— The Baroness Brown of Cambridge, DBE, FREng; ✉ Aston University, Aston Triangle, Birmingham B4 7ET (☎ 0121 204 4884)

BROWN OF EATON-UNDER-HEYWOOD, Baron (Life Peer UK 2004), of Eaton-under-Heywood in the County of Shropshire; Sir Simon Denis Brown; kt (1984), PC (1992); s of Denis Baer Brown (d 1981), and Edna Elizabeth, *née* Abrahams; *b* 9 April 1937; *Educ* Stowe Sch, Worcester Coll Oxford (BA); *m* 31 May 1963, Jennifer, da of (Robert) Prosper Gedye Buddicom (d 1968); 1 da (Abigail b 1964), 2 s (Daniel b 1966, Benedict 1969); *Career* called to the Bar Middle Temple 1961 (Harmsworth scholar, bencher 1980), recorder of the Crown Court 1979–84, first jr treas counsel Common Law 1979–84, judge of the High Court of Justice (Queen's Bench Div) 1984–92, Lord Justice of Appeal 1992–2004, a Lord of Appeal in Ordinary 2004–09, a Justice of the Supreme Court 2009–12; vice-pres Court of Appeal (Civil Div) 2001–03; intelligence services cmmr 2000–06; Liveryman Worshipful Co of Butchers; hon fell Worcester Coll Oxford 1993; *Recreations* golf, theatre, reading; *Clubs* Denham Golf, Church Stretton Golf, Garrick; *Style*— The Rt Hon the Lord Brown of Eaton-under-Heywood, PC; ✉ House of Lords, London SW1A 0PW

BROWNBILL, HE Timothy Patrick (Tim); *Career* diplomat; Maritime, Aviation and Environment Dept FCO 1979–82, commercial attaché Lagos 1982–85, vice-consul Madrid 1986–89, Info Dept FCO 1989–92, dep head of mission Vilnius 1992–94, EU Enlargement Negotiations FCO 1994–96, second sec (commercial/economic) Havana 1996–99, head of resources EU Directorate FCO 1999–2000, seconded as int trade dir for Yorks and Humber Yorks Forward 2000–02, ambass to Nicaragua 2002–04, head of UK trade services Düsseldorf 2004–08, consul gen Ho Chi Minh City 2008–11, Asst Mgmnt Dept Estates and Security Directorate FCO 2012–14, ambass to the Repub of Guinea 2014–; *Style*— HE Mr Tim Brownbill; ✉ c/o FCO (Conakry), King Charles Street, London SW1A 2AH

BROWNE; *see also:* Gore Browne

BROWNE, Anthony; s of Patrick Browne, and Gerd Browne; *Educ* Univ of Cambridge; *m* Paula Higgins; 1s (Theodore b 18 May 2005), 1 da (Isabella b 18 May 2005); *Career* business analyst BoozAllen and Hamilton 1988–89, various media roles incl prodr Uden Assocs 1989–92, business reporter, economics reporter and acting economics corr BBC Radio and TV 1992–97, economics corr, dep business ed, health ed and environment ed The Observer 1997–2002, environment ed, Brussels corr and chief political corr The Times 2002–07, dir Policy Exchange 2007–8, policy dir London Mayor's Office 2008–12, chief exec Br Bankers' Assoc 2012–; *Style*— Anthony Browne, Esq; ✉ British Bankers' Association, Pinners Hall, 105–108 Old Broad Street, London EC2N 1EX

BROWNE, Anthony Edward Tudor; s of Jack Browne, and Doris May Browne; *b* 11 September 1946, Sheffield, Yorks; *Educ* Leeds Coll of Art (BA); *Children* 1 s (Joseph b 14 Oct 1982), 1 da (Elen b 1 Sept 1984); *Career* medical artist Royal Infirmary Victoria Univ of Manchester 1968–70, designer Gordon Fraser Cards 1971–88, children's author and illustrator 1975–; writer and illustrator-in-residence Tate Britain Gallery 2001–02; Children's Laureate 2009–11; Hans Christian Andersen Award 2000; *Books* Bear Hunt (1979), Bear Goes to Town (1982), Willy the Wimp (1984), Willy the Champ (1985), The Little Bear Book (1988), A Bear-y Tale (1989), Willy and Hugh (1991), Willy the Wizard (1995), Willy the Dreamer (1997), Willy's Pictures (2000); picture books: Through the Magic Mirror (1976), A Walk in the Park (1977, published as Voices in the Park 1998, Kurt Maschler Award), Look What I've Got! (1980), Gorilla (1983, Kurt Maschler Award and Kate Greenaway Medal), Piggybook (1986), I Like Books (1989), Things I Like (1989), The Tunnel (1989), Changes (1990), Zoo (1992, Kate Greenaway Medal), The Big Baby: A Little Joke (1993), My Dad (2001), Animal Fair (2002), The Shape Game (2003), Into the Forest (2004), My Mum (2005), Silly Billy (2006), My Brother (2007), Little Beauty (2008), Me and You (2010); as illustrator: The Visitors Who Came to Stay (by Annalena McAfee, 1984), Knock, Knock! Who's There? (by Sally Grindley, 1985), Kirsty Knows Best (by Annalena McAfee, 1987), Alice's Adventures in Wonderland (by Lewis Carroll, 1988, Kurt Maschler Award), Trail of Stones (by Gwen Strauss, 1990), The Night Shimmy (by Gwen Strauss, 1992), The Daydreamer (by Ian McEwan, 1994), The Topiary Garden (by Janni Howker, 1995); *Style*— Anthony Browne, Esq; ✉ c/o Walker Books, 87 Vauxhall Walk, London SE11 5HJ

BROWNE, Anthony Percy Scott; s of Percy Basil Browne (d 2004), and Pamela, *née* Exham (d 1951); *b* 8 January 1949; *Educ* Eton, ChCh Oxford (MA); *m* 8 May 1976, Annabel Louise, *née* Hankinson; 3 da (Eleanor b 9 Sept 1981, Cornelia b 17 May 1983, Molly b 29 Nov 1985); *Career* dir Christie's 1978–96, sr conslt Christie's Int plc 1996–; chm Br Art Market Fedn 1996–; memb: Cultural Industries Export Advsy Gp 1998–2001, Ministerial Advsy Panel on Illicit Trade 1999–2003, Bd European Fine Art Fndn 1999–, Advsy Panel Goodison Review 2003, Cncl American Museum in Britain 2011–; tstee Raise from Ruins 1978–80; vice-chm Art Fortnight London 2004–05; hon assoc Soc of Fine Art Auctioneers 2005; *Recreations* fishing, gardening; *Clubs* Turf, Pratt's; *Style*— Anthony Browne, Esq; ✉ British Art Market Federation, 10 Bury Street, London SW1Y 6AA (☎ 020 7389 2148, fax 020 7839 6599)

BROWNE, Benjamin Chapman; s of Benjamin Chapman Browne (d 1968), of Balsham, Cambs, and Marjorie Grace Hope, *née* Hope-Gill (later Lady Wade; d 2001); *b* 18 May 1953; *Educ* Eton, Trinity Coll Cambridge (MA); *m* 28 July 1979, Sara Katharine, da of Brian Pangbourne, of Liss, Hants; 2 s (Benjamin Chapman b 22 Dec 1982, Edward Pangbourne b 1 April 1985), 1 da (Rebecca Katharine b 24 April 1989); *Career* admitted slr 1978; Lovell White and King 1976–79, Morrell Peel and Gamlen Oxford 1979–81; Clyde and Co: joined 1981, ptnr London 1985–2001, res ptnr Dubai 1989–90; ptnr (specialising in shipping and trade) Shaw and Croft 2001–07, ptnr Thomas Cooper 2007–; memb: Br Maritime Law Assoc, Comite Maritime Internationale, Lloyd's Salvage Gp; subscriber Average Adjusters Assoc; *Recreations* walking, gardening, football; *Style*— Benjamin Browne, Esq; ✉ The Old Vicarage, Church Road, Steep, Petersfield, Hampshire GU32 2DB (☎ 01730 233050); Thomas Cooper, Ibex House, 42–47 Minories, London EC3N 1HA (☎ 020 7481 8851, fax 020 7480 6097, e-mail ben.browne@thomascooperlaw.com, website www.thomascooperlaw.com)

BROWNE, Benjamin James; QC (1996); s of Percy Basil Browne (d 2004), and Jenefer Mary, *née* Petherick (d 2009); *b* 25 April 1954; *Educ* Eton, Christ Church Oxford (MA); *m* 30 May 1987, Juliet Mary, da of Maj Geoffrey Beresford Heywood; 1 s (Samuel James Timothy b 14 July 1992), 1 da (Matilda Jane b 4 Oct 1989); *Career* called to the Bar Inner Temple 1976; recorder 1998–, head of chambers 2 Temple Gardens 2005–; *Recreations* country pursuits, gardening; *Clubs* Boodle's; *Style*— Benjamin Browne, Esq, QC; ✉ 2 Temple Gardens, Temple, London EC4Y 9AY (☎ 020 7822 1200, fax 020 7822 1300)

BROWNE, HE Dr Carolyn; da of Brig Christopher Charles Lloyd Browne (d 1972), and Margaret, *née* Howard; *b* 19 October 1958, Yorks; *Educ* Univ of Bristol (BSc), Linacre Coll Oxford (DPhil); *Career* diplomat; desk offr Repub of Ireland FCO 1986–87, second sec then first sec Moscow 1988–91, EU Dept FCO 1991–93, UK Mission to the UN NY 1993–97, dep head Southern European Dept FCO 1997–99, head Human Rights Policy Dept FCO 1999–2002, UK rep Brussels 2002–05, advsr to Dir of Int Security FCO 2005–06, ambass to Repub of Azerbaijan 2007–11, ambass to Kazakhstan 2013–; *Style*— HE Dr Carolyn Browne

BROWNE, (John) Colin Clarke; s of Ernest Browne, JP (d 1964), of Lisburn, Co Antrim, N Ireland, and Isobel Sarah, *née* McVitie (d 1996); *b* 25 October 1945; *Educ* Wallace HS Lisburn, Trinity Coll Dublin (BA); *m* 3 March 1984, Karen Lascelles Barr, da of Ian Barr (d 1995), of Edinburgh; 1 s; *Career* joined Post Office 1969, head of Bd Secretariat Post Office 1977–80, dir Chm's Office BT 1981–85, chief exec Broadband Servs BT 1985–86, dir of corp relations BT 1986–94, dir of corp affrs BBC 1994–2000; ptnr Maitland Consultancy 2000–09, fndr and ceo Colin Browne Strategic Communications Ltd 2009–; former dir MTV Europe and chm Children's Channel; non-exec dir Centre for Effective Dispute Resolution (CEDR) 2012–, chm Voice of the Listener and Viewer (VLV) 2012–; memb: Cncl ISBA 1990–94, Health Educn Authy (later Health Devpt Agency) 1996–2003, Spongiform Encephalopathy Ctee (SEAC) 2003–04, Communications Consumer Panel 2008–13; tstee: BBC Children in Need 1994–2000, One World Broadcasting Tst 1997–2002, IIC 1998–2000; dir Cwlth Broadcasting Assoc 1997–2000; memb Govt Communications Review Gp 2003; FIPR; *Recreations* sport, music, reading; *Clubs* Reform, Hurlingham; *Style*— Colin Browne, Esq; ☎ 07733 103800, e-mail colin@colinbrowne.com

BROWNE, Desmond John Michael; QC (1990); s of Sir Denis Browne, KCVO, FRCS (d 1967), of London, and Lady Moyra Browne, DBE, *née* Ponsonby; *b* 5 April 1947; *Educ* Eton, New Coll Oxford; *m* 1 Sept 1973, Jennifer Mary, da of Frank Wilmore, of Brierfield, Lancs; 2 da (Natasha b 1974, Harriet b 1976); *Career* called to the Bar Gray's Inn 1969 (bencher 1999, treas 2015), recorder of the Crown Court 1991–2008; chm Bar Cncl 2009, pres Cncl of the Inns of Court 2016; hon memb Australian Bar Assoc 2009; *Recreations* Australiana, Venice, the South Downs; *Clubs* Brooks's, Beefsteak; *Style*— Desmond Browne, Esq, QC; ✉ 5 Gray's Inn Square, Gray's Inn, London WC1R 5AH (☎ 020 7242 2902, fax 020 7831 2686)

BROWNE, Henry; s of Henry Clarence Browne (d 1974), and Veva Helen, *née* Symons (d 1978); *b* 11 July 1944; *Educ* Felsted, Gstaad International; *m* 30 May 1969, Marion Carole, da of Charles Anthony Wenninger (d 1991), of Poole, Dorset; 1 da (Juliette Caroline b 30 Nov 1971), 1 s (Stephen Henry b 15 Dec 1975); *Career* chm Falcon Holdings plc 1974–; Freeman City of London 1990, Liveryman Worshipful Co of Painter-Stainers 1991; *Recreations* golf; *Clubs* RAC, Moor Park Golf; *Style*— Henry Browne, Esq

BROWNE, Jeremy; s of HE Sir Nicholas Browne, KBE, CMG, *qv*, and Diana, née Aldwinckle; *b* 17 May 1970; *Educ* Univ of Nottingham; *Partner* Rachel Binks; 1 da; *Career* former Parly asst to Alan Beith MP, Dewe Rogerson 1994–96, dir of press and broadcasting Lib Dem Pty 1997–2000, Edelman Communications Worldwide 2000–02, ReputationInc 2003–04; Parly candidate (Lib Dem) Enfield Southgate 1997, MP (Lib Dem) Taunton 2005–15; min of state FCO 2010–12, min of state Home Office 2012–; memb Advsy Bd Reform 2005–; *Style*— Jeremy Browne, Esq; ✉ House of Commons, London SW1A 0AA

BROWNE, Brig Michael Edward; CBE (1994), TD (and three Bars), DL (1989); s of John Edward Stevenson Browne, CBE (d 1976), and Muriel May, *née* Lambert (d 1965); *b* 6 December 1942; *Educ* Uppingham; *m* 11 Dec 1970, Susan Elizabeth, da of Sir Hugh Neill, CBE; 2 da (Anna Jane b 27 April 1974, Nicola Catherine b 6 Sept 1975); *Career* TA 1961–94, cmd 3 WFR 1982–84, Brig TA UKLF 1991–94; admitted slr 1966, dep coroner Retford Dist 1970–80, dep dist judge Supreme Ct of Judicature 1986–2013; former chm Bassetlaw Cons Assoc; chm: Reserve Forces Assoc 1993–96 (pres 1999–2004), E Midlands Reserve Forces and Cadets Assoc (RFCA) 1994–2003; pres CIOR (Interallied Confedn of Reserve Offrs) 1996–98, chm Cncl Reserve Forces and Cadets Assoc 2004–08; memb Law Soc 1966; *Recreations* tennis; *Style*— Brig Michael Browne, CBE, TD, DL; ✉ Firdene, Church Street, Headon, Retford, Nottinghamshire DN22 0RD (☎ 01777 249552); Cannon Square, Retford, Nottinghamshire DN22 6PB (☎ 01777 703827, fax 01777 870, mobile 07774 233223, e-mail me.browne@btinternet.com)

BROWNE, His Hon Judge (James) Nicholas; QC (1995); s of James Christopher Browne, MC (d 1952), of London, and Winifred Jessie, *née* Pirie; *b* 25 April 1947; *Educ* Cheltenham Coll, Univ of Liverpool (LLB); *m* 28 March 1981, Angelica Elizabeth (Her Hon Judge Mitchell, d 2006), da of Sir George Mitchell, CB, QC, and Lady Elizabeth Mitchell; 2 da

(Emily Elizabeth b 27 Nov 1981, Cassandra Lucy b 10 Dec 1983); *Career* called to the Bar Inner Temple 1971 (Duke of Edinburgh entrance scholar, bencher 2002), criminal practice Midland Circuit and SE Circuit, recorder of the Crown Court (Midland Circuit) 1993–2006 (asst recorder 1990–93), circuit judge (SE Circuit) 2006–; chm Code of Practice Appeal Bd Assoc of the Br Pharmaceutical Industry 2000–06; memb: Criminal Bar Assoc, Midland Circuit; *Recreations* squash, cricket, theatre, spending time with family and friends; *Clubs* Cumberland Lawn Tennis, Garrick; *Style—* His Hon Judge Browne, QC; ✉ e-mail nbrowneqc@hotmail.com

BROWNE OF BELMONT, Baron (Life Peer UK 2006), of Belmont in the County of Antrim; Wallace Hamilton Browne; s of Gerald Browne, and Phyllis Hamilton, *née* Smyth; *b* 29 October 1947, Belfast; *Educ* Campbell Coll Belfast, Queen's Univ Belfast (BSc); *Career* biology teacher Rainey Endowed Sch Magherafelt 1970–2000; memb (DUP) Belfast City Cncl 1985– (alderman 1993), MLA (DUP) E Belfast 2007–11; Lord Mayor of Belfast 2005–06; sits in House of Lords as crossbench peer 2006–; tstee Somme Assoc; memb NASUWT 1972; High Sheriff Belfast 2002–03; *Recreations* golf, football, cricket, rugby; *Clubs* Army and Navy; *Style—* The Lord Browne of Belmont; ✉ House of Lords, London SW1A 0PW

BROWNE OF LADYTON, Baron (Life Peer 2010), of Ladyton in Ayreshire and Arran; Rt Hon Desmond (Des) Browne; PC (2005); *Career* MP (Lab) Kilmarnock and Loudoun 1997–2010, PPS to Sec of State for Scotland 1998–2001, PPS to Min of State for NI 2000, Parly under-sec of state NI Office 2001–03, min of state Dept of Work and Pensions 2003–04, min of state Home Office 2004–05, chief sec to the Treasy 2005–07, sec of state for def 2007–08, sec of state for Scot 2007–08; *Style—* The Rt Hon the Lord Browne of Ladyton; ✉ House of Lords, London SW1A 0PW

BROWNE OF MADINGLEY, Baron (Life Peer UK 2001), of Madingley in the County of Cambridgeshire; Sir (Edmund) John Phillip Browne; kt (1998); s of late Edmund Browne, and Paula Browne; *b* 20 February 1948, Hamburg, Germany; *Educ* King's Sch Ely, Univ of Cambridge (MA), Stanford Univ (MS); *Career* British Petroleum Company plc: joined as univ apprentice 1966, various exploration and prodn posts Anchorage, NY, San Francisco, London and Canada 1969–83, gp treas and chief exec BP Finance International 1984–86, exec vice-pres and chief fin offr Standard Oil Co Ohio 1987–89 (chief fin offr 1986–87); BP Amoco plc (formerly BP plc): chief exec and md 1989–95, main bd dir 1991–2007, gp chief exec 1995–2007; managing ptnr Riverstone LLP 2007–; non-exec dir: Redland plc 1993–96, SmithKline Beecham plc 1996–99, Intel Corporation 1997–2006, Goldman Sachs 1999–2007; memb Supervisory Bd Daimler Chrysler AG 1998–2001; Govt's Lead Non Exec Bd Membs 2010–; pres: Royal Acad of Engrg 2006–11, BAAS 2006–07; former chm Advsy Bd Judge Business Sch Cambridge, emeritus chm Advsy Bd Stanford Grad Sch of Business, chm Blavatnik Sch of Govt Oxford 2011–; former vice-pres Bd Prince of Wales Business Leaders Forum; chm of tstees Queen Elizabeth Prize for Engrg 2011–; tstee: Br Museum 1995–2005, Tate Galls 2007–; chm Tate Gallery 2009–; Gold Medal Inst of Mgmnt 2001, Prince Philip Medal RAE 1999; hon fell St John's Coll Cambridge; Hon LLD: Univ of Dundee, Notre Dame Univ, Thunderbird; Hon DSc: Univ of Hull, Leuven Univ, Cranfield Univ, Univ of Buckingham, Imperial Coll London, Univ of Warwick, Univ of Surrey, Arizona State Univ; Hon DEng: Heriot-Watt Univ, Colorado Sch of Mines, Queen's Univ Belfast, Aston Univ; Hon DTech Robert Gordon Univ, Hon DUniv Sheffield Hallam, Hon Chem Tech Mendeleyev Univ Moscow; FIMM 1987, FREng 1993, CCMI (CIMgt 1993), FRS 2006, FInstP, FInstPet, Hon FIChemE, Hon FIMechE, Hon FRSC, Hon FGS, FAAAS 2003, Hon FICE, Hon FCGI; *Books* Beyond Business (2010), Seven Elements that Changed the World (2013), The Glass Closet: Why Coming Out Is Good Business (2014); *Recreations* ballet, opera, collecting pre-Colombian artefacts, Venetian books of the 17th and 18th centuries; *Clubs* Athenaeum, Savile; *Style—* The Rt Hon the Lord Browne of Madingley, FRS, FREng; ✉ Riverstone LLP, 3 Burlington Gardens, London W1S 3EP (✆ 020 3206 6303, e-mail jbrowne@riverstonellc.com)

BROWNING, Baroness (Life Peer UK 2010) Angela Frances Browning; da of late Thomas Pearson, and late Linda Chamberlain; *b* 4 December 1946; *Educ* Reading Coll of Technol, Bournemouth Coll of Technol; *m* 1968, David Browning; 2 s; *Career* teacher of home economics in adult educn 1968–74, auxiliary nurse 1976–77, freelance conslt to mfrg indust 1977–85, mgmnt conslt specialising in trg, finance and corp communications 1985–92; MP (Cons): Tiverton 1992–97, Tiverton and Honiton 1997–2010; PPS Dept of Employment 1993–94, Parly sec Min of Agric Fisheries and Food 1994–97, oppn spokeswoman on education and disability 1997–98, shadow trade and industry sec 1999–2000, shadow Ldr of the House 2000–01, oppn spokeswoman on constitutional affrs until 2001, electoral cmmr 2010–11, min of state Home Office 2011–; dep chm Cons Pty 2005–07 (vice-chm 2001–05); dir Small Business Bureau 1985–94 and 1997–99, chm Women into Business 1988–92, memb Dept of Employment Advsy Ctee for Women's Employment 1989–92, govt co-chm Women's Nat Cmmn 1996–97, memb Advsy Ctee on Business Appts 2014– (chair 2015–); Parly candidate (Cons) Crewe and Nantwich 1987, former chm Western Area CPC (and memb CPC Nat Advsy Ctee); pres Inst of Home Economics 1997–2000, vice-pres Inst Sales & Mktg Mgmnt 1997–; nat vice-pres Alzheimers Disease Soc 1997–, vice-pres Nat Autistic Soc; FInstSMM; *Style—* The Baroness Browning; ✉ House of Lords, London SW1A 0PW

BROWNING, (Walter) Geoffrey (Geoff); s of Lt Walter Samuel Browning (d 1992), and Dorothy Gwendoline, *née* Hill (d 1987); *b* 6 November 1938; *Educ* Burnage GS Manchester; *m* 1, 20 June 1964 (m dis 1982), Barbara; 2 da (Helen b 11 May 1965, Claire b 22 April 1969), 1 s (Matthew b 18 Sept 1967), 1 adopted s (Jon b 16 March 1972); m 2, 17 Aug 1983, Pauline Ann, da of William Wilkinson (d 1998); 2 da (Alexandra b 7 June 1984, Danielle b 9 Sept 1985); *Career* chartered accountant; asst gp sr KPMG (formerly Peat Marwick Mitchell and Co) 1961–63 (articled clerk 1955–60), div co sec The Steetly Co Ltd 1963–64, fin dir Syd Abrams Ltd 1964–69, jt md Boalloy Ltd 1969–90; dir: Marling Industries plc 1990–92, Ardsley Ltd 1992–, Habib European Bank Ltd 1995–2012; underwriting memb Lloyd's 1980–96; FCA; *Recreations* sailing, golf, horses; *Style—* Geoff Browning, Esq; ✉ Beech Barn, Slegaby Ride, Slegaby, Isle of Man IM4 5BW

BROWNING, Prof George Gordon; s of George Gordon Browning, of Glasgow, and Janet Smith Ballantyne, *née* Money; *b* 10 January 1941; *Educ* Kelvinside Acad, Univ of Glasgow (MB ChB, MD); *m* 1971, Annette Campbell, da of William Mallinson; 2 da (Gillian Gordon b 26 Jan 1973, Jennifer Gordon b 24 Oct 1974), 1 s (Grigor Gordon b 20 Sept 1978); *Career* former appts: resident house surgn and physician then research fell Dept of Surgery Western Infirmary Glasgow, MRC Wernher-Piggott travelling fell Harvard Univ and Massachusetts Eye and Ear Infirmary, sr registrar Glasgow Trg Scheme; sr lectr then titular prof in otorhinolaryngology Univ of Glasgow 1990–99; conslt otologist MRC Inst of Hearing Research Glasgow Royal Infirmary 1978–2003, hon conslt N Glasgow Tst 1978–, hon conslt in charge Dept of Otorhinolaryngology and Scottish Sch of Audiology Glasgow Royal Infirmary 1989–99; ed Clinical Otolaryngology 2004–13; visiting scholar Sch of Public Health Harvard Univ 1989; Royal Soc of Med: chm Academic Bd 2001–03, vice-pres 2005–07, memb Section of Otology (pres 1999–2000; memb: Otorhinolaryngological Research Soc (sec 1983–86, pres 1992–94), Br Soc of Academics in Otolaryngology (sec 1992–94, pres 1994–99), Br Soc of Otolaryngologists, Scottish Otolaryngological Soc; Leon Goldman Medal Univ of Cape Town 1991, Walter Jobson Horne Prize BMA 1998, George Davey Howells Meml PrizeUniv of London 2000; FRCSEd 1970, FRCSGlas 1976; *Books* Clinical Audiology and Otology (1986, 2 edn 1998), Updated ENT (3 edn, 1994), Otoscopy: A structured approach (1995), Picture Tests in Otolaryngology (jtly, 1999), Scott-Brown's Otorhinolarygology: Head and NEck Surgery (jt ed, 7 edn 2008); author of numerous articles in learned jls; *Recreations* silversmithing, skiing, swimming; *Style—* Prof George G Browning; ✉ MRC/CSO Institute of Hearing Research, Scottish Section, Glasgow Royal Infirmary, New Lister Building, 10–16 Alexandra Parade, Glasgow G31 2ER

BROWNING, Helen; OBE (1998); *Career* farmer 1350 acre organic livestock and arable farm Wilts; formerly: food and farming dir Soil Assoc, dir of external affrs Nat Tst; chief exec Soil Assoc 2011–; chair Food Ethics Cncl; *Style—* Ms Helen Browning, OBE; ✉ Soil Association, South Plaza, Marlborough Street, Bristol BS1 3NX

BROWNING, John; *b* 5 June 1956; *Educ* Crown Woods Sch Eltham, Kingston Univ; *m* Linda; 1 s (James Stephen), 1 da (Virginia Elizabeth); *Career* Henry Bath Ltd 1979, Metallgesellschaft Ltd 1986, Kleinwort Benson Ltd 1989, Barclays Capital 2004, Bear Sterns Asia 2007, Newedge Asia 2008; dir London Metal Exchange 2002–04; FRSA; *Clubs* RAC; *Style—* John Browning, Esq; ✉ Newedge Group, Level 35, Three Pacific Palce, Queens Road East, Hong Kong

BROWNING, Prof Keith Anthony; s of James Anthony Browning (d 1972), and Amy Hilda, *née* Greenwood (d 2004); *b* 31 July 1938, Sunderland; *Educ* Commonweal GS Swindon, Imperial Coll London (state scholarship, BSc, PhD, DIC); *m* 4 August 1962, Ann Muriel, *née* Baish; 2 da (Michelle Ann b 19 March 1967, Jacqueline Claire b 15 Sept 1968), 1 s (Julian James b 25 June 1971); *Career* meteorologist; research atmospheric physicist Air Force Cambridge Research Labs USA until 1966, princ meteorological offr Meteorological Office Radar Research Lab 1966–74, chief scientist Nat Hail Research Experiment Nat Center for Atmospheric Research USA 1974–75, chief meteorological offr Meteorological Office Radar Research Lab 1975–84; Meteorological Office: dep dir Physical Research 1985–89, dir of research 1989–91, memb Bd of Dirs 1989–91, dir Jt Centre for Mesoscale Meteorology (JCMM) Univ of Reading 1992–2003; prof of meteorology Univ of Reading 1995–2003, now emeritus; visiting prof Univ of Leeds 2007–; NERC: memb Cncl 1984–87, dir Univs Weather Research Network (UWERN) 1997–2003, dir Univs Facility for Atmospheric Measurements (UFAM) 2000–03, memb various ctees; chm: Int Symposia on Nowcasting (under auspices of Int Assoc of Meteorology and Atmospheric Physics) 1981, 1984 and 1987, Working Gp 1 Inter-Agency Ctee for Global Environmental Change 1990, Task Gp 7 Second World Climate Conf Geneva 1990, UK Interagency Atmospheric Radar Working Gp 1992, Global Energy and Water Cycle Experiment (GEWEX) Cloud System Study 1992–95, Scientific Prog Ctee European Conf on Global Energy and Water Cycles 1993–94, World Weather Research Prog Int Conf on Quantitative Precipitation Forecasting 2002; co-ordinator European Cloud Resolving Modelling Prog 1996–98; memb: American Meteorological Soc (AMS) Severe Local Storms Ctee 1965–67, Inter-Union Cmmn on Radio Meteorology 1975–78, Int Cmnn on Cloud Physics 1976–84, Cncl and Policy Advsy Ctee European Orgn for the Exploitation of Meteorological Satellites (EUMETSAT) 1986–90, Advsy Panel on Environmental Research Central Electricity Research Labs 1986–90, World Climate Research Prog Sci Steering Gp GEWEX 1988–97, Jt World Meteorological Orgn (WMO)/Int Cncl of Scientific Unions (ICSU) Scientific Ctee World Climate Research Prog 1990–94, Review Panel Aust Bureau of Meteorology Research Centre 1992, Scientific Steering Ctee WMO World Weather Research Prog 1996–2005; RMS: student memb 1956–59, fell 1959–, vice-pres 1979–81, 1987–88 and 1990–91, pres 1988–90, chartered meteorologist 1994–2013, hon memb 2006, fndr memb Accreditation Bd (chm 1994–97), sometime memb Cncl; memb Academia Europaea 1989–; foreign assoc US Nat Acad of Engrg 1992–; ARCS 1959, fell AMS 1975 (hon memb 2010), FRS 1978; *Awards* Air Force Cambridge Research Labs: Superior Performance Award 1964, Award for Special Service Accomplished 1965; RMS: L F Richardson Prize 1965, Buchan Prize 1972, William Gaskell Meml Medal 1982, Symons meml lectr 1998, Symons Gold Medal 2001; L G Groves Meml Prize for Meteorology MOD 1969; AMS: Meisinger Award 1974, Jule G Charney Award 1984, Carl Gustaf Rossby Medal 2003; Charles Chree Medal and Prize Inst of Physics 1981; *Publications* Nowcasting (ed), Global Energy and Water Cycles (co-ed); author of over 200 peer-reviewed articles in learned jls in the areas of mesoscale meteorology, severe storms, frontal precipitation, radar meteorology and nowcasting; *Recreations* home, garden, walking, photography, piano, weather research; *Style—* Prof Keith Browning, FRS

BROWNJOHN, Alan Charles; s of Charles Henry Brownjohn (d 1985), of London, and Dorothy, *née* Mulligan (d 1976); *b* 28 July 1931; *Educ* Univ of Oxford (MA); *m* 1 (m dis 1969), Shirley Toulson; 1 s; m 2 (m dis 2005), Sandra Willingham; *Career* formerly sch teacher and lectr in English; freelance author and poet 1979–; chm Poetry Soc 1982–88; poetry critic: New Statesman 1968–76, Encounter 1977–80, Sunday Times 1990–2013; reg contrib to TLS and BBC Radio poetry progs; memb Cncl of Mgmnt Arvon Fndn 1973–2002; memb: Writers' Guild of GB, Soc of Authors; Cholmondeley Award for Poetry 1979, Soc of Authors travelling scholarship 1985, Special Award Books Ctee Writers' Guild of GB 2007; FRSL, fell English Assoc; *Books* Torquato Tasso (trans, 1985), The Way You Tell Them (1990, Authors' Club prize), Horace (trans, 1996), The Long Shadows (published in Romanian, 1996, Br edn 1997), A Funny Old Year (novel, 2001), Windows on the Moon (novel, 2009); poetry: Collected Poems (1988, new edn 2006), The Observation Car (1990), In the Cruel Arcade (1994), The Cat without E-Mail (2001), The Men Around Her Bed (2004), Ludbrooke and Others (2010), The Saner Places: Selected Poems (2011), A Bottle, and Other Poems (2015); anthologies: First I Say This (ed), New Poems 1970–71 (ed with Seamus Heaney and Jon Stallworthy), New Poetry 3 (ed with Maureen Duffy); *Recreations* walking, travelling, left-wing censoriousness; *Style—* Alan Brownjohn, Esq; ✉ 2 Belsize Park, London NW3 4ET (✆ 020 7794 2479); c/o Rosica Colin Ltd, 1 Clareville Grove Mews, London SW7 5AH (✆ 020 7370 1080)

BROWNJOHN, John Nevil Maxwell; s of Gen Sir Nevil Charles Dowell Brownjohn, GBE, KCB, CMG, MC (d 1973), and Isabelle, *née* White (d 1984); *Educ* Sherborne, Lincoln Coll Oxford (MA); *m* 19 Nov 1968, Jacqueline Sally Brownjohn, MBE, da of Geoffrey Byrd (d 1952), and Louise Leigh-Pemberton (d 1960); 1 da (Emma b 1969), 1 s (Jonathan b 1971); *Career* literary translator, screenwriter; cmmnd Somersetshire LI 1948, served Royal W African Frontier Force 1948–49; chm Exec Ctee Translators' Assoc Soc of Authors 1976; Schlegel-Tieck Special Award 1979, US PEN Goethe-House Prize 1981, Schlegel-Tieck Prize 1993, US Christopher Award 1995, US Helen and Kurt Wolff Prize 1998, Schlegel-Tieck Prize 1999; *Books* over 160 book translations from German and French incl: The Night of the Generals (1963), Klemperer Recollections (1964), The Poisoned Stream (1969), The Human Animal (1971), The Boat (U-Boat) (1974), Willy Brandt Memoirs (1978), A German Love Story (1980), Momo (1985), The Marquis of Bolibar (1989), Love Letters from Cell 92 (1994), Acts: The Autobiography of Wolfgang Wagner (1994), The Karnau Tapes (1997), Heroes Like Us (1997), The 13 and a Half Lives of Captain Bluebear (2000), Hidden Hitler (2001), Winston Churchill (2003), My Wounded Heart (2004), Please, Mr Einstein (2006), Elizabeth I and Mary Stuart (2007), The Sinner (2007), A Perfect Waiter (2008), Night Work (2008), A Question of Time (2009), The Alchemaster's Apprentice (2009), Sailing by Starlight (2010), Bad Karma (2010), Splinter (2011), The Hour of the Jackal (2011), Léon and Louise (2011), The Eye-Collector (2012), The Camera Killer (2012), The Labyrinth of Dreaming Books (2012), Pull Yourself Together (2013), Almost Like Spring (2013), Catalyst (2014), A Price to Pay (2014), The Bible Hunter (2014), The Last Voyage of Sigismund Skirk (2015), Fishers of Souls (2015), Auntie Poldi and the Sicilian Lions (2016), The Draper's Daughter (2016); *Screen Credits* Tess (in collaboration with Roman Polanski and Gérard Brach, 1980),

The Boat (1981), Pirates (1986), The Name of the Rose (1986), The Bear (1989), Bitter Moon (in collaboration with Roman Polanski, 1992), The Ninth Gate (in collaboration with Roman Polanski, 1999); *Recreations* music; *Style*— John Brownjohn, Esq; ✉ Bookend House, Hound Street, Sherborne, Dorset DT9 3AA (☎ and fax 01935 814553, e-mail johnbrownjohn@tinyworld.co.uk)

BROWNLEE, Alistair Edward; MBE (2013); bro of Jonathan Brownlee, *qv*; *b* 23 April 1988; *Educ* Bradford GS, Univ of Leeds (BSc), Leeds Met Univ; *Career* triathlete; achievements incl: Gold medal World Championships 2009, Silver medal European Championships 2009, Gold medal European Championships 2010. Gold medal (team) World Championships 2011, Gold medal European Championships 2011, Gold medal World Championships 2011, Gold medal Olympic Games 2012, Gold medal Olympic Games 2016; *Style*— Mr Alistair Brownlee, MBE

BROWNLEE, Jonathan Callum; bro of Alistair Brownlee, *qv*; *b* 30 April 1990; *Educ* Bradford GS, Univ of Leeds; *Career* triathlete; achievements incl: Gold medal (sprint distance triathlon) World Championships 2010 and 2011, Gold medal (team triathlon) World Championships 2011, Silver medal World Championships 2011, Bronze medal Olympic Games 2012, Gold medal World Championships 2012, Gold medal Olympic Games 2016; *Style*— Mr Jonathan Brownlee

BROZZETTI, Gianluca; *b* 4 March 1954; *Educ* Univ of Perugia; *Career* various positions: Procter & Gamble, McKinsey & Co, Gucci Group; exec dir Watch and Jewellery Div rising to exec vice-pres Fragrance Div Bulgari Group, pres and ceo Louis Vuitton Malletier 1999–2001, group ceo Asprey & Garrard 2001–05, ceo Asprey 2005–07, ceo Roberto Cavalli Gp 2009–14; *Style*— Gianluca Brozzetti, Esq

BRUCE; *see also:* Cumming-Bruce

BRUCE, Hon Adam Robert; WS (1999); yr s of The Earl of Elgin and Kincardine, KT, CD, *qv*, and Victoria Mary, da of Dudley George Usher, MBE, TD; *b* 18 January 1968; *Educ* Glenalmond Coll, Balliol Coll Oxford (MA, pres Union 1989), Univ of Edinburgh (LLB); *m* Donna Maria Sofia Giovanna Rose, da of The Prince of Belmonte and Muro Leccese; 2 s; *Career* slr; dir of public policy McGrigors 1998–2006, ceo Airtricity UK 2006–08, global head of corporate affrs Mainstream Renewable Power 2008–; dir Westminster Forum 2000–; chm RenewableUK (BWEA) 2007–10; chm Offshore Wind Prog Bd 2012–, chm Seastar Industrial Alliance 2014–; memb: Arbuthnott Cmmn, Exec Ctee SCDI 2007–09, Bd EWEA 2008–14 (vice-pres 2013–14), Bd GWEC 2008–, MPLS Devpt Bd Univ of Oxford 2010–; tstee: Policy Inst 2006–08, St Andrew's Fund for Scots Heraldry 2007–, Mitsubishi UFJ Tst Oxford Fndn 2014–; memb Royal Co of Archers (HM's Bodyguard for Scotland); Finlaggan Pursuivant 2006–08, HM Unicorn Pursuivant of Arms 2008–12, HM Marchmont Herald of Arms 2012–; FRSA, FSA (Scot), OStJ 2014; *Clubs* New (Edinburgh), Pratt's; *Style*— The Hon Adam Bruce, WS; ✉ Mainstream Renewable Power, Arena House, Arena Road, Sandyford, Dublin 18, Ireland

BRUCE, (Robert) Andrew; s of Robert Bruce (d 1965), and Betty, *née* Bowen (d 1988); *b* 23 June 1949, Cardiff; *Educ* Pembroke Coll Cambridge (MA), Manchester Business Sch (MBA); *m* (m dis); 4 s (Robert b 29 April 1978, James b 17 Dec 1979, Alexander b 1 Oct 1984, Edward b 3 May 1987); *Career* J P Morgan: joined 1973, petroleum and project finance 1974–82, corporate finance SW USA 1982–86, head of risk J P Morgan Securities 1986–88, head of corporate financing 1988–91, European head of credit 1991–93; Barclays plc: risk dir and memb Exec Ctee BZW/Barclays Capital 1993–98, gp credit risk dir 1998–2015 (ret); dir: Clearstream 1996–2015, Witan Investment Trust plc 2003–14; *Recreations* sailing, skiing, golf; *Clubs* Royal Southern Yacht; *Style*— Andrew Bruce, Esq; ✉ R A Bruce, 1 Rigault Road, Fulham, London SW6 4JJ (e-mail r.andrewbruce@gmail.com)

BRUCE, Christopher; CBE (1998); s of Alexander Bruce (d 1970), and Ethel, *née* Parker; *b* 3 October 1945, Leicester; *Educ* Benson Stage Acad Scarborough, Ballet Rambert Sch London; *m* 1967, Marian, da of Frank Meadowcroft, BEM (d 1969); 2 s (Mark Sebastian b 1968, Thomas Benjamin b 1970), 1 da (Molly Ellen b 1975); *Career* choreographer; formerly dancer, debut with London Ballet 1963; Ballet Rambert (later Rambert Dance Co): joined as dancer 1963, leading dancer in modern roles 1966 (roles incl The Poet in Cruel Garden, Prospero in The Tempest and Pierrot in Pierrot Lunaire), choreographer 1969, assoc choreographer 1975–87, assoc dir 1975–79, artistic dir 1994–2003; roles danced with English Nat Ballet incl Tchaikovsky/Drosselmeyer in The Nutcracker and title role in Petrouchka, assoc choreographer Eng Nat Ballet 1986–91; resident choreographer Houston Ballet 1989–98 (assoc choreographer 1998–); works as choreographer for Ballet Rambert incl: George Frideric (debut, music by Handel) 1969, Ancient Voices of Children 1975, Cruel Garden (with Lindsay Kemp) 1977, Ghost Dances 1981, Requiem 1982, Intimate Pages 1984, Ceremonies 1986; works for Eng Nat Ballet incl: Land 1985, The World Again 1986, The Dream is Over 1987, Symphony in Three Movements 1989; works for Houston Ballet incl: Guatama Buddha 1989, Journey 1990, Nature Dances 1992, Hush 2006; works for Rambert Dance Co: Crossing 1994, Meeting Point 1995, Quicksilver 1996, Stream 1996, Four Scenes 1998, God's Plenty 1999, Grinning in Your Face 2001, A Steel Garden 2005, Some Sort of Island Dance 2015; works for other companies incl: Unfamiliar Playground (Royal Ballet) 1974, Cantate (Tanz Forum Cologne) 1981, Village Songs (Nederlands Dans Theater) 1981, Silence is the End of our Song (Royal Danish Ballet) 1984, Remembered Dances (Scottish Ballet) 1985, Les Noces (Gulbenkian Ballet Lisbon) 1989, Il Ballo della Ingrate Agrippina and Venus and Adonis (Kent Opera), Rooster (Geneva Ballet) 1991, Three Songs-Two Voices (Royal Ballet) 2005, Shift (Ballet Central) 2007, Dance at the Crossroads (Ballet Mainz) 2007; new ballets created: Kingdom (Geneva) 1993, Moonshine (Nederlands Dans Theater) 1993, Waiting (London Contemporary Dance Theatre) 1993, Ten Poems (Ballet Kiel Germany) 2009, Für Alina (Ballet Central), Dream (Nat Dance Wales) 2012, Shadows (Phoenix Dance Theatre) 2014, Morning and Moonshine (Ballet Central) 2015, Some Sort of Island Dance (Rambert School) 2015; subject of BBC documentary 1978; hon visiting prof Univ of Exeter 2009; Evening Standard Award for Dance 1974, Prix Italia 1982, International Theatre Inst Award for Dance 1993, Evening Standard Ballet Award for Outstanding Artistic Achievement 1996, De Valois Award for outstanding contribution to Dance Critics' Circle Nat Dance Awards 2003, Rheinische Post Theater Oscar (for An Evening of Work by Christopher Bruce (Theater Krefeld-Mönchengladbach) 2004, Bst Choreography Critic's Choice Award 2010; hon life memb Amnesty Int 2002; Hon Dr Art De Montfort Univ 2000, Hon DLitt Univ of Exeter 2001; *Style*— Christopher Bruce, Esq, CBE; ✉ c/o Rambert Dance Co, 99 Upper Ground, London SE1 9PP

BRUCE, David Ian Rehbinder; s of Ian Stuart Rae Bruce, MC (d 1967), and Reinhildt Hilda Henriette Reinholdtsdotter, *née* Baroness Rehbinder; *b* 16 August 1946; *Educ* Eton, Oriel Coll Oxford (MA); *m* 4 Dec 1976, Anne Margaret Turquand (Muffyn), da of Col David Frank Turquand Colbeck, OBE (d 1995); 2 s (Edward, Ian (twins) b 1984); *Career* chartered accountant; Peat Marwick Mitchell & Co 1968–72; Cazenove & Co: investment analyst 1972–79, conslt Ctee to Review the Functioning of Fin Inst 1977–79; Royal Dutch/Shell Gp: asst treas advsr Shell Int Petroleum Co Ltd 1979–80, mangr fin planning Shell Canada Ltd 1980–83, treas & controller Shell UK Ltd 1983–86; exec dir fin and admin The Stock Exchange 1986–90, gp fin dir Guinness Mahon Holdings plc 1990–93, dir of fin Lloyd's of London 1993; chm Bolingbroke Mgmnt Consultancy Ltd 1995–; former memb Hundred Gp, memb Tech Ctee of the Assoc of Corporate Treasurers 1988–; Freeman City of London 1977, Liveryman Worshipful Co of Merchant Taylors 1980; FCA, AIIMR, FCT; *Recreations* music, opera (spectator), shooting, fishing; *Clubs* Pratt's, White's; *Style*— David Bruce, Esq; ✉ 5 Bolingbroke Grove, London SW11 6ES (☎ 020 8673 1434, fax 020 7787 8144); office (☎ 020 7771 0065)

BRUCE, Fiona Claire; MP; *née* Riley; *b* 26 March 1957; *Educ* Burnley HS for Girls, Howell's Sch Llandaff, Univ of Manchester, Chester Coll of Law; *m* Richard; 2 s (Samuel, Daniel); *Career* admitted slr 1981; fndr and sr ptnr Fiona Bruce LLP 1988–; memb Law Soc 1979; cncllr Warrington BC 2004–10, MP (Cons) Congleton 2010–; chair Human Rights Cmmn Cons Pty; patron Evangelical Alliance; *Recreations* music, travel, countryside; *Style*— Mrs Fiona Bruce, MP; ✉ House of Commons, London SW1A 0AA

BRUCE, Fiona Elizabeth; da of John Bruce, and Rosemary Bruce; *Educ* Int Sch Milan, Aske's Girls' Sch, Br Inst Paris (scholar), Hertford Coll Oxford (MA); *Career* broadcaster; BBC: reporter Newsnight 1996–98, presenter Six O'Clock News 1999–, presenter 10 O'Clock News 2002–; presenter: Antiques Show 1998–2000 and 2009–, Crimewatch 2000–08, Real Story 2003–06, Call My Bluff 2003; patron Touch UCHL, supporter Refuge; ambass: Childline, Prince's Tst, Action Medical Research, Wellbeing of Women; *Recreations* playing with my children; *Style*— Ms Fiona Bruce; ✉ c/o Avalon Management, 4a Exmoor Street, London W10 6BD (☎ 020 7598 7321)

BRUCE, Prof Ian Waugh; CBE (2004); s of Thomas Waugh Bruce (d 1980), and Una Nellie, *née* Eagle (d 1987); *b* 21 April 1945; *Educ* King Edward VI Sch Southampton, Central HS Arizona, Univ of Birmingham (BSocSci); *m* 19 June 1971, Anthea Christine (Tina), da of Dr P R Rowland, of London; 1 da (Hannah b 20 Dec 1976), 1 s (William Waugh (Tom) b 18 May 1979); *Career* apprentice chem engr Courtaulds 1964–65, mktg trainee then mangr Unilever 1968–70, appeals and PR offr then asst dir Age Concern England 1970–74, dir Nat Centre for Volunteering 1975–81, controller of secretariat then asst chief exec Borough of Hammersmith and Fulham 1981–83, vice-pres RNIB 2003– (dir gen 1983–2003); Cass Business Sch (formerly City Univ Business Sch): visiting prof 1991–, pres Centre for Charity Effectiveness 2010– (fndr dir 1991–2010, formerly known as VOLPROF Centre for Vol Sector and Not-for-Profit Mgmnt); chm Coventry Int Centre 1964, memb Arts Cncl of GB Art Panel, Art Film Ctee and New Activities Ctee 1967–71, conslt UN Div of Social Affrs 1970–72; spokesman: Artists Now 1973–77, Nat Good Neighbour Campaign 1977–79; founding sec Volunteurope Brussels 1979–81, advsr BBC Community Progs Unit 1979–81, co-chm Disability Benefits Consortium 1987–2001; memb: Exec Ctee NCVO 1978–81 and 1990–94, Cncl Ret Execs Action Clearing House 1978–83, Advsy Cncl Centre for Policies on Ageing 1979–83, Educn Advsy Cncl IBA 1981–83, Steering Ctee Disability Alliance 1985–92, Exec Ctee Age Concern Eng 1986–92, Nat Advsy Cncl on Employment of Disabled People 1987–98, Bd Central London TEC 1990–97 (dep chm 1996–97), Ctee Nat Giving Campaign 2001–04; chair Res Ctee 2001–04; Univ of Birmingham: Cncl 1994–2000, Ct 2001–; co-fndr KnowHow NonProfit 2008, sec World Nonprofit Academic Centres' Cncl 2008–10, chair Centre Directors Gp Int Soc of Third Sector Research 2008–10, vice-pres Int Cncl of Volunteerism, Civil Soc and Social Economy Research Assocs 2012–, fndr chair Charity Mktg Special Interest Gp of UK CIM 2013–, chair Richmond Soc 2013–; Sir Raymond Priestley Expeditionary Award Univ of Birmingham 1968, UK Charity Outstanding Achievement Award 2001 and 2003; Hon DSocSc Univ of Birmingham 1995; memb ICA, MIMgt 1975, FIMgt 1981, CIMgt 1991, FRSA 1991; *Publications* Public Relations and the Social Services (1972), Patronage of the Creative Artist (jtly, 1974, 2 edn 1975), Blind and Partially Sighted Adults in Britain (1991), Managing and Staffing Britain's Largest Charities (jtly, 1992), Management for Tomorrow (jtly, 1993), Access to Written Information (jtly, 2001), Employment and Unemployment Among People with Sight Problems in the UK (jtly, 2003), The Art of Raising Income (2010), Charity Marketing – Meeting Need through Customer Focus (4 edn, 2011); author of papers on visual impairment, voluntary and community work, older people, contemporary art and marketing; *Recreations* the arts, the countryside; *Style*— Prof Ian Bruce, CBE; ✉ Ormond House Cottage, Ormond Road, Richmond, Surrey TW10 6TH; Cass Business School, 106 Bunhill Row, London EC1Y 8TZ (☎ 020 7040 8781)

BRUCE, Kenneth Frederick Charles; s of Kenneth Frederick Bruce, and Anne Barlow, *née* Agnew; *b* 4 June 1975, Morecambe; *Educ* Univ of Southampton; *m* Kerinna Kerr; 2 s (George Bruce, Tom Bruce), 1 da (Keria Bruce); *Career* estate agent and entrepreneur; sales dir Enfields 1999–2006, co-owner (with bro Michael Bruce) and sales dir Burchell Edwards 2006–11, fndr Purplebricks.com (with Michael Bruce) 2014–; *Recreations* cinema, gardening, horse racing, music, travel, walking; *Style*— Kenny Bruce, Esq

BRUCE, Kenneth Robertson (Ken); s of Peter Smith Bruce (d 1984), and Williamina McKenzie, *née* Dunbar (d 2000); *b* 2 February 1951; *Educ* Hutchesons' Boys' GS Glasgow; *m* 1 (m dis), Fiona Frater; 2 s (Campbell McKenzie b 20 Nov 1979, Douglas Robertson b 23 March 1981); m 2, (m dis), Anne Gilchrist; 1 da (Kate Anne b 15 Oct 1992); m 3, 16 Sept 2000, Kerith Coldham; 2 s (William Murray b 5 Jan 2002, Charles Gregor b 10 Feb 2008), 1 da (Verity Isobel b 1 April 2005); *Career* broadcaster; BBC staff announcer 1976–80 (progs incl: Good Morning Scotland, SRO Road Show, Ken Bruce's Saturday (BBC Radio Scot), Midday Concert (BBC Radio 3), Music To Remember (BBC Radio 4); freelance broadcaster 1980–, own daily prog BBC Radio Scot 1980–84; BBC Radio 2: reg dep work 1982–83, own Saturday night show 1984, own daily morning prog 1985–90 and 1991–, presenter daily late night prog 1990; weekly prog BBC World Service 1986–93, presenter Breakaway (BBC Radio 4) 1990–92; main presenter Nat Music Day 1992–95; other progs incl: The 'What If' Show, The ABC Quiz, Pop Score, Comedy Classics (BBC Radio 2), Freewheeling, Pick of the Week (BBC Radio 4), Friday Night is Music Night (BBC Radio 2), regular appearances Countdown (Channel 4); commentaries: Commonwealth Games 1986, Olympic Games Seoul 1988, Eurovision Song Contest (BBC Radio 2) 1988–; events incl: Wings and Strings, Voice of Musical Theatre 2000, Proms in the Park; inducted into Radio Acad Hall of Fame 2008; *Publications* Tracks of My Years (autobiography, 2009); *Recreations* films, reading, music, theatre; *Style*— Ken Bruce, Esq; ✉ c/o Jo Gurnett Personal Management, 12 Newburgh Street, London W1F 7RP (☎ 020 7440 1850, fax 020 7287 9642)

BRUCE, Robert Charles; s of late Maj James Charles, MC (and Bar), and Enid Lilian, *née* Brown; *b* 5 May 1948; *Educ* Belmont House, Solihull Sch, City of London Coll (BSc); *Career* trainee accountant Edward Moore and Sons 1971–75; Accountancy Age: staff writer and news ed 1976–81, ed 1981–90, assoc ed 1990–93; The Times: accountancy columnist 1992–99, accountancy ed 1999–2001; ed: Corporate Financier 1998–2004, Balance Sheet 1999–2004; writer to The Prince of Wales Accounting for Sustainability Project 2007; Accountancy Journalist of the Year 1995, overall winner Inst of Internal Auditors (IIA) Millennium Award for excellence in business and mgmnt press journalism 2000, IIA Award for excellence in business journalism 2001, shortlisted Tax Journalist of the Year 2001, Inst of Financial Accountants (IFA) Business Finance Journalist of the Year 2004, finalist Tax Writer of the Year 2006, winner corporate governance category Excellence in HR Journalism 2008; FRSA; *Books* Winners – How Small Businesses Achieve Excellence (1986), ICAS: 150 Years – a Celebration (2004); *Recreations* cricket, buying books, watching swifts; *Clubs* MCC, BCC; *Style*— Robert Bruce, Esq; ✉ 87 Marylands Road, London W9 2DS (☎ 020 7286 0211, e-mail robertbruce@ntlworld.com)

BRUCE, Steve Roger; s of Joseph Bruce, of Newcastle upon Tyne, and Sheenagh, *née* Creed; *b* 31 December 1960; *Educ* Benfield Comp Sch Newcastle upon Tyne; *m* Janet, da of Lesley Smith; 1 s (Alex b 28 Sept 1984), 1 da (Amy b 24 May 1987); *Career* professional footballer and manager; player: Gillingham 1978–84, Norwich City 1984–87 (League Cup 1985), Manchester United 1987–96 (capt 1994–96, FA Cup 1990, 1994 and 1996, European Cup Winners' Cup 1991, League Cup 1992, FA Premier League Championship 1993, 1994 and 1996, Charity Shield 1993 and 1994), Birmingham City 1996–98; player/mangr Sheffield United FC 1998–99; mangr: Huddersfield Town FC 1999–2001, Birmingham City FC 2001–07, Wigan Athletic FC 2007–09, Sunderland AFC 2009–11, Hull City FC 2012–; England: 8 youth caps, 1 B cap; *Style*— Steve Bruce, Esq

BRUCE, Prof Dame Victoria Geraldine (Vicki); DBE (2015, OBE 1997); da of Charles Frederick Bruce, and Geraldine Cordelia Diane, *née* Giffard; *b* 4 January 1953; *Educ* Church HS Newcastle, Newnham Coll Cambridge (MA, PhD); *Career* demonstrator Dept of Psychology Univ of Newcastle upon Tyne 1977–78; Univ of Nottingham: lectr in psychology 1978–88, reader 1988–90, prof of psychology 1990–92; Univ of Stirling: prof of psychology 1992–2002, dep princ (research) 1995–2002; vice-princ and head Coll of Humanities and Social Sci Univ of Edinburgh 2002–08, head School of Psychology Univ of Newcastle; pres Euro Soc for Cognitive Psychology 1996–98 (memb 1987–, memb Ctee 1994–), chm Psychology Panel 1996 and 2001, chair Panel K 2008 Research Assessment Exercise; memb: Neurosciences and Mental Health Bd MRC 1989–92, ESRC 1992–96 (chm Research Programmes Bd 1992–96), SHEFC 1995–2001; memb Editorial Advsy Bd Psychological Research 1988–; memb Editorial Bd: Euro Jl of Cognitive Psychology 1988–, Visual Cognition 1993–, Applied Cognitive Psychology 1994–95; ed British Jl of Psychology 1995–2000; consulting ed Jl of Experimental Psychology: Applied 1994–2001; memb: Experimental Psychology Soc 1980– (memb Ctee 1986–89), Psychonomic Soc 1988–; FBPsS 1989 (hon fell 1997), CPsychol 1989, FRSE 1996, FBA 1999 (vice-pres Public Engagement 2011–); *Publications* Visual Perception: Psychology and Ecology (jtly, 1985, 4 edn 2003), Recognising Faces (1988), Visual Cognition: computational, experimental and neuropsychological perspectives (jtly, 1989), Face Recognition (ed, 1991), Processing Images of Faces (ed jtly, 1992), Processing the Facial Image (ed jtly, 1992), Object and face recognition (ed jtly, 1994), Perception and Representation (jtly, 1995), Unsolved Mysteries of Mind: tutorial essays in cognition (ed, 1996), In the Eye of the Beholder: The Science of Face Perception (with A W Young , *qv*, 1998); also author of numerous articles and papers in learned jls; *Recreations* dogs, walking, games; *Style*— Prof Dame Vicki Bruce, DBE, FBA, FRSE; ✉ School of Psychology, Ridley Building 1, Queen Victoria Road, Newcastle upon Tyne NE1 7RU

BRUCE OF BENNACHIE, Baron (Life Peer UK 2015) of Bennachie, of Torphins in the County of Aberdeen; **Rt Hon Sir Malcolm Gray Bruce;** kt (2012), PC (2006); s of late David Stewart Bruce, of Wirral, and late Kathleen Elmslie, *née* Delf; *b* 17 November 1944; *Educ* Wrekin Coll, Univ of St Andrews (MA), Univ of Strathclyde (MSc), Univ of Middx (CPE); *m* 1, 1969 (m dis 1992), Veronica Jane, da of Henry Coxon Wilson, of West Kirby, Wirral; 1 s (Alexander b 1974), 1 da (Caroline b 1976); *m* 2, 1998, Rosemary Elizabeth, da of Peter Arthur Vetterlein, of Beckenham, Kent; 2 da (Catriona b 1999, Emma b 2004), 1 s (Alasdair b 2002); *Career* trainee journalist Liverpool Daily Post, buyer Boots Ltd, res info offr NESDA, journalist and publisher Aberdeen Petroleum Publishing Ltd; called to the Bar Gray's Inn 1995; Parly candidate (Lib): North Angus and Mearns Oct 1974, West Aberdeenshire 1979; MP (Lib 1983–88, Lib Dem 1988–2015) Gordon 1983–2015; Lib spokesman Energy 1986–87, Alliance spokesman Employment 1987, Lib spokesman Trade and Indust 1987–88, SLD spokesman Natural Resources 1988–89; Lib Dem spokesman: Environment and Natural Resources 1989–90, Scotland 1990–92, Treasy and Econ Affrs 1994–99 (also Treasy and Civil Serv 1994–95), Trade and Indust; chm Lib Dem Parly Pty 1999–2001, Lib Dem shadow sec of state for the Environment, Food and Rural Affrs 2001–02, dep ldr Lib Dem Parly Pty 2014–; chair Int Devpt Select Ctee 2005–; memb: Scottish Select Ctee 1983–87, Trade and Industry Ctee 1987–89 and 1992–94, Treasy Ctee 1994–98, Standards and Privileges Select Ctee 1999–2001, Parly Assembly Cncl of Europe 1999–2005, Liaison Ctee 2005–, ctees on arms efforts controls 2006–, Jt Ctee on the Nat Security Strategy 2011–; pres Scot Lib Dems 2000– (ldr 1988–92); occasional journalist and broadcaster; vice-pres: Nat Deaf Children's Soc, Action on Hearing Loss (formerly Royal Nat Inst for the Deaf, former tstee); rector Univ of Dundee 1984–87; *Style*— The Rt Hon the Lord Bruce of Bennachie; ✉ House of Commons, London SW1A 0AA

BRUCE-JONES, Tom Allan; CBE (2003); s of Tom Bruce-Jones (d 1984), of Blairlogie, Stirlingshire, and Rachel Inglis, *née* Dunlop (d 2002); *b* 28 August 1941; *Educ* Charterhouse, Lincoln Coll Oxford (BA); *m* 1, 1965 (m dis 1980), R Normand; 1 da (Caroline b 23 Nov 1966), 1 s (Tom b 8 Sept 1968); *m* 2, 6 March 1981, Stina Birgitta, da of Harry Ossian Ahlgren (d 1982), of Helsinki; *Career* dir Price and Pierce (Woodpulp) Ltd 1973–77, vice-pres Georgia-Pacific International Inc 1977–79; James Jones and Sons Ltd: jt md 1979–87, md 1987–97, chm 1995–; chm SWL Ltd 2005–16 (dir 1990–2005); dir Stella-Jones Inc (Montreal) 1993– (chm 1994–); forestry cmmr 1996–2003, pres Western European Inst for Wood Preservation 1998–2001; consul for Finland Glasgow 1994–2015; Knight (First Class) Order of the Lion of Finland 2003; *Recreations* fishing, golf, music; *Clubs* Hon Co of Edinburgh Golfers; *Style*— Tom Bruce-Jones, Esq, CBE; ✉ 18 Park Terrace, Glasgow G3 6BY; James Jones & Sons Ltd, Broomage Avenue, Larbert, Stirlingshire FK5 4NQ (☎ 01324 562241, fax 01324 556642, e-mail t.brucejones@jamesjones.co.uk)

BRUCE-RADCLIFFE, Godfrey Martin; s of Roy Bruce-Radcliffe (d 1976), and Joyce Evelyn, *née* Shewring (d 1996); *b* 19 June 1945; *Educ* King's Coll Taunton, Guildford Coll of Law; *m* 5 Oct 1974, Claire Miller; 2 c (Edward b 9 Aug 1976, Helen b 2 Nov 1982); *Career* articled clerk Trower Still & Keeling (now Trowers and Hamlins), admitted slr 1970, ptnr D J Freeman 1978–94 (joined 1977), ptnr Hobson Audley 1994–2002, ptnr Thomas Eggar 2002–06, conslt Thomas Eggar 2007–09; memb London Regnl Cncl CBI 1999–2005; Freeman City of London 1986, Liveryman Worshipful Co of Basketmakers 1998–2009, Liveryman Worshipful Co of Loriners 2004; memb Law Soc 1970; *Books* Property Development Partnerships (co-author, 1994), Practical Property Development and Finance (1996), Encyclopaedia of Forms and Precedents (contrib author, Vol 38 (2) 2000), Development and the Law: A Guide for Construction and Property Professionals (2005); *Recreations* sailing, walking, gardening, music; *Style*— Godfrey Bruce-Radcliffe, Esq; ✉ Ellacombe, 21 Anstey Lane, Alton, Hampshire GU34 2NB (e-mail gbruceradcliffe@icloud.com)

BRUCK, Steven Mark; *Educ* Hendon GS, Univ of Southampton (BSc), LSE (MSc); *Career* articled clerk Chalmers Impey CAs 1969–72, gp accountant Halma plc 1972–73, special projects accountant Overseas Containers Ltd 1973–75, Pannell Fitzpatrick 1975–78, ptnr Mercers Bryant 1978–84, corp fin ptnr Pannell Kerr Forster 1984–97, ptnr Blick Rothenberg 1997–2013; chm Delbanco Meyer & Co Ltd 2000–03; chm Belsize Square Synagogue 1998–2003, vice-chm Edgwarebury Cemetery 2013–; FCA 1972; *Recreations* family, theatre, cycling; *Style*— Steven M Bruck, Esq

BRUCKNER, Dr Felix Ernest; s of late William Bruckner, of London, and late Anna, *née* Hahn; *b* 18 April 1937, Mikulov, Czechoslovakia; *Educ* London Hosp Med Coll Univ of London (MB BS); *m* 24 June 1967, Rosalind Dorothy, da of late George Edward Bailey, of Herts; 2 s (James b 1974, Thomas b 1976), 1 da (Catherine b 1981); *Career* conslt physician and rheumatologist St George's Hosp London 1970–2002; pres Rheumatology and Rehabilitation Section RSM 1994–95; FRCP; *Publications* Death on the Koh-i-noor (crime fiction, 2012), In The Footsteps of the Whitechapel Slasher (crime fiction, 2013), Death on the House (crime fiction, 2014); numerous chapters and papers on rheumatological subjects; *Recreations* music, bridge, reading, writing fiction; *Clubs* RSM; *Style*— Dr Felix Bruckner; ✉ 12 Southwood Avenue, Kingston upon Thames, Surrey KT2 7HD (☎ 020 8949 3955)

BRUDENELL, Thomas Mervyn; s of Edmund Crispin Stephen James George Brudenell (d 2014), of Deene Park, Corby, Northants, and Marian Cynthia, *née* Manningham-Buller (d 2013), da of 1 Viscount Dilhorne; *b* 12 August 1956; *Educ* Eton; *m* 1, 5 May 1984, Venetia Jane (d 1993), da of Maj Robert Patricius Chaworth-Musters (d 1992); 2 da (Sophia b 12 April 1985, Victoria b 11 Feb 1987); *m* 2, 27 June 1996, Mrs Amanda J Skiffington, da of Alick David Yorke Naylor-Leyland, MVO (d 1991), and the Countess of Wilton; *Career* called to the Bar Inner Temple 1977; *Recreations* shooting, stalking, bridge, racing, golf; *Clubs* White's, Pratt's, Royal St George's Golf, Swinley Forest Golf; *Style*— Thomas Brudenell, Esq; ✉ 86a Tachbrook Street, London SW1V 2NB (☎ 020 7932 0291); Lark Hall, Fordham, Ely, Cambridgeshire CB7 5LS (☎ 01638 720590); Queen Elizabeth Building, Temple, London EC4Y 9BS (☎ 020 7797 7837, e-mail t.brudenell@qeb.co.uk); Felley Priory, Jacksdale, Nottinghamshire NG16 5FJ (☎ 01773 811324)

BRUDNIZKI, Martin; s of Andre Brudnizki, and Karin Brudnizki Gamrell; *b* 1966, Stockholm; *Educ* Stockholm Univ (BA), The American Univ London (BA); *Career* interior designer and interior architect; Wolfson Design 1993–94, David Gill Galleries 1995, David Collins Studio, 1995–99, fndr Martin Brudnizki Design Studio 2000–; fndr And Objects; patron Sir John Soane's Museum; *Recreations* opera, reading, travel, walking, theatre, ballet, art, charity work; *Clubs* Soho House, The Academicians' Room (RA), The Club at the Ivy, 5 Hertford Street; *Style*— Martin Brudnizki, Esq; ✉ Martin Brudnizki Design Studio, Unit 1G Chelsea Reach, 79–89 Lots Road, London SW10 0RN (☎ 020 7376 7555, e-mail studio@mbds.com, website www.mbds.com, Twitter @MBDS_News)

BRUETON, Dr Martin John; s of Neville Frederick William Brueton (d 1981), of Bristol, and Nancy Rushton, *née* Baldwin; *b* 2 February 1944; *Educ* Bristol GS, Bart's Med Sch (MB BS, MD, FRCP, FRCPCH, DCH), Univ of Birmingham (MSc); *m* May 1967, Patricia Ann, da of Geoffrey Oliphant May (d 1994), and Jean, *née* Heyward (d 1986); 2 da (Nicola Ann b 18 June 1969, Catherine Jane b 16 March 1975), 1 s (Mark Richard b 25 May 1971); *Career* jr registrar Bart's 1970–71 (house physician 1968), sr registrar Ahmadu Bello Univ Zaria Nigeria 1971–73, lectr in paediatrics Univ of Birmingham/Children's Hosp Birmingham 1973–78, sr lectr and hon conslt paediatrician Westminster Children's Hosp 1979–93, hon conslt paediatrician Chelsea and Westminster, Charing Cross and Royal Brompton Hosps and reader in child health Imperial Coll Sch of Med (Charing Cross and Westminster Med Sch until merger 1997) 1979–2001, conslt paediatric gastroentorologist Chelsea and Westminster and St Mary's Hosps 2001–07, emeritus conslt paediatric gastroenterologist Chelsea and Westminster Hosp 2007–, clinical dir Women and Children's Directorate Chelsea and Westminster Healthcare NHS Tst 1994–95; regularly invited to lecture at overseas univs and to participate in meetings/working gps in the fields of paediatric gastroenterology and nutrition; hon reader in child health Imperial Coll Faculty of Med London 2001–, Wellcome Tst jr research fell 1976; chm Children's Hosp Tst Fnd 1991–2011; memb Br Soc of Paediatric Gastroenterology Hepatology and Nutrition (pres 1998–2001); FRCP, FRCPCH (offr for higher specialist training 1997–2002); *Books* Diseases of Children in Subtropics and Tropics (jt ed, 1991), Practical Paediatric Therapeutics (jtly, 1991); *Recreations* tennis, music, theatre; *Clubs* RSM; *Style*— Dr Martin Brueton; ✉ The Cleve, Castle Hill, Woodgreen, Fordingbridge, Hampshire SP6 2AX (☎ 01725 512324)

BRUGES, Jason David; s of John Edward Bruges, and Lynne, *née* Harris; *b* 15 September 1972, Rochford, Essex; *Educ* Tring Sch, Oxford Brookes Univ (BA), Bartlett Sch of Architecture UCL (Dip); *m* 23 Oct 2004, Katayoun Ghahremani; *Career* Foster Asia 1994–95, Sir Norman Foster & Ptnrs 1995–98, sr designer Imagination 1999–2001, fndr and creative dir Jason Bruges Studio 2001–; artist in residence Veuve Clicquot 2008; teacher and visiting lectr: Westminster Univ, UCL, RCA, Middx Univ, Oxford Brookes Univ, Univ of Plymouth, Southern Californian Inst of Architecture and Design Research Lab, Architectural Assoc; sometime lectr: BAFTA, Inst of Physics, ELDA, ICA; exhbns: RIBA, SCIARC, SCP, Victoria Miro Gallery, Habitat (Brilliant), Venice Film Festival, Selfridges, V&A, Tate Britain, Millennium Galleries, London Fashion Week, UBS/Tate Modern London Architectural Biennale, Center for Architecture NY 2007; first artist cmmn for Olympic Park 2010 2008; contrib V&A's 150th Anniversary Album 2007; work featured in numerous pubns; jt nominee Interactive BAFTA 2004, Int Lighting Design Award (for Hotel Puerta America) 2006, highly commended Special Projects Lighting Design Awards 2009, Workplace Category Design Week Awards 2009, nominated (with pd3) D&AD Award 2009, nominated Essance of the 21st Century Wallpaper Courvoisier Award 2009, nominated Design Award Germany 2009, nominated mentor Nesta Creative Business Mentor Award 2009, voted amongst top 50 influential people DesignWeek Top 50 2009; memb BAFTA 2004; *Recreations* food and wine, architecture, interaction design, time based art, dynamic and kinetic art; *Clubs* Shoreditch House (fndr memb); *Style*— Jason Bruges, Esq; ✉ Jason Bruges Studio, Unit 2.08, The Tea Building, 56 Shoreditch High Street, London E1 6JJ (☎ 020 7012 1122, fax 020 7012 1199, e-mail jason@jasonbruges.com)

BRUGES, Katharine Georgia (Kate); da of Christopher John Farara, of Guildford, Surrey, and Alison Mary, *née* Duguid; *b* 19 November 1962; *Educ* Woking Grammar Sch, Woking Sixth Form Coll, Newnham Coll Cambridge (MA); *m* 7 Sept 1991, Richard Michael Bruges, s of Maj Michael Bruges; 3 s (Max b 16 June 1993, Harry b 16 June 1995, Jim b 17 July 1999); *Career* J Walter Thompson: joined as graduate trainee 1984, youngest bd appointment 1989, currently talent dir; memb IPA Cncl 2011; FIPA 2005; *Recreations* riding, pantomime, gardening; *Style*— Mrs Kate Bruges; ✉ JWT, 1 Knightsbridge Green, London SW1X 7NW (☎ 020 7656 7000, fax 020 7656 7010, e-mail kate.bruges@jwt.com)

BRUGHA, Prof Traolach Seán; s of Ruairi Brugha, of Dublin, and Maire, *née* MacSwiney; *b* 6 January 1953; *Educ* Gonzaga Coll Dublin, UCD (MB BCh, MD); *m* 3 April 1976, Máire Nic Eoghain; 3 da (Rossa Eoghain, Lia Patricia, Cillian Traolach); *Career* registrar in psychiatry St Vincent's Hosp Elm Park Dublin 1979–80, registrar then sr registrar Bethlem and Maudsley Hosp London 1980–87, clinical scientist MRC Social Psychiatry Unit London 1982–87, hon lectr in psychiatry Inst of Psychiatry London 1984–87, sr lectr Univ of Leicester 1987–2000, prof of psychiatry Univ of Leicester 2000–, hon conslt psychiatrist Leicester Health Authy 1987–, seconded as SMO Dept of Health London 1995–97; FRCPsych 2002 (MRCPsych 1981); *Recreations* photography, cycling, music; *Style*— Prof Traolach Brugha; ✉ Department of Psychiatry, University of Leicester, Leicester (☎ 0116 225 6295, fax 0116 225 6235)

BRUINVELS, Canon Peter Nigel Edward; er s of Capt Stanley Bruinvels (d 2012), and Ninette Maud, *née* Kibblewhite (d 2001); *b* 30 March 1950, Dorking, Surrey; *Educ* St John's Sch Leatherhead, Univ of London (LLB), Cncl of Legal Educn; *m* 20 Sept 1980, Alison Margaret, da of Maj David Gilmore Bacon, of Lymington, Hants; 2 da (Alexandra Caroline Jane b 6 April 1986, Georgina Emma Kate b 20 Oct 1988); *Career* princ Peter Bruinvels Assocs (media mgmnt corp communications and public affrs conslts) 1986–, managing ed Bruinvels News & Media (press and broadcasting agents) 1993–, political commentator, freelance journalist and author 1987–; special external advsr DTI 1993–95, memb Child Support and Social Security Appeals Tbnls 1994–99; Church Cmmr 1992–; OFSTED Denominational Schs S48/SIAS RE Inspector 1994–; co-opted business representative memb Surrey LEA 1997–2007, exec offr Surrey CC Civilian-Military Partnership Bd 2013–; MP (Cons) Leicester E 1983–87, memb Cons Home Office and NI Ctees 1983–87; jt vice-chm: Cons Urban Affrs and New Towns Ctee 1984–87, Cons Educn Ctee 1985–87; promoter Crossbows Act 1987; campaign co-ordinator gen election Eastbourne 1992, Parly candidate The Wrekin 1997 (prospective Parly candidate 1995);

memb Cons NUEC 1976–81, vice-chm SE Area Conservatives 1977–79, pres Dorking Conservatives 1995–; chm Church Army Remuneration Ctee 1999–2004, dir Church Army 1999–2004, vice-chm Guildford Diocesan Bd of Educn 2008– (chm 2005–08); ind lay chm NHS Complaints Procedure 1999–2005; pres NW Midlands CIM 1997–98; chm Surrey Schools Orgn Ctee 2000–07, chm Surrey Jt Services' Charities Ctee 2004–; county field offr Surrey The Royal Br Legion 2002–12, county mangr Sussex Royal Br Legion 2011–12, project offr Nat Armed Forces Day Guildford 2015–; non-exec dir E Elmbridge and Mid Surrey PCT 2002–07; hon sec Surrey Military Appeals Ctee (formerly Surrey County Appeals Ctee) 2002–; elected memb Guildford Crown Nominations Cmmn 2003, elected memb Surrey Assembly 2010–13; memb: Guildford Diocesan Synod 1974– (vice-pres 2003–13), Gen Synod C of E 1985–, Bd of Patrons 1985–, Parly Legislative Ctee (C of E) 1991–96 and 2000– (dep chm 2011–), Gen Synod Bd of Educn 1996–2007, Bd of Govrs Church Cmmns 1998– (Mgmnt Advsy Ctee 1999–2009), House of Bishops Clergy Discipline (Doctrine) Gp 1999–, Dearing Implementation Follow-Up Gp 2001–, Cathedrals Fabric Cmmn for England 2006–, Surrey SACRE 2013–; dep chm Nominations and Governance Ctee Church Cmmrs 2009–, dep chm SE England Veterans and Pensions Advsy Ctee 2014–, dep chm Church Cmmrs Pastoral Ctee 2015–; lay canon Guildford Cathedral 2002– (memb Cncl 2003–); regnl fundraiser SE ABF Solders' Charity 2013–; govr Univ of York St John 1999–2007, admissions adjudicator Surrey LEA 1999–2007, memb Ct Univ of Sussex 2001–08, memb Coll of Canons 2002–, govr Whitelands Coll Roehampton Univ 2007– (chm of govrs 2009–12), memb Cncl Royal Alexandra & Albert Sch Reigate 2009–, memb Cncl Roehampton Univ 2009–12, dir Guildford Diocesan Educn Tst (GDET) 2012, exec offr Kent CC Civilian-Military Partnership Bd 2016–; memb: SE England War Pensions Ctee 2003–, Cncl Queen Victoria Clergy Fund 2006– (vice-chm Cncl 2010–, chm 2016–), Church Cmmrs Assets Ctee 2014–; Ofsted SIAS denominational schs S48 RE inspr 1994–; Freeman City of London 1980; fell Industry and Parl Tst; FRSA, FCIM, MCIJ, MCIPR; *Books* Zoning in on Enterprise (1982), Light up the Roads (1984), Sharing in Britain's Success: A Study in Widening Share Ownership Through Privatisation (1987), Investing in Enterprise: A Comprehensive Guide to Inner City Regeneration and Urban Renewal (1989); *Recreations* politics in the C of E, political campaigning, the media, freedom marches by the military; *Clubs* Carlton, Inner Temple, Corporation of Church House, Jersey Wildlife Preservation; *Style—* Canon Peter Bruinvels; ✆ 01306 887082, mobile 07721 411688

BRUMMELL, David; CB (2005); s of Ernest Brummell (d 1997), and Florence Elizabeth, *née* Martin (d 2002); *b* 18 December 1947; *Educ* Nottingham HS, Queens' Coll Cambridge; *Career* articled clerk then asst slr Simmons & Simmons 1971–75; local govt: Devon CC 1975–77, W Sussex CC 1977–79; Govt Legal Service: Office of Fair Trading 1979–84, Treasy Advsy Division 1984–86, Dept of Energy Advsy Division 1986–89, Treasy Slr's Litigation Division 1989–2000 (head of division 1995–2000), legal secretary to the law officers 2000–; *Recreations* music, tennis, walking, languages, poetry; *Clubs* Athenaeum, Thames Hare & Hounds; *Style—* David Brummell, Esq, CB; ✉ The Legal Secretariat to the Law Officers, Attorney General's Chambers, 9 Buckingham Gate, London SW1E 6JP (✆ 020 7271 2401, fax 020 7271 2431)

BRUMMELL, HE Paul; CMG (2016); s of Robert George Brummell (d 1992), and June Brummell (d 2002); *b* 28 August 1965; *Educ* St Albans Sch, St Catharine's Coll Cambridge (MA); *m* 9 June 2012, Adriana Mitsue Ivama; 1 s (George Sussumi b 20 Aug 2013); *Career* joined HM Dip Serv 1987, third later second sec Islamabad 1989–92, FCO 1993–94, first sec Rome 1995–2000, dep head Eastern Dept FCO 2000–01, ambass to Turkmenistan 2002–05, ambass to Kazakhstan 2005–09 (concurrently non-resident ambass to Kyrgyzstan), high cmmr to Barbados 2009–13 (concurrently non-resident high cmmr to Antigua and Barbuda, Dominica, Grenada, St Kitts and Nevis, St Lucia and St Vincent and the Grenadines 2009–13, concurrently perm rep to Orgn of Eastern Caribbean States (OECS) and plenipotentiary rep to the Caribbean Community (CARICOM) 2010–13, consul-gen to the Dutch Caribbean 2011–13), ambass to Romania 2014–; *Books* Turkmenistan: The Bradt Travel Guide (2005), Kazakhstan: The Bradt Travel Guide (2008); *Recreations* travel writing; *Style—* HE Mr Paul Brummell, CMG; ✉ c/o Foreign & Commonwealth Office (Bucharest), King Charles Street, London SW1A 2AH (Twitter @paulbrummell)

BRUMMER, Alexander; s of Michael Brummer, of Brighton, E Sussex, and Hilda, *née* Lyons; *b* 25 May 1949; *Educ* Brighton Hove & Sussex GS, Univ of Southampton (BSc), Univ of Bradford Mgmnt Centre (MBA); *m* 26 Oct 1975, Patricia Lyndsey, da of Saul Leopold Magrill; 1 da (Jessica Rachel b 5 Jan 1978), 2 s (Justin Adam b 29 Sept 1980, Gabriel Joseph b 30 Dec 1981); *Career* journalist; De La Rue Company 1971–72, Haymarket Publishing 1972–73; The Guardian: fin corr 1973–79, Washington corr 1979–85, Washington bureau chief 1985–89, foreign ed 1989, fin ed 1990–99, assoc ed 1998–99; ed Financial Mail on Sunday 1999–2000, City ed Daily Mail 2000–; *Awards* Best Foreign Corr in US Overseas Press Club 1989, Financial Journalist of the Year British Press Awards 1999, Best City Journalist Media Awards 2000, Sr Financial Journalist Wincott 2001, Newspaper Journalist of the Year Work Fndn 2002, Business Journalist of the Year World Leadership Forum 2006, Business Journalist of the Year London Press Club 2010; hon doctorate Univ of Bradford 2014; *Books* American Destiny (jt author, 1985), Hanson: A Biography (1994), Weinstock: The Life and Times of Britain's Premier Industrialist (1998), The Crunch (2008), The Great Pensions Robbery (2010), Britain for Sale (2012), Bad Banks (2014); *Recreations* reading, antiques; *Style—* Alexander Brummer, Esq; ✉ Associated Newspapers, Northcliffe House, Derry Street, London W8 5TS (✆ 020 7938 6000, e-mail alex.brummer@dailymail.co.uk)

BRUMMITT, Nick; *Career* internet entrepreneur; ceo and fndr cybermarket.co.uk 2002–09, dir and fndr Wowcher.co.uk 2009–11, dir and ceo Magic Future Media 2011–, fndr and prop Fabfob.com 2012–, fndr and ceo Gcard 2014–; *Style—* Nick Brummitt, Esq

BRUNDLE, Martin John; s of late Alfred Edward John Brundle, and Alma, *née* Coe; *b* 1 June 1959; *Educ* King Edward VII GS Kings Lynn, Norfolk Coll of Arts and Technol; *m* Elizabeth Mary; 1 da (Charlotte Emily b 9 May 1988), 1 s (Alexander Martin b 7 Aug 1990); *Career* motor racing driver and TV presenter; began racing aged 12, turned professional 1984; Formula One teams driven for: Tyrrell, Zakspeed, Williams, Brabham, Benetton, McLaren, Ligier, Jordan; drove for Jaguar in World Sportscar Championship 1985–91; Le Mans driver: Toyota 1998–99, Bentley 2001; achievements incl: runner-up Br Formula 3 1983, fifth place in first ever grand prix 1984, world sportscar champion 1988, winner Le Mans 24-hr Race 1990, runner-up Italian Grand Prix 1992, third place Br, French, Japanese and Australian Grands Prix 1992, third place San Marino Gp 1993, runner-up Monaco Grand Prix 1994, third place Belgian Grand Prix 1995; currently presenter and commentator Sky Sports F1; chm: Grand Prix Drivers Assoc 1994–96, Br Racing Drivers' Club 2000–04; awards: Grovewood Award for most promising young driver in Cwlth 1982, Segrave Trophy for exceptional performance on land or sea 1988, Br Racing Drivers' Club Gold Star 1988 and 2004, RTS Sports Commentator of the Year Award 1998, 1999, 2005 and 2007, BAFTA 2006, 2007 and 2008; *Publications* Working the Wheel (2004), Martin Brundle Scrapbook (2013); *Recreations* motor cycling, helicopter flying; *Clubs* British Racing Drivers', BARC; *Style—* Martin Brundle, Esq

BRUNNER, Kate; QC (2015); *b* 5 August 1972, London; *m* 28 May 2004, Robin Pargeter; 2 da (Millie Josephine b 13 Jan 2006, Edie Grace Elliott b 5 March 2007); *Career* called to the Bar Inner Temple 1997; recorder 2012, pt-time judge of the Upper Tbnl (Administrative Appeals Chamber) 2014; *Style—* Ms Kate Brunner, QC; ✉ Albion Chambers, Broad Street, Bristol BS1 1DR

BRUTON, (Victoria) Jane; da of Roger Bruton (d 2000), and Glynnis, *née* Boardman; *b* 21 March 1968, Wigan, Lancs; *Educ* The Byrchall HS Ashton-in-Makerfield, Winstanley Coll Wigan, Univ of Nottingham (BA), City Univ (Dip Journalism); *m* 23 Aug 1996, Johnathan Whitehead; 2 s (Arthur Louis b 8 July 2001, Jonah Alexander b 21 July 2004); *Career* journalist; sub ed then writer Chat 1991–92, freelance 1993–94, dep ed Wedding and Home 1994–97, assoc ed Prima 1997; ed: Living etc 1998–2002, Eve 2002–04, Grazia 2004–; dep ed and Lifestyle dir of the Daily Telegraph 2015–; Ed of the Year BSME 2004, 2006 and 2010, Magazine of the Year PPA 2008, Ed's Ed BSME 2008; fndr memb and tstee Trees for Cities; *Style—* Ms Jane Bruton; ✉ Grazia, Endeavour House, 189 Shaftesbury Avenue, London WC2H 8JG

BRYAN, Felicity Anne (Mrs Alexander Duncan); da of Sir Paul Bryan, DSO, MC (d 2004), and Betty Mary, *née* Hoyle (d 1968); *b* 16 October 1945; *Educ* Courtauld Inst of Art, Univ of London; *m* 23 Oct 1981, Alexander Duncan, s of Patrick Duncan (d 1967), and Cynthia Duncan; 1 da (Alice Mary b 1982 d 2004), 2 s (Maxim Paul b 1983, Benjamin Patrick b 1987); *Career* journalist: Financial Times 1968–70, The Economist 1970–72; literary agent and dir Curtis Brown Ltd 1972–88, fndr The Felicity Bryan Agency 1988–; Fndr Stern Fellowship with the Washington Post; memb Ct Oxford Brookes Univ; sponsor Oxford Literary Festival, patron Woodstock Literary Festival, tstee Equilibrium – The Bipolar Fndn; *Books* The Town Gardener's Companion (1982), A Garden for Children (1986), Nursery Style (1989); *Recreations* opera, ballet, gardening, travel, entertaining; *Style—* Ms Felicity Bryan; ✉ Felicity Bryan Associates, 2A North Parade, Banbury Road, Oxford OX2 6LX (✆ 01865 513816, fax 01865 310055, website www.felicitybryan.com)

BRYAN, Rex Victor; s of Bertram Henry Bryan (d 1970), of Purley, Surrey, and Annie Ella Margaret, *née* King; *b* 2 December 1946; *Educ* Wallington GS, Jesus Coll Oxford (MA); *m* 1, 31 July 1971 (m dis 1981), Catherine, da of Samuel Carbery, of Ballymena, Co Antrim, NI; 1 s (Roland Patrick b 1977); m 2, 9 Aug 1982, Mary Elizabeth, da of Brendan Joseph O'Toole, of Frinton-on-Sea, Essex; 2 s (Adam Francis b 1985, Thomas Edward b 1988), 2 da (Victoria Louise b 1986, Leonora Rose b 1991); *Career* called to the Bar Lincoln's Inn 1971, head of chambers 1986–2003, recorder of the Crown Court 1994–; *Recreations* DIY, horticulture; *Style—* Rex Bryan, Esq; ✉ 5 Pump Court, Temple, London EC4Y 7AP (✆ 020 7353 2532, fax 020 7353 5321)

BRYANT, Chris; MP; s of Rees Bryant, and Anne Gracie, *née* Goodwin (d 1993); *b* 11 January 1962; *Career* MP (Lab) Rhondda 2001–; Parly under-sec of state for Europe and Asia 2009–10; shadow ldr of the House 2015–16; *Style—* Chris Bryant, Esq, MP; ✉ House of Commons, London SW1A 0AA (✆ 020 7219 8315, fax 020 7219 1792)

BRYANT, Prof Christopher Gordon Alastair; s of Gordon Douglas Clifford Bryant (d 1975), of Bristol, and Edna Mollie, *née* Shrubb (d 1996); *b* 14 April 1944; *Educ* Kingston GS, Univ of Leicester (BA, MA), Univ of Southampton (PhD); *m* Elizabeth Mary, da of George Thomas Martyn Peters; 2 da (Catherine Elizabeth, Lucy Ann); *Career* tutorial asst Dept of Sociology Univ of Leicester 1965–66; Univ of Southampton: asst lectr in sociology 1966–68, lectr 1968–76; Univ of Salford: sr lectr in sociology 1976–82, chm Dept of Sociology 1982–90, prof of sociology 1982–2010, dir Inst for Social Research 1993–98, dean Faculty of Arts, Media and Social Sciences 1999–2003, pro-vice-chllr (research) 2004, emeritus prof 2010–; visiting fell: Ohio State Univ Columbus 1981, Univ of Utrecht 1986–91; guest prof Univ of Frankfurt 1973, visiting prof Central European Univ Warsaw 1996–99, O'Donnell lectr Univ of Wales 2010; memb: Br Sociological Assoc 1966– (memb Exec Ctee 1987–91, chm Pubns Ctee 1989–91), Advsy Bd Central European Univ Warsaw 1999–2003; memb Editorial Bd: Br Jl of Sociology 1991–2000, International Sociology 1992–2004, Polish Sociological Review 2000–07; FAcSS 2014 (AcSS 2005); *Books* Sociology in Action (1976), Positivism in Social Theory and Research (1985), What Has Sociology Achieved? (1990), Giddens' Theory of Structuration (1991), The New Great Transformation? (1994), Practical Sociology (1995), Democracy, Civil Society and Pluralism in Comparative Perspective (1995), Anthony Giddens: Critical Assessments (4 vols, 1997), The Contemporary Giddens (2001), The Nations of Britain (2006); *Recreations* watching football, theatre, concerts, walking, seeing friends, fine and decorative arts; *Style—* Prof Christopher Bryant; ✉ e-mail chris.bryant1@ntlworld.com

BRYANT, Prof Greyham Frank; s of Ernest Noel Bryant (d 1981), and Florence Ivy, *née* Russell (d 1974); *b* 3 June 1931; *Educ* Univ of Reading (BSc), Imperial Coll London (PhD); *m* 2 July 1955, Iris Sybil, da of Albert Edward Jardine (d 1980); 2 s (Mark Greyham b 2 Jan 1963, David Nicholas b 18 Aug 1966); *Career* sr scientific offr Br Iron and Steel Res 1959–64; Imperial Coll London: research fell 1964–67, reader in industrial control 1975–82, prof of control 1982–, res dir and co-fndr Interdisciplinary Research Centre in Systems Engrg 1989–96, sr research fell 1997–; chm: Broner Conslts 1979–88, Greycon Consls 1985–97; dir Circulation Research 1989–2007; MIEE, FIMA, FREng 1988; *Books* Automation of Tandem Mills (jtly), Multivariable Control System Design Techniques; *Recreations* music, oil painting; *Clubs* Athenaeum; *Style—* Prof Greyham Bryant, FREng; ✉ 18 Wimborne Avenue, Norwood Green, Middlesex UB2 4HB (✆ 020 8574 5648); Department of Electrical Engineering, Imperial College, London SW7 2AZ

BRYANT, Prof John Allen; s of Joseph Samuel Bryant (d 1996), of Croydon, Surrey, and (Beatrice Maud) Patricia, *née* Wallace-Page (d 1990); *b* 14 April 1944; *Educ* Whitgift Sch Croydon, Queens' Coll Cambridge (BA, MA, PhD); *m* 27 July 1968, Marjorie Joan, da of Maj Gerald C G Hatch (d 1983), of Hingham, Norfolk; 2 s (Mark b 1 Jan 1972, Simon b 3 Jan 1974); *Career* research fell UEA 1969–70, lectr Univ of Nottingham 1970–74, reader Univ Coll Cardiff 1982–85 (lectr 1974–77, sr lectr 1977–82), prof of biological sciences Univ of Exeter 1985– (head of biology 1986–91, prof emeritus 2001–), visiting prof West Virginia State Univ 1999–2007; Soc for Experimental Biology: memb Cncl 1981–87 and 1992–2005, hon sec 1983–87, memb Cell Biology Ctee 1988–97, vice-pres 2001–03, pres 2003–05; memb: Plant Sci and Microbiology Ctee SERC 1986–89, Bd of Dirs E African Inst for Scientific Res and Devpt 1991–99, Professional and Educn Ctee Biochemical Soc 1994–97; memb Editorial Bd Sci and Christian Belief; chm Christians in Science 2001–07; FRSA 1989, FRSB 2014 (FIBiol 1986, CBiol 1984, MIBiol 1970); *Publications* over 100 research papers and review articles/chapters; author/co-author/ed/co-ed of 19 books incl: Functional Biology of Plants (with Martin Hodson, 2012), Beyond Human (2013); *Recreations* cross-country (formerly at intercounty level) and road running, birdwatching, walking; *Style—* Prof John Bryant; ✉ e-mail j.a.bryant@exeter.ac.uk

BRYANT, Dr John Martin; s of William George Bryant (d 1969), and Doris, *née* Martin (d 1972); *b* 28 September 1943; *Educ* West Monmouth Sch Pontypool, St Catharine's Coll Cambridge (state scholarship), Univ of Wales (DSc); *m* 28 August 1965, Andrea Irene, da of John Leslie Emmons; 2 s (David John b 21 February 1967, Matthew James b 1 February 1971), 1 da (Catherine Jane b 26 July 1969); *Career* grad trainee Steel Co of Wales 1965–67; British Steel plc (now Corus Gp plc): asst mangr Port Talbot 1967–70, technical mangr 1970–73, departmental mangr 1973–76, personnel mangr 1976–78, works mangr 1978–88, project mangr 1982–88, dir of Coated Products 1988–90, md of Tin Plate 1990–92, md of Strip Products 1992–96, exec dir 1996–99, chief exec British Steel plc 1999–, jt chief exec Corus Gp plc 1999–2000; pres British Steel Trico Hldgs 1995–2001; chm: European Profiles Ltd 1992–95, PMF Ltd 1992–95, chm Welsh Water 2013–; dir: ASW Gp plc 1993–95, Bank of Wales plc 1996–2001; non-exec dir: Welsh Water plc 2001–14, Glas Cymru 2001–14, Costain Gp plc 2002–13; memb Occupational Health Advsy Ctee 1988–94; CEng 1993, FIM 1993, FREng 2000; *Recreations* rugby, cricket, walking, reading, opera, theatre, family; *Clubs* Crawshays Welsh RFC, Bridgend Lawn Tennis and Squash; *Style—* Dr John Bryant; ✉ e-mail drjmbryant@aol.com

BRYANT, Karina Louise; da of Derek Payne, and Nicola Bryant; *b* 27 January 1979, Kingston, London; *Career* judoka; achievements incl: Silver medal European Junior Championships 1995, 1996 and 1997, Gold medal World Junior Championships 1996 and 1998, Gold medal European Junior Championships 1998, Gold medal European Championships 1998, Bronze medal (+78kg class) World Championships 1999, Gold medal (+78kg class) European Championships 2000, Silver medal (open class) World Championships 2001, Bronze medal (open class) European Championships 2001, Silver medal (open class) and Bronze medal (+78kg class) World Championships 2003, Gold medal (+78kg class) European Championships 2003, Silver medal (+78kg class) European Championships 2004, 2 Silver medals (+78kg class and open class) World Championships 2005, Gold medal (+78kg class) European Championships 2005, Silver medal World Championships 2009, Bronze medal European Championships 2010, Bronze medal (+78kg class) European Championships 2012, Bronze medal (+78kg class) Olympic Games 2012; BOA Olympic Judo Athlete of the Year 2009; *Clubs* Camberley Judo; *Style*— Miss Karina Bryant; ✉ website www.karinabryant.com, Twitter @karinabryantgb

BRYANT, Michael Sydney; s of Sydney Cecil Bryant (d 1977), of Keynsham, Avon, and Lily May, *née* Jefferies; *b* 16 March 1944, Bristol; *Educ* Bristol GS, Univ of Exeter, City of London Coll; *m* 1 Oct 1994, Sheila Daviron; *Career* Estate Duty Office Inland Revenue 1965–70, assoc dir Bevington Lowndes Ltd 1970–75, mktg dir Rathbone Brothers plc 1975–97; chm Hambro Fraser Smith Ltd 1997–2000; taxation and fin conslt 1997–; contrib: Daily Telegraph, Sunday Times, Money Mktg, Taxation; memb Cncl FIMBRA 1986–88 and 1990–91, chm Insurance and Compensation Ctee FIMBRA, memb Tax Ctee IFAA, memb Securities Inst IAC Ctee 1998–; Compagnon du Beaujolais 1982–; IBRC 1977; *Recreations* food, wine, bridge, travel; *Clubs* Carlton, Cercle de Deauville; *Style*— Michael Bryant, Esq; ✉ Rue St Nicol, 14600 Honfleur, France (☎ 00 33 2 31 89 07 51, fax 00 33 2 31 89 16 30, e-mail michael.bryant@wanadoo.fr)

BRYCE, Andrew John; s of John Robert Murray Bryce, of Lymington, Hants, and Eileen Josephine, *née* Denham; *b* 31 August 1947; *Educ* Thorpe GS Norwich, Univ of Newcastle upon Tyne (LLB), Coll of Law Lancaster Gate; *m* 1, 1972 (m dis 1994), Karalee Frances Lovegrove; 1 s (Alexander Henry b 22 June 1977), 1 da (Lucy Charlotte b 21 May 1980); m 2 (m dis 2005), 1994, Rosalind Beverley Hardy; 1 s (Matthew Cameron b 2 Oct 1986); *Career* CMS Cameron McKenna slrs (formerly Cameron Markby Hewitt): articled clerk 1969–71, admitted slr 1971, ptnr 1973–94; in practice specialising in environmental law Andrew Bryce & Co 1994–; UK Environmental Law Assoc: fndr memb 1986, vice-chm 1987–88, chm 1988–91, memb Cncl 1986–96, hon life memb 2007–; former vice-chm Planning and Environmental Sub-Ctee City of London Law Soc; non-exec dir Augean plc 2005–; memb Law Soc 1973; *Recreations* bird watching, travel, decorative arts, music, sailing; *Clubs* Essex Birdwatching Soc, BTO, RSPB, Cambridge Bird; *Style*— Andrew Bryce, Esq; ✉ Andrew Bryce & Co, Unit 23, Cambridge Science Park, Milton Road, Cambridge CB4 0EY (☎ 01223 437011, fax 01223 437012, e-mail bryce@ehslaw.co.uk, website ehslaw.co.uk)

BRYCE, Gordon Craigie; s of George Bryce (d 1970), and Annie Macleod (d 1982); *b* 30 June 1943, Edinburgh; *Educ* George Watsons Coll Edinburgh, Edinburgh Coll of Art (DA); *m* 1, 1966 (m dis 1976), Margaret Lothian; 2 s (Jon Oliver b 1968, Toby Garrad b 1969); m 2, 1984, Hilary Duthie; 2 da (Emma Louise b 1984, Alice Victoria b 1992), 1 s (Simon Nicholas b 1988); *Career* studied under Sir Robin Philipson and Sir William Gillies; head of fine art Grays Sch of Art 1986–95 (lectr in printmaking 1968–86); full time artist 1995–; RSW 1976, RSA 1995 (ARSA 1976); *Awards* RSA Chalmers Bursary 1965, RSA Keith Prize 1965, winner Pernod Scottish Acad Competition 1967, Arts Cncl Award 1968 and 1971, RSA Latimer Award 1969, May Marshall Brown Award 1977, maj Arts Cncl Award 1980, Educations Inst of Scotland Award 1981, Shell Expo Premier Award 1982, Sir William Gillies travelling scholarship 1984, Scottish Postal Bd Award 1986, Regional Award Discerning Eye Exhbn Mall Galleries London 2013; *Solo Exhibitions* New 57 Gallery 1966 and 1968, Absalom Gallery 1968, Richard Demarco Gallery 1971, Univ of Aberdeen 1972, McMurray Gallery London 1977, Royal Edinburgh Hosp 1978, Univ of Edinburgh 1984, Sue Rankin Gallery London 1986–93, Thackeray Gallery London 1986–2013, Grape Lane Gallery York 1988, Kingfisher Gallery Edinburgh 1988, Yperifanos Gallery NY 1988, Macaulay Gallery Stenton E Lothian 1989–94, Ancrum Gallery 1990, Rendezvous Gallery Aberdeen 1990, 1992 and 1996, Bruton Gallery Bath 1993, Thackeray Rankin Gallery London 1993, Jorgensen Fine Art Dublin 1994, Corrymella Scott Gallery Newcastle 1994, The Scottish Gallery 1996, Aitken Dott Ltd Edinburgh 1996–2004 and 2006; *Work in Public Collections* incl: Scottish Nat Gallery of Modern Art, Scottish Arts Cncl, Aberdeen Arts Cncl, Edinburgh Civic Collection, Fife Educn Authy, Royal Edinburgh Hosps Collection, Carnegie Dunfermline Tst, Nat Tst for Scotland, Charterhouse Gp London, Flemings Collection, Seaforth Maritime Museum Aberdeen, BP, Argyle Securities London, Elf Oil, Mobile Oil, Bank of Scotland, Enterprise Oil plc, RSA, Grampian Television, George Watsons Coll Edinburgh, Perth Museum and Art Gallery, Darlington Borough Art Collection, The Turcan Connell Collection; *Recreations* fly fishing; *Style*— Gordon Bryce, Esq; ✉ Sylva Cottage, 2 Culter House Road, Milltimber, Aberdeen AB1 0EN (☎ 01224 733274); Thackeray Gallery, 18 Thackeray Street, Kensington Square, London W8 5ET (☎ 020 7937 5883, fax 020 7937 6965, e-mail enquiries@thackeraygallery.com, website www.thackeraygallery.com)

BRYDEN, William Campbell Rough (Bill); CBE (1993); s of late George Bryden, and Catherine Bryden; *b* 12 April 1942; *Educ* Greenock HS; *m* 1, 1970 (m dis 1989), Hon (Monica) Deborah, *née* Morris, da of 3 Baron Killanin, MBE, TD; 1 s (Dillon Michael George b 1972), 1 da (Mary Kate b 1975); m 2, 2008, Angela More; *Career* television/theatre director; documentary writer Scottish TV 1963–64; asst dir: Belgrade Theatre Coventry 1965–67, Royal Court Theatre London 1967–69; assoc dir: Royal Lyceum Theatre Edinburgh 1971–74, Royal National Theatre 1975; head of drama television BBC Scotland 1984–94; dir: Cottesloe Theatre (Nat Theatre) 1978–80, Royal Opera House Covent Garden (productions include Parsifal 1988 and The Cunning Little Vixen 1990, 2003 and 2010), Bernstein's Mass (Guildhall Sch of Music & Drama) 1987, A Life in the Theatre (Haymarket) 1989, The Ship (Glasgow)1990, The Big Picnic (Glasgow) 1994, A Month In the Country (West End) 1995, Uncle Vanya (West End) 1996, The Mysteries (RNT) 1999, The Silver Tassie (ENO) 2000 (revival 2002), The Good Hope (RNT) 2001, The Creeper (West End) 2006, Small Craft Warnings (Arcola London) 2008; radio 2003–13 incl: HMS Ulysses, The Charge of the Light Brigade, Daisy Miller, The Plutocrat, The Last Tycoon; exec producer BBC TV: Tutti Frutti (by John Byrne) 1987 (best series BAFTA awards), The Play on One (series) 1989; dir The Shawl (by David Mamet) BBC TV 1989; winner: Dir of the Year (Laurence Olivier Awards) 1985, Best Dir Award (Evening Standard) for The Mysteries Nat Theatre 1985, Assoc and Drama Magazine Awards 1986, Gulliver Award; Hon DUniv: Queen Margaret Coll Edinburgh 1989, Stirling 1991; memb bd Scottish TV 1979–85; *Plays* Willie Rough (1972), Benny Lynch (1974), Old Movies (1977), The Long Riders (screenplay, 1980), The Ship (1990), The Big Picnic (1994); *Recreations* music; *Style*— Bill Bryden, Esq, CBE; ✉ c/o Independent Talent Group, 40 Whitfield Street, London W1T 2RH (☎ 020 7636 6565, fax 020 7323 0101)

BRYDON, Donald Hood; CBE (2004, OBE 1993); s of James Hood Brydon (d 1975), and Mary Duncanson, *née* Young; *b* 25 May 1945; *Educ* George Watson's Coll Edinburgh, Univ of Edinburgh (BSc); *m* 1996, Corrine; 1 da (Fiona b 1975), 1 s (Angus b 1977); *Career* research asst Dept of Economics Univ of Edinburgh; investment mangr: Airways Pension Scheme (British Airways), Barclays Bank; dir Barclays Investment Management, chm (formerly chief exec) BZW Investment Management Ltd, dep chief exec BZW 1994–96; chm: BZW Private Equity 1994–96, Axa Investment Managers SA 1997–2001, Axa Real Estate Investment Managers SA 1998–2001, Royal Mail Gp 2009–, Sage plc 2012–; chm: Amersham 2003–04 (non-exec dir 1997–2004), Smiths Gp plc 2004–13, Taylor Nelson Sofres 2006–09, LifeSight Ltd 2015–; non-exec dir: London Stock Exchange 1991–98, Edinburgh UK Tracker Trust plc 1996–2006, AXA UK plc 1997–2001, Allied Domecq plc 1997–2005, Scottish Power plc 2003–07; chm: Institutional Shareholders Ctee 1989–90, Fund Mangrs Assoc 1999–2001, Code Ctee Panel on Takeovers and Mergers 2001–06, Financial Servs Practitioner Panel 2001–03 (dep chm 2003–04), London Metal Exchange 2003–11, ifs Sch of Finance 2006–, Medical Research Cncl 2012–; vice-chm Nat Assoc of Pension Funds 1988–90, memb Auditing Practices Bd 1991–94, pres Euro Asset Mgmnt Assoc 1999–2001; chm: EveryChild 2003–07, David Rattray Memorial Tst (UK) 2008–11, Chance to Shine Fndn 2014–; ldr Bracknell DC 1977–80; AIIMR 1972; *Books* Economics of Technical Information Services (jtly, 1972), Pension Fund Investment (jtly, 1988); *Recreations* golf, reading, deltiology; *Clubs* Caledonian; *Style*— Donald Brydon, Esq, CBE; ✉ Royal Mail Group, 100 Victoria Embankment, London EC4Y 0HQ (☎ 020 7449 8099)

BRYDON, Rob (né Robert Brydon Jones); MBE (2013); s of Howard Jones, and Joy Brydon Jones; *b* 3 May 1965, Port Talbot; *Educ* Porthcawl Comp Sch, Welsh Coll of Music and Drama; *m* 2006, Claire, *née* Holland; 4 c; *Career* actor; early career as radio and TV presenter and voiceover artist; nat tour Rob Brydon Live 2008–09; single Islands In The Stream 2009 (official Comic Relief single with Sir Tom Jones, Ruth Jones and Robin Gibb, UK no 1); *Television* as writer and actor: Marion and Geoff 2000 (Br Comedy Award Best Newcomer, RTS Best Newcomer, South Bank Award Best Drama, Broadcasting Press Guild of GB Best Entertainment, also stage show West End and Edinburgh Festival), Human Remains 2000 (Br Comedy Award Best Actor, Banff TV Festival Best Comedy), A Small Summer Party 2001, Director's Commentary 2004, The Keith Barret Show 2004 (also stage show nat tour), Rob Brydon's Annually Retentive (BBC 3) 2006–07, The Trip (BBC 2) 2010 and (US) 2011, The Rob Brydon Show (BBC 2) 2010–; as actor incl: Eleven Men Against Eleven 1995, Cold Lazarus 1996, The Way We Live Now 2001, Murder in Mind 2002, Black Books 2002, Cruise of the Gods 2002, Marple: 4.50 from Paddington 2004, Kenneth Tynan: In Praise of Hardcore 2005, Little Britain (BBC 1) 2005, Gavin and Stacey (BBC 2) 2007–09, Heroes and Villains: Napoleon (BBC 1) 2007, Rob Brydon's Identity Crisis (BBC 4) 2008, The Gruffalo (voice, BBC 1) 2009, The Gruffalo's Child (voice, BBC 1) 2011, The Best of Men 2012, The Trip to Italy (BBC 2) 2014, The Brink (HBO) 2015, Gangsta Granny (BBC 1) 2014, Room on the Broom (voice, BBC 1) 2014; regular panellist QI (BBC 1), host Would I Lie To You? (BBC 1) 2009–, host The Guess List (BBC 1) 2014, Sunday Night at the Palladium (ITV) 2014, Neil Diamond For One Night Only (ITV) 2014, Tom Jones and Rob Brydon: One Big Night for Children in Need (BBC 1) 2016; *Films* Lock, Stock and Two Smoking Barrels 1998, Twenty Four Hour Party People 2002, Mirrormask 2005, A Cock and Bull Story 2005, Cinderella 2015, The Huntsman 2016; *Radio* panellist I'm Sorry I Haven't A Clue (BBC Radio 4); *Theatre* incl: The Painkiller (Lyric Theatre Belfast) 2011, A Chorus of Disapproval (Harold Pinter Theatre) 2012, Future Conditional (The Old Vic) 2015, The Painkiller (Garrick) 2016; *Books* Small Man in a Book (autobiography, 2011); *Style*— Mr Rob Brydon, MBE; ✉ c/o Maureen Vincent, United Agents Ltd, 12–26 Lexington Street, London W1F 0LE (☎ 020 3214 0800, fax 020 3214 0801, website www.robbrydon.com)

BRYER, (Alastair) Robin Mornington; s of Gp Capt Gerald Mornington Bryer, OBE, AFC (d 1994), and Joan Evelyn, *née* Grigsby (d 1994); *b* 13 May 1944; *Educ* Dauntsey's Sch West Lavington, King's Coll Durham (BA); *m* 16 Sept 1976, Jennifer Sheridan, da of Lt-Col Richard Sheridan Skelton, OBE; 1 s (William b 1977); *Career* sr planning asst Hampshire CC 1967–73, ptnr Inland and Waterside Planners 1973–77, ind chartered town planner (one of the first in private practice) assisting landowners, developers, MPs, conservation bodies and govt depts 1977–; award winner: Tomorrow's New Communities Competition 1991, Best Small Project Class Daily Telegraph Individual Home Builder Awards 1997; exhibited in architectural section of RA 1980, guest lectr Hellenic Travellers' Club 1980–96; chm PEST (Tory pressure gp) 1966–68, memb Consultancy Bd RTPI 1980–83; chm Old Dauntseians' Assoc 1985–86; Freeman City of London 1987, Guildsman City Guild of Old Mercers 1988; MRTPI 1973; *Books* Jolie Brise, A Tall Ships Tale (1982, 2 edn 1997), Roving Commissions (ed 1983–86), Hair, Fashion and Fantasy down the Ages (2000, Chinese edn 2003), Jack: A literary biography of John Connell (2007); *Recreations* sailing; *Clubs* Royal Cruising (sr memb), Royal Lymington Yacht; *Style*— Robin Bryer, Esq; ✉ Princes Place, Closworth, Yeovil, Somerset BA22 9RH (☎ 01935 872268, fax 01935 873341)

BRYMER, Timothy; s of Jack Brymer (d 2003), and Joan, *née* Richardson; *b* 7 November 1951, London; *Educ* Dulwich Coll, Coll of Air Training, Coll of Law; *m* 10 Aug 1985, Helen, *née* Cahill; 1 s (Toby James b 22 Jan 1987), 1 da (Lucy Alexandra b 7 Sept 1990); *Career* admitted slr 1977; slr specialising in aviation and aerospace law; sr ptnr Brymer Marland & Co 1985–90; ptnr and head of aviation gp: CMS Cameron McKenna 1991–2004, Clyde & Co 2004–; author of articles in insurance and aviation publications; trained as commercial pilot Br Overseas Airways Corp (BOAC); founding memb Lawyers Flying Assoc, memb Guild of Pilots and Air Navigators; *Recreations* tennis, squash, cycling, flying (holds pilot's license); *Style*— Timothy Brymer, Esq; ✉ Flambards, Northdown Road, Woldingham, Surrey CR3 7BB (☎ 01883 652245, fax 01883 652821, e-mail tim.brymer@gmail.com); Clyde & Co, The St Botolph Building, 138 Houndsditch, London EC3A 7AR (e-mail tim.brymer@clydeco.com)

BRYNING, Charles Frederick; s of Frederick Bryning (d 1982), of Norbreck, Blackpool, and Dorothy Edith Bryning; *b* 17 July 1946; *Educ* Arnold Sch Blackpool; *m* 29 April 1983, Katrina Carol, da of John Carol Boris Ely, of Lytham St Anne's; 1 s (Simon b 1983); *Career* CA; ptnr Jones Harris & Co 1972–, chief exec Alexander Walker Gp of Cos 1987–91; FCA; *Style*— Charles Bryning, Esq; ✉ 17 St Peters Place, Fleetwood, Lancashire FY7 6EB (☎ 01253 874255, e-mail charles.bryning@jones-harris.co.uk)

BRYSON, Bill; Hon OBE (2006); *b* 1951, Des Moines, IA; *Educ* Drake Univ IA; *m*; 4 c; *Career* travel writer; formerly newspaper journalist: chief copy ed business section The Times, dep nat news ed business section The Independent; cmmr English Heritage, pres Campaign to Protect Rural England 2007–; chllr Univ of Durham 2005–11; James Cameron Meml Lecture City Univ 2005; Hon DCL Univ of Durham 2004; *Books* travel writing: The Lost Continent (1989), Neither Here Nor There (1991), Notes From a Small Island (1995, adapted for TV 1998, voted best portrayal of England World Book Day 2003), A Walk in the Woods (1997), Notes From a Big Country (1998), Down Under (2000), African Diary (charity book for CARE Int, 2002); other books incl: Mother Tongue (1990), Made In America (1994), Bryson's Dictionary of Troublesome Words (2002), A Short History of Nearly Everything (2003, winner General Prize Aventis Prizes for Science Books 2004, shortlisted Samuel Johnson Prize 2004), The Life and Times of the Thunderbolt Kid (memoir, 2006), Shakespeare: The World as Stage (2007), Bryson's Dictionary for Writers and Editors (2008), Icons of England (2008), At Home: A Short History of Private Life (2010), One Summer: America 1927 (2013); *Style*— Bill Bryson, Esq, OBE; ✉ c/o Doubleday, Transworld Publishers, 61–63 Uxbridge Road, London W5 5SA

BUBB, Nicholas Henry (Nick); s of John William Edward Bubb, of Orsett, Essex, and Diana Rosemary, *née* Willetts; *b* 24 March 1955; *Educ* Gillingham GS, ChCh Oxford (MA); *m*

10 April 1982, Susan Mary, da of Joan Dare, of Richmond, Surrey; 1 s (Alexander Benjamin Thomas b 1985), 1 da (Amy Louise Harriet b 1988); *Career* retailing analyst: Rowe & Pitman & Co 1977–79, Citicorp Scrimgeour Vickers (formerly Kemp-Gee & Co and Scrimgeour Kemp-Gee) 1979–88 (ptnr 1983), Morgan Stanley 1988–95 (exec dir), Mees Pierson 1996–97, SG Securities 1997–2002, Evolution Securities 2003–06, Pali Int 2007–09, Arden Partners 2010–11; fndr Bubb Retail Consultancy Ltd; memb KPMG-Ipsos Retail Think-Tank; author The Daily Retailer blog; *Recreations* cricket, travel, golf, reading, films, wine, horse racing; *Clubs* Oriental, Riverside Sports Chiswick, MCC; *Style*— Nick Bubb, Esq; ✉ 6 Orchard Rise, Richmond, Surrey TW10 5BX (e-mail nicholas_bubb@hotmail.com)

BUBB, Sir Stephen John Limrick; kt (2011), JP; s of John William Edward Bubb, of Orsett, Essex, and Diana Rosemary, *née* Willatts; *b* 5 November 1952, Wigmore, Kent; *Educ* Gillingham GS, ChCh Oxford (MA); *Career* economist NEDO 1975–76, res offr TGWU 1976–80, negotiations offr NUT 1980–87, head of pay negotiations for local govt Assoc of Metropolitan Authorities 1987–95, founding dir Nat Lottery Charities Bd 1995–2000, chief exec ACEVO 2000–16, sec-gen euclid (European network of third sector ldrs) 2007–15, dir Charity Futures 2016–; fndr dir Metropolitan Authorities Recruitment Agency 1990–95, ind assessor for govt appts 1999–, memb Cabinet Sec's Hons Advsy Ctee 2005–10; chm Adventure Capital Fund 2006–16, chm Social Investment Business 2008–; memb Tyson Task Force on Non-Exec Dir Appts 2002; memb Cwlth Civil Soc Advsy Ctee 2008–12; memb W Lambeth HA 1982–89, non-exec memb Lambeth, Lewisham and Southwark HA 1998–2002, govr Guy's & St Thomas' Fndn Tst (chm Strategy Ctee 2004–07), chief whip Lambeth Cncl 1982–86, youth court magistrate Inner London 1980–2000, founder chm Lambeth Landmark 1982–88; pt/t tutor Open Univ 1982–87; chm City of Oxford Orchestra 1993–95, vice-patron Alms Houses Assocs 2012, tstee Helen and Douglas House 2014–; FCIPD; *Publications* People are Key (2003), And Why Not? Tapping the Talent of Not-For-Profit Chief Executives (2004), Only Connect: A Leader's Guide to Networking (2005), Choice and Voice (2006), Public Matters (contrib, 2007), Building Castles in the Air (2007), At Tipping Point: the third sector leading from recession to recovery (2009), Rediscovering Charity (2012), Winterbourne View: Time for Change (2015); *Recreations* genealogy, travel, fine art and fine wine, Anglican church, making a difference; *Clubs* Oxford and Cambridge; *Style*— Sir Stephen Bubb, JP; ✉ Armada Cottage, Thames Street, Charlbury, Oxfordshire OX7 3QQ; Association of Chief Executives of Voluntary Organisations (☎ 020 7014 4600, e-mail sirstephenbubb@gmail.com)

BUCCLEUCH AND QUEENSBERRY, 10 and 12 Duke of (S 1663 and 1684); Sir Richard Walter John Montagu Douglas Scott; KBE (2000), DL; s of 9 and 11 Duke of Buccleuch and Queensberry, KT, VRD, JP (d 2007), and Jane McNeill (d 2011); *Educ* Eton, ChCh Oxford; *m* Lady Elizabeth Marian Frances Kerr, da of 12 Marquess of Lothian, KCVO (d 2004); 2 da (Lady Louise Jane Therese b 1982, Lady Amabel Clare Alice b 1992), 2 s (Walter John Frances, Earl of Dalkeith, b 2 Aug 1984, Lord Charles David Peter b 1987); *Heir* s, Earl of Dalkeith; *Career* a page of honour to HM Queen Elizabeth the Queen Mother 1967–69, Capt Gen Queen's Own Body Guard for Scotland (Royal Co of Archers) 2011–; district cncllr Nithsdale 1984–90; dir Border Television 1989–90; pres: Royal Scottish Geographical Soc 1999–2005, Nat Tst for Scotland 2002–12; memb: Nature Conservancy Cncl 1989–92, Scottish Natural Heritage 1992–95 (chm SW Bd), Millennium Cmmn 1994–2002; nat memb for Scotland Ind Television Cmmn 1990–95 (dep chm 1996–98); regimental tstee King's Own Scottish Borderers 1987–2006, memb Cncl Winston Churchill Meml Tst 1993–2005; tstee: Heritage Lottery Fund 2000–05, Nat Heritage Meml Fund 2000–05, Royal Collection Tst 2011–; pres Georgian Gp 2015–; Hon Col 52 Lowland 6 Battalion Royal Regiment of Scotland 2011–16; FRSE, FSA; *Style*— The Duke of Buccleuch and Queensberry, KBE, DL, FRSE; ✉ Bowhill, Selkirk TD7 5ET; Boughton House, Kettering, Northamptonshire NN14 1BJ; Drumlanrig Castle, Thornhill, Dumfriesshire DG3 4AQ

BUCHAN, District Judge; (James Alexander) Bruce; s of James Welsh Ross Buchan (d 1982), and Phyllis Clare, *née* Buckle (d 1990); *b* 4 May 1947; *Educ* Fulneck Boys Sch, Univ of Birmingham (LLB); *Career* admitted slr; ptnr Dibb Lupton Broomhead 1975–92, district judge 1992–; nat chm Young Slrs' Gp Law Soc 1982–83; memb Law Soc, hon memb Leeds Law Soc; *Recreations* walking and golf; *Clubs* LSI Leeds, Headingly Golf (Leeds); *Style*— District Judge Buchan; ✉ Dewsbury County Court, Eightlands Road, Dewsbury, West Yorkshire WF13 2PE (☎ 01924 465860)

BUCHAN, Colin Alexander Mason; s of G H Buchan, of Scotland, and H Buchan, *née* Stewart; *b* 6 December 1954; *Educ* St John's Coll Johannesburg, INSEAD (AMP), Univ of the Witwatersrand (BComm); *m* 28 March 1980, Susan, *née* Monahan; 3 da (Kirsten b 28 Oct 1984, Alexandra b 27 Dec 1987, Caitlin b 6 May 1990); *Career* with African Finance Corp 1980–84; md SG Warburg South Africa 1984–87, md SG Warburg Far East 1987–94, appointed dir SG Warburg plc 1995, memb Exec Bd SBC Warburg 1995, global head of equities and memb Gp Mgmnt Bd UBS AG 1999–2001; memb Bd: Merrill Lynch World Mining Tst 2001–, Royal Bank of Scotland Gp plc 2002–11, Standard Life Investments 2002–11 (chm 2008–11), Standard Life Gp 2008–14, Wood Mackenzie 2008–09; dir: Royal Scot Nat Orch 2002–08, Scottish Chamber Orch 2012–, TTT Moneycorp Ltd 2012–; fell Chartered Inst of Bankers Scotland; *Recreations* hill walking, farming pedigree Aberdeen Angus cattle; *Clubs* Rand, Oriental, Hong Kong, New; *Style*— Colin Buchan, Esq

BUCHAN, Dennis Thorne; s of David S Buchan; *b* 25 April 1937; *Educ* Arbroath HS, Dundee Coll of Art (DA); *m* 1965 (m dis 1976), Elizabeth, *née* Watson; 1 da (Wendy), 1 s (John MacGregor); *Career* artist; lectr Duncan of Jordanstone Coll of Art 1965–94; memb Dundee Group Artists Ltd 1975–81; convenor Royal Scottish Academy 177th Annual Exhbn 2003; RSA 1991 (ARSA 1975) *Solo Exhibitions* Douglas and Foulis Gall 1965, Saltire Soc (Edinburgh Festival) 1974, Compass Gall 1975, A Span of Shores (Compass Gall Glasgow) 1994, Traquair House 1996, Various Experiences (Pentagon Business Centre Glasgow) 2001, 2000+ (Meffan Gall Forfar) 2005, Compass Gall Glasgow 2006; *Group Exhibitions* Five Dundee Painters 1961, + – 30 (Hunterian Museum and tour) 1964, Six Coastal Artists (Demarco Gall) 1965, Scottish Contemporary Painting (Aberdeen Art Gall) 1970, Seven Painters in Dundee (Scottish Nat Gall of Modern Art, McManus Gall) 1972, Painters in Parallel (Scottish Arts Cncl Festival Exhbn) 1978, Kindred Spirits (Ancrum Gall) 1990, Compass Contribution (Tramway) 1990, Scottish Contemporary Painting (Flowers East) 1993, Paperworks (Seagate Gall) 1993, Artists in Angus (Meffan Gall) 1993, Five Scottish Artists (Centre d'Art en L'Ile Geneva) 1994, The RSA in London (Albermarle Gall) 1999, RSA Connections (Edinburgh Festival) 1999 and 2000, invited painter Brechin Arts Festival 2007; *Collections* Edinburgh Hosp Gp, Dundee Coll of Educn, Kingsway Tech Coll, Univ of Leicester, Scottish Arts Cncl, Dundee Museum and Art Galls, Vincent Price Collection, Aberdeen Royal Infirmary; *Awards* Keith Prize RSA 1962, Latimer Award RSA 1963, Arts Cncl Award 1973, William McCaully Award for most distinguished work in RSA Exhbn 1988, William Gillies Bequest Fund Award RSA 1991; *Style*— Dennis Buchan, Esq, RSA

BUCHAN, (Hon) (Charles Walter) Edward Ralph; 2 s of 3 Baron Tweedsmuir, and his 2 wife Barbara Howard, *née* Ensor (d 1969); *b* 5 August 1951; *Educ* Magdalen Coll Sch Oxford, Univ of Southampton (BSc); *m* 27 Nov 1982, Fiona Jane, da of Capt E P Carlisle, of Llanigon, Hay-on-Wye; 1 s (William b 1984), 3 da (Annabel b 1986, Laura b 1988, Amilia b 1992); *Career* Hill Samuel Bank Ltd: joined 1977, dir 1985–96, md 1993–96; exec dir West LB Panmure Ltd 1999–; formerly md Close Brothers Corporate Finance Ltd, non-exec dir Tibbett & Britten Gp plc; FCA 1976; *Clubs* Travellers; *Style*— Edward Buchan, Esq

BUCHAN, Hon James Ernest; 3 s of 3 Baron Tweedsmuir, *qv*, and Barbara Howard, *née* Ensor (d 1969); *b* 11 June 1954; *Educ* Eton, Magdalen Coll Oxford (MA); *m* 1986, Lady Evelyn Rose Phipps, da of 4 Marquess of Normanby, KG, CBE (d 1994); 2 da (Elizabeth Blanche b 1989, Rose Barbara Averil b 1995), 1 s (Nicholas Adam b 1992); *Career* Financial Times: corr Saudi Arabia 1978–80, corr Bonn 1982–84, columnist Lex Column 1984–86, corr NY 1987–90; contrib Independent on Sunday Review 1990–94, chief book critic Spectator 1990–94; Harold Wincott Award for Business Journalism 1986; FRGS, FRAS, FRSL; *Books* The House of Saud (with Richard Johns and David Holden, 1981), A Parish of Rich Women (1984, Whitbread First Novel Award, Yorkshire Post Award, David Higham Award), Davy Chadwick (1987), Slide (1990), Heart's Journey in Winter (1995, Guardian Fiction Award), High Latitudes (1996), Frozen Desire (1997, Duff Cooper Prize), A Good Place to Die (1999), Capital of the Mind (2003), Adam Smith and the Pursuit of Perfect Liberty (2006), The Gate of Air (2008), Days of God: The Revolution in Iran (2012); *Style*— The Hon James Buchan; ✉ c/o Caroline Dawnay, United Agents Limited, 12–26 Lexington Street, London W1F 0LE (☎ 020 3214 0800, fax 020 3214 0801, website www.unitedagents.co.uk)

BUCHANAN; *see also:* Macdonald-Buchanan

BUCHANAN, Alistair John; s of John James Buchanan (d 1983), and Phoebe Leonora, *née* Messel (d 1952); *b* 13 December 1935; *Educ* Eton, New Coll Oxford; *m* 1, 1959, Louise Parker (d 1961); m 2, 1963, Prof Ann Buchanan, MBE, *qv*, da of Raymond Alexander Baring (d 1967); 3 da (Katie, Tessa, Helen); *Career* 2 Lt 2 Bn Coldstream Guards 1954–56; Layton-Bennett Billingham & Co 1959–62, Allen Harvey & Ross Ltd 1962–81, A Sarasin & Co Ltd 1980–87, chm Cater Allen Holdings plc 1981–85, md Morgan Grenfell Govt Securities 1985–87, dep chm and md Mees & Hope Securities Holdings Ltd 1987–91; chm: Premium Management Ltd 1989–2000, Lorne House Trust Ltd 1991–2006; dir: LIFFE 1981–84, Heritage of London Trust Ltd 1982–98, Eyecare Products plc 1994–97, Mannin Industries Ltd; Master Worshipful Co of Vintners 1999–2000; *Recreations* golf, gardening (family rep Nymans Gardens 1987–); *Clubs* White's, Cavalry and Guards, Swinley Forest Golf; *Style*— Alistair Buchanan, Esq; ✉ 11 London Place, Oxford OX4 1BD (☎ 01865 424576)

BUCHANAN, Sir Andrew George; 5 Bt (UK 1878), of Dunburgh, Stirlingshire; KCVO (2011); s of Maj Sir Charles James Buchanan, 4 Bt (d 1984), and Barbara Helen (d 1986), da of Lt-Col Rt Hon Sir George Frederick Stanley, GCSI, GCIE, CMG; *b* 21 July 1937; *Educ* Eton, Trinity Coll Cambridge, Wye Coll London; *m* 26 April 1966, Belinda Jane Virginia, DL, da of Donald Colquhoun Maclean and wid of Gresham N Vaughan (d 1964); 1 da (Laura Evelyn (Mrs James Mayes) b 1967), 1 s (George Charles Mellish b 1975), 1 step s, 1 step da; *Heir* s, George Buchanan; *Career* 2 Lt Coldstream Guards 1956–58, Major cmd A Sqdn Sherwood Rangers Yeo (TA) 1971–74, Hon Col B Sqdn (Sherwood Rangers Yeo) Queen's Own Yeomanry 1989–94, Hon Col Notts Army Cadet Force 1991–; farmer; High Sheriff Notts 1976–77; chm Bd of Visitors HM Prison Ranby 1983–84; HM Lord-Lt Notts 1991–2012 (DL 1985); KStJ 1991; *Recreations* walking, forestry, gardening; *Clubs* Boodle's; *Style*— Sir Andrew Buchanan, Bt, KCVO; ✉ Hodsock Priory Farm, Blyth, Worksop, Nottinghamshire S81 0TY (☎ 01909 591227, e-mail andrew.buchanan@hodsockpriory.com)

BUCHANAN, Prof (Robert) Angus; OBE (1993); s of Robert Graham Buchanan (d 1975), of Sheffield, and Bertha Buchanan, MBE, JP, *née* Davis (d 1975); *b* 5 June 1930; *Educ* High Storrs GS Sheffield, St Catharine's Coll Cambridge (MA, PhD); *m* 10 Aug 1955, Brenda June, da of George Henry Wade (d 1955), of Sheffield, and Doris Elsie Wade (d 1971); 2 s (Andrew Nassau b 1958, Thomas Claridge b 1960); *Career* Nat Serv RAOC 1948–50, GHQ FARELF 1949–50; educn offr Royal Fndn of St Katharine Stepney 1956–60, co-opted memb London CC Educn Ctee 1958–60; Univ of Bath: formerly lectr, sr lectr and reader, prof 1990–95 (emeritus 1995–), dir Centre for the History of Technol, Science and Soc 1964–; visiting prof ANU 1981, visiting lectr Wuhan People's Republic of China 1983, Jubilee prof Chalmers Univ Sweden 1984; royal cmmr Royal Cmmn for Historical Monuments 1979–93, memb Properties Ctee Nat Tst 1974–2001; pres: Assoc for Industrial Archaeology 1975–77 and 2003–10, Newcomen Soc for History of Engrg and Technol 1981–83, Int Ctee for the History of Technol 1993–97 (sec gen 1981–93); vice-pres Soc of Antiquaries of London 1995–99; chm Bath Branch Historical Assoc 1987–90, dir Nat Cataloguing Unit for the Archives of Contemporary Scientists 1987–95; Hon DSc Chalmers Univ Sweden 1986; Leonardo da Vinci Medal Soc for the History of Technol 1989; hon fell Science Museum 1992–; FRHistS 1978, FSA 1990, FRSA 1993–99; *Books* Technology and Social Progress (1965), Industrial Archaeology of the Bristol Region (jtly, 1969), Industrial Archaeology in Britain (1972), Industrial Archaeology of the Stationary Steam Engine (jtly, 1976), History and Industrial Civilisation (1979), Industrial Archaeology of Central Southern England (jtly, 1980), The Engineers – A History of the Engineering Profession in Britain 1750–1914 (1989), The Power of the Machine (1992), Brunel: The Life and Times of Isambard Kingdom Brunel (2002), Landscape with Technology (ed, 2011); *Recreations* walking, rambling, travelling; *Style*— Prof R Angus Buchanan, OBE, FSA; ✉ 13 Hensley Road, Bath BA2 2DR (☎ 01225 311508); Centre for the History of Technology Science and Society, University of Bath, Claverton Down, Bath BA2 7AY (e-mail hssraab@bath.ac.uk)

BUCHANAN, Prof Ann Hermione; MBE (2012); da of Raymond Alexander Baring (d 1967); *b* 21 May 1941, Winchester, Hants; *Educ* Univ of Southampton (PhD), Univ of Oxford (MA), Univ of Bath (CQSW); *m* 1963, Alistair John Buchanan, *qv*; 3 da (Katie b 1965, Tessa b 1967, Helen b 1972); *Career* dir Oxford Centre for Research into Parenting and Children, prof in social work Univ of Oxford; tstee: Family Welfare Assoc 2000–08, Baring Fndn 2000–12, Oxon Community Fndn 2006–16, Grandparent Plus 2014–; memb Cncl ESRC 2007–13, chair Evaluation Ctee 2010–13; fell St Hilda's College Oxford; Hon DLL Univ of Bath 2013; AcSS 2009 (memb Cncl 2011–); *Publications* incl: Cycles of Child Maltreatment (1996), Promoting the Emotional Well-being of Children (2000), Families in Conflict (2001), What Works for Troubled Children (2003), Fertility Rates and Population Decline: No Time for Children? (2013), Grandfathers: global perspectives (2016); over 70 papers in peer-reviewed jls; *Recreations* family, travel, gardening; *Style*— Prof Ann Buchanan, MBE; ✉ 11 London Place, Oxford OX4 1BD (☎ 01865 424576, e-mail ann.buchanan@spi.ox.ac.uk)

BUCHANAN, Cameron Roy Marchand; MSP; s of late Maj Alexander Bell Watson Buchanan, MC, TD, of Woking, Surrey, and Katharine Norma, *née* Stiles; *Educ* St Edward's Sch Oxford, Sorbonne; *m* 1, 11 May 1973 (m dis), Diana Frances, da of Hugh Wilson Jones (d 1979); 1 da (Tanya Katharine b 18 Sept 1974), 1 s (Alexander Cameron b 4 April 1977); m 2, 13 July 2009, Emma Margaret, *née* Wallis; *Career* George Harrison & Co Edinburgh Ltd 1985–1999; MSP (Cons) Lothian 2013–; Scottish Entrepreneur of the Year 1992; memb Leith High Constables, pres Bespoke Tailors Benevolent Assoc; Freeman Worshipful Co of Merchants Edinburgh; *Recreations* skiing, golf, tennis; *Clubs* New (Edinburgh), Hon Co of Edinburgh Golfers; *Style*— Cameron Buchanan, Esq, MSP; ✉ Calax House, 2 Douglas Gardens, Edinburgh EH4 3DA (☎ 0131 220 5775, fax 0131 225 6317, e-mail cameron@cameronbuchanan.com)

BUCHANAN, Dr David John; *b* 27 December 1945; *Educ* Royal HS Edinburgh, Univ of St Andrews (BSc, PhD, DSc); *m* Joan; 1 da (b 1972), 1 s (b 1974); *Career* research assoc Culham Lab UKAEA 1971–73; British Coal (formerly NCB): head of Geophysics Group Mining Research and Development Establishment (MRDE) 1974–82, head of data processing Doncaster Mining Dept 1982–83, head Mining Sciences Division MRDE 1983–87, mangr of tech strategy/dep head of research HQ Tech Dept 1987–89, head of mining research 1989–90, dir of research and scientific servs 1990–93; dir of Int Mining Consultants Ltd (IMCL) 1994–95, chief exec/accounting offr Health and Safety Lab (HSL) 1995–; non-exec dir Complete Computing Ltd 1979–; special prof Dept of Mineral Resources Engrg Univ of Nottingham; past chm Energy Industries Research Liaison Ctee; memb: Safety in Mines Research Advsy Bd, Soc of Exploration Geophysicists, European Assoc of Exploration Geophysicists; FIMMM, CEng, FREng 1997; *Awards* Best Paper in Geophysics Soc of Exploration Geophysicists 1980, JJ Thomson Premium IEE 1980, Elimco/McArthur Award Inst of Mining Engrs 1988, WM Thornton Medal Inst of Mining Electrical and Mining Mechanical Engrs 1992; *Publications* Coal Geophysics (jt ed) and author of 56 technical papers in a variety of jls; *Recreations* golf, reading, travel; *Style—* Dr David Buchanan, FREng

BUCHANAN, Prof Dennis Langston; s of Langston Llewellyn Buchanan (d 1954), and Georgina Vera, *née* Wheatley; *b* 15 April 1947; *Educ* Cambridge High, Rhodes Univ (BSc), Univ of Pretoria (MSc), Univ of London (PhD), Imperial Coll London (DIC); *m* 17 Dec 1970, Vaughan Elizabeth, da of Fritz Reitz Hayward, of Port Elizabeth; 1 s (James George), 1 da (Alexandra Claire); *Career* Union Corp Ltd South Africa 1969–73, res fell Univ of Witwatersrand 1978–79 (res asst 1976–77), prof of mining geology Royal Sch of Mines Imperial Coll London 1984–97 (res asst 1976–77, lectr 1980–83, emeritus prof and sr research fell 1997–); ind consulting mining geologist and dir Altyn-Tas Jt Venture Kazakhstan 1994, fndr and dir IC-FinEval Ltd 2000; vice-pres Inst of Mining and Metallurgy 1995; CEng 1976, FGS (SA) 1986, FIMMM 1989; *Books* Platinum Group Element Exploration (1988); *Recreations* jogging; *Clubs* Royal Sch of Mines Assoc, Chaps; *Style—* Prof Dennis Buchanan; ✉ Department of Earth Science and Engineering, Imperial College, London SW7 2BP (☏ 020 7594 6440, fax 020 7594 7444, e-mail d.buchanan@imperial.ac.uk)

BUCHANAN, James Meredith; s of Donald Geoffrey Buchanan (d 1978), and Violet Hetherington, *née* Bell; *b* 4 March 1943; *Educ* Haberdashers' Aske's, St George's Hosp Med Sch Univ of London (MB BS, AKC); *m* 4 May 1974, Judith, da of James Edward Spence (d 1997), of Sedgefield, Co Durham; 3 da (Helen, Charlotte, Sarah); *Career* registrar: Norfolk and Norwich Hosp 1972, St Mary's Hosp Portsmouth 1973; sr registrar St George's Hosp London 1974–77 (house offr posts 1967), conslt orthopaedic surgn Sunderland Gp of Hosps 1977–; hon clinical lectr Univ of Newcastle upon Tyne 1979; author of paper in RCS annals and multiple presentations on HA hip arthroplasty; LRCP 1967, FRCS 1972, fell Br Orthopaedic Assoc 1977; *Recreations* rugby football; *Clubs* Blaydon RUFC; *Style—* James Buchanan, Esq; ✉ 8 Grange Terrace, Stockton Road, Sunderland, Tyne & Wear SR2 7DF (☏ 0191 5100 555, fax 0191 2841 599, e-mail buchanan@dial.pipex.com)

BUCHANAN, Nigel James Cubitt; CVO (2012); s of Rev Basil Roberts Buchanan (d 1987), of Cambridge, and Elene, *née* Cubitt (d 2005); *b* 13 November 1943; *Educ* Denstone Coll; *m* 6 July 1968, (Katherine) Mary, da of Prof Sir Arthur Llewellyn Armitage (d 1984); 2 da (Katherine Lucy b 21 Sept 1975, Elizabeth Mary b 15 May 1978), 1 s (James Kenyon b 20 Nov 1979); *Career* PricewaterhouseCoopers (formerly Price Waterhouse before merger): ptnr 1978–2001, Euro dir Fin Servs Practice 1988–97, vice-chm World Financial Servs Practice 1989–97, memb Bd E European Firm 1994–97, sr client ptnr 1994–2001; chm Amlin Underwriting Ltd 2013–16; non-exec dir: Leopold Joseph Hldgs plc 2001–04, Amlin plc 2004–13 (sr ind dir), Butterfield Bank (UK) Ltd 2004–14; memb Ethics Standards Bd Accounting Fndn 2001–03; memb Bd Outward Bound Tst 2002–11 (dep chm 2005 and 2008), tstee Adventure Learning Schs 2010–; lay memb Fin Ctee UCL 2002–09, chm of govrs Aldwickbury Sch 2004–09; Freeman City of London 2001, Liveryman Worshipful Co of Tylers and Bricklayers 2001; FCA; *Books* Accounting for Pensions (jtly), PW/Euromoney Debt Equity Swap Guide (jtly); *Recreations* tennis, golf; *Clubs* Carlton; *Style—* Nigel Buchanan, Esq, CVO; ✉ Longwood, 16 Park Avenue South, Harpenden, Hertfordshire AL5 2EA (☏ 01582 763076, fax 01582 760559)

BUCHANAN, Robin William Turnbull; s of Iain Buchanan, and Gillian Pamela, *née* Hughes-Hallett; *b* 2 April 1952; *Educ* Harvard Business Sch (Baker scholar, MBA); *m* 1986, Diana Tei Tanaka; 2 c (Rowan Hisayo Lindsay b 2 June 1989, Iain James Tei-An b 26 Feb 1993); *Career* Deloitte Touche Tohmatsu (formerly Mann Judd Landau) 1970–77, American Express International Banking Corp 1979–82; Bain & Co Inc: Bain Capital 1982–84, managing ptnr London 1990–96, sr ptnr London 1996–2007, sr advsr 2007–; dean and pres London Business Sch 2007–09; chm Michael Page Int plc 2011–15; non-exec dir: Liberty International plc 1997–2008, Shire plc (formerly Shire Pharmaceuticals Gp plc) 2003–08, Schroders plc 2010–, Lyondell Basell NV 2011–; sr advsr Coller Capital Ltd 2010–; memb: Northern Meeting, Highland Soc, Professional Standards Advsy Bd IOD, Int Advsy Cncl Recipco; tstee Trees for Life 2014–; fell Salzburg Seminar; Liveryman Worshipful Co of Ironmongers; FCA, FRSA; *Recreations* farming, forestry, shooting, collecting old children's books; *Clubs* Pilgrims; *Style—* Robin Buchanan, Esq; ✉ Bain & Company, 40 Strand, London WC2N 5RW (e-mail robin.buchanan@bain.com)

BUCK, Karen Patricia; MP; *b* 30 August 1958; *Educ* Chelmsford County HS, LSE (BSc, MA, MSc); *Career* head of research OUTSET 1979–83, with London Borough of Hackney 1983–87, health policy offr Lab Party 1987–92, actg head Campaigns Dept Lab Party 1994–95 (dep head 1993–97); MP (Lab): Regent's Park and Kensington N 1997–2010, Westminster N 2010–; chair London Gp of Lab MPs 1998–2005, Parly under sec of state Dept of Transport 2005–; memb Social Security Select Ctee 1997–2001, memb Work and Pensions Select Ctee 2001–05, chair All-Pty Parly Gp on Childcare 2004–05; memb: Westminster City Cncl 1990–97; chair of govrs Wilberforce Sch 1992–99; *Style—* Ms Karen Buck, MP; ✉ House of Commons, London SW1A 0AA; constituency office (☏ 020 8968 7999, fax 020 8960 0150, e-mail k.buck@rpkn-labour.co.uk)

BUCK, Louisa; da of late Sir Antony Buck, QC, and Judy Breakell, *née* Grant; *b* 10 July 1960; *Educ* Queensgate Sch London, Girton Coll Cambridge (BA), Courtauld Inst of Art Univ of London (MA); *Children* 2 s (Alfred Benedict b 7 Jan 1992, Francis George b 10 April 2002), 1 da (Nancy Eleanor b 23 March 1995); *Career* freelance author, lectr, broadcaster and journalist; freelance lectr on Twentieth Century Art 1983–84 (Tate Gallery, Sotheby's fine art courses, art courses in London and Europe), Tate Gallery 1984–85 (cataloguer of John Banting and Edward Burra material, curator of exhibition of Bantings graphic work, public lectr), ran Bonhams Modern Pictures Dept 1985; freelance journalist, broadcaster lectr and researcher 1986–; arts correspondent, contrib ed and visual arts correspondent The Art Newspaper; contrib to: New Statesman & Society, Guardian arts pages, Tatler, Vogue, Marie Claire, The Evening Standard; radio 1988–90: visual arts critic LBC, currently visual art reviewer Front Row BBC Radio 4; lectr on Twentieth Century art design and culture: Tate Gallery, RCA, Saatchi Collection, Univ of Reading, ICA; *Books* author of catalogue essays for: A Salute to British Surrealism (Minories Gallery Colchester, 1985), The Surrealist Spirit in Britain (Whitford & Hughes, 1988), Sylvia Ziranek: Ici Villa Moi (Watermans Arts Centre, 1989), Jacqueline Morreau: Paradise Now (Odette Gilbert Gallery, 1990), Meret Oppenheim retrospective Barcelona, Relative Values or What's Art Worth? (jtly, 1990), Something the Matter: Helen Chadwick, Cathy de Monchaux, Cornelia Parker (Saô Paulo Bienal, 1994), The Personal Political Art of Grayson Perry (Stedelijk Museum Amsterdam 2002), Tableau Vivant: Jane Simpson (Centre for Contemporary Art Malaga, 2004); Moving Targets: A User's Guide to British Art Now (1997), Moving Targets 2: A User's Guide to British Art Now (2000), Owning Art: The Contemporary Art Collector's Handbook (co-author, 2006), Commissioning Contemporary Art: A Handbook for Curators, Collectors and Artists (2012); *Recreations* gardening, swimming, travelling; *Style—* Ms Louisa Buck; ☏ 020 7737 0511, fax 020 7274 6087, e-mail louisa@louisabuck.co.uk)

BUCK, Michele; *Career* controller of drama United Prodns 1997–2001 (credits incl: Oliver Twist, Hornblower, Where the Heart Is, Without Motive, The Turn of the Screw, In the Name of Love, Innocents, Hearts and Bones), controller of drama ITV Prodns 2001–07 (credits incl: Housewife 49, William and Mary, Lewis, Marple, Poirot, Walk Away and I Stumble, The Last Detective, The History of Mr Polly, Family, Night and Day, Sex Traffic, Ballet Shoes, Dracula, Casanova), fndr and jt md Mammoth Screen 2007–15 (credits incl Parade's End, Endeavour, Lost in Austen, Wuthering Heights, Christopher and his Kind), ceo Company Pictures All3Media 2015–; *Style—* Ms Michele Buck; ✉ All3Media, Berkshire House, 168–173 High Holborn, London WC1V 7AA

BUCKBY, Anthony Jonathan; MBE (1996); s of Gordon Harry Buckby (d 1985), of Worcs, and Muriel, *née* Darby; *b* 1 September 1951; *Educ* King's Sch Worcester (scholar), Univ of Nottingham (BA), Univ of Essex (MA); *m* Giuliana, da of Mario Salvagno; *Career* teacher of English in UK, Germany and Italy 1974–76, reader Univ of Naples 1978–79, asst dir of studies Br Cncl Naples 1979–82 (teacher 1976–78, teacher trainer 1978–79), sch dir Br Inst of Florence 1987–90 (acad advsr 1982–86), dir Br Cncl Bologna 1990–96, dir Language Servs Br Cncl 1996–2000, dep dir Br Cncl Italy 2000–; *Books* Variety (jtly, 1985); *Recreations* gardening; *Style—* Anthony Buckby, Esq, MBE; ✉ Via Urbana 156, 00184 Rome, Italy; Faircroft, Aberedw, Builth Wells, Powys; The British Council, Via Quattro Fontane 20, 00184 Rome, Italy

BUCKINGHAM, Bishop of 2003–; Rt Rev Dr Alan Thomas Lawrence Wilson; s of Alan Thomas Wilson (d 1990), of Sevenoaks, Kent, and Anna Maria Magdalena, *née* Amfer (d 1994); *b* 27 March 1955, Edinburgh; *Educ* Sevenoaks Sch, St John's Coll Cambridge (open scholar, MA), Wycliffe Hall Oxford (CertTheol), Balliol Coll Oxford (DPhil); *m* 14 July 1984, Lucy Catherine Janet, *née* Richards; 3 da (Catherine Joanna b 10 May 1986, Stephanie Julia b 26 Dec 1987, Anna Maria b 12 Oct 1998), 2 s (Stewart Thomas b 21 March 1995, Nicholas James (twin) b 21 March 1995); *Career* ordained: deacon 1979, priest 1980; non-stipendiary min then asst curate Eynsham 1978–82, priest i/c St John's Caversham and asst curate Caversham and Mapledurham 1982–89, vicar St John the Baptist Caversham 1989–92, subst chaplain HMP Reading 1990–92, rector Sandhurst 1992–2003, area dean of Sonning 1998–2003, hon canon ChCh Oxford 2002–03; memb: Ecclesiastical Law Soc, Howard League for Penal Reform, Nat Tst, Oxford Dicesan Ctee for Racial Justice 2005–, Diocesan Bd of Social Responsibility 2006–, Diocesan Partnership in World Mission 2006–; pres Padstones Housing Tst 2004–; Eton Dorney Tst 2003–; memb Cncl Wycombe Abbey Sch 2008–, govr Cressex Community Sch 2008–; *Recreations* running, art and design, photography, singing, France, modern history, penal affairs, adult education, new and social media; *Style—* The Rt Rev the Bishop of Buckingham; ✉ Sheridan, Grimms Hill, Great Missenden, Buckinghamshire HP16 9BG (☏ 01494 862163, fax 01494 890508, e-mail alan.wilson49@btopenworld.com and bishopbucks@oxford.anglican.org)

BUCKINGHAM, Prof Julia Clare; da of Jack William Harry Buckingham (d 1991), of Feock, Cornwall, and Barbara Joan, *née* Baker; *b* 18 October 1950; *Educ* St Mary's Sch Calne, Univ of Sheffield (BSc), Univ of London (PhD, DSc); *m* 1974, Simon James Smith, s of Sidney George Smith (d 1973); *Career* sr lectr in pharmacology Royal Free Hosp Sch of Med 1980–87 (research fell Dept of Pharmacology 1974–80), prof and head Dept of Pharmacology Charing Cross and Westminster Med Sch London 1988–97, Imperial Coll London at Hammersmith Hosp: head Dept of Neuroendocrinology, vice-chm Academic Div of Neuroscience and Psychological Med 1997–2003, non-clinical dean for med 2000–03, dep head (non-clinical) Undergraduate Med 2002–, prof of pharmacology, head Academic Div of Neuroscience and Mental Health 2003–07; Imperial Coll London: pro-rector (educn) 2007–10, pro-rector (educn and academic affrs) 2010–12, vice-chllr and pres Brunel Univ London 2014–; chm SCORE 2013–16; memb Cncl Sch of Pharmacy Univ of London 2001–05; chm Bioscientifica Ltd 2002–05; ed-in-chief Jl of Neuroendocrinology 2004–08; memb Cncl Biosciences Fedn 2008–09, tstee and memb Cncl Royal Soc of Biology; tstee STEMNET 2016–; memb Bd Universities UK 2014– (treas 2016–), dir Nat Centre for Univs and Business 2016–; Gaddum Meml Prize Br Pharmacological Soc 1994 (hon fell 2014) Soc Medal Soc for Endocrinology 1994, sr sci advsr 2012–14; hon fell Br Soc for Neouroendocrinology 2014; AstraZeneca Women in Pharmacology Prize Br Pharmacology Soc 2009; memb: Soc for Endocrinology 1975 (treas 1996–2001, gen sec 2005–09, chm 2009–11, pres 2011–12, sr scientific advsr 2012–, chm Nominations Ctee 2013–), Br Pharmacological Soc 1977 (pres 2004–05, fell 2004), Br Soc for Neuroendocrinology 1980, Physiological Soc 1980, Soc for Meds Research 1980, Br Neuroscience Assoc 1985, Biochemical Soc 1988, Royal Inst 2011 (tstee 2011–16, chm Science and Educn Ctee 2011–16, memb Finance Ctee 2011–16); memb Treasy's Ctee Imp Coll Health Ptnrs 2013– (dir 2014–); govr: KCS Wimbledon 1993–97, St Mary's Sch Calne 2003–; Hon DSc Univ of Sheffield 2013; FRSA 1995, FCGI 2009, FRSB 2009 (memb Cncl 2009–); *Recreations* music, skiing, sailing; *Clubs* Riverside, Athenaeum; *Style—* Prof Julia Buckingham; ✉ Brunel University London, Kingston Lane, Middlesex UB8 3PH (☏ 10895 274000)

BUCKINGHAM, Lisa; OBE (2011); *m* Anthony Gray; 2 da (Natasha b 14 Nov 1990, Camille b 23 Jan 1993); *Career* The Guardian: dep city ed 1994–96, city ed 1996–2000; dep ed then ed Financial Mail on Sunday 2000–; FRSA; *Style—* Ms Lisa Buckingham, OBE; ✉ Institute of Directors, 116 Pall Mall, London SW1Y 5ED

BUCKLAND, Christopher Robert; s of Claude Buckland (d 1987), of Burnley, Lancs, and Vera, *née* Greenwood (d 1949); *b* 4 January 1944, Burnley, Lancs; *Educ* Burnley GS, Univ of Birmingham (BSocSc); *Career* reporter Daily Mail Manchester 1964–65 (Belfast 1965–66); Daily Mirror: reporter Dublin 1966–70, bureau chief Belfast 1970–72, home affrs corr London 1972–74, chief political corr 1974–76, corr Washington DC 1976–78, head of US Bureau 1978–81, foreign ed London 1981–82; political ed: Sunday People 1982–85, Today 1985–89; The Express: asst ed (political and foreign) 1989–95, assoc ed and political columnist 1995–98; political columnist Sunday Mirror 1998–2001; News of the World: political columnist 2001–03, special corr 2003–06; special corr The Sun 2006–; *Recreations* music, piano, racing, soccer spectating, travel; *Clubs* Garrick; *Style—* Christopher Buckland; ✉ Press Gallery, House of Commons, London SW1A 0AA (☏ 020 7219 4700); ☏ and fax 020 8340 4453, e-mail expressbk@aol.com

BUCKLAND, David; s of Denis Buckland, of Sydling St Nicholas, Dorset, and Valarie Buckland; *b* 15 June 1949; *Educ* Hardy's GS, Deep River HS, London Coll of Printing; *Partner* Siobhan Davies, CBE , *qv*; 2 c (Piera b 15 Oct 1984, Sean b 13 April 1986); *Career* designer, artist and film-maker; short film Dwell Time broadcast BBC1 Dance for Camera Season 1996, presented one-man show Nat Portrait Gallery London 1999; cmmn incl: MasterCard, Vanguard Insurance, Royal Caribbean; set and costume designs: Siobhan Davies Dance Co, Royal Ballet, Rambert Dance Co, Second Stride, Compagnie Cré-Ange; work in public collections incl: Nat Portrait Gallery London, Center Georges Pompidou Paris, Metropolitan Museum NY, Getty Collection LA; Cape Farewell expedition (environmental sailing voyage to High Arctic, in partnership with Geographical Assoc, NESTA and Southampton Ocoeanography Centre): dir 2003 and 2004, launched new GCSE geography course 2003, winner NESTA Award 2003 and Arts Cncl Award 2004; video installation This Side to Body 2002; Northern Arts Fellowship 1972, Kodak Award 1980, Nesta Award 2001; *Books* David Buckland (mongraph, 1989),

Performances (2000), The Last Judgement (with Sir Antony Caro, 2000); *Recreations* sailing; *Style*— David Buckland, Esq; ✉ Cape Farewell, University of the Arts Chelsea, 16 John Islip Street, London SW1P 4JU

BUCKLAND, Gerald David; s of Francis G Buckland (d 1994), of Cheshunt, Herts, and Elizabeth, *née* Hamilton-Allen (d 1998); *b* 22 March 1948; *Educ* St Ignatius' Coll, E Herts Coll; *m* 27 May 1975, Paula, da of Mark Gandy (d 1989); 2 da (Marianne Paula Elizabeth b 10 Feb 1980, Isabella Louise Geraldine b 9 June 1983), 1 s (Anthony Francis Gerald b 3 Jan 1988); *Career* press offr BP Chemicals Ltd 1977–80, PR coordinator BP Int Ltd 1980–82, PR mangr Marathon Int Petroleum Inc 1982–88, corporate rels dir TVS Entertainment plc 1988–91, md Sunrise Media Communications 1991–94, chief exec The Buckland Consultancy UK Ltd 1994–; memb: RTS, CIPR, BAFTA; *Recreations* French, Dutch, Romanian; *Clubs* Groucho; *Style*— Gerald Buckland, Esq; ✉ Le Haut Clairvaux, 86140 Scorbe Clairvaux, France (☎ 00 33 6 17 57 34 78, e-mail gerrybuckland@mac.com)

BUCKLAND, Robert James; QC, MP; *b* 1968, Llanelli, Dyfed; *Educ* Univ of Durham; *m* 1997, Sian; 1 da (Millicent b 2002 (twin)), 1 s (George b 2002 (twin)); *Career* called to the Bar Inner Temple 1991; tenant Iscoed Chambers Swansea until 1999, 30 Park Place Cardiff 1999–2007, Apex Chambers Cardiff 2007; recorder Crown Court 2009–; QC 2014; MP (Cons) Swindon S 2010–; HM Solicitor Gen for England and Wales 2014–; memb: Commons Justice Select Ctee 2010–13 &14, Commons Ctee on Standards 2012–14, Commons Ctee on Privileges 2012–14, Jt Ctee on Human Rights 2013–14; jt sec 1922 Ctee 2012–14; chair Cons Human Rights Cmmn 2011–14, chm Exec Ctee Soc of Cons Lawyers 2013–; *Recreations* reading, watching cricket and rugby, running about with my family; *Clubs* Carlton, Llanelli Cons, Swindon Cons; *Style*— Robert Buckland, Esq, QC, MP; ✉ House of Commons, London SW1A 0AA (☎ 020 7219 7168, website www.robertbuckland.co.uk, Twitter @robertbuckland)

BUCKLAND, Sir Ross; kt (1997); s of William Arthur Haverfield Buckland, and Elizabeth, *née* Schmitzer; *b* 19 December 1942, Sydney, Australia; *Educ* Sydney Boys' HS; *m* 22 Jan 1966, Patricia Ann, da of William Stephen Bubb, of Warriewood, NSW, Aust; 2 s (Sean William b 1968, Mark Charles b 1970); *Career* held various positions in companies engaged in banking, engrg, office equipment and food industry 1958–66; dir fin and admin Elizabeth Arden Pty Ltd 1966–73, md Kellogg (Aust) Pty Ltd 1978 (various positions 1973–77), pres and ceo Kellogg Salada Canada Inc 1979–80, vice-pres Kellogg Co USA, chm Kellogg Company of Great Britain Ltd to 1990 (dir European Operations), gp chief exec Uniq plc (formerly Unigate plc) 1990–2001; pres: Food & Drink Fedn 1987–89, Inst of Grocery Distribution 1997–99, Nat Aust Bank Europe Ltd 1999–2002; non-exec dir: Allied Domecq plc 1998–2004, RJB Mining plc 1995–99, Mayne Gp Ltd 2001–04, Goodman Fielder Ltd 2001–03, Clayton Utz 2001–08; memb Medical Research Cncl 1998–2001; hon fell Inst of Logistics 1996; CIMgt, FICS, FCPA, FIGD; *Recreations* walking, reading; *Clubs* Royal Sydney Golf; *Style*— Sir Ross Buckland; ✉ e-mail ross.buckland@bigpond.com

BUCKLAND-WRIGHT, Prof (John) Christopher; s of John Buckland-Wright (d 1954), of Dunedin, NZ, and Mary Elizabeth, *née* Anderson (d 1976); *b* 19 November 1945, London; *Educ* Lycée Français de Londres, KCL (BSc, AKC, PhD), Univ of London (DSc); *m* 1, 11 Nov 1975, Rosalin (d 2012), da of Charles W G T Kirk, OBE (d 1986); 2 da (Helen b 1977, Alexandra b 1978); m 2, 6 April 2013, Jane, da of Norman J A Foster (d 1994); *Career* asst head Dept of Comparative Osteology Centre for Prehistory and Paleontology Nairobi Kenya 1966–67, teacher Lycée Français de Londres 1971–72, anatomy lectr St Mary's Hosp Med Sch London 1973–76; Guy's Hosp Med Sch London: lectr 1976–80, sr lectr 1980–89, reader in radiological anatomy 1989–97, prof of radiological anatomy 1997–2008; Guy's Hosp: head Macroradiographic Res Unit Guy's Hosp 1981–88, head Arthrology Unit 1988–96, chm Applied Clinical Anatomy 1996–2008; lectr Medical Artists Assoc 2007–13; memb Int Cmmn on Radiation Units and Measurements 1987–93; first Jessie Dobson lectr RCS 1984, Fifth B Shine lectr in rheumatology Technion Haifa 1994, Vicary lectr RCS 1999; pioneered med applications of high definition macroradiography and new methods for radiography of the human knee, developed standardised radiographic procedures now employed internationally for clinical trials in knee osteoarthritis, developed novel methods for measuring changes in joint structure including cancellous bone changes in arthritic joints, first to report beneficial effect of bisphosphonate treatment in knee osteoarthritis; author of over 200 scientific pubns radiography and its application to the study of bone and arthritis; Freeman City of London 1980; Worshipful Co of Barbers: Liveryman 1980, Hon Librarian 1984–2006 (recreated Co's historic library of 1540 to 1745), memb Ct of Assts 2000, Renter Warden 2004, Middle Warden 2005, Upper Warden 2006, Master 2007–08, Dep Master 2008–09; memb: Anatomy Soc 1974–2005, Br Soc of Rheumatology 1984–2005, Br Inst of Radiology 1992–2005 (Immation-Mayneord Meml lectr 1998), Osteoarthritis Res Soc 1992–2008; fell Br Assoc of Clinical Anatomists 1996–2009, hon fell Medical Artists Assoc 2009; *Publications* Cockerel Cavalcade (1988), The Engravings of John Buckland Wright (1990), Bathers and Dancers (1993), Baigneuses (1995), Surreal Times (2000), Endeavours and Experiments (2004), To Beauty (2007), Sensuous Lines (2014, Best British Book for 2014 British Book Design and Production Awards 2014); exhibn catalogues: John Buckland Wright The Surrealist Years 1934–54 (1999), John Buckland Wright The Golden Cockerel Years (2001), John Buckland Wright For My Own Pleasure (2003); *Recreations* fine art and antiquarian books, drawing, painting, walking; *Clubs* City Livery; *Style*— Prof Christopher Buckland-Wright; ✉ Acer House, Vicarage Road, East Budleigh, Budleigh Salterton, Devon EX9 7EF (e-mail cbucklandwright@aol.com)

BUCKLEY, Prof Adrian Arthur; s of Arthur Penketh Buckley (d 1977), and Beatrice May Buckley (d 1953); *b* 28 December 1938; *Educ* Poole GS, Univ of Sheffield and Open Univ (BA), Univ of Bradford (MSc), Free Univ Amsterdam (PhD); *m* 6 August 1966, Jenny Rosalie Buckley (d 1977); 2 s (Peter James Scott b 24 Dec 1971, David John Scott b 4 April 1974); *Career* Corp Fin Charterhouse Bank 1971–73, gp treas Redland plc 1973–79, prof Cranfield Sch of Mgmnt 1986– (joined 1980); FCA 1963, FCT 1985; *Books* Multinational Finance (1986, 5 edn 2004), The Essence of International Money (1990, 2nd 1996), International Capital Budgeting (1996), International Investment – Value Creation and Appraisal: Real Options Approach (1998), Corporate Finance Europe (1998), Financial Crisis (2011), International Finance (2012); *Recreations* skiing, walking, theatre; *Style*— Prof Adrian Buckley; ✉ Cranfield School of Management, Cranfield University, Cranfield, Bedford MK43 0AL (☎ 01234 751122, fax 01234 751806, e-mail adrian.buckley@cranfield.ac.uk)

BUCKLEY, Edgar Vincent; CB (1999); s of Michael Joseph Buckley (d 1983), and Mary, *née* Byrne (d 1998); *b* 17 November 1946; *Educ* St Ignatius Coll London, NW Poly London, Birkbeck Coll London (BA, PhD); *m* Frances Jacqueline, da of late Dr Harry A Cheetham; 3 da (Martha Jane b 11 July 1974, Hannah Katharine b 30 June 1981, Emmeline Jessica b 11 Feb 1987), 2 s (Edgar Jonathan Christopher b 29 June 1976, William Nicholas Quentin b 11 Nov 1978); *Career* MOD: asst dir Strategic Systems Fin 1980–84, asst dir Nuclear Policy 1984–86, head Resources and Progs (Navy) 1986–90, RCDS 1990, head Def Arms Control Unit 1991–92; def cnsllr UK Delgn to NATO 1992–96, asst under sec of state (Home and Overseas) MOD 1996–99, asst sec gen (planning and operations) NATO 1999–2003, sr vice-pres European mktg Thales 2003–; *Recreations* running, swimming; *Style*— Edgar Buckley, Esq, CB

BUCKLEY, Ian Michael; s of Frank Leslie Buckley (d 1973), and Edith Mary, *née* Brown; *b* 16 November 1950; *Educ* Bradfield Coll, Univ of Southampton (BSc); *m* 20 July 1974, Sarah Ann, da of Arthur William Sale; 2 da (Anna Louise b 11 April 1978, Camilla Alice b 8 Aug 1981); *Career* chartered accountant Peat Marwick Mitchell & Co 1972–82 (articled clerk 1972–75); Smith and Williamson: joined 1982, ptnr and dir of securities 1983–86, gp chief exec 1986–95; chief exec EFG Private Bank Ltd 1997–98 (dir 1995, also md Asset Mgmnt subsid), chief exec Tenon Gp plc 2000–03; Rathbone Bros plc: dir 2001–11, memb Gp Exec Ctee 2003–14, special advsr 2015–; non-exec dir Miller Insurance Services LLP; dep chm Family Assurance Friendly Soc; FCA 1975; *Style*— Ian Buckley, Esq

BUCKLEY, Prof Richard Anthony; s of late Alfred Buckley, of Southampton, and late Dorothy Iris, *née* Neale; *b* 16 April 1947; *Educ* Queen Elizabeth GS Wakefield, Merton Coll Oxford (MA, DPhil), Univ of Oxford (DCL); *m* 1993, Alison Mary, *née* Jones; 1 da (Olivia b 26 Nov 1995); *Career* called to the Bar Lincoln's Inn 1969; lectr in law KCL 1970–75, fell and tutor in law Mansfield Coll Oxford 1975–93, prof of law Univ of Reading 1993–2008 (emeritus prof 2008–); writer of various articles for legal periodicals, memb Edtorial Bd Rights of Way Law Review 1993–2001 (ed 1991–93); Leverhulme res fell 2001; DCL 2006; *Books* The Law of Nuisance (1981, 3 edn 2013), The Modern Law of Negligence (1988, 3 edn 1999), Salmond and Heuston on Torts (21 edn, with R F V Heuston, 1996), Illegality and Public Policy (2002, 3 edn 2013), The Law of Negligence (2005), The Law of Negligence and Nuisance (2011); *Recreations* walking, swimming, working; *Style*— Professor Richard Buckley; ✉ School of Law, Foxhill House, University of Reading, PO Box 217, Whiteknights Road, Reading RG6 7BA (e-mail r.a.buckley@reading.ac.uk)

BUCKLEY, Prof Roger John; s of Frederick William Buckley (d 1997), of Mersham, Kent, and Eileen, *née* Street (d 2007); *b* 11 January 1945; *Educ* Plymouth Coll, Exeter Coll Oxford, St Thomas' Hosp Med Sch (MA, BM BCh); *m* 1 (m dis), Elizabeth Arnold, da of William Joseph Arnold Sykes (d 1986), of Speldhurst, Kent; 1 da (Harriet b 1974), 1 s (Adam b 1978); m 2, Lesley, *née* Reading; *Career* house surgn St Thomas' Hosp London 1970, sr registrar Westminster Hosp 1978; Moorfields Eye Hosp: res surgical offr 1975, conslt ophthalmologist 1981–2004, dir Contact Lens and Prosthesis Dept 1983–97, hon conslt ophthalmologist 2004–; prof of ocular med: City Univ 1997–2005, Anglia Ruskin Univ 2005–; hon visiting specialist Addenbrooke's Hosp Cambridge 2007–14; memb: BSI Contact Lens Ctee 1984–89, Ctee on Dental and Surgical Materials DHSS 1983–94, Gen Optical Cncl 1988–2007, Expert Advsy Panel Ctee on Safety of Medicines 1994–2005; pres: Med Contact Lens Assoc 1989–92, Br Contact Lens Assoc 2003–04; vice-pres Int Soc for Contact Lens Research 1993–99; hon med advsr: Musicians' Benevolent Fund 1991–2007, Royal Soc of Musicians 1994–2007, Br Assoc for Performing Arts Med 1995–2007; Delius Soc: chm 2000–08, vice-pres 2008–; author of a number of papers and chapters on the cornea, contact lenses, ocular allergy and music; ATCL 1964, FRCS 1978, FRCOphth 1989, Hon FCOptom 2002; *Recreations* music, gardening; *Clubs* RSM; *Style*— Prof Roger Buckley; ✉ Vision and Eye Research Unit, Anglia Ruskin University, East Road, Cambridge CB1 1PT (☎ 01223 363271, e-mail Roger.Buckley@anglia.ac.uk)

BUCKLEY, Prof Stephen; s of Leslie Buckley (d 1972), of Leicester and Nancy Throsby (d 1989); *b* 5 April 1944; *Educ* City of Leicester Boys' GS, King's Coll Newcastle, Univ of Durham (BA), Univ of Reading (MFA); *m* 1973, Stephanie James; 1 da (Scarlet Matilda b 1973), 1 s (Felix Rupert b 1978); *Career* artist in residence King's Coll Cambridge 1972–74, ind work 1974–; prof of fine art Univ of Reading 1994–2009; over 60 one man shows worldwide to date incl retrospective MOMA Oxford 1985 and Yale Center for British Art Newhaven 1986; prizewinner at: John Moores Liverpool Exhbn 1974 and 1985, Chichester Nat Art Exhbn 1975, Tolly Cobbold Exhbn 1977; work in collections of: Arts Cncl England, British Cncl, Tate Gallery, V&A, Contemporary Arts Soc, Aberdeen Art Gallery, City Art Gallery Bristol, Walker Art Gallery Liverpool, Whitworth Art Gallery Manchester, Southampton City Art Gallery, Metropolitan Museum NY, MOMA Caracas, Australian Nat Gallery Canberra, Nat Gallery Wellington NZ, Kettle's Yard Gallery Univ of Cambridge; in collaboration with Rambert Dance Co 1987 and 1989; *Style*— Prof Stephen Buckley; ✉ Austin Desmond Fine Art, Pied Bull Yard, London WC1B 3BN (website www.stephenbuckley.com)

BUCKMAN, Dr Laurence; s of Allan Buckman (d 1979), and Toni Buckman (d 1978); *b* 19 March 1954, London; *Educ* Univ Coll Sch, Univ Coll Hosp Med Sch; *m* 14 June 1978, Elise, *née* Sider; 2 s (Simon b 1981, Robert b 1983); *Career* hosp dr 1977–83; GP: Borehamwood 1984–93 (trainee 1983–84), Temple Fortune London 1993–; tutor Dept of Primary Care UCL Med Sch 1984–; chm GP Ctee BMA 2007–13 (memb 1991–2014); author of many articles and broadcaster about medicine, medical politics and the NHS; FRCGP 2001; *Recreations* music, photography, cycling; *Style*— Dr Laurence Buckman; ✉ e-mail l.buckman@ntlworld.com

BUCKNALL, Alison Lucy (Ali); *née* Blackford; da of Lt Col Thomas George Blackford (d 2002), and Anthea Jean, *née* Martin; *b* 27 October 1962, Sussex; *Educ* The Royal Sch Bath, Royal Holloway Coll Univ of London (BA); *m* 18 Dec 1993, Richard Kenneth Lowndes Bucknall; 2 s (Jake Casper Lowndes b 19 Aug 1996, Max Harry Holden b 6 Oct 2000), 1 da (Sophie Tara Kate b 30 April 1998); *Career* advtg account planner Collett Dickenson and Pearce 1983–89, planner Elgie Stewart Smith 1989–90, planner and assoc dir WCRS 1990–95, bd planning dir D'Arcy 1995–2003; Leo Burnett: bd planning dir 2003–05, exec planning dir 2005–08; planning dir Elvis Communications 2008–, owner/fndr Ali Bucknall Planning and Research 2008–; conslt: Effectiveness Partnership 2008–, Kitchen-8 2008–; memb: Mktg Soc, Account Planning Gp, Market Research Soc, Women in Advtg Communications London (WACL); APG Account Planning Awards: highly commended 1995, silver and bronze 2001, gold 2003; *Recreations* reading, travelling; *Clubs* Union; *Style*— Mrs Ali Bucknall; ✉ 75 St Julian's Farm Road, London SE27 0RJ (e-mail ali@alibucknall.com)

BUCKNALL, Dr Clifford Adrian (Cliff); s of Eric Bucknall, of Berkswell, W Midlands, and Elsie Constance, *née* Whittaker; *b* 25 February 1956; *Educ* Leamington Coll, KCL, Westminster Med Sch London (MB BS, MD); *m* 1, 30 July 1983 (m dis 1996); 2 s (Sam b 1984, Tom b 1986); m 2, 22 Nov 1997, Clare, *née* Collis; 2 da (Sophie Charlotte b 2002, Phoebe Holly b 2004); *Career* house surgn Warwick 1979–80, house physician Westminster 1980, sr house physician Nottingham 1980–82, research fell Guy's Hosp 1982–84, registrar Brighton 1984–85, registrar then locum sr registrar KCH 1985–87, sr registrar in cardiology Guy's Hosp 1987–89, conslt cardiologist KCH and Dulwich Hosps 1989–92, conslt cardiologist Guy's and St Thomas' Trust (formerly GKT) 1993– (dir of cardiac services 1993–97 and 2002–05); CMO Royal & Sun Alliance 1993–2000; memb Br Cardiac Soc; FRSM 1979, MRCS 1979, FRCP 1994 (MRCP 1982, LRCP 1979), FESC 1997; *Books* Horizons In Medicine no 1 (contrib, 1989); *Recreations* hockey, tennis, swimming; *Style*— Dr Cliff Bucknall; ✉ c/o 6th Floor, St Olaf House, London Bridge Hospital, 27 Tooley Street, London SE1 2PR (☎ 020 7407 0292)

BUCKS, Peter; OBE (2012); s of Nathan Bucks (d 1959), and Winifred José Beryl, *née* Hooper (d 1959); *b* 30 September 1947; *Educ* Sevenoaks Sch, Univ of Southampton (BSc); *m* 1973, Sarah Ann, da of Leslie Bernard Dobson (d 1983); 2 s (Oliver b 1978, Toby b 1982), 1 da (Eleanor b 1980); *Career* merchant banker; dir Hill Samuel Bank Ltd 1987–98, non-exec dir British Marine Managers Ltd 1997–2000; sr fin advsr Office of Gas and Electricity Markets 1997–2008, corp fin advsr Office of Water Services 2000–06; non-exec bd memb: Office of Rail Regulation 2004–14, Water Servs Regulation Authy 2006–11, Market Operator Servs Ltd 2015–; chm Open Water Markets Ltd 2014–15; Hon FSI, FRSA, Hon FCISI; *Style*— Peter Bucks, Esq, OBE; ✉ Bryants Farm, Dowlish Wake,

Ilminster, Somerset TA19 0NX (☎ 01460 52441, mobile 07710 746356, e-mail peter.bucks@bryantsfarm.co.uk)

BUCKS, Simon; s of Nathan Bucks (d 1960), of Oxted, Surrey, and Josie, *née* Hooper (d 1960); *b* 31 July 1952; *Educ* Clifton, Open Univ (BA); *m* 1, 1976 (m dis), Rita, *née* Goldberg; m 2, 1981, Cheryl Armitage *née* Davey; 1 da (Anna), 1 s (Jonathan); *Career* South West News Service Bristol 1972–75, journalist HTV West Bristol 1975–81, sub-ed then chief sub-ed ITN 1981–87, programme ed Weekend News 1987–89, programme ed News At Ten 1989–92, ed Lunchtime News and sr programme ed ITN 1992–94, controller of programmes London News Network 1996–99 (head of news 1994–96), assoc ed Sky News 2004–15; conslt and ptnr Armitage Bucks Communications 1999–; ceo Services Sound and Vision Corp 2015–; dir Soc of Eds (pres 2008); vice-chm Defence, Press and Broadcasting Advsy Ctee 2008–15, chm Media Side 2008–15; *Style*— Simon Bucks, Esq; ✉ 16 Micheldever Road, London SE12 8LX (☎ 020 8297 2858)

BUCKWELL, Allan Edgar; s of George Alfred Donald Buckwell, of Timsbury, Avon, and Jessie Ethel Neave (d 1989); *b* 10 April 1947; *Educ* Gillingham GS, Univ of London (BSc), Univ of Manchester (MA); *m* 1, (m dis 1990); 2 s (Andrew Simon b 1967, Timothy James b 1971); m 2, 9 July 1997, Elizabeth Mitchell; *Career* lectr Univ of Newcastle upon Tyne 1973–84, prof of agric economics Univ of London 1984–99, emeritus prof of agric economics Imperial Coll London 2002–; policy dir CLA 2000–12; sr research fell Inst for European Environmental Policy; pres: European Assoc of Agric Economists 1993–96, Agric Econs Soc 2004–05; *Books* Costs of the Common Agricultural Policy (with D R Harvey, K Parton and K J Thompson, 1982), Chinese Grain Economy and Policy (with Cheng Liang Yu, 1990), Agricultural Privatisation, Land Reform and Farm Restructuring in Central Europe (with J F M Swinnen and E Mathijs, 1997); *Style*— Allan Buckwell

BUCZACKI, Prof Stefan Tadeusz; s of Tadeusz Buczacki (d 1978), and Madeleine Mary Cato, *née* Fry (d 2000); *b* 16 October 1945, Derby; *Educ* Ecclesbourne Sch Duffield, Univ of Southampton (BSc), Linacre Coll Oxford (DPhil); *m* 1970, Beverley Ann, da of Sidney Charman; 2 s (Julian Nicholas Edward b 10 Nov 1973, Simon James Alexander b 25 March 1977); *Career* princ scientific offr Nat Vegetable Res Station Wellesbourne 1970–84, freelance broadcaster and author, public speaker, expert witness and garden designer 1984–; ptnr Stefan Buczacki Associates Landscape and Garden Design 2001–13; hon prof in plant pathology Liverpool John Moores Univ; pres E Midlands Assoc for Science Educn 1996–97; gardening corr: The Guardian 1986–95, Sunday Mirror 1993–96, Manchester Evening News 1997–2009; weekly columnist: Amateur Gardening 1974–97, Garden News 1997–; contrib Oxford Dictionary of National Biography, contrib to magazines, newspapers and learned jls; chm Pershore Forum Ctee and memb Local Consultancy Bd Pershore Coll; tstee: Brogdale Horticultural Tst, Hestercombe Gardens Tst (chm Estates Ctee), North of England Zoological Soc/Chester Zoo, Dawlish Gardens Tst; patron: Parrs Wood Rural Studies Centre, Langdon Gardens Tst, Warwick Castle Gardens Tst, Friends of Hestercombe Garden, Southport Flower Show; memb: Bd of Advsrs Gardeners' Royal Benevolent Soc, British Mycological Soc (pres 1999–2000, vice-pres 1994, Benefactor's Medal 1996), Int Trg Fund, CABI Int, Broadcasting Ctee Soc of Authors; hon fell CABI Bioscience, hon fell Warks Colls; Veitch Meml Medal (Gold) RHS 2010, Lifetime Achievement Award Garden Media Guild 2013; Hon DUniv Derby, Hon DLitt Univ of Southampton; CBiol, FRSB, CHort, FCIHort, FLS, ARPS; *Radio* incl: Gardeners' Question Time 1982–94 (chm 1993–94), The Gardening Quiz (originator, writer and presenter) 1988–93, Classic Gardening Forum (presenter) 1994–97; *Television* incl: Gardeners' Direct Line 1983–85, Gardeners' World 1990–91, That's Gardening 1989–92, Chelsea Flower Show 1990–91, Bazaar 1989–93, Good Morning 1992–96, Stefan Buczacki's Gardening Britain 1996, Stefan's Garden Roadshow 1997–98 and 2000, Open House 1998–2002, Learn to Garden with Stefan Buczacki 1999, Stefan's Ultimate Gardens 2001, Gardens of Kent 2009, Celebrity University Challenge 2013; *Theatre* John Cage Musicircus (Barbican and BBC Symphony Orch) 2004 and (ENO) 2012; *Books* Collins Guide to the Pests, Diseases and Disorders of Garden Plants (jt, 1981, 4 edn 2014), Gem Guide to Mushrooms and Toadstools (1982), Collins Shorter Guide to the Pests, Diseases and Disorders of Garden Plants (jt, 1983), Zoosporic Plant Pathogens (ed, 1983), Beat Garden Pests and Diseases (1985), Gardener's Questions Answered (1985), Three Men in a Garden (jt, 1986), Ground Rules for Gardeners (1986), Beginners Guide to Gardening (1988), Creating a Victorian Flower Garden (1988), Garden Warfare (1988), New Generation Guide to the Fungi of Britain and Europe (1989), A Garden for all Seasons (1990), Understanding Your Garden (1990), The Essential Gardener (1991), Dr Stefan Buczacki's Gardening Hints (1992), The Plant Care Manual (1992), The Budget Gardening Year (1993), Mushrooms and Toadstools of Britain and Europe (1993), The Gardeners' Handbook (ed, 1993), Best Climbers (1994), Best Foliage Shrubs (1994), Best Shade Plants (1994), Best Soft Fruit (1994), Best Water Plants (1995), Best Herbs (1995), Best Roses (1996), Best Container Plants (1996), Classic FM Garden Planner (jtly, 1996), Stefan Buczacki's Gardening Britain (1996), Best Garden Doctor (1997), Best Summer Flowering Shrubs (1997), Best Winter Plants (1997), Best Geraniums (1998), Best Clematis (1998), Best Pruning (1998), Stefan Buczacki's Gardening Dictionary (1998), Photoguide to the Pests, Diseases and Disorders of Garden Plants (jt, 1998), Stefan Buczacki's Plant Dictionary (1999), Best Fuchsias (1999), Best Evergreen Trees and Shrubs (1999), First Time Gardener (2000), Essential Garden Answers (2000), Best Ground Cover (2000), Best Rock Garden Plants (2000), Best Kitchen Herbs (2000), Best Water Gardens (2000), Plant Problems – Prevention and Control (2000), Hamlyn Encyclopaedia of Gardening (2002), Fauna Britannica (2002), The Commonsense Gardener (2004), Young Gardener (jtly, 2006), Garden Natural History: New Naturalist No 102 (2007), Collins Wildlife Gardener (2007), Churchill and Chartwell (2007), National Trust Chartwell Guide (2010), Collins Fungi Guide (2012), The Herb Bible (2015), My darling Mr Asquith: the extraordinary life and times of Venetia Stanley (2016); *Recreations* gardening, fishing, travel, live theatre, fine music, Derbyshire porcelain, book collecting, kippers, photography, my classic Jaguars; *Clubs* Garrick; *Style*— Prof Stefan Buczacki; ✉ Prospect House, Clifford Chambers, Stratford-upon-Avon, Warwickshire CV37 8HX (☎ 01789 298106, fax 01789 292450, e-mail info@stefanbuczacki.co.uk, website www.stefanbuczacki.co.uk)

BUDD, Sir Colin Richard; KCMG (2002, CMG 1991); s of late Bernard Wilfred Budd, QC, and Margaret Alison Budd, MBE, *née* Burgin; *b* 31 August 1945; *Educ* Kingswood Sch Bath, Pembroke Coll Cambridge; *m* 1971, Agnes, *née* Smit; 1 da (Francesca b 1979), 1 s (Nicholas b 1986); *Career* HM Dip Serv: CO 1967–68, asst private sec to Min without Portfolio 1968–69, third sec Warsaw 1969–72, second sec Islamabad 1972–75, first sec FCO 1976–80, head of Chancery The Hague 1980–84, asst private sec to Sec of State FCO 1984–87, on secondment Euro Secretariat Cabinet Office 1987–88, head of Chancery Bonn 1989–92, chef de cabinet to Sir Leon Brittan (vice-pres EC) 1993–96, dep sec Cabinet Office 1996–97, econ and EU dir FCO 1997–2001, ambass to Netherlands 2001–05, cmmr Cmmn for Racial Equality 2006–07; lay memb QC Selection Panel 2009–13, memb PM's Advsy Ctee on Business Appointments 2010–15; *Recreations* running, mountains, music; *Style*— Sir Colin Budd, KCMG; ✉ e-mail acbudd@hotmail.com

BUDENBERG, Robin; CBE (2015); *Career* qualified CA Price Waterhouse; joined SG Warburg 1984, subsequently with SBC Warburg, UBS Warburg and latterly UBS, chief exec then chm UK Financial Investments 2009–; *Style*— Robin Budenberg, CBE; ✉ UKFI, 100 Parliament Street, London SW1A 2BQ

BUDGE, David; s of Alistair Budge, of Wick, and Elizabeth, *née* Henderson; *b* 18 October 1957; *Educ* Wick HS, Glasgow Coll (SHND, Dip Industrial Admin); *m* 5 Aug 1983, Christine Margaret, da of James Deans Rankin (d 1970); 2 da (Alexandra, Catherine), 1 s (Andrew John); *Career* res exec Consensus Res Pty Brisbane 1979–80, press offr Wolf Electric Tools Ltd London 1980–81, dir PR Consultants Scotland 1987–94 (joined 1982), ptnr Budge Newton 1994–98, md Budge PR 1998–; vice-chair Glasgow Cncl on Alcohol; winner IPR Sword of Excellence 1986; FCIPR; DipCAM; *Recreations* tennis, badminton; *Clubs* Blantyre Sports; *Style*— David Budge, Esq; ✉ 2 Dunclutha Drive, Bothwell G71 8SQ (☎ 01698 852900, fax 0141 553 1119, e-mail david.budge@budgepr.com)

BUDGE, Prof Ian; s of John Elder Budge (d 1985), of Edinburgh, and Elizabeth, *née* Barnet (d 1979); *b* 21 October 1936; *Educ* Wardie Sch Edinburgh, George Heriot's Sch Edinburgh, Univ of Edinburgh, Yale Univ; *m* 17 July 1964, Judith Beatrice Ruth, da of Richard Franklin Harrison (d 1973), of Preston, Lancs; 1 s (Gavin b 1965), 1 da (Eileen Elizabeth b 1968); *Career* lectr Univ of Strathclyde 1963–66, prof (now emeritus) Univ of Essex 1977– (formerly lectr, sr lectr, reader); visiting prof: Univ of Wisconsin Madison 1969–70, Euro Univ Inst Florence 1982–85, Univ of Calif Irvine 1989, Wissenschaftzentrum Berlin 1990, Universitat Autónoma Barcelona 1991, Netherlands Inst for Advanced Study in the Social Sciences (NIAS) 1995–96, SUNY Binghampton 1998, ANU 2001; exec dir Euro Consortium for Political Res 1979–83; European Consortium for Political Research Lifetime Achievement Award 2013; FRSA; *Books* jtly: Scottish Political Behaviour (1966), Belfast: Approach to Crisis (1973), Voting and Party Competition (1978), Explaining and Predicting Elections (1983), The New British Political System (1988); Parties and Democracy (1990), Party Policy and Coalition Government (1992), Parties, Policies and Democracy (1994), The New Challenge of Direct Democracy (1996), The Politics of the New Europe (1997), Mapping Policy Preferences (2001), New British Politics (2004), Elections, Parties, Democracy: Conferring The Median Mandate (2005) Mapping Policy Preferences II (2006), Organizing Democratic Choice (2012); *Recreations* gardening, walking, travel, Italy, Scotland, opera, reading; *Style*— Prof Ian Budge; ✉ 4 Oxford Road, Colchester, Essex CO3 3HW (☎ 01206 546622); Department of Government, University of Essex, Colchester CO4 3SQ (☎ 01206 872149, fax 01206 873598, e-mail budgi@essex.ac.uk)

BUDGE, Keith Joseph; s of William Henry Budge (d 1976), and Megan, *née* Parry; *b* 24 May 1957; *Educ* Rossall Sch, UC Oxford (MA, PGCE); *m* 1983, Caroline; 2 s (Alastair b 1987, Joseph b 1990), 1 da (Lara b 1991); *Career* asst master: Eastbourne Coll 1980–84 and 1989–91, Marlborough Coll 1984–88; instr in English The Stevenson Sch Pebble Beach Calif 1988–89, housemaster (Cotton House) Marlborough Coll 1991–95, headmaster Loretto Sch 1995–2000, headmaster Bedales Sch 2001–; memb HMC; *Recreations* walking, fishing, theatre, reading; *Clubs* Vincent's (Oxford), Lansdowne; *Style*— Keith Budge, Esq; ✉ Headmaster, Bedales School, Steep, Petersfield, Hampshire GU32 2DG (☎ 01730 711551, fax 01730 300500, e-mail head@bedales.org.uk)

BUENFELD, Prof Nick; *Educ* BSc, MSc, PhD, DIC; *Career* Dept of Civil and Environmental Engrg Imperial Coll London: reader 1998–2000, prof of concrete structures 2000–, head of dept 2011–; provided guidance to the designers or constructors of: Los Angeles Cathedral, Great Man-Made River Project Libya, Channel Tunnel, Tsing Ma and Tsing Lung Bridges Hong Kong, many other projects; author of more than 150 refereed publns and four patents; FREng 2011, FICE 2011 (MICE 1984), FIStructE 2012, CEng, HonFICT 2015; *Clubs* Campden Hill Lawn Tennis, Alleyn; *Style*— Prof Nick Buenfeld; ✉ Department of Civil and Environmental Engineering, Imperial College, London SW7 2BU (e-mail n.buenfeld@imperial.ac.uk)

BUERK, Michael Duncan; s of Capt Gordon Charles Buerk (d 1975), and Betty Mary Buerk (d 1962); *b* 18 February 1946; *Educ* Solihull Sch; *m* 9 Sept 1968, Christine, da of late Bernard Joseph Lilley, of Hereford; 2 s (Simon, Roland (twins) b 30 Nov 1973); *Career* BBC TV News: joined 1973, energy corr 1976–79, Scotland corr 1979–81, special corr 1981–82, corr and presenter 1982–83, Africa corr 1983–87, presenter 1987–2003; presenter: Moral Maze (BBC Radio 4) 1990–, 999 (BBC 1) 1993–2002, The Choice (BBC Radio 4) 1998–2011; judge Costa Book Award 2008; *Awards* RTS Television Journalist of the Year 1984, RTS Int News Award 1984, George Polk Award (US) Foreign TV Reporting 1984, Nat Headlines Award (US) 1984, Int News/Documentary Award Monte Carlo Festival 1984, BAFTA News & Documentary Award 1985, James Cameron Meml Award 1987, Glaxo Science Writer of the Year Award 1989; *Recreations* oenophily; *Style*— Michael Buerk, Esq

BUFFONG, Michael; *b* 11 February 1964, London; *Career* artistic dir Talawa Theatre Co 2012–; prodns for Talawa incl: God's Property (Soho Theatre and The Albany), The Serpent's Tooth (Almeida Theatre and Shoreditch Town Hall), All My Sons (Manchester Royal Exchange Theatre), King Lear (Manchester Royal Exchange and Birmingham Rep); other prodns incl: Moon on a Rainbow Shawl (RNT), A Raisin in the Sun (Manchester Royal Exchange), One Flew Over the Cuckoo's Nest (Liecester Curve), Crawling in the Dark (Almeida Theatre), Private Lives (Manchester Royal Exchange), To Kill a Mockingbird (W Yorks Playhouse and Birmingham Rep), Little Sweet Thing (Hampstead Theatre); *Style*— Michael Buffong, Esq; ✉ Talawa Theatre Company, 53–55 East Road, London N1 6AH; c/o Cathy King, Independent Talent (☎ 020 7636 6565, e-mail cathyking@independenttalent.com)

BUFORD, William Holmes (Bill); s of William Holmes Buford, Jr, of Jonesboro, Louisiana, and Helen McCollough Shiel, of NYC; *b* 6 October 1954; *Educ* Univ of Calif Berkeley (BA), King's Coll Cambridge (Marshall scholar, MA); *m* 1, 6 July 1991 (m dis 2000), Alicja, *née* Kobiernicka; m 2, 18 Oct 2002, Jessica Hawkins Green; 2 s (George Ely, Frederick Hawkins (twins) b 24 Sept 2005); *Career* ed Granta 1979–95, publisher Granta Books 1989–95, chm Granta Publications Ltd until 1995, literary and fiction ed New Yorker 1995–2002, staff writer New Yorker 2006–; *Books* Among the Thugs (1991), The Granta Book of Travel Writing (ed, 1992), The Granta Book of Reportage (1993), The Granta Book of The Family (ed, 1995), Heat: An Amateur's Adventures as Kitchen Slave, Line Cook, Pasta-Maker and Apprentice to a Danté-Quoting Butcher in Tuscany (2006); *Style*— Bill Buford, Esq; ✉ The New Yorker, 4 Times Square, New York, NY 10036, USA (☎ 00 1 212 286 2860, fax 00 1 212 997 7852)

BUGDEN, Paul William; s of Frederick William Bugden, and Rosemary Anne Matilda Winifred Bugden (d 1995); *b* 18 April 1953; *Educ* Merchant Taylors', Univ of Kent (BA); *m* 14 Feb 1984, Nicola Ann, da of Peter Raynes, OBE; 1 s (James William b 22 March 1985), 1 da (Jessica Lucy b 29 Sept 1986); *Career* articled clerk Russell-Cooke Potter & Chapman 1976–77; Clyde & Co: articled clerk 1977–78, admitted slr 1978, based Hong Kong 1981–84, ptnr 1982–2013; memb: Law Soc, Br Insurance Law Assoc; *Recreations* cycling, reading, theatre, running; *Clubs* Bramley Golf, Cranleigh Cycle; *Style*— Paul Bugden, Esq

BUGEJA, Martin Timothy; s of late Capt Paul Bugeja, and Lina, *née* Aquilina; *b* 27 June 1957, Malta; *Educ* St Edward's Coll Malta; *m* 21 Feb 1977, Joanna Juliet, *née* McNally; 1 s (Tom b 17 May 1984), 1 da (Emma b 7 Sept 1985); *Career* fndr and md Sunspot Tours Mercury Direct 1980–; *Recreations* playing: golf, tennis, walking, bridge; watching: football, rugby; *Style*— Martin Bugeja, Esq; ✉ The Five Gables, East Street, Mayfield, East Sussex TN20 6TZ (e-mail mbugeja@sunspottours.com)

BUGGY, Niall Michael; s of Martin William Buggy (d 1985), of Ireland, and Kathleen Veronica, *née* Bourke (d 2004); *b* 3 October 1948; *Educ* Sandy Mount HS, Brendan Smith Acad, Abbey Theatre Sch; *Career* actor; joined Abbey Sch aged 15, various roles incl Trofimov in The Cherry Orchard, The Seagull; *Theatre* incl: Crucible Theatre Sheffield: Stanley in The Birthday Party, Estragon in Waiting for Godot; RNT: Lucius O'Trigger in The Rivals, Scandal in Love for Love, Gal in Rough Crossing; other roles incl: Christie Mahon in Playboy of The Western World (Actor of the Year Award), Seamus Shields in Shadow of A Gunman (Young Vic, nominated for Helen Hayes Award), Memoir (Dublin and London), Spokesong (King's Head, Plays and Players' Award for Best Newcomer 1978), Baron Tusenbach in Three Sisters (Harvey Award), Major General in Pirates of Penzance (Best Supporting Actor Award), Casimir in Aristocrats (winner Clarence Derwent, Time Out and Obie Awards), Bluntschli in Arms and the Man, Player King in Hamlet, Captain Boyle in Juno and the Paycock (TMA Regional Theatre Best Actor Award), Dead Funny (Vaudeville, Olivier Award for Best Comedy Performance 1995), Song at Sunset (one man show, Hampstead 1996, NY 1997), The Misanthrope (Young Vic), No Man's Land (Gate, Dublin), Give Me Your Answer Do (Hampstead), Uncle Vanya (Gate Dublin and NY, Best Actor Irish Theatre Awards), The Weir (Royal Court, Broadway, Perth and Sydney), The Beckett Festival (Barbican), Snogging Ken (Almeida), The Importance of Being Oscar (one man show, NY 2001), John Bull's Other Island (Tricycle), Mr Nobody (Soho), An Inspector Calls (Playhouse Theatre), Guys and Dolls (Piccadilly), The Gigli Concert (Finborough Theatre), A Kind of Alaska (Gate Notting Hill), Translations (Broadway), Gentrification (Druid Theatre Galway), Afterplay (Sydney Festival, Gate Theatre Dublin, Edinburgh Festival), Haunted (Royal Exchange, Bath, Belfast, Dublin, Brighton), Penelope (Galway, Edinburgh Festival) 2010, Druid Murphy (Galway, Lincoln Centre NY, Cork, Kennedy Centre Washington and Dublin Theatre Festival) 2012, The Hanging Garden (Abbey Theatre) 2013, Translations (English Touring Theatre) 2014, The Importance of Being Earnest (West End) 2014, The Invisible (Bush Theatre) 2015, You Never Can Tell (Abbey Theatre) 2015–16; *Television* incl: Once in a Lifetime, The Gathering Seed, The Citadel, Red Roses for Me, The Promise, The Little Mother, Chinese Whispers, The Full Wax, 99–1, Little Napoleon, Agony Again, Upwardly Mobile, Father Ted, Lucy Sullivan is Getting Married, Grease Monkeys, Cruise of the Gods, Family Affairs, Malice Aforethought, Lewis, Dalziel and Pascoe; *Films* incl: Zardoz, Portrait of the Artist as a Young Man, Alien 3, Playboys, King David, Close My Eyes, Anna Karenina, The Butcher Boy, Sweeney Todd, That Time, Spin the Bottle, Morality Play, The Libertine, Mamma Mia, Brideshead Revisited, The Duel, Mr Turner; *Style—* Niall Buggy, Esq; ✉ c/o Sally Long-Innes, Independent Talent Group, Oxford House, 76 Oxford Street, London W1D 1BS (☎ 020 7636 6565)

BUHLMANN, Jerry; *b* 26 November 1959, London; *Career* Young & Rubicam 1980–83, media mangr WCRS Advertising 1983–89, prop and md BBJ 1989–99; Aegis Gp plc: pres Carat International 2000–03, ceo EMEA 2003–08, ceo Aegis Media 2008–10, memb Bd 2008–10, ceo 2010–13; ceo Dentsu Aegis Network 2013–; *Recreations* road cycling, triathlon, skiing, Chelsea FC, rugby, fine wine; *Style—* Jerry Buhlmann, Esq; ✉ Dentsu Aegis Network, 10 Triton Street, Regent's Place, London NW1 3BF

BUITER, Prof Willem Hendrik; CBE (2000); s of Harm Geert Buiter, of Groningen, Netherlands, and Hendrien, *née* van Schooten; *b* 26 September 1949, The Hague, The Netherlands; *Educ* European Sch Brussels, Univ of Amsterdam, Emmanuel Coll Cambridge (BA), Yale Univ (MA, MPhil, PhD); *m* 1, 4 August 1973 (m dis 1985, remarried 18 April 1988, m dis 1998) Jean, da of Alan Simeon Archer, and Elizabeth Archer; 1 s (David Michael Alejandro b 22 Feb 1991), 1 da (Elizabeth Lorca b 6 August 1993); m 2, 5 June 1998, Anne, da of Edwin Luther Sibert, Jr; *Career* asst prof of public and int affrs Princeton Univ 1975–76 and 1977–79, lectr in economics LSE 1976–77, prof of economics Univ of Bristol 1980–82, Cassel prof of economics with special reference to money and banking LSE 1982–85, Juan T Trippe prof of economics Yale Univ 1990–94 (prof of economics 1985–89), appointed prof of int macroeconomics Univ of Cambridge 1994, appointed prof of political economy Univ of Amsterdam 2000, prof of European political economy LSE 2005–10; chief economist European Bank for Reconstruction and Devpt 2000–05, chief economist Citigroup 2010–; memb Monetary Policy Ctee Bank of England 1997–2000; research assoc Nat Bureau of Economic Research 1979, research fell Centre for Economic Policy Research 1983–, Irving Fisher visiting prof Yale Univ 1983–88, visiting prof Univ of Groningen 1986 and 1988, visiting prof LSE 1987–88, adjunct sr fell Cncl on Foreign Rels 2014, adjunct prof of economics Sch of Int and Public Affrs Columbia Univ 2015–; specialist advsr House of Commons Select Ctee on the Treasy and Civil Serv 1980, chair Cncl of Economic Advsrs Dutch Parl 2005–07; advsr Goldman Sachs Int 2005–; conslt: AT&T 1976, Oxford Analytica Ltd 1977, IMF 1985–, World Bank 1986–, Inter-American Devpt Bank 1992–, EBRD 1994–; assoc ed: World Politics 1978, Economic Jl 1980–85; jt winner Sanwa Monograph on Int Financial Markets Award 1993, Dr Hendrik Muller Prize (Netherlands prize for Social Sciences) 1995, N G Person Medal for contributions to economics 2000; corresponding memb Royal Netherlands Acad of Sciences 1989, memb Int Inst of Public Finance 1993, memb Cncl Royal Economic Soc 1997; hon doctorate Univ of Amsterdam 2012; FBA 1998; *Books* Temporary and Long-Run Equilibrium (1979), Budgetary Policy, International and Intertemporal Trade in the Global Economy (1989), Macroeconomic Theory and Stabilization Policy (1989), Principles of Budgetary and Financial Policy (1990), International Macroeconomics (1990), Financial Markets and European Monetary Cooperation – The Lessons of the 92–93 ERM Crisis (with G Corsetti and P Pesenti, 1997); author of numerous articles in learned jls and also of book reviews, comments and discussions, and of the Maverecon blog 2007–09; *Recreations* tennis, science fiction and phantasy, poetry; *Style—* Prof Willem Buiter, CBE, FBA; ✉ Citigroup Global Markets Inc, 388 Greenwich Street, New York NY10013, USA (☎ 001 212 816 2363, e-mail willem.buiter@citi.com, website http://willembuiter.com)

BULFIELD, Prof Grahame John; CBE (2001); s of Frederick Robert Bulfield (d 1956), of Cheshire, and Madge, *née* Jones (d 1968); *b* 12 June 1941; *Educ* King's Sch Macclesfield, Univ of Leeds (BSc), Univ of Edinburgh (Dip Animal Genetics, PhD); *Career* Fulbright fell and NIH postdoctoral fell Dept of Genetics Univ of Calif 1968–70, research assoc Inst of Animal Genetics Univ of Edinburgh 1971–76 (SRC resettlement fell 1970–71), lectr and convenor of med genetics Dept of Genetics Univ of Leicester 1976–81, head of genetics gp AFRC Poultry Res Centre 1981–86, head of station and assoc dir Edinburgh Res Station Inst of Animal Physiology and Genetic Res 1988–93 (head of gene expression gp 1986–88), dir and chief exec Roslin Inst 1993–2002; Univ of Edinburgh: hon fell Dept of Genetics 1981–90, hon prof Div of Biological Science Univ of Edinburgh 1990–2002, vice-princ, head Coll of Sci and Engrg and prof of animal genetics 2002–08, emeritus prof of genetics 2008–; memb: Genetical Soc 1971– (memb Ctee 1980–83 and 1986–90), Advsy Ctee on Genetic Modification 1990–96, Advsy Bd Partnerships UK 2002–03, Bd Scottish Agricultural Coll 2007–, Shell Animal Testing Review Panel 2010–; chair RSE/BBSRC Enterprise Fellowship Panel 2010–; fndr ed Genes and Development 1987–90; memb: Home Office Animal Proceedures Ctee 1998–2006, Research and Knowledge Transfer Ctee Scottish Funding Cncl 2002–07; author of research papers and book chapters on biochemical and molecular genetics; Hon DSc: Univ of Edinburgh 2000, Univ of Abertay 2003; FRSE 1992, CBiol, FSB 1995, Hon FRASE 1999; *Recreations* fell walking, cricket, genealogy; *Style—* Prof Grahame Bulfield, CBE, FRSE

BULKELEY; *see:* Williams-Bulkeley

BULKIN, Dr Bernard J; s of Jacob Bulkin (d 1992), and Beatrice, *née* Kotkofsky (d 1990); *b* 9 March 1942, Trenton, NJ, USA; *Educ* Poly Inst of Brooklyn (BS), Purdue Univ (PhD); *m* 14 July 2002, Vivien, *née* Rose; 1 da (Anna b 31 Aug 1970), 2 s (Noah b 31 May 1977, David b 21 July 1979); *Career* postdoctoral fell Eidgenössische Technische Hochschule Zürich 1966–67, prof City Univ of NY 1967–75; Poly Inst of NY: dean of arts and sciences 1975–81, vice-pres 1981–85; Standard Oil of Ohio: dir analytical and environmental science 1985–87, dir R&D Sohio Oil 1987–88; BP plc: head Products Div 1989–92, R&D dir BP Oil 1992–97, dir manufacturing and supply 1993–97, vice-pres environmental affrs 1997–2000, chief scientist 2000–03; professorial fell New Hall Cambridge 2004–, ptnr Vantage Point 2004–, chm AEA Technology plc 2005–09, non-exec dir Severn Trent plc 2006–, chm Chemrec AB 2007–12, chm Pursuit Dynamics plc 2012–, non-exec dir Ludgate Investments Ltd 2012–; chair Office of Renewable Energy UK Dept of Energy and Climate Change 2010–; author of more than 125 papers and two books; Oscar Foster Award 1973, Coblentz Award 1975, Soc for Applied Spectroscopy Gold Medal 1978; FRSC 1989, FRSA 1995, FEI 1998; *Recreations* horseback riding; *Clubs* Reform; *Style—* Dr Bernard Bulkin; ✉ e-mail bbulkin@vpcp.com

BULL, David; s of J W Bull; *Educ* Univ of Reading (BA, MA); *Career* various positions at academic and science publishers incl: Routledge, Thomson, Chapman & Hall, Taylor & Francis; dir of journals Palgrave (formerly Macmillan Press); *Publications* Marketing Explained (1997); author of numerous articles for industry publications; *Recreations* my children, writing, reading, music; *Style—* David Bull, Esq; ✉ Macmillan Publishers Ltd, Houndmills, Basingstoke RG21 6XS (☎ 01256 329242, e-mail d.bull@palgrave.com)

BULL, David Neill; CBE (2015); s of Denis Albert Bull (d 1986), of Grays, Essex, and Doreen Lilian, *née* Durham; *b* 21 June 1951; *Educ* Palmer's Sch for Boys Grays, Univ of Sussex (BA), Univ of Bath (MSc); *m* 1978, Claire, da of Peter Grenger; 1 da (Kate b 1984); *Career* public affrs offr Oxfam 1979–84, exec dir Environment Liaison Centre (Kenya) 1984–87, gen sec World University Service (WUS) UK 1987–90, dir Amnesty International UK 1990–99, exec dir UK Ctee for UNICEF 1999–2016; memb: Exec Ctee (vol) The Refugee Cncl 1987–90, Bd (vol) PAN UK 1987–99, Exec Ctee ACEVO 1994–98; *Books* A Growing Problem: Pesticides and the Third World Poor (1982), The Poverty of Diplomacy: Kampuchea and the Outside World (1983); blog www.worldtorights.org; *Style—* David Bull, CBE; ✉ e-mail davidnbull@gmail.com, website www.worldtorights.org, Twitter @DavidNBull

BULL, Deborah Clare; CBE (1999); da of Rev (Michael) John Bull, of Suffolk, and Doreen Audrey, *née* Plumb; *b* 22 March 1963; *Educ* The Royal Ballet Sch, Academie de Danse Classique de Monte Carlo; *Career* Royal Ballet 1981–2001 (soloist 1986, princ 1992), creative dir ROH2 2002–08, creative dir ROH 2008–12, dir of cultural partnerships KCL 2012–, asst princ Culture and London Engagement KCL 2015–; major dance roles incl: Rite of Spring, La Bayadère, Sleeping Beauty, Agon, Steptext, Giselle, Song of the Earth, Don Quixote, In the Middle, Somewhat Elevated, Swan Lake; created major roles in: Still Life at the Penguin Café, Pursuit, Piano, Fearful Symmetries; memb cast: In the Middle, Somewhat Elevated (Laurence Olivier Award 1993); guest performances: Italy, Canada, Japan, N America; organised and performed in An Evening of British Ballet at The Sintra Festival 1994 and 1995; addressed Oxford Union 1996, delivered Arts Cncl Annual Lectr 1996, dir Artists' Devpt Initiative at ROH, columnist The Daily Telegraph, writer/presenter Dance Ballerina, Dance (BBC2) 1998; presenter: Travels with My Tutu (four part series, BBC2) 2000, Breaking the Law (5 part series, BBC Radio 4) 2001, Law in Order (5 part series BBC Radio 4) 2002, The Dancer's Body (three part series, BBC2) 2002, Saved for the Nation, Artsworld 2006, Hothouse Kids (BBC Radio 4) 2009, Deborah Bull's Dance Nation (BBC Radio 4) 2012, Dancing for Russia (Sky Arts) 2014; regular presenter live broadcasts BBC1 and BBC2; memb: Bd South Bank Centre 1997–2003, Arts Cncl of England 1998–2005, Bd of Govrs BBC 2003–06, Artistic Ctee Prix de Lausanne 1997–2012, Fndn of the Prix de Lausanne 2012–, Arts and Humanities Research Cncl 2012–; winner Prix de Lausanne 1980, voted one of the Dancers of the Year by readers of Dance and Dancers 1991 and 1992, Olivier Award nomination for Outstanding Achievement in Dance (for Steptext at ROH) 1996; vice-pres Br Science Assoc 2015–; patron Nat Osteoporosis Soc; Hon Dr: Univ of Derby 1998, Sheffield Hallam Univ 2001, Open Univ 2005, Univ of Kent 2010; *Books* The Vitality Plan (1998), Dancing Away – A Covent Garden Diary (1998), The Faber Guide to Classical Ballets (2004), The Everyday Dancer (2011); *Recreations* literature, music, neurology, physiology, nutrition, people; *Style—* Miss Deborah Bull, CBE; ✉ c/o Rosemary Scoular, United Agents, 12–26 Lexington Street, London W1F 0LE (website www.kcl.ac.uk/cultural/index.aspx, Twitter @BullDeborah or @CulturalKings)

BULL, Sir George Jeffrey; kt (1998); s of Michael Herbert Perkins Bull (d 1965), and Hon Noreen Madeleine Hennessy (d 2004), da of 1 Baron Windlesham; *b* 16 July 1936, London; *Educ* Ampleforth; *m* 7 Jan 1960, Jane Fleur Thérèse (Tessa), da of Patrick Freeland (d 1977); 4 s (Sebastian b 1960, Rupert b 1963, Justin b 1964, Cassian b 1966), 1 da (Tamsin b 1972); *Career* Lt Coldstream Gds 1954–57, served in Ger and UK; Dorland Advertising Ltd 1957, Twiss Browning and Hallowes wine merchants 1958, md Gilbey Vintners Ltd 1970, md Int Distillers and Vintners UK Ltd 1973, md IDV Europe Ltd 1977, dep md IDV Ltd 1982, dir Grand Metropolitan Ltd 1985, chief exec Grand Metropolitan Drinks Sector and IDV Ltd 1987, chm and chief exec IDV Ltd 1984–1992; Grand Metropolitan plc: gp chief exec 1993–95, gp chm 1995–97; jt gp chm Diageo plc (following merger with Guinness plc) 1997–98 (non-exec dir 1998–2000), chm J Sainsbury plc 1998–2004; non-exec dir: United News and Media plc (formerly United Newspapers plc) 1993–98, BNP Paribas UK Holdings 2000–04, The Maersk Co Ltd 2001–06, Marakon Assocs 2002–06; dir Br Overseas Trading Bd 1990–95; memb: Exec Ctee GMFA 1992–94, President's Ctee CBI 1993–1996, BACC Advsy Bd 1994–98, Ctee Westminster Cathederal Centenary Appeal 1995–96; chm: Wine and Spirit Assoc of GB 1975–76, Ampleforth Bi-centenary Appeal 1999–2004; pres Wine & Spirit Benevolent Soc 2000–01; dir US Adv Educ Fndn 1994–98, founding dir The Mktg Cncl 1995–2000; pres Advtg Assoc (AA) 1996–2000; vice-pres Mencap 2000– (chm Jubilee Appeal Ctee 1995–98); chm Old Codgers Assoc 2006–; dir/sec Chapel Annunciation Furneux Pelham 2010–13; Mktg Hall of Fame 1998; hon pres Perkins Bull Collection Inc 2008–; patron Keepers of the Quaich 1996–2005 (Grand Master 1995–96), confrater Ampleforth Abbey 2005–, patron Caritas Anchor House Project 2010–; Freeman City of London 1995, Freeman Worshipful Co of Distillers 1995–; FRSA 1992–98, Hon FCIM 1995 (vice-pres 1994), hon fell Mktg Soc 1997 (memb 1997); Chevalier de la Legion d'Honneur 1994, Chevalier du Tastevin 2005; *Recreations* golf, photography; *Clubs* The Pilgrims, Cavalry and Guards', Royal Worlington Golf (memb Cncl 2008–11), Nulli Secundus; *Style—* Sir George Bull; ✉ The Old Vicarage, Arkesden, Saffron Walden, Essex (☎ 01799 550445, e-mail george.j.bull@btinternet.com)

BULL, Prof (Roger) John; CBE (2002); *b* 31 March 1940; *Educ* Churcher's Coll Petersfield, LSE (BSc); *m* 1964, Margaret Evelyn, *née* Clifton; 1 s, 1 da; *Career* student accountant then systems accountant Ford Motor Co 1958–62, lectr II in accounting NE London Poly 1965–66, res fell Dept of Educn and Science/ICAEW 1966–67, sr lectr in accounting NE London Poly 1967–68, princ lectr in accounting Trent Poly 1968–72, head Sch of Accounting and Applied Economics Leeds Poly 1972–84, vice-chllr and chief exec Univ of Plymouth 1989–2002 (dep 1985–89); chm LSC Devon and Cornwall 2002–08, chm Plymouth Hosps NHS Tst 2002–10; chm Dartington Coll of Arts 2003–08; dep chm Universities Superannuation Scheme (USS) Ltd 2004–14; author of pubns in accounting and academic mgmnt; FCCA 1976 (ACCA 1962); *Recreations* music, gardening; *Style—* Prof John Bull, CBE; ✉ 3 Westmoor Park, Tavistock, Devon PL19 9AA

BULLEN, James Edward; s of Albert Edward Bullen (d 1977), and Doris Josephine, *née* McHale (d 1976); *b* 26 March 1943; *Educ* Univ of London (LLB); *m* 1, 1973 (m dis 1984); m 2, 27 Sept 1985, Mary, da of late Patrick Keane; 1 s (William James b 1986); *Career* called to the Bar Gray's Inn 1966, memb Senate of Inns of Ct and Bar 1979–82, recorder (Western Circuit) 1997–; *Recreations* music, reading, walking, horse riding; *Clubs* Garrick, RAC; *Style—* James Bullen, Esq; ✉ 1 Paper Buildings, Temple, London EC4Y 7EP

BULLMORE, Prof Edward Thomas; s of Jeremy Bullmore, CBE, *qv*, of London, and Pamela Audrey, *née* Green; *b* 27 September 1960; *Educ* Westminster, ChCh Oxford (MA, Ida Mary Henderson scholar), Univ of London (MB BS, PhD); *m* 13 Dec 1992, Mary, da of Arthur Pitt; 3 s (Alfred b 1993, Sidney b 1996, Ferdinand b 2001); *Career* house offr Bart's and Hackney Hosps 1985–86, lectr in med Univ of Hong Kong 1987–88, SHO in psychiatry St George's Hosp London 1989–90, registrar, hon sr registrar then conslt psychiatrist Bethlem Royal & Maudsley Hosp London 1990–99, conslt psychiatrist Cambs and Peterborough Mental Health NHS Tst and Addenbrooke's Hosp Cambridge 1999–; Wellcome Tst advanced research trg fell Inst of Psychiatry 1996–99 (Wellcome Tst research trg fell and hon lectr 1993–96); Univ of Cambridge: prof of psychiatry 1999–, dir of fMRI Wolfson Brain Imaging Centre 2000–05, professorial fell Wolfson Coll 2002–10, head Dept of Psychiatry Univ of Cambridge 2014–; vice-pres Experimental Medicine and head Clinical Unit Cambridge GlaxoSmithKline 2005–13, vice-pres Immunopsychiatry GlaxoSmithKline 2013–; clinical dir MRC/Wellcome Tst Behavioural & Clinical Neurosciences Inst 2005–, dir R&D Cambs and Peterborough Fndn NHS Tst 2011–, co-chair Cambridge Neuroscience 2013–, sr investigator Nat Inst for Health Research (NIHR) 2014, chair Cambridge Health Imaging 2015–; memb MRC Neurosciences and Mental Health Bd 2002–06; dep ed Biological Psychiatry 2011; author of articles on brain mapping, statistics and psychiatry; Denis Hill Prize Inst of Psychiatry 1992, Br Neuropsychiatry Prize 1994; FMedSci 2008, FRCPsych 2009 (MRCPsych 1992), FRCP 2010 (MRCP 1989); *Publications* Fundamentals of Brain Network Analysis (2016); *Style*— Prof Ed Bullmore; ✉ University of Cambridge, Department of Psychiatry, Herchel Smith Building for Brain and Mind Sciences, Cambridge CB2 0SZ (☎ 01223 336583, fax 01223 336581, e-mail etb23@cam.ac.uk)

BULLOCK, Gareth Richard; s of George Haydn Bullock, of Richmond, Surrey, and Veronica, *née* Jackson; *b* 20 November 1953; *Educ* Marling Sch Stroud, St Catharine's Coll Cambridge (MA); *m* 3 Sept 1983, Juliet Lucy Emma, da of Maj Cyril Vivian Eagleson Gordon, MC, of Winterbourne Gunner, Wilts; 3 s (Joshua b 1985, Marcus b 1987, Caspar b 1992); *Career* vice pres Citibank NA London 1984 (joined 1977), exec dir Swiss Bank Corp Investment Banking Ltd 1984–90, gp md UBS Phillips & Drew 1990–92, head of corporate banking Société Générale 1993–96; Standard Chartered Bank: joined 1996, formerly ceo Africa and gp chief info offr, currently dir and gp head of strategy; non-exec dir Spirax-Sarco Engineering plc 2005–; memb: Ctee St Catharine's Coll Soc, RSPB; *Publications* Euronotes and Euro-Commercial Paper (1987); *Recreations* second-hand book collecting, ornithology; *Style*— Gareth Bullock, Esq

BULLOCK, Hon Matthew Peter Dominic; yst s of Baron Bullock (Life Peer); *b* 9 September 1949; *Educ* Magdalen Coll Sch Oxford, Peterhouse Cambridge; *m* 1970, Anna-Lena Margareta, da of Sven Hansson, of Uppsala, Sweden; 1 s, 2 da; *Career* banker; dir of risk mgmnt Banking Div Barclays Bank plc 1993–94 (joined 1974); BZW Ltd: dir of debt capital mkts 1994–96, md Investment Banking Div 1996–97; md Treasy Relationship Mgmnt Barclays Capital Group 1997–99, chief exec Norwich and Peterborough Building Society 1999–2011, chm Building Societies Assoc, memb Financial Services Practitioner Panel 2001–07, non-exec dir and chair of audit Cambridge Univ Hospitals Fndn Tst 2010–13, chm Tranforming Pathology Partnership 2013–; chm Int House Tst 2011–14; master St Edmund's Coll Cambridge 2014–; *Recreations* gardening, reading, walking; *Clubs* Oxford and Cambridge; *Style*— The Hon Matthew Bullock; ✉ Easby House, High Street, Great Chesterford, Saffron Waldon, Essex CB10 1PL

BULLOCK, Peter Bradley; s of William H Bradley Bullock, of Benson, Oxon; *b* 9 June 1934; *Educ* Dudley GS, QMC London (BSc); *m* 1958, Joyce Frances Muriel, da of Horace Rea (d 1957); 2 da (Claire Elizabeth Bradley (Mrs Locke), Penelope Jane Bradley (Mrs Hembrow)); *Career* md Flymo Ltd (memb of Electrolux Group Sweden), jt md Electrolux Group UK until 1983; chief exec: James Neill Holdings plc 1983–89, Spear & Jackson Int plc 1985–89; chm: London & Geneva Securities Ltd 1990–2001, The Paterson Photax Gp Ltd 1992–94, James Dickie plc 1993–98, Scala Collections Ltd (Artigiano) 1997–2006; non-exec dir: 600 Gp plc 1989–2004, Wetherby Consultants Ltd 1990–96, Syltone plc 1990–99, Bison Bede Ltd 1997–98; Queen's Award: for Export 1966 and 1982, for Technol 1979 and 1983; CEng, MEI, MCIM; *Recreations* France, Hannibal's route over the Alps; *Clubs* Leander, Phyllis Court; *Style*— Peter Bullock, Esq; ✉ 5 Old Brewery Lane, Henley-on-Thames RG9 2DE (e-mail genelond1@aol.com)

BULLOCK, Susan Margaret; CBE (2014); da of John Robert Bullock (d 1994), of Cheadle Hulme, Cheshire, and Mair, *née* Jones (d 2000); *b* 9 December 1958, Davenham, Cheshire; *Educ* Cheadle Hulme Sch, Royal Northern Coll of Music (Jr Sch), Royal Holloway Coll London (BMus), Royal Acad of Music (LRAM), National Opera Studio; *m* 1, (m dis 2008), Lawrence Archer Wallington, singer, s of Rev Christopher Wallington (d 1988); m 2, 2009, Richard Berkeley-Steele, s of Brian Steele; *Career* soprano; memb Glyndebourne Festival Chorus 1983–84, princ soprano English National Opera 1985–89; has performed with numerous major orchs incl: London Philharmonic, Royal Philharmonic, Royal Liverpool Philharmonic, BBC Nat Orch of Wales, BBC Scottish Symphony, Bournemouth Symphony, London Mozart Players, CBSO, Philharmonia, Hallé, Manchester Camerata, BBC Philharmonic, Czech Philharmonic, Sydney Symphony, Melbourne Symphony, Tokyo Philharmonic, BBC Symphony, NHK Tokyo, Hong Kong Philharmonic; regularly performs at overseas festivals incl Beaune, Istanbul, Aix-en-Provence, Prague Spring Festival; broadcasts regularly at the Proms and with BBC Concert Orch; hon fell Royal Holloway Univ of London; FRAM; int opera roles incl: Brünnhilde (ROH, Vienna State Opera, Frankfurt, Melbourne, Tokyo, Lisbon, Toronto, Perth, Budapest Deutsche Oper Berlin), Elektra (ROH, La Scala Milan, Brussels, Frankfurt, Stuttgart, Rouen, Dresden, Tolouse, Metropolitan Opera, Washington DC, Opera North, Florence, Sao Paulo, Hong Kong, Toronto; other notable roles incl: Marie in Wozzeck (ROH), title role in Gloriana (ROH), Isolde (Frankfurt, Verona, Rouen, Bochum, ENO, Opera North, Munich), Emilia Marty in V?c Makropulos (Frankfurt); other int appearances: Teatro Colon Buenos Aires, Spoleto Festival Italy and USA, Perth Festival Australia, Theater an der Wien Vienna, Prague Spring Festival, New Israeli Opera, Flanders Opera, Bergen Festival, Glyndebourne Festival, Houston Grand Opera, Portland Opera, Bayerische Staatsoper, Teatro de la Maestranza Seville, ENO; *Recordings* incl: The Mikado (with ENO under Peter Robinson) 1988, Street Scene (with ENO under Carl Davis) 1989, Mahler's 8th Symphony (with London Philharmonic under Klaus Tennstedt) 1990, La Traviata/Acting (BBC TV, directed by Jonathan Miller), The Little Sweep (Thames TV), The Mikado (Thames TV), solo album 1994, Songs (La Nouvelle Musique Consonante) 1995, A Little Water Music 1997, Hindemith Sancta Susanna and Songs (with BBC Philharmonic under Yan Pascal Tortelier) 1998, Magda Sorel in The Consul, Lady Billows in Albert Herring 2002, Requiem Daffyd Bullock 2002, recital with Malcolm Martineau 2006, Salome (with Charles Mackerras) 2007; *Awards* Royal Over-Seas League Singers Award, Decca/Kathleen Ferrier Prize, Worshipful Co of Musicians' Silver Medal, Premio Pegaso Spoleto Festival Italy, Royal Philharmonic Soc Singers Award 2008, Green Room Award for Outstanding Performance in a Leading Role by Female Singer 2009; *Recreations* theatre, films, playing the piano, cooking, reading, jazz; *Style*— Ms Susan Bullock, CBE; ✉ c/o Harrison Parrott Ltd, 5–6 Albion Court, Albion Place, London W6 0QT (☎ 020 7229 9166, e-mail info@harrisonparrott.co.uk, website www.harrisonparrott.co.uk)

BULMER-THOMAS, Prof Victor Gerald; CMG (2007), OBE (1998); s of Ivor Bulmer-Thomas, CBE (d 1993), and Joan, *née* Bulmer; *b* 23 March 1948; *Educ* Univ of Oxford; *m* 7 Sept 1970, Barbara Ann, da of James Swasey; 2 s (Hadrian b 30 Nov 1972, Rupert b 3 May 1978), 1 da (Bianca b 11 Sept 1979); *Career* res fell Fraser of Allander Inst 1975–78; Univ of London: lectr QMC 1978–88, reader Queen Mary & Westfield Coll 1988–90, prof of econ Queen Mary & Westfield Coll 1990–98 (emeritus prof 1998–), dir Inst of Latin American Studies 1992–98; dir Chatham House (RIIA) 2001–06 (assoc fell 2007–); hon res fell Inst for the Study of the Americas 2004–13; hon res fell Inst of Latin American Studies 2014–; visiting prof Florida Int Univ Miami 2007–10, sr distinguished fell Sch of Advanced Study 2007–, hon prof Inst of the Americas UCL 2012–; non-exec dir JP Morgan Brazil Investment Tst; incl: Input-Output Analysis: Sources, Methods and Applications for Developing Countries (1982), The Political Economy of Central America Since 1920 (1987), Studies in the Economics of Central America (1988), Latin America in Perspective (1991), The Economic History of Latin America Since Independence (1994, 3 edn 2014), Reflexiones sobre la Integración Centroamericana (1997); as ed incl: Britain and Latin America: A Changing Relationship (1989), Central American Integration, Report for the Commission of the European Community (and co-author,1992), Mexico and the North American Agreement: Who will Benefit? (co-ed, 1994), Growth and Development in Brazil: Cardoso's Real Challenge (co-ed, 1995), Rebuilding the State: Mexico After Salinas (co-ed, 1996), The New Economic Model in Latin America and its Impact on Income Distribution and Poverty (1996), Thirty Years of Latin American Studies in the United Kingdom (1997), Integración Regional en Centroamérica, San José (1998), The United States and Latin America: the New Agenda (co-ed, 1999), Regional Integration in Latin America and the Caribbean: the Political Economy of Open Regionalism (2001), The Cambridge Economic History of Latin America (2 vols, co-ed, 2006), The Economic History of the Caribbean since the Napoleonic Wars (2012), The Economic History of Belize: from 17th Century to Post-Independence (co-author, 2012), Empire without a Name: Past, Present and Future of the United States (2017); *Recreations* tennis, kayaking, underwater photography, chamber music; *Clubs* Athenaeum; *Style*— Prof Victor Bulmer-Thomas, CMG, OBE; ✉ The Royal Institute of International Affairs, Chatham House, 10 St James's Square, London SW1Y 4LE

BULSTRODE, Prof Christopher John Kent; CBE (2016); s of John Christopher Bulstrode (d 1994), and Jacqueline Mary Bulstrode; *b* 5 January 1951; *Educ* Radley, UC Oxford (open scholar, MA), Univ of Cambridge (MA), Univ of Oxford (BM BCh); *Partner* Dr Victoria Louise Hunt, *née* Ashley-Taylor; 2 s (Harry b 1982, John-James b 1985), 1 da (Jennifer Jane b 1988); 3 step s (James, Glynn, Adam), 1 step da (Eloise); *Career* postgrad: Ethiopian refugee prog Sudan 1977, Univ of Dar es Salaam 1978; GP: Kenya 1978, London and Edinburgh 1979–88; prof of trauma and orthopaedics Univ of Oxford 1988–; memb Cncl: RCSEd 2000–11, RCS 2003–11, GMC 2004–07; Maj RAMC 2007–11; voluntary work: Doctors of the World, Medecins du Monde, Save the Children Fund, DFID (Afghanistan, Haiti, Gaza, Nepal, Bangladesh, Sudan, Sri Lanka, India, USSR, Kenya, Malawi, Tanzania, Ukraine, Sierra Leone); expedition dr: Antarctica (3 times), Everest; Sir Robert Menzies travelling fell 1981, Sir Herbert Seddon Orthopaedic Research Prize 1984, BOA European travelling fell 1986, Cutler's Prize for surgical instrument design 1986, Pres's medal Br Orthopaedic Research Soc 1987, ABC travelling fell 1988, AO travelling fell 1993; Hunterian prof RCS 1995; FRCS 1982, FRCSEd 1982, FRCS in Orthopaedics (FRCSOrth) 1992; *Publications* Oxford Textbook of Trauma and Orthopaedics (ed-in-chief, 2002 and 2006), Bailey & Love Textbook of Surgery (23–26 edns), Orthopaedics at a Glance (2007); *Recreations* sailing, gardening, ornithology, family activities; *Clubs* Vincents; *Style*— Prof Christopher Bulstrode, CBE; ✉ Cherryford, Martinhoe, Nr Parracombe, Devon EX31 4QP

BUNBURY; *see also:* Richardson-Bunbury

BUNBURY, Sir Michael William; 13 Bt (E 1681), of Stanney Hall, Cheshire; KCVO (2005), DL (Suffolk 2004); s of Sir (John) William Napier Bunbury, 12 Bt (d 1985), and late Margaret Pamela, *née* Sutton; *b* 29 December 1946; *Educ* Eton, Trinity Coll Cambridge (MA); *m* 1976, Caroline Anne, da of Col Anthony Derek Swift Mangnall, OBE; 1 da (Katherine Rosemary (Mrs Daniel Webster) b 1978), 2 s (Henry Michael Napier b 1980, Edward Peter b 1986); *Heir* s, Henry Bunbury; *Career* landowner and farmer (1100 acres), fin advsr; conslt Smith & Williamson 1997– (ptnr 1974–97, chm 1986–93); chm: HarbourVest Global Private Equity Ltd 1997–, Duchy of Lancaster 2000–05 (memb Cncl 1993–2005), B H Global Ltd 2013–; dir: Fleming High Income Investment Tst plc 1995–97, JP Morgan Claverhouse Investment Tst plc 1996–2015 (chm 2005–15), Foreign and Colonial Investment Tst plc 1998–2012, Investco Perpetual Select Tst plc 2008–; memb Exec Ctee CLA 1992–97 and 1999–2004; chm Taxation Ctee 1999–2003 (chm Suffolk Branch Ctee 1995–97); pres Suffolk Agric Assoc 2000–02; High Sheriff Suffolk 2006–07; *Recreations* shooting; *Clubs* Boodle's; *Style*— Sir Michael Bunbury, Bt, KCVO, DL; ✉ Naunton Hall, Rendlesham, Woodbridge, Suffolk IP12 2RD (☎ 01394 460235); 25 Moorgate, London EC2R 6AY (☎ 020 7131 4000)

BUNCE, Charlie; s of Michael Bunce, of London, and Tina, *née* Simms; *b* 26 December 1962; *m* 1994, Corinne, *née* D'Souza; 2 da; *Career* TV prodr; head of features and formats Leopard Films 2011–15, exec prodr Red House Television 2015–; *Television* incl: Esther, Holiday, That's Life!; series prodr: Watchdog, Weekend Watchdog, Mysteries, Living Dangerously; exec prodr This Morning 2001–02, exec ed The Granada Academy 2002–03, series ed Property Ladder 2003; exec prodr: Grand Designs 2004–11, The Stirling Prize 2008–09, Accidental Heroes 2008, Great British Railway Journeys 2009–11, Four Rooms 2010–11, Squeamish 2011, Tourettes: I Swear I Can Sing 2012, Let Me Entertain You 2012, Trade Your Way to the USA 2012–13; *Radio* prodn credits incl: Loose Ends, Midweek, Desert Island Discs, Woman's Hour; *Books* Great British Railway Journeys (2011); *Style*— Charlie Bunce, Esq; ✉ e-mail charlie.freshstartproductions@gmail.com

BUNDY, Prof Alan Richard; CBE (2012); s of Stanley Alfred Bundy (d 1994), and Joan Margaret Bundy; *b* 18 May 1947; *Educ* Heston Secdy Modern, Springgrove GS, Univ of Leicester (BSc, PhD); *m* 23 Sept 1967, Josephine, da of John Maule; 1 da (Rachel b 26 Nov 1970); *Career* tutorial asst Univ of Leicester 1970–71; Univ of Edinburgh: research fell 1971–74, lectr 1974–84, reader 1984–87, professorial fell 1987–90, prof 1990–, head of Div of Informatics 1998–2001; SD Insight Award 1986; IJCAI Distinguished Service Award 2003, IJCAI Research Excellence Award 2007, CADE Herbrand Award 2007; fell American Assoc for Artificial Intelligence 1990, fell Artificial Intelligence and Simulation of Behaviour 1997–, fell European Coordinating Ctee for Artificial Intelligence 1999, FRSE 1996, FBCS 2002, FIEE 2005, FREng 2008, FRS 2012, fell Assoc for Computing Machinery 2015; *Books* Artificial Intelligence: An Introductory Course (1978), The Computer Modelling of Mathematical Reasoning (1983), The Catalogue of Artificial Intelligence (1984), Eco-Logic: Logic based approaches to ecological modelling (1991), Rippling: Meta-Level Guidance for Mathematical Reasoning (jtly, 2005); *Recreations* beer making, valley walking; *Style*— Prof Alan Bundy, CBE, FRSE, FRS, FREng; ✉ School of Informatics, University of Edinburgh, Informatics Forum, 10 Crichton Street, Edinburgh EH8 9AB (☎ 0131 650 2716, fax 0131 650 6513, e-mail a.bundy@ed.ac.uk, website http://homepages.inf.ed.ac.uk/bundy/)

BUNKER, Prof Christopher Barry; s of Dr Nigel Vincent Delahunty Bunker, MBE (d 1967), and Joy, *née* Bolsover; *b* 22 November 1956; *Educ* Wycliffe Coll (top scholar), St Catharine's Coll Cambridge (Kitchener scholar, MA, MD, Sir Walter Langdon Brown Prize), Westminster Med Sch London (Kitchener scholar, MB BS); *m* 1991, Anna Christina, yst da of Dr J Kurowski, of Hull; 2 da (Minette b 1992, Matilda b 1995); *Career* currently: conslt dermatologist Univ Coll Hosps London, St Luke's Hosp for the Clergy and King Edward VII Hosp for Officers, prof UC London; Sir Jules Thorn res fell 1988–90; pres Br Assoc of Dermatologists 2012–14, memb Cncl RCP 2012–14, UK Bd memb European Acad of Dermatovenereology (EADV) 2014–; hon sec Br Skin Fndn (BSF)

2015–; Gold Award American Acad of Dermatology (Historical Poster section) 1991, Bristol Cup Br Assoc of Dermatologists 1998, John Thornton Ingram Lecture RCP 2001 and 2015, Dowling Orator 2010; MRCS, FRCP; *Publications* author of numerous original papers and articles; *Clubs* Garrick; *Style*— Prof Christopher Bunker; ⊠ King Edward VII Hospital, Beaumont Street, London W1G 6AA (✆ 020 7794 5943)

BUNKER, Christopher Jonathan; *s* of Jonathan William Bunker, and Beryl Kathleen Rose, *née* Wood; *b* 16 December 1946; *Educ* Ilford County HS, KCL; *m* 9 Sept 1972, Julia Doris, da of Arthur James Seymour Russell (d 1954); 2 da (Jennifer b 1978, Elizabeth b 1982); *Career* accountant; fin dir Westland Group plc 1987–96, gp fin dir Tarmac plc 1996–2000, gp fin dir Thames Water plc (latterly Water Div RWE AG) 2000–04; non-exec dir: DS Smith plc 2003–, Travis Perkins plc 2004–, Xansa plc 2006–; formerly non-exec dir: Mowlem plc, Baltimore Technologies plc; *Style*— Christopher Bunker, Esq

BUNNEY, John Herrick; OBE (1997); *b* 2 June 1945; *m* Pamela Anne Simcock; 1 s (b 1973), 1 da (b 1976); *Career* second sec FCO 1971–73, MECAS 1971–73, first sec Damascus 1974–78, FCO 1978–80, dep head of mission and consul Sana'a 1981–83, FCO 1983–87, first sec (political) Tunis 1987–90, FCO 1990–93, cnsllr Riyadh 1993–97, FCO 1997–2000, advsr Dept of Safeguards IAEA Vienna 2000–03, co dir 2004–; *Clubs* Savile, Rye, Royal Blackheath Golf; *Style*— John H Bunney, Esq, OBE

BUNTON, Christopher John; *s* of John Bunton, and Marian Helen, *née* Gotobed; *b* 22 February 1948; *Educ* Charterhouse, Trinity Coll Cambridge (MA), London Grad Sch of Business Studies (MBA); *m* 10 May 1975, Jane Melanie, da of Anthony J S Cartmell; 2 s (Anthony, Michael); *Career* with Gulf Oil Corp 1973–1985, gp treas Cordiant plc (previously Saatchi & Saatchi plc) 1986–97, dir Westcape Corporate Finance 1998–; tstee and treas Ataxia UK 2001–13; vice-pres ACT 2001 (memb Council 1987–89 and 1997–2001); *Recreations* music; *Clubs* Hawks' (Cambridge); *Style*— Christopher Bunton, Esq; ⊠ Westcape Corporate Finance, 12 The Chowns, West Common, Harpenden, Hertfordshire AL5 2BN (✆ 01582 769543, e-mail cbunton@westcape.co.uk)

BUONAGUIDI, David Mervyn; *s* of Gianfranco Buonaguidi, of Esher, Surrey, and Karen, *née* Petersen; *b* 13 August 1964; *Educ* City of London Freemans' Sch Ashtead Surrey, Epsom Sch of Art and Design Epsom Surrey (DATEC graphics); *Career* advtg art dir: TBWA 1984–85, Wight Collins Rutherford Scott 1985–88, Howell Henry Chaldecott Lury 1988–91, J Walter Thompson 1991–92, Howell Henry Chaldecott Lury 1992–93; jt creative dir St Luke's (formerly Chiat/Day) 1993–98, creative dir Channel Four TV Corporation 1998–2000, co-fndr and creative dir Karmarama Ltd 2000–; *Style*— David Buonaguidi, Esq

BURBIDGE, Eileen; MBE (2015); *Educ* Univ of Illinois at Urbana-Champaign; *Career* engrg assoc GTE Telephone Ops, engrg assoc Verizon Wireless (formerly GTE Mobilnet) 1994–95, market devpt mangr Apple Computer 1995–96, gp mangr Market Devpt Sun Microsystems 1996–99, dir Business Devpt Openwave Systems 1999–2000, dir Business Devpt 12 Entrepreneuring 2000–01, vice-pres Marketing and Business Devpt Embedded Internet Solutions Inc 2001–02, dir Worldwide Account Mgmnt/ dir Project Mgmnt Office Palmsource 2003–04, dir Product Skype 2004–05, dir Communication Products Yahoo! 2005–06, contractor (Social Search) Yahoo! 2007, advsr Ambient Sound Investments 2007–, non-exec dir Technology and Innovation The National Archives 2008–09, co-fndr White Bear Yard 2009–, ptnr Passion Capital 2011–; Mayor of London tech ambass 2014–, chair Tech City UK 2015–, special envoy HM Treasy 2015–, memb PM's Business Advsy Gp 2015–; *Style*— Ms Eileen Burbidge, MBE; ⊠ Passion Capital, 2nd Floor, White Bear Yard, 144a Clerkenwell Road, London EC1R 5DF

BURBIDGE, Sean; *Career* began career as apprentice chef Sutton Arms Stokesley 1993, chef de partie rising to sous chef Restaurant Gordon Ramsay 2003–08, Gordon Ramsay au Trianon Versaille 2008–10, head chef Petrus 2010– (Michelin star 2011–); *Style*— Sean Burbidge, Esq; ⊠ Petrus, 1 Kinnerton Street, Knightsbridge, London SW1X 8EA

BURCH, Monica; da of Fraser Burch, and Katia Hajicristofis; *b* York; *Educ* Queens Sch Rheindahlen, Pembroke Coll Oxford, Guildford Coll of Law, Nottingham Trent Univ; *m* Paul Lister; 3 c; *Career* trainee Theodore Goddard 1988, Dewey Ballantine 1996–97, ptnr Addleshaw Goodard 1999–2016 (sr ptnr and chair 2010–16); recorder (civil) 2010–; non-exec dir Channel 4 Corporation 2010–; dir Prime (charity) 2012–15, chair The Mentoring Fndn 2015–; *Style*— Ms Monica Burch; ⊠ Addleshaw Goddard, Milton Gate, 60 Chiswell Street, London EC1Y 4A

BURCHELL, Prof Brian; *s* of Kenneth and Grace Burchell; *b* 1 October 1946; *Educ* Univ of St Andrews (BSc), Univ of Dundee (PhD); *m* 1973, Ann, *née* Kinsella; 1 s (Colin James b 1978), 1 da (Karen Jane b 1982); *Career* post doctoral research fell Univ of Dundee 1972–74, lectr in biochemistry Loughborough Univ 1974–75; Univ of Dundee: lectr in biochemistry 1976–78, Wellcome Tst research leave fell 1978–80, Wellcome Tst sr lectr in biochemistry 1980–88, head of biomedical medicine 1988–96, prof of med biochemistry 1988–, head of molecular and cellular pathology 1999–; Ninewells Hosp Dundee: clinical dir of biochemical med 1990–96, dir human genetics 1996–; hon prof of biochemistry Univ of St Andrews 1991–; Morton J Rodman distinguished lectr in pharmacology Rutgers Univ USA 1994; ACB Fndn Award 1997; chm Int Scientific Advsy Ctee ISSX 1997; pres Euro Soc of Biochemical Pharmacology 2000–; FRCPath 1997, FRSE 1997; *Publications* author of more than 200 papers and reviews in learned jls; *Recreations* golf; *Clubs* Scots Craig GC; *Style*— Prof Brian Burchell, FRSE; ⊠ Department of Molecular & Cellular Pathology, Ninewells Medical School, Dundee University, Dundee DD1 9SY (✆ 01382 632164, fax 01382 633952, e-mail b.burchell@dundee.ac.uk)

BURDEN, Richard; MP; *s* of late Kenneth Burden, and late Pauline Burden; *b* 1 September 1954; *Educ* Wallasey Tech GS, Bramhall Comp Sch, St John's Coll of FE Manchester, Univ of York (BA), Univ of Warwick (MA); *m* (sep), Jane Slowey; 2 step da, 1 step s; *Career* pres York Univ Students' Union 1976–77, dist offr W Midlands Dist NALGO 1981–92 (branch organiser N Yorks branch 1979–81); Parly candidate (Lab) Meriden 1987, MP (Lab) Birmingham Northfield 1992–, PPS to Jeff Rooker, MP, as Food Safety min then Pensions min 1997–2001, advsr on motorsport to min of state for Sport (Richard Caborn, MP) 2002–07, shadow Transport min 2013–; memb House of Commons Euro Standing Ctee 1996–97, chm All-Pty Parly Gp on Electoral Reform 1997–, chm All-Pty Parly Motor Gp 1998–, chair Br-Palestine All-Pty Gp 2001–, chm W Midlands Select Ctee 2009–10, vice chair Lab Friends of Palestine and the ME, chm All-Pty Parly Jordan Gp 2010–13, memb Ctee on Arms Export Controls 2010–; sec: All-Pty Parly Water Gp 1994–97, PLP Trade and Indust Ctee 1996–97 (vice-chm 1995–96); chair Lab Campaign for Electoral Reform 1996–98 (vice-chair 1998–); fndr sec Jt Action on Water Services (JAWS) to oppose water privatisation 1985–90; chm Birmingham Gp of Lab MPs, vice-chair Lab Middle East Cncl 1995–96, fndr memb Bedale Lab Pty 1980; memb: W Midlands Regnl Assembly, Trade and Industry Select Ctee 2001–05, Int Devpt Select Ctee 2005–13, Socialist Health Assoc, Lab Housing Gp, Fabian Soc, Co-op Pty, Electoral Reform Soc; *Recreations* motor racing, travel, cinema, reading, food; *Clubs* Kingshurst Lab, Austin Sports and Social, Austin Branch British Legion, 750 Motor; *Style*— Richard Burden, MP; ⊠ House of Commons, London SW1A 0AA (✆ 020 7219 2318, constituency office 0121 477 7746, e-mail richard.burden.mp@parliament.uk, website www.richardburden.com)

BURDON, (Gerald) Desmond Patrick; *s* of Dr David Joseph Burdon (d 1987), and Kathrine, *née* O'Reilly (d 1986); *b* 12 June 1956, Damascus, Syria; *Educ* Notre Dame Int Sch Rome, Poly of NE London; *m* 28 Dec 2001, Pauline, *née* McCoy; *Career* photographer; numerous int clients; memb Assoc of Photographers (former chm Awards Ctee 1984–89 and vice-chm Cncl); *Awards* Ilford Advtg Photographer of the Year, Kodak Calendar Award,

AOP awards 1997, 1999, 2000 and 2001; *Style*— Desmond Burdon; ⊠ website www.desmondburdon.com

BURDON, Prof Roy Hunter; *s* of Ian Murray Burdon (d 1956), and Rose Carnegie Burdon (d 1962); *b* 27 April 1938; *Educ* Glasgow Acad, Univ of St Andrews (BSc), Univ of Glasgow (PhD); *m* 4 Sept 1962, Margery Grace; 2 s (Ian J, Keith A); *Career* Univ of Glasgow: asst lectr 1959–63, lectr 1964–68, sr lectr 1968–74, reader in biochemistry 1974–77, titular prof in biochemistry 1977–89; post doctorate and res fell Univ of NY 1963–64, guest prof of microbiology Polytechnical Univ of Denmark Copenhagen 1977–78, prof of molecular biology Univ of Strathclyde 1985–97 (chm Dept of Bioscience and Biotechnology 1986–88, prof emeritus 1997–); chm: Br Coordinating Ctee Biotechnol 1991–93, Scientific Advsy Ctee European Fedn of Biotechnology 1991; The Biochemical Soc: hon meetings sec 1981–85, hon gen sec 1985–89, chm 1989–92; treas European Soc for Free Radical Research 1994–97; govr W of Scotland Coll of Agric, pres Milngavie Art Club 2001–02, pres Probus Club of Strathendrick 2010–11; accredited lectr Nat Assoc of Decorative and Fine Arts Socs 2015; FIBiol 1987, FRSE 1975, FRSA 2013; *Books* RNA Biosynthesis (1976), Molecular Biology of DNA Methylation (1985), Free Radical Damage and its Control (1994), Genes and the Environment (1999), The Suffering Gene (2003), Menace sur nos Gènes (2005); *Recreations* painting (group and one-person exhbns), golf, clarinet/saxophone playing in local orchestras, memb Strathendrick Singers; *Style*— Prof Roy Burdon, FRSE; ⊠ 28 Station Road, Killearn G63 9NY (✆ 01360 551726)

BURFORD, Earl of; Charles Francis Topham de Vere Beauclerk; does not use courtesy title; *s* and *h* of 14 Duke of St Albans, *qv*; *b* 22 February 1965; *Educ* Sherborne, Hertford Coll Oxford; *m* 29 Dec 1994 (m dis 2001), Louise Ann Beatrice Fiona, eldest da of Col Malcolm Vernon Robey; 1 s (James Malcolm Aubrey Edward de Vere (does not use courtesy title) b 2 Aug 1995); *Career* fndr De Vere Soc; tstee Stringer Lawrence Meml Tst; appointed vice-chm (jt) The Royal Stuart Soc 1989; pres Shakespeare Oxford Soc 1995–97, co-fndr Shakespeare Acad 2015; Parly candidate (Democratic Party) Kensington & Chelsea by-election 1999; Liveryman Worshipful Co of Drapers; *Publications* Nell Gwyn: A Biography (2005), Shakespeare's Lost Kingdom (2010), Piano Man: A Life of John Ogdon (2014), Take Physic, Pomp (2016); *Style*— Charles Beauclerk; ⊠ e-mail c.beauclerk446@btinternet.com. website www.whowroteshakespeare.com

BURGE, Prof (Peter) Sherwood; OBE (2005); *s* of Graham Mowbray Burge (d 1974), and Anne Elizabeth, *née* Batt; *b* 8 July 1944; *Educ* Lancing, Royal Free Hosp Sch of Med, London Sch of Hygiene & Tropical Med (MB BS, MSc, MD); *m* 1, 18 Aug 1968 (m dis), Dr Anne Willard, da of Canon James Stanley Willard (d 1988), Essex; 2 s (Cedd b 1974, Chad b 1977); *m* 2, 6 May 2009, Geraldine Anne, da of Gerald Alwyn Forrest, of Somerset; *Career* lectr in Dept of Clinical Immunology Cardiothoracic Inst London 1976–80, conslt physician Solihull Hosp 1980–93, conslt chest physician Birmingham Heartlands Hosp 1980–, dir Occupational Lung Disease Unit Birmingham 1980–2015; prof of occupational med Univ of Birmingham; chm Sci Ctee on ISOLDE trial in COPD; numerous sci pubns on: occupational lung diseases, indoor air quality and sick building syndrome, asthma and bronchitis and interstitial lung diseases; temporary advsr to WHO, NATO and EEC on indoor air quality and occupational lung disease; memb Acad of Indoor Air Science 1997; MRCS 1969, MFOM 1984, FRCP 1985, FFOM 1991, FRCPEd 2002, fell European Respiratory Soc 2014; *Recreations* punt racing, skiing, gardening; *Style*— Prof Sherwood Burge, OBE; ⊠ Birmingham Heartlands Hospital, Bordesley Green East, Birmingham B9 5SS (✆ 0121 424 2000, fax 0121 772 0292, e-mail sherwood.burge@heartofengland.nhs.uk)

BURGESS, (Thomas Lionel) Ashley; *s* of Harry Severs Burgess (d 1953), and Marjorie, *née* Raines (d 1982); *b* 24 May 1933, Thornton-le-Dale, N Yorks; *Educ* Shrewsbury; *m* 19 April 1958, Margaret Gillian, *née* Naylor; 2 da (Victoria Jane b 30 July 1959, Sara Gillian b 22 Feb 1961); *Career* Nat Serv cmmnd RNVR Seatime HMS Indefatigable, HMS Leeds Castle; founding dir Criddle-Burgess Feeds Ltd 1969–87, dir Whitegate Leisure plc, fndr and chm Burgess Group plc, founding dir BDVH Hldgs Ltd; former memb Nat Cncl and NE chm UK Agricultural Trade Assoc; memb Scarborough Hosps Ctee 1960–69, vice-chm N Yorks HA 1992–95, chm Scarborough and NE Yorks NHS Tst 1995–97; pres Royal Soc of St George 1979–85, govr Merchant Adventurers City of York 1989–99; Univ of York: memb Ct 2000–, Morrell fellowship 2008; chm Macmillan Nurse Appeal Scarborough and Ryedale; benefactor: RNLI (Walmer Lifeboat 'James Burgess'), Cleathorpes Lifeboat James Burgess II, Univ of York (James Burgess scholarships); memb Campaign Bd Rotunda Museum 2005–06, chair Ocean Youth Tst NE 2008–14, chair Antibiotic Research UK; pres Ryedale Cons Assoc 2003–07 (chm 1990–93), memb Yorks Cons Business Cncl, life govr RNLI, pres Bradford Small Animal Soc; *Recreations* nearly all forms of sport, history, politics, chess; *Clubs* Farmers, Ganton Golf, Royal Naval Sailing Assoc; *Style*— Ashley Burgess, Esq

BURGESS, James Christopher Appleyard; *s* of Christopher Gerald Burgess, of Suffolk, and Bridget Vaughan, *née* Parry-Jones; *b* 7 July 1957, Colchester, Essex; *Educ* Radley, Coll of Law Lancaster Gate; *m* 6 June 1980, Penelope, *née* Jacobs; 2 s (Benjamin, Toby (triplets) b 24 Sept 1987), 1 da (Tabitha (triplet) b 24 Sept 1987); *Career* admitted slr 1981; Bolton and Lowe 1977–81, Plummer & Co 1981–85, Plummer Tilsey & Ptnrs 1985–89, Burgess Cheves & Ptnrs 1985–87, Pitmans 1989–2008, Field Seymour Parkes 2008–; memb Law Soc; *Recreations* shooting, tennis, skiing; *Clubs* Leander; *Style*— James Burgess, Esq; ⊠ Magpie Farm, Yattendon, Berkshire RG18 0XX (✆ 01635 200440, e-mail jcaburgess@live.co.uk); Field Seymour Parkes, 1 London Street, Reading, Berkshire RG1 4QW (✆ 0118 951 6252, fax 0118 950 2704, e-mail james.burgess@fsp-law.com)

BURGESS, Rear Adm John; CB (1987), LVO (1975); *s* of Albert Burgess (d 1957), of Coventry, Warks, and Winifred, *née* Evans; *b* 13 July 1929; *Educ* RNEC, RNC Greenwich (advanced engrg); *m* 21 June 1952, Avi (d 2015), da of William Johnson-Morgan (d 1953), of Coventry, Warks; 2 da (Sara b 14 Jan 1958, Jenny (Mrs Andersson) b 6 Aug 1960); *Career* RN Serv 1945–; HMS: Aisne, Maidstone, Theseus, Implacable, Cumberland, Caprice; cmmnd 1952, lectr in Thermodynamics RNEC 1962–65, HMS Victorious, appt Cdr 1968, nuclear design and manufacture Rolls Royce 1968–70, naval staff Washington DC 1970–72, Royal Yacht Britannia 1972–75, head Forward Design Gp Ship Dept 1975–77, appt Capt 1976, naval asst to Controller Navy 1977–79, OC HMS Defiance 1979–81, OC HMS Sultan 1981–83, appt Adm 1983, md HM Docky Rosyth 1984–87; dir: Rolls Royce 1987– (special projects, business devpt), Rolls Royce Nuclear Ltd, Rolls Royce and Associates Ltd; contrib various papers for professional socs and periodicals; memb: naval charities, local church socs, conservation socs; Hon Freeman New Orleans 1974; CEng, FIMechE, FIMarEst; *Recreations* sailing, golf, music, theatre; *Clubs* Cawsand Bay Sailing (pres), Rame Gig (vice-pres); *Style*— Rear Adm John Burgess, CB, LVO; ⊠ Bay House, Combe Park Close, Cawsand, Cornwall PL10 1PW

BURGESS, His Hon Judge John Edward Ramsay; *b* 11 March 1956; *Educ* St Edward's Sch Oxford, Univ of Exeter (LLB); *Career* called to the Bar Middle Temple 1978; practising barr 1978–2002, recorder 2000–02 (asst recorder 1995–2000), circuit judge (Midland Circuit) 2002–, resident judge Derby Combined Court Centre 2008–16 (hon recorder 2009–16); *Style*— His Hon Judge Burgess; ⊠ c/o Midland Circuit Office, Priory Courts, 33 Bull Street, Birmingham B4 6DW

BURGESS, Melvin; *s* of Chris Burgess, of Haworth, and Helen Burgess; *b* 25 April 1954; *Children* 1 s (Oliver b 26 April 1989), 1 da (Pearl b 15 June 1991); *Career* children's writer; various jobs incl: bus conductor, brick layer, fndr own business (marbling onto fabric for fashion indust); memb Soc of Authors 1991; *Books* Cry of the Wolf (1990), Burning Issy (1992), An Angel for May (1992), The Baby and Fly Pie (1993), Loving

April (1994), The Earth Giant (1994), Tiger, Tiger (1996), Junk (1996, Guardian Award for Children's Fiction 1996, Library Assoc Carnegie Medal 1997, shortlisted Whitbread Children's Book Award 1997), Kite (1997), The Copper Treasure (1998), Bloodtide (1999), Old Bag (1999), The Ghost Behind the Wall (2000), Billy Elliot (2001, novelisation of the film), Lady (2001), Doing It (2003); *Recreations* walking, nature, cooking; *Style*— Melvin Burgess

BURGESS, Michael John Clement; OBE (2009); s of David Clement Burgess (d 1966), and Dr Ethne Nannette Moira Barnwall, *née* Ryan (d 2002), of Kingston upon Thames; *b* 31 March 1946; *Educ* Beaumont Coll, KCL; *m* 31 July 1971, Catherine Vivian, da of late Vivian John Du Veluz Gout, of Mulhausen, Germany; 2 da (Alexandra b 1974, Nicola b 1976), 1 s (Peter b 1980); *Career* admitted slr 1970 (non-practising 2013–); conslt McNamara Ryan Weybridge 1986–2012 (ptnr 1972–86); coroner Surrey 1986–2011 (asst dep coroner 1979–86), coroner of the Queen's Household 2002–13 (dep coroner 1991–2002), lead coroner UK DVI 2008–12; asst coroner: Berks 2011–, Surrey 2011–, W Sussex 2011–, Norfolk 2013–; coroners trg course dir Judicial Coll 2013–; pres SE England Coroners Soc 1990–91, hon sec Coroners Soc of England and Wales 1993–2003 (asst sec 1991–93, legal sec 2010–13); pres West Surrey Law Soc 1985–86 (hon treas 1979–84), memb Catholic Union 1974–, chm Fin Ctee and memb Parish Cncl St Francis de Sales RC Church Hampton 1974–2012, helper (formerly gp ldr and SE regnl chm) Handicapped Children's Pilgrimage Tst; Freeman: City of London, Worshipful Co of Feltmakers 1967; memb: Law Soc 1970, Coroners' Soc 1979; *Publications* Coroners Title to Halsbury's Laws of England (jtly, 1996), Coroners' Society Practice Notes for Coroners (1998), Coroners' Bench Book (2003 and 2007), Jervis on Coroners (jt ed, 13 edn 2012–), Coroners' Bench Book (for Judicial Coll); various articles and advices to and for coroners covering issues incl conduct in court; *Recreations* reading, art, music, gardening, water-colour painting; *Clubs* Surrey Law; *Style*— Michael Burgess, Esq, OBE; ✉ 49 Ormond Avenue, Hampton, Middlesex TW12 2RY

BURGESS, (David) Patrick Henry; OBE (2015, MBE 2002), DL (W Sussex 2014); s of David Clement Burgess (d 1966), and Dr Ethne Nanette Burgess, *née* Ryan (d 2002); *b* 31 October 1944, Cheam, Surrey; *Educ* Wimbledon Coll, Beaumont Coll, Gonville & Caius Coll Cambridge (MA); *m* 1994, Margaret Ann, *née* Mosey; by previous m, 2 s (Barnaby b 1971, Edmund b 1973), 1 da (Elizabeth b 1976); *Career* admitted slr 1972; with Gouldens 1972–2003 (sr ptnr 1997–2003), ptnr Jones Day 2003–04; non-exec chm Liberty Int plc (now Intu Properties plc) 2008– (non-exec dir 2000–); non-exec dir: Strand Partners Ltd 1994–2007, First Technology plc 1997–2006 (sr dir), Standard Bank London plc 2000–15; chm Thrombosis Research Inst, sometime regnl chm Handicapped Children's Pilgrimage Tst, chm Caius House Battersea, tstee Chichester Cathedral Devpt Tst, sometime chm Cncl St John Ambulance Sussex and hon legal counsel to Most Venerable Order of St John 2007–; chm Friends of Arundel Cathedal, chm Bulldog tst 2008–13; High Sheriff W Sussex 2013–14; chllr Order of St John 2014; Past Master Worshipful Co of Feltmakers, Liveryman City of London Slrs Co; memb Law Soc; GCStJ 2014 (OStJ 2003, CStJ 2008), Knight Grand Cross of the Holy Sepulchre 2014; *Publications* incl Unlocking Growth: a venture capital study (2001); *Recreations* rowing, sailing, shooting, history, poetry, architecture; *Clubs* Boodle's, Leander, Royal Thames Yacht; *Style*— Patrick Burgess, Esq, OBE, DL; ✉ Shopwyke Hall, Chichester, West Sussex PO20 2AA (☎ 01243 771177); Rowe & Wilkie (e-mail dphb@roweandwilkie.co.uk)

BURGESS, Prof Sir Robert George; kt (2010), DL; s of George Burgess, and Olive, *née* Andrews; *b* 23 April 1947, Sherborne, Dorset; *Educ* Bede Coll Durham (Teachers' Cert), Univ of Durham (BA), Univ of Warwick (PhD); *m* 1974, Hilary, da of Rev H R Joyce; *Career* Univ of Warwick: lectr 1974–84, sr lectr 1984–88, dept chair 1985–88, dir Centre for Educnl Devpt Appraisal and Research (CEDAR) 1987–99, prof of sociology 1988–99, chm Faculty of Social Sciences 1988–91, fndr chm Grad Sch 1991–95, sr pro-vice-chllr 1995–99; vice-chllr Univ of Leicester 1999–2014; ESRC: memb Research Resources Bd 1991–96, memb Cncl 1996–2000, chm Postgrad Trg Bd 1997–2000 (memb 1989–93, vice-chm 1996–97); fndr chm UK Cncl for Grad Educn 1993–99; pres: Br Sociological Assoc 1989–91, Assoc for the Teaching of the Soc Sciences 1991–99, SRHE 2013–; chair: HEFCE Quality Assessment Ctee 2001–03, E Midlands Univs Assoc 2001–04, ESRC Funding Cncls Teaching and Learning Research Prog 2003–09, UUK/Guild HE Measuring and Recording Student Achievement (on credit and honours degree classification – the Burgess Gp) 2003–, Research Information Network 2004–11, UCAS 2005–11 (memb Bd 2001–11), HE Acad Bd 2007–14 (memb Bd 2003–14), Bd GSM London 2015–; memb: HEFCE review of postgrad educn 1995–96, CVCP review of clinical academic careers 1996–97, HEFCE Research Libraries Strategy Gp 2001–02, Jt Equality Steering Gp 2001–03, Br Library Bd 2003–10, Ctee HEFCE Quality Assurance Learning and Teaching 2003–07, Quality Assurance Agency (QAA) Implementation Gp on Postgrad Educn, School Teacher Review Body 2015–; chair Nat Centre for Social Research 2012–; Hon DLitt Staffordshire Univ 1998, Hon DUniv Northampton 2007, Hon EdD De Montfort Univ 2013, Hon LLD Univ of Leicester, Hon DCL Durham Univ 2016; memb BERA; FAcSS 2000; *Books* Experiencing Comprehensive Education (1983), In the Field (1984), Education, Schools and Schooling (1985), Sociology, Education and Schools (1986), Implementing In-Service Education (jtly, 1993), Research Methods (1993), Reflections of the University of Leicester (jtly, 2010); also ed of 20 books on methodology and education; *Recreations* walking, music, art, sculpture and some gardening; *Style*— Prof Sir Robert Burgess, DL; ✉ Feldon House, Lower Brailes, Banbury, Oxfordshire OX15 5HS (e-mail sirbobburgess@outlook.com)

BURGESS, Robert Lawie Frederick (Robin); OBE (2008), DL (1998); s of Sir John Burgess (d 1987), and Lady Burgess, *née* Gillieron (d 2012); *b* 31 January 1951; *Educ* Trinity Coll Glenalmond; *m* 20 Sept 1986, Alexandra Rosemary, da of W A Twiston-Davies, of Hereford; 1 s (James), 3 da (Rose, Catherine, Rachel); *Career* 2 Lt The King's Own Royal Border Regt 1969–72; chief exec C N Group Ltd (formerly Cumbrian Newspapers Group Ltd) 1985–2016 (non-exec chm 2016–); pres Newspaper Soc 1996–97; dir: Cumberland and Westmorland Herald Ltd 1985–, Border TV plc 1987–2000; High Sheriff Cumbria 2006–07; *Clubs* Garrick, Army and Navy; *Style*— R L F Burgess, Esq, OBE, DL; ✉ C N Group Ltd, Dalston Road, Carlisle, Cumbria CA2 5UA

BURGESS, Sally; *Career* opera and concert singer; mezzo-soprano; *Roles* with ENO incl: Carmen (debut, subsequently performed role at Bregenz Festival, Zürich, Berlin, NZ, Met Opera NY, Paris Bastille), Judith in Bluebeard's Castle, Charlotte in Werther, Octavian in Der Rosenkavalier, Mrs Begbick in Mahagonny, Herodias in Salome, Dulinée in Don Quixote, Azucena in Trovatore, Mistress Quickly in Sir John in Love 2006; other operatic roles incl: Fricka in Die Walküre (Scottish Opera), Amneris in Aida (Scottish Opera), Dido in The Trojans (Opera North), Laura in La Gioconda (Opera North), Azucena in Il Trovatore (Opera North), Margareta in Genoveva (Opera North), Ottavia in The Coronation of Poppea (WNO, also BBC), Eboli in Don Carlos 1998, Kabanicha in Katya Kabanova (Munich Staatsoper) 1999, Fricka in Das Rheingold (Geneva Opera) 1999, Mere Marie in Dialogue of the Carmelites by Poulenc (WNO) 1999, Die Walküre 2000, Baba the Turk, Rake's Progress 2002, Fortunata in Satyricon (Opera Nancy and Vlaamse Opera) 2004, Hanna Glawari in Merry Widow (Met Opera NY) 2004, Judith in Duke Bluebeard's Castle (Houston and Opera North) 2005, Carmen (Christchurch NZ) 2005, Fricka in Die Walkure (Marseille) 2007, Kabanicka in Katya Kabanova (Opera North) 2007, Mistress Quickly in Falstaff (Scottish Opera) 2008, Herodias in Salome (Welsh Nat Opera) 2008; other performances incl: Liverpool Oratorio (world and American première, recorded with EMI), The Voyage by Philip Glass, Sorceress in Dido and Aeneas (recorded with Chandos and broadcast BBC TV), Showboat with Opera North and RSC (nominated Best Actress in a Musical Olivier Awards), Sally Burgess's Women (one woman jazz show, Lyric Theatre Hammersmith), Amelia in Mark-Anthony Turnage's Twice Through the Heart, Pierrot Lunaire (Almeida Theatre London) 2006; *Recordings* incl: Showboat, West Side Story, The King & I, works of Howard Ferguson, works of Delius, Sally Burgess sings Jazz (with husband Neal Thornton), The Other Me (jazz), Happy Talk: the Life and Works of Richard Rodgers, Judith Bartok's Duke Bluebeard's Castle and Herodias Salome; *Style*— Ms Sally Burgess; ✉ c/o Jenny Rose, AOR Management, 6910 Roosevelt Way NE, PMB 221, Seattle, WA 98115, USA (☎ 00 1 206 729 6160, e-mail aormanagement@gmail.com)

BURGESS, Sir (Joseph) Stuart; kt (1994), CBE (1984); *b* 20 March 1929, Barnsley, Yorks; *Educ* Barnsley Holgate GS, UCL (BSc, PhD); *m* 1955, Valerie Ann, *née* Street; 1 da (Jacqueline Ann b 23 March 1959), 1 s (Timothy Stuart b 6 Oct 1961); *Career* The Radiochemical Centre Ltd 1953–61, UKAEA Risley 1961–62, Amersham International plc 1962–89 (chief exec 1979–89), pres Amersham Corp USA 1975–77, conslt Immuno International AG Vienna 1990–96; chm: Oxford RHA 1990–94, Immuno UK Ltd 1993–96, Anglia & Oxford RHA 1994–98, Finsbury Worldwide Pharmaceutical Tst plc 1995–2004, Haemonetics Corp USA 1998–2003, Chartered Mgmnt Inst Bd of Companions 1999–2002; dir Anagen plc UK 1993–97; vice-pres Asthma UK 2008– (vice-chm 2000–07); fell UCL 1994; FRSC 1960, CIMgt 1986; *Recreations* theatre, music, travel; *Clubs* RSM, RSA; *Style*— Sir Stuart Burgess, CBE

BURGESS, Rev Dr Stuart John; CBE (2009); s of Frederick John Burgess (d 1993), and Winifred May, *née* Gowan (d 2002); *b* 18 March 1940, Birmingham; *Educ* Moseley GS Birmingham, St Peter's Coll, Wesley Coll Leeds, Univ of London (BD), Univ of Nottingham (MEd, MTh); *m* 17 July 1965, Elisabeth, *née* Fowler; 2 da (Alison Jane b 13 Sept 1968, Kathryn Elisabeth b 13 May 1970); *Career* chaplain Univ of Nottingham 1970–81, chaplain Univ of Birmingham 1981–89, chair York and Hull Methodist Dist 1989–2004, pres Methodist Church of GB 1999–2000; rural advocate; chair: Countryside Agency 2004–06, Cmmn for Rural Communities 2005–13; memb: Ethics Ctee Dept of Work Pensions, Patient Liaison Gp BMA, Ct Univ of Nottingham, Passenger Focus Bd 2013–; Hon MA Univ of Birmingham 1989; Hon DD: Univ of Hull 2001, Lambeth and Oxford 2003; Hon DUniv Birmingham 2006, Hon PhD Univ of Glos 2008; *Publications* Spiritual Journey of John Wesley (1980), Reflections on the Stations of the Cross (1991), Coming of Age: Challenges and Opportunities for the 21st Century (1999); *Recreations* music, tennis, travel; *Clubs* Liberal; *Style*— The Rev Dr Stuart Burgess, CBE; ✉ The Wesley, 83–101 Euston Street, London NW1 2EZ (☎ 07900 608249, e-mail stuart@micentre.com)

BURGH, 8 Baron (E 1529) Alexander Gregory Disney Leith; s of 7 Baron Burgh (d 2001); *b* 16 March 1958; *m* 1984 (m dis 1998), Catharine Mary, da of David Parkes; 2 s (Hon Alexander James Strachan b 1986, Hon Benjamin David Willoughby b 1988), 1 da (Hon Hannah Elizabeth Rose b 1990); m 2, 1999, Emma Jane, da of Martin Burdick; 1 s (Hon Peter Martin Vincent b 2002), 1 da (Hon Charlotte Alice Romi b 2004); *Heir* s, Hon Alexander James Leith; *Career* ptnr St James's Place Wealth Mgmnt; *Style*— The Rt Hon the Lord Burgh; ✉ Les Reviers, Steam Mill Lane, Guernsey GY4 6NJ

BURGH, Anita, Lady; Anita Lorna Leith; *née* Eldridge; da of Frederick Clements Eldridge (d 1973), and Alice Milner (d 1989); *b* 9 June 1937; *Educ* Chatham GS; *m* 29 Aug 1957 (m dis 1982), 7 Baron Burgh (d 2001); 2 s, 1 da; partner, William Westall Jackson; 1 da (Kate Rosalind Scarlett b 25 March 1971); *Career* novelist 1987–; patients' advocate Cure Parkinson's Tst 2010; memb Ctee SW Fundraising Innovation CPT 2012; memb: Romantic Novelists' Assoc 1987, Soc of Authors 1990, The Historical Novelists Assoc; Outstanding Achievement Award Romantic Novelists' Association 2016; *Publications* Loves Me, Loves Me Not (contrib, 2009); *Novels* as Anita Burgh: Distinctions of Class (1987), Love the Bright Foreigner (1988), The Azure Bowl (1989), The Golden Butterfly (1990), The Stone Mistress (1991), Advances (1992), Overtures (1993), Avarice (1994), Lottery (1995), Breeders (1996), The Cult (1997), On Call (1998), The Family (1999), Clare's War (2000), Exiles (2001), The House at Harcourt (2002), The Visitor (2003), The Broken Gate (2004), Heart's Citadel (2005), The Breached Wall (2007); as Annie Leith: Tales From Sarson Magna: Molly's Flashings (1991), Hector's Hobbies (1994); *Recreations* bulldogs and nattering; *Style*— Anita Burgh; ✉ c/o The Mic Cheetham Agency, 11–12 Dover Street, London W1X 3PH (☎ 020 7495 2002, fax 020 7495 5777, e-mail miccheetham@compuserve.com, website www.anitaburgh.com)

BURGHES, Prof David Noel; s of Edmund Noel Burghes (d 1944), and Lilian Mary, *née* Luckhurst; *b* 21 March 1944; *Educ* Christ's Coll Finchley, Univ of Sheffield (BSc, PhD); *m* 21 Sept 1968, Jennifer Jean, da of Dr Donald Harry Smith (d 1971); 4 s (Andrew b 1970, Christopher b 1972, Jamie b 1974, Timothy b 1975); *Career* asst lectr Dept of Applied Mathematics Univ of Sheffield 1970–71 (jr res fell 1968–70), lectr Sch of Mathematics Univ of Newcastle 1972–75, dir Cranfield Centre for Teacher Servs Cranfield Inst of Technol 1980–81 (lectr 1975–79); Univ of Exeter: prof of educn 1981, dir Centre for Innovation in Mathematics Teaching 1986, dir Kassel Project (int comparative study in sch mathematics) 1994–99, dir Mathematics Enhancement Project 1996, dir Int Project in Maths Attainment (IPMA) 1998; Univ of Plymouth: prof of educn 2005–, seconded as dir Nat Centre for Excellence in the Teaching of Mathematics 2005–06, dir Int Comparative Study in Maths Teacher Training 2007–09; memb Govt Numeracy Task Force 1997–98; author and co-author of over twenty books on mathematics and educn mathematics dir Spode Group 1980–2000; chm Indust and Educn Maths Ctee DTI 1985–88, founding ed jl Teaching Mathematics and its Applications 1985–, chair Teaching Core Maths CFBT 2014–16; FIMA 1970; *Recreations* music, travelling; *Style*— Prof David Burghes

BURGIN, Prof Victor; s of Samuel Burgin (d 1991), of Sheffield, S Yorks, and Gwendolyn Ann, *née* Crowther (d 1973); *b* 24 July 1941; *Educ* Firth Park GS for Boys Sheffield, Sheffield Coll of Art (NDD), RCA (ARCA), Yale Univ (MFA); *m* 1, 1964 (m dis), Hazel Patricia, da of Louis Rowbotham; 2 s (Julian Alexander b 1967, Gaius Louis b 1970); m 2, 1988, Francette Marie-Anne, da of Guy Edouard Pacteau; *Career* lectr: Sch of Fine Art Trent Poly 1965–73, Sch of Communication Central London Poly 1973–88, Bd of Studies in Art History Univ of Calif Santa Cruz 1988–95, Bd of Studies in History of Consciousness Univ of Calif Santa Cruz 1995–2001; prof emeritus of history of consciousness 2001–; Millard prof of fine art Goldsmiths Coll London 2001–; US/UK Bicentennial Arts Exchange fell NY 1976–77, Deutsche Akademische Austausdienst fell Berlin 1978–79; Hon DUniv Sheffield Hallam 2005; *Solo Exhibitions* incl: ICA London 1976, Stedelijk van Abbemuseum Eindhoven 1977, MOMA Oxford 1978, DAAD Gallery Berlin 1979, Musée de la Ville de Calais 1981, Zwiczek Polskich Artsow Fotografickow Warsaw 1981, Impressions Gallery of Photography York 1984, Renaissance Soc at the Univ of Chicago 1986, Albert and Vera List Visual Arts Centre Cambridge MA 1986, Orchard Gallery Derry 1986, Kettles Yard Cambridge 1986, ICA London 1986, Nat Gallery of Aust Canberra 1988, Film in the Cities St Paul 1989, Musée d'Art Moderne Villeneuve d'Ascq 1991, Centre for Research in Contemporary Art Univ of Texas at Arlington 1993, Univ at Buffalo Art Gallery/Research Centre in Art + Culture 1995, Mücsarnok Museum Budapest 1997, Galerie Fotohof Salzburg 1998, Yerba Buena Centre for the Arts San Francisco 1998–99, Weimar 99 Cultural Festival 1999, Architectural Assoc London 2000, Fundació Antoni Tàpies Barcelona 2001, Arnolfini Bristol 2002, LisboaPhoto Lisbon 2003, Cornerhouse Manchester 2003; *Group Exhibitions* incl: When Attitudes Become Form (ICA London) 1969, Information (MOMA NY) 1970, Guggenheim

Int Exhbn (Solomon R Guggenheim Museum NY) 1971, The British Avant-Garde (NY Cultural Center) 1971, 36 Biennale de Venezia 1972, Documenta 5 (Museum Fredericianum and Neue Galerie Kassel) 1972, The New Art (Hayward Gallery London) 1972, Contemporanea (Parcheggio di Villa Borghese Rome) 1973, Art and Politics (Gallerie Bochum) 1974, Victor Burgin/ Art and Language (Musée d'Art er d'Industrie Saint-Etienne) 1975, Arte Inglese Oggi 1960–76 (Palazzo Reale Milan) 1976, Hayward Annual (Hayward Gallery London) 1977, Europe in the Seventies (Art Inst of Chicago) 1977, Kunst im Sozialen Kontext (Badische Kunstverein Karlsruhe) 1980, The Third Biennale of Sydney (Art Gallery of New South Wales) 1980, Three Perspectives in Photography (Hayward Gallery London) 1980, Photographic Image in Contemporary Art (Nat MOMA Tokyo) 1984, The Turner Prize (Tate Gallery London) 1987, Photography and Art (LA Co Museum and touring) 1987, Écran Politiques (Musee d'Art Contempoarain de Montreal) 1987, Berlinart 1961–1987 (MOMA NY) 1987, The British Edge (ICA Boston) 1987, British Art in the Twentieth Century (Royal Acad of Arts London) 1987, Difference: On Sexuality and Representation (New Museum of Contemporary Art NY) 1987, The Future of the Metropolis (Triennale di Milano) 1988,; The Art of Photography: 1839–1989 (Museum of Fine Arts Houston and touring) 1989, On the Art of Fixing a Shadow: One Hundred and Fifty Years of Photography (Art Inst of Chicago and touring) 1989, L'art conceptuel, une perspective (Musée d'Art Moderne de la Ville de Paris) 1989, 1965–75: Reconsidering the Object of Art (The Museum of Contemporary Art LA) 1995–96, 3e Biennale de Lyon 1995–96, Hall of Mirrors: Art and Film Since 1945 (The Museum of Contemporary Art LA) 1996, Photography after Photography (Kunsthalle München and touring) 1996, Text & Image (Frankfurter Kunstverein and MOMA Bolzano) 1996, Face á l'Histoire 1933–66 (Centre Georges Pompidou Paris) 1996–97, The Impossible Document: Photography and British Conceptual Art 1967–76 (Camerawork Gallery London) 1997, Notorious: Art and Cinema (MOMA Oxford and touring) 1999, Blast to Freeze (Kunstmuseum Wolfsburg) 2002, Sans commune mesure, Image et texte dans l'art actuel (Musee d'Art Moderne Lille) 2002, I Promise It's Political (Museum Ludwig Cologne) 2002, Rapture: art's seduction by fashion since 1970 (Barbican London) 2002–03, L'Art au Futur Anterieur (Musée de Grenoble) 2004, The Last Picture Show:Artists Using Photography 1960–1982 (Walker Art Centre Minneapolis) 2004, Eblouissement (Jeu de Paume Paris) 2004, Artists' Choice (ICA London) 2004; *Work in Public Collections* incl: MOMA NY, New York Public Library, LA Co Museum of Art LA, Museum of Contemporary Art LA, Walker Art Centre Minneapolis, Tate Gallery London, V&A London, Arts Cncl Collection London, Centre Georges Pompidou Paris; *Books* Work and Commentary (1973), Thinking Photography (1982), Between (1986), The End of Art Theory (1986), Passages (1991), In/Different Spaces (1996), Some Cities (1996), Venise (1997), Shadowed (2000), Victor Burgin (2001), Relocating (2002), The Remembered Film (2004); *Style*— Prof Victor Burgin

BURKE, Cordell Aguilla; s of Ickford Aguilla Burke (d 1999), and Geraldine Margaret, *née* Crump; *b* 20 September 1957, Leicester; *Educ* Gateway Sch Leicester, Loughborough Coll of Art, Wimbledon Sch of Art; *m* 2 June 1984, Julie Ann, *née* Mitchell; 1 da (Christella Marie b 7 Jan 1985), 1 s (Lewis John b 9 June 1987); *Career* art dir: Latham Braley Cowan 1980–83, Benton & Bowles 1983–85, Lowe Howard-Spink 1985–86, BMP Business 1986–89; jt creative dir Ash Gupta Communications London 1989–91, dep creative dir/head of art Saatchi & Saatchi Direct 1991–93, freelance 1993–94; sr art dir Ogilvy & Mather Direct 1994–97; OgilvyOne Worldwide: dep creative dir/bd dir 1997–98, creative dir 1998–2003, exec creative dir/managing ptnr 2003–06, gp creative ptnr Ogilvy Gp UK 2006; exec creative dir Tequila London 2006–09, creative dir Cordscom 2009–10, creative managing ptnr and dir Bigdog Agency (formerly Balloon Dog) 2010–; DMA: memb Creative Cncl 1998–, memb Awards Ctee 2006–; chm Campaign Direct Awards Judges 2006; jt chm Graeme Robertson Tst (GRT) 2016–; Creative Circle Silver 1988, 7 DMA Golds and 13 DMA Silvers 1997–2013, Campaign Direct Silver 2000, Cannes Lion 2002, DMA Echo Silver 2005, John Caples Bronze 2005, Univ of Arts Black 100+ Achievers 2007, Brand Republic Digital Awards (Rev Awards) 2013–16; MIDM 2003; *Books* Shared Beliefs (contrib, 2002); *Recreations* football; *Style*— Cordell Burke, Esq; ✉ Bigdog Agency, 36 Percy Street, London W1T 2DH (e-mail cordell.burke@bigdogagency.com)

BURKE, David Patrick; s of Patrick Burke (d 1965), and Mary, *née* Walsh (d 1980); *b* 25 May 1934, Liverpool; *Educ* St Francis Xavier's Coll Liverpool, CCC Oxford (MA), RADA; *m* 20 March 1971, Anna, da of Arthur Calder-Marshall; 1 s (Tom Liam b 30 June 1981); *Career* actor; memb Br Actors Equity; *Theatre* RSC 1986–87: Hector in Troilus and Cressida, Bessemenow in Philistines, Melons; NT 1988–91: William Goodchild in The Strangeness of Others, Zeal-of-the-Land Busy in Bartholomew Fair, Ghost and First Gravedigger in Hamlet, Mr Voysey in The Voysey Inheritance, Reverend John Hale in The Crucible, Watch on the Rhine; Birmingham Rep: Measure for Measure, The Devil is an Ass; Hampstead Theatre (and West End): Bodies, Rocket to the Moon; other credits incl: Othello (Young Vic), A Flea in her Ear (Thorndike), Slow Dance on the Killing Ground (Greenwich) 1991, Claudius and Ghost in Hamlet (Riverside Studios) 1992, The Colonel in States of Shock (Salisbury Playhouse) 1993, Simonides in Pericles (RNT) 1994, New England (RSC) 1994, The Woman In Black (Fortune) 1995, Kent in King Lear (RNT) 1997, Copenhagen (RNT) 1998–99, Old Gaunt in Richard II (Almeida) 2000, Further than the Furthest Thing (Tricycle Theatre) 2001, The Wind in the Willows (narrator, ROH) 2002–03, The Three Sisters (West End) 2003, The Rivals (Bristol Old Vic) 2004, Mary Stuart (Donmar) 2005, John Gabriel Borkman (Donmar) 2007, The Sea (Haymarket Theatre) 2008, Afterlife (RNT) 2008, Oedipus (RNT) 2008, Hippolitus (tour) 2009, Hamlet (Donmar) 2009, The Prince of Homburg (Donmar) 2010, Danger: Memory (Jermyn Street Theatre), Choir Boy (Royal Ct) 2012, Roots (Donmar Warehouse) 2013; *Television* Dr Watson in The Adventures of Sherlock Holmes, Ron Fisher in Casualty, James Maybrick in The James Maybrick Case, Crown Court, Holly and Inheritance, Sir John Crowborough in The House of Eliott, Sir Arthur Stanley in Hickory Dickory Dock, Oedipus in An A-Z of Greek Democracy, Kipling, Two Days in the Love of Michael Reagan, Barlowe at Large, Love School, Fair Trading on the Dance Ground, Esther Waters, Pope Pius XII, The Murder Machine, The Comedians, A Winter's Tale, Nannie, Henry VI Parts 1 and 2, Richard III, Dreams, Secrets, Beautiful Lies, Run for the Life Boat, Taking Liberties, The Woodlanders, Hotel in Amsterdam, Hine and Crimes of Passion, Rooms, Hammer and Sickle, Quiet as a Nun, The Guardian, Villain, Bertie and Elizabeth, Waking the Dead, Casualty, Inspector Lynley, Secret Histories, De Vauzesnes in Mesmer (film) 1993, King Lear (film) 1998, The Regicides 2004, Cathedral 2004, Dalziel and Pascoe 2004, Boy Soldiers 2004, Ghost Story 2005, The Musketeers (BBC) 2013; *Film* The Woman in Black 2011, Christ The Lord 2014; *Books* Celia's Secret (with Michael Frayn, 2000); *Recreations* gardening, walking, cinema, music, reading; *Style*— David Burke; ✉ c/o Scott Marshall Management (☎ 020 7637 4623)

BURKE, David Thomas (Tom); CBE (1997); s of Jeremiah Vincent Burke, DSM (d 1990), and Mary, *née* Bradley (d 1998); *b* 5 January 1947; *Educ* St Boniface's Coll Plymouth, Univ of Liverpool (BA); *Career* lectr: Carlett Park Coll 1970–71, Old Swan Tech Coll 1971–73; Friends of the Earth: local gps co-ordinator 1973–75, exec dir 1975–79, dir special projects 1979–80, vice-chm 1980–81; dir The Green Alliance 1982–91 (memb Exec Ctee 1979–82, tstee 1997–2016), special advsr to Sec of State for the Environment 1991–97, environmental advsr BP plc 1997–2001, environmental policy advsr Rio Tinto plc 1996–, advsr Central Policy Gp Office of the Dep PM 2002, sr advsr to Foreign Sec's special rep on climate change 2006–12; non-exec dir Earth Resources Res 1975–88; memb: Waste Mgmnt Advsy Cncl 1976–80, Packaging Cncl 1978–82, Exec Ctee NCVO (also chm Planning and Environment Gp) 1984–89, UK Nat Ctee Euro Year of the Environment 1986–88, Exec Ctee Euro Environmental Bureau 1988–91 (policy advsr 1978–88), Co-operative Insurance Servs Environment Tst Advsy Ctee 1990–92, Cncl RSA 1990–92 (memb Environment Ctee 1989–96), Exec Bd World Energy Cncl Cmmn 1990–93, Cncl English Nature 1999–2005; chm Review of Environmental Governance in NI 2006–07; sr assoc Cambridge Prog for Sustainability Leadership 2010–; founding dir E3G 2004– (appointed chair 2013); chm China Dialogue Tst 2016–; visiting prof Imperial Coll London 1997–, hon prof Faculty of Law UCL 2003–; chm Editorial Bd Environmental Data Services (ENDS) 2005–12; hon visiting fell Manchester Business Sch 1984–86, visiting fell Cranfield Sch of Mgmnt 1990–94; tstee Borough Market Tstees 1999–2001; numerous radio and TV broadcasts, scriptwriter Crumbling Britain (BBC Radio 4) 1983; Parly candidate (SDP): Brighton Kemptown 1983, Surbiton 1987; Royal Humane Soc Testimonial on Parchment 1969 (on Vellum 1966); UNEP Global 500 laureate; FRSA 1987, FEI 2007, Hon FSE 2011; *Books* incl: Europe Environment (1981), Pressure Groups in the Global System (1982), Ecology 2000 (co-author and picture ed, 1984), The Gaia Atlas of Planetary Management (contrib, 1984), The Green Capitalists (with John Elkington, 1987), Green Pages (with John Elkington and Julia Hales, 1988), Ethics, Environment and the Company (with Julie Hill, 1990), The Fragile City (with Charles Landry, 2014); *Recreations* birdwatching, landscape photography, military history, walking; *Clubs* Reform; *Style*— Tom Burke, Esq, CBE; ✉ Studio 2, Clink Wharf Studios, Clink Street, London SE1 9DG (☎ 020 7357 9146, mobile 07710 627616); E3G, 47 Great Guildford Street, London SE1 0ES (☎ 020 7593 2020, e-mail tom.burke@e3g.org and tom.burke2@btinternet.com)

BURKE, Frank Desmond; *b* 23 March 1944; *Educ* Newcastle (MB BS); *m* Linda Margaret; 2 s (Richard b 1972, Timothy b 1979), 1 da (Sarah b 1975); *Career* fell in hand surgery: Louisville Kentucky 1976, Iowa City 1977; conslt hand surgn Derbyshire Royal Infirmary 1981–; visiting prof of hand surgery Med Scis Dept Univ of Derby; sec Br Soc for Surgery of the Hand 1989 (pres 1997), pres Br Assoc of Hand Therapists 1989, memb American Soc of Surgery of The Hand 1989, archivist Int Fedn of Societies for Surgery of the Hand 2011; FRCS 1972; *Books* Principles of Hand Surgery (with D A McGrougher and P J Smith, 1990); *Style*— Frank Burke, Esq; ✉ The Hand Unit, Royal Derby Hospital, Uttoxeter Road, Derby DE22 3NE (☎ 01332 290480)

BURKE, Gregory; s of Brian Joseph Burke, of Dunfermline, and Elizabeth, *née* Innes,; *b* 2 August 1968; *Educ* Bayside Comp Gibraltar, St Columba's HS Dunfermline, Univ of Stirling; *Partner* Lorraine Ann Forbes; *Career* writer; early career fulfilling variety of roles in minimum wage economy; *Plays* Gagarin Way (performed Traverse Theatre Edinburgh, RNT, Arts Theatre London and worldwide) 2001 (First of the Fringe Firsts Edinburgh Festival 2001, Critics Circle Awards Most Promising Playwright 2002, Barclays/TMA Awards Best New Play 2002, Meyer-Whitworth Award Best New Play 2002), The Straits (Paines Plough Theatre Co) 2003, Debt (NT) 2004, On Tour (Royal Court Upstairs) 2005, Black Watch (Traverse Theatre Edinburgh) 2006; *Recreations* absorbing culture in all its guises; *Clubs* Dunfermline Athletic FC; *Style*— Gregory Burke, Esq

BURKE, (Michael) Ian; s of Ron Burke, of Morecambe, Lancs, and Rosemary, *née* Gannor; *b* 2 June 1956, Liverpool; *Educ* Imperial Coll London (BSc), London Business Sch (MSc); *m* 22 Sept 1979, Jane, *née* McGuinness; 1 da (Jennie b 27 Dec 1983), 1 s (Paul b 4 Feb 1987); *Career* various roles Bass plc 1991–98 (incl: md Holiday Inn, md Gala Clubs); ceo: Thistles Hotels plc 1998–2003, Holmes Place Health Clubs 2003–06, Rank Gp plc 2006–; dir Business in Sport and Leisure; ACMA; *Recreations* fell walking, cycling, philosophy; *Style*— Ian Burke, Esq; ✉ Rank Group plc, Statesman House, Stafferton Way, Maidenhead, Berkshire SL6 1AY (☎ 01628 504000, fax 01628 504042, e-mail ian_burke@rank.com)

BURKE, Sir James Stanley Gilbert; 9 Bt (I 1797), of Marble Hill, Galway; s of Sir Thomas Stanley Burke, 8 Bt (d 1989), and Susanne Margaretha, *née* Salvisberg (d 1983); *b* 1 July 1956; *m* 1980, Laura, da of Domingo Branzuela, of Catmon, Cebu, Philippines; 1 s (Martin James b 1980), 1 da (Catherine Elizabeth b 1982); *Heir* s, Martin Burke; *Style*— Sir James Burke, Bt; ✉ Bleierstrasse 14, 8942 Oberrieden, Switzerland (website www.jbexe-coaching.ch)

BURKE, Prof Philip George; CBE (1993); s of Henry Burke (d 1969), of South Woodford, London, and Frances Mary, *née* Sprague (d 1980); *b* 18 October 1932; *Educ* Wanstead Co HS London, UC Exeter (BSc London), UCL (Granville studentship, PhD); *m* 29 Aug 1959, Valerie Mona, da of Harold William Martin (d 1987), of Eastbourne, E Sussex; 4 da (Helen Frances b 1961, Susan Valerie b 1963, Pamela Jean b 1964, Alice Charlotte b 1973); *Career* research asst UCL 1956–57, asst lectr Computer Unit Univ of London 1957–59; research assoc Lawrence Radiation Lab Univ of Calif Berkeley: Alvarez Bubble Chamber Gp 1959–61, Theory Gp 1961–62; successively research fell, princ sci offr then sr princ sci offr Theoretical Physics Div UK Atomic Energy Authy Harwell 1962–67; Queen's Univ Belfast: prof of mathematical physics 1967–98 (prof emeritus 1998–), head Dept of Applied Mathematics and Theoretical Physics 1974–77, dir Sch of Mathematics and Physics 1988–90; head of Theory and Computational Sci Div Daresbury Lab (jt appt) 1977–82; founding ed Computer Physics Communications 1969–79 (hon ed 1979–), series ed (with H Kleinpoppen) Physics of Atoms and Molecules 1974–2004, series ed Springer Series on Atomic Optical and Plasma Physics 2005–; memb: Physics Ctee SRC 1967–71, Synchrotron Radiation Research Ctee SRC 1971–75, Atlas Computer Ctee SRC 1973–76, Jt Policy Ctee on Advanced Res Computing 1988–90, Cncl SERC 1989–94, Cncl Royal Soc 1990–92, Nuclear Research Advsy Cncl MOD 1997–2008; chm: Synchrotron Radiation Panel SRC 1969–71, Comput Physics Gp Euro Physics Soc 1976–78, Sci Bd Computer Ctee SRC 1976–77 and 1984–86, Computer Bd Computer Conslt Cncl 1983–85, Atomic, Molecular and Optical Physics Div Inst of Physics 1987–90, Allocations and Resources Panel Jt Research Cncls Advanced Research Computing Ctee 1988–89, SERC Scientific Computing Advsy Panel 1989–94, SERC Supercomputing Mgmnt Ctee 1991–94 (memb Advsy Bd for Res Cncls Supercomputing Sub-Ctee 1991–94), Jt Research Cncls High Performance Computing Mgmnt Ctee 1996–98; Guthrie Medal and Prize Inst of Physics 1994, Sir David Bates Prize Inst of Physics 2000, Will Allis Prize American Physical Soc 2012; Hon DSc: Univ of Exeter 1981, Queen's Univ Belfast 1999; fell UCL 1986; FInstP 1970, fell American Physical Soc 1970, MRIA 1974, FRS 1978; *Books* Atomic Processes and Applications (jtly, 1976), Potential Scattering in Atomic Physics (1977), Atoms in Astrophysics (jtly, 1983), Electron Molecule Scattering and Photoionisation (jtly, 1988), Atomic and Molecular Processes: An R-Matrix Approach (jtly, 1993), Theory of Electron-Atom Collisions: Part I – Potential Scattering (jtly, 1995), Photon and Electron Collisions with Atoms and Molecules (jtly, 1997), R-matrix Theory of Atomic Collisions (2011); author of many papers in learned jls; *Recreations* walking, reading, listening to music; *Style*— Prof Philip G Burke, CBE, FRS, MRIA; ✉ Brook House, Norley Lane, Crowton, Northwich, Cheshire CW8 2RR (☎ 01928 788301); (e-mail p.burke@qub.ac.uk)

BURKE, Simon; s of Vincent Paul Burke (d 1989), and Beryl Mary, *née* Cregan; *b* 25 August 1958, Dublin; *Educ* St Mary's Coll Dublin; *Career* trainee accountant Binder Hamlyn 1976–82, various positions from supervisor to sr mangr Coopers & Lybrand 1982–87, corp fin mangr Virgin Gp plc 1987–88, md Virgin Retail Ltd 1988–94, chief exec Virgin Our Price 1994–96, chief exec Virgin Entertainment Gp 1996–99, chief exec and subsequently chm Hamleys plc 1999–2003; chm: Majestic Wine plc 2005–10 (non-exec dir 2000–05), Superquinn (Ireland) 2005–10, HobbyCraft 2010–14, Mitchells & Butlers plc 2010–11, Bathstore.com 2012–14, The Light Cinema Gp 2015–, Blue Diamond Gp

2015–; dir: BBC 2011–, Co-op Gp 2014–; tstee Nat Gallery 2003–11; FCA (Ireland); *Recreations* 17th Century Dutch art, flying (pilot's licence), history; *Style*— Simon Burke, Esq; ✉ Field House, Chiswick Mall, London W4 2PR

BURKHARDT, Prof (George) Hugh; s of Dr (George) Norman Burkhardt (d 1991), of Manchester, and Caroline Mary, *née* Bell; *b* 4 April 1935; *Educ* Manchester Grammar, Balliol Coll Oxford (BA), Univ of Birmingham (PhD); *m* 21 Dec 1955 (m dis 1995), Diana Jeanette, da of Stapley Farmer (d 1970); 2 s (Roger b 1960, Tansen, formerly Ian b 1963), 1 da (Jan b 1962); *Career* res fell: Columbia Univ 1958–59, Caltech 1959–60; lectr then sr lectr in mathematical physics Univ of Birmingham 1960–76, prof of mathematical educn Univ of Nottingham 1976–92; dir Shell Centre for Mathematical Educn 1976–92, dir Balanced Assessment for the Mathematics Curriculum and other int projects 1992–; chm International Society for Design and Development in Educn 1999–2010; visiting prof: UCLA 1968–69, CERN 1964–66 and 1973–74, UC Berkeley 1992–95 and 2010–, Michigan State Univ 1997–; memb: Jt Mathematical Cncl of the UK 1979–85 (treas 1982–85), Nat Curriculum Mathematical Working Gp 1987–88; nat memb Int Cmmn on Mathematics Instruction 1980–88; Prize for Lifetime Achievement Int Soc for Design and Development in Educn 2013, Emma Castelnuovo Award Int Cmmn on Mathematics Instruction 2015; *Books* Dispersion Relation Dynamics (1969), The Real World and Mathematics (1981), Problem Solving – A World View (1988), Curriculum – towards the Year 2000; *Recreations* oboe, theatre, dance, music; *Style*— Prof Hugh Burkhardt; ✉ e-mail hugh.burkhardt@nottingham.ac.uk

BURLAND, James Alan; s of James Glyn Burland, and Elizabeth Beresford, *née* Thompson (d 1978); *b* 25 September 1954; *Educ* King Henry VIII Sch Coventry, Univ of Bath (BSc, BArch), Cert of HE in Professional Music Performance, Univ of Cambridge; *Career* architect; Arup Assocs 1978–86, Philip Cox Richardson Taylor and Partners Sydney 1986–90, dir and princ architect Arup Assocs 1996– (re-joined 1990) (projects incl: Stockley Park Heathrow, Bedford HS Jr Sch, Durham New Coll, City of Manchester Stadium, Johannesburg Athletics Stadium, Glasgow Nat Arena, Plantation House London), fndr BURLAND TM (projects incl: Ealing Studios, Providence Row Refuge and Convent Dept, Pinewood and Shepperton Film Studios, Falcon Wharf Thameside Apartments, Bermondsey St Market, conslt to Terrell Ltd to set up Terrell Associates Engineering Architecture); private cmmns The Body Shop Bath, Liverpool and Brighton 1982–83; current projects incl: Billiardrome, extension to Edward Jenner Unit Gloucester Royal Hosps, Camden Market, Project Collage – creative media settlement and permanent film studio backlot, house at Middleton-on-Sea W Sussex; roof extension tutor Univ of Sydney 1987–88; memb Nat Tst; RIBA 1983, CA, ARB; *Publications* Crowd Engineering for High Capacity Venues (1992), Hillsborough Disaster (1994, now unavailable); *Recreations* music, cycling; *Clubs* London RC (cycling, pres and co-fndr); *Style*— James Burland; ✉ Burland TM (e-mail jb@burlandtm.com, website www.burlandtm.com)

BURLAND, Prof John Boscawen; CBE (2005); s of John Whitmore Burland (d 1994), and Margaret Irene, *née* Boscawen (d 1986); *b* 4 March 1936; *Educ* Parktown Boys' HS Johannesburg, Univ of the Witwatersrand (BSc, MSc, DSc), Emmanuel Coll Cambridge (PhD); *m* 30 March 1963, Gillian Margaret, da of John Kenneth Miller (d 1981); 2 s (David 1965, Timothy 1967), 1 da (Tamsin 1969); *Career* engr Ove Arup and Ptnrs London 1961–63; Building Res Estab: SSO, PSO 1966–72, SPSO head Geotechnics Div 1972–79, asst dir DCSO 1979–80; visiting prof Univ of Strathclyde 1973–82; ICSTM: prof of soil mechanics 1980–2001, sr research investigator 2001–, emeritus prof of soil mechanics 2001–, fell 2004–; vice-pres ICE 2002–05, memb Cncl Royal Acad of Engrg 1994–97; commendatore Ordine della Stella di Solidarieta' Italiana 2003, memb Academia Europea, foreign memb US Nat Acad of Engrg 2016; Hon DEng Heriot-Watt Univ 1994, Hon DSc Univ of Nottingham 1998, Hon DEng Univ of Glasgow 2001, Hon DSc Univ of Warwick 2003, Hon DSc Univ of the Witwatersrand 2007, Hon DSc Univ of Hertford 2011; hon fell: Emmanuel Coll Cambridge 2004, Univ of Cardiff 2005; FIStructE 2001 (MIStructE 1976), FREng 1981, FICE 1982 (MICE 1969, recently elected hon fell), FRS 1997, FCGI 1997; *Recreations* golf, sailing, painting; *Style*— Prof John Burland, CBE, FRS, FREng; ✉ Department of Civil Engineering, Imperial College London, South Kensington Campus, London SW7 2AZ (✆ 020 7594 6079, fax 020 7594 5934, e-mail j.burland@imperial.ac.uk)

BURLEY, Philip George; s of Victor George Burley (d 1989), and Blanche Clara, *née* Coleman (d 1962); *b* 31 December 1943; *Educ* Whitgift Sch Croydon, Univ of the Arts London; *m* 8 June 1974, Christine Elizabeth, da of Istvan Komaromy, of Shirley, Surrey; 3 da (Victoria b 1976, Elisabeth b 1979, Georgina b 1981); *Career* musician 1961–63, md Joint Marketing and Publishing Services Ltd 1970 (graphic designer 1963–69), fndr ptnr Design Counsellors and Incentive Counsellors 1971, fndr ptnr and creative dir The Incentive Group 1972, chm The Quadrant Group 1982, chm and chief exec Excelsior Group Productions Ltd 1989–, exec prodr The Darling Buds of May 1990–93, exec prodr A Touch of Frost 1992–2010, exec prodr and prodr Pride of Africa 1997, exec prodr My Uncle Silas 2001; composer of music for theatre and TV incl title music for The Darling Buds of May 1990 (Ivor Novello Award for Best TV Theme Music 1991); festival dir Polesden Lacey Festival 1999–2002; chief barker Variety Club of GB 1999; govr Guildford Sch of Acting 2002–10, chm Bd of Govrs Quest Acad Croydon 2010–15, pres Whitgiftian Assoc 2013, chm Old Whitgiftian Assoc 2014–; *Books* Views from the Back of a Taxi (2010); *Recreations* music, theatre, art, reading, golf; *Clubs* Kingswood Golf and Country, Beaverbrook Golf and Country; *Style*— Philip Burley, Esq; ✉ Excelsior Group Productions Limited, The Mint House, Headley, Surrey KT18 6QA (✆ 01372 362740, mobile 07970 426704)

BURN, (Bryan) Adrian Falconer; s of Reginald Falconer Burn (d 1981), and Kathleen Ruth, *née* Davis (d 2002); *b* 23 May 1945; *Educ* Abingdon Sch; *m* 1968, Jeanette Carol; 4 c (Clare b 1976, Victoria b 1979, Katharine b 1983, James b 1985); *Career* chartered accountant Whinney Murray 1968–72 (articled clerk 1964–68); Binder Hamlyn: joined 1973, ptnr 1977, managing ptnr 1988–97; ptnr Arthur Andersen (following merger) 1994–99; chm: Atlas Group Holdings Ltd 1999–2002, Search Holdings Ltd 2000–06; non-exec dir: Brent International plc 1994–99, Era Group plc 1999–2001, Wolff Olins 1999–2001, G E Capital Bank Ltd 1999–2008, Richards Butler 1999–2006, Strutt and Parker 1999–2006, Pinewood Shepperton plc 2000–11, Smart and Cook Hldgs 2004–07, Acertec plc 2006–09, G E Money Home Lending Ltd 2007–; treas and tstee NSPCC 1999–2008; tstee Royal Br Legion 2009–, chm of govrs Abingdon Sch Fndn 2013–; FCA (ACA 1968); *Clubs* Roehampton; *Style*— Adrian Burn, Esq

BURN, Prof Sir John; kt (2010); s of Henry Burn, of West Auckland, Co Durham, and Margaret, *née* Wilkinson; *b* 6 February 1952; *Educ* Barnard Castle GS, Univ of Newcastle upon Tyne (BMedSci, MB BS, MD); *m* 5 Aug 1972, Linda Marjorie, da of Charles Frederick Wilson, of Winston, Darlington, Co Durham; 1 da (Danielle Louise b 17 Aug 1977), 1 s (James Richard David b 20 Sept 1981); *Career* jr med trg Newcastle teaching hosps 1976–80, MRC clinical scientific offr Inst of Child Health London 1981–82, hon sr registrar in clinical genetics Gt Ormond St Hosp 1981–84, conslt clinical geneticist Royal Victoria Infirmary Newcastle 1984–91; Univ of Newcastle upon Tyne: clinical lectr 1984–91, prof of clinical genetics 1991–, head Div of Human Genetics 1992–98; exec dir Life Knowledge Park, med dir and head Inst of Human Genetics, lead clinician NHS North East 2009–13; chm UK Cancer Family Study Gp 1996–2002, chair Br Soc for Genetic Medicine 2011–13; memb: gen sec Clinical Genetics Soc of GB 1989–95, Ctee on Clinical Genetics RCP 1991–93, Bd Euro Soc of Human Genetics 1995–99, Human Genetics Cmmn 1999–2005; chair Int Soc for Gastrointestinal Hereditary Tumours (InSIGHT) 2003–05, vice-pres European Soc of Human Genetics 2008 (pres 2006–07), chair Genetics Specialty Gp NIHR 2008–15, chief med offr and chm QuantuMDx Ltd 2008–, dir NIHR Collaborative Gp for Genetics in Healthcare 2010–16, chair Br Soc for Human Genetics (now Br Soc for Genetic Medicine) 2011–13, non-exec memb Bd NHS Eng 2014–, chair Rare Disorders Registries and Databases Advsy Gp Dept of Health 2015–; FRCP 1989 (MRCP 1978), FRCPCH 1997, FRCOG 1998, FMedSci 2000, FRCPEd 2003; *Publications* Long Term Effects of Aspirin on Cancer Risk in Carriers of Hereditary Colorectal Cancer: the CAPP2 randomised controlled trial (jtly, 2011); over 250 peer reviewd pubns; *Recreations* running, golf, playing drums; *Style*— Prof Sir John Burn; ✉ Institute of Genetic Medicine, Newcastle University, Central Parkway, Newcastle upon Tyne NE1 3BZ

BURN, (Adrian) Lachlan; *b* 4 April 1951; *Educ* Univ of Bristol (LLB); *Career* slr; Linklaters: articled clerk 1974–76, slr 1976–82, ptnr 1982– (Paris office 1982–87, capital markets 1987–); memb: Legal and Documentation Ctee Int Capital Marktes Assoc, Legal Risk Review Ctee Bank of England 1991–92, Advsy Ctee Listing Authy 1999–2011, Financial Markets Law Ctee 2002–06, Primary Markets Gp London Stock Exchange; gen ed Capital Markets Law Jl 2006–; *Recreations* music, literature, travel; *Style*— Lachlan Burn, Esq; ✉ Linklaters, One Silk Street, London EC2Y 8HQ (✆ 020 7456 4614, fax 020 7456 2222, e-mail lburn@linklaters.com)

BURNAND, Hugo; s of Peter Burnand, of Hungerford, Berks (d 2015), and Susan, *née* Gordon (d 1964); step-s of Ursy Burnand, photographer; *b* 24 September 1963, Cannes, France; *Educ* Cheam Sch, Harrow Sch; *m* 22 May 1993 (m dis 2015), Louisa, *née* Hallifax; 1 s (Fergus b 1994), 3 da (Lily b 1996, Una b 1998, Maya b 2000); *Career* became freelance professional photographer 1991, Tatler 1993–; subjects incl: HM The Queen, TRH The Prince of Wales and The Duchess of Cornwall, TRH Prince William and Prince Harry, HRH Princess Alexandria, President Bill Clinton, President Mikhail Gorbachev, Sir Dennis and Baroness Thatcher, David Hockney, Ruth Rendall (Baroness Rendell of Babergh, CBE), Victoria Beckham, Imelda Staunton, Santa and Simon Seabag Montefiore, Linda Evangelista, Sienna Miller, Spike Milligan, Uma Thurman, Michael Jackson; official photographer for the marriage of HRH The Prince of Wales to Camilla Parker Bowles, the marriage of HRH Prince William of Wales to Catherine Middleton, and the marriage of David Cameron, to Samantha Cameron, *née* Sheffield, *qqv*; *Style*— Hugo Burnand, Esq; ✉ 1 Powis Mews, London W11 1JN (✆ 020 7229 2297, e-mail hugo@hugofoto.com, website www.hugofoto.com)

BURNELL-NUGENT, Adm Sir James Michael; High Sheriff Devon 2015–, KCB (2004), CBE (1999); s of Cdr A F Burnell-Nugent, DSC, RN, and Gian Mary, *née* Alexander; *b* Stutton, Suffolk; *Educ* Stowe, CCC Cambridge (MA); *m* Mary *née* Woods; 1 da (Henrietta), 3 s (Anthony, Rupert, Tom); *Career* RN: joined 1971, Capt HMS Olympus (submarine) 1978, Capt HMS Conqueror (submarine) 1984–86, Capt 1990, Capt Second Frigate Sqdn and Capt HMS Brilliant 1992–93 (Bosnia), Cdre 1994, Capt HMS Invincible 1997–99 (Gulf, Kosovo), Rear Adm 1999, Asst Chief of Naval Staff 1999–2001, memb Admiralty Bd 1999–2001 and 2003–07, Cdr UK Maritime Forces and ASW Striking Force 2001–02 (Iraq, Afghanistan), Second Sea Lord and C-in-C Naval Home Command 2003–05, Flag ADC to HM The Queen 2003–05, Vice-Adm 2003, Vice-Adm of the UK 2005–07, Adm 2005, C-in-C Fleet and NATO Cdr Maritime Component Northwood 2005–07, ret 2008; chm Aerospace, Defence and Maritime Practice Regester Larkin 2013–; vice-chm Annual Nat Service for Seafarers 2014–; dir: Orchard Leadership 2008–, Plymouth Marine Lab 2008–, Qineteq 2010–; int strategic advsr to: Shell 2008–, Evercore Partners 2008–, OCIMF 2009–, RiskIntelligence 2012 (chm Advsy Bd 2012–), Sonardyne 2014–; chm Witt Ltd 2016–; pres HMS Ganges Assoc 2009–; govr Stowe Sch 2008–, dir St George's House Windsor Castle 2014–; Queen's Gold Medal, Max Horton Prize; yr bro Trinity House 2004; Freeman City of London 1999; High Sheriff of Devon 2015–16; hon fell CCC Cambridge 2005, sr fell One Earth Future Fndn 2012; Companion Inst of Leadership and Mngmnt 2005; *Publications* Leadership in the Office (1996), Keeping an Eye on the Cost of Government (2006), My Royal Navy Scrapbook (2014), Frank Nugent and Arthur Burnell, Brothers-in-Law in the Great War (2016); *Recreations* living in the country; *Clubs* IoD; *Style*— Adm Sir James Burnell-Nugent, KCB, CBE; ✉ The Naval Secretary, Leach Building, Whale Island, Portsmouth

BURNETT, Alexander John (Sandy); s of George David Burnett (d 2000), and Margaret Marion Elizabeth, *née* Miller; *b* 29 October 1964, Bute; *Educ* Glasgow Acad, St Catharine's Coll Cambridge (MA); *m* 29 Oct 1994, Clare Elizabeth, *née* Gibbons; 1 s (Robbie b 5 July 1995), 1 da (Anna b 18 April 1997); *Career* freelance musical dir for regnl theatres, RSC, RNT and West End 1987–94; radio presenter: BBC Radio 3 1994–2007 (incl: Proms 1996–2006, Edinburgh Int Festival morning concerts 2000–05, Morning on 3 2003–07), Lyric FM RTÉ 1999– (incl Calling the Tune 1999–2002), Grace Notes BBC Radio Scotland 2001–02; conductor and jazz double bassist; *Style*— Sandy Burnett, Esq

BURNETT, (Ronald) Bruce Owen; s of Lt Col Ronald John Burnett, OBE, of Bentworth, Hants, and Stella Ruth, *née* Cundy; *b* 17 April 1959; *Educ* Denstone Coll, Univ of London (BA); *m* 1, 2 Nov 1991 (m dis 2002), Pippa Lesley, da of Sqdn Ldr Leslie Sands; m 2, 22 May 2004, Fiona Jane, da of John Sutherland; 1 da (Siena Isabella Phoebe b 11 Oct 2004); *Career* Rowntree Mackintosh: sales rep 1981–82, nat accounts exec 1982–83, trade devpt exec 1983–84, trade mktg/sales promotion mangr 1984–85, asst nat sales mangr 1985–86, brand mangr 1986–87, sr brand mangr 1987–89, gp mktg mangr 1989–91; Trebor Bassett (subsid of Cadbury Schweppes): mktg mangr 1991–92, mktg gen mangr 1992–93, mktg dir 1993–97; gp commercial dir Communication Innovation Group; md: Creative Concept Development Ltd, Origin8 International Sourcing Ltd, Global Sponsorship Management Ltd 1997–2000; ceo i2i Face to Face Marketing Ltd 2001–, ceo i2i Marketing 2008–; *Recreations* dressage, polo, mountaineering, photography, art and architecture, antiques; *Clubs* Cowdray Park Polo, Cirencester Park Polo, Beaufort Polo, Longdole Polo; *Style*— Bruce Burnett, Esq

BURNETT, Sir Charles David; 4 Bt (UK 1913), of Selborne House, Co Borough of Croydon; s of Sir David Burnett, 3 Bt, MBE, TD (d 2002); *b* 18 May 1951; *Educ* Harrow, Lincoln Coll Oxford; *m* 21 Oct 1989 (m dis), Victoria Joan, er da of James Simpson, of Rye, E Sussex; 1 da (Roberta Elizabeth b 24 July 1992); m 2, 2 Sept 1998, Kay Rosemary, *née* Naylor; 1 da (Isabel Louise b 23 Jan 2004); *Career* international insurance broker; *Recreations* wine, fishing, travel, shooting; *Clubs* Brooks's, Turf, 106; *Style*— Sir Charles Burnett, Bt; ✉ 25 Marloes Road, London W8 6LG (✆ 020 7975 2546, fax 020 7975 2840)

BURNETT, Charles John; s of Charles Alexander Urquhart Burnett (d 1977), of Fraserburgh, Aberdeenshire, and Agnes, *née* Watt; *b* 6 November 1940; *Educ* Fraserburgh Acad, Gray's Sch of Art Aberdeen (DA), Aberdeen Coll of Educn, Univ of Edinburgh (MLitt, 1992); *m* 29 April 1967, Aileen Elizabeth, da of Alexander Robb McIntyre (d 1982), of Portsoy, Banffshire; 1 da (Sara b 1969), 2 s (Sandy b 1972, John b 1976); *Career* Advertising Dept House of Fraser 1963–64, Exhibitions Div Central Office of Information 1964–68, asst curator Letchworth Museum and Art Gallery 1968–71, head of design Nat Museum of Antiquities of Scotland 1971–85, curator of fine art Scot United Servs Museum Edinburgh Castle 1985–96, chamberlain Duff House Banff 1997–2004; heraldic advsr Girl Guide Assoc Scotland 1978–2010, vice-pres Soc of Antiquaries of Scot 1992–95 (memb Cncl 1986–88), memb Bd Heraldry Soc of Ireland 1986–90, pres Heraldry Soc of Scot 2003–15 (vice-pres 1987–2003, pres emeritus 2015–); librarian Priory of the Order of St John in Scot 1987–98; tstee St Andrews Fund for Socts Heraldry 2001–14, chm Banff Preservation and Heritage Soc 2002–10, chm Pitsligo Castle Tst 2010–14 (vice-chm 2003–10), memb Bd Banff Renaissance Project 2008–10; pres 27th Int Congress for Genealogical and Heraldic Sciences 2006; numerous pubns on Scottish history and heraldry; HM Offr of Arms: Dingwall Pursuivant 1983, Ross Herald 1988–2010, Ross Herald Extraordinary 2011–15; tstee Bield Retirement Housing Tst 1992–96; first hon memb Dorothy Dunnett Readers' Assoc 2006; hon citizen State of Oklahoma USA 1989; convenor Companions of the Order of Malta 1991–94; Queen's Golden Jubilee Medal 2002, Queen's Diamond Jubilee Medal 2012; FSA Scot 1964, AMA 1972, FHS Scot 1989; KStJ 1991 (CStJ 1982, OStJ 1974, SBStJ 1972); Knight of the Order of St Maurice and St Lazarus 1999, Knight of the Royal Order of Francis I 2002; *Books* The Honours of Scotland (jtly, 1993), Scotland's Heraldic Heritage (jtly, 1997), The Order of St John in Scotland (jtly, 2000), Stall Plates of the Most Ancient and Most Noble Order of the Thistle in the Chapel of the Order within St Giles' Cathedral, The High Kirk of Edinburgh (jtly, 2001), Officers of Arms Within the Realm of Scotland 1290–2016 (2016); *Recreations* reading, visiting places of historic interest; *Clubs* Banff Town and County, Royal Scots Edinburgh; *Style—* Charles J Burnett, Esq; ✉ Seaview House, Portsoy, Banffshire AB45 2RS; Court of the Lord Lyon, HM New Register House, Edinburgh EH1 3YT (☎ 0131 556 7255)

BURNETT, Prof Charles Stuart Freeman; s of Donald Stuart Burnett, and Joan, *née* Freeman; *b* 26 September 1951; *Educ* Manchester Grammar, St John's Coll Cambridge (BA, PhD), LGSM; *m* 1, 1985 (m dis 1991), Mitsuru Kamachi; *m* 2, 1995, Tamae Nakamura; 2 s (Ken Stuart b 21 Sept 1995, Miki Jo b 30 Dec 1997); *Career* jr research fell St John's Coll Cambridge 1975–79, sr research fell Warburg Inst London 1979–82, Leverhulme research fell Dept of History Univ of Sheffield 1982–84 and 1985, prof Warburg Inst London 1999– (lectr 1985–99); distinguished visiting prof Univ of Calif Berkeley 2003, visiting prof Univ of Munich 2009; Brauer fell Univ of Chicago 2008, corresponding fell Medieval Acad of America 2014; FBA 1998; *Publications* Jesuit Plays on Japan and English Recusancy (with M Takenaka, 1995), Magic and Divination in the Middle Ages: Texts and Techniques in the Islamic and Christian Worlds (1996), The Introduction of Arabic Learning into England (1997), Arabic into Latin in the Middle Ages: The Translators and their Intellectual and Social Context (2009), Numerals and Arithmatic in the Middle Ages (2010); also author of over 150 articles in learned jls; *Recreations* playing music (viola, piano, viola da gamba, shakuhachi); *Style—* Prof Charles Burnett, FBA; ✉ Warburg Institute, Woburn Square, London WC1H 0AB (☎ 020 7862 8949, e-mail charles.burnett@sas.ac.uk)

BURNETT, David Henry; s of G D Burnett, CBE, TD, of Surrey, and F A Burnett; *Educ* Tonbridge, Churchill Coll Cambridge (MA); *Career* gp gen mangr and chief operating offr Global Banking and Markets HSBC Bank plc; *Style—* David H Burnett, Esq; ✉ Faircroft, Vale of Health, London NW3 1AN; HSBC Bank plc, 8 Canada Square, London E14 5HQ

BURNETT, David John Stuart; s of John Edward Burnett (d 1989), and Margaret Kathleen (*née* Cole); *b* 6 February 1958; *Educ* Oundle, Peterhouse Cambridge; *m* 1988, Anne, da of C J C Humfrey (d 1993); 1 s (Joe Alexander Stuart b 9 Aug 1990), 1 da (Laura Frances Kathleen b 16 June 1992); *Career* Rowe & Pitman 1979–86 (ptnr 1985–86); dir S G Warburg Securities Ltd 1986–95, md SBC Warburg 1995–98; TT International: managing ptnr 1998–2005, ptnr 2005–; chm Smart & Cook Hldgs 2006–07, chm Children's Support Services Ltd 2013–; dir: BMS Finance 2006–13, Copperdime 2010–15; chm: Venue Retail Ltd 2010–14, Nene Valley Brewery Ltd 2012–, Tap and Kitchen Ltd 2014–, Captured Hldgs 2014–; *Style—* David Burnett, Esq; ✉ Hall Farm, Wigsthorpe, Northamptonshire PE8 5SE (☎ 01832 720488); 49 Montagu Mansions, London W1U 6LD (☎ 020 7935 1372); TT International, 62 Threadneedle Street, London EC2R 8HP (☎ 020 7509 1230)

BURNETT, Hon Mr Justice; Sir Ian Duncan Burnett; kt (2008); s of David John Burnett, and Maureen Burnett, *née* O'Brien; *b* 28 February 1958; *Educ* St John's Coll Southsea, Pembroke Coll Oxford (MA); *m* 2 November 1991, Caroline Ruth Monks; 1 s (Robert Andrew b 4 Feb 1998), 1 da (Helen Alexandra b 12 June 2003); *Career* called to the Bar Middle Temple 1980 (Astbury scholar, bencher 2001), jr counsel to the Crown (common law) 1992–98, QC 1998, recorder 2000–08 (asst recorder 1998–2000), head of chambers 1 Temple Gardens 2003–08, judge of the High Court of Justice (Queen's Bench Div) 2008–, presiding judge Western Circuit 2011–; dep chm Security Vetting Appeals Panel 2009–; hon fell Pembroke Coll Oxford 2008; *Publications* Asylum and Human Rights Handbook (with Anna Kotzeva, Lucy Murray and Robin Tam, QC, *qv*, 2008), Judicial College Guidelines for the Assessment of General Damages; *Recreations* history, silver, music, wine; *Style—* The Hon Mr Justice Burnett; ✉ Royal Courts of Justice, Strand, London WC2A 2LL (☎ 020 7947 7895)

BURNETT, Baron (Life Peer UK 2006), of Whitchurch in the County of Devon; John Patrick Aubone Burnett; *Educ* Ampleforth, Commando Trg Centre Royal Marines, Britannia Royal Naval Coll Dartmouth, Coll of Law London; *m* 1971, Elizabeth (Billie); 2 s, 2 da; *Career* Royal Marines 1964–70: troop cdr 42 Commando RM Borneo 1965–66, troop cdr and second in command company 40 Commando RM Far East and Middle East 1967–69, ret as Lt; qualified as slr 1975, ptnr then sr ptnr Burd Pearse Slrs Okehampton 1976–97; farmer 1976–98: memb cncl Devon Cattle Breeders' Soc 1985–97, winner Devon Cattle Breeders Soc Nat Herd Competition 1989; MP (Lib Dem) Devon W and Torridge 1997–2005; Lib Dem spokesman on legal affairs 1997–2002, memb Finance Bill Ctee 1998–2005, Lib Dem shadow Attorney General 2002–05; conslt Stephens & Scown 2005–; memb: Revenue Law Ctee Law Soc 1984–96, Royal Marines Assoc (N Devon Branch), Royal Br Legion; *Style—* The Rt Hon the Lord Burnett; ✉ Stephens & Scown, Curzon House, Southernhay West, Exeter EX1 1RS (☎ 01392 210700, fax 01392 274010, e-mail commerce.exeter@stephens-scown.co.uk)

BURNETT, Prof Sir Keith; kt (2013), CBE (2004); *Educ* Jesus Coll Oxford (BA, DPhil); *Career* former chm of physics Univ of Oxford, head Div of Mathematical, Physical and Life Sciences Univ of Oxford 2005–07, vice-chllr Univ of Sheffield 2007–; FRS 2001; *Style—* Prof Sir Keith Burnett, CBE, FRS; ✉ Vice-Chancellor's Office, University of Sheffield, Western Bank, Sheffield S10 2TN

BURNETT, Richard Leslie; MBE (2008); s of Sir Leslie T Burnett, Bt, CBE (d 1955), of Godstone, Surrey, and Joan, *née* Humphery; *b* 23 June 1932; *Educ* Eton, RCM, King's Coll Cambridge; *m* Katrina Eveline, *née* Hendrey; *Career* concert pianist, specialising in fortepianos (early pianos) 1970–; fndr and dir Finchcocks Museum; *Recordings* incl: Schubert's Die Schöne Müllerin (with Nigel Rogers) and Die Winterreise, Haydn's Sonatas, The Romantic Fortepiano, Clementi's Fortepiano Works, Beethoven's Violin Sonatas and Songs, Hummel's Violin and Piano Works, Mozart Piano Quartets, Mendelssohn's Clarinet Works, Brahms' Clarinet Trio; *Style—* Richard Burnett, Esq, MBE; ✉ Finchcocks, Goudhurst, Kent TN17 1HH (☎ 01580 211702, fax 01580 211007)

BURNETT, Timothy Adrian John; s of late Lt-Col Maurice John Brownless Burnett, DSO, DL, of Dalton, N Yorks, and late Crystal Henrietta Deschamps, *née* Chamier; *b* 12 April 1937; *Educ* Eton, Trinity Coll Cambridge (BA); *m* 15 July 1961, (Catherine Barbara) Jean, da of Dr Julius Harald Beilby (d 1978), of Bedale, N Yorks; 1 da (Henrietta b 1962), 1 s (James b 1964); *Career* 2 Lt Coldstream Gds 1956–58; asst keeper Dept of Manuscripts Br Museum 1961, manuscripts librarian Br Library 1986–97, conslt Robert Holden Ltd Fine Art Agents 1997–2015, conslt Omnia Art Ltd Fine Art Agents 2015–; owner Dunsa Manor Estate, tstee Kiplin Hall Tst, tstee The Fan Museum; FSA 2005; *Books* The Rise and Fall of a Regency Dandy, The Life and Times of Scrope Berdmore Davies (1981), Byron, Childe Harold Canto III (1988), Browning, The Ring and The Book (1998, 2000, 2004), Catalogue of the Ashley Manuscripts (1999); *Recreations* architectural history, travel, sailing, shooting, fishing; *Clubs* Beefsteak, Pratt's, Royal Yacht Sqdn; *Style—* Timothy Burnett, Esq, FSA; ✉ 11 Highbury Place, London N5 1QZ (☎ 020 7226 6234, e-mail tajburnett@aol.com); Dunsa Manor, Dalton, Richmond, North Yorkshire DL11 7HE; Omnia Art Ltd Fine Art Agents, 13 Old Burlington Street, London W1S 3AJ (☎ 020 7437 6010, fax 020 7437 1733)

BURNHAM, Rt Hon Andrew (Andy); PC (2007), MP; *b* 7 January 1970; *Educ* Fitzwilliam Coll Cambridge (MA); *m* 2000, Marie-France van Heel; 1 s, 2 da; *Career* journalist Baltic Publishing 1992–94, researcher to Tessa Jowell, MP 1994–97, Parly offr NHS Confedn 1997, advsr to Football Task Force 1997–98, special advsr to Rt Hon Chris Smith, MP 1998–2001, MP (Lab) Leigh 2001–; memb Health Select Ctee 2001–03, formerly PPS to Rt Hon David Blunkett, MP, Parly sec Home Office 2005–06, min of state Dept of Health 2006–07, chief sec to the Treasy 2007–08, sec of state for culture media and sport 2008–09, sec of state for health 2009–10, shadow sec of state for educn 2010–11, shadow sec of state for health 2011–15, shadow home secretary 2015–16; chair Supporters Direct 2002–05; memb Co-op Pty, affliated to Unison and TGWU; *Recreations* football, rugby league, cricket; *Clubs* Everton FC, Leigh Centurions RLFC; *Style—* The Rt Hon Andy Burnham, MP; ✉ Constituency Office, 10 Market Street, Leigh, Lancashire WN7 1DS (☎ 01942 682353, e-mail andy.burnham.mp@parliament.uk); House of Commons, London SW1A 0AA

BURNHAM, 7 Baron (UK 1903); Harry Frederick Alan Lawson; 7 Bt (UK 1892); s of 6 Baron Burnham (d 2005), and Hilary Margaret, *née* Hunter; *b* 22 February 1968, London; *Educ* Eton; *Career* with Evening Standard 1988–95, investment mangr Williams de Broë plc 1996–2000, investment mgmnt dir Brewin Dolphin Ltd 2000–13 (gp fund dir 2002–), ceo Ashcourt Rowan Asset Mgmnt; pres Salt Hill Soc; Liveryman Worshipful Co of Gunmakers; FCSI (MSI 2007); *Recreations* shooting, oenology, tobogganing, horse and greyhound racing, golf; *Clubs* Turf, Pratt's, St Moritz Toboggan, City Livery, Burnham Beeches Golf; *Style—* The Rt Hon the Lord Burnham

BURNS, Sir (Robert) Andrew; KCMG (1997, CMG 1992); s of Robert Burns, CB, CMG (d 1971), and Mary, *née* Goodland; *b* 21 July 1943; *Educ* Highgate Sch, Trinity Coll Cambridge (MA); *m* 19 July 1973, Sarah, JP, da of Peter Cadogan (d 1962), and Joan, *née* Banbury (d 1979); 2 s ((Robert) Duncan b 29 May 1975, Thomas Alexander Luckwell b 15 March 1977), 1 step da (Ella Jane Kenion b 23 Nov 1968); *Career* HM Dip Serv: third sec UK Mission to UN 1965, second sec New Delhi 1967–71, first sec FCO and UK delg Conf on Security and Co-operation in Europe 1971–75, first sec and head of Chancery Bucharest 1976–78, private sec to Perm Under Sec FCO 1979–82, cnsllr (info) Washington 1983–86, head of British info services NY 1983–86, head S Asian Dept FCO 1986–88, head News Dept FCO 1988–90, asst under sec of state (Asia) FCO 1990–92, ambass to Israel 1992–95, dep under sec of state (non-Europe and trade) FCO 1995–97, consul-gen to Hong Kong Special Admin Regn and Macao 1997–2000, high cmmr to Canada 2000–03, UK envoy for post-Holocaust issues 2010–15; dir: JP Morgan Chinese Investment Tst 2003–16, Aberdeen All Asia Investment Tst 2008–13, Aberdeen Japan Investment Tst 2013–16; chm Canada-UK Colloquia 2013– (hon pres 2008–13), memb Br N American Ctee 2004–13; chm Cncl Royal Holloway Univ of London 2004–11, tstee UK Fndn of Univ of Br Columbia 2005–10, chm Ctee of Univ Chairs 2008–11 (dep chm 2007–08), tstee Canadian Studies Fndn 2008–14; chm Exec Ctee Anglo-Israel Assoc 2004–05 and 2008–11, pres China Assoc 2008–14, memb Ctee Hong Kong Soc 2008–11; chm Bar Standards Bd 2015–; memb Devpt Bd The Sixteen 2007–14; int govr BBC 2005–06; chm: Hestercombe Gardens Tst 2005–, Advsy Cncl Br Expertise 2006–10 (memb 2003–13); chair Int Polar Fndn UK 2006–; memb Bd of Govrs GSMD 2011–; chair Int Holocaust Remembrance Alliance 2014–15; fell Center for Int Affairs Harvard Univ 1982–83, Portland fell 2004; FRSA; *Books* Diplomacy, War and Parliamentary Democracy (1985); *Recreations* choral singing, theatre, walking; *Clubs* Garrick, RAC, Hong Kong, Royal Over-Seas League; *Style—* Sir Andrew Burns, KCMG; ✉ Walland Farm, Wheddon Cross, Minehead, Somerset TA24 7EE

BURNS, Andrew Philip; QC (2015); s of Chris Burns, and Lynne Burns, *née* Docker; *b* 8 April 1971, Bromsgrove; *Educ* Downing Coll Cambridge; *m* 1995, Ruth, *née* Farries; 2 s (Jamie, Alistair); *Career* called to the Bar 1993; recorder of the Crown Ct; head Chambers Pupillage Ctee 2007–12, memb Professional Conduct Ctee Bar Standards Bd 2007–13, memb Middle Temple Educn Ctee 2009–13; Scout ldr 2013–; *Publications* Law of Reinsurance (2013), Discrimination Law (gen ed, 2015); *Style—* Andrew Burns, Esq, QC; ✉ Devereux Chambers, Devereux Court, London WC2R 3JH (Twitter @AndrewBurnsQC)

BURNS, Angela Jane; AM; *m* Andrew Stuart Burns; 2 da (Katie, Daisy); *Career* memb Nat Assembly for Wales (Cons) Carmarthen W and S Pembrokeshire 2007–, former shadow min for environment and planning, shadow min for fin and public serv delivery 2007–08, shadow min for tport and regeneration 2008–11, shadow min for educn 2011–, assembly cmmr 2011–; Memb to Watch ITV Wales Yearbook Award 2007; *Recreations* sailing, riding, travel; *Style—* Mrs Angela Burns, AM; ✉ c/o Tomos Davies, political advisor (☎ 029 2089 8593 or 0300 200 7243, e-mail tomos.davies@assembly.wales, website www.angelaburns.org.uk)

BURNS, Conor; MP; s of Thomas Burns, of Puerto Banus, Spain, and Kathleen, *née* Kennedy; *b* 24 September 1972, Belfast; *Educ* St Columba's Coll St Albans, Univ of Southampton (BA); *Career* co sec De Havilland Global Knowledge Distribution plc 1998–2004, rgnl sales mangr Zurich Advice Network 2004–05, assoc dir PLMR 2008–10; MP (Cons) Bournemouth West 2010–, PPS NI Office 2010–12, memb Culture Media and Sport Select Ctee 2012–15, PPS Treasy 2015–; *Recreations* cooking, swimming, snooker; *Clubs* Southern Parishes, Westbourne, Kinson Conservative; *Style—* Conor Burns, Esq, MP; ✉ Bournemouth West Conservatives, 135 Hankinson Road, Bournemouth, Dorset BH9 1HR; House of Commons, London SW1A 0AA (☎ 020 7219 7021, e-mail conor.burns.mp@parliament.uk, website www.conorburns.com, Twitter @conor_burns.mp)

BURNS, Julian Delisle (Jules); *b* 18 September 1949; *Career* Granada TV: joined as mangr Regnl Programmes 1976, head Programme Servs 1987–88, dir Business Affrs 1988–93 (also co sec and responsible for Personnel 1993), dir (Main Bd) Programme and Mgmnt Servs and md Granada Enterprises Dec 1993–94, jt md Granada TV and md Divnl Ops 1995, jt md Granada Productions 1996–2000, md ops Granada Media 2000–02; chief operating offr ALL3MEDIA 2003–; non-exec dir Liverpool FC; *Style—* Jules Burns, Esq; ✉ mobile 07768 725116

BURNS, Nica; OBE (2013); *Educ* Haberdashers Aske's, UCL (LLB), Webber Douglas Acad of Dramatic Art; *Career* artistic dir Donmar Warehouse 1983–89, dir and prodr Foster's Edinburgh Comedy Awards (formerly Perrier Awards) 1984–, prodn dir Really Useful Theatres 1993–2005, owner and chief exec Nimax Theatres Ltd (comprising 6 West End theatres) 2005–; chair King's Head Theatre Club 1995–2005, dir Sadler's Wells Fndn 1995–2012, vice-pres Soc of London Theatre 2011–13 (pres 2008–11); Private Business Woman of the Year Private Business Awards 2013; fell UCL 2007; *Style—* Ms Nica Burns, OBE; ✉ Nimax Theatres Ltd, 11 Maiden Lane, London WC2E 7NA (website www.nimaxtheatres.com)

BURNS, Sir, Rt Hon Simon Hugh McGuigan; kt (2015), PC (2011), MP; s of late Maj Brian Stanley Burns, MC, and late Shelagh Mary Nash; *b* 6 September 1952; *Educ* Christ the King Sch Accra Ghana, Stamford Sch, Worcester Coll Oxford (BA); *m* 1982 (m dis); 1 da (Amelia b 1987), 1 s (Bobby b 1991); *Career* political asst to Rt Hon Mrs Sally Oppenheim, MP 1975–81, dir What to Buy Ltd 1981–83, conf organiser IOD 1983–87;

MP (Cons): Chelmsford 1987–97, Chelmsford W 1997–2010, Chelmsford 2010–; PPS to: Rt Hon Tim Eggar, MP 1989–93, Rt Hon Mrs Gillian Shephard, MP 1993–94; asst Govt whip 1994–95, a Lord Cmmr to HM Treasy (Govt whip) 1995–96, Parly under sec of state Dept of Health 1996–97; oppn spokesman on: social security 1997–98, environment 1998–99, health 2001–05; oppn whip 2005–10, min of state for health 2010–12, min of state for tport 2012–13; *Recreations* photography, travelling, American politics; *Clubs* Chelmsford Conservatives (patron); *Style—* The Rt Hon Sir Simon Burns, MP; ✉ House of Commons, London SW1 (☎ 020 7219 3000)

BURNS, Baron (Life Peer UK 1998), of Pitshanger in the London Borough of Ealing; Sir Terence Burns; GCB (1995), kt (1983); s of Patrick Owen Burns, and Doris Burns; *b* 13 March 1944; *Educ* Houghton-le-Spring GS, Univ of Manchester (BA), London Business Sch; *m* 1969, Anne Elizabeth Powell; 1 s, 2 da; *Career* chief econ advsr to Treasy and head Govt Econ Serv 1980–91, perm sec to Treasy 1991–98; chm: Financial Services and Markets Jt Cmmn 1999, Ctee of Inquiry into Hunting with Dogs 2000, Nat Lottery Cmmn 2000–01; ind advsr on the Govt's BBC Charter Review 2003–, head Football Assoc structural review 2005; chm: Glas Cymru (Welsh Water) 2001–, Abbey National plc 2002– (dep chm 2001), Marks and Spencer plc 2006–08 (dep chm 2005), Channel 4 Television Corporation 2010– (chm-designate 2009–10); non-exec dir: Legal and General 1999–2001 (chm Audit Ctee 2000–01), Pearson plc 1999–, The British Land Co plc 2000–05, Banco Santander SA 2004–; dir Queens Park Rangers FC 1996–2001; vice-pres Royal Economic Soc 1992–, pres Soc of Business Economists 1999– (vice-pres 1985–99), NIESR 2003– (govr 1998–2003); memb Bd of Mgmnt Manchester Business Sch 1993–98; chair Governing Body Royal Acad of Music 2002– (memb 1998–), chm of tstees Monteverdi Choir and Orchestra 2001–07 (tstee 1998–2007); fell London Business Sch 1989–, visiting fell Nuffield Coll Oxford 1991–97; CIMgt 1992; *Recreations* soccer (spectator), golf, music; *Clubs* Reform; *Style—* The Rt Hon the Lord Burns, GCB; ✉ House of Lords, London SW1A 0PW (☎ 020 7219 0312, e-mail burnst@parliament.uk)

BURNS, Prof Thomas (Tom); CBE (2006); *b* 20 September 1946, Belfast; *Educ* Univ of Cambridge (MB BChir, MD), Univ of London (DSc); *Career* fndn prof of social and community psychiatry St George's Hosp Med Sch Tooting until 2003, prof of social psychiatry Univ of Oxford 2003–14, fell Kellogg Coll Oxford 2003–14 (emeritus fell 2014–); past chm Social and Community Section RCPsych; FRCPsych; *Books* Psychological Management of the Physically Ill (ed with J Hubert Lacey, 1989), Assertive Outreach in Mental Health: A Manual for Practitioners (with Mike Firn, 2002), Community Mental Health: A Guide to Current Practices (2004), Psychiatry: A very short introduction (2006), Shorter Oxford Textbook of Psychiatry (6 edn with Phil Cowen and Paul Harrison, 2012) Our Necessary Shadow: The Nature and Meaning of Psychiatry (2013), Psycotherapy: A very short introduction (with Eva Burns-Lundgren, 2015); *Style—* Prof Tom Burns, CBE; ✉ Department of Psychiatry, University of Oxford, Warneford Hospital, Oxford OX3 7JX

BURNS, Rt Rev Thomas Matthew (Tom); s of William James Burns (d 1998), and Louisa Mary, *née* McGarry (d 1998); *b* 3 June 1944; *Educ* St Mary's Coll Blackburn, Winslade Sch Clyst St Mary, The Monastery Paignton, Heythrop Coll London (BD), Coll of Commerce & Technol Hull (Dip Business Studies), Open Univ (BA); *Career* ordained RC priest Soc of Mary (Marist Fathers) 1971 (ordinand 1965–71), curate St Anne's Parish Whitechapel London 1973–74, head of economics St Mary's GS Sidcup 1974–78, head of economics and social scis St Mary's Sixth Form Coll Blackburn 1979–86, chaplain Royal Navy 1986–92, bursar gen Soc of Mary (Marist Fathers) Rome 1992–93; Royal Navy: initial sea trg chaplain 1994–95, establishment co-ordinating chaplain HMS Nelson and HM Naval Base Portsmouth 1995–96, RN dir Armed Forces' Chaplaincy Centre Amport House 1996–98, princ RC Chaplain to the RN and Vicar Gen 1998–2002, dir Naval Chaplaincy Serv (Trg & Progs) 1998–2000, dir Naval Chaplaincy Serv (Manning) 2000–02, Bishop of the Forces 2002–08, Bishop of Menevia 2008–; Queen's Honorary Chaplain (QHC) 1998–2002; episcopal advsr Catholic Police Force Guild of England & Wales, memb Bishops' Conf Dept of Int Affrs; dir RN Handicapped Children's Pilgrimage Tst 1998–2002, bishop promoter (dir and tstee) Apostleship of the Sea 2002, dir, tstee and memb Bd St Luke's Centre Manchester 2006; MIMgt; *Publications* Index of Laws of the Game of Rugby Football (ed and compiler); *Recreations* rugby assessor/advisor; *Style—* The Rt Rev Tom M Burns, SM; ✉ Diocese of Menevia, 27 Convent Street, Greenhill, Swansea SA1 2BX (☎ 01792 644017, e-mail bishop@menevia.org)

BURNSIDE, Graham Mathieson; WS (1984); s of John Young Burnside, of Newtongrange, Midlothian, and (Mary) Ishbel, *née* Sim; *b* 23 March 1954, Edinburgh; *Educ* George Heriot's Sch Edinburgh, Univ of Edinburgh (Muirhead prize, LLB), LTCL; *Career* admitted slr 1978; trainee slr Dundas & Wilson 1976–78, slr Nat Coal Bd/CIN Properties Ltd 1978–82; Tods Murray LLP (formerly Tods Murray WS): slr 1983–84, ptnr 1984–2014, head Banking Dept 1999–2014, chm 2010–14; conslt Shepherd and Wedderburn LLP 2014–; memb Advsy Bd Islamic Finance Cncl UK; author of articles in professional jls on Scots law and on aspects of securitisation and of Islamic finance; govr St Columba's Hospice until 2015 (hon vice-pres 2015–), chm New Town Concerts Soc 2015–, dir St Mary's Music Sch Edinburgh; *Recreations* opera, organ playing, hill walking; *Clubs* Scottish Arts; *Style—* Graham Burnside, WS; ✉ Shepherd and Wedderburn LLP, 1 Exchange Crescent, Conference Square, Edinburgh EH3 8UL (☎ 0131 228 9900, e-mail graham.burnside@shepwedd.co.uk)

BURNSIDE, Prof John; *b* 19 March 1955, Dunfermline; *Educ* Cambridge Coll of Arts and Technol; *Career* writer; prof of creative writing Univ of St Andrews; *Poetry* The Hoop (1988, Scottish Arts Cncl Book Award 1988), Common Knowledge (1991, Scottish Arts Cncl Book Award 1991), Feast Days (1992, Geoffrey Faber Meml Prize 1994), The Myth of the Twin (1995), Swimming in the Flood (1995), A Normal Skin (1997), The Asylum Dance (2000, Whitbread Book Award Poetry Award 2000), The Light Trap (2002), The Good Neighbour (2005), Selected Poems (2006), Gift Songs (2007), The Hunt in the Forest (2009), Black Cat Bone (2011, Petrarca-Preis 2011, Forward Prize 2011, T S Eliot Prize 2011), All One Breath (2014); *Fiction* The Dumb House (1997), The Mercy Boys (1999, Encore Award 1999), Burning Elvis (2000), The Locust Room (2001), Living Nowhere (2003), The Devil's Footprints (2007), Glister (2008), A Summer of Drowning (2011); *Creative Non-Fiction* A Lie About My Father (2006, Prix Zepter, Saltire Soc Scottish Book of the Year Award 2006, Corine Literature Prize 2011), Waking up in Toytown (2010), I Put A Spell On You (2014); *Style—* Prof John Burnside; ✉ c/o David Miller, Rogers, Coleridge & White Ltd, 20 Powis Mews, London W11 1JN

BURNSTOCK, Prof Aviva Ruth; da of Prof Geoffrey Burnstock, *qv*, of London, and Nomi, *née* Hirschfeld; *b* 1 September 1959; *Educ* King Alfred Sch Hampstead, Univ of Sussex (BSc), Courtauld Inst of Art (Dip Conservation, PhD); *m* 1988, Hugh, s of Dr Stephen Sebag-Montefiore; 2 s (Saul, Abraham), 1 da (Esther); *Career* paintings conservator Art Gall of NSW Sydney 1984–85, scientist National Gallery London 1986–92, currently head Dept of Conservation and Technol Courtauld Inst of Art; memb Int Inst of Conservation 1981–; *Style—* Prof Aviva Burnstock; ✉ Department of Conservation and Technology, The Courtauld Institute of Art, Somerset House, Strand, London WC2R 0RN (☎ 020 7848 2192, e-mail aviva.burnstock@courtauld.ac.uk)

BURRAGE, Kenneth Walter; *b* 27 April 1939; *Educ* Churcher's Coll Petersfield, Guildford and Wimbledon Tech Coll (ONC, HNC); *m*; 3 c; *Career* British Railways Bd: signal engrg Southern Region 1956–77, regnl signal engr Western Region 1977–81, chief signal and telecommunications engr London Midland Region 1981–88, dir of signal and telecommunications engrg Bd HQ 1989–92 (dep dir 1988–89), dir of engrg standards Bd HQ 1992–94, memb BRT Bd 1993–94, controller Safety Standards Railtrack plc 1994–95; dir Westinghouse Signals Ltd 1995–99 (dep md 1998–99), chief exec Inst of Railway Signal Engineers 1999–2006 (memb Cncl 2010–16); memb Cncl Engrg Cncl 1992–96 (memb Working Party on Unification of Engrg profession, chm Implementation Panel for Risk Code), memb Cncl IEE 1994–97; FREng, FIET, Hon FIRSE; *Recreations* music, motorsport, walking, ornithology; *Style—* Kenneth Burrage, Esq; ✉ Institution of Railway Signal Engineers, Floor 4, 1 Birdcage Walk, London SW1H 9JJ (☎ 020 7808 1180, fax 020 7808 1196)

BURRAS, Stephanie; CBE (2014); *Educ* St Catharine's Coll Cambridge; *Career* formerly slr, ptnr Pinsenst Slrs 2001–04, fndr and chief exec Ahead Partnership 2004–; memb Bd Leeds City Region Local Enterprise Partnership 2011–; *Style—* Ms Stephanie Burras; ✉ Ahead Partnership, 1 Park Row, Leeds LS1 5AB (www.aheadpartnership.org.uk)

BURRELL, His Hon Judge (Francis) Gary; QC (1996); *b* 7 August 1953, Belfast; *Educ* Belfast Boys' Model, Univ of Exeter (LLB); *m* 4 Aug 1979, Heather Burrell; 3 c (Sam, Edward, Alex); *Career* called to the Bar Inner Temple 1977 (bencher 2002), recorder of the Crown Ct 1996– (asst recorder 1992), dep High Court judge 2001, circuit judge (Western Circuit) 2009–; specialist in personal injury, crime, and clinical negligence litigation; memb Bar Cncl; *Publications* author of various articles in periodicals; *Recreations* sailing, fly fishing; *Style—* His Hon Judge Burrell, QC; ✉ Southampton Combined Court, London Road, Southampton

BURRELL, Michael Ian; s of Sydney Burrell, of Haslemere, Surrey, and Mary, *née* Smith; *b* 25 June 1950; *Educ* Godalming Co GS, St Peter's Coll Oxford (MA); *Career* journalist Durham Advertiser 1971–72, local govt corr Evening Argus Brighton 1972–73, lobby corr Westminster Press 1973–83, Profile PR 1983–86; chm Grayling Political Strategy Brussels 1990–2002, chm Westminster Strategy 2000–02 (md 1986–2000), vice-chm The Grayling Group 2000–02 (chief exec 1991–2000), European chm Public Affairs Edelman 2002–04, vice-chm Edelman Europe 2004–11, vice-chm public affrs Europe APCO Worldwide 2011–12 (sr counsel 2013–14), ind conslt 2013–; non-exec dir Connect Communications 2013–; chm Assoc of Professional Political Consultants 1999–2002 and 2011–14, sr advsr European Centre for Public Affairs 2005–2013 (dep chm 2005–13); Outstanding Contribution to European Public Affrs European Public Affrs Award 2009; *Publications* Lobbying and the Media: Working with Politicians and Journalists; various articles on lobbying Westminster, Whitehall and the European Union; *Recreations* doing nothing in the sunshine; *Style—* Michael Burrell, Esq; ✉ e-mail michael.burrell@mail.com; Michael Burrell Associates, 46 Wilmington Avenue, London W4 3HA (☎ 020 8742 1903)

BURRIDGE, Rev Canon Prof Richard Alan; s of Alan Burridge (d 2000), of Exmouth, Devon, and Iris Joyce, *née* Coates (d 1994); *b* 11 June 1955; *Educ* Bristol Cathedral Sch (County scholar), UC Oxford (MA), Univ of Nottingham (CertEd, DipTh, PhD); *m* 1, 1 Sept 1979 (m dis 2009), Susan Burridge, *née* Morgan; 2 da (Rebecca b 5 Aug 1986, Sarah b 1 March 1988); m 2, 20 April 2014, Megan Warner; *Career* classics master and house tutor Sevenoaks Sch 1978–82, curate St Peter and St Paul Bromley Parish Church 1985–87, Lazenby chaplain and pt/t lectr Depts of Theology and Classics and Ancient History Univ of Exeter 1987–94; KCL: dean and hon lectr Dept of Theology and Religious Studies 1994–, prof of biblical interpretation 2008–; canon theologian Salisbury Cathedral 2013–; lecture tour to American univs and seminaries 1993, St Matthiastide lectr Bristol 1994, Boundy meml lectr Univ of Exeter 1993, preacher Univ Sermon Univ of Oxford 1994, inaugural lecture KCL 1995, commissary for Bishop of the High Veld Church of the Province of Southern Africa 1997–2009, lecture tour to South African univs, seminaries and churches 1998, 2014 and 2015; chair Bishop of Southwark's Theological Gp 2004–10; memb: Cncl of Mgmnt St John's Coll Nottingham Ltd 1986–99, Cncl of Reference Monarch Publications 1992–2000, Gen Synod C of E 1994–2015, Studiorum Novi Testamenti Societas (SNTS) 1995–, Soc for the Study of Theology (SST) 1995–, Soc of Biblical Literature (SBL) 1995–, Church Cmmrs' Ethical Investment Advsy Gp 2008– (dep chair 2010–15); Archbishop of Canterbury's rep at II World Pastoral Congress Rome 2005; gen ed People's Bible Commentary Series 1997–; chm Eric Symes Abbot Meml Fund 1994–, chm Christian Evidence Soc 2000– (tstee 1994–), external examiner to SW Ministry Trg Course 1995–99, theological advsr for the film Miracle Maker 1995–2000, chm C of E's Educnl Validation Panel 1996–2004, Gen Synod rep Ptnrs in Mission Consultation for the Province of W Africa at Accra 1998, tstee King George VI and Queen Elizabeth Fndn of St Catherine's Cumberland Lodge 1998–2008, advsr and writer New Millennium Experience Co Greenwich Dome 1998–2000; reg contrib BBC TV and radio, World Serv and ITV; Ratzinger Prize for Theology 2013 (jtly); FKC 2002; *Publications* Sex Therapy: Some Ethical Considerations (1985), What are the Gospels? A Comparison with Graeco-Roman Biography (1992, paperback reprint 1995, revised edn 2004), Four Gospels, One Jesus? (1994, reprinted in USA 1996, 1999 and 2014, reprinted in UK 1997 and 2000, revised edn 2005, SPCK Classic edn 2013), Where Shall We Find God? (1998), John (1998, revised edns 2008 and 2013), Faith Odyssey (2001, 2 edn 2003), Jesus Now and Then (2004), Imitating Jesus: An Inclusive Approach to New Testament Ethics (2007); *Recreations* golf, swimming, music, cycling, being with my family; *Style—* Rev Canon Prof Richard Burridge; ✉ The Dean's Office, King's College London, Strand, London WC2R 2LS (☎ 020 7848 2333, e-mail dean@kcl.ac.uk, website www.kcl.ac.uk/dean/)

BURRILL, Timothy Peckover; yr s of Lyonel Peckover Burrill, OBE (d 1983), and Marjorie Sybil, *née* Hurlbutt (d 1976); *b* 8 June 1931; *Educ* Eton, Sorbonne; *m* 1, 1959 (m dis 1966), Philippa, o da of Maurice Hare; 1 da (Rebecca Nina b 1961); m 2, 1968 (m dis 1989), Santa, er da of John Raymond; 2 da (Jemima Lucy b 1970, Tabitha Sara b 1974), 1 s (Joshua Hal Peckover b 1973); *Career* film prodr; served Grenadier Gds 1949–52; jr mgmnt Cayzer Irvine & Co 1952–56; entered film indust 1956, joined Brookfield Productions 1965, md Burrill Productions 1966–2013, dir World Film Services 1967–69, first prodn admin Nat Film and TV Sch 1972; md: Allied Stars (responsible for Chariots of Fire) 1980–81, Pathé Productions Ltd 1994–99; dir: Artistry Ltd (responsible for Superman and Supergirl films) 1982, Central Casting 1988–92; conslt: Nat Film Devpt Fund 1980–81, The Really Useful Gp 1989–90; UK film industry rep on Eurimages 1994–96; chm: BAFTA 1980–83 (vice-chm 1979–81), Film Asset Development plc 1987–94, First Film Fndn 1989–98, Prodn Trg Fund 1993–2001; vice-chm The Producers' Assoc (PACT) 1993–94 (memb Exec Ctee 1990–2001); dir Br Film Cmmn 1997–99; prodr memb: Cinematograph Films Cncl 1980–83, Gen Cncl ACTT 1975–76, Exec Ctee Br Film and TV Prodrs' Assoc 1981–90; memb: UK Govt's Middleton Ctee on Film Finance 1996, Le Club des Producteurs Européens 1996–98, Bd Int Fedn of Film Prodrs Assoc 1997–2001, UK Govt's Film Policy Review 1997–98, European Film Acad 1997–; govr: Nat Film and TV Sch 1981–92, Royal Nat Theatre 1982–88; films incl: Fourth Protocol, Supergirl, Tess, Oliver Twist, La Vie en Rose, The Ghost; *Recreations* gardening, theatre; *Style—* Timothy Burrill, Esq; ✉ 19 Cranbury Road, London SW6 2NS (☎ 020 7736 8673, fax 020 7731 3921, mobile 07785 298680, e-mail timothy@timothyburrill.co.uk)

BURROUGHS, Philip Anthony; s of Anthony John Burroughs (d 2011), and Brenda Mabel, *née* Downing; *b* 2 October 1955; *Educ* Hemel Hempstead GS, Univ of Bristol (LLB); *m* 23 July 1977, Katharine Mary, da of Douglas Campbell Doughty, of Tring, Herts; 1 da (Rebecca b 1982), 1 s (Alastair b 1984); *Career* admitted slr 1980; asst slr Freshfields 1980–83; ptnr: Lawrence Graham 1985–93 (asst slr 1983–85), Coudert Brothers 1993–2000, McGrigors London (formerly KLegal) 2000–11; non-exec dir Hilstone Property Investments Ltd 2004–12, dir and co sec Chase Green Devpts Ltd 2010–; chm Langleys

Round Table 1988–89 (memb 1984); govr Berkhamsted Sch 2010–14; memb Law Soc; *Recreations* travel, Dorset, Isles of Scilly, Barbados, sports cars, fine dining, 60s and 70s popular music, jukebox, reading, wine, gardening, family, golden retriever; *Style—* Philip Burroughs, Esq

BURROW, Dr Charles Thomas; s of Richard Burrow, of Lancaster, and Ivy Reta, *née* Coates; *b* 22 September 1945; *Educ* Lancaster Royal GS, Univ of Liverpool (MB ChB); *m* Ann Jane, da of William George Frederick Gunstone (d 1977); 1 s (Michael b 1987), 2 da (Katharine b 1976, Lucy b 1977); *Career* lectr Univ of Liverpool 1975–77, conslt pathologist Univ Hosp Aintree (formerly Walton Hosp) Liverpool 1978–; FRCPath 1988 (MRCPath 1976); *Style—* Dr Charles Burrow; ✉ University Hospital Aintree, Lower Lane, Liverpool L9 7AL (☎ 0151 525 5980)

BURROW, Robert Philip; s of Robert F Burrow, and Rosalind, *née* Hughes; *b* 24 March 1951; *Educ* St George's Coll Weybridge, Fitzwilliam Coll Cambridge (MA); *m* 21 July 1984, Angela Mary, da of Henry Cornelius Bourne Hill; 2 s (Matthew Robert Henry b 5 June 1985, Simon Richard Philip b 20 July 1987), 1 da (Julia Rosamund Mary b 28 June 1991); *Career* admitted slr 1975; slr: Clifford Turner 1975–76 (articled clerk 1973–75), Linklaters & Paines 1976–78; dir RIT Management Ltd 1979; md: J Rothschild & Co 1981–85, Transcontinental Service Group NV 1983–88; ptnr SJ Berwin & Co 1985–2007, chief exec Chelsfield Ptnrs LLP 2007– (chm Chelsfield Ptnrs LLP 2013–, chief exec Chelsfield Advsrs LLP); chm: Control Components Ltd 1983; non-exec dir Quindell plc 2005–; memb Law Soc; *Style—* Robert P Burrow, Esq; ✉ Chelsfield LLP, 50 Hans Crescent, London W1K 4NJ (☎ 020 7290 2388)

BURROWES, David John Barrington; MP; s of John Burrowes (d 1986), and Mary Burrowes; *b* 12 June 1969, Barnet; *Educ* Highgate Sch, Univ of Exeter (LLB), Coll of Law London; *m* 1997, Janet, *née* Coekin; 4 s (Barnaby (twin) b 27 Aug 1997, Dougal b 1 May 1999, Noah b 24 Sept 2004, Toby b 15 April 2007), 2 da (Harriet (twin) b 27 Aug 1997, Dorothy b 21 Feb 2001); *Career* admitted slr 1994; trainee slr Turner and Debenhams 1991–93, slr Shepherd Harris and Co 1994–2005 (conslt 2005–), MP (Cons) Enfield Southgate 2005– (Parly candidate (Cons) Edmonton 2001); cncllr (Cons) Enfield BC 1994–2006; vice-pres Edmonton Cons Assoc, tstee and co-fndr Cons Christian Fellowship; memb Law Soc; *Publications* Moral Basis of Conservatism (1991), Such a Thing as Society: Maggie's Children (2006), Were you up for Twigg? (2006), Forgotten: The children of addicts (2006), Breakdown Britain (2007), Breakthrough Britain (2007), Cord Blook Transplantation: Meeting the Unmet Demand (2012), A Better Future for Families: The importance of family-based interventions in tackling drug and alcohol problems (2012); *Recreations* sport enthusiast (football and cricket); *Style—* David Burrowes, Esq, MP; ✉ 1C Chaseville Parade, Chaseville Park Road, London N21 1PG (☎ 020 8360 0234, e-mail david@davidburrowes.com, website www.davidburrowes.com); House of Commons, London SW1A 0AA (☎ 020 7219 8144, fax 020 7219 5289)

BURROWS, Prof Desmond David; *b* 11 July 1930; *Educ* Queen's Univ Belfast (MB BCh, BAO, MD); *m* 17 Dec 1958, Marie, *née* Madden; *Career* house offr Royal Victoria Infirmary 1953–54, asst lectr Dept of Pathology Queen's Univ Belfast 1954–56, sr registrar in dermatology Royal Victoria Hosp 1958–60 (registrar in dermatology 1956–58), MRC research fell Inst of Dermatology London 1960–61, conslt dermatologist Royal Victoria Hosp 1961– (chm Med Div 1981–83); Queen's Univ Belfast: memb Faculty of Med 1981–, hon lectr in dermatology 1985–, hon prof Clinical Med Sch 1990–; memb: Central Conslts and Hosp Specialities Ctee BMA 1980–82, Scientific Advsy Ctee Gen (Internal) Med and Related Specialities DHSS 1986; chm: Med Exec Ctee Royal Gp of Hosps 1984–86, Med Specialities Ctee Postgraduate Cncl NI 1989–; sec: Irish Dermatological Soc 1965–71, Euro Soc for Contact Dermatitis 1986–90 (memb Cncl 1987); pres: Irish Assoc of Dermatologists 1975–77, Euro Soc of Contact Dermatology 1990–92, Br Assoc of Dermatologists 1991–92 (memb Cncl 1975–77 and 1980–86); chm Br Contact Dermatitis Gp 1983–86 (memb Exec Ctee 1981–89); memb Cncl: Ulster Medical/Legal Soc 1976–78, Int League of Dermatological Socs 1981–88, Euro Environmental and Contact Dermatitis Gp 1985–96, BMA 1986–87, RCPEd; memb Editorial Bd: Contact Dermatitis – Environmental and Occupational Dermatitis 1985–99, Jl of the American Acad of Dermatology 1990–97, Jl of the Euro Acad of Dermatology and Venereology, Bollettino di Dermatologia Allergologia e Professionale; Sir Archibald Gray Medal for Outstanding Service to British Dermatology 2009; invited lectr at 50-year celebration of Irish Assoc of Dermatologists Dublin 2015; hon memb: Finnish Soc of Dermatology 1986, Swedish Dermatological Soc 1986, American Dermatology Assoc 1987, Academia Espanola de Dermatologia 1988, N American Clinical Dermatology Soc 1993, Br Assoc of Dermatologists 1993, Norwegian Dermatological Soc (corresponding memb); memb: Ulster Med Soc, Dowling Dermatological Soc, St John's Hosp Dermatological Soc; FRCPEd 1969 (MRCPEd), FRCP Dublin 1982, FRCP 1986; *Books* Chromium: Metabolism and Toxicity (1983); author of various book chapters and numerous published papers; *Recreations* golf; *Clubs* Corrigan; *Style—* Prof Desmond Burrows; ✉ Apartments 66/67, Stranmillis Wharf, Lockview Road, Belfast BT9 5GN (☎ 028 9038 1669, mobile 07785 250521, e-mail desmond.burrows1@ntlworld.com)

BURROWS, Peter Malcolm Grant; s of late John Grant Burrows, of Holywell, N Wales, and Elizabeth Eleanor, *née* Fryte; *b* 14 December 1952, Singapore; *Educ* Holywell GS, Univ of Aberystwyth; *m* 26 Sept 1981, Louise Elizabeth, da of Dr W G Wenley; 1 da (Clare Elizabeth b 1 March 1984); *Career* articled clerk Philip Jones Hillyer & Jackson Chester 1975–77, slr Winter Wilkinson St Neots & St Ives 1977–87; Norton Rose: joined 1987, ptnr 1989–, mangr Commercial Property and Planning Dept 1994–2000, mangr London real estate team 2003–07, head of China practice 2008–13, head of Russia practice 2011–13; sr conslt DaHui Lawyers Beijing 2013–; Freeman: City of London, City of London Slrs' Co 1987; memb Law Soc 1977; *Recreations* travel; *Style—* Peter Burrows, Esq; ✉ DaHui Lawyers, 3720 China World Tower, 1 Jianguomenwai Avenue, Beijing 100004, China (www.dahuilawyers.com)

BURROWS, Prof Philip Nicholas; s of Nicholas Charles Ernest Burrows, of Chorley, Lancs, and Winefred Grace Hart, *née* Coyle (d 2003); *b* 22 July 1964, Chorley, Lancs; *Educ* Oriel Coll Oxford (MA, DPhil); *Career* research scientist MIT 1989–98, PPARC advanced fell Univ of Oxford 1998–2002, sr lectr, reader and prof of physics Queen Mary Univ of London 2002–05, prof of accelerator physics John Adams Inst Univ of Oxford 2006–; sr research fell Jesus Coll Oxford; visiting scholar Stanford Univ; CPhys 1990, FInstP 2004, fell American Physical Soc 2008; *Recreations* music, the arts, travel, photography; *Style—* Prof Philip Burrows; ✉ John Adams Institute, Particle Physics, Keble Road, Oxford OX1 3RH (☎ 01865 273451, fax 01865 273417, e-mail p.burrows@physics.ox.ac.uk)

BURSELL, His Hon Canon Rupert David Hingston; QC (1986); s of Rev Henry Bursell (d 1983), and Cicely Mary, *née* Pawson (d 1977); *b* 10 November 1942; *Educ* St John's Sch Leatherhead, Univ of Exeter (LLB), St Edmund Hall Oxford (MA, DPhil), St Stephen House Oxford; *m* 1 July 1967, Joanna Ruth, da of Maj Robert Peter Davies Gibb (d 1999); 2 s (Michael Hingston b 1970, James David Hingston b 1972), 1 da (Polly Joanna Hingston b 1976); *Career* called to the Bar Lincoln's Inn 1968, circuit judge (Western Circuit) 1988–2003, official referee, judge of the Technol and Construction Ct 1992–08, designated civil judge 1998, sr circuit judge 2003–08, ret 2008; ordained: deacon 1968, priest 1969; hon curate: St Marylebone 1968–69, St Mary The Virgin Almondsbury 1969–71, St Francis Bedminster 1971–83, Christ Church, St Stephen Bristol 1983–88, St Mary The Virgin Cheddar 1993–2011, gen licence to officiate Dio of Oxford 2011–; chllr, vicar gen and official princ: Dio of Durham 1989–, Dio of Bath & Wells 1992–93, Dio of St Albans 1992–2002, Dio of Oxford 2002–14 (chllr emeritus 2014–); hon canon ChCh Oxford 2011–13; dep chllr: Dio of York 1994–2007, Dio of St Albans 2003–13; hon chaplain 3 Vol Mil Intelligence Bn 1996–2001; *Books* Atkins Court Forms (contrib Ecclesiastical Law), Halsbury's Laws of England: Cremation and Burial and Ecclesiastical Law (contrib), Principles of Dermatitis Legislation (contrib), Crown Court Practice (jtly), Liturgy, Order and the Law; *Recreations* church music, military history, archaeology of Greece, Turkey and the Holy Land; *Clubs* MCC; *Style—* His Hon Canon Rupert Bursell, QC; ✉ Pear Tree Cottage, Hatchet Leys Lane, Thornborough, Buckinghamshire MK18 2BU (☎ 01280 822995, e-mail rdhb@xaipe.eu)

BURSTEIN, Joan; CBE (2006); da of Ashley Harvey Jotner (d 1956), and Mary, *née* Pleeth (d 1956); *b* 21 February 1926; *Educ* Henrietta Barnet Sch, Hampstead Garden Suburb; *m* Sidney Burstein (d 2010); 1 da (Caroline b 1949), 1 s (Simon b 1951); *Career* opened Browns: South Molton St 1970, Sloane St 1976; introduced many designers to London, Donna Karan, Giorgio Armani, Ralph Lauren, Calvin Klein, Romeo Gigli; V&A Award for Outstanding Achievement in Fashion 2006; Hon Dr Univ of the Arts London 2007; *Style—* Mrs Joan Burstein, CBE; ✉ Browns, 27 South Molton Street, London W1K 5RD (☎ 020 7514 0000, fax 020 7408 1281, e-mail buyingoffice@brownsfashion.com)

BURSTOW, Paul Kenneth; s of Brian Seymour Burstow, and Sheila, *née* Edmonds; *b* 13 May 1962; *Educ* Glastonbury HS for Boys Carshalton, Carshalton Coll, South Bank Univ (BA); *m* 11 Nov 1995, Mary; 3 c; *Career* Assoc of Lib Dem Cnclls: cncllrs' offr 1989–92, campaigns offr 1992–96, acting political sec 1996–97; MP (Lib Dem) Sutton and Cheam 1997–2015; Lib Dem spokesman on disabled people 1997–98, chief spokesman on local government 1997–99, Lib Dem shadow min for older people 1999–2003, chief spokesman on health 2003–05, chief whip 2006–10, min of state for health 2010–; chm All-Pty Parly Gp on Back Pain, chm All-Pty Parly Gp on Health and Wellbeing in Schs, co-chm All-Pty Parly Gp on Older People, vice-chm All-Pty Disablement Gp, vice-chm All-Pty Gp on ME, sec All Pty Gp on Parkinsons, memb All-Pty Parly Gp on Personal Soc Servs Panel; dep ldr London Borough of Sutton 1994–97 (cncllr 1986–2002); *Recreations* walking, cycling, cooking, working out in gym; *Clubs* National Liberal; *Style—* Paul Burstow, Esq; ✉ 234 Gander Green Lane, Cheam SM3 9FQ (website www.paulburstow.org.uk)

BURT, Prof Alastair David; s of George Hoggan Burt, of Glasgow, and Iris Helen Forrest Burt; *b* 9 March 1957; *Educ* Hummersknott GS Darlington, Eastwood HS Glasgow, Univ of Glasgow (BSc, MB ChB, MD); *m* 29 Dec 1980, Alison Carol, *née* Tweedlie; 1 da (Jennifer Alison b 24 Oct 1984), 1 s (Stuart Alastair b 20 Aug 1988); *Career* jr house offr in gen med Western Infirmary Glasgow 1981–82, jr house offr in gen surgery Royal Infirmary Glasgow 1982, SHO and registrar in pathology Western Infirmary Glasgow 1982–85, Peel travelling research fell Lab for Cell Biology and Histology Free Univ of Brussels 1985–86, registrar and sr registrar in pathology Western Infirmary Glasgow 1986–89; Newcastle Univ: sr lectr in pathology 1989–95, personal professorship in hepatopathology 1995–98, prof of pathology and head Sch of Clinical and Lab Sciences 1998–2005; head of clinical service Dept of Cellular Pathology 1999–2005 Newcastle upon Tyne Hosps NHS Tst; latterly dean of clinical medicine Newcastle Univ; exec dean Faculty of Health Sciences Univ of Adelaide 2014–; visiting prof Univ of Otago 1993; ed Basic Sciences Section Hepatogastroenterology 1994–97, ed-in-chief Liver 1998–2002, asst ed Gastroenterology Research and Practice 2008–; memb: Editorial Bd Jl of Hepatology 1995–97, Editorial Bd Jl of Gastroenterology and Hepatology 1996–2005, Ctee on Pubn Ethics 1999–2002, Int Advsy Bd Med Molecular Morphology 2002–, Advsy Bd Clinical Science 2002–, Editorial Advsy Bd Jl of Pathology 2006– (reviews ed 1994–97), Editorial Bd World Jl of Gastroenterology 2007–, Editorial Bd Liver Disease Review 2009–, Editorial Bd World J Hepatol 2010– (ed-in-chief histopathology 2012–); memb: Int Hepatopathology Gp 1995–, Research Assessment Exercise 2008 Panel A Subpanel 5, REF 2014 Sub Panel 1; treas and tstee Pathological Soc of GB and I 2003–12; memb: Br Assoc for the Study of the Liver 1990–, Int Assoc for the Study of the Liver 1990–, European Assoc for the Study of the Liver 1991–, American Assoc for the Society of Liver Diseases 1992–, Caledonian Soc Gastroenterology 1993–, NY Acad of Sciences 1995–97, Assoc of Profs of Pathology 1996–, Laennec Soc 1999–, Br Soc of Gastroenterology 2003–, Int Acad of Pathologists (Br Div); corresponding memb Hans Popper Hepatopathology Soc 1991–, perm memb Int Gastro-Surgical Club 1993–, hon memb Cuban Soc of Pathology 1997, fndr memb European Club for Liver Cell Biology 2000–, hon life memb Glasgow Univ Medico-Chirurgical Soc; Bellahouston Medal Univ of Glasgow 1992, C L Oakley lectr Pathological Soc of GB and I 1993, Ishak meml lectr 2005, Vincent McGovern meml lectr 2007; FRSB 1996 (MIBiol 1991), FRCPath 1997 (MRCPath 1988), FRCP 2009, FRCPA 2014, fell Australian Acad of Health and Med Scis 2015; *Books* Pathology of the Liver (jtly, 3 edn 1994, 4 edn 2001, First Prize/Highly Commended Medical Book Awards, ed-in-chief 5 edn 2007, 6 edn 2012), Multiple Choice Questions in Clinical Pathology (jtly, 1995), Liver Inflammation and Fibrogenesis (1996), Muir's Textbook of Pathology (14 edn); *Recreations* music (baroque and contemporary classic), cooking; *Clubs* Athenaeum; *Style—* Prof Alastair D Burt; ✉ Faculty of Health Sciences, Barr Smith Building, North Terrace Campus, University of Adelaide, Adelaide, SA 5000, Australia (☎ 0061 8 8313 5193, e-mail alastair.burt@adelaide.edu.au)

BURT, Alistair James Hendrie; PC (2013), MP; s of James Hendrie Burt and Mina Christie Robertson; *b* 25 May 1955, Manchester; *Educ* Bury GS, St John's Coll Oxford, Chester Coll of Law; *m* 1983, Eve Alexandra Twite; 1 s, 1 da; *Career* slr; memb London Borough of Haringey 1982–84; MP (Cons): Bury North 1983–97, Beds NE 2001–; PPS to Rt Hon Kenneth Baker MP 1985–90, Parly under-sec of state for Social Security 1992–95, min of state DSS 1995–97, shadow min for Educn and Skills 2001–02, PPS to Iain Duncan Smith 2002–03, PPS to Michael Howard 2003–05, shadow min for communities and regeneration 2005–07, shadow min for local govt and regeneration 2007–08, oppn asst chief whip 2008–10, dep chm (devpt) Cons Pty 2008–10, Parly under-sec of state FCO 2010–13, min of state for health 2015–; sponsor min for Manchester and Salford 1994–97; sr search conslt Whitehead Mann GKR plc 1997–2001; vice-pres Tory Reform Gp; *Recreations* family, modern art, music, sport, gardening; *Clubs* Biggleswade Athletic; *Style—* The Rt Hon Alistair Burt, MP; ✉ House of Commons, London SW1A 0AA (☎ 020 7219 8132, e-mail alistair.burt.mp@parliament.uk, website www.alistair-burt.co.uk)

BURT, David Jeffery; OBE (1985); *b* 24 March 1935; *Career* non-exec dir Deutsch Corp NY; chm: Optical Consumer Complaints Cncl, High Ground EBA LLP Mentoring Services; sr advsr Wendel Gp Paris; Liveryman Worshipful Co of Spectacle Makers 1993; FIPM, FRSA; *Recreations* sculptor (exhibited at RA Summer Exhbn), classic rally driver, farmer, squash player; *Style—* David Burt, Esq, OBE; ✉ e-mail djburt@highgroundeba.co.uk

BURT, Maxwell John (Max); s of Dr Nicholas Burt (d 1988), and Margaret, *née* Anderson; *b* 16 December 1964, London; *Educ* Westminster, Univ of Bristol (BA); *m* 1, Lucy, *née* Eadie; m 2, Justine O'Brien; *Career* Abbott Mead Vickers BBDO 1988–91, Butterfield Day Devito Hockney 1991–92, Abbott Mead Vickers BBDO 1992–96, D'Arcy Masius Benton & Bowles 1996–99, Good 2003–08, Disability Consulting 2009–12, Max Burt Consulting 2012–; tstee Diversability 2009–13, tstee WheelEasy 2013–; Best Paper Award MRS 1995, Grand and Gold Awards AME Int Advtg & Mktg Effectiveness Awards 1995, Grand Prix and Gold Award IPA Advtg Effectiveness Awards 1996, Stelios Disabled Entrepreneur of the Year 2007; memb: MRS 1989, AQRP 1989, APG 1989, D&AD 1995, IPA 1996, Mktg Soc 1997; *Recreations* collecting signed photographs; *Style—* Max Burt, Esq; ✉ e-mail max@maxburt.com

BURT, Sir Peter Alexander; kt (2003); s of Robert Wallace Burt (d 1970), of Longniddry, E Lothian, and May Henderson, *née* Rodger (d 1991); *b* 6 March 1944; *Educ* Merchiston Castle Sch Edinburgh, Univ of St Andrews (MA), Univ of St Andrews (LLD), Univ of Pennsylvania (Thouron scholar, MBA); *m* 23 April 1971, Alison Mackintosh, da of John M Turner, OBE (d 1991), of Kilmarnock; 3 s (Michael Wallace b 1975, Hamish Jonathan b 1978, Angus Moncrieff b 1984); *Career* Hewlett Packard Co Palo Alto Calif 1968–70, Conversational Software Ltd Edinburgh 1970–74, Edward Bates & Sons Edinburgh 1974; Bank of Scotland: joined 1975, asst gen mangr Int Div 1979–84, divnl gen mangr Int Div 1984–85, jt gen mangr Int Div 1985–88, chief gen mangr and chm Mgmnt Bd 1988–96, appointed main bd dir 1995, chief exec 1996–2001, dep chm HBOS plc 2001–03; chm Gleacher Shacklock 2000–08, non-exec chm ITV plc 2004–07, chm Promethean Investments LLP 2005–; non-exec dir: Shell Transport & Trading 2002–04, Royal Dutch Shell 2004–06; dir Templeton Emerging Markets Investment Trust plc 2004–; chm Int Centre for Mathematical Sciences 2006–; FCIB (Scotland), FRSE; *Recreations* golf, tennis, skiing, reading; *Clubs* Royal & Ancient, Hon Co of Edinburgh Golfers, Gullane Golf; *Style—* Sir Peter Burt

BURT OF SOLIHULL, Baroness (Life Peer UK 2015), of Solihull in the County of West Midlands Lorely Burt; *b* 10 September 1954; *Educ* High Arcal GS, Univ of Swansea, Open Univ (MBA), FT Non-exec Dir Dip; *m* Richard; 1 da, 1 step s; *Career* sometime asst govr HM Prison Service, personnel trg mangr, business conslt and md of small business in adult trg, mktg and financial servs; Parly candidate (Lib Dem) Dudley S 2001, MP (Lib Dem) Solihull 2005–15; PPS to chief sec to the Treasy 2012–; chair Lib Dem Parly Pty, memb federal exec Lib Dem Pty 2012–; former cncllr (Lib Dem) Dudley MBC; former memb: Lib Dem Fed Policy Ctee, W Midlands Regional Exec; govt champion Women in Enterprise 2014; Int Luminary Award Women's Business Enterprise Nat Cncl 2009; fell Institute of Sales and Mktg Mgmnt (ISMM); *Style—* The Baroness Burt of Solihull; ✉ House of Lords, London SW1A 0PW (☎ 020 7219 8269, e-mail burtl@parliament.uk, website www.solihull-libdems.org.uk, Twitter @LorelyBurt)

BURTON, Amanda; *b* 10 October 1956, Derry, NI; *Educ* Ballougry Primary Sch, Londonderry HS, Manchester Poly Sch of Theatre; *m* (m dis); 2 da (Phoebe Marie, Brid Irina); *Career* actress; Hon DLitt Univ of Ulster 2006; FRSA; *Theatre* incl: Playhouse Theatre Lancaster, Octagon Theatre Bolton; *Television* incl: Brookside (Channel Four) 1982–86, Boon (Central) 1988, Inspector Morse (Zenith), A Casualty of War 1990, The Greek Myths – Theseus and the Minotaur (Jim Henson Organisation) 1990, Stay Lucky (Yorkshire), Lovejoy (BBC), Minder (Thames), Medics (Granada), Peak Practice (Central) 1993–95, Silent Witness (BBC) 1996–2004, The Precious Blood (Screen 2) 1996, The Gift (Screen 1) 1998, Forgotten (LWT) 1999, Little Bird (Granada) 2000, The Whistle Blower (BBC) 2001, Bears in Idaho (BBC documentary), Helen West (ITV) 2002, Pollyanna (ITV) 2003, The Commander 2003, 2004 and 2007, Miss Marple 2006, Waterloo Road 2009–10, Masterchef 2014, Midsomer Murders 2014, The Dog with the Woman 2015, The Level 2016; *Film* Bronson 2009; *Awards* Nat TV Awards 1998, 1999 and 2001, Festival of TV Monte Carlo 1999, Woman of the Year Irish Tatler 2004; *Clubs* Whippet, BAFTA; *Style—* Ms Amanda Burton; ✉ c/o Denee De Emmony, Independent Talent Group, 40 Whitfield Street, London W1T 2RH

BURTON, Amanda Jane; da of Michael Charles Pearson Burton, of N Yorks, and Ann Margaret Burton, of Suffolk; *b* 3 January 1959; *Educ* Queen Ethelburga's Harrogate, Bradford Girls' GS, Univ of Durham (BA), Coll of Law Guildford; *Career* slr Slaughter and May 1982–86, asst co sec Tiphook plc 1986–90, co sec Ratners Gp plc 1990–92; Meyer International plc: co sec 1992–97, legal and corp servs dir 1997–2000; Clifford Chance: regnl chief operating offr 2000–07, dir of global business servs 2006–10, chief operating offr 2010–14; non-exec dir: Fresca Gp Ltd 1998–2010, UCM Timber plc 2002–03, Galliford Try plc 2005–14, Monitise plc 2014–, Copthorne Hldgs Ltd 2014–, HSS Hire Gp plc 2015–; tstee Battersea Dogs and Cats Home 2010– (vice-chm 2014); memb Law Soc; *Recreations* travel, painting, theatre, museums; *Clubs* Annabel's; *Style—* Miss Amanda Burton; ☎ 07881 588798, e-mail burtonamanda001@gmail.com

BURTON, Anthony George Graham; s of Donald Graham Burton (d 1960), and Irene, *née* Trotter (d 1992); *b* 24 December 1934; *Educ* King James's GS Knaresborough, Univ of Leeds; *m* 28 March 1959, Pip, da of Walter Sharman (d 1961); 2 s (Jonathan b 1961, Nicholas b 1964), 1 da (Jenny b 1963); *Career* freelance writer and broadcaster; *Books* incl: A Programmed Guide to Office Warfare (1969), The Jones Report (1970), The Canal Builders (1972, 4 edn 2005), The Reluctant Musketeer (1973), Canals in Colour (1974), Remains of a Revolution (1975, 2 edn 2001), The Master Idol (1975), The Navigators (1976), The Miners (1976), Josiah Wedgwood (1976), Canal (with Derek Pratt, 1976), Industrial Archaeological Sites of Britain (1977), A Place to Stand (1977), Back Door Britain (1977), The Green Bag Travellers (with Pip Burton, 1978), The Past at Work (1980), The Rainhill Story (1980), The Past Afloat (1982), The Shell Book of Curious Britain (1982), The Changing River (1982), The Waterways of Britain (1983), The National Trust Guide to Our Industrial Past (1983), The Rise and Fall of King Cotton (1984), Walking the Line (1985), Wilderness Britain (1985), Britain's Light Railways (jtly, 1985), Britain Revisited (1986), The Shell Book of Undiscovered Britain and Ireland (1986), Landscape Detective (jtly, 1986), Opening Time (1987), Steaming Through Britain (1987), Walking Through History (1988), Walk the South Downs (1988), The Yorkshire Dales and York (1989), The Great Days of the Canals (1989), Astonishing Britain (1990), Cityscapes (1990), Slow Roads (1991), The Railway Builders (1992), Canal Mania (1993), The Grand Union Canal Walk (with Neil Curtis, 1993), The Railway Empire (1994), The Rise and Fall of British Shipbuilding (1994, 2 edn 2013), The Dales Way (1995), The Cotswold Way (1995), The West Highland Way (1996), The Southern Upland Way (1997), William Cobbett: Englishman (1997), The Wye Valley Walk (1998), The Caledonian Canal (1998), Best Foot Forward (1998), The Cumbria Way (1999), The Wessex Ridgeway (1999), Thomas Telford (1999), Weekend Walks Dartmoor and Exmoor (2000), Weekend Walks The Yorkshire Dales (2000), Traction Engines (2000), Richard Trevithick (2000), Weekend Walks in the Peak District (2001), The Orient Express (2001), The Anatomy of Canals: The Early Years (2001), The Daily Telegraph Guide to Britain's Working Past (2002), The Anatomy of Canals: the Mania Years (2002), The Daily Telegraph Guide to Britain's Maritime Past (2003), Hadrian's Wall Walk (2003), The Anatomy of Canals: Decline and Renewal (2003), On the Rails (2004), The Ridgeway (2005), The Cotswold Way (2007), Tracing Your Shipbuilding Ancestors (2010), Canal 250 (2011), The Navvies (2012), The Miners (2013), Life on the Canal (2013), Life on the Railway (2013), Life in the Mine (2013), Life in the Mill (2013), Life on the Farm (2013), Matthew Boutlon (2013); *Recreations* steam engines, boats, walking, beer; *Style—* Anthony Burton, Esq; ✉ e-mail anthonyggburton@btinternet.com

BURTON, Caroline M; *Career* joined Guardian Royal Exchange 1973, variously investment mangr (Stock Exchange Overseas), md Guardian Asset Management Ltd and md Guardian Unit Managers Ltd, gp exec dir (investment) Guardian Royal Exchange plc 1990–99; chm TR Property Investment Tst (formerly non-exec dir); non exec dir: Rathbone Bros plc 2003–12, Liverpool Victoria Friendly Soc 2011–, Blackrock Smaller Companies Investment Tst plc 2011–; memb Hermes Property Unit Tst Appt Ctee 2006–; *Style—* Ms Caroline Burton

BURTON, Charles Philip Henry; s of Sir George Vernon Kennedy Burton, CBE, DL (d 2009), and Sarah Katherine, *née* Tcherniavsky; *b* 6 December 1952; *Educ* Charterhouse, Univ of Exeter (BA); *m* 2 Nov 1985, Susanna Louise, da of Peter Henry Buller; 2 da (Sophie Mary, Rose Elizabeth (twins) b 7 July 1993); *Career* economist Beecham Pharmaceuticals Ltd 1974–75; CBI 1975–85: head industrial trends and economic forecasting, dep dir Economic Directorate; business devpt mangr Wharton Econometric Forecasting Assocs Ltd 1985–88, chief exec Business Strategies Ltd 1996–2003 (jt md 1988–96), md Micromarketing Div Experian Ltd 2003–08, dir Oxford Economics Ltd 2008–, chm Sofia Property Fund Ltd (formerly Lewis Charles Sofia Property Fund Ltd) 2008–; fell Soc of Business Economists (memb Cncl 1996–, hon treas 1997–2006), memb Econ Advsy Ctee Univ of Strathclyde 1996–2006, memb Scottish Economic Conslts Gp Sottish Govt; FRSA; *Books* Competition and Markets (1990); *Recreations* music, history, photography; *Clubs* RAC, MCC; *Style—* Charles Burton, Esq; ✉ Oxford Economics Limited, Broadwall House, 21 Broadwall, London SE1 9PL (☎ 020 7803 1400, fax 020 7936 9231)

BURTON, (Anthony) David; CBE (1992); s of Leslie Mitchell Burton (d 1967), and Marion, *née* Marsh (d 1976); *b* 2 April 1937; *Educ* Arnold Sch Blackpool; *m* 30 May 1964, Valerie, da of Harry Swire, of Burnley, Lancs; 2 da (Judith Alison b 1966, Anne Louise b 1968), 1 s (Michael John b 1971); *Career* Nat Serv RAPC 1955–57; chief dealer Bank of America NT & SA 1967–72, exec dir S G Warburg & Co Ltd 1979–92; LIFFE: fndr memb Working Party 1979, dir 1980–94, chm Membership & Rules Ctee 1982–88, dep chm 1985–88, chm 1988–92; chm: S G Warburg Futures & Options Ltd 1988–92, Marshalls Finance Ltd (int money brokers) 1989–98, Ludgate 181 Ltd 1999–2002, Ludgate 181 (Jersey) Ltd 2002–11, Ludgate Investments Ltd 2004–10, Beechwood House Finance Ltd 2004–11, Ashley House plc 2004–07, Ashley House Properties Ltd 2005–07, The 181 Fund Ltd 2011–; fndr memb Assoc of Futures Brokers and Dealers 1986–88; memb: Br Invisible Exports Cncl 1988–90, Euro Ctee Br Invisibles 1990–92; dir: British Invisibles 1992–93, The Securities Inst 1992–93; non-exec dir Car Crash Line Gp plc 2003–05; memb Governing Bd City Res Project 1991–94; Freeman City of London 1984, Liveryman Worshipful Co of Glass Sellers 1984; FCIB, FCT; *Books* collector, lectr and writer on: early English glass c 1600–1800, English blackjacks and leather bottles c 1550–1700, early German Rhenish pottery c 1500–1650, Antique Sealed Bottles 1640–1900 and the families who owned them (2015); *Recreations* fine wine, travel, sport, music, opera; *Style—* David Burton, Esq, CBE; ✉ e-mail david@burton1.com

BURTON, David Gowan; s of Reginald Frank Burton (d 1967), of Woodford Green, Essex, and Nellie Erwin, *née* Biggs (d 1991); *b* 3 April 1943; *Educ* McEntree Tech Sch; *m* 8 Aug 1970, Hilary Kathleen, da of Canon Robert Smith; 2 s (Matthew Edward Gowan b 21 Oct 1972, Simon James Gowan b 19 May 1983), 1 da (Emma Claire b 8 Sept 1975); *Career* articles with Keens Shay Keens & Co 1960–65, Thomson McLintock 1965–73 (latterly sr mangr), sr mangr Neville Russell & Co (now Mazars) 1973–75; Touche Ross & Co (now Deloitte LLP): sr mangr 1975–79, ptnr 1979–93, seconded from London to IOM 1983–91, estab Green Field office IOM 1985, ptnr Cambridge office 1991–93; estab private consultancy and corp fin practice 1993; dir: IDEM Holdings Ltd 1999–2002, City Life Ltd 1999–2002, SigmaQC Ltd 2001–09; chm: Ossys Holdings Ltd 1999–2004, Globaltech Solutions Ltd 2002–09, Aon Alexander and Alexander UK Pensions Tstees Ltd 2006–12 (dir 2001–), Aon UK Pension Scheme 2006–12, Hirco plc 2006–, Aon Retirement Plan 2012–; founding ptnr Argyll Assocs 2004–, assoc ptnr Lancea Ptnrs Ltd 2005–; memb Advsy Bd Campbell Lutyens & Co Ltd (Corp Fin Boutique) 1993–2003; chm Combined Britons Pension Plan 2006–12; memb Bd of Mgmnt Springboard Housing Assoc 1993–99, memb Bd of Tstees St Francis Hospice Havering-Atte-Bower 2001–; chm of tstees: Jubilee Centre, Relationships Fndn 1996–2002; treas Church Army 1995–2000; govr Chigwell Sch 1992–2002; Liveryman Worshipful Co of CAs in England and Wales; FCA 1976 (ACA 1965), FRSA 1993; *Recreations* family, golf, walking, gardening, farming; *Clubs* New (Edinburgh) Chigwell Golf; *Style—* David Burton, Esq; ✉ 3 The Green, Woodford Green, Essex IG8 0NF (☎ 020 8505 5402, mobile 07976 713662, e-mail burton.d@btinternet.com)

BURTON, Diane Elizabeth (Di); da of Victor St Clair Yates, of Durban, South Africa, and Betty, *née* Woolliscroft; *b* 26 July 1954, Johannesburg; *Educ* Univ of the Witwatersrand (BA), Huddersfield Poly (PGCE), Damelin Mgmnt Sch Johannesburg (DipPR); *m* 1979, Andrew Thomas Guy Burton; 1 da (Sarah St Clair b 1980), 1 s (Rupert Thomas b 1982); *Career* emigrated to UK 1985, dir Moss International Ltd 1988–89, md Cicada PR Ltd 2002–15, currently dir Di Burton Ltd; sr lectr Leeds Business Sch 1992–94, Faculty of Media Univ of Leeds 1994–2001, conslt fell Univ of Leeds 1998–, external examiner Northumbria Univ 2015–19; memb Mktg Standards Lead Body for Dept for Educn and Employment NVQ Devpt; memb Cncl IPR 1998–2003; memb Cabinet Office Govt Communications Review Team; tstee: Harrogate Theatre, Northern Aldborough Festival; Business Personality of the Year Ackrill Media Gp Business Awards 2005, listed in PR Week's PowerBook 2010–13; hon fell Leeds Trinity UC Leeds; MInstD 1989 (chm Export Award Scheme); *Recreations* tennis, yoga, gardening; *Clubs* Reform, Two Percent; *Style—* Mrs Di Burton, FCIPR, FCIPD; ✉ website www.diburton.uk, Twitter @Di_Burton

BURTON, Dr Frances Rosemary; da of Maj Richard Francis Heveningham Pughe, DFC, ERD (d 1990), of Ridlington, Norfolk, and Pamela Margaret, *née* Coates (d 1978); *b* 19 June 1941; *Educ* St Mary's Convent Bishop's Stortford, Tortington Park Arundel, Lady Margaret House Cambridge, St Anne's Coll Oxford, Univ of London (LLB), Univ of Leicester (LLM, MA), Liverpool John Moores Univ (PhD); *m* 1, 26 Oct 1963 (m dis 1973), Robert Scott Alexander (later Baron Alexander of Weedon, QC (Life Peer), d 2005), s of Samuel James Alexander (d 1965), of Fleet, Hants; 2 s (David Robert James b 1964, William Richard Scott b 1969), 1 da (Mary Frances Anne b 1966); m 2, 28 Nov 1975 (m dis 1991), David Michael Burton (d 2000), s of Frank Raymond Burton (d 1965), of Wellington, Salop; 2 da (Jane Richenda Frances b 1979, Charlotte Alice Octavia b 1981); *Career* called to the Bar Middle Temple 1970 (Harmsworth Major Entrance Exhibition, ad eundem Lincoln's Inn 1972); in practice Chancery Bar 1973–75 and 1989–2012, mediator 2000–, family arbitrator 2014–; tutor for Bar and Law Soc examinations, lectr and tutor Dept of Law and Faculty of Business City of London Poly 1989–93, dir of Bar courses BPP Law Sch 1992–93 (memb Advsy Bd 1993–2000), sr lectr in Law London Guildhall Univ 1993–2001, lectr Coll of Law of England and Wales 2001–02, princ lectr UWE 2002–08, co-dir Centre for Family Law and Practice London Met Univ 2009–13 (research fell 2010–13), co-dir Int Centre for Family Law, Policy and Practice (www.famlawandpractice.com) 2013–; visiting assoc lectr Bucks New Univ 2012–, visiting lectr Middlesex Univ 2014–15, visiting lectr Aston Univ 2014–15; dep traffic cmmr S Eastern and Metropolitan Eastern and Western Traffic Areas 1996–2002, legal chm Residential Property Tbnl Service (formerly London Rent Assessment Panel) 1997–2011, judicial chm Tport Tbnl 2002–09, judge Upper Tbnl (Administrative Appeals Chamber) 2009–11; vice-pres Assoc of Women Barristers 2003– (memb Ctee 1996–, hon treas 1998–99, vice-chair 1999–2001, chair 2001–03); author of legal text books; govr Westminster Coll 1969–73; numerous fundraising activities incl: Justice Br Section Int Cmmn of Jurists 1963–2000, Peckham Settlement 1973–85, Jubilee Sailing Tst 1985–, Cancer Res Campaign 1986–87, Duke of Edinburgh's Award Scheme 1987; chm Ctee Justice Ball 1983 and 1985, memb Exec Ctee Big Bang City Ball 1986; MCIArb 2014; *Books* Family Law Textbook (1988, revised edn 1990), Bar Final General Paper Textbook (1990), Family Law – Documents, Forms and Precedents (1992), Criminal Litigation (jtly, 1994, 3 edn 1997), Family Law and Practice (1996), Guide to the Family Law Act 1996 (1996), Teaching Family Law (jtly, 1999), Family Law Textbook (2003), ILEX Family Law Manual (2004), Core Statutes on Family Law (2005, 11 edn 2016), Family Law (2012, 2 edn 2015); *Recreations* opera, history, archaeology; *Clubs* Oxford and Cambridge; *Style—* Dr Frances Burton; ✉ 10 Old Square, Lincoln's Inn, London WC2A 3SU (☎ 020 7405 0758, fax 020 7831 8237, mobile 07775 655088, e-mail frb@frburton.com)

BURTON, Frank Patrick; QC (1998); s of Robert Burton; *b* 19 June 1950; *Educ* Salesian Coll Farnborough, Univ of Kent (BA), LSE (PhD), City Univ (Dip Law); *m* 1983, Caroline Reid; 3 c (Daniel b 1 July 1984, Thomas b 8 Jan 1986, Tamar b 8 Sept 1987); *Career* lectr 1976–82, called to the Bar 1982 (bencher 2004), recorder 2000– (asst recorder 1999), dep judge of the High Court of Justice 2010; chm Law Reform Ctee Bar Cncl 2003–, chm Personal Injury Bar Assoc 2004– (exec memb 1996–, vice-chm 2002–04); *Publications* The Politics of Legitimacy, Official Discourse (with P Carlen), Personal Injury Limitation Law (1994), Medical Negligence (1995); *Recreations* reading, sport, Suffolk; *Style—* Frank Burton, Esq, QC; ✉ 12 King's Bench Walk, Temple, London EC4Y 7EL (☎ 020 7583 0811, fax 020 7583 7228, e-mail burton@12kbw.co.uk)

BURTON, Gerald; s of Edward Neville Burton (d 1985), of Kelsall, Cheshire, and Mary Elizabeth, *née* Bull (d 1977); *b* 12 August 1938, Weaverham, Cheshire; *Educ* Liverpool Collegiate GS; *m* 1, 1963 (m dis 2000), Gillian Margaret, da of John Dean Wilson (d 1986), of West Kirby, Cheshire; 3 s (John, James, Andrew), 1 da (Deborah); m 2, 2000, Carol Jane, da of Tom Moody (d 2001), of Driffield, E Yorks; *Career* Kidsons Impey (now Baker Tilly) chartered accountants: joined 1961, ptnr 1965, sr ptnr 1989–92; ptnr Cozumel Management Services 1993–2004; chief exec WRVS 1992–2002; dir: Regent House Properties Ltd 1993–, Bellerive Ltd 2007–, DRT Lease Ltd 2007–, Regent House Properties (Romania) Ltd 2007–14, Lebada Hotel (Bucharest) Inc 2007–14; non-exec dir: Bradford and Bingley Building Soc London region 1994–97, Bethlem Maudsley NHS Tst 1994–99, Oxfordshire HA 2000–02; Freeman City of London 1980, Hon Asst and Liveryman Worshipful Co of Basketmakers 1982; FCA; *Recreations* golf, music, wine; *Clubs* City Livery; *Style—* Gerald Burton, Esq; ✉ Le Village, Cazaril-Tambourès, 31580, France (☎ 00 33 9 6521 7723, e-mail gerry.burton1@wanadoo.fr)

BURTON, Sir Graham Stuart; KCMG (1999, CMG 1987); s of Cyril Stanley Richard Burton (d 1982), and Jessie Blythe Burton (d 1992); *b* 8 April 1941; *Educ* Sir William Borlase's Sch Marlow; *m* 30 Jan 1965, Julia Margaret Lappin; 1 da (b 1966), 1 s (b 1967); *Career* HM Dip Serv; FO 1961, Abu Dhabi 1964, ME Centre for Arabic Studies 1967, Kuwait 1969, FCO 1972, Tunis 1975, UK Mission to UN 1978, cnsllr Tripoli 1981, FCO 1984–87, consul-gen San Francisco 1987–90; ambass to: UAE 1990–94, Indonesia 1994–97; high cmmr to Nigeria and non-resident ambass to Benin 1997–2001; dir Gulf of Guinea Energy Ltd 2006–09, advsr Control Risks Gp 2001–12, dir W Africa Business Assoc 2004–10, dir Magadi Soda 2001–9; tstee Sightsavers Int 2005–09 (vice-pres 2014–), tstee Chalker Fndn 2005–; *Recreations* most sports, golf, travel, classical music, America; *Clubs* MCC; *Style—* Sir Graham Burton, KCMG; ✉ e-mail burtongsjm@aol.com

BURTON, Ian Richard; s of Jack Burton (d 1971), of Manchester, and Faie Burton (d 2002); *Educ* Whittingeham Coll Brighton; *m* 1973, Sarah Ruth, da of Reginald Ashbrook; 1 da (Lissa Rachel b 1975), 1 s (Jack David b 1978); *Career* admitted slr 1971; ptnr Nigel Copeland Glickman 1971–82, fndr and sr ptnr Burton Copeland Manchester 1982–2001, fndr and sr ptnr BCL Burton Copeland London 1991–; memb: Law Soc 1971, Int Bar Assoc, Assoc of Regulatory and Disciplinary Lawyers (ARDL), Commercial Fraud Lawyers Assoc (CFLA), American Bar Assoc (ABA); *Recreations* family, opera; *Clubs* RAC, Mark's; *Style—* Ian Burton, Esq; ✉ BCL Burton Copeland, 51 Lincoln's Inn Fields, London WC2A 3LZ (☎ 020 7430 2277, fax 020 7430 1101, e-mail ianburton@bcl.com)

BURTON, (Sara) Jocelyn Margarita Elissa; da of Wing Cdr Roland Louis Ernest Burton, AFC (ret), of Correze, France, and Sian Joan, *née* Gwilliam Evans (d 1980); *b* 10 January 1946; *Educ* St Clare's Sch Devon, Lady Margaret House Cambridge, Sir John Cass Coll Central Sch of Art; *Career* Diamonds Int award 1968, first solo exhibition Archer Gallery Dover St 1971, modern silver collection for Jean Renet Bond St 1970–75; pieces in many public and private collections throughout world; works incl: silver table fountain for Worshipful Co of Fishmongers 1975, Fitzwilliam Cup 1984, centrepiece for Sir Roy Strong V&A; Prince Phillip City and Guilds Gold Medal for Services to Silversmithing 2003; Freeman: City of London 1974, Worshipful Co of Goldsmiths; *Recreations* playing harpsichord, travel, reading; *Clubs* Blacks, Academy; *Style—* Miss Jocelyn Burton; ✉ 50C Red Lion Street, Holborn, London WC1R 4PF (☎ 020 7405 3042, fax 020 7831 9324, e-mail jocelynburton@hotmail.com)

BURTON, John Michael; MBE (2013); s of Gerald Victor Burton, of Northampton, and Kathleen Blodwyn, *née* Harper; *b* 21 May 1945; *Educ* Oxford Sch of Architecture, DipArch; *m* 11 Sept 1971, Sally, da of Norman Donaby Bason (d 1987), of Northampton; 1 da (Amy Victoria b 17 Jan 1975), 1 s (Thomas Donaby b 19 April 1977); *Career* architect; sr ptnr Purcell, Architects; conservation of: Wingfield Coll 1972–74, Lavenham Guildhall 1973–94, Holy Trinity Church Long Melford 1974–, Melford Hall 1975–96, Flatford Mill for Nat Tst 1979–85, Colchester Castle 1980–90, Newnham Coll Cambridge 1984–94, St Mary's Thaxted 1988–, Manor House Bury St Edmunds 1990–94, Hunsdon House Herts 1990–96; conservation advsr to the Crown Urban Estate; Surveyor to the Fabric of Canterbury Cathedral 1991–2014 (Surveyor Emeritus 2014–), cmmr Cathedral Fabric Cmmn for England 1996–2006, Surveyor of the Fabric of Westminster Abbey 1999–2012, (Surveyor Emeritus 2012–); pres Cathedral Architects Assoc 1996–99, chm Redundant Churches Uses Ctee Chelmsford; memb Diocesan Advsy Ctee: Chelmsford 1975–, St Edmundsbury & Ipswich 1987–98; govr Kent Inst of Art & Design 1993–2000; memb: Inst of Historic Building Conservation, Church Cmmrs Redundant Churches Ctee, English Heritage Places of Worship Panel, Historic Built Environment Advsy Ctee 1998–2002, Cncl Nat Tst 2007–12, Eastern Region Advsy Bd Nat Tst 2012–; vice-chm Georgian Gp 2014–; chm Colchester Arts Centre 1985–90, dir Mercury Theatre Bd Colchester 1998–2005; Freeman City of London 1996, Liveryman Worshipful Co of Masons 1996 (Master 2013–14), Liveryman Worshipful Co of Carpenters 2007; memb IHBC, RIBA, AABC; *Recreations* skiing, woodwork, archaeology; *Clubs* Athenaeum; *Style—* John M Burton, Esq, MBE; ✉ 50 Creffield Road, Colchester, Essex CO3 3HY (☎ 07970 097415)

BURTON, Simon; s of Peter Burton, of London, and Sheila Burton; *Educ* Emanuel Sch London, Merton Coll Oxford, Ashridge Business Sch; *Partner* Lesley Bainsfair; *Career* House of Lords: clerk 1988–, successively clerk in the Jl Office, Public Bill Office and Ctee Office, seconded to Cabinet Office as private sec to Chief Whip 1996–99, responsible for EU scrutiny 2000–07, responsible for internet strategy 2001–05, HR dir and memb Bd 2007–; Cabinet Office assessor for Far Stream Grad Prog 2008–; *Recreations* House of Lords: clerk 1988–, successively clerk in the Jl Office, Public Bill Office and Ctee Office, seconded to Cabinet Office as private sec to Chief Whip 1996–99, responsible for EU scrutiny 2000–07, responsible for internet strategy 2001–05, HR dir and memb Bd 2007–; Cabinet Office assessor for Far Stream Grad Prog 2008–; govr Dulwich Hamlet Jr Sch 2008–; *Style—* Simon Burton, Esq; ✉ House of Lords, London SW1A 0PW (☎ 020 7219 3185, fax 020 7219 6715)

BURTON-CHADWICK; *see:* Chadwick

BURTON-RACE, John William; s of Denys Arthur Race, and Shirley, *née* Manning; *b* 1 May 1957; *Educ* St Mary's Coll Southampton, Highbury Tech Coll (City & Guilds 706/1, 706/2), Portsmouth Poly (HCITB Cert of Apprenticeship), Westminster Coll; *Career* apprentice Wessex Hotel Winchester 1973–75, commis Quaglino's Hotel Meurice London 1975–76, first commis Chewton Glen Hotel 1976–78, chef Olivers Midhurst 1978–79, chef tournant La Sorbonne Oxford 1979–82, private chef MacKenzie-Hill Property Development International 1982–83, sous chef Les Quat'Saisons Oxford 1983–84, head chef and mangr Le Petit Blanc Oxford 1984–86, chef, md and chm L'Ortolan Shinfield 1986–2000, chef John Burton-Race at Landmark Hotel London 2000–02, in France (French Leave) 2002–03, prop The New Angel Dartmouth 2004–07; memb: Chambre Syndicate de Haute Cuisine Française, Restaurateurs' Assoc of GB; *Awards* Mumm prizewinner 1987, Acorn Award Caterer and Hotelkeeper Magazine, Best in Britain Award Ackerman Guide, five stars AA, three stars Egon Ronay, Restaurant of the Year Egon Ronay 1991, included in Relais Gourmand, five out of five Good Food Guide 1990–94, four and a half out of five Good Food Guide 1995–97, eighteen out of twenty and three red toques Gault Millau Guide, two Michelin stars 1991–96, 1999 and 2001 (one star 1987–90), Personalité de l'Année Chef Lauréat Paris 1991, one Silver and two Gold medals Madrid Euro Olympics 1992, Grand Prix de l'Art de la Cuisine Int Acad of Gastronomy 1994, Chef of the Year Caterer and Hotelkeeper Magazine 1995, 8 out of 10 Good Food Guide 1999, one Michelin star 2005, AA Restaurant of the Year (England) 2005–06; *Television* series advsr and conslt to Chef (starring Lenny Henry, *qv*, BBC1); contrib: Best Fish, Best Game, Best Chocolate series 1987, Master Chefs of Europe 1988, Great British Chefs 1989, Great European Chefs 1990, French Leave 2003, Great British Menu (BBC) 2006, Kitchen Criminals (BBC) 2007, Britain's Best Dish (ITV) 2007, I'm a Celebrity, Get Me out of Here! (ITV) 2007; *Books* Recipes from an English Masterchef (1994), French Leave (2003); *Recreations* Jaguar motor sports, fishing, shooting; *Clubs* 190 Queen's Gate, Acorn; *Style—* John Burton-Race, Esq

BURY, Dr Robert Frederick (Bob); s of William George Bury, and Evelyn Winifred, *née* Liggins; *b* 10 August 1948; *Educ* Kettering GS, Univ of London (BSc), Middx Hosp Med Sch (MB BS); *m* 18 Nov 1972, Linda Joyce, da of Samuel Hart; 3 s (Nicholas b 1974, Mathew b 1977, Tom b 1984), 1 da (Kate b 1976); *Career* MO RAF Med Branch 1971–88: med cadetship 1971–73, surgn PMRAF Hosp 1974–79 (55 Field Surgical Team 1976–77), radiologist 1979–88; conslt radiologist nuclear med 1988–, dir of radiology Leeds Teaching Hosps Tst 1996–99; ed: RCR Newsletter 1992–2004, Clinical Radiology 2006– (asst ed 1990–95, dep ed 1995–2006); FRCS 1978, FRCR 1983; *Books* Radiology: A Practical Guide (1988), Imaging Strategy: A guide for clinicians (with Dr Richard Fowler, 1992), Myocardial Perfusion Scintigraphy: From Request to Report (with Catherine Dickinson, Karen Sheard and Penny Thorley, 2008); *Recreations* hill walking, fishing, writing; *Style—* Dr Bob Bury; ✉ Department of Nuclear Medicine, Leeds General Infirmary, Great George Street, Leeds LS1 3EX (☎ 0113 392 6471, fax 0113 392 2598, e-mail bobbury@gmail.com)

BUSBY, Richard Anthony; s of Ronald Arthur Busby (d 1991), of Bromley, Kent, and Sheila Annora, *née* Fitzherbert (d 1998); *b* 4 June 1950; *Educ* St Dunstan's Coll, Univ of Essex (BA); *m* 1, 24 July 1977 (m dis 1983), Karen, da of Ian Barr, of Edinburgh; m 2, 5 July 1985 (m dis 2006), Kathleen, da of Daniel Henebury (d 1984); 1 s (Lucas b 2006), 2 step s (Rhys b 1997, Brandon b 1997); m 3, 3 May 2006, Sarah, da of Gareth Lewis; *Career* articled clerk Touche Ross 1968–69, asst prodn mangr Hodder & Stoughton 1973–76, mktg mangr Futura Publications 1976–77, md C & C Communications 1977–85, chm and ceo Strategic Sponsorship Ltd 1985–93, ceo BDS Sponsorship Ltd 1993–; memb Variety Club of GB; involved with various environmental and charitable orgns; FRSA; *Publications* Measuring Successful Sponsorship (report); *Recreations* reading, current affairs, art, theatre, opera, sport, jazz and cinema; *Style—* Richard Busby, Esq; ✉ BDS Sponsorship Ltd, 2 Hat and Mitre Court, London EC1 4EF (☎ 020 7689 3333, e-mail rbusby.bds@sponsorship.co.uk)

BUSCOMBE, Dr John Richard; s of Richard John Buscombe, MBE, of South Mundham, W Sussex, and Jacqueline Doreen, *née* Beet (d 2014); *b* 7 December 1959; *Educ* Price's GS Fareham, London Hosp Med Coll (MB BS), UCL (MSc, MD); *m* 25 July 1981, Jacqueline Ann, da of Dr Ronald Phillip Smith; 1 da (Ruth Hazel b 21 Dec 1989), 1 s (Peter Leonard b 18 Oct 1992); *Career* registrar and lectr in nuclear med Middlesex Hosp 1988–92, conslt in nuclear med Royal Free Hosp 1994–2010, conslt in nuclear med Cambridge Univ Hosps 2010–; prof of nuclear med Univ of Pretoria SA 2010–; scientific advsr Int Atomic Energy Authy, memb Europa Donna, chair of tstees Care for St Anne's; memb Worshipful Co of Parish Clerks; FRCPEd 1998, FRCP 1999, FRCR 2011; *Recreations* travel, teaching, eating then dieting; *Style—* Dr John Buscombe; ✉ Addenbrooke's Hospital, Cambridge CB2 0UU (☎ 01223 217185, e-mail john.buscombe@addenbrookes.nhs.uk)

BUSH, Catherine (Kate); CBE (2013); *b* 30 July 1958; *Career* singer and songwriter; debut single Wuthering Heights 1978 (UK no 1); albums: The Kick Inside 1978 (reached UK no 3), Lionheart 1978 (UK no 6), Never For Ever 1980 (UK no 1), The Dreaming 1982 (UK no 3), Hounds of Love 1985 (UK no 1), The Whole Story 1986 (compilation, UK no 1), The Sensual World 1989 (UK no 2), This Woman's Work 1990 (box set), The Red Shoes 1993 (UK no 2), Aerial 2005, Director's Cut 2011 (UK no 2), 50 Words for Snow 2011 (UK no 5); Ivor Novello Award 1978–79, Best British Female Artist BRIT Awards 1987; film The Line, The Cross and The Curve (premiered London Film Festival) Nov 1993; *Style—* Miss Kate Bush, CBE

BUSH, Charles Martin Peter; s of Dr J P Bush (d 1993), and E M Bush, *née* Farnsworth; *b* 28 June 1952; *Educ* Melbourne GS, Univ of Melbourne, Trinity Coll Oxford (MA); *m* April 1977, Mary, *née* Nevin, da of R W Nevin; 3 s (Michael b 1979, Andrew b 1981, Paddy b 1984); *Career* teacher Aylesbury GS 1975–78 (head of pure mathematics 1977–78), head of mathematics Abingdon Sch 1978–82; Marlborough Coll: head of mathematics 1982–89, boarding housemaster 1988–93; headmaster Eastbourne Coll 1993–2005, headmaster Oundle Sch 2005–15; memb HMC 1993–2015; *Publications* co-author SMP Revised Advanced Mathematics (1989–90); *Recreations* cricket, golf, reading, fell-walking; *Clubs* MCC (Marylebone and Melbourne), East India, Lansdowne; *Style—* Charles Bush, Esq; ✉ Oundle School, The Great Hall, Oundle, Peterborough PE8 4GH (☎ 01832 277142, e-mail headmaster@oundleschool.org.uk)

BUSH, Paul Anthony; OBE (2007); s of Anthony Clive Bush (d 1998), and Beatrice Catherine Bush (d 1997); *b* 11 June 1958; *Educ* South Wigston HS, Gateway Boys' Sch Leicester, Borough Road Coll of Physical Educn, Dunfermline Coll of Physical Educn Edinburgh (Dip Sports Coaching); *m* 15 April 1989, Katriona Christine, da of late James Edward Bayley; *Career* accounts clerk Gen Accident Life Assurance Co 1978–79, trainee surveyor Dist Valuer's Office Leicester 1979–81, chief coach Leics Amateur Swimming Assoc 1979–81, swimming devpt offr/chief coach City of Bradford Met Cncl 1982–84, chief coach City of Leicester Swimming Club 1984–87, swimming devpt offr Leeds Leisure Servs 1987–92, gen sec Br Swimming Coaches Assoc 1986–92, chm Br Swimming Grand Prix 1987–88 (sec 1987–90), dir of swimming Amateur Swimming Assoc 1992–96, asst head of development Sports Cncl 1996–97, ptnr Sporting Initiatives 1997–, chief exec Scottish Swimming 1998–2004; Event Scotland: int sports event mangr 2004–05, dep chief exec 2005–07, chief operating offr 2007–; currently dir of events Visit Scotland; sr team mangr England Swimming Team 1989–98, gen mangr England Swimming Team Cwlth Games Auckland 1990, GB Swimming Team mangr Olympic Games Barcelona 1992, dep chef de mission BOA Holland European Youth Olympics 1993, dir of swimming Cwlth Games Victoria Canada 1994, chef de mission BOA Bath European Youth Olympics 1995, dir of swimming Olympic Games Atlanta 1996, GB Swimming Team mangr European Championships Seville 1997, GB Swimming Team mangr World Championships Perth 1998, gen team mangr Scottish Cwlth Games team 2000–02, chef de mission Scottish Cwlth Games Team 2003–06, chair Cwlth Games Scotland 2015–; conslt Gezira Sporting Club Egypt 1982 and 1983, tech dir Euro Jr Swimming and Diving Championships 1989 and 1992; dir of aquatics Universiade Sheffield 1991 (rep FISU Tech Ctee 1991); bd dir World Swimming Coaches Assoc 1994–98; event dir Leeds Cycling Events (incl World Cyclo Cross Championships 1992) 1991–92, chair E of Scotland Inst of Sport 2006–, bd dir UK Sport Major Events Gp 2008–14; memb: Exec Ctee and Swimming Ctee Yorks Amateur Swimming Assoc 1991–92, Swimming Ctee North Eastern Counties Amateur Swimming Assoc 1990–92, Swimming Ctee Amateur

Swimming Assoc 1991–96; bd dir: Edinburgh Int Festival 2008–, Highland 2007 2008–, Business Club Scotland 2009–13; govr Gateway Boys' Sch 1996–99; memb: Br Inst of Sports Coaches 1987–, Inst of Swimming Teachers and Coaches 1980–, Br Swimming Coaches Assoc 1981– (hon life fell 1992), Inst of Leisure and Amenity Mgmnt 1992–; fell Br Inst of Sports Administrators; *Books* Take up Swimming (jtly, 1989), author of numerous articles in Swimming Times; *Recreations* most sports (especially golf, swimming and walking), travel, theatre, gardening, food and drink; *Style—* Paul Bush, Esq, OBE; ✉ Ochil Paddocks, Burnfoot, Glendevon, Dollar, Perthshire FK14 7JY (☎ 0131 472 2296, fax 0131 472 2310, e-mail pbush@bshsport.demon.co.uk)

BUSH, Prof Ronald; s of Raymond Bush (d 1988), and Esther, *née* Schneyer (d 1979); *b* 16 June 1946; *Educ* Univ of Pennsylvania (BA), Univ of Cambridge (BA), Princeton Univ (MA, PhD); *m* 14 Dec 1969, Marilyn; 1 s (Charles b 26 May 1979); *Career* assoc prof of English Harvard Univ 1979–82 (asst prof 1974–79), prof of English Caltech 1985–97 (assoc prof 1982–85), Drue Heinz prof of American literature Univ of Oxford 1997–13 (Drue Heinz prof emeritus 2013–); NEH fellowship 1977–78 and 1992–93, fell Exeter Coll Oxford 1994–95, fell American Civilization Harvard 2004, distinguished visiting Hurst prof Washington Univ St Louis 2013, emeritus research fell St John's Coll Oxford 2013–, sr research fell Inst of English Studies Sch of Advanced Studies Univ of London 2013–, visiting scholar American Acad in Rome 2014 and 2015; *Books* The Genesis of Ezra Pound's Cantos (1976), T S Eliot: A Study in Character and Style (1983), T S Eliot: The Modernist in History (1991), Prehistories of the Future (1995), Claiming the Stones (2002); *Recreations* tennis, travel; *Style—* Prof Ronald Bush; ✉ St John's College, Oxford OX1 3JP (☎ 01865 277300, e-mail ron.bush@ell.ox.ac.uk)

BUSH, Prof Stephen Frederick; s of Albert Edward Bush (d 1982), and Winifred May, *née* Maltby (d 1995); *b* 6 May 1939; *Educ* Isleworth GS, Trinity Coll Cambridge (MA, PhD, sr scholar and res scholar), MIT (SM), Univ of Manchester (MSc); *m* 26 Oct 1963, Gillian Mary, da of Reginald Charles Layton (d 2001), of Thorpe Bay, Essex; 1 s (James Henry b 1970), 1 da (Jane Elizabeth b 1972); *Career* mangr Process Technology Gp ICI Corporate Laboratory 1969–72, mangr Systems Technol Dept ICI Europa Ltd 1972–79; UMIST (now Univ of Manchester): prof of polymer engrg 1979–2004, head Polymer Engrg Div 1980–2000, chm Dept of Mech Engrg 1982–83 and 1985–87, dir Centre for Manufacture 2000–05, prof of process manufacture 2004–05, emeritus prof 2006–; fndr and md Prosyma Research Ltd 1987–, chm and co-fndr N of England Plastics Processors Consortium 1990–2000, int rep Polymer Processing Soc 1993–2001, memb Editorial Bd Int Industrial and Systems Engrg 2005–; dir SME Process Manufacture Centre 1996–2006; chm Applied Mechanics Ctee SERC 1985–87, vice-chm Campaign for Ind Britain 1991–98, memb Schs Examination and Assessment Ctee for Technol 1992–94; chm NEPPCO Ltd 2000–06 (dir 2006–07), memb Advsy Bd Business Innovation Center Univ of Massachusetts 2007–; policy advsr UKIP 2007–10 (Parly candidate 2010); fndr and ed britain-watch.com 2009–; 20 granted patents on polymer composites (incl SAFIRE, Viscor and Smartform), chemical processes and healthcare products 1976–; Sir George Nelson Prize 1960, NATO Research Studentship MIT 1960–61, Moulton Medal 1969, Sir George Beilby Medal and Prize 1979, Dupont Industrial Product Design of the Year 2005, Hanson Medal 2011, finalist Inst of Economic Affrs Brexit Prize 2014; FIMechE (memb Cncl 1978–81), FIChemE 1993; FPRI (memb Cncl 1985–87), FIMMM 1993, FRSA 1998; *Technical Publications* incl: Prediction and Measurement of Chemical Oscillations (1969), Determination of Chemical Kinetics Mechanisms (with P Dyer, 1976), Macromolecular Chemistry (contrib, 1980), Polymer Engineering (contrib, 1984), Biological and Synthetic Networks (contrib with J M Methven, 1986), New Processes for Production of Polymer Composites (1990), Systems Concepts and Technological Change (1994), Long Glass Fibre Reinforcement of Thermoplastics (1999), Scale Order and Complexity in Polymer Processing (2000), New Processes for Smart Materials (with D R Blackburn, 2003), Technoeconomic Models for New Products and Processes (2005), Renewable Energy: Squaring the Circle (with D R MacDonald, 2011), and over 160 other scientific pubns and int conference presentations on mathematical modelling, economics of manufacture, and polymer and chemical engrg; *Political Publications* Britain's Future: Independence or Extinction – No Middle Way (1989), Models for 16–19 Education: More Matter less Art (1990), The Meaning of the Maastricht Treaty (with G M Bush, 1992), Business, Industry and a New Relationship with the European Union (1998), The Importance of Manufacture to the Economy (2000),University Admissions and Fees (2004), Produce and Prosper (2010), Averting Catastrophe: Ensuring the Security of Britain's Energy Supplies (with D R MacDonald, 2011), Band of Brothers: Recovering the English Nation (2012), Britain Revitalised and Independence Regained (2014), Britain's Referendum Decision and its Effects (2016), and over 130 articles and letters in the nat press on political, industrial and educational matters; *Recreations* hill walking, British imperial and military history, music, tennis, travel; *Clubs* Manchester Statistical Soc (memb Cncl 2001–07), Royal Economic Soc; *Style—* Prof Stephen Bush; ✉ website http://stephenbush.net and www.britain-watch.com; Prosyma Research Ltd, PO Box 599, Thurston, Bury St Edmunds IP31 3TS (☎ 01359 271704, fax 01359 271852, e-mail stephenbush@technomica.co.uk or s.f.bush@prosyma.co.uk)

BUSHELL, Michael David (Mickey); MBE (2013); s of Pete Bushell, and Shelley Bushell; *b* 8 June 1990, Shrewsbury, Salops; *Career* Paralympic athlete; achievements incl: Silver medal (100m) Paralympic Games 2008, Silver medal (100m) and Bronze medal (200m) Athletics World Championships 2011, Gold (100m) Paralympic Games 2012; *Style—* Mr Mickey Bushell, MBE

BUSHILL-MATTHEWS, Philip; *b* 1943, Droitwich; *Educ* Malvern Coll, UC Oxford (MA), Harvard Business Sch (Advanced Mgmnt Program), Univ of Leicester (BA); *m* Angela; 3 c; *Career* joined Unilever 1965, seconded to Thomas Lipton Inc USA 1976, nat accounts dir Birds Eye Sales Ltd 1977–80, md Iglo Portugal 1980–81, sales dir Birds Eye Walls Ltd 1981–88, dir Van den Bergh & Jurgens Ltd 1988–91, md Red Mill Snack Foods Ltd Wednesbury and Red Mill Co BV Netherlands 1991–99; MEP (Cons) West Midlands 1999–2009, ldr Cons MEPs 2008; vice-chm Coventry and Warks NHS Partnership Tst 2012–14; FInstD; *Publications* The Gravy Train (2003), Who Rules Britannia? (2005); *Recreations* theatre, reading, enjoying the countryside, archaeology; *Clubs* Harbury Village; *Style—* Philip Bushill-Matthews, Esq; ✉ e-mail bushillm@outlook.com

BUSS, Nicola Sian (Nicky); da of Dr David Buss, and Heather, *née* Parr; *b* 14 October 1967; *Educ* Farnborough Hill Convent Coll, Magdalen Coll Oxford (entrance scholar, Demy scholar, MA Philosophy & Psychology, Alec Varley Psychology Prize); *Career* Booz Allen & Hamilton/OC & C Strategy Consulting 1988–90, bd dir Planning Dept Saatchi & Saatchi Advertising 1991–94 (APG Gold Creative Planning Award for British Airways Club World, first prize AMSO Research Effectiveness Award), vice-pres Strategy and Planning MTV Europe 1994–96, exec planning dir and managing ptnr Ammirati Puris Lintas London 1996–99; memb: MRS 1991, Account Planning Gp 1991, Media Research Gp 1995; *Publications* AMSO Research Works (1992), Greener Communications (1993), Creative Planning, Outstanding Advertising (1994); *Recreations* sailing, music, fashion; *Clubs* Harbour; *Style—* Ms Nicky Buss

BUSSELL, Darcey Andrea; CBE (2006, OBE 1995); da of Philip Michael Bussell, and Andrea Pemberton, *née* Williams; *b* 27 April 1969; *Educ* Arts Educnl Sch, Royal Ballet Sch; *m* 1997, Angus Forbes; 2 da (Phoebe Olivia b 2001, Zoe Sophia b 2004); *Career* ballerina; appeared in 1986 and 1987 Royal Ballet Sch performances, joined Sadler's Wells Royal Ballet (now Birmingham Royal Ballet) 1987; Royal Ballet: joined as soloist 1988, first soloist 1989, princ 1989–2006, princ guest artist 2006–07; also international guest performances with various other cos incl Balleto della Scala 2005–06, subject of Omnibus (BBC) 1998; memb Bd of Dirs Sydney Dance Co 2008–; Hon DLitt Univ of Oxford 2009; *Performances* first professional leading role Myrthe in Giselle; classical repertory incl: Odette/Odile in Swan Lake, Princess Aurora in The Sleeping Beauty, Sugar Plum Fairy in The Nutcracker, Nikiya and Gamzatti in La Bayadère, title role in Giselle, Raymonda in Raymonda Act III; Sir Kenneth MacMillan ballets: cr role of Princess Rose in The Prince of the Pagodas, cr role of Masha in Winter Dreams 1991 (Farewell pas de deux created in advance for her and Irek Mukhamedov and performed at the HM Queen Elizabeth the Queen Mother's 90th Birthday Tribute and Royal Opera House 1990, also televised), title role in Manon, Juliet in Romeo and Juliet, leading role in Song of the Earth, leading role in Elite Syncopations, Agnus Dei role in Requiem, Mitzi Caspar in Mayerling; Balanchine ballets incl: appeared in Royal Ballet's first performances of Rubies and Stravinsky Violin Concerto, princ roles in Agon, Symphony in C, Tchaikovsky pas de deux, Duo Concertant, Serenade and Ballet Imperial, Terpsichore in Apollo, Siren in Prodigal Son; leading roles in other major ballets incl: Sir Frederick Ashton's Cinderella, Monotones II, Les Illuminations (role of Sacred Love), William Forsythe's In the Middle Somewhat Elevated 1992 and Hermann Schmerman 1993, first Royal Ballet performance of Glen Tetley's La Ronde (role of Prostitute), Dame Ninette de Valois' Checkmate (role of Black Queen), Galanteries, David Bintley's The Spirit of Fugue (cr leading role), Enigma Variations (role of Lady Mary), Ashley Page's Bloodlines (cr leading role), Twyla Tharp's Mr Worldly Wise (cr role of Mistress Truth-on-Toe) 1995, and Push Comes to Shove, Dances with Death (cr role) 1996, ...now languorous, now wild..., Pavane pour une infante défunte (cr role), Amores (cr role), Towards Poetry (cr role), Anastasia (role of Kschessinska) 1996, Push Comes to Shove 1997, La Bayadere (Kirov Ballet and Australian Ballet) 1998, Towards Poetry 1999, Serenade 1999, Lento 1999, Barber Violin Concerto 2000, Les Rendezvous 2000, The Concert 2000, There where she loves 2000, Dance Variations 2000, Lilac Garden (role of Caroline) 2000, Beyond Bach 2002, In the middle, somwhat elevated (role of Sylvie) 2002, Tryst 2002, Gong 2002, Sylvia (title role) 2004, A Month in the Country (role of Natalia Petrovna) 2005, La Fete Étrange (role of Bride) 2005, Tanglewood 2005, Le Jeune Homme et la Mort 2006, Homage to The Queen (role of Queen of the Air) 2006, The Four Temperaments 2006, DGV 2006, Kiss 2006, Theme and Variations 2007; guest performances with NYC Ballet and Tokyo Ballet; judge Strictly Come Dancing (BBC1) 2012– (guest judge 2009); *Awards* Prix de Lausanne 1986, Dancer of the Year Dance and Dancers magazine 1990, Most Promising Artiste of 1990 Variety Club of GB, Evening Standard Award 1991, Olivier Award (for In the Middle Somewhat Elevated) 1992; *Publications* incl: The Young Dancer (1994), Life in Dance (jtly, 1999), Pilates for Life (2005, also DVD), Dance Body Workout (2007), Magic Ballerina series (2008–10); *DVDs* Winter Dreams (1992), Mayerling (1994), Great Pas de Deux (2004), The Prince of the Pagodas (2005), La Bayadere (2006), Le Jeune Homme et la Mort (jtly, 2006), Sylvia (2007), Viva La Diva (2008); *Style—* Miss Darcey Bussell, CBE; ✉ The Royal Ballet, Royal Opera House, Covent Garden, London WC2E 9DD

BUSSEY, Ed; *Educ* Emmanuel Coll Cambridge (MA), INSEAD; *Career* sub-lt RN 1987–91, diplomat FCO 1992–2000, founding team memb and global mktg dir figleaves.com 2000–07, e-commerce advsr PCCW Hong Kong 2007, chief operating offr ZYB 2007–08, non-exec dir Clash Media 2008–10, interim ceo Clash Media 2010–11, fndr and ceo Quill Content 2010–; advsy memb Bd Mr & Mrs Smith Boutique Hotels 2007–, advsr Bd Secret Sales 2009; memb UKTI Catalyst 2011–16; ✉ Quill, 5th Floor, Holden House, 57 Rathbone Place, London W1T 1JU (☎ 020 3290 6150, website www.quillcontent.com)

BUSSON, Andre Arpad; *b* 27 January 1963, France; *Children* 2 s (Arpad Flynn, Aurelius Cy), 1 da (Rosalind Altalune Thurman-Busson); *Career* fndr and chm EIM Gp; founding tstee and chm ARK, founding tstee Theodora Children's Tst; *Style—* Andre Arpad Busson, Esq; ✉ EIM (United Kingdom) Ltd, 5 Savile Row, London W1S 3BP(☎ 020 7290 6100, fax 020 7290 6113)

BUSUTTIL, Prof Anthony; OBE; s of Anthony Busuttil (d 1973), of Malta, and Maria, *née* Vassallo (d 1978); *b* 30 December 1945; *Educ* St Aloysius' Coll Malta; *m* 31 Aug 1969, Angela, da of Angelo Bonello (d 1979), of Gozo; 3 s (Godwin b 1970, Christopher b 1973, Joseph b 1978); *Career* lectr in pathology Univ of Glasgow 1971–76, conslt pathologist Lothian Health Bd 1976–87, currently emeritus regius prof of forensic med Univ of Edinburgh (sr lectr in pathology 1976–87), contrib to several chapters on gastroenterology, genitourinary and forensic pathology; Euro Cncl for Legal Med; memb BMA; DMJ(Path); fell Br Assoc of Forensic Med, FRCPath, FRCPE, FRCPGlas, FRSSA, FRCSEd, FFFLM; memb Order of Merit (Malta) 1998, Knight Holy Sepulchre; *Publications* Clinical Forensic Medicine, Paediatric Forensic Medicine & Pathology, Scenes Crime Investigation; *Recreations* classical music, reading; *Clubs* RSM; *Style—* Prof Anthony Busuttil, OBE; ✉ 78 Hillpark Avenue, Edinburgh EH4 7AL (☎ 0131 336 3241, e-mail tony@busuttil.demon.co.uk)

BUTCHER, Ian George; s of George Wilfred Robert Butcher, of Winchmore Hill, London, and Joyce Patricia, *née* Payne; *b* 13 April 1950; *Educ* Winchmore Sch, City of London Coll; *m* 1, 15 Sept 1978 (m dis 2001), Sarah Jane, da of Donald Percy Jeffery, of Halton, Bucks; 2 da (Emma b 1981, Kellie b 1984), 1 s (Harry b 1987); m 2, 7 April 2001, Elizabeth Dundee Jones, *née* Davis; *Career* Touche Ross & Co (chartered accountants) 1969–74, exec dir County Bank Ltd 1974–84, fin dir Addison Page plc 1984–86, corp devpt dir Addison Conslt Group plc 1986–87, gp fin dir Charles Barker plc 1987–89, chm Lefax Publishing Ltd 1984–88, dir Whitehead Mann Group plc 1989–2002, chief fin offr Cambridge Disply Technol Ltd 2002–04, ptnr MWM Consulting Ltd 2004–; FCA; *Recreations* cricket, music, reading, theatre, ballet, wine; *Clubs* MCC, RAC; *Style—* Ian G Butcher, Esq; ✉ e-mail iangbutcher@hotmail.com

BUTCHER, Stephen James; s of Geoffrey Cecil Butcher (d 2006), and Audrey Ray, *née* Vince (d 1985); *b* 25 February 1952; *Educ* Stonyhurst, St John's Coll Oxford (BA); *m* 11 Nov 1989, Jane Mary, da of Dr Toby Thorne; 2 da (Catherine Mary b 18 April 1992, Eleanor Margaret b 16 Dec 1995), 1 s (John Geoffrey b 1 April 1998); *Career* md Academic Div Cassell 1995–98, gen mangr Unitary Business Edexcel 1998–2002, chief exec Eduserv 2002–; *Style—* Stephen Butcher, Esq; ✉ Eduserv, Royal Mead, Railway Place, Bath BA1 1SR (☎ 01225 474348, e-mail stephen.butcher@eduserv.org.uk)

BUTE, 7 Marquess of (GB 1796); Sir John Colum Crichton-Stuart; 12 Bt (S 1627); also Lord Crichton (S 1488), Earl of Dumfries, Viscount of Air, Lord Crichton of Sanquhar and Cumnock (S 1633), Earl of Bute, Viscount Kingarth, Lord Mountstuart, Cumra(e) and Inchmarnock (S 1703), Baron Mountstuart of Wortley (GB 1761), Baron Cardiff of Cardiff Castle (GB 1776), Earl of Windsor and Viscount Mountjoy (GB 1796); Hereditary Sheriff and Coroner of Co Bute, Hereditary Keeper of Rothesay Castle; patron of 9 livings; s of 6 Marquess of Bute, KBE (d 1993), and his 1 w, (Beatrice) Nicola Grace, *née* Weld-Forester; *b* 26 April 1958; *m* 1 (m dis 1993), Carolyn, da of Bryson Waddell (d 1975); 2 da (Lady Caroline b 1984, Lady Cathleen b 1986), 1 s (John Bryson, Earl of Dumfries b 21 Dec 1989); m 2, Serena Solitaire Wendell, da of Maj Jac Wendell; 1 da (Lady Lola Affrica b 23 June 1999); *Heir* s, Earl of Dumfries; *Career* motor racing driver (as Johnny Dumfries) 1980–91; British Formula Three champion 1984, runner-up FIA European Formula Three Championship 1984, contracted to Ferrari Formula One team as test driver 1985, number two driver for John Player Special Team Lotus 1986, works driver for World Champion Sports Prototype Team Silk Cut Jaguar 1988 (jt winner Le Mans 1988), lead driver for Toyota GB World Sports Prototype Championship 1989 and 1990;

Style— The Marquess of Bute; ✉ Mount Stuart, Rothesay, Isle of Bute PA20 9LR (☎ 01700 503877)

BUTLER, Alan Edward; s of Albert Frederick Butler (d 1978), of Clacton on Sea, Essex, and Lillian Elizabeth, *née* Carlson (d 1969); *b* 6 December 1940; *Educ* Raine's Fndn GS, UCL (BSc); *m* 27 Nov 1981, Gail Katharine; 2 s (Richard b 1984, James b 1990); *Career* md: Carl Byoir and Associates Ltd 1975–85 (dir 1970), Communications Strategy Ltd 1985–86, Countrywide Communications Ltd 1987–93; managing ptnr Kudos Communications 1993–, conslt Kudos Consulting Dubai 1994–2000, dir YTJ Pacific Singapore 1994–; chm Wentworth Gate Management Co Ltd 1999–; former chm: Strangers Gallery NW Surrey House of Commons Dining Club, PRCA; Freeman City of London, Liveryman Worshipful Co of Marketors 1988–; memb Mktg Soc; MBCS, MIPRA, FIPR, FInstD; *Recreations* most sports; *Style*— Alan Butler, Esq

BUTLER, Dr Anthony David (Tony); s of Bernard Reuben Butler (d 1975), and Ethel Elizabeth, *née* Butter; *b* 7 April 1945, Newmarket, Suffolk; *Educ* Soham GS, Univ of Leicester (BSc), UC Wales Aberystwyth (MSc), Univ of Kent (PhD); *m* 14 April 1971, Rosemary Jane, da of Samuel Leight Medlar; *Career* workforce planner Civil Service Dept 1969–75, OECD conslt Athens 1971–72, statistician Dept of Environment 1975–82, head of Traffic Census Unit Dept of Transport 1982–88; Dept of Environment: project mangr for water privatisation 1988–90, head of business devpt and procurement 1990–93; dir of corp affrs HM Inspectorate of Pollution 1993–96, head of mgmnt services CPS 1996–98, dep DG Advertising Standards Authority and sec Ctee of Advertising Practice 1998–2001; chm Advtg Bodies Tstees Ltd 2001–, memb Mktg Codes Interpretation Panel Int C of C 2001–03; non-exec memb: Bd Nat Patient Safety Agency 2001–07, HM Inspectorate of Probation 2001–02; lay memb: Preliminary Investigation Ctee RCVS 2001–07, Ethics Ctee Univ of Chichester 2009–; author of several papers on statistical manpower planning, construction price indicies, evidence of seat belt wearing and automated traffic counting; Scout fell 2009; memb Ctee Friends of Greenwich Park; life memb: RSPB, British Museum, National Trust, WWF, Greenwich Soc, English Heritage, WWT; CStat RSS; *Recreations* swimming, choral singing, theatre, foreign travel, bird watching, gardening; *Style*— Dr Tony Butler; ✉ 19 Maidenstone Hill, Greenwich, London SE10 8SY (☎ 020 8692 7845, e-mail anthonybutler06@btinternet.com)

BUTLER, David John; s of John Carrol Butler (d 1979), of Sunderland, and Doris, *née* Stockdale; *b* 28 September 1952; *Educ* Bede Sch Sunderland, Sunderland Coll of Art; *Career* painter, printmaker, publisher and art conslt 1985; ed: Making Ways 1985, 1987 and 1992, Artists Newsletter 1985–95; devpt dir AN Publications 1995–99; freelance writer and ed 1985–; dir 'Round Midnight – an Inquiry into the State of the Visual Arts in the UK 1996, co-dir Interrupt Symposia: the role of artists in socially engaged art symposia 2003; coordinator Life Work Art Univ of Newcastle Sch of Art and Culture 2003; *Books* Live Art (jt ed, 1991), Across Europe (1992), Art of Negotiation (jt ed, 2007); *Style*— David Butler; ✉ Fine Art Department, School of Arts and Cultures, University of Newcastle upon Tyne, The Quadrangle, Newcastle upon Tyne NE2 1HQ (☎ 0191 222 6052, e-mail david.butler@ncl.ac.uk)

BUTLER, Dawn; MP; *b* 1969, Forest Gate, London; *Educ* Waltham Forest Coll of FE (Dip); *Career* early career as systems analyst Johnson Matthey, exec Employment Serv and recruitment offr Public Service Union, nat race and equality min GMB 1995–2005; MP (Lab) Brent South 2005–10 and Brent Central 2015–, PPS to Jane Kennedy MP (as Min for Health) 2005–06, memb Ctee for Modernisation of the House of Commons, memb DCSF Ctee, chair All Pty Parly Gp on Youth Affrs; hon pres Br Youth Cncl; MP of the Year Women in Public Life Award 2009; *Recreations* salsa dancing, spending time with family; *Style*— Ms Dawn Butler, MP

BUTLER, Dr Eamonn Francis; s of Richard Henry Bland Butler (d 1977), of Shrewsbury, and Janet Provan Butler (d 2001); *b* 3 January 1952; *Educ* Univ of Aberdeen, Univ of St Andrews (MA, PhD); *m* 1986, Christine Anna, da of Giuseppe Pieroni; 2 s (Richard Cosmo b 1988, Joseph Felix b 1990); *Career* economist; res assoc US House of Representatives 1976–77; dir Adam Smith Inst 1978–; asst prof of philosophy Hillsdale Coll Michigan 1977–78; ed The Broker 1979–87; memb Bd Assoc of Private Enterprise Educn 2012–; memb Mont Pelerin Soc 1984– (vice-pres 2008–10, sec 2012–); Hon DLitt Heriot Watt Univ 2013; *Publications* Forty Centuries of Wage and Price Controls (jtly, 1979), Hayek: His Contribution to the Social and Economic Thought of Our Time (1983), Milton Friedman: A Guide to His Economic Thought (1985), Ludwig von Mises: Fountainhead of the Modern Microeconomics Revolution (1989), Adam Smith: A Primer (2007), The Best Book on the Market (2008), The Rotten State of Britain (2009), The Alternative Manifesto (2010), Ludwig von Mises: A Primer (2010), Milton Friedman (2011), The Condensed Wealth of Nations (2011), Public Choice: A Primer (2012), Friedrich Hayek (2012), Foundations of a Free Society (2013), The Economics of Success (2014), Classical Liberalism: A Primer (2015), Magna Carter: A Primer (2015); with Madsen Pirie: Test Your IQ (1983), Boost Your IQ (1990), The Sherlock Holmes IQ Book (1995), IQ Puzzlers (1995); articles published in various newspapers and jls; *Recreations* archaeology, antiquarian books and prints; *Style*— Dr Eamonn Butler; ✉ The Adam Smith Institute, 23 Great Smith Street, London SW1P 3BL (e-mail eamonn.butler@adamsmith.org.uk, website www.eamonnbutler.com, Twitter @eamonnbutler)

BUTLER, Gwendoline; *Educ* Haberdashers' Aske's, Lady Margaret Hall Oxford (BA); *m* Dr Lionel Butler (decd), historian and author; 1 da (Lucilla b 1955); *Career* crime writer and novelist, lectr and broadcaster; author of over 70 books, series characters detectives Sir John Coffin, Charmian Daniels, Maj Mearns and Sgt Denny, also writes under pseudonym Jennie Melville; historical crime reviewer Crime Time magazine 1999–2002; memb Ctee and chm of judges of Gold Dagger Awards Crime Writers' Assoc, judge Ellis Peters Historical Crime Competition 2000; Silver Dagger Award Crime Writers' Assoc (for Coffin for Pandora) 1974, Romantic Novelists' Award (for The Red Staircase) 1981, Ellery Queen Short Story Award; sec Detection Club 1992–95; *Style*— Mrs Gwendoline Butler

BUTLER, Ian John; s of Donald Butler, and Eileen, *née* Green; *b* 26 February 1954; *Educ* Mexborough GS, Central Sch of Art & Design (BA Sculpture), Univ of Liverpool (BA Architecture), Poly of Central London (DipArch); *m* 1980, Theresa Mary, da of Patrick Tomlins; 3 s (David George b 1989, Peter John b 1991, George Patrick b 1997); *Career* architect; Powell Moya & Partners 1980, Llewelyn-Davies Weeks 1982–84, RMJM London Ltd 1985–91, RMJM Hong Kong Ltd 1991–2005 (latterly md), managing ptnr Northern Office Sheppard Robson 2005–14, dir and head of transportation architecture Aecom 2014–; project architect several large complex building projects in Kong Kong and London; RIBA 1984; memb: ARBUK 1983, Hong Kong Inst of Architects 1993, Hong Kong Architects Registration Bd 1993; *Recreations* photography, golf; *Style*— Ian Butler, Esq

BUTLER, James Walter; MBE (2009); s of Walter Arthur Butler (d 1942), and Rosina Harriet, *née* Kingman (d 1967); *b* 25 July 1931; *Educ* Maidstone GS, Maidstone Sch of Art, St Martin's Sch of Art; *m* 1 (m dis); 1 da (Kate b 12 Dec 1966); m 2, 1975, Angela Elizabeth, da of Col Roger Berry, and Mrs Lisa Berry; 4 da (Rosie b 23 Aug 1975, Saskia b 12 April 1977, Candida b 24 April 1979, Aurelia b 11 Aug 1983); *Career* sculptor; tutor of sculpture and drawing City and Guilds London Art Sch 1960–75; works in public places: portrait statue Pres Kenyatta Nairobi 1973, Monument to Freedom Fighters of Zambia Lusaka 1975, sculpture of Burton Cooper Staffs 1977, Meml to King Richard III Leicester 1980, portrait statue Field Marshal Earl Alexander of Tunis Wellington Barracks London 1985, bronze sculpture Skipping Girl Harrow 1985, Dolphin Fountain Dolphin Sq London 1987, portrait statue Sir John Moore and Figures of Rifleman and Bugler Sir John Moore Barracks Winchester 1986, portrait statue John Wilkes New Fetter Lane London, Wilkes Univ Pennsylvania 1988, bronze sculpture The Leicester Seamstress Leicester 1990, portrait head Sir Hugh Wontner Savoy Hotel London 1990, War Memorial to Royal Electrical and Mechanical Engineers Arborfield 1992, portrait statue Thomas Cook Leicester 1994, bronze sculpture The Stratford Jester Stratford-upon-Avon 1994, portrait statue James Henry Greathead Cornhill London 1994, meml statue Reg Harris (sprint cycling champion) 1995, portrait statue Billy Wright, CBE Molineux Wolverhampton 1996, D Day Memorial to Green Howard Regt Crepon Normandy 1996, portrait bust of Sir Nicholas Bacon St Albans Sch 1996, portrait statue of James Brindley canal engineer Coventry Canal Basin 1998, Fountain, Child and Whale KK Women's and Children's Hosp Singapore, portrait statue of Duncan Edwards Dudley, portrait bust of Robert Beldam, CBE CCC Cambridge 2000, Fleet Air Arm Memorial Victoria Embankment Gardens London 2000, portrait bust of R J Mitchell RAF Club London, portrait bust of Roy Chadwick RAF Club London, portrait statue of Jack Walker Blackburn Rovers FC, portrait statue of Stan Cullis Wolverhampton Wanderers FC, Great Seal of the Realm 2001, portrait bust of Queen Elizabeth The Queen Mother Butchers' Co 2008, portrait head of Prof Michael Farthing St Georges Hosp Tooting 2009, statue of HM Queen Elizabeth II commissioned to celebrate her 90th birthday and to commemorate the signing of the Magna Carta in Runnymede 2015; Rainbow Meml Div Fere En Tardenois France 2011; RA 1972 (ARA 1964), RWA, FRBS; *Books* James Butler: A Collector's Personal View (Bby John Meulkens, 2006); *Recreations* astronomy; *Clubs* The Arts; *Style*— James Butler, Esq, MBE, RA; ✉ Valley Farm, Radway, Warwickshire CV35 0UJ (☎ 01926 641938, fax 01926 640624)

BUTLER, Dr Paul; s of Frank William Butler (d 1966), and Elizabeth, *née* Wright (d 1993); *b* 4 June 1952; *Educ* Cotham GS, UCL (BSc), Westminster Med Sch (MB BS); *m* 28 Jan 1978, Janet Ann Butler, da of Percival Jack Barber, of Sawbridgeworth, Herts; 1 da (Claire b 19 Dec 1980), 1 s (David b 20 Oct 1982); *Career* med registrar rotation Leicester AHA 1979, trainee in radiodiagnosis Manchester RHA 1983, sr registrar neuroradiology Manchester Royal Infirmary; conslt neuroradiologist: London Clinic, King Edward VII's Sister Agnes Hosp, Bart's and London NHS Tst (ret); currently conslt neuroradiologist in full time practice; Freeman City of London, Liveryman Worshipful Soc of Apothecaries; memb Br Soc of Neuroradiologists, MRCP 1979, DMRD 1983, FRCR 1983; *Publications* Imaging of the Nervous System (ed, 1990), Applied Radiological Anatomy (ed, 1999, 2 edn 2012), Endovascular Neurosurgery (ed, 1999); *Recreations* gardening; *Style*— Dr Paul Butler; ✉ 45 Queen Anne Street, London W1G 9JF

BUTLER, Peter Robert; *b* 17 May 1949; *Educ* Southend HS, Univ of Bristol (BSc); *m* Linley; 1 s (Simon b 1980), 1 da (Rachel b 1984); *Career* articled clerk and accountant Touche Ross & Co 1970–75; BOC Gp plc: investigations accountant BOC Ltd London 1975–77, fin dir/fin mangr BOC Ltd Far East Singapore 1977–79, fin controller Oilfield Servs 1980, mangr Corp Fin (Welding) 1980–83, gp commercial mangr (Welding) 1983–84; British Sugar plc and Berisford International plc: joined as gp ops controller 1984–86, assoc dir Fin S & W Berisford 1987–88, fin dir British Sugar plc and Bristar Food and Agribusiness Div 1988–90, chief fin offr and exec dir Berisford International plc 1991–93; gp fin dir Hi-Tec Sports plc 1993–95; corp focus dir Hermes Pensions Management Ltd 1996–2004, chief exec Hermes Focus Asset Management Ltd 1998–2004, fndr ptnr emeritus GO Investment Ptnrs LLP (formerly Governance for Owners LLP) 2004–; chm Essex and Southend Sports Tst 2002–, chm Southend Cricket Festival Ctee 2003–10, Gen Ctee Essex CCC; FCA 1979 (ACA 1973); *Recreations* cricket, football (Southend United FC, former player/manager Old Southendians FC Veterans XI), France, New Zealand; *Clubs* MCC, Essex CCC, Southend United FC, Singapore CC; *Style*— Peter Butler, Esq

BUTLER, His Hon Judge Philip Andrew; *b* 13 April 1957, Manchester; *Educ* St Peter's GS Manchester, Univ of Manchester (LLB, LLM); *Career* called to the Bar Middle Temple 1979 (Harmsworth scholar); barr 1979–2009, circuit judge (Northern Circuit) 2009–, designated civil judge Cumbria and Lancs 2011–; KHS 1999, KCHS 2006, KCSHS 2012; *Style*— His Hon Judge Butler; ✉ c/o The Law Courts, Ring Way, Preston PR1 2LL

BUTLER, Robin Noël Holman; s of George Noël Butler (d 1969), of Honiton, and Marjorie Blanche, *née* Dunn (d 1993); *b* 26 April 1943; *Educ* Allhallows Sch; *m* 17 Feb 1995 (m dis 1997), Wendy, da of Arthur Knott; m 2, 31 July 2003, Carol Zenia, da of Francis James Hunter; *Career* schoolmaster 1961–63, family antiques business 1963–, specialist in antique wine accessories, memb Br Antique Dealers' Assoc 1970–2000 (memb Cncl 1984–87); *Books* Arthur Negus Guide to English Furniture (1978), Book of Wine Antiques (1986), The Albert Collection – 500 Years of British & European Silver (2004), Great British Wine Accessories 1550–1900 (2009); *Recreations* photography, cooking, listening to people and making friends; *Style*— Robin Butler, Esq; ✉ 18 Churchill Avenue, Haverhill, Suffolk CB9 0AA (☎ 07831 194997, e-mail mhb@me.com)

BUTLER, Dame Rosemary Janet Mair; DBE (2014); da of Godfrey McGrath, of Llangibby, Monmouthshire, and Gwyneth, *née* Jones (d 1997); *b* 21 January 1943; *Educ* St Julian's HS S Wales; *m* 18 Dec 1966, Derek Richard Butler; 2 da (Kate Rebecca b 1968 d 2013, Helen Alice b 1970); *Career* qualified chiropodist; cncllr (Lab) Newport BC and County BC 1973–99, mayor of Newport 1989–90; memb Nat Assembly for Wales (Lab) Newport West 1999–2016; min for educn and children Nat Assembly for Wales 1999–2000, memb Ctee of the Regions of the EU 2001–07, chair Culture, Welsh Language and Sport Ctee 2003–07, chair Legislation Ctee 1 until 2011, elected presiding offr Nat Assembly for Wales 2011–16 (dep presiding offr 2007–11); hon life memb Newport Sports Cncl, life memb Newport Cricket Club, fndr memb Newport Women's Aid, patron Caerleon Festival; fndr Newport-Kutaisi Twinning Assoc, hon citizen Repub of Georgia 1997; hon fell Univ of Wales Newport 2000, hon fell Cardiff Met Univ 2012; hon dr Univ of S Wales; *Style*— Dame Rosemary Butler, DBE; ✉ National Assembly for Wales, Cardiff Bay, Cardiff CF99 1NA (☎ 0300 200 7104, website www.rosemarybutleram.com, Twitter @rosemarybutler)

BUTLER, Rt Rev Dr Thomas Frederick; s of Thomas John Butler (decd), and Elsie, *née* Bainbridge (decd); *b* 5 March 1940; *Educ* Univ of Leeds (BSc, MSc, PhD), Coll of the Resurrection Mirfield; *m* Barbara Joan, *née* Clark; 1 s (Nicholas Roland b 1967), 1 da (Anna Clare b 1969); *Career* ordained: deacon 1964, priest 1965; curate: St Augustine's Wisbech 1964–66, St Saviour's Folkestone 1966–68; lectr and chaplain Univ of Zambia 1968–73, actg dean Holy Cross Cathedral Lusaka Zambia 1973, chaplain to Univ of Kent at Canterbury 1973–80, archdeacon of Northolt 1980–85, area bishop of Willesden 1985–91, bishop of Leicester 1991–1998, bishop of Southwark 1998–2010, ret; actg diocesan bishop of Bradford 2014, hon asst bishop Dio of Leeds; memb House of Lords 1996–2010; Hon LLD Univ of Leicester 1996, Hon DSc Loughborough Univ 1997, Hon LLD De Montfort Univ 1998, Hon DLitt South Bank Univ 2005, Hon DD Univ of Kent 2005; CEng, MIEE, FKC 2008; *Publications* Just Mission (with Barbara Butler, 1992), Just Spirituality in a World of Faiths (with Barbara Butler, 1996); *Recreations* walking, reading; *Style*— The Rt Rev Dr Tom Butler

BUTLER, Prof William Elliott; s of William Elliott Butler (d 1996), of Black Mountain, N Carolina, and Maxine Swan Elmberg (d 2009); *b* 20 October 1939, Minneapolis, MN, USA; *Educ* American Univ Washington DC (BA), Johns Hopkins Univ Baltimore (MA), Harvard Law Sch (JD), Sch of Law Inst of State and Law Russian Acad of Sciences (LLM), Johns Hopkins Univ (PhD), Univ of London (LLD); *m* 1, 2 Sept 1961, Darlene Mae Johnson (d 1989); 2 s (William Elliott III, Bradley Newman); m 2, 6 Dec 1991, Maryann Elizabeth Gashi; *Career* research asst Washington Centre of Foreign Policy

B

Research Johns Hopkins Univ 1966–68, research assoc in law Harvard Law Sch and Assoc Russian Research Centre Harvard 1968–70; Univ of London: reader in comparative law 1970–76, prof of comparative law 1976–2005, emeritus prof 2005–, dean Faculty of Laws UCL 1977–79, dean Faculty of Laws Univ of London 1988–90; John Edward Fowler Distinguished Prof of Law Dickinson Sch of Law Pennsylvania State Univ 2005–; counsel Clifford Chance 1992–94, ptnr White & Case 1994–96, ptnr CIS Law Firm PricewaterhouseCoopers 1997–2001, ptnr Phoenix Law Associates CIS 2002–11; visiting scholar: Moscow State Univ 1972 and 1980, USSR Acad of Sci 1976, 1981, 1983, 1984, and 1988, Mongolian State Univ 1979; memb: Cncl SSEES 1973–88 and 1989–93 (vice-chm 1983–88), Exec Cmmn Russian Assoc of Maritime Law 2008–; Speranskii prof of int and comparative law and dean 1994–2004, Faculty of Law Moscow Sch of Social and Econ Sci 1994–; visiting prof: NY Univ Law Sch 1978, Ritsumeikan Univ 1985, Harvard Law Sch 1986–87, Washington and Lee Law Sch 2005; memb Faculty Governing Cncl Sch of Int Affrs Penn State 2007–, memb Univ Senate Penn State 2008–; coordinator UCL-USSR Acad of Sci Protocol on Co-operation in Social Sci 1981–, dir The Vinogradoff Inst UCL 1982–, lectr Hague Acad of Int Law 1985, memb Ctee of Mgmnt Inst of Advanced Legal Studies Univ of London 1985–88, govr City of London Poly 1985–89, visiting fell Research Centre for Int Law Univ of Cambridge 1991–92, Leverhulme Research Grant 1991–92; ed East European and Russian Yearbook of International and Comparative Law 2007–, co-ed Jl of Comparative Law 2008–, author of more than 100 books, 900 articles, reviews, and translations on int and comparative law, especially Soviet and Russian law and other CIS legal systems, bookplates, and bibliography; GI Tunkin Medal Russian Int Law Assoc 2003, Medal for Fidelity to Law Supreme Court of Ukraine 2012; sec The Bookplate Soc 1978–86 (foreign sec 1988–94), fndr ed: The Bookplate Jl 1983–92 (co-ed 1989–92), Bookplate International 1994–, Sudebnik 1996–2007, Russian Law 2004–09, Law of Ukraine 2011–; VP Fed Int des Sociétés d'Amateurs d'Ex-Libris 1984–86 (exec sec 1988–); memb: Dist of Columbia Bar, Bar of US Court of Appeals for Dist of Columbia, Bar of US Supreme Court, Cncl Cole Corette and Abrutyn (London and Moscow) 1989–92, Russian Acad of Nat Sciences (section Russian Encyclopaedia) 1992–, EC Jt Task Force for Law Reform in the CIS 1992–93, Nat Acad of Sciences Ukraine 1992–, Russian Court of Int Commercial Arbitration 1995–, Bar of Uzbekistan 1996–, Bar of Russia 1997–, Russian Acad of Legal Sciences 1999–, Learned Cncl 2004–, Kazakhstan Int Arbitrage 2012, Int Commecial Arbitration Ct of Ukraine 2013; special counsel USSR Cncl of Ministers Cmmn for Econ Reform 1989–91; tstee Hakluyt Soc 2004–; Hon LLD Kiev Univ of Law 2012; hon memb: All Union Soc of the Book (USSR) 1989, Soviet Maritime Law Assoc (USSR) 1990, USSR Union of Jurists 1990; memb Associé Int Acad of Comparative Law 1983, memb American Law Inst 2009; FRSA 1986, FSA 1989; *Publications* Russian Law (3 edn 2009), Russia and the Law of Nations in Historical Perspective (2009), The Russian Legal Practitioner (2011), Russian Public Law (3 edn 2013); *Recreations* book collecting, bookplate collecting, bee-keeping; *Clubs* Cosmos, Grolier; *Style—* Prof William Butler, FSA; ✉ e-mail webakademik@aol.com or web15@psu.edu

BUTLER OF BROCKWELL, Baron (Life Peer UK 1998), of Herne Hill in the London Borough of Lambeth; Sir (Frederick Edward) Robin Butler; KG (2003), GCB (1992, KCB 1988), CVO (1986), PC (2004); s of Bernard Daft Butler, and Nora, *née* Jones, of St Annes on Sea, Lancs; *b* 3 January 1938; *Educ* Harrow, UC Oxford (MA); *m* 1962, Gillian Lois, da of Dr Robert Galley, of Teddington, Middx; 2 da (Hon Sophie b 1964, Hon Nell b 1967), 1 s (Hon Andrew b 1968); *Career* private sec to: Rt Hon Edward Heath 1972–74, Rt Hon Harold Wilson 1974–75; princ private sec to Rt Hon Margaret Thatcher 1982–85, second perm sec HM Treasy 1985–87, Sec of the Cabinet and Head of the Home Civil Service 1988–98; master UC Oxford 1998–2008; memb Royal Cmmn on Reform of House of Lords 1999, chm Review of Intelligence on Weapons of Mass Destruction 2004; non-exec dir: ICI plc 1998–2008, HSBC Holdings plc 1998–2008; ind chm King's Health Ptnrs 2009–15; chm of govrs: Harrow Sch 1987–91, Dulwich Coll 1997–2003; hon memb Worshipful Co of Salters; *Recreations* competitive games, opera; *Clubs* Anglo-Belgian, Athenaeum, Brooks's, Beefsteak, MCC, Oxford and Cambridge; *Style—* The Rt Hon Lord Butler of Brockwell, KG, GCB, CVO, PC; ✉ House of Lords, London SW1A 0PW

BUTLER-SLOSS, Baroness (Life Peer UK 2006), of Marsh Green in the County of Devon; Rt Hon Dame (Ann) Elizabeth Oldfield Butler-Sloss; GBE (2005, DBE 1979), PC (1987); da of Hon Mr Justice Cecil Havers (d 1977), High Court judge (Queen's Bench Div), and Enid, *née* Snelling (d 1956), and sister of Baron Havers, PC, QC (d 1992); *b* 10 August 1933; *Educ* Wycombe Abbey; *m* 1958, Joseph William Alexander Sloss (later Butler-Sloss); 2 s, 1 da; *Career* called to the Bar Inner Temple 1955 (reader 1997, treas 1998), registrar Principal Registry Probate Div (subsequently Family Div) 1970–79, judge of the High Court of Justice (Family Div) 1979–88, a Lord Justice of Appeal 1988–99, pres Family Div 1999–2005; Parly candidate (Cons) Lambeth Vauxhall 1959; sometime vice-pres Medico-Legal Soc, memb Judicial Studies Bd 1985–89, chm Cleveland Child Abuse Inquiry 1987–88; past pres Cwlth and English Bar Assoc; former chm Security Cmmn; vice-chm Cncl KCL 1992–97, memb Cncl Wycombe Abbey Sch 1992–1997, chllr UWE 1993–, govr Merchant Taylor's Sch Moor Park; chm Advsy Cncl St Paul's Cathedral 2001–, chm Cmmn appointing the Archbishop of Canterbury 2002; pres Grandparents' Assoc, vice-pres Hospicare Exeter; visitor St Hilda's Coll Oxford, fell Sarum Coll 2004; hon fell: St Hilda's Coll Oxford, Peterhouse Cambridge 2007; Hon DLitt Loughborough Univ 1992; Hon LLD: Univ of Hull 1989, Keele Univ 1991, Univ of Bristol 1991, Univ of Exeter 1992, Brunel Univ 1992, Univ of Central England 1994, Univ of Manchester 1995, Univ of Greenwich 1999, Univ of Cambridge 2000, UAE 2001, Univ of Liverpool 2001, Univ of Ulster 2004, Open Univ, Univ of London 2004, Buckingham Univ 2006; hon memb Merchant Taylors Co 2003; hon bencher NI Inns of Court, hon memb American Law Inst; FKC 1991; Hon FRCP 1992, Hon FRCPsych 1992, Hon FRCPCH, Hon FRSM 1997; *Style—* The Rt Hon the Lady Butler-Sloss, GBE, PC

BUTLER-WHEELHOUSE, Keith Oliver; s of Kenneth Butler-Wheelhouse (d 1998), and May, *née* Page (d 1981); *b* 29 March 1946, Walsall; *Educ* Queen Mary's GS Walsall, Grey HS Port Elizabeth, Port Elizabeth Univ, Witwatersrand Univ Johannesburg (BCom), Grad Sch of Business Univ of Cape Town; *m* 15 Dec 1973, Pamela Anne, *née* Bosworth Smith; 2 s (Duncan b 4 April 1981, Andrew b 3 Feb 1985); *Career* various assignments in manufacturing, product devpt, finance and sales and mktg Ford Motor Co 1965–85, led MBO of General Motor's South African business, chm and chief exec Delta Motor Corporation South Africa 1987–92, chief exec and worldwide pres Saab Automobile Sweden 1992–96, chief exec Smiths Gp plc UK 1996–2008; currently: non-exec chm Chamberlin plc, non-exec dir Plastics Capital; previously non-exec dir Sainsbury's Atlas Copco; Citizen of the Year Port Elizabeth 1988; *Recreations* tennis, swimming, surfing, golf; *Clubs* Johannesburg Country, Fancourt, St Francis Bay and Humewood (all South Africa), Moor Park, Sunningdale, R&A, Queen's; *Style—* Keith Butler-Wheelhouse, Esq; ✉ The Orchard, Sudbury Hill, Harrow on the Hill, London HA1 3NA (☎ 020 8864 7300, mobile 07768 275320)

BUTLIN, Martin Richard Fletcher; CBE (1990); s of Kenneth Rupert Butlin (d 1965), and Helen Mary, *née* Fletcher, MBE (d 1998); *b* 7 June 1929; *Educ* Rendcomb Coll, Trinity Coll Cambridge (MA), Courtauld Inst of Art Univ of London (DLit); *m* 31 Jan 1969, Frances Caroline, da of Michael Anthony Chodzko (d 1997); *Career* Nat Serv RAMC; asst keeper Tate Gallery 1955–67, keeper Historic Br Collection Tate Gallery 1967–89; involved in selection and cataloguing of exhibitions on Blake and the Ancients, author of numerous articles and reviews for magazines; FBA 1984; *Publications* incl: A Catalogue of the Works of William Blake in the Tate Gallery (1957, 3 edn 1990), Samuel Palmer's Sketchbook of 1824 (1962, 2 edn 2005), Turner Watercolours (1962), Turner (with Sir John Rothenstein, 1964), Tate Gallery Catalogues, The Modern British Paintings, Drawings and Sculpture (with Mary Chamot and Dennis Farr, 1964), The Later Works of JMW Turner (1965), William Blake (1966), The Blake-Varley Sketchbook of 1819 (1969), The Paintings of J M W Turner (with Evelyn Joll, 1977, 2 edn 1984, Mitchell Prize 1978), The Paintings and Drawings of William Blake (1981), Aspects of British Painting 1550–1800 from the collection of the Sarah Campbell Blaffer Foundation (1988), William Blake in the collection of the National Gallery of Victoria (with Tedd Gott, 1989), Turner at Petworth (with Mollie Luther and Ian Warrell, 1989), The Oxford Companion to J M W Turner (ed with Evelyn Joll and Luke Herrmann, 2001), William Blake's Watercolour Inventions in Illustration of The Grave by Robert Blair (with Morton D Paley, 2009); *Recreations* opera, ballet, travel; *Style—* Martin Butlin, Esq, CBE, FBA; ✉ 74C Eccleston Square, London SW1V 1PJ

BUTT, Prof John; OBE (2013); s of Wilfrid Roger Butt, of Stratford-upon-Avon, Warks, and Patricia Doreen Butt; *b* 17 November 1960, Solihull, Warks; *Educ* Solihull Sch, King's Coll Cambridge (MA, MPhil, PhD); *m* 22 July 1989, Sally Ann, *née* Cantlay; 4 s (Christopher Andrew b 26 March 1992, James Arthur b 23 June 1994, Angus Alastair b 6 April 1999, Fergus Alexander b 2 June 2004), 1 da (Victoria Ailidh b 11 Sept 1996); *Career* temp lectr Univ of Aberdeen 1986–87, research fell Magdalene Coll Cambridge 1987–89, assoc prof of music and univ organist Univ of Calif Berkeley 1989–97, univ lectr in music Univ of Cambridge 1997–2001 (fell King's Coll), Gardiner prof of music Univ of Glasgow 2001–; recorded 11 CDs for Harmonia Mundi on organ and harpsichord, 4 CDs for Linn Records of choral and orchestral music by Bach and Handel, other recordings with Koch, Centaur and Delphian; W H Scheide Award American Bach Soc 1992, Dent Medal RMA 2003, Classic FM/Gramophone Award (Baroque Vocal) 2007 (for recording of Handel's Messiah with Dunedin Consort), MIDEM (Cannes) Classical Award (Baroque Music) 2008 (for Messiah recording); FRCO 1977, FRSE 2003, FBA 2006; *Books* Bach Interpretation (1990), Bach Mass in B Minor (1991), Music Education in the German Baroque (1994), Cambridge Companion to Bach (1997), Playing with History (2002), Cambridge History of Seventeenth-Century Music (co-ed), Bach's Dialogue with Modernity (2010); *Recreations* reading, hill walking; *Style—* Prof John Butt, OBE; ✉ Music, School of Culture and Creative Arts, University of Glasgow, 14 University Gardens, Glasgow G12 8QQ (☎ 0141 330 4571, mobile 07970 632685, e-mail john.butt@glasgow.ac.uk)

BUTT, Michael Acton; OBE (2011); s of Leslie Acton Kingsford Butt and Mina Gascoigne Butt; *b* 25 May 1942; *Educ* Rugby, Magdalen Coll Oxford, INSEAD France (MBA); *m* 1, 1964 (m dis 1986), Diana Lorraine, *née* Brook; 2 s; m 2, 1986, Zoé Benson; *Career* joined Bland Welch Group 1964, dir Bland Payne Holdings 1970, chm Sedgwick Ltd 1983–87, dep chm Sedgwick Group plc 1985–87, chm and chief exec Eagle Star Holdings plc 1987–91, dir BAT Industries plc 1987–91, chm and chief exec Eagle Star Insurance Co 1987–91; dir: Marceau Investissements SA (France) 1987–95, Mid Ocean Ltd (pres and chief exec) 1992–98, Phoenix Securities Ltd 1992–95, Bank of NT Butterfield Bermuda 1996–2002, XL Capital Ltd 1998–2002; chm AXIS Capital Holdings Ltd 2002– (dir 2012–); tstee: Monte Verdi Tst London 1989–2000, Bermuda Biological Station for Research 1996–2007; dep chm Exec Ctee Bermuda Underwater Exploration Inst 1997–2001; memb: Bd INSEAD France, Instituto Nazionale delle Assicurazioni (INA) Rome 1994–99; Liveryman Worshipful Co of Insurers; *Recreations* tennis, opera, reading, family, the European Movement; *Clubs* Travellers, Mid Ocean (Bermuda), Royal Bermuda Yacht (Bermuda), Coral Beach and Tennis (Bermuda), Tuckers Point; *Style—* Michael Butt, Esq, OBE; ✉ Leamington House, 50 Harrington Sound Road, Hamilton Parish CR04, Bermuda (☎ 00 441 293 1378, fax 00 441 293 8511); AXIS Speciality Limited, PO Box HM 1254, Hamilton HM FX, Bermuda (☎ 00 441 496 2600, fax 00 441 405 2720, e-mail michael.butt@axis.bm)

BUTTERFIELD, Leslie Paul; CBE (2007); s of Leslie John Butterfield (d 1983), and Ruth, *née* Andräs (d 2010); *b* 31 August 1952; *Educ* NE London Poly (BA), Lancaster Univ (MA); *m* 14 May 1988 (m dis), Judy Mary Tombleson; partner Penny Harris; 1 da (Alexa), 1 s (Cerian); *Career* advertising exec and branding conslt; account planner and assoc dir Boase Massimi Pollitt Ltd 1975–80, planning dir Abbott Mead Vickers Ltd 1980–87, chm Partners BDDH (formerly Butterfield Day Devito Hockney) 1987–2001, ceo Butterfield8 2001–03, managing ptnr Ingram 2003–07, ceo Butterfield Ptnrs 2007–08, chief strategy offr Interbrand Gp 2008–; IPA Effectiveness Award 1984 and 2000; FIPA 1988; *Books* Excellence in Advertising (1997, 2 edn 1999), Understanding the Financial Value of Brands (1998), AdValue (2003), Enduring Passion: The story of the Mercedes-Benz brand (2005); *Style—* Leslie Butterfield, Esq, CBE; ✉ 324 Green Valley Villas, 1500 Ha Mi Road, Chang Ning District, Shanghai 200336, China (☎ 0086 139 1807 5596, e-mail leslie.butterfield@interbrand.com)

BUTTERFIELD, Hon Sarah Harriet Anne (Hon Mrs Willetts); da of Baron Butterfield, OBE (d 2000), and Isabel Ann Foster, *née* Kennedy; *b* 28 August 1953, London; *Educ* Sherborne Sch for Girls, Univ of Edinburgh (BA), Ruskin Sch of Fine Art and Drawing Univ of Oxford, Univ of Bristol (DipArch); *m* 19 April 1986, Rt Hon David Lindsay Willetts, MP, *qv*, s of John Roland Willetts, of Birmingham; 1 da, 1 s; *Career* architect 1978–86: California, Bristol, London; illustrator for Experimental Psychology Dept Cambridge Univ 1976–78, art critic Oxford Mail 1978; currently working as an artist; art reviewer Art and Entertainment Prog LBC 1999–2002; exhibitions incl: RCA 1978, Mall Galleries 1980, 1984, 1986 and 1988, Young Contemporaries Agnews 1988, Richmond Gallery London 1990, Roy Miles Gallery London 1991 and 1994, one-man shows Cadogan Contemporary London 1991, 1994 and 1997, Discerning Eye 1997, group show dfn Gallery NY 2000, one-man show 27 Cork St London 2001, group show The View – an Exhibition about Richmond Hill Orleans House Gallery Twickenham 2003, gp show Albemarle Gallery London 2004, one-man show Albemarle Gallery London 2005, official artist on Royal tour by HRH The Prince of Wales and HRH The Duchess of Cornwall on their visit to Egypt, Saudi Arabia and India 2006, Frost and Reed Gallery 2011 and 2012; paintings on permanent view at: British Airways Terminal 4 Heathrow Airport, Gatwick Airport, Wimbledon Lawn Tennis Museum, The Prudential, Trust House Forte Hotels (Exeter and Yorks); Egerton Coghill Landscape Award 1976, Windor & Newton Award 1978, finalist Hunting Gp Art Competition 1987, commended Spector Three Cities Competition 1988; actress: Joan Fielding in Catherine Cookson's Tillie Trotter (ITV) 1999, appearances in Stop, Look, Listen (Channel 4); memb: Equity, ARB; *Books* Word Order Comprehension Test (with Dr Gillian Fenn); *Clubs* Hurlingham; *Style—* The Hon Sarah Butterfield

BUTTERFILL, Sir John Valentine; kt (2004); s of George Thomas Butterfill (d 1980), and Elsie Amelia, *née* Watts (d 1974); *b* 14 February 1941; *Educ* Caterham Sch, Coll of Estate Mgmnt London; *m* 1965, Pamela Ross, da of Frederick Ross-Symons; 3 da (Natasha (Mrs Toby Rougier) b 1969, Samara (Mrs Roger Jones) b 1974, Jemima (Mrs Darsh Dhillon) b 1976), 1 s (James b 1975); *Career* chartered surveyor; valuer Jones Lang Wootton 1962–64, sr exec Hammerson Gp 1964–69, dir Audley Properties Ltd (Bovis Gp) 1969–71, md St Paul's Securities Gp 1971–76, dir Micro Business Systems Ltd 1977–79, sr ptnr Curchod & Co Chartered Surveyors 1977–92, dir Pavilion Services Group Ltd 1992–94, conslt Curchod & Co 1992–, chm Conservation Investments Group, pres European Properties Associates; MP (Cons) Bournemouth W 1983–2010 (Euro Parly candidate London S Inner 1979, Parly candidate Croydon NW by-election 1981); vice-chm

Backbench Tourism Ctee 1985–88 (sec 1983–85), sec Backbench Trade and Industry Ctee 1987–88 and 1990; PPS to: Sec of State for Energy 1988–89, Sec of State for Tport 1989–90, Min of State for NI 1991–92; memb: Trade and Industry Select Ctee 1992–2001, Chm's Panel 1997–, Ct of Referees 1997–; vice-chm: Fin Ctee 1992–2000, Euro Affrs Ctee 1992–97; chm All-Pty Gp on Occupational Pensions 1992–; dep chm Euro Democrat Forum 1981–87, vice-chm Foreign Affairs Forum 1983–92, chm Cons Gp for Europe 1989–92; Parly conslt to BIIBA 1992–97, Parly advsr to BVCA 1994–2001; memb Cncl of Mgmnt PDSA 1990–; memb Ct Univs of Reading, Southampton and Exeter; memb Cncl of Mgmnt People's Dispensary for Sick Animals; FRICS 1974; *Recreations* skiing, tennis, bridge, music; *Style—* Sir John Butterfill

BUTTERWORTH, David; s of John Butterworth (d 1971), and Annie May, *née* Claughton (d 2003); *b* 24 October 1943; *Educ* Audenshaw GS, UCL (BSc(Eng)); *m* 2 Aug 1966, Pauline Patricia, da of Leonard Morgan; 1 s (Richard David b 9 Feb 1968); *Career* AEA Technology Harwell: res scientist/engr 1965–69, section ldr 1969–76, gp ldr 1977–89, md Heat Transfer and Fluid Flow Serv 1989–95 (sr consIt 1995–2008); visiting engr MIT 1976–77; visiting prof: Univ of Bristol 1993–2005, Cranfield Univ 1995–2002; Royal Acad of Engrg visiting prof Aston Univ 1996–2001; gen sec Aluminium Plate-Fin Heat Exchanger Mfrs' Assoc 1995–2008; D Q Kern Award for industrial application of heat transfer technol American Inst of Chem Engrs 1986; chm Heat Transfer Steering Gp Engrg Sciences Data Unit 1986–94, pres UK Heat Transfer Soc 1988–89; memb: Cncl and Engrg Practice Ctee Inst of Chem Engrs 1989–92 (also hon librarian), Scientific Cncl Int Centre for Heat and Mass Transfer 1990–2006, Int Ctee Royal Acad of Engrg 1993–96, UK Nat Ctee for Heat Transfer 1996–2007, Cncl Herb Soc UK 2004–07; tstee Root & Branch 2008–16, community ambass for Abingdon 2014–; CEng 1969, FIChemE 1985, FREng 1991, Eur Ing 1991, FRSA 1993, CSci 2005; *Books* Introduction to Heat Transfer (1977), Two Phase Flow and Heat Transfer (jt ed, 1977, 1978 and 1979, also published in Russian 1980), Design and Operation of Heat Exchangers (jt ed, 1992); *Recreations* painting, cooking, website design; *Style—* David Butterworth, FREng; ✉ e-mail davebutterworth@aol.com

BUTTERWORTH, Jon-Allan; *b* 6 February 1986, Sutton Coldfield, Birmingham; *Career* RAF weapons technician 2002–07, injured in Iraq 2009; Paralympic cyclist; achievements incl: Silver medal (1km time trial) Para-Cycling Europa Cup 2010, Gold medal (1km time trial) Para-Cycling Track World Championships 2011, Gold medal (1km time trial) Para-Cycling Track World Championships 2012, 3 Silver medals (team sprint, individual 4km pursuit and 1km time trial) Paralympic Games 2012, Silver medal (1km time trial) and Bronze medal (individual 4km pursuit) Track World Championships 2013; *Recreations* cinema, dining out, snowboarding; *Style—* Mr Jon-Allan Butterworth; ✉ website www.j-butterworth.com

BUTTERWORTH, Nicholas Gerald; s of Gerald Leonard Butterworth, and Margaret, *née* Cooke; *b* 28 January 1958, Wimbledon; *Educ* Worth Sch, Poly of the South Bank (BSc); *m* 9 Sept 1983, Geraldine Serena, *née* Ruiz; 1 s (Robert Gerald b 11 Dec 1987), 1 da (Serena Catherine b 24 May 1989); *Career* dir DTZ Debenham Tie Leung 1989–2001, ceo Jackson-Stops & Staff 2001–; chm Worth Old Boys' Soc; Liveryman Worshipful Co of Founders 1996, Freeman City of London 1997; MRICS 1983; *Recreations* historic houses, shooting, motoring; *Clubs* East India; *Style—* Nicholas Butterworth, Esq; ✉ Whitmoor Court, Whitmoor Lane, Sutton Green, Guildford, Surrey GU4 7QB (☎ 01483 562534); Jackson-Stops & Staff, 17C Curzon Street, London W1J 5HU (☎ 020 7664 6644, fax 020 7664 6645, e-mail nbutterworth@jackson-stops.com)

BUTTON, Jenson; MBE (2010); s of John Button, and Simone Lyons; *b* 19 January 1980, Frome, Somerset; *Career* Formula One racing driver; winner Br Kart Super Prix 1989, winner Br Cadet Kart Series 1990, winner Br Open and Br Cadet Kart Series 1991, winner Br Open and Br Jr TKM Kart Series 1992, winner Br Open Kart Series 1993, fourth place Br Jr Kart Series 1994, winner races in Jr Intercontinental A Euro Series and Jr Intercontinental A Italian Winter Kart Series 1994, winner Sr ICA Italian Kart Series 1995, youngest ever runner-up World Formula A Kart Series 1995, third place World Cup 1996, third place American Kart Series 1996, winner Euro Supercup A Kart Series 1997, winner Ayrton Senna Meml Cup Suzuka 1997, winner Br Formula Ford Series 1998 (also winner Formula Ford Festival), second place Euro Formula Ford Series (Haywood Racing) 1998, third place Br Formula 3 Series 1999 (top rookie driver); Formula One: Williams 2000 (Grand Prix debut, best qualifying position third place, eighth place in Driver's Championship), seventeenth place Benetton 2001, Renault F1 2002 (seventh place Driver's Championship), Lucky Strike BAR Honda 2003–04 (Driver's Championship: ninth place 2003, third place 2004), BAR Honda 2005 (ninth place Driver's Championship), Honda Racing F1 Team 2006–08 (winner Hungarian Grand Prix 2006; Driver's Championship: sixth place 2006, fifteenth place 2007, eighteenth place 2008), Brawn GP 2009 (winner: Australian Grand Prix 2009, Malaysian Grand Prix 2009, Bahrain Grand Prix 2009, Spanish Grand Prix 2009, Monaco Grand Prix 2009, Turkish Grand Prix 2009; Formula One World Champion 2009), McLaren 2010– (winner: Australian Grand Prix 2010, Chinese Grand Prix 2010, Canadian Grand Prix 2011, Hungarian Grand Prix 2011, Japanese Grand Prix 2011, Australian Grand Prix 2012); *Recreations* triathlons, cars, scuba diving; *Clubs* Br Racing Drivers; *Style—* Jenson Button, Esq, MBE; ✉ website www.jensonbutton.com, Twitter @the_real_jb

BUTTRESS, (Talfryn) David; *b* 9 March 1976, Wales; *Educ* Croesyceiliog Comp Sch Gwent, Middlesex Univ Business Sch (BA); *Career* various sales and mgmnt positions Coca-Cola Enterprises Ltd 1998–2006, co-fndr and md Just-Eat.co.uk Ltd 2006–13, ceo JUST EAT Gp 2013–; angel investor: Minicabster 2011, Rock Pamper Scissors 2013, Dipstix.co.uk 2013; advsr UK govt; Entrepreneur of the Year Investor Allstars 2014, Top CEOs Glassdoor 2016; *Recreations* rugby, cricket, golf, dog lover; *Style—* David Buttress, Esq; ✉ JUST EAT, Fleet Place House, 2 Fleet Place, London EC4M 7RF (e-mail david.buttress@justeat.com, website www.justeat.com)

BUXTON, Adam Offord; *b* 7 June 1969, London; *Educ* Westminster, Cheltenham Coll of Art; *m* Sarah; 2 s (Frank, Natty), 1 da (Hope); *Career* comedian, radio presenter, writer and actor; stand-up incl I, Pavel (Edinburgh Festival) 2005, presenter BUG – The Evolution of Music Video (BFI Southbank) 2007–; *Television* as writer and presenter (with Joe Cornish) incl: The Adam and Joe Show (Channel 4) 1996–2001 (RTS Best Newcomers Award 1998), Adam & Joe's Fourmative Years (Channel 4) 1997, Adam & Joe's Wonky World Of Animation (Channel 4) 2000, Adam and Joe's American Animation Adventure (Channel 4) 2001 presenter (with Joe Cornish) Adam and Joe Go Tokyo! (BBC3 and BBC1) 2003; *Radio* presenter (with Joe Cornish): Saturday Lunchtime Show XFM 2005–06, Breakfast Show BBC 6Music 2007, Saturday Morning Show BBC 6Music 2007– (Best Radio Prog Broadcasting Press Guild Award 2008, 3 Silver Sony Awards 2009, Gold Sony Award 2010, Silver Sony Award 2012); presenter Adam Buxton's Big Mix Tape BBC 6Music (Best Radio Show BT Digital Award 2010); *Film* Stardust 2007, Hot Fuzz 2007, Son of Rambow 2007; *Books* The Adam & Joe Book (1999); *Style—* Mr Adam Buxton; ✉ c/o Emily Rees Jones, PBJ and JBJ Management, 22 Rathbone Street, London W1T 1LA (website www.adam-buxton.co.uk)

BUXTON, Hon Lucinda Catherine; 2 da of Baron Buxton of Alsa, KCVO, MC, DL (Life Peer), *qv*, and Pamela Mary, *née* Birkin; *b* 21 August 1950; *Educ* New Hall Sch Chelmsford; *Career* wildlife cinematographer/dir; has made 18 TV films for Survival Wildlife series and 3 TV films for Partridge Films Ltd; sr prodr Z-Axis Corporation 1997–, European conslt; vice-pres Concept 2 1999, ceo C2 Imaginations 2000–02; tstee Falkland Islands Appeal; vice-pres: Falkland Islands Assoc, UK Falkland Islands Ctee; memb S Georgia Assoc, memb Ctee Trisan da Cunha Assoc; Media Award 1982, Cherry Kearton Award RGS 1983; FRGS; *Books* Survival in the Wild (1980), Survival – South Atlantic (1983); *Recreations* tennis, gardening; *Style—* The Hon Lucinda Buxton; ✉ 7 Vicarage Crescent, London SW11 3LP (☎ 020 7350 1241, mobile 07952 884249, e-mail cindy.buxton@zaxis.com)

BUZAN, Prof Barry Gordon; s of Gordon Buzan, and Jean, *née* Burn; *b* 28 April 1946; *Educ* Univ of Br Columbia (BA), LSE (PhD); *m* 1973, Deborah Skinner; *Career* research fell Inst of Int Rels Univ of Br Columbia 1973–75; Univ of Warwick: lectr 1976–83, sr lectr 1983–88, reader 1988–90, prof 1990–95; prof of int studies Univ of Westminster 1995–2002, prof of int rels LSE 2002– (Montague Burton prof 2008–12, emeritus prof 2011–); visiting prof Grad Sch of Int Rels Int Univ of Japan 1995, Olof Palme visiting prof Sweden 1997–98; hon prof: Jilin Univ 2003–, Univ of Copenhagen 2005–, China Foreign Affrs Univ 2015–; British Int Studies Assoc: vice-chm 1986–87, chm 1988–90; int vice-pres Int Studies Assoc 1993–94; project dir Copenhagen Peace Research Inst 1988–2003; ed Millennium 1971–72, ed Euro Jl of Int Relations 2004–07; Francis Deak Prize American Jl of Int Law 1982; FBA 1998, AcSS 2001; *Books* Seabed Politics (1976), People States and Fear: the National Security Problem in International Relations (1983, revised edn 2007), An Introduction to Strategic Studies: Military Technology and International Relations (1987), The European Security Order Recast: Scenarios for the Post-Cold War Era (jtly, 1990), The Logic of Anarchy: Neorealism to Structural Realism (with Charles Jones and Richard Little, 1993), Identity, Migration and the New Security Agenda in Europe (jtly, 1993), The Mind Map Book (with Tony Buzan, 1993), Security: A New Framework for Analysis (jtly, 1998), Anticipating the Future: Twenty Millennia of Human Progress (with Gerald Segal, 1998), The Arms Dynamic in World Politics (with Eric Herring, 1998), International Systems in World History: Remaking the Study of International Relations (with Richard Little, 2000), Regions and Powers: The Structure of International Security (with Ole Waever, 2003), From International to World Society? English School Theory and the Social Structure of Globalization (2004), The United States and the Great Powers: World Politics in the Twenty-First Century (2004), International Society and the Middle East (co-ed with Ana Gonzalez-Pelaez, 2009), The Evolution of International Security Studies (with Lene Hansen, 2009), Non-Western International Relations Theory (co-ed with Amitav Acharya, 2010), Bringing Soiology to International Relations (co-ed with Mathias Albert and Michael Zürn, 2013), An Introduction to the English School of International Relations: The Societal Approach (2014), Contesting International Society in East Asia (co-ed with Yongjin Zhang, 2014), The Global Transformation: History, Modernity and the Making of International Relations (with George Lawson, 2015); also author of numerous articles and book chapters; *Recreations* chess, gardening; *Style—* Prof Barry Buzan, FBA; ✉ e-mail b.g.buzan@lse.ac.uk

BUZASI, Carla; da of Michael Bevan, and Cherry, *née* Jackson; *b* 7 October 1979, Stroud, Glos; *Educ* Stroud HS, Univ of Warwick; *Career* asst ed Swarovski Magazine Redwood Publishing 2002–03, writer Glamour.com, Vogue.com, GQ.com and CNTraveller.com Condé Nast Digital 2003–04, dep ed Glamour.com 2004–06, assoc ed/online ed Marie Claire 2006–10, ed-in-chief Huffington Post UK 2011–14, global chief content offr WGSN 2014–; Ed of the Year Online Media Award 2012 and 2013, Media Innovator of the Year Br Media Award 2012; *Style—* Ms Carla Buzasi; ✉ e-mail carla@wgsn.com, website www.carlabuzasi.com

BUZZARD, Sir Anthony Farquhar; 3 Bt (UK 1929), of Munstead Grange, Godalming, Surrey; s of Rear Adm Sir Anthony Wass Buzzard, 2 Bt, CB, DSO, OBE (d 1972), and Margaret (d 1989), da of Sir Arthur Knapp, KCIE, CSI, CBE; *b* 28 June 1935; *Educ* Charterhouse, ChCh Oxford (MA), Bethany Theological Coll (MA Th); *m* 1970, Barbara Jean, da of Gordon Arnold, of Michigan; 3 da (Sarah Jane b 1971, Claire Judith b 1974, Heather Elizabeth b 1988); *Heir* bro, Timothy Buzzard; *Career* modern languages teacher at American School in London 1974–81, lectr in theology Atlanta Bible Coll Morrow Georgia (formerly Oregon Bible Coll Illinois) 1982–; articles on Christology & Eschatology in various theological journals, fndr of Restoration Fellowship; speaker Focus on the Kingdom (radio worldwide); fndr Peachtree Wind Quintet Georgia USA 2015; Hon PhD Asia Theological Seminary; *Books* The Coming Kingdom of the Messiah: A Solution to the Riddle of the New Testament (1987), The Doctrine of the Trinity: Christianity's Self-Inflicted Wound (1994), Our Fathers Who Aren't in Heaven: The Forgotten Christianity of Jesus the Jew (1995), The Law, The Sabbath and New Testament Christianity (2005), The Amazing Aims and Claims of Jesus: What You Didn't Learn in Church (2006), Jesus was not a Trinitarian: Recovering the Creed of Jesus (2007); *Recreations* music; *Style—* Sir A F Buzzard, Bt; ✉ 175 West Lake Drive, Fayetteville, GA 30214, USA (☎ 00 1 770 964 1571, fax 00 1 770 964 1571, e-mail anthonybuzzard@mindspring.com, website www.restorationfellowship.org)

BYAM SHAW, Matthew; *Career* former actor, currently theatre prodr; co-fndr Playful Prodns 2010– (prodns incl: Enron (West End and Broadway), Red (Broadway), Krapp's Last Tape (Duchess), Yes, Prime Minister (Gielgud, tour and Apollo), Flare Path (Theatre Royal Haymarket), The Audience (Gielgud Theatre), Frost/Nixon (Gielgud Theatre), The Weir (Wyndham's Theatre), Wolf Hall and Bring Up The Bodies (Aldwych Theatre), Sweeney Todd (Adelphi Theatre), Hay Fever (Noël Coward Theatre); *Style—* Matthew Byam Shaw, Esq; ✉ Playful Productions, Fourth Floor, 41–44 Great Queen Street, London WC2B 5AD

BYATT, Andrew Keir Campbell; *b* 1 October 1959; *Educ* Wellington, Univ of Bristol (BSc), UCL (MSc), CNAA; *Career* BBC: prodr The Swarm (part of Wildlife on One series) 1992–93 (festival winner Semina Internacional de Cine Cientifico Palme D'Or Antibes Underwater Film Festival 1994), prodr Really Wild Guide to Britain 1994, prodr Besieged (part of Wildlife on One series) 1994–95 (Wildscreen Best Series 1998), prodr Incredible Journeys 1995–96, prodr The Humpback – Seiner of the Sea (part of Wildlife on One Specials series) 1995–97, prodr The Blue Planet 1998–2001 (Best Documentary Series BPG TV Awards 2002, Best TV Prog Radio and TV Viewers Choice 2002, Documentary Prog of the Year TRIC Awards 2002, Diver of the Year Diver Magazine 2002), series prodr Monsters We Met 2001–02, co-dir Deep Blue (cinematic release of The Blue Planet) 2002–03, series prodr Amazon Abyss 2005, prodr Ocean Deep (part of Planet Earth series) 2006; head of dive team BBC Natural History Unit 1995–; FGS; *Publications* The Blue Planet (WHSmith Illustrated Book of the Year 2002, Best Educnl Book Br Book Awards 2002, Pubn of the Year Diver Magazine 2002); *Recreations* diving, sailing, skiing and ski mountaineering, photography; *Style—* Andrew Byatt, Esq

BYATT, Dame Antonia Susan (A S Byatt); DBE (1999, CBE 1990); da of His Hon Judge John Frederick Drabble, QC (d 1983), and Kathleen Marie Bloor (d 1984); *b* 24 August 1936; *m* 1, 1959 (m dis 1969), Sir Ian Byatt, *qv*; 1 da (Antonia b 1960), 1 s (Charles b 1961 d 1972); m 2, 1969, Peter John Duffy; 2 da (Isabel b 1970, Miranda b 1973); *Career* teacher: Westminster Tutors 1962–65, Extra-mural Dept Univ of London 1962–71; pt/t lectr Dept of Lib Studies Central Sch of Art and Design 1965–69, lectr Dept of English UCL 1972–81, tutor for admissions Dept of English UCL 1980–82 (asst tutor 1977–80), sr lectr Dept of English UCL 1981–83; full-time writer 1983–; regular reviewer and contrib to press, radio and TV; external assessor in lit Central Sch of Art and Design, external examiner UEA; judge Booker Prize 1974; chm Ctee of Mgmnt Soc of Authors 1984–88 (chair 1986–88); memb: Panel of Judges Hawthornden Prize, BBC's Social Effects of TV Advsy Gp 1974–77, Communications and Cultural Studies Bd CNAA 1978–84, Creative and Performing Arts Bd 1985–87, Kingman Ctee on English Language 1987–88, Advsy Bd Harold Hyam Wingate Fellowship 1988–92, Lit Advsy Panel Br Cncl

1990–98, London Library Ctee 1990–, Bd Br Cncl 1993–98; assoc Newnham Coll Cambridge 1977–82; Premio Malaparte Award Capri 1995, Mythopoeic Fantasy Award for Adult Literature (for The Djinn in the Nightingale's Eye) 1998, Toepfer Fndn Shakespeare Prize for contributions to British Culture 2002, Blue Metropolis Int Literary Grand Prize (Canada) 2009; Hon DLitt: Univ of Bradford 1987, Univ of Durham 1991, Univ of York 1991, Univ of Nottingham 1992, Univ of Liverpool 1993, Univ of Portsmouth 1994, Univ of London 1995, Univ of Cambridge 1999, Univ of Sheffield 2000, Univ of Oxford 2007; hon fell: Newnham Coll Cambridge 1999, London Inst 2000, UCL 2004, Univ of Kent 2004; fell English Assoc 2004, FRSL, Hon FRSA 2009; Chevalier de l'Ordre des Arts et des Lettres (France) 2003; *Books* as A S Byatt: The Shadow of the Sun (1964, reissued 1991), Degrees of Freedom (1965, reissued 1994), The Game (1967), Wordsworth and Coleridge in their Time (1970, reissued as Unruly Times 1989), The Virgin in the Garden (1978), Still Life (1985, PEN Macmillan Silver Pen of Fiction), Sugar and Other Stories (1987), Possession: A Romance (1990, Booker Prize, Irish Times/Aer Lingus Int Fiction Prize, filmed 2002), George Eliot: The Mill on the Floss (ed), George Eliot: Selected Essays and Other Writings (ed, 1990), Passions of The Mind (essays, 1991), Angels and Insects (1992, filmed 1996), The Matisse Stories (1993), The Djinn in the Nightingale's Eye: Five Fairy Stories (1994), Imagining Characters (with Ignês Sodré, 1995), Babel Tower (1996), The Oxford Book of English Short Stories (ed, 1998), Elementals: Stories of Fire and Ice (1998), The Biographer's Tale (2000), On Histories and Stories (2000), Ovid Metamorphosed (contrib, 2000), Portraits in Fiction (2001), The Bird Hand Book (jtly, 2001), A Whistling Woman (2002), Little Black Book of Stories (short stories, 2003), O Henry Prize Stories (contrib short story The Thing in the Forest, 2003), Memory (anthology, ed with Harriet Harvey Wood, 2008), The Children's Book (2009), Moving Pictures (2009); author of varied literary criticism, articles, prefaces, reviews and broadcasts; *Style*— Dame Antonia Byatt, DBE, FRSL; ✉ c/o Rogers, Coleridge and White, 20 Powis Mews, London W11 1JN

BYATT, Sir Ian Charles Rayner; kt (2000); s of Charles Rayner Byatt (d 1944), and Enid Marjorie Annie, *née* Howat (d 1977); *b* 11 March 1932, Preston, Lancs; *Educ* Kirkham GS, St Edmund Hall Oxford (BA), Nuffield Coll Oxford (DPhil), Harvard Univ; *m* 1, 4 July 1959 (m dis 1969), Antonia Susan (Dame Antonia Byatt, DBE, FRSL, *qv*), da of His Hon Judge J F Drabble, QC (d 1982); 1 da ((Helen) Antonia b 1960), 1 s (Charles Nicholas John b 1961, d 1972); m 2, 12 Dec 1997, Prof Deirdre Kelly, *qv*, da of Francis Kelly (d 1998); 2 step s (Eoin Matthew Parker b 1978, Lochlinn Francis Parker b 1980); *Career* serv RAF 1950–52; lectr in economics Univ of Durham 1958–62, economic conslt HM Treasy 1962–64, lectr LSE 1964–67, sr economic advsr DES 1967–69, dir of economics and statistics Miny of Housing (later DOE) 1969–72, dep chief economic advsr HM Treasy 1978–89 (head of public sector economics 1972–78), DG of Water Servs 1989–2000, co sec-gen Fndn for Int Studies on Social Security 2001–02; sr assoc Frontier Economics 2000–; memb Productivity Panel HM Treasy 2000–06; pres Economic and Business Educnl Assoc 1998–2001; non-exec dir RSM Audit UK LLP (formerly Baker Tilly Audit LLP) 2014–; vice-pres Strategic Planning Soc 1993–; chm Water Industry Cmmn for Scotland 2005–11; memb: Cncl of Mgmnt NIESR 1996–2002, Bd of Advsrs St Edmund Hall Oxford 1998–2003, Bd of Mgmnt Int Inst of Public Fin 1987–90 and 2000–06, Cncl Regulatory Policy Inst 2001–07, Int Advsy Ctee Public Utilities Research Center Univ of Florida 2001–, Advsy Panel to Water Industry Cmmr for Scot 2002–04, Advsy Panel on Reform of Water Servs in NI 2003–06; govr Birkbeck Coll London 1997–2005, pres Human City Inst Birmingham 1999–2002, tstee Acad of Youth 2001–05, chm of tstees David Hume Inst Edinburgh 2008–11; chm Friends of Birmingham Cathedral 1999–2015, memb Cncl Birmingham Cathedral 2003–14 (chm Finance Ctee of Chapter 2012–14); memb Holy Cross Centre Tst 1983–2002 (patron 2006–); Freeman City of London; fell Birkbeck Coll London, hon fell St Edmund Hall 2007; Hon DUniv: Brunel, Central England; Hon DSc: Aston Univ 2005, Univ of Birmingham 2007; memb Royal Econ Soc, CIMgt, Hon FIWEM, Hon FCIPS; *Publications* British Electrical Industry 1875–1914 (1979); chapters in books and articles in jls; *Recreations* painting and married life; *Clubs* Oxford and Cambridge; *Style*— Sir Ian Byatt; ✉ 34 Frederick Road, Birmingham B15 1JN (☎ 0121 689 7946, fax 0121 454 6438, e-mail ianbyatt@blueyonder.co.uk); 17 Thanet Street, London WC1H 9QL (☎ 020 7388 3888); Frontier Economics, 71 High Holborn, London WC1V 6DA (☎ 020 7031 7067, fax 020 7031 7001, e-mail ian.byatt@frontier-economics.com)

BYERS, His Hon Charles William; o s of Baron Byers, OBE, PC, DL (Life Peer, d 1984), and Joan (Lady Byers, d 1998); *b* 24 March 1949; *Educ* Westminster, ChCh Oxford; *m* 1, 8 July 1972 (m dis 1995), Suzan Mary, o da of Aubrey Kefford Stone (d 1980); 2 s (Jonathan Charles b 11 April 1975, George William b 19 Nov 1977); m 2, 10 Feb 2002, Mary Louise Elizabeth Ilett, da of John Ilett, of Hyde, Cheshire; *Career* called to the Bar Gray's Inn 1973; recorder of the Crown Court 1993–99, circuit judge (SE Circuit) 1999–2014, ret; *Recreations* craft, the countryside, sailing, water skiing; *Style*— His Hon Charles Byers

BYFIELD, Stephen Keith; s of Keith James Byfield, of Richmond, N Yorks, and Patricia Betty, *née* Smith; *b* 29 April 1963; *Educ* Richmond Sch, Univ of Leeds (BA); *m* 3 Aug 1991, Valérie Amparro Lucienne, da of Robert Legras; 2 da (Sophie b 1987, Heloïse b 1995), 1 s (Christopher b 1996); *Career* political researcher 1983; with Ian Greer Associates 1985–87, dir Profile Political Relations Ltd 1987–90, fndr and md PPS Group Ltd 1990–; *Recreations* exercise and sports; *Clubs* RAC; *Style*— Stephen Byfield, Esq; ✉ PPS Group, 69 Grosvenor Street, London W1K 3JW (☎ 020 7529 1700, fax 020 7629 7514, mobile 07836 611503, e-mail stephen.byfield@ppsgroup.co.uk)

BYFORD, Baroness (Life Peer UK 1996), of Rothley in the County of Leicestershire; Hazel Byford; DBE (1994); da of Sir Cyril Osborne MP, and Lady Osborne; *Educ* St Leonard's Sch St Andrews, Moulton Agric Coll Northampton; *m* 1962, C Barrie Byford (d 2013); 1 da, 1 s (decd); *Career* former farmer; Cons shadow minister for food, farming and rural affrs House of Lords 1998–2007 (shadow minister for environment 1998–2003); *Recreations* golf, reading, bridge; *Clubs* Farmers'; *Style*— The Rt Hon the Baroness Byford, DBE; ✉ House of Lords, London SW1A 0PW (☎ 020 7219 3095, e-mail byfordh@parliament.uk)

BYFORD, Mark; s of Sir Lawrence Byford, CBE, QPM, DL, and Muriel, *née* Massey; *b* 13 June 1958; *Educ* Lincoln Christ's Hosp Sch, Univ of Leeds (LLB); *m* Hilary Bleiker; 2 s (Sam b 1986, Harry b 1994), 3 da (Molly b 1988, Flora b 1992, Lily b 1996); *Career* regnl journalist BBC North 1979–82, asst news ed BBC South 1982–87, news ed BBC West 1987–88, home news ed BBC News and Current Affrs 1988–89, head of centre Leeds BBC North 1989–90; BBC Regnl Broadcasting: asst controller 1990–91, controller 1991–94, dep md 1994–96, dir of regnl broadcasting BBC Broadcast 1996–98; dir BBC World Service 1998–2002, dir BBC World Serv and Global News 2002–04, dep DG and head of journalism BBC 2004–11; govr Univ of Winchester 2014–; tstee RNLI 2012–; fell Radio Acad 2000; *Books* A Name on a Wall (2013); *Recreations* family life, entertaining close friends, football, cricket, rock music, tennis, swimming, fell walking, cinema, theatre, visiting cathedrals, collecting rock memorabilia; *Style*— Mark Byford, Esq

BYGRAVE, Clifford; s of Fred Bygrave (d 1993), and Beatrice Rose, *née* Bonnick (d 2006); *b* 24 May 1934, Markyate, Herts; *Educ* Luton GS; *m* 15 July 1961, Jean Elizabeth, da of Edward Neale (d 1986); 3 da (Angela Joy b 1964, Paula Jane b 1968, Heather Alison b 1972); *Career* RNVR 1955–59; chartered accountant; ptnr: Hillier Hills Frary & Co 1962–81, Arthur Young (now Ernst & Young) 1981–96, sole practitioner 1996–2011; memb: Mgmnt Ctee Beds, Bucks and Herts Soc of Chartered Accountants 1971–2016 (pres 1975–76, 1993–94, 2005–06 and 2006–07), Cncl ICAEW 1980–2003 (chair: Trg Standards Bd, Investigation Ctee, Professional Standards Office, Fin Servs Authorisation Ctee, Ethics Ctee, CCAB Ethics Ctee, The CA Jt Ethics Ctee); represented UK accounting bodies on Int Fedn of Accountants Ethics Ctee and ICAEW on Ethics Ctee Fédération des Experts Comptables Européens (FEE) Brussels; vice-chm and non-exec dir Luton and Dunstable Hosp NHS Tst 2001–15; int lectr on corp ethics, presented paper XIV World Congress; nat treas and tstee Boys' Brigade, tstee of a number of local charitable tsts; Freeman City of London, Clerk Worshipful Co of Chartered Accountants 1996–2009 (Jr Warden 2010–11, Sr Warden 2011–12, Master 2012–13); FCA 1958, ATII 1964; *Recreations* golf, soccer; *Clubs* Farmers', Ashridge Golf; *Style*— Clifford Bygrave, Esq; ✉ The Rustlings, Valley Close, Studham, Dunstable, Bedfordshire LU6 2QN (☎ 01582 872070, e-mail rustlingscb@gmail.com)

BYLES, Daniel Alan (Dan); *b* June 1974, Hastings, E Sussex; *Educ* Warwick Sch, Univ of Leeds, RMA Sandhurst; *Career* Regular Army Offr 1996–2005; MP (Cons) Warks N 2010–15; vice-pres Corp Devpt Living PlanIT 2015–; chair SmarterUK 2015–; FRGS; *Style*— Dan Byles, Esq; ✉ House of Commons, London SW1A 0AA (website www.danbyles.co.uk, Twitter @danielbyles)

BYLES, David Warner; s of Charles Humphrey Gilbert Byles (d 1970), of Kemsing, Kent, and Pamela Beatrice Byles; *b* 6 April 1954; *Educ* Sevenoaks Sch, Univ of Kent (BA); *m* 1981, Susan Jane, da of Edward Fowles; 1 da (Jennifer Mary b 1985), 1 s (Thomas Edward b 1988); *Career* advtg exec; asst to Co Sec HP Drewry (Shipping Consultants) Ltd 1976–77; Benton & Bowles: graduate trainee 1977–78, media exec 1978–79, media gp head 1979–81; J Walter Thompson: dep media gp mangr 1981–82, media gp mangr 1982–83, asst media dir 1983–87, bd dir media 1987–89, media dir 1989–95, media dir Latin America (Mexico) and worldwide media dir working on Kellogg's account 1995; accounts handled for JWT incl: Nestlé Rowntree, NatWest, Thomson Holidays, St Ivel, Kellogg; fndr and ldr Mindshare 1998–; RAF Special Flying award 1970–71; memb RSPB 1985, MIPA 1988; *Recreations* ornithology, motorcycling, scuba diving; *Clubs* RAC; *Style*— David Byles, Esq

BYLES, Tim; CBE (2006); s of Charles Humphrey Gilbert Byles, and Pamela Beatrice Byles; *m* 1985, Shirley Elizabeth Rowland; 3 s; *Career* mgmnt trainee corp planning Marketing Dept British Gas 1980–84; English Tourist Bd: mangr Mgmnt Servs 1984–85, asst dir of devpt 1985–88; dir of economic devpt Kent CC 1988–96, chief exec Norfolk CC 1996–2006, chief exec Partnerships for Schs 2006–; *Recreations* music, swimming, church; *Style*— Tim Byles, Esq, CBE

BYLLAM-BARNES, Joseph Charles Felix Byllam; s of Cyril Charles Byllam-Barnes (d 1976), of Ashtead, Surrey, and Barbara Isabel Mary, *née* Walls (d 2003); *b* 30 August 1928; *Educ* The Modern Sch Streatham, Shaftesbury, City of London Freemen's Sch; *m* 1 April 1978, Maureen Margaret Mary, da of Maj Claude Montague Castle, MC (d 1940), of Hampstead, London; *Career* RAMC 1946–49, i/c Mil and Public Health Servs Eritrea 1948–49; with Barclays Bank plc 1945–92 (Head Office inspr 1976–92); banking law conslt 1992–2000; elected memb Ct of Common Cncl City of London 1997–2004; govr City of London Freemen's Sch 1999–2004; vice-pres Royal Soc of St George City of London Branch (chm 1994–95, hon sec 1995–2011); pres: Farringdon Ward Club 1990–91, United Wards Club of the City of London 2002–03, Ward of Cheap Club 2003–04, City Livery Club 2005–06 (hon sec 1996–98); vice-chm London Rivers Assoc 2001–04; memb: Bluebell Railway Preservation Soc, Brighton Atlantic Project Ctee 2000–, Castle Baynards Ward Club, HAC, RUSI, IOD; Oblate Quarr Abbey 1963; Freeman City of London 1983, Master Guild of Freemen of the City of London 2000–01 (memb Ct of Assts 1990); Liveryman: Worshipful Co of Upholders 1984 (treas 1984–2010, memb Ct of Assts 1986, Master 1993–94), Worshipful Co of Fletchers 1995, Worshipful Co of Int Bankers 2008; FCIB, FFA, FRSA; KMCO 2011; *Recreations* music, opera, study of law and theology; *Clubs* Carlton, Guards Polo, City Livery Yacht (ctee memb 1990–2010), Surrey CCC; *Style*— Joseph Byllam-Barnes, Esq, KMCO; ✉ Walsingham House, Oldfield Gardens, Ashtead, Surrey KT21 2NA (☎ 01372 277667, fax 01372 271533, e-mail byllam-barnes@zen.co.uk)

BYNOE, Ian Kellman; OBE (2009); s of Harold Gore Bynoe (d 1970), and Sheila Mary, *née* Hay (d 2007); *b* 6 March 1953, Leamington Spa, Warks; *Educ* Monkton Combe Sch, Univ of Durham (BA), Coll of Law Guildford; *m* 22 April 1995, Denise, *née* Stevens; *Career* admitted slr 1977; slr Small Heath Community Law Centre Birmingham 1977–81, asst slr then ptnr David Gray & Co Slrs 1981–87, slr Springfield Advice and Law Centre Springfield Psychiatric Hosp London 1988, legal offr then legal dir and head Legal Dept MIND (Nat Assoc for Mental Health) 1988–94, self-employed public policy researcher (incl for IPPR), legal and practice trainer and conslt, and pt/t slr Scott Moncrieff, Harbour and Sinclair 1994–98; Police Complaints Authy: memb 1998–2001, second dep chm 2001–02, first dep chm 2002–04; cmmr Ind Police Complaints Cmmn 2004–09, ind complaints assessor Dept for Tport and its Exec Agencies 2010–14; memb: Mental Health and Disability Sub-Ctee Law Soc 1989–94, BMA Working Party on the Health Needs of Remand Prisoners 1989–91, Legal and Parly Ctee Royal Assoc for Disability and Rehabilitation 1990–93, Ctee of Patrons (formerly Bd of Dirs) Revolving Doors Agency 1991–2004, Mentally Disordered Offender Sub-Ctee Mental Health Fndn 1992–94, Nat Advsy Ctee on Mentally Disordered Offenders Home Office/Dept of Health 1993–94, Working Party on Code of Practice on Advocacy with Older People Centre for Policy on Ageing 1994–95, Ind Ctee on the Role and Responsibilities of the Police Policy Studies Inst/Police Fndn 1993–96, Ctee on Reform of Coroners' Servs Liberty/Inquest 2002, Home Office Review of Misconduct Action Against Ethnic Minority Police Offrs 2002–03; govr Royal United Hosps Bath NHS Fndn Tst 2014–; memb: Legal Action Gp 1974, Law Soc 1977; FRSA 1993; *Publications* Equal Rights for Disabled People: The case for a new law (jtly, 1991), Treatment, Care and Security: Waiting for change (1992), Beyond the Citizen's Charter: New directions in social rights (1996), How to Comply with the Disability Discrimination Act 1995: An essential guide for solicitors (1997), Rights to Fair Treatment (1997), A Human Rights Commission: The options for Britain and Northern Ireland (jtly, 1998), Mainstreaming Human Rights in Whitehall and Westminster (jtly, 1999); contrib of chapters to books and author of articles in jls and professional and nat press; *Recreations* cycling, walking, classical music, singing, gardening; *Style*— Ian Bynoe, Esq, OBE; ✉ Brook House, Prestleigh Lane, Prestleigh, Shepton Mallet, Somerset BA4 4NG (☎ 01749 830810, e-mail ian.bynoe@btinternet.com)

BYRNE, Dorothy; *Educ* Univ of Manchester (BA), Univ of Sheffield (Dip); *Career* prodr/dir World in Action (Granada) 1989–96, ed The Big Story (ITV) 1996–98 (dep ed 1994–96), head of news and current affairs Channel 4 2003–; visiting prof Sch of Journalism Univ of Lincoln 2005–16, prof De Montfort Univ Leicester 2016–; *Style*— Ms Dorothy Byrne; ✉ Channel 4, 124 Horseferry Road, London SW1P 2TX

BYRNE, Prof James Vincent; s of Wing Cdr Vincent George Byrne (d 1978), and Hon Nona Georgette, *née* Lawrence (d 2012); *b* 13 October 1950; *Educ* Nautical Coll Pangebourne, St Mary's Hosp Med Sch (MB, BS), Univ of London (MD); *m* 1975, Juliet Elizabeth Anson, *née* Bailey; 1 da (Rowena Catherine Anson b 1977), 3 s (Thomas Vincent Lawrence b 1979, George Henry St Clare b 1982, Henry Charles Mogridge b 1985); *Career* conslt neuroradiologist: Atkinson Moreley Hosp 1988–90, Radcliffe Infirmary Oxford 1991–2006, John Radcliffe Hosp Oxford 2006–16; clinical lectr: St George's Hosp Med Sch 1988–90, Univ of Oxford 1994– (reader 2003, prof 2006); med dir Lodestone Patient Care Ltd 1994–2004, med dir Oxford Endovascular Ltd 2016–; ed-in-chief Neuroradiology 2004–10, ed-in-chief European Jl of Radiology 2016–; dir Catholic Building Soc 1989–98; Flude

Memorial Prize Br Inst of Radiology 1997, Hunterian lectr RCS 1999; FRCS 1979, FRCR 1986; *Publications* Endovascular Treatment of Intracranial Aneurysms 1998, A Textbook of Interventional Neuroradiology 2002, Tutorials in Endovascular Neurosurgery and Interventional Neuroradiology (2012); *Recreations* skiing, fishing, sailing, gardening; *Clubs* RAC, Pall Mall; *Style*— Prof James Byrne, ⊠ Hawkyard House, New Street, Chipping Norton, Oxfordshire OX7 5LJ (☎ 01608 642504); Nuffield Department of Surgical Sciences, John Radcliffe Hospital, Headley Way, Oxford OX3 9DU (e-mail james.byrne@nds.ox.ac.uk)

BYRNE, Joe; MLA; *Educ* Queen's Univ Belfast; *Career* former lectr in economics and business; MLA (SDLP) W Tyrone 1998–2003 and 2011–; *Style*— Joe Byrne, Esq, MLA; ⊠ Northern Ireland Assembly, Parliament Buildings, Belfast BT4 3XX

BYRNE, John Edward Thomas; s of John Byrne (d 1979), and Violet Mary, *née* Harris (d 1999); *b* 16 February 1935; *Educ* Kilkenny Coll, Mountjoy Sch Dublin, Trinity Coll Dublin (BA, MB BCh, BAO); *m* 23 Nov 1963, Margaret Elizabeth Ross, da of William Albert Wilson (d 1975); 2 da (Katharine b 1969, Johanna b 1971); *Career* house surgn and house physician Dr Steeven's Hosp Dublin 1961–62, house surgn RNTE Hosp Golden Sq 1963, anatomy lectr and demonstrator St Mary's Hosp Med Sch 1966–67, fell in otology Wayne State Univ Detroit 1973, conslt in otolaryngology Belfast City Hosp 1974–2000, civilian conslt in otolaryngology HM Forces NI 1974–2010; external examiner to constituent colls Nat Univ of Ireland, examiner RCSI (otolaryngology), author of various pubns on blast injury to ears; memb: ORS, Irish Otolaryngological Soc (hon ed Proceedings 1974–93, pres 1994), Ulster Med Soc, Br Cochlear Implant Gp, TCD Assoc; FRCSI 1970; *Books* Scott/Brown's Otolaryngology (contrib, 1997); *Recreations* sailing, maritime history, gardening, theatre; *Clubs* Kildare St and Univ, Strangford Lough Yacht, RSM; *Style*— John Byrne, Esq; ⊠ Mulroy Lodge, Ballymenoch Park, Holywood BT18 0LP (☎ 028 9042 3374, e-mail jetb@btinternet.com)

BYRNE, Rt Hon Liam; PC (2008), MP; *b* 2 October 1970; *Educ* Univ of Manchester, Harvard Business Sch (Fulbright Scholar); *m* Sarah; 3 c (Alex, John, Elizabeth); *Career* joined Lab Pty 1985; began career at Andersen Consulting, moving to NM Rothschilds, co-fndr EGS Gp 2000; advsr Lab Pty 1996–97; MP (Lab) Birmingham Hodge Hill 2004– (by-election), Parly under sec of state for care services 2005–06, min of state Home Office 2006–08, min for the West Midlands 2007–08, min of state HM Treasury 2008, min Cabinet Office and Chllr of the Duchy of Lancaster 2008–09, chief sec to the Treasury 2009–10, shadow min Cabinet Office 2010–11, shadow sec for work and pensions 2011–; memb: Amicus, Fabian Soc, Co-op Soc; assoc fell Social Market Fndn; *Style*— The Rt Hon Liam Byrne, MP; ⊠ House of Commons, London SW1A 0AA

BYRNE, Lisa; da of Narinder Palta, of York, and Philomena, *née* Fleming (d 2001); *b* 12 April 1970, Shrewsbury, Salop; *Educ* Bar Convent Sch York, Goldsmiths Coll London; *m* 18 March 2006, David Byrne; 1 da (Brontë Philomena b 26 Jan 2008); *Career* OK! magazine: feature writer 1998–, dep ed 2002–04, ed 2004–; freelance writer: Mail on Sunday, Sunday Mirror, Sunday People, Chat; fundraiser for Children with Leukaemia; *Recreations* walking the dog (cocker spaniel called Diggerley), social events, theatre; *Style*— Mrs Lisa Byrne; ⊠ The Northern & Shell Building, Number 10 Lower Thames Street, London EC3R 6EN (☎ 020 8612 7066, fax 020 8612 7305, email lisa.byrne@express.co.uk)

BYRNE, His Hon Judge Michael David; s of late Gerard Robert Byrne, and Margaret Doreen, *née* Charlton; *b* 7 December 1945; *Educ* St Edward's Coll Liverpool, Univ of Liverpool (BA, LLB); *m* 1985, Felicity Jane, *née* Davies; *Career* called to the Bar 1971; barr 1971–2002, recorder 1992–2002 (asst recorder 1989–92), circuit judge (Northern Circuit) 2002–; non-exec dir Ashworth Special Hosp 1996–97 (chm Mangrs Advsy Ctee 1989–98), vice-chm Ashworth Special HA 1997–98; chm of govrs St Edward's Coll Liverpool 1995– (govr 1993–); *Recreations* music, literature, theatre, travel; *Style*— His Hon Judge Byrne; ⊠ Preston Combined Court Centre, The Law Courts, Ring Way, Preston PR1 2LL

BYROM, Peter John; s of John Byrom (d 1988), and Mary, *née* Hinch (d 2004); *b* 23 June 1944; *Educ* Perse Sch, Univ of Southampton (BSc); *m* 2 June 1987, Melanie Signe, da of John Palmer; 3 da (Nicola Christa b 20 June 1987, Olivia Signe b 31 March 1989, Serena Melanie b 1 Oct 1993); *Career* Arthur Andersen & Co 1966–72; chm: Leeds Life Assurance Ltd 1994–96, Domino Printing Sciences plc 1996–, Molins plc 1999–2009; dep chm T&N plc 1989–96; dir: N M Rothschild & Sons Ltd 1972–96, Peter Black Holdings plc 1984–2001, Adwest Group plc 1989–94, China Investment Trust plc 1995–98, Rolls-Royce plc 1997–2013, Wilson Bowden plc 1998–2007, Amec plc 2005–11; tstee Southampton Univ Devpt Tst 1998–2010; Freeman City of London 1989, Liveryman Worshipful Co of Goldsmiths 1993; FCA, FRAeS 1999; *Clubs* Bosham Sailing, Kandahar Ski, Brooks's; *Style*— Peter Byrom, Esq; ⊠ Chalton Priory, Chalton, Hampshire PO8 0BG (☎ 023 9259 5181)

BYROM, Dr Richard John; s of Richard Byrom (d 1961), of Bury, and Bessie, *née* Jardin; *b* 12 October 1939; *Educ* Denstone Coll, Univ of Manchester (BA, MPhil), Univ of Huddersfield (PhD); *m* 4 April 1964, Susan Hope, da of Richard Clegg (d 1984), of Gwydir; 2 s (Peter b 1965, David b 1968), 1 da (Joy b 1967); *Career* private architectural practice 1964–2016, Byrom Clark Roberts Architects Surveyors and Consulting Engrs Manchester; chm Register Architects Accredited in Building Conservation 2003–06; ISVA: chm Building Surveying Ctee 1986–90, chm Manchester and Dist Branch 1995; JP 1973–2000; reader Hawkshaw Parish Church 1964–; govr Bolton Sch 1997–2013; RIBA 1965 (chm President's Ctee on Arbitration 1999–2002), FCIArb 1977 (chm NW Branch CIArb 1998–2000), FSVA 1976, FRICS 2000; *Recreations* industrial history; *Clubs* St James's (Manchester); *Style*— Dr Richard J Byrom; ⊠ Byrom Clark Roberts Ltd, Washbrook House, Old Trafford, Manchester M32 0FP (☎ 0161 875 0600)

BYRON, 13 Baron (E 1643); Robert James Byron; 2 (but only surviving) s of 12 Baron Byron (d 1989), and his 2 w, Dorigen Margaret, *née* Esdaile (d 1985); *b* 5 April 1950; *Educ* Wellington, Trinity Coll Cambridge; *m* 1979, Robyn Margaret, da of John McLean, of Hamilton, NZ; 3 da (Hon Caroline b 1981, Hon Emily b 1984, Hon Sophie b 1986), 1 s (Hon Charles Richard Gordon b 1990); *Heir* s, Hon Charles Byron; *Career* barr 1974; admitted slr 1978; ptnr Holman Fenwick & Willan 1984–; *Style*— The Rt Hon the Lord Byron

BYWATER, Isabella; da of Tom Stacey, of London, and Caroline, *née* Clay; *b* 6 October 1957; *Educ* Tunbridge Wells Girls GS, Godolphin & Latymer Sch, Cambridge Coll of Arts and Technol, Motley Sch of Theatre Design; *m* 1 (m dis), Michael Bywater, s of late Dr Keith Bywater; 1 da (Benedicta May b 12 July 1984); *m* 2, Christopher Simon Sykes, s of late Sir Richard Sykes; *Career* opera designer and director; former: prop maker, scene painter; *Theatre* designs incl: Titus Andronicus 1987, A Midsummer Night's Dream 1992, A Doll's House 1992, Of Mice and Men 1992, The Tempest 1993, All My Sons 1993, School for Wives 1993, Twelfth Night 1994, Hedda Gabler 1996, The Cherry Orchard (Crucible Theatre Sheffield) 2007, Faust (Mariinsky, St Petersburg) 2013 (also dir); *Opera* UK prodns incl: The Barber of Seville 1982, Nabucco 1982, Il Tabarro 1983, Soeur Angelica 1983, Gianni Schicci 1983, The Turn of The Screw 1983, Eugene Onegin 1984, Andrea Chenier 1984, The Flying Dutchman 1987, Belshazzar 1987, The Duenna 1991, Madama Butterfly 1992, La Finta Giardinera 1994, King Arthur 1995, The Marriage of Figaro 1996, The Elixir of Love 1996, The Emperor of Atlantis 1997, The Dictator 1997, Il Re Pastore 1999, Snegourochka 2001, Don Pasquale (Covent Garden Opera) 2004, Elixir of Love (ENO) 2010, Aida (Royal Albert Hall) 2012, Aida (Royal Albert Hall) 2012, Rutherford and Son (Northern Broadsides) 2013; overseas prodns incl: Cavalleria Rusticana (Stockholm Royal Opera) 1991, Pagliacci (Stockholm Royal Opera) 1991, The Elixir of Love (W Aust Opera, Qland Opera and Victoria State Opera) 1995, Ezio (Theatre des Champs Elysees Paris) 1995, La Traviata (Opera NI Belfast) 1996, (Vancouver) 2010 and (NYC Opera) 2011, Fidelio (Opera NI Belfast) 1996, The Masked Ball (Opera Monte Carlo) 1998, Nabucco (Zurich Opera) 1998, I Puritani (Bayerischer Staatsoper Munich) 2000, Ermione (Santa Fe Opera) 2000, Don Pasquale (Teatro Maggio Musicale di Firenze) 2001 and (La Scala Milan) 2012, Eugene Onegin (Santa Fe Opera) 2002, The Makropulos Case (Stockholm Royal Opera) 2003, Die Entführung aus dem Serail (Zurich Opera) 2003, L'Elisir D'Amore (Stockholm Royal Opera) 2003 and (NYC Opera) 2006, Falstaff (New Nat Theatre Tokyo) 2004, Clemenza di Tito (Zurich Opera) 2005, Entführung aus dem Serail (Ancona) 2005, Jenufa (Glimmerglass USA) 2006, Der Rosenkavalier (New Nat Theatre Tokyo) 2007, Fidelio (Aarhus) 2007, Die Entführung aus dem Serail (Cagliari) 2007, La Boheme (ENO) 2009, La Traviata (Glimmerglass USA) 2009, La Boheme (Cincinnati) 2011, A Midsummer Night's Dream (Mariinsky St Petersburg) 2011 (Best Opera Production Zoloty Sofit 2011); dir and designer Gounod's Faust (Mariinsky Theatre St Petersburg) 2013, Lucia Di Lammermoor (Danish National Opera 2014), La Boheme (San Diego Opera 2015), La Traviata (Mariinsky 2015); *Recreations* sculpture, philosophy, biking; *Style*— Ms Isabella Bywater; ⊠ c/o Judy Daish, 2 St Charles Place, London W10 6EG (☎ 020 8964 8811, website www.isabellabywater.com)

BYWATER, John; *b* Leeds; *Career* chartered surveyor; early career with British Rail, Leeds Corporation, Joshua Tetley and Burton Gp (latterly md Burton Property Tst then head of retail Donaldsons), md Hammerson UK and exec dir Hammerson plc 1998–2007, md Caddick Devpts 2007–; non-exec dir: Workspace Gp plc, Low Carbon Workplace plc, Opera North, Realis Estates; chair Harrogate Symphony Orchestra, chair Canal and River Tst; FRICS; *Recreations* music, tennis, golf, family, playing the violin; *Style*— John Bywater, Esq; ⊠ Caddick Developments Limited, Castlegarth Grange, Scott Lane, Wetherby, Yorkshire LS22 6LH (website www.caddickdevelopments.co.uk)

C

C

CAAN, James (né Nazim Khan); CBE (2015); *b* 1960, Lahore, Pakistan; *Educ* Harvard Business Sch; *Career* entrepreneur; fndr Alexander Mann 1985 (sold 2002), co-fndr Humana Int 1993 (sold 1999), co-fndr AMS 1999 (sold 2002), fndr Hamilton Bradshaw 2004; co-chair Ethnic Minority of the Business Task Force 2009–; panel memb Dragon's Den (BBC 2) 2007–10; fndr James Caan Fndn 2006; BT Enterprise of the Year Award 2001, PricewaterhouseCoopers Entrepreneur of the Year 2003, Entrepreneur of the Year Asian Jewel Awards 2003, Man of the Year and Asian Businessman of the Year GG2 Leadership and Diversity Awards 2008; *Books* The Real Deal (2008); *Style—* James Caan, Esq, CBE; ✉ Hamilton Bradshaw, 23 Grosvenor Street, London W1K 4QL

CABLE, Rt Hon Sir (John) Vincent (Vince); kt (2015), PC (2010); s of (John) Leonard Cable (d 1981), and Edith, *née* Pinkney; *b* 9 May 1943, York; *Educ* Nunthorpe GS York, Univ of Cambridge (BA, pres Cambridge Union), Univ of Glasgow (PhD); *m* 1 Maria Olympia, *née* Rebelo (d 2001); 2 s (Paul, Hugo), 1 da (Aida); m 2, 2004, Rachel *née* Wenban-Smith; *Career* fin offr Kenya Treasy (ODI/Nuffield fell) 1966–68, lectr in econs Univ of Glasgow 1968–74, first sec Diplomatic Serv 1974–76, dep dir Overseas Devpt Inst 1976–83, special advsr to late Rt Hon John Smith, MP as Sec of State for Trade 1979, special advsr (dir) Cwlth Secretariat 1983–90, advsr to Brundtland Cmmn on environment and devpt 1986, head Econs Prog Chatham House 1993–95, chief economist Shell (International) 1995–97, MP (Lib Dem) Twickenham 1997–2015; memb Treasy Select Ctee 1999, Lib Dem shadow Chllr of the Exchequer 2003–10, dep ldr 2006–10, acting ldr 2007, sec of state for business innovation and skills 2010–15; pres Bd of Trade 2010–; former chair All Pty Police Gp, chair All Pty Victims of Crime Gp; cncllr (Lab) Glasgow City Cncl 1971–74; contested: Glasgow Hillhead (Lab) 1970, York (Lib Dem) 1983 and 1987, Twickenham (Lib Dem) 1992; visiting fell: Nuffield Coll Oxford, LSE; *Publications* Protectionism and Industrial Decline (1983), Private Foreign Investment and Development (jtly, 1987), Trade Blocs (jtly, 1994), The World's New Fissures, The Politics of Identity (Demos, 1994), Global Superhighways (1995), China and India, The Emerging Giants (1995), Globalisation and Global Governance (1999), Multiple Identity (2005), The Storm (2009), Free Radical (2009), Tackling the Fiscal Crisis (2009); *Recreations* dancing (ballroom and latin); *Clubs* British Legion (Twickenham); *Style—* The Rt Hon Sir Vince Cable; ✉ 2a Lion Road, Twickenham TW1 4JQ (☎ 020 8892 0215, e-mail cablev@parliament.uk, website www.vincentcable.org.uk); House of Commons, London SW1A 0AA; Constituency Office

CADBURY, Sir (Nicholas) Dominic; kt (1997); *Career* Cadbury Schweppes plc: joined 1964, memb Bd 1975, gp chief exec 1983–93, chm 1993–2000; chm: The Economist 1993–2003, Wellcome Tst 2000–06, Misys plc 2005–09 (non-exec dir 2000–09); jt dep chm EMI Gp plc 1999–2004 (non-exec dir 1998–2004), non-exec dep chm New Star Asset Mgmnt Gp plc 2005–07; chllr Univ of Birmingham 2002–; *Style—* Sir Dominic Cadbury

CADBURY, Peter Hugh George; 3 s of (John) Christopher Cadbury, of Rednal, Birmingham, by his 1 w, Honor Mary, *née* Milward (d 1957); *b* 8 June 1943; *Educ* Rugby; *m* 1969, Sally, er da of Peter Frederick Strouvelle, of Cape Town, South Africa; 1 da (Eleanor (Duchess of Argyll) b 1973), 1 s (Simon b 1975); *Career* admitted slr, with Linklaters & Paines 1965–70, with Morgan Grenfell 1970–97 (dir 1977–97, dep chm 1992–97); chm: Henderson Smaller Companies Investment Trust plc 1989–2003, Close Brothers Corporate Finance Ltd 1997–99, Peter Cadbury & Co 1999–, DTZ Corporate Finance Ltd 2002–08; dir: SMG plc 1998–2001, Celltech plc 2003–06; sr advsr: Kleinwort Benson, Tata Consultancy Services; memb Pilgrims Assoc; FRSA, FRGS; *Clubs* Boodle's, Lansdowne, Beefsteak; *Style—* Peter Cadbury, Esq; ✉ PA Sue Ellis (☎ 01920 464569, e-mail sue@petercadbury.com)

CADDICK, Paul; s of Albert Caddick, and Nora, *née* Higinson; *b* 25 July 1950, Castleford, W Yorks; *Educ* Castleford Secdy Modern, Castleford GS, Leeds Coll of Building, Sheffield Poly (BSc); *m* 30 Sept 1974, Alexandra, *née* Hartley; 1 da (Alexandra Victoria (Mrs Hulme) b 26 Dec 1977), 1 s (John Paul b 17 June 1981); *Career* Sir Lindsay Parkinson's 1966–69, Dowsett Engrg Construction 1969–74, W Yorks CC 1974–77, John Laing Construction 1977–80, fndr and chm Caddick Gp 1980–; MICE 1977, memb Inst of Municipal Engrs 1977; *Style—* Paul Caddick, Esq; ✉ Oakgate Group plc, Oakgate House, 25 Market Place, Wetherby, West Yorkshire LS22 6LQ; Caddick Group, Castlegarth Grange, Scott Lane, Wetherby, West Yorkshire LS22 6LH

CADDY, David Henry Arnold Courtenay; s of Colonel John Caddy, of Melbourne, Australia and Highgate Village, London, and Elizabeth, *née* Day; *b* 22 June 1944; *Educ* Eton; *m* 1, 24 July 1971 (m dis 2000), Valerie Elizabeth Margaret, da of Dr Kelly Swanston, of Helmsley, N Yorks; 1 s (Julian b 1972), 1 da (Henrietta b 1978); m 2, 15 Sept 2000, Susan Lougher Jermine, da of Gwynne Lougher Porter, of Cyncoed, Glamorgan; *Career* articled to Layton Bennett Billingham and Co London 1962–68, qualified chartered accountant 1968; PricewaterhouseCoopers (formerly Coopers & Lybrand before merger) 1968–2000: ptnr Liberia 1974, managing ptnr Liberia 1974–77, ptnr UK 1977–2000, regnl chm UK South and East 1993–98; memb Ctee: London Soc of Chartered Accountants 1980, Cncl of Ptnrs Coopers & Lybrand 1989–97, Bd of Coopers & Lybrand 1994–97; fin dir Numasters.com 2000–, ptnr Hadleigh Partners 2011–; dir: Meyer Timber Gp Ltd 2011–15, Bolton Aerospace Ltd 2011–17, Thomas Bolton Ltd 2012–14, Hadleigh Industrial Estates Ltd 2012–15, The Meade Family Office Ltd 2014–; treas and govr Reed's Sch 2006–15; ICAEW 1968, ICA (Ghana) 1983, ICA (Nigeria) 1983; *Recreations* horse racing (racehorse owner), art, golf, swimming, walking, reading, opera, theatre; *Clubs* Boodle's, Leander; *Style—* David Caddy, Esq; ✉ 79B Iverna Court, Kensington, London W8 6TU (☎ 020 7937 2035); 104/392A Toorak Road, Toorak, Victoria 3142, Australia

CADMAN, Deborah; OBE; *Educ* BSc, MA, MSc; *Career* chief exec St Edmundsbury BC 2002–08, chief exec East of England Devpt Agency 2008–11, chief exec Suffolk CC 2011–; *Style—* Ms Deborah Cadman, OBE; ✉ Suffolk County Council, Endeavour House, 8 Russell Road, Ipswich IP1 2BX (e-mail deborah.cadman@suffolk.gov.uk)

CAHILL, (Paul) Jeremy; QC (2002); s of late Dr Tim Cahill, and late Mary O'Mahony; *b* 28 January 1952, Birmingham; *Educ* Ratcliffe Coll Leicester, Univ of Liverpool; *m* 25 June 2010, Bettina, *née* Lugge; 2 da (Jenni Rachel b 6 Dec 1985, Eleanor Felicity b 12 April 1989); *Career* called to the Bar Middle Temple 1975 (Blackstone exhibitioner); practising barr No5 Chambers; memb: Planning and Environmental Bar Assoc, Compulsory Purchase Assoc; memb Grand Order of the Badgers; *Recreations* conversation, West Cork; *Clubs* Copt Heath Golf, RAC; *Style—* Jeremy Cahill, Esq, QC; ✉ No5 Chambers (Birmingham, London and Bristol) (☎ 0870 203 5555, e-mail jc@no5.com)

CAHILL, Kevin; CBE (2007); *Career* head of educn RNT 1982–91; Comic Relief: dir of educn and info 1991, dir of communications 1992, dep dir (creative) 1993, dir 1994, chief exec 1997, pres Comic Relief Inc; former bd pres Charity Projects Entertainment Fund 2007, pres America Gives Back, former memb UK Bd Malaria No More, former memb Fundraising Ctee Manchester United Fndn; former chair Trinity Coll London; former chair: Gate Theatre 1988–2008, Cncl Drama Centre 1989–1992, Advsy Ctee ACU; former memb Bd Young Vic, former tstee Int Broadcasting Tst; chllr Univ of Nottingham 2014–; Hon DLitt Nottingham Trent Univ; *Style—* Kevin Cahill, Esq, CBE; ✉ Comic Relief UK, Camelford House, 87–90 Albert Embankment, London SE1 7TP (☎ 020 7820 5555, fax 020 7820 5500)

CAHILL, Her Hon Judge Sally Elizabeth Mary; QC (2003); *b* 12 November 1955; *Educ* Harrogate Ladies' Coll, Univ of Leeds (LLB); *Career* called to the Bar Gray's Inn 1978; practising barr specialising in family law 1978–2004, former tenant Park Lane Chambers Leeds; recorder 2000–04 (asst recorder 1997–2000), circuit judge (North Eastern Circuit) 2004–; *Style—* Her Hon Judge Cahill, QC; ✉ c/o Leeds Combined Court Centre, Oxford Row, Leeds LS1 3BG

CAHILL, Teresa Mary; da of Henry Daniel Cahill (d 1948), of Rotherhithe, London, and Florence, *née* Dallimore (d 1964); *b* 30 July 1944; *Educ* Notre Dame HS Southwark, Guildhall Sch of Music & Drama, London Opera Centre; *m* 1, 1971 (m dis 1978), John Anthony Kiernander; m 2, 11 Nov 2005, Prof Robert Saxton, *qv*; *Career* opera and concert singer; Glyndebourne debut 1969, Covent Garden debut 1970, La Scala Milan 1976, Philadelphia Opera 1981, Liceo Barcelona 1991, specialising in Mozart & Strauss; concerts: all the London orchestras, Boston Symphony Orch, Chicago Symphony Orch, Vienna Festival 1983, Berlin Festival 1987, Bath Festival 2000, Rotterdam Philharmonic 1984, Hamburg Philharmonic 1985, West Deutscher Rundfunk Cologne 1985; promenade concerts BBC Radio & TV; recordings incl Elgar, Mozart, Strauss and Mahler for all major cos; recitals and concerts throughout Europe, USA and the Far East; examiner and vocal adjudicator Masterclasses, external examiner Univ of Reading 1992–95; masterclasses: Univ of Oxford 1995–, Univ of Durham 2013; artistic advsr Nat Mozart Competition 1997–2002, masterclasses and memb Int Jury S'Hertogenbosch Vocal Concours 1998 and 2000, masterclass Peabody Inst Baltimore USA 1999, adjudicator Live Music Now 1988– (music advsr 2000–), jury memb Kathleen Ferrier Competition 1988, adjudicator YCAT 1989–, adjudicator the Royal Overseas League Competition 1985–89, 1992, 1995, 2000 and 2008; prof of singing Trinity Coll of Music; govr Royal Soc of Musicians 2000–05, 2006–11 and 2013–; Silver medal Worshipful Co of Musicians, John Christie award 1970; AGSM, LRAM; *Publications* career archive housed in the British Library; *Recreations* cinema, theatre, travel, reading, collecting things, sales from car boots to Sotheby's, photography; *Clubs* Royal Over-Seas League (hon memb); *Style—* Ms Teresa Cahill; ✉ 65 Leyland Road, London SE12 8DW (website www.teresacahill.net)

CAHN, Sir Andrew Thomas; KCMG (2009, CMG 2001); s of Robert Wolfgang Cahn, FRS, and Patricia Lois, *née* Hanson; *b* 1 April 1951; *Educ* Bedales, Trinity Coll Cambridge (BA); *m* 1976, Virginia, da of David Fordyce Beardshaw; 1 da (Jessica b 1983), 2 s (Thomas b 1986, Laurence b 1994); *Career* civil servant; MAFF 1973–76, FCO 1976–77, MAFF 1977–81 (private sec to Perm Sec 1977–78), first sec perm rep to EC (FCO) 1982–84, Cabinet of Lord Cockfield (as vice-pres of EC) 1985–88, MAFF 1988–92; princ private sec: to chllr of Duchy of Lancaster 1992–94, to min for Agric Fisheries and Food 1994–95; under-sec Cabinet Office 1995–97, chef de cabinet to Rt Hon Neil Kinnock as cmmr for Tport then vice-pres and cmmr for Admin Reform 1997–2000; dir of govt and industry affrs BA 2000–06, chief exec UK Trade and Investment 2006–11, acting perm sec BERR 2009; vice-chm Nomura Int plc 2011–; non-exec dir Cadbury Ltd 1990–92; chair Advsy Bd Huawei (UK) 2011–14, memb Franchise Bd Lloyds of London 2011–, non-exec dir General Dynamics UK 2012–, non-exec dir Huawei Technologies (UK) Ltd 2015–; memb Advsy Bd Br American Business 2007–11, memb Int Advsy Cncl Asia House 2011–, memb Advsy Bd Univ of the Arts 2012–, chair Int Trade and Investment Gp City of London 2013–16, memb Fin Services Trade & Investment Bd 2013–15; govr Bedales Sch 1993–98; tstee: Gatsby Fndn 1996–, Royal Botanic Gardens Kew 2002–07, Inst for Govt 2008–, Arvon Fndn 2011–, Japan Soc 2011–13, TheCityUK 2012– (chair Int Trade and Investment Gp 2013–); chair WWF UK 2014–; assoc memb BUPA 2012–; FRSA 1979; *Recreations* family, reading, mountains; *Clubs* RAC, Hampstead Golf, St-Cyr Haut Poitou; *Style—* Sir Andrew Cahn, KCMG; ✉ Nomura International plc, 1 Angel Lane, London EC4R 3AB (☎ 020 7102 7050, e-mail andrew.cahn@nomura.com)

CAIE, Prof Graham; CBE (2015); s of William Caie, and Adeline Caie; *b* 3 February 1945; *Educ* Univ of Aberdeen (MA), McMaster Univ (MA, PhD); *m* Ann Pringle Abbott; *Career* Univ of Copenhagen until 1990, prof and chair of English language Univ of Glasgow 1990–2012 (clerk of Senate and vice-princ 2008–12, hon prof fell); memb: English Panel AHRC, Literature Ctee Scottish Arts Cncl, Cncl Dictionary of the Older Scottish Tongue, Bd Scottish Language Dictionaries, AHRC Peer Review Coll; UK rep Bd ALLEA (Fedn of All European Acads); panelist Research Assessment Exercise, vice-pres Scottish Text Soc, dep chair Bd and tstee Nat Library of Scotland, sec European Soc for the Study of English, chair Swedish Research Cncl Linnaeus Awards, fell Japanese Soc for Medieval Studies, tstee Faculty of Advocates Abbotsford Book Collection; QAA institutional reviewer, memb Advsy Ctee Br Cncl (Scotland), observer Lloyds TSB Fndn for Scotland; memb Ct Queen Margaret Univ; founding fell English Assoc 1999, FRSE 2004 (vice-pres 2011), FRSA; *Books* incl: The Judgement Day Theme in Old English Poetry (1976), Bibliography of Junius XI Manuscript (1976), The Old English Poem: Judgement Day II (2000), The European Sun: Proceedings of the 7th International Conference on Medieval and Renaissance Scottish Language and Literature. (co-ed, 2001), The Power of Worlds: Essays in Lexicography, Lexicology and Semantics (co-ed, 2006), Medieval Texts in Context (2008); many articles on medieval English studies and codicology; *Clubs* Malt Whisky (Edinburgh); *Style—* Prof Graham Caie, CBE

CAINE, Jeffrey; *Educ* Central Fndn Boys' GS London, Univ of Sussex (BA), Univ of Leeds (MA); *Career* writer for film and TV; film: GoldenEye 1995, Inside I'm Dancing 2004, The Constant Gardener 2005; TV incl Dempsey & Makepeace 1985, Gods and Kings 2014 (co-writer), Time Out of Mind (story credit) 2015; creator: The Chief 1990, BodyGuards 1996; *Novels* The Cold Room (1976), Heathcliff (1977); *Clubs* Groucho;

Style— Jeffrey Caine, Esq; ✉ c/o Diana Tyler, MBA Ltd, 62 Grafton Way, London W1T 5DW

CAINE, Sir Michael (né Maurice Joseph Micklewhite); kt (2000), CBE (1992); s of late Maurice Micklewhite, and Ellen Frances Marie Micklewhite; *b* 14 March 1933; *Educ* Wilson's GS Peckham; *m* 1, 1955 (m dis), Patricia Haines; 1 da; m 2, 1973, Shakira Baksh; 1 da; *Career* actor; served Army Berlin and Korea 1951–53; asst stage mangr Westminster Repertory Horsham Sussex 1953, actor Lowestoft Repertory 1953–55, Theatre Workshop London 1955, numerous TV appearances 1957–63; awarded Special Award for Contribution to British Film Evening Standard British Film Awards 1999; *Films* incl: A Hill in Korea 1956, How to Murder a Rich Uncle 1958, Zulu 1964, The Ipcress File 1965, Alfie 1966, The Wrong Box 1966, Gambit 1966, Hurry Sundown 1967, Woman Times Seven 1967, Deadfall 1967, The Magus 1968, Battle of Britain 1968, Play Dirty 1968, The Italian Job 1969, Too Late the Hero 1970, The Last Valley 1971, Get Carter 1971, Zee & Co 1972, Kidnapped 1972, Pulp 1972, Sleuth 1973, The Black Windmill 1974, Marseilles Contract 1974, The Wilby Conspiracy 1974, Fat Chance 1975, The Romantic Englishwoman 1975, The Man who would be King 1975, Harry and Walter Go to New York 1975, The Eagle Has Landed 1976, A Bridge Too Far 1976, Silver Bears 1976, The Swarm 1977, California Suite 1978, Ashanti 1979, Beyond The Poseidon Adventure 1979, The Island 1979, Dressed to Kill 1979, Escape to Victory 1980, Death Trap 1981, Jigsaw Man 1982, Educating Rita 1982, The Honorary Consul 1982, Blame it on Rio 1984, Water 1985, The Holcroft Covenant 1985, Hannah and Her Sisters 1986, Mona Lisa 1986, The Fourth Protocol 1987, The Whistle Blower 1987, Surrender 1987, Jaws The Revenge 1987, Without a Clue 1988, Dirty Rotten Scoundrels 1988, Bullseye 1989, Mr Destiny 1990, A Shock to the System 1990, Noises Off 1992, Blue Ice 1992, The Muppets Christmas Carol 1992, On Deadly Ground 1994, Bullet to Beijing 1994, Blood and Wine 1995, 20,000 Leagues under the Sea 1996, Curtain Call 1997, Shadowrun 1997, Little Voice 1997, The Debtor 1998, The Cider House Rules 1998, Quills 1999, Shiner 2000, Miss Congeniality 2000, Last Orders 2000, Quick Sands 2000, The Quiet American 2001, Austin Powers – Gold Member 2002, The Actors 2002, Second-Hand Lions 2003, The Statement 2003, Around the Bend 2004, The Weather Man 2004, Batman Begins 2005, Bewitched 2005, Prestige 2006, Flawless 2006, Children of Men 2006, Sleuth 2007, The Dark Knight 2008, Is There Anybody There? 2008, Harry Brown 2009, Inception 2010, Cars 2 2011, Gnomeo and Juliet 2011, Journey 2: The Mysterious Island 2012, The Dark Knight Rises 2012, Mr Morgan's Last Love 2012; films for TV: Jack The Ripper 1988, Jekyll and Hyde 1989, World War II: When Lions Roared 1994, Mandela and De Klerk 1996; *Awards* incl: Best Supporting Actor Oscar (for Hannah and her Sisters) 1987, Best Actor BAFTA (for Educating Rita) 1987, Golden Globe (for Little Voice) 1999, Eros Special Award British Film Awards 1999, Best Supporting Actor Oscar (for Cider House Rules) 2000, Best Supporting Actor Golden Globe (for Cider House Rules) 2000; *Books* Not Many People Know That (1985), Not Many People Know This Either (1986), Moving Picture Show (1988), Acting In Film (1990), What's It All About? (autobiography, 1992); *Recreations* cinema, theatre, travel, gardening; *Style—* Sir Michael Caine, CBE; ✉ c/o Independent Artists, Oxford House, 76 Oxford Street, London W1D 1BS (☎ 020 7636 6565, fax 020 7323 0101)

CAINE, Seth Fargher; s of Edwin Seth Caine (d 1964), and Anne, *née* Fargher; *b* 3 June 1956, Brighton, Sussex; *Educ* King William's Coll Castletown, Univ of Nottingham (LLB), Coll of Law Chester; *m* 28 Aug 1997, Joanne, *née* Sayle; 1 da (Georgia Blaa b 20 Nov 1998); *Career* slr; articled clerk Stanley Evans, Oates & Co slrs 1980–82, asst slr Metropolitan Police London 1983–85, head of branch Post Office Slr's Dept 1985–90; Cains Advocates: advocate 1990–94, ptnr 1994–, head of litigation 2000–; memb Editorial Advsy Bd Insolvency Intelligence Jl; memb Cncl IOM Law Soc 2005–, memb Assoc of Contentious Tst and Probate Specialists, memb Human Rights Inst; *Publications* International Commercial Fraud (contrib, 2002); *Recreations* rugby, music, reading; *Clubs* Ronnie Scott's; *Style—* Seth Caine, Esq; ✉ Cains Advocates, 15–19 Athol Street, Douglas, Isle of Man IM1 1LB (☎ 01624 638356, fax 01624 638333, e-mail seth.caine@cains.com)

CAINES, Michael Andrew; MBE (2006); s of Peter Anthony Caines (d 2014), and Patricia Caines (d 1995); *b* 3 January 1969; *Children* Joseph, Hope, India; *Career* chef; Ninety Park Lane 1987–89, Le Manoir aux Quat'Saisons 1989–91, La Côte-d'Or France 1992–93, Joël Robuchon France 1993–94, exec chef Gidleigh Park Devon 1994–, fndr, operational ptnr and dir Michael Caines Restaurants (formed to run The Food and Beverage at Michael Caines at The Royal Clarence Hotel) 1999, co-fndr, operational ptnr and dir ABode Hotels; Chef of the Year The Independent 1994, Relais Gourmand 1998, Michelin star 1998, 2 Michelin stars 1999, 5 out of 5 AA Rosettes 1998, 9 out of 10 Good Food Guide 1998, 8 out of 10 Good Food Guide 1999, Traditions and Qualite 2000 entry for Gidleigh Park, Hotel and Caterer Chef of the Year 2001, AA Chef's Chef of the Year 2007; Hon LLD St Loye's Sch of Health and Sciences 2004; *Books* Michael Caines At Home (2013); *Recreations* motorsport, skiing; *Style—* Michael Caines, Esq, MBE; ✉ The Richard Stone Partnership, London W1W 6XD (☎ 020 7497 0849, website www.michaelcaines.com, Twitter @michaelcaines)

CAIRD, Prof George; s of George Bradford Caird (d 1984), and Viola Mary, *née* Newport; *b* 30 August 1950; *Educ* Magdalen Coll Sch Oxford, Royal Acad of Music (LRAM, ARCM), Nordwestdeutsche Musikakademie Detmold, Peterhouse Cambridge (MA); *m* 1, 1974 (m dis), Sarah Verney; 3 s (Adam Benjamin b 23 April 1977, Oliver Ralph b 22 June 1978, Edmund George b 4 July 1989), 1 da (Iona Katharine Mary b 10 July 1991); m 2, 2001, Jane Amanda Salmon; 1 da (Elizabeth Jane b 7 May 2004); *Career* freelance oboist 1972–, memb Albion Ensemble 1976–, memb Acad of St Martin-in-the-Fields 1984–92; Royal Acad of Music: prof 1984–93, head Woodwind 1987–93, head Instrumental Studies 1990–93; princ Birmingham Conservatoire Birmingham City Univ 1993–2010, artistic dir Rotterdam Classical Music Acad Codarts Rotterdam 2011–; sec Fedn of Br Conservatoires (formerly Ctee of Princs of Conservatoires) 1998–2003, pres Incorporated Soc of Musicians 2004–05, sec-gen Assoc of European Conservatoires 2005–10, pres Barbirolli Int Oboe Competition 2008–, pres Birmingham Conservatoire Assoc 2012–; chm: Music Educn Cncl 2001–04, MEC 2001–04; tstee: Symphony Hall Birmingham 1998–2010, Youth Music 2004–10, Countess of Munster Musical Tst 2007–; memb: Ctee Br Double Reed Soc, Exec Ctee Music Educn Cncl 1997–2010, chair Nat Assoc of Youth Orchs 2005–10; memb: Royal Soc of Musicians, Incorporated Soc of Musicians (chm Birmingham Centre 1996–99, pres 2003–04), W Midlands Arts Bd 1999–2002; FRAM 1989 (ARAM 1985), FRSA 1993, Hon FLCM 1999, FRCM 1999, FRNCM 2004; *Recordings* incl: Mozart and Beethoven Quintets (Albion Ensemble) 1981, Kenneth Leighton Veris Gratia 1986, Mozart Serenade K361 (Albion Ensemble) 1989, Beethoven and Hummel Octets 1999, 20th Century English Music for Oboe and Piano 1999, An English Renaissance for Oboe and Strings 2004, Benjamin Britten: Six Metamorphoses after Ovid 2007, Martinu Piano Quartet 2009; *Publications* articles on music education, woodwind music and the oboe music of Benjamin Britten incl: Benjamin Britten and Ovid's Metamorphoses (The Double Reed Vol 29 No 3, 2006), Dorothy Gow Quintet for Oboe and Strings (ed with Stephen Powell, 2007); *Recreations* reading, theatre, languages, travel, sport, walking; *Style—* Professor George Caird; ✉ Codarts Rotterdam, Kruisplein 26, 3012 Rotterdam, The Netherlands (☎ 0031 10 217 1106, e-mail georgecaird50@gmail.com)

CAIRD, John Newport; s of late Rev George Bradford Caird and Viola Mary, *née* Newport; *b* 22 September 1948; *Educ* Selwyn House Sch Montreal, Magdalen Coll Sch Oxford, Bristol Old Vic Theatre Sch; *m* 1, 1972 (m dis 1982), Helen Frances Brammer; m 2, 1982 (m dis 1990), Ann Dorzynski; 1 da (Joanna b 29 Jan 1983), 2 s (Benjamin b 10 Oct 1984, Samuel b 8 July 1987); m 3, 1990, Frances Ruffelle (m dis 1994); 1 da (Eliza b 18 April 1988), 1 s (Nathaniel b 17 June 1990); m 4, 1998, Maoko Imai; 1 s (Yoji b 19 Oct 1998), 2 da (Miyako b 18 Jan 2000, Yayako b 14 March 2002); *Career* director, writer and producer of plays, opera and musical theatre; hon assoc dir RSC 1990–, fndr and dir Caird Co 2001–06, princ guest dir Royal Dramatic Theatre Stockholm 2009–; fell Welsh Coll of Music and Drama, fell Mansfield Coll Oxford; Hon DLitt UEA; *Theatre* assoc dir Contact Theatre Manchester 1974–76: Look Back in Anger, Downright Hooligan, Krapp's Last Tape, Twelfth Night; fndr (with Steven Barlow and others) Circle of Muses touring music theatre gp; dir The Changeling (Univ of Ottawa) 1975, Last Resort (Sidewalk Theatre Co) 1976, Regina v Stephens (Avon Touring Co) 1976; resident dir RSC 1977–82: Dance of Death 1977, Savage Amusement 1978, Look Out Here Comes Trouble 1978, Caucasian Chalk Circle 1979, Nicholas Nickleby (co-dir with Trevor Nunn in London, NY and LA) 1980, 1982 and 1986, Naked Robots 1981, Twin Rivals 1981, Our Friends in the North 1982, Peter Pan (co-dir with Trevor Nunn) 1982–84; assoc dir RSC 1982–90: Twelfth Night 1983, Romeo and Juliet 1983, The Merchant of Venice 1984, Red Star 1984, Philistines 1985, Les Miserables (co-dir with Trevor Nunn in London, NY, Tokyo, Sydney and worldwide) 1985–, Every Man in His Humour 1986, Misalliance 1986, A Question of Geography 1987, The New Inn 1987, As You Like It 1989, A Midsummer Night's Dream 1989, The Beggar's Opera 1992, Columbus and the Discovery of Japan 1992, Antony and Cleopatra 1992; dir: Song and Dance (London) 1982, As You Like It (Stockholm, for TV 1985) 1984, Siegfried & Roy Spectacular (Las Vegas) 1989, Zaïde (Batignamo) 1991, The Beggar's Opera (RSC, Barbican) 1993, Trelawny of the Wells (RNT) 1993, Life Sentences (Second Stage Theatre NY) 1993, The Seagull (RNT) 1994, Watch your Step (Her Majesty's Theatre) 1995, Henry IV (also adaptor for BBC) 1995, The Millionairess (UK tour) 1995, Stanley (RNT and Broadway) 1996, (worldwide) 1998–2001, Money (RNT) 1999, Jane Eyre (Broadway) 2000, Hamlet (RNT and World tour) 2000, A Midsummer Night's Dream (Royal Dramatic Theatre Stockholm) 2000, Humbleboy (RNT, West End) 2001 (NY) 2003, Twelfth Night (Royal Dramatic Theatre Stockholm) 2002, What the Night is For (Comedy Theatre) 2002, Rattle of a Simple Man (Comedy Theatre) 2004, Becket (Theatre Royal Haymarket), Macbeth (Almeida Theatre) 2005, Don Carlos (WNO) 2005, (Toronto) 2007 and Houston Grand Opera 2012, Beggar's Opera (Nissay Theatre Tokyo and WOWOW TV) 2005 and (Osaka) 2008, Twin Spirits (writer and dir, ROH) 2006, Dance of Death (Royal Dramatic Theatre Stockholm) 2007, A Midsummer Night's Dream (New National Theatre Tokyo) 2007 and 2009, Aida (WNO) 2008, Private Lives (theatre Crié Tokyo) 2008, Merry Wives of Windsor (Royal Dramatic Theatre Stockholm) 2009, Jane Eyre (Nissay Theatre Tokyo) 2009 and 2012, Daddy Long Legs (Ventura CA and US tour), Tosca (HGO) 2010, Candide (Imperial Theatre Tokyo) 2010, The Tempest (Royal Dramatic Theatre Stockholm) 2010, Romeo and Juliet (Royal Dramatic Theatre Stockholm) 2011, Don Giovanni (WNO) 2011, Daddy Long Legs (Tokyo, London and US tour) 2012, Jane Eyre (Tokyo) 2012, La Bohème (Houston Grand Opera) 2012, (Canadian Opera Co) 2013 and (San Fransisco Opera) 2014, Tosca (LA Opera) 2013, Parsifal (Chicago Lyric Opera) 2013, Little Miss Scrooge (Ventura CA) 2013, Gertrud (Royal Dramatic Theatre Stockholm) 2014, At Home in the World (Sendai & Tokyo, staged for Ashinaga Ikneikai & Vassar Coll) 2014; staged for Worldwide Fund for Nature: Religion and Nature Interfaith Ceremony (Assisi) 1986, Sacred Gifts for a Living Planet (Bhaktapur, Nepal) 2000; as prodr: new writing festivals 2001–02 (Gatehouse Theatre 2001, Jerwood Space 2002 and 2003, Pleasance Theatre 2002, Soho Theatre 2002), Robin Hood (RNT) 2002–03, Theatre Cafe (Arcola Theatre) 2004, Arab-Israeli Cookbook (Gate Theatre) 2004, New Directions (Theatre Royal Haymarket) 2004, The Lemon Princess (West Yorkshire Playhouse) 2005; writer and dir: Beethoven The Kingdom of the Spirit (a concert for actor and string quartet) 1986, Children of Eden (with music and lyrics by Stephen Schwartz, London and worldwide) 1991, Jane Eyre (with lyrics and music by Paul Gordon, Toronto, La Jolla and Broadway) 1996 and (Nissay Theatre Tokyo) 2009, Candide (with music by Leonard Berstein, RNT) 1999, Daddy Long Legs (with lyrics and music by Paul Gordon) 2002, Kinshu (adapted from Teru Mitamoto, Tokyo) 2007 and 2009, Brief Encounter – An Opera (music by André Previn, Houston Grand Opera) 2009; *Awards* SWET Award 1980, Tony Award for Best Dir 1982 (both for Nicholas Nickleby), Tony Award for Best Dir 1986 and 1987 (for Les Miserables), Lawrence Olivier Award for Most Outstanding Musical (for Candide) 2000, Critics Outer Circle Award (for Stanley), Nipon Engeki Kogyo Kyukai Award (for Kinshu & Beggar's Opera) 2007, Kikuta Kazuo Theatre Award for Special Achievement in Japanese Theatre, LA Ovation Award for Book of a Musical (for Daddy Long Legs) 2010; *Publications* Peter Pan (1993, 2 edn, 1998), Children of Eden (1997), The Beggar's Opera (with Ilona Sekacz, 1999), Jane Eyre (2003), Candide (2003), Theatre Craft (2010); *Recordings* Les Miserables (1985, and further cast recordings worldwide), Children of Eden (1991), The Beggar's Opera (1992), Jane Eyre (1998), Candide (2000), Daddy Long Legs (2010, Japanese recording 2014), Brief Encounter (2011); *Recreations* music, birds, children; *Clubs* Ivy; *Style—* John Caird, Esq; ✉ Church House, 10 South Grove, Highgate, London N6 6BS (website www.johncaird.com); UK agent Michael McCoy (☎ 020 7636 6565); UK literary agent Gordon Wise (☎ 020 7393 4400); US agent Seth Glewen (☎ 001 212 634 8124)

CAIRD, Richard Francis; s of Prof Francis Irvine Caird, of Oxford, and Angela Margaret Alsop (d 1983); *b* 20 January 1958; *Educ* Glasgow Acad, New Coll Oxford (BA), Coll of Law Guildford; *m* 1985, Helen Vanessa, da of Anthony Simpson; 1 da (Julia Margaret b 1 July 1989), 1 s (James Francis b 27 Jan 1992); *Career* articled clerk Radcliffes & Co 1980–82; Wilde Sapte: asst slr 1983–87, ptnr 1987–98, head Litigation Dept 1994–98; head of legal and compliance Commerzbank Global Equities 1998–2005, ptnr Denton Wilde Sapte 2005–; memb Law Soc; *Recreations* sport, theatre, reading; *Style—* Richard Caird, Esq; ✉ Denton Wilde Sapte, 5 Chancery Lane, Clifford's Inn, London EC4A 1BU

CAIRNCROSS, Dame Frances Anne; DBE (2015); *see:* McRae, Frances Anne; *Style—* Dame Frances Anne Cairncross, DBE

CAIRNES, (Simon) Paul Steven; s of Edward Michael Hornby Cairnes, and Audrey Mary, *née* Stevens; *b* 19 December 1957; *Educ* Christ Coll Brecon, UCW Aberystwyth (LLB); *Career* barr; called to the Bar Gray's Inn 1980 (NSW Aust 1989); memb: Barrs Euro Gp 1989–, Personal Injury Bar Assoc 2000–, Planning and Environmental Bar Assoc 2005–; *Recreations* sailing, skiing, music, travelling; *Style—* Paul Cairnes, Esq; ✉ 3 Paper Buildings, Temple, London EC4Y 7EU (☎ 020 7353 8192, fax 020 7353 6271, e-mail paul.cairnes@3paper.co.uk)

CAIRNS, Alun Hugh; MP; s of Hewitt John Cairns, and Margaret, of Clydach, Swansea; *b* 30 July 1970; *Educ* Ysgol Gyfun Ddwyieithog Ystalyfera, Univ of Wales; *m* 1996, Emma Elizabeth, da of Martin Graham Turner; *Career* Business Devpt Conslt Lloyds Bank Gp, Lloyds TSB South Wales Compliance Conslt; Cons Pty: memb Swansea West Assoc 1987–, Mid and West Wales Euro-Constituency Cncl rep for Swansea West 1990, Assoc dep treas 1993, memb Wales Area Cncl 1994, dep chm Wales Area Young Cons 1995, chm Policy Advsy Gp 1996–97, Parly candidate Gower 1997, Economic Spokesman for Wales 1997, memb Nat Assembly for Wales South Wales West 1999–2011, shadow min for educn 2007–08, shadow min for local govt 2008–09, opposition chief whip and spokesman on industry, tourism and culture 2009–11, under sec of state for Wales 2014–16, sec of state for Wales 2016–; MP (Cons) Vale of Glamorgan 2010–; radio panel memb and commentator; *Recreations* skiing, shooting, cycling; *Style—* Alun Cairns, Esq, MP; ✉ House of Commons, London SW1A 0AA

CAIRNS, Christine Wilson; da of late Thomas Cairns, of Saltcoats, Scotland, and late Christine Dawson Galloway, *née* Wilson; *b* 11 February 1959; *Educ* Ardrossan Acad, RSAMD; *m* 13 July 1991, John David Peter Lubbock, *qv*, s of late Michael Ronald Lubbock and late Diana Lubbock *née* Crawley; 2 s (Adam Thomas b 28 Nov 1991, Alexander Michael b 30 June 1993); *Career* mezzo-soprano; performed with orchs incl: Berlin Philharmonic, LA Philharmonic, London Philharmonic, Royal Philharmonic, LSO, Vienna Philharmonic, BBC Scottish, Cleveland and Philadelphia Orchs, Euro Community Youth Orch; worked with conductors incl: Sir Colin Davis, André Previn, Vladimir Ashkenazy, Yuri Temirkanov, Simon Rattle, Christoph von Dohnányi, John Lubbock; currently giving concerts to raise money for autism, recorded fund-raising CD Songs for Alexander (2002), chm and fndr Music for Autism; teacher (singing) Birmingham Conservatoire 2000–; *Recordings* incl: Mendelssohn's Midsummer Night's Dream (with André Previn and the Vienna Philharmonic) 1986, Prokofiev's Alexander Nevsky (with André Previn and the LA Philharmonic) 1986, Mendelssohn's Die Erste Walpurgisnacht (with Christoph von Dohnányi and the Cleveland Orch) 1988; *Style—* Ms Christine Cairns; ✉ 7 Warborough Road, Shillingford, Oxfordshire OX10 7SA (website www.musicforautism.org.uk)

CAIRNS, David Howard; OBE (1995); s of David Lauder Cairns (d 2008), of Birmingham, and Edith, *née* Rose; *b* 4 June 1946; *Educ* Cheadle Hulme Sch, LSE (MSc); *m* 1 May 1980, Stella Jane, da of Stanley Cecil Askew, DSO, DFC (d 1996); *Career* chartered accountant; Pannell Kerr Forster 1964–71, Carlsberg Brewery Ltd 1971–72, Black & Decker Ltd 1972–75, ptnr Stoy Hayward 1975–85, sec gen Int Accounting Standards Ctee 1985–94, dir Int Fin Reporting 1995–2013; conslt World Bank Centre for Financial Reporting Reform (Vienna) 2009–13; LSE: PD Leake fell 1973–75, visiting fell 1995–2004, visiting prof 2004–12; visiting prof Univ of Edinburgh Business Sch 2012–15; memb: Financial Reporting Review Panel 2006–14; pres Thames Valley Soc of Chartered Accountants 1979–80; chm of tstees Turville Village Hall Northend 2008–11 and 2014–, chm Turville Parish Cncl 2009–; FCA 1974 (ACA); *Recreations* cricket, collecting contemporary British paintings, music; *Clubs* Turville Park Cricket, Henley Rugby; *Style—* David Cairns, Esq, OBE; ✉ Bramblewood, Turville Heath, Henley-on-Thames, Oxfordshire RG9 6JY (☎ 01491 638296, e-mail david@cairns.co.uk)

CAIRNS, HE David Seldon; Sharon Anouk; 1 da, 1 s; *Career* diplomat; Nomura Int 1992–93; FCO: joined 1993, desk offr Security Policy Dept 1993–95, second sec Commercial Tokyo 1995–99, head of public diplomacy Europe Command 1999–2000, private sec to mins for Africa and N Americas 2000–02, head WTO Section Geneva 2002–06, dir of trade and investment Tokyo 2006–10, dir Estates and Security Corp Services 2010–15, ambass to Sweden and dir Nordic Baltic Region 2015–; *Style—* HE Mr David Cairns; ✉ c/o FCO (Stockholm), King Charles Street, London SW1A 2AH

CAIRNS, Fiona; *m* Kishore Patel, *qv*; *Career* luxury cake maker; co-fndr Fiona Cairns Ltd 1986, clients incl Harrods, Selfridges, Waitrose, Fortnum and Mason, The Conran Shop, Eat Your Hearts Out, the wedding cake for the marriage of HRH Prince William of Wales to Catherine Middleton; *Books* Bake and Decorate (2010), The Birthday Cake Book (2011), Seasonal Baking (2013); *Style—* Ms Fiona Cairns; ✉ Fiona Cairns Ltd, 8 Churchill Way, Fleckney, Leicestershire LE8 8UD

CAIRNS, Joyce Winifred; da of Lt-Col Robert William Cairns, MBE, TD, (d 1972), and Marjorie Helen, *née* Dickson (d 1983); *b* 21 March 1947; *Educ* Mary Erskine Sch for Girls Edinburgh, Gray Sch of Art Aberdeen (dip and post dip), RCA (MA), Goldsmiths Coll London (ATC); *m* 1, 1975, Christopher George Dowland; m 2, 1980, Arthur James Watson; m 3, 1989, Capt Robert Kemp Hamilton Cunningham; *Career* artist and lectr; lectr Grays Sch of Art Aberdeen 1976–2004; visiting lectr: Glasgow Sch of Art, Duncan of Jordanston Coll of Art Dundee; fell Glos Coll of Art & Design, fell Cheltenham Coll of Art & Design; Scottish Arts Cncl: memb Art Ctee 1986–89, memb Awards Panel 1981–83 and 1987–90; tstee Hospitalfield House Arbroath 2007–; memb: Aberdeen Artists Soc 1978 (first woman pres), Royal Scottish Soc of Painters in Watercolours 1979; ARSA 1985, RSA 1998 (memb Cncl 2008–11, chm Gen Purposes Ctee 2014–17, ex officio Cncl 2014–17, dep pres 2015–18); *Solo Exhibitions* Compass Gallery Glasgow 1980, ESU Edinburgh 1981, Peacock Printmakers Aberdeen 1981, Art Space Galleries Aberdeen 1984, Perth Museum and Art Gallery 1986, 369 Gallery Edinburgh 1986, The Third Eye Gallery Glasgow 1987, Talbot Rice Gallery Univ of Edinburgh 1991, Peacock Gallery Aberdeen 1991, Odette Gilbert Gallery London 1991, Kirkcaldy Art Gallery & Museum 1992, An Lanntair Stornoway 1992, Lamont Gallery 1993, Elektra Fine Art Toronto, Roger Billcliffe Gallery Glasgow 1995, Rendezvous Gallery Aberdeen 1998, 2004 and 2008, The Weem Gallery Pittenweem 2003, Peacock Visual Arts Aberdeen 2003, Aberdeen Art Gallery and Museum 2006; *Work in Public Collections* Aberdeen Art Gallery, Scottish Arts Cncl, Univ of Aberdeen, Fife Regnl Cncl, Graves Art Gallery & Museum Sheffield, Edinburgh City Arts Centre, Lanarkshire CC, Univ of Strathclyde, The Contemporary Arts Soc, BBC, Glasgow Art Gallery & Museum, Perth City Art Gallery and Museums, Glasgow MOMA, Flemings Bank, McMaster Museum Hamilton Ontario Canada, The Royal Scottish Academy, Nat Museums of Scotland, Aberdeen Asset Mgmnt, Grays Sch of Art Robert Gordon Univ, Nat Museums of Scotland (War Museum, Edinburgh Castle), Victor Meml Tst; *Awards* incl: Carnegie Travelling Scholarship, First Prize Arbroath Art Competition, ESU Scholarship to USA, Anstruther Award RCA, E Q Henriques Gift RCA, Latimer Award RSA, bursary Scottish Arts Cncl, First Prize Morrison Portrait Competition 1989, May Marshall Brown Award RSW, W P J Burness Award RSA, First Prize Shell Expro, Sir William Gillies Travel Bursary 1997, second prize Shell Expo 2002, Maude Gemmell Hutchison Award RSA 2006; *Publications* Joyce Cairns: War Tourist (illustrated anthology, 2006); *Recreations* eating, walking, swimming, reading; *Clubs* Royal Tayside Yacht; *Style—* Ms Joyce W Cairns, RSA, RSW; ✉ Bay House, 36 Dundee Road, West Ferry, Dundee DD5 1HY (website www.joycecairns.co.uk)

CAIRNS, Richard James; s of Brian Cairns, and Christina Cairns; *b* 2 July 1966, Nairobi, Kenya; *Educ* Oratory Sch Reading, Lady Margaret Hall Oxford (MA); *Career* usher Magdalen Coll Sch Oxford 1999–2005, headmaster and chief exec Brighton Coll 2006–; govr: King's Coll Sch Wimbledon, Kingsford Community Sch London, London Acad of Excellence Newham; memb Ct Univ of Sussex; FRSA 2006; *Recreations* travel; *Clubs* East India, Lansdowne; *Style—* Richard Cairns, Esq; ✉ Headmaster's House, Brighton College, Eastern Road, Brighton, East Sussex BN2 0AL

CAIRNS, Dr Roger John Russell; s of Arthur John Cairns (d 1982), and Edith Anne, *née* Russell (d 1979); *b* 8 March 1943; *Educ* Ranelagh Sch, Univ of Durham (BSc), Univ of Bristol (MSc, PhD); *m* 20 July 1966, Zara Corry, da of Herbert Bolton (d 1970); 2 s (Nigel b 1969, Alistair b 1973), 1 da (Kirsten b 1975); *Career* oilfield water mgmnt BP 1978–81, planner Qatar General Petroleum Corp 1981–83; md: Trafalgar House Oil and Gas Ltd (tech and commercial dir 1983–89), Hardy Oil and Gas plc 1989–97; chm and ceo CEDAR International plc 1997–2009; non-exec dir Sodra Petroleum AB 1998–2001; memb Cncl IP 1999–2003, chm EI Discussion Gp Ctee 1998–2005; Enhanced Recovery Systems Ltd: sr technical advsr 2000–06, md 2006–09, vice-chm 2009–10; non-exec dir Technip 2003–07; pres NSPCC Bucks 2001–09 (chm NSPCC Full Stop Campaign Ctee in Berks and Bucks 1998–2002); memb SPE; FRSC, FInstPet, life fell Royal Instn of GB; *Recreations* theatre and music, wine, tennis, reading, chess; *Clubs* RAC; *Style—* Dr Roger Cairns; ✉ High Larch, Lewis Lane, Chalfont Heights, Gerrard's Cross, Buckinghamshire SL9 9TS (e-mail cairoilcon@aol.com)

CAIRNS, 6 Earl (UK 1878); Simon Dallas Cairns; CVO (2000), CBE (1992); also Baron Cairns (UK 1867) and Viscount Garmoyle (UK 1878); s of 5 Earl Cairns, GCVO, CB (d 1989); *b* 27 May 1939; *Educ* Eton, Trinity Coll Cambridge; *m* 4 Feb 1964, Amanda Mary, o da of late Maj Edgar Fitzgerald Heathcoat-Amory, RA; 3 s (Hugh Sebastian, Viscount Garmoyle b 1965, Hon (David) Patrick b 1967, Hon Alistair Benedict b 1969); *Heir* s, Viscount Garmoyle, *qv*; *Career* formerly with J A Scrimgeour; S G Warburg Gp plc: md 1979–85, dir 1985–95, vice-chm 1985–87, jt chm 1987–91, chief exec and dep chm 1991–95; chm: BAT Industries plc 1996–98 (dir 1990–), Allied Zurich 1998–2000 (also vice-chm Zurich Financial Services and Zurich Allied AG), Celtel Int BV 2006–10 (dep chm 2004–06); dir Fresnillo plc 2008–14; chm: VSO 1981–92, ODI 1994–2002, Commonwealth Development Corp (latterly CDC Group plc then Actis) 1995–2005, Commonwealth Business Cncl 1997–2002, Charities Aid Fndn 2003–10; tstee Diana Princess of Wales Meml Fund 1998–2006, dir Mo Ibrahim Fndn 2006–; curator Univ of Oxford Chest 1995–2000; receiver gen Duchy of Cornwall 1990–2000; memb Ct of Assts Worshipful Co of Fishmongers; *Clubs* Turf; *Style—* The Rt Hon Earl Cairns, CVO, CBE

CAITHNESS, 20 Earl of (S 1455); Malcolm Ian Sinclair; 15 Bt (S 1631), PC (1990); also Lord Berriedale (S 1592); s of 19 Earl of Caithness (d 1965), and his 2 w Madeleine Gabrielle, *née* de Pury (d 1990); *b* 3 November 1948; *Educ* Marlborough, RAC Cirencester; *m* 1, 1975, Diana Caroline (d 1994), da of Maj Richard Coke, DSO, MC, DL (gs of 2 Earl of Leicester); 1 da (Lady Iona b 1978), 1 s (Alexander James Richard, Lord Berriedale b 1981); m 2, 2004, Leila Jenkins; *Heir* s, Lord Berriedale; *Career* Savills 1972–78, Brown and Mumford 1978–80, dir of various companies 1980–84; a Lord in Waiting and Government Whip 1984–85, under sec for transport 1985–86; min of state: Home Office 1986–88, Dept of the Environment 1988–89, HM Treasy 1989–90 (Paymaster Gen), FCO 1990–92, Dept of Tport 1992–94; conslt to and non-exec dir of various companies 1994–; conslt Victoria Soames Ltd (former dir), md Clan Sinclair Tst 1999–; tstee Queen Elizabeth Castle of May Tst (and various other trusts); FRICS; *Style—* The Rt Hon the Earl of Caithness, PC; ✉ House of Lords, London SW1A 0PW

CALAM, Prof Derek Harold; CBE (2016, OBE 1997); s of Richard Hellyer Calam (d 1993), of Northwood, and Winifred Ella, *née* Nortier (d 1986); *b* 11 May 1936; *Educ* Christ's Hosp, Wadham Coll Oxford (MA, DPhil); *m* 15 Sept 1965, Claudia (d 2015), da of Gerald Marcus Summers (d 1967); 2 s (Duncan b 1969, Douglas b 1973), 1 da (Josephine b 1971); *Career* Nat Serv 2 Lt RA 1954–56; Nat Inst for Med Res 1962–66 and 1969–72, Rothamsted Experimental Station 1966–69, Euro co-ordinator Nat Inst for Biological Standards and Control 1994–2001 (joined 1972, head Chemistry Div 1975–94), author of numerous pubns in jls; memb: Br Pharmacopoeia Cmmn 1982–2005 (vice-chm 1995–98, chm 1998–2005), Euro Pharmacopoeia Cmmn 1988–2005 (first vice-chm 1995–98, chm 1998–2001), Nat Biological Standards Bd 2002–09, Cmmn on Human Medicines 2005–13; visiting prof Univ of Strathclyde 1998–; MHRA Shirley Norton Lectr 2014; expert advsr WHO 1984–; hon memb Br Inst of Regulatory Affairs 1999; Hon DSc Univ of Strathclyde 2003; CChem, FRSC 1977, Hon MRPharmS 1992, FRSA 2000; *Recreations* walking, travel; *Style—* Professor Derek Calam, CBE; ✉ Orchard House, 6 Milton Road, Pewsey, Wiltshire SN9 5JJ

CALDECOTT, Andrew Hilary; QC (1994); s of Andrew Caldecott, CBE (d 1990), and Zita, *née* Belloc; *b* 22 June 1952; *Educ* Eton, New Coll Oxford (BA); *m* 1977, Rosamond Ashton, *née* Shuttleworth; 2 s (Harry b 1981, Edmund b 1985), 2 da (Zita b 1983, Xanthe 1991); *Career* called to the Bar Inner Temple 1975 (bencher 2004); specialist advsr Jt Parly Ctee on the Draft Defamation Bill 2011; play Higher than Babel staged at Bridewell Theatre 1999; *Style—* Andrew Caldecott, Esq, QC; ✉ 1 Brick Court, Temple, London EC4Y 8BY (☎ 020 7353 8845)

CALDER, Prof Muffy; OBE (2010); da of Carmen Van Thomas (d 1996), and Lois, *née* Hallen; *b* Shawinigan, Canada; *Educ* Univ of Stirling (BSc), Univ of St Andrews (PhD); *m* 1998, David Calder; *Career* research appointments at Univ of Edinburgh and Univ of Stirling; Univ of Glasgow: prof 1988–, head Dept of Computing Science 2003–; memb Scottish Science Advsy Ctee (SSAC); author of over 50 scientific pubns; FRSE 2003, FIEE 2003; *Recreations* long-distance, hill running; *Clubs* Westerlands Cross Country; *Style—* Prof Muffy Calder, OBE; ✉ Department of Computing Science, University of Glasgow, Glasgow G12 8QQ (☎ 0141 330 4969, e-mail muffy.calder@glasgow.ac.uk)

CALDER, Rachel Elisabeth; da of Richard Calder, of USA, and Elisabeth, *née* Baber; *b* 25 January 1961, Derby; *Educ* Fyling Hall Sch Whitby, Univ of Hull (BA); *m* 30 March 1996, Daniel Kunkle; 2 s (Jack b 19 April 1995, Milo b 14 Jan 1998), 1 da (Matilda b 8 Oct 2001); *Career* Andre Deutsch 1982–83; literary agent: Curtis Brown Gp 1987–91, The Sayle Literary Agency (formerly Tessa Sayle Agency) 1991–; *Style—* Ms Rachel Calder; ✉ The Sayle Literary Agency, 1 Petersfield, Cambridge CB1 1BB (☎ 01223 303035, fax 01223 301638, e-mail rachel@sayleliteraryagency.com)

CALDERWOOD, Robert; *b* 11 October 1953; *Educ* Camphill Sr Secdy Sch, Glasgow Coll of Technol (HND in Business Studies), Inst of Health Serv Mangrs (DipHSM), Univ of Aberdeen (Cert in Health Economics); *m*; 1 s; *Career* admin trainee NHS 1971–74, various admin posts Argyll and Clyde Health Bd 1974–85; Gtr Glasgow Health Bd: various hosp admin posts, dir of property and strategic planning 1988–91, unit gen mangr Southern Gen Hosp Unit 1991–93; chief exec: Southern Gen Hosp NHS Tst 1993–97, South Glasgow Univ Hosps NHS Tst 1998–2004, GGHB South Glasgow Univ Hosps Div 2004–06; chief operating off NHS Gtr Glasgow and Clyde Acute Servs Div 2006–09, chief exec NHS Gtr Glasgow and Clyde 2009–; non-exec dir: Skills for Health 2012, NHS Nat Services Scotland 2013; hon prof Adam Smith Business Sch Univ of Glasgow 2013; Companion Inst of Healthcare Mgmnt; *Recreations* golf; *Style—* Robert Calderwood, Esq; ✉ JB Russell House, Gartnavel Royal Hospital, 1055 Great Western Road, Glasgow G12 0XH (☎ 0141 201 4642, e-mail robert.calderwood@ggc.scot.nhs.uk)

CALDICOTT, Dame Fiona; DBE (1996); *née* Soesan; da of Joseph Maurice Soesan (d 1999), of Coventry, Warks, and Elizabeth Jane, *née* Ransley (d 2007); *b* 12 January 1941; *Educ* City of London Sch for Girls, St Hilda's Coll Oxford (MA, BM BCh); *m* 5 June 1965, Robert Gordon Woodruff Caldicott, s of Capt Gordon Ezra Woodruff (d 1941), of Louisville, KY; 1 da (Lucy Woodruff b 1968), 1 s (Richard Woodruff b 1971 d 1990); *Career* conslt psychiatrist Univ of Warwick 1979–85, conslt psychotherapist Uffculme Clinic 1979–96, sr clinical lectr in psychotherapy Univ of Birmingham 1982–96, unit gen mangr Mental Health Unit Central Birmingham HA 1989–91, dir Adult Psychiatric and Psychotherapy Services S Birmingham HA 1991–94, med dir S Birmingham Mental Health NHS Tst 1994–96; princ Somerville Coll Oxford 1996–2010, memb Cncl Univ of Oxford 1998–2009, pro-vice-chllr Univ of Oxford 2001–10 (chm Conf of Colls 2003–05); chm: Section of Psychiatry Union of Euro Med Specialists 1996–99, Nat Info Governance Bd 2011–13, Review Info Governance 2012–13, Ind Info Governance Oversight Panel 2013–; memb: Conf (now Acad) of Med Royal Colls and their Faculties in UK 1993–96 (chm 1995–96), Central Manpower Ctee BMA 1977–89 and 1996–97, Med Workforce Advsy Ctee 1991–2001, Nat Advsy Ctee on Mentally Disordered Offenders 1993–96, Standing Ctee on Postgrad Med Educn 1993–99, Broadcasting Standards Cmmn 1996–2001; conslt advsr to Cmmrs for High Security Psychiatric Care 1996–2000; RCPsych: chm Manpower Ctee 1981–89, sub dean 1987–90, dean 1990–93, pres 1993–96; pres Guild of Health Writers 1996–99; chm Bd Med Ed BMA 1996–2000, chm Mgmnt Ctee Nat Counselling Service for Sick Doctors 1999–2005; pres Br Assoc of Counselling Psychotherapy 2000–06; tstee Nuffield Tst 1998–2008; elected memb GMC 1999–2003; non-exec dir: Coventry Building Soc 1997–2001, Oxford Radcliffe Hospitals NHS Tst 2002– (chm 2009–); nat data guardian for health and social care Dept of Health 2014–;

lay memb Cncl Univ of Warwick 2010–, memb Cncl UN Univ 2010; govr: Univ of Oxford, Cheltenham Coll 2000–05, Rugby Sch 2005–08; memb Czech Psychiatric Soc 1994; hon conslt psychiatrist S Birmingham Mental Health NHS Tst 1996–2012; hon fell St Hilda's Coll Oxford 1996, hon fell Somerville Coll Oxford 2010; Hon DSc Univ of Warwick 1996, Hon MD Univ of Birmingham 1997; FRCPsych 1985, FRSM 1990, fell Acad of Med Singapore 1994, FRCP 1995, FRCPI 1996, FRCGP 1996, FMedSci 1998; *Publications* Caldicott Report on Patient Identifiable Data (1997), Caldicott Review of Information Governance (2013); *Clubs* RSM; *Style*— Dame Fiona Caldicott, DBE; ✉ 27 High Street, Warwick, Warwickshire CV34 4AX (e-mail fiona.caldicott@some.ox.ac.uk)

CALDWELL, Prof John; s of Gilbert Reginald Caldwell (d 1990), and Marian Elizabeth Caldwell (1992); *b* 4 April 1947, Hillingdon, Middx; *Educ* Chelsea Coll London (BPharm), St Mary's Hosp Med Sch London (PhD), Univ of London (DSc); *m* 13 Sept 1969, Rev Jill Caldwell, *née* Gregory; 2 s (David George Mawdsley b 2 June 1975, James Alexander Gregory b 17 Nov 1979); *Career* Imperial Coll Faculty of Med (St Mary's Hosp Med Sch until merger 1997): lectr in biochemistry 1972–74, lectr in biochemical pharmacology 1974–78, sr lectr in biochemical pharmacology 1978–82, reader in drug metabolism 1982–88, prof of biochemical toxicology 1988–2002, head Dept of Pharmacology and Toxicology 1992–97, dean Imperial Sch of Med at St Mary's 1995–97, head Div of Biomedical Sciences 1997–2002, head of undergraduate med 2000–02; Univ of Liverpool: dean Faculty of Med 2002–10, pro-vice chllr 2007–12, prof emeritus 2012–; chm Mid-Staffordshire NHS Fndn Tst 2012–15; chair: Scientific Ctee N W Cancer Res Fund 2003–09, MorEx Devpt Partners 2008–, Health Educn Eng Thames Valley 2014–; non-exec dir: St Mary's Hosp NHS Tst 1995–98, Huntingdon Life Sciences plc 1997–2003, Cheshire and Merseyside Strategic HA 2003–06, North West Strategic HA 2006–11, Eden Biopharma Group Ltd 2004–10, Liverpool Science Park Ltd 2007–11; fndr and dir Amedis Pharmaceuticals Ltd 2000–02, md Drouzin Therapies Ltd 2014–; memb: WHO Task Gp on principles for the safety assessment of food additives and contaminants in food 1987, Int Expert Advsy Ctee Centre for Bio-Pharmaceutical Sciences Univ of Leiden 1989, MAFF Steering Gp for Food Surveillance 1993–96, Scientific Advsy Bd Merlin Venture Fund 1996–2004, Ctee on Safety of Meds 1999–2005, Nuffield Cncl for Bioethics Working Pty on Pharmacogenetics 2001–03; scientific advsr on peroxisomal proliferation Dijon Groupement d'Interet Scientifique Universite-Industrielle (appointed by French Miny of HE and Research) 1988–93, conslt for evaluation of chemicals for their carcinogenicity to humans Int Agency for Res on Cancer Lyon 1997–2000; Sterling-Winthrop distinguished prof Univ of Michigan 1995; prestige lectr Univ of Bradford 1996; author of numerous pubns on drug metabolism incl papers, invited contribs and 11 edited books; European ed and fndr Chirality 1989– (Assoc of American Publishers Award for Best New Jl in Science, Technol and Med 1991); past or present memb 17 editorial bds; membership of learned socs incl Int Soc for the Study of Xenobiotics (memb Cncl 1986–90, pres 1994–95, hon life memb 2001–); tstee: Edgar Lawley Fndn 1997–2002, Francis Holland Educnl Tst 1998–2002, Westlakes Research Inst Cumbria 2003–05; hon memb Canadian Soc for Pharmaceutical Scis 2002–; Hon MRCP 1998; CBiol, FSB 1992; *Recreations* reader St Marylebone PC 1997–2002, Venice, rugby football, motor racing; *Clubs* Athenaeum, London Welsh RFC; *Style*— Prof John Caldwell; ✉ c/o The Athenaeum, 107 Pall Mall, London SW1Y 5ER

CALDWELL, Dr Neil Edward; s of Robert Aldridge Caldwell (d 1999), of Barrow-in-Furness, Cumbria, and Kathleen Constance, *née* Barnard; *b* 17 April 1952, London; *Educ* Dr Challoner's GS Amersham, UCW Aberystwyth (BSc), Poly of Wales (PhD); *m* 1977, Betsan Charles, *née* Jones; 1 da (Catrin Lowri Iorwerth b 1978), 1 s (Owain Rhys Iorwerth b 1980); *Career* vice-pres Aberystwyth Guild of Students 1973–74, pres NUS Wales 1975–77, res student Poly of Wales (now Univ of Glamorgan) 1977–82; National Trust warden: for Ll?n 1982–85, for Gower 1985–88; dir: Campaign for the Protection of Rural Wales 1988–94, Prince of Wales' Ctee 1994–96, The Prince's Trust – Bro 1996–99, exec dir The Prince's Tst Cymru 1999–2000, ind community regeneration conslt 2000–11, ret; former ed Rural Wales Magazine; memb: European Environmental Bureau 1988–2000, Bd ENTRUST 1996–2002, SW Wales Economic Forum 1999–2004, Bd Wales Cncl for Voluntary Action 2000–10, Aggregates Levy Sustainability Fund for Wales; chair Participation Cymru; former memb Welsh Language Bd; vice-chair Wales Wildlife and Countryside Link 1991–99; FRSA; *Books* Discovering Welshness (contrib, 1992), Environment of Wales (contrib, 1993), An Icon for Modern Wales: Realising the Benefits of the National Botanic Garden (2001); *Recreations* walking, sailing, reading, travelling; *Clubs* Pembrokeshire Yacht Club; *Style*— Dr Neil Caldwell; ✉ 19 Picton Terrace, Carmarthen SA31 3BX (☎ 01267 234529, mobile 07866 740203, e-mail neilecaldwell@gmail.com)

CALEB, Ruth Irene; OBE (2004); da of Emilio Caleb (d 1963), and Edith, *née* Pordes (d 1983); *b* 13 May 1942; *Educ* Church HS Newcastle upon Tyne, Bristol Old Vic Theatre Sch; *m* 1978, Martin Landy; 1 da (Francesca b 1979), 1 s (Jonathan b 1983); *Career* actress 1962–65; BBC: asst floor mangr 1965–67, prodn mangr 1967–72, assoc prodr 1972–79, prodr 1979–89, exec prodr BBC Drama 1989–2010, head of Drama Wales 1992–96, acting head of Drama Gp 1997, currently freelance exec prodr BBC TV Drama Gp; Alan Clarke Award for outstanding creative contribution to TV 2001, Columbia Tristar Award for Women in Film 2001, Women in Film and Television Eon Productions Lifetime Achievement Award 2012; Hon Dr of Arts Oxford Brooks Univ; memb: RTS, BAFTA; FRSA; *Television* Bread or Blood 1980, Month of the Doctors 1981, The Mountain and the Molehill 1982, Night on the Tyne 1983, Out of Love 1984, Stanley Spencer 1984, The Burston Rebellion 1986 (ACE Award LA, Samuel G Engel Award, Reims Award), Sweet As You Are 1988 (Silver Hugo Chicago, ACE Award LA, BANFF, RTS Writer Award), Ms Rymney Valley 1988, Can You Hear Me Thinking? 1988, Testimony of a Child 1990, Morphine & Dolly Mixtures 1990, Count of Solar 1991, Keeping Tom Nice 1991, Close Relations 1992 (Reims Award, ACE nomination), Black & Blue 1992, Civvies 1992, The Lost Language of Cranes 1992 (Sodom to Hollywood Award Turin, Golden Gate Award, BAFTA nomination), Friday on my Mind 1993, The Old Devils 1993 (Golden Gate Award, BAFTA Cymru Award), The Cormorant 1993, Selected Exits 1994, Pat & Margaret 1995 (Nymph D'Or Monte Carlo, Critics Award Monte Carlo, Reims Award), Street Life 1996, Trip Trap 1996, Bravo 2 Zero 1998, Big Cat 1998, Nice Girl 2000, Last Resort 2001 (Michael Powell Award for Best New Br Film Edinburgh Int Film Festival, Best Feature Thessalonica Film Festival, Best Feature Film Gijon Film Festival), Care 2001 (Best Single Drama BAFTA, Golden Rembrandt, Prix Italia for Single Drama), When I Was 12 2002 (Best Single Drama BAFTA), Tomorrow La Scala! 2002 (Best Made for TV Movie Award BANFF TV Festival, Best Single Drama Independent Award), Out of Control 2002 (Michael Powell Award for Best New Br Film Edinburgh Int Film Festival, Best Single Drama RTS, Best One Off Drama Broadcast Awards, Signis Prize Monte Carlo TV Festival), The Other Boleyn Girl 2003, Rehab 2003, Bullet Boy 2004, Red Dust 2004, England Expects 2004, Love and Hate 2004, Judge John Deed 2004–07, Shooting Dogs 2005, Four Last Songs 2006, Shiny Shiny Bright New Hole in My Heart 2006, Born Equal 2006, Learners 2007, Walters War 2008, A Short Stay in Switzerland 2009 (Broadcasting Award for Single Drama, BAFTA nomination), The Last Days of Lehman Brothers 2009, Money 2010, The Whale 2013, A Poet in New York 2014 (nominated Broadcast Award 2015); *Style*— Ms Ruth Caleb, OBE

CALEDON, 7 Earl of (I 1800); Nicholas James Alexander; KCVO (2015), JP; Baron Caledon (I 1790), Viscount (I 1797); s of 6 Earl of Caledon (d 1980), by his 2 w, Baroness Anne (d 1963), da of Baron Nicolai de Graevenitz (Grand Duchy of Mecklenburg-Schwerin 1847, Russia (Tsar Nicholas I) 1851); *b* 6 May 1955; *Educ* Gordonstoun; *m* 1, 1979 (m dis 1985), Wendy Catherine, da of Spiro Nicholas Coumantaros, of Athens; m 2, 19 Dec 1989, Henrietta Mary Alison, er da of John Newman, of Compton Park, Compton Chamberlayne, Wilts; 1 s (Frederick James, Viscount Alexander b 15 Oct 1990), 1 da (Lady Leonora Jane b 26 May 1993); m 3, 2 Feb 2008, Amanda Cosbie Sara Cayzer, yr da of John Squire of Gaucin, Spain, and Mrs Ticehurst, of Chelsea, London; *Heir* s, Viscount Alexander; *Career* HM Lord Lieutenant for Co Armagh 1989–; chm Caledon Estates; *Recreations* travel, skiing, flying; *Clubs* Corviglia Ski, Helicopter Club of Ireland, White's, Armagh Co; *Style*— The Rt Hon the Earl of Caledon, KCVO; ✉ Caledon Castle, Caledon, Co Tyrone (☎ 028 3756 8232)

CALIGARI, Prof Peter Douglas Savaria; s of Flt Lt Kenneth Vane Savaria Caligari, DFM (d 2003), of Worcester, and Mary Annetta, *née* Rock; *b* 10 November 1949, Rinteln, Germany; *Educ* Hereford Cathedral Sch, Univ of Birmingham (BSc, PhD, DSc); *m* 1, 23 June 1973 (m dis); 2 da (Louise b 13 Jan 1978, Helena b 26 Sept 1980); m 2, 29 Dec 2007, Andrea Veronica Moreno González; 2 da (Constanza b 16 April 1992, Francisca b 6 June 1997); *Career* res fell Univ of Birmingham 1974–81 (res asst 1971–74), princ scientific offr Scottish Crop Res Inst 1984–86 (sr scientific offr 1981–84), prof of agric botany Univ of Reading 1986–2006 (head Dept of Agric Botany 1987–98), prof titular Inst de Ciências Biológicas Univ of Talca Chile 2002–15 (dir 2004–09); md BioHybrids Gp; memb Comité de Xpertos Beca de Presidente de la República de Chile 2006–07; dir: Genberries Ltda 2008–, Sumatra Bioscience pta Ltd 2008–11, Sustainable Plant Nutrition Ltd 2010–14, Bioscience Private Ltd (Singapore) 2012–13, Corporación Centro de Genómica Nutricional Agroacuicola 2012–, BioSing Private Ltd (Singapore) 2013–, Verdant Bioscience Private Ltd (Singapore) 2013–, PT Timbang Deli Indonesia 2014–; dir and chm Bd of Dirs Ghana Sumatra Ltd 2008–12, dir and chm NG Seeds SA (Chile) 2013– (chm Bd 2013–); sr ed Heredity 1988–91 (jr ed 1985–88), memb Editorial Bd Euphytica 1991–, chm Pubns Ctee XVIIth Int Genetics Congress (1993) 1991–93, memb Editorial Bd Turkish Jl of Agriculture and Forestry 2013–; vice-pres Inst of Biology, chm Science Policy Bd 1999–2002; memb: Conf of Agric Profs 1986–2002, Governing Body Plant Science Research Ltd 1991–94, Governing Cncl John Innes Centre 1994–99, European Cncl for the Volcani Centre 1999–2002, Assoc of Applied Biologists, EUCARPIA (Euro Assoc for Res in Plant Breeding), Euro Assoc for Potato Res, Genetics Soc (ex officio ctee memb 1985–91), Int Assoc for Plant Tissue Culture (IAPTC), Sociedad de Genética de Chile, Int Lupin Assoc, La Asociación para la Cooperación en Investigaciones Bananeras en el Caribe y en América Tropical (ACORBAT); FRSA 1990, FRSB 1998 (CIBiol); memb Int Soc for Horticultural Sci (2014–), memb Academia Chilena de Ciencias Agronómicas (2013–); *Books* Selection Methods in Plant Breeding (with I Bos, 1995, 2 edn 2008), Compositae Vol II Biology and Utilisation (ed with N Hind, 1996), Cashew and Coconuts: Trees for Life (ed with C P Topper et al, 1999), Wheat Taxonomy: the legacy of John Percival (ed with P E Brandham, 2001), Introduction to Plant Breeding (with J Brown, 2008), Plant Breeding (with J Brown and H Campos, 2014); numerous scientific articles, book chapters and reports; *Style*— Prof Peter DS Caligari; ✉ 5 Poniente 244, Entre 14 y 15 Sur, Loteo San Agustin, Talca, Chile (☎ 00 56 99 452 2 451, e-mail peter.caligari@verdantbioscience.com)

CALLAGHAN, Rev Brendan Alphonsus; SJ; s of Dr Alphonsus Callaghan (d 1975), and Dr Kathleen Callaghan, *née* Kavanagh (d 1997); *b* 29 July 1948; *Educ* Stonyhurst, Heythrop Coll, Campion Hall Oxford (MA), Univ of Glasgow (MPhil), Heythrop Coll London (MTh); *Career* voluntary serv teacher Zimbabwe 1966–67; Soc of Jesus: joined 1967, ordained priest 1978, memb Formation Cmmn 1990–, formation asst to provincial 2002–07; superior: Brixton Jesuit Community 1993–94, Merrivale Community KwaZulu-Natal 1997–98, Wimbledon Jesuit Community 1998–2005, Clapham Jesuit Community 2007–08; master Campion Hall Univ of Oxford 2008–13 (master of novices 2014–); clinical psychologist: Glasgow Southern Gen Hosp 1974–76, Middx Hosp 1976–79; conslt various orders and dioceses 1975–, conslt Catholic Marriage Advsy Cncl 1981–; Heythrop Coll London: lectr in psychology 1980– (also Allen Hall Chelsea 1981–87), memb Academic Bd 1982–97, memb Governing Body 1982–97, 1998–99 and 2012–, princ 1985–97 (actg princ 1998–99), sr lectr 2007–08, visiting lectr 2008–, fell 2009; Univ of London: chm Bd of Examiners Theology and Religious Studies 1987–89, memb Schs Examination Bd 1987–97, memb Collegiate Cncl and Senate 1989–94, memb Cncl 1994–97 and 1997–98; memb Governing Body: Campion Hall Oxford 1985–95, Inst of Med Ethics 1989–2002 (hon asst then assoc dir 1976–89, gen sec 1998–2002), Syon House Angmering 1985–97; memb: Academic Advsy Ctee Jews Coll 1993–97, Ctee for People in Higher Educn RC Bishop's Conf of Eng and Wales 1985–97, Centre for the Study of Communication and Culture Univ of Santa Clara (chm) 1990–2000, Inst of St Anselm 1991–98, Family Res Tst 1991–2000, Ctee Bishop John Robinson Fellowship 1993–2002, Ethics Ctee Westminster Pastoral Fndn 1994–2002, Local Research Ethics Ctee St Thomas' Hospital 1989–2002 (dep chm 1989–97), Ethics Ctee St Joseph's Hospice 2011–; visiting lectr: St Joseph's Inst of Theology Kwazulu-Natal 1987 and 1997–98, Imperial Coll London 1990–, KCL 1991–94; visiting prof Fordham Univ NY 1990, visiting scholar Weston Sch of Theology Cambridge Mass 1992; chm Govrs Digby Stuart Coll Roehampton Univ of Surrey (formerly Roehampton Inst London) 1998–2002; patron Inst of Ecumenical Studies Prague Czech Republic 1995–; memb: (int affiliate), Progressio (formerly Catholic Inst for Int Rels), CND, Int Assoc for the Psychology of Religion; Hon FCollT; *Publications* Life Before Birth (co-author, 1986); author of various articles, book reviews and poetry in jls; *Recreations* photography, long distance walking, poetry; *Style*— The Rev Brendan Callaghan, SJ; ✉ Manresa House, 10 Albert Road, Birmingham B17 0AN (e-mail brendancsj@jesuits.net)

CALLAHAN, J Loughlin (Lough); s of John G P Callahan, Lt-Col US Air Force (d 1992), of Dayton, Ohio, and Marie, *née* Loughlin (d 1995); *b* 18 January 1948; *Educ* Holy Cross Coll Worcester Massachusetts (BA), Harvard Law Sch (Juris Dr, cum laude); *m* 5 May 1973, Mary, da of Vincent Reilly (d 1969), of Tinton Falls, New Jersey; 1 s (Christopher b 1974), 1 da (Denise b 1976 d 1996); *Career* law Davis Polk & Wardwell NY 1972–80; investment banking dir: S G Warburg & Co Ltd 1983–86, S G Warburg Securities 1986–92; investment mgmnt dir Mercury Asset Mgmnt Ltd 1992–99, investment mgmnt conslt 1999–; pres: The Europe Fund Inc 1996–99, The United Kingdom Fund Inc 1996–99; dir: International Primary Market Assoc 1986–91 (vice-chm 1988–91), Euroclear Clearance System Société Cooperative 1991–93, Tribune Tst plc 1999–; chm The European Technology and Income Co Ltd 2000–02; conslt Fin Services Office Ernst & Young 1999–; dir Assoc of Investment Tst Companies 2001–; *Recreations* art, music, theatre and tennis; *Clubs* Chelsea Arts; *Style*— Lough Callahan, Esq; ✉ 7 Spencer Hill, London SW19 4PA (☎ 020 8947 7726, fax 020 8947 1772, e-mail lough@maryandlough.com)

CALLANAN, Baron (Life Peer UK 2014), of Low Fell in the County of Tyne and Wear Martin Callanan; *b* 8 August 1961; *Educ* Heathfield Sr HS, Newcastle Poly (BSc); *m* 1997, Jayne, *née* Burton; 1 s (Joseph b 1995); *Career* MEP (Cons) NE England 1999–2014; ldr Cons MEPs 2010–11, ldr European Conservatives and Reformists Gp European Parl 2011–14; cncllr Tyne & Wear CC 1983–86, cncllr Gateshead MBC 1987–96; project engrg mangr Scottish & Newcastle Breweries 1986–98; *Style*— The Lord Callanan; ✉ House of Lords, London SW1A 0PW

CALLERY, Simon Laurence Christopher; s of Christopher Thomas Callery, and Shirley Fay, *née* Tennant; *Educ* Bloxham Sch, Campion Sch Athens, Berkshire Coll of Art & Design, S Glamorgan Inst of Higher Educn (BA); *Children* 2 s, by Paola Piccato; (Andreas Alessandro Christopher b Sept 1995, Lewis Ettore b May 2000); *Career* artist; *Solo*

Exhibitions E14 SE10 (Free Trade Wharf London) 1991, Simon Callery (Anderson O'Day Gallery London) 1993 and 1994, Galleria Christian Stein Turin 1994–, Anthony Wilkinson Fine Art London 1996, Oxford Univ Museum of Nat History 1997, Pitt Rivers Museum Oxford 1997, Art Now 19 (Tate Gallery London, Kohn Turner Gallery LA) 1999, Philippe Casini Gallery Paris 2001, Philippe Casini Gall Paris 2001 and 2002, Segsbury Project Dover Castle 2003; *Group Exhibitions* incl: New Contemporaries (ICA London) 1983, National Eisteddfod (S Wales, prizewinner) 1986, Strictly Painting (Cubitt St Gallery London) 1993, John Moores 18 (Walker Art Gallery Liverpool, prizewinner) 1993, Young British Artists III (Saatchi Gallery) 1994, Landscapes (Ex-Lanificio Bona Torino) 1994, About Vision (MOMA Oxford) 1996–97, Khoj (Br Cncl New Delhi India) 1997, Sensation (touring Royal Acad of Art exbn) 1997–99, Fact & Value (Charlottenborg Copenhagen) 2000, Paper Assets (British Museum) 2001, Colour White (De La War Pavillion Bexhill), Multiples Object de Desir (Musee des Beaux-Arts Nantes); *Awards* Arts Cncl Young Artists grant 1983 and 1984, Gold Medal Nat Eisteddfod S Wales; *Style—* Simon Callery, Esq

CALLOW, Simon; CBE (1999); s of Neil Francis Callow (d 1973), and Yvonne Mary, *née* Guise (d 2015); *b* 15 June 1949; *Educ* London Oratory GS, Queen's Univ Belfast, Drama Centre London; *m* June 2016, Sebastian Fox; *Career* actor, director and writer; govr London Inst 2000, tstee Theatres Tst 2004; fell Univ of the Arts 2010; Freedom of the City of London 2011; Hon DLL: Queen's Univ Belfast 1999, Univ of Birmingham 2000, Kingston Univ 2015; hon doctorate Open Univ 2010; *Theatre* roles incl: The Resistable Rise of Arturo Ui (Half Moon) 1978, Titus Andronicus (Bristol Old Vic), Mary Barnes (Royal Court) 1978, Plumbers Progress (Prince of Wales), As You Like It (NT) 1979, title role in Amadeus (NT) 1979, Sisterly Feelings (NT), Verlaine in Total Eclipse (Lyric Hammersmith), Lord Are in Restoration (Royal Court) 1981, Beastly Beatitudes (Duke of York's) 1981, Lord Foppington in The Relapse (Lyric Hammersmith) 1983, On The Spot (Watford and West End) 1984, Melancholy Jacques (Traverse and Bush), Kiss of the Spiderwoman (Bush) 1985, Faust (Lyric Hammersmith) 1988, Single Spies (NT and Queens' Theatre) 1988 and 1989, The Destiny of Me (also dir, Haymarket Leicester) 1993, The Alchemist (Birmingham and RNT) 1996, The Importance of Being Oscar (Savoy) 1997, Chimes at Midnight 1998, The Mystery of Charles Dickens (West End, Broadway and world tour), Through the Leaves (Southwark Playhouse and West End) 2003, The Holy Terror (West End and tour) 2004, Woman in White (West End) 2006, Aladdin (Richmond) 2006, Present Laughter 2006, Merry Wives the Musical 2006, Equus (nat tour) 2008, There Reigns Love (Stratford Ontario) 2008, A Festival Dickens (Edinburgh Fringe Festival) 2008, Peter Pan (Richmond) 2008, Pozzo in Waiting For Godot (tour and Theatre Royal Haymarket) 2009, Dr Marigold and Mr Chops (Riverside Studios) 2009 and (nat tour) 2011, The Man From Stratford (tour, Edinburgh and Riverside Studios) 2010, Toby Belch in Twelfth Night (NT) 2010, Being Shakespeare (Trafalgar Studios) 2011 and 2012, (Brooklyn Academy of Music and Chicago Shakespeare Theatre) 2012 and (Harold Pinter Theatre) 2014, Pauline in Tuesday at Tesco's (Assembly Hall Edinburgh) 2011, A Christmas Carol (Arts Theatre London) 2011 and 2012, The Mystery of Charles Dickens (Playhouse Theatre), The Man Jesus (Lyric Theatre Belfast) 2013 and (nat tour and West End) 2014, Inside Wagner's Head (also writer, Linbury Studios Royal Opera House) 2013, Chin-Chin (Cesareo) (nat tour) 2013, Juvenalia (Edinburgh) 2014, Pauline in Tuesday at Tesco's (New York) 2015; *as director* incl: Loving Reno (Bush) 1984, The Passport (Offstage) 1985, Amadeus (Clwyd) 1986, The Infernal Machine (Lyric Hammersmith) 1986, Cosi fan Tutte (Luzern, Switzerland) 1987, Shirley Valentine (West End/Broadway) 1988, Die Fledermaus (Scottish Opera) 1988–89, Carmen Jones (Old Vic) 1991, Shades (West End) 1992, My Fair Lady (nat tour) 1992, Il Trittico (Broomhill) 1995, La Calisto, Glimmerglass (NY) 1996, Les Enfant du Paradis (RSC) 1996, Il Turco in Italia (Broomhill) 1997, HRH (Playhouse) 1997, The Pajama Game (Birmingham Rep, Princess of Wales Toronto, West End) 1999, The Consul (Holland Park Opera) 1999, Jus' Like That (West End) 2003, Everyman (Norwich Festival) 2003, Le Roi Malgré Lui (Grange Park) 2003, The Magic Flute (Holland Park) 2008, A Christmas Carol (also librettist, Houston Grand Opera) 2014; *Television* BBC incl: Instant Enlightenment Inc VAT, Man of Destiny, Juvenilia, La Ronde, All the World's a Stage, Deadhead, David Copperfield (serial) 1986, Cariani and the Courtesan 1987, Old Flames 1989, Patriot Witness, Trials of Oz, Femmes Fatale, Crime and Punishment, Woman in White 1997, An Audience with Charles Dickens 1996 and A Christmas Dickens 1997; other credits incl: Wings of Song (Granada), Bye Bye Columbus (Greenpoint), Chance in a Million (Thames) 1983 and 1985–86, Scarecrow and Mrs King (Warner Bros), Handel (film, Channel 4), The Christmas Tree (YTV), Inspector Morse (Central), Trials, Retribution, Hans Christian Anderson 2001, Galileo's Daughter 2002, Miss Marple 2005, Dr Who 2005, Roman Mysteries 2006, Poirot (ITV) 2013, Plebs 2014, Space Age 2014, Outlander 2015, The Rebel (series) 2016; *Radio* incl documentaries on: Charles Laughton (1987), Michéal macLiammóir (1992), Orson Welles (1999); dir Tomorrow Week 1999, The Man Who Came to Dinner 2000, The Judas Kiss 2000, I'll Be George 2001, Third Soldier 2004, Put Money in Thy Purse 2005 and Single Spies 2006; *Film* Amadeus 1983, A Room with a View 1986, The Good Father 1986, Maurice 1987, Manifesto 1988, Mr and Mrs Bridge 1991, Crucifer of Blood, Postcards from the Edge 1991, Soft Top Hard Shoulder 1992, Four Weddings and a Funeral 1994, Jefferson in Paris 1995, Le Passager Clandestin 1995, When Nature Calls 1995, England My England 1995, Victory 1995, Bedrooms and Hallways 1998, Shakespeare in Love 1998, No Man's Land 2000, A Christmas Carol 2000, Thunderpants 2001, The Civilisation of Maxwell Bright 2003, Bright Young Things 2003, The Phantom of the Opera 2004, Bob the Butler 2005, Surveillance 2006, Arn the Warrior 2007, Chemical Wedding 2008, Late Bloomers 2010, Love in the Kitchen 2011, Acts of Godfrey 2012, Golden Years 2015, Mindhorn 2015, The Viceroy's House 2015; also dir: The Ballad of the Sad Café 1991; *Books* Being an Actor (1984, 2 edn 2003), A Difficult Actor: Charles Laughton (1987), Shooting the Actor (1990, 2 edn 2003), Acting in Restoration Comedy (1991), Orson Welles: The Road to Xanadu (1995), The National (1997), Love is Where it Falls (1999), Oscar Wilde and His Circle (2000), Charles Laughton's Night of the Hunter (2000), Henry IV Part One (2002), Henry IV Part Two (2003), Dickens's Christmas (2003), Hello Americans (2006), My Life in Pieces (2010), Charles Dickens and the Great Theatre of the World (2012), Orson Welles: One Man Band (2015); *Audio* incl: Shooting the Actor (1992), Fairy Tales (by Oscar Wilde, 1995), Handful of Dust (1995), Dance to the Music of Time (1995), Swann's Way (1996), The Road to Xanadu (1996), The Witches (1997), The Twits (1998), The Plato Papers (1999), London: A Biography (2000), What Ho Jeeves (2000), English Passengers (2001), Jeeves (series, 2003), Death in Venice (2004), Shakespeare (2005), The Aeneid (2006), Practical Cats (2008), My Life in Pieces (2010), Charles Dickens and the Great Theatre of the World (2012); *Style—* Simon Callow, Esq, CBE; ✉ c/o Suzanne Lazenbury, 2 Tooveys Mill Close, Kings Langley, Hertfordshire WD4 8AG

CALLUM, Ian S; *b* 1954, Dumfries, Scotland; *Educ* Lanchester Poly, Aberdeen Art Coll, Glasgow Sch of Art, RCA (MA); *Career* Ford 1979–90, TWR Design 1990–99 (designs incl: Aston Martin DB7, Aston Martin Vanquish, Aston Martin DB7 Vantage, Nissan R390), design dir Jaguar 1999– (designs incl: XK, XF, F-Type); Assoc of Scottish Motoring Writers Jim Clark Meml Award 1995 and 2006, Autocar Designer of the Year Award 2001, Walpole Award for Br Design Talent 2008, hon fellowship and Gerald Frewer Meml Trophy Inst of Engrg Designers 2008, Auto Express UK Person of the Year Award 2009, Top Gear Man of the Year Award 2012, Automotive Interiors Expo Global Interior Designer of the Year Award 2013, Britweek LA Global Design Icon Award 2013, Scottish Automotive Hall of Fame 2015, Minerva Medal Chartered Soc of Designers (CSD) 2014; hon doctorate: Acad of Art Univ San Francisco 2000, De Montfort Univ 2002, Abertay Univ 2006, Birmingham City Univ 2011, Univ of Glasgow 2012; Hon FRIBA 2006, RDI 2007; *Style—* Ian Callum, Esq; ✉ Jaguar Cars, Abbey Road, Whitley, Coventry CV3 4LF

CALMAN, Prof Sir Kenneth Charles; KCB (1996), DL (Glasgow 2009); s of Arthur MacIntosh Calman (d 1951), and Grace Douglas, *née* Don; *b* 25 December 1941; *Educ* Allan Glens Sch Glasgow, Univ of Glasgow (BSc, MB ChB, PhD, MD, MLitt); *m* 8 July 1967, Ann, *née* Wilkie; 1 s (Andrew John b 5 Feb 1970), 2 da (Lynn Ann b 16 Nov 1971, Susan Grace b 6 Nov 1974); *Career* lectr in surgery Univ of Glasgow 1968–74, res fell Chester Beatty Inst London 1972–74, prof of oncology Univ of Glasgow 1974–84, dean of postgrad med 1984–89, chief med offr England Dept of Health 1991–98 (chief med offr Scotland 1989–91); vice-chllr and warden Univ of Durham 1998–2007, chllr Univ of Glasgow 2006–; chm NHS Genetics Educn Ctee 2004–08, chm Risk Advsy Gp Health Protection Agency 2004–, pres Inst of Medical Ethics 2005–10, pres BMA 2008–09; chm Cmmn on Scottish Devolution 2008–09, chm Glasgow Sci Centre 2008–10; memb: Unilever Ethics Ctee 2005–09, Bd Moredun Research Inst 2006–08, Scottish Sci Advsy Ctee 2007–08; memb Bd Macmillan Cancer Relief 1999–2004, tstee Cancer Research UK 2007–, chm Nat Cancer Research Inst 2008–11; nat pres Boys' Brigade 2007–11; dep chair and tstee Br Library 2006–15 (chm Audit Ctee), chm Nat Tst for Scotland 2010–15; Hon DUniv: Stirling 1991, Open Univ 1996, Paisley 1997; Hon DSc: Univ of Strathclyde 1993, Univ of Westminster 1995, Glasgow Caledonian Univ 1995, Univ of Glasgow 1996, Brighton Univ 2000, Univ of Durham 2008; Hon MD: Univ of Nottingham 1994, Univ of Birmingham 1996; Hon LLD Univ of Aberdeen 2005; FRCS, FRCP, FRCGP, FRCPATH, FRCR, FFPHM, FFPM, FRCOG, FRCSI, FRSM, FMedSci, FRSE 1979; *Books* Healthy Respect (with RS Downie, 2 edn 1994), The Potential for Health (1998), A Study of Story Telling, Humour and Learning in Medicine (2000), Medical Education: Past, present and future (2006), A Doctor's Line, Scottish Literature and Medicine (2014); *Recreations* gardening, golf, cartoons; *Style—* Prof Sir Kenneth Calman, KCB, DL, FRSE; ✉ University of Glasgow, Glasgow G12 8QQ (✆ 0141 330 4250)

CALTHORPE; *see:* Anstruther-Gough-Calthorpe

CALVER, Giles Christian; s of Peter Edwin Calver (d 2003), and Patricia Rosemary Calver; *b* 5 December 1958, Gibraltar; *Educ* St Joseph's Coll Ipswich, Gilberd Sch Colchester, Whitelands Coll London (BA), Univ of Western Ontario (MA); *m* 1 (m dis); 2 s (Rory Christian b 8 Dec 1991, Jake Harry b 8 July 1994); m 2, 16 Oct 2016, Luisa Manetta; *Career* account mangr rising to account supervisor Ogilvy & Mather Direct 1985–87, account supervisor DMB&B Direct 1987–89, account dir Pearson Paul Haworth Nolan 1989–90, co-fndr Lippa Pearce Design 1990–2006 (also md), planning dir Sedley Place 2010–; memb Design Business Assoc, memb D&AD; *Publications* Retail Graphics (2001), What is Packaging Design? (2004), Terminal 5: Transforming Heathrow (2008); *Recreations* reading, film, the arts, swimming, cycling, cinema, music, travel; *Style—* Giles Calver, Esq; ✉ 5 St Aubyns Road, Portslade, Brighton, East Sussex BN41 1AB (✆ 01273 410 804, e-mail gilescalver@hotmail.com)

CALVER, Simon John; s of Brian David Calver, of Kingskerswell, Devon, and Pamela Kathleen, *née* Smith; *b* 24 July 1964, Gloucester; *Educ* Sir Thomas Rich's Sch Gloucester, Univ of Hull (BSc), IOD (Cert); *m* 26 July 2014, Catharine Lisa, *née* Roberts; 1 s (Monty James b 26 Aug 2011), 1 da (Nieve Elizabeth b 16 Dec 2012); *Career* Unilever Plc 1985–89, Deloitte's 1989–91, vice pres UK/Ireland and int sales ops Pepsi Cola Int 1991–2000, vice pres UK/Ireland Dell Inc 2000–03, chief operating offr and pres Riverdeep plc 2003–05, chief exec LOVEFiLM Int Ltd 2005–12, chief exec Mothercare plc 2012–14, founding ptnr BGF Venutres 2015–; fndr and chm Calforce Ltd 2004–; chm: Moo.com 2014–, ChemistDirect.co.uk 2014–, Gousto Ltd 2015–; chm UK Business Angels Assoc 2015–; winner Sunday Times Tech Track Mgmnt Team 2007, finalist Ernst & Young Entrepreneur of the Year 2008, London and SE winner Ernst & Young Entrepreneur of the Year 2009, CBI Growth Co of the Year 2009, winner Sunday Times Buy Out Track 2011, winner UKV CA Large Exit (London and SE) 2011, named in Sunday Times Maserati 100 supporting next generation of entrepreneurs; memb Marketing Soc 1995, FInstD 1996, FRSA, CCIM; Success The LOVEFiLM Way (2013); *Recreations* collecting wine, cycling, shooting, rugby, skiing; *Clubs* Soho House, George, Second Home; *Style—* Simon Calver, Esq; ✉ The Lawns, Nightingales Lane, Chalfont St Giles, Buckinghamshire (✆ 01494 264949, e-mail simonjohncalver@yahoo.co.uk, website www.moo.com); BGF Ventures plc, 21 Palmer Street, London SW1H 0AD (e-mail simon@bgfventures.com, website www.bgfventures.com)

CALVERLEY, 3 Baron (UK 1945); Charles Rodney Muff; s of 2 Baron Calverley (d 1971); *b* 2 October 1946; *Educ* Moravian Boys' Sch Fulneck; *m* 1, 1972 (m dis 2000), Barbara Ann, da of Jonathan Brown, of Colne, Lancs; 2 s (Hon Jonathan Edward Brown b 1975, Hon Andrew Raymond Brown b 1978); m 2, 2008, Jenifer, da of late Leslie Green; *Heir* s, Hon Jonathan Brown; *Career* formerly with City of Bradford Police, memb W Yorkshire Police 1963–1996, seconded to RUC; took seat (Lib Dem) in House of Lords 1997; *Clubs* Parliamentary Sports and Social (hon life memb); *Style—* The Rt Hon the Lord Calverley; ✉ 36a Dunrossil Street, Wembley Downs, Perth 6019, Western Australia (✆ 0061 8 6162 0820)

CALVERLEY, Prof Peter Martin Anthony; s of Peter Calverley, and Jennifer, *née* Taylor; *b* 27 November 1949; *Educ* Queen Elizabeth GS Blackburn, Univ of Edinburgh (MB ChB); *m* 28 June 1973, Margaret Elizabeth, da of William Tatam, of Grantham, Lincs; 4 s (Adam Richard, James Iain (twins) b 1977, Robert Andrew b 1979, Thomas Peter b 1981); *Career* house offr Edinburgh 1973–74, SHO Dept of Med Leicester 1975–76, clinical fell MRC 1977–79, sr registrar Dept of Med Univ of Edinburgh 1979–85, MRC (Can) travelling fell McGill Univ Montreal 1982–83; currently: hon conslt physician Aintree Hosps Liverpool, emeritus prof of med (pulmonary rehabilitation) Univ of Liverpool; assoc ed: Thorax until 2010, Euro Respiratory Jl 2000–05, American Jl of Respiratory and Critical Care Medicine; chm Br Sleep Soc 2000–02; memb WHO/NHLBI Steering Ctee for Global Initiative in Obstructive Lung Disease, chair Respiratory Speciality Gps MHR CRN; Hon DSc 2010; memb: American Thoracic Soc, Assoc of Physicians of GB and Ireland; fell European Respiratory Soc (FERS); FRCP, FRCPE, FMedSci 2011; *Recreations* travel, skiing and talking; *Style—* Prof Peter Calverley; ✉ Clinical Science Centre, University Hospital Aintree, Longmoor Lane, Aintree, Liverpool L9 7AL (✆ 0151 529 5886, fax 0151 529 5888)

CALVERT, Prof (Alan) Hilary; *b* 18 February 1947; *Educ* Univ of Cambridge (BA, MB BChir, MD), Chelsea Coll London (MSc); *m*; 3 c; *Career* house physician St Charles' Hosp London 1972–73, house surgn Northwick Park Hosp Harrow Middx 1973, SHO Renal Unit Royal Free Hosp London 1973–74, SHO in med Royal Marsden Hosp London 1974, locum registrar Renal Unit Royal Free Hosp Oct-Dec 1974; Royal Marsden Hosp: research fell 1975–77, hon sr registrar 1977–80, hon conslt in med Div of Med 1980–85, hon conslt Div of Med 1985–89; Inst of Cancer Research: lectr 1977–80, sr lectr 1980–85, reader in clinical pharmacology and team leader Clinical Pharmacology Team Drug Devpt Section 1985–89; Univ of Newcastle upon Tyne: prof of clinical oncology and dir Cancer Research Unit 1989–2009, head Dept of Oncology 1990–2009; dir of cancer drug discovery and devpt UCL Cancer Institute 2009–, prof of cancer therapeutics UCL; formerly memb: SW Thames Head and Neck Co-operative Gp, MRC Bladder Cancer Chemotherapy Sub-gp, Advsy Panel Beatson Laboratories, Scientific Ctee Leukaemia Research Fund; currently memb: Phase I Clinical Trials Ctee Cancer Research Campaign, Drug Devpt Ctee and

Pharmacokinetics and Metabolism Gp Euro Orgn for Research on Treatment of Cancer (memb Advsy Panel 1979); memb: Int Agency for Research on Cancer Working Gp on the Evaluation of the Carcinogenic Risk of Chemicals to Humans 1980, EORTC/Nat Cancer Inst (USA) Liaison Ctee 1988, EORTC/NCI/CRC Coordinating Ctee; author of over 200 pubns in the field of cancer therapeutics; ed-in-chief Cancer Chemotherapy and Pharmacology, assoc ed Cancer Surveys; memb Editorial Bd: Anticancer Drug Design, Cancer Topics, Biochemical Pharmacology; numerous invited lectures in Europe, USA, Canada and NZ; memb: Br Assoc for Cancer Research, American Assoc for Cancer Research, Assoc of Cancer Physicians, American Soc of Clinical Oncology, Euro Soc of Med Oncology (invited memb), NY Acad of Scis (invited memb); FRCP 1988 (MRCP 1975, accreditation in med oncology 1987), fell Acad of Medical Sciences 2001; *Style—* Prof Hilary Calvert; ✉ UCL Cancer Institute, Paul O'Gorman Building, 72 Huntley Street, London WC1E 6BT

CALVERT, Jonathan; *Educ* Ackworth Sch Pontefract, Univ of Leeds (BA); *Career* journalist; The Western Mail 1991–93, reporter Insight The Sunday Times 1993–95, investigations ed The Observer 1995–2000, asst ed (investigations) Sunday and Daily Express 2000–01; The Sunday Times: rejoined 2001, dep news ed 2003–05, ed Insight 2005–; over 20 top journalism awards incl 3 times Scoop of the Year; *Books* The Ugly Game: The Qatari Plot to Buy the World Cup (with Heidi Blake, 2015); *Recreations* cinema, cricket, gardening, music, opera, reading, skiing, tennis, travel; *Style—* Jonathan Calvert, Esq; ✉ c/o Capel and Land, 29 Wardour Street, London W1D 6PS (☎ 020 7782 5035, e-mail jonathan.calvert@sunday-times.co.uk, Twitter @JCalvertST)

CALVERT, Prof Peter Anthony Richard; s of Raymond Calvert (d 1959), of Helen's Bay, Co Down, and Irene Calvert, MP, *née* Earls (d 2000); *b* 19 November 1936; *Educ* Campbell Coll Belfast, Queens' Coll Cambridge (MA, PhD), Univ of Michigan (MA); *m* 1, 1962 (m dis 1987), Diana Elizabeth Farrow; 2 c; m 2, 1987, Susan Ann, da of Leonard John Milbank, of Slough, Berks; 2 s; *Career* Regular Army (NI Enlistment) 1955–57; teaching fell Univ of Michigan 1960–61; Univ of Southampton: lectr 1964–71, sr lectr 1971–74, reader in politics 1974–83, prof of comparative and international politics 1984–2002, emeritus prof 2002; visiting lectr Univ of Calif Santa Barbara 1966, res fell Charles Warren Center for Studies in American History Harvard Univ 1969–70, visiting prof Dept of Politics and Sociology Birkbeck Coll London 1984–85; memb Cambridge City Cncl 1962–64, co-opted memb Dorset Educn Ctee 1984–89; FRHistS 1972; *Books* The Mexican Revolution 1910–1914: The Diplomacy of Anglo American Conflict (1968, 2 edn 2008), Latin America: Internal Conflict and International Peace (1969), A Study of Revolution (1970), Revolution (Key Concepts in Political Science) (1970), Mexico (1973), The Mexicans: How They Live and Work (1975), The Concept of Class (1982), The Falklands Crisis: The Rights and the Wrongs (1982), Politics Power and Revolution: An Introduction to Comparative Politics (1983), Revolution and International Politics (1984), Guatemala, A Nation in Turmoil (1985), The Foreign Policy of New States (1986), The Process of Political Succession (ed, 1987), The Central American Security System: North-South or East-West? (ed, 1988, 2 edn 2008), Argentina: Political Culture and Instability (jtly, 1989), Latin America in the Twentieth Century (jtly, 1990, 2 edn 1993), Revolution and Counter-Revolution (1990), Political and Economic Encyclopaedia of South America and the Caribbean (ed, 1991), Sociology Today (jtly, 1992), An Introduction to Comparative Politics (1993), The International Politics of Latin America (1994), Politics and Society in the Third World (jtly, 1995), The Resilience of Democracy (ed jtly, 1999), The South, the North and the Environment (jtly, 1999, 2 edn 2001), Comparative Politics: An Introduction (2002), Border and Territorial Disputes of the World (ed, 2004), A Political and Economic Dictionary of Latin America (2004), Civil Society in Democratization (jt ed, 2004), Politics and Society in the Developing World (jtly, 2007), Terrorism, Civil War and Revolution (2010), Mexico, One Hundred Years of Revolution (2012), The King of the Land of Flopdoodle (fiction, 2012); *Recreations* non-jarring exercise; *Style—* Prof Peter Calvert; ✉ 19 Queens Road, Chandlers Ford, Eastleigh SO53 5AH (☎ 023 8025 4130); School of Social Sciences, Politics and International Relations, University of Southampton, Highfield, Southampton SO17 1BJ (e-mail pcpol@soton.ac.uk)

CALVIN, Michael; s of Charles Calvin, of Watford, and Margaret, *née* Platts; *b* 3 August 1957; *Educ* Watford GS; *m* Lynn-Marie, da of Oliver Frank Goss; 3 s (Nicholas b 17 April 1987, Aaron b 15 April 1989, William b 20 Jan 1995), 1 da (Lydia Joy b 27 July 1997); *Career* Watford Observer 1974–77, Hayters Sports Agency 1977–79, chief sports writer Westminster Press Newspapers 1979–83, sports reporter Thames TV 1983–84; Daily Telegraph: gen sports feature writer 1984–86, chief sports feature writer 1986–96; sr sports writer The Times 1997–98, chief sports feature writer Mail on Sunday 1998–2002, chief sports writer Sunday Mirror 2007–11, chief sportswriter Independent on Sunday 2011–; md Calvin Communications (sports consultancy) 1996–2002, dep dir Eng Inst of Sport 2002–07, ceo Integr8 Communications 2007–; memb winning British team Camel Trophy off-road rally around Amazon basin 1989, finished third on yacht Hofbrau Lager in British Steel Challenge round the world yacht race 1992–93; winner Seagrave Medal for Outstanding Achievement 1990; ldr Daily Telegraph sports writing team Newspaper of the Year in Sport for Disabled Media Awards 1991, 1992, 1993 and 1994; Sports Reporter of the Year 1992, Sports Journalist of the Year 1992, special award for services to yachting journalism 1994, Sports Reporter of the Year (highly commended) 1998, Sports Reporter of the Year 1999, Sports Story of the Year 2000, Sports Journalist of the Year (commended) 2009, Sports Columnist of the Year (highly commended) 2012; memb Sport Writers Assoc; *Books* Cricket Captaincy (1978), Only Wind and Water (1997), Family: Life, Death and Football (2010, 2 edn 2012), The Nowhere Men (2013, Sports Book of the Year 2014), Proud (with Gareth Thomas, 2014, Sports Book of the Year 2015), Living On The Volcano (2015); *Recreations* innocent adventure; *Clubs* Cape Horners', Royal Ocean Racing; *Style—* Michael Calvin, Esq; ✉ e-mail calvins01@btinternet.com; literary agent Paul Moreton (e-mail paul@bell-lomax.co.uk)

CAMBER, Richard Monash; s of Maurice Camber (d 1991), of Glasgow, and Libby Camber (d 1981); *b* 22 July 1944; *Educ* Glasgow HS, Univ of Edinburgh (MA), Univ of Paris, Univ of London; *m* 26 Oct 1970, Hon Angela Felicity, da of Baroness Birk (Life Peer), by her husband Ellis Birk; 2 da (Alice b 1974, Chloe b 1980), 1 s (Thomas b 1980); *Career* asst keeper Dept of Medieval and Later Antiquities Br Museum 1970–78; dir: Sotheby's London 1983–87, Sotheby's, Sotheby's International; conslt Euro Works of Art 1988–; FSA; *Recreations* reading, listening to music (particularly opera); *Style—* Richard Camber, Esq, FSA

CAMBRIDGE, Archdeacon of; *see:* Beer, Ven John

CAMERON, (John) Alastair; *see:* Abernethy, Hon Lord

CAMERON, (Allan) Alexander; QC (2003); s of Ian Donald Cameron (d 2010), and Mary Fleur, *née* Mount; *b* 27 August 1963, London; *Educ* Eton, Univ of Bristol (LLB); *m* 19 May 1990, Sarah Louise, *née* Fearnley-Whittingstall; 1 da (Imogen Clare b 3 Oct 1992), 1 s (Angus Ewan b 8 Oct 1994); *Career* called to the Bar 1986; currently head of chambers at 3 Raymond Buildings; memb: Criminal Bar Assoc, Int Bar Assoc, Fraud Lawyers' Assoc, Assoc of Regulatory and Disciplinary Lawyers; *Recreations* various; *Clubs* White's, Queen's, MCC; *Style—* Alexander Cameron, Esq, QC; ✉ 3 Raymond Buildings, Gray's Inn, London WC1R 5BH

CAMERON, Prof Dame Averil Millicent; DBE (2006, CBE 1999); *née* Sutton; *b* 8 February 1940, Leek, Staffs; *Educ* Westwood Hall Girls' HS Leek, Somerville Coll Oxford (exhibitioner, Passmore Edwards scholar, Rosa Hovey scholar, state student, MA, DLitt), UCL (PhD); *m* 1962 (m dis 1980), Alan Douglas Edward Cameron; 1 s, 1 da; *Career* KCL: asst lectr in classics 1965–68, lectr in classics 1968–70, reader in ancient history 1970–78, prof of ancient history 1978–89, memb Cncl 1982–85, head Dept of Classics 1985–89, fell 1987–, prof of late antique and Byzantine studies 1989–94, dir Centre for Hellenic Studies 1989–94, chair Humanities Res Centres 1992–94; warden Keble Coll Oxford 1994–2010; pro-vice-chllr Univ of Oxford 2001–10; chair: British Nat Byzantine Ctee 1983–89, Roman Soc Schs Ctee 1986–88, Classics Sub-Ctee Univ of London Arts Review 1987, Univ of London Byzantine Library Subject Sub-Ctee 1990–94; pres London Assoc of Classical Teachers 1988–90; memb: Cncl British Acad 1983–86, JACT Ancient History Ctee 1985–89, Ctee of Mgmnt and Fin Ctee Warburg Inst 1986–93; business mangr Dialogos Hellenic Studies Review 1994, memb Bd of Mgmnt Inst of Classical Studies 1990–94; ed Jl of Roman Studies 1985–90; visiting asst prof Columbia Univ NYC 1967–68, visiting memb Inst of Advanced Study Princeton 1977–78, Sather prof of classical literature Univ of Calif Berkeley 1986, visiting prof Collège de France 1987, distinguished visitor Inst of Advanced Study Princeton 1992, Lansdowne lectr Univ of Victoria 1992; chm Prosopography of the Byzantine Empire 1997–2005, co-dir Late Antiquity and Early Islam Project 1989–2004; pres Soc for the Promotion of Roman Studies 1995–98, Cncl for Br Research in the Levant 2004–, Ecclesiastical History Soc 2005, Fédération Internationale des Études Classiques 2009–14; chm: Cathedrals Fabric Cmmn 1999–2005 (vice-chm 1996–99), Review Gp on the Royal Peculiars 1999–2000, Inst of Classical Studies 2002–05, Oxford Centre for Byzantine Research 2010–; Hon DLitt: Univ of Warwick 1996, Univ of St Andrews 1998, Queen's Univ Belfast 2000, Lund Univ 2001, Univ of Aberdeen 2003, Univ of London 2005; corresponding memb Akademie der Wissenschaften zu Göttingen 2006, corresponding fell Byzantine Reserach Centre Aristotle Univ of Thessaloniki 2011; FBA 1981, FSA 1981; *Books* Procopius (abridged trans, 1967), Agathias (1970), Corippus In Laudem Iustini minoris libri quattuor (1976), Continuity and Change in Sixth-Century Byzantium (collected articles, 1981), Images of Women in Antiquity (ed with Amelie Kuhrt, 1983, revd 1993), Constantinople in the Eighth Century: the Parastaseis Syntomoi Chronikai (ed with Judith Herrin et al, 1984), Procopius and the Sixth Century (1985), The Greek Renaissance in the Roman Empire (ed with Susan Walker, 1989), History as Text (ed, 1989), Christianity and the Rhetoric of Empire (Sather lectr, 1991), The Byzantine and Early Islamic Near East I: Problems in the Literary Sources (ed with Lawrence I Conrad, 1992), Storia dell'età tardoantica/L'antiquité tardive (1992), The Later Roman Empire: Fontana History of the Ancient World (1993), The Mediterranean World in Late Antiquity AD 395–600: Routledge History of Classical Civilization (1993, 2 edn 2011), The Byzantine and Early Islamic Near East II: Land Use and Settlement Patterns (ed with Geoffrey King, 1994), The Byzantine and Early Islamic Near East III: States, Resources and Armies (ed, 1995), Changing Cultures in Early Byzantium (1996), Cambridge Ancient History vol XIII (ed with Peter Garnsey, 1997), Eusebius, Life of Constantine (with S G Hall, 1999), Cambridge Ancient History vol XIV (ed with Michael Whitby and Bryan Ward-Perkins, 2000), Fifty Years of Prosopography (ed, 2003), Cambridge Ancient History vol XII (ed with Alan Bowman and Peter Garnsey, 2006), The Byzantines (2006), Keble Past and Present (with Ian Archer, 2008), Doctrine and Debate in the East Christian World (ed with Robert Hoyland, 2011), Late Antiquity on the Eve of Islam (ed, 2013), Byzantine Matters (2014), Dialoguing in Late Antiquity (2014), Arguing it Out: Discussion in Twelfth-Century Byzantium (2016); author of many articles in jls, etc; *Style—* Prof Dame Averil Cameron, DBE, FBA, FSA; ✉ Keble College, Oxford OX1 3PG

CAMERON, Her Hon Judge Barbara Alexander; *Career* called to the Bar 1979; dep district judge 2000, recorder 2000, circuit judge (South Eastern Circuit) 2007–; *Style—* Her Hon Judge Cameron; ✉ c/o The South Eastern Circuit, 289–293 High Holborn, London WC1V 7HZ

CAMERON, Rt Hon David William Donald; PC (2005); s of Ian Donald Cameron (d 2010), and Mary Fleur Cameron; *b* 9 October 1966; *Educ* Eton, BNC Oxford (BA); *m* 1 June 1996, Samantha Gwendoline, *qv*, da of Sir Reginald Sheffield, Bt, DL, *qv*; 2 s (Ivan Reginald Ian b 8 April 2002 d 2009, Arthur Elwen b 14 Feb 2006), 2 da (Nancy Gwendoline Beatrice b 19 Jan 2004, Florence Rose Endellion b 24 Aug 2010); *Career* with Cons Research Dept 1988–92, special advsr HM Treasy, then with Home Office, then head of corp affrs Carlton Communications plc; MP (Cons) Witney 2001–16; shadow dep ldr of the house 2003–04, shadow local govt min and head of policy co-ordination 2004–05, shadow educn sec 2005, ldr Cons Pty 2005–16 (ldr HM Oppn 2005–10), Prime Minister, First Lord of the Treasury and Minister for the Civil Service 2010–16; memb Home Affrs Select Ctee 2001–05; *Style—* The Rt Hon David Cameron; ✉ House of Commons, London SW1A 0AA

CAMERON, Rt Rev Gregory; *see:* St Asaph, Bishop of

CAMERON, Prof Iain Thomas; s of Maj James David Cameron (d 1993), of Preston, and Stella, *née* Turner (d 1999); *b* 21 February 1956; *Educ* Hutton GS, Univ of Edinburgh (BSc, MB ChB, MD), Univ of Cambridge (MA); *m* 1, 1983 (m dis); 2 da (Sarah b 22 Aug 1985, Fiona b 6 Jan 1988); m 2, 1992, Heidi, da of Dr Alan Francis Wade (d 1995); 1 s (James b 7 April 1993), 1 da (Mhairi b 13 July 1995); *Career* clinical and scientific training posts in Edinburgh, Melbourne and Cambridge 1980–92; regius prof of obstetrics and gynaecology Univ of Glasgow 1993–99; Univ of Southampton: prof of obstetrics and gynaecology 1999–, head Sch of Med 2004–10, Univ Cncl 2004–07 and 2009–12, chm Wellbeing of Women Research Advsy Ctee 2003–08, dean Faculty of Medicine 2010–; non-exec dir Univ Hosp Southampton NHS Fndn Tst 2011–; chm: Part 1 MRCOG MCQ Sub-Ctee RCOG 1996–99, Meetings Ctee RCOG 2000–03; specialist advsr menorrhagia Nat Inst for Clinical Effectiveness (NICE) 2000; memb: British Fertility Soc 1991, Soc for Gynecologic Investigation 1996, The 1942 Club 1998, Human Fertilisation and Embryology Authy 2001–06, Expert Advsy Network Health Technol Assessment Prog 2004–12, MRC Coll of Experts 2005–10, Exec Ctee Medical Schs Cncl 2006–16 (chair 2013–16), Advsy Bd UK Clinical Research Collaboration (UKCRC) 2008–, Clinical Academic Staff Advsy Gp Univs and Colls Employers Assoc 2008–13, Bd UK Research Integrity Office (UKRIO) 2009–13, Wessex Acad Health Sci Network Bd 2012–, NIHR Advsy Bd 2013–, Health Educ Eng Medical Advsy Gp 2013–, Medical Educ UK Scrutiny Gp 2014–; Advsy Bd NIHR 2013–16, Medical Advsy Gp Health Educn England 2013–16; ed-in-chief Reproductive Medicine Review 1999–2002; FRCOG, FRCPEd, MRANZCOG, FHEA, FRSB; *Publications* numerous books and articles on reproductive medicine, menstrual disorders and the endometrium; *Recreations* solo piping; *Clubs* Athenaeum; *Style—* Prof Iain T Cameron; ✉ Faculty of Medicine, South Academic Block, Southampton General Hospital, Tremona Road, Southampton SO16 5YD (☎ 02381 206581, e-mail itc@soton.ac.uk)

CAMERON, Ivy; *b* 25 January 1948; *Educ* Rolle Coll of Educn Exmouth (CertEd), LSE (Dip Industrial Relations and Trade Union Studies); *Career* English teacher Bristol LEA and TEFL Lérida Spain 1969–72; Banking Insurance and Finance Union: area organiser W Midlands, negotiating offr Int Banks, asst sec, nat negotiator 1972–90; ptnr Cameron Woods Assocs 1990–93; memb: Trade Union Congress Women's Ctee 1984–90, EEC's IRIS Training Network; England rep to European Women's Lobby; German Marshall Fund fell Cornel Univ NY 1980, visiting fell Industrial Relations Pembroke Coll Oxford 1989; FRSA 1993; author of numerous articles in a variety of nat newspapers and int TU and mgmt magazines; *Recreations* singing, dancing, reading, walking, cross-country skiing; *Style—* Ms Ivy Cameron; ✉ Cameron Woods Associates Ltd, Prospect House, 5

C

Hill Road, Clevedon BS21 7NE (☎ 01275 342660, fax 01275 342661, e-mail directors@ cameron-woods.co.uk)

CAMERON, John Alastair Nigel (Johnny); s of Col Sir Donald Cameron of Lochiel, KT, CVO, TD, 26 Chief of Clan (d 2004), and Margaret, née Gathorne-Hardy (d 2006); *b* 24 June 1954, Inverness; *Educ* Harrow, ChCh Oxford (BA), MIT (MSc); *m* 27 May 1982, Julia Rosemary, née Wurtzburg; 2 s (Hamish b 1985, Robert b 1991), 1 da (Kirsty b 1987); *Career* Jardine Matheson & Co 1976–80, McKinsey & Co 1981–83, County NatWest 1983–88, Dresdner Kleinwort Benson 1988–98, chief exec corporate banking and financial markets then chm global markets Royal Bank of Scotland 1998– (memb Bd 2006–), dir Citizens Bank USA 2004–; fell Inst of Scottish Bankers; *Recreations* golf, tennis, shooting; *Clubs* Pratt's, New (Edinburgh); *Style*— Johnny Cameron, Esq; ✉ Micheldever, Hampshire SO21 3DF (☎ 01962 774254); Royal Bank of Scotland, 135 Bishopsgate, London (☎ 020 7334 1478, e-mail john.cameron@rbs.com)

CAMERON, John Bell; CBE; s of Capt John Archibald, MC (d 1960), and Margaret (d 1974); *b* 14 June 1939; *Educ* Dollar Acad; *m* 24 July 1964, Margaret, da of James Clapperton, OBE (d 1977); *Career* pres: NFU of Scotland 1979–84 (first long-term pres), UK Hereford Cattle Soc 2003–04, Scottish Beef Cattle Assoc 2005–, Scottish Nat Sheep Assoc 2005–, Moredun Research Inst 2009–; chm: EEC Sheepmeat Ctee 1983–90, World Meats Gp 1983–93, UK Sheep Consultative Ctee 1984–86, United Auctions Ltd 1988–92, Scottish Beef Cncl 1997–2001, Livestock Standards Ctee 2004–; memb Bd: BR 1988–95 (chm BR Scotland 1988–95), SW Trains 1995–2010, Island Line 1995–2010; chm Bd of Govrs Dollar Acad; Hon Dr of Technol (Railway) 1998; FRAgS, fell Scottish Agric Coll (FSAC); *Recreations* flying, shooting, swimming; *Style*— John Cameron, Esq, CBE; ✉ Balbuthie Farm, Leven, Fife (☎ 01333 730210)

CAMERON, Prof Keith Colwyn; s of Leonard George Cameron (d 1969), and Ethel Cameron (d 1999); *b* 1 April 1939; *Educ* Jones' West Monmouth Sch, Univ of Exeter (BA), Univ of Cambridge (CertEd), Université de Rennes (LèsL, Docteur de l'univ); *m* 4 Aug 1962, Marie-Edith Françoise, da of Francis Marie-Joseph Briens (d 1978), of I et V, France; 3 da (Anne b 1963, Cécilia, b 1964, Virginia b 1968); *Career* asst lectr Univ of Aberdeen 1964–66; Univ of Exeter: lectr 1966–76, sr lectr 1976–88, reader 1988–94, dean Faculty of Arts 1991–94 and 1997–98, prof of French and Renaissance studies 1994–2001, prof emeritus 2001–; gen ed: Exeter Textes littéraires 1970–2001, CALL 1990–2001 (hon asst ed 2001–), European Studies 1993–2004, Europa 1994–2004; ed Seizieme Siecle 2004–09; dir: Exeter Tapes 1972–2004, Elm Bank Pubns 1972–2004; hon vice-pres Euro Movement Devon Branch, hon pres Cercle Culturel du Pays de Grasse (CCPG); FRHistS; Chevalier dans l'Ordre des Palmes Académiques; *Books* Montaigne et l'humour (1966), Agrippa d'Aubigné (1977), Henri III – a Maligned or Malignant King? (1978), Montaigne and his Age (1981), René Maran (1985), B Palissy, Recepte véritable (1988), Concordance de Du Bellay (1988), Computer Assisted Language Learning (1989), From Valois to Bourbon (1989), Louise Labé: Renaissance Poet and Feminist (1990), Humour and History (1993), The Nation: Myth or Reality? (1994), The Literary Portrayal of Passion through the Ages: An Interdisciplinary View (1996), Multimedia CALL: Theory and Practice (1998), National Identity (1999), CALL: Media, Design and Applications (1999), Concordance de Ph. Desportes (2000), CALL: The Challenge of Change (2001), The Changing Face of Montaigne (2003), Jean Boucher: La Vie et Faits Notables de Henry de Valois (2003), P Le Loyer: La Néphélococugie (2004), Vocabulaire et Création Poétique (2013); *Recreations* theatre, walking, travel; *Style*— Prof Keith Cameron; ✉ Villa Effra, 31 avenue Aimé Martin, 06200 Nice, France (e-mail k.c.cameron@exeter.ac.uk)

CAMERON, Dr Lisa; MP; da of Sandra Cameron, stepda of Campbell McCulloch; *b* 8 April 1972, Glasgow; *Educ* BA, MSc, DClinPsy; *m* 17 Oct 2009, Mark Horsham; 2 da (Olivia b 17 Oct 2008, Charlotte b 14 Aug 2013); *Career* conslt forensic and clinical psychologist: NHS Greater Glasgow 1999–2001, NHS Lanarkshire 2001–04, The State Hosp 2004–06, NHS Greater Glasgow and Clyde 2006–15; risk assessor RMA Scotland 2012–15; memb Health and Care Professions Cncl; memb Br Psychological Soc 1995; MP (SNP) E Kilbride, Strathaven and Lesmahagow 2015–; *Recreations* cinema, opera, reading; *Clubs* Rotary Lanark; *Style*— Dr Lisa Cameron, MP; ✉ 510, 1 Parliament Street, Westminster, London (e-mail lisa.cameron.mp@parliament.uk, Twitter @LisaCameronSNP)

CAMERON, Pam; MLA; *Career* MLA (DUP) S Antrim 2011–; *Style*— Mrs Pam Cameron, MLA; ✉ Northern Ireland Assembly, Parliament Buildings, Belfast BT4 3XX

CAMERON, Samantha Gwendoline; da of Sir Reginald Adrian Berkeley Sheffield, Bt, DL, *qv*, and Annabel Astor, née Jones; *b* 18 April 1971, London; *Educ* Sch of St Helen and St Katherine Abingdon, Marlborough, Camberwell Coll of Arts, Bristol Poly (BA); *m* 1 June 1996, Rt Hon David William Donald Cameron, MP, *qv*; 2 s (Ivan Reginald Ian b 8 April 2002 d 2009, (Arthur) Elwen b 14 Feb 2006), 2 da (Nancy Gwendoline Barbara b 19 Jan 2004, Florence Rose Endellion b 24 Aug 2010); *Career* creative dir Smythson of Bond St 1997–; *Style*— Mrs Samantha Cameron; ✉ Smythson of Bond Street, 40 New Bond Street, London W1S 2DE (☎ 020 7629 8558, e-mail samanthacameron@ smythson.com)

CAMERON OF DILLINGTON, Baron (Life Peer UK 2004), of Dillington in the County of Somerset; Sir Ewen James Hanning Cameron; kt (2003), DL (Somerset 1989); s of Maj Allan Cameron, MBE, JP, DL, of Munlochy, Ross-shire, and Mary Elizabeth, née Vaughan-Lee; *b* 24 November 1949; *Educ* Harrow, Univ of Oxford (MA); *m* 1975, Caroline Anne, da of H D Ripley (d 1967), sometime chm of Willis Faber & Dumas insurance brokers; 3 s (Hon Ewen Allan Hanning b 10 July 1977, Hon James Alexander Hanning 14 May 1979, Hon Angus Derek Hanning b 19 March 1983), 1 da (Hon Flora Elisabeth Patricia b 13 Oct 1986); *Career* cross-bench memb House of Lords (memb Agriculture, Fisheries, Energy and Environment Sub-Ctee 2005–09 and 2010–15, chair All Pty Parly Gp for Agriculture and Devpt 2009–, memb EU Select Ctee 2012–15, memb Science and Technol Ctee 2015–); owner and mangr Dillington Estate Somerset; fndr and chm Orchard Media Ltd (commercial radio stations) 1989–99; chm: Lets Go Travel Ltd 1998–2006, Airports Direct Travel Ltd 2006–; nat pres CLA 1995–97, chm Countryside Agency 1999–2004, UK Govt rural advocate 2000–04, memb UK Round Table for Sustainable Devpt 1997–2000, chair Strategy Advsy Bd UK Global Food Security Prog 2011–, chair Advsy Cncl Centre of Ecology and Hydrology (Wallingford); pres UK Guild of Agricultural Journalists 2010–15; pres Somerset Fedn of Young Farmers' Clubs 1990–91, chm Somerset Strategic Partnership 2004–11, dir Royal Bath and West Soc 2008–15 (pres 2006–07); chair Charity Property Assoc 2005–; High Sheriff Somerset 1986–87; Hon LLD Univ of Exeter 2004; FRICS 1992, FRAgS 1996, FRSA 1996; *Recreations* golf, windsurfing, shooting; *Style*— The Rt Hon the Lord Cameron of Dillington, DL; ✉ Dillington Estate, Ilminster, Somerset TA19 9EG (☎ 01460 54614)

CAMERON OF LOCHBROOM, Baron (Life Peer UK 1984), of Lochbroom in the District of Ross and Cromarty; Kenneth John Cameron; PC (1984), QC (1972); s of Hon Lord (John) Cameron, KT, DSC (d 1996), and his 1 w, Eileen Dorothea, née Burrell (d 1943); *b* 11 June 1931; *Educ* Edinburgh Acad, Univ of Oxford (MA), Univ of Edinburgh (LLB); *m* 1964, Jean Pamela, da of late Col Granville Murray; 2 da (Hon Victoria Christian (Hon Mrs Fraser) b 1965, Hon Camilla Louise b 1967); *Career* served RN 1950–52; advocate 1958, Lord Advocate of Scotland 1984–89, senator Coll of Justice 1989–2003; chm Industrial Tbnls Scotland 1966–81, pres Pensions Appeal Tbnl Scotland 1976–84 (chm 1975), chm Ctee for Investigation in Scotland of Agric Mktg Schemes 1980–84; chm Royal Fine Art Cmmn for Scotland 1995–2005; chllr's assessor Univ of Edinburgh 1997–2010; Hon FRIAS 1994, FRSE 1990, Hon RSA 2004; *Clubs* New (Edinburgh); *Style*— The Rt Hon the Lord Cameron of Lochbroom, PC, QC, FRSE; ✉ House of Lords, London SW1A 0PW

CAMERON WATT, Ewen; s of Prof Donald Cameron Watt, *qv*, and Marianne Ruth Grau; *b* 24 June 1956; *Educ* St Paul's, Oriel Coll Oxford (BA); *m* 8 Jan 1983, Penelope Ann Cameron Watt, *qv*, da of Robert Henry Weldon, of Stone, Bucks; 2 da (Heather Frances b 31 Dec 1991, Flora Imogen b 4 Sept 1995); *Career* ptnr E B Savory Milln 1979–85, divnl dir SG Warburg Securities (formerly Rowe & Pitman) 1986–90, dir SG Warburg Securities 1990, head of global research, head of strategic investment then chm Central Strategy Gp BlackRock (formerly Merrill Lynch Asset Mgmnt) 2000–; *Recreations* walking, travel, Scottish watercolours; *Clubs* Vincent's (Oxford); *Style*— Ewen Cameron Watt, Esq

CAMERON WATT, Penelope Ann (Penny); da of Robert Henry Weldon, and Brenda Marianne, née Jones; *b* 10 May 1959; *Educ* Clifton HS Bristol, St Hugh's Coll Oxford (MA); *m* 8 Jan 1983, Ewen Cameron Watt, *qv*, s of Prof Donald Cameron Watt, *qv*, of London; 2 da (Heather Frances b 31 Dec 1991, Flora Imogen b 4 Sept 1995), 1 s (Fergus Robert b 2 June 1999); *Career* EB Savory Milln 1980–82, Wico Galloway and Pearson 1982–84, Kleinwort Benson 1984–87, investment mangr Robert Fleming 1987, dir Indosuez Asia Investment Services 1990; Oxford School of Business English Ltd 2002–; *Recreations* travel, walking, Japanese language; *Style*— Mrs Penny Cameron Watt; ✉ e-mail penny.watt@osbe.org.uk, website www.osbe.org.uk

CAMFIELD, Barry George; *b* 1 September 1950, Barking, London; *m* 17 May 1972, Ann, née Hayles; 1 s (Peter James b 24 Nov 1972), 1 da (Julie Ann (Mrs Layland) b 2 May 1975); *Career* Tport and Gen Workers Union 1975–2007 (asst gen sec 2000–07); currently vice-pres Campaign for Trade Union Freedom; memb: SE England Devpt Agency 1999–2005, Gen Cncl and Exec Ctee TUC 2000–07, Bd Olympic Delivery Authy 2007–; memb educn offr Australian Nursing and Midwifery Fedn (SA Branch) 2013–15; *Style*— Barry Camfield, Esq; ✉ Olympic Delivery Authority, One Churchill Place, Canary Wharf, London E14 5LN

CAMI, Aziz; s of Viktor Cami, of Vienna, and Francesca Cami; *b* 1 November 1950; *Educ* Ravenswood Sch for Boys, Camberwell Sch of Art, London Coll of Printing; *m* 15 June 1991, Jean, née Hedley; *Career* graphic designer; asst: Moura George Briggs 1973, Ken Briggs and Associates 1974; dir PIC Design 1976; fndr: C S & S Design 1978, The Partners 1983 (part of WPP Gp); creative dir Kantar (part of WPP) 2008; pres D&AD 1992–93; memb Exec Cncl Design Business Assoc 1992–93; winner of more than 140 creative awards incl D&AD Yellow Pencils, DBA Design Effectiveness Awards, Art Dir's Club of NY and Communication Arts; Hon Dr of Design Univ of Wolverhampton; FCSD, FRSA; *Recreations* music, art, photography, olive farming; *Clubs* Mosimann's; *Style*— Aziz Cami; ✉ 11 Eaton Place, London SW1X 8BN (☎ 07769 743610, e-mail aziz.cami@mac.com, website www.casaloreto.co.uk)

CAMLEY, Mark; s of Martin Camley, and Frances, née MacPherson; *b* 11 June 1964, Glasgow; *Educ* Univ of Edinburgh (MA); *m* 5 April 2002, Camilla, née Rosier; 2 da (Francesca b 3 March 2011, Helena b 1 Feb 2013); *Career* dir Crown Court 1999–2001, customer serv dir Court Serv 2001–03, dir Supreme Court Gp 2003–05, chief exec The Royal Parks 2005–12, dir of park operations London Legacy Devpt Corp 2012–13, exec dir park operations and venues London Legacy Devpt Corp 2013–; chm The Parks Alliance; ind advsr Poplar Harca; tstee Bromley by Bow Centre; *Recreations* art, culture, sport; *Clubs* Royal Household Football; *Style*— Mark Camley, Esq; ✉ London Legacy Development Corporation, Level 10, 1 Stratford Place, Montfichet Road, London E20 1EJ (☎ 020 3288 1857, mobile 07972 078775, e-mail markcamley@londonlegacy.co.uk, website www.londonlegacy.co.uk

CAMM, Prof (Alan) John; s of John Donald Camm, and Joan Camm; *b* 11 January 1947; *Educ* Guy's Hosp Med Sch London (BSc, MB BS, MD); *m* 1987, Joy-Maria, LVO née Frappell; 1 s, 1 da; *Career* Guy's Hosp London: house surgn 1971, house physician 1971–72, jr registrar 1972, jr lectr in med 1972–73, registrar in cardiology 1973–74; clinical fell in cardiology Univ of Vermont 1974–75; Bart's London: Br Heart Fndn res registrar 1975–76, sr registrar 1977–79, Wellcome sr lectr and hon conslt cardiologist 1979–83, Sir Ronald Bodley Scott prof of cardiovascular med 1983–86; Prudential prof of clinical cardiology St George's Hosp Med Sch London 1986–2012 (head Div of Cardiology); ed Europace, ed Clinical Cardiology; pres Arrhythmia Alliance 2003, past chm Jt Cardiology Ctee RCP, fndr and tstee Atrial Fibrillation Assoc 2008, dir European Heart Research Fndn 2008, pres-elect European Heart Rhythm Assoc 2015; past memb Cncl: RCP, Br Cardiac Soc (past pres); tstee World Soc of Arrhythmias, tstee Drug Safety Research Unit; past tstee: Crawley and Jersey Research Unit, American Coll of Cardiology 2006, N American Soc of Pacing and Electrophysiology, Int Soc of Cardiac Pacing and Electrophysiology; Queen's Hon Physician (QHPc) 1982; Distinguished Teacher Award Heart Rhythm Soc 2001, Berzelius Medal Swedish Cardiac Soc 2005, Cardiostim Medal 2006, Gold Medal European Soc of Cardiology 2006, Mackenzie Medal Br Cardiovascular Soc 2008, Maseri-Florio Award American Coll of Cardiology 2014; Freeman City of London 1982, Liveryman Worshipful Soc of Apothecaries 1982; MRCS 1971, fell American Coll of Cardiology (FACC) 1981, FRCP 1984 (LRCP 1971, MRCP 1973), FESC 1988, FRCP 1988, fell Cncl of Geriatric Cardiology (FAGC) 2000, fell American Heart Assoc (FAHA) 2001, FRCPEd 2003, FMedSci 2004, fell Heart Rhythm Soc 2006, FRCPGlas 2011; CStJ 1990; *Publications* First Aid – Step by Step (1978), Pacing for Tachycardia Control (1983), Heart Disease in the Elderly (1984 and 1994), Clinical Electrophysiology of the Heart (1987), Heart Disease in Old Age (1988 and 1990), Clinical Aspects of Arrhythmias (1988), Diseases of the Heart (1989 and 1995), Heart Rate Variability (1995), Atrial Fibrillation for the Clinician (1995), Antiarrhythmic Drugs (1995), Transvenous Defibrillation and Radiofrequency Ablation (1995), Nonpharmacological Management of Atrial Fibrillation (1997), Evidence Based Cardiology (1998, 2003 and 2010), Drug-Induced Long QT Syndrome (2003), Chronic Infection, Chlamydia and Coronary Heart Disease (1999), Atrial Fibrillation (2000), Drug-Induced Long QT Syndrome (2003), Cardiovascular Risk Associated with Schizophrenia and its Treatment (2003), ABC of Clinical Electrocardiography (2003, 2 edn 2008), Acquired Long QT Syndrome (2004), Clinical Electrophysiology of the Heart (2004, 2 edn 2011), Dynamic Electrocardiography (2004), European Society of Cardiology Textbook on Cardiovascular Medicine (2006, 2 edn 2009), Heart Rate Slowing by If Current Inhibition (2006), Comprehensive Electrocardiology (2010), Clinical Cardiology – Current Practice Guidelines (2013, 2 edn 2015), Guide to Clinical Cardiology (2016); approx 1250 papers in major jls; *Recreations* collector of prints, watercolours and antiques, model railway enthusiast; *Clubs* Oriental, RSM; *Style*— Prof A John Camm; ✉ St George's University of London, Cranmer Terrace, Tooting, London SW17 0RE (e-mail jcamm@sgul.ac.uk)

CAMOYS, 7 Baron (E 1384; called out of abeyance 1839); (Ralph) Thomas Campion George Sherman Stonor; GCVO (1998), PC (1997), DL (Oxon 1994); s of 6 Baron Camoys (d 1976), and Mary Jeanne, née Stourton (d 1987); the Stonors inherited the Barony through a Mary Biddulph who m Thomas Stonor 1732, descended from an earlier Thomas Stonor and Jeanne, da of John de la Pole, Duke of Suffolk, thus descending from Geoffrey Chaucer, the poet; *b* 16 April 1940; *Educ* Eton, Balliol Coll Oxford; *m* 11 June 1966, Elisabeth Mary Hyde, o da of Sir William Hyde Parker, 11 Bt; 3 da (Hon Alina (Hon Mrs Barrowcliff) b 1967, Hon Emily (Countess of Stair) b 1969, Hon Sophia (Baroness Moritz von Hirsch) b 1971), 1 s (Hon (Ralph) William Robert Thomas b 10 Sept 1974); *Heir* s, Hon William Stonor; *Career* md Rothschild Intercontinental Bank Ltd

1969–75, with Amex Bank Ltd 1975–78, md Barclays Merchant Bank 1978–84, dir Barclays Bank plc 1984–94, chief exec Barclays de Zoete Wedd Holdings Ltd 1986–87 (dep chm 1987–98), dep chm Barclays Capital 1997–98; dir 3i Group 1991–2002, dep chm Sotheby's Holdings Inc 1994–97, dir Perpetual plc 1994–2000, dir Brit Grolux Ltd 1994–; Lord Chamberlain of The Queen's Household 1998–2000 (Permanent Lord in Waiting to HM The Queen 2000, Lord in Waiting 1992–98); cmmr Eng Heritage 1984–87, memb Royal Cmmn on Historical MSS 1987–94; consultor Extraordinary Section of the Administration of the Patrimony of the Holy See 1991–2006; memb Court of Assts Fishmongers' Co (Prime Warden 1992–93); Hon DLitt Univ of Sheffield 2001; hon fell St Edmund's Coll Cambridge 2016; 1 class Order of Gorkha Dakshina Bahu (Nepal) 1980, GCSG 2006; *Recreations* the arts, family; *Clubs* Boodle's, Leander, Pilgrims; *Style*— The Rt Hon the Lord Camoys, GCVO, PC, DL; ✉ Stonor Park, Henley-on-Thames, Oxfordshire RG9 6HF (☎ 01491 638644)

CAMPBELL, Aileen Elizabeth; MSP; da of Peter Campbell, of Coupar Angus, Perthshire, and Ann, *née* Webster; *b* 18 May 1980, Perth; *Educ* Perth Acad, Univ of Glasgow (MA); *Partner* Fraser White; *Career* copy asst Construction Magazine Keystone 2003–04, ed Keystone 2004–05, editorial asst Scottish Standard Newspaper 2005; parly asst to Nicola Sturgeon, MSP, *qv*, 2005–06, parly asst to Shona Robison, MSP, *qv*, 2006–07; MSP (SNP): S of Scot 2007–11, Clydesdale 2011–; min for local govt and planning 2011, min for children and young people 2011–16, min for public health and sport 2016–; *Recreations* reading, music, football (St Johnstone FC); *Style*— Ms Aileen Campbell, MSP; ✉ Kirkton Chambers, 12 Kirkton Street, Carluke ML8 4AB (☎ 0131 348 6707, fax 0131 348 6709, e-mail aileen.campbell.msp@parliament.scot)

CAMPBELL, Rt Hon Alan; PC (2014), MP; s of Albert Campbell, and Marion, *née* Hewitt; *b* 8 July 1957, Consett, Co Durham; *Educ* Blackfyne Secdy Sch Consett, Univ of Lancaster, Univ of Leeds, Newcastle Poly; *m* Jayne, *née* Lamont; *Career* MP (Lab) Tynemouth 1997–; PPS to: Rt Hon Lord MacDonald of Tradeston, CBE, PC, *qv* 2001–03, Rt Hon Adam Ingram, MP, *qv* 2003–05, asst Govt whip 2005–06, a Lord Cmmr of HM Treasy (Govt whip) 2006–08, parly under-sec of state (crime reduction) Home Office 2008–10, dep shadow chief whip 2010–; *Style*— The Rt Hon Alan Campbell, MP; ✉ Constituency Office, 99 Howard Street, North Shields, Tyne & Wear NE30 1NA (☎ 0191 257 1927, fax 0191 257 6537); House of Commons, London SW1A 0AA (☎ 020 7219 3000, e-mail campbellal@parliament.uk)

CAMPBELL, Alan William; s of William James Campbell, and Jennifer Anne Campbell; *b* 9 May 1983, Coleraine, NI; *Educ* Coleraine Academical Inst for Boys, Welbeck Sixth Form Defence Coll, Royal Military Coll Shrivenham, Open Univ Business Sch; *m* Juilet Anna, *née* Parkinson; 1 da; *Career* 3-time Olympic rower, Bronze medal (single sculls) Olympic Games 2012; achievements incl: Silver medal (single sculls) World Championships 2009, Bronze medal (single sculls) World Championships 2010, Bronze medal (single sculls) World Championships 2011; *Clubs* The Tideway Scullers School; *Style*— Mr Alan Campbell; ✉ website www.alancampbellgb.com

CAMPBELL, Alastair John; s of Donald Campbell, of Embsay, N Yorks, and Elizabeth Howie, *née* Caldwell; *b* 25 May 1957; *Educ* City of Leicester Boys' Sch, Gonville & Caius Coll Cambridge (MA); *Partner* Fiona Millar; 2 s (Rory b 23 Oct 1987, Calum b 29 July 1989), 1 da (Grace b 30 April 1994); *Career* trainee reporter Tavistock Times and Sunday Independent Truro Mirror Group Training Scheme 1980–82, freelance reporter London 1982–83, reporter Daily Mirror 1983–85, news ed Sunday Today 1985–86, reporter Daily Mirror 1986; Sunday Mirror: political corr 1986–87, political ed 1987–89, columnist 1989–92; Daily Mirror: political ed 1989–93, columnist 1992–93; presenter Week in Westminster (BBC) 1992–94, asst ed (politics) and columnist Today 1993–94, columnist Tribune 1993–, political commentator LBC 1993–94; press sec to Tony Blair as Ldr Lab Pty 1994–97, chief press sec Tony Blair as PM 1997–2003, PM's dir of communication and strategy 2001–03; *Recreations* bagpipes, Burnley FC; *Style*— Mr Alastair Campbell

CAMPBELL, (Ian) Angus; s of Lt Col Duncan Lorne Campbell, MBE, MC (d 2005), and Christine Marion, *née* Phillipps (d 2006); *b* 4 September 1949, London; *Educ* Shebbear Coll N Devon, Poole Tech Coll, RMA Sandhurst, Army Sch of Flying (Army Flying Wings); *m* 20 Aug 1977, Carola Claire, *née* Schulte; 2 da (Marion Francis b 12 July 1979, Anthea Claire b 7 May 1982); *Career* Auckland Herd Improvement Assoc NZ 1970–72; army offr and helicopter pilot Br Army Air Corps 1974–79: 658 Squadron and 662 Squadron W Germany, UNFICYP Aviation Flight UN Cyprus, emergency tours S Armagh and Belfast City (Army Air Corps Commendation), Suffield Battle Gp Training Canada, second-in-cmd 16 Flight Army Air Corps; farmer Preston Hill N Dorset 1980–; cncllr Dorset CC 1989–93 and 2001–13 (vice-chm Dorset Educn Ctee 1992–93, dep ldr and portfolio responsibility for educn and roads, transport and regnl strategy 2002–06, ldr 2006–13), cncllr N Dorset Dist Cncl 1999–2011 (ldr 1999–2003); N Dorset Cons Assoc: chm 1998–2001 and 2002–03, pres 2004–14; memb and exec memb S W Regnl Assembly, memb Local Govt Assoc (memb Local Govt Exec 2010–13); chm: Strategic Ldrs Bd for the SW 2008–11, SW Cncls 2011–13, Lord Chllr's Advsy Ctee on Justices of the Peace for Dorset 2014–; pres 2014–: Dorset County Priory Gp of St John, Dorset Branch Army Benevolent Fund, Dorset SSAFA, Dorset Army Cadet League, Dorset Historic Churches Tst, Dorset Youth Assoc; jt pres Somerset and Dorset Marine Soc and Sea Cadets 2014–; patron 2014–: Dorset Child and Family Counselling Tst, Dorset Community Action, Dorset Community Fndn, Dorset County Arts in Hosp Somerset, Dorset Air Ambulance, Friends of Salisbury Cathedral, Dorset Safewise, Wessex Branch Western Front Assoc; HM Lord-Lieutenant Dorset 2014–; *Recreations* game shooting, fly fishing, writing; *Style*— Angus Campbell; ✉ Preston Hill Farm, Iwerne Minster, Blandford, Dorset DT11 8NL (☎ 01747 811219, e-mail prestonhil@aol.com); Dorset County Council, County Hall, Colliton Park, Dorchester, Dorset DT1 1XJ

CAMPBELL, Archibald Greig (Archie); s of William Greig Campbell (d 1986), and Isabel Hamilton, *née* Gordon (d 1961); *b* 17 March 1934; *Educ* Kelvinside Acad (capped for Scotland in rugby), Univ of Glasgow; *m* 1, 1960 (m dis 1986), Madge Eileen, *née* Baillie; 3 da (Deborah Elaine b 1963, Angela Gillian b 1965, Claire Patricia b 1967); *m* 2, 1986, Teresa Lois, *née* Kingsbury; *Career* Touche Ross (latterly Deloitte & Touche): joined 1958, regnl ptnr Asia Pacific Region Singapore 1975–78, dir Int Servs New York 1978–81, regnl ptnr Europe 1981–90, dep regnl dir Special Projects Europe 1990–92, dep ceo Central/Eastern Europe 1992–94; sr ptnr Campbell Fin Consits 1992–; MICAS 1958, ACA 1977, ICA Hong Kong 1978, ICA Malaysia 1978, ICA Singapore 1978; *Recreations* golf, tennis; *Clubs* Loch Lomond Golf, St George's Hill Golf, Castle Royal Golf, Oaks Country (FL); *Style*— Archie Campbell, Esq; ✉ Water's Edge, Loddon Drive, Wargrave, Berkshire RG10 8HL; 362 MacEwen Drive, Osprey, Florida 34220, USA

CAMPBELL, (Mary Lorimer) Beatrix; OBE (2009); da of James William Barnes, of Carlisle, Cumbria, and Catharina Johana, *née* Lorier; *b* 3 February 1947; *Educ* Harraby Secdy Modern Sch, Carlisle HS, AA; *m* 28 Oct 1968 (m dis 1978), Bobby Campbell (d 1997); *Career* journalist: Morning Star 1967–76, Time Out 1979, City Limits 1981–87; freelance reporter: New Statesman, The Guardian, The Observer, Marxism Today; columnist: The Independent 1993–95, The Guardian 1995–; broadcaster: I Shot My Husband and No One Asked Me Why (documentary, Channel 4), Listening to the Children (documentary, Channel 4), Vice and Virtue (Radio 4); cmmr Women's Nat Cmmn 2008–; candidate (Green Pty) Gen Election 2010; memb: Women's Liberation Movement, Communist Party; *Books* Sweet Freedom (with Anna Coote, 1981), Wigan Pier Revisited (1984, winner of Cheltenham Literary Festival), The Iron Ladies – Why Women Vote Tory (1987, winner of Fawcett Prize), Unofficial Secrets – The Cleveland Child Sex Abuse Case (1988, new edn 1998), Goliath – Britain's Dangerous Places (1993), Diana, Princess of Wales – How Sexual Politics Shook the Monarchy (1998), And All the Children Cried (with Judith Jones, commissioned by West Yorkshire Playhouse, 2002), Blame (with Judith Jones, commissioned by Sphinx Theatre Co, 2007), Agreement! The State, Conflict and Change in Northern Ireland (2008), End of Equality (forthcoming); *Style*— Ms Beatrix Campbell, OBE; ✉ mobile 07866 370769, e-mail beatrixcampbell@yahoo.com

CAMPBELL, Charles Alexander MacArthur; *b* 26 May 1977, London; *Career* dep ed Literary Review 2001–04, asst agent Johnson & Alcock Ltd 2004, literary agent Ed Victor Ltd 2005–14, dir Kingsford Campbell Ltd 2014–; *Books* Scapegoat: A History of Blaming Other People (2011), The Authors XI: A Season of English Cricket from Hackney to Hambledon (2013); *Recreations* cricket; *Clubs* The Authors CC; *Style*— Charlie Campbell, Esq; ✉ Kingsford Campbell Ltd, 38A Minford Gardens, London W14 0AN (☎ 020 7603 5695, e-mail charlie@kingsfordcampbell.com, Twitter @scapegoatcc)

CAMPBELL, HE Christopher John; *b* 12 April 1963, London; *Educ* Wimbledon Coll; *m* HE Sharon Isabel Campbell; *Career* diplomat; N America Dept FCO 1982–84, Sec of State's Private Office 1984–85, accountant Khartoum 1985–88, third sec immigration Dhaka 1988–92, third sec mgmnt Jakarta 1992–95, desk offr Polar Regions Section Overseas Territories Dept FCO 1995–98, second sec commercial Caracas 1999–2003, second sec external relations policy UK Del NATO Brussels 2003–07, strategy mangr Int Military Capacity Building Conflict Gp FCO 2008–09, head of peacekeeping Conflict Gp FCO 2009–11, non-resident ambass to Nicaragua 2011–15, ambass to the Dominican Repub 2015–; *Style*— HE Mr Christopher Campbell

CAMPBELL, Christopher Robert James (Chris); s of late Kenneth James Campbell, and Barbara Muir Kirkness Campbell; *b* 1 December 1958; *Educ* Daniel Stewart's and Melville Coll Edinburgh, Univ of Edinburgh (LLB); *m* 10 Sept 1983, Katharine Mairi, da of Archibald Macdonald; 1 s (Andrew Archibald Kenneth b 16 Nov 1988), 1 da (Victoria Barbara Dorothy b 8 April 1991); *Career* Dundas & Wilson CS: apprentice 1980–82, asst 1982–87, ptnr 1987–, ptnr i/c Glasgow office 1991–96, dep managing ptnr 1995–96, managing ptnr 1996–2005; dir of legal servs and dep gen counsel then gp gen counsel Royal Bank of Scotland Gp 2005–; *Recreations* golf, cycling, football, photography; *Clubs* Murrayfield Golf (Edinburgh), Royal Scottish Automobile; *Style*— Chris Campbell, Esq

CAMPBELL, Prof Sir Colin Murray; kt (1994), DL (Notts 1996); s of late Donald Campbell, and late Isobel Campbell; *b* 26 December 1944; *Educ* Robert Gordon's Coll Aberdeen, Univ of Aberdeen (LLB); *Children* 1 da (Victoria Louise b 1979), 1 s (Andrew William Roger b 1982); *Career* lectr: Faculty of Law Univ of Dundee 1967–69, Dept of Public Law Univ of Edinburgh 1969–73; Queen's Univ Belfast: prof of jurisprudence 1974–88, dean Faculty of Law 1977–80, pro-vice-chllr 1983–87; vice-chllr Univ of Nottingham 1988–2008; dir HEFCE E Univ Holding Co 2001–; chm: Qubis Ltd 1983–88, Lace Market Development Co 1989–97, Zeton Ltd 1990; non-exec dir Swiss Re GB 1999–2005; memb: Cncl Soc for Computers and Law 1973–88, Standing Advsy Cmmn on Human Rights for NI 1977–80, Legal Aid Advsy Ctee NI 1978–82, Mental Health Legislation Review Ctee NI 1978–82, UGC 1987–88, Nottingham Devpt Enterprise 1988–91, UFC Scottish Ctee 1989–93; chm: Ind Advice Gp on Consumer Protection in NI 1984, NI Econ Cncl 1987–94, Human Fertilization and Embryology Authy 1990–94, Med Workforce Standing Advsy Ctee 1991–2001, Food Advsy Ctee 1994–2001, Human Genetics Advsy Cmmn 1996–99; memb: HEFCE 1992–97, Inquiry into Police Responsibilities and Rewards 1992–93, Trent RHA 1992–96; vice-chm CVCP 1992–93; HM First Cmmr for Judicial Appts 2001–06; Hon LLD: Univ of Aberdeen 2001, Shanghai Jiao Tong 2006, Univ of Lincoln 2008, Univ of Nottingham 2008; *Books* Law & Society (co-ed, 1979), Do We Need a Bill of Rights? (ed, 1980), Data Processing and the Law (ed, 1984); contrib numerous articles in books and periodicals; *Recreations* sport, walking, music, reading; *Style*— Prof Sir Colin Campbell, DL

CAMPBELL, Darren; MBE (2005); *b* 1975; *Career* athlete; memb Sale Harriers; achievements at 100m: Gold medal European Junior Championships 1991, Silver medal World Junior Championships 1992, semi-finalist World Championships Athens 1997, winner National Championships 1998, Gold medal European Championships Budapest 1998, Bronze medal European Championships Munich 2002, Bronze medal World Championships Paris 2003; achievements at 4x100m: Gold medal European Junior Championships 1991, Gold medal World Junior Championships 1992, Bronze medal World Championships Athens 1997, Gold medal European Championships Budapest 1998, Gold medal Cwlth Games Kuala Lumpur 1998, Silver medal World Championships Seville 1999, Gold medal Cwlth Games Manchester 2002, Gold medal European Championships Munich 2002, Gold medal Olympic Games Athens 2004, Gold medal European Championships Copenhagen 2006; achievements at 200m: Gold medal European Junior Championships 1991, Silver medal World Junior Championships 1992, Silver medal Olympic Games Sydney 2000, Bronze medal Cwlth Games Manchester 2002; former footballer with Newport FC; *Style*— Darren Campbell, MBE; ✉ c/o Sue Barrett, Nuff Respect, The Coach House, 107 Sherland Road, Twickenham, Middlesex TW1 4HB (☎ 020 8891 4145, fax 020 8891 4140, website www.nuff-respect.co.uk)

CAMPBELL, David Allan; s of James Campbell, and Jean Campbell; *b* 9 December 1959, Ayr, Scotland; *Educ* William Hulme's GS Manchester, Univ of Bristol (LLB); *m* 8 June 1991, Susan, *née* Jenkins; 1 s (Ewan James b 14 March 1994), 1 da (Isabella Grace Caitlin b 2 Feb 2001); *Career* slr; ptnr Sansbury Campbell, chm SW Regnl Duty Slr Ctee 1995–, chief assessor Law Soc criminal litigation accreditation scheme 2001–06; memb Law Soc 1985; *Style*— David Campbell, Esq; ✉ Sansbury Campbell, 6 Unity Street, Bristol BS1 5HH (☎ 0117 926 5341, fax 0117 922 5625, e-mail dcampbell@sansburycampbell.co.uk)

CAMPBELL, David Lachlan; s of Archibald Campbell, and Jean Campbell; *b* 4 September 1959, Glasgow; *Educ* Washington Univ St Louis MO (AB, MBA); *m* 15 July 1995, Tracey Helen, *née* Adams; 3 s, 1 da; *Career* General Mills US until 1982, Pepsi-Cola NY and London 1982–86, joined Virgin Entertainment Group 1986, i/c Virgin's Euro TV post prodn cos until 1992, chief exec Virgin Radio 1993–2000 (dir 1992–2000), chief exec Ginger Media 1997–2000, vice-chm Ministry of Sound 2001–02, chief exec Visit London 2003–05, pres and chief exec AEG Europe 2005–11, dir Formula One 2011–12, chief exec Wagamama Gp 2013–; dir Sports & Entertainment 2012–; Freeman City of Glasgow, memb Guild of Hammermen of Glasgow; memb Mktg Gp of GB 2008; *Recreations* family, travelling, live music and sports; *Clubs* Soho House; *Style*— David Campbell, Esq; ✉ e-mail dc@thecampbells.co.uk

CAMPBELL, Donald Angus; s of William Alexander Campbell, of Elgin, Moray, and Williamina Scott, *née* Allan; *b* 10 April 1948; *Educ* Elgin Acad, Univ of Edinburgh (BSc, MB ChB); *m* 9 Sept 1972, Görrel Anna Kristina, da of (Stig Ture) Olof Sahlberg, of Sweden; 1 s (Alasdair Olof b 7 Oct 1981); *Career* neurosurgn: Karolinska Sjukhuset 1972, Royal Infirmary of Edinburgh 1972–73 and 1978; surgn: Köpings Lasarett 1973–76, King's Coll London 1976–77, Royal Marsden Hosp 1977–78; neurosurgn Walton Hosp Liverpool 1981–84, conslt neurosurgn to W Midlands RHA 1984–96, in full time private practice 1996–; med supt Svenska Londondoktorer 15 Harley Street; res papers on: chronic pain, epilepsy, head injury, meningiomas, stereotactic surgery; hon pres Headway Staffs; FRCS 1977, FRCSEd 1977, FRSM 1977; *Recreations* model aircraft engineering, parachuting, private pilot, photography; *Clubs* Soc of Model Aeronautical Engrs; *Style*— Donald Campbell, Esq; ✉ c/o Susan Thayer-Lewis, 48 Willow Road, Charlton Kings, Cheltenham GL53 8PQ (☎ 01242 526836); 15 Harley Street, London W1N 1DA (☎ 020

7636 7780); Sussex Nuffield Hospital, Woodingdean, East Sussex BN2 6DX (☎ 01273 624488, e-mail bellerophon@msn.com)

CAMPBELL, Emily Jane; *née* Hayes; da of (Alfred) Graham Hayes, of Ince Blundell, Merseyside, and Sheila Frances, *née* Pemberton (d 2001); *b* 13 January 1966, Liverpool; *Educ* Merchant Taylors' Crosby, Westminster, Clare Coll Cambridge (BA), London Coll of Fashion (Dip Clothing Technol), Yale Univ Sch of Art (MFA); *m* 31 May 1997, Edward Shanklin Campbell, s of Thomas Philip Campbell (d 1996), and Anne Campbell; 2 s (Arthur Shanklin b 29 Nov 1998, Edward Graham b 15 July 2001); *Career* pattern cutter Jean Muir 1989–91, designer Pentagram Design NY 1994–96, head of design and architecture Br Cncl 1996–2008, dir of design RSA 2008–11, dir of progs Creative Educn Tst 2011–; tstee: Aspire, Westminster Opera Co; *Style—* Ms Emily Campbell; ✉ RSA, 8 John Adam Street, London WC2N 6EZ (☎ 020 7930 5115, e-mail emily.campbell@rsa.org.uk)

CAMPBELL, Francis Martin; s of Daniel Campbell, of Warrenpoint, Co Down, and Brigid, *née* Cosgrove (d 1995); *b* 20 April 1970, Newry, Co Down; *Educ* Queen's Univ Belfast (BA), TCD, Katholieke Univ of Leuven Belgium (MA), Jagieollian Univ Krakow, Univ of Pensylvania (Thouron fell, MA); *Career* EU enlargement desk FCO 1997 and 1998–99, UN Security Cncl NY 1997–98, policy advsr PM's Policy Unit 1999–2001, private sec to the PM 2001–03, first sec (external) Br Embassy Rome 2003–05, sr dir of policy Amnesty Int 2005, ambass to the Holy See 2005–11, dep high cmmr Karachi and dir UKTI Pakistan 2011–13, head Policy Unit FCO 2013–; President's Medal Catholic Univ of America 2009; Hon DUniv Queen's Univ Belfast 2009, Hon PhD Catholic Univ of Steubenville USA, Hon PhD Fordham Univ NY, Hon PhD Inst of Technol and Business Pakistan 2013; *Publications* Federalism Doomed (contrib chapter, 2002), The Catholic Church and the International Policy of the Holy See (contrib, 2008), Pierre d'Angle No 14/2008 (contrib, 2008); *Recreations* reading, walking, travelling; *Style—* Mr Francis Campbell

CAMPBELL, Gregory; MP, MLA; *b* 15 February 1953; *m* Frances; 1 s, 3 da; *Career* MP (DUP) Londonderry E 2001–; MLA (DUP) Londonderry E 1998–; min for regnl devpt until 2001 (resigned), min Dept of Culture, Arts and Leisure 2008–09; *Style—* Gregory Campbell, Esq, MP, MLA; ✉ House of Commons, London SW1A 0AA; Constituency Office, 25 Bushmills Road, Coleraine BT52 2BP (☎ 028 7032 7327, fax 028 7032 7328); Constituency Office, 6–8 Catherine Street, Limavady BT49 9DB (☎ 028 7776 6060, e-mail DUPColeraine@parliament.uk)

CAMPBELL, Hugh Hall; QC (Scot 1983); s of William Wright Campbell (d 1992), of Cambuslang, Lanarkshire, and Marianne Doris Stewart, *née* Hutchison (d 1988); *b* 18 February 1944; *Educ* Glasgow Acad, Glenalmond Coll, Exeter Coll Oxford (BA), Univ of Edinburgh (LLB); *m* 1969, Eleanor Jane, da of Sydney Charles Hare (d 1990), of Stoke Poges; 3 s (Benjamin b 1972, Timothy b 1975, Thomas b 1978); *Career* advocate Scottish Bar 1969, standing jr counsel to Admty 1976; FCIArb 1986; hon citizen of Antigua and Barbuda 2010; *Recreations* carnival, wine, music; *Clubs* Hon Co of Edinburgh Golfers; *Style—* H H Campbell, Esq, QC; ✉ 12 Ainslie Place, Edinburgh EH3 6AS (☎ 0131 225 2067)

CAMPBELL, Prof Ian William; s of William Campbell (d 1991), of Fife, and Janet Campbell (d 1991); *b* 23 November 1945; *Educ* Buckhaven HS, Univ of Edinburgh (BSc, MB ChB); *m* 1970, Catherine McEwan, *née* Burgess; 2 da (Lorna Jane b 3 April 1975, Christina Kate b 13 Dec 1980), 1 s (Alastair John b 17 Jan 1978); *Career* conslt physician Victoria Hosp Kirkcaldy 1978–, hon sr lectr in med Univ of Edinburgh 1978–, hon prof of biological and med sci Univ of St Andrews 1995–; chm: Scot Ctee Br Diabetic Assoc 1991–95, Scot Study Gp for the Care of the Young Diabetic 1993–97; memb Cncl RCPEd; presented papers and invited lectures (principally in field of diabetes mellitus) worldwide; 3rd Croom Lecture RCPEd 1977, J K Bekaert Meml Lecture Univ of Antwerp 1990, John Mathewson Shaw Endowed Lecture Belfast 1994; FRCPEd, FRCPGlas; *Books* Diagnosis and Management of Endocrine Diseases (jtly, 1981), Complications in Diabetes: Diabetic Retinopathy (jtly, 1992), Fast Facts: Diabetes Mellitus (jtly, 1996); also author of 200 papers in scientific jls and textbooks; *Recreations* squash, golf, classical music; *Clubs* Lundin Sports; *Style—* Prof Ian Campbell; ✉ Strathearn, 19 Victoria Road, Lundin Links, Fife KY8 6AZ (☎ 01333 320533); Victoria Hospital, Hayfield Road, Kirkcaldy, Fife KY2 5AH (☎ 01592 643355, fax 01592 647069)

CAMPBELL, Sir James Alexander Moffat Bain; 9 Bt (NS *ca* 1668), of Aberuchill, Perthshire; s of Sir Colin Moffat Campbell, 8 Bt, MC (d 1997); *b* 23 September 1956; *Educ* Stowe; *m* 6 Feb 1993, Carola Jane, yr da of George Denman, of Stratton House, Stoney Stratton, Somerset; 2 da (b 10 Nov 1994 and 16 May 1996), 1 s (b 1999); *Heir* s, Colin Campbell; *Career* Capt Scots Gds ret 1983, Capt London Scottish 1/51 Highlanders 1984–87; insurance broker 1983–2001 and 2007– (insurance conslt 2001–05); farmer 2001–; *Recreations* trees, excavating; *Style—* Sir James Campbell, Bt; ✉ Kilbryde Castle, Dunblane, Perthshire (☎ 01786 824897)

CAMPBELL, James Farquhar Robin; s of Robin John Ronald Campbell, of Invernesshire, and Alison Barbara Rose, *née* Cave-Browne; *b* 26 November 1958; *m* 30 March 1985, Marina Caroline Vere, *née* Norton; 2 da (Ishbel b 30 Nov 1988, Isla b 16 Sept 1997), 2 s (Guy b 17 March 1991, Hugh (twin) b 16 Sept 1997); *Career* served 1 Bn Queen's Own Highlanders 1977–87 (ret as Capt); with: Towry Law & Co 1987–88, MIM Britannia 1988, Perpetual 1989–94; md: Jupiter Unit Trust 1994–98, ABN AMRO Fund Managers 1998–99, Artemis Unit Tst Mangrs 1999–; dir: Perpetual Unit Trust Managers 1989–94, Jupiter Asset Management 1994–98, ABN AMRO Asset Management 1998–99, Union Jack (Trading) Ltd; memb Queen's Body Guard for Scotland (Royal Co of Archers); *Recreations* bagpipes, farming, golf, field sports; *Style—* James Campbell, Esq

CAMPBELL, Jennifer Bernice (Jenny); *née* Sproson; da of Philip Norgrove Sproson, of Romiley, Cheshire, and Dorothy Bernice, *née* Petch (d 1999); *b* 5 October 1961, Hyde, Cheshire; *Educ* Manchester HS for Girls, Sheffield Hallam Univ (Dip); *m* 1983, Andrew Charles Campbell; 2 s (Richard Andrew b May 1988, Thomas William b Aug 1992); *Career* exec NatWest then RBS 1978–2010 (retail, commercial and corporate divisions), md Hanco ATM Systems Ltd 1996–10, ceo Your Cash Gp Ltd 2010–; memb LINK Scheme's Network Membs Cncl, elected memb LINK Scheme's Governance and Performance Ctee, non-exec dir LINK Scheme Ltd; involved with: Tomorrow's People, Young Enterprise, New Entrepreneurs Fndn; Ernst and Young Entrepreneur of the Year finalist 2011 and 2013, Silver Award winner Turnaround Entrepreneur of the Year category GB Entrepreneur Awards 2013, Vitalise Businesswoman of the Year Award 2014/15; Freeman Guild of Entrepreneurs; *Recreations* Flatcoated Retriever breeder under the Ronevorg kennel name and judge; *Clubs* Ernst and Young Alumni, Flatcoated Retriever Soc; *Style—* Mrs Jennifer Campbell; ✉ Your Cash Group Ltd, Willow House, Milton Keynes MK14 6EU (☎ 01908 574109, e-mail ceo@yourcash.com, websites www.yourcash.com and www.jennybcampbell.com, Twitter @jennybcampbell)

CAMPBELL, Jim; *Career* dir Energy Devpt Unit Dept for Business, Enterprise and Regulatory Reform; *Style—* Jim Campbell, Esq; ✉ Department for Business, Enterprise and Regulatory Reform, 1 Victoria Street, London SW1H 0ET

CAMPBELL, Prof John; OBE (1993); s of Clarence Preston Campbell (d 1979), and Catherine Mary, *née* Crossley (d 2007); *b* 2 December 1938; *Educ* Gateway Sch Leicester, Fitzwilliam Coll Cambridge (MA), Univ of Sheffield (MMet), Univ of Birmingham (PhD, DEng); *m* 1, Jacqueline Pamela, *née* Harrison; 1 da (Zoe Elizabeth); m 2, Sheila Margaret, *née* Taylor; step s, Richard Bacon, MP; *Career* graduate trainee Tube Investments Ltd 1963–64, British Iron and Steel Research Assoc 1967–70, Fulmer Research Inst 1970–78; UNIDO: Cairo 1973, Lahore 1976, tech dir Cosworth R&D Ltd 1978–85, tech dir Cosworth Castings Ltd 1984–85; Triplex Alloys Ltd: tech dir 1985–89, R&D dir 1989–91; dir Campbell Technology 1988–, dir Castings Technology International (CTi) 2015–; non-exec dir: Cast Metals Development Ltd 1992–96, Alfer Ltd 1994–95, Alloy Technologies Ltd 1996–2000, Westley Group 1997–2004; Univ of Birmingham: visiting prof 1989–92, prof of casting technology 1992–2004, emeritus prof 2004–; chm VK Educnl Foundry Trust 1989–2006; ACTA Metallurgica lectr 1992–94, Hoyte Meml lectr AFS Annual Congress 2012; memb Editorial Bd: Cast Metals jl 1988–2009, Materials Science & Technology jl 1991–2002; hon dir Light Metals Founders Assoc R&D Ltd 1987–94; fell Inst of Cast Metal Engrs 1985; memb American Foundry Soc 1990; Sir Jonathan North Gold Metal 1957–58, Wilkinson Medal Staffs Iron and Steel Inst 1990, AFS Hall/Heroult Award 1997, IBF MM Hallett Medal 1999, AFS Howard F Taylor Award 2000, Merton C Flemings Award 2003, Bruce Chalmers TMS Award 2004, E J Fox Medal 2010; annual John Campbell Medal Award launched by Inst of Cast Metal Engrs 2010; Liveryman Worshipful Co of Founders; FREng 1991; *Books* Castings (1991, 2 edn 2003), Castings Practice (2004), Concise Castings (2010), Complete Casting Handbook (2011, 2 edn 2015), Quality Castings: a personal account of the development of the Cosworth Casting Process (2015); *Recreations* music, walking, writing; *Style—* Prof John Campbell, OBE, FREng; ✉ 6 Old Market Court, Ledbury HR8 2GE (☎ 01531 636077); Department of Metallurgy and Materials, The University of Birmingham, Birmingham B15 2TT (e-mail jc@campbelltech.co.uk)

CAMPBELL, John Donington; OBE (2008); s of Maj John Donington Campbell (d 2001), of Heathfield, E Sussex, and Edith Jean, *née* Crick; *b* 23 April 1959; *Educ* Harrow, RMA Sandhurst; *m* 4 June 1988, Catriona Helen Cecelia, da of John Spence Swan (d 2004), of Letham, Fife; 1 da (Iona Helen b 18 Feb 1996), 2 s (Charles John b 9 Dec 2000, James Donington b 18 July 2002); *Career* cmmnd Royal Scots Dragoon Guards 1979, ADC to General Offr Cmd Scot 1985–87; Phoenix Burners Ltd 1977–79, Ivory and Sime plc 1987–89; md: Instate plc 1989–91, Framlington Pensions Management 1991–93, Latchly Management Ltd 1996–2000, State Street Corporation 2000–16; dir: Cursitor Management Ltd 1993–98, Scottish Financial Enterprise 2001–09 (chm 2004–09); memb Financial Services Strategy Gp 2003–05, dep chm Financial Services Advsy Bd 2005–09, memb EU Advsy Gp City of London Corp 2005–10; tstee Inst of Business Ethics 1995–2008, memb Advsy Bd Univ of Edinburgh Mgmnt Sch 2004– (chm 2007–), tstee Regimental Tst Royal Scots Dragoon Guards 2010–; hon vice-pres Border Bothie Assoc 2002–; govr Sedbergh Sch 2015– (chm Investment Ctee 2016–); FRSA 2006; *Recreations* country pursuits, tobogganing, exercise; *Clubs* New (Edinburgh), St Moritz Tobogganing; *Style—* John Campbell, Esq, OBE; ✉ Currburn, Yetholm, Roxburghshire TD5 8PT

CAMPBELL, Prof John Joseph; *b* 2 November 1956, Glasgow; *Educ* Univ of Stirling (BA), Univ of Calgary (MA), The Queen's Coll Oxford, Wolfson Coll Oxford (BPhil, John Locke prize), BNC Oxford, ChCh Oxford (DPhil); *Career* Univ of Oxford: research lectr ChCh 1983–86, fell and tutor New Coll 1986–2001, reader in philosophy 1997–2001, fell CCC 2001–, Wilde prof of mental philosophy 2001–, Willis S and Marion Slusser prof of philosophy Univ of California at Berkeley 2004–; visiting assoc prof UCLA 1988, visiting fell King's Coll Research Centre Cambridge 1990 and 1991, visiting fell Research Sch of Social Sciences ANU 1991–92, Br Acad research reader 1995–97, distinguished visitor in cognitive science Univ of Calif Berkeley 1996, fell Center for Advanced Study in the Behavioural Sciences Stanford Univ 2003–04; memb Steering Ctee Leverhulme Project on Consciousness and Self-Consciousness 1996–; European Soc for Philosophy and Psychology: memb Steering Ctee 1995–98, prog chair 1996–98, memb Bd 1999–, pres 2003–06; Guggenheim fell 2011, NEH fell 2011; Whitehead lectures at Harvard 2009, Simon Lectures Toronto 2011, Carnap Lectures in Germany 2015;; *Books* Berkeley's Puzzle (with Quassim Cassam, 2014); *Publications* Past, Space and Self (1994), Reference and Consciousness (2002); author of numerous articles in learned jls; *Style—* Prof John Campbell; ✉ Department of Philosophy, 314 Moses Hall #2390, University of California, Berkeley, CA 94720–2390, USA

CAMPBELL, Dr John Malcolm; s of Malcolm Rider Campbell (d 1991), of London and latterly Wiltshire, and Sheila Stuart, *née* Robertson (d 1979); *b* 2 September 1947; *Educ* Charterhouse, Univ of Edinburgh (MA, PhD); *m* 1, 1972 (m dis 2008), Alison Elizabeth, da of Thomas Archibald and Olive McCracken; 1 da (Robin Alexandra b 1981), 1 s (Patrick McCracken b 1983); m 2, 2013, Kirsty Hogarth, da of Stanley and Alison Palmer; *Career* freelance historian/biographer; memb Soc of Authors; author of book reviews for The Times, TLS, Independent, Sunday Telegraph, Mail on Sunday, etc; *Books* Lloyd George: The Goat in the Wilderness (1977, second prize Yorkshire Post Award for Best First Book), F E Smith, First Earl of Birkenhead (1983), Roy Jenkins: A Biography (1983), Nye Bevan and the Mirage of British Socialism (1987), The Experience of World War II (ed, 1989), Makers of the Twentieth Century (series ed, 1990–91), Edward Heath: A Biography (1993, NCR Award for Non-Fiction 1994), Margaret Thatcher, Vol 1: The Grocer's Daughter (2000), Margaret Thatcher, Vol 2: The Iron Lady (2003), If Love Were All...: The Story of Frances Stevenson and David Lloyd George (2006), Pistols at Dawn: Two Hundred Years of Political Rivalry from Pitt and Fox to Blair and Brown (2009), Roy Jenkins: A Well-Rounded Life (2014, shortlisted for Samuel Johnson Prize 2014); *Recreations* tennis, golf, theatre, music, amateur dramatics/directing; *Clubs* Society of Authors, Canterbury Golf; *Style—* Dr John Campbell; ✉ No 1 The Green, Littlebourne, Kent CT3 1UU (e-mail johncampbell_@hotmail.com)

CAMPBELL, John Park; OBE (2000); s of Keith Campbell (d 1950), and Joan, *née* Park (d 1985); *b* 1 April 1934, Gourock, Glasgow; *Educ* Strathallan Sch Perthshire; *m* 3 Apr 1957, Catherine, *née* Kent; 1 da (Karen b 31 March 1958), 3 s (Ian b 26 Dec 1960, Keith 12 July 1963, Colin 14 Oct 1974); *Career* farmer 1950–, owner 15,000 acre farm (all acquired in own lifetime), now Peeblesshire's largest landowner and farmer, world's largest free range egg prodr; vice-pres Royal Highland and Agricultural Soc Scotland, vice-pres Royal Higland Soc 2011, warden Neidpath Castle 2011; convenor Tweeddale DC 1979–88, candidate Scottish Parl 1999; UK Farm Business of the Year 2004 and 2012, category winner Entrepreneur of the Year 2004, Entrepreneur of the Year Scotland 2010, Br Free Range Egg Prodrs Lifetime Achievement Award 2010, Int Egg Person of the Year 2011; former JP; Nuffield Farming Scholar; FRAgS (past chm); *Clubs* Farmers; *Style—* John Campbell, Esq, OBE; ✉ Glenfyne, Stobo, Peebles EH45 8NP (☎ 01721 740214)

CAMPBELL, (Alastair) John Wilson; OBE (2015); s of Wilson William Campbell (d 1975), and Pearl Gray, *née* Ackrill (d 2005); *b* 18 February 1947; *Educ* King's Sch Canterbury, Sidney Sussex Coll Cambridge (MA); *m* 25 Feb 1972, Sarah Jane, da of Patrick Philip Shellard (d 1982); 2 s (Milo b 1974, Rollo b 1978), 1 da (Coco b 1976); *Career* exec NM Rothschild & Sons Ltd 1969–72, dir Noble Grossart Ltd 1973–88, md McLeod Russel plc 1979–82, sr ptnr and co-fndr Campbell Lutyens & Co Ltd 1988–; *Clubs* Reform, New (Edinburgh); *Style—* John Campbell, Esq, OBE; ✉ 10 Campden Hill Gate, Duchess of Bedford's Walk, London W8 7QH (☎ 020 7795 6445); Campbell Lutyens & Co Ltd, 3 Burlington Gardens, London W1S 3EP (☎ 020 7439 7191, fax 020 7432 3749)

CAMPBELL, Lucy B; *née* Barnett; da of James Allen Barnett (d 1999), of Portland, OR, and Jane, *née* Dodge (d 1952); *b* 26 January 1940; *Educ* Nightingale Bamford Sch NYC, The Garland Coll Boston MA; *m* 1, 1959 (m dis 1963), Clifford Smith, Jr, s of Clifford Smith (d 1961), of Rockport, Maine; 2 s (Clifford Allen b 24 Aug 1960, Grafton Dodge b 3 Dec 1961); m 2, 1965 (m dis 1981), Colin Guy Napier Campbell, s of Archibald Campbell (d 1975), of London; 2 da (Georgina Dorothy b 24 Jan 1969, Tessa Sylvia b 3 April 1971); *Career* fine art dealer; proprietor Lucy B Campbell Fine Art London (founded 1984) and

Lucy B Campbell Ltd New York; exhibitions: The Fine Art and Antiques Fair Olympia London 1995–2003, The British Antique Dealers' Fair Duke of York's HQ London May 1995, The San Francisco Fall Antiques Show 1987–94, Art London 2004–09, Art Antiques London 2010–15, Lapada Art and Antiques Fair 2012–15; memb: The Pilgrims, Le Confédération Internationale des Négociants en Oeuvres d'Art (CINOA), Lapada Modern (Assoc of Art and Antique Dealers), Br Antique Dealers Assoc (BADA); *Publications* Anna Pugh (2007); *Style—* Mrs Lucy B Campbell; ✉ Lucy B Campbell Fine Art, 3 The Village, 101 Amies Street, London SW11 2JW (☎ 020 7727 2205, fax 020 7229 4252, e-mail lucy@lucybcampbell.co.uk, website www.lucybcampbell.com)

CAMPBELL, Malcolm; s of Malcolm Brown Campbell (d 1940), and Helen Munro, *née* Carruthers (d 1992); *b* 3 January 1934; *Educ* Glenalmond Coll; *m* 1, 25 Sept 1960 (m dis 1977), Fiona, *née* McLaren; 3 s (Colin b 30 Sept 1961, David b 19 April 1963, Graham b 6 March 1967); m 2, 18 Feb 1983, Susan Elizabeth Patten, da of Sydney David (d 1965), of Mid Glamorgan; 1 s (James b 29 June 1984), 1 step da (Elizabeth b 7 Oct 1975); *Career* Nat Serv RA 1953–55; chm Malcolm Campbell Ltd 1969– (joined 1955, sales mangr 1959, sales dir 1961, md 1966); dir and pres Glasgow C of C 1995, memb Cncl Br Chambers of Commerce 1995–96; winner Scottish Special Free Enterprise Award by Aims of Indust 1988; memb: Bd of Govrs Queen's Coll Glasgow 1989–93, Court Glasgow Caledonian Univ 1993–98 (chm 1996–98); dir The Merchants House of Glasgow 1998–; Freeman City of London 1978, Liveryman Worshipful Co of Fruiterers 1978; *Recreations* golf (Western Gailes capt 1974), sailing; *Clubs* Royal and Ancient (St Andrews), Prestwick, Western; *Style—* Malcolm Campbell, Esq; ✉ e-mail malcolmcampbellltd@btinternet.com

CAMPBELL, Mandie Jane; CBE (2014); *b* 7 December 1965, Bristol; *Career* Home Office: dir of drugs, alcohol and community safety until 2012, chief operating offr Border Force 2012–14, DG of immigration enforcement 2014–; *Style—* Ms Mandie Campbell, CBE; ✉ Home Office, 2 Marsham Street, London SW1P 4DF

CAMPBELL, Margaret Jane (Mrs Margaret Bain); da of Dr Colin Campbell, MBE, of Wendover, Bucks, and Daphne E M, *née* Robbins; *b* 15 June 1957; *Educ* Aylesbury HS, Royal Coll of Music; *m* 22 Dec 1990, Christopher Bain; 3 s, 1 da; *Career* princ flute: City of Birmingham Symphony Orchestra 1977–86, Orchestra of the Royal Opera House Covent Garden 1986; prof of flute Trinity Laban Conservetoire of Music and Dance 2011–; Nat Fedn of Music Socs Award for Young Concert Artists 1981; ARCM; *Style—* Ms Margaret Campbell; ✉ 90 Haven Lane, Ealing, London W5 2HY (☎ 020 8998 6246, e-mail m@campbellbain.co.uk)

CAMPBELL, Michael David Colin Craven; MBE (2008), DL (Hants 1994); s of Bruce Colin Campbell (d 1980), and Doris, *née* Craven-Ellis (d 2006); *b* 12 December 1942; *Educ* Radley; *m* 6 April 1967, Linda Frances, da of Charles Brownrigg (d 1982); 2 da (Alexandra Jane (Mrs James Andrew) b 1968, Laura Grace (Mrs Hugh Montgomery) b 1977), 1 s (Jamie Loudoun Craven b 1970); *Career* Ellis Campbell Group: md 1977–2009, chm 1987–; memb and tstee Small Business Bureau 1999–2004 (patron 1983–98); memb Hants CC 1983–87; chm of govrs Treloar Sch and Coll 1993–98; chm: Whitchurch Silk Mill Tst 1986–98, Treloar Tst 1993–2002, Hants Community Fndn 2006–10; tstee: Hants Building Preservation Tst 1984–2007, Hants Garden Tst 1986–, Hants Bobby Tst 1999–2010; Cdre Royal Yacht Squadron 2009–13; Yr Bro Trinity House 2009; High Sheriff Hants 2008–09; *Recreations* shooting, sailing, escaping to Scotland; *Clubs* Boodle's, Royal Yacht Squadron, Highland Soc of London, Bembridge Sailing; *Style—* Michael Campbell, Esq, MBE, DL; ✉ Shalden Park House, Shalden, Alton, Hampshire GU34 4DS (☎ 01256 381821, fax 01256 381921)

CAMPBELL, (Henrietta) Nina Sylvia; da of John Archibald Campbell (d 1974), and Elizabeth, *née* Pearth (d 1996); *b* 9 May 1945; *Educ* Heathfield Sch Ascot; *m* 1 (m dis 1978), Andrew Guy Louis De Chappuis Konig; 1 da (Henrietta Lucy Elizabeth b 1973), 1 s (Maximillian John b 1976); m 2 (m dis 1991), John Henry Deen; 1 da (Alice Nina b 1982); *Career* interior designer; apprenticeship with John Fowler of Colefax & Fowler; own interior decoration business and shop 1974–; cmmns for many private residences in UK and abroad incl: Sunninghill Park (for Duke and Duchess of York), new sales rooms Christie's London, Hotel de Vigny Paris, Mark's Club London, Hotel Balzac Paris, Parc Victor Hugo Paris; former tstee V&A; patron Museum of Design and Domestic Architecture (MODA); govr: Heathfield Sch, Bath Spa Univ 2013–14; Women Who Most Influenced Style Internationally Award Night of Stars 1990 (Fashion Gp Int), Waterford Wedgwood Hospitality Award 2000, runner-up Best of the Best Award 2001 (for the Loire Silk Collection) London Design Week 2001, Christopher Guy Design Icon Award 2014; Hon DUniv Middlesex; FBIDA, FRSA; *Books* Elsie de Wolfe – A Decorative Life (1992), Nina Campbell on Decoration (1996), Decorating Secrets (2000), Nina Campbell Interiors (2013); *Style—* Miss Nina Campbell; ☎ 020 7225 0644, e-mail info@ninacampbell.com, website www.ninacampbell.com

CAMPBELL, Paddy (Patricia Ann); da of Tom Webster (Daily Mail cartoonist, d 1963), and Ida Shelley, *née* Michael (d 1991); *b* 10 July 1940; *Educ* La Sainte Union des Sacrées Coeurs Highgate, RADA; *m* 1 Jan 1965, John Charles Middleton Campbell, s of Lord Campbell of Eskan; 3 da; *Career* fashion designer; began career as actress, entered fashion industry 1974, estab own business and opened first shop St Christopher's Place 1979, opened second shop Beauchamp Place 1984, signed licensing deal with Japanese co 1985, wholesaling since 1990, opened third shop Wimbledon; patron (former vice-pres) The Women of the Year Lunch (raising money for Gtr London Fund for the Blind, former chm); FRSA 1996; *Style—* Mrs Paddy Campbell; ✉ 8 Gees Court, St Christopher's Place, London W1M 5HQ (☎ 020 7493 5646)

CAMPBELL, Dr Philip; *Educ* Univ of Bristol, QMC London, Univ of Leicester (PhD); *Career* postdoctoral research asst Dept of Physics Univ of Leicester 1977–79, physical sciences ed Nature 1982–88 (asst ed 1979–82), founding ed Physics World 1988–95, ed-in-chief Nature and Nature Pubns 1995–, memb Bd of Dirs Nature Publishing Gp; hon prof Peking Union Medical Coll 2009; tstee MQ: Tranforming Mental Health; Hon DSc Univ of Leicester 1999, Hon DSc Univ of Bristol 2008; hon fell Queen Mary Univ of London 2009; FRAS, FInstP; *Recreations* music; *Style—* Dr Philip Campbell; ✉ Nature, The Macmillan Building, 4–6 Crinan Street, London N1 9XW

CAMPBELL, (Alistair) Robert Macbrair; s of Dr Bruce Campbell, OBE, and Margaret Campbell; *b* 9 May 1946; *Educ* Marlborough, Univ of Aberdeen (BSc); *m* 7 Sept 1968, Frances Rosemary, *née* Kirkwood; 1 s (Tomas b 11 Aug 1971), 2 da (Chloe b 5 July 1973, Nancy b 15 May 1977); *Career* md Blackwell Science Ltd 1987–2000, pres Blackwell Publishing 2000–07, sr publisher Wiley-Blackwell 2007–2015; chm: STM Assoc 1998–2000, INASP 2004–09, CrossRef 2008–10, River Thame Conservation Tst 2012–; ALPSP Award for Contrib to Scholarly Publishing 2009; hon memb Br Ecological Soc 2011–; Hon DUniv Oxford Brookes 2005; FIBiol 2007; *Books* A Guide to the Birds of the Coast (1976), Microform Publishing (1979), Journal Publishing (1997), Journal Production (1992), Academic and Professional Publishing (2012); *Recreations* fly fishing, Scottish history, conservatism; *Style—* Robert Campbell, Esq; ✉ e-mail rcampbell192@live.com

CAMPBELL, Roderick Alexander McRobie; MSP; *b* Edinburgh; *Educ* Reading Sch, Exeter Univ, Univ of Glasgow, Univ of Strathclyde; *Career* advocate; MSP (SNP) Fife NE 2011–; *Style—* Roderick Campbell, Esq, MSP; ✉ The Scottish Parliament, Edinburgh EH99 1SP

CAMPBELL, Ronnie; MP; s of Ronald Campbell, and Edna, *née* Howes; *b* 14 August 1943; *Educ* Ridley HS; *m* 17 July 1967, Deirdre, da of Edward McHale (d 1976); 5 s (Edward b 1968, Barry b 1971, Shaun b 1973, Brendan b 1973, Aiden b 1977), 1 da (Sharon b 1969); *Career* former miner, chm Bates NUM; MP (Lab) Blyth Valley 1987–; memb Public Admin Ctee 1997–; cncllr: Blyth Borough Cncl 1969–74, Blyth Valley DC 1974–88; *Style—* Ronnie Campbell, MP; ✉ House of Commons, London SW1A 0AA

CAMPBELL, Dr Sir Simon Fraser; kt (2015), CBE (2006); s of William Fraser Campbell (d 1953), and Ellen Mary, *née* Casey (d 1998); *b* 27 March 1941; *Educ* Univ of Birmingham (BSc, PhD); *m* 1966, Jill, *née* Lewis; 2 s (Duncan John b 1970, Douglas Simon b 1973); *Career* res fell and visiting lectr Universidade de São Paulo Brazil 1970–72; Pfizer Central Research: staff chemist 1972–78, mangr Discovery Chem 1978–83, dir Discovery Chem 1983–92, gp dir Medicinals Discovery 1992–93, vice-pres Medicinals Discovery 1993–96, sr vice-pres Worldwide Discovery and Medicinals R&D Europe 1996–98, dir and memb Bd Pfizer; co-ed Current Opinion in Drug Discovery and Devpt 1998–2004; visiting prof Univ of Leeds 1996–99; memb: SERC Organic Chem Sub-Ctee 1988–91, SERC Sci Bd 1992–94, R&D Ctee Assoc of Br Pharmaceutical Industry 1994–96, Academic Advsy Bd for Chem Univ of Kent 1994–96, Review Panel for Wellcome SHOWCASE Awards 1997, Editorial Bd Perspectives in Drug Discovery and Design 1995–98, Industrial Advsy Bd Dept of Chem Univ of Bristol 1998–2001, Advsy Cncl Save Br Sci 1998–, Cncl Univ of Kent 1999–2007, RSC Steering and Co-ordinating Ctee 1999–2001, BP Technol Advsy Cncl 2000–04, RSC Cncl 2003–07; pres RSC 2004–06; chair MMV Expert Scientific Advsy Ctee for Malaria 1999–2003; RSC Award for Medicinal Chem 1989, E B Hershberg Award for Important Discoveries in Medicinally Active Substances ACS 1997, Industrial Research Inst (US) Achievement Award 1997, CIA Individual Achievement Award 2006, Galen Medal 2007; Hon DSc: Univ of Kent 1999, Univ of Birmingham 2004, Univ of St Andrews 2008; ACS, FRSC 1985 (pres 2004–06), FRS 1999, FMedSci 2002; *Publications* over 120 scientific publications and patents; *Clubs* Athenaeum; *Style—* Dr Sir Simon Campbell, CBE, FRS, FMedSci

CAMPBELL OF AIRDS, Alastair Lorne; er s of Brig Lorne Campbell of Airds, VC, DSO, OBE, TD (d 1991), and (Amy) Muriel Jordan, *née* Campbell (d 1950); *b* 11 July 1937; *Educ* Eton, Sandhurst; *m* 1960, Mary Ann, da of Lt-Col (George) Patrick Campbell-Preston, MBE; 4 c; *Career* Argyll and Sutherland Highlanders 1957–63, Royal Green Jackets TA 1964–69; md Waverley Vintners Ltd 1977–83; chm Christopher and Co Ltd 1975–83, chief exec Clan Campbell 1984–; HM Unicorn Pursuivant of Arms, memb Ct of the Lord Lyon 1987–, memb Queen's Body Guard for Scotland (Royal Co of Archers); memb Priory Chapter Scotland (Order of St John of Jerusalem) 1996; memb Cncl Nat Tst for Scotland 1996–2001; hon res fell Univ of Aberdeen 1996–2001; *Publications* History of Clan Campbell (3 vols), Two Hundred Years – The History of the Highland Society of London, History of the Queen's Body Guard for Scotland – The Royal Company of Archers (co-author); *Style—* Alastair Campbell of Airds

CAMPBELL OF LOUGHBOROUGH, Baroness (UK Life Peer 2008), of Loughborough in the County of Leicestershire; Susan Catherine (Sue) Campbell; CBE (2003, MBE 1991); *Educ* Long Eaton GS, Bedford Coll of Physical Educn, Univ of Leicester (Dip, MEd); *Career* physical educn teacher Whalley Range GS Manchester 1970–72, dep dir of physical educn Sch of Educn Univ of Leicester 1972–76, lectr Dept of Physical Educn and Sports Science Univ of Loughborough 1976–80, regnl offr East Midlands Region Sports Cncl 1980–84; Nat Coaching Fndn: dep chief exec 1984, chief exec 1985–95; chief exec Youth Sport Tst 1995–2005 (chair 2005–), non-political advsr Dept for Culture, Media and Sport and Dept for Educn and Skills 2000–03; UK Sport: reform chair 2003–05, chair 2005–13; sits in House of Lords as ind crossbench peer 2008–; Int Olympic Ctee President's Prize 1998; hon fell Leeds Poly 1990, hon fell Sheffield Poly 1991, Companion Inst of Sport and Recreation Managers 1994, hon life memb Central Cncl of Physical Recreation 1998, hon life memb Br Advsrs and Lectrs of Physical Educn 1998; Hon DEd: Cncl for Nat Academic Awards 1992, De Montfort Univ 1996, Univ of Leicester 2000; Hon DSc Univ of Brighton 1993, Hon DTech Loughborough Univ 1997; hon doctorate: Bedford Univ, Leeds Met Univ 2006, City & Guilds 2010, Univ of Exeter 2010, Endicott Coll Boston USA 2011, Queen's Univ Belfast 2013; *Style—* The Baroness Campbell of Loughborough, CBE; ✉ Youth Sport Trust, Sport Park, 3 Oakwood Drive, Loughborough LE11 3QF

CAMPBELL OF PITTENWEEM, Baron (Life Peer UK 2015) of Pittenweem in the County of Fife; Rt Hon Sir (Walter) Menzies Campbell; CH (2013), kt (2004), CBE (1987), PC (1999), QC (Scot 1982); s of George Alexander Campbell, and Elizabeth Jean Adam, *née* Phillips; *b* 22 May 1941; *Educ* Hillhead HS Glasgow, Univ of Glasgow (MA, LLB), Stanford Univ; *m* 1970, Elspeth Mary Grant-Suttie, da of Maj-Gen R E Urquhart, CB, DSO; *Career* admitted advocate 1968, advocate depute 1977–80, standing jr counsel to the Army in Scotland 1980–82; pt/t chm: VAT Tbnl 1984–87, Med Appeal Tbnl 1985–87; memb: Legal Aid Central Ctee 1983–86, Broadcasting Cncl for Scotland 1984–87, Scottish Legal Aid Bd 1986–87; Parly candidate (Lib): Greenock and Port Glasgow 1974 (both Gen Elections), E Fife 1979, NE Fife 1983; MP (Lib 1987–88, Lib Dem 1988–) Fife NE 1987–2015; Lib then Lib Dem spokesman on sport 1987–; Lib Dem spokesman on: defence 1988–95, foreign affairs and defence 1995–, foreign affairs, defence and Europe 1997–; Lib Dem shadow foreign sec 1997–2006, ldr Lib Dems 2006–07 (dep ldr 2003–06); memb House of Commons: Trade and Industry Select Ctee 1990–92, Defence Select Ctee 1992–99, Foreign Affrs Ctee 2007–, Intelligence and Security Ctee 2007–; ldr UK Delgn to the NATO Parly Assembly; capt UK athletics team 1965 and 1966, competed in Olympic Games Tokyo 1964 and Cwlth Games 1966, UK 100 metres record holder 1967–74; memb 2012 Olympic Bd; *Clubs* Reform, Nat Lib; *Style—* The Rt Hon the Lord Campbell of Pittenweem, CH, CBE, PC, QC; ✉ 9 Lynedoch Place, Edinburgh, EH3 7PX

CAMPBELL OF STRACHUR, David Niall MacArthur; 25 Chief of the MacArthur Campbells of Strachur; s of (Ian) Niall MacArthur Campbell of Strachur (d 2000); *b* 15 April 1948; *Educ* Eton, Exeter Coll Oxford; *m* 1974, Alexandra Wiggin, Marquesa de Muros, da of Sir Charles Wiggin, KCMG, DFC, AFC, Marques de Muros (d 1977); 1 s (Charles Alexander, Yr of Strachur, b 26 May 1977), 1 da (Iona Margot (Mrs Geoffrey Hemphill) b 15 Jan 1979); *Career* int publishing dir Hachette (Paris) 1982–90, md éditions du Chêne 1986–90, publisher Everyman's Library 1990–; chm Scala Publishers 1998–2012; fndr FromVineyardsDirect.com; Chevalier de la Legion d'Honneur 2007; *Clubs* Beefsteak, Pratt's, White's; *Style—* David Campbell of Strachur; ✉ 23K Warwick Square, London SW1V 2AB; Barbreck House, By Lochgilphead, Argyll PA31 8QW

CAMPBELL OF SURBITON, Baroness (Life Peer UK 2007), of Surbiton in the Royal Borough of Kingston upon Thames; Dame Jane Susan Campbell; DBE (2006, MBE 2000); da of Ronald James Campbell (d 1987), and Jessie Mary, *née* Ball; *b* 19 April 1959, Kingston Hill, Surrey; *Educ* Hatfield Poly (BA), Univ of Sussex (MA); *m* 1, 27 June 1987 (husb d 1993); m 2, 17 Sept 2000, Roger Symes; *Career* equal opportunities liaison offr GLC 1984–86, disability trg devpt offr London Boroughs Disability Resource Team 1986–87, dir of trg London Boroughs Disability Resource Team 1988–94, co-dir Nat Centre for Ind Living 1996–2000 (now tstee); chair: Social Care Inst for Excellence 2001–05, Independent Living Review Expert Panel Office of Disability Issues 2006–07; cmmr: Disability Rights Cmmn 2000–07, Equality and Human Rights Cmmn 2006–09 (chair Disability Ctee 2006–09); sits in House of Lords as crossbench peer 2007–, cmmr House of Lords Appointments Cmmn 2008–13, chair All Party Parly Disability Gp 2008–14, memb Parly Jt Select Ctee on Human Rights 2010–12, memb Parly Select Ctee on the Equality Act 2010 and Disability 2015–16, chair Ind Living Strategy Gp (parliamentary initiative) 2016–; chair Br Cncl of Disabled People 1991–95, patron Nat Disability Arts Collection and Archive (NDACA), patron Just Fair (UK); memb Editorial Bd Br Jl of Social Work 2007–11; Mayor's Community Award Kingston-upon-Thames 1994, Lifetime Achievement Award Liberty Human Rights 2012; Hon LLD Univ of Bristol 2002, Hon

DUniv Sheffield Hallam Univ 2003, Hon DUniv Birmingham 2009; *Publications* Disability Equality Training (jtly, 1991), Disability Politics (jtly, 1996), Disabled People and the Right to Life (jtly, 2008); *Recreations* theatre, cinema, gardening; *Style—* Baroness Campbell of Surbiton, DBE; ✉ House of Lords, London SW1A 0PW (☎ 020 7219 5124, e-mail campbellljs@parliament.uk); website www.baronesscampbellofsurbition.com

CAMPBELL-SAVOURS, Baron (Life Peer UK 2001), of Allerdale in the County of Cumbria; Dale Norman Campbell-Savours; s of John Lawrence, and Cynthia Lorraine Campbell-Savours; *b* 23 August 1943; *Educ* Keswick Sch, Sorbonne Paris; *m* 1970, Gudrun Kristin Runolfsdottir; 3 s; *Career* formerly co dir; Parly candidate (Lab) Darwen Feb and Oct 1974, MP (Lab) Workington 1979–2001 (also contested by-election 1976); front bench spokesman: overseas devpt 1991–92, agriculture 1992–94, ret; memb: Public Accounts Ctee 1980–91, Procedure Ctee 1983–91, Member's Interests Select Ctee 1983–92, Agriculture Select Ctee 1994–96, Standards and Privileges Ctee 1996–2001, Intelligence and Security Ctee 1997–2001; memb UNISON 1970–; *Publications* The case for the Supplementary Vote (1990), The case for the University of the Lakes (1995); *Style—* The Rt Hon the Lord Campbell-Savours

CAMPION, David Bardsley (Barry); s of Norman Campion (d 1987), and Enid Mary, *née* Bardsley (d 1991); *b* 20 March 1938; *Educ* Shrewsbury; *m* 1, 1962 (m dis 1972), Victoria Wild; 1 s (Mark), 1 da (Sarah); m 2, 1979, Sally, da of Frank Walter Manning Arkle; *Career* dir Wheatsheaf Distribution and Trading 1968–78, dir Linfood Holdings 1978–81, chm Food Div CWS Ltd 1982–87, chief exec Monarchy Foods Ltd 1987–90: chm: BAF Securities Ltd (dir 1972–), Meridian Foods Ltd 1990–97, Wilsons of Holyhead 1991–98, Burgess Supafeeds 1996–2004, Gott Foods Ltd 1996–2001, Gold Star (Natural Fruit Juices) Ltd 1997–98, Opus Europe Ltd 1999–2001, Wholebake Ltd 2001–11; dep chm Gold Crown Foods Ltd 1993–94; dir: Snackhouse plc 1990–2001, West Trust plc 1991–93, Sutton Hoo Produce Ltd 1995–98, Freshers Foods Ltd 2005–, Oscar Pet Foods Ltd 2010–, Maggi Maggi UK Ltd 2012–; MInstD 1972, FIGD 1983; *Recreations* golf, cricket, travel; *Clubs* MCC, Delamere Forest Golf, Royal Birkdale Golf, Holyhead Golf, Trearddur Bay Sailing, Farmers', Grosvenor; *Style—* Barry Campion, Esq; ✉ 4 South Close, High Street, Tarporley, Cheshire CW6 0DP (e-mail campion@monarchy.freeserve.co.uk)

CAMPION-SMITH, (William) Nigel; s of H R A Campion-Smith (d 2015), and Moyra, *née* Campion (d 2001); *b* 10 July 1954; *Educ* King George V Sch Southport, Royal GS High Wycombe, St John's Coll Cambridge (MA); *m* 31 July 1976, Andrea Jean, da of Edward Willacy, of Hale Barns, Cheshire; 1 da (Dr Joanna b 1983), 2 s (Jonathan b 1985, Timothy b 1990); *Career* admitted slr 1978; ptnr Travers Smith Braithwaite 1982–97, ptnr Latham & Watkins 2000–14 (counsel 2015–); Law Soc 1978; *Style—* Nigel Campion-Smith, Esq; ☎ 020 7710 1070, fax 020 7374 4460

CANADY, Diane Elizabeth; da of late Jimmy Roger Canady, of High Wycombe, Bucks, and Kathleen Ann, *née* Knight; *b* 22 May 1954; *Educ* USAF Central HS USA, High Wycombe Tech Coll, Univ of Essex (BA, MA); *m* 2 Dec 1977, Brian Armistead, s of Douglas Armistead; 1 s (Benjamin James b 25 May 1981); *Career* grad trainee McCann Erickson advtg 1977–81, account supr Royds Advertising 1981–82, account dir NCK Advertising 1982–83, gp product mangr Levi Strauss 1983–84, bd dir Geers Gross 1984–91, client servs dir and exec bd dir rising to managing ptnr Publicis 1991–97, md Publicis Dialogue 1997–; lectr in advtg for CAM course Coll of Distributive Trades; memb: Bd Cosmetic Exec Women, WACL and Fragrance Fndn; patron Women of the Year Luncheon; *Recreations* music, interior decorating, reading, cooking; *Style—* Ms Diane Canady; ✉ Publicis Dialogue, 82 Baker Street, London W1M 2AE (☎ 020 7935 4426, fax 020 7830 3290, mobile 07860 702140)

CANBY, Michael William; s of Clarence Canby (d 2004), and Mary Frances, *née* Drake (d 2008); *b* 11 January 1955; *Educ* Buckhurst Hill County HS, Univ of Cambridge (MA, LLB); *m* 6 Sept 1980, Sarah, da of John Houghton Masters (d 1965), and Mary, *née* Dymond; 1 s (Philip Charles Houghton b 1988), 1 da (Harriet Georgina Mary b 1991); *Career* admitted slr 1980; Linklaters: New York office 1982–84, ptnr 1986–, Paris office 1989–95; memb Law Soc; *Style—* Michael Canby, Esq; ✉ c/o Linklaters, One Silk Street, London EC2Y 8HQ (☎ 020 7456 2000, fax 020 7456 2222, e-mail michael.canby@linklaters.com)

CANDY, Lorraine; da of Anthony Butler, and Vivienne Butler; *b* 8 July 1968; *Educ* NCTJ Proficiency Test 1988; *Career* journalist; The Cornish Times 1990, reporter The Sun Showbiz section 1990, feature writer The Daily Mirror 1990–93, women's ed The Sun Feb-Aug 1993, women's ed Today Newspaper 1993–95, dep ed Marie Claire 1995–97, dep ed Saturday Magazine The Times 1997–98, ed B Magazine 1998–99, features ed The Times 1999–2000, ed Cosmopolitan 2000–04, ed Elle 2004–; *Recreations* family; *Style—* Mrs Lorraine Candy

CANDY, Nick; *Career* property developer; co-fndr (with bro, Christian Candy) Candy & Candy; *Style—* Nick Candy, Esq; ✉ Candy & Candy, Rutland House, Rutland Gardens, London SW7 1BX

CANN, (John William) Anthony; s of Dr John Cann (d 1991), and Enid Grace, *née* Long (d 2003); *b* 21 July 1947; *Educ* Old Malthouse Sch Swanage, Shrewsbury, Univ of Southampton (LLB); *m* 6 Jan 1973, Anne, da of Harold Thorswald Clausen (d 1994), of Johannesburg; 2 s (John Harold b 25 Nov 1973, Robert Charles b 13 Aug 1984), 1 da (Sally Elizabeth b 10 Jan 1978); *Career* admitted slr 1972; Linklaters 1970–2006: asst slr 1972–78, NY office 1975–82, ptnr 1978–2006, head Corp Dept 1995–2000, sr ptnr 2001–06; co-head M&A and Corp Practice Gp of Linklaters & Alliance 1998–2001; memb Advsy Ctee CAB Battersea 1973–75, non-exec dir and chm Remuneration Ctee Connect Gp plc 2006–16, non-exec dir and chm Remuneration Ctee Panmure Gordon & Co plc 2007–, dir Social Investment Business Ltd 2008–16, strategic advsr Kinstellar LLP 2008–; tstee Social Investment Business Fndn 2006–16, chm Changing Faces 2007–09, govr Haberdashers' Aske's Fedn 2007–11, govr Haberdashers' Adams' Fedn 2011– (chm 2013–); Freeman City of London Slrs Co 1978, Liveryman and Asst Haberdashers' Co; *Books* Mergers & Acquisitions Handbook (Part D), Mergers and Acquisitions in Europe (United Kingdom); *Recreations* travel, photography, sports, sailing; *Clubs* Athenaeum, MCC, Trojans; *Style—* Anthony Cann, Esq; ✉ Langrick, 13 Murray Road, Wimbledon, London SW19 4PD (☎ 020 8946 6731, e-mail anthony.cann@yahoo.com)

CANNADINE, Prof Sir David Nicholas; kt (2009); *b* 7 September 1950; *Educ* King Edward's Five Ways Sch Birmingham, Clare Coll Cambridge (MA, Robbins prize), St John's Coll Oxford (DPhil); *m* Prof Linda Colley; *Career* res fell St John's Coll Cambridge 1975–77, fell and Coll lectr in history Christ's Coll Cambridge 1977–88 (dir of studies in history 1977–83, tutor 1979–81, memb Coll Cncl 1979–88, fell steward 1981–88), lectr in history Univ of Cambridge 1980–88 (asst lectr 1976–80, memb Faculty Bd of History 1983–85), prof of history Columbia Univ 1988–98 (memb Univ Senate 1989–90, chm Dept Personnel Ctee 1991–92, memb Governing Body Soc of Fells 1992–98, Moore collegiate prof 1992–98); Inst of Historical Research Univ of London: dir 1998–2003, Queen Elizabeth the Queen Mother prof of Br history 2003–08; distinguished sr fell Sch of Advanced Study Univ of London 2008–,Whitney J Oates sr scholar Humanities Cncl Princeton Univ 2008–; visiting memb Sch of Historical Studies Inst for Advanced Study Princeton 1980–81, assoc fell Berkeley Coll Yale Univ 1985–, visiting prof Birkbeck Coll London 1995–97, visiting fell Whitney Humanities Center Yale Univ 1995–98; a cmmr English Heritage 2001–; gen ed: Studies in Modern History 1979–, Penguin History of Britain 1989–, Penguin History of Europe 1991–; advsy ed Complete Edition of the Works of W S Gilbert 1988–, ed Historical Research 1998–2003; memb Editorial Bd: Urban History Yearbook 1979–83, Past and Present 1983–, Midland History 1985–88, Rural History 1995–, Prospect 1995–, Library History 1998–; fell J P Morgan Library NY 1992–98; chm John Ben Snow Prize Ctee Conf on Br Studies 1993; memb: Cncl Urban History Gp 1980–88, Advsy Cncl Centre for the Study of Soc and Politics Kingston Univ 1997, Advsy Cncl Warburg Inst 1998–2003, Advsy Bd Inst of Contemporary Br History 1998–2003, Advsy Cncl PRO 1999–2004, Advsy Cncl Inst of US Studies 1999–2004, Advsy Cncl Inst of English Studies 2000–, Advsy Cncl Inst of Latin American Studies 2000–04, Eastern Regnl Ctee Nat Tst 2001–, Advsy Cncl Inst for Study of the Americas 2004–, Govt's Ind Review of the 30-Year Rule 2007–08; historical advsr Ian Fleming Centenary Exhbn Imperial War Museum 2007–08; vice-pres Br Record Soc 1998–, vice-pres Royal Historical Soc 1998–2003, pres Worcestershire Historical Soc 1999–; tstee: Parliament History 1998–, London Jl 1998–, Kennedy Meml Tst 2000–, Nat Portrait Gallery 2001–, Br Empire and Cwlth Museum 2003–; patron Attingham Tst 2006–; govr Ipswich Sch 1982–88; T S Ashton Prize in Economic History 1977, Agricultural History Silver Jubilee Prize 1977, Lionel Trilling Prize 1991, Governors' Award 1991, Dean's Distinguished Award in the Humanities Columbia Univ 1996, Tercentenary Medal Soc of Antiquaries 2008; Hon DLitt: UEA 2001, South Bank Univ 2001, Univ of Birmingham 2002; hon prof Univ of London 2008–; FRHistS 1981, FRSA 1998, FRSL 1999, FBA 1999; *Books* Lords and Landlords: The Aristocracy and the Towns 1774–1967 (1980), Patricians, Power and Politics in Nineteenth Century Towns (ed, 1982), Exploring the Urban Past: Essays in Urban History by H J Dyos (co-ed, 1982), Rituals of Royalty: Power and Ceremonial in Traditional Societies (co-ed, 1987), The Pleasures of the Past (1989), Blood, Toil, Tears and Sweat: Winston Churchill's Famous Speeches (ed, 1989), The First Modern Society: Essays in English History in Honour of Lawrence Stone (co-ed, 1989), The Decline and Fall of the British Aristocracy (1990), G M Trevelyan: A Life in History (1992), Aspects of Aristocracy: Grandeur and Decline in Modern Britain, (1994), History and Biography: Essays in Honour of Derek Beales (co-ed, 1996), Class in Britain (1998), History in Our Time (1998), Ornamentalism: How the British saw their Empire (2001), In Churchill's Shadow: Confronting the past in modern Britain (2002), What is History Now? (ed, 2002), History and the Media (ed, 2004), Mellon: An American Life (2006), The National Portrait Gallery: A Brief Outline History (2007), Empire, The Sea and Global History: Britain's Maritime World 1763–1833 (ed, 2007), Making History Now and Then: Discoveries, Controversies and Explorations (2008); also author of numerous book chapters and articles in learned jls; *Style—* Prof Sir David Cannadine; ✉ PA Jennifer Wallis (☎ 020 7862 8755, e-mail jennifer.wallis@sas.ac.uk); Department of History, Dickinson Hall, Princeton University, Princeton, NJ 08544–1017, USA

CANNING, Alison Mary; da of Dr William Carbis Canning, of Knowle, W Midlands, and Bertha Sheila, *née* McGill; *b* 15 April 1959; *Educ* Marlborough, Westminster Univ (BA), City Univ Business Sch (MBA); *m* 23 Sept 1994 (m dis 1997), Richard Albert Moore; *Career* Burson-Marsteller PR: graduate trainee rising to vice-pres/client servs mangr NY 1983–88, bd dir London 1988–89; fndr md Cohn & Wolfe PR London 1989–94, ceo Burson-Marsteller UK 1994–96, fndr md First & 42nd (mgmnt consultancy) 1997–2001, pres int ops Edelman Worldwide 2001–03, fndr dir Burns-Canning Ltd (brand consultancy), fndr dir By Its Nature (brand consultancy) 2012–14, gp mktg dir City Football Gp 2014–; *Recreations* diving, fishing, sailing, opera; *Style—* Ms Alison Canning; ✉ e-mail alison@byitsnature.com

CANNING, Hugh Donaldson; s of David Donaldson Canning, of Whissendine, Leics, and Olga Mary, *née* Simms; *b* 28 May 1954; *Educ* Oakham Sch, Pembroke Coll Oxford (BA), UC Cardiff (Dip Theatre Studies); *Career* regular contrib The Western Mail 1977–82, freelance writer 1979 (Music & Musicians, Opera, Times Higher Educn Supplement), freelance contrib on music The Guardian 1983–87, music critic London Daily News 1987, music critic and feature writer (contract) The Guardian 1987–89, chief music critic Sunday Times 1989–; contrib and memb Editorial Bd Opera magazine; opera critic The Listener (until closure); Critic of the Year 1994 (Br Press Awards) 1995; memb Critics' Circle; *Recreations* theatre, music, eating out, watching tennis; *Style—* Hugh Canning; ✉ The Sunday Times, 1 Pennington Street, London E1 9XN

CANNING, HE Mark; CMG (2009); *b* 15 December 1954; *Educ* Downside Sch, Univ of London (MBA); *m* 2004, Cecilia Kenny; 1 da (b 2004); *Career* entered HM Diplomatic Serv 1973, Freetown 1975–77, Georgetown 1982–86, Chicago 1986–88, Jakarta 1993–97, cnsllr FCO 2000, Kuala Lumpur 2001–06, ambass to Burma 2006–09, ambass to Zimbabwe 2009–11, ambass to Indonesia 2011–14, ret; career memb HM Diplomatic Serv; currently sr advsr Bell Pottinger; s of John Canning, and Paul Canning; *Recreations* sport, sea fishing, history; *Clubs* Royal Overseas-League; *Style—* HE Mr Mark Canning, CMG; ✉ c/o Royal League, 1 Park Place, London SW1 (e-mail markcanning@aldwickpartners.com)

CANNON, Fiona; OBE (2011); da of John Cannon (d 2002), and Joan, *née* Henvey; *b* 7 January 1964, London; *Educ* Bishop Thomas Grant Sch London, Univ of Leeds (BA); *Partner* David Langan; 1 s (Joseph b 8 April 2000), 1 da (Jessica b 14 Dec 2001); *Career* Pepperell Unit Industrial Soc (now Work Fndn) 1987–89, freelance conslt 1989–90, head of equality and diversity Lloyds TSB Gp 1990–; cmmr Equal Opportunities Cmmn 2000–07 (dep chair 2006–07), dir of Equality and Diversity Lloyds Banking Gp 2009–; chair Practitioners Gp Taskforce on Racial Equality IPPR 2003–04; chm and fndr memb Employers for Childcare 1992–99, fndr memb Employers for Work-Life Balance 2000–03 (chm Steering Gp), dir Agile Future Forum 2013–; fndr memb Race for Opportunity Campaign 1995; memb: Ministerial Advsy Gp on Work-Life Balance 2001–02, Work and Parents Taskforce 2001–; *Recreations* reading, travelling; *Style—* Ms Fiona Cannon, OBE; ✉ Lloyds Banking Group, PO Box 112, Canons House, Canons Way, Bristol BS99 7LB (☎ 020 7522 5666, fax 0117 943 3945, e-mail fiona.cannon2@lloydstsb.co.uk)

CANNON, Prof Paul Stephen; OBE (2014); s of John James Peter (d 2004), and Betty, *née* Carter (d 1996); *b* 28 October 1953; *Educ* Edmonton County GS, Univ of Southampton (BSc, MSc, PhD); *m* 14 May 1976, Vivian Avis, da of James Frederick Goodwin (d 2008); 1 da (Ruth Avis b 27 Sept 1981), 1 s (Thomas James b 23 Oct 1984); *Career* engr; with RAE 1981–93, fndr Radio Science and Propagation Gp (later Centre for Propagation and Atmospheric Research) 1993, individual merit and fell DERA (Defence Evaluation and Research Agency) 1993–2002; QinetiQ: tech dir Communications Dept 2000–02, sr fell 2002, chief scientist Communications Div 2004–08, univs partnership dir 2004–05; visiting prof Center for Atmospheric Research Univ of Massachusetts 1989–90, pt/t chair Communications and Atmospheric Sciences Univ of Bath 1998–2011, visiting chair in engrg Univ of Birmingham 2007–11, pt/t chair Radio Science and Systems Univ of Birmingham 2011–, dir Poynting Inst Univ of Birmingham 2011–14 (memb Engrg Policy Ctee 2011–14); NATO-AGARD (Advsy Gp for Aerospace Research and Devpt): nat rep Electromagnetic Propagation Panel and Sensors and Propagation Panel 1993–97, vice-chair and chair designate Sensors and Propagation Panel 1996–97; chair: UK-Canada-Norway-Sweden Doppler and Multipath Sounding Network (DAMSON) Project 1993–2000, Nat Facilities Funding Ctee PPARC 2000–2002; co-chair US/UK Memorandum of Understanding (MOU) on Effects of the Ionosphere on C3I Systems 1996–2001, chair URSI Commn G Ionospheric Radio Propagation 2005–08 (vice-chair 2002–05); URSI: national rep Commn G 1993–99, national chair UK 2008–11, vice-pres and treas 2011–14, pres 2014–17; assoc ed URSI Radio Science Bulletin 2002–04, ed Radio Science jl 2009–14; IEE: memb Cncl 2003–06, member Antennas and Propagation Professional Network Exec 2003–04, memb Defence Science Advsy Cncl 2014–; FREng (memb Engrg Policy Ctee 2011–14), FIET, CEng, MAGU (American Geophysical Union); *Publications* author of numerous articles in jls;

Recreations photography, travelling, American presidential history; *Style*— Prof Paul Cannon, OBE, FREng; ✉ University of Birmingham, Edgbaston, Birmingham B15 2TT (☎ 0121 414 4323, mobile 07990 564772, e-mail p.cannon@bham.ac.uk, website www.birmingham.ac.uk/staff/profiles/eese/cannon-paul.aspx)

CANNON, (Jack) Philip; s of William George Cannon (d 1973), of Perranporth, Cornwall, and Charlotte Loraine, *née* Renoir (d 1984); *b* 21 December 1929; *Educ* Falmouth GS, Dartington Hall, Royal Coll of Music; *m* 1, 15 July 1950, Jacqueline Playfair Laidlaw (d 1984), da of Hugh Alexander Lyon Laidlaw; 1 da (Virginia Shona Playfair b 29 June 1953); m 2, 5 Nov 1997, Jane, Baroness Buijs van Schouwenburg, da of Stanley Dyson; *Career* composer; dep prof Royal Coll of Music 1953–59, lectr in music Univ of Sydney 1959–60, prof of composition Royal Coll of Music 1960–95; author of many articles for music jls; compositions incl: Morvoren (opera) 1964, String Quartet (winner of Grand Prix and Prix de la Critique Paris) 1965, Oraison Funèbre de L'Ame Humaine (symphony cmmnd by ORTF) 1971, Lacrimae Mundi (cmmnd by Gulbenkian Fndn for Music Gp of London) 1972, Son of Man (symphony cmmnd by BBC to mark Britain's entry to the EC) 1973, The Temple (cmmnd by The Three Choirs Festival) 1974, Te Deum (cmmnd by HM The Queen for St George's Day) 1975, Logos (clarinet quintet cmmnd by BBC for Silver Jubilee) 1977, Lord of Light Requiem (cmmnd by The Three Choirs Festival) 1980, Cinq Supplications sur une Bénédiction (cmmnd by RF) 1983, Dr Jekyll and Mr Hyde (cmmnd by BBC TV), A Ralegh Triptych (cmmnd by The Three Choirs Festival) 1992, Septain (in memoriam John Ogdon) 1993, Piano Quintet (for John Lill and the Medici String Quartet) 1994, Symphony (for BBC Philharmonic) 1996, Symphony for the Millennium 2000, Faith (cmmnd by St Martin's Chamber Choir Denver) 2012; all works (original manuscripts, pubns etc) held in the Cannon Archive Bodleian Library Oxford; memb: Royal Philharmonic Soc, ISM, Br Acad of Composers and Songwriters; Bard of Gorsedd Kernow 1997; FRCM 1971; *Recreations* exploring comparative philosophies, travel; *Clubs* Savile, Chelsea Arts; *Style*— Philip Cannon, Esq; ✉ Elmdale Cottage, Marsh, Aylesbury, Buckinghamshire HP17 8SP (☎ 01296 613157)

CANNON-BROOKES, Dr Peter; s of Victor Montgomery (Joe) Cannon Brookes (d 2004), and Nancy Margaret, *née* Markham Carter (d 1994); *b* 23 August 1938; *Educ* Bryanston, Trinity Hall Cambridge (MA), Courtauld Inst of Art Univ of London (PhD); *m* 13 April 1966, Caroline Aylmer, da of Lt Col John Aylmer Christie-Miller, CBE, TD, DL (d 2007), of Manor House, Bourton-on-the-Hill, Glos; 1 s (Stephen William Aylmer b 1966), 1 da (Emma Wilbraham Montgomery b 1968); *Career* keeper Dept of Art: City Museum and Art Gallery Birmingham 1965–78, Nat Museum of Wales 1978–86; fndr ed International Journal of Museum Management and Curatorship 2003– (ed 1981–2003), dir museum servs Stipple Database Services Ltd 1986–89, conslt curator The Tabley House Collection Univ of Manchester 1988–, int museum conslt 1990–; Int Cncl of Museums: memb Exec Bd UK Ctee 1973–81, pres Int Art Exhibitions Ctee 1977–79 (Exec Bd 1975–81), vice-pres Conservation Ctee 1978–81 (Exec Bd 1975–81); memb: Welsh Arts Cncl 1979–84 (memb Craft Ctee 1983–87, memb Art Ctee 1979–85), Projects and Orgns Ctee Crafts Cncl 1985–87; pres: Welsh Fedn of Museums 1980–82, S Wales Art Soc 1980–87; memb: Town Twinning Ctee Birmingham Int Cncl 1968–78, Birmingham Dio Synod 1970–78, Birmingham Dio Advsy Ctee for Care of Churches 1972–78, Edgbaston Deanery Synod 1970–78 (lay jt chm 1975–78), Abingdon Deanery Synod 1999–2007 and 2009–, Oxford Diocesan Synod 2003–07, Oxford Diocesan Bd of Educn 2004–07; JP: Birmingham 1973–78, Cardiff 1978–82; Liveryman Worshipful Co of Goldsmiths 1974 (Freeman 1969); FMA, Fell Int Inst of Conservation (FIIC), FRSA; *Books* European Sculpture (with H D Molesworth, 1964), Baroque Churches (with C A Cannon-Brookes, 1969), Lombard Painting (1974), After Gulbenkian (1976), The Cornbury Park Bellini (1977), Michael Ayrton (1978), Emile Antoine Bourdelle (1983), Ivor Roberts-Jones (1983), Czech Sculpture 1800–1938 (1983), Paintings from Tabley (1989), The Painted Word (1991), William Redgrave (1998), The Godolphin Arabian (2005), Pantaloon (2011); *Recreations* cooking, growing vegetables, photography; *Clubs* Athenaeum; *Style*— Dr Peter Cannon-Brookes; ✉ Thrupp Farm, Abingdon, Oxfordshire OX14 3NE (☎ 01235 520595, e-mail cannonbrookesassociates@gmail.com)

CANOSA MONTORO, Francisco Octavio (Frank); s of Dr Francisco Canosa Lorenzo, and Elisa, *née* Montoro de la Torre; *b* 28 May 1951; *Educ* Columbia Univ NY (BA), Fordham Univ NY (JD); *m* 1, Dec 1972 (m dis 1975), Gloria de Aragón; m 2, 15 Sept 1979, Belinda Mary, da of Lt-Col Charles Reginald Clayton Albrecht, OBE, TA, of Pulborough, W Sussex; 2 da (Alexandra Elisa b 12 Jan 1983, Isabel Christina b 20 June 1985); *Career* asst to pres Bank of America NY 1975, asst vice-pres Manufacturers Hanover Trust Co NY 1978; Bank of America International Ltd London: vice-pres 1980, exec dir 1985, head corp fin UK and Europe 1987–89; vice-pres and sr mktg offr Bankers Trust Co 1989–92, first vice-pres and head of private banking Banca della Svizzera Italiana 1992–95, sr vice-pres and head of the branch and of private banking Bank Julius Baer & Co Ltd 1995–2000, md and ceo Julius Baer International Ltd 2000–04, conslt ABN Amro Bank NV Private Banking 2005–07, conslt SG Hambros 2007–11, special advsr Bd Newton Investment Mgmnt Ltd 2012–; chm Private Banking Ctee BBA 1996–2003; memb: Finances Ctee CAFOD 2001–06, Fin Advsy Gp Douai Abbey Tst 2001–, Advsy Panel PricewaterhouseCooper 2005–09; US Dept of State: public memb Selection Bd 2006 and 2009, public memb Dept Sr Review Bd 2007; visiting prof Univ of Buckingham 2005–, visiting prof EDHEC Nice 2010–, lectr in wealth mgmnt and int financial regulation Cass Business Sch City Univ London; various broadcasts on private banking and various aspects relating to Cuba for the BBC, writer and presenter of series Cuba!Cuba! (Radio 4) 2000; memb: Advsy Cncl Philharmonia Orchestra 2001–, Public Membs Assoc of the Foreign Serv (Washington DC) 2006–; FRSA 2006, chartered fell Chartered Inst for Securities and Investment 2006 (memb Examination Bd 2009–, memb Disciplinary Bd 2010–, chief CPD advsr 2010–); *Clubs* RAC, Nuevo, Madrid; *Style*— Frank Canosa Montoro, Esq

CANTER, Prof David Victor; s of Chaim Yizchak (Harry) Canter (d 1960), and Coralie Lilian, *née* Hyam (d 1970); *b* 5 January 1944; *Educ* Liverpool Collegiate GS, Univ of Liverpool (BA, PhD), Univ of Huddersfield (MA); *m* 10 Nov 1967, Sandra Lorraine, da of late Alfred Smith; 2 da (Hana b 1970, Lily Rebecca b 1979), 1 s (Daniel b 1972); *Career* visiting lectr Birmingham Sch of Architecture 1967–70, visiting res fell Tokyo Univ 1970–71, lectr Univ of Strathclyde 1970–71 (res fell Building Performance Res Unit 1965–70); Univ of Surrey: lectr 1972–78, reader 1978–83, personal chair in applied psychology 1983–87, chair of psychology 1987–94, head of dept 1987–91, academic head of dept 1991–94; prof of psychology Univ of Liverpool 1994–, dir Centre for Investigative Psychology Univ of Liverpool 1998–2009 (emeritus prof 2009–), prof of psychology and dir Int Research Centre for Investigative Psychology Univ of Huddersfield 2009–; managing ed Jl of Environmental Psychology 1981–2001, founding and managing ed Jl of Investigative Psychology and Offender Profiling 2007–, managing ed Contemporary Social Science 2010–, fndr and managing ed Crime Psychology Review 2015; series ed: Ethnoscopes – Current Challenges in the Environmental Social Sciences 1988–, Int Library Psychology 2004–, Benchmark 2004–, Successful Studying 2006–, Psychology Crime and Law 2006–, Contemporary Issues in Social Science; numerous contribs to newspapers, jls, TV and radio; writer, prodr and presenter Mapping Murder (six part TV documentary); chm Psychologists for Peace 1985–88, pres Int Acad of Investigative Psychology 2008; memb: Res Cncl for Complementary Med, London Advsy Bd Salvation Army, CND; Golden Dagger Award for non-fiction 1994, Anthony Award for non-fiction 1995, Lifetime Achievement Award John Jay Coll of Criminal Justice NY 2016; Freeman City of Quito 1985; Hon MD 1987, hon memb Japanese Inst of Architects 1970; FBPsS 1975, FAPA 1985, FIMgt 1985, CPsychol 1988, FAcSS, FRSA 2000, hon fell Psychological Assoc of SA 2004, Hon FBPS 2008, FRSM 2009, FHEA 2012; *Books* Architectural Psychology (1970), Psychology for Architects (1974), Psychology and the Built Environment (1974), Environmental Interaction (1975), The Psychology of Place (1977, e-edn 2016), Designing for Therapeutic Environments (with S Canter, 1979), Fires and Human Behaviour (1980, revised 1990), Psychology in Practice (with S Canter, 1982), Facet Theory: Approaches to Social Research (1985), The Research Interview: Uses and Approaches (1985), Environmental Social Psychology (1986), Environmental Perspectives (1988), Environmental Policy Assessment and Communication (1988), New Directions in Environmental Participation (1988), Periballontike Psychologia (in Greek, 1988), Football In Its Place (with M Comber and D Uzzell, 1989), Empirical Approaches to Social Representations (with G Breakwell, 1993), Criminal Shadows (1994), The Faces of Homelessness (1995), Psychology in Action (1996), Criminal Detection and the Psychology of Crime (with L Alison, 1997), Interviewing and Deception (with L Alison, 2000), The Social Psychology of Crime (with L Alison, 1999), Profiling in Policy and Practice (with L Alison, 1999), Profiling Property Crimes (with L Alison, 2000), Mapping Murder (2003), Becoming an Author (with G Fairbairn, 2006), Principles of Geographical Offender Profiling (with D Youngs, 2007), Applications of Geographical Offender Profiling (with D Youngs, 2007), Psychology and Law (2008), Criminal Psychology (2008), Investigative Psychology: Offender Profiling and the Analysis of Criminal Action (with D Youngs, 2009), The Face of Terrorism: Interdisciplinary Perspectives (2009), Safer Sex in the City: The Experience and Management of Street Prostitution (with M Ioannou and D Youngs, 2009), Forensic Psychology: a Very Short Introduction (2010), Forensic Psychology for Dummies (2012), Biologising the Social Sciences (with D Turner, 2013), Social Science Perspectives on Climate Change (2015); *Recreations* musical composition, collage, horticulture; *Style*— Prof David Canter; ✉ e-mail dvcanter@btinternet.com, website www.davidcanter.com; c/o Doreen Montgomery, Rupert Crew Limited, 6 Windsor Road, London N3 3SS (☎ 020 8346 3000)

CANTERBURY, Archdeacon of; *see:* Watson, Ven Sheila

CANTERBURY, Dean of; *see:* Willis, Very Rev Robert Andrew

CANTERBURY, Archbishop of 2013–; Most Rev and Rt Hon Justin Portal Welby; *b* 6 January 1956; *Educ* Eton, Trinity Coll Cambridge, Univ of Durham; *Career* curate Chilvers Coton and Astly 1992–95, rector Southam 1995–2002, vicar Ufton 1996–2002, canon residentiary Coventry Cathedral 2002–07, sub-dean Int Centre for Reconciliation 2005–07, priest-in-charge Holy Trinity Coventry 2007, dean Liverpool Cathedral 2007–11, bishop of Durham 2011–13; *Style*— The Most Rev and Rt Hon the Lord Archbishop of Canterbury; ✉ Lambeth Palace, London SE1 7JU

CANTLAY, Charles Peter Thrale; s of Peter Allen Cantlay, and Elizabeth Ann Cantlay; *b* 4 February 1954; *Educ* Radley, Oriel Coll Oxford (BA); *m* 1985, Sandra Jane; *Career* Alexander Howden Reinsurance Brokers Ltd: joined 1976, dir Marine Div 1983–86, md Marine Div 1986–92; ceo 1992–97; AON Group Ltd: chm Marine and Energy Reinsurance Div 2000– (dep chm 1997–2000), dep chm AON Reinsurance UK, head ReSpecialty; Liveryman Worshipful Co of Haberdashers; *Recreations* golf, hockey, skiing; *Clubs* Tandridge Golf, Oxted Hockey; *Style*— Charles P T Cantlay, Esq; ✉ AON Group Ltd, 8 Devonshire Square, London EC2M 4PL (☎ 020 7623 5500, fax 020 7216 3211)

CANTOR, (Prof) Brian; CBE (2013); *b* 11 January 1948; *Educ* Manchester Grammar, Christ's Coll Cambridge (MA, PhD), Univ of Oxford (MA); *m* 1, 1967 (m dis 1979), m 2, 1981 (widowed 1993); 2 s; *Career* research fell/lectr in materials science Sch of Engrg Univ of Sussex 1972–81; Dept of Materials Univ of Oxford: lectr in metallurgy 1981–91, reader in materials processing 1991–95, head of dept 1995–2000, Cookson prof of materials 1995–2002, head Div of Mathematical and Physical Sciences 2000–02; lectr then sr research fell Jesus Coll Oxford 1985–95, professorial fell St Catherine's Coll Oxford 1995–2002, vice-chllr Univ of York 2002–13, vice-chllr Univ of Bradford 2013–; dir Oxford Centre for Advanced Materials and Composites Univ of Oxford 1990–95; univ visiting fell Dept of Mechanical Engrg Northeastern Univ Boston USA 1976, Br Cncl fell Dept of Metallurgy Banaras Hindu Univ India 1980, industrial fell GE Research Labs Schenectady USA 1982; memb Bd: Isis Innovation Ltd 2000–02, Amaethon Ltd 2004–06; conslt: Alcan Int Research Labs 1986–94, Rolls-Royce plc 1996–2015; ed advsr/series ed: Inst of Physics Publications 1983–2006, Taylor & Francis 2006–08; ed Progress in Materials Science 1988–; memb Bd: Worldwide Universities Network 2002–13, Yorks Univs 2002–, White Rose 2002–13, Nat Early Music Centre 2002–13, York Science Park (Innovation Centre) Ltd 2004–06, Nat Science Learning Centre 2004–13, Yorks Innovation (formerly Yorks Science) 2004–10, Nat Media Museum 2013–, Bradford Producer City 2013–, UK Coll of Business and Computing 2016–; memb: World Technol Network 2002–, York Economic Partnership 2007–13, Leeds Local Economic Partnership 2011–13; chm UUK Employers Pensions Forum 2011–13, vice-pres (research) Cncl Royal Acad of Engrg 2009–13; Rosenhain Medal Inst of Materials 1993, Ismanam Prize 1998, Platinum Medal Inst of Materials 2002, Lifetime Achievement Award York Press 2011; hon prof: Northeastern Univ Shenyang PRC 1996–, Nat Inst of Metals, Chinese Acad of Sciences 1998–, Zhejiang Univ Hangjiao 2003–, Nanjing Univ 2008– Indian Inst of Science Bangalore 2013–; hon memb Indian Inst Metallurgists 2010; memb: American Inst of Mining and Metallurgical Engrs 1980, Academia Europea 1999; CEng 1979, FIM 1989 (MIM 1970), FRMS 1993, FREng 1998, FInstP 1999, CCMI 2008; *Books* Rapidly Quenched Metals III (ed, 1978), A Tribute to J W Christian (ed jtly, 1992), Thermal Analysis of Advanced Materials (ed jtly, 1994), Stability of Microstructure in Metals and Alloys (jtly, 2 edn, 1996), Aerospace Materials (jt ed, 2001), Solidification and Casting (jt ed, 2002), Metal and Ceramic Matrix Composites (jt ed, 2003), Rapidly Quenched Metals 11 (jt ed, 2004), Novel Nanocrystalline Alloys and Magnetic Nanomaterials (jt ed, 2004), Automotive Materials (jt ed, 2008); also author of numerous articles in learned jls; *Style*— Brian Cantor, CBE; ✉ University of Bradford, Richmond Road, Bradford, Yorkshire BD7 1DP (☎ 01274 233012, website www.brad.ac.uk)

CAPALDI, Dr Michael John; *b* 22 May 1958; *Educ* Bedford Sch, UEA (BSc), Univ of Manchester (PhD); *m* 1 April 1989, Bryony Elizabeth, *née* Pearce; 3 s (Benjamin b 16 April 1991, Duncan b 8 June 1993, Dominic b 24 July 2007); *Career* sr research offr (paediatrics and neonatal med) Royal Postgrad Med Sch Hammersmith Hosp 1983–84, section ldr Advanced Drug Delivery Research (ADDR) Unit Ciba Geigy Pharmaceuticals 1984–87, sales rep rising to sr project mangr Smith Kline and French (later SmithKline Beecham Pharmaceuticals) 1987–92, gp and European mktg mangr Drug Devpt Services (DDS) Amersham International plc 1992–93, sales and mktg dir (N America) DDS Amersham Life Sciences Inc 1993–96, head of gp mktg Cell Biology/DDS Amersham International plc 1996, business devpt dir Core Group plc 1996–98, exec vice-pres strategic mktg Nycomed Amersham plc 1998–2000, commercial dir Oxford Asymmetry International plc 2000; ceo: Synaptica Ltd 2000–03, Scancell Ltd 2004–06, Hunter-Fleming Ltd 2006–08; dir Edinburgh BioQuarter 2010–15, ceo Sunergos Innovations Ltd 2015–; non-exec dir: Stealthyx Therapeutics Ltd, Roslin Cells Ltd; memb UK Pharmaceutical Licensing Gp; former ed Pharmaceutical Forum: International Topics in Drug Devpt; former memb Sec of State for Scotland's Business Bd 2011–15, memb Regnl Advsy Bd Scottish Enterprise East 2014–; MInstD, MRI, FRMS; *Publications* author of over 10 pubns in scientific jls and books 1982–86; *Recreations* golf, skiing, squash, walking, family; *Style*— Dr Michael Capaldi

CAPELLINO, Ally (aka Alison Lloyd); *b* 1956; *Educ* Middx Poly (BA); *Career* fashion designer; Courtaulds Central Design Studio 1978–79, estab Ally Capellino 'Little Hat' (initially selling accessories) 1979, developed clothing and sold Ally Capellino label internationally (Italy, USA, Japan) 1980–86, introduced menswear and children's wear collections 1986, first showed London (men's and womenswear) 1986, opened first store Soho 1988, launched diffusion sportswear collection 'Hearts of Oak' 1990, launched diffusion collection 'ao' 1996 at Serpentine Gallery, opened Ally Capellino shop in Sloane Avenue London 1997, formed Capellino Design Ltd 1999, redesigned Girl Guides and Brownie uniform 1999, launched Ally Capellino womenswear leather accessories collection 2000, launched 'A for Ally Capellino' womenswear collection for Debenhams 2001, redesigned Brownies uniform 2002, developed menswear accessories collection 2002, opened showroom and design studio Shoreditch 2002, opened Shoreditch boutique and launched business online 2005, designed artists' bag range for Tate Modern Gallery 2006, collaboration with Apple 2008, 30 Years exhbn The Wapping Project featuring the 'Wall of Bags' 2010, second shop opens on Portobello Road 2011, Bags for Bikes range launched 2012, Bums on Seats London Design Festival Project V&A Museum and Ally Capellino shops 2013, London Design Festival collaboration with architect Seng Watson 'Polyomino' 2014, third shop opens in Marylebone 2015; *Style*— Ms Alison Lloyd

CAPIE, Prof Forrest Hunter; s of Daniel Forrest Capie (d 1975), and Isabella Ferguson, *née* Doughty (d 1996); *b* 1 December 1940, Glasgow; *Educ* Nelson Coll NZ, Univ of Auckland NZ (BA), LSE (MSc, PhD); *m* 11 Feb 1967, Dianna Dix, da of William John Harvey, of Auckland, NZ; *Career* economics tutor LSE 1970–72; lectr: Dept of Economics Univ of Warwick 1972–74, Sch of Economics Univ of Leeds 1974–79; Centre for Banking and Int Fin City Univ: lectr 1979–82, sr lectr 1982–83, reader 1983–86, prof of economic history 1986–2004, head of dept 1988–92, official historian Bank of England 2004–10, prof emeritus 2009–; ed Economic History Review 1993–99; memb: Economic History Soc 1970 (memb Cncl 1986–), Cliometric Soc 1986; FRSA; *Books* The British Economy Between the Wars (with M Collins, 1983), Depression and Protectionism, Britain Between the Wars (1983), Monetary History of the United Kingdom 1870–1970: Data Sources and Methods (with A Webber, 1985), Financial Crises and the World Banking System (ed with G E Wood, 1986), Monetary Economics in the 1980s: Some Themes from Henry Thornton (ed with G E Wood, 1988), Major Inflations in History (ed, 1991), Have the Banks Failed British Industry? (1992), Protectionism in World Economy (1992), The Future of Central Banking (with Charles Goodhart, 1994), Monetary Economics in the 1990s (with G E Wood, 1996), The Lender of Last Resort (with G E Wood, 2007), The Bank of England 1950s to 1979 (2010), Money Over Two Centuries (with G E Wood, 2012); *Recreations* golf, music, theatre; *Clubs* Travellers, Political Economy, Hampstead Golf, MCC; *Style*— Prof Forrest Capie; ✉ 2 Fitzroy Road, Primrose Hill, London NW1 8TZ (☎ 020 7722 7456); Faculty of Finance, Cass Business School, 106 Bunhill Row, London EC1Y 8TZ (☎ 020 7040 8730, e-mail f.h.capie@city.ac.uk)

CAPLAN, Jonathan Michael; QC (1991); s of (Malcolm) Denis Caplan (d 2005), and Jean Hilary, *née* Winroope (d 1985); *b* 11 January 1951, London; *Educ* St Paul's, Downing Coll Cambridge (Harris open scholar); *m* 7 March 1993, Selena Anne, *née* Peskin; 2 s (James, Alexander), 1 da (Natasha); *Career* called to the Bar Gray's Inn 1973 (Holker scholar, bencher 2000); recorder of the Crown Court 1995– (asst recorder 1990–95); chm Bar Cncl Ctee on Televising the Courts 1989, chm Public Affrs Ctee Bar Cncl 1990–92; adjudicator for Dubai Broadcasting and Publishing Standards Tbnl; memb Editorial Bd Jl of Criminal Law; chm BAFTA Management Ltd, chm BAFTA Hong Kong Advsy Bd; patron Wiener Library; MCIArb 2003; *Books* The Confait Confessions (1977), The Bar on Trial (1978), Disabling Professions (1979); *Recreations* tennis, Thai and Khmer art, collecting manuscripts and historical newspapers, ufology, reading, writing, music, horse racing (flat), cinema; *Clubs* Queen's, Alfred's; *Style*— Jonathan Caplan, Esq, QC; ✉ 1st Floor, 5 Paper Buildings, Temple, London EC4Y 7HB (☎ 020 7583 6117, fax 020 7353 0075, e-mail jcaplanqc@gmail.com)

CAPLAN, Simon Anthony; s of late Malcolm Denis Caplan and Jean Hilary, *née* Winroope; *b* 13 December 1946; *Educ* Carmel Coll; *m* 6 Sept 1970, Yolande Anne, da of Simon Albert (d 1978) and Phyllis Green (d 1982); 1 da (Amanda b 1971), 1 s (Benjamin b 1974); *Career* Deloittes (Touche Ross) 1965–70; jt fndr Fin Advice Panels (within CAB), fndr Caplan Montagu Assoc Chartered Tax Advisers and Accountants, chm and chief exec Transmedia Pictures, Transmedia Int Releasing and Pictures in Motion Corp; Gen Cmmr of Income Tax 1988–95 (ret); JP 1986–95 (ret); Freeman of the City of London 1980; memb: BAFTA, RTS, FTII, FCCA (FAPA); *Publications* Gibraltar: International Financial Centre; *Recreations* cinema, theatre, art and antique collecting; *Clubs* Naval and Military, The Hospital Club, Soho House; *Style*— Simon A Caplan, Esq; ✉ Ground Floor, 29 Harley Street, London W1G 9QR

CAPLEHORN, Peter Leslie; s of Leslie Gilbert George Caplehorn (d 1994), and Glades, *née* Rankin (d 1986); *b* 23 October 1951; *Educ* Carisbrooke GS IOW, Portsmouth Sch of Architecture; *m* 13 Sept 1991 (m dis 2004), Sally Anne, *née* Hare; 1 da (Katie b 10 May 1996); *Career* architect; worked in Winchester and Isle of Wight and own practice until 1980; Scott Brownrigg + Turner: joined 1980, assoc dir 1988–, divnl dir 1996–, tech dir 2000–, currently responsible for tech standards, specification and health and safety; projects incl: Concept 2000 Farnborough 1986 (Civic Tst Award 1987), Manchester Airport Y2 1990–93, new HQ Eastern Electricity 1996–98; chair health and safety Exec Bd CIC; BSI: memb Standards Policy and Strategy Ctee, chair CB- Ctee, chair CB10 Ctee, dep chair BRAC Ctee; ARB 1978, RIBA 1978 (memb Cncl 2009–); *Publications* Whole Life Costing – a new approach (2012); *Recreations* sailing, skiing, photography; *Style*— Peter Caplehorn, Esq; ✉ 12 Glyncastle, Caversham, Reading, Berkshire RG4 7XF; Scott Brownrigg, 46–48 Portsmouth Road, Guildford, Surrey GU2 4DU (☎ 01483 568686, mobile 07801 050404, fax 01483 575830, e-mail p.caplehorn@scottbrownrigg.com)

CAPNER, Gareth Roger John; s of John Hammond Capner (d 1973), and Clarice May, *née* Gibbins (d 1971); *b* 14 May 1947; *Educ* Taunton Sch, Univ of Sheffield (BA, MA); *m* 2 Jan 1971, Susan Mary, da of Arthur Snell, of Lincs (d 1994); *Career* princ planning offr Berkshire CC 1973–79; Barton Willmore Partnership: assoc 1979–81, ptnr 1981–85, sr planning ptnr 1985–96, sr ptnr 1996–2008; business conslt 2008–; chm HMG Housing Design Awards; MIMgt 1978, FRTPI 1983 (MRTPI 1974); *Recreations* boating, shooting, wine grower, squash; *Style*— Gareth Capner, Esq; ✉ Dunley House, Dunley, Whitchurch, Hampshire RG28 7PU (☎ 01256 892876, mobile 07850 491320, e-mail capneresq@btinternet.com); Trafalgar Place, Lymington, Hampshire SO41 9BN

CARAYOL, René; MBE (2004); *Career* entrepreneur, bd dir, business advsr, author and speaker; past clients incl: World Economic Forum, McKinseys, Barclays Bank, Tesco, PM's Delivery Unit; former bd dir IPC Magazines and PEPSI UK, md IPC Electric; e-chm e-photomail.com; non-exec dir Inland Revenue, chief exec Carayol Ltd; lectr and speaker worldwide; contrib to TV and radio documentaries and business news: BBC TV, Channel 4 and Sky, BBC Radio 4, BBC Radio 5 Live; columnist Observer; *Style*— René Carayol, Esq, MBE; ✉ c/o Jill Thorn, 3 Victoria Rise, Hilgrove Road, London NW6 4TH (☎ 01707 646 731, fax 01707 851 259, e-mail rene@carayol.com, website www.carayol.com)

CARBERRY, Kay; CBE (2007); da of Sean Carberry (d 2000), and Sheila, *née* McCormack (d 2006); *b* 19 October 1950, Dublin; *Educ* Royal Naval Sch Malta, Univ of Sussex (BA); *Family* 1 s (Joe b 17 July 1983); *Career* secdy sch teacher 1973–76, research asst NUT 1976–78; TUC: policy offr 1978–83, sr policy offr 1983–88, head of equal rights 1988–2003, asst gen sec 2003–16; cmmr: Equal Opportunities Cmmn 1999–2007, Cmmn for Equality and Human Rights 2006–12, Low Pay Cmmn 2012–; tstee People's History Museum; *Recreations* theatre, arts, swimming; *Style*— Ms Kay Carberry, CBE; ✉ Trades Union Congress, Congress House, Great Russell Street, London WC1B 3LS (☎ 020 7467 1266, fax 020 7467 1277, e-mail kcarberry@tuc.org.uk)

CARDALE, David Michael; s of Brig W J Cardale, OBE (d 1986), of Bury St Edmunds, Suffolk, and Audrey Vere, *née* Parry-Crooke (d 1996); *b* 26 December 1947, London; *Educ* Eton, Univ of Essex (BA), INSEAD (MBA); *m* 31 Aug 1985, Fionna, *née* MacCormick; 1 s (Hugo William b 7 March 1989), 2 da (Natasha Lucy Vere b 19 Dec 1990, Alicia Daisy Catherine b 11 May 1993); *Career* dir County NatWest 1983–90 (N American rep 1981–83), dir NatWest Ventures 1990–95; chm Oxford Community Internet Holdings plc 1999–2001 (non-exec dir 1997–99); co-fndr and chm global3digital Ltd 1999–2014, chm: City of London Investment Gp plc 2012– (non-exec dir 2006–12), Supervisory Bd Hosking Ptnrs LLP 2015–, Solar Options for Schools Ltd 2016–; non-exec dir: Sphere Investment Trust plc 1988–96, The Emerging Markets Country Investment Trust plc 1994–2000, Toolex International NV (Sweden) 1995–2001; *Recreations* skiing, trail hunting, tennis, walking; *Clubs* Hurlingham; *Style*— David Cardale, Esq; ✉ Aldacre House, Shipton Moyne, Tetbury GL8 8QE (☎ 01666 880349, e-mail db@snow.co.uk, website www.betterhomes4all.org.uk)

CARDEW, Anthony John; s of late Dr Martin Philip Cardew, and late Anne Elizabeth, *née* Foster; *b* 8 September 1949; *Educ* Bishop Wordsworth's Sch Salisbury, Marlborough; *m* 10 Dec 1971, Janice Frances, da of Alec Anthony Smallwood (d 1985); 1 s (James), 1 da (Sarah); *Career* chief reporter Surrey Mirror 1968–70, news reporter UPI 1970–71, fin corr Reuters 1971–74, dir then head of fin PR Charles Barker Ltd 1974–83, chm Grandfield Rork Collins 1985–91 (dir 1983–91), chm Cardew Group 1991–; *Recreations* book collecting, walking, grandchildren, theatre; *Clubs* London Library, Athenaeum; *Style*— Anthony Cardew, Esq; ✉ Cardew Group, Albemarle House, 1 Albemarle Street, London W1S 4HA (☎ 020 7930 0777, fax 020 7925 0647)

CARDIGAN, Earl of; David Michael James Brudenell-Bruce; s and h of 8 Marquess of Ailesbury; *b* 12 November 1952; *Educ* Eton, Rannoch, RAC Cirencester; *m* 1, 1980 (m dis), Rosamond Jane (d 2012), er da of Capt Winkley, of Bruton, Somerset, and Mrs Jane Winkley, of Pewsey, Wilts; 1 s (Thomas, Viscount Savernake b 1982), 1 da (Lady Catherine b 1984); m 2, 2011, Mrs Joanne Hill, of Phoenix, Arizona; 1 da (Lady Sophie b 2013); *Heir* s, Viscount Savernake; *Career* 31 Hereditary Warden of Savernake Forest (position created in 1067) 1987–, owner mangr Savernake Forest; sec Marlborough Conservatives; memb exec Devizes Constituency Conservative Assoc; *Recreations* scuba diving, motorcycling; *Style*— Earl of Cardigan; ✉ Savernake Lodge, Savernake Forest, Marlborough, Wiltshire (e-mail davidcardigan1@gmail.com)

CARDINAL, His Hon Judge Martin John; s of Ralph William Cardinal, of Sutton Coldfield, W Midlands, and Ella Winifred, *née* Austin; *b* 10 June 1952, Birmingham; *Educ* Magdalene Coll Cambridge (exhibitioner, Dame Rebecca Flower Squire scholar, MA, Magdalene Coll Law Prize); *m* 22 Oct 1977, Janet Dorothy, *née* Allnutt; 1 s (Stephen James b 20 Dec 1980), 1 da (Deborah Jane b 10 Dec 1984); *Career* admitted slr 1977; ptnr: Wood Amphlet Wild & Co 1978–85, Anthony Collins 1985–94, dist judge 1994–2004 (dep dist judge 1992–94), recorder 2000–04 (asst recorder 1997–2000), circuit judge (Midlands Circuit) 2004–; legal memb Mental Health Review Tbnl 1987–94; *Books* Matrimonial Costs (2000, 2 edn 2007); *Recreations* walking, swimming, gardening, lay reader; *Style*— His Hon Judge Cardinal; ✉ Brimingham County Court, 33 Bull Street, Birmingham B4 6DS (☎ 0121 250 6392)

CARDOZO, Prof Linda Dolores; OBE (2014); da of Felix Elia Cardozo (d 1971), of London, and Olga Annette, *née* Watts (d 1992); *b* 15 September 1950; *Educ* Haberdashers' Aske's, Acton Tech Coll, Univ of Liverpool (MB ChB, MD); *m* 13 July 1974, Stuart Ian Hutcheson, s of Ian Steen Hutcheson (d 1994); 2 da (Melissa b 27 Feb 1989, Juliet b 27 July 1990), 1 s (Marius (twin) b 27 July 1990); *Career* house offr and SHO in obstetrics and gynaecology Liverpool, res registrar in urodynamics St George's Hosp London 1976–78, conslt obstetrician and gynaecologist specialising in female urinary incontinence King's Coll Hosp 1985– (registrar then sr registrar 1979–85), prof of urogynaecology KCL 1994–; memb Editorial Bd of several jls; pres ACPWH 1995–; chm: Continence Fndn UK 1998–2006, Br Menopause Soc 2001–03, Br Soc of Urogynaecology 2001–06 (founding chm); pres European Urogynaecological Assoc (EUGA) 2011–15; int fells rep Cncl RCOG 2001–07 and 2010–; memb: RSM (pres Section of Obstetrics and Gynaecology 2001–02), BMA, Int Urogynaecology Assoc (pres 1999–2000), Int Continence Soc (chm Educn Ctee 2002–08, exec offr and memb Advsy Bd); FRCOG 1991 (MRCOG 1980); *Publications* author of 23 books incl: Basic Urogynaecology (1993), Urogynaecology (1997), Urinary Incontinence in Primary Care (2000), Textbook of Female Urology and Urogynaecology (2001, 3 edn 2010 (Best New Edn of an Edited Medical Book Soc of Authors and RSM)); author of more than 500 publications relating to urogynaecology; *Recreations* theatre, bridge, gardening, scuba diving, skiing, water skiing; *Style*— Prof Linda Cardozo, OBE; ✉ The Sloes, Potter Street Hill, Pinner, Middlesex HA5 3YH (☎ 020 8866 0291, fax 020 8866 0129, e-mail linda@lindacardozo.co.uk); King's College Hospital, Denmark Hill, London SE5 9RS (☎ 020 7737 4000); 8 Devonshire Place, London W1G 6HP (☎ 020 3299 9000, fax 020 7224 2797)

CARDWELL, Paul; s of Charles Alexander Cardwell, and Irene Julia-Ann, *née* Moodie; *b* 10 June 1952; *m* May 1984, Christina Hughes, da of Fergus Hughes Boyter; 2 da (Rebecca Caterina Madelaine Macdonald b 15 March 1986, Amelia Iona Francis b 29 Aug 1988); *Career* with advtg agencies: Foote Cone & Belding 1978–79, Young & Rubicam 1979–85, Publicis 1985–87; bd dir Leo Burnett 1987–89, joint chm and creative dir GGK London 1993–95 (creative dir 1989–93), creative dir Doner Cardwell Hawkins 1995–2010, European creative dir Armando Testa 2010–11, exec creative dir Brand Union 2011–; contrib Horizon (BBC) and Channel 4 as freelance documentary writer through Brand X Ltd; winner (1991): Gold Medal The One Show NY, Lion D'Or Cannes Advtg Festival, Gold Award Art Dirs' Club of Europe, ITV Award, Gold and Silver Br TV Advtg Awards, Silver D&AD Award; memb: D&AD 1979, Royal Photographic Soc 1990, The Photographers Gallery 1991; *Books* The Race Against Time – The Story of Sport Aid (1988); *Recreations* theatre, travel, reading, photography; *Style*— Paul Cardwell, Esq

CARDWELL, Emeritus Prof Richard Andrew; s of Lt Cdr Albert Cardwell RN (d 1995), and Mary Margarethe, *née* Knight (d 2012); *b* 16 July 1938; *Educ* Helston GS, Univ of Southampton (BA, DipEd), Univ of Nottingham (PhD); *m* 29 July 1961, Oithona Shaguine (Bunty), da of Edgar Treadwell (d 1968); *Career* lectr UCW Aberystwyth 1965–67 (asst lectr 1964–65); Univ of Nottingham: lectr 1967–74, sr lectr 1974–78, reader 1978–83, prof of modern Spanish lit and head Dept of Hispanic Studies 1983–96, emeritus prof 2003–; visiting prof: Johns Hopkins Univ 1992, Univ of Colorado; memb: Assoc of Br Hispanists, Anglo-Catalan Soc; corresponding memb Real Academia Sevillana de Buenas Letras Seville and Granada Spain; Boy Scouts' Assoc Silver Cross for Gallantry and Royal Humane Soc Testimonial on Vellum for Gallantry 1958, Emma Dangerfield Prize for Best Byron Study 2007; Freeman City of London 2012, Liveryman Worshipful Co of Glaziers and Painters of Glass 2012; *Books* Blasco Ibáñez's La Barraca (1972 and 1995), Juan Ramón Jiménez: The Modernist Apprenticeship (1977), Espronceda (1981), Gabriel García Márquez: New Readings (1987), Virgil: Essays for the Bimillennium (1987), Literature and Language (1989), Espronceda: Student of Salamanca (1990), Qué es el Modernismo? (1992), Zorrilla: Centennial Readings (1994), Sánchez Rodríguez (1996), Lord Byron the European (1997), ed Reception of British Authors in Europe: Byron Volume (2005); also edns of Juan Ramón Jiménez; author of more than 130 articles and 22 books and edns; *Recreations* writing, research, conversation with intelligent women; *Style*— Emeritus Prof Richard A Cardwell; ✉ The Yews, 6 Town Street, Sandiacre, Nottingham NG10 5DP (☎ 0115 939 7316); Department of Spanish, Portuguese and Latin American Studies, University of Nottingham, University Park, Nottingham NG7 2RD (☎ 0115 951 5796/5800, fax 0115 951 5814, e-mail richard.cardwell@nottingham.ac.uk)

CARE, Daniel Stuart (Danny); *b* 2 January 1987, Leeds, Yorks; *Educ* Prince Henry's GS Otley; *Career* rugby union player; clubs: Leeds Tykes 2003–06, Harlequins 2006–; England: 25 caps, debut 2008; *Style*— Mr Danny Care; ✉ c/o Harlequins, Twickenham Stoop Stadium, Langhorn Drive, Twickenham TW2 7SX

CAREW, 7 Baron (I 1834 and UK 1838); Patrick Thomas Conolly-Carew; s of 6 Baron Carew, CBE (d 1994), and Lady Sylvia Gwendoline Eva Maitland (d 1991), da of 15 Earl of Lauderdale; *b* 6 March 1938; *Educ* Harrow, RMA Sandhurst; *m* 30 April 1962, Celia Mary, da of Col Hon (Charles) Guy Cubitt, CBE, DSO, TD; 3 da (Hon Virginia Mary (Hon Mrs McGrath) b 1965, Hon Nicola Rosamond (Hon Mrs de Montfort) b 1966, Hon Camilla Sylvia b 1969 (Hon Mrs Newman)), 1 s (Hon William Patrick b 1973); *Heir* s, Hon William Conolly-Carew; *Career* late Capt Royal Horse Guards (The Blues, served in UK, Cyprus and Germany), former int show jumping rider; represented Ireland in European Three Day Event Championships 1959, 1962 and 1967 and World Championships 1966; memb Irish Olympic Three Day Event team: Mexico 1968, Munich 1972, Montreal 1976; pres: Equestrian Fedn of Ireland 1979–84 (vice-pres 1985–), Ground Jury Three Day Event Olympic Games Barcelona 1992 and Olympic Games Atlanta 1996, Irish Horse Trials Soc 1998–2013; chm Three Day Event Ctee FEI (memb Bureau) 1989–97 (hon memb Bureau 1997), former memb Cncl and tstee World Horse Welfare, dir Castletown Fndn; FEI Gold Medal for Three Day Eventing, Equestrian Fedn of Ireland Badge of Honour; *Recreations* all equestrian sports, shooting, cricket, bridge; *Clubs* Kildare St and Univ (Dublin); *Style*— The Rt Hon the Lord Carew; ✉ The Garden House, Donadea, Naas, Co Kildare, Ireland (☎ 00 353 458 68204, fax 00 353 458 61105)

CAREW POLE, Sir (John) Richard Walter Reginald; 13 Bt (E 1628), of Shute House, Devonshire; OBE (2000), DL (Cornwall 1988); s of Col Sir John Gawen Carew Pole, 12 Bt, DSO, TD (d 1993), and Cynthia Mary Burns, OBE (d 1977); *b* 2 December 1938; *Educ* Eton, RAC Cirencester; *Heir* s, Tremayne Carew Pole; *Career* late Coldstream Gds; memb Devon and Cornwall Ctee Nat Tst 1978–83, pres Surf Life Saving Assoc of GB 1978–87; High Sheriff Cornwall 1979; pt/t dir SW Electricity Bd 1981–90, regnl dir Portman Building Society 1989–91; pres Royal Cornwall Agric Show 1981, chm Devon and Cornwall Police Authy 1985–87; pres RHS 2001–06 (memb Cncl 1999–2006), vice-pres Garden History Soc 1999–; govr: Seale Hayne Agric Coll 1979–89, Plymouth Coll 1981–96; dir Theatre Royal Plymouth 1985–97; Cornwall CC: cncllr 1973–93, chm Planning and Employment Ctee 1980–84, chm Finance Cmmn 1985–89, chm Property Ctee 1989–93; tstee: Nat Heritage Memorial Fund 1991–2000, Tate Gallery 1993–2003, Eden Project 1996–2007, Tst House Charitable Fndn 1999–2009, Pilgrim Tst 2000–08; tstee and chm Capital Campaign Ctee Royal Acad of Arts 2007–; pres Devon & Cornwall Record Soc 1999–2000; chm Combined Universities in Cornwall Steering Ctee 2000–03; memb Countryside Cmmn 1991–96; Liveryman Worshipful Co of Fishmongers (memb Ct of Assts 1993–, Prime Warden 2006–07); ARICS 1969; *Recreations* walking, contemporary pictures, gardening; *Style*— Sir Richard Carew Pole, Bt, OBE, DL; ✉ Clift Barn, Antony, Torpoint, Cornwall PL11 3AA (☎ and fax 01752 814914)

CAREY, Sir de Vic Graham; kt (2002); s of Michael Carey (d 1964), of Guernsey, and Jean, *née* Bullen (d 1975); *b* 15 June 1940; *Educ* Bryanston, Trinity Hall Cambridge (MA), Caen Univ; *m* 22 June 1968, Bridget, da of Maj John Lindsay Smith (ka 1943); 2 s (Perrin b 1971, Julius b 1980), 2 da (Jenette b 1974, Henrietta b 1979); *Career* slr Supreme Court of Judicature 1965, advocate Royal Court of Guernsey 1966, in private practice 1966–76, people's dep States of Guernsey April-Dec 1976; Guernsey: HM Slr-Gen 1977–82, HM Attorney-Gen 1982–92, HM Receiver-Gen 1985–92, Dep Bailiff 1992–99, Bailiff 1999–2005, Lt Bailiff of the Royal Court 2005–12, judge Court of Appeal 2005–12; Jersey: judge of the Court of Appeal 2000–05, Cmmr of the Royal Court 2006–10; QC 1989; memb Gen Synod C of E 1982–98, chm House of Laity Winchester Diocesan Synod 1993–97, vice-chair Guernsey Children's Convenor and Tbnl Bd 2010–16; *Style*— Sir de Vic Carey; ✉ Les Padins, St Saviour, Guernsey GY7 9JJ (☎ 01481 264587)

CAREY, Godfrey Mohun Cecil; QC (1991); s of Dr Godfrey Fraser Carey, LVO (d 1972), and Prudence Loveday, *née* Webb (d 1977); *b* 31 October 1941; *Educ* Eton; *m* 1, 1965 (m dis 1975), Caroline Jane; 1 da (Miranda b 1967), 2 s (Sebastian Fraser b 1969, d 1971, Hugo b 1972); m 2, 1978 (m dis 1985), Dorothy; 1 da (Lucy b 1978); *Career* legal asst Rolls Royce 1966–70; called to the Bar Inner Temple 1969 (bencher 2000); recorder of the Crown Court 1986–, memb Mental Health Review Tribunal 2000–12; *Recreations* tennis, jazz, Aztec culture; *Clubs* Boodle's; *Style*— Godfrey Carey, Esq, QC; ✉ 5 Paper Buildings, Temple, London EC4Y 7HB (☎ 020 7583 6117, fax 020 7353 0075, e-mail gmohuncc@gmail.com)

CAREY, Prof John; s of Charles William Carey (d 1965), and Winifred Ethel, *née* Cook (d 1967); *b* 5 April 1934; *Educ* Richmond and East Sheen County GS, St John's Coll Oxford (MA, DPhil); *m* 1960, Gillian Mary Florence, da of Reginald Booth (d 1968); 2 s (Leo b 1974, Thomas b 1977); *Career* 2 Lt E Surrey Regt 1953–54; Harmsworth sr scholar Merton Coll Oxford 1957–58, lectr ChCh Oxford 1958–59, Andrew Bradley jr res fell Balliol Oxford 1959–60; tutorial fell: Keble Coll Oxford 1960–64, St John's Coll Oxford 1964–75; Merton prof of English literature Univ of Oxford 1975–2001; princ book reviewer Sunday Times 1977–, author of articles in Modern Language Review, Review of English Studies etc; chm of judges: Booker Prize 1982 and 2003, WHSmith Literary Prize 1996–2003, Man Booker Int Prize 2005; hon fell: St John's Coll Oxford 1991, Balliol Coll Oxford 1992; FRSL, FBA 1996; *Books* The Poems of John Milton (ed with Alastair Fowler, 1968, 2 edn 1997), Milton (1969), The Private Memoirs and Confessions of a Justified Sinner (ed, 1970), The Violent Effigy: a Study of Dickens' Imagination (1973, 2 edn 1991), Thackeray: Prodigal Genius (1977), John Donne: Life, Mind and Art (1981, 2 edn 1990), Original Copy: Selected Reviews and Journalism 1969–1986 (1987), The Faber Book of Reportage (ed, 1987), The Intellectuals and the Masses (1992), The Faber Book of Science (ed, 1995), The Faber Book of Utopias (ed, 1999), Pure Pleasure: A Guide to the 20th Century's Most Enjoyable Books (2000), What Good are the Arts? (2005), William Golding: The Man Who Wrote Lord of the Flies A Life (2009, James Tait Black Meml Prize 2010), The Unexpected Professor: An Oxford Life in Books (2014); *Recreations* swimming, gardening, beekeeping; *Style*— Prof John Carey, FBA; ✉ Brasenose Cottage, Lyneham, Oxfordshire OX7 6QL; 57 Stapleton Road, Headington, Oxford OX3 7LX (☎ 01865 764304); Merton College, Oxford OX1 4JD (☎ 01865 281266)

CAREY, Peter Philip; s of Percival Stanley Carey (d 1984), and Helen Jean Carey (d 1991); *b* 7 May 1943; *Educ* Geelong GS Aust; *m* 1 (m dis), Leigh Weetman; m 2, 16 March 1985 (m dis 2005), Alison Margaret, da of Stanley Newnham Summers (d 1987); 2 s (Sam Summers Carey b 1986, Charley Carey Summers b 1990); m 3, 20 Nov 2007, Frances Coady; *Career* writer; teacher Princeton and NY Univs, exec dir MFA in Creative Writing Hunter Coll New York 2003–; Hon DLitt Univ of Queensland 1989, Hon DHL New Sch NY 1998, Hon DLitt Monash Univ 2000; memb American Acad of Arts and Letters 2016; FRSL; Order of Australia 2012; *Awards* NSW Premier Award for Lit 1979 and 1980, Miles Franklin Award 1980, 1989 and 1998, Nat Book Cncl Award 1980 and 1985, Victorian Premier Award 1985, Age Book of the Year Award 1985, Booker Prize 1988 and 2001, Cwlth Prize 1998 and 2001; *Books* The Fat Man in History (1979), Bliss (1980), Illywhacker (1985), Oscar and Lucinda (1988), The Tax Inspector (1991), The Unusual Life of Tristan Smith (1994), Jack Maggs (1997), True History of the Kelly Gang (2000), My Life as a Fake (2003), Wrong About Japan (2005), Theft: A Love Story (2006), His Illegal Self (2008), Parrot and Olivier in America (2010), The Chemistry of Tears (2012), Amnesia (2014); *Recreations* swimming, laughing; *Style*— Peter Carey, Esq; ✉ website www.petercareybooks.com

CAREY OF CLIFTON, Baron (Life Peer UK 2002), of Clifton in the City and County of Bristol; George Leonard Carey; PC (1991); s of George Thomas Carey, and Ruby Catherine, *née* Gurney; *b* 13 November 1935; *Educ* Bifrons Secdy Modern Sch, London Coll of Divinity, KCL (ALCD, BD, MTh, PhD); *m* 25 June 1960, Eileen Harmsworth, da of Douglas Cunningham Hood; 2 da (Hon Rachel Helen b 30 May 1963, Hon Elizabeth Ruth b 26 Oct 1971), 2 s (Hon Mark Jonathan b 28 Feb 1965, Hon Andrew Stephen b 18 Feb 1966); *Career* Nat Serv 1954–56, served Egypt, Shaibah Iraq; curate St Mary's Islington 1962–66; lectr: Oakhill Theol Coll London 1966–70, St John's Theol Coll Notts 1970–75; vicar St Nicholas's Church Durham 1975–82, princ Trinity Coll Bristol 1982–87; bishop of Bath and Wells 1987–91, archbishop of Canterbury 1991–2002; memb House of Lords 1991–; presentation fell KCL 1996; memb Cncl Bath Int Art Festival, patron and pres of many organizations; Freeman: City of Wells 1990, City of Canterbury 1992, City of London 1997; Hon DD: Univ of Kent, Univ of Durham, Univ of Bath, Univ of Nottingham, Open Univ, City Univ, Notre Dame Univ USA, Sewanee Univ USA, Southwest Univ USA; distinguished fell Library of Congress Washington DC; *Books* I Believe in Man (1975), God Incarnate (1976), The Great Acquittal (1980), The Church in The Market Place (1984), The Meeting of The Waters (1985), The Gate of Glory (1986, updated and reissued 1992), The Message of the Bible (1986), The Great God Robbery (1989), I Believe (1991), Sharing a Vision (1993), Spiritual Journey (1994), My Journey, Your Journey (1996), Canterbury Letters to the Future (1998), Jesus (2000), Know the Truth (autobiography, 2004); *Recreations* walking, reading, music, family life; *Style*— The Rt Rev and Rt Hon the Lord Carey of Clifton, PC

CAREY-ELMS, Marsha Marilyn; OBE (2012), JP (Brentford 1982); da of James Frederick Carey (d 1992), and Carolyn Mary, *née* Fordham (d 1989); *b* 11 June 1946; *Educ* Tottenham Co GS, Bedford Coll London (BA), Brunel Univ (PGCE), Univ of Reading (MA); *Children* 1 da (Lily Elizabeth Laura b 17 Nov 1975), 1 s (Edward James b 20 Nov 1979); *Career* teacher rising to dep head Featherstone HS 1969–89, dep head Magna Carta Sch Surrey 1989–93, head Kendrick Sch Reading 1993–, conslt head Ashmead Sch Reading 1997, exec headteacher Kendrick Fedn (Reading Girls' Sch and Kendrick Sch) 2007–12; pres Assoc of Maintained Girls' Schs (AMGS) 2003, memb SHA Exec 1995–99 (memb Cncl 2004–08), memb Bd of Tstees NFER 1995–2008, chair Berks Assoc of Secdy Heads 2009–12, day chair W London Magistrate Advsy Ctee 2012–; author of various SHA/ASCL pubns on equal opportunities and leadership; Sue Ryder Teacher of the Year Bucks, Berks and Oxon 2013; FRSA; *Recreations* art, antiques, food, family; *Clubs* Landsdowne, Phyllis Court Henley; *Style*— Mrs Marsha Carey-Elms, OBE; ✉ e-mail marshaelms@sky.com

CARINGTON, Hon Rupert Francis John; DL (Bucks 2005); s and h of 6 Baron Carrington, *qv*; *b* 2 December 1948; *Educ* Eton, Univ of Bristol; *m* 12 Sept 1989, Daniela, da of Flavio Diotallevi; 1 s (Robert b 7 Dec 1990), 2 da (Francesca b 24 July 1993, Isabella Iona b 19 May 1995); *Career* dir: Morgan Grenfell International 1983–87, Hartwell plc 1990–2000, JP Morgan Fleming Smaller Companies Investment Trust (formerly The Fleming Smaller Companies Investment Trust plc) 1990–2004, Morgan Shipley Ltd 2001–07, Sete Technical Services SA 2002–, Alger Associates Inc 2012–, Viridis Real Estate Services Ltd 2012–, Abdul Latif Jameel United Real Estate Instalment Co Ltd 2013–16, ret; chm: Korea Asia Fund Limited 1990–2000, Schroder Asia Pacific Fund plc 1995–2016 (ret), Schroder Emerging Countries Fund plc 1996–2003, Vietnam Infrastructure Ltd 2012–; memb Dubai UK Trade and Economic Ctee 1997–2005; chm: Bucks CLA 2002–05, Bucks Strategic Partnership 2002–08, Carington Estates Ltd 2004–; memb Cncl Univ of Buckingham 2003–06; High Sheriff Bucks 2002–03; *Clubs* White's, Pratt's; *Style*— The Hon Rupert Carington, DL; ✉ Manor Farm, Church End, Bledlow, Buckinghamshire HP27 9PD (☎ 01844 274461)

CARLAW, Jackson; MSP; *b* 12 April 1959; *Educ* Glasgow Acad; *Career* MSP (Cons): W of Scotland 2011–, Eastwood 2016–; dep ldr Scottish Cons Pty 2011–; *Style*— Jackson Carlaw, Esq, MSP; ✉ The Scottish Parliament, Edinburgh EH99 1SP

CARLILE OF BERRIEW, Baron (Life Peer UK 1999), of Berriew in the Co of Powys Alexander Charles (Alex) Carlile; CBE (2012), QC; *b* 12 February 1948, Ruabon, Derbyshire; *Educ* Epsom Coll Surrey, KCL (LLB), Inns of Court Sch of Law; *m* 1, 1968 (m dis), Frances, da of Michael Soley; 3 da; m 2, 2007, Alison Levitt, QC, da of David Levitt, OBE, FRIBA, and Her Hon Judge Christian Bevington; *Career* Parly candidate (Lib) Flintshire E Feb 1974 and 1979, chm Welsh Lib Pty 1980–82, MP (Lib then Lib Dem) Montgomery 1983–97, former ldr Welsh Lib Dems and spokesman on Welsh Affrs, Justice and Home Affairs; a recorder of the Crown Court, former hon recorder of the City of Hereford, bencher Gray's Inn, former dep judge of the High Court; Ind Reviewer of Terrorism Legislation 2001–11; pres Howard League for Penal Reform 2008–12, pt/t chm Competition Appeal Tbnl 2005–13; chm Lloyds Enforcement Bd; dep chief steward Hereford 2009–; fell Industry and Parliament Tst; tstee White Ensign Assoc; Hon LLD: Univ of S Wales, Manchester Met Univ, Hungarian Inst of Criminology; FKC; *Publications* author of numerous reports on terrorism and on penal policy; *Recreations* politics, football; *Clubs* Athenaeum; *Style*— The Lord Carlile of Berriew, CBE, QC; ✉ House of Lords, London SW1A 1PW (☎ 020 7219 3000, fax 020 7404 1405, e-mail carlilea@parliament.uk)

CARLISLE, Anthony Edwin Charles Glen; s of George Geddes Glen Carlisle (d 1980), and Dorothy Louise, *née* Pickering; *b* 10 March 1947; *Educ* Charterhouse, Univ of Sussex (BA); *m* Nancy Susan, *née* Hayward; *Career* Lintas Advertising 1968–70; Dewe Rogerson Ltd: joined 1970, chief exec and dep chm 1986–95, exec chm 1995–98; exec dir Incepta Gp plc (and dir Citigate Dewe Rogerson) 1998–; non-exec dir CSR plc 2005–; Freeman City of London, Liveryman Worshipful Co of Glovers; MIPA, memb PRCA; *Recreations* travel, books, music, wine; *Style*— Anthony Carlisle, Esq

CARLISLE, 13 Earl of (E 1661); George William Beaumont Howard; Master of Ruthven; also Viscount Howard of Morpeth, Baron Dacre of Gillesland (both E 1661) and 13 Lord Ruthven of Freeland (S 1651); s of 12 Earl of Carlisle, MC, DL (d 1994), and Hon Ela Hilda Aline Beaumont (d 2002), da of 2 Viscount Allendale, KG, CB, CBE, MC; *b* 15 February 1949; *Educ* Eton, Balliol Coll Oxford (MA); *Heir* bro, Hon Philip Howard; *Career* joined 9/12 Royal Lancers 1967, Lt 1970, Capt 1974, Maj (Prince of Wales, Royal Armoured Corps) 1981–87; Parly candidate (Lib) Easington Co Durham 1987, Euro Parly candidate Northumbria 1989, Parly candidate (Lib Dem) Leeds W 1992; sec British-Estonian All-Pty Parly Gp 1997–, memb House of Lords All-Pty Defence Gp; Order of Marjamaa (1 class) Estonia 1998; *Clubs* Beefsteak; *Style*— The Rt Hon the Earl of Carlisle

CARLISLE, Hugh Bernard Harwood; QC (1978); s of William Harwood Carlisle, FRCS, FRCOG (d 1979), and Joyce Carlisle; *b* 14 March 1937; *Educ* Oundle, Downing Coll Cambridge (MA); *m* 1964, Veronica Marjorie, da of George Arthur Worth, MBE, DL (d 1994), of Manton, Rutland; 1 s, 1 da; *Career* Nat Serv 2 Lt RA; called to the Bar Middle Temple 1961 (bencher 1985), jr treasy counsel (personal injuries cases) 1975–78, inspr Dept of Trade Inquiry into Bryanston Finance Ltd 1978–87, memb Criminal Injuries Bd 1982–2000, recorder of the Crown Court 1983–2002, dep high court judge 1984–2002, inspr Dept of Trade Inquiry into Milbury plc 1985–87, head of chambers 1988–2001, judge Upper Tbnl 2009–12; pres Tport Tnbl 1997–2009; *Recreations* fly-fishing, croquet;

Clubs Garrick, Hurlingham (chm 1982–85); *Style*— Hugh Carlisle Esq, QC; ✉ Temple Garden Chambers, 1 Harcourt Buildings, Temple, London EC4Y 9DA (✆ 020 7583 1315, fax 020 7353 3969)

CARLISLE, Bishop of 2009–; Rt Rev James William Scobie Newcome; DL (Cumbria); *b* 24 July 1953, Aldershot; *Educ* Marlborough (exhibitioner), Trinity Coll Oxford (MA, exhibitioner, Laurence Binyon prize), Selwyn Coll Cambridge (MA, scholar), Ridley Hall Cambridge; *m* Sept 1977, Alison Margaret; 2 s (Edward John b 1984, Alexander Charles b 1988), 2 da (Clare Rosamonde b 1986, Anna Jane b 1991); *Career* ordained 1978; asst curate All Saints Leavesden 1978–82 (ATC chaplain), minister Bar Hill Church 1982–94, rural dean North Stowe Deanery 1993–94, residentiary canon Chester Cathedral 1994–2002, proctor in convocation Gen Synod 2000–02, bishop of Penrith 2002–09; tutor Ridley Hall Cambridge 1983–94, diocesan dir of ordinands and lay ministry advsr 1994–2000, dir adult educn and trg Chester Dio 1996–2002; chm Dio Bd for Ministry and Trg; Clerk of the Closet 2014–; pres Cncl St John's Coll Durham, lead bishop for URC, memb Sage Gp and Bishops' MDR Gp, pres Churches Together in Cumbria, nat chaplain Royal British Legion; chm NW bishops, lead Bishop on healthcare, chm Nat Stewardship Ctee, chair Rose Cncl Fndn; numerous broadcasting and speaking engagements, various articles and contributions to reviews; memb Soc for Study of Christian Ethics; *Recreations* squash (Trinity Oxford and Selwyn Cambridge 1st Fives), cross country running, hill walking, history of art, novels, films, cricket (St Albans, Ely and Chester Dio teams), restoring furniture; *Clubs* Athenaeum; *Style*— The Rt Rev the Bishop of Carlisle, DL; ✉ Bishop's House, Ambleside Road, Keswick, Cumbria CA12 4DD (e-mail bishop.carlisle@carlislediocese.org.uk)

CARLISLE, Sir Kenneth Melville; kt (1994); s of Maj Kenneth Ralph Malcolm (Peter) Carlisle, TD (d 1983), and Hon Elizabeth Mary McLaren (d 1991), er da of 2 Baron Aberconway, CBE; *b* 25 March 1941; *Educ* Harrow, Magdalen Coll Oxford; *m* July 1986, Carla, da of A W Heffner, of Maryland USA; 1 s (Sam Fenimore Cooper b 28 Jan 1989); *Career* called to the Bar 1965; with Brooke Bond Liebig 1966–74; farmer; MP (Cons) Lincoln 1979–97, an asst Govt whip 1987–88, a Lord Cmmr of the Treasy (Govt whip) 1988–90; Parly under sec: Miny of Defence 1990–92, Miny of Transport 1992–93; memb Public Accounts Ctee 1995; memb Cncl: RSPB 1985–87, RHS 1996–2006, Suffolk Wildlife Tst 2007–14; tstee World Land Tst 2009–15; *Recreations* gardening, wildlife and conservation; *Style*— Sir Kenneth Carlisle

CARLOWAY, Rt Hon Lord Colin John MacLean Sutherland; PC (2008); s of Eric Alexander Cruickshank Sutherland, and Mary, *née* Macaulay; *b* 20 May 1954; *Educ* Edinburgh Acad, Univ of Edinburgh (LLB); *m* 1988, Jane Alexander Turnbull; 2 s; *Career* admitted to Faculty of Advocates 1977, advocate depute 1986–89, QC (Scot) 1990, treas Faculty of Advocates 1994–2000, a senator of the Coll of Justice 2000–, Lord Justice Clerk and pres Second Div Court of Session 2012–16, Lord Justice Gen and Lord Pres Court of Session 2016–; *Clubs* Scottish Arts (Edinburgh); *Style*— The Rt Hon Lord Carloway; ✉ Supreme Courts, Parliament House, Edinburgh EH1 1RQ (✆ 0131 225 2595, fax 0131 225 8213)

CARLTON, Vivienne Margaret; da of John Carlton, and Phyllis Florence Kaye, *née* Minchin; *b* 28 September 1947; *Educ* Herts & Essex HS Bishop's Stortford, Trent Park Coll, Univ of London; *m* 1985 (m dis 2001), Julian Charles Bray, *qv*; 1 s (William Charles b 18 Aug 1989); *Career* account dir: Biss Lancaster plc 1980–82, Opus PR Ltd 1982–84; dir: Osca plc 1985–86, Leadenhall Associates Ltd 1986–91, NTN Television News Ltd 1988–90; princ Carlton Consulting 1991–; non-exec dir Queen Victoria Hosp NHS Tst 1999–2004; MIPR, FInstD (chm Central London IOD 1999–2004), MIMgt; *Recreations* theatre, interior design; *Style*— Ms Vivienne Carlton

CARLTON-PORTER, Robert William; s of Francis William Porter, of Derbys, and Cyrilla, *née* Carlton; *b* 29 November 1944; *Educ* St Helens Derby; *m* 9 Oct 1987, Angela, da of William Jenkins, of Hereford; 1 s (Alexander William b 8 Aug 1988); *Career* fin dir Hoechst UK Ltd 1973–83, fin dir English China Clays plc 1983–92, dir of a number of unlisted cos; non-exec dir: Newport Holdings plc (former chm), Rok plc (former chm), Michelmersh Brick Holdings plc, Hawtin plc (former chm); former chm Chartered Assoc of Corp Treasurers, former memb Stock Exchange Pre-emption Ctee; former govr and treas Kingswood Sch Bath; former external examiner Univ of Exeter; ACIB 1968, FCIM 1973, FIMgt 1976, FCT 1979 (fndn fell); *Recreations* antiques, philately, gardening, charity work; *Style*— Robert Carlton-Porter, Esq; ✉ 4 Laggan House, College Road, Bath BA1 5RY (✆ 01225 484220)

CARLUCCIO, Antonio Mario Gaetano; OBE (2006); s of Giovanni Carluccio (d 1978), and Maria, *née* Trivellone (d 1992); *b* 19 April 1937, Vietri Sul Mare, Italy; *Educ* Roland Matura Schule Vienna; *m* 22 Dec 1981 (m dis 2009), Priscilla Marion, da of Gerard Rupert Conran; *Career* restaurateur, food writer and broadcaster; former corr Gazzetta del Popolo and La Stampa Turin, resident in Germany 1963–75, wine merchant England 1975–81; restaurateur Neal Street Restaurant 1981–2007, proprietor (with wife) Carluccio's food retailers 1992– (conslt 2008–); memb Guild of Food Writers; hon assoc Altagamma Int Hon Cncl 2005; Commendatore dell'Ordine al Merito della Repubblica Italiana 1998; *Television* Antonio Carluccio's Italian Feasts (six part series, BBC 2, winner World Food Media Award 1997) 1996, Antonio Carluccio's Southern Italian Feast (six part series, BBC 2) 1998, Two Greedy Italians 2011 and 2012, Masterchef Australia, judge Masterchef UK Final 2014, Carluccio's 6 Seasons (SBS Australia) 2015; co-winner James Beard Award for Best National Television Food Journalism Program USA 1999; *Books* An Invitation to Italian Cooking (1986), A Passion for Mushrooms (1989), A Passion for Pasta (1993), Antonio Carluccio's Italian Food (book of TV series, 1996, winner BBC Good Food Best Book Award 1997), Carluccio's Complete Italian Feast (1997), Carluccio's Complete Italian Food (1997), Southern Italian Feast (1998), Antonio Carluccio's Vegetables (2000), Antonio Carluccio Goes Wild (2001), An Invitiation to Italian Cooking (2002), Antonio Carluccio's Complete Mushroom Book (2003), Antonio Carluccio's Italia (2005), Carluccio's Complete A-Z of Italian Food (2007), Antonio Carluccio's Simple Cooking (2009), My Kitchen Table – Antonio Carluccio: 100 Pasta Recipes (2011), Two Greedy Italians (with Gennaro Contaldo, 2011), Antonio Carluccio: The Collection (2012), A Recipe For Life (2012), Two Greedy Italians Eat Italy (with Gennaro Contaldo, 2012), Antonio Carluccio's Pasta (2014, 2 edn 2016); DVDs incl: Antonio Carluccio's Italian Feast (2010), Carluccio's 6 Seasons (2015); *Style*— Comm Antonio Carluccio, OBE

CARLYLE, Robert; OBE; *b* 14 April 1961, Glasgow; *Educ* Glasgow Arts Centre; *m* 28 Dec 1997, Anastasia Shirley; 3 c; *Career* actor; fndr memb Rain Dog Theatre Co; *Television* incl: The Part of Valour 1981, The Bill 1984, Cracker 1993, Hamish Macbeth 1995, Looking After Jo Jo 1998, Hitler: The Rise of Evil 2003, Gunpowder, Treason & Plot 2003, Human Trafficking 2005, Born Equal 2006, The Last Enemy 2008, 24: Redemption 2008, Stargate Universe 2009–, Once Upon a Time 2011–16; *Films* Silent Scream 1990, Riff-Raff 1990, Safe 1993, Being Human 1993, Priest 1994, Go Now 1995, Trainspotting 1996, Carla's Song 1996, Face 1997, The Full Monty 1997, Ravenous 1999, Angela's Ashes 1999, Plunkett & Macleane 1999, The World is Not Enough 1999, The Beach 2000, To End All Wars 2000, The 51st State 2000, Once Upon a Time in the Midlands 2001, Black and White 2001, Dead Fish 2003, Marilyn Hotchkiss' Dance School 2004, In Like Flynn 2004, Eragon 2006, Flood 2007, 28 Weeks Later 2007, I Know You Know 2008, Stone of Destiny 2008, The Tournament 2009, California Solo 2012, Barney Thomson 2015; *Theatre* Othello (TAG), Cuttin' a Rug (Dundee), To Mean City (7:84), City (TAG), Nae Problem (7:84), Dead Dad Dog (Traverse Theatre); *Style*— Robert Carlyle, Esq, OBE; ✉ c/o Hamilton Hodell, 20 Golden Square, London W1F 9JL (✆ 020 7636 1221, fax 020 7636 1226, website www.hamiltonhodell.co.uk)

CARMAN, Charlotte Nina Hermione (Charlie); da of George Carman (d 2001), and Jacqueline Storm, *née* Wild (d 2001); *b* 3 March 1970; *Educ* James Allen's Girls' Sch, Pembroke Coll Cambridge (MA); *Career* Longman Publishers: sales and mktg co-ordinator 1991–92, ed 1992–94, commissioning ed 1994–95; Boxtree: commissioning ed 1995–97, sr ed 1997–98; ed dir Channel 4 Books 1998–2000, ed dir FilmFour Books 1999–2000, publisher Channel 4 and FilmFour Books 2000–, memb Mgmnt Bd Pan Macmillan Gp; *Books* The FilmFour Book of Film Quotes (2000); *Clubs* Soho House; *Style*— Ms Charlie Carman; ✉ Macmillan, 20 New Wharf Road, London N1 9RR (✆ 020 7014 6000, fax 020 7014 6023)

CARMICHAEL, Rt Hon Alexander Morrison (Alistair); MP, PC (2013); s of Alexander Calder Carmichael, and Mina Neil, *née* McKay; *b* 15 July 1965; *Educ* Islay HS, Univ of Aberdeen (LLB, DipLP); *m* 19 Sept 1987 Kathryn Jane, da of Prof J Frederick Eastham; 2 s (Alexander Frederick Bethune b 31 March 1997, Simon Robin Calder 23 March 2001); *Career* hotel mangr 1984–89, dep procurator fiscal 1993–96, slr private practice 1996–2001; MP (Lib Dem) Orkney and Shetland 2001–; comptroller of HM Household (dep chief whip) 2010–13, sec of state for Scotland 2013–15; elder Church of Scot; memb Law Soc of Scot 1995–; *Recreations* music, theatre; *Style*— The Rt Hon Alistair Carmichael, MP; ✉ Shetland Constituency Office, 171 Commercial Street, Lerwick, Shetland ZE1 0HX (✆ 01595 690044); Orkney Constituency Office, 31 Broad Street, Kirkwall, Orkney KW15 1DH (✆ 01856 876541)

CARMICHAEL, Andrew James; s of James Horsfall Elliott Carmichael, MD, FRCR, DMRD, of Liverpool, and late Maureen Catherine Carmichael, JP, *née* McGowan; *b* 8 August 1957; *Educ* St Edward's Coll Liverpool, Downing Coll Cambridge (MA); *Career* Linklaters: articled clerk 1979–81, slr 1981, ptnr 1987–; *Recreations* art, theatre; *Style*— Andrew Carmichael, Esq; ✉ Linklaters, One Silk Street, London EC2Y 8HQ (✆ 020 7456 2000, fax 020 7456 2222)

CARMICHAEL, Keith Stanley; CBE (1981); s of Stanley Carmichael (d 1949), of Bristol, and Ruby Dorothy, *née* Fox (d 1980); *b* 5 October 1929; *Educ* Charlton House Sch, Bristol GS; *m* 1958, Cynthia Mary, da of John David Robert Jones (d 1971); 1 s (Richard John Carmichael b 1968); *Career* qualified CA 1951, ptnr Wilson Bigg and Co 1957–69; dir: H Foulks Lynch & Co Ltd 1957–69, Radio Rentals Ltd 1967–69; sole practitioner 1968–81 and 1990–, managing ptnr Longcrofts 1981–90; memb Monopolies and Mergers Cmmn 1983–92, Lloyd's underwriter 1979–90; memb Editorial Bd Simons Taxes 1970–82; pres Hertsmere Cons Assoc until 2015; chm then pres Bd of Govrs Royal Masonic Sch for Girls 1984–2010; tstee RMIG Endowment Tst 1984–2010; fndr memb Soc of Share and Business Valuers; pres Gen Bd Grand Lodge of Mark Masons in England and Wales 1991–2006 (Holder of Service to Mark Masonic Medal); memb Ct of Assts Worshipful Co of Chartered Accountants until 1996; FCA, FInstD, FTII, TEP, FRICS 2010–15; CStJ 2001; *Books* Spicer and Peglers Income Tax (1965), Ranking Spicer and Peglers Executorship Law and Accounts (ed, 1965–87), Corporation Tax (1966), Capital Gains Tax (1966), Taxation of Lloyd's Underwriters (with P Wolstenholme, 1988), Strategic Tax Planning (contrib, 1991); *Recreations* gardening, reading, golf; *Clubs* Carlton (dep chm 1989–95, tstee 1999–), MCC, Lord's Taverners; *Style*— Keith Carmichael, Esq, CBE; ✉ 117 Newberries Avenue, Radlett, Hertfordshire WD7 7EN (✆ 01923 855098, fax 01923 855654); Flat 1, Princess Court, Bryanston Place, London W1H 7FP (✆ 020 7258 1577, fax 020 7258 1578)

CARMICHAEL, (William) Neil; MP; s of Thomas Lynn Bell Carmichael (d 1996), and Eleanor Carmichael; *b* 15 April 1961, Stannington, Northumberland; *Educ* St Peter's Sch York, Univ of Nottingham (BA); *m* June 1995, Laurence Jagodzinski; 1 s (James b 16 Sept 1996), 2 da (Alicia, Rebecca b 22 Feb 1998 (twins)); *Career* cncllr Northumberland CC 1989–93, MP (Cons) Stroud 2010–, chair Educn Select Ctee 2015–; took Antarctic Act through Parliament 2013, chair Cons Europe Gp; memb RIIA 1992; *Recreations* gardening, golf, motorsport, reading, travel, classic tractors; *Style*— Neil Carmichael, Esq, MP; ✉ Southveiw, Park End, Stroud GL5 4BB (✆ 01453 299096); House of Commons, London SW1A 0AA (e-mail neil.carmichael.mp@parliament.uk, Twitter @Stroud_Neil)

CARNAC; *see:* Rivett-Carnac

CARNALL, Dame Ruth; DBE (2011, CBE 2004); *Career* began career as fin dir and chief exec of various NHS orgns 1976, dir Departmental Change Prog Dept of Health 2003–04, freelance conslt 2004–06, chief exec London NHS 2007– (interim chief exec 2006); *Style*— Dame Ruth Carnall, DBE; ✉ NHS London, Southside, 105 Victoria Street, London SW1E 6QT

CARNARVON, 8 Earl of (GB 1793); George (Geordie) Reginald Oliver Molyneux Herbert; s of 7 Earl of Carnarvon (d 2001); *b* 10 November 1956, London; *Educ* Eton, St John's Coll Oxford (BA); *m* 1, 16 Dec 1989 (m dis 1997), Jayne M, eldest da of K A Wilby, of Cheshire, and Princess Frances Colonna di Stigliano, of Ashford, Co Wicklow; 1 da (Lady Saoirse b 2 June 1991), 1 s (George, Lord Porchester b 13 Oct 1992); m 2, 18 Feb 1999, Fiona Aitken, da of Ronnie Aitken (decd) and Frances Aitken (decd); 1 s (Hon Edward b 10 Oct 1999); *Heir* s, Lord Porchester; *Career* a page of honour to HM The Queen 1969–73; PA to Hon Peter Morrison, MP 1986–87, computer conslt/estate mgmnt 1976–92; founder shareholder: Telecom Express Ltd 1992–96, Digital People Ltd 1996–98; former dir Azur plc; patron Greenham Common Tst 1994–, ptnr Highclere Enterprises LLP 2003–, chm Corn Exchange Newbury Tst 2009–11, patron Langa Langa Scholarship Fund 2009; regnl chm (Thames & Chilterns) Historic Houses Assoc 2010–; pres NW Hants Cons Assoc 2012–; *Recreations* riding, shooting, skiing, cricket, stalking and hill walking, horse racing and breeding, art, gardening, farming and conservation; *Clubs* White's; *Style*— The Rt Hon the Earl of Carnarvon; ✉ e-mail lordcarnarvon@highclerecastle.co.uk

CARNE, Dr Christopher Alan; s of Colin Ewing Carne, of London, and Philippa, *née* Trouton; *b* 31 October 1953; *Educ* Bryanston, Middx Hosp Med Sch (MB BS), Univ of London (MD), Univ of Cambridge (MA); *m* 1992, Julia Warnes; 1 s (Daniel b 1993), 1 da (Tulla b 2002); *Career* lectr genito-urinary med Middx Hosp Medical Sch 1984–87, conslt genito-urinary med Addenbrooke's Hosp Cambridge 1987–, assoc lectr Faculty Clinical Med Cambridge 1988–; former asst ed Genito-Urinary Medicine, former assoc ed Sexually Transmitted Infections; chm British Cooperative Clinical Gp 1999–2006 (sec 1993–99), chair Nat Audit Gp Br Assoc for Sexual Health and HIV (BASHH) 2008–10 (hon sec 2004–08, vice-chair 2010–); memb: STD Advsy Gp HEA 1990–92, Working Pty on HIV/AIDS Funding Dept of Health 1991, HIV and AIDS Clinical Trials Working Pty MRC 1991–94, Cncl MSSVD 1992–95 and 1999–2002, Working Pty on Koerner Coding in Genito-urinary Med Dept of Health 1994, Steering Gp UK Register of HIV Seroconverters 1994–2006, Specialist Advsy Ctee in Genito-urinary Med 1998–2002, Jt Specialty Ctee in Genito-urinary Med RCP 2007–10; memb BMA 1978, MSSVD 1983; FRCP; *Books* Aids (1987, 3 edn 1989); *Recreations* walking, bridge, playing clarinet; *Style*— Dr Christopher Carne; ✉ Clinic 1A, Addenbrooke's Hospital, Hills Road, Cambridge CB2 2QQ (✆ 01223 217774, fax 01223 217807, e-mail christopher.carne@addenbrookes.nhs.uk)

CARNE, Mark; *Educ* Univ of Exeter; *Career* former exec vice-pres ME and N Africa Royal Dutch Shell, chief exec Network Rail 2014–; ind govr Falmouth Univ; FIMechE; *Style*— Mark Carne, Esq; ✉ Network Rail, Waterloo General Offices, London SE1 8SW

CARNEGIE, Phillip; s of James Carnegie, and Kirsty, *née* Rose; *b* 28 November 1972, Aberdeen; *m* 22 Oct 2010, Lesley, *née* Livingston; 2 da (Laura b 24 July 1988, Emma b 23 Oct 1992); *Career* formerly worked in Germany: Villa Hammerschmide, Landhaus

Stricker, Söl'ring-Hof; Inverlochy Castle Hotel: sous chef 2003–09, head chef 2009– (Michelin star 2009–, 3 AA Red Rosettes); involved with Great British Chefs; *Style*— Phillip Carnegie, Esq; ✉ Inverlochy Castle Hotel, Torlundy, Fort William PH33 6SN

CARNEGY, Christopher Roy; s of Julian Roy Carnegy, of New Malden, Surrey, and Vivien, *née* Kay-Menzies; *b* 9 December 1961; *Educ* Kingston GS, Univ of Southampton; *Career* presenter Radio Victory Portsmouth 1984–86, prog controller Ocean Sound Southampton 1986–92, md Spire FM Salisbury 1992–96, chief exec The Local Radio Co 1996–2000, md SouthCity FM Southampton 2000–04, broadcaster BBC World Service 2002–05, mangr Express FM 2005–09, managing ed BBC Radio Solent 2009–13, ed BBC Local TV 2013–; sometime freelance broadcaster LBC, IRN and TVS; nominated for Best Local Radio Prog Sony Radio Awards 1986, winner Sony Radio Award Best Local Radio Station 1994, winner One World Broadcasting Award 1999, winner Andrew Cross Awards 1999; UK rep Govt of Tristan da Cunha 2015–; FRSA; *Recreations* boating, flying; *Clubs* Royal Southampton Yacht; *Style*— Christopher Carnegy, Esq; ✉ Broadcasting House, Havelock Road, Southampton SO14 7PW (☎ 02380 631311, e-mail chris.carnegy@bbc.co.uk)

CARNEGY, Dr Patrick Charles; *see:* Northesk, 15 Earl of

CARNOCK, 5 Baron (UK 1916); Adam Nicolson; s of Nigel Nicolson; *b* 12 September 1957; *Educ* Eton, Magdalene Coll Cambridge; *m* 1, 1982 (m dis 1992), Olivia Fane; 3 s; m 2, 1992, Sarah Raven; 2 da; *Career* writer; former journalist and columnist Sunday Times, Sunday Telegraph and Daily Telegraph; *Television* incl: Atlantic Britain (Channel 4) 2004, Homer's Landscapes (BBC Radio 3) 2008, Sissinghurst (BBC 4) 2009, When God Spoke English: The Making of the King James Bible (BBC 4) 2011, The Century That Wrote Itself (BBC 4) 2013, Britain's Whale Hunters (BBC 4), 2014; *Radio* incl: Homer's Landscapes (BBC Radio 3) 2008, A Cretan Spring (with Sarah Raven, BBC Radio 3) 2009, Dark Arcadias (BBC Radio 3) 2011; FRSL 2005; *Books* The National Trust Book of Long Walks (1981), Long Walks in France (1983), Frontiers (1985, Somerset Maugham Award), Wetland (1987, PBFA Topography Prize), Two Roads to Dodge City (jtly, 1988), Prospects of England (1990), Restoration: Rebuilding of Windsor Castle (1997), Regeneration: The Story of the Dome (1999), Perch Hill: A New Life (2000), Mrs Kipling (2001), Sea Room (2001), Power and Glory (2003, RSL W H Heinemann Prize), Seamanship (2004), Men of Honour: Trafalgar and the Making of the English Hero (2005), Earls of Paradise (2008), Sissinghurst: An Unfinished History (2008), Arcadia: The Dream of Perfection in Renaissance England (revised edn of Earls of Paradise, 2009), The Smell of Summer Grass (updated edn of Perch Hill, 2011), The Gentry: Stories of the English (2011), The Mighty Dead: Why Homer Matters (2014); *Recreations* walking, sailing; *Style*— Adam Nicolson; ✉ Perch Hill Farm, Brightling, Robertsbridge, East Sussex TN32 5HP (e-mail adam@shiantisles.net)

CARNWATH, Dame Alison Jane; DBE (2014); *Educ* Howells Sch Denbigh, Univ of Reading (BA), Univ of Munich; *Career* CA; KPMG 1975–80, Lloyds Bank International 1980–83, J Henry Schroder & Co 1983–93, ptnr Phoenix Securities 1993–97, md Donaldson Lufkin Jenrette 1997–2000; chm: Vitec Gp plc 1999–2004, Mgmnt Bd Livingbridge Equity Ptnrs LLP 2005–; ind chm MF Global 2007–10; non-exec dir: Dwr Cymru 2001–07, Man Gp plc 2001–13, Friends Provident plc 2002–07, Gallaher Gp plc 2003–07, Land Securities plc 2004– (chm 2008–), Paccar Inc 2005–, Zurich Insurance Gp 2012–; dir Barclays Bank plc 2010–12, dir BASF (SE) 2014–; memb Advsy Bd Xfi Centre for Finance and Investment Univ of Exeter 2004–; Hon LLD Univ of Reading 2010, Univ of Exeter 2015; ACA 1980, FRSA 1989; *Recreations* skiing, music; *Style*— Dame Alison Carnwath, DBE; ✉ The Old Dairy, Sidbury, East Devon EX10 0QR

CARNWATH, Francis Anthony Armstrong; CBE (1997); s of Sir Andrew Hunter Carnwath, KCVO, DL (d 1995), and Kathleen Marianne, *née* Armstrong (d 1968); bro of Rt Hon Lord Justice Carnwath, CVO, *qv*; *b* 26 May 1940; *Educ* Eton (Oppidan scholar), Trinity Coll Cambridge; *m* 1 March 1975 (sep), Penelope Clare, da of Sir Charles Henry Rose, 3 Bt (d 1965); 2 da (Flora Helen b 1976, Catriona Rose b 1978 d 1985), 1 s (Alexander Patrick b 1980); *Career* dir Baring Bros and Co Ltd 1979–89, chm Ravensbourne Registration Services Ltd 1981–89, dep dir The Tate Gallery 1990–94, advsr National Heritage Memorial Fund 1995–97 (actg dir 1995), chief exec Greenwich Fndn for the Royal Naval Coll 1997–2002; dir Foreign Anglican Church and Educational Assoc Ltd 1973–96 (co sec 1973–85); tstee and treas Shelter Nat Campaign for the Homeless 1968–76 (dep chm 1973–76); treas: VSO 1979–84, Friends of Tate Gallery 1985–90; tstee: Phillimore Estates 1982–, Whitechapel Art Gallery 1994–2000, Musgrave-Kinley Outsider Arts Tst 1994–2011 (chm 1999–2011), Royal Armouries 2000–07; chm: Henley Soc (Civic Amenity Tst Soc) 1984–88, Spitalfields Historic Bldg Tst 1984–2000, Commemorative Plaques Panel English Heritage 1995–2002, Thames 21 2003–, Yorkshire Sculpture Park 2004–12, Nat Tst Architectural Panel 2004–10; memb: London Advsy Ctee English Heritage 1990–99, Bd Spitalfields Festival 2002–12; Master Worshipful Co of Musicians 1995–96; Hon FTCL 2002, Hon RCM 2004; *Recreations* music, the arts, gardening, walking; *Clubs* Garrick, Beefsteak; *Style*— Francis Carnwath, Esq, CBE; ✉ 26 Lansdowne Gardens, London SW8 2EG (☎ 020 7627 2158)

CARNWATH OF NOTTING HILL, Lord, of Notting Hill in the London Borough of Kensington and Chelsea; Rt Hon Sir Robert John Anderson Carnwath; kt (1994), CVO (1995), PC (2002); s of Sir Andrew Hunter Carnwath, KCVO, DL (d 1995), and Kathleen Marianne, *née* Armstrong (d 1968); bro of Francis Carnwath, *qv*; *b* 15 March 1945; *Educ* Eton, Trinity Coll Cambridge (MA, LLB); *m* 18 May 1974, Bambina, da of G D'Adda, of Bergamo, Italy; *Career* called to the Bar 1969; jr counsel to Revenue 1980–85, QC 1985–94, attorney-gen to HRH The Prince of Wales 1988–94, judge of the High Court of Justice (Chancery Div) 1994–2002, a Lord Justice of Appeal 2002–12, Sr Pres of Tbnls 2007–12 (sr pres designate 2004–07), a Justice of the Supreme Court 2012–; chm Law Cmmn 1999–2002; author of various legal pubns; chm Britten-Pears Fndn 2001–09; Freeman Worshipful Co of Musicians; hon fell Trinity Coll Cambridge 2013–; Hon FRAM 1994; *Recreations* viola, singing, tennis, golf; *Style*— The Rt Hon Lord Carnwath of Notting Hill, CVO; ✉ Supreme Court, Parliament Square, London SW1P 3BD

CARPANINI, Prof David Lawrence; s of Lorenzo Carpanini (d 2004), and Gwenllian Carpanini (d 1990); *b* 22 October 1946; *Educ* Glan Afan GS Port Talbot, Gloucestershire Coll of Art and Design (DipAD), RCA (MA), Univ of Reading (Art Teacher's Cert); *m* 1972, Jane Carpanini, *qv*; 1 s (Noel Dominic b 22 Aug 1977); *Career* artist and teacher; dir of art Kingham Hill Sch 1972–79, dir of art Oundle Sch 1979–86, sr lectr in art and design W Midlands Coll of HE 1986–89, head Dept of Art and Design Sch of Educn Univ of Wolverhampton (formerly Wolverhampton Poly) 1989–2000, prof of art Univ of Wolverhampton 1992–2000; pres Royal Soc of Painter-Printmakers 1995–2003, vice-pres Royal Soc of Br Artists 1982–86; subject of documentaries: Every One a Special Kind of Artist (Channel 4) 1984, David Carpanini (HTV) 1987, Elinor-Glamorgan (HTV) 1988, Zoom pm (WDR Cologne) 1989, Artist of Wales (Lifestyle Prodns Ltd (Cable TV)) 1991, A Word In Your Eye (HTV) 1997, A Visit to the Eisteddfod (HTV) 1998, Visions of the Valleys (BBC 4) 2015; de Lazlo Medal RBA 1980; Hon RWS 1996, Hon RBSA 2002; RBA 1976, RWA 1977, RE 1979, NEAC 1983, RCA 1992; *Solo Exhibitions* incl: Paintings, Etchings, Drawings (John Hansard Gallery Univ of Southampton) 1972, Paintings and Drawings at the John Nevill Gallery 1973, Paintings (Bristol Arts Centre) 1975, Etchings (The Arts Club London) 1982, Paintings and Drawings (Tegfryn Gallery) 1982, Etchings (Park Gallery Cheltenham) 1982, Paintings and Etchings (Ceri Richards Gallery Taliesin Art Centre UC Swansea) 1983, Paintings and Etchings (Business Art Galleries at the Royal Acad) 1984, permanent display of combined GLC and ASTMS (now MSF) collection of David Carpanini works at MSF HQ London and mgmnt coll Bishop's Stortford 1984–, Paintings and Etchings (East Gate Gallery Warwick) 1986, Paintings and Etchings (Mostyn Gallery Llandudno) 1988, Paintings and Etchings (Rhondda Heritage Park) 1989, Paintings 1968–88 (Walsall Museum and Art Gallery) 1989, David Carpanini Paintings and Prints (Attic Gallery Swansea) 1994 and 1998, The Royal Cambrian Acad Conwy 1998, 'Welsh Impressions' Etchings (St David's Hall Cardiff) 1999, New Drawings and Etchings (Taliesin Art Centre) 1999, Etchings and Drawings (Pam Schomberg Gallery) 2000, Paintings and Prints (Attic Gallery Swansea) 2001, Paintings, Etchings, Drawings (Attic Gallery Swansea) 2002, New Etchings (APW Gallery Melbourne) 2004, Attic Gallery Swansea 2005, Recent Paintings, Drawings and Etchings (Attic Gallery Swansea) 2008, Recent Etchings (St David's Hall Cardiff) 2009, Etchings (Oriel Plas Glyn-y-Weddw Gallery Llanbedrog, Rhondda Heritage Park Trehafod and Pontardawe Arts Centre) 2010, New Paintings, Drawings and Etchings (Attic Gallery Swansea) 2011, David L Carpanini, A Painter Printmaker and His World (retrospective 1964–2014, Royal Leamington Spa Art Gallery and Museum) 2014, New Paintings, Etchings and Drawings (Attic Gallery Swansea) 2014, The Kyffin Collection and Other Drawings by David Carpanini (Attic Gallery Swansea) 2014; *Two Person Exhibitions* with Jane Carpanini: Yarrow Gallery Oundle 1979, David and Jane Carpanini Paintings 1968–80 (Welsh Arts Council Exhbn) 1980, Paintings, Etchings and Watercolours (Queen Elizabeth Theatre Gallery Oakham) 1987, Paintings, Etchings and Drawings (Albany Gallery Cardiff) 1991, Rhondda Heritage Park Gallery 1994; also Paintings and Etchings with Richard Bawden RE (Royal Exchange Theatre Gallery Manchester) 1993, Print Noir with Peter Freeth and John Duffin (Bankside Gallery London) 2001; *Group Exhibitions* incl: Royal Acad Summer Exhbn 1973–, Royal W of England Acad Annual Exhbn 1973–, Royal Soc of Br Artists Annual Exhbn 1975–, Industrial Soc exhbn London 1974, The Artist in Society (Whitechapel Gallery London and Ulster Museum Belfast) 1978, Twelve Regular RA Exhibitors (Patricia Wells Gallery) 1979, Royal Soc of Painter-Etchers and Engravers Annual Exhbn 1979–, Six Welsh Artists: A View of Wales (Ceri Richards Gallery Swansea as part of National Eisteddfod) 1982, NEAC Annual Exhbn 1983–, Tradition and Innovation in Printmaking Today (national touring) 1985–86, Int Contemporary Art Fair (Olympia and Bath, with Bankside Gallery) 1985–, Contemporary Printmakers (Cadogan Fine Arts London) 1986–, Glynn Vivian Art Gallery Swansea 1986, Reflections of Summer (Bankside Gallery London) 1987, Contemporary Art Soc for Wales Collection (National Museum of Wales Cardiff) 1987, The Face of Wales (seven artists, tour of Wales) 1987–88, 20th Century Br Art Fair (with Fosse Gallery) 1988, Bristol Open Printmaking Exhbn (Royal W of England Acad) 1988, various exhbns of gallery artists Fosse Gallery (John Lindsey Fine Art) 1988–, British Printmaking Today (Br Cncl touring former Soviet Union) 1989–91, Wales Art Fair (Cardiff, with Albany Gallery) 1990 and (also with Attic Gallery) 1991, Art 90 Fair (Olympia, with Fosse Gallery) 1990, Albany Gallery 25th Anniversary Exhbn of Gallery Artists 1990, Past and Present RAs and RA Exhibitors (John Noott 20th Century Broadway) 1991, Welsh Coalmining – The End of an Era (New Gallery Swansea as part of Swansea Festival) 1991, Invited Members of the RE and RWS (Gorstella Gallery Chester) 1991, The NEAC in Wales (Albany Gallery Cardiff) 1992, Invited Members of the RE (Shell International London) 1992, RWS Open Exhbn (Bankside Gallery) 1993, Invited Members and Guests Royal Cambrian Acad 1993, Fedn of Br Artists National Print Exhbn (Mall Galleries) 1994–2003, Paintings, Drawings and Prints by Invited Artists (Gorstella Gallery Chester) 1994, Labour Intensive (City Gallery Leicester) 2000, What Makes Wales (Nat Museum of Wales Cardiff) 2001, Wrexham Print International 2001, Urban Perspectives (New Ashgate Gallery) 2001; *Work in Collections* incl: Ashmolean Museum Oxford, Fitzwilliam Museum Cambridge, Nat Museum of Wales, Nat Library of Wales, Newport Museum and Art Gallery, Glynn Vivian Art Gallery Swansea, Contemporary Art Soc for Wales, UC Swansea, Coleg Harlech, National Coal Board, Britoil, British Steel plc, Rank Xerox, Redpath Mining Corp Ontario, ASTMS (now MSF), Dept of the Environment, Royal Coll of Art, GLC, HM The Queen Windsor, numerous private collections in Europe, N America, Australia and Saudi Arabia; *Awards* Royal Instn Annual Scholarship for Engraving 1969, Catto Gallery Award RWS Open Exhbn 1993, first prize Daler Rowney Award RWS Open Exhbn 1995; *Recreations* opera, travel; *Style*— Prof David Carpanini; ✉ Fernlea, 145 Rugby Road, Milverton, Leamington Spa, Warwickshire CV32 6DJ (☎ 01926 430658); c/o The Bankside Gallery, 48 Hopton Street, Blackfriars, London SE1 9JH (☎ 020 7928 7521, fax 020 7928 2820); c/o The Attic Gallery, 37 Pockets Wharf, Maritime Quarter, Swansea SA1 3XL (☎ 01792 653387)

CARPANINI, Jane; da of Derrick Stanley Allen (d 2004), and Joan Allen; *b* 13 October 1949; *Educ* Bedford HS, Luton Coll of Technol Sch of Art, Faculty of Art & Design Brighton Poly (DipAD), Sch of Education Univ of Reading (Art Teacher's Cert); *m* 1972, Prof David Lawrence Carpanini, *qv*, s of Lorenzo Carpanini (d 2004); 1 s (Noel Dominic b 22 Aug 1977); *Career* artist; art teacher: The High Sch Bedford 1972–73, Bishops Cleeve Comp 1973–76, Oundle Sch 1980–86 (pt/t); head of art and design King's HS for Girls Warwick 1987–97; hon treas Royal Watercolour Soc 1998–2003 (hon treas 1983–86, vice-pres 1992–93); RWA 1977, RWS 1978, RBA 1978, RCA 1992; *Television Documentaries* A Word in Your Eye (HTV) 1997; *Solo exhibitions* Watercolours and Drawings (Bristol Art Centre) 1975, Watercolours (Patricia Wells Gallery Thornbury Bristol) 1976, Watercolours and Drawings (Tegfryn Gallery) 1982, Watercolours (Ceri Richards Gallery Univ Coll Swansea) 1983, Watercolours of Wales (Nat Museum of Wales) 1984, Watercolours by Jane Carpanini (Warwick Museum) 1990, Watercolours (Albany Gallery Cardiff) 1991, Attic Gallery 2007; *Exhibitions with David Carpanini* David and Jane Carpanini Paintings 1968–80 (Welsh Arts Council Exhbn) 1980, Yarrow Gallery Oundle 1979, Rhondda Heritage Park Gallery 1994; *Group exhibitions* incl: Royal W of England Acad Summer Exhbn annually 1973–, RA Summer Exhbn 1974–80, Royal Soc of Br Artists Exhbn annually 1975–88, Royal Soc of Painters in Watercolours annual London and tourning exhbns 1978–, Twelve Regular RA Exhibitors (Patricia Wells Gallery Thornbury) 1979, The Native Land (Welsh Arts Cncl Exhbn Mostyn Gallery Llandudno) 1980, Mason Watts Fine Art Warwick 1990 and 1993, Royal Cambrian Academy Annual Exhbn 1993, invited members of the RWS exhbn Gorstella Gallery Chester 1994; *Work in collections* incl: Nat Library of Wales, Nat Museum of Wales, Br Nat Oil Museum, Dixons Photographic, Diploma Collection of RWS, Burnley Building Society, Coleg Harlech, HM The Queen Windsor, numerous private collections; commissions: numerous paintings of independent schools and Oxford and Cambridge Colleges for Contemporary Watercolours Ltd; *Awards* Hunting Group Prize for watercolour of the year by a Br artist 1983; *Recreations* opera, travel; *Style*— Mrs Jane Carpanini; ✉ Fernlea, 145 Rugby Road, Milverton, Leamington Spa, Warwickshire CV32 6DJ (☎ 01926 430658); c/o The Bankside Gallery, 48 Hopton Street, Blackfriars, London SE1 9JH (☎ 020 7928 7521, fax 020 7928 2820); c/o The Attic Gallery, 37 Pockets Wharf, Maritime Quarter, Swansea SA1 3XL (☎ 01792 653387)

CARPENTER, Prof Barry; CBE (2016, OBE 2001); s of Gerald Carpenter, and Betty, *née* Lawrence; *b* 10 April 1955, Cradley Heath, W Midlands; *Educ* Rowley Regis GS, Westminster Coll Oxford (CertEd), Univ of London (Dip), Univ of Nottingham (MPhil), Anglia Ruskin Univ (PhD); *m* 19 Aug 1978, Susan, *née* Cookson; 1 s (Matthew b 1 Oct 1980), 2 da (Katie b 23 July 1984, Grace b 9 March 1993); *Career* headteacher Blythe Sch Warwickshire 1982–89, inspr of schools Solihull 1989–93, dir Centre for Special Educn Westminster Coll Oxford 1993–98, chief exec Sunfield Worcs 1998–2009, dir Children with Complex Learning Difficulties and Disabilities Research Project 2009–12; chair: My Life Housing Tst, Nat Forum Girls with Autism; fndr Nat Forum for Neuroscience in Special Educn; dir Books Beyond Words; visiting prof 2012–; fell Harris Manchester Coll Oxford; memb: RSA 1998, RSM 2001; *Books* Enabling Access: Effective Teaching and Learning for Pupils with Learning Difficulties (Times Educational Award Special Needs Book of the Year, 1996), Educating Children and Young People With Fetal Alcohol Spectrum Disorders (with Carolyn Blackburn and Jo Egerton, 2012), Fetal Alcohol Spectrum Disorders Interdisciplinary perspectives (ed, with Carolyn Blackburn and Jo Egerton, 2013), Engaging Learners with Complex Learning Difficulties and Disabilities (jtly, 2015); *Recreations* gardening, music (singing), travel, athletics, hen keeping; *Clubs* Navy and Military; *Style—* Professor Barry Carpenter, CBE; ✉ www.barrycarpentereducation.com

CARPENTER, Prof (Mary) Christine; *née* Johnston; da of Kemball Johnston (d 1987), and Gertrud (Trude), *née* Porges (d 1991); *b* 7 December 1946, Oxford; *Educ* Perse Sch for Girls Cambridge (govrs scholar), Newnham Coll Cambridge (MA, PhD); *m* 8 Aug 1969, Roger Carpenter; 1 s (James b 31 July 1976), 1 da (Alison b 8 March 1979); *Career* Univ of Cambridge: freelance tutor and lectr various colls and Faculty of History 1976–79, fell and coll lectr New Hall 1979–2005, univ asst lectr 1983–88, univ lectr 1988–95, reader in medieval English history 1995–2005, prof of medieval English history 2005–14, professorial fell New Hall 2005–08, Faculty of History rep for the Prince's Teaching Inst until 2014, appointed Ford's Lectr Univ of Oxford 2015–16; assoc ed Oxford DNB 1994–2002; James Ford special lectr Univ of Oxford 1996, guest lectr Moscow State Univ 2006; memb Editorial Bd The Fifteenth Century, memb Medieval Sources Advsy Panel TNA (now discontinued), memb Bd of Dirs Anglo American Legal Tradition (AALT), memb AHRC Review Panel; co-ed Cambridge Univ Press Studies in Medieval Life and Thought; Royal Historical Soc Whitfield Prize 1992; Br Acad Leverhulme sr research fell 2002–03; AHRC maj research grants 1999–2008; memb Cncl Francis Holland Schs until 2014; FRHistS (1982); *Publications* Locality and Polity: a study of Warwickshire landed society 1401–1499 (1992), Kingsford's Stonor Letters and Papers 1290–1483 (ed,1996), The Wars of the Roses: politics and the constitution in England c1437–1509 (1997 and repeat edns), The Armburgh Papers (ed, 1998), Calendars of Inquisitions Post Mortem XXII-XXVI (gen ed and dir of project, 2003–10), Political Culture in Late Medieval Britain (ed with L Clark, 2004), various articles, reviews and chapters in books; *Recreations* music (concerts and opera), theatre, film, visiting art galleries, exhibitions and buildings and places of historical and artistic interest, reading, watching football, walking; *Style—* Prof Christine Carpenter; ✉ Faculty of History, West Road, Cambridge CB3 9EF (☎ 01223 335314, e-mail mcc1000@cam.ac.uk)

CARPENTER, David Iain; RD (1994); s of Jeffrey Frank Carpenter (d 2008), and Joyce Cumming, *née* Mitchell; *b* 14 October 1951; *Educ* Sutton GS, BRNC Dartmouth, Heriot-Watt Sch of Architecture Edinburgh (DipArch); *m* 20 Jan 1979, Anne Richmond, da of Dr Norman John McQueen (d 1993); 4 s (Angus b 1980, Edward b 1981, Alexander b and d 1983, Simon b 1984); *Career* offr RN 1974–78, RNR 1979–2006 (head Public Affrs Branch 1996–98); architect J & F Johnston & Partners 1982–88 (assoc dir 1987), in own practice David Carpenter Architect Edinburgh 1988–96; architect Northwood Devpt Team 1996–2004, chief ops support Multi-National Div SE Iraq (MND (SE)) Basrah 2004–05, Project Neptune Faslane 2005–11; David Carpenter Architect 2011–; memb and chm Sea Cadet Assoc in Scotland 2012–; *Recreations* sailing, sketching, reading; *Clubs* Army and Navy, Langstone Sailing; *Style—* David Carpenter, Esq; ✉ David Carpenter Architect, 3 Argyle Park Terrace, Edinburgh EH9 1JY (☎ 0131 229 1383, e-mail davidcarpenterarchitect@gmail.com)

CARPENTER, Dr (George) Iain; s of George Anthony Carpenter (d 1967), of Horsmonden, Kent, and Dr Annie Pack MacKinnon; *b* 2 June 1950; *Educ* Christ's Hosp, Univ of Edinburgh (BSc, MD); *m* 1, 22 Feb 1970 (m dis 1982), (Marie) Catrine, da of Gaston Bauer, of Anglet, France; 1 da (Violaine b 1 May 1976), 1 s (Edward b 24 May 1979); m 2, 11 June 1983, Bridget Mary, da of Robert Charles Combley, of Headington, Oxford; 1 da (Annie b 18 Aug 1984), 1 s (James b 30 Jan 1986); *Career* sr registrar in geriatric med: Brighton Gen Hosp 1978–80, Bolingbroke 1980–81, St George's Hosp 1980–81; conslt geriatrician Royal Hampshire Co Hosp and St Paul's Hosp Winchester 1981–95 (also conslt in rehabilitation med 1990–95); regnl med advsr and dir of screening Beaumont Med Serv 1986–89, dir ICS Med Ltd 1989–91, sr lectr in health care of the elderly King's Coll Sch of Med and Dentistry 1995–, assoc dir and reader (older people) Centre for Health Services Studies Univ of Kent 2001–; memb: Br Geriatric Soc, BMA; FRCP 1993, FRCPEd 1994; *Books* All of Us – Strategies for Health Promotion for Old People (jtly, 1989), Housing, Care and Frailty (jtly, 1990), Assessment in Continuing Care Homes: Towards a National Standard Instrument (jtly, 1996), RAI Home Care (RAI-HC) Assessment Manual (jtly, 1996), Care of Older People – A Comparison of Systems in North America, Europe and Japan (jtly, 1999); *Recreations* walking, swimming, scuba diving, windsurfing, radio controlled model aircraft; *Style—* Dr Iain Carpenter; ✉ Centre for Health Service Studies, George Allen Wing, The University of Kent at Canterbury, Kent CT2 7NF (☎ 01227 827760)

CARR, Her Hon Judge (Elizabeth) Annabel; QC (1997); da of William John Denys Carr (d 1991), and Norah Betty, *née* Boot; *b* 14 November 1954; *Educ* Queenswood Sch Hatfield, Univ of Sheffield (LLB); *Children* 1 da (Hannah Betty), 1 s (Marcus John); *Career* called to the Bar Gray's Inn 1976, recorder 1996–2001, circuit judge 2001–; *Recreations* family, travelling, theatre; *Style—* Her Hon Judge Carr, QC

CARR, David Hugh; s of Tom Carr, and Katherine Mary, *née* Bull; *b* 11 October 1960, Northallerton, N Yorks; *Educ* Richmond Sch, Oriel Coll Oxford (exhibitioner, BA); *m* 14 May 1994, Julia May, *née* Dodd; 3 s (Robert James b 22 Nov 1994, Oliver Ben b 23 Aug 1999, Jonathan Adam b 2 Jan 2001); *Career* trainee then actuary Friends' Provident 1982–86, corporate pensions advsr The Wyatt Co 1986–87, property analyst Hillier Parker 1987–88; co-fndr and dir: Hazell Carr Training 1988–, Hazell Carr plc 1997–; Entrepreneur of the Year (Southern Region) 2003; supporter: London Chorus, Oxfam, Action Aid, Br Humanist Assoc; memb Co of Mercers, Grocers and Haberdashers Richmond; FIA 1988; *Recreations* singing (memb London Chorus), playing piano (Dip London Coll of Music), Concept 2 rowing, mountain biking, wine; *Style—* David Carr, Esq; ✉ Hazell Carr, Kings Reach, 38–50 Kings Road, Reading RG1 3AA (☎ 0118 951 3700, fax 0870 762 7281, e-mail david.carr@hazellcarr.com)

CARR, Francis Christopher (Fred); s of Allan Eric John Carr (d 2002), of San Francisco, and Elizabeth Constance, *née* Hope-Jones (d 1989); *b* 6 March 1945; *Educ* Eton, Keble Coll Oxford (BA); *m* 7 May 1983, Corinna Elizabeth, da of Lt Cdr Cedric Wake-Walker, of Rogate, Hants; 2 da (Polly b 1985, Matilda b 1987); *Career* memb London Stock Exchange 1971, ptnr Smith Rice and Hill 1973, dir Capel-Cure Myers 1979–89; chief exec: W I Carr (Investments) Ltd 1991–93, Carr Sheppards Crosthwaite Ltd 1993–2004; chm: M & G High Income Investment Trust plc 1997–, The City of Oxford Geared Income Tst plc 1998–2005, India Capital Growth Fund Ltd 2009–; dir: Investec Capital Accumulator Tst plc 2005–09, SVM UK Active Fund plc 2006–11; vice-pres Nat Gardens Scheme; FCSI 2005; *Recreations* fishing, shooting, aquatics, cooking; *Clubs* White's, Pratt's, Chelsea Arts, Leander, Vincent's (Oxford), City of London; *Style—* Fred Carr, Esq; ✉ e-mail fcarr@fredneedle.com

CARR, Henry James; QC (1998); s of Malcolm Lester Carr (d 1984), of Liverpool, and Dr Sara Carr, *née* Leigh; *b* 31 March 1958; *Educ* King David Sch Liverpool, Hertford Coll Oxford (BA), Univ of British Columbia (LLM); *m* 22 Sept 1988, Jan Mary, da of Maj Richard Alfred Dawson, of Harrogate; 3 s (Oliver b 1989, Harry b 1991, Charlie b 1994); 1 da (Lily b 1997); *Career* called to the Bar Gray's Inn 1982; memb Cncl and Bd Intellectual Property Inst; *Books* Protection of Computer Software in the United Kingdom (1986, co-author 2 edn with R Arnold, 1992); *Recreations* tennis, swimming, skiing; *Clubs* RAC, Harbour, Hurlingham; *Style—* Henry Carr, Esq; ✉ 11 South Square, Gray's Inn, London WC1R 5EY (☎ 020 7405 1222, fax 020 7242 4282)

CARR, Jimmy; s of Nora Mary Carr, *née* Lawlor (d 2001); *b* 15 September 1972, London; *Educ* Burnham GS, Royal GS High Wycombe, Gonville & Caius Coll Cambridge; *Partner* Karoline Copping; *Career* comedian; memb: Equity 2002, BAFTA 2004; *Performances* stand up incl: The Royal Variety Show 2002, Edinburgh Fringe Festival, Kilkenny Comedy Festival, Montreal Comedy Festival, Aspen Comedy Festival, Late Night with Conan O'Brien 2003, 2004, 2005 and 2006, The Tonight Show with Jay Leno 2003–05, Comedy Central Special 2004; *Television* Your Face or Mine (2 series) 2003, Distraction (UK 2 series, US 2 series) 2003–04, guest on Parkinson 2004, guest host Have I Got News for You 2004, panellist Question Time 2004, guest on Friday Night with Jonathan Ross 2004, 2005, 2006 and 2007, co-presenter 10 O'Clock Live 2011; *Films* Confetti 2006, Stormbreaker 2006, Alien Autopsy 2006, I Want Candy 2007; *Awards* nominee Perrier Award 2002, Billy Marsh Award 2003, Best Stand Up Time Out Comedy Award 2003, Best On Screen Newcomer RTS Award 2003, Best Gameshow Silver Rose (for Your Face or Mine) 2003, nominee Best Presenter Golden Rose of Montreux (for Distraction) 2004, Best Stand-up Br Comedy Award 2006; *Recreations* tennis, enjoying all the trappings c-list celebrity life brings (attending parties, premieres and the like); *Clubs* Groucho; *Style—* Jimmy Carr, Esq; ✉ c/o Hannah Chambers, Chambers Management Ltd, 39–41 Parker Street, London WC2B 5PQ (☎ 020 7796 3588, fax 020 7796 3676, mobile 07803 126177, e-mail hannah@chambersmgt.co.uk)

CARR, Joanne (Jo); da of Ian Carr, of Andover, Hants, and Beryl, *née* Messenger; *b* 27 September 1968; *Educ* Harrow Way Comp Sch Andover, Univ of Birmingham (BA); *m* James Battersby; 2 s (Ned, Will); *Career* teacher Kyoto 1990–92, conslt Corporate Communications Ltd Hong Kong 1992–95, PR conslt QBO (now Bell Pottinger) 1995–2005 (dep md 2003–05), dir Teamspirit PR 2006–08, jt managing ptnr Seventy Seven PR 2008–11, fndr and managing ptnr Hope and Glory PR 2011–; *Style—* Ms Jo Carr; ✉ Hope and Glory PR, The Spitfire Building, 71 Collier Street, London N1 9BE

CARR, Sir Peter Derek; kt (2007), CBE (1989), DL (Durham 1997); s of George William Carr (d 1972), and Marjorie, *née* Tailby; *b* 12 July 1930; *Educ* Fircroft Coll Birmingham, Ruskin Coll Oxford, Garnett Coll London; *m* 12 April 1958, Geraldine Pamela, da of Alexander Quarrier Ward, of Babbacombe, Devon; 1 s (Steven John b 1959), 1 da (Alyce b 1963); *Career* Nat Serv Mountain Rescue Serv RAF 1951–53; site mangr construction industry 1944–60, sr lectr in mgmnt Thurrock Coll 1964–69, advsr Nat Bd for Prices and Incomes 1967–69, dir Cmmn on Industrial Rels 1969–74, section dir ACAS 1974–78, Dip Serv cnsllr Br Embassy Washington DC 1978–83, regnl dir DOE (Northern) and ldr Govt City Action Team 1983–89; chm: Northern Screen Cmmn 1989–2002, Northern RHA 1990–94, Co Durham Devpt Co 1990–2001, NHS Supra Regnl Services Advsy Gp 1993–94, Durham County Waste Management Co 1993–2011, Occupational Pensions Bd 1994–97, Newcastle & North Tyne HA 1998–2002, Northern Regnl Awards Ctee NHS 2002–03, Northumberland, Tyne & Wear SHA 2002–06, NE Health Forum 2003–08, Northern Ctee on Clinical Excellence Awards 2004–07, NE Regnl SHA 2006–12, NE Cmmn on Rural Health 2008–11, NHS Tst Devpt Authy 2012–16; visiting fell Univ of Durham 1990–2000; memb Ct Univ of Newcastle upon Tyne 2005–; Hon DSc Univ of Sunderland 2009, Hon LLD Univ of Teesside 2011, Hon LLD Univ of Northumbria 2012; *Books* Worker Participation and Collective Bargaining in Europe, Industrial Relations in the National Newspaper Industry, It Occurred to Me; *Recreations* cabinet making, cycling, cooking, grandchildren, the history of the United States; *Clubs* Royal Over-Seas League, RSM; *Style—* Sir Peter D Carr, CBE, DL; ✉ NHS Trust Development Authority, Chairman's Office, Waterfront 4 Goldcrest Way, Newcastle upon Tyne, NE15 8NY (☎ 020 74 84 9469)

CARR, Rodney Paul (Rod); CBE (2010, OBE 2005); s of Capt George Paul Carr, of Whatton-in-the-Vale, Nottingham (d 2004), and Alma, *née* Walker (d 1960); *b* 10 March 1950; *Educ* Carlton Le Willows GS Nottingham, Univ of Birmingham (BSc); *m* 21 July 1971, Lynne Alison, da of Charles Wilfred Ashwell; 1 da (Joanne b 17 Oct 1979), 1 s (David b 15 Feb 1982); *Career* yachtsman; instr London Borough of Haringey 1972–75, chief instr and dep dir Nat Sailing Centre Cowes IOW 1979–81 (instr 1975–79), memb winning Br Admirals Cup team 1981, chief racing coach (yachting) Royal Yachting Assoc 1984– (olympic coach 1981–92), olympic team mangr 1992–97; coach to: J Richards and P Allam Flying Dutchman Class Bronze medal Olympic Games LA 1984, M McIntyre and B Vaile Star Class Gold medal Olympic Games Seoul 1988; mangr of: Ben Ainslie, John Merricks and Ian Walker (Silver medallists Olympic Games Atlanta 1996); dep chef de mission GB Olympic Team Sydney 2000, chief exec Royal Yachting Assoc 2000–10 (racing mangr 1987–2000), sports conslt 2010–; field of play mangr Sailing LOCOG 2010–12; chair UK Sport 2013– (memb Bd 2005–13); memb Bd: Weymouth and Portland Nat Sailing Acad 2008– (currently dep chair), Outward Bound Tst 2009–15, 1851 Tst 2014–, English Inst of Sport 2015–, Stem Crew 2016–; tstee John Merrick's Sailing Tst 1997–; pres North London Sailing Assoc; hon life memb Royal Yachting Assoc 2010; yr bro Trinity House 2006; Hon MBA Southampton Inst 2002; *Recreations* sailing, music, long-distance walking; *Clubs* Royal Thames Yacht, Emsworth Slipper Sailing, Hayling Island Sailing; *Style—* Rod Carr, Esq, CBE; ✉ Riverfield, Lumley Road, Emsworth, Hampshire PO10 8AA (☎ 01243 370204, e-mail rod@coachone.co.uk)

CARR, Sir Roger Martyn; kt (2011); *b* 22 December 1946; *Educ* Nottingham HS, Nottingham Poly; *m* Stephanie; 1 da; *Career* various appts Honeywell, gen mgmnt appts various engrg cos until 1982; Williams plc: gp md 1988–94, chief exec 1994–2000; chm: Thames Water plc 1999–2000, Chubb plc 2000–02, Mitchells & Butlers plc 2003–08, Centrica plc 2004–13, Cadbury plc (formerly Cadbury Schweppes plc until demerger) 2008–10 (non-exec dir 2001–10, dep chm 2003–08), BAE Systems plc 2014–; sr advsr Kohlberg Kravis Roberts Co Ltd; non-exec dir Bank of England 2007–14 (dep chm 2011–14); vice-chm BBC Tst 2015–; visiting fell Said Business Sch Oxford; dep pres then pres CBI 2011; CIMgt, FRSA, FCIS 2013; *Style—* Sir Roger Carr; ✉ BAE Systems, Stirling Square, 6 Carlton Gardens, London SW1Y 5AD

CARR, His Hon Judge Simon; *b* 9 August 1961, Stafford; *Educ* Perse Sch Cambridge, Univ of Southampton (LLB); *m* 7 April 1990, Stephanie Farrimond; *Career* called to the Bar 1984; Goldsmith Chambers 1985–94, 9 Gough Square chambers 1994–2009, circuit judge (South Eastern Circuit) 2009–14 and (Western Circuit) 2014–; chair Global Ethics Ctee and Global Tstees Jane Goodall Inst; *Recreations* hockey, scuba diving, travel; *Clubs* Spencer Hockey; *Style—* His Hon Judge Simon Carr; ✉ c/o Truro Combined Court, Edward Street, Truro TR1 2PB (e-mail hhj.simon.carr@ejudiciary.net)

CARR, Hon Mrs Justice; Dame Sue Carr; DBE (2013), QC (2003); *Educ* Trinity Coll Cambridge (MA); *Career* called to the Bar 1987; practising barr specialising in general commercial law and professional liability, took silk 2003; arbitrator and accredited mediator; complaints cmmr Int Criminal Court The Hague 2012–13; recorder Crown Court, master Inner Temple, judge of the High Court of Justice (Queen's Bench Division) 2013– (nominated judge of the Commercial Court and Technol and Construction Court); presiding judge Midland Circuit 2016–; chm: Professional Negligence Bar Assoc 2008–09, Complaints Ctee Bar Standards Bd 2008–10; memb: Chancery and Commercial Bar Assoc, Investigatory Powers Tribunal 2013–15, Judicial Coll Bd; *Publications* Jackson & Powell: Professional Liability Precedents (gen ed and contrib author, 2000), Where

There's a Will There's a Damages Claim (2001); *Style*— The Hon Mrs Justice Carr; ✉ Royal Courts of Justice, Strand, London WC2A 2LL

CARR-LOCKE, Andrew Charles Philip; s of Lionel Charles Carr-Locke (d 1998), and Elsie Marjorie, *née* Wright; *b* 2 June 1953; *Educ* Whitgift Sch Croydon, Univ of Warwick (BSc); *m* 18 Aug 1979, Elizabeth Clare, *née* Hall; 2 da (Katherine Elizabeth b 1 April 1984, Sarah Ann b 20 Feb 1986); *Career* Europe finance dir consumer business Eastman Kodak 1974–85, finance dir Bowater Scott/Scott Ltd 1985–95, European finance dir United Distillers 1996–98, gp finance dir Courtaulds Textiles plc 1998–2000, gp finance dir George Wimpey plc 2001–07; exec chm Countryside Properties 2010–14; non-exec dir: AWG plc 2003–07, Venture Prodn plc 2008–09, Royal Mail Hldgs plc 2009–10, Dairy Crest plc, Grainger plc; memb 100 Gp 2001–07; FCMA 2006 (ACMA 1974); *Recreations* golf, tennis, travel; *Clubs* RAC, Tandridge Golf; *Style*— Andrew Carr-Locke, Esq; ✉ carr.locke@btinternet.com

CARRAGHER, Jamie; s of Philly Carragher, of Liverpool, and Paula Carragher; *b* 28 January 1978, Liverpool; *m* 1 July 2005, Nicola; 1 s (James b 11 Nov 2002), 1 da (Mia b 14 May 2004); *Career* former professional footballer; Liverpool FC: debut v Middlesbrough 1996, 508 appearances, winners FA Youth Cup 1996, League Cup 2001 and 2003, FA Cup 2001, UEFA Cup 2001, European Super Cup 2001 and UEFA Champions League 2005 (finalists 2007); England: 38 caps (also 27 Under 21 caps), debut v Hungary 1999, memb squad European Championship 2004, memb squad World Cup 2010; football pundit Sky Sports 2013–; *Style*— Mr Jamie Carragher

CARRAGHER, Patrick Matthew; MBE (2016); s of Thomas A Carragher (d 1977), and Eileen M Carragher; *b* 21 September 1957; *Educ* St Catharine's Coll Cambridge (BA); *m* 1990, Alexandra; 2 da (Charlotte Maeve and Maria); *Career* gen sec Br Assoc of Colliery Mgmnt 1996– (full time offr 1981–); involved in a number of coal industry orgns incl Coal Soc, Coal Industry Social Welfare Orgn among others; *Recreations* squash, cinema, music; *Style*— Patrick Carragher, Esq, MBE; ✉ BACM-TEAM, Danum House, 6A South Parade, Doncaster, South Yorkshire DN1 2DY (☎ 01302 815551, fax 01302 815552, e-mail gs@bacmteam.org.uk)

CARRICK, Julia; OBE (2014); *b* Colchester, Essex; *Children* 2 da (Arabella Boardman, Charlotte-Sophia Boardman); *Career* BBC World Service 1979–85, fndr, publisher and global dir FT How To Spend It magazine 1985–2015; Walpole Br Luxury: fndr and chief exec 1990–2013, global ambass 2013; chief exec Julia Carrick Luxury Consultancy Ltd 2013–; publisher Country & Town House 2013–; global luxury adviser Bell Pottinger 2013–, luxury and retail advsr Cream UK 2015–, memb Bd Livoos 2015–; *Clubs* Hurlingham, Home House, Guards Polo; *Style*— Ms Julia Carrick, OBE; ✉ e-mail julia@juliacarrickluxury.com; Country & Town House, Chelsea Gate Studios, 115 Harwood Road, London S16 4QL (☎ 020 7873 3802, e-mail julia@countryandtownhouse.co.uk)

CARRICK, Michael; *b* 28 July 1981, Wallsend, Tyneside; *Career* professional footballer; clubs: West Ham United 1997–2004 (winners FA Youth Cup Final 1999, first team debut 1999, loaned to Swindon Town 1999 and Birmingham City 2000), Tottenham Hotspur 2004–06, Manchester United 2006– (winners FA Premiership 2007, 2008, 2009, 2011 and 2013, winners UEFA Champions League 2008); England: 28 caps, debut v Mexico 2001, memb squad World Cup 2006 and 2010; *Style*— Michael Carrick, Esq; ✉ c/o Manchester United FC, Old Trafford, Manchester M16 0RA

CARRINGTON, Baron (Life Peer UK 2013), of Fulham in the London Borough of Hammersmith and Fulham; Matthew Hadrian Marshall Carrington; s of late Walter Hadrian Marshall Carrington, and late Dilys Mary Gwyneth Carrington; *b* 19 October 1947; *Educ* French Lycée London, Imperial Coll London (BSc), London Business Sch (MSc); *m* 1, 29 March 1975, Mary Lou (d 2008), da of late Robert Darrow, of Columbus, OH; 1 da (Victoria b 11 June 1981); m 2, 15 Oct 2011, Margaret Ann Stitt; *Career* prodn foreman GKN Sankey 1969–72; banker: First National Bank of Chicago 1974–78, Saudi International Bank 1978–87; MP (Cons) Fulham 1987–97, PPS to Rt Hon John Patten MP as sec of state for Educn 1992–94, memb Treasy and Civil Serv Select Ctee 1994–96, chm Treasy Select Ctee 1996, asst Govt whip 1996–97; London rgnl chm Cons Pty 2005–08; chm Outdoor Advertising Assoc 1998–2002, chief exec Retail Motor Industry Fedn 2002–06, dep chm and dir Gatehouse Bank plc 2007–; non-exec dir Arab Br C of C 2011–; *Recreations* cooking, political history; *Style*— The Lord Carrington of Fulham; ✉ House of Lords, London SW1A 0PW

CARRINGTON, Nigel Martyn; s of Thomas Ronald Carrington, and Vera Carrington; *b* 1 May 1956; *Educ* Brighton Coll, St John's Coll Oxford (BA, pres Oxford Univ Law Soc), Courtauld Inst (PGDHA); *m* 2 Jan 1988, Elisabeth Buchanan; 1 s, 2 da; *Career* slr and ptnr Baker & McKenzie 1979–2000: articled clerk 1979–81, assoc 1981–87, ptnr 1987–2000, managing ptnr London 1994–98, memb Int Exec Ctee 1998–2000, chm European Renl Cncl 1998–2000; McLaren Gp Ltd: md 2000–05, dep chm 2005–07; vice-chllr Univ of the Arts London 2008–; non-exec dir: UCL Hosps NHS Fndn Tst 2005–08, Hornby plc 2007–14; tstee: Crisis 2005–11 (treas 2005–08), English Concert 2005– (chm 2006–12), Independent Opera 2006–10, Cass Sculpture Fndn 2015–; chm: Jeans for Genes 2006–08, Henry Moore Fndn 2014–; tstee and dir Universities UK 2015–; dir Creative Industries Fedn 2014–; govr: N London Collegiate Sch 2008–15, Int Students House 2009–; *Books* Acquiring Companies and Businesses in Europe (1994); *Recreations* swimming, skiing, music, wine; *Clubs* RAC, Chelsea Arts; *Style*— Nigel Carrington, Esq; ✉ University of the Arts London, 272 High Holborn, London WC1V 7EY (☎ 020 7514 6002)

CARRINGTON, 6 Baron (I 1796, GB 1797); Peter Alexander Rupert Carrington; KG (1985), GCMG (1988, KCMG 1958), CH (1983), MC (1945), PC (1959); sits as Baron Carington of Upton (Life Peer UK 1999), of Upton, Co Nottinghamshire; s of 5 Baron Carrington, JP, DL (d 1938, n of 3 Baron, KG, GCMG, PC, JP, DL, sometime MP High Wycombe, and also 1 and last Marquess of Lincolnshire, govr of New South Wales, Lord Great Chamberlain of England and Lord Privy Seal) by his w, Hon Sybil, da of 2 Viscount Colville of Culross; *b* 6 June 1919; *Educ* Eton, RMC Sandhurst; *m* 1942, Iona (d 2009), yr da of Sir Francis Kennedy McClean, AFC (d 1955); 1 s (Hon Rupert), 2 da (Hon Mrs de Bunsen, Hon Virginia); *Heir* s, Hon Rupert Carington, *qv*; *Career* served as Maj Grenadier Gds NW Europe; Parly sec Miny of Agric and Fisheries 1951–54, MOD 1954–56, high cmmr to Australia 1956–59, First Lord of Admiralty 1959–63, min without portfolio and ldr of House of Lords 1963–64, ldr of oppn House of Lords 1964–70 and 1974–79; sec of state: for defence 1970–74, Dept of Energy 1974; min of aviation supply 1971–74; sec of state for foreign and Cwlth affrs and min of overseas devpt 1979–82; chm Cons Party 1972–74, sec gen NATO 1984–88, chm EC Peace Conf on Yugoslavia 1991–92; chm GEC 1983–84 (dir 1982–84); dir: Christie's International plc 1988–98 (chm 1988–93), The Telegraph plc 1990–2004; non-exec dir Chime Communications 1993–99; JP Bucks 1948, DL 1951; fell Eton 1966–81; memb Int Bd United World Colls 1982–84, chm Bd of Tstees V&A 1983–88; chllr: Order of St Michael and St George 1984–94, Univ of Reading 1992–2007, Order of the Garter 1994–2013 (pres 1994–); pres: Pilgrims 1983–2002, VSO 1993–98; hon fell St Antony's Coll Oxford 1982, hon bencher Middle Temple 1983, hon elder Brother Trinity House 1984; Hon LLD Univs of: Leeds 1981, Cambridge 1981, Philippines 1982, S Carolina 1983, Aberdeen 1985, Harvard 1986, Sussex 1989, Reading 1989, Buckingham 1989, Nottingham 1993, Birmingham 1993; Hon DCL: Univ of Newcastle upon Tyne 1998, Univ of Oxford 2003; Hon DSc Cranfield 1983, Hon DUniv Essex; Liveryman Worshipful Co of Clothworkers; *Books* Reflect on Things Past – The Memoirs of Lord Carrington (1988); *Clubs* Pratt's, White's; *Style*— The Rt Hon the Lord Carrington, KG, GCMG, CH, MC, PC; ✉ The Manor House, Bledlow, Princes Risborough, Buckinghamshire HP27 9PB (☎ 01844 343499, office tel 01844 274292)

CARRINGTON, Prof Simon Robert; s of Robert Carrington (d 1996), of Suffolk, and Jean, *née* Hill (d 1991), of Wilts; *b* 23 October 1942; *Educ* ChCh Cathedral Choir Sch Oxford, The King's Sch Canterbury, King's Coll Cambridge, New Coll Oxford; *m* 2 Aug 1969, Hilary Elizabeth, da of Leslie Stott (d 1964); 1 da (Rebecca b 1971), 1 s (Jamie b 1973); *Career* emeritus prof Yale Univ; freelance conductor, teacher and adjudicator; dir The King's Singers 1968–93; 72 CDs for EMI and BMG, tours worldwide, concerts, workshops and master classes; regular TV appearances worldwide incl: Live at the Boston Pops 1983, BBC TV Series The King's Singers Madrigal History Tour 1984, ABC TV (USA) The Sound of Christmas from Salzburg 1987, 8 appearances on the Johnny Carson Tonight Show (NBC TV, USA) 1983–90; 25th Anniversary concerts worldwide 1993; festival dir Barbican Summer in the City Festivals 1988–89, Grammy nomination USA 1986; prof, dir of choral activities and artist in residence Univ of Kansas 1994–2001, dir of choral activities New England Conservatory Boston USA 2001–03, prof and choral dir Yale Univ Inst of Sacred Music and Sch of Music 2003–09; visiting prof of conducting Univ of Birmingham 2016–; choral conductor, clinician and memb int juries at events incl: Tokyo Cantat, Leipzig Int Choral Festival, Santa Fe Desert Chorale, Trinity Church Wall St NY, Sarteano Conducting Inst Italy, Europa Cantat Barcelona, World Symposium, Argentina, Annual Yale Summer Sch conducting course 2006–; hon doctorate New England Conservatory 2014; FRSA; *Books* The King's Singers – a Self Portrait (1981); Simon Carrington Choral Series Alliance Music and GIA, Rehearsing a Choir – the Cambridge Companion to Choral Music; *Recreations* vintage cars, inland waterways, gardens, trees, walking, jogging; *Clubs* Royal Soc of Musicians; *Style*— Prof Simon Carrington; ✉ Puy Calvel, 46240 Lamothe Cassel, France; 50d Clapham Common Southside, London SW4 9BX (e-mail sc@simoncarrington.com, website www.simoncarrington.com)

CARROLL, Ben; s of Joseph Carroll, of Harrow, Middx, and Margaret, *née* O'Carroll; *b* 5 May 1945; *Educ* London Oratory; *m* 13 May 1967, Rosemary-Anne, da of Morris Tucker; *Career* Scottish Widows Fund & Life Assurance Soc 1964–66, Keith Shipton (Life & Pensions) Ltd 1966–68; Noble Lowndes & Partners Ltd 1968–93: md Noble Lowndes International Ltd 1986, md Employee Benefits 1988, md Personal Fin Servs 1990–93 (author of papers on behalf of firm); chief exec Bain Hogg Financial Services Ltd 1994, chm Bain Hogg Asset Management Ltd 1994, md Towry Law Financial Planning Ltd 1995, sales dir Corp Pensions Prudential 1998–2000, sr ptnr Carroll Consulting 2000–; head of qualifications Securities Inst 2001–02, dir of membership Securities Inst 2002–03; chm Syndaxi Financial Planning 2004–; dir: Towry Law plc, IFA Promotion Ltd 1993–96, IFA Assoc Ltd 1994, The Ideas Lab 2002–, Network Exams 2004–05, Dalbar Europe 2004–; chm Soc of Fin Advsrs 1993–95 (dir 1992–98); memb Memb Ctee PIA 1994–97, memb Disciplinary Tbnl Panel for Actuarial Profession 2005–; tstee David Rattray Meml Tst (UK); MSI, FPMI (pres 1987–89), FCII, assoc Personal Finance Soc (APFS); *Recreations* golf, travel, opera, theatre, modern films, walking; *Clubs* Croham Hurst Golf; *Style*— Ben Carroll, Esq; ✉ Springhurst Close, Shirley, Surrey CR0 5AT

CARROLL, John; s of Sean Carroll, of Bentley, nr Doncaster, and Norah, *née* Coombes; *b* 15 April 1964; *Educ* St Peter's HS Doncaster; *m* 17 Nov 1989, Tracy, da of John Hunter; 2 da (Danielle b 29 Oct 1990, Lauren b 4 Jan 1994); *Career* flat race jockey 1981–, best season 94 winners 1993; achievements: winner of Molecomb Stakes Group Three Goodwood 1988, winner of Cocked Hat of the North 1991, runner up Heinz 57 Group One Phoenix Park, winner Flying Childers Stakes Group Two on Paris House 1991, winner Newbury Sales Super Sprint Trophy on Paris House 1991, winner King George V Handicap on Learmont (Royal Ascot) 1993; winner Palace House Stakes Group Three: on Paris House 1993, on Mind Games 1995; winner Temple Stakes Group Two: on Paris House 1993, on Mind Games 1995; winner Norfolk Stakes Group Three on Mind Games; two winners inaugural Dubai World Cup Meeting 1996, winner 1000 Guineas Dubai 2002, winner Stanley Leisure Sprint Cup (Group I) on Invincible Spirit 2002; *Recreations* shooting, fishing, playing football, golf; *Style*— John Carroll, Esq; ✉ The Paddocks, 279 Park Lane, Preesall, Blackpool, Lancashire FY6 0LT (☎ 01253 812299, mobile 07889 860797)

CARROLL, Prof John Edward; s of Sidney Wentworth Carroll (d 1959), and May Doris, *née* Brand; *b* 15 February 1934; *Educ* Oundle, Queens' Coll Cambridge (BA, MA, PhD, ScD); *m* Vera Mary, *née* Jordan; *Career* princ scientific offr Servs Electronic Res Laboratory 1961–67; Univ of Cambridge Engrg Dept: lectr 1967–76, reader 1976–83, prof 1983–2001 (emeritus prof 2001–), head of Electrical Div 1992–99; chm Cncl School of Technology Univ of Cambridge 1996–99; fell Queens' Coll Cambridge 1967–; FIEE 1965, FREng 1985; *Books* Hot Electron Microwave Generators (1970), Semiconductor Devices (1974), Rate Equations in Semiconductor Electronics (1985), Distributed Feedback Semiconductor Lasers (1998), Ether Space-time & Cosmology (contrib, Vol 1 2008, Vol 2 2009); *Recreations* DIY, caring, reading, quantum theory; *Style*— Prof John Carroll, FREng; ✉ Queen's College, University of Cambridge, Silver Street, Cambridge CB3 9ET (☎ 01223 335511, fax 01223 335577, e-mail jec1000@cam.ac.uk)

CARROLL, His Hon Michael John; s of late Matthew Carroll, and late Gladys, *née* Hensman; *b* 26 December 1948; *Educ* Shebbear Coll, City of London Business Sch (BA), Cncl of Legal Educn; *m* 24 Aug 1974, Stella, da of Thomas Reilly; 3 da (Erin, Joanna (decd)), 2 s (Matthew, Padraig); *Career* called to the Bar Gray's Inn 1973; recorder 1994–96 (asst recorder 1990), circuit judge (SE Circuit) 1996–2016, dep circuit judge 2016–; *Recreations* reading, football; *Style*— His Hon Michael Carroll; ✉ 2 Dr Johnson's Building, Temple, London EC4Y 7AY

CARRUTHERS, (Philip) Anthony (Tony); s of Donald Carruthers (d 1983), and Beatrice Ada, *née* Tremain (d 1987); *b* 29 November 1934; *Educ* Homelands Tech HS Torquay, S Devon Tech Coll Torquay; *m* 4 April 1964, Sheila Mary, da of Rowdon Atkins (d 1956), and Kathleen Atkins, *née* Mooney (d 1971), of Torquay, Devon; 1 da (Anne-Marie Carole (Mrs A Adams, JP) b 1966); *Career* RN 1951–54, RNR 1954–59; dir: Charles Moxham & Co Ltd 1960–68 (joined 1954), Moxhams of Torquay Ltd (Barlow Gp) 1968–72, Thos Barlow Motors Ltd 1970–72, Barlow Handling Ltd 1972–94 (co sec 1975–94), Barlow Handling (Properties) Ltd 1973–94, Barlow Handling Gp Ltd 1975–94, Thos Barlow (Holdings) Ltd (Materials Handling Div of J Bibby & Sons plc) 1985–94, Barlow Pension Tst Ltd 1986–2005, DD Lamson plc 1990–94; memb Employment Tbnls England and Wales 1992–2005, memb and voluntary advsr Pension Advsy Serv (OPAS) London 1994–2004; memb Henley Royal Regatta 1976–, memb Henley Town & Visitors Regatta 2007–, friend of Henley Festival of Music and Art 1990–, memb Fleet Air Arm Officers Assoc, memb NADFAS, memb Fellowship of the Motor Industry; Freeman City of London, Liveryman Worshipful Co of Gold and Silver Wyre Drawers; FInstD 1968–2008; *Recreations* home computers, gardening, theatre, music, opera, Probus, eating out, wine, enjoying retirement; *Clubs* Leander (memb ctee 1996–2000, treas 2000–05), Phyllis Court, Henley; *Style*— Tony Carruthers, Esq; ✉ St Marymead, Beverley Gardens, Wargrave, Berkshire RG10 8ED (☎ 0118 940 2693, fax 0118 940 6208, e-mail tony@devoniantq.me.uk)

CARSBERG, Sir Bryan Victor; kt (1989); s of Alfred Victor Carsberg (d 2002), of Chesham Bois, Bucks, and Maryllia Cicely, *née* Collins (d 1996); *b* 3 January 1939; *Educ* Berkhamsted, LSE (MSc); *m* 1960, Margaret Linda, da of Capt Neil McKenzie Graham (d 1966); 2 da (Debbie, Sarah); *Career* in sole practice as chartered accountant 1962–64, lectr in accounting LSE 1964–68, visiting lectr Grad Sch of Business Univ of Chicago 1968–69, prof of accounting Univ of Manchester 1969–81 (dean Faculty of Econ and

Social Studies 1977–78), visiting prof of business admin Univ of Calif Berkeley 1974, asst dir of res and technical activities Financial Accounting Standards Bd USA 1978–81, Arthur Andersen prof of accounting LSE 1981–87, dir of research (pt/t) ICAEW 1981–87, visiting prof of accounting LSE 1987–89, pt/t prof of accounting London Business Sch 1995–98; DG of telecommunications OFTEL 1984–92, DG Office of Fair Trading 1992–95, sec gen International Accounting Standards Ctee 1995–2001, chm Pensions Compensation Bd; memb Cncl ICAEW 1975–79, dep chm Accounting Standards Bd 1990–92 (memb 1990–94); dir: Economists Advsy Gp 1976–84, Economist Bookshop 1981–91, Philip Allan Publishers 1981–92 and 1995–, Nynex CableComms 1996–97, Cable and Wireless Communications 1997–2000, MLL Telecoms 1999–2002, RM plc 2002–12, Novae Gp plc (formerly SvB Hldgs plc) 2003–15, Inmarsat 2005–, Actual Experience plc 2014–; memb: Bd Radiocommunications Agency 1990–92, Cncl Univ of Surrey 1990–92, Cncl Loughborough Univ 1999–2011 (chm 2001–11); CAs Founding Society's Centenary award 1988, Sempier Award IFAC 2002; Hon MA Univ of Manchester 1973, hon fell LSE 1990; Hon ScD UEA 1992, Hon DLitt Loughborough Univ 1994, Hon DUniv Essex 1995, Hon LLD Univ of Bath 1996, Hon DBA Nottingham Trent Univ 2008; Hon FIA 2000, Hon RICS 2010; FCA 1970; *Books* An Introduction to Mathematical Programming for Accountants (1969), Modern Financial Management (with H C Edey, 1969), Analysis for Investment Decisions (1974), Indexation and Inflation (with E V Morgan and M Parkin, 1975), Economics of Business Decisions (1975), Investment Decisions under Inflation (with A Hope, 1976), Current Issues in Accountancy (with A Hope, 1977), Topics in Management Accounting (with J Arnold and R Scapens, 1980), Current Cost Accounting (with M Page, 1983), Small Company Financial Reporting (with M Page and others, 1985); *Recreations* theatre, opera, music, gardening, physics; *Style*— Sir Bryan Carsberg

CARSLAKE, Hugh Bampfield; s of John Carslake, DL (d 1991), and Dorothea Jeanne, *née* Nesbitt; *b* 15 November 1946; *Educ* West House Sch Birmingham, Rugby, Trinity Coll Dublin (BA, LLB), Coll of Law; *m* 10 Oct 1970, June Helen, da of George Pratt McVitty; 6 c; *Career* slr; articled clerk Freshfields 1970–72, Shakespeare Martineau (formerly Martineau Johnson) Birmingham 1974– (sr ptnr 2004–07), NP 1981; tstee Worcester Cathedral Appeal 1988–2009, chm The Barber Inst of Fine Arts Univ of Birmingham 1989–, memb Cncl Univ of Birmingham 1991–2000; registrar Dio of Birmingham 1992–; chm of govrs King's Sch Worcester 2001–; memb: Law Soc, Ecclesiastical Law Soc, Notaries Soc, Lunar Soc, STEP; pres City of Birmingham Choir 2003–; *Recreations* music and family; *Style*— Hugh Carslake, Esq; ✉ Shakespeare Martineau, No1 Colmore Square, Birmingham B4 6AA (☎ 0121 214 0486)

CARSLAW, Debbie Patricia; da of John Murray Carslaw, of Gloucester, and Patricia Emily, *née* Smith; *b* 26 August 1961, Gloucester; *Educ* Ribston Hall GS for Girls Gloucester, Univ of Leeds (Margaret Harrison Simpson prize, LLB); *Career* slr; ptnr: Wilde Sapte 1996–98, Denton Wilde Sapte 1998–2002, Sidley Austin 2003–; cases incl the acquisition of Canary Wharf Gp plc and the construction of the BBC Building in Portland Place London; memb: Law Soc, RA; supporter Terrence Higgins Tst; *Recreations* contemporary art (owner Madder139 Gallery), walking, cycling, music, dance; *Style*— Miss Debbie Carslaw; ✉ Sidley Austin, Woolgate Exchange, 25 Basinghall Street, London EC2V 5HA (☎ 020 7360 3608, fax 020 7626 7937, e-mail dcarslaw@sidley.com)

CARSON, Ciaran Gerard; s of William Carson, of Belfast, and Mary Ellen, *née* Maginn; *b* 9 October 1948; *Educ* St Mary's Christian Brothers' Sch, Queen's Univ Belfast (BA); *m* 16 Oct 1982, Deirdre, da of Patrick Shannon; 2 s (Manus b 5 April 1986, Gerard 29 Oct 1987), 1 da (Mary Ellen b 3 Oct 1990); *Career* poet and prose writer; traditional arts offr Arts Cncl of NI 1975–98; Gregory Award 1976, Alice Hunt Bartlett Award 1988, Irish Times/Aer Lingus Award 1990, T S Eliot Poetry Prize 1993; *Books* poetry: The New Estate (1976), The Irish For No (1987, Alice Hunt Bartlett Award), Belfast Confetti (1989, Irish Times Irish Literature Prize for Poetry), First Language (1993, T S Eliot Prize), Opera Et Cetera (1996), The Alexandrine Plan (1998), The Twelfth of Never (1998), Selected Poems (2001), Breaking News (2003), The Midnight Court (2006), For All We Know (2008), Collected Poems (2009), Until Before After (2010), On the Night Watch (2010), In the Light Of (2013), From Elsewhere (2015, shortlisted for the Forward Prize); non-fiction: The Pocket Guide to Irish Traditional Music (1986), Last Night's Fun (1996), The Star Factory (1997, Yorkshire Post Book Award), Shamrock Tea (2001), Dante Alighieri: The Inferno (translator, 2002); *Recreations* playing traditional music; *Style*— Ciaran Carson, Esq

CARSON, Neil Andrew Patrick; OBE (2016); s of Patrick Carson, and Sheila Margaret Rose Carson; *b* 15 April 1957, London; *Educ* Emanuel Sch, Coventry Univ (BSc); *m* 1988, Helen Barbara; 2 s (Peter Charles b 23 Dec 1992, Philip Robert b 5 May 1994), 1 da (Hannah Constance b 9 Oct 1997); *Career* Johnson Matthey plc: dir Catalytic Systems Div 1997, exec dir Catalysts Div 1999, exec dir Catalysts and Precious Metals Div 2003, chief exec 2004–14; non-exec dir AMEC plc 2011–, chm TT Electronics plc 2015–, sr ind dir and chair remco Amecfw, sr ind dir and chair remco Pay Point plc; jt chm (with Michael Fallon, MP, *qv*), Chemistry Growth Partnership 2013–; hon pres SCI 2015–; Liveryman Goldsmiths Co 2009 (Ct Asst); Hon DBA Anglia Ruskin Univ 2011; *Recreations* watching rugby, skiing, family; *Style*— Neil Carson, Esq, OBE; ✉ TT Electronics plc, 12 to 18 Queens Road, Weybridge, Surrey KT13 9XB (☎ 01223 891591)

CARSON, Dr (Thomas) Richard; s of Johnston Carson (d 1961), of Co Fermanagh, and Rebecca, *née* Farrell (d 1958); *Educ* Portora Royal Sch (Seale open scholar), Queen's Univ Belfast (Sullivan open scholar, BSc, PhD); *m* 1971, Ursula Margaret Mary, *née* Davies; 1 s (David Richard b 1973); *Career* theoretical physicist/astrophysicist; lectr Dept of Natural Philosophy Univ of Glasgow, sr scientific offr AWRE Aldermaston, currently hon reader in astrophysics Univ of St Andrews; sometime: conslt Atomic Weapons Research Establishment Aldermaston, visiting fell and prof Univ of Colorado, sr res assoc NASA Inst for Space Studies NY, visiting staff memb Los Alamos Nat Laboratory Univ of Calif, visiting prof Aust Nat Univ Canberra; memb: Int Astronomical Union 1966, American Astronomical Soc 1968, NY Acad of Sciences 1989; fndr memb Euro Astronomical Soc 1991; FRAS 1959; former: jr and sr 1 mile champion ATC (NI Cmd), co-holder NI and All Ireland 4 x 440 yards relay record; *Books* Atoms and Molecules in Astrophysics (ed with M J Roberts, 1972), also author of numerous research papers, reviews and articles in scientific literature; *Recreations* skiing, tennis, swimming, reading French prose and German verse, listening to Lieder and classical music; *Style*— Dr Richard Carson

CARSON, William Hunter Fisher (Willie); OBE (1983); s of Thomas Whelan Carson, and Mary Hay; *b* 16 November 1942; *Educ* Riverside Sch Stirling; *m* 1, 1963 (m dis 1979), Carole Jane Sutton; 3 s (Antony Thomas, Neil John, Ross William); m 2, 5 May 1982, Elaine, da of John B Williams; *Career* former racehorse jockey (ret 1997); currently racing mangr to Prince Ahmed Bin Salman 1997–; apprentice to: Capt G Armstrong 1957–63 (first winner Catterick 1962), Fred Armstrong 1963–66; first jockey to: Lord Derby 1967, Dick Hern 1977–97; appointed Royal jockey 1977; major races won: 2000 Guineas 4 times (High Top 1972, Known Fact 1980, Don't Forget Me 1987, Nashwan 1989), Oaks 4 times (Dunfermline 1977 for HM The Queen, Bireme 1980, Sun Princess 1983, Salsabil 1990), Derby 4 times (Troy 1979, Henbit 1980, Nashwan 1989, Erhaab 1994), King George VI and Queen Elizabeth Diamond Stakes 4 times (Troy 1979, Ela-Mana-Mou 1980, Petoski 1985, Nashwan 1989), St Léger 3 times (Dunfermline 1977 for HM The Queen, Sun Princess 1983, Minster Son 1988), the Eclipse twice (Nashwan 1989, Elmaamul 1990), Ascot Gold Cup 1983 (Little Wolf), 1000 Guineas 1990 (Salsabil); champion jockey 1972, 1973, 1978, 1980, 1983; has ridden over 100 winners every season since 1972 (except 1984 when injured), became third most successful Br jockey with 3,882 wins Aug 1990 (incl over 100 group one races), only jockey to ride and breed Classic winner (Minster Son, St Leger 1988); Swindon Town FC: dir 1997–, head of PR 1997–, chm 2001–; racing pundit BBC 1997–; Hon Dr Univ of Stirling 1998; *Style*— Willie Carson, Esq, OBE; ✉ Minster House, Barnsley, Cirencester, Gloucestershire

CARSS-FRISK, Monica; QC (2001); *Educ* Univ of London (LLB), Univ of Oxford (BCL); *Career* called to the Bar Gray's Inn 1985; practising barr specialising in administrative and public law, employment law and human rights 1986–; jt head of chambers Blackstone Chambers 2012–; pt/t tutor in law UCL 1984–87, memb Treasy Slrs Supplementary Common Law Panel 1997–99, jr counsel to the Crown (A Panel); memb Cncl of Justice; frequent participant in conferences on public law, human rights and employment law; *Publications* contrib: Halsbury's Laws of England: Constitutional Law and Human Rights (vol 8, 2 edn 1996), Butterworth's Human Rights Law and Practice (1999 and 2004), European Employment Law in the UK (2001); *Style*— Ms Monica Carss-Frisk, QC; ✉ Blackstone Chambers, Blackstone House, Temple, London EC4Y 9BW (☎ 020 7583 1770, fax 020 7822 7350, e-mail clerks@blackstonechambers.com)

CARSWELL, Douglas; MP; s of John Wilson Carswell, OBE, FRCS, and Margaret, *née* Clark; *b* 3 May 1971, London; *Educ* Charterhouse, UEA, KCL; *m* Clementine, *née* Bailey; *Career* with Invesco Asset Mgmnt 1999–2003, memb Cons Party Policy Unit 2004–05, MP (Cons): Harwich 2005–10, Clacton 2010–14 (Parly candidate (Cons) Sedgefield 2001); MP (UKIP) Clacton (by-election) 2014–; nominated Spectator Magazine Parliamentarian of the Year 2009; *Publications* Paying for Localism (2003), Direct Democracy: an agenda for a new model party (2005), The Localist Papers (2007), The Plan: 12 Months to Renew Britain (2008); *Recreations* gardening, blogging; *Clubs* Clacton Cons; *Style*— Douglas Carswell, Esq, MP; ✉ House of Commons, London SW1A 0AA (website www.talkcarswell.com); Constituency Office ☎ 01255 423112

CARSWELL, Baron (Life Peer UK 2004), of Killeen in the County of Down; Sir Robert Douglas Carswell; kt (1988), PC (1993); s of Alan Edward Carswell (d 1972), of Belfast, and Nance Eileen, *née* Corlett (d 2000); *b* 28 June 1934; *Educ* Royal Belfast Academical Inst, Pembroke Coll Oxford (MA), Univ of Chicago Law Sch; *m* 1961, Romayne Winifred, *qv*, da of James Ferris, JP, of Co Down; 2 da (Catherine, Patricia); *Career* called to the Bar NI 1957, English Bar (Gray's Inn) 1972, counsel to Attorney Gen for NI 1970–71, QC 1971, sr Crown counsel in NI 1979–84, judge of the High Court of NI 1984–93, Lord Justice of Appeal NI 1993–97, Lord Chief Justice of NI 1997–2004, a Lord of Appeal in Ordinary 2004–09; bencher Inn of Court of NI 1979; hon bencher: Gray's Inn 1993, King's Inns Dublin 1997; chm Law Reform Advsy Ctee NI 1989–97; govr Royal Belfast Academical Instn 1967–2004 (chm 1986–97, pres 2004–), pro-chllr and chm Cncl Univ of Ulster 1984–94, chllr Dioceses of Armagh and of Down and Dromore 1990–97; *Recreations* golf; *Clubs* Ulster Reform (Belfast); *Style*— The Rt Hon the Lord Carswell, PC

CARSWELL, Lady; Romayne Winifred Carswell; CVO (2010), OBE (1988), JP (2000); da of James Ferris, JP (d 1960), and Eileen Ferris, JP, *née* Johnston (d 2010); *Educ* Victoria Coll Belfast, Queen's Univ Belfast; *m* 11 July 1961, Baron Carswell, PC (Life Peer), *qv*; 2 da (Catherine b 5 March 1963, Patricia b 2 Dec 1967); *Career* former memb NI Civil Serv; dep chm Police Complaints Bd for NI (subsequently Ind Cmmn for Police Complaints) 1983–94 (memb 1977–83); pt/t memb: Standing Advsy Cmmn on Human Rights 1984–86, Industrial Tbnls 1987–97; pres: Friends of the Ulster Museum 1996–2011, Ulster Soc for the Protection of the Countryside 2010–15; vice-pres Belfast branch Royal Naval Assoc 2010; tstee Ulster Historical Fndn 1992–2003 (dep chm 1997–2000), tstee Winston Churchill Meml Tst 2002–09, convener Project Ctee Ulster Architectural Heritage Soc 1991–2000; memb: Bd of Govrs Victoria Coll Belfast 1979–99 (dep chm 1995–99), Ards Historical Soc, Ulster Wildlife Tst; HM Lord-Lt Co Borough of Belfast 2000–09 (DL 1997–2000); Hon Capt Royal Naval Reserve 2005–13; DStJ 2010 (CStJ 2000); *Style*— The Lady Carswell, CVO, OBE

CARTE, Brian Addison; TD (1976); s of late James Carte; *b* 7 August 1943; *Educ* St Lawrence Coll Ramsgate, Wharton Business Sch Univ of Pennsylvania; *m* 1969, Shirley Anne, da of Lt-Col W H Brinkley; 2 da; *Career* Co Cdr Queen's Regt TA, Maj GSO II HQ London Dist, asst project offr DTA and C, RARO 1987; dir County Bank Ltd 1976–85, md National Westminster Insurance Services Ltd 1985–89, chief exec Lombard North Central plc 1989–96 (dir 1996–97); chm Motability Finance Ltd 1992–95, dep chm First National Bank plc 1998–2003, chm Caffyns plc 2003–08 (non-exec dir 1996–2003); non-exec dir: PPP Ltd 1996–99, Fletcher King plc 1997–2002, Royal Automobile Club Ltd 1998–99, Cardif Pinnacle plc 2009–12; govr Motability 1992–2014; former pres Assoc of Corp Treasurers; Freeman and Liveryman Worshipful Co of Scriveners; FCIB, FCT, FRSA, FIMI; *Recreations* golf, shooting, opera; *Clubs* New Zealand Golf, RAC; *Style*— Brian Carte, Esq, TD; ✉ Fairfield Lodge, Hardwick Close, Knott Park, Oxshott, Surrey KT22 0HZ

CARTER, Sir David Craig; kt (1996); s of Horace Ramsay Carter, and Mary Florence, *née* Lister; *b* 1 September 1940; *Educ* Univ of St Andrews (MB ChB), Univ of Dundee (MD); *m* 23 Sept 1967, Ilske Ursula, da of Wolfgang August Luth (d 1945), of Riga, Latvia; 2 s (Adrian b 5 Jan 1969, Ben b 3 Nov 1970); *Career* St Mungo prof of surgery Univ of Glasgow 1979–88, regius prof of clinical surgery Univ of Edinburgh 1988–96; surgn to HM The Queen in Scotland 1993–97, CMO for Scotland 1996–2000; former memb: Biomedical Research Ctee Scottish Home and Health Dept, Br Broadcasting Cncl Scotland, Cncl RCSEd, Int Surgical Gp; chm: Scottish Fndn for Surgery in Nepal 1987–2010, Scottish Cncl for Postgrad Med Educn 1990–96, Bd of Science BMA 2002–05, Queens Nursing Inst Scot 2002–10, Health Fndn 2003–08, Bd for Academic Medicine 2004–16, Managed Service Network for Neurosurgery 2009–14; pres: Int Hepato-Biliary and Pancreatic Assoc 1988–89, Surgical Research Soc 1996–97, Assoc of Surgns of GB and I 1996–97, BMA 2001–02; vice-princ Univ of Edinburgh 2000–02, chm Scientific Advsy Ctee Cancer Research Campaign 2000–02, pres BMA 2001–02, vice-pres Royal Soc Edinburgh 2000–03, govr PPP Healthcare Fndn 2001–03, memb Sci Exec Bd Cancer Research UK 2002–04, tstee and vice-chm Cancer Research UK 2004–07; overseas assoc Inst of Medicine USA 1998–; Gold Medal: RCSEd 2000, BMA 2006, RSE 2008; Hon DSc: Univ of St Andrews, Queen Margaret UC Edinburgh, Univ of Aberdeen, Univ of Edinburgh, Inst of Cancer Research, Univ of London; hon sec: Br Jl of Surgery 1991–95, James IV Assoc of Surgns 1990–96; Hon LLD Univ of Dundee, Hon DSc Univ of Hull 2010; Hon FRCSI, Hon FACS, Hon FRACS, Hon FRCGP, Hon FRCPS (Glas), Hon CSHK 2003, Hon FRCP 2005; FRCSEd, FRCPEd, FRCSGlas, FRCS (Eng), FFPHM 1998, fell Acad Med Sci 1998; fell American Surgical Assoc 2000, FRSE; awarded Gorka Dakshim Bahu (Nepal, 1999); *Books* Peptic Ulcer (1983), Principles and Practice of Surgery (1985, 2 edn 1989), Atlas of General Surgery (1986, 2 edn 1996), British Journal of Surgery (co-ed, 1986–91), Perioperative Care (1988), Pancreatitis (1989), Surgery of the Pancreas (1993 and 1997), Rob & Smith's Operative Surgery series (co-ed); *Recreations* gardening, philately, music; *Clubs* New (Edinburgh); *Style*— Sir David Carter, FRSE; ✉ 19A Buckingham Terrace, Edinburgh EH4 3AD (☎ 0131 332 5554)

CARTER, (William) George Key; CBE, DL (W Midlands 1996); s of Lt-Col William Tom Carter, OBE, JP (d 1956), and Georgina Margaret, *née* Key (d 1986); *b* 29 January 1934; *Educ* Warwick Sch; *m* 30 June 1965, Anne Rosalie Mary, da of Trevor Acheson-Williams Flanagan (d 1987); 1 da (Louisa Mary-Anne b 1968), 1 s (Alexander Corfield Key b 1971); *Career* 2 Lt 16/5 The Queen's Royal Lancers 1958–60 (asst Adj 1959); qualified CA 1957; Price Waterhouse: joined 1956, mangr 1963, ptnr 1966, sr ptnr (W Midlands) 1982–94;

C

pres: Birmingham C of C and Industry 1993–94, Worcs Branch ESU 1998–2003; chm: W Midlands Devpt Agency 1989–95, Black Country Development Corp 1994–98; vice-chm: Birmingham Mktg Partnership 1993–95, Birmingham Children's Hosp NHS Tst 1996–2003; dir Birmingham Economic Devpt Partnership 1991–95; memb: Ferrous Foundry Industry Advsy Ctee 1974–80, Pharmacist Review Bd 1980–97, Cncl W Midlands CBI 1988–98, Advsy Bd Univ of Birmingham Business Sch 1993–2000, N Worcs HA 1994–96, Cncl Aston Univ 1995–98; feoffee and govr Old Swinford Hosp Sch 1986–2000; chm: Cncl Order of St John W Midlands 1994–2001, Lunar Soc 1996–99 (chm 1999–2001); High Sheriff W Midlands 1998–99; FCA 1957, FRSA 1993; *Books* The Work of the Investigating Accountant; *Recreations* golf, gardening; *Clubs* Cavalry and Guards'; *Style*— George Carter, Esq, CBE, DL, CStJ, FCA; ✉ The Old Rectory, Elmley Lovett, Droitwich, Worcestershire WR9 0PS (✆ 01299 851251, e-mail wgkcarter@btinternet.com)

CARTER, Gillian; *Educ* Jersey Coll for Girls; *Career* journalist; features writer Sunday Mirror 1993–95, dep ed Woman magazine 1995–99, ed Family Circle 2000–02; BBC Good Food: dep ed 2003–04, editorial dir 2004–; *Style*— Ms Gillian Carter; ✉ BBC Good Food, 44 Vineyard House, Brook Green, London W6 7BT (e-mail gillian.carter@bbcgoodfoodmagazine.com)

CARTER, John; s of Eric Gordon Carter (d 1991), and Mercia Gertrude, née Edmonds (d 2008); *b* 3 March 1942; *Educ* Twickenham Sch of Art, Kingston Sch of Art, British Sch in Rome; *m* 11 July 1986, Belinda Juliet, da of Alan Cadbury; *Career* artist; memb Cathedrals Fabric Cmmn for England; RA 2007; *Solo Exhibitions* incl: Redfern Gallery 1968, 1971, 1974, 1977, 2010 and 2013, Univ of Reading 1979, Nicola Jacobs Gallery 1980, 1983, 1987 and 1990, Retrospective 1965–83 1983, Warwick Arts Tst 1983, Moris Gallery Tokyo 1987 and 1989, Gallery Yamaguchi Osaka 1989, Sumi Gallery Okayama 1989, Galerie Hoffmann Friedberg 1990, 2008 and 2014, Knoedler Gallery London 1991, Galerie Wack Kaiserslautern 1991, 2002, 2007, 2012 and 2015, Museum Moderner Kunst Landkreis Cuxhaven 1994, Belloc Lowndes Fine Art Chicago 1995, Gudrun Spielvogel Galerie Munich 1995, 1999, 2008 and 2013, Ecole Superiere des Arts Visuels de la Cambre Brussels 1995, Francis Graham-Dixon Gallery London 1996, Galerie Lattemann Darmstadt 1996 and 2003, Galerie St Johann Saarbrücken 1998 and 2009, Slade Gallery UCL 2002, Espace Fanal Basle 2002, 2010 and 2014, Gallery Benoot Knokke-Zoute 2003, Artmark Galerie, Spital am Pyhrn, The Blue Gallery London 2004, Konstruktiv Tendens Stockholm 2005 and 2008, Galerie Konkret Martin Wörn 2006, De Vierde Dimensie Plasmolen 2007 and 2011, Galerie La Ligne Zurich 2011 and 2013, Tennant Gallery RA 2013, Galerie Leonhard Graz 2014, Fondation Louis Moret Martigny 2014; *Group Exhibitions* incl: New Generation Whitechapel Gallery 1966, New British Painting and Sculpture UCLA Art Galleries LA and USA tour, British Painting Hayward Gallery 1974, British Art Show Mappin Art Gallery Sheffield and tour 1979, The British Cncl Collection Serpentine Gallery 1980, British Art 1940–80 The Arts Cncl Collection Hayward Gallery 1981, British Art Show Birmingham Museum and tour 1984, New Works on Paper Br Cncl and world tour 1984, Die Ecke Galerie Hoffmann Friedberg 1986, Britannica – 30 ans de Sculpture Musée André Malraux Le Havre 1988, The Presence of Painting Aspects of British Abstraction 1957–88 Mappin Art Gallery and tour 1988, Britse Sculptuur 1960–88 Museum van Hedendaagse Kunst Antwerp 1989, Arte Constructivo y Sistematico Centro Cultural de la Villa Madrid 1989, 1000 Kubikzentimeter Geom Minituren Wilhem-Hack-Museum Ludwigshafen 1990, Universal Progression Manege Moscow 1990, Piccolo Formato Arte Struktura Milan 1990, Geometrisk Abstraktion X Konstruktiv Tendens Stockholm 1991, Royal Acad of Arts Summer Exhbn 1992 and annually from 2002, Aspects de la Mouvance Construite Internationale Musée des Beaux Arts Verviers 1993, Skulptur und Architektur: Ein Diskurs T H Lichtwiese Darmstadt 1993, Interférences Musée des Beaux-Arts Mons, Blick über den Armelkanal Pfalzgalerie Kaiserslautern 1994, Kunstmuseum Thun 1996, Mondiale Echo's Mondriaanhuis Amersfoort 2000, Das Entgrenzte Wilhelm-Hack-Museum Ludwigshafen 2002, Mesures Art International (Musée Matisse Le Cateu-Cambresis); *Awards* Leverhulme travelling scholarship to Italy 1963, Peter Stuyvesant Fndn travel bursary to USA 1966, Arts Cncl awards 1977 and 1979; *Style*— John Carter, Esq, RA; ✉ 71A Westbourne Park Road, London W2 5QH; c/o Edition & Galerie Hoffmann, Görbel Heimer Mühle, D-61169 Friedberg, Germany (✆ 00 49 6031 2443); c/o Redfern Gallery, 20 Cork Street, London W1S 3HL (✆ 020 7734 1732)

CARTER, Prof Joy; DL (Hampshire, 2013); *b* 26 December 1963, Fleetwood, Lancs; *Educ* Durham Univ (BSc), Univ of Lancaster (PhD); *m* Martin; 4 s (Jonathan, Jeremy, Joshua, Jared); *Career* lectr and reader in environmental geochemistry and health Postgraduate Research Inst for Sedimentology Univ of Reading 1981–99; Univ of Derby: asst dean of science, prof of environmental geochemistry and health, and dir of science research and consultancy 1999–2000, dean of science, prof of environmental geochemistry and health, and dir of science research and consultancy 2000–02, pro-vice-chllr Univ of Glamorgan 2002–06, vice-chllr Univ of Winchester 2006–; memb Editorial Bd Times Higher Educn (THE); memb Bd: HE Quality Assurance Agency (QAA, incl Audit and Nominations Ctees), UCAS; chair: Supporting Professionalism Admissions (SPA), GuildHE; memb Educnl Advsy Gp Mary Rose Tst; patron: Education Uganda, Winchester Cathedral Fundraising Campaign, Carroll Centre Winchester, Hampshire Writers Soc, Winchester Action on Climate Change; vice-pres Winchester YMCA, pres Winchester City Tst, memb Int Women's Forum; hon fell Oxford Centre for Animal Ethics; pres Int Soc for Environmental Geochemistry and Health 2002–08; FGS; *Recreations* fashion, gardening, antiques, cycling with my dog; *Style*— Prof Joy Carter, DL; ✉ West Wing, The Old Rectory, Park Lane, Abbots Worthy, Winchester, SO21 1DT (✆ 01962 881530) ; University of Winchester, Sparkford Road, Winchester, Hampshire SO22 4NR (✆ 01962 827222, e-mail joy.carter@winchester.ac.uk, website www.winchester.ac.uk)

CARTER, Gen Sir Nicholas Patrick; KCB (2014), CBE (2003, OBE 2000, MBE 1996), DSO (2011); *b* 11 February 1959; *Career* cmmnd Royal Green Jackets 1978 (served NI, Cyprus, Germany and GB), mil asst to Chief of the Gen Staff 1994, CO 2nd Bn Royal Green Jackets 1998 (deployed to Bosnia and Kosovo), Hon Dep Col The Rifles 2007, Dir Army Resources and Plans 2006, Gen Offr Commanding 6th Div 2009 (deployed to Afghanistan), DG Land Warfare 2011, Dep Cdr Int Security Assistance Force (ISAF) 2012, Cdr Land Forces 2013, Chief of the Gen Staff 2014–; *Style*— Gen Sir Nicholas Carter, KCB, CBE, DSO, ADC Gen; ✉ Ministry of Defence, Whitehall, London SW1A 2HB

CARTER, Peter; QC (1995); s of Tom Carter, and Winifred Carter, of Huddersfield, W Yorks; *b* 8 August 1952; *Educ* King James' GS Huddersfield, UCL (LLB); *m* 1973, Caroline Ann, da of Leslie Hugh Adams; 1 s (Jonathan Edwin b 3 Nov 1988); *Career* called to the Bar Gray's Inn 1974 (bencher 2003); chair Bar Human Rights Ctee, govr Br Inst of Human Rights, memb Legal Section Amnesty; memb: Criminal Bar Assoc (sec 1985–89), Inst of Advanced Legal Studies; *Books* Offences of Violence; *Recreations* poetry, sport, walking; *Style*— Peter Carter, Esq, QC; ✉ 18 Red Lion Court, London EC4A 3EB; Park Court Chambers, 16 Park Place Leeds LS1 2SJ

CARTER, Dr Peter John; OBE (2006); s of Reginald John Carter (d 1982), and Mary Doreen Carter; *Educ* Univ of Birmingham (MBA, PhD), RMN, RGN; *m* Lilian; 2 da (Catherine b 13 March 1971, Elizabeth b 22 Jan 1973); *Career* head of personnel SW Herts HA 1980–83, commissioning mangr S Beds HA 1990–92 (dir of ops 1986–90); chief exec: NW London Mental Health NHS Tst 1995–98 (dir of ops 1993–95), Brent Kensington Chelsea and Westminster Mental Health NHS Tst 1998–99, Central and NW London Mental

Health NHS Tst 1999–2007, RCN 2007–15; ind mgmnt conslt 2015–; memb PM's Cmmn on the Futures of Nursing 2009–10, memb various ctees incl Review Panel examining prescribing practice in the UK, expert witness in health related litigation; vice-pres Inst of Customer Services 2014; visiting prof: KCL, Anglia Ruskin Univ; President's Medal RCPsych 2011; Hon Col 203 Field Hosp 2011; Hon DSc Univ of Herts 2010, hon doctorate Edge Hill Univ 2013; memb RCN, MIPD; Hon FRCGP 2014; *Publications* Abuse of the Doctor – Patient Relationship (contrib, 2010); *Recreations* rugby, scuba diving and most other sports, music, opera, cycling, gardening, ballet; *Clubs* Harpenden RFC; *Style*— Dr Peter Carter, OBE; ✉ e-mail carterp118@hotmail.com

CARTER, Philip Mark (Phil); s of Brian Carter, of Norwich, Norfolk, and Barbara Mary, née Herod; *b* 26 September 1955; *Educ* Thorpe GS Norwich, Great Yarmouth Coll of Art, Norwich Sch of Art (BA), RCA (MA); *m* 1984, Deborah, da of David Catford; 1 s (Joseph b 1985), 1 da (Caitlin b 1989); *Career* designer Minale Tattersfield & Partners 1980–83, fndr ptnr/creative dir Carter Wong 1984–; work featured in various pubns incl: D&AD Annual 1983, 1985, 1988, 1989, 1990, 1994, 1995, 1999, 2000, 2001, 2002, 2003, 2004 and 2005, Graphis Annual 1996; designer of both Unilever ice cream 'heartmark' and FIA Formula One F1 Championship logos; D&AD Silver Award (Heal's Corp Identity) 1983, Media Natura Award (Marine Conservation Identity) 1988, DBA Design Effectiveness Awards winner 1999, 2003, 2014 and 2016, D&AD Silver Award nomination 2002 and 2003, Design Week Award 2003; external assessor: Bath Coll of HE 1991–96, Kingston Univ 1994–97, Dept of Communication Art and Design RCA, UC Falmouth 2009–12; speaker ICOGRADA 4 Designers Conference 2015, numerous lectures at various insts; memb: Exec Ctee D&AD 1992–94, D&AD Jury 2000, 2002, 2003, 2004 and 2005, DBA, SCR RCA; *Books* 1057: Cycle Lane Markings (2011), A Cycling Lexicon: Bicycle Headbadges (2013); *Recreations* swimming, cycling, tennis; *Clubs* Chelsea Arts; *Style*— Phil Carter; ✉ Carter Wong, 29 Brook Mews North, London W2 3BW (✆ 020 7569 0000, mobile 07787 533925, fax 020 7569 0001, e-mail p.carter@carterwongdesign.com, website www.carterwongdesign.com)

CARTER OF BARNES, Baron (Life Peer UK 2008), of Barnes in the London Borough of Richmond upon Thames; Stephen Andrew Carter; CBE (2007); s of Mr and Mrs G R Carter, of Pitlochry; *b* 12 February 1964; *Educ* Univ of Aberdeen (LLB), Harvard Business Sch (AMP); *m* Anna Maria, da of Kevin and Joan Gorman; 1 s (Max Gorman Alexander b 11 Oct 1996), 1 da (Ellie Gorman Imogen b 7 Feb 1999); *Career* md/ceo JWT UK Gp Ltd 1995–2000; md and chief operating offr NTL UK and Ireland 2000–03, chief exec Ofcom 2003–07, gp chief exec Brunswick Gp 2007–08; PM's chief of strategy and princ advsr and min for technol 2008–09; gp ceo Informa plc 2013–; formerly: non-exec dir Travis Perkins, non-exec dir Royal Mail, chm Mktg Gp of GB; currently: exec vice-pres Alcatel Lucent, non-exec dir Informa plc, vice-pres Unicef UK, chm Ashridge Business Sch; *Style*— The Lord Carter of Barnes, CBE; ✉ House of Lords, London SW1A 0PW

CARTER OF COLES, Baron (Life Peer UK 2004), of Coles in the County of Hertfordshire; Patrick Robert Carter; s of late Robert Stanley Edward Carter; *b* 9 February 1946; *Educ* Brentwood Sch, Univ of Durham (BA); *m* 1969, Julia K H, née Bourne; 2 da (Esther Jenny b 1973, Sasha Beatrice b 1976); *Career* exec dir MAI plc 1975–85, chief exec and md Westminster Health Care 1985–99 (fndr 1985), chm Sport England 2002–06; non-exec dir Prison Service 1998–2002; chm Govt Review of: Cwlth Games 2002, English Stadium (Wembley) 2002, Nat Athletics, Payroll Services, Criminal Record Bureau 2003, Court Estates 2004; memb: Productivity Panel HM Treasy 2000–, Gen Bd Home Office 2002–06, London 2012 Ltd 2003–12, Competition and Co-operation Panel 2014–; chair NHS procurement & efficiency bd; *Style*— The Lord Carter of Coles; ✉ House of Lords, London SW1A 0PW

CARTER OWERS, Hannah; da of Michael Carter, of Fulham, and Deborah Doyle, of Oxfordshire; *b* 28 April 1976, Sheffield; *Educ* James Allen's Girls' School London, Oxford Brookes Univ (DipAD), Glasgow Sch of Art (BA); *m* 18 July 2009, Nicholas Owers; 2 c; *Career* designer Conran Design Gp 1998–2001, designer Four IV 2001–03, dir Universal Design Studio 2003–; visiting lectr: Univ of the Arts London, Oxford Brookes Univ; designs featured in pubns incl: Elle Decoration, Icon, Pol Oxygen Design Directory, Blueprint, Design Week and Building Design (all 2005–07), WWD, Design Week, Luxury Briefing, Campaign and On Office (all 2008), Dezeen, Obras Semana, Frame, Glass Magazine and Living Etc (all 2010), Blueprint, Metropolis Magazine, Luxury Briefing, Elle Decoration, Frame, Interior World, Creative Review and Retail Focus (all 2011), Elle Decoration, Inside Magazine and Design Week (all 2012), Dezeen, Surface Magazine and Monocle (all 2014), On Office, Monocle, Disegno and Design Week (all 2015); *Books* designs featured in: Ultimate London Design (2006), New Exhibition Design (2010), Detail in Retail (2012), Power Shop 2: New Retail Design (2010), Space 2: Workplace (2012), Detail in Contemporary Retail Design (2012), Detail in Contemporary Office Design (2013); *Recreations* cinema, fashion, skiing, travel, walking, drawing, food and dining; *Style*— Ms Hannah Carter Owers; ✉ Universal Design Studio, 37–42 Charlotte Road, London EC2A 3PG (e-mail hannah@universaldesignstudio.com, website www.universaldesignstudio.com)

CARTER-STEPHENSON, George Anthony; QC (1998); s of Raymond M Stephenson, and Brenda S Carter; *b* 10 July 1952; *Educ* Arnold Sch Blackpool, Univ of Leeds (LLB); *m* 1974, Christine Maria; 1 s (Christian James b 31 Jan 1977), 1 da (Sarah Louise b 22 April 1981); *Career* called to the Bar Inner Temple 1975; jt head of chambers 2009–; *Recreations* motorcycling, theatre, cinema, music; *Style*— George Carter-Stephenson, Esq, QC; ✉ 25 Bedford Row, London WC1R 4HD (✆ 020 7067 1500, fax 020 7067 1507)

CARTLEDGE, Graham Stanley; CBE (2008), DL (Notts); s of Thomas S Cartledge (d 1967), and Doris B Cartledge (d 1991); *b* 7 January 1947; *Educ* Magnus Boys GS Newark, Leics Sch of Architecture (DipArch); *m* 31 July 1972, Jo, da of J W Booth; 2 s (Ben b 17 March 1978, Tom b 15 June 1979), 1 da (Amy b 21 July 1984); *Career* architect; sr ptnr Gordon Benoy & Partners 1975–88 (merged with Fitch & Co); chm Benoy (int award-winning architecture and design firm with projects in around 60 countries across the world 1992–; co-fndr with wife Jo Benoy Fndn 2007; ambass Wildlife Tsts; High Sheriff of Nottinghamshire 2014–15; Hon DDes De Montfort Univ, Hon DArch Univ of Nottingham; RIBA 1972; *Recreations* golf, cricket, football; *Style*— Graham Cartledge, Esq, CBE, DL; ✉ Benoy Ltd, 1 Monkwell Square, London EC2Y 5BL (✆ 020 7726 8999, e-mail graham.cartledge@benoy.com)

CARTLEDGE, Prof Paul Anthony; s of Marcus Raymond Cartledge (d 1990), and Margaret Christobel Cartledge (d 2000); *b* 24 March 1947; *Educ* St Paul's (fndn scholar), New Coll Oxford (Ella Stephens open scholar, MA, DPhil); *Career* Craven fell Univ of Oxford 1969–70, Salvesen jr res fell Univ Coll Oxford 1970–72, lectr in classics New Univ of Ulster 1972–73, lectr in classics Trinity Coll Dublin 1973–78, lectr in classical civilization Univ of Warwick 1978–79; Univ of Cambridge: lectr in classics 1979–93, fell Clare Coll 1981– (professorial fell 1999–, pres of the fellowship 2011–14, AG Leventis sr research fell 2014–), reader in Greek history 1993–99, prof of Greek history 1999–2008, chm Faculty of Classics 2001–02, A G Leventis prof of Greek culture 2008–14; Hellenic Parl global distinguished prof NYU 2006–10; invited speaker at numerous int confs and symposia; pres Cambridge Philological Soc 1994–96, memb Br Ctee for the Reunification of the Parthenon Marbles, pres Jt Assoc of Classical Teachers 2011–13; awarded Leverhulme Tst research grant 1982; Hon PhD (Economics) Univ of Thessaly Greece 2011; FSA 1980, FRSA 2007; Gold Cross of Order of Honour (Greece) 2002, Hon Citizen of Sparta Greece 2005; *Books* Sparta and Lakonia: a regional history 1300–362 BC (1979, 2 edn 2001), CRUX: Essays in Greek History presented to G E M de Ste. Croix on his 75th birthday (co-ed and contrib, 1985), Agesilaos and the Crisis of Sparta (1987), Hellenistic and Roman Sparta: a tale of two cities (jtly, 1989, revised edn 2001), Aristophanes and his Theatre of the Absurd (1990, revised edn 1999), NOMOS: Essays in Athenian Law, Politics and Society (co-ed and contrib, 1990), L Bruit Zaidman & P Schmitt Pantel: Religion in the Ancient Greek City (ed and trans, 1992), The Greeks. A Portrait of Self and Others (1993, 2 edn 2002), Hellenistic Constructs: Essays in culture, history, and historiography (co-ed and contrib, 1997), The Cambridge Illustrated History of Ancient Greece (creator, ed and contrib, 1997, revised edn 2002), Xenophon: Hiero the Tyrant and Other Treatises (jtly, 1997, revised edn 2006), KOSMOS: Essays in Athenian Order, Conflict and Community (co-ed and contrib, 1998), Democritus and Atomistic Politics (1998), The Greeks: Crucible of Civilization (2000), Spartan Reflections (2001), Money, Labour and Land. Approaches to the economies of ancient Greece (co-ed and contrib, 2001), The Spartans: An Epic History (2002, 2 edn 2003), Alexander the Great: The hunt for a new past (2004), Thermopylae: The Battle That Changed the World (2006), Eine Trilogie über Demokratie (2008), Ancient Greek Political Thought in Practice (2009), Ancient Greece: A History in Eleven Cities (2009), Responses to Oliver Stone's Alexander: Film, History, and Cultural Studies (co-ed, 2010), Ancient Greece: A Very Short Introduction (2011), The Cambridge World History of Slavery Vol I (co-ed and contrib, 2011), After Thermopylae: The Oath of Plataea and the End of the Greco-Persian Wars (2013), Democracy: A Life (2016); *Recreations* theatre, ballet, opera; *Clubs* Athenaeum; *Style*— Prof Paul Cartledge; ✉ Clare College, Cambridge CB2 1TL (☎ 01223 333200, fax 01223 845808, e-mail pac1001@cam.ac.uk); Faculty of Classics, Sidgwick Avenue, Cambridge CB3 9DA (fax 01223 335409)

CARTWRIGHT, Jim; s of Jim Cartwright, of Farnworth, Lancs, and Edna, *née* Main; *b* 27 June 1958; *Educ* Harper Green Secdy Sch Farnworth; *m* Angela Louise, da of Samuel Jones; 2 s (James Lewis b 22 Oct 1984, Samuel Aaron b 2 May 1998), 2 da (Georgina Lucy b 12 June 1996, Charlotte Emily (twin) b 2 May 1998); *Career* writer; *Plays* Road (performed Royal Court Theatre 1986–87, adapted for BBC TV 1987), Baths (radio, 1987), Vroom (film on Channel 4, 1988), Bed (RNT 1989), TWO (Octagon Bolton and Young Vic London 1989–90), June (BBC TV 1990), Wedded (BBC TV 1990), The Rise and Fall of Little Voice (RNT then Aldwych 1992), I Licked a Slag's Deodorant (Royal Court at the Ambassadors 1996), Prize Night (Royal Exchange 1999), Hard Fruit (Royal Court 2000), Strumpet (BBC 2002), Vacuuming Completely Nude In Paradise (BBC 2002); *Awards* for Road: Samuel Beckett Award, Drama Magazine Award, jt winner George Devine Award and Plays and Players Award, Golden Nymph Award for Best Film at Monte Carlo TV and Film Festival; for TWO: Manchester Evening News Theatre Award for Best New Play; for The Rise and Fall of Little Voice: Best Comedy Evening Standard Drama Awards 1992, Best Comedy Laurence Olivier Awards 1993; *Style*— Jim Cartwright, Esq; ✉ AJ Associates, Department C, Higher Healey House, Higher House Lane, White Coppice, Chorley, Lancashire PR6 9BT

CARTWRIGHT, Prof Nancy Delaney; *b* 24 June 1944; *Educ* Univ of Pittsburgh (BS), Univ of Illinois (Carnegie fell, Danforth fell, Woodrow Wilson fell, PhD); *Career* asst prof of philosophy Univ of Maryland 1971–73; Stanford Univ: asst prof of philosophy 1973–77, assoc prof 1977–83, prof 1983–91, chair Philosophy Dept 1988–90; LSE: prof of philosophy, logic and scientific method 1991–, dir Centre for Philosophy of Nat and Social Science 2006–08; prof of philosophy Univ of Calif San Diego 1997–; visiting lectr Univ of Cambridge 1974, visiting asst prof UCLA 1976, visiting assoc prof Princeton Univ 1978, visiting prof Univ of Pittsburgh 1984, short term visiting prof Univ of Oslo 1993 and 1994; fell: Center for Interdisciplinary Research (ZiF) Bielefeld Germany 1976–77 (memb Advsy Bd 1993–), Philosophy of Science Center Univ of Pittsburgh 1982–83 and 1984, Wissenschaftskolleg Berlin 1987–88 (memb Advsy Bd 1991–96); pres: Soc for Exact Philosophy 1985, American Assoc of Univ Profs Stanford Chapter 1986–87, Philosophy of Science Assoc 2008–10, Pacific Div American Philosophical Assoc 2008–09; MacArthur Fndn Award 1993; memb Deutsche Akademie der Naturforscher Leopoldina 1999–; Old Dominion fell Princeton Univ 1996; memb: American Acad of Arts and Scis 2001, American Philosophical Soc 2004; FBA 1996; *Books* How the Laws of Physics Lie (1983), Nature's Capacities and their Measurement (1989), Otto Neurath: Philosophy between Science and Politics (jtly, 1995), The Dappled World – A Study of the Boundaries of Science (1999), Measuring Causes: Invariance, Modularity and Causal Markov Condition (2000), Hunting Causes and Using Them: Studies in Philosophy and Economics (2007), Causal Powers: What Are They? Why Do We Need Them? What Can be Done with Them and What Cannot? (2007); also author of numerous articles in learned jls; *Style*— Prof Nancy Cartwright, FBA; ✉ Department of Philosophy, Logic, and Scientific Method, London School of Economics and Political Science, Houghton Street, London WC2A 2AE (☎ 020 7955 7341/7901, fax 020 7955 6845)

CARTWRIGHT, His Hon Judge Nicolas Frederick; s of Geoffrey Cartwright (d 2013), and Christa, *née* Hillebrand (d 1983); *Educ* Malvern Coll, King Edward's Sch Birmingham, Univ of Liverpool; *m* 31 May 1991, Penelope, *née* Martyn-Smith; 1 s (Edward b 13 May 1993), 2 da (Molly b 25 June 1995, Emma b 3 March 1998); *Career* called to the Bar 1986; dep dist judge Magistrates' Ct 2005, recorder 2009, circuit judge (Midland Circuit) 2015–; *Style*— His Hon Judge Cartwright

CARTWRIGHT, Sally Amanda; OBE (2001); da of Dennis Cartwright (d 1990), and Eileen Sergeant Cartwright (d 1979); *b* 8 May 1944; *Educ* Merton House Sch Keymer; *m* 1, 23 Feb 1973, John William Robinson; m 2, 29 Feb 1980, John Brian Hutchings; *Career* IPC Magazine: asst publisher 1979–82, publisher 1983–86; md: Capital Magazine 1987, Harmsworth Publications (pt of Assoc Newspapers) 1988–90; publishing dir Hello! magazine 1990–2009; pres Women's Advtg Club of London 1992–93, assoc Women of the Year Luncheon; chm: PPA 1998–2000, Environmental Ctee Int Fedn of the Periodical Press (FIPP), Newstrade Jt Industry Gp 2008–09, Audit Bureau of Circulations 2010–; memb Cncl Advtg Standards Authy 2007–; church warden St Peter ad Vincola Broad Hinton; *Recreations* reading, embroidery, skiing, swimming, opera, theatre; *Clubs* Ski Club of GB (chm and pres 2001–05); *Style*— Ms Sally Cartwright, OBE; ✉ ABC, Saxon House, 211 High Street, Berkhamsted, Hertfordshire HP4 1AD (☎ 01442 870800)

CARTWRIGHT, Stacey; *Career* Pricewaterhouse until 1988 (qualified CA), various finance positions incl dir of finance and corp devpt then commercial dir Media Div Granada Gp plc 1988–99, chief fin offr Egg plc 1999–2004, chief fin offr Burberry plc 2004–08, exec vice-pres Burberry plc 2008–13, chief exec Harvey Nichols 2014–; *Style*— Ms Stacey Cartwright; ✉ Harvey Nichols, 109 – 125 Knightsbridge, London SW1X 7RJ

CARTY, Austin Timothy; s of Dr Thomas James Augustine (Gus) Carty (d 1975), of Glasnevin, Dublin, and Dr Catherine Anne Carty, *née* Quinn (d 1981); *b* 22 June 1941; *Educ* Belvedere Coll Dublin, UCD (MB BCh, BAO); *m* 23 Sept 1967, Prof Helen Carty, DL, *qv*, da of Roland Moloney (d 1971), of Dun Laoghaire, Co Dublin and Dungarvan, Co Waterford; 1 s (Timothy b 1968), 2 da (Jennifer b 1970, Sarah b 1973); *Career* conslt radiologist Liverpool HA 1974–2004 (ret), med dir Royal Liverpool Univ Hosp NHS Tst 1991–95; pres Liverpool Med Inst 1990–91; hon staff pres Liverpool Med Students' Soc 1999–2000; FRCR, FRCPI; *Recreations* opera and classical music, wine, salmon fishing, paintings; *Clubs* Athenaeum, Leander, Artists' (Liverpool, pres 1996–97, tstee 2004–), Twenty (Liverpool), Innominate (Liverpool); *Style*— Mr Austin Carty; ✉ 6 Grosvenor Road, Cressington Park, Liverpool L19 0PL (☎ 0151 427 6727, e-mail austincarty@btinternet.com)

CARTY, Prof Helen; DL (Merseyside 2005); da of Roland Moloney (d 1971), of Dublin, and Honor, *née* Frame (d 1982); *b* 12 May 1944; *Educ* St Mary's Arklow Co Wicklow, UCD (MB BCh, BAO); *m* 23 Sept 1967, Austin Carty, *qv*, s of Dr Thomas J A Carty (d 1975), of Dublin, and Dr Catherine Quinn (d 1981); 1 s (Timothy Mark b 13 Oct 1968), 2 da (Jennifer Ann b 29 Aug 1970, Sarah Lucy b 7 Feb 1973); *Career* house offr and med registrar Mater Hosp Dublin 1967–71, registrar in radiology St Thomas' Hosp London 1971–74, sr registrar Broadgreen Hosp Liverpool 1974–75, clinical dir radiology Alder Hey Hosp Liverpool 1977–2001 (conslt radiologist 1975–2004); prof of paediatric radiology Univ of Liverpool 1996–2004; chm Intercollegiate Standing Ctee on Nuclear Med London 1989–95; pres Liverpool Med Instn 1993–94; RCR: sometime memb Bd of Faculty, Cncl and Educn Bd, examiner Final Fellowship 1988–91; memb Steering Ctee for monitoring Nat Breast Screening Prog Dept of Health 1987–96, warden RCR 1998–2002, pres Euro Congress of Radiology 2003–04 (chm Exec Bd 2004–05), memb Cncl Univ of Liverpool 2012–15, memb Fdn Tst Liverpool Cathedral 2012–; patron Sefton Cncl for Voluntary Services 2013; High Sheriff Merseyside 2011–12; *Books* Imaging Children: A Textbook of Paediatric Radiology (jt ed and author of several chapters, 1994; 2 edn, ed-in-chief and author of chapters, 2004), Emergency Paediatric Radiology (1999), Paediatric Ultrasound (ed, 2000), The Encyclopedia of Medical Imaging – Vol VII: Paediatrics (2001); *Recreations* birdwatching, theatre, cooking, wood carving and turning; *Style*— Prof Helen Carty, DL; ✉ 6 Grosvenor Road, Cressington Park, Liverpool L19 0PL (☎ 0151 427 6727, email helen.carty1@btinternet.com)

CARUSO, Adam; *b* 8 February 1962, Montreal, Canada; *Educ* McGill Univ Montreal; *m* Helen Thomas; 1 s (Sol Caruso Thomas); *Career* architect; early career with Florian Beigel and Arup Assocs; co-fndr (with Peter St John) Caruso St John Architects 1990–; major projects: New Art Gallery Walsall, Brick House London, Stortorget Sweden, Gagosian Gallery London, Museum of Childhood London, Nottingham Contemporary, Tate Britain, new chancel for St GAllen Cathedral; prof of architecture Univ of Bath 2002–04; teacher: Univ of N London 1990–2000, Grad Sch of Design Harvard Univ 2005; visiting prof: Acad of Architecture Mendrisio Switzerland 1999–2001, LSE 2005–08, ETH Zürich 2007–09 (prof of architecture and construction 2011–); *Publications* Almost Everything (2008), The Feeling of Things (2008), Gardens of Experience (2010); *Style*— Adam Caruso; ✉ Caruso St John Architects, 1 Coate Street, London E2 9AG (☎ 020 7613 3161, fax 020 7729 6188)

CARVEL, Bertie; *b* 6 September 1977; *Educ* Univ of Sussex (BA), RADA; *Career* actor; *Theatre* incl: Revelations (Hampstead Theatre) 2003, Professor Bernhardi (Oxford Stage Co) 2005, Rose Berndt (Oxford Stage Co) 2005, Coram Boy (NT) 2005 (revived 2006), The Life of Galileo (NT) 2006, The Man of Mode (NT) 2007, Parade (Donmar Warehouse) 2007, The Pride (Royal Court) 2008 (Best Achievement in an Affiliate Theatre Olivier Awards 2009), Rope (Almeida Theatre) 2009, Matilda The Musical (RSC and West End) 2010– (Best Performance in a Musical TMA Award 2011, Best Actor in a Musical Olivier Award 2012), Doctor Dee (Manchester Int Festival) 2011, Damned by Despair (NT) 2012, Bakkhai 2015 (nominated Best Supporting Actor in a Play Whatsonstage Awards 2015); *Television* incl: Hawking 2004, Agatha Christie: A Life in Pictures 2004, Beethoven 2005, Doctor Who 2007, Sherlock 2010, Just William 2010, The Crimson Petal and the White 2011, Hidden 2011, Babylon 2014, Doctor Foster 2015, Jonathan Strange and Mr Norrell 2015; *Film* Les Misérables 2012; *Style*— Mr Bertie Carvel; ✉ c/o Hamilton Hodell, 20 Golden Square, London W1F 9JL

CARVELL, John Edward; s of Robert Charles Carvell (d 1984), and Ivy, *née* Dutch (d 1987); *b* 30 May 1946; *Educ* Perth Acad, Univ of St Andrews (MB ChB), Univ of Dundee (MMSc); *m* 22 July 1972, Carol, da of Gilbert D Ritchie, of Broughty Ferry, Dundee; 1 da (Claire b 1976), 1 s (Robin b 1979); *Career* registrar in orthopaedics Royal United Hosps Bath 1976–77, sr registrar in orthopaedics Nuffield Orthopaedic Centre Oxford and John Radcliffe Hosp Oxford 1978–83, conslt orthopaedic and trauma surgn Salisbury Dist Hosp 1983–2001 (emeritus conslt spinal and orthopaedic surgn 2001–), hon visiting conslt Royal United Hospital Bath 2002–08; sr MO Larkhill Point-to-Point Racecourse 2001–06; BMA: chm Wessex Regnl Conslts and Specialists Ctee 1997–2001 (hon sec 1994–97), chm of divn (Salisbury) 2010–, memb CCSC 2001–08, chm Orthopaedic Sub-Ctee CCSC 2003–08 (rep 1995–99 and 2001–), memb Private Practice and Medico-Legal Ctees 2006–07; Br Orthopaedic Assoc: memb Cncl 2002–04, chair Medico-Legal Ctee 2003–07 (memb 2001–03), memb Professional Practice Ctee 2002–08; public govr Salisbury NHS Fndn Tst 2006–15 (lead govr 2009–11), chm Spinal Task Force DOH 2008–13, chair Clinical Devpt Gp Spines Br Orthopaedic Assoc/RCS 2012–, memb Nat Orthopaedic Project Team DOH, chm CRG Complex Spinal Surgery DOH 2012–13; tutor RCS 1996–2000; dist pres Arthritis Research Campaign 1985–2010; emeritus memb Int Soc of Arthroscopy Knee Surgery and Orthopaedic Sports Med; chair Salisbury Ind Hosp Tst; memb: Salisbury Community Choir, Laudamus Choral Gp, Guild of Stewards Salisbury Cathedral; FRCSEd 1976, FRCS (ad eundem) 1997, Cardiff Univ Accredited Expert Witness (CUEW) Cardiff Univ 2005, FBOA 1983, fell Br Scoliosis Soc 1988, elected fell BMA 2009; *Recreations* music, gardening, hill walking, opera, wildlife; *Clubs* Royal Perth Golfing Soc and County and City Club; *Style*— John Carvell, Esq; ✉ Newstead, 143 Bouverie Avenue South, Salisbury, Wiltshire SP2 8EB (☎ 01722 330519)

CARVER, (James) John; s of James Carver, and Jean Mary, *née* Kerry; *b* 28 September 1957; *Educ* Dulwich Coll, Canterbury Coll of Art; *m* 1, 1987; m 2 1997; *Career* md designate J Carver & Co 1977–79, account exec International Marketing & Promotions (pt of the Masius Gp) 1979–81, creative exec Promotional Marketing Limited (pt of O & M) 1981–82, creative art dir and writer 1982–85, creative dir and fndr ptnr The Leisure Process 1985–97, fndr Harry Monk creative consultancy 1998, currently co-fndr and exec creative dir Cunning; winner various advtg prizes and awards from the music indust and mktg/advtg sector 1985–91; *Books* Duran Duran (1985), Michael Jackson (1985); *Recreations* marlin fishing, hot air ballooning, historic car racing, classic car collecting, carp fishing, aerobics, Thai boxing, travel, origami, Ntse Tui and wakebayne (mental arts), natural healing, skydiving, running marathons; *Style*— John Carver

CARVER, Wyndham Houssemayne; s of Capt Edmund Squarey Carver, DSC, RN (d 2001), and Freda Wilmot Houssemayne, *née* Du Boulay (d 1970); *b* 4 May 1943; *Educ* Malvern Coll, Harvard Business Sch (PMD); *m* 1 (m dis), Jocelyn Mary Anne, da of Graham Rogers, of Hyde, Hants; m 2, Shona Leslie, da of Maj Ian McKillop, of East Cholderton, Hants; 3 da (Verity b Nov 1979, Lucy b Oct 1982, Tamsin b 7 Sept 1985); *Career* International Distillers & Vintners (subsid of Grand Metropolitan, now Diageo plc) 1965–97, Hunters and Frankau Ltd 1997–2001; non-exec directorships, business consultancy and mentoring 2001–; *Recreations* tennis, golf, forestry, shooting, travel; *Clubs* Boodle's, IoD; *Style*— Wyndham Carver, Esq; ✉ Rondle Wood House, Milland, Liphook, Hampshire GU30 7LA (☎ 01730 821397, office 01730 821136)

CARVILLE, Fiona Mary; *née* Gordon; da of Cdr David Leslie Gordon (d 1984), and Anne Josephine, *née* Haywood (d 1999); *b* 2 June 1951, London; *Educ* Hurst Lodge Sunningdale, Beechlawn Tutorial Coll Oxford; *m* 2 June 2001, Thomas Edward Carville; *Career* dir: Brook-Hart Advertising Ltd 1980–85, Hewland Consultants International Ltd 1980–85; md and fndr First Public Relations Ltd 1985–2012; owner The Pink Cottage Boutique Bed and Breakfast Suffolk; MCIPR, MIPA; *Recreations* cinema, gardening, horse racing, music, reading, travel; *Clubs* Morton's; *Style*— Mrs Fiona Carville; ☎ 07826 911697, e-mail fiona.carville@btinternet.com, website www.lavenhampink.com, Twitter @lavenhampink

CARWARDINE, Prof Richard John; s of John Francis Carwardine (d 2005), and Beryl, *née* Jones (d 2001); *b* 12 January 1947, Cardiff; *Educ* Monmouth Sch, CCC Oxford (William Jones exhibitioner, MA), The Queen's Coll Oxford (Ochs-Oakes sr scholar, DPhil), Univ of Calif Berkeley; *m* 17 May 1975, Dr Linda Margaret Kirk; *Career* historian; Univ of Sheffield: lectr, sr lectr then reader in American history 1971–94, prof of history 1994–2002, dean Faculty of Arts 1999–2001; Univ of Oxford: Rhodes prof of American history 2002–09, fell St Catherine's Coll 2002–09 (hon fell 2009–), Ramsey Murray lectr Selwyn Coll 2010, pres Corpus Christi Coll 2010–, hon fell Queen's Coll 2010–, pro-vice-chllr 2012–; visiting asst prof Syracuse Univ NY 1974–75, visiting fell Univ of N Carolina at Chapel Hill 1989, Birkbeck lectr Trinity Coll Cambridge 2004, Stenton lectr Univ of Reading 2004, Harry Allen lectr Inst for the Americas Univ of London 2006, distinguished lectr Organization of American Historians 2006–, Stewart fell Princeton Univ 2011, Watson lectr Br Library 2013, Roger Anstey lectr Univ of Kent 2015; Arthur Miller American Studies Prize 1997, Lincoln Prize 2004, Bicentennial Order of Lincoln The Lincoln Acad of Illinois 2009; Leverhulme Tst Res Fellowship 2001–04, Huntington Library Res Fellowship 2014; memb Advsy Bd Lincoln Studies Center Knox College Illinois 2009–, founding memb Cncl for the Defence of Br Univs 2013; memb Ed Bd: Jl of Ecclesiastical History 1991–, American Nineteenth Century History 2000–, The Papers of Abraham Lincoln 2013–; ed advsr BBC History Magazine 2000–; memb Advsy Cncl Sulgrave Manor 2003–, memb Pilgrims Soc 2009–; Freeman Haberdashers Co 2011–; Diploma of Honor Lincoln Memorial Univ Tennessee 2013, Hon DLitt Univ of Sheffield 2015; FRHistS 1983, FBA 2006, founding FLSW 2010; *Publications* Transatlantic Revivalism: Popular Evangelicalism in Britain and America 1790–1865 (1978), Evangelicals and Politics in Antebellum America (1993), Lincoln (2003, revised edn 2006), The Global Lincoln (jtly, 2011); author of numerous articles in learned jls; *Recreations* acting, theatre-going, walking, gardening, watching rugby; *Clubs* Oxford and Cambridge; *Style—* Prof Richard Carwardine, FBA; ✉ Corpus Christi College, Merton Street, Oxford OX1 4JF (☎ 01865 276700, e-mail president@ccc.ox.ac.uk)

CARWOOD, Andrew; s of Thomas George Carwood (d 1973), and Daisy Ninnes (d 1991); *b* 30 April 1965; *Educ* John Lyon Sch Harrow, St John's Coll Cambridge (choral scholar); *Career* singer and conductor; artistic dir Edington Music Festival 1991–97; winner Gramophone Early Music Award 1995, 2006, 2007 and 2010, winner Gramophone Record of the Year 2010; hon fell Acad of St Cecilia, hon fell Guild of Singers and Musicians; FRSCM 2016; *Singer* choral scholar St John's Coll Cambridge 1983–86; lay clerk: Christ Church Oxford 1987–90, Westminster Cathedral 1990–95; solo and consort work with: The Tallis Scholars, The Sixteen, The English Concert, The King's Concert, Finzi Singers, Oxford Camerata, Parley of Instruments, Collegium Musicum 90, City of London Sinfonia, Orch of the Age of Enlightenment, The Monteverdi Choir, Choeur de la Chapelle Royale, Pro Cantione Antiqua, Gabrieli Consort, Acad of Ancient Music, The Schütz Choir; *Conducting* artistic dir The Cardinall's Musick 1989–, dir of music The London Oratory 1995–2000, dir The Edington Schola Cantorum 1998–2010, jt princ guest conductor The BBC Singers 2006–10, dir of music St Paul's Cathedral 2007–; *Recordings* as singer: works by Hassler, Vivaldi, Purcell, Haydn, Warlock, Howells, Janá?ek, Headington; as conductor: works of Ludford, Fayrfax, Cornysh, Merbecke, Tallis, Parsons, Byrd, Palestrina, Guerroro, Victoria, Lassus, H Praetorius, Allegri, Mozart, Harris; *Recreations* theatre, British comedy, wine; *Style—* Andrew Carwood, Esq; ✉ c/o Ben Rayfield, Rayfield Allied, Southbank House, Black Prince Road, London SE1 7SJ (☎ 020 3176 5500, e-mail info@rayfieldallied.com)

CARY, Anthony Joyce; CMG (1997); s of Sir Michael Cary, GCB, and Lady (Isabel) Cary; *b* 1 July 1951, London; *Educ* Eton, Trinity Coll Oxford (MA), Stanford Business Sch (Harkness fell, MBA); *m* 1975, Clare, *née* Elworthy; 3 s (Sam b 1978, Tom b 1980, Arthur b 1983), 1 da (Harriet b 1985); *Career* entered HM Dip Serv 1973; served: Br Military Government Berlin 1974–77, Policy Planning Staff FCO 1978–80, EC Dept FCO 1982–84; private sec to min of state FCO 1984–86, head of Chancery Kuala Lumpur 1986–88, on loan to Cabinet of Sir Leon Brittan (later Baron Brittan of Spennithorne, PC, QC, DL (Life Peer) European Cmmn 1989–92, head EU Dept FCO 1993–96, cnsllr Washington DC 1997–99, on loan as chef de cabinet to Rt Hon Chris Patten, CH (now The Rt Hon the Lord Patten of Barnes, CH, PC, *qv*), European Cmmn 1999–2003, ambass to Sweden 2003–07, high cmmr to Canada 2007–10, exec dir Queen's-Blyth Worldwide 2011–13, Cwlth Scholarship cmmr 2012–; hon pres Canada-UK Cncl 2010–; *Style—* Mr Anthony Cary, CMG; ✉ The Old Vicarage, 97A Knatchbull Road, London SE5 9QU (e-mail antcary@gmail.com)

CARY-ELWES, Charles Gervase Rundle; s of Lt-Col Oswald Aloysius Joseph Cary-Elwes (d 1994), and (Elisabeth) Pamela Rundle, *née* Brendon (d 1996); *b* 8 November 1939; *Educ* Ampleforth, Sorbonne, Trinity Coll Oxford (MA); *m* 2 April 1972, Angela Jean, da of Maj Eric Rowland, TD, TA (d 1960); 1 da (Lucy b 1974), 1 s (James b 1976); *Career* stockjobber Durlacher Oldham Mordaunt Godson 1962–65, in film prodn 1965–74, Peat Marwick Mitchell & Co Chartered Accountants 1975–79, corporate finance exec Grieveson Grant & Co 1980–83, Exco International plc 1983–85; chm Br America's Cup Challenge plc 1984; dir: British & Commonwealth Holdings plc 1986–89, Leopold Joseph & Sons Ltd 1991–93, Woolton Elwes Ltd 1993–2004, Orion Publishing Group Ltd 1994–2003, London Colonial Hldgs Ltd 1997–; Research, Recommendations and Electronic Voting plc (RREV) 2003–05; hon treas Keats Shelley Memorial Assoc; FCA, CIT; *Recreations* golf, jazz piano, theatre, travel; *Clubs* Athenaeum, Rye Golf; *Style—* Charles Cary-Elwes, Esq

CASE, Prof (Richard) Maynard; s of John (Jack) Case (d 1985), of Stockport, Cheshire, and Joycelyn Mary, *née* Ashcroft (d 2000); *b* 23 July 1943; *Educ* Stockport GS, King's Coll Durham (BSc), Univ of Newcastle upon Tyne (MRC scholar, PhD); *m* 1, 22 Dec 1967, Gillian Mary (d 1997), da of John Guy (d 2011); m 2, 2 April 2001, Miriam Diane, da of Frank Basil Shaftoe (d 2013); 1 s (Samuel Thomas b 17 Dec 2004); *Career* Dept of Physiology Univ of Newcastle upon Tyne: lectr 1967–75, sr lectr 1975–76, reader 1976–79; Univ of Manchester: prof of physiology 1979–2011, head Dept of Physiology 1980–86, head Dept of Physiological Scis 1986–90, dean Sch of Biological Scis 1990–94 and 2001–04, assoc vice-pres 2006–11; lectr Inst of Physiology Aarhus Univ 1970–71, Northern regnl tutor Open Univ 1973–75, lectr Dept of Physiology Univ of Sydney 1976–77; res leave fell Wellcome Tst 1994–97; memb: Animal Scis and Psychology Sub-Ctee Biological Scis Ctee SERC 1981–84, Res and Med Advsy Ctee Cystic Fibrosis Res Tst 1982–87, Grants Ctee A Cell Bd MRC 1983–87, Scientific and Res Awards Ctee Br Digestive Fndn 1989–93, Biochemistry and Cell Biology Ctee BBSRC 1994–96; managing ed Cell Calcium 1978–99; memb Editorial Bd: Gut 1984–87, Yonsei Med Jl 1986–, Pancreas 1986–92; Br Soc of Gastroenterology: Res Medal 1981, chm Basic Scis Section 1986–88, memb Res Ctee 1991–93; chm Gastrointestinal Cmmn Int Union of Physiological Scis 1993–2002; Daiwa Prize Daiwa Anglo-Japanese Fndn 1994; memb: Physiological Soc (memb Ctee 1996–2000), Biochemical Soc, Soc for Experimental Biology, Br Biophysical Soc, Br Soc for Cell Biology, Euro Pancreatic Club (memb Cncl 1983–85 and 1992–95, pres 1985); *Books* Stimulus-Secretion Coupling in the Gastrointestinal Tract (co-ed, 1976), Electrolyte and Water Transport across Gastrointestinal Epithelia (co-ed, 1982), Secretion: Mechanisms and Control (co-ed, 1984), Variations in Human Physiology (ed, 1985), EPC – European Pancreatic Club Extracts (ed, 1985), The Exocrine Pancreas (ed, 1990), Human Physiology: Age, Stress and the Environment (2 edn of Variations in Human Physiology, co-ed, 1994); author of over 160 articles in learned scientific journals; *Recreations* Italy, gardening, classical music; *Style—* Prof Maynard Case; ✉ Faculty of Life Sciences, University of Manchester, Michael Smith Building, Oxford Road, Manchester M13 9PT (e-mail maynard.case@manchester.ac.uk)

CASEMENT, Ann D Elizabeth; *Educ* Sorbonne Univ Paris (Dip French), LSE (BSc), Westminster Fndn (Dip), Univ of London; *Career* NY State licensed pyschoanalyst; Jungian analyst; psychiatric placement St Mary Abbotts Hosp London 1979–82; chair UK Cncl for Psychotherapy 1998–2001; lectr and teacher in Jungian psychoanalysis & psychotherapy and anthropology; England corr NAAP News NY; memb: Programme Ctee Int Congress Int Assoc of Analytical Psychology, House of Lords Working Pty on Statutory Regulation of Psychotherapy, Editorial Bd Jung Jl San Francisco, Intake Ctee Br Psychoanalytic Cncl 2009–10, Editorial Bd Jl of Analytical Psychology, Editorial Bd Quadrant, Gradiva Awards Ctee NY 2013; sr memb Br Assoc of Psychotherapists, assoc memb Jungian Psychoanalytic Assoc NY; memb: Br Psychological Soc, Int Neuro-Psychoanalytic Soc, Nat Assoc for the Advancement of Psychoanalysis USA, Int Assoc of Analytical Psychology Zurich 1985 (chair Organizing Ctee for their Int Conf in Cambridge 2001, memb Exec Ctee, chair Ethics Ctee); memb Int Cncl Metropolitan Opera NY; FRAI 1976, FRSM 2005; *Books* Post-Jungians Today (ed, 1998), Carl Gustav Jung (2001), Who Owns Psychoanalysis? (ed, 2004), The Idea of the Numinous (2006), Who Owns Jung (2007); chapters in: Psicologica Analytica Contemporanea, Handbook of Individual Therapy, When a Princess Dies, Globalized Psychotherapy, The Handbook of Jungian Psychology, Jungian Psychoanalysis, Critically Engaging CBT in an Age of Happiness; articles and book reviews for The Economist and others; *Clubs* Analytical Psychology; *Style—* Mrs Ann Casement; ✉ 3D Hans Crescent, London SW1X 0LN (e-mail adecasement@gmail.com)

CASEWELL, Prof Mark William; s of William John Ivor Casewell (d 1951), of Hants, and Phyllis Rebecca, *née* Raymond (d 1976); *b* 17 August 1940; *Educ* Royal Masonic Sch, Univ of London (BSc, MB BS, MD); *m* 1, 8 July 1967 (m dis 1972), Carolle Anne, da of Richard Eaton, of Portsmouth, Hants; m 2, 9 Dec 1995, Rosa Coello, da of Alfredo Coello of Orense, Spain; *Career* house physician St Bartholomew's Hosp 1965–66, asst pathologist Univ of Cambridge 1967–70, sr lectr and hon conslt in microbiology (former lectr) St Thomas' Hosp 1971–81, reader and hon conslt in microbiology The London Hosp 1982–84, prof and head of Dulwich Public Health Laboratory and Med Microbiology King's Coll Sch of Med and Dentistry 1984–97, emeritus prof Univ of London 1997–; ind conslt on use of antibiotics in food animals 1997–; memb AIDS Advsy Gp King's Healthcare 1985–97; memb Editorial Bd: Jl of Hosp Infection, Jl of Antimicrobial Chemotherapy; chm Hosp Infection Soc 1987–91 (fndr memb 1979, scientific sec 1979–85); MRCS 1965, LRCP 1965, FRCPath 1986 (MRCPath 1975), Hon FRCP 1999 (Hon MRCP 1994); *Books* Hospital Infection Control: Policies and Practical Procedures (jtly with J Philpott-Howard, 1994); chapters in: Skin Microbiology: Relevance to Clinical Infection (1981), Recent Advances in Infection (1982), Quality Assurance Principles and Practice in the Microbiology Laboratory (1999), Antibiotic and Chemotherapy (2001); *Publications* numerous contribs incl: BMJ, Jl of Clinical Pathology, Jl of Hospital Infection, Jl of Antimicrobial Chemotherapy; *Recreations* cooking, Spain, very fast cars; *Clubs* Porsche GB, Fountain (Barts), Real Madrid FC, Tate Modern; *Style—* Prof Mark Casewell; ✉ 43 Primrose Gardens, London NW3 4UL (☎ and fax 020 7586 3181, e-mail mark.casewell@zen.co.uk); Department of Infectious Diseases, Guy's, King's and St Thomas' School of Medicine, Bessemer Road, London SE5 9RS (fax 020 7346 3404)

CASEY, Gavin Frank; *b* 18 October 1946; *Career* chartered accountant Harmood Banner & Co 1965–69, Cooper Brothers & Co 1970–71, various appts rising to dep chief exec County Natwest Ltd 1972–89, fin dir and chief operating offr Smith New Court plc 1989–95, chief admin offr int equities Merrill Lynch International Ltd (following takeover of Smith New Court) 1995–96, chief exec London Stock Exchange plc 1996–2000; chm: Tragus Holdings 2002–05, EDM Gp 2004–11, Integrated Dental Hldgs 2006–08; dir: Abingdon Capital 2004–06, Tellings Golden Miller 2004–05; dep chm Corp Fin Advsy Bd PricewaterhouseCoopers LLP 2001–; Freeman City of London, memb Worshipful Co of Chartered Accountants in England and Wales; FCA 1970; *Recreations* horse racing, shooting, theatre; *Clubs* City of London, Turf; *Style—* Gavin Casey, Esq

CASEY, Dame Louise; DBE (2016), CB (2008); *b* 29 March 1965; *Career* DG troubled families Dept for Communities and Local Govt 2011–; *Style—* Dame Louise Casey, DBE, CB; ✉ Department for Communities and Local Government, Eland House, Bressenden Place, London SW1E 5DU

CASEY, HE Nigel Philip; MVO; *Educ* Balliol Coll Oxford (BA); *m* Clare Casey; 1 s, 1 da; *Career* diplomat; desk offr Know How Fund (Hungary, Bulgaria) FCO 1991–93, vice-consul (political/aid/press) Johannesburg 1993–95, private sec to HM Ambass Washington 1996–98, head Nuclear and Missile Defence Section Security Policy Dept FCO 1999–2000, head G8 and OECD Section Economic Policy Dept FCO 2001, head External Section Moscow 2003–06, political counsellor New Delhi 2007–09, dep high cmmr New Delhi 2009–11, ambass to Bosnia and Herzegovina 2011–; *Style—* HE Mr Nigel Casey, MVO; ✉ c/o FCO (Sarajevo), King Charles Street, London SW1A 2AH

CASEY, Prof Patricia Rosarie; da of James Casey (d 1991), of Co Cork, and Margaret Casey; *b* 27 October 1952; *Educ* Presentation Convent Fermoy, UC Cork (MD); *m* John McGuiggan, barr-at-law; 2 s (James b 29 Nov 1987, Gavan b 19 Aug 1991); *Career* MRC research fell MRC Unit for Epidemiological Studies in Psychiatry Royal Edinburgh Hosp 1982–84, statuatory lectr in psychiatry Regnl Hosp Cork 1984–91, prof of psychiatry Univ Coll Dublin/Mater Hosp Dublin 1991–; ed Advances in Psychiatric Treatment; elected memb: Irish Med Cncl 1994–, Cncl Royal Coll of Psychiatrists 1995–; FRCP, FRCPsych, fell Irish Coll of Physicians; *Publications* A Guide to Psychiatry in Primary Care (1990, 4 edn 2010), Social Function: the hidden axis of psychiatric diagnosis (1990), Psychiatry and the Law (with P Brady, A Dillon and C Craven, 1999, 2 edn 2010), From the Heart (2004); contrib to 22 books and 150 editorials/ review articles/ original papers; *Recreations* listening to classical music, cooking, writing for newspapers; *Style—* Prof Patricia Casey; ✉ Department of Psychiatry, Mater Hospital, Eccles Street, Dublin 7, Ireland (☎ 00 353 1 803 2176, fax 00353 1 830 9323, e-mail apsych@mater.ie)

CASEY, Robert Bernard (Ben); s of Thomas Casey (d 2008), and Marie, *née* Wilson (d 2010); *b* 19 October 1949, Preston, Lancs; *Educ* St Ignatius Sch Preston, Harris Coll Preston, Blackpool Coll of Technol and Design; *Career* typographer Horniblow Cox-Freeman 1969–71; designer: Berkoff Assoc 1971–72, Conway Gp Graphics 1972–74, Gask & Hawley 1974–77; lectr: Blackburn Coll of Technol and Design 1977–78, Preston Poly 1978–84; head of Sch Lancs Poly 1984–85, sr tutor Sch of Communication Arts London 1985–86, co-fndr and creative dir The Chase 1986–; dir Etc Urban 2011–; prof of visual communication Univ of Central Lancs 2002–; external examiner: Staffs Poly 1991–95, Manchester Poly 1992–96, Bretton Hall Univ of Leeds 1997–2001, Manchester Met Univ 2001–05, Northumbria Univ 2005–09, Blackpool and The Fylde Coll Lancaster Univ 2013–, Falmouth Univ 2013–; govr Salford Coll of Technol 1991–92; awards incl: NY Festival of Advertising and Print Grand Award for Creativity, Cannes Lions, D&AD, Design Week, Clio, NY Art Directors Club, Football League Award Design and Innovation; MCSD 1977, memb D&AD 1982 (dir 1992–96, chair Educn Gp 1992–96, chair D&AD North 2005–10); *Publications* The Chase by The Chase (How a Design Company Thinks it Thinks) (1993); *Recreations* football (spectator); *Style—* Ben Casey, Esq; ✉ The Chase, 1 North Parade, Parsonage Gardens, Manchester M3 2NH (☎ 0161 832 5575, fax 0161 832 5576, e-mail benc@thechase.co.uk)

CASH, Sir Andrew J; kt (2009), OBE (2001); *Educ* Bristol GS, UEA (BA, DCL), Univ of Leeds; *m* Debora; 1 s (Thomas), 1 da (Rebecca); *Career* Nat Mgmnt Training Scheme, asst sector admin Leicester Royal Infirmary 1980–83, dep unit admin Doncaster Royal Infirmary 1983–85, gen mangr Community Unit Rotherham Health Authy 1985–89, chief exec Rotherham Gen Hosps NHS Tst 1989–94, regnl dir of performance NHS Exec Trent 1994–96; chief exec: Northern Gen Hosp NHS Tst Sheffield 1996–2001, Sheffield Teaching Hosps NHS Tst 2001–04, Sheffield Teaching Hosps NHS Fndn Tst 2004–; head Millennium Exec Team Dept of Health 1999–2000, nat chair Fndn Tst Network 2004–06, director general provider devpt NHS Dept of Health 2006–07, chair NHS Employer's Pay Policy Bd 2012, vice-chair NHS Confedn 2013, chair Shelford Gp 2014–15; Hon Col 212 (Yorks) Field Hosp (Volunteers) 2009; MIPM 1980, MHSM 1983; *Style*— Sir Andrew J Cash, OBE; ✉ 1 The Paddock, Tickhill, Doncaster, South Yorkshire DN11 9HS (☎ 01302 743034, mobile 07798 607843, e-mail andrewcash7@gmail.com); Sheffield Teaching Hospitals NHS Foundation Trust, Trust Headquarters, 8 Beech Hill Road, Sheffield S10 2SB (☎ 0114 271 2358, e-mail andrew.cash@sth.nhs.uk)

CASH, Sir William Nigel Paul (Bill); kt (2014), MP; s of Capt Paul Trevor Cash, MC (ka Normandy 1944), and Moyra Margaret Elizabeth, *née* Morrison; *b* 10 May 1940; *Educ* Stonyhurst, Lincoln Coll Oxford (MA); *m* 1965, Bridget Mary, da of James Rupert Lee; 2 s (William Cash, *qv*, Samuel), 1 da (Laetitia); *Career* slr William Cash and Co; MP (Cons): Stafford 1984–97, Stone 1997–; shadow attorney gen 2001–03, shadow sec of state constitutional affairs 2003; memb Select Ctee on Euro Legislation 1985–; chm All-Pty Parly Ctee: on E Africa 1988–2000, on Complementary and Alternative Medicine 1991–97, on Kenya 1997–, on Uganda 1997–, on Malaysia 2006–; chm Cons Backbench Ctee Euro Affrs 1989–91; jt chm All Pty Jazz Gp 1991–2000, chm All-Pty Jubilee Campaign for Reduction of Third World Debt 1998–, chm All-Pty Ctee on Sanitation and Water in the Third World 2008–, chm European Scrutiny Ctee 2010– (memb 1985–), memb Jt Ctee on Privilege 2013; successfully promoted Int Devpt (Gender Equality) Act 2014; chm Maastricht Referendum Campaign and ldr Maastricht Rebellion and Gt Coll Gp 1990s; fndr and chm: European Fndn, European Jl; KStJ (Malta); *Books* A Democratic Way to European Unity, Arguments against Federalsim (1990), Against a Federal Europe – The Battle for Britain (1991), Europe – The Crunch (1992), Vision of Europe (contrib, 1993), Are We Really Winning on Europe? (1995), Response to Chancellor Kohl (1996), The Blue Paper (1996), British and German National Interests (1998), Britain and Europe, Challenging Questions for Tony Blair, Kenneth Clarke and Michael Heseltine (1999), Associated but not Absorbed (2000), The European Constitution: A Political Timebomb (2003), The Strangulation of Britain and British Business (2004), The Challenge for the Conservative Party – the Future for Britain and Europe (2004), It's the EU Stupid (2011), The EU Single Market (with Hon Bernard Jenkin, MP, 2012), John Bright: Statesman, Orator, Agitator (2012), From Brussels with Love (with Radomir Tylecote, 2016); monthly editorials Euro Jl 1993–; *Recreations* cricket, jazz, heritage, cutting red tape; *Clubs* Carlton, Vincent's (Oxford), Garrick; *Style*— Sir William Cash, MP; ✉ The Tithe Barn, Upton Cressett, Bridgnorth, Shropshire WV16 6UH (☎ 01746 714307); House of Commons, London SW1A 0AA (☎ 020 7219 6330)

CASH, William Rupert Paul; s of Sir William Nigel Paul (Bill) Cash, MP, *qv*, and Bridget Mary, *née* Lee; *b* 1 September 1966, London; *Educ* Westminster, Magdalene Coll Cambridge; *m* 1, 2003 (m dis 2007), Ilaria Bulgari; m 2, 2008 (m dis 2010), Dr Vanessa Neumann; m 3, 2014, Lady Laura Cathcart; 1 da (Cosima Elizabeth Rose b 24 June 2015); *Career* West Coast corr The Times 1991–93, US special corr Daily Telegraph 1994–98, contrib ed Evening Standard Magazine 2001–, fndr and ed-in-chief Spear's 2005–; heritage and tourism spokesman UKIP 2014–; memb Devpt Bd Churches Conservation Tst; Ed of the Year PPA Ind Publisher Award 2007 and 2008; memb: Historic Houses Assoc 2004, RSL; *Publications* Memoirs of a Hollywood Correspondent (1993), The Third Woman (2001), The Green Room (Observer Critic's Choice Edinburgh Festival, 2000); *Recreations* cricket, skiing, real tennis, theatre; *Clubs* 5 Hertford St, Annabel's, Lords and Commons Cricket, Free Foresters; *Style*— William Cash, Esq; ✉ Upton Cressett Hall, Bridgnorth, Shropshire WV16 6UH (☎ 01746 714616, mobile 07703 532501, e-mail williamrpcash@googlemail.com, website www.uptoncressetthall.co.uk)

CASHMAN, Baron (Life Peer UK 2014), of Limehouse in the London Borough of Tower Hamlets Michael Maurice Cashman; CBE (2013), MEP (Lab) West Midlands; s of John Cashman, of London, and Mary Alvena, *née* Clayton; *b* 17 December 1950, Limehouse, London; *Educ* Cardinal Griffin Secdy Modern, Gladys Dare's Sch; *Partner* Paul Cottingham (civil partnership 11 March 2006) (d 2014); *Career* actor in theatre, musical theatre, TV, films and radio 1963–99, first role in Oliver 1963, other roles incl Colin in EastEnders (BBC), Horst in RNT prodn of Bent, Noises Off (Mobil Touring Theatre) 1995 and Prospero in The Tempest (Shared Experience Theatre) 1997; MEP (Lab) W Midlands 1999–; memb Lab Pty 1975–, memb Lab Pty NEC 1998– (chair 2011–12), auditor European PLP 1999–, co-pres LGBT European Parly Intergroup; cncllr and hon treas Br Actors' Equity 1994–98, memb Bd Shared Experience Theatre 1998–2000; founding dir Stonewall Gp (chm 1988–96); patron: European Policy Network, Friends and Families for Lesbians and Gays, Volunteering England, Volunteering Europe, Hereford and Worcester Lesbian and Gay Switchboard (HWLGS), Nat Secular Soc, Int Performers Aid Tst 2016–; tstee and fndr The Paul Cottingham Trust, tstee Evelyn Norris Tst; Hon Doctorate Univ of Staffordshire 2007; special serv award from American Assoc of Physicians for Human Rights 1998, nominated EV50 most influential actors 2002, nominated EV50 politician of the year, named as one of 20 most influential gays in the UK by The Observer, MEP of the Year Award 2011 and 2013, Lifetime Achievement Award for Diversity and Equality European Diversity Awards, IGLA Appreciation Award for Equality 2014, Lifetime Achievement Award West Midlands LGBTI, number 11 on the Guardian newspaper's World Power list of 100 most influential LGBTI people 2014; FRSA 1996; *Recreations* travel, photography; *Style*— The Lord Cashman, CBE, MEP; ✉ House of Lords, London SW1A 0PW (e-mail cashmanm@parliament.uk)

CASHMORE, Claire Georgina Katie; da of Duncan J Cashmore, and Brigid C, *née* O'Beirne; *b* 21 May 1988, Redditch, Worcs; *Educ* Univ of Leeds; *Career* Paralympic swimmer; achievements incl: 2 Bronze medals (100m backstroke, 200m individual medley) Paralympics Athens 2004, Gold medal 200m individual medley Br Championships 2004, 2 Silver medals (50m freestyle and 100m freestyle) Br Championships 2004, Bronze medal 50m freestyle Visa Paralympic World Cup 2006, 2 Silver medals (100m breaststroke and 400m medley relay) World Championships 2006, Silver medal 100m freestyle Paralympic World Cup 2007, Bronze medal women's 100m breaststroke Paralympics Beijing 2008, Gold medal relay (new world record) and 2 Bronze medals (100m breaststroke and 50m freestyle) European Championship Reyjkavik 2009, 2 Gold medals (100m individual medley and 400m medley relay, both new world records) and 2 Silver medals (100m breaststroke and 200m individual medley) World Shortcourse Rio 2009, 2 Silver medals (100 metres breaststroke, 400 m freestyle relay and 400 medley relay) World Longcourse Championships Eindhoven 2010, 2 Gold medals (100m medley relay (new world record) and 4x100m freestyle relay (new European record)), Silver medal 100m breaststroke (new British record) and 2 Bronze medals (200m individual medley and 100m butterfly) European Championship Berlin 2011, 2 Silver medals (4x100m medley relay and 100m breaststroke) and Bronze medal 4x100m freestyle relay Paralympics London 2012, 2 Gold medals (4x100m freestyle relay and 4x100m medley relay (new world record)) Silver medal (100m breaststroke), and Bronze medal (200m individual medley) World Championships Montreal 2013, 2 Gold medals (100m breaststroke and medley relay) European Championships 2014, Gold medal (4x100m medley relay) European Championships Funchal 2016, 2 Bronze medals (100m breaststroke and 100m butterfly) European Championships Funchal 2016, selected for Rio Paralympic Games 2016; Br Paralympic athlete rep Br Paralympic Assoc Athlete Cmmn; BBC Midlands Young Disabled Sports Person of the Year 2004; Worcester County Founders Prize 2004, ITV Midlander of the Year 2004, N Power Young Female Achiever Award 2004, Ambass of Excellence Midlands Excellence Award 2008/09; work for DKH Legacy Tst and Youth Sport Tst; ambass Reach; Hon LLD Univ of Leeds 2013; *Clubs* Leeds City Swimming, Wyre Forest Swimming, British Para Swimming, National Performance Centre Manchester; *Style*— Ms Claire Cashmore; ✉ c/o Duncan Cashmore, 61 Hillgrove Crescent, Kidderminster, Worcestershire DY10 3AR (☎ 01562 750505, e-mail duncan.cashmore@blueyonder.co.uk)

C

CASHMORE, Prof Roger John; CMG (2004); s of Cyril John Charles Cashmore, of Dudley, Worcs, and Elsie May, *née* Jones; *b* 22 August 1944; *Educ* Dudley GS, St John's Coll Cambridge (MA), Balliol Coll and UC Oxford (DPhil, Weir jr res fell, 1851 res fell); *m* 6 Aug 1971, Elizabeth Ann, da of Rev S J C Lindsay; 1 s (Christopher John Hrothgar Lindsay-Cashmore b 1976); *Career* res assoc Stanford Linear Accelerator Centre Calif 1969–74; Univ of Oxford: res offr 1974–78, lectr ChCh 1976–78, sr res fell Merton Coll 1977–79, tutorial fell Balliol Coll and univ lectr in physics 1979–90, reader in experimental physics 1990–91, prof of experimental physics 1991–2003; dep DG and dir of research CERN Geneva 1999–2003, princ BNC Oxford 2003–11, chm UKAEA 2010–; SERC sr res fell 1982–87, guest scientist Fermilab Chicago 1986–87, visiting prof Vrije Univ Brussels 1982; chm: Scientific Ctee of Laboratorie Nazional de Gran Sasso 2004–10; CV Boys Prize Inst of Physics 1983, Alexander Von Humboldt Fndn Humboldt Research Award 1995–96; memb Academia Europa 1992; FInstP 1985, FRSA 1996, FRS 1998; *Recreations* sports, wine; *Style*— Prof Roger Cashmore, CMG, FRS; ✉ UK Atomic Energy Authority, Culham Science Centre, Abingdon, Oxfordshire OX14 3DB (☎ 01235 466608, e-mail roger.cashmore@physics.ox.ac.uk)

CASKEN, Prof John; *b* 15 July 1949; *Educ* Barnsley and Dist Holgate GS, Univ of Birmingham (BMus, MA), Univ of Durham (DMus), Acad of Music Warsaw; *Career* lectr in music Univ of Birmingham 1973–79, fell in composition Huddersfield Poly 1980–81, lectr in music Univ of Durham 1981–92, prof of music Univ of Manchester 1992–2008 (emeritus prof 2008–); compositions incl: Tableaux des Trois Ages 1976, Orion Over Farne 1984, Maharal Dreaming 1989, Darting the Skiff 1992, Sortilège 1996, Symphony (Broken Consort) 2004, Rest-ringing for string quartet and orchestra 2005, Concerto for orchestra 2007; concertos: Masque 1982, Erin 1982, Cello Concerto 1990, Violin Concerto 1994, Distant Variations 1997, That Subtle Knot for violin, viola and orchestra 2012, Apollinaire's Bird for oboe and orchestra 2013; opera: Golem (chamber opera) 1986, God's Liar 1996; vocal: Ia Orana, Gauguin 1978, Firewhirl 1979, Still Mine 1991, Sharp Thorne 1992, To the Lovers' Well 2001, Farness (three poems of Carol Ann Duffy) 2006, Chansons de Verlaine 2006, The Dream of the Rood 2008, Deadly Pleasures 2009; choral: To Fields We Do Not Know 1984, Three Choral Pieces 1990, 1991 and 1993, In the Bleak Mid-winter 2008, The Knight's Stone 2011, Magnificat and Nunc Dimittis 2012, Returning from the Tomb 2013, Memorial 2014; instrumental and ensemble: Kagura 1972, Music for the Crabbing Sun 1974, Thymehaze 1976, Amarantos 1977, String Quartet No 1 1981, Vaganza 1985, Salamandra 1986, Piano Quartet 1989, String Quartet No 2 1993, Infanta Marina 1993, Après un silence 1997, Piano Trio 2000, Blue Medusa 2002, Choses en Moi for string quartet 2003, Shadowed Pieces for violin and piano 2006, Amethyst Deceiver for solo oboe 2009, Inevitable Rifts for string quintet 2009, Sacrificium for organ 2009, Winter Reels 2010; recordings on: NMC Ancora, Metier Sound and Vision, Champs Hill Records, Resonus, Nimbus, Deux-Elles, Wergo, EMI Classics, Toccata Classics, Herald, ECM, Priory Records, USK, Meridian; first Britten Award for Golem 1990, Northern Electric Performing Arts Award 1990, Gramophone Award for Golem (recording) 1991, Fondation Prince Pierre de Monaco Prize for Still Mine 1993, Br Composer Award for Vocal Music (for The Dream of the Rood) 2009; Hon DMus Univ of Birmingham 2011, Hon DCL Univ of King's Coll Halifax Nova Scotia; FRNCM; *Publications* Transition and Transformation in the Music of Witold Lutoslawski (1975), The Visionary and the Dramatic in the Music of Witold Lutoslawski (2000), review article Polish Music Since Szymanowksi (by Adrian Thomas, 2005), Contemporary Classical Music: The Grit in the Oyster (in Manchester Memoirs 2014); *Recreations* visual arts, church architecture, gardening, rural landscapes, painting; *Style*— John Casken; ✉ c/o Sam Rigby, Schott Music Publishers, 48 Great Marlborough Street, London W1F 7BB (☎ 020 7534 0751, fax 020 7534 0759, e-mail john@casken.myzen.co.uk, website www.schott-music.com)

CASS, Sir Geoffrey Arthur; kt (1992); s of Arthur Cass (d 1982), of Darlington and Oxford, and Jessie, *née* Simpson (d 1967); *b* 11 August 1932; *Educ* Queen Elizabeth GS Darlington, Jesus Coll Oxford (MA), Dept of Social and Administrative Studies Oxford, Nuffield Coll Oxford, Jesus Coll Cambridge (MA), Clare Hall Cambridge; *m* 1957, Olwen Mary, JP, DL, da of late William Leslie Richards, of Brecon; 4 da (Fiona (Mrs Patrick Allen), Karen (Mrs Gavin Clunie), Miranda (Mrs John Hosking), Fleur (Mrs Philip Clegg); *Career* cmmnd PO RAFVR (Oxford Univ Air Sqdn) 1954, Nat Serv PO 1958, Flying Offr 1960, Air Min Directorate Work Study RAF 1958–60; conslt PA Mgmnt Conslts 1960–65; private mgmnt conslt: British Communications Corp, Controls and Communications Ltd 1965; md George Allen & Unwin 1967–71 (dir 1965–67); dir: Controls and Communications Ltd 1966–69, Chicago Univ Press (UK) Ltd 1971–86; chief exec Cambridge Univ Press 1972–92 (sec the Press Syndicate 1974–92, Univ Printer 1982–83 and 1991–92, conslt 1992–); dir Weidenfeld Publishers Ltd 1972–74; dir: Newcastle Theatre Royal Tst 1984–89, American Friends Royal Shakespeare Theatre 1985–2000, Cambridge Theatre Co 1986–95, Theatres Tst 1991–2000, Marc Sinden Productions 2000–02; memb Restoration Appeal Ctee Theatre Royal Bury St Edmunds 2002–; The All England LTC (Wimbledon) Ltd 1997–99, The All England Lawn Tennis Ground plc 1997–99, fndr memb Inigo Productions 1996–, tstee and guardian Shakespeare Birthplace Tst 1982– (life tstee 1994–); chm: RSC 1985–2000 (govr 1975–, dep pres 2000–), Royal Shakespeare Theatre Tst 1983– (fndr dir 1967–); Lawn Tennis Assoc of GB: memb Cncl 1976–, memb Mgmnt Bd 1985–90 and 1993–2000, chm Nat Ranking Ctee 1990–99, memb Int Events Ctee 1991–93, memb Nat Trg and Int Match Ctee 1982–90 and 1992–93 (chm 1985–90), memb Reorganisation Working Pty 1984–85 and 1994–99 (chm), dep pres 1994–96, pres and chm Cncl 1997–99; Wimbledon Championships: memb Ctee of Mgmnt 1990–2002, memb Jt Fin Ctee 1993–2002 (chm 1997–99), Jt Fin Bd 1989–93; govr Perse Sch for Girls Cambridge 1997–98 (chm Bd of Govrs 1978–88); memb: Governing Syndicate Fitzwilliam Museum Cambridge 1977–78, Univ of Cambridge Ctee and Exec Sub-Ctee of Mgmnt of Fenners 1976–, Exec Ctee Univ of Cambridge Careers Service Syndicate 1982–2002 (memb 1977–2002); pres Macmillan Cancer Relief Cambridgeshire 1998–, chm Univ of Cambridge ADC Theatre Appeal 2000–, chm Univ of Cambridge Sports Centre Appeal 2001–, patron Cambridge Rowing Tst 2001–, tstee Univ of Cambridge Fndn 1998–; Oxford tennis blue 1953, 1954 and 1955 (sec 1955), Oxford badminton blue 1951 and 1952 (capt 1952); chm Cambridge Univ Lawn Tennis Club 1977–, pres Cambridgeshire Lawn Tennis Assoc 1980–82; played Wimbledon Championships: 1954, 1955, 1956, 1959; played in inter-county lawn tennis championships for Durham Co (singles champion 1951) then for Cambridgeshire (singles champion 1976) 1952–82, represented RAF 1958–59; Br Veterans Singles (45 and over) champion Wimbledon 1978; memb Br Veterans Int Championships Dubler Cup Team: Barcelona 1978, Milano Marittima 1979 (Capt); hon Cambridge tennis blue 1980; fell Clare Hall Cambridge 1979; hon fell Jesus Coll Oxford 1998; life FInstD 1968, FIIM (formerly FIWM) 1979, CCMI (CIMgt 1980), FRSA 1991; Chevalier de l'Ordre des Arts et des Lettres (France) 1982; *Recreations* lawn tennis, theatre; *Clubs* All England Lawn Tennis and

Croquet (hon memb 2000), Hurlingham, Queen's (hon memb 1997), Hawks' (Cambridge; hon memb), IOD, Int Lawn Tennis of GB, The 45 (hon memb), Cambridge Univ Lawn Tennis, West Hants LTC (hon memb 2000–), Veterans Lawn Tennis GB; *Style*— Sir Geoffrey Cass; ✉ Middlefield, Huntingdon Road, Girton, Cambridge CB3 0LH

CASS, Marilyn Lal Ross; da of Garrett Taylor Lionel Maurice Graham, of Bath, and Lal Elizabeth Joan, *née* Norton; *b* 26 February 1954, Trowbridge, Wilts; *Educ* Royal Sch Bath, Univ of Exeter (BA, PGCE), Univ of Bath (MA); *m* 6 Aug 1977, Geoffrey Philip Cass; 2 s (Philip Tristan b 12 Sept 1980, David Alexander b 25 Sept 1982); *Career* cmmnd Army 1973, travel and various posts incl hotel mgmnt, libraries and voluntary work 1979–89, geography teacher, housemistress and head of modern studies Royal Sch Bath 1992–97, dep head Redland HS Bristol 1997–2000, headmistress Shrewsbury HS 2000–12; former memb GSA (former memb HMC/GSA Professional Devpt Ctee); former memb Cncl Univ of Birmingham, voluntary work Nat Tst Educn and Univ of the Third Age; memb Drapers Co Shrewsbury; *Recreations* skiing, travel, walking, reading; *Clubs* Lansdown, Univ Women's; *Style*— Mrs Marilyn Cass

CASS, Richard Martin; s of Edward Charles Cass, of Cheshire, and Hazel Rosemary; *b* 25 May 1946; *Educ* High Wycombe GS, Sheffield Univ (BArch, MA); *m* 1977, Judith Claire, da of Dr Linton Morris Snaith, of Newcastle upon Tyne; 2 s (Simon b 1983, Alexander b 1986); *Career* architect and landscape architect; dir Brian Clouston and Ptnrs 1979–82; Cass Assocs: princ 1982–, ptnr 1989–2013; dir Cass Projects Ltd 2001–13, dir CPL Mgmnt Ltd 2001–13; cmmr Cmmn for Architecture and the Built Environment 2008–11; memb: NW Regnl Design Review Panel 2007–09, London 2012 Olympics Design Review Panel 2007–11; tstee Heritage Works Building Preservation Tst 2008, chm and tstee The Cass Fndn 2012–; Design Cncl Commission for Architecture and the Built Environment (CABE) Built Environment Expert 2013–; awards incl: Civic Tst Centre Vision Award 2002, RIBA Award 2002, Landscape Inst Award 2005; *Recreations* music, theatre, gardening, sailing, reading; *Style*— Richard M Cass, Esq; ✉ The Cass Foundation, Osborne House West, 13 Fulwood Park, Liverpool L17 5AD (☎ 0151 727 7614)

CASSEL, Sir Timothy Felix Harold; 4 Bt (UK 1920), of Lincoln's Inn, City of London, QC (1988); s of His Hon Sir Harold Cassel, 3 Bt, TD, QC (d 2001); *b* 30 April 1942; *Educ* Eton; *m* 1, 1971 (m dis 1975), Mrs Jenifer Samuel, da of Kenneth Bridge Puckle; 1 da (Natalia Hermione b 1972), 1 s (Alexander James Felix b 25 May 1974); m 2, 1979 (m dis 2007), Ann, (Baroness Mallalieu, QC (Life Peer), *qv*), only da of Sir William Mallalieu; 2 da (Hon Bathsheba Anna b 1981, Hon Cosima b 1984); *Heir* s, Alexander Cassel; *Career* called to the Bar Lincoln's Inn 1965 (bencher 1994); jr prosecutor for the Crown of the Central Criminal Court 1978, asst boundary cmmr 1979, sr prosecutor for the Crown 1986; *Recreations* country sports, opera, skiing; *Clubs* Garrick, Turf; *Style*— Sir Timothy Cassel, Bt, QC

CASSERLEY, Dominic James Andrew; s of Christopher Casserley, and Pamela, *née* Lockett; *b* 23 December 1957, Gosport, Hants; *Educ* Univ Coll Sch London, Jesus Coll Cambridge (BA); *m* 1986, Nancy, *née* Broadbent; 2 s (Edward b 1988, Henry b 1991), 1 da (Isabel b 1995); *Career* exec investment mangr then M&A Morgan Grenfell & Co 1979–83; McKinsey & Co: assoc 1983–87, princ 1987–93, dir 1993–, ldr Gtr China Practice 1994–99, ldr European Banking & Securities Practice 1999–2003, managing ptnr UK & Ireland 2003–10, global head of investment banking 2011–; memb US Task Force on Market Mechanisms 1987; memb Bd: Manhattan Theatre Club 1991–94, Donmar Theatre 2003–11, NT 2011–; chm: Action on Addiction 2007–, Charities Aid Fndn 2010–; memb Cncl Univ of Cambridge 2011–; *Books* Facing up to the Risks: How Financial Institutions Can Survive and Prosper (1993, 4 edn 1997), Banking in Asia, The End of Entitlement (jtly, 1999); *Recreations* tennis, travelling; *Clubs* Reform, MCC, Queen's, Univ (NY), Field (Greenwich CT); *Style*— Dominic Casserley, Esq; ✉ McKinsey & Company, 1 Jermyn Street, London SW1Y 4UH (☎ 020 7839 8040, e-mail dominic_casserley@mckinsey.com, website www.mckinsey.com)

CASSIDY, Bryan Michael Deece; s of William Francis Deece Cassidy (d 1986), and Kathleen Selina Patricia, *née* Geraghty (d 1989); *b* Leicester; *Educ* Ratcliffe Coll Leicester, Sidney Sussex Coll Cambridge (MA); *m* 27 Aug 1960, Gillian Mary, da of Austen Patrick Bohane (d 1988); 2 da (Katherine b 1961, Siobhan b 1962), 1 s (Dominic b 1964); *Career* cmmnd RA 1955–57 (Malta and Libya), HAC 1957–62; with Ever Ready, Beechams and Reed Int; memb Cncl CBI 1981–84, dir gen Cosmetic Toiletry and Perfumery Assoc 1981–84; Parly candidate Wandsworth Central 1966, memb GLC (Hendon N) 1977–85 (oppn spokesman on industry and employment 1983–84); MEP (Cons): Dorset E and Hampshire W 1984–94, Dorset and E Devon 1994–99; former Cons spokesman on Legal Affairs and Citizens' Rights Ctee; memb Econ & Monetary Affrs & Industrial Policy Ctee, memb European Economic and Social Ctee 2002–14; vice-pres Euro Parly delgn to USA; fndr Cassidy and Associates 1999–; memb Advsy Bd Euro Performance Inst Brussels 1999–2002; assignments for BESO: Estonia 2000, Mongolia 2002; dir Studies for Hawksmere Brussels Briefings; Woodrow Wilson fell at various USA Univs; lectr and conslt on the EU, chm Section for the Single Market Prodn and Consumption European Economic and Social Ctee Brussels 2012–14; *Publications* Hawksmere European Lobbying Guide, Industry Europe (regluar contib); *Recreations* country pursuits, theatre, reading; *Clubs* Carlton; *Style*— Bryan Cassidy, Esq; ✉ 11 Esmond Court, Thackeray Street, Kensington, London W8 5HB (☎ 020 7937 3558, e-mail bmdcassidy@aol.com)

CASSIDY, Michael John; CBE (2004); s of Francis Cassidy, and Vera Rosina, *née* Valler; *b* 14 January 1947; *Educ* Downing Coll Cambridge (BA), City Univ Business Sch (MBA); *m* 1, 7 Sept 1974 (m dis 1988), Amanda Fitzgerald; 2 da (Kate b 1977, Annabel b 1979), 1 s (Thomas b 1981); m 2, 7 June 1997, Amelia, da of George Simpson (d 1985); 2 da (Georgia Rose b 30 Sept 1997, Netanya Sylvie b 16 Sept 2002); *Career* ptnr: Maxwell Batley Slrs 1971–2002 (sr ptnr 1991–2002), DJ Freeman Slrs 2002–03, Hammonds 2003–05; conslt: Olswang Slrs 2003–04, DLA Piper Slrs 2005–12, Armstrong Bonham-Carter 2007–; chm: Askonas Holt Ltd 2002–, Hemingway Properties Ltd 2003–06, Bulgarian Land Devpt plc 2006–07, Trinity Capital plc 2006–09, Ebbsfleet Devpt Corp 2014–; dir British Land Co plc 1996–2007; non-exec dir: UBS Ltd until 2015, Crossrail Ltd 2008–, P2P Global Investments plc 2014–; memb: Bd Int Financial Servs London (IFSL) 2007–10, London Pension Fund Authy 2007–13; memb Corp of London Cncl 1980– (chm Planning and Communications Ctee 1986–89, chm Policy and Resources Ctee 1992–97, chm Property Investment Bd 2009–13, chm Investment Bd 2013–15), estates ctee chm London Inst 1999–2005, chm Barbican Arts Centre 2000–03, memb Development Bd City Univ 2000–05, pres London C of C and Industry 2005–07 (memb Bd 2004), chm Museum of London 2005–13, chm Homerton Univ Hosp Fndn Tst 2006–13; Master Worshipful Co of Slrs; Hon Degree: City Univ 1996, South Bank Univ 1996; hon fell London Business Sch; memb Law Soc 1971; FRSA, Hon FRIBA; *Recreations* classical music; *Style*— Michael Cassidy, Esq, CBE; ✉ 202 Cromwell Tower, Barbican, London EC2Y 8DD

CASSIDY, Nigel Peter; s of Rev Albert Cassidy (d 1970), and Hilda May, *née* Newport (d 1996); *b* 26 December 1954; *Educ* Thames Valley GS, Univ of Portsmouth, London Coll of Printing; *m* Ann, da of Donald Clark (d 1995); 2 da (Ruth, Claire); *Career* Dimbleby Newspapers 1972–74; BBC: Radio Sussex 1974–77, Radio London 1978–86, Current Affrs Dept BBC TV 1986–87, Radio News 1987–88, Parly Unit 1988–89, business presenter and TV reporter 1989–, business correspondent Today programme 1995–2002, author 2004–, Europe business corr 2009–15, breakfast presenter Share Radio 2015–; business media content prodr, freelance broadcaster and media coach 2015–; chair: (deviser and co-writer) The Board Game 1992–2001 (New York Radio Festival Medal), Newstalk, Workplace, Shelf Lives, Tricks of the Trade, Workers Without Frontiers, Paying for Old Age, The Global Sell Off, The Climate Change Challenge, The Narrowcasters, World Business Report, Your Money; *Publications* Starting Out: How to Choose a Career (2004), Jumpstart Your Career (2006), Battenberg Britain (2009); *Recreations* writing, gardening, food, continental canal and riverboating; *Style*— Nigel Cassidy; ☎ 07802 724520, e-mail nigelcassidy@hotmail.com

CASSIDY, Dr Sheila Anne; da of Air Vice Marshal John Reginald Cassidy, CBE (d 1974), and Barbara Margaret, *née* Drew; *b* 18 August 1937; *Educ* Our Lady of Mercy Coll Parramatta, Univ of Sydney, Univ of Oxford (MA, BM BCh); *Career* Radcliffe Infirmary 1963–68, Leicester Royal Infirmary 1968–71, went to Santiago Chile to work in Assistencia Publica in emergency hosp and church clinic 1971, detained for 2 months for treating wounded revolutionary, tortured and expelled 1975, writer and human rights worker 1975–77, student Ampleforth Abbey 1977–78, novice St Bernard's Convent Slough 1978–80, SHO Dept of Radiotherapy Plymouth Gen Hosp 1980–82, med dir St Lukes Hospice Plymouth 1982–93; Plymouth Gen Hosp: specialist in palliative care 1993–96, specialist in psychosocial oncology 1996–2002, psychotherapist; UKCncl for Psychotherapy (UKCP) registered psychotherapist; regular writer, broadcaster and preacher, lectr on med and religious issues throughout UK and abroad; Valiant for Truth Media Award Order of Christian Unity, Templeton Prize for Religion 1995; Freedom City of Plymouth 1998; Hon DSc Univ of Exeter 1991, Hon DLitt Cheltenham and Glos Coll of HE (via CNNA), Hon DM Univ of Plymouth 2001; memb Br Psychosocial Oncology Soc; *Books* Audacity to Believe (1977), Prayer for Pilgrims (1979), Sharing the Darkness (1989), Good Friday People (1991, special award Collins Religious Book Award), Light from The Dark Valley (1994), The Loneliest Journey (1995), The Creation Story (1996), Made for Laughter (2006), Confessions of a Lapsed Catholic (2010), Lent is for Loving (2012); *Recreations* writing, sewing, painting, entertaining, TV; *Style*— Dr Sheila Cassidy; ✉ 7 The Esplanade, The Hoe, Plymouth PL1 2PJ

CASSIDY, (Michael) Stuart; s of John Michael Cassidy, and Jacqueline Eleanor, *née* Allison, of Sheringham, Norfolk; *b* 26 September 1968, Erith, Kent; *Educ* White Lodge, Royal Ballet Sch, Royal Acad of Dance (Dip); *m* 1993, Nicola Jane, *née* Searchfield; 2 s (Sean William b 1998, Alexander Michael b 2001); *Career* principal dancer; Royal Ballet: Siegfried in Swan Lake, Romeo in Romeo and Juliet, Prince in Sleeping Beauty, Prince of The Pagodas, Nutcracker and Cinderella, Solor in La Bayadère, Lescaut in Manon, Basilio in Don Quixote, Colas in La Fille Mal Gardée, Jean de Brienne in Raymonda, Gloria, Song of the Earth, Galanteries, Persuit, Pas de Six, Elite Syncopations; cr roles in David Bintley's Spirit of Fugue and Ashley Page's Piano; Ashton's Pas de Deux in the opera Die Fledermaus (BBC2) 1990; fndr memb K Ballet Co (touring Japan and Europe) 1999– (asst dir 2011); Nora Roche Award 1984, Prix de Lausanne Professional Prize 1987; *Recreations* classic cars, music (all types), computers, food; *Style*— Stuart Cassidy, Esq

CASSON, HE John; CMG (2014); s of Rev D C Casson, and Mrs H M Casson, of Norfolk; *b* 4 June 1971; *Educ* Queen's Coll Cambridge (BA), Christ's Coll Cambridge (DipTh); *m* Dec 2000, Kathryn Casson; *Career* diplomat; research asst Divinity Faculty Univ of Cambridge 1996–98; desk offr EU Dept FCO 1998–99, second sec UK Representation to the EU Brussels 1999, desk offr (Conflict Prevention and Peacekeeping) UN Dept FCO 2000, private sec to the ambass Washington 2000–02, first sec (Political) Washington 2002–05, sr policy advsr HM Treasy 2005–07, dep head of mission Amman 2007–09, head Near East and N Africa Dept FCO 2009–10, private sec to the PM 2010–14, ambass to Egypt 2014–; *Recreations* walking, kayaking, baseball, poems; *Style*— HE Mr John Casson, CMG; ✉ c/o FCO (Cairo), King Charles Street, London SW1A 2AH (Twitter @FCOJohnCasson)

CASSON, Prof Mark Christopher; s of Rev Stanley Christopher Casson (d 1988), and Dorothy Nowell, *née* Barlow (d 1974); *b* 17 December 1945; *Educ* Manchester Grammar, Univ of Bristol, Churchill Coll Cambridge; *m* 26 July 1975, Janet Penelope, da of William Louis Close (d 1961); 1 da (Catherine Mary b 1984); *Career* Dept of Economics Univ of Reading: lectr 1969–77, reader 1977–81, prof 1981–, head of dept 1987–94; chm Business Enterprise Heritage Tst 2000–; memb Cncl Royal Economic Soc 1985–90; pres Assoc of Business Historians 2007–08; Freeman City of London, memb Worshipful Co of Arts Scholars; fell Acad of Int Business 1993, FRSA 1996; *Books* Introduction to Mathematical Economics (1973), The Future of the Multinational Enterprise (1976), Alternatives to the Multinational Enterprise (1979), Youth Unemployment (1979), Unemployment: A Disequilibrium Approach (1981), The Entrepreneur: An Economic Theory (1982), Economics of Unemployment: An Historical Perspective (1983), Growth of International Business (1983), Economic Theory of the Multinational Enterprise: Selected Papers (1985), Multinationals and World Trade (1986), The Firm and the Market: Studies in Multinational Enterprise and the Scope of the Firm (1987), Enterprise and Competitiveness: A Systems View of International Business (1990), Multinational Corporations (1990), Entrepreneurship (1990), Economics of Business Culture: Game Theory, Transaction Costs and Economic Performance (1991), Global Research Strategy and International Competitiveness (1991), International Business and Global Integration (1992), Multinational Enterprises in the World Economy (1992), Industrial Concentration and Economic Inequality (1993), Entrepreneurship and Business Culture (1995), The Organization of International Business (1995), Theory of the Firm (1996), Information and Organization: A New Perspective on the Theory of the Firm (1997), Culture, Social Norms and Economics (1997), Institutions and the Evolution of Modern Enterprise (1998), Economics of Marketing (1998), Economics of International Business (2000), Enterprise and Leadership (2000), Cultural Factors in Economic Growth (2000), Oxford Handbook of Entrepreneurship (2006), Economics of Networks (2008), The World's First Railway System (2009), The Multinational Enterprise Revisited (2009), Entrepreneurship: Theory, Networks, History (2010), Markets and Market Institutions: Their Origin and Evolution (2011), The Entrepreneur in History (2013), History of Entrepreneurship: Innovation and Risk-taking (2013), Large Databases in Economic History (2013), Theory of International Business: Economic Models and Methods (2016); *Recreations* book collecting, railway history, drawing in pastel, church activities; *Style*— Prof Mark Casson; ✉ 6 Wayside Green, Woodcote, Reading RG8 0QJ (☎ 01491 681483); Department of Economics, University of Reading, Box 218, Reading RG6 6AH (☎ 0118 931 8227, fax 0118 975 0236, telex 847813, e-mail m.c.casson@reading.ac.uk)

CASSONI, Maria Luisa (Marisa); da of Nicola Ugo Dante Cassoni, of London, and Leonita Greco Cassoni; *b* 27 December 1951; *Educ* Sacred Heart Convent London, St Benedict's Sch Ealing, Imperial Coll London (BSc); *Career* early career as hosp physicist, teacher, market researcher, cashier and sales asst; Deloitte Haskins & Sells: trainee accountant then accountant-in-charge London 1975–79, audit sr then sr mangr Milan 1979–84, corp fin mangr 1984–86; Prudential Gp: fin ops mangr then fin controller Prudential Property Services Ltd 1986–91, fin controller then fin dir Prudential Home Service Div 1991–94, fin dir Prudential UK Div 1994–98; gp fin dir Britannic Assurance plc 1998–2001, gp fin dir Royal Mail Gp plc 2001–05, finance dir John Lewis Partnership 2006–; non-exec dir: Severn Trent plc 2001–, WSP Gp plc 2006–; memb Accounting Standards Bd; govr Peabody Tst; ARCS, ACA 1979; *Recreations* travel, skiing, theatre, opera; *Style*— Ms Marisa Cassoni

CASTELL, Sir William Martin (Bill); kt (2000), LVO (2004); s of William Gummer Castell, and Gladys Castell, *née* Doe; *b* 10 April 1947; *Educ* St Dunstan's Coll, City of London Coll (BA); *m* 1971, Renice, *née* Mendelson; 2 da, 1 s; *Career* chartered accountant Spicer & Pegler 1971–75; Wellcome plc: fin controller Europe 1976–79, controller fin and admin continental Europe Africa and Asia 1979–81, md Wellcome Biotech 1982–87, commercial dir 1987–89; chief exec Amersham plc 1990–2004, ceo and pres GE Healthcare (formerly Amersham plc) 2004–06, vice-chm General Electric Co 2004–06 (dir 2006–), chm Wellcome Tst 2006–; non-exec dir: Marconi plc (formerly General Electric Co plc) 1997–2002, British Petroleum 2006–; visiting fell Green Coll Oxford 1993–; memb: MRC 2001–04, Bd Inst of Life Sciences Univ of Michigan 2003–06; chm: Design Dimension Educnl Tst 1994–99, Regeneration Through Heritage 1997–2000, The Prince's Tst 1998–2003; tstee Natural History Museum 2004–08; Outstanding Achievement Award ICAEW 2004; Hon DCL Univ of Oxford 2005; hon memb Academia Europea Assoc in support of Russian Science and Educn 1996; FCA 1980 (ACA 1974); *Recreations* int affairs, shooting, golf, walking, tennis; *Clubs* Athenaeum; *Style*— Sir William Castell, LVO; ✉ Wellcome Trust, 215 Euston Road, London NW1 2BE (☏ 020 7611 8888, fax 020 7611 8545)

CASTLE, Andrew Nicholas; s of Frank James Castle (d 1985), and Lyn Mathers, *née* Pollock; *b* 15 November 1963; *Educ* Huish's GS Taunton, Millfield, Wichita State Univ USA (BA); *m* 18 May 1991, Sophia Anna Stuart Runham; 2 da (Georgina b 11 Dec 1992, Claudia b 30 July 1994); *Career* television presenter and former tennis player; memb: GB Davis Cup team 1986–91, Euro Cup team 1986–90, GB Olympic team Seoul 1988 and Barcelona 1992; nat singles champion 1987, 1989 and 1991, nat doubles champion 1987 and 1989–91, reached third round US Open (lost to Boris Becker) 1987, finalist Korean Open Grand Prix 1988, winner Dunlop Masters of Japan 1988; doubles champion: Rye Brook (NY), Madeira, Cherbourg, Singapore, Nagoya, Adelaide, Korea, Malaysian Open; presenter Skysports: basketball, PGA European Tour, tennis; presenter GMTV 2000–10, commentator ATP Tour Highlights Show (TWI); contrib: Sunday Times, The Observer, The Guardian; *Clubs* International Club of GB, All-England Lawn Tennis and Croquet; *Style*— Andrew Castle, Esq; ✉ c/o M&C Saatchi Merlin, 36 Golden Square, London W1F 9EE

CASTLE, Rt Rev Brian Colin; *see:* Tonbridge, Bishop of

CASTLE STEWART, 8 Earl (I 1800) Arthur Patrick Avondale Stuart; 15 Bt (S 1628); also Baron Castle Stuart (I 1619), and Viscount Castle Stuart (I 1793); s of 7 Earl Castle Stewart, MC (d 1961), and Eleanor May (d 1992), da of Solomon R Guggenheim, of New York; *b* 18 August 1928; *Educ* Eton, Trinity Coll Cambridge; *m* 1952, Edna (d 2003), da of William Edward Fowler; 1 s, 1 da; m 2, 2004, Gillian, DL, da of Frederick William Savill, of Blaby, Leics; *Heir* s, Viscount Stuart; *Career* late Lt Scots Gds; vice-pres Solomon R Guggenheim Museum NY 1967–97, pres emeritus Advsy Bd Peggy Guggenheim Museum Venice 2013– (vice-pres 1980–2011, pres 2011–13); FCMI; *Recreations* art, reading, forestry, music, gardening, opera, travel, walking; *Clubs* Carlton; *Style*— The Rt Hon the Earl Castle Stewart; ✉ Stuart Hall, Stewartstown, Co Tyrone, BT71 5AE (☏ 028 8773 8208)

CASTLEDEN, Prof (Christopher) Mark; s of Dr Leslie Ivan Mark Castleden (d 1984), and Joan, *née* Smith; *b* 22 July 1944; *Educ* UCS, Bart's and Univ of London (MB BS, MD); *m* Julie Dawn; 3 da (Emily Jayne b 1972, Lorraine b 1975, Caroline b 1975), 1 s (Luke b 1991); *Career* RCP: memb 1972, memb Geriatrics Ctee 1979–85, fell 1984, prof 1987–98, prof emeritus 1998; chm: Advsy Sub-Ctee Geriatrics Med Tst 1981, Regl Educn Ctee on Geriatric Med 1994–96; dir of CME/CPD Br Geriatrics Soc 1998–2003 (chm Scientific Ctee 1994–97); memb: Ctee Safety of Meds 1984–86, Advsy Ctee on NHS Drugs 1991–99, Advsy Bd for the Registration of Homeopathic Products 2007–11; *Recreations* sailing, gardening, antiques, reading; *Style*— Prof Mark Castleden; ✉ Oaklands, East Village, Crediton, Devon EX17 4BY (e-mail markcastleden@hotmail.com)

CASTRO, Dr John Edward; s of Edward George Castro, of Norfolk, and Ivy Leuze Castro; *b* 10 August 1940; *Educ* Barnet GS, UCL (scholar, BSc, Suckling Prize for anatomy), UCH Med Sch (Fanny Magrath scholar in surgery, MRCS, LRCP, MB BS, MS, PhD, Sir Frances Walshe Prize in neurology, Erichson Prize for practical surgery); *m* 1 (m dis), Sylvia Rosemary Barber; 1 s (Ashley John b 1967), 2 da (Naomi Jane b 1970, Rebecca Elizabeth b 1973); m 2, Pamela Elizabeth, da of Rev Preb John Clifford Dale; *Career* house surgn UCH July-Dec 1965 (house physician Jan-June 1965), GP 1966; sr house surgn: Accident Service Luton and Dunstable Hosp Jan-June 1967, Hammersmith Hosp July-Dec 1967; res fell and hon urological registrar RPMS 1968–69, rotating surgical registrar Norfolk and Norwich Hosp 1969–71, scientific worker 1971–73 (Nat Inst for Med Res Mill Hill and Clinical Res Centre Harrow), res grant Cancer Res Campaign 1975, Arris-Gale lectr RCS 1975, hon conslt urologist Hammersmith Hosp 1975–79 (sr surgical registrar urology 1973–75), sr lectr in urology RPMS 1975–79 (tutor in surgery and lectr in immunology 1973–75), conslt urologist and transplant surgn 1979–; Patey Prize Surgical Res Soc 1973 and 1975, Univ Medal Univ of Hiroshima 1975, Ethicon Travel fellowship 1977; memb: Int Transplant Soc, BMA, Br Assoc of Urological Surgeons, European Dialysis and Transplantation Assoc, Euro Assoc of Urology; fndr memb Br Transplantation Soc, FRSM, FRCS (Edinburgh) 1968, FRCS (Eng) 1970; *Books* Treatment of Benign Prostate Hypertrophy and Neoplasia (1974), Immunology for Surgeons (1976), Immunological Aspects of Cancer (1978), Treatment of Renal Failure (1980); *Recreations* gardening, cooking, collecting card cases; *Clubs* Chelsea Clinical Soc; *Style*— Dr John Castro; ✉ The Old Vicarage, Fressingfield, Eye, Suffolk IP21 5QL (☏ 01379 586537)

CATCHPOLE, Andrew; s of David John Catchpole, of Bath, and Jennifer Susan, *née* Roskruge; *b* 1 October 1966, Devon; *Educ* King's Coll Taunton, Goldsmiths Coll London (BA), London Inst (Dip Publishing); *m* 1 Dec 2001, Miranda, *née* Mather; *Career* early work with Oddbins and Bloomsbury Publishing; wine ed Channel 11 1996–97, dep ed Harpers Wine and Spirit Weekly 1997–99, food and drink ed Ampersand Magazine 2000–01, ed Hot Magazine 1999–2002, wine corr Daily Telegraph 2001–05; freelance food, wine, travel and restaurant writer, lectr and broadcaster 2000–; memb Circle of Wine Writers 1998–; *Recreations* cooking, sailing, photography; *Style*— Andrew Catchpole, Esq; ✉ c/o Miranda Mather (☏ 01273 227089, mobile 07949 078614); e-mail andrew.catchpole@virgin.net

CATES, Armel Conyers; s of Conyers Seely Cates (d 1965), of Guildford, Surrey, and Jacqueline Maude, *née* Geoffroy (d 1988); *b* 3 May 1943; *Educ* Charterhouse, Univ of Southampton (LLB); *m* 8 July 1967, Pamela Susan, da of Colin Huson Walker, of Barrington, Cambs; 2 s (Tom b 1974, Sam b 1978), 1 da (Ilaria b 1980); *Career* articled to Theodore Goddard (London) and Vinters (Cambridge) 1967–69, admitted slr 1969; asst slr Coward Chance 1970–72, Clifford-Turner 1972–75, ptnr Clifford Chance 1975–2002 (conslt 2002–); non-exec dir The Law Debenture Corp plc 2001–12; former editorial advsr International Financial Law Review; tstee Charterhouse in Southwark; memb Law Soc 1969; Liveryman Worshipful Co of Slrs; *Recreations* golf, tennis, photography; *Clubs* Royal Worlington and Newmarket Golf; *Style*— Armel Cates, Esq; ✉ Graves Farm, Catmere End, Saffron Walden, Essex CB11 4XG

CATHCART, 7 Earl (UK 1814); Charles Alan Andrew Cathcart; also 16 Lord Cathcart (S *circa* 1447), Baron Greenock and Viscount Cathcart (both UK 1807); s of 6 Earl Cathcart, CB, DSO, MC (d 1999); *b* 30 November 1952, London; *Educ* Eton; *m* 1981, Vivien Clare, o da of Francis Desmond McInnes Skinner, of Snetterton, Norfolk; 1 da (Lady Laura Rosemary b 11 June 1984), 1 s (Alan George, Lord Greenock b 16 March 1986); *Heir* s, Lord Greenock; *Career* cmmnd Scots Gds 1972–75; CA Ernst and Whinney 1976–83, Hogg Robinson plc 1983, dir Gardner Mountain and Capel-Cure Agencies Ltd 1987–94, Murray Lawrence Holdings Ltd 1995–96; dir RGA Holdings Ltd and RGA Capital Ltd 1998–2010, currently dir Vivien Greenock Ltd; Cons whip and spokesman for local govt, DEFRA and NI House of Lords 2007–13; cncllr for Breckland DC 1998–2007; memb Queen's Body Guard for Scotland (Royal Co of Archers); ACA; *Clubs* Pratt's; *Style*— The Rt Hon the Earl Cathcart

CATLING, Prof Brian David; s of Leonard Frederick Catling, of London, and Lilian Alice Catling; *b* 23 October 1948; *Educ* NE London Poly, RCA; *m* 1; 1 s (Jack Ishmael b 19 Dec 1983); m 2; 1 da (Florence Pike b 13 April 1989), 1 s (Finn Bell b 23 Nov 1990); *Career* artist and poet; visiting lectr: Jan Van Eyck Akademie Maastricht Netherlands 1980–84, Chelsea Sch of Art, Royal Acad, Vestlandets Kunsteakademi Bergen Norway, Kunsteakademi Trondheim Norway; Henry Moore fell in sculpture Norwich Sch of Art 1982–85, tutor in sculpture RCA 1983–90, princ lectr in sculpture Brighton Poly, head of sculpture Ruskin Sch of Drawing and Fine Art 1991–, fell Linacre Coll Oxford 1991, prof of fine art Univ of Oxford; winner Paul Hamlyn Fndn Award for Visual Art 2001; hon fell Dartington Sch of Arts; *Solo Exhibitions* incl: Air Gallery London 1977, Camden Arts Centre London 1979, Arnolfini Gallery Bristol 1980, Norwich Sch of Art Gallery 1982–84, Atlantis Gallery London 1984, South Hill Park Arts Centre Berkshire 1984, Liefsgade 22 Copenhagen 1986, Hordaland Kunstnercentrum Bergen 1987, Matt's Gallery London 1987, Neue Gallerie Sammlung Ludwig Aachen 1988, MOMA Oxford 1989, At the Lighthouse (Matt's Gallery London) 1991, Gallerie Satellite Paris 1993, TEN Gallery Fukuoka Japan 1993, The Blindings (Serpentine Gallery London), A Conceptual Telescope for Bergen (cmmnd public sculptures over five sites) 1994, Window (installed sculpture for Br Embassy Dublin) 1995, Cyclops (video installation, Galerie Satellite Paris, South London Gallery, Museet for Samtidskunst Oslo, Project Gallery Leipzig) 1995–97, Vanished! a video seance (with Tony Grisoni, Ikon Gallery Birmingham and South London Gallery) 1999, Palermo Apport Tables (Bluecoat Arts Centre Liverpool) 2000, Cyclops (Inst Friedrichsbau Bühl) 2002, Trans-Art Trondheim 2002, ANTIX (16 night performance installation, Matt's Gallery London) 2006, Ingleby Gallery Edinburgh 2008; *Group Exhibitions* incl: Albion Island Vortex (Whitechapel Gallery London) 1974, Imagination is the Venom (Ikon Gallery London) 1981, Art and the Sea (Arnolfini Gallery Bristol and ICA London) 1982, Nordic Winter Symposium (Geilo) 1982, Bookworks (V&A Museum London) 1988, MOBSHOP IV (Viborg and Malmö Kunsthaller Sweden) 1989, Upturned Art (Pitt Rivers Museum Oxford) 1990, Nylistasfnid (The Living Art Museum Reykjavik) 1990, 3 Artists from Oxford (St Catherine's Coll Oxford and Kobe Japan) 1993, Oak Repels Lightning (Science Museum London) 1998, Small Acts at the Millennium 2000; *Performance Works* incl: Miltonian Ghost Dance (Whitechapel Gallery London) 1980, Spogelsemasse (Leifscade 22 Copenhagen) 1986, five performances (cmmnd by MOMA Oxford) 1989, Two Works for Trondheim (Trondelac Arts Centre Trondheim Norway) 1990, Refined White (Tate Gallery London) 1993, Augenlied (Schloss Plüschow Art Centre Mecklenburg) 1993, Sunflint (Artifact Gallery Tel Aviv) 1993, Hidden Cities (bus tour, Laboratory Gallery Oxford) 1995, Clepsydra (South London Gallery) 1996, Freiwild Festival (Halle) 1996, Madrid Festival 1997, One Night Stands (Norwich Gallery) 1997, Hush (Slaughter House Gallery) 1997, Night of the Living Tongues (Cambridge) 1997, Flylkingen (Stockholm) 1997, Science Museum London 1997, Bergen Performance Festival 1997, Stadt Gallerie Berne 1998, Virus (Freiwild Festival Halle) 1998, Nat Review of Live Art (Glasgow) 2000–02, Steder: More Places For Ever (Lillehammer) 2002, The Boulavards (Den Bosch) 2002, Acts of Faith and Generosity (La Bisbal) 2002, The Wolf (Greenland tour) 2003, Halle Cyclops (Handel-Festspiele Halle Saale) 2005, Mellom himmel og hav (performance festival Bergen) 2005, Art Space Tetra Fukuoka 2007, AIAV (Yamaguchi) 2007, Fresh Festival South Hill Park 2007, Alma Enterprises London 2007, The Rail (Ikon Gallery Birmingham) 2007, Long Breath (Maschinehaus Essen) 2007; fndr The Wolf in the Winter int performance collective 2001 (performances cmmned: Wurttenberischer Kunstverien Stuttgart 2002, Nat Review of Live Art Glasgow 2003, La Bisbal Californaia 2005, South London Gallery 2006); *Commissions* Presence (BBC Braodcasting House) 2002, Shuffle (for Variety exhbn, Delaware Pavilion Bexhill on Sea) 2005, monument at site of execution Tower of London (Historic Royal Palaces cmmn) 2006; *Publications* The First Electron Heresy (1977), Vorticegargen (1979), Pleides in Nine (1981), Vox Humana (1984), Das Kranke Tier (1984), The Tulpa Index (1986), Lair (1987), Boschlog (1988 and 1989), The Stumbling Block (1990), Future Exiles (1991), The First London Halo (1994), Thyhand (1994), The Blindings (1995), Large Ghost (2001), Late Harping (2001), Thyhand (2001); poem The Stumbling incl in OUP Anthology of 20th Century British and Irish Poetry (2001); subject of Tending the Vortex: the Works of B Catling (by Simon Perrill, 2001); *Style*— Prof Brian Catling; ✉ Ruskin School of Drawing & Fine Art, 74 High Street, Oxford OX1 4BG (☏ 01865 276940, e-mail brian.catling@ruskin-school.ox.ac.uk)

CATON, Brian; *b* 28 July 1950; *Career* trade unionist; joined Prison Service 1977; Prison Offrs Assoc (POA, now Professional Trades Union for Prison Correctional and Secure Psychiatric Workers): memb Branch Ctee HMP Wakefield 1979 and 1994 (health and safety rep 1979, branch sec 1980–89), memb NEC 1989 (vice-chair 1990–94), asst sec 1996–2000, gen sec 2000– (also ed Gatelodge magazine, sec to various POA ctees, memb Cncl of Civil Service Unions Superannuation Sub-Ctee, memb Review of Pensions Jt Working Gp); TUC: press offr Wakefield 1983, vice-pres and political offr Wakefield 1984, pres Wakefield 1986–89, gen sec Wakefield 2000–, currently memb Gen Cncl, memb Lesbian and Gay, Bisexual and Transsexual Ctee, memb Nat Trades Cncl TUC Ctee; currently exec memb Cncl European Fedn of Employees in Public Serv (also pres Justice Gp); memb Lab Pty; *Style*— Brian Caton, Esq; ✉ POA, Cronin House, 245 Church Street, Edmonton, Middlesex N9 9HW (☏ 020 8803 0255, fax 020 8803 1761, e-mail gs@poauk.org.uk)

CATON, Martin; *Career* MP (Lab) Gower 1997–2015; *Style*— Martin Caton, Esq; ✉ House of Commons, London SW1A 0AA (☏ 020 7219 5111/2078); constituency office: 9 Pontardulais Road, Gorseinon, Swansea (☏ 01792 892100, fax 01792 892375)

CATON, Dr Valerie; da of Robert Caton (d 1996), and Florence Amy, *née* Aspden; *b* 12 May 1952, Darwen, Lancs; *Educ* Blackburn HS for Girls, Univ of Bristol (BA, PhD), Reading Grad Sch (MA); *m* 5 Sept 1987, David Mark Harrison; 1 da (Isobel b 29 May 1992), 1 s (Thomas b 5 Nov 1994); *Career* diplomat; tutor in French Univ of Exeter 1978–80; joined FCO 1980, with UK Perm Representation to the EU Brussels then second then first sec (EC affrs) Brussels 1982–84, desk offr Southern Africa Dept FCO 1984–86, dep head policy planners FCO 1986–88, first sec (political) Paris 1988–92, dep head of mission and consul-gen Stockholm 1993–96, cnsllr (financial and economic) Paris 1997–2001, sr assoc memb St Antony's Coll Oxford 2001–02, head Environment Policy Dept FCO 2002–04, head Climate Change and Energy Gp FCO 2004–06, ambass to Finland 2006–10; *Publications* France and the Politics of EMU (2002); author of articles on Raymond Queneau; *Recreations* walking, riding, theatre, collecting first editions by P G Wodehouse and Mark Twain; *Style*— Dr Valerie Caton; ✉ c/o FCO, King Charles Street, London SW1A 2AH (☏ 00 358 2286 5222, fax 00 358 2286 5284)

CATOR, Albemarle John; s of John Cator, of Woodbastwick, Norfolk, and Elizabeth Jane, *née* Kerrison; *b* 23 August 1953; *Educ* Harrow; *m* 1, 29 Nov 1980 (m dis 1992), Fiona Mary, da of Robert Edgar Atheling Drummond; 2 s (John b 1983, Robert Henry b 1985); m 2, 17 May 1995 (m dis 2014), Victoria Katherine, da of Maj-Gen David Pank, CB; 2 s (Christian David b 22 Sept 1996, Sebastian Edward b 20 Feb 1999); *Career* Lt Scots Guards 1971–74; with Samuel Montagu 1975–84, exec dir Chemical Bank International Ltd 1984–88, exec dir Chemical Securities Ltd 1988–91, vice-pres Chemical Bank 1988–91; NatWest Capital Markets Ltd: exec dir 1991–95, md 1995–97; chm AC European Finance Ltd 1997–2003; dir: ECU Gp plc 2004–08, Longleat Enterprises Ltd 2004–, Easi-Rad Ltd 2008–12; *Recreations* sailing, shooting, skiing; *Clubs* RYS, Pratt's; *Style*—

C

Albemarle Cator, Esq; ✉ Woodbastwick Hall, Woodbastwick, Norwich, Norfolk NR13 6HL

CATOR, Charles; s of Peter Cator (d 2006), and Katharine, *née* Coke; *b* 1 October 1952, London; *Educ* Eton, Univ of Bristol; *Career* joined Christie's 1973, dep chm Christie's Europe 1995–2000, co-chm Christie's Int UK Ltd 2001–06, dep chm Christie's Int 2007–; *Publications* contrib on subject of furniture to: Jl of the Furniture History Society, Apollo, Dictionary of English Furniture Makers 1660–1840, Country Life, Star Pieces (2009); *Recreations* gardening, opera, architecture and design; *Clubs* White's, Brooks's; *Style*— Charles Cator, Esq; ✉ Christie's, 8 King Street, London SW1Y 6QT (☎ 020 7389 2355, fax 020 7389 2869, e-mail ccator@christies.com)

CATOR, James; *b* 31 January 1980; *Educ* Univ of Leeds (BSc); *Career* digital mktg mangr Eagle Rock Entertainment 2009–12, mangr content partnerships – music YouTube 2012–14, chief operating offr Mixmag Media Network 2014–; *Recreations* cinema, music; *Style*— James Cator, Esq; ✉ Twitter @jamescator

CATT, Michael John (Mike); OBE (2011, MBE 2004); s of James Ernest Catt, of Port Elizabeth, South Africa, and Anne Gillian, *née* Crowther; *b* 17 September 1971; *Educ* Grey HS Port Elizabeth; *m* Dec 2001, Allison Hastie; 2 da (Evie b 2002, Erin b 2009); *Career* rugby union back; club: Bath 1993–2004 (Courage League Champions 1996, winners Pilkington Cup 1996, winners Heineken European Cup 1998), London Irish 2004–; England: 75 caps, debut v Wales 1994, memb squad World Cup 1995, 1999, 2003 (champions) and 2007 (finalists), winners Grand Slam 1995 and Six Nations Championship 2000 and 2001, ret from ints 2007; memb Br Lions tour to SA 1997 and Aust 2001; Bath Player of the Year 1994, Most Promising Player of the Year Award 1995, Guinness Player of the Year 2005, London Irish Player of the Year 2006; *Recreations* socialising, golf; *Style*— Mike Catt, Esq, OBE

CATTANEO, Peter; *Educ* RCA; *Career* director; attached to Paul Weiland Film Co to direct commercials 1991; *Television* Diary of a Teenage Health Freak II (Limelight/Channel Four) 1992, The Bill (Thames Television) 1992, The Full Wax (BBC) 1992–93; *Film* True or False – The Big Easy 1989, Two 12 Minute Films 1990, Dear Rosie 1990, Say Hello to the Real Dr Snide 1990, Loved Up 1995, The Full Monty 1997, Lucky Break 2001; *Style*— Peter Cattaneo, Esq

CATTERALL, John Stewart; s of John Bernard Catterall (d 1965), and Eliza, *née* Whitiker; *b* 13 January 1939; *Educ* Blackpool Tech Coll Sch of Art; *m* 18 Sept 1965, (Ann) Beryl, da of Edgar Watkin Hughes; 2 s (Andrew b 4 Aug 1969, Stewart b 3 Feb 1971); *Career* Nat Serv band memb 12 Royal Lancers 1958–60; dep auditor Preston CBC 1966–68, sr accountant Derby CBC 1968–70, mgmnt and chief accountant Cambs and Isle of Ely CC 1970–73, asst co treas Cambs CC 1973–76, dist treas Southampton & SW Hants HA 1976–78, area treas Hants AHA 1978–82, regnl treas NE Thames RHA 1982–85; dep dir fin mgmnt Dept of Health and head Health Serv CIPFA 1985–88, dir consultancy for health 1988–89; md and chief exec C International Ltd 1989–92, dir Healthcare Consultancy Capita plc 1992–93, md C & T Ltd 1993–2001, dir Agenda Planning and Research 2002–11, former dir The C&T Partnership, ret 2014; memb CIPFA; *Books* ebooks: The Price of Fear, Bellman's Folly, The Anderton Legacy; *Recreations* golf, tennis; *Style*— John Catterall, Esq; ✉ 18 Lipizzaner Fields, Whiteley, Fareham Hampshire PO15 7BH (☎ 01489 881309, mobile 07407 280398, e-mail johnscatterall@gmail.com)

CATTERSON, Her Hon Judge Marie Thérèse; da of late James Joseph Catterson, and Rosemary, *née* McCarthy; *b* 14 October 1948; *Educ* Wyggeston Girls' GS Leicester, UCL (LLB); *m* 4 Aug 1984; 2 da; *Career* called to the Bar Gray's Inn 1972; recorder of the Crown Court 1996–2001, circuit judge (SE Circuit) 2001–; *Style*— Her Hon Judge Catterson; ✉ The Crown Court at St Albans, Bricket Road, St Albans, Hertfordshire AL1 3JW (☎ 01727 753220, fax 01727 753221)

CATTO, Hon Alexander Gordon; 2 s (by 1 m) of 2 Baron Catto; *b* 22 June 1952; *Educ* Westminster, Trinity Coll Cambridge; *m* 1981, Elizabeth Scott, da of late Maj T P Boyes, MC, of Whitford, Devon; 2 s (Thomas Innes Gordon b 1983, Alastair Gordon b 1986), 1 da (Charlotte Gordon b 1988); *Career* vice-pres Morgan Guaranty Trust Co of New York 1980–85; dir: Yule Catto & Co plc 1981–, Morgan Grenfell & Co Ltd 1986–88; md: Lazard Bros & Co 1988–94, CairnSea Investments Ltd, other private and public cos; *Style*— The Hon Alexander Catto; ✉ Yule Catto & Co plc, Temple Fields, Harlow, Essex CM20 2BH (☎ 01279 442791)

CATTO, Prof Sir Graeme Robertson Dawson; kt (2002); s of Dr William Dawson Catto (d 2005), and Dora Elizabeth, *née* Spiby (d 1978); *b* 24 April 1945, Aberdeen; *Educ* Robert Gordon's Coll Aberdeen, Univ of Aberdeen (MB ChB, MD, DSc), Harvard Univ; *m* 14 July 1967, Joan, da of James Alexander Sievewright (d 1958), of Aberdeen; 1 da (Sarah b 1970), 1 s (Simon b 1972); *Career* house offr Aberdeen Royal Infirmary 1969–70, Harkness fell in med Harvard Med Sch 1975–77; Univ of Aberdeen: lectr in med 1970–75, sr lectr in med 1977–88, prof of med and therapeutics 1988–2000, dean Faculty of Clinical Med 1992–95, vice-princ and dean Faculty of Med & Med Sciences 1995–98, vice-princ 1998–2000; hon conslt physician and nephrologist Grampian Health Bd 1977–2000, co-ordinator of clinical services Acute Services Unit Grampian Health Bd 1988–92, vice-chm Aberdeen Royal Hosps NHS Tst 1992–99, hon physician Guy's and St Thomas' Hosp NHS Tst, vice-princ KCL and dean GKT 2000–05 (pro-vice-chllr Univ of London 2003–05), prof of medicine Univ of Aberdeen and hon conslt physician and nephrologist NHS Grampian 2005–09; govr: PPP Healthcare Med Tst 2001–02, Qatar Science Technol Park 2003–07; pres: GMC 2002–09 (chm Educn Ctee 1999–2002), Assoc for the Study of Medical Educn 2009–13; memb Scottish Higher Educn Funding Cncl 1996–2002, chief scientist NHS Scotland 1997–2000, treas Acad of Med Scis 1998–2001, chm Scottish Stem Cell Network 2008–11, chm HE Better Regulation Gp Univs UK 2009–12, memb Cmmn on Assisted Dying 2010–11, advsr Medical and Dental Defence Union of Scotland 2010–13, memb Governance Bd Capita Clinical 2011–12, chm Dignity in Dying 2012–15 (patron 2015–); pres Coll of Medicine 2010–14; memb: SE London Strategic HA 2002–05, Cncl for the Regulation of Healthcare Professionals 2003–08, Assoc of Physicians of GB and I, Qatar Cncl for Healthcare Practitioners 2014–; chm Robert Gordon's Coll Aberdeen 1995–2005, chm of dirs Lathallan Sch Angus 2012–; Burgess of Guild City of Aberdeen; Hon LLD Univ of Aberdeen 2002; Hon DSc: Univ of St Andrews 2003, Robert Gordon Univ 2004, Univ of Kent 2007, South Bank Univ 2008, Univ of London 2009, Univ of Brighton 2010; Hon MD Univ of Southampton 2004, Hon MD Univ of Buckingham 2015; Hon FRCGP, Hon FRCSE; FRCP, FRCPEd, FRCPGlas, FMedSci, FRSE, FKC 2005, Hon FFPhM 2008, FAcadMEd 2012; *Books* Clinical Nephrology (1988), Transplant Immunology (1993); *Recreations* hill walking; *Clubs* Royal Northern and University, Athenaeum; *Style*— Prof Sir Graeme Catto, FRSE; ✉ Maryfield, Glenbuchat, Strathdon, Aberdeenshire AB36 8TS (☎ 01975 641317, e-mail gcatto@btinternet.com)

CATTO, 3 Baron (UK 1936); Sir Innes Gordon Catto; 3 Bt (UK 1921); s (by 1 m) of 2 Baron Catto (d 2001); *b* 7 August 1950; *Educ* Grenville Coll, Shuttleworth Agric Coll; *m* 29 March 2014, Ali Farhan Negyal; *Career* dir Caledonian Opera Co; *Style*— The Rt Hon the Lord Catto; ✉ Flat 17, Centre Point Flats, St Giles High Street, London WC2H 8LW

CATTRALL, Peter Jeremy; s of late Ralph W Cattrall, and late Sally Cattrall; *b* 8 January 1947; *Educ* King's Sch Canterbury, Trinity Coll Oxford (MA); *m* 26 April 1975, Amanda Jane Maria, da of Maj Gen W N J Withall, CB, and Pamela Withall, of Wiltshire; 1 s (Charles David b 1 March 1980), 1 da (Sarah Louise b 21 Sept 1982); *Career* former sch master Holmewood House Kent; admitted slr 1974, asst slr Knocker and Foskett Kent 1974–77, slr/oil and gas lawyer to Esso UK plc / Exxon Corp 1977–2000; slr and legal advsr to EMC Ltd and Saipem UK 2001–03, conslt to Carroll Insurance Gp 2000–, sometime conslt to Mitsui and other cos; memb nominated tstee dir ExxonMobil Pension Tst Ltd 2013–; memb: Oxford Union, Law Soc; memb Kent Co squash team 1970–78; MEI; *Recreations* golf, swimming, squash doubles, watching sport, travel, reading, music, current affairs; *Clubs* Oxford and Cambridge, MCC, Rye, Jesters, Free Foresters, I Zingari, Stragglers of Asia, Arabs, Band of Brothers, Yellowhammers, Harlequins, Vincent's, Beckenham Cricket; *Style*— Peter Cattrall, Esq; ✉ 21 Whitmore Road, Beckenham, Kent (home ☎ 020 8658 7265, e-mail petercattrall@hotmail.com); office ☎ 020 7623 2228

CAULFIELD, Maria; MP; *Career* MP (Cons) Lewes 2015–; *Style*— Ms Maria Caulfield, MP; ✉ House of Commons, London SW1A 0AA

CAUTE, (John) David; JP (1993); *b* 16 December 1936; *Educ* Edinburgh Acad, Wellington, Wadham Coll Oxford (MA, DPhil); *m* 1, 1961 (m dis 1970), Catherine Shuckburgh; 2 s; m 2, 1973, Martha Bates; 2 da; *Career* served Army Gold Coast 1955–56; novelist and historian; Henry fell Harvard Univ 1960–61, fell All Souls Oxford 1959–65, visiting prof NY and Colombia Univs 1966–67, reader in social and political theory Brunel Univ 1967–70, Regent's lectr Univ of Calif 1974, visiting prof Univ of Bristol 1985; literary ed New Statesman 1979–80, co-chm Writers' Guild 1981–82; FRSL 1998, FRHistS 2013; *Novels* At Fever Pitch (1959, Authors' Club Award, John Llewelyn Rhys Prize), Comrade Jacob (1961), The Decline of the West (1966), The Occupation (1971), The Baby-Sitters (as John Salisbury, 1978), Moscow Gold (as John Salisbury, 1980), The K-Factor (1983), News From Nowhere (1986), Veronica or the Two Nations (1988), The Women's Hour (1991), Dr Orwell and Mr Blair (1994), Fatima's Scarf (1998), Doubles (2016); *Plays* Songs for an Autumn Rifle (1961), The Demonstration (1969), The Fourth World (1973); *Radio Plays* Fallout (1972), The Zimbabwe Tapes (1983), Henry and the Dogs (1986), Sanctions (1988), Animal Fun Park (1995); *Non-Fiction* Communism and the French Intellectuals 1914–1960 (1964), The Left in Europe Since 1789 (1966), Essential Writings of Karl Marx (ed, 1967), Fanon (1970), The Illusion (1971), The Fellow-Travellers (1973, revised edn 1988), Cuba, Yes ? (1974), Collisions – Essays and Reviews (1974), The Great Fear – The Anti-Communist Purge under Truman and Eisenhower (1978), Under the Skin – The Death of White Rhodesia (1983), The Espionage of the Saints (1986), Sixty-Eight – The Year of the Barricades (1988), Joseph Losey: A Revenge on Life (1994), The Dancer Defects – The Struggle for Cultural Supremacy During the Cold War (2003), Marechera and the Colonel (2009), Poitics and the Novel during the Cold War (2009), Isaac and Isaiah: The Covert Punishment of a Cold War Heretic (2013); *Style*— David Caute, Esq; ✉ 41 Westcroft Square, London W6 0TA

CAVALIER, David John; s of John Richard Cavalier, of Bloxwich, Birmingham, and Jackie Orama, *née* Wheatley; *b* 12 February 1962; *Educ* Mandeville County Secdy Sch, Aylesbury Coll of Further Educn (City and Guilds Certs, Cert of Royal Inst of Health and Hygiene), Ealing Coll of Higher Educn (City and Guilds Cert); *m* 2 Feb 1985, Susan Caroline, da of Ronald Dorsett; 2 da (Jennifer b 22 Oct 1988, Alexandra b 24 Oct 1995), m 2, 1 June 2000, Jo-Anne Karen, da of Sidney Bibby; 2 da (Françoise Molly-Anna b 30 Jan 2002, Beatrice Millie Helena b 19 Dec 2006); *Career* commis chef Royal Garden Hotel 1979–81, first commis chef Grosvenor House Hotel 1981–82, chef de partie Dorchester Hotel 1982–84, sous chef Auberge du Mail France 1984, first sous chef Berkeley Hotel 1984–85; chef and proprietor: Pebbles Restaurant 1985–87, Cavalier's Restaurant 1987–; head chef: The Bell Inn Aston Clinton 1992–93, L'Escargot 1993–95; jt proprietor Chapter One 1996–, proprietor Memo restaurant 1996–, exec chef Mosimanns 1999–2000, High Holborn 2000–01, food innovation dir Charlton House 2001–; winner: Gold medal (potato work) Hotel Olympia, Gold medal for best exhibit in jr class, finalist Young Chef of the Year competition 1987; awarded: 4 rosette AA Guide, 2 star Michelin Guide, black clover Ackerman Guide, 1 star Egon Ronay; memb Restaurant Assoc GB 1985; *Recreations* classic cars, fishing; *Style*— David Cavalier, Esq; ✉ Old School House, 72 Station Road, Chinnor, Oxfordshire OX39 4PZ

CAVALIER, Stephen; s of Kenneth Cavalier, and Marion, *née* Hussey; *b* 26 February 1962, St Albans, Herts; *Educ* Univ of Oxford (BA); *Children* 2 s (Cameron b 22 Nov 1990, Keir b 8 Oct 1992); *Career* slr; Thompsons: joined as slr 1987, head Employment Rights Unit 1996, client dir 2003, ceo 2007–; former chair Industrial Law Soc; memb Lab Pty 1979–; *Publications* Transfer of Undertakings (1997 and 2006); *Recreations* politics, football; *Clubs* Tottenham Hotspur FC; *Style*— Stephen Cavalier, Esq; ✉ Thompsons, Congress House, Great Russell Street, London WC1B 3LW (☎ 020 7290 0007, e-mail stephencavalier@thompsons.law.co.uk)

CAVALIER, Stephen Ronald (Steve); s of Ronald Ernest Cavalier, of Romford, Essex, and Jean, *née* Chinery; *b* 25 June 1952; *Educ* Harold Hill GS Essex, Colchester Sch of Art; *m* 1 Sept 1979, Christine, da of William Alfred Guerrier; 1 da (Clare Jean b 31 Aug 1982), 1 s (James William b 11 Feb 1985); *Career* photographer; asst with advertising photographers London 1971–77, fndr Steve Cavalier Studios 1977– (Central London then moving to St John's Wood); Gold and Silver Awards Design and Art Directors' Assoc, Gold and Silver Campaign Press Awards, Gold Award The One Show NY, commendation Benson & Hedges Gold Award 1990, Silver Award Campaign Poster Awards 1995; memb: Assoc of Photographers (formerly Assoc of Fashion, Advertising and Editorial Photographers), D&AD; *Style*— Steve Cavalier, Esq; ✉ Steve Cavalier Studios (☎ 07787 545054, e-mail steve@stevecavalier.co.uk, website www.stevecavalier.co.uk)

CAVALIER-SMITH, Prof Thomas (Tom); s of Alan Cavalier-Smith (d 1976), and Mary Cavalier-Smith (d 2006); *b* 21 October 1942, London; *Educ* Gonville & Caius Coll Cambridge (maj open scholar, MA) KCL (PhD), Open Univ (BA); *m* 1, 1967, Gillian; m 2, Ema, *née* Chao; 2 da (Jane b 1964, Rose Mary b 1994), 1 s (Neal b 1966); *Career* guest investigator Rockefeller Univ 1967–69; KCL: lectr 1969–82, reader in biophysics 1982–89; prof of botany Univ of British Columbia 1989–99; Univ of Oxford: research prof NERC 1999–2007, prof of evolutionary biology 2000–; fell Canadian Inst for Advanced Research 1998–2007; Int Prize for Biology 2004, Linnean Medal for Zoology 2007, Frink Medal Zoological Soc of London 2008; FRSC 1997, FRS 1998, FRSA, FLS, FIBiol; *Publications* Biology, Society and Choice (ed with J P Hudson. 1982), The Evolution of Genome Size (ed, 1985); author of over 200 scientific articles and book chapters; *Recreations* reading, natural history; *Style*— Prof Thomas Cavalier-Smith; ✉ Department of Zoology, University of Oxford, South Parks Road, Oxford OX1 3PS (e-mail tom.cavalier-smith@zoo.ox.ac.uk)

CAVALIERO, Dr Glen; s of Clarence John Cavaliero (d 1958), and Mildred Osborne Cavaliero, *née* Tilburn (d 1950); *b* 7 June 1927, Eastbourne, E Sussex; *Educ* Tonbridge, Magdalen Coll Oxford (MA), St Catharine's Coll Cambridge (MA, PhD); *Career* poet; staff memb Lincoln Theol Coll 1956–61; St Catharine's Coll Cambridge: research fell 1967–71, fell commoner 1986; pres The Powys Soc; FRSL 1986; *Publications* incl: The Ancient People (poems, 1973), John Cowper Powys: Novelist (1973), Paradise Stairway (poems, 1977), The Rural Tradition in the English Novel (1977), A Reading of E M Forster (1979), Elegy for St Anne's (poems, 1982), Charles Williams: Poet of Theology (1983), The Supernatural and English Fiction (1995), Steeple on a Hill (poems, 1997), The Alchemy of Laughter (2000), Ancestral Haunt (poems, 2002), The Justice of the Night (poems, 2007), Towards the Waiting Sun (poems, 2011); *Style*— Dr Glen Cavaliero; ✉ St Catharine's College, Cambridge CB2 1RL

CAVANAGH, John Eric; s of Charles Cavanagh, and Jean Burns Cavanagh; *b* 27 December 1964; *Career* broadcaster, musician, writer and radio prodr; presenter BBC Radio 1990–, wide range of material across the BBC network incl the Radio One Rock Show and

Music Machine (Radio 3) and shows on BBC Scotland and World Service; memb Electroscope (over 100 titles released) 1996–2000 and 2011–; Phosphene (music project) 2000– (albums: Long Meadow Felt Company 2001, Projection 2003, The Plum, the Orange and the Matchbox 2005, Phoenix Trees 2007, Are You Sitting Comfortably? 2008); collaborations incl work with: The Poets & Andrew Loog Oldham, Mount Vernon Arts Lab, Hefner, Isobel Campbell, Lol Coxhill, Bridget St John, Bill Wells, Nalle, Aube (Japanese performance artist), Colleen, Colour Match by Simon Patterson Tate Modern; prodr/co-prodr of records by Rab Noakes, Barbara Dickson, Family Elan, Trembling Bells and others; English language stadium announcer for all four winter Olympic and Paralympic ceremonies Sochi Russia 2014, announcer of introductory films to all sports Cwlth Games Glasgow 2014; *Publications* The Piper at the Gates of Dawn (2003); *Recreations* vintage analogue sound instruments and recording, travel, wine, cinema; *Clubs* BBC, Pastelism, Joe Meek Appreciation Soc; *Style*— John Cavanagh, Esq; ✉ BBC Radio One, Glasgow G12 8DG (e-mail john.cavanagh@bbc.co.uk, website www.johncavanagh.co.uk)

CAVANAGH, John Patrick; QC (2001); s of Dr Gerry Cavanagh (decd), of Welford-on-Avon, Warks, and Anne, *née* Kennedy; *b* 17 June 1960, Belfast; *Educ* Warwick Sch, New Coll Oxford (open scholar, MA), Clare Coll Cambridge (LLM), Univ of Illinois Coll of Law; *m* 6 May 1989, Suzanne Fiona (Suzie), da of Harry Tolley; 3 da (Sophie Marie b 1 Oct 1990, Emma Rosanne b 19 March 1992, Isabelle Grace b 29 Dec 1996), 1 s (John Patrick b 27 Sept 1994); *Career* called to the Bar Middle Temple 1985; Treasy counsel (B Panel) 1997–2001; pt/t lectr New Coll Oxford 1984–86; memb editorial team: Tolley's Employment Handbook 1998–2005 (jt ed), Harvey on Industrial Relations and Employment Law 2000–04, Butterworth's Local Government Law; frequent speaker and writer on employment law and public law issues; chair Employment Law Bar Assoc 2005–07; memb: Administrative Law Bar Assoc, Commercial Bar Assoc; *Recreations* family, reading, music, football; *Style*— John Cavanagh, Esq, QC; ✉ 11 King's Bench Walk, Temple, London EC4Y 7EQ (☎ 020 7632 8500, fax 020 7583 9123, e-mail cavanagh@11kbw.com, website www.11kbw.com)

CAVE; *see:* Haddon-Cave

CAVE, Sir John Charles; 5 Bt (UK 1896), of Cleve Hill, Mangotsfield, Co Gloucester, Sidbury Manor, Sidbury, Co Devon, and Stoneleigh House, Clifton, Bristol; DL (Devon 2001); o s of Sir Charles Edward Coleridge Cave, 4 Bt (d 1997); *b* 8 September 1958; *Educ* Eton, RAC Cirencester; *m* 1984, Carey Diana, er da of John Lloyd (d 2010); 2 s (George Charles b 8 Sept 1987, William Alexander b 7 May 1992), 1 da (Alice Elizabeth b 28 June 1989); *Heir* s, George Cave; *Career* High Sheriff Devon 2005, Vice Lord-Lt Devon 2007; *Clubs* MCC, Farmers, Army and Navy; *Style*— Sir John Cave, Bt, DL; ✉ Sidbury Manor, Sidmouth, Devon EX10 0QE

CAVE, Prof Terence Christopher; CBE (2013); s of Alfred Cyril Cave (d 1979), and Sylvia Norah, *née* Norman (d 1989); *b* 1 December 1938; *Educ* Winchester, Gonville & Caius Coll Cambridge (MA, DPhil); *m* 1, 31 July 1965 (m dis 1990), Helen Elizabeth; 1 s (Christopher b 1969), 1 da (Hilary b 1970); m 2, Kirsti, *née* Sellevold; *Career* lectr Univ of St Andrews 1963–65 (asst lectr 1962–63), sr lectr Univ of Warwick 1970–72 (lectr 1965–70), fell and tutor St John's Coll Oxford 1972–2001 (emeritus res fell 2001–14, emeritus fell 2014–), prof of French literature Univ of Oxford 1989–2001 (emeritus prof 2001–); visiting posts: Cornell Univ 1967–68, Univ of Calif Santa Barbara 1976, Univ of Virginia 1979, Princeton Univ 1984, Univ of Trondheim 1991, Univ of Alberta Edmonton 1992, Univ of Paris 7 1995 and 2002, UCLA 1997, NYU 2003, Univ of Oslo 2006; Balzan Prize for Literature since 1500 2009; Hon DLit Univ of London 2007; visiting fell All Souls Coll Oxford 1971; hon sr res fell Inst of Romance Studies London, memb Royal Norwegian Soc of Sciences and Letters; hon fell Gonville & Caius Coll Cambridge, hon fell Queen Mary Univ of London 2010; memb Academia Europaea, memb Norwegian Acad of Science and Letters; FBA; Chevalier dans l'Ordre National du Mérite (France); *Books* Devotional Poetry in France (1969), The Cornucopian Text (1979), Recognitions (1988), Pré-histoires (1999), Pré-histoires II (2001), How to Read Montaigne (2007), Mignon's Afterlives (2011), Thinking with Literature (2016); *Recreations* music, languages; *Style*— Prof Terence Cave, CBE, FBA; ✉ St John's College, Oxford OX1 3JP (☎ 01865 280176, fax 01865 277435, e-mail terence.cave@sjc.ox.ac.uk)

CAVELL, His Hon Judge John James; *b* 1 October 1947; *Educ* King Edward's Sch Stourbridge, Churchill Coll Cambridge (MA); *Career* called to the Bar Middle Temple 1971; practising barr 1971–94, recorder 1991–94, circuit judge (Midland Circuit) 1994–; *Style*— His Hon Judge Cavell; ✉ c/o Midland Circuit Office, Priory Courts, 33 Bull Street, Birmingham B4 6DW

CAVENAGH-MAINWARING, Charles Rafe Gordon; s of Capt Maurice Kildare Cavenagh-Mainwaring, DSO, RN, and Iris Mary, *née* Denaro; *Educ* Downside; *m* 20 Oct 1973 (m dis), Rosemary Lee, da of Capt Thomas Lee Reay Hardy (d 1982), of London; 1 s (Rupert William b 1976); *Career* Lt RM Reserve 1964–67, Lt HAC (RHA) 1967–73, transferred to RARO 1974; dir Hinton Hill Underwriting Agents Ltd 1987–89, conslt Allied Dunbar 1990–96, fin advsr Eggar Forrester 1996–97; social researcher Nat Centre for Social Research (NatCen) 2002–; bd memb Atlantic Cncl (NATO Support Gp) 1997–, memb Insurance Brokers Registration Cncl 1997–2000, memb European-Atlantic Gp; memb RUSI 2012–; Knight of Honour and Devotion Sovereign Mil Order of Malta (Cross of Merit 2010), Knight of Justice of the Sacred Mil Order of Constantine of St George; *Recreations* skiing, watching rugby union football, tennis; *Clubs* Hurlingham, Harlequins RFC, HAC Mess; *Style*— Charles Cavenagh-Mainwaring, Esq

CAVENDISH, Lucy; da of Edward Patrick James Cavendish (d 2000), and Pamela, *née* Iles; *b* 16 December 1966; *Children* 1 s (Raymond Stanley Ellison b 1996); *Career* journalist; ed Observer Food Monthly until 2002, interviewer and features writer Evening Standard 2002–; *Style*— Ms Lucy Cavendish

CAVENDISH, Mark; MBE (2011); *b* 21 May 1985, Douglas, IOM; *Career* cyclist; early career as track cyclist, professional road racing cyclist 2007–; memb: Team Sparkasse 2006, T-Mobile Team 2007, Team Columbia 2008–; achievements as track cyclist incl: winner team pursuit Br Nat Track Championships 2004 and 2005, Gold medal points race Under 23s European Championships 2005, Gold medal madison World Championships LA 2005 (with Rob Hayles) and Manchester 2008 (with Bradley Wiggins), Gold medal (rep IOM) scratch race Cwlth Games Melbourne 2006, winner madison Br Nat Track Championships 2008, competed madison Olympic Games Beijing 2008, Silver medal omnium Olympic Games 2016; achievements as road cyclist incl: stage winner Tour of Berlin 2005, winner Br Nat Circuit Race Championships 2005, winner (points) Tour of Britain 2006 and 2007, winner stages 4 and 5 Tour of Berlin 2006 (second place overall), winner Grote Scheldeprijs 2007 and 2008, winner (points) Four Days of Dunkirk 2007, winner (points) Volta a Catalunya 2007, winner stage 4 Ster Elektrotoer 2007, winner (points) Post Danmark Rundt 2007, winner (points) Eneco Tour of Benelux 2007, winner Stage 3 Circuit Franco-Belge 2007, debut Tour de France 2007, winner stages 2 and 3A Three Days of De Panne 2008, winner prologue Tour de Romandie 2008, winner stage 5 Ster Elektotoer 2008, winner stages 4 and 13 Giro d'Italia 2008 (fourth (points)), winner stages 5, 8, 12 and 13 Tour de France 2008, winner stages 5, 6, 11, 18 and 20 Tour de France 2010; *Style*— Mark Cavendish, Esq, MBE

CAVENDISH OF FURNESS, Baron (Life Peer UK 1990), of Cartmel in the County of Cumbria; Richard Hugh Cavendish; DL (Cumbria 1988); s of late Capt Richard Edward Osborne Cavendish, DL; *b* 2 November 1941; *Educ* Eton; *m* 1970, Grania Mary, da of Brig Toby St George Caulfeild, CBE; 1 s, 2 da; *Career* int merchanting and banking London 1961–71, dir Holker Estate Gp of Cos, chm 1971–2015, dir UK Nirex Ltd 1993–99; High Sheriff of Cumbria 1978, cncllr Cumbria CC 1985–90; a Lord in Waiting (Govt whip) 1990–92; memb: Select Ctee on Croydon Tramlink Bill 1992–93, EU Sub-Ctee B (Energy, Indust and Tport) 2001–04, House of Lords Select Ctee on the EU 2001–, Assoc of Cons Peers; cmmnr Historic Buildings and Monuments Cmmn (English Heritage) 1992–98; pres Dry Stone Walling Assoc of GB; chm Morecambe and Lonsdale Cons Assoc 1975–78, chm of govrs St Anne's Sch Windermere 1983–89, chm Lancs and Cumbria Fndn for Med Res 1994–96, co-fndr St Mary's Hospice Ulverston (chm 2003–09); Liveryman Worshipful Co of Fishmongers; FRSA 1988; *Publications* A Time to Plant (2012); *Recreations* gardening, National Hunt racing, shooting, fishing, reading, travel; *Clubs* Brooks's, White's, Pratt's, Beefsteak; *Style*— The Lord Cavendish of Furness, DL; ✉ Low Frith, Cark-in-Cartmel, Cumbria LA11 7PP (☎ 01539 59999 home 01539 558123, e-mail cavendish@holker.co.uk)

CAVENDISH OF LITTLE VENICE, Baroness (Life Peer UK 2016), of Little Venice, of Mells in the County of Somerset; Camilla Cavendish; *Educ* BNC Oxford (MA), John F Kennedy Sch of Govt Harvard Univ (MPA); *Career* assoc ed, columnist and chief ldr writer The Times 2002–12, assoc ed, columnist The Sunday Times 2013–15, head Downing Street Policy Unit 2015–; author Cavendish Review into the Care Workforce, commissioned by Sec of State for Health 2013; tstee: Thames Festival Tst 2000–07, Policy Exchange 2002–, Early Years Fndn Tst 2012–; non-exec Care Quality Commission 2013–; Paul Foot Award 2008, Campaigning Journalist of the Year Br Press Award 2009, Harold Wincott Sr Financial Journalist of the Year 2012; *Style*— The Baroness Cavendish of Little Venice; ✉ 10 Downing Street, London SW1A 2AA

CAVILL, Henry William Dalgliesh; *b* 5 May 1983, Jersey; *Educ* Stowe; *Career* actor; *Film* incl: The Count of Monte Cristo 2002, I Capture the Castle 2003, Tristan + Isolde 2006, Stardust 2007, Immortals 2011, Superman: Man of Steel 2012; *Television* incl The Tudors 2007–10; *Style*— Henry Cavill, Esq; ✉ c/o United Agents, 12–26 Lexington Street, London W1F 0LE (☎ 020 3214 0800, website www.unitedagents.co.uk)

CAWDRON, Peter Edward Blackburn; *m* 1968, Diana Anderson; 2 s (Nicholas, Benjamin), 1 da (Emily); *Career* with: Peat Marwick Mitchell 1961–70, S G Warburg & Co Ltd 1970–77, D'Arcy MacManus & Masius (advtg agency) 1977–83; Grand Metropolitan plc: joined 1983, gp planning dir 1983–87, gp strategy development dir 1987–97, main bd dir 1993–97; non-exec chm: Capital Radio plc 2002–05, GCap 2005–, Punch Taverns plc 2007– (non-exec dir 2003–); dep chm and sr non-exec dir Compass Group plc (formerly non-exec dir) 1999–; non-exec dir: Capita Group 1997–, Johnston Press 1998–, ARM Hldgs plc 1998–, Christian Salvesen plc 1997–, Arla Foods UK plc 2000–06; *Style*— Peter Cawdron, Esq

CAWKWELL, Paul G J; s of Geoffrey Cawkwell, and Louise, *née* Langan; *b* 3 October 1969, Dagenham, Essex; *Educ* Campion Sch Hornchurch, Havering Coll of FE; *m* 29 Oct 1994, Tina, *née* Evans; 2 da (Grace b 23 Dec 1995, Lily b 30 Sept 1998); *Career* Coutts & Co 1986–91, Hambros Bank Ltd 1991–93; joined HM Prison Service 1993, dep govr HMP Wellingborough 2002–03, dep govr HMP Norwich 2004–06, govr HMP Blundeston 2006–08, first govr HMP Bure 2009–10, govr HMP Whitemoor 2010–13, govr HMP Wayland 2016–; joined NI Prison Service 2013, dir of offender policy and operations NI Prison Service 2013–15; Ind Review of Extremism Ministry of Justice 2015; *Publications* Independent Review of Extremism in Prisons and Probation (2016); *Style*— Paul Cawkwell, Esq

CAWLEY, Dr Michael Ian David Setchell; RD; s of late William Miller Seddon Cawley, CBE, of Bexhill, E Sussex, and late Edith Mary, *née* Setchell; *b* 14 October 1935; *Educ* Caterham Sch, Bart's Med Coll Univ of London (MB BS, MD); *m* 1997, Alison Lindsey, *née* Chapman; 2 da (Imogen Edith b 31 Aug 1998, Helena Alice b 24 July 2000); *Career* Nat Serv Lt and Capt RAMC 1960–62, surgn Lt Cdr RNR 1970–90; house offr 1959–60: Norwich, Bournemouth, Bart's; med registrar 1962–68: Bart's, Lewisham Hosp London; Aylwen res fell Bart's 1965–66, sr registrar and tutor in med Bristol Royal Hosp 1968–70, ARC visiting res fell Univ of Texas at Dallas 1971–72, lectr in rheumatology Univ of Manchester 1970–73; conslt physician rheumatology: Wrightington Hosp 1973–74, Southampton Univ Hosps 1974– (clinical tutor 1979–82, hon sr lectr 1990–); hon civilian conslt advsr to RN 1989–, visiting conslt Princess Elizabeth Hosp Guernsey 1997–; author of papers and chapters on rheumatic diseases; memb: Ctee on Rheumatology RCP 1983–89 (dist tutor 1987–93), Cncl Br Soc of Rheumatology 1986–88, Central Conslts and Specialists Ctee BMA 1986–93, Cncl BMA 1996–98, Cncl RCP 1998–2001; vice-pres Rheumatology Section RSM 1999–2001; Heberden Roundsman Br Soc for Rheumatology 1992; pres S Wales S West and Wessex Rheumatology Club 1986–89; memb: American Coll of Rheumatology, Br Soc for Rheumatology, Br Soc for Immunology, Bone and Tooth Soc; Liveryman Worshipful Soc of Apothecaries 1990 (Freeman 1982, memb Livery Ctee 2004–07); FRCP 1979 (MRCP), FRSM; *Recreations* classical music, sailing, skiing; *Clubs* Royal Lymington Yacht, Royal Naval Sailing Association, Royal Southampton Yacht, Ski Club of Great Britain; *Style*— Dr Michael Cawley; ✉ Paddock Cottage, Bramshaw, Lyndhurst, Hampshire SO43 7JN (☎ 01794 390934, secretary tel and fax 01722 238399, e-mail midscl@googlemail.com)

CAYLEY, Dr (Arthur) Charles Digby; s of Dr Forde Everard de Wend Cayley, MBE, of Thames Ditton, Surrey, and Eileen Lillian, *née* Dalton; *b* 8 November 1946; *Educ* Middx Hosp Med Sch London (MB BS); *m* 1 Nov 1969, Jeanette Ann, da of George Richard Avery (d 1968), of Plymouth, Devon; 3 s (George b 1971, Adam b 1975, Seth b 1980); *Career* sr registrar in geriatric med and hon lectr Middx Hosp 1974–76, conslt physician in med of the elderly NW London Hosps NHS Tst and Brent PCT 1976– (clinical dir med and care of the elderly 2001–, assoc med dir 2002–), med dir London NW Hosps NHS Tst 2013–; recognised teacher Univ of London, hon clinical sr lectr ICSTM London; President's Medal Br Geriatrics Soc 2012; *Books* Hospital Geriatric Medicine (1987); *Recreations* walking, listening to classical music; *Style*— Dr Charles Cayley; ✉ Department of Medicine for the Elderly, Central Middlesex Hospital, Acton Lane, London NW10 7NS (☎ 020 8453 2184, fax 020 8961 1827, e-mail charles.cayley1@nhs.net)

CAYTON, William Henry Rymer (Harry); CBE (2014, OBE 2001); s of Dr H Rymer Cayton (d 1989), and Mrs Marion Cayton (d 1999); *b* 27 March 1950; *Educ* Bristol Cathedral Sch, New Univ of Ulster (BA), Univ of Durham (Dip), Univ of Newcastle upon Tyne (BPhil); *Career* teacher: King's Sch Rochester 1972–73, Dame Allan's Sch Newcastle upon Tyne 1973–76, Northern Counties Sch for the Deaf 1976–80; National Deaf Children's Soc: educn offr 1980–82, dir 1982–91; elected hon life memb European Fed of Deaf Children's Assocs 1991, chief exec Alzheimer's Soc 1991–2003, dir Patients and Public Dept of Health 2003–07, chief exec Professional Standards Authy (formerly Cncl for Healthcare Regulatory Excellence) 2007–, chair Nat Info Governance Bd for Health and Social Care 2008–11; vice-chair Consumers in NHS Research and Devpt 1998–2003; social care advsr Macmillan Cancer Support 2003–14; tstee: Hearing Research Tst 1985–2005, Comic Relief 2005– (chair UK Grants Ctee 2014–); memb: Alzheimer Europe 1998–2002, Central R&D Ctee NHS 1999, NHS Modernisation Bd 2000–03, Press Recognition Panel 2014–; fell Faculty of Public Health 2007; Distinguished Grad Award Univ of Ulster 2003, Alzheimer Europe Award 2004, Lifetime Achievement Award RCPsych 2007; Canadian Cwlth fell 1982; *Publications* Alzheimers and other Dementias (2002); author of numerous essays and articles; *Recreations* Old Master drawings, music, cooking and eating; *Clubs* Athenaeum; *Style*— Harry Cayton, Esq, CBE; ✉ 24 Barlby Gardens, North Kensington,

London W10 5LW; Professional Standards Authority, 157–159 Buckingham Palace Road, London SW1W 9SP (☎ 020 7389 8030)

CAYZER, Hon Charles William; s of 2 Baron Rotherwick (d 1996); *b* 26 April 1957; *Educ* Harrow; *m* 1, 1985, Amanda Cosbie Sara, 2 da of John Squire, of Marbella, Spain; 1 da (Victoria Amanda b 22 June 1989), 1 s ((Charles) William b 14 July 1991); m 2, 1 March 2013, Sarah Jane Mancini; *Career* late The Life Guards; dir: Caledonia Investments plc, The Cayzer Trust Company Ltd, The Sloane Club Group Ltd; *Style*— The Hon Charles Cayzer; ✉ Brize Lodge, Leafield, Oxfordshire OX7 3DD

CAYZER-COLVIN, Jamie Michael Beale; s of Michael Keith Beale Colvin MP (d 2000), and Hon Nichola, *née* Cayzer (d 2000); *b* 1 April 1965, London; *Educ* Gordonstoun, RMA Sandhurst, Henley Mgmnt Coll (MBA); *m* 31 Oct 1992, Esther Anne Mary, *née* Tree; 2 da (Mollie Isabella Elizabeth b 30 Sept 1995, Lily Georgia Daphanne b 8 April 1999); *Career* Lt Grenadier Gds 1985–89, Close Bros plc 1989–90 (non-exec dir 2008–12), Whitbread Beer Co 1991–92, Amber Ind Holdings plc 1992–95, exec dir Caledonia Investments plc 1995–; non-exec dir: Polar Capital Hldgs plc 2000–, Rathbone Bros plc 2002–07, Eddington Capital Mgmnt 2003–11, Ermtage Ltd 2006–11; former non-exec dir Indian Capital Growth Fund plc; chm: Henderson Smaller Companies Investment Tst 2011–, RHS Pension Fund 2013–, tstees Heritage of London Tst 2012–, Gateway to India 2012–; former chm of tstees Children's Fire and Burns Tst; *Recreations* family, country and gardens; *Clubs* Boodles; *Style*— Jamie Cayzer-Colvin, Esq; ✉ The Manor House, Milton Lilbourne, Pewsey, Wilshire SN9 5LQ; Caledonia Investments plc, Cayzer House, 30 Buckingham Gate, London SW1E 6NN (☎ 020 7802 8080, e-mail jamie.cayzer-colvin@caledonia.com, website www.caledonia.com)

CAZALET, Hon Lady (Camilla Jane); *née* Gage; da of 6 Viscount Gage, KCVO, by his 1 w, Hon Imogen Grenfell; *b* 12 July 1937; *Educ* Benenden; *m* 24 April 1965, Sir Edward Stephen Cazalet, DL, *qv*; 2 s, 1 da; *Career* dir Lumley Cazalet 1967–2002; tstee Glyndebourne Arts Tst 1978–2004; memb Cncl: Friends of Covent Garden 1977–2005 (memb Mgmnt Ctee 1994–2000), RNT Cncl 1997–2008 (memb Bd 1991–97); govr Royal Ballet 2000–08; *Recreations* visual and performing arts, music, tennis; *Style*— The Hon Lady Cazalet; ✉ Shaw Farm, Plumpton Green, East Sussex BN7 3DG (☎ 01273 890207, fax 01273 890358); Flat 10, 41 Stanhope Gardens, London SW7 5QY (☎ 020 7244 6182, fax 020 7341 4496)

CAZALET, Sir Edward Stephen; kt (1988), DL (E Sussex 1989); s of Peter Victor Ferdinand Cazalet, JP, DL (d 1973), the race horse trainer, and his 1 w, Leonora, *née* Rowley, step da of Sir P G Wodehouse; *b* 26 April 1936; *Educ* Eton, ChCh Oxford; *m* 24 April 1965, Hon Camilla Jane (Hon Lady Cazalet, *qv*), da of 7 Viscount Gage, KCVO (d 1982); 2 s (David b 1967, Hal b 1969), 1 da (Lara b 1973); *Career* subaltern Welsh Guards 1954–56; called to the Bar Inner Temple 1960 (bencher 1985); QC 1980, recorder of the Crown Court 1985–88, judge of the High Court of Justice (Family Div) 1988–2000; chm: Horse Race Betting Levy Appeal Tbnl 1979–88, CAB Royal Courts of Justice 1993–97, Br Agencies for Adoption and Fostering 2000–05, Jockey Club Appeal Bd 2001–05, Injured Jockeys Fund; tstee Winston Churchill Meml Tst 2005–10; fell Eton Coll 1989–2004; *Recreations* riding, ball games, chess; *Clubs* Garrick; *Style*— Sir Edward Cazalet, DL; ✉ Shaw Farm, Plumpton Green, Lewes, East Sussex BN7 3DG

CAZALET, (Charles) Julian; s of Vice Adm Sir Peter Grenville Lyon Cazalet, KBE, CB, DSO, DSC (d 1982), of Newick, E Sussex, and Lady Beatrice Elise, *née* Winterbotham; *b* 29 November 1947; *Educ* Uppingham, Magdalene Coll Cambridge (MA); *m* 29 Nov 1986, Jennifer Clare, da of Maurice Nelson Little (d 1985), of Laverton, Glos; 1 s (Charles b 1987), 1 da (Fleur b 1989); *Career* ptnr Cazenove & Co Investment Bankers 1978–2001, md corp fin Cazenove & Co Ltd 2001–05, md corp fin JP Morgan Cazenove 2005–07; dir: Herald Investment Tst plc 2008– (chm 2009–), Deltex Medical Gp plc 2008–, Charles Taylor plc 2008–15, Private Equity Investor plc 2012–; chm The Lindsell Train Investment Tst plc 2015– (formerly dir); memb Cncl White Ensign Assoc Ltd 2003–; chm Imperial War Graves Endowment Fund 2010– (former tstee); govr Cothill House Sch 2005–13; tstee: Greenham Common Tst 2011–, Uppingham Sch 2012–, tstee HMS Victory Preservation Co 2012–; FCA 1977; *Recreations* golf, skiing, stalking; *Clubs* City Univ (chm 1994–2012), Wisley Golf, Brooks's, Hurlingham; *Style*— Julian Cazalet, Esq; ✉ 38 Norland Square, London W11 4PZ (☎ 020 7727 1756, fax 020 7792 2358, e-mail julian@cazalet.org.uk)

CAZENOVE, Bernard Michael de Lerisson; TD; s of David Michael de Lerisson Cazenove (d 1988), and Euphemia, *née* Maclean (d 1997); *b* 14 June 1947; *Educ* Radley, RMA Sandhurst; *m* 19 Dec 1971, Caroline June, da of Richard Moore (d 1963), of Wellington, NZ; 2 s (Richard b 1974, George b 1977), 1 da (Edwina b 1984); *Career* cmmnd Coldstream Guards 1967, ADC to HE Govr Gen of NZ 1971, transferred Parachute Regt (TA) 1973, Hon Col 4 Bn Parachute Regt 1999–2006; ptnr Cazenove & Co 1982–2001 (joined 1973), md Cazenove Gp 2001–2004; memb Ct of Patrons RCS (Royal Coll of Surgns of Eng) 2004; govr Forest Sch; hon fell Darwin Coll Cambridge 2005; tstee: Airborne Forces Security Fund, Ulysses Tst; Liveryman Worshipful Co of Dyers; *Clubs* White's, Pratt's, Rock Sailing, Flyfishers, Kandahar Ski, St Enodoc Golf; *Style*— Bernard Cazenove, Esq, TD; ✉ Brocas, Ellisfield, Basingstoke, Hampshire RG24 2QS

CECIL, Desmond Hugh; CMG (1995); s of Dr Rupert Cecil, DFC, and Rosemary, *née* Luker; *b* 19 October 1941; *Educ* Magdalen Coll Sch Oxford, The Queen's Coll Oxford (MA); *m* 1964, Ruth Elizabeth, *née* Sachs; 3 s, 1 da; *Career* studied violin, viola and oboe with Profs Max Rostal in Berne and Joy Boughton in London, subsequently violinist and oboist in Switzerland (leader Neuchâtel Chamber Orch 1965–70); HM Dip Serv 1970–95: second sec London 1970–73, first sec Bonn 1973–74, FCO 1974–76, press offr Mission to UN Geneva 1976–80, FCO 1980–85, cnsllr and chargé d'Affaires Vienna 1985–89, FCO 1989–92, on secondment with Bd of P&O European Ferries 1992, under sec FCO 1992–95; sr advsr to: BT 1996–97, British Nuclear Fuels plc 1996–2006, Marconi 1998–2001; advsr Bd Nuclear Mgmnt Ptnrs Ltd 2008 and 2014–16; chm Arena Pal Ltd 2002–03, UK rep and sr vice-pres AREVA 2006– (expert chair 2012–); antiquarian book dealer 1997–; memb Advsy Cncl Park Lane Gp 2015–; dir and tstee Jupiter Orch London 1996–2002; Royal Philharmonic Soc: memb Cncl 1995–2005, chm Sponsorship Ctee, hon co-treas; memb Cncl Britain-Russia Centre 1998–2000; int rep Gstaad Menuhin Festival and Acad 2001–; memb Cncl and tstee Voices for Hospices 2000–04, advsr Russia Arts Help Charity Moscow 2000–05; tstee Norbert Brainin Fndn Asolo 2004–09, tstee then dir London Philharmonic Orchestra 2005–; memb: Mensa 1968–2005, Sherlock Holmes Soc of London 1970–, Kingston Chamber Music Soc 1990–, Panel 2000 Germany Project Bd 1999–2000, Br-German Assoc 2001–05, Bd Int Mendelssohn Fndn Leipzig 2001– (chm UK Friends 2005–), Appeal Ctee later Devpt Ctee The Queen's Coll Oxford 2005–, Bd Nuclear Industry Assoc 2010–, Official Monetary and Financial Institutions Forum (OMFIF) Advsy Bd 2013–; Distinguished Friend of Oxford University Award 2012; Freeman Worshipful Co of Musicians 2015–; *Recreations* playing music and cricket, downhill skiing, chess, antiquarian travel books; *Clubs* Athenaeum (chm Wine Ctee 1999–2002, chm Gen Ctee 2003–06, tstee 2008–), MCC (European cricket advsr 1998–2002), Claygate Cricket (life vice-pres); *Style*— Desmond Cecil, Esq, CMG; ✉ 38 Palace Road, East Molesey, Surrey KT8 9DL (☎ 020 8783 1998, e-mail desmondcecil1@gmail.com)

CEENEY, Natalie Anna; CBE (2010); da of Anthony Ceeney, of Bath, and Jacqueline Ceeney; *b* 22 August 1971, Harlow, Essex; *Educ* Newnham Coll Cambridge (MA, Jemima Clough Prize); *m* Dr Simon Chaplin; *Career* pres Univ of Cambridge Students' Union 1990–91, business mangr Northwick Park Hosp 1992–94, contracts mangr Herts HA 1994–96, directorate mangr medicine Gt Ormond St Hosp 1996–98, engagement mangr McKinsey & Co 1998–2001, dir ops and servs Br Library 2001–05, chief exec Nat Archives (keeper of the public records and historic manuscripts cmmr) 2005–10, chief exec and Chief Ombudsman Financial Ombudsman Service 2010–13, head Customer Standards HSBC UK 2014, ceo HM Courts and Tribunals Service 2015–; Information World Review Information Professional of the Year 2008; *Recreations* cycling, rugby, film, literature; *Style*— Ms Natalie Ceeney, CBE; ✉ HM Courts and Tribunals Service, 102 Petty France, London SW1H 9AJ (e-mail natalie.ceeney@hmcts.gsi.gov.uk)

CELLAN-JONES, (Nicholas) Rory; s of James Cellan-Jones, of Kew, Surrey, and Sylvia, *née* Parish; *b* 17 January 1958; *Educ* Dulwich Coll, Jesus Coll Cambridge (BA); *m* 7 April 1990, Diane Coyle, *qv*; 2 s (Adam Joseph b 13 Sept 1990, Rufus Gareth b 11 July 1998); *Career* BBC TV: researcher Look North BBC Leeds 1981–83, sub ed TV News London, asst prodr Newsnight, prodr TV News Special Projects 1983–85, reporter BBC Wales Cardiff 1986–88, reporter Breakfast Time 1988, business reporter TV News and Money Programme 1989–, internet corr BBC TV News 1999– (business corr 1994–); *Style*— Rory Cellan-Jones, Esq; ✉ BBC, MediaCityUK, Salford, M50 2EQ (☎ 020 8624 8992)

CHADLINGTON, Baron (Life Peer UK 1996), of Dean in the County of Oxfordshire; Peter Selwyn Gummer; s of Rev Canon Selwyn Gummer (d 1999), and (Margaret) Sybille Vera, *née* Mason (d 1993); bro of Rt Hon the Lord Deben, *qv*; *b* 24 August 1942; *Educ* King's Sch Rochester, Selwyn Coll Cambridge (MA); *m* 23 Oct 1982, Lucy Rachel, da of Antony Ponsonby Dudley-Hill (d 1969); 3 da (Hon Naomi b 10 Jan 1984, Hon Chloe b 17 Nov 1985, Hon Eleanor b 5 Aug 1988), 1 s (Hon James b 4 Aug 1990); *Career* Portsmouth and Sunderland Newspaper Gp 1964–65, Viyella Int 1965–66, Hodgkinson & Partners 1966–67, Industrial & Commercial Fin Corp 1967–74, Shandwick Int plc 1974–2000 (fndr and chief exec 1974–94, chm 1994–2000), chm International PR 1998–2000, chief exec and dir Huntsworth plc 2000–15 (gp client advsr 2015–); chm: Oxford Resources 1999–2002, Chadlington Consultancy 1999–, guideforlife.com 2000–02, Hotcourses 2000–04, Action on Addiction 2000–07 (tstee 1999–2000), LAPADA 2011–; non-exec dir: CIA Group plc (now Tempus plc) 1990–94, Halifax Building Society (now Halifax plc) 1994–2001 (non-exec dir London Bd 1990–94), Britax Childcare Hldgs Ltd 2005–11; dir: Walbrook Club Ltd 1999–2004, Black Box Music Ltd 1999–2001, Hill Hay Saddle Ltd 2002–; chm: Understanding Industry Tst 1991–96, Marketing Gp of GB 1993–95, ROH 1996–97; non-exec memb: NHS Policy Bd 1991–95, Arts Cncl of England (formerly Arts Cncl of GB) 1991–96 (chm Arts Cncl Lottery Bd 1994–96); memb: House of Lords 1996– (memb EU Sub-Ctee B (Energy, Industry and Tport) 2000–03), Cncl Cheltenham Ladies' College 1998–2003, Bd of Tstees Atlantic Partnership 1999–, Bd of Tstees American Univ 1999–2001, Mending Broken Hearts Appeal Ctee Br Heart Fndn 2010–; govr Ditchley Fndn 2008–; Inst of PR President's Medal 1988, PR Week Award for outstanding individual contribution to PR 1994, Ernst & Young Entrepreneur of the Year Master Entrepreneur London Region 2008; hon fell Bournemouth Univ 1999; *Recreations* opera, cricket, rugby; *Clubs* White's, Garrick, MCC, Carlton, Walbrook; *Style*— The Lord Chadlington; ✉ House of Lords, London, SW1A 0PW

CHADWICK, Dr Derek James; s of Dennis Edmund Chadwick (d 1955), and Ida Chadwick (d 1979); *b* 9 February 1948; *Educ* St Joseph's Coll Blackpool, Keble Coll Oxford (Pfizer industrial scholar, open scholar, sr scholar, BA, BSc, MA, DPhil); *m* 20 Dec 1980, Susan (d 2002), da of Dr (Hugh) Alastair Reid, OBE (d 1983); 2 s (Andrew John b 1984, (Frederick) Mark b 1986); *Career* ICI fell Univ of Cambridge 1972–73, Prize fell Magdalen Coll Oxford 1973–77, Royal Soc European exchange fell ETH-Zürich 1975–77, lectr, sr lectr then reader Univ of Liverpool 1977–88, dir The Novartis Fndn (formerly The Ciba Fndn) London 1988–2008; Emilio Noelting visiting prof École Nationale Supérieur Mulhouse 1988, visiting prof Univ of Trondheim 1995–2012; vice-chm Assoc of Medical Research Charities 1994–2000; cncl memb Cncl for the Central Lab of the Research Cncls 2002–07; memb: Steering Ctee Media Resource Serv Scientists' Inst for Public Information NY 1989–96, Scientific Ctee Louis Jeantet Fndn Geneva 1989–98; sec Hague Club of Dirs of European Fndns 1993–97; Liveryman Worshipful Soc of Apothecaries 1990; FRSC 1982, Hon FRCP 2009; *Books* contrib to: Aromatic & Heteroaromatic Chemistry (1979), Comprehensive Heterocyclic Chemistry (1984), The Research and Academic Users' Guide to the IBMPC (1988), Physical and Theoretical Aspects of 1H-Pyrroles (1990); author of over 100 pubns incl papers in learned jls, book chapters and computer progs; *Recreations* gardening, music, bridge; *Style*— Dr Derek Chadwick; ✉ 4 Bromley Avenue, Bromley, Kent BR1 4BQ (☎ 020 8460 3332, e-mail derekchadwick@hotmail.com)

CHADWICK, Julian William Mark; s of Douglas Herbert Chadwick (d 2009), and Elizabeth Mary, *née* Evans (d 1994); *b* 3 January 1957; *Educ* Royal GS High Wycombe, ChCh Oxford (MA); *Career* admitted slr 1982; ptnr: Gamlens 1985–90, Penningtons 1990–07 (managing ptnr Newbury Office), Thomas Eggar LLP 2007–15 (chm 2012–15), Irwin Mitchel LLP 2015–; memb Nat Taxation Ctee CLA; former: jt master West Welsh Foot Beagles, sr master Christ Church and Farley Hill Beagles; currently master Palmer Marlborough Beagles; sec and hon slr Newbury Spring Festival; former chm Latin Mass Soc, former chm Marie-Louise von Motesiczky Charitable Tst; tstee: Orpheus Fndn, CIEL(UK); memb: Assoc of Masters of Beagles and Harriers, Berks County Ctee CLA, Vice-Chllr's Circle Univ of Oxford; memb Law Soc; Liveryman Worshipful Co of Glass Sellers, Freeman City of London; Knight of Justice SMOM; *Recreations* field sports, music; *Clubs* Travellers; *Style*—Julian Chadwick, Esq; ✉ Irwin Mitchell LLP, Mercantile House, 18 London Road, Newbury, Berkshire RG14 1JX (☎ 01635 571000, e-mail julian.chadwick@irwinmitchell.com); Bryntawel, Drefach, Llanbydder, Ceredigion SA40 9SY (☎ 01570 480267)

CHADWICK, Dr Priscilla; da of Prof Sir Henry Chadwick (d 2008); *b* 7 November 1947; *Educ* Oxford HS, Clarendon Sch N Wales, Girton Coll Cambridge (MA), Univ of Oxford (PGCE), Univ of London (MA, PhD); *Career* head of RE: St Helen's Sch Northwood 1971–73, Putney HS 1973–78, St Bede's C of E/RC Comp Redhill 1979–82; dep head Twyford C of E HS Acton 1982–85, headteacher Bishop Ramsey C of E Sch Ruislip 1986–91, dean of educnl devpt South Bank Univ 1992–96, princ Berkhamsted Collegiate Sch 1996–2008, chair Dioceses Cmmn 2008–10; chm HMC 2005; memb: Eng Anglican/RC Ctee 1981–2006, BBC/ITC Central Religious Advsy Ctee 1983–93, Youth Crime Ctee NACRO 1988–94, Cncl Goldsmiths Coll London 1991–97; chair Culham St Gabriel's Tst 1984–; govr: King's Sch Canterbury 1990–97, Westminster Sch 1998–; vice-chair of govrs Uppingham Sch 2013–; Hon DEd Univ of Hertfordshire 2006, Hon LLD Univ of Roehampton 2011; FRSA 1992; *Publications* Schools of Reconciliation (1994), Shifting Alliances: the partnership of Church and State in English education (1997); author of articles in various educnl jls; *Recreations* music, the arts, world travel; *Clubs* East India; *Style*— Dr Priscilla Chadwick

CHAIN, Julia; *Educ* Univ of Cambridge; *Career* slr; Shearman and Sterling NY 1982–84, Herbert Smith 1984–93, managing ptnr Garretts 1994–98 (joined 1993), gen counsel Bd T-Mobile UK 1998–2003, strategic conslt Jomati Conslts 2003–; cmmr Cmmn for Racial Equality, memb Academic Cncl BPP plc, tstee Jewish Assoc for Business Ethics, memb Bd Jewish Chronicle, memb Bd of Mgmnt Golders Green Synagogue, tstee Norwood Ravenswood; *Style*— Ms Julia Chain; ✉ Jomati Ltd, 3 Amen Lodge, Warwick Lane, London EC4M 7BY (☎ 020 7248 1045)

CHAITOW, Christopher John Adam; s of Boris Reuben Chaitow (d 1995), and of Elizabeth, *née* Rice (d 1980); *b* 19 January 1943; *Educ* Worthing HS; *m* 18 May 1974, Susan Patricia, da of George Joseph Foley, of Cardiff; 1 da (Ella b 1983), 1 s (Daniel b 1984); *Career* research/institutional sales Northcote & Co 1964–70, ptnr Beamish & Co 1970–75, returned to institutional sales Northcote & Co 1975–79; technical analyst: Simon & Coates

1979–86, Chase Manhattan Securities 1986, Morgan Grenfell Securities 1986–88; dir Value and Momentum Research and Chartroom UK 1989–92, technical analyst Credit Lyonnais Laing 1992–94, dir and head of technical analysis Robert Fleming Securities 1995–99, technical analyst Collins Stewart 1999–; fell STA, MSI; *Recreations* music, golf; *Style—* Christopher Chaitow, Esq; ✉ Caroline House, 29–30 Alwyne Road, London N1 2HW (☎ 020 7226 4471)

CHAKRABARTI, Baroness (Life Peer UK 2016), of Kennington in the London Borough of Lambeth Shami Chakrabarti; CBE (2007); da of Syamalendou Chakrabarti, and Shyamali, *née* Chattergee; *b* 16 June 1969, London; *Educ* Bentley Wood HS Harrow, LSE; *Career* called to the Bar Middle Temple 1994; Legal Advsr's Branch Home Office 1996–2001; Liberty: in-house counsel 2001–03, dir 2003–16; chllr Univ of Essex 2014–; shadow AG 2016–; visiting fell Mansfield Coll Oxford, visiting prof Univ of Manchester; tstee BFI; *Books* On Liberty (2014); *Recreations* cinema, theatre; *Style—* The Baroness Chakrabarti, CBE; ✉ 39 Essex Chambers, 81 Chancery Lane, London WC2A 1DD; speaking agents c/o Jeremy Lee Speakers' Agency, 14 Berners Street, London W1T 3LJ; literary agent c/o Wylie Agency, 17 Bedford Square, London WC1B 3JA

CHAKRABARTI, Sir Sumantra (Suma); KCB (2006); s of Hirendranath Chakrabarti, and Gayatri, *née* Rudra; *Educ* City of London Sch, New Coll Oxford (BA), Univ of Sussex (MA); *Career* economist Govt of Botswana 1981–83, official Overseas Devpt Admin 1984–96, leader Treasy team 1997–98, dep dir budget and public fin Treasy 1998, dir Performance and Innovation Unit Cabinet Office 1998–99, head Economic and Domestic Secretariat (EDS) Cabinet Office 2000–01, subsequently DG Regnl Progs DFID, perm sec DFID, perm sec Miny of Justice; Hon LLD Univ of Sussex 2004; hon fell New Coll Oxford 2004, hon bencher Middle Temple; FRSA; *Recreations* Indian history, soul music, football; *Style—* Sir Suma Chakrabarti, KCB; ✉ e-mail psecretary1@justice.gsi.gov.uk

CHALAYAN, Hussein; MBE (2006); *b* 12 August 1970, Nicosia, Cyprus; *Educ* Central St Martins (BA); *Career* fashion designer; design dir TSE NY 1998–2001, creative dir Asprey 2001–04, appointed creative dir Puma 2008–10, designer Vionnet (demi-couture line) 2013–, collaboration with Mavi 2013; head prof Fashion Dept Univ of Applied Arts Vienna 2014–; costume design: Current/See Michael Clark Co 1998, Handel's Messiah (John Jay Coll Theater NY) 1999, In the Spirit of Diaghilev 2009; work featured in numerous exhibitions and shows incl: The Tangent Flows (final year collection bought by Browns boutique London) 1993, Cartesia (first solo collection, West Soho Galleries London) 1994, Temporary Interface (Tokyo and Kobe) 1994, Nothing/Interscope (winner inaugural Absolut Vodka Absolut Creation Award) 1995, Jam – Style + Music + Media (Barbican Art Gallery) 1996, The Cutting Edge Exhibition (V&A) 1997, Addressing the Century: 100 Years of Art & Fashion (Hayward Gallery) 1998–99, Visions of the Body: Fashion or Invisible Corset (Kyoto Costume Inst) 1999, Echoform Exhibition (Fast Forward San Francisco, Atlantis Gallery London, Festival des Jeunes Createurs Hyeres, Exposing Meaning in Fashion Through Presentation NY and Fast Forward Vienna) 1999, Airmail Clothing (Musee de la Mode Palais du Louvre) 1999, La Beauté (installation, Avignon) 2000, Century City (installation, Tate Modern) 2001, Egofugal (7th Int Istanbul Biennial and Tokyo Opera City) 2001, Great Expectations (Design Cncl installation, Grand Central Terminal NY) 2001, London Designers (Museum at FIT NY) 2001, Radical Fashion (V&A) 2001, Goddess: The Classical Mode Exhibition (Museum of Modern Art NY and Mode Museum Antwerp) 2003, Hussein Chalayan 10 Years of Work Retrospective Exhibition (Groniger Museum Netherlands and Wolfsburg Germany) 2005, Anglomania: Tradition and Transgression in British Fashion (MET Museum NY) 2006, Skin and Bones: Parallel Practices in Fashion and Architecture (Museum of Contemporary Art LA, Nat Art Centre Tokyo and Somerset House London) 2007–08, Tomorrow Now When Design Meets Science Fiction (Musee d'Art Moderne Grand-Duc Jean Luxembourg) 2007, Superheroes Fashion and Fantasy (Costume Inst Met Museum of Luxembourg) 2007, Dichter op de huid (Nat Glasmuseum Leerdem/Fort Asperen Netherlands) 2008, Hussein Chalayan: From Fashion and Back (a comprehensive selection of 15 years of work exhibited at Design Museum London, Museum of Contemporary Art Tokyo and Istanbul Modern) 2009–10, Arnham Mode Biennale (Arnhem Netherlands) 2009, The Art of Fashion (Museum Boijmans van Beuningen Rotterdam Netherlands) 2009, Fashion Narratives Exhibition (Musée des Arts Décoratifs Paris) 2011, Glasstress Exhibition (Istituto Veneto di Scienze Lettere ed Arti Italy) 2013 and (London Coll of Fashion) 2013–14 ; collections shown bi-annually at Paris Fashion Week 2001–; Design Star Honoree Fashion Gp Int NY 2007, Br Insurance Designs of the Year Award 2008, Outstanding Lifetime Achievement to Design FX Int Interior Design Award 2009, Royal Designer for Industry Award 2013; nominated: Lloyds Designer of the Year Award 1995, 1996 and 1997, Avant Garde Designer Award VH1 Fashion Awards 1998, Designer of the Year Br Fashion Awards 1999 and 2000, Prince Philip Design Award 2009; *Books* Hussein Chalayan (2011); *Style—* Hussein Chalayan, Esq, MBE; ✉ Chalayan LLP, 109–123 Clifton Street, London EC2A 4LD (☎ 020 7613 3914, website www.chalayan.com, e-mail press@chalayan.com, Twitter @husseinchalayan)

CHALDECOTT, Axel James; s of John James Chaldecott, of Beltinge, Kent, and Alix Mathilde, *née* Von Kauffmann (d 2001); *b* 11 December 1954; *Educ* Charterhouse, Canterbury Coll of Art (BA); *m* 14 Feb 1987, Claire, da of Kenneth Evans; *Career* art dir: Ogilvy & Mather 1977–80, Crawfords 1980–81, Gold Greenlees Trott 1981–85; creative gp head Wight Collins Rutherford Scott 1985–87, co-fndr and creative ptnr HHCL and Partners 1987–2003 (awards incl Agency of the Decade Campaign magazine 2001), co-fndr SMLXL 2003–; JWT: global creative chief HSBC account 2005–; *Style—* Axel Chaldecott, Esq

CHALK, Alex; MP; *b* 8 August 1976; *Educ* Magdalen Coll Oxford (BA), City Univ London (DipLaw); *Career* MP (Cons) Cheltenham 2015–; *Style—* Alex Chalk, Esq, MP; ✉ House of Commons, London SW1A 0AA

CHALK, Gilbert John; s of Ronald Arthur Chalk (d 1993), of Chorleywood, Herts, and Elizabeth, *née* Talbot; *b* 21 September 1947; *Educ* Lancing, Univ of Southampton (BSc), Lancaster Univ (MA), Columbia Univ NY (MBA); *m* 12 April 1975 (m dis 1999), Gillian Frances Audrey, da of Sir Gervase Blois, 10 Bt (d 1967); 2 s (Alexander John Gervase b 1976, Christopher Harry Gilbert b 1985), 1 da (Nicola Elizabeth b 1978); m 2, 26 Jan 2001, Verena Elizabeth Burrowes; *Career* dir: Centaur Communications Ltd 1981–98, Hambros Bank Ltd 1984–94, Hambro Gp Investments 1988–94; md Hambro European Ventures Ltd 1987–94, sr advsr ECI Ventures Ltd 1994–95, sr advsr ABSA Bank (UK) Ltd 1998–99 (head of corp fin 1995–98), ptnr Baring Private Equity Partners 1999–2005; chm: Baring English Growth Fund 2000–10, Parkside Int Ltd 2000–04, Image Scan Hldgs plc 2008–09, Castle Private Equity AG 2008–, Aurora Russia Ltd 2013–16 (dir 2011–13); dir: Secure Mail Services Ltd 2002–06, Constantine Gp plc 2004–12, Vantage Goldfields Ltd 2011–; Parly candidate (Cons) Strangford 1997; *Recreations* tennis, riding, skiing; *Clubs* City, Queen's, Turf, Berkshire Golf; *Style—* Gilbert Chalk, Esq; ✉ 103 Elgin Crescent, London W11 2JF (☎ 020 7727 1981)

CHALKE, Rev Stephen John (Steve); MBE (2004); s of Victor Joseph Chalke (d 1993), and Ada Elizabeth, *née* Wroth; *b* 17 November 1955; *Educ* Spurgeon's Coll London; *m* 23 Aug 1980, Cornelia Marta, da of Otto Reeves (d 1996); 2 da (Emily Louise b 5 July 1982, Abigail Lucy b 9 June 1986), 2 s (Daniel John b 5 Feb 1984, Joshua Thomas b 12 May 1988); *Career* writer and television/radio broadcaster, charity founder; ordained as Baptist minister 1981; founding dir Oasis Tst 1985, fndr Faithworks, sr minister Oasis Church Waterloo 2003–, fndr Oasis Community Learning 2005– (currently sponsoring 44 academies), fndr Stop the Traffik 2006–, appointed UN.GIFT special advsr on community action against human trafficking 2008–; individual Templeton UK Award 1997 (for contrib made in the field of the advancement of spiritual values); hon fell Sarum Coll Salisbury 2005; hon dr of arts Staffs Univ 2015; *Television* appearances on Sunday Morning (ITV Networked), GMTV, The Time The Place, First Light, Songs of Praise; presenter Changing Places BBC Radio 4; numerous commentaries on charity, social action, poverty and homelessness, education and anti-human trafficking; nat charity projects incl: Christmas Cracker, Get Up and Give & Motivation Weekend (in assoc with GMTV); *Publications* The Complete Youth Manual (1987), Christmas Cracker (1990), Understanding Teenagers (1991), The Christian Youth Manual (1992), Making A Team Work (1995), More Than Meets the Eye (1995), I Believe in Taking Action (1995), The Truth About Suffering (1996), Sex Matters (1996), How to Succeed as a Parent (1997), Get Up And Give (1998), Managing Your Time (1998), New Era, New Church? (1999), He Never Said (2000), Parent Talk (2000), Faithworks (2001), Faithworks Stories of Hope (2001), Faithworks Unpacked (2002), Intimacy and Involvement (2003), 100 Proven Ways to Transform Your Community (2003), The Lost Message of Jesus (2003), Trust: A Radical Manifesto (2004), Intelligent Church: A Journey Towards Christ-Centered Community (2006), Change Agents: 25 hard-learned lessons in the art of getting things done (2007), Apprentice: Walking The Way of Christ (2009), Stop The Traffik: People Shouldn't be Bought and Sold (2009), Being Human (2015); The Parentalk Guide series ed: The Parentalk Guide to the Childhood Years (1999), The Parentalk Guide to the Teenage Years (1999), The Parentalk Guide to the Toddler Years (1999), The Parentalk Guide to your Child and Sex (2000), The Parentalk Guide to Being a Mum (2000), The Parentalk Guide to Being a Dad (2000), The Parentalk Guide to Sleep (2001), The Parentalk Guide to Your Child and Food (2001), The Parentalk Guide to The First Six Weeks (2001), The Parentalk Guide to Being a Grandparent (2001), The Parentalk Guide to Great Days Out (2001), The Parentalk Guide to Brothers and Sisters (2002), The Parentalk Guide to Working Parents (2002), The Parentalk Guide to Your Child and the Internet (2003), The Parentalk Guide to Primary School (2003); also regular contrib to newspapers and magazines incl: The Mail on Sunday, The Guardian, Hello, Woman's Weekly, The Sun, The Times, Times Educational Supplement; *Recreations* gym, swimming, running (Guinness World Record for Most Money Raised by a Marathon Runner 2005, 2007 and 2011); *Style—* The Rev Steve Chalke, MBE; ✉ Oasis UK, The Oasis Centre, 75 Westminster Bridge Road, London SE1 7HS (☎ 020 7921 4241, fax 020 7921 4201)

CHALKER OF WALLASEY, Baroness (Life Peer UK 1992), of Leigh-on-Sea in the County of Essex; Lynda Chalker; PC (1987); *née* Bates; da of late Sidney Henry James Bates, and late Marjorie Kathleen Randell; *b* 29 April 1942, Hitchin, Herts; *Educ* Roedean, Univ of Heidelberg, Westfield Coll London, Central London Poly; *m* 1, 1967 (m dis 1973), Eric Robert Chalker (chm Greater London Young Conservatives 1966–67); m 2, 1981 (m ds 2003), Clive Landa (chm Tory Reform Gp 1979–82 and chm Young Cons 1972–74); *Career* statistician Research Bureau Ltd (Unilever subsid) 1963–69, market researcher Shell Mex & BP Ltd 1969–72, chief exec Int Div Louis Harris International 1972–74; chm Gtr London Young Cons 1969–70, nat vice-chm Young Cons 1970–71; MP (Cons) Wallasey 1974–92; memb BBC Gen Advsy Ctee 1975–79, oppn spokesman for Social Servs 1976–79; Parly under sec of state: DHSS 1979–82, Tport 1982–83; min of state: Tport 1983–86, FCO 1986–97, for Overseas Devpt 1989–97; ind conslt on Africa and Devpt to business and public sector 1997–; chm: LSHTM 1998–2006, Africa Matters Ltd 1998–, Medicines for Malaria 2006–11; non-exec dir: Capital Shopping Centres plc 1997–2000, Freeplay Energy Holdings 1997–2007, Landell Mills Ltd 1999–2003, Ashanti Goldfields Co 2000–04, Group Five Ltd 2001–12, DCI 2002–03, Unilever plc 2004–07 (advsy dir 1998–2004), Equator Exploration Ltd 2005–07; memb Int Advsy Bd: Lafarge & Cie 2004–, Merchant Bridge & Co 2006–, Merchant Int Gp (MIG) 2007–08; memb Africa Advsy Bd Renaissance Gp; hon fell: Liverpool John Moores Univ, Queen Mary & Westfield Coll London, Univ of East London, Univ of Liverpool, London Sch of Hygiene and Tropical Medicine; Hon Dr: Univ of Westminster, Cranfield Univ, Univ of Bradford, Univ of Warwick; Hon LLD Univ of Cape Town; hon memb RGS, Hon FRSS, Hon FIHT; *Recreations* theatre, driving, game and environmental conservation; *Style—* The Rt Hon Baroness Chalker of Wallasey; ✉ House of Lords, London SW1A 0PW (☎ 020 7976 6850, fax 020 7976 4999)

CHALLACOMBE, Prof Stephen James; s of Kenneth Vivian Challacombe (d 2007), of Sudbury, Suffolk, and Caryl Graydon, *née* Poore (d 1986); *b* 5 April 1946, London; *Educ* Culford Sch, Guy's Hosp Dental Sch (state scholar, Malleson Prize for Student Research, BDS), Univ of London (PhD); *m* 2 Aug 1969, Tina, da of Bishop Frank Cocks, CB, and Barbara Cocks; 1 s (Benjamin James b 8 June 1973), 1 da (Fiona Lucy b 8 May 1976); *Career* Dept of Oral Immunology and Microbiology Guy's Hosp Med and Dental Schs: research fell 1971–72, lectr 1972–76, sr lectr 1976–85; reader in oral immunology Univ of London 1985–88, prof of oral med Univ of London 1988–; UMDS (GKT since 1998): sub dean of dental studies Guy's Hosp Med and Dental Schs 1983–87, head Dept of Oral Med and Pathology 1986–2005, postgrad sub dean (dental) 1992–2002, dir of postgrad studies 1998–2003, chm Div of Oral Med, Pathology, Microbiology and Immunology GKT Dental Inst 1998–2005, dir of external relations KCL Dental Inst 2004–12; sr research fell and asst prof Dept of Immunology Mayo Clinic Rochester MN 1978–79 (Edward C Kendall Research Fellowship), external conslt Specialised Caries Research Centre Dows Inst of Dental Research Coll of Dentistry Univ of Iowa 1984–91, visiting prof Dept of Oral Biology Univ of Calif San Francisco 1995; hon conslt in oral immunology and microbiology Guy's Hosp 1982–2012, control of infection offr Guy's Dental Hosp 1984–2000, conslt in diagnostic microbiology, cytology and immunology Lewisham and N Southwark HA (now Guy's and St Thomas' Hosp NHS Tst) 1984–, dir Centre for the Study of Oral Manifestations of HIV Infection Guy's Hosp 1990–2000; hon conslt in oral med to UK Armed Forces 1998–2012; memb Clinical Dentistry Research Assessment Exercise Panels HEFCE 1996–97 and 1999–2001 (also vice-chm), memb Cncl Br Sjogren's Syndrome Assoc; pres: Br Soc for Oral Med 1995–97, Br Soc for Dental Research (Br Div IADR) 2000–02 (treas 1993–2001), Odontological Section RSM 1996–97 (treas 1992–95), Metropolitan Branch BDA 1999, IADR 2003–04 (pres Experimental Pathology Gp 1998–99, vice-pres 2001, pres-elect 2002); memb: Br Soc for Immunology, RSM, Br Soc for Oral Pathology, Int Assoc for Oral Pathology, Br Soc of Oral Med, European Assoc for Oral Med (treas 1997–2005, pres 2010–12), Int Soc for Mucosal Immunology; author or co-author of 10 books, over 225 peer-reviewed scientific pubns and 150 other pubns; Colgate Research Prize Br Div IADR 1977, Newland-Pedley Travelling Scholarship Guy's Hosp Med and Dental Schs 1978, Basic Research in Oral Science Award IADR 1981, Cwlth Travelling Scholarship 1990, Distinguished Scientist Award for Experimental Pathology IADR 1997; pres: Guy's Hosp (now GKT) Swimming and Water Polo Club 1985–2005, Guy's Hosp RFC (now Guy's, King's and St Thomas' Hosps RFC) 1991–2001; DSc (hc) 2010; LDSRCS 1968, FRCPath 1992 (MRCPath 1981), FDSRCSE 1994, FMedSci 1998, FDSRCS 2005, FKC 2010; *Publications* Food Allergy and Intolerance (2 edn, ed, with J Brostoff, 2002), The Mouth and AIDS: lessons learned and emerging challenges in global oral health (ed, with A R Tappuni, 2016); *Recreations* golf, tennis, rugby, sailing, swimming; *Clubs* MCC, Savage, Nobody's Friends, Royal Blackheath Golf, Felixstowe Ferry Golf, Hunterian Soc (pres 2006–07), Athenaeum; *Style—* Prof Stephen Challacombe; ✉ 101 Mycenae Road, Blackheath, London SE3 7RX (☎ 020 8858 7933); King's College London

Dental Institute, King's College London, Guy's Hospital, London SE1 9RT (☎ 020 7188 4373, fax 020 7188 1159, e-mail stephen.challacombe@kcl.ac.uk, website http://kclpure.kcl.ac.uk/portal/stephen.1.challacombe.html)

CHALLIS, Dr Christine Joyce; OBE (2003); da of Bernard Arthur Black (d 1995), of Nottingham, and Nora Alice, *née* Willoughby (d 1985); *b* 24 February 1940; *Educ* Queen Ethelburga's Sch Harrogate, Nottingham HS for Girls, Bedford Coll London (BA), QMC London (PhD); *m* 4 Jan 1967, Christopher Edgar Challis, *qv*, s of Edgar Challis; *Career* pt/t tutor in history Univ of London, public relations offr Castlefield Textiles 1964–69; Univ of Leeds: admin asst 1969–72, asst sec 1972–74, dep sec 1974–83; pt/t CVCP admin trg offr for UK univs 1980–83, sec LSE 1983– (sec and dir of admin 2001–03); dir: Enterprise LSE, LSE LETS, VELSE, Southern Universities Management Services, Univs Superannuation Scheme Ltd 1989–97 (dir Audit Ctee), LSE Fndn Inc (pres 2002–04), LSE Gurukul Prog 2002–04; chm: UK Organising Gp for UK/Swedish Univ Registrars and Secretaries Link, Univs Superannuation Scheme Ltd Audit Ctee 1999–2006 (ind memb 1997–99); UK and Ireland rep Heads of Univs Mgmnt and Admin in Europe 1997–; memb: South Bank Univ Human Resources Ctee, South Bank Univ Hon Fells Ctee, South Bank Univ Renumeration Ctee, Advsy Cncl Civil Serv Coll 1986–89, Steering Ctee Assoc of Heads of Univ Administrators 1989–94, Careers Advsy Bd Univ of London 1991–96, Trg and Mgmnt Ctee Univ of London 1991–96, South Bank Univ Audit Ctee 1992–96, SAUL Negotiating Ctee, Frank Knox Fellowship Selection Panel, Euro Round Table for Sr Univ Administrators in Europe 1998–2003, Academic Advsy Bd Mills & Reeve 2003–06, Bd European Strategic Mgmnt of Univ (ESMU) 2003–07 (chm ESMU-HUMANE Winter Sch for Sr Administrators in Europe 2003–08); contrib to historical and univ jls and publications; govr: Fulneck Girls' Sch Pudsey W Yorks 1973–83, South Bank Univ 1995–2003; hon fell LSE 2004; churchwarden All Saints' Church Nether Silton 2006–; FRSA; *Recreations* music, vernacular architecture; *Clubs* Athenaeum; *Style*— Dr Christine Challis, OBE; ✉ Old Manor House, Nether Silton, Thirsk, North Yorkshire YO7 2JZ (☎ 01609 883375, e-mail cjchallis@ns.eclipse.co.uk)

CHALLIS, Dr Christopher Edgar; s of Edgar Challis (d 1957), of Leeds, and Hilda May, *née* Elsworth (d 1989); *b* 5 February 1939; *Educ* Cockburn HS Leeds, Univ of Bristol (BA, CertEd, PhD); *m* 4 Jan 1967, Dr Christine Joyce Challis, OBE, *qv*, da of Bernard Arthur Black, of Nottingham; *Career* Univ of Leeds: asst lectr 1964–67, lectr 1967–78, sr lectr 1978–82, reader 1982–2001, chm of the sch 1988–91; ed Br Numismatic Journal 1980–89; vice-pres Br Numismatic Soc 1995–2009 (pres 1988–93), tstee UK Numismatic Tst 1988– (pres 2000–); memb Royal Mint Advsy Ctee on the Design of Coins, Medals, Seals and Decorations 1991–98; John Sanford Saltus Gold Medal of Br Numismatic Soc 1992; FRHistS 1970, FSA 1987, FRSA 1991; *Books* The Tudor Coinage (1978), A New History of the Royal Mint (ed, 1992); *Recreations* travelling; *Style*— Dr Christopher Challis, FSA; ✉ Old Manor House, Nether Silton, Thirsk, North Yorkshire YO7 2JZ (☎ 01609 883375)

CHALLIS, Prof Richard; *b* 24 November 1945, Beaconsfield, UK; *Educ* Imperial Coll London (BSc, PhD); *Career* clinical engr Guy's Hosp London 1973–78, professor visitante Federal Univ of Rio de Janeiro 1978–80, lectr in bioengineering and physiology Univ of London 1980, lectr, sr lectr and prof of engrg physics Keele Univ until 1998, head Sch of Electrical and Electronic Engrg Univ of Nottingham 1998–2003, prof of ultrasonic engrg Univ of Nottingham 2003–15 (emeritus prof 2015–), prof of non-destructive evaluation Imperial Coll London 2012–15 (emeritus prof 2015–); CEng, CPhys, fell British Inst of Non-Destructive Testing (FBINDT), FIET, FInstP, FREng 2004; *Style*— Prof Richard Challis; ✉ Rosemead, 7 The Village, Keele, Staffordshire ST5 5AD (e-mail challis.science@gmail.com)

CHALMERS, Judith; OBE (1994); da of David Norman Chalmers, FRICS (d 1953), and Millie Locke, *née* Broadhurst (d 1993); *b* 10 October 1937; *Educ* Withington Girls' Sch Manchester, LAMDA; *m* 3 Jan 1964, Neil Durden-Smith, OBE, *qv*, s of Anthony James Durden-Smith, FRCS (d 1963); 1 da (Emma (Mrs Gordon Dawson) b 4 March 1967), 1 s (Mark b 1 Oct 1968); *Career* began broadcasting in Manchester BBC Children's Hour at age of 13 (while still at school); interviewer/presenter many radio and TV programmes in North and then London from 1960 with BBC; joined Thames TV with own afternoon programme 1972; first series of travel programme Wish You Were Here...? 1973–2003; developed own idea for home interest programme Hot Property; joined Radio 2 to host own daily programme 1990; reporter Castle in the Country (BBC 2) 2005, contrib Breakfast BBC TV; commentator for many royal and state occasions; travel ed Woman's Realm; past memb Nat Consumer Cncl; memb Peacock Ctee on Broadcasting; pres emeritus Lady Taverners; vice-pres Holiday Care Service; memb British Guild of Travel Writers; Freeman City of London; *Books* Wish You Were Here ...? 50 of the Best Holidays (1987), At Home and Away with Judith Chalmers (2001, 2002, 2003, 2004 and 2005), Wish You Were Here...? Now and Then (2008); *Recreations* watching rugby and cricket; *Clubs* Mosimann's, The Lord's Taverners; *Style*— Miss Judith Chalmers, OBE; ✉ c/o Jane Wynbourne (☎ 07831 598422, e-mail jane@wynbourne.fsnet.co.uk)

CHALMERS, Sir Neil Robert; kt (2001); s of William King Chalmers, and Irene Margaret, *née* Pemberton; *b* 19 June 1942, London; *Educ* KCS Wimbledon, Magdalen Coll Oxford (MA), St John's Coll Cambridge (PhD); *m* 28 Feb 1970, Monica Elizabeth Byanjeru, *née* Rusoke; 2 da (Emily Anne Nsemere b 5 Dec 1970, Louise Jane Kobuyenje b 11 Oct 1978); *Career* lectr in zoology Makerere UC Kampala Uganda 1966–69, scientific dir Nat Primate Res Centre Nairobi Kenya 1969–70; Open Univ: lectr, sr lectr then reader in biology 1970–85, dean of sci 1985–88; dir Natural History Museum (previously Br Museum (Natural History)) 1988–2004, warden Wadham Coll Oxford 2004–12; pres: Assoc for the Study of Animal Behaviour 1989–92, Marine Biology Assoc UK 2002–07, Inst of Biology 2004–06; chair Nat Biodiversity Network Tst 2005–12; tstee St Andrews Prize for the Environment 2002–10; hon fell: Birkbeck Coll London 2002, KCS Wimbledon 2003; Hon DSc Univ of Plymouth 2004; FZS, FLS, FIBiol, FRSA 1988; *Books* Social Behaviour in Primates (1979), contrib numerous papers on animal behaviour to various jls; *Recreations* music, golf; *Clubs* Oxford and Cambridge; *Style*— Sir Neil Chalmers; ✉ Wadham College, Oxford OX1 3PN (☎ 01865 277931, fax 01865 277964)

CHALMERS, Dr Robert James Guille; s of James Alexander Chalmers (d 1998), of Oxford, and Lois Guille, *née* Taudevin (d 1980); *b* 18 November 1950; *Educ* St Edward's Sch Oxford, Middx Hosp Med Sch (MB BS); *m* 1 Oct 1988, Elizabeth Joyce, da of Leonard Cater (d 1980), of Balwest, Cornwall; *Career* conslt dermatologist: Royal Bolton Hosp 1983–2009, Salford Royal Hospitals NHS Trust 1983–2013, Manchester Royal Infirmary 1983–2013, hon conslt dermatologist Salford Royal Hosps NHS Tst and Central Manchester Hosps Tst 2013–; co-chair and managing ed Dermatology Topic Advsy Gp Int Classification of Diseases Revision Project WHO Geneva 2009–; FRCP; *Books* Rook's Textbook of Dermatology (ed, 9 edn 2016); *Recreations* travelling, playing the bassoon; *Clubs* Royal Society of Medicine; *Style*— Dr Robert Chalmers; ✉ 16 Oaker Avenue, Manchester M20 2XH (e-mail r.chalmers@man.ac.uk)

CHAMBERLAIN, Andrew Michael John; s of Alan Chamberlain (d 2000), and Patricia, *née* Stevens; *b* 14 February 1963, Lytham, Lancs; *Educ* King Edward VII Sch Lytham, Univ of Nottingham (BA), Trent Poly; *m* 28 Aug 1999, Cathy, *née* Wienholdt; 1 s (James (twin) b 16 Sept 2005), 1 da (Anna (twin) b 16 Sept 2005); *Career* slr; articled clerk then slr Freshfields 1986–92, DLA 1993–95 (ptnr 1994), ptnr Addleshaw Goddard 1995–2013, ptnr and nat head of employment DWF LLP 2013–; memb Law Soc; *Recreations* golf, music, family, watching all major sports; *Clubs* Royal Automobile, Royal Lytham & St Anne's Golf, Wilmslow Golf; *Style*— Andrew Chamberlain, Esq; ✉ DWF LLP, 1 Scott Place, 2 Hardman Street, Manchester M3 3AA (☎ 0161 603 5000, e-mail andrew.chamberlain@dwf.co.uk)

CHAMBERLAIN, Arthur; s of Lt-Col Arthur Chamberlain, MC, TD (d 1986), of Edgbaston, Birmingham, and Elizabeth Susan, *née* Edwards (d 1986); *b* 20 February 1952; *Educ* Milton Abbey, Oxford Brookes Univ; *m* 1, 18 June 1988 (m dis 1993), Dominique Jane Patricia; 1 da (b 17 Oct 1991); m 2, 6 Dec 1997, Vivien Elizabeth, *née* Visser, of Cape Town, South Africa; 2 s (Arthur b 2 Oct 1998, William Louis b 19 July 2000); *Career* Bank of London and South America Ecuador 1975–76, Bank of London and Montreal Guatemala 1976–77, Lloyds Bank International London 1977–79, dir Banco La Guaira International Venezuela 1979–82, md Lloyds Bank Nigeria Ltd 1982–84, sr corp mangr Lloyds Bank plc London 1984–2000, relationship dir Corporate Banking Lloyds TSB 2001–03; dir Barton Advisory Services Ltd, investment dir Beer and Partners Ltd 2003–10; Freeman City of London; Liveryman: Worshipful Co of Gunmakers, Worshipful Co of Cordwainers; MInstD; *Recreations* shooting, fishing, travel, photography; *Clubs* Shikar, Hurlingham; *Style*— Arthur Chamberlain, Esq; ✉ 20 Settrington Road, London SW6 3BA (e-mail chamberlain@bartonadvisory.com)

CHAMBERLAIN, Dr Michael Albert John; s of Frederick Chamberlain (d 1980), and Mary, *née* O'Hare (d 1975); *b* 9 May 1948, Liverpool; *Educ* Univ of Manchester (BA, MA), Florida State Univ (PhD); *m* 1, 16 June 1973 (m dis 1978), Jane Margaret, *née* Pickering; m 2, 2 June 1978, Noreen, *née* Laurie; 2 da (Laura Mary b 14 Nov 1978, Dr Charlotte Ann b 16 June 1980); *Career* specialist writer on econ affairs and economist ITN 1973–76, ed Campaign magazine 1976–78, fndr ed/publisher Marketing Week and md Centaur Business Publishing 1978–89, head of new media United Newspapers plc 1994–96, dir Informed Sources Int 1996–97, vice-pres and head of media Arthur D Little 1998–2000, ptnr and industry ldr IBM Business Consltg Servs EMEA 2001–04, chm BMJ Publishing Gp Ltd and dir BMA 2004–14, alternate chm and dir British National Formulary (BNF) 2004–14, chm RCN Publishing Co Ltd 2013–; non-exec dir Alphameric plc 2000–08; tstee: Breathlessness Res Charitable Tst 2000–07, MedFASH 2006–14; FRSM; *Publications* Interactive Marketing (contrib, 1996), Mad Cow Crisis: Health and the Public Good (contrib, 1998); *Recreations* clay shooting; *Clubs* The Solus; *Style*— Dr Michael A Chamberlain; ✉ 11 Gloucester Row, Clifton, Bristol BS8 4AW (☎ 0117 317 9645, mobile 07775 816762, e-mail michaelcham1@aol.com)

CHAMBERLAIN, (Leslie) Neville; CBE (1990); s of Leslie Chamberlain (d 1970), and Doris Anne, *née* Thompson; *b* 3 October 1939; *Educ* King James GS Bishop Auckland, King's Coll Durham; *m* 13 April 1971, Joy Rachel, da of Capt William Wellings (d 1979); 3 da (Louise b 1972, Elizabeth b 1974, Christina b 1981), 1 s (Andrew b 1984); *Career* UKAEA: mgmnt trainee 1962–64, health physicist Springfields 1964–67, res scientist Capenhurst 1967–71; mangr URENCO 1971–77; BNFL: works mangr Springfields 1977–81, enrichment business mangr Risley 1981–84, dir Enrichment Div Risley 1984–86; British Nuclear Fuels plc Risley: chief exec 1986–96, dep chm 1995–99; chm: Br Energy Assoc 1998–2001, TEC Nat Cncl 1999–2001, Manufacturing Inst 2002–, URENCO Ltd 2002–05, Cheshire and Warrington Economic Alliance 2005–10, Northern Way 2006–09, Cheshire Business Ldrs 2010–; non-exec dir Essar Oil Ltd 2013–14; memb Int Nuclear Energy Acad (chm 2001–03); Melchett Medallist 1989; Hon DSc: Univ of Salford 1989, Univ of Chester 2012; hon fell: Inst of Nuclear Engrg, Euro Nuclear Soc; Freeman City of London; CIMgt, FInstP, FInstE, FRSA; *Recreations* racing, swimming, music, fell walking; *Clubs* Athenaeum; *Style*— Neville Chamberlain, Esq, CBE; ✉ Oaklands, 2 The Paddock, Hinderton Road, Neston, South Wirral, Cheshire CH64 9PH (☎ 0151 353 1980)

CHAMBERLAIN, Peter Edwin; s of late Dr Eric Alfred Charles Chamberlain, OBE, and Susan Winifred Louise, *née* Bone; *b* 25 July 1939; *Educ* Royal HS, Univ of Edinburgh (BSc), RNC Manadon, RNC Greenwich, RCDS; *m* 27 July 1963 (sep), Irene May, *née* Frew; 2 s (Mark b 1964, Paul b 1965), 1 da (Louise b 1970); partner, Annamaria Tarallo; *Career* MOD 1963–92: asst constructor ship and submarine design ME and Bath 1963–68, constructor 1968–69, submarine construction Birkenhead 1969–72, ship structures R&D Dunfermline 1972–74, mgmnt of Postgrad Progs of Naval Architecture UCL 1974–77, Ship Design Bath 1977–78, chief constructor and head of Secretariat to DG Ships 1978–80, Surface Ship Forward Design Bath 1980–82, asst sec head of Secretariat to MGO London 1984–85, under sec dir gen Future Material Programmes 1985–87, dep controller Warship Equipment 1987–88, chief Underwater Systems Exec 1988–89, head Def Res Agency Implementation Team 1989–92; BAe Systems: engrg dir Systems and Services 1992–99, dir ANZAC WIP (Weapons Improvement Prog) BAe Land and Sea Systems 1999, dir of engrg Sea Systems Gp 2002; dir Timely Solutions Ltd 2000–06, dir Pal Faena SRL 2002–; memb Royal Acad of Engrg Ctees: Programmes 1991–94, International 2001–04; memb Int Cncl on Systems Engrg (INCOSE) 1994–; RCNC 1960, FRINA 1986, FREng 1988; *Recreations* maintaining a small part of rural Italy, visual arts, poetry, opera, recreational computing; *Style*— Peter Chamberlain, FREng; ✉ Via San Martino 7, 06057 Monte Castello di Vibio (PG), Italy (e-mail peter@paifaena.com)

CHAMBERLIN, Richard Alexander; s of John Alexander Chamberlin, MC, of Lenham, Kent, and Kathleen Mary, *née* Fraser (d 1990); *b* 1 July 1951; *Educ* The King's Sch Canterbury, Jesus Coll Cambridge (BA); *m* 1977, Mary-Angela, da of Norman William Stoakes Franks, of Folkestone, Kent; 2 da (Zoe b 1977, Naomi b 1979); *Career* articled Clerk Wedlake Bell 1973–75, admitted slr 1975, ptnr Freshfields 1981– (joined 1976); memb Worshipful Co of Solicitors; memb Law Soc; *Recreations* archaeology, sailing; *Clubs* Leander, Kent Archaeological Soc, Cambridge Soc (Kent Branch); *Style*— Richard Chamberlin, Esq; ✉ Freshfields, 65 Fleet Street, London EC4Y 1HS

CHAMBERS, Andrew David; s of (Lewis) Harold Chambers (d 1963), of Brundall, Norfolk, and Florence Lilian, *née* Barton (d 1979); *b* 7 April 1943; *Educ* St Albans Sch, Hatfield Coll Durham (BA), London South Bank Univ (PhD); *m* 1, 1969 (m dis 1984), Mary Elizabeth Ann Kilbey; 2 s (Gregory b 1976, Thomas b 1979); m 2, 2 Oct 1987, Celia Barrington, da of Rev Hugh Pruen, of Old Bolingbroke, Lincs; 2 da (Chloë b 1988, Phoebe b 1992), 2 s (Theo b 1990, Cosmo b 1992), 1 step s (Henry b 1985); *Career* audit sr Arthur Andersen & Co 1965–69, admin exec Barker & Dobson 1969–70, systems gp mangr fin United Biscuits 1970–71; City Univ Business Sch: lectr computer applications in accountancy 1971–74, Leverhulme sr res fell internal auditing 1974–78, sr lectr audit and mgmnt control 1978–83, prof of internal auditing 1983–93, admin sub-dean 1983–86, dean 1986–91 (acting dean 1985–86), emeritus prof 1993–; prof of audit and control Univ of Hull 1994–98; non-exec chm Harlequin IT Services 1998–1999; dir: National Home Loans plc (now Paragon Group of Companies plc) 1991–2003, National Mortgage Bank 1991–92, Management Audit 1991–, Pilgrim Health NHS Tst 1996–2000, FTMS Online 1999–2002; visiting prof in computer auditing Univ of Leuven Belgium 1980–81 and 1991–92, Prof of Int Auditing (pt/t) London South Bank Univ 2004–13, academic dir FTMSGlobal 2014–; warden Northampton Hall City Univ 1983–86 (dep warden 1972–76); memb: Cncl BCS 1979–82, Educn Training & Technol Transfer Ctee Br Malaysian Soc 1987–91, Corp Govt Ctee ICAEW 2004–06, Auditing Practices Bd 2006–09; chair Corporate Governance and Risk Mngmnt Ctee ACCA 2006–10; ed: International Jl of Auditing 1997–2003, Internal Control Newsletter 1997–2005, Corporate Governance Newsletter 1998–2004; govr Islington Green Sch 1989–91; JJ Morris Award for Distinguished Service of the Inst of Internal Auditors UK and Ireland 2008, Bradford Camus Memorial Award of the Inst of Internal Auditors Inc 2014; Liveryman Worshipful Co of Loriners; Eur Ing, CEng, FBCS, CITP, FCCA, FCA, FIIA, FRSA; *Books* Keeping Computers Under Control (with O J Hanson, 1975), Internal Auditing (1981), Computer Auditing (1981), Effective Internal Audits (1992), Auditing the IT Environment (with G

Rand, 1994), Auditing Contracts (with G Rand, 1994), Internal Auditing (ed, 1996), The Operational Auditing Handbook – Auditing Business Processes (with G Rand, 1997, 2 edn 2010), Leading Edge Internal Auditing (with J Ridley, 1998), Chambers Corporate Governance Handbook (2002, 6 edn 2014), Tolley's Internal Auditor's Handbook (2005, 2 edn 2009); *Recreations* family; *Clubs* Reform, Travellers; *Style—* Prof Andrew Chambers; ✉ e-mail ac@m-a.myzen.co.uk

CHAMBERS, Christopher Michael; s of Walter Michael Chambers (d 1996), of Glos, and Marlis, *née* Stiefel (d 1978); *b* 28 June 1961, Warks; *m* 19 May 1990, Alexa Adderley, da of Sir Michael Hodson, Bt; 3 da (Lara Adderley b 25 June 1992, Gemma Marlis b 8 April 1994, Anna Isabel b 5 March 1998); *Career* dir BZW Securities until 1997, dir de Zoete and Bevan Ltd until 1997, md and head European Equity Capital Markets Credit Suisse First Boston (Europe) Ltd until 2002, ceo Man Investments 2002–05, dir Man Gp plc 2003–05, policy advsr to HRH The Prince of Wales' Charities Office 2005–08, chm Jelmoli Hldgs AG Zurich 2007–10, chm Helvetic Consultancy Ltd 2012–, exec chm Lonrho Ltd 2013–, vice chm Cembra Money Bank AG Switzerland 2013–16, chm GVO Investment Mgmnt Ltd 2014–15, chm Moneta Money Bank Czech Repub 2016–; non-exec dir: Hansa Aktiengesellschaft 2015–, Swiss Prime Site AG Zurich 2009–, Evolution Gp plc 2009–12, Pendragon plc 2013–, Oxford Sci Innovation Plc 2015–; memb Supervisory Bd: GE Money Bank Switzerland 2010–14, Berenberg Bank AG Switzerland 2012–; sr advsr real estate Lone Star Europe 2011–; govr Kensington Prep Sch 2002–13; FRSA; *Recreations* skiing, shooting; *Clubs* Turf, Hurlingham; *Style—* Christopher Chambers, Esq; ✉ 1 Napier Avenue, London SW6 3PS

CHAMBERS, Daniel (Dan); s of Michael Chambers, *qv*, and Florence Ruth, *née* Cooper; *b* 13 September 1968; *Educ* William Ellis Sch, UC Sch, BNC Oxford (BA); *Partner* Rebecca Cotton; *Career* journalist Evening Standard 1991–92, researcher/asst prodr Panorama, Dispatches and Equinox 1992–96, dir Equinox Sun Storm 1996, dir Equinox Russian Roulette 1997; Sci Dept Channel 4: dep commissioning ed 1998–99, ed Channel 4 1999–2001; Channel 5 (now Five): controller of factual progs 2001–03 (devised History Strand Revealed (2002 RTS Best History for Dambusters), cmmnd World War I in Colour, Kings & Queens), dir of programmes 2003–06; govr London Int Film Sch 2006–; author of play Selling Out (dir by Sir Alan Ayckbourn, CBE, *qv*); *Recreations* photography, scuba diving, television watching; *Clubs* Ski-Slovenia (fndr memb); *Style—* Dan Chambers, Esq

CHAMBERS, David Phillip; s of Joseph Christopher Chambers (d 1994), and Bernadette Mary, *née* Costello (d 1978); *b* 2 August 1953; *Educ* Beaufoy Sch Lambeth, Slough Coll of Further Educn (City and Guilds Basic Cookery), Ealing Coll of Further Educn (City and Guilds Chefs Dip), Westminster Coll of Further Educn; *m* 7 March 1987, Helena, da of Branko Nikola Jovicich; 2 da (Zoe Anne b 17 April 1975, Amy Louise b 21 Aug 1978), 1 s (Liam Christie b 12 Nov 1992); *Career* apprentice chef: Piccadilly Hotel 1969–70, St Ermins Hotel 1970–71; chef tournant St Ermins Hotel 1971–72, chef saucier East Indian Sports and Public Schools Club 1972, Claridges Hotel 1973–74 (commis poissonier, commis saucier), chef gardemanger St Ermins Hotel 1974; sous chef: Mullard House 1974–75, Army and Navy Club 1975–76, Carlton Tower Hotel 1976–78; executive chef Portman Intercontinental 1980–81 (sous chef rising to first sous chef 1978–80), exec chef Le Restaurant Dolphin Square 1981, first sous chef Hyatt Carlton Tower 1981–82, chef de cuisine Dukes Hotel 1982–85; exec head chef: Le Meridien Piccadilly 1985–94, London Hilton on Park Lane 1994–97, chef and dir Rules (London's oldest restaurant) 1997–2004, exec chef Mount Wolseley Hotel Tullow 2004–; various TV appearances; awards for the Oak Room Restaurant: one Michelin Star, three AA rosettes, one Star Egon Ronay, 4/5 Good Food Guide, 17/20 and three Toques Gault Millau; awards for Windows Roof Restaurant: three AA rosettes, 3/5 Good Food Guide, 16/20 and two Toques Gault Millau, voted Best Game Restaurant 1999 Quantum Publications Ltd; Rules voted British Restaurant of the Year Tio Pepe Carlton London Awards 2003; sr academician mentor Acad of Culinary Arts; memb: Conseil Culinaire Français (Palmes Culinaires), Guilde des Fromagers Compagnon de Saint-Uguzon; Maitrise Escoffier; *Recreations* cooking, reading, shooting; *Style—* David Chambers, Esq

CHAMBERS, Guy; s of Colin Chambers, of Oxon, and Pat Carroll; *b* 12 January 1963, Hammersmith, London; *Educ* King David Liverpool, Guildhall Sch of Music; *m* 6 Aug 1999, Emma; 3 da (Isis b 19 May 2000, Gala b 8 Dec 2003, Celeste b 9 May 2008), 1 s (Marley b 11 Oct 2002); *Career* songwriter, prodr and musician; early career as keyboard player with artists incl Julian Cope and The Waterboys, joined World Party 1986, formed The Lemon Trees 1993–95; co-writer, co-prodr and musical dir with Robbie Williams, *qv* 1997–, albums incl Life Thru A Lens, I've Been Expecting You (Best Produced Album Int Managers Forum Award 1998), Sing When You're Winning, Swing When You're Winning and Escapology, numerous singles incl Angels, Millennium, Strong, No Regrets, Let Me Entertain You, She's the One/It's Only Us and Rock DJ; prodr and songwriter for numerous artists incl: Anastacia, Andrea Bocelli, Beverley Knight, Busted, Caro Emerald, Carole King, Darren Hayes, David Archuleta, Delta Goodrem, Diana Ross, Eros Ramazzotti, Example, Hilary Duff, James Blunt, Jamie Cullum, Jessica Simpson, Jewel, INXS, The Isis Project, Katie Melua, Katy B, Kylie Minogue, Marlon Roudette, Miles Kane, Natasha Bedingfield, Rachel Stevens, Rufus Wainwright, Skin, Texas, The Wanted, Tina Turner, Tokio Hotel, Sir Tom Jones, Will Young, *qqv*; Ivor Novello Awards 1998 (three) and 1999, 3 Brit Awards, Q Classic Songwriter Award, MMF Best Produced Record Award 1998; *Clubs* Groucho, Soho House, RAC; *Style—* Guy Chambers, Esq; ✉ c/o Sleeper Sounds, 1–3 Middle Row, London W10 5AT (e-mail dylan@sleepersounds.com)

CHAMBERS, Prof John Boyd; s of Dr Kenneth Boyd Chambers, and Taissia, *née* Petrova; *b* 28 December 1954; *Educ* Tonbridge (entrance scholar), Pembroke Coll Cambridge (entrance scholar, MA, MD), KCH London (MB BChir); *Career* Br Heart Fndn jr fell KCH London 1985–89, lectr and hon sr registrar Guy's Hosp 1989–91, sr lectr and hon conslt in cardiology Guy's and St Thomas' NHS Tst and KCL 1991–, conslt cardiologist Maidstone Hosp 1994–2002, prof of clinical cardiology KCL 2009–; Guy's and St Thomas' Hosp: estab clinical echocardiographic res 1991, fndr Valve Study Gp 1998, head of non-invasive cardiology 2001–; lead clinician regnl cardiology audit 1998–2000; Br Soc of Echocardiography: memb Cncl 1993–98 and 2000–06, pres 2003–05, chief examiner 1995–98, chm Educn Ctee 1996–98, memb Trg and Res Ctees; memb: Int Panel Canadian Guidelines on Valve Surgery, Nucleus Working Gp on Valve Disease Euro Soc of Cardiology, Ctee on Prosthetic Heart Valves BSI 1991–, Ctee on Prosthetic Heart Valves ISO 2001–, int ctees on imaging native and prosthetic valve disease; chair Int Ctee for Standards in Care of Heart Valve Disease; fndr memb Soc for Valve Disease, pres Br Heart Valve Soc 2010–13; memb Editorial Bd Br Jl of Clinical Practice 1991–, ed Jl of Heart Valve Disease 1995–2004 (memb Editorial Bd 1994–), estab syllabus for training in heart valve disease; fell Euro Soc of Cardiology 1997, fell American Coll of Cardiology 1997; FRCP 1996 (MRCP 1982); *Publications* Acute Medicine: a Practical Guide to Medical Emergencies (jtly, 1990, 5 edn 2016), Echocardiography: an International Review (jt ed, 1993), Clinical Echocardiography (1995), Echocardiography in Primary Care (1996), A Slide Atlas of Echocardiography (1997), Echocardiography: Guidelines for Reporting (jtly, 1998, 3 edn 2016); numerous original chapters and articles; *Recreations* studio ceramics; *Style—* Prof John Chambers; ✉ Cardiothoracic Centre, St Thomas' Hospital, London SE1 7EH (☎ 020 7188 1047, fax 020 7188 1011, e-mail jboydchambers@aol.com)

CHAMBERS, Lucinda Anne; da of Michael and Anne Chambers; *b* 17 December 1959; *Educ* Convent of the Sacred Heart Woldingham; *m* 1991, Simon Crow; 2 s (Theo b 4 Feb 1993, Gabriel b 1 March 2004); 1 other s (Toby Knott b 23 Feb 1988); *Career* sr fashion ed Elle Magazine UK 1986–88, fashion dir Vogue Magazine 1992– (former exec fashion ed); *Style—* Miss Lucinda Chambers; ✉ Vogue Magazine, Vogue House, Hanover Square, London W1S 1JU

CHAMBERS, Michael; s of Jack Chambers (d 1987), and Gerda, *née* Eisler (d 2001); *b* 30 November 1941; *Educ* William Ellis GS, LSE (BSc); *m* 1967 (m dis 1999), Florence; 2 s (Daniel, *qv*, b 1968, Jesse b 1973), 1 da (Hannah b 1976); *Career* lectr in sociology Univ of Ife Ibadan Nigeria; called to the Bar Lincoln's Inn 1966; practising barr 1966–69, head Legal Dept Monsanto UK 1972–73; chief exec: Orbach & Chambers Ltd (book and magazine publishers) 1969–, Chambers & Partners (recruitment agency) 1973–; producer Orbach & Chambers Records Ltd 1977–79; ed: Chambers Legal Directories 1989–, Commercial Lawyer (jl) 1995–, The Chambers Gallery 2003–; *Books* London: the Secret City (1973), There was a Young Lady... A Book of Limericks (1978); *Recreations* jazz trumpet; *Style—* Michael Chambers, Esq; ✉ Chambers & Partners, Saville House, 23 Long Lane, London EC1A 9HL (☎ 020 7606 1300, fax 020 7606 0906, website www.chambersandpartners.com)

CHAMBERS, Nicholas Mordaunt; QC (1985); s of Marcus Mordaunt Bertrand Chambers, and Lona Margit, *née* Gross (d 1987); *b* 25 February 1944; *Educ* King's Sch Worcester, Hertford Coll Oxford; *m* 1966, Sarah Elizabeth, da of Thomas Herbert Fothergill Banks; 2 s, 1 da; *Career* called to the Bar Gray's Inn 1966 (bencher 1994), recorder of the Crown Court 1987–99, dep High Court judge 1994–99; mercantile judge: (Wales & Chester Circuit) 1999–2005, (Wales) 2005–12; mediator and arbitrator 2012–; chm Inc Cncl of Law Reporting 2001–; *Recreations* illustration, writing, sketching; *Clubs* Garrick, Lansdowne; *Style—* Nicholas Chambers, Esq, QC; ✉ Brick Court Chambers, 7–8 Essex Street, London WC2R 3LD (☎ 020 7379 3550)

CHAMBERS, Peter; *b* 14 March 1990, Coleraine, NI; *Educ* Oxford Brookes Univ; *Career* rower; achievements incl: Gold medal (lightweight pair) U23 World Championships 2011, Silver medal (lightweight four) Olympic Games 2012; *Clubs* Oxford Brookes Univ Boat; *Style—* Mr Peter Chambers

CHAMBERS, Richard Scott; s of Eric Chambers, of Coleraine, NI, and Gillian, *née* Cregan; *b* 10 June 1985, Belfast; *Educ* Coleraine Academical Inst, Oxford Brookes Univ; *m* 18 Sept 2009, Abigail, *née* Buggs; 1 s (Joshua Scott b 18 Oct 2011), 1 da (Alexandra Laurina b 9 May 2014); *Career* rower; achievements incl: Gold medal (lightweight four) World Championships 2007, Gold medal (lightweight four) World Championships 2010, Bronze medal (lightweight four) World Championships 2011, Silver medal (lightweight four) Olympic Games 2012, Bronze medal (lightweight double) World Championships 2013, Bronze medal (lightweight four) World Championships 2014; *Clubs* Leander; *Style—* Mr Richard Chambers; ✉ e-mail rschambers10@gmail.com, Twitter @rschambers10gb

CHAMBERS, Robert George; s of Peter Bertram Chambers (d 2008), and Wendy, *née* Randall; *b* 30 May 1954, Cambridge; *Educ* Oundle, Univ of Hull (BSc); *m* 16 May 1987, (Christine) Belinda, da of Roy Johnson, of Littlington, Herts; 2 s (Nicholas Timothy George b 6 Dec 1989, Charles Robert b 10 Aug 1993), 1 da (Serena Daisy b 13 Dec 1990); *Career* ptnr Wedd Durlacher Mordaunt and Co 1985–86 (joined 1976); ceo Chambers Farming Gp Ltd 2009–; exec dir: Barclays de Zoete Wedd 1986–89, ABN AMRO Hoare Govett 1989–2001, TradeRisks 2010–11; exec dir UBS 2001–08; dep chm Stock Exchange Benevolent Fund 2008–15, sec Stock Exchange Benevolent Fund 2015–; chm Cokenach Cricket Club; MSI 1988 (memb Stock Exchange 1980); *Recreations* shooting, fishing, cricket (level II cricket coach), golf, tennis, Olympics Games Maker 2012, Help for Heroes Big Battlefield Bike Ride 2010 and 2013; *Clubs* MCC, Royal Worlington Golf, Jockey Club Rooms (Newmarket), City of London; *Style—* Robert Chambers, Esq

CHAMBERS, Prof Robert John Haylock; OBE (1995); *b* 1 May 1932; *m* Jennifer; 3 c; *Career* res assoc IDS Univ of Sussex 1997– (fell 1972–97); memb visiting faculty Admin Staff Coll Hyderabad India 1989–91; varied experience incl rural field res India, Kenya and Sri Lanka and participatory rural appraisal devpt and trg; formerly: evaluation offr UNHCR Geneva, lectr Univ of Glasgow, prog offr Ford Fndn New Delhi, memb Band Aid/Live Aid Project Ctee; tstee Action Aid 1993–2000 and 2002–08; sometime conslt: Aga Khan Fndn, Asian Devpt Bank, Br Cncl, FAO, Ford Fndn, Consultative Gp for Int Agric Res, House of Commons, Int Inst for Environment and Devpt, ILO, INTRAC, League of Red Cross and Red Crescent Socs, Swedish Int Devpt Agency, Swiss Devpt Cooperation, ODA, World Bank; Hon DLitt UEA, Hon DSocS Univ of Edinburgh, Hon DLitt Univ of Sussex, hon doctorate Erasmus Univ Rotterdam; *Books* incl: Settlement Schemes in Tropical Africa (1969), Managing Rural Development – Ideas and Experience from East Africa (1974), Seasonal Dimensions to Rural Poverty (jt ed, 1981), Rural Development – Putting the Last First (1983), Managing Canal Irrigation – Practical Analysis from South Asia (1988), To the Hands of the Poor – Water and Trees (jtly, 1989), Farmer First – Farmer Innovation and Agricultural Research (jt ed, 1989), Challenging the Professions: frontiers for rural development (1993), Whose Reality Counts? Putting the first last (1997), Voices of the Poor: Crying Out for Change (jtly, 2000), Participatory Workshops: a Source Book of 21 Sets of Ideas and Activities (2002), Ideas for Development (2005), Revolutions in Development Inquiry (2008), Provocations for Development (2012), Into the Unknown: Explorations in Development Practice (2014); *Recreations* mountaineering, jogging; *Style—* Robert Chambers; ✉ Institute of Development Studies, University of Sussex, Brighton BN1 9RE (☎ 01273 606261, fax 01273 621202/691647)

CHAMBERS, Sarah; *Career* former head Automotive Unit DTI, former dir of licensing Oftel, chief exec Postal Services Cmmn (Postcomm) 2004–08, dir of consumer and competition policy Dept for Business, Innovation and Skills 2008–; *Style—* Ms Sarah Chambers

CHAMBERS, Stuart John; s of Reginald Chambers, and Eileen Chambers; *b* 25 May 1956, Seria, Brunei; *Educ* Friends Sch Great Ayton, UCL (BSc); *m* 1984, Nicolette, *née* Horrocks; 1 s, 2 da; *Career* with Shell 1977–88, with Mars Corp 1988–96; Pilkington plc: gp vice-pres (mktg) Bldg Products 1996–97, gen mangr Pilkington UK Ltd 1997–98, md Primary Products Europe 1998–2000, pres Bldg Products Worldwide 2000, gp chief exec 2002–06; chief exec Pilkington Gp Ltd 2006–; NSG Gp: dir Nippon Sheet Glass Co 2006–, gp chief operating offr 2007–08, gp chief exec 2008–09; chm: Rexam plc 2012–16, ARM Hldgs plc 2014–; non-exec dir: Associated British Ports (Hldgs) plc 2002–06, Smiths Gp plc 2006–12 (chm Remuneration Ctee 2006–12), Manchester Airport Gp 2010–12, Tesco plc 2010–15 (chm Remuneration Ctee 2010–15), Tesco Personal Finance 2012–14; memb Takeover Panel 2016–; *Recreations* sailing, tennis, rugby union; *Style—* Mr Stuart Chambers; ✉ Foxfields, Peover Lane, Chelford SK11 9AL

CHAMBERS, Dr Timothy Lachlan (Tim); OBE (2009), JP (Bristol 1993), DL (2012); b Seamus Rory Dorrington, s of late Mary Teresa; adopted s of Victor Lachlan Chambers (d 1970), and Elsie Ruth, *née* Reynolds (d 2002); *b* 11 February 1946, Croydon, Surrey; *Educ* Wallington Co GS, KCL and KCH Univ of London (LRCP MRCS, MB BS); *m* 9 Oct 1971, (Elizabeth) Joanna, DL, da of John Carrington Ward (d 1989); 2 da (Catherine Louise (Mrs Peter Chapman) b 1973 (d 2007), Rachel Elizabeth (Mrs Simon Hatch) b 1976), 1 s (Oliver Lachlan Dorrington b 1978); *Career* consulting physician and nephrologist Bristol Royal Hosp for Children 1979–2010; Univ of Bristol: sr clinical lectr in child health 1979–2010, a clinical dean 1983–90, memb Governing Bd Inst of Child Health 1987–97, memb Ct 1994–99; dep med dir Southmead Health Servs NHS Tst 1994–96; pres: Union of Nat Euro Paediatric Socs and Assocs 1990–94, Bristol Medico-Chirurgical Soc 1996–97, Bristol Div BMA 1999–2000, SW Paediatric Club 2004–06, Bristol Medico-Legal Soc 2007–09; RCP: past censor, cncllr; RCPCH: hon sec (BPA) 1984–89, hon sec Int Bd 1998–2000; RCPEd regnl advsr (SW England) 1996–2001; sec of state's appointee: Bd of Govrs

Hosps for Sick Children (London) Special HA 1993–94, Ctee on Safety of Meds 1999–2005 (memb Paediatric Meds Working Gp and Expert Advsy Gp 2000–05 and 2008–12); Advsy Bd on the Registration of Homoeopathic Products 2000–14 (chair 2003–14); a UK delg to Paediatric Ctee European Medicines Agency 2008–12; present and past examiner to UK and int diploma and degree awarding bodies; sometime memb and chm professional advsy ctees at home and abroad; conslt in paediatrics to MOD 1985–2010, civilian conslt advsr (paediatrics) to MDG (RN) 1992–2012; Lt Col RAMC (V) 1997–2010 (cmmnd 1984), Somerset Cadet Bn (The Rifles) ACF (Bn MO) 2001–12; clinical dir 243 (The Wessex) Field Hosp 2006–08, non-regimental memb HAC 2013, vice-chm County of City of Bristol Wessex RFCA 2015–; tstee: Royal Med Benevolent Fund 1998–2004, Education and Resources for Improving Childhood Continence (ERIC) 2006–14 (actg chm of tstees 2012–14); reader and eucharistic min RC Cathedral Church of SS Peter and Paul Clifton 1992–, Master Bristol Guild of Catholic Drs 2006–08, Oblate of Downside 2010–; NSPCC Bristol: chm 2011–14, vice-pres 2014–; hon vice-pres Guild of Friends of Bristol Royal Hosp for Children 2010–; ambass: Girlguiding Bristol and S Gloucs 2010–, Alabaré Christian Care and Support Bristol 2010–; govr Redland HS Bristol 2011–16 (chair 2012–16); memb: European Soc for Paediatric Nephrology 1978–, Philosophical Soc Oxford 1990–; hon memb British Assoc for Paediatric Nephrology 2011; membre correspondant de la Société Française de Pédiatrie 1994, Cadet Forces Medal 2011, Queen's Diamond Jubilee Medal 2012, Pontifical Cncl for Health Care Workers Good Samaritan Medal 2013; County of Bristol: High Sheriff 2009–10, Vice Lord-Lt 2012–; DSc (hc) Univ of Bristol 2016; Freeman City of London 1982, Liveryman Worshipful Soc of Apothecaries 1984 (memb Ct of Assts 2000–, Master 2011–12), Liveryman Worshipful Co of Barbers 2012 (Freeman 2004); FRSM 1979 (pres Sections of Paediatrics 1994–95 and United Services (now Military Medicine) 2001–03, hon ed 1997–2001, a vice-pres 2001–03), FRCP 1983, FRCPEd 1985, FRCPI 1995 (fell Faculty of Paediatrics 1989), Hon FSLCPaed 2002, Hon FRCPCH 2014; Commander of the Military and Hospitaller Order of St Lazarus of Jerusalem 2013; *Publications* Fluid Therapy in Childhood (1987), Clinical Paediatric Nephrology (chapter, 1986 and 1994), author of contribs to scientific and lay literature; *Recreations* wonder; *Clubs* Athenaeum, Victory Services, MCC (assoc), Clifton (Bristol), Bristol Savages (Green Feather), Gloucs CCC, Somerset CCC, Surrey CCC, Friends of Arundel Castle CC, Galle Face Hotel, Colombo, Officers' Mess 243 (The Wessex) Field Hosp (Volunteers) (hon memb), Royal Marines Reserves Mess (Bristol) (hon memb); *Style*— Dr T L Chambers, OBE, JP, DL, FRCP; ✉ 4 Clyde Park, Bristol BS6 6RR (☎ 01179 742814)

CHAMBERS, Tony; s of Joseph Chambers (d 1991), and Anne, *née* Findley; *b* 4 September 1963, Liverpool; *Educ* De la Salle GS, Central St Martins Sch of Art; *m* 2012, Georgia Dehn; 1 da (Olive Joe b 22 May 2013); *Career* designer then art ed The Sunday Times Magazine 1986–1996, art dir British GQ magazine 1997–2002; Wallpaper* magazine: creative dir 2003–06, ed-in-chief 2007–; twice Periodical Publishers Assoc Awards Art Director of the Year, BSME New Ed of the Year 2008, BSME Mark Boxer Award for Outstanding Editorial Contribution to Magazines 2015; Wallpaper*, Room: Inside Contemporary Interiors, Restaurant and Bar Design; *Recreations* art and photography, architecture, food and wine, keen footballer; *Clubs* Walbrook; ✉ 603 Gilbert House, Barbican, London EC2Y 8BD; Wallpaper* Magazine, Blue Fin Building, 110 Southwark Street, London SE1 0SU (☎ 020 314 8775, e-mail tony_chambers@wallpaper.com)

CHAMPION, Jonathan Martin (Jon); s of David Yeo Champion, of York, and Maureen Ray, *née* Wilby; *b* 23 May 1965; *Educ* Archbishop Holgate's GS York, Trinity and All Saints' Coll Leeds (BA); *m* 1 Oct 1994, Anna Clare, *née* Clarke; 1 da (Emily Susannah b 6 July 1995), 3 s (Benjamin Henry b 2 Feb 1998, Harry George b 20 Oct 1999, William James b 7 Sept 2002); *Career* sports broadcaster; sports reporter BBC Radio Leeds 1988–89, presenter BBC Night Network 1989, presenter/commentator BBC Radio Sport 1990–96 (incl: occasional presenter Sports Report, presenter Champion Sport Radio 5, worked at World Cups 1990, 1994 and 1998 and Olympic Games 1992, 1996 and 2000); football commentator Match of the Day BBC TV 1995–2001 (incl World Cup 1998 and Olympic Games Sydney 2000), cricket commentator Test Match Special Radio 4, football commentator ITV 2001– (incl World Cup 2002, 2006 and 2010, also princ commentator Rugby World Cup 2007 and 2015), sr commentator Setanta Sports 2007–09, chief commentator ESPN 2009– (incl World Cup 2014); *Recreations* music (piano and violin player), fell walking, cycling, cricket, golf; *Clubs* Worcs CCC; *Style*— Jon Champion, Esq; ✉ c/o Melissa Chappell, I Will Know Someone (☎ 07768 878975, e mail mel@iwillknow someone.com)

CHAMPION, Robert (Bob); MBE; s of Bob Champion (d 1987), and Phyllis Doreen Champion (d 2010); *b* 4 June 1948; *Educ* Earl Haig Sch Guisborough; *m* 1, Oct 1982 (m dis 1985); 1 s (Michael Robert b 1983); m 2, Oct 1987 (m dis 1998); 1 da (Henrietta Camilla b 1988); *Career* jockey and racehorse trainer; one of the four top jockeys of the 1970s, recovered from cancer to win 1981 Grand National on Aldaniti (portrayed by John Hurt in film Champions 1984); fndr Bob Champion Cancer Tst; Hon DCL UEA 2004, Hon LLD Univ of Teesside 2005; BBC Sports Personality of the Year Helen Rollason Award 2011; *Books* Champion Story; *Recreations* riding; *Style*— Bob Champion, MBE; ✉ e-mail bob@bobchampion.co.uk and bob@bobchampion.com, website www.bobchampion.com

CHANCE, Alan Derek; s of Derek Arthur Chance (d 1997), of Funtington, W Sussex, and Kay, *née* Renshaw (d 1988); *b* 12 April 1951; *Educ* Eton, Merton Coll Oxford (MA); *m* 30 May 1981, Sarah Elizabeth, da of (William) Denis Delany, of Funtington, W Sussex; 2 s (Benjamin b 1984, Thomas b 1987); *Career* dir Streets Financial Ltd 1979–83, chm Chance Plastics Ltd 1978–87; md: Money Marketing Ltd 1983–86, The Moorgate Group plc 1988–89 (dir 1986); ptnr Chance Jarosz 1990–93; chm AML Communications 2011–; dir: Allison Mitchell Ltd 1992–2011, Lawpack Publishing Ltd 2003–06, Giveacar Ltd 2010–; *Recreations* skiing, backgammon, croquet; *Clubs* Hurlingham; *Style*— Alan Chance, Esq; ✉ Allison Mitchell Ltd, Holland House, 1–4 Bury Street, London EC3A 5AW (☎ 020 7469 2525)

CHANCE, Michael Edward Ferguson; CBE (2009); s of John Wybergh Chance (d 1984), of London, and Wendy Muriel Chance (d 1970); *b* 7 March 1955; *Educ* Eton, King's Coll Cambridge (MA); *Career* opera and concert singer; princ singer Kent Opera 1984–88, BBC Promenade Concerts 1985–; appearances/debuts incl: Lincoln Centre NY 1985, La Scala Milan 1985, Lyon Opera 1985 (Andronico in Tamerlano), Paris Opera 1988 (Ptolomeo in Giulio Cesar), Glyndebourne Festival 1989 (Oberon in A Midsummer Night's Dream), Netherlands Opera 1990 (Anfinomo in Il Ritorno D'Ulisse), Sao Carlo Lisbon 1991 (Gofredo in Rinaldo), Royal Opera House Covent Garden 1992 (Apollo in Death in Venice), ENO 1992 (Anfinomo in Return of Ulysses), Scottish Opera 1992 (title role in Julius Caesar), Australian Opera Sydney 1993 (Oberon in A Midsummer Night's Dream); has made over 130 recordings; *Style*— Michael Chance, Esq, CBE; ✉ c/o Ingpen and Williams Ltd, Ingpen & Williams, 7 St George's Court, 131 Putney Bridge Road, London SW15 2PA

CHANCELLOR, Alexander Surtees; CBE (2012); s of Sir Christopher John Chancellor, CMG (d 1989), and Sylvia Mary, OBE (d 1996), eld da of Sir Richard Paget, 2 Bt, and his 1 w, Lady Muriel Finch-Hatton, CBE, only da of 12 Earl of Winchilsea and Nottingham; *b* 4 January 1940; *Educ* Eton, Trinity Hall Cambridge; *m* 1964, Susanna, da of Martin Debenham, JP (3 s of Sir Ernest Debenham, 1 Bt, JP, and Cecily, niece of Rt Hon Joseph Chamberlain); 2 da; *Career* Reuters News Agency 1964–74, ed The Spectator 1975–84, asst ed The Sunday Telegraph 1984–86; dep ed The Sunday Telegraph 1986, US ed The Independent 1986–88, ed The Independent Magazine 1988–92, writer The New Yorker 1992–93, assoc ed The Sunday Telegraph 1994–95, ed The Sunday Telegraph Magazine 1995, columnist The Guardian 1996–2012, currently columnist The Spectator and ed The Oldie 2014–; *Books* Some Times in America (1999); *Clubs* Garrick, Chelsea Arts; *Style*— Alexander Chancellor, Esq, CBE

CHANDE, Manish; *Career* co-fndr and chief exec Trillium Gp 1997–2000, memb Bd Land Securities plc 2000–02, co-fndr and chief exec Mountgrange Capital plc 2002–09, co-fndr and sr ptnr Mountgrange Investment LLP; non-exec dir: National Car Parks Ltd 2002–05 (chm), Property Fund Management plc 2002–04, Mitie Gp 2002–06; cmmr English Heritage 2003–11; tstee: Windsor Leadership Tst 2005–09, London Clinic 2007–, Canal and River Tst 2012–; *Style*— Manish Chande, Esq; ✉ Mountgrange Investment Management LLP, 6 Cork Street, London W1X 3NX

CHANDLER, Prof Richard John; s of John Harris Chandler (d 1987), of Stamford, Lincs, and Agnes Mary Chandler (d 1961); *b* 20 September 1939; *Educ* Stamford Sch, Loughborough Univ of Technol (BSc), Univ of Birmingham (MSc, PhD); *m* 19 Oct 1963, Eunice, da of Bertie Thomas Howes; 2 s (Simon John b 19 June 1966, Mark Richard b 20 April 1969); *Career* res fell Univ of Birmingham 1965–68; Imperial Coll London: lectr 1969–81, reader in soil mechanics 1981–90, prof of geotechnical engrg 1990–2003, emeritus prof of geotechnical engrg 2003–; chm Tstees and Editorial Bd Br Birds Jl; DSc(Eng) Univ of London 1990; FGS 1965, FICE 1989, FREng 2001; *Publications* North Atlantic Shorebirds (1989), Slope Stability Engineering (1991), Shorebirds of the Northern Hemisphere (2009); author of many papers on engrg, especially soil mechanics, and many articles on field ornithology; *Recreations* ornithology, climbing; *Clubs* Fell and Rock Climbing Club of the English Lake District, British Ornithologists; *Style*— Prof Richard Chandler; ✉ 4 Kings Road, Oundle, Northamptonshire PE8 4AX

CHANDOS, 3 Viscount (1954 UK); Thomas Orlando Lyttelton; sits as Baron Lyttelton of Aldershot (Life Peer UK 2000), of Aldershot, Co Hampshire; s of 2 Viscount Chandos (d 1980, himself ggs of 4 Baron Cobham) and Caroline (da of Sir Alan Lascelles, who was in his turn gs of 4 Earl of Harewood); *b* 12 February 1953; *Educ* Eton, Worcester Coll Oxford; *m* 19 Oct 1985, Arabella Sarah Lucy, da of Adrian Bailey; 2 s (Hon Oliver Antony b 21 Feb 1986, Hon Benedict b 30 April 1988), 1 da (Hon Rosanna Mary b 19 March 1990); *Heir* s, Hon Oliver Lyttelton; *Career* corp fin dir Kleinwort Benson 1985–93, exec dir Botts & Co 1994–; chm: Capital and Regional Properties plc 2000–10 (non-exec dir 1993–2010), The Television Corporation 2004–06; non-exec dir: Lopex 1993–, Chrysalis Group plc 1994–96; dir Social Market Fndn; formerly: govr Nat Film and TV Sch, memb Gen Advsy Cncl IBA; *Style*— The Viscount Chandos

CHANG, Dr Jung; née Er-Hong; da of Shou-Yu Chang (d 1975), of Yibin, China, and De-Hong Xia, *née* Bao-Qin Xue; *b* 25 March 1952; *Educ* No 4 Middle Sch Chengdu (oldest state sch in China, founded 141 BC), Sichuan Univ (BA), Ealing Coll of HE, Univ of York (PhD, first person from Communist China to receive PhD from British instn); *m* 26 July 1991, Jon Arthur George Halliday; *Career* author; Hon DLit Univ of Buckingham 1996; Hon Dr: Univ of York 1997, Univ of Warwick 1997, Open Univ 1998, Bowdoin Coll 2005; *Books* Wild Swans – Three Daughters of China (1992, NCR Book Award 1992, Writers' Guild of GB Best Non-Fiction Award 1992, Fawcett Soc Book Award 1992, Book of the Year 1993, Humo's Gouden Bladwijzer Belgium 1993 and 1994, Bjørnsonordenen Den Norske Orden for Lit Norway 1995), Mao: the Unkown Story (with Jon Halliday, 2005), Empress Dowager CIXI: The Concubine Who Launched Modern China (2013); *Recreations* reading, travelling, swimming, gardening; *Style*— Dr Jung Chang; ✉ c/o Aitken Alexander Associates, 18–21 Cavaye Place, London SW10 9PT (☎ 020 7373 8672, fax 020 7373 6002, e-mail reception@aitkenalexander.co.uk)

CHANNON, Prof Keith Michael; *b* Lincoln; *Career* Field Marshal Earl Alexander of Tunis prof of cardiovascular med Univ of Oxford, hon conslt cardiologist John Radcliffe Hosp Oxford, dir of research and devpt Oxford Univ Hosps; chm Br Atherosclerosis Soc, assoc ed Heart Journal; *Publications* on clinical cardiology, coronary artery disease and cardiovascular biology; *Style*— Prof Keith Channon; ✉ Department of Cardiovascular Medicine, John Radcliffe Hospital, Oxford OX3 9DU (☎ 01865 572783, fax 01865 572784, e-mail keith.channon@cardiov.ox.ac.uk)

CHANT, (Elizabeth) Ann; CB (1997); da of Capt Harry Charles Chant (d 1945), and Gertrude, *née* Poel (d 1998); *b* 16 August 1945, Blackpool; *Educ* Blackpool Collegiate Sch; *Career* Nat Assistance Bd Lincoln 1963–66, Miny of Social Security Lincoln 1966–70, NHS Whitley Cncl DHSS London 1970–72, DHSS Lincoln 1972–74, DHSS Regnl Office Nottingham 1974–82, mangr DHSS Sutton-in-Ashfield 1982–83, DHSS HQ London 1983–85, princ private sec to perm sec DHSS 1985–87, head Records Branch DSS Newcastle upon Tyne 1987–89, head Contributions Unit DSS 1990–91, chief exec Contributions Agency DSS 1991–94, chief exec Child Support Agency DSS 1994–97; Reviews of Public Tst Office and Legal Services ombudsman Lord Chancellor's Dept 1999, chm Inland Revenue 2004 (dep chm 2000–04), DG HM Revenue and Customs 2005, dep dir of charities The Office of HRH The Prince of Wales 2005–11; md Business in the Community 1997–99, exec memb Bd Industrial Soc 1993–2000; tstee: Garfield Weston Tst for St Paul's Cathedral 2010–, Fndn Years Tst 2012–; lay govr London South Bank Univ 2000–09; *Recreations* friends, music (especially opera), theatre; *Clubs* Athenaeum; *Style*— Miss Ann Chant, CB; ✉ The Athenaeum, Pall Mall, London SW1Y 5ZX

CHANTER, Rev Canon Anthony R; s of Charles Harry Chanter (d 1989), of Jersey, CI, and Eva Marjorie, *née* Le Cornu (d 1966); *b* 24 October 1937; *Educ* Hautlieu Sch Jersey, Salisbury Theol Coll, Open Univ (BA), Univ of London (MA); *m* 10 Sept 1966, Yvonne, da of Flt Lt William Reid (ka 1944); 2 da (Fiona b 31 May 1968, Alison b 15 May 1975); *Career* priest vicar Lincoln Cathedral 1970–73; headmaster: Bishop King Sch Lincoln 1970–73, Grey Court Sch Ham Richmond upon Thames 1973–77, Bishop Reindorp Sch Guildford 1977–84; dir of educn Dio of Guildford 1984–2001, hon canon Guildford Cathedral 1984–2001 (canon emeritus 2002–); memb Educn Ctee Surrey CC 1984–2001, dir Guildford Diocesan Bd of Fin; memb Nat Assoc of Headteachers; *Books* Student Profiling (co-author 1980); *Recreations* golf, cricket, country skiing, iconography, music, opera; *Clubs* MCC, Ham Manor Golf; *Style*— The Rev Canon Anthony Chanter; ✉ Thalassa, 62 Sea Avenue, Rustington, West Sussex BN16 2DJ (☎ 01903 774288, e-mail tonychanter@hotmail.com)

CHANTLER, Sir Cyril; kt (1996); s of Fred Chantler (d 1957), of Blackpool, and Marjorie, *née* Clark; *b* 12 May 1939; *Educ* Wrekin Coll, St Catharine's Coll Cambridge (BA), Guy's Hosp Med Sch London (MB BChir), Univ of Cambridge (MD); *m* 1963, Shireen M Saleh; 2 s (Paul Frederick b 29 July 1965, Jonathan Mark b 22 June 1967), 1 da (Nariane Emma b 24 May 1970); *Career* Guy's Hosp: sr lectr in paediatrics and conslt paediatrician 1971–2000, chm Mgmnt Bd and unit gen mangr 1985–88; prof of paediatric nephrology Guy's Hosp Med Sch 1980–2000 (emeritus prof 2001–), princ UMDS 1992–98 (clinical dean 1989–92), dean GKT 1998–2000, vice-princ KCL 1998–2000; pro-vice-chllr for med Univ of London 1997–2000, chm Cncl Heads of UK Med Schs 1998–99; MRC: memb external staff 1967, clinical research fell 1967–69, travelling fell Univ of Calif 1971; co-ed Paediatric Nephrology 1986–96, memb Editorial Bd Jl of the American Medical Assoc 2002–11; chair: Scientific Advsy Ctee Fndn for the Study of Infant Deaths 1987–90, Great Ormond St Hosp for Sick Children 2001–08, Beit Meml Fellowships for Med Research 2004–09, King's Fund London 2004–10, Shared Medical Record Ctee NHS Connecting for Health 2005–06, Clinical Advsy Gp NHS London 2007–08, UCL Ptnrs Academic Health Scis Partnership 2009–14 (hon fell 2014–); ind chm NHS Eng Audit Ctee for Quality and Clinical Risk 2013–14, chm Complex Primary Care Practice Prog Bd Barking Havering and Redbridge Clinical Commissioning Gps 2014–, non-exec dir Private Healthcare

Information Network 2015–; memb: Registration Ctee Euro Dialysis and Transplant Assoc 1975–80, Cncl Euro Soc for Paediatric Nephrology 1978–81, Academic Bd Br Paediatric Assoc 1983–86, NHS Policy Bd 1989–95, Cncl Renal Assoc 1981, Grants Cncl Br Kidney Patients' Assoc 1985–2010, GMC 1994–2003 (chm Standards Ctee 1997–2003), Public Sector Advsy Panel Doctors.net.uk 2007–14, Advsy Bd Inst of Healthcare Optimisation Boston US 2013–15; med advsr Children Nationwide Med Research Fund 1986–2005; RCP: fell 1977, lectr 1987, pro-censor 1989, censor 1990, Harveian orator 2002; pres Br Assoc of Med Mangrs 1991–97; James Spence medallist RCPCH 2005, Ira Griefer Award Int Pediatric Nephrology Assoc 2007; memb: Cncl Southwark Cathedral 2000–, Bd of Govrs London South Bank Univ 2002–05; non-exec dir By the Bridge 2006–15; tstee: Dunhill Medical Tst 2001–09, Media Standards Tst 2006–15, Complex Care Practice Bd 2015–; vice-chm Nat Maternity Review 2016–; Hon DUniv: Lille 1998, South Bank 1999, London 2005, Kent 2009, UCL 2012; hon memb American Paediatric Soc 1991, foreign assoc memb Inst of Med Nat Acad of Sci USA 1999; FRCP 1977, FRCPCH 1996, FKC 1998, FMedSci 1999; *Publications* jt author of reports for Br Assoc of Paediatric Nephrology: Future Care of Children with Renal Failure (1975), Siting of Units to Care for Children with Chronic Renal Failure (1980); contrib to scientific literature on paediatrics, kidney disease and management in the NHS, author of Govt review on plain packaging of tobacco products 2014; *Recreations* golf, walking, reading, opera; *Clubs* Athenaeum; *Style*— Sir Cyril Chantler; ✉ 22 Benbow House, New Globe Walk, London SE1 9DS (☎ 020 7401 3246)

CHANTLER, Paul Anthony; s of Peter Victor Chantler, of Tunbridge Wells, Kent, and Joy Edith, *née* Austin; *b* 12 October 1959; *Educ* Skinners' Sch Tunbridge Wells; *Career* trainee reporter Kent & Sussex Courier 1978–82, reporter Kent Messenger 1982–83, sr reporter Kent Evening Post 1983–84, journalist and presenter Invicta Radio 1984–88, news ed Southern Sound 1988–89, breakfast show presenter BBC Wiltshire Sound 1989; Chiltern Radio Network: head of news 1989–90, prog controller 1990–92, gp prog dir 1992–95; md Network News 1991–95, chief exec Galaxy Radio 1994–96, gp prog dir Essex Radio Gp 1996–2000, prog dir Talksport 2000, gp prog dir Wireless Gp 2000–01, radio prog conslt (GMG Radio, Smooth Radio, EMAP Radio, Century FM, Metro Radio, Hallam FM, Newstalk Ireland) 2002–, sr ptnr United Radio Conslts 2006–12; Radio Ideas Bank: chm 2010–, radio prog consIt 2012–; content consIt Premier Christian Radio 2013–; UK Commercial Radio Programmer of the Year 1997; *Books* Local Radio Journalism (1992 and 1997), Basic Radio Journalism (2003), Essential Radio Journalism (2008), Hang The DJ? (2011), Twibel (2012 and 2014); *Recreations* pop music, reading, travel, wine and food, driving; *Clubs* Radio Acad; *Style*— Paul Chantler, Esq; ✉ 1 Candle Cottages, Stoney Lane, Hailsham, East Sussex BN27 2AP (☎ 07788 584888, e-mail chantler@aol.com, website www.paulchantler.com, Twitter @paulchantler)

CHAPMAN, Prof Antony John; s of Arthur Charles Chapman (d 1997), of London, and Joan Muriel, *née* Brown (d 1997), of Canterbury; *b* 21 April 1947, Canterbury, Kent; *Educ* Milford Haven GS, Bexley GS, Univ of Leicester (BSc, PhD); *m* 1 June 1985, Siriol Sophia Jones, da of Cledan David, of Llanddowror; 2 s (David Charles Luke b 1987, Luke Christopher David b 1989), 2 da (Harriet Emily Siriol b 1991, Madeleine Sophie Elizabeth b 1993); *Career* sr lectr UWIST Cardiff 1978–83 (lectr 1971–78); Univ of Leeds: prof 1983–98, head Dept of Psychology 1983–91, dir Centre for Applied Psychological Studies 1987–90, dean of science 1992–94, pro-vice-chllr 1994–98, visiting prof 1998–2003, pt/t secondment to CVCP Academic Audit Unit 1990–94; DETR-DTLR-DFT Child Pedestrian Safety consIt 1993–2004; prof Univ of Wales 1998–; vice-chllr/pres and chief exec Cardiff Met Univ (formerly Univ of Wales Inst Cardiff) 1998–, sr vice-chllr and chief exec Univ of Wales 2004–07; dir BPS Communications Ltd 1979–, fndr dir Sound Alert Ltd 1994; Prince of Wales Award for Innovation 1997, Design Cncl Millennium Product Awards for Sound Localizer (emergency vehicles) and Localizer Beacon (fire egress); dir: Quality Assurance Agency for HE 2000–06 and 2011–, Cardiff Business Technol Centre 2000–, Univs and Colls Employers Assoc 2002–06, Leadership Fndn for HE 2003–07, Univs and Colls Admission Serv 2007–11, HE Acad 2009–; chm: Br Psychological Soc Qualifying Examination 1986–90, Assoc of UK Heads of Psychology Depts 1990–92, UK Deans of Science Ctee 1993–94, ESRC Research Studentships Open Competition 1993–95, ESRC Research Recognition Exercise 1993–96, Jls Ctee Br Psychological Soc 1995–98, ESRC Psychology Area Panel 1996–2001, HE Wales 2002–04, HE Wales Tst 2002–04, Quality Assurance Agency Access Recognition and Licensing Ctee 2003–06 and 2015–, Quality Assurance Agency Ctee for Wales 2004–06 and 2013–, Academic Accreditation Cmmn, Singapore Assoc Private Schs and Colls 2009–12, Academic Cncl HE Acad 2009–11; assoc ed Br Jl of Devpt Psychology 1983–88, memb Editorial Bd Jl of Organizational Behaviour 1988–92, co-ed Current Psychology 1989–2013 (ed-in-chief 1985–89), ed Br Jl of Psychology 1989–95, memb Editorial Ctee Br Jl of Educational Psychology 1991–95; pres: Br Psychological Soc 1988–89, Psychology Section BAAS 1993–94, Assoc Learned Socs in the Social Sciences 1995–98; vice-pres Univs UK 2002–04 (memb Bd 2002–06); vice-chm ESRC Trg Bd 1995–96; memb: Ctee European Assoc of Deans of Science 1993–94, Exec Bd Int Soc for Research in Humor 1993–98, Bd NEAB 1994–98, HEFCE Psychology Advsy Gp 1997–2000 (memb Research Assessment Exercise Panel (Psychology) 1992 and 1996), Royal Soc Scientific Unions Ctee 1999–2002, Cncl CBI Wales 1999–2004, 2006–12 and 2013–, Cncl Industry and HE 2002–12, Leadership Cncl Nat Centre for Univs and Business 2012–, Cncl Cardiff C of C 2004–07, Cncl All Pty Parly Univs Gp 2004–, Advsy Bd London Sch of Commerce 2007–11 and 2016, Advsy Bd Cardiff Business Cncl 2013–16, Advsy Bd Assoc of Arab Univs 2014–; advsr Bd of Govrs S Australia Mgmnt Inst 2009–12; govr Bramhope Primary Sch W Yorks 1997–98, vice-pres Cardiff Business Club 2007–; memb Ct Cardiff Univ 1993–, memb Ct Aberystwyth Univ 1998–; memb Worshipful Livery Co of Wales, memb Worshipful Livery Guild 2014–; Hon DSc Univ of Leicester 2008, Hon DLitt Cardiff Met Univ 2016; CPsychol 1989, FRSA 1997, fndr FAcSS 1999, Hon FBPsS 1999 (FBPsS 1978), fell Inst of Welsh Affrs 2007–08 and 2010–, FIoD 2015, FLSW; *Publications* 15 jt books incl: Humour and Laughter: Theory, Research and Applications (1976, 2 edn 1995), Models of Man (1980), Friendship and Social Relations in Children (1980, 2 edn 1995), Road Safety: Research and Practice (1981), Pedestrian Accidents (1982), Noise and Society (1984), Cognitive Processes in the Perception of Art (1984), Psychology and Social Problems (1984), Elements of Applied Psychology (1994), Psychology and Law (1994, 2 edn 2015), Cognitive Science, Vols I, II and III (1995), Biographical Dictionary of Psychology (1997); co-ed 11 special issues of journals and sr ed 3 book series, Psychology for Professional Groups, Psychology in Action, International Library of Critical Writings in Psychology; author of articles in books and learned jls; *Recreations* family, music, cricket, soccer; *Clubs* Athenaeum, Cardiff and County; *Style*— Prof Antony J Chapman; ✉ Hill House, 95 Cyncoed Road, Cardiff CF23 6AE (☎ 07768 035304, e-mail ajchapman@gmail.com)

CHAPMAN, Cathy; *b* 1950, London; *Career* dir of food product devpt and direction Marks & Spencer Gp plc 2011–; *Style*— Ms Cathy Chapman; ✉ Marks & Spencer Group plc, Waterside House, 35 North Wharf Road, London W2 1NW

CHAPMAN, Christine; da of late John Price, and late Jean Price; *b* 7 April 1956; *Educ* Porth County Girls' Sch, Univ of Wales Aberystwyth (BA), South Bank Poly (Dip), Univ of Wales Cardiff (MScEcon, MPhil), Univ of Swansea (PGCE); *m* 1981, Dr Michael Chapman, s of late Don Chapman, and Mai Chapman; 1 da (Rhiannon b 3 June 1983), 1 s (Stephen b 1 Oct 1985); *Career* Mid Glamorgan: Community Services Agency 1979–80, Careers (careers advsr) 1980–92, Educn Business Partnership 1992–93; teacher trg 1993–94, consIt 1995–96, co-ordinator Torfaen Educn Business Partnership 1996–99; secdy sch teacher, pt/t tutor; memb Nat Assembly for Wales (Lab Co-op) Cynon Valley 1999–2015, dep min for educn and lifelong learning and finance, local govt and public servs 2005–07; chair: Objective One Prog Monitoring Ctee 2000–05, Petitions Ctee 2009–11, Children and Young People Ctee 2011–13, Communities, Equality and Local Govt Ctee 2013–; memb Ctee of the Regions 2008–12; memb: Inst of Careers Guidance (memb Nat Cncl 1992–94), Co-operative Pty; *Recreations* walking, theatre; *Style*— Ms Christine Chapman; ✉ Cynon Valley Constituency Office, Bank Chambers, 28A Oxford Street, Mountain Ash, Rhondda Cynon Taff CF45 3EU (☎ 01443 478098, fax 01443 478 311); National Assembly for Wales, Cardiff Bay, Cardiff CF99 1NA (☎ 029 2089 8364, fax 029 2089 8365, e-mail christine.chapman@wales.gov.uk)

C

CHAPMAN, Christopher Henry George (Kit); MBE (1989); s of Peter Francis Chapman (d 1997), of Taunton, Somerset, and Georgette (Etty), *née* Rosi (d 2004); *b* 10 March 1947; *Educ* Taunton Sch, Univ of Surrey (BSc, pres Food and Wine Soc); *m* 1971, (Marie) Louise Anne, da of late Peter Edward Guiver; 2 s (Dominic Alexander Pierre b 1973, Nicholas Mark Christopher b 1975); *Career* in advertising 1969–76 (latterly with Benton and Bowles Ltd); prop The Castle Hotel Taunton 1980–; chm Prestige Hotels 1985–87; dir: Orchard Media Ltd 1992–99, Taunton Forward Ltd 2014–; columnist Caterer and Hotelkeeper 1983–88; writer and presenter: Simply the Best: A Celebration of British Food (12 films for ITV and Channel 4) 1991 and 1993, Of Madeleines and Other Masterpieces (arts prog, BBC Radio 2) 1994, Diary of an Innkeeper (6 part documentary series for Carlton TV, inspired by book An Innkeeper's Diary) 2003, Keep It In The Family (1 part of a 4 part documentary series on BBC 2, produced by TwoFour Broadcast); chm Commercial Membs' Gp West Country Tourist Bd 1980–86; ministerial appointee Exmoor Nat Park Ctee 1979–81; memb: Leisure Industries Econ Devpt Ctee NEDC 1987–89, Bd Somerset TEC 1989–94; chm ArtsTaunton, dir Passion for Somerset; visiting sr fell Sch of Mgmnt Studies Univ of Surrey 1999; Freeman City of London 1984; *Awards* Ward Cavendish Trophy for the Small Business Award 1980 and 1981, British Airways and BTA Award for Overseas Mktg 1981, Caterer and Hotelkeeper Awards (CATEYS) Tourism Award 1987, Good Hotel Guide César Award for Best Town Hotel 1987, CATEYS Best Ind Mktg Campaign for BRAZZ 1999, Best Out-of-Town Restaurant for The Castle Tatler Restaurant Awards 2002, VisitBritain 4 Star Gold Award 2008; *Books* Great British Chefs (1989, shortlisted André Simon Book Award 1990), Great British Chefs 2 (1995, Guild of Food Writers Michael Smith Award 1996), An Innkeeper's Diary (1999), My Archipelago (2010, Kindle edn 2013); *Recreations* good food and wine, walking the Quantocks with the dogs, my grandchildren; *Clubs* Garrick; *Style*— Kit Chapman, Esq, MBE; ✉ The Castle Hotel, Taunton, Somerset TA1 1NF (☎ 01823 272671, fax 01823 336066, e-mail chapman@the-castle-hotel.com, website www.the-castle-hotel.com)

CHAPMAN, Prof Christopher Hugh; s of John Harold Chapman (d 1999), of Milton-under-Wychwood, Oxon, and Margaret Joan, *née* Weeks (d 2001); *b* 5 May 1945, Sutton, Surrey; *Educ* Latymer Upper Sch, Christ's Coll Cambridge (MA, PhD); *m* 1 June 1974, Lillian, da of Michael Tarapaski, of Redwater, Canada; 1 s (Timothy b 26 May 1978), 1 da (Heather b 24 June 1981); *Career* asst prof Dept of Geology and Geophysics Univ Calif Berkeley 1972–73, assoc prof Dept of Physics Univ of Alberta 1973–74 (asst prof 1969–72), Green scholar Univ of Calif San Diego 1978–79, prof Dept of Physics Univ of Toronto 1980–84 and 1988–90 (assoc prof 1974–80), prof of geophysics Dept of Earth Sciences Univ of Cambridge 1984–88, scientific advsr Schlumberger Cambridge Research 1991–2005 (consIt 2005–); hon prof of theoretical seismology Dept of Earth Sciences Univ of Cambridge 2006–12 (hon emeritus prof of theoretical seismology 2012–); Royal Astronomical Soc Gold Medal (Geophysics) 2013; memb SEG, FRAS, FAGU; *Publications* Fundamentals of Seismic Wave Propagation (2004); *Recreations* sailing, photography; *Style*— Prof Christopher Chapman; ✉ 7 Spinney Drive, Great Shelford, Cambridge CB22 5LY (☎ 01223 845007); Schlumberger Gould Research, High Cross, Madingley Road, Cambridge CB3 0EL (☎ 01223 325434)

CHAPMAN, Sir David Robert Macgowan; 3 Bt (UK 1958), of Cleadon, Tyne & Wear; DL; s of Col Sir Robert (Robin) Chapman, 2 Bt, CBE, TD, JP, DL (d 1987), and Barbara May, *née* Tonks; bro of Peter Stuart Chapman, *qv*; *b* 16 December 1941; *Educ* Marlborough, Grenoble Univ, McGill Univ Montreal (BCom); *m* 19 June 1965, Maria Elizabeth de Gosztonyi-Zsolnay, da of Dr Nicholas de Mattyasovszky-Zsolnay, of Ottawa, Canada; 1 s (Michael Nicholas b 1969), 1 da (Christina Elisabeth b 1970); *Heir* s, Michael Chapman; *Career* stockbroker; chm Stock Exchange NE Region Advsy Gp 1991–98; first vice-pres Merrill Lynch Int Bank Ltd 1999–2002; chm: Northern Enterprise (General Partner) Ltd 2000–, Northern Rock Asset Mgmnt Pension Scheme (formerly Northern Rock Pension Scheme) 2004–13, chm Virgin Money 2011 Pension Scheme 2011–, chm Virgin Money Ind Governance Ctee 2015–; dir: Wise Speke Ltd 1987–99 (ptnr Wise Speke & Co 1971–87), Breathe North Ltd 1988–95, British Lung Fndn 1989–94, Team General Partner (chm) 1993–2012, Montfort Press Ltd 1994–95, Northern Rock plc (formerly Northern Rock Building Society) 1996–2004, Sunderland City Radio Ltd 1997–98, Gordon Durham Holdings Ltd 1997–98, High Gosforth Park Ltd 1999–2004, NES General Partner Ltd 1999–, Zytronic plc 2000–, NE Regional Investment Fund Two Ltd 2001–09, CNE General Partner Ltd 2001–; consIt UBS Wealth Management Ltd 2002–12; chm CBI NE Region 2000–02 (dep chm 2003–05), dep chm Advsy Bd Finance for Business NE 2009–; memb Cncl: The Stock Exchange 1979–88, Univ of Durham (chm Ustinov Coll (grad soc) 2001–04); memb: The Greenbury Ctee 1995, Northern Regnl Cncl CBI 1996–2006, NE Regnl Investment Fund Ltd 1999–2009, NE Regnl Investment Fund Three Ltd 2004–09, Northern Business Forum Ltd 2003–05; chm Northumbria Coalition against Crime 1995–2000; tstee Northern Rock Fndn 2002–16; High Sheriff Tyne & Wear 1993–94; *Recreations* travel, tennis, reading; *Clubs* Northern Counties (Newcastle), Victory Services (London); *Style*— Sir David Chapman, Bt, DL; ✉ Pinfold House, 6 West Park Road, Cleadon, Sunderland, Tyne & Wear SR6 7RR (☎ 0191 536 7887)

CHAPMAN, Dinos; *b* 1962, London; *Educ* Ravensbourne Coll of Art (BA), RCA (MA); *Career* artist, in partnership with brother Jake Chapman, *qv*, fndr Chapman FineART London, curated Some of My Best Friends are Geniuses (Ind Art Space London) 1996; shortlisted Turner Prize 2003; *Selected Two-Person Exhibitions* We Are Artists (Hales Gallery London and Bluecoat Gallery Liverpool) 1992, The Disasters of War (Victoria Miro Gallery London) 1993, Mummy & Daddy (Galeria Franco Toselli Milan) 1994, Great Deeds Against the Dead (Victoria Miro Gallery London) 1994, Five Easy Pissers (Andréhn-Schiptjenko Gallery Stockholm) 1995, Bring Me the Head of Franco Toselli! (Ridinghouse Editions London) 1995, Zygotic acceleration, biogenetic, de-sublimated libidinal model (enlarged x 1000) (Victoria Miro Gallery London) 1995, Gavin Brown's Enterprise NY 1995, Chapmanworld (ICA London) 1996, Zero Principle (Giò Marconi Milan) 1996, P-House Tokyo 1996, Chapmanworld (Grazer Kunstverein Graz) 1997, Six Feet Under (Gagosian Gallery NY) 1997, Galerie Daniel Templon Paris 1998, Disasters of War (White Cube London) 1999, Jake & Dinos Chapman (Fig 1 London) 1999, Jake & Dinos Chapman GCSE Art Exam (The Art Ginza Space Tokyo) 2000, Jake & Dinos Chapman (Kunst Werke Berlin) 2000, Jackie & Denise Chapwoman. New Work (Modern Art London) 2001, Jake and Dinos Chapman (Groninger Museum) 2002, Work from the Chapman Family Collection (White Cube London) 2002, Jake & Dinos Chapman (Museum Kunst Palast Düsseldorf) 2003, The Rape of Creativity (Modern Art Oxford) 2003, Jake & Dinos Chapman (Saatchi Gallery London) 2003, The Marriage of Reason and Squalor (Centro de Arte Contemporáneo Malaga and Dunkers Kulturhaus Sweden) 2004, Insult to Injury (Kunst Sammlungen der Veste Coburg) 2004, The New and Improved Andrex Works (Thomas Olbricht Collection Essen) 2004, Explaining Christians to Dinosaurs (Kunsthaus Bregenz) 2005, Bad Art for Bad People (Tate Liverpool) 2006, When Humans Walked the Earth (Tate Britain) 2007; *Selected Group Exhibitions* Great Deeds Against the Dead (Andrea Rosen Gallery NY) 1994, Liar (Hoxton Square London) 1994, The Institute of Cultural Anxiety: Works from the Collection (ICA London) 1995, General Release: Young British Artists (Venice Biennale Scuola di San Pasquale Venice) 1995, Brilliant! New Art from London (Walker Art Center Minneapolis and Museum of Contemporary Art Houston) 1995, Young British Artists (Roslyn Oxley Gallery Sydney) 1996, Florence Biennale 1996, Gothic (ICA Boston) 1997, Minor Sensation (Victoria Miro Gallery London) 1997, Body (Art Gallery of NSW Sydney) 1997, Sensation: Young British Artists from the Saatchi Collection (Royal Acad of Arts London) 1997, Future, Present, Past (Venice Biennale) 1997, Wounds: Between Democracy and Redemption in Contemporary Art (Moderna Museet Stockholm) 1998, Heaven: An Exhbn that will break your heart (Kunsthalle Düsseldorf and Tate Gallery Liverpool) 1999, Sex and the British – Slap and Tickle (Galerie Thaddeaus Ropac Salzburg and Galerie Thaddaeus Ropac Paris) 2000, Ant Noises II (Saatchi Gallery London) 2000, Out There (White Cube London) 2000, The Pölstar Art Programme (Leicester Square London) 2000, Apocalypse: Beauty and Horror in Contemporary Art (Royal Acad of Arts London) 2000, Nervous Kingdom (Bluecoat Gallery Liverpool) 2000, ManMoMa. A Thick Bloke Kicking a Dog to Death (International 3 Summer Fête Fairfield Manchester) 2000, Jake & Dinos Chapman and Francisco Goya y Lucientes (The Power Plant Toronto) 2000, Disasters of War. Francisco de Goya, Henry Darger and Jake and Dinos Chapman (PS1 Contemporary Art Center NY) 2000, Paper Assets: Collecting Prints and Drawings 1996–2001 (British Museum London) 2001, Francisco Goya and Jake and Dinos Chapman: The Disasters of War (Musée des Beaux-Arts de Montréal) 2001, Art Crazy Nation Show (Milton Keynes Gallery) 2002, Rapture: Art's Seduction by Fashion since 1970 (Barbican Gallery London) 2002, Fran el Greco till Dali (Nationalmuseum Sweden Stockholm) 2003, Mars. Art and War (Neue Galerie am Landesmuseum Joanneum Graz) 2003, Summer Exhbn (Royal Acad of Arts London) 2003 (Charles Wollaston Award), The Turner Prize (Tate Britain London) 2003, Gewalt (Loushy Art & Editions Tel Aviv) 2004, Mike Kelley: The Uncanny (Tate Liverpool) 2004, At War (Centre de Cultura Contemporània de Barcelona) 2004, After Images (Neues Museum Weserburg Bremen) 2004, Deliver Us From Evil (Matthew Marks Gallery NY) 2004, The Charged Image (Joseloff Gallery CT) 2004, Paper Democracy: Contemporary Art in Editions on Paper (Edificio Cultura Inglesa Sao Paulo) 2004, The Christmas Exhibition (Edinburgh Printmakers) 2004, Critic's Choice (FACT Liverpool) 2005, Mixed-up Childhood: An Exhibition for Grown-ups (Auckland Art Gallery) 2005, Glasgow International Festival of Contemporary Visual Art (Glasgow Print Studio) 2005, Body: New Art from the UK (Vancouver Art Gallery) 2005, Bidibidobidiboo: La Collezione Sandretto Re Rebaudengo (Turin) 2005; *Work in Public Collections* Deste Fndn Athens, Rubell Family Collection, Saatchi Collection, Walker Art Centre Minneapolis, British Museum, Simmons & Simmons London, The Israel Museum Jerusalem, Groninger Museum, Museum Kunst Palast Düsseldorf, MOMA NY; *Style*— Dinos Chapman, Esq; ✉ c/o White Cube, 144–152 Bermondsey St, London SE1 3TQ

CHAPMAN, His Hon Judge Frank Arthur; s of Dennis Arthur Chapman, of Culcheth, Warrington, Cheshire, and Joan, *née* Dickinson; *b* 28 May 1946; *Educ* Newton-le-Willows GS, UCL (LLB, LLM, Brigid Cotter Prize 1994); *m* 27 July 1968, Mary Kathleen, da of late Edwin Keith Jones, and Marion Jones, of Pontypool, Gwent; 1 da (Rachel Lynn (now Mrs D Heron) b 12 March 1971), 1 s (Thomas William Lawson b 21 Oct 1973); *Career* called to the Bar 1968, practised Midland & Oxford Circuit 1969–91, asst recorder 1982–86, recorder 1986–92, circuit judge (Midland & Oxford Circuit) 1992–97, res judge Wolverhampton Court 1997–2007, sr circuit judge 2002–, resident judge Birmingham Crown Court 2007–; memb Bar Cncl 1989–91; *Recreations* mountaineering, angling, travel; *Style*— His Hon Judge Chapman; ✉ Midland & Oxford Circuit, 2 Newton Street, Birmingham B4 7LU

CHAPMAN, Frank Watson; s of Thomas Chapman (d 1965), of Bournemouth, Dorset, and Beatrice, *née* Padgett (d 1976); *b* 7 November 1929; *Educ* Swindon Coll, Marine Sch of South Shields; *m* 18 March 1955, Wendy Joanna, da of Roger Philip Holly (d 1972), of Switzerland; 1 da (Susie b 1956), 1 s (Thomas b 1963); *Career* cadet MN 1946; deck offr: Union Steamship Co NZ 1951–54, Royal Mail Lines 1954–58, Cunard Steamship Co 1958–62; salesman Telephone Rentals 1962; fndr and md 1964: Bahamas Properties Ltd, Sovereign Travel Ltd; purchased Loch Rannoch and Forest Hills Hotels Scotland 1974, fndr Multi-Ownership & Hotels Ltd 1975 (thereby becoming fndr of Timeshare in UK), 2 devpts in Wales 1978, 3 devpts Forest Hills Hotel 1980, sold co to Barratt Devpts plc 1982 (md until 1988); fndr and chm Sovereign Travel & Leisure Gp plc 1988–, chm The Timeshare Cncl 1995–, dir Rusort Devpt Orgn (RDO), dir Acell SpA; *Recreations* travel, gardening, reading, swimming; *Style*— Frank Chapman; ✉ Moulsey House, 11 Wolsey Road, East Molesey, Surrey KT8 9EL (☎ 020 8783 9437); Sovereign Travel & Leisure Group plc, 74 High Street, Wimbledon Village, London SW19 5EG (☎ 020 8879 7199)

CHAPMAN, Ian Stewart; s of Francis Ian Chapman, of Cheam, Surrey, and Marjory Stewart, *née* Swinton; *b* 15 January 1955; *Educ* Cranleigh Sch, Univ of Durham (BA, 1 XI Cricket); *m* Maria, da of late Daniel Samper; 1 s (Gabriel Ian Daniel b 22 July 1983), 2 da (Sabrina Stewart Burdett b 11 Nov 1986, Natalya Alexa Campbell b 5 Nov 1990); *Career* publisher; asst on shop floor W H Smith Paris 1974–75; trainee: Doubleday & Co Inc NY 1980–81, Berkley Publishers The Putnam Group NY May-Nov 1981; editorial asst William Morrow & Co Inc NY 1981–82, ed rising to editorial dir Hodder & Stoughton Ltd London 1983–87, publishing dir Pan Books Ltd rising to gp publisher Pan Macmillan Ltd 1987–94, md Macmillan General Books 1994–99; Simon & Schuster: md and ceo 2000–13, chief exec and publisher 2013–; *Recreations* golf, walking, skiing, gym, reading, cinema, travel, music, opera; *Clubs* Garrick, MCC; *Style*— Ian S Chapman, Esq; ✉ Benedict House, Staplecross Road, Northiam, East Sussex TN31 6JJ (☎ 01580 830222, fax 01580 830027); Simon & Schuster UK Ltd, 1st Floor, 222 Gray's Inn Road, London WC1X 8HB (☎ 020 7316 1910, fax 020 7316 0331, e-mail ian.chapman@simonandschuster.co.uk)

CHAPMAN, Jake; *b* Cheltenham, 1966; *Educ* Grange Hill Comp, Hastings Sch of Art, Poly of London (BA), RCA (MA), London Marathon 1991; *Career* artist, in partnership with brother Dinos Chapman, *qv*; fndr Chapman FineART London; curated Some of My Best Friends are Geniuses (Ind Art Space London) 1996; shortlisted Turner Prize 2003; memb: Secret Police, CIA, FBI, MI5, MFI; professorship (mail-order); professional bodies: arms, legs, feet back (bad), etc; key to Hastings; *Selected Two-Person Exhibitions* We Are Artists (Hales Gallery London and Bluecoat Gallery Liverpool) 1992, The Disasters of War (Victoria Miro Gallery London) 1993, Mummy & Daddy (Galeria Franco Toselli Milan) 1994, Great Deeds Against the Dead (Victoria Miro Gallery London) 1994, Five Easy Pissers (Andréhn-Schiptjenko Gallery Stockholm) 1995, Bring Me the Head of Franco Toselli! (Ridinghouse Editions London) 1995, Zygotic acceleration, biogenetic, de-sublimated libidinal model (enlarged x 1000) (Victoria Miro Gallery London) 1995, Gavin Brown's Enterprise NY 1995, Chapmanworld (ICA London) 1996, Zero Principle (Giò Marconi Milan) 1996, P-House Tokyo 1996, Chapmanworld (Grazer Kunstverein Graz) 1997, Six Feet Under (Gagosian Gallery NY) 1997, Galerie Daniel Templon Paris 1998, Disasters of War (White Cube London) 1999, Jake & Dinos Chapman (Fig 1 London) 1999, Jake & Dinos Chapman GCSE Art Exam (The Art Ginza Space Tokyo) 2000, Jake & Dinos Chapman (Kunst Werke Berlin) 2000, Jackie & Denise Chapwoman. New Work (Modern Art London) 2001, Jake and Dinos Chapman (Groninger Museum) 2002, Work from the Chapman Family Collection (White Cube London) 2002, Jake & Dinos Chapman (Museum Kunst Palast Düsseldorf) 2003, The Rape of Creativity (Modern Art Oxford) 2003, Jake & Dinos Chapman (Saatchi Gallery London) 2003, The Marriage of Reason and Squalor (Centro de Arte Contemporáneo Malaga and Dunkers Kulturhaus Sweden) 2004, Insult to Injury (Kunst Sammlungen der Veste Coburg) 2004, The New and Improved Andrex Works (Thomas Olbricht Collection Essen) 2004, Explaining Christians to Dinosaurs (Kunsthaus Bregenz) 2005, Bad Art for Bad People (Tate Liverpool) 2006, When Humans Walked the Earth (Tate Britain) 2007; *Selected Group Exhibitions* Great Deeds Against the Dead (Andrea Rosen Gallery NY) 1994, Liar (Hoxton Square London) 1994, The Institute of Cultural Anxiety: Works from the Collection (ICA London) 1995, General Release: Young British Artists (Venice Biennale Scuola di San Pasquale Venice) 1995, Brilliant! New Art from London (Walker Art Center Minneapolis and Museum of Contemporary Art Houston) 1995, Young British Artists (Roslyn Oxley Gallery Sydney) 1996, Florence Biennale 1996, Gothic (ICA Boston) 1997, Minor Sensation (Victoria Miro Gallery London) 1997, Body (Art Gallery of NSW Sydney) 1997, Sensation: Young British Artists from the Saatchi Collection (Royal Acad of Arts London) 1997, Future, Present, Past (Venice Biennale) 1997, Wounds: Between Democracy and Redemption in Contemporary Art (Moderna Museet Stockholm) 1998, Heaven: An Exhbn that will break your heart (Kunsthalle Düsseldorf and Tate Gallery Liverpool) 1999, Sex and the British – Slap and Tickle (Galerie Thaddeaus Ropac Salzburg and Galerie Thaddaeus Ropac Paris) 2000, Ant Noises II (Saatchi Gallery London) 2000, Out There (White Cube London) 2000, The Pölstar Art Programme (Leicester Square London) 2000, Apocalypse: Beauty and Horror in Contemporary Art (Royal Acad of Arts London) 2000, Nervous Kingdom (Bluecoat Gallery Liverpool) 2000, ManMoMa. A Thick Bloke Kicking a Dog to Death (International 3 Summer Fête Fairfield Manchester) 2000, Jake & Dinos Chapman and Francisco Goya y Lucientes (The Power Plant Toronto) 2000, Disasters of War. Francisco de Goya, Henry Darger and Jake and Dinos Chapman (PS1 Contemporary Art Center NY) 2000, Paper Assets: Collecting Prints and Drawings 1996–2001 (British Museum London) 2001, Francisco Goya and Jake and Dinos Chapman: The Disasters of War (Musée des Beaux-Arts de Montréal) 2001, Art Crazy Nation Show (Milton Keynes Gallery) 2002, Rapture: Art's Seduction by Fashion since 1970 (Barbican Gallery London) 2002, Fran el Greco till Dali (Nationalmuseum Sweden Stockholm) 2003, Mars. Art and War (Neue Galerie am Landesmuseum Joanneum Graz) 2003, Summer Exhbn (Royal Acad of arts London) 2003 (Charles Wollaston Award), The Turner Prize (Tate Britain London) 2003, Gewalt (Loushy Art & Editions Tel Aviv) 2004, Mike Kelley: The Uncanny (Tate Liverpool 2004), At War (Centre de Cultura Contemporània de Barcelona) 2004, After Images (Neues Museum Weserburg Bremen) 2004, Deliver Us From Evil (Matthew Marks Gallery NY) 2004, The Charged Image (Joseloff Gallery CT) 2004, Paper Democracy: Contemporary Art in Editions on Paper (Edificio Cultura Inglesa Sao Paulo) 2004, The Christmas Exhibition (Edinburgh Printmakers) 2004, Critic's Choice (FACT Liverpool) 2005, Mixed-up Childhood: An Exhibition for Grown-ups (Auckland Art Gallery) 2005, Glasgow International Festival of Contemporary Visual Art (Glasgow Print Studio) 2005, Body: New Art from the UK (Vancouver Art Gallery) 2005, Bidibidobidiboo: La Collezione Sandretto Re Rebaudengo (Turin) 2005; *Work in Public Collections* Deste Fndn Athens, Rubell Family Collection, Saatchi Collection, Walker Art Centre Minneapolis, British Museum, Simmons & Simmons London, The Israel Museum Jerusalem, Groninger Museum, Museum Kunst Palast Düsseldorf, MOMA NY; Razzle; *Recreations* drugs, fast cars, molecular biology; *Clubs* Water Mark, Harpo, Variety, Seal; *Style*— Prof Jake Chapman; ✉ c/o White Cube, 144–152 Bermondsey St, London SE1 3TQ

CHAPMAN, James Alfred (Jim); s of John Chapman, and Judith, *née* Hunt; *b* 28 December 1987, Norwich; *Educ* UEA (BSc); *m* 30 Sept 2015, Tanya Burr; *Career* social influencer, blogger and model; owner j1mmyb0bba YouTube channel 2010– (currently over 2.5m subscribers); style columnist GQ; *Recreations* cinema, fashion, motorsport, music, reading, travel, gym; *Style*— Jim Chapman, Esq; ✉ c/o Gleam Futures, 6th Floor, 60 Charlotte Street, London W1T 2NU (e-mail hello@jimchapman.co.uk, website www.jimchapman.co.uk, Twitter @JimChapman)

CHAPMAN, Jennifer (Jenny); MP; *b* 25 September 1973; *Educ* Hummersknott Sch Darlington, Queen Elizabeth Sixth Form Coll Darlington, Brunel Univ, Univ of Durham (MA); *Career* cncllr Darlington Borough Cncl 2007–10, MP (Lab) Darlington 2010–; *Style*— Mrs Jenny Chapman, MP; ✉ 40a Coniscliffe Road, Darlington DL3 7RG; House of Commons, London SW1A 0AA

CHAPMAN, Jennifer Mary; da of Peter Norman Johnson (d 2007), of Royston, Herts, and Agnes Mabel, *née* Taylor (d 1989); *b* 19 February 1950; *Educ* St Albans HS; *m* 1, 1971 (m dis 1979), Paul Robin Moncrieff Westoby; 2 da (Frances b 1974, Anna b 1976); m 2, 1980 (m dis 2016), Geoffrey Richard Chapman; 1 da (Quinta b 1990); *Career* NCTJ apprenticeship Westminster Press 1968–72, Heart of England Newspapers 1972–73, Coventry Evening Telegraph 1974, Mid-Anglia Newspapers 1976–80, fndr Multi Media PR consultancy 1980–; co-fndr Chapman and Vincent Literary Agents (formerly Media House) 1995–; currently business ed Cambridge News, currently ed Cambridge Business (Santander SME/Enterprise Title of the Year 2014 and 2015); Midlands Journalist of the Year 1974, Business and Financial Journalist of the Year UK Regnl Press Awards 2005, Wincott Nations and Regions Journalist of the Year 2013; memb: Soc of Authors 1982, English PEN 1993; MIPR 1986; *Books* The Geneva Touch (thriller, as Lydia Hitchcock, 1982), The Long Weekend (novel, 1984), Mysterious Ways (novel, 1985), Not Playing the Game (novel, 1986), Regretting It (novel, 1987), The Last Bastion – the case for and against women priests (1989), Barnardo's Today (foreword by HRH the Princess of Wales, 1991), Victor Ludorum (novel, 1991), Made in Heaven (1993), Jeremy's Baby (novel, 2001), I Know Who You Are (novel, 2012); *Style*— Mrs Jennifer Chapman; ✉ 18 Saxon Road, Cambridge CB5 8HS (e-mail jenny.chapman@cambridge-news.co.uk)

CHAPMAN, Prof John Newton; s of John Avi Chapman (d 1978), and Nora, *née* Newton (d 1982); *b* 21 November 1947, Sheffield; *Educ* King Edward VII Sch Sheffield, St John's Coll Cambridge (exhibitioner, scholar, Wright Prize, MA), Fitzwilliam Coll Cambridge (PhD); *m* 23 Sept 1972, Judith Margaret, *née* Brown; 1 da (Catherine Helen b 2 Dec 1977), 1 s (Christopher John b 26 March 1980); *Career* research fell Fitzwilliam Coll Cambridge 1971–74; Univ of Glasgow: lectr Dept of Natural Philosophy 1974–84, reader Dept of Natural Philosophy 1984–88, prof Dept of Physics and Astronomy 1988–, head of dept 2001–06, dean Faculty of Physical Sciences 2008–10, head Coll of Science and Engrg 2010–14; assoc ed Jl of Physics D, Applied Physics 1993–2002 (memb Editorial Bd 1989–93), memb Editorial Bd: Jl of Magnetism and Magnetic Materials 1990–2008, Materials Science and Engineering Reports 2009–; EPSRC: memb 2003–08, memb Coll, chm Advanced Magnetics Prog Mgmnt Panel 1998–2000, memb Audit Ctee 2003–08; chm: Electron Microscopy and Analysis Gp Inst of Physics 1982–83 (memb 1977–79, hon sec 1981–83), UK Magnetics Chapter IEEE 1992–94; memb: Magnetism Gp Inst of Physics 1990–94, Mgmnt Gp UK Magnetics Soc 1995–2001, Advsy Bd Max Planck Inst fur Mikrostrukturphysik 1998–2009, IT, Electronics and Communications Task Force DTI 1999–2000, LINK Evaluation Panel on Storage and Displays DTI 2001–06, Magnetic Soc Adcom IEEE 2005–10; distinguished visitor Univ of Western Aust 1995, distinguished lectr IEEE Magnetics Soc 2003, visiting prof Nat Univ of Singapore 2008; FRSE 1991, FIEEE 2010, FInstP; *Publications* 300 scientific papers; *Recreations* tennis, hill walking, photography, music; *Style*— Prof John N Chapman; ✉ Kelvin Building, University of

Glasgow, Glasgow G12 8QQ (☎ 0141 330 4462, fax 0141 330 2359, e-mail john.chapman@glasgow.ac.uk)

CHAPMAN, Prof (Stephen) Jonathan; s of Stephen Cyril Chapman, of N Yorks, and Pauline Mary Chapman; *b* 31 August 1968, Keighley, W Yorks; *Educ* South Craven Sch Crosshills, Merton Coll Oxford (BA), St Catherine's Coll Oxford (DPhil); *m* 1 Dec 1996, Aarti; 1 s (Tarun Stephen b 11 Aug 2000), 1 da (Maya Yasmin b 19 April 2002); *Career* postdoctoral research fell Stanford Univ 1992, Nuclear Electric research fell St Catherine's Coll Oxford 1993–95, Royal Soc univ research fell St Catherine's Coll Oxford 1995–99, prof of mathematics and its applications Mansfield Coll Oxford 1999–; author of pubns in learned jls; Richard C Diprima Prize Soc for Industrial and Applied Maths (SIAM) 1994, Whitehead Prize London Mathematical Soc 1998, Julian Cole Prize SIAM 2002; *Recreations* bridge, golf; *Style—* Prof Jonathan Chapman; ✉ Mathematical Institute, 24–29 St Giles', Oxford OX1 3LB (☎ 01865 270507, fax 01865 250515, e-mail chapman@maths.ox.ac.uk)

CHAPMAN, Kenneth James; s of Kenneth Roland Chapman, of Lincoln, and Marie Louise, *née* Robinson; *b* 14 September 1950; *Educ* Hornchurch GS, The Sweyne Sch Rayleigh, Univ of Wales (BSc, DipTP); *m* 31 Aug 1970, Pamela Margaret, da of Alan Henry Sertin, of Midsomer Norton, Avon; 2 s (Mark b 1974, Daniel b 1979), 1 da (Kelly b and d 1977); *Career* Glamorgan CC 1972–73, Mid Glamorgan CC 1974–75, Monmouth BC 1975–79, Edwin H Bradley & Sons Ltd 1979–81, managing ptnr Chapman Warren 1981–2000; dir: RPS Group plc 2000–04, Meadfleet Ltd 2004–, Sports Solutions GB Ltd 2006–; chm Swindon Town FC 1990–91, dir Cirencester Town FC; memb Cncl Swindon C of C and Industry; govr Wootton Bassett Sch; MRTPI 1978, MIMgt 1979, FRSA 2000; *Recreations* professional and non-league football, commemorative china and Dinky car collecting; *Style—* Kenneth Chapman, Esq; ✉ 16 Tutt Close, Fernwood, Newark NG24 3UL (☎ 01636 640211)

CHAPMAN, Nigel; CMG (2008); s of Norman Chapman (d 2008), and Maureen, *née* Bungey; *b* 14 December 1955, Southampton; *Educ* Univ of Cambridge (MA); *m* 1984, Margaret Farrar; 2 da (Clare b 8 Feb 1985, Grace b 11 Dec 1987); *Career* BBC: trainee 1977, former prodr Nationwide, Newsnight and Breakfast News, ed Public Eye 1989–92, head of centre SE Elstree 1992–94, head of broadcasting Midlands and E 1994–96, controller BBC English Regions 1996–99, dir BBC Online 1999–2000, dir BBC World Service 2004–09 (dep dir 2000–04), chair World Service Tst 2002–09, ceo Plan International 2009–; chair Plan (UK) 2003–09, tstee Shelter UK 2012–; *Recreations* cricket, music, reading, travel, walking, soccer; *Style—* Nigel Chapman, Esq, CMG; ✉ 34 Chalfont Road, Oxford OX2 6TH (☎ 07850 763708, e-mail nigelchapman@ymail.com); Plan International HQ, Duke Court, Duke Street, Woking, Surrey GU21 5BH (☎ 01483 755155, e-mail nigel.chapman@plan_international.org, website www.planinternational.org)

CHAPMAN, Nigel Peter; s of Lt Col Sidney Rex Chapman, MC, of Lincs, and Joan Mary, *née* Bates; *b* 31 January 1950; *Educ* Kimbolton Sch; *m* 26 Sept 1981, Heather Elizabeth, da of James Lindsay, of London; 3 s (Nicolas b 1982, Daniel b 1984, Cullan b 1999), 2 da (Jennifer b 1987, Clare b 1990); *Career* CA; md: LHM plc 1991–, Alias Hotels 1999–2004, Four Winds Resorts plc 2003–, Luxury Family Hotels plc 2004–06; *Recreations* tennis, cricket; *Clubs* Reform; *Style—* Nigel P Chapman, Esq; ✉ Four Winds Resorts, Carpenters Buildings, Carpenters Lane, Cirencester, Gloucestershire GL7 1EE (mobile 07710 504804, e-mail nigel.chapman@fourwindsresorts.com, website www.fourwindsresorts.com)

CHAPMAN, Peter Stuart; s of Sir Robin Chapman, Bt (d 1987), and Lady (Barbara) Chapman (d 2007); bro of Sir David Chapman, Bt, DL, *qv*; *b* 24 August 1944; *Educ* Trinity Coll Cambridge (MA), LSE (MSc); *m* 4 Aug 1972, Joan; 1 s (Christopher b 9 Oct 1974), 3 da (Vicky b 18 Dec 1977, Katherine b 13 Aug 1980, Rachel b 28 December 1981); *Career* research assoc Centre for Urban and Regnl Studies Univ of Birmingham 1967–69, asst research offr Sociological Research Section Miny of Housing and Local Govt 1969–70, asst ed Built Environment The Builder Gp 1970–72, devpt asst Peabody Tst 1972–73, housing and social planning conslt Llewelyn-Davies, Weeks, Forestier-Walker & Bor 1973–75, princ housing offr Admin & Resource Control London Borough of Hammersmith and Fulham 1975–79, asst dir of housing and property servs (devpt) RBK&C 1979–85, princ conslt Urban Renewal Consultancy KMG Thomson McLintock 1985–87, dir of housing and urban renewal consultancy CIPFA Services Ltd 1987–88; dir: Chapman Hendy Assocs Ltd 1988–2000, HACAS Chapman Hendy Ltd, HACAS Gp Ltd and Tribal HCH 2000–06, Assettrust Housing Ltd 2003–12; princ Peter S Chapman Consltg 2007–, dir Royal Borough of Kensington and Chelsea Tenant Mgmnt Orgn 2007–16; chm: Octavia Fndn 2009–15, Kensington Dragons FC 2012–, Friends of the Museum of Archaeology and Anthropology Cambridge, Advsy Ctee MMC Ventures London Fund; former special advsr House of Commons Environment, Tport and Regnl Affrs Ctee; fell Chartered Inst of Housing, fell Royal Anthropological Inst; *Publications* Local Housing Companies Implementation Manual (co-ed); *Recreations* tennis, walking, theatre, cinema; *Style—* Peter S Chapman, Esq; ✉ Peter S Chapman Consulting (e-mail peterschapman@chapmanlondon.com)

CHAPMAN, Dr Roger William Gibson; s of late Lt-Col Roy Chapman, OBE, and Margaret Gibson, *née* Abraham; *b* 16 February 1949; *Educ* Whitchurch GS Cardiff, Bart's Med Sch London (BSc, MD, MB BS); *m* 24 April 1972, Gillian Patricia, da of Dr James C Prestwich (d 1969), of Portsmouth; 3 s (James b 1977, Andrew b 1979, George b 1983), 1 da (Emily b 1987); *Career* house physician Bart's 1974–76, med registrar Southampton 1976–78, med lectr Liver Unit Royal Free Hosp 1978–81, conslt gastroenterologist and hepatologist John Radcliff Hosp Oxford 1987– (sr registrar 1981–87); sec Br Assoc for the Study of the Liver 1990–93; FRCP; *Books* Topics in Gastroenterology (co-ed and written with Dr D P Jewell, 1985), Drugs for the Gut (1997), Hepatobiliary Medicine (2003); *Recreations* tennis, golf, skiing, cinema; *Style—* Dr Roger Chapman; ✉ Department of Gastroenterology, John Radcliffe Hospital, Headington, Oxford OX3 9DU (☎ 01865 228756, fax 01865 751100, e-mail roger.chapman@ndm.ox.ac.uk)

CHAPMAN, Prof Stephen Kenneth (Steve); CBE (2016); *b* 12 May 1959; *Educ* Newcastle Univ (BSc, PhD); *Career* Univ of Edinburgh: lectr then sr lectr 1985–95, prof of biological chemistry 1996, head Sch of Chemistry 2000, vice-princ of planning, resources and research policy 2006; princ and vice-chllr Heriot-Watt Univ 2009–; author of over 200 research pubns; RSC Interdisciplinary Award 2001; FRSE, FRSC; *Style—* Prof Steve Chapman, CBE

CHAPPATTE, Philippe Paul; s of Joseph Chappatte (d 1998), and Sallie van Zwanenberg; *b* 6 October 1956; *Educ* Bryanston, Univ of Oxford (MA), Université Libre de Bruxelles (Licencie Spéciale en Droit Européen); *m* 22 June 1985, Sarah Jane; 3 c (Sam b 29 Dec 1986, Jessica b 23 March 1989, Hannah b 26 April 1997); *Career* slr; with Slaughter and May 1980–; specialises in competition law; pres and co-fndr European Competition Lawyers Forum; *Recreations* skiing; *Style—* Philippe Chappatte, Esq; ✉ Slaughter and May, 1 Bunhill Row, London EC1Y 8YY (☎ 020 7090 4424, fax 020 7090 5000, e-mail philippe.chappatte@slaughterandmay.com)

CHAPPELL, Julie Louise Jo; OBE; da of John Chappell, and Kathryn Chappell; *Educ* Brasenose Coll Oxford (BA); *Career* diplomat; Africa Directorate (Equatorial) Central Africa Desk, FCO 1999–2000, 2 sec political/economic Amman 2000–03, secondment to Coalition Provisional Authy Baghdad 2003–04, secondment to State Dept Washington 2004, head NATO Section Security Policy Dept FCO 2004–06, regnl conflict advsr Addis Ababa 2006–08, ambass to Guatemala and non-resident ambass to El Salvador and Honduras 2009–12; *Recreations* keen lacrosse player; *Style—* Ms Julie Chappell, OBE; ✉ c/o FCO, King Charles Street, London SW1A 2AH

CHAPPLE, Brian John; s of Capt John Ernest Chapple (d 1977), and Mildred, *née* Fairbrother (d 1988); *b* 24 March 1945; *Educ* Highgate Sch, RAM (GRSM, LRAM, ARAM); *m* 20 Dec 1973, Janet Mary, *née* Whittaker-Coldron; 1 da (Rosalind Bailey); *Career* composer; compositions incl: Trees Revisited 1970, Hallelujahs 1971, Scherzos 1970 (premiered Proms Royal Albert Hall 1976), 5 Blake Songs, Praeludiana 1973 (premiered Royal Festival Hall), Green and Pleasant 1973 (BBC Monarchy 1000 Prize), Veni Sancte Spiritus 1974, In Ecclesiis 1976, Piano Concerto 1977, Cantica 1978 (cmmnd Highgate Choral Soc), Venus Fly Trap 1979 (cmmnd London Sinfonietta), Little Symphony 1982 (cmmnd Haydn Society), Lamentations of Jeremiah 1984, Piano Sonata 1986 (cmmnd Dartington Int Summer Sch), Magnificat 1987 (cmmnd Highgate Choral Soc), Confitebor 1989, In Memoriam 1989, Tribute I and II 1989 and 1990, Requies 1991, Missa Brevis 1991 (cmmnd St Paul's Cathedral), Three Motets 1992, Songs of Innocence 1993 (cmmnd Finchley Children's Music Gp), Ecce Lignum Crucis 1993, Holy Communion Service in E 1993 (cmmnd St John the Baptist, Chipping Barnet), Ebony and Ivory 1994, A Bit of a Blow 1996, Magnificat and Nunc Dimittis The St Paul's Service 1996 (tercentenary celebrations cmmnd St Paul's Cathedral), Tribute for Jo Klein 1997, Songs of Experience 1998 (cmmnd Finchley Children's Music Gp), Burlesque 2000, A Birthday Suite for John 2002, Viola Suite 2004, Tribute for JMC 2004, Bagatelles Diverses 2005, God's Love Come Among Us 2005, Three For Two 2007, Swing's the Thing 2007, Three Sacred Pieces 2007, Three Lenten Motets 2007, Missa Brevis Exoniensis (premiered Exeter Cathedral) 2009, What Child Is This 2009, Six Bagatelles 2011, Safe Where I Cannot Lie Yet (premiered Buckfast Abbey) 2012, Home and Dry 2013, A Hymn to God the Father (cmmnd for New Music Wells) 2014, Beautiful Soup 2016, Psalm 23 2016; anthems and canticles for New Coll Oxford, Canterbury Cathedral and St Paul's Cathedral, children's songs, piano and instrumental music; PRS, MCPS; *Style—* Brian Chapple, Esq; ✉ c/o Chester Novello, 14–15 Berners Street, London W1T 3LJ

CHAPPLE, Glen; *b* 23 January 1974; *Career* professional cricketer; Lancashire CCC 1992– (capt 2008–); England: memb U18 team to Canada 1991, U19 tour to NZ 1991, Pakistan 1992 and India 1993, A tour to India 1995, 52 Twenty20 appearances; *Recreations* golf, football (Liverpool supporter); *Style—* Glen Chapple, Esq; ✉ c/o Lancashire CCC, Old Trafford, Manchester M16 0PX (☎ 0161 848 7021)

CHAPPLE, Prof (Alfred) John Victor; s of Alfred Edward Chapple (d 1942), and Frances Lilian, *née* Taylor (d 1972); *b* 25 April 1928; *Educ* St Boniface's Coll Plymouth, UCL (BA, MA); *m* 6 Aug 1955, Kathleen, da of James Sheridan Bolton (d 1979); 4 s (Andrew b 1958, John b 1960, James b 1964, Christopher b 1967), 1 da (Clare b 1962); *Career* Nat Serv RA 1946–49: 2 Lt 1947, short serv cmmn as Lt; res asst Yale Univ 1955–58, asst Univ of Aberdeen 1958–59, asst lectr, lectr then sr lectr Univ of Manchester 1959–71 (hon prof of English 1998–2000), prof of English Univ of Hull 1971–92 (dean of Arts 1980–82, pro-vice-chllr 1985–88), visiting fell Corpus Christi Coll Cambridge 1992; memb Int Assoc of Profs of English 1986–, memb Gaskell Soc 1975– (chm 1990–97, pres 1998–2005, patron 2013–); *Books* The Letters of Mrs Gaskell (ed with Arthur Pollard, 1966, new issue 1997), Documentary and Imaginative Literature 1880–1920 (1970), Elizabeth Gaskell: A Portrait In Letters (1980, new issue 2007), Science and Literature in the Nineteenth Century (1986), Private Voices: the Diaries of Elizabeth Gaskell and Sophia Holland (ed with Anita Wilson, 1996), Elizabeth Gaskell: the Early Years (1997), Further Letters of Mrs Gaskell (ed with Alan Shelston, 2000, new issue 2003), S Johnson, Lives of the Poets (contrib, 2010); *Recreations* music, wine, gardening, calligraphy; *Style—* Prof John Chapple; ✉ 8 Lomax Close, Lichfield (☎ 01543 251964, e-mail javckc@dsl.pipex.com)

CHAPPLE, His Hon Judge Roger Graham; s of Robert William Chapple (d 1997), and Elsie Mary, *née* Hubbard (d 1995); *b* 28 August 1951, London; *Educ* Univ of Leeds (LLB), Inns of Court Sch of Law; *Career* called to the Bar Gray's Inn 1974; barr specialising in gen common law Francis Taylor Bldg Temple 1974–94, dep judge advocate 1994–95, asst judge advocate gen 1995–2004, recorder 2000–04 (asst recorder 1999–2000), circuit judge (South Eastern Circuit) 2004–, sr circuit judge 2007–, resident judge Middx Guildhall Crown Court 2005–07, resident judge Inner London Crown Court 2007–, bencher Gray's Inn 2009–; sr judge Sovereign Base Areas Court Cyprus 2007–; memb Worshipful Co of Musicians; *Recreations* all types of music (especially opera), travel; *Style—* His Hon Judge Chapple; ✉ c/o Judicial Secretariat for the London & South East Regions, First Avenue House, 42–49 High Holborn, London WC1V 6WP (e-mail hhjchapple@gmail.com)

CHAPPLE, Sean; s of Brian Edward William John Chapple, and Valerie Ann, *née* Giles; *b* 10 October 1967, Isleworth, Middx; *Educ* Harwich Secdy Comp; *Career* RM 1984–2008 (completed Commando trg 1985, received Offr Cmm 2002, Capt RM); dir Team Development and Training Ltd 2007–10, co-fndr and chief operating offr Scimitar Security Ltd 2010–; maritime security advs Kuwait Oil Sector 2010–; explorer: ldr Erukenya Expdn 1987 (lightweight mountaineering climb Mt Kenya), equipment mangr Karakoram Expdn 1991 (lightweight mountaineering climb Yazghill Sar, Pakistan), expdn ldr Grand Canyon Ironman Challenge 1992 (270 mile cycle over San Francisco mountains, 40 mile trek through Grand Canyon, 106 mile run through Painted Desert, 4 mile swim at Flagstaff), ldr Northern Trail Expdn 1994 (ski crossing of Rondane NP Norway), ldr Icelandic 500 Expdn 1995 (first ski crossing of Iceland from W to E), ldr Frozen Fields expdn 1996 (ski expdn to Beechy Is to pay tribute to last resting place of RM William Braine of the ill-fated 1875 Franklin Expdn), ldr Polar Connection Expdn 1997, ldr Polar North Expdn 1998 (first RM attempt to ski unaided to geographical N Pole), ldr Polar Quest Expdn 2006–07 (ski to magnetic N Pole and geographical S Pole unsupported), first military expdn to S Pole since Capt Scott; Keeling Trophy for outstanding achievements for expdn ldrship and planning; FRGS, FInstLM, MCGI; *Publications* No Ordinary Tourist (1996), Polar Quest (2007), High Performance Teams (2009); *Recreations* hill walking, Polar history, genealogy, painting; *Style—* Sean Chapple, Esq; ✉ e-mail sean@seanchapple.co.uk, website www.seanchapple.co.uk

CHAPPLE-HYAM, Peter William; s of William Henry Chapple-Hyam, of Itchington, Warwicks, and Mary Constance, *née* Mann; *b* 2 April 1963; *Educ* Princethorpe Coll; *m* 24 June 1990, Jane Fiona, da of Andrew Sharpe Peacock; *Career* racehorse trainer; Young Trainer of the Year 1991 and 1992; trained winner of: The Derby, 2,000 Guineas and Irish 2000 Guineas (all 1992), Italian Derby 1993, Irish 2000 Guineas 1994 and 1995, Hong King Cup 2002 (based in Hong Kong 1999–2003); *Recreations* soccer, cricket, tennis; *Style—* Peter Chapple-Hyam, Esq; ✉ website www.peterchapplehyam.com

CHARAP, Emeritus Prof John Michael; s of Samuel Lewis Charap (d 1995), and Irene, *née* Shaw (d 1984); *b* 1 January 1935; *Educ* City of London Sch, Trinity Coll Cambridge (MA, PhD); *m* 11 June 1961, Ellen Elfrieda (d 2013), da of Eric Kuhn (d 1986); 1 s (David b 1965); *Career* res assoc: Univ of Chicago 1959–60, Univ of Calif Berkeley 1960–62; memb Inst for Advanced Study Princeton 1962–63, lectr in physics Imperial Coll London 1964–65 (sr scientific offr 1963–64); Queen Mary Univ of London: reader in theoretical physics 1965–78, prof of theoretical physics 1978– (now emeritus), head Dept of Physics 1980–85, dean Faculty of Science 1982–85, pro princ 1987–89, vice-princ 1989–90; Univ of London: chm Bd of Studies in Physics 1976–80, memb Senate 1981–94, memb Ct 1989–94, memb Cncl 1994–2000; memb: American Physical Soc 1960, European Physical Soc 1980; FInstP 1979, CPhys 1988; *Publications* Explaining the Universe: The New Age of Physics (2002), Covariant Electrodynamics: A Concise Guide (2011); *Recreations* walking, talking; *Clubs* Chelsea Arts; *Style—* Emeritus Prof John Charap; ✉ e-mail j.m.charap@gmail.com

CHARING, Rabbi Douglas Stephen; *b* 1945, London; *Educ* Leo Baeck Coll London; *m* Oct 1972, Eve; 1 s (Benjamin); *Career* ordained rabbi 1970; former: rabbi to progressive synagogues in N and W London and Leeds, visiting rabbi Bristol & The West Progressive Synagogue, pt/t dir Jewish Information Serv, pt/t lectr Theol and Religious Studies Dept Univ of Leeds and Gtr Manchester Police Coll, specialist advsr Theol and Religious Studies Bd CNAA, memb Planning Ctee Centre for the Study of Judaism and Jewish/Christian Rels, pt/t dir Concord Multi-Faith Resources Centre, visiting rabbi Sha'arei Shalom Synagogue Manchester, conslt Int Consultancy on Religion, Educn and Culture; currently: dir Jewish Educn Bureau (fndr), tutor Greenwich Univ, specialist assessor Higher Educn Funding Cncl for Wales, visiting rabbi Bradford Synagogue, accredited lectr Potchefstroom Univ of Christian Higher Educn SA, hon sec Leeds Living Heritage Centre, visiting lectr Northern Ordination Coll; memb: Inter-European Cmmn on Church and Sch, Cncl of Christians and Jews, World Congress of Faiths, Inter-Faith Network, Cncl of Reform and Liberal Rabbis, Advsy Ctee Nat Community Folktale Centre, Christian-Jewish Consultation of the United Reformed Church, Bd of Dirs Anne Frank Educnl Tst UK, Exec Cncl for Religious Educn, Professional Cncl for Religious Educn, Assoc of Religious Educn Insprs, Advsr & Conslts (AREIAC), Soc for Storytelling, Network of Biblical Storytellers, fell Leo Baeck Coll 2008; *Publications* incl: Comparative Religions (jtly, 1982, reprinted 1984 and 1991, renamed as Six World Faiths, 1996), The Jewish World (1983, reprinted 1985, 1992, 1995 and 1996), Visiting a Synagogue (1984, reprinted 1988), The Torah (1993), Religion in Leeds (contrib, 1994), Renewing the Vision (contrib, 1996), Judaism (2003), Great Reform Lives (contrib, 2010); writer of Rabbinic stories for children on BBC TV; *Style—* Rabbi Douglas Charing; ✉ 8 Westcombe Avenue, Leeds LS8 2BS (☎ 0345 567 4070, fax 0844 873 1046, e-mail rabbi@jewisheducationbureau.co.uk)

CHARING CROSS, Archdeacon of; *see:* Jacob, Ven Dr William Mungo

CHARKIN, Richard Denis Paul; s of Frank Charkin (d 1963), and Mabel Doreen, *née* Rosen (d 2005); *b* 17 June 1949; *Educ* Haileybury and ISC, Trinity Coll Cambridge (MA), Harvard Business Sch; *m* 7 Aug 1972, Susan Mary, da of Sidney William Poole; 2 da (Emily b 1973, Boo b 1977), 1 s (Toby b 1975); *Career* Oxford University Press: med ed 1974–76, head of Sci and Med Div 1976–80, head of Reference Div 1980–84, md Academic Div 1984–88; exec dir Octopus Publishing Group 1988–; chief exec: Reed Consumer Books 1990–94, Reed International Books 1994–95 (formerly with Reed Elsevier (UK) Ltd), Current Science Group 1995–96, Macmillan Ltd 1997–2007; exec dir Bloomsbury plc 2007–; pres Publishers Assoc 2004–05, formerly Publishers Assoc rep Fedn of European Publishers, currently pres Int Publishers Assoc, pres The Book Soc 2015–; non-exec dir Inst of Physics Publishing 2009–; visiting prof Univ of the Arts London; tstee Common Purpose Charitable Tst; *Publications* Charkin Blog: The Archive (2008), The Lowdown: top tips for wannabe CEOs (2009); *Recreations* cricket, music, art; *Clubs* Chelsea Arts; *Style—* Richard Charkin, Esq; ✉ Bloomsbury Publishing plc, 50 Bedford Square, London WC1B 3DP

CHARLES, Caroline (Mrs Malcolm Valentine); OBE (2002); *b* 18 May 1942; *Educ* Sacred Heart Convent Woldingham, Swindon Coll of Art; *m* 8 Jan 1966, Malcolm Valentine; 2 c (Kate, Alex); *Career* fashion designer; apprentice to Michael Sherard British Couture Curzon St London 1960, worked for Mary Quant London 1961, estab Caroline Charles London 1963; exhibitor V&A Summer Exhbn 1989; memb British Colour & Textile Group; Yardley Young Designer Award NY 1964, Evening Standard Design Award 1978; *Books* Weekend Wardrobe, 50 Years in Fashion; *Recreations* travel, theatre, tennis; *Style—* Ms Caroline Charles, OBE; ✉ 56–57 Beauchamp Place, London SW3 1NY (☎ 020 7225 3197, fax 020 7589 4029, website www.carolinecharles.co.uk)

CHARLES, Jonathan; s of Henry Simon Charles, of Nottingham, and Diane Betty, *née* Lewis; *b* 9 July 1964; *Educ* Nottingham Boys' HS, Oriel Coll Oxford; *Career* editorial trainee ITN 1986–87; BBC: joined as reporter 1987, New York corr 1988, Europe reporter Paris 1989–90, Europe business corr Brussels 1990–94, Europe corr Frankfurt 1995, presenter BBC World News until 2011, dir of comms European Bank for Reconstruction and Devpt 2011–; *Recreations* music, skiing, art, literature, films, cookery; *Clubs* Frontline, BAFTA; *Style—* Jonathan Charles, Esq

CHARLES, Paul; *Educ* Nottingham HS for Boys, Manchester Met Univ; *Career* presenter and reporter BBC News (TV and radio) 1990–2000, head of communications Misys plc 2000–03, dir of communications Eurostar 2003–06, dir of communications Virgin Atlantic 2006–09, chief operating offr Lewis PR 2010–11, co-fndr and ceo Perowne Charles Communications 2011–16, fndr and CEO the PC Agency 2016–; PR Week PR Professional of the Year 2004, listed in every PR Week PowerBook 2006–16, listed in London Evening Standard's Most Influential 1000 People 2011 and 2012; *Clubs* Arts, Dover Street, Electric House; *Style—* Paul Charles, Esq; ✉ The PC Agency, 99c Talbot Road, London W11 2AT (☎ 020 7768 0001, e-mail pc@pc.agency, website www.pc.agency, Twitter @ppaulcharles)

CHARLES, Peter Dominic; MBE (2013); s of Kenneth Charles (d 1970), of Liverpool, and Julia, *née* Norton (d 1975); *b* 18 January 1960; *Career* professional show jumper; winner individual Grand Prix Royal Int Horse Show 1986, memb World Cup winning team Brussels 1986, winner Individual Grand Prix World Cup Meeting Holland 1987 and 1990; winner: Irish Jumping Derby 1993, British Grand Prix Olympia 1993, British Horse Master Championship Royal Windsor 1994, indoor Grand Prix Glasgow 1994, Grand Prix France 1995, Gold medal (individual jumping) European Championships 1995, Gold medal (team jumping) European Championships 2001, Gold medal (team jumping) Olympic Games 2012 (representing GB); memb winning Nations Cup Team: Belgium, Ireland and Canada 1988, Switzerland, Germany and Canada 1989, Germany 1990, Ireland 1992, France 1994, Germany, Canada and Ireland 1995; competed for Eire Barcelona Olympics 1992 and World Championships Holland 1994; *Style—* Peter Charles, Esq, MBE; ✉ c/o British Show Jumping Association, British Equestrian Centre, Stoneleigh Park, Kenilworth, Warwickshire CV8 2LR (☎ 024 76696516)

CHARLES, Susan Jane; da of Alfred Norman Harris, of Solihull, and Esme Joyce, *née* Skey; *b* 2 January 1959; *Educ* Tudor Grange Girls' GS, Solihull Sixth Form Coll, St Catherine's Coll Oxford (MA, Swimming half blue), Cranfield Sch of Management (PR Week scholar, MBA), Chartered Inst of Marketing (DipM); *m* 1 Sept 1992, Prof Ian George Charles; *Career* pre-doctoral res asst Univ of Leicester 1981–84 (res demonstrator 1984–85); Kempsters Communications Gp: tech conslt 1984–85, PR tech writer 1985, PR account exec 1985–87, PR dir 1987–89, gp business dir 1989–91; md and chm De Facto Consultants Ltd 1991–98 (managed PR launch of Dolly the sheep), princ conslt Charles Consultants 1991–2004, chief exec HCC De Facto Gp plc 1997–2001, fndr and ceo Northbank Communications Ltd 2002–07, managing ptnr Life Sciences Instinctif Ptnrs (formerly College Hill Assocs) Ltd 2007–, dir Instinctif Ptnrs (Australia) Pty Ltd 2012–; non-exec chm Bang Communications Ltd 1991–99; dir: Genus Communications Ltd 1994–97, BioScape Ltd 1994–97, Int Career Alternatives for Scientists 2001–03, Axia Therapeutics Ltd 2002–04; tstee Jane Goodall Inst (UK) 2009–11; MCIM, MCIPR; *Style—* Mrs Susan Charles

CHARLES, Hon Mr Justice; Sir (Arthur) William Hessin Charles; kt (1998); s of Arthur Attwood Sinclair Charles (d 2001), and Dr May Davies Charles, *née* Westerman (d 2005), of Frith Common, Worcs; *b* 25 March 1948; *Educ* Malvern Coll, Christ's Coll Cambridge (MA); *m* 22 June 1974, Lydia Margaret, da of John Barlow Ainscow, of Ambleside, Cumbria; 1 s (Simon b 1980), 1 da (Florence b 1983); *Career* called to the Bar Lincoln's Inn 1971; jr counsel to the Crown Chancery 1986–89, first jr counsel to the Treasy in Chancery matters 1989–98, judge of the High Court of Justice 1998–, pres Upper Tbnl (Admin Appeals Chamber) 2012–, vice-pres Ct of Protection 2014–; *Recreations* golf; *Clubs* Hawks' (Cambridge), Denham Golf; *Style—* The Hon Mr Justice Charles; ✉ c/o Royal Courts of Justice, The Strand, London WC2A 2LL

CHARLESWORTH, Anita; *Educ* Univ of Westminster (BA), Univ of York (MSc); *Career* Dept of Health 1990–95, SmithKline Beecham 1995–98, HM Treasy 1998–2007, chief analyst Dept for Culture, Media and Sport 2008–10, chief economist Nuffield Tst 2010–; non-exec dir Islington PCT; tstee Tommy's; *Style—* Mrs Anita Charlesworth

CHARLESWORTH, David Anthony; s of David Harold Charlesworth, MBE (d 1970), and Jessie Vilma, *née* Waldron (d 1970); *b* 19 July 1936; *Educ* Haileybury and ISC; *m* 1970 (m dis 1975), Carol Ann, *née* Green; partner Charles David Micklewright FRSA (civil partnership, 2005); *Career* Capt RAPC; dir and sec: Grandring Ltd 1964–72, Sika Contracts Group of Cos 1965–76, Surban Trading Co Ltd 1968–; dir: SGB Group 1973–76, Johnson and Avon Ltd 1977–82, Michael Ashby Fine Art Ltd 1978–84, NHM Agency Holdings Ltd 1982–91, Michael Watson (Management) Ltd 1983–87, P J Dewey (Agencies) Co 1983–91, Shaftesbury Mews Co Ltd 1984–97 and 2006–, Nelson Hurst & Marsh Agencies Ltd 1985–90, Jardine (Lloyd's Agencies) 1990–91, Rimmer Properties Limited 1990–92, Glenrand Marsh Ltd 1992–95, Andrew Wallas & Marsh Ltd 1994–98; underwriting memb of Lloyd's 1975–2002; memb Eurotunnel Shareholder Ctee 2002–06; tstee Mickworth Charitable Tst 2004–; elected hon life fell IOD 2013; *Recreations* listening to Mozart, reading biographies, genealogy, symmetry; *Clubs* IOD; *Style—* David Charlesworth, Esq; ✉ 1 Shaftesbury Mews, London W8 6QR (☎ 020 7937 3550)

CHARLTON, (Richard Wingate) Edward; s of Col Wingate Charlton, OBE, DL, of Great Canfield Park, Takeley, Essex, and Angela Margot, *née* Windle; *b* 3 May 1948; *Educ* Eton, Univ of Neuchâtel; *m* 1 Feb 1979, Claudine Marie Germaine, da of Maître Hubert Maringe (d 1988), of Champlin, Premery, Nievre, France; 1 s (Andrew b 9 Nov 1981), 2 da (Emma b 29 Sept 1985, Jessica b 28 April 1989); *Career* Frere Cholmeley & Co Slrs 1968–73, Swales & Co Slrs 1974–76, Hambros Bank 1977–81, exec dir Banque Paribas London 1981–88, md Banque Internationale à Luxembourg London 1988–2002, dir HSBC Private Bank 2005–10, sr advsr Citibank Int 2010–; non-exec dir Williams; various co directorships; slr of the Supreme Court 1976; Freeman City of London, memb Ct of Assts Worshipful Co of Merchant Taylors; MInstD; *Recreations* various active sports, cinema and family pursuits; *Clubs* White's, Turf, City of London; *Style—* Edward Charlton, Esq

CHARLTON, (William Wingate) Hugo; s of Lt Col D R W G Collins-Charlton, OBE, MBE, DL, and Angela Margot, *née* Windle; *b* 23 September 1951; *Educ* Eton, Univ of York (BA); *m* 1, 21 Oct 1978 (m dis 1984); m 2, 21 July 1994, Jane Louise, da of Donald Frank Sidnell; 2 da (Lavinia Sophie b 1 May 1997, Isabella Alice b 16 June 1999); *Career* called to the Bar Gray's Inn 1978; Distillers Co 1977–84, in practice as barrister 1986–; Inns of Court and City Yeomanry 1987–94; Green Pty: law offr 1991–97, home affairs spokesman 1998–2005, chair 2003–05; memb Criminal Bar Assoc, memb Barreau Pénal International, advsr Environmental Law Fndn, memb Panel Special Tbnl for Lebanon; documentary films as prodr and presenter incl: Bingol Ballot Bazaar (2010), The Song of the Quetzal (2013); chair of tstees Widows for Peace through Democracy; Freeman City of London, Liveryman Worshipful Co of Merchant Taylors; *Publications* A Guide to Council Tax Appeals; *Recreations* riding, skiing, scuba, hermetism; *Clubs* Bosham Sailing; *Style—* Hugo Charlton, Esq; ✉ 1 Gray's Inn Square, London WC1R 5AA (☎ 020 7405 0001, fax 020 7405 0002, e-mail hugo@gn.apc.org)

CHARLTON, Louise; da of John Charlton, and Patricia Mary Crawford, *née* Hulme; *b* 25 May 1960; *m* 1985, Andrew, s of David Durant; 2 s (Sam b 10 Sept 1991, Jack b 14 Feb 1996), 1 da (Olivia b 16 Aug 1993); *Career* Broadstreet Associates 1984–87, founding ptnr Brunswick Group LLP 1987– (gp sr ptnr 2004–); non-exec dir RPS Gp; tstee Nat History Museum; *Recreations* family; *Style—* Ms Louise Charlton; ✉ Brunswick Group Ltd, 15–17 Lincoln's Inn Fields, London WC2A 3ED (☎ 020 7404 5959)

CHARLTON, Mervyn; s of Rowland Charlton (d 1986), and Madge Louise, *née* Eaton; *b* 2 July 1945; *Educ* Loughton Coll of FE (Art Fndn Course), Nottingham Art Coll (BA); *m* 1982, Ann, da of John James Hewitson; 1 s (Conrad Alexander b 1 March 1986); *Career* artist-in-residence: Holly Head Jr Sch (South Hill Park Artist in Schs Project) 1981, Guildford House 1983, Hammond Middle Sch Surrey (in conjunction with SE Arts) 1994, Windlesham Village Infant Sch (sponsored by SE Arts)1996, Long Cross Sch Slough 1996, ATD Fourth World Charity (workshops and exhbn) 1998–99, St Catherine's Sch Bramley 2001, BBC Big Arts Week Thames Ditton Junior Sch 2002; Gulbenkian Printmaker award 1983; *Solo Exhibitions* Moira Kelly Fine Art 1981 and 1982, Festival Gallery Bath 1983, Sally Hunter/Patrick Seale Fine Art 1985, Anne Berthoud Gallery 1988, Sally Hunter Fine Art 1989, South Hill Park Arts Centre Bracknell 1991, Boundary Art Gallery London 1992, The Economist London 1994, The Yehudi Menuhin Sch 1994, Lewis Elton Gallery Univ of Surrey Guildford 2004, Exhibit A Gallery Frome 2009, The Chapel Row Gallery Bath 2010, FSA Canary Wharf London 2011, Mott MacDonald Fleet Place London; *Group Exhibitions* incl: Metro Show (Docklands Art Gallery) 1980, London Summer Show (Whitechapel Art Gallery) 1980, Third and Fourth Nat Exhibition Tours (Tolly Cobbald) 1981 and 1983, Subjective Eye Midland Gp (Nottingham and tour) 1981–82, Leicestershire Schs Exhibition 1982, Whitechapel Open (Whitechapel Gallery) 1982, 1983 and 1984, The London Gp (Camden Arts Centre and tour) 1982, Eight in the Eighties (NY) 1983, Royal Academy Summer Exhibition 1984, Guildford House Summer Show Guildford 1984, London Group Show (RCA) 1984, Bath Festival Show 1984 and 1987, Curwen Gallery 1984, Open House (City Gallery Arts Tst Milton Keynes) 1984, Quintin Green Gallery London 1985, Side By Side (Nat Art Gallery Kuala Lumpur and Br Cncl tour) 1986, Vorpal Gallery (NY) 1987, The Circus Comes to Town (Northern Centre for Contemporary Art Sutherland and tour) 1987, Mixed Summer Show (Thumb Gallery) 1987–90, CAS Art Market (Smith's Gallery) 1990–91 and 1992, Boxes and Totems (England & Co) 1990, Anne Berthoud Gallery 1990, Ikon Gallery Group Touring Exhibition 1991, 1st Reading Arts Festival 1992, Touch of Red (Boundary Gallery London) 1992, Art for Sale (Whiteleys, in conjunction with The Guardian) 1992–93, Contemporary Art Fair London 1993, Royal Acad Summer Exhibition London 1993, The New Ashgate Gallery 1993, Interiors (Open Show Towner Art Gallery Eastbourne) 1993, Christmas Show (Boundary Gallery) 1993, East West Gallery London 1993, CAS Festival Hall London 1994, The Colour Blue Boundary Gallery London 1995, ojects of obsession (Boundary Gallery) 1996, Strange Encounters (Sally Hunter Fine Art London) 1996, Working Images (Archiutti and Cable & Wireless London), Christmas Show Boundary Gallery London 1998, Art Fair Business Design Centre Boundary Gallery 1998–2000, 50over50 (Univ of Brighton) 2006, Brian Sinfield Gallery Burford 2006, Plumbline Gallery St Ives 2006, Surrey Open Art Exhbn (The Lightbox Gallery Woking) 2008 and (Black Swan Open Arts Competition Frome) 2009, Courcoux Gallery Stockbridge 2010, Four and Twenty Artists (Rook Lane Chaple Frome) 2011, Julian Hartnell Gallery Summer Show 2012; *Work in Collections* incl: Achim Moeller Ltd, BP, Unilever, Euro Parl Luxembourg, Leics Schs, Blond Fine Art, Guildford House, Nat Art Gallery Kuala Lumpur, South East Arts, Halton Roy Productions/Howard Guard Productions, England & Co Art Gallery, Electra Management Trust Ltd, Lady Antonia Fraser, Geoffrey Robinson QC, Lady Patricia Gibberd, Tim Sayer, Nancy Balfour, Coopers & Lybrand, Boundary Gallery, The Economist Building London, John Allen, Peter Dicks, Avia Willment, Standerwick Court, Freshfields Bruckhaus Deringer, Josie Reed Chaple Row

Gallery Bath, Sir Gerald Acher, CBE, LVO and Lady Acher, FSA Canary Wharf, Patrick Hughes, Sarah Long (Long & Ryle Gallery); *Publications* subject of articles in publications incl Apollo, London Portrait, Artscribe, Arts Review and Art Monthly; *Recreations* interest in non-western belief systems and their religious expressions and in exotic art in general, walking, travel, reading; *Style*— Mervyn Charlton, Esq; ✉ 1 Rose Cottages, Downside Bridge Road, Cobham, Surrey KT11 3EJ (☎ 07830 715081, e-mail mervyncharlton@icloud.com, website www.mervyncharlton.co.uk)

CHARLTON, Michael; *b* 14 April 1965, Cardiff; *Educ* Loughborough Univ of Technol (BSc); *Career* qualified CA KPMG; chief exec Think London; ACA; *Style*— Michael Charlton, Esq

CHARLTON, Peter John; s of J V Charlton (d 2001), and S M Charlton; *b* 16 December 1955; *Educ* Royal GS Newcastle upon Tyne, UCL (LLB), Coll of Law; *m* 1980 (m dis 2008), Rosemary, *née* Markham; 2 s (Christopher b June 1983, John b Oct 1984), 1 da (Elizabeth b Aug 1987); *Career* Clifford Chance LLP (formerly Coward Chance): articled clerk 1979, corp fin ptnr 1986, managing ptnr corp London 1993, managing ptnr London region 2000–05, global head of corporate practice 2005–08, managing ptnr Asia Region 2008–; winner Ptnr of the Year The Lawyer Awards 2001; involved with numerous orgns incl London First and Br Chilean C of C; memb Law Soc 1979; *Recreations* golf, travel; *Style*— Peter Charlton, Esq; ✉ Clifford Chance, 28th Floor, Jardine House, One Connaught Place, Hong Kong (☎ 00 852 282 5888, fax 00 852 2825 8800, e-mail peter.charlton@cliffordchance.com)

CHARLTON, Philip; OBE (1987); s of late George Charlton, of Chester, and Lottie, *née* Little (d 1976); *b* 31 July 1930; *Educ* City GS Chester; *m* 27 June 1953, Jessie (d 2008), da of Joseph Boulton (d 1966), of Chester; 1 da (Margaret b 1959), 1 s (Philip John b 1962); *Career* Nat Serv RN 1947–49; gen mangr: Chester Savings Bank 1966–75, TSB Wales and Border Counties 1975–81; chief gen mangr Central Bd Trustee Savings Bank 1982–83 (dep chief gen mangr 1981–82); dir: TSB Computer Services (Wythenshawe) Ltd 1976–81, TSB Trust Co Ltd 1979–82, TSB Holdings Ltd 1982–86, TSB Group Computer Services Ltd 1981–84, Central Trustee Savings Bank 1982–86; chief gen mangr TSB England and Wales 1983–85, dir TSB England and Wales 1985–87, gp chief exec TSB Group plc 1986–89 (non-exec dep chm 1990–91), chm Philip Charlton Associates Ltd 1991–96; vice-pres Inst of Bankers 1991– (memb Cncl 1982–, dep chm 1988–89, pres 1990–91); memb Bd of Admin: Int Savings Banks Inst Geneva 1985–91 (vice-pres 1985–91), Euro Savings Bank Gp Brussels 1989–91; FCIB, CIMgt, FRSA; *Clubs* Chester City, RAC; *Style*— Philip Charlton, Esq, OBE; ✉ Apartment 48, Rowton, Boughton Hall, Filkins Lane, Boughton CH3 5BG

CHARLTON, Susannah Karen; da of Bryan Michael Charlton, and Valerie, *née* Henderson; *Educ* Fairfield GS Bristol, Sorbonne, UCL (BA), Birkbeck Coll London (Cert), Bartlett Sch of Architecture UCL (MSc); *Partner* Irene Roele (civil partnership Sept 2012); *Career* editorial asst rising to sr ed QPD (first UK paperback book club) then managing ed World Books Book Club Assocs 1982–96, publisher Telegraph Books 1997–2002, mangr guidebooks English Heritage 2002–04, publisher (books and RHS online) Royal Horticultural Soc 2004–10, conslt 2011–; dir Twentieth Century Soc 2002–08; memb Soc of Bookmen 2000; *Recreations* travel, history of art and architecture, swimming, walking, theatre, gardening, reading; *Clubs* Dining; *Style*— Ms Susannah Charlton

CHARMLEY, Prof John Denis; s of John Charmley (d 1977), and Doris, *née* Halliwell (d 1990); *b* 9 November 1955; *Educ* Rock Ferry HS, Pembroke Coll Oxford (open scholar, MA, A M P Read scholar, DPhil); *m* 1, 1977 (m dis 1992), Ann Dorothea; 3 s (Gervase Nicholas Edward, Gerard Timothy John (twins) b 8 Jan 1980, Christian Francis Robin (Kit) b 14 June 1989); m 2, 1992 (m dis 2003), Lorraine, da of K G Charles, MBE; m 3, 2004, Rachael Heap; *Career* UEA: lectr 1979–93, sr lectr 1993–96, reader in English history 1996–98, prof of modern history 1998–2016, dean Sch of History 2002–16, assoc dean of research 2003–10, head Sch of History 2003–13, assoc dean of enterprise 2005–16, head Sch of Music 2009–14, dir of employability 2013–16; visiting fell Churchill Coll Cambridge 1985, Fulbright prof Westminster Coll Fulton MO 1992–93; scriptwriter Peace In Our Time (Channel 4) 1989; chm Mid Norfolk Cons Assoc 1999–2003, pres Norfolk and Norwich Historical Assoc 2001–16, vice-chair Cons History Gp 2003–, dir Norwich Heritage and Regeneration Tst 2010–15, dir East Anglian Film Archive 2011–14, dir Centre of East Anglian Studies 2013–14, head Inst for Interdisciplinary Humanities 2013–16; election agent for Richard Bacon, MP South Norfolk 2005 and 2010; FRHistS 1986, fell Historical Assoc 2015; *Books* Duff Cooper (1986, Yorkshire Post Best First Book Prize 1986), Lord Lloyd and the Decline of the British Empire (1987), Chamberlain and the Lost Peace (1989), Churchill – The End of Glory (1993), Churchill's Grand Alliance (1995), A History of Conservative Politics 1900–1996 (1996), Splendid Isolation? (1999), The Princess and the Politicians (2005), A History of Conservative Politics since 1830 (2008); *Recreations* reading, writing letters, dining out; *Clubs* Norfolk; *Style*— Prof John Charmley; ✉ c/o Felicity Bryan, 2A North Parade, Oxford OX2 6PE (☎ 01865 513816)

CHARNLEY, William Francis; Duke of Aymer, granted by letters patent 29 Nov 2012 by HRH Prince Davit Bagrationi Mukhran Batonishvili, head of Royal House of Georgia, Marquess of Quarlton 2015, Count of Darsie 2015, Viscount Turton 2015; s of Louis Charnley (d 2001), and Pauline Mary, *née* Matthews; *b* 21 August 1960, Wigan; *Educ* Rivington and Blackrod GS, Bolton Inst of Technol (HND), Sheffield City Poly (Postgrad Dip Co Admin), Lancaster Univ (LLB), Manchester Poly (Law Soc Finals), Univ of Cambridge (MA); *m* 1999, Kathryn Patricia, da of James Mylrea, of Toronto, Canada; 1 s (Piers Augustus William b 21 Sept 1999), 1 da (Henrietta Blythe Venetia b 14 June 2001); *Heir* s, Piers; *Career* articled clerk Slater Heelis 1985–87, corp fin ptnr Booth & Co Leeds 1989–94 (slr 1987–89), corp fin ptnr Corp Dept Simmons & Simmons 1994–98, ptnr McDermott Will & Emery 1998–2007, ptnr Mayer Brown 2007–12, ptnr King & Spalding 2012–; dir C D Bramall plc 2000–04, dir Bank & Clients plc 2014–; fell Hughes Hall Cambridge 2003–; chm External Devpt Bd Lancaster Univ 2002–; hon fell Law Faculty Lancaster Univ; tstee Children's Heart Surgery Fund (charity) 1992–2001; memb Appeals Ctee Canine Partners, memb Advsy Bd Grange Park Opera; Freeman City of London; Liveryman: Worshipful Co of Drapers (Jr Warden 2010–11, Second Master Warden 2014–15, Master Warden 2015–16, Master 2016–17), Worshipful Co of Slrs, Worshipful Co of Chartered Secretaries and Administrators, Worshipful Co of Int Bankers; memb Law Soc 1987, FCIS; Knight Grand Cross of the Order of the Eagle of Georgia and the Seamless Tunic of Our Lord Jesus Christ, Knight Grand Cross of the Order of St Michael of the Wing, Hereditary Knight of the Royal Portuguese House of Bragança, Knight Commander with Plaque of the Order of the Immaculate Conception of Vila Viçosa; *Recreations* Scottish Impressionist art, keeping fit, country pursuits, music, food, wine; *Clubs* City of London, Brooks's, Pingus, Jockey Club Rooms, Pratt's, Oxford & Cambridge; *Style*— William Charnley, Esq; ✉ 31 Chapel Street, London SW1X 7DD

CHARNOCK, (Frederick) Mark Luckhoff; s of Frederick Niven Charnock, of Cape Town, South Africa, and Alta Anna, *née* Luckhoff; *b* 20 June 1945; *Educ* Diocesan Coll Cape Town, Univ of Cape Town (MB ChB); *m* 8 April 1970, Margaret Isobel, da of Frances Neale Murray, of Cape Town, South Africa; 1 da (Annabel b 1982), 1 s (Alasdair b 1984); *Career* house offr: Queen Charlotte's Hosp 1971, Samaritan Hosp 1975–76; registrar and sr registrar Bart's 1977–80; currently: conslt obstetrician and gynaecologist Radcliffe and Churchill Hosp Oxford, hon sr lectr Univ of Oxford; examiner: RCOGS, RCS, Univs of Oxford, Cambridge, and London; memb and cncllr: RCOG 1983–89, RCS; sec: Section O & G RSM 1989–90, Br Gynaecological Cancer Soc 1999–; Liveryman Worshipful Soc of Apothecaries 1989, Freeman City of London 1985; FRCS (Eng), FRCS(Ed), FRCOG; *Recreations* tennis, skiing, reading, opera, art; *Style*— Mark Charnock, Esq; ✉ Manor Farm House, Bletchingdon, Oxfordshire OX5 3DP (☎ 01869 350149)

CHARONE, Barbara; *b* Chicago, IL; *Educ* Northwestern Univ USA (BA); *Career* writer/journalist for pubns incl Sounds and Rolling Stone 1974–83, PR Warners 1983–2000, co-fndr (with Moira Bellas, *qv*) MBC (PR co) 2000– (clients incl: Madonna, REM, Russell Brand, Rod Stewart, Kasabian, Mark Ronson, Paolo Nutini, Pearl Jam, Depeche Mode, Rufus Wainwright, Stereophonics, Martha Wainwright, Olly Murs, Robert Plant, Ray Davies); MW Press Award 2006 and 2009; *Books* Keith Richards: Life as a Rolling Stone (1978); *Recreations* Chelsea FC; *Clubs* Ivy, Groucho; *Style*— Ms Barbara Charone; ✉ MBC, Warm Seas House, 23 Wellington Road, London NW8 9SL (e-mail bc@mbcpr.com)

C

CHARTRES, Rt Rev Sir Richard John Carew; KCVO (2009); *see:* London, Bishop of

CHASE, Prof Howard Allaker; s of Peter Howard Chase, and Phoebe Farrar, *née* Winn (d 2007); *b* 17 November 1954, London; *Educ* Westminster, Magdalene Coll Cambridge (exhibitioner, Bundy scholarship, Mynors Bright prize, MA, PhD), Univ of Cambridge (ScD); *m* 1, 30 Jan 1982 (m dis), Penelope Jane, *née* Lewis; 1 s (George Howard b 14 Oct 1984), 1 da (Charlotte Elizabeth Chase b 1 June 1986); m 2, 17 May 2003, Dawn Christine, *née* Leeder; *Career* with Gen Electric Co 1971–72; Univ of Cambridge: postdoctoral res asst Dept of Biochemistry 1978–81, res fell St John's Coll 1978–82, res assoc Dept of Chemical Engrg 1982–83, lectr in chemical engrg 1986–96 (asst lectr 1984–86), reader in biochemical engrg 1996–2000, head Dept of Chemical Engrg 1998–2006, prof of biochemical engrg 2000– (personal professorship), head Sch of Technol 2010–14; Magdalene Coll Cambridge: bye-fell 1977–78, fell 1984–, dir of studies in chemical engrg and lectr in natural sciences 1984–, tutor for grad students 1987–93, sr tutor 1993–96, tutor 1996–98; Dept of Chemical and Biochemical Engrg UCL: visiting prof 1991–92, hon res fell 1993–; memb Editorial Bd: Biotechnology and Bioengineering, Jl of Bioscience and Bioengineering; conslt to firms with interests in biochemical engrg; dir Enval Ltd 2006–, dir Girl on a Bike Ltd 2007–; SERC Advanced Fellowship 1983 (not taken up), Royal Soc 1983 Univ Res Fellowship 1983–84 (at Dept of Chemical Engrg Univ of Cambridge), Sir George Beilby Medal and Prize Soc of Chemical Industry, RSC and Inst of Metals 1993, BOC Environmental Award IChemE Awards 2001, Donald Medal IChemE 2010; fell Philosophical Soc Cambridge; CEng, CChem, CSci, MRSC 1987, MIBiol 1991, FIChemE 1998, FREng 2005; *Publications* author of numerous articles published in learned jls; *Recreations* food and drink, travel; *Clubs* The Pickprops (Cambridge); *Style*— Professor Howard Chase; ✉ Magdalene College, Cambridge CB3 0AG; Department of Chemical Engineering and Biotechnology, University of Cambridge, Pembroke Street, Cambridge CB2 3RA (☎ 01223 334799, fax 01223 334796, e-mail hac1000@cam.ac.uk)

CHASE, Robert Henry Armitage; s of Philip Martin Chase (d 1987), of Foxley, Norfolk, and Jean Alison, *née* Barr (d 1976); *b* 10 March 1945; *Educ* Ipswich Sch; *m* 1972, Moya, da of Dr William Jones (d 1985), of Shotley Bridge, Co Durham; 2 s (Patrick William Armitage b 1975, Thomas Martin b 1986), 1 da (Ella Kathleen b 1977); *Career* chartered accountant; Vol Serv Nigeria 1963; articled clerk Lovewell Blake & Co Norwich 1964–69, with Cooper Brothers London and Kenya 1969–76, fin dir Mackenzie (Kenya) Ltd 1976, asst md GEC Hong Kong 1982–86 (fin dir 1981–82), chief fin offr Orient Overseas (Holdings) Ltd 1986–89, dir Furness Withy & Co Ltd 1987–90, gp md and memb Ctee Automobile Assoc 1990–97, non-exec dir London Transport 1996–99, ceo Albert Abela Gp 2002–03, non-exec dir Intelligent Processing Solutions Ltd 2007–09, ptnr Quantum Capital Ptnrs 2008–, dir Smith & Williamson 2008–09, dir Footstep Hldgs Ltd 2010–, chm Stratus Transport Connections Ltd 2010–12; chm International Assoc of Financial Executives Insts 1995; Liveryman Worshipful Co of Information Technologists 1990, Freeman City of London 1991; FCA 1969, MCT 1984, FIoT 2005; *Recreations* golf, shooting, vintage automobiles; *Clubs* Hong Kong, Muthaiga; *Style*— Robert Chase, Esq; ✉ Garden Cottage, Upper Farringdon, Alton, Hampshire GU34 3DT (e-mail rhachase@gmail.com)

CHASE, Rodney Frank; CBE (2000); s of Norman Maxwell Chase, and Barbara, *née* Marshall; *b* 12 May 1943; *Educ* Univ of Liverpool (BA); *Career* BP plc: joined 1964, various posts in marketing, oil trading and shipping distribution 1964–81, dir (exploration and prodn) BP Australia 1982–85, gp treas 1986–89, ceo BP Exploration US 1989–92, an md 1992–98, chm and ceo BP America 1992–94, dep gp chief exec 1998–2003; chm Petrofac 2005–, dep chm and sr non-exec dir Tesco plc 2002–; non-exec dir: Computer Sciences Corp 2001–, Nalco Co 2005–, Tesoro Corp 2006–; sr advsr Lehman Bros 2003–; *Recreations* golf, skiing; *Style*— Rodney Chase, Esq, CBE

CHASSAY, Tchaik; s of Arthur Arcade Chassay (d 1970), and Margot Epstein; *b* 14 September 1942; *m* 1975, Melissa North; 1 s (Clancy), 1 da (Dixie); *Career* architect; year out (AA) Ram Karmi Associates Tel Aviv; Edward Cullinan Architects 1969–81 (latterly sr ptnr), fndr Tchaik Chassay Architects 1982, co-fndr (with Malcolm Last) Chassay + Last Architects 1997; co-fndr: Zanzibar Club (1975), 192 Restaurant (1982), The Groucho Club (1984); vice-pres AA 1986–; former lectr and visiting tutor: Faculty of Architecture Univ of Cambridge, Bristol and Hull Univs, Oxford and Thames Polys, AA; former external examiner Dept of Architecture and Interior Design RCA, currently external examiner Univ of Central England Birmingham; assessor Civic Tst Awards 1981 and 1983; *Recreations* travel, tennis; *Clubs* Groucho; *Style*— Mr Tchaik Chassay; ✉ Chassay + Last Architects, Berkeley Works, Berkley Grove, London NW1 8XY (☎ 020 7483 7700)

CHATAWAY, Mark Denys; s of late Rt Hon Sir Christopher Chataway, and Anna Maria, *née* Lett; *b* 21 March 1960; *Educ* Troy State Univ Alabama (BSc), NY Univ (MSc); *Partner* Chris Nial (civil partnership 2007); *Career* programme dir WRNG Atlanta USA 1980–82, exec prodr WMCA NY 1982–83, dir of communications GMHC (the AIDS Serv and Educn Fndn USA) 1983–84, vice-pres heading Med Info Div Van Vechten and Associates NY 1984–87; Hill and Knowlton (UK): dir Special Servs Div 1987–89, md Mktg Communications Div 1990, md Eurosciences Communications Div 1991–93; owner/dir Hyderus Cyf 2002–; princ Interscience Communications 1993–2000, chm Baird's Communication Mgmnt Conslts Ltd 2002–, advsr Int AIDS Vaccine Initiative 1996–, memb Scientific Advsy Gp Population Scis Div Rockefeller Fndn NY 1997–2001, sr cnsllr Edelman Health Europe 2000–03, Bd of Ambassadors Nat AIDS Tst 2001–, conslt World Vision Int 2002–, advsr Population Programme Hewlett Fndn 2003–, memb Govt of SA Review Panel on Vaccines 2007, tstee US Nat AIDS Fndn 2008–12, memb Bd Engender Health 2012–, memb Ind Advsy Bd Amplify Change 2014–; former freelance TV journalist for Turner Broadcasting/CNN (US) and TV-AM, former freelance radio assignments for BBC, Ind Radio News (UK), CBS and Capital Radio (South Africa); author of feature or news articles for various UK and US publications; memb Sardis Chapel Ynysddu; memb Chartered Inst of Journalists; *Recreations* physical fitness, languages, running, church activities; *Clubs* Frontline, Royal Over-Seas League; *Style*— Mark Chataway, Esq; ✉ Baird's Communication Management Consultants Ltd, 34 Heol Maindee, Cwmfelinfach, Ynysddu, Casnewydd NP11 7HR (☎ 01495 200321, e-mail mark.chataway@bairdsmc.com, Twitter @markcha)

CHATER, Prof Keith Frederick; s of Frederick Ernest Chater (d 1987), and Marjorie Inez, *née* Palmer (d 2009); *b* 23 April 1944; *Educ* Trinity Sch of John Whitgift, Univ of Birmingham (BSc, PhD); *m* 1966, Jean, da of Frederick Arthur Wallbridge (d 2005), and Ellen, *née* Bennett (d 1998); 1 da (Alison Clare b 23 April 1970), 3 s (Simon Frederick b 24 Sept 1972, Julian David b 17 July 1978, Timothy Felix b 8 Aug 1980); *Career* John

Innes Centre (formerly John Innes Inst): scientist 1969–, dep head 1989–98, head Genetics Dept 1998–2001, head Molecular Microbiology Dept 2001–04, emeritus fell 2004–; hon prof: UEA 1988, Chinese Acad of Sciences Inst of Microbiology 1998, Huazhong Agric Univ 2000, Newcastle Univ 2006; Fulbright scholar Harvard Univ 1983, Fred Griffith Review Lecture (Soc for Gen Microbiology) 1997, Leeuwenhoek Lecture (Royal Soc) 2005; memb: Soc for Gen Microbiology 1975, CND, Norfolk and Norwich Naturalists Assoc, Norfolk Contemporary Art Soc, Friends of the Royal Academy, Butterfly Conservation; FRS 1995; *Books* Genetic Manipulation of Streptomyces (one of 10 co-authors, 1985), Genetics of Bacterial Diversity (jt ed with Prof Sir D A Hopwood, *qv*, 1989), Practical Streptomyces Genetics (one of five co-authors, 2000); *Recreations* bird-watching, art, gardening, cooking; *Style—* Prof Keith Chater, FRS; ✉ 6 Coach House Court, Norwich NR4 7QR (☎ 01603 506145); John Innes Centre, Norwich Research Park, Colney, Norwich NR4 7UH (☎ 01603 450297, fax 01603 450045, e-mail keith.chater@jic.ac.uk)

CHATER, Stephen Paul; s of John Charles Chater, of Byfleet, Surrey, and Patricia Norby, *née* Oakes; *b* 2 March 1956; *Educ* Hartlepool GS, ChCh Oxford (MA); *m* 10 Sept 1988, Susan Frances Margaret, da of late Charles Harborne Stuart, of Combe, Oxon; 1 s (Anthony Charles Thomas b 10 Aug 1996); *Career* slr; ptnr: Allen & Overy 1979–2003, Addleshaw Goddard 2003–10, Postlethwaite Slrs 2011–; memb: Law Soc, Soc of Genealogists, Durham CCC, Surrey CCC; *Recreations* music, genealogy, cricket; *Clubs* Reform; *Style—* Stephen Chater, Esq; ✉ Postlethwaite Solicitors Ltd, 9 Staple Inn, London WC1V 7QH (☎ 020 3818 9420)

CHATTERJEE, Mira; da of Dr Haradlan Chatterjee (Capt IMS/IAMC SEAC, Burma Star), of Chigwell, Essex, and Kamala, *née* Banerjee; *b* 19 April 1948; *Educ* City of London Sch for Girls; *m* 19 April 1980, Dr Gautam Chaudhuri, s of Dr Punendu Chandhuri, of Calcutta; 1 da (Sarada b 28 Jan 1981); *Career* called to the Bar Middle Temple 1973, in practice SE circuit; memb Guild of Scholars; FRSA; *Recreations* reading, philosophy; *Style—* Miss Mira Chatterjee; ✉ Maya Cottage, 7 Chase Lane, Chigwell, Essex IG7 6JW

CHATTERTON DICKSON, Robert Maurice French; s of Capt W W F Chatterton Dickson, RN, and Judy, *née* French; *b* 1 February 1962; *Educ* Wellington, Magdalene Coll Cambridge (exhibitioner); *m* 1995, Teresa Bargielska Albor; 2 da, 1 step da, 1 step s; *Career* diplomat; former investment analyst and portfolio mangr Morgan Grenfell Asset Management Ltd, entered HM Dip Serv 1990, Security Policy Dept FCO 1990–91, second sec (Chancery and info) Manila 1991–94, SE Asian Dept FCO 1994–95, UN Dept FCO 1995–96, first sec (press and public affrs) Washington 1997–98, private sec to HM Ambass Washington 1998–2000, Security Policy Dept FCO 2000–03, Iraq Policy Unit FCO 2003, ambass to Macedonia 2004–07, jt head CounterTerrorism Dept FCO 2007–10, HM consul gen Chicago 2010–13, dep ambass Kabul 2013–; *Recreations* history, sailing, fresh air; *Clubs* Bosham Sailing; *Style—* Robert Chatterton Dickson, Esq; ✉ c/o Foreign & Commonwealth Office, King Charles Street, London SW1A 2AH

CHATTINGTON, Barry John; s of John William Chattington (d 1967), of Kent, and Rose Amelia, *née* Darlington; *b* 24 April 1947; *Educ* Dartford Tech High Sch; *Career* film ed 1963–66, film dir 1972–; md: Goldcrest Facilities Ltd 1988, Elstree Studios, Roger Cherrill Ltd, Cherry Video Ltd 1991; chm: Renaissance Productions Ltd, Money Spark Ltd; works incl: numerous long and short films for Paul McCartney, Pink Floyd and others, drama series for US TV, major documentary for Kuwait TV, charity films with the Prince of Wales and the Princess Royal; memb Br Kinematograph Sound & TV Soc 1963; chm: Directors' Guild of GB 1985–86, Producers' and Directors' Section ACTT 1985–86; Br delegate on Federation Européene des Industries Techniques de l'Image et du Son; *Awards* 4 Golden Halos from S Calif Motion Picture Cncl, Silver award NY Int Film and TV Festival 1982, numerous D&AD commendations, nomination Best Design BAFTA Interactive 1999; *Publications* David Lean: An Intimate Portrait (2001); *Clubs* Groucho, Variety, Reform, Chelsea Arts; *Style—* Barry Chattington, Esq; ✉ mobile 07831 570516, e-mail barry_chattington@hotmail.com

CHATTO, Lady Sarah Frances Elizabeth; *see: Royal Family Section; née* Armstrong-Jones

CHAUDHURI, Amit Prakash; s of Nages Chandra Chaudhuri, and Bijoya, *née* Nandi Majumdar; *b* 15 May 1962; *Educ* Cathedral and John Connon Sch Bombay, UCL (BA), Balliol Coll Oxford (Dervorguilla scholar, DPhil); *m* 12 Dec 1991, Rosinka Shubhasree, da of Shiva Ranjan Khastgir; *Career* writer; Harper-Wood studentship for English poetry and literature St John's Coll Cambridge 1992–93, Creative Arts fell Wolfson Coll Oxford 1992–95, Leverhulme special research fell Faculty of English Univ of Cambridge 1997–99, prof of contemporary literature Univ of E Anglia 2006–; fiction and poetry have appeared in London Review of Books, The Observer, London Magazine and Oxford Poetry; contrib articles and reviews to TLS, London Review of Books, The Guardian, The Observer, The Spectator, Vogue, The New Yorker, Granta and other jls; bursary Kathleen Blundell Trust; Arts Cncl Writers Award 1994; trained singer N Indian classical tradition (released albums on HMV 1992 and 1994); FRSL 2009; *Books* A Strange and Sublime Address (1991, Betty Trask Award Soc of Authors, runner-up Guardian Fiction Award, Cwlth Writer's Prize for Best First Book (Eurasia)), Noon in Calcutta (contrib, anthology, 1992), New Writing 2 (contrib, British Cncl anthology, eds Malcolm Bradbury and Andrew Motion, 1993), Afternoon Raag (1993, Encore Award Soc of Authors 1994, Southern Arts Lit Prize 1994, runner-up Guardian Fiction Award 1993), Vintage Book of Indian Writing: 1947–97 (ed with Salman Rushdie and Elizabeth West, 1997), Freedom Song (1998), Freedom Song: Three Novels (1999, Los Angeles Times Book Award for Fiction 2000), A New World (2000, Sahitya Akademi Award Govt of India 2002), Picador Book of Modern Indian Literature (ed, 2001), Real Time (short stories, 2002), D H Lawrence and Difference (2003), The Immortals (2009), Clearing a Space (essays, 2008), On Tagore: Reading the Poet Today (2010, W Bengal Govt's Rabindra Puraskar); *Style—* Amit Chaudhuri, Esq; ✉ c/o Peter Straus, Rogers, Coleridge and White Ltd, 20 Powis Mews, London W11 1JN (website www.amitchaudhuri.com, Twitter @amitchaudhuri)

CHEAL, (Martin) Jonathan (Cedric); s of Wilfrid Cheal (d 1987), and Barbara, *née* Ledgard (d 2010); *b* 30 June 1950, Crawley, W Sussex; *Educ* Gt Walstead Sch Lindfield, St Lawrence Coll Ramsgate, L'École des Roches Verneuil, Coll of Law Chester and Guildford; *m* 11 July 1986, Miriam Diana, da of Maj W P Mead Royal Irish Fusiliers; 2 da (Diana Juliet b 28 June 1988, Hermione Claudia b 20 June 1990), 1 s (Henry Hugh Ogden b 2 July 1993); *Career* admitted slr 1976; slr specialising in agricultural property with particular interest in rights of way cases; slr Hong Kong 1976–82, legal advsr CLA 1983–87, ptnr and head of agriculture Thrings Slrs 1987–2010, Mogers Drewett LLP (formerly Dyne Drewett Slrs) 2010–; memb Ctee CLA, currently pres Somerset CLA; memb: Prayer Book Soc, Royal Soc of St George, Inst of Public Rights of Way and Access Mgmnt; memb: Agric Law Assoc, Law Soc; *Books* as Pelham Witherspoon: The Drink-Spotty Book (1984), The High-Spotty Book (1985); *Recreations* stage, books, music, topography, military history, cricket; *Style—* Jonathan Cheal, Esq; ✉ Mogers Drewett LLP, Bishopbrook House, Cathedral Avenue, Wells, Somerset BA5 1FD (☎ 01749 342323, fax 01749 345016, e-mail jcheal@md-solicitors.co.uk)

CHEESMAN, Dr Clive Edwin Alexander; s of Wilfrid Henry Cheesman (d 1994), and Elizabeth Amelia, *née* Hughes (d 1993); *b* 21 February 1968, London; *Educ* Latymer Upper Sch, Oriel Coll Oxford (MA), Scuola Superiore di Studi Storici Università di San Marino (PhD), City Univ (Dip Law); *m* 8 April 2002, Roberta, *née* Suzzi Valli; *Career* called to the Bar Middle Temple 1996 (Harmsworth maj exhibitioner and Astbury scholar); special asst and curator Dept of Coins and Medals Br Museum 1990–2000, Rouge Dragon Pursuivant Coll of Arms 1998–, lectr in ancient history Birkbeck Coll London 2002–03; jt ed The Coat of Arms 2004–; visiting fell Oriel Coll Oxford 2007–; memb Lord Chancellor's Forum on Historical Manuscripts 2011–; advsr Portable Antiquities Scheme DCMS 2004–; memb Oriel Coll Devpt Bd (formerly Oriel Coll Devpt Tst) 2006–, tstee Thames Explorer Tst 2006–; FSA 2011; *Books* Rebels, Pretenders and Impostors (jtly, 2000), The Armorial of Haiti (ed, 2007); *Style—* Dr Clive Cheesman; ✉ The College of Arms, Queen Victoria Street, London EC4V 4BT (☎ 020 7236 2191, fax 020 7248 6448, e-mail rougedragon@college-of-arms.gov.uk)

CHEETHAM, Anthony John Valerian; s of Sir Nicolas John Alexander Cheetham, KCMG (d 2002), of London, and Jean Evison, *née* Corfe; *b* 12 April 1943; *Educ* Eton, Balliol Coll Oxford (BA); *m* 1, 1969 (m dis), Julia Rollason; 2 s (Nicolas b 1971, Oliver b 1973), 1 da (Flavia b 1976); m 2, 1979 (m dis 1996), Rosemary de Courcy; 2 da (Emma b 1981, Rebecca b 1983); m 3, 1997, Georgina Capel; *Career* editorial dir Sphere Books 1968; md: Futura Publications 1973, Macdonald Futura 1979, Century Hutchinson 1985–89; fndr and chm Century Publishing 1982–85, chm and chief exec Random Century Group 1989–91, fndr and ceo The Orion Publishing Group 1991–2003, exec chm Quercus Publishing plc 2006–09 (non-exec chm 2005–06), dir Atlantic Books 2009–12, fndr and exec chm Head of Zeus 2013–; *Books* Richard III (1972); *Recreations* reading, music, trees, gardening; *Style—* Anthony Cheetham, Esq

CHEETHAM, Prof Juliet; OBE (1995); da of Col Harold Neville Blair (d 1989), of London, and Isabel, *née* Sanders (d 1988); *b* 12 October 1939; *Educ* Univ of St Andrews (MA), Univ of Oxford; *m* 26 April 1965, (Christopher) Paul Cheetham, s of Robert Cheetham, of Wallasey; 1 s (Matthew b 1969), 2 da (Rebecca b 1972, Sophie b 1983); *Career* probation offr 1959–65, lectr in applied social studies and fell Green Coll Oxford 1965–85, prof and dir Social Work Research Centre Univ of Stirling 1986–95 (prof emeritus 1995–); co-ordinator Scottish Higher Educn Funding Cncl 1996–97, social work cmmr Mental Welfare Cmmn for Scotland 1998–2005, memb Mental Health Tbnl for Scotland 2005–, inspr Social Work Inspection Agency 2006–; memb: Ctee of Enquiry into the Working of the Abortion Act 1971–74, Cmmn for Racial Equality 1977–84, Social Security Advsy Ctee 1983–84; *Books* Social Work with Immigrants (1972), Unwanted Pregnancy and Counselling (1977), Social Work and Ethnicity (1982), Social Work with Black Children and their Families (1986), Evaluating Social Work Effectiveness (1992), The Working of Social Work (1997); *Recreations* canal boats; *Style—* Prof Juliet Cheetham, OBE; ✉ St Margaret's Gatehouse, 7A Restalrig Road South, Edinburgh EH7 6LF (☎ 0131 661 0948)

CHEETHAM, Rt Rev Dr Richard Ian; *see:* Kingston, Bishop of

CHEEVERS, Anthony William (Tony); s of Thomas Joseph Cheevers (d 1984), and Jessie, *née* Strahan; *b* 1 May 1956, Barnet, Herts; *Educ* Finchley GS, Royal Holloway Coll, Univ of London (BMus); *Career* joined BBC 1978; Music Dept BBC Radio 3: prodr 1984–90, ed Speech and Music 1991–93, ed Music Talks and Documentaries 1993–95; head of radio Mentorn Radio 1995–2001, freelance prodr 2001–02, ed BBC Radio 3 2002–; memb Opera Panel Olivier Awards 2006–07; *Publications* CageTalk: Dialogues with and about John Cage (contrib, 2006); *Recreations* tennis, opera, music, cinema, travel; *Style—* Tony Cheevers, Esq; ✉ BBC Radio 3, Room 3015, BBC Broadcasting House, London W1A 1AA (☎ 020 7765 4404, e-mail tony.cheevers@bbc.co.uk)

CHEFFINS, Prof Brian Robert; s of Ronald Cheffins, and Sylvia, *née* Green; *b* 21 January 1961; *Educ* Univ of Victoria BC Canada (BA, LLB), Univ of Cambridge (LLM); *m* 10 Oct 1992, Joanna Hilary, *née* Thurstans; 2 da (Hannah Victoria b 24 May 1998, Lucy Sylvia b 9 Feb 2002); *Career* memb Bar of Br Columbia 1985–2011; Univ of Br Columbia Canada: asst prof 1986–91, assoc prof 1991–97, prof 1997; SJ Berwin prof of corp law Univ of Cambridge and professorial fell Trinity Hall Cambridge 1998–, fell European Corp Governance Inst 2005–; visiting prof Harvard Law Sch 2002, visiting prof Columbia Law Sch 2016; visiting fell: Wolfson Coll/Centre for Socio-Legal Studies Univ of Oxford 1992–93, Duke Law Sch/Duke Global Markets Center 2000, Stanford Law Sch 2003; John S Guggenheim Meml Fellowship 2002–03, Fasken Martineau visiting sr scholar Faculty of Law Univ of Br Columbia 2013, Thomas McCraw Business History Fell Harvard Business Sch 2014, Leverhulme Major Research Fellowship 2016–18; *Books* Company Law: Theory, Structure & Operation (1997), The Trajectory of (Corporate Law) Scholarship (2004), Corporate Ownership and Control: British Business Transformed (2008), The History of Modern US Corporate Governance (ed, 2011); *Style—* Prof Brian Cheffins; ✉ Faculty of Law, University of Cambridge, 10 West Road, Cambridge CB3 9DZ (☎ 01223 330084, e-mail brc21@cam.ac.uk)

CHEFFINS, John Patrick; CBE (2007); s of Edward Michael Cheffins (d 2003), and Sheila Marion, *née* Doolin (d 2004); *b* Redhill, Surrey; *Educ* Perse Sch Cambridge, UMIST (BSc), Tuck Business Sch Dartmouth Coll NH; *m* 1980, Janet Marie, *née* Dessertine; 2 s (Patrick b 1981, Martin b 1983); *Career* joined as undergrad apprentice Rolls-Royce Ltd 1967; Rolls-Royce (Canada) Ltd: prodn control mangr 1975–80, vice-pres ops 1980–86, vice-pres mktg 1986–89, pres 1989–91; pres and ceo Rolls-Royce Industries Canada Inc 1991–93; Rolls-Royce plc: dir civil engine business 1993–98, pres civil aerospace 1998–2001, chief operating offr 2001–; memb Cncl Soc of Br Aerospace Cos (SBAC); Francois-Xavier Bagnould Prize for Aerospace 2001; FRAeS, FREng; *Recreations* skiing, shooting, fly fishing; *Style—* John Cheffins, Esq, CBE; ✉ Rolls-Royce plc, 65 Buckingham Gate, London SW1E 6AT (☎ 020 7227 9195, fax 020 7227 9120, e-mail john.cheffins@rolls-royce.com)

CHELL, Edward B; s of Charles Robert Chell, and June Beryl, *née* Silversides; *Educ* Hipperholm Boys' GS, Univ of Newcastle upon Tyne (BA), RCA (MA); *Career* artist; work in numerous private collections; Lloyds Printmaker Award 1987, Hunting Group Award First Prize Winner 1988, Br Inst Fund Award 1988; *Solo Exhibitions* exhibitions incl: Newcastle Poly Gallery 1989, Blason Gallery London 1990, Anthony Wilkinson Fine Art London 1995, Galerie Thieme + Pohl Darmstadt 1996, Galerie Bugdahn und Kaimer Düsseldorf 1997 and 2000, Anthony Wilkinson Gallery London 2001; *Group Exhibitions* incl: Promenade des Anglais (Galerie Ralph Debarrn Nice) 1994–95, Lead & Follow (Atlantis Gallery London and tour) 1994–95, 7th Open Exhibition (Oriel Mostyn Gallery Llandudno) 1995, John Moores 19 (Walker Art Gallery Liverpool) 1995, White Out (Curwen Gallery London) 1995, Hunting Group Prize Winners Exhibition (RCA) 1997, East 96 (Norwich Gallery) 1997, Black, Grey & White (Galerie Bugdahn und Kaimer Düsseldorf) 1997, Whitechapel Open (Delfina Gallery London) 1997, Foil (Bedford Hill Gallery London) 1997, Shuttle (Anthony Wilkinson Fine Art London) 1997, John Moores 20 (Walker Art Gallery Liverpool) 1997, Host (Tramway Gallery Glasgow) 1998, Whitechapel Open (Whitechapel Art Gallery London) 1998, Tech (Jason & Rhodes Gallery London) 1998, Foil (Stanley Picker Gallery Kingston) 1998, Tech (Galerie EOF Paris) 1998, Near (MOMA Sharjar UAE) 1998, The Vauxhall Gardens (Norwich Gallery) 1998, Zwischenraum #1 (Galerie Bugdahn und Kaimer Düsseldorf) 1999, Zwischenraum #2 (Galerie Bugdahn und Kaimer Düsseldorf) 1999, Now Showing (Houldsworth Fine Art London) 1999, Chora (Underwood Street Gallery London, Abbott Hall Gallery Kendal, Bracknell Gallery and Hot Bath Gallery Bath) 1999–2000, The Wreck of Hope (Nunnery Gallery London, also jt curator) 2000, FOIL (Gallery Westland Place London, Falmouth Sch of Art Gallery and Herbert Read Gallery KIAD Canterbury) 2001, Record Collection (VTO Gallery London and Euro tour) 2001, British Abstract Painting 2001 (Flowers East Gallery London) 2001, Paradise Valley (LUSAD) 2001, Yes. I am a long way from home (Wolverhampton Art Gallery, The Nunnery London, Northern Gallery for Contemporary Art and Herbert Read Gallery Canterbury) 2003, Will and Compulsion (Broadbent Fine Art London) 2004, John Moores 23 (Walker Art Gallery Liverpool) 2004; *Work in Public Collections* Arts Cncl of GB, Arthur Andersen & Co London, Northern Arts Assoc, Northumberland County Libraries, Grizedale Forrest Soc, Bede Gallery Jarrow, People's

Theatre Newcastle upon Tyne, British Telecom, Laing Art Gallery Newcastle upon Tyne, American Express London, RCA, Newcastle Poly Gallery, TI Group London; *Solo Catalogues* Parmenides Dilemma (1990), Vanishing Point (2000); *Recreations* mycology, cultural history, packaging and graphics, natural sciences; *Style*— Edward Chell, Esq; ✉ Anthony Wilkinson Gallery, 242 Cambridge Heath Road, London E2 9DA (☎ 020 8980 2662, fax 0870 128 6531, e-mail info@anthonywilkinsongallery.com); Galerie Bugdahn und Kaimer, Düsseldorfer Strasse 6, 40545 Düsseldorf, Germany (☎ 0049 211 329140, fax 0049 211 329147, e-mail bugdahn.kaimer@t-online.de)

CHELMSFORD, Dean of; *see:* Judd, Very Rev Peter Somerset Margesson

CHELMSFORD, 4 Viscount (UK 1921) Frederic Corin Piers (Kim) Thesiger; s of 3 Viscount (d 1999); *b* 6 March 1962; *Career* early career as TV prodr; fndr Webcast Ltd 1996, co-fndr Gossiptel 2003; currently md TTL; former conslt: Virgin Management, idesk plc, Chyron Corporation, Dentsu, NTT, Fuji Television; memb Advsy Bd XConnect; fndr memb Internet Telephony Service Providers Assoc 2004– (currently vice-chair); *Style*— The Rt Hon the Viscount Chelmsford

CHELSOM, Peter Anthony; s of Reginald Chelsom (d 1970), and Catherine Chelsom (d 1977); *b* 20 April 1956; *Educ* Wrekin Coll, Central Sch of Drama; *Career* actor; leading roles: RSC, NT, Royal Court; TV incl: Sorrell and Son, Woman of Substance, Christmas Present; writer and dir of films incl: Treacle (BAFTA nomination), Hear My Song 1992 (Best Newcomer Evening Standard Film Awards), Funny Bones 1994 (The Peter Sellers Award for Comedy Evening Standard Awards 1995), The Mighty 1997, Town and Country 1999, Serendipity 2001, Shall We Dance 2004, Hannah Montana: The Movie 2009; dir of commercials; memb: BAFTA, DGA, WGA, American Acad of Motion Pictures Arts and Sciences; *Clubs* RAC; *Style*— Peter Chelsom, Esq

CHELTENHAM, Archdeacon of; *see:* Ringrose, Ven Hedley Sidney

CHENEVIX-TRENCH, Jonathan Charles Stewart; s of Anthony Chenevix-Trench (d 1979), and Elisabeth, *née* Spicer (d 1992); *b* 24 March 1961, Bradfield; *Educ* Eton, Merton Coll Oxford (BA); *m* 30 May 1998, Lucy, *née* Ward; 2 da (May Lygon Gillespie, Evie Laura), 2 s (Jack Ward Lygon, Max Gerald Lefroy); *Career* Morgan Stanley: joined 1984, head of fixed income in Europe 1999–2004, global head of interest rates and foreign exchange 2000–05, chm Institutional Securities Gp Operating Ctee Europe 2004–05, chm Morgan Stanley Int 2006–07, chief operating offr Institutional Securities Gp 2007; chm Ashdown Capital 2008–; co-fndr African Century Gp; govr Royal Ballet Sch; *Recreations* reading, outside activities, gardening, entomology; *Clubs* Pratts, White's, Traveller's; *Style*— Jonathan Chenevix-Trench, Esq; ✉ Madresfield Court, Malvern, Worcestershire WR13 5AJ (☎ 01684 573024)

CHERNS, Penelope Ann (Penny); da of Albert Bernard Cherns (d 1987), and Barbara Simone, *née* Brotman (d 2003); *b* 21 May 1948; *Educ* N London Collegiate Sch, Univ of Kent (BA), Drama Centre London (Dip Directing), LSE (MSc); *Career* director; numerous teaching appts incl: LAMDA, RADA Drama Centre, WSCAD, Royal Coll of Music, Trent Poly, Loughborough Univ, Oslo, Univ of Iowa, Juilliard Sch NY, Guildhall Sch of Drama, Nat Film Sch, Cultura Inglesa Sao Paolo Brazil, Anglo Inst Montevideo Uruguay, Amsterdam Int Theatre Workshop, Institut del Teatr Barcelona, Brandeis Univ USA, Yale Univ USA, Central Sch of Speech and Drama; Theatre and Conflict workshop, fndr Dramatic Solutions 1997, currently head MA in Classical Acting for the Professional Theatre LAMDA; script conslt: Channel 4 1987, Warner Sisters (Hothouse Warner Sisters 1989), Family Pride (Channel 4) 1993; *Theatre* Hello and Goodbye Pal Joey 1974, Stop The World 1975, My Fair Lady 1975, West Side Story 1976 (all Northcott Theatre Exeter), Smile for Jesus (ICA and Sheffield Crucible Studio) 1976, A Winter's Tale 1977, Guys and Dolls 1977, Cabaret 1977 (all Gateway Theatre Chester), Queen Christina (RSC) 1977, School for Clowns (Haymarket Leicester) 1977, Dusa, Fish, Stas and Vi (Bristol Old Vic) 1977, Wreckers (7:84) 1977, Prodigal Father (Soho Poly) 1978, Kiss Me Kate 1978, Beaux Stratagem 1978, Alice 1978 (all Nottingham Playhouse), You Never Can Tell 1978, Side By Side By Sondheim 1979 (both Palace Theatre Watford), Julius Caesar 1979, Teeth 'n' Smiles 1979 (both Nottingham Playhouse), Trees in the Wind (7:84) 1979, Heroes 1979, Statements (Bristol Old Vic) 1980, Letters Home 1980, Strangers 1981 (all New End), Chicago 1981, Pinocchio 1981 (both Newcastle Playhouse), Mourning Pictures (Monstrous Regiment) 1981, The Boyfriend (Churchill Theatre Bromley) 1982, Duet for One (Br Cncl India Tour) 1983, A Day In The Death of Joe Egg (Haymarket Leicester) 1984, Vigilantes (Asian Co-op Theatre) 1985, Alarms (Monstrous Regiment 1986, Riverside Studios 1987) Panorama (The King's Head) 1988, The Millionairess (Greenwich) 1988, Iranian Nights (Royal Court) 1989, Revelations (Traverse Edinburgh) 1992, Tant Per Tant Shakespeare (Barcelona) 1995, The Odd Couple (York Theatre Royal) 1997, Birth of Pleasure (Rosemary Bransch) 1997, A Doll's House (Harrogate) 1998, The Wolf Road (Gate Theatre) 1998–99, Perfect Day (Haymarket Basingstoke) 2000, No Man's Land (ACT Theatre USA) 2012, Twelfth Night (Schoolhouse Theater Connecticut) 2012; *Television and Film* for Channel 4: Letters Home 1982, The Inner Eye (asst prodr only) 1986, Iranian Nights 1989, Bite the Ball 1989, Mixing It 1990; for BBC: Prisoners of Incest (Horizon) 1983, Battered Baby (Horizon) 1985, Home Front 1988, And The Cow Jumped Over The Moon 1990; other credits incl: Clients and Professionals and Managing Change (Melrose Film Productions) 1990; *Recreations* travel, languages, swimming; *Style*— Ms Penny Cherns; ✉ e-mail penelope.cherns@virgin.net

CHERRY, John Mitchell; QC (1988); s of John William (Jack) Cherry (d 1967), of Cheshunt, Herts, and Dorothy Mary, *née* Maybury (d 1975); *b* 10 September 1937; *Educ* Cheshunt GS; *m* 7 Oct 1972, Eunice Ann; 2 s (Troy Alexander b 10 July 1968 d 1995, Matthew John b 13 April 1971), 2 da (Suzanne Marie, Katherine Ann (twins) b 3 Jan 1970); *Career* called to the Bar Gray's Inn 1961; recorder of the Crown Court 1987–2003 (asst recorder 1984–87); memb: Criminal Injuries Compensation Bd 1989–2002, Mental Health Review Tbnl 2002–07; *Recreations* cricket, rugby, food, wine; *Style*— John Cherry, Esq, QC; ✉ Winterton, 163 Turkey Street, Bulls Cross, Enfield, Middlesex EN1 4RJ (☎ 01992 719018); Lamb Chambers, Lamb Building, Temple, London EC4Y 7AS (☎ 020 7797 8300, fax 020 7797 8308)

CHERRY, Paul David; s of Peter Harold Cherry, of Weston Manor, Herts (d 2002), and Joanna Alice, *née* Pryor; *b* 15 April 1961, Weston, Herts; *Educ* Eton, RAC Cirencester; *m* 26 May 1985, Carolina Davina, *née* Nall-Cain; 1 s (Alexander David b 17 Feb 1988), 1 da (Harriet Alice b 18 Oct 1989); *Career* High Sheriff Herts 2008–09; *Recreations* field sports, skiing; *Style*— Paul Cherry, Esq; ☎ 01462 790425, fax 01462 790219, e-mail paulcherrytree@hotmail.com

CHERRY, Prof Richard John; s of Leslie George Cherry (d 1970), and Dorothy Emily, *née* Tasker (d 1969); *b* 3 January 1939, Hitchin; *Educ* Hitchin Boys GS, St John's Coll Oxford (BA), Univ of Sheffield (PhD); *m* 23 June 1962, Georgine Mary, da of George Walter Ansell; 2 s (Simon Richard b 1965, Matthew James b 1972); *Career* scientific offr SERL 1960–64, scientist Unilever Res 1964–70, res fell Dept of Chemistry Univ of Sheffield 1970–73, privat dozent Dept of Biochemistry ETH Zürich 1973–82, prof of biological chemistry Univ of Essex 1982–2004 (emeritus prof 2004–); memb Editorial Bd: Biochemical Journal 1984–91, European Journal of Biophysics 1984–91, Progress in Lipid Research 1990–97; co-ordinator SERC Membranes Initiative 1989–93; memb: Molecular and Cell Panel Wellcome Tst 1988–91, Biochemistry and Cell Biology Ctee BBSRC 1994–96; Ruzicka prize for chem Switzerland 1981; memb: Biochemical Soc 1971, Biophysical Soc 1973; ARPS 2007; *Books* Techniques for the Analysis of Membrane Proteins (with C I Ragan, 1986), New Techniques of Optical Microscopy and Microspectroscopy (1991), Structural and Dynamic Properties of Lipids and Membranes (with P J Quinn, 1992); *Recreations* photography, gardening, music; *Style*— Richard Cherry; ✉ Department of Biological Sciences, University of Essex, Colchester CO4 3SQ (☎ 01206 872244, fax 01206 873598)

CHERRYMAN, John Richard; QC (1982); s of Albert James Cherryman (d 1963), and Mabel, *née* Faggetter; *b* 7 December 1932; *Educ* Farnham GS, LSE (LLB), Harvard Law Sch; *m* 18 Sept 1963, Anna, da of Edward Greenleaf Collis; 3 s (Oliver b 1964, Nicholas b 1966, Rupert b 1968), 1 da (Louise b 1971); *Career* called to the Bar Gray's Inn 1955 (bencher 1989); property litigation specialist, recorder and dep High Court judge 1985–97, ret from practice 2006; *Recreations* restoring property in France, gardening, trying to play the piano; *Style*— John Cherryman, Esq, QC

CHESHER, Prof Andrew Douglas; s of Douglas George Chesher (d 1980), of Croydon, Surrey, and Eileen Jessie, *née* Arnott; *b* 21 December 1948; *Educ* Whitgift Sch, Univ of Birmingham (G Henry Wright Prize, Birmingham C of C Prize); *m* 1, 1971 (m dis), Janice Margaret Elizabeth, *née* Duffield; 2 s (James Richard b 21 July 1976, Thomas Andrew b 27 Dec 1978); m 2, 2000, Valérie Marie Rose Jeanne, da of Claude Pierre Lechene; 2 da (Jacqueline Rose b 1 July 2004, Joséphine Hannah b 5 Jan 2006); *Career* res assoc Acton Soc 1970–71, lectr in econometrics Univ of Birmingham 1971–83; Univ of Bristol: prof of econometrics 1984–99, head Dept of Economics 1987–90 and 1996–98; UCL: prof of economics 1999–, William Stanley Jevons prof of economics and economic measurement 2013–; chair Res Grants Bd ESRC 2001–05; dir Centre for Microdata Methods and Practice 2001–, govr NIESR 2002–; memb: Nat Food Survey Ctee 1987–, Cncl Royal Econ Soc 1998–2004, ESRC 2001–05, Cncl Econometric Soc 2012–16; co-ed Econometric Soc Monographs series 2001–09; assoc ed: Econometric Reviews 1986–87, Econometric Theory 1990–93, Econometrica 1990–96 and 2000–03, Jl of Econometrics 1995–2003, Economics Jl 1997–2000, Jl of the Royal Statistical Soc A 1999–2001; referee for numerous learned jls; involved in numerous nat and int seminars and confs; foreign hon memb American Economic Assoc 2011; fell Econometric Soc 1999, FBA 2001, pres Royal Economic Soc 2016–17 (memb Cncl and Exec Ctee 2016–18); *Publications* Vehicle Operating Costs: Evidence from Developing Countries (jtly, 1987); articles, working papers and reports; *Style*— Prof Andrew Chesher; ✉ Glebe Lodge, 289 Hills Road, Cambridge CB2 8RP; Department of Economics, University College London, Gower Street, London WC1E 6BT (e-mail andrew.chesher@ucl.ac.uk)

CHESHIRE, Sir Ian Michael; kt (2014); s of Don Cheshire, and Pamela Cheshire; *b* 6 August 1959, Miri, Malaysia; *Educ* King's Sch Canterbury, Christ's Coll Cambridge (MA, economics scholar); *m* 1 Sept 1984, Kate, *née* Atherton; 2 s, 1 da; *Career* exec dir Kingfisher plc 2000– (gp chief exec 2008–), chief exec B&Q plc 2008; non-exec dir: HIT plc 1998–2000, Bradford & Bingley plc 2004–08; sr ind dir Whitbread plc 2011–; lead non-exec dir Dept of Work and Pensions 2011–; chair Advsy Bd Cambridge Inst for Sustainability Leadership; chm of tstees MediCinema, chair of govrs Ernest Devin Coll 2003–09; FRSA, MInstD; *Recreations* family, books, music, sailing (badly); *Clubs* Reform, Bembridge Sailing, Hurlingham; *Style*— Sir Ian Cheshire

CHESHIRE, Prof Jenny; *Educ* LSE (BA), Univ of Reading (PhD); *Career* lectr rising to sr lectr Birkbeck Coll London 1983–91, prof of English linguistics Univ of Fribourg and Univ of Neuchâtel Switzerland 1991–96, prof of linguistics Queen Mary & Westfield Coll London (now Queen Mary Univ of London) 1996–; Erskine visiting fell Univ of Canterbury Christchurch NZ 1995 and 2001; memb Editorial Bd: English WorldWide, Int Jl of Applied Linguistics, Jl of Multilingual and Multicultural Devpt, Jl of Sociolinguistics, Language in Society, Multilingua, Te Reo; FBA 2011; *Books* Variation in an English Dialect: A Sociolinguistic Study (1982), Describing Language (jtly, 1986, 2 edn 1994), Dialect in Education: Some European Perspectives (jtly, 1989), Dialect and School in the European Countries (jtly, 1989), English around the World: Sociolinguistic Perspectives (ed, 1991), Taming the Vernacular: From Dialect to Written Standard Language (co-ed, 1997), A Reader in Sociolinguistics Volume 1: Multilingualism and Variation (co-ed, 1998), A Reader in Sociolinguistics Volume 2: Gender and Discourse (co-ed,1998), Social Dialectology (co-ed, 2003); author of c70 articles in peer-reviewed jls and edited collections; *Style*— Prof Jenny Cheshire; ✉ Department of Linguistics, School of Languages, Linguistics and Film, Queen Mary, University of London, Mile End Road, London E1 4NS

CHESHIRE, Dr (Christopher) Michael; s of Gordon Sydney (d 1983), of Birmingham, and Vera, *née* Hepburn; *b* 18 July 1946; *Educ* West Bromwich GS, Univ of Manchester (BSc, MB ChB); *m* 1 Aug 1970, Jane Mary, da of Claude Cordle, of Norwich; 1 da (Amy Tamsin b 1 April 1977), 1 s (Jonathan Christopher b 5 Nov 1980); *Career* house offr Manchester Royal Infirmary and Hope Hosp Salford 1976–77 (pharmacist 1969–71), SHO Central and S Manchester Hosps 1976–79, lectr in geriatric med Univ of Manchester 1979–83, conslt physician in gen and geriatric med Manchester Royal Infirmary and Barnes Hosp 1983, dean of clinical studies Manchester Med Sch 1991–93; Central Manchester Health Care Tst: med dir 1993–97, dir of educn 1997–, dir of postgrad med educn 2000–05; clinical head of intermediate care Central Manchester PCT 2005–07; clinical vice-pres RCP London 2007– (censor 2005–07); memb: Br Geriatrics Soc (chm NW branch), British Assoc of Med Mangrs; FRCP 1990; *Recreations* gardening, swimming; *Style*— Dr Michael Cheshire; ✉ 38 The Crescent, Davenport, Stockport, Cheshire SK3 8SN (☎ 0161 483 2972); The Royal Infirmary, Oxford Road, Manchester (☎ 0161 276 3517, e-mail mike.cheshire@cmmc.nhs.uk)

CHESSHYRE, (David) Hubert Boothby; CVO (2004, LVO 1988); s of Col Hubert Layard Chesshyre (d 1981), and (Katharine) Anne, *née* Boothby (d 1995); *b* 22 June 1940; *Educ* King's Sch Canterbury, Trinity Coll Cambridge (MA), ChCh Oxford (DipEd); *Career* former vintner and language teacher; green staff offr at Investiture of Prince of Wales 1969, Rouge Croix Pursuivant 1970–78, on staff of Sir Anthony Wagner as Garter King of Arms 1971–78, Chester Herald of Arms 1978–95, Norroy and Ulster King of Arms 1995–97, Clarenceux King of Arms 1997–2010; Registrar Coll of Arms 1992–2000; lay clerk Southwark Cathedral 1971–2003, lately lectr for NADFAS and Speaker Finders; memb: Westminster Abbey Architectural Advsy Panel 1985–98, Fabric Commission 1998–2003; hon genealogist Royal Victorian Order 1987–2010, sec of the Order of the Garter 1988–2003; memb: HAC 1964–65 (fired salute at funeral of Sir Winston Churchill 1965), Soc of Genealogists 1968–, Bach Choir 1979–93, Madrigal Soc 1980–, London Docklands Singers 2002; Freeman City of London 1975, Liveryman Worshipful Co of Musicians 1995 (Freeman 1994); fell Heraldry Soc 1990 (memb Cncl 1973–85), FSA 1977; *Books* Heraldry of the World (ed, 1973), The Identification of Coats of Arms on British Silver (1978), The Green, A History of the Heart of Bethnal Green (with A J Robinson, 1978), Heralds of Today (with Adrian Ailes 1986, new edn 2001), Dictionary of British Arms Medieval Ordinary Vol I (jt ed with T Woodcock, 1992), Garter Banners of the Nineties (1998), The Most Noble Order of the Garter, 650 Years (with P J Begent, 1999); *Recreations* singing, gardening, motorcycling; *Style*— Hubert Chesshyre, Esq, CVO, FSA; ✉ 12 Pensioners Court, Charterhouse Square, London EC1M 6AU (☎ 020 7253 4222)

CHESTER, Bishop of 1996–; Rt Rev Peter Robert Forster; s of Thomas Forster (d 1991), of Birmingham, and Edna, *née* Russell; *b* 16 March 1950; *Educ* Tudor Grange GS for Boys Solihull, Merton Coll Oxford (MA), Univ of Edinburgh (BD, PhD), Edinburgh Theol Coll; *m* 1978, Elisabeth Anne, da of Rev Dr Eric Stevenson; 2 da (Inge b 1979, Helen b 1985), 2 s (Thomas b 1981, Douglas b 1993); *Career* curate Mossley Hill Parish Church Liverpool 1980–82, sr tutor St John's Coll Durham 1983–91, vicar Beverley Minster 1991–96; memb House of Lords 2001–; *Recreations* tennis, woodwork, family life, gardening; *Style*— The

C

Rt Rev the Lord Bishop of Chester; ✉ Bishop's House, Abbey Square, Chester CH1 2JD (☎ 01244 350864, fax 01244 314187)

CHESTER, Richard Waugh; MBE (1999); s of Cyril Waugh Chester (d 1999), and Margaret, *née* Dally (d 2010); *b* 19 April 1943, Hutton Rudby, N Yorks; *Educ* Friends' Sch Great Ayton, Huddersfield Coll of Technol (ARCM), Royal Acad of Music (FRAM, GRSM); *m* 12 Dec 1970, Sarah, da of Thomas Arthur Leopold Chapman-Mortimer (d 1979); 1 s (Matthew b 1973), 2 da (Lucy b 1976, Emily b 1979); *Career* flautist; fndr memb Nash Ensemble 1964; BBC NI Orchestra 1965–67; princ flautist and soloist; Scottish Nat Orchestra 1967–87; fndr memb Cantilena, dir Nat Youth Orchestras of Scotland 1987–2007; hon chm World Fedn of Amateur Orchestras; fndr memb and past pres European Fedn of Nat Youth Orchestras, fndr ctee memb World Youth Orchestra Conference, former vice-chm Making Music Scotland, former memb Scottish Arts Cncl; former chm St Mary's Music Sch Edinburgh; tstee: Dewar Arts Awards, NYOS Endowment Tst, Agar Tst, Lochaber Music Sch, Acting for Charities Tst, Scottish Schools Orch Tst; adjudicator, examiner and trainer; *Recreations* walking, reading; *Style*— Richard Chester, Esq, MBE; ✉ Milton of Cardross, Port of Menteith, Stirling (☎ 01877 385634, e-mail mail@rchester.co.uk)

CHESTERFIELD, Archdeacon of; *see:* Garnett, Ven David Christopher

CHESTERMAN, Alex; OBE (2016); *b* 9 January 1970, London; *Educ* London Univ; *Career* co-fndr LOVEFiLM 2003–07, fndr and ceo Zoopla Property Gp plc 2008–; *Style*— Alex Chesterman, Esq, OBE; ✉ Zoopla Property Group Plc, Harlequin Building, 65 Southwark Street, London SE1 0HR

CHESTERTON, Fiona Mary; da of Clarence Herbert Chesterton (d 1977), and Mary Biddulph, *née* McDonald (d 2009); *b* 19 May 1952, Leicester; *Educ* Wyggeston Girls' GS Leicester, Lady Margaret Hall Oxford (BA); *m* 1 Jan 1980, Howard Anderson (d 2012); 2 da (Sarah Elizabeth b 26 June 1984, Rachel Clare b 22 April 1987); *Career* BBC: news trainee 1975–77, TV news scriptwriter 1977–79, prodr TV current affairs esp Nationwide 1979–87, ed London Plus 1987–89, ed Newsroom South East 1989–91, ed Bi-Media South East 1991–92; commissioning ed Daytime Ch4 TV 1996–98 (dep commissioning ed news & current affrs 1992–96), commissioning ed for adult educn BBC 1998, controller Adult Learning BBC 2000–03; dir TV Skillset 2006–08; vice-chair Broadcasting Support Services 1998–2006; educn and trg memb Cncl RTS 2007–12 (memb 2000–04); non-exec dir Cambs & Peterborough Mental Health NHS Tst 2004–06, tstee Nat Extension Coll until 2010, memb E of England Ctee Heritage Lottery Fund 2002–08; tstee and hon sec Beds, Cambs, Northants and Peterborough Wildlife Tst 2010–, Little Gidding Tst 2010–, Indie Trg Fund (ITF) 2010–; FRSA, FRTS; *Recreations* swimming, choral singing, theatre-going; *Style*— Ms Fiona Chesterton; ✉ e-mail fchesterton@hotmail.com, Twitter @fionachesterton

CHEVALIER, Tracy; *b* 1962; *Educ* Oberlin Coll OH (BA), UEA (MA); *m*; 1 s; *Career* writer; former reference book ed; hon doctorate: Oberlin Coll OH 2013, UEA 2013; FRSL 2008; *Books* The Virgin Blue (1997), Girl with a Pearl Earring (1999, film adaptation 2003), Falling Angels (2001), The Lady and the Unicorn (2003), Burning Bright (2007), Remarkable Creatures (2009), The Last Runaway (2013), At the Edge of the Orchard (2016), Reader, I Married Him (ed, 2016); *Style*— Ms Tracy Chevalier; ✉ c/o Jonny Geller, Curtis Brown, Haymarket House, 28–29 Haymarket, London SW1Y 4SP (☎ 020 7393 4400, e-mail hello@tchevalier.com)

CHEVALLIER, Andrew Bretland; s of Lt Cdr John Bretland Chevallier, RN (d 1995), of Barnston, Wirral, Merseyside, and Rosemary Catherine, *née* Wylie; *b* 20 February 1953; *Educ* Tonbridge, Univ of Warwick (BA), NE London Poly (postgrad cert in educn), Sch of Phytotherapy Hailsham Sussex (cert of herbal med); *m* 1985, Maria Mercedes, *née* Uribe; 1 s by prev m (Leon b 26 Aug 1978), 1 step da (Tamara Davidson-Uribe b 6 Aug 1980); *Career* in private practice as conslt med herbalist 1985–, tutor and examiner in pharmacology Sch of Phytotherapy 1987–93 (tutor and supervisor Sch Trg Clinic 1988–93), lectr in herbal med Middlesex Univ 1994–95, sr lectr in herbal med and professional advsr BSc in herbal med Middx Univ 2000– (sr lectr in herbal med and prog ldr 1995–2000); med herbalist memb Multi Disciplinary Complementary Health Practice St Leonard's Hosp London 1990–95; Nat Inst of Med Herbalists: a dir and student liaison offr 1989–91, vice-pres and dir of educn 1991–, pres 1994–96, chm Nat Inst of Med Herbalists Educnl Fndn 1996–; memb Cncl Natural Med Soc 1993–96, chm Cncl for Complementary and Alternative Med 1996–98 (memb 1991–), vice-chm Euro Herbal Practitioners Assoc 2001–; fell Nat Inst of Med Herbalists 1997 (memb 1985); *Publications* Herbal First Aid (1993), Herbal Teas: A Guide for Home Use (1994), Encyclopaedia of Medicinal Plants (1996, revised edn 2001), Fifty Vital Herbs (1998), Hypericum – The Natural Anti-Depressant and More (1999); *Style*— Andrew Chevallier, Esq; ✉ 282 Saint Paul's Road, London N1 2LH

CHEVSKA, Maria Elizabeth; da of Klemens Skwarczewski (d 1985), and Susan Skwarczewska (d 2007); *b* 30 October 1948; *Educ* Our Lady's Convent Abingdon, Oxford Poly, Byam Shaw Sch of Art (London Univ of the Arts); *m* Gary Melville Thomas (d 1985); *Career* artist; prof of fine art Ruskin Sch of Art Univ of Oxford (fell Brasenose Coll); *Solo Exhibitions* incl: Air Gallery London 1982, Midland Group Nottingham 1985, Chapter Gallery Cardiff 1986, Bernard Jacobson Gallery London 1987, Anderson O'Day Gallery London 1989, 1990, 1992 and 1994, Mummery & Schnelle Gallery London 1990, 1996, 2001, 2004, 2006 and 2009, Warehouse Gallery Amsterdam 1993, Angel Row Gallery Nottingham 1994, Kunstmuseum Heidenheim 1997, Galerie Awangarda BWA Wroctaw 1997, Museum Goch 1997, Abott Hall Art Gallery and Museum Cumbria 1999, Wateroven Galerie Vlissingen 2000, Galerie Philippe Casini Paris 2000, 2002 and 2006, Maze Galerie Turin 2000, Maison de la Culture Amiens 2002 (also Caen and Bagneux 2003), Wetterling Stockholm 2002, Kunst Punkt Berlin 2003, Moca London 2005, Slought Fndn PA 2005, Musée Clamecy France 2006, Yet (Gallery Kalhama and Piippo Helsinki) 2008, And (Modernism Inc San Francisco) 2010, Guest from the Future (Galerie 8 London) 2011, From the Diary of a Fly (Mummery and Schnelle London) 2013, Dubious to Reason (VANE Newcastle) 2014; *Group Exhibitions* incl: Art and the Sea (John Hansard Gallery Univ of Southampton, ICA London) 1981, British Drawing (Hayward Annual London) 1982, Whitechapel Open (Whitechapel Gallery London) 1983–92, Gulbenkian Fndn Award Winners' Prints (touring GB and Ireland) 1983, New Blood on Paper (MOMA Oxford) 1983, Landscape Memory and Desire (Serpentine Gallery London) 1984, XXII Int Festival of Painting (Chateau Musée Music Grimaldi) 1990, Crossover (Anderson O'Day Gallery) 1993, British Painting (Arts Cncl Collection, Royal Festival Hall) 1993, Museo Pigorini Rome 1994, New Painting (touring Darlington, Newcastle and Norwich) 1994, Permission to Speak (Worcester City Museum and Art Gallery, touring Derby and Peterborough) 1994, White Out (Curwen Gallery London) 1995, Museum of Art Bacau 1998, Presencing (Eagle Gallery London) 1998, Chora (London and touring) 1999, Marianne Hollenbach Gallery Stuttgart 2001, STOFF (Stadtische Galerie Albstadt) 2002, Independence (South London Gallery) 2003, Translator's Notes (London) 2003, Lekker (APT London) 2005, Weiss (Rokunstbau Sacrow Palace Berlin) 2007, Gleichheit-Rowno (Program Gall Warsaw) 2008, Travelling Light (London and Venice) 2009, A Thousand Yard Stare (Artspace Gallery London) 2010, Eye of the Blackbird (Tank London) 2011, The Dark Would (Summerhall Edinburgh and Bury Art Museum) 2013/14, Do You Believe in Angels (MO Space Manila and Equator Arts Singapore) 2014, Painting About Painting (Simmons & Simmons London and Hillsboro Fine Art Dublin) 2014, Crowd, the artist's book (i'klectik London) 2015, Abstract Apartment London 2015; *Work in Public Collections* Arts Cncl of GB, Bolton City Art Gallery, Gulbenkian Fndn, Br Cncl, World Bank, Contemporary Art Soc, New Hall Coll Cambridge, NatWest Art Collection, Oldham Gallery, Heidenheim Museum, Bachau Museum, Brasenose Coll Oxford, Bury Art Museum; *Awards* Arts Cncl of GB Award 1977 and 2005, Gtr London Arts Assoc Award 1979 and 1984, Gulbenkian Fndn Printmakers' Award 1982, Austin Abbey Award British Sch Rome 1994, Br Cncl 2002 and 2005, Arts Cncl of England 2004, DACS 360 Artists Legacy 2015/16; *Publications* Spoken Image (texts by Rene Hirner and Jorg Becker, 1997), Company (text by Tony Godfrey, 1999), Eh (text by Ann Hindry, 2002), subject of mongraph Vera's Room: The Art of Maria Chevska (texts by Helen Cixous and Tony Godfrey, 2005), Chris Townsend, To Confuse the Twentieth Century (catalogue essay, 2011), Guest From the Future (collab, 2011), Hélène Cixous, Peintures: Ecrits sur l'art (2012), The Dark Would (ed by Phillip Davenport, 2013); *Style*— Ms Maria Chevska; ✉ e-mail mchevska@yahoo.com or maria.chevska@bnc.ox.ac.uk, website www.mariachevska.com

CHEW, (Gaik) Khuan; *b* 10 October 1956; *Educ* Roedean, Bath HS GPDST, Univ of London (BMus), RAM, Trinity Coll of Music, London Coll of Furniture, Inchbald Sch of Design (Dip Interior Design); *Career* interior designer (construction and bldg indust); design dir David Hicks International plc 1986–88, in practice Khuan Chew and Associates (Dubai, Hong Kong, London) 1993–; int projects incl: Hilton Int Hotel Cardiff, PortemilioAll-Suite Hotel Beirut, Okura Hotel Tokyo, Jumeirah Beach Resort Hotel Dubai (Condé Nast Hotel of the Year 1999), Burj Al Arab Tower Hotel Dubai, Madinat Jumeirah Dubai, Jumeirah Beach Club (refurbishment) Dubai, Dubai Int Airport, Ghantoot Royal Palace Abu Dhabi, Hilton Int Hotel Budapest (voted Best Architecture Design), Castillo Son Vida Majorca, Arabian Ranches Dubai, Abdul Aziz Yacht, Private Royal Palace Riyadh, Four Seasons Hotel Hong Kong, Mandarin Oriental Hotel Prague, Dubai Metro, Marco Polo Yacht, St Regis Hotel Tianjin, Swissotel Istanbul, Westin Chaoyang Beijing, Jumeirah Hotel Shanghai; FCSD, FRSA; *Style*— Miss Khuan Chew; ✉ 235, 2nd Floor, B Block, Al Shafour Building, Al Quaz, PO Box 72103, Dubai, UAE; Unit 901–903 9F, 663 Kings Road, Prosperity Milenia Plaza, North Point, Hong Kong; KCA International Designers Ltd, Unit 1.11, Canterbury Court, Kennington Park, 1–3 Brixton Road, London SW9 6DE (☎ 020 7582 8898, fax 020 7582 8860)

CHEYNE, David Watson; s of Brig William Watson Cheyne, DSO, OBE (d 1970), and Laurel Audrey, *née* Hutchison (d 1986); *b* 30 December 1948; *Educ* Stowe, Trinity Coll Cambridge (MA); *m* 22 April 1978, (Judith) Gay McAuslane, da of late David Anstruther Passey; 3 s (Alexander William David b 25 Nov 1980, Rory Alistair Watson b 22 Aug 1984, Rupert Valentine Hutchison b 20 Feb 1989); *Career* Linklaters LLP (formerly Linklaters & Paines): articled clerk 1972–74, asst slr 1974–80, ptnr 1980–, head Corporate Dept 2000–05, sr corporate ptnr 2005–06, sr ptnr 2006–11, conslt 2011–14, dir Blackrock World Mining Investment Tst plc 2012–; vice-chm EMEA Moelis & Co 2011–14; memb: City of London Slrs' Co 1980, Law Soc; *Recreations* shooting, fishing, collecting antiques; *Style*— David Cheyne, Esq; ✉ 19 Ladbroke Gardens, London W11 2PT (☎ 020 7908 1901); Linklaters, One Silk Street, London EC2Y 8HQ (☎ 020 7456 2000, fax 020 7456 2222)

CHICHESTER, Giles Bryan; s of Sir Francis Charles Chichester KBE (d 1972), and Sheila Mary, *née* Craven (d 1989); *b* 29 July 1946, London; *Educ* Westminster, ChCh Oxford (MA); *m* 1979, Virginia; 2 s (George b 1981, Charles b 1990), 1 da (Jessica b 1984); *Career* trainee Univ of London Press and Hodder & Stoughton 1968–69, mangr family business Francis Chichester Ltd 1969–94 (chm 1994–); contested: ILEA election Fulham Parly constituency 1986, Hammersmith and Fulham BC election 1986; PA to chm Cons Pty Orgn (Lord Tebbit) gen election campaign 1987; campaign asst to Sir Gerard Vaughan MP 1992; MEP (Cons): Devon and E Plymouth 1994–99, SW England 1999–2004, SW England and Gibraltar 2004–14; ldr Cons MEPs 2007–08 (dep chm 2010–13); chm: St James's Place Assoc (conservation/environment) 1980–, St James's Ward Ctee Westminster 1982–84 (memb 1975–88 and 1989–96), Westminster Branch Small Business Bureau (fndr) 1983–88, Hammersmith Cons Assoc 1984–87, London W European Constituency Cncl 1987–88, Foreign Affairs Forum 1987–90 (hon treas 1985–87), Dr Edwards' and Bishop King's Estate Charity 1990–93, Political Ctee Carlton Club 1992–95 (hon sec 1988–92), Industry Research and Energy Ctee European Parl 2004–07; pres European Energy Forum (formerly European Energy Fndn) 2004–14 (vice-pres 1995–2004), pres Delegation of European Parl for Relations with Australia and New Zealand 2007–08 and 2008–09; memb: Advsy Ctee Gtr London CPC 1984–91 (GP Ctee 1989–91), Nat Advsy CPC (co-opted) 1987–90 and 1994–97, Exec Ctee Cons Nat Union 1988–90 and 1997–98, Gen Cncl Cons Gp for Europe 1991–95, Exec Cncl Parly Gp for Energy Studies 1994–; tstee: United Charities of St James's Church Piccadilly 1977–97, 6s & 7s Club 1980–2008, Hammersmith United Charities (caring for the elderly) 1985–95; primary sch govr: Tower Hamlets 1983–86, Hammersmith 1983–2000; memb Cncl Air League 1995–2000; sporting career: rowed for sch, coll and England VIIIs (jr trials medal in VIIIs for Oxford), capt and navigator across N Atlantic 1978, 1979 and 1981, and S Indian Ocean 1979; MRIN, FRGS 1972; *Recreations* rowing, sailing, snooker, vegetarian cooking; *Clubs* London Rowing, Pratt's, Royal Western Yacht of England, Royal Yacht Sqdn; *Style*— Giles Chichester, Esq; ✉ Longridge, West Hill, Ottery St Mary, Devon EX11 1UX (☎ 01404 812889, e-mail g.chichester@btinternet.com); 9 St James's Place, London SW1A 1PE (☎ 020 7493 0932, fax 020 7409 1830)

CHICHESTER-CLARK, Sir Robert (Robin); kt (1974); s of Capt James Jackson Lenox-Conyngham Chichester-Clark, DSO (and Bar), DL, MP, and Marion Caroline Dehra, *née* Chichester (later Mrs Charles Edward Brackenbury); bro of Penelope Hobhouse, *qv*; *b* 10 January 1928; *Educ* Magdalene Coll Cambridge (BA); *m* 1, 6 Nov 1953 (m dis 1972), Jane Helen, o da of Air Marshal Sir (Robert) Victor Goddard, KCB; 1 s, 2 da; m 2, 1974, Caroline, o child of Col Anthony Bull, CBE, RE, of London; 2 s; *Career* MP (UUP) Londonderry City and Co 1955–74, PPS to Financial Sec to HM Treasy 1958–59, Lord Cmmr of the Treasy 1960–61, comptroller of HM Household 1961–64; chief oppn spokesman on: NI 1964–70, Public Bldg and Works 1965–70, The Arts 1965–66; min of state Dept of Employment 1972–74; memb Cncl of Europe 1959–61, delg WEU 1959–61; mgmnt conslt; dir: Alfred Booth and Co 1975–86, Welbeck Group Ltd; chm: Restoration of Appearance and Function Tst 1988–2000, Arvon Fndn 1997– (chm 1997–2001, jt pres 2001–); tstee: RPO Development Tst 1993–95, The House of Illustration (formerly Quentin Blake Gall of Illustration) 2002–08; Hon FIIM (formerly FIWM); *Clubs* Brooks's; *Style*— Sir Robin Chichester-Clark

CHIDGEY, Baron (Life Peer UK 2005), of Hamble-le-Rice in the County of Hampshire; David William George Chidgey; s of late Cyril Cecil Chidgey, of Bruton, Somerset, and Winifred Hilda Doris, *née* Weston; *b* 9 July 1942; *Educ* Brune Park Sch, Royal Naval Coll Portsmouth, Portsmouth Poly (Dip Civil Engrg); *m* 1964, April Carolyn, da of Glyn Idris-Jones; 1 s (Hon David Ryan b 1965), 2 da (Hon Joanna Louise b 1969, Hon Caitlin Victoria b 1971); *Career* grad mech and aeronautical engr The Admiralty 1958–64, sr highways and civil engr motorway design and construction Hants CC 1965–72; Brian Colquhoun and Partners Consltg Engrs 1973–94: princ engr traffic mgmnt studies 1973–78, dir Ireland and chief tech advsr Dept of Tport and Dublin Tport Authy integrated tport planning 1978–88, assoc ptnr (projects totalling over £200m) Repub of Guinea 1979–85, assoc ptnr and dir responsible for Central and Southern England (incl facilities mgmnt of 13 military bases for MOD) 1988–94; MP (Lib Dem) Eastleigh 1994–2005; Lib Dem spokesman on: Employment and Training 1995, Transport 1995–97, DTI 1997–99; memb: Speaker's Chm's Panel 2001–06, Foreign Affrs Ctee 1999–06, jt Ctee on Human Rights 2003–06; memb Assoc of Consulting Engrs of Ireland 1993; CEng 1971, MCIT

1983, FIHT 1990, FIEI 1990, FICE 1993; *Recreations* golf, reading; *Clubs* National Liberal; *Style*— The Rt Hon the Lord Chidgey; ✉ House of Lords, London SW1A 0PW (☎ 020 7219 6944, fax 020 7219 2810)

CHILCOTT, HE Dominick John; CMG; s of Lt Col Michael-John Chilcott, and Rosemary, *née* Hopkins; *b* 17 November 1959, Hong Kong; *Educ* Greyfriars Hall Oxford; *m* Jane Elizabeth, *née* Bromage; 1 da, 3 s; *Career* diplomat; asst desk offr Southern African Dept FCO 1982–83, Turkish language trg 1984, third then second sec Ankara 1985–88, head of section Central African Dept FCO 1988–89, desk offr for EU regnl policy and Gibraltar Europe Directorate FCO 1990–92, head Political Section Lisbon 1993–95, asst private sec to Foreign Sec FCO 1996–98, consellor for external rels UK Repesentation to the EU Brussels 1998–2002, dir Iraq Policy Unit FCO 2002–03, dir for Europe (bilateral rels and resources) FCO 2003–06, high cmmr Sri Lanka and Maldives 2006–07, dep head of mission Washington 2008–11, ambass to Iran 2011, ambass to Ireland 2012–; *Recreations* music, walking, gym; *Style*— HE Mr Dominick Chilcott, CMG; ✉ c/o FCO (Dublin), King Charles Street, London SW1A 2AH (Twitter @DChilcottFCO)

CHILCOTT, Robert (Bob); *b* 9 April 1955; *Educ* King's Coll Cantab, RCM; *Career* composer and choral conductor; princ guest conductor BBC Singers 2002–; *Compositions* incl: Salisbury Vespers 2009, Requiem 2010, The Angry Planet 2012, St John Passion 2013, Five Days That Changed the World 2013; *Books* St John Passion (2013); *Style*— Bob Chilcott, Esq; ✉ Choral Connections, 14 Stevens Close, Prestwood, Great Missenden, Buckinghamshire HP16 0SQ (e-mail val@choralconnections.com, website www.bobchilcott.com, Twitter @bobchilcott)

CHILD, Graham Derek; s of Albert Edward Child (d 1992), of Aldridge, Staffs, and Phyllis, *née* Wooldridge (d 1973); *b* 24 June 1943; *Educ* Bedford Sch, Worcester Coll Oxford (MA); *Career* Slaughter and May: asst slr 1968–75, ptnr 1976–95, resident ptnr Frankfurt 1993–95, Slaughter and May visiting fell in Euro competition law Lincoln Coll Oxford 1995–2002, visiting prof Faculté de droit Univ of Paris II 2000–02, supernumerary fell Lincoln Coll Oxford 2002–; chm Ladbroke Assoc 2011–; *Books* Common Market Law of Competition (with C W Bellamy QC, 1978); *Recreations* travel, walking; *Clubs* Reform, Hurlingham, Highgate Golf, Soc of Cons Lawyers, Carlton; *Style*— Graham Child, Esq

CHILD, Sir (Coles John) Jeremy; 3 Bt (UK 1919), of Bromley Palace, Bromley, Kent; s of Sir (Coles) John Child, 2 Bt (d 1971), and Sheila, *née* Mathewson (d 1964); *b* 20 September 1944; *Educ* Eton, Poitiers Univ (Dip); *m* 1, 1971 (m dis 1976), Deborah Jane, da of Henry Percival Snelling; 1 da ((Honor) Melissa b 1973); m 2, 1978 (m dis 1987), Jan Todd, yst da of Bernard Todd, of Kingston upon Thames, Surrey; 1 da (Leonora b 25 July 1980), 1 s ((Coles John) Alexander b 10 May 1982); m 3, 1987, Elizabeth, yst da of Rev Grenville Morgan, of Canterbury, Kent; 1 da (Eliza Caroline b 29 Jan 1989), 1 s (Patrick Grenville b 3 Jan 1991); *Heir* s, Alexander Child; *Career* actor; trained Bristol Old Vic Theatre Sch; memb Cncl Shakespeare's Globe Theatre; *Theatre* 3 plays Royal Court, Misalliance (Mermaid), Scenes from an Execution (with Glenda Jackson, Almeida), Dr Richard Warren in The Madness of George III (RNT); West End: Conduct Unbecoming (Queen's), Donkey's Years (Globe), Oh Kay and An Ideal Husband (Westminster), Plenty (Albery), Ying Tong (New Ambassadors) 2005; Out of Order (Far East tour) 1995, The Deep Blue Sea (Royal Theatre Northampton), The Seduction of Ann Boleyn (Nuffield Southampton), Pride and Prejudice (tour), Denial (Bristol Old Vic) 2000, The Circle 2002, An English Tragedy (Palace Theatre Watford); *Television* incl Father Dear Father, Wings, Glittering Prizes, Edward and Mrs Simpson, The Jewel in the Crown, Edge of Darkness, Fairly Secret Army, First Among Equals, Game Set and Match, Fools Gold, Harnessing Peacocks, Demob, Sharpe's Enemy, Frank Stubbs, Dance to the Music of Time, Love in a Cold Climate, A Touch of Frost, Doc Martin, Midsomer Murders, Falklands Play, Casualty, Judge John Deed, Amnesia, Eastenders, Thatcher – The Long Road to Finchley, Doctors, Katy Brand Show; *Films* incl: High Road to China 1982, Give My Regards to Broad Street 1984, Taffin 1987, A Fish Called Wanda 1988, The Madness of George III 1994, Regeneration 1996, Whatever Happened to Harold Smith? 1995, Don't Go Breaking My Heart 1997, Lagaan (Bollywood) 2000, Laisser Passez 2000, South Kensington 2001, Wimbledon 2004, Separate Lies 2004, Foster 2010, The Iron Lady 2011; *Recreations* travel, gardening; *Clubs* Garrick; *Style*— Sir Jeremy Child, Bt

CHILD, Prof John; s of Clifton Child (d 1994), and Hilde, *née* Hurwitz (d 1999); *b* 10 November 1940; *Educ* Purley GS (state scholar), St John's Coll Cambridge (scholar, MA, PhD, ScD); *m* 1965, Dr Elizabeth Anne Mitchiner, da of Geoffrey Mitchiner; 1 s (Martin Edmund b 12 Jan 1970), 1 da (Caroline Marianne b 10 April 1973); *Career* personnel offr and systems analyst Rolls Royce Ltd 1965–66, research fell Aston Univ 1966–68, sr research offr London Business Sch 1968–73, prof of organizational behaviour Aston Univ 1973–91, dean Aston Business Sch 1986–89, Guinness prof (later Diageo prof) of mgmnt studies Univ of Cambridge 1991–2000; fell St John's Coll Cambridge 1991–2000; chair of commerce Univ of Birmingham 2000–09 (emeritus chair of commerce 2009–); visiting prof Euro Inst for Advanced Studies in Mgmnt 1971–75, visiting prof Sun Yat-sen Univ Guangzhou China; dean and dir China-Euro Community Mgmnt Inst Beijing China 1989–90, dir Judge Inst of Mgmnt Studies Univ of Cambridge 1992–93, dir Centre for Int Business and Mgmnt 1995–98; ed-in-chief Organization Studies 1992–96; memb Mgmnt and Industrial Relations Ctee SSRC 1978–82; memb: Br Sociological Assoc 1962, Acad of Int Business 1993; Acad of Mgmnt: memb 1977, distinguished lectr 1980, 1991 and 2000, fell 2002; Hon Dr Helsinki Sch of Economics 1996, Hon Dr Corvinus Univ Budapest 2009, Hon Dr Aston Univ 2013, Hon Dr Aalborg Univ 2016; fell Br Acad of Mgmnt 2002 (fndr memb 1987, Lifetime Achievement Award 2015), FBA 2006, fell Acad of Int Business 2009; *Publications* author of 22 books incl: Management in China (1994), Strategies of Co-operation (jtly, 1998), The Management of International Acquisitions (jtly, 2001), Organization (2005, 2 edn 2015), Co-operative Strategy (jtly, 2005), Corporate Co-evolution (jtly, 2008), The Evolution of Organizations (2012), The Dynamics of Corporate Co-evolution (jtly, 2013), Knowledge, Organization and Management (jtly, 2013); also author of numerous articles; *Recreations* dinghy sailing, hill walking, bridge; *Clubs* Earlswood Lakes Sailing; *Style*— Prof John Child; ✉ Tudor Croft, Tanners Green Lane, Earlswood, Solihull, West Midlands B94 5JT (e-mail j.child@bham.ac.uk)

CHILD, John Frederick; s of Frederick George Child (d 1980), and Doris Frances, *née* Henley; *b* 18 April 1942; *Educ* King Edward's Sch Bath, Univ of Southampton (BA), Sidney Sussex Coll Cambridge (scholar, LLB (now LLM)), Univ of Columbia Leiden (Dip American Law); *m* 1, 2 Sept 1972, Dr Jean Alexander (d 2007), da of Dr Albert Alexander Cunningham, of Esher, Surrey; 2 s (Andrew b 25 May 1974, Jeremy b 11 May 1977); m 2, 3 July 2011, Angie Louise; *Career* called to the Bar Lincoln's Inn 1966 (Droop scholar and Tancred common law student); Chancery barr; memb Hon Soc of Lincoln's Inn, supervisor in law Sidney Sussex Coll Cambridge 1966–78; memb: Chancery Bar Assoc; *Books* Vol 19 (Sale of Land) Encyclopaedia of Forms and Precedents (main contrib 4 edn), Accumulation and Maintenance Settlements, Encyclopaedia of Forms and Precedents, Vol 40(3) (2006); *Recreations* walking, foreign travel; *Style*— John Child, Esq; ✉ Wilberforce Chambers, 8 New Square, Lincoln's Inn, London WC2A 3QP (☎ 020 7306 0102, fax 020 7306 0095, e-mail jchild@wilberforce.co.uk, website www.wilberforce.co.uk/child.html)

CHILD, Judith; *Career* headteacher Clitheroe Royal GS 2004–; *Style*— Mrs Judith Child; ✉ Clitheroe Royal Grammar School, Chatburn Road, Clitheroe BB7 2BA

CHILDS, David; *Educ* Sheffield Univ (LLB), UCL (LLM); *Career* Clifford Chance: ptnr 1981–, managing ptnr 2006–; *Style*— David Childs, Esq; ✉ Clifford Chance, 10 Upper Bank Street, London E14 5JJ

CHILDS, Robert Simon; s of Walter Childs (d 1991), and Patricia Rose, *née* Carton; *b* 21 June 1951, Brentwood, Essex; *Educ* St Joseph's Coll Ipswich, Bedford Coll London (BA); *m* 5 Aug 1977, Mary, *née* James; 2 s (Benjamin Joseph James b 19 Nov 1980, Joshua William James b 31 Oct 1983), 1 da (Alexandra Mary b 20 Sept 1987); *Career* Hiscox Group: joined as dep underwriter 1986, underwriter Syndicate 33 1993–2001, chief underwriting offr 2001–03, currently gp chm; chm Lloyd's Market Assoc 2003–05, chm War, Civil War and Financial Guarantee Sub-Ctee, memb Worldwide Markets Bd, memb Authorisation Ctee and memb Cncl Lloyd's of London; former chm Advsy Bd Sch of Mgmnt Royal Holloway Univ; tstee Enham, chm Bermuda Soc; hon fell Royal Holloway Univ of London 2008; *Recreations* tennis, sailing; *Clubs* Royal Bermuda Yacht; *Style*— Robert Childs, Esq; ☎ 020 7448 6009

C

CHILES, Adrian; *b* 21 March 1967, Hagley, Worcs; *Educ* Univ of London; *Career* early career as sports reporter for pubns incl News of the World; presenter: Financial World Tonight (Radio 4) 1993–94, Wake Up to Money (Radio Five Live), 6–0-6 (Radio Five Live), Chiles on Saturday (Radio Five Live, Gold Medal Sony Radio Awards), Working Lunch (BBC2), The Apprentice: You're Fired (BBC2) until 2010, Match of the Day 2 (BBC2) until 2010, The One Show (BBC1) 2007–10, Daybreak (ITV) 2010–11, football coverage ITV 2010–14, 5 Live Drive (Radio Five Live) 2013–14, 5 Live Daily (Radio Five Live) 2014–; *Style*— Adrian Chiles, Esq; ✉ c/o Avalon Management, 4a Exmoor Street, London W10 6BD

CHILSTON, 4 Viscount (UK 1911); Alastair George Akers-Douglas; also Baron Douglas of Baads; s of late Capt Ian Stanley Akers-Douglas (gs of 1 Viscount Chilston), by his 2 w, Phyllis Rosemary; suc kinsman, 3 Viscount Chilston, 1982; *b* 5 September 1946, Tunbridge Wells; *Educ* Ashdown House, Eton; *m* 1971, Juliet Anne, da of late Lt-Col Nigel Lovett, of The Old Rectory, Inwardleigh, Okehampton, Devon; 3 s (Hon Oliver Ian b 1973, Hon Alexander Hugh b 1975, Hon Dominic b 1979); *Heir* s, Hon Oliver Akers-Douglas; *Career* film producer; *Style*— The Rt Hon the Viscount Chilston; ✉ Tichborne Cottage, Tichborne, Arlesford, Hampshire SO24 0NA (☎ 01962 734010, fax 01962 734409, e-mail alastair@littlescreen.com)

CHILTON, Dr Robert (Bob); OBE (2007); *Educ* Downing Coll Cambridge; *Career* dir Local Govt Studies Audit Cmmn 1989–2001, interim cmmr for transport Transport for London; chief exec: Local Govt Cmmn 1995–96, Gtr London Authy 1999–2001; chair Standards Bd for England, non-exec dir Waste & Resources Action Prog (WRAP), vice-chair Bd Nat Consumer Cncl 2001–08, chair E Thames Gp, ind memb Bd Office of Information Cmmn, ind memb Home Office Audit Ctee, memb Bd Central Police Trg and Devpt Authy 2001–07; dep chair Phonepayplus; *Style*— Dr Bob Chilton, OBE

CHILVERS, Prof Edwin Roy; s of Derek John Chilvers, of Ipswich, Suffolk, and Marjorie Grace, *née* Bugg; *b* 17 March 1959; *Educ* Deben HS Felixstowe, Univ of Nottingham Med Sch (BMedSci, BM BS), Univ of London (PhD), Univ of Leicester, Univ of Edinburgh, Univ of Cambridge (MA, ScD); *m* 26 June 1982, Rowena Joy, *née* Tyssen; 1 da (Caroline b 1985), 2 s (Timothy b 1987, Alastair b 1992); *Career* Wellcome Tst sr clinical fell, hon sr lectr then reader Univ of Edinburgh 1992–98, hon conslt physician Edinburgh Royal Infirmary 1992–98; Univ of Cambridge: prof of respiratory med 1998–, hon conslt physician Addenbrooke's and Papworth Hosps 1998–, fell St Edmund's Coll 1999–, dir Clinical Academic Trg Office (CATO) Sch of Clinical Medicine, dep head Dept of Medicine; non-exec dir Papworth Hosp NHS Tst 2003–07; FRCPEd 1995, FRCP 1999 (MRCP 1985), FHEA 2007, FMedSci 2007; *Publications* Davidson's Principles and Practice of Medicine (ed, 17 edn 1995, 18 edn 1999, 19 edn 2002); author of papers on neutrophil cell biology and signalling; *Recreations* reading, music; *Style*— Prof Edwin Chilvers; ✉ Department of Medicine, University of Cambridge School of Clinial Medicine, Box 157, Addenbrooke's Hospital, Cambridge CB2 0QQ (e-mail erc24@cam.ac.uk)

CHIN, Joanna Louise; *née* Harris; da of Michael John Harris, of Bedworth, Warks, and Christine Mary, *née* Yendell; *b* 13 July 1961, Shipston-on-Stour, Warks; *Educ* Kings High Sch Warwick, King Henry VIII GS Coventry, Univ of Manchester (BA); *m* 8 Aug 1987, Philip Chin; 1 s (Alexander Philip b 27 Dec 1987 (twin)), 1 da (Anneliese Mei b 27 Dec 1987 (twin)); *Career* co-fndr Langland 1991; Everywoman Modern Muse Project 100 Founding Muses; finalist NatWest Everywoman Awards 2009 and 2015; patron Sebastian's Action Tst; *Recreations* pilates; *Style*— Mrs Joanna Chin; ✉ e-mail joanna@joannachin.co.uk, Twitter @joannalchin

CHIODINI, Prof Peter Leslie; s of Leslie Chiodini (d 1990), of London, and Catherine Beatrice, *née* Coleman (d 2001); *b* 27 October 1948; *Educ* Dunstable GS, KCH Med Sch (BSc, PhD, MB BS); *m* 5 Sept 1981, Jane Heather, da of Alan Edgar Bennett (d 2015); 2 s (James Peter b 13 Jan 1986, Jonathan Peter b 19 Aug 1988); *Career* house physician KCH 1978, house surgn Royal Sussex Co Hosp 1979; SHO: St James's Hosp 1979–80, Royal Marsden Hosp 1980; med registrar: St George's Hosp 1981, Broadgreen Hosp 1981–82; sr registrar East Birmingham Hosp 1982–85, conslt parasitologist Hosp for Tropical Diseases 1985–, dir PHE Malaria Reference Lab 2003–; hon prof LSHTM; Stephen Whittaker prize West Midlands Physicians' Assoc 1984, Medicine-Gilliland travelling fell 1985; fell Linnean Soc 2005–; MRCS, FRSTM&H 1970 (memb Cncl 1987–90 and 2002–05), FRCP 1992 (LRCP, MRCP), FRCPath 1996, FRCP(Glas) 2008 (fell Faculty of Travel Medicine 2006, dean Faculty of Travel Medicine 2009–12); *Recreations* cathedrals, running; *Style*— Prof Peter Chiodini; ✉ 9 Lavenham Drive, Biddenham, Bedford MK40 4QR; Department of Clinical Parasitology, Hospital for Tropical Diseases, Mortimer Market, London WC1E 6JB (☎ 020 7387 4411 ext 75418, fax 020 7383 0041, e-mail peter.chiodini@uclh.nhs.uk)

CHIPMAN, Dr John Miguel Warwick; CMG 1999; s of Lawrence Carroll Chipman (decd), and Maria Isobel, *née* Prados (decd); *b* 10 February 1957, Montreal; *Educ* Westmount HS Montreal, Harvard Univ (BA), LSE (MA), Balliol Coll Oxford (MPhil, DPhil); *m* 28 June 1997, Lady Theresa Manners, da of 10 Duke of Rutland (d 1999); 2 s (Ivor, Warwick (twins) b 24 Dec 2000); *Career* DG and chief exec IISS 1993– (res assoc 1983–84, asst dir 1987–90, dir of studies 1990–93); res assoc Atlantic Inst for Int Affrs Paris 1985–87; special advsr to Chm Reliance Industries (Mumbia), memb Bd of Dirs Abraaj Gp (Dubai); conslt with regular speaking engagements; *Books* NATO's Southern Allies (1988), French Power in Africa (1989); numerous chapters in books, scholarly articles and newspaper editorial pieces; *Recreations* tennis, skiing, riding; *Clubs* White's, Brooks's, Beefsteak, Garrick, Harvard (NY); *Style*— Dr John Chipman, CMG; ✉ IISS, Arundel House, 13–15 Arundel Street, Temple Place, London WC2R 3DX (☎ 020 7395 7676, fax 020 7395 9186)

CHIPPERFIELD, Sir David Alan; kt (2010), CBE (2004); s of Alan John Chipperfield, and Peggy, *née* Singleton; *b* 18 December 1953; *Educ* Wellington Sch, Kingston Sch of Art, Architectural Association (AADipl); *m* Dr Evelyn Stern; 3 s (Chester, Gabriel, Raphael), 1 da (Celeste); *Career* architect; princ David Chipperfield Architects 1984–; visiting prof: Harvard Univ 1987–88 (visiting lectr 1986–87), Univ of Naples 1992, Univ of Graz 1992, École Polytechnique Fédérale de Lausanne 1993–94, Staatliche Akademie der Bildenden Künste Stuttgart 1995–2001, London Inst 1997–; Norman R Foster visiting prof of architectural design Yale Univ 2011; Mies van der Rohe Chair Escola Tècnica 2001; fndr and dir 9H Gallery London 1985; curator 13th Int Architecture Exhibition of the Venice Biennale 2012; tstee Architectural Fndn London 1992–97, tstee Sir John Soane's Museum London 2014–; projects incl: Tak Design Centre Kyoto Japan 1989, private museum Tokyo 1991, River and Rowing Museum Henley-on-Thames 1997, Ernstings Service Centre Münster Germany 2002, Gormley Studio London 2003, Figge Art Museum US 2005, EMV Housing Madrid Spain 2005, Des Moines Public Library US 2006, America's Cup Building Valencia 2006, Museum of Modern Literature Marbach 2006, Freshfields

Bruckhaus Deringer office building Amsterdam 2006, BBC Scotland Headquarters Glasgow 2006, Liangzhu Culture Museum China 2007, Empire Riverside Hotel Hamburg 2007, Gallery building Am Kupfergraben 10 Berlin 2007, Kivik Pavilion Sweden 2008, Campus Audiovisual Barcelona 2008, Ninetree Village Hangzhou 2008, Neues Museum Berlin 2009, City of Justice Barcelona 2009, Anchorage Museum US 2009, Rockbund Art Museum Shanghai 2010, Kaufhaus Tyrol Dept Store Innsbruck 2010, Museum Folkwang Essen 2010, Turner Contemporary Gallery Margate 2011, The Hepworth Wakefield 2011, Peek & Cloppenburg flagship store Vienna 2011, MBA building Hautes Etudes Commerciales Jouy en Josas France 2012, Cottage Place London 2012, Café Royal London 2012, Saint Louis Art Museum USA 2013, Europaallee 21 Zurich 2013, Joachmistrasse 11 Berlin 2013, Museo Jumex Mexico City 2013, Fayland House Buckinghamshire 2013, One Pancras Square London 2013, Valentino new store concept (various locations); current projects incl: new entrance building Museum Island Berlin, San Michele Cemetery Venice, Palace of Justice Salerno, Ravelins of Castelo Sforzesco Milan, Rockbund Project Shanghai, Colville Towers London, Portland House London, Al Shaqab Hotel Doha, De Vere Gardens London, Canada Water London, Elizabeth House London, Neue Nationalgalerie Berlin, Haus Der Kunst Munich, Kunsthaus Zurich, Amorepacific Headquarters Seoul, Nobel Center Stockholm, Bryant Park Tower NY, Selfridges Dept Store London, Metropolitan Museum of Art NY Modern and Contemporary Wing; Royal Designer for Industry 2006; hon fell AIA 2007, hon memb Bund Deutscher Architekten 2007; RIBA 1982, RA 2008; *Awards* Andrea Palladio Prize 1993, RIBA Regnl Award 1996 and 1998, Civic Trust Award 1999, Tessenow Gold Medal Award 1999, Royal Fine Art Cmmn Tst/Br Sky Broadcasting Best Building (England) 1999, RIBA Category Award 1999, RIBA Award 2002, 2003 and 2004, Leaf Award 2006, AIA Regnl Awards 2006, RIBA European and International Awards 2007, RIBA Stirling Prize 2007, RIBA Nat and European Awards 2008, RIBA Int Award 2009, RIBA European and Int Awards 2010, Wolf Prize in the Arts (Architecture) 2010, Grosse Nike 2010, Europa Nostra Grand Prix 2010, RIBA Royal Gold Medal 2011, EU Prize for Contemporary Architecture – Mies van der Rohe Award 2011, RIBA European and Int Award 2011, RIBA Award 2012, Civic Trust Award 2012, AIA UK Chapter Excellence in Design Award 2012, Praemium Imperiale 2013, RIBA Nat and European Awards 2014, AIA UK Chapter Excellence in Design Award 2015; *Books* Theoretical Practice (1994), El Croquis: David Chipperfield, Architectural Works (1998, 3 edn 2006), David Chipperfield: Architectural Works 1990–2002 (2003), David Chipperfield: Idea e Realta (2005), Motta – David Chipperfield (2007), Neues Museum Berlin (2009), Form Matters (2009), El Croquis: David Chipperfield: Architectural Works 2007–2010 (2010), David Chipperfield Architects (2013), El Croquis: David Chipperfield: Architectural Works 2010–2014 (2014); *Style*— Sir David Chipperfield, CBE; ✉ David Chipperfield Architects, 11 York Road, London SE1 7NX (☎ 020 7620 4800, e-mail info@davidchipperfield.co.uk, website www.davidchipperfield.com)

CHIPPINDALE, Christopher Ralph; s of Keith Chippindale, and Ruth Chippindale; *b* 13 October 1951; *Educ* Sedbergh, St John's Coll Cambridge (BA), Girton Coll Cambridge (PhD); *m* 1976 (m dis 2008), Anne, *née* Lowe; 2 s, 2 da; civil partner, 2008, Justice Oleka; *Career* ed: Penguin Books, Hutchinson Publishing Group 1974–82, Antiquity 1987–97; res fell in archaeology Girton Coll Cambridge 1985–87, asst curator Cambridge Univ Museum of Archaeology and Anthropology 1987–13, reader in archaeology Univ of Cambridge 2001–13, Emeritus reader in archaelogy Univ of Cambridge 2015–; *Books* Stonehenge Complete (1983, 1994, 2004 and 2011), Who Owns Stonehenge? (1990), The Archaeology of Rock Art (1998); *Recreations* gardening, thinking what to do next; *Style*— Christopher Chippindale, Esq; ✉ 46 High Street, Chesterton, Cambridge CB4 1NG (e-mail cc43@cam.ac.uk)

CHISHOLM, Sir John Alexander Raymond; kt (1999); *b* 27 August 1946; *Educ* Univ of Cambridge (MA); *m*; 2 c; *Career* apprentice Vauxhall Motors Luton 1964–69; Scicon Ltd: analyst and programmer London 1969–74, managing conslt and fndr memb Milton Keynes Branch 1974–76, gp mangr 1976–79; CAP Scientific: fndr 1979–81, md 1981–86, memb Bd Cap Group plc 1986–88, md UK 1988–91; Sema Gp plc; chief exec Defence Evaluation and Res Agency 1991–2001; QinetiQGroup plc: chief exec 2001–05, chm 2005–06, non-exec chm 2006–10, ret; chm MRC 2006–; non-exec dir: ExproInt plc 1994–2003, Bespak plc 1999–2006; pres IET 2005–06; CEng, FIEE, FREng 1996, FRAeS, FIP; *Style*— Sir John Chisholm, FREng

CHISHOLM, Malcolm; MSP; *b* 7 March 1949; *Educ* Univ of Edinburgh (MA, DipEd); *m*; 3 c; *Career* former teacher of English Castlebrae HS and Broughton HS; MP (Lab): Edinburgh Leith 1992–97, Edinburgh N and Leith 1997–2001; Parly under-sec of state Scottish Office 1997 (resigned); MSP Edinburgh N and Leith 1999–; dep min for Health and Community Care 2000–01, min for Health and Community Care 2001–04, min for Communities 2004–06; memb Educnl Inst of Scotland; *Style*— Malcolm Chisholm, Esq, MSP; ✉ The Scottish Parliament, Edinburgh EH99 1SP

CHISHOLM, Melanie (aka Melanie C); *b* 12 January 1974; *Career* singer and actress; fndr memb (with Victoria Beckham, *qv*, Emma Bunton, Melanie Brown (Mel B) and Geri Halliwell) Spice Girls 1993; *Albums* with Spice Girls (in excess of 40m albums sold worldwide): Spice 1996 (UK no 1), Spiceworld 1997 (UK no 1, platinum UK, double platinum US, no 1 in Holland, Norway, Denmark, New Zealand, Finland and Austria), Forever 2000; solo: Northern Star 1999, Reason 2003, Beautiful Intentions 2005, This Time 2007, The Sea 2011, Stages 2012; *Singles* with Spice Girls incl: Wannabe 1996 (debut single, UK no 1, first all-girl group to attain position since the Supremes 1964, 4m copies sold worldwide, no 1 in 31 territories incl American Billboard (first UK act to attain position on debut single) 1997), Say You'll Be There 1996 (UK no 1), 2 Become 1 1996 (UK Christmas no 1), Mama/Who Do You Think You Are (double A-side) 1997 (UK no 1, thus first ever band to go to no 1 in the UK with first 4 singles), Spice Up Your Life 1997 (UK no 1), Too Much 1997 (UK Christmas no 1), Stop 1998 (UK no 2), Viva Forever 1998 (UK no 1), Goodbye 1998 (UK Christmas no 1), Holler/Let Love Lead The Way (double A-side) 2000 (UK no 1); solo: When You're Gone (with Bryan Adams) 1998, Goin' Down 1999, Northern Star 1999, Never Be The Same Again (with Lisa Lopes) 2000 (UK no 1), I Turn To You 2000 (UK no 1), If That Were Me 2000, Here It Comes Again 2003, On The Horizon 2003, Next Best Superstar 2005, I Want Candy 2007; *Film* Spiceworld The Movie 1997; *Theatre* Blood Brothers (West End) 2009–10, Jesus Christ Superstar (UK tour) 2012–; *Awards* Best Video (for Say You'll Be There) and Best Single (for Wannabe) Brit Awards 1997, two Ivor Novello song writing awards 1997, Best Br Band Smash Hits Show 1997, three American Music Awards 1998, Special Award for International Sales Brit Awards 1998, Outstanding Contribution to Music Brit Awards 2000, Brits Performance of 30 Years Brit Award 2010, Best Supporting Actress in a Musical Whatsonstage Award 2013 (for Jesus Christ Superstar); *Style*— Melanie C; ✉ c/o MBC PR, Wellington Building, 28–32 Wellington Road, London NW8 9SP

CHISHOLM, Paul William; *Career* various mgmnt positions in New England Telephone & Telegraph Co and AT&T Corp 1974–85, vice-pres Shawmut Bank Boston 1985–88, vice-pres and gen mangr Teleport Communications Boston Inc 1988–92, md COLT Telecommunications 1992–95, pres and ceo COLT Telecom Group plc 1996–; first chm Other Licensed Operators Gp 1993–95; *Style*— Paul Chisholm, Esq

CHITTENDEN, Rear Adm Timothy Clive (Tim); s of Frederick William John Chittenden (d 1993), and Pauline Beryl, *née* Cockle (d 1978); *b* 25 May 1951, Woodford; *Educ* Chatham House GS, Churchill Coll Cambridge (MA, Shooting half blue), RN Engrg Coll (MSc), RNC Greenwich (Dip Nuclear Engrg); *m* 2 Feb 1974, Clare Anne, da of David Style; 3 da (Sarah b 1975, Victoria b 1977, Alice b 1982); *Career* Marine Engr Offr HMS Warspite 1982–85, Marine Engr Offr HMS Talent 1988–90, asst dir Nuclear Safety MOD (PE) 1990–93, production manager Clyde Submarine Base Faslane 1993–94, Capt 1994, conducted MOD Dual Nuclear Regulation Study 1994–95, asst dir Business and Safety Chief Strategic Systems Directorate MOD 1995–97, asst dir S&T Update MOD 1997–99, dir in Service Submarines Ship Support Agency MOD DLO 1999–2000, ldr Submarine Support IPT Warship Support Agency 2000–03, Rear Adm 2003, COS (Support) to CINCFLEET 2003–05; BAESYSTEMS Submarines: astute prog dir 2005–07, assurance dir 2007–11; non-exec dir Sellafield Ltd 2007–; pres Nuclear Inst 2013–16; Inst Nuclear Engineers Prize 1975; Freeman Worshipful Company of Carmen 2004; MINucE 1982, FNucI 2005, FIMechE 2001 (MIMechE 1988), CEng 1988; *Recreations* sailing and dinghy racing (RYA coastal skipper), hill walking, 0.22 target rifle shooting, reading, listening to music; *Clubs* Bassenthwaite Sailing, Hawks' (Cambridge), RN and RM Rifle, RNSA, Old Gaffers Assoc; *Style*— Rear Adm Tim Chittenden; ✉ Sellafield Ltd, Seascale, Cumbria CA20 1PG

CHITTY, Alison Jill; OBE (2004); da of Ernest Hedley Chitty, and Irene Joan Waldron; *b* 16 October 1948; *Educ* King Alfred Sch London, St Martin's Sch of Art, Central Sch of Art and Design, Arts Cncl scholar; *Career* theatre designer; Victoria Theatre Stoke-on-Trent 1970–79 (designed over 40 prodns, head of design 4 years), dir Motley Theatre Design Course 2000– (co-dir 1992–2000), design conslt Rose Theatre Kingston 2007–08; Retrospective exhibition: Design Process 1970–2010 Nat Theatre 2010; Hon Dr Univ of Staffordshire 2005, Hon Dr Univ of the Arts 2013; Mischa Black Award 2007, Young Vic Award 2008; fell Birkbeck Coll 2011; RDI 2009; *Theatre* RNT incl: A Month in the Country, Don Juan, Much Ado About Nothing, The Prince of Homburg, Danton's Death, Major Barbara, Kick for Touch, Tales from Hollywood, Antigone, Martine, Venice Preserv'd, Fool for Love, Neaptide, Antony and Cleopatra, The Tempest, The Winter's Tale, Cymbeline, Cardiff East; RSC incl: Tartuffe, Volpone, Breaking the Silence, Romeo and Juliet; other prodns incl: Old King Cole (Theatre Royal Stratford East), Orpheus Descending (Haymarket), The Rose Tattoo (Playhouse), Ecstasy and Uncle Vanya (Hampstead Theatre), Measure for Measure and Julius Caesar (Riverside Studios), The Way South (Bush), Carmen Jones and Lennon (Crucible Sheffield), Rememberance of the Past (RNT) 2000 (Olivier Award 2001), Hamlet (RSC) 2001, Luther (RNT) 2001, Scenes from the Big Picture (RNT) 2003, The Merchant of Venice (Chichester) 2004, The Master and Margarita (Chichester) 2004, Days of Wine and Roses (Donmar Warehouse) 2005, King Lear (Chichester) 2005, Two Thousand Years (RNT) 2005, The Voysey Inheritance (RNT) 2006 (Best Costume Designer Lawrence Olivier Award 2007), The Vortex (UK tour and Apollo Theatre) 2007–08, Uncle Vanya (Rose Theatre Kingston and UK tour) 2008, Ecstasy (Hampstead and West End) 2011, Grief (RNT) 2011, A Provincial Life (NT Wales) 2012; *Opera* The Marriage of Figaro (Opera North), New Year (Houston Grand Opera), BowDown/Down by the Green Wood Side (Southbank), The Siege of Calais (Wexford), The Vanishing Bridegroom (St Louis Opera Theatre), Gawain (ROH), Falstaff (Gothenburg Music Theatre), Jenufa (Dallas Opera) 1994, Billy Budd (Grand Theatre Geneva) 1994, Blond Eckbert (Santa Fé Opera) 1994, Khovanshchina (ENO) 1994 (Best Opera Prodn Lawrence Olivier Award 1995), Billy Budd (ROH) 1995 (Best Opera Prodn Lawrence Olivier Award 1995), Modern Painters (Santa Fé Opera) 1995, Arianna (ROH) 1995, Billy Budd (Bastille Opera Paris) 1996, The Mask of Orpheus (Royal Festival Hall) 1996, Die Meistersinger von Nürnberg (Danish Royal Opera Copenhagen) 1996, Misper (Glyndebourne) 1997, Turandot (Bastille Opera Paris) 1997, Billy Budd (Dallas Opera and Houston Grand Opera) 1997–98, The Flying Dutchman (Bordeaux Opera) 1998, Tristan and Isolde (Seattle Opera) 1998, The Bartered Bride (ROH at Sadlers Wells) 1998, Julius Caesar (Bordeaux Opera) 1999, Otello (Bavarian Opera Munich) 1999 and 2013, Dialogues of the Carmelites (Santa Fé Opera) 1999, Aida (Grand Theatre Geneva) 1999, Tristan and Isolde (Lyric Opera Chicago) 2000, The Last Supper (Staats Oper Berlin and Glyndebourne) 2000, Ion (Aldeburgh Festival and Almeida Opera) 2000, Billy Budd (Seattle and Tel Aviv) 2000, Jenufa (San Francisco) 2000, La Vestale (ENO) 2002, Bacchae (RNT) 2002, Original Sin (Crucible Sheffield) 2002, Cavalleria Rusticana (Royal Albert Hall) 2002, Pagliacci (Royal Albert Hall) 2002, Khovanshchina (ENO) 2003, L'Enfant et les Sorlileges (Maastricht) 2003, Cosi Fan Tutti (ENO) 2003, The Flying Dutchman (Vilnius) 2004, The Io Passion (Aldeburgh Festival, Almeida Opera, Bregenz and UK tour) 2004, Billy Budd (Washington) 2004, Jenufa (Dallas Opera) 2004, Tangier Tattoo (Glyndebourne) 2005, Midsummer Marriage (Chicago Lyric Opera) 2005, Carmen (Greek Nat Opera) 2007, The Minotaur (ROH) 2008 and 2013, The Flying Dutchman (Bergen) 2008, Adrianna's Fall (Cologne) 2008, Hippolyte et Aricie (Reis Opera Holland) 2009, Semper Dolors, Semper Dowland/The Corridor (Aldeburgh Festival, Queen Elizabeth Hall and Bregenz) 2009, La Forza del Destino (Holland Park Opera) 2010, Rigoletto (La Fenice Venice and Reggio Emelia) 2010, Betrothal in a Monastery (Toulouse and Paris) 2011, Madame Butterfly (Oslo) 2012, Rigoletto (Venice) 2012, Nabucco (La Scala Milan and ROH) 2013, The Minotaur (ROH) 2013, Parsifal (ROH) 2013, Billy Budd (LA Opera) 2014, The Pirates of Penzance (ENO) 2015, Betrothal in a Monastery (Toulouse) 2015, The Corridor/The Cure (Aldeburgh Festival and Linbury Theatre ROH) 2015, Nabucco (Barcelona) 2015, Theodora (Theatre Champs Elysées Paris) 2015, The Pirates of Penzance (Luxembourg/ Caen/ Saarbruken) 2015, The Corridor/ The Cure (Holland Festival) 2016; *Film* Blue Jean, Aria, Life is Sweet, Black Poppies (BBC), Naked, Secrets and Lies (Palm d'Or Cannes), The Turn of the Screw (BBC); *Style*— Ms Alison Chitty, OBE, RDI; ✉ c/o Rayfield Allied, Southbank House, Black Prince Road, London SE1 7SJ (☎ 020 7589 6243, fax 020 7662 1720)

CHOAT, Jonathan Martin Cameron; *Educ* Dulwich Coll, Univ of London (BA); *Career* former mktg positions: Lever Bros, Texaco, J Lyons, Burmah Oil; currently fndr and chm Nexus Communications Gp, chm The Justin de Blank Co (restaurateurs); Freeman City of London, Liveryman Worshipful Co of Fruiterers; FRSA; *Style*— Jonathan Choat, Esq; ✉ Comberton House, Comberton, Ludlow, Shropshire SY8 4HE; Nexus Communications Group, 52A Cromwell Road, London SW7 5BE (☎ 020 7052 8812, fax 020 7052 8889)

CHODEL, Peter; s of Stanislaw Chodel (d 1978), of Mirfield, W Yorks, and Helena, *née* Naczenko; *b* 15 April 1956; *Educ* Mirfield Secdy Modern, Batley Art Sch, Central Sch of Art and Design (BA); *m* 1 Aug 1981, Vanessa, da of James Fredrick Lowery King, OBE; 1 s (Fredrick Stanislaw b 9 Feb 1988), 1 da (Molly Irena b 15 Feb 1990); *Career* freelance designer Mitchell Beazley Books 1979; designer: Observer Magazine 1979 (summer vacation placement 1978), Stadden Hughes Ltd 1980–84; design dir Michael Peters Group plc (Annual Reports Ltd, Right Angle, Michael Peters Corporate Literature, Michael Peters Literature) 1984–91, creative dir Addison Design Company Ltd 1991–; judge D&AD Awards 1994 and 2000; *Awards* D&AD award (for Yorkshire TV Good Companions Brochure 1981), MEAD Annual Report Show awards (for Michael Peters Group 1984 annual report 1985 and for Prestwich Holdings plc 1986 annual report 1987), Business Magazine/Price Waterhouse Annual Report of the Year award (for Tesco plc 1990); *Recreations* home and family, things Medieval; *Style*— Peter Chodel, Esq; ✉ 20 Finsen Road, Camberwell, London SE5 9AX (☎ 020 7274 3848); Addison Corporate Marketing Ltd, 2 Cathedral Street, London SE1 9DE (☎ 020 7403 7444, fax 020 7403 1243, e-mail peter.chodel@addison.co.uk)

CHOI, Christopher (Chris); s of Denis Choi, and Gloria, *née* Stephenson; *Educ* Univ of Nottingham (LLB); *Career* broadcaster; prodr That's Life (BBC1) 1991–93, presenter/reporter Watchdog (BBC 1) 1993–97, reporter Holiday (BBC 1) 1993–98, presenter You and Yours (Radio 4) 1997–98, presenter Radio Five Live 1997–99, consumer ed ITV News 1999–; *Recreations* argument, social drinking, country activities; *Style*— Chris Choi, Esq; ✉ ITN, 200 Gray's Inn Road, London WC1X 8XZ (☎ 020 7833 3000, fax 020 7430 4302, e-mail chris.choi@itn.co.uk)

CHOLMONDELEY, 7 Marquess of (UK 1815); David George Philip Cholmondeley; KCVO (2007); also Viscount Cholmondeley of Kells (I 1661), Baron Cholmondeley of Namptwich (E 1689), Viscount Malpas and Earl of Cholmondeley (GB 1706), Baron Newborough (I 1715), Baron Newburgh (GB 1716), and Earl of Rocksavage (UK 1815); o s of 6 Marquess of Cholmondeley, GCVO, MC (d 1990); *b* 27 June 1960; *Educ* Eton, La Sorbonne Paris; *m* 25 June 2009, Rose, da of Timothy Hanbury, of Wembury, Devon; 2 s (Alexander Hugh George (Earl of Rocksavage), Lord Oliver Timothy George b 12th Oct 2009 (twins)); *Heir* s, Earl of Rocksavage; *Career* a page of honour to HM The Queen 1974–76; jt Hereditary Lord Great Chamberlain of England 1990–; *Style*— The Most Hon the Marquess of Cholmondeley; ✉ Cholmondeley Castle, Malpas, Cheshire (☎ 01829 22202); Houghton Hall, King's Lynn, Norfolk

CHOO, Jimmy; Hon OBE (2003); s of Kee-Yin Choo, of Penang, Malaysia, and Ah-Yin Moo Choo, of Penang, Malaysia; *b* 15 November 1952; *Educ* Cordwainer Coll; *Career* shoe designer; started own label 1988; has designed for the Royal Shakespeare Co and for the films Goldeneye (featuring character James Bond) and French Kiss; clients incl royalty, film stars, pop stars and many other celebrities; visiting prof London Inst 2001–; Best Accessories Award Bridal Awards 1989, Accessory Designer of the Year Br Fashion Awards 2000 (nominated 6 times 1989–94), Gold Award Assoc of Colls 2000; Hon Dato given by Sultan of Pahang for contribution to Malaysia; Hon Liveryman Worshipful Co of Cordwainers 2004; *Style*— Jimmy Choo, Esq, OBE; ✉ Jimmy Choo Couture, 18 Connaught Street, London W2 2AF (☎ 020 7262 6888)

CHOPE, Christopher Robert; OBE (1983), MP; s of His Hon Judge Robert Charles Chope (d 1988), and Pamela, *née* Durell (d 2004); *b* 19 May 1947; *Educ* Marlborough, Univ of St Andrews (LLB); *m* Christine, *née* Hutchinson; 1 s (Philip Robert), 1 da (Antonia); *Career* called to the Bar 1972; ldr Wandsworth BC 1979–83 (memb 1974–83); MP (Cons): Southampton Itchen 1983–92, Christchurch 1997–; Parly under sec of state: DOE 1986–90, Dept of Transport 1990–92; oppn frontbench spokesman on: tport, housing and construction 1997–98, trade and industry 1998–99, Treasy 2001–02, tport 2002–05; a vice-chm Cons Pty 1997–98, chm Cons Way Forward 2002–, memb 1922 Exec Ctee 2005–; memb: Health and Safety Cmmn 1993–97, Local Govt Cmmn 1994–95, House of Commons Trade and Industry Ctee 1999–, Speaker's Panel of Chm 2005–, Select Ctee on Procedure 2005–, UK delgn to Cncl of Europe 2005–; conslt Ernst & Young 1992–98; *Style*— Christopher Chope, Esq, OBE, MP; ✉ House of Commons, London SW1A 0AA (☎ 020 7219 3000)

CHOPE, Dr John Norman; JP (Devon); s of William Pearse Chope (d 2007), and Kathleen Mary, *née* Calvert (d 1955); *b* 27 June 1948; *Educ* Waverley GS Birmingham (awarded Reserved Cadetship Dartmouth RNC), Univ of Bristol (Associated Dental Co scholar, BSc, BDS, MRC Award, L E Attenborough Medal, George Fawn Prize), LDS RCS Eng, MFDGP (UK); *m* 1970, Susan Mary, da of Clinton and Kathleen Le Page; 1 da (Jenny Kathleen b 28 Sept 1976); *Career* trainee dental technician 1965, dental pathology res technician Univ of Birmingham 1966; neurophysiologist USA and subsequently Sudan (helped found Khartoum Dental Sch) 1969 and 1973, SHO (oral surgery) United Bristol Hosps 1973; assoc dental surgn: Backwell Somerset 1973, Stockwood Bristol and Shepton Mallet Somerset 1973–74; princ dental surgn and dental practice owner: Holsworthy Devon 1974–, Hartland Devon 1975–2008, Bude Cornwall 1981–90, Okehampton Devon 1983–98; hypnotherapist 1977–; conslt to Veterinary Drug Co plc 1996–98, dental medico-legal expert 2006–; conf lectr on practice mgmnt, business skills, communication, marketing dental health, the dental team and training; ed: Code of Practice (dental business quarterly) 1995–2004, CODE business advice sheets (series) 1995–2004; memb Editorial Bd: Dentistry 2000, t-dental.com 2000–; formerly: memb N Devon Dist and SW Regnl Dental Advsy Ctees, chm N Devon BDA, memb N Devon Dental Postgrad Ctee, chm Confedn of Dental Employers 1995–2004; currently: fndr memb, bd memb and treas SW Div Faculty of Gen Dental Practitioners (UK) RCS Eng, fndr memb and memb Ctee N Devon Independent Dental Practitioners' Gp; elected memb GDC 1996–2009, chm GDC Standards Ctee 2005–08, memb GDC Investigating Ctee 2006–12; expert professional panel memb Family Health Servs Appeal Authy 2001–10, professional memb Health, Educn and Social Care Chamber of First Tier Tnbl Miny of Justice 2010–; ind medical-legal dental expert for civil claims 2006–; memb numerous professional socs incl: BDA, RSM, FGDP (UK), RCS, FDI, AOG; farmer/landowner 1976–, proprietor small specialist bldg co 1976–; chm: Speke Valley Services Ltd 1979– (t/a Firmadenta 1993–96 dental wholesalers and mktg co), Codental Products Ltd (dental service co for voluntary soc) 1995–2001, The Penroses Consultancy Ltd (business and mgmnt consultancy) 1997–2000; columnist for Dentistry 2002–09; memb: CLA, Magistrates' Assoc, Cwlth Magistrates' and Judges' Assoc; *Publications* numerous publications on neurophysiology of taste receptors, therapeutic lasers, dental bodies corporate, dental health marketing, dental business management; *Recreations* architecture, building, structural design, writing, sketching, drawing, natural history, animal husbandry, gardening, swimming, walking, skiing, theatre; *Style*— Dr John Chope; ✉ Delivery 1, Hartland, Devon EX39 6DZ

CHOUDHURY, Akhlaq; QC (2015); *Educ* Univ of Glasgow (BSc), Univ of London (LLB); *Career* called to the Bar 1992; recorder (SE Circuit) 2009; *Style*— Akhlaq Choudhury, Esq, QC; ✉ 11 Kings Bench Walk, Temple, London EC4Y 7EQ

CHOUDHURY, Anwar Bokth; s of Afruz Bokth Choudhury, and Ashrafun Nessa Choudhury; *b* 15 June 1959, Sylhet, Bangladesh; *Educ* Univ of Salford (BSc), Univ of Durham (MBA); *m* Jan 2001, Momina; 2 c (Umar, Amani); *Career* princ engr Siemens Plessey 1985–89, strategist and conslt RAF 1990–94, asst dir MOD 1995–99, dir Cabinet Office 2000–03, high cmmr to Bangladesh FCO 2004–08, dir of int insts FCO 2008–; memb RIIA; *Recreations* bridge, cricket, cinema; *Style*— Mr Anwar Choudhury; ✉ Foreign & Commonwealth Office, King Charles Street, London SW1A 2AH

CHOW, Alex; *b* Malaysia; *Career* head chef Kai Mayfair 2004– (Michelin star 2009–); *Style*— Mr Alex Chow; ✉ Kai Mayfair, 65 South Audley Street, London W1K 2QU

CHOW, Andre; s of John Chow, and Joanne, *née* Chen; *b* 3 February 1980, Oxford; *Educ* Imperial Coll London (MB BS, BSc, PhD); *m* 6 June 2011, Regine Tan; *Career* gen surgical trainee 2004–13; co-fndr and chief operating offr Touch Surgery 2013–; MRCS; *Recreations* skiing, travel, walking, climbing; *Style*— Dr Andre Chow; ✉ Touch Surgery, 17–18 Haywards Place, London EC1R 0EQ

CHOW, Dr Anthony; *Educ* The Royal Free Hosp Sch (MB BS, BSc, MD); *Career* conslt cardiologist and hon sr lectr Univ Coll Hosp, hon conslt cardiologist Royal Berkshire Hosp, Barnet Chase Farm NHS Tst and Wellington Hosp, clinical lead in arrhythmias and sudden death Thames Valley; finalist: Euro Soc of Cardiology Young Ivestigator 2000, Rosanni Degani Young Investigator Award 2000; memb: American Heart Assoc, Br Cardiac Soc; FRCP; *Books* Pacemakers and Defibrillators: all you wanted to know (2005); *Recreations* racket sports, theatre, country walks, fishing; *Style*— Dr Anthony Chow; ✉ The Heart Hospital, UCLH, 16–18 Westmoreland Street, London W1G 8PH

CHOW, Sir C K; kt (2000); *b* 9 September 1950; *Educ* Univ of Wisconsin (BS), Univ of Calif (MS), Chinese Univ of Hong Kong (MBA), Harvard Business Sch (AMP); *Career* research engr Climax Chemical Co New Mexico 1974–76, process engr Sybron Asia Ltd Hong Kong 1976–77; The BOC Gp plc: various sr positions in Hong Kong and Australia 1977–86, pres BOC Japan 1986–89, gp mangr England and USA Gases Business Devpt 1989–91, regnl dir North Pacific 1991–93, chief exec Gases 1993–96, md 1994–97; chief exec GKN plc 1997–2001, ceo Brambles Industries plc 2001–03, ceo MTR Corp Ltd 2003–; chm Standard Chartered Bank (Hong Kong) Ltd 2004–; non-exec dir: Standard Chartered Bank (Hong Kong) Ltd 1997–2008, Anglo American plc 2008–; pres Soc of Br Aerospace Companies Ltd 1999; Int Exec of the Year Acad of Int Mgmnt 2001, Exec of the Year DHL/SCMP Business Awards in Hong Kong 2006, Dir of the Year Hong Kong IOD 2006, Best ceo in Hong Kong FinanceAsia Magazine 2009 and 2010; Hon DEng; Hon FHKIE, FIChemE, FCGI, Hon FIET, FCILT; *Style*— Sir C K Chow

CHOW-STUART, Alexander; *see:* Stuart, Alexander Charles

CHOWDHURY, Ajay; s of Manindra Narayan Chowdhury, of New Delhi, India, and Indira, *née* Kumar; *b* 29 April 1962, Delhi, India; *Educ* Sydenham Coll of Economics Bombay (BComm), Wharton Sch Univ of Pennsylvania (MBA), Central Sch of Speech and Drama London (Dip), Metropolitan Film Sch (Dip); *m* 1, 1 July 1995 (m dis 2012), Elizabeth McDonnell; 2 da (Layla Catriona b 4 April 1997, Eva Maya b 13 Oct 2000); m 2, 9 Aug 2015, Angelina Melwani; *Career* mgmnt trainee IBM 1983–84, conslt then mangr Bain & Co 1986–91, successively gp devpt mangr, md United Interactive, dir United Broadcasting & Entertainment and ceo LineOne United News & Media 1991–99, pres and ceo NBC Internet Europe 2000, co-fndr and managing ptnr IDG Ventures Europe 2000–06, gen ptnr Acacia Capital Ptnrs 2006–07, ceo ENQII plc 2007–11, ceo ComQii 2011–13, ceo Seatwave 2013–14, ptnr and md BCG Digital Ventures 2015–; chm Shazam Entertainment 2002–05, non-exec dir Virtual Internet plc until 2002, dir Empower Interactive 2003–06, dir Lionhead 2004–06; artistic dir Rented Space Theatre Co, dir Museums, Libraries and Archives Cncl 2000–06, tstee 24 Hour Museum 2003–06, dir Arts Cncl London 2009–13, dep chm BSAC 2013–, non-exec dir DCMS 2013–; *Recreations* music, diving, books, theatre, film; *Style*— Ajay Chowdhury, Esq; ✉ 30D South Hill Park, London NW3 2SB (☎ 020 8452 2234, e-mail ajay@ajaychowdhury.com)

CHOWN, Christopher Richard; s of Dr Charles Stanley Malcolm Chown, of Betws-y-Coed, Gwynedd, and Elisabeth Annan, *née* Dickson (d 1978); *b* 29 June 1957; *m* 25 June 1988, Gunna, da of Heine á Trødni (d 1987), of Grønlandsfekagid, Faroe Islands; 1 step s (Peder b 7 June 1970), 1 step da (Tania b 29 May 1966); *Career* audit jr Peat Marwick Mitchell 1980–81, rebuilt and converted derelict house in Clapham 1982–83, kitchen asst teacher La Petite Cuisine Sch of Cookery Richmond 1983–84, commis chef Terrace Restaurant Dorchester 1984, sous chef Restaurant Riesbächli Zürich Switzerland 1984–85; converted and opened Plas Bodegroes 1986, bought and refurbished The Hole in the Wall Restaurant 1994; *Awards* Good Food Guide Gwynedd Newcomer of the Year 1988, Michelin Red M 1989, Taste of Wales Restaurant of the Year 1990, Good Food Guide Highest Rated Restaurant in Wales 1990–96, 1995, AA Guide Rosette for Cooking 1991 (three rosettes 1992, 1993, 1994 and 1995), Michelin Star 1991, 1992, 1993, 1994 and 1995 (the only one in Wales), Good Hotel Guide César Award 1992; memb N Wales Tourism Mktg Bureau 1986–, treas Llyn Peninsula Tourist Assoc 1986–88, memb Taste of Wales 1989–, memb Dwyfor Business Forum Ctee 1992; *Recreations* photography, architecture, gardening, music and opera; *Style*— Christopher Chown, Esq; ✉ Plas Bodegroes Ltd, Pwllheli, Gwynedd LL53 5TH (☎ 01758 612363, fax 01758 701247)

CHOY, Prof Ernest Ho Sing; s of Kim Hung Choy, of Hong Kong, and Foo Chun Fok Choy; *b* 15 June 1961; *Educ* Sutton Valence, Univ of Wales Coll of Med (MB BCh, MD); *m* 30 July 1999, Christina Bik Fun Mok; 1 da (Catrina b 2 Oct 2000); *Career* house physician Merthyr Tydfil Hosp 1985–86, house surgn Wrexham Maelor Hosp 1986, SHO (A&E) Walsall Gen Hosp 1986–87, SHO (Gen Med) Wrexham Maelor Hosp 1987–88, med registrar Maidstone Hosp 1989, registrar in rheumatology Rheumatology Unit Guy's and Lewisham Hosps 1989–90, research fell Rheumatology Unit UMDS Guy's Hosp 1990–93, lectr in clinical and academic rheumatology King's Coll Sch of Med and Dentistry (KCSMD) and UMDS 1993–98, conslt sr lectr in rheumatology and head of therapeutic rheumatology Academic Dept of Rheumatology Guy's, King's and St Thomas Hosps Sch of Med 1998–; prof of rheumatology and head Section of Rheumatology Cardiff Univ Sch of Medicine 2011–; chm Arthritis Research Campaign Clinical Trial Collaboration, expert advsr NICE, memb Standing Ctee Rheumatology and Rehabilitation section RSM 1992–95; memb: Br Soc for Rheumatology, Br Soc of Immunology, American Coll of Rheumatology; hon memb Hong Kong Soc of Rheumatology; FRCP 2002 (MRCP 1988); *Publications* author of numerous articles and book chapters; *Recreations* classical music, visiting galleries and exhibitions of early 20th century art, tennis, golf; *Style*— Prof Ernest Choy; ✉ Cardiff University School of Medicine, Tenovus Building, Heath Park, Cardiff CF14 4XN (☎ 029 2068 7092, fax 029 2068 7303)

CHRIS, Oliver Graham; s of Valerie Chris, and Robert Chris; *Career* actor; *Television* incl: The Office (BBC 2) 2001, Green Wing (Channel 4) 2004–06, Nathan Barley (Channel 4) 2005, The It Crowd (Channel 4) 2006, Bonkers (ITV) 2007, Silent Witness (BBC 1) 2011, Breathless (ITV) 2013, Bluestone 42 (BBC 3); *Theatre* incl: The Taming of the Shrew (Wilton's Music Hall) 2007, Well 2008, A Midsummer Night's Dream (Rose Theatre Kingston) 2010, Season's Greetings (NT) 2010, One Man, Two Guvnors (NT, Adelphi, Broadway) 2011, Great Britain (NT) 2014, Closer (Donmar Warehouse) 2015, King Charles III (Almeida, Wyndham's and Broadway) 2014–16; *Film* incl: The Gathering 2002, The Other Boleyn Girl 2003, Bridget Jones: The Edge of Reason 2004, Huge 2010, Scandalous Lady W (BBC 2) 2015; *Style*— Oliver Chris, Esq; ✉ Twitter @OliverChris

CHRISFIELD, Lawrence John (Larry); s of Sydney George Chrisfield (d 1977), and Minnie, *née* Underwood (d 1999); *b* 31 March 1938; *Educ* St Olave's and St Savior's GS; *m* Patricia Maureen, *née* Scoble; 4 c (Cindy Jane b 1961, Susan Melinda b 1962, Carol Ann b 1964, David Alexander b 1967); *Career* articled clerk, accountant Merrett Son and Street 1955–63, tax sr, mangr Arthur Young McClelland Moores & Co 1963–72, UK tax mangr Unilever plc 1972–74, ptnr Ernst & Young (formerly Arthur Young) 1975–97 (mangr 1974–75); currently ind tax conslt; dir: GTS Films Ltd, Rainmaker Films Ltd, Vine Media Ltd; FCA 1963, CTA 1963; *Recreations* theatre, photography; *Style*— Larry Chrisfield, Esq; ✉ 29 The Meadow, Chislehurst, Kent BR7 6AA (☎ and fax 020 8468 7730)

CHRISTIAN, Clive; OBE (2012); *b* 12 July 1951, Scotland; *Children* 3 da (Victoria b 22 Feb 1978, Juliana (Mrs Mark Allen, Jr) b 12 March 1982, Alice b 18 Sept 1985); *Career* fndr and chm Clive Christian plc 1978–; Outstanding Perfume Presentation Fifi Award Fragrance Fndn 2006, House and Garden Designers' Best Award 2007, Guinness world record for world's most expensive perfume 2008, Outstanding Contribution to Educn and Innovation of the Perfume Industry Fifi Award Fragrance Fndn 2009; memb: Rotary Int (Hon Lifetime Rotarian, Hon Paul Harris Fell), Walpole; *Recreations* art, architecture, music; *Clubs* Morton's, Home House, Annabel's; *Style*— Clive Christian, Esq, OBE

CHRISTIAN, Dominic Gerard; s of Denis Ambrose Christian, and Marie Stephenson Christian, *née* Falconer; *b* 12 October 1960, York; *Educ* St Joseph's Coll Ipswich, UEA (BA); *m* August 1993, Catherine (Kate), *née* Birch; 1 s (Joey b 11 Nov 1994), 1 da (Julia b 10 July 1997); *Career* J K Buckenham 1984–89, Greig Fester Ltd 1989–97 (dir 1995); Benfield Gp 1997–2010: memb PLC Bd 2004, ceo Int Div 2005–10, ceo Benfield Ltd 2005–10; co-ceo Aon Benfield Gp 2010–, ceo Aon UK Ltd 2013–; pres IIL 2016; memb Cncl Lloyd's 2014, chm Lloyd's Tercentenary Tst; dir Juvenile Diabetes Research Fndn, memb Norfolk Churches Tst; memb Ct of Common Cncl Lime Street Ward 2016; MInstD; *Recreations* my children would say: football, tennis, Norfolk, history, church architecture, trees, lakes, cats and family; *Clubs* Nat Lib, The Wimbledon, Reepham Tennis, Historic Royal Palaces, Globe Theatre; *Style*— Dominic Christian, Esq

CHRISTIAN, Louise; *Career* admitted slr 1978; specialises in personal injury, clinical negligence and public law; with Lovell White and King Slrs until 1979, slr Plumstead Community Law Centre 1979–81, advsr to GLC Police Ctee 1981–84, co-fndr and ptnr Christian Khan Slrs (formerly Christian Fisher Slrs) 1985–10 (conslt 2010–); has represented victims of the Marchioness disaster and of the Paddington, Southall, Potters Bar and Cumbrian rail crashes, British detainees in Guantanamo Bay and Marina Litvinenko; sr fell Coll of Personal Injury Law; chair: Liberty, INQUEST; memb Bd Centre for Corporate Accountability, memb Personal Injury and Clinical Negligence Panel Law Soc; tstee Article 19; Hon Dr Staffordshire Univ 2003; Legal Aid Personality of the Year LAPG/Independent Lawyer 2004, Liberty/Law Soc/Justice Human Rights Award 2004 for outstanding contribution to defending the rule of law; *Publications* Inquests: a Practitioners Guide (co-author, 2002); *Style*— Ms Louise Christian; ✉ Christian Khan, 5 Gower Street, London WC1E 6HA (☎ 020 7631 9500, e-mail louisec@christiankhan.co.uk)

CHRISTIANS, Sharon Jane; da of John Hlywka (d 1982), and Rose Theresa, *née* Yastrzhembsky (d 1990); *b* 6 October 1951; *Educ* Notre Dame Coll Sch Canada, Carleton Univ of Ottawa Canada (BA); *m* 18 Aug 1988, Ian Douglas Christians, s of Douglas Tamplin Christians, of Swansea, Wales; *Career* researcher and speech writer House of Commons Ottawa 1972–75, dir Ontario Youth Secretariat 1975–76, fed affrs analyst Canadian Inst of CA 1976–78; dir of public affrs: Northern Pipeline Agency Alaska Highway Gas Pipeline Project Canada 1978–80, Ontario Energy Corporation 1980–82; mangr International Communications General Electric USA 1982–88; dir of corporate affrs: THORN EMI plc 1988–90, Stanhope Properties plc 1990–91; dir of corporate affrs and sec to the Bd Amersham International plc 1991–93, exec vice-pres of corp affrs EMI Group plc (formerly THORN EMI) 1994–98, dir Client Communications McKinsey and Co Incorporated UK 1998–; non-exec dir: Ashford Hosp NHS Tst Middx 1992–94, HMV Group Ltd 1997–98; FRSA 1990, memb Investor Rels Soc 1994; *Recreations* music, tennis, languages; *Style*— Mrs Sharon Christians; ✉ McKinsey and Co Incorporated UK, 1 Jermyn Street, London SW1 4UH (☎ 020 7839 8040, e-mail sharon_christians@mckinsey.com)

CHRISTIANSEN, Rupert Elliott Niels; s of Michael Robin Christiansen (d 1983), and Kathleen Gertrude, *née* Lyon (d 2004); *b* 6 September 1954; *Educ* Millfield, King's Coll Cambridge (MA, MLitt), Columbia Univ (Fulbright Scholar); *Partner* Ellis Woodman (civil partnership Jan 2009); *Career* arts ed Harpers & Queen 1988–95, dep arts ed The Observer 1990–93; opera critic: The Spectator 1989–96, Daily Telegraph 1996–; dance critic Mail on Sunday 1996–; Somerset Maugham Prize 1989; dir Gate Theatre 1995–; memb Ctee London Library 1989–92 and 1995–, memb Int Jury Birgit Nilsson Prize 2011–; tstee Charleston Tst 1999–2011; FRSL 1997; *Books* Prima Donna (1984), Romantic Affinities (1988), The Grand Obsession (ed, 1988), Tales of the New Babylon (1994), Cambridge Arts Theatre (ed, 1997), The Visitors: Culture Shock in 19th Century Britain (2000), Arthur Hugh Clough: The Voice of Victorian Sex (2001), Pocket Guide to Opera (2002), Who Was William Shakespeare? (2003), The Complete Book of Aunts (2006), Once More with Feeling (2007), I Know You're Going to be Happy (2013); *Recreations* swimming, skiing, walking; *Clubs* Two Brydges Place; *Style*— Rupert Christiansen, Esq, FRSL; ✉ c/o United Agents, 12–26 Lexington Street, London W1F 0LE (☎ 020 3214 0800, fax 020 3214 0801, website www.unitedagents.co.uk)

CHRISTIANSEN, Sophie Margaret; OBE (2013, MBE 2009); da of Karl Christiansen, of Sunningdale, Berks, and Caroline, *née* Elliott; *b* 14 November 1987, Ascot, Berks; *Educ* Royal Holloway London (MSc); *Career* Paralympic equestrian; achievements incl: Bronze medal (championship test) Paralympic Games 2004 (youngest rider at age 16), 3 Gold medals European Championships 2005, Gold medal and Bronze medal World Para Dressage Championships 2007, 2 Gold medals (freestyle and team event) and Silver medal (individual championship test) Paralympic Games 2008, 2 Gold medals and Silver medal Para European Championships 2009, 2 Gold medals and Silver medal World Equestrian Games 2010, 3 Gold medals (freestyle test, championship test and team event) Paralympic Games 2012, 3 Gold medals European Championships 2013, 2 Gold medals (championship test and team event) and Silver medal (freestyle) World Equestrian Games 2014, 3 Gold medals European Championships 2015; hon fell Royal Holloway London 2012; *Style*— Ms Sophie Christiansen, OBE; ✉ website www.sophiechristiansen.co.uk, Twitter @SChristiansen87, Facebook sophiechristiansenobe

CHRISTIE, Gus; s of Sir George Christie, of Ringmer, E Sussex, and Lady Mary, *née* Nicholson; *b* 4 December 1963, Lewes, Sussex; *Educ* St Aubyns Rottingdean, Eton, KCL; *m* 1 (m dis); 4 s (Jackson, Romulus (twins) b 17 Jul 1996, Alexander b 30 Jan 2000, Ivo b 29 Apr 2001); m 2, 19 Dec 2009, Danielle de Niese; 1 s Bacchus William Anderson b 4 June 2015; *Career* early career in wildlife filmmaking, trg with Partridge Films, freelance cameraman 1992, films incl Buffalo, The African Boss, Red Monkeys of Zanzibar and New Fox in Town; exec chm Glyndebourne Productions Ltd 2000–; dir South-East Arts; awards for Glyndebourne: Royal Philharmonic Soc Audience Devpt Award (Zoe, Last Supper, La Boheme, Don Giovanni) 2000, Opera Award (Fidelio) 2001 South Bank Show Opera Award (Pelleas et Melisande) 2000 and (Giulio Cesare) 2005, Theatrical Mgmnt Assoc Award Outstanding Achievement in Opera (Tristan und Isolde) 2003; TMA Award for Glyndebourne Season 2009, Int Emmy Award for Best Arts Programme for BBC documentary 'Gareth Goes to Glyndebourne 2011, Royal Philharmonic Soc Music Award for Learning and Participation (Imago) 2014; *Recreations* sport (cycling, cricket, tennis, golf, football), nature, green energy, music; *Style*— Gus Christie, Esq; ✉ Glyndebourne, Lewes, East Sussex BN8 5UU (☎ 01273 812321, fax 01273 812783, e-mail gus.christie@glyndebourne.com)

CHRISTIE, Nan Stevenson; da of James Cowan Christie, of Ayr, and Henrietta, *née* Rock (d 1988); *b* 6 March 1948; *Educ* Ayr Acad, RSAMD, London Opera Centre; *m* 16 June 1972, Andrew S Hendrie, s of William Hendrie; 1 s (Ross b 2 July 1983); *Career* soprano; operatic debut as Fiametta in The Gondoliers (Scottish Opera), Covent Garden debut as First Esquire in Parsifal; toured in Switzerland, Portugal, Germany, Poland and Japan, princ guest artist Frankfurt Opera; worked with conductors incl: Claudio Abbado, André Previn, Sir John Pritchard, Sir Bernard Haitink, Sir Simon Rattle, Sir Alexander Gibson, John Mauceri, Michael Gielen; prof of singing and head of classical voice Goldsmiths Coll London, estab amateur opera co Operagold 2004 (dir and prodr: Venus & Adonis 2004, Dido and Aeneas 2005, the Magic Flute 2006, Carmen 2007, Peter Grimes 2008, Marriage of Figaro 2009, Rigoletto 2010, La Bohème 2011, La Traviata 2012, Die Zauberflote 2014, Die Fledermaus 2015; dir A Midsummer Night's Dream); dir of professional prodns: Carmen (Meantime Opera Greenwich) 2007, Peter Grimes 2008; James Caird travelling scholarship, Peter Stuyvesant scholarship, Countess of Munster scholarship, Peter Styvesant scholarship, James Caird travelling scholarship, Countss of Munster scholarship; *Roles* incl: Pamina in The Magic Flute (Eng Music Theatre, Opera de Nancy), Sophie in Tom Jones (Eng Music Theatre), Xenia in Boris Godunov (Scot Opera), Flora in The Turn of the Screw (Scot Opera), Galla in The Cataline Conspiracy (Scot Opera), Tytania in A Midsummer Night's Dream (Scot Opera, Opera North), Susanna in The Marriage of Figaro (Scot Opera, Frankfurt Opera), Despina in Cosi fan Tutte (Scot Opera, Netherlands Opera, Glyndebourne), Frasquita in Carmen (Edinburgh Festival, Earls Court, Japan), Oscar in Un Ballo in Maschera (Frankfurt Opera), Marie in Die Soldaten (Frankfurt Opera), Euridice in Orpheus in the Underworld (ENO), Countess Adele in Count Ory (ENO), Adele in Die Fledermaus (ENO), Queen of Night in The Magic Flute (Scot Opera, Marseille, ENO), Arbace in Mitridate (La Fenice Venice, Italian debut), Blonde in Mozart's Die Entführung aus dem Serail (Scot Opera, Frankfurt Opera), Oscar in Verdi's Un Ballo in Maschera (Bonn Opera), Peter Maxwell Davies' Dr of Myddfai (WNO, World Première) William Bolcom's Songs of Innocence & Experience (Royal Festival Hall, Eurp Première), Madame Herz in Ser Schauspieldirektor (BBC), Cunegonde in Candide (London Symphony Orchestra), Frasquita in Carmen (Edinburgh Festival), Despina in Cosi Fan Tutte (Glyndebourne), Carlotta in The Phantom of the Opera (HM Theatre Haymarket); *Recordings* audio incl: La Vita Nuova (with the Nash Ensemble and Nicholas Maw), Anthology of Italian Opera, Gli Orazie ed i Curiazi, Melancholia (by Dusapin, with Orchestra de Lyon), Dr of Myddfai (by Peter Maxwell Davies, with WNO), Parsifal (ROH); video incl: various Gilbert and Sullivan, Gianetta in The Gondoliers, Aline in The Sorcerer, title role in Princess Ida; DVD incl L'Enfant et les Sortileges (Glyndebourne); *Recreations* painting, reading, gardening; *Style*— Ms Nan Christie; ✉ e-mail nanchristie@hotmail.co.uk

CHRISTIE-MILLER, Andrew William Michael; o s of Maj Samuel Vandeleur Christie-Miller, CBE (d 1968), of Clarendon Park, Wilts, and Esmée Antoinette Fraser, *née* Hutcheson; *b* 22 September 1950; *Educ* Eton, RAC Cirencester (Dip Rural Estate Mgmnt, Dip Advanced Farm Mgmnt); *m* 6 Feb 1976 (m dis 2014), Barbara, da of Maj Charles Alexander Neil (d 1959), of London; 2 da (Rebecca Claire b 1976, Victoria Phoebe b 1978), 1 s (Alexander William Henry b 1982); *Career* Spicer & Pegler 1970–73, Savills 1978–82; chm Grainfarmers Ltd; memb Wilts CC 1985–93; chm Game Conservancy Tst 2000–06; High Sheriff Wilts 1996–97; ARICS 1979; *Recreations* shooting, travel, conservation; *Clubs* White's; *Style*— Andrew Christie-Miller, Esq; ✉ 2 Halsey Street, London SW3 2QH (☎ 07799 114850, e-mail andrewchristiemiller@gmail.com)

CHRISTMAS, Colin Adrian; s of R F Christmas, and M Haskey; *b* 11 December 1938; *Educ* Forest Sch, architectural colls Essex and London; *m* 31 March 1962, Elisa Curling, da of H H Curling Hope; 1 da (Laura b 14 Oct 1966), 1 s (Paul b 7 Feb 1968); *Career* with Sir Giles Gilbert Scott Son and Partner 1959–63; work on: Liverpool Cathedral, Bankside Power Station; Fitzroy Robinson Partnership: designer/planner 1963, ptnr 1987–92, conslt 1992–; architectural and historic conslt Covent Garden Market and Royal Exchange 1997–; designs for shopping, office, residential and industrial complexes in UK and abroad incl Palace Garden Shopping Centre Enfield and Pinners Hall City of London; responsible for design and implementation of extension and refurbishment of Royal Exchange London 1983–91 and Pinners Hall City of London; Civic Tst commendation for Watling Court, Design Award Chancery House Sutton, Stone Fedn commendation and City Heritage Award for Royal Exchange; *Books* The Caliphs Design (conslt, ed by Paul Edwards, 1986), The Royal Exchange (contrib, 1997); *Recreations* east coast sailing, music, travel, art; *Style*— Colin Christmas, Esq; ✉ 33 The Drive, North Chingford, London E4 7AJ (☎ and fax 020 8529 0925, e-mail cchristmas321@btinternet.com); 31 Woodrolfe Park, Tollesbury, Maldon CM9 8TB

CHRISTOPHER, (Phyllis) Ann; da of William Christopher (d 1986), of Rickmansworth, Herts, and Phyllis, *née* Vennall (d 2005); *b* 4 December 1947; *Educ* Watford Girls GS, Harrow Sch of Art, W of Eng Coll of Art (Dip AD); *m* 19 July 1969, Kenneth Harold Cook, s of Harold Gilbert Cook (d 2005), of Oldland Common, nr Bristol; *Career* sculptor; numerous gp and solo exhibitions 1969–; works in public collections incl: Bristol City Art Gallery, Univ of Bristol, Glynn Vivian Art Gallery Swansea, Royal W of Eng Acad, Chantrey Bequest Royal Acad, Harrison Weir Collection London, Br Museum, Contemporary Art Soc, Corcoran Art Gallery Washington DC, Pallant House Gallery Chichester; commissions incl: Corten Sculpture (4.9m) Marsh Mills Plymouth 1996, Bronze Sculpture (2.4m) Linklaters & Paines London 1997, Bronze Sculpture (3m) private garden Great Barrington USA 1998, Corten Sculpture (5.5m) Port Marine Bristol 2001, Bronze Sculpture (2.2m) private garden Albi France 2002; RA 1989 (assoc 1980), FRBS 1992; *Publications* Ann Christopher (monograph published by RA, 2016); *Recreations* cinema, travel, architecture; *Style*— Miss Ann Christopher, RA; ✉ website www.pangolinlondon.com

CHRISTOPHER, Baron (Life Peer UK 1998), of Leckhampton in the County of Gloucestershire; Anthony Martin Grosvenor (Tony) Christopher; CBE (1984); s of George Russell Christopher (d 1951), and Helen Kathleen Milford, *née* Rowley (d 1971); *b* 25 April 1925; *Educ* Cheltenham GS, Westminster Coll of Commerce; *m* 1962, Adela Joy Thompson; *Career* chm Trades Union Unit Trust Mangrs Ltd 1983; political and PR conslt 1989–; Inland Revenue Staff Fedn: asst sec 1957–60, asst gen sec 1960–74, jt gen sec 1975, gen sec 1976–88; chm Civil Serv Bldg Soc 1958–87, pres TUC Gen Cncl 1988–89 (memb 1976–89); memb: Bd Civil Serv Housing Assoc 1958–96 (vice-chm 1988–96), Cncl of Nat Assoc for Care and Resettlement of Offenders 1956–98 (chm 1973–98), Home Sec's Advsy Cncl for Probation and After-Care Ctee 1966–79, Home Sec's Working Party on Treatment of Habitual Drunken Offenders 1969–71, Cncl of Policy Studies Inst, Cncl Inst of Manpower Studies, Econ Social Res Cncl 1985–88, TUC Gen Cncl 1976–89, TUC Econ Ctee 1977–89, TUC Educn Ctee 1977–85, TUC Employment Policy and Orgn Ctee 1979–89, TUC Int Ctee 1982–89, TUC Media Working Group 1979–89 (chm 1985–89), TUC Fin Gen Purposes Ctee 1984–89, TUC Educn and Trg Ctee 1985–86, Tax Consultative Ctee 1974–88, Royal Cmmn on Distribution of Income and Wealth 1979–80, IBA 1978–83, Broadcasting Complaints Cmmn 1989–96, Audit Cmmn 1989–95, GMC 1989–94, Ind Inquiry into Rover Cowley Works Closure Proposals 1990; tstee Inst for Public Policy Res (treas 1991–94); chm: NEDO Tyre Ind Econ Devpt Ctee 1983–84, Alcoholics Recovery Project 1970–76; FRSA 1989; *Books* Policy for Poverty (jtly, 1970), The Wealth Report (jtly, 1979); *Recreations* gardening, reading, music; *Clubs* Beefsteak, Wig and Pen; *Style*— The Lord Christopher, CBE; ✉ c/o T U Fund Managers Ltd, Congress House, Great Russell Street, London WC1B 3LQ; House of Lords, London SW1A 0PW

CHRISTOPHERS, Dr Richard Henry Tudor (Harry); CBE (2012); s of Richard Henry Christophers (d 1991), of Canterbury, Kent, and Constance Clavering, *née* Thorp (d 1987); *b* 26 December 1953; *Educ* Canterbury Cathedral Choir Sch, King's Sch Canterbury, Magdalen Coll Oxford; *m* 2 June 1979, Veronica Mary, da of Francis Vincent Hayward; 2 da (Antonia Lucy Mary b 30 Nov 1984, Cecilia Mary b 1 March 1991), 2 s (Dominic James b 18 March 1987, Sebastian John b 14 April 1989); *Career* conductor; South Bank debut 1983, Salzburg Festival debut 1989, Proms debut 1990, Opera debut (Lisbon Opera) 1994, Musikverein debut 1998, Concertgebiuw Amsterdam debut 1999, ENO debut 2000; conductor and fndr The Sixteen (choir and period instrument orchestra); orchs conducted incl: Deutsche Kammerphilharmonie, Orch of the Age of Enlightenment, City of London Sinfonia, English Chamber Orch, Northern Sinfonia, BBC Philharmonic, London Symphony Orch, Hallé Orch, Academy of St Martin-in-the-Fields, Royal Liverpool Philharmonic, San Francisco Symphony Orchestra, Handel and Haydn Soc of Boston, Granada Symphony Orchestra, Orquesta Comunidad de Madrid; princ guest conductor Granada Symphony Orchestra; artistic dir Handel & Haydn Soc Boston 2008; Classic FM Gramaphone Artist of the Year Award 2009; Hon DMus Univ of Leicester 2008; hon fell Magdalen Coll Oxford 2009, hon fell Royal Welsh Acad for Music and Drama 2009; *Recordings* numerous recordings with The Sixteen incl: Taverner's Festal Masses Vols I-VI (1984–93) and Missa Gloria Tibi Trinitas (1989, Grand Prix du Disque), Monteverdi's Masses (1987) and Vespers (1988), Handel's Messiah (1989, Grand Prix du Disque), Byrd's Mass à 5 (1989) and Mass à 4 (1990), Poulenc's Figure Humaine (1990), Bach's St John Passion (1990), Palestrina's Missa Papae Marcelli (1990), 20 Century Christmas Collection (1990), Eton Choirbook Vols 1–5 (1991–95, Vol 1 winner Gramophone Award 1992), Handel's Alexander's Feast (1991, Deutschen Schallplatten, 1992), Purcell's Fairy Queen

(1991), Sheppard's Sacred Music Vols 1–4 (1990–92), 20 Century American Collection (1991), Britten's Choral Music Vols 1–3 (1992–93, Vol 2 Deutschen Schauplatten, 1993), Bach's Christmas Oratorio (1993), Handel's Israel in Egypt (1993), Bach's B Minor Mass (1994), Stravinsky's Symphony of Psalms with the BBC Philharmonic (1995, Diapason d'Or 1995), Handel's Esther (1996), Messiaen's Cinq Rechants (1996), Handel's Samson (1997), Scarlatti's Stabat Mater (1997), Victoria's Sacred Music Vols 1–3 (1997–98), Buxtehude's Membra Jesu Nostri (2001), Renaissance (2004, Classical Brit Award 2005), Victoria's Requiem (2004), Ikon (2005), Music from the Sistine Chapel (2007), A Mother's Love (2007), Streams of Tears (2008), Faure's Requiem (2008), Handel's Messiah (2008), Handel Coronation Anthems (Gramaphone Award 2009); *Television and DVDs* BBC Sacred Music Series 1 (2007) and Series 2 (2009), God's Composer (2011), Monteverdi (2015); video Handel's Messiah in Dublin (1992); *Recreations* cooking, Arsenal FC; *Style—* Dr Harry Christophers, CBE; ✉ c/o The Sixteen Limited, Quadrant House, 10 Fleet Street, London EC4Y 1AU (☎ 020 7936 3420, e-mail info@thesixteen.org.uk, website www.thesixteen.com)

CHRUSZCZ, Charles Francis; QC (1992); s of Jan Franciszek Chruszcz, of Cheadle, Cheshire, and Kathleen Whitehurst; *b* 19 November 1950; *Educ* Brookway HS, QMC London (LLB); *m* Margaret Olivia, da of John Chapman; 3 s (Alexander John b 30 Aug 1977, Edward Charles b 26 March 1979, Thomas Robert b 20 May 1981); *Career* called to the Bar Middle Temple 1971, entered chambers at Peters St Manchester 1973, recorder of the Crown Court 1991– (asst recorder 1986–91); *Recreations* keen interest in lacrosse, rugby, reading, music, politics and the outdoors; *Style—* Charles Chruszcz, Esq, QC; ✉ Exchange Chambers, 7 Ralli Court, Westriverside, Manchester M3 5FT (☎ 0161 833 2722)

CHRYSTAL, Prof (Kenneth) Alexander (Alec); s of Kenneth Hugh Chrystal (d 1945), and Dorothy Bell, *née* Anderson (d 2003); *b* 21 January 1946, Wallasey, Merseyside; *Educ* Oldershaw GS Wallasey, Univ of Exeter (BA), Univ of Essex (MA, PhD); *m* 1, 4 April 1972 (m dis 1978); 1 s (Mark Kenneth James b 1972); m 2, 29 July 1995, Alison Anne Wigley; *Career* lectr: Univ of Manchester 1971–72, Civil Serv Coll 1972–75; econ advsr HM Treasy 1975–76, lectr Univ of Essex 1976–84, visiting prof Univ of Calif Davis 1979–80, visiting scholar Federal Reserve Bank of St Louis 1983–84, prof of economics Univ of Sheffield 1984–88, prof of monetary economics City Univ Business Sch 1988–99 (head Dept of Banking Fin 1996–97), sr advsr Bank of England 1997–2001, prof of money and banking City Univ Business Sch (now Sir John Cass Business Sch) 2001–09 (prof emeritus 2009–); FSS 1967, FRSA 1995; *Books* Controversies in Macroeconomics (1979), Political Economics (with J Alt, 1983), Exchange Rates and the Open Economy (ed with R Sedgwick, 1987), Introduction to Positive Economics (with R G Lipsey, 1995), Economics for Business and Management (with R G Lipsey, 1997), Principles of Economics (with R G Lipsey, 1999), Economics (with R G Lipsey, 10 edn 2004, 11 edn 2007, 12 edn 2011, 13 edn 2015); *Recreations* music, travel, economics; *Style—* Prof Alec Chrystal; ✉ 6 Montague Road, Cambridge CB4 1BX (☎ 01223 352134); Sir John Cass Business School, City of London, 106 Bunhill Row, London EC1Y 8TZ (☎ 020 7040 0159, e-mail a.chrystal@city.ac.uk)

CHRYSTIE, Dr Kenneth George; s of Gordon Buchanan Chrystie (d 1993), and Winifrede Mary Chrystie (d 1993); *b* 24 November 1946, Glasgow; *Educ* Univ of Glasgow (LLB, PhD), Univ of Virginia; *m* 11 June 1975, Mary Harrison Chrystie, *née* Kirkpatrick; 1 s (Patrick William Gordon b 19 Nov 1978), 2 da (Kate Helen b 18 June 1980, Lindsay Elizabeth b 21 July 1983); *Career* lawyer McClure Naismith; non-exec dir: Murgitroyd plc, Nautricity Ltd, L'Escargot Ltd; chm Discipline Ctee ICAS; memb Law Soc of Scotland; past pres Royal Glasgow Inst of the Fine Arts; chm Hugh Fraser Fndn, dir Glasgow Science Centre; FRSA; *Publications* Encyclopaedia of Scots Law (contrib, 1988), International Handbook on Contracts of Employment (contrib, 1988); *Recreations* golf, tennis, skiing; *Clubs* Prestwick Golf, Glasgow Art, Glasgow Golf; *Style—* Dr Kenneth Chrystie; ✉ 2 Redlands Road, Glasgow G12 0SJ (☎ 0141 339 2757, e-mail kgchrystie@icloud.com)

CHU, Dr Anthony Christopher; s of Yu-Chang Chu, of Bexley, Kent, and Frances Nelly Chu; *b* 13 May 1951; *Educ* Alleyn's Sch Dulwich, Guy's Hosp Med Sch (BSc, MB BS); *m* 11 March 1978 (m dis 1987), Sian Meryl, da of John Daniel Griffths, of Hailey, Oxon; 2 da (Jessica Louise b 1979, Alexandra Mary b 1980); m 2, 30 Dec 1989, Jenny Frances, da of Robert Morris, of Haughley Green, Suffolk; 2 da (Natasha Victoria and Caroline Frances b 1999), 1 s (James Andrew Portman b 1999); *Career* various posts NHS 1975–80, sr staff assoc coll of physicians and surgns Columbia Presbyterian Hosp New York 1980–81, sr registrar St John's Hosp for Skin Diseases 1981–82; sr lectr (also conslt dermatologist and Wellcome sr res fell): Royal Post Grad Med Sch Hammersmith Hosp, St John's Hosp for Skin Diseases 1982–89; sr lectr and conslt dermatologist Imperial Coll Sch of Med at Hammersmith Hosp (Royal Postgrad Med Sch until merger) and Ealing Hosp 1989–2005, conslt dermatologist, hon sr lectr and head of dermatology Hammersmith Hosps Tst and Ealing Hosp 2005–; prof of dermatologic oncology Univ of Buckingham 2010; memb and sec: Int Histiocyte Soc, Br Assoc of Univ Teachers of Dermatology; chm Acne Support Gp; Freeman City of London 1991, Liveryman Worshipful Soc of Apothecaries 1989; FRCP 1993 (MRCP 1978); *Recreations* horticulture, painting; *Style—* Dr Anthony Chu; ✉ Unit of Dermatology, Imperial College School of Medicine, Hammersmith Hospital, Du Cane Road, London W12 0NN (☎ 020 8383 3264, e-mail a.chu@imperial.ac.uk)

CHUNG, Dan; s of Thiam Chung, of Costock, Leics, and Pearl, *née* Yeo; *b* 29 May 1971, Loughborough, Leics; *Educ* Univ of Plymouth (BSc), Sheffield Coll (NCTJ); Tania Anin Branigan; 1 s Zan Tarit Chung Branigan; *Career* photographer: Reuters Ltd 1997–2003, The Guardian 2003–13; cameraman CNBC 2014–15, ed Newshooter.com 2015–; memb Guild of Television Cameramen; Nikon Press Photographer of the Year 2002, Photographer of the Year Picture Eds Award 2004, What The Papers Say Photographer of the Year 2004 and 2005, Nikon Celebrity Photographer 2005, James Cameron Meml Special Award 2006; *Publications* contrib: The Art of Sport (2002), Guardian Yearbook (2003), The State of the World (2006), Photojournalism: The World's Top Photographers (2006); *Recreations* music, travel; *Style—* Dan Chung, Esq; ✉ e-mail photographer@gmail.com; The Guardian, Kings Place, 90 York Way, London N1 9GU (☎ 020 7713 4161, fax 020 7239 9951, e-mail dan.chung@guardian.co.uk)

CHUNG, Prof (Kian) Fan; s of Young Cheong Chung (d 1991), and Ah-Lime Cheung Kam Cheong; *b* 12 February 1951; *Educ* Royal Coll Curepipe Mauritius (Gold Medal Chamber of Agric, Govt Mauritius scholar), Middx Hosp Med Sch Univ of London (Thomas Meyerstein scholar, Harold Boldero scholar, MB BS, MD, DSc), MRC (Dorothy Temple Cross scholar); *m* 9 July 1977, Soop-Chin Claire, da of Ng Kee Kwong; 3 da (Joanne b 20 April 1982, Katie b 16 Feb 1991, Annabelle b 1 March 1996); *Career* house offr Hammersmith & Middlesex Hosp and Radcliffe Infirmary Oxford 1975–78, chief resident Hosp Cantonal Geneva 1978–79, sr registrar Charing Cross Hosp 1979–83, visiting sci Univ of Calif 1983–85, currently prof of respiratory med Nat Heart and Lung Inst ICSTM (sr lectr and reader in respiratory med 1987–96); hon conslt physician Royal Brompton and Harefield NHS Tst, sr fell Nat Inst of Health Research; visiting prof: Changgung Univ Hosp Taiwan 1997, Univ of Natal SA 1998, Univ of WA 1999, Guangzhou Respiratory Inst 2014–16, Jiaotong Univ Med Sch 2015–17; princ investigator: Severe Asthma Research Project, MRC-Asthma UK Centre for Asthma, UBIOPRED Severe Asthma Project; sr investigator Nat Inst for Health Research 2010; memb Editorial Bd: Euro Respiratory Jl 1995–99, American Jl of Respiratory and Critical Care Med 1996–2003, Jl of Euro Soc of Allergy and Clinical Immunology 1999–2005, Euro Jl of Clinical Pharmacology 2000–, Therapy in Respiratory Disease 2001–, Respirology 2007–, Euro Jl of Pharmacology 2008–, Lancet Respiratory Medicine 2013–; res awards: Wellcome Tst 1995–, MRC 1999–, Nat Inst of Health 2001–; memb: Br Thoracic Soc 1986–, American Thoracic Soc 1986–, Euro Respiratory Soc 1987– (memb: Exec 1998–, Sci Ctee 2001–, Prog Ctee Annual Congress 1999–), Br Pharmacological Soc 1987–, American Coll of Chest Physicians 1989–, Prog Ctee World Asthma Meeting Chicago 2001, Br Guidelines on Asthma Mgmnt Nat Asthma Campaign 2001; co-chm Euro Asthma Congress Moscow 2001, chair 7th Int Symposium on Cough 2012; Sadoul Lectr at European Respiratory Soc 2014; FRCP 1992; *Publications* Therapeutics of Respiratory Disease (co-author, 1994), Asthma: Mechanisms and Protocols (co-ed, 2000), Clinicians' Guide to Asthma (2002), Cough: Causes, Mechanisms and Treatment (co-ed, 2003), Airway smooth muscle in asthma and COPD (2008), Pharmacology and Therapeutics of Cough (co-ed, 2009), Pharmacology and Therapeutics of Airways Disease (2010); author of 400 scientific pubns; *Recreations* table tennis, travel, history; *Style—* Prof Fan Chung; ✉ National Heart and Lung Institute, Imperial College, Dovehouse Street, London SW3 6LY (☎ 020 7594 7959, fax 020 7351 8126, e-mail f.chung@imperial.ac.uk)

CHUNN, Louise; da of Jeremiah Alfred Chunn, of Auckland, NZ, and Yvonne Chunn; *b* 24 July 1956; *Educ* St Joseph's Convent Otahuhu, Baradene Coll Remuera, Univ of Aukland (BA); *m* 1, Aug 1981 (m dis), Dominic Anthony Free; 1 s (Charlie b 11 March 1986), 1 da (Alice b 23 June 1988); m 2, April 2001, Andrew John Anthony; 1 da (Isabel b 14 June 2000); *Career* ed Just Seventeen 1985–86, dep ed Elle 1986–89; The Guardian: ed Women's Page 1989–94, ed Madame Figaro 1993–95, assoc features ed 1994–95; Vogue: assoc ed 1995–96, features dir 1996–97, dep ed 1997–98; ed: ES Magazine 1998–2000, InStyle magazine 2002–06 (dep ed 2001–02), Good Housekeeping 2006–08, Psychologies 2009–; fndr memb Women in Journalism; fndr welldoing.org 2012; tstee UK Friends Univ of Auckland 2010–; *Style—* Ms Louise Chunn; ☎ 020 8930 8906, e-mail louisechunn@welldoing.org, website http://welldoing.org

CHURCH, Jonathan; CBE (2015); s of Tony Church, of Nottingham, and Marielaine, *née* Douglas; *b* 4 March 1967; *Educ* Frank Weldon Comp Nottingham, Clarendon Coll of FE Nottingham; *m* Yvonne Thomson; 4 da; *Career* theatre director and producer; asst dir Nottingham Playhouse 1990–91 (asst prodr 1992), artistic dir Triptych Theatre Co 1993–97, assoc dir Derby Playhouse 1994–95, artistic dir Salisbury Playhouse 1995–99, assoc dir Hampstead Theatre 1999–2001, artistic dir Birmingham Rep 2001–06, artistic dir Chichester Festival Theatre 2006–; *Theatre* as dir, West End prodns incl: Taken at Midnight (Theatre Royal Haymarket), Singin' in the Rain (Palace Theatre), The Resistable Rise of Arturo Ui (Duchess Theatre), Of Mice and Men (Savoy Theatre and Old Vic), The Witches (Wyndhams Theatre), A Busy Day (Lyric Theatre), Nicholas Nickleby (Gielgud Theatre); as co-prodr, West End prodns incl: Guys and dolls (Savoy Theatre), Gypsy (Savoy Theatre), Stevie (Hampstead Theatre), The Pajama Game (Shaftesbury Theatre), Private Lives (Gielgud Theatre), Kiss Me Kate (Old Vic), Sweeney Todd (Adelphi Theatre), Love Story (Duchess Theatre), ENRON (Coward Theatre BAM and Broadway); theatre as dir, national prodns incl: Mack and Mabel, Singin in the Rain, The Grapes of Wrath, The Crucible, The Witches, Of Mice and Men, The Diary of Anne Frank, Hobsons Choice, God and Stephen Hawking, Romeo and Juliet, The Circle and Master Class; theatre as di, international producns incl: Singin in the Rain (Tokyo, Australia, New Zealand), The Last Confession (Toronto, Los Angeles, Perth, Brisbane, Adelaide, Melbourne, Sydney), The Life and Adventures of Nicholas Nickleby (Princess of Wales Theatre Toronto); theatre as dir, other producns incl: Mack and Mabel (Chichester), Taken at Midnight (Chichester), Amadeus (Chichester), The Resistable Rise of Arturo Ui (Chichester), Singin in the Rain (Chichester), The Critic/The Real Inspector Hound (co-directed with Sean Foley, Chichester), The Grapes of Wrath (Chichester), The Circle (Chichester), Hobsons Choice (Chichester), Pravda (Chichester), Nicholas Nickleby (co-directed with Philip Franks Chichester), The Life of Galileo, Promises and Lies, Elizabeth Rex, Hobsons Choice, Of Mice and Men, Private Lives, Closer, Peter Pan, The David Hare Triliogy, The Norman Conquests, The Crucible, The Witches (Birmingham Rep), A Busy Day (Bristol Old Vic), You Be Ted and Ill Be Sylvia (Hampstead Theatre), The Crucible (Birmingham Old Rep), The Norman Conquests, The Rover, The Banished Cavaliers, The Merchant of Venice, The Rehearsal, The Double Inconstancy, Disappearances, Racing Demon, The Cherry Orchard, Romeo and Juliet, The Alchemical Wedding, Colombe (Salisbury Playhouse), Angels Rave On and Saint Oscar (Nottingham Playhouse), Educating Rita and Oleanna (Salisbury Playhouse and Chichester Festival Theatre), Top Girls, Plymouth Theatre Royal, Time and the Conways (Colchester Mercury), Frankie and Johnny in the Claire de Lune, Two, Someone Wholl Watch Over Me, The Importance of Being Earnest, Absurd Person Singular, and Oleanna (Derby Playhouse), The Bear and The Ballad of Reading Gaol (Sheffield Crucible), Magnetic North (West Yorkshire Playhouse), In Lambeth (Lyric Hammersmith Studio and Nottingham Playhouse), The Broken Heart (Lyric Hammersmith Studio) and Comic Cuts (Derby Playhouse, Bristol Old Vic and Lyric Hammersmith Studio); *Style—* Jonathan Church, CBE; ✉ Chichester Festival Theatre, Oaklands Park, Chichester, West Sussex PO19 6AP (☎ 01243 784437)

CHURCH, Prof Roy Anthony; s of William Alfred Church (d 1973), of Kettering, and Lillian Gertrude Church (d 1990); *b* 21 February 1935; *Educ* Kettering GS, Univ of Nottingham (BA, PhD); *m* 10 Oct 1959, Gwenllian Elizabeth, da of James Whyte Martin (d 1984), of Kettering; 3 s (Benjamin b 1964, Joseph b 1969, Thomas b 1970), 1 da (Naomi b 1980); *Career* economic historian; BBC 1958–60, Purdue Univ Indiana USA 1960–61, Univ of Washington Seattle USA 1961–62, Univ of Br Columbia Vancouver Canada 1962–63, Univ of Birmingham 1963–72; UEA: prof of economic and social history 1972–, pro-vice-chllr 1986–89, dean Sch of History 1997–1999; visiting research fell Univ of Canberra 1998, Wellcome special research fell 1999–2003; pres Assoc of Business Historians; memb: Cncl of Econ History Soc, Econ and Social Research Cncl; govr History of Advertising Trust; FRHistS 1972; ed Economic History Review 1982–90; *Books* Economic and Social Change in a Midland Town 1815–1900: Victorian Nottingham (1966), Kenricks in Hardware: A Family Business, 1790–1965 (1969), The Great Victorian Boom (1975), Herbert Austin: The British Motor Car Industry to 1941 (1979), The Dynamics of Victorian Business (ed, 1980), The History of the British Coal Industry, Volume 3: 1830–1913, Victorian Pre-eminence (1986, Wadsworth Prize), The Rise and Decline of the British Motor Industry (1994), Strikes and Solidarity: Coalfield Conflict in Britain 1889–1966 (with C E Outram, 1999), Burroughs Wellcome & Co: Knowledge, Trust, Profit and the Transformation of the British Pharmaceutical Industry 1880–1940 (with E M Tansey, 2007), Pharmaceutical Innovation, Contested Organizational Cultures, and the Triumph of Philanthropy (2015); *Recreations* tennis, badminton, fell walking, theatre; *Style—* Prof Roy Church; ✉ School of History, University of East Anglia, Norwich (☎ 01603 456161)

CHURCH, William Henry; s of Henry Albion Church (d 1981), and Iris Edith, *née* Duddy (d 1986); *b* 23 July 1946; *Educ* St Joseph's Coll Ipswich, King's Coll, Univ of London (MB BS); *m* 6 Jan 1973, Jane Ann, da of Hugh Parry, of Aberdaron, Gwynedd; 3 s (Edward b 1974, James b 1976, Martin b 1977), 1 da (Sarah b 1981); *Career* sr registrar in ophthalmology Royal Victoria Infirmary Newcastle upon Tyne 1984–88, conslt ophthalmologist Aberdeen Royal Infirmary 1988–; mountaineering achievements: first solo ascent N Face Mount Kenya 1969, first ascent N face Koh-i-Mondi Afghanistan with P Boardman, M Wragg and C Fitzhugh 1972, first ascent Chong Kumdan I (7,071m) E Karakoram India with D Wilkinson, N McAdie and J Porter 1992, 11 first ascents in

Eastern Greenland Alps with David Wilkinson and Brian Davison 2004; MRCP 1975, FRCS 1983, FRCOphth 1991; *Recreations* mountaineering, rock climbing, skiing, fly fishing; *Clubs* Alpine; *Style*— William Church, Esq; ⊠ Aberdeen Royal Infirmary, Foresthill, Aberdeen AB9 2ZB (☏ 01224 681818, ext 52422)

CHURCHER, Neville John (Nev); MBE (1996); s of Nigel Churcher, of Gosport, and Eileen Helen, *née* Ryman; *b* 22 May 1945; *Educ* Portsmouth GS, Portsmouth Sch of Architecture; *m* 1970, Marilyn Jean (Maz), da of Anthony John Stapleton; 2 c (Joe b 1972, Eppie b 1976); *Career* architect specialising in early years and primary educn and one-off houses on small and difficult sites; with Hampshire CC 1978–2010, currently in private practice; awards assessor, pt/t educator; RIBA 1980, FCSD 1996, FRSA 1996; *Awards* for Jamaica Cottage 1975; for Woodlea Sch: The Educn Award 1992, RIBA President's Building of the Year Award 1993, BBC Design Awards Arch and Environment and Designer of the Year Awards 1994; for offices and gardens Old Churcher's Coll at Petersfield: Civic Tst Award 1996, BDA Public Building Award 1998; for Whiteley Primary School: RIBA Award 2002; Civic Tst Award 2003, BDA Sustainability Award 2003; *Recreations* old competition cars, wooden gliders and boats, classical, jazz and world music, photography; *Clubs* VSCC, Midland Automobile; *Style*— Nev Churcher, Esq, MBE; ⊠ Jamaica Cottage, Jamaica Place, Gosport, Hampshire PO12 1LX (☏ 023 9252 7202)

CHURCHILL, Caryl Lesley; da of Robert Churchill, and Jan, *née* Brown; *b* 3 September 1938; *Educ* Trafalgar Montreal Canada, LMH Oxford; *m* David Richard Harter; 3 s (Joe b 1963, Paul b 1964, Rick b 1969); *Career* playwright; wrote: one-act play Downstairs (produced by Oriel Coll Oxford) 1958, Having A Wonderful Time (Questors Theatre) 1960, Easy Death (Oxford Playhouse) 1962; BBC radio plays incl: The Ants (Third Prog) 1962, Lovesick 1967, Identical Twins 1968, Abortive 1971, Not..Not..Not..Not Enough Oxygen 1971, Schreber's Nervous Illness 1972 (subsequently adapted for stage, King's Head Theatre Islington), Henry's Past 1972, Perfect Happiness 1973; BBC TV plays incl: The Judge's Wife 1972, Turkish Delight 1974, The After Dinner Joke 1978, Crimes 1982; other stage plays incl: Owners (Theatre Upstairs, Royal Court) 1972, Objections To Sex And Violence (Royal Court) 1975, Light Shining in Buckinghamshire (Joint Stock UK tour, Theatre Upstairs, Royal Court) 1976, Vinegar Tom (Monstrous Regt UK tour, ICA Theatre) 1976, Traps (Theatre Upstairs, Royal Court) 1977, Cloud 9 (Joint Stock UK tour, Royal Court 1978 and 1980, 2 years Off-Broadway), Three More Sleepless Nights (Soho Poly and Theatre Upstairs, Royal Court) 1980, Top Girls (Royal Court, New York Shakespeare Festival Theatre) 1982–83, Fen (Joint Stock UK tour, Almeida Theatre, New York Shakespeare Festival Theatre) 1983–84, Softcops (RSC, The Barbican) 1984, A Mouthful of Birds (with David Lan, Joint Stock UK tour, Royal Court) 1986, Serious Money (Royal Court, Wyndhams Theatre, New York Shakespeare Festival then Broadway) 1987–88, Ice Cream (Royal Court) 1989, Ice Cream with Hot Fudge (Public Theatre) 1989, Mad Forest (Central Sch of Speech and Drama London, Nat Theatre Bucharest, Royal Court) 1990, Lives of the Great Poisoners (with Orlando Gough and Ian Spink, Second Strike UK tour, Riverside Studios) 1991, The Skriker (RNT) 1994, Thyestes (trans, Royal Court Theatre Upstairs) 1994, Hotel (Second Stride, The Place) 1997, This is a Chair (Royal Court) 1997, Blue Heart (Out of Joint, Royal Court and tour) 1997, Far Away (Royal Court, Albery) 2000, A Number (Royal Court) 2002, Drunk Enough to Say I Love You? (Royal Court) 2006, Seven Jewish Children (Royal Court) 2009; *Awards* incl: Obie for Cloud 9 1982, Obie for Top Girls 1983, Hollywood Dramalogue Critics Award for Cloud 9, Susan Blackburn Award 1984 and 1987, Best Play Olivier Award, Best Comedy Evening Standard Award and the Plays and Players Award all for Serious Money 1987; *Style*— Ms Caryl Churchill; ⊠ Casarotto Ramsay Ltd, Waverley House, 7–12 Noel Street, London W1F 8GQ (☏ 020 7287 4450, fax 020 7287 9128)

CHURCHILL, Jane (Lady Charles Spencer-Churchill); da of Hon Mark Wyndham, and Hon Mrs Wyndham, *née* Winn; *b* 17 January 1948; *m* 9 Dec 1970, Lord Charles Spencer-Churchill; 3 s (Rupert b 26 Nov 1971, Dominic b 15 Dec 1979, Alexander b 9 June 1983); *Career* interior designer; began at Colefax & Fowler, fndr and owner gift shop Treasure Island until 1982, fndr fabric and wallpaper shop Jane Churchill Design 1982 (sold to Colefax & Fowler 1989); fndr Jane Churchill Interiors Ltd (projects incl interiors in UK, Europe, USA, Aust and Caribbean); with Annie Charlton: presenter TV series Finishing Touches (Granada) and author of accompanying book, home furnishings conslt to Next plc and Hunters of Brora, designer Simplicity Patterns 1994–, designer Pimlico Road (for cos incl Drexel Heritage, Frederick Cooper and Tynedale, Sherrill Furniture and NDI); memb Advsy Bd Liberty's plc 2008–, memb Int Cncl Wallace Collection 2010; TV guest: Elsa Klensh Style (CNN), Dream Home (GMTV); *Style*— Jane Churchill; ⊠ Jane Churchill Interiors Ltd, 81 Pimlico Road, London SW1W 8PH (☏ 020 7730 8564, fax 020 7823 6421, e-mail jchurchill@janechurchillinteriors.co.uk, website www.janechurchillinteriors.com)

CHURCHILL, Lawrence; CBE (2010); s of Austin Churchill (d 1969), and Kathleen, *née* Keating (d 1993); *b* 5 August 1946, Birkenhead; *Educ* Birkenhead Sch, St John's Coll Oxford (MA); *m* 7 Sept 1991, Karen, da of Arnold Darcy, and Mary Darcy; 2 da (Charlotte Mary Kathleen, Sophie Janet Tonia (twins) b 16 March 2000); by previous m, 1 s (Andrew Mark b 23 Aug 1973), 1 da (Emma Jane b 3 May 1975); *Career* systems analyst Procter & Gamble Ltd 1969–73, systems analyst rising to exec dir Allied Dunbar Assurance plc 1973–91 (memb Bd 1985–91), joined National Westminster Bank plc 1991 (held several internal directorships 1992–98), fndr chief exec NatWest Life 1992–96, md NatWest Life & Investments 1995–98, chm and md UNUM Ltd 1998–2002, chief exec UK, Irish and int life Zurich Fin Services 2002–04, chair Pensions Protection Fund 2004–10. chm Nat Employment Savings Tst Corporation 2010–15, chm Financial Services Compensation Scheme 2012–; non-exec dir: Monkton/Good Energy plc 2004–12, Huntswood 2005–06, The Children's Mutual 2005–10, Bupa 2009– (sr ind dir 2015–); dir PIA 1994–97, dir ABI 1996–98 (memb Life Insurance Cncl 1994–96 and 2000–04), non-exec dir Fin Ombudsman Serv 2002–05, memb Bd for Actuarial Standards 2006–12, chm Ind Governance Gp Prudential UK 2015–; chm Applegate Marketplace 2015–; memb Ministerial Advsy Gp Incapacity Benefit Reform 2003–05, memb Disability Advsy Gp Nat Employment Panel, vice-pres Employment Opportunities; tstee Royal Soc of Arts 2000–02, tstee Int Longevity Centre UK 2007–, govr Pensions Policy Inst 2010– (chm 2016–), tstee Age UK 2015–; memb Chartered Inst of Technol Professionals, affiliate Inst of Risk Mgmnt, MBCS, MCMI, FRSA; *Recreations* rugby, bridge, opera, gardening; *Clubs* Oxford & Cambridge; *Style*— Lawrence Churchill, Esq, CBE; ⊠ e-mail lawrence.churchill@thechurchillsonline.com

CHURCHILL, Dr Sophie; OBE (2011); da of Dr John Race, of Abingdon, Oxon, and Eva, *née* Carabine; *b* 1963, Braintree; *Educ* CCC Oxford (BA), Univ of Birmingham (DPhil); *Children* 2 s (Ben b 1985, Owen b 1989), 1 da (Emily b 1986); *Career* dir Birmingham City Pride 2000–03, chief exec RegenWM 2003–06, chief exec Nat Forest Co 2006–14; pres Royal Forestry Soc 2015– (vice-pres 2013–15), chair TREE AID; fndr The Corpse Project 2015–; visiting fell Univ of Derby 2014; hon fell Inst of Chartered Foresters 2012; FRSA 2015; *Style*— Dr Sophie Churchill, OBE; ⊠ 16 Bevin House, Butler Street, Bethnal Green, London E2 0RW (☏ 07973 529603, e-mail sophiechurchill505@gmail.com, website www.thecorpseproject.net, Twitter @churchillsophie)

CHURCHMAN, Michael Anthony; s of Richard John Churchman (d 1978), of Islington, London, and Mary, *née* Bradley (d 2001); *b* 6 February 1952; *Educ* St Ignatius Coll London, Worcester Coll Oxford (MA); *m* 1974, Christine Elizabeth, da of Bryan Bernard George Dyer, of Lowestoft, Suffolk; 3 s (Anthony Laurence b 4 Aug 1979, Christopher Michael b 28 July 1981, Alexander Richard b 19 Nov 1986); *Career* account exec Young and Rubicam 1973–75, account mangr Benton and Bowles 1975–77, account supervisor Lintas 1977–79, account dir Wasey Campbell Ewald 1979–83; bd dir: AAP Ketchum 1983–87, Grey Ltd 1987–89; md PML Creative Strategy 1990–91, fndr Churchmans Marketing Communications Ltd 1991–; counsellor ESU 2012–; memb: Advertising Advsy Ctee ITC, Cncl of Nat Advertising Benevolent Soc 1975–, Oxford Business Alumni 2000–; chair of tstees Citizens Advice Maidenhead & Windsor 2013–; govr English-Speaking Union 2015–; FIPA 1989 (MIPA 1982), FInstD (dip in co mgmnt 1988); *Publications* Principled Persuasion in Employee Communication (2015); *Recreations* travel, reading, book collecting, classical music; *Style*— Michael Churchman, Esq; ⊠ 20 Rutland Place, Maidenhead, Berkshire SL6 4JA (☏ 01628 639404, e-mail mike@churchmans.com)

CICLITIRA, Prof Paul Jonathan; s of Dennis J Ciclitira, and Grace, *née* Cooksley (d 2003); *b* 7 July 1948; *Educ* Wycliffe Coll, Bart's Med Sch (MB BS), Univ of Cambridge (MD, PhD); *m* Dr Diane Watson; 1 da (Katherine Anne b 1989), 1 s (James Alexander b 1992); *Career* SHO in gen med: Rochford Hosp 1972–73 (house offr 1971), Bart's 1973–74 (house offr in gen surgery 1971), Royal Marsden Hosp 1975; hon sr registrar Addenbrooke's Hosps 1977–80 (med registrar 1975–77), trg fell MRC Lab of Molecular Biology Cambridge 1980–83 (Drummond nutrition fell 1977–80), hon sr registrar Guy's Hosp 1980–83; UMDS Guy's and St Thomas' Hosp Tst: sr res fell Wellcome Tst 1983–89, sr lectr and hon conslt physician 1983–, prof of gastroenterology 1994–, head of Research Unit The Rayne Inst; memb: Darwin Coll Cambridge, Editorial Bd Clinical and Experimental Immunology; Br Soc of Gastroenterology Res Medal 1986, Br and Eire Socs of Gastroenterology and Lilly Res Award 1988, Euro Soc of Gastroenterology and Lilly Res Award 1989; memb: Assoc of Physicians of the UK, Biochemical Soc, Br Soc of Gastroenterology (memb Nutrition Ctee), Br Soc of Immunology, Euro Soc of Clinical Investigation, Med Res Soc of GB, Soc of Cell Biology; FRSM, FRCP 1991 (MRCP); *Publications* author of various pubns in learned jls particularly on coeliac disease; *Recreations* squash, swimming, theatre, cooking, wine tasting; *Clubs* Athenaeum, Chelsea Arts, Groucho; *Style*— Prof Paul J Ciclitira; ⊠ Gastroenterology Unit, UMDS, The Rayne Institute, St Thomas' Hospital, London SE1 7EH (☏ 020 7928 9292 ext 3063, fax 020 7620 2597)

CIERACH, Lindka Rosalind Wanda; da of Edek (Edward) Cierach, MBE (d 1992), and Diana Rosemary, *née* Wilson; f mapped large tracts of Africa, decorated for Battle of Monte Cassino with highest Order of Virtuti Military, Kirzyz Walecznych, Star medal 1939–44, Star Italian Campaign, Star of Monte Cassino, Star Defense MBE; *b* June 1952; *Educ* Uganda, Convent of the Holy Child Jesus St Leonards and Mayfield, London Coll of Fashion; *Career* fashion designer; worked for Vogue magazine, established couture house 1984, designed wedding dress for Duchess of York's wedding on 23 July 1986, launched ready-to-wear collection 1987, currently designs couture for int client base; contrib to gala fashion shows for charities incl: Unicef, Leukaemia Research, Martletts Hosp; appearances in TV series incl Ladette to Lady (ITV) 2006, designer for TV specials incl Lesley Garrett Tonight (BBC 2) 1998; patron Full of Life; Designer of the Year Award 1987; *Recreations* music, films, reading, walking, boating, safari, meditation; *Style*— Lindka Cierach; ⊠ The Studio, 1c Clareville Grove, London SW7 5AU (☏ 020 7373 3131, fax 020 7373 1675, e-mail lindka@lindka-cierach.co.uk, website www.lindka-cierach.co.uk)

CIPOLLA, Prof Roberto; s of Salvatore Cipolla, of Agrigento, Italy, and Concetta, *née* Criminisi; *b* 3 May 1963, Solihull; *Educ* Solihull Sixth Form Coll, Queens' Coll Cambridge (fndn scholar, BA), Univ of Pennsylvania (MSE), Osaka Univ of Foreign Studies (Dip Japanese), Univ of Electrocommunications Tokyo (Monbusho scholar, MEng), Balliol Coll Oxford (IBM research studentship, DPhil); *m* 9 Sept 2000, Maria Cristina Bordin, da of Oreste Bordin; 1 da (Francesca Sofia b 1 Aug 2002); *Career* research asst Valley Forge Research Center PA, visiting researcher Electrotechnical Lab Tsukuba Japan, Lady Wolfson research fell St Hugh's Coll Oxford 1990–92, Toshiba fell Toshiba R&D Centre Kawasaki 1991–92; Univ of Cambridge: lectr in engrg 1992–97, reader of info engrg 1997–2000, prof of info engrg 2000–; Jesus Coll Cambridge: fell 1992–, actg praelector 1994 and 1996, fell steward 1998–99, currently dir of studies, organiser Sculpture in the Close exhbn 1994, curator of works of art 1998; scientific advsr: Sci and Technol Agency Japan 1996, Nanyang Technological Univ Singapore (distinguished visitor 1994 and 1999), Univ of Bologna 2003–; external examiner UCL; dir Toshiba Research Europe Ltd; FIET 2009 (formerly MIET), MIEEE; *Publications* incl: Active visual inference of surface shape (1995), Computer vision for human-machine interaction (1998), Visual motion of curves and surfaces (2000), Mathematics of surfaces (2000); more than 300 contribs to int jls and confs; *Recreations* photography (Seeking Gandhara exhbn Tokyo 1992), wine, Japanese language and culture, tennis, cycling; *Style*— Prof Roberto Cipolla; ⊠ Jesus College, Cambridge CB5 8BL; Department of Engineering, University of Cambridge, Cambridge CB2 1PZ (☏ 01223 332849, fax 01223 332662, e-mail cipolla@eng.cam.ac.uk)

CIPRIANI, Danny; *b* 2 November 1987, Roehampton, London; *Educ* Whitgift Sch Croydon; *Career* professional rugby union player; London Wasps: joined 2003, debut 2004, winners Heineken Cup 2007, Guinness Premiership 2008; Melbourne Rebels 2010–12, Sale Sharks 2012–; England: 7 caps, debut v Wales 2008, also Croydon rep at Under 16 (capt), Under 19, and Saxons level; *Style*— Danny Cipriani, Esq

CIULLI, Dr Franco; s of Antonio Ciulli, of Verona, Italy and Sydney, Aust, and Gabriella Ciulli (d 1981); *b* 19 August 1960; *Educ* St Ignatius Coll Sydney, Univ of Verona (MD); *Children* Alessandro, Francesco, Valentina; *Career* transplant surgn Papworth Hosp 1991, sr registrar Glasgow Royal Infirmary 1993, sr transplant fell St Vincent's Hosp Sydney 1994, conslt cardiothoracic surgn Sheffield 1995, conslt cardiothoracic surgn Bristol 1999, clinical dir Cardiothoracic Surgery Bristol Royal Infirmary 2000–; special interests in beating heart coronary artery bypass surgery, mitral valve repair and minimally invasive surgery, surgical ablation for atrial fibrillation; memb: Soc of Cardiothoracic Surgns of GB and I 1998, European Soc of Cardiothoracic Surgns 1998; memb RYA 2001; *Publications* Essentials of Thoracic and Cardiac Surgery (jt ed, 2003); *Recreations* sailing, tennis, general aviation; *Clubs* Bristol Lawn Tennis and Squash; *Style*— Dr Franco Ciulli; ⊠ Level 7 Bristol Heart Institute, Bristol Royal Infirmary, Bristol BS2 8HW (☏ 01173 426661 (secretary), fax 0117 042 0496, e-mail franco.ciulli@uhbristol.nhs.uk)

CLACHER, Ray; *Career* commercial dir Gieves Ltd 2002–09, brand md Trinity Ltd 2009–12, md Gieves & Hawkes 2012–; *Style*— Ray Clacher, Esq; ⊠ Gieves & Hawkes, 1 Savile Row, London W1S 3JR

CLAGUE, Andrew Charlesworth; s of John Charlesworth Clague, of Canterbury, Kent, and Margaret Elsie, *née* Musgrave; *b* 15 May 1951; *Educ* St Edmund's Sch Canterbury, Kent Inst of Design (DipArch); *m* 1 (m dis 1991); 2 s (James Charlesworth, Nicholas Charlesworth), 2 da (Anna Genevieve, Isabel Lucy); *Career* sr ptnr Clague (architects, urban designers, historic buildings consultants and interior designers) London Faringdon, Canterbury (HQ) and Harpenden Herts, fndr and dir Countryman Properties Ltd 1986–; vice-pres Practice RIBA 1998–99; RIBA: chm Canterbury and Dist 1989–91, memb Cncl 1995–2001, chm SE Region 1996–98; memb Rotary Club (Canterbury), pres Round Table (Canterbury and Dist) 1997–98 (chm 1990–91); govr Kent Inst of Art and Design 2000–05; pres St Edmund's Soc 2002–03; AABC; *Recreations* yachting, music; *Clubs* Royal Dart Yacht, Royal Thames Yacht; *Style*— Andrew Clague, Esq, RIBA; ⊠ 2 Lime Tree House, Old Dover Road, Canterbury, Kent CT1 3NY; Clague, 62 Burgate, Canterbury, Kent CT1 2BJ (☏ 01227 762060, fax 01227 762149)

CLANCARTY, 9 Earl of (I 1803); Nicholas Power Richard Le Poer Trench; also Viscount Clancarty (UK 1823), Baron Kilconnel (I 1797), Viscount Dunlo (I 1801), Baron Trench (UK 1815), Marquis of Heusden in the Kingdom of the Netherlands (1818); s of Hon Power Edward Ford Le Poer Trench (yst s of 5 Earl; d 1975), and Jocelyn Louise, *née* Courtney (d 1962); suc uncle, 8 Earl of Clancarty 1995; *b* 1 May 1952; *Educ* Westminster, Ashford GS, Plymouth Poly, Univ of Colorado, Sheffield Poly; *Career* artist/film-maker; *Style*— The Rt Hon the Earl of Clancarty; ✉ e-mail clancarty@hotmail.com

CLANCY, Claire; *née* Coates; da of Douglas Coates, and Teresa Coates; *b* 14 March 1958, Rayleigh, Essex; *Educ* Dartford GS for Girls, Open Univ (BA); *m* 1994, Michael Clancy (d 2010); *Career* Manpower Services Cmmn 1977–88, Dept of Employment 1988–90, chief exec Powys TEC 1990–92, Govt Office for South West 1992–96, dir of policy and planning Companies House 1996–97, dir Patent Office 1999–2002, registrar of companies and chief exec Companies House 2002–07, chief exec and clerk Nat Assembly for Wales 2007–; *Recreations* horse riding, dressage, walking; *Style*— Mrs Claire Clancy; ✉ National Assembly for Wales, Cardiff Bay, Cardiff CF99 1NA (☎ 0300 200 6230, e-mail claire.clancy@assembly.wales, website www.assembly.wales)

CLAPP, Peter Michael; s of Percival Dennis Clapp (d 1994), of Exmouth, Devon, and Lily, *née* Duck (d 1988); *b* 12 March 1943; *Educ* Exeter Sch, Dept of Architecture Hammersmith Coll of Art and Building (DipArch, RIBA Sir Bannister Fletcher Silver Medal); *m* 26 Sept 1964, Ann; 2 s (Giles Benedict b 25 Dec 1966, Adam Julian b 10 Oct 1968); *Career* architect and designer; own practice and RIBA res award 1964–67, assoc ptnr in various practices incl Whinney McKay Lewis and Louis de Soissons 1968–74, Architect's Dept London Borough of Camden 1975–80; W H Smith: responsible for Do-it-All building prog 1981–82, dep chief architect 1983–86, design mangr 1987–92 (with overall responsibility for all design, architecture, advtg, art purchasing and corp identity); chief architect Sport England 1996–2001 (princ architect 1992–96) (responsible for multi-disciplinary team advising on buildings, funded by the Sport England Lottery Fund); design conslt 2001–; 2 Civic Tst Awards 1981, DOE Good Design in Housing Award 1982; Civic Tst assessor 1982–; visiting lectr: London Business Sch, RCA, Templeton Coll Oxford; ARIBA 1966 (memb Cncl 1972–75), FCSD 1991; *Recreations* landscape photography, theatre, music, walking; *Style*— Peter Clapp, Esq; ✉ 12 Jeffrey's Place, London NW1 9PP (☎ 020 7267 2445, e-mail peterclapp@ukonline.co.uk)

CLAPPERTON, (Alexander) Wallace Ford; s of Alexander Clapperton (d 1943), of Edinburgh, and Kathleen Nora, *née* Ford (d 1991); *b* 22 July 1934; *Educ* Charterhouse; *m* 27 March 1965, Catherine Anne, da of Sir Henry Horsman, MC (d 1966), of Bermuda; 1 da (Alison Nicola b 1967), 1 s (Graeme Alexander Ford b 1969); *Career* Nat Serv RCS 1957–59; ptnr de Zoete and Bevan stockbrokers (formerly de Zoete and Gorton) 1963–86, dir Barclays de Zoete Wedd Securities Ltd 1986–92; non-exec chm Scantronic Holdings 1992–95, non-exec dir Henderson TR Pacific Investment Trust 1992–2003; MICAS; *Recreations* golf, skiing; *Clubs* Hon Co of Edinburgh Golfers, Denham Golf, Woburn Golf, City of London; *Style*— Wallace Clapperton, Esq; ✉ Heron Path House, Heron Path, Chapel Lane, Wendover, Buckinghamshire HP22 6NN (☎ 01296 620421)

CLAPPISON, James; s of late Leonard Clappison, and late Dorothy Clappison; *b* 14 September 1956; *Educ* St Peter's Sch York, The Queen's Coll Oxford (scholar); *m* 6 July 1984, Helen Margherita, *née* Carter; 1 s, 3 da; *Career* called to the Bar 1981; MP (Cons) Hertsmere 1992–2015 (Parly candidate Barnsley E 1987, Euro Parly candidate Yorks S 1989 Parly candidate Bootle May and Nov 1990 (by-elections)); PPS to min of state Home Office 1994–95, Parly under-sec of state Dept of the Environment 1995–97; oppn front bench spokesman: on home affrs (crime, immigration and asylums) 1997–99, for educn 1999–2000, for treasy 2000–01; shadow min for work 2001–02, shadow min for Treasy 2002–03; *Clubs* Carlton; *Style*— James Clappison, Esq; ✉ House of Commons, London SW1A 0AA

CLAPTON, Eric Patrick; CBE (2004, OBE 1995); *b* 30 March 1945; *Educ* St Bede's Sch Surrey, Kingston Coll of Art; *m* 1, 1979 (m dis 1988), Patti Harrison; 2 c by subseq ptnr (Conor b 1987 d 1991, Ruth b 1985); m 2, 2002, Melia McEnery; 1 da (Julie Rose); *Career* guitarist and singer; has worked with Howlin' Wolf, Steve Winwood, The Beatles, The Rolling Stones, Pete Townshend, Elton John, Phil Collins and others; joined Yardbirds as lead guitarist 1963, recorded album Five Little Yardbirds (live, 1964), joined John Mayall's Bluesbreakers 1965; albums with John Mayall: Lonely Years (1965), Blues Breakers (1966, reached UK no 6); formed Cream 1966; albums with Cream: Fresh Cream (1967, UK no 6), Disraeli Gears (1967, UK no 5), Wheels Of Fire (1968, UK no 3), Goodbye (1969, UK no 1), The Best Of Cream (compilation, 1969, UK no 6), Live Cream (live, 1970, UK no 4), Live Cream – Vol 2 (live, 1972, UK no 15); formed Blind Faith 1969, recorded album Blind Faith (1969, UK no 1); started solo career 1970, formed Derek & The Dominoes 1970, recorded albums Layla And Other Love Songs (1970, US no 16), Derek & The Dominoes In Concert (live, 1973, UK no 36); solo albums: Eric Clapton (1970, UK no 17), History Of Eric Clapton (1972, UK no 20), Eric Clapton's Rainbow Concert (live, 1973, UK no 19), 461 Ocean Boulevard (1974, UK no 3), There's One In Every Crowd (1975, UK no 15), E C Was Here (live, 1975, UK no 14), No Reason To Cry (1976, UK no 8), Slowhand (1977, UK no 23), Backless (1978, UK no 18), Just One Night (1980, UK no 3), Another Ticket (1981, UK no 18), Time Pieces – The Best Of Eric Clapton (1982, UK no 20), Money And Cigarettes (1983, UK no 13), Backtrackin' (compilation, 1984, UK no 29), Behind The Sun (1985, UK no 8), August (1986, UK no 3), The Cream Of Eric Clapton (compilation, UK no 3), Crossroads (box set, 1988), Journeyman (1989, UK no 2), 24 Nights (live, 1992), Unplugged (1992, UK no 3), Stages (1993), From the Cradle (1994), Crossroads 2: Live in the 70s (1996), Pilgrim (1998), Riding with the King (2000), Reptile (2001), Eric Clapton Live (2002), The Road to Escondido (with JJ Cale, 2006), Live from Madison Square Garden (with Steve Winwood, 2009); has worked on numerous film soundtracks incl: Tommy, The Colour Of Money, Lethal Weapon, Rush; *Awards* incl: winner Grammy award for Best Male Rock Vocal (for Bad Love) 1991, Variety Club Best Recording Artist of 1992, six Grammy awards 1993, winner Grammy award for Best Traditional Blues Recording (for From the Cradle) 1995, winner Grammy awards for Record of the Year and Best Male Pop Vocalist (for Change the World) 1997, winner Grammy award for Best Male Pop Vocal (for My Father's Eyes) 1999; *Style*— Eric Clapton, CBE

CLARE, John Charles; CBE (2004); s of Sidney Charles Clare (d 1990), of Great Yarmouth, and Joan Mildred, *née* Hall (d 1997); *b* 2 August 1950, Great Yarmouth; *Educ* Great Yarmouth GS, Univ of Edinburgh (BSc); *m* 22 June 1974, Anne, *née* Ross; 2 s (Tony Charles b 20 July 1976, Andy James b 12 Nov 1981); *Career* various sales and mktg roles Mars Ltd 1972–82, mktg dir Ladbrokes Racing Div 1982–85, md Dixons Ltd 1986 (mktg dir 1985), md Dixons Stores Gp Ltd and dir Dixons Gp plc 1988, chief exec Dixons Gp plc (now Dixons Retail plc) 1994–2007; chm: JobCentrePlus 2006–12, Dreams plc 2008–11, JJB Sports 2010–11, Capital and Regional plc 2010–, Comet 2012; dir: Hammersons plc 1988–2009, Dyson Ltd 2007–12; regent Univ of Edinburgh 2011–; *Recreations* boating, sports, music; *Style*— John Clare, Esq, CBE

CLARE, Jonathan; s of John Clare, and Sheila, *née* Crush; *b* 25 July 1954; *Educ* Windsor GS, Lancaster Univ (BA); *Partner* Celeste Warner; *Career* business and fin journalist 1975–86 (Morgan Grampian, Investors Chronicle, Birmingham Post, The Times, Daily Mail), Streets Financial 1986–88, fndr and dep md Citigate Communications Group 1988–98, md Citigate Dewe Rogerson (following merger) 1998–; memb: Int Spinal Research Tst, Cruising Assoc, RNLI, RHS, RYA, MIPR; *Recreations* mountain walking, sailing, skiing, reading; *Style*— Jonathan Clare, Esq; ✉ Citigate Dewe Rogerson, 3 London Wall Buildings, London EC2M 5SY

CLARE, Mark Sydney; *b* 10 August 1957; *m* 26 July 1980, Alison; 1 s (David), 2 da (Nicola, Emily); *Career* fin mangr GEC-Marconi 1985–88; STC plc: gp fin mangr 1989–90, fin controller Telecoms System Div 1990, asst fin dir STC Telecommunications 1990–91; fin controller Telecoms Systems Gp Nortel 1991–92, fin dir STC Submarine Systems Nortel 1992–94, gp fin controller British Gas plc 1994–97, gp fin dir Centrica plc 1997–2000, dep chief exec Centrica plc 2000–06, md British Gas Residential Energy 2002–06, gp chief exec Barratt Developments plc 2006–15; non-exec dir BAA plc until 2006; FCMA; *Recreations* tennis, fast cars, gadgets; *Clubs* Brooks's; *Style*— Mark Clare, Esq; ✉ Barratt Developments plc, 14–17 Market Place, London W1W 8AJ

CLARE, Michael George (Mike); DL (Bucks 2011); s of Thomas Clare (d 1967), of Beaconsfield, Bucks, and Betty, *née* Jeffries (d 2000); *b* 8 February 1955, Beaconsfield; *Educ* High Wycombe Coll; *m* 27 Oct 1979, Carol, *née* Ballingall; 2 s (Thomas b 31 Dec 1984, Edward b 2 April 1986), 2 da (Rebecca b 13 Aug 1991, Hannah b 13 Oct 1992); *Career* branch mangr Williams Furniture 1976–78, area mangr Hardys Furniture 1978–80, area mangr Perrings Furniture 1980–84, sales dir W H Deanes Furniture 1984–86, chief exec Dreams plc 1987–2008, chm Today Retail Ltd 2009, managing ptnr Cygnus LLP 2009, exec chm Clarenco LLP 2009–; patron Chalfonts Community Coll, enterprise fell Prince's Tst, patron Clare Business Sch, chm of tstees Clare Fndn 2009; Ernst & Young Regnl Entrepreneur of the Year 2002; Liveryman City of London 2002, Liveryman Worshipful Company of Furniture Makers; Hon DUniv Bucks New Univ 2009; FInstD; *Recreations* travelling the world, making dreams a reality; *Clubs* Beaconsfield 41, Annabel's; *Style*— Mike Clare, Esq, DL; ✉ Clarenco LLP, Clarenco House, Ibstone Road, Stockenchurch HP14 3EF

CLARE, (Rear Adm) Roy Alexander George; CBE (2007); s of John Arnold Clare (d 1978), and Ludmilla, *née* Nossoff (d 2002); *b* 30 September 1950, Hammersmith, London; *Educ* St George's GS Cape Town, BRNC Dartmouth, RN Staff Coll, RCDS; *m* 1, 1979, Leonie (Mimi), *née* Hutchings (d 1979); m 2, 1981, Sarah Catherine Jane, da of Anthony Parkin; 1 s (Oliver Christopher George b 16 June 1984), 2 da (Philippa Anne Elizabeth b 16 Sept 1986, Louisa Jane Natasha b 1 Feb 1990); *Career* jr seaman 1966, midshipman 1970; chief mate yacht 'Adventure' Whitbread Round the World Yacht Race 1973–74; co: HMS Bronington 1980–81 (second in command 1975–77), HMS Birmingham 1987–89, HMS York and 3 Destroyer Sqdn 1991–92, HMS Invincible 1996–97, BRNC 1998–99 (fndr Britannia Museum, led opening of BRNC to paying visitors 1998); Rear Adm (NATO appt) 1999–2000, dir Nat Maritime Museum 2000–07, chief exec Museums, Libraries and Archives Cncl 2007–11 (memb Bd 2006–07), dir Auckland War Meml Museum NZ 2011–17, maritime research sabbatical UK 2017–; memb Bd Creative and Cultural Skills Sector Skills Cncl 2005–07, memb Bd Qualifications and Curriculum Devpt Agency 2009–11; vice-pres Bronington Tst 1999–2002 (tstee 1989–99), pres Midland Naval Offrs Assoc 2000–02; fndr Britannia Museum, tstee Naval Review 1999–2011, tstee Britannia Assoc 2001–04; memb: Assembly Univ of Greenwich 2001–07, Greenwich Forum 2001–07, Bd Museums Aotearoa 2014–16 (chair 2015–16); Hon DLitt Univ of Greenwich 2007; Sword of Honour 1972, Queen's Silver Jubilee Medal 1977, GSM 1977 and 1989; Freeman: City of London 2001, Worshipful Co of Shipwrights 2002, Worshipful Co of Clockmakers 2004; CCMI 2001–11, FRSA 2005–08, FRIN 2005–08; *Books* Bronington – The Last of Britain's Wooden Walls (ed, 1996); *Recreations* family, sailing, walking, maritime research; *Clubs* Anchorites, RN Sailing Assoc, RN of 1765 and 1785, Royal Yacht Sqdn (naval memb); *Style*— Roy Clare, CBE; ✉ http://uk.linkedin.com/in/royclare, Twitter @swatchway, Instagram @royclarenz

CLARIDGE, Prof Michael Frederick; s of Frederick William Claridge (d 1965), of Rugby, Warks, and Eva Alice, *née* Jeffery (d 1969); *b* 2 June 1934; *Educ* Lawrence Sheriff Sch Rugby, Keble Coll Oxford (MA, DPhil); *m* 30 Sept 1967, (Lindsey) Clare, da of Gilbert Hellings (d 1973), of Shipton-under-Wychwood, Oxon; 2 s (John, Robert), 1 da (Elin); *Career* UC Cardiff: lectr in zoology 1959–76, reader in entomology 1977–83, personal chair in entomology 1983–89, acting head of zoology 1987–88; Univ of Wales Cardiff: head Sch of Pure and Applied Biology 1989–94, prof of entomology 1989–2000, emeritus prof of entomology 2001–; pres: Linnean Soc of London 1988–91 (memb Cncl 1984–91), Systematics Assoc 1991–94 (memb Cncl 1984–87), Royal Entomological Soc 2000–02 (memb Cncl 1971–74, 1998–2010 and 2012–, editorial offr 2002–10); memb British Ecological Soc (memb Cncl 1976–79); Linnean Medal for Zoology 2000; FLS, FRES, FIBiol; *Books* The Leafhoppers and Planthoppers (contrib, 1985), The Organization of Communities, Past and Present (contrib, 1987), Prospects in Systematics (contrib, 1988), Handbook for the Identification of Leafhoppers and Planthoppers of Rice (jtly, 1991), Evolutionary Patterns and Processes (contrib, 1993), Planthoppers: Their Ecology and Management (contrib, 1993), Species the Units of Biodiversity (ed and contrib, 1997), Insect Sounds and Communication (ed and contrib, 2005), Insect Biodiversity Science and Society (contrib, 2009), Contemporary Debates in Philosophy of Biology (contrib, 2009); *Recreations* cricket, music, natural history; *Clubs* The Entomological; *Style*— Prof Michael Claridge; ✉ 84 The Hollies, Quakers Yard, Treharris, Mid Glamorgan CF46 5PP (e-mail claridge@cardiff.ac.uk)

CLARK; *see also:* Chichester-Clark, Stewart-Clark"

CLARK, Adrian; *b* 20 May 1957; *Educ* King Edward VI GS Retford, Peterhouse Cambridge (exhibitioner), Coll of Law; *Career* slr; Slaughter and May 1981–86; Ashurst: joined 1986, seconded to Panel on Takeovers and Mergers 1988–90, ptnr 1990–, head Corp Dept 2004–10; tstee Churches Conservation; *Publications* British and Irish Art 1945–1951 (2010), Queer Saint. The Cultured Life of Peter Watson (2015); *Clubs* MCC, Brooks's; *Style*— Adrian Clark, Esq; ✉ Ashurst, Broadwalk House, 5 Appold Street, London EC2A 2HA (website www.britishandirishart.co.uk)

CLARK, Anthony Richard; s of Noel Edmund Clark, and Marianne Edith, *née* Sayres; *b* 4 April 1958, Hammersmith, London; *Educ* Downside, Univ of Manchester (BA Drama, Dip Playwriting); *m* 1984, Delia Mary, da of John Goddard; 4 c (Anna Magdalene, Gabriel James, Eleanor Pearl, Crispin Lee); *Career* director and writer; dir Orange Tree Theatre Richmond 1981–83, artistic dir Contact Theatre Manchester 1984–89, assoc artistic dir Birmingham Rep Theatre Co 1990–2001, artistic dir Hampstead Theatre 2003–10, freelance; head of MA directors course East 15 univ of essex 2010–13, head of BA Directing Drama Centre 2014–; Central St Martins head of course MA directing drama centre 2013–; *Theatre* Contact Theatre prodns incl: Face Value, Two Wheel Tricycle, McAlpine's Fusiliers, Green, Homeland, Mother Courage and her Children, Blood Wedding, A Midsummer Night's Dream, The Duchess of Malfi, To Kill a Mockingbird (European Premiere), Oedipus Rex; Birmingham Rep incl: The Seagull, Macbeth, Of Mice and Men, Saturday Sunday Monday, Cider with Rosie (nat tour), The Threepenny Opera, The Pied Piper, My Mother Said I Never Should, The Grapes of Wrath, The Atheist's Tragedy, The Playboy of the Western World, Peter Pan, Pygmalion, The Red Balloon, The Entertainer, Gentlemen Prefer Blonds, Julius Caesar, St Joan; new plays incl: Belonging, The Slight Witch, My Best Friend, Silence, All That Trouble That We Had, Home Truths, True Brit, Rough, Playing by the Rules, Nervous Women, Syme (co-prodn with RNT studio), Paddies, Confidence; Hampstead Theatre prodns incl: The Maths Tutor, Revelations, When the Night Begins, Osama the Hero, A Single Act, Nathan the Wise, Taking Care of Baby, Life After Scandal, Turandot, Lucky Seven, Amongst Friends; freelance dir incl: Dr Faustus (Young Vic), To Kill a Mockingbird (Greenwich), The Snowman (Leicester Haymarket), The Red Balloon (Bristol Old Vic and RNT), The Day After Tomorrow (RNT), Mother Courage and her Children (RNT), The Wood Demon (Playhouse), Loveplay (RSC), Tender (Hampstead Theatre), Edward III (RSC); as writer plays incl: Hand it to Them, Wake, The Power of Darkness (Orange Tree), Tidemark (RSC Thoughtcrimes Festival), A Matter of Life and Death (RNT), Green, Our Brother David (Watford Palace), The Eighth Continent (Tristan Bates); as writer musical adapts incl: The Snowman, The Little Prince, The Red Balloon (all Contact Theatre Manchester), The Pied Piper, Pinocchio (both Birmingham Rep), Winnie the Witch; *Awards* RSC Buzz Award 1979, Manchester Evening News Best Prodn Award (for To Kill a Mockingbird) 1984, TMA/Martini Award for Best Dir (for The Atheist's Tragedy) 1994, TMA/Martina Award for Best Show for Children and Young People (for The Red Balloon) 1995, Mentorn First Night Prodn Award (for Playing by the Rules); *Publications* The Power of Darkness (trans Tolstoy, 1987), The Red Balloon (1997), Pinocchio (2001), Winnie the Witch (2002), The Pied Piper (2003), Little Wolf's Book of Badness (2008), Our Brother David (2012); *Style*— Anthony Clark, Esq; ✉ c/o Catherine King, Independent Talent Group, Oxford House, 76 Oxford Street, London W1N 0AX (☎ 020 7636 6565, website www.anthonyclarktheatre.com)

CLARK, Antony Roy; *b* 7 November 1956; *Educ* St Andrew's Coll Grahamstown S Africa, Rhodes Univ (BA, HDE), Downing Coll Cambridge (MA); *m* 1981, Dr Brigitte Jennifer Lang; 1 s, 2 da; *Career* teacher Westerford HS Cape Town 1984–90; headmaster: St Joseph's Marist Coll Cape Town 1992–94, St Andrew's Coll Grahamstown 1994–2002, Gresham's Sch 2002–08, Malvern Coll 2008–; *Style*— Antony Clark, Esq; ✉ Malvern College, College Road, Worcestershire WR14 3DF

CLARK, Brian Stephen; s of Stephen Wilfred Clark (d 1974), and Florence Sybil Elizabeth, *née* Webb; *b* 11 August 1936; *Educ* Willesden Co GS, LSE (LLB); *m* 17 Feb 1962, Rita, *née* Jones; 2 s (Stephen Nicholas b 2 Oct 1963, Andrew Simon b 26 July 1966); *Career* admitted slr 1961; Goodman Derrick & Co 1958–69 (articled clerk, asst slr, ptnr), exec International Management Group (IMG) London 1969–71, sr corp ptnr Nabarro Nathanson 1988–93 (ptnr 1971–93), dir of European legal affrs IMG 1993–2000 (conslt to IMG 2000–13), Monaco Sport and Mgmnt SAM 2006–; memb Law Soc; *Recreations* golf, photography, opera; *Style*— Brian Clark, Esq; ✉ Monaco Sport and Management SAM, Est-Ouest 24 Boulevard Princesse Charlotte, MC98000, Monaco (☎ 00377 93 104250, fax 00377 93 104251, e-mail brian@clarkassociates.co.uk)

CLARK, Prof Charles Victor; s of Dennis Clark, and Margaret, *née* Slowther; *b* 11 August 1956; *Educ* George Heriot's Sch Edinburgh, Univ of Edinburgh (BSc, MB ChB, MD, ChM, DSc, LLM); *m* 15 Dec 1983, Maureen, da of James Corr (d 1978); *Career* sr surgical registrar Moorfields Eye Hosp London 1986–88, conslt ophthalmic surgn Royal Infirmary of Edinburgh and sr lectr in ophthalmology Univ of Edinburgh 1988–91, prof of ophthalmology and dir Glaucoma Servs Univ of Queensland 1991–94, prof of educn Griffith Univ Queensland 1995–; md: Charles V Clark Med Pty Ltd 1991–02, Orion Eye Centre 2003–05, Dr Charles V Clark Ltd 2005–; conslt ophthalmic surgn London Diabetes and Lipid Centre 2003–05, conslt ophthalmic surgeon London 2005–; specialist in glaucoma, diabetic eye disease and nutrition; author of 12 books and over 80 scientific papers; memb: Assoc for Eye Res, Oxford Ophthalmological Congress, Clinical Autonomic Res Soc; fell RMS 1979, FRCSEd 1985, FRCOphth 1988, CBiol, FIBiol 1991, fell Royal Aust Coll of Ophthalmologists 1991, fell Royal Aust Coll of Surgns 1992, fell American Acad of Opthalmology 1992, fell Aust Inst of Biology 1994, FSA Scot 2000; *Recreations* photography, music, theatre, rugby football; *Style*— Prof Charles Clark

CLARK, His Hon Judge Christopher Harvey; QC (1989); s of Harvey Frederick Beckford Clark, of Southampton, Hants, and Winifred Julia, *née* Caesar; *b* 20 December 1946; *Educ* Taunton's Sch Southampton, The Queen's Coll Oxford (MA); *m* 25 March 1972 (m dis 2004), Gillian Elizabeth Ann, da of Anthony Mullen; 1 s (Patrick Harvey b 1974), 2 da (Melanie Julia b 1976, Lucy Elizabeth b 1980); m 2, 5 June 2004, Wendy Gaye Keith, da of Harvey Heyworth; *Career* called to the Bar Gray's Inn 1969 (bencher 2000–11); memb Western Circuit 1970–, asst recorder 1982–86, recorder of the Crown Court 1986–2005, head Pump Court Chambers 2001–05, circuit judge 2005–, resident judge Truro Combined Court 2012– (hon recorder 2015); memb Wine Ctee Western Circuit 1985–90, chm Fees and Legal Aid Ctee Western Circuit 1989, pres Dorset Branch Magistrates Assoc 2007–11; chllr Dio of Winchester 1993–, dep chllr Dio of Chichester 1995–2006, dep chllr Dio of Salisbury 1997–2007, chllr Dio of Portsmouth 2003–13 (dep chllr 1994–2003); hon legal advsr to the Hampshire Assoc of Parish and Town Cncls 1996–99, memb Ecclesiastical Judges Assoc Standing Ctee 1996–2004, memb Legal Advsy Cmmn Gen Synod 1996–2001; chm Stockbridge Dramatic Soc 1977–2007 (pres 2007–11), memb Longstock Parish Cncl 1979–2002, youth club organiser (The Longstock Tadpoles) 1981–90, pres City of Winchester Tst 2007–11; licensed reader C of E 1998–; *Recreations* grandchildren, golf, fishing, swimming, gardening, walking, bird-watching, reading; *Clubs* Flyfishers; *Style*— His Hon Judge Christopher Harvey Clark, QC; ✉ Truro Combined Court, Courts of Justice, Edward Street, Truro TR1 2PB (☎ 01872 267420)

CLARK, Dr David Findlay; OBE (1990), DL (Banffshire 1992); s of Rev Dr David Findlay Clark (d 1966), and Annie, *née* McKenzie (d 1963); *b* 30 May 1930; *Educ* Banff Acad, Univ of Aberdeen (MA, PhD); *m* 9 Oct 1954, Janet Anne, da of Gavin M Stephen, of Brechin, Angus; 2 da (Morag Anne (Mrs Baptie) b 1955, Linda Jane (Mrs Wimble) b 1958); *Career* Flying Offr RAF 1951–53, RAFVR 1953–57; psychologist Leicester Industrial Rehabilitation Unit 1953–56, princ clinical psychologist Leicester Area Clinical Psychology Serv 1960–66 (sr clinical psychologist 1956–60), dir and top grade clinical psychologist Grampian Health Bd 1966–90, clinical sr lectr Dept of Mental Health Univ of Aberdeen 1966–, conslt clinical psychologist in private practice 1990–96; former: chm Div of Clinical Psychology Br Psychological Soc (memb Cncl), memb Health Serv Planning Cncl, town and co cncllr Banff and Banffshire, Safeguarder (under terms of SWK Scotland Act) 1985–2001; Hon Sheriff Grampian and Highlands and Islands at Banff 1979–; FBPsS 1969, ARPS 1991; *Books* Help, Hospitals and the Handicapped (1984), One Boy's War (1997), Stand by Your Beds (2001), Remember Who You Are! (2007), Chancer! (2008); contrib to major textbooks and author of numerous jl articles; *Recreations* golf, photography, painting, guitar, piano, travel, writing; *Clubs* Duff House Royal Golf, Banff Rotary (past pres); *Style*— Dr David Clark, OBE, DL; ✉ Glendeveron, 8 Deveron Terrace, Banff AB45 1BB (☎ 01261 812624, e-mail drdavidfindlayclark@btinternet.com)

CLARK, Derek Roland; MEP; s of Horace William Alfred (d 1984), and Doris Alice, *née* Beer (d 1984); *b* 10 October 1933, Bristol; *Educ* Bristol Cathedral Sch, Redland Trg Coll (Cert), St Luke's Coll Univ of Exeter (Cert, Dip); *m* 26 May 1973, Rosemary Jane, *née* Purser; *Career* teacher of sci Air Balloon Hill Secdy Modern Bristol 1954–62, head Sci Dept Cherry Orchard Secdy Sch Northampton 1962–74 (tutor exam courses 1968–74, sr master 1970–74), sr head of house Lings Upper Sch Northampton 1974–85, sr teacher Falcon Manor Sch Towcester 1985–93; MEP (UK Independence) E Midlands 2004–, memb Ctee on Employment and Social Affrs European Parl; UK Independence Party: chm Northants Branch 1995–2004, chm E Midlands Regnl Ctee 1996–2003, memb NEC 2001–04, party sec 2002–04; assoc Coll of Preceptors 1971; memb (non-singing) World Festival Choir; *Recreations* rugby (union) and cricket (but past playing days), travel, gardening; *Clubs* Northampton Saints RFC; *Style*— Derek Clark, Esq, MEP; ✉ 31 Tall Trees Close, Northampton NN4 9XZ (☎ 01604 766064, e-mail derekrclark@hotmail.co.uk); Rowan House, 23 Billing Road, Northampton NN1 5AT (☎ 01604 620064, fax 01604 636002, e-mail mep_eastmids@hotmail.com)

CLARK, Dingle Charles; s of Dr Charles Clark (d 1995), of Eltham, London, and Marcelle Pamela, *née* Marrable; *b* 7 June 1959; *Educ* Eltham Coll, Univ of Southampton (BSc), Central London Poly (Dip Law); *m* 15 April 1989, Caroline, da of John Patrick Hough, of Blackheath; 1 da (Charlotte Annabel Felicity b 18 Jan 1991), 3 s (Angus Lorne b 27 March 1993, Hugo Charles Alexander b 24 Sept 1995, James Archie b 15 Oct 1997); *Career* called to the Bar Middle Temple 1981, asst dep coroner (Essex) 1993–96; pt/t lectr: Cncl of Legal Educn 1987–, City Univ (Inns of Ct Sch of Law) 2002–; cncllr London Borough of Greenwich 1982–90 (Cons chief whip 1985–90); dir Original Holloway Friendly Soc Gloucester 1991–94; govr Woolwich Coll 1990–92; *Recreations* golf, football (Charlton Athletic supporter); *Clubs* Royal Blackheath Golf, Frinton Golf, Frinton Meml; *Style*— Dingle Clark, Esq; ✉ Goldsmith Building, Temple, London EC4Y 7AX (☎ 020 7353 9328, fax 020 7583 5255)

CLARK, Prof Frank; CBE (1991); *b* 17 October 1946; *m*; 2 da; *Career* clerical trainee Bd of Mgmnt Royal Cornhill and Associated Hosps 1965–67, higher clerical offr Kingseat Hosp 1967–69, hosp sec Canniesburn and Schaw Hosps 1970–71 (dep hosp sec 1969–70), admin Glasgow Royal Infirmary 1974–77 (dep hosp sec Glasgow Royal Infirmary and Sub-Gp 1971–74), dist gen admin Gtr Glasgow Health Bd Eastern Dist 1981–83 (asst dist admin 1977–81); dir Appeal Ctee West of Scotland Postgrad Dental Educn Centre 1981–83; Lanarkshire Health Bd: dist admin Hamilton and E Kilbride Unit 1983–84, dir of admin servs Hamilton and East Kilbride Unit June-Sept 1984, sec to the Bd 1984–85, gen mangr 1985–96; gen mangr Lothian Health Bd May-Dec 1990; dir Strathcarron Hospice 1996–2006, convener Scottish Cmmn for the Regulation of Care 2006–10, chair Social Care and Social Work Improvement Scotland 2010–11, chair Care Inspectorate 2011–; non-exec dir: VAMW Homes Ltd, VAMW Training Ltd 1996–2000; hon prof Dept of Nursing and Midwifery Univ of Stirling 1997–; memb: Working Pty on the Introduction of General Mgmnt at Unit Level 1984–85, Advsy Gp on New Devpts in Health Care 1984–90, Nat Specialist Servs Advsy Ctee (NSSAC) 1985–90, Scottish Health Mgmnt Efficiency Gp 1985–91, Univ Grants Ctee (Scottish Sub-Ctee) 1987–89, Working Pty on Community Med in Scotland (The Robertson Report) 1988–89, Working Pty on the Future of Dental Educn in Scotland (The McCallum Report) 1988–89 (Sec of State appt to 3 Memb Working Pty), Univs Funding Cncl (Scottish Ctee) 1989–91, Chief Scientists Health Serv Res Ctee 1989–93, Scottish Health Serv Advsy Cncl (Sec of State appt) 1990–93, Scottish Health Bd Gen Managers Gp 1990– (vice-chm 1990–93 and 1995, chm 1993–95) Advsy Gp on Acute Serv (successor body to NSSAC) 1990–93, Nat Nursing Strategy Gp 1990–93, West of Scotland Dental Educnl Tst Distance Learning Unit Appeal Ctee 1992–93, Scottish Overseas Health Support Policy Bd 1990–96, Jt Working Gp on Purchasing 1992–96, Bd New Lanarkshire Ltd 1992–97, Scottish Implementation Gp Jr Doctors' and Dentists' Hours of Work 1992–96, Scottish Cncl for Postgraduate Med and Dental Educn 1993–96, Editorial Advsy Bd Health Bulletin 1993–96, Scottish Health Services Mgmnt Centre Implementation Gp 1993–95, Strategy Gp R&D Strategy for NHS in Scotland 1994–96, Cncl of Mgmnt Scottish Partnership Agency 1998–2001 (dep chm 1999), Ind Hospices Rep Ctee Help the Hospices 1999–2001, Ministerial Advsy Panel on the Strategic Devpt of Mgmnt and Decision Making in NHS Scotland 2002, Scottish Social Services Cncl 2006–, Ind Scrutiny Gp 2009, Capaburgh Review Gp 2010, Bd Healthcare Improvement Scotland 2011–, Scotland Social Services Cncl 2011–, Healthcare Improvement Scotland 2011–; chm: Working Pty on Introduction of Hay Grading System to the NHS in Scotland 1989–90, Jt Mgmnt Exec/Gen Mangrs Manpower Gp 1990–93, West of Scotland Health Service Res Network 1990–95, Lanarkshire Drugs Action Team 1995–96, Scottish Hospices Forum 1998–2001, Central Scotland Health Care NHS Tst 1999, Forth Valley Primary Care NHS Tst 1999, Forth Valley NHS Bd 2002–03, Scottish Partnership for Palliative Care 2003– (hon treas 2001–03), Delivery Gp Scottish Acad for Health Policy and Mgmnt; head of Ministerial Taskforce Tayside Health Bd 2000; vice-chm of govrs Queen's Coll Glasgow 1988–93; memb Glasgow Dental Alumnus Assoc 1983; Rotary Paul Harris Fellowship 2011; MHSM DipHSM 1974; *Clubs* Rotary of Cumbernauld; *Style*— Prof Frank Clark, CBE; ✉ 7 Heatherdale Gardens, Head of Muir, Stirlingshire FK6 5JN (☎ 01324 824214)

CLARK, Gerald Edmondson; CMG (1989); s of Edward John Clark, and Irene Elizabeth Ada, *née* Edmondson; *b* 26 December 1935; *Educ* Johnston GS Durham, New Coll Oxford (MA); *m* 1967, Mary Rose Organ; 2 da; *Career* joined FO 1960, Hong Kong 1961, Peking 1962–63, FO 1964–68, Moscow 1968–70, FCO 1970–73, head of Chancery Lisbon 1973–77, Cabinet Office 1977–79, seconded to Barclays Bank International 1979–81, commercial cnsllr Peking 1981–83, FCO 1984–87, UK ambass to IAEA and other international orgns in Vienna 1987–92, sr civilian dir RCDS 1993, sec-gen Uranium Inst 1994–2000; gen sec Energy Strategists Consultancy Ltd 2001–14, chm Int Nuclear Energy Acad (INEA) 2013–14 (sec 2001–12); currently nuclear advsr to Pell Frischmann Gp; fell Energy Inst 1998–; *Recreations* geology, teaching Russian, nuclear science, conversation; *Clubs* Athenaeum; *Style*— Gerald Clark, Esq, CMG; ✉ e-mail geraldeclark@aol.com

CLARK, Gillian Margaret Rose; *née* Lockwood; da of Cyril Geoffrey Gunning Lockwood (d 1981), and Vera Irene Lockwood, *née* Marchant (d 1991); *b* 15 January 1949; *Educ* Varndean GS for Girls, Ashridge Mgmnt Coll (City Univ) (MBA); *m* 16 Oct 1982, Philip Stephen Clark; 1 da (Juliette Annabelle b 11 March 1984); *Career* chartered insurer 1989; Eagle Star (now Zurich Financial Services): joined as accident underwriting clerk 1968, head clerk Chatham branch 1972–74, accident underwriting superintendent Maidstone 1974–81, underwriting superintendent UK 1981–82, asst planning mangr 1982–83, asst mktg mangr 1983–86, mktg servs mangr 1986–88, mktg mangr UK Gen Div 1988–90, business devpt mangr 1990–91, divnl dir 1991–98, dir of Implementation and Integration Zurich Financial Services 1998–99, e-commerce coordination dir 1999–2001, non-exec dir Prophit Share Ltd 1999–2004, conslt Zurich Financial Services 2001–03, exec mentor and mgmnt conslt 2003–12; FCII 1974, AIPM 1979, MCIM 1986, memb Soc of Fellows London 1987, DipMktg, MInstM; *Recreations* golf; *Clubs* Naunton Downs Golf; *Style*— Mrs Gillian Clark; ✉ Hill Barn, Cowley, Gloucestershire GL53 9NJ (☎ 01242 870555)

CLARK, Prof Gordon Leslie; s of Bryan Victor Clark (d 2009), and Florence Lesley, *née* Cowling; *b* 10 September 1950; *Educ* Monash Univ Melbourne (BEcon, MA), McMaster Univ Hamilton (Benefactors scholar, PhD), Univ of Oxford (MA, DSc); *m* 1972, Shirley Anne, *née* Spratling; 1 s (Peter b 1988); *Career* Ford fell in urban studies McMaster Univ 1976–78, asst prof John F Kennedy Sch of Govt and Grad Sch of Design Harvard Univ 1978–83, assoc prof Dept of Geography Center for Urban Studies and Center for Organisation Studies Univ of Chicago 1983–85, prof Heinz Sch of Public Policy and Management Center for Labor Studies and Center for Economic Devpt Carnegie Mellon Univ Pittsburgh 1985–91; Monash Univ Melbourne 1990–94: prof and head Dept of Geography and Environmental Science and Grad Sch of Environmental Science, dir Inst of Ethics and Public Policy Grad Sch of Govt, head Faculty of Arts 1993, memb Advsy Bd Nat Key Center in Industrial Relations Grad Sch of Management, Sir Louis Matheson visiting prof 2009–; Univ of Oxford: fell St Peter's Coll 1995–2012, Halford Mackinder prof of geography 1995–2012, head of sch 2003–08, fell Saïd Business Sch 2000–03 and 2013–, prof and dir Smith Sch of Enterprise and Environment 2013–, fell St Edmund Hall; academician Learned Socs for the Social Sciences 2000–; memb Academic Panel Nat Assoc of Pension Funds 2001–, govr Pensions Policy Inst 2002–; fell Lincoln Land Inst Cambridge MA 1981–82, Andrew Mellon fell Nat Acad of Scis 1981–82, fell Acad of Soc Scis Australia 1993–, fell Monash Univ 2012; Distinguished Alumni Award McMaster Univ 1998, Conference Medal Royal Australian Inst of Planners 1988, Chllr's Medal Univ of Calif 2000; FBA 2005; *Books* Interregional Migration, National Policy and Social Justice (1983), State Apparatus: Structures and Language of Legitimacy (jtly, 1984), Judges and the Cities: Interpreting Local Autonomy (1985), Regional Dynamics: Studies in Adjustment Theory (jtly, 1986), Unions and Communities Under Siege: American

Communities and the Crisis of Organized Labor (1989), Multiculturalism, Difference and Postmodernism: Image and Representation in Australia (co-ed, 1993), Pensions and Corporate Restructuring in American Industry: A Crisis of Regulation (1993), Management Ethics: Theories, Cases and Materials (co-ed, 1995), Asian Newly Industrialized Economies in the Global Economy: Corporate Strategy and Industrial Restructuring in the 1990s (jtly, 1995), Accountability and Corruption (co-ed, 1997), Pension Fund Capitalism (2000), The Oxford Handbook of Economic Geography (co-ed, 2000), European Pensions & Global Finance (2003), Global Competitiveness and Innovation (jtly, 2004), The Oxford Handbook of Pensions and Retirement Income (co-ed, 2006), The Geography of Finance (jtly, 2007), Managing Financial Risk (co-ed, 2009), Saving for Retirement (jtly, 2012), Sovereign Wealth Funds (jtly, 2013), International Investors in Global Markets (jtly, 2017); also author of numerous papers and articles in learned jls; *Clubs* Athenaeum; *Style*— Prof Gordon L Clark; ✉ Oxford University Centre for the Environment, South Parks Road, Oxford OX1 3QY (☎ 01865 285067, e-mail gordon.clark@smithschool.ox.ac.uk)

CLARK, Graham Ronald; s of Ronald Edward Clark (d 2003), and Annie, *née* Eckersley (d 1984); *b* 10 November 1941, Littleborough, Lancs; *Educ* Kirkham GS, Loughborough Coll of Educn (DLC), Loughborough Univ (MSc); *m* 1, 9 April 1966 (m dis 1975), Susan, da of late Walter George Fenn, of Oxford; m 2, 31 March 1979, Joan Barbara, da of Albert Frederick Lawrence (d 1955), of Dunstable, Beds; 1 step da (Sarah Elisabeth b 8 Oct 1965); *Career* tenor; teacher and dir of PE 1964–69; sr regnl offr The Sports Cncl 1971–75; princ Scottish Opera 1975–77, debut London Bomarzo (ENO) 1976, princ ENO 1978–85 plus guest appearances (22 princ roles) 1986–2014; freelance 1985–; int venues 1976– incl: Bayreuther Festspiele Germany (16 seasons and 122 performances as Loge and Mime in Der Ring des Nibelungen (two prodns), David in Die Meistersinger von Nürnberg, Steuermann in Der fliegende Holländer, Melot and Seemann in Tristan und Isolde) 1981–92 and 2001–04, The Met Opera NY (15 seasons and 82 performances as Herodes in Salome, Steva in Jenufa, Captain Vere in Billy Budd, Bégearss in The Ghosts of Versailles (world première), Hauptmann in Wozzeck (two prodns), Albert Gregor in The Makropulos Case, Loge and Mime in Der Ring des Nibelungen, Prinz/Kammerdiener/Marquis in Lulu, Tanzmeister in Ariadne auf Naxos) 1985–2010, ROH, Glyndebourne Festival, WNO, Scottish Opera, Opera North, Northern Ireland Opera, Chelsea Opera, Opera Rara, Aix-en-Provence, Amsterdam, Barcelona Gran Teatre del Liceu, Berlin Deutsche Oper, Berlin Deutsche Staatsoper, Bilbao, Biwako, Bonn, Brussels La Monnaie, Catania, Chicago Lyric, Dallas, Dublin, Frankfurt, Geneva, Hamamatsu, Hamburg, Los Angeles, Madrid Teatro Real, Madrid La Zarzuela, Matsumoto, Milan La Scala, Munich, Nagoya, Nice, Paris Opéra Bastille, Paris Théâtre du Châtelet, Paris Théâtre des Champs Élysées, Paris Palais Garnier, Rome, Salzburg Festspiele, San Francisco, Seville, Stockholm, Tokyo Bunka Kaikan, Tokyo NHK, Toronto, Toulouse, Turin, Vancouver, Vienna Staatsoper, Yokohama, Zurich 1976–2016; concerts and festivals incl: Proms, Amsterdam, Antwerp, Bamberg, Berlin, Brussels, Canaries, Chicago, Cologne, Copenhagen, Edinburgh, Lucerne, Milan, Paris, Rome, Tel Aviv, Washington; recordings with: BBC, BMG, Challenge Classics, Chandos, Decca, Deutsche Grammophon, EMI, Erato, Etcetera, EuroArts, Oehms Classics, Opera Rara, Opus Arte, Philips, Sony, Teldec, The Met, WDR; videos and DVDs incl: The Ghosts of Versailles (Met Opera NY), Der Ring des Nibelungen (Bayreuther Festspiele), Der fliegende Hollander (Bayreuther Festspiele), Die Meistersinger von Nürnberg (Bayreuther Festspiele), Der Ring des Nibelungen (Gran Teatre del Liceu Barcelona), Der Ring des Nibelungen (De Nederlandse Opera Amsterdam), Lady Macbeth of Mtsensk (Gran Teatre del Liceu Barcelona), Khovanshchina (Gran Teatre del Liceu Barcelona), The Makropulos Case (Canadian Opera Toronto), Ariadne auf Naxos (Opéra National de Paris), Wozzeck (Deutsche Staatsoper Berlin), Wozzeck (Met Opera NY), The Rake's Progress (Glyndebourne Festival), debut actor as Socrates in Plato's Apology The Trial of Socrates (Grand Théâtre de Luxembourg) 2011; over 400 Wagner performances and recordings incl over 275 performances (Loge and Mime) in Der Ring des Nibelungen; Laurence Olivier Award for Mephistopheles in Busoni's Doktor Faust at ENO 1986, 3 nominations for Outstanding Individual Achievement in Opera incl EMMY for Bégearss in The Ghosts of Versailles at The Met 1983, 1986 and 1993, Sir Reginald Goodall Award The Wagner Soc London 2001, Sherwin Award The Wagner Soc of Southern California 2009; Hon DLitt Loughborough Univ 1999, Hon BSc Loughborough Univ 2009; *Recreations* sports; *Clubs* Garrick; *Style*— Graham Clark; ✉ c/o Ingpen & Williams Ltd, 7 St George's Court, 131 Putney Bridge Road, London SW15 2PA (☎ 020 8874 3222, fax 020 8877 3113, website www.ingpen.co.uk and www.grahamclark.org)

CLARK, Rt Hon Greg; PC (2010), MP; *b* 1967, Middlesbrough; *Educ* Univ of Cambridge, LSE (PhD); *m* Helen; 2 da, 1 s; *Career* Boston Consulting Gp, chief advsr commercial policy BBC, special advsr to Ian Lang MP (Sec of State for Trade and Industry) 1996–97, dir of policy Cons Pty 2001–05; MP (Cons) Tunbridge Wells 2005–; min of state for decentralisation Dept for Communities and Local Govt 2010–12, financial sec to the Treasy 2012–13, min of state for cities and constitution 2013–15, min for science and universities 2014–15, sec of state for communities and local govt 2015–16, sec of state for business, energy and industrial strategy 2016–; *Style*— The Rt Hon Greg Clark, MP; ✉ House of Commons, London SW1A 0AA (e-mail greg@gregclark.org)

CLARK, Gregor Munro; CB (2006); s of Ian Munro Clark (d 1995), of Keills, Isle of Jura, and Norah Isobel, *née* Joss (d 1998); *b* 18 April 1946; *Educ* Queen's Park Sr Secdy Sch Glasgow, Univ of St Andrews (LLB); *m* 1, 30 March 1974, Jane Maralyn (d 1999), da of Leslie John Palmer (d 1972); 1 s (Aidan Benedikt b 1979), 2 da (Flora Daisy Louise b 1982, Madeleine Alexandra Rose b 1984); m 2, 21 Feb 2000, Alexandra Groves, da of Duncan McIntyre Miller (d 2013); *Career* admitted Faculty of Advocates 1972, in practice 1972–74; Lord Advocate's Dept: joined 1974, asst parly draftsman then dep parly draftsman 1974–79, Scottish parly counsel and asst legal sec 1979–99, counsel to the Scottish Law Cmmn 1995–2000 and 2006–, Scottish parly counsel to the Scottish Exec 1999–2002 and 2005–06, Scottish parly counsel to UK Govt 2002–05; *Recreations* piano, Scandinavian languages and literature, walking; *Clubs* New (Edinburgh); *Style*— Gregor Clark, Esq, CB; ✉ 18 Rocheid Park, Inverleith, Edinburgh EH4 1RU (☎ 0131 315 4634); Scottish Law Commission, 140 Causewayside, Edinburgh EH9 1PR (☎ 0131 6625219)

CLARK, Guy Wyndham Nial Hamilton; JP (Inverclyde, 1981–2007); s of Capt George Hubert Wyndham Clark (d 1978), and Lavinia Maraquita Smith, *née* Shaw Stewart (d 1971); *b* 28 March 1944; *Educ* Eton, Mons OCS; *m* 1967, Brighid Lovell Greene; 2 s, 1 da; *Career* cmmnd Coldstream Gds 1962–67; investment mangr Murray Johnstone Ltd Glasgow 1973–77, ptnr RC Greig & Co (stockbrokers) Glasgow 1977–86, dir Greig Middleton & Co Ltd (stockbrokers) 1986–97, md Murray Johnstone Private Investors Ltd 1997–2001, md Aberdeen Private Investors Ltd 2001–06, sr divnl dir Bell Lawrie Investment Mgmnt 2006–08; vice-chm JP Advsy Ctee for Inverclyde 1990–2003, vice-pres West Lowland Bn Army Cadet Force League 2007–; memb Exec Ctee Erskine Hosp for Ex-Servicemen 1981–97, patron Accord Hospice 2007–, hon patron Inc Glasgow Renfrewshire Soc 2007–, pres SSAFA Forces Help Renfrewshire, East Renfrewshire & Inverclyde Branch 2007–, hon pres St Columba's Sch 2008–, pres Lowland Reserve Forces & Cadets Assoc 2014; Lord-Lt Renfrewshire 2007– (Vice Lord-Lt 2002–07, DL 1987–2002); memb Int Stock Exchange 1983, FCSI 2008 (MSI 1992); *Recreations* country sports, gardening; *Clubs* Turf, Western (Glasgow), MCC; *Style*— Guy Clark, Esq, JP, FCSI; ✉ Braeton House, Inverkip, Renfrewshire, PA16 0DU (☎ 01475 520619)

CLARK, Prof Ian; s of Alexander Buchanan Clark (d 1984), and Amanda, *née* Vangsnes (d 1995); *b* 14 March 1949; *Educ* Hamilton Acad (Dux Gold Medal), Univ of Glasgow (MA), Australian Nat Univ (PhD); *m* 1970, Janice, *née* Cochrane; 1 da (Paula), 1 s (Steven); *Career* lectr Univ of Western Australia 1974–81 (sr lectr 1981–84); Univ of Cambridge: fell Selwyn Coll Cambridge 1985–97 (hon fell 2000), teaching fell Defence Studies 1984–88, asst dir Studies in Int Relations 1988–97, dep dir Centre of Int Studies 1993–97; Univ of Wales Aberystwyth: prof of int politics 1998–2014, E H Carr prof 2008–14; prof of int relations Univ of Queensland 2014–; visiting prof Nanyang Technol Univ Singapore 2014–; memb Br Int Studies Assoc 1980–, memb IISS 1990–; Leverhulme major res fell 2001, ESRC professorial fell 2007–10; FBA 1999 (memb Cncl 2001–04, chair political studies 2005–08, chair research posts 2005–11), founding FLSW 2010; *Publications* Waging War (1988), Nuclear Diplomacy and the Special Relationship (1994), Globalization and Fragmentation (1997), Globalization and International Relations Theory (1999), The Post-Cold War Order (2001), Legitimacy in International Society (2005), International Legitimacy and World Society (2007), Hegemony in International Society (2011), The Vulnerable in International Society (2013), Waging War (2015); *Recreations* hill walking, being a grandfather; *Style*— Prof Ian Clark

CLARK, Katy; *b* 3 July 1967; *Career* solicitor then head of memb legal servs Unison; MP (Lab) Ayrshire N and Arran 2005–15; *Style*— Ms Katy Clark; ✉ House of Commons, London SW1A 0AA

CLARK, Keith; s of Douglas William Clark (d 1967), of Chichester, W Sussex, and Evelyn Lucy, *née* Longlands; *b* 25 October 1944; *Educ* Chichester HS for Boys, St Catherine's Coll Oxford (MA); *m* 1 (m dis); 1 s (Nicholas Howard Douglas b 1980), 1 da (Katherine Sara Amy b 1984); m 2, 15 Dec 2001, Helen Patricia, da of James Paterson, of Kent; *Career* slr; Clifford Chance: joined 1971, ptnr 1977–, sr ptnr 1993–2001, various mgmnt appts; int gen counsel Morgan Stanley 2002–; memb: Law Soc 1971, Slrs' Benevolent Soc, Int Bar Assoc; *Recreations* hiking, family, modern art, modern jazz; *Style*— Keith Clark, Esq; ✉ Morgan Stanley, 25 Cabot Square, Canary Wharf, London E14 4QA

CLARK, Lance; s of Tony Clark (d 1994), and Eileen Clark (d 1999); *b* 30 April 1936; *Educ* Univ of Oxford (BA), Harvard Univ, INSEAD; *m* 6 Dec 2003, Ying; 2 c (Yoyi b 12 June 2004, Umei b 17 Aug 2006); *Career* md: Clarks Ltd, Clarks Ireland, Clarks Australia, Padmore & Barnes, Barkers; chm: Edward Green, Terra Plana; fndr and mangr Soul of Africa; Irish Export Award 1966, Drapers Award for contribution to industry 2005; *Recreations* painting, art, tennis, swimming, skiing; *Clubs* Lansdowne; *Style*— Lance Clark, Esq; ✉ Unit 14, 2 Archie Street, London SE1 3JT (fax 020 7357 8565, e-mail lancelotclark@yahoo.co.uk); Terra Plana, 124 Bermondsey Street, London SE1 3TX (☎ 020 7407 3758)

CLARK, Prof Leslie Arthur; OBE (2001); s of Arthur George Clark, of Chadwell Heath, Essex, and Lilian Rosina, *née* Procter; *b* 3 May 1944; *Educ* Ilford Co HS for Boys, Univ of Sheffield (Cicely Courtauld scholar, BEng, PhD, Mappin medal); *m* 29 Dec 1973, Helen Rose, da of William Ireson Tripp; 2 da (Laura Jane b 18 March 1977, Georgina Ann b 2 Dec 1980); *Career* res engr in design Cement and Concrete Assoc 1968–78; Sch of Civil Engrg Univ of Birmingham: lectr 1978–86, sr lectr 1986–91, prof of structural engrg 1991–, pro-vice-chllr (estates and infrastructure) 2005–09; pres IStructE 1998–99; FIStructE 1986 (MIStructE 1975), FREng 1994, FICE 1995 (MICE 1973), Hon FICT 2001; *Books* Concrete Bridge Design (1983), Concrete Slabs: Analysis and Design (1984); *Recreations* cricket, football, jazz music; *Clubs* MCC; *Style*— Prof Leslie Clark, OBE, FREng

CLARK, Martin Charles; s of John Clark (d 1998), and Ann, *née* Green; *b* 15 January 1976, Chelmsford, Essex; *Educ* Campion Sch Hornchurch, Thurrock Coll Grays (BTEC), Sheffield Hallam Univ (BA), RCA (MA); *m* 21 Sept 2002, Rosie, *née* Hill; 1 da (Kitty Winter b 25 Sept 2003), 1 s (Oscar Felix b 4 July 2006); *Career* art curator; club promoter The Store, Takin' Note, Sound Advice (all in Sheffield) 1998–2000, record buyer and DJ The Store 1999–2000, info asst Tate Modern 2000–01, gall intern Kapinos Gall Berlin 2001, exhbns curator and tutor Herbert Read Gall Kent Inst of Art and Design 2001–05, exhbns curator Arnolfini Bristol 2005–07, artistic dir Tate St Ives 2007–; *Exhibitions* Marks out of 10 (S1 Artspace Sheffield) 1999, Quitters (Democracy! RCA Gall London) 2000, Felix Gonzales Torres (Serpentine Gall London) 2000, Playing Amongst the Ruins (RCA Gall) 2001, No Timewasters (Zandra Rhodes Gall Rochester) 2002, Daniel Guzman – I Am In The World With You (Herbert Read Gall Canterbury and Vilma Gold London) 2002, Art is very much like rock and roll... (Zandra Rhodes Gall Rochester) 2002, The Exhibition Began with a Scandal (Lenbachaus Museum Munich) 2002, Billy Childish – 25 Years of Being Childish (George Rodger Gall Maidstone and Window Gall Central St Martins London) 2002, The Greatest Show on Earth (Metropole Gall Folkestone) 2003, MODEL: (Zandra Rhodes Gall Rochester) 2003, Michael Stevenson – To Our German Friend (Vilma Gold London) 2003, Ursula Biemann (George Rodger Gall Maidstone) 2003, Adam Chodzko – Design for a Carnival (Herbert Read Gall Canterbury) 2003, Candyland Zoo (Herbert Read Gall Canterbury) 2004, The Hollows of Glamour (Herbert Read Gall Canterbury) 2004, David Claerbout (Herbert Read Gall Canterbury) 2004, Will there be a last letter (co-curator, Horsebridge Whitstable) 2004, Europa – Artists Film and Video from the Centre of Europe (co-curator, Tate Modern) 2004, Michael Stevenson – Rakit (Herbert Read Gall Canterbury and Neuer Aachner Kunstverein Aachen) 2004, Growing Up Absurd – The Problems of Youth in the Organized System (Herbert Read Gall Canterbury) 2005, This storm is what we call progress (co-curator, Arnolfini Bristol) 2005, Mark Titchner- IT IS YOU (Arnolfini Bristol) 2006, Deimantas Narkevicius – Once in the XX Century (Arnolfini Bristol) 2006, Albert Oehlen – I Will Always Champion Bad Painting (Arnolfini Bristol) 2006, Pale Carnage (Arnolfini Bristol) 2007, Henri Gaudier Brzeska (Arnolfini Bristol) 2007, Brian Griffiths – The Man Who Loved Islands (Arnolfini Bristol) 2007, Eileen Quinlan and Cheyney Thompson – TBA (Arnolfini Bristol) 2007, Lucy McKenzie – 10 Years of Robotic Mayhem (Arnolfini Bristol) 2007, Jonty Lees – Lodger (Tate St Ives) 2007, Hans-Peter Feldmann (Arnolfini Bristol) 2007; *Style*— Martin Clark, Esq; ✉ Tate St Ives, Porthmeor Beach, St Ives, Cornwall TR26 1TG (☎ 01736 791103, e-mail martin.clark@tate.org.uk)

CLARK, Matthew David; s of David Clark, of Billericay, Essex, and Patricia, *née* Hollis; *b* 9 November 1966, Reading, Berks; *Educ* Anglo European Sch Ingatestone, Oxford Brookes Univ (Dip), Blakemores; *m* 4 Sept 2004, Sarah, *née* Case; 3 s (Samuel b 30 April 1994, Felix b 8 April 2002, Oscar b 14 Sept 2003); *Career* fin dir: BNL Advtg 1989–90, Reay Keating Hamer 1990–95, Mellors Reay & Ptnrs 1995–99; gp chief fin offr and ptnr Mother Hldgs Ltd 1999–; hon treas NABS 2002–04; tstee Shelter from the Storm 2010–; MIPA 1992; *Recreations* running, cycling, travelling, wine; *Clubs* Soho House, Century, Shoreditch House, Eight, Ivy; *Style*— Matthew Clark, Esq; ✉ 32 Avenue Road, London N6 5DW (☎ 020 8340 7271, e-mail m@tthewclark.com); Mother Holdings Limited, 10 Redchurch Street, London E2 7DD (☎ 020 7012 1800, fax 020 7012 1989)

CLARK, Dr Michael Llewellyn; *b* 17 June 1935; *Educ* W Monmouth GS Pontypool Monmouthshire, KCL, St George's Hosp Med Sch Univ of London (LRCP, MB BS, MD); *m* 2 c; *Career* house physician: Neurological Unit Atkinson Morley's Hosp London 1959–60, Brompton Hosp London 1960; jr med specialist HM Forces QAMH Millbank London 1960–63; St George's Hosp London: house physician 1958, house surgn Surgical Unit 1958–59, med registrar 1963–66, clinical res registrar Med Unit 1964–66, sr registrar in med 1968; fell in gastroenterology Philadelphia Gen Hosp Univ of Pennsylvania 1966–68; Bart's London: clinical res asst and hon lectr in med 1969–70, sr lectr in med Bart's Med Coll 1970–93, postgrad sub-dean Bart's Med Coll 1974–80, head Gastroenterology

Dept 1986–91; City & Hackney Health Dist: conslt physician 1970–93, unit gen mangr Hackney Unit 1985–88, unit gen mangr City Unit 1988–90, dir of res and clinical devpt 1990–92; conslt physician: St Leonards Hosp 1970–84, Hackney Hosp 1984–85, Princess Grace Hosp 1990– (chair of clinical governance 1995–2014); postgraduate co-ordinator Royal Hosps Tst 1994–2003, reg teacher for MRCP examination; author of numerous published articles in learned jls; MRCS, FRCP 1975 (MRCP); *Books* Clinical Medicine (jtly, 1987, 1990, 1994, 1998, 2002, 2005, 2009 and 2012); *Style—* Dr Michael Clark; ✉ 4 Palace Court, 26 The Broadway, Cheam, Surrey SM3 8AZ (☎ 020 8643 5378, e-mail michaelclark467@hotmail.com)

CLARK, His Hon Judge Neil Andrew; s of Andrew Clark, and Margaret, *née* Rae (d 2004); *b* 26 November 1964, Sunderland; *Educ* Bede Sch Sunderland, Univ of Leeds (LLB); *m* 20 Nov 1998, Susan Mary, *née* Godley; *Career* called to the Bar Inner Temple 1987 (master of the bench 2012); recorder 2005, pt/t judge Mental Health Review Tbnl 2008–, circuit judge North Eastern Circuit 2012–; *Recreations* supporter Sunderland AFC, cricket, horse racing, Scotland; *Clubs* Durham CCC; *Style—* His Hon Judge Neil Clark; ✉ Leeds Combined Court Centre, The Courthouse, 1 Oxford Row, Leeds LS1 3BG

CLARK, Paul Evans; s of Harry Frederick Clark, of Derby, and Joyce Evelyn, *née* Margetts; *b* 18 March 1946; *Educ* Bemrose GS Derby, Univ of Manchester (LLB); *m* 25 July 1970 (dis), Jane Mary, da of Edmund Patrick Flowers; 2 s (Guy Edmund b 22 Feb 1977, Ben Thomas b 28 July 1980), 2 da (Nina Jane b 13 Dec 1972, Lucy Anna b 25 March 1975); m 2, 26 May 2000, Susan Roxana, da of Frederick White; *Career* admitted slr 1970; asst slr Rubinstein Nash & Co 1970–72 (articled clerk 1968–70), asst slr Property Dept Linklaters & Paines 1972–83, D J Freeman 1984–2003 (joined 1984, ptnr 1985, head of property 1990–2000), conslt Cripps Harries Hall LLP 2003–; memb Law Soc 1970; *Publications* The Conveyancer and Property Lawyer (conveyancing ed); *Recreations* pianist, music, church membership, reading; *Style—* Paul Clark, Esq; ✉ Cripps Harries Hall LLP, Wallside House, 12 Mount Ephraim Road, Tunbridge Wells, Kent TN1 1EG (☎ 01892 515121, fax 01892 544878, e-mail paul.clark@crippslaw.com)

CLARK, Paul Richard; s of Henry Clark (d 1981), and Daphne, *née* Andreazzi; *b* 7 November 1962, London; *Educ* Univ of Reading (BA, MPhil); *m* July 2003, Tracey, *née* Adamson; 1 s (Harry b 1 March 1996), 1 da (Eleanor b 24 May 1999); *Career* Prudential Investment Management (PIM) 1986–89, sr surveyor Donaldsons 1990, assoc dir DTZ Debenham Tie Leung 1990–99, dir Hemingway Properties Ltd 1999–2001, dir ISG Occupancy Ltd (now Dunlop Haywards) 2001–03, chief surveyor Church Commissioners for England 2003–; dir Real Service Ltd; memb Investors Property Forum, memb Residential Ctee Br Property Fedn; MRICS 1989; *Recreations* cricket, golf, theatre, cinema; *Style—* Paul Clark, Esq; ✉ Church House, Great Smith Street, London SW1P 3AZ (☎ 020 7898 1634, fax 020 7898 1153)

CLARK, Dr Peter John Alleguen; OBE (1993); s of Dr Kenneth Clark (d 1971), and Kitty Matilda, *née* Ruffle (d 1990); *b* Sheffield, S Yorks; *Educ* Loughborough GS, Southend HS for Boys, Keele Univ (BA), Downing Coll Cambridge, Univ of Leicester (PhD); *m* 1, 1968 (m dis 1980), Isobel, *née* Rankin; 1 s (John Paul Jeremy b 1972); m 2, 1980, Theresa Mary Philomena Brown, *née* Alleguen; 1 step da (Kate Philomena b 1968), 2 s (Gabriel Edwin Alleguen b 1981, Nathaniel Luke Alleguen b 1983); *Career* mathematics teacher Ankara Coll and teacher of English British Council 1962–63, tutorial asst Dept of History Univ of Leicester 1964–66, lectr in general studies Duncan of Jordanstone Coll of Art 1966–67; British Council: trg 1967–68, Jordan 1968–70, MECAS 1970–71, Sudan 1971–77, London 1977–80, Yemen 1980–84, Tunisia 1984–88, UAE 1988–92, dir Syria 1992–97, advsr Middle East and North Africa Dept 1997–99, dir Middle East Cultural Advsy Services 1998–; memb Middle East Studies Assoc 1993; conslt ed Banipal; chair Advsy Panel Br Centre for Literary Translation 2000–02; tstee: Karim Rida Said Fndn 1999–2004, Int Prize for Arabic Fiction 2007–13; conslt AMAR Int Charitable Fndn 2000–01 (ceo 2002–04); memb Methodology Soc, chm Frome Soc for Local Study 2011–16; FRGS 1982, FIL 1993; *Books* Three Sudanese Battles (1977), Karari (trans, 1980), Henry Hallam (1982), Marmaduke Pickthall British Muslim (1986, 2 edn 2016), Dubai Tales (trans, 1991), Thesiger's Return (1992), A Balcony Over Fakihani (trans, 1993), Sabriya (trans, 1995), Grandfather's Tale (trans, 1998), Arabic Literature Unveiled: Challenges of Translation (2000), Pearl-Fishing in the Gulf: A Kuwaiti Memoir (trans, 2000), The Iraqi Marshlands – A Human and Environmental Study (co-ed with Emma Nicholson, 2002), Memory of the Flesh (trans, 2003), Sardines and Oranges (ed, 2005), The Woman of the Flask (trans, 2005), The Lefties' Guide to Britain (ed, 2005), Istanbul (2010), Coffeehouse Footnotes (2010), Emerging Arab Voices 1 (ed, 2010), Dickens's London (2012), Emerging Arab Voices 2 (ed, 2012), Dickens: London into Kent (2013), Damascus Diaries (2015), Emirates Diaries (2016); *Recreations* writing book reviews, grandfatherhood, walking in hills; *Style—* Dr Peter Clark, OBE; ✉ 71 Nunney Road, Frome, Somerset BA11 4LF (☎ 01373 300310, e-mail mecas@blueyonder.co.uk)

CLARK, Prof Robin Jon Hawes; CNZM (2004); s of Reginald Hawes Clark, JP (BCom), of Christchurch, NZ, and Marjorie Alice, *née* Thomas; *b* 16 February 1935, Rangiora, NZ; *Educ* Christ's Coll Christchurch, Canterbury UC Univ of NZ (BSc, MSc), UCL (PhD, DSc); *m* 30 May 1964, Beatrice Rawdin Clark, JP, da of Ellis Rawdin Brown (d 1978); 1 da (Victoria b 23 June 1967), 1 s (Matthew b 14 Dec 1971); *Career* UCL: asst lectr 1962, lectr 1963–71, reader 1972–81, prof 1982–88, dean of sci 1988–89, head Dept of Chem 1989–99, Sir William Ramsay prof 1989–, memb Cncl 1991–94, fell 1992; senator Univ of London 1988–93; chm: 11th Int Conf on Raman Spectroscopy London 1988, Advsy Ctee Ramsay Meml Fellowships Tst 1989–2009, Steering Ctee Int Confs on Raman Spectroscopy 1990–92; memb Cncl Royal Soc 1993–94; sec Royal Inst of GB 1998–2004; visiting prof: Columbia 1965, Padua 1967, Western Ontario 1968, Texas A and M 1978, Bern 1979, Fribourg 1979, Auckland 1981, Odense 1982, Sydney 1985, Bordeaux 1988, Pretoria 1991, Würzburg 1997, Indiana 1998, Thessaloniki 1999; Royal Soc of Chemistry lectr: Tilden 1983–84, Nyholm 1989–90, Thomas Graham 1991, Harry Hallam 1993 and 2000, Liversidge 2003–04, Sir George Stokes Award 2009–10; Kresge-Hooker lectr Wayne State Univ 1965, Frontiers in Chemistry lectr Case-Western Reserve Univ 1978, John van Geuns lectr Univ of Amsterdam 1979, Firth lectr Univ of Sheffield 1991, Carman lectr SA Chemical Inst 1994, Moissan lectr ENSC Paris 1998, Leermakers lectr Wesleyan Univ 2000, Hassel lectr Univ of Oslo 2000, Royal Soc UK-Canada Rutherford lectr 2000, Ralph Anderson lectr Worshipful Co of Horners 2003, Benezra-Kern lectr Inst Chimie Strasbourg 2008, Royal Soc Bakerian lectr 2008, Sir Lionel Denny lectr Barber Surgns Co 2009, Minerva lectr Scientific Instrument Makers Co 2011, Rutherford lectr Univ of Canterbury New Zealand 2013, first jt lectr RSC/ RA 2013, Tribute to Lord Lewis Cambridge 2014, Soc of Chemical Industries Public Lecture 2015; tstee: Ramsay Meml Fellowships Tst 1994– (vice-chm 2006–), Univ of Canterbury NZ Tst 2004– (chm 2005–); govr Haberdashers' Aske's Sch 1995–98; Joannes Marcus Marci Medal (Czech Spectroscopy Soc) 1998, Inaugural Biennial Franklin-Lavoiser Prize, Maison de la Chimie (Paris) and the Chemical Heritage Fndn (Philadelphia) 2009; T K Sidey Medal (Royal Soc NZ) 2001; Hon DSc Canterbury Univ NZ 2001; memb Academia Europaea 1990; Hon FRSNZ 1989, FRSC 1969, FRS 1990, FRSA 1992, Hon FRI 2004, foreign fell Nat Acad of Scis India 2007, int memb American Philosophical Soc 2010; *Books* The Chemistry of Titanium and Vanadium (1968), The Chemistry of Titanium Zirconium and Hafnium (1973), The Chemistry of Vanadium Niobium and Tantalum (1973), Advances in Spectroscopy Vols 1–26 (co ed, 1975–98), Raman Spectroscopy (co ed, 1988); also author of more than 530 scientific papers; *Recreations* golf, bridge, music, theatre, travel; *Clubs* Athenaeum, Porters Park, Lucretians; *Style—* Prof Robin Clark, CNZM, FRS; ✉ 3a Loom Lane, Radlett, Hertfordshire WD7 8AA (☎ 01923 857899); Christopher Ingold Laboratories, University College London, 20 Gordon Street, London WC1H 0AJ (☎ 020 7679 7457, fax 020 7679 7463, e-mail r.j.h.clark@ucl.ac.uk)

CLARK, Rodney; OBE (2001); *b* 7 September 1944; *Educ* Andover GS, UCL; *m*; *Career* mangr family furniture removals business 1965–67, gen asst Welfare Dept Hampshire CC 1967–68, Israeli Kibbutz 1968–69, admin asst Welfare Dept London Borough of Camden 1969–71; London Borough of Islington then Camden and Islington AHA: administrator Personal Health Servs 1971–72, opened and managed Highbury Grange Health Centre 1972–74, sr administrator Islington Sch Health Serv 1974–77, capital projects mangr Islington Health Dist 1977–78; projects administrator RNID 1978–81, chief exec Sense (Nat Deafblind and Rubella Assoc) 1981–2001; chm: SIGN (Nat Soc for Mental Health and Deafness) 1994–, Christopher Brock Charitable Tst 1994–, Br Dyslexia Assoc 2002–05, Parents Autism Campaign for Educn (PACE) 2003–05, Woodford Fndn 2003–; vice-chm Hearing Conservation Cncl 2001–, sec Deafblind International 1987–2001; treas: European Deafblind Network 1989–2001, UK Cncl on Deafness 1995–2003; tstee: Whitefields Devpt Tst 1996–2005, KIDS 1997–2005, Royal Sch for Deaf Children Margate 2005–06, Richmond Charitable Tst 2005–; conslt in mgmnt and devpt to the voluntary sector 2001–; mgmnt speaker at seminars and confs for voluntary organisations; *Recreations* choral singing, tennis, swimming, walking, theatre, opera and concerts; *Style—* Rodney Clark, Esq, OBE; ✉ 31 Sutton Road, Shrewsbury, Shropshire SY2 6DL (☎ 01743 358998, e-mail rod.clark@virgin.net)

CLARK, Prof Stephen Richard Lyster; s of David Allen Richard Clark (d 1986), and Mary Kathleen, *née* Finney (d 1992); *b* 30 October 1945; *Educ* Nottingham HS, Balliol and All Souls Colls Oxford (MA, DPhil); *m* 1 July 1972 (Edith) Gillian, da of Prof John Callan James Metford, of Bristol; 1 s (Samuel b 1974), 2 da (Alexandra b 1976, Verity b 1985); *Career* fell All Souls Coll Oxford 1968–74, lectr in moral philosophy Univ of Glasgow 1974–83 (Gifford lectr 1982); Univ of Liverpool: prof of philosophy 1984–2009, dean Faculty of Arts 1995–98; Stanton lectr Univ of Cambridge 1987–89, Wilde lectr Univ of Oxford 1990, Scott Holland lectr 1992, Read Tuckwell lectr Univ of Bristol 1994, Alan Richardson fell Univ of Durham 1999; Leverhulme major research fellowship 2003–06, hon research fell Univ of Bristol 2011–; memb: Farm Animal Welfare Cncl 1997–2002, Animal Procedures Ctee 1998–2006; ed Jl of Applied Philosophy 1990–2001, assoc ed Br Jl for the History of Philosophy 2010–; *Books* Aristotle's Man (1975), The Moral Status of Animals (1977), The Nature of the Beast (1982), From Athens to Jerusalem (1984), The Mysteries of Religion (1986), La Naturaleza De La Bestia (1987), Money, Obedience and Affection (ed, 1989), Civil Peace and Sacred Order (1989), A Parliament of Souls (1990), God's World and the Great Awakening (1991), How to Think about the Earth (1993), How to Live Forever (1995), Animals and their Moral Standing (1997), God, Religion and Reality (1998), The Political Animal (1999), Biology and Christian Ethics (2000), G K Chesterton: Thinking Backwards, Looking Forwards (2006), Understanding Faith: Religious Belief and its Place in Society (2009), Ancient Mediterranean Philosophy (2012), Plotinus: myth, metaphor and philosophical practice (2016); *Recreations* science fiction, computers; *Style—* Prof Stephen R L Clark; ✉ 49 Bellevue Crescent, Bristol BS8 4TF (e-mail srlclark@liv.ac.uk)

CLARK, Terrence Michael; s of Douglas Gordon Clark, of Littlehampton, W Sussex, and Doris, *née* Landymore; *b* 5 May 1946; *m* 29 May 1976, Sally-Marie, da of Ronald Strange, of Ripley, Surrey; 2 s (Paul b 1967, Tobias b 1989), 1 da (Rebecca b 1983); *Career* artist craftsman in metals; ed Br Blacksmith Magazine 1980–84, ed Artist Blacksmith magazine 1999–2009; chm Br Artist Blacksmiths' Assoc 2009–11 (vice-chm 1992–94); organiser and chm The Int Blacksmithing Conf 1985; first artsmith to have a gate accepted by the Royal Acad Ctee under sculpture 1986; toured Missouri, Kansas and Texas lecturing and demonstrating blacksmiths skills 2002, taken USA blacksmithing masterclasses 2008, 2010 and 2011; Environmental Project Award for Sculptural Railings Runnymede Cncl 1997 and 2001, Godalming Tst Civic Design Award 1998, winner Waverley Design Awards 1999, Worshipful Co of Blacksmiths Joint Tonypandy Award 2009; Freeman City of London 1997, Liveryman Worshipful Co of Blacksmiths 2011 (fell (Silver medal) 1995); *Exhibitions* incl: Towards a New Iron Age V&A 1982, New York Craft Centre 1982, Br Artist Blacksmiths' Assoc Exhibitions 1983–92, Int Metalwork and Sculpture Exhibition Friedrichshafen W Germany 1987, Fe – an exploration of iron through the senses 1995–96; won Addy Taylor Cup awarded by Worshipful Co of Blacksmiths 1983, Hot Metal 1998; *Commissions* HH Sheik Mohammed Bin Rashid Al Maktoum 1984–95, Guildford Cathedral 1985, public sculpture Horsham Cncl 1994, 50m x 4m public cmmn High St Godalming 1995, external and internal work Grace Barrand Studio Nutfield 1995, 3 pairs of gates Dorneywood 1995, gates and railings Brasenose Coll Oxford 1996, Restoration Work Chancellor's residence Dorneywood 1997, gates Town Hall Chester 1998, gates and screens Geffrye Museum London 1998, stainless steel entrance Chelsea Flower Show 1998, 7 metre high sculpture Staines 1998, 3 public art sculptures Leatherhead 1999, public art sculpture Staines 1999, public art sculpture Guildford 1999, gates Jesus Coll Oxford 2000, sculpture Regents Coll London 2000; *Books* Towards a New Iron Age (1982), Schmeidearbeiten von Heute (1986), Art From The Fire (1986), Art for Architecture (1987), Metal-Handwerk & Technik (1987); *Recreations* holder of pilot's licence, skiing, golf; *Style—* Terrence Clark, Esq; ✉ Wildfields Farm, Woodstreet Village, Guildford, Surrey GU3 3BP (☎ 01483 235244, fax 01483 236456, e-mail terrence@artsmith.co.uk, website www.artsmith.co.uk)

CLARK, Sir Timothy Charles (Tim); KBE (2014); *Educ* Univ of London; *Career* Br Caledonian 1972–75, Gulf Air 1975–1985, Emirates 1985– (joined as head of airline planning 1985, pres 2003–); md Sri Lankan Airlines 1998–2008; chm Emirates Airline Fndn; Gold Award Royal Aeronautical Soc 2009, Leader of the Year Airline Business and Flightglobal Achievement Awards 2011, Centre for Aviation (CAPA) Legends Award 2013 (and inducted into CAPA hall of fame); hon doctorate Middlesex Univ 2011, hon doctorate Northumbria Univ 2015; FRAeS; Officier de la Légion d'Honneur 2009; *Style—* Sir Tim Clark, KBE; ✉ Emirates Group HQ, PO Box 686, Dubai

CLARK, Prof Timothy John Hayes (Tim); *b* 18 October 1935; *Educ* Christ's Hosp, Guy's Hosp Med Sch London (BSc, MRCS, LRCP, MB BS, MD); *m*; 4 c; *Career* house offr: Guy's Hosp 1961, Brompton Hosp 1961–62, Hammersmith Hosp 1962–63, Nat Hosp for Nervous Diseases London 1963; fell in med Johns Hopkins Hosp Baltimore 1963–64, registrar Hammersmith Hosp 1964–66; Guy's Hosp: sr lectr Depts of Med and Physiology 1966–68, hon sr registrar 1966–68, conslt physician 1968–90, prof of thoracic med UMDS 1977–90; specialist advsr to Social Servs Ctee House of Commons 1980–81 and 1984–85, conslt in thoracic med to the CMO Dept of Health 1985–90; Royal Brompton Hosp: conslt physician 1990–98 (pt/t 1970–90), prof of pulmonary med Nat Heart and Lung Inst 1990–; dean: Guy's Campus 1984–86, United Dental and Med Schs 1986–89 (govr 1982–90), Nat Heart and Lung Inst 1990–97; pro-rector Imperial Coll and dep princ Imperial Coll Sch of Med 1995–97, pro-rector (educational quality) Imperial Coll 1997–2000, provost Imperial Coll at Wye 2000–2001, pro-rector (admissions) 2001–02; pro-vice-chllr for med and dentistry Univ of London 1987–89; special tstee Guy's Hosp 1982–89; pres Br Thoracic Soc 1990–91; memb: Lambeth Southwark and Lewisham AHA 1978–82, Lewisham and N Southwark HA 1982–85, SE Thames RHA 1985–87, Systems Bd MRC 1985–88, Royal Brompton Hospital NHS Tst 1993–98; fell: City and Guilds Inst, King's Coll London; hon prof Xian Med Coll Xian China 1985–; FRCP 1973; *Publications* author of over 200 textbooks, articles and papers on respiratory medicine; *Clubs* MCC; *Style—* Prof Tim Clark; ✉ 8 Lawrence Court, London NW7 3QP (☎ 020 8959 4411)

CLARK, Timothy Nicholas (Tim); s of Sir Robert Clark (d 2013), and Andolyn Marjorie Beynon, *née* Lewis; *b* 9 January 1951, London; *Educ* Sherborne, Pembroke Coll Cambridge (MA); *m* 24 Aug 1974, Caroline, *née* Moffat; 2 s (Nicholas b 1979, Richard b 1984); *Career* Slaughter and May: joined 1974, ptnr 1983, sr ptnr 2001–08; co-fndr BCKR 2013–; sr ind dir Big Yellow plc, sr advsr G3; sr advsr Chatham House, vice-chair Business for New Europe, memb Int Advsy Cncl Uria Menendez 2008, memb Advsy Bd Centre for European Reform 2010; chair Economist Tst 2009, chm Royal Air Sqdn 2010; memb Bd RNT; govr Bradfield Sch until 2011, tstee Geoffrey de Havilland Flying Fndn, memb Nat Gallery Devpt Ctee, memb governing body ICC UK, chair WaterAid UK 2013; memb Law Soc 1976; *Recreations* flying, Italy, history, theatre, football, cricket; *Clubs* Royal Air Sqdn; *Style*— Tim Clark, Esq

CLARK OF CALTON, Baroness (Life Peer UK 2005), of Calton in the City of Edinburgh; Dr Lynda Margaret Clark; QC (Scot 1989); *Educ* Univ of St Andrews (LLB), Univ of Edinburgh (PhD); *Career* lectr in law Univ of Dundee 1973–76, called to the Scottish Bar 1977, called to the Bar Inner Temple 1990; Bd Memb Scottish Legal Aid Bd 1990–93; Parly candidate (Lab) NE Fife 1992, MP (Lab) Edinburgh Pentlands 1997–2005, advocate-gen for Scotland 1999–, memb Select Ctee on Pub Admin 1997–; memb Ct Univ of Edinburgh 1995–97; *Style*— The Rt Hon the Lady Clark of Calton, QC; ✉ House of Lords, London SW1A 0PW

CLARK OF WINDERMERE, Baron (Life Peer UK 2001), of Windermere in the County of Cumbria; David George Clark; PC (1997), DL (Cumbria 2007); s of George Clark, and Janet, of Askham, Cumbria; *b* 19 October 1939; *Educ* Windermere GS, Univ of Manchester (BA, MSc), Univ of Sheffield (PhD); *m* 1970, Christine, da of Ronald Kirkby, of Grasmere, Cumbria; 1 da; *Career* former forester, lab asst, student teacher, univ lectr; Parly candidate (Lab) Manchester Withington 1966; MP (Lab): Colne Valley 1970–74 (also contested Oct 1974), South Shields 1979–2001; oppn spokesman on agric and food 1973–74, oppn spokesman on defence 1980–81, oppn front bench spokesman on the environment 1981–87, memb Shadow Cabinet 1986–97; chief oppn spokesman on: agric and rural affairs 1987–92, defence, disarmament and arms control 1992–97; chllr of the Duchy of Lancaster 1997–98; ldr UK delgn to NATO 2001–05; dir: Homeowners Friendly Soc 1989–97 and 1999–2009, Thales plc 1999–2011, Carlisle United (1921) Ltd, Sellafield Ltd 2007–15; chm Forestry Cmmn 2001–09; visiting prof of history and politics Univ of Huddersfield 2013–; fell Univ of Cumbria 2009–; *Books* Industrial Manager (1966), Radicalism to Socialism (1981), Victor Grayson (1985), We Do Not Want the Earth (1992), The Labour Movement in Westmorland (2012), Voices from Labour's Past (2015), Grayson: The Man and the Mystery (2016); *Style*— The Rt Hon the Lord Clark of Windermere, PC, DL

CLARKE, Alan; s of Thomas Clarke (d 2009), and Mary, *née* Carson; *b* 10 April 1951, Lurgan; *Educ* Univ of Ulster (BSc), Scottish Hotel Sch (MSc), Univ of Strathclyde (MSc); *m* 12 Sep 1979, Mary, *née* Marks; 1 da (Emma b 19 March 1986); *Career* head Devon Tourism 1986–90, dir of mktg Edinburgh and Lothians Tourist Bd 1990–97, chief exec Aberdeen and Grampian Tourist Bd 1997–2001, chief exec NI Tourist Bd 2001–14, princ Alan Clark Tourism 2014–; memb: Bd Historic Environment Scotland 2015–; FCIM, FIDM, FIoD; *Recreations* cricket, gardening, music, travel, walking; *Style*— Alan Clarke, Esq; ✉ 118 Findhorn Place, Edinburgh EH9 2PB (☎ 0131 668 4975, e-mail talanclarke@gmail.com)

CLARKE, Alison Jane; da of Leonard William Clarke, of Cheltenham, Glos, and Florence, *née* Pitt; *b* 17 October 1960; *Educ* Pate's GS for Girls, Bulmershe Coll, Univ of Reading (BA); *m* 6 May 1995, Nigel Andrew Mogridge, s of Ralph John Mogridge; 1 da (Isabel b 28 June 2001); *Career* graduate trainee Pedigree Petfoods; Welbeck Golin/Harris Communications (Shandwick Welbeck from May 1998): account exec 1985–90, bd dir 1990–, dep md 1993–96, md 1996–97, chief exec 1997–99; chief exec Weber Shandwick Asia Pacific 2000–02, gp business dir Huntsworth plc 2003–11, ceo Grayling UK & Ireland 2011–15, fndr Alison Clarke Communications 2015–; chm PRCA 2012–14; FCIPR 1999 (MCIPR 1989, pres 2000–); *Recreations* theatre, opera; *Style*— Ms Alison Clarke; ✉ website www.alisonclarke.co.uk

CLARKE, Andrew Bertram; QC (1997); s of Arthur Bertram Clarke, and Violet Doris, *née* Lewis; *b* 23 August 1956, Nantwich, Cheshire; *Educ* Crewe Co GS, KCL (LLB, AKC), Lincoln Coll Oxford (BCL); *m* 1 Aug 1981, Victoria Clare, da of Kelsey Thomas; 1 s (Christopher Harding b 1985), 2 da (Judith Ellen b 1987, Alexandra Clare b 1990); *Career* called to the Bar Middle Temple 1980; head Littleton Chambers 2006–14; *Recreations* football, cricket, gardening and wine; *Clubs* Gloucestershire CCC; *Style*— Andrew Clarke, Esq, QC; ✉ Littleton Chambers, 3 King's Bench Walk North, Temple, London EC4Y 7HR (☎ 020 7797 8600, fax 020 7797 8699)

CLARKE, Prof Angus John; *b* 20 December 1954, London; *Educ* King's Coll Cambridge (BA), Univ of Oxford (BM, BCh, DM); *Career* house offr John Radcliffe Hosp 1979–80, SHO general medicine Peterborough Dist Gen Hosp 1980–81, SHO in paediatrics S Manchester Hosps 1981–82, SHO in neonatal medicine Bristol Maternity Hosp 1982–83, registrar in general and neonatal paediatrics S Glamorgan HA 1983–85, research assoc Section of Medical Genetics Univ of Wales Coll of Medicine and registrar in paediatrics S Glamorgan Hosps 1985–86, research assoc and (hon) sr registrar in Depts of Human Genetics and Child Health Univ of Newcastle upon Tyne 1987–89; Univ of Wales Coll of Medicine: clinical sr lectr and hon conslt clinical geneticist Dept of Medical Genetics 1989–, reader 1996–2000, prof 2000–; chm Medical Advsy Bd Ectodermal Dysplasia Soc 1998–, CMO rep for Wales on Human Genetics Cmmn 2004–; memb: Research Advsy Bd Wellbeing of Women 2003–06, Editorial Bd Communication & Medicine 2003–, Medical Advsy Panel Rett Syndrome Assoc UK; FRCP 1994 (MRCP 1982), FRCPCH 1997; *Publications* Genetic Counselling: practice and principles (ed, 1994), Culture, Kinship and Genes (jt ed, 1997), Genetics, Society and Clinical Practice (jtly, 1997), The Genetic Testing of Children (ed 1998), Risky Relations. Family and Kinship in the Era of New Genetics (jtly, 2006), Living with the Genome (jt ed, 2006); articles in professional jls; *Style*— Prof Angus Clarke; ✉ Institute of Medical Genetics, University Hospital of Wales, Cardiff CF14 4XN

CLARKE, Barry James; s of Robert Clarke, of Olney, Bucks, and Carol, *née* Lodge; *b* 10 May 1970, Derby; *Educ* Redborne Sch Ampthill, Univ of Manchester (BA, Bradford scholar, TF Tout Prize), Coll of Law Chester (CPE, LSFE), LSE (MSc Econ); *m* 22 Aug 1992, Dr Kathryn Walters; 2 da, 1 s; *Career* admitted slr 1996; Russell Jones & Walker: ptnr 2002–07, conslt 2007–10; fee paid employment judge 2005–10, fee paid immigration judge 2006–10, nat chm Employment Lawyers' Assoc 2006–08, arbitrator ACAS 2007–10, salaried employment judge 2010–15, regnl employment judge for Wales 2015–; memb Statutory Ctee Equality and Human Right Cmmn 2007–10; Wig and Pen Prize 1996, commended Asst Slr of the Year The Lawyer Awards 2002; *Books* Challenging Racism (ed, 2002); *Recreations* music, cycling, keep fit, technology, history; *Style*— Barry Clarke, Esq; ✉ Employment Tribunals, Caradog House, 1–6 St Andrews Place, Cardiff CF10 3BE (☎ 02920 678100, e-mail barry.clarke@judiciary.gsi.gov.uk)

CLARKE, Brian; s of Edward Ord Clarke, (d 1979), and Lilian, *née* Whitehead; *b* 2 July 1953; *Educ* Clarksfield Sch Oldham, Oldham Sch of Arts and Crafts (jr scholarship), Burnley Sch of Art, N Devon Coll of Art and Design (DipAD); *m* Elizabeth Cecila, da of Rev John Finch; 1 s (Daniel John Finch b 11 Feb 1989); *Career* artist, architectural stained glass artist; memb Cncl Winston Churchill Meml Tst 1985– (tstee 2007–), tstee and memb Ctee Robert Fraser Fndn 1990, tstee The Ely Stained Glass Museum 1995–2008; visiting prof of architectural art UCL 1993–, sole executor the estate of Francis Bacon 1998–; memb Ctee DRC Cmmn for Architecture and the Built Environment 2000–05, tstee The Lowe Educational Charitable Fndn 2001–, govr Capital City Acad 2001–, chm Architecture Fndn 2007– (tstee 2002–07); subject of numerous publications and catalogues; Hon Liveryman Worshipful Co of Glaziers and Master Glass Painters 2012; Hon DLitt Univ of Huddersfield 2007; FRSA 1988, Hon FRIBA 1993; *Selected Exhibitions* Glass/Light Exhibition (Festival of the City of London with John Piper and Marc Chagall) 1979, New Paintings Constructions and Prints (RIBA) 1981, Paintings (Robert Fraser Gallery Cork Street) 1983, 1976–86 (Seibu Museum of Art Tokyo) 1987, Malerei und Farbfenster 1977–88 (Hessiches Landesmuseum) 1988, Intimations of Mortality (Galerie Karsten Greve Köln Germany), Paintings (Indar Pasricha Gallery New Delhi) 1989, Into and Out of Architecture (Mayor Gallery London) 1990, Architecture and Stained Glass (Sezon Museum of Art Tokyo) 1990, Architecture and Light (Ingolstadt Germany, in assoc with Future Systems) 1992, Designs on Architecture (Oldham Art Gallery) 1993, New Paintings (The Mayor Gallery London) 1993, Paintings and Stained Glass Works in Architecture (The Tony Shafrazi Gallery NY), Paintings and Stained Glass Works in Architecture (The Tony Shafrazi Gallery NY) 1995, Brian Clarke Linda McCartney (Musée Suisse du Vitrail au Château de Romont and the German Museum for Stained Glass) 1997–98, 80 Artistes autour du Mondial (Galerie Enrico Navarra Paris) 1998, Fleurs de Lys, exhibition of new paintings (Faggionato Fine Arts London) 1999, Flowers for New York – a tribute to New York in stained glass and painting on canvas (The Corning Gallery Steuben NY) 2002, Transillumination (Tony Shafrazi Gallery NY) 2003, Lamina (Gagosian Gallery London) 2005, Don't Forget The Lamb (Phillips de Pury NY) 2008, Brian Clarke Works on Paper (Phillips de Pury and Co space at the Saatchi Gallery London) 2011, The Quick and the Dead (Gemeentemuseum Den Haag Netherlands) 2011, Atlantes and Astragals (Christie's London) 2011, Love Him More (Kristy Stubbs Gallery Dallas TX) 2011–12, Between Extremities (Pace Gallery NY) 2013, Brian Clarke: Born Oldham 1953 (Oldham Gallery 2013), Piper & Clarke – Stained Glass: Art or Anti-Art (Verey Gallery and Eton College) 2013–14, Spitfires and Primroses (Pace London) 2015, A Strong, Sweet Smell of Incense: A Portrait of Robert Fraser (curator, Pace London) 2015; *Selected Works* St Gabriel's Church Blackburn 1976, All Saints Church Habergham 1976, Queen's Medical Centre Nottingham 1978, Olympus Optical Europa GmbH Headquarters Building Hamburg 1981, King Kahled Int Airport Riyadh 1982, The Buxton Thermal Baths 1987, The Lake Sagami Country Club Yamanishi (in assoc with Arata Isozaki) 1988, The New Synagogue Darmstadt 1988, Victoria Quarter Leeds 1989, stage designs for Paul McCartney World Tour 1989, Cibreo Restaurant Tokyo 1990, Glaxo Pharmaceuticals Stockley Park Uxbridge 1990, Stansted Airport (in assoc with Sir Norman Foster) 1991, The Spindles Shopping Centre Oldham 1991–93, España Telefonica Barcelona 1991, The Carmelite London 1992, 100 New Bridge St London 1992, façade of Hotel de Ville des Bouches-du-Rhones Marseille (with Will Alsop) 1992–94, The Glass Dune – Hamburg (with Future Systems) 1992, EAM Building Kassel 1992–93, design of stadia sets for Paul McCartney New World Tour 1993, design of stage sets for The Ruins of Time (a ballet in tribute to Rudolph Nureyev by the Dutch National Ballet) 1993, The New Synagogue Heidelberg 1993, SMS Lowe The Grace Building NY 1994, Crossrail Paddington London (design) 1994, Schadow Arkaden Düsseldorf 1994, Norte Shopping Rio de Janeiro 1995, Rye Hosp Sussex (with Linda McCartney) 1995, Valentino Village Noci 1996, Kinderhaus Regensburg 1996, Centre Villa-Lobos São Paulo (design) 1997, Willis Corroon Building Ipswich 1997, RWE Essen (refurbishment of lobby) 1997, Offenbach Synagogue (curved glass wall and thorah shrine) 1997, Heidelberg Cathedral (design) 1997, Obersalbach 1997, Pfizer Pharmaceuticals NY 1997, Chicago Sinai 1997, Warburg Dillon Read Stamford CT (stained glass cone) 1998, Al Faisaliah Centre Riyadh (in assoc with Lord Foster of Thames Bank) 2000, Olympus Optical Europa GmbH (new HQ building) Hamburg 2000, Pfizer Pharmaceuticals NY 2001, West Winter Garden Heron Quays London (design) 2001, Hotel and Thalassotherapy Centre Nova Yardinia 2002, Pfizer Pharmaceuticals NY 2003, Ascot Racecourse 2003, Pyramid of Peace Astana Kazakhstan (design with Lord Foster of Thames Bank) 2005, Jermyn St Apax Partners London 2007, Gesamtkunstwerk Regents Park London 2010, Linkopings Domkyrke Sweden 2010, Apostolic Nunciature London 2010; *Awards* Churchill fellowship in architectural art 1974, Art and Work award special commendation 1989, Europa Nostra award 1990, The Leeds Award for Architecture Special Award for Stained Glass 1990, The Euro Shopping Centre Award 1995, BDA Auszeichnung guter Bauten Heidelberg 1996, Comite d'Honnour Fondation Vincent Van Gogh Arles France 2001; *Publications* Architectural Stained Glass (ed, 1979), The Two Cultures (portfolio, 1981), Brian Clarke (by Martin Harrison, 1981), Brian Clarke: Paintings (1983), Brian Clarke: Works 1977–85, Elan Vital (by Juni Ito, 1987), Brian Clarke: Malerei und Farbfenster 1977–1988 (1988), Brian Clarke (1990), The Parts of the Sum: Brian Clarke (1990), Brian Clarke: Into and Out of Architecture (1994), Brian Clarke: Architectural Artist (1994), Les Vitraux de la Fille Dieu de Brian Clarke (1997), Brian Clarke/ Linda McCartney – Collaborations (1997), Fleurs de Lys: Brian Clarke (1997), Brian Clarke – Projects (1998), Brian Clarke – Transillumination (2002), Brian Clarke Lamina (2005), Brian Clarke – Don't Forget the Lamb (2008), Brian Clarke – Cristophe (2009), Brian Clarke – WORK (2009), Brian Clarke – Life and Death (by Stefan Trümpler, 2010), Brian Clarke – Works on Paper (by Bettina von Hase, 2011), Brian Clarke – Atlantes and Astragals (by Martin Harrison and Hans Janssen, 2011), Between Extremities (by Martin Harrison and Robert C Morgan, 2013) Piper & Clarke – Stained Glass: Art or Anti-Art (by David Fraser Jenkins, Michael Meredith and Martin Harrison, 2014), Brian Clarke: Spitfires and Primroses 2012–14 / Works 1977–85 (2015), A Strong Sweet Smell of Incense: A Portrait of Robert Fraser by Brian Clarke (2015); *Recreations* reading, hoarding; *Style*— Brian Clarke, Esq; ✉ website www.brianclarke.co.uk

CLARKE, Prof Bryan Campbell; s of Robert Campbell Clarke (d 1941), of Sywell, Northants, and Gladys Mary, *née* Carter (d 1987); *b* 24 June 1932; *Educ* Fay Sch Southborough Mass, Magdalen Coll Sch Oxford, Magdalen Coll Oxford (MA, DPhil); *m* 20 Aug 1960, Dr Ann Gillian, da of Prof John Jewkes, CBE (d 1988), of Boar's Hill, Oxford; 1 s (Peter b 1971), 1 da (Alexandra b 1975); *Career* PO RAF 1951–52; Univ of Edinburgh: asst in zoology 1959–63, lectr in zoology, reader in zoology 1969–71; Univ of Nottingham: prof of genetics 1971–, research prof 1994– (emeritus 1997); SERC sr res fell 1976–81; vice-pres: Genetical Soc 1981, Linnean Soc 1983–85, Soc for the Study of Evolution (USA) 1990, Zoological Soc of London 1998; scientific expeditions to: Morocco 1955, Polynesia 1962, 1967, 1968, 1980, 1982, 1986, 1991, 1994 and 2000; chm: Biological Sciences Panel HEFCE 1992–98, Cncl Royal Soc 1994–96; hon res fell Nat History Museum 1993–; chm of tstees Charles Darwin Tst 2000–06, co-fndr Frozen Art Project 2002 (tstee 2007–); ed: Heredity 1977–84, Proceedings of the Royal Soc Series B 1989–93; Linnean Medal for Zoology 2003, Darwin-Wallace Medal 2008, Darwin Medal of the Royal Soc 2010; int memb American Philosophical Soc 2003, hon foreign memb American Acad of Arts and Scis 2004; FRS 1982; *Books* Berber Village (1959), The Evolution of DNA Sequences (ed, 1986), Frequency-Dependent Selection (ed, 1988); *Recreations* painting, archaeology; *Clubs* RAF; *Style*— Prof Bryan Clarke, FRS; ✉ Linden Cottage, School Lane, Colston Bassett, Nottingham NG12 3FD (☎ 01949 81243); School of Biology, University Park, Nottingham NG7 2RD (☎ 0115 9513 0339)

CLARKE, Catherine; *Career* former trade publishing dir OUP, agent and md Felicity Bryan Assocs; *Style*— Ms Catherine Clarke; ✉ Felicity Bryan Associates, 2A North Parade, Oxford OX2 6LX

CLARKE, Christopher Alan; s of Harry Alston Clarke (d 1979), and Isobel Corsan, *née* Kay; *b* 14 May 1945, Edinburgh; *Educ* Oakham, Selwyn Coll Cambridge (MA), London Business Sch (MSc (now known as MBA)); *m* 1, 4 Sept 1971 (m dis 1976), late Jessica Mary Pearson; m 2, 9 Dec 1978, Charlotte, *née* Jenkins; 1 da (Katherine b 1981), 1 s (Henry b 1984); *Career* Shell Int Petroleum 1967–73, IDJ Ltd 1973–74, Arbuthnot Latham & Co Ltd 1974–82 (dir 1978–82), md Arbuthnot Latham Asia Ltd 1979–82; dir: Samuel Montagu & Co Ltd 1982–96, HSBC Investment Banking 1996–98; non-exec dir: The Weir Gp plc 1999–2008, Omega Underwriting Holdings plc 2005–06, Omega Insurance Holdings Ltd 2006–10; dep chm Competition Cmmn 2004–10 (memb 2001–10); dir, hon treas and tstee Classics for All Ltd 2014–; *Recreations* golf, fishing, reading, wine; *Clubs* Berkshire Golf; *Style*— Christopher Clarke, Esq

CLARKE, Christopher George; s of Philip George Clarke (d 1991), and José Margaret Clarke (d 1979); *b* 18 September 1944; *Educ* Radley; *m* 1 June 1968, Jane, *née* Ellis; 2 da (Natasha Jane b 12 June 1970, Vanessa Clare b 5 April 1973); *Career* articled clerk Hodgson Morris & Co Chartered Accountants 1963–67 (qualified 1967), investment mangr Wm Brandts 1968–72, investment mangr JH Vavasseur London 1972–74; Henderson Investors: joined 1974, dir Henderson Administration Ltd 1976–, dir Henderson Administration Gp plc 1983–1998; dir Witan Investment Co plc 1993–2006 (md 1993–2000); non-exec dir Investec Wealth & Investment (formerly Rensburg Sheppards plc) 1999– (chm 2003–14); memb Cncl Radley Coll 1989–2009 (vice-chm 2004–09); *Style*— Christopher Clarke, Esq; ✉ e-mail cgclarke22@btinternet.com

CLARKE, Christopher John David; s of Maj John Herbert Thomson Clarke (d 1983), and Hazel, *née* Chapman (d 1988); *b* 21 March 1950; *Educ* Fettes, Coll of Law London; *m* 4 April 1992, Catherine, *née* Shuttlewood; 1 da (Lucy b 9 Dec 1992), 1 s (Rory b 22 Feb 1994); *Career* admitted slr England and Hong Kong 1974; Denton Hall: ptnr Hong Kong 1978–84, ptnr London 1984–92, sr ptnr Asia 1992–99; sr and managing ptnr Asia CMS Cameron McKenna 1999–2003; DLA Piper: sr commercial litigation ptnr Asia 2003–08, managing ptnr Hong Kong 2008–; dir: Arnhold Holdings Ltd, Baltrans Holdings Ltd; memb: Int Bar Assoc, Law Assoc; *Recreations* travel, food, family; *Clubs* Hong Kong, China; *Style*— Christopher J D Clarke, Esq

CLARKE, Rt Hon Lord Justice; Rt Hon Sir Christopher Simon Courtenay Stephenson; kt (2005), PC (2015); yr s of Rev John Stephenson Clarke (d 1982), and Enid Courtenay, *née* Manico; *b* 14 March 1947; *Educ* Marlborough, Gonville & Caius Coll Cambridge (MA); *m* 14 Sept 1974, Caroline Anne, da of Prof Charles Montague Fletcher, CBE; 2 da (Henrietta b 16 Aug 1977, Louisa b 21 June 1979), 1 s (Edward b 31 May 1981); *Career* called to the Bar Middle Temple 1969 (bencher 1991); advocate of the Supreme Court of the Turks and Caicos Is 1975, QC 1984, head of chambers Brick Court Chambers 1990–2005, recorder of the Crown Court 1990–2005, judge Court of Appeal of Jersey and Guernsey 1998–, judge of the High Court of Justice (Queen's Bench Div) 2005–14 (dep judge 1993–2005), Lord Justice of Appeal 2015–; judge Court of Ecclesiastical Causes Reserved 2015–; counsel to Bloody Sunday Inquiry 1998–2004; chm Ctee of Inquiry of States of Guernsey into Barnett Christie (Fin) Ltd 1985–87; cncllr Int Bar Assoc 1988–91, chm Commercial Law Bar Assoc 1993–95, memb Bar Cncl 1993–99; FRSA 1994; *Clubs* Brooks's, Hurlingham; *Style*— The Rt Hon Lord Justice Christopher Clarke; ✉ c/o Royal Courts of Justice, Strand, London WC2A 2LL

CLARKE, Prof Colin Graham; s of Harold William Clarke (d 1994), and Ivy Gladys, *née* Vaughan (d 2002); *b* 21 October 1938, Worcester; *Educ* Jesus Coll Oxford (Collins exhibitioner, MA), Univ of Oxford (DPhil, DLitt); *m* 1962, Gillian, da of Frederick Grice; 1 s (Aidan Vaughan b 1965), 1 da (Veronica Helen b 1967); *Career* research assoc Research Inst for the Study of Man NY 1963–64; Univ of Liverpool: Leverhulme research fell in geography 1964–66, lectr Dept of Geography and Centre for Latin American Studies 1966–74, sr lectr 1974–77, chm Bd of Geographical Studies 1975–76, reader in geography and Latin American studies 1977–81, memb Senate and Academic Planning Ctee 1979–81; Univ of Oxford: lectr in urban and social geography 1981–97, chm Anthropology and Geography Faculty Bd 1991–93 (vice-chm 1989–91), prof of urban and social geography 1997–2003, head of dept Sch of Geography and the Environment 1998–2002, emeritus prof of geography 2003; official fell Jesus Coll Oxford 1981 (sr research fell 2003–06, emeritus fell 2006); visiting asst prof Dept of Geography Univ of Toronto 1967–68, visiting lectr Dept of Geography Univ of Leeds 1970–71, visiting prof Instituto de Geográfia Universidad Nacional Autónoma de México 1982, visiting prof Facultad de Humanidades Universidad Central Caracas 1988; assoc fell Centre for Caribbean Studies Univ of Warwick 1983–93, visiting sr research fell Max Planck Inst for the Study of Religious and Ethnic Diversity 2011–12; memb: Latin American Field Ctee Oxfam 1971–77, Co-ordinating Cncl for Area Studies Assocs 1980–84 and 1993–95, Comité Scientifique Centre d'Etude de Geographie Tropicale (CNRS) Bordeaux 1990–92, Area Studies Panel for Coursework Awards ESRC 1993, Latin American Studies Panel HEFCE Research Assessment Exercise 1996; pres d'honneur Assoc for European Research on Central America and the Caribbean 1988– (memb Exec Ctee 1985–86, chm 1986–88), pres Soc for Latin American Studies 1993–95 (memb Ctee 1990–93), life memb Soc for Caribbean Studies 2004 (sec 1977–79 and 1983–84, chm 1978–80), memb Inst of Br Geographers 1961– (sec Population Study Gp 1968–71); ed Liverpool Centre for Latin American Studies monograph series 1970–73 and 1976–81, ed Bulletin of Latin American Research 1992–97 (memb Editorial Bd 1981–92); memb: Editorial Advsy Bd Jl of Latin American Studies 1977–89, Comision Dictaminadora Editorial del Instituto de Geográfia Universidad Nacional Autónoma de México 1982–92, Conseil Scientifique Cahiers d'Outre-mer 1988–, Conseil Scientifique Iles et Archipels 1988–, Editorial Bd European Review of Latin American and Caribbean Studies 1990–2001, Int Advsy Bd Third World Planning Review 1991–2001; Gold Medal RSGS 1999; *Publications* Jamaica in Maps (1974), Kingston, Jamaica: Urban Development and Social Change, 1692–1962 (1975), Caribbean Social Relations (ed, 1978), A Geography of the Third World (jtly, 1983, 2 edn 1996), Geography and Ethnic Pluralism (jt ed, 1984), East Indians in a West Indian Town: San Fernando Trinidad 1930–1970 (1986), Cambio Social y Económico en Latinoamerica: Perspectivas Geográficas (jt ed, 1986), Politics, Security and Development in Small States (jt ed, 1987), South Asians Overseas: Migration and Ethnicity (jt ed, 1990), Society and Politics in the Caribbean (ed, 1991), Class, Ethnicity and Community in Southern Mexico: Oaxaca's Peasantries (2000), Kingston, Jamaica: Urban Devolopment and Social change 1692–2002 (2006), Decolonizing the Colonial City: Urbanization and Stratification in Kingston, Jamaica (2006), Post-Colonial Trinidad: An Ethnographic Journal (jtly, 2010), War's Nomads: A Mobile Radar Unit in Pursuit of Rommel During the Western Desert Campaign 1942–3 (jt ed, 2015), Race, Class, and the Politics of Decolonization: Jamaica journals, 1961 and 1968 (2015); also author of book contribs and papers and articles published in learned jls; *Recreations* theatre, opera, music; *Clubs* Royal Over-Seas League; *Style*— Prof Colin Clarke; ✉ Jesus College, Oxford OX1 3DW (e-mail colin.clarke@ouce.ox.ac.uk)

CLARKE, David; s of Dennis Percy Clarke, of Himbleton, Worcs, and Vera, *née* Timpson; *b* 19 March 1954; *Educ* Sevenoaks Sch, Bromsgrove Sch, Univ of Bristol Sch of Architecture (BA(Arch), DipArch); *m* 21 May 1983, Victoria, da of late Peter Kysylicia; 1 s (Jonathan David b 1987); *Career* architect; Watkins Gray Woodgate International 1977–79, Peterborough Devpt Corp 1979–82; Building Design Partnership (BDP) Sheffield office: joined 1986, assoc 1988–97, architect dir 1997–; projects incl White Rose Centre Leeds (Br Cncl of Shopping Centres New Shopping Centre Award 1997 and Int Cncl of Shopping Centres commendation New Centre Category 1998); memb ARCUK, RIBA; *Recreations* windsurfing, motor cars, cycling; *Style*— David Clarke, Esq

CLARKE, Hon Sir David Clive; kt (2003), DL (Merseyside 2011); s of Philip George Clarke (d 1991), and José Margaret, *née* Fletcher (d 1979); *b* 16 July 1942; *Educ* Winchester, Magdalene Coll Cambridge (MA); *m* 2 Aug 1969, Alison Claire, da of Rt Rev (Percy) James Brazier (d 1989); 3 s (Andrew b 1970 d 1993, Jonathan b 1972, Edward b 1975); *Career* called to the Bar Inner Temple 1965; in practice Northern Circuit until 1993 (treas 1988–92), QC 1983, recorder of the Crown Court 1981–93, circuit judge (Northern Circuit) 1993–1997, sr circuit judge and hon recorder of Liverpool 1997–2003, judge of the High Court of Justice (Queen's Bench Div) 2003–10, presiding judge Northern Circuit 2006–09; an asst surveillance cmmr 2010–; memb Criminal Justice Consultative Cncl 1999–2003, memb UK Donation Ethics Ctee 2014–16; Hon LLD Univ of Liverpool 2004, hon fell Liverpool John Moores Univ 2007; *Recreations* canals, sailing, swimming; *Clubs* Trearddur Bay Sailing (Anglesey); *Style*— The Hon Sir David Clarke, DL

CLARKE, David Edwin; DL (West Midlands 2014); s of Ernest Wilfred Clarke (d 1972), and Irene Elisabeth, *née* Bennett (d 1974); *b* 7 March 1953; *Educ* Solihull Sch Warks, Abington HS PA USA; *m* 10 Sept 1977, Nicola Jayne, da of John Frank Cordwell; 2 da (Hannah Jayne b 10 Jan 1982, Caroline May b 18 Aug 1984); *Career* reporter Birmingham Post & Mail Group 1974–78, PRO Midlands Electricity Bd 1978–79, exec Priority PR 1979–80, md Graham Rote & Co Ltd 1983–86 (dir 1981–83), md Clarke Associates UK Ltd 1986–, chm Edelman Public Relations Network (UK) 1994–98; chm Miss Macaroon CIC 2015–; nat hon treas IPR 1986–89; chm Birmingham Forward 2000–02 (dir 1997–); dir Birmingham Settlement 1992–2001, chm Birmingham Business Breakfast Club 1994–99, dir Marketing Birmingham 2001–07; Barker Variety Club of Great Britain 1998–2007; chm Judges Midlands Business Awards 2001–06; cncl memb: Birmingham C of C and Industry, Birmingham Civic Soc (chm 2009–13); guardian Birmingham Assay Office 2013–, warden Birmingham Assay Office 2015–; FCIPR (FIPR 1991, MIPR 1973); *Books* The Rabbit Guide to Birmingham (2004), City Life (2007); *Recreations* walking, travel, keep fit, Birmingham Baltis, sailing; *Clubs* Birmingham and Edgbaston Debating Soc (pres 2016–); *Style*— David Clarke, Esq, DL; ✉ Pinley Cottage, Pinley, Claverdon, Warwickshire CV35 8NA (☎ 01926 84 2266); Clarke Associates UK Ltd, The Old School House, Chapel Lane, Wythall, Birmingham B47 6JX

CLARKE, Hon Mr Justice Frank Clarke; s of Ben Clarke (d 1963), of Walkinstown, Dublin, and Sheila, *née* Bailey (d 1996); *b* 10 October 1951, Dublin; *Educ* Drimnagh Castle Christian Bros Sch, NUI Dublin (UCD) (BA), King's Inns Sch of Law; *m* 29 Dec 1977, Prof Jacqueline Hayden; 1 s (Ben b 13 July 1986), 1 da (Charlotte b 14 Sept 1988); *Career* called to the Bar King's Inns Dublin 1973 (bencher 1995–); sr counsel 1985, judge of the High Court of Ireland 2004–12, judge of the Supreme Court of Ireland 2012–; twice appointed by Supreme Court as counsel to argue Article 26 references; memb: Bar Cncl of Ireland 1977–85 and 1987–95 (vice-chair 1992, chair 1993–95), Cncl Int Bar Assoc 1996–2004 (co-chair Forum for Barrs and Advocates 1999–2003), Cncl of King's Inns 1997–2004 (chair 1999–2004); chair Referendum Cmmn on Lisbon Referendum 2009–10; hon memb: Canadian Bar Assoc 1994, Australian Bar Assoc 2003; chair Irish Legal Terms Advsy Ctee 2015–; pres Irish Soc for European Law 2015–; judge in residence Griffith Coll Dublin 2010–; adjunct prof Trinity Coll Dublin 2012–, adjunct prof Univ Coll Cork 2015–; memb Bd Leopardstown Racecourse 1995–2006 (chair 2003–05), memb Turf Club and Irish Nat Hunt Steeplechase Ctee 1999– (dep sr steward 2003–05), memb Bd of Horse Racing Ireland 2003–05; *Recreations* horse racing, music; *Clubs* Turf (Dublin); *Style*— The Hon Mr Justice Frank Clarke; ✉ The Supreme Court, Fourt Courts, Dublin 7, Ireland (☎ 00 353 1 888 6000, fax 00 353 1 872 5669, e-mail fclarke@courts.ie)

CLARKE, (Charles) Giles; CBE (2012), DL (Somerset 2004); s of Charles Nigel Clarke, and Stella Rosemary Clarke; *b* 29 May 1953, Bristol; *Educ* Rugby, Oriel Coll Oxford (MA), Damascus Univ; *m* Judy; 1 s (Jack); *Career* fndr: Majestic Wine 1981, Pet City 1990, Safestore plc 1998, Westleigh Investments; chm: Amerisur Resources, Ironveld, Kennedy Ventures, Sovereign Mines; chm: Somerset CCC 2002–08, ECB 2007–15 (pres 2015–); dir Int Cricket Cncl 2007– (chair Pakistan Task Team 2010–, chair Finance and Commercial Ctee 2011–); memb Nat Cncl Learning and Skills Cncl 2002–07; *Recreations* wine, scuba diving, shooting, moorland management; *Clubs* MCC, Army and Navy; *Style*— Giles Clarke, Esq, CBE, DL; ✉ The England and Wales Cricket Board, Lord's Cricket Ground, London NW8 8QZ

CLARKE, Graham Neil; s of Henry Charles Owen Clarke, MVO (d 1996), and Doris May, *née* Morgan (d 2002); *b* 23 July 1956; *Educ* Rutherford Sch London, RHS, Sch of Horticulture Wisley; *m* 2 Feb 1980, Denise Carole, da of Robert Fraser Anderson; 2 da (Rebecca Sarah b 1990, Helena Charlotte b 1994); *Career* gardener: Buckingham Palace 1975–76, Royal Parks Nursery 1976; Amateur Gardening: sub-ed 1976–79, chief sub-ed 1979–81, dep ed 1981–86; ed: Home Plus Magazine 1985, Amateur Gardening 1986–98; ed IPC Gardening Magazines (gp ed 1993–95): Amateur Gardening, Your Garden, The Gardener, special projects ed 1995–98, ed at large 1998–99; GMC Publications: devpt ed 1999–2000, editorial mangr 2000–2002; freelance publishing and horticultural conslt 2002–04, ed Horticulture Week 2004–05, conslt 2005–06 chm Hamdene Horticultural Publishing Servs Ltd 2006–; memb Exec Ctee: RHS Garden Club 1975–82, Garden Writers' Guild 2005–, Commercial Horticulture Assoc 2005–09, Royal Parks Guild 2006–; prodr and presenter Hosp Radio London and Bournemouth 1976–89; FLS, FCIHort; *Books* Step-By-Step Pruning (1984), A-Z of Garden Plants (1985), Autumn/Winter Colour in the Garden (1986), Your Gardening Questions Answered (1987), The Complete Book of Plant Propagation (1990), The Ultimate House Plant Handbook (1996), Beginner's Guide to Water Gardening (2002), Collins Practical Gardener: Water Gardening (2004), Collins Practical Gardener: Pruning (2005), Success with Roses (2007), Success with Shade-Loving Plants (2007), Success with Sun-Loving Plants (2007), Success with Water Gardens (2007), Success with Water-Saving Gardens (2007), Success with Acid-Loving Plants (2008), Success with Alkaline-Loving Plants (2008), The Organic Fruit and Vegetable Gardener's Year (2008), Coastal Gardening (2009), Success with Small-Space Gardening (2009), Success with Alpine Gardening (2009), The Organic Herb Gardener (2010), Growing for Food and Colour (2012); *Recreations* gardening, writing, genealogy; *Clubs* RHS Gardens; *Style*— Graham Clarke, Esq; ✉ Hamdene House, 127 Magna Road, Bearwood, Bournemouth, Dorset BH11 9NE (e-mail gra.clarke@virgin.net)

CLARKE, Graham Staward; TD (1971); s of Douglas Staward Clarke (d 1949), and Beatrice, *née* Auld (d 1988); *b* 16 March 1937; *Educ* St Bees Sch Cumberland, Emmanuel Coll Cambridge (MA); *m* 1964, Rita Elisabeth Karoline, da of Oskar Becker (d 1961); 1 da (Tessa b 1965), 1 s (Douglas b 1968); *Career* Maj RA, Euro theatre; gp fin dir: Telex Computers Ltd 1972–75, Coles Cranes Ltd 1976–81, Fairey Holdings Ltd 1981–84; md Energy and Military Engrg Div Fairey Holdings Ltd 1984–86; chm: Fairey Engineering Ltd 1984–86, Elequip Ltd 1984–86, Bourn Management Consultants Ltd 1985–2000; dir: Fairey Holdings Ltd 1981–86, Fairey Developments Ltd 1981–86, Fairey Construction Ltd 1984–86, Mathews and Yates Ltd 1984–86, Fairey Nuclear Ltd 1984–86, Begley Engineering Ltd 1984–91, Nightingale Secretariat plc 1991–95; chm and md: Bourn Developments 1986–2008, Bourn Properties Ltd 1997–2000, Bourn Investments Ltd 1999–; prop Bourn Estates 1980–; chm Fedn of Oxshott Residents and Associations (memb Mgmnt Ctee 1988–2011); involved with town planning, community, environment and green belt issues in Surrey 1993–98; FCA, FRSA; *Recreations* bridge, travel, geo-politics, business management; *Clubs* RAC, IOD; *Style*— Graham S Clarke Esq, TD;

✉ Bourn Investments Ltd, Bourn Reach, 9 Montrose Gardens, Oxshott, Surrey KT22 OUU (☎ 01372 843445, fax 01372 842216, e-mail graham.clarke37@btconnect.com)

CLARKE, Henry Benwell; s of Stephen Lampard Clarke (d 1984), of Hastings, and Elinor Wade, *née* Benwell (d 1974); *b* 30 January 1950; *Educ* St John's Sch Leatherhead, South Bank Poly (BSc), Imperial Coll London (MSc, DIC, British Airways prize for MSc); *m* 18 Aug 1973, Verena Angela, da of late Dennis Howard Lodge; 1 da (Jessamy Anne b 1976), 4 s (Samuel John b 1977, Timothy Michael b 1980, Philip Andrew b 1982, Jonathan Peter b 1992); *Career* British Rail Property Bd: S Region 1972–78, NW Region 1978–82, E Region 1982–85, regnl estate surveyor and mangr Midland Region 1985–86, chief estate surveyor HQ 1986–87, nat devpt mangr 1987–88; The Crown Estate Cmmn: dep chief exec 1988–92, actg chief exec and accounting offr 1989; jt md People and Places International 1993–2004, md People and Places Property Consultants Ltd 1993–2004; conslt Anthony Green and Spencer 1993–, princ Henry Clarke Associates 2004–; memb Bd: People and Places Architects Ltd 1993–2004, Broadway Malyan Healthcare Ltd 1994–96, Mouchel Parkman Property Mgmnt Ltd 1995–97, Lewisham Is...Ltd 1997–2001, The Rail Estate Consultancy Ltd 1998–, Crowmead Properties Ltd 1998–, The Greater Bristol Light Railway Ltd 1999–2001, Children's Crystal Palace Ltd 1999–2004, Telecom Property Ltd 1999–2009, Crystal Palace Devpt Co Ltd 2000–04, Kings Yard Devpts Ltd 2004, Intelligent Business Space Ltd 2004–08, C-Space Ltd 2005–, Jackson Green Ltd 2006–, Model Bus Co Ltd 2006–, Revetment Ltd 2008–, Aquobex Ltd 2013–; memb: Cncl Christian Union for Estate Profession 1983–88, Gen Cncl Br Property Fedn 1989–92, Bd Youth With a Mission (Eng) 1990–, Br Cncl of Shopping Centres 1990–92, British Urban Regeneration Assoc 1992–, Urban Village Forum 1992–, Bd Mercy Ships UK 1997–, Bd Mercy Ships Int 2015–; tstee: Moggerhanger House Preservation Tst 1998–2005, Railway Children 2002–, Lindow Miny Tst 2003–, BCF Harpenden Tst 2004–; judge Nat Railway Heritage Awards 2013–; Freeman City of London 2008, Liveryman Worshipful Co of Plumbers 2009; MIMgt 1975, ACIArb 1979, FRICS 1986 (ARICS 1973), MInstD 1993; *Publications* author of various articles in periodicals; *Recreations* reading, walking, classic public transport, architecture, church; *Style*— Henry Clarke, Esq; ✉ Rail Estate, 12 Bridge Wharf, 156 Caledonian Road, London N1 9UU (☎ 020 7837 1114, fax 020 7713 0328, e-mail henryclarke@railestate.co.uk)

CLARKE, Jane; da of Michael David Hilborne-Clarke (d 1999), and Margaret, *née* Lythell; *Educ* Norwich HS for Girls, UCL (BA), Slade Film Unit Slade Sch of Fine Art (postgrad research); *Children* 1 da (Amelia Frances Clarke Trevette b 6 Sept 1986); *Career* journalist Time Out magazine and freelance and lectr RCA Sch of Film and TV 1978–80, film programmer BFI 1980–82, freelance film programmer Barbican Arts Centre Cinema 1982; TV-am 1982–88: ed Henry Kelly Saturday Show 1984–85, features ed Good Morning Britain 1985–86, ed After Nine 1987–88; series ed Children First Granada Television 1989, prodr The Other Side of Christmas Thames Television 1989, series ed New Living and dep ed Living Now New Era Television Ltd 1990, controller features Westcountry Television 1991–95, dep dir BFI 1995–97 (actg dir Oct-Dec 1997), chief exec BAFTA 1998, head TV and Radio Section FCO Public Diplomacy Dept 1999–2002, head FCO Strategy and Programmes Public Diplomacy Policy Dept 2002–04, head of internal communications FCO 2005–06, head of communications Sport England 2006–08, head of communications Kent CC 2008–11; writer under the name Jane Lythell; *Books* Move Over Misconceptions – Doris Day Re-appraised (with Diana Simmonds, 1980); as Jane Lythell: The Lie of You (novel, 2014), After the Storm (novel, 2015), Woman of the Hour (novel, 2016); *Recreations* literature, football (Tottenham Hotspur FC), walking; *Clubs* Tottenham Hotspur FC; *Style*— Ms Jane Clarke; ✉ e-mail clarke.jane22@gmail.com, website http://chroniclesofchloegreene.blogspot.com, Twitter @janelythell; c/o Gaia Banks (literary agent), Sheil Land Associates Ltd (☎ 020 7405 9351, e-mail info@sheilland.co.uk, website www.sheilland.co.uk)

CLARKE, Prof John; s of Victor Patrick Clarke (d 1995), of Cambridge, and Ethel May, *née* Blowers (d 1978); *b* 10 February 1942; *Educ* Perse Sch for Boys Cambridge, Univ of Cambridge (BA, MA, PhD, ScD); *m* 15 Sept 1979, Grethe, da of Hartwig Fog Pedersen (d 1990), of Copenhagen; 1 da (Elizabeth Jane b 1980); *Career* postdoctoral fell Univ of Calif 1968–69, princ investigator Materials Sciences Div Lawrence Berkeley Laboratory 1969–; Univ of Calif Berkeley: asst prof 1969–71, assoc prof 1971–73, prof of physics 1973–, Luis W Alvarez meml chair for experimental physics 1994–; visiting appts: Cavendish Laboratory Cambridge 1972 and 1979, HC Orsted Inst Copenhagen 1972, 1979 and 1985, Univ of Karlsruhe Germany 1978, CEN Saclay France 1986, visiting fell Clare Hall Cambridge 1989, 150th anniversary visiting prof Chalmers Univ of Technol Gothenburg 2009, 2010, 2011, 2012, 2013, 2015 and 2016, Morris Loeb lectr in physics Harvard Univ 2012; faculty research lectr Univ of California Berkeley 2005; by-fell Churchill Coll Cambridge 1998; Alfred P Sloan Fndn Fellowship 1970–72, Adolph C and Mary Sprague Miller Res Professorship 1975–76, 1994–95 and 2007–08, John Simon Guggenheim Fellowship 1977–78, Wallenberg Fndn Fellowship Chalmers Univ of Technol Gothenburg 2003 and 2008, Russell Marker Lectures Penn State Univ 2013, Miller Lecture Univ of Notre Dame; Charles Vernon Boys Prize Br Inst Physics 1977, Soc of Exploration Geophysics Award for best paper in geophysics (with T D Gamble and W M Goubau) 1979, Technology Magazine Technology 100 Award (with Gamble and Goubau) 1981, Distinguished Teaching Award Univ of Calif Berkeley 1983, Award for Sustained Outstanding Res in Solid State Physics in Dept of Energy's 1986 Materials Sciences Res Competition, Calif Scientist of the Year 1987, Fritz London Meml Award for Low Temperature Physics 1987, Federal Laboratory Consortium Award for Excellence in Technol Transfer 1992, Dept of Energy Div of Materials Sciences Award for Solid State Physics – Significant Implications for DOE Related Technols 1992, Electrotechnology Transfer Award Inst of Electrical and Electronic Engrs Activities Bd 1995, Joseph F Keithley Award for Advances in Measurement Sci The American Physical Society 1998, Comstock Prize in Physics Nat Acad of Sci 1999, IEEE Cncl on Superconductivity Award for Significant and Continuing Contributions to Applied Superconductivity 2002, The Scientific American 50 Award 2002, Olli V Lounasmaa Prize Finnish Acad of Arts and Scis 2004, Hughes Medal Royal Soc 2004, Outstanding Performance Award Lawrence Berkeley Nat Laboratory 2010, The Berkeley Citation 2011; hon fell Christ's Coll Cambridge 1997; fell: AAAS 1982, American Physical Soc 1985, American Acad of Arts and Sciences 2015; FRS 1986, FInstP 1999, foreign memb Royal Soc of Arts and Scis Gothenburg 2007, foreign assoc Nat Acad of Sciences 2012; *Publications* approx 460 papers in learned jls; *Style*— Prof John Clarke, FRS; ✉ Department of Physics, 366 LeConte Hall, University of California, Berkeley, CA 94720-7300, USA (☎ 00 1 510 642 3069)

CLARKE, Prof John Charles; s of Percy Charles Clarke (d 1998), of Brackley, Northants, and Gladys May, *née* Gibbard (d 1967); *b* 18 January 1947; *Educ* Magdalen Coll Sch Brackley, Wadham Coll Oxford (minor scholar, MA, DPhil); *m* 1976, Celia Imogen, da of Cecil Ralph Wathen (d 1976); *Career* fell All Souls Coll Oxford 1967–1976, 1979–86, 1995–, sr lectr in history Univ Coll at Buckingham 1976–84, lectr in history Wadham Coll Oxford 1979–86; Univ of Buckingham: reader in history 1984–, dean of humanities 1994–, prof of history 1994–; *Books* George III (1972), The Age of Cobbett (1976), The Book of Buckingham (1984), British Diplomacy and Foreign Policy (1989), The Book of Brackley (1987), Yesterday's Brackley (1990); *Recreations* railways; *Style*— Prof John Clarke; ✉ Dean Faculty of Humanities, University of Buckingham, Yeomanry House, Hunter Street, Buckingham MK18 1EG (☎ 01280 820294)

CLARKE, Very Rev John Martin; s of Roland Clarke (d 1993), and Edna, *née* Hay; *b* 20 February 1952; *Educ* West Buckland Sch, Hertford Coll Oxford (MA), New Coll Edinburgh (BD), Edinburgh Theol Coll; *m* 1985, Cressida, da of Norman Nash; 2 s (Benedict b 1989, Edmund b 1992), 1 da (Esther b 1993); *Career* asst curate The Ascension Kenton 1976–79, precentor St Ninian's Cathedral Perth 1979–82, info offr and communications advsr to the Gen Synod Scottish Episcopal Church 1982–87, Philip Usher Meml scholar Greece 1987–88, vicar St Mary's Battersea 1989–96, princ Ripon Coll Cuddesdon 1997–2004, canon and prebendary Lincoln 2000–2004, dean of Wells 2004–; *Recreations* walking, reading, music; *Style*— The Very Rev the Dean of Wells; ✉ The Dean's Lodgings, 25 The Liberty, Wells, Somerset BA5 2SZ

CLARKE, Rear Adm John Patrick; CB (1996), LVO, MBE; s of Frank Clarke (d 1965), and Christine Margaret, *née* Sendell (d 1996); *b* 12 December 1944; *Educ* Epsom Coll, BRNC Dartmouth; *m* 1, 1969 (m dis), Ann, da of Bishop A G Parham; 1 s (b 1971), 2 da (b 1973, b 1977); m 2, 1998, Mrs J J Salt; *Career* Capt HMS Finwhale 1976, Capt HMS Oberon 1977, Capt HMS Dreadnought 1979–81, cmdg offr Submarine COs Qualifying Course 1981–83, Exec Offr HM Yacht Britannia 1985–86, Capt Submarine Sea Trg 1986–89, Capt 7 Frigate Sqdn and HMS Argonaut 1989–90, Asst Dir Naval Staff Duties 1990–91, Dir Naval Warfare 1992, Dir Naval Mgmnt and CIS 1993–94, Flag Offr Trg and Recruiting 1994–96, Hydrographer of the Navy and chief exec UK Hydrographic Office 1996–2001, chief exec Br Marine Fedn 2001–06; lay adjudicator Solicitors Regulation Authy 2008–13; hon RICS; *Recreations* golf, sailing; *Clubs* RNSA, Yeovil Golf; *Style*— Rear Adm John Clarke, CB, LVO, MBE

CLARKE, Keith Edward; s of late Albert Clarke, and late Eileen Clarke; *b* 1940, London; *Educ* Alleyne's GS, Nunthorpe GS York, Univ of Bradford (BEng), Imperial Coll London (Dip Computing Sci, MPhil), London Business Sch; *m* 1965, Barbara (d 2013); 1 s (Vaughan), 1 da (Julie); *Career* Miny of Technol 1969–70, various research posts rising to dir BT Laboratories 1970–92, sr vice-pres Engrg BT N America San José CA 1992, various dir-level posts on technol strategy for BT plc 1992–2000; BABT: exec dir 2000, conslt 2001–; dir: Cellnet 1989–92, BT (CBP) Ltd 1989–95, Br Approvals Bd for Telecommunications 1992–2000, BABT Inc 2000, Hermont (Hldgs) Ltd 2001–03; memb: DTI Advsy Ctee on Flat Screen Displays Technol 1985–87, Editorial Advsy Bd Telematics and Informatics Jl 1989–98, various IEE ctees incl Standards Policy Ctee 1992–93, EC Parly Gp for Engrg Devpt 1996–2000, Gen Engrg Ctee Royal Acad of Engrg 1997–2000, EU ACTS Res Monitoring Panel 1998–99, Bd Fedn of Electronic Industries 1998–2000, City of London Adult Advsy Gp 2010–; chm: Industrial Advsy Bd Univ of Bradford 1992–97, EU High Level Strategy Gp for IT Standards 1998; author of numerous articles in professional jls, sometime lectr various educnl estabs, occasional broadcaster; winner Charles Babbage Premium Instn of Electronic and Radio Engrs 1983; Liveryman Worshipful Co of Engrs, Liveryman Worshipful Co of Info Technologists (sec IT Industry Panel 2003–05); City of London adult advsy gp 2010–; FIEE, FBCS, FCMI, FREng 1995; *Publications* 62 professional papers and book contributions; *Recreations* cruising, theatre, London history; *Clubs* City Livery Yacht, Windsor Yacht (past Cdre), Cripplegate Ward; *Style*— Keith Clarke, Esq, FREng; ✉ e-mail keclarke22@gmail.com

CLARKE, Rt Hon Kenneth Harry; CH (2014), PC (1984), QC (1980), MP; s of Kenneth Clarke, of Nottingham; *b* 2 July 1940; *Educ* Nottingham HS, Gonville & Caius Coll Cambridge (pres Cambridge Union); *m* 1963, Gillian Mary, da of Bruce Edwards, of Sidcup, Kent; 1 s, 1 da; *Career* called to the Bar Gray's Inn 1963 (bencher 1989); MP (Cons) Rushcliffe 1970–; oppn spokesman: on social servs 1974–76, on industry 1976–79; Parly under sec Dept of Tport 1979–82, min of state (health) DHSS 1982–85, HM paymaster-gen and min for employment 1985–87, chllr of the Duchy of Lancaster and min for trade and industry 1987–88, sec of state for health 1988–90, sec of state for education and science 1990–92, home sec 1992–93, chllr of the Exchequer 1993–97, shadow sec for business, enterprise and regulatory reform 2009–10, sec of state for justice and Lord Chllr 2010–12, min without portfolio 2012–14; Cons Pty leadership challenger 1997, 2001 and 2005; chm Cons Pty Democracy Task Force 2005–10; dep chm British American Tobacco plc 1998–2008, dir Independent News and Media (UK) 1999–2010, Independent News and Media plc 2007–10; *Recreations* modern jazz, bird watching, watching football (Nottingham Forest FC), cricket and motor racing; *Style*— The Rt Hon Kenneth Clarke, CH, QC, MP; ✉ House of Commons, London SW1A 0AA (☎ 020 7219 3000)

CLARKE, Prof Kieran; da of Kevin James O'Leary (d 1992), and Barbara Christophers Scott; *b* 15 May 1951, Adelaide, Australia; *Educ* Flinders Univ S Australia (BSc), Univ of Queensland (PhD); *partner* 10 April 1971, Warwick John Clarke; *Career* clinical biochemist Repatriation Gen Hosp S Australia 1974–76, res asst Griffith Univ Queensland and Univ of Queensland 1978–86, lectr in physiology and pharmacology Sch of Sci Griffith Univ 1987, sr res fell in med and tutor in medical physiology Harvard Med Sch USA 1988–89 (visiting fell 1985), adjunct prof Dept of Physiology Univ of Ottawa 1990–92, assoc res offr and gp ldr Biomedical NMR Nat Res Cncl Canada 1990–91; Univ of Oxford: Br Heart Fndn sr research fell 1992, assoc dir Br Heart Fndn Gp 1996, sr departmental teaching assoc Dept of Biochemistry 1996–2003, dir Magnetic Resonance Lab 1998–, Br Heart Fndn princ scienist 2001–, dir Cardiac Metabolism Research Gp Univ Lab of Physiology 2003–, currently prof of physiological biochemistry; fndr and non-exec dir TdeltaS Ltd 2005–; memb: Int Soc for Heart Res 1981, Int Soc for Magnetic Resonance in Med 1987 (memb Dynamic NMR Spectroscopy Study Gp), Basic Sci Cncl American Heart Assoc 1987, Br Soc for Cardiovascular Res 1991, Biochemical Soc 1994, Soc for Cardiovascular Magnetic Resonance 1998; memb: Project Grants Ctee Br Heart Fndn 2002–05; holder of various European and US patents; referee for scientific and med jls; grant reviewer for int bodies; numerous res articles in professional jls and book contribs; American Heart Assoc Howard B Sprague fell 1989; *Style*— Prof Kieran Clarke; ✉ Department of Physiology, Anatomy & Genetics, University of Oxford, Parks Road, Oxford OX1 3PT (☎ 01865 282248, fax 01865 282272, e-mail kieran.clarke@dpag.ox.ac.uk)

CLARKE, (Victor) Lindsay; s of Victor Metcalfe Clarke (d 1972), of Halifax, W Yorks, and Clara, *née* Bell; *b* 14 August 1939; *Educ* Heath GS Halifax, King's Coll Cambridge (BA); *m* 1, 1961 (m dis 1972), Carolyn Pattinson; 1 da (Madeleine Sara b 1966); m 2, 1980, Phoebe Clare Mackmin, *née* Harris; *Career* novelist; sr master ODA Secdy Sch Ghana 1962–65, lectr Great Yarmouth Coll of Further Educn 1965–67, co-ordinator of Liberal Studies Norwich City Coll 1967–70, co-dir Euro Centre Friends World Coll 1970–79, currently assoc lectr Univ of Wales (writer in residence 1995); creative conslt: Pushkin Tst 1998, Interalia 2012, Olivier Mythodrama 2013; memb PEN Int 1989; *Radio Dramas* Cathal of the Woods (1994), A Stone from Heaven (1995); *Books* Sunday Whiteman (1987), The Chymical Wedding (Whitbread award for fiction, 1989), Alice's Masque (1994), Essential Celtic Mythology (1997), Parzival and the Stone from Heaven (2001), The War at Troy (2004), The Return from Troy (2005), Stoker (poems, 2006), The Water Theatre (2010), The Gist: A Celebration of the Imagination (ed, 2012); *CDs* Twelve Songs for Parzival (lyrics, 2011); *Recreations* life drawing, divination, shooting pool; *Style*— Lindsay Clarke, Esq; ✉ c/o United Agents Ltd, 12–26 Lexington Street, London W1F 0LE

CLARKE, Lorna; da of Lincoln and Norma Gayle; *b* 8 March 1962; *Career* news reporter: Radio Humberside 1986, Metro Radio 1986, BBC Radio Cornwall 1987; prodr: Radio London, Everyman BBC TV 1987, Caribbean Service BBC World Service 1988, GLR 1989; prog dir: Kiss 100 1990–97, EMAP Radio SA 1997–98; BBC: successively ed Music

Entertainment, head of mainstream music and head of daytime programming BBC Radio One, currently head BBC Talent; current memb Radio Academy; memb Ctee Shelter; Commercial Radio Programmer of the Year 1996; *Style—* Miss Lorna Clarke; ✉ e-mail lorna.clarke@bbc.co.uk

CLARKE, Prof Malcolm Alistair; s of Kenneth Alfred William Clarke (d 1973), and Marion, *née* Rich (d 1967); *b* 1 April 1943; *Educ* Kingswood Sch Bath, St John's Coll Cambridge (MA, LLB, PhD); *m* 1968, Eva, *née* Nathan; 2 s (Timothy b 1972, Nicholas b 1975); *Career* asst Inst De Droit Comparé Paris 1965–6, res fell Fitzwilliam Coll Cambridge 1966–68, lectr Univ of Singapore 1968–70, fell St John's Coll Cambridge 1970–; Univ of Cambridge: lectr 1970–97, reader 1997–99, prof 1999–; memb: Br Maritime Law Assoc, Br Insurance Law Assoc; memb Great St Mary's Church Cambridge; *Books* Aspects of the Hague Rules (1976), Shipbuilding Contracts (ed and contrib, 2 edn 1992), Contracts for the Carriage of Goods (contrib, 1993), International Encyclopedia of Comparative Law (contrib, vol 3 1996), Policies and Perceptions of Insurance (1997), Contracts of Carriage by Air (2002, 2 edn 2010), The International Carriage of Goods by Road: CMR (2003, 6 edn 2013), The Law of Contract, Part 4: Vitiating Factors (contrib, 2003, 4 edn 2010, Butterworths series), Contracts of Carriage by Land and Air (jtly, 2004, 2 edn 2008), Policies and Perceptions of Insurance in the Twenty-First Century (2005), The Law of Insurance Contracts (2006, 6 edn 2009); *Recreations* cycling, walking, photography, music; *Style—* Prof Malcolm Clarke; ✉ St John's College, Cambridge CB2 1TP (☎ 01223 338600)

CLARKE, Martin Peter; *b* 26 August 1964; *Educ* Univ of Bristol; *m* Veronica; *Career* various positions with Daily Mail 1986–95, news ed The Mirror 1995; ed: The Scottish Daily Mail 1995–97, The Scotsman 1997–98; ed-in-chief: Scottish Daily Record & Sunday Mail Ltd 1998–2000, Ireland on Sunday 2001–04; exec ed Mail on Sunday 2004–06, ed Mail Online 2006–; *Recreations* football, newspapers; *Style—* Martin Clarke, Esq

CLARKE, Rt Hon Lord Matthew Gerard; PC (2008), QC (Scot 1989); s of Thomas Clarke (d 1978), and Ann, *née* Duddy (d 1984); *Educ* Holy Cross HS Hamilton, Univ of Glasgow (Francis Hunter scholar, Chartered Inst of Secretaries scholar, Cunninghame bursar, LLB, MA); *Career* admitted slr Scotland 1972, admitted memb Faculty of Advocates 1978; lectr Faculty of Law Univ of Edinburgh 1972, standing jr counsel Scot Home and Health Dept 1983–89, Senator Coll of Justice 2000–13; pt/t chm Industrial Tbnls 1987–2000; chm Br Cncl's Law and Governance Ctee (Scotland) 2001–; judge Court of Appeals Jersey and Guernsey 1996–2000; memb: Consumer Credit Licensing Appeal Tbnl 1976–2000, Estate Agents Tbnls 1980–2000, UK Delgn Cncl of Euro Bars and Law Socs 1989–99 (ldr 1993–96), Trademarks Appeal Tbnl 1996–2000; hon fell Faculty of Law Univ of Edinburgh 1995–; *Books* The Unfair Contract Terms Act 1977 (1978), Sweet & Maxwell Encyclopaedia of Consumer Law (Scottish ed, 1978–85), Company Law: The European Dimension (contrib, 1991), EC Legal Systems (contrib, 1992), Green's Guide to European Law in Scotland (contrib, 1996), McPhail's Sheriff Court Practice (contrib, 1999), Court of Session Practice (contrib, 2005); *Recreations* travel, opera, chamber music, the music of Schubert; *Style—* The Rt Hon Lord Clarke, QC; ✉ Parliament House, Edinburgh EH1

CLARKE, Melanie-Ann (Mel); da of Stephen Clarke, of Taverham, Norwich, and Brenda, *née* Burgess; *b* 2 September 1982, Norwich; *Educ* Taverham HS, Norwich City Coll (Dip); *Career* Paralympic archer; achievements incl: European Champion 2002, Nat Champion 2003, second European Grand Prix (able bodied) 2003, World Champion 2005, world ranked number one 2005, third European Championships 2006, second Br Championships 2006, fifth World Championships 2007, Team World Champion (Gold medal) 2007, world ranked number two 2007, Bronze medal (open individual compound) Paralympics Beijing 2008, Gold medal (team event) and Silver medal (individual event) World Championships 2009, Silver medal (open individual compound) AAE Arizona Cup 2010, Silver medal (open team compound) European Para-Archery Championships 2010, Silver medal (open team compound) Arizona Cup 2012, Silver medal (open individual compound) Paralympics London 2012, Bronze medal (individual event) World Championships 2013; shot eleven national, eight paralympic and four team world records; Norfolk sporting ambass; ldr Girl Guides Assoc; *Recreations* art, swimming; *Style—* Miss Mel Clarke; ✉ 119 Nightingale Drive, Taverham, Norwich, Norfolk (☎ 01603 868836, mobile 078584 293263, e-mail melclarkearchery@googlemail.com)

CLARKE, (Christopher) Michael; CBE (2009); s of Patrick Reginald Rudland Clarke, of Helmsley, N Yorks, and Margaret Catherine, *née* Waugh; *b* 29 August 1952; *Educ* Felsted, Univ of Manchester (BA); *m* 1 July 1978, Deborah Clare, da of Paul Wilfred Cowling; 2 s (Oliver Paul b 29 June 1984, Alexander Patrick b 19 April 1986), 1 da (Emily Louisa b 15 Sept 1992); *Career* art asst York Art Gallery 1973–76, res asst Br Museum 1976–78, asst keeper i/c prints Whitworth Art Gallery Univ of Manchester 1978–84; Scottish Nat Gallery: asst keeper 1984–87, keeper 1987–2000, dir 2001–; visiting fell: Paul Mellon Center for Studies in Br Art Yale Univ 1985, Clark Art Inst Williamston MA 2004; FRSE 2008; Chevalier de l'Ordre des Arts et des Lettres (France) 2004, Cdr Order of the Dannebrog Denmark 2012; *Books* The Tempting Prospect: A Social History of English Watercolours (1981), The Arrogant Connoisseur: Richard Payne Knight (co ed with Nicholas Penny, 1982), The Draughtsman's Art: Master Drawings in the Whitworth Art Gallery (1982), Lighting Up The Landscape: French Impressionism And Its Origins (1986), Corot And The Art Of Landscape (1991), Eyewitness Art: Watercolour (1993), Corot, Courbet und die Maler von Barbizon (co ed with Christoph Heilmann and John Sillevis, 1996), The Concise Oxford Dictionary of Art Terms (2001), Monet: The Seine and the Sea (with Richard Thomson, 2003); *Recreations* golf, music; *Clubs* R&A; *Style—* Michael Clarke, Esq, CBE; ✉ Scottish National Gallery, The Mound, Edinburgh EH2 2EL (☎ 0131 624 6511, fax 0131 220 0917)

CLARKE, Prof Michael Gilbert; CBE (2000), DL (Worcs 2000); s of Canon Reginald Gilbert (Rex) Clarke (d 1993), of Kirkby Lonsdale, Cumbria, and Marjorie Kathleen, *née* Haslegrave (d 1991); *b* 21 May 1944; *Educ* Queen Elizabeth GS Wakefield, Univ of Sussex (BA, MA); *m* 1 July 1967, Angela Mary, da of John Bowen Cook (d 1988), of Easingwold, N Yorks; 2 da (Joanna Mary (Mrs Gavin Hill) b 1970, Lucy Elizabeth (Mrs Mark Mathieson) b 1972), 1 s (Thomas John Kempe b 1980); *Career* teaching asst Univ of Essex 1967–78, lectr and dir of studies in politics Univ of Edinburgh 1969–75, dep dir policy planning Lothian Regnl Cncl 1977–81 (asst dir 1975–77), chief exec Local Govt Trg Bd 1981–90, chief exec The Local Govt Mgmnt Bd 1990–93; Univ of Birmingham: head Sch of Public Policy 1993–98, pro-vice-chllr 1998–2003, vice-princ 2003–2008, prof emeritus 2008; pres: Worcester Civic Soc 1999–, Herefordshire and Worcestershire Community First 2005–; chair Birmingham Royal Ballet 2009–; memb Gen Synod C of E 1990–93 and 1995–, memb Dioceses Cmmn 2008– (chair 2011–); lay canon Worcester Cathedral 2001–10 (canon emeritus 2010); tstee: Elgar Fndn 2008–, Barber Inst 2008–, Three Choirs Festival 2014–, Hult Int Business Sch 2015–; govr: The King's Sch Worcester 2006–, Univ of Worcester 2007–15, Ashridge 2010–15, Univ of Birmingham Sch 2012– (chair 2012–); fell Ashridge Coll 2015–; Hon MA Univ of Worcester 2003, Hon DLitt Univ of Aston 2009, Hon DUniv Univ of Birmingham 2014; FRSA 1992; *Publications* books, academic jls and press contributions on local and national govt; *Recreations* gardening, music, history, grandchildren; *Clubs* Reform; *Style—* Canon Prof Michael Clarke, CBE, DL; ✉ Millington House, 15 Lansdowne Crescent, Worcester WR3 8JE (☎ 01905 617634)

CLARKE, Dr Michael John (Mike); s of George Fredrick Albert Clarke (d 2007), and Barbara Patricia Clarke; *b* 2 January 1960, Dartford, Kent; *Educ* Gravesend GS, Univ of Oxford (MA), Univ of Southampton (PhD); *m* 1982, Naomi Joan; 2 da; *Career* Nature Conservancy Cncl 1981–88; RSPB: conservation mangr 1988–91, regnl dir SE England 1991–98, operations dir 1998–2010, chief exec 2010–; FRSA 1990; *Recreations* birds and wildlife, archaeology, slow food; *Style—* Dr Mike Clarke; ✉ RSPB, The Lodge, Potton Road, Sandy, Bedfordshire SG19 2DL (☎ 01767 680551, e-mail mike.clarke@rspb.org.uk, website www.rspb.org.uk)

CLARKE, Nicky; OBE (2007); s of William Clarke, of London, and Irene, *née* Lignu; *b* 17 June 1958; *Educ* Archbishop Tenisons GS; *m* Lesley, *née* Gale; 1 s (Harrison b 13 May 1986), 1 da (Tellisa b 25 Oct 1988); *Career* hairdresser; Leonard of Mayfair 1974–76, Stafford and Frieda 1976–80, John Frieda 1980–90, Nicky Clarke 1990–; *Awards* incl: Br Hairdresser of the Year, London Hairdresser of the Year (three times), Session Hairdresser of the Year (twice), World Master Award Art and Fash Gp USA, Most Newsworthy Hairdresser Worldwide Int Beauty Show NY, Hairdresser of the Year Fellowship of Br Hairdressing, Image of the Year (twice), Golden Scissors Award Fellowship of Br Hairdressing; *Publications* Hair Power (1999); *Recreations* skiing (water and snow), indoor rock climbing, tennis, squash, keep fit, scuba diving; *Style—* Nicky Clarke, Esq, OBE; ✉ 11 Carlos Place, London W1K 3AX (☎ 020 7491 4700, e-mail nicky@nickyclarke.com)

CLARKE, Noel; *b* 6 December 1975, London; *Educ* Univ of N London; *Career* actor, dir and screenwriter; Orange Rising Star Award BAFTA 2009; *Television* as actor incl: Metrosexuality 1999, Auf Wiedersehen, Pet 2002–04, Doctor Who 2005–08; *Film* as actor incl: Kidulthood (also writer) 2006, Adulthood (also writer and dir) 2008, Heartless 2009, Doghouse 2009, Centurion 2010, Huge 2010, 4.3.2.1 (also writer and dir) 2010; *Style—* Noel Clarke, Esq; ✉ c/o Independent Talent Group, 40 Whitfield Street, London W1T 2RH

CLARKE, Oz; *Educ* Canterbury Choir Sch, King's Sch Canterbury, Pembroke Coll Oxford (MA); *Career* wine writer and broadcaster; co-presenter Food & Drink BBC TV and numerous other shows incl several drinks series with James May and Hugh Dennis as well as shows on music, politics, sport, travel, fashion and antiques, Oz and Armonico Drink to Music (wine and music concerts) 2016; *Books* incl: Oz Clarke's Wine Guide, Oz Clarke's New Classic Wines, Oz Clarke's Wine Atlas, Microsoft Wine Guide, Grapes and Wines, Oz Clarke's Pocket Wine Book, Oz Clarke's Bordeaux, Oz Clarke's Grapes and Wines, History of Wine in 100 Bottles, Oz Clarke's 250 Best Wines, Oz Clarke's Encyclopaedia of Wine, Oz Clarke's Let Me Tell You About Wine; *Recreations* any sport, virtually any music, the great outdoors (especially Britain's wonderful coastline), theatre, railways, time to contemplate life; *Style—* Oz Clarke, Esq; ✉ c/o Limelight, 10 Filmer Mews, 75 Filmer Road, London SW6 7JF (☎ 020 7384 9950)

CLARKE, Peter Lawrence; s of George David Clarke, of Bramshill, Berks, and June, *née* Bray; *b* 28 October 1954, Hitchin, Herts; *Educ* Culford Sch Bury St Edmunds, Queen's Coll Cambridge; *m* 12 June 1993, Prunella, *née* Townsend-Green; 1 da (Tabitha Laura Alice b 21 Jan 1995), 1 s (Barnaby George Oliver b 30 Oct 1996); *Career* admitted slr 1985; Slaughter and May 1985–86, Morgan Grenfell & Co Ltd 1986–88, Citicorp Investment Bank 1988–91, head of M&A Nikko Securities 1991–93; Man Gp plc: head of corporate finance 1993–2000, memb Bd 1997–, gp finance dir 2000–07, dep ceo 2005–07, ceo 2007–; *Recreations* tennis, country sports; *Style—* Peter Clarke, Esq; ✉ Man Group plc, Sugar Quay, Lower Thames Street, London EC3R 6DU

CLARKE, Peter Lovat; JP (1970); s of Harold Clarke (d 1945), of Warrington, and Alice Taylor (d 1992); *b* 25 July 1934; *Educ* Ellesmere, Open Univ (BA); *m* 1956, Audrey Christine, da of Walter Jonathan Elston, of Cheshire; 3 s (John b 1956, Simon and Timothy (twins) b 1964), 1 da (Denise b 1959); *Career* dir: The Greenalls Group plc (chm Gilbert & John Greenall Ltd), The Greenalls Group Pension Trustees Ltd; former chm North and Mid-Cheshire TEC Ltd, dir Warrington Community Health Care (NHS) Tst until 1996; Liveryman Worshipful Co of Distillers 1979; ACIS 1959, FCIMA 1963, CCIM 1992; *Recreations* golf, music, reading, swimming; *Clubs* Knutsford Golf, Wine and Spirit Over 40, Punt, Old Codgers, Majority, Walton Investment, Pickwick; *Style—* Peter Clarke, Esq; ✉ Brook House, Cann Lane South, Appleton, Warrington, Cheshire WA4 5NJ (☎ 01925 261660)

CLARKE, His Hon Judge Peter William; QC (1997); s of Judge Edward Clarke, QC (d 1989), and Dorothy May, *née* Leask (d 1996); *b* 29 May 1950; *Educ* Sherborne, Inns of Court Sch of Law; *m* 9 Sept 1978; Victoria Mary, da of Michael Francis Gilbert, CBE, TD (d 2006); 2 c (Edward Benedict, Jessica Alice); *Career* called to the Bar Lincoln's Inn 1973 (bencher 2003); recorder to the Crown Court 1991–2009 (asst recorder 1987), circuit judge (South Eastern Circuit) 2009–; *Recreations* losing at tennis to my children, skiing, golf, photography, enjoying my wife's paintings; *Clubs* Garrick; *Style—* His Hon Judge Peter Clarke, QC; ✉ c/o The South Eastern Circuit, 289–293 High Holborn, London WC1V 7HZ

CLARKE, Phil; *Career* ed of comedy Talkback Productions until 2003, head of comedy and entertainment Objective Productions 2003–13 (exec prodr of scripted comedy incl Fresh Meat, Peep Show, Star Stories and Pete Versus Life), head of comedy Channel 4 2013–; *Style—* Phil Clarke, Esq; ✉ Channel 4, 124 Horseferry Road, London SW1P 2TX

CLARKE, Richard Allen; s of Allen Lee Clarke, of London, and Anne Clarke; *b* 19 August 1942; *Educ* Aldenham, The Architectural Assoc Sch (AADipl); *m* 11 May 1968, Mary Mildred Irene, da of Dr James Francis Hanratty, OBE, of London; 2 s (Jason b 1970, Dominic b 1979), 2 da (Antonia b 1973, Louisa b 1976); *Career* architect; ptnr Clifford Tee & Gale 1977– (joined 1974); Freeman City of London 1964; RIBA; *Recreations* shooting, gardening; *Style—* Richard Clarke, Esq; ✉ Clifford Tee & Gale, 5 Eccleston Street, London SW1W 9LY

CLARKE, Most Rev Richard Lionel; *see:* Armagh, Archbishop of

CLARKE, Prof Roger Howard; CBE (2005); *b* 22 August 1943; *Educ* King Edward VI Sch Stourbridge, Univ of Birmingham (BSc, MSc), Univ of Westminster (PhD); *m* 15 Oct 1966, Sandra Ann; 1 s, 1 da; *Career* res offr CEGB 1965–77; National Radiological Protection Bd: head of nuclear power assessments 1978–82, Bd sec 1983–87, dir 1987–2003; visiting prof Centre for Environmental Technology ICSTM London 1991–2002, visiting prof in radiation and environmental protection Dept of Physics Univ of Surrey 1993–; chm Int Cmmn on Radiological Protection 1993–2005; memb: CEC Gp of Experts in Basic Safety Standards for Radiation Protection 1987–2003; UK delg to UN Sci Ctee on Effects of Atomic Radiation 1990–2003; US Health Physics Soc William Morgan Award 1994, RSM Ellison-Cliffe Medal 1996, Hanns-Lagendorff Medal, Deutscher Strahlenschutzärtze 2002, medal of the French Assembly 2005; hon vice-pres Instn of Nuclear Engrs 2002, hon fell Soc of Radiological Protection; Hon DUniv Surrey 2004; Hon FRCR; *Publications* Carcinogenesis and Radiation Risk: A Biomathematical Reconnaissance (with W V Mayneord, 1977); author of numerous papers in scientific lit; *Recreations* theatre, gardening, travel; *Style—* Prof Roger Clarke, CBE; ✉ Corner Cottage, Woolton Hill, Newbury, Berkshire RG20 9XJ (☎ 01635 253957, e-mail clarke.rogerh@btopenworld.com)

CLARKE, Sally Vanessa; MBE (2009); da of Brian Trent Clarke, of Surrey, and Sheila Margaret, *née* Coomber; *b* 6 January 1954; *Educ* Guildford HS, Croydon Tech Coll (Dip Hotel and Catering Ops); *Career* studied and worked in Paris (Cordon Bleu Advanced Cert) 1974–75, asst cook Leiths Good Food Catering Co 1976–77, head teacher and demonstrator Leiths Sch of Food and Wine 1977–79, moved to Los Angeles to work with Michael McCarty and helped set up Michaels Santa Monica 1979, asst cook and asst night mangr Michaels Santa Monica Calif and West Beach Cafe Venice Calif 1980–83; opened: Clarke's in London 1984, & Clarke's 1988, & Clarke's Bread 1989; *Books* Sally Clarke's Book, Recipes from a Restaurant, Shop and Bakery (1999, Glenfiddich

Food Book of the Year 2000); *Recreations* cooking, eating, drinking good wine, opera; *Style*— Miss Sally Clarke, MBE; ✉ Clarke's, 124 Kensington Church Street, London W8 4BH (☎ 020 7221 9225, fax 020 7229 4564, e-mail restaurant@sallyclarke.com)

CLARKE, Sharon D; *b* 1966, London; *Career* actress and singer; *Theatre* incl: Guys and Dolls 1996, Rent (Shaftesbury Theatre) 1998, Fame 1999, The Lion King (Lyceum Theatre) 2000–02, Chicago 2004, We Will Rock You (Dominion Theatre) 2004, Once in This Island (Birmingham Repertory Theatre), Hairspray (Shaftesbury Theatre) 2010, Ghost (Manchester Opera House and Piccadilly Theatre) 2011, The Amen Corner (NT) 2013 (Best Actress in a Supporting Role Olivier Award 2014); *Television* incl: Holby City 2005–08, The Shadow Line 2011; *Style*— Ms Sharon D Clarke; ✉ c/o Sandra Boyce Management, 1 Kingsway House, Albion Road, London N16 0TA

CLARKE, Stephen; *b* 15 September 1967, Belfast; *Educ* Queen's Univ Belfast (BEng); *Partner* Michael Galway (civil partnership June 2012); *Career* Dixons Stores Gp 1989–94, Ladbroke Gp 1994–95, Optus Communications Sydney 1995–2000, head of product mktg Argos 2001–04; WH Smith plc: mktg dir high street retail 2004–06, commercial and mktg dir 2006–08, md high street retail 2008–13, chief exec 2013–; *Style*— Stephen Clarke, Esq; ✉ WH Smith plc, Victoria House, Bloomsbury Square, London WC1B 4DA

CLARKE, Susanna; *b* 1959, Nottingham; *Educ* St Hilda's Coll Oxford; *Career* writer; previously worked in non-fiction publishing incl Gordon Fraser and Quarto; taught English in Turin and Bilbao; ed cookery list Simon and Schuster 1993–2003; *Books* Jonathan Strange and Mr Norrell (2004, Best Novel Hugo Award 2005, World Fantasy Award 2005, shortlisted Whitbread First Novel, shortlisted Guardian First Book Award), The Ladies of Grace Adieu and Other Stories (2006); *Style*— Miss Susanna Clarke; ✉ c/o literary agent: Jonny Geller, Curtis Brown (e-mail jonny@curtisbrown.co.uk)

CLARKE, Rt Hon Thomas (Tom); PC (1997), CBE (1980), JP (Lanark 1972); s of James Clarke, and Mary, née Gordon; *b* 10 January 1941; *Educ* Columba HS, Coatbridge and Scottish Coll of Commerce; *Career* former asst dir Scottish Film Cncl; memb Coatbridge Cncl 1964–74, provost Monklands DC 1974–82, pres Convention of Scottish Local Authorities 1978–80 (vice-pres 1976–78); MP (Lab): Coatbridge and Airdrie 1982–83, Monklands W 1983–97, Coatbridge and Chryston 1997–2015; sponsor: Disabled Persons' Act 1986, Int Devpt (Reporting and Transparency) Act 2006; memb Shadow Cabinet 1992–97; chief oppn spokesman: on Scottish affrs 1992–93, on devpt and co-operation 1993–94, on disabled people's rights 1994–97; min for film and tourism Dept for Culture, Media and Sport 1997–98; govr BFI; *Books* Managing Third World Debt (co-author); *Style*— The Rt Hon Tom Clarke, CBE; ✉ House of Commons, London SW1A 0AA

CLARKE, (George) Timothy Horace De Courquetaine; s of late Denis Horace Hilary Clarke, of Powick, Worcs, and Louise Marie, née Schlincker; *b* 20 April 1949; *Educ* Oundle, St John's Coll Cambridge (MA); *m* 2 Sept 1989, Henrietta Barbara, da of Alexander Neilson Strachan Walker, CMG (d 1980); 1 s (Matthew Alexander Henry b 24 April 1994), 1 da (Veronica Julia b 31 July 1996); *Career* admitted slr 1974; ptnr Linklaters 1982–; *Recreations* gardening, reading, France; *Style*— Timothy Clarke, Esq; ✉ Linklaters, One Silk Street, London EC2Y 8HQ (☎ 020 7456 2000, fax 020 7456 2222)

CLARKE, Trevor; MLA; *Career* MLA (DUP) S Antrim 2007–; *Style*— Trevor Clarke, Esq, MLA; ✉ Northern Ireland Assembly, Parliament Buildings, Belfast BT4 3XX (☎ 028 9446 3273)

CLARKE OF HAMPSTEAD, Baron (Life Peer UK 1998), of Hampstead in the London Borough of Camden; Anthony James (Tony) Clarke; CBE (1998); *b* 17 April 1932; *Educ* Hampstead, New End & St Dominic's RC Sch Kentish Town, Ruskin Coll Oxford (by correspondence); *Career* Nat Serv Royal Signals 1950–52; Post Office: successively telegraph boy, postman then sorter until 1979; CWU (formerly Union of Post Office Workers): memb Ctee Hampstead 1953–62, branch sec 1962–69, memb District Cncl (London) Ctee 1964–68, memb Exec Ctee London District Cncl 1965–79, district orgnr 1968–70, sec (London all grades) 1972–79 (dep sec 1970–72), memb Exec cncl 1975, nat ed UPW Jl 1979–82, dep gen-sec 1982–93; Lab Pty: chm 1992–93, memb NEC, chm Int Ctee 1986–93; Cncllr London Borough of Camden 1971–78, Parly candidate Hampstead Feb and Oct 1974; memb: London Trades Cncl 1965–69, TUC Disputes Panel 1972–93, TUC SE Regl Cncl 1974–79; tstee Post Office Pension Funds 1991–97; tstee RAF Museum Hendon 2001–10; KStG 1994; *Style*— The Lord Clarke of Hampstead, CBE; ✉ House of Lords, London SW1A 0PW (☎ 020 7219 1379)

CLARKE OF STONE-CUM-EBONY, Rt Hon Baron (Life Peer UK 2009), of Stone-cum-Ebony in the County of Kent; Sir Anthony Peter Clarke; kt (1993), PC (1998); s of Harry Alston Clarke (d 1979), and Isobel, née Kay; *b* 13 May 1943; *Educ* Oakham Sch, King's Coll Cambridge; *m* 7 Sept 1968, Rosemary, da of K W Adam, of Barnham, W Sussex; 2 s (Ben b 7 Jan 1972, Thomas b 20 June 1973), 1 da (Sally b 3 June 1977); *Career* called to the Bar Middle Temple 1965 (bencher 1987); QC 1979, recorder of the Crown Court 1985–92, judge of the High Court of Justice 1993–98, a Lord Justice of Appeal 1998–2005, Master of the Rolls 2005–09, Justice of the Supreme Court 2009–; conducted: Thames Safety Inquiry 1999, Marchioness and Bowbelle Inquiries 2000; arbitrator Lloyd's and ICC, wreck cmmr and memb Chambre Arbitrale Maritime until 1992; *Recreations* tennis, golf, holidays, bridge; *Style*— The Lord Clarke of Stone-cum-Ebony; ✉ Supreme Court, Middlesex Guildhall, London

CLARKSON, Jeremy Charles Robert; s of Edward Grenville Clarkson, of Doncaster, and Shirley Gabrielle, née Ward; *b* 11 April 1960; *Educ* Repton; *m* Frances Catherine, da of Maj Robert H Cain, VC; 2 da (Emily Harriet b 21 July 1994, Katya Helena b 24 Nov 1998), 1 s (Finlo Robert Edward b 14 March 1996); *Career* trainee journalist Rotherham Advertiser 1978–83, fndr Motoring Press Agency 1983; presenter: Top Gear (BBC) 1989–99 and 2002–15, Jeremy Clarkson's Motorworld (BBC) 1995 and 1996, Extreme Machines (BBC) 1998, Robot Wars (BBC), Clarkson (BBC) 1998, 1999 and 2000, Clarkson's Car Years (BBC) 2000, Speed (BBC) 2001, Meet The Neighbours (BBC) 2002, Great Britons: Brunel (BBC) 2003, For Valour (BBC) 2003, Greatest Raid of All Time 2007; fndr BBC Top Gear Magazine 1993; columnist: The Sunday Times 1993–, The Sun 1995–; *Style*— Jeremy Clarkson, Esq

CLARKSON, Prof (Peter) John; s of Alan Geoffrey Clarkson, and Monica Ruth, née Lightburne; *b* 11 November 1961, Oswestry, Salop; *Educ* Trinity Hall Cambridge (BA, Rex Moir Prize, Baker Prize, Charles Lamb Prize, PhD); *m* 13 Aug 1988, Mary Susan Joan, née Moore; 2 da (Alice Mary b 6 June 1989, Hannah Miriam b 13 June 1991), 2 s (David John b 19 Oct 1994, Patrick Edward b 1 Jan 2001); *Career* gp ldr PA Consulting Gp 1988–95; Univ of Cambridge: lectr in engrg design 1995–2001, dir Cambridge Engrg Design Centre 1997–, reader in engrg design 2001–04, prof of engrg design 2004–; fell Trinity Hall Cambridge 1995– (vice-master 2009–13); Pres's Medal Ergonomics Soc 2005; Thatcher Bros Prize IMechE 2006, William Floyd Medal Inst of Ergonomics and Human Factors 2010, Inst lectr Inst of Ergonomics and Human Factors 2013; Hon Dr KU Leuven 2012; memb: Design Soc 2001, ASME 2002; foreign memb Royal Swedish Acad of Engrg Sciences (IVA) 2013; FIET 2004, FIED 2011, FREng 2012; *Books* Countering Design Exclusion: An Introduction to Inclusive Design (jtly, 2003), Inclusive Design: Design for the Whole Population (jt ed, 2003), Design Process Improvement: A Review of Current Practice (jt ed, 2005), Inclusive Design Toolkit (jt ed, 2007), Design for Inclusivity: A Practical Guide to Accessible, Innovation and User-centred Design (jt ed, 2007); *Recreations* music, cycling; *Style*— Prof P John Clarkson; ✉ Department of Engineering, University of Cambridge, Trumpington Street, Cambridge CB2 1PZ (☎ 01223 748246, fax 01223 332662, e-mail pjc10@eng.cam.ac.uk, website http://www-edc.eng.cam.ac.uk/people/pjc10.html)

CLARKSON, Patrick Robert James; QC (1991); s of Cdr Robert Anthony Clarkson, LVO, of Crudwell House, Wiltshire, and Sheila Clarissa, née Neale; *b* 1 August 1949; *Educ* Winchester; *m* 26 July 1975, Bridget Cecilia Doyne (d 2013), da of Col Robert Harry Doyne (d 1965); 2 s (Benjamin Robin b 1978, William Patrick b 1985), 1 da (Georgia Emily b 1980); *Career* called to the Bar Lincoln's Inn 1972, recorder of the Crown Court 1996; memb Hon Soc of Lincoln's Inn and Inner Temple; *Recreations* country; *Clubs* Boodle's, MCC; *Style*— Patrick Clarkson, Esq, QC; ✉ 84 Kingfisher House, Juniper Drive, Battersea Reach, London SW18 1TY

CLARKSON, Dr Peter David; MBE (2010); s of Maurice Roland Clarkson (d 1992), and Jessie née Baker (d 2015); *b* 19 June 1945; *Educ* Epsom Coll, Univ of Durham (BSc), Univ of Birmingham (PhD); *m* 1974, Rita Margaret, née Skinner; 1 da; *Career* geologist with British Antarctic Survey 1967–89: wintered in Halley Bay Antarctica 1968 and 1969, base cdr 1969, Antarctic field seasons in Shackleton Range (ldr 3 times) 1968–78, in S Shetland Islands 1974–75, ldr in Antarctic Peninsula 1985–86; exec sec Scientific Ctee on Antarctic Research 1989–2005, emeritus assoc Scott Polar Research Inst 2005–; articles on Antarctic geology; UK advsr to PROANTAR Brazil 1982; hon sec Trans-Antarctic Assoc 1980–95 (tstee 1995–2017, chm 2006–17); Polar Medal 1976, FGS 1979; *Publications* 100 Natural Wonders of the World (jtly, 1995, 2 edn 2004), Volcanoes (2000), 100 Great Wonders of the World (jtly, 2004), Science in the Snow (jtly, 2011); *Recreations* walking, woodworking, photography, music, all matters Antarctic, lecturing on Antarctic cruise ships; *Clubs* Antarctic; *Style*— Dr Peter Clarkson, MBE; ✉ Scott Polar Research Institute, Lensfield Road, Cambridge CB2 1ER (☎ 01223 336531, fax 01223 336549, e-mail pdc3@cam.ac.uk)

CLARRICOATS, Prof Peter John Bell; CBE (1996); s of John Clarricoats, OBE (d 1969), of London, and Alice Cecilia, née Bell (d 1982); *b* 6 April 1932; *Educ* Minchenden GS, Imperial Coll London (BSc, PhD, DSc); *m* 1, 6 Aug 1955 (m dis 1963), (Mary) Gillian Stephenson, da of George Gerald Hall (d 1971), of Leeds; 1 s (Michael b 1960), 1 da (Alison b 1962); *m* 2, 19 Oct 1968, Phyllis Joan, da of Reginald Blackburn Lloyd (d 1989), of Newton Abbot; 2 da (Angela b 1969, Caroline b 1969); *Career* scientific staff GEC 1953–59; lectr: Queen's Univ of Belfast 1959–62, Univ of Sheffield 1962–63; prof Univ of Leeds 1963–67; Queen Mary Univ of London 1968–: dean of engrg 1977–80, head of electronic engrg 1979–96, govr 1976–79 and 1987–90; chm: IEE Electronics Div 1979, Br Nat Ctee for Radio Sci 1985–89, Defence Scientific Advsy Cncl 1997–2000, Technology Bd Filtronia plc 1997–2003, numerous conferences on microwaves and antenna; distinguished lectr IEEE Antenna and Propagation Soc 1986–88; Coopers Hill Meml Prize (IEE) 1964, Measurement Prize (IEE) 1989, JJ Thomson Medal (IEE) 1989, European Microwave Prize 1989, Millennium Medal (IEEE) 2000, Distinguished Achievement Award (IEEE) 2001, European Microwave Medal 2005, J R James Meml Prize European Assoc of Antennas and Propagation) 2011, Sir Frank White Medal (Royal Acad of Engrg) 2015; Hon DSc: Univ of Kent 1993, Aston Univ 1995; vice-pres: IEE 1989 (hon fell 1993), International Union of Radio Science 1993; FInstP 1964, FIEE 1968, FIEEE 1968, FCGI 1980, FREng 1983, FRS 1990; *Books* Microwave Ferrites (1960), Corrugated Horns for Microwave Antennas (1984), Microwave Horns and Feeds (1994); *Recreations* classical music; *Style*— Prof Peter Clarricoats, CBE, FRS, FREng; ✉ The Red House, 3 Grange Meadows, Elmswell, Suffolk IP30 9GE (☎ 01359 240585); School of Electronic Engineering and Computer Science, Queen Mary, University of London, Mile End Road, London E1 4NS (e-mail clarricoats@icloud.com)

CLARY, Prof Sir David Charles; kt (2016); s of Cecil Raymond Clary (d 1979), and Mary Mildred, née Hill (d 2012); *b* 14 January 1953; *Educ* Colchester Royal GS, Univ of Sussex (BSc), CCC Cambridge (PhD), Magdalene Coll Cambridge (ScD); *m* 1975, Heather Ann, da of Trevor Vinson; 3 s (James b 1979, Simon b 1981, Nicholas b 1984); *Career* IBM World-Trade postdoctoral fell San José 1977–78, postdoctoral fell Univ of Manchester 1978–80, res lectr in chemistry UMIST 1980–83; Dept of Chemistry Univ of Cambridge: demonstrator 1983–87, lectr 1987–93, reader in theoretical chemistry 1993–96; Magdalene Coll Cambridge: fell 1983–96, dir of studies in natural scis 1988–96, sr tutor 1989–93; UCL: prof of chemistry 1996–2002, dir of Centre for Theoretical and Computational Chemistry; Univ of Oxford: head of division of mathematical and physical sciences 2002–05, prof of chemistry 2002–, fell St John's Coll 2002–05, pres Magdalen Coll 2005–; chief scientific advsr FCO 2009–13; visiting fell: Univ of Colorado, Canterbury Univ NZ, Hebrew Univ Jerusalem, Univ of Sydney, Université de Paris Sud, Univ of Calif Berkeley, National Univ of Singapore; George B Kistiakowsky Lectr Harvard Univ 2002, Kenneth Pitzer lectr Univ of Calif Berkeley 2004, Burton Meml lectr Imperial Coll 2004, Paul Grandpierre lectr Columbia Univ 2004, Thomas Graham lectr UCL and RSC 2004, Charles Coulson lectr Univ of Georgia 2009, IBM Hursley lectr Univ of Southampton 2009, Einstein prof Chinese Acad of Sciences 2014, Noel Hush lectr Univ of Sydney 2014; Royal Soc of Chemistry: Meldola Medal 1981, Marlow Medal Faraday Div 1986, Corday-Morgan Medal 1989, Tilden lectr 1998, Prize for Chemical Dynamics 1998, Polanyi Medal 2004, Liversidge Award 2010; Hon DSc Univ of Sussex 2011; memb Int Acad of Quantum Molecular Scis 1998 (Annual Medal 1989); hon fell Magdalene Coll Cambridge 2005, 50th anniversary fell Univ of Sussex 2012; FRSC 1997 (pres Faraday Div 2006–09 (vice-pres 1997–2000), memb Cncl 1990–93 and 1994–2001)), FInstP 1997, FRS 1997 (memb Cncl 2003–05), fell APS 2003, foreign hon memb American Acad of Arts and Scis 2003, fell AAAS 2003, FRSA 2005; *Publications* ed Chemical Physics Letters; author of papers in scientific jls on chemical physics and theoretical chemistry; *Recreations* family, football, foreign travel; *Style*— Prof Sir David Clary, FRS; ✉ Magdalen College, Oxford OX1 4AU

CLARY, Julian Peter McDonald; s of Peter John Clary, and Brenda, née McDonald; *b* 25 May 1959; *Educ* St Benedict's Sch Ealing, Goldsmiths Coll London (BA); *Career* comedian and entertainer; *Theatre* Bravo in Splendid's (Lyric) 1995; numerous tours and live shows; *Television* shows/appearances for LWT incl: Saturday Night Live, Trick or Treat; for Channel Four incl: Sticky Moments with Julian Clary, Sticky Moments on Tour with Julian Clary, Desperately Seeking Roger, Terry & Julian, Brace Yourself Sydney; for BBC incl: Wogan, Open Air, Paramount City, All Rise for Julian Clary, Brassen Hussies (Screen Two), It's Only TV But I Like It 1999, Who Do You Think You Are? (BBC 1) 2005, National Lottery (BBC 1) 2006, The Underdog Show (BBC 2) 2007; for Sky TV incl: Prickly Heat 1999; *Radio* Big Fun Show (Radio 4), Intimate Contact with Julian Clary (Radio 1), With Great Pleasure (Radio 4), Just a Minute (Radio 4); *Film* Carry on Columbus 1992, Baby Juice Express 2002; *Recordings* Leader of the Pack (10 Records/Virgin) 1988, Wandrin' Star (Wonderdog Records Ltd) 1990; *Video* Julian Clary aka The Joan Collins Fan Club – The Mincing Machine 1989, The Best of Sticky Moments, My Glittering Passage 1993; *Books* My Life with Fanny the Wonder Dog, How to be a Real Man (1992), A Young Man's Passage (2005), Murder Most Fab (2007), Devil in Disguise (2009); *Recreations* housework, chickens and other rural pursuits; *Style*— Julian Clary, Esq; ✉ c/o International Artistes Drama, 4th Floor, 197 High Holborn, London, London WC1V 7BD (☎ 020 7025 0600)

CLASE, HE Nicola; *m* Dr Andrew Schenkel; *Career* Swedish diplomat; ambass to the Ct of St James's 2010–; *Style*— HE Ms Nicola Clase; ✉ Embassy of Sweden, 11 Montagu Place, London W1H 2AL

CLASPER, Michael; CBE (1995); s of Douglas Clasper (d 1992), and Hilda Clasper; *b* 21 April 1953; *Educ* Bede Sch Sunderland, St John's Coll Cambridge (MA); *m* 6 Sept 1975, Susan Rosemary; 1 da (Jacqueline Sarah b 21 July 1983), 2 s (Matthew Dennis Owen b 16 Jan 1986, Christopher Duncan b 28 Feb 1989); *Career* BR 1974–78; Procter & Gamble Ltd: joined as brand asst 1978, subsequently various posts in advtg then advtg dir 1985–

88, gen mangr Holland 1988–91, md and vice-pres UK 1991–95, regnl vice-pres laundry Europe 1995–98, pres Europe fabric and home care 1998–99, pres global home care 1999–2001; BAA plc: dep chief exec 2001–03, chief exec 2003–06; operating md Terra Firma Capital Ptnrs 2007–08; chm: HM Revenue & Customs 2008–12, Which? Ltd 2008–, Coats Gp plc 2014–; non-exec dir ITV plc 2006–14, sr ind dir Serco plc 2014–; chm Marketplace Taskforce 2005–08, memb Nat Employment Panel 2006–08; memb Advsy Bd Judge Inst Univ of Cambridge 1994–2003; memb HRH The Prince of Wales' Business and the Environment prog 2000–07; govr RSC 2011–; pres CMIT 2014–; *Recreations* theatre, walking, skiing, tennis, golf; *Style*— Michael Clasper, Esq, CBE

CLAUGHTON, John Alan; s of Ronald Kirby Claughton, and Patricia May, *née* Dobell (d 2003); *b* 17 September 1956, Leeds; *Educ* Bradford GS (govrs' scholar), King Edward's Sch Birmingham (fndn scholar, King Edward's scholar), Merton Coll Oxford (postmastership, MA, Cricket blue, capt Oxford Univ CC); *m* 13 April 1993, Alexandra Mary Benbow, *née* Dyer; 3 s (James Ian b 23 March 1994, Thomas Hugh b 24 Jan 1996, Samuel John Benbow b 24 Sept 2000); *Career* professional cricketer Warks CCC 1979–80, corporate finance advsr N M Rothschild & Sons 1980–82, schoolmaster Bradfield Coll 1982–84, Eton Coll 1984–2001 (master i/c cricket 1985–96, house master 1997–2001), headmaster Solihull Sch 2001–05, chief master King Edward's Sch Birmingham 2006–16 (Tatler Public School Head of the Year 2016); memb HMC, memb Educational Advsy Gp Sutton Tst; govr: Highgate Sch, Wellington Coll, Selly Oak Tst Sch; *Publications* Herodotus and the Persian Wars (2008), Aristophanes' Clouds (2012); *Recreations* travel (to Italy), ballet, classical literature, sport; *Style*— John Claughton, Esq; ✉ Vince House, 341 Bristol Road, Edgbaston, Birmingham B5 7SW (✆ 0121 472 0652); King Edward's School, Edgbaston Park Road, Birmingham B15 2UA (✆ 0121 472 1672, e-mail jac@kes.org.uk)

CLAVELL-BATE, Michael; s of Frederick Clavell-Bate, and Barbara, *née* Dean; *b* 25 March 1966; *Educ* Fishermore Catholic Sch, Univ of Newcastle upon Tyne (LLB), Chester Coll of Law; *m* 2 Sept 1989, Judith, *née* Sharples; 2 da (Hannah b 25 May 1994, Elia b 25 Jan 1998); *Career* admitted slr 1990; Eversheds: joined 1988, ptnr 1997, currently sr ptnr and head of commercial litigation Eversheds North; memb Cncl Law Soc, pres Manchester Law Soc 2001–02; *Recreations* shooting, tennis; *Style*— Michael Clavell-Bate, Esq; ✉ Eversheds, Eversheds House, 70 Great Bridgewater Street, Manchester M1 5ES (✆ 0845 497 9797)

CLAXSON, Nick; s of David Claxson, and Angela, *née* Gunn; *b* 22 March 1977, Frimley, Surrey; *Educ* Brighton Hill Community Sch Basingstoke, Queen Mary's Coll Basingstoke, Bournemouth Univ; *m* 21 July 2001, Victoria, *née* Smith; 2 s (Oliver David b 5 April 2004, Thomas Andrew b 20 July 2006); *Career* md: Comtec Enterprises Ltd 1999–, DP Direct Ltd and DP (Direct Mail) Ltd 2007–; *Clubs* Sussex Polo (dir); *Style*— Nick Claxson, Esq; ✉ Comtec House, Albert Road North, Reigate, Surrey RH2 9EL (✆ 0845 899 1400, fax 0845 899 1401, e-mail nick.claxson@comtec.com)

CLAXTON, Prof Guy; s of Eric Lennox Claxton (d 1990), and Ruby Mary, *née* Pinnock (d 1999); *b* 20 June 1947, London; *Educ* King's Sch Worcester, Trinity Hall Cambridge (scholar, MA), Magdalen Coll Oxford (DPhil); *m* 2008, Judith Nesbitt; *Career* lectr in educn: Inst of Educn Univ of London 1974–79, Chelsea Coll London 1979–86; sr lectr in educn KCL 1986–90, founding faculty Schumacher Coll Dartington 1990–93, prof Univ of Bristol 1993–2008, prof and dir Centre for Real-World Learning Univ of Winchester 2008–13 (emeritus prof 2013–); visiting prof KCL 2013–; FBPsS 1986, FAcSS, CPsychol, FRSA; *Books* Hare Brain, Tortoise Mind (1997), Wise Up (1999), Building Learning Power (2002), The Wayward Mind (2005), What's the Point of School? (2008), New Kinds of Smart (with Bill Lucas, 2010), The Learning Powered School (jtly, 2011), Expansive Education (with Bill Lucas and Ellen Spencer, 2012), Intelligence in the Flesh (2015); *Style*— Prof Guy Claxton; ✉ Centre for Real-World Learning, University of Winchester SO22 5HT (e-mail guy.claxton@winchester.ac.uk)

CLAY, David Nicholas; s of late John Clay, and late Edith Mary Clay; *b* 18 January 1944; *Educ* Ellesmere Coll, KCL (LLB), Liverpool John Moores Univ (LLM); *Career* slr; sr ptnr Dodds Ashcroft Liverpool 1986 (articled clerk 1966), merged with Davies Wallis Foyster 1988; *Style*— David Clay, Esq; ✉ DWF, 5 Castle Street, Liverpool, L2 4XE (✆ 0151 907 3000, fax 0151 907 3030, e-mail david.clay@dwf.co.uk)

CLAY, Lindsey; da of Michael John Clay (d 2000), of Distington, Cumbria, and Patricia Anne, *née* Dunn; *b* 28 November 1965, Workington, Cumbria; *Educ* St Bees Sch Cumbria, Jesus Coll Cambridge (MA); *m* 29 Dec 2000, Matthew White; 2 da (Lydia Esme b 25 July 2000, Xanthe Olivia b 30 Sept 2003); *Career* Clarke Hooper Consulting 1989–92, gp account dir McCann Communications 1992–94, bd account dir McCann Erickson 1994–97; JWT (J Walter Thompson): bd account dir 1997–99, managing ptnr 1999–2001, dir of account mgmnt 2001–06, dep md 2005–06, chief talent offr 2006–07; Thinkbox: mktg dir 2007–10, md 2011–, ceo 2013–; dir Br Television Advertising Awards (Br Arrows) 2010–; chair Trg and Devpt Ctee WACL 2007–11 (hon sec 2011–12); Steering Ctee Rank Fellowship WACL: vice-pres 2014–15, pres 2015–16, currently chair; Media Industry Body of the Decade 2013 (with Thinkbox); memb: IPA, Mktg Gp of GB (MGGB); fell Mktg Soc 2014; *Recreations* club sec Weston Park Netball; *Clubs* WACL (vice-pres 2014–15, pres-elect 2015–16); *Style*— Ms Lindsey Clay; ✉ Thinkbox, Manning House, 22 Carlisle Place, London SW1P 1JA (e-mail lindsey.clay@thinkbox.tv)

CLAYDEN, Dr Graham Stuart; s of Colin Stewart Clayden (d 1985), of Bournemouth, and Amy Joyce, *née* Burrough; *b* 8 January 1947; *Educ* Bournemouth Sch, Univ of London (MD); *m* 15 Aug 1970, Christine, da of Reginald Thomas Steele (d 1980); 1 s (Jonathan Stuart b 1972), 1 da (Anna Francesca b 1974); *Career* sr registrar in paediatrics Hosp for Sick Children Gt Ormond St 1977, sr lectr and hon conslt in paediatrics St Thomas' Hosp 1977–89, reader in paediatrics and hon conslt GKT (formerly UMDS) 1989–; procensor RCP, memb Exec Ctee Royal Coll of Paediatrics and Child Health; founding govr Br Paediatric Computer and Info Gp; FRCP 1984 (MRCP 1972); *Books* Treatment and Prognosis in Paediatrics (1988), Catechism in Paediatrics (1987), Constipation in Childhood (1991), Illustrated Paediatrics (1996); *Recreations* choral singing, bassoon; *Style*— Dr Graham Clayden; ✉ Paediatric Unit, GKT Medical School, Lambeth Palace Road, London SE1 7EH (✆ 020 7928 9292, ext 3046)

CLAYDEN, Phillippa; da of Alan John Clayden, of Truro, Cornwall, and Pauline Vivien, *née* Dye; *b* 4 August 1955, Muswell Hill, London; *Educ* Creighton Comp, Hackney Stoke Newington Coll of Further Educn, Central Sch of Art & Design (BA), Royal Acad of Art (Post Grad Dip); *Career* artist; study of drawing with Cecil Collins 1977–83, fndr tutor and curator Young Visions: An Extravaganza of Extraordinary Art 1979–2014, freelance lectr in univs, corporations and art orgns around Britain 1982–, dir of art Islington Arts Factory 1989–2005, adult painting and life drawing The Sternberg Centre 2005–13; memb: Royal Acad Schs Alumni, Penwith Soc of Artists, Plymouth Soc of Artists; *Exhibitions* incl: New Contemporaries 1977, solo show Camden Art Centre 1978, Premiums Show RA Dipl Gallery 1981 and 1982 (winner Landseer prize and Dorothy Morgan prize), RA Summer Show 1982–90 and 2001, solo show Southampton City Art Gallery 1988, Berkeley Square Gallery 1988, Blim Sanat Gallery Istanbul 1995, solo show Boundary Gallery 1993, 1995, 1997 and 2002, Plymouth Museum Gallery 2000–04, Penwith Soc of Artists Cornwall 2005, Burlington Arcade 2006, Cork St Gallery 2008, Lynne Painter Stainers London 2010, Thaxted Church Essex 2010, Penwith Gallery St Ives 2011, Traquair Gallery Truro 2013–; *Publications* Landscape Painting (by Kimm Stevens), exhibition catalogues by John Russell Taylor; *Recreations* walking, gardening; *Style*— Ms Phillippa Clayden; ✉ Holly Tree House,

No 9 The Parade, Truro, Cornwall TR1 1QE (✆ 07900 317874, e-mail phillippa-c@hotmail.co.uk, website www.phillippaclayden.co.uk)

CLAYDON, Jonathan (Jon); s of Reginald Claydon, of Sydney, Australia, and Pauline, *née* Cox; *b* 19 April 1961, Farnborough, Kent; *Educ* Dulwich Coll, Univ of Durham (LLB); *Partner* Annie Woolf; 3 da (Hope b 25 Aug 1995, Kezia b 5 Sept 1997, Edith 16 Sept 2006), 1 s (James b 28 Aug 2003); *Career* trader/desk head Cargill Geneva 1987–90, ceo Claydon Heeley 1990–2000, chm Claydon Heeley and Agency Republic 2001–07, chm and ptnr Work Club 2007–; chm and ptnr: Grapple Mobile, Upcast Social Advertising, Work Angel Technology; chm and ptnr Havas Work Club 2007–; chm Yuno Juno Digital freelance recruitment; patron and memb Mktg Bd NSPCC; patron NSPCC and Royal Fndn; *Style*— Jon Claydon; ✉ c/o Work Club, Axe & Bottle Court, 70 Newcomen Street, London SE1 1YT

CLAYTON, Adam; s of Brian Clayton, and Josephine (Joe) Clayton; *b* 13 March 1960; *Educ* Castle Park Sch Dalkey, St Columba's Coll Rathfarnham; *Career* bass guitarist and fndr memb U2 1978– (with Bono, The Edge, and Larry Mullen, Jr, *qqv*); first U2 release U23 (EP) 1979; *Albums* Boy 1980, October 1981, War 1983 (entered UK chart at no 1), Under A Blood Red Sky 1983 (live album), The Unforgettable Fire 1984 (entered UK charts at no 1), Wide Awake in America 1985, The Joshua Tree 1987 (entered UK charts at no 1, fastest selling album ever in UK, Album of the Year Grammy Awards 1987), The Joshua Tree Singles 1988, Rattle & Hum 1988 (entered UK charts at no 1), Achtung Baby 1991, Zooropa 1993 (no 1 in 18 countries, Best Alternative Album Grammy Awards 1993), Pop 1997 (no 1), The Best of 1980–1990 1998, All That You Can't Leave Behind 2000 (no 1, Best Rock Album Grammy Awards 2002), The Best of 1990–2000 2002, How To Dismantle An Atomic Bomb 2004 (Album of the Year and Best Rock Album Grammy Awards 2006), U218 Singles 2006, No Line on the Horizon 2009; *Singles* incl: Fire 1981, New Year's Day (first UK Top Ten hit) 1983, Pride (In the Name of Love) 1984, Unforgettable Fire 1985, With or Without You 1987, I Still Haven't Found What I'm Looking For 1987, Where The Streets Have No Name 1987 (Best Video Grammy Awards 1989), Desire (first UK no 1 single) 1988 (Best Rock Performance Grammy Awards 1989), Angel of Harlem 1988, When Love Comes to Town 1989, All I Want Is You 1989, Night & Day (for AIDS benefit LP Red Hot & Blue) 1990, The Fly (UK no 1) 1991, Stay 1993, Discotheque (UK no 1) 1997, Staring at the Sun 1997, Sweetest Thing 1998, Beautiful Day (UK no 1) 2000 (Record of the Year, Song of the Year and Best Rock Performance by a Duo or Group with Vocal Grammy Awards 2001), Stuck in a Moment You Can't Get Out Of 2001 (Best Song by a Pop Duo or Group Grammy Awards 2002), Elevation 2001 (Best Rock Performance by a Duo or Group with Vocal Grammy Awards 2002), Walk On 2001 (Record of the Year Grammy Awards 2002), Electrical Storm 2002, Vertigo (UK no 1) 2004 (Best Rock Performance by a Duo or Group with Vocal, Best Rock Song and Best Short Form Music Video Grammy Awards 2004), Sometimes You Can't Make It On Your Own (UK no 1) 2005 (Song of the Year, Best Rock Duo or Group Vocal and Best Rock Song Grammy Awards 2006), City of Blinding Lights 2005 (Best Rock Song Grammy Awards 2006), All Because of You 2005, the Saints are Coming 2006, Window in the Skies 2007, Get on Your Boots 2009, Magnificent 2009, I'll Go Crazy If I Don't Go Crazy Tonight 2009, Ordinary Love 2013 (Best Original Song – Motion Picture Golden Globe Award 2014); *Film* Rattle & Hum 1988; *Tours* incl: UK, US, Belgium and Holland 1980, UK, US, Ireland and Europe 1981–83, Aust, NZ and Europe 1984, A Conspiracy of Hope (Amnesty International Tour) 1986, Joshua Tree tour 1987, Rattle & Hum tour 1988, Zoo TV tour (played to 5 million people) 1992–93, Popmart Tour 1997–98, Elevation 2001 tour 2001, Vertigo tour 2005; also appeared at: Live Aid 1985 (Best Live Aid Performance Rolling Stone Readers' Poll 1986), Self Aid Dublin, Smile Jamaica (Dominion Theatre, in aid of hurricane disaster relief) 1988, New Year's Eve concert Dublin (broadcast live to Europe and USSR) 1989; performed at venues incl: Wembley Stadium, Madison Square Garden NY, Longest Day Festival Milton Keynes Bowl, Croke Park Dublin, Sun Devil Stadium AZ; *Awards* Best Band Rolling Stone Readers' Poll 1986 (also jt winner Critics' Poll), Band of the Year Rolling Stone Writers' Poll 1984, Best International Act BPI Awards 1989 and 1990, Best Live Act BPI Awards 1993, Best International Group Brit Awards 2001, Outstanding Contribution to the Music Industry Brit Awards 2001, Outstanding Song Collection Ivor Novello Awards 2003, Golden Globe Award (for Hands that Built America) 2003, Oscar nomination (for Hands that Built America) 2003; *Publications* U2 by U2 (2006); *Style*— Adam Clayton, Esq

CLAYTON, Charles; s of late Charles Harry Clayton, of Overstrand, Norfolk, and Elizabeth, *née* Appleyard-Entwisle (d 1999); *b* 27 January 1947; *Educ* The Royal Sch Armagh, Queen Elizabeth GS Middleton, Moseley Hall GS Cheadle, Loughborough Univ (BSc), Westminster Theological Seminary Philadelphia (MA); *m* 17 Oct 1970, Anne, da of late Frank Wharton; 2 da (Rachel Fiona b 2 March 1973, Victoria Elizabeth b 9 Oct 1975); *Career* civil engr City Engineers' Dept Glasgow 1970–72, Scottish area dir The Navigators 1980–84 (area rep 1972–80), sabbatical study USA 1984–86, southern regnl leader The Navigators 1986–89, exec dir World Vision UK 1989–2003, gp chief exec Shaftesbury Housing Gp 2003–04, nat dir World Vision Jerusalem/West Bank/Gaza 2004–09, chief exec Primary Trauma Care Fndn 2010–, dir Oxford Leaders Ltd 2010–; MCMI 1993, FInstD 1995, FRSA 1995; *Publications* Let The Reader Understand (1994); *Recreations* walking, sailing, church activities; *Style*— Charles Clayton, Esq; ✉ 2-B Blenheim Drive, Oxford OX2 8DG (e-mail charles99clayton@gmail.com)

CLAYTON, John Reginald William; *b* 3 December 1950; *Educ* King Edward VI Camp Hill Sch, Downing Coll Cambridge (MA, Rugby blue); *Career* admitted slr 1976; previously co sec and dir Legal Secretariat Guardian Royal Exchange plc; co sec and gp sr counsel Invensys plc; *Clubs* East India, Hawks' (Cambridge); *Style*— John Clayton, Esq

CLAYTON, Richard Anthony; QC (2002); s of Dennis Lloyd Clayton (d 1969), of London, and Patricia Estelle, *née* Morris; *b* 25 May 1954; *Educ* Westminster, New Coll Oxford; *m* 1 (m dis 1987); 2 s (Benjamin Daniel, Jack James); *m* 2, 27 April 1994, Anne Bernadette Burns; *Career* called to the Bar Middle Temple 1977; S Islington Law Centre 1980–82, Osler Hoskin & Harcourt Toronto Canada 1983; visiting fell Centre for Public Law Univ of Cambridge 2001–; memb Ctee Legal Action Gp 1985–, assoc fell and chair Constitutional and Admin Law Bar Assoc; *Books* Practise and Procedure at Industrial Tribunals (1986), Civil Actions Against the Police (2 edn 1992, 3 edn 2004), A Judicial Review Procedure (2 edn, 1996), Police Actions; a practical guide (2 edn, 1996), Law of Human Rights (2000); *Recreations* reading, theatre, cinema, travel; *Style*— Richard Clayton, Esq, QC; ✉ 4–5 Gray's Inn Square, London WC1R 5AH

CLAYTON, Robert; s of Colin Clayton, and Rose Ann Clayton; *b* 23 July 1970; *Educ* Wintringham Sch Grimsby, Grimsby Coll of Technol (BTEC); *m* 18 Sept 1999, Sara Louise, *née* Wilson; 2 da (Imogen Olive b 8 May 2001, Liberty Molly Clayton b 15 August 2004); *Career* commis chef Menage à Trois Restaurant 1988–89, demi chef Heath Lodge Hotel 1989–90, demi chef Chez Nico 1990–91, head chef Hunstrete House Hotel 1991–97, Priory Hotel Bath 1997–2005, Merchant Inns plc 2005–09, First Sight Estates and Clayton's Kitchen, Clayton's Kitchen Restaurant 2013; chef conslt and outside caterer; *Awards* finalist Chef of the Year 1994 and 1995, second place Roux Scholarship 1996 (finalist 1994), AA 3 Rosettes 1995 and 1996, Michelin Star 1996–; *Recreations* jogging, fly fishing, shooting; *Style*— Robert Clayton, Esq; ✉ 4 & 6 Pen Hill Road, Weston, Bath BA1 4ED (✆ 01225 311017, mobile 07870 156099, e-mail claytonfamily@hotmail.co.uk)

CLAYTON-SMITH, David Charles; s of late John Anthony Clayton-Smith, of Lichfield, Staffs, and Winifred Mary, *née* Elvy; *b* 5 November 1953; *Educ* Malvern Coll, Kingston Poly (BA), Dip Accounting and Fin; *m* 7 Nov 1987, Katharine Clare, da of Dr Owen Jones; 3

da (Philippa Clare b 11 July 1989, Eleanor Jane b 23 Dec 1990, Joanna Mary b 13 March 1997); *Career* Courage Ltd: md (Take Home Trade) 1987–88, exec dir sales and mktg 1989–91, gp exec dir mktg 1992–93; mktg and merchandise dir Do it All Ltd 1993–98, dir of mktg Boots the Chemist 1998–2000, mktg and merchandise dir Halfords Ltd 2000–03; chair Highwood Brewery Ltd 2008–11; dir: Handbag.com 1999–2006, Andrum Ltd 2007–, Health Insights Ltd 2009–14, Fairtrade Int; non-exec dir: Imagesound plc 2006–08 and 2014–16, Frimley Park Hospital 2013–16; chair: Fairtrade Fndn 2008–13, NHS Surrey 2010–13, Jupiter Design 2010–12, NHS Sussex 2012–13, KSS Academic Health Science Network 2013–, Thames Valley Housing Assoc 2014–, East Sussex Healthcare NHS Tst; dir Advtg Standards Bd of Fin (ASBOF) 1998–2004; memb Exec Ctee Advtg Assoc 1989–90; chm Ctee of Advtg Practice CAP 1996–98; memb Nat Cycling Strategy Bd 2002–03; Freeman: Worshipful Co of Brewers 1990, City of London 1992; fell Industry and Parl Tst 1998; fndr emeritus memb Marketing Gp GB, sr assoc memb RSM, fell Mktg Soc; *Recreations* family, gardening, motor racing; *Style—* David Clayton-Smith, Esq; ✉ 4 Winchester Close, Esher, Surrey KT10 8QH (☎ 07973 778821)

CLAYTON-WELCH, Prof Anthony Roy (Tony); s of Flt Lt Roy Hector Welch, AFC, AE, of Flamstead, Herts, and Barbara Joan, *née* Clayton; *b* 5 September 1942, Sleaford Grantham, Lincs; *Educ* St Albans Abbey Sch, Poly of Central London (DipArch), Carpenters Sch (scholarship); *m* 4 Feb 1967, Kathleen Margaret, da of Henry Samuel Norman, of Wembley Park, Middx; 1 s (Bruno b 20 Oct 1975), 1 da (Sophie b 27 Sept 1977); *Career* architect; TA Offr Trg Corps 1962–64; London ptnr Melich & Welch Florida USA 1970–74, fndn ptnr Renton Welch Partnership 1974–96; appointed church architect Diocesan Advsy Cncl (DAC) 1996–; adjudicator and ctee memb Royal Jubilee Tst and Prince's Tst; awards incl: Carpenters Award 1965, Civic Design Award 1987, 2002, 2003, 2004 and 2005, Educational Award 1988, Environment and Access Awards 1991, Heritage Trust Awards 2001, 2002, 2003, 2004 and 2006; educnl bldg advsr: DfEE, DOW, RBKC; vice-chm Local Bd Sch Govrs St John's Sch Stanmore, dir/tstee Bishop's Meadow Tst 2010; RIBA 1966, FInstD 1995; *Books* 3-D Structural Model Analysis of Space Frames (1967), Rationalised Constructions (1970), Herts CC Educational Building – An Appraisal 1942–70 (1986), Harmonic Proportion (2009); *Recreations* chess, astronomy, sub-tropical plant cultivation and landscaping, voice-overs; *Clubs* The Arts, Morton's; *Style—* Prof Tony Clayton-Welch, RIBA; ✉ The Milking Barn, Shackleford, Surrey GU8 6BU (☎ 01483 813823, e-mail twa_architects@btinternet.com)

CLEAL, Adam Anthony; *b* 10 March 1956; *Educ* Allhallows Sch, Univ of Leeds (LLB); *m* 11 Aug 1984, Noreen, da of George Monger; 2 s (Charles Anthony b 16 Aug 1986, George Hugo b 22 Aug 1992), 1 da (Harriet Catherine b 14 March 1989); *Career* trainee slr 1979–81, slr 1982–91, ptnr Allen & Overy LLP 1991– (head of real estate gp 2000–15); Freeman City of London; *Recreations* music, opera, fine wine, scuba diving, cycling; *Clubs* Reform, MCC; *Style—* Adam Cleal, Esq; ✉ Allen & Overy LLP, One Bishops Square, London E1 6AD (☎ 020 3088 0000, fax 020 3088 0088)

CLEARY, His Hon Judge Anthony Simon Lissant; s of late Bruce Cleary, and Patricia North, *née* Beardmore; *b* 21 January 1946, London; *Educ* Fettes, Univ of Sheffield (LLB); *m* 1 (m dis 1971), Georgina Clark; 2 da (Sophie b 1968, Alexia b 1969 (twin), 1 s (Damian b 1969 (twin); m 2, 30 Nov 1974, Carmel Catherine, *née* Briddon; 1 s (Dominic b 1988); *Career* admitted slr 1971; district judge 1986, recorder 1991, circuit judge (Midland Circuit) 2006–, dep High Court judge 2011–; tutor judge Judicial Studies Bd 1999–2010; lay clerk Coventry Cathedral 1986–; *Publications* The Family Court Practice (gen ed, 1993–), Nobody Comes (2014); *Recreations* choral singing, rifle shooting, gymnasium; *Clubs* Armonico Consort; *Style—* His Hon Judge Cleary; ✉ c/o Midland Circuit Office, Priory Courts, 33 Bull Street, Birmingham B4 6DW

CLEARY, (Anthony) Shaun; *m* Kathryn; 6 c; *Career* diplomat; South America Dept FCO 1989–90, political offr S Africa 1990–93, head NATO Team and Baltic/Balkans Team FCO 1994–97, budget environment and energy counsellor UK Delgn to the OECD Paris 1998–2002, dep head Aviation Maritime and Energy Dept FCO 2003–04, dep consul gen Basra 2004–05, head Capability Review Team and Spending Review Team FCO 2005–07, financial planning dir E Surrey NHS Tst 2007, asst dir of protocol and dep ldr Cabinet Office Review Team FCO 2008, acting high cmmr Fiji 2009, head Flu Crisis Unit Consular Crisis Gp FCO 2009, high cmmr to Mozambique 2010–14, dep head Counter Extremism Gp FCO 2015; *Style—* Mr Shaun Cleary; ✉ c/o FCO, King Charles Street, London SW1A 2AH

CLEAVE, Brian Elseley; CB (1994), Hon QC (1999); s of Walter Edward Cleave (d 1986), and Hilda Lillian, *née* Newman (d 1974); *b* 3 September 1939, Ilford, Essex; *Educ* Eastbourne Coll (Duke of Devonshire's scholar), Univ of Exeter (LLB, Lloyd Parry prize, Bracton prize), Kansas Univ, Univ of Manchester; *m* 10 Feb 1979, Celia Valentine, da of Maurice Lovel Burton Williams, MBE, and Patricia Cawood Williams; *Career* articled clerk Wilkinson, Howlett & Moorhouse 1963–66, student Coll of Law 1965–66, admitted slr 1966, asst slr Wilkinson, Howlett & Durham 1966–67; Solicitor's Office Inland Revenue: legal asst 1967–72, sr legal asst 1972–78, asst slr 1978–86, princ asst slr 1986–90, slr of Inland Revenue 1990–99; called to the Bar Gray's Inn 1999; sr legal advsr EU-Tacis Taxation Reform Project Moscow Phase 1 2000–02 and Phase 2 2003–05, sr legal advsr EU-Tacis Assistance to Tax Administration of Ukraine Project Kiev 2006–07, legal conslt to Govt of United Repub of Tanzania and Revolutionary Govt of Zanzibar 2008–09; memb Inst for Fiscal Studies; memb Int Fiscal Assoc; FRSA 1995; *Publications* The Impact of the OECD and UN Model Conventions on Bilateral Tax Treaties (contrib, 2012), Tax Rules in Non-Tax Agreements (contrib, 2012); various contributions to British Tax Review, European Taxation and Bulletin for International Taxation; *Recreations* travel, music, photography, theatre; *Style—* Brian Cleave, Esq, CB, QC

CLEAVER, Sir Anthony Brian; kt (1992); s of William Brian Cleaver (d 1969), and Dorothea Early Cleaver (d 1989); *b* 10 April 1938, London; *Educ* Berkhamsted Sch, Trinity Coll Oxford (MA); *m* 1, 1962, Mary Teresa, *née* Cotter (d 1999); 1 s (Paul Anthony b 31 Aug 1972), 1 da (Caroline b 14 Nov 1977); m 2, 2000, Jennifer Guise Lloyd Graham; *Career* IBM United Kingdom Ltd: trainee instr 1962, conslt systems engr 1968, branch mangr 1969; asst to vice-pres (devpt) IBM World Trade Corporation USA 1973–74; IBM UK: dist mangr 1974–76, sales dir 1976–77, divnl dir 1977–80; IBM Europe: gp dir 1980, vice-pres (mktg and servs) 1981–82; IBM UK: gen mangr 1982–86, chief exec 1986–92, chm 1990–94; chm: UK Atomic Energy Authy 1993–96, General Cable plc 1995–98 (non-exec dir 1994–95), AEA Technology plc 1996–99 (non-exec chm 1999–2001), The Strategic Partnership Ltd 1996–2000, MRC 1998–2006, The Baxi Partnership Ltd 1999–2000, IX Europe plc 1999–2007, SThree 2000–10, UK eUniversities Worldwide Ltd 2001–04, Working Links (Employment) Ltd 2003–08, Nuclear Decommissioning Authy 2004–07, Engineering UK (was ETB) 2007–10; non-exec dir: General Accident Fire and Life Assurance Corporation plc 1988–98, Smith & Nephew plc 1993–2002, The Cable Corporation 1995–97, Lockheed Martin Tactical Systems UK Ltd 1995–99, Lockheed Martin UK Ltd 1999–2007; dir Nat Computing Centre 1977–80; memb Univ of Oxford Devpt Prog Advsy Bd 1999–2004; memb Cncl: Templeton Coll Oxford 1982–93, Policy Studies Inst 1985–89, RIPA 1986–89; memb Bd: Centre for Econ & Environmental Devpt 1985–98 (dep chm 1989–98), Assoc for Business Sponsorship of the Arts 1986–98, American C of C 1987–90, ENO 1988–2000 (dep chm 1998–2000), Royal Coll of Music 1998–2007 (chm 1999–2007); chm Business in the Environment 1989–99, dep chm Business in the Community 1992–2000 (memb Pres's Ctee 1986–92); memb: BOTB 1988–91, Presidents' Ctee CBI 1988–92, Nat Trg Task Force 1989–92, ACBE 1991–93, NACETT 1994–98, Ctee on Standards in Public Life 1997–2003, Govt Panel for Sustainable Devpt 1998–2000, Singapore Br Business Cncl 1999–2000 and 2003–04; chm: RSA Inquiry into Tomorrow's Company 1992–95, Industrial Devpt Advsy Bd 1993–99, Independent Assessors of TECs 1994–98, Cncl for Excellence in Mgmnt and Leadership 2000–02, Asia Pacific Advsrs (Trade Ptnrs UK) 2000–03, Novia Financial plc 2007–; pres: Classical Assoc 1995–96, Involvement and Participation Assoc 1997–2002, Inst of Mgmnt 1999–2000, Business Commitment to the Environment 2000–13; chm Nat Environment Research Cncl 2014–; chm of govrs Birkbeck Coll London 1989–98; UN Environment Prog Global 500 Roll of Honour 1989; Worshipful Co of Information Technologists 1987 (Liveryman 1994), Worshipful Co of Musicians 2003 (Master 2013); Hon LLD: Univ of Nottingham 1991, Univ of Portsmouth 1996; Hon DSc: Cranfield Univ 1995, Univ of Hull 2002, City Univ 2002; Hon DTech London Met Univ 2003, Hon DUniv Middlesex Univ 2003; hon fell Trinity Coll Oxford 1989, hon fell Birkbeck Coll London 1999, fell City and Guilds Inst 2004, hon fell Univ of Central Lancs 2007; FBCS 1976, FCIM (currently vice-pres), Hon FCIPS 1996, FRCM 2009, Hon FREng 2011, Hon FICE 2013; *Recreations* music, opera, cricket, reading; *Clubs* RAC, MCC, Lord's Taverners, Serpentine Swimmers, Athenaeum; *Style—* Sir Anthony Cleaver; ✉ e-mail a.cleaver1@btinternet.com

CLEESE, Alyce Faye; *née* McBride; da of Albert Clinton McBride (d 1973), and Frances Fay, *née* Mitchell (d 1962); *b* 28 October 1944; *Educ* Oklahoma State Univ USA (BSc), Baylor Univ (MA, MSc), Univ of London Inst of Educn (DPMC), Tavistock Inst; *m* 1, 22 Jan 1966, Martin Davis Eichelberger, Jr, s of Martin Davis Eichelberger; 2 s (Martin Davis III b 28 Sept 1969, Clinton Charles b 14 March 1973); m 2, 28 Dec 1992, John Marwood Cleese, *qv*; *Career* teacher secdy sch 1962–69, teaching asst to Dean of Special Educn Baylor Univ 1974–75, educnl psychologist Waco Ind Sch Dist Texas 1975–78, child psychotherapist Notre Dame Clinic 1981–87; teacher in secdy sch for emotionally disturbed children 1980–83, teacher of children with med and emotional problems ILEA 1983–84; child psychotherapist: Tavistock Clinic, Chalcot Sch; educnl psychologist Educn Records Bureau NY; psychotherapist and psychologist: American Sch of London, American Embassy, Tasis Sch Thorpe Park Surrey; in private practice: Holland Park, Kensington and Chelsea; currently psychological conslt Archer Films and Lifetime Prodns; visiting sr tutor Massachusetts Gen Hosp Harvard Med Educn Dept of Psychiatry 2005–11; founding memb Jr League of London 1978; memb: Republicans Abroad, Int Jr League Assoc of Child Psychotherapy 1986, Ctee Freud Museum Limited Edn Print Portfolio Display 1997, Visitors' Ctee Leonardis Klinik (site tours of HIV clinic and special schools in Ethiopia) 2000; relief worker Direct Relief to Ethiopia 2001; tstee Esalen Inst Big Sur CA 2005–2010, tstee Tarongo Zoo Sydney Australia 2006–09; co-fndr lunchtime lectures RGS (fndr memb and conslt), co-fndr Sunday lectures Wine Cask Santa Barbara 2001–02; judge Books for a Better Life Award Publisher's Guild 2000–02; Leadership Award for the Advancement of Mental Health Sch of Educn Oklahoma State Univ 2006, Distinguished Alumnae Hall of Fame Oklahoma State Univ 2007, Award for Outstanding Contributions in the Advancement of Mental Health Harvard Med Sch & Massachusetts Gen Hosp Psychiatry Service Endowment for Psychotherapies 2007; ABPS 1980, fell American Psychological Assoc 1980, fell American Med Psychotherapist Assoc 1987, memb RSM 1988, assoc fell Br Psychological Soc 1988; *Publications* Comparative Education of Gifted Children in France (1979), Corporate Education of Gifted Children in the USSR (1979), A Case Study of Maladjusted Children in a London Day School (1983), How to Manage your Mother (1999, Publisher's Guild Award, MS Soc Winner); also Another Revolutionary – A Case Study of Psychotherapy With a Five Year Old Rastafarian Boy; Santa Barbara Magazine profiles; *Recreations* yoga; *Clubs* Arts, Groucho; *Style—* Mrs Alyce Faye Eichelberger Cleese; ✉ website www.alycefaye.com

CLEESE, John Marwood; s of Reginald Cleese (né Cheese), and Muriel Cleese; *b* 27 October 1939; *Educ* Downing Coll Cambridge (MA); *m* 1, 1968 (m dis 1978), Connie Booth; 1 da (Cynthia); m 2, 1981 (m dis 1990), Barbara Trentham; 1 da (Camilla); m 3, 1992 (m dis 2008), Alyce Faye Eichelberger, *qv*, formerly w of David Eichelberger; 2 step s; m 4, 2012, Jennifer Wade; *Career* comedian, writer and actor; started making jokes professionally 1963, started on British TV 1966; fndr and former dir Video Arts Ltd; Hon LLD Univ of St Andrews, A D White prof-at-large Cornell Univ 1999–; *Television* series incl: The Frost Report 1966, At Last the 1948 Show 1967, Monty Python's Flying Circus 1969–73, Fawlty Towers 1975, Look at the State We're In! (BBC) 1995, The Human Face 2001; *Films* incl: Interlude 1968, The Magic Christian 1969, And Now For Something Completely Different 1971, Romance with a Double Bass 1974, Monty Python and the Holy Grail 1975, Life of Brian 1979, Privates on Parade 1982, The Meaning of Life 1983, Silverado 1985, Clockwise 1986, A Fish Called Wanda 1988, Erik the Viking, Frankenstein 1993, Jungle Book 1994, The Wind In The Willows 1996, Fierce Creatures 1997, George Of The Jungle 1997, Parting Shots 1998, The Out-of-Towners 1999, The World is Not Enough 1999, Isn't She Great 2000, Harry Potter and the Philosopher's Stone 2001, Rat Race 2001, Die Another Day 2002, Harry Potter and the Chamber of Secrets 2002; *Books* Families and How to Survive Them (with Dr Robin Skynner, 1983), The Golden Skits of Wing Commander Muriel Volestrangler FRHS and Bar (1984), The Complete Fawlty Towers (with Connie Booth, 1989), Life and How to Survive It (with Dr Robin Skynner, 1993), The Human Face (with Brian Bates, 2001); *Recreations* gluttony and sloth; *Style—* John Cleese, Esq; ✉ c/o David Wilkinson Associates, 115 Hazlebury Road, London SW6 2LX (☎ 020 7371 5188, fax 020 7371 5161)

CLEGG, Rt Hon Nicholas William Peter (Nick); PC (2008), MP; s of Nicholas P Clegg, and Hermance Eulalie, *née* Van den Wall Bake; *b* 7 January 1967; *Educ* Westminster, Robinson Coll Cambridge (MA), Univ of Minnesota, Coll of Euro Bruges (MA); *m* Sept 2000, Miriam, *née* González Durántez; 3 s; *Career* trainee journalist The Nation magazine NY 1990, conslt GJW Govt Relations London 1992–93, EC official Relations with New Independent States 1994–96, memb EC Cabinet Office of Lord Brittan of Spennithorne 1996–99, MEP (Lib Dem) E Midlands 1999–2004, MP (Lib Dem) Sheffield Hallam 2005–; Lib Dem spokesperson for: FCO 2005–06, home affrs 2006–07; ldr Lib Dems 2007–15, dep Prime Minister and Lord Pres of the Cncl 2010–15; David Thomas Prize FT 1993; *Recreations* skiing, theatre; *Style—* The Rt Hon Nick Clegg, MP; ✉ House of Commons, London SW1A 0AA

CLEGG, Simon Paul; CBE (2006, OBE 2001); s of Peter Vernon Clegg, and Patricia Anne Clegg; *b* 11 August 1959, Harlington, Beds; *Educ* Stowe, RMA Sandhurst; *m* Hilary Anne, da of Brig John Davis; 1 da (Lucinda Elizabeth b 6 April 1990), 1 s (Toby James b 21 Jan 1992); *Career* army offr RHA 1981–89; dep gen sec BOA 1989–97, chief exec European Youth Olympic Games (Bath) 1995, chief exec BOA 1997–2009, chief exec Ipswich Town FC 2009–13, md Zeus Int Mgmnt 2014–; non-exec dir: London Olympic Bid Co 2003–05, London Olympic Games Organising Ctee 2005–09; exec bd memb BOA 2013–; conslt Madrid 2020 Olympic bid 2013–, chief operating offr Baku 2015 Organising Ctee 2014–15, chief operating offr Expo 2020 Dubai 2016–; mangr Br Biathlon Team 1984–87; Olympic and Olympic Winter Games: Team GB official 1988, dep chef de mission Team GB 1992, 1994 and 1996, chef de mission Team GB 1998, 2000, 2002, 2004, 2006 and 2008; chm GB Badminton 2013–; Br Sports Journalists Assoc JL Manning Award 2008; hon doctorate Univ Campus Suffolk 2011; Dostlug Order (Azerbaijan) 2015; *Recreations* skiing, golf; *Clubs* Cavalry and Guards', Leander; *Style—* Simon Clegg, Esq, CBE

CLEGG, William; QC (1991); s of Peter Hepworth Clegg, and Sheila, *née* Needham; *b* 5 September 1949; *Educ* St Thomas Moore HS for Boys, Univ of Bristol (LLB); *m* 1, 5 Oct

1974 (m dis 2002), Wendy Doreen, da of George Chard; 1 s (Peter William Christopher), 1 da (Joanna Sheila); m 2, 2008, Gay, da of Edward Hutchings; *Career* called to the Bar Gray's Inn 1972, in practice SE Circuit, memb SE Circuit Ctee 1990–, recorder of the Crown Court 1992–, head of chambers 1995–, chm Essex Bar Mess 1998–2001; *Recreations* squash, cricket; *Clubs* Sudbury Racquets, Garrick, Our Society, MCC; *Style—* William Clegg, Esq, QC; ✉ 2 Bedford Row, London WC1R 4BU (☎ 020 7440 8888, fax 020 7242 1738)

CLEGG LITTLER, George Gordon Vysokovsky; s of late George Clegg Littler, OBE, TD, of Ibiza, Spain, and Barbara Noble Meidell-Andersen, *née* Gordon, of Bergen, Norway; *b* 1 May 1950; *Educ* Bradfield, Coll of Law; *m* 1, 25 April 1981 (m dis 1986), Emma, da of Sir John Greville Stanley Beith, KCMG; m 2, 19 May 1990, Sarah Long, *qv*, da of Viscount Long; 1 s (Alexander George Richard b 17 Jan 1996), 1 da (Xenia Charlotte Marina b 15 April 1999); *Career* slr; ptnr Simmons & Simmons 1985–2015 (joined 1981); memb Law Soc; memb Exec Ctee Supporting Wounded Veterans; *Recreations* contemporary art, association football, my garden; *Clubs* Brooks's; *Style—* George Littler, Esq; ✉ 20 Oakley Gardens, London SW3 5QG (☎ 020 7352 3555)

CLEGG LITTLER, Hon Mrs Sarah; *see:* Long, Sarah Victoria

CLEMENS, Prof Michael J (Mike); s of Thomas Truscott Clemens, of Camborne, Cornwall, and Doris Edith, *née* Osborne; *b* 25 May 1947, Camborne, Cornwall; *Educ* Truro Sch, Univ of Bristol (BSc, Albert Fry meml prize for sci), Sch of Biological Scis Univ of Sussex (DPhil); *m* 17 Oct 1970, Virginia Marion, da of late Victor James Pain; *Career* Beit meml research fell Nat Inst for Med Research London 1970–73, research assoc and Fulbright-Hays travel scholar Dept of Biology MIT 1973–74, Royal Soc Mr and Mrs John Jaffé fell Div of Biochemistry Nat Inst for Med Research London 1974–76; St George's Hosp Med Sch: lectr Dept of Biochemistry 1976–78, sr lectr 1978–87, reader 1987–89, prof of biochemistry Div of Biochemistry Dept of Cellular and Molecular Scis 1990–91, prof of biochemistry and immunology 1991–96 and 1997–2007, hon prof 2007–; sr research fell in biochemistry Sch of Life Scis Univ of Sussex 2007–11 (visiting prof fell 2011–); scientific sec MRC Working Pty on Interferon in Cancer Therapy 1975–80; external examiner (2 MB course) Univ of Cambridge 1998–2001, PhD examiner numerous UK univs, assessor Aust Research Cncl; memb Editorial Bd: Int Jl of Biochemistry and Cell Biology 1995–2005, Jl of Interferon and Cytokine Research 1996–2009; managing ed Euro Jl of Biochemistry 1988–97; Cancer Research Campaign Career Devpt Award 1980–86; chm Mgmnt Ctee Brighton Early Music Festival; memb: Biochemical Soc, Int Soc for Interferon and Cytokine Research, American Assoc for Cancer Research; *Books* Cytokines (Medical Perspective Series) (eds A P Rea and T Brown, 1991), Protein Phosphorylation in Cell Growth Regulation (ed, 1996); also author of over 150 published scientific papers and review articles in learned jls; *Recreations* performing vocal and instrumental music of the Renaissance and Early Baroque (memb Brighton Consort and E Sussex Bach Choir), jazz saxophone, photography, gardening, walking; *Style—* Prof Mike Clemens; ✉ School of Life Sciences, University of Sussex, Falmer, Brighton BN1 9QG (☎ 01273 872680, *Website* www.sussex.ac.uk/profiles/33914, www.bremf.org.uk/index.htm)

CLEMENT, John; s of Frederick Clement, and Alice Eleanor Clement; *b* 18 May 1932; *Educ* Bishop's Stortford Coll; *m* 1956, Elisabeth Anne, *née* Emery; 1 da (Anne Catherine Bloomfield b 4 June 1957), 2 s (John Emery b 6 April 1959, Richard Frederick b 10 Dec 1965); *Career* Howard Dairies Westcliff on Sea 1949–64, United Dairies London Ltd 1964–69, asst md Rank Leisure Services Ltd 1969–73, chm and chief exec Unigate plc 1976–91; chm: The Littlewoods Organisation plc 1982–90, Culpho Consultants 1991–, Tuddenham Hall Foods 1991–, Anglo American Insurance Co Ltd 1993–94 (dir 1991–94), Ransomes plc 1993–98, King's Coll Cambridge (business expansion scheme) 1993–98, Nat Car Auctions 1995–98, Dresdner RCM Second Endowment Policy Tst plc 1995– (dir 1993–); dir: Eagle Star Holdings 1981–84, NV Verenigde Bedrijven Nutricia 1981–92, Jarvis Hotels Ltd 1994–2004; memb Securities Investment Bd 1986–89; chm: Children's Liver Disease Fndn 1982–95, Br Liver Tst 1992–99; chm of govrs Framlingham Coll 1991–2001 (govr 1982–2001); High Sheriff Suffolk 2000–01; FIGD 1979; *Recreations* shooting, sailing, bridge, rugby, tennis; *Clubs* Cumberland Lawn Tennis, Royal Harwich Yacht, Royal Danish Yacht; *Style—* John Clement, Esq; ✉ Tuddenham Hall, Tuddenham, Ipswich, Suffolk IP6 9DD (☎ 01473 785099, e-mail johnclement@keme.co.uk)

CLEMENT, Dr Michele Ingrid; da of Maj Joseph Cyril Clement (d 1984), and Joyce Mona Clement (d 2007); *b* 18 September 1951; *Educ* Queenswood Sch, UCL (BSc), UCH (MB BS); *Family* 2 s (Edward Harry Clement Corn b 1983, Charles Joseph Clement Corn b 1985); *Career* med qualifications and house post UCH; jr med posts: King's Coll Hosp 1977–78, UCH 1978–79; dermatology trg: St John's Hosp 1980, King's Coll Hosp 1980–87; conslt dermatologist Bromley Hosps NHS Tst 1987–2014; FRCP 1994 (MRCP 1978); *Books* Topical Steroids for Skin Disorders (1987); *Style—* Dr Michele Clement

CLEMENT-JONES, Baron (Life Peer UK 1998), of Clapham in the London Borough of Lambeth; Timothy Francis Clement-Jones; CBE (1988); s of Maurice Llewelyn Clement-Jones (d 1988), of Haywards Heath, W Sussex, and Margaret Jean, *née* Hudson; *b* 26 October 1949; *Educ* Haileybury, Trinity Coll Cambridge (MA); *m* 1, 14 June 1973, Dr Vicky Veronica Clement-Jones (d 1987), fndr of Cancerbackup (now merged with MacMillan Cancer Support), da of Teddy Yip, of Hong Kong; m 2, 15 July 1994, Jean Roberta Whiteside; 1 s (Harry Alexander b 1 March 1998); *Career* slr; articled clerk Coward Chance 1972–74, assoc Joynson-Hicks & Co 1974–76, corp lawyer Letraset International Ltd 1976–80, asst head (later head) Legal Servs LWT Ltd 1980–83, legal dir retailing div Grand Met plc 1984–86, gp co sec and legal advsr Kingfisher plc 1986–95; dir Political Context Ltd 1996–99, chm Context Gp Ltd 1997–2009; ptnr Independent Corporate Mentoring (ICM) 1996–99; DLA Piper (int law firm): co-chm global govt rels practice 1999–2009, ptnr int business rels 2010–12, London managing ptnr 2011–; vice-pres Eurocommerce (Euro Retail Fedn) 1992–95; chm: Assoc of Lib Lawyers 1982–86, Lib Pty 1986–88; Liberal Democrats: chm Fed Fin Ctee 1991–98, dir Euro Election Campaign 1992–94, vice-chm Gen Election Group 1994–97, chm Lib Dem London Mayoral Assembly Campaign 2000 and 2004, federal treas 2005–10; House of Lords: Lib Dem spokesman on Health 1998–2004, Lib Dem spokesman on culture, media and sport 2004–10, vice-chm All-Pty Autism Gp 2000–10, dep chm All-Pty China Gp 2005–, vice-chm All-Pty Turkey Gp 2010–, vice-chm All-Pty UAE Gp 2010–, memb Communications Select Ctee 2010–15, Lib Dem spokesman on creative industries 2015–, memb Nat Policy on the Built Environment Select Ctee 2015–; chm Crime Concern Advsy Bd 1981–95, chm Lambeth Crime Prevention Tst 2004–09; memb Ctee 48 Gp Club; chm of tstees Treehouse (sch and centre of excellence for children with autism) 2000–08, tstee Cancer BACUP 1986–2008, pres Ambitious about Autism (formerly Treehouse) 2010–, tstee Barbican Centre Tst 2012–; chm Cncl Sch of Pharmacy Univ of London 2008–12, memb Cncl UCL 2012, memb Cncl Heart of the City 2013–; Freeman City of London 2012; memb Law Soc, FRSA, fell PRCA, fell CIPR; *Recreations* walking, running, travelling, reading, eating, talking, the arts; *Clubs* Arts; *Style—* Lord Clement-Jones, CBE; ✉ House of Lords, London SW1A 0PW (☎ 020 7219 3660, e-mail clementjonest@parliament.uk)

CLEMENTI, Sir David Cecil; kt (2004); s of Air Vice Marshal Cresswell Montagu Clementi, CB, CBE, and Susan, da of late Sir (Edward) Henry Pelham, KCB; gs of Sir Cecil Clementi, GCMG (d 1947); *b* 25 February 1949; *Educ* Winchester, Univ of Oxford (MA), Harvard Business Sch (MBA); *m* 23 Sept 1972, Sarah Louise (Sally), da of Dr Anthony Beach Cowley; 1 da (Anna b 26 Nov 1976), 1 s (Tom b 17 April 1979); *Career* with Arthur Andersen & Co 1970–73; qualified as CA 1973; Kleinwort Benson Ltd: joined 1975, dir 1981, chief exec 1994–97, vice-chm 1997; dep govr Bank of England 1997–2002; chm: Prudential plc 2002–08, King's Cross Central (partnership to develop 67-acre Central London scheme) 2008–, World First 2011–, Virgin Money Hldgs 2011–15; non-exec dir Rio Tinto plc 2003–10; tstee ROH 2006–14; memb Worshipful Co of Mercers; *Recreations* sailing, ballet; *Clubs* Royal Yacht Sqdn; *Style—* Sir David Clementi; ✉ Virgin Money, 1 Eagle Place, London SW1Y 6AF (☎ 020 7111 0096)

CLEMENTS, Nicholas David Beckwith (Nick); s of Desmond Lyle Clements (d 2000), of Wells, Somerset, and Rosemary Jill, *née* Beckwith; *b* 11 November 1958; *Educ* Rossall Sch, Liverpool John Moores Univ; *m* 7 Sept 1996, Michaela, *née* Rosner; 1 s (Luke Beckwith b 2001); *Career* buyer Transocean Gp 1979–81, media planner/buyer Tony Rowse Media 1981–85, sr account mangr Foote Cone and Belding 1985–87, client servs dir/int business dir S P Lintas 1987–95, int bd account dir Bates Dorland 1995–99, ceo Atlas Advertising Ltd 1999, former global dir JWT, currently business devpt dir Barrett Howe plc; tstee CRISIS; MIPA, memb Mktg Soc, memb D&AD; *Recreations* cricket, golf, riding; *Clubs* Buck's, MCC; *Style—* Nick Clements, Esq

CLEMENTS, Paul Michael; s of Stanley Clements, and Edna, *née* Garber; *b* 29 April 1953; *Educ* Haberdashers' Aske's, Univ of Birmingham (LLB); *m* 1, 4 June 1983 (m dis 1995), Pamela Anne, da of Robert David Poulton Hughes; 1 s (Simon Lewis b 11 June 1985); m 2, 1 June 1996 (m dis 1999), Melinda, da of John Pinfold; m 3, 7 May 2005, Elaine, da of George Scribens; *Career* admitted slr 1977; litigation asst Bird & Bird 1977–79; RadcliffesLeBrasseur (and predecessor firms): litigation asst 1979–80, salaried ptnr 1980–84, equity ptnr 1985–2004, head Litigation Dept 1988–89 and 1991–2004, managing ptnr 1989–91, head Commercial Dispute Resolution Dept 2002–04; head of dispute resolution Rooks Rider 2004–09, ptnr Sprecher Grier Halberstam LLP 2009–; recorder SE Circuit 1997– (asst recorder 1992–97); memb: Law Soc, London Slrs' Litigation Assoc; Liveryman Worshipful Co of Broderers; *Recreations* amateur drama participant, rugby, opera, classical music; *Style—* Paul M Clements, Esq

CLEMMOW, Richard Gordon Menzies; s of David Clemmow, and Frances Clemmow, of Cambs; *b* 25 June 1955; *Educ* Sevenoaks Sch, Jesus Coll Cambridge (BA); *m* 19 December 1995, Jana Bennett, *qv*, da of late Gordon Bennett; 2 c (Alexandra b 1 August 1991, Skomer b 26 May 1994); *Career* researcher House of Commons 1981–82, offr London Borough of Islington 1982–83; BBC: general trainee 1983–85, with News and Current Affrs Dept (responsibilities incl This Week Next Week, Newsnight, Panorama) 1985–86; with ITN (script writer, chief sub-ed and prog ed Channel 4 News) 1986–92, BBC 1992–2002 (dep ed Newsnight, ed daily parly progs, ed Live Budget/Conference coverage, dep head Political Progs Dept, managing ed News Progs Dept, head of News Progs Dept), dir of factual programmes Carlton 2002–04, head of factual progs TWI 2004–06, md Juniper 2006–; winner of Best Topical Feature RTS Awards 1989; *Recreations* mountain climbing, cycling, cooking; *Style—* Richard Clemmow, Esq; ✉ Juniper, 52 Lant Street, London SE1 1RB (☎ 020 7407 9292, fax 020 74707 3940, website www.junipertv.co.uk)

CLEMMOW, Simon Phillip; s of Phillip Charles Clemmow, of Cambridge, and Joan Alicia, *née* Watkins; *b* 30 June 1956, Cambridge; *Educ* Perse Sch Cambridge, Univ of Reading (BA); *m* 1987, Elizabeth Danuta, *née* Kaminska; 1 s (Nicholas Kazik b 1989), 1 step da (Eva Charlotte b 1972); *Career* account planner GGT 1983–88, co-fndr Simons Palmer Denton Clemmow & Johnson 1988 (co sold to Omnicom 1997), exec planning dir TBWA GGT Simons Palmer (later TBWALondon) 1997–99, ceo TBWALondon 1999–2001 (also memb TBWAWorldwide Bd), co-fndr Clemmow Hornby Inge (now CHI & Partners) 2001; *Recreations* restoring old properties, researching and writing local history, playing the drums in a band; *Clubs* The Union, Brocket Hall; *Style—* Simon Clemmow, Esq; ✉ CHI & Partners, 7–9 Rathbone Street, London W1T 1LY (☎ 020 7462 8500, fax 020 7462 8501, mobile 07764 199666, e-mail simon.clemmow@chiandpartners.com)

CLEOBURY, Nicholas; s of Dr John Frank Cleobury, of Chartham, Kent, and Brenda Julie, *née* Randall; bro of Stephen Cleobury, *qv*; *b* 23 June 1950; *Educ* King's Sch Worcester, Worcester Coll Oxford (MA); *m* 4 Nov 1978, Heather Noelle, da of Noel Kay (d 1980); 1 s (Simon Randall b 23 Oct 1979), 1 da (Sophie Noelle b 12 Dec 1981); *Career* asst organist: Chichester Cathedral 1971–72, Christ Church Oxford 1972–76, conductor Schola Cantorum of Oxford 1973–77; chorus master Glyndebourne Opera 1977–79, asst dir BBC Singers 1978–80, princ conductor of opera RAM 1981–87, dir Aquarius 1983–92, artistic dir Cambridge Festival 1992, music dir Broomhill 1990–94; 1980–: int conductor working throughout UK, Europe, Scandinavia, USA, Canada, Australia, Singapore and Hong Kong, regular TV and BBC Radio and Prom and Classic FM appearances, numerous commercial recordings; princ guest conductor Gävle Orch (Sweden) 1989–91, princ conductor Britten Sinfonia 1991–2004, guest conductor Zurich Opera House 1992–2006, music dir Oxford Bach Choir 1998–2015, artistic advsr Berkshire Choral Festival 2002–08, artistic dir Mozart Ways (Canterbury) 2003–07, assoc dir Orchestra of the Swan 2004–08, princ conductor John Armitage Meml (JAM) 2006–, fndr princ conductor Sounds New 2007–14 (artistic dir 1997–2007), artistic dir Mid Wales Opera 2009–17, artistic dir Britten in Oxford 2013, head Opera Queensland Conservatorium Brisbane 2016–; lectr, teacher and speaker, tstee Schola Cantorum Oxford, tstee YouthMusic; hon fell Christ Church Univ Canterbury; FRCO 1968 (Limpus Prize); Hon RAM 1985; *Recreations* theatre, cricket, reading, walking, food, wine; *Clubs* Lord's Taverners, MCC; *Style—* Mr Nicholas Cleobury; ✉ e-mail nicholascleobury@btinternet.com

CLEOBURY, Stephen John; CBE (2009); s of late Dr John Frank Cleobury, of Chartham, Canterbury, and late Brenda Julie, *née* Randall; bro of Nicholas Cleobury, *qv*; *b* 31 December 1948; *Educ* King's Sch Worcester, St John's Coll Cambridge (MA, MusB); *Children* 4 da (Suzannah Helen b 1973, Laura Elizabeth b 1976, Olivia Eleanor b 2003, Frances Johanna b 2009); *Career* organist St Matthew's Church Northampton, dir of Music Northampton GS 1971–74, sub-organist Westminster Abbey 1974–78, master of music Westminster Cathedral 1979–82, fell, organist and dir of music King's Coll Cambridge 1982–, conductor Cambridge Univ Musical Soc 1983–2016, chief conductor BBC Singers 1995–2006 (conductor laureate 2006–); also works in Europe, America and Australasia, regular TV and radio performances; recordings with EMI, Decca Records, Signum, Priory, Columns Classics, Collins Classics and King's Coll; pres: Inc Assoc of Organists 1985–87, Cathedral Organists' Assoc 1988–90, Royal Coll of Organists 1990–92 (hon sec 1981–90), Friends of Cathedral Music 2016–, Herbert Howells Soc 2016–; Hon DMus Anglia Ruskin Univ; memb Advsy Bd Royal Sch of Church Music 1981–2007; memb ISM, FRCO 1968, FRCM, FRSCM 2008, FGCM; *Recreations* reading; *Style—* Stephen Cleobury, Esq, CBE; ✉ King's College, Cambridge CB2 1ST (☎ 01223 331224, fax 01223 331890, e-mail choir@kings.cam.ac.uk)

CLEREY, (Christopher) Kevin Nelson; s of Colin Charlton Clerey (d 1996), of Guernsey, CI, and Margaret Elizabeth, *née* Nelson (d 2006); *b* 2 February 1957; *Educ* Sedbergh (Capt running VIII), Bristol Poly; *m* 3 Oct 1981, Amanda Jean, da of Ronald Charles Houslip (d 2008); 2 s (Duncan Christopher Houslip b 18 May 1983, David Alasdair b 16 Sept 1985), 1 da (Helen Jean Alice b 19 July 1990); *Career* Coopers & Lybrand 1976–77, EDG (Europe) Ltd 1977–78; Credit Suisse Trust Ltd Guernsey: joined 1981, dir 1985–, md 1990–94, chm and ceo 1997–2009; md: Credit Suisse Trust Switzerland 1994–2009, Credit Suisse Trust Holdings Ltd 1994–2006, IPG Switzerland GmbH 2012; dir: Credit Suisse Fund Administration 1988–2005, Credit Suisse Trust Ltd IOM 1988–2009, Credit Suisse Trust Ltd Gibraltar 1991–97, Inreska Insurance 1992–2000, Credit Suisse Trust Ltd Bahamas 1999–2009, Credit Suisse Trust Singapore 2001–09; fndr Clerey Assocs of Switzerland 2010; co sec Guernsey Colour Laboratories 1981–97; sec: Guernsey Branch Inst of Chartered Secs 1981–85, Old Sedberghians Club (CI Branch) 1992–94; FCIS 1983,

MInstD 1991, TEP 1998; *Recreations* fell and alpine walking, tennis, video editing, genealogy, skiing, cycling; *Clubs* Old Sedberghians, Klosters Tennis; *Style—* Kevin Clerey, Esq; ✉ Bildweg 16, 7250 Klosters, Switzerland (e-mail kevin@clerey.com)

CLERK OF PENICUIK, Sir Robert Maxwell; 11 Bt (NS 1679), of Penicuik, Midlothian; OBE (1995), DL (1995); s of Sir John Dutton Clerk, 10 Bt, CBE, VRD (d 2002), and Evelyn Elizabeth, *née* Robertson; *b* 3 April 1945; *Educ* Winchester, Univ of London (BSc); *m* 1970, Felicity Faye, yr da of George Collins, of Bampton, Oxon; 1 da (Julia Elizabeth b 1973), 2 s (George Napier b 1975, Edward James b 1986); *Career* ptnr Smiths Gore chartered surveyors; Lord-Lt Midlothian (2013); Brig Queen's Body Guard for Scotland (Royal Co of Archers); *Recreations* field sports, landscape gardening, beekeeping; *Clubs* New (Edinburgh); *Style—* Sir Robert M Clerk, Bt, OBE

CLEUGH, Christopher Joseph (Chris); s of Leslie Major Cleugh, of Crosby, Liverpool, and Frances Mary, *née* Ferguson; *b* 15 May 1952; *Educ* St Mary's Coll Crosby, BSc, Univ of Hull (MSc); *m* 29 June 1974, Christina Linda (Tina), da of late Christy Dorman, of Castleknock, Dublin; 2 s (Damien Paul b 18 Nov 1976, Gerard Norman b 23 July 1979), 2 da (Francesca Margaret b 11 April 1978, Carmel Linda b 8 June 1981); *Career* asst sci teacher St Kevin's RC Comp Kirkby 1975–76; St Mary's Coll Crosby: chemistry and maths teacher 1976–86, head of sixth form and dep headmaster 1986–93, actg headmaster 1991; headmaster: St Anselm's Coll Birkenhead 1993–2001, St Benedict's Sch Ealing 2002–; chm Catholic Independent Schs Conference 2014–16; memb: SHA 1989, HMC 1993; chm of tstees St Mary's Coll Crosby, govr St Columba's Coll St Albans 2009–; memb St Vincent de Paul Soc; BP International Chemicals Prize 1972; JP: Wirral 2000–01, Ealing 2002–12 and supplementary list 2012–; *Recreations* cycling, reading, walking; *Clubs* East India; *Style—* Chris Cleugh, Esq; ✉ St Benedict's School, 54 Eaton Rise, Ealing, London W5 2ES (☎ 020 8862 2010, fax 020 8862 2007, e-mail ccleugh@stbenedicts.org.uk)

CLEVERDON, Dame Julia Charity; DCVO (2008, CVO 2003), CBE (1996); (Mrs John Garnett); da of Douglas Cleverdon (d 1987), of London, and Elinor Nest Lewis (d 2003); *b* 19 April 1950; *Educ* Camden Sch for Girls, Newnham Coll Cambridge (BA); *m* 1, 30 June 1973 (m dis), Martin Ollard; m 2, 3 April 1985, (William) John Poulton Maxwell Garnett, CBE (d 1997), s of Maxwell Garnett (d 1960); 2 da (Charity b 1982, Victoria b 1985); *Career* dir of educn The Industrial Soc 1981–87; Business in the Community: md 1988–91, chief exec 1992–2008, vice-pres 2008–; dir Julia Cleverdon Ltd; special advsr Prince's Charities 2008–, chair Teachfirst, bd tstee NCVO, chair Newnham Campaign Advsy Bd, chair RWE NPower Corporate Responsibility Ctee; *Recreations* gardening, cooking, junk shops; *Style—* Dame Julia C Cleverdon, DCVO, CBE; ✉ 8 Alwyne Road, London N1 2HH

CLEVERLY, James; TD, MP; *b* 4 September 1969, Lewisham, London; *Educ* Thames Valley Univ; *Career* memb London Assembly GLA (Cons) London 2008–, ambass for youth London Mayor's Office 2009–10, chm London Waste and Recycling Bd 2010–12, chm London Fire and Emergency Planning Authy 2012–15; chm London Local Resilience Forum 2012–15; MP (Cons) Braintree 2015–; *Clubs* Carlton; *Style—* James Cleverly, TD, MP; ✉ GLA, City Hall, The Queen's Walk, London SE1 2AA (e-mail james.cleverly@london.gov.uk); House of Commons, London SW1A 0AA (☎ 020 7219 3000, e-mail james.cleverly.mp@parliament.uk)

CLEWS, Michael Graham; s of late Reginald Alan Frederick Clews, of Bristol, and Alwine Annie, *née* Adams; *b* 11 October 1944; *Educ* Kingswood GS, Oxford Sch of Architecture (DipArch); *m* 24 July 1971, Heather Jane, da of late Douglas Charles Sharratt, of Coventry; 2 da (Camilla b 1976, Helena b 1985), 2 s (Charles b 1978, Jonathan b 1983 d 1984); *Career* architect; fndr ptnr Clews Architectural Partnership (now Acanthus Clews Architects) 1972–; works incl historic buildings: Champneys, Sulgrave Manor Visitors' Centre; conslt to DOE on historic buildings 1984–87 (historic buildings survey Oxfordshire, Warwickshire and Northamptonshire); pilot project for computerisation of historic building records for English Heritage; Oxford diocesian surveyor; architect to Llandaff and Coventry Cathedrals; ARIBA; *Recreations* sailing, golf; *Style—* Michael Clews, Esq; ✉ Acanthus Clews Architects, Acanthus House, 57 Hightown Road, Banbury, Oxfordshire OX16 9BE

CLIFF, Prof Andrew David; s of Alfred Cliff (d 1965), and Annabel, *née* McQuade (d 1975); *b* 26 October 1943; *Educ* Grimsby Wintringham Boys' GS, King's Coll London (state scholar, BA), Northwestern Univ Illinois (MA), Univ of Bristol (PhD, DSc 1982); *m* 1964, Margaret, da of Arthur Blyton; 3 s (Ross Andrew b 6 Sept 1966, Michael Peter b 28 July 1968, Timothy Edward b 12 April 1972); *Career* Northwestern Univ: Fulbright scholar, teaching asst in geography 1964–65, head teaching asst in geography 1965–66; lectr in geography Univ of Bristol 1969–72 (research assoc 1968–69), prof of theoretical geography Univ of Cambridge 1997– (univ lectr in geography 1973–91, MA 1973, reader in theoretical geography 1991–97), head of dept 1999–2001, chair Sch of Physical Scis 2001–03, pro-vice-chllr 2004–10; Christ's Coll Cambridge: dir of studies and Coll lectr 1973–, fell 1974–; visiting scholar: WHO 1989, 1990, 1994 and 1995, Epidemiology Program Office US Centres for Disease Control and Prevention Atlanta GA 1990, 1991 and 1993; memb Academia Europaea 2002; FSS 1968, FBA 1996, CGeog 2002; *Books* Spatial Autocorrelation (with J K Ord, 1973), Elements of Spatial Structure: A Quantitative Approach (jtly, 1975), Locational Analysis in Human Geography (with P Haggett and A E Frey, Locational Models and Locational Methods both form pts I and II of this book, 1977), Spatial Processes: Models and Applications (with J K Ord, 1981), Spatial Diffusion: An Historical Geography of Epidemics in an Island Community (jtly, 1981), Spatial Components in the Transmission of Epidemic Waves through Island Communities: the spread of Measles in Fiji and the Pacific (with P Haggett, 1985), Spatial Aspects of Influenza Epidemics (with P Haggett and J K Ord, 1986), Atlas of Disease Distributions: Analytic Approaches to Epidemiological Data (with P Haggett, 1988, 2 edn, 1992), London International Atlas of AIDS (with M R Smallman-Raynor and P Haggett, 1992), Measles: an Historical Geography of a Major Human Viral Disease from Global Expansion to Local Retreat, 1840–1990 (with P Haggett and M R Smallman-Raynor, 1993), Diffusing Geography (ed jtly, 1995), Deciphering Epidemics (with P Haggett and M R Smallman-Raynor, 1998), Island Epidemics (with P Haggett and M R Smallman-Raynor, 2000), War Epidemics (with M R Smallman-Rayner, 2004), World Atlas of Epidemic Diseases (with P Haggett and M R Smallman-Rayner, 2004), Poliomyelitis: A World Geography (with M R Smallman-Raynor and P Haggett, 2006), Emerging Infectious Diseases (with M R Smallman-Raynor, P Haggett et al, 2009), Atlas of Epidemic Britain: a Twentieth Century Picture (with M R Smallman-Raynor, 2012), Oxford Textbook of Infectious Disease Control (with M R Smallman-Raynor, 2013); also author of numerous related papers; *Recreations* watching Grimsby Town FC, old roses, theatre; *Style—* Prof Andrew Cliff, FBA; ✉ Department of Geography, University of Cambridge, Downing Place, Cambridge CB2 3EN

CLIFF, HE Ian Cameron; OBE (1991); s of Gerald Shaw Cliff (d 1970), of Wakefield, and Dorothy, *née* Cameron (d 1999); *b* 11 September 1952; *Educ* Hampton GS, Magdalen Coll Oxford; *m* 2 July 1988, Caroline Mary, da of Noel Redman; 1 s (Richard b 27 March 1989), 2 da (Louise b 24 Dec 1993, Julia b 14 May 2001); *Career* history master Dr Challoner's GS Amersham 1975–79; joined FCO 1979, first sec Khartoum 1982–85, FCO 1985–89, first sec UK mission New York 1989–93, dir exports to Middle East DTI 1993–96, dep head of mission Vienna 1996–2001, ambass to Bosnia and Herzegovina 2001–05, ambass to Sudan 2005–07, UK perm rep to Orgn for Security and Co-operation in Europe (OSCE) Vienna 2007–11, ambass to Repub of Kosovo 2011–15, chargé d'affaires Zagreb 2015–16; *Recreations* railways, music, theatre, philately; *Style—* HE Mr Ian Cliff, OBE; ✉ c/o Foreign & Commonwealth Office, King Charles Street, London SW1A 2AH

CLIFFE, His Hon Judge Graham; s of Donald Joe Cliffe (d 1997), and Edna, *née* Kennedy (d 1982); *b* 3 January 1948, Huddersfield, W Yorks; *Educ* King James' GS Huddersfield, Univ of Manchester (LLB); *m* 22 Aug 1970, Isla, *née* Preston; 2 s (James b 2 March 1973, Thomas b 16 Dec 1982), 2 da (Emma b 11 Jan 1976, Sally b 19 Feb 1984); *Career* admitted slr 1972; county court registrar 1988, district judge 1991, recorder 1998, circuit judge (North Eastern Circuit) 2000–, dep judge of the High Court 2001–; *Recreations* walking, reading, cricket, grandchildren, Huddersfield Town AFC; *Clubs* Catenian Assoc, Old Almondburians CC; *Style—* His Hon Judge Cliffe; ✉ c/o Leeds Combined Court Centre, 1 Oxford Row, Leeds LS1 3BG (☎ 0113 306 2800)

CLIFFORD, Daniel; s of Tony Clifford, and Denise, *née* Wynn; *b* 6 August 1973, Canterbury, Kent; *Educ* Canterbury HS; *m* Valerie, *née* Arnou; 3 da (Shannon b 29 May 1999, Fay b 18 Oct 2000, Saffron b 28 Sept 2003); 2 da with Deborah Fox Lilly (May b 13 May 2009, April b 29 April 2010); *Career* commis chef Howfield Manor Hotel and Restaurant Canterbury 1989–92, first commis chef The Bell Inn Aston Clinton 1992, demi-chef de partie The Box Tree Ilkley 1992–93, chef de partie Millers Harrogate 1993, sous chef Provence Restaurant Hordle 1993–95, chef de partie Jean Bardet Restaurant Tours 1995–96, sr sous chef Rascasse Leeds 1996–98, head chef Midsummer House Restaurant Cambridge 1998– (2 Michelin Stars, Egon Ronay 2 Stars, AA Guide 5 Rosettes (Best Wine List of the Year runner-up 2003–05), Good Food Guide County Restaurant of the Year 2005, Square Meal BMW Award Best Out of Town Restaurant 2005, Cambridge Local Secrets Best Fine Dining Restaurant 2004 and 2005, Harpers & Queen Best Outside London Restaurant Award 2005 (Chef of the Year nomination 2005), Tatler Restaurant Awards Best Restaurant Outside London 2006, Best Overall Restaurant Local Secrets Restaurant Awards 2006); television appearances incl Great British Menu (BBC 2) 2012 (winner, cooked main course for the Olympic Banquet); *Style—* Daniel Clifford, Esq; ✉ Midsummer House, Midsummer Common, Cambridge CB4 1HA (☎ 01223 369299, fax 01223 302672)

CLIFFORD, David Robert; s of late Mark Clifford, and late Dorothy Emily, *née* Lee; *b* 14 September 1952; *Educ* Dr Morgan's GS Bridgwater, Univ of Wales Inst of Science and Technol (BSc); *m* 1, 13 Sept 1975 (m dis 2001), Audrey Elizabeth, *née* Potter; 1 s (John David b 14 May 1980), 1 da (Rachel Elizabeth b 23 Dec 1983); m 2, 20 Oct 2007, Sarah Elizabeth, *née* Hyde; *Career* vice-pres compensation and benefits Bank of America NT & SA 1978–86, personnel dir Citicorp Scrimgeour Vickers Ltd 1986–88, personnel dir Citicorp Investment Bank Ltd 1988–92, ptnr KPMG 1992–99, gp HR dir Robert Fleming & Co Ltd 2000, ptnr Ernst & Young 2000–04, exec vice-pres global reward ABN Amro NV 2005–08, dir David Clifford Consulting Ltd; memb Chartered Inst of Personnel Mgmnt; *Recreations* skiing, family activities; *Style—* David Clifford, Esq

CLIFFORD, Nigel Richard; s of John Clifford (d 1995), of Emsworth, Hants, and Barbara Dorothy Clifford; *b* 22 June 1959, Emsworth, Hants; *Educ* Downing Coll Cambridge (MA), Univ of Strathclyde (MBA), DipM, DipCAM; *m* 1989, Jeanette, *née* Floyd; 2 s (Aidan b 1990, Brendan b 1992), 1 da (Caitlin b 1995); *Career* British Telecommunications plc 1981–92: commercial mangr 1981–84, product mangr 1984–85, gp product mangr 1985–87, gen mangr BT International Operator Servs 1987–90, sr strategist 1990, head of business strategy BT Mobile 1990–92; chief exec Glasgow Royal Infirmary Univ NHS Tst 1992–98, sr vice-pres (service delivery) Cable & Wireless Communications Ltd 1998–2000, ceo Tertio Hldgs Ltd 2000–04, ceo Symbian Ltd 2005–08, ceo Procserve, ceo Ordnance Survey 2015–; non-exec dir Anite plc, non-exec dir Alliance Pharma; fndr tstee Herald Fndn for Women's Health; FRGS, FRSA, FCMI; *Recreations* running, walking, kayaking; *Clubs* Morpeth Comrades Club and Institute Union; *Style—* Nigel Clifford, Esq

CLIFFORD OF CHUDLEIGH, 14 Baron (E 1672) Thomas Hugh Clifford; DL; Count of the Holy Roman Empire; s of 13 Baron Clifford of Chudleigh (d 1988), and Katharine, Lady Clifford of Chudleigh (d 1999); *b* 17 March 1948; *Educ* Downside; *m* 1, 15 Dec 1980 (m dis 1993), (Muriel) Suzanne, yr da of Maj Campbell Austin; 1 da (Hon Georgina Apollonia b 1983), 2 s (Hon Alexander Thomas Hugh b 24 Sept 1985, Hon Edward George Hugh b 1988); m 2, 21 Nov 1994, Clarissa Anne, da of His Honour Anthony Charles Goodall, MC, DL (d 2001), of Moretonhampstead, Devon; *Heir* s, Hon Alexander Clifford; *Career* late Capt Coldstream Gds, served Norway, Turkey, Berlin, Ireland, British Honduras (Belize); former mangr: The Clifford Estate Co, Ugbrooke Enterprises, Ugbrooke Reception Enterprise; KSOM; *Style—* Capt the Rt Hon the Lord Clifford of Chudleigh, DL; ✉ The Old Stables, Ugbrooke Park, Chudleigh, South Devon TQ13 OAD (☎ 01626 852179)

CLIFT, Prof Roland; CBE (2006, OBE 1994); s of Leslie William Clift, of Wallington, Surrey, and Ivy Florence Gertrude, *née* Wheeler; *b* 19 November 1942; *Educ* Trinity Sch of John Whitgift Croydon, Trinity Coll Cambridge, McGill Univ Montreal; *m* 1, 1968, Rosena Valory, da of Robert Bruce Davison; 1 da (Vanessa b 14 July 1972); m 2, 1979, Diana Helen, da of William Reginald Dermot Manning; 2 s (Julian William Dermot b 2 Oct 1979 d 1997, Adrian Manning b 3 July 1982); *Career* tech offr and chem engr ICI Ltd 1964–67; McGill Univ Montreal: lectr 1967–70, asst prof 1970–72, assoc prof 1972–75; lectr in chem engrg Imperial Coll London 1975–76; Univ of Cambridge: lectr in chem engrg 1976–81, fell Trinity Coll 1978–81, praelector 1980–81; Univ of Surrey: prof of chem engrg 1981–92, head Dept of Chem and Process Engrg 1981–91, prof of environmental technology and dir Centre for Environmental Strategy 1992–2005, distinguished prof 2002–08, emeritus prof 2008–; visiting prof Università di Napoli 1973–74, visiting prof Environmental System Analysis Chalmers Univ Sweden 1999–, adjunct prof Univ of Br Columbia Canada 2009–; pres Int Soc for Industrial Ecology (ISIE) 2008–10 (exec dir 2011–14); ed-in-chief Powder Technology 1987–95; chm: Process Engrg Ctee SERC 1989–90, Clean Technol Unit SERC and AFRC 1990–94, Engrg Research Bd AFRC 1992–94; memb BBSRC 1994–96; dir: Climfar Associates Ltd 1986–2008, Particle Consultants Ltd 1988–2005, Blackrock New Energy Investment Tst 2000–10, Industrial Ecology Solutions Ltd 2001–07; memb: UK Ecolabelling Bd 1992–99, Comité des Sages on LCA and Ecolabelling European Cmmn 1993–98, Tech Opportunities Panel EPSRC 1994–98, Royal Cmmn on Environmental Pollution 1996–2005, Science Advsy Cncl DEFRA 2006–11; expert advsr Science and Technol Ctee House of Lords 2004–05; Henry Marion Howe Medal American Soc for Metals 1976, Moulton Medal Inst of Chem Engrs 1979, Sir Frank Whittle Medal Royal Acad of Engrg 2003, Hanson Medal IChemE 2008, Society Award Int Soc for Industrial Ecology 2015; hon citizen Augusta GA 1987; FIChemE 1984 (MIChemE 1979), FREng 1986; *Books* Bubbles, Drops and Particles (with J R Grace and M E Weber, 1978, reprinted 2005), Fluidization (ed with J F Davidson and D Harrison, 1985), Slurry Transport using Centrifugal Pumps (with K C Wilson and G R Addie, 1992, 3 edn 2005), Gas Cleaning at High Temperatures (ed with J P K Seville, 1993), Processing of Particulate Solids (with J P K Seville and U Tüzün, 1997), Sustainable Development in Practice: Case Studies for Engineers and Scientists (ed with A Azapagic and S Perdan, 2004), Taking Stock of Industrial Ecology (ed with A Druckman, 2015); *Recreations* thinking, arguing; *Clubs* Athenaeum; *Style—* Prof Roland Clift, CBE, FREng; ✉ 93 Peperharow Road, Godalming, Surrey GU7 2PN (☎ 01483 417922); Centre for Environmental Strategy, University of Surrey, Guildford, Surrey GU2 7XH (☎ 01483 689271, fax 01483 686671, e-mail r.clift@surrey.ac.uk)

CLIFTON, Bishop of (RC) 2001–; Rt Rev Declan Lang; *b* 15 April 1950, Cowes, IOW; *Educ* Ryde Sch, St Edmund's Coll Ware, Royal Holloway Coll London (BA); *Career* ordained priest 1975; asst priest St John's Cathedral Portsmouth 1975–79, chaplain St Edmund's

C

Comp Sch Portsmouth 1975–79, chllr and sec to bishop of Portsmouth 1979–83, parish priest Our Lady, Queen of Apostles Bishop's Waltham 1983–87, parish priest Sacred Heart Bournemouth 1987–90, moderator of the Curia Diocese of Portsmouth 1990, admin St John's Cathedral Portsmouth 1990–96, a vicar gen Dio of Portsmouth 1996–2001, parish priest St Edmund Abingdon 1996–2001; adult religious educn advsr Religious Educn Cncl 1983–90 (co-prodr Parish Project), sometime chaplain Portsmouth Gp pilgrimage to Lourdes, former chair Working Pty on Clergy Appraisal Bishop's Conf/ Nat Conf of Priests; *Style—* The Rt Rev the Bishop of Clifton; ✉ St Ambrose, North Road, Leigh Woods, Bristol BS8 3PW (☎ 0117 973 3072, fax 0117 973 5913)

CLIFTON, Rita Ann; CBE (2014); da of Arthur Leonard Clifton (d 1970), of Marlow, Bucks, and Iris Mona, *née* Hill; *b* 30 January 1958; *Educ* High Wycombe HS, Newnham Coll Cambridge (MA); *Partner* Brian Martin Astley; 2 da; *Career* D'Arcy MacManus & Masius advtg agency 1979–81, Saatchi & Saatchi 1981–82, J Walter Thompson 1983–86; Saatchi & Saatchi: sr account planner 1986–89, bd dir 1989, gp planning dir 1990–92, dir of strategic planning 1992–95, vice-chm 1995–97; chief exec Interbrand brand consultancy 1997–, chm 2002–; non-exec dir: Dixons Retail plc 2003–, Bupa 2010–; non-exec chm Populus Ltd 2004–, chm Conservation Volunteers (formerly BTCV) 2011–; visiting prof Henley Business Sch 2006–; memb: Bd of Advsrs Judge Business Sch Univ of Cambridge, Editorial Bd Jl of Brand Mgmnt, Sustainable Devpt Cmmn, Business Advsy Bd Duke of Edinburgh's Award, Advsy and Assurance Panel BP's Carbon Offset Prog 2006–; pres Women's Advertising Club of London 1997–98; dir Henley Festival 2010–, tstee WWF (UK); memb: RSA, IPA, Account Planning Gp, Marketing Soc, Marketing Gp of GB; pres MRS; *Style—* Ms Rita Clifton, CBE

CLIFTON-BROWN, Geoffrey; MP; s of Robert Clifton-Brown, and Elizabeth Clifton-Brown (d 2006); *b* 23 March 1953; *Educ* Eton, RAU Cirencester; *m*; 1 s, 1 da; *Career* chartered surveyor PSA Dorchester 1975, investment surveyor Jones Lang Wootton 1975–79, md own farming business Norfolk 1979–; MP (Cons): Cirencester and Tewkesbury 1992–97, Cotswold 1997–; PPS to Rt Hon Douglas Hogg 1995–97; oppn whip DETR 1999–2001; oppn spokesman for: environment, food and rural affrs 2001, transport, local govt and the regions 2001–02, local govt and the regions 2002–04; oppn whip 2004–05, asst chief whip 2005, shadow min for trade and foreign affrs 2005–; vice-chm Cons Pty with responsibility for the Int Office 2010–15, chm House of Commons Ctee of Selection 2010–15; memb: Environment Select Ctee 1992–95, Public Accounts Ctee 1997–99;vice-chm N Norfolk Constituency Cons Assoc 1986–91; Freeman City of London; Liveryman Worshipful Co of Farmers; FRICS; *Publications* Privatising the State Pension – Secure Funded Provision for All (Bow Group); *Recreations* fishing, rural pursuits; *Clubs* Carlton, Farmers'; *Style—* Geoffrey Clifton-Brown, Esq, MP, FRICS; ✉ House of Commons, London SW1A 0AA

CLINTON, Robert George; CVO (2008); s of George Thomas Clinton, and Mary Josephine, *née* Harris; *b* 19 August 1948; *Educ* Beaumont Coll Windsor, Brasenose Coll Oxford (MA); *m* 28 Aug 1981, Annita Louise, *née* Bennett; 1 s (Thomas Mark George), 1 da (Joanna Marika Alice); *Career* slr; sr ptnr Farrer & Co 2002–08, conslt 2008–12; chm Tony Blair Faith Fndn, dir Early Resolution CIC, tstee Wessex Youth Tst; memb Law Soc 1975; *Recreations* sailing, travel; *Clubs* Garrick; *Style—* Robert Clinton, Esq, CVO; ✉ 85 Richmond Avenue, London N1 0LX (☎ 020 7609 8336, e-mail rgclinton@hotmail.co.uk)

CLINTON-DAVIS, Baron (Life Peer UK 1990), of Hackney in the London Borough of Hackney; Stanley Clinton Clinton-Davis; PC (1998); s of Sidney Davis; assumed the surname of Clinton-Davis by Deed Poll 1990; *b* 6 December 1928; *Educ* Hackney Downs Sch, Mercers Sch, KCL; *m* 1954, Frances Jane, *née* Lucas; 1 s, 3 da; *Career* Parly candidate: Portsmouth Langstone 1955, Yarmouth 1959 & 1964; cncllr (Hackney) 1959–71, Mayor Hackney 1968–69; MP (Lab) Hackney Central 1970–83, Parly under sec Trade 1974–79; oppn frontbench spokesman on: Trade 1979–81, Foreign and Cwlth Affrs 1981–83; memb Cmmn of Euro Communities (responsible for tport, environment and nuclear safety) 1985–89, princ spokesperson for the oppn on Tport in the House of Lords and supporting spokesman on trade and indust and on foreign affrs 1990–97, min for trade DTI 1997–98; slr 1953–; conslt on Euro and environmental law and affrs with SJ Berwin & Co slrs 1989–97 and 1998–; conslt: Euro Cockpit Assoc 1990–97, Soc of Lab Lawyers 1990–; vice-pres: Soc of Lab Lawyers 1987–, Chartered Inst of Environmental Health; hon memb Exec Cncl of Justice, exec memb Inst of Jewish Affairs 1993–97; memb UN Selection Ctee UNEP-Sasakawa Environment Award 1989– (chm 1999–); chm: Refugee Cncl 1989–96 (pres 1996–97), Advsy Ctee on protection of the sea 1989–97 and 1998–2001 (pres 2001–), Packaging Standards Cncl until 1996; memb: GMBH, Advsy Panel CIS Environ Tst until 1997; pres: Br Multiple Sclerosis Soc (Hackney Branch) until 1997, UK Pilots Assoc (Marine) until 1997, Assoc of Municipal Authorities until 1997, Inst of Travel Mgmnt until 1997, Br Airline Pilots Assoc until 1997 and 1998–, Aviation Environment Federation until 1997; tstee Int Shakespeare Globe Centre until 1997; memb Panel 2000; Grand Cross Order of Leopold II (Belgium) for servs to the EC 1990; Hon Dr Poly Univ of Bucharest; fell: Queen Mary & Westfield Coll London, KCL; fell Chartered Institution of Water and Environmental Management; *Books* Report of a British Parliamentary Delegation to Chile (jtly, 1982); contrib to books and jls on environment issues; *Recreations* reading political biographies, golf, watching assoc football; *Style—* The Rt Hon Lord Clinton-Davis, PC; ✉ House of Lords, London SW1A 0PW; DTI: (☎ 020 7215 5501)

CLISSITT, Benedict Paul (Ben); s of Adrian Clissitt (d 2002), and Audrey, *née* Hull; *b* 18 March 1967, Leeds, W Yorks; *Educ* St Michael's Sch Stevenage, UCL (BA), Sch of Communication Arts; *m* 19 Feb 2005, Paula Cocozza; 1 da (Elsa Blanche b 25 Nov 2007); *Career* sports journalist; dep sports ed Independent on Sunday 1995–96 (asst sports ed 1993–95); The Guardian: asst sports ed 1996–98, dep features ed 1998–2000, sports ed 2000–08; head of sport The Guardian, The Observer and guardian.co.uk 2008–10; digital dir (visual journalism) Daily Telegraph (joined 2010); The Bedside Guardian (ed, 2007); *Recreations* football (watching), wine, opera, travel; *Style—* Ben Clissitt, Esq; ✉ Daily Telegraph, 111 Buckingham Palace Road, London SW1 0DT

CLIVAZ, Brian Melville Winrow-Campbell; s of Anthony Constant Clivaz, and Glynneth, *née* Williams; *b* 7 May 1960, Brighton; *Educ* Woking Co GS, Thames Valley Univ (renamed Univ of West London); *Career* entrepreneur; varied hotel experience 1976–81 (The Dorchester Hotel London, L'Hotel Plaza Athenee Paris, L'Hotel Meurice Paris, The Hyde Park Hotel London, Dubai International Hotel UAE); md: The Old Lodge Restaurant Ltd (Michelin Star, Egon Ronay Star, numerous other awards) 1981–88, ACA Catering Services 1986–88; gen mangr The Fourways Inn Bermuda 1988–90; md: Simpson's-in-the-Strand Ltd 1990–97, Berkeley Adam Ltd 1995–2005, Home House Ltd 1995–2005, Mayfair Valley Ltd 2000–07, Scott's Restaurant Ltd 2002–2004, By Recommendation Ltd, The Arts Club (London) Ltd (ceo 2005–12); prop L'Escargot Ltd 2014–; dir: Crowbarn Ltd, Malman Ltd, The Arts Club (property) Ltd), Devonshire Club Ltd 2014–; chm CPG and Ptnrs, chm Langan's Brasserie 2012–15; hon memb Savoy Gastronomes, pres Reunion des Gastronomes 1997–99; co-organiser The Times World Chess Championship 1993, dir The World Memory Championships 1993–; vice-pres The Brain Tst 1993–; hon treas The Philidor Soc; co-fndr The Staunton Soc, chm The Whitebait Soc; memb: Br Hospitality Assoc (memb Club Panel), Restaurateurs Assoc of GB (past memb Nat Ctee), Royal Academy of Culinary Arts, Les Arts de la Table, The Chopin Soc; Hon MBA Univ of West London; Freeman: City of London 1994, Worshipful Co of Cooks; FRSA, FIH; Knight Order of Merit Royal House of Savoy, Knight of the Order of Francis I; *Recreations* gardening, collecting old cookery books, chess; *Clubs* Arts, Black's, Devonshire, Groucho, Home House, Keeper's House, Quo Vadis; *Style—* Brian Clivaz, Esq; ✉ 48 Greek Street, London W1D 4EF (☎ 020 494 1318, e-mail brian@clivaz.com)

CLIVE, Prof Eric McCredie; CBE (1999); s of Robert M Clive (d 1971), and Mary, *née* McCredie (d 1976); *b* 24 July 1938; *Educ* Stranraer Acad, Stranraer HS, Univ of Edinburgh (MA, LLB), Univ of Michigan (LLM), Univ of Virginia (SJD); *m* 6 Sept 1962, Kay, da of Rev Alastair McLeman (d 1940); 4 c (Gael b 6 Sept 1963 d 1996, Alastair M M b 19 March 1965, Sally b 22 March 1968, Rachel b 9 Sept 1969); *Career* slr; Univ of Edinburgh: lectr 1962–69, sr lectr 1969–75, reader 1975–77, prof of Scots law 1977–81, visiting prof 1999–; memb Study Gp on a European Civil Code 2000–09; memb Scottish Law Commission 1981–99; Hon Dr Univ of Osnabrück 2008, Hon LLD Univ of Edinburgh 2016; FRSE 1999; *Books* Law of Husband and Wife in Scotland (1974, 4 edn 1997), Scots Law for Journalists (jtly 1965, 5 edn 1988), Principles, Definitions and Model Rules of Euroepan Private law (jtly, 2008); *Style—* Prof Eric Clive, CBE, FRSE; ✉ School of Law, University of Edinburgh, Old College, South Bridge, Edinburgh (☎ 0131 650 9588, e-mail eric.clive@ed.ac.uk)

CLOGHER, Bishop (RC) of 2010–; Most Rev Liam Seán MacDaid; s of William John MacDaid (d 1968), and Mary Ellen, *née* Kerrigan (d 1993); *b* 19 July 1945, Dublin; *Educ* St Macartan's Coll Monaghan, St Patrick's Coll Maynooth (BA, BD, HDipEd), UC Dublin (Dip); *Career* St Macartan's Coll Monaghan: teacher and dean of studies 1970–77, careers and guidance counsellor 1978–81, pres 1981–90; chm Cncl of Priests Clogher Dio 1988–96, diocesan sec and communications offr 1993–2010, chllr of diocese 1994–2010; tutor in counselling Catholic Marriage Advsy Cncl 1978–85; chaplain to His Holiness 2002; fndr memb AMCSS (Assoc of Mgmnt of Catholic Secdy Schs); chm Cncl for Marriage and the Family Irish Episcopal Conference 2014; *Recreations* swimming, walking, cycling; *Clubs* St Joseph's GFC; *Style—* The Most Rev the Bishop of Clogher; ✉ Bishop's House, Monaghan, Co Monaghan, Ireland (e-mail diocesanoffice@clogherdiocese.ie, website www.diocesanoffice@clogherdiocese.ie)

CLOONEY, Amal; *née* Alamuddin; *b* 3 February 1978, Beirut; *Educ* Dr Challoner's HS, Hertford Coll Oxford (exhibitioner, Shrigley Award, BA/LLB), NYU Sch of Law (Jack J Katz Memorial Award, LLM); *m* 2014, George Clooney; *Career* called to the Bar: NY 2002, Inner Temple 2010, barr specialising in int law and human rights; trainer Int Bar Assoc, devised and delivered training programmes to UN investigators and Bahraini judges, prosecutors and police; lectr: Univ of N Carolina 2007, Hague Academy of Int Law 2009; guest lectr New Sch NY 2012; visiting prof Columbia law Sch; speaker: Chatham House 2012, Int Centre for Transitional Justice NY 2011; devised and delivered training programmes to UN investigators and Bahraini judges, prosecutors and police; *Publications* The Special Tribunal for Lebanon: Law and Practice (co-ed with D Tolbert, 2013); *Style—* Mrs Amal Clooney; ✉ Doughty Street Chambers, 54 Doughty Street, London WC1N 2LA

CLORE, Melanie Sarah Jane; da of Martin Clore, of London, and Cynthia Clore; *b* 28 January 1960; *Educ* Channing Sch Highgate, Univ of Manchester (BA); *m* 22 July 1994, Yaron Meshoulam; 1 s (Theo Felix Clore b 18 May 1996), 1 da (Martha Lily Clore b 27 June 1998); *Career* Sotheby's: graduate trainee 1981, jr cataloguer in Impressionist and Modern Art Dept 1982, auctioneer 1985–, dep dir 1986–88, dir 1988–91, sr dir 1991–, head of Impressionist and Modern Art Dept Europe 1992–, co-chm Worldwide Impressionist and Modern Art Dept 2001–, chm Sotheby's Europe 2011– (memb Bd 1994–, dep chm 1997–2011); tstee: Whitechapel Art Gallery 1988–98, Tate 2004–08; *Recreations* travel, cinema; *Style—* Ms Melanie Clore; ✉ Impressionist and Modern Art Department, Sotheby's, 34–35 New Bond Street, London W1A 2AA (☎ 020 7293 5394, fax 020 7293 5932)

CLOSE, Prof Frank; OBE; *Educ* Univ of St Andrews, Magdalen Coll Oxford (DPhil); *m*; 2 da; *Career* postdoctoral fell Stanford Univ, research CERN Geneva 1973–75, research physicist rising to head Theoretical Physics Div Rutherford Appleton Lab 1975–2001, concurrently head of communication and public educn activities CERN Geneva 1997–2000, prof of physics Univ of Oxford 2001–11 (emeritus 2011–), fell and tutor in physics Exeter Coll Oxford 2001–11 (emeritus 2011–), prof of astronomy Gresham Coll London 2001–04; vice-pres BAAS until 2000; delivered Royal Instn Christmas Lectures 1993, Kelvin Medal Inst of Physics 1996, Michael Faraday Medal Royal Soc 2014; *Books* incl: An Introduction to Quarks and Partons (1979), The Cosmic Onion: Quarks and the Nature of the Universe (1983), The Particle Explosion (with Michael Marten and Christine Sutton, 1987), End: Cosmic Catastrophe and the Fate of the Universe (1988), Spectroscopy of Light and Heavy Quarks (ed with Ygo Gastaldi and Robert Klapisch, 1989), Too Hot to Handle: The Story of the Race for Cold Fusion (1990), Lucifer's Legacy: The Meaning of Asymmetry (2000), The Particle Odyssey: A Journey to the Heart of the Matter (with Michael Marten and Christine Sutton, 2002), Particle Physics: A Very Short Introduction (2004), The New Cosmic Onion (2007), The Void (2007), Antimatter (2009), Neutrino (2010), The Infinity Puzzle (2011), Half Life (2015), Nuclear Physics: A Very Short Introduction (2016); *Recreations* playing real tennis, writing, walking, singing, chasing solar eclipses, Peterborough United; *Clubs* Oxford Univ Real Tennis, Radley Real Tennis; *Style—* Prof Frank Close, OBE; ✉ Exeter College, Oxford OX1 3DP

CLOSE, James; s of Russell Close, and Helene, *née* Lewin; *b* 17 October 1979, Bishop Auckland, Co Durham; *Educ* Barnard Castle Sch; *Career* chef-prop Raby Hunt Inn Co Durham 2009– (Michelin star 2013–); *Style—* James Close, Esq; ✉ Grove Cottage, Hamsterley, Bishop Auckland, County Durham DL13 3NL (☎ 01358 488203); The Raby Hunt Inn and Restaurant with Rooms, Summerhouse, Nr Darlington, Co Durham DL2 3UD (e-mail enquiries@rabyhuntrestaurant.co.uk, Twitter @rabyhunt)

CLOSE, Seamus; OBE (1997); s of late James Close, and late Kathleen, *née* Murphy; *b* 12 August 1947; *Educ* St Malachy's Coll Belfast, Coll of Business Studies (Dip Business Studies); *m* 15 April 1978, Deirdre, da of late Barney McCann; 3 s (Christopher b 9 Feb 1979, Brian b 5 July 1981, Stephen b 13 Jan 1984), 1 da (Natasha b 27 July 1987); *Career* memb Lisburn BC 1973–2011 (mayor 1993–94); Alliance Pty: chm 1981–82, dep ldr 1991–2001; memb NI Assembly 1982–86, MLA (Alliance) Lagan Valley 1998–2007; key negotiator: Brooke-Mayhew Talks 1991–92, Good Friday Agreement 1996–98; delg: Atkins Conf on NI 1980, NI Forum for Peace and Reconciliation 1994–95, NI Forum for Political Dialogue 1996; dir S D Bell & Co Ltd 1986–; Hon Freeman City of Lisburn 2010; *Recreations* sports, family, current affairs; *Style—* Seamus Close, Esq, OBE

CLOUGH, Dr Chris; s of George Clough (d 1996), of Knaresborough, and Daisy, *née* Elsdon-Howard; *b* 30 August 1953, London; *Educ* Univ of Manchester (MB, ChB); *m* 17 March 1979, Lyn, *née* Griffiths; 1 da (Sophie Laura b 18 March 1980), 2 s (Jonathan James b 5 Jan 1982, Joshua Edward b 25 May 1984); *Career* registrar Hull Royal Infirmary 1976–79, research fell Mount Sinai Med Centre NY 1980–81, sr registrar Midland Centre for Neurology and Neurosurgery Birmingham 1982–88, conslt neurologist Brook Regnl Neuroscience Centre 1989–95, dir King's Regnl Neuroscience Centre 1991–98, conslt neurologist KCH 1994– (med dir 1998–2003), chief med advsr SE London RHA 2003–05, med dir RCP 2005–08; chair Nat Clinical Assessment Team 2009–14; memb: Doctors' Forum Dept of Health 2002, External Reference Gp Nat Serv Framework for Long-term Conditions Dept of Health 2002; Liversedge Prize 1982; FRCP 1992 (MRCP 1978); *Publications* Parkinson's Disease Fast Facts (2004), Training Tomorrow's Physicians (2005); author of papers on Parkinson's disease, restless legs and lumbar puncture 1977–;

Recreations tennis, Spurs fan, walking, cinema; *Clubs* Fabian Soc, Labour Party; *Style—* Dr Chris Clough

CLOUGH, Mark Gerard; QC (1999); *b* 13 May 1953; *Educ* Ampleforth, Univ of St Andrews (MA); *m* Joanne Elizabeth, *née* Dishington; 2 s, 1 da; *Career* called to the Bar Gray's Inn 1978, slr advocate Supreme Court of England and Wales 1996; slr 1995– (specialising in: EU law, competition law and sectoral regulation, int trade law); ptnr Ashurst 1995–2006, ptnr Addleshaw Goddard LLP 2006–10, ptnr Brodies LLP Edinburgh 2011–14 (head of competition and EU law Public Law and Regulation Div Litigation Dept, conslt 2013), specialist counsel EU and competition law 2014–, sr counsel Dentons Brussels 2014–; chm Slr's Assoc of Higher Court Advocates (SAHCA) 2003–06; dir: European Maritime Law Organisation, Slynn Fndn; memb: Advsy Bd Br Inst of Int and Comparative Law Competition Law Forum 2005–11, IBA Anti-trust and Int Trade Law Ctee; chm EU Ctee Law Soc 2010–13, Scottish Law Soc rep in UK delegation to CCBE 2014–; memb Editorial Bd: European Competition Jl, Int Trade Law and Regulation Jl; dir Camden People's Theatre; memb Cncl Euro Law Inst; *Publications* books incl: Shipping And EC Competition Law (1990), EC Merger Regulation (1995) and Butterworth's European Community Law Service EC Anti-Dumping, Subsidies And Trade Barrier Regulation Sections (1997), Trade and Telecoms (2002); contributed articles to numerous journals and chapters to books; *Recreations* golf, tennis, theatre, poetry, shooting; *Clubs* Travellers, New (Edinburgh); *Style—* Mark Clough, Esq, QC

CLOUGH, Peter; s of Michael Clough, of St Ives, Cornwall, and Stella, *née* Ripley (d 1989); *b* 3 March 1967, St Ives, Cornwall; *Educ* Humphry Davy Sch Cornwall, UC Cardiff (LLB); *m* 18 Nov 2005, Annie, *née* Walshe; 2 da (Lottie b 3 Aug 1997, Olivia b 31 Oct 1999), 1 s (Xavier b 23 Sept 2003); *Career* head of litigation and dispute resolution Osborne Clarke; slr specialising in technology, energy and natural resources and financial servs; *Recreations* veteran motorsport, sailing, scuba diving, tennis, travel; *Style—* Peter Clough, Esq; ✉ Osborne Clarke, 2 Temple Back East, Temple Quay, Bristol BS1 6EG (☎ 0117 917 4060, fax 0117 917 4061, e-mail peter.clough@osborneclarke.com)

CLOVER, Charles Robert Harold; s of Harold Percy Clover (d 1973), and Diana Patricia, *née* Hutchinson Smith (d 1975); *b* 22 August 1958; *Educ* Westminster, Univ of York (BA); *m* Pamela Anne, da of Leonard C Roberts; 2 s (Duncan Harold Cairns, Thaddeus John Charles); *Career* asst ed The Spectator 1979; Daily Telegraph: reporter Peterborough Column 1982, rock critic 1983–86, TV critic and feature writer 1986–87, environment corr 1987–89, environment ed 1989–2008; columnist Sunday Times 2009–; nat journalist Media Nature's Br Environment and Media Awards 1989, 1994 and 1996; dir The Fish Film Co 2007–, chm Blue Marine Fndn 2011–16, exec dir Blue Marine Fndn 2016–; chm Dedham Vale Soc 2008–; *Books* Highgrove (with HRH The Prince of Wales, 1993), The End of the Line (2004, special award André Simon Meml Fund Book Awards 2004, Derek Cooper Award Guild of Food Writers 2005, Biosis Award for Communicating Zoology Zoological Soc of London, made into feature-length documentary film 2009, Puma Award 2011); *Recreations* fly fishing; *Clubs* The Farmers; *Style—* Charles Clover, Esq; ✉ e-mail crhclover@gmail.com

CLUCKIE, Prof Ian David; *b* 20 July 1949; *Career* with W S Atkins Swansea 1966–72, with Central Water Planning Unit Reading 1974–76, lectr Univ of Birmingham 1976–88, prof of water resources Univ of Salford 1988–97 (chm Civil Engrg Dept 1991–96), academic dir Salford Civil Engrg Ltd 1989–97, dir Telford Research Inst 1993–94 and 1996–97, prof of hydrology and water mgmnt (dir of Water and Environmental Mgmnt Research Centre) Univ of Bristol 1997–; emeritus prof of engrg Swansea Univ 2015; chm: Aquatic Atmospheric and Physical Sciences Ctee 1991–94 (memb Research Grants and Trg Awards Ctee 1988–91), EPSRC Flood Risk Mgmnt Research Consortium (FRMRC) 2003–; memb: NERC Ctee, Terrestrial and Freshwater Sciences Ctee, Marine Sciences Ctee, Atmospheric Sciences Ctee, various HE ctees 1991–94, European Environmental Research Orgns 1998–; China Friendship Medal 2015, Academician Chinese Acad of Engrg (CAE) 2015; pres Int Ctee on Remote Sensing 2007–11; FRSA 1993, FREng 1997; *Books* Hydrological Applications of Weather Radar (co author with C G Collier, 1991); author of various contributions to learned jls; *Recreations* sailing, hill walking; *Clubs* Royal Yachting Assoc (RYA), Royal Welsh Yacht (RWYC); *Style—* Professor Cluckie, FREng; ✉ PVC (Science and Engineering), Room 201, Singleton Abbey, Swansea University, Singleton Park, Swansea SA2 8PP (e-mail i.d.cluckie@swansea.ac.uk)

CLUFF, John Gordon (Algy); s of Harold Cluff (d 1989), and Freda Cluff; *b* 19 April 1940; *Educ* Stowe; *m* 1993, Blondel, *née* Hodge; 3 s (Harry b 30 Dec 1993, Philip Randolph Macartney b 4 July 1996, Charles b 7 Feb 2002); *Career* Mil Serv: Lt Grenadier Gds 1959–62, Capt Gds Parachute Co 1962–64, serv W Africa, Cyprus, Malaysia; chm and chief exec Cluff Mining plc 1996–2004, chm Cluff Gold Ltd 2004–; chm: Apollo Magazine, The Spectator until 2004; Parly candidate (Cons) Ardwick Manchester 1966; chm Cmmn on the Cwlth 2001; tstee Anglo-Hong Kong Tst, a dir The Centre for Policy Studies, chm The War Memls Tst a govr Cwlth Inst; *Clubs* White's, Pratt's, Beefsteak, Royal Yacht Sqdn, The Brook (New York), Rand (Johannesburg), Special Forces; *Style—* J G Cluff, Esq

CLUGSTON, John Westland Antony; DL; s of Leonard Gordon Clugston, OBE, DL (d 1984), and Sybil Mary Bacon (d 1981); *b* 16 May 1938; *Educ* Sandroyd, Gordonstoun; *m* 1, Patricia, da of Gordon Columba Harvey (d 1994); 2 s (Alistair b 1970, David b 1972), 2 da (Linda b 1973, Christina b 1976); m 2, Jane Elizabeth Ann (d 1996), da of Charles Burtt Marfleet (d 1967); m 3, Fiona Margaret Yuill Baillie, da of Lt-Col James Yuill Ferguson, MBE, MC, and Margaret Ferguson; *Career* Lt Sherwood Rangers Yeo (TA); apprentice: at Huttenwerk Rheinhausen A G Iron and Steel Works Germany 1958–60, Lorraine Escaut Iron and Steel Works at Mont-St-Martin and Senelle France 1960–61; dir: Clugston Holdings Ltd 1964, Roadstone Div 1965–68 (dir for all subsidiary cos 1970), E Bacon & Co 1985; chm: Roadstone Div 1969, Reclamation Div and St Vincent Plant Ltd 1980; gp chm: Colvilles Clugston Shanks (Holdings) Ltd, Colvilles Clugston Shanks Ltd 1984, Clydesdale Excavating and Construction Co Ltd 1987–; dir: Appleby Gp Ltd 1983, Market Rasen Racecourse Ltd 1995–2008; chm and md: Clugston Holdings Ltd 1984 (gp vice-chm and md 1978), Clugston Gp Ltd 1991–; past pres Humberside branch Br Inst of Mgmnt, pres Lincolnshire Iron and Steel Inst 1989–90, pres Hull and Humber C of C and Shipping 2005–06; chm S Humberside Business Advice Centre, former memb Cncl British Aggregates Construction Materials Industry; pres Humberside Scout Cncl (formerly exec chm), chm Lincoln Cathedral Preservation Cncl, former chm of govrs Brigg Prep Sch; High Sheriff Humberside 1992–93; Freeman City of London, Master Worshipful Co of Paviors 1996–97 (Liveryman 1965, memb Ct of Assts 1986, Upper Warden 1996); assoc Inst of Quarrying, MInstD, FCIHT 1984; *Recreations* shooting, fishing, tennis, music; *Style—* J W A Clugston, Esq, DL; ✉ The Old Vicarage, Scawby, Brigg, Lincolnshire DN20 9LX (☎ 01652 657100); Clugston Group Ltd, St Vincent House, Normanby Road, Scunthorpe, North Lincolnshire DN15 8QT (☎ 01724 843491, fax 01724 282853, e-mail group@clugston.co.uk, website www.clugston.co.uk)

CLUTTERBUCK, Prof David; s of Leslie Herbert Clutterbuck, and Doris Violet, *née* Maylett; *b* 4 June 1947; *Educ* Christ's Coll Finchley, Westfield Coll London (BA), KCL (PhD); *m* 16 May 1970, Pauline Sandra, *née* Neudegg; 4 s (Simon b 1974, Alan b 1976, Daniel b 1979, Jonathan b 1986); *Career* Dept of Immigration Home Office 1968–69, ed Journal of the British Nuclear Energy Society (ICE) 1969–70, news ed (technol) New Scientist 1970–73, assoc ed rising to managing ed/ed-in-chief International Management 1973–83; fndr ed: Issues magazine 1984–90, Strategic Direction and Technology Strategies 1985–89, Marketing Business 1988–90; Euro ed On Achieving Excellence 1989–92; chm ITEM Group Ltd (communications project mgmnt co) 1982–, sr ptnr Clutterbuck Associates (mgmnt consultancy) 1983–; dir: The European Mentoring Centre 1991–2000, Mentoring Directors Ltd, Boardroom Effectiveness Ltd 1995–97, Clutterbuck, Palmer, Schneider 1996–98, Nothing Publishing Ltd 1999–; co-fndr and dir European Mentoring and Coaching Cncl 2000– (hon vice-pres 2008–); public sector clients incl: NHS, Dept of Work and Pensions, Dept of Employment, Inland Revenue, DTI, DSS, BR Systems, Cabinet Office, ONS, BIS, NHSI, Transport for London; private sector clients incl: ASDA, British American Tobacco, Brooke Bond Foods, Shell, British Aerospace, Coates Viyella, Audit Cmmn, Kellogg, Whitbread, Gillette, BT, HSBC, Actis, Standard Chartered Bank, Petronas, Barclays, Anglo-American, Rank, Oracle, Mencap, Facebook; also leader various in-house research programmes; chair Int Standards for Mentoring Progs in Employment, special ambass European Mentoring and Coaching Cncl, int bd memb Int Mentoring Assoc; assoc prof Int Mgmnt Centres (IMCB); visiting prof: Sheffield Hallam Univ 2000–, Oxford Brookes Univ, York St John Univ; Hon DLitt IMCB; MInstD, FCIPD, FRSA; *Publications* incl: How to be a Good Corporate Citizen (1981), The Tales of Gribble the Goblin (1983), New Patterns of Work (1985), Everyone Needs a Mentor (1985, 4 edn 2004), Clore: The Man and his Millions (1986), Businesswoman (1987), Turnaround (1988), The Makers of Management (1990), Making Customers Count (1991), Inspired Customer Service (1993), The Independent Board Director (with Peter Waine, *qv*, 1993), The Power of Empowerment (1994), Charity as a Business (1995), Mentoring in Action (1995), The Winning Streak Mark II (1997), Learning Alliances (1998), Learning Teams (1998), Mentoring Executives and Directors (1999), Doing it Different (1999), Mentoring and Diversity (2001), Implementing Mentoring Schemes (2001), Talking Business (2002), Managing Work-Life Balance (2003), The Situational Mentor (2004), Techniques for Coaching and Mentoring (2005, revised edn 2016), Making Coaching Work (2005), Coaching the Team at Work (2007), Techniques for Coaching and Mentoring Vol 2 (2009), Virtual Coach, Virtual Mentor (2009), Further Techniques for Coaching and Mentoring (2009), Developing Successful Diversity Mentoring Programmes (2012), The Talent Wave (2012), Coaching Supervision (2016), Sage Handbook of Mentoring (2016), Mentoring new Parents at Work (2016), Building and Sustaining a Coaching Culture (2016); also author of numerous articles and papers; *E-books* Making the Most of Developmental Mentoring (2013), Powerful Questions for Coaches and Mentors (2013), Writing your First Book (2013), Beyond Goals (2013), The Leader's Guide to Being Coached (2014); *Videos* Beyond the Winning Streak (1989), The Service Dimension (1991), Creating Tomorrow's Company Today (1993), The Mentor Dimension (1994); *Recreations* travel writing, comedy; *Clubs* Spice (Special People on Ice); *Style—* Prof David Clutterbuck; ✉ David Clutterbuck Partnership, Woodlands, Tollgate, Maidenhead, Berkshire SL6 4LJ (☎ 07747 012334, e-mail david@davidclutterbuckpartnership.com, website www.davidclutterbuckpartnership.com)

CLUTTON, (Bernard Geoffrey) Owen; s of Maj Arthur Henry Clutton, MC (d 1979), and Joyce, *née* Worthington (d 2002); *b* 3 March 1951; *Educ* St Aidans Coll Grahamstown, Univ of the Witwatersrand (BA, LLB), Univ of Oxford (BCL); *m* 12 Oct 1979, Rosemary Elizabeth, da of Geoffrey Thomas Skett (d 2013); 1 s (William Edward Henry b 28 March 1988), 1 da (Alice Elizabeth Katherine b 5 Aug 1990); *Career* admitted slr 1980; ptnr Macfarlanes LLP 1984–2011 (conslt 2011–); President's Certificate Nat Playing Fields Assoc; Liveryman Worshipful Co of Slrs; memb Law Soc; CTA, STEP (founding memb); *Style—* Owen Clutton, Esq; ✉ Macfarlanes LLP, 20 Cursitor Street, London EC4A 1LT (☎ 020 7831 9222, fax 020 7831 9607, telex 296381, e-mail owen.clutton@macfarlanes.com)

CLUTTON-BROCK, Prof Timothy Hugh (Tim); *b* 13 August 1946; *Educ* Rugby, Magdalene Coll Cambridge (MA, PhD, ScD); *Career* Game Dept Zambia 1964–65, researcher Sub-Dept of Animal Behaviour Madingley Cambridge (and field work in Tanzania and Uganda) 1969–70, NERC res fell Animal Behaviour Res Gp Univ of Oxford 1972–73, lectr in biology Sch of Biological Scis Univ of Sussex 1973–76, sr res fell in behavioural ecology Res Centre King's Coll Cambridge 1976–80; Dept of Zoology Univ of Cambridge: fndr Large Animal Res Gp 1980, SERC advanced res fell 1981–83, Royal Soc sr res fell in biology 1983–88, univ lectr 1987–91, reader in animal ecology 1991–, prof of animal ecology 1994–, Prince Phillip chair of ecology and evolutionary biology 2007–13; co-fndr and dir Wildlife Consultants Ltd 1976–86, chm Deer Specialist Gp IUCN 1980–91; res projects incl: primate ecology, the evolution of mammalian breeding systems, natural and sexual selection, the evolution of sexual care, population regulation in ungulates, management of deer populations; memb Editorial Bd: Jl of Animal Ecology, Behavioural Ecology, Behavioural Ecology and Sociobiology; jt ed Princeton Univ Press Monograph series in behavioural ecology; contrib to various radio and TV progs (incl script for BBC Horizon prog on Rhum and four series of Meerkat Manor); Scientific Medal Zoological Soc of London 1984, C Hart Merriam Award American Soc of Mammalogists 1991, Frink Medal 1998, Marsh Award Br Ecological Soc 1998, Darwin Medal Royal Soc; hon doctorate: Univ of Zurich, Univ of Pretoria; FRS 1993; *Publications* Primate Ecology (ed, 1977), Current Problems in Sociobiology (ed, 1982), Red Deer – Behaviour and Ecology of Two Sexes (jtly, 1982, Wildlife Soc of America best book award), Rhum – the Natural History of an Island (ed jtly, 1987), Reproductive Success – Studies of Individual Variation in Contrasting Breeding Systems (ed, 1988), Red Deer in the Highlands (jtly, 1989), The Evolution of Parental Care (1991), Meerkat Manor: Flower of the Kalahari, Mammal Societies (2016); author of around 350 articles in learned jls; popular articles in New Scientist, Nat Geographic, Natural History and The Field; *Style—* Prof Tim Clutton-Brock, FRS; ✉ Large Animal Research Group, Department of Zoology, Downing Street, Cambridge CB2 3EJ (☎ 01223 336605)

CLWYD, Rt Hon Ann; PC (2004), MP; da of Gwilym Henri Lewis, and Elizabeth Ann Lewis; *b* 21 March 1937; *Educ* Holywell GS, The Queen's Sch Chester, UC Bangor; *m* 1963, Owen Dryhurst Roberts (d 2012); *Career* former journalist The Guardian and The Observer, reporter BBC; Parly candidate (Lab) Denbigh 1970 and Gloucester Oct 1974, MEP (Lab) Mid and W Wales 1979–84, MP (Lab) Cynon Valley 1984–; oppn front spokesperson on educn and women's affrs 1987–88, shadow sec on overseas devpt 1989–92, shadow Welsh sec 1992, shadow nat heritage sec 1992–93, oppn front bench spokesperson on employment 1993–94, oppn front bench spokesperson on foreign affrs 1994–95, dep to John Prescott 1994–95, chair PLP 2005–06 (vice-chair 2001–05); memb Select Ctee on Int Devpt 1997–2005, chm All-Pty Gp on Human Rights 1997–, memb Select Ctee on Strategic Export Controls on Arms Sales 2000–05, chair All-Pty Parly Iraq Gp, vice-chair All-Pty Parly Gp on Coalfield Communities; former chair UK gp Inter-Parly Union chair Ctee on Middle East Questions and on Coordinating Ctee of Women Parliamentarians); chair International Campaign on Iraqi War Crimes (INDICT) 1997–2003, PM's special envoy to Iraq on human rights 2003–; memb Arts Cncl and vice-chm Welsh Arts Cncl 1975–79; memb Royal Cmmn on NHS 1977–79; memb Lab NEC 1983–84; Backbencher of the Year BBC/House Magazine Awards 2003, Backbencher of the Year Spectator Awards 2003, Campaigning Politician of the Year Channel 4 Political Awards 2004, Communicator of the Year Wales Yearbook Political Awards 2005; hon fell Univ of Wales Bangor, hon degree NE Wales Inst of HE, Hon LLD Trinity Coll Carmarthen; White Robe of the Gorsedd of Bards Nat Eisteddfod of Wales 1991; *Style—* The Rt Hon Ann Clwyd, MP; ✉ Constituency Office, 4th Floor, Crown Buildings, Aberdare CF44 7HU; House of Commons, London SW1A 0AA (☎ 020 7219 3000, fax 020 7219 5943)

C

COADY, Chantal; OBE (2014); da of Anthony Coady (d 1975), and Sybil, *née* Bateman; *b* 17 April 1959; *Educ* St Leonards-Mayfield Convent of the Holy Child Jesus, Mary Datchelor Sch, St Martin's Sch of Art, Camberwell Sch of Art (BA); *m* Nov 1992, James Booth; 1 s (William Fergus b 26 Feb 1997), 1 da (Emilia Sybil Esther b 17 May 1999); *Career* opened Rococo Chocolates 1983, fndr Campaign for Real Chocolate 1986, fndr (with Nicola and Alan Porter) Chocolate Society 1990; treas Bonnington Square Garden Assoc, supporter Sense; fndr memb Acad of Chocolate 2005; Chocolate Oscar Award for Best Chocolate Book Eurochocolate Festival Perugia 1996, winner Best Chocolate Book Gourmand Awards 2003, Academy of Chocolate Special Award for 25 Years of Rococo 2008, winner Walpole Brands of Tomorrow 2010, winner Outstanding Service to the Chocolate Industry FCIA (Fine Chocolate Industry America) 2011, Chocolatier of the Year Academy of Chocolate 2011 and 2012, merit award Int Chocolate Awards 2013, Ruby Award 2014; *Books* Chocolate – Food of the Gods (1993), The Chocolate Companion (1995, translated into six languages, revised 2006), Real Chocolate (2003, shortlisted for Cookery Book of the Year Guild of Foodwriters 2004), Rococo: Mastering the Art of Chocolate (2012); *Recreations* food, wine, music, photography, spending time with family in London and Provence, gardening, urban bee-keeping, sustainability in cocoa farming, part owner of Grococo Farm in Grenada with the Grenada Chocolate Co; *Clubs* Bluebird, Arts, Dover Street; *Style—* Ms Chantal Coady, OBE; ✉ Rococo Chocolates, 5 Motcomb Street, London SW1X 8JU (website www.rococochocolates.com); c/o Michael Alcock, Johnson & Alcock, Clerkenwell House, 45–47 Clerkenwell Green, London EC1R 0HT (☎ 020 7251 0125)

COAKER, Vernon; MP; *Career* MP (Lab) Gedling 1997–; formerly: PPS to Stephen Timms, MP, *qv*, PPS to Rt Hon Estelle Morris, MP, *qv*; asst whip 2003–05, Govt whip 2005–06, Parly under sec of state Home Office 2006–08, min of state for security, counter-terrorism, crime and policing 2008–09, min of state for schs and learners 2009–10, shadow sec of state for NI 2011–13 & 2015–, shadow sec of state for defence 2013–15; *Style—* Vernon Coaker, Esq, MP; ✉ House of Commons, London SW1A 0AA (☎ 020 7219 3000, fax 0115 920 4500, e-mail vernon.coaker.mp@parliament.uk, website www.vernon-coaker-mp.co.uk, Twitter @vernon_coakermp)

COAKHAM, Prof Hugh Beresford; s of William Coakham (d 1973), and Evelyn Grace, *née* Cale; *b* 17 September 1944; *Educ* Windsor GS, UCL (BSc), UCH (MB BS); *m* 1, 15 May 1972, Elspeth Margaret, da of Harold Macfarlane; 1 da (Simone b 29 May 1977), 2 s (Alexander b 22 Dec 1978, Jonathan b 24 April 1982); m 2, 11 Sept 1992, Janet James, da of George McKie; *Career* conslt neurosurgeon Frenchay Hosp and Bristol Royal Infirmary 1980–2006, dir Brain Tumour Res Laboratory 1980–86, clinical dir Imperial Cancer Res Fund Paediatric and Neuro-Oncology Group 1990–96, emeritus prof of neurosurgery Univ of Bristol 1993–; memb Editorial Bd: Br Jl of Neurosurgery 1991, Clinical Neurosurgery 1992, Pan-Arab Jl of Neurosurgery 1998, Neurosurgical Revue; memb: Soc of Br Neurological Surgns, Br Neuropathological Assoc, Br Neuro-Oncology Gp, Euro Assoc of Neurosurgical Soc; author of numerous published papers in int jls of neurosurgery and cancer research; Heart of Gold Award BBC TV 1988 (for NHS fundraising), ABI Medical Award 1991, Hunterian prof Royal Coll of Surgns 1993, listed in Best Doctors Guide 1999, American Assoc of Neuropathologists Moore Award 2006, first prize Presentation to American Assoc of Neurological Surgeons 2009; FRCS 1974, FRCP 1991 (MRCP); *Books* Recent Advances in Neuropathology (contrib, 1985), Tumours of the Brain (contrib, 1986), Biology of Brain Tumours (contrib, 1986), Medulloblastoma: Clinical and Biological Aspects (contrib, 1986), Progress in Surgery – Vol 2 (contrib, 1987), Progress in Paediatric Surgery – Vol 22 (contrib, 1989), Cranial Base Surgery (ed, 2000); *Recreations* jazz saxophone, shooting; *Clubs* Clifton; *Style—* Prof Hugh Coakham; ✉ Neurosurgical Clinic, Spire Bristol Hospital, Redland Hill, Bristol BS6 6UT (☎ 0117 980 4075)

COATES; *see also:* Milnes Coates

COATES, Clive; s of John Alfred Henry Coates (d 1963), and Sonja, *née* van Blaaderen (d 1995); *b* 21 October 1941; *Educ* St Paul's Sch London, Westminster Hotel Sch (Student of the Year 1964); *m* 1, 1965 (m dis 1983), Rosalind, *née* Cohen; 1 da (Emma Jane b 1966), 1 s (Ben Jonathan b 1968); m 2, 1984 (m dis 1994), Juliet Trestini, eld da of David Burns, MW; *Career* promotions mangr IEC Wine Soc of Stevenage 1967–73, dir Genevieve Wine Cellars 1973–75, exec dir Wines Div British Transport Hotels 1975–81, dir Les Amis du Vin (UK) 1981–84, fndr ed The Vine (monthly fine wine magazine, 241 issues) 1985–2005 (special commendation Wine Guild of GB 1992), concurrently ind writer on wine, lectr and conslt; Glenfiddich Trophy for Trade Wine Writer of the Year 1980, Ruffino/Cyril Ray Meml Prize for writing on Italian wine 1994, Rame D'Or for Services to French wine 1994, Lanson Wine Writer of the Year and Champagne Writer of the Year 1998; MW 1971 (chm Educn Ctee 1985, memb Cncl 1976–82 and 1990–93); Chevalier de l'Ordre du Mérite Agricole 1994; *Books* Claret (1982), The Wines of France (1990), Grands Vins, The Finest Châteaux of Bordeaux (1995), Côte D'Or – A Celebration of the Great Wines of Burgandy (1997, André Simon, James Beard and Clicquot Awards for Best Book of the Year, Prix des Arts et des Lettres Burgundian Confrérie du Tastevin), The Wine Lover's Companion to Burgandy (1997), Encyclopaedia of the Wines and Domaines of France (2000), The Wines of Bordeaux (2004), The Great Wines of France (2005), The Wines of Burgundy (2008), My Favorite Burgundies (2013); *Recreations* music, cooking, visiting old churches, watching athletics and cricket, lying by a pool in the south of France with a good book; *Style—* Clive Coates, Esq; ✉ website www.clive-coates.com

COATES, Denise; CBE (2012); da of Peter Coates; *Career* fndr and chief exec bet365 2000–; *Style—* Ms Denise Coates, CBE; ✉ bet365, Hillside, Festival Way, Stoke-on-Trent, Staffs. ST1 5SH

COATES, James Richard; CB (1992); s of William Richard Coates (d 1974), and Doris Coral, *née* Richmond (d 1992); *b* 18 October 1935; *Educ* Nottingham HS, Clare Coll Cambridge (major scholar, MA); *m* 22 March 1969, (Helen) Rosamund, da of John William Rimington, MBE (d 1996); 1 s (Nicholas Benjamin b 14 Nov 1972), 1 da (Beatrice Emma b 28 May 1975); *Career* Miny of Tport: asst princ 1959–63, princ Road Safety and Channel Tunnel Divs 1963–69, private sec to Min 1969–71; DOE: asst sec 1972–77, Urban Tport Policy Div 1972–75, Directorate of Civil Accommodation (PSA) 1975–77, under sec 1977–83, dir of civil accommodation 1977–79, dir London Region (PSA) 1979–83; Dept of Tport: under sec 1983–, Highways Policy and Prog Directorate 1983–85, Railways Directorate 1985–91, Urban and Gen Directorate 1991–94, Urban and Local Tport Directorate 1994–95; independent conslt 1995–; Liveryman Worshipful Co of Carmen 2009; FCIT 1996, FCILT 2004; *Recreations* reading, listening to music, looking at buildings; *Style—* James Coates, Esq, CB; ✉ 10 Alwyne Road, London N1 2HH (☎ 020 7359 7827)

COATES, Prof John Henry; s of James Henry Coates (d 1970), of Australia, and Beryl Lilian, *née* Lee (d 1952); *b* 26 January 1945; *Educ* Australian Nat Univ (BSc), Ecole Normale Superieure Paris, Univ of Cambridge; *m* 8 Jan 1966, Julie Mildred, da of Henry Basil Turner (d 1988); 3 s (David b 3 Jan 1970, Stephen b 7 Nov 1971, Philip b 22 June 1973); *Career* asst prof Harvard Univ 1969–72, assoc prof Stanford Univ 1972–75, lectr Univ of Cambridge 1975–77; prof: Australian Nat Univ 1977–78, Université de Paris XI (Orsay) 1978–85; prof and dir of mathematics École Normale Superieure Paris 1985–86; Univ of Cambridge: fell Emmanuel Coll 1975–77 and 1986–, Sadleirian prof of pure mathematics 1986–2012, head Dept of Pure Mathematics and Mathematical Statistics 1991–97; pres London Mathematical Soc 1988–90, vice-pres Int Mathematical Union 1991–95; Dr (hc) École Normale Superieure Paris 1997, Dr (hc) Heidelberg Univ 2012; FRS 1985; *Style—* Prof John Coates, FRS; ✉ 104 Mawson Road, Cambridge CB1 2EA (☎ 01223 740260); Department of Pure Mathematics and Mathematical Statistics, University of Cambridge, 16 Mill Lane, Cambridge CB2 1SB (☎ 01223 337989, fax 01223 337920, e-mail j.h.coates@dpmms.cam.ac.uk)

COATES, Michael Odiarne; s of Gordon Lionel Coates (d 1990), of Oxted, Surrey, and Dorothy Madeleine, *née* Nelson (d 2003); *b* 4 July 1938; *Educ* Haileybury and ISC; *m* 20 April 1963, Frances Ann, da of Harold P S Paish; 2 da (Annabel Frances b 29 March 1965, Rebecca Jane b 21 Jan 1967); *Career* qualified chartered quantity surveyor 1962, sr ptnr Gardiner and Theobald 1979–2000 (ptnr 1966–); Past Master Worshipful Co of Chartered Surveyors, memb Worshipful Co of Masons; FRICS 1971; *Recreations* wife and family, sports; *Clubs* Boodle's; *Style—* Michael Coates, Esq; ✉ The Square House, Aldingbourne, West Sussex PO20 3TS (☎ 01243 545076)

COATES, Prof Nigel; s of Douglas Coates, of Great Malvern, Worcs, and Margaret Trigg; *b* 2 March 1949; *Educ* Hanley Castle GS Malvern, Univ of Nottingham (BArch), Architectural Assoc London (AADipl, year prize, Italian Govt scholarship to Univ of Rome); *Career* architect and designer; unit master Architectural Assoc 1979–89, fndr memb Narrative Architecture Today (NATO) 1983–86, course master Bennington Coll Vermont USA 1980–81; fndr ptnr: Branson Coates Architecture (with Doug Branson) 1985–2006, Nigel Coates Designs 1987–, Nigel Coates Ltd 2009–; art dir Slamp 2009–; TV features incl: Building Sites (BBC 2) 1989, Omnibus (BBC 1) 1992; work featured in numerous int pubns and jls; lectr worldwide; prof of architectural design RCA 1995–(currently head Dept of Architecture); external examiner: Bartlett Sch of Architecture and Architectural Assoc 1993–94, Dept of Architecture Univ of Cambridge 2000–02; memb Advsy Bd ICA 1987–89, chm Architecture Ctee V&A 2003; columnist Independent on Sunday 2003–; tstee Architecture Fndn 2000–; memb Soc of Authors; *Projects* with Branson Coates: Arca di Noe Japan 1988, Katharine Hamnett Shop London 1988, Hotel Otaru Marittimo Japan 1989, Nishi Azabu Wall Tokyo 1990, Taxim Nightclub Istanbul 1991, Art Silo Building Tokyo 1993, La Forêt and Nautilus Restaurants Schiphol Airport Amsterdam 1993, shops for Jigsaw women and men's fashion in UK, Ireland and Japan, new depts for Liberty store Regent's Street, Bargo bar Glasgow 1996, gallery extention of Geffrye Museum London 1998, Nat Centre for Popular Music Sheffield 1999, Body Zone Millennium Dome Greenwich 2000, Inside Out (Br Cncl int travelling exhbn) 2001, Marketing Suite and Roman Amphitheatre display London 2002; Living Bridge Exhbn Royal Acad 1996, Erotic Design Exhbn Design Museum 1996, Br Exhbn Lisbon '98, Powerhouse::uk Horseguards Parade London 1998, House to Home Exhbn Houses of Parliament 2004; with Nigel Coates Ltd: Middle and Over Wallop Restaurant Glyndebourne 2009; *Design Commissions* Metropole and Jazz furniture collections (for Rockstone) 1986, Noah collection (for SCP) 1988, Female, He-man and She-woman mannequins (for Omniate) 1988, Tongue chair (for SCP) 1989, carpet collection (for V'soske Joyce) 1990, Slipper chair (for Hitch Mylius) 1994, collection of mannequins (for Stockman London) 1994, David collection (for Liberty) 1995, glassware (for Simon Moore) 1997, Oyster Furniture Collection (for Lloyd Loom of Spalding) 1998–, OXO sofa system (for Hitch Mylius) 1998, Fiesolani glassware collection (for Salvati) 2002, Tête á Tête furniture and glassware collection (for Fornasetti) 2002, Dafne lamps (for Slamp) 2003, Shoom bowl (for Alessi) 2004, Lighting Collections (Slamp) 2005–, Veneziani Collections (A V Mazzega) 2008–, Scubism Collection (Fratelli Boffi) 2008–, Pandada Table (Pandamoneum auction WWF) 2009, Cloudelier (Swarovski Crystal Palace) 2009, Rollover and Loop Collections (Varaschin) 2009, Tulipino Vases (Simon Moore) 2009, Animalia (Fratelli Boffi) 2010; *Exhibitions* incl: British Pavilion (Venice Biennale) 2000, Latent Utopias (Graz) 2002, Micro Utopias (Valencia Bienual) 2003, Vextacity (Fabbrica Europa Florence) 2003, Hypnerotosphere (Venice Biennale) 2008, Battersea Gods Home Super Contemporary Exhibition (Design Museum) 2009, Baroccabilly (Galleria Camera 16 Milan) 2010; work exhibited in London, Milan, NY, Paris and Tokyo and in the collections of V&A London, Cooper-Hewitt NY and FRAC Orleans France; *Awards* Inter-Design Award for contrib to Japanese cities through architectural work 1990; with Branson Coates: finalist BBC Design Awards 1994, finalist invited competition for luxury highrise apartments Beirut 1995, invited competition for Millennium Markers Richmond 1995, winner of Concept House (Oyster House) 1998; *Publications* Guide to Ecstacity (2003), Collidoscope (2004); *Monographs* The City in Motion, Rick Poyner (1989), Nigel Coates: Body Buildings and City Scapes, Jonathan Glancey, Cutting Edge series (1999); *Recreations* contemporary art, video making, motorcycling, Italian language and culture; *Clubs* Groucho, Blacks; *Style—* Prof Nigel Coates

COATES, Prof Philip David; s of Frank Coates (d 1983), of Leeds, and Elsie, *née* Tyreman (d 2003); *b* 20 September 1948; *Educ* Cockburn HS Leeds, Imperial Coll London (BSc), Univ of Leeds (MSc, PhD); *m* 3 July 1971, Jane Margaret, da of Robert (Sandy) McNab (d 1994); 3 da (Emma Caroline b 8 March 1975, Charlotte Ruth b 14 Nov 1977 d 2014, Laura Jane b 2 Sept 1984), 1 s (John Philip b 6 Aug 1986); *Career* post-doctoral res fell in physics Univ of Leeds 1976–78; Univ of Bradford: lectr in manufacturing systems engrg 1978–81, lectr in mechanical engrg 1981–84, sr lectr in mechanical engrg 1984–89, reader 1989–90, prof of polymer engrg Dept of Mechanical and Medical Engrg/IRC in Polymer Sci and Technol Univ of Bradford 1990–, dir Polymer Insights 1994–, assoc dir IRC in Polymer Sci and Technol 1996–, pro-vice-chllr Research Innovation & Knowledge Transfer 2004–11; dir: Jt Lab Polymer Micro Processing Sichuan Univ 2010, Polymer IRC 2011–, UK-China Advanced Materials Inst 2012–, MeDe Innovation Centre for Innovative Manufacturing of Medical Devices 2013–; hon prof Sichuan Univ 2008, hon prof Beijing Univ of Chemical Technol 2009–, Famous Overseas Scholar China 2010–, High End Foreign prof Sichuan 2010–, Molecular Sciences Forum prof Chinese Acad of Sciences 2010; conslt various cos 1979–, dir Medilink (Y&H) Ltd 2005–, dir Cogent SSC Ltd 2006–10; tech assessor DTI 1993–99; memb: Polymers and Composites Ctee SERC 1989–92, Structural Composites Ctee DTI/SERC Link 1989–1994; chm Polymer Processing and Engrg Ctee Inst of Materials 1989– (memb Polymer Soc Bd 2000–); chief ed Plastics, Rubber and Composites 2004– (ed 1999–2004); organiser of 18 int confs in polymer field; Competitive Res Fellowship Sci Research Cncl 1976–78, Silver Medal Plastics and Rubber Inst 1982 and 1987, Personal Res Award Wolfson Fndn 1988, Thatcher Bros Prize IMechE 1995, Netlon Award Inst of Materials 1999, Swinburne Award IMMM 2008, Composites Award IMMM 2009; memb Nat Bureau of Foreign Experts China 2012–; FIM 1987, FIMechE 1990, FREng 1995; *Publications* Concise Encyclopedia of Polymer Processing (contrib, 1992), Encyclopedia of Advanced Materials (contrib, 1994), Polymer Process Engineering (ed, 1997– (biennial)), Solid Phase Processing of Polymers (ed, 2000), Neutron-Mapping Polymer Flow: Scattering, Flow Visualization and Molecular Theory, Science, 301, 1691–1695 (with Bent, L R Hutchings, R W Richards, T Gough, R Spares, I Grillo, O G Harlen, D J Read, R S Graham, A E Likhtman, D J Groves, T M Nicholson, T C B McLeish, 2003); author of over 300 scientific pubns; *Recreations* family, playing various musical instruments, computers; *Style—* Prof Philip Coates, FREng; ✉ University of Bradford, Bradford BD7 1DP (☎ 01274 234540, fax 01274 234525, e-mail p.d.coates@bradford.ac.uk, websites www.polyeng.com, www.polymerirc.org, www.ukchina-amri.com, www.bradford.ac.uk)

COATES, Dame Sally Anne; DBE (2013); da of Francis George Coates (d 1966), and Emilie Margaret Coates (d 2000); *b* 15 April 1953, London; *Educ* Convent of the Sacred Heart, Maidstone Girls' Grammar, Inst of Educn (BEd), South Bank Univ (MA); *m* 7 Oct 1995, Serge Ernest Cefai; 3 s (Benjamin b 21 Oct 1978, Theodore b 19 April 1989, Nathan 29 March 1997), 1 da (Gabrielle b 13 Nov 1984); *Career* head teacher Sacred Heart Camberwell 2005–08, head teacher Burlington Danes Acad 2008–14, dir of secdy acads

(South) United Learning 2014–; chair of ind reviews: Teacher Standards 2011–, Teacher Skills Tests 2012–, Prison Educn 2016–; *Books* Headstrong – 11 Lessons of School Leadership (2015); *Recreations* cinema, fashion, reading, travel; *Style*— Dame Sally Coates, DBE; ✉ United Learning, Fairline House, Nene Valley Business Park, Oundle PE8 4HN

COATS, Percy Murray; s of Percy Murray Coats (d 1968), and Lizzie Burroughs Blance (d 1980); *b* 8 January 1941, Lerwick, Shetland; *Educ* Highgate Sch, Bishop Vesey's GS Sutton Coldfield, Univ of London, St George's Hosp (MB BS, DCH); *m* 20 Sept 1975, Margaret Elisabeth Joan, da of Donald Clarence Ashley; 3 da (Louise b 1976, Caroline b 1978, Maria b 1981), 1 s (Edward b 1980); *Career* Surgn Lt RN 1966–72; Queen Charlotte's and Chelsea Hosp for Women 1973–74, King's Coll Hosp 1974–80, conslt obstetrician and gynaecologist SW Surrey Health Dist 1980–2001, dist tutor in obstetrics and gynaecology SW Surrey, med dir Surrey County Hosp NHS Tst 1995–97 (dir Obstetrics and Gynaecology Dept 1990–95), conslt emeritus Royal Surrey County Hosp, special professional interest ultrasound and subfertility; author of specialist medical papers; Liveryman Worshipful Soc of Apothecaries; memb BMA; MRCP, FRCS 1974, FRCOG 1988; *Publications* specialist medical papers; *Recreations* fly fishing; *Clubs* Royal Soc of Med, Carlton; *Style*— Percy M Coats, Esq; ✉ Fairacre, Horsham Road, Bramley, Surrey GU5 0AW (e-mail p.coats@btinternet.com)

COBB, Stephen William Scott; kt (2013), QC (2003); s of Sir John Cobb (d 1977), of Harrogate, N Yorks, and Joan Mary, *née* Knapton; *b* 12 April 1962, Sheffield; *Educ* Winchester, Univ of Liverpool (LLB); *m* 16 Dec 1989, Samantha, *née* Cowling; 1 da (Isabel b 31 Jan 1992), 2 s (James b 2 Jan 1994, Edward b 4 March 1997); *Career* called to the Bar Inner Temple 1985 (bencher 2011); recorder 2004–12, dep High Court judge 2009–12, appointed to the High Court Bench (Family Div) 2013; chm Family Law Bar Assoc 2010–11 (hon life vice-pres 2013); memb: Family Justice Cncl 2004–09, Professional Advsy Gp Nat Youth Advocacy Serv; tstee Gingerbread; fell Int Acad of Matrimonial Lawyers; *Publications* Essential Family Practice (ed, 2000, 2001 and 2002), Clarke Hall and Morrison on Children (ed, 2006–09), Halsbury's Laws of England Vol 5(2) (contrib); *Recreations* sailing, family; *Clubs* Bembridge Sailing, Hurlingham; *Style*— Sir Stephen Cobb, QC; ✉ c/o Royal Courts of Justice, Strand, London WC2A 2LL

COBBE, Prof Stuart Malcolm; s of Brian Morton Cobbe, OBE (d 1991), and Catherine Mary, *née* Caddy (d 1985); *b* 2 May 1948; *Educ* Royal GS Guildford, Univ of Cambridge (MA, MD), St Thomas' Hosp Med Sch (MB BChir); *m* 11 Dec 1970, Patricia Frances, da of George Bertram Barrett, of London; 3 da (Lindsay Ann, Heather Jane (twins) b 21 Aug 1974, Sarah Caroline b 9 May 1977); *Career* gen med trg in Nottingham, Birmingham, Worthing and St Thomas' Hosp London 1972–76, registrar in cardiology Nat Heart Hosp London 1976–77, res fell in cardiology Cardiothoracic Inst London 1977–79, sr registrar in cardiology John Radcliffe Hosp London 1979–81, res fell Univ of Heidelberg Germany 1981–82, clinical reader John Radcliffe Hosp Oxford 1982–85, Walton prof of med cardiology Univ of Glasgow 1985–2008, conslt cardiologist NHS Greater Glasgow & Clyde 1985–2012; author of over 270 scientific papers and 90 editorials, reviews and chapters on cardiac metabolism, cardiac arrhythmias, coronary prevention and other cardiac topics; memb: Br Cardiac Soc, Assoc of Physicians of GB and I; FRCP, FRCPG, FMedSci, FRSE; *Recreations* cycling, sailing, Scottish country dancing; *Style*— Prof Stuart Cobbe; ✉ Department of Medical Cardiology, Royal Infirmary, 10 Alexandra Parade, Glasgow G31 2ER (☎ 0141 211 4722, fax 0141 552 4683, e-mail stuart.cobbe@clinmed.gla.ac.uk)

COBBOLD, 2 Baron (UK 1960), of Knebworth, Co Hertford; David Antony Fromanteel Lytton Cobbold; DL (Herts 1993); er s of 1 Baron Cobbold, KG, GCVO, PC (d 1987); assumed by Deed Poll 1960 the additional surname of Lytton before his patronymic; *b* 14 July 1937; *Educ* Eton, Trinity Coll Cambridge (BA); *m* 7 Jan 1961, Christine Elizabeth, 3 da of Maj Sir Dennis Frederick Bankes Stucley, 5 Bt (d 1983); 3 s (Hon Henry Fromanteel b 1962, Hon Peter Guy Fromanteel b 1964, Hon Richard Stucley Fromanteel b 1968, a Page of Honour to HM The Queen 1980–82), 1 da (Hon Rosina Kim b 1971); *Heir* s, Hon Henry Lytton Cobbold; *Career* NATO flying in Canada, served in RAF 1955–57; Bank of London and S America 1962–72, Finance for Industry 1974–79, BP 1979–87, TSB England and Wales plc 1987–88; md Gaiacorp UK Ltd 1989–94; dir: 39 Production Co Ltd 1987–2000, Hill Samuel Bank Ltd 1988–89, Close Brothers Gp plc 1993–2000, Stevenage Leisure Ltd 1999–2002, English Sinfonia Ltd 1999–2002, Shuttleworth Tst 1999–2002; chm: Lytton Enterprises Ltd 1970–, Stevenage Community Tst 1990–2006; hon treas Historic Houses Assoc 1988–97, govr Union of Euro Historic Houses Assocs 1993–97; crossbench memb House of Lords until 2015 (ret); Univ of Herts: pres Devpt Ctee 1992–2005, memb Bd of Govrs 1993–2005; tstee: Pilgrim Tst 1993–2010, Knebworth House Educn and Preservation Tst 2001–; FACT 1983; *Style*— The Lord Cobbold, DL; ✉ Park Gate House, Knebworth, Hertfordshire SG3 6QD (☎ and fax 01438 817455, website www.knebworthhouse.com)

COBBOLD, Hon Rowland John Fromanteel; yr s of 1 Baron Cobbold, KG, GCVO, PC; *b* 20 June 1944; *Educ* Eton, Trinity Coll Cambridge (MA); *m* 3 June 1969, Sophia Augusta, da of late B N White-Spunner; 1 s, 1 da; *Career* Lt Kent and Co of London Yeo (TA); with BOAC/Br Airways 1966–80, Swire Group 1980–94; chm Ecco Tours Ltd 1995–2015, chm Followme2 Ltd 2015–; dir Cathay Pacific Airways 1987–94, regnl dir Hong Kong Tourist Assoc 1994–97, dir Air Partner plc 1996–2004, dir Groundstar Ltd 1999–2004; dir Swindon and Marlborough NHS Tst 2003–08, dep chm Great Western Hosps NHS Fndn Tst 2008–12; *Style*— The Hon Rowland Cobbold; ✉ The Old Mail House, East Garston, Hungerford, Berks RG17 7HN

COBDEN, Dr Irving; s of Manuel Cobden, of Newcastle upon Tyne, and Fay, *née* Alexander; *b* 18 May 1950; *Educ* Royal GS Newcastle upon Tyne, Univ of Newcastle Med Sch (MB BS, MD); *m* 1, 1972 (m dis 1991), Jennifer Deborah, da of Mark Gilbert; 3 da (Sarah b 1975, Gemma b 1977, Laura b 1982); m 2, 1992, Carolyn Michelle, da of Kenneth Collett; 2 da (Imogen b 1994, Josephine b 1996); *Career* conslt physician N Tyneside Health Centre 1985–, clinical tutor in postgrad med 1986–92, clinical lectr in med Univ of Newcastle upon Tyne 1992–, clinical dir of med North Tyneside Hospital 1994–98, med dir Northumbria Healthcare NHS Tst 1998–2002, sr med advsr Dept of Health 2002–, hon clinical reader Hull-York Med Sch 2004–, med dir Tees, E and N Yorks Ambulance Service 2004–; Wyeth USA travelling fell 1988; contrib many pubns on gastroenterology; hon fell Société Royale Belge de Gastro Enterologie; MRCP 1976, FRCP 1991; *Recreations* bridge, angling, travel, golf; *Style*— Dr Irving Cobden; ✉ North Tyneside Hospital, Rake Lane, North Shields, Tyne & Wear NE29 8NH (☎ 0191 2932581, e-mail irving.cobden@northumbria-healthcare.nhs)

COBHAM, Viscountess Penelope; CBE (2014); da of Roy Cooper (d 1980), and Dorothy, *née* Henshall (subsequently Mrs Turner, d 2006); *b* 2 January 1954, Manchester; *Educ* St James's Sch Malvern; *Career* ptnr Hagley Hall recreation 1979–1994, chm Triton Television Ltd 1989–92, dir Chrysalis Radio London Ltd 1994–2000, chm Chrysalis Radio Midlands Ltd 1993–2007; conslt Ernst & Young 1997–2009; advsr Citi Private Bank 2010–11, advsr CTN Communications 2013–14; chm Advsy Bd Highland Gp Int 2010–14, dep chm Advsy Bd Pagefield 2013; dep chm Visit Britain 2005–09 (memb Bd 2003–), chm Visit England 2009–; cmmr: English Heritage 1989–92, Countryside Cmmn 1991–92, Museums and Galleries Cmmn 1993–2000; memb LGA Ind Cmmn on economic growth and the future of public services in non-metropolitan England 2014; special advsr to Sec of State for Nat Heritage 1992, tstee V&A 1993–2003; memb Bd: HHA 1985–, Historic Royal Palaces Bd 1990–98, LAPADA 1993–94, London Docklands Devpt Corporation 1993–99; memb Strategy Bd Linley 2015–; chm Museum Prize Tst 2006–; chm of tstees: Civic Tst 1999–2003, Art Fund Prize for Museums & Galleries 2002–; chm Br Casino Assoc 1999–2009, memb Cncl Nat Tst 2004–10, dir Bd Historic Houses Assoc, pres Midlands Woman of the Year, memb Bd Birmingham Museums Tst 2012–16, tstee Shakespeare Birthplace Tst 2013–; *Recreations* historic buildings, gardening; *Style*— Penelope, Viscountess Cobham, CBE; ✉ 198 Hagley Road, Stourbridge, West Midlands DY8 2JN (☎ 01384 377517, e-mail canalhse@aol.com)

COCHAND, Charles MacLean (Chas); s of Louis Emile Cochand, and Morna Aldous, *née* Maclean; *b* 2 May 1951, Montreal, Canada; *Educ* Aiglon Coll Chesieres Villars, Univ of Western Ontario (BA); *m* 6 July 1982, Judith Ann, da of John David Harrison, QC, OBE; 3 s (Nicholas John b 1984, Matthew Charles b 1986, Alexander Maclean b 1989); *Career* called to the Bar Middle Temple 1978; in criminal law practice Western Circuit; *Recreations* writing, sailing, skiing, scouting; *Clubs* Eagle Ski (Gstaad); *Style*— Chas M Cochand, Esq; ✉ The Chambers of W Mousley QC, 2 King's Bench Walk, Temple, London EC4 YDN (e-mail clerks@2kbw.com)

COCHRANE, James Michael Thomas; CBE (2013); s of Maj-Gen J Rupert Cochrane, CB, CBE (d 1978), and Hilary, *née* Standen (d 2002); *b* 21 May 1944, Sevenoaks, Kent; *Educ* Marlborough, Clare Coll Cambridge (MA), London Business Sch (MSc); *m* 1975, Dr Maggie Cochrane, *née* Powell; 4 da (Caroline b 20 May 1976, Alison b 18 Oct 1977, Isabel b 7 Feb 1980, Susannah b 18 May 1982); *Career* Shell Chemicals UK 1965–69, md UK and vice-pres Europe Bristol Myers Squibb (formerly Squibb Pharma) 1971–90, dir Europe Wellcome plc 1990–95, dir int GlaxoWellcome plc 1995–2001, chm SW London SHA 2002–06, chm Br Red Cross 2007–12; vice-chair TNT NV 1998–2007; memb Bd LSHTM 2001–08, treas and memb Bd St George's Univ of London 2006–11 (hon fell 2013), chm NHS Innovations London 2007–12, memb Bd Medicines for Malaria Venture 2007–12, cmmr Cmmn on the Voluntary Sector and Ageing 2013–15; assoc memb BUPA; tstee Raleigh Int 2007–14; *Recreations* walking, skiing; *Style*— James Cochrane, Esq, CBE; ✉ e-mail jmtcochrane@gmail.com

COCHRANE, Judith; MLA; *Educ* Queen's Univ Belfast (MBA), Robert Gordon Univ (BSc); *Career* MLA (Alliance) Belfast E 2011–; *Style*— Mrs Judith Cochrane, MLA; ✉ Northern Ireland Assembly, Parliament Buildings, Stormont, Belfast BT4 3XX

COCHRANE, Keith; CBE (2016); *Educ* Univ of Glasgow (BAcc); *m* 1998, Fiona Margaret, *née* Armstrong; 1 s, 1 da; *Career* CA 1989; early career with Arthur Andersen, gp chief exec Stagecoach Holdings plc 1996–2002, dir of gp financial reporting Scottish Power 2003–06; The Weir Gp plc: gp finance dir 2006–09, chief exec 2009–; sr ind dir Carillion plc 2015–, lead non-exec dir Scotland Office 2015–; Hon DSc Univ of Strathclyde 2013; FRSE 2016; *Recreations* golf, music, reading, travel; *Clubs* Royal Perth Golfing Soc, The Golf House; *Style*— Keith Cochrane, Esq, CBE

COCHRANE, Sir (Henry) Marc Sursock; 4 Bt (UK 1903), of Woodbrook, Old Connaught, Bray, Co Wicklow, Lisgar Castle, Bailieborough, Co Cavan, and Kildare Street, City of Dublin; s of Sir Desmond Oriel Alastair George Weston Cochrane, 3 Bt (d 1979), and Yvonne, *née* Sursock; *b* 23 October 1946; *Educ* Eton, Trinity Coll Dublin (BBS, MA); *m* 28 June 1969, Hala, 2 da of Fouad Mahmoud Bey es-Said, of Beirut; 2 s (Alexander Desmond Sursock b 1973, Patrick Talal b 1976), 1 da (Faiza Maria Rosebud b 1971); *Heir* s, Alexander Cochrane; *Career* hon consul gen for Ireland in Lebanon 1979–84; dir: Hambros Bank Ltd 1979–85, GT Management plc/LGT Asset Mgmnt 1985–98, INVESCO 1998–99, Henderson Global Investors 2000–; tstee Chester Beatty Library and Gallery of Oriental Art Dublin; *Recreations* electronics, skiing, shooting; *Clubs* Annabel's, Ham & Petersham Rifle and pistol; *Style*— Sir Marc Cochrane, Bt; ✉ Woodbrook, Bray, Co Wicklow, Republic of Ireland (☎ 00 3531 2821421); Palais Sursock, Beirut, Lebanon

COCHRANE, Prof Peter; OBE (1999); s of Colin Cochrane, of Sutton-in-Ashfield, Notts, and Gladys, *née* Keeton; *b* 11 July 1946; *Educ* Trent Poly (BSc, IEE Prize of the Year), Univ of Essex (MSc, PhD, DSc); *m* 1, 2 May 1971, Brenda (d 2003); 2 da (Catherine b 24 Sept 1973, Sarah b 16 Dec 1974), 2 s (Richard b 27 Nov 1981, Paul b 25 Aug 1987); m 2, 8 Oct 2005, Jane; *Career* student engr British PO 1969–73 (technician system maintenance 1962–69), head of gp British PO Research Labs 1979–83 (exec engr 1973–79); British Telecom: head of section BTRL 1983–87, divnl mangr Optical Networks BTRL 1987–91, divnl mangr systems research BT Labs 1991–93, gen mangr BT Research Labs 1993–94, head of BT Labs Advanced Research 1994–99, chief technologist 1999–2001; co-fndr and dir Concept Labs California 1998–, dir Picosecond Pulse Labs Colorado 1999–2006, co-founding dir Knowledge Vector NC 2003–; non-exec dir iBookers 1999–2003; pt/t lectr People's Coll of Further Educn Nottingham 1972, visiting prof CNET Lannion Univ France 1978, visiting industrial prof Poly of East London 1980–90, scientific collaborator Univ of Liège 1981–91, industrial visiting fell UNCW at Bangor 1985–90; visiting prof: Univ of Essex 1988–2001, Opto-electronics Research Centre Univ of Southampton 1991–98, Telecommunications & IT Systems Centre UCL 1994–2000, Queen Mary Coll London 2005–08, Univ of Herts 2012–; hon prof of communication & electronics and memb Ct Univ of Kent 1991–99; Collier Chair for the Public Understanding of Science and Technology Univ of Bristol 1999–2001; external examiner: CNAA MSc in Info Systems Robert Gordon's Inst of Technol 1990–93, CNAA BSc in Electrical Engrg Nottingham Poly 1991–94; memb Computer Science Corporation Advsy Bd 1996–99; occasional lectr and presenter on telecommunication matters worldwide; author of over 700 scientific papers, patents, articles, edited books and chapters; Hon DUniv Essex 1996; Hon DTech: Staffordshire Univ 1996, Robert Gordon Univ 1999, Univ of Abertay Dundee 2004; Hon DEng: Nottingham Trent Univ 1999, Brunel Univ 2002; FIEE 1987 (MIEE 1977), FIEEE 1992 (MIEEE 1983, sr memb 1987), FREng 1994 (CEng 1977), memb NY Acad of Scis 1995, FRSA; *Recreations* swimming, running, walking, music, reading, flyfishing; *Style*— Prof Peter Cochrane, OBE, FREng; ✉ Cochrane Associates, Suffolk (☎ 07747 863013, e-mail peter@ca-global.org)

COCHRANE, Polly Clare; da of Christopher Cochrane QC, and Caroline, *née* Carey; *b* 5 April 1964, London; *Educ* St Paul's Girls Sch (scholar), Univ of Cambridge (MA); *m* 16 Dec 2004, Tom Sykes; 2 s (Finley b 5 Nov 2000, Oscar b 7 May 2003); *Career* account mangr WCRS 1988–90, account dir Cowan Kemsley Taylor 1990–92, communications mangr Vanity Fair 1992–93, prodct mangr The Observer and devpt mangr Guardian Media Gp 1993–96, head of advtg and promotions Channel 5 TV 1996–98, dir mktg Channel 4 TV 1998–; dir Freeview, non-exec dir Dept of Communities and Local Govt; memb Mktg Gp of GB 2007–; winner of numerous awards for mktg innovation, creativity, effectiveness and planning; *Recreations* travel, film; *Clubs* Soho House; *Style*— Ms Polly Cochrane; ✉ Channel 4, 124 Horseferry Road, London SW1P 2TY (☎ 020 7396 4444)

COCHRANE-DYET, Fergus; OBE (2015); s of Lt-Col I G C Cochrane-Dyet, of Dumfries, and R A Cochrane-Dyet, *née* Carpenter; *b* 16 January 1965, Germany; *Educ* Felsted Sch, Jesus Coll Oxford, Univ of Durham, SOAS, Univ of Exeter; *m* 1987, Susie, *née* Aram; 3 s (James b 24 Feb 1990, Alex b 4 Nov 1991, William b 5 Oct 1996); *Career* HM Diplomatic Serv: joined 1987–, served in Lagos then Abuja Nigeria 1990–94, head Br Interests Section Tripoli Libya 1996–97, head commercial section Jakarta Indonesia 1998, dep consul gen Sydney Aust 1998–2001, chargé d'affaires Conakry Guinea 2001–02, chargé d'affaires Kabul Afghanistan 2002, dep head Africa Dept (Southern) FCO 2002–04, dep high cmmr to Zambia 2004–07, dep head Helmand Afghanistan 2007, high cmmr to Seychelles 2007–09, high cmmr to Malawi 2009–11, dep head Helmand Afghanistan 2012, ambass to Liberia 2013–15, head Int Skills FCO 2015–; *Recreations* scuba diving, running, films, books; *Style*— Fergus Cochrane-Dyet, Esq, OBE; ✉ c/o FCO, King Charles Street, London SW1A 2AH

COCKBURN, Charles Christopher; s and h of Sir John Elliot Cockburn, 12 Bt, *qv*, and Glory Patricia, *née* Mullings; *b* 19 November 1950; *Educ* Emanuel Sch, City of London Poly (BA), Garnett Coll London (CertEd); *m* 1, 1978, Beverly J (d 1999), o da of B Stangroom (d 1995), of Richmond, Surrey; m 2, 1985, Margaret Ruth, da of Samuel Esmond Bell (d 1999), of Bury Green, Herts; 2 s (Christopher Samuel Alexander b 24 March 1986, William James John b 26 Feb 1996), 1 da (Charlotte Elspeth Catherine (twin) b 24 March 1986); *Career* lectr; conslt in govt relations, ed Financial Regulation Review, chm Portcullis Research Ltd (govt relations conslts); visiting lectr (lobbying major) INSEEC; chm Speakability; MCIPR, MInstD; *Recreations* cycling, song-writing, travelling; *Clubs* IOD, Twickenham Rowing; *Style*— Charles Cockburn, Esq; ✉ Portcullis Public Affairs, 11 Haymarket, St James, London SW1Y 4BP (☎ 020 7368 3100, e-mail charles.cockburn@portcullispublicaffairs.com)

COCKBURN, William; CBE (1989), TD (1980); s of Edward Cockburn (d 1986), of Edinburgh, and Alice, *née* Brennan (d 1983); *b* 28 February 1943; *Educ* Holy Cross Acad Edinburgh (Dip); *m* 25 July 1970, Susan Elisabeth, da of Maj William Phillpots, MBE; 2 da (Rachel b 1974, Rebecca b 1977); *Career* TA Royal Logistic Corps Postal and Courier Serv 1968, Hon Col 1990, Hon Col Cmdt 1996–2007; PO: Glasgow 1961, PA to Chm 1971–73, asst dir of fin and planning 1973–77, dir of central planning 1977–78, dir postal fin 1978–79, dir London Postal Region 1979–82, memb PO Bd 1981, memb for Fin Counter Servs and Planning 1982–84, memb for Royal Mail Ops 1984–86; md Royal Mail 1986–92, chief exec The Post Office 1992–95, chm International Postal Corporation 1994–95; chief exec W H Smith Group plc 1996–97 (dir 1995–97), gp md British Telecommunications plc 1997–2001; non-exec chm Parity Group plc 2001–04, non-exec dep chm Business Post Group plc 2002–; non-exec dir: Watkins Holdings Ltd 1985–93, Lex Service plc 1993–2002, Whitbread plc 1995 (resigned Nov), Centrica plc 1996–99; dep chm AWG plc 2003–06; non-exec memb Bd Business in the Community 1990–2003, memb Cncl The Industrial Soc 1992–2002, govr Euro Fndn for Quality Mgmnt 1992–95, chm Sch Teachers' Review Body 2002–08, chm Sr Salaries Review Bd 2008–, non-exec dir Exec Ctee Army Bd 2008–11; Freeman City of London 1980; CIMgt 1995; FCIT 1991, FRSA 1992; *Style*— William Cockburn, Esq, CBE, TD

COCKCROFT, Dr Barry; CBE (2010); *Educ* Univ of Birmingham; *Career* Dept of Health: dep chief dental offr 2002–05, acting chief dental offr 2005–06, chief dental offr 2006–; *Style*— Dr Barry Cockcroft, CBE; ✉ Office of the Chief Dental Officer, Department of Health, Richmond House, 79 Whitehall, London SW1A 2NS

COCKELL, Sir Merrick Richard; kt (2010); *b* 16 June 1957; *Career* trader F M Barshall Ltd 1977–82, fndr and dir Abingdon Cockell Ltd 1982–2006; dir Localis Research Ltd 2008– (chm 2009–), exec chm Cratus Communications Ltd 2014–, sr advsr PA Consulting Gp 2014–; cncllr Kensington and Chelsea Royal Borough Cncl 1986–2015 (chm of educn 1992–95, Cons chief whip 1995–2000, ldr 2000–13); memb London Governance Cmmn 2004–06, chm London Cncls 2006–10, chm Local Govt Assoc 2011–14, chm Crossrail 2 Growth Cmmn 2015–; chm Cons Cncllrs' Assoc 2008–11, memb Bd Cons Pty 2008–11; memb Bd London Pension Fund Authy 2010– (dep chm 2013–15, chm 2015–), chm UK Municipal Bonds Agency 2015–; govr Chelsea Acad 2008–14, govr Kensington Aldridge Acad 2014–; Hon Col 41 (Princess Louise's Kensington) Sqdn 38 Signal Regt (voluntary) 2012–; Freeman City of London 2008; *Clubs* Chelsea Arts; *Style*— Sir Merrick Cockell; ✉ c/o LPFA, 2nd Floor, 169 Union Street, London SE1 0LL (☎ 020 7369 6006, e-mail mrc@cockell.co)

COCKER, Victor; CBE (2000); s of Harold Nathan Cocker (d 2001), and Marjorie Cocker (d 1986); *b* 30 October 1940, Sheffield; *Educ* King Edward VII GS Sheffield, Univ of Nottingham (BA); *m* 24 Aug 1963, Jennifer Muriel, *née* Nicholls; 2 da (Jane Andrea (Mrs Nutt) b 13 Nov 1965, Susan Frances (Mrs Williams) b 2 May 1967); *Career* economist; North West Gas 1963–68, West Midlands Gas 1968–74, head of corporate planning Severn Trent Water Authy 1974–89; Severn Trent Water Ltd: md 1991–95, chair 1995–2000; gp chief exec Severn Trent plc 1995–2000; chair: Waste and Resources Action Prog (WRAP) 2000–08, Cncl WaterAid 2001–07 (tstee 1996–2007), Aga Foodservice Gp 2004–08 (non-exec dir 2000–08); non-exec dir Modern Waste 2008; memb Cncl: RNLI (vice pres 2011), RSA 2004; memb Bd of Govrs Birmingham City Univ 2009–, pro-chllr and dep chm Birmingham City Univ 2011–14; Freeman City of London, Liveryman Worshipful Co of Water Conservators; Hon DUniv Central England 2006; Hon FCIWM 2004, FCIWEM, FCMI, FRSA; *Recreations* Fakenham Ramblers (sec), North Norfolk U3A (vice-chair), national hunt racing; *Style*— Victor Cocker, Esq, CBE; ✉ Aldercarr, Bayfield, Holt, Norfolk NR25 7JW

COCKING, Prof Edward Charles Daniel; s of Charles Edward Cocking (d 1965), and Mary, *née* Murray (d 1994); *b* 26 September 1931; *Educ* Buckhurst Hill Co HS, Univ of Bristol (BSc, PhD, DSc); *m* 6 Aug 1960, Bernadette, da of Frank Keane (d 1948); 1 s (Sean Daniel b 1961), 1 da (Sarah Anne b 1966); *Career* Civil Serv Cmmn res fell 1956–59; Univ of Nottingham: lectr in plant physiology 1959–66, reader in botany 1966–69, prof of botany 1969–97 (emeritus 1997–), head Dept of Botany 1969–91; memb: Bd of Tstees Royal Botanic Gardens Kew 1983–93, Cncl Royal Soc 1986–88; memb Governing Body Rothamsted Experimental Station 1991– (chm 1999–2003, memb Lawes Agric Tst Ctee 1987–91), memb Lawes Agric Tst Co 1999–2015; Royal Soc assessor AFRC 1988–90, memb Cncl AFRC 1990–94 (chm Plants & Environment Res Ctee); tstee Uppingham Sch 1997–2007; Leverhulme Tst res fell 1995–97 (emeritus res fell 2000–02); Lifetime Achievement Award Univ of Toledo USA 2004; memb Academia Europaea 1993, hon memb Hungarian Acad of Scis 1995, fell Indian Acad Agric Sciences 2000, fell World Innovation Fndn 2003; FRS 1983; *Books* Introduction to the Principles of Plant Physiology (with W Stiles, 1969); *Recreations* walking, travelling by train, gothic architecture (A W N Pugin), occassional chess; *Style*— Prof Edward Cocking, FRS; ✉ 30 Patterdale Road, Woodthorpe, Nottingham NG5 4LQ; Centre for Crop Nitrogen Fixation, Life Science Building, University of Nottingham, Nottingham NG7 2RD (☎ 0115 951 3056)

COCKLE, Ted; *b* 17 August 1972, Wendover, Bucks; *Educ* Aylesbury GS, Univ of Bristol; *m* Joanne, *née* Reid; 1 s (Larry b 26 Feb 2007), 1 da (Thandie b 15 Oct 2008); *Career* Sony 1995–2005, co-pres Island Records UK 2008–13 (joined 2005), pres Virgin EMI Records UK 2013–; *Style*— Ted Cockle, Esq; ✉ Virgin EMI Records, 364 Kensington High Street, London W14 8NS

COCKS, David John; QC (1982); *Educ* Univ of Oxford (MA); *Career* called to the Bar Lincoln's Inn 1961, head of chambers 5 King's Bench Walk, recorder of the Crown Court; chm Criminal Bar Association 1985–88; *Style*— David Cocks, Esq, QC; ✉ 18 Red Lion Court, London EC4A 3EB (☎ 020 7520 6000)

COCKS, Dr Leonard Robert Morrison (Robin); OBE (1999), TD (1979); s of Ralph Morrison Cocks (d 1970), and Lucille Mary, *née* Blackler (d 1996); *b* 17 June 1938; *Educ* Felsted, Hertford Coll Oxford (MA, DPhil, DSc); *m* 31 Aug 1963, Elaine Margaret, da of Canon J B Sturdy; 1 s (Mark b 1964), 2 da (Zoe b 1967, Julia b 1970); *Career* 2 Lt RA 1957–59, active serv Malaya; scientist Nat History Museum 1965– (Keeper of Palaeontology 1986–98), cmmr Int Cmmn on Zoological Nomenclature 1980–2000; visiting prof Imperial Coll London 1997–2001; sec Geological Soc 1985–89 (pres 1998–2000); visitor Oxford Univ Museum 1997–2008; pres: Palaeontological Assoc 1986–88 (Lapworth Medal 2010), Palaeontographical Soc 1994–98, Geologists' Assoc 2004–06; Pingat Jasa Malaysian Medal 2012; CGeol, FGS; *Books* The Evolving Earth (1981), Encyclopedia of Geology (2005), Earth History and Palaeogeography (2016), contrib to over 190 articles in sci jls on geology and palaeontology; *Style*— Dr Robin Cocks, OBE, TD; ✉ Department of Earth Sciences, Natural History Museum, Cromwell Road, London SW7 5BD (☎ 020 7942 5140, e-mail r.cocks@nhm.ac.uk)

COCKSHAW, Sir Alan; kt (1992); s of John Cockshaw (d 1986), and Maud, *née* Simpson (d 1996); *b* 14 July 1937; *Educ* Farnworth GS, Univ of Leeds (BSc); *m* 17 Dec 1960, Brenda, da of Fred Payne; 1 s (John Nigel b 1964), 3 da (Elizabeth Ann b 1967, Sally Louise b 1970, Catherine Helen b 1979); *Career* chief exec: Fairclough Civil Engineering Ltd 1978–85, Fairclough-Parkinson Mining Ltd 1982–85; AMEC plc: dir 1983–97, chief exec 1984–88, chm 1988–97; chm: Overseas Projects Bd 1992–95, Oil & Gas Projects & Supplies Office 1994–97, Manchester Millennium Ltd 1996–2003, Shawbridge Management Ltd 1996–, Roxboro Gp plc 1997–2005, English Partnerships 1998–2001, Commission for New Towns 1998–2001, Major Projects Assoc 1998–2004, New East Manchester Ltd 1999–2002, Cibitas Ltd 2003–, HPR Hldgs Ltd 2003–; chm and dir Br Airways Regnl 1999–2003; non-exec dep chm NORWEB plc 1992–95, non-exec dir The New Millennium Experience Co Ltd 1997–2000, dir Pidemco/Capitaland Ltd Singapore 1999–2005; memb British Overseas Trade Bd 1992–95; life pres North West Business Leadership Team 1997–, pres ICE 1997–98 (sr vice-pres 1996–97); chm of Govrs Bolton Sch 1997–2009; Hon DEng UMIST 1997, Hon DSc Univ of Salford 1998; FREng 1986; *Recreations* rugby (both codes), cricket, walking, gardening; *Style*— Sir Alan Cockshaw, FREng; ✉ e-mail sac@shawbridge.co.uk

CODARIN, Judith; da of William Ernest Walker (d 1971), of Thornham, N Norfolk, and Mary Eileen Jacob; *b* 8 July 1946; *Educ* Kings Lynn HS for Girls, Norwich Sch of Art, Birmingham Coll of Art; *m* Armando Codarin, s of Venceslao Codarin; 1 da (Melanie Maria b 8 Dec 1973), 1 s (Pierre Daniel b 28 April 1980); *Career* design conslt; architectural asst Casson Conder & Partners; freelance res and commercial illustrating, designing and concept presentation and development for cos incl: Conran Design Group, Fitch, McColl, Ryman, Franco Nadali Ltd, Baker Sayer; practises as Codarin Associates Interior Designers & Design Management for nat and int clients 1988–; lectr in interior design: South East Essex Coll 1993–2000 and 2005–11 (former govr for design industry), Chelsea Sch of Art 2001–; author of numerous published articles and courses; CSD: fell 1998, past chm Interiors Gp; *Recreations* walking, swimming, landscape gardening, holidaying with the family; *Style*— Mrs Judith Codarin; ✉ Codarin Associates Interior Designers & Design Management, 14 Riviera Drive, Southend on Sea, Essex SS1 2RB

CODY, Sebastian; s of Stephen Cody (d 1990), and Maria, *née* Schenker-Angerer (d 2008); *b* 6 October 1956; *Educ* King Alfred Sch Hampstead, Univ of Vienna, Univ of York (BA), Nat Film Sch (trained as dir); *m* 1997, Annabel, *née* Cole; 2 da (Elsa b 31 July 1999, Rosa b 23 Aug 2002), 1 s (Christopher b 30 May 2004); *Career* researcher BBC TV 1979–81; prodr and dir: Why Do I Believe You... 1983, Before His Very Eyes 1984; staff prodr Royal Opera House Covent Garden 1985, ed After Dark (Channel 4, BBC) 1987–2003; freelance writer and conslt 1979–; exec prodr Open Media 1987–; progs: The Secret Cabaret 1990–92, James Randi – Psychic Investigator 1991, Opinions 1993–94, Brave New World 1994, Is This Your Life? 1995–96, The Mediator 1995, Natural Causes 1996, Suez 1996, Secrets of the Psychics 1997, Mossad: The Spy Machine 1998; assoc prodr Top Ten Monks (HBO) 2010; co-fndr InView (BFI online social history of Britain) 2009; album Chant: Music For Paradise 2008 (Gold Disk); memb Sr Advsy Bd 21st Century Tst 1996–2009; memb Editorial Bd Jl of Political Marketing 2002–; visiting fell Rothermere American Inst Univ of Oxford 2000–04, sr assoc memb St Antony's Coll Oxford 2004, assoc fell Rothermere American Inst Univ of Oxford 2005–11, visiting research assoc Oxford Univ Centre for the Environment (ECI) 2011–; special advsr to the dir Int Inst for Applied Systems Analysis (IIASA) 2005–; *Clubs* Garrick, Savile, Jockey (Vienna), St Johann's (Vienna); *Style*— Sebastian Cody, Esq; ✉ Open Media, 38 Berkeley Square, London W1J 5AE (☎ 020 7603 9029, website www.openmedia.co.uk)

COE, Gerry; s of Jack Turland Sanders Coe, and Sarah Jane, *née* McCabe; *b* 29 April 1948, Desborough, Northants; *m* 17 Sept 1976, Lorna, *née* Mayne; 1 da (Emma Jane b 18 March 1981); *Career* photographer; prodr of fine art images for both home and office; only Irish winner of AGFA UK and Ireland Portrait Photographer of the Year Award, first ever double BIPP Peter Grugeon Award winner; first ever winner of a BIPP fellowship for iPhone Photography; FBIPP, FMPA, FRPS, FSWPP, first quadruple fell in Ireland for pictorial/illustrative photography, hon fell BIPP 2016; *Publications* contributions to many articles and magazines; *Recreations* mostly photographic, walking, reading, computer studies; *Clubs* Bangor & North Down Camera; *Style*— Gerry Coe; ✉ COE- photographer, 14 Morningside, Bangor BT20 5PD (mobile 07846 871704, e-mail gerrycoe@fastmail.fm, website www.gerrycoe.co.uk, www.coe-artworks.co.uk and www.iphone-art.co.uk)

COE, Jonathan; s of Roger Frank Coe, of Birmingham, and Janet Mary Kay; *b* 19 August 1961; *Educ* King Edward's Sch Birmingham, Trinity Coll Cambridge (BA), Univ of Warwick (MA, PhD); *m* 1989, Janine McKeown; 2 da (Matilda b Sept 1997, Madeline b Nov 2000); *Career* writer; memb Soc of Authors 1995; FRSL 2012; Chevalier de l'Ordre des Arts et des Lettres 2004; *Awards* Mail on Sunday John Llewellyn Rhys Prize 1995, Prix du Meilleur Livre Etranger 1996, Writer's Guild Best Fiction Award 1997, Prix Médicis Etranger 1998, Bollinger Everyman Wodehouse Prize 2001, Premio Arzobispo San Clemente 2003, Samuel Johnson Prize 2005; *Books* The Accidental Woman (1987), A Touch of Love (1989), The Dwarves of Death (1990), What A Carve Up! (1994), The House of Sleep (1997), The Rotters' Club (2001), Like a Fiery Elephant: The Story of B S Johnson (2004, Samuel Johnson Prize 2005), The Closed Circle (2004), The Rain Before It Falls (2007), The Terrible Privacy of Maxwell Sim (2010), Lo Specchio dei Desideri (2012), Expo 58 (2013), The Story of Gulliver (2013); *Style*— Jonathan Coe, Esq; ✉ c/o Tony Peake, Peake Associates, PO Box 66726, London NW5 9FE (☎ 020 7681 4307, fax 0870 141 0447, e-mail tony@tonypeake.com)

COE, Her Honour Judge Rosalind; QC (2008); *Career* called to the Bar 1983; recorder 2003, circuit judge (Midland Circuit) 2011–, bencher (Middle Temple) 2013; *Style*— Her Honour Judge Coe, QC; ✉ Nottingham Crown Court, 60 Canal Street, Nottingham NG1 7EL

COE, Baron (Life Peer UK 2000), of Ranmore in the County of Surrey; Sir Sebastian Newbold Coe; CH (2013), KBE (2006, OBE 1990, MBE 1981); s of Peter Coe, and Angela, *née* Lall (d 2005); *b* 29 September 1956; *Educ* Tapton Sch Sheffield, Loughborough Univ (BSc); *m* 23 Aug 1990 (m dis), Nicola McIrvine; 2 da (Hon Madeleine Rose b 8 July 1992, Hon Alice India Violet b 25 Sept 1998), 2 s (Hon Harry Sebastian Newbold b 29 Sept 1994, Hon Peter Henry Christopher b 31 May 1996); *Career* former athlete; broke 12 world records incl 800m (holder until 1997), 1500m and 1 mile, Gold medal 1500m Olympic Games 1980 and 1984, Silver medal 800m Olympic Games 1980 and 1984, Gold medal 800m World Cup 1981, Gold medal 800m Euro Championships 1986, ret 1990; MP (Cons) Falmouth and Camborne 1992–97; PPS to Roger Freeman: as min of state for defence 1994–95, as Chllr of the Duchy of Lancaster 1995–96; PPS to Michael Heseltine as dep PM 1995–96, Govt whip 1996–97; chief of staff and private sec to Rt Hon William Hague, MP as Ldr of the Oppn 1997–2001; chm and pres London 2012 Olympic Games bid 2004–05 (vice-chm 2003–04), chm LOCOG (London Organising Ctee of the Olympic Games and Paralympic Games) 2005–12, chm British Olympic Assoc 2012–; memb Sports Cncl of GB 1983– (vice-chm 1986), chm Sports Cncls Olympic Review 1985–86; memb: Health Educn Authy (formerly Health Educn Cncl) 1986–, Athletes Cmmn, Med Cmmn Int Olympic Ctee 1987–2002, Cncl Int Assoc of Athletics Fedns (IAAF) 2003–; assoc memb Académie Des Sports France 1982–; steward Br Boxing Bd of Control 1994–; global advsr Nike, columnist Daily Telegraph; pres Amateur Athletics Assoc of England until 2004, founding memb Laureus World Sports Acad; Kiphuth fell Yale Univ 1982, Hon DTech Loughborough Univ 1985, Hon DSc Univ of Hull 1988; hon fell Univ of Wales Inst 2008; *Books* Running Free, Running for Fitness with Peter Coe (1983), The Olympians (1984, 2 edn 1996), The Winning Mind: My Inside Track on Great Leadership (2009); *Clubs* East India and Sportsman's; *Style*— The Lord Coe, CH, KBE; ✉ CSM, Southside, 6th Floor, 105 Victoria Street, London SW1E 6QT (☎ 020 7593 5231, e-mail sara@csm.com)

COE, Stephen; s of Richard Gerald Coe (d 1964), of Brentwood, Essex, and Mary, *née* Fox (d 1961); *b* 6 Feb 1943, Khartoum; *Educ* Brentwood Sch, London Coll of Printing; *m* 1965 (m dis 1975); 1 s (Simon b 1966), 1 da (Elinor b 1976); *Career* photographer; freelance for Picture Agency until 1963, own studio 1963–93, freelance fine art photographer 1993–; current project African film and book: Dinesen & Finch Hatton; features incl: various cmmns in Vogue 1961–63, American 6 Fleet in Mediterranean, Cassius Clay (Muhammad Ali), covers for Queen and About Town magazines, posters of African landscapes for Athena; authored image 'Surreal Reflected Eye, 1964' appropriated as 'Untitled' 1983 by Richard Prince; advtg campaigns incl: Heinz soup posters 1963–66, Tern Shirts, Remington, Volkswagen, Rolls Royce, COI, Samaritans, Red Cross, Microsoft 1996; exhbns incl: Little Squares of Hampstead 1987, NW3 and Beyond (London, Africa & Scandinavia) 1988, Spirit of Hampstead (Burgh House London) 1994, Awesome Tones & Moments (Burgh House London) 1997, rephotograph (Seeing Things Exhbn V&A) 2002; work in private collections in London, Paris, Melbourne, Nairobi, Sweden and throughout USA; initial memb: Advtg Film and Video Prodrs Assoc (formerly Advtg Film Prodrs Assoc) 1967, Assoc of Photographers (formerly AFAEP) 1969 (vice-chm 1973–74); memb Pilgrims to Willoughby Res Assoc Heath & Old Hampstead; memb Players and Playwrights; *Awards* Master Photographers Assoc Shield, Layton Award (for Heinz campaign) 1963, various D&AD awards 1965–76, One Show Award (USA) 1966, Communication Art Award (USA) 1966, Venice Film Festival Award (Diploma) 1968, D&AD Silver Award, Creative Circle Award, Brit Press Award and two Grand Slam Awards for COI campaign Put Your Fingers over Headlights 1976; *Publications* Africa Adorned (with Angela Fisher, 1983), Lazy Afternoon (fine art print), Hampstead Memories (2000); articles in Br Jl of Photography; *Recreations* cinema, music, lighting design, memb local initiatives on restoration of Victorian street lighting, conservation and tree mgmnt etc, architectural woodwork, creative writing, hill and coastal walking, tennis, creative recycling, browsing, antiquarian books; *Clubs* White Elephant on the River, Club Rollei (Jersey); *Style*— Stephen Coe, Esq; ✉ e-mail stephencoe@telia.com

COELHO, George Arjun; s of George Victor Coelho (d 1999), of India, and Rani, *née* Krishnamachari (d 1997); *b* 8 June 1952; *Educ* American Univ (BS), George Washington Univ (MBA); *m* 20 April 1995, Margo, da of Robert O'Brien, of California, and Jo Ann, *née* Ulloa (d 1989); *Career* asst vice-pres Bank of America Airlines and Aerospace Gp 1978–80; vice-pres: Union Bank of Switzerland 1980–86, Nomura Securities 1987–90; asst treas M&A and strategic investments Intel Corp 1990–95, vice-pres Intel International 1995–99, ptnr Benchmark Capital Europe 2000–08, md Good Energies (UK) 2008–; memb Bd TiE UK (charter memb); tstee George Washington Univ, memb Bd of Advsrs Sch of Business George Washington Univ, life memb Ognisko Polskie, life fell RSA; *Recreations* bass guitar, skiing, shooting, classic rallying; *Clubs* Home House, Century; *Style*— George A Coelho; ✉ e-mail gacoelho@aol.com

COEY, Prof (John) Michael David; s of David Stuart Coey (d 1993), and Joan Elizabeth, *née* Newsam (d 2003); *b* 24 February 1945, Belfast; *Educ* Tonbridge Sch, Univ of Cambridge (BA), Univ of Manitoba (PhD), Institut Nat Polytechnique Grenoble (Diplôme d'Habilitation), Univ of Dublin (ScD); *m* 1 Sept 1973, Wong May; 2 s (James b 1978, Dominic b 1985); *Career* chargé de recherche CNRS Grenoble 1971–78, IBM Yorktown Heights 1976–77, successively lectr, assoc prof, prof of experimental physics, Eramus Smith's prof of natural and experimental philosophy and prof emeritus TCD 1978–; visiting academic appts: IBM Yorktown Heights 1979, Inst of Physics Peking 1980, McGill Univ Montreal 1982, Univ of Bordeaux 1984, Centre d'Études Nucléaires (CEN) Grenoble 1985, Johns Hopkins Univ 1986, Univ of Paris VI 1992, Univ of Calif San Diego 1997, Florida State Univ 1998, Univ of Paris XI 1998, Le Mans Univ 1999, 2001 and 2003, Univ of Strasbourg 2006 and 2015, Nat Univ of Singapore 2012–, Beihang Univ Peking 2014–; advsy ed: Physical Review Letters, Jl of Magnetism and Magnetic Materials, Materials Science and Engrg B; fndr and dir Magnetic Solutions Ltd 1994; Charles Chree Medal and Prize Inst of Physics 1997, Fulbright fell 1997; fell Trinity Coll Dublin 1982, Dr (hc) Institut Nat Polytechnique Grenoble 1994; fell American Mineralogical Soc 1995, fell American Physical Soc 2000, foreign assoc Nat Acad of Sciences 2005; FInstP 1984, MRIA 1987 (vice-pres 1989–90), FRS 2003; *Publications* Magnetic Glasses (with K Moorjani, 1984), Current Topics in Magnetism (1987), Structural and Magnetic Phase Transitions in Minerals (1988), Concerted European Action on Magnets (ed, 1989), Rare Earth Iron Permanent Magnets (1996), Permanent Magnetism (with R Skomski, 1999), Magnetism and Magnetic Materials (2010); also over 600 research and review papers in refereed jls; *Recreations* gardening; *Style*— Prof Michael Coey; ☎ 00 353 1 896 1470, fax 00 353 1 671 1759, e-mail jcoey@tcd.ie

COFFEY, Ann; MP; *b* 31 August 1946; *Educ* Nairn Acad, Bodmin GS, Bushey GS, South Bank Poly, Walsall Coll of Educn, Univ of Manchester (BSc, MSc); *m* 1 (m dis); m 2 Peter Saraga 1998; 1 da; *Career* social worker: Birmingham 1972–73, Gwynedd 1973–74, Wolverhampton 1974–75, Stockport 1977–82, Cheshire 1982–88; team ldr (fostering) Oldham Social Servs 1988–92; MP (Lab) Stockport 1992– (Parly candidate (Lab) Cheadle 1987); oppn whip 1995–96, oppn frontbench spokesperson on health (community care and social servs) 1996–97; PPS to: Rt Hon Tony Blair, MP, *qv*, 1997–98, Rt Hon Alistair Darling, MP, *qv*, 1998–; memb Select Ctee Modernisation; cncllr Stockport DC 1984–92 (ldr Lab gp 1988–92); memb USDAW; *Recreations* photography, drawing, cinema, swimming, reading; *Style*— Ann Coffey, MP; ✉ House of Commons, London SW1A 0AA

COFFEY, Dr Thérèse Anne; MP; *Educ* UCL (BSc, PhD); *Career* Mars Inc 1997–2009, property finance manager BBC 2009; MP (Cons) Suffolk Coastal 2010–; *Style*— Dr Thérèse Coffey, MP; ✉ House of Commons, London SW1A 0AA

COGBILL, Alan; *b* 1 December 1952; *Educ* Exeter Coll Oxford; *m* Vivienne Cogbill, *née* Dews; 1 s, 1 da; *Career* joined Civil Serv 1974, Home Office 1974–91, various positions rising to finance dir Lord Chllr's Dept (latterly Miny of Justice) 1992–2005, dir Wales Office 2005–09, chief exec Local Govt Boundary Cmmn for England 2009–14; assoc UCL Constitution Unit 2015–; tstee Avenues 2015–; *Style*— Alan Cogbill, Esq; ✉ e-mail alancogbill@blueyonder.co.uk

COGDELL, Prof Richard John; s of Harry William Frank Cogdell (d 1991), and Evelyn, *née* Passmore; *b* 4 February 1949; *Educ* Royal GS Guildford, Univ of Bristol (BSc, PhD); *m* 20 June 1970, Barbara, *née* Lippold; 1 da (Lucy Miriam), 1 s (Jesse Simon); *Career* postdoctoral res Cornell Univ 1973–74, sr fell Dept of Biochemistry Univ of Washington 1974–75; Dept of Botany Univ of Glasgow: lectr in biochemistry 1975–86, sr lectr 1986, head of dept 1987–93, titular prof 1988, Hooker chair of botany 1993–; dir Inst of Molecular, Cell & Systems Biology and dep head Coll of Medical, Veterinary and Life Sciences Univ of Glasgow; EMBO fell Univ of Göttingen 1977; visiting res fell: Univ of Calif 1979, Univ of Illinois 1980; visiting prof: Univ of Munich 1983, Univ of Calif 1986, Univ of Paris-Sud 2004; pres Int Soc for Carotenoid Research; memb: Biochemical Soc, Br Photobiology Soc, American Photobiology Soc, Scottish and Newcastle Bioenergetics Gp; memb bd govrs Scottish Crop Research Inst; dir Mylnefield Research Services Ltd, dir Mylnefield Holdings Ltd, tstee Mylnefield Tst, tstee TGAC (The Genome Analysis Centre) 2011–13, chair Scientific Advsy Bd Max Planck Inst; guest lectr award Max Planck Inst for Radiation Chemistry Germany 1997; Alexander von Humboldt Research Prize 1996, Diawa Adrian Prize Tokyo 2001; author of numerous scientific pubns; chm Glasgow McIntyre Begonia Tst 2002–; FRSE 1991, FRS 2007, FRSA 2009, FSB 2011; *Recreations* cricket, opera, travel; *Style*— Prof Richard Cogdell, FRSE, FRS, FRSA; ✉ Institute of Molecular, Cell & Systems Biology, College of Medical, Veterinary and Life Sciences, University of Glasgow, Glasgow G12 8QO (e-mail richard.cogdell@glasgow.ac.uk)

C

COGHLAN, Terence Augustine; QC (1993); s of Austin Coghlan (d 1981), of Horsted Keynes, W Sussex, and Ruby, *née* Comrie; *b* 17 August 1945; *Educ* Downside, Perugia, Univ of Oxford (MA); *m* 11 Aug 1973, Angela, da of Rev F E Westmacott (d 1987), of Barsham, Suffolk; 1 s (Thomas Alexander b 1975), 2 da (Candida Mary b 1978, Anna Frances b 1988); *Career* RAFVR (Oxford Univ Air Sqdn) 1964–67; film extra 1967–68 (speaking part as Heinkel bomber pilot in Battle of Britain 1968); called to the Bar Inner Temple 1968 (scholar, bencher 2005); in practice 1968–, recorder of the Crown Court 1985–2010; memb Ct of Appeal Mediation Panel 1998–, tbnl judge Mental Health Review Tbnl 2000–15; dir: City of London Sinfonia 1973–2010, Temple Music Fndn 2005–13; chm St Endellion Festivals Tst 2012–; MCIArb; *Recreations* music, birdwatching, cycling, walking around old churches with Pevsner, cooking, skiing; *Clubs* Omar Khayyam, Les Six, MCC; *Style*— Terence Coghlan, Esq, QC; ✉ e-mail terence.coghlan@1cor.com

COGHLIN, Rt Hon Sir Patrick; kt (1997), PC (2009); s of James Edwin Coghlin (d 1959), and Margaret van Hovenberg, *née* Brown (d 1977); *b* 7 November 1945; *Educ* Royal Belfast Academical Instn, Queen's Univ Belfast (LLB), Christ's Coll Cambridge (Dip Criminology); *m* 6 Aug 1971, Patricia Ann Elizabeth, da of Robert Young; 3 da (Jennifer Elaine b 9 April 1974, Caroline Laura b 28 Dec 1975, Sara Gail Rhodes b 6 March 1981), 1 s (Richard James b 1 Aug 1978); *Career* called to the Bar: NI 1970, England and Wales 1975, Republic of Ireland 1993, NSW 1993; jr crown counsel NI 1983–85, QC (NI) 1985, dep County Court judge 1983–94, sr crown counsel NI 1993–97, judge of the High Court of Justice NI 1997–2008, a Lord Justice of Appeal NI 2008–15; NI judicial appointments cmmr 2008–15; vice-chm Mental Health Review Tbnl NI 1986–97, memb Law Reform Advsy Ctee NI 1989–93, vice-pres VAT Tbnl NI 1990–93, chm Exec Cncl of the Bar NI 1991–93, pres Lands Tbnl NI 1999–2015, dep chm Boundary Cmmn for NI 1999–2002, memb Cncl Assoc of European Competition Law Judges 2002–; hon bencher Gray's Inn 2000; *Recreations* reading, travelling, rugby, squash; *Clubs* Royal Ulster Yacht, Bangor Rugby and Cricket, Ballyholme Bombers Football, Ulster Perennials Rugby, Kildare Street & University; *Style*— The Rt Hon Sir Patrick Coghlin; ✉ The Royal Courts of Justice, Chichester Street, Belfast BT1 3JF (☎ 028 902 35111)

COGILL, Julie Antoinette; *née* Berry; da of Arthur Harold Berry (d 1971), of Blackburn, Lancs, and Mary Margaret Berry (d 1991); *b* 25 August 1945; *Educ* Notre Dame GS Blackburn, Univ of Liverpool (BSc), KCL (MA, EdD); *m* 1967 (m dis 2008); 3 c (Adelene Mary b 1968, Eleanor Ruth b 1969, Geoffrey Owen b 1971); *Career* head of mathematics and asst head Tolworth Girl's Sch 1980–87, chief educn offr BBC 1991–2001 (educn offr 1987–88); currently educn media conslt, md Framerstamp; FRSA; *Publications* You Can Use an Interactive Whiteboard, Star Maths Ys 1–6: Starters, Star Maths Ys 1–6: Puzzles and Problems, Star Maths Ys 1–6: Tools, Scholastic Primary Science: Move It, Force Factor, Healthy Habitats (2011), Scholastic 100 Science Lessons Year 5 (2014); *Recreations* walking, stamp collecting, picture framing, travelling; *Style*— Dr Julie Cogill; ☎ 020 8663 1501, e-mail juliecogill@hotmail.com, websites www.juliecogill.co.uk and www.framerstamp.com

COHEN; *see also:* Waley-Cohen

COHEN, Andrew; s of Geof Cohen (d 2007), and Barbara, *née* Briscoll; *b* 1 January 1973, Essex; *Educ* Univ of Manchester (BSc), Imperial Coll London (MSc); *m* 9 Feb 2003, Anna, *née* Mishcon; 2 s (Benjamin Harry b 2 Oct 2003, Theodore George b 29 March 2009), 1 da (Martha Esme b 6 April 2005); *Career* BBC: series prod Edge of Life 1995–2005, ed Horizon 2005–10, head of science 2010–; prodr: Tomorrow's World, Brain Story, How to Build a Human, Horizon; exec prodr: Wonders of the Solar System 2010, Inside the Human Body 2011, Planet Dinosaur 2011; hon lectr Univ of Machester; RTS Award 2011, Peabody Award 2011, Broadcasting Press Guild Award 2011, Outstanding Alumnus Award 2012; Wonders of the Solar System (2010), Wonders of the Universe (2011), Wonders of Life (2012); *Recreations* running, cycling, cooking; *Style*— Andrew Cohen, Esq; ✉ BBC Science, New Broadcasting House, Portland Place, London W1A 1AA

COHEN, Dr Andrew Timothy; s of John Alan Cohen (d 2009), and Audrey Pamela Cohen (d 1974); *b* 11 July 1952; *Educ* Leeds GS, Leeds Med Sch (MB ChB); *m* 1, 1977 (m dis 1991); m 2, 1997, Alison Jane, *née* Pittard; 2 da (Hannah b 9 Jan 1999, Rachel b 29 March 2000); *Career* lectr in anaesthesia Univ of Manchester 1980–83, instr anaesthesiology Univ of Michigan 1982–83; Leeds Teaching Hosps: conslt anaesthetist, clinical dir Intensive Care Unit 1983–96, div dir Cinical Support Servs 1996–98; hon sr lectr Univ of Leeds; memb Editorial Bd Jl of Intensive Care Soc 2012–; memb: BMA, Intensive Care Soc, Med Protection Soc, Assoc Anaesthetists, Cncl Intensive Care Soc 1997–2004 (hon sec 2002–04), Nat Clinical Reference Gp Adult Critical Care 2013–16; examiner: Royal Coll of Anaesthetists 1996–2008, European Dip in Intensive Care Medicine 2006–13; chair of examiners Faculty of Intensive Care Med 2014–; DRCOG 1977, FFARCS 1979, FFICM (fell Faculty of Intensive Care Med) 2011; *Recreations* wine, horse riding, skiing, scuba diving, information technology; *Style*— Dr Andrew T Cohen; ✉ 3 Bluecoat Court, Collingham, Wetherby, West Yorkshire LS22 5NH; Intensive Care Unit, St James's Hospital, Beckett Street, Leeds LS9 7TF (☎ 0113 243 3144)

COHEN, Arnaldo; s of Eliazar Cohen (d 1985), of Brazil, and Rachel, *née* Ainbinder; *b* 22 April 1948, Rio de Janeiro, Brazil; *Educ* Colegio Pedro II Rio de Janeiro, Sch of Music Fed Univ of Rio de Janeiro, Sch of Engrg Fed Univ of Rio de Janeiro; *m* (m dis); 1 s (Gabriel b 12 Oct 1976); m 2, 30 March 2012, Karina Maucha; *Career* pianist, former memb Amadeus Piano Trio; performed with orchs incl: Philadelphia, Cleveland, Royal Philharmonic, Philharmonia, Bavarian Radio, Santa Cecilia, Suisse-Romande, City of Birmingham Symphony, Rotterdam Philharmonic; worked with conductors incl: Kurt Masur, Kurt Sanderling, Yehudi Menuhin, Klaus Tennstedt; appeared at venues incl: Royal Festival Hall, La Scala Milan, Champs-Elysées Paris, Concertgebouw Amsterdam, Musikverein Vienna; taught at Sch of Music Federal Univ of Rio de Janeiro and RNCM Manchester (fell 2000), given masterclasses in Italy, Switzerland, Brazil, USA, England and others, prof Royal Acad of Music 2002–, prof of music Jacobs Sch of Music Indiana Univ (prof with tenure 2004–); artistic dir Portland Piano Int; memb jury various int competitions incl: Busoni Competition, Liszt Competition, Chopin Competition (Warsaw); 1st prize: Beethoven Competition 1970, Busoni Competition 1972; *Recordings* incl: Chopin works (1978), Liszt works (1991 and 1997), Brahms works (1997), Schumann works (1997), Brasiliana (2002); Liszt solo works and Liszt Piano Concertos & Totentanz with Sao Paulo State Symphony Orchestra; *Books* Ilha Deserta; *Recreations* football; *Style*— Arnaldo Cohen, Esq; ✉ e-mail arnaldocohen@gmail.com, website www.portlandpiano.org

COHEN, Arnold Judah; s of Samuel Cohen (d 1982), and Leah, *née* Sperling; *b* 17 December 1936; *Educ* Grocers' Co Sch, Gateshead Talmudical Coll; *m* 1, Ruth (d 1977), da of Leo Kremer, of Zurich; m 2, Sara, da of S D Kaminski, of Brussels; 4 s (Daniel b 25 May 1965, Joseph b 30 July 1968, Moshe Broner b 11 Oct 1970, Avigdor Broner b 13 Sept

1971), 1 da (Mrs Yudit Eytan b 7 Dec 1974); *Career* Cohen Arnold & Co Chartered Accountants: articled clerk 1958–62, ptnr 1962–75, sr ptnr 1975–; lectr in economics and accounting Westminster Coll 1968–72, lectr in Talmudics Hillel House 1968, lectr in Jewish civil law Hasmonean HS 1981–86; pres Fedn of Synagogues 1989–2001 (treas 1986–89); FCA 1967 (ACA 1962), ATII 1967, MInstD 1978–91; *Books* An Introduction to Jewish Civil Law (1990), An Introduction to Jewish Matrimonial Law (2009); monographs: The Rabbi who helped Columbus (1972), The Miracle Worker of London (1973); *Recreations* research into Jewish Civil Law, boating; *Style*— Arnold Cohen, Esq; ✉ Cohen Arnold & Co, 1075 Finchley Road, London NW11 0PU (☎ 020 731 0777, fax 020 8731 0778)

COHEN, Ben Christopher; MBE (2004); n of George Cohen (memb England football World Cup team 1966); *b* 14 September 1978, Northampton; *Educ* Kingsthorpe Upper Sch Northampton; *m* Abbie, *née* Blayney; 2 da (Harriette, Isabelle b 2008 (twins)); *Career* rugby union player (wing); clubs: Northampton Saints RUFC until 2007 (winners Heineken Cup 2000), Brive (France) 2007–09, Sale Sharks 2009–11, ret; England: 57 caps, scored two tries on debut v Ireland 2000, jt leading try scorer Six Nations Championship 2000, winners Six Nations Championship 2000, 2001 and 2003 (Grand Slam 2003), ranked no 1 team in world 2003, winners World Cup Aust 2003; memb squad Br Lions tour to Aust 2001; currently chm Ben Cohen Stand Up Fndn; *Style*— Ben Cohen, Esq, MBE

COHEN, Cheryl; *b* London; *Career* dir London Farmers' Markets 2000–; fndr Tottenham Ploughman Community Festivals; *Recreations* walking, writing, photography, event organisation for local community, Tottenham Ploughman; *Style*— Ms Cheryl Cohen; ☎ 07814 030647, e-mail info@tottenhamploughman.com, website www.tottenhamploughman.com, blog http://queenofmarkets.blogspot.co.uk, Twitter @queenofmarkets, @tottenhamplough and playdaysldn; London Farmers' Markets, 11 O'Donnell Court, Brunswick Centre, London WC1N 1NY (e-mail cheryl@lfm.org.uk, website www.lfm.org.uk)

COHEN, Ven Clive Ronald Franklin; s of Ronald Arthur Wilfred Cohen, MBE, and Janet Ruth Lindsay, *née* Macdonald; *b* 30 January 1946, London; *Educ* Tonbridge, Salisbury and Wells Theol Coll; *m* June; 1 da, 4 s (1 s decd); *Career* asst master Edinburgh House Sch 1965–67, Midland Bank 1967–79; asst curate Esher 1981–85, rector of Winterslow 1985–2000, rural dean of Alderbury 1989–93, hon canon and prebend Salisbury Cathedral 1992–2000, archdeacon of Bodmin 2000–11 (archdeacon emeritus 2011–), chapter canon Exeter Cathedral 2011–, acting archdeacon of Totnes 2014–15; ACIB 1971; *Publications* Crying in the Wilderness (1994), So Great a Cloud (1995), The Life and Works of John Dalbiac Luard (1830–1860): Soldier and Artist (in Jl of the Soc for Army Historical Research, 2015), Brothers in War: George (1788–1847) and John (1790–1875) Luard: Paths to Waterloo (in ...a damned nice thing... the nearest run thing you ever saw in your life: A Peninsular and Waterloo Anthology (to mark 200th anniversary of Waterloo), 2015); *Recreations* researching life of John Dalbiac Luard (painter 1830–60) and other members of the Luard family, (researching) British wars 1807–1860; *Style*— The Ven Clive Cohen; ✉ 86 Moor View Drive, Teignmouth, Devon TQ14 9UZ

COHEN, Danny; *Career* Channel 4: factual commissioning ed for the launch of E4 2000–01, commissioning ed then head of documentaries 2001–06, head of E4 and head of factual entertainment 2006–07; controller BBC 3 2007–10, controller BBC 1 2010–13, dir BBC TV 2013–15; *Style*— Danny Cohen, Esq; ✉ BBC Broadcasting House, Portland Place, London W1A 1AA

COHEN, Prof Jonathan; s of Dr Norman A Cohen (d 2009), and Ruth N, *née* Kimche (d 2016); *b* 11 October 1949; *Educ* William Ellis GS, Univ of London (BSc, MB BS, MSc); *m* 6 Jan 1974, Dr Noemi Cohen, da of Richard Weingarten (d 1968), of India; 1 da (Joanna b 1979), 1 s (Richard b 1981); *Career* formerly prof and head Dept of Infectious Diseases Imperial Coll Sch of Med at Hammersmith Hosp (Royal Postgrad Med Sch until merger 1997) and hon conslt physician Hammersmith Hosp, dean Brighton and Sussex Med Sch 2002–13, pres Int Soc for Infectious Diseases 2014–; non-exec dir King's Coll Hospital Fndn Tst 2015–; author of scientific papers and contribs to books on infection and infectious disease; tstee Arthritis Research UK 2016–; hon fell Faculty of Intensive Care Medicine, Hon MD Brighton and Sussex Med Sch; FRCP, FRCPath, FRCPEd, FMedSci; *Recreations* skiing, photography; *Style*— Prof Jonathan Cohen; ✉ e-mail j.cohen@bsms.ac.uk

COHEN, Jonathan Lionel; QC (1997); s of Hon Leonard Cohen, OBE, and Eleanor Lucy, *née* Henriques; *b* 8 May 1951; *Educ* Eton, Univ of Kent at Canterbury (BA); *m* 1983, Bryony Frances, *née* Carfrae; 2 s, 1 da; *Career* called to the Bar Lincoln's Inn 1974 (bencher 2004–), recorder 1997–, head of chambers 2003–12, dep judge of the High Court (Family Div) 2005–; memb Mental Health Review Tbnl 2000–; govr: Skinners' Sch for Girls 1994–2002, Judd Sch Tonbridge 2002–06, Tonbridge Sch 2006– (chm 2007–); memb Ct of Assts Worshipful Co of Skinners 2000– (Master 2005–06); *Recreations* cricket, golf, theatre; *Clubs* Refreshers Cricket, MCC, Garrick, Swinley Forest Golf; *Style*— Jonathan Cohen, QC; ✉ 4 Paper Buildings, Temple, London EC4Y 7EX (☎ 020 7427 5200, fax 020 7353 4979)

COHEN, Lawrence Francis Richard; QC (1993); s of Harris Cohen of Willesden, and Sarah *née* Rich; *b* 4 November 1951; *Educ* Preston Manor Sch, Univ of Birmingham (LLB), Inns of Court Sch of Law; *m* 24 May 1986, Alison Jane, da of Dr Rowland Patrick Bradshaw of Cobham, Surrey; 1 da (Sophie 1987), 1 s (Leo b 1989); *Career* called to the Bar Gray's Inn 1974; recorder 1998– (asst recorder 1995–98); memb: Chancery Bar Association, Insolvency Lawyers Association, Commercial Bar Association (COMBAR); ACIA 1986; *Recreations* reading, cycling; *Style*— Lawrence F R Cohen, Esq, QC; ✉ 24 Old Buildings, Lincoln's Inn, London WC2A 3UP (☎ 020 7404 0946, fax 020 7405 1360)

COHEN, Dr Martin; s of Prof Desmond Cohen, and Prof Brenda Almond; *b* Brighton; *Educ* Univ of Sussex (BA), Univ of Exeter (PhD); *Career* ed The Philosopher (Jl of the Philosophical Soc) 1995–; memb Quantificational Aesthetics Working Gp; first person to swim River Wharfe from Bolton Abbey to Ilkley 1996; memb Mortagne Cattle Processing Plant Advocates Assoc; *Books* 101 Philosophy Problems (1999), Political Philosophy: from Plato to Chairman Mao (2001), Adam Smith and the Wealth of Nations (2001), 101 Ethical Dilemmas (2002), Wittgenstein's Beetle (2005), No Holiday (2006) Philosophical Tales (2008), Philosophy for Dummies (2010), How to Live (2014), Critical Thinking Skills for Dummies (2015), Paradigm Shift (2015); *Recreations* axioms of set theory, inverse-propositional logic, felicific calculus, scrabble (in Latin); *Style*— Dr Martin Cohen; ✉ Dr Martin Cohen Editor, the Philosopher, (website www.the-philosopher.co.uk)

COHEN, Michàl; *b* 2 April 1964, Ladysmith, Kwazulu-Natal; *Educ* Univ of Kwazulu-Natal, Univ of Westminster; *Career* project architect Gerraghty Little and McCaffery Architects, Durban and Koski Solomon Ruthven Architects London 1989–94, co-fndr and dir Walters & Cohen Architects 1994–; RIBA competitions architectural advsr 2007–, panelist CABE education design reviews 2009–11, built environment expert Design Cncl Cabe 2012–; tutor and examiner Univ of Nottingham 2012–, delivers lectures at numerous academic institutions nationally; tstee Portsmouth Naval Base Property Tst 2008–; RIBA Award for Redbrook Hayes Sch Staffs 2007, AJ Woman Architect of the Year (with Cindy Walters, *qv*) 2012, BCSE 'Jonathan Ibikunle' School Architect of the Year 2012, BCSE Award for Hylands Primary Sch 2012, BCSE Award for Elm Park Primary Sch 2012, RIBA S W Award for Colston's Girls' Sch 2012, RIBA London Award for arts centre at Lady Eleanor Holles Sch 2014, RIAS Award and Scottish Design Award for Lairdsland Primary Sch Glasgow 2016; memb: ARB, RIBA, RSA; *Style*— Ms Michàl Cohen; ✉ Walters & Cohen Architects, 2 Wilkin Street, London NW5 3NL (website www.waltersandcohen.com)

COHEN, Prof Sir Philip; kt (1998); s of Jacob D Cohen, of London, and Fanny, *née* Bragman; *b* 22 July 1945; *Educ* Hendon Co GS, UCL (BSc, PhD); *m* 17 Feb 1969, Patricia Townsend, da of Charles H T Wade, of Greenmount, Lancs; 1 da ((Suzanne) Emma b 1974), 1 s (Simon Daniel b 1977); *Career* SRC/NATO fell Univ of Washington Seattle 1969–71; Univ of Dundee: lectr in biochemistry 1971–78, reader in biochemistry 1978–81, prof of enzymology 1981–84 and 2012–, Royal Soc research prof 1984–2010, dir MRC Protein Phosphorylation Unit 1990–2012; dir Wellcome Trust Biocentre 1997–2007, founding dir Scottish Inst for Cell Signaling 2008–12; fell UCL 1993; author of over 500 articles in learned jls; tstee Robert T Jones Jr Meml Tst 2000–; Hon DSc: Univ of Abertay 1998, Univ of Strathclyde 1999, Univ of St Andrews 2005; Hon MD Linkoping Univ Sweden 2004; Hon LLD: Univ of Debrecen Hungary 2004, Univ of Dundee 2007; Hon DSc Universidad Autonoma di Madrid Spain 2016; hon pres Br Biochemical Soc 2006–08 (hon memb 2003), foreign assoc US Nat Acad of Sciences 2008, hon memb American Soc of Toxicology 2010, elected corresponding memb Australian Acad of Science 2014; FRS 1984, FRSE 1984, Hon FRCPath 1998, FMedSci 1999; *Awards* Colworth Medal Br Biochemical Soc 1977, Anniversary Prize Fedn of Euro Biochemical Socs 1977, CIBA Medal Br Biochemical Soc 1991, Prix van Gysel Belgian Royal Acads of Med 1992, Bruce Preller Prize Royal Soc of Edinburgh 1993, Dundee City of Discovery Rosebowl Award 1993, Prix Louis Jeantet de Médecine (Geneva) 1997, Datta Medal of the Fedn of Euro Biochemical Socs 1997, Croonian Lecture Royal Soc 1998, Pfizer innovation award for Europe 1999, named by ISI as third most highly cited UK based scientist of 1990s), Sir Hans Krebs Medal Fedn of Euro Biochemical Societies 2001, Bristol Myers Squibb Distinguished Achievement Award in Metabolic Res 2002, World's Second Most Cited Scientist in Biology and Biochemistry 1992–2003, Debrecen Award for Molecular Medicine 2004, Royal Medal Royal Soc of Edinburgh 2004, Queen's Anniversary Award for HE 2006, Rolf Luft Prize Karolinska Inst Sweden 2006, Royal Medal Royal Soc 2008, Leading Individual Contrib to the Life Sciences in Scotland 2009, Scottish Enterprise Soc for Bimolecular Sciences Achievement Award 2009, MRC Millennium Medal 2013, Albert Einstein World Award of Science World Cultural Council 2014; *Books* Control of Enzyme Activity (1976, 2 edn 1983, trans into German, Italian, Russian and Malay), Molecular Aspects of Cellular Regulation (series ed); *Recreations* bridge, chess, golf, natural history; *Clubs* Isle of Harris Golf, Royal and Ancient Golf Club of St Andrews; *Style*— Prof Sir Philip Cohen, FRS, FRSE; ✉ Inverbay Bramblings, Invergowrie, Dundee DD2 5DQ (☎ 01382 562 328, mobile 07885 423623); College of Life Sciences, University of Dundee, Dundee (☎ 01382 384238, fax 01382 223778)

COHEN, Robert; s of Raymond Cohen, and Anthya, *née* Rael; *b* 15 June 1959; *Educ* Purcell Sch, Guildhall Sch (Cert Advanced Solo Studies); *m* 1 Aug 1987, Rachel, *née* Smith; 4 s (Joshua b 4 Sept 1992, Isaac b 13 May 1994, Joseph b 15 May 1996, Louis b 16 July 1999); *Career* concert cellist and conductor; concerto debut Royal Festival Hall 1971; cellist Fine Arts Quartet 2012; recital debuts: Wigmore Hall 1976, NY 1979, LA 1979, Washington DC 1979; many TV and radio appearances incl subject of documentary (Thames TV) 1979; gives master classes in: USA, Europe, Scandinavia, Australia, UK, NZ, Israel; prof Royal Acad of Music 1998–, prof of advanced cello and chamber music Conservatorio Della Svizzera Italiana Lugano 2000–11; curator HiBrow.TV 2009; launched Cello Clinic and Cohen Pod Talks 2009; patron Beauchamp Music Club, dir Charleston Manor Festival 1989–2012, fell Purcell Sch for Young Musicians; memb Inc Soc of Musicians; Hon RAM 2009; *Performances* major concerto tours since 1980: USA, Europe, Eastern Europe, Scandinavia, Israel, UK, NZ, Aust and Japan; orchs: all major Br orchs, Detroit Symphony, Minnesota Orch, Swiss Romande, Rotterdam Philharmonic, Helsinki Philharmonic, Leipzig Gewandhaus, Netherlands Philharmonic, Oslo Philharmonic, ECYO, Sydney Symphony, Sapporo Symphony; working with conductors incl: Abbado, Dorati, Jansons, Marriner, Masur, Muti, Otaka, Rattle, Sinopoli; conductor and directing guest of several European chamber orchs 1992– (symphony orchs 2000–); chamber ptnrs incl: Amadeus Quartet, Massimo Quarta, Peter Donohoe, Heini Kärkkäinen, Cohen Trio, Yehudi Menuhin; *Recordings* Elgar Cello Concerto (silver disc), Dvorák Cello Concerto, Tchaikovsky Rococo Variations, Grieg Sonata/Franck Sonata, Rodrigo Concerto En Modo Galante, Saint-Saens Piano Quintet, Piano Quartet and Barcarolle (with Fine Arts Quartet and C Ortiz) 2012, Lutoslawski Cello Concerto (Sinfonia Varsovia Maksymiuk) 2013; virtuoso cello music: Locatelli Sonata, Chopin Intro and Polonaise Brillante, Dvorák Rondo, Popper 3 pieces, Beethoven Triple Concerto (with F P Zimmerman and W Manz), Dvorák Complete Piano Trios (with Cohen Trio), Schubert String Quintet (with Amadeus Quartet), Bach 6 Solo Suites, Howard Blake Diversions 1991, Elgar Concerto 1993, Bliss Concerto 1994, Walton Concerto 1995, Britten 3 Solo Suites 1997, Morton Feldman Concerto 1998, Britten Cello Symphony 1998, Sally Beamish Cello Concerto River 1999, H K Gruber Cello Concerto 2003, Tchaikovsky Souvenir de Florence (with the Endellion String Quartet); recording contract (7 years) with Decca/Argo 1992–; *Awards* Suggia prize 1967–71, Martin Tst award 1973–75, winner Young Concert Artists Int Competition NY 1978, Piatigorsky prize USA 1978, winner UNESCO Int Competition Czechoslovakia 1980; *Recreations* photography, alternative medicine, healing, philosophy; *Clubs* Inst of Advanced Motorists, Royal Soc of Musicians; *Style*— Robert Cohen, Esq; ✉ e-mail office@robertcohen.info, website www.robertcohen.info and www.fineartsquartet.com

COHEN, Sir Ronald Mourad; kt (2001); s of Michael Mourad Cohen (d 1997), and Sonia Sophie, *née* Douek (d 2013); *b* 1 August 1945; *Educ* Orange Hill GS London, Exeter Coll Oxford (MA, pres Oxford Union), Harvard Business Sch (MBA, Henry fellowship); *m* 1, Dec 1972 (m dis 1975), Carol Marylene, da of Gérard Belmont, of Geneva; m 2, Dec 1983 (m dis 1986), Claire Enders, *qv*, da of Thomas Enders, of New York; m 3, 5 March 1987, Sharon Ruth, da of Joseph Harel, of Tel Aviv; 1 da (Tamara Jennifer Harel-Cohen b 7 Oct 1987), 1 s (Jonathan Michael Harel-Cohen b 3 June 1991); *Career* conslt McKinsey & Co (UK and Italy) 1969–71, chargé de mission Institut de Développement Industriel France 1971–72, fndr chm Apax Partners Worldwide LLP 1972–2005; chm Bridges Ventures 2002–12, fndr and chm The Portland Tst 2003–, chm Portland Capital LLP 2006–09, chm Big Soc Capital 2011–13; fndr dir: British Venture Capital Assoc (former chm) 1983, Euro Venture Capital Assoc 1985, City Gp for Smaller Cos (now Quoted Cos Alliance) 1992; dir: NASDAQ Europe 2001–03, Social Finance UK 2007–11, Social Finance USA 2011–, Social Finance Israel 2013–, Harvard Mgmnt Co 2012–15; fndr and vice-chm EASDAQ 1995–2001; chm: DTI Tech Stars Steering Ctee 1997–99, Social Investment Task Force HM Treasy 2000–10, Social Impact Investment Taskforce (established by the G8) 2013–15; memb: CBI Wider Share Ownership Ctee 1988–90, Stock Exchange Working Pty on Smaller Cos 1993, CBI City Advsy Gp 1993–99, Exec Ctee Centre for Economic Policy and Research 1996–99, Inst for Social and Economic Policy in the Middle East Kennedy Sch Harvard Univ 1997–98, Advsy Bd Fulbright Cmmn 1997–99, SFA, Univ of Oxford Investment Ctee 2007–14; tstee and memb Exec Ctee IISS 2005–10; vice-chm Ben Gurion Univ 2002–; memb: Dean's Bd of Advsrs Harvard Business Sch 2003–08 and 2010–, Chllr's Ct of Benefactors Univ of Oxford 2003–, Harvard Bd of Overseers 2007–13; tstee Br Museum 2007–12; Lib candidate Kensington North Gen Election 1974 and London West for Euro Parl 1979; hon fell Exeter Coll Oxford 2000; *Books* The Second Bounce of the Ball: Turning Risk into Opportunity (2007); *Recreations* music, art, tennis, travel, theatre, cinema; *Clubs* Athenaeum, RAC,

Queen's; *Style*— Sir Ronald Cohen; ✉ 42 Portland Place, London W1B 1NB (☎ 020 7182 7801, fax 020 7182 7897)

COHEN, Shimon; s of Louis Cohen, of Stanmore, Middx, and Elaine, *née* Liss; *b* 24 May 1960; *Educ* Llanedeyrn HS Cardiff, Univ of Manchester; *m* 24 July 1994, Jessica Dana, da of Sydney Ann Blair, of New York; 3 da; *Career* ceo Office of the Chief Rabbi 1983–90, sr conslt Bell Pottinger Consultants 1990–2000, ceo Bell Pottinger Public Relations 2000–04, fndr and ceo The PR Office 2004–; dir Jewish Chronicle Newspaper Ltd 1994–2003; MIPR, FRSA; *Recreations* theatre, dining; *Clubs* RAC; *Style*— Shimon Cohen, Esq; ✉ The PR Office, 720 Highgate Studios, 53–79 Highgate Road, London NW5 1TL (☎ 020 7284 6969, website www.theproffice.com)

COHEN OF PIMLICO, Baroness (Life Peer UK 2000), of Pimlico in the City of Westminster; Janet Cohen; da of George Edric Neel (d 1952), and Mary Isabel, *née* Budge; *b* 4 July 1940; *Educ* South Hampstead HS, Newnham Coll Cambridge (BA); *m* 1 (m dis); m 2, 18 Dec 1971, James Lionel Cohen, s of Dr Richard Henry Lionel Cohen, CB, of Cambridge; 2 s (Henry b 1973, Richard b 1975), 1 da (Isobel b 1979); *Career* articled clerk Frere Cholmeley 1963–65, admitted slr 1965, ABT Assoc Cambridge MA 1965–67, John Laing Construction 1967–69, princ (later asst sec) DTI 1969–82; dir: Cafe Pelican Ltd 1983–90, Charterhouse Bank Ltd 1987–2000 (joined 1982); non-exec chm: BPP Holdings plc 2002–06 (non-exec dir 1994–2006), Inviseo Media Hldgs 2007–09; vice-chair Yorkshire Building Soc 1991–99; non-exec dir: John Waddington plc 1994–97, London and Manchester Corporation plc 1997–98, United Assurance Gp plc 1999–2000, Defence Logistics Organisation 1999–2005, Management Consulting Gp 2004–11, London Stock Exchange plc 2001–13; advsy dir HSBC Investment Bank 2000–02, TRL Electronics 2005–06, Freshwater UK plc 2007–09 (non-exec chm 2007–09); memb Expert Panel on the Strategic Defence Review 1997–98, chm Sub-Ctee A EU Ctee 2006–10; pres Combustion Engrg Assoc 2006–08; pres BPP UC of Professional Studies 2007–15, chllr BPP Univ 2013–; chm House of Lords Audit Ctee 2015–16; memb Bd of Govrs BBC 1994–99; chm Cambridge Arts Theatre Tst 2007–15, chm Parl Choir 2006–07; writer; hon fell: St Edmund's Coll Cambridge 2001, Lucy Cavendish Coll Cambridge 2008; *Books* Deaths Bright Angel (as Janet Neel, 1988, John Creasey Award for Best First Crime Novel), Death on Site (1989), Death of a Partner (1991), The Highest Bidder (as Janet Cohen, 1992), Death Among the Dons (1993), Children of a Harsh Winter (as Janet Cohen, 1994), A Timely Death (1996), To Die For (1998), O Gentle Death (2000), Ticket to Ride (2005); *Recreations* writing, theatre; *Style*— Baroness Cohen of Pimlico; ✉ House of Lords, London SW1A 0PW

COHN-SHERBOK, Rabbi Prof Daniel Mark (Dan); s of Bernard Cohn-Sherbok, of Denver, Colorado, and Ruth Cohn-Sherbok; *b* 1 February 1945; *Educ* E Denver HS, Williams Coll MA (BA), Hebrew Union Coll Cincinnati (MA, DD), Wolfson Coll Cambridge (MLitt, PhD); *m* 19 Dec 1976, Lavinia Charlotte Cohn-Sherbok, *qv*, da of late Graham Heath; *Career* ordained rabbi 1971; chaplain Colorado State House of Representatives 1971; lectr in theology Univ of Kent 1975–97 (dir Centre for the Study of Religion and Society 1982–90); visiting prof: Univ of Essex 1993–94, Univ of Wales Lampeter 1994–97 (prof of Judaism 1997–2009, emeritus prof of Judaism 2011–), Univ of Middx 1994–2001, Univ of Wales Bangor 1998, Univ of Vilnius 2000, Univ of Durham 2002, Trinity UC 2007, St Mary's Univ 2008, Charles Univ Prague 2008, York St John Univ 2011–; hon prof Univ of Aberstwyth 2010–, visiting research fell Heythrop Coll Univ of London 2011–, hon fell Centre of Religions for Peace and Reconciliation Univ of Winchester 2013–; memb Arts and Humanities Peer Review Coll; fell Hebrew Union Coll 1972, corresponding fell Acad of Jewish Philosophy 1978, visiting fell: Wolfson Coll Cambridge 1991, Harris Manchester Coll 2002; visiting scholar: Mansfield Coll Oxford 1994, Oxford Centre for Postgrad Hebrew Studies 1994; memb London Soc for the Study of Religion 1981; finalist Times Preacher of the Year 2001, RA Friends design competition winner 2015; *Books* On Earth As It Is In Heaven (1987), The Jewish Heritage (1988), Holocaust Theology (1989), A Dictionary of Christianity and Judaism (1990), Rabbinic Perspectives on the New Testament (1990), Blackwell's Dictionary of Judaica (1991), Israel (1992), The Crucified Jew (1992), Atlas of Jewish History (1993), The Jewish Faith (1993), The American Jew (1994), Judaism and Other Faiths (1994), The Future of Judaism (1994), Jewish and Christian Mysticism (1994), Jewish Mysticism: An Anthology (1995), Modern Judaism (1996), The Hebrew Bible (1996), Biblical Hebrew For Beginners (1996), Mediaeval Jewish Philosophy (1996), Fifty Key Jewish Thinkers (1996), After Noah (1997), The Jewish Messiah (1997), Consice Encyclopedia of Judaism (1998), Understanding the Holocaust (1999), Messianic Judaism (2000), Holocaust Theology: A Reader (2001), Interfaith Theology: A Reader (2001), Anti-Semitism (2002), Judaism: History, Belief and Practice (2003), The Vision of Judaism: Wrestling with God (2004), Pursuing the Dream: A Jewish-Christian Conversation (2005), Dictionary of Jewish Biography (2005), An Encyclopedia of Judaism and Christianity (2005), The Paradox of Antisemitism (2006), The Politics of Apocalypse: The History and Influence of Christian Zionism (2006), The Palestine Israeli Conflict (2008), Dictionary of Kabbalah and Kabbalists (2009), Judaism Today (2010), Introduction to Zionism and Israel (2011), The Palestinian State: A Jewish Justification (2012), An Illustrated History of Judaism (2013), Love, Sex and Marriage (2013), Debating Palestine and Israel (2014), The Athenaeum Sketches (2014), Why Can't They Get Along? (2015), Sensible Religion (2015), Debating Palestine and Israel (2015), The Athenaeum Sketches (2015); *Recreations* keeping cats, walking, drawing cartoons; *Clubs* Athenaeum, Lansdowne; *Style*— Rabbi Prof Dan Cohn-Sherbok; ☎ 01570 470409, mobile 07814 851666, e-mail cohnsherbok@googlemail.com

COHN-SHERBOK, Lavinia Charlotte; da of Graham Heath (d 1969); *b* 1952, Surrey; *Educ* Benenden Sch, Girton Coll Cambridge, Univ of Kent at Canterbury; *m* 19 Dec 1976, Rabbi Prof Dan Cohn-Sherbok, *qv*; *Career* writer; girls' tutor King's Sch Canterbury 1980–87, princ West Heath Sch Sevenoaks 1987–93; *Publications* A History of Jewish Civilisation (1997), Routledge Who's Who in Christianity (1998), A Campus Conspiracy (2006), Degrees R'Us (2007), The Whistleblower (2008), The Campus Trilogy (2010), The Philosopher Cat (2014); with Dan Cohn-Sherbok: The American Jew (1994), A Short History of Judaism (1994), Jewish and Christian Mysticism (1994), A Short Reader of Judaism (1996), A Short Introduction to Judaism (1997), Encyclopedia of Judaism and Christianity (2006), What Do You Do When Your Parents Live Forever? (2007), The Philosopher Cat (2014); Judaism ed Encyclopedia of World's Religions; *Clubs* Lansdowne; *Style*— Mrs Lavinia Cohn-Sherbok; ✉ e-mail lcohnsherbok@hotmail.com

COID, Dr Donald Routledge; s of late Charles Routledge Coid, and late Marjory Macdonald Coid, *née* Keay; *b* 13 June 1953; *Educ* Bromley GS for Boys, Harrow Co Sch for Boys, Univ of Nottingham (BMedSci, BM BS), London Sch of Hygiene and Tropical Med (MSc), Univ of NSW; *m* 1985, Susan Kathleen Ramus, da of Clifford Roy Crocker; 1 da (Joanna Fleur Julia b 6 Dec 1987), 2 adopted da (Amber Ramus b 4 Feb 1976, Holly Ramus b 21 Sept 1978); *Career* house physician Univ Dept of Therapeutics Nottingham July 1976–77, house surgn Univ Dept of Surgery Nottingham 1977, SHO in gen med Brook Hosp London 1977–78, locum med offr Medic International Ltd London 1978–79, research asst (clinical epidemiology) Dept of Community Med Middx Hosp Med Sch 1979, field MO Eastern Goldfields Section Royal Flying Doctor Serv of Aust 1979–80, MO Community and Child Health Servs Kalgoorlie Western Aust 1981–82, regional dir of public health Eastern Goldfields Western Aust 1982–85 (med superintendent Kalgoorlie Regional Hosp 1984–85); Fife Health Bd: community med specialist 1985–89, conslt in public health 1990–92, asst gen mangr 1992–93; chief admin med offr, dir of public health and exec dir Tayside Health Bd 1994–98, conslt in health servs research Univ of Dundee 1998–2001, public health conslt Grampian Health Bd 1999–2001, dir of med servs Armadale Health Serv W Aust 2001–06, exec dir of med servs Wide Bay Health Serv Dist Queensland 2006–09, public health physician Population Health Services Bundaberg Queensland 2009–10, regnl medical dir China, Taiwan, Mongolia and remote territories Int SOS 2010–12, dir and medical specialist Donald Coid Consultants Pty Ltd 2012–, dir of med servs St John of God Murdoch Hospital Western Aust; medical advsr Travel Vaccination and Medical Centre S Western Australia 2010; hon sr lectr Univ of Dundee 1994–2001; memb: Christian Church, Royal Aust Coll of Med Admins 1985, Br Schools' Exploring Soc, Aust Faculty of Public Health Med, Aust Med Assoc; FFPHM 1996, FRCPEd 1997, FRSPH 1997; *Publications* various articles on public health and related topics; *Recreations* public health theory, golf, cricket, dancing, piano and singing, cycling; *Clubs* Royal & Ancient Golf (St Andrews), New Golf (St Andrews), Cottesloe Golf (Western Australia); *Style*— Dr Donald R Coid; ✉ 131 Churchill Avenue, Subiaco, Western Australia 6008, Australia (☎ 0061 98 9382 2496, e-mail dcoid@internode.on.net)

C

COJOCARU, Alina; *b* Bucharest, Romania; *Educ* Ukrainian State Ballet Sch Kiev, Royal Ballet Sch (Prix de Lausanne scholarship); *Career* ballet dancer; formerly with Kiev Ballet, princ Royal Ballet 2001– (joined 1999); guest dancer: Kirov Ballet, American Ballet Theatre, Royal Danish Ballet, Hungarian Nat Ballet, Paris Opera Garnier, Romanian Nat Ballet, Bolshoi Ballet (debut La Sylphide); organiser ballet galas Bucharest 2007, patron Hospices of Hope (also organised charity galas 2008); Pentru Merit Gradul de Cavaler (Romania) 2002; *Performances* with Kiev Ballet incl: Kitri, Aurora, Cinderella, Clara, Swanilda; with Royal Ballet incl: Sugar Plum Fairy, Nikiya, Kitri, Juliet, Giselle, Odette, Odile, Mary Vetsera, Aurora, Tatiana, Olga in Onegin, Titania in The Dream, Manon, Raymonda, Cinderella, Vera in A Month in the Country, La Sylphide pas de deux, The Leaves are Fading, Scènes de ballet, Ondine, Symphonic Variations, The Veriginous Thrill of Exactitude, Symphony in C, This House Will Burn Down, Les Saisons; *Awards* Best Female Dancer: Critics' Circle Dance Awards 2002, Int Movimentos Tanz Preis 2004, Benois de la Dance 2004, Nijinsky Award 2004; *Style*— Ms Alina Cojocaru; ✉ c/o The Royal Ballet, Royal Opera House, Covent Garden, London WC2E 9DD

COKE, Edward Peter; s of Lt Cdr John Hodson Coke, RN, of East Stour, Dorset, and Kathleen Mary, *née* Pennington (d 2000); *b* 12 October 1948; *Educ* St John's Coll Southsea, Univ of Warwick (LLB), Inns of Court Sch of Law; *m* 1, 6 July 1968 (m dis 1994), Josephine Linette, da of Frederick Francis Kennard (d 1987); 1 s (Dominic Francis), 2 da (Sarah Marie, Jessica Mary); m 2, 9 June 2007, Wendy Jane, da of Richard Newcomb; *Career* trainee mangr W Woolworth 1966–69, postman PO 1969–71, sr advsy offr Consumer Protection Dept W Midlands CC; called to the Bar Inner Temple 1976; tenant St Ive's Chambers 1977– (head of chambers 1990–2000 (re-elected 1997)), recorder of the Crown Court 2005–; memb: Midland Circuit, Criminal Bar Assoc; dir Conviction Pictures Ltd 2002; memb crew yacht Portsmouth Times Round the World Yacht Race 2000–01; *Recreations* theatre, cinema, walking, fly fishing; *Style*— Edward Coke, Esq; ✉ St Ive's Chambers, Whittal Street, Birmingham B4 6DH (☎ 0121 236 0863, fax 0121 236 6961, e-mail edcoke@mac.com)

COLACICCHI, Clare Elizabeth Vivienne; da of Richard Clutterbuck, of Worcs, and Gillian, *née* Harding; *b* 3 August 1958, Leamington Spa, Warks; *Educ* Queens Gate Sch London, Somerville Coll Oxford; *m* June 1982, William Colacicchi; 3 da (Cecilia Mary Elizabeth b 18 April 1988, Lucy Anne Isabella b 17 Sept 1990, Caroline Daisy b 16 July 1993); *Career* admitted slr 1983; articled clerk then asst slr Macfarlanes 1981–89; Hewitsons: slr 1989, ptnr 1990–, sr ptnr 2015–; worldwide chm Soc of Tst and Estate Practitioners 2003–04; memb Law Soc 1983; *Recreations* theatre, gardening; *Style*— Mrs Clare Colacicchi; ✉ Hewitsons, Elgin House, Billing Road, Northampton NN1 5AU (☎ 01604 233233, fax 01604 627941, e-mail clarecolacicchi@hewitsons.com)

COLBOURNE, Christopher Richard Leslie (Chris); s of Robert Henry Colbourne, of Chichester, and Jane Freda, *née* Gardner; *b* 19 November 1947; *Educ* Lexington HS Mass, Boston Univ (BA), AA Sch of Architecture (AADip); *m* 1977, Anne Louise, da of James McElhatton; 1 s (Tom Robert b 25 Jan 1980), 1 da (Clare Rosina b 22 April 1987); *Career* Llewelyn-Davies Weeks: architect, planner and devpt dir 1974–78, assoc 1977; dir Tibbalds Monro (formerly Tibbalds Colbourne Partnership) 1978–96; Masterworks Devpt Corp: dir devpt Europe 1998–2001, vice-pres NY 2001–; RIBA: memb Cncl 1976–, chm London Region 1992–93, vice-pres Public Affairs 1994–96, dep DG 1996–98, dir RIBA Insurance Agency Ltd 1998–, dir Jt Contracts Tbnl Ltd 1998–; chm communications Cwlth Assoc of Architects 2000–; teacher Brunel Univ; external examiner: Kingston Univ, Bartlett Sch of Architecture UCL; Freeman City of London, Liveryman Worshipful Co of Chartered Architects; *Recreations* sailing, skiing; *Style*— Chris Colbourne, Esq; ✉ Masterworks Development Corporation, 56 West 45th Street, 4th Floor, New York, NY 10036, USA

COLCHESTER, Prof Alan Charles Francis; s of John Sparrow Colchester (d 1981), of East Chiltington, E Sussex, and Norah Diana Taylor, *née* Pengelley (d 2013); *b* 4 October 1947, Swatow, China; *Educ* Haileybury, BNC Oxford (BA), UCH London (BM BCh), Inst of Neurology London (PhD), Univ of Oxford (MA); *m* 17 Aug 1974, Nicola Jane, da of Edward Rocksborough Smith (d 1989), of Briantspuddle, Dorset; 2 da (Nancy b 1979, Emily b 1981), 1 s (Rupert b 1984); *Career* research MO RAF Inst of Aerospace Med Farnborough 1978–81, registrar in neurology The London Hosp 1982–83, sr registrar in neurology Atkinson Morley's and St George's Hosps 1983–87, sr lectr UMDS 1987–96, conslt neurologist Guy's Hosp London and E Kent Hosps Tst 1987–2014, lead clinican for neurosciences E Kent Hosps 2002–05; prof of clinical neuroscience and med image computing Univ of Kent at Canterbury 1999–2009; memb Cncl of Govrs E Kent Hosps Tst 2012–14; research and publications in med image computing, Creutzfeld-Jakob disease, BSE, stroke, and image guided surgery; chm XIIth Int Conf on Info Processing in Med Imaging 1991; chm Int Mgmnt Bd conference series and pres Int Soc Med Image Computing and Computer Assisted Intervention Cambridge 1999–2007; patron Human BSE Fndn 1997–2009; FRSM 1983, FRCP 1993; *Style*— Prof Alan Colchester; ✉ The Old Rectory, Stowting, Kent TN25 6BE (e-mail a.colchester@gmail.com)

COLCHESTER, Charles Meredith Hastings; s of Rev Capt Halsey Sparrowe Colchester, CMG, OBE (d 1995), and Rozanne Felicity Hastings, *née* Medhurst; *b* 12 January 1950, London; *Educ* Dragon Sch Oxford, Radley, Magdalen Coll Oxford (BA, Arden scholar); *m* 3 July 1976, Dr Serena Laura Peabody, da of Hon John M W North (d 1987), of Wickhambreaux, Kent; 3 s (Alexander North Peabody b 1981, Benjamin Medhurst Pawson b 1983, Zachary Wheatland Maynard b 1988), 3 da (Tamara Sarah Sparrowe b 1985, Talitha Chloë Jacob b 1991, Zoë Francesca Tatiana b 1995); *Career* dir: Global Enterprises Ltd Bahrain 1973–75, Zoremel Ltd Ajman UAE 1975–79; ME dir Collingwood of Conduit Street 1976–82; dir: The Well Tst 1978, The Initiative Project Tst 1980, Well Marine Reinsurance Advisors Ltd 1986–94, Tear Fund 1989–94, Riding Lights Tst 2004–16, Doha Int Family Inst 2005–2015, Metal and Butter Co Ltd; Christian Action Res and Educn (CARE): chm of campaigns 1982, gen dir 1987–2004, int dir 2004–08, Care for Europe (AISBL) 1990–2008, gen dir CARE for the Family 1997–2008; chm: Centre for Bioethics and Public Policy 1998–2001, P & P Tst 1998–, Christian Inspiration Tst 2000–15; pres: Reconciliation and Peace Fndn 2005–15, Office of Int Diplomacy (US and Canada) 2005–16; chm of tstees Dolphin Sch Tst 1988–; tstee Swinfen Charitable Tst 1999–16, patron Epiphany Tst 2009–, tstee Hope for Entoto Tst 2013–15; church warden: Holy Trinity Church Brompton 1977–93, St Paul's Anglican Fellowship 1996–2000, St Mary's Bryanston Square 2000–12; *Recreations* family, water colouring, travel, reading, cooking, singing; *Clubs* Travellers, Bath and County Club; *Style—* Charles Colchester, Esq; ☎ 07778 156642, e-mail president@theoid.org)

COLCLOUGH, Prof Christopher Louis; s of Frederick Colclough (d 2003), and Margaret, *née* McMellon (d 2009); *b* 10 July 1946, Glossop, Derbys; *Educ* Univ of Bristol (BA, Powesland Meml Prize in Economics), CCC Cambridge (Dip, PhD); *m* Sarah Elizabeth, *née* Butler; 1 s (Giles Louis b 15 Jan 1989); *Career* economic advsr Miny of Fin and Devpt Planning Govt of Botswana (appointed by Br Govt) 1971–75, fell Inst of Devpt Studies Univ of Sussex 1975–2004 (professorial fell 1994), dir Educn for All Global Monitoring Report UNESCO Paris 2002–04, prof of the economics of educn and dir Centre for Cwlth Educn Univ of Cambridge 2005–08, professorial fell CCC Cambridge 2006–13 (life fell 2014–), Cwlth prof of educn and devpt and dir Centre for Educn and Int Devpt Univ of Cambridge 2008–13, emeritus prof of educn and int devpt Univ of Cambridge 2014–; managing ed economics Jl of Devpt Studies 1989–2004, memb Bd Int Jl of Educnl Devpt 1990–; delg Task Force 3 Millennium Devpt Project UNDP 2002–05, chair Educn Expert Gp Global Governance Initiative World Economic Forum Davos 2002–06; memb: Devpt Studies Panel HEFCE Research Assessment Exercise 2008 2004–08, Educn Advisory Ctee UK Nat Cmmn for UNESCO 2004–06; dir: Research Consortium on Educational Outcomes and Poverty 2005–10; pres Br Assoc for Int and Comparative Educn 2004–05; tstee Educn and Devpt Forum 2011–15 (chair Bd of Tstees 2014–15); hon doctorate Univ of Leuven (Belgium) 2010; *Publications* The Political Economy of Botswana: A Study of Growth and Distribution (co-author, 1980), States or Markets? Neo-Liberalism and the Development Policy Debate (co-ed, 1991), Educating All the Children: Strategies for Primary Schooling in the South (co-author, 1993), Public Sector Pay and Adjustment: Lessons from Five Countries (ed, 1997), Marketizing Education and Health in Developing Countries: Miracle or Mirage (ed, 1997), Achieving Schooling for All in Africa: Costs, Commitment and Gender (co-author, 2003), Education Outcomes and Poverty: a Reassessment (ed, 2012); lead author of int reports incl: Gender and Education for All: The Leap to Equality (2003), Education for All: The Quality Imperative (2004); author of numerous articles in refereed books and jls incl: Journal of Educational Development, Journal of International Development, World Development, Journal of Development Studies, Development Policy Review, International Affairs, Journal of Modern African Studies, Comparative Education, Compare, Prospects; *Recreations* playing the piano and cello, opera, walking in the Pennines; *Style—* Prof Christopher Colclough; ✉ Corpus Christi College, Cambridge CB2 1RH (e-mail cc413@cam.ac.uk); Little Hallands, Norton, Seaford, East Sussex BN25 2UN (☎ 01323 896101)

COLCLOUGH, Rt Rev Michael John; s of Joseph Colclough (d 2012), and Beryl, *née* Dale (d 1969); *b* 29 December 1944; *Educ* Stanfield Tech HS 1957–65, Univ of Leeds (BA), Cuddesdon Theol Coll; *m* 24 Sept 1983, Cynthia Flora Mary, da of Joseph Christopher de Sousa, MBE; 2 s (Edward Joseph, Aidan Michael); *Career* curate: St Werburgh Burslem 1971–75, St Mary S Ruislip 1975–79; vicar of St Anselm Hayes 1979–86, area dean of Hillingdon 1985–92; priest-in-charge St Margaret and St Andrew Uxbridge and St John Uxbridge Moor 1986–88, team rector of Uxbridge 1988–92, archdeacon of Northolt 1992–94, personal asst to the Bishop of London 1994–96, priest-in-charge St Vedast-alias-Foster London 1994–96, priest-in-charge St Magnus the Martyr London 1995–96, dep priest in Ordinary to HM The Queen 1995–96, bishop of Kensington 1996–2008, canon residential St Paul's Cathedral 2008–13; hon asst bishop Diocese of London 2008–, hon asst bishop Diocese of Gibraltar Europe 2013–, bishop in residence St Paul's Church Knightsbridge 2014–; dean of univ chaplains 1994–96; chair Dioceses of London and Southwark Penal Concerns Gp 1996–2008, vice-pres Everychild 1998–2002; patron: Micro-Loan Fndn 1999–2008, London Care Connections 2003–08, Shooting Star Tst 2004–08, West London Action for Children 2005–08, Hoffman Fndn 2005–08; chaplain Worshipful Co of Mercers 2010–; *Recreations* English countryside, family, reading; *Style—* The Rt Rev Michael Colclough; ✉ 12 Grosvenor Court, Sloane Street, London SW1X 9PF (☎ 020 3612 3135, e-mail michaeljcolclough@gmail.com)

COLDMAN, (David) John; *b* 27 June 1947; *Educ* Selhurst GS Croydon; *m* 7 Sept 1979, Nicola Anne, *née* Teuten; 2 s (Charles William Edward b 18 June 1984, Thomas Frederick John b 11 May 1994), 1 da (Katharine Elizabeth Jayne b 27 January 1988); *Career* Greig Fester 1963–81, asst dir Alwen Hough Johnson Ltd 1981–84; Benfield Gp Ltd: dir 1985–86, md 1986–96, chm 1996–2008; chm Brit Insurance Holdings plc 1996–2000, dep chm Lloyd's of London 2001–06; non-exec dir Improvement Fndn Ltd 2006–07, non-exec chm Roodlane Medical Ltd 2007–11, chm Omega Insurance Hldgs Ltd 2010–12, dir Arthur J Gallagher & Co 2014–, non-exec dir Arthur J Gallagher Hldgs (UK) Ltd 2016–; govr Tonbridge Sch 2005–13, chm Tonbridge Sch Devpt Gp; Liveryman Worshipful Co of Skinners, Freeman City of London; FInstD, CCMI 2002 (MIMgt 1995); *Recreations* country sports, reading, theatre; *Clubs* Boodle's, RAC, City of London; *Style—* John Coldman, Esq; ✉ Hasilwood House, 62 Bishopsgate, London EC2N 4AW (☎ 020 7826 4006, fax 020 7826 4000)

COLE, Dr Anthony Paul; JP (1996); s of Bernard Joseph Cole, ISO (d 1948), and Mary Veronica, *née* Ryden (d 1987); *b* 23 January 1939; *Educ* St Boniface Coll, Univ of Bristol (MB ChB); *m* 1, 24 July 1970, Elizabeth Mary (d 2007), da of Leonard Vaughan-Shaw (d 1957); 2 da (Sarah b 27 July 1971, Alice b 11 May 1979), 2 s (Nicholas b 7 June 1973, Matthew b 24 Oct 1976); m 2, 16 May 2009, Kathleen Mary, *née* Webb (formerly Mrs Smith); *Career* conslt paediatrician Worcester Royal Infirmary 1974, sr clinical tutor Univ of Birmingham 1986; govr St Richard Hospice; med dir Lejeune Clinic; fndr pres Worcestershire Medico Legal Soc; memb Br Paediatric Assoc 1974, chm Medical Ethics Alliance 2000–; Schindler Prize 2014; chm Catholic Union of GB 2000–; Master Guild of Catholic Doctors 1994; FRCP 1983, FRCPCH 1997; KCHS 1991, KSG, KCSG 2011; *Publications* Looking for Answers, Ethics and Wisdom in Medicine (ed); *Recreations* music, sailing, golf; *Clubs* Catenians, Royal Commonwealth Soc; *Style—* Dr Anthony Cole; ✉ Leawood, Bell Lane, Broadheath, Worcestershire WR15 8QX (☎ 01886 853308, e-mail worcestercoles@aol.com)

COLE, Ashley; *b* 20 December 1980, Stepney, London; *m* 2006 (m dis 2010), Cheryl, *née* Tweedy; *Career* footballer; clubs: Arsenal FC 2000–06 (over 200 appearances, winners FA Premiership 2002 and 2004, FA Cup 2002, 2003 and 2005 (finalists 2001)), Chelsea FC 2006– (winners: FA Cup 2007 and 2009, Carling Cup 2007, Community Shield 2009, Europa League 2013; finalists UEFA Champions League 2008); England: 107 caps, debut v Albania 2001, memb squad World Cup 2002, 2006 and 2010, memb squad European Championship 2004, ret 2014; *Publications* My Defence (autobiography, 2006); *Style—* Mr Ashley Cole

COLE, Joe; *b* 8 November 1981, Islington, London; *m* 20 June 2009, Carly Zucker; 1 da (Ruby b March 2010); *Career* professional footballer; clubs: West Ham United 1999–2003, Chelsea 2003–10 (winners FA Premiership 2005 and 2006 (runners up 2004 and 2007), League Cup 2005 and 2007, FA Charity/Community Shield 2005 and 2009, FA Cup 2007 and 2009, finalists UEFA Champions League 2008), Liverpool 2010–13, Lille 2011–12 (on loan), West Ham United 2013–; England: 53 caps, 10 goals, debut v Mexico 2001, memb squad World Cup 2002, 2006 and 2010, memb European Championship 2004; *Style—* Mr Joe Cole; ✉ c/o West Ham United FC, Boleyn Ground, Green Street, Upton Park, London E13 9AZ

COLE, Margaret; *Educ* New Hall (now Murray Edwards) Cambridge (MA); *Career* ptnr Stephenson Harwood 1990–95, White & Case 1995–2005, md of enforcement and fin crime and memb Bd FSA 2005–12, gen counsel and client risk offr PricewaterhouseCoopers 2012–; tstee Inst for Fiscal Studies 2012–; Hon LLD Coll of Law 2012; *Style—* Miss Margaret Cole

COLE, Martina; *b* 30 March 1959; *Educ* Grays Convent; *Career* novelist; patron Chelmsford Women's Aid; hon doctorate: Univ of East London 2008, Anglia Ruskin Univ; memb Crime Writer's Assoc (CWA); *Books* Dangerous Lady (1992, TV adaptation 1995), The Ladykiller (1993), Goodnight Lady (1994), The Jump (1996, TV adaptation 1998), The Runaway (1998), Two Women (1999), Broken (2000), Faceless (2001), Maura's Game (2002), The Know (2003), The Graft (2004), The Take (2005, Crime Novel of the Year Br Book Award 2006), Close (2006), Faces (2007), The Business (2008), Hard Girls (2009), The Family (2010), The Faithless (2011), The Life (2012), Revenge (2013); *Clubs* Gerry's; *Style—* Martina Cole; ✉ c/o Darley Anderson Literary, TV and Film Agency, Estelle House, 11 Eustace Road, London SW6 1JB (☎ 020 7385 6652, fax 020 7386 5571); Little Freddie Productions, The Village Shop, The Street, Inghtham, Kent TN15 9HH (☎ 01732 886342, mobile 07768 353011, e-mail martina@littlefreddie.tv, website www.littlefreddie.tv)

COLE, His Hon Judge Nicholas Arthur; s of John C P Cole, of Warwickshire (d 2016), and Moira J Cole (d 2015); *b* 21 March 1968; *Educ* Nottingham HS, Univ of Birmingham (BSc), Nottingham Law Sch (CPE), Inns of Court Sch of Law (Bar Vocational Course); *m* 2 Sept 1995, Joanne, *née* Ellis; 2 s (b 2007); *Career* called to the Bar 1993; head St Ives Chambers Birmingham 2013–15; recorder 2009, circuit judge (Midland Circuit) 2015–; *Recreations* motorsport, skiing, travel; *Style—* His Hon Judge Nicholas Cole

COLE, Simon; *Educ* Univ of Manchester; *Career* Manchester Piccadilly Radio: presenter and prodr 1983–86, head of progs 1986–87; fndr PPM Radiowaves (ind prodn sector of Manchester Piccadilly Radio) 1987–89, fndr ptnr The Unique Broadcasting Co 1989–2000, gp chief exec UBC Media Gp 2000–, ceo 7digital Gp plc 2014–; dir Audioboo Ltd 2010–; govr Central Sch of Ballet 2009– (chm Campaign Cncl 2009–); fell Radio Acad 2001; *Style—* Simon Cole; ✉ 7digital, 69 Wilson Street, London EC2A 2BB (website www.about.7digital.com)

COLE, HE Timothy Marcus (Tim); s of John Chantler Cole, and Elsie Anne, *née* Dawkins; *Educ* Warwick Sch, Univ of Durham; *m* Clare, *née* Parkes; 2 c (Jonathan, Zea); *Career* diplomat; Christian Aid: asst European community offr 1993–95, sr prog offr Great Lakes region 1995–97, head of Great Lakes region 1997–99; prog dir Democratic Repub of Congo Save the Children UK 1999–2001; FCO: head of global economic issues Economic Policy Dept 2001–02, Africa policy co-ordinator Pan-Africa Policy Unit 2002–03, head Pan-Africa Policy Unit 2003–05, dep head of mission Maputo 2006–09, dep head of mission Harare 2009–12, ambass to Cuba 2012–; *Recreations* golf, music, skiing, walking; *Style—* HE Mr Tim Cole; ✉ c/o Foreign & Commonwealth Office (Havana), King Charles Street, London SW1A 2AH

COLE-HAMILTON, Emeritus Prof David John; s of Lt Cdr Anthony Mervyn Cole-Hamilton (d 2010), and Monica Mary, *née* Cartwright (d 1954); *b* 22 May 1948; *Educ* Haileybury, Univ of Edinburgh (BSc, PhD); *m* 1, 25 Aug 1973 (m dis 2008), Elizabeth Ann, da of Bruce Lloyd Brown (d 2002); 2 s (Alexander Geoffrey b 22 July 1977, Nicholas Anthony Michael b 23 May 1986 (twin)), 2 da (Rose Monica Elizabeth b 17 June 1979, (Sian) Fiona Non (twin) b 23 May 1986); m 2, 20 Dec 2009, Rosemary Elizabeth, da of late Dr Robert Semple; *Career* temp lectr Imperial Coll London 1975–78 (post doctoral fell 1974–75), sr lectr Univ of Liverpool 1983–85 (lectr 1978–83), Irvine prof of chemistry Univ of St Andrews 1985–2014 (emeritus prof 2014–); chm: Chemistry Sectional Ctee Royal Soc of Edinburgh 1994–95, Chemistry Section Br Assoc for the Advancement of Science 1995–96; 370 pubns on organometallic chemistry and homogeneous catalysis; RSC: Corday Morgan medallist 1983, Sir Edward Frankland fell 1984–85, Industry Award for Organometallic Chemistry 1998, Tilden Lectureship 2000–01, Sir Geoffrey Wilkinson Prize Lectureship 2005–06; runner-up Museums and Galleries Cmmn Award for Innovation in Conservation 1995, runner-up Acad Award IChemE 2001; pres European Assoc of Chemical and Molecular Sciences (EuCheMS) 2014– (vice-pres and pres-elect 2013–14); FRSE 1988, FRSC (memb Cncl 2009–13, chm Audit Ctee 2011–13, pres Dalton Div 2013–); *Books* Reactions of Organometallic Compounds with Surfaces (ed, 1989), Catalyst Separation, Recovery and Recycling: Chemistry and Process Design (ed, 2006); *Style—* Emeritus Prof David Cole-Hamilton, FRSE; ✉ School of Chemistry, University of St Andrews, St Andrews, Fife KY16 9ST (☎ 01334 463805, fax 01334 463808, e-mail djc@st-and.ac.uk)

COLEBROOK, Miles William Merrill; s of Peter Merrill Colebrook, MC, JP (d 1999), of Princes Gate, Ascot, and Joyce Hay, *née* Ruthven (d 1969); *b* 14 January 1948; *Educ* Shrewsbury, Ann Arbor Univ Michigan; *m* 1 Sept 1973 (m dis); 1 da (Lucy b 1977) 2 s (Thomas b 1978, George b 1987); m 2, 12 June 1997, Teresa Celdran, *née* Degano; *Career* J Walter Thompson: media exec 1966–70, account exec 1970–78, bd dir 1978–85, md 1985–88, pres and chief exec Europe 1988–96, int gp pres JWT Worldwide 1996, chm JWT Asia-Pacific 2001; FIPA 1990; *Recreations* shooting, skiing, cooking; *Style—* Miles Colebrook, Esq

COLEMAN, Adrian Michael; s of Brian Francis Coleman, of Malvern, Worcs, and Jean, *née*, Batten; *b* 10 October 1963, Cardiff; *Educ* Malvern Coll, Univ of Manchester; *m* 16 Sept 1989 (m dis 2007), Kathryn Sara, *née* Lyttle; 3 da (Ella Bethan b 5 Feb 1996, Clara Mae b 2 April 1998, Eve Harriet b 31 May 2003); *Career* bd dir IMP 1988–93, ptnr HHCL 1993–2000, ceo AMD 2000–02, chm Vallance Carruthers Coleman Priest (VCCP) 2002–; MIPA, memb Mktg Soc; *Recreations* golf, tennis, cricket, rugby; *Clubs* R&A, St George's Hill, Royal Cinque Ports, St Stephens; *Style—* Adrian Coleman, Esq; ✉ VCCP, Greencoat House, Francis Street, London SW1P 1DH (☎ 020 7592 9331, fax 020 7592 7465, e-mail adrianc@vccp.com)

COLEMAN, Brenda Anne (Mrs Tarquin Gorst); da of late Gordon Barton Coleman, and Moira, *née* Vogt; *b* 28 September 1959, Sao Paulo, Brazil; *Educ* Harrow Co GS, KCL (LLB, intermediate scholar in law, AKC), Coll of Law Lancaster Gate; *m* 7 Sept 1991, Tarquin Harold Gorst, s of late Sir John Gorst; 3 s (Thomas Barton b 18 Aug 1992, Charles William Eldon b 23 Feb 1994, Rupert Edward Lowndes b 17 July 1995); *Career* slr Slaughter and May 1984–89 (articles 1982–84); ptnr: Herbert Smith (Tax Dept) 1991–98, Allen & Overy (Tax Dept) 1998–2009, Weil Gotshal & Manges (Tax Dept) 2009–13, Ropes & Gray (Tax Dept) 2013–; author various articles in jls; memb: City of London Slrs' Co, Law Soc; *Recreations* swimming, tennis, reading; *Style—* Ms Brenda Coleman; ✉ e-mail brenda.coleman@ropesgray.com

COLEMAN, Brian John; AM; s of John and Gladys Coleman; *b* 25 June 1961; *Educ* Queen Elizabeth's Boys Sch Barnet; *Career* London Borough of Barnet: cnclr 1998–2014, cabinet memb for environment 2002–04, Mayor's Escort 2002–03, dep mayor 2004–05, cabinet memb for community safety 2006–09, mayor 2009–10, cabinet memb for environment 2010–12; GLA: memb London Assembly (Cons) Barnet and Camden 2000–12, dep ldr Cons Gp 2002 and 2004, dep mayor's escort 2003–04, chm London Assembly 2004–05 and 2006–07 (dep chm 2005–06 and 2007–08); ldr Cons Gp 2000–, chm London Fire and Emergency Planning Authy 2008–12 (dep chm 2000–08); jt pres London Home and Water Safety Cncl 2001–, memb and Cons ldr N London Waste Authy 2002–08 (chm 2006–08); currently planning and political conslt; dep chm Chipping Barnet Cons Assoc 1999–2002; govr: Christchurch Sch Finchley 1993–2002, Ravenscroft Sch 1996–2012, Queen Elizabeth Boys Sch Barnet 2005–10; asst govr London District Rotary 2016–; memb: Church Cncl Finchley Methodist Church 1981–2003, Ctee Friends of Finchley Meml Hosp 1981–2016, Hendon and Edgware District Scouts 2004–09, Barnet CHC 1991–94; tstee Finchley Charities 2001–; pres Barnet Scouts 2009–12; Hon Dr Univ of Middx

2008; Freeman City of London, Liveryman Worshipful Co of Farriers 2008; FRSA; *Recreations* opera, theatre; *Clubs* Finchley Rotary, Rotary Club of Barnet; *Style*— Councillor Brian Coleman, AM, FRSA; ✉ 1 Essex Park, Finchley, London N3 1ND (e-mail bjc25@hotmail.co.uk)

COLEMAN, David; *see:* Firth, David

COLEMAN, Prof David Anwyll; s of Matthew Anthony Coleman (d 1961), and Mary Helena, *née* Anwyll (d 1984); *b* 26 June 1946; *Educ* St Benedict's Sch Ealing, The Queen's Coll Oxford (MA, Dip Human Biology), LSE (PhD); *m* 2 Aug 1974, Sarah Caroline, *née* Babington; 3 da (Caroline Jane b 26 Aug 1976, Margaret Clare b 4 June 1978, Katherine Mary Louise b 28 Dec 1979); *Career* VSO Nigeria 1968–69, lectr in physical anthropology UCL 1970–80; Univ of Oxford: lectr in demography 1980–, reader in demography 1996–, prof of demography 2002–, fell St John's Coll 2002–13, prof emeritus 2014–; special advsr Home Office and DoE 1987–87, conslt Home Office, conslt UN, hon advsr Migration Watch UK; memb: Br Soc for Population Studies 1974, Int Union for the Scientific Study of Population 1981 (memb Cncl 1997–), Galton Inst 1990, Population Assoc of America 2000; jt ed European Jl of Population 1992–2000; Parly candidate (Cons) Islington N 1983; FRSS 1998; *Publications* 8 books incl: The British Population: Patterns, Trends and Processes (with J Salt, 1992); author of approx 150 scientific papers; *Recreations* music, amateur astronomy, naval history; *Style*— Prof David Coleman; ✉ 13 Crick Road, Oxford OX2 6QL (☎ 01865 558453); Department of Social Policy and Intervention, Barnett House, Wellington Square, Oxford OX1 2ER (☎ 01865 270345, fax 01865 270324)

COLEMAN, Jenna-Louise; *b* 27 April 1986, Blackpool, Lancs; *Educ* Arnold Sch Blackpool (head girl); *Career* actress; *Television* Emmerdale 2005–09, Waterloo Road 2009, Room at the Top 2010, Dancing on the Edge 2012, Titanic 2012, Doctor Who 2012–; *Film* Captain America: The First Avenger 2011; *Style*— Ms Jenna-Louise Coleman; ✉ c/o Conor McCaughan, 10a Christina Street, London EC2A 4PA

COLEMAN, John; s of Peter Coleman, of Sawbridgeworth, Herts, and Katherine Jane Drummond Bailey Napier; *b* 17 June 1952; *Educ* Hyndland Sr Secdy Sch, Univ of Glasgow (Bachelor of Accountancy, Arthur Young Medal); *m* 5 Oct 1974, Maureen Sheila Helen, da of David Venters (d 1989); 2 s (Euan Stuart b 24 Jan 1986, Neil Scott b 17 Aug 1988); *Career* various fin appts Procter & Gamble Ltd 1974–79, various fin appts Oil Tools International Ltd 1979–83; The Burton Group plc: dep fin dir 1983–86, md Top Shop Retail Ltd 1986–90, md Top Shop/Top Man 1990–91, md Dorothy Perkins Retail Ltd 1991–93; chief exec Texas Homecare 1993–95, main bd dir Ladbroke Group plc (parent co of Texas until 1995) 1993–95, chief exec House of Fraser plc 1996–2006; chm: Aga Foodservice Gp 2008–, Holidaybreak plc 2010–; non-exec dir Travis Perkins 2005–; CIMA 1977; *Style*— John Coleman, Esq

COLEMAN, (Elisabeth) Kay (Mrs Rodney Graves); OBE (1994); da of Harvey Wild (d 1999), of Prestbury, Cheshire, and Ann, *née* Sutcliffe (d 1977); *b* 28 December 1945; *Educ* Brentwood Girls' Sch; *m* 1, 1971 (m dis 1985); 1 s (Julian Graham b 1973), 1 da (Lisa-Kay b 1975); m 2, 1993, Rodney Michael Graves, s of Brian William Graves; *Career* mgmnt trainee Harveys & Co (Clothing) Ltd 1962–68, flight stewardess BOAC (Br Airways) 1968–73; Harveys of Oldham (formerly Harveys & Co Ltd): chief exec 1985–2001, non-exec dir 2001–; non-exec dir British Regional Airlines Gp plc 1998–2001; vice-chm Cons Pty 2001–06; memb: Armed Forces Pay Review Body 1996–2002, Bd of Govrs Manchester Metropolitan Univ 1996–2002; *Recreations* opera, tennis, horse racing; *Style*— Mrs Kay Coleman, OBE; ✉ Mere Hall, Mere, Cheshire WA16 0WY (e-mail kaycoleman@merehall.net); Harveys of Oldham, Glodwick Road, Oldham OL4 1YU (☎ 0161 624 9535, fax 0161 627 2028)

COLEMAN, Martin Andrew; s of Joseph Coleman (d 1990), and Betty, *née* Yarrow (d 1975); *b* 19 November 1952, London; *Educ* Preston Manor HS Wembley, Worcester Coll Oxford (BA, BCL); *m* 19 April 1991, Heather Ishbel, *née* MacLeod; 2 da (Olivia Betty b 20 July 1992, Kirsten Eilidh Miriam b 20 Feb 1998), 1 s (Alasdair Calum Joseph b 29 May 1996); *Career* lectr in law Brunel Univ 1979–89; Norton Rose: ptnr 1991, managing ptnr Brussels office 1991–96, global head of competition and regulation 1997–; memb: Law Soc 1979, Legal Services Consultative Panel 2006–; *Publications* The Competition Act 1998 (1999); *Recreations* travel, modern novels; *Style*— Martin Coleman, Esq; ✉ Norton Rose, 3 More London Riverside, London SE1 2AQ (☎ 020 7283 6000, fax 020 7283 6500, e-mail martin.coleman@nortonrose.com)

COLEMAN, His Hon Nicholas John; s of Leslie Earnest Coleman (d 1955), and Joyce Coleman (d 1990); *b* 12 August 1947; *Educ* Royal Pinner Sch, Univ of Liverpool (LLB); *m* April 1971, Her Hon Judge Isobel Plumstead; 1 s (Thomas George Bartholomew b 5 March 1978), 2 da (Victoria Alice Beatrice b 13 Feb 1982, Flora Nancy Joyce b 5 July 1985); *Career* called to the Bar Inner Temple 1970 (bencher 2005); lectr Inns of Court Sch of Law 1970–72; recorder 1989–98 (asst recorder 1986–89), circuit judge 1998–2015, ret, resident judge Peterborough Crown Court 2001–09; judicial memb Parole Bd for England and Wales 2004–16, judicial memb Restricted Patients Panel 2012–; *Recreations* sport, reading, theatre, films; *Clubs* MCC, Hunstanton Golf, Hampstead and Westminster Hockey; *Style*— His Hon Nicholas Coleman

COLEMAN, Peter John; *b* 9 June 1954; *Educ* Sch of Arch Brighton Poly (BA, DipArch, Crown Prize for Schs of Arch); *m*; 3 c; *Career* architect; formerly with: Phippen Randall and Parks, Chamberlain Powell and Bon, Manning & Clamp; dir Building Design Partnership 1989– (joined 1981, specializing in the design of various shopping environments); memb: Br Cncl of Shopping Centres (BCSC), ICSC (Int Cncl of Shopping Centres); speaker AJ Conf on Retail Regeneration 2006; jury memb BCSC Awards; Retail Architect of the Year 2004; RIBA; *Projects* incl: St James' Quarter Edinburgh, Elements Livington Scotland, Westgate Oxford, Eden Quarter Kingston, urban regeneration of new retail quarter Sheffield, Chapelfield regeneration Norwich, masterplanning of waterfront city in Melbourne Aust, retail projects in Europe incl Tres Aguas Madrid; other completed retail devpt schemes incl: redevelopment New Cathedral Street Manchester, West Quay Southampton, upgrading and extending Brent Cross Shopping Centre, Via Catarina Oporto, Lancer Square Kensington Church Street, Tunsgate Square Guildford; *Exhibitions* 21 New Architects (Design Centre) 1984; *Books* Shopping Environments: Evolution, Planning and Design (2006); *Recreations* tennis, cycling; *Style*— Peter Coleman; ✉ BDP, 16 Brewhouse Yard, Clerkenwell, London EC1V 4LJ (☎ 020 7812 8081, fax 020 7812 8399, e-mail peter.coleman@bdp.com)

COLEMAN, Prof Roger; s of Ronald Coleman, of Finchingfield, Essex, and Grace, *née* Thomas (d 1994); *b* 20 March 1943; *Educ* Ealing GS, Univ of Edinburgh (MA), Edinburgh Sch of Art (Andrew Grant scholar, Dip Art); *m* 1, 1964 (m dis), Alison Fell, *qv*; 1 s (Ivan b 1967); m 2, 1995, Sally Reilly; *Career* visiting lectr Dept of Liberal Studies Bradford Regional Coll of Art 1967–68, lectr Dept of Liberal Studies Leeds Sch of Art and Design 1967–70, sr lectr Dept of Humanities St Martin's Sch of Art and Design 1970–72; fndr memb: Community Press London (printing and publishing co-op) 1972–73, Pitsmoor Builders Sheffield (bldg/design co-op) 1973–75; joiner and wood-machinist John Brignell & Co Ltd Cambridge (specialist joinery and restoration) 1975–76, ptnr Coleman & Hollis Cambridge (furniture and joinery design) 1976–82, conslt and freelance designer 1982–85, dir and project mangr Community Construction & Design Ltd 1984–91, co-dir London Innovation Ltd (R&D co with expertise in design and devpt of socially and environmentally desirable products) 1985–2003; RCA: sr research fell and dir DesignAge prog and co-ordinator Euro Design for Ageing Network 1991–99, dir Helen Hamlyn Res Centre 1999–2008, prof of inclusive design 2003–2008, prof emeritus 2008–; numerous invited conf papers and lectures at home and abroad incl Kelmscott Lectr 1992, contrib academic and professional jls; featured in Designers: Making Money or Making Sense (through work of London Innovation) BBC 2 1987; co-fndr, advsr and memb Bd Welfare State International 1968–2006, chair Jury RSA Student Design Awards 2002–06; currently landscape photographer and furniture maker/designer; Sir Misha Black Award for Innovation in Design Educn 2001; hon doctorate Catholic Univ of Leuven 2012; FRCA 1996, FRSA 1999; *Exhibitions* One Rock (Lanternhouse Ulverston Cumbria) 2003, Flat Earth (Old Fire Engine House Ely) 2006 and (Exhibit London) 2007, A Short Walk on the Lark (Old Fire Engine House Ely) 2008, Vandanges d'Images (Sancerre France) 2010, New Directions (Old Fire Engine House Ely) 2012, A Husk of Hares (travelling exhibition (Wishbech Museum, March Museum, Babylon Gallery, Ely), with writer Sue Welfare and painter John Wiltshire) 2013, Between Countries (Old Fire Engine House Ely), with Sally Reilly 2014; *Books* The Art of Work (1988), Designing for our Future Selves (ed, 1993), Design für die Zukunft (1997), The Methods Lab: User Research for Design (1999), Moving On: The Future of City Transport (jtly, 2000), Living Longer: The New Context for Design (2001), Inclusive Design: Design for the Whole Population (jtly, 2003), Design for Patient Safety: A System-Wide Design-Led Approach to Tackling Patient Safety in the NHS (jtly, 2004), Design for Patient Safety: Future ambulances (jtly, 2006), Design for Inclusivity (jtly, 2007); *Style*— Prof Roger Coleman; ✉ website www.rogercolemanphotography.com

COLEMAN, Sylvia May; da of Capt Gordon Barton Coleman, of Harrow, Middx, and Marie Jessie Therese, *née* Vogt; *b* 10 December 1957; *Educ* Harrow Co GS for Girls, Univ of Birmingham (LLB), Coll of Law Lancaster Gate; *Career* admitted slr 1982; Stephenson Harwood 1980–85, co lawyer Gallaher Ltd 1985–86, dir of corp business affrs and co sec Sony Music Entertainment (UK) Ltd (formerly CBS Records) 1987–95, sr vice-pres business affrs Sony Music Entertainment Europe 1995–2005, sr vice-pres business affrs EMI Music 2005–11; dir bwin.party Digital Entertainment plc 2013–16; chm of tstees Chicken Shed Theatre Co 1995–2011, tstee Reprieve 2011–16; Advsy Cncl Denville Hall 2014–; *Recreations* dance, music; *Clubs* Soho House; *Style*— Miss Sylvia Coleman; ✉ 19 Coulson Street, London SW3 3NA

COLEMAN, Terence Francis Frank (Terry); s of Jack Coleman (d 1978), of Poole, Dorset, and Doreen, *née* Grose; *b* 13 February 1931; *Educ* 14 schs, Univ of London (LLB); *m* 27 June 1981, Vivien Rosemary Lumsdaine Wallace, *qv*; 1 da (Eliza b 1983), 1 s (Jack b 1984); *Career* journalist: Poole Herald, Savoir Faire (ed), Sunday Mercury, Birmingham Post; reporter, arts corr, chief feature writer The Guardian 1961–74, special writer Daily Mail 1974–76; The Guardian: chief feature writer 1976–78, New York corr 1981, special corr 1982–89; assoc ed The Independent 1989–91; Feature Writer of the Year Br Press Awards 1983, Journalist of the Year Granada Awards 1987; FRSA; *Books* The Railway Navvies (1965, revised edns 2001 and 2015, Yorkshire Post Prize for the Best Book of the Year), A Girl for the Afternoons (1965), Providence and Mr Hardy (with Lois Deacon, 1966), The Only True History (collected journalism, 1969), Passage to America (1972), The Liners (1976), An Indiscretion in the Life of an Heiress (ed 1976), The Scented Brawl (collected journalism, 1978), Southern Cross (1979), Thanksgiving (1981), Movers and Shakers (collected interviews, 1987), Thatcher's Britain (1987), Empire (1994), Nelson: Man and Legend (2001, shortlisted Marsh Biography Prize), Olivier: The Authorised Biography (2005), The Old Vic: Story of a Great Theatre (2014); reprinted articles in The Bedside Guardian Vols 13–37, The Bedside Years (2001) and Great Interviews of the 20th Century (2008); *Recreations* cricket, opera, circumnavigation; *Clubs* MCC; *Style*— Terry Coleman, Esq; ✉ 18 Clapham Common North Side, London SW4 0RQ (☎ 020 7720 2651, e-mail colemanterry@hotmail.co.uk)

COLEMAN, Dr Vernon Edward; s of late Edward Coleman, and late Kathleen Coleman; *b* 18 May 1946; *Educ* Univ of Birmingham (MB ChB); *m* 3 Dec 1999, Donna Antoinette Davidson; *Career* GP NHS 1972–83; ed Br Clinical Jl 1972–74, ed European Medical Jl 1984–; launched world's first medical software for personal computers 1983; publisher: EMJ Books, Chilton Designs, Blue Books; TV presenter, columnist numerous nat magazines and newspapers; Hon DSc, hon prof holistic med and hon chllr Open Int Univ Sri Lanka; FRSA; *Books* author of over 100 books incl fiction and non-fiction; *Recreations* books, cycling, golf, cricket, travel, sitting in cafés; *Clubs* MCC, National Liberal; *Style*— Dr Vernon Coleman; ✉ e-mail vernon@vernoncoleman.com, website www.vernoncoleman.com

COLEMAN-SMITH, Ashton John (Ash); s of Richard Coleman-Smith, and Edna, *née* Roach; *Educ* Queen Elizabeth HS Northumberland, Univ of Newcastle upon Tyne (BA); *m* Pamela Anne, da of Hugh Griffith Davies; 1 s (Toby b 2 June 1992), 1 da (Hannah b 4 July 1994); *Career* mktg exec Med Sickness Soc 1984–86, account dir Charles Barker 1988–92, former div md Hill & Knowlton (bd dir 1992–2000), md Edelman PR Worldwide 2000–02, md Cohn and Wolfe 2002–05, md EMEA Ogilvy PR 2005–10, mktg dir Berwin Leighton Paisner 2010–; FRSA, IPR, ICCO; *Recreations* running, archaeology field research (papers published); *Style*— Ash Coleman-Smith; ✉ Berwin Leighton Paisner LLP, Adelaide House, London Bridge, London EC4R 9HA (☎ 020 7760 4311, e-mail ash.coleman.smith@blplaw.com)

COLEMAN-SMITH, Brian Francis; s of Derek Gordon Coleman-Smith of Putney, London, and Patricia Edwina Cronin (d 1972); *b* 26 October 1944; *Educ* Emanuel Sch; *m* 19 Oct 1984, Frances Mary, da of John Alexander Gladstone; 1 step da (Alison Hysom b 13 June 1970), 2 step s (Douglas Croxford b 22 Jan 1973, Bruce Croxford b 21 Sept 1979); *Career* northern fin advertisement mangr The Guardian 1976–79, advertisement dir Financial Weekly 1979–81, fin sales dir The Guardian 1981–85; dir: Burson-Marsteller Financial 1985–91, Burson-Marsteller Ltd 1989–91; fndr md Smith Franklin Ltd 1991–94, dir Binns & Co Public Relations Ltd 1994–2002, exec vice-chm Beattie Financial 2002–05, currently dir Cubitt Consulting; *Recreations* sport, theatre, cinema, classical music; *Style*— Brian Coleman-Smith, Esq; ✉ Cubitt Consulting, The West Wing, Somerset House, Strand, London WC2R 1LA (☎ 020 7367 5100, e-mail brian.colemansmith@cubitt.com)

COLERIDGE, David Ean; s of late Guy Cecil Richard Coleridge, MC, and Katherine Cicely Stewart Smith; *b* 7 June 1932; *Educ* Eton; *m* 1955, Susan, *née* Senior; 3 s (one of whom, Nicholas Coleridge, *qv*); *Career* Lloyd's underwriter; non-exec dir Highway Insurance Holdings plc (chm 1994–96); chm Lloyd's 1991–92 (dep chm 1985, 1988 and 1989); Liveryman Worshipful Co of Grocers; *Recreations* racing, golf, early English watercolours, family; *Style*— David Coleridge, Esq; ✉ 37 Egerton Terrace, London SW3 2BU (☎ 020 7581 1756)

COLERIDGE, Geraldine Margaret (Gill) (Mrs David Leeming); da of Antony Duke Coleridge (d 2000), and June Marion, *née* Caswell; *b* 26 May 1948, Surrey; *Educ* Queen Anne's Sch Caversham, Marlborough Secretarial Coll Oxford; *m* 18 May 1974, David Roger Leeming; 2 s (Robert b 5 Oct 1978, Toby b 12 Aug 1981); *Career* sales and publicity mangr Sidgwick & Jackson 1968–70, publicity dir Chatto & Windus 1970, dir Anthony Sheil Associates 1973–87, literary agent and dir Rogers, Coleridge and White Ltd 1987–2014 (chm 2014–); memb Royal Literary Fund Ctee, past pres Assoc of Authors' Agents; *Recreations* reading, opera, gardening, travel; *Style*— Gill Coleridge; ✉ Rogers, Coleridge and White Limited, 20 Powis Mews, London W11 1JN (☎ 020 7221 3717, fax 020 7229 9084, e-mail gill@rcwlitagency.com)

COLERIDGE, Nicholas David; CBE (2009); s of David Ean Coleridge, *qv*, and Susan, *née* Senior; *b* 4 March 1957; *Educ* Eton, Trinity Coll Cambridge; *m* 22 July 1989, Georgia, eldest da of George Metcalfe and Mrs John Ungley; 3 s (Alexander James b 22 May 1991, Frederick Timothy b 14 Jan 1993, Thomas Maximillian b 21 Dec 1998), 1 da (Sophie

C

Cecily b 14 March 1996); *Career* assoc ed Tatler 1980–82, columnist Evening Standard 1982–84, ed Harpers and Queen 1986–89 (assoc ed 1984–86), currently md Condé Nast Publications (editorial dir 1989) and pres Condé Nast Int 2012–; memb Cncl Royal Coll of Art 1995–2000; chm: Br Fashion Cncl 2000–03, Fashion Rocks Prince's Tst 2003, Periodical Publishers Assoc 2004–06, Campaign for Wool 2014– (dep chair 2009–14), V&A Museum 2015– (tstee 2012–15); Young Journalist of the Year 1984, Mark Boxer Award for Lifetime Achievement and Editorial Excellence 2001, Marcus Morris Award 2013; *Books* Tunnel Vision (collected journalism, 1982), Shooting Stars (1984), Around the World in 78 Days (1984), The Fashion Conspiracy (1988), How I Met My Wife and Other Stories (1991), Paper Tigers (1993), With Friends Like These (1997), Streetsmart (1999), Godchildren (2002), A Much Married Man (2006), Deadly Sins (2009), The Adventuress (2012); *Recreations* sunbathing, shuttlecock; *Clubs* George, 5 Hertford St, Annabel's; *Style*— Nicholas Coleridge, Esq, CBE; ✉ Condé Nast, Vogue House, Hanover Square, London W1S 1JU (☎ 020 7499 9080)

COLERIDGE, Hon Mr Justice; Sir Paul James Duke Coleridge; kt (2000); s of James Bernard Coleridge (d 1991), and Jane Evelina, *née* Giffard; *b* 30 May 1949; *Educ* Cranleigh, Coll of Law London; *m* 6 Jan 1973, Judith Elizabeth, da of Hugh Trenchard Rossiter; 1 da (Alice b 19 Sept 1974), 2 s (William b 7 July 1976, Edward b 22 Oct 1980); *Career* called to the Bar Middle Temple 1970, in practice at Queen Elizabeth Bldg 1970–85 and 1989–2000, QC 1993, judge of the High Court of Justice (Family Div) 2000–; int legal advsr Baron Hans Heinrich Thyssen-Bornemisza Lugano Switzerland 1985–89; *Recreations* Dorset, gardening, motorbikes; *Clubs* MCC; *Style*— The Hon Mr Justice Coleridge; ✉ Royal Courts of Justice, Strand, London WC2A 2LL

COLES, Ian Ronald; s of Ronald Frederick Coles, of Mexborough, S Yorks, and Rosena, *née* Haigh; *b* 12 September 1956; *Educ* Mexborough GS, Univ of Cambridge (BA), Harvard Univ (LLM); *m* 27 March 1988, Bethann, da of Bernard Firestone (d 1989); 2 da (Katharine Emma Mary b 15 Aug 1990, Hannah Elizabeth Jane b 20 Jan 1998), 1 s (Benjamin Charles Frederick b 16 Oct 1992); *Career* called to the Bar Lincoln's Inn 1979; attorney NY State Bar 1983; lectr in law City of London Poly 1978–80; Mayer Brown and Platt: assoc NY and London 1981–86, ptnr London 1986–99, ptnr-in-charge 1999–2002; European fin gp head and memb London Exec Ctee Mayer Brown Int LLP 2002–09 (memb Global Partnership Bd 2009–16, co-head of project finance and head of Africa and mining practices 2009–); *Recreations* music, wine, books, skiing, football; *Clubs* IOD, Hurlingham; *Style*— Ian Coles, Esq; ✉ Mayer Brown International LLP, 201 Bishopsgate, London EC2M 3AF (☎ 020 3130 3205, fax 020 3130 8774, e-mail icoles@mayerbrown.com)

COLES, Joanna Louise; da of Michael Edward Coles, and Margaret Coles; *b* 20 April 1962; *Educ* Prince Henry's Comprehensive Sch Otley, UEA (BA); *m* Peter Godwin; 2 s; *Career* dep literary ed The Spectator 1986–89 (graduate trainee 1984–86), news/feature writer Daily Telegraph 1989; The Guardian: news/feature writer until 1991, arts corr 1991–93, columnist 1993–, weekly Guardian interview 1996–, head NY bureau The Times until 2001, features ed then articles ed New York magazine 2001–04, exec ed More 2004–06, ed-in-chief Marie Claire (US edition) 2006–; broadcaster 1993– (incl contrib ABC, CNN and MSNBC), launch presenter Radio 4 mediumwave 1993–95; founding memb American Friends of the Royal Court Theatre; *Publications* Three of Us (co-author); *Style*— Ms Joanna Coles

COLES, Ronald John; s of late Reginald Herbert Coles, and late Mary McAlpine McLeish, *née* Leslie; *b* 18 July 1944; *Educ* Wellingborough GS, Sunderland Coll of Educn, Univ of Leeds; *m* 22 Nov 1969, Stefanie, da of late Richard Ewart Smith; 1 da (Melanie b 11 June 1973), 1 s (Toby b 4 Aug 1975); *Career* BBC Radio: prodr local and network radio 1969–75, trg instr radio prodn techniques 1975–76, prog organiser Nottingham 1976–78, mangr Sheffield 1978–80; md: Radio Trent Ltd 1980–89, Midlands Radio plc 1989–92; radio conslt 1992–; md: Investors In Radio Ltd 1996–98, Radio 106FM Ltd 1996–98; dir of radio Saga Gp 1999–2007; Assoc of Ind Radio Contractors: chm Labour Relations Ctee 1982–83, elected to Cncl 1982–92 (chm 1986–87), chm of finance 1988–92; chm Radio Academy 1995–98 (memb Cncl 1989–98, vice-chm 1994–95, fell 1998–); ed The Beekeepers' Annual 1993–97; alumni fell Univ of Sunderland 2010; FRSA 2001; *Recreations* beekeeping, golf, broadcasting; *Style*— Ronald Coles, Esq; ✉ Manor Farm, Main Street, Upton, Newark, Nottinghamshire NG23 5ST (☎ 01636 812289, e-mail ron208@btinternet.com)

COLEY, (Susan) Gaynor; da of Kenneth Matthews, of Usk, Gwent, and Eileen, *née* Wheeldon (d 2002); *b* 22 July 1958, Wales; *Educ* Croesyceiliog Sch Gwent, UCL (BSc Econ), Inst of Educn London (PGCE); *m* 3 Sept 1988, Nicholas Coley; *Career* Touche Ross & Co 1982–87, KPMG 1987–90, finance dir Horizon Farms 1990–92, dir of finance Univ of Plymouth 1992–97, md Eden Project 1997–2013, dir of public programmes Royal Botanic Gardens Kew 2013–; non-exec dir Atlantic Broadcasting 2005–09; govr Cornwall Coll 1998–2003; Finance Team of the Year Accountancy Age 2001, Best All Rounder SW Region ICAEW 2005, CBI Real Business First Women Award in Tourism and Leisure 2009; ACA 1986; *Recreations* reading, gardening, interior design, walking the dog; *Style*— Mrs Gaynor Coley

COLGAN, Michael Anthony; OBE (2010); s of James Colgan, and Josephine, *née* Geoghegan; *b* 17 July 1950, Dublin; *Educ* Trinity Coll Dublin (BA); *Career* theatre prodr and dir; dir Abbey Theatre Dublin 1974–78, co mangr Irish Theatre Co 1977–78; Dublin Theatre Festival: mangr 1978–80, artistic dir 1981–83, memb Bd of Dirs 1983–; artistic dir Gate Theatre Dublin 1983– (also memb Bd); exec dir Little Bird Films 1986–89, co-fndr Blue Angel Film Co 1999 (prodrs The Beckett Film Project 2000 Channel 4 and RTÉ (Best Drama Award South Bank Show 2002, US Peabody Award 2003) and Celebration by Harold Pinter Channel 4 2006); artistic dir Parma Festival 1982; theatre prodns incl: Faith Healer (Dublin and NY), I'll Go On, Juno and the Paycock, Salomé, 6 Beckett Festivals Dublin, NY, London and Sydney (all 19 Samuel Beckett stage plays), 4 Pinter Festivals Dublin and NY; world premieres incl: Molly Sweeney, Afterplay, Shining City, The Home Place, First Love (dir); prodr Two Lives (TV drama, RTÉ) 1986; chm St Patrick's Festival 1996–99; memb Bd: Millennium Festivals Ltd, Laura Pels Fndn NY 2000–04; memb: Irish Arts Cncl 1989–94, Governing Authy Dublin City Univ, Irish Cancer Soc 2011–12; Sunday Independent Arts Award 1985 and 1987, Nat Entertainment Award 1996, People of the Year Award 1999, Irish Times Theatre Lifetime Achievement Award 2006; Dr of Laws (hc) Trinity Coll Dublin; Chevalier dans l'Ordre des Arts et des Lettres 2007; *Recreations* middle distance running, chamber music; *Clubs* Groucho, Residence (Dublin), Club at the Ivy; *Style*— Michael Colgan, Esq, OBE; ✉ The Gate Theatre, Cavendish Row, Dublin 1, Ireland (☎ 00 353 1 874 4368, e-mail michael.colgan@gate-theatre.ie, website www.gate-theatre.ie)

COLIN, John Fitzmaurice; s of Bishop Gerald Fitzmaurice Colin (d 1995), of Louth, Lincs, and Iris Susan Stuart, *née* Weir; *b* 8 March 1942; *Educ* KCL (MB BS), Westminster Med Sch Univ of London (MS); *m* 20 July 1974, Christel Elizabeth, da of Franciskus Kern (d 1981), of Ziegenhain, W Germany; 3 da (Katharine b 1976, Alexandra b 1979, Anna b 1981); *Career* surgn; Westminster Hosp: house physician 1965–66, sr registrar 1975–79; conslt surgn Norfolk & Norwich Univ Hosp NHS Tst (formerly United Norwich Hosps) 1979–, tutor RCS 1983–89; memb: Cncl Assoc of Surgns of GB and I, Vascular Surgical Soc; memb and vice-chm SAC in General Surgery 1996–2001; LRCP, FRCS; *Recreations* fishing, tennis; *Clubs* Strangers (Elm Hill Norwich); *Style*— John Colin, Esq

COLIN-THOMÉ, Prof David Geoffrey; OBE (1997); s of William James Charles Colin-Thomé (d 1987), and Pearl Erin Colin-Thomé (d 2013); *b* 5 October 1943, Badulla, Sri Lanka; *Educ* Univ of Newcastle upon Tyne Med Sch (MB BS); *m* 7 June 1969, Christine Mary, da of Francis Bernard Simpson; 1 s (Antony Mark b 2 Jan 1970), 1 da (Nicola Jill b 18 March 1972); *Career* hosp serv NE Eng 1967–71: house offr in surgery and med, SHO in paediatrics and obstetrics and gynaecology, paediatric registrar Newcatle upon Tyne Teaching Hosp; GP Castlefields Health Centre Runcorn 1971– (pt/t 1994–, managing ptnr 1987–98); primary care advsr Mersey Regnl HA 1992–94, pt/t dir of primary care NW Regnl Office NHSE 1994–96 (primary care advsr 1998–2001), pt/t SMO Primary Care Directorate Scot Office 1997–98, dir of primary care London Regnl Office NHSE 1998–2001 (primary care advsr 2001–02), primary care advsr Dorset Community Tst and Dorset HA 1998–2001; Dept of Health: nat clinical dir for primary care 2001–07, nat dir of primary care 2007–10, ret; ind healthcare conslt; hon prof: Manchester Centre for Public Policy and Mgmnt 2002– (hon fell 1988–2002), Sch of Health Univ of Durham 2003–; DRCOG, DCH 1971; FRCGP 1990 (MRCGP 1973), MHSM 1998, FFPHM 2002, Hon FFGDP 2005, FRCP 2006; *Publications* Fundholding Management Handbook (ed); author of articles, papers and contribs to books on subjects relating to primary care and on clinical resource mgmnt and clinical inappropriateness; *Recreations* travelling overseas, eclectic tastes in music, dance, theatre, films and books; *Clubs* RSM; *Style*— Prof David Colin-Thomé, OBE; ✉ Hunter House, Bainbridge Lane, Eshott, Morpeth, Northumberland NE65 9FD (e-mail david@dctconsultingltd.co.uk)

COLKER, Richard Frank; s of Frank Colker (d 1986), of Grosse Pointe Woods, Michigan, USA, and Marjorie, *née* Humphry (d 1993); *b* 5 October 1945; *Educ* Michigan State Univ USA (BA), Georgetown Univ; *Children* 3 da (Emilie b 1980, Jennifer b 1982, Stephanie b 1985); *Career* served US Army until 1968; Wells Fargo Bank San Francisco US 1969–72 (London 1973–75), vice-pres corp fin Banque de la Société Financière Européenne Paris 1976–83, md investment banking Kidder Peabody Int London 1983–90, interim chm Balmoral Hotel Gp 1990, managing ptnr Colker Gelardin & Co 1990–, interim chm and ceo Havas Paris 2005; private investor; *Recreations* golf, classical music, European history; *Clubs* Royal St George's Golf (Kent), White's (London), Royal Co Down Golf; *Style*— Richard Colker, Esq; ✉ e-mail rfcolker@gmail.com

COLLENDER, His Hon Andrew Robert; QC (1991); s of John Talbot Collender (d 1966), and Kathleen Collender (d 2014); *b* 11 August 1946; *Educ* Mount Pleasant Boys' HS Zimbabwe, Univ of Bristol (LLB); *m* 26 Oct 1974, Titia (d 2013), da of Reinier Tybout, of Holland; 2 s (Guy b 1979, Paul b 1981); *Career* called to the Bar Lincoln's Inn 1969; recorder of the Crown Court 1993–2006, dep judge of the High Court 1998–, head of chambers 2002–05, circuit judge (SE Circuit) 2006–16, sr judge Sovereign Base Area Cyprus 2007–16, presiding judge Sr Judges' Ct Sovereign Base Area Cyprus 2014–16; *Recreations* violin, sailing; *Clubs* Bosham Sailing; *Style*— His Hon Andrew Collender, QC; ✉ 57 Clarendon Drive, Putney, London SW15 1AW

Collet, Robert Thomson (Robin); s of Robert Alan Collet (d 1979), of Epsom, and Jean Edith Isobel, *née* Thomson (d 1993); *b* 26 November 1939; *Educ* Malvern Coll, Pembroke Coll Cambridge (MA); *m* 6 May 1972, Olivia Diana Mary, da of Leonard Clough-Taylor; 1 da (Eloise b 1974), 1 s (Henry b 1977); *Career* chartered accountant; dir Tilhill Forestry Ltd 1979–92, gp fin dir Addis Ltd 1992–, dir PKG Holdings Ltd 1998–, dir Internet Digital Media Ltd; Freeman City of London 1964, memb Worshipful Co of Coopers 1964; FCA 1966, FInstD 1993, FRSA 1996; *Recreations* golf, skiing, walking; *Style*— Robin Collet, Esq; ✉ The School House, Wimble Hill, Crondall, Farnham, Surrey GU10 5KL (☎ 01252 850824); Addis Ltd, Conbar House, Mead Lane, Hertford, Hertfordshire SG13 7AS (☎ 01992 584221, fax 01992 553050, e-mail robin.collet@btopenworld.com)

COLLEY, Prof Linda Jane; CBE (2009); da of Roy Colley, and Marjorie Colley; *b* 13 September 1949, Chester; *Educ* Univ of Bristol (BA, George Hare Leonard Prize in History), Girton Coll Cambridge (MA, PhD); *m* Prof David Cannadine; *Career* jt lectr King's Coll and Newnham Coll Cambridge 1978–79, fell and lectr in history Christ's Coll Cambridge 1979–82, dir of studies in history Christ's Coll Cambridge 1981–82; Yale Univ USA: asst prof of history 1982–85, tenured assoc prof of history 1985–90, sr faculty fell 1987, memb Humanities Advsy Ctee 1988–94, dir grad studies Dept of History 1988–90, dir Lewis Walpole Library 1988–96, prof of history 1990–92, memb Exec Ctee Dept of History 1991–93, Richard M Colgate prof of history 1992–98, memb Cncl on West European Studies 1993–97; Leverhulme res prof and sch prof in history LSE 1998–2003, Shelby MC Davis 1958 prof of history Princeton Univ 2003–; Eugenie Strong res fell Girton Coll Cambridge 1975, res fell Huntington Library California, Morse fell Yale Univ 1983, visiting fell St John's Coll Cambridge 1988, fell Whitney Humanities Center Yale Univ 1991, Hooker distinguished visiting prof McMaster Univ 1999, Birkeland fell Cullman Center 2013–14; Trevelyan lectr Cambridge 1997, Wiles lectr Queen's Univ Belfast 1997, Ford Special lectr Oxford 1999, Prime Minister's Millennium lectr 10 Downing St 1999, Bateson lectr Oxford 2003, Nehru lectr LSE 2003, Chancellor Dunning Tst lectr Queen's Univ Kingston Ontario 2004, Byrn lectr Vanderbilt Univ 2005, annual lecture in int history LSE 2006, annual lecture in imperial and maritime studies Nat Maritime Museum 2007, Pres's lecture Princeton Univ 2007, Bosley-Warnock lecture Univ of Delaware 2010, Gordon B Hinckley lecture Univ of Utah 2010, IESHR annual lecture Univ of Delhi 2011, Coffin meml lecture Inst of the Americas 2012, Max Weber lecture European Univ 2012, Margaret Macmillan lecture Univ of Toronto 2013, Ralph Miliband lecture LSE 2014, Magna Carta lecture Royal Holloway Univ of London 2014, Donald W Sutherland memorial lecture in legal history Univ of Iowa 2014, annual Magna Carta lecture Royal Holloway Univ of London 2014, Robbs lectures Univ of Auckland NZ 2015, Aylmer lecture Univ of York 2015, Gomes lecture Emmanuel Coll Cambridge 2015, Thomas Jefferson Fndn lecture Univ of Virginia 2016, Lowell Humanities lecture Boston Coll 2016, John Mackintosh lecture Univ of Edinburgh 2016; sr fell Nat Humanities Center 2006; guest curator Taking Liberties: The Struggle for Britain's Freedom and Rights exhibition at Br Library 2008–09; memb: Editorial Bd Jl of Modern History 1983–86, Editoral Bd Eighteenth Century Studies 1987–90, Editoral Bd Jl of Br Studies 1990–, Cncl of North American Conf on Br Studies 1995–98, Advsy Cncl Paul Mellon Centre for Studies in Br Art 1998–2003, Cncl Tate Gallery 1999–2003, Br Library Bd 1999–2003, Editorial Bd London Review of Books 1999–, Research Ctee Br Museum 2013–, Steering Gp to Review Research Exercise Framework (REF) UK 2016–; fell Cullman Center of Scholars and Writers NY Public Library 2013–14; hon degrees: South Bank Univ 1999, Univ of Essex 2004, UEA 2005, Univ of Bristol 2006, Univ of Hull 2012; FRHistS 1988, FBA 1999, FRSL 2005, fell Academia Europaea 2010; *Publications* In Defiance of Oligarchy: The Tory Party 1714–1760 (1982), Namier (1989), Britons: Forging the Nation 1707–1837 (1992, Wolfson Prize 1993), Captives: Britain, Empire and the World 1600–1850 (2002), The Ordeal of Elizabeth Marsh: A Woman in World History (2007), Taking Stock of Taking Liberties: A Personal View (2008), Acts of Union and Disunion (based on a series of 15 lectures delivered on BBC Radio 4, 2014); also author of numerous essays, chapters, and articles; *Recreations* travel, looking at art, swimming; *Clubs* Princeton (NY); *Style*— Prof L Colley, CBE, FBA, FRSL; ✉ Department of History, Princeton University, 129 Dickinson Hall, Princeton, NJ 08544–1017, USA (e-mail lcolley@princeton.edu); literary agent: Gill Coleridge, RCW Ltd, London (website www.lindacolley.com)

COLLIE COUSINS, Philippa Jane Elizabeth Caroline; da of Alexis John Poole Cousins, and Jean, *née* Berry; *Educ* Our Lady's Convent Sch Cardiff, Univ of Warwick, Nat Film Sch Beaconsfield, Br Inst Florence, Univ of Westminster; *m* 8 May 1999, David Andrew Collie, s of Dr Bertie Harold Guy Collie; 1 da (Isabella b 29 Jan 2000), 1 s (Lucas b 26 April 2001); *Career* TV and film writer, prodr and dir; dir: Celtic Prodns 1990–2000,

Ruby Films 2001–02; head of prodn BBC Drama Commissioning 2006–08, head of devpt and prodr Hartwood Films West 2008–10, head of devpt and exec prodr Fresh Pictures Jamie Oliver Gp 2010–; Xbox and app games dir and developer; dir of commercials for brands incl: Glenmorangie Whiskey, Tropicana Orange Juice, Time Out, Family Planning (Bronze Arrow Best Newcomer Br TV Awards); memb: Prodrs Alliance in Film and TV (PACT) 1992–, Nat Film and TV Grad Soc 1992–, Warwick Univ Grad Soc 1998–; patron: Tate, Demos, Plan Int; sch govr Sch's Building Panel Univ of Westminster; govr: Kensington Acad St Charles Sixth Form, Directors UK; called to the Bar Lincoln's Inn 2006; *Film* Tom Jones: The Voice Made Flesh, Jazz on the Beacons, The Mask, The Enchanted Castle (writer and dir, nomination Best Documentary BAFTA Awards), Car Boot Sale, The Deadness of Dad (Best Short Film BAFTA Awards, Best New Dir Galway Film Festival, Best Short Film Celtic Film and TV Festival), Happy Now? (Best Feature Film Variety Critics Choice), Mansworld (exec prodr), Hereafter (exec prodr), Edwina Mountbatten (exec prodr); *Publications* incl: Battle of the Allies (Young Poet of the Year 1977), Kissing with Confidence (play, winner Silver Baird 1985), The Deadness of Dad (1998), Happy Now? (2002), Small Island (2009), White Girl (2009); *Recreations* tropical snorkelling, politics, poetry; *Clubs* Electric House, Notting Hill; *Style*— Mrs Philippa Collie Cousins; ✉ Fresh Pictures, 19/21 Nile Street, London N1 7LL (✆ 07798 524646, e-mail philippac.c@talk21.com)

COLLIER, Charles; *b* 20 September 1974, Norwich; *Educ* Emmanuel Coll Cambridge (BA); *Career* lawyer; agent Tavistock Wood; clients incl: Eva Green, Olga Kurylenko, Alicia Vikander, Dominic West, Ronan Bennett, Lily James; prodr, credits incl: Top Boy, Irish Myths; *Style*— Charles Collier, Esq; ✉ Tavistock Wood, 45 Conduit Street, London W1S 2YN

COLLIER, David Gordon; OBE (2015); s of John Collier, and Pat, *née* Healy; *b* 22 April 1955, Leicester; *Educ* Loughborough GS, Loughborough Univ (BSc); *m* 12 July 1980, Jennifer, *née* Pendleton; 1 da (Zoe b 8 Aug 1983), 2 s (Simon b 5 Nov 1984, Mark b 15 July 1988); *Career* dep mangr Adams Sports Centre Wem 1979–80, dep sec mangr Essex CCC 1980–83, chief exec Glos CCC 1983–86, mktg mangr Sema Gp plc 1986–88, sr vice-pres American Airlines/Sabre 1988–95, md Servisair plc 1995–97, chief exec Leics CCC 1997–99, chief exec Notts CCC 1999–2004, chief exec ECB 2005–14, chief exec Rugby League Int Fedn 2015–; int hockey umpire; memb Exec Bd and chm Int Hockey Rules Bd Int Hockey Fedn, ind memb UK Sport Major Event Panel 2007–15; chm Hix Mgmnt Gp 2015–; Sydney Friskin Award 2003; hon doctorate Loughborough Univ 2014; *Recreations* cricket, hockey, golf; *Style*— David Collier, Esq, OBE; ✉ The Rugby League International Federation, 20 Fitzroy Square, London (✆ 07917 271818)

COLLIER, Air Vice-Marshal James Andrew (Andy); CB (2005), CBE (1995); s of Charles Robert Collier (d 1952), and Cynthia, *née* Walsh (d 2014); step s of Paul Scott (d 2003); *b* 6 July 1951; *Educ* Headlands Sch Swindon, Van Mildert Coll Durham (BSc); *m* 18 Nov 1972, Judith, *née* Arnold; 1 da (Ruth b 27 Oct 1978); *Career* cmmnd RAF 1972, Sqdn Ldr 1980, staff course 1987 (winner Brooke-Popham Essay Prize), Wing Cdr 1987, Gp Capt 1991, Air Cdre 1998, Air Vice Marshal 2003; *Recreations* golf, making bread, following test match cricket and rugby, reading (science and historical fiction); *Clubs* RAF; *Style*— Air Vice-Marshal J A Collier, CB, CBE

COLLIER, John Spencer; s of James Bradburn Collier, of Bramhall, Cheshire, and Phyllis Mary Collier; *b* 4 March 1945; *Educ* Cheadle Hulme Sch, Trinity Coll Cambridge (BA); *m* 25 March 1972, Theresa Mary, da of Charles John Peers; 2 s (Barnaby James b 26 March 1973, Edward John b 19 Dec 1977), 1 da (Amy Louise b 16 Feb 1975); *Career* tutor in geography KCL 1967–69; Price Waterhouse: student, mangr then sr mangr London and Aust 1969–81, ptnr Aberdeen 1981–84, ptnr Newcastle upon Tyne 1984–92; chief exec: The Newcastle Initiative 1992–95, Lowes Gp plc 1995–96, sec gen ICAEW 1997–2002 (memb Cncl 1991–97 and 2003–11), dir Clive & Stokes International 2004–11, ptnr Grosvenor Clive and Stokes 2011–; treas Wordsworth Tst 2004–; FCA (ACA 1972), MICAS 1981; *Publications* The Corporate Environment (1995); *Recreations* art, mountains and marathons; *Clubs* Travellers; *Style*— John Collier, Esq; ✆ 07710 269795, e-mail john.s.collier@btinternet.com

COLLIER, His Hon Judge Peter Neville; QC (1992); s of Arthur Neville Collier (d 1990), of Hull, and Joan Audrey, *née* Brewer; *b* 1 June 1948; *Educ* Hymers Coll Hull, Selwyn Coll Cambridge (MA); *m* 1972, Susan Margaret, da of John Williamson; 2 s (Andrew James Neville b 6 Sept 1975, Richard John Stephen b 13 Sept 1978); *Career* called to the Bar Inner Temple 1970 (bencher 2002); in practice NE Circuit 1973–2007 (ldr 2002–05), recorder of the Crown Court 1988–2007, dep High Court judge (Family Div) 1998–, sr circuit judge 2007–, resident judge Leeds Combined Court 2007–, hon recorder Leeds 2007–; chllr: Diocese of Wakefield 1992–2006, Diocese of Lincoln 1998–2006, Diocese of York 2006–; lay canon York Minster 2001–, memb York Minster Cncl 2001– (chm 2005–), vicar general Province of York 2008–; *Recreations* walking, reading, music; *Style*— His Hon Judge Collier, QC; ✉ Leeds Combined Court Centre, 1 Oxford Row, Leeds LS1 3BG

COLLIER, Stephen; *Career* barr until 1982; BMI Healthcare Ltd: joined 1982, then corp lawyer, exec dir Ross Hall Hosp Glasgow, int dir, commercial dir and gen counsel, strategy dir 2011, gp chief exec 2011–; treas Bar Cncl 2011–13, chm NHS Ptnrs Network 2013–; *Style*— Stephen Collier, Esq; ✉ BMI Healthcare Ltd, 3 Paris Garden, Southwark, London SE1 8ND

COLLIN, Jack; s of John Collin, and Amy Maud, *née* Burton; *b* 23 April 1945; *Educ* Consett GS, Univ of Newcastle upon Tyne (MB BS, MD), Mayo Clinic USA, Univ of Oxford (MA); *m* 17 July 1971, Christine Frances, da of Albert Proud (d 1973), of Durham; 1 da (Beth b 1974), 3 s (Neil b 1976, Graham b 1980, Ivan b 1985); *Career* registrar in surgery Newcastle 1971–80, research fell Mayo Clinic USA 1977, Arris and Gale lectr RCS 1976, European fell Surgical Research Soc 1979, Moynihan travelling fell Assoc of Surgeons 1980, reader in surgery Oxon 1980–, conslt surgn John Radcliffe Hosp, professorial fell Trinity Coll Oxford, Hunterian Prof RCS 1988–89; non-exec dir Nuffield Orthopaedic Centre NHS Tst 1990–93; David Dickson Research Prize 1973, Jacksonian prizewinner RCS 1979, Jobst Prize Vascular Surgical Soc 1990, James IV travelling fell 1993; Assoc of Surgeons of GB and I: memb Cncl 1999–, dir of educn 2001–; memb: Dist Research Ctee, Regnl Med Advsy Ctee, Bd of Faculty Clinical Medicine (chm 1990–92), Governing Body and Bursarial Ctee Trinity Coll, Gen Purposes Ctee Faculty of Clinical Med; examiner: in surgery Univ of Oxford, in anatomy RCS; memb: Vascular Surgical Soc 1982 (memb Cncl 1992–94), European Vascular Surgical Soc 1988, Int Soc of Surgeons 1994, European Surgical Assoc 1994; FRCS 1972; *Recreations* food, family, gardening; *Style*— Mr Jack Collin; ✉ Nuffield Department of Surgery, John Radcliffe Hospital, Oxford OX3 9DU (✆ 01865 221 282/286, fax 01865 221117, e-mail jack.collin@nds.ox.ac.uk)

COLLIN, Prof (John) Richard Olaf; s of Dr John Olaf Collin, MB, BChir (d 2000), of Forest Row, E Sussex, and late Ellen Vera, *née* Knudsen (d 2001); *b* 1 May 1943; *Educ* Charterhouse, Univ of Cambridge (MA, MB); *m* 1993, Dr Geraldine O'Sullivan (d 2013); 2 da (Sophie b 1994, Olivia b 1996); *Career* ophthalmic surgeon with conslt appts to Moorfields Eye Hosp and Hosp for Sick Children Gt Ormond St 1981 and King Edward VII Hosp 1993; special interest in eyelid surgery; hon prof of ophthalmology UCL and Inst of Ophthalmology Univ of London 2008–; Master Oxford Opthalmological Congress 1997–98; pres: Br Ocular Plastic Surgery Soc 2002–05, European Soc of Oculo Plastic and Reconstructive Surgery 2003–05; Liveryman: Worshipful Soc of Apothecaries, Worshipful Co of Coachmakers & Coach Harness Makers; FRCS, DO; *Books* publications on ophthalmic plastic surgery incl: A Manual of Systematic Eyelid Surgery (1983, 2 edn 1989, 3 edn 2006), Colour Atlas of Ophthalmic Plastic Surgery (1995, 3 edn 2007); *Recreations* sailing, shooting, tennis, hunting, opera; *Clubs* Royal Ocean Racing, Hurlingham; *Style*— Prof Richard Collin; ✉ 67 Harley Street, London W1G 8QZ (✆ 020 7486 2699, fax 020 7486 8626, e-mail email@richardcollinsurgery.co.uk)

COLLINGE, (Richard) Paul; s of Graham Collinge (d 1965), and Winifred Mary, *née* Farley (d 1969); *b* 26 June 1946; *Educ* (Architectural) Thames Poly (ATP); *m* (m dis 1991); 1 da (Emma b 23 Oct 1972), 2 s (Jake b 2 May 1974, Luke b 14 Sept 1976); *Career* princ Aldington Craig & Collinge 1986– (ptnr from 1979); external examiner N London Poly Sch of Architecture 1986–89, assessor RIBA awards 1988, external examiner Oxford Brookes; tutoring at many schools of architecture including: Bath, Brighton, Cambridge, Cardiff, Dundee, Newcastle, Nottingham, N London, Oxford Brookes, Plymouth, Portsmouth, Queen's Belfast; selected in 1985 as one of the 40 under 40 young architects; design awards received: RIBA award 1987, 1991 (two awards) and 1995 (commendation 1978), DoE Good Housing award 1978, Civic Tst awards 1978, 1987 and 1988 (commendation 1992), Brick Devpt Assoc Biennial award 1979, 1991 and 1998 (commendation 1991), CSD Malcolm Dean award 1996, 1997 and 2000, highly commended RIBA Downland Prize 1998, Small Projects Award BCO Nat Awards 2007, S of England and S Wales BCO Regnl Awards 2007, Best Housing between 1970 and 1980 in GB Award DoE 2008; RIBA 1972, MCSD 1984, memb Brick Devpt Assoc 1998, memb Assoc of Conslt Architects (memb Bd); *Recreations* wine, good food, cricket, golf, landscape gardening, reading, walking; *Clubs* Dinton Cricket, Oxfordshire Golf, Carrick Golf (Loch Lomond); *Style*— Paul Collinge, Esq; ✉ Aldington Craig & Collinge, The Byre Albury Court, Albury, Thame, Oxfordshire OX9 2LP (✆ 01844 339911, fax 01844 339922, e-mail pc@aldingtoncraigandcollinge.com)

COLLINGHAM, Christopher Eric; s of Harold Eric Collingham, of Carlton-in-Lindrick, Notts, and Olive, *née* Radcliffe; *b* 4 August 1952; *Educ* Henry Harland Sch Worksop, Granville Coll Sheffield; *m* 5 July 1975, Michele Kathleen, da of Eric Keep, of Carlton in Lindrick, Notts; *Career* BBC: communications engr 1971–78, mangr special projects 1978–82; chief engr TV-am plc 1983–89 (joined 1982), md Broadcast Projects Ltd 1989–, tech dir Channel S TV 1990–93, controller Engrg and Ops Channel 5 Broadcasting Ltd 1996–2001, dir of engrg Pearson TV 2001–02; currently vice-pres Technology and Facilities The Hospital Gp (joined as dir of facilities 2002); memb RTS; *Recreations* gliding, power flying; *Style*— Christopher Collingham, Esq; ✉ Pilgrims Landing, The Hamlet, Potten End, Berkhamstead, Hertfordshire HP4 2RD

COLLINGRIDGE, Prof Graham Leon; s of Cyril Leon Collingridge, and Marjorie May, *née* Caesar; *b* 1 February 1955; *Educ* Enfield GS, Univ of Bristol (BSc), Univ of London (PhD); *m* 1992 (m dis 2009), Catherine Rose; 2 s, 2 da; *Career* res fell Univ of British Columbia 1980–82, sr res offr Dept of Physiology and Pharmacology Univ of New South Wales 1983; reader Univ of Bristol 1990 (lectr 1983–90); prof and head Dept of Pharmacolgy Univ of Birmingham 1990–94; Univ of Bristol: prof of neuroscience 1994–, head Dept of Anatomy 1996–98, dir MRC Centre for Synaptic Plasticity 1999–; ed-in-chief Neuropharmacology 1993; memb Grant Panel: MRC, Wellcome Tst, Royal Soc; fndr Euro Dana Alliance for the Brain 1999; pres Br Neuroscience Assoc 2007–; CBiol, FIBiol 1997, FMedSci 1998, FRS 2001, fell Br Pharmacological Soc 2005; *Recreations* skiing, football, running; *Style*— Prof Graham Collingridge; ✉ School of Physiology and Pharmacology, University of Bristol, Bristol BS1 3NY (✆ 01173 313153, e-mail anglc@bris.ac.uk)

COLLINGS, Matthew; *b* 1955; *Educ* Finchden Manor Therapeutic Community, Byam Shaw Sch of Drawing and Painting, Goldsmiths Coll London; *Family* 1 da (Babette Semmer b 24 Aug 1989); m, 22 July 2000, Emma, da of Richard Biggs; *Career* artist, writer and television presenter; ed Artscribe Int 1983–87, prodr and presenter The Late Show (BBC) 1988–96, presenter The Turner Prize (Channel 4) 1997–; writer and presenter: This is Modern Art (Channel 4) 1999, Hello Culture (Channel 4) 2001, Matt's Old Masters (Channel 4) 2003, Impressionism: Revenge of the Nice 2005, The Me Generation: Artists' Self Portraits 2005; *Books* Blimey! From Bohemia to Britpop: The London Artworld from Francis Bacon to Damien Hirst (1997), It Hurts: New York Art from Warhol to Now (1998), This is Modern Art (1999), Art Crazy Nation: The Post Blimey Art World (2001), British Abstract Painting (introduction, 2001), Sarah Lucas (2002), Matt's Old Masters: Titian, Rubens, Veláquez, Hogarth (2003); *Style*— Matthew Collings

COLLINGS, Peter Glydon; s of late Alfred James Collings, of Poole, Dorset, and late Margot Lavinia, *née* Harper; *b* 4 November 1942; *Educ* Worksop Coll; *m* 1 Sept 1967, Rosemary Anne, da of Henry William Wesley-Harkcom (d 1966); 2 da (Sarah Jane b 1968, Emma Louise b 1970); *Career* asst regnl mangr Old Broad St Securities Ltd Birmingham 1970–75, regnl mangr Grindlays Industrial Finance Ltd Birmingham 1976–82, chief exec W Midlands Enterprise Ltd 1982–2000, princ Wellesley Consulting 2000–12, head of corp fin W Midlands Haines Watts 2002–03, fin dir UK Biofuels (Midlands) Ltd 2003–04, gp fin dir Aston Manor Brewery Co Ltd 2005–07; dir: Tangye Ltd 1986–87, Fairne Textile Holdings Ltd 1986–2000, Raydyot Ltd 1987–2000, E R Hammersley & Co Ltd 1989–91, Jeenay plc 1990–97, D H Haden plc 1991–2000, G R Smithson & Co Ltd 1992–96, Somers Handling plc 1992–96, Airfield Estates Ltd 1992–2000, Butler Group plc 1994–2004, Excalibur Manufacturing Jewellers Ltd 1995–97, Clayton Holdings Ltd 1995–2002, Barker Ellis Silver Company Ltd 1996–97, Payton Pepper Ltd 1996–97, LAP Electrical Ltd 1998–99, Venetian Blind Manufacturing Company Ltd 1998–99, Vit-Tec Enamel Ltd 1998–2000, Hipkiss Holdings Ltd 1998–2002, A F Holdings Ltd 1998–2002, Precision Engineering (Worcester) Ltd 2000–02, Richardson Oseland Ltd 2000–02, Procam Tooling Ltd 2001–02, Technolink (UK) Ltd 2006–12; Birmingham and W Midlands Soc of Chartered Accountants: hon sec 1999–2000, dep pres 2000–01, pres 2001–02; memb: Br Venture Capital Assoc Regnl Ctee 1995–2001, Midlands Regn Electricity Consumers Ctee 1996–2001, Ctee Old Worksopian Soc 1996–2001, Corp Fin Faculty Exec Ctee 1998–2003; hon treas St Michael and All Angels Church Knighton-on-Tame 2009–, memb Tame Valley North PCC 2011–; FCA 1966; *Recreations* rugby football, cricket, theatre, opera, jazz; *Clubs* Sutton Coldfield RFC (vice-pres), Warwickshire CCC; *Style*— Peter Collings, Esq; ✉ Green Cottage, Woodgates Green, Knighton-on-Teme, Tenbury Wells, Worcestershire WR15 8LX (✆ 01584 781584, e-mail petercollings@wellesley.org.uk)

COLLINGWOOD, Charles Henry; s of Henry Ernest (Jack) Collingwood (d 1994), and Evelyn Mary (Molly), *née* Atherton (d 1999); *b* 30 May 1943; *Educ* Sherborne, RADA; *m* 13 Nov 1976, Judy Bennett; 1 da (Jane Molly b 4 June 1979), 2 step s (Toby Daniel Scott-Hughes b 20 March 1967, Barnaby William Scott-Hughes b 23 Jan 1969); *Career* radio and television actor; *Theatre* extensive repertory work in Guildford, Canterbury, Derby, Liverpool and Harrogate; roles incl: William Featherstone in How The Other Half Loves (Greenwich) 1973, Cocklebury-Smythe in Dirty Linen (Arts) 1979–80, Philip in Relatively Speaking (Globe Theatre Co: Hong Kong, Singapore, Bangkok) 1996, touring own show Laughter and Intrigue (with Judy Bennett); *Television* numerous shows incl: Undermanning (co-host with Bernard Manning), The Bretts, Hannay, Inspector Morse, For The Greater Good, Chief, Tonight at 8:30, Up The Garden Path, The Upper Hand, Hot Metal, Trouble in Mind, 10%ers, Telly Addicts, Call My Bluff, White Teeth, Midsomer Murders, Countdown; over 20 years continual work for BBC Sch TV as presenter, actor and commentator: 3 series of Castles Corner (with Roy Castle), 3 series with Harry Worth, 2 series with Jack Smethurst, 4 series of Stilgoes Around (with Richard Stilgoe); subject of This is Your Life 2003; *Radio* numerous leading roles in BBC Radio Drama notably Brian Aldridge in The Archers 1975–, Just a Minute, Quote, Unquote; *Books* The Book of the Archers (co-author, 1994); *Recreations* cricket, golf, fishing and gardening; *Clubs* MCC, Stage Cricket, Cryptics Cricket, Stage Golf Soc, Cross Arrows Cricket, RAC; *Style*— Charles Collingwood, Esq; ✉ c/o NSM, The Nightingale Centre, 8 Balham Hill, London SW12 9EA (☎ 020 8772 0100)

COLLINGWOOD, Paul David; MBE (2006); *b* 26 May 1976, Shotley Bridge, Co Durham; *Career* cricketer (all-rounder); Durham CCC: one day debut 1995, first class debut 1996, more than 100 first class appearances; England: 48 test caps, 161 one-day appearances, 14 Twenty20 appearances, capt one-day team 2007–08, one-day debut v Pakistan Edgbaston 2001, test debut v Sri Lanka Galle 2003, memb squad ICC World Cup South Africa 2003 and WI 2007, capt squad Twenty20 World Cup 2007; *Style*— Mr Paul Collingwood, MBE; ✉ Durham County Cricket Club, County Ground, Riverside, Chester-le-Street, County Durham DH3 3QR

COLLINS, Adrian John Reginald; s of John Reginald Mauldon Collins, MBE, and Jennifer Anne, *née* Wasey; *b* 29 May 1954; *Educ* Leys Sch Cambridge; *m* 2, 6 Aug 1984 (m dis); 1 s (Mark John Ford), 1 da (Seil Charlotte); m 3, 28 July 1994 (m dis 2012); 2 s (Robert Jonathan Mauldon b 20 Nov 1994, Theodore Oliver Mauldon b 1 Nov 1996); m 4, 16 May 2012, Jennifer, *née*Reid; *Career* chief exec: Gartmore Investment 1974–84, Royal Trust Asset Management Ltd 1985–90, Fincorp International Ltd 1984–, Lazard Investors Ltd 1994–96; formerly with Buchanan Capital Management Ltd; dep chm ITG Europe 1998–2000, dir Strand Partners Ltd 2003–07, chm Liontrust 2010–; memb Bd: City Natural Resources High Yield Tst plc, New City High Yield Tst plc; *Style*— Adrian Collins, Esq

COLLINS, Aletta Rachel; da of Michael John Collins, of Lower Street, Cavendish, Suffolk, and Sonja Anne, *née* O'Hanlon; *b* 12 April 1967; *Educ* LCDT; *Career* choreographer; memb 4D Performance Group 1987–88, cmmnd Place Portfolio choreographer 1988, choreographer Phoenix Dance Co Leeds (Digital Dance award) 1988, res choreographer Place Theatre 1988–89, dancer and choreographer LCDT 1990, currently choreographer Aletta Collins Dance Co; work incl: Kool Down (Somerset House), His Dark Materials (RNT), The Tempest (ROH), The Cunning Little Vixen (Bregenz Festival and San Francisco Opera), Jenufa (Opera North), King Priam (Opera North, ENO and Flanders), La Boheme (Stuttgart), Carmen (Earl's Court), The Second Mrs Kong (Glyndebourne Festival Opera), Samson et Dalila (Bregenz Festival and Amsterdam), Aladdin (co-writer and dir, Bristol Old Vic), The Barber of Seville (Savoy Theatre), Bash (Citizen's Theatre Glasgow), Jesus Christ Superstar (Lyceum), Honk! (Scarborough, Royal National Theatre and Boston USA); film incl: The Girl in the Red Dress, Regina, The Man Who Knew Too Little; *Style*— Ms Aletta Collins

COLLINS, Andrew John; s of John William Collins, and Christine, *née* Ward; *b* 4 March 1965; *Educ* Weston Favell Upper Sch Northampton, Nene Coll Northampton, Chelsea Sch of Art; *Career* freelance illustrator 1987–88, features ed New Musical Express 1991–92 (asst art ed 1988–89, staff writer 1990–91), staff writer Vox magazine 1990–91; features ed: Select magazine Jan-Sept 1993, Q magazine Oct 1993–95; ed: Empire 1995, Q magazine 1995–97; film ed Radio Times 2001–; BBC: co-writer and performer Fantastic Voyage Radio 5 1993, weekly series Collins and Maconie's Hit Parade (with Stuart Maconie, Radio 1) 1994 (Sony Gold Radio Award 1995), presented (with Stuart Maconie) Mercury Music Prize and Brit Awards (Radio 1) 1994, 1995, 1996 and 1997, regular appearances on the Mark Radcliffe show (Radio 1); appeared in own weekly satire slot (with Stuart Maconie) for Naked City (C4) 1994; presenter: Collins and Maconie's Movie Club (with Stuart Maconie, ITV) 1997–98, Back Row (BBC Radio 4) 2000–02, Teatime (6 Music) 2002–05, The Day the Music Died (BBC Radio 2) 2004–08, Chart Show (BBC 6 Music) 2005–07, weekend shows (BBC 6 Music) 2005–12, Banter (BBC Radio 4) 2006–08, Telly Addict (Guardian website) 2011–16 and (YouTube) 2016–, Saturday Night at the Movies (Classic FM) 2015–; writer: Family Affairs (Channel 5) 1997–99, Eastenders (BBC 1) 1999–2002, Grass (with Simon Day, BBC 3 and BBC 2), Not Going Out (with Lee Mack, BBC 1, RTS Breakthrough Award 2007, Rose D'Or 2007), Mr Blue Sky (BBC Radio 4) 2011–12, Gates (Sky Living) 2012, Common Ground (Sky Atlantic) 2013; script ed: The Persuasionists (BBC 2) 2010, Little Crackers (Sky 1) 2011, Badults (BBC 3) 2012–14, Man Down (C4) 2013, Drifters (E4) 2014; Thames TV Bursary 1986, nominated Writers' Guild of GB Award 1993; patron Thomas's Fund; hon fell Univ of Northampton; *Publications* Still Suitable for Miners: The Official Biography of Billy Bragg, Where Did It All Go Right? (memoir), Friends Reunited, Heaven Knows I'm Miserable Now (memoir), That's Me in the Corner (memoir), End of a Century (ed), Gogglebook: The Wit and Wisdom of Gogglebox; *Recreations* cats, music, film, cooking, trivia, military history, nutrition, bird watching; *Style*— Andrew Collins; ✉ e-mail happy@wheredidital1goright.com

COLLINS, Prof Brian Stanley; CB (2011); *b* 3 October 1945, Orpington, Kent; *Educ* Chislehurst and Sidcup GS, Univ of Oxford; *Career* formerly: int dir of IT Clifford Chance, head of info systems Wellcome Tst, dir of Sci and Technol and chief scientist GCHQ; chief scientific advsr Dept for Business, Innovation and Skills and Dept for Tport 2006–11; prof of info systems Cranfield Univ 2003–11, currently prof of engrg policy UCL; *Recreations* golf; *Style*— Prof Brian Collins, CB, FREng; ✉ University College London, Gower Street, London WC1E 6BT (e-mail brian.collins@ucl.ac.uk)

COLLINS, Charles Douglas; s of Prof Douglas Henry Collins, OBE (d 1964), of Sheffield, and Jean, *née* Wright; *b* 18 March 1939, Harrogate, N Yorks; *Educ* St Edward's Sch Oxford, Queens' Coll Cambridge (MA, MB BChir), Univ of Sheffield (MB ChM); *m* 5 June 1965, Jhoann Temlett, da of Jack Marke (d 1977), of Huish Champflower, Somerset; 2 s (James b 8 Dec 1969, William b 15 July 1974), 1 da (Victoria b 11 Feb 1971); *Career* conslt surgn in Taunton 1973–2004, med dir Taunton and Somerset NHS Tst 1991–95; regnl advsr RCS 1990–97, med advsr WPA 1994–2016; memb: BMA 1963–, Cncl RCS (Eng) 1995–2003; memb Cncl Nat Tst 2003–12; FRCS 1967, FRCSEd (ad hominem) 2001; *Recreations* equestrian pursuits; *Style*— Charles Collins, Esq; ✉ Crowcombe House, Crowcombe, Taunton, Somerset TA4 4AE (☎ 01984 618266, e-mail charlesdcollins@hotmail.com)

COLLINS, Christopher Douglas; *b* 19 January 1940; *Educ* Eton; *m* 1976, Susan Anne, *née* Lumb; 1 s, 1 da; *Career* Hanson plc: joined 1989, main bd dir 1991–, dir of corp devpt 1991–95, vice-chm 1995–98, chm 1998–; dir: The Go-Ahead Gp plc 1999–, Alfred McAlpine plc 2000–; chm: Forth Ports plc 2000–, Old Mutual plc 2005– (dir 1999–2005); articled clerk Peat Marwick Mitchell 1959–65, amateur steeplechase jockey 1965–75, md Goya Ltd 1968–75 (dir 1975–80), represented GB in 3-day equestrian events 1974–80, steward of Jockey Club 1980–81, memb Horse Race Betting Levy Bd 1982–84; chm: Br 3-Day Equestrian Team Selection Ctee 1981–84, Aintree Racecourse Ltd 1983–88, Nat Stud 1986–88; ACA 1965; *Recreations* riding, skiing; *Clubs* Jockey, White's; *Style*— Christopher Collins, Esq; ✉ Old Mutual plc, Old Mutual Place, 2 Lambeth Hill, London EC4V 4GG (☎ 020 7002 7000)

COLLINS, Claudine; da of Michael Collins, of London, and Zilda, *née* Lessman; *b* 14 June 1968, London; *Educ* St Helens Sch Northwood Middx, Watford Coll (Dip); *Career* planner/buyer Squires Robertson Gill 1988–93, gp head CIA Medianetwork 1993–95, assoc dir Media Business 1995–99; Mediacom: dir 1999–, managing ptnr and head of press 2007–, md 2012–; *Clubs* The George, Soho House; *Style*— Ms Claudine Collins; ✉ MediaCom, 124 Theobalds Road, London WC1X 8RX

COLLINS, Damian Noel Thomas; MP; *b* 4 February 1974, Northampton; *Educ* St Benet's Hall Oxford (MA); *m* 2004, Sarah, *née* Richardson; 1 da (Claudia b 2007), 1 s (Hugo b 2009); *Career* dir M&C Saatchi 1998–2008, sr counsel Lexington Communications 2008–10; MP (Cons) Folkestone and Hythe 2010–, PPS to Sec of State for NI 2012–; *Clubs* Cons, MCC, Lord's Taverners; *Style*— Damian Collins, Esq, MP; ✉ Folkestone and Hythe Conservative Association, 4 West Cliff Gardens, Folkestone, Kent CT20 1SP; House of Commons, London SW1A 0AA

COLLINS, David; s of John Edward Collins, and Helen, *née* Kennedy; *Educ* St Conleths Coll Dublin, Bolton Sch of Architecture (BArch), Trinity Coll Dublin; *Career* architect; qualified 1980; founded David Collins Associates 1985; designed restaurants incl: Mirabelle, Quo Vadis, Claridges Bar, J Sheekey, The Blue Bar at The Berkeley; memb bd Crusaid 1998–, memb Sargent Cancer Fund, patron Gilda's Club; ARIA 1986, DBA; *Books* The New Hotel (2001); *Recreations* travelling, writing, composing, collecting 20th century furniture, reading; *Style*— David Collins, Esq; ✉ David Collins Architecture & Design, 7 Chelsea Wharf, Lots Road, London SW10 0QJ

COLLINS, David Stuart; s of James Henry Collins, of Dalkeith, Midlothian, and Hilda, *née* Oldfield (d 1977); *b* 24 February 1945; *Educ* Fazakerley Comprehensive Liverpool, Liverpool Coll of Commerce; *m* 14 Oct 1967, Penelope Noël, da of Herbert Lancelot Charters, of Maghull, Liverpool; 1 s (Mark Stuart b 1977), 1 da (Nicola Caroline b 1980); *Career* Granada Publishing Ltd: mangr South Africa 1974–77, area sales mangr North Africa, ME, India and Pakistan 1977–81, trade mangr 1981–83; export sales mangr Harrap Ltd 1983–84 (sales dir 1984–91), Columbus Books Ltd 1986–91, md Verulam Publishing Ltd 1992–; *Recreations* travel, walking, reading, swimming, good conversation; *Style*— David Stuart Collins, Esq; ✉ 152A Park Street Lane, Park Street, St Albans, Hertfordshire AL2 2AU (☎ 01727 873866, e-mail verulampub@yahoo.co.uk)

COLLINS, David-John (D-J); s of David Collins, and Rosemary Collins; *b* 11 September 1971, Tunbridge Wells; *Educ* BA, MA; *m* 2005, Alison, *née* James; 2 da (Martha, Emily); *Career* vice-pres of public policy and communications Google until 2013 (joined 2006), co-fndr and managing ptnr Milltown Ptnrs (communications and policy advsy firm) 2013–; *Style*— D-J Collins, Esq; ✉ Milltown Partners, 22 Cross Keys Close, London W1U 2DW

COLLINS, (Andrew) Dominic John Bucke; s of Preb John Collins, and Diana, *née* Kimpton; *b* 26 December 1956, London; *Educ* Marlborough; *m* July 1993, Caroline, *née* Braine; 2 da (Cornelia b 2 May 1994, Cressida b 26 July 1996), 1 s (Benedict b 18 June 1999); *Career* joined Bland Payne Ltd 1976, joined Lloyd Thompson Ltd 1984 (ceo 1997), dir Jardine Lloyd Thompson plc 1997–2006, chm R K Harrison Ltd 2007–15, chm Hyperion Gp 2015–; non-exec dir Tribal Group plc 2002–05; *Style*— Dominic Collins, Esq

COLLINS, Mrs Michael; (Lesley) Elizabeth; *see:* Appleby, (Lesley) Elizabeth

COLLINS, Evelyn Jane; CBE (2008); *b* 16 January 1959, Dublin, Repub of Ireland; *Educ* Univ of Sheffield (LLB), Univ of Toronto (MA), Queen's Univ Belfast (LLM); *Career* various positions Equal Opportunities Cmmn 1982–98 (incl nat expert European Cmmn 1990–92), chief exec Equal Opportunities Cmmn for NI 1998–99, chief exec Equality Cmmn for NI 2000–; chair Bd Equinet 2013– (memb 2011–); fell: German Marshall Fund 1986, Cwlth Study Conference 1992; LLD (hc) Univ of Ulster 2014; FRSA; *Style*— Dr Evelyn Collins, CBE; ✉ Equality Commission for Northern Ireland, Equality House, 7–9 Shaftesbury Square, Belfast BT2 7DP

COLLINS, Hannah; da of Clifford Collins, of Horsham, W Sussex, and Christine Collins; *b* 10 August 1956; *Educ* Lady Eleanor Holles Sch, Slade Sch of Fine Art UCL (Dip Fine Art) Fulbright-Hays scholar to USA; *partner* John Egan; 1 s (Echo Collins Egan b 29 Feb 1988); *Career* artist and photographer; lectr in fine art Chelsea Sch of Fine Art London, prof of art in photography and new media Univ of Calif Davis 2001–04; shortlisted Turner Prize 1993; *Solo Exhibitions* incl: Film Stills (Matt's Gallery London) 1986, Heart and Soul (Ikon Gallery Birmingham) 1988, Viewpoints (Walker Art Centre Minneapolis) 1989, Stairway to Heaven (Hacienda Club Manchester) 1989, Stonefree (Tinglado II Tarragona) 1991, Signs of Life (3rd Istanbul Biennale) 1992, Signs of Life (Leo Castelli Gallery NY) 1994, Slow Time (Galeria Helga de Alvear Madrid) 1995, A Worldwide Case of Homesickness (Irish MOMA Dublin) 1996, Filming Things (Centre National de Photographie Paris) 1997, True Stories (Leo Castelli Gallery NY) 1998, Life on Film (Galeria Joan Prats Barcelona) 1999, Hotel of Being (Galeria Joan Prats Barcelona) 2002, La Mina / The Mind – The Gypsy Project (Nelson Gallery Davis CA and Printemps en Septiembre Toulouse) 2003 and (Vox Image Contemporaine Montreal) 2004, Another City Not My Own (Peer Fndn London) 2003, El Olor del Jazmín (Galería Javier López Madrid) 2005, A Future Life (Galería Joan Prats Barcelona) 2006, Moving Image (Gering & López Gallery NY) 2007; *Group Exhibitions* incl: Antidotes to Madness (Riverside Studios London) 1986, The British Edge (ICA Boston) 1987, Australian Biennale (Sydney and Melbourne) 1988, Aperto '88 (Venice Biennale Italy) 1988, Une Autre Objectivité (Centre Nationale des Arts Plastiques Paris) 1989, Polaroid Works (V&A Museum London) 1989, British Artists in Russia (Kiev and Moscow) 1990, Art and Photography (Modern Art Museum Kyoto and MOMA Tokyo) 1990, Turner Prize Exhibition (Tate Gallery London) 1993, A Positive View (Saatchi Gallery London) 1994, Warworks (V&A Museum London and Canadian Center for Photography Toronto) 1995–96, Prospect 96 (Frankfurt) 1996, Surroundings (Tel Aviv Museum of Art) 1997, Contact (city poster project, Cardiff) 1998, Chime: Thinking Aloud (Kettles Yard Cambridge, Cornerhouse Manchester and Camden Arts Centre London) 1998, Invisible Museum (House Cairo) 1999, Opening Exhibition (Tate Modern London) 2000, New Works (Museo Reina Sofia Madrid) 2001, Acquired Works (Irish MOMA Dublin) 2002, Buscando la Vida (35mm feature film, Sitges Film Festival Barcelona) 2002, After the News (Centre de Cultura Contemprània Barcelona) 2003, Wunderkammer The Artificial Kingdom, The Collection (Usher Gallery City and County Museum Lincolnshire) 2005; *Work in Public Collections* EPolaroid Int, Arts Cncl of GB, Br Cncl, Walker Art Center Minneapolis, V&A Museum London, Fonds Régional d'Art Contemporain (FRAC) Rhone Alpes, Fonds Régional d'Art Contemporain (FRAC) Lyon , Fonds Régional d'Art Contemporain (FRAC) Bretagne, Fonds National d'Art Contemporain (FNAC), Museo Reina Sofia Madrid, Tate Gallery London; *Publications* Finding, Transmitting, Receiving (2007); *Style*— Ms Hannah Collins; ✉ website www.hannahcollins.net

COLLINS, Joan Henrietta; DBE (2015, OBE 1997); Dame; da of Joseph William Collins (d 1988), and his 1 w, Elsa, *née* Bessant (d 1962); sis of Ms Jackie Collins; *Educ* Francis Holland Sch, St Margaret's Middx, RADA; *m* 1, May 1954 (m dis 1957), Maxwell Reed, actor (d 1974); m 2, May 1963 (m dis), Anthony Newley, actor; 1 s (Alexander b 8 Sept 1965), 1 da (Tara b 12 Oct 1963); m 3, Feb 1972 (m dis 1983), Ron Kass, film prodr; 1 da (Katyana b 20 June 1972); m 4, Nov 1985 (m dis 1987), Peter Holm; m 5, Feb 2002, Percy Gibson; *Career* film and television actress since 1951; guest ed Christmas edn Marie Claire 1993; *Theatre* incl Last of Mrs Cheyne 1980, A Doll's House, Skin of Our Teeth, Claudia and David, 7th Veil, The Praying Mantis, Private Lives (Aldwych Theatre and US tour/Broadway) 1990, Love Letters (US tour) 2000, Over the Moon (Old Vic London) 2002, Full Circle (UK nat tour) 2004, An Evening with Joan Collins (one woman show, nat tour) 2005, Legends (USA tour) 2006; *Television* Br TV incl: Tales of the Unexpected, The Persuaders; US TV incl: Star Trek 1975, Batman 1975, The Moneychangers 1976, Mission Impossible 1976, Police Woman 1976, Starsky and Hutch 1978, Space 1999 1979, Fantasy Island 1981, The Making of a Male Model 1983, My Life as a Man 1984, Dynasty 1981–89, Sins 1985, Monte Carlo 1986, Rosanne 1991, Mamas Back 1992, Annie – A Royal Adventure 1995, Hart to Hart (TV film) 1995, Pacific Pallisades (series) 1997, Will & Grace 2000, These Old Broads (TV film) 2000, Footballers Wives 2006, Hotel Babylon 2006, Miss Marple 2009, Rules of Engagement 2010; *Films* Br films incl: The Road to Hong Kong 1962, Can Hieronymus Merkin Ever Forget Mercy Humppe and Find True Happiness 1969, I Believe In You, Adventures of Sadie, Decameron Nights, Good Die Young, Cosh Boy, Turn the Key Softly, Tales From the

Crypt 1972, The Big Sleep 1977, The Stud 1978, The Bitch 1979, Decadence 1993, In the Bleak Mid-Winter 1995, The Clandestine Marriage 1998; US films incl: Land of the Pharaohs 1954, The Virgin Queen 1955, The Opposite Sex 1956, Rally Round the Flag Boys 1958, The Bravados, 7 Thieves, Esther and the King 1960, Joseph Amazing Technicolour Dreamcoat, Decadence 1994, In the Bleak Midwinter (aka A Midwinter's Tale) 1995, Annie II: A Royal Adventure 1996, Clandestine Marriage 1998, The Flintstones: Viva Rock Vegas 1999, Ozzie 2001, Ellis in Glamourland 2004, Fetish 2010, Saving Santa 2013, Molly Moon – The Incredible Hypnotist 2014; *Awards* Hollywood Women's Press Club Golden Apple Award 1982, Golden Globe Best Actress in a TV Drama Award (Alexis in Dynasty) 1983, People's Choice Most Popular Actress Award 1983 and 1984, Golden Nymph Award Monte Carlo Television Festival 2001, Best Actress NY Int Film Festival 2010; *Books* Past Imperfect (1978), Joan Collins' Beauty Book (1982), Katy – A Fight for Life (1983), Prime Time (1988), Love and Desire and Hate (1990), My Secrets (1994), Too Damn Famous (1995), Second Act (1996), My Friends' Secrets (1999), Star Quality (2002), Misfortune's Daughters (2004), Joan's Way: Looking Good and Feeling Great (2006), The World According to Joan (2011), Passion for Life (2013); *Recreations* travelling, collecting 18 century antiques, writing, photography; *Style*— Dame Joan Collins, DBE; ✉ c/o Peter Charlesworth, 67 Holland Park Mews, London W11 3SS (☎ 020 7792 4600, e-mail info@petercharlesworth.co.uk)

COLLINS, Sir John Alexander; kt (1993); s of Maj John Constantine Collins, of Bodmin, Cornwall, and Nancy Isobel, *née* Mitchell; *b* 10 December 1941; *Educ* Campbell Coll Belfast, Univ of Reading (BSc); *m* 24 April 1965, Susan Mary, da of Robert Reid Hooper, of Wimborne, Dorset; 1 da (Helen b 18 June 1968), 1 s (Robert b 18 May 1970); *Career* joined Shell 1964, various appts Kenya, Nigeria and Colombia, chm and chief exec Shell UK Ltd 1990–93; chief exec Vestey Group Ltd 1993–2001; chm: Cantab Pharmaceuticals 1996–99, National Power plc 1998–2000 (non-exec dir 1996–2000), chm DSG int plc 2002–09 (dep chm 2001–02); non-exec dir: British Sky Broadcasting Group plc 1994–97, NM Rothschild & Sons Ltd 1995–2005, Peninsular and Oriental Steam Navigation Co 1998–2006, Stoll Moss Theatres Ltd 1999–2000, Rothschild Continuation Holdings AG 1999–2010, 3i Infrastructure plc 2009–14, Blue Diamond Ltd 2014–; chm: Advsy Ctee on Business and the Environment 1991–93, DTI/DEFRA Sustainable Energy Policy Advsy Bd 2001–07; pres The Energy Inst 2005–07; CIMgt; *Recreations* theatre, sailing; *Clubs* Royal Yacht Squadron; *Style*— Sir John Collins; ✉ Le Repos Au Coin, La Fosse, St Martin, Guernsey GY4 6EB

COLLINS, John Joseph; s of Patrick Collins (d 1982), of Killiney, Dublin, and Mary Josephine, *née* O'Brien (d 1954); *b* 23 May 1944; *m* 1, 1970 (m dis 1998), (Eline) Mary, da of James Cullen (d 1978); 2 s (Patrick James, Paul Ivor), 1 da (Aisling Mary); m 2, 1998, Jamela, *née* Clooney (m dis 2003); 1 s (Glenn Michael); *Career* called to the Bar King's Inns Ireland 1967 (in practice 1967–71), called to the Bar Middle Temple 1971; fndr chambers at 11 South Square Gray's Inn 1980; fndr and head of chambers in: Lewes 1987, Hastings and Chichester 1996; called to the Aust Bar in Supreme Court of NSW 1989; memb Ctee Int Bar Assoc 1990–, chm Int Assoc of Irish Lawyers 1992–2008; *Recreations* reading, walking, swimming; *Style*— John Collins, Esq; ✉ Westgate Chambers, 64 High Street, Lewes, East Sussex BN7 1XG (☎ 01273 480510, fax 01273 483179, e-mail jcwestgate@aol.com, website www.westgate-chambers.co.uk)

COLLINS, John Morris; s of Emmanuel Cohen, MBE (d 1980), of Leeds, and Ruby Cohen (d 1988); *b* 25 June 1931, Horsforth, Leeds; *Educ* Leeds GS, The Queen's Coll Oxford (MA); *m* 19 March 1968, Sheila, da of David Brummer (d 2005), of Hendon, London; 1 da (Simone Natalie (Mrs Baxter) b 1974); *Career* called to the Bar Middle Temple 1956; dep co ct judge 1970–71, asst recorder 1971, dep circuit judge 1972–80, recorder of the Crown Court 1980–98, jt head of (Zenith) chambers 2001–02 (sole head of chambers 1966–2001); *Publications* Summary Justice (1963) and numerous legal articles; *Recreations* walking, communal work; *Style*— John M Collins, Esq; ✉ 14 Sandhill Oval, Leeds LS17 8EA (☎ 0113 268 6008); Zenith Chambers, 10 Park Square, Leeds LS1 2LH (☎ 0113 245 5438, fax 0113 242 3515, website www.zenithchambers.co.uk)

COLLINS, Dr John Vincent; s of Thomas Ernest Collins (d 1987), of Denham, Bucks, and Zillah Phoebe, *née* Jessop (d 1997); *b* 16 July 1938; *Educ* Univ of London (BDS, MB BS, MD), Guy's Hosp, St Mary's Hosp, Westminster Hosp; *m* 1, 1963 (m dis), Helen Eluned, da of William Alan Cash; 1 s (Jonathan James b March 1972), 1 da (Philippa Helen b Sept 1977); m 2, Sept 2009, Hilary Anne Booker, da of David Broadbent Johnston; *Career* house physician Guy's Hosp 1966–67, house surgn 1966–67, SHO in neurology St Mary's Hosp 1967, med registrar 1968–70, sr med registrar Westminster and Brompton Hosp 1970–72, sr lectr in med and conslt physician Bart's Med Coll 1973–76; conslt physician: Royal Brompton and National Heart Hosps (now Royal Brompton Hosp) 1976–2003, Riverside HA 1979–2003, Lister Hosp; med dir Chelsea and Westminster Hosp 1994–2003, conslt physician and dir of professional devpt and educn Benenden Hosp 2008–12, med dir Lister Hosp 2008–14; sr med advsr Benenden Healthcare Soc 1979–2011 gp med advsr Smith and Nephew 1989–2010; hon conslt Royal Hosp Chelsea 1979–2003; *Recreations* tennis, drawing, painting; *Style*— Dr John Collins; ✉ Royal Brompton Hospital, Sydney Street, London SW3 6NP (☎ 020 7881 4168, fax 020 7881 4167)

COLLINS, Sir Kevan; kt (2015); s of Arthur Collins (d 2015), and Thelma *née* Townrow; *b* 8 December 1960, Rinteln, Germany; *Educ* Lancaster Univ, Univ of Leeds (doctorate); *Partner* Theophilus Jones; *Career* chief exec London Borough of Tower Hamlets 2005–11, chief exec Education Endowment Fndn 2011–; *Style*— Sir Kevan Collins; ✉ The Education Endowment Foundation, 9th Floor, Millbank Tower, 21–24 Millbank, London SW1P 4QP

COLLINS, Dr (Nicholas) Mark; s of John Anthony Collins (d 2004), and Mary, *née* Humphries; *b* 23 April 1952, Cheltenham, Glos; *Educ* Rendcomb Coll Cirencester (scholar), Wadham Coll Oxford (BA), Imperial Coll London (PhD), Open Univ (Cert, Dip, MBA); *m* 30 Oct 1982, Melanie Margaret, *née* Stephens; 1 da (Charlotte Daisy b 23 Oct 1986), 1 s (George Benjamin b 17 June 1989); *Career* Centre for Overseas Pest Res ODA 1974–80, Int Centre for Insect Physiology and Ecology Kenya 1980–82, Int Union for the Conservation of Nature 1982–88; World Conservation Monitoring Centre 1988–2000; UN Environment Prog: dir UNEP World Conservation Monitoring Centre 2000–04, princ UNEP Div of Environmental Policy Implementation 2004–05; dir Cwlth Fndn 2005–11, visiting fell Univ of Westminster 2011–12; HM Inspr of Zoos 1990–2000; memb: Darwin Initiative Expert Ctee 2001–06 and 2012–15, Total Fndn for the Biodiversity of the Sea Paris 2003–06, Int Advsy Cncl Inst of Cwlth Studies Univ of London 2005–11; chm: Cambridge Sustainable City 1996–2002, Cambridge and Peterborough Sustainable Devpt Round Table 2003–04; tstee: Fauna & Flora Int 1989–98 (chair Cambridge Gp 1996–2002), Wildscreen Tst 1997–2004, Galapagos Conservation Tst 2006– (chair 2011–), Friends of the Cwlth Fndn 2007–11, The Round Table 2007–15, Earthwatch Inst 2011– (vice-chm 2012–15); Busk Medal RGS 2000; *Publications* ed and contrib to 11 books incl: Threatened Swallowtail Butterflies of the World (1985), The Last Rain Forests (1990), The Conservation Atlas of Tropical Forests (co-ed, 1991 and 1992), From Hook to Plate: the State of Marine Fisheries; author of more than 140 published papers and articles; *Recreations* natural history, sailing; *Clubs* Geographical; *Style*— Dr Mark Collins; ✉ West Acre, 49 West Street, Comberton, Cambridge CB23 7DS (e-mail collinsmark@gmail.com)

COLLINS, Mark William Gerard; s of William Henry Collins, of Sheffield, S Yorks, and Oonagh Sheila Maria, *née* Lissenden; *b* 14 May 1953, Sheffield, S Yorks; *Educ* De La Salle Coll Sheffield; *m* 30 Oct 1985, Elisabeth Jayne, *née* Frith; 1 s (Alexander William James b 10 May 1987), 1 da (Emma Elisabeth Alexandra b 18 Oct 1988); *Career* Moore Fletcher & Co: articled clerk 1971–76, audit mangr 1977–80; Sheffield Insulation Ltd: joined 1980, gp financial controller 1985–87, dir 1987–90; finance dir and co sec Brooke Industrial Holdings plc 1990–96; Cattles plc: chief accountant 1996–99, finance dir 1999–2001, treasy and risk dir 2001–09; memb Cncl CBI Yorkshire and Humber; FCA 1983 (ACA 1977); *Recreations* travel, golf, motor sport; *Clubs* Walbrook, Abbeydale Golf; *Style*— Mark Collins, Esq; ✉ Whitelow House Farm, Whitelow Lane, Dore, Sheffield S17 3AG (☎ 01142 369208, fax 01142 360159, e-mail mwgc@hotmail.co.uk)

COLLINS, Michael Geoffrey; QC (1988); s of (Francis) Geoffrey Collins (d 1982), of Scottburgh, South Africa, and Margaret Isabelle, *née* Harper-Gow (d 1989); *b* 4 March 1948; *Educ* Peterhouse Marandellas Rhodesia, Univ of Exeter (LLB); *m* 13 April 1985, Bonnie Gayle Bird, da of John Wilbur Bird (d 1988), and Frances Ratliff Bird (d 1995), of New Albany, Indiana; *Career* called to the Bar Gray's Inn 1971 (bencher 1999); recorder of the Crown Court 1997–2001, special legal conslt Fulbright & Jaworski LLP Washington DC 2002–; *Books* Private International Litigation (contrib, 1988); *Recreations* golf, tennis, watercolour painting, amateur dramatics; *Clubs* Woking Golf; *Style*— Michael Collins, Esq, QC; ✉ Fulbright & Jaworski LLP, 801 Pennsylvania Avenue NW, Washington DC 20004–2623, USA (☎ 1 202 662 4527, fax 1 202 662 4643, e-mail mcollins@fulbright.com); Essex Court Chambers, 24 Lincoln's Inn Fields, London WC2A 3EG (☎ 020 7813 8000, fax 020 7813 8080)

COLLINS, Prof Michael John; MBE (2015); s of Frederick Allenby Collins, and Gwendoline Violet, *née* Hersey-Walker; *b* 27 January 1962; *Educ* Royal Coll of Music (ARCM); *m* 1997 (m dis 2006), Isabelle van Keulen; 1 s (Simon Jan b 1999, Rose Jane b 2000); *Career* clarinettist; with Nash Ensemble 1982–88; principal clarinet: London Sinfonietta 1982–, Philharmonia Orch 1988–95; prof: Royal Coll of Music 1985–, Royal Acad of Music 1996–; Carnegie Hall debut (with Philharmonia) 1992; soloist Last Night of the Proms 1995, soloist with Russian Nat Orch BBC Proms 1996; currently princ conductor City of London Sinfonia; ambass Pancreatic Cancer UK (PCUK); winner: BBC TV Young Musician of the Year 1978, Leeds Nat Competition for Musicians 1980, Int Rostrum of Young Performers UNESCO 1985, Worshipful Co of Musicians Medal 1980, Tagore Gold Medal Royal Coll of Music; awarded Hon RAM 1997, FRCM 2010; *Recreations* record collecting, walking, travel; *Style*— Prof Michael Collins, MBE; ✉ 8 Vale Wood Drive, Farnham, Surrey GU10 3HW (☎ 01252 795715, e-mail collinsclarinet@icloud.com)

COLLINS, Dr Michael Lawrence; s of Sidney Collins, of Leeds, and Essie, *née* Gross; *b* 26 May 1943; *Educ* Roundhay Sch Leeds, Univ of Leeds Sch of Med (MB ChB); *m* 27 June 1971, Jackie, da of Theodore Hall, of Leeds; 1 s (Spencer b 1974), 1 da (Antonia (Mrs James Rubin) b 1977); *Career* house surgn and SHO United Leeds Hosps 1969–72, teaching fell Univ of Br Columbia 1972–73, registrar Leeds Maternity Hosp and Hosp for Women 1973–76, specialist in gynaecological endocrinology and infertility McMaster Univ Med Centre 1977–79, princ gen practice Middx 1980–84, specialist practice in gynaecological endocrinology 1980–, med advsr Well Woman Clinics 1980–, clinical dir Lynbrook Hosp 1992–94, lectr in med gynaecology; ed Gynaecology and Infertility Digest; memb: Hillingdon FPC 1980–84, Hillingdon Local Med Ctee 1980–84, Hillingdon Brunel Univ Liaison Ctee; MDU, Assoc of Profs in Gynecology and Obstetrics; memb: BMA, RSM; *Recreations* art, photography, writing, antiquarian books, croquet; *Clubs* Phyllis Court, Henley; *Style*— Dr Michael Collins; ✉ Melnick House, Ascot, Berkshire SL5 5BN; 144 Harley Street, London W1G 7LD (e-mail dr.collins@consultant.com)

COLLINS, Neil Adam; s of Clive Dinant Collins, and Joan Collins; *Educ* Uppingham, Selwyn Coll Cambridge; *m* 1, 1981 (m dis 1994), Vivien Goldsmith; 1 da (Alice Laura b 30 July 1982); m 2, 1999, Julia Barnes; 1 da (Fleur Joan), 1 s (Arthur Jeremy); *Career* journalist: Daily Mail 1974–79; city ed: Evening Standard 1979–84, The Sunday Times 1984–86, The Daily Telegraph 1986–2005; fly fishing corr The Spectator 2002–04; columnist: Evening Standard 2005–09, Reuters 2009–10, FT 2012–; dir: Templeton Emerging Markets Investment Tst 2006–, Dyson James Ltd 2006–07, Finsbury Growth & Income Investment Tst 2008–; Fin Journalist of the Year 2002; *Style*— Neil Collins, Esq; ✉ 12 Gertrude Street, London SW10 0JN (☎ 07836 256674, e-mail neilcollins10@gmail.com)

COLLINS, Patrick Michael; s of Patrick John Collins (d 1990), of London, and Julia Ann, *née* Canty (d 1988); *b* 23 November 1943; *Educ* St Joseph's Acad Blackheath; *m* 1969, Julie Kathleen, da of Leslie Gordon Grundon; 3 s (Michael Patrick b 19 Sept 1970, Daniel Timothy b 7 Feb 1972, Patrick Joseph Gerard b 13 Jan 1983), 1 da (Mary Julie b 31 Dec 1974); *Career* sports writer; cub reporter Kentish Mercury 1962–65; sports writer: Sunday Citizen 1965–67, News of the World 1967–78; sports columnist: London Evening News 1978–80, London Evening Standard 1980–82; chief sports writer Mail on Sunday 1982–2015, sports columnist Punch 1990–92; memb English Sports Cncl 1999–2002, pres Br Sports Journalists' Assoc 2015–; Br Sports Journalist of the Year 1989, 1990, 1997, 2002 and 2008; commendations: Br Press Awards 1978, 1987, 1988, 1991, 1993, 1996, 1998, 1999, 2001 and 2003, Sports Cncl Awards 1979, 1985, 1986, 1988, 1992, 1994, 1996, 1998, 2000, 2001, 2002, 2003, 2004, 2006, 2007, 2010, 2012 and 2013; Br Magazine Columnist of the Year 1990, Sports Feature Writer of the Year Br Sports Journalism Award 1993, 2002 and 2004, Sports Columnist of the Year Br Sports Journalism Award 1999, 2000, 2004, 2006 and 2012; former sports rep: Kent rugby union XV, London schs athletics team; *Books* The Sportswriter (1996), Among the Fans (2011); *Recreations* watching cricket, family; *Style*— Patrick Collins, Esq; ✉ e-mail collinspatk@yahoo.co.uk; Mail on Sunday, Northcliffe House, 2 Derry Street, London W8 5TS (☎ 020 7938 6000)

COLLINS, Dr Peter Donald Bruce; s of Douglas Collins (d 1984), and Marjorie, *née* Reynolds (d 2007); *b* 3 January 1939; *Educ* William Hulme's GS Manchester, Univ of Bristol (Lacrosse colours, BSc, PhD); *m* 1970, Margaret, *née* Purnell; 2 s (Andrew Richard Purnell b 1974, Nigel Antony Lawrence b 1976); *Career* research fell Univ of Calif Berkeley 1963–65; Univ of Durham: lectr in theoretical physics 1965–73, sr lectr 1973–83, reader 1983–98, dean Faculty of Science 1988–91, pro-vice-chllr 1991–97, sub warden 1994–97; chm Higher Edcn Support for Industry in the North (HESIN) 1993–97, chm Foresight North East 1997–2006; dir: Regnl Technol Centre (North) 1990–97, County Durham Development Co 1994–97, Durham Univ Investment Ltd and subsidiary cos 1994–2002, Northern Infomatics Applications Agency 1995–97, Gentoo Gp Ltd 2007–10; chm Houghton and Hetton Housing Co Ltd 2001–06; chm of govrs Houghton Kepier Sch 1997–2014; vice-chm Sunderland Schools' Forum 2003–06, chm Hetton Local History Gp 2009–; memb American Physical Soc 1964–; FRSA 1991, FInstP 1992; *Books* Regge Poles in Particle Physics (with E J Squires, 1967), Regge Theory and High Energy Physics (1976), Hadron Interactions (with A D Martin, 1984), Particle Physics and Cosmology (with A D Martin and E J Squires, 1989); *Recreations* cricket, gardening, house restoration, railway modelling; *Clubs* Durham CCC; *Style*— Dr Peter Collins

COLLINS, Richard Denis James; s of Patrick Joseph Collins (d 1993), and Kathleen, *née* O'Mahony (d 1992); *b* 15 February 1942, Co Cork, Ireland; *Educ* Bray Nat Boys Secdy Sch Co Dublin, Our Lady of Grace Secdy Sch Charlton London, SE London Tech Sch Deptford, Coll of Estate Mgmnt Reading and London; *m* Noreen, *née* O'Keeffe; 2 da (Catherine Marie b 31 Aug 1964, Amanda Jane b 5 Sept 1966), 1 s (Robert John b 4 March 1972); *Career* surveyor; Morden College Estates 1958–63, Purvis & Purvis Architects and Surveyors 1963–64, GLC/ILEA 1964–68, chief building surveyor London Borough of Bexley 1968–72, ptnr Kennedy & Partners 1972–2001 (sr ptnr 1982); former dir and chm Dunlop Haywards Ltd; dir and chm: Kennedy Properties Ltd, Kennedy and Partners Ltd, Kennedy Haywards Ltd, Kennedy and Partners (UK) Ltd, Construction Consultants Consortium Ltd, Swan New Homes Ltd, Erinaceous (Ireland) Ltd; currently dir: Kennedy Woodward Allen Ltd; Charlton Athletic FC Ltd (also life pres and former chm), Charlton Athletic Hldgs Ltd, PDR Ventures Ltd, Sundridge Park Golf Club Ltd, Building Control Charity; RICS: former pres Building Surveyors Div, chm Construction Design and Economics Practice Panel, memb various ctees and panels; various appts as arbitrator; dir and former pres Bexley and Greenwich C of C; former memb London Rent Assessment Panel Leasehold Valuation Tbnl; conslt to FA of Ireland; Irish Businessman of the Year 2002; Freedom of the City of London 1993; memb: Soc of Construction Law, Adjudication Soc; FRICS 1968, FCIArb 1971, FBEng 1974, MAE 1991, FInstD 1986; *Recreations* flying light aircraft (holds private pilot's licence), football, golf; *Clubs* Sportair Flying, Sundridge Park Golf, Charlton Athletic FC; *Style—* Richard Collins, Esq; ✉ 5 Kinnaird Avenue, Bromley, Kent BR1 4HG (☎ home 020 8290 1779, mobile 07866 674233, e-mail rdc@kennedysurveyors.com)

COLLINS, Sir Rory Edwards; kt (2011); s of late Jack Collins, and late Catherine, *née* Burke; *b* 3 January 1955, Hong Kong; *Educ* Dulwich Coll, George Washington Univ Washington DC (BSc), Univ of London (LMSSA), St Thomas' Hosp Med Sch London (MB BS), Univ of Oxford (MSc, MA); *m* Barbara Casadei; *Career* Dept of Cardiovascular Med John Radcliffe Hosp Oxford: research asst (hon SHO, registrar then sr registrar) 1981–91, hon conslt in public health 1991–; Univ of Oxford: joined Clinical Trial Service Unit (CTSU) and Epidemiology Studies Unit Nuffield Dept of Clinical Med 1981, co-dir (with Prof Sir Richard Peto, *qv*) CTSU 1986–, Br Heart Fndn prof of med and epidemiology 1996–; fell St Cross Coll 2013–; fell Green Coll 1997–; co-dir MRC Directly Supported Team 1996–; chief exec UK Biobank 2005–; head Nuffield Dept of Population Health 2013; memb: Br Atherosclerosis Soc 1986–, Br Cardiac Soc 1986–, American Coll of Cardiology 1991–, Br Hypertension Soc 1993–, European Soc of Cardiology 1994–, Assoc of Physicians 1998–, American Heart Fndn 1999–; Hon Medal Polish Card Soc 1994, European Award for Excellence in Stroke Research (jtly) 1995, Prix Raymond Bourgine for Achievement in Cancer Research (jtly) 1996, Fothergill Medal Med Soc of London (jtly) 1998, Sr Aspirin Award 2000 (jtly), Queen's Anniversary Prize for Research 2005; FRCPEd 2002, Mackenzie Medal Br Cardiovascular Soc 2014, ESC Gold Medal 2014; *Style—* Sir Rory Collins; ✉ 15 Godstow Road, Wolvercote, Oxford OX2 8AJ (☎ 01865 557636); Clinical Trial Service Unit and Epidemiological Studies Unit, University of Oxford, Richard Doll Building, Old Road Campus, Roosevelt Drive, Oxford OX3 7LF (☎ 01865 743834, fax 01865 743985, e-mail secretary@ctsu.ox.ac.uk)

COLLINS, Roy William; s of Charles Albert Collins (d 1987), and Lilian Maud, *née* Williamson (d 1960); *b* 17 July 1948; *Educ* SE Essex Co Tech HS; *m* 1, 1971 (m dis 1975), Barbara Anne, *née* Askew; m 2, 1987, Sheila Anne, da of Leslie Arthur Love; 1 da (Lucy Elizabeth b 3 Jan 1987); *Career* gen reporter Barking Advertiser 1967, sports ed Express & Independent Walthamstow 1967–68, sports writer Essex & East London Newspapers 1968–69, sports columnist Evening Echo Southend 1969–74, freelance sports and news features journalist Fleet Street 1974–79, gen sports writer then columnist Sunday People 1979–83, freelance sports and gen journalist 1983–86, chief sports writer and columnist Today 1986–95 (following paper's closure), sports columnist The People 1996–2000, freelance writer The Guardian 2000–03, football corr Sunday Telegraph 2003–; memb: SWA, Football Writers' Assoc; *Recreations* tennis, running, chess, pubs, horse racing; *Clubs* Nothing Writers' Overseas Dining (treas), Coolhurst Tennis; *Style—* Roy Collins, Esq; ✉ 48 Rosebery Road, Muswell Hill, London N10 2LJ (☎ 020 8883 6706, e-mail roycol@aol.com)

COLLINS, Scott; *Career* restaurateur; formerly worked in banking and IT sales; prop: The Castle Camberwell, The Clarence Balham (Pub of the Year Evening Standard 2006); prop with Yianni Papoutsis: MEATliquor (London, Brighton, Leeds, Singapore, Bristol, Islington, East Dulwich, Croydon), MEATmarket Covent Garden, MEATmission Hoxton, CHICKENliquor Brixton, Hobo Beer Co Ltd; *Books* The MEATliquor Chronicles (jtly, 2014); *Style—* Scott Collins, Esq

COLLINS, Sheila Mary; da of Peter Gilbert Stuart Dawson, of Ringwood, Hants, and Mary Violet, *née* Rabbetts (d 1992); *b* 10 March 1952; *Educ* Dorchester GS for Girls, UCL (LLB), Coll of Law Lanchester Gate London; *m* John Brook Collins; 1 da (Michelle Mary Elizabeth b 1984), 1 s (Dominic John Luke b 8 March 1986); *Career* admitted slr 1976; practice mangr Messrs Harold G Walker & Co Slrs Bournemouth 1996–; chair Royal Bournemouth & Christchurch Hosps NHS Tst 1997– (non-exec dir 1991–97); treas Young Slrs Gp Bournemouth 1981–85, hon sec Bournemouth and Dist Law Soc 1985–; independent lay visitor Hesley Gp of Schs 1992–95; memb: Law Soc of England and Wales 1976, Soc of Tst and Estate Practitioners 1996; *Recreations* horse riding, quiz team member, wine appreciation; *Style—* Mrs Sheila Collins; ✉ Royal Bournemouth & Christchurch Hospitals NHS Foundation Trust, Castle Lane East, Bournemouth, Dorset BH7 7DW

COLLINS, Tim William George; CBE (1996); s of William Alfred Collins (d 1997), and Diana Mary Collins; *b* 7 May 1964; *Educ* Chigwell Sch, LSE (BSc(Econ)), King's Coll London (MA); *m* July 1997, Clare, da of Geoffrey Benson; 1 s (Christopher); *Career* special advsr: DOE 1989–90, Dept of Employment 1990–92; press sec to PM gen election 1992 and leadership election 1995, dir of communications Cons Pty 1992–95, business conslt WCT Live Communications Ltd 1995–97; MP (Cons) Westmorland and Lonsdale 1997–2005; oppn whip 1998–99, sr vice-chm Cons Pty 1999–2001, shadow min for the Cabinet Office 2001–02, shadow Tport sec 2002–03, shadow educn sec 2003–; memb Cons Pty Policy Bd 2001–02; *Recreations* theatre, cinema, reading; *Style—* Tim Collins, Esq, CBE; ✉ 112 Highgate, Kendal, Cumbria LA9 4HE (☎ 01539 721010, e-mail listening@timcollins.co.uk)

COLLINS, Prof Vincent Peter; s of James Vincent Collins (d 1989), of Dublin, and Mary Ann, *née* Blanche (d 2002); *b* 3 December 1947; *Educ* St Fintains HS Dublin, UCD (MB BCh, BAO), Karolinska Inst Stockholm (MD); *Career* jr hosp and research posts Regnl Hosp Limerick, Mater Hosp Dublin, Stockholm's Cancer Soc and Karolinska Inst Stockholm 1971–74, various med appts and research posts in pathology Karolinska Inst and Hosp Stockholm 1974–97; latter appts: prof of pathology (with particular responsibility for neuropathology) Univ of Gothenburg Sweden 1990–94, prof of tumour pathology Karolinska Inst Stockholm 1994–97, sr conslt pathologist and latterly chm Dept of Oncology-Pathology Karolinska Hosp Stockholm 1994–97, head of clinical research Ludwig Inst Stockholm 1986–98; current appts: prof of histopathology and morbid anatomy Univ of Cambridge 1997–2014 (emeritus prof 2014–), hon conslt in histopathology Addenbrooke's Hosp Cambridge 1997–2014; memb: Bd Stockholm Cancer Soc 1995–2017 (latterly chm), Scientific Bd Biol, Bd Swedish Childhood Cancer Fund 1996–2015 (latterly chm); Minerva Prize Minerva Fndn Stockholm 1987, Joanne Vandenberg Hill Award and William O Russell Lectureship in Anatomical Pathology Anderson Hosp and Tumor Inst Univ of Texas 1990, research fell Japan 1991, Lucien J Rubenstein Neuropathology Research Lectureship Virginia Neurological Inst Univ of Virginia 1994, 2000 and 2010, Roll of Honour Int Union Against Cancer (UICC) 1996, Linse Bock Visiting Professorship in Neuro-Oncology Mayo Clinic Rochester Minnesota 1997, Takao Hoshino Lectureship Univ of Calif San Francisco 1998; memb various professional orgns incl: Int Soc of Neuropathology, Br Neuropathological Soc, Euro Soc of Pathology, NY Acad of Scis; FRCPath 1996 (MRCPath 1988), FMedSci 2002, fell European Acad of Cancer Sciences 2009; *Publications* author of numerous pubns in learned jls; memb Editorial Bd Neuropathology & Applied Neurobiology; memb Int Editorial Bd (Section on Pathology and Pathological Anatomy) Excerpta Medica; *Recreations* sailing, skiing, music; *Style—* Prof V Peter Collins; ✉ Department of Histopathology, Box 235, Addenbrooke's Hospital, Hills Road, Cambridge CB2 0QQ (☎ 01223 336072, fax 01223 586670, e-mail vpc20@cam.ac.uk)

COLLINS OF HIGHBURY, Baron (Life Peer UK 2011), of Highbury in the London Borough of Islington; Raymond Edward Harry (Ray) Collins; s of late Harry Collins, and late Isabel Collins; *b* 21 December 1954; *Educ* Matthew Arnold Sch Staines, Richmond Coll, Univ of Kent at Canterbury (BA); *m* 21 Dec 2005, Rafael Ballesteros (civil partnership converted); *Career* TGWU (now UNITE): memb 1972–, asst librarian 1972–74, specialist asst educn 1974–77, policy advsr and special asst to the Gen Sec 1980–84, nat admin offr 1984–99, asst gen sec 1999–2008, memb Branch Ctee and Staff Negotiating Ctee; Lab Pty: memb 1970–, memb Nat Policy Forum 1997–2003, memb Nat Constitution Ctee 2001–08, gen sec 2008–11, dir Lionel Cook Meml Fund 2008–; House of Lords: memb All Party Parly Gp Governance Gp, memb All Party Parly Gp London Gp, memb All Party Parly Gp Humanist Gp, memb Inter-Parly Union, oppn whip 2011–, oppn front bench spokesperson work and pensions 2012–13, oppn front bench spokesperson int devpt and foreign affrs 2013–; memb Governing Body Ruskin Coll Oxford; patron: Positive East, Stonewall; *Recreations* swimming, reading, cinema, supporter of Arsenal FC; *Style—* The Lord Collins of Highbury; ✉ House of Lords, London SW1A 0PW (☎ 020 7219 1675, website www.labourlords.org.uk, Twitter @lord_collins)

COLLINS RICE, Rowena; da of John Frederick (Jack) Collins, of Letchworth Garden City Herts, and Hilda, *née* Campbell; *b* 24 April 1960, Dundee, Scotland; *Educ* Westbourne Sch Glasgow, Hertford Coll Oxford (BA); *m* 9 Aug 1986, Hugh Robert; 2 s (Benedict Gabriel b 25 Sept 1991, Clement Gregory b 21 Jan 1997); *Career* Home Office 1985–91 and 1995–2003, Treasy Slr's Dept 1992–95; admitted slr 1995; Dept Constitutional Affairs 2003–05, legal dir (tax law) HMRC 2005–07, legal dir DCA 2007–08, DG democracy, constitution and law and chief legal offr Miny of Justice 2008–10, DG constitution Dep PM's Gp Cabinet Office 2010–11, sec Leveson Inquiry into Culture, Practices and Ethics of the Press 2011–12, DG Attorney Gen's Office and legal sec to the Law Offrs 2013–; *Style—* Ms Rowena Collins Rice; ✉ Attorney General's Office, 20 Victoria Street, London SW1H 0NF (☎ 020 7271 2401, e-mail rowena.collins-rice@attorneygeneral.gsi.gov.uk, website www.gov.uk/government/organisations/attorney-generals-office)

COLLINSON, Alicia Hester; da of His Hon Judge Richard Jeffreys Hampton Collinson (d 1983), and Gwendolen Hester, *née* Ward; *b* 12 August 1956; *Educ* Birkenhead HS, St Hugh's Coll Oxford (MA, MPhil); *m* 23 April 1988, Rt Hon Damian Howard Green, MP, *qv*, s of Howard Green, KSG; 2 da (Felicity b 1990, Verity b 1993); *Career* called to the Bar Middle Temple 1982 (Harmsworth scholar); memb Bar Cncl 1990–93; memb Ct of Common Cncl Corporation of London 1991–94; dep chllr Diocese of Gloucester 2013–; Freeman City of London; *Publications* Tough Love: A Critique of the Domestic Violence, Crime and Victims Bill 2003 (2004), Politics for Partners: How to live with a politican (2007); *Clubs* Oxford Union; *Style—* Miss Alicia Collinson; ✉ 2 Harcourt Buildings, Temple, London EC4Y 9DB (☎ 0844 561 7135, fax 020 7353 6968); Harcourt Chambers, Churchill House, St Aldates Courtyard, 38 St Aldates, Oxford OX1 1BN (fax 01865 791585, e-mail acollinson@harcourtchambers.co.uk)

COLLINSON, Prof Leonard; DL (Merseyside 2002); s of Sidney Lupton Collinson (d 1987), and Jane, *née* Crooks (d 1999), of Immingham; *b* 30 March 1934, Grimsby; *Educ* Humberstone Fndn Sch Cleethorpes, Univ of Nottingham (Dip); *m* 17 Sept 1955, Shirley Grace, da of Ernest Frederick Funnell (d 1962); 2 s (Christopher b 1956, Andrew b 1962); *Career* Nat Serv RAF 1952–54; organiser Nat Cncl of Lab Colls 1954–58, personnel mangr rising to dep nat mangr Bakery Div Co-operative Gp 1958–66, dir manpower Plessey Telecommunications and Office Systems 1966–71, fndr and exec chm Collinson Grant Group 1971–96; chm: European Consortium of Mgmnt Consults 1991–97, Newsco Pubns 1994–99, Grosvenor Career Services 1996–98, Central Plastics 2000–04, Industry Northwest 2002–04; dir: Collinson Grant Gp 1971–2010, United Gas Industries 1975–82, Wormald Int Holdings 1979–83, RAD Sheep Sportswear 2006–09; CBI: memb Smaller Firms Cncl 1980–86, memb NW Regnl Cncl 1987–93 and 1998–, memb Nat Cncl 1995–98; chm Private Sector Partners 2001–04 and 2008–11, dir and chm Forum of Private Business 2004–08 (dir 1994–2001); dir: Manchester TEC 1989–92, Univs Superannuation Scheme 1989–2004; tstee Merseyside Ecumenical Cncl for Mission in the Economy 1966–, memb Ct Univ of Manchester 1994–2004, chm Manchester Diocesan Cncl for Church in the Economy 1994–99, memb Rgnl Economic Forecasting Panel 2003–11, Jt Economic Cncl for North West 2008–10; dep chm NW Regnl Assembly 2001–02; tstee People's History Museum 1994–2014; hon prof Univ of Central Lancashire 2007 (hon fell 2005); FCIM 1967, FCIPD 1970, FIC/CMC 1980, CCMI 1985, FRSA 1990, Br Acad of Mgmnt 2004; *Books* Employment Law Keynotes (with C M Hodkinson, 1985), Manual for Small Business (1983), The Line Manager's Employment Law (16 edns since 1978), Start and Manage Your Own Business (2009); *Recreations* football, postcards, politics; *Clubs* RAC; *Style—* Prof Leonard Collinson, DL; ✉ Suite 2, Moorfield House, 2a Moorside Road, Swinton, Manchester M27 0EW (☎ 0161 794 9538, fax 0161 794 1594, e-mail lcollinson@colgranhouse.com)

COLLIS, Pamela Caroline Neild; da of Michael Neild Collis, MBE, of Beds, and Shirley Ann, *née* Strong; *b* 9 March 1957; *Educ* Rosemead Sch for Girls Littlehampton Sussex, Univ of Bristol (LLB), Guildford Coll of Law; *m* 22 Dec 1987, Joseph Sinyor, s of Samuel Sinyor; 2 s (Joshua Samuel Michael b 17 Nov 1988, Benjamin Jonathon b 30 June 1990); 1 da (Jessica Claire Rachael b 1 Jan 1994); *Career* asst slr Herbert Smith 1981–82 (articled clerk 1979–81); Kingsley Napley: joined 1982, ptnr 1985–99, head Family Law Dept 1989–99; accredited memb Family Law Panel Law Soc, memb Resolution; trained collaborative lawyer and memb Collaborative Forum London; fell Acad of Int Matrimonial Lawyers (co-chair Surrogacy Ctee); *Recreations* sailing, cycling, reading, opera, walking; *Style—* Miss Pamela Collis; ✉ HowardKennedyFsi, 19 Cavendish Square, London W1A 2AW (☎ 020 7663 8669, fax 020 3350 3351)

COLLIS, HE Simon; *Career* diplomat; 2 sec Bahrain 1981–84, ME spokesperson News Dept FCO 1984–86, NY 1986, dep head of mission Tunis 1988–90, Gulf War Emergency Unit FCO 1990–91, New Delhi 1991–94, dep head Near East and North Africa Dept FCO 1994–96, dep head of mission Amman 1996–99, secondment to BP 1999–2000, consul-gen Dubai 2000–04, consul-gen Basra 2004–05, ambass to Qatar 2005–07, ambass to Syria 2007–12, ambass to Iraq 2012–14, ambass to Saudi Arabia 2015–; *Style—* HE Mr Simon Collis; ✉ c/o FCO (Riyadh), King Charles Street, London SW1A 2AH

COLLIS, Terrence Ivor; *b* 1 February 1954; *Educ* Laxton GS Oundle, Univ of Durham (BSc); *m* 21 Oct 1989, Sarah Lilian Anderson, CBE, da of Derek Anderson; 1 s (Benjamin Ivor b 7 May 1991), 1 da (Sophie Helena b 14 April 1993); *Career* press serv exec Nicholas Mendes & Associates 1975–76, press and PRO Barlow Handling Ltd 1976–78, press offr Lucas Group 1978–81, sr PR exec Hawker Siddeley Group 1981–85; Vickers plc: media rels mangr 1985–87, dep dir of public affrs 1988, dir of public affrs 1988–92; md Bell Pottinger Financial (formerly Lowe Bell Financial) 1992–97, dir of corp affrs and memb Exec Mgmnt Ctee National Westminster Bank plc 1997–2000, dir of gp corp communications Lloyds TSB Gp plc 2000–05, dir of communications Food Standards Agency 2006–; vice-chm and tstee Br Red Cross 2004–; FIPR 2002 (MIPR 1988); *Recreations* wicket-keeping, astronomy; *Clubs* Pimlico Astronomical Soc, Mortlake Casuals Cricket; *Style—* Terrence Collis, Esq

COLLON, Nicholas William Hyde; s of Michael Collon, and Jo Collon; *b* 7 February 1983, Kingston-upon-Thames; *Educ* Eton, Clare Coll Cambridge; 4 Sept 2010, Jane Mitchell; *Career* fndr and princ conductor Aurora Orchestra; 2013 debuts: The Magic Flute (ENO), Jonathan Harvey's Wagner Dream (WNO), Rape of Lucretia (Glyndebourne on Tour);

guest conductor: Philharmonia, City of Birmingham Symphony Orchestra, LSO, BBC and Royal Philharmonics, Munich Chamber Orchestra, Spanish Nat Orchestra, Orchestre National d'Ile de France, Bournemouth Symphony, BBC Nat Orchestra of Wales, Northern Sinfonia, Academy of Ancient Music, Auckland Philharmonia, Ensemble Intercontemporain; lead New Moves series; Best Ensemble Royal Philharmonic Soc Award 2011, Critics' Circle Award for Exceptional Young Talent 2012; *Style*— Nicholas Collon, Esq; ✉ c/o Janet Marsden, International Classical Artists, Dunstan House, 14a St Cross Street, London EC1N 8XA

COLMAN, Sir Anthony Colman; kt (1992); s of Solomon Colman (d 1991), and Helen, *née* Weiss (d 1987); *b* 27 May 1938; *Educ* Harrogate GS, Trinity Hall Cambridge (BA, MA); *m* 23 Aug 1964, Angela Barbara, da of Hyman Glynn (d 1984), of London; 2 da (Deborah b 1967, Rosalind b 1971); *Career* Nat Serv Instr RAEC 1957–59; called to the Bar Gray's Inn 1962 (bencher 1986); in commercial practice 1963 (specialising in shipping, int trade and insur), QC 1977, chm ctees of enquiry and disciplinary ctees at Lloyd's 1982–84, recorder of the Crown Court 1985, dep High Court judge 1987, judge of the High Court of Justice (Queen's Bench Div) 1992–2007, judge i/c Commercial List 1996–97, dep chief justice Dubai Int Financial Centre (DIFC) Court 2010– (judge 2007–10); int commercial arbitrator 2007–; judge conducting investigation into loss of MV Derbyshire 1999–2000, cmmr to Govt of Trinidad and Tobago conducting Public Enquiry into Clico and HCU 2010–; advsr to Czech Republic on commercial litigation 2000–2001; accession advsr to European Cmmn: on Czech Republic 2002, on Slovakia 2003; memb Bar Cncl 1989–92; chm: Commercial Bar Assoc 1991–92 (treas 1989–91), The British-Bulgarian Law Assoc 1993–96; pres Trinity Hall Assoc 1998–99; hon pres Societate di Mediazone Rome 2003–, princ Faculty of Mediation and vice-pres Acad of Experts 2004–; FCIArb 1978; *Books* Mathew's Practice of the Commercial Court (2 edn 1965), The Practice and Procedure of the Commercial Court (1983, 2 edn 1986, 5 edn 2000), The Encyclopaedia of International Commercial Litigation (gen ed and contrib, 1 edn 1991); *Recreations* tennis, gardening, painting; *Style*— Sir Anthony Colman; ✉ c/o 24 Lincolns Inn Fields, London WC2A 3EG

COLMAN, Prof David Robert; OBE (2003); s of Colin Robert Colman, of London, and Jessica Ada, *née* Gregson (d 1972); *b* 14 May 1940; *Educ* Bury GS, Latymer Upper Sch, Wye Coll London (BSc), Univ of Illinois (MS), Univ of Manchester (PhD); *m* 9 Aug 1969, Susan, da of William Blundell (d 1952); 2 da (Lucy b 1974, Sophie b 1976); *Career* res asst Univ of Illinois 1963–65, tech advsr Govt of Malawi 1972–73, visiting prof Cornell Univ 1978–79; Univ of Manchester: lectr 1965–74, sr lectr 1974–79, prof 1979–, head Sch of Economic Studies 1994–97 and 1999–; chm Exec Agric Economics Soc 1980–83 and 1989–91 (pres 1994–95); pres IAAE 2006–09; memb: AES 1965, IAEA 1974 (AAEA 1968); *Books* The United Kingdom Cereals Market (1972), Principles of Agricultural Economics (1989), Economics of Change in Less-Developed Countries (3 edn, 1994); *Recreations* badminton, fishing, philately, theatre, food and drink; *Style*— Prof David Colman, OBE; ✉ 11 Brooklyn Crescent, Cheadle, Cheshire SK8 1DX (e-mail david.colman@man.ac.uk)

COLMAN, Sir Michael Jeremiah; 3 Bt (UK 1907), of Gatton Park, Gatton, Surrey; s of Sir Jeremiah Colman, 2 Bt (d 1961); *b* 7 July 1928; *Educ* Eton; *m* 29 Oct 1955, Judith Jean Wallop, da of late Vice Adm Sir Peveril Barton Reibey William-Powlett, KCB, KCMG, CBE, DSO; 3 da (Olivia Helena Judith (Mrs Patrick J Whitworth) b 1956, Victoria Rose (Mrs Matthew S Persson) b 1960, Alice Mary (Mrs Timothy A C Page) b 1965), 2 s (Jeremiah Michael Powlett b 1958, John Powlett b 1962); *Heir* s, Jeremiah Colman; *Career* chm Reckitt and Colman plc 1986–95 (dir 1970–95); first church estates cmmr Church Commissioners 1993–99; dir Foreign & Colonial Ventures Advisors Ltd 1988–99 (dir Private Equity Tst 1995–2002); dir: UK Centre for Economic and Environmental Devpt 1985–1999 (chm 1996–99); chm Trade Affrs Bd 1982–84, memb Cncl Chemical Industries Assoc; memb Cncl: Royal Warrant Holders 1977–2012 (pres 1984); Trinity House: assoc 1984–93, memb Lighthouse Bd 1984–93, Younger Brother 1994–; memb Gen Cncl and Finance Ctee King Edward's Hosp Fund for London 1978–2004, special tstee for St Mary's Hosp 1988–99; tstee The Royal Fndn Grey Coat Hosp 1989–2004; memb Cncl The Scouts' Assoc 1985–2000; Sr Asst Worshipful Co of Skinners (memb Ct of Assts 1985–2007, Master 1991); tstee Allchurches Tst Ltd 1994–2008; Hon LLD Univ of Hull 1993; awarded Archbishop of Canterbury's Cross of St Augustine; *Recreations* farming, forestry, golf, shooting; *Clubs* Cavalry and Guards'; *Style*— Sir Michael Colman, Bt; ✉ Dairy Hill House, Malshanger, Basingstoke, Hampshire RG23 7ET (☎ 01256 780252)

COLMAN, Olivia; *b* 30 January 1974; *Educ* Bristol Old Vic Theatre Sch; *Career* actress; London Film Critics Circle Award for Br Actress of the Year 2012; *Television* incl: That Mitchell and Webb Situation 2001, Peep Show 2003–, Green Wing 2004–06, Look Around You 2005, That Mitchell and Webb Look 2006–08, Grow Your Own 2007, The Time of Your Life 2007, Hancock and Joan 2008, Consuming Passion 2008, Beautiful People 2008–09, Rev 2010–11, Twenty Twelve 2011–12 (Best Female Performance in a Comedy Programme BAFTA 2013), Exile 2011, Accused 2012 (Best Actor (Female) RTS Award, Best Supporting Actress BAFTA 2013), Broadchurch 2013 and 2015, Run 2013, The Suspicions of Mr Whicher (Series 2) 2013, The Thirteenth Tale 2013, The 7.39 2014, The Secrets 2014, Mr Sloane 2014, The Night Manager 2016; *Film* incl: Hot Fuzz 2007, Tyrannosaur 2011 (Sundance Film Festival World Cinema Special Jury Prize for Breakout Performance 2011, Br Ind Film Award for Best Actress 2011, Best Actress London Evening Standard Br Film Award 2012), The Iron Lady 2011, Hyde Park on Hudson 2012, I Give It A Year 2013, Cuban Fury 2014, Locke 2014, Pudsey 2014, The Lobster 2015, London Road 2015; *Style*— Ms Olivia Colman; ✉ c/o United Agents, 12–26 Lexington Street, London W1F 0LE

COLMAN, Dr Richard Douglas; s of the late Jack Douglas Colman, of Huby, N Yorks, and the late Muriel, *née* Longden; *b* 5 March 1949; *Educ* Ansdell County Secdy Modern Lytham St Annes, King Edward VII Lytham St Annes, Magdalene Coll Cambridge (MA, MB BChir), Bart's Med Coll, Univ of Hull (Cert Moral Philosophy), Univ of Manchester; *m* 17 March 1979, Mary Janet van der Westhuizen, da of Dr Fiona Waugh; 3 da (Rose Mary Fiona b 10 Sept 1983, Bethany Ellen b 19 May 1985, Shannon Elizabeth b 31 May 1992), 2 s (Jack Pieter Dale b 24 Feb 1987, Rowan Richard Grant b 27 June 1989); *Career* vocational trg in gen practice, ind med practice 1985–2014, ret (challenged UK law on restrictions on advtg, lost High Court judgement but appealed to European Court of Human Rights, subsequently accepted friendly settlement with Govt following GMC's removal of restrictions at insistence of DTI 1993), former occupational physician NE, now ret; memb GMC 1994–99; DipRCOG, MRCGP, DOccMed, AFOM; *Publications* Occupational Medicine Vol 56 No 4 (contrib, 2006), The Right Thing? The Life, Travels and Some Revelations of an English Doctor (autobiography, 2015); *Recreations* outdoor activities, practical self sufficiency, judo (coach and area referee), conservation (tenant of the NT), bee keeper; *Clubs* Hawks' (Cambridge), Ryedale Judo, Ryedale Beekeepers Assoc (treas); *Style*— Dr Richard Colman; ✉ Cowl House, Bransdale, Fadmoor, York YO62 7JW (☎ 01751 432342, e-mail richardcol@doctors.org.uk)

COLQUHOUN, Dr Andrew John; s of Maj Kenneth James Colquhoun, MC (d 1990), and Christine Mary, *née* Morris; *b* 21 September 1949; *Educ* Tiffin Sch, Univ of Nottingham (BSc), Univ of Glasgow (PhD), City Univ (MBA), Roehampton Univ (PGDip); *m* 1, 22 Feb 1975 (m dis 2009), Patricia, da of John Beardall; 1 s (Simon James b 1976), 1 da (Helen Elizabeth b 1978); m 2, 12 May 2011, Stephanie Donaldson, da of Flight Lt Ralph Williams, DFC (d 1951); *Career* FCO: joined 1974, served London and ME, seconded to Cabinet Office 1981–83, Planning Staff 1983–84; Shandwick Consultants 1984–86 (seconded to ICAEW), sec and chief exec ICAEW 1990–97 (dir of educn and trg 1987–90); sec Consultative Ctee of Accountancy Bodies 1990–97; DG RHS 1999–2006; chm: Nat Horticultural Forum 2002–12, SEEDA Horticulture Working Gp 2006–10; non-exec dir NERC 2007–12, non-exec dir OHPA 2010–12; cnsllr in private and charitable practice 2009–; memb Rail Passengers Ctee for Southern England 1998–2003, chair Investigation Ctee ICAEW 2009–15, chair Farming and Rural Issues for the South East 2010–15; lay memb Univ of Nottingham Cncl 1999–2006; author of various articles on horticulture, accountancy, educn and recruitment; *Recreations* gardening, bird watching, reading, walking, country life; *Style*— Dr Andrew Colquhoun; ✉ Studio House, 64 Croft Road, Hastings, Sussex TN34 3HE (☎ 01424 442546)

C

COLQUHOUN, Barry John (BJ); s of Alan John Colquhoun, and Elsie Vera, *née* Chinn; *b* 19 July 1947, Greenock, Inverclyde; *Educ* St Crispin's Wokingham; *Career* photographer; dir art and advtg El Arenal Palma de Mallorca 1966–67, private art cmmns throughout the Caribbean and USA 1967–68, lectr on creative black and white photographic techniques 1970–75, freelance journalist, lectr and conslt on 100% digital imaging 1997–; past pres and memb cncl Lytham St Annes Photographic Soc; Distinction of the Photographic Alliance of GB (DPAGB) 2003; FRPS (ARPS); *Recreations* property repairs and maintenance; *Style*— BJ Colquhoun, Esq; ✉ ALBA Co (Digital Imaging), 154 St Andrews Road South, St Annes-on-Sea, Lancashire FY8 1YA (☎ 01253 720217, e-mail bjc.albaco@btinternet.com and bjc@bjc100.co.uk)

COLQUHOUN, Prof David; *b* 19 July 1936, Birkenhead, Merseyside; *Educ* Univ of Leeds (BSc), Univ of Edinburgh (PhD); *m* April 1976, Margaret Anne, *née* Boultwood; 1 s (Andrew Stuart b 24 Dec 1984); *Career* asst lectr Dept of Pharmacology Univ of Edinburgh 1962–64, visiting asst then assoc prof Dept of Pharmacology Yale Univ Sch of Med 1964–72, sr lectr Dept of Physiology and Biochemistry Univ of Southampton 1972–75 (acting head of dept 1974–75), sr lectr in pharmacology St George's Hosp Med Sch 1976–79; UCL: reader of pharmacology 1979–83, prof 1983–, A J Clark chair 1985–2004, dir Wellcome Laboratory for Molecular Pharmacology 1993–2004; visiting scientist Dept of Physiology and Biophysics Univ of Washington 1974, visiting prof Max Planck Institut für Medizinische 1990–91; memb: Editorial Bd Jl of Physiology 1974–81, Sir Ronald Fisher Meml Ctee 1975– (tstee Meml Fund), Sectional Ctee Royal Soc 1988–91 (chm 1990), Editorial Bd Royal Soc Pubns 1989, Academia Europaea 1992; J C Krantz prize lectr Univ of Maryland 1987, Alexander von Humboldt prize 1990, Riker lectr Oregon Health Sci Univ 2008; hon fell UCL 2004; FRS 1985; *Publications* Lectures on Biostatistics (1970); many papers in scientific jls; *Style*— Prof David Colquhoun, FRS; ✉ e-mail d.colquhoun@ucl.ac.uk, website dcscience.net

COLQUHOUN OF LUSS, Lady; Katharine Anne Colquhoun of Luss; *née* Mears; da of Arthur Christopher Mears (d 1989), and Heather Rosemary, *née* Hilton; *b* 17 November 1954, Maidenhead, Berks; *Educ* Canberra C of E Girls GS, Univ of Melbourne (BEd, Dip); *m* Oct 1989, Sir Malcom Colquhoun of Luss, Bt, s of Sir Ivor Colquhoun of Luss, Bt, DL (d 2008); 1 s (Fergus b 15 May 1991), 1 da (Georgina b 4 Feb 1993); *Career* teacher 1976–83; Broomwood Hall Sch: fndr 1984, headmistress 1984–2005, princ 2006–; co-fndr (with husb, Sir Malcolm Colquhoun of Luss) and co-princ Northcote Lodge Sch 1993–; *Recreations* flying, flower arranging, reading; *Clubs* Turf, West London Flying, Hurlingham; *Style*— Lady Colquhoun of Luss (professionally known as Katharine Colquhoun); ✉ Broomwood Hall School, 68–74 Nightingale Lane, London SW12 8NR (☎ 020 8682 8826, email k.colquhoun@northwoodschools.com)

COLQUHOUN-DENVERS, Nicholas John Arthur; s of HE John Dalrymple Colquhoun-Denvers, Australian Consul-Gen, of Bombay, India, and Winifred May, *née* Mitchell; *b* 5 January 1949, Cuckfield, Sussex; *Educ* Christ Church Coll, Perth; *m* 20 May 1978, Anne Patricia, da of Maj Charles Walter Douglas Wellesley Alexander (d 1983), late of 3 Carabiniers and Royal Scots Dragoon Gds; *Career* sec to Chm Australian Public Service Bd Canberra 1966–69; offr RA served BAOR, Hong Kong, N Ireland Lt 1969–77, ret; with Adnan Khashoggi's Triad Corporation 1977–85; md: CLC 1985–87, Hurlingham (Management) Ltd 1987–; ceo Horizon Energy (UK) Ltd (formerly FAL Energy (UK) Ltd); Gen Service Medal 1971; chm: Ham Polo Club 1995–, Hurlingham Polo Assoc 2008–12; pres Fedn of Int Polo 2014–; *Recreations* polo, shooting; *Clubs* Guards Polo, Ham Polo (chm 1995–), Annabel's, Mosimann's; *Style*— Nicholas J A Colquhoun-Denvers, Esq; ✉ Dorchester Court, 77 Sloane Street, London SW1X 9SE (☎ 020 7259 5654/6808); Horizon Energy (UK) Limited, The Bridge, 334 Queenstown Road, London SW8 4NP (☎ 020 7486 2600, fax 020 7486 2700, mobile 078 8055 5555, e-mail cd@fal.uk.com)

COLTART, Dr (Douglas) John; s of Frank Joseph John Coltart (d 1974), and Hilda Kate, *née* Moore (d 2010); *b* 7 October 1943; *Educ* Hardye's Sch Dorchester, Bart's Med Sch London (MD); *m* 7 May 1977 (m dis 2004), Linda Maitland, da of Stuart Douglas Luxon, of Riversdale, Bucks; 1 s (Rupert b 4 July 1978), 3 da (Cordelia b 7 Feb 1980, Clementine b 23 Sept 1982, Christianna b 19 June 1991); *Career* conslt physician and cardiologist Royal Masonic Hosp London 1974, conslt physician to St Luke's Hosp for The Clergy 1975 and St Dunstan's Hosp for the Blind 1980; currently: emeritus conslt physician and cardiologist Guy's and St Thomas' Hosps London, conslt cardiologist King Edward VII Hosp, clinical dir of cardiac servs Guy's and St Thomas' Hosp, conslt physician to Met Police, civilian conslt in cardiology to the Army; visiting prof: univs in Middle East and Far East, Stanford Univ USA; author of chapters in textbooks of med and over 250 scientific pubns; pres Cardiology Section RSM, sec Br Cardiac Soc, vice-pres Postgrad Fedn, memb Exec Bds Br Heart Fndn Coronary Prevention Gp, past pres RSM (Cardiology); memb: Br Cardiac Soc, Med Defence Union; Buckston Browne Prize Harveian Soc; Liveryman Worshipful Soc of Apothecaries, Freeman City of London; FRCP, FACC, FESC; *Books* Cardio-vascular Pharmacology (textbook); *Recreations* athletics, tennis, keep fit; *Clubs* Fountain; *Style*— Dr John Coltart; ✉ 47 Weymouth Street, London W1G 8NE (☎ 020 74865787, mobile 07940 816851, fax 020 7486 5470, e-mail johncoltart@btconnect.com); Wyvis View, Kinkell House Hotel, Easter Kinkell, Conon Bridge, Rosshire IV7 8HY

COLTART, His Hon Judge Simon Stewart; s of Gilbert McCallum Coltart, of Lindfield, W Sussex, and Mary Louise, *née* Kemp; *b* 3 September 1946; *Educ* Epsom Coll, Univ of Leeds (LLB); *m* 8 March 1973, Sarah Victoria, da of John Claude Birts; 3 s (Mark Cresswell, Edward John (twins) b 23 Nov 1974, William James b 3 June 1978); *Career* called to the Bar Lincoln's Inn (Eastham Sch) 1969; jr SE Circuit Bar Mess 1970–71, jr Sussex Bar Mess 1973–86, recorder SE Circuit Bar Mess 1987–90, recorder 1987–91, circuit judge (SE Circuit) 1991–; memb Parole Bd 1997–2003; govr: Stoke Brunswick Sch 1991–2006 (chm 2002–06), Oundle Sch 2003–09; memb Ct of Assts Worshipful Co of Grocers 1991 (Freeman 1975, Liveryman 1984, Master 1999); *Recreations* sailing, golf, fishing shooting; *Clubs* Boodle's, Royal Yacht Sqdn, Bar Yacht, Rye Golf, Sussex; *Style*— His Hon Judge Coltart; ✉ Lewes Combined Court, High Street, Lewes, East Sussex BN7 1YB

COLTRANE, Robbie; OBE (2006); s of Dr Ian Baxter McMillan (d 1969), of Rutherglen, Glasgow, and Jean Ross, *née* Howie; *b* 31 March 1950; *Educ* Trinity Coll Glenalmond, Glasgow Sch of Art (Dip Drawing and Painting); *Children* 1 s, 1 da; *Career* actor; BAFTA Best Actor nomination for Tutti Frutti 1987, Evening Standard Peter Sellers Award for contribution to Br film comedy 1990; involved with: Lab Pty, Amnesty, Greenpeace, Friends of the Earth, CND; hon pres Heriot-Watt Univ; *Theatre* toured univs with the San Quentin Theatre Workshop 1974–75, John Byrne's Slab Boys and Threads (Traverse Theatre Edinburgh) 1975–79, Snobs and Yobs (Edinburgh Festival) 1980, Your Obedient Servant (one man show on Dr Samuel Johnson, Lyric Hammersmith) 1987, Mistero Buffo 1990; *Television* incl: Alfresco (2 series), A Kick Up the Eighties, The Lenny Henry Show,

The Comic Strip Presents (various programmes), Laugh I Nearly Paid My Licence Fee, The Young Ones (several guest roles), Tutti Frutti (lead role), Blackadder III (guest role) and Blackadder Xmas Special, Robbie Coltrane Special, GLC and S Atlantic Raiders (Comic Strip Presents), Mistero Buffo 1990, Alive and Kicking 1991, Coltrane in a Cadillac (ITV) 1993, Cracker (Granada 1993–95, winner Broadcast Press Guild Best Actor Award 1994, BAFTA Best TV Actor Award 1994, 1995 and 1996, RTS Best Male Performance Award 1994, Cable Ace USA Award for Best Actor 1995), Silver Nymph (Best Performance TV Series, Monte Carlo 1994, FIPA Award for Best Actor Nice 1994), The Ebb Tide 1997, Coltrane's Planes and Automobiles 1997, Alice in Wonderland, The Plan Man 2002, Cracker (special episode) 2005, Robbie Coltrane's B-Road Britain (ITV) 2007, Murderland (ITV) 2009, Lead Balloon 2011, The Hunt for Tony Blair 2011, Yes Prime Minister 2012, Comic Strip: Five Go to Rehab 2012; co-writer (with Morag Fullarton) and dir Jealousy (short film for BBC2); *Film* incl: Scrubbers 1982, The Supergrass (Comic Strip feature film) 1984, Defence of the Realm 1985, Revolution 1985, Caravaggio 1985, Absolute Beginners 1985, Mona Lisa 1985, Eat the Rich 1987, The Fruit Machine 1987, Danny Champion of the World 1988, Henry V (as Falstaff) 1988, Let It Ride 1988, Nuns on the Run 1989, Perfectly Normal 1989, The Pope Must Die 1990, Oh What a Night 1991, Huck Finn 1992, Goldeneye 1995, Buddy 1996, Montana 1997, Frogs For Snakes 1997, Message in a Bottle 1998, The World is Not Enough 1999, On the Nose 2000, From Hell 2000, Harry Potter and the Philosopher's Stone 2001, Harry Potter and the Chamber of Secrets 2002, Harry Potter and the Prisoner of Azkaban 2004, Ocean's Twelve 2005, Harry Potter and the Goblet of Fire 2005, Stormbreaker 2005, Provoked 2005, Harry Potter and the Order of the Phoenix 2007, The Brothers Bloom 2007, Gooby 2008, The Tales of Despereaux 2008, Harry Potter and the Half Blood Prince 2009, Harry Potter and the Deathly Hallows 2010, Great Expectations 2011, Effie 2011, Arthur Christmas 2011, Brave 2012; *Recreations* vintage cars, painting, sailing, clubs, playing piano; *Clubs* Groucho, Colony Room, Moscow, Glasgow Arts, Soho House; *Style*— Robbie Coltrane, Esq, OBE; ✉ c/o Belinda Wright, CDA, 167–169 Kensington High Street, London W8 6SH (☎ 020 7373 3323, fax 020 7373 1110)

COLVILE, Oliver Newton; MP; *b* 26 August 1959; *Educ* Stowe; *Career* MP (Cons) Plymouth Sutton & Devonport 2010–; *Style*— Oliver Colvile, Esq, MP; ✉ House of Commons, London SW1A 0AA

COLVIN, Andrew James; s of Gilbert Russell Colvin, OBE, and Dr Beatrice Colvin; *b* 28 April 1947; *Educ* LLM; *m* 1971, Helen Mary, *née* Ryan; 3 da (Clare b June 1975, Fiona b March 1979, Sarah b March 1982), 1 s (Simon b May 1977); *Career* admitted as slr 1975; articled clerk then asst town clerk London Borough of Ealing 1971–82, dep town clerk and borough slr Royal Borough of Kensington and Chelsea 1982–89, the Comptroller and City Slr The Corp of London 1989–; Vice-Chamberlain of London; pres City of London Arizona Educnl Tst Inc; advsr: LBA 1985, AMA 1990, ALG 1996; govr: St Gregory's RC Sch 1989–92, Cardinal Wiseman RC Sch 1992–98; Freeman City of London 1989; *Recreations* sailing, cycling, music; *Style*— Andrew Colvin, Esq; ✉ The Comptroller and City Solicitor, The Corporation of London, PO Box 270, Guildhall, London EC2P 2EJ (☎ 020 7606 3030 ext 1660)

COLVIN, Prof Brian Trevor; s of Clifford James Leslie Colvin (d 1990), of Sevenoaks, and Ivy Emmeline, *née* Goodchild (d 1996); *b* 17 January 1946; *Educ* Sevenoaks Sch, Clare Coll Cambridge (MA, MB BChir), London Hosp Med Coll; *m* 21 Aug 1971, Kathryn Frances, former HM ambass to The Holy See, da of Ernest Osborne (d 1966); *Career* conslt haematologist: St Peter's Hosp Gp and Inst of Urology 1977–86, Barts and the London NHS Tst 1977–2009, ret; dir of postgrad med and dental educn Royal Hosps Tst 1996–99, dean Queen Mary's Sch of Medicine and Dentistry 1998–2008, hon prof Queen Mary Univ of London, medical dir haemophilia Pfizer Europe 2008–15; dir Clinical Pathology Accreditation Ltd 1998–2004; memb: Standing Ctee of Membs RCP 1973–77, Ctee Br Soc for Haematology 1983–86, Med Advsy Ctee Haemophilia Soc 1993–2007; chm: Haemostasis and Thrombosis Sub-Ctee BCSH 1991–94, Steering Ctee UK Nat External Quality Assurance Scheme (NEQAS) in Blood Coagulation 1992–96 and 2005–11, UK Haemophilia Centre Dirs Orgn 1993–96, Panel of Examiners in Haematology RCPath 1994–99, Nat Quality Assurance Advsy Panel in Haematology 1996–98, Ethics Ctee RCPath 2004–08; pres Cncl Pathology Section RSM 1996–98; pres Barts and The London Alumnus Assoc 2007–11; Queen Mary Univ of London Coll Medal 2012; Liveryman Worshipful Soc of Apothecaries; memb BMA; FRCPath 1988 (MRCPath 1976), FRCP 1990 (MRCP 1972), FRSM 1989–2008; *Publications* author of various papers, articles and contrib to books incl Haematology Pocket Consultant (with A C Newland, 1988); *Recreations* foreign travel, opera, cricket; *Clubs* MCC; *Style*— Prof Brian Colvin; ✉ Alumnus Office, Queen Mary University of London, Mile End Road, London E1 4NS (☎ 020 7882 7423, fax 020 7882 3706, e-mail b.t.colvin@qmul.ac.uk)

COLVIN, Prof Calum Munro; OBE (2001); s of Dr David Colvin, CBE, of Edinburgh, and Elma; *b* 26 October 1961, Glasgow; *Educ* North Berwick HS, Duncan of Jordanstone Coll of Art Dundee (diploma in sculpture), RCA London (MA); *m* 11 Aug 1988, S J Colvin (*née* Moore); 1 da (Heather b 1992), 2 s (Robbie David Nichol b 1993, Finlay b 1998); *Career* artist; prof of fine art photography Univ of Dundee 2001; exhibited widely incl Orkney, LA and Ecuador; work in collections incl: Met MOMA NY, Museum of Fine Art Houston TX, V&A, Scottish Nat Portrait Gallery Edinburgh, Gallery of Modern Art Glasgow; awards incl: Photographers Gallery Brandt Award 1987, RPS gold medal 1989, 13th Higashikawa Overseas Photographer Prize 1997, Leverhulme scholarship 2000, Creative Scotland Award 2000, Leverhulme Tst Research Fellowship 2000, Carnegie Tst Award 2002, Critics Award for Theatre in Scotland (set design) 2003; *Publications* Constructed Narratives (1986), Calum Colvin (1990), The Seven Deadly Sins & the Four Last Things (1993), Sacred & Profane (1998), Ossian – Fragments of Ancient Poetry (2002); *Style*— Prof Calum Colvin, OBE; ✉ c/o Open Eye Gallery, 34 Abercromby Place, Edinburgh EH3 6QE (☎ 0131 557 1020, mobile 07603 274694, website www.calumcolvin.com)

COLVIN, Holly; da of Ian Colvin, and Louise, *née* Steel; *b* 7 September 1989, Chichester; *Educ* Westbourne House, Brighton Coll, Univ of Durham; *Career* cricketer; Sussex WCCC 2005–; England: Test debut v Aust 2005, memb Ashes-winning side 2005 and 2008, memb World Cup-winning side 2009, memb touring squad Aust 2008; *Style*— Miss Holly Colvin; ✉ The England and Wales Cricket Board, Lord's Cricket Ground, London NW8 8QZ

COLWYN, 3 Baron (UK 1917); Sir (Ian) Anthony; 3 Bt (UK 1912), CBE (1989); s of 2 Baron Colwyn (d 1966); *b* 1 January 1942; *Educ* Cheltenham Coll, Univ of London (BDS, LDS, RCS); *m* 1, 1964 (m dis 1977), Sonia Jane, er da of Peter Henry Geoffrey Morgan; 1 da (Hon Jacqueline b 5 March 1967), 1 s (Hon Craig Peter b 13 Oct 1968); m 2, 1977, Nicola Jeanne, da of Arthur Tyers; 2 da (Hon Kirsten b 17 Jan 1981, Hon Tanya b 14 Jan 1983); *Heir* s, Hon Craig Hamilton-Smith; *Career* dental surgeon 1966–2007; chm: Dental Protection Ltd 1995–2001, Project Hope 1997–2001, Action against Hunger 2000–01; elected Conservative in House of Lords, pres Parly All-Pty Gp for Complementary and Integrated Healthcare 1989–, chm Offices Sub-Ctee on Refreshment 1997–2004 and 2013–15, memb Science and Technol Sub-Ctee III (complementary medicine 2000–01), memb Select Ctee on EU Sub-Ctee G 2004–07, memb Sci and Technol Select Ctee 2007–11, dep chm of ctees and dep speaker 2007–; memb All-Pty Jazz Appreciation Gp 1990– (co-chair), chair All-Pty Gp for Emergency Ambulance and Paramedic Servs 2011–12; memb Cncl Medical Protection Soc; pres: Natural Medicines Soc 1988–2005, Arterial Health Fndn 1993–2004, Soc for Advancement of Anaesthesia in Dentistry 1995–97; patron: Blackie Fndn, Res Cncl for Complementary Medicine; life patron: Cheltenham Rugby Club, Colwyn Bay Rugby Club; former patron Eastman Research Inst; musician, bandleader; FRSM; *Recreations* riparian activities, golf; *Clubs* Ronnie Scotts, 606 Jazz, Leander, Hennerton Golf; *Style*— The Rt Hon the Lord Colwyn, CBE; ✉ House of Lords, London SW1A 0PW (☎ 020 7219 3000)

COLWYN-THOMAS, Anthony (Tony); s of Bertie Colwyn-Thomas, of Bridgend, and Brenda, *née* Kendrick; *b* 5 October 1956; *Educ* Ogmore GS, Univ of Southampton (BSc); *m* (m dis); 2 s (Owain b 19 Dec 1986, Trystan b 1 July 1988); *Career* qualified as chartered accountant KPMG 1978–82, internal auditor and fin accountant Bass plc 1982–85, gp fin accountant Trusthouse Forte plc 1985–87, co accountant Hamells (subsid of C & A) 1987–88, fin controller/co sec ACL (subsid of Standard Chartered Bank plc) 1988–93, mangr Business Planning and Risk Mgmnt Halifax Mortgage Services Ltd 1993–96, fin control conslt Pearl Assurance plc 1997, gp fin mangr HFC Bank plc (subsid of HSBC plc) 1998–2003, md Cetelem (UK) Ltd (subsid of BNP Paribas) 2004–06 (fin dir 2003–04), dep head Int Accounting BNP Paribas SA (France) 2006–08, ceo Cetelem Thailand 2009, gen mangr BNP Paribas Personal Finance Greece 2010–11, dep ceo BNP Paribas Personal Finance Netherlands 2011–; former chm Cardiff and Dist Soc of Chartered Accountants; former memb: Cncl ICAEW, Ctee S Wales Dist Soc of Chartered Accountants, Br Jr Chamber Cardiff; FCA 1991 (ACA 1981); *Recreations* travel, local history, sport; *Style*— Tony Colwyn-Thomas, Esq

COMBER, Abigail; *Career* BA: started at BA Holidays 1992, sr mktg roles since 2002, head of brands and mktg 2012–15, head of customer 2015–; fell Mktg Acad, fell Mktg Soc; *Style*— Ms Abigail Comber

COMBER, Darren Edwin; s of Gary Edwin Comber, of Maidstone, Kent, and Maree Rosalie, *née* Hickmott; *b* 14 August 1966; *Educ* W Kent Coll of FE, Univ of Plymouth (BA), UCL (DipArch); *m* 1996, Anja, *née* Hemstra; 3 s (Tias b 4 Oct 2000, Kaspar, Nicklaus (twins) b 23 Dec 2002); *Career* architect; Scott Brownrigg: joined 1995, appointed main bd dir 2002, ceo 2010–; Camden Soc of Architects Design Excellence Award, work commended Civic Tst Awards 2000; former violinist Maidstone Youth Orch; ARB 1992, RIBA 1992, FRSA 2011; *Recreations* skiing, golf, motorsport; *Clubs* Reform, Soho House; *Style*— Darren Comber, Esq

COMFORT, Nicholas Alfred Fenner; s of Dr Alex Comfort (d 2000), of Cranbrook, Kent, and Ruth Muriel, *née* Harris (d 2000); *b* 4 August 1946; *Educ* Highgate Sch, Trinity Coll Cambridge (exhibitioner, MA); *m* 1, 1970 (m dis 1988), Deborah Elliott; 1 da (Caroline Sarah b 1 June 1974), 1 s (John Miles b 23 July 1977); m 2, 1990 (m dis 2009), Corinne Reed; 1 s (Alexander Thomas Reed b 18 Aug 1994); m 3, 2014, Jeanette Owens, *née* Crosby; *Career* municipal corr Morning Telegraph Sheffield 1968–74; Daily Telegraph: Midlands corr 1974–75, Washington bureau 1976–78, political staff writer 1978–87, ldr writer 1987–89; political ed Independent on Sunday 1989–90, political ed The European 1990–91, political ed Daily Record 1992–95, obiturist Daily Telegraph 1995–, conslt Politics International 1996–97, conslt European presentation DTI 2000–01, special advsr to sec of state for Scotland 2001–02, govt affrs advsr QinetiQ plc 2003–06, govt advsr Unisys 2008–09, assoc Bellenden Public Affrs 2015–; memb: Railway Study Assoc, Omnibus Soc; *Publications* The Tunnel: The Channel and Beyond (co-author, 1987), Brewer's Politics: A Phrase and Fable Dictionary (1993), The Lost City of Dunwich (1994), The Mid-Suffolk Light Railway (1998), Politico's Guide to How to Handle the Media (2003), The Politics Book (2005), The Channel Tunnel and its High-Speed Links (2006), Surrender: How British Industry Gave Up The Ghost 1952–2012 (2012), The Regional Railways Story (with Gordon Pettitt, 2015); *Recreations* music, cricket, Sheffield United FC; *Clubs* Athenaeum, Essex CCC; *Style*— Nicholas Comfort, Esq; ✉ 129 Croydon Road, London SE20 7TT (☎ 07979 958753, e-mail nc65464@yahoo.com)

COMINS, David; s of Jack Comins (d 2002), of Scarborough, N Yorks, and (Mabel) Marjorie, *née* Rowbotham (d 1973); *b* 1 March 1948, Scarborough, Yorks; *Educ* Scarborough HS for Boys (head boy, rugby capt), Downing Coll Cambridge (MA), Cambridge Inst (PGCE); *m* 22 July 1972, (Christine) Anne, da of Thomas Brian Speak (d 2003); 2 da (Laura b 4 Sept 1976, Amy b 20 April 1980), 1 s (Robert b 3 June 1978); *Career* asst maths teacher: Mill Hill Sch 1971–75, Strathallan Sch 1975–76; Glenalmond Coll: asst maths teacher 1976–80, head of maths 1980–85, dir of studies 1985–89; dep head Queen's Coll Taunton 1989–94 (head of maths 1991–94), rector Glasgow Acad 1994–2005, maths teacher Shenzhen Coll of Int Educn China 2005–07; chm HMC Scottish Div 2001, memb Gen Teaching Cncl of Scotland 1974, memb HMC 1994; memb Tayside Expedition Panel (Duke of Edinburgh's Award); Winston Churchill fell 1981 (for expedition to Peruvian Andes); *Recreations* mountaineering, killer su doku, ballet; *Clubs* Alpine; *Style*— David Comins, Esq; ✉ Flat 6, Block 8, Kirklee Gate, Glasgow G12 0SZ (☎ 0141 337 6897, e-mail d.comins@hotmail.co.uk)

COMPSTON, Prof (David) Alastair Standish; CBE (2016); s of Dr Nigel Dean Compston, CBE, MD, FRCP (d 1986), and Diana Mary, *née* Standish (d 2015); *b* 23 January 1948; *Educ* Rugby, Middx Hosp Med Sch London (MB BS, PhD); *m* 21 July 1973, Juliet Elizabeth, da of Sir Denys Page (d 1978); 1 da (Polly Clare b 5 Nov 1981); *Career* various hosp appts 1971–82, conslt neurologist Univ Hosp of Wales Cardiff 1982–86; prof of neurology: Univ of Wales Coll of Med Cardiff 1987–88, Univ of Cambridge 1989–2015; professorial fell Jesus Coll Cambridge 1990–, hon conslt neurologist Addenbrooke's Hosp Cambridge 1989–2015, head Dept of Clinical Neurosciences 2004–15; chm MRC Cambridge Centre for Brain Repair 1990–2000; ed: Jl of Neurology 1989–99, Brain 2004–13; pres Assoc for Br Neurologists 2009–11; FRCP 1986, FRSA 1997, FMedSci 1998, FIBiol 2000, foreign memb Nat Acad of Medicine of the USA (formerly Inst of Medicine Nat Academia of the USA) 2012–, foreign memb Nat Acad of Sciences of Germany Leopoldina 2008–, FRS 2016; *Publications* McAlpine's Multiple Sclerosis (4 edn 2005); also author of articles in periodicals on human and experimental demyelinating disease; *Recreations* being outside, antiquarian books; *Clubs* Garrick; *Style*— Prof Alastair Compston, CBE; ✉ Mead House, West Wickham Road, Horseheath, Cambridge CB21 4QA (☎ 01223 893414); University of Cambridge Neurology Unit, Level 5, Addenbrooke's Hospital, Hills Road, Cambridge CB2 0QQ (☎ 01223 217091, fax 01223 336941, e-mail alastair.compston@medschl.cam.ac.uk)

COMPTON, HE Eugenie Tshiela; da of Albert Gregoire Kamba, of Kananga, Democratic Repub of Congo, and Marie Goretti Nkanu, *née* Tshifutshiela; *b* 20 January 1962, Kananga, Democratic Repub of Congo; *Educ* Collège Catholique de Tshiolimba Democratic Repub of Congo, Univ Catholique de Kinshasa Democratic Repub of Congo, Univ de Liège Belgium, Univ of Westminster; *m* 16 March 1991, Guy Robin Compton; 2 s (Jack b 24 Aug 1990, Roy b 21 Jan 1999), 1 da (Gabrielle b 5 Nov 1992); *Career* dep nat rep 1987–96, masters degree student Univ of Westminster 1996–98, rep Rassemblement Congolais pour la Démocratie (RCD) 1998–2003, dep nat designateé 2003–05, ambass to the Ct of St James's 2005–; memb Int Assembly for French Language, pres Amani Forum; Prix de Journaliste Congolais 1995; *Books* Diamond, Politics and I; *Style*— HE Mrs Eugenie Tshiela Compton; ✉ Embassy of the Democratic Republic of the Congo, 281 Gray's Inn Road, London WC1X 8QF (☎ 020 7278 9825, fax 020 7833 9967, e-mail t-compton@hotmail.co.uk)

COMPTON, Richard Clephane; DL (N Yorks 2007); s of Robert Edward John Compton (d 2009), and Ursula Jane, *née* Kenyon-Slaney (d 2012); *b* 1957; *Educ* Harrow, RAC Cirencester; *m* 1982, Lucinda Jane Astell *née* Hohler; 2 s (Orlando Edward de Grey b 1986, Ludovic Hugh b 1989), 1 da (Theodosia Alexandra b 1992); *Career* pres HHA 2013– (dep pres 2008–13); chm of Govrs Harrow 2009–; High Sheriff N Yorks 2010;

Recreations heritage, cricket, golf, skiing, country issues; *Clubs* White's, Pratt's, Swinley Forest Golf, I Zingari Cricket (Freeman 2012); *Style*— Richard Compton, Esq, DL; ✉ Newby Hall, Ripon, Yorkshire HG4 5AE (☎ 01423 322583, e-mail richard.c@newbyhall.com, website www.newbyhall.com); Historic Houses Association, 2 Chester Street, London SW1X 7BB

COMPTON MILLER, Richard Maurice McEwen; s of Sir John Compton Miller (d 1992), of Crown Office Row, London, and Mary Baird-Smith (d 1998), of Wheathampstead, Herts; *b* 18 March 1945, Brocket Hall, Hertfordshire; *Educ* Westminster, New Coll Oxford (MA, ed Cherwell); *Partner* Nicola Muir; *Career* called to the Bar Inner Temple 1969; co-fndr Advise 1968, trainee property developer Star (GB) Hldgs 1970, journalist Daily Express, Daily Mail, Sunday Times, Harper's & Queen and Evening Standard 1972–78, ed In Town column Evening News and Evening Standard 1978–82, freelance feature writer (incl ed People column Daily Express) 1982–85, ed William Hickey column, TV critic and sr feature writer Daily Express 1985–95, freelance feature writer Daily Mail, Daily Express, Independent and Sunday Express 1995–2011, art critic London Magazine 1998–2003, ed property column Evening Standard 2000–11, property columnist The Hill 2007–09; dir Marine Court Freeholders Ltd; chm and co-fndr Leonard Tst 1996–, memb Ctee Hair and Beauty Benevolent 1996–, memb Ctee New Coll Soc 2006–; fundraiser: Scope, London Press Club, Coram; *Publications* Who's Really Who (ed, 1983–97); *Recreations* partying, dabbling with property, collecting antiques, playing bridge and backgammon, listening to rock'n'roll; *Clubs* Biographers', The Andrew Robson Bridge; *Style*— Richard Compton Miller, Esq; ✉ c/o Andrew Lownie Literary Agency, 36 Great Smith Street, London SW1P 3BU

COMYNS, District Judge Jacqueline Roberta; da of late Jack Fisher, and late Belle, *née* Offenbach (d 1994); *b* 27 April 1943; *Educ* Hendon Co GS, LSE (LLB); *m* 29 Aug 1963, Dr Malcolm John Comyns, s of Louis Comyns (d 1962); 1 s (David b 13 Aug 1975); *Career* called to the Bar Inner Temple 1969, in practice SE Circuit, district judge (Magistrates' Court) 1982–, recorder of the Crown Court 1991–2002; *Recreations* travel, theatre, swimming; *Style*— District Judge Comyns; ✉ Thames Magistrates Court, Bow Road, London E3 4DJ (☎ 020 8271 1202)

CONBOY, Prof Martin; *b* 1953, Liverpool; *Educ* Univ of Durham (BA), Inst of Educn Univ of London (MA, PhD); *m* Simone; 1 da (Lara); *Career* former lectr Inst for English and American Studes Univ of Potsdam Germany, prof of journalism history Univ of Sheffield 2005–; memb Int Editorial Bd: Journalism Studies, Media History, Journalism: Theory Practice and Criticism; The Press and Popular Culture (2002), Journalism: A Critical History (2004), Tabloid Britain: Constructing a Community Through Language (2006), The Language of the News (2007), The Language of Newspapers: Socio-historical Perspectives (2010), Journalism in Britain: A Historical Introduction (2011), How Journalism Uses History (2012), Journalism Studies: The Basics (2013); co-ed Journalism Studies: Key Texts series; *Style*— Prof Martin Conboy; ✉ Department of Journalism Studies, University of Sheffield, 18–22 Regent Street, Sheffield S1 3NJ (e-mail m.conboy@sheffield.ac.uk)

CONDON, Baron (Life Peer UK 2001), of Langton Green in the County of Kent; Sir Paul Condon; kt (1994), QPM (1989); *Educ* St Peter's Coll Oxford (MA); *m*; 1 da, 2 s; *Career* Metropolitan Police: joined 1967, served various stations in East End 1967–72, St Peter's Coll Oxford 1972–75, uniformed Inspr West End 1975–78, Chief Inspr Community Relations Branch 1978–81, Supt Bethnal Green 1981–82, staff offr to Sir David McNee as Cmmr 1982–84, Sr Cmd Course Police Staff Coll 1984; Asst Chief Constable Kent Constabulary 1984–87, Dep Asst Cmmr i/c W London then Asst Cmmr i/c personnel and trg Metropolitan Police 1987–89, Chief Constable Kent 1989–93, Cmmr Metropolitan Police 1993–2000; dir Int Cricket Cncl Anti-Corruption Unit 2000–; non-exec dir Securicor plc 2000–; hon fell St Peter's Coll Oxford; CIMgt 1992, FRSA 1992; *Recreations* swimming, horse riding, reading; *Style*— The Rt Hon the Lord Condon, QPM

CONGDON, Prof Timothy George (Tim); CBE (1997); s of Douglas George Congdon, of Colchester, Essex, and Olive Emma, *née* Good; *b* 28 April 1951; *Educ* Colchester Royal GS, St John's Coll Oxford (open scholar, BA), Nuffield Coll Oxford; *m* 18 June 1988, Dorianne, da of Percy Preston-Lowe; 1 da (Venetia Andrea Dorianne b 30 July 1991); *Career* economics staff The Times 1973–76, chief economist L Messel & Co 1976–87 (ptnr 1980–86), chief UK economist Shearson Lehman 1987–88; Lombard Street Research: md 1989–2001, chief economist 2001–05; Party candidate (UKIP) Forest of Dean 2010, runner-up UKIP leadership election 2010, economics spokesman UKIP 2010–14; non-exec chm SBW Insurance Research 1994–97; non-exec dir: Invesco Recovery Tst 1991–2008, Highland Timber 1997–2005; memb HM Treasy Panel of Ind Forecasters 1992–97; hon prof Cardiff Business Sch 1990–2006, visiting prof City Univ Business Sch 1997–2004, visiting research fell LSE 2005–07; Univ of Buckingham: dir Inst of Int Monetary Research 2014–15, prof of economics 2014–, chm Inst of Int Monetary Research 2015–; hon sec Political Economy Club 1999–2010, chm Freedom Assoc 2011–14; MSI, FRSA 1990, Hon FIA 2002; *Books* Monetarism: Essay in Definition (1978), Monetary Control in Britain (1982), The Debt Threat (1988), Monetarism Lost (1989), Reflections on Monetarism (1992), Money and Asset Prices in Boom and Bust (2005), Keynes, the Keynesians and Monetarism (2007), Central Banking in a Free Society (2009), How to Stop the Recession (2009), Money in a Free Society (2011), Privatise the BBC (2015); *Recreations* opera, chess, reading; *Clubs* RAC; *Style*— Prof Tim Congdon, CBE; ✉ Huntley Manor, Huntley, Gloucestershire GL19 3HQ (☎ 01452 830840, e-mail timcongdon@btinternet.com)

CONKLIN, Margery (Margi); da of Theodore E Conklin, of Gardiner, NY, and Susan Meadows Conklin; *b* 31 May 1972, Schenectady, NY; *Educ* Cobleskill Central HS NY, Medill Sch of Journalism Northwestern Univ IL (BSJ); *Partner* Christopher J Yates; *Career* journalist; early career as reporter on local newspapers and prodn asst on local TV USA, reporter The Journal Newcastle upon Tyne 1994–95, features writer rising to features ed Take A Break 1996–1998, features ed then asst ed New Woman 1998–2000, ed Celebrity Looks 2000–01 (shortlisted New Ed of the Year BSME Awards 2001), dep ed Elle 2001–03 (actg ed Jan-April 2002), dep ed InStyle 2003–04, ed New Woman 2004–05, actg ed Wedding 2006–; *Style*— Ms Margi Conklin; ✉ New Woman, Endeavour House, 189 Shaftesbury Avenue, London WC2H 8JG (☎ 020 7208 3727, e-mail margi.conklin@emap.com)

CONLAN, John Oliver; s of Eugene J Conlan, of Dublin, Ireland, and Bridgid, *née* Hayes; *b* 13 July 1942; *Educ* Thurles Christian Brothers Sch Ireland; *m* 19 March 1968, Carolyn Sylvia, da of Raymond Ingram, of Luton, Beds; 3 da (Tara Louise b 1972, Amanda Carolyn (Mrs Richard Otley) b 1973, Alison Theresa b 1980); *Career* md: EMI Leisure 1980–81, Trust House Forte Leisure 1981–83; chief exec First Leisure Corporation plc 1988–97 (md 1983–88), chm Tiger Tiger Ltd (formerly Chorion plc then Urbium plc) 1997–, chm Barracuda plc 2002–; dir: Blue Green SA, London Irish Holdings; *Recreations* golf; *Style*— John Conlan, Esq

CONLON, James; *b* 1950, New York City; *Educ* Juilliard Sch; *Career* conductor; music dir Cincinnati May Festival 1979–, music dir Rotterdam Philharmonic 1983–91, chief conductor Cologne Opera 1989–98, music dir Gürzenich Orchestra Cologne 1989–2002, gen music dir City of Cologne, princ conductor Paris Nat Opera 1996–2004, music dir designate Ravinia Festival Chicago 2004–; worked with orchs incl: NY Philharmonic (debut 1974), Chicago Symphony, Boston Symphony, Philadelphia Orch, Cleveland Orch, Nat Symphony, Berlin Philharmonic, Staatskapelle Dresden, London Philharmonic, LSO, BBC Symphony, Orchestre de Paris, Orchestre National de France, Munich Philharmonic, RSO-Berlin, Orchestre de la Suisse Romande, Orchestra di Santa Cecilia, European Community Youth Orch, Orch of the Kirov Opera, Bayerische Rundfunk Orch; repertoire of over 70 operas and 200 symphonic works incl: Die Zauberflöte (Met Opera debut 1976 over 200 performances), Don Carlos (ROH Covent Garden debut 1979), I Pagliacci (Opéra de Paris debut 1982), La Forza del Destino (Chicago Lyric Opera debut 1988), Oberon (Milano La Scala debut 1992), Der Fliegende Holländer, Pelléas et Mélisande, Lady Macbeth of Mtzensk, Die Entführung aus dem Serail, Semiramide, Don Giovanni, Cosi fan Tutte, Le Nozze di Figaro, Lohengrin, Aida, La Bohème, Boris Godunov, Carmen, Jenufa, Khovanschina, Salomé, Tosca, La Traviata, Il Trovatore, Peter Grimes, Macbeth, Tristan und Isolde, Die Meistersinger, Tannhäuser, Das Rheingold, Die Walkyrie, Siegfried, Götterdämmerung, Parsifal, Wozzeck, Otello, Falstaff, Rigoletto, Luisa Miller, Il Trittico, Turandot, Madame Butterfly, Nabucco, Rosenkavalier, Elektra, Simon Boccanegra, Un Ballo in Maschera, Cavalleria Rusticana; Zemlinsky Prize 1999; Hon Dr Juillard Sch 2004; Commandeur de l'Ordre des Arts et des Lettres (France) 2004 (Officier 1996), Chevalier de la Légion d'Honneur (France) 2001; *Style*— James Conlon, Esq

C

CONNAGHAN, John Gerard; CBE (2015); s of John Connaghan (d 1984), and Mary, *née* Hendry; *b* 2 September 1954; *Educ* St Mungo's Acad, Glasgow Caledonian Univ (BA), Univ of Strathclyde (DMS, MBA); *m* 1 Oct 1983, Evelyn Joyce, da of J W B Steven, of Flode, Dornoch; 3 s (Christopher b Oct 1986, James b Dec 1988, Paul b March 1990), 1 da (Ruth b 6 Feb 1994); *Career* Wm Collins & Sons Ltd 1977–79; Charles Letts (Scotland) Ltd Edinburgh 1979–87, Greater Glasgow Health Bd 1987–93; chief exec: Victoria Infirmary Tst 1992–94, Western General Hospitals NHS Tst 1994–99, Fife Acute Hospitals Tst 1999; led Scottish Govt drive to improve NHS Scotland performance: dir of NHS delivery Scottish Govt 2006–11, dir of NHS workforce and performance Scottish Govt 2011–14, chief operating offr NHS Scotland 2015– (leading nat programme to create six new diagnostic and treatment centres in Scotland with responsibilities for ehealth and technology enabled care); dir: Maggies Cancer Charity 1997–2007, Opex Ltd 1998–; *Recreations* hockey (mangr Scotland Veterans 2006–, selected to represent Scotland in Veterans Hockey World Cup Australia 2016), hill walking, cycling, fine wines, golf, reading; *Clubs* Blairgowrie Golf; *Style*— John Connaghan, Esq, CBE; ✉ e-mail connaghan2000@yahoo.com

CONNAL, (Robert) Craig; QC (2002); s of James Brownlee Connal (d 2000), and Jean Elizabeth, *née* Polley; *b* 7 July 1954, Brentwood, Essex; *Educ* Hamilton Acad, Univ of Glasgow (LLB); *m* 29 June 1976, Mary Ferguson, *née* Bowie; 2 da (Lindsay Chalmers b 18 Oct 1981, Gillian Melissa b 13 Nov 1984); *Career* admitted: slr 1977, slr-advocate (civil) 1996, slr-advocate (criminal) 2004, slr England and Wales 2006, slr-advocate (all courts) 2006; ptnr McGrigors LLP 1980–2012 (head of commercial litigation 2002–07, sr litigation ptnr and UK head of advocacy 2007–12), ptnr Pinsent Masons LLP 2012– (head Advocacy, Litigation and Regulatory 2014–); memb Cncl Royal Faculty of Procurators in Glasgow 1995–98, memb Scottish Law Cmmn Working Party on Partnership Law 2000–03; author of articles in professional jls and general press; external examiner Univ of Aberdeen 2001–05; NITA certified advocacy trainer, certified specialist in arbitration; Law Soc of England and Wales Slr Advocate of the Year 2012; memb: Law Soc of Scotland (convenor Higher Rights Course), Law Soc of England and Wales, Soc of Slrs in Supreme Court, Scottish Law Agents' Soc, International Bar Assoc, vice-chm (Scotland) Br Irish Commercial Bar Assoc, Notary Public; *Publications* Stair Memorial Encyclopaedia of Scots Law (contrib, 1986); *Recreations* rugby referee, food and wine, gardens (not gardening); *Clubs* Whitecraigs Rugby; *Style*— R Craig Connal, Esq, QC; ✉ Pinsent Masons LLP, 141 Bothwell Street, Glasgow G2 7EQ (☎ 0141 567 8400, fax 0141 567 8401, e-mail craig.connal@pinsentmasons.com)

CONNAUGHTON, Richard Michael; s of Thomas Connaughton (d 1981), of Huntingdon, and Joan Florence, *née* Lisher (d 1979); *b* 20 January 1942; *Educ* Duke of York's Royal Military Sch Dover, RMA Sandhurst, Univ of Cambridge (MPhil), Lancaster Univ (PhD); *m* 12 June 1971, (Annis Rosemary) Georgina, da of Capt George Frederic Matthew Best, OBE, RN (d 1994), and Rosemary Elizabeth, *née* Brooks, of Dorset; 1 s (Michael b 1972), 1 da (Emma b 1974); *Career* RMA Sandhurst 1960–61, III Co RASC (Guided Weapons) W Germany 1962–64, 28 Co Gurkha Army Serv Corps Hong Kong 1965–67, Jr Ldrs' RCT Taunton 1967–69, 28 Sqdn Gurkha Tport Regt Hong Kong 1969–71 (Adj 1971–73), student Army Staff Coll Camberley 1974, GS0 2 Co-ord MVEE Chertsey 1975–76, cmd 2 Sqdn RCT W Germany 1977–79, 2 i/c Logistic Support Gp Regt Aldershot 1979–81, cmd 1 Armd Div Tport Regt RCT W Germany 1982–84, memb Directing Staff Army Staff Coll Camberley and Australian Army Cmd and Staff Coll Fort Queenscliff Victoria 1984–86, Col Tport HQ BAOR W Germany 1987–89; def fellowship St John's Coll Cambridge 1989–90, Colonel Defence Studies 1990–92, exec dir National & International Consultancy 1992–; FIMgt 1981, FCIT 1989; *Books* The War of The Rising Sun and Tumbling Bear: The Russo-Japanese War 1904–05 (1989, revised edn 2003), The Republic of the Ushakovka (1990), Military Intervention in the 1990s: a New Logic of War (1992), To Loose the Bands of Wickedness (contrib, ed Nigel Rodley, 1992), The Changing Face of Armed Conflict: Today and Tomorrow (1994), Shrouded Secrets: Australia's Mainland War with Japan 1942–44 (1994), The Nature of Future Conflict (1995), The Battle for Manila 1945 (with Drs Anderson and Pimlott, 1995), Celebration of Victory (1995), Descent into Chaos (1996), MacArthur and Defeat in the Philippines (2001), Military Intervention and Peacekeeping: The Reality (2001), Omai: The Prince Who Never Was (2003), A Brief History of Modern Warfare (2009), A Dorset Parish Remembers 1914–1919 (ed, 2014), A Dorset Parish Remembers 1939–45 (ed, 2015); *Recreations* writing, family tennis; *Style*— Mr Richard Connaughton; ✉ Wallhayes, Nettlecombe, Bridport, Dorset DT6 3SX (☎ 01308 485002, fax 01308 485446, e-mail richard.m.connaughton@lineone.net, website www.connaughton.org.uk)

CONNAUGHTON, Shane; s of Brian Connaughton (d 1983), and Elizabeth, *née* Moylett (d 1979); *b* 4 April 1941; *Educ* St Tiarnachs Clones, Bristol Old Vic Theatre Sch; *m* Ann-Marie, da of Paul Hammersley-Fenton; 1 da (Tara b 17 March 1974), 1 s (Tom b 10 March 1979); *Career* writer; actor in repertoire and Nat Theatre London and Abbey Theatre Dublin; Hennessy Award for Irish Fiction 1985, The Irish Post Award 1987; *Novels* A Border Station (1989, shortlist GPA Literary Award), The Run of the Country (1991); *Plays* Sir Is Winning (1977, NT), Weston Coyney Cowboy (1975, Stoke-on-Trent), George Davis is Innocent OK (1976, Half Moon), Divisions (1981, Dublin Theatre Festival), Lily (1984, The Irish Co); *Screenplays* Every Picture Tells A Story (Channel 4), Dollar Bottom (1981, Oscar Best Short Film), My Left Foot (1990, Oscar nomination Best Adapted Screenplay), The Playboys (1992), O Mary This London (1994), The Run of the Country (1995), Tara Road (2005), various others for BBC and ITV; *Recreations* smelling flowers, my wife; *Style*— Shane Connaughton, Esq

CONNELL, Douglas Andrew; *b* 18 May 1954, Callander, Perthshire; *Educ* McLaren HS Callander, Univ of Edinburgh (LLB); *m* 1 Oct 1983, Marjorie Elizabeth; 2 s (Richard Thomson b 28 Nov 1984, Nicholas Alastair b 19 June 1987); *Career* admitted slr 1976; ptnr Dundas & Wilson 1979–97; Turcan Connell: jt sr ptnr 1997–2013, sr ptnr 2013–; chair Museums Galleries Scotland 2012–; gen cncl assessor Ct of Univ of Edinburgh 2007–11; memb Scottish Ctee Historic Houses Assoc, tstee Historic Scotland Fndn, former chm Recognition Ctee Museums Galleries Scotland, tstee Buildings of Scotland Tst; patron: Nat Galleries of Scotland, Nat Museums of Scotland; former chm Lottery Ctee Scottish Arts Cncl, former chm Edinburgh Book Festival; former memb Ct Univ of St Andrews; *Style*— Douglas Connell, Esq; ✉ Turcan Connell, Princes Exchange, 1 Earl

Grey Street, Edinburgh EH3 9EE (☎ 0131 228 8111, fax 0131 228 8118, e-mail douglasconnell@turcanconnell.com)

CONNELL, Prof John Muir Cochrane; s of William Connell, and Betty Nicol; *b* 10 October 1954, Irvine, Scotland; *Educ* Univ of Glasgow (MB ChB, MD); *m* 1978, Lesley Armstrong; 3 s, 1 da; *Career* registrar in gen med and endocrinology Univ Dept of Med Western Infirmary Glasgow 1980–83, clinical scientist MRC Blood Pressure Unit Western Infirmary Glasgow 1983–86, visiting research fell Howard Florey Inst for Experimental Physiology and Med Univ of Melbourne 1986–87, sr clinical scientist MRC Blood Pressure Unit Western Infirmary Glasgow 1987–95 (also hon conslt physician), hon prof of med Faculty of Med Univ of Glasgow 1993, prof of endocrinology Univ of Glasgow 1996–2009; Univ of Dundee: dean of medicine 2009–11, vice-princ and head Coll of Medicine, Dentistry and Nursing 2012–; sec Assoc of Physicians of GB and Ireland 2001–; sr ed Clinical Endocrinology 2005–, author of over 200 peer-reviewed papers and over 20 book chapters in specialist endocrine and cardiovascular textbooks; R D Wright lectr High Blood Pressure Cncl of Aust 1994, Richard Underwood Meml Lecture Harvard Univ and Brigham & Women's Hosp 1999, Croonian Lecture RCP 2000, lectr Clinical Endocrinology Tst 2008; Soc Endocrinol Medal 2005; MRCP 1979, FRCPGlas 1990, FMedSci 1999, FRCPEd 2002, FRSE 2002; *Recreations* golf, family, literature; *Clubs* New Golf (St Andrews); *Style*— Prof John Connell; ✉ Ninewells Hospital and Medical School, Dundee DD1 9SY

CONNELL, Josephine Lilian (Jo); OBE (2012), DL (Herts); da of Charles Kingsley Williams (d 2005), and Jean Elaine, *née* Hannay (d 2008); *b* 26 January 1948, Windsor, Berks; *m* 28 June 1975, Michael Patrick Connell; 1 s (Christopher Michael b 7 Nov 1976), 1 da (Alison Emma b 27 Sept 1978); *Career* gp md Xansa plc 1997–2003; non exec dir: THUS Gp plc 2001–07, London Bridge Software Hldgs plc 2003–04, Synstar plc 2003–04, Cornwell Mgmnt Conslts plc 2004–07, @UK plc 2005–08, RM plc 2007–14; chm Help the Aged 2004–09, vice-pres Age UK 2009–; chm Hospice St Francis Berkhamsted Herts 2004–10, chm OFCOM Advsr Ctee for Older and Disabled People 2010–, chm Communications Consumer Panel 2012–; chm of govrs and pro-chllr Univ of Herts 2007–13, tstee Herts Community Fndn 2010–, chm WCIT Charity 2012–; Master Worshipful Co of Info Technologists 2008–09; Hon DLitt Univ of Herts 2014; FBCS, CEng; *Style*— Mrs Josephine Connell, OBE, DL; ☎ 07775 714110, e-mail jo@mpconnell.demon.co.uk

CONNELLY, Kevin Aloysius Scott; *b* 27 August 1957; *Educ* St Mary's Marist Fathers Coll Middlesbrough; *Career* mangr McCoys Restaurant Northallerton 1979–90; full time comedy writer and performer 1990–; appearances and contribs to radio and TV progs incl Dead Ringers BBC Radio 4 and BBC 2 (Best Radio Comedy Sony Awards 2001, Best Radio Comedy TV and Radio Comedy Awards 2002); after dinner speaker, supporter Comic Heritage Fndn; *Clubs* Lord's Taverners, Naval; *Style*— Kevin Connelly, Esq; ✉ c/o Jane Morgan Management Ltd, Argentum, 2 Queen Caroline Street, London W6 9DX (☎ 020 3178 8071, e-mail enquiries@janemorganmgt.com)

CONNER, Angela Mary (Mrs Bulmer); da of late Judge Cyril Conner, and Mary Stephanie, *née* Douglass; *Educ* spent much of childhood travelling; *m* John Frederick Bulmer; 1 da (Georgia Bulmer Ferreira); *Career* sculptor; worked for Dame Barbara Hepworth UK then full-time painter and sculptor; researched and developed use of water, sun and wind for abstract mobile sculptures in contemporary art; FRBS; *Collective Exhibitions* incl: Gimpel Fils NY, Met Museum NY, Browse and Darby London, Istanbul Biennale, Lincoln Centre NY, Jewish Art Museum NY, Washington Museum, Economist Plaza London, Hirschl Gallery London, Galerie Piece Unique Paris, Chicago Arts Fair, Carnegie Museum Pittsburgh, Nat Portrait Gall London, Royal Acad, Art Dubai, Christies Art Fair, Artefiera Bologna; *Important Public and Private Works* incl: centrepiece water mobile lent to Downing St for state dining table), tallest mobile sculpture in Europe Dublin, large water mobile Chatsworth, three works for Lincoln Center NYC, Great Tipper Germany, multiple water mobile sculptures for Horsham Town Centre, Victims of Yalta Meml (Brompton Rd London), water sculpture and co-designed Plaza Heinz Hall Pittsburgh, water sculptures for King Fahid, 20ft water mobile Aston Univ, 30ft water mobile Economist Plaza St James's London, 20ft water mobile for Fidelity, 85ft mobile water arch Longleat, largest indoor mobile in Europe Lovells London, etc; numerous private cmmns eg Duke of Devonshire Collection, Gunter Sachs, Mrs Henry Ford II, President Chirac, etc; *Portraits* incl: statues of de Gaulle, Sir Noel Coward (London, NY and Jamaica), Philippe De Montebello (ret dir Met Museum NYC); busts: HRH The Prince of Wales, HM The Queen, HM Queen Elizabeth the Queen Mother, Lucien Freud, Lord Sainsbury, Drue Heniz, Duke of Devonshire, Harold Macmillan (Earl of Stockton), Sir John Betjeman, Sir John Tavener, Dame Janet Baker, Rab Butler (House of Commons), Paul Mellon, Sir Peter O'Sullevan, Sir Alec Douglas Home, Lord Rothschild, Sir Tom Stoppard, etc; *Awards* incl: Honor Award of American Inst of Architects, Best Br Equestrian Sculptor Award Br Sporting Art Tst; winner various competitions incl: Lexington Airport Int Competition, Hereford City Nat Competition, W Midlands Arts Nat Competition for Aston Univ, Darlington Art Centre Competition; *Recreations* breeding and showing Morgan horses, co-founded the breed in Britain; *Style*— Angela Conner; ✉ George and Dragon Hall, Mary Place, London W11 4PL (☎ 020 7221 4510, fax 020 7243 1167, e-mail angela.conner@which.net, website www.angelaconner.co.uk)

CONNER, Rt Rev David John; KCVO (2010); s of William Ernest Conner (d 1989), and Joan Millington, *née* Cheek (d 1994); *b* 6 April 1947; *Educ* Erith GS, Exeter Coll Oxford (Symes exhibitioner, MA), St Stephen's House Oxford; *m* 10 July 1969, Jayne Maria, da of Lt-Col George E Evans, OBE; 2 s (Andrew David b 1970, Jonathan Paul b 1972); *Career* chaplain St Edward's Sch Oxford 1973–80 (asst chaplain 1971–73), team vicar Wolvercote with Summertown Oxford 1976–80, sr chaplain Winchester Coll 1980–86, vicar St Mary the Great with St Michaels Cambridge 1987–94, rural dean of Cambridge 1989–94, bishop of Lynn 1994–98, dean of Windsor and register of the Most Noble Order of the Garter 1998–; bishop to The Forces 2001–09, hon chaplain to Pilgrims 2002–12; hon fell Girton Coll Cambridge 1995; *Recreations* reading and friends; *Style*— The Rt Rev David Conner, KCVO; ✉ The Deanery, Windsor Castle, Berkshire SL4 1NJ (☎ 01753 865561, fax 01753 819002, e-mail deansprivatesecretary@stgeorges-windsor.org)

CONNERY, Sir Sean Thomas; kt (2000); s of Joseph Connery, and Euphamia Connery; *b* 25 August 1930; *m* 1, 29 Nov 1962 (m dis 1974), Diane (who m 3, 1985, Anthony Shaffer, playwright), da of Sir Raphael West Cilento (d 1985), and former w of Andrea Volpt; 1 s (Jason Connery b 1963); m 2, Jan 1975, Micheline Roquebrune; *Career* actor, fell: Royal Scottish Academy of Music and Drama, BAFTA; Freeman City of Edinburgh 1991; Hon DLitt Heriot-Watt Univ 1981; Golden Globe Cecil B De Mille Lifetime Achievement Award 1996, Lifetime Achievement Award Palm Springs Int Film Festival 2001; films incl: Tarzan's Greatest Adventure 1959, The Longest Day 1962, Dr No 1963, From Russia With Love 1964, Goldfinger 1965, Thunderball 1965, A Fine Madness 1966, You Only Live Twice 1967, Shalako 1968, Diamonds are Forever 1971, Murder on the Orient Express 1974, The Man Who Would be King 1975, Outland 1981, Never Say Never Again 1983, Highlander 1986, The Name of the Rose 1986, The Untouchables 1987, The Presidio 1988, Indiana Jones – The Last Crusade 1989, The Hunt For Red October 1990, Family Business 1990, Highlander II 1991, Robin Hood Prince of Thieves 1991, The Russia House 1991, The Medicine Man 1992, Just Cause 1995, King Arthur in First Knight 1995, The Rock 1996, the voice of Draco in Dragonheart 1996, The Avengers 1998, Entrapment 1998, The James Bond Story 1999, Finding Forrester 2000, The League of Extraordinary Gentlemen 2003; *Style*— Sir Sean Connery

CONNOCK, Stephen Leslie; MBE (1999); s of Leslie Thomas Connock, of Peterborough, Cambs, and Gladys Edna, *née* Chappell; *b* 16 November 1949; *Educ* Univ of Sheffield (BA), LSE (MPhil); *m* 18 Aug 1973, Margaret Anne, da of Richard Bolger, of Palmers Green, London; 2 s (Adrian b 1981, Mark b 1985); *Career* Philips Electronics: industrial relations mangr 1979–85, mgmnt devpt mangr 1985–87; gen mangr human resources Pearl Assurance plc 1987–92, customer and corp affrs dir Eastern Group plc (formerly Eastern Electricity plc) 1992–97, chm Inst of Customer Service 1996–2001, chm The Garland Appeal (fndn in honour of Linda McCartney), managing partner Integrys Ltd, people dir easyJet plc 2003–05, dir of gp HR Aggreko plc 2006–08, gp HR dir Nat Express Gp plc 2009–14, gp HR advsr CPP Gp plc 2015; chm: Albion Music Ltd, Albion Film Series, Rydal Records, Braga Santos Foundation; MCIPD 1973; *Books* Industrial Relations Training for Managers (1981), Cost Effective Strategies in Industrial Relations (1985), H R Vision – Managing a Quality Workforce (1991), Ethical Leadership (1995), There was a Time – RVW in Photographs (ed, 2003), The Complete Poems of Ursula Vaughan Williams (ed, 2003); *Recreations* music (vice-pres Ralph Vaughan Williams Soc, vice-pres Joyful Co of Singers), writing, football (Spurs), cricket (Surrey); *Clubs* Reform; *Style*— Stephen Connock, Esq, MBE

CONNOLLY, Billy; CBE (2003); *b* 24 November 1942; *m* 1990, Pamela Stephenson; 3 da (Daisy, Amy, Scarlett); from previous m; 1 s (Jamie), 1 da (Cara); *Career* comedian, actor, musician, playwright and presenter; started work as apprentice welder, began show business career with Gerry Rafferty and The Humblebums; as playwright The Red Runner (Edinburgh Fringe) 1979; Freeman City of Glasgow 2010; *Theatre* The Great Northern Welly Boot Show (Palladium), Die Fledermaus (Scottish Opera) 1978, The Beastly Beastitudes of Balthazar B (West End) 1982, What About Dick? 2007 and 2012; *Television* Film '72–2008 1972–2008 (39 appearances), Just Another Saturday 1975, Parkinson 1975–2007 (9 appearances), The Elephant's Graveyard 1976, The South Bank Show 1979, This Is Your Life 1980, Worzel Gummidge: A Cup o' Tean an' a Slice o' Cake 1980, Concert for Kampuchea 1981, An Audience with Billy Connelly 1984, Tickle on the Tum 1984, Weekend in Wallop 1984, Androcles and the Lion 1984, Aspel & Company 1985, Live Aid 1985, Supergran: Supergran and the Course of True Love 1985, Omnibus – Comic Relief 1986, The the North of Katmandu 1986, The Hunting of the Snark 1987, Nelson Mandela 70th Birthday Tribute 1988, Minder 1989, Return to Nose and Beak (Comic Relief), HBO special (with Whoopi Goldberg) 1990, Dreaming 1990, Good Morning Britain 1991, Pale Blue Scottish Person 1991, South Bank Show Special (25th Anniversary commemoration) 1992, Down Among the Big Boys (BBC) 1993, Late Show with David Letterman 1993 and 1997, Clive James 1994, Head of the Class, Billy, Billy Connolly's World Tour of Scotland (6 part documentary) 1994, A Scot in the Arctic 1995, The Big Picture (BBC) 1995, Dennis the Menace: Dennis Ahoy 1996, Pearl: Billy Returns 1996, Billy Connolly's World Tour of Australia 1996, Sean Connery: An Intimate Portrait 1997, Sean Connery: Close Up 1997, The Rosie O'Donnell Show 1997, Whatever Happened to? Clement and La Frenais 1997, Erect for 30 Years 1998, The Roseanne Show 1998, Tracey Takes On: Culture 1998, Veronica's Closet: Veronica's Got a Secret 1998, 3rd Rock from the Sun: Dial M for Dick 1999, Gentleman's Relish 2000 (BBC), Comic Relief Short Pants 2001, Comic Relief: Say Pants to Poverty 2001, Prince Charming 2001, Rove Live 2001, The Ray Martin Show 2001, World Tour of England, Ireland and Wales 2002, Airport 2002, Billy Connolly a BAFTA Tribute 2002, Judi Dench a BAFTA Tribute 2002, Ultimate Fights from the Movies 2002, Comic Relief 2003, The Big Hair Do 2003, Dolly Parton: Platinum Blonde 2003, ESPN Fly Fishing Show with John Barrett 2003 and 2007, Julie Walters a BAFTA Tribute 2003, Overnight 2003, The Hollywood Greats 2003, The Importance of Being Famous 2003, The Late Late Show 2003, Tinseltown TV 2003, World Tour of NZ 2004, A Terrible Tragedy 2004, Comedy Central Presents: 100 Greatest Stand-Ups of all Time 2004 (no 73), Last CAll with Carson Daly 2004, Late Show with Conan O'Brien 2004, The Daily Show with Jon Stewart 2004 and 2006, Avenue of the Stars: 50 Years of ITV 2005, Britain's Finest: Actors 2005, Britain's Finest: Actresses 2005, Good Sharma 2005, Ivor Cutler: Looking for Truth with a Pin 2005, Preal Time with Bill Maher 2005, Canada AM 2006, Enough Rope with Andrew Denton 2006, The Late Late Show with Craig Ferguson 2006, Comic Relief 2007: The Big One 2007, Comic Relief Does Fame Academy 2007, Happy Birthday Elton! From Madison Square Gardens 2007, Kenny Everitt: Licence to Laugh 2007, Late Night with Conan O'Brien 2007, Parkinson: The Final Conversation 2007, New Heroes of Comedy 2008, Ronnie Drew: September Song 2009, Journey to the Edge of the World 2009, Route 66 2011, House MD 2012, The Tonight Show with Jay Leno 2013, The Late Late Show with Craig Ferguson 2013, Billy Connolly's Big Send Off 2013; *Films* incl: The Secret Policeman's Ball 1979, Absolution (with Richard Burton) 1979, The Secret Policeman's Other Ball 1982, Blue Monkey 1984, Bullshot 1984, Water (with Michael Caine, *qv*) 1984, The Return of the Musketeers 1989, The Big Man (with Liam Neeson) 1989, Crossing the Line 1990, Dreaming 1990, Indecent Proposal 1993, Pocahontas (animation) 1995, Billy Big Bones in Treasure Island (Muppet Movie) 1996, William Brodie in Deacon Brodie (BBC Film) 1996, Ship of Fools 1997, Middleton's Changeling 1997, Paws 1997, Beverly Hills Ninja 1997, Mrs Brown (with Judi Dench, *qv*) 1997, Still Crazy 1998, The Imposters 1998, The Debt Collector 1999, An Everlasting Piece 2000, Beautiful Joe 2000, The Boondock Saints 2000, Columbo: Murder with Too Many Notes 2001, Gabriel & Me 2001, White Oleander 2002, Who Is Cletis Tout? 2002, Man Who Sued God 2002, The Rutles 2: Can't Buy Me Lunch 2003, Overnight 2003, Timeline 2003, The Last Samurai 2003, Lemony Snicket: A Series of Unfortunate Events 2004, The Aristocrats 2005, F*ck 2005, The Snow Goose 2006, Open Season 2006, Garfield – A Tail of Two Kitties 2006, Fido 2007, Good Sharma 2007, The X-Files: I Want To Believe 2008, The Boondock Saints II: All Saints Day 2009, Open Season 2 2009, Gulliver's Travels 2010, The Hobbit: An Unexpected Journey 2012, Brave 2012, Quartet 2012, The Hobbit: There and Back Again 2013, What We Did On Our Holiday 2013, Wild Oats 2014; *Videos* numerous releases incl: Connolly 1975, Big Banana Feet 1976, Billy Connolly in Concert 1978, Bite your Bum 1981 (Music Week and Record Business Award 1982), 25 BC, Billy and Albert, An Audience with Billy Connolly, Billy Connolly Live, Hand-Picked by Billy Connolly 1982, The Pick of Billy Connolly 1982, An Audience with Billy Connolly 1985, Billy and Albert 1987, Live at Hammersmith 1991, Live' 94, World Tour of Scotland 1995, Two Bites of Billy Connolly 1995, A Scot in The Arctic 1995, World Tour of Australia 1996, Two Night Stand 1997, Erect for 30 Years 1998, One Night Stand/Down Under (Live 99) 1999, Billy Connolly – The Greatest Hits 2001, World Tour of England, Ireland and Wales 2002, Billy Connolly Live 2002, Handpicked by Billy 2003, Bites Yer Bum 2003, Billy Connolly's World Tour of NZ 2004, Billy Connolly Live in NY 2006, Billy Connolly – The Essential Collection 2006, Billy Connolly Live – Was It Something I Said? 2007, Journey to the Edge of the World 2009, Billy Connolly The Man Live in London 2010, Billy Connolly: You Asked For It 2011; *Albums* numerous releases incl: The Great Northern Welly Boot Show (incl no 1 hit DIVORCE), Pick of Billy Connolly (gold disc) 1982, Billy Connolly's Musical Tour of NZ 2004; *Books* Gullible's Travels (1982), Journey to the Edge of the World (2009); subject of: Billy (by Pamela Stephenson, 2001), Bravemouth (by Pamela Stephenson, 2003); *Style*— Billy Connolly, Esq, CBE; ✉ c/o Steve Brown, Tickety-boo Limited, 2 Triq Il-Barriera, Balzan BZN1200, Malta (☎ 00 356 2155 6166, fax 00 356 2155 7316, e-mail tickety-boo@tickety-boo.com)

CONNOLLY, Prof Joseph Edward; s of Patrick Joseph Connolly (d 1985), and Kathryn Mary, *née* Mcnaney (d 2009); *b* 15 June 1950; *Educ* Cornell Univ (AB), Harvard Univ (MBA); *Career* second vice-pres Continental Bank London 1975–81, gp head Bank of

Boston London 1981–83, sr analyst Moody's Investors NY 1984–86, dir Euro Ratings Ltd London 1986–88, vice-pres and gp head Citibank London 1988–99, exec dir UBS-Warburg London and Zurich 1999–2004, ceo Connolly Associates (CH) 2004–; non-exec dir J M Huber Fin Servs Ltd 2000–04, princ and non-exec dir Mulvaney Capital Mgmnt Lt 2007–10, non-exec dir Unitas Ltd 2009–11 and 2013–; dir Princeton Center for Economic Studies 1995–99, Willard Brown distinguished prof of global finance and Islamic finance American Univ in Cairo 2005–07, distinguished prof of corp finance Ecole Nationale des Ponts et Chauseés Paris 2007–14, prof of economics and Islamic finance Fordham Univ NYC 2010–, distinguished fell Finance and Ethics Sorbonne Paris 2012–; US cmmr UK-US Bilateral Cmmn for Fulbrights 2005–12, cmmr for the public Middle State Cmmn for HE Philadelphia 2012–; memb: Swiss Bankers Assoc 1999–2006, Advsy Bd Islamic Inst of Banking and Insurance in London 2006–, Advsy Bd Scholar Rescue at Inst of Int Educn NYC 2007–; hon fell Centre for Islamic Finance Swiss Banking Inst Univ of Zurich; dir Wealth Mgmnt Congress 2003–04; tstee Richmond The American Int Univ of London 2003–09, tstee and dir Assoc of MBAs 2012–13, tstee Harvard Library of NYC; *Books* The International Data Communications Market; *Recreations* racing, looking at pictures, skiing; *Clubs* Harvard (NY, London, Zurich and Boston), Kildare St and Univ (Dublin); *Style—* Prof Joseph Connolly; ✉ 52A Eaton Place, London SW1X 8AL (☎ 020 7245 1223, e-mail josconnolly@yahoo.com); 83 Montvale Avenue, Woburn, Massachusetts, USA

CONNOLLY, Sarah Patricia; CBE (2010); da of Gerald Joseph Connolly, DSO (d 1995), and Jane, *née* Widdowson; *b* 13 June 1963; *Educ* Queen Margaret's York, Clarendon Coll Nottingham, RCM (DipRCM (piano and voice), ARCM); *m* 1998, Carl Talbot; 1 da (Lily Jane Talbot b 6 May 2003); *Career* studied under David Mason and now with Gerald Martin Moore; former memb BBC Singers, joined Glyndebourne Festival Chorus 1992, opera début as Annina in Der Rosenkavalier (WNO) 1994; appeared on My Night with Handel (Channel 4), numerous broadcasts BBC Radio; nominated Olivier Award for Outstanding Achievement in Opera 2006; FRCM 2008, FRSA; *Performances* opera roles: Messenger in Monteverdi's Orfeo (ENO), title roles in Handel's Xerxes (ENO) and Ariodante (NY City Opera, Richard Gold Debut Award 2000, ENO, dir David Alden 2002), Ruggiero in Handel's Alcina (ENO), Susie in The Silver Tassie (world premiere by Mark Anthony Turnage, ENO, South Bank Show Award 2001), Nerone in L'Incoronazione di Poppea Monteverdi (Maggio Musicale, Florence), Ottavia in L'incoronazione di Poppea, Dido in Dido and Aeneas, Ino and Juno in Semele (San Francisco Opera), Romeo in I Capuleti ei Montecchi (NYC Opera) 2001, Lucretia in Britten's The Rape of Lucretia (Aldeburgh Festival, ENO, filmed for BBC, South Bank Show Award 2002), Sesto in Giulio Cesare (Paris Opera, with Minkowski), Juno in Handel's Semele (Theatre des Champs Elysées Paris) 2004, Lucretia (Bayerische Staatsoper Munich) 2004, title role in Giulio Cesare (Glyndebourne) 2005, Annio in Mozart's La Clemenza di Tito (Met Opera NY) 2005, Purcell's Dido and Aneas (La Scala Milan) 2006, Octavian in Der Rosenkavalier (Scottish Opera) 2006, alto in Bach's St Matthew's Passion (Glyndebourne Festival) 2007, Octavian in Der Rosenkavalier (ENO) 2008, Purcell's Dido and Aneas (ROH), Nerone in L'incoronazione di Poppea (Liceu Barcelona) 2009, La Mort de Cleopatre (The Hall Manchester), Brangene in Tristan und Isolde (Glyndebourne Festival Opera) 2009; concert roles: Mozart's Requiem (with Acad of St Martin's in the Field under Sir Neville Marriner), Bach's B minor Mass and Bach Cantatas (with Philippe Herreweghe and Berlin Philharmonie), Wigmore Hall Recital début (with Julius Drake) 1998, Bach Cantatas (with Collegium Vocale and Philippe Herreweghe in Concertgebouw, Amsterdam), Elgar's Dream of Gerontius (under Edo de Waart, Sydney, and Mark Elder with LPO), Mark Anthony Turnage's Twice Through the Heart (with London Sinfonietta under Markus Stenz), Queen of Sheba in Handel's Solomon (with Ivor Bolton at Maggio Musicale, Florence), Marguerite in Berlioz's Damnation de Faust (Perth Festival Aust), world premiere of Rime d'Amore ('Rhyme of Love', with Giuseppe Sinopoli, Rome), Berlioz's Les Nuits d'Été (Vienna Konzerthaus and Concertgebouw, with Acad of Ancient Music under Christopher Hogwood), Mahler's Kindertodenlieder (with Daniel Harding and Mahler Chamber Orchestra), St Matthew Passion (with Sir Colin Davis), Haydn Harmoniemesse (with Sir Simon Rattle), Mozart Dominicus Mass (Salzburg Festival debut) 2002, Mahler's Das Lied von der Erde (Concertgebouw Orch under Daniel Harding) 2006, Mahler's Rucker Lieder (with Mark Elder and Hallé Orch) 2006, Elgar's The Kingdom (with Mark Elder and The Hallé) 2007, Elgar's Dream of Gerontius (Boston Symphony Orch under Sir Colin Davis) 2008; *Recordings* Bach Cantatas (with Philippe Herreweghe and Collegium Vocale), Rameau's Les Fêtes d'Hebe (with Les Art Florissants under William Christie, Gramophone Award for Early Opera 1998), Vivaldi's Juditha Triumphans (with King's Consort under Robert King), Vaughan Williams Sir John in Love (with Richard Hickox), Schoenberg's Das buch der hängenden gärten (with Iain Burnside) 2002, Heroes and Heroines (Handel, with The Sixteen and Harry Christophers) 2004, Mahler's Des Knaben Wunderhorn (with Philippe Herreweghe and Orch des Champs Elysées, Edison Award for Vocal Performance), The Exquisite Hour, Giulio Cesare (Glyndebourne) 2005, vocal solist in film Children of Men 2006, Mozart's Mass in C Minor (Paul McCreesch and Gabrieli Consort); *Recreations* animals, reading, jazz and classical piano playing, films, theatre; *Style—* Miss Sarah Connolly, CBE; ✉ c/o Askonas Holt, Lincoln House, 300 High Holborn, London WC1V 7JH (e-mail sue.spencer@askonasholt.co.uk)

CONNOR, (Jill) Alexandra; da of John Connor, and Ella Crossley, *née* Worthington; *Educ* Harrogate Ladies Coll, Yorks; *m* (m dis); *Career* writer, artist and television presenter; one woman exhibitions: Marina Henderson Gallery, Richmond Gallery; work cmmnd by RSC and Aspreys; former presenter Past Masters on This Morning, featured in documentary 40 Minutes (BBC); subject of many articles in national newspapers and magazines, numerous appearances on TV, regular BBC radio slots; FRSA; *Books* non-fiction: The Wrong Side of the Canvas (1989), Rembrandt's Monkey (1991), Private View (2002); fiction: The Witch Mark (1986), Thomas (1987), The Hour of the Angel (1989), The Mask of Fortune (1990), The Well of Dreams (1992), The Green Bay Tree (1993), Winter Women: Midsummer Men (1994), The Moon is My Witness (1997), Midnight's Smiling (1998), Green Baize Road (1999), An Angel Passing Over (2000), Hunter's Moon (2001), The Sixpenny Winner (2002), A Face in the Locket (2003), The Turn of the Tide (2004), The Tailor's Wife (2005), The Lydgate Widow (2006), The Soldier's Woman (2008), The Jeweller's Niece (2010); as Alexandra Hampton: The Experience Buyer (1994), The Deaf House (1995); medical thrillers: Bodily Harm (1998), Cipher (1999), The Watchman's Daughter (2007); as Alex Connor: The Rembrandt Secret (2011), Legacy of Blood (2012), The Memory of Bones (2012), Isle of the Dead (2013), The Caravaggio Conspiracy (2013), The Bosch Deception (2014), Conspirazione Caravaggio (2016); *Recreations* collecting antiques and rare art books; *Style—* Alexandra Connor, FRSA; ✉ Braganza, 142 Longhill Road, Ovingdean, Near Brighton, East Sussex BN2 7BD (e-mail alexandra@alexandra-connor.co.uk, websites www.alexandra-connor.com, www.alexconnorthrillers.com, www.alexandraconnor-artist.com)

CONNOR, Clare Joanne; OBE (2006, MBE 2004); da of Michael Connor, of Brighton and Hove, Sussex, and Norma, *née* Harwood; *b* 1 September 1976, Brighton; *Educ* Brighton Coll (academic scholar), Univ of Manchester (BA); *Career* cricketer; Sussex: capt 1996–2006, coach women's team and jr teams 2003–06, winners County title 2003, 2004 and 2005; England: debut 1995, capt 2000–06, memb Ashes winning team 2005 (after 42 years held by Australia), ret from int cricket 2006; head of England women's cricket ECB 2008–; player Lashings World XI 2006 (first woman to sign professional terms); chair Women's Ctee ICC 2011–; memb: Cricket Ctee ICC, Bd Sport England, Cmmn on Future of Women's Sport; sports columnist for Observer, presenter and interviewer The Cricket Show (Channel 4), reporter Test Match Special (BBC Radio 4) 2003–05; ambass: Women's Sports Fndn, Chance to Shine scheme ECB; Vodafone England Cricketer of the Year 2002, runner-up Sunday Times Sportswoman of the Year 2005; *Recreations* reading, travelling, theatre; *Style—* Ms Clare Connor, OBE; ✉ ECB, Lord's Cricket Ground, London NW8 8QZ (☎ 020 7432 1200, mobile 07721 728394, e-mail clare.connor@ecb.co.uk)

CONNOR, Howard Arthur; s of Arthur Albert William Connor (d 1969, Sgt RAF), of Chingford, London, and Winifred Edith, *née* Rugg (d 1983); *b* 31 January 1938; *Educ* Richmond House Sch Chingford, Chingford Co HS; *m* 23 July 1960, Dorothy Myrtle, da of Frederick Hobbs (d 1981), of Chingford, London; 2 da (Alison b 1964, Melinda b 1966); *Career* chartered accountant; dir G H Attenborough and Co Ltd; memb and former chm Broxbourne Parliamentary Cons Assoc Business Gp; chartered tax advsr; FCA, CTA; *Recreations* tennis, bridge, golf, badminton; *Clubs* Rotary of Hoddesdon (former pres), Broxbourne Bridge (hon auditor); *Style—* Howard Connor, Esq

CONNOR, Leslie John; s of William John Connor (d 1980), of Lancs, and Doris Eliza, *née* Neild (d 2000); *b* 23 April 1932; *Educ* St Mary's Coll Crosby, Univ of Liverpool (BA), Calif Univ of Advanced Studies (MBA); *m* 1951, Jean Margaret, da of Roger Pendleton, of Lancs; 2 da (Christine Lesley b 1964, Hilary Elaine b 1968); *Career* exec trainee C & A Modes 1956–58, Great Universal Stores 1958–63, Connor Finance Corporation Ltd 1963–, md Leisure and General Holdings Ltd 1970–73, fndr and chm First Castle Electronics plc 1973–86; dir: Connor Finance Corporation Ltd, W J Connor Properties Ltd; Br Show Pony Soc (BSPS): memb Cncl 1978–83, treas 1979–83, show pres 1994–; *Books* The Managed Growth of a Quoted British Public Company, The Working Hunter Pony (jtly); *Recreations* showing horses, farming, antiques, porcelain and painting, walking, writing, golf; *Clubs* Farmers'; *Style—* Leslie Connor, Esq; ✉ Greenacres, Bowker's Green Farm, Bowker's Green, Aughton, Lancashire L39 6TA; Connor Finance Corporation Ltd, Bowker's Green Court, Bowker's Green, Aughton, Lancashire L39 6TA (☎ 01695 424200, fax 01695 424109, e-mail connor.finance@btinternet.com)

CONNOR, Dr (Ryan) Stephen (Steve); OBE (2013); *Educ* Univ of Surrey (LLB); *Career* called to the Bar Inner Temple; fndr and ceo Nat Centre for Domestic Violence 2002–; chair CPS Hate Crime Scrutiny Panel 2008–10; Police/ACPO accredited trainer 2007–, Judicial Studies Bd accredited trainer 2009–; fell City Univ London; Nat Hero Award 2008; *Recreations* fishing; *Style—* Dr Steve Connor, OBE; ✉ National Centre for Domestic Violence, Edgeborough House, Upper Edgeborough Road, Guildford, Surrey GU1 2BJ (e-mail steve.connor@ncdv.org.uk, website www.ncdv.org.uk)

CONNOR, Vincent; s of Stanley Connor (d 2005), and Mary Patricia, *née* McAlindon (d 1973); *b* 17 April 1964, Glasgow; *Educ* Univ of Glasgow (LLB, DipLP); *m* 14 Sept 1996, Gillian Johnston; *Career* admitted slr 1989; trainee then asst slr Hughes Dowall 1987–90; ptnr: McGrigors 1995–98 (asst slr 1990–93, assoc 1993–95), Pinsent Masons 1998–; memb Law Soc of Scotland 1989; accredited construction law specialist and mediator Law Soc of Scotland; *Recreations* music, cinema; *Clubs* Foreign Correspondents (Hong Kong), Fringe (Hong Kong), The China (Hong Kong); *Style—* Vincent Connor, Esq; ✉ Pinsent Masons, 50th Floor, Central Plaza, 18 Harbour Road, Hong Kong (☎ 00852 2521 5621)

CONNORS, Dr Steven George; s of Stanley George Connors, of Cardiff, and Jeanne, *née* White; *b* Cardiff; *Educ* Llanrumney HS Cardiff, UC Swansea (BA, PhD); *m* 22 Aug 1981, Elizabeth Anne, *née* Dawson; 2 s (Owain James, Cullen George Stuart); *Career* teacher of English Denstone Coll 1981–86, head of English Queen's Coll Taunton 1986–91, head of English, housemaster of the int centre and head of boarding Sevenoaks Sch 1991–2000, dep head Christ's Hosp Horsham 2000–05, headmaster Monmouth Sch 2005–15; govr Sherborne Girls; *Recreations* reading, theatre-going, hill walking; *Clubs* East India, Devonshire, Sports and Public Schools, Lansdowne; *Style—* Dr Steven Connors; ✉ e-mail stevenconnors465@gmail.com

CONRAD, His Hon Judge Alan David; QC (1999); s of Maurice Conrad (d 1990), and Peggy Rose Conrad; *b* 10 December 1953; *Educ* Bury GS, BNC Oxford (BA); *m* 1982 (m dis 1999), Andrea, *née* Williams; 1 s (Jonathan b 23 June 1988), 1 da (Anna b 1 Dec 1990); m 2, Julie, *née* Whittle; *Career* called to the Bar 1976, recorder 1997, practising barrister specialising in criminal law; memb Middle Temple Criminal Bar Assoc; *Recreations* reading, travel, food and drink, cricket; *Clubs* Lancashire CCC; *Style—* His Hon Judge Conrad, QC; ✉ Liverpool Crown Court, The Queen Elizabeth II Law Courts, Derby Square, Liverpool L2 1XA

CONRAD, Henrietta; *Educ* Yale Univ; *Career* fndr and co-dir (with Sebastian Scott, *qv*) Princess Productions 1996–; prodns incl: Friday Night Project, The Search, The Wright Stuff, Get Me The Producer; *Style—* Ms Henrietta Conrad; ✉ Princess Productions, Third Floor, Whiteley's Centre, 151 Queensway, London W2 4SB

CONRAD, Peter John; s of Eric Conrad (d 1989), and Pearl Conrad (d 1999); *b* 11 February 1948, Hobart, Tasmania; *Educ* Hobart HS, Univ of Tasmania (BA), Univ of Oxford (MA); *Career* fell All Souls Coll Oxford 1970–73, tutor in English literature ChCh Oxford 1973–2011, reviewer and feature writer The Observer; Hon DLitt Univ of Tasmania 1993; FRSL 1974, hon fell Australian Acad of the Humanities 2004; *Publications* The Victorian Treasure House (1973), Shandyism (1977), Romantic Opera and Literary Form (1978), Imagining America (1980), Television: The Medium and its Manners (1982), The Art of the City (1984), Everyman History of English Literature (1985), A Song of Love and Death (1987), Down Home (1988), Where I Fell to Earth (1990), Underworld (1992), Feasting with Panthers (1994), To Be Continued (1996), Modern Times Modern Places (1998), The Hitchcock Murders (2000), Orson Welles (2003), At Home in Australia (2003), Tales of Two Hemispheres (2004), Creation: Artists, Gods and Origins (2007), Islands (2009), Verdi and/or Wagner (2011), How the World Was Won (2014), Mythomania (2016); *Style—* Peter Conrad, Esq; ✉ c/o United Agents, 12–26 Lexington Street, London W1F 0LE

CONRAN, Jasper Alexander; OBE (2008); s of Sir Terence Conran, and Shirley Ida Conran; bro of Sebastian Conran, *qqv*; *b* 12 December 1959; *Educ* Bryanston, Parsons Sch of Design NY; *Career* md and designer Jasper Conran Ltd 1978–; tstee: Wallace Collection, Architecture Fndn; visiting prof Herriot-Watt Univ; Fil d'Or (Int Linen award) 1982 and 1983, British Fashion Cncl Designer of the Year award 1986–87, Fashion Gp of America award 1987, Laurence Olivier Costume Designer of the Year award 1991 for Jean Anouilh's The Rehearsal (Almeida Theatre 1990, Garrick Theatre 1990–91), British Collections award British Fashion Awards 1991; Hon DLitt Herriot-Watt Univ, hon dr of civil law UEA; *Publications* Jasper Conran Country (2010); *Style—* Jasper Conran, Esq, OBE; ✉ Jasper Conran Ltd, 1–7 Rostrevor Mews, Fulham, London SW6 5AZ (☎ 020 7384 0800, fax 020 7384 0801)

CONRAN, Sebastian Orby; s of Sir Terence Conran, and Shirley Conran, OBE; bro of Jasper Conran, OBE, *qqv*; *b* 5 April 1956, London; *Educ* Bryanston Sch Dorset, Central St Martins Coll of Art and Design; *m* Gertrude; 2 s (Sam, Max); *Career* Wolf Olins 1979–81, head of product design Mothercare 1981–86, fndr Sebastian Conran Associates 1986 (merged with Conran Gp to form Conran & Ptnrs 1999, currently md Studio Conran (brand and merchandise devpt div), re-established Sebastian Conran Associates 2009); ceo: Consequential Robotics Ltd; dir: Conran & Ptnrs Ltd, Inclusiviti Ltd, Bike Republic Ltd, Universal Expert LLP, Sheffield Robotics; chair: Design Special Interest Gp Innovate UK, Design Action in Scotland; former chm: Home Office Design & Technol Alliance,

Advsy Bd Creative Industries Knowledge Transfer Network TSB UK; visiting prof of design Central Ct Martins, former visiting prof Univ of Arts London, designer in residence Univ of Sheffield, visiting fell Robotics Faculty Univ of Bristol; tstee: Conran Fndn, Bryanston Sch; former tstee D&AD, former tstee Design Cncl, founding tstee Design Museum; ambass: ACID (Anti Copying in Design), ICAN (children's communication charity), Bristol Aerospace Design Museum; Liveryman Worshipful Co of Pewterers; hon fell: Univ of the Arts London, Bournemouth Univ of the Arts, Inst of Minerals, Materials and Mining; Hon DArts Univ of Hertfordshire, Hon DTech Loughborough Univ; hon FRCA, FRSA, FIoP, FCSD, memb D&AD; *Publications* Contemporary Furniture (1997), Contemporary Lighting (1998); *Recreations* cooking, gardening; *Style*— Mr Sebastian Conran; ✉ Sebastian Conran Associates, 2 Munden Street, West Kensington, London W14 0RH

CONRAN, Shirley Ida; OBE (2004); da of W Thirlby Pearce, and Ida Pearce; *b* 21 September 1932; *Educ* St Paul's Girls' Sch; *m* 1955 (m dis 1962), as his 2 w, Terence Orby Conran (now Sir Terence); 2 s (Sebastian Conran, Jasper Conran, *qqv*); *Career* designer/writer; co fndr Conran Fabrics Ltd 1957, memb Selection Ctee Design Cncl 1961, first woman ed Observer Colour Magazine 1964–69, woman ed Daily Mail 1968; fndr pres: Mothers in Mgmnt 1998–, Work-Life Balance Tst 2000–; fndr Maths Action 2004–; *Books* Superwoman (1974), Superwoman Year Book (1975), Superwoman in Action (1977), Futures (with E Sidney), Lace (1982), The Magic Garden (1983), Lace 2 (1984), Savages (1987), The Amazing Umbrella Shop (1990), Down with Superwoman (Penguin, 1990), Crimson (1992), Tiger Eyes (1994), The Revenge (1997), Money Stuff, a simple, complete maths course (ebook, 2014), Money $tuff, International Edition (ebook, 2015); *Style*— Ms Shirley Conran, OBE

CONRAN, Sir Terence Orby; kt (1983); *b* 4 October 1931; *Educ* Bryanston, Central Sch of Arts & Crafts; *m* 2, 1955 (m dis 1962), Shirley Ida Pearce (Shirley Conran); 2 s (Jasper Conran, Sebastian Conran, *qqv*); m 3, 1963 (m dis 1996), Caroline Herbert (the cookery writer Caroline Conran); 2 s, 1 da; m 4, 2000, Victoria Davis; *Career* designer, retailer, restaurateur; currently chm: The Conran Shop Ltd 1976–, Jasper Conran Ltd 1982–, Benchmark Ltd 1989–, Blue Print Café Ltd 1989–, Terence Conran Ltd 1990–, Conran Shop Holdings Ltd 1990– (shops in London, Paris, NY, Hamburg, Tokyo, Nagoya, Fukuoka), Le Pont de la Tour Ltd 1991–, Quaglino's Restaurant Ltd 1991–, Butlers Wharf Chop House Ltd 1992–, Conran Shop SA 1992–,Conran & Partners Ltd (formerly CD Partnership Ltd) 1993–, Conran Holdings Ltd 1993–, Mezzo Ltd 1993–, The Bluebird Store Ltd 1994–, Conran Restaurants Ltd 1994–, Conran Shop (Marylebone) Ltd 1996–, Conran Shop (Germany) Ltd 1997–, Afterdecide Ltd 1997–, Guastavino's Inc 1997–, Conran Distribution SARL Ltd 1997–, Conran Collection Ltd 1997–, Conran Properties (Marylebone) Ltd 1997–, Coq d'Argent Ltd 1997–, Conran Shop (Manhattan) Inc 1997–, Great Eastern Hotel Co Ltd 1997–2005, Orrery Restaurant Ltd 1997–, Sartoria Restaurant Ltd 1997–, Zinc Bar & Grill Ltd 1997–, Atlantic Blue SNC 1998–, Conran Finance Ltd 1998–; currently dir: Conran Ink Ltd 1969–, Conran Roche Ltd 1980–, Conran Octopus Ltd 1983–, Bibendum Restaurant Ltd 1986–, Michelin House Devpt Co Ltd 1989–, Michelin House Investment Co Ltd 1989–; jt chm Ryman Conran Ltd 1968–71; Habitat/Storehouse group: fndr 1971, chm Habitat Group Ltd 1971–88, chm Habitat France SA 1973–88, chm J Hepworth and Son Ltd 1981–83 (dir 1979–83), chm Habitat Mothercare plc (following merger) 1982–88, chm Richard Shops Ltd 1983–87, chm Heal and Son Ltd 1983–87, chm and chief exec Storehouse plc (following merger of Habitat/Mothercare with British Home Stores) 1986–88 (chm only 1988–90, non-exec dir 1990), dir BhS plc 1986–88; also formerly dir: RSCG Conran Design (formerly Conran Design Group/Conran Associates) 1971–92, The Neal Street Restaurant 1972–89, Conran Stores Inc 1977–88, Electra Risk Capital Group plc 1981–84, Savacentre Ltd 1986–88; memb: Royal Cmmn on Environmental Pollution 1973–76, Cncl RCA 1978–81 and 1986–, Advsy Cncl V&A 1979–83, Bd of Tstees V&A 1984–90, Assoc for Business Sponsorship of the Arts; estab Conran Fndn for Design Educn and Res 1981; chm Design Museum 1992– (tstee 1989–), vice-pres FNAC 1985–89, pres D&AD Awards 1989; provost RCA; Hon Dr RCA 1996, Hon DSc London Southbank Univ 2007; Commandeur de l'Ordre des Arts et des Lettres (France) 1991; Hon FRIBA 1984, FSIAD; *Awards* Daily Telegraph/Assoc for Business Sponsorship of the Arts Award to Habitat Mothercare 1982, SIAD Medal 1982, RSA Bicentenary Medal 1984, RSA Presidential Medal for Design Mgmnt to Conran Gp, RSA Presidential Award for Design Mgmnt to Habitat Designs 1975; *Books* The House Book (1974), The Kitchen Book (1977), The Bedroom and Bathroom Book (1978), The Cook Book (with Caroline Conran, 1980), Terence Conran's New House Book (1985), Conran Directory of Design (1985), Plants at Home (1986), The Soft Furnishings Book (1986), Terence Conran's France (1987), Terence Conran's DIY By Design (1989), Terence Conran's Garden DIY (1991), Toys and Children's Furniture (1992), Terence Conran's Kitchen Book (1993), The Essential House Book (1994), Terence Conran on Design (1996), The Conran Cookbook (1997, rev edn of The Cook Book), The Essential Garden Book (with Dan Pearson, 1998), Easy Living (1999), Chef's Garden (1999), Terence Conran on Restaurants (2000), Terence Conran on London (2000), Small Spaces (2001), Classic Conran (with Vicki Conran), Storage, Bathrooms, Kitchens, How to Live in Small Spaces, Designers on Design (with Max Fraser), Intelligence Made Visible (with Stephen Bayley), Eat London (with Peter Prescott), Outdoors (with Diarmuid Gavin), Inspiration (with Stafford Cliff); *Recreations* gardening, cooking; *Style*— Sir Terence Conran; ✉ Terence Conran Ltd, 22 Shad Thames, London SE1 2YU (☎ 020 7378 1161, fax 020 7403 4309)

CONROY, Stephen Alexander; s of Stephen James Conroy (d 1993), of Renton, Dunbartonshire, and Elizabeth Ann, *née* Walker; *b* 2 March 1964; *Educ* St Patrick's HS Dunbarton, Glasgow Sch of Art (BA, Harry McLean Bequest, Jock McFie award, postgrad award); *Career* artist; solo exhibitions: Marlborough Fine Art London 1989, 1992 and 1999 (and tour 1989), Glasgow Art Gallery & Museum 1989, Whitworth Art Gallery Manchester 1989, Marlborough Gallery NY 1995 and 2003, Everard Read Gallery Johannesburg SA 1996, Marlborough Galleria Madrid 1997, Musée Granet Aix-en-Provence 1998, FIAC Paris 2000, Marlborough Graphics London 2003, Schloss Gottorf Schleswig Germany 2003; gp exhibitions incl: The Vigorous Imagination – New Scottish Art (Scottish Nat Gallery of Modern Art, Edinburgh) 1987, The New British Painting tour USA 1988, Scottish Art Since 1990 (Scottish Nat Gallery of Modern Art Edinburgh and The Barbican London) 1989, Glasgow's Great British Art Exhibition 1990, Through The Artists Glass (Marlborough Graphics London) 1991, Scottish Art since 1900 (Gallery of Modern Art Edinburgh) 1992, The Portrait Now (Nat Portrait Gallery London) 1993, The Line of Tradition (Royal Scot Acad Edinburgh) 1994, An American Passion (Glasgow Museum and Royal Coll of Art London) 1994, Su Carta – On Paper (Galleria D'Arte Il Gabbiano Rome) 1996, Mirror Image (National Gallery London) 1998, L'Ecole de Londres (Musée Maillol Paris) 1998; work in the collections of: Aberdeen Art Gallery, The British Cncl, Birmingham Art Gallery, Contemporary Art Soc, Metropolitan Museum of Art NY, RCS, Robert Fleming Holdings Ltd, Scottish Nat Gallery of Modern Art, Scottish Nat Portrait Gallery, Southampton Art Gallery, Nat Portrait Gallery; awarded Grand Prix de Monte Carlo International Painting Prize 1998; *Style*— Stephen Conroy, Esq; ✉ Marlborough Fine Art, 6 Albemarle Street, London W1X 4BY (☎ 020 7629 5161, fax 020 7629 6338)

CONRY, Rt Rev Kieran Thomas; *b* 1 February 1951, Coventry, Warks; *Educ* Cotton Coll, Ven English Coll Rome, Gregorian Univ Rome (PhB, STB); *Career* ordained priest 1975; teacher Cotton Coll 1976–80, private sec to Archbishop Bruno Heim then to Archbishop Luigi Barbarito 1980–88; appointed monsignor 1984; priest Leek parish 1988, admin St Chad's Cathedral 1990, dir Catholic Media Office 1994–2001, priest St Austin's parish Stafford 2001, bishop of Arundel and Brighton 2001–14; memb Nat Conf of Priests 1988–93 (vice-chm 1992–93), chm Birmingham City Centre Churches 1992–93, trainer of counsellors Catholic Marriage Care 1993–2000; *Style*— The Rt Rev Kieran Conry; ✉ High Oaks, Old Brighton Road, Pease Pottage, West Sussex RH11 9AJ

CONSTABLE, Neil; *Career* RSC 1987–2003, exec dir Almeida Theatre 2003–10, chief exec Shakespeare's Globe 2010–; tstee Shakespeare Birthplace Tst, tstee Royal Theatrical Support Tst, govr GSM, memb SOLT; govr Clifton Coll; FGSM 2011, CCMI 2012; *Style*— Neil Constable, Esq; ✉ Shakespeare's Globe, 21 New Globe Walk, London SE1 9DT

CONSTABLE, Paule; da of Wing Cdr Paul Constable, RAF, AFC, and Evelyn Rose Hadley; *b* 9 November 1966; *Educ* Goldsmiths Coll London; *m* Ian Richards; 1 da (Morgan Jezebel Richards b 14 May 1996), 1 s (Bram Willoughby Moon Richards b 6 August 1998); *Career* lighting designer; assoc dir Nat Theatre, assoc Lyric Hammersmith, assoc Matthew Bourne's New Adventures; appts as lighting electrician incl: Midnight Design Ltd 1988–1990, Opera 80 (dep) 1990, Edinburgh Int Theatre (chief for Churchill Theatre 1990, dep chief for Playhouse Theatre 1991), English Shakespeare Co (chief) 1990–91, Rose English's The Double Wedding (prodn, LIFT) 1991, Shared Experiences UK tour of Anna Karenina (prodn) 1991, Rosie Lee (prodn) 1992, Mayfest (chief) 1992; appts as prodn mangr incl: International Workshop Festival 1990, Theatre de Complicité's The Winters Tale (UK tour) 1992, Theatre de Complicité's The Street of Crocodiles (World tour) 1993–94; tstee Cmmn to Promote Ribald Discourse Amongst Lighting Designers; memb Assoc of Lighting Designers; fell Goldsmiths Coll; hon fell: Rose Bruford Colll, Central Sch of Speech and Drama; colleague Liverpool Inst for Performing Arts; *Theatre* prodns incl: The Resistable Rise of Arturo Ui (7:84 Scotland) 1991, Scotland Matters (7:84 Scotland) 1992, The Street of Crocodiles (Theatre de Complicité/RNT (Olivier Award nomination for Best Lighting Design 1993)) 1992, Billy Liar (RNT Mobil touring prodn) 1992, India Song (Theatr Clwyd) 1993, Bondagers (Traverse and Donmar Warehouse) 1993, The Three Lives of Lucie Cabrol (Theatre de Complicité) 1994, Omma, Oedipus and the Luck of Thebes (Young Vic) 1994, The Slab Boys Trilogy (Young Vic) 1994, Out of a House Walked a Man (Theatre de Complicité/RNT) 1994, A Minute Too Late (Theatre de Complicité) Lucky (David Glass Mime Ensemble) 1995, Spring Awakening (RSC) 1995, Tartuffe (Royal Exchange) 1995, The Jungle Book (Young Vic) 1995, Henry IV (parts I & II, English Touring Theatre) 1996, A Christmas Carol (Lyric Hammersmith) 1996, Oliver Twist, The Servant, The Dispute, Pericles, The Prince of Homburg, The Mysteries (RSC) 1997, The Caucasian Chalk Circle (RNT) 1997, Beckett Shorts (RSC) 1997, Waves, Three Sisters, The Weir (Royal Court Upstairs) 1997, Morebinyon Tales (Young Vic and Broadway) 1997, Uncle Vanya (RSC/Young Vic) 1998, Haram and the Sea of Stories (RNT) 1998, Amadeus (Old Vic) 1998, Blasted, Little Foxes, Poor Superman, Saint Joan, War Horse (Tony Award), The Light Princess, The Curious Incident of the Dog in the Night-time (Olivier and Tony Awards), Vernon God Little, Behind the Beautiful Forevers, Wonder.Land, Don Carlos (Olivier Award), The Chalk Garden (Olivier Award), The Cripple of Inishmaan, His Dark Materials (Olivier Award), Wolf Hall, This House; *Opera* Magic Flute (Opera North) 1994 and 1997, Death of the Carmelites (Guildhall School) 1995, Worthur (English Touring Opera) 1995, Life with an Idiot (ENO) 1995, Ines de Castro (Scottish Opera) 1996, Don Giovanni (WNO) 1996, Sweeny Todd (Opera North) 1998, Fidelio (Wellington Int Festival NZ) 1998, Carmen, Faust, Rigoletto, The Marriage of Figaro, The Magic Flute, Macbeth and numerous prodns for Royal Opera House, Glyndebourne, ENO, Met Opera NY, Scottish Opera, Opera National du Rhin, WNO and throughout Europe, N America, Aust and NZ; *Dance* incl: The Goldberg Variations, Seven Deadly Sins (Royal Ballet), Naked (Ballet Boyz), La Baiser de la Fe (Birmingham Royal Ballet), Sleeping Beauty, Dorian Gray and Play Without Words (all Matthew Bourne); *Awards*: Opera Award for Lighting 2013 (first recipient), White Light Award for Lighting Design 2013 (for Curious Incident of the Dog in the Night-Time), Hospital Award for Contribution to Theatre 2015, Helpmann Award 2015 (for Les Miserables Aust), LA Drama Desk Award (for Sleeping Beauty, Les Miserables and War Horse), NY Critics Circle Award and Drama Desk Award (for War Horse and Curious Incident of the Dog in the Night-Time on Broadway); *Recreations* travel, cricket, running, mountains, surf; *Style*— Ms Paule Constable

CONSTANCE, Angela; MSP; *b* 15 July 1970, Blackburn, W Lothian; *Educ* Univ of Glasgow, Univ of Stirling; *Career* social worker 1997–2007; cncllr W Lothian Council 1997–2007; MSP (SNP): Livingston 2007–11, Almond Valley 2011–; Scottish Govt: min for skills and lifelong learning 2010–11, min for children and young people 2011, min for youth employment 2011–; Scottish Govt: cabinet sec for training, youth and women's employment 2014–16, cabinet sec for educn and lifelong learning 2014–16, cabinet sec for communities, social security and equalities 2016–; *Style*— Ms Angela Constance, MSP; ✉ The Scottish Parliament, Edinburgh EH99 1SP; Unit 4, Ochil House, Owen Square, Livingston EH54 6QF (☎ 01506 460403, e-mail angela.constance.msp@parliament.scot)

CONSTANT, Richard Ashley Meyricke; MBE (1983); s of Maj Ashley Henry Constant (d 1985), and Mabel Catherine (Kate), *née* Meyricke (d 1972); *b* 25 November 1954, Alberta, Canada; *Educ* King's Sch Canterbury, RMA Sandhurst, Univ of Durham (BA); *m* 1984, Melinda Jane, da of late H J Davies; 2 s (Llewelyn Ashley Meyricke b 1985, Tristam Ashley Meyricke b 1987), 2 da (Sophia Louise Meyricke, Rosanna Catherine Meyricke (twins) b 1989); *Career* cmmnd Royal Green Jackets 1973, ret with the rank of Maj; merchant banker Robert Fleming & Co Ltd 1985–89; chief exec Gavin Anderson & Company UK Ltd 1999–, chm and chief exec Gavin Anderson Worldwide 2000–09, pres and ceo Kreab Gavin Anderson 2009–12, chm Bara Kali Ltd 2013–; non-exec dir: Austin Reed Gp plc 1992–2001, Fibrowatt Ltd 1992–2005, Homeland Renewable Energy Inc 2007–, Living PlanIT SA 2010–; dir: Samburumburu Ltd (Kenya) 2003–, Africa Rising Gp Ltd; vice-chm Global Reputation.com Inc 2013–; dep chm LFA2014 (Laikipia Farmers Assoc) 2014–; snr advr GEOREACH Ltd 2014–; COO Living PlanITSA 2015–; tstee Help for Heroes 2007–; *Recreations* shooting, eventing, fishing; *Clubs* Royal Green Jackets, Muthaiga Farmers, Turf, Rumuruti; *Style*— Richard Constant, Esq, MBE; ✉ Sosian Ranch, Rumuruti, PO Box 6, Kenya (e-mail Richard@RichardConstant.com)

CONSTANTINE, David John; s of William Bernard Constantine, of Deganwy, N Wales, and Bertha, *née* Gleave; *b* 4 March 1944; *Educ* Manchester Grammar, Wadham Coll Oxford (BA, DPhil); *m* 9 July 1966, Helen Frances, da of Richard Stanley Best; 1 da (Mary Ann b 27 Nov 1968), 1 s (Simon Martin b 1 Oct 1972); *Career* sr lectr in German Univ of Durham 1979–80 (lectr 1969–79), fell in German The Queen's Coll Oxford 1980–2000; fndr memb Durham Cyrenians charity for homeless (sec 1972–80); jt ed Modern Poetry in Translation 2003–12; FRSL 2007; *Books* poetry: A Brightness to Cast Shadows (1980), Watching for Dolphins (1983, Alice Hunt Barlett Award), Madder (1987, Southern Arts Literature Prize), New and Selected Poems (1991), Caspar Hauser (1994), The Pelt of Wasps (1998), Something for the Ghosts (2002), Collected Poems (2004), Nine Fathom Deep (2009), Elder (2014); fiction: Davies (1985), Back at the Spike (1994), Under the Dam (2005), The Shieling (2009), Tea at the Midland (2012, Frank O'Connor Award 2013); trans: Selected Poems of Friedrich Hölderlin (1990, new edn 1996), Goethe's Elective Affinities (1994), Kleist: Selected Writings (1997), Hölderlin's Sophocles (2001), H M Enzensberger: Lighter than Air (2002), Goethe: Faust Part I (2005), Goethe, Faust Part II (2009), Goethe: The Sorrows of Young Werther (2012), Bertolt Brecht: Love Poems (with Tom Kuhn, 2014), Volker Braun: Rubble Flora (with Karen Leeder, 2014); biography: Hölderlin (1988), Fields of Fire, A Life of Sir William Hamilton (2001);

academic works: Early Greek Travellers and the Hellenic Ideal (1984, Runciman Prize), The Literary Agenda: Poetry (2013); *Recreations* walking; *Style*— David Constantine, Esq; ✉ 1 Hill Top Road, Oxford OX4 1PB (e-mail david.constantine@queens.ox.ac.uk)

CONSTANTINIDES, Prof Anthony George; s of George Anthony Constantinides, and Paraskeve Constantinides Skaliondas; *b* 1 January 1943; *Educ* The Pancyprian Gymnasium, Univ of London (BSc, PhD); *m* 21 Dec 1968, Pamela Maureen, da of Anthony Robert Bowman (ka 1940); 1 s (George Anthony b 21 Oct 1975); *Career* sr research fell PO Research Dept 1968–70, prof in signal processing Imperial Coll of Science and Technol 1983– (lectr then reader 1970–83), hon visiting prof Inst of Archaeology UCL; author of six books and over 200 papers in learned jls on aspects of digital signal processing; FIEE 1985, FRSA 1986, FIEEE 1997 (MIEEE 1978), FREng 2004; Officier dans l'Ordre des Palmes Académiques (France); *Recreations* reading; *Style*— Prof Anthony Constantinides; ✉ Imperial College London, Department of Electrical and Electronic Engineering, Exhibition Road, London SW7 2BT (☎ 020 7594 6233)

CONSTANTINOU, Achilleas; s of Nicos Constantinou (d 1971), of London, and Efthymia, *née* Cleanthous; *b* 21 April 1948; *Educ* Arnos Secdy Modern Sch Southgate, Waltham Forest Tech Coll, KCL (LLB); *m* Androulla, da of George Georgallides; 3 s (Alexander Nicholas b 21 June 1981, Nicholas George b 3 May 1982, Marcus Aristos b 18 July 1990), 1 da (Lana Marie b 4 Aug 1984); *Career* started fashion business Aristos of London with late bro Aristos at 45 Carnaby St in 1966, joined family co full time in 1971, by 1973 owned 6 retail outlets in Carnaby St and Oxford St, a wholesale showroom in Great Portland St and headquarters in Marylebone, subsequently added retail stores in Duke St (London) and Lausanne, Switzerland, and franchised stores in Chicago and Washington DC; relocated showrooms to Mortimer St and subsequently to larger premises in Highgate N London; now focuses exclusively on designing, manufacturing, wholesaling and retailing exclusive ladies special occasionwear under the Ariella brands; was honoured by a royal visit by Princess Anne in 1992 to celebrate co's 25th anniversary; chm and ceo Ariella Fashions Ltd & Group of Cos (two Woman Fashion Awards for Best Cocktail Dress and Best Evening Dress 1985, Br Apparel Export Award 1996, Queen's Award for Export Achievement 1998, UK Fashion Export Award 2008, UKFT Fashion Export Award 2010, HSBC Business Thinking Award 2010, finalist UKFT Fashion Award 2013 and 2014), launched Ariella Couture label 2012 and Ariella London retail brand 2015, opened flagship stores at Brent Cross 2015 and Bluewater 2016 and multiple retail outlets within House of Fraser, Oxford Street, Westfield, Shepherd's Bush and selected stores countrywide, as well as e-stores with Debenhams, John Lewis, House of Fraser and ariella.com online; fndr Br Fashion & Design Protection Assoc 1974 (which succeeded in gaining copyright protection extended to cover original fashion garment designs in 1980), advsr to Govt on amendments to Design Copyright and Patents Act 1988, UK rep EEC meeting of Assoc Européene des Industries de L'Habillement, fndr memb Fashion Indust Action Gp (responsible for formation of Br Fashion Cncl (BFC)), fndr memb and dir Br Fashion Cncl 1984–2010, former chm BFC Mainstream Ctee, former memb Advsy Bd London Fashion Exhibition, memb Bd of Management and former chm of the Women's Wear Exec Ctee Br Knitting and Clothing Export Cncl (BKCEC, now UK Fashion Exports), memb Grad Fashion Week Advsy Bd 2007, memb UK Fashion and Textiles Assoc 2009; memb Bd Skillset UK 2007; memb Finance Ctee UKFT 2010, memb Bd UKFT 2011; memb Gray's Inn; *Books* Memorandum on the Law of Copyright, Design Protection (contrib); *Recreations* charitable fundraising, historic cars, property developments, backgammon; *Style*— Achilleas Constantinou, Esq; ✉ Ariella House, 94–96 Great North Road, London N2 0NL (☎ 020 8883 7288, e-mail ac@ariella.co.uk, website www.ariella.com)

CONTE HELM, Marie; *b* 13 November 1949, New York City; *Educ* City Univ of NY (BA), East West Center Univ of Hawaii (MA); *Career* lectr art history Leeward Community Coll Hawaii 1973–74, cultural offr Japan Info Centre Embassy of Japan London 1975–79, lectr in art history Sunderland Poly 1979–86, head Japanese Studies Div and reader in Japanese studies Univ of Sunderland 1986–94, reader in Japanese studies Univ of Northumbria 1994–99; visiting prof Univ of Northumbria 1999–; The Daiwa Anglo-Japanese Fndn: dir 1999–2000, DG 2000–11; exec dir UK-Japan 21st Century Gp 2011–; memb: British Assoc for Japanese Studies (hon sec 1992–94), Royal Soc for the Encouragement of Arts, Manufacturers and Commerce; memb Cncl Japan Soc 1992–96 and 2003–09, memb Educn Ctee Japan Festival 1991 1989–91 (N Regnl Ctee 1988–91), memb Ctee Japan Language Assoc 1990–94, chair Anglo-Japanese Women's Soc 1990–94; memb Culture and E Asian Working Gp of UK-Japan 2000 Gp 1992–; HEFCE subject assessor South and East Asian Studies 1996–99; *Books* Japan and the North East of England – From 1862 to the Present Day (1989, a Financial Times Book of the Year 1989, Japanese edn 1991), The Japanese and Europe: Economic and Cultural Encounters (1996); author of numerous articles and reviews; *Style*— Prof Marie Conte Helm

CONTI, Thomas A (Tom); s of Alfonso Conti (d 1961), of Paisley, Renfrewshire, and Mary McGoldrick (d 1979); *b* 22 November 1941; *Educ* Royal Scottish Acad of Music; *m* 1967, Katherine Drummond, da of Wilson George Drummond Tait, of Edinburgh; 1 da (Nina b 1973); *Career* actor, director and novelist; *Theatre* began 1960; London appearances incl: Savages (Royal Court and Comedy) 1973, The Devil's Disciple (RSC Aldwych) 1976, Whose Life Is It Anyway? (Mermaid and Savoy) 1978 (also NY 1979), They're Playing Our Song (Shaftesbury) 1980, Romantic Comedy (Apollo) 1983, Jeffrey Bernard Is Unwell (Lyric) 1990, The Ride Down Mount Morgan (Wyndhams) 1991, Present Laughter (also dir) 1993, Chapter Two (Gielgud) 1996, Jesus my Boy (Apollo)1998; as director: Last Licks (Broadway) 1979, Before the Party (Oxford Playhouse and Queen's) 1980, The Housekeeper (Apollo) 1982; *Television* incl: Madame Bovary, The Norman Conquests, The Glittering Prizes, The Quick and the Dead (TV film), The Beatte Klarsfeld Story (mini-series), Wright Verdicts (USA), Cinderella and Me, I Was a Rat, Donovan; *Film* incl: Galileo 1974, Flame 1974, Eclipse 1975, Full Circle 1977, The Duellists 1977, The Wall 1980, Merry Christmas Mr Lawrence 1983, Reuben Reuben 1983, American Dreamer 1984, Heavenly Pursuits 1985, Saving Grace 1985, Miracles 1986, Beyond Therapy 1987, Two Brothers Running 1988, That Summer of White Roses 1989, Shirley Valentine1989, Someone Else's America 1994, XSUB Down 1996, Something to Believe In 1996, Out of Control 1997, The Enemy 2000, Derailed 2004, Paid 2004, Beyond Friendship 2005, The Tempest 2010; *Awards* for Whose Life Is It Anyway?: Best Actor in a New Play SWET 1978, Best Stage Actor Variety Club of GB 1978, Tony for Best Actor 1979; *Books* The Doctor (2004); *Clubs* Garrick; *Style*— Tom Conti Esq

CONTRERAS, Prof Dame (Carmen) Marcela; DBE (2007); da of Dr Juan Eduardo Contreras (d 1995), of Coelemu, Chile, and Elena Mireya, *née* Arriagada; *b* 4 January 1942; *Educ* Dunalastair Br Sch for Girls Santiago Chile, Sch of Med Univ of Chile (clinical/immunology scholar, BSc, LMed, Medico-Cirujano, MD); *m* 1968 (m dis 1997); 1 s (Claudio b 10 Nov 1968), 1 da (Carolina b 1 May 1972); *Career* trg prog in internal med, immunology and immunohaematology (Univ of Chile) Univ Hosp J J Aguirre and Hosp San Juan de Dios Santiago 1968–72, lectr in immunology and immunohaematology Centre of Immunohaematology Univ Hosp J J Aguirre Santiago 1971–72, Br Cncl scholar Royal Postgraduate Med Sch and MRC Blood Gp Unit London 1972–74, head Immunohaematology Lab North London Blood Transfusion Centre Edgware 1974–78, sr registrar in haematology St Mary's Hosp London and Northwick Park Hosp Harrow 1978–80; North London Blood Transfusion Centre London: dep dir 1980–84, chief exec/med dir 1984–95; exec dir London and SE Zone Nat Blood Serv 1995–99, dir of diagnostics, development and research Nat Blood Serv 1999–; prof of transfusion med Royal Free and Univ Coll Hosp Med Sch 1998–, visiting prof Faculty of Applied Sciences Univ of the West of England 2004–; memb Cncl: Int Soc of Blood Transfusion (pres 1996–98), RCPath (chm Sub-Ctee on Transfusion Med 1994–95 and 1999–2001); pres Section of Pathology RSM 1992–94, pres Br Blood Transfusion Soc 2000–02; review ed Vox Sanguinis 1987–95 and 2003– (ed-in-chief 1996–2003), assoc ed Transfusion Alternatives In Transfusion Medicine 1989–96 and 1999–; memb Editorial Bd: Transfusion Medicine 1990–, Transfusion Medicine Reviews 1993–, Blood Reviews 1995–; hon sr lectr St Mary's Hosp London 1999–, hon memb MRC Blood Gp Unit; memb: bd of dirs NATA, Br Soc for Haematology, BMA, American Assoc of Blood Banks (AABB), Int Soc of Blood Transfusion (ISBT), Br Blood Transfusion Soc (BBTS), RSM (Sections of Pathology and Immunology), Euro Sch of Transfusion Med, Euro Cord Blood Banking Gp; hon academic Faculty of Medicine Univ of Buenos Aires 1989, Paul Harris fell Rotary Fndn of Rotary Int 1990, honoured guest lectr Hong Kong Red Cross Blood Transfusion Soc 1993; Zoutendyk Medal Univ of Johannesburg 1995, H R Nevanlinna Medal Helsinki 2002, ISBT Award for outstanding contrib to blood transfusion and transfusion medicine 2004, ACOBASMET & Gp CIAMT Transfusion Medicine Award 2004, AABB/BBTS/ISBT Int Women in Transfusion Award 2005; hon memb: Chilean Soc for Haematology 1990, Brazilian Soc for Haemotherapy 1993; FRCPEd 1992, FRCPath 1997 (MRCPath 1988), FRCP 1998, fell Acad Med Sci 2003; *Books* Blood Transfusion in Clinical Med (jtly, 8 edn 1987, 10 edn 1997), ABC of Transfusion (1990, 3 edn 1998), Blood Transfusion: The Impact of New Technologies (1990); author of over 300 pubns in the field of transfusion med; *Recreations* opera, theatre, walking, reading, training in developing countries, riding; *Clubs* International Medical, Haematology Travellers'; *Style*— Prof Dame Marcela Contreras, DBE

CONVILLE, Clare Benedicta; da of David Conville, of Blandford Forum, Dorset, and Margaret, *née* Bury (d 1967); *b* 14 October 1959, London; *Educ* Cranborne Chase Sch, Westminster, Univ of Bristol; *m* 1, 26 Oct 1984 (m dis), Simon Pell; m 2, 4 Aug 1989 (sep), Jonathan Riley; 2 s (Thomas b 18 Aug 1988, Edward b 14 Sept 1991), 1 da (Mary b 4 Aug 1993); *Career* Random House Children's Books: publicity and mktg dir 1989–91, publishing dir 1991–93; agent A P Watt 1993–2000, fndr and dir Conville & Walsh Ltd 2000–; *Recreations* reading, listening to classical music, bikram yoga; *Clubs* Academy; *Style*— Miss Clare Conville; ✉ Conville & Walsh Limited, Haymarket House, 28–29 Haymarket, London SW1Y 4SP (☎ 020 7393 3030, fax 020 7393 4210, e-mail clare@convilleandwalsh.com)

CONWAY, Dr Ashley V; *b* 7 September 1956; *Educ* St Edward's Sch Oxford, Univ of Southampton (BSc), Univ of London (PhD); *m* 7 July 1984, Martine Louise, *née* Jeronimus; 2 da (Emily Louise b 29 Aug 1987, Catherine May b 25 April 1993), 1 s (Joseph Jeronimus b 15 March 1989); *Career* psychologist specialising in therapy for trauma, anxiety and stress-related illness; sec Univ Psychology Soc 1977–79, hon psychologist Charing Cross Hosp 1985–95, psychologist Devonshire Clinic London 1986–91, trauma conslt PPC UK Ltd 1993–98; pt/t med res examining mind/body interactions 1985–, memb Cncl Hypnosis and Psychosomatic Med RSM 1998–; author of numerous published papers on related subjects in med and psychological jls; FRSM 1998; *Style*— Dr A V Conway; ✉ 150 Harley Street, London W1G 7LQ (☎ 020 3075 3150, e-mail drashley.conway@gmail.com, website www.drashleyconway.com)

CONWAY, Prof Sir Gordon Richard; KCMG (2005), DL (East Sussex 2006); s of Cyril Gordon Conway (d 1977), of Kingston, Surrey, and Thelma, *née* Goodwin (d 1992); *b* 6 July 1938; *Educ* Kingston GS, Kingston Tech Coll, Univ of Wales Bangor (BSc), Univ of Cambridge (DipAgSc), Univ of West Indies Trinidad (DTA), Univ of Calif Davis (PhD); *m* 20 March 1965, Susan Mary, da of Harold Mumford, of Winchester, Hants; 1 s (Simon Goodwin b 10 Feb 1967), 2 da (Katherine Ellen, Zoe Martha (twins) b 2 March 1973); *Career* entomologist State of Sabah Malaysia 1961–66, statistician Inst of Ecology Univ of Calif 1966–69; Univ of London: res fell and lectr Dept of Zoology & Applied Entomology Imperial Coll 1970–76, reader in environmental mgmnt 1976–80, prof of environmental technol 1980–88, chm Centre for Environmental Technol 1980–86 (dir 1977–80), dir Sustainable Agric Prog Int Inst for Environment and Devpt 1986–88; rep for India, Nepal and Sri Lanka The Ford Foundation New Delhi 1989–92, vice-chllr Univ of Sussex 1992–98 (now emeritus prof), pres Rockefeller Fndn NY 1998–2004, chief scientific advsr DfID 2004–09, prof of int devpt Imperial Coll London 2004– (visiting prof 1989–2004); pres RGS 2006–09; chm: Bd IDS 1992–98, Runnymede Cmmn on British Muslims and Islamaphobia 1996–98, Bd Visiting Arts 2005–09, UK Collaborative on Devpt Scis 2007–09, Montpellier Panel 2010–16; memb Royal Cmmn on Environmental Pollution 1984–88, dir Agriculture 4 Impact Imperial Coll London 2009–, memb Bd African Agricultural Technology Fndn 2010–15, memb Bd of Dirs Lawes Agricultural Tst 2011–, memb Kirkhouse Tst 2012–, memb Bd Meridian Inst 2012–; co-chm Living Cities 1999–2003; hon fell Univ of Wales Bangor, fell Imperial Coll London, Hon LLD Univ of Sussex, Hon DSc Univ of West Indies Trinidad, Hon DSc Univ of Brighton, Hon DUniv Open Univ; Hon FIBiol, FCGI, FAAAS, FRS, Hon FREng 2008; *Books* Pest and Pathogen Control (1980), After The Green Revolution (jtly, 1989), Unwelcome Harvest (jtly, 1991), The Doubly Green Revolution (1997), One Billion Hungry: Can we feed the world? (2012), African Farmers in the Digital Age (jtly, 2016); *Recreations* travel, music; *Clubs* Reform; *Style*— Prof Sir Gordon Conway, KCMG, DL, FRS, Hon FREng; ✉ Imperial College, 15 Princes Gardens, London SW7 1NA

COOGAN, Steve; *b* 14 October 1965, Manchester; *Educ* Manchester Poly; *Career* comedian, actor and writer; co-fndr Baby Cow Productions 1999; Showbusiness Personality of the Year Variety Club Awards 1999, Perrier Award 1992 *Television* incl: Spitting Image (various voices) 1984, Paul Calf's Video Diary 1993, The Day Today 1994, Knowing Me, Knowing You with Alan Partridge 1994, Paul Calf's Wedding Video (Three Fights, Two Weddings and a Funeral) 1994, Coogan's Run 1995, The Tony Ferrino Phenomenon 1997, I'm Alan Partridge 1998–2002, Dr Terrible's House of Horrible 2001, Paul and Pauline Calf's Cheese and Ham Sandwich 2003, The Private Life of Samuel Pepys 2003, The All Star Comedy Show 2004, I Am Not an Animal 2004, Saxondale 2005, The Trip 2010 (Best Male Performance in a Comedy Prog BAFTA 2011), Mid Morning Matters with Alan Partridge 2010–11, Welcome to the Places of My Life 2012 (Best Male Performance in a Comedy Programme BAFTA 2013); *Radio* incl: On the Hour (BBC Radio 4) 1991–92 (Best Radio Comedy Br Comedy Awards 1992), Knowing Me, Knowing You with Alan Partridge (BBC Radio 4) 1992–93; *Film* incl: The Indian in the Cupboard 1995, The Wind in the Willows 1996, The Parole Officer 2001 (also writer), 24 Hour Party People 2002, Around the World in 80 Days 2004, A Cock and Bull Story 2005, Marie Antoinette 2006, Hot Fuzz 2007, Tropic Thunder 2008, In The Loop 2009, Night at the Museum 2: Battle of the Smithsonian 2009, Percy Jackson & the Olympians: The Lightning Thief 2010, Ruby Sparks 2012, Despicable Me 2 2013, Alan Partridge: Alpha Papa 2013 (also writer), Philomena 2013 (also writer, Best Adapted Screenplay BAFTA 2014); *Style*— Steve Coogan; ✉ c/o Baby Cow Productions, 77 Oxford Street, London W1D 2ES (☎ 020 7399 1267, fax 020 7399 1262, website www.babycow.co.uk)

COOK, Alan Ronald; CBE (2006); s of late Ronald Joseph Cook, and Dorothy, *née* Wills; *b* 23 September 1953, Wembley, Middx; *Educ* Ealing GS for Boys; *m* 20 Sept 1970, Anita, *née* Kelleher; 2 s (Christopher b 23 April 1978, Martin b 6 March 1986), 1 da (Jennifer b 10 April 1981); *Career* Prudential Assurance Co Ltd 1970–93, sr vice-pres Jackson National Life USA 1993–96; Prudential Assurance Co Ltd: acquisitions dir 1996–97, md gen insurance 1997–99, md retail insurance ops 1999–2000, chief exec insurance servs

C

2000–01, chief operating offr UK and Europe 2001–02; chief exec National Savings and Investments 2002–06, md Post Office Ltd 2006–10; govr Inst of Financial Servs 2005–08; chm Permanent TSB Gp Hldgs (formerly Irish Life and Permanent Gp Hldgs) 2011–; non-exec dir: Sainsbury's Bank 2011–, MetLife Europe 2013–; chm Highways Agency 2011–14; non-exec dir: Financial Ombudsman Service 2008–11, Dept for Transport 2009–14, Office of Fair Trading 2010–11; chm Action for ME 2010–; chm Univ of Bedfordshire 2011–; Freeman City of London, memb Worshipful Co of Insurers 2005; FCII 1975, FRSA 2000, FCIM 2005; *Recreations* family, fell walking, swimming; *Style*— Alan Cook, Esq, CBE; ✉ e-mail alan.cook@orchard-grange.co.uk

COOK, Alastair Nathan; CBE (2016, MBE 2011); *b* 25 December 1984, Gloucester; *Educ* Bedford Sch; *Career* cricketer; Essex CCC 2003–; England: 75 Test caps (capt 2012–), 45 one day int appearances (capt 2011–), 2 Twenty20 appearances, Test debut v India Nagpur 2006, one day int debut v Sri Lanka Old Trafford 2006, capt under 19 team World Cup 2004; NBC Denis Compton Award 2003, 2004 and 2005, Cricket Writers' Club Young Cricketer of the Year 2005, Professional Cricketers Assoc Young Player of the Year 2005 and 2006; *Style*— Alastair Cook, Esq, CBE; ✉ England and Wales Cricket Board, Lord's Cricket Ground, St John's Wood Road, London NW8 8QZ

COOK, Alistair Copland Campbell; s of George Arthur Campbell Cook (d 1978), of Edinburgh, and Margaret Maule, *née* McMurtrie (d 1987); *b* 3 July 1953; *Educ* Daniel Stewart's Coll Edinburgh, Univ of Aberdeen (BSc), Univ of Strathclyde; *m* 22 June 1979, Dr Glynis Elizabeth, da of Douglas Cruickshank Watson; 3 s (Stuart b 9 Dec 1982, Richard b 7 Dec 1984, Graeme b 19 June 1988); *Career* articled clerk Touche Ross & Co Edinburgh 1976–80, mangr Price Waterhouse Hong Kong 1980–84, sr mangr Price Waterhouse London 1984–87, fin dir and co sec D'Arcy Masius Benton & Bowles Ltd London 1987, chief fin offr DMB&B Holdings Ltd (UK, Ireland and Middle East) 1990–95, chief fin offr Ammirati Puris Lintas UK/Northern Europe 1996–2000; McCann-Erickson: sr vice-pres and regnl fin dir Central and Eastern Europe 2000–02, exec vice-pres and chief fin offr EMEA 2003–06; divnl chief fin offr Chime Communications plc 2008–10, chief fin offr Spark44 Worldwide (jt venture with Jaguar Land Rover) 2011–; memb Fin Ctee EACA 1998–2006; tstee and hon treas Int Family Health 1996–2003; MICAS 1979, MIPA 1990, FRSA 2005; *Recreations* golf, motoring, tennis, travel, Scottish art; *Clubs* RAC, Hever Golf, Hong Kong Cricket; *Style*— Alistair C C Cook, Esq; ✉ 4 Drummond Hall, Swaylands, Penshurst, Kent TN11 8DF (☎ 01892 871421); Spark44 Worldwide, Morelands, 5–23 Old Street, London EC1V 9HL (☎ 020 3150 0044)

COOK, Christopher Paul; s of Edward Peter Cook, of Great Broughton, N Yorks, and Joyce, *née* Layland; *b* 24 January 1959; *Educ* Barnard Castle Sch, Univ of Exeter (BA, combined arts prize, Gladys Hunkin poetry prize), RCA (MA, J Andrew Lloyd scholar, John Minton travel award), Accademia di Belle Arti Bologna (Italian Govt scholar); *m* (m dis) Jennifer Jane, da of Edward John Mellings; 2 s (Matthew b 13 Jan 1983, Samuel b 3 Nov 1988); *Career* artist, poet; Univ of Plymouth: sr lectr 1992–, assoc prof 2010–; visiting lectr RCA 1990–99; guest artist Stadelschule Frankfurt-am-Main 1991, visiting artist Academie van Beeldende Kunsten Rotterdam 1992, visiting fell Ruskin Sch Univ of Oxford 1993, distinguished visiting artist Calif State Univ Long Beach 1994, visiting artist BHU Varanasi India 1995, Arts Cncl residency Eden Project Cornwall 2001, visiting artist Univ of Memphis 2004, Bogliasco fell Liguria Italy 2013; PAS scholar Br Sch at Rome 2008–09; Br Cncl Award 2004, Daiwa Award 2005, AHRC Award Yokohama Triennial 2005, Br Cncl Award Beijing 2006; *Solo Exhibitions* incl: Camden Arts Centre 1985, Br Cncl Amsterdam 1985, Spacex Gallery Exeter 1986, Galleria Maggiore Bologna 1987, Benjamin Rhodes Gallery 1988, 1990 and 1993, The Cleveland Gallery Middlesbrough 1989, Plymouth Arts Centre 1989, Stadelschule Frankfurt-am-Main 1991, Kasteel van Rhoon Rotterdam 1992, Darlington Arts Centre 1992, Oldham Museum 1992, Northern Centre for Contemporary Art Sunderland 1994, Collins Gallery Glasgow 1995, Angel Row Nottingham 1995, Plymouth City Museum 1995, Galerie Helmut Pabst Frankfurt 1995 and 1999, Jason & Rhodes Gallery 1996, Haugesund Kunstforening 1997, De Beyerd Breda 1999, Heidelberger Kunstverein 2000, Bundanon Tst North Nowra 2000, Hirschl Contemporary Art London 2000 and 2001, Ferens Hull 2001, Towner Eastbourne 2001, Koraalberg Gallery Antwerp 2002, EZG Galerie Frankfurt 2003, Art Museum Memphis 2004, Mary Ryan Gallery NY 2004 and 2007, Yokohama Museum 2005, Today Art Museum Beijing 2007, Eyestorm UK (with Susan Derges) 2007, Fine Art Soc 2009, Mary Ryan Gallery NY 2010, Ryan Lee Gallery NY 2013, Art First London 2014; *Group Exhibitions* incl: The Sheffield Open (Mappin Gallery) 1985, The Camden Annual 1984 1985 (first prizewinner), Romantic Visions (Camden Arts Centre) 1988, Minories Colchester 1988, Figure 2 – A Personal Mythology (Welsh Arts Cncl tour) 1988, Met Museum of Art NY 1989, Eros in Albion (Casa Masaccio San Giovanni Valdarno) 1989, 3 Ways (Br Cncl/RCA tour to Eastern Europe) 1990–94, Modern Painters (Manchester City Art Gallery) 1990, Da Bacon a Oggi (Palazzo Vecchio Florence) 1991, EAST (The Norwich Gallery) 1991, Bristol City Museum 1992, Camouflage (Br Cncl tour) LA 1994, 27e Festival International de la Peinture Cagnes-sur-Mer 1995, European Union Artists (Univ of Bangkok) 1995, de Peus a Terra (Galeria 4RT Barcelona) 1996, John Moores XXI (Walker Art Gallery Liverpool) 1999 (prizewinner), West by South West (Kunstforening Stavanger) 1999, Kunstenkunst (Stade Museum Hamburg) 2001, East of Eden (Spacex Gallery Exeter) 2002, Crossing Borders (Morley Gallery London) 2003, Site and Situation (Univ of Southern Calif LA) 2003, Yale Center for British Art 2005, Leaded (Univ of Richmond touring exbhn USA) 2007, Trace and Transience (CCANW Devon) 2007, Tempo Real (Br Sch at Rome) 2008, Spazi Aperti (Accademia di Romania Rome) 2009, Dust on the Mirror (Djanogly Gallery Nottingham) 2010 and (ICA Singapore) 2011, Drawings for the New Century (Minneapolis Museum of Art USA) 2011, Grey (Fitzwilliam Museum Cambridge) 2011, John Moores Liverpool 2014; *Poetry* incl: New Nerves (1983), The Choosing and other Poems (1984), A Mythic Cycle (1989), A Lowdown Ecstasy (1991), Pilgrimage III (Into Night) (1992), Dust on the Mirror (1997), For and Against Nature (2000), A Thoroughbred Golden Calf (2003), Falls at Ono on the Kiso Road (2014); *Style*— Christopher Cook, Esq; ✉ e-mail c1cook@plymouth.ac.uk, website www.cookgraphites.com

COOK, Christopher William Batstone; s of Cecil Batstone Cook (d 1965), and Penelope, *née* Mayall (d 2003); *b* 21 January 1951; *Educ* Eton; *m* 15 July 1978 (m dis 1991), Margaret Anne, da of Maj John Christopher Blackett Ord (d 1996), of Whitfield Hall, Northumberland; 1 da (Emma b 1980), 2 s (Edward b 1982, Benjamin b 1983); m 2, 11 April 1997, Emma Caroline Faber, *née* Miller-Stirling; *Career* Lloyd's broker; dir C T Bowring & Co (Insurance) Ltd 1980–91, md Marsh & McLennan Worldwide 1988–91, chief exec Johnson and Higgins (Aviation) 1991–98, md Aviation and Space J & H Marsh McLennan 1998–, md Marsh Aviation 1999–2004; *Recreations* shooting, stalking, fishing; *Style*— Christopher W B Cook, Esq; ✉ 45 Eland Road, London SW11 5JX (☎ 020 7228 5937, fax 020 7350 2998, mobile 07889 829410, e-mail cwb.cook@freeserve.uk)

COOK, David Julian; CB (2015); s of Stanley Cook, and Dorothy Mary, *née* Daft; *b* 15 July 1962; *Educ* Colchester Royal GS, Merton Coll Oxford (MA), Coll of Law London; *m* 10 Sept 1988, Christine Margaret Alice, da of late Keith Roy Barnard; 2 s (Jonathan William David b 13 May 1995, Matthew Henry David b 12 Dec 2001), 1 da (Katherine Sarah Elizabeth b 1 April 1999); *Career* articled clerk then slr Freshfields 1988–91; Office of the Parly Counsel: asst counsel 1991–95, sr asst counsel 1995–99, dep Parly counsel 1999–2003, Parly counsel 2003–, on secondment as head of drafting team Tax Law Rewrite Project Inland Revenue 2003–05, second Parly counsel 2007–; *Recreations* walking, archaeology, tennis, Victorian novels; *Style*— David Cook, Esq, CB

COOK, Prof Gordon Charles; s of Charles Francis Cook (d 1983), and Kate, *née* Grainger, formerly Kraninger (d 1979); *b* 17 February 1932, Wimbledon; *Educ* Wellingborough GS, Kingston upon Thames GS, Raynes Park GS, Royal Free Hosp Sch of Med London (BSc, MB BS, MRCS, LRCP, MD, DSc, Charlotte Brown prize, Cunning award, Legg award); *m* 1963, Elizabeth Jane, da of late Rev Stephen Noel Agg-Large, of Longparish, Hants; 3 da (Rosamund Elizabeth b 7 June 1967, Caroline Jane b 10 June 1969, Susanna Catherine b 23 July 1973), 1 s (David Charles Stephen (twin) b 10 June 1969); *Career* cmmnd RAMC (Capt), seconded Royal Nigerian Army 1960–62; various appts Royal Free, Hampstead Gen, Royal Northern, Brompton and St George's Hosps 1958–63, lectr Royal Free Hosp Sch of Med and Makerere UC Uganda 1963–69; prof of med and conslt physician: Univ of Zambia 1969–74, Univ of Riyadh 1974–75, Univ of Papua New Guinea 1978–81; sr MO MRC 1975–76, sr lectr in clinical scis London Sch of Hygiene and Tropical Med 1976–97; hon conslt physician: Hosp for Tropical Diseases and UCLH 1976–97, St Luke's Hosp for the Clergy 1988–2009; visiting prof UCL 2000– (hon sr lectr in tropical med and infectious diseases 1981–2000), hon lectr in clinical parasitology Bart's Med Coll 1992–; research assoc Wellcome Tst Centre for the History of Medicine 1997–2002; visiting prof Univs of Basrah, Mosul and Doha; memb Editorial Bd: Jl of Infection (ed 1995–97), Postgraduate Medical Jl, Transactions of the Royal Society of Tropical Medicine and Hygiene; examiner RCP 1977–84; pres: Royal Soc of Tropical Med and Hygiene 1993–95, Osler Club of London 1993–95, Fellowship of Postgrad Med 2000–07 (memb Cncl 1989–2007, vice-pres 1996–2000), History of Med Section RSM 2003–04 (vice-pres 1994–96); vice-pres Erasmus Darwin Fndn Lichfield 2011– (chm 1994–2011); tstee Bookpower (formerly Educnl Low-Priced Sponsored Texts (ELST)) 1996–2011; Seamen's Hosp Soc: hon archivist 2002–, hon life govr 2007–; research assoc Greenwich Maritime Inst Univ of Greenwich 2003–; memb Exec Ctee and examiner Faculty of History and Philosophy of Medicine and Pharmacy 1997–, memb Cncl Galton Inst 2005–09; vice-chair Friends of the Florence Nightingale Museum 2005–09; Frederick Murgatroyd meml prize RCP jtly 1973; Hugh L'Etang Prize RSM 1999; Freeman City of London, Liveryman Worshipful Soc of Apothecaries 1981 (examiner Worshipful Soc of Apothecaries of London 1997–); memb various professional bodies incl: RSM 1962, MRS 1965, Br Soc of Gastroenterology 1968, Physiological Soc 1971, Assoc of Physicians of GB and I 1973, Med Soc of London 1976, Br Soc for the Study of Infection 1982, Soc of Authors 1985 (memb Cncl Med Writers' Gp 1995–, chm 1997–99), BMA, Harveian Soc, Hunterian Soc, JCHMT 1987–93; FRCP 1972, FRACP 1978, FLS 1989, FRCPE 2002, MRCS; *Publications* Acute Renal Failure (jt ed, 1964), Tropical Gastroenterology (1980), 100 Clinical Problems in Tropical Medicine (jtly, 1987, 2 edn 1998), Communicable and Tropical Diseases (1988), Parasitic Disease in Clinical Practice (1990), From the Greenwich Hulks to Old St Pancras: a history of tropical disease in London (1992), Gastroenterological Problems from the Tropics (ed, 1995), Travel-associated Disease (ed, 1995), Manson's Tropical Diseases (ed, 20 edn 1996, 21 edn 2003, 22 edn 2009), Victorian Incurables: A History of the Royal Hospital for Neuro-Disability, Putney (2004), John MacAlister's Other Vision: A History of the Fellowship of Postgraduate Medicine (2005), The Incurables Movement: An Illustrated History of The British Home (2006), Tropical Medicine: An Illustrated History of the Pioneers (2007), Disease in the Merchant Navy: A History of the Seamen's Hospital Society (2007), Health-care For All: History of a 'third world' dilemma (2009), Caribbean Diseases: Doctor George Low's expedition in 1901–02 (2009), Twenty-Six Portland Place: the early years of the Royal Society of Tropical Medicine and Hygiene (2011), Torrid Disease: memoirs of a tropical physician in the late twentieth century (2011), Origin of a Medical Specialty: the Seaman's Hospital Society and Tropical Medicine (2012), The Tropical Disease that Never Existed: A History of Sprue (2013), National Service Fifty Years Ago: Life of a Medical Conscript in West Africa (2014), The Rise and Fall of a Medical Speciality: London's Clinical Tropical Medicine (2014), Before the 'Germ Theory': A History of Cause and Management of Infectious Diseases Before 1900 (2015), Disease and Sanitation in Victorian Britain: lessons for the 'third world' (2015), The Milk Enzyme: Adventurers with the Human Lactase Polymorphism (2016), History of malabsorption in a warm environment (2016); *Recreations* walking, cricket, baroque and classical music, history (medical and scientific), philately; *Clubs* Athenaeum, MCC, Baconian (St Albans; pres 1995–96); *Style*— Prof Gordon Cook; ✉ 11 Old London Road, St Albans, Hertfordshire AL1 1QE (☎ 01727 869000)

COOK, Lindsay Mary; da of Francis John Cook (d 1972), and Elsie Mary, *née* Gilliatt; *b* 24 July 1951; *Educ* Havelock Comp Sch Grimsby, Open Univ (BA); *m* 1 May 1987, Tony Wilkinson, s of Ernest Wilkinson; 2 s (Rory b 14 Aug 1988, Gray b 27 Jan 1991); *Career* trainee journalist Grimsby Evening Telegraph 1969–74, reporter and consumer writer Morning Telegraph Sheffield 1974–76, freelance writer Sunday Times 1976–77, freelance contrib Money Mail (pt of Daily Mail) 1977–79, United Newspapers London 1977–86 (number 3 on newsdesk, features dept, dep London ed 1984), personal finance ed The Daily Telegraph 1986–89; The Times: money ed 1990–93, dep business ed 1993–94, business ed 1994–97; managing ed The Express 1997–98, gp managing ed and dir Express Newspapers 1998–2001 (editorial devpt dir 1998–2001), media conslt 2001–03, editorial dir CMP Information 2004–; Personal Finance Journalist of the Year 1987; *Books* The Money Diet, Three Months To Financial Fitness (1986), Working Mum: The Survival Guide (2000); *Recreations* food, theatre; *Style*— Miss Lindsay Cook; ✉ 10 Duncan Terrace, London N1 8BZ (mobile 07831 237030, fax 020 7837 4509)

COOK, Malcolm Roderick Grant; s of Harold Cook, of Warwickshire, and Brenda Eileen, *née* Moore; *b* 29 November 1955; *Educ* Univ of Bath (BSc Econ); *m* Ann Cook; 1 da (Victoria Ann b 12 March 1989); *Career* chartered accountant; Arthur Young Chartered Accountants 1977–84, gp accountant F H Thomkins plc 1984–86, business servs gp mangr Arthur Young 1986–87; Pannell Kerr Forster Birmingham: business servs gp mangr 1987–89, ptnr 1989–, managing ptnr 1991–; dir Birmingham Press Club Ltd; MInstD, ACA; *Style*— Malcolm Cook, Esq; ✉ Pannell Kerr Forster, New Guild House, 45 Great Charles Street, Queensway, Birmingham B3 2LX (☎ 0121 212 2222, fax 0121 212 2300, mobile 078 3159 0025)

COOK, Prof Nicholas John; s of John Manuel Cook (d 1994), and Enid May, *née* Robertson (1976); *b* 5 June 1950, Athens, Greece; *Educ* Univ of Cambridge (BA, MA, PhD), Univ of Southampton (BA); *m* 14 Feb 1975, Louise Catherine Bridget, da of Harry Elgie; 1 da (Chloe b 1984), 1 s (Christopher b 1987); *Career* lectr Univ of Hong Kong 1982–90; Univ of Southampton: prof of music 1990–99, research prof 1999–2003; prof of music then professorial research fell Royal Holloway Univ of London 2004–09, dir AHRC Research Centre for the History and Analysis of Recorded Music 2004–09, 1684 prof of music Univ of Cambridge 2009–; Br Acad Wolfson prof 2014–; DHL Univ of Chicago 2013; FBA 2001, fell Acad of Europe 2010; *Books* A Guide to Musical Analysis (1987), Musical Analysis and the Listener (1989), Music, Imagination and Culture (1990), Beethoven: Symphony No 9 (1993), Analysis Through Composition: Principles of the Classical Style (1996), Analysing Musical Multimedia (1998), Music: A Very Short Introduction (1998, revised edn 2000), The Schenker Project: Culture, Race and Music Theory in Fin-de-siècle Vienna (2007), Beyond the Score: Music as Performance (2013); co-edited and co-authored books and author of numerous articles; *Style*— Prof Nicholas Cook; ✉ Faculty of Music, West Road, Cambridge CB3 9DP

COOK, Patrick Donald; s of Donald George Herbert Cook (d 1992), of Henley-on-Thames, Oxon, and Doreen Elizabeth, *née* Simpson; *b* 11 July 1956; *Educ* Abingdon Sch, Pembroke Coll Oxford (MA); *m* 10 Oct 1981, Caroline Elizabeth, da of John Andrew Graves, of Barnstaple, Devon; 3 da (Megan Elizabeth b 25 April 1986, Florence Emma b 4 Oct

1989, Imogen Amy b 25 Nov 1994), 1 s (Charles Patrick (twin) b 25 Nov 1994); *Career* admitted slr 1981; ptnr Osborne Clarke 1986–, licensed insolvency practitioner 1989–; memb: Law Soc 1981, Insolvency Lawyers Assoc 1989, Insolvency Practitioners Assoc 1989, R3 Soc of Business Recovery Professionals 1989; *Recreations* sports (various), theatre, reading, gardening; *Style*— Patrick Cook, Esq; ✉ Osborne Clarke, One London Wall, London EC2Y 5EB

COOK, Prof Paul Derek; MBE (1985); s of James Walter Cook, and Florence, *née* Jefferay; *b* 12 March 1934; *Educ* QMC London (Sir John Johnson scholar, BSc, PhD); *m* 1954, Frances Ann, *née* James; 4 da; *Career* res scientist: MRC 1960–62, Middx Hosp Med Sch 1962–65; chm and md Scientifica-Cook Ltd 1962–; Brunel Univ: prof of laser technol 1986–97, prof of laser physics 1986–91, prof of environmental sci 1992–97; scientific advsr to: min for the Environment and Countryside DoE 1990–92, British Gas 1990–93; laser conslt BAe 1986–; responsible for design and devpt of numerous laser systems used in med and mil estab throughout world, originator and inventor of Laser Guidance Systems for weapon alignment in Tornados, contrib to Europe's first laser gyroscope, invented laser instrument that improves motor safety by detecting and correcting night myopia, established world's first Night Vision Clinic for treating night blindness disorders 1986, developed (and registered for patent) Reaction Time Exerciser Measurement Gauge (a means of registering and improving the response time of motor vehicle drivers and sports people) 2007; fndr and pres The Br Sci and Technol Tst (helping disabled children worldwide) 1985–96, originator Lena Appeal (sending med aid to sick children in Russia) 1991, fndr and pres Sci and Technol Tst (presenter Animal SciTech Awards) 2002; dep chm Conserve (Cons Govt Environmental Gp) 1990–92; envoy to Boris Yeltsin 1992; UK pres Japanese Zen Nippon Airinkai 1978–81; CEng, MIEE 1963; *Recreations* breeding and rearing exotic Japanese carp, inventing, experimenting with ideas, especially those related to improving safety on the roads, passion for early automobile number plates; *Style*— Prof Paul Cook, MBE; ✉ 252A Acton Lane, Chiswick, London W4 5DJ

COOK, Prof Sir Peter Frederic Chester; kt (2007); s of Maj Frederick William Cook, and Ada, *née* Shaw (d 1986); *b* 22 October 1936, Southend-on-Sea, Essex; *Educ* Ipswich Sch, Bournemouth Sch, Bournemouth Coll of Art, AA Sch of Architecture (AADipl); *m* 1960 (m dis 1990), Hazel, *née* Fennell; m 2, 1990, Dr Yael Reisner; 1 s (Alexander Guy b 1990); *Career* architect and teacher; asst in various offices in London and Bournemouth 1956–63, Taylor Woodrow Design Gp 1962–64, fndr memb Archigram Gp 1963–76, ptnr Cook and Hawley Architects 1979, prof of architecture HBK Städelschule Frankfurt-am-Main 1984–2002, Bartlett prof of architecture UCL 1990– (chm Bartlett Sch of Architecture 1990–2004), design princ HOK International 2004–, jt prof of architecture Royal Acad 2005–; projects incl: Graz Kunsthaus 2003, Vienna Univ of Economics Law Sch 2013, Bond Univ (Queensland) Architecture Sch 2013; work featured in numerous worldwide exhbns; advsr numerous architectural schools worldwide; chief designer extension of the Municipality of Pinto Madrid 2003–; dir ICA 1970–72, fndr dir Art Net 1972–79; Hon DTech Lund Univ Sweden 2011; memb: Euro Acad of Sci and Art 1998; RIBA 1968, RSA 1970, RA 2003; Commandeur de l'Ordre des Arts et des Lettres (France) 2002; *Awards* winner first prize for: old people's housing 1963, Monaco centre 1970, solar housing 1980, museum in lower Australia 1996, Graz Kunsthaus (now under construction) 2000; Los Angeles Medal American Inst of Architecture 1989, Jean Tschumi Medal Int Union of Architects 1998, Royal Gold Medal RIBA 2002, Gustav Eiffel Prize Ecole Spéciale d'architecture Paris 2005; *Books* Architecture: Action and Plan (1966), Experimental Architecture (1972), New Spirit in Architecture (1991), Six Conversations (1995), Primer (1998), Power of Contemporary Architecture (1999), Paradox of Contemporary Architecture (2001), Drawing: The Motive Force of Architecture (2008, revised edn 2013); *Recreations* listening to music, restaurants, gossip, walking; *Clubs* Arts; *Style*— Prof Sir Peter Cook; ✉ 54 Compayne Gardens, London NW6 3RY (☎ 07812 044063, e-mail peter.cook@ucl.ac.uk); Cook Robotham Architecture Bureau, 50A Rosebery Avenue, London EC1R 4RP (e-mail peter@crabstudio.net, website www.crab-studio.com)

COOK, Prof Peter John; CBE (1996); s of late John and Rose Cook, of Sale, Cheshire; *b* 15 October 1938; *Educ* Chorlton GS, Univ of Durham (BSc, DSc), ANU Canberra (MSc), Univ of Colorado Boulder (PhD); *m* 1961, Norma Irene; 2 s (John b 24 Nov 1964, Julian b 20 July 1968); *Career* geologist: Univ of Cambridge Gornergletcher Glaciological Expedition 1959, Univ of Durham Spitsbergen Expedition (ldr) 1960, Oil Search Gp Aust Bureau of Mineral Resources (BMR) 1961–64, Aust Nat Antarctic Res Expedition 1964–65, Phosphate Section BMR 1966–69; sr geologist Phosphate and Marine Geology BMR 1969–76, sr res fell in econ geology Res Sch of Earth Sciences ANU 1976–82 (chm of Faculty 1978–79, visiting fell 1982–90 and 1995), visiting fell Resource Systems Inst East-West Center Univ of Hawaii 1979, chief scientist BMR Div Continental Geology 1982–89, assoc dir BMR 1989–90, dir British Geological Survey 1990–98, exec dir Aust Petroleum Co-op Res Centre 1998–2003, chief exec CO2CRC 2003–11, chief exec CO2CRC Technologies 2003–11; dir PJC International 1998–, dir MineXchange Pty Ltd 2000–; conslt: Astrogeology Div US Geological Survey 1967, Le Nickel Exploration 1977, Agrico Chemical Co 1980, Esso Exploration 1981–82; prof Institut de Geologie Universite Louis Pasteur Strasbourg 1989; chm: ACT Div Geological Soc of Aust 1972–73, Consortium for Ocean Geosciences of Aust Univs 1980–82, Cwlth-state Hydrogeological Ctee 1983–87, Tech Prog Int Sedimentological Congress 1983–86; memb: Indian Ocean Working Gp Int Union of Geology and Geophysics 1974–78, Geosciences Delgn to China Aust Acad of Sciences 1978, Cncl Aust Inst of Marine Sciences 1979–85, Advsy Ctee Centre for Remote Sensing Univ of NSW 1985–90, Review Ctee Dept of Geology James Cook Univ 1987, Advsy Cncl Aust Nuclear Sci and Technol Orgn 1986–90, Advsy Bd Inst of Engrg Surveying and Space Geodesy Univ of Nottingham 1990–98, Geological Museum Advsy Panel Natural History Museum 1990–98, Advsy Bd Univ of Manchester, Earth Sciences Ctee NERC 1991–98, Advsy Bd Global Sedimentary Geology Prog 1991–96, Bd Mineral Industry Research Orgn 1991–98, Bd of Patrons Earth Centre Edinburgh 1992–98, Earth Science and Technol Bd NERC 1994–98; Adrian fell Univ of Leicester 1992–98, professorial fell Univ of Melbourne 2011–; chm: UNESCO/IOC Prog of Ocean Sci in Relation to Non-Living Resources 1985–2001, Forum of Dirs of Euro Geological Surveys 1997; chair Australian Cncl of Learned Academies Review of Unconventional Gas 2012–13; pres: Aust Geoscience Cncl 1987–88, Euro Geo Surveys 1995–96 (vice-pres 1997); memb: American Assoc of Petroleum Geologists, Geological Soc London, Geological Soc of Aust (chm 1972–73), Int Rels Ctee Australian Acad of Technol, Sci and Engrg 2001–05; Geological Soc of London Cope Medal 1997, Centenary Medal 2001, German Geological Soc Leopold von Buch Medal 2004, Aust Petroleum Exploration Assoc Lewis G Weeks Gold Medal 2004, French Order of Merit 2005, Greenman Award Int Energy Agency GHG Prog 2010, Peter Cook Centre for CSS Research Univ of Melbourne created in recognition of contribution to science 2012; fell Australian Acad of Technol, Sci and Engrg (FTSE) 1998, fell Geological Soc Aust 2007; *Publications* Sedimentology & Holocene History of a Tropical Estuary (1978), Phosphate Deposits of the World (1986), Australia: Evolution of a Continent (1990), Continental Shelf Limits: the scientific and legal interface (2000), IPCC Special Volume: Carbon Dioxide Capture and Storage (co-ordinating lead author, 2005), Clean Energy Climate and Carbon (2012), Engineering Energy: Unconventional Gas Production (2013), Geologically Storing Carbon: Learning from the Otway Project Experience (2014); author of 130 papers and articles in learned jls; *Recreations* skiing, walking, history, travel; *Clubs* Geological Soc, Commonwealth; *Style*— Prof Peter J Cook, CBE, FTSE; ✉ Forrest, Canberra, ACT 2603, Aus (☎ +61262396504, fax +61262396049, e-mail pjcook@pjcinternational.com, www.petercook.unimelb.edu.au)

COOK, Susan Lorraine (Sue); *née* Thomas; da of William Arthur Thomas, of Ickenham, Middx, and Kathleen May, *née* Prow; *b* 30 March 1949, Ruislip, Middx; *Educ* Vyner's GS Hillingdon, Univ of Leicester (BA, DLitt); *m* 1, 20 May 1981 (m dis 1987), John Christopher Williams, s of Leonard Williams (d 1988), of The Monkey Sanctuary, Looe, Cornwall; 1 s (Alexander Charles (Charlie) b 12 Oct 1982); partner 1986–2001, William James Macqueen; 1 da (Megan Jane Emily b 30 March 1988); m 2, 27 Aug 2004, Ian Sharp, s of Frederick Sharp, of Clitheroe, Lancs; *Career* radio prodr and broadcaster Capital Radio 1974–76, radio presenter of You and Yours, Making History, documentaries and topical features for BBC Radio 4 and World Service, reporter and presenter for BBC TV's Nationwide 1979–83; presenter BBC TV: Pebble Mill at One, Breakfast Time, Out of Court, Holiday, Crimewatch UK (until 1995), Daytime Live, Having a Baby, Children in Need Appeal, That's the Way the Money Goes, Omnibus at the Proms, The Story of the London Sinfonietta, Maternity Hospital, The Children's Royal Variety Performance, The Write Lines (BBC Oxford) 2009–; presenter Collectors' Lot and Hampton Court Palace (Channel 4), exec prodr Tracker (starring Ray Winstone) 2011; patron: Br Wireless Fund for the Blind, Rainbow Tst, Children's Liver Disease Fndn, Chipping Norton Literary Festival 2012–; ambass Prince's Tst; *Books* Accident Action (jtly, 1978), Crimewatch UK (jtly, 1987), The Crimewatch Guide to Home Security and Personal Safety (1988), On Dangerous Ground (fiction, 2006), Force of Nature (fiction, 2008); *Recreations* tennis, singing, spending time at home with the family; *Clubs* Arts; *Style*— Miss Sue Cook; ✉ John Miles Organisation, Cadbury Camp Lane, Clapton-in-Gordano, Bristol BS20 7SB (☎ 01275 854675, e-mail sue@suecook.com, website www.suecook.com); c/o Juliet Pickering, Blake Friedmann Literary, Film & TV Agency, 1st Floor Selous House, 5–12 Mandela Street, London NW1 0DU (☎ 020 7387 0842, fax 020 7691 6926, e-mail juliet@blackfriedmann.co.uk)

COOK, William (Bill); s of William James Cook, of Eltham, London, and Lillian Maud, *née* Avery; *b* 19 November 1955, London; *Educ* Colfe's GS; *m* 5 Nov 1988, Diana Helen (formerly Mrs Sangway); 1 da (Louise Sarah b 13 April 1980); *Career* Dept of Trade 1974–77, private sec to Stanley Clinton Davis MP 1977–79, private sec to Reginald Eyre MP 1979–80, DTI 1980–84, Cabinet Office 1984–87, HM Treasy 1987, Ernst & Young 1987–99 (ptnr 1994–99); Capgemini: variously head of public sector, finance dir, commercial dir and sales dir 1999–2009, ceo techology services 2009–11, ceo consulting services 2011–12, dir Bd Capgemini UK plc; dir Bd Working Links Ltd, dir Bd Sogeti Ireland Ltd; *Recreations* golf, cricket, bridge; *Clubs* Feldon Valley Golf, Long Compton Cricket, Old Colfeians Assoc; *Style*— Bill Cook, Esq; ✉ Capgemini UK, 40 High Holborn, London EC1N 2PB (☎ 07891 158934, e-mail billanddianac@aol.com)

COOKE, Dr Alistair Basil; OBE (1988); *see:* Lexden, Lord

COOKE, Christopher Edward Cobden; s of Reginald Garforth Cooke (d 1991), of Marlow, Bucks, and Phyllis Mary Blackburn, *née* Wilde (d 1992); *b* 18 April 1944; *Educ* King William's Coll IOM, Univ of Southampton (LLB); *m* 26 July 1969, (Greta) Yvonne, da of Raymond Vere Alberto (d 1979); 3 da (Lisa b 25 May 1971, Lucy b 11 March 1973, Lindy b 19 Jan 1977); *Career* slr; ptnr Rooks Rider (formerly Rooks & Co) London 1970– (currently sr ptnr); memb Int Ctee Soc of Tst and Estate Practitioners; memb: Law Soc 1969, Holborn Law Soc 1988, Int Tax Planning Assoc, Soc of Tst and Estate Practitioners; Freeman: City of London 1966, City of Monroe Louisiana 1986; Liveryman Worshipful Co of Makers of Playing Cards 1966; *Recreations* skiing; *Style*— Christopher Cooke, Esq; ✉ Rooks Rider, Challoner House, 19 Clerkenwell Close, London EC1R 0RR (☎ 020 7689 7000, fax 020 7689 7001, mobile tel 077 8522 5196, e-mail ccooke@rooksrider.co.uk)

COOKE, His Hon Judge David John; s of Matthew Peterson Cooke, of Rugby, and Margaret Rose; *b* 23 August 1956; *Educ* Lawrence Sheriff Sch Rugby, Trinity Coll Cambridge (MA); *m* 31 March 1979, Susan Margaret, da of Albert Arthur George, of Rugby; 1 s (Stephen b 1984), 1 da (Helen b 1986); *Career* slr; ptnr Pinsents (now Pinsent Masons) 1982–2001; district judge 2001–08, specialist circuit judge Chancery Div 2008–; hon bencher Lincoln's Inn 2016; memb: Law Soc; *Recreations* sailing, golf, competitive swimming; *Clubs* Olton Golf; *Style*— His Hon Judge David Cooke; ✉ Birmingham Civil Justice Centre, Bull Street, Birmingham B4 6DW

COOKE, Prof David John; s of John McKay Cooke (d 2001), of Glasgow, and Esther Doonan, *née* Burch (d 1982); *b* 13 July 1952; *Educ* Larbert HS, Univ of St Andrews (BSc), Univ of Newcastle upon Tyne (MSc), Univ of Glasgow (PhD); *m* 28 Sept 1979, Janet Ruth, da of Francis Salter; 2 da (Rachael Elizabeth b 2 Sept 1988, Esther Jane b 26 Feb 1991); *Career* basic grade clinical psychologist: Northumberland AHAs 1974–76, Greater Glasgow Health Bd 1976–78; sr clinical psychologist Gartnavel Royal Hosp Glasgow 1978–83; Douglas Inch Centre: princ clinical psychologist 1984, top grade clinical psychologist 1984–2007 (with greater responsibility 1989–); prof of forensic psychology Dept of Psychology Glasgow Caledonian Univ 1992–; visiting prof: Univ of Glasgow 1997–2001, Univ of Bergen 2006–, La Trobe Univ Melbourne Aust; Cropwood fell Inst of Criminology Univ of Cambridge 1986; Sr Award for outstanding lifetime contribution to forensic psychology Div of Forensic Psychology BPsS 2006, Medal of David the Invincible of the Armenian Philosophical Acad 2012; FBPsS 1986, FRSE 2004; *Books* Psychology in Prisons (with P Baldwin and J Howison, 1990), Treatment as an Alternative to Prosecution (1990), Psychological Disturbance in the Scottish Prison System: Prevalance, Precipitants and Policy (1994), Predicting Recidivism in a Scottish Prison Sample (with C Michie, 1997), International Perspectives on Psychopathy (with A Forth, J Newman and R Hare, 1997), Psychopathy: Theory, Research and Implications for Society (with A Forth and R Hare, 1998); *Recreations* sailing, cooking, opera, music, skiing, travel; *Clubs* Loch Lomond Sailing; *Style*— Prof David Cooke; ✉ Glasgow Caledonian University, Cowcaddens Road, Glasgow G4 0BA (☎ 0141 331 3019, fax 0141 211 8005, e-mail djcooke@rgardens.vianw.co.uk)

COOKE, (Sally) Del; da of Eirwyn (Tom) Rowlands, and Marlene, *née* Samson; *b* 3 September 1958, London; *Educ* Univ of Bristol (BSc), Univ of Nottingham (PGCE), Univ of Leicester (MBA), Nat Coll of Teaching and Leadership (NPQH); *m* July 1980, David W Cooke; 3 s (Ben b 15 March 1983, Sam b 22 Dec 1984, Toby b 6 June 1988); *Career* teacher TP Riley Community Sch W Mids 1980–82, teacher Coll of Richard Collyer Horsham 1990–96, teacher, head of maths, housemistress, dep head, actg head then head Cranleigh Sch 1993–2007, head Sir William Perkins's Sch Surrey 2007–14, head The Henrietta Barnett Sch 2014–; team inspr Ind Schs Inspectorate 2007–14, vice-chair Educn Ctee GSA 2011–14, memb Jt Assoc Curriculum Gp 2011–14; govr Halstead Prep Sch 2007–14; *Recreations* music, reading, church; *Style*— Mrs Del Cooke; ✉ The Henrietta Barnett School, Central Square, Hampstead Garden Suburb, London NW11 7BN (☎ 020 8458 8999, e-mail dcooke@hbschool.org.uk)

COOKE, Dominic; CBE (2014); s of Malcolm Cooke, and Gloria Solomon, *née* Turower; *b* 1 February 1966, London; *Educ* Westminster City Sch, Univ of Warwick (BA); *Career* theatre dir; assoc dir Royal Court Theatre 1998–2002 (prodns incl: Plasticine, The People are Friendly, Fucking Games, Redundant, Spinning into Butter, Fireface, Other People, This is a Chair, Identical Twins), assoc dir RSC 2002–07 (prodns incl: The Malcontent, Cymbeline, Macbeth, As You Like It, Postcards from America, The Crucible (Best Dir Olivier Awards 2006), The Winter's Tale, Pericles), artistic dir Royal Court Theatre 2007–13 (prodns incl: Aunt Dan & Lemon, The Fever, Seven Jewish Children, Wig Out!, Now

Or Later, War & Peace/Fear & Misery, Rhinoceros, The Pain and the Itch); other theatre incl: Noughts and Crosses (RSC and tour), Autogeddon (Assembly Rooms Edinburgh, Fringe First Award 1991), Arabian Nights (Young Vic, UK and world tour, New Victory Theatre NY, TMA Award 2000), By the Bog of Cats (Wyndham Theatre), The Eccentricities of a Nightingale (Gate Dublin), The Weavers, Hunting Scenes From Lower Bavaria (Gate Dublin), The Bullet (Donmar Warehouse), Afore Night Come, Entertaining Mr Sloane (Theatr Clwyd), The Importance of Being Earnest (Atlantic Theatre Festival Canada), Caravan (Nat Theatre of Norway), My Mother Said I Never Should (Oxford Stage Co and Young Vic), Kiss of the Spider Woman (Bolton Octagon), Of Mice and Men (Nottingham Playhouse); opera incl: The Marriage of Figaro (Manchester Evening News Award 1990), The Magic Flute (Welsh National Opera), I Capuleti e I Montecchi and La Bohème (both Grange Park Opera); *Publications* Arabian Nights (1998), Noughts and Crosses (2007); *Style—* Dominic Cooke, Esq, CBE

COOKE, Hon Mr Justice; Sir Jeremy Lionel Cooke; kt (2001); s of Eric Edwin Cooke, of Warlingham, Surrey, and Margaret Lilian, *née* Taylor; *b* 28 April 1949; *Educ* Whitgift Sch Croydon, St Edmund Hall Oxford (open exhibition, MA, Rugby blues 1968 and 1969); *m* 24 June 1972, Barbara Helen, da of Geoffrey Curtis Willey, of Wallington, Surrey; 2 da (Emily b 3 June 1978, Josie b 28 March 1980), 1 s (Samuel b 29 June 1984); *Career* admitted slr 1973, called to the Bar Lincoln's Inn 1976 (Droop scholar, bencher 2001); slr Coward Chance 1973–76; QC 1990, recorder 1998–2001 (asst recorder 1994–98), head of chambers 2000–01, judge of the High Court of Justice (Queen's Bench Div Commercial Ct) 2001–, presiding judge South Eastern Circuit 2007–11, judge in charge Commercial Court 2012–; memb Advsy Bd Int Assoc for English in Law and Insurance 2013–; reader C of E 2001–; memb Harlequins RFC 1970–75; *Recreations* foozling at golf, learning to sing; *Clubs* National, Vincents (Oxford); *Style—* The Hon Mr Justice Cooke; ✉ Commercial Court, Royal Courts of Justice, 7 Rolls Building, Fetter Lane, London EC4A 1NL

COOKE, Cdre Jonathan Gervaise Fitzpatrick; OBE (1983); s of Rear Adm John Gervaise Beresford Cooke, CB (d 1976), and Helen Beatrice, *née* Cameron; *b* 26 March 1943; *Educ* Summerfields Oxford, Marlborough, RNC Dartmouth; *m* 9 April 1983, Henrietta Lorraine Deschamps, da of late Maj Saunders Edward Chamier, MC, of Wadhurst, E Sussex; 2 da (Arabella b 1984, Serena b 1985), 1 s (Hugo b 1987); *Career* joined RN 1961; cmd three submarines (HMS Rorqual 1974–76, HMS Churchill 1981–82, HMS Warspite 1980–84), Cdr submarine sea trg 1984–86, Capt 3 Submarine Sqdn 1986–89, Br Naval Attaché Paris 1990–92, RCDS 1993, Cdre MOD and ADC 1993–96; chief exec Leathersellers' Co 1996–2009; dir: Anglo-Siberian Oil Co 1998–2003, Bayfield Energy Hldgs 2011–13; govr Leathersellers Fedn of Schs 1996–2015 (chm 2008–14), chm Leather Conservation Centre Northampton 2009–; tstee Hosp of Sr Cross 2011–; Yr Bro Trinity House 1994; Cdr de l'Ordre Nationale de Mérite (France) 1992; *Recreations* tennis, golf, gardening; *Clubs* Naval and Military; *Style—* Cdre Jonathan Cooke, OBE, RN; ✉ Downstead House, Morestead, Winchester, Hampshire SO21 1LF (☎ 01962 777765, mobile 07714 759270, e-mail jonathan.cooke@btinternet.com)

COOKE, Justin; s of Graham Cooke, and Jane, *née* Featherstone; *b* 18 June 1972, Huntingdon, Cambs; *Educ* London Business Sch, Univ of Manchester; *m* 11 July 2003, Jaime, *née* Halliday; 1 da (Alberta b 29 Dec 2008), 2 s (Gibson b 4 Aug 2010, Montgomery b 30 March 2013); *Career* fndr and ceo Fortune Cookie 1997–2012, ceo UK Possible 2012–15, venture ptnr Northzone 2015–; non-exec dir FutureLearn 2014–; memb No. 10 Gov Digital Bd GREAT Campaign; memb Digital Bd Br Museum 2012–; lifetime ambass Br Interactive Media Assoc 2008 (chair 2009–); listed in Wired 100 2012, memb Digital Hall of Fame 2013; *Recreations* cinema, gardening, music, travel; *Style—* Justin Cooke, Esq; ✉ Bayham Hall, Bayham Abbey, Tunbridge Wells TN3 8BG (☎ 01892 891594, mobile 07710 070020, e-mail justin.cooke@gmail.com, Twitter @justincooke); Northzone, 6–8 Kingly Court, London W1B 5PW

COOKE, His Hon Judge Nicholas Orton; QC (1998); only surviving s of Mr B O Cooke, of Rogerstone, nr Newport, and Mrs V Cooke, *née* Price (d 2014); *b* 1 July 1955; *Educ* King Edward's Sch Birmingham, UCW Aberystwyth (Sweet and Maxwell Prize); *m* 1979, Jean Ann, da of late Mr W H Tucker; *Career* called to the Bar Middle Temple 1977 (Blackstone entrance exhbn 1976); practising barr Wales & Chester Circuit 1978–2007, recorder 1997–2007 (asst recorder 1994–97), sr circuit judge 2007–, resident judge Cardiff Crown Court 2007–12, recorder of Cardiff 2008–12, dep High Court judge Queen's Bench Div 2010–, judge Central Criminal Court 2012–; dep pres Mental Health Review Tnbl for Wales 1999–; chm Bristol and Wales Chancery Bar Assoc, chm Wales Public Law and Human Rights Assoc; Church in Wales: memb Governing Body 1999–2012, judge of the Provincial Court 2004–, chllr Dio of St David's 2005–; Freeman City of London 2014, Liveryman Worshipful Co of Fan Makers 2014; *Recreations* hockey, theatre; *Style—* His Hon Judge Cooke, QC; ✉ Central Criminal Court, Old Bailey, London EC4M 7EH

COOKE, Nigel; *b* 17 July 1973, Manchester; *Educ* Nottingham Trent Univ (BA), RCA (MA), Goldsmiths Coll London (PhD); *Career* artist; *Solo Exhibitions* Chapman Fine Arts London 2000, Modern Art London 2002 and 2005, Art Now Tate Britain 2004, Andrea Rosen Gallery NY 2004, Blum and Poe LA 2005; *Group Exhibitions* Interesting Painting (City Racing London) 1997, New Contemporaries 98 (Camden Arts Centre and tour) 1998, Glory (Br Cncl Window Gallery Prague) 1999, Wooden Heart (Avco London) 2000, Homage to the Budokan (Foyles Gallery London) 2000, A Sport & a Pastime (Greene Naftali Inc NY) 2001, Tattoo Show (Modern Art London) 2001, Melodrama (Israel and Spain) 2002, Still Life (Br Cncl Chile, Venezuela, Argentina and Columbia) 2002–03, Exploring Landscape (Andrea Rosen Gallery NY) 2003, Dirty Pictures (The Approach London) 2003, I See a Darkness (Blum and Poe LA) 2003, Contemporary Drawing (Jack Hanley Gallery San Francisco) 2003, Painting (Gallery Somme Tel Aviv), Frass (122 Leadenhall St London), Gewalt (Loushy Art and Editions Tel Aviv); *Style—* Nigel Cooke, Esq; ✉ e-mail modernart@easynet.co.uk, website www.modernartinc.com

COOKE, (William) Peter; CBE (1997); s of Douglas Edgar Cooke, MC (Lt Durham LI, d 1964), of Gerrards Cross, Bucks, and Florence May, *née* Mills (d 1986); *b* 1 February 1932; *Educ* Kingswood Sch Bath, Merton Coll Oxford (MA); *m* 1, 22 April 1957, Maureen Elizabeth (d 1999), da of Dr E A Haslam-Fox (d 1975) of Holmes Chapel, Cheshire; 2 s (Nicholas b 1959, Andrew b 1964), 2 da (Caroline b 1960, Stephanie b 1970); *m* 2, 20 Aug 2005, Julia Mary Bain, *née* Warrack; *Career* Nat Serv RA 1951; joined Bank of England 1955; seconded: to Bank for International Settlements Basle Switzerland 1958–59, as PA to md IMF Washington DC 1961–65, as sec City Takeover Panel 1968–69; Bank of England: first dep chief cashier 1970–73, advsr to Govrs 1973–76, head Banking Supervision 1976–85, assoc dir 1982–88; chm: City EEC Ctee 1973–80, Ctee on Banking Regulations and Supervisory Practices Bank for International Settlements Basel Switzerland 1977–88, Price Waterhouse World Regulatory Advsy Practice 1989–97; dir: Safra Republic Holdings SA 1989–99, Alexander & Alexander Services Inc 1994–96, Financial Security Assurance (UK) Ltd 1994–2009, Bank of China International Holdings 1997–98, The Housing Finance Corporation 1997–2003, Bank of China International (UK) Ltd 1998–, State Street Bank (UK) Ltd 1998–2006, HSBC Republic Holdings 2000–01, Bank of China Ltd 2004–07, Medicapital Holdings plc 2006–11, Assured Guaranty Ltd 2009–12; advsr PricewaterhouseCoopers 1997–2002; chm Merton Soc 1979–95 (pres 1995–98); memb Bd: The Housing Corporation 1989–97 (chm 1997), Eng Churches Housing Gp 1977–93, Salzburg Seminar 1990–2004; memb Cncl Chatham House 1992–2005 (dep chm 1998–2005); govr: Pangbourne Coll 1982–2002, Kingswood Sch 1990–2002, Gayhurst Sch 2010–14 (chm 2011–14); hon fell Merton Coll Oxford 1997; *Recreations* music, golf, travel; *Clubs* Reform, Denham Golf; *Style—* Peter Cooke, Esq, CBE; ✉ Oak Lodge, Maltmans Lane, Chalfont St Peter, Gerrards Cross, Buckinghamshire SL9 8RP (☎ 01753 886236, e-mail email@petercooke.co.uk)

COOKE, Peter Stephen; s of Henry Peter Cooke (d 1988), and Patricia Jean Cooke, *née* Wearing; *b* 13 April 1948; *Educ* Guildford Royal GS, Univ of Southampton (BSc); *m* 1, 24 July 1971 (m dis 1989), Patricia Ann, da of Robert Frederick Meredith; 2 da (Alexander b 1978, Amy b 1979); *m* 2, 15 July 1989, Elizabeth Margaret, da of Glyndwr Thomas; 1 s (George Henry b 1991); *Career* slr; legal advsr to Engrg Employers' Fedn 1978–83, managing ptnr Theodore Goddard 1984– (currently head Employment and Employee Benefits Gp); memb Worshipful Co of Slrs 1989; memb Law Soc; *Books* Croners Employment Law (1980), Croners Industrial Relations Law (contrib 1989); *Recreations* music, cycling and sailing; *Style—* Peter Cooke, Esq; ✉ 302 Cromwell Tower, Barbican, London EC2Y 8DD; Theodore Goddard, 150 Aldersgate Street, London EC1A 4EJ (☎ 020 7606 8855, telex 884678, fax 020 7606 4390)

COOKE, Dr Richard Kennedy Gordon; s of Alfred Gordon Cooke (d 1992), and Mary Eluned, *née* Mason (d 2003); *b* 23 April 1950; *Educ* St Paul's Cathedral Choir Sch, Monkton Combe Sch, King's Coll Cambridge; *m* 31 May 1980 (m dis 2004), Alison Mary, da of Hon (Arthur) Maxwell Stamp (d 1984); 2 da (Florence Mary b 10 Sept 1982, Hannah Marian b 4 May 1984), 1 s (Maxwell Richard Gordon b 3 Nov 1985); partner, Christina Mariam Astin; 1 da (Emily Freya b 17 Oct 2004), 1 s (Wilfred Gregor b 14 Nov 2006); *Career* conductor; conductor Cambridge Univ Chamber Orch and asst conductor Cambridge Univ Music Soc 1972–73, dir of choral music Tiffin Sch Kingston upon Thames 1974–81, conductor London Philharmonic Choir 1982–91, chorus master Opéra de Lyon 1992–95, music dir Royal Choral Soc 1995–; other appointments incl: dir of music St Columb Festival 1969–90, asst conductor Gemini Opera 1974–80, music dir Univ of Essex Choir 1981–, music dir Canterbury Choral Soc 1984–, asst chorus master London Symphony Chorus 1976–82, fndr and music dir Canterbury Choral Soc Youth Choir 2007–; various conducting in Europe and Scandinavia incl: Gothenburg Symphony Orchestra, Opéra de Lyon, Aix-en-Provence Festival; Hon Doctorate Univ of Essex 1996, Hon DMus Univ of Kent 2010; *Recordings* as conductor incl: Orff Carmina Burana (with RPO and Royal Choral Soc) 1995, Last Night of the Proms (with RPO and Canterbury Choral Soc) 1996, Elgar The Apostles (Philharmonia and Canterbury Choral Soc) 2005; as chorus master incl: Brahms Requiem (LPO under Klaus Tennstedt) 1986, Mahler Symphony No 8 (with LPO under Tennstedt, Grammy nomination) 1987, Cherubini Mass (with LPO under Riccardo Muti) 1987, Vaughan Williams Sea Symphony (with LPO under Bernard Haitink) 1989; *Recreations* reading, surfing, politics, hill-walking, cycling; *Style—* Dr Richard Cooke; ✉ 11, Lincoln Avenue, Canterbury CT1 3YD (☎ 01227 652031)

COOKE, His Hon Roger Arnold; s of Stanley Gordon Cooke (d 1994), of Nether Alderley, Cheshire, and Frances Mabel, *née* Reading (d 2001); *b* 30 November 1939, Upton, Birkenhead; *Educ* Repton, Magdalen Coll Oxford (MA); *m* 16 May 1970, Hilary, da of Eric Robertson (d 1993), of Shorwell, IOW; 2 s (James b 1972, Thomas b 1975), 2 da (Elizabeth (Mrs Lees) b 1973, Mary (Mrs Leatherman) b 1979); *Career* called to the Bar Middle Temple 1962 (Astbury scholar), ad eundem Lincoln's Inn 1967 (bencher 1994); practised at the Chancery Bar 1963–89, head of Chambers 1985–88, jt head of Chambers 1988–89, recorder 1987–89 (asst recorder 1982–87), circuit judge (SE Circuit) 1989–2005 (dep circuit judge 2005–07); authorised to sit as judge of the High Court: Chancery Div 1992–, Queen's Bench Div 1994; pt/t students offr Lincoln's Inn 1976–80, hon sec Chancery Bar Assoc 1979–89; memb: Inns of Court Advocacy Training Ctee 1995–2004, Advocacy Studies Bd 1996–2000; churchwarden: Little Berkhamsted 1979–94, St Mary Ashwell 2000–07; memb Fin and Gen Purposes Ctee Broxbourne Cons Assoc 1986–89; govr The Pines Sch Hertford 1988–96 (chm 1990–95); Freeman (by purchase) City of London 1986; memb Inst Conveyancers 1983; *Publications* A Portrait of Lincoln's Inn (contrib); *Recreations* gardening, photography, travel, history, old buildings, food; *Clubs* Athenaeum; *Style—* His Hon Roger Cooke; ✉ c/o Radcliffe Chambers, 11 New Square, Lincoln's Inn, London WC2A 3QB

COOKE, Sir Ronald Urwick (Ron); kt (2002); s of Ernest Oswald Cooke (d 1949), and Lilian, *née* Mount (d 1948); *b* 1 September 1941; *Educ* Ashford GS, UCL (BSc, MSc, PhD, DSc); *m* 4 Jan 1968, Barbara Anne, da of Albert Henry Baldwin (d 1969), of Petts Wood, Kent; 1 s (Graham Stephen b 1971), 1 da (Emma Louise b 1974); *Career* Dept of Geography UCL: lectr 1961–75, reader 1975, prof and head of dept 1981–91, dean of arts 1991–92, vice-provost 1991–93; vice-chllr Univ of York 1993–2002; Bedford Coll London: prof 1975–81, dean of sci 1978–80, vice-princ 1979–80; co-fndr, dir and chm Geomorphological Services Ltd 1980–90; cmmr US-UK Fulbright Cmmn 1995–2000; tstee Nat Sci Museum 2002–10, chm Jt Info Systems Ctee 2004–09; chm: Kew at Castle Howard Arboretum Tst 2002–11, York's Local Strategic Partnership 2007–12, York Civic Tst 2008–12 (vice-chair 2012–); dir Visit York 2012–15, tstee Ryedale Festival 2015–; govr: Watford Boys' GS, Watford Girls' GS 1985–92; hon fell: UCL 1993, Royal Holloway and Bedford New Coll 1993; Hon DCL Univ of Kent 2004, Hon DPhil Univ of Glos 2004, Hon DUniv York 2005; Hon Freeman City of York 2006; memb: Inst of Br Geographers (pres 1991–92), HEFCE 1997–2003, RGS (pres 2000–03), FAcSS; *Books* incl: Geomorphology in Deserts (with A Warren, 1973), Geomorphology in Environmental Management (with J C Doornkamp, 1974, 2 edn 1990), Arroyos and Environmental Change in the American Southwest (with R W Reeves, 1976), Environmental Hazards in Los Angeles (1984), Urban Geomorphology in Drylands (with D Brunsden, J C Doornkamp and DKC Jones, 1982), Desert Geomorphology (with A Warren and A S Goudie, 1993), Crumbling Heritage (with G Gibbs, 1993); *Clubs* Merchant Adventurers; *Style—* Sir Ron Cooke

COOKE, Stephen Giles; s of late Basil Cooke, and Dora Cynthia, *née* Richards; *b* 30 July 1946; *Educ* Stamford Sch, Leicester Sch of Architecture; *m* Jane Lesley, da of late Cowper Fredrick Ide; 2 s (Henry Stephen b 1975, James Cowper b 1979); *Career* articled clerk Clay Allison & Clark Worksop Notts, admitted slr 1971; Withers: joined 1971, ptnr 1973–2012, conslt 2012–; dir: Ockenden International (refugee charity), Buccleuch Living Heritage Tst, London Handel Soc; *Books* Inheritance Tax and Lifetime Gifts (1987); *Recreations* music, the countryside, gardening; *Clubs* Garrick; *Style—* Stephen Cooke, Esq; ✉ The Pond House, Well, Hook, Hampshire RG29 1TL; Withers LLP, 16 Old Bailey, London EC4M 7EG (☎ 020 7597 6000, fax 020 7597 6543)

COOKE, Stephen John; s of Robert Cooke (d 1995), and Barbara Cooke (d 2000); *b* 7 March 1959; *Educ* Lincoln Coll Oxford (MA); *Career* slr; Slaughter and May: joined 1982, NY office 1989–90, ptnr 1991–, head of M&A 2001–16, sr ptnr 2016–; composer and musician; film China's Stolen Children 2007; television incl: The Dying Rooms 1995, Innocents Lost 1997, Slavery 2000, Old 2002, Reporters at War 2003, Bulgaria's Abandoned Children 2007, Chosen 2008, War Child 2011, Kashmir's Torture Trial 2012, Land of Hope and Glory (series) 2016; various radio; *Books* Takeovers (1997); *Clubs* Groucho, Athenaeum; *Style—* Stephen Cooke, Esq; ✉ Slaughter and May, 1 Bunhill Row, London EC1Y 8YY (☎ 020 7090 3261, e-mail stephen.cooke@slaughterandmay.com)

COOKLIN, Susan; *b* 4 April 1960, Leicester; *Career* sr exec Barclays Gp plc 2002–06, group chief info offr Network Rail 2009–; non-exec dir Leeds Met Univ 2011–; finalist MIT CIO Innovation Award 2012, UKIT CIO of the Year 2012; *Style—* Ms Susan Cooklin; ✉ Network Rail, Kings Place, 90 York Way, London N1 9AG

COOKSEY, Sir David James Scott; kt (1993), GBE (2007); s of late Dr Frank Sebastian Cooksey, CBE, of Suffolk, and Muriel Mary, *née* Scott; *b* 14 May 1940; *Educ* Westminster,

St Edmund Hall Oxford (MA, hon fell 1995); *m* 1, 1973 (m dis 2003), Janet Clouston Bewley, da of Dr Ian Aysgarth Bewley Cathie, of Glos; 1 s (Alexander b 1976), 1 da (Leanda b 1974); m 2, 2011, Mary Ann Julie Phylis Lutyens, da of late John Stuart Patrick Drabble; *Career* chm: Advent Venture Ptnrs 1987–2006 (md 1981–87), Bespak plc 1995–2004 (dir 1993–2004); a dir of the Bank of England 1994–2005 (chm non-exec dir ctee 2001–05); dir: British Venture Capital Association 1983–89 (chm 1983–84, hon pres 2012), William Baird plc 1995–2002, Establishment Investment Tst plc 2002–15 (chm 2011–15), Resolution plc 2004–08, European Venture Capital Association 2004–07 (chm 2005–06), Procserve Ltd 2011–13; non-exec chm: Diamond Light Source Ltd 2002–08, London & Continental Railways 2006–11, Eurasian Natural Resources Corporation plc 2007–09, Francis Crick Inst 2008–, UK Financial Investments Ltd 2009–12, Bechtel Ltd 2009–, Aegate Hldgs Ltd 2013–; memb Advsy Cncl SVP Global LLP 2012–; memb Innovation Advsy Bd DTI 1988–93; chm: Audit Cmmn for Local Govt and the NHS in England and Wales 1986–95, Local Govt Cmmn 1995–96, UK Clinical Research Collaboration Industry Reference Gp Dept of Health 2004–10, State Honours Ctee 2005–10, Cooksey Review of UK Health Research HM Treasury 2006; pro-chllr Univ of Southampton 2008–13 (memb Cncl 1993–2003); govr Wellcome Tst 1995–99; tstee: Mary Rose Tst 1993–2001 (chm 1996–2001); Liveryman Worshipful Co of Info Technologists; Hon DBA Kingston Univ 1996, Hon DSc Univ of Southampton 2008, Hon DSc UCL 2011; hon fell: Univ of Wales Cardiff 1998, Imperial Coll 2008, King's Coll 2012; hon fell British Assoc; FRSA, Hon FMedSci; *Publications* Biosciences 2015 (2003), A Review of UK Health Research Funding (2006), Biosciences 2015, Review and Refresh (2009); *Recreations* sailing, performing and visual arts; *Clubs* Boodle's, Royal Yacht Squadron, Royal Thames Yacht; *Style—* Sir David Cooksey, GBE; ✉ c/o Francis Crick Institute, Gibbs Building, 215 Euston Road, London NW1 2BE (☎ 020 7611 2097)

COOKSON, Clive Michael; s of Richard Clive Cookson, and Ellen, *née* Fawwaz; *b* 13 February 1952; *Educ* Winchester, BNC Oxford (BA); *m* 8 April 1978, Caroline Davidson; 1 s (Robert b 9 Oct 1984), 1 da (Emma b 10 July 1986); *Career* sci journalist; trainee journalist Luton Evening Post (Thomson Regional Newspapers) 1974–76, American ed (in Washington) Times Higher Education Supplement 1977–81 (science corr 1976–77), technol corr The Times 1981–83, sci and med corr BBC Radio 1983–87, sci ed Financial Times 1991– (technol ed 1987–90); Feature Writer of the Year (UK Technol Press Awards) 1988 and 1989, Glaxo Sci Writer of the Year 1994 and 1998; *Style—* Clive Cookson, Esq; ✉ The Financial Times, 1 Southwark Bridge, London SE1 9HL (☎ 020 7873 4950, e-mail clive.cookson@ft.com)

COOL, Kenton Edward; s of John Cool, and Maggie Cool; *b* 30 July 1973; *Educ* Univ of Leeds (BSc); *m* 2 Aug 2008, Jazz, *née* Black; 1 da (Saffron b 30 June 2010), 1 s (Willoughby b 2 Oct 2012); *Career* mountain climber; first European to summit Mount Everest eleven times, first non-Asian to summit Everest twice in one week, sent the first Tweet from the summit of Mt Everest, only Briton to have skied down two 8000m mountains, completed more than 18 expeditions to the greater ranges, first person to climb Nuptse, Everest and Lhotse in one continuous trip, fulfilled Olympic pledge in 2012 by taking a 1924 Olympic Gold Medal to the top of Everest and personally thanked Lord Coe for his efforts; contrib to Alpine Jl and American Alpine Jl; patron: Br Exploring Soc, Porters' Progress; *Clubs* Alpine, Explorers; *Style—* Kenton Cool, Esq; ✉ website www.kentoncool.com, Twitter @kentoncool

COOLS-LARTIGUE, Dominic; s of Marie-José Cools-Lartigue, of London; *b* London; *Children* 1 s (Remy b 6 Oct 2008); *Career* music promoter and mangr 1995–2011, fndr Street Feast 2012–, fndr and ceo Modern Assembly 2015–; *Recreations* cinema, fashion, music, reading, travel, food, print publishing; *Clubs* Power 1000 (London's Most Influential People) Evening Standard 2013–15; *Style—* Dominic Cools-Lartigue, Esq; ✉ website www.modernassembly.tv, Twitter @DomCools

COOMBE, Donald Howard; MBE (1992), JP (1973); er s of Howard James Coombe (d 1988) and Rose May *née* Tate (d 1997); *b* 21 October 1927; *Educ* Northbrook C of E Sch Lee, Roan Sch Greenwich, Univ of the World (MA); *m* 5 June 1948, Betty Joyce, da of George William Adie (d 1938); 2 s (Richard Howard b 25 April 1953, David b 8 Oct 1958); *Career* RN 1942–47, hon cmmn to Adm Texas Navy 1976, hon cmmn to Gen Washington 2001; chm: RTC Ltd (Lloyd's Brokers) 1971–; fndr chm: Coombe Tst Fund, Coombe Holiday Tst Fund (both registered charities for Needy Children); life memb Royal Soc of St George; former cmmr Scouts Assoc (Silver Acorn); hon attorney-gen N Carolina, chm of bench 1982, cmmr Income Tax 1978–85; Grand Offr (Freemasons) United Grand Lodge of England, Grand Chamberlain Mediaeval Knights of London 2002; Freeman: City of London 1970, City of Dallas Texas 1976; Liveryman Worshipful Co of Poulters 1978; Paul Harris fell Rotary; ACII; Order of St George (Sweden) 1974; *Books* The Geezer Wiv the Flahr; *Recreations* charity fundraising, social work, boxing; *Clubs* Three Rooms, Naval and Military; *Style—* Donald H Coombe, Esq, MBE, JP; ✉ 1 Thornes Close, Beckenham, Kent BR3 6QT (☎ 020 8658 2714); Lloyd's of London, Lime Street, London EC3M 7HA

COOMBE, John David; s of Sidney Coombe; *b* 17 March 1945; *Educ* Haberdashers' Aske's, Univ of London (BSc); *m* 1970, Gail Alicia, *née* Brazier; 3 da; *Career* CA; gp treas The Charterhouse Group plc 1976–84, mangr fin and treasy Charter Consolidated plc 1984–86, md fin and main bd dir Glaxo Holdings plc 1992–95 (fin controller 1986–92), fin dir Glaxo Wellcome plc 1995–2000, chief financial offr GlaxoSmithKline plc 2000–05, chm Hogg Robinson Gp plc 2006–16, chm Home Retail Gp plc 2012– (dir 2006–12); dir: Supervisory Bd Siemens AG 2003–08, HSBC Holdings plc 2005–14, GUS plc 2005–06; chm Hundred Gp of Fin Dirs 1999–2001; memb Accounting Standards Bd 1996–2003; *Clubs* Carlton; *Style—* John Coombe, Esq; ☎ 07901 828741

COOMBES, Prof (Raoul) Charles Dalmedo Stuart; s of Col R C Coombes, MC, of Aldbourne, Wilts, and Doreen Mary, *née* Ellis; *b* 20 April 1949; *Educ* Douai Sch, St George's Hosp Med Sch (MB BS), UCL (PhD, MD, BS); *m* 27 July 1984, Caroline Sarah, da of David Oakes, of St Helens, Merseyside; 2 s (Jack Raoul b 1985, Charles David b 1992), 2 da (Sophie Flora b 1987, Matilda Rose b 1989); *Career* house physican and SHO in med and surgery St George's and associated hosps London 1971–73, SHO Radiotherapy Dept and research registrar Endocrine Unit Hammersmith Hosp 1973–74, MRC clinical res fell Inst of Cancer Research and Endocrine Unit Hammersmith Hosp 1974–76; Royal Marsden Hosp: registrar then clinical scientist and sr registrar 1976–80, sr lectr and hon conslt physican 1980–87; sr clinical scientist Ludwig Inst for Cancer Res 1980–87, conslt physician, med oncologist and head Clinical Oncology Unit St George's Hosp and hon sr lectr St George's Hosp Med Sch 1987–90, prof of med oncology and head Dept of Medical Oncology 1990–97, dean of research Charing Cross and Westminster Med Sch 1993–97, co-dir Cancer Servs and Clinical Haematology Directorate Hammersmith Hosps Tst 1994–, head Dept of Cancer Medicine Imperial Coll Sch of Med 1997–, hon conslt med oncologist Hammersmith Hosps Tst 1999–, prof of med oncology and dir Cancer Research (UK) Labs Hammersmith Hosp 1999–; co-ordinator of nat and int trials for Int Collaborative Cancer Gp; memb: SW Thames Regnl Cancer Gp, Br Breast Gp 1988; memb: Br Assoc Cancer Res 1988, American Assoc Cancer Res 1988, Endocrine Soc of GB, NY Acad of Sciences, European Soc for Clinical Oncology, Assoc of Cancer Physicians, European of Medical Oncology, American Assoc for the Advancement Science; FRCP 1983 (MRCP 1973), FMedSci 2001; *Publications* Breast Cancer Management (jt ed, 1981), New Endocrinology of Cancer (jt ed, 1986), New Targets in Cancer Therapy (1994); author of more than 400 papers on breast cancer; *Recreations* painting; *Style—* Prof Charles Coombes; ✉ Imperial College School of Medicine at Hammersmith Hospital, Du Cane Road, London W12 (☎ 020 8383 5828, fax 020 8383 5830, e-mail c.coombes@ic.ac.uk)

COOMBS, Prof Graham H; *b* 22 September 1947; *Educ* UCL (BSc, PhD); *Career* research fell Biological Lab Univ of Kent 1972–74; Dept of Zoology Univ of Glasgow: lectr 1974–86, sr lectr 1986–88, reader 1988–90, titular prof 1990–95, head of dept 1991–94; Inst of Biomedical and Life Sciences Univ of Glasgow: head Parasitology Lab Div of Molecular and Cellular Biology 1994–95, with Div of Infection & Immunity 1995–2006, personal professorship in biochemical parasitology 1995–2006, dep dir Glasgow Biomedical Research Centre 2005–06, head Strathclyde Inst of Pharmacy and Biomedical Sciences Univ of Strathclyde 2006–; pres: Br Section Soc of Protozoologists, Br Soc of Parasitology 2008–; UK rep Int Cmmn of Protozoology; MRC: memb Physiological Med and Infections Bd 1999–2003, memb Cross Bd Gp 2000–04; Seymour H Hutner Prize Soc of Protozoologists 1986; FRSE 1993; *Publications* incl: Trypanosomiasis and leishmaniasis: Biology and Control (jt ed, 1997), Evolutionary Relationships among Protozoa (jt ed, 1998); author of more than 190 papers, articles and reviews, particularly on subjects relating to protozoan parasites; *Style—* Prof Graham H Coombs; ✉ Strathclyde Institute of Pharmacy and Biomedical Sciences, University of Strathclyde, 161 Cathedral Street, Glasgow G4 0RE (☎ 0141 548 2155, fax 0141 552 2562, e-mail graham.coombs@strath.ac.uk, website www.strath.ac.uk/sipbs)

COOMBS, Martyn; *Educ* Univ of Reading (BSc), Warwick Business Sch (MBA); *Career* previously: pres Japan Perkin Elmer, vice-pres Amersham plc; chief exec Asterand plc 2007–; *Style—* Martyn Coombs, Esq; ✉ Asterand plc, 2 Orchard Road, Royston, Hertfordshire SG8 5HD

COOPER; *see also:* Astley-Cooper

COOPER, Alan Guthlac; s of late John Carr Cooper, of Harrogate, N Yorks, and late Veronica Dora, *née* Ludolf; *b* 23 August 1955, Chelmsford; *Educ* Brentwood Sch, Univ of Durham (BA); *m* 17 July 1990, Carol, da of late Alexander Beattie; 2 s (Matthew Guthlac b 30 Sept 1991, Samuel Alexander b 3 July 1993), 2 da (Rebecca Aimi b 26 May 1995, Abigail Flora b 30 Jan 1997); *Career* British Market Research Bureau Ltd 1977–80, sr researcher rising to planning dir Leo Burnett Advertising Ltd 1980–84, sr planner rising to assoc dir Gold Greenlees Trott Ltd 1984–88, bd/planning dir DDB Needham Ltd 1988; Simons Palmer Clemmow Johnson Ltd: bd/planning dir 1989–97, head of planning 1993–97, chm Account Planning Gp 1996–98; planning dir TBWA Simons Palmer (following merger) 1997–98; md Brand Vitality Ltd 1999–2004; HPI Research: ptnr 2000–07, exec ptnr 2007–16; lead conslt Home Strategic 2014–; Marketing Soc Brand of the Year Award 1993; IPA Advertising Effectiveness Award 1986 and 1994; memb MRS; *Books* Advertising Works (contrib Vol 4, 1987 and Vol 8, 1995), Understanding Brands (1996), How To Plan Advertising (ed, 1997), CBI Communications Handbook (contrib, 1997), Admap (contrib, 2001, 2005 and 2013), Isle of Man Summits (2016); *Recreations* horticulture, hill walking, Fulham FC, organiser of IOM Real Ale Festival; *Clubs* IOM TT Marshals Assoc, CAMRA; *Style—* Alan Cooper, Esq; ✉ Bramble Brae, Quarterbridge Road, Douglas, Isle of Man IM2 3RH (☎ 01624 623220, e-mail thealancooper@manx.net)

COOPER, Dr Andrew Michael; s of Peter Cooper (d 2011), and Eileen Mildred, *née* Billings (d 2006); *b* 31 October 1958, Leek, Staffs; *Educ* Longton HS Stoke-on-Trent, City of Stoke-on-Trent Sixth Form Coll, Univ of Leeds Sch of Med (MB ChB, DRCOG, PGCertMedEd); *m* 1 July 1989, Ann, da of Roy Rossington; 1 s (Michael David b 20 Jan 1992), 1 da (Bethan Sarah b 23 June 1997); *Career* house offr Leeds Gen Infirmary 1982–83, SHO A&E Cardiff Royal Infirmary 1983–84, SHO obstetrics and gynaecology Llandough Hosp Cardiff 1984–85, S Glamorgan Vocational Trg Scheme for Gen Practice 1985–87, ptnr Fairwater Health Centre Cardiff 1987–; clinical teacher Univ of Wales Coll of Med 1998; prog dir Cardiff Specialty Trg Prog for Gen Practice Univ of Wales Coll of Med Dept of Postgraduate Studies 1992–; RCGP: memb Welsh Cncl 1989–97, memb Central Cncl 1990–95, treas SE Wales Faculty 1991–94, chm SE Wales Faculty 1994–97, memb Patient Liaison Gp 1994–95, provost SE Wales Faculty 1997–2000, examiner for membership 2007–, assessor for IMAP 2010–; memb: RCP/RCPsych Working Pty on Care of Elderly Patients with Mental Illness 1994–95, UK Alcohol Forum 2000; memb BMA 1982, memb RSM 1989; FRCGP 1999 (MRCGP 1987); *Recreations* golf, cricket, skiing, travel, music; *Style—* Dr Andrew Cooper; ✉ Fairwater Health Centre, Plasmawr Road, Fairwater, Cardiff CF5 3JT (☎ 029 2056 6291, fax 029 2057 8870, e-mail geirwen@mac.com)

COOPER, Prof Sir Cary Lynn; kt (2014), CBE (2001); s of Harry Cooper, of LA, USA, and Caroline Lillian, *née* Greenberg; *b* 28 April 1940; *Educ* Fairfax Sch LA, Univ of Calif (BS, MBA), Univ of Manchester (MSc), Univ of Leeds (PhD); *m* 1, 1970 (m dis 1984), (Edna) June Taylor; 1 s (Hamish Scott b 1972), 1 da (Natasha Beth b 1974); m 2, 1984, Rachel Faith Davies; 2 da (Laura Anne b 1982, Sarah Kate b 1985); *Career* lectr in psychology Univ of Southampton 1967–73; UMIST: prof of mgmnt educn methods 1975–79, prof of organisational psychology 1979–98, pro-vice-chllr 1995–99, dep vice-chllr 2000–02, BUPA prof of organisational psychology and health 1998–2003; Lancaster Univ: distinguished prof of organisational psychology and health 2003–15, pro-vice-chllr 2004–10 and 2012–15; temp advsr: WHO and ILO 1982–84, Home Office (on police stress) 1982–84; memb Bd of Tstees American Inst of Stress 1984–, pres Br Acad of Mgmnt 1986–90 and 1999–2004, treas Int Fedn of Scholarly Assoc of Mgmnt 1990–92; ed Jl of Organizational Behavior 1980–98, ed Stress and Health 2009–13 (co-ed 1992–2009); chm Business and Mgmnt RAE Panel HEFCE 1996 and 2001; pres: Inst of Welfare Officers 1999–, ISIS 2000, Br Assoc of Counselling and Psychotherapy 2006–12 (vice-pres 2000–05, pres 2006–12), RELATE 2011–; chair AcSS 2009–15, chair Global Agenda Cncl on Chronic Disease World Economic Forum 2009–10; ambass The Samaritans 2000–12; dir Robertson Cooper Ltd; broadcaster; Myers Lecture Br Psychological Soc 1986, Lord Dearing Lifetime Achievement Award in HE 2010; memb American Psychosomatic Assoc, fell American Acad of Mgmnt 1997 (Distinguished Service Award 1998, memb Bd of Govrs 2001–03), hon fell European Acad of Occupational Health Psychology 2010, hon fell Instn of Occupational Safety and Health 2012; hon prof of psychology Univ of Manchester 1986–2003; 50th Anniversary prof of organizational psychology and health 2015–; Hon DLitt Heriot-Watt Univ 1998, Hon DBA Wolverhampton Univ 1999, Hon DSc Aston Univ 2002, Hon Dr Univ of Middlesex 2003, Hon DSc Univ of Sheffield 2010, Hon DL Univ of Bath 2014; CIMgt 1997, FRSA, FBPsS, FRSM, FRSH, FBAM, FAcSS 2000, Hon FFOM 2005, Hon FRCP 2006, Hon FFOM of RCP of Ireland 2008, Hon FBPsS 2010, pres Br Acad of Mgmnt 2015–, pres CIPD 2016–; *Books* incl: T-Groups (jtly, 1971), Theories of Group Processes (1976), Developing Social Skills in Managers (1976), Stress at Work (jtly, 1978), Executives Under Pressure (jtly, 1978), Behavioural Problems in Organisations (1979), Learning From Others in Groups (1979), The Executive Gypsy (1979), Current Concerns in Occupational Stress (1980), The Stress Check (1980), Improving Interpersonal Relations (1981), Psychology and Management (jtly, 1982), Management Education (jtly, 1982), Stress Research (1983), Public Faces, Private Lives (jtly, 1984), Working Women (jtly, 1984), Psychology for Managers (jtly, 1984), Change Makers (jtly, 1985), Man and Accidents Offshore (jtly, 1986), International Review of Industrial and Organisational Psychology (jtly, 1986–2004), Pilots Under Stress (jtly, 1986), Women and Information Technology (jtly, 1987), Pressure Sensitive (jtly, 1988), High Flyers (jtly, 1988), Living with Stress (jtly, 1988), Early Retirement (jtly, 1989), Career Couples (jtly, 1989), Managing People at Work (jtly, 1989), Understanding Stress (jtly, 1990), Stress Survivors (jtly, 1991), Industrial and Organizational Psychology Vols 1 and 2 (1991), Stress and Cancer (1991), Accidents and Stress in the Offshore Oil and Gas Industry (jtly, 1991),

Relax: Dealing with Stress (jtly, 1992), Shattering the Glass Ceiling (jtly, 1992), Total Quality and Human Resource Management (jtly, 1992), Women's Career Development (jtly, 1992), Stress in the Dealing Room (jtly, 1993), The Workplace Revolution (jtly, 1993), Business Elites (jtly, 1994), Creating Healthy Work Organizations (jtly, 1994), Trends in Organizational Behavior (jtly, 1994), Work Psychology (jtly, 1995), Managing Mergers, Acquistions and Strategic Alliances (jtly, 1996), Handbook of Stress, Medicine, and Health (1996), Managing Workplace Stress (jtly, 1997), Blackwell Encyclopaedia of Management (12 vols, 1997, 2004 and 2014), Balancing Your Career, Family and Life (jtly, 1998), Personality: Critical Concepts in Psychology (jtly, 4 volumes, 1998), Dealing with the New Russia (jtly, 1998), Concise Encyclopedia of Management (jtly, 1999), Stress and Strain (jtly, 1999, 2 edn 2003), Industrial and Organisational Psychology: Theory and Practice (jtly, 2000), Strategic Stress Management (jtly, 2000), Who's Who in the Management Sciences (2000), Classics in Management Thought (2 vols, 2000), Organizational Stress (jtly, 2001), Handbook of Organizational Culture and Climate (jtly, 2001), Managerial, Occupational and Organizational Stress Research (2001), FT Guide to Executive Health (jtly, 2002), Creating a Balance (jtly, 2003), The Employment Relationship (jtly, 2003), Managing the Risk of Workplace Stress (jtly, 2003), Shut Up and Listen (jtly, 2004), Leadership and Management in the 21st Century (2004), Handbook of Stress Medicine and Health (2004), Stress: A brief history (jtly, 2004), Work-Life Integration (jtly, 2005), Work (jtly, 3 vols, 2005), Research Companion for Occupational Health Psychology (jtly, 2005), Business and the Beautiful Game (jtly, 2005), Managing the Emotions in Mergers and Acquisitions (jtly, 2005), Managing Value Based Organizations (jtly, 2006), Happy Performing Managers (jtly, 2006), Inspiring Leaders (jtly, 2006), How to Deal with Stress (jtly, 2007), Positive Organizational Behavior (jtly, 2007), Surviving the Workplace (jtly, 2007), Organizational and Work Psychology (jtly, 2008), Positively Responsible (jtly, 2008), Managing Executive Health (jtly, 2008), Employee Well-Being and Support (jtly, 2008), Building More Effective Organizations (jtly, 2008), Oxford Handbook of Personnel Psychology (jtly, 2008), Oxford Handbook of Organizational Wellbeing (jtly, 2009), New Directions in Organizational Behaviour (2009), Sage Handbook of Organizational Behaviour (jtly, 2009), Open Source Leadership (jtly, 2009), Workplace Psychological Health (jtly, 2009), Missing Pieces: Seven Ways to Improve Employee Wellbeing (jtly, 2009), Employee Morale (jtly, 2009), Handbook of Managerial Behaviour and Occupational Health (jtly, 2009), Research Companion on Corruption in Organizations (jtly, 2009), International Handbook of Work and Health Psychology (jtly, 2009), Mental Capital and Wellbeing (jtly, 2009), Organizational Stress Management (jtly, 2010), Risky Business (jtly, 2010), The Science of Occupational Health (jtly, 2010), How To Deal With Stress: Creating Success (jtly, 2010), Wellbeing: Productivity and Happiness at Work (jtly, 2011), Doing the Right Thing: The Importance of Wellbeing (jtly, 2012), Stress in Turbulent Times (jtly, 2012), Wellbeing and Work (jtly, 2012), Organizational Behaviour for Dummies (jtly, 2012), Downsizing (jtly, 2012), International Handbook of Workplace Trauma Support (jtly, 2012), Improving Organizational Interventions for Stress & Wellbeing (jtly, 2012), The Innovative Imperative in Health Care Organizations (jtly, 2012), 50 Things You Can Do to Manage Stress at Work (jtly, 2013), Building Resilience for Success (jtly, 2013), The Psychology of the Recession (jtly, 2013), Aging, Work & Society (jtly, 2013), From Stress to Wellbeing (2013), Wellbeing in Children and Families (jtly, 2014), Wellbeing in Later Life (jtly, 2014), Work & Wellbeing (jtly, 2014), Interventions & Policies to Enhance Wellbeing (jtly, 2014), Boundary Spanning in Organisations (jtly, 2014), The Economics of Wellbeing (jtly, 2014), Wellbeing & The Environment (jtly, 2014), Solving the Strategy Delusion (jtly, 2015), The Economic Crisis and Occupational Stress (jtly, 2015), Do We Need HR? (jtly, 2015), Stress Management in the Construction Industry (jtly, 2015), Handbook of Stress and Health (jtly, 2016), Advances in Mergers and Acquisitions (jtly, 2016); *Recreations* worrying about my children and their future, Russian literature, walking 10,000 steps a day, celebrating in Manchester City FC, following politics; *Style*— Prof Sir Cary L Cooper, CBE; ✉ 25 Lostock Hall Road, Poynton, Cheshire (☎ 01625 871 450); Manchester Business School, University of Manchester, Booth Street West, Manchester M15 6PB (☎ 0161 275 6371, e-mail cary.cooper@manchester.ac.uk)

COOPER, Hon Clare Antonia (Artemis); only da of 2 Viscount Norwich, CVO, *qv*; *b* 22 April 1953; *Educ* Camden Sch for Girls, St Hugh's Coll Oxford (BA); *m* 1 Feb 1986, Antony Beevor, *qv*, s of John Grosvenor Beevor, OBE (d 1987); 1 da (Eleanor Allegra Lucie (Nella) b 19 Jan 1990), 1 s (Adam John Cosmo b 10 Feb 1993); *Career* writer; tstee: London Library 1994–2002, 999 Club 2004–11; administrator Duff Cooper Prize 1993–; Chevalier de l'Ordre des Arts et des Lettres (France) 1997; *Books* A Durable Fire: The Letters of Duff and Diana Cooper (ed, 1983), Cairo in The War 1939–45 (1989), Mr Wu and Mrs Stitch: The Letters of Evelyn Waugh and Diana Cooper (ed, 1991), Watching in the Dark – A Child's Fight for Life (1992), Paris after the Liberation 1944–49 (with Antony Beevor 1994), Writing at the Kitchen Table: The Authorised Biography of Elizabeth David (1999), Patrick Leigh Fermor, An Adventure (2012), Elizabeth Jane Howard, A Dangerous Innocence (2016); *Recreations* walking, cooking, reading, peering into other people's windows; *Clubs* Literary Soc, Grillion's; *Style*— Ms Artemis Cooper; ✉ e-mail ac@artemiscooper.com, website www.artemiscooper.com

COOPER, David John; s of John Alec Cooper, of London, and late Norma May, *née* Kennard; *b* 4 July 1951; *Educ* Green Sch, Univ of London (CertEd, BEd); *Career* analyst Unilever plc 1967–71, chemistry master Barking Abbey 1974–75, business devpt and mktg exec Baxter Inc 1975–79, mktg exec Smith and Nephew Ltd 1979–82, business devpt and mktg exec LIG Int Ltd, dir Pfizer Inc 1984–87, corporate financier Robert Fleming 1987–88, fndr and md DCA (high technology business devpt consultancy) 1974–; memb Maritime Volunteer Service; Freeman City of London 1985, Liveryman Worshipful Co of Marketors 1985; confrerie des chevaliers du sacavin; FIMgt 1984, FInstD 1984, FCInstM 1984, MCInstB 1987, FRSA 1990, MIMC 1994, MSCI 1994; *Clubs* Athenaeum, Army & Navy, Loophole (fndr), City Livery Yacht (Cdre); *Style*— David J Cooper, Esq; ✉ DCA, 2nd Floor, 14 Austin Friars, London EC2N 2HE (☎ 020 3145 1575, fax 020 3292 1525, e-mail davidcooper@dca-uk.com)

COOPER, Derek Anthony (Tony); s of Donald Cooper (d 1985), and Freda, *née* Sheridan (d 1991); *b* 11 December 1943; *Educ* Whitehaven GS, Univ of Edinburgh (BSc); *m* 23 Sept 1967, June, da of Thomas Iley; 2 da (Yvette b 23 March 1969, Nichola b 11 Feb 1971), 2 s (David b 4 Nov 1973, Edward Lois b 11 July 1989); *Career* forest offr Forestry Cmmn 1967–77; Inst of Professional Civil Servants: negotiations offr 1977–81, asst sec 1981–84, asst gen sec 1984–88, dep gen sec 1988–91; gen sec Engrs and Mangrs Assoc 1991–2001, jt gen sec Prospect 2001–02; non-exec cmmr: Postal Services Cmmn 2000–, Forestry Cmmn 2000–; chm Nuclear Industry Assoc (formerly Br Nuclear Industry Forum) 2002–04, chm Combined Nuclear Pension Plan Trustees Ltd 2006–, non-exec memb Nuclear Decommissioning Authority 2004–; DTI: memb Energy Advsy Panel 1993–2003, non-exec memb Strategy Bd 2002–04, memb Investment Ctee 2002–04; memb: Energy Consultative Ctee EU 1992–95, DETR/TU Sustainable Devpt Ctee 1995–2000, Gen Cncl TUC 1996–2000; chm PPP Consultancy Ltd; dir: Aid Transport Ltd 1993–2000, Way Ahead Training Ltd 1995–2000; *Recreations* sailing, hill walking; *Style*— Tony Cooper, Esq

COOPER, Edward James Oswald; s of Derek Cooper (d 2002), of Eynsford, Kent, and Julia, *née* Vinson; *b* 12 June 1959, London; *Educ* Tonbridge, Univ of Bristol (LLB), Guildford Law Coll; *m* 27 Nov 1992, Atinuke Olubunmi Alake (Bobbie), *née* Akinboro; 3 s (Oliver, Jonathan, Reuben); *Career* slr; Simmons & Simmons 1982–85 (joined as trainee), Russell Jones and Walker 1985– (ptnr and head Employment Dept 1988–); nat practice gp ldr employment Slater & Gordon 2012–15, nat practice gp ldr orgns and membs (employment) Slater & Gordon 2015–; winner Employment Team of the Year Lawyer Awards 2000, 2002 and 2006 (2nd place 2007); *Publications* Encyclopaedia of Forms and Precedents (Trade Union Section, 2005); *Recreations* jazz saxophone, reading, tennis, swimming; *Clubs* MCC, Crocodiles Cricket (fndr memb and capt), Mange Tout Book (fndr memb); *Style*— Mr Edward Cooper; ✉ e-mail edward.cooper@slatergordon.co.uk

COOPER, Eileen; OBE (2016); *b* 1953; *Educ* Goldsmiths Coll London, Royal Coll of Art; *m* Malcolm Southward; 2 s (b 1984 and 1986); *Career* artist; pt/t tutor Printmaking Dept Royal Coll of Art; artist in residence Dulwich Picture Gallery London 1998–99, AHRB Award for Ceramic Work 1999; RA 2001, RE 2001; *Solo Exhibitions* Air Gallery 1979, House Gallery 1981, Blond Fine Art 1982, 1983 and 1985, Artspace Gallery Aberdeen 1985, Castlefield Gallery Manchester 1986, Artsite Gallery Bath 1987, Benjamin Rhodes Gallery London 1988, 1989 (Works on Paper), 1990, 1992 and 1994, Lifelines (touring England) 1993–94, Sadlers Wells Theatre London 1994, Bohun Gallery Oxon 1995, Graphic Work (touring Darlington and Harrogate 1996, Benjamin Rhodes Gallery London 1997), Graphic Work (Bridport Arts Centre) 1998, Open Secrets 1998, Art First (Cork Street London) 1998, Second Skin (Wolverhampton Museum and touring and Nottingham & Towner Museum Eastbourne) 1999, Dulwich Picture Gallery (work made from collection) 2000, Art First (new paintings, London 2000), Passions: New Work on Paper (Art First NY and Art First London) 2002, Eileen Cooper 50 (new paintings and drawings; celebration of the artist's 50th birthday) 2003; *Group Exhibitions* numerous gp exhbns since 1974 incl: The Essential Myth (Philip Graham Contemporary Art London) 1994, Figuratively Speaking (Atkinson Gallery Somerset) 1995, Cabinet Art (Jason & Rhodes London) 1996, An American Passion (RCA London) 1995, Spirit on the Staircase (100 years of print publishing at RCA and V&A London) 1996–97, Down to Earth (Lamont Gallery London and The Body Politik Wolverhampton 1997), From the Interior, Chinese & British Artists touring show 1997–98, British Figurative Art Part 1 (Flavers East London) 1997, Monotypes (Art Space Gallery London) 1997, RA Summer Show 1998, Figure of Eight (New Arts Gallery Bantam Connecticut) 1999, Hand to Hand (new porceline ceramics, Shipley Art Gallery Gateshead) 1999, Mixing It (new ceramic work with Annie Turner, Midlands Arts Centre Birmingham and touring) 1999, AA First in Print (Art First London) 2001, RA Summer Show 2001, 10x10 (Art First London) 2001, Starting a Collection (Art First London) 2002, RA Summer Show 2002, From Little Acorns 2002; *Public Collections* incl: Open Univ, Imperial Coll London, British Cncl, Kunsthalle Nuremberg (Purchase prize), Arts Cncl of GB, Contemporary Arts Soc, Cleveland Gallery, V&A Museum, Whitworth Art Gallery Manchester, Towner Art Gallery Eastbourne, Unilever plc, TI Group plc, Br Museum Soc, Manchester City Art Galleries, Harvard USA; *Major Commissions* incl: Staircase Project (ICA London) 1982, The Art (tv prog BBC Educn) 1993, Inside Art (C4) 1994, cover and illustrations for Carol Anne Duffy's Meeting Midnight 1999; subject of 'Eileen Cooper: Between the Lines' by Martin Gayford (2015); *Style*— Ms Eileen Cooper, OBE

COOPER, Granville John; s of Joseph Cooper (d 2000), of Tibshelf, Derbys, and Edna May, *née* Slack (d 1989); *b* 1 May 1940; *Educ* Tupton Hall GS, Univ of N London (BSc); *Career* microwave engr GEC Applied Electronics Laboratories 1963–67, dep engrg mangr NATO Phase II Satellite Terminal Project 1968–69, project mangr Scot Naval Satellite Communications (SATCOM) project 1971–73 (engrg mangr 1970–71), divnl mangr SATCOM Marconi Space and Defence Systems Ltd 1973–76, tech dir McMichael Ltd 1977–85 (joined 1976), md Vistek Electronics Ltd 1986–96, chm Vistek Group 1996–98, dir Deltatel Ltd; CPhys, CEng, FIEE, FInstP, FREng 1994; *Recreations* work, science, music, opera; *Style*— Granville Cooper, Esq, FREng; ✉ Springfield, 21 Lower Road, Higher Denham, Uxbridge UB9 5EB

COOPER, Dr Griselda Mary; OBE (2006); da of Dr Charles James Constantine Davey (d 2001), and Dr Gwyneth June Davey, *née* Pearson (d 2011); *b* 8 April 1949; *Educ* Bath HS, Univ of Birmingham (MB ChB); *m* 31 Aug 1973, Dr Brian Thomas Cooper, s of Dr Andrew Matthew Cooper (d 1979); 1 da (Charlotte b 1987); *Career* sr lectr in anaesthesia Univ of Bristol 1981–87, conslt anaesthetist Dunedin Public Hosp NZ 1985–86, sr lectr in anaesthesia Univ of Birmingham 1988–09; FRCA (vice-pres 2004–05 and 2006–7); *Recreations* walking, gardening, cookery, skiing; *Style*— Dr Griselda Cooper, OBE; ✉ 6 Lord Austin Drive, Grange Park, Marlbrook, Bromsgrove, Worcestershire B60 1RB (☎ 0121 445 2727)

COOPER, Prof Helen; da of Sir Peter Kent, and Betty, *née* Hood; *b* 6 February 1947; *Educ* New Hall Cambridge (MA, PhD), Univ of Oxford (LittD); *m* 18 July 1970, Dr Michael Cooper (d 2007); 2 da (Katy b 8 Jan 1973, Anne b 1 May 1976); *Career* tutorial fell in English UC Oxford 1978–2004 (first woman fell since Coll's fndn in 1249, tutor for admissions 1985–89, sr tutor 1997–2000, emeritus fell 2004–, hon fell 2014–), prof Univ of Oxford 1996–2004 (chair English Faculty 1990–93), prof of Medieval and Renaissance English Univ of Cambridge 2004–14 (chair Faculty Bd of English 2010–12), fell Magdalene Coll Cambridge 2004– (life fell 2014–); distinguished visiting mediaevalist Univ of Connecticut 1991; Br Acad res readership 2000–02; delivered lectures and papers at numerous univs and conferences in UK, Europe, USA, Japan and India; ed Old and Middle English language and literature Medium Aevum 1989–2001; pres New Chaucer Soc 2000–02; Hon DLitt Washington and Lee Univ 2001; FBA 2006; *Publications* Pastoral: Mediaeval into Renaissance (1978), The Structure of the Canterbury Tales (1983, reprinted 1992), Oxford Guides to Chaucer: The Canterbury Tales (1989, 2 edn 1996), The Long Fifteenth Century: Essays for Douglas Gray (co-ed with Sally Mapstone, 1997), Sir Thomas Malory: Le Morte Darthur (ed, 1998), The English Romance in Time (2004), Shakespeare and the Medieval World (2010); numerous articles on Chaucer, Gower, the Gawain-poet, romance, Wyatt, Spenser, Shakespeare et al; numerous reviews incl articles in TLS and London Review of Books; *Style*— Prof Helen Cooper, FBA; ✉ Magdalene College, Cambridge CB3 0AG (e-mail ehc31@cam.ac.uk)

COOPER, Imogen; CBE (2007); da of Martin Cooper (d 1986), and Mary, *née* Stewart (d 1998); *b* 28 August 1949; *Educ* Paris Conservatoire (Premier Prix); *m* 1982 (m dis 2002), John Batten; *Career* pianist; regular performer at Proms since televised debut 1975, first UK pianist and first woman to appear in South Bank Piano Series 1975, regular performer with all major orchs; orchestral engagements with: Berlin Philharmonic, Vienna Philharmonic, Boston Symphony, New York and Los Angeles Philharmonic Orchs; int tours incl: Austria, Italy, Germany, Australasia, Holland, France, Scandinavia, Spain, USA, Japan; *Recordings* incl: six CDs of Schubert, the piano works of Schubert's last six years, Schumann, Haydn, Mozart and Beethoven with Wolfgang Holzmair, Mozart double and triple piano concertos with Alfred Brendel, Schubert Trios and Arpeggione with Raphaël Oleg and Sonia Wieder-Atherton, Imogen Cooper & Friends (solo, chamber and lieder works), Mozart Concertos with Northern Sinfonia (aria); *Recreations* hill walking, architecture, cooking; *Style*— Imogen Cooper, CBE

COOPER, Janet; *b* 18 May 1959; *Educ* Univ of Leeds (LLB), London Business Sch; *Career* slr; ptnr and global head employee incentives Linklaters 1991–2011, ptnr Tapestry 2011–; dir: Employee Share Ownership Centre 1991–2011, Global Equity Orgn 1999– (vice-chair 2003–); dir ifsProShare Faculty Bd 2005–; co-fndr Share Schemes Advanced Studies Gp 1992–, course dir ICSA Cert Employee Share Plans; memb Cncl Roehampton Univ 2012–; tstee: UN Women NC UK 2009–15 (vice-chair 2012–15), RNLI 2014; memb CIPD Vice Pres Reward Panel 2012–14; memb Law Soc 1984; FRSA 2010, FCIPD 2012, FCIS 2015; *Publications* Tolley's Directors Remuneration (1996), The Executive Remuneration

Review (2015); *Recreations* family and friends, human rights, opera and theatre, skiing and travelling; *Clubs* Inst of Business Ethics, Int Women's Forum; *Style—* Ms Janet Cooper; ✉ e-mail janet.cooper@tapestrycompliance.com

COOPER, Hon Jason Charles Duff Bede; s and h of 2 Viscount Norwich; *b* 27 October 1959; *Educ* Eton, New Coll Oxford (BA), Oxford Brookes Univ (BA, Dip Arch); *Career* architect, designer, journalist; RIBA; *Recreations* piano, travel, skiing; *Style—* Jason Cooper; ✉ 14 Alexander Street, London W2 5NT (✆ 020 7727 3104)

COOPER, Jilly; OBE (2004); da of Brig W B Sallitt, OBE (d 1982), and Mary Elaine, *née* Whincup (d 1997); *b* 21 February 1937; *Educ* Godolphin Sch Salisbury; *m* 7 Oct 1961, Leo Cooper (d 2013), s of Leonard Cooper (d 1997), of Yorks; 1 s (Matthew Felix b 5 Sept 1968), 1 da (Emily Maud Lavinia b 13 June 1971); *Career* writer; former cub reporter Middlesex Independent Brentford 1955–57, followed by several jobs incl info offr, puppy fat model and switch board wrecker; newspaper columnist: Sunday Times 1969–82, Mail on Sunday 1982–87; winner of Lifetime Achievement Award British Book Awards 1998; hon degree Glocs Univ 2009, hon degree Anglia Ruskin Univ 2011; *Books* author of 40 books incl: Class (1979), Animals in War (1983), The Common Years (1984), Riders (1985), Rivals (1988), Polo (1991), The Man Who Made Husbands Jealous (1993), Araminta's Wedding (1993), Appassionata (1996), Score! (1999), Pandora (2002), Wicked! (2006), Jump! (2010), Mount! (2016); *Recreations* wild flowers, reading, mongrels, merry making, music and rescued greyhounds; *Style—* Mrs Leo Cooper, OBE; ✉ c/o Vivienne Schuster, Curtis Brown, Haymarket House, 28–29 Haymarket, London SW1Y 4ST (✆ 020 7393 4400)

COOPER, John; s of Kenneth Cooper, of Manchester, and Irene, *née* Wright; *b* 29 April 1955; *Educ* Manchester Grammar, Royal Coll of Music (ARCM), King's Coll Cambridge (MA), Heythrop Coll, Univ of London (MA); *m* 5 Oct 1983, Jane Mary, da of late Alan Arthur Kingshotte, of Strawberry Hill, Middx; 1 da (Charlotte b 28 Aug 1984), 1 s (Benedict b 26 April 1988); *Career* admitted slr 1979, avocat au barreau de Paris 1992; ptnr Lovell White & King 1985–88 (articled clerk 1977), ptnr Hogan Lovells (formerly Lovell White Durrant) 1988–2011, conslt Memery Crystal 2011–, co sec Kuwait Energy plc 2012–15; dir CFT Conslts Ltd 2011–, dir Kothari Investment Partnership Fund Inc 2014–; Freeman Worshipful Co of Slrs 1981; memb Law Soc; *Recreations* golf, horse racing, wine, music; *Style—* John Cooper, Esq; ✉ e-mail cooperjohn888@gmail.com

COOPER, John Gordon; QC (2010); s of John Gordon Cooper, of Wolverhampton, and Mary, *née* Hallam (d 1992); *b* 15 September 1958, Wolverhampton; *Educ* Regis Comp Sch, Univ of Newcastle upon Tyne (LLB, Butterworth Prize, Badminton blue), Cncl of Legal Educn; *Career* writer, barrister and broadcaster (in practice 25 Bedford Row London, named in Bar Nat Directory as one of the most highly regarded and leading barristers in London (top 40)); called to the Bar Middle Temple 1983 (advocacy trainer 2009–, bencher 2012), called to the Aust Bar NSW 1989 and Victoria 2014, lawyer Clifford Chance 1989, chief counsel to the Statute Law Revision Soc 2002–14, sr prosecutor for Attorney-General 2003–07, called to the Gibraltar Bar 2013; cases incl: defended in Leah Betts Ecstasy trial, employees rep BCCI litigation, Lord Ahmed vs Govt regarding privacy action, rep families in Deepcut Barracks case, appeal advsr in Jill Dando case, appeal advsr in R vs Whitewind (infanticide) case, advsr to families in Hercules and Nimrod aircraft cases v Govt, represents small shareholders in Northern Rock litigation, defended in R v Page (Buckingham Palace fraud) 2009, advising in appeal against conviction of Dr Crippen 2010, Dr David Kelly Judicial Review 2011, Twitter Joke Trial, Occupy St Paul's, R v Marrache (significant int fraud) 2013–14, representing family of deceased Jacintha Saldahna (nurse at King Edward VII Hosp) 2014; advised Law Cmmn on reform of the law of murder 2007 and expert evidence 2008, provided evidence to House of Lords Select Ctee on Communications Regarding Social Media 2014; legal advsr to: Lab Pty 1994–2003, Treasy 1997–2003 (Shadow Treasy 1993–97), Louise Woodward Campaign, Manjit Basuta Campaign 1999, FO 2003–; advsr to Slovakian oppn in Gen Election, advsr to Shadow AG and Shadow Slr-Gen 2014–, special advsr to Home Affairs Select Ctee 2015; judicial cmmr Children First Cmmn 2000–02; sec Lab Media Ctee; memb: Bar Cncl (co-opted) 1981–84 and 2000–14, Bar Human Rights Ctee 2002–, Bar Working Pty on Broadcasting in the Courtroom (co-author of paper), Coroners and Justice Bill 2009; Criminal Bar Assoc spokesperson Bar Cncl 2003–13, vice-chair Bar Cncl Public Affrs Ctee 2008–10; leading lawyer The Times Law Panel 2009–, dir of media Halsbury Law Exchange 2009–; memb: Fundraising Ctee Sheriffs and Recorders Fund for Ex-Offenders 2008–, Bar Conference Organising Bd 2008–, Bd of Tstees Prisoners of Conscience 2011–, Advsy Bd Law Faculty Newcastle Univ 2014–, Advsy Bd Big Brother Watch 2015–; chm Advsy Bd Trust the Market 2013–; visiting prof of law Cardiff Univ 2011; commended Barrister of the Year Lawyer Awards 1998, shortlisted Human Rights Barrister of the Year 2008, cited Pro Bono Barrister of the Year 2008, Lawyer of the Year Political and Public Life Awards 2015; contested (Lab): Surrey NW 1987, Amber Valley 1992; cnclr Watford 1990–94; pres and chm Nat Exec League Against Cruel Sports 1995– (memb 1992–), fell Oxford Centre for Animal Ethics 2008; memb Civic Theatre Tst Palace Theatre Watford 1991; academic advsr: London Law Review 2006–, UCL Jurisprudence Review 2007–; fndr creative writing course Poly of Central London (now Univ of Westminster) 1984, ed Criminal Bar Quarterly 1999–, memb Editorial Bd Wildlife Guardian (BBC Magazine of the Year 1998), memb Editorial Bd Catalyst (political think-tank) 1999–2014, bi-weekly columnist Justis.com 1999–2004, columnist The Times 1999–2009, feature writer Sunday Express 2004–, columnist New Law Jl 2007–, writer The Observer 2008–, conslt ed Criminal Law & Justice Weekly 2010–, columnist The Independent 2013–; writer: The Cure (Royal Court Theatre), Burning Point (Tricycle Theatre Kilburn), The Cured (Finborough Arms Theatre), The Law Lord (Screen Two film, BBC), The Advocates (3 part drama, Scottish TV), The Bill (contrib, Thames), Cutting Loose (LWT), Too Few to Mention (Channel 4), The Trial of Charles Stuart (Globe Theatre), To the Death (Bush Theatre); contrib: Legal Eagles (BBC Radio WM), Presenter (BBC Radio), The Talking Show (Channel 4), Street Legal (Channel 4), Talkback (Sky TV), The Moral Maze (Radio 4), Kangaroo Court (Endemol), Teens on Trial (Channel 4), Law in Action (BBC Radio 4), presenter Mindfield (BBC), Newsnight Special: Trial of the Allies (co-presenter, BBC) 2006, The Trial of Dick Turpin (Five), In My View (Al-Jazeera) 2010, Reunion (Radio 4) 2011, panellist Any Questions (Radio 4) 2013, guest Unreliable Evidence (Radio 4) 2014; res diarist The Lawyer 1992–2002, various TV appearances as legal expert; assoc prodr Zenith North; Freeman City of London (Coopers Co) 2013; FRSA 2009; *Publications* Planning and Environmental Law Bulletin (1991), Police and Criminal Evidence Act (2000), Judicial Review (2000), Cruelty – An Analysis of Article 3 (2000), The Courts Bill (2003), Domestic Violence, Crime and Victims (2004), Encyclopedia of Data Protection & Privacy (co-editor, 2004–), Animal Abuse and Human Violence (2009), Inquests (2010); *Recreations* photography, working out, football, the English Civil War; *Clubs* Chelsea Arts, Groucho, Home House, Wolverhampton Wanderers FC, Royal Gibraltar Yacht; *Style—* John Cooper, Esq; ✉ Parsonage Farm, Dairy Way, Abbots Langley, Hertfordshire WD5 0QJ (✆ and fax 01923 291264, website www.john-cooper.info); 25 Bedford Row, London WC1R 4HD (✆ 020 7067 1500, e-mail johncooperqc@sky.com, Twitter @John_Cooper_QC); agent: Paul Stevens, Independent Talent, 76 Oxford Street, London W1

COOPER, John Kaye; s of Ernest James Cooper, of Swillington, W Yorks, and Doreen Annie, *née* Kaye (d 1990); *b* 20 May 1947; *Educ* Rothwell GS, RSAMD; *m* 1 (m dis); 1 da (Gemma Lys b 1 Oct 1970); m 2, 1979, Charlotte Nerys Anne, da of Rev Canon Stephen Jackson; 2 s (Adam b 27 Oct 1980, Simon b 15 June 1982); *Career* cameraman Scottish Television 1967, floor mangr Thames Television 1968–71, prodn mangr Yorkshire Television 1971–76, drama prodr Tyne Tees Television 1976–77, prodr/dir Entertainment Dept LWT 1977–83, prodr/dir Limehouse Television 1983–84, controller of entertainment TVS 1984–87, independent prodr and md John Kaye Cooper Productions 1988–90, controller of entertainment and comedy LWT 1990–95, md Talent Television 1995–2002, creative dir Talent TV 2002–08, controller of entertainment ITV plc 2008–14; prodr Euro '96 Opening Ceremony Wembley Stadium; prodr numerous progs and series incl: Stanley Baxter Specials 1979–81, Stanley Baxter series 1982 (BAFTA Best Light Entertainment Prog 1982), Russ Abbot's Madhouse 1981–84, Save the Children with Michael Crawford 1988, Surgical Spirit (dir) 1988–89, That's Showbusiness 1990, BAFTA Craft Awards 1990, Cluedo 1990, Royal Variety Performance 1991, 1993, 1995, 2009, 2011–13 and 2015, Time After Time 1994–95, Audience with Alf Garnett 1997, 50th British Academy Film Awards 1998, British Academy TV Awards 1998, Alan Davies – Urban Trauma 1998, Our Vera 1999, The Villa 1999–2003, Bill Bailey – Bewilderness, TV Scrabble; exec prodr: Gladiators, Barrymore, The Brian Conley Show, Second Thoughts and Br Comedy Awards 1990–95, Test the Nation (BBC 1) 2002–07, What Did ITV Do For Me 2005, Piers Morgan's Life Stories (ITV) 2008–09, X Factor, Britain's Got Talent, The Cube, Take Me Out, Harry Hill's TV Burp, Ant & Dec's Saturday Night Takeaway, Catchphrase, The Brits and Classical Brits (ITV) 2008–14, Royal Variety Performance 2009, 2011, 2012 and 2013, An Audience with Michael Buble 2010, Brit Icons – Sir Elton John 2013; exec prodr numerous TV specials for ITV incl: Rod Stewart, Michael Buble, Phil Collins, Katherine Jenkins, Lionel Ritchie, Westlife; memb: RTS, BAFTA; *Recreations* supporting Leeds United; *Clubs* Ivy; *Style—* John Kaye Cooper, Esq

COOPER, Julie Elizabeth; MP; da of Robert Calder, and Teresa, *née* Smith; *b* 20 June 1960, Nelson, Lancs; *Educ* Edge Hill Coll of HE (BA), PGCE; *m* 28 July 1984, Brian Cooper; 1 s (David Robert b 13 Jan 1986), 1 da (Anna Elizabeth b 21 June 1988); *Career* formerly English teacher and pharmacy director; MP (Lab) Burnley 2015–; *Style—* Ms Julie Cooper, MP; ✉ 4 Keirby Walk, Burnley BB11 2DE (✆ 01282 425744); House of Commons, London SW1A 0AA (e-mail julie.cooper.mp@parliament.uk, website www.juliecooperforburnley.co.uk, Twitter @JulieForBurnley)

COOPER, Malcolm Ashton; s of Peter Ashton Cooper (d 1995), and Elisabeth, *née* Ward; *b* 28 July 1959, Exeter, Devon; *Educ* Univ of Birmingham (BA), Univ of Staffs (MPhil), Univ of Central England (Dip); *m* 1997, Dr Claire Frances Kenwood; *Career* Field Archaeology Unit Univ of Birmingham 1984–88, Hereford and Worcester CC 1988–93; English Heritage: inspector of ancient monuments 1993–96, head of Thames and Chilterns team and cathedrals team 1996–97, head of North and East London team 1997–98, dep dir London region 1998–2000, regnl dir North West region 2000–04, planning and devpt dir North 2004–05; chief inspector Historic Scotland 2005–11, dir Malcolm A Cooper Consulting 2011–12; special advsr Royal Incorporation of Architects in Scotland 2011–12; hon research fell Univ of Edinburgh Sch of History, Classics and Archaeology, visiting fell Univ of York 2011–, visiting lectr Moffett Centre Glasgow Caledonian Univ 2011–12; memb: Inst of Field Archaeologists 1987, MCIM 1992; FSA 2003, FSA Scot 2005, FRSA 2007, Hon FRIAS 2010, memb IHBC 2011; *Publications* Managing Archaeology (jt ed, 1995); *Recreations* classical and contemporary guitar; *Style—* Malcolm Cooper, Esq; ✉ The Croft, Irthington, Carlisle CA6 4NJ (✆ 01697 508638)

COOPER, Mark; s of Sir Frank Cooper, and Lady Peggy Cooper; *b* 14 November 1952, London; *Educ* Jesus Coll Cambridge (MA), Univ of Sussex (MA); *m* 2003, Sian Non Davies; 3 s (Luke b 6 July 1986, Cian b 10 Dec 1988, Evan b 31 May 1997), 1 da (Ceri b 8 Feb 2000); *Career* BBC: joined 1990, rising to creative head of music entertainment until 2013, head of music television BBC Studios 2013–; credits incl: Later...With Jools Holland, BBC Proms, Britannia series of documentaries, coverage of Glastonbury, Reading Festival and Radio 1's Big Weekend; *Recreations* cinema, cricket, reading; *Style—* Mark Cooper, Esq; ✉ BBC Western House, 99 Great Portland Street, London W1A 1AA

COOPER, Michael John; OBE (1997); s of Stanley Donald Cooper (d 1978), of Norwich, Norfolk, and Evelyn Joyce, *née* Norgate; *b* 5 April 1949; *Educ* Sutton HS, Univ of York (BA, PGCE); *m* 23 Aug 1975, Gillian Mary, *née* Isted; 2 s (David John b 11 June 1981, Simon John b 14 Jan 1983); *Career* VSO Chassa Secdy Sch Zambia 1972, dir of biology Mill Hill Sch London 1974–78 (teacher 1973–74), dep head upper sch Moulsham HS Chelmsford 1978–81, dep headteacher Valley Sch Worksop 1982–85, headteacher Hillcrest Sch Hastings 1985–90, princ Br Sch in the Netherlands 1990–99, headteacher Latymer Sch London 1999–; hon vice-pres Confedn of Br Schs in the European Communities, additional memb HMC; memb Bd of Govrs: Enfield Coll, Middlesex Univ; MIBiol 1971, FRSA 1990; *Recreations* walking, gardening, swimming, reading; *Clubs* East India; *Style—* Michael Cooper, Esq, OBE; ✉ The Latymer School, Haselbury Road, Edmonton, London N9 9TN (✆ 020 8807 2470, e-mail cpr@latymer.co.uk)

COOPER, Natasha; *see:* Wright, (Idonea) Daphne

COOPER, Neil Hunter; s of Keith Hunter Cooper (d 1977), and Margaret Anne, *née* Golden (d 2002); *b* 30 June 1947; *m* Marion Louise, *née* Woodward; 1 s (Ewan Charles Hunter), 1 da (Louise Elizabeth Anne (Mrs Tobias Duffin)); *Career* Government Insolvency Service 1966–72, public practice 1972–2015; dir Trutta Ltd; ret ptnr ZolfoCooper LLP; past pres Assoc Européenne de Practiciens des Procedures Collectives, pres Insol Int; conslt with World Bank, UNCITRAL, ADB, OECD, EBRD and Insol Int on int insolvency law reform, hon life pres INSOL Europe; regular speaker at professional and commercial confs on insolvency law and practice; FCCA, FIPA, FSPI, FRSA; *Books* Tolley's European Insolvency Guide, Recognition and Enforcement of Cross-Border Insolvency; *Recreations* classical music, opera, fly fishing, bird watching, photography; *Clubs* Athenaeum; *Style—* Neil Cooper, Esq; ✉ 10 Fleet Place, London EC4M 7RB (✆ 020 7332 5211, fax 020 7332 5001, e-mail neilc@trutta.co.uk)

COOPER, Paul; *b* 30 July 1965, York; *Educ* Archbishop Holgate's GS York, York Coll of Arts and Technol; *Career* photographer; trainee serv engr rising to product mktg mangr Azlan plc (formerly ADT Ltd) 1984–94, fndr Bailey-Cooper Photography 1995; commercial sector chm PPQB 2006–07; dir of qualifications Master Photographer's Assoc 2014– (nat pres 2011–12); FBIPP, FMPA; *Awards* over 150 awards incl BIPP Gold awards and UK Fuji Film Wedding & Portrait Awards; Master Photographers Assoc: UK Master Photographer of the Year 1999, UK Digital Photographer of the Year 2000, UK Commercial Photographer of the Year 2002, UK Fashion Photographer of the Year 2002, Awards of Excellence in Digital, Avant Garde Wedding and Under 5s categories, BIPP Peter Grugeon Award for Fellowship 2003, BIPP UK Commercial Photographer of the Year 2003, BIPP Photographer of the Year 2003, Qualified European Photographer Fedn of European Photographers 2003; hon fell Masters Photographers Assoc 2014; *Style—* Paul Cooper, Esq; ✉ Bailey-Cooper Photography, 4 Geldof Road, Huntington, North Yorkshire YO32 9JT (✆ 01904 416684, e-mail pc@baileycooper.co.uk)

COOPER, Paul Antony; s of Raymond Dennis Cooper, of Oxford, and Margaret, *née* Gingell; *b* 6 February 1953, Oxford; *Educ* The Oxford Sch, Selwyn Coll Cambridge (MA); *m* 2 Oct 1976, Nicola Francesca, *née* Jarvis; 3 s (Nicholas Guy David b 12 June 1981, Robert Antony Douglas b 1 April 1984, David Paul Edward b 22 Nov 1988); *Career* admitted slr 1977; trainee slr then slr Boodle Hatfield 1975–78, slr Norton Rose 1978–80, ptnr Bevan Ashford 1981–97 (slr 1980–81), ptnr Osborne Clarke 1997–; Corporate Lawyer of the Year Western Daily Press 2004, 2005 and 2006; memb Law Soc 1977; *Recreations* E-type Jaguar, running, wine; *Clubs* Commanderie de Bordeaux; *Style—* Paul

C

Cooper, Esq; ✉ Osborne Clarke, 2 Temple Back East, Temple Quay, Bristol BS1 6HE (☎ 0117 917 4252, fax 0117 917 4253, e-mail paul.cooper@osborneclarke.com)

COOPER, Philip Anthony Robert; s of Stanley Ernest Cooper, and Amy May, *née* Coleman; *b* 13 January 1950; *Educ* Felsted, Univ of Leeds (BSc), Univ of Cambridge (MA); *m* 1, 17 July 1976 (m dis 2000), (Elizabeth) Jane, da of Dr Harold Leslie Keer Whitehouse; 2 da (Harriet Amy Jane b 1980, Emily Sarah Rose b 1982), 1 s (Oliver Edward Keer b 1986); m 2, 17 Sept 2005, Ana; *Career* lectr Sch of Architecture Univ of Cambridge 1974–78, engr Harris and Sutherland (London and Cambridge) 1978–2003, tech dir Cameron Taylor Bedford Civil and Structural Engineers 2003–09, prof of structural design (first in UK) Univ of Leeds 1986–91; dir of structures Cambridge Architectural Research Ltd 2009–; lectr: Architectural Assoc 1993–, Univ of Cambridge; visiting prof Bath Univ; engr to the Royal Acad of Arts; memb Cathedrals Fabric Cmmn for Eng; FIStructE, FICE; *Recreations* tennis, music, windsurfing, furniture making; *Style—* Philip Cooper, Esq; ✉ 7 Quarry Crescent, Hastings TN34 3SD (☎ 01424 423354); Cambridge Architectural Research Ltd, 25 Gwydir Street, Cambridge CB1 2LG (☎ 01223 460475, fax 01223 464142, e-mail philip.cooper@carltd.com)

COOPER, R A; *see:* Austin-Cooper, Richard Arthur

COOPER, Prof Rachel Faith Davies; OBE (2012); da of David Withers (d 1973), of Leicester, and Elizabeth, *née* Parkes (d 1982); *b* 26 November 1953, Derby; *Educ* Staffordshire Poly (BA), Manchester Poly (PhD); *m* 1, 1974 (m dis 1982); m 2, 1984, Cary Cooper; 2 da (Laura Ann b 1 Nov 1982, Sarah Kate b 2 March 1985); *Career* freelance designer and pt/t lectr in design 1976–91, research fell Manchester Poly 1978–82, prof Salford Univ 1995–2005 (research fell 1991–95), prof Lancaster Univ and dir Lancaster Inst for the Contemporary Arts 2006–; memb Cncl AHRC 2005–; strategic advsr EPSRC 2002–05; FRSA; *Publications* The Design Agenda (1995), The Design Experience (2003), The Design and Construction Process (2004), Designing Sustainable Cities (2010); *Recreations* gardening; *Style—* Prof Rachel Cooper, OBE

COOPER, Prof Richard Anthony; s of Arthur Charles Cooper, and Joan Mary, *née* Cutter; *b* 12 January 1947, York; *Educ* Manchester Grammar, New Coll Oxford (BA, DPhil, Lacrosse half blue); *m* 1, 1973, Clara Maria Florio; 2 s (Edward b 1977, Alexander b 1981); m 2, 2012, Emanuela Tandello; *Career* lectr in French Lancaster Univ 1971; Univ of Oxford: fell BNC 1977, reader in French 1996, prof of French 1998, chair Faculty Bd 2012–; memb Académie des Sciences, Belles Lettres et Arts Lyon 1997, memb Institut des Sciences de l'Homme Lyon; Commandeur dans l'Ordre des Palmes Académiques 1996, Commendatore dell'Ordine al Merito della Repubblica Italiana 2003; *Publications* Rabelais et L'Italie (1991), Litterae in Tempore Belli (1997), The Entry of Henri II into Lyon, September 1548 (1997), Marguerite de Navarre, Chretiens et Mondains, poemes epars (2007), Jean Du Bellay, Poemata (jtly, 2007), Jean Maugin, Le premier livre de l'histoire et ancienne chronique de Gerard d'Euphrate (2012); *Recreations* sport, wine, gardening; *Clubs* Vincent's (Oxford), Athenaeum; *Style—* Prof Richard Cooper; ✉ 26 Polstead Road, Oxford OX2 6TN (☎ 01865 510030); Brasenose College, Oxford OX1 4AJ (☎ 01865 277864, e-mail richard.cooper@bnc.ox.ac.uk)

COOPER, Dr Richard Michael; s of late Harry Cecil Cohen, of London, and Sadie, *née* Speier; *b* 25 November 1940; *Educ* Belmont, Mill Hill Sch, Charing Cross Hosp (Gynaecology Prize, Forensic Med Prize); *m* Dawne Cooper (d 2014); 1 s (Adam b 31 July 1968), 2 da (Louise b 6 May 1972, Gabrielle b 22 Nov 1972); *Career* house appts at Charing Cross Hosp and Mount Vernon Hosp; princ in gen practice: 74 Brooksby's Walk London 1966–70, 71 Amhurst Park London 1970–76; in private practice 17 Harley St London 1966–; med conslt: WPP Advertising, Zurich Assurance Co and various other companies; med examiner numerous insurance cos, conslt med offr Pinnacle and Catlin Insurance Cos, approved med examiner for all major cruise lines; memb Cncl Ind Doctors' Forum (also educn offr); fell: Assurance Med Soc (also sec), Hunterian Soc; FRSM 1969; *Recreations* family, broadcasting, fundraising and other communal activities, writing med articles, foreign travel; *Clubs* Old Millhillians, Knightsbridge Speakers'; *Style—* Dr Richard M Cooper; ✉ 35 West Hill Park, Highgate, London N6 6ND (☎ 020 8342 8818); 17 Harley Street, London W1G 9QH (☎ 020 7580 3324, 020 7636 3126, website www.17harleystreet.co.uk)

COOPER, Robert Francis; KCMG (2013, CMG 1997), MVO (1975); s of Norman Cooper (d 1966), and Frances Cooper (d 1999); *b* 28 August 1947; *Educ* Delamere Sch Nairobi, Worcester Coll Oxford (BA), Univ of Pennsylvania (MA); *Career* HM Dip Serv 1970, FCO 1970–71, Language Study 1971–73, Br Embassy Tokyo 1973–77, FCO 1979–82, seconded to Bank of England 1982–84, UK rep to EC Brussels 1984–87, head Far Eastern Dept FCO 1987–89, head of Policy Planning Staff 1989–92, British Embassy Bonn 1993–98, dir Asia Pacific FCO 1998–99, on loan to Cabinet Office 1999–2001, govt special rep on Afghanistan 2001–02, DG for external affrs EU Cncl Secretariat 2002– ; Order of the Sacred Treasure (4 Class, Japan) 1975; *Publications* The Breaking of Nations (2003); *Recreations* bicycles, ballroom bridge and the Bard; *Style—* Sir Robert Cooper, KCMG, MVO

COOPER, Robert George; s of Alan Cooper, and Helen Cooper; *b* 8 September 1950; *Educ* Univ of Hull (BA); *Children* 2 da (Zoe b 1984, Emily b 1987); *Career* station asst BBC Radios Humberside and Merseyside 1972–74, prodr of Alan Bleasdale's Scully... series for Radio City Liverpool 1974–76, stage mangr Victoria Theatre Stoke-on-Trent 1977, radio drama prodr for BBC (incl radio plays by Anthony Minghella, Jimmy McGovern, Stewart Parker, William Trevor and Neil Jordan), head of TV drama BBC Northern Ireland 1989–2004 (prodr: Truly Madly Deeply 1990 (BAFTA nomination 1992), Love Lies Bleeding 1993, The Precious Blood 1996 (Emmy nomination 1996, BAFTA nomination 1997), Divorcing Jack 1997, Rebel Heart 2000, As The Beast Sleeps 2002; exec prodr: Ballykissangel 1995–2001 (BAFTA nomination 1997, RTS award 1997), The Hanging Gale 1995 (BAFTA nomination 1996, FIPA award 1996), Dance Lexie Dance 1997 (Oscar nomination 1998), Amongst Women 1998 (BAFTA nomination 1999, BANNF award 1999), Eureka Street 1999, Messiah 2001–08 (Monte Carlo TV Festival Award 2002), Sinners 2002 (Monte Carlo TV Festival Award 2002, Shanghai TV Festival Awards 2002), Holy Cross 2003 (Shanghai TV Festival Award 2004, RTS nomination 2004), Gunpowder, Treason and Plot 2004), dir Great Meadow Prodns 2004– (exec prodr: Margaret Thatcher: The Long Walk To Finchley 2008 (Broadcasting Press Guild Award, BAFTA nomination, RTS nomination), Margaret 2009, When Harvey Met Bob 2010 (IFRA Award), Room at the Top 2012 (BAFTA Award 2013, RTS nomination 2013), Wodehouse In Exile 2013); *Recreations* making furniture; *Clubs* BAFTA; *Style—* Robert Cooper; ✉ Great Meadow Ltd (☎ 020 7733 7621, website www.greatmeadowprods.com)

COOPER, Prof Robin Hayes; s of Dennis Joffre Cooper, and Marjorie, *née* Wilding; *b* 23 December 1947; *Educ* Corpus Christi Coll Cambridge (MA), Univ of Massachusetts (PhD); *m* 14 June 1985, Elisabet Britt, da of Gunnar Engdahl; 2 da (Anna Julia b 12 May 1986, Maria Emily b 19 March 1991); *Career* lectr in English language Univ of Freiburg 1969–71; Univ of Massachusetts: teaching asst in linguistics and TEFL 1971–73, research asst in natural language semantics 1973–75; asst prof Dept of Linguistics: Univ of Texas 1975–76, Univ of Massachusetts 1976–77; assoc prof Dept of Linguistics Univ of Wisconsin 1981–87 (asst prof 1977–81); docent Dept of Linguistics and Phonetics Lund Univ 1984–87; Univ of Edinburgh: reader Dept of Artificial Intelligence and Centre for Cognitive Science 1989–92 (lectr 1986–89), princ investigator Human Communication Research Centre 1989–96, reader Centre for Cognitive Science 1992–96; prof of computational linguistics Univ of Gothenburg 1995–2012, dir Swedish Nat Grad Sch of Language Technol 2001–12, sr prof of computational linguistics Univ of Gothenburg 2012–; Stanford Univ: Mellon fell in linguistics and philosophy 1980–81, fell Center for Advanced Study in the Behavioural Sciences 1981–82; Guggenheim fell 1986–87; fil dr hc Uppsala 2006; FBA 1993, fell Royal Soc of Arts and Sciences Göteborg 1996, MAE 2009; *Books* Quantification and Syntactic Theory (1983), Situation Theory and its Applications Vol 1 (jt ed, 1990), Language in Flux: Dialogue Coordination, Language Variation, Change and Evolution (jt ed, 2008); *Recreations* yoga, music; *Style—* Prof Robin Cooper, FBA; ✉ Bigatan 1, S-431 39 Mölndal, Sweden (☎ 00 46 31 82 94 38); Department of Philosophy, Linguistics and Theory of Science, University of Gothenburg, Box 200, S-40530, Göteborg, Sweden (☎ 00 46 31 786 2536, fax 00 46 31 786 4853, e-mail cooper@ling.gu.se)

COOPER, Rosie; MP; *b* 5 September 1950; *Career* cncllr Liverpool City Cncl 1973–2000, Lord Mayor of Liverpool 1992–93; dir Merseyside Centre for Deaf People; MP (Lab) Lancashire W 2005– (Parly candidate (Lab) Liverpool Broadgreen 1992); Hon Alderman Liverpool City Cncl 2011; *Style—* Ms Rosie Cooper, MP; ✉ House of Commons, London SW1A 0AA

COOPER, Rt Hon Yvette; PC (2007), MP; da of Tony Cooper, and June, *née* Iley; *b* 20 March 1969; *Educ* Eggars Comp, Alton Sixth Form Coll, Balliol Coll Oxford (BA), Harvard Univ (Kennedy Scholar), LSE (MSc); *m* 10 Jan 1998, Rt Hon Edward Balls, MP, *qv*; 1 s, 2 da; *Career* economic researcher for late John Smith, MP as shadow Chllr of the Exchequer 1990–92, policy advsr to Bill Clinton presidential elections 1992, policy advsr to Lab Treasy team 1993–94, research assoc Centre for Economic Performance LSE 1994–95, econ columnist and ldr writer The Independent 1995–97, MP (Lab) Pontefract and Castleford 1997–, Parly under-sec of state and min for Public Health 1999–2002, Parly sec Lord Chllr's Dept 2002–03, Parly sec ODPM 2003–05, min for housing and planning ODPM 2005–06, min of state Dept for Communities and Local Govt 2006–07, min of state for Housing 2007–08, chief sec to the Treasury 2008–09, sec of state for work and pensions 2009–10, shadow foreign sec and min for women and equalities 2010–11, shadow home sec and min for women and equalities 2011–15; *Recreations* swimming, gardening; *Style—* Ms Yvette Cooper, MP; ✉ House of Commons, London SW1A 0AA (☎ 020 7219 5080, e-mail coopery@parliament.uk, website www.yvettecooper.com)

COOPER OF WINDRUSH, Baron (Life Peer UK 2014), of Windrush, of Chipping Norton in the County of Oxfordshire Andrew Cooper; *Educ* LSE (BSc Econ); *Career* head of research Soc for Market R&D 1994–96,dir of strategy Cons Pty 1997–99, fndr and strategy dir Populus 2003–; memb Mgmnt Ctee Br Polling Cncl 2005–; *Publications* Wrong Again (1997), Blue Tomorrow (contrib, 2001), From the Ashes (contrib, 2005); *Style—* The Lord Cooper of Windrush; ✉ Populus, Northburgh House, 10 Northburgh Street, London EC1V 0AT

COOTE, Prof John Haven; s of Albert Ernest Coote (d 1967), of Enfield, and Gladys Mary Elizabeth, *née* Noble; *b* 5 January 1937; *Educ* Enfield GS, Chelsea Coll, Royal Free Hosp Sch of Med, Univ of London (BSc, PhD), Univ of Birmingham (DSc), Jagiellonian Univ Kraców (Dip Faculty of Med); *m* 28 Dec 1974, Susan Mary, da of Dr William Hawkins Hylton (d 1989), of Clevedon; 1 s (Edward John b 1976), 2 da (Rachel Elizabeth b 1978, Naomi Caroline b 1981); *Career* Univ of Birmingham: lectr 1967, sr lectr 1970, reader 1977, prof of physiology and head of dept 1984–2003, Bowman prof of physiology 1985–2003, head Sch of Basic Med 1988–91, emeritus prof 2003–; hon lectr Royal Free Hosp Sch of Med 1966; visiting prof: Tokyo 1974, Chicago 1988, Shanghai 1989, Heidelberg 1992, in cardiology Glenfield Hosp Univ of Leicester 2003–, in biomedical scis Univ of Warwick 2003–, Univ of Nankai China 2004; hon conslt in physiology NHS Dudley AHA 1978–82; chair Ethics Ctee QinetiQ Ltd 1998–2008; chair Editorial Bd Experimental Physiology; memb: Ctee Physiological Soc 1976–80, Soc for Experimental Biology 1976–, Ethics Ctee Defence Evaluation and Research Agency 1998–, Cncl British Heart Fndn 1998–2003, Physiologica Soc 2002–, Defence Science Advy Cncl 2003–; Carl Ludwig Distinguished Lecture Award American Physiological Soc 2003; hon memb Physiological Soc 2004–, civil conslt Applied Physiology RAF; FRSB 1988, CBiol 1988, memb NY Acad of Sciences 1991, FRGS 2004, hon fell Br Physiological Soc 2012; *Recreations* running, mountaineering (Birmingham Med Res Expeditionary Soc); *Clubs* Univ of London Graduate Mountaineering; *Style—* Prof John Coote; ✉ School of Clinical and Experimental Medicine, College of Medical and Dental Sciences, University of Birmingham, Birmingham B15 2TJ (☎ 0121 414 6916, fax 0121 414 6924, e-mail j.h.coote@bham.ac.uk); home ☎ 0121 427 5037

COPE, Jerry; s of Michael Ewart Cope, and Maureen Ann, *née* Casey; *b* 30 November 1951; *Educ* St Paul's, Jesus Coll Cambridge (MA), Univ of Warwick (MSc, MBA); *m* 19 Oct 1985, Dianne Elizabeth Gilmour; 1 s (Jonathan b 21 Nov 1989); *Career* Post Office: joined 1973, early roles in personnel and line mgmnt, gen mangr London 1988, dir gp strategy 1993, full time memb Bd 1996, gp md strategy and int 1998; md UK Royal Mail 2002–03; dir Camelot 2000–03, chair t-three Ltd (formerly HRS Ltd) 2004–, chair PLCWW 2008–; chair Prison Service Pay Review Body 2005–11, chair NHS Pay Review Body 2011–, tstee RMSE Pension Plan 2015–; chair Bd of Govrs Kingston Univ 2002–07, non-exec dir GCDA 2007–12, dir English Bridge Union 2011–; chair London South Bank Univ 2015–; *Recreations* supporting Fulham FC, bridge, arts, cooking, avoiding the gardening; *Clubs* Hurlingham; *Style—* Jerry Cope, Esq; ✉ 24 Auckland Road, London SE19 2DJ

COPE, Jonathan; CBE (2003); *b* 1963; *Educ* White Lodge Royal Ballet Sch; *m* Maria Almeida; 1 da (Anoushka), 1 s (Joseph); *Career* ballet dancer; princ Royal Ballet 1987–90 (joined 1982), business career 1990–92, returned to Royal Ballet 1992; leading roles (with Royal Ballet) incl: Prince in Swan Lake, The Sleeping Beauty and The Nutcracker, Solor in La Bayadère, Albrecht in Giselle, Romeo and Juliet, Le Baiser de la Fée, The Prince of the Pagodas, Cinderella, Palemon in Ondine, Serenade, Agon, Apollo, Opus 19/ The Dreamer, The Sons of Horus, Young Apollo, Galanteries, The Planets, Still Life at the Penguin Café, The Spirit of Fugue, Concerto, Gloria, Requiem, Triad, A Broken Set of Rules, Pursuit, Piano, Grand Pas Classique, Monotones, Crown Prince Rudolph in Mayerling, Woyzeck in Different Drummer, Second Friend and Foreman in The Judas Tree, Anastasia, Beliaev in A Month in the Country, The Poet in Illuminations, Birthday Offering, La Valise, Air, Monotones II, Thaïs, Armand in Marguerite and Armand, Fox in Renard, Fearful Symmetries, ...now languorous, now wild..., Symphony in C (partnering Sylvie Guillem), Duo Concertant, Jean de Brienne in Raymonda Act III, Remanso, Seranade, The Firebird, Andantino Boy in Les Biches, The Lover in Lilac Garden, If This Is Still A Problem, Dances with Death, Pavane Pour une Infante Défunte, Sawdust and Tinsel, Words Apart, Tidelines, Cry Baby Kreisler, 3:4, The Crucible, Dance Variations, Tryst, There Where She Loves, Des Grieux in Manon, Beyond Bach, Por Vos Muero, Escamillo in Carmen; various TV perfomances with Royal Ballet; South Bank Show Dance Award 2003; *Style—* Jonathan Cope, Esq, CBE; ✉ The Royal Ballet, Royal Opera House, Covent Garden, London WC2E 9DD (☎ 020 7240 1200, fax 020 7212 9121)

COPE, Wendy Mary; OBE (2010); da of Fred Stanley Cope (d 1971), of Kent, and Alice Mary, *née* Hand (d 2004); *b* 21 July 1945, Erith, Kent; *Educ* Farringtons Sch Chislehurst, St Hilda's Coll Oxford (MA), Westminster Coll Oxford (DipEd); *m* 8 May 2013, Lachlan Mackinnon; *Career* primary sch teacher: London Borough of Newham 1967–69, ILEA 1969–86 (seconded to Contact Newspaper as Arts and Reviews ed 1982–84, pt/t teacher 1984–86); freelance writer 1986–; Cholmondeley Award for Poetry 1987, Michael Braude Award American Acad of Arts and Letters 1995; Hon DLitt: King Alfred's Coll Winchester/Univ of Southampton 1999, Oxford Brookes Univ 2003; FRSL; *Books* Making

Cocoa for Kingsley Amis (1986), Twiddling Your Thumbs (1988), The River Girl (1991), Is That The New Moon? Poems by Women Poets (ed, 1988), Serious Concerns (1992), The Orchard Book of Funny Poems (ed, 1993), The Funny Side (ed, 1998), The Faber Book of Bedtime Stories (ed, 2000), If I Don't Know (2001), Heaven on Earth: Happy Poems (ed, 2001), George Herbert: Verse and Prose (ed, 2002), Two Cures for Love: selected poems 1979–2006 (2008), Going for a Drive (2010), Family Values (2011), Time for School (2013), Life, Love and the Archers (2014); *Recreations* playing the piano; *Style—* Ms Wendy Cope, OBE, FRSL; ✉ c/o Faber & Faber, Bloomsbury House, 74–77 Great Russell Street, London WC1B 3DA (☎ 020 7927 3800)

COPE OF BERKELEY, Baron (Life Peer UK 1997), of Berkeley in the County of Gloucestershire; Sir John Ambrose Cope; kt (1991), PC (1988); s of late George Arnold Cope, MC, FRIBA, and Mrs Catherine Cope; *b* 13 May 1937, Leicester; *Educ* Oakham Sch Rutland; *m* 1969, Djemila, da of late Col P V Lovell Payne, and late Mrs Tanetta Blackden, of the American Colony of Jerusalem; 2 da (Lucinda (Mrs Lopresti), Nicola (Mrs Haine)); *Career* cmmd RA 1955–57, then TA; chartered accountant; Parly candidate (Cons) Woolwich E 1970; MP (Cons): S Glos 1974–83, Northavon 1983–97; asst Govt whip 1979–81, a Lord Cmmr of the Treasury 1981–83, dep chief whip and treas HM's Household 1983–87, min of state Dept of Employment and minister for Small Firms 1987–89, min of state Northern Ireland 1989–90, dep chm Cons Pty 1990–92, Paymaster Gen 1992–94; oppn spokesman on NI House of Lords 1997–98, oppn spokesman on Home Affrs House of Lords 1998–2001, oppn chief whip House of Lords 2001–07; tstee: War Memls Tst, Friends of Edward Said, National Conservatory of Music UK; FCA; *Recreations* a Derby Bentley motor car; *Clubs* Beefsteak, Pratt's, Carlton, Tudor House Chipping Sodbury; *Style—* The Rt Hon Lord Cope of Berkeley; ✉ House of Lords, London SW1A 0PW (e-mail copej@parliament.uk)

COPELAND, Prof John Richard Malcolm; s of Lorenzo Copeland (d 1982), and Kathleen Mary, *née* Hopkinson (d 1970); *b* 14 October 1932, Stoke-on-Trent; *Educ* Newcastle under Lyme HS, Emmanuel Coll Cambridge (MA, MD, ScD), Univ of London (academic DPM); *m* 1963, Mary Bridget, da of Thomas O'Dwyer; 2 da (Caroline Mary Teresa b 1964, Veronica Anne Louise b 1965), 1 s (Andrew Thomas John b 1967); *Career* West End Hosp for Neurology and Neurosurgery London 1962–64, Maudsley Hosp 1964–76, lectr and sr lectr in psychiatry Inst of Psychiatry London 1969–76 (UK dir US/UK Diagnostic Project 1970–77), hon lectr Guy's Hosp 1970–76; Univ of Liverpool: prof and head Dept of Psychiatry 1976–97, founding dir Inst of Human Ageing 1981–97, hon conslt psychiatrist North Mersey Community Tst 1976–97; head: Collaborating Centre on Ageing, World Fedn for Mental Health, Inst of Human Ageing 1993–97; Sandoz lectr Basle 1990, Maudsley Bequest lectr RCPsych, Hakone lectr Japan 1998; advsr WHO, advsr and visiting prof Univ of Garounis (Libya) 1980–90; chm Jt Ctee on Higher Psychiatric Trg in the Br Isles 1988–91, chair Mgmnt Ctee European Concerted Action on Depression in Older Age Eurodep 1993–2005; pres World Fedn Mental Health 2007–09 (treas 1999–2003, chair World Mental Health Day 2003–05, chair Disaster Response Initiative 2005–, fndr and chair World Fedn Mental Health UK), chair WFMH Great Push for Mental Health 2010– and originator of the People's Charter for Mental Health sponsored by WFMH 2013 and the Movement for Global Mental Health, Sharma-Copeland Partnership for the Global Mental Health Assessment and Treatment Tool (GMHAT) 2010–; memb: Advsy Bd on the Conferment of Titles Univ of London 1991–97, Sci Ctee Int Inst of Psychosocial and Social Economic Research Univ of Maastricht 1990–2005, Research Ctee Alzheimers Disease Soc UK 1990–99, chm Academic Old Age Psychiatry Assoc 1998–2006, Steering Ctee MRC Cognitive Function and Ageing Study, Mgmnt Ctee MRC AGENET Foresight Initiative 1996–2001; Gold medal Yonsei Univ Coll of Med (Korea); Lifetime Achievement Award Indian Neuroscience Gp 2003, Personality of the Year EUTHAMI Europe 2015; memb European Psychogeriatric Assoc; FRCPsych 1977, FRCP 1980, FRSM (memb Cncl Section on Geriatrics and Gerantology 1992–97); *Books* Psychiatric Diagnosis in New York and London (jtly, 1972), The Mind and Mood of Ageing: The Mental Health Problems of the Community Elderly in New York and London (jtly, 1983), Alzheimer's Disease: Potential Therapeutic Strategies (ed, 1992), Principles and Practice of Geriatric Psychiatry (sr ed, 2 edn 2002); *Recreations* porcelain, Victorian house maintenance; *Clubs* Oxford and Cambridge; *Style—* Emeritus Prof John Copeland; ✉ Liverpool University Div of Psychiatry, Section of Old Age Psychiatry, St Catherine's Hospital, Birkenhead, Wirral CH42 0LQ (☎ 0151 488 7291, fax 0151 653 3441, e-mail jrmcop@btinternet.com)

COPELAND, Katherine; MBE (2013); *b* 1 December 1990, Ashington, Northumberland; *Educ* Yarm Sch; *Career* rower; achievements incl: Gold medal (lightweight single scull) World U23 Rowing Championships 2011, Gold medal (lightweight double sculls) Olympic Games 2012; *Clubs* Tees Rowing; *Style—* Ms Katherine Copeland, MBE

COPELAND, Councillor Michael Stewart; MLA, GSM (NI); s of George Copeland, and Emily, *née* Spence; *b* 23 June 1954, Belfast; *Educ* Lisnasharragh Secdy Sch, RMA Sandhurst; *m* 1979, Sonia Christina, *née* Moore; 1 da (Sarah), 1 s (Matthew); *Career* carpenter William Copeland & Sons Ltd 1970, offr HM Armed Forces 1972, sales mangr MoDorc Sales Ltd 1979–81, co dir 1981–84, md 1984, MLA (UUP) Belfast E 2003–07 and 2011–; *Recreations* reading, music; *Clubs* The Original Seven; *Style—* Councillor Michael Copeland, MLA; ✉ Room 276, Parliament Buildings, Stormont, Ballymiscaw BT4 3XX (e-mail michael.copeland@mla.niassembly.gov.uk, website www.michaelcopelandmla.com)

COPELAND, Stephen Andrew; s of Derek Copeland, of Nantwich, Cheshire, and Peggy, *née* Strangward; *b* 7 May 1946; *Educ* Nantwich GS, St Bartholomew's Hosp Med Sch London (MB BS); *m* 3 April 1972, Jennifer Ann, da of Dr John Almeyda, KSG (d 1986); 1 da (Sara Clare b 26 Feb 1973), 1 s (Matthew Scott b 17 March 1976); *Career* sr registrar Bart's 1975–79, clinical lectr Royal Nat Orthopaedic Hosp 1978, conslt orthopaedic surgn Royal Berkshire Hosp Reading 1979–2002, dir Reading Shoulder Unit 2002–12 (currently emeritus pres); past pres Euro Shoulder and Elbow Surgery Soc, chm Int Bd of Shoulder and Elbow Surgeons, corresponding memb American Shoulder and Elbow Soc; former: pres Br Shoulder and Elbow Soc, memb Cncl Orthopaedic Section RSM; memb Editorial Bd JBJS; developed own design of shoulder replacement; author of papers on shoulder surgery; hon memb Spanish, Australian, S African, Brazilian, Argentinian and S Korean Shoulder Surgery Socs, ABC travelling fell; *Books* Surgical Reconstruction in Rheumatoid Disease (1993), Operative Shoulder Surgery (1995), Shoulder Surgery (1996), Stiffness in the Upper Limb (1997); *Recreations* cars, garden; *Style—* Stephen Copeland, Esq; ✉ Springfield House, Shepherds Green, Henley-on-Thames, Oxfordshire RG9 4QR; Berkshire Independent Hospital, Wensley Road, Coley Park, Reading, Berkshire (☎ 0118 902 8063, e-mail stephen.copeland@btinternet.com)

COPEMAN, Dr Peter William Monckton; s of William Sydney Charles Copeman, CBE, TD, JP, MA, MD, FRCP (d 1970), and Helen, *née* Bourne (d 1980); head of the Copeman family, formerly of Sparham, Norfolk (see Burke's Landed Gentry, 18 Edn, Vol III, 1972); *b* 9 April 1932; *Educ* Eton, CCC Cambridge (MA, MD, Copeman medal 1973), St Thomas' Hosp; *m* 19 May 1973, Lindsey Bridget, da of late David Vaughan Brims, of Heddon Hall, Northumberland; 3 da (Mary (Mrs Rose) b 1975, Louisa (Mrs Elder) b 1977, Caroline (Mrs Barrow) b 1980), 1 s (Andrew b 1980); *Career* emeritus consIt physician for diseases of the skin i/c Dept of Dermatology Westminster and Westminster Children's Hosp; research fell Mayo Clinic USA 1968; Wellcome research fell 1969–73; clinician and researcher; hon conslt dermatologist St Luke's Hosp for the Clergy London; Willan librarian RCP; hon sr lectr Westminster Med Sch; former memb Gen and Exec Ctees The Game Conservancy (co-fndr Research Planning Ctee 1971), tstee Arthritis Research UK (formerly Arthritis Research Campaign) 1970–2004 (vice-pres 2004), The Soc of the Faith; co-patron (with A R C Copeman) Living of St James the Less Hadleigh Essex; co-patron and tstee St Mary's Bourne St London 1969–2015 (churchwarden 1970–95); Liveryman Worshipful Soc of Apothecaries, Freeman City of London; fell or memb: Br Assoc of Dermatologists, Med Soc of London, Hunterian Soc, Osler Club, RSM, European Soc of Clinical Investigation, Soc for Investigative Dermatology Inc, American Fedn for Clinical Research; FRCP 1975; memb Hosp Ctee Military and Hospitaller Order of St Lazarus of Jerusalem 1960–71; OStJ (memb Hosp Ctee 1972–99); *Publications* On Cutaneous Diseases: Robert Willan (book and CD-Rom, 1998); author of textbook chapters, and 150 papers in int jls on original research in gen med, dermatology and history of med; *Recreations* field sports, improving the landscape (Laurent Perrier Conservation Award finalist); *Clubs* Athenaeum (past chm Wine Ctee), Old Etonian Rifle (Capt VIII 1950), Univ Pitt (Cambridge); *Style—* Dr Peter Copeman; ✉ 20 Spencer Park, London SW18 2SZ (☎ 020 8874 7549); Abshiel Farm, Morpeth, Northumberland NE65 8QN

C

COPLAND, Dr Geoffrey Malcolm; CBE (2007); s of Cyril Charles Copland (d 1984), and Jessie, *née* Ogden; *b* 28 June 1942; *Educ* Fitzmaurice GS Bradford-on-Avon, Merton Coll Oxford (open postmastership, Harmsworth sr scholar, MA, DPhil); *m* 1, 1967, Janet Mary Todd; 1 da (Heidi Louise b 1970), 1 s (Alistair Hugh b 1973); m 2, 1985, Dorothy Joy Harrison; *Career* postdoctoral research Yale Univ 1967–69; Univ of London: postdoctoral research Queen Mary Coll 1969–71, lectr in physics Queen Elizabeth Coll 1971–80, dean of studies Goldsmiths Coll 1981–87; Univ of Westminster (formerly Poly of Central London): dep rector 1987–95, rector and vice-chllr 1995–2007; govr Harrow Coll 1995–2003; chm Thomas Wall Tst; memb cncl Edexcel Fndn 1998–2003, tstee and memb Cncl CIHE (Cncl for Industry and Higher Educn) 1999–2007, chm Univs and Colleges Employers Assoc (UCEA) 2002–06; UUK (formerly CVCP): memb Cncl 1998–2007, vice-pres 2003–07, chm England and NI Cncl 2003–07; govr: Int Student House 2002–, Trinity Laban Conserrvatoire of Music and Dance 2007– (vice-chair 2012–), Univ of Bedfordshire 2007–14, Trinity Coll London 2012–; pres Assoc Sandwich Educn of Trg (ASET) 2006–; Hon DSc Univ of Westminster 2008; FInstP 2003 (MInstP 1974), FRSA 1990, FGCL 2000, Hon FTCL 2000; *Publications* author of research papers and review articles in various academic jls; *Recreations* walking, gardening, cricket; *Clubs* Oxford and Cambridge; *Style—* Dr Geoffrey Copland, CBE; ✉ 24 The Broadway, Wheathampstead, St Albans, Hertfordshire AL4 8LN (☎ 01438 833663, e-mail coplang494@aol.com)

COPLAND, (William) Michael Ainslie; s of William Oranmore Copland (d 1980), of Tarporley, Cheshire, and Ethel Ainslie, *née* Bond; *b* 17 April 1947; *Educ* Sedbergh, St Catherine's Coll Oxford (MA), DMS; *m* 9 May 1970, Elizabeth Proctor, da of Edgar Anthony Francis; 1 s (Christopher Ainslie b 31 Jan 1974), 1 da (Sarah Elizabeth b 19 July 1975); *Career* editorial asst FMT Editorial & Writing Services Ltd 1970–73, PR mangr Inst of Mktg 1973–75, gp communications exec Giltspur Ltd 1975–77, dir of advtg and PR Burroughs Machines Ltd 1979–83 (PR mangr 1977–79), media rels mangr STC plc 1983–86, md Brodeur A Plus (formerly A Plus Group Ltd PR) 1992–98 (dir 1986–), md Brodeur Worldwide EMEA 1998–; memb Bd of Mgmnt PRCA; MCIM 1991; *Recreations* tennis, walking, Amnesty International; *Style—* Michael Copland, Esq; ✉ Brodeur A Plus, New Tithe Court, 23 Datchet Road, Slough, Berkshire SL3 7PT (☎ 01753 790700, fax 01753 790701)

COPLAND-GRIFFITHS, Dr Michael Charles; s of Lt Cdr (Frederick) Charles Brandling Copland-Griffiths, MBE, of Bramley Cottage, Trowle House, Wingfield, Trowbridge, Wilts, and Mary Esmah Elizabeth, *née* Fry; *b* 7 November 1946; *Educ* Bradfield Coll, Anglo-Euro Coll of Chiropractic (Dr of Chiropractic, Best All-round Student Award); *m* 1, 28 Aug 1976 (m dis 1980), (Lorna) Penelope, da of John Napthine, of Spondon, Derbys; m 2, 6 Dec 1980 (m dis 2005), Noelle Mary (Penny), da of Herbert Bexon Spencer (d 1989), of Horton, Dorset; m 3, 18 Nov 2006, Larysa, da of Vasyl Senyk, of Tryduby, Ukraine; 1 s (Alexander Charles b 16 Sept 2007), 1 da (Anna Victoria b 7 Dec 2010); *Career* chiropractor; memb Faculty Anglo-Euro Coll of Chiropractic 1977–81 (memb Cncl 1978–80); Br Chiropractic Assoc: memb Cncl 1979–91 and 1993–97, asst sec 1979–85, pres 1985–87, vice-pres 1993–94, Br rep Euro Chiropractors' Union 1986–87, memb Fin and Gen Purposes Ctee 1986–88 and 1993–94 (chm 1986–87), chm Parly Ctee 1987–90 and 1994–97 (memb 1987–97), President's Award for outstanding serv to the profession 1991, Western Provident Assoc Cup for servs to the chiropractic profession 1996; dir Chiropractic Registration Steering Group Ltd 1992–97 (chm 1994–97, memb Safe and Competent Practice Working Pty 1994–95); memb: Advsy Ctee and Educn Ctee Inst for Complementary Med 1982–85, Bd of Advsrs Jl of Alternative and Complementary Med 1986–99; vice-pres Anglo Euro Coll of Chiropractic Alumni Assoc 1982–91; Cncl for Complementary and Alternative Med: memb Ctee 1984–89, vice-chm 1986–89; Gen Chiropractic Cncl: chm Cncl 2002–06 (memb 1997–2007), chm Code of Practice Working Gp 1997–99, memb Standards of Proficiency Working Gp 1997–99, memb Professional Conduct Ctee 1999–2002 and 2006–07, memb Chiropractic Clinical Effectiveness Ctee 2000–02, memb Common Codes Virtual Gp 2000–02, memb Education Ctee 2002–06, memb Resource Mgmnt Ctee 2002–06, memb Communications Strategy Working Gp 2002–04, memb Health Ctee 2006–07; memb Cncl for Healthcare Regulatory Excellence (formerly Cncl for the Regulation of Healthcare Professionals) 2003–06; fell Royal Coll of Chiropractors 1999, fell Br Chiropractic Assoc 2005, fell European Acad of Chiropractic 2007; *Books* Dynamic Chiropractic Today – The Complete and Authoritative Guide (1991); *Recreations* history, natural history, British heritage, country living, organic gardening; *Style—* Dr Michael Copland-Griffiths; ✉ Trowle House, Wingfield, Trowbridge, Wiltshire BA14 9LE (☎ 01225 752199); Healthcare 2000 Clinics, Trowle House, Wingfield, Trowbridge, Wiltshire BA14 9LE 01225 752199, fax 01225 769842, e-mail mccg@healthcare2k.co.uk, website www.healthcare2k.co.uk)

COPLEY, Paul MacKriell; s of Harold Copley (d 1971), of Denby Dale, W Yorks, and Rene, *née* Hudson (d 1994); *b* 25 November 1944, Denby Dale, W Yorks; *Educ* Penistone GS, Northern Counties Coll of Educn (Assoc Drama Bd Teachers' Cert); *m* 7 July 1972, (Primula) Natasha Mary Menzies, da of Lt-Col John Menzies Pyne (d 1965); *Career* actor and writer; *Theatre* incl: For King and Country 1976 (Olivier Award for Actor of the Year in a New Play, plays and Players Award for Most Promising Actor), Sisters 1978, Whose Life is it Anyway? 1979, Rita Sue And Bob Too 1982, Other Worlds 1983, Fool in King Lear 1987 (with Anthony Quayle as Lear), Twelfth Night (tour of Iraq, Pakistan, Ethiopia, Sudan and Zimbabwe) 1987–88, Prin 1989, The Awakening 1990, I Thought I Heard a Rustling 1991, The Mortal Ash 1994, The Servant (Martini TMA Regional Theatre Award for Best Actor in a Supporting Role) 1995, With Every Beat 1995, When we are Married 1996, Celaine 1999, The Mysteries (RNT) 2000, The Contractor 2001, Sing Yer Heart Out for the Lads (RNT) 2002, Got To Be Happy (Bush Theatre) 2003, Billy Liar (tour) 2004, Breathing Corpses (Royal Court) 2005, Ghosts (Gate Theatre London) 2007, In Extremis, The Frontline and King Lear (Shakespeare's Globe) 2007–08, Lulu (Gate Theatre London) 2010, If So, Then Yes (Jermyn Street) 2010, The Last Cuckoo (LBT Huddersfield and Wilde Theatre Bracknell) 2010, Winterlong (Royal Exchange Studio and Soho Theatre) 2011, Lear in King Lear (RSC YPS tour to theatres in UK and US) 2012, Home (Arcola) 2013; *Television* incl: Days of Hope 1974, Chester Mystery Plays 1976, Treasure Island 1977, Travellers 1978, Cries from Watchtower 1979, Death of a Princess 1980, A Room for the Winter 1981, The Gathering Seed 1983, The Bird Fancier 1984, Dangerous Journey 1985, Oedipus at Colonus 1986, Gruey 1987, Young Charlie Chaplin 1988, Testimony of a Child 1989, Landmarks – Christopher

Columbus 1990, Collision Course 1991, Stay Lucky 1991, Heartbeat 1992, Rides II 1992, Harry 1993, Cracker (series 1, 2, 3) 1993–95, A Pinch of Snuff 1993, Roughnecks 1994, Peak Practice (series 3) 1994, Sloggers 1995, This Life 1996, The Lakes 1997, Hornblower 1998–99, The Lakes II 1998, Queer as Folk 1999, Silent Witness 1999, In Deep 2001, Hornblower II 2001, Clocking Off II 2001, Nice Guy Eddie 2002, Dalziel & Pascoe 2002, Horn Blower III 2003, Burn It 2003, The Key 2003, How Clean is your House? 2003–05 (narrator), Born and Bred 2004, Inspector Lynley Mysteries 2004, New Tricks 2004, Messiah III 2004, Best Friends 2004, Dead Man Weds 2005, A Most Mysterious Murder 2005, Waking the Dead 2005, Life on Mars 2006, The Street 2006, Shadow in the North 2007, Coronation Street 2007, The Bill 2008, Holby City 2008, George Gently 2009, Torchwood III: Children of Earth 2009, The Royal 2009, Doctors 2009, Survivors 2009, Casualty 2009 (four episodes), The Bill 2010, Rowntree – Life Without Work 2010, Downton Abbey (seasons 2–6) 2011–15, White Heat 2012, In With the Flynns 2012, Last Tango in Halifax (series 1–3) 2012–15, Midsomer Murders 2013, Vera IV 2014, British Gardens in Time (narrator) 2014, Code of a Killer 2015, Inside No. 9 – 12 Days of Christine 2015, The Sound of Music – Live 2015, Call the Midwife 2016, Moving On – Passengers 2016, Suspects 2016, Doctors 2016, Reg 2016; *Films* incl: Alfie Darling 1974, A Bridge Too Far 1976, Zulu Dawn 1979, Doll's Eye 1982, Ends and Means 1984, War and Remembrance 1987, The Pile Rats 1988, How's Business 1991, The Remains of the Day 1993, Jude 1996, Driven 1998, Blow Dry 2000, A Distant Mirage 2008, Sniff 2008, Acquiescence 2009, The Day My Nan Died 2012, Tea Time in Howarth 2013, The Nest Egg 2014, A Special Guest 2015; *Radio* incl: The Marshalling Yard 1986, The Pilgrim's Progess 1988, Jesus 1990, The Fight For Barbara 1991, Tolkien's Smith of Wooton Major 1992, Vlad the Impaler 1992, That Summer 1993, Sons and Lovers 1994, The Snow Queen 1995 , King St Junior 2003 (12th Series), Markurell 1998, Ironhand 1999, Challenged 2000, Bad Weather 2000, Ernest's Tower 2001, Heart/Attack 2002, Saturday Night and Sunday Morning 2003, Serjeant Musgrave's Dance 2003, Selby – Death of a Coalfield 2004, Selby – Life After the Pits 2005, Witness 2007, Snow in July 2008, Words and Music (Radio 3) 2009–10, Everyone Quite Likes Justin 2010–11, I Before Bee 2011, Disconnected 2011, The Last Executioner 2011, EQL Justin 2012, The Morpeth Carol (Radio Academy Award for Drama) 2013, Tom Wrigglesworth's Hang Ups 2013–14, Stories in the Stars 2014, Jane Gardam Stories 2015, Sylvia's Lovers 2016, The Winter's Tale 2016; audio book: Adam Bede (Penguin), Sons and Lovers (Penguin); *Writing* incl: Hitch (1976), Pillion (1977), Viaduct (1979), Tapster (1981), Fire Eaters (1984), Calling (1986), On Mayday (1987), Shakespeare in Africa (1990), Sally's Tree (1992), Tipperary Smith (1993), King St Junior (1998), Words Alive! (1998), Odysseus and the Cyclops and Pardoner's Tale for Heinemann Educ Literacy Worlds – Plays (1999), Loki the Mischief Maker (2000), Jennifer Jenks (2000), The Royal Court Theatre Inside Out (contrib, 2007), Close-Up Magic – 40 Years at the Bush Theatre (contrib, 2011); *Recreations* swimming, motorcycling, travel, photography; *Style*— Paul Copley, Esq; ✉ c/o AHA Talent Ltd (theatrical agent) or The Joneses (voice-over agent), 74 Clerkenwell Road, London EC1M 5QA (☎ 020 7250 1760, e-mail mail@ahatalent.co.uk); c/o Casarotto Ramsay Ltd (literary agent), Waverley House, 7–12 Noel Street, London W1F 8GQ (☎ 020 7287 4450)

COPLEY, Robert Anthony; s of Anthony Copley, DL (d 2000), and Bridget Griselda Kemble, *née* Emmott; *b* 29 January 1960; *Educ* Sherborne; *m* 1, 25 Oct 1986 (m dis 2010), Diana, da of Charles Talbot Rhys Wingfield, DL; 1 s (Jack Anthony Talbot b 6 Oct 1989), 1 da (Alice Florence Hastings b 2 Feb 1992); m 2, 9 Aug 2012, Tara, da of Derek Rastrick (d 2010) and Roberta; *Career* Christie's: head Furniture Dept 1995, dep chm 2000–, int head Furniture Dept 2007–; *Style*— Robert Copley, Esq; ✉ Christie's, 8 King Street, London SW1Y 6QT (☎ 020 7389 2353, fax 020 7389 2225, e-mail rcopley@christies.com)

COPLEY, Tom; AM; *b* 11 May 1985; *Educ* Bishop Wordsworth's Sch Salisbury, Univ of Nottingham; *Career* formerly with Searchlight Educnl Tst, memb London Assembly (Lab) Londonwide 2012–; patron LGBT Lab, tstee Br Humanist Assoc; tstee New Diorama Theatre; *Style*— Tom Copley, Esq, AM; ✉ London Assembly, City Hall, The Queen's Walk, London SE1 2AA (website www.tomcopley.com, Twitter @TomCopley)

COPLIN, Prof John Frederick; CBE (1996); *b* 29 October 1934; *Educ* Bablake Sch Coventry, Imperial Coll London (BSc); *m* 1957, Jean Fowler; 3 s (Stephen b 1965, Richard b 1966, David b 1970); *Career* Rolls-Royce: joined as grad apprentice Derby 1956, grad of the year 1958, chief designer RB211 1968–77, asst engrg dir Aero-Div 1977, dir of technol 1978, dir of design 1983, dir of new products engrg Rolls-Royce plc 1987, md Rolls-Royce Business Ventures Ltd 1988–91; UK advsr to Indonesian min of state for Research and Technol Jakarta 1991–99, chm and chief exec Hiflux Ltd 2000–15; Fellowship of Engrg: memb Cncl 1981–84, memb F & GP Ctee 1985–88; chm Aerospace Technol Bd MOD 1984–85 (memb 1980–83); memb: Advsy Cncl for Applied R&D 1983–86, Def Scientific Advsy Cncl MOD 1984–85; assoc fell Univ of Warwick, visiting prof of principles of engrg design Univ of Oxford 1989–91, visiting prof Imperial Coll London 1998–2008; Akroyd Stuart Award 1966 (with G L Wilde) and 1985, James Clayton Prize (with Frank Turner); life story held by British Library; FREng 1980, FCGI, FRAeS, FIMechE, FRSA; *Publications* author of numerous tech papers and articles worldwide; *Style*— Prof John Coplin, CBE, FREng; ✉ Swan Lodge, 27d Radwell Road, Milton Ernest, Bedford, Bedfordshire MK44 1SH (☎ 01234 589618, e-mail jcoplin@dsl.pipex.com)

COPPEN, Luke Benjamin Edward; s of Canon Martin Coppen, and Christine, *née* Stevens; *b* 8 February 1976, Basingstoke, Hants; *Educ* Cricklade Tertiary Coll Andover, SOAS (BA), Univ of Wales Cardiff (Dip Journalism Studies); *m* 14 Aug 2004, Marlena, *née* Marciniszyn; 2 da (Grace Teresa b 4 Nov 2006, Sophia Elizabeth b 24 Nov 2010); *Career* film ed The London Student 1996–97; The Catholic Herald: reporter 1998–2000, dep ed 2000–04, ed 2004–; Faith in Brief columnist The Times 2001–05; *Recreations* travel, food, film; *Style*— Luke Coppen, Esq; ✉ The Catholic Herald, Herald House, Lambs Passage, Bunhill Row, London EC1Y 8TQ (☎ 020 7448 3606, fax 020 7256 9728, e-mail luke@catholicherald.co.uk)

COPPEN, Dr Michael James; s of Dr Alec James Coppen, of Epsom, Surrey, and Gunhild Margaretta, *née* Andersson; *b* 3 December 1953; *Educ* Epsom Coll, Royal Free Hosp Univ of London (MB BS); *m* 3 Sept 1983, Dr Regina Goh, da of Goh Choe Jim (d 1987); 1 da (Victoria Jade b 3 Sept 1991), 1 s (Daniel James Michael b 25 Nov 1993); *Career* sr house offr (later registrar) Guy's Hosp 1979–82, sr registrar UCH and Whittington Hosp 1982–87, conslt histopathologist Mayday Univ Hosp 1987–; FRCPath 1996 (MRCPath 1985); memb: Assoc Clinical Pathologists, British Soc of Clinical Cytology; *Articles* incl: Chrohn's Disease of the Appendix (1988), Coexistent Crone's Disease and Sigmoid Diverticulosis (1989), Giant Cell Arteritis Presenting as Limb Caudication (1989), Chronic Periaortitis Presenting As Common Bile Duct Obstruction (1991), Audit of Necropsies in a British District General Hospital (1992), Histoplasmosis of the Central Nervous System (1992), A Case of Warthin's Tumour with Co-existent Hodgkin's Disease (1993), Predication of the Histologic Grade of Breast Carcinoma by Fine Needle Aspiration Cytology (1994), Changes in Oestrogen Receptor, Progesterone Receptor and pS2 Expression in Tamoxifen-resistant Breast Cancer (1995), The Role of Thyroid Fine Needle Aspirate Cytology in a District General Hospital Setting (1995), Isolated Arteritis of the Uterine Cervix (1996), A Six-Year Follow up of Cervical Cytology in 329 Women from Croydon after Loop Excisional Biopsies (1997); pubns incl Evaluation of Buffy Coat Microscopy for the Early Diagnosis of Bacteraemia (1981); *Recreations* golf, reading, music; *Clubs* RAC, Hole in One; *Style*— Dr Michael Coppen; ✉ Department of Histopathology, Mayday Hospital, Mayday Road, Thornton Heath, Surrey (☎ 020 8401 3000 ext 5014, e-mail mcoppen@doctors.org.uk)

COPPOCK, Lawrence Patrick; s of Eric Francis Coppock, of Harrogate, and Betty Winifred, *née* Wilson; *b* 27 January 1952; *Educ* Royal GS, King George V GS; *m* 1 May 1982, Gillian Mary, da of Richard Charles Darby, of Stratford-on-Avon; 2 da (Katherine b 1984, Victoria b 1987), 1 s (Richard b 1993); *Career* chartered accountant Coopers & Lybrand 1971–75, gp fin dir Heron Motor Group 1983–84, gp fin controller Heron Corporation plc 1985, fin and ops dir HP Bulmer Drinks Ltd 1986–88, fin dir B & Q plc 1988–94, gp fin dir Hunter Timber Group Ltd 1994–95, fin dir Sunsail International plc 1996–98, fin dir Haskins Group 1998–2000, gp fin dir and bd advsr MFI Furniture Gp plc 2000–05, fin dir Weir Services Ltd 2006, chief fin offr Wyndeham Press Gp Ltd 2007–09, gp fin dir JJB Sports plc 2009–11, chief fin offr Jemella Ltd 2011–; chm Broadreach Retail Services Ltd 1992–94, chm Girl Heaven Ltd 2000–01; dir Nicholas King Homes plc 2000–05, dir Close Mgmnt Servs Ltd 2000–; govr Kings' Sch Winchester; FCA 1980; *Recreations* skiing, tennis, club motor racing; *Clubs* East India; *Style*— Lawrence Coppock, Esq

CORBETT, Gerald Michael Nolan; DL (Herts 2015); s of John Michael Nolan Corbett (d 1982), of Sedlescombe, E Sussex, and Pamela Muriel, *née* Gay; *b* 7 September 1951; *Educ* Tonbridge, Pembroke Coll Cambridge (fndn scholar, MA), London Business Sch (MSc), Harvard Business Sch (Exchange scholarship); *m* 19 April 1976, Virginia Moore, da of Neill Newsum, of Warham, Norfolk; 3 da (Sarah b 4 June 1979, Olivia b 13 Nov 1982, Josephine b 5 Oct 1984), 1 s (John b 20 Jan 1981); *Career* Boston Consulting Gp 1975–82; Dixons Gp plc: gp fin controller 1982–85, corporate fin dir 1985–87; gp fin dir Redland plc 1987–94, gp fin dir Grand Metropolitan plc 1994–97, chief exec Railtrack plc 1997–2000; chm: Woolworths Gp plc 2001–07, Holmes Place plc 2003–06, SSL International plc 2005–10, Britvic plc 2005–, Moneysupermarkets.com plc 2007–14, Betfair plc 2012–16, Towry 2012–14, MCC 2015–, Segro plc 2016–; non-exec dir: MEPC plc 1995–98, Burmah Castrol plc 1998–2000, Greencore Gp plc 2004–10, Numis plc 2009–14 (chm 2014–); chm RNID 2007–13, chm St Albans Cathedral Music Tst 2010–, vice-chm Herts Community Fndn 2011–13 (chm 2014–), chm St Albans Cathedral Appeal (Alban Britain's First Saint) 2014–; memb Cncl High Sheriff's Assoc 2008–11; chm of govrs Abbot's Hill Sch 1997–2002, govr Univ of Luton 2002–04; High Sheriff Herts 2010–11; Freeman City of London 1987; FRSA; *Recreations* country pursuits, golf; *Clubs* Downhill Only, MCC, Oxford and Cambridge, Aldeburgh Golf; *Style*— Gerald Corbett, Esq, DL; ✉ Holtsmere End Farm, Redbourn, Hertfordshire AL3 7AW

CORBETT, Prof Greville G; *b* 23 December 1947; *Educ* Univ of Birmingham (BA, MA, PhD), Univ of Belgrade, Univ of Moscow; *Children* 3 s; *Career* Univ of Surrey: lectr Dept of Linguistic and International Studies 1974–85, reader in Russian 1985–88, prof of linguistics and of Russian language 1988–2000, fndn research prof of linguistics and of Russian language 2000–, distinguished prof 2002–; pres Linguistics Assoc of GB 1994–97 (sometime memb chair Linguistics RAE Panel), memb Cncl Philological Soc 1993–98, memb Research Grants Bd ESRC 1994–98; memb Bd of Consltg Eds Jrnl of Linguistics; Russian Linguistics, Morphology (formerly Yearbook of Morphology); hon memb Linguistic Soc of America 2014; author of numerous jl articles; univ research fellowship Univ of Melbourne 1980–81, ESRC research fellowship 2002–04; FBA 1997, AcSS 2000, AE (2008); *Books* Predicate Agreement in Russian (1979), Hierarchies, Targets and Controllers: Agreement Patterns in Slavic (1983), Computers, Language Learning and Language Teaching (jtly, 1985), Gender (1991), Heads in Grammatical Theory (jt ed, 1993), The Slavonic Languages (jt ed, 1993), Agreement (ed, 1999), Number (2000), The Syntax-Morphology Interface: A study of syncretism (jtly, 2005), Agreement (2006), A Dictionary of Archi: Archi-Russian-English (jtly, 2007), Deponency and Morphological Mismatches (jt ed, 2007), Case and Grammatical Relations: Studies in honor of Bernard Comrie (jt ed, 2008), Defective Paradigms: missing forms and what they tell us (jt ed, 2010), Features: perspectives on a key notion in linguistics (jt ed, 2010), Features (2012), Canonical Morphology and Syntax (jt ed, 2013), Periphrasis: The role of syntax and morphology in paradigms (jt ed, 2013), The Expression of Gender (ed, 2014), Understanding and measuring morphological complexity (jt ed, 2015); *Recreations* music; *Clubs* Lions; *Style*— Prof Greville G Corbett, FBA; ✉ Surrey Morphology Group, School of English and Languages, University of Surrey, Guildford, Surrey GU2 7XH

CORBETT, James Patrick; QC (1999); s of Patrick Francis Corbett (d 1999), and Kathleen Mary Corbett, of Welford, Northants; *b* 10 May 1952; *Educ* Sloane Sch Chelsea, Univ of Exeter (LLB, LLM), Inns of Court Sch of Law (Duke of Edinburgh scholarship, Ashworth scholarship); *m* 1979, Barbara Janet, *née* Willett; 4 da (Anna b 1982, Alice b 1986, Katharine, Rose (twins) b 1988), 1 s (James b 1984); *Career* called to the Bar Inner Temple 1975; practising barrister 1977– (Midland & Oxford Circuit), recorder 2000 (asst recorder 1996); lectr in law Univ of Leicester 1975–77; Bar of Ireland 1981, Bar of Northern Ireland 1994, Bar of New South Wales 2002, Bar of Anguilla 2002, Bar of St Kitts and Nevis 2004, Bar of British Virgin Islands 2004; memb Lincoln's Inn (ad eundem) 1998; Parly candidate (SDP): Erewash 1983, Staffordshire Moorlands 1987; European Parly candidate Cheshire E 1984; former memb Gas Consumers Cncl and special advsr on competition and consumer affairs; chm Welford Parish Cncl 1988–92 and 1996–2001; Freeman City of London 2000; Liveryman: Worshipful Co of Arbitrators 2000, Worshipful Co of Bowyers 2003; FCIArb 1997, FHKIArb 2001, FSIArb 2002; *Recreations* jazz, cinema, rugby league; *Clubs* Athenaeum; *Style*— James Corbett, Esq, QC; ✉ Serle Court Chambers, 6 New Square, Lincoln's Inn, London WC2A 3QS (☎ 020 7242 6105, fax 020 7405 4004)

CORBETT, (Richard) Panton; s of Richard William Corbett, TD (d 1987), and Doris Vaughan, *née* Kimber (d 1991); *b* 17 February 1938; *Educ* Sunningdale, Eton, Aix en Provence Univ; *m* 1, 28 April 1962 (m dis 1973), Leila Francis, *née* Wolsten-Croft; 1 s (Oliver b 1965); m 2, 11 July 1974, Dame Antoinette Sibley, DBE, *qv*, da of E G Sibley (d 1991), and W M Sibley (d 2002) of Birchington on Sea; 1 s (Isambard b 1980), 1 da (Eloise b 1975); *Career* 2 Lt Welsh Gds 1957; dir Singer and Friedlander Holdings plc 1973–98; dir: Interfinance and Investment Corporation 1974–80, First British American Corporation Ltd 1976–93, Saxon Oil plc 1980–86, Tex Holdings 1987–2007, Peninsula TV 1989–93, Haynes Publishing Group plc 1993–2009, South Staffordshire Gp plc 1993–2011 (formerly South Staffordshire Water Holdings), SPG Media Gp plc 1995–2004; chm Alternative Investment Market (AIM) London Stock Exchange 1995–98; dir Royal Opera House Tst 1989–95, tstee Royal Ballet Benevolent Fund 1985–2002, memb Exec and chm Fin Ctee Royal Acad of Dance 1988–2005, chm Finance Ctee and tstee Dancers Career Devpt Tst 2002–14; High Sheriff of Shropshire 2000–01; Freeman City of Shrewsbury 1979, Freeman City of London 2000; FRAD; *Publications* numerous articles in magazines incl The Banker, Management Today; *Recreations* tennis, opera, fishing; *Clubs* Boodle's, Queen's; *Style*— Panton Corbett, Esq; ✉ 24 Chapel Street, London SW1X 7BY (☎ 020 7235 4506, fax 020 7235 9565, e-mail panton.corbett@btinternet.com)

CORBETT, Peter George; s of Dr John Hotchkins Corbett (d 1999), and Patricia Kathleen, *née* Hope (d 1998); *b* 13 April 1952; *Educ* Liverpool Coll, Liverpool Coll of Art and Design (fndn), Manchester Regnl Coll of Art and Design (BA Hons); *Career* artist (oil on canvas); poet, poems incl in numerous anthologies; memb: Creative Minds Arts Gp Ctee 1978–81, New Age Festival Organising Ctee 1983 and 1984; lead singer and fndr memb rock band Aquarian 1983–85, composer and musical dir Dr F and The TV Kids (Unity Theatre Liverpool) 1985, fndr memb Merseyside Contemporary Artists Mgmnt Ctee (formerly Liverpool Acad of Arts) 1988, chm and fndr memb Merseyside Visual Arts Festival 1989–90, originator Liverpool European Capital of Culture 2008 1996–97, ambass

Liverpool European Capital of Culture 08 2006; hon prof: Académie des Sciences Humaines Universelles Paris 1993, St Lukas Acad Memmelsdorf Germany 1998; life fell and hon prof of fine art Inst of Co-ordinated Research Victoria Aust 1994; memb: Nat Artists Assoc 1988–89 (chm Merseyside Branch), Maison Internationale des Intellectuels Paris 1994, Design and Artists Copyright Soc; former memb Abstract Artists Organisation London; fndr memb: Order of St Francis Liberal Catholic Church, American Order of Excellence in the Fields of Painting and Poetry American Biographical Inst 2003; Peter G Corbett Award Fndn 2007 estab by American Biographical Inst; American Biographical Inst Minister of Culture 2003, numerous other awards from American Biographical Inst (incl Genius Laureate of the UK in the field of art and culture 2005); other awards incl: Cert of Merit Int Biographical Centre Cambridge1988, Purchase Prize Merseyside Contemporary Artists Exhbn Albert Dock Liverpool 1988, Dip winner Int Open Scottish Poetry Competition 1998, Outstanding Achievement Award Albert Einstein Int Acad Fndn 1998, Int German Art Prize, Van Gogh Award and Gold Medal, and Friedrich Hölderin Award and Gold Medal for Poetry St Lukas Acad Memmelsdorf Germany 2000, Int Poet of Merit Award Int Soc of Poets USA 2002, Int Peace Prize United Cultural Convention USA 2002, World Lifetime Achievement Award ABI USA 2002, Int Soc of Poets' Poet of the Year 2003 (nominated 1997), Poet of the Year Int Soc of Poetry USA 2003, Best Poems and Best Poets of the Year Int Library of Poetry 2004, Greatest Minds of the Twentieth Century Diploma ABI USA 2006, competition finalist Poetry Rivals 2011 Forward Press 2012 (for poem Here It Comes Again); 1st XV hooker Waterloo RUFC Liverpool 1973–74; *Solo Exhibitions* incl: Anglican Cathedral Liverpool 1988, Atkinson Gallery Southport 1995, Retrospective of Paintings 1987–2002 (part of Liverpool Biennial of Contemporary Art Senate House Gallery Univ of Liverpool) 2004, Florence Biennale of Contemporary Art (representing the UK) 2007, A Transformative Vision (Liverpool Biennial of Contemporary Art) 2008, Liverpool Biennial of Contemporary Art 2008 and 2010, Liverpool Hope Univ Cornerstones Gallery 10th Anniv Exhibition 2014, Victoria GAllery & Museum The Univ of Liverpool Retrospective 'Metamorphosis' 2015; *Group Exhibitions* incl: Surreal Objects Exhibition (Tate Gallery Liverpool) 1989, Mixed Exhibition (Liverpool Univ Art Gallery) 2002, Influences and Innovations (Agora Gallery NY) 2002, Lexmark European Art Prize – UK Finalists (Air Gallery London) 2004, Mixed Exhibition (Liverpool Univ Art Gallery) 2004, Florence Biennale of Contemporary Art 2007, Liverpool Hope Univ Tenth Anniversary Exhibn (Cornerstone Gall) 2014; *Work in Collections* paintings in public collections: Univ of Liverpool Art Collection, Atkinson Gallery Southport, Hope Univ Liverpool; paintings in private collections in USA, Netherlands, Aust, Germany, Britain, Spain, Nigeria and France; created The Liverpool Dream plaque Liverpool City Centre 2007; *Publications* Tales From Erewhon (2001), The Pool of Life (2003); contrib to The International Whos Who in Poetry (2007) and numerous creative jls incl Forward Press (2004–), 2000 Outstanding Intellectuals of the 21st Century (2016), Dictionary of International Biography (2016); *Recreations* musical composition, playing the piano, meditation, yoga, contemporary dance; *Style*— Peter Corbett, Esq; ✉ Flat 4, 7 Gambier Terrace, Hope Street, Liverpool L1 7BG (☎ 0151 709 4045, website www.petercorbett.co.uk)

CORBETT, Dr Richard Graham; MEP; s of Harry Graham Corbett, and Kathleen Zita Bryant; *b* 6 January 1955, Southport; *Educ* Farnborough Rd Sch Southport, Int Sch Geneva, Trinity Coll Oxford (BA), Univ of Hull (PhD); *m* 1, 1984, Inge van Gaal; 1 s; m 2, 1989, Anne de Malshe; 2 da; *Career* worked in voluntary sector for youth orgns 1977–81, civil servant 1981–89, dep sec-gen Socialist Gp European Parl 1994–96 (policy advsr 1989–94), advsr to Elisabeth Gigou (European Parl rep at Amsterdam Treaty Inter-Governmental Conf); MEP (Lab): Merseyside West 1996–99, Yorks and Humber 1999–2009 and 2014–; European Parl: memb Environment and Consumer Protection Ctee 1997–99, memb Constitutional Ctee 1997– (vice-pres 1997–99, Socialist Gp spokesman 1999–2009), memb Econ and Monetary Affrs Ctee 1999–, memb Civil Liberties Ctee 2004–; European Parl rapporteur on: Constitutional Treaty 2004, Lisbon Treaty 2008, overhauling Parliament's Rules of Procedure 2002 and 2009; Lab Pty: memb 1973–, memb Gen Mgmnt Ctee of CLP 1975–76, memb Regnl Exec Ctee NW Region 1997–98, memb Yorks and Humber Regnl Bd 1999–, memb Nat Policy Forum 2001–03, 2007–09 and 2014–, dep ldr Lab MEPs 2006–09 and 2014–; pres Jeunesse Européenne Fédéraliste 1979–81, pres Links Europa 1998–03, vice-pres European Movement, vice-pres Local Govt Gp for Europe, memb Steering Gp Yorks and Humber in Europe, chair Labour Movement for Europe 2009–10; memb GMB (pres GMB MEPs); advsr on institutional matters and on relations with the European Parl for Herman Van Rompuy (pres European Cncl) 2010–14; Silver Medal European Parl 1996; *Publications* A Socialist Policy for Europe (1985), The Treaty of Maastricht: From Conception to Ratification (1992), The European Parliament's Role in Closer EU Integration (1998), Combating Mythology and Changing Reality: the debate on the future of Europe (pamphlet, 2001), The European Parliament (8 edn 2011), The European Union: How Does It Work? (4 edn, 2015); numerous chapters in books and articles in newspapers and learned jls incl the annual review on institutional devpts for Jl of Common Market Studies 1992–98; *Style*— Dr Richard Corbett, MEP; ✉ European Parliament, 1047 Brussels, Belgium (e-mail richard.corbett@europarl.europa.eu)

CORBIN, Christopher John (Chris); OBE (2014); s of Frederick Christopher Corbin (d 1959), of Bournemouth, Dorset, and Vera, *née* Copperwaite (d 1984); *b* 1 March 1952, Bournemouth, Dorset; *Educ* St Christopher's Sch Bournemouth, Kingsley Secdy Modern Bournemouth; *m* 1982, Francine, *née* Checinski; 2 c (James, Amy (twins) b 8 Nov 1988); *Career* restaurateur; mangr Langan's Brasserie London; dir and prop (with Jeremy King, OBE, *qv*): Caprice Holdings Ltd 1981–2000 (restaurants opened incl: Le Caprice 1981, The Ivy 1990, J Sheekey 1998), The Wolseley 2003–, St Alban 2006–, The Delaunay 2011–, Brasserie Zedel 2012, Colbert 2012; chm: Who's Cooking Dinner?, Leuka; Caterer and Hotelkeeper Restaurateur of the Year 1993 (jtly), Entrepreneurs of the Year (with Jeremy King, 2013); Hon BSc Univ of W London 2014; *Recreations* eating out, art history, life drawing, meditation; *Clubs* RAC, Groucho; *Style*— Chris Corbin, Esq, OBE; ✉ 11 Crescent Grove, London SW4 7AF (☎ 020 7978 2628, fax 020 7978 2629, e-mail chris@chriscorbin.co.uk)

CORBIN, Jane; da of Aubrey George Corbin (d 1989), and Olive May, *née* Amery; *b* 16 July 1954; *Educ* King's Coll London (BA); *m*; 2 c; *Career* television correspondent and presenter; early career with Granada TV and Thames TV, foreign corr Channel 4 News 1983–88; BBC Television News & Current Affrs 1988–; sr corr Panorama (BBC1) 1988–; presenter: Behind the Headlines (BBC2) 1991–93, The Money Programme (BBC2) 1995–96; corr Election Night Special 1992, occasional presenter BBC news bulletins; *Assignments* for Channel 4 News incl: US presidential election 1984, assassination of Indira Gandhi (last journalist to interview her) and subsequent election of Rajiv Gandhi 1984–85, return of Benazir Bhutto to Pakistan 1988; for Panorama incl: fall of the Berlin Wall 1989, environmental effect of Chernobyl disaster 1990, Red Army's quashing of Azerbaijani rebellion, Cambodia ten years after Year Zero 1988, Iraqi weapons of mass destruction progs 1989–93, newly liberated Kuwait 1991, Iranian nuclear weapons prog 1993, Bosnia 1993, Norwegian involvement in Israeli/Palestinian peace accord (The Norway Channel) 1993, return of Yasser Arafat to Gaza 1994, investigation of war crimes at Srebrenica Bosnia 1996, investigation of death of Diana Princess of Wales 1997, The Killing of Kosovo 1999; *Awards* four RTS TV Journalism Awards, Rainier Award Monte Carlo TV Festival (for The Poisoned Land, The Dying Sea) 1990, Emmy nomination for Best Investigative Journalist (for Saddam's Secret Arms Ring) 1992; *Books* The Norway Channel (1994); *Recreations* sleeping, gardening, cooking; *Style*— Ms Jane Corbin

CORBOULD, Neil; *b* 24 December 1962, Blackheath, London; *Career* special effects supervisor; films incl: Licence to Kill 1989, Cliffhanger 1993, Leon 1994, The Fifth Element 1997 (Best Special Visual Effects BAFTA 1997), Saving Private Ryan 1998 (Best Special Visual Effects BAFTA 1998), Entrapment 1999, Gladiator 2000 (Best Visual Effects Acad Award 2000, Las Vegas Film Critics Soc Award 2000), Vertical Limit 2000, The Mummy Returns 2001, Black Hawk Down 2001, The Day After Tomorrow 2004 (Best Special Visual Effects BAFTA 2005), King Arthur 2004, Kingdom of Heaven 2005, Superman Returns 2006 (Phoenix Film Critics Soc Award 2006), Blood Diamond 2006, Fred Claus 2007, National Treasure: Book of Secrets 2007, Clash of the Titans 2010, Pirates of the Caribbean: On Stranger Tides 2011, War Horse 2011, Wrath of the Titans 2012, Snow White and the Huntsman 2012, Zero Dark Thirty 2012, World War Z 2013, RED 2 2013, Gravity 2013 (Best Special Visual Effects BAFTA 2014, Best Visual Effects Acad Award 2014, Visual Effects Soc (VES) Award 2014, Satellite Award 2014, Las Vegas Critics Soc Award 2014, Phoenix Film Critics Soc Award 2014, Acad of Science Fiction Fantasy & Horror Films Saturn Award 2014, Broadcast Film Critics Assoc Critics Choice Award 2014, Florida Film Critics Circle Award 2014, Online Film Critics Soc Award 2014); memb: Acad of Motion Picture Arts and Sciences, BAFTA, Visual Effects Soc, BECTU; *Recreations* cinema, music, reading, tennis, travel; *Clubs* Wentworth; *Style*— Neil Corbould, Esq; ✉ Neil Corbould Special Effects, Pinewood Studios, Pinewood Road, Iver Heath, Buckinghamshire SL0 0NH (☎ 01753 656415, e-mail gmcorbould@aol.com, website www.ncsfx.com)

CORBY, Peter John Siddons; s of John Siddons Corby (d 1955), and Helen Anna, *née* Ratray (d 1974); *b* 8 July 1924; *Educ* Taplow GS; *m* 1, 1950 (m dis 1959), Gail Susan Clifford-Marshall; 2 s (Mark b 1950, Michael b 1951); m 2, 1960, Ines Rosemary, da of Dr George Anderson Mandow (d 1991); 1 s (John b 1962); *Career* RAFVR 1942–48; created manufactured and marketed many products incl The Corby Electric Trouser Press (1961); non-exec dir various cos (plc and private) 1950–; memb Lloyd's 1974–; Freeman City of London 1977, Liveryman Worshipful Co of Marketors 1978; FInstD 1955; *Recreations* sailing, bridge; *Clubs* Ocean Cruising, Island Sailing, Yacht Club de France; *Style*— Peter Corby, Esq; ✉ The Sloop, 89 High Street, Cowes, Isle of Wight PO31 7AW (☎ 01983 292188, fax 01983 291598, e-mail pjscorby@icloud.com)

CORBYN, Jeremy Bernard; MP; s of David Benjamin Corbyn, and Naomi Loveday, *née* Jocelyn; *b* 26 May 1949; *Educ* Adams GS Newport; *Career* memb Haringey Borough Cncl 1974–83, NUPE area offr 1975–83; MP (Lab) Islington N 1983–, memb Select Ctee on Social Security 1991–97; ldr Labour Pty and HM Oppn 2015–; chm: London Gp of Lab MPs 1992–96, PLP Health and Social Security Ctee 1985–89, PLP Northern Ireland Ctee 1985–89 and 1990–96; memb All Party Parly Gp on: Campaign for Nuclear Disarmament Parliamentary Gp (chair), Liberation, Human Rights (vice-chair), Latin America (vice-chair), Mexico (treas), Cycling; memb Parly Gp: RMT, PCS, CWU, RMT, Socialist Campaign; chair Parly Campaign for Nuclear Disarmament Gp, chair and memb Nat Cncl CND, memb Lab CND, chair Liberation, chair and memb Steering Ctee Stop the War Coalition; tstee: Highbury Vale Blackstock Tst, Dalit Solidarity Campaign; patron Mitford Under Fives; *Recreations* running, allotment, reading; *Style*— Jeremy Corbyn, MP; ✉ House of Commons, London SW1A 0AA

CORDEN, James Kimberly; OBE (2015); *b* 18 August 1978; *Career* actor and presenter; *Theatre* incl History Boys (RNT) 2004 and (Broadhurst Theatre Broadway) 2006, One Man, Two Guvnors (Nat Theatre and Broadway) 2011; *Television* as actor incl: Boyz Unlimited 1999, Fat Friends 2000–04, Teachers 2001–03, Gavin & Stacey 2007–09 (also writer), Horne and Corden 2009 (also writer), The Gruffalo 2009, The Wrong Mans 2013 (also writer); co-presenter BRIT Awards 2009, host A League of Their Own (Sky1) 2010–, presenter BRIT Awards 2011 and 2012, presenter The Late Late Show 2015–, presenter Tony Awards 2016; *Film* incl: Starter for 10 2006, History Boys 2006, Lesbian Vampire Killers 2009, Animals United 2010, Gulliver's Travels 2010, The Three Musketeers 2011, Begin Again 2013, One Chance 2013, Into the Woods 2014, Kill Your Friends 2015, The Lady in the Van 2015, Norm of the North 2016, Trolls 2016; *Awards* Best Comedy Newcomer Br Comedy Awards 2007; for Gavin & Stacey: Best New TV Comedy Br Comedy Awards 2007, Best TV Comedy Br Comedy Awards 2008, Best TV Comedy Writers Guild Award 2008, Best Comedy Performance BAFTA 2008, Sky+ Audience Award for Prog of the Year BAFTA 2008, Best Comedy/Entertainment Prog Broadcasting Press Guild Award 2008, South Bank Award for Comedy 2008, Most Popular Comedy Prog Nat Television Award 2010; Best Actor in a Play Tony Award 2012 (for One Man, Two Guvnors); *Style*— Mr James Corden, OBE

CORDER, Michael; s of Michael Borman (d 2000), and Beryl Margaret Borman (now Mrs Coleman); *b* 17 March 1955, London; *Educ* Royal Ballet Sch; *Partner* Jonathan Walsh (civil partnership 4 Aug 2007); *Career* choreographer; formerly ballet dancer, joined Royal Ballet 1973, also performed with Sadler's Wells Royal Ballet, Royal Danish Ballet, Dutch Nat Ballet, Aust Ballet and Joffrey ballet; princ dancing roles incl: Siegfried in Swan Lake, the Prince in The Nutcracker, Albrecht in Giselle, James in La Sylphide, Basil in Don Quixote, Franz in Coppelia, Red Knight in deValois's Checkmate, Romeo and Mercutio in Cranko's Romeo and Juliet; as choreographer creator of over fifty original works incl: Rhyme Nor Reason (Royal Ballet) 1978, L'Invitation au Voyage (Royal Ballet) 1982 (nominated Olivier Award), St Anthony Variations (Sadler's Wells Royal Ballet) 1983, The Wand of Youth (Sadler's Wells Royal Ballet) 1985 (nominated Olivier Award), Ancient Airs and Dances (Northern Ballet Theatre) 1986, Romeo and Juliet (Norwegian Nat Ballet) 1992, Danses Concertantes (Hong Kong Ballet) 1993 and (Boston Ballet) 2000, Cinderella (English Nat Ballet) 1996 (Evening Standard Award for Outstanding Prodn 1996, Best New Dance Prodn Olivier Awards 1997), Masquerade (Royal Ballet) 1999, Dance Variations (Royal Ballet) 2000, Melody on the Move (English Nat Ballet) 2003 (Best Choreography Critics' Circle Nat Dance Award 2003), 'Water' in Homage To The Queen (Royal Ballet) 2006, The Snow Queen (English Nat Ballet) 2007, Orpheus (Royal Ballet of Flanders) 2008, Le Baiser de la Fee (Birmingham Royal Ballet) 2008; dir of dance English Nat Ballet Sch 2009–; *Recreations* swimming, gardening, music, theatre; *Style*— Michael Corder, Esq; ✉ c/o Gavin Barker, Gavin Barker Associates, 2D Wimpole Street, London W1G 0EB (☎ 020 7499 4777, e-mail gavin@gavinbarkerassociates.co.uk)

CORDER, Simon; *b* 11 February 1960, London; *Career* lighting designer 1984–; clients incl: NT, RSC, ENO, Scottish Opera, WNO, Lumiere & Son, Cholmondeleys, Night Safari Singapore, La Scala Milan; Special Projects Award Lighting Design Awards 2006, nomination Olivier Awards 2004; memb Assoc of Lighting Designers; *Recreations* cycling, gadgets; *Clubs* London Cycling Campaign; *Style*— Simon Corder; ✉ 112 Blackstock Road, London N4 2DR (mobile 07973 552348, e-mail simon@simoncorder.com, website www.simoncorder.com)

CORDINGLEY, David; s of Robert Cordingley (d 2005), and Annie, *née* Powell (d 2009); *b* 27 October 1952, Morecambe, Lancs; *Educ* Lancaster Royal GS, St Peter's Coll Oxford (open scholar, MA, PGCE), UEA (MA); *m* 17 Nov 1992, Patricia, *née* Lobo; 1 s (Timothy b 23 Dec 1993); *Career* VSO teacher Basseterre HS St Kitts 1974–76, teacher Tonbridge Sch Kent 1976–79, head of science Navrongo Secdy Sch Ghana 1979–81, teacher Island Sch Hong Kong 1981–86, mathematics teacher Weald Sch (Millinghust) 2015–; Br Cncl: London 1986–87, asst rep Malawi 1987–88; first sec Br High Cmmn Delhi 1988–92; Br Cncl: business devpt mangr Manchester 1993–97, project mangr Nairobi 1997–2000, country dir Vietnam 2000–04, regnl dir Americas and Australasia London 2004–05, country dir Brazil 2005–09, country dir South Africa 2010–13; *Recreations* transport, reading, sport; *Style*— David Cordingley, Esq; ✉ e-mail dcordingley@btinternet.com

CORDINGLEY, Maj Gen Patrick Anthony John; DSO (1991); s of Maj Gen John Edward Cordingley, and Ruth Pamela, *née* Boddam-Whetham; *b* 6 October 1944; *Educ* Sherborne, RMA Sandhurst; *m* 1968, Melissa, da of James Eric Crawley, OBE; 2 da (Antonia b 1972, Miranda b 1974); *Career* CO 5 Royal Inniskilling Dragoon Gds 1985–87 (cmmnd 1965), Bde Cdr 7 Armd Bde (Desert Rats) 1988–91, GOC 2nd Division 1992–96, Sr Br Loan Serv Offr Sultanate of Oman 1996–2000, Col Royal Dragoon Gds 2000–04, Hon Col Bristol Univ OTC 2000–05; Bronze Star (US) 1991, Order of Oman 2000; chm: MMI Res 2001–08, Defence and Security Forum 2002–, Cavalry and Guards' Club 2002–04; govr Sherborne Sch 2001– (chm of govrs Int Coll); chm of tstees Gilbert White's House and the Oates Museum 2002–08; Freeman: City of London, Worshipful Co of Ironmongers (memb Ct 2000–, Master 2010–11); DSc (hc) Univ of Hull 2007; OStJ 1992; FRGS; *Books* Captain Oates: Soldier and Explorer (1982), In the Eye of the Storm (1996); *Recreations* country pursuits, whale and dolphin watching; *Clubs* Cavalry and Guards'; *Style*— Maj Gen Patrick Cordingley, DSO, DSc; ✉ c/o Cavalry and Guards' Club, 127 Piccadilly, London W1J 7PX (e-mail pajc@onetel.com)

CORDINGLY, Dr David Michael Bradley; s of Rt Rev Eric William Bradley Cordingly, MBE (d 1976), and Mary Eileen, *née* Mathews; *b* 5 December 1938; *Educ* Christ's Hosp, Oriel Coll Oxford (MA), Univ of Sussex (DPhil); *m* 8 May 1971, Shirley Elizabeth, da of Ian Gibson Robin and Shelagh Marian, *née* Croft; 1 s (Matthew), 1 da (Rebecca); *Career* graphic designer and typographer 1960–66, teacher in Jamaica 1966–67, exhibition designer British Museum 1968–71, keeper of Art Gallery and Museum Brighton 1971–78, asst dir The Museum of London 1978–80; Nat Maritime Museum: asst keeper 1980–86, keeper of pictures 1986–89, head of exhibitions 1989–93; writer 1993–; contrib articles: Burlington Magazine, The Connoisseur, Apollo Magazine, History Today; FRSA 1974; Order of the White Rose (Finland) 1986; *Books* Marine Painting in England (1974), Painters of the Sea (1979), Nicholas Pocock (1986), Captain James Cook, Navigator (ed, 1988), Pirates, Fact and Fiction (1992), Life among the Pirates: The Romance and The Reality (1995), Pirates, an Illustrated History (1996), Ships and Seascapes, an Introduction to Maritime Prints, Drawings and Watercolours (1997), Heroines and Harlots: Women at Sea in the Great Age of Sail (2001), Billy Ruffian: The Bellerophon and the Downfall of Napoleon (2003), Cochrane the Dauntless (2007), Spanish Gold (2011); *Clubs* Athenaeum, Chichester Yacht; *Style*— Dr David Cordingly; ✉ 2 Vine Place, Brighton, East Sussex BN1 3HE

CORDY, Timothy Soames; s of John Knutt Cordy, and Margaret Winifred, *née* Sheward; *b* 17 May 1949; *Educ* Dragon Sch Oxford, Sherborne, Univ of Durham (BA), Univ of Glasgow (MPhil); *m* 1974, Dr Jill Margaret Tattersall; 2 c; *Career* asst city planning offr Leicester City Cncl 1980–85 (joined 1974), Communauté Urbaine de Strasbourg 1978–79, asst chief exec Bolton Municipal Borough Cncl 1985–87, chief exec Royal Soc for Nature Conservation 1987–94, dir Town and Country Planning Assoc 1994–96, dir Global to Local Ltd; author of articles on housing renewal, sustainable devpt and nature conservation; memb Bd: UK 2000, Volunteer Centre UK; MRTPI 1976, FRSA 1991; *Recreations* music, food, France; *Style*— Timothy Cordy, Esq

COREN, Anne; da of Michael Maximilian Kasriel (d 1981), and Isabel, *née* Koss (d 1996); *Educ* North London Collegiate Sch, Royal Free Hosp Sch of Med Univ of London (MB BS); *m* 14 Oct 1963, Alan Coren (d 2007), s of Sam Coren (d 1989); 1 s (Giles, *qv*, b 1969), 1 da (Victoria b 1972); *Career* Nat Heart Hosp, Charing Cross Hosp, sr registrar Middx Hosp, conslt anaesthetist Moorfields Eye Hosp; memb: Assoc of Anaesthetists, RSM; fell Coll of Anaesthetists, FRCA; memb BMA; *Style*— Dr Anne Coren; ✉ e-mail anne.coren@sky.com

COREN, Giles Robin Patrick; s of Alan Coren (d 2007), and Dr Anne Coren, *qv*, *née* Kasriel; *b* 29 July 1969, London; *Educ* Westminster (capt Fives), Keble Coll Oxford (BA, Fives half blue); *m* 24 April 2010, Esther, *née* Walker; 1 da (Kitty b 3 Feb 2011), 1 s (Samuel b 6 May 2013); *Career* The Times: feature writer 1994–97, columnist 1999–, restaurant critic 2001–; ed-at-large Esquire, contrib ed Tatler; presenter: The F-Word (Channel 4) 2005, Movie Lounge (Five) 2006, Animal Farm (Channel 4) 2006, Tax The Fat (More4) 2006 (also writer), The Supersizers Go... (BBC2) 2007–09, Giles and Sue Live The Good Life (BBC2) 2010, Giles and Sue's Royal Wedding (BBC2) 2011, Our Food (BBC2) 2012, Eat to Live Forever (BBC2) 2015, Back in Time for Dinner (BBC2) 2015, Back in Time for Christmas (BBC2) 2015, Back in Time for the Weekend (BBC2) 2016, My Failed Novel (Sky Arts) 2016; Best Food and Drink Writer British Press Awards 2005, Fortnum & Mason Restaurant Writer of the Year 2016; *Books* Against the Odds: An Autobiography (with James Dyson, *qv*, 1997), Winkler (novel, 2005), Anger Management for Beginners (2010), How to Eat Out (2012); *Recreations* fives, cricket, writing; *Clubs* Queen's Park Rangers, MCC; *Style*— Giles Coren, Esq; ✉ The Times, 3 Thomas More Square, London E98 1XY (☎ 020 7782 5000, e-mail giles.coren@thetimes.co.uk, Twitter @gilescoren)

CORFIELD, Corrie Kear; da of late Bernard Corfield, and Molly Corfield; *b* 28 April 1961; *Educ* Stratford-upon-Avon GS for Girls, Goldsmiths Coll London (BA); *Career* studio mangr BBC World Service 1984–87 (trainee studio mangr 1983–84), announcer and newsreader BBC World Service 1987–88, announcer and newsreader BBC Radio 4 1988–91 and 1995–; newsreader Radio 702 Johannesburg SA and prodr Canadian Broadcasting Co (based in SA) 1991–1995; *Recreations* skiing, gardening, cryptic crosswords; *Style*— Ms Corrie Corfield; ✉ BBC Radio 4, Broadcasting House, London W1A 1AA (☎ 020 7765 2821, e-mail corrie.corfield@bbc.co.uk, Twitter @corrie_corfield)

CORK, Richard Graham; s of Hubert Henry Cork, of Bath, and Beatrice Hester, *née* Smale; *b* 25 March 1947; *Educ* Kingswood Sch Bath, Trinity Hall Cambridge (MA, PhD); *m* 1970, Vena, da of James Jackson; 2 s (Adam James b 1974, Joe John b 1980), 2 da (Polly Beatrice b 1975, Katy Anna b 1978); *Career* author, critic, historian, exhibition organiser and broadcaster; art critic: Evening Standard 1969–77 and 1980–83, The Listener 1984–90, The Times 1991–2002, New Statesman 2003–07; Lethaby lectr RCA 1974, ed Studio International 1975–79, Durning-Lawrence lectr UCL 1987, Slade prof of fine art Univ of Cambridge 1989–90, Henry Moore fell Courtauld Inst of Art 1992–95; John Llewelyn Rhys Meml Prize 1976, Sir Banister Fletcher Award 1985, Nat Art Fund Award 1995; memb: Editorial Bd Tate – The Art Magazine, Advsy Ctee Hayward Gallery until 1996, Ctee Contemporary Art Soc until 1997, Fine Arts Advsy Ctee British Cncl until 1997, Trafalgar Square Vacant Plinth Advsy Gp 1999–2000, St Paul's Cathedral Font Selection Ctee 1999–2000, Paul Mellon Centre for Br Art Advsy Cncl 1999–2005, Diana Princess of Wales Memorial Fountain Design Ctee 2000–02, Syndic Fitzwilliam Museum Cambridge 2002–14, Maggie's Art Gp 2009–, Editorial Bd RA Magazine 2010–; chm Visual Arts Advsy Panel Arts Cncl 1995–98; tstee Public Art Devpt Tst until 1996; elector to Slade professorship of fine art Cambridge, selector Sunderland Gateway Cmmn 1999–2000, Watson Gordon lectr Univ of Edinburgh 2005, Turner Lecture Turner Contemporary Margate 2013; judge: Turner Prize 1988, Nat Art Collections Fund Awards 1994, Citibank Photography Prize 1997, NatWest Painting Prize 1998, John Moores Prize 1999, Charles Wollaston Award 1999, Times/Artangel Open 1999–2000, Art 2000 Commission 1999–2000, Jerwood Drawing Prize 2001, BBC Churchill Memorial 2003–04, Trafalgar Square Crib Sculpture 2005, Blind Art 2006, St Martin-in-the-Fields East Window and Altar 2006–07, Rouse Kent Public Art Award 2006–07, Open Art Chichester 2007–08, Darwin Canopy Cmmn (Nat History Museum) 2008, Wollaston Award Royal Acad 2008, RIBA Norman Foster Travelling Scholarship 2009; hon fell Royal Acad 2011, Jack Goldhill Award for Sculpture Royal Acad 2013, Wollaston Award Royal Acad 2014,

RWS Contemporary Watercolour Competition 2015; *Exhibitions* organiser of various exhbns incl: Critic's Choice (Tooth Gallery) 1973, Beyond Painting and Sculpture (Arts Cncl) 1973, Vorticism and Its Allies (Hayward Gallery) 1974, Sculpture Now: Dissolution or Redefinition? (RCA) 1974, Art for Whom? (Serpentine Gallery) 1978, David Bomberg Retrospective (Tate Gallery) 1988, The Last Days of Mankind (Altes Museum Berlin) 1994, A Bitter Truth (Barbican Art Gallery) 1994, A Life of Their Own (Lismore Castle Arts Ireland) 2008, Wild Thing: Epstein, Gaudier-Brzeska, Gill (Royal Acad) 2009–10; co-organiser: Arte Inglese Oggi (Palazzo Reale Milan) 1976, Un Certain Art Anglais (Musée d'Art Moderne Paris) 1979, British Art in the Twentieth Century (Royal Acad) 1987, The British Art Show 4 (Manchester, Edinburgh and Cardiff) 1995–96; North Meadow Art Project (Millennium Dome) 2000; *Publications* Vorticism and Abstract Art in the First Machine Age (vol 1 1975, vol 2 1976), The Social Role of Art: Essays in Criticism for a Newspaper Public (1979), Art Beyond the Gallery in Early Twentieth Century England (1985), David Bomberg (1987), Architect's Choice: Art in Architecture in Great Britain since 1945 (with Eugene Rosenberg, 1992), A Bitter Truth: Avant-Garde Art and the Great War (1994), Bottle of Notes: Claes Oldenburg/Coosje van Bruggen (1997), Jacob Epstein (1999), Everything Seemed Possible: Art in the 1970s (2003), New Spirit, New Sculpture, New Money: Art in the 1980s (2003), Breaking Down the Barriers: Art in the 1990s (2003), Annus Mirabilis? Art in the Year 2000 (2003), Michael Craig-Martin (2006), Wild Thing: Epstein, Gaudier-Brzeska, Gill (2009), The Healing Presence of Art: A History of Western Art in Hospitals (2012), Face to Face: Interviews with Artists (2015); contrib numerous essays to art magazines and exhbn catalogues; *Recreations* enjoying my family, looking at art, walking, going to the cinema; *Style*— Richard Cork, Esq; ✉ email richardcork@hotmail.com

CORK AND ORRERY, 15 Earl of (I 1620) and (I 1660) respectively; John Richard Boyle; also Baron Boyle of Marston (GB 1711), Baron Boyle of Youghal (I 1616), Viscount Dungarvan (I 1620), Viscount Boyle of Kinalmeaky, Baron of Bandon Bridge and Baron Boyle of Broghill (I 1628), Earl of Orrery (I 1660); s of 14 Earl (d 2003); *b* 3 November 1945, London; *Educ* Harrow, BRNC Dartmouth; *m* 1973, Hon Rebecca Juliet Noble, yst da of Baron Glenkinglas (Life Peer; d 1984); 2 da (Lady Cara Mary Cecilia (Mrs James Willoughby) b 16 June 1976, Lady Davina Claire Theresa (Mrs Christopher Knight) b 10 Dec 1978), 1 s (Rory Jonathan Courtenay, Viscount Dungarvan (twin) b 10 Dec 1978); *Heir* s, Viscount Dungarvan; *Career* Lt Cdr RN (ret); dir E D & F Man Sugar Ltd London, ret 2006; dir MapAction 2007–14; tstee and chm Chichester Cathedral Restoration and Devpt Tst 2008–, hereditary life govr Soc for the Advancement of the Christian Faith; memb Cncl Int Dendrology Soc; *Recreations* sailing, skiing, country sports; *Clubs* Boodle's, RYS, Castaways; *Style*— The Rt Hon the Earl of Cork and Orrery; ✉ Lickfold House, Petworth, West Sussex GU28 9EY

CORKREY, Michael Christopher; s of Thomas Edward Lawrence Corkrey, of Moulsoe, Bucks, and Carole Martha, *née* Snape; *b* 24 November 1962; *Educ* Wootton Upper Sch, Bedford Coll of HE (DA), Leeds Poly (BA), Royal Acad Schs (post-dip painting, Henfield Award, Worshipful Co of Painter-Stainers' Prize, De Segonzac Travelling Scholarship); *Career* artist; *Solo exhibition* Seascapes (Sarah Myerscough Fine Art London) 2004, Undertow (Sarah Myerscough Fine Art London) 2006, New Seascapes (Sarah Myerscough Fine Art London) 2007, Sea Change (Sarah Myerscough Fine Art London) 2008, Wave Breaking Over Rock (Sarah Myerscough Fine Art London) 2013; *Group exhibitions* John Player Portrait Award Exhbn (Nat Portrait Gall) 1986, 1987 and 1989, BP Portrait Award Exhbn (Nat Portrait Gall) 1990, 1991 and 1992, Three Young Painters (New Grafton Gall) 1990, Portrait Painters (Wyndham Fine Art) 1992, 1993 and 1994, Five (Atlantis Gall) 1993, Hunting/Observer Art Prizes Exhbn 1993, Hunting Group Art Prizes Exhbn 1994, 1995, 1997 and 1999, Figure it Out (Harrogate Art Gallery) 1996, Summer Show (Offer Waterman London) 1997, Line Up (gf2 London) 2001, S.O.A.P. Artists (Gallery Fine London) 2001, Wall to Wall (Sarah Myerscough Fine Art) 2002, Waterline (Sarah Myerscough Fine Art) 2002, To be Continued... (gf2) 2002, Art 2002 (gf2) 2002, London Art Fair (Sarah Myerscough Fine Art) 2003, 2005, 2006, 2007, 2008, 2009, 2010, 2011 and 2012, Art London (Sarah Myerscough Fine Art) 2003 and 2004, Miniatures (Sarah Myerscough Fine Art) 2003, Initmacy (Sarah Myerscough Fine Art) 2004, Toronto Art Fair (Sarah Myerscough Fine Art) 2006, 2007 and 2008, 20/21 British Art Fair (Saray Myerscough Fine Art) 2009, 2010 and 2011, 20/21 Art Fair 2010, 2011 and 2012, Br Art Fair (Sarah Myerscough Fine Art) 2012 and 2013, London Art Fair 2013, Paris Art Fair 2013, Summer Salon (Rarity Gallery Mykonos) 2014; *Portraits* incl: Jeffrey Bernard 1992, Keith Miller 1993, The Earl Spencer 1993; *Awards* Elizabeth Greenshield Fndn Award 1990, First Prize Hunting Gp Art Prizes 1994; *Style*— Michael Corkrey, Esq; ✉ e-mail michaelcorkrey@hotmail.co.uk, website www.michaelcorkrey.com

CORLEY, Elizabeth Pauline Lucy; CBE (2015); *Career* Sun Alliance 1975–85, Coopers & Lybrand 1985–93, Mercury Asset Mgmnt (later Merrill Lynch Investment Mgmnt) 1993–2004; Allianz Global Investors: ceo Europe 2005–12, global ceo 2012–16; non-exec dir: Financial Reporting Cncl, Pearson plc, BAE Systems plc; *Books* detective novels incl: Requiem Mass (1998), Fatal Legacy (2000), Grave Doubts (2006), Innocent Blood (2008), Dead of Winter (2013); *Style*— Ms Elizabeth Corley, CBE

CORLEY, Paul; *b* 1950; *Educ* Bablake Sch Coventry, Worcester Coll Oxford (BA); *Career* graduate trainee journalist Westminster Press 1972–75, sr feature writer Thomson Newspapers Newcastle upon Tyne 1975, journalist Look North BBC North East 1976–78, regnl features prodr BBC North East 1978–80, current affrs prodr BBC TV London 1980–82, prodr The Tube live music magazine prog (winner various int awards incl TV Times special award for innovation) Tyne Tees TV Newcastle upon Tyne 1982–84, dir of progs and exec prodr of all network progs Border TV Carlisle 1984–91, dir of progs North East TV (bidding for NE franchise) 1991, controller of factual progs Carlton Television 1991–95, md Carlton Broadcasting 1995–96, controller of factual progs ITV Network 1996–97, chief exec Border TV 1998–2000, md GMTV 2001–07; *Style*— Paul Corley, Esq

CORLEY, Roger David; CBE (1993); s of Thomas Arthur Corley (d 1989), and Erica, *née* Trent (d 2003); *b* 13 April 1933; *Educ* Hymers Coll Kingston upon Hull, Univ of Manchester (BSc); *m* 14 May 1964, Dr Brigitte, da of Leo Hubert Anton Roeder (d 1977); 3 s (Dr Martin b 1966, Dr Kevin b 1969, Dr Steffan b 1971); *Career* Nat Serv Sub Lt RNVR 1954–56; Clerical Medical and General Life Assurance Society: joined 1956, investment mangr 1961–72, actuary 1972–80, dir 1975–96, dep gen mangr 1980–82, gen mangr 1982, md 1991–95; chm: St Andrew's Group plc 1995–2003, Pharos SA 1995–2006; dir: Korea Asia Fund 1990–2000, Lands Improvement Hldgs plc 1994–1999, City of Westminster Arts Cncl 1994–2003, Br Heart Fndn 1995–2004, Med Defence Union Ltd 1996–2004, Fidelity Investments Life Insurance Ltd 1997–2012, RGA Reinsurance UK Ltd 1998–2012; memb Fin Services Cmmn (Gibraltar) 1995–2000; Inst of Actuaries: fell 1960, memb Cncl 1976–94, hon sec 1980–82, vice-pres 1985–88, pres 1988–90; memb Cncl Int Actuarial Assoc 1983–98 (vice-pres 1990–98); Freeman City of London 1979, memb Ct of Assts Worshipful Co of Actuaries 1985–2011 (Liveryman 1979, Sr Warden 1991–92, Master 1992–93); FIA 1960, DGVM 1975, FRSA 1990; *Recreations* music, theatre, opera, visual arts, books, travel; *Clubs* Gallio, Actuaries; *Style*— Roger Corley, Esq, CBE; ✉ e-mail roger@corleys.org.uk

CORMACK, Ian Donald; s of Andrew Gray Cormack (d 1993), of Falmouth, Cornwall, and Eliza Cormack; *b* 12 November 1947; *Educ* Falmouth GS, Pembroke Coll Oxford (MA, fndn fell); *m* 1, 14 Sept 1968, (Elizabeth) Susan (d 1994), da of Mark Tallack (d 1976), of

Penryn, Cornwall; 1 s (James Mark Ian b 1975), 1 da (Sally Elizabeth b 1979); m 2, 12 Sept 1997, Caroline Castleman, of South Africa, da of Norman Westcott; *Career* Citibank NA: joined 1969, dir SCAM 1976–78, head of Euro Trg Centre 1979, personnel dir N Europe 1980–84, head Financial Instns Gp UK 1984–88, head Financial Instns Gp Europe 1989–95, country corp offr UK 1993–98, global industry head Investment Industry 1996–2000; chm Citicorp UK Pension Fund 1980–89; ceo (Europe) American Int Gp Inc 2000–02, with Cormack Tansey Partners (conslts) 2002–05, chm Entertaining Finance Ltd 2006–12, memb Advsy Bd Millennium Associates AG 2003–06, chm Aberdeen Growth Opportunities VCT2 plc 2005–09, chm Maven Investment and Growth 4 VCT plc 2005–, chm Carbon Reductions Int Ltd 2006–12, chm Bank Trg & Devpt Ltd 2006–08, Phoenix Life Hldgs Ltd 2011–, chm Temporis Capital 2011–; dep chm Qatarlyst 2009–12, dep chm Qatar Insurance Services Ltd 2009–12; non-exec dir: Aspen Insurance Hldgs Bermuda 2003–13, American Assocs of NT Inc 2003–08, Klipmart Corp 2003–07, Mphasis BFL Ltd 2004–05, Nat Angels Ltd 2004–, Phoenix Gp Hldgs (formerly Pearl Gp Ltd) 2005–, Qatar Financial Centre 2006–12, Europe-Arab Bank plc 2008–09, Bloomsbury Publishing plc 2011–15, Xchanging plc 2012–, Partnership plc 2013–, Hastings Gp Hldgs plc 2015–; sr ind dir Phoenix Gp plc 2013–; Assoc of Payment Clearing Systems (APACS): memb Cncl 1985–96, chm Risk Steering Gp 1990–91, memb Settlement Risk Gp 1991–93; London Stock Exchange: memb Securities Settlement Bd 1990–92, chm TAURUS Monitoring Gp 1992–93, memb CREST Task Force 1993; chm: Woolnoth Soc City of London 1990–92, CHAPS 1993–96; memb: Bd Cedel SA Luxembourg 1985–96, Clearing House Formation Ctee (LSE) 1989–91, Cncl ABSAL 1993–96, Chllr's City Promotion Panel 1995–2001, Devpt Bd Oxford Business Sch 1999–2003, Devpt Cncl NT 2000–12, Advsy Gp Pembroke Coll Oxford; *Recreations* skiing, golf, fly fishing, theatre; *Clubs* RAC; *Style*— Ian Cormack, Esq; ✉ 24 Kensington Court Gardens, London W8 5QF (☎ 020 7937 1407, fax 020 7795 6930); West Hyes Barn, Guildford Road, Rudgwick, West Sussex RH12 3BX (☎ 01403 823002); 14 Egret Lane, Steenberg, Constantia, South Africa; 7–10 Adam Street, The Strand, London WC2N 6AA (☎ 020 7520 9230, e-mail ian@idcormack.com)

CORMACK, Baron (Life Peer UK 2010), of Enville in the County of Staffordshire; Sir Patrick Thomas Cormack; kt (1995), DL (Staffs 2011); s of Thomas Charles Cormack, of Grimsby, and Kathleen Mary Cormack; *b* 18 May 1939; *Educ* St James's Choir Sch Grimsby, Havelock Sch Grimsby, Univ of Hull; *m* 1967, Kathleen Mary, da of William Eric McDonald, of Aberdeen; 2 s; *Career* second master St James's Choir Sch Grimsby 1961–66, former English master and asst housemaster Wrekin Coll, head of History Dept Brewood GS Stafford; MP (Cons): Cannock 1970–74, Staffs S Feb 1974–2010; PPS to jt Parly Secs DHSS 1970–73; chm: All-Pty Ctee Widows and One Parent Families 1974, Cons Pty Arts and Heritage Ctee 1979–83, All-Pty Heritage Ctee 1979–2010 (pres 2010–), Br-Croatian Parly Gp 1992–97, Br-Bosnian Parly Gp 1992–97 and 2001–10, Br-Finnish Parly Gp 1992–2010, NI Affrs Ctee 2005–10; memb: Select Ctee Educn Science and Arts 1979–83, Speaker's Panel of Chm in the House of Commons 1983–98, Foreign Affrs Ctee 2001–03; chm: House of Commons Works of Art Ctee 1987–2000, Cons Party Arts and Heritage Advsy Ctee 1988–99; dep shadow ldr House of Commons 1997–2000; rector's warden St Margaret's Westminster 1978–90, Parly warden 1990–92; visiting Parly fell St Antony's Coll Oxford 1994, visiting sr scholar Univ of Hull 1995–; ed House Magazine 1981–2004 (life pres 2005–), int pres First Magazine 1994–; govr ESU 1999–2007; vice-pres Lincolnshire Churches Tst 1983–, sr vice-pres Public Monument and Sculpture Assoc 2010–, chm Historic Lincoln Tst 2012–, vice-chm Heritage in Danger; memb: Historic Buildings Cncl 1979–85, Faculty Jurisdiction Cmmn 1981–84, Royal Cmmn on Historical Manuscripts 1981–2003, Cncl Winston Churchill Meml Tst 1983–93, House of Commons Cmmn 2002–05, Nat Archives Cncl 2003–06, Cncl for Br Archaeology, House of Lords Works of Art Ctee 2013–; pres: Staffs Historic Churches Tst 1998–2012, Staffs Parks and Gardens Tst 2006–, Prayer Book Soc 2011–; tstee: Historic Churches Preservation Tst (now Nat Churches Tst) 1972–2005 (vice-pres 2005–), History of Parliament Tst 1983– (chm 2001–); vice-pres Tennyson Soc 2011–; memb Gen Synod C of E 1995–2005; Freeman City of London, Liveryman Worshipful Co of Glaziers & Painters of Glass; Hon DLitt Univ of Hull 2011, Hon LLD Catholic Univ of America 2011; FSA (vice-pres 1994–98), FRHistS 2010, hon fell Historical Assoc 2010; hon citizen of Texas; Cdr Order of the Lion of Finland 1998; *Books* Heritage in Danger (1976), Right Turn (1978), Westminster Palace and Parliament (1981), Castles of Britain (1982), Wilberforce the Nation's Conscience (1983), English Cathedrals (1984), Responsible Capitalism (ed, 2010); *Recreations* visiting old churches, fighting philistines, not sitting on fences; *Clubs* Athenaeum; *Style*— The Lord Cormack, DL

CORMACK, Prof Robert John; s of John Cormack (d 1979), and Christina, *née* Milne (d 1992); *b* 14 December 1946; *Educ* Montrose Acad, Univ of Aberdeen (MA), Brown Univ; *m* 1, 1973 (m dis 2009), Dr Elisabeth Charlotte Fischer, da of Ludwig Fischer; 2 da (Kelly Ann b 16 July 1976, Flutra b 1 Jan 2000 (adopted 2003)), 1 s (Nicholas John Ludwig b 17 May 1979); m 2, 2010, Norma Ruth Hurley, da of Patrick Rogan; *Career* Brown Univ USA 1969–73 (Woodrow Wilson fell 1972–73); Queen's Univ Belfast: lectr in sociology 1973–87, sr lectr 1987–92, reader 1992–95, prof 1995–, dean Faculty of Economics and Social Sciences 1993–95, pro-vice-chllr 1995–2001, memb Joint Information Systems Cmtee (JISC) 1997–2006, memb Universities Scotland 2001–09, memb ILT Nat FEIls Advisy Panel 2000–01, memb Bd of Govs Stranmillis Coll 1996–2001; hon sex Sociological Assoc of Ireland 1976–7; principal UHI Millennium Inst 2001–09; conslt Fair Employment Cmmn Standing Advsy Cmmn on Human Rights, memb Cncl Soc for Research into HE; expert contrib confs on HE Cncl of Europe; chm Belfast CAB 1989–93; memb Highland Ctee IOD; DLitt (hc) Cape Breton Univ 2009, Dr (hc) Univ of Edinburgh 2009; fell Univ of the Highlands and Islands 2012; tstee The Ireland Chair of Poetry, the Arts Cncl of NI and the ROI; memb of Court Queen Margaret Univ 2010–16; tstee Royal Soc of Edinburgh 2013–16, tstee David Hume Inst 2015; FRSA 1999, FRSE 2008; *Books* Religion, Education and Employment (co-ed, 1983), Education and Social Policy in Northern Ireland (co-ed, 1987), Discrimination and Public Policy in Northern Ireland (co-ed, 1991), After the Reforms (co-ed, 1993); and numerous articles on higher education, equality of opportunity, and Northern Ireland; *Recreations* relaxing in the Garfagnana Tuscany; *Clubs* New (Edinburgh); *Style*— Prof Robert Cormack; ✉ 16B Glencairn Crescent, Edinburgh EH12 5BT (☎ 0131 346 0490, e-mail rjc@fastmail.fm)

CORNELL, David; s of Henry Arthur Cornell (d 1949), of London, and Edith Rose, *née* Short (d 1989); *b* 18 September 1935; *Educ* Central Sch of Art, Harrow Sch of Art, Acad of Fine Art Univ of Pennsylvania; *m* 1 (m dis) 2 s (Darren b 1963, Simon b 1965); m 2, Geraldine Anne, *née* Condron; 2 s (Paul b 1983, Steven b 1985); *Career* sculptor and medallist; mil serv in 42 Commando Royal Marines; won Royal Mint nat selection and was appointed coin and medal engraver 1965, dir of sculpture John Pinches Ltd, int dir Franklin Mint; collaborations incl work with Henry Moore, Pablo Picasso, Salvador Dali, Marc Chagall, Lord Mountbatten and Sir John Betjeman; specialises in official portraits of the Royal Family; designs for int coinage incl: Bahamas, Bermuda, China, Falkland Islands, New Zealand, Turkey and UAE; commissions incl: portrait cameos of the children of the Dutch Royal Family, birthday portrait of HM Queen Elizabeth the Queen Mother, portrait of Diana Princess of Wales, retirement bronze of Lestor Piggott, Unicorn bronze for Wellcome Fndn HQ, set of sovereigns depicting the Kings and Queens of England and their coats of arms, life-size bronze of Sir Arthur Conan Doyle, life-size portraits of Leonardo Di Caprio and Kate Moss, 21st birthday portrait of HRH Prince William, works for Royal Doulton, Welsh Porcelain, Spink, Coalport, Franklin Mint, Wedgwood, Richard Borek and the Richmond Herald of Arms, life size bust of Robert Burns, meml coin of Princess Diana; won nat competition to design a 50p coin for the 2012 London Olympics (judo); formerly judge at Goldsmiths and Silversmiths Art Cncl Awards of GB; vice-pres Soc of Portrait Sculptors 1977–, FRSA, FRBS; *Selected Exhibitions* Royal Acad London 1967, San Diego USA 1969, Krakow 1970, 14th Int Medaille Cologne 1975–79, Soc of Portrait Sculptors Mall Galleries London 1979, Guildhall London 1980, Hall Place Kent 1982, Palk Walk Galleries London 1983, Plazzotta Studio London 1984, Cadogan Gall London 1985, Blackheath Gall London 1986 and 1991, Harrods Fine Art Gall London 1987, St Albans Arts Festival 1988, Llewellyn Alexander London 1989, Seymours Gardens Surrey 1990, Henry Brett Gall Paris 1992, Woodlands Gall 1993, RBS London 1994, London Contemporary Art 1995, Docklands Gall London 1996, Alwin Davis Tunbridge Wells 1997 and 1998, Sausmarez Manor Guernsey 1999, Tokyo Japan 1999, Sausmarez Manor Guernsey 2000, Wales Fine Art 2001–, Chepstow Nat Sculpture Festival Belvoir Castle 2001–, Newnham Paddox Duridston Art Parks Canterbury 2001–, The Garden House Wrexham 2001–, Nevill Gall Canterbury 2001–, one man show Adam Gall Wales 2004, Abbey House Gardens Malmesbury 2007; *Recreations* brown belt at judo, swimming, running, clay shooting; *Style*— David Cornell, Esq; ✉ e-mail davidcornell1@aol.com, website www.davidcornell.com

C

CORNELL, Peter Charles Edward; s of Sydney Page Cornell (d 1997), and Marjorie Joan, *née* Edwards (d 1998); *b* 5 October 1952, Tonbridge, Kent; *Educ* Tonbridge Sch, Univ of Exeter, Chester Coll of Law; *m* Bernadette, *née* Conway; 1 s (Tom b 22 Nov 1985), 3 da (Kate b 16 July 1987, Stephanie b 2 May 1989, Isabel b 25 Sept 1991); *Career* trainee Clifford Chance 1975–78; managing ptnr Clifford Chance: Singapore office 1983–85, Madrid office 1990–2000, Barcelona office 1993–2000, Europe 1995–2000; global managing ptnr Clifford Chance 2001–06; guest lectr: Harvard Business Sch, Madrid Business Sch; Lawyer of the Year Legal Business 2007; *Recreations* family, sport; *Clubs* Roehampton, La Moraleja (Madrid), Club de Campo (Madrid); *Style*— Peter Cornell, Esq; ✉ Cornell Institute, 71 Camino Ancho, Madrid 28109, Spain

CORNER, HE Diane Louise; da of Capt A J Corner, of Winchester, Hants, and Marjorie, *née* Ashcroft; *b* Sept 1959, Preston; *Educ* Winchester County HS for Girls, Petery Symonds' Coll, Univ of Bristol; *m* 20 Sept 1986, Peter Stocker; 4 da (Claudia b 1989, Olivia b 1991, Katharine b 1994, Eleanor b 2004); *Career* diplomat; FCO 1982–85, 2 sec chancery Kuala Lumpur 1985–88, conference support offr NY 1988, 1 sec Central and South Africa Dept FCO 1989–91, Cabinet Office (secondment) 1991–93, dep head British Embassy Office Berlin 1994–98, dep head Cncl of Europe Dept FCO 1998–2000, cnsllr and dep high cmmr Harare 2001–03, head Employment Policy Dept FCO 2003–04, chief assessor Civil Service Selection Bd Cabinet Office 2004–05, dir PRISM Prog then dir Shared Services Prog FCO 2005–08, Catlin Underwriting Agencies (secondment) 2008, acting high cmmr to Sierra Leone 2008–09, high cmmr to Tanzania 2009–13, ambass to Democratic Repub of the Congo 2013–; *Recreations* reading, walking, riding; *Clubs* Cercle Hippique de Kinshasa; *Style*— HE Ms Diane Corner; ✉ c/o FCO (Kinshasa), King Charles Street, London SW1A 2AH (Twitter @HMADianeCorner)

CORNER, Prof Dame Jessica; DBE (2014); *Educ* KCL (PhD); *Career* dir Centre of Cancer and Palliative Care Studies and dep dean of nursing Inst of Cancer Research Royal Marsden Hosp 1996–2008; Univ of Southampton: prof of cancer and palliative care 2008–, dean of health sciences 2010–15; pro-vice-chllr (Research and Knowledge Exchange) and prof of cancer and supportive care Univ of Nottingham 2016–; FMedSci; *Style*— Prof Dame Jessica Corner, DBE, FMedSci; ✉ The University of Nottingham, Executive Office, Trent Building, University Park, Nottingham NG7 2RD

CORNER, Timothy Frank; QC (2002); s of Frank Herbert Corner (d 1983), and June Ruby, *née* Benson (d 2007); *b* 25 July 1958, Salford; *Educ* Bolton Sch, Magdalen Coll Oxford (Demy, MA, BCL); *Career* called to the Bar Gray's Inn 1981 (bencher 2007); recorder 2004–; Dep High Court Judge 2008–; chair Advsy Panel on Standards for the Planning Inspectorate 2006–10, chm Planning and Environment Bar Assoc 2008–; *Clubs* Athenaeum; *Style*— Timothy Corner, Esq, QC; ✉ 4–5 Gray's Inn Square, Gray's Inn, London WC1R 5AH (☎ 020 7404 5252)

CORNICK, Roger Courtenay; s of William Charles Cornick (d 1968), of Singapore, and Cynthia Avisa Louise, *née* Courtenay; *b* 13 February 1944; *Educ* various army schs in Egypt, Queen Elizabeth's Sch Crediton Devon; *m* 8 July 1995, Susan Mary (Susie); 2 da (Kate Elizabeth b April 1979, Victoria Rose b Feb 1981); *Career* trainee Royal Insurance Group 1963–68, rep Abbey Life Assurance Co 1968–70, asst dir Hambro Life Assurance Ltd 1970–77, dir Crown Financial Management Ltd 1977–80, ptnr Courtenay Manning Partners 1980–83, dep chm and gp mktg dir Perpetual plc 1982–2000; non-exec dir Aberdeen Asset Management 2004– (chm 2009–); tstee River and Rowing Museum; *Recreations* golf, tennis, skiing, theatre; *Clubs* Riverside, Royal Mid-Surrey Golf Club, Queenwood Golf Club, The Berkshire Golf Club; *Style*— Roger Cornick, Esq

CORNISH, Alan Stewart; s of Alfred Stewart Cornish (d 1980), of Orpington, Kent, and Ann Selina, *née* Westgate (d 2000); *b* 27 April 1944; *Educ* Beckenham and Penge GS; *m* 8 March 1969, Daphne Elisabeth, da of Charles Gordon Saunders; 3 s (Nigel b 1972, Graham b 1975, Iain b 1982); *Career* gp fin controller Associated Communications Corporation plc 1975–82, vice-pres Euro regnl office RCA Records 1982–84, gp chief exec Good Relations Group plc 1984–86, gp md Lowe Bell Communications Ltd 1986–89, chm and chief exec Deal Holdings Ltd 1989–90, chm Cornish Ltd 1989–98, chief fin offr Hilton International 1992–95, gp chief exec Eurobell (Holdings) plc 1996–2000, chief exec Deutsche Telekom Ltd 1997–99, dir Cable Communications Assoc 1996–99, dep chm MORI 2000–04; chm: Management Team Ltd 2001–04, Unitel Communications Ltd 2001–02, Azzurri Communications Ltd 2003–07, Local Press Ltd 2004–05, Telecity plc 2004–05, Eurotel Ltd 2008–09; London Borough of Bromley: cncllr 1974–80, dep ldr 1976–78, dep mayor 1978–79; fndr memb Orpington Dist Guide Dogs for the Blind Assoc; FCMA 1976 (assoc 1971), FCMI 1978, FInstD 1986; *Recreations* sport; *Clubs* local golf; *Style*— Mr A S Cornish; ✉ Aspens, 42 Oxenden Wood Road, Chelsfield Park, Orpington, Kent BR6 6HP (☎ 01689 856880, e-mail alan@cornish.name)

CORNISH, Charles T (Charlie); s of Charlie Cornish, of Strathaven, Strathclyde, and late Isabel, *née* McEwan; *b* 30 November 1959, Hamilton, Strathclyde; *Educ* Univ of Strathclyde (BA), Inst of Personnel and Devpt (Dip); *m* Margo; 1 s (Calum), 3 da (Eilidh, Katie, Fiona); *Career* chief exec West of Scotland Water 2001 (customer services dir 1997); RWE Thames: global business performance dir 2001, chief operating offr UK 2003; md United Utilities NW and gp bd (P2C) exec dir United Utilities 2004–10, chief exec Manchester Airports Gp plc 2010–; dir Young Enterprise UK, chm Young Enterprise NW, memb Mersey Employment Coalition; *Recreations* golf, football; *Style*— Charlie Cornish, Esq

CORNISH, Prof William Rodolph; CMG (2013), Hon QC (1997); s of Jack Rodolph Cornish (d 1978), and Elizabeth Ellen, *née* Reid (d 2007); *b* 9 August 1937; *Educ* St Peter's Coll Adelaide, Univ of Adelaide (LLB), Univ of Oxford (BCL), Univ of Cambridge (LLD); *m* 25 July 1964, Lovedy Elizabeth, da of Edward Christopher Moule (d 1942); 1 s (Peter b 1968), 2 da (Anna b 1970, Cecilia b 1972); *Career* lectr in law LSE 1962–68, reader QMC London 1969–70, prof of English law LSE 1970–90, prof of law Univ of Cambridge 1990–95, dir Centre for Euro Legal Studies 1991–94, Herchel Smith prof of intellectual property law Univ of Cambridge 1995–2004, pres Magdalene Coll Cambridge 1998–2001; external academic memb Max Planck Inst for Innovation and Competition Munich 1989–; bencher Gray's Inn 1998; FBA 1984; *Books* The Jury (2 edn, 1970), Law and Society in England 1750–1950 (1989), Intellectual Property: Patents, Copyright, Trade Marks and Allied

Rights (8 edn, 2013), Oxford History of the Laws of England Vols XI-XIII: 1820–1914 (jtly); *Style*— Prof William Cornish, CMG, QC, FBA; ✉ Magdalene College, Cambridge CB3 0AG

CORNWELL, Bernard; OBE (2006); s of William Oughtred, of British Columbia, Canada, and Dorothy Cornwell; *b* 23 February 1944; *Educ* Monkton Combe Sch, Coll of St Mark and St John London (BA); *m* 1970 (m dis 1976), Lindsay Leworthy; 1 da (Antonia b 4 Oct 1971); m 2, 1980, Judy Cashdollar; *Career* prodr Current Affairs BBC TV 1971–76, head Current Affairs BBC Northern Ireland 1976–79, ed News Thames TV 1979–80; freelance writer 1981–; *Books* Sharpe's Eagle, Sharpe's Gold, Sharpe's Company, Sharpe's Sword, Sharpe's Enemy, Sharpe's Honour, Sharpe's Regiment, Sharpe's Siege, Sharpe's Rifles, Sharpe's Revenge, Sharpe's Waterloo, Sharpe's Devil, Sharpe's Battle, Sharpe's Tiger, Sharpe's Triumph, Sharpe's Fortress, Sharpe's Trafalgar, Sharpe's Prey, Sharpe's Havoc, Sharpe's Escape, Rebel, Copperhead, Battle Flag, The Bloody Ground, Redcoat, Wildtrack, Sea Lord, Crackdown, Stormchild, Scoundrel, The Winter King, Enemy of God, Excalibur, Stonehenge, Harlequin, Gallows Thief, Vagabond, Heretic, The Last Kingdom, The Pale Horseman, Lords of the North Country, Sword Song, The Burning Land, Azincourt, Captivate, Kill or Destroy; *Recreations* sailing, scuba diving, swimming; *Style*— Bernard Cornwell, Esq, OBE; ✉ c/o Toby Eady Associates Ltd, 9 Orme Court, London W2 4RL (✆ 020 7792 0092, fax 020 7792 0879, e-mail bc@bernardcornwell.net, website www.bernardcornwell.net)

CORNWELL, David John Moore; *see:* Le Carré, John

CORNWELL, Judy Valerie; da of Darcy Nigel Barry Cornwell (d 1967), of Australia, and Irene, *née* McCullen (d 1996); *b* 22 February 1940; *Educ* Convent of Mercy Australia, Lewes GS; *m* 18 Dec 1960, John Kelsall Parry, *qv*, s of Edward Parry (d 1983), of Loughborough; 1 s (Edward Dylan b 20 June 1965); *Career* actress and author; pres: Relate (Brighton) 1988–94, Nat Assoc of Deaf Children (E Sussex) 1984–97, Brighton and Hove Entertainment Mangrs' Assoc 1998–2000; chm Brighton Alcohol Recovery Shelter (BARS) 1983–95; memb: Bd West Pier Tst 1974–89, Cncl Equity 1982–85, Bd Inst of Alcohol Studies 1983–91; memb: Equity 1955, Soc of Authors 1986, PEN 1989, Royal Soc of Literature 1994; JP Brighton and Hove 1985–97; *Television* Younger Generation plays 1961 (nominated Tommorrow's Star Actress Daily Mirror 1961), Call Me Daddy (Emmy Award) 1967, Moody and Pegg 1974, Cakes and Ale 1974 (nominated Best Actress SFTA), The Good Companions 1980, Keeping Up Appearances 1990–95; *Radio* The Navy Lark 1962, The Scan 1999; *Theatre* Oh! What A Lovely War 1963, RSC season at Stratford-upon-Avon 1972, Bed Before Yesterday 1976, Rose (NZ tour) 1981, The Government Inspector 1988, The Cemetery Club 1993, Romeo and Juliet 1997, Miss Marple in A Murder is Announced (nat tour) 2015–16; *Films* Wuthering Heights 1971, Santa Claus The Movie 1985, Persuasion 1994, David Copperfield 1999; *Books* Cow and Cowparsley (1985), Fishcakes at the Ritz (1989), Seventh Sunrise (1993), Fear and Favour (1996), Adventures of a Jellybaby (autobiography, 2005); *Recreations* travel, philosophy, reading; *Style*— Ms Judy Cornwell; ✉ c/o Gareth Owen, Infinite Artists LLP, Room 105, Pinewood Studios, Iver Heath, Buckinghamshire SL0 0NH

CORNWELL, Prof Keith John; *b* 4 April 1942; *Educ* Rickmansworth GS, City Univ (BSc, PhD), Heriot-Watt Univ (DEng); m; 2 c; *Career* apprentice then engrg designer J G Slatter Ltd 1959–65, lectr Middlesex Poly 1965–70; Heriot Watt Univ: successively lectr, reader then prof and head Dept of Mech Engrg 1970–93, dean of engrg 1993–96, dir of quality 1996–2003, head Sch of Mathematical and Computing Sciences 2003–06, head Dubai Campus; chm C-MIST Ltd 2009–14, ptnr A1 Classic Cars LLP 2009–; author of over 100 pubns; CEng, FIMechE; *Style*— Prof Keith Cornwell; ✉ Ivanlea, Main Road, Dirleton, East Lothian EH39 5EA (e-mail cornwellmail@gmail.com)

CORNWELL, Rupert Howard; s of Ronald Cornwell (d 1975), of Maidenhead, and Jean Margaret Cornwell; *b* 22 February 1946; *Educ* Winchester, Magdalen Coll Oxford (BA); *m* 1, April 1972, Angela Doria; 1 s (Sean b Oct 1974); m 2, March 1988, Susan Jean, da of Samuel Smith, of Edwardsville, Illinois; *Career* journalist; Reuters: joined London 1968, Paris 1969, Brussels 1969–70, Paris 1970–72; Financial Times: joined 1972, Foreign Desk 1972, Paris Bureau 1973–76, lobby corr Westminster 1976–78, Rome corr 1978–83, Bonn corr 1983–86; The Independent: joined 1986, Moscow corr 1987–91, former Washington corr from 1991, currently with The Independent; Foreign Correspondent of the Year Granada 1988, David Holden prize 1989; *Books* God's Banker, The Life of Roberto Calvi (1983); *Recreations* foreign languages, cricket, travel; *Style*— Rupert Cornwell, Esq; ✉ The Independent, 2 Derry Street, London W8 5TT

CORP, Rev Ronald Geoffrey; OBE (2012), SSC; s of Geoffrey Charles Corp, and Elsie Grace, *née* Kinchin; *b* 4 January 1951, Wells, Somerset; *Educ* Blue Sch Wells, ChCh Oxford (MA), Univ of Southampton (DipTheol); *Career* librarian, prodr and presenter BBC Radio 3 1973–87; composer: various choral works, And All the Trumpets Sounded (cantata) performed 1989, Laudamus (cantata) 1994, Cornucopia 1997, Piano Concerto performed 1997, A New Song 1999, Mary's Song 2001, Adonai Echad 2001, Missa San Marco 2002, Dover Beach 2003, Forever Child 2004, Guernsey Postcards 2004, String Quartet no 1 (The Bustard) 2008, String Quartet no 2 2009, Symphony 2009, The Ice Mountain (children's opera) 2010, Dhammapada 2010, String Quartet no 3 2011, Things I Didn't Say 2011, Songs of the Elder Sisters 2011, The Yellow Wallpaper 2011, Crawhall (clarinet quintet) 2012, Lullaby for a Lost Soul (2013), Cello Concerto (2014), The Pelican (chamber opera 2014), Fields of the Fallen (WWI song cycle) 2014; conductor: Highgate Choral Soc 1984–, London Chorus (formerly London Choral Soc) 1985–, New London Orch 1988–, New London Children's Choir 1991–; dir of choir (Jr Dept) RCM 1993–95; dir New London Collegium 1994–96; various recordings with New London Orch and New London Children's Choir, extensive discography on Hyperion, Dutton Epoch and Stone Records; vice-chm Musicians Benevolent Fund 2000– (chm Educn Ctee 2003–), vice-pres The Sullivan Soc, patron Bracknell Choral Soc, patron Oundle Festival; non-stipendiary min St Mary's Kilburn with St James' West End Lane 1998–2002, non-stipendiary asst curate Christ Church Hendon 2002–07, asst priest St Alban's Holborn 2007–; Freeman Worshipful Co of Musicians 2007, Freeman City of London 2007; Hon DMus Anglia Ruskin Univ 2012, Hon DMus Univ of Hull 2014; *Books* The Choral Singer's Companion (1987 and 2000); *Recreations* reading; *Style*— The Rev Ronald Corp, OBE, SSC; ✉ Bulford Mill, Bulford Mill Lane, Cressing, Essex CM77 8NS (e-mail ronald.corp@btconnect.com)

CORRICK, Philip; s of Frank Corrick (d 1999), of Sidmouth, Devon, and Violet, *née* Willey (d 1991); *b* 30 March 1954; *Educ* Sidmouth Secdy Modern Sch, Exeter Coll (City & Guilds); *m* Karen, *née* Geddes; 1 s (Cameron b 16 Dec 1996), 1 da (Olivia b 20 Jan 1999); *Career* jr sous chef Claridges Hotel London 1979–80, sous chef The Berkeley Knightsbridge 1980–84, exec chef Westbury Hotel London 1984–87, exec chef (all restaurants) Grosvenor House Park Lane 1989–90, exec chef Royal Automobile Club 1990–; affiliate memb Académie Culinaire de France (now Acad of Culinary Arts) 1986, memb Assoc Culinaire Française 1995; Trusthouse Forte Chef of the Year 1988, finalist Meilleur Ouvrier de Grande Bretagne 1991, Maitrise Escoffier Award (Conseil Culinaire) 1998, Cordon Culinaire Award (Conseil Culinaire) 2006, Disciple of Auguste Escoffier Award 2007; hon fell Thames Valley Univ 2009; *Recreations* music, swimming; *Clubs* Barnsdale Country; *Style*— Philip Corrick, Esq; ✉ 4 Alston Court, Langtoft, Peterborough PE6 9RU (✆ 01778 380269); The RAC, 89–91 Pall Mall, London SW1Y 5HS (✆ 020 7747 3377, e-mail chef@royalautomobileclub.co.uk)

CORRIE, His Hon Thomas Graham Edgar Corrie; s of John Alexander Galloway Corrie, OBE, MC (d 1986), of Chobham, Surrey, and Barbara Phyllis, *née* Turner (d 2008); *b* 18 December 1946; *Educ* Eton (King's Scholar), BNC Oxford (MA); *m* 17 July 1971, Anna, da of John Logsdail; 2 da (Tamsin Laura b 12 Dec 1974, Alice Kate Marguerite b 6 Nov 1976), 1 s (Matthew John Galloway b 4 June 1981); *Career* called to the Bar Gray's Inn 1969; in practice 1971–94, circuit remembrancer 1988–94, recorder 1988–94, circuit judge (Midland & Oxford Circuit) 1994–2014 (ret), dep circuit judge 2014–16; pres Oxford Medico-Legal Soc 2011– (chm 1999–2011); Freeman City of London; *Recreations* gardening, cycling; *Clubs* Frewen (Oxford); *Style*— His Hon Thomas Corrie; ✉ Oxford Combined Court Centre, St Aldates, Oxford OX1 1TL (✆ 01865 264200)

CORRIGAN, Prof (Francis) Edward (Ed); s of Anthony Corrigan (d 1994), and Eileen, *née* Ryan (d 2011); *b* 10 August 1946, Birkenhead, Merseyside; *Educ* St Bede's Coll Manchester, Christ's Coll Cambridge (MA, PhD); *m* 18 July 1970, Jane Mary, *née* Halton; 2 da (Anna Louise b 16 July 1972, Laura Jane b 13 July 1982); 2 s (David Noel b 22 Dec 1974, Richard Francis b 11 July 1984); *Career* academic; Univ of Durham: Addison Wheeler Fell 1972–74, CERN Fell 1974–76, lectr in applied mathematics 1976, sr lectr 1982, Sir Derman Chistopherson Fndn fell 1983–84, reader 1987, prof of mathematics 1992–99, visiting prof in the Centre for Particle Theory 1999–2002; prof of mathematics and head of dept Univ of York 1999–2008 and 2011–15, princ Collingwood Coll and prof in mathematical sciences Univ of Durham 2008–11; awarded Daiwa-Adrian Prize 1998; hon ed Jl of Physics A 1999–2003; memb: London Mathematical Soc 1989, IMA 1998; FRS 1995, FInstP 1999, FIMA 2013; *Publications* articles on mathematics and theoretical physics in numerous learned jls; *Recreations* squash, piano, walking; *Style*— Prof Edward Corrigan, FRS; ✉ Department of Mathematics, University of York, Heslington, York YO10 5DD (✆ 01904 323074)

CORRIGAN, District Judge Peter William; s of William Corrigan (d 2008), and Dorothy, *née* Bird (d 1993); *b* 28 March 1949; *Educ* Clifton, Univ of Leeds (LLB); *m* 26 Feb 1987, Meriel; 3 s (James, Edward, Christopher), 1 da (Sara); *Career* slr; articled clerk and asst slr Wansbrough Willey and Hargrave until 1976, ptnr Porter Dodsons 1976–99; district judge: Torquay and Plymouth 1999–2005, Weston-super-Mare, Taunton and Bristol 2005–, Yeovil and Taunton 2012–; memb Law Soc; *Recreations* golf, general sport, current affairs, reading and theatre; *Clubs* Remedy Oak; *Style*— District Judge Corrigan

CORRIGAN, Richard; *b* 10 February 1964, Ireland; *m* Maria; 1 da, 2 s; *Career* restaurateur and chef; trainee chef Kirwin Hotel Co Meath and Kylemore Hotel Co Cavan 1978–81, chef de partie various hotels in Holland 1981–85; head chef: The Meridien Hotel Picadilly 1985–86, Blandford St W1 1986–87, Mulligan's Mayfair, Bentleys W1, Fulham Road (Michelin star); launched Searcy's Barbican 1996 (formed partnership with Searcy's), prop and chef Lindsay House Soho 1997–2009 (Michelin Star 1999–2008, Outstanding London Chef Carlton London Restaurant Awards 2000), prop and chef Corrigan's Mayfair 2008–, prop and chef Virginia Park Lodge 2013–; conslt BA Culinary Cncl, Slowfood UK, Irish Youth Fndn; *Books* From the Waters and the Wild (1999); *Recreations* reading, gardening, shooting; *Clubs* Groucho; *Style*— Richard Corrigan, Esq

CORRIGAN, Thomas Stephen; OBE (1999); s of Thomas Corrigan (d 1992), and Renée Victorine, *née* Chaborel (d 1994); *b* 2 July 1932; *Educ* Beulah Hill; *m* 1963, Sally Margaret, da of George Ernest Everitt (d 1980), and Kathleen, *née* Sympson (d 2009); 2 da; *Career* chartered accountant; chm: Inveresk Group plc 1974–83 (md 1971–83), Havelock Europa plc 1983–89, Post Office Users' Nat Cncl 1984–94, Rex Stewart Group plc 1987–91, Rex Stewart Tst 1989–97, Direct Mail Accreditation and Recognition Centre 1995–97; also dir various other cos; pres Br Paper and Board Industry Fedn 1975–77, vice-pres European Confedn of Pulp, Paper and Packaging Industries 1981–82; chm 2change 2003–10; memb ind judging panel Charter Mark Awards Cabinet Office 2001–03 (advsr and chief assessor 1994–2000), memb London Award Panel Prince's Tst 2001–, chief assessor Queen's Award for Int Trade 2002–11; memb Investment Ctee Printing Charity 2005–; Master Worshipful Co of: Makers of Playing Cards 1978–79, Stationers and Newspaper Makers 1990–91 (gave Annual Livery Lecture 1976), Marketors 1995; *Recreations* golf, tennis, bridge; *Clubs* MCC, R&A, Walton Heath Golf; *Style*— Thomas Corrigan, Esq, OBE; ✉ 57 Marsham Court, Marsham Street, London SW1P 4JZ (✆ 020 7828 2078)

CORRY, Dan; *b* 4 December 1959; *Career* economist Dept of Employment 1984–86, economist Treasy 1986–89, advsr Lab Pty Front Bench economics team 1989–92, sr economist IPPR 1992–97, special advsr to Sec of State for Trade and Indust 1997–2001, special advsr to Sec of State for Transport, Local Govt and the Regions 2001–02, dir New Local Govt Network 2002–05, special advsr to Sec of State for Educn 2005–06, special advsr to Sec of State for Communities and Local Govt 2006, chair Cncl of Economic Advisers HM Treasy 2006–07, head Policy Unit PM's Office 2007–08, sr policy advsr on economy PM's Office 2008–10, dir Economics Segment FTI Consulting 2011, ceo New Philanthropy Capital 2011–; fndr ed IPPR Jl New Economy; *Publications* author of several books on the regulation of utilities; numerous essays and articles on economic policy and public spending, political economy, and the role of the market in professional sport; several pamphlets on new localism, PPPs and aspects of local govt; *Style*— Dan Corry, Esq

CORSTON, Baroness (Life Peer UK 2005), of St George in the County and City of Bristol; Jean Ann Corston; PC (2003); *née* Parkin; da of late Charles (Laurie) Parkin, and late Eileen Parkin; *b* 5 May 1942, Hull; *Educ* Yeovil Girls' HS, LSE (LLB 1989), Inns of Court Sch of Law; *m* 1, 1961, Christopher Corston; 1 s, 1 da; m 2, 1985, Prof Peter Townsend (d 2009); *Career* called to the Bar Inner Temple 1990; organiser Taunton Lab Pty 1974–76, regnl organiser SW Regn Lab Pty 1981–85 (asst regnl organiser 1976–81), asst nat agent London 1985–86, sec Lab Pty Annual Conf arrangements 1985–86, MP (Lab) Bristol E 1992–2005; PPS to sec of state for Educn and Employment 1997–2000; memb Select Ctee on: Agric 1992–95, Home Affrs 1995–97; chair All-Pty Gp on Parenting, sec All-Pty Parly Child Support Agency Monitoring Gp 1993–97, chair Jt Ctee on Human Rights 2001–05, chair All Pty Gp on Women in the Penal System 2009–; memb House of Lords Sub-Ctee on Justice, Institutions and Consumer Affrs 2012 (chair 2013–14), chair House of Lords Ctee on Social Mobility in the Transition from School to Work 2015–16; PLP: chair 2001–05, vice-chair 1997–98 and 1999–2000, co-chair PLP Women's Gp 1992–97, chair Children and the Family Gp 1995–97, chair Civil Liberties Gp 1997–2005; chair Cwlth Women Parliamentarians 2000, chair Fawcett Soc Cmmn on Women in the Criminal Justice System 2007–08; vice-chair and tstee Parliament Choir 2011–; memb: Unite, Exec Ctee Cwlth Parly Assoc UK 1999–2005 and 2011–16, CPA UK 2011–14; FRSA 2008; *Publications* The Corston Report: A Review of Women with Particular Vulnerabilities in the Criminal Justice System (2007); *Recreations* gardening, reading; *Style*— The Rt Hon the Lady Corston, PC

CORY, Charlotte Polly; da of Charles Peveril Phillips (d 1981), and Hilda May Flax, *née* Battle (d 1976); *b* 23 September 1956; *Educ* N London Collegiate Sch, Univ of Bristol (BA), Univ of York (DPhil); *m* 1, April 1988 (m dis), Robert Cory; m 2, June 2009, Prof Arthur Kevin Parrott; *Career* novelist, playwright and artist; dir Inst of Advanced Visitorian Studies; exhbns incl: Mercer Art Gallery Harrogate 2006 and 2013, Rhg Gallery 2007, La Maison des Gourmands Arles 2008, The Circus of Light 2009, Globe Theatre 2012, Royal Acad Summer Exhbn 2012, 2014 and 2016, Brontë Parsonage Museum 2013, Long & Ryle Gallery 2014, Woolff Gallery 2016; curator Charlotte Brontë at the Soane 2016; works in Royal Collection; represented by Woolff Gallery Charlotte Street (www.woolffgallery.com); *Books* An ABC in Black & White (1987), The Unforgiving (1991), The Laughter of Fools (1993), The Guest (1996), The Visitors (All clichés conserved) (2007), Thinking of Leaving Your Husband? (2011), You Animal, You (2012), Pursued by a Bear (2012), Capturing the Brontës (2013), A Visitorian Jane Eyre (2016),

Los Que No Perdonan (2016); *Plays* The Day I Finished Off Charlotte Brönte, The Wonderful World of Allaetitia, Mangosteen Mania, Something Sort Of, Don't Ask Me, The Brave New World of Allaetitia, Snap, The Great Snarling, Thinking of Leaving Your Husband?, Find the Perfect Partner 4 U Dot Com (2012), Charlotte Brontë in Babylon (BBC Radio 4, 2016); *Recreations* wirehaired fox terriers, toy theatre, cultivating monkey puzzles and rare roses, exploring France; *Clubs* Visitorian Soc; *Style*— Charlotte Cory; ✉ c/o David Godwin, David Godwin Associates, 55 Monmouth Street, London WC2H 9DG (☎ 020 7240 9992); e-mail charlotte@charlottecory.com, website www.charlottecory.com

CORY-SMITH, Alexi; da of Michael Glen Cory-Smith, of London, and Cristina, *née* Macdonald; *b* 8 December 1967, London; *Educ* Queen Mary Coll Univ of London (LLB), Coll of Law (CPE, LPC); *Career* IRS Records 1992–96, law student 1997–2001, Virgin Records 2001–05, Simkins LLP 2005–08, Lee and Thompson LLP 2009–11; exec vice-pres BMG UK 2011–; *Recreations* cinema, music, opera, reading, travel, walking, polo, food and wine; *Clubs* Soho House, Union; *Style*— Miss Alexi Cory-Smith; ✉ BMG UK, 8th Floor, 5 Merchant Square, London W2 1AS (☎ 020 3214 1210, e-mail alexi.cory-smith@bmg.com, website www.bmg.com)

COSFORD, Prof Paul Anthony; CB (2016); *Educ* St Mary's Hosp Med Sch Imperial Coll London (MB BS); *Career* regnl dir of public health NHS E of England 2006–10, dir Health Protection Services Health Protection Agency 2010–13, dir for health protection and med dir Public Health England 2013–; *Style*— Prof Paul Cosford, CB

COSH, (Ethel Eleanor) Mary; da of Arthur Lionel Strode Cosh (d 1952), and Ellen, *née* Janisch (d 1931); *Educ* Clifton HS Bristol, St Anne's Coll Oxford (MA); *Career* freelance writer, historian, architectural historian and lectr; contrib to: The Times, TLS, Glasgow Herald, Country Life, Spectator, Highbury & Islington Express, Islington Tribune; memb all nat conservation orgns, former memb Ctee Soc of Architectural Historians of GB; vice-pres Islington Soc, vice-pres Islington Archaeology and History Soc (former chm); tstee Islington Museum; FSA 1987; *Books* The Real World (fiction, 1961), Inveraray and the Dukes of Argyll (with late Ian Lindsay, 1973), A Historical Walk through Clerkenwell (2 edn, 1987), With Gurdjieff in St Petersburg and Paris (with late Anna Butkovsky, 1980), A Historical Walk through Barnsbury (1981, revised 2 edn 2001), The Squares of Islington (Part I 1990, Part II 1993), The New River (revised edn, 2001), Edinburgh: The Golden Age (2003), A History of Islington (2005), 53 Cross Street (jtly, 2007); *Recreations* architecture, opera, reading, historical research, travel; *Style*— Mary Cosh, FSA; ✉ 10 Albion Mews, London N1 1JX (☎ 020 7607 9305)

COSSLETT, Andrew; *b* 1955; *Educ* Victoria Univ of Manchester (BA, MA); *m*; 2 c; *Career* various mktg positions Unilever plc 1979–90, successively mktg dir Schweppes GB, chm Cadbury Schweppes Aust, ceo Asia Pacific (confectionery), md GB and Ireland and pres EMEA Cadbury Schweppes plc 1990–2005, chief exec InterContinental Hotels Gp plc 2005–11, ceo Fitness First 2012–; non-exec chm: Duchy Originals Ltd, England Rugby 2015–; *Recreations* rugby, tennis, golf, music; *Style*— Andrew Cosslett, Esq

COSSONS, Sir Neil; kt (1994), OBE (1982); s of Arthur Cossons (d 1963), of Beeston, Notts, and Evelyn Edith, *née* Bettle (d 1986); *b* 15 January 1939; *Educ* Henry Mellish GS Nottingham, Univ of Liverpool (BA, MA); *m* 7 Aug 1965, Veronica, MBE, DL, da of Henry Edwards (d 1986), of Liverpool; 2 s (Nigel b 1966, Malcolm b 1972), 1 da (Elisabeth b 1967); *Career* curator of technology Bristol City Museum 1964–69, dep dir City of Liverpool Museums 1969–71; dir: Ironbridge Gorge Museum Tst 1971–83, Nat Maritime Museum 1983–86, Science Museum 1986–2000; Collier prof in public understanding of science Univ of Bristol 2001–02; cmmr Historic Bldgs and Monuments Cmmn (English Heritage) 1989–95 and 1999–2000 (chm 2000–07); pres: Museums Assoc 1981–82, Assoc of Ind Museums 1983– (chm 1977–83), Assoc for Science Educn 1996, RGS Inst of Br Geographers 2003–06; memb: BBC Gen Advsy Cncl 1987–90, Design Cncl 1990–94, Cncl Fndn for Manufacturing and Industry 1993–97, Br Waterways Bd 1995–2001; pro-provost and chm Cncl RCA 2007–15 (govr 1989–2015, hon fell 1989, sr fell 2015), govr ICSTM 1989–93; tstee: Mary Rose Tst 1983–2000, Civic Tst 1987–93, HMS Warrior Tst 1988–99, Heritage Lottery Fund 2016–; Newcomen Soc: memb 1963–, Dickinson Meml Medal 2001, pres 2002–03, fell 2010; Freeman City of London 1983; memb Comité Scientifique Conservatoire National des Arts et Métiers 1991–2000; Norton Medlicott Medal Historical Assoc 1991, President's Medal Royal Acad of Engrg 1993, Maitland Medal IStructE 2002; Hon: DSocSc Univ of Birmingham 1979 (hon prof 1994–), DUniv Open Univ 1984, DLitt Univ of Liverpool 1989, DLitt Univ of Bradford 1991, DLitt Nottingham Trent Univ 1994, DUniv Sheffield Hallam Univ 1995, DLitt UWE 1995, DSc Univ of Leicester 1995, DLitt Univ of Bath 1997, DArts De Montfort Univ 1997, DUniv York 1998, DSc Univ of Nottingham 2000, DLitt Univ of Greenwich 2004; hon fell RCA; FSA 1968, FMA 1970, CIEE 1991, CIMgt 1996, Hon CRAeS 1996, Hon FRIBA 2002, Hon MSCI 2002, Hon FCIWEM 2002, hon fell BSA 2007; *Books* Industrial Archaeology of the Bristol Region (with R A Buchanan, 1968), Industrial Archaeology (1975, 1987 and 1993), Ironbridge: Landscape of Industry (with H Sowden, 1977), The Iron Bridge: Symbol of the Industrial Revolution (with B S Trinder, 1979, 1989 and 2002), Management of Change in Museums (ed, 1985), Making of the Modern World (ed, 1992), Perspectives on Industrial Archaeology (ed, 2000), England's Landscape series (series ed, 2006), Liverpool: Seaport City (with Martin Jenkins, 2011); *Clubs* Athenaeum; *Style*— Sir Neil Cossons, OBE; ✉ The Old Rectory, Rushbury, Shropshire SY6 7EB (☎ 01694 771603, e-mail nc@cossons.org.uk)

COSTALL, Prof Brenda; da of John Costall (d 2012), and Eileen Stella, *née* Austin; *b* 12 September 1947; *Educ* Kesteven and Grantham Girls' Sch, Univ of Bradford (BPharm, PhD, DSc); *m* 1, 13 Dec 1969 (m dis 2008), Robert John Naylor, s of John Edwin Naylor; m 2, 23 July 2010, David Edward Atack, s of Edward Atack; *Career* Univ of Bradford: research fell MRC 1972–73, lectr in pharmacology 1973–79, sr lectr in pharmacology 1979–83, reader in neuropharmacology 1983–85, prof of neuropharmacology 1985–, pro-vice-chllr (planning and resources) 1990–92, sr pro-vice-chllr (planning and resources) 1992–94, dep vice-chllr (with special responsibility for research, planning and resources) 1994–98, head Sch of Pharmacy 1998–2004; cnslt in educn and pharmaceutical devpts Marley Hall 2007–; memb: Br Pharmacological Soc, Brain Research Assoc, Collegium Internationale Neuro-Psychopharmacologicum, Euro Coll of Neuropsychopharmacology, New York Acad of Sciences, Gen Pharmaceutical Cncl Accreditation Team; FRSM; *Recreations* managing a large Jacobean property, collecting antique furniture and paintings, love of arts; *Style*— Prof Brenda Costall; ✉ Marley Hall, Marley, Bingley, West Yorkshire BD16 2DN (☎ 01535 680419, mobile 07725 962160, e-mail b.costall@yahoo.co.uk)

COSTELLO, Dr John Francis; s of William Francis Costello (d 1987), of Dublin, and Sarah, *née* O'Donoghue (d 1968); *b* 22 September 1944; *Educ* Belvedere Coll Dublin, UCD, Mater Hosp Dublin (MB BCh, BAO, MD); *m* 1, 11 Nov 1972 (m dis 1986), Dr Christine White, da of Wilfred White, and Irene White; 3 s (Declan b 12 Aug 1973, Manus b 26 Feb 1976, Hugh b 5 July 1980); m 2, 5 July 1996, Susanna, da of late Nicholas Clarke; 2 s (William b 8 Jan 1997, Charlie b 4 April 1998); *Career* house staff Mater Hosp Dublin 1968–69, SHO St Stephen's Hosp, Royal Northern Hosp, Royal Postgrad Med Sch and Hammersmith Hosp 1970–72, registrar Brompton Hosp 1972–74, lectr Dept of Med Univ of Edinburgh and Royal Infirmary 1974–75, asst prof of med, attending physician and dir Pulmonary Function Laboratory San Francisco Gen Hosp and Univ of Calif 1975–77, conslt physician in gen med with special interest in respiratory disease King's Coll Hosp London 1978–2003 (med dir 1991–94), sr lectr in med GKT (previously King's Coll of Med and Dentistry) 1982–2003, clinical dir of acute servs Camberwell HA 1988–91 (chm of conslts 1989–91), clinical dir of med King's Healthcare Tst 1997–2003 (med dir and memb Bd 1991–94), dir Dept of Respiratory Med King's Coll Sch of Med 1982–98, clinical dir Sackler Inst for Pulmonary Pharmacology 1993–2003; conslt Skanska UK 2015–; memb Bd Health Care Projects 2008–11; chm: Capital Hospitals Ltd (rebuilding Barts and the Royal London) 2006–, Bd of Tstees Ind Doctors Fedn Educnl Tst 2006–15; author of numerous scientific papers, reviews, books and chapters on aspects of respiratory disease; FRCP, FRCPI, FRSM (fndr pres Respiratory Section 1991–93); *Recreations* golf, opera, reading; *Clubs* Royal Wimbledon Golf, Garrick; *Style*— Dr John Costello; ✉ 12 Melville Avenue, London SW20 0NS (☎ 020 8879 1309, fax 020 8947 7090, e-mail jfcostello@btinternet.com); Cromwell Hospital, Cromwell Road, London SW5 0TU (☎ 020 7460 5795, fax 020 7460 5790)

COSTELLOE, Paul; *b* Dublin; *Educ* Blackrock Coll Dublin, design coll Dublin; *m* Anne; 6 s, 1 da; *Career* fashion designer; design asst Jacquest Sterel Paris 1969–71, designer Marks & Spencer 1972, chief house designer A Rinascente Milan 1972–74, designer Anne Fogerty NY, Pennaco NY and Trimfit Philadelphia 1974–79, own design house 1979–; company currently sells in the UK, Ireland, Europe, Scandinavia and N America under Paul Costelloe Collection and Dressage labels; designer of British Airways uniform 1994–2004, designer of European Ryder Cup team uniform 2006–, designer of England Women's cricket team uniform 2008–; memb London Designer Collection UK 1980–93; Hon DLitt Univ of Ulster; *Awards* Fil d'Or 1987, 1988 and 1989, nominee Br Designer of the Year 1989, Woman's Jl Designer of the Year 1990, Stazenbreau Designer of the Year 1991; *Books* Over the Moon, The People's Princess (contrib); *Clubs* Chelsea Arts, Groucho, Stephen's Green Hibernian, Home House, Irish; *Style*— Mr Paul Costelloe; ✉ Ladieswear: Paul Costelloe Design Ltd, 57 Gloucester Place, London W1U 8JU (☎ 020 7224 1927); Menswear: Berwin & Berwin Ltd, 2nd Floor, Eastgate House, 16–19 Eastcastle Street, London W1W 8DA (☎ 020 7637 1560, websites www.paulcostelloeman.co.uk and www.paulcostelloe.com)

COSTER, Malcolm David; *b* 29 June 1944; *Career* exec ptnr Coopers & Lybrand 1986–94, pres EMEA UNISYS Corp 1994–97; chm: UNISYS Ltd 1986–94, Fiberweb plc 2006–, MTL Instruments Gp plc, DMW Gp; non-exec dir Universe Gp plc; *Style*— Malcolm Coster, Esq; ✉ Fiberweb plc, 1 Victoria Villas, Richmond on Thames, London TW9 2GW

COTTAM, Graeme Robin; *b* 1955; *Educ* Reed's Sch Cobham, Univ of Bristol (LLB), Coll of Law; *Career* called to the Bar Middle Temple 1978, pupillage 1978–79; Price Waterhouse 1979–85, Arthur Andersen & Co 1985–86; Price Waterhouse: sr mangr London 1986–90, tax ptnr Eastern Europe 1990–91, tax ptnr NY 1991–94, tax ptnr London 1994–98; princ GR Cottam & Co (business consits) 1998–; dir Leonard X Bosack and Bette M Kruger Fndn 2001–05; tstee: Southwark Festival 1995–99, Borough High Street Amenity Fndn 1997–2005, Chawton House Library 2000–04 (dir 2004–06), London Library 2007–11 (vice-chm 2008–11); treas Women's Health Concern 2008–09; FCA 1993 (ACA 1983), FRSA 2005; *Publications* Chawton House Library (2005); contribs to tax jls and other professional publications; *Recreations* books, theatre, music, film; *Style*— Graeme Cottam, Esq; ✉ Parson's Farm, Warren Corner, Froxfield, Hampshire GU32 1BJ (☎ 01730 827586, fax 01730 827314)

COTTAM, Harold; s of Rev Canon Frank Cottam (d 1974), and Elizabeth, *née* Wilson (d 1982); *b* 12 October 1938, London; *Educ* Bedford Sch; *m* 1962, Lyn, *née* Minton; 2 da (Hilary Anne b 25 Jan 1965, Rachel Marjorie b 21 May 1966); *Career* head of corp planning SmithKline Beecham UK 1964–66, commercial dir for Spain Simon Engineering Group 1966–68; Ernst & Young (and preceding firms): ptnr 1968–92, managing ptnr UK 1986–92, chm Ernst & Young pan-European consultancy gp 1992–93, chm Ernst & Young CASE Services (International) Paris 1992–93; chm: Haden MacLellan Holdings plc 1992–97, Anglo United plc 1993–96, Rebus Group plc 1996–99, Britannic Gp plc 1996–2004; ptnr Investor Relations Devpt 2002–08; dir Allied Colloids Group plc 1992–97, dir Pentwyn Renewables Ltd 2012–; FCA (ACA 1960); *Recreations* music, tennis, farming; *Style*— Harold Cottam, Esq; ✉ 8a Burton Mews, London SW1W 9EP (☎ 020 7730 5016)

COTTAM, Dr Hilary; da of Harold Cottam, and Malin Cottam; *b* 25 January 1965; *Educ* St Hugh's Coll Oxford (BA), Univ of Sussex (MPhil), Open Univ (DPhil); *m* 21 August 2004, Nigel Carter; 1 da (b 21 Dec 04); *Career* with REST (Ethiopia) Khartoum Sudan 1987–89, CARE Int Dominican Republic 1989–91, urban social policy specialist World Bank Washington DC USA 1993–95, fndr dir School Works Ltd 1998–2001, dir The Do Tank Ltd 1999–, dir Design Cncl 2001–06, founding dir Participle Ltd 2007–; visiting fell LSE 1998–99; Top 100 Int Creative Business Award BT/Henley Mgmnt Centre 2001; associate Demos, memb Cncl CARE Int; FRSA 2001; *Publications* author of articles in numerous newspapers, magazines and jls; *Recreations* my allotment, modern dance, architecture, film, walking; *Style*— Dr Hilary Cottam; ✉ 8A Burton Mews, London SW1W 9EP

COTTAM, Maj-Gen Nicholas J; CB, OBE; *Career* Royal Green Jackets, GOC 5 Div 2003–05, Military Sec 2005–08; *Style*— Maj-Gen N J Cottam, CB, OBE; ✉ c/o Regimental Headquarters, The Rifles, Peninsula Barracks, Romsey Road, Winchester SO23 8TS

COTTER, Baron (Life Peer UK 2006), of Congresbury in the County of Somerset; Brian Joseph Michael Cotter; *b* 24 August 1936; *Educ* Downside; *m* Eyleen; 2 s, 1 da; *Career* Nat Serv army; in business for 40 years latterly co md; MP (Lib Dem) Weston-super-Mare 1997–2005 (Parly candidate Weston-super-Mare 1992); House of Commons: memb Lib Dem Trade and Industry team (spokesman on small business) 1997–2005, Lib Dem spokesperson on small businesses and skills; former: vice-chm All-Pty Gp on Retail Industry, vice-chm All-Pty Gp on Small Business, sec All-Pty China Gp, treas All-Pty Autism Gp; Lib Dem dist cncllr and chm Cncl Youth Ctee 1986–90; memb: Lib Dem Parly Candidates Assoc, Assoc of Lib Dem Cncllrs, Amnesty Int, Green Lib Dems, Ct Univ of Bristol, Consultative Ctee Weston Foyer; patron Somewhere To Go Project, nat patron Surf (Rwandan widows charity); former memb Weston Community Health Cncl; *Style*— The Lord Cotter; ✉ e-mail cotterb@parliament.uk

COTTERRELL, Prof Roger Brian Melvyn; s of Walter Leslie Cotterrell (d 1977), and Hilda Margaret, *née* Randle (d 1970); *b* 30 November 1946, Selly Oak, Birmingham; *Educ* King Edward VI Camp Hill Sch Birmingham, UCL (LLB, LLM), Birkbeck Coll Univ of London (MSc Soc), Univ of London (LLD); *m* 1969, Ann Zillah Poyner; 1 s (David Roger b 1974), 1 da (Linda Ann Margaret b 1975); *Career* lectr in law Univ of Leicester 1969–74; QMC (then Queen Mary and Westfield Coll Univ of London, now Queen Mary Univ of London): lectr in law 1974–78, sr lectr in law 1978–85, reader in legal theory 1985–90, acting head Dept of Law 1989–90, prof of legal theory 1990–2005, head Dept of Law 1990–91, dean Faculty of Laws 1993–96, anniversary prof of legal theory 2005–; visiting prof and Jay H Brown Centennial Faculty fell in law Univ of Texas 1989, George Lurcy lectr Amherst Coll Massachusetts 1989; visiting prof: Univ of Lund 1996, Katholiek Universeit Brussel and Facultés Universitaires Saint Louis Brussels 1996–97, Int Inst for the Sociology of Law Onati Spain 2003 and 2004; memb: Ctee of Heads of Univ Law Schs 1993–96, Ct of Govrs Univ of Leicester 2000–03, Res Assessment Exercise Law Panel and Sub-Panel 1999–2001 and 2005–08, Law Assessment Ctee Flemish Interuniversity Cncl Belgium 2006–07; tstee Law and Soc Assoc 1996–99; Lifetime Achievement Award Socio-legal Studies Assoc 2013; FBA 2005, FAcSS 2014; *Books* The Sociology of Law: An Introduction (1984, 2nd edn 1992), Law, Democracy and Social Justice (jt ed, 1988), The Politics of Jurisprudence: A Critical Introduction to Legal Philosophy (1989, 2nd edn 2003), Law and Society (ed, 1994), Process and Substance: Butterworth Lectures on

Comparative Law (ed, 1994), Law's Community: Legal Theory in Sociological Perspective (1995), Emile Durkheim: Law in a Moral Domain (1999), Sociological Perspectives on Law (ed, 2 vols 2001), Bass Lines: A Life in Jazz (jt author, 2002), Law in Social Theory (ed, 2006), Law, Culture and Society: Legal Ideas in the Mirror of Social Theory (2006), Living Law: Essays in Legal and Social Theory (2008), Emile Durkheim: Justice, Morality, Politics (ed, 2010), Authority in Transnational Legal Theory: Theorising Across Disciplines (jt ed, 2016); *Recreations* listening to and writing about music, exploring cities, European cinema; *Style—* Prof Roger Cotterrell; ✉ Department of Law, Queen Mary University of London, Mile End Road, London E1 4NS (☎ 020 7882 3946, fax 020 8981 8733, e-mail r.b.m.cotterrell@qmul.ac.uk)

COTTINGHAM, Barrie; s of John Cottingham, of Sheffield, and Eleanor, *née* Price; *b* 5 October 1933; *Educ* Carfield Sch Sheffield; *m* 5 Oct 1957, Kathleen, da of John Ernest Morton (d 1945), of Sheffield; 1 s (Nigel David b 13 Dec 1964), 1 da (Michelle Jayne b 5 Aug 1962, d 1998); *Career* RAF 1955–57, cmmnd PO 1956; Coopers & Lybrand 1957–95: ptnr 1964, memb UK Bd 1974–93, exec ptnr i/c of the regions 1986–93; chm: SIG plc 1993–2004, Cattles plc 1995–; memb Bd: VP plc 1996–, Dew Pitchmastic plc 1997–; pres Sheffield and Dist Soc of CAs 1964; FCA 1955, ATII 1965; *Recreations* squash, golf, watching rugby and cricket, opera; *Clubs* Naval and Military; *Style—* Barrie Cottingham, Esq; ✉ Cattles plc, Kingston House, Centre 27, Business Park, Woodhead Road, Batley WF17 9TD (☎ 01924 444466, fax 01924 448366)

COTTIS, Matthew; s of John Cottis, of Wantage, Oxon, and Janie, *née* Moon; *b* 13 May 1962, Epping, Essex; *Educ* King Alfred's Sch Wantage, Keble Coll Oxford (BA); *m* 5 May 2000, Ann Marie, *née* Arstall; 2 da (Joanna b 26 March 1993, Isabel b 27 Aug 1997); *Career* admitted slr 1987; Hogan Lovells: joined 1985, ptnr 1993–, head of int banking practice 2009–; *Recreations* golf, walking, travel; *Clubs* Chislehurst Golf; *Style—* Matthew Cottis, Esq; ✉ Hogan Lovells, 50 Holborn Viaduct, London EC1A 2DY (☎ 020 7296 5482, fax 020 7296 2000, e-mail matthew.cottis@hoganlovells.com)

COTTLE, Gerry; s of Reginald Brookes Cottle (d 1975), of Highbury, London, and Joan Miriam, *née* Ward (d 1993), of Streatham, London; *b* 7 April 1945; *Educ* Rutlish Sch Wimbledon; *m* 7 Dec 1968, Betty, da of James Fossett (d 1972), of Henley-in-Arden; 3 da (Sarah b 1970, April b 1973, Juliette b 1976), 1 s (Gerry b 20 Jan 1981); *Career* ran away from school and joined a small circus becoming juggler and equestrian 1961, formed Gerry Cottle's Circus 1974; flew complete circus to Oman for Sultan's birthday 1976; overseas tours 1981–84: Bahrain, Iran, Shajah, Iceland, Hong Kong, Macáu, Singapore, Malaysia; currently world's most travelled circus, touring 46 weeks a year, touring Moscow State Circus in UK 1995–, touring Circus of Horrors in UK and overseas 1995, touring Cottle and Austen Combined Circus in UK 1999, touring Chinese State Circus in UK 2000–; prop Wookey Hole Caves Somerset 2004; memb: Variety Club of GB, Assoc of Circus Proprietors of GB 1973–; *Recreations* horse riding, collecting show business memorabilia; *Style—* Gerry Cottle, Esq; ✉ The Mill, Wookey Hole, Wells, Somerset BA5 1BB (☎ 01749 672243, fax 01749 677749)

COTTON, Diana Rosemary (Mrs R B Allan); QC (1983); da of Arthur Frank Edward Cotton (d 1990), of Herts, and Muriel, *née* John (d 1986); *b* 30 November 1941; *Educ* Berkhamsted Sch for Girls, Lady Margaret Hall Oxford (exhibitioner, MA); *m* 1966, Richard Bellerby Allan, *qv*, s of John Bellerby Allan (d 1985), of Oxon; 2 s (Jonathan b 1972, Jeremy b 1974), 1 da (Joanna b 1977); *Career* called to the Bar Middle Temple 1964 (bencher 1990); memb Midland Circuit, recorder of the Crown Court 1982–2011; asst boundary commissioner 2000; memb: Criminal Injuries Compensation Bd 1989–2000, Criminal Injuries Compensation Appeals Panel 1996–2008, Bar Cncl 1997–99, Mental Health Ind Review Tbnl for restricted cases 1997–2008; tbnl judge Tbnls Service Criminal Injuries Compensation 2008–13, tbnl judge Tbnls Service Mental Health 2008–11; *Recreations* family, sport, gardening; *Style—* Miss Diana Cotton, QC

COTTON, Fearne; *b* 3 September 1981, London; *m* Jesse Wood, s of Ronnie Wood, *qv*; 1 s (Rex Rayne b 21 Feb 2013); *Career* television and radio presenter; *Television* incl: Diggit 1998–2001, The Saturday Show 2001–03, Smile 2002–04, Comic Relief Does Fame Academy 2003, Top of the Pops (BBC) 2004–06, Live 8 2005, Children in Need 2005–, Comic Relief 2005–, The Extra Factor (ITV2) 2007, Holly and Fearne Go Dating 2007 (with Holly Willoughby, *qv*), Celebrity Juice 2008–; *Radio* BBC Radio 1: early morning show 2005–07, Chart Show 2007–09, Live Lounge 2009– (Best Music Prog Sony Radio Acad Gold Award 2012); *Style—* Ms Fearne Cotton; ✉ c/o James Grant Group Ltd, 94 Strand On The Green, Chiswick, London W4 3NN

COTTON, John Nicholas; s of Sir John Cotton, KCMG, OBE, and Mary Bridget, *née* Connors; *b* 6 August 1941; *Educ* Downside, Merton Coll Oxford (MA); *m* 1 (m dis 1976), Caroline, da of Michael Stoop, MC; 1 s (Tanguy b 1969); m 2, Martine, da of Roland du Roy de Blicquy; 1 da (Charlotte b 1981), 1 s (Edward b 1986); *Career* Samuel Montagu London 1963–65, Spencer Thornton Belgium 1965–68, vice-pres Loeb Rhoades Belgium 1968–72, exec dir Cogefon Belgium 1972–77; md: Edwin H Bradley Belgium 1977–80, Banque Belge Ltd London 1980–92, Mercury Asset Management (latterly Merrill Lynch Investment Mgmnt) 1992–2003; chm Queensborough Steel Co Ltd 1989–97, ptnr Dalton Strategic Partnership LLP 2003–, memb Advsy Bd Close Trustees (Switzerland) LLP 2003–06; vice-chm Anglo-Belgian C of C 1992; *Clubs* Boodle's, Eagle (Gstaad); *Style—* John Cotton, Esq; ✉ 19 Bourne Street, London SW1W 8JR (☎ and fax 020 7730 1685, e-mail jncotton8@yahoo.co.uk)

COTTON, Oliver; s of Robert Cotton, of London, and Ester, *née* Bonessen; *b* 20 June 1944; *Educ* Chiswick Poly, Drama Centre London; *m* 1, Catherine, *née* Stevens; 1 da (Abigail b 1969); m 2, Irene, *née* Gorst; 1 da (Sophie b 1986); *Career* actor and writer; stage debut Off Broadway NY 1966, The National Theatre 1966–68, Royal Court 1966–75, repertory at Cheltenham and Watford 1969–72, RSC 1975, NT 1975–79, RSC 1988–89, RNT 1990–91; *Theatre* prodns incl: Teddy in The Homecoming (Garrick) 1978, James Leeds in Children of a Lesser God (Albery) 1982, David in Benefactors (Vaudeville) 1984, David in That Summer (Hampstead) 1987, Butterfly Kiss (world premiere, Almeida) 1994, Dr Ostermark in Strindberg's The Father (tour) 1995; Wet Weather Cover (writer only) 1994–95 and 2010, Frank in Educating Rita (tour) 1996, lead role in King Lear (Southwark Playhouse) 1996, Tom Sergent in Skylight 1997, Jack Kent in Blast From the Past (W Yorkshire Playhouse) 1998, Robert Chiltern in An Ideal Husband (Haymarket Theatre) 1998, Agamemnon in Troilus and Cressida (RNT) 1999, Lord Glossmore in Money (RNT) 1999, Suslov in Summer folk (RNT) 1999, Wet Weather Cover (writer, Tiffany Theatre LA) 1999, Lockit in The Villains Opera (NT) 2000, Hubert in Life x 3 (NT and Old Vic) 2000–01, Malvolio in Twelfth Night (Globe prodn at Middle Temple Hall) 2002, the Mayor in Brand (RSC Stratford and Theatre Royal Haymarket) 2003, Seth Lord in The Philadelphia Story (Old Vic) 2005, Northumberland in Richard II (Old Vic) 2005; as writer: Man Falling Down (Shakespeares' Globe) 2005, Valverde in Royal Hunt of the Sun (NT) 2006, Clifford in Piano Forte (Royal Court) 2006, Charles in The Clean House (nat tour) 2008, Van Ruijven in The Girl with a Pearl Earring (West End) 2008, Gabriel in Gates of Gold (Library Theatre Manchester) 2009, Casy in Grapes of Wrath (Chichester Festival Theatre) 2009, title role in Henry IV (Globe) 2010, A Flea in her Ear (Old Vic) 2010–11, The Syndicate (Chichester Festival Theatre) 2011, Barefoot in the Park 2012, King Arthur by Purcell (Manchester and Paris) 2012; Jim in Passion Play (Duke of York's Theatre), Billy in Daytona (Theatre Royal, Haymarket) *Television* incl: Cesare Borgia in The Borgias 1980, Ford in The Party 1987, Giles in Room at the Bottom 1988, Anderez in Boon 1989, Gregorie Rolf in Poirot 1989, Neville Nunn in Redemption 1991, Max Erstweiler in The Camomile Lawn 1991, Alan Cromer in Westbeach 1992 and 1993, Fireworks 1993, Space Cops 1994, Harry 1994, Sharpe's Battle 1994, The Story of Joseph 1994, Joseph Chamberlain in Rhodes 1995, Gregory Watling in Wokenwell 1996, Declan in The Preston Front 1997, Augelini in Innocents 2000, Maurice Phillips in Judge John Deed 2001, Dalziel and Pascoe 2002, Casualty 2003, Sir Charles Stewart in Waking the Dead 2003, Artoym Bia Toulos in Murder Investigation Team 2004, Midsomer Murders 2005, Sensitive Skin 2005–06, Mr Dovic in Hotel Babylon 2006, Donald in The Commander 2007, Aetius in Atilla 2007, Michael Heseltine in Margaret (BBC) 2008; as writer A Touch of Frost (episode Hit and Run); *Radio* Jocylin in The Spire 2005; *Films* incl: John the Disciple in The Day Christ Died 1979, Monks in Oliver Twist 1981, Priabin in Firefox 1982, Katis in Eleni 1985, Landis in Hiding Out 1987, Roccafino in The Sicilian 1987, Harana in Columbus – The Discovery 1992, King Heroac in Son of Pink Panther 1992, Paulo Lusano in The Innocent Sleep 1994, Charles Elliot in The Opium Wars 1996, Hrothgar in Beowulf 1997, Merino in The Dancer Upstairs 2000, Ron Wood in Baby Blue 2000, Stein in Jimmy Figg 2001, Moshe in The Gisella Perl Story 2002, Jack the Ripper in Shanghai Knights 2002, Regulus in Bonehunter 2002, Metaclfe in Colour Me Kubrick 2004, Duke in Rain Dogs 2004, Tooting Broadway 2011; as writer: Singing for Stalin 1994–95, Daytona 2000, Deadtime 2005, Diamond Geezer 2006, 24 Hours from Tulse Hill 2006, The Pier (short film), Wet Weather Cover The Movie 2009, Deadline 2009, The Dark Knight Rises 2012 *writing* Sans Souci (stage play); *Recreations* classical guitar, listening to music, talking, running, writing; *Style—* Oliver Cotton, Esq; ✉ c/o Dallas Smith, United Agents Ltd, 12–26 Lexington Street, London W1F 0LE (☎ 020 3214 0800, fax 020 3214 0801, website www.unitedagents.co.uk); e-mail oliver36@btopenworld.com

COTTON, Richard Selkirk; s of A G Cotton, of Bicester, Oxon, and V M, *née* Woolley (d 1993); *b* 29 March 1947, Woodstock, Oxon; *Educ* Univ of London (BSc, Dip Farm Business Admin); *Partner* Penelope Rankin; *Career* chartered surveyor; Cluttons: resident ptnr Middle East 1977–87, managing ptnr 2001–03, sr ptnr 2003–09; property dir Residential Land 2010–; Master Worshipful Co of Chartered Surveyors 2006–07; FRICS; *Recreations* theatre, travel, tennis, bridge; *Style—* Richard Cotton, Esq; ✉ 21c Sunderland Terrace, London W2 5PA (☎ 020 7727 0313)

COTTON, Robert George (Bob); OBE (2003); s of A G Cotton, of Oxford, and V H Cotton, *née* Wholley (d 1993); *b* 26 August 1948, Woodstock, Oxon; *Educ* Colston's Sch Bristol, Univ of Surrey; *Career* with Trust House Forte and Gardner Merchant 1975–98 (latterly dir of corporate affrs, communications and strategic planning), tourism advsr to DCMS 1999–2000, chief exec Br Hospitality Assoc 2000–; chm: Best Practice Forum DTI, Hospitality Skills Acad; memb Bd: Tourism Alliance, Tourism South East, Arora Hldgs; pres Hospitality Action; tstee: Springboard UK, PM Tst; Master Innholder 2001, Special Catey Award Caterer & Hotelkeeper 2002, Arena Accolade 2003; Hon MA London Met Univ 2005; hon fell Thames Valley Univ, visiting fell Bournemouth Univ; FHCIMA; *Style—* Bob Cotton, Esq, OBE; ✉ British Hospitality Association, Queens House, 55–56 Lincoln's Inn Fields, London WC2A 3BH (☎ 0845 880 7744, fax 020 7404 7799)

COTTON, Simon; *Educ* Univ of Strathclyde; *Career* mktg offr Motherwell Bridge 1995–97, dir Russell Europe Ltd 1997–2008, md Carron Phoenix Ltd 2008–10, head Strategic Mktg Franke Kitchen Systems Gp 2010–11, pres Colored Sinks Franke 2011–13, chief exec Johnstons of Elgin 2013–; *Style—* Simon Cotton, Esq

COUCHMAN, Martin; OBE (2005); s of Frederick Alfred James Couchman (d 1970), and Pamela Mary, *née* Argent (d 2007); *b* 28 September 1947; *Educ* Sutton Valence, Exeter Coll Oxford (MA); *m* 29 Oct 1983, Carolyn Mary Constance, da of Victor Frow Roberts (d 1987), of Childer Thornton, Cheshire; 3 s (Edmund Frederick Martin b 1985, William Thomas James b 1987, Nicholas Robert David b 1992), 1 da (Annie Elizabeth Constance b 1989); *Career* bldg industry 1970–77; Nat Econ Devpt Office: indust advsr 1977–84, head of admin 1984–87, on secondment as UK dir of Euro Year of the Environment 1987–88, sec to Nat Econ Devpt Cncl 1988–92; chm CBI Sectoral Employment Issues Ctee 2000–10; dep chief exec British Hospitality Assoc 1993–2016, chm Social Affrs Euro Hotel and Restaurant Confedn (HOTREC) 2001–13 (memb Exec Ctee 1997–2000); memb Green Alliance 1988–; FRSA 1987; *Recreations* amateur dramatics, Anglo-Saxon history, armchair archaeology; *Style—* Martin Couchman, Esq, OBE; ✉ Kangles, Sevenoaks Road, Pratt's Bottom, Orpington, Kent BR6 7SE

COULSON, The Hon Mr Justice; Sir Peter David William Coulson; kt (2008), QC (2001); s of David Coulson, and Pamela, *née* Shorter; *b* 31 March 1958, London; *Educ* The Pilgrims' Sch Winchester, Lord Wandsworth Coll Hants, Univ of Keele (BA); *m* 25 May 1985, Veronica, *née* Lachkovic; 1 s (Thomas David Peter b 30 July 1989), 2 da (Joanna Clare b 1 June 1991, Kate Mary b 28 Dec 1997); *Career* barr Keating Chambers 1984–2004, recorder 2002–04, sr circuit judge 2004–08, judge of the High Court of Justice (Queen's Bench Div) 2008–; Sir Malcolm Hilberry Award Gray's Inn 1982; ACIArb; *Publications* Lloyds Professional Negligence Law Reports (founding ed, 1999), Professional Negligence and Liability (chapter, 2000), The Technology and Construction Court (2006); *Recreations* comedy, British art (1750–1950), renovating a castle in France; *Clubs* Travellers, Santa Monica Flyers; *Style—* The Hon Mr Justice Coulson; ✉ Technology and Construction Court, St Dunstan's House, 133–137 Fetter Lane, London EC4A 1HD (☎ 020 7947 6497, e-mail peter.coulson@hmcourts-service.gsi.gov.uk)

COULSON-THOMAS, Prof Colin Joseph; s of Joseph Coulson Thomas, of Mullion, Cornwall, and Elsie Coulson Thomas; *Educ* Helston GS, LSE (Trevennon exhibitioner), London Business Sch (MSc), Univ of London (DPA, MSc(Econ)), Univ of Southern Calif (AM), Univ of SA (MPA), Aston Univ (PhD), PCL (MA), DipM, DipCAM; *m* (m dis 1992), Margaret Anne, *née* Grantham; 2 da (Yvette May b 1978, Vivien Jane b 1980); 1 s (Trystan Joseph b 1991); *Career* articled clerk Neville Hovey Gardner & Co 1970–73 (qualified CA 1973), conslt Coopers and Lybrand Associates Ltd 1975–77, research exec IOD 1977–78; ed/publisher Professional Administration (ICSA) 1978–81; head of pubns and PR ICSA 1980–81, publishing dir (Periodicals) Longman Group Ltd 1981–84; mangr corp affrs Rank Xerox UK Ltd 1984–87; chm: Adaptation Ltd 1994– (chm and ceo 1987–94), Attitudes Skills and Knowledge Ltd 1994–2003, ASK Europe plc 1995–2003, ASK Multimedia Ltd 1995–98, Policy Publications Ltd 1995–, Cambridge Management Centres plc 1998–2003, Cotoco Ltd 1998–, Creative Database Projects Ltd 2000–01; non-exec dir: NHS Peterborough 2009–13 (chair Audit and Governance Ctee 2009–11), NHS Cambridgeshire 2011–13; chm Bryok Systems 2008–; chm Gp Risk Ctee United Church Schs Tst/ United Learning Tst 2012–13, chm Audit and Risk Ctee United Learning 2013–; chm Elms Global Ltd 2013–; corp affrs advsr BIM 1987–91, memb Home Office Partnership Advsy Bd 1993–94, leader and co-ordinator COBRA Project (EC) 1994–95, assoc dir The Chamberlain Partnership 2003–05; visiting research fell IT Inst Univ of Salford 1987–95, head of exec progs Univ of Southern Calif UK Prog 1987–88, dir of external affrs Euro Business Sch 1987–88, visiting fell Aston Business Sch 1988–93 (fndr dir Centre for the Professions 1988–89), sr visiting research fell City Univ Business Sch 1991–94, The Willmott Dixon prof of corp transformation Univ of Luton 1994–97 (dean Faculty of Mgmnt Univ of Luton 1994–97), visiting prof Univ of Luton 1998–2000, prof and head Centre for Competitiveness Univ of Luton 2000–06, prof of direction and leadership Univ of Lincoln 2005–09, visiting prof Univ of Bedfordshire 2006–09, prof Univ of Greenwich 2009–, adjunct visitng prof Dept of Geopolitics and Int Relations Manipal Univ 2011–; sr assoc judge Inst Univ of Cambridge 1994–97, Hooker distinguished visiting prof McMaster Univ 1995, visiting prof East China Univ of Science and Technology Shanghai 1996, visiting prof Mgmnt Devpt Inst India 1997–2000, distinguished visiting prof e-TQM Coll Dubai 2008; govr Moorfields Eye Hosp 1978–88, dep chm London Electricity Consultative Cncl 1980–86; memb: Cncl for Professions Supplementary to Med 1982–89, Nat Biological Standards Bd 1985–94; rep govr Peterborough and Stamford Hospitals NHS Fndn Tst 2010–; treas Central London Branch BIM 1977–79; chm: Crossbencher (Parly Liaison) Prog 1977–80, Public Affrs Ctee Inst of Mktg 1979–80; memb Ctee London Soc of Chartered Accountants 1979–81; pres Soc of Co and Commercial Accountants 1984–85 (memb Cncl 1978–86), vice-pres Soc of Conservative Accountants 1990– (sec 1978–83, chm 1983–90); memb: Cncl IPR 1983–86 (chm Professional Practices Ctee 1985–86), Professional Devpt Ctee IOD 1989–97, Professional Standards Ctee and Chartered Accreditation Bd IOD 1997–2002, Bd of Examiners IOD 1998–2009, Professional Accreditation Ctee 2003–09, Corp Governance and Risk Mgmnt Ctee ACCA 2006–11, ACCA Governance, Risk and Performance Global Forum 2011–; memb Cncl Conflict Res Soc 1974–76, treas The Beauchamp Lodge Settlement 1976–77, cncllr London Borough of Greenwich 1977–82, memb Greenwich Community Health Cncl 1977–80, govr Eltham Green, Kidbrooke, Roan and Charlton Schs 1977–81, memb Cncl Anglo-Brasilian Soc 1978–81, contested (Cons) Easington General Election 1983; chm: Bow Group and Bow Publications 1982–83, Focus Group 1981–82 (pres 1983–86); memb Cncl: Royal Cwlth Soc 1981–85, Parly Info Technol Ctee 1987–96 and 1997–2002, Fndn for Sci and Technol 1987–92; lay memb Gen Osteopathic Cncl 2013–16 (chm Educn and Registration Standards Ctee 2013–16); chllr and professorial fell Sch for the Creative Arts 2015–; tstee Community Network 1989–2011; memb Nat Trade and Indust Forum 1993–2002; judge: Sword of Excellence Awards 1990–92, BT Award for Innovation in Electronic Trading 1993–99 (chm 1995–99), eBusiness Innovations Awards 2000– (chm 2000–); Change Agent and Transformation Leader Award 2012, Meritorious Service Medal (MSMLJ) Order of St Lazarus 2015; Freeman City of London 1978; memb Worshipful Co of: Chartered Secs and Administrators 1978, Bakers 1984; DG (UK and Europe) IOD India 2013–; FCA 1979, FCIS 1984, FSCA 1978, FCCA 1980, FMS 1984, FITD 1989, FIPR 1990, FIPM 1991, Hon FAIA 2003, FCIM 2006, FRGS, FRSA; *Publications* A Guide to Business Schools (1975), Company Administration Made Simple (1975), Public Relations: A Practical Guide (1979), Public Relations is Your Business (1981), Marketing Communications (1983), The 'New Professionals' (BIM, 1988), The Responsive Organisation, People Management, the challenge of the 1990s (with Richard Brown, BIM, 1989), Too Old at 40? (BIM, 1989), Beyond Quality: Managing the Relationship with the Customer (with Richard Brown, BIM, 1990), The Complete Spokesperson (with Peter Bartram, 1990), The Flat Organisation: Philosophy and Practice (with Trudy Coe, BIM, 1991), Creating the Global Company – Successful Internationalisation (1992), Transforming the Company (1992, w edn 2002), Creating Excellence in the Boardroom: A Guide to Shaping Directorial Competence and Board Effectiveness (1993), Developing Directors: Building An Effective Boardroom Team (1993), Business Process Re-engineering: Myths and Realities (ed, 1994), The Responsive Organisation: Re-engineering new patterns of work (gen ed, 3 vols, 1995), The Competitive Network (exec ed, 1996), The Future of the Organization (1997), Winning Major Bids – The Critical Success Factors (exec ed, 1997), Developing Strategic Customers and Key Accounts (exec ed, 1998), Individuals and Enterprise (1999), Winning Business Series of Reports (exec ed, 1999–2001), Developing a Corporate Learning Strategy (1999), The Information Entrepreneur (2000), Shaping Things to Come (2001), Pricing for Profit (2002), Winning New Business: the critical success factors (jt author, 2003), The Knowledge Entrepreneur (2003), How to Make Your Case to the Media (jtly, 2006), Winning Companies, Winning People (2007), Developing Directors: a handbook for building an effective boardroom team (2007), Talent Management 2 (2012), Transforming Public Services (2012), Transforming Knowledge Management (2013); *Recreations* country life, boating, the music of the Rolling Stones; *Clubs* City Livery; *Style*— Prof Colin Coulson-Thomas; ✉ Adaptation Ltd, Mill Reach, 12 Mill Lane, Water Newton, Peterborough Cambridgeshire PE8 6LY (e-mail colinct@tiscali.co.uk or colin@coulson-thomas.com)

COULTER, Michael Daley; s of Thomas Coulter (d 1976), of Glasgow, and Elizabeth, *née* Daley (d 1991); *b* 29 August 1952; *Educ* Holy Cross HS Hamilton; *m* 27 Aug 2007, Catherine M Lord; 2 s (Luke b 21 Jan 1981, Eliot b 18 Feb 1987), 2 da (Ruth b 8 April 1983, Sophie b 23 May 1985); *Career* dir of photography 1985–; winner BAFTA Scotland Award for outstanding contribution to film and TV 1997; memb: BSC 1988, AMPAS 1995; supporter Amnesty Int; *Film* incl: No Surrender 1985, The Good Father 1985, Housekeeping 1987, The Dressmaker 1988, Where Angels Fear To Tread 1991, The Long Day Closes 1992, Being Human 1993, Four Weddings and a Funeral 1993 (BSC nomination), Neon Bible 1995, Sense and Sensibility 1996 (Oscar and BAFTA nominations 1996, BSC nomination 1997) , Eskimo Day (for TV) 1996, Fairy Tale: A True Story 1997, Notting Hill 1998, Mansfield Park 1999, Killing Me Softly 2000, Love Actually 2003, The Bank Job 2008; *Recreations* cinema, movies, walking, reading, watching football; *Style*— Michael Coulter, Esq; ✉ c/o McKinney Macartney Management, Gable House, 18–24 Turnham Green Terrace, London W4 1QP (☎ 020 8995 4747, fax 020 8995 2414, website www.michael-coulter.com)

COUNT, Dr Brian Morrison; s of Douglas John Count, of Suffolk, and Ethel Sarah, *née* Goodwin; *b* 18 February 1951; *Educ* Bungay GS, King's Coll Cambridge (BA), Univ of Exeter (PhD); *m* 1975, Jane Elizabeth, *née* Hudson; 3 s (Michael Andrew b 8 May 1978, David Brian b 3 January 1981, Jonathan Peter b 22 October 1985); *Career* CEGB: research offr 1974–84, with Corp Planning Dept 1984–86, planning mangr 1986–90; National Power plc: dir of projects 1990–93, dir of power generation 1993–96, dir of ops and technol 1996–99, memb Bd 1996–2000, md of UK business 1999–2000; Innogy plc: chief operating offr 2000–01, ceo 2001–03; ceo RWE Trading 2003–05; non-exec chm Ceres Power 2008– (non-exec dir 2007–), chm Progressive Energy, non-exec dir Eskom; memb Industrial Devpt Advsy Bd DTI 2004–; FRSA 1980, FInstP 1997, CEng 1997; *Recreations* rugby, fly fishing, golf; *Clubs* Newbury Rugby, Sandford Springs Golf; *Style*— Dr Brian Count

COUPER, Prof Heather Anita; CBE (2007); da of George Couper Elder Couper (d 1998), and Anita, *née* Taylor (d 1984); *b* 2 June 1949; *Educ* St Mary's GS, Univ of Leicester (BSc), Univ of Oxford; *Career* mgmnt trainee Peter Robinson Ltd 1967–69, res asst Cambridge Observatories 1969–70, lectr Greenwich Planetarium 1977–83, broadcaster and writer on astronomy and sci 1983–, Gresham prof of astronomy 1993–96; cmmr Millenium Cmmn 1994–2007; dir Pioneer Film and TV Productions 1988–99; astronomy columnist The Independent; presenter of and contrib to many radio programmes incl Seeing Stars (BBC World Serv); pres: Br Astronomical Assoc 1984–86, Jr Astronomical Soc 1987–89; Hon DLitt Loughborough Univ 1991, Hon DSc Univ of Hertfordshire 1994, Hon DSc Univ of Leicester 1997; FRAS 1970, FInstP 1998, CPhys 1998; *Television* Channel 4: The Planets 1985, The Stars 1988, Avalanche 1995, Raging Planet 1998, Killer Earth 1998, Stormforce 1998, Universe 1999, Space Shuttle: Human Time Bomb 2003; Horizon Special: A Close Encounter of the Second Kind (BBC 2) 1992; Pioneer Productions: The Neptune Encounter (ITV) 1989, ET Please Phone Earth 1992, Space Shuttle Discovery 1993, Electric Skies 1994, Arthur C Clarke: The Visionary (Discovery Channel Europe) 1995, Wonders of Weather (Discovery Channel Europe and Learning Channel USA) 1995, On Jupiter (Discovery Channel America and Channel 4) 1995, Black Holes (Discovery Channel USA, ABC Aust, Channel 4) 1997, Stephen Hawking: Profile (BBC) 2002; *Radio* presenter and scriptwriter Red Planet (BBC Radio 4) 2003, Worlds Beyond (BBC Radio 4) 2005, Arthur C Clarke: The Science and the Fiction (BBC Radio 4) 2005, Britain's Space Race (BBC Radio 4) 2007, Cosmic Quest (series, BBC Radio 4) 2008; *Books* over 40 pubns incl: The Space Scientist series, The Universe, The Restless Universe, The Stars, The Planets, The Space Atlas, How the Universe Works, Guide to the Galaxy, Black Holes, Big Bang, Is Anybody Out There?, To the Ends of the Universe, Universe, Mars: The Inside Story, Extreme Universe, Philips Stargazing (annual series), The History of Astronomy, The Story of Astronomy, The Astronomy Bible, The Secret Life of Space; *Recreations* travel, the English countryside, wine, food, music; *Clubs* Groucho; *Style*— Prof Heather Couper, CBE; ✉ David Higham, 7th Floor, Waverley House, 7–12 Noel Street, London W1F 8GQ (e-mail dha@davidhigham.co.uk, web www.davidhigham.co.uk)

C

COUPLAND, (William) James; s of late William Arthur Coupland, and late Patricia Anne, *née* Martin; *b* 25 May 1957; *Educ* KCS Wimbledon; *m* 13 Sept 1980, Helen Jane, da of late Charles Alfred Everett; 3 s (Christopher Everett, Benjamin Jake b 1981, Joshua James b 1987); *Career* dir Shearson American Express Ltd 1982–92, md Shearson Lehman Metals Ltd 1985–93, dir Shearson Lehman Hutton Commodities Tokyo Ltd, sr vice-pres Shearson Lehman Hutton Inc 1986–93, chm Shearson Lehman Hutton Commodities (now Lehman Brothers Commodities Ltd) 1987–93; dir The London Metal Exchange Ltd 1992–93, sr vice-pres Kidder Peabody International Ltd 1993–94, dir Deutsche Sharps Pixley Metals Ltd 1994–95, Standard Bank plc 1995–2015 (head of metals 1995–2012, head of commodities 2012–15), dir Standard Resources China Ltd; dir LME Hldgs Ltd and London Metal Exchange 2005–12; FRSA; *Recreations* tennis, golf, painting; *Style*— James Coupland, Esq; ✉ 5 Durrington Park, Wimbledon, London SW20 8NU (e-mail jim.coupland@live.co.uk)

COURT, Catherine Mary (Cathy); OBE (2014); *Career* co-fndr and dir Netmums.com 2000–14; *Style*— Mrs Cathy Court, OBE; ✉ Henry Wood House, 2 Riding House Street, London W1W 5BA (website www.netmums.com)

COURT, Louise; *Children* 2 s; *Career* showbiz writer Express Newspapers until 1990, asst ed Woman's Own 1990–94, Best 1994–2005 (ed 1998–2005), editorial dir ACP-NatMag 2005–07, ed Cosmopolitan 2007–; *Style*— Ms Louise Court; ✉ Cosmopolitan, The National Magazine Company, National Magazine House, 33 Broadwick Street, London W1F 0DQ

COURT, Pamela Mary (Pam); da of Thomas Richardson (d 2004), of Gosforth, Newcastle upon Tyne, and Kathleen, *née* Carroll; *b* 10 November 1954; *Educ* Gosforth Grammar, Dorset House Coll of Occupational Therapy (Dip Occupational Therapy), PCL (BSc), City Univ (MHM); *m* 17 Sept 1977, David Court, s of James Court (d 1990), of Moreton Morrell, Warks; 2 da (Rebecca b 4 Nov 1985, Kathryn b 15 Nov 1988); *Career* occupational therapist: Spinal Injuries Unit Hexam Hosp, Stroke Unit St Pancras Hosp, Camden Rehabilitation Centre (head occupational therapist); Waltham Forest HA: head occupational therapist Whipps Cross Hosp until 1986, dist occupational therapist 1986–91, therapy servs mangr 1991–93; Forest Healthcare NHS Tst: dir Women and Children's Servs and Learning Disabilities and Mental Health and Med Care Gp 1993–98, dep dir of ops Primary and Community and Mental Health Servs 1996–98, serv dir Women and Children's Servs 1996–98, actg operational dir Primary and Community Servs, Community and Primary Care Servs, Learning Disabilities and Women's and Children's Servs 1998–2000, dir of ops Primary, Community Women and Children and Mental Health Servs 2000–01; project dir Chingford (estab Wanstead and Woodford PCT) 2000–01, chief exec Harlow PCT 2001–06, actg chief exec Uttlesford PCT 2004, chief exec NHS SW Essex (formerly SW Essex PCT) 2006–10, chief exec lead for transition Essex PCT 2010–11, chief exec Saint Francis Hospice Havering-atte-Bower 2011–; memb Essex and E of England Leadership Devpt (NHS); former vice-chair Harlow 2020 Local Strategic Partnership, non-exec dir Princes Alexandra Hosp NHS Tst Harlow 2016–; *Recreations* walking, reading, cooking, gardening; *Style*— Mrs Pam Court; ✉ Saint Francis Hospice, The Hall, Havering-atte-Bower, Romford, Essex RM4 1QH (☎ 01708 753319, e-mail pamcourt@sfh.org.uk)

COURT-BROWN, Prof Charles Michael; s of William Michael Court-Brown, OBE (d 1968), and Caroline Gordon Stephen, *née* Thom; *b* 3 February 1948; *Educ* George Watson's Coll Edinburgh, Univ of Aberdeen (BSc), Univ of Edinburgh (MD, MB ChB); *m* 6 July 1974, Jacqueline Yek Quen, da of To Leong Mok; 1 s (Michael b 1988), 1 da (Johanna b 1979); *Career* conslt orthopaedic surgn 1985–, pt/t sr lectr Dept of Orthopaedic Surgery Univ of Edinburgh 1985, conslt orthopaedic surgn Lothian Health Bd 1992–; prof of orthopaedic trauma Univ of Edinburgh 2000; chm Scottish Orthopaedic Research Tst; fndr memb Br Trauma Soc; fell BOA, FRCS 1979, BORS 1983, FRCSEd (Orth) 1984; *Books* External Skeletal Fixation (1984), Atlas of Intramedullary Nailing of the Tibia and Femur (1991), Management of Open Fractures (1996), Tibia and Fibula (1997), Mastercases in Orthopaedic Surgery (1999), Trauma (2006), Fractures in Adults (ed, 6 edn 2006, 7 edn 2010); *Recreations* house building, cooking; *Style*— Professor Charles Court-Brown

COURTENAY, Sir Thomas Daniel (Tom); kt (2001); s of Thomas Henry Courtenay (d 1984), of Hull, and Annie Eliza, *née* Quest (d 1962); *b* 25 February 1937, Hull; *m* Isabel; *Career* actor; *Theatre* numerous performances from 1960–; venues incl The Old Vic Theatre, Royal Exchange Theatre, various locations in the West End and Broadway; *Television* incl: The Old Curiosity Shop 1994, Young Indiana Jones 1995, Pretending To Be Me 2003, Ready When You Are Mr McGill 2003, Little Dorrit 2008, Unforgotten 2015; *Films* incl: Private Potter 1962, The Loneliness of the Long Distance Runner 1962 (BAFTA winner), Billy Liar 1963 (BAFTA nomination), King and Country 1964 (BAFTA nomination), Operation Crossbow 1965, Doctor Zhivago 1965 (Oscar nomination), King Rat 1965, Night of the Generals 1967, The Day the Fish Came Out 1967, A Dandy in Aspic 1968, Otley 1969, One Day in the Life of Ivan Denisovich 1970, To Catch a Spy 1971, Keep Your Fingers Crossed 1971, I Heard the Owl Call my Name 1973, The Dresser 1983 (Oscar nomination, BAFTA nomination, Golden Globe winner), Me and the Girls 1985, Absent Friends 1985, Leonard Part 6 1987, Happy New Year 1987, The Last Butterfly 1990, Let Him Have It 1991, Redemption 1991, The Boy from Mercury 1996, A Rather English Marriage 1998, Whatever Happened to Harold Smith? 1999, Last Orders 2001, Nicholas Nickleby 2003, Flood 2007, The Golden Compass 2007, Quartet 2012, 45 Years 2015 (Silver Bear Berlin Film Festival); *Books* Dear Tom (2000); *Style*— Sir Tom Courtenay; ✉ c/o Jonathan Altaras Associates, 11 Garrick Street, London WC2E 9AR

COURTENAY-LUCK, Dr Nigel Stephen; s of Gerald Harold Courtenay-Luck (d 1969), and Margaret Elizabeth Mary, *née* Bishop (d 1983); *b* 2 December 1952; *Educ* Kingsway-Princeton Coll, St George's Hosp and Chelsea Coll London (BSc), Royal Post Grad Med Sch Univ of London (PhD); *m* 27 July 1975, Maria, *née* Lombardi; 1 s (Giovanni Gerald b 3 Aug 1979), 2 da (Santina Rosa b 23 June 1986, Francesca Aurora b 9 March 1992); *Career* researcher ICRF 1981–84; Hammersmith Hosp London: sr researcher 1984–87 (Unilever research scholar), lectr in immunology 1987–99; co-fndr Antisoma (now Antisoma plc) 1991, chief scientific offr Antisoma Research Ltd 2003– (tech dir 1991–2003); sr lectr Imperial Coll Sch of Med London 2001; PhD examiner Univ of London 2004–; co-ordinator European Sch of Oncology 1989, scientific advsr Bio-Industry Assoc 1993–98; author of more than 30 papers in oncology and immunology jls and of 8 chapters in books; more than 50 invited lectures in UK and abroad; Eureka Award DTI 1993, Smart Award DTI 1998; memb: Inst of Biology 1980–, Br Soc of Immunology 1991–, American Soc of Clinical Oncology 2004–; FRSM 1999; *Recreations* walking, travelling, skiing, ski-jetting, family activities; *Clubs* Courtenay Soc, Powderham Castle

(Devon), David Lloyd's; *Style*— Dr Nigel Courtenay-Luck; ✉ Antisoma Research Ltd, Hanger Lane, London W5 3QR (☎ 020 8799 8200, fax 020 8799 8201)

COURTENAY-STAMP, (David) Jeremy; s of David Courtenay-Stamp, and Helen Annette, *née* Smith; *b* 25 April 1962; *Educ* Blundell's (scholar), LSE (LLB); *m* Elizabeth Ann, *née* Crawford; 2 da (Georgina Louise b 31 March 1993, Alexandra Isobelle b 22 April 1995); *Career* ptnr Macfarlanes 1992– (joined 1984, currently head Commercial Section); memb: Worshipful Co of Dyers, City of London Solicitors Co, Law Soc; ACA 1986; *Recreations* golf, scuba, skiing, sailing, tennis, squash; *Clubs* Chelsea Harbour; *Style*— Jeremy Courtenay-Stamp, Esq; ✉ Macfarlanes, 10 Norwich Street, London EC4A 1BD (☎ 020 7831 9222, fax 020 7831 9607)

COURTNEY, Prof James McNiven; s of George Courtney (d 1972), of Glasgow, and Margaret, *née* McNiven (d 1980); *b* 25 March 1940; *Educ* Whitehall Sr Secdy Sch Glasgow, Univ of Glasgow (BSc), Univ of Strathclyde (PhD), Univ of Rostock (Dr sc nat); *m* 26 June 1965, Ellen Miller, da of James Copeland; 1 da (Margaret Ellen Louise b 28 March 1966), 2 s (James George b 28 June 1969, David William b 3 Aug 1975); *Career* rubber technologist: Maclellan Rubber Ltd 1962–65, Uniroyal Ltd 1965–66; Univ of Strathclyde: postgrad student 1966–69, lectr Bioengineering Unit 1969–81, sr lectr 1981–85, reader 1986–89, prof 1989–; Int Soc for Artificial Organs (sec treas 1994), Int Faculty for Artificial Organs 1995 (tenured prof 1992); Rudolf Virchow prize 1986, Univ of Rostock prize of honour 1987; EurChem 1994; FRSC 1977, FIM 1993; *Books* Artificial Organs (ed, 1977), Biomaterials in Artificial Organs (ed, 1984), Progress in Bioengineering (ed, 1989); *Recreations* football supporter (Glasgow Rangers); *Style*— Prof James M Courtney

COURTNEY, Rohan Richard; OBE (2008); s of Arthur Richard Courtney (d 2002), of Chingford, London, and Cecelia, *née* Harrington (d 2006); *b* 28 January 1948, Chingford, London; *Educ* William Morris GS London; *m* 12 Jan 1974 (m dis 2004), Marilyn, da of Ernest Arthur Charles Goward (d 1972), of Waltham Cross, Herts; 1 s (Liam b 1975), 1 da (Siân b 1977); *Career* banker and co director; National Provincial Bank London 1965–68; mangr: Rothschild Intercontinental Bank Ltd London 1968–75, Amex Bank Ltd London 1975–76; asst dir Amex Bancom Ltd Hong Kong 1976–78, md Euro Asian Fin (Hong Kong) Ltd Hong Kong 1978–80, sr mangr Creditanstalt Bankverein London 1980–82, gen mangr State Bank of NSW London 1982–90, md Rohan Courtney & Partners Ltd 1990–96, gp chief exec Robert Fraser & Co Ltd 1991–92, dir and co-fndr UCG Partnership Ltd 2005–12, dir UCG Engrg Ltd 2007–08; chm: Associated Australian Banks in London 1988, Br Overseas Cwealth Banks Assoc 1990, Sterling Trust plc 1992–94 (dir 1991–94), Swaine Adeney Brigg Ltd 1993–94, International Pacific Securities plc 1993–96, West 175 Media Gp 1996–2001, Sanctuary Music Productions plc 1997–98, Chartfield Fund Management plc 1997–98, Project Leaders Int Ltd 2002–07, Creative Realisation Ltd 2002–03, Britain-Australia Soc 2003–06 (dep chm 2001–03), Stockval Hldgs plc 2007–08, World UFO Ltd 2007–, Artemis Energy plc 2007–09, Clean Coal Ltd 2008–, Africa Oil Exploration Ltd 2012–14, Koralis Entertainment Inc 2014–; dep chm: Galleon Holdings plc 2001–03 (non-exec 1999–2001); chief exec Turnbulls Group Ltd 2002–03; non-exec dir: Tullow Oil plc 1993–2007, Boisdale plc 1993–2005, Inn Business Group plc 1995–97, London Chamber of Commerce and Industry Commercial Educn Tst 2002–03, Education Development International plc 2002–03, Corac Gp plc 2010–14; sr ptnr Courtney and ptnrs LLP 2015–; memb The Cook Soc 1989–2007 (chm 2000); tstee: Sir Robert Menzies Educational Tst 1999–2013, Brit-Oz E-Pals Tst 2005–10 (chm tstees), UCG Assoc 2009–15 (chm of tstees 2009–13); Freeman City of London, Liveryman Worshipful Co of Woolmen 1990–2010; *Publications* Underground Coal Gasification (chapter in The Coal Handbook (2013)); *Clubs* Hong Kong CC; *Style*— Rohan Courtney, Esq, OBE; ✉ 4 Westbourne Place, Farnham, Surrey GU9 8EF (mobile 07879 498544, e-mail rohan.courtney@gmail.com)

COURTOWN, 9 Earl of (I 1762); James Patrick Montagu Burgoyne Winthrop Stopford; also (sits as) Baron Saltersford (GB 1796), Baron Courtown (I 1758), Viscount Stopford (I 1762); s of 8 Earl of Courtown, OBE, TD, DL (d 1975); *b* 19 March 1954; *Educ* Eton, Berkshire Agric Coll, RAC Cirencester; *m* 6 July 1985, Elisabeth Dorothy, yr da of Ian Rodger Dunnett, of Pinders, Broad Campden, Glos; 2 da (Lady Rosanna Elisabeth Alice b 13 Sept 1986, Lady Poppy Patricia Lilly b 19 Oct 2000), 1 s (James Richard Ian Montagu, Viscount Stopford b 30 March 1988); *Heir* s, Viscount Stopford; *Career* land agent; landscape contractor; ARICS; Lord in Waiting (Govt whip) 1995–97 and 2015–, oppn whip 1997–2000; former govt spokesman for Home Office, Scotland and Transport, govt spokesman for business, innovation and skills, culture, media and sport, FCO, int devpt; *Style*— The Rt Hon the Earl of Courtown; ✉ House of Lords, London SW1A 0PW

COUSINS, Jeremy Vincent; QC (1999); s of Eric Cousins of Headington, and Joyce, *née* Gurl; *b* 25 February 1955; *Educ* Oxford Sch, Univ of Warwick (LLB); *m* 27 July 1993, Jane, da of Dr John Owens, FRCPsych, of Sutton Coldfield; 2 s, 1 da; *Career* called to the Bar Middle Temple 1977, asst recorder 1996, recorder 2000; chm: Midland Bar Assoc 2002–, Commercial Gp St Philip's Chambers 2003–; sidesman and memb Parochial Church Cncl St Anne's Moseley; *Recreations* wine, France and Italy; *Style*— Jeremy Cousins, Esq, QC; ✉ St Philip's Chambers, 55 Temple Row, Birmingham B2 5LS (☎ 0121 246 7000, fax 0121 246 7001)

COUSINS, John Stewart; s of L R Cousins (d 1976), and Margaret Betty Kate, *née* Fry (d 2001); *b* 31 July 1940; *Educ* Brentwood Sch, Britannia RNC Dartmouth, Jesus Coll Cambridge (MA); *m* 1, 26 Oct 1970 (m dis 1979), Anne Elizabeth, da of Patrick O'Leary (d 1976); 1 da (Charlotte b 1973); m 2, 28 Dec 1979, Geraldine Anne, da of Col Thomas Ivan Bowers, CBE, DSO, MC* (d 1980); *Career* RN 1958–62, Sub Lt 1960, served Far East in HMS Belfast and HMS Maryton; Kleinwort Benson Ltd: joined 1966, Far East rep Tokyo 1970–73, md Hong Kong 1973–78; fin advsr to chm Porodisa Gp Indonesia 1979–80, ptnr de Zoete and Bevan 1980–85, dir Barclays de Zoete Wedd Securities 1985–92, md Barclays de Zoete Wedd Equities Ltd, chief exec BZW Puget Mahé SA Paris; dir: Corney & Barrow Group Ltd, Baring Emerging Europe plc 1994–2011; chm Int Equities Ctee London Stock Exchange 1990–92; ASIP, MSI; *Recreations* racing, rugby, cricket, field sports; *Clubs* Brooks's, Caledonian; *Style*— John Cousins, Esq; ✉ 73 Redcliffe Gardens, London SW10 9JJ (☎ and fax 020 7373 1919); Lamarie, 46140 Luzech, France (☎ and fax 00 33 5 65 20 11 95)

COUSINS, Eur Ing Raymond John Randal; s of Henry George Cousins (d 1983), and Freda Isabella, *née* Roberts; *b* 14 July 1938; *Educ* Alleyn's Sch Dulwich, King's Coll London (BSc); *m* 28 Dec 1963, Ruth Imogen, da of William Charles Vigurs (d 1982); 2 da (Fiona Mary b 4 Oct 1967, Kirstie Ann b 6 Oct 1969); *Career* civil engr; sr ptnr Cyril Blumfield and Ptnrs 1988– (ptnr 1973–); chm Assoc of Consltg Engrs 1997–98; govr: Dulwich Coll 1991–95, Alleyn's Sch 1991–2008 (chm 2002–08); tstee Dulwich Estate 1989–2004 (chm 1997–98); Master Worshipful Co of Woolmen 1993–94 (Liveryman 1973, clerk 1975–87, memb Court of Assts 1986–2013), Master Worshipful Co of Engrs 2002–03 (Liveryman and memb Ct of Assts 1983–2008, Asst Clerk 1983–98; CEng, FICE, FIStructE, FConsE; *Recreations* golf, ornithology, hill walking; *Clubs* Athenaeum, Dulwich and Sydenham Hill Golf; *Style*— Eur Ing Raymond J R Cousins; ✉ 33 Hitherwood Drive, London SE19 1XA (☎ 020 8670 4673, e-mail cyril.blumfield@btinternet.com); Cyril Blumfield & Partners (☎ and fax 020 8761 0072)

COUSINS, Richard; s of late Philip Cousins, and late Marian Cousins; *b* 29 March 1959; *Educ* Univ of Sheffield (BSc), Univ of Lancaster (MA); *m* 1982, Caroline, *née* Thorpe (d 2015); 2 s; *Career* OR Dept Cadbury Schweppes PLC 1981–84, corporate planning BTR (Newey and Eyre) 1984–90; BPB PLC: corporate planning 1990–92, gp finance controller 1992–95, gen mangr packaging 1995–96, md Abertay 1996–98, pres BPB Westroc (Canada) 1998–2000, chief exec 2000–05; gp chief exec Compass Gp PLC 2006–; non-exec dir: P&O PLC 2005–06, HBOS PLC 2007–09, Reckitt Benckiser Gp PLC 2009–14, non-exec dir Tesco PLC 2014–; *Recreations* cricket, walking, Scotland; *Style*— Richard Cousins, Esq; ✉ Compass Group PLC, Compass House, Guildford Street, Chertsey, Surrey KT16 9BQ (☎ 01932 573000, fax 01932 569956)

COUSSINS, Baroness (Life Peer UK 2007), of Whitehall Park in the London Borough of Islington; Jean Elizabeth Coussins; da of Walter Leonard Coussins (d 1973), and Jessica, *née* Hughes (d 1996); *b* 26 October 1950, London; *Educ* Godolphin & Latymer Sch, Newnham Coll Cambridge (MA); *Children* 2 da (Anna b 1978, Claudia b 1988), 1 s (Matthew b 1981); *Career* UNA 1973–75, NCCL 1975–80, dep dir Child Poverty Action Gp 1980–83, sr educn offr ILEA 1983–88; Cmmn for Racial Equality: dir Social Policy 1988–94, dir Equality Assurance 1994–96; ceo The Portman Gp 1996–2006; memb: Crime Prevention Panel DTI 1999, Scottish Ministerial Advsy Gp on Alcohol Problems 2001–06, BBFC 2002–05, ASA 2003–09, PM's Strategy Unit Advsy Gp 2003–04, Dept of Health Taskforce on Consumers and Markets 2004, Alcohol Educn & Research Cncl 2004–07, Better Regulation Cmmn 2004–07, Corporate Responsibility Bd Camelot; ind consl on corporate responsibility 2006–; chair All Pty Parly Gp on Modern Languages 2008–; fndr memb and chair Maternity Alliance 1980s; author of numerous pamphlets, articles and chapters in books; pres: Money Advice Tst 2010–, Peru Support Gp 2012–; patron On the Shoulders of Giants Theatre Co 2008–; vice-pres Chartered Inst of Linguistics; assoc fell and memb Governing Body Newnham Coll Cambridge 2002–05, govr Channing Sch 2007–12, hon fell UCL 2010–, hon fell Newnham Coll Cambridge 2015–; President's Medal Br Acad 2013; *Books* Taking Liberties (1977), Shattering Illusions (co-author, 1986); *Recreations* family, travel, food, swimming; *Clubs* Fulham FC; *Style*— The Rt Hon the Baroness Coussins

COUTTIE, Baroness (Life Peer UK 2016), of Downe in the County of Kent; Philippa Marion Couttie (Philippa Roe); da of James Kenneth Roe, and Marion Audrey, *née* Keyte; *Educ* Roedean, St Andrews Univ; *m* 20 Sep 2002, Stephen Couttie; 1 s (Angus James Jack), 1 da (Genevieve Patricia Marion); *Career* ldr Westminster City Cncl since 2012; co-fndr Wearne PR 1987–90, chief exec Cornerstone Communications 1990–92, prop and ceo PR Consultants 1992–99, assoc dir J Henry Schroder 1999–2000, dir Citigroup Securitisation Divn 2000–06; Westminster City Cncl: cncllr 2006–, memb Children's Services Overview & Scrutiny Ctee, memb Planning & City Devpt Ctee 2006–07, memb School Govrs Appt Ctee 2007–08, dep cabinet memb Children's Services 2007–08, memb Resources and Corporate Services Overview & Scrutiny Ctee 2007–08, dir Local Educn Partnership 2008, memb Cabinet (Housing) 2008–11, memb Cabinet (Finance) 2011–12, ldr 2012–; head Educn Team Private Finance Panel Conservative Party 1997–99, head Treas Team James Ctee 2004–05, chm Public Sector Efficiency Subgroup Econ Competitive Policy Group 2006–07, chair West End Partnership Bd 2012–, chm Westminster Health & Wellbeing Bd 2012–13; memb: London Crime Reduction Bd 2012–, Bd Royal Parks 2012–, LGA Housing & Environment Bd 2013–, Cncl Canal & River Tst 2013–, London Enterprise Panel 2014–, LEP Infrastructure Gp 2014–; patron Breast Cancer Haven 2004–12, Macmillan Cancer Support 2004–12, govr Centre for Young Musicians 2007–08, memb Cncl Imperial Coll London 2006–14 (chm Audit Ctee 2008); *Recreations* skiing, travelling, reading, ancient history, antiquities, opera; *Style*— The Baroness Couttie; ✉ Westminster City Council, 64 Victoria Street, London SW1E 6QP

COUTTS, Anne Jane; da of Rev Alistair Sutherland, of Watlington, Oxfordshire, and Mysie, *née* Dunn; *b* 19 April 1956, Watford, Herts; *Educ* Univ of Warwick (BSc, PGCE, MEd); *m* 2 Sept 1978, Ian Alexander Coutts; 2 da (Amy b 22 Aug 1983, Rachael b 22 April 1985); *Career* dep head Edgbaston C of E Coll 1989–92; headteacher: Eothen Sch Caterham 1992–95, Sutton HS (GDST) 1995–2003, Headington Sch Oxford 2003–10; memb: HMC, ISI Inspectorate, QCA Ctee Advsy Gp on Research into Assessment and Qualifications (AGRAQ); *Recreations* photography, saxophone, cooking, reading, choral singing; *Clubs* Lansdowne; *Style*— Mrs Anne Coutts

COUTTS, Derek James; s of Donald James Coutts, and Margaret Joan Coutts; *Educ* William Morris Sch London, Colchester Art Sch, Royal Coll of Art London (ARCA); *Children* 2 s (Jonathan James, Julien Mignonac); *Career* freelance photographer 1966–75, commercials dir 1975–; recipient of numerous advertising awards from D&AD, Cannes, etc; *Clubs* Groucho; *Style*— Derek Coutts

COUTTS, (Thomas) Gordon; QC (Scot 1973); s of Thomas Coutts (d 1976), and Evelyn Gordon Coutts; *b* 5 July 1933; *Educ* Aberdeen GS, Univ of Aberdeen (MA, LLB); *m* 1 Aug 1959, Winifred Katherine, da of William Alexander Scott (d 1982); 1 s (Julian b 1962 d 2008), 1 da (Charlotte b 1964); *Career* passed Advocate 1959, standing jr counsel to Dept of Agric and Fisheries (Scot) 1965–73; chm: Industrial Tbnls 1972–2003, Med Appeal Tbnls 1984–2006, VAT Tbnls 1990–96, Financial Services and Markets Tbnl 2001–08; temp judge Court of Session Scot 1991–2004, vice-pres (Scot) VAT and Duties Tbnls 1996–2008; called to the Bar Lincoln's Inn 1995; FCIArb; chm Faculty Services Ltd 1989–93 (exec dir 1974–84); *Recreations* historical studies, travel, stamp collecting; *Clubs* New (Edinburgh), Bruntsfield Links Golf (Edinburgh); *Style*— T Gordon Coutts, Esq, QC; ✉ 6 Heriot Row, Edinburgh EH3 6HU (☎ 0131 556 3042, fax 0131 556 5947)

COUTTS, Herbert; MBE (2008); Bailie of Dolphinstoun; s of late Herbert Coutts, and Agnes, *née* Boyle; *b* 9 March 1944; *Educ* Morgan Acad Dundee; *m* 24 Dec 1970, Angela Elizabeth Mason, da of late Henry Smith; 1 s (Christopher b 10 Feb 1976), 3 da (Antonia b 17 Nov 1971, Naomi b 12 April 1977, Lydia b 31 Dec 1980); *Career* keeper of antiquities and bygones Dundee Museum 1968–71 (asst keeper 1965–68), supt of Edinburgh City Museums 1971–73, city curator Edinburgh City Museums and Galleries 1973–94; City of Edinburgh Cncl: head of museums and galleries 1994–97, head of heritage and arts 1997–98, acting dir of recreation 1998–99, dir of recreation 1999–2001, dir of culture and leisure 2001–07; major projects: City of Edinburgh Art Centre 1980, Museum of Childhood Extension 1986, The People's Story Museum 1989, City of Edinburgh Art Centre Extension 1992, Newhaven Heritage Museum 1994, Makars' Court (Scotland's Poets Corner) 1998, Scott Monument Restoration 1999, Usher Hall Restoration 1999; vice-pres Museum Assts Gp 1967–70; memb: Govt Ctee on Future of Scotland's National Museums and Galleries 1978–80 (report published 1981), Cncl of Museums Assoc 1977–78 and 1986–88, Bd of Scottish Museums Cncl 1971–74 and 1986–88, Registration Ctee Museums and Galleries Cmmn 1989–2000, Bd Museums Training Inst 1995–98, Bd Cultural Heritage NTO 1998–2005, Scottish Catholic Heritage Cmmn 2006–, Bd Order of Malta Dial-a-Journey 2007– (chm 2010–); museums advsr to Convention of Scottish Local Authorities 1986–90; tstee: Paxton House 1988–2002 and 2007–, E Lothian Community Devpt Tst 1989–2009, Dunbar Community Cncl 2007–, Dunbar Community Devpt Tst 2007–, Nat Galleries of Scotland 2007–11, Battle of Prestonpans (1745) Tst 2007– (vice-chair 2010–), Scottish Catholic Heritage Collections Tst 2011–; chm Scottish Battlefields Tst 2015–; chm Wheelchair Accessible Vehicle Enterprise Ltd 2010–16; external examiner Univ of St Andrews 1993–97; contested (Lab) S Angus 1970; AMA 1970, FSA Scot 1965, FMA 1976; SBStJ 1977, KM 2009; Bailie of Dolphinstoun; *Publications* Ancient Monuments of Tayside (1970), Tayside Before History (1971), Edinburgh – An Illustrated History (1975), Huntly House (1980), Lady Stair's House (1980), Museum of Childhood (with John Heyes, 1986), The Pharaoh's Gold Mask (1998); exhibition catalogues incl: Edinburgh Crafts (with R A Hill, 1973), Aince a Bailie Aye a Bailie (1974), Gold of The Pharaohs (ed, 1988), Sweat of the Sun – Gold of Peru (ed, 1990), Dinosaurs Alive (ed, 1990), Golden Warriors of the Ukranian Steppes (ed, 1993), Star Trek – The Exhibition (ed, 1995), Quest for a Pirate (ed, 1996), Gateway to the Silk Road: Cultural Relics from the Han to the Tang Dynasties from Xi'an, China (ed, 1996), Faster, Higher, Stronger: An Exhibition about the Olympic Dream (ed, 1997); author of professional and academic papers and popular articles; *Recreations* gardening, swimming, music, family; *Style—* Herbert Coutts, Esq, MBE, Bailie of Dolphinstoun; ✉ Kirkhill House, Queen's Road, Dunbar, East Lothian, EH42 1LN (☎ 01368 863113, e-mail coutts826@btinternet.com)

COUZENS, Air Vice-Marshal David Cyril; s of Cyril Couzens (d 1982), and Joyce, *née* Walker (d 2000); *b* 15 October 1949; *Educ* Ecclesbourne Sch, Churchill Coll Cambridge (MA), RAF Coll Cranwell, Loughborough Univ (Dip), Open Univ Business Sch (MBA); *m* 1977, Deborah, *née* Cawse; 1 s, 1 da; *Career* RAF: initial trg 1968–72, practical aircraft and weaponry appts 1972–88, personnel mgmnt 1988–89, Superintendent of Armament 1990–91, MOD Support Policy (Operational Requirements) 1991–94, Air Cdre 1995, CIS HQ Strike Command 1995–97, Dir Logistics Information Strategy 1997–98, Air Vice-Marshal 1998, Air Offr Logistics Information and Indust Interface Study 1998–99, DG Defence Logistics (CIS) 1999–2000, DG Defence Logistics (IS) 2000–01, DG Capability (DLO) 2001–02, COS Surgn Gen 2002–03, SDS (Air) RCDS 2003–; pres Combined Servs and RAF Rugby League; CEng 1979, FIMechE 1991, memb RCDS 1994, FRAeS 1995 (pres 2010–11); *Recreations* hill walking, gardening, music; *Clubs* RAF; *Style—* Air Vice-Marshal David Couzens

COVENEY, Michael William; s of William Coveney, and Violet Amy, *née* Perry; *b* 24 July 1948; *Educ* St Ignatius Coll, Worcester Coll Oxford; *m* Susan Monica Hyman; 1 s (Thomas Geoffrey b 16 Dec 1977); *Career* ed Plays and Players 1975–78 (asst ed 1973–75), theatre critic and dep arts ed Financial Times 1981–89 (contrib 1972–80), theatre critic The Observer 1990–97, theatre critic Daily Mail 1997–2004; *Books* The Citz (1990), The Aisle is Full of Noises (1994), Knight Errant (with Robert Stephens, 1995), The World According to Mike Leigh (1996), Cats on a Chandelier (1999), Ken Campbell: The Great Caper (2011), Maggie Smith: A Biography (2015); *Recreations* music, travel, running; *Style—* Michael Coveney, Esq; ✉ c/o AP Watt, United Agents, 12–26 Lexington Street, London W1F 0LE

COVENEY, Prof Peter Vivian; s of Prof James Coveney (d 2013), and Patricia Yvonne, *née* Townsend; *b* 30 October 1958; *Educ* Beechen Cliff Sch Bath, Lincoln Coll Oxford (BA), Princeton Univ (Jane Eliza Procter fell), Merton Coll Oxford (sr scholar, MA), Keble Coll Oxford (Sir Edward P Abraham jr res fell, DPhil); *m* 9 May 1987, Samia Antonios Néhmé, da of Antonios Néhmé; 1 da (Elena b 22 Oct 1993), 1 s (Christopher b 12 March 1999); *Career* Wiener-Anspach fell Free Univ of Brussels 1985–86, sr coll lectr in physical chemistry Keble Coll Oxford 1987–88, lectr in physical chemistry Univ of Wales Bangor 1987–90; Schlumberger Cambridge Res Cambridge: prog ldr 1990–93, sr scientist 1993–98; prof and head of physical chemistry and dir Centre for Computational Science Queen Mary Univ of London 1999–2002, prof of physical chemistry and dir Centre for Computational Science UCL 2002–, co-dir UCL e-Science Centre of Excellence 2004–06, dir UCL Computational Life and Medical Sciences Network 2010–14; special invited lectr Dept of Applied Mathematics and Theoretical Physics Queen's Univ Belfast 1989–90, scholar in residence Inst for Science, Engrg and Public Policy Portland OR 1993, visiting fell in theoretical physics Wolfson Coll Oxford 1996–2000, visiting sr res fell UMIST 1997–2000, visiting scholar Dept of Mathematics Tufts Univ USA 2005–06, hon prof of computer science UCL 2005–, prof adjunct Yale Sch of Medicine Yale Univ 2011–; chair: UK Collaborative Computational Projects Steering Panel 2005–, UK High-End Computing Strategy Ctee Working Gp on HEC Strategic Framework Review 2005–06, UK e-Science All Hands Meeting 2008, Strategy for the UK Research Computing Ecosystem 2011, Willett's Report Editorial Bd on High Performance Computing and e-Infrastructure 2011, UK Govt E-Leadership Cncl 2012–; memb: Scientific Steering Ctee Isaac Newton Inst Univ of Cambridge 2004–08, JISC Ctee for Support of Research 2005–07, UK High-End Computing Strategy Ctee 2005–10; acad-nominated expert advsr UK PM's Cncl for Science and Technol 2012–13; ed: Jl of Computational Science, Computer Physics Communications & Philosophical Transactions Royal Soc A; author and ed of articles in books and scientific jls; holder of 7 patents for technical inventions; memb: American Physical Soc (USA) 1985, Soc of Petroleum Engrs 1993; assoc memb Center for Advanced Mathematical Sciences American Univ of Beirut 1999–; CChem 1988, CPhys 1988, FRSC, FInstP; *Books* The Arrow of Time (with Roger Highfield, 1990), Frontiers of Complexity (with Roger Highfield, 1995), Computational Biomedicine (with Marco Viceconti, Vanessa Diaz and Peter Hunter, 2014); *Recreations* football, squash, swimming; *Style—* Prof Peter Coveney; ✉ Centre for Computational Science, Department of Chemistry, University College London, 20 Gordon Street, London WC1H 0AJ (☎ 020 7679 4560, fax 020 7679 7463, e-mail p.v.coveney@ucl.ac.uk, website http://ccs.chem.ucl.ac.uk)

COVENTRY, Dean of; *see:* Irvine, Very Rev John

COVILLE, Air Marshal Sir Christopher Charles Cotton; KCB (2000, CB 1995); *Educ* RAF Coll Cranwell, Open Univ (BA), RAF Staff Coll Bracknell, RCDS; *m* Irene; 1 s, 2 da; *Career* joined RAF 1964; pilot (Lightning) 5 Sqdn, instr Operational Conversion Unit, pilot (Phantom) 43 Sqdn 1973, served Phantom Operational Conversion Unit RAF Coningsby, fighter specialist Central Tactics and Trials Org 1977, PSO to UKMILREP NATO HQ Brussels, OC Ops Wing RAF Stanley Falkland Islands, Cdr 111 (Fighter) Sqdn RAF Leuchars 1983–85, Gp Capt Air HQ 11 Gp Strike Command, Cdr RAF Coningsby, Air Cdre Flying Trg HQ Support Command, promoted Air Vice-Marshal 1992, AOC Trg Units 1992–94, AOC Trg Gp Personnel and Trg Command 1994, Asst Chief of Defence Staff Operational Requirements (Air Systems) 1994–98, Dep C-in-C Allied Forces Central Europe (re-titled Allied Forces N Europe 2000) 1998–2001, Air Memb for Personnel and C-in-C Personnel and Trg Command 2001–03; defence advsr to BT (Defence) 2003–09, sr defence advsr Rockwell Collins UK 2005–09; chm Westland Helicopters 2005–11; chm C4 Defence and Aerospace Ltd 2003–09, chm C4 Defence and Security Ltd 2010–; sr defence and security advsr to EMC (UK) 2010–; FCIPD, FRAeS; *Recreations* flying, shooting, mountaineering; *Style—* Air Marshal Sir Christopher Coville, KCB; ✉ Royal Air Force Club, 128 Piccadilly, London W1J 7PY

COWAN, David Neville; s of Roy Neville Cowan (d 1987), of Heyshott, W Sussex, and Dorne Margaret, *née* Burgoyne-Johnson (d 1998); *b* 21 May 1950, London; *Educ* Marlborough, Univ of Bath (BSc, BArch); *m* 23 Aug 1975, Gillian Judith, da of David Hay Davidson, OBE (d 1983), of Lymington, Hants; 2 s (Jonathan b 1979, Christopher b 1988); *Career* architect 1975–; dir: Cowan Architects (formerly David Cowan Associates) 1989– (formed 1983), Charterfield Group of Cos 1985–, dir Dignity Access 2014; memb: SPAB, Panel of Architects Chichester Dio; author of papers on designing for the elderly and disabled, expert witness to the Courts on disability housing; dir Nat Conservation Conf 1999–2005, tstee Sussex Heritage Tst 2005–15; RIBA 1976, FRSA 2006; *Recreations* skiing, sailing, shooting; *Clubs* Army & Navy; *Style—* David N Cowan, Esq; ✉ Oak Tree Cottage, Nursery Lane, Maresfield, East Sussex; Cowan Architects, 9–10 Old Stone Link, Ship Street, East Grinstead, West Sussex (☎ 01342 410242, e-mail dnc@cowan-architects.co.uk)

COWAN, Prof Edward James (Ted); s of William Cowan (d 1987), and Margaret, *née* MacBryde (d 1997); *b* 15 February 1944, Edinburgh; *Educ* Univ of Edinburgh (MA); *m* 1, 14 Dec 1963, Alison Shirley, *née* Dawson; 2 da (Karen b 26 April 1964, Morna b 1 Dec 1965), 1 s (David b 18 Oct 1966); *m* 2, 15 Jan 2004, Lizanne Frances, *née* Henderson; *Career* lectr in Scot history Univ of Edinburgh 1967–79, prof of history and chair of Scot studies Univ of Guelph Ontario 1979–93, prof of Scot history Univ of Glasgow 1993– (dir Crichton Campus Dumfries 2005–); Scot Arts Cncl Award 1978; FRSE 2004; *Publications* Montrose for Covenant and King (1977), The Ballad in Scottish History (2000), Alba: Celtic Scotland in the Medieval Era (2000), Scottish History: The Power of the Past (2002), For Freedom Alone: The Declaration of Arbroath 1320 (2004); *Recreations* hill walking, bird watching, folk music; *Style—* Prof Ted Cowan; ✉ Dalarran House, Balmaclellan, Castle Douglas DG7 3PP (☎ 01644 420839); University of Glasgow, Crichton Campus, Bankend Road, Dumfries DG1 4ZL (☎ 01387 702042, fax 01387 702043, e-mail ted.cowan@crichton.gla.ac.uk)

COWAN, Graham Kerr; s of Robert Kerr Cowan, and Agnes Una, *née* McKinlay; *b* 30 January 1964, Edinburgh; *Educ* George Watson's Coll Edinburgh, Univ of Edinburgh (BVMS, MRCVS); *m* 12 Sept 1992, Fay Cowan, *qv*; 2 s (Kerr McMillan b 25 April 1996, Ruadhan McKinlay b 30 Sept 1997); *Career* vet surgn 1986–94, hotelier Glenapp Castle 1994–2015 (AA Hotel of the Year for Scot & NI 2005–06, Luxury Hotel of the Year Hotel Review Scot 2005, Castle Hotel of the Year Hotel Review Scot 2006), hotelier McMillan Hotels Ltd 1994–, dir Peebles Hotel Hydropathic 2008–; *Style—* Graham Cowan, Esq; ✉ Barbados Villa, Station Road, Wigtown, Dumfries and Galloway DG8 9DZ

COWAN, Matthew Alexander; s of Ian Alexander Cowan, of Bristol, and Jacqueline, *née* Matthews; *b* 31 March 1967, Bristol; *Educ* Bristol GS, Univ of Exeter (BSc, BA), Coll of Law Guildford; *m* 2 Oct 1993, Shammima Bibi, *née* Golaup; 1 da (Hannah Bibi b 3 Sept 1997), 1 s (Adam Ali Alexander b 21 Dec 2001); *Career* slr; ptnr: Olswang 1998–2003 (joined 1993), Clyde & Co 2004–07, Payne Hicks Beach 2007–11, Bracher Rawlins LLP 2011–; memb Law Soc; *Recreations* reading, gardening, classic cars; *Style—* Matthew Cowan, Esq; ✉ Bracher Rawlins LLP, 77 Kingsway, London WC2B 6SR

COWAN, Michael John Julian; s of Kenneth Christopher Armstrong Cowan (d 1955), and Flora Muriel, *née* Stewart (d 2011); *b* 24 June 1952; *Educ* Midhurst GS Sussex, Churchill Coll Cambridge (MA); *m* 26 Sept 1981, Hilary Jane, da of Albert Edward Slade (d 1987); 2 da (Eleanor Josephine, Philippa Rose), 1 s (Christopher David Andrew); *Career* investment advsr NM Rothschild & Sons Ltd 1973–78, investment dir Lazard Bros & Co Ltd 1979–87, princ Morgan Stanley International 1987–95, sr ptnr Silchester International Investors LLP 1995–; fell Churchill Coll Cambridge; FCSI; *Recreations* golf, tennis, DIY; *Style—* Michael Cowan, Esq, FCSI; ✉ Silchester International Investors LLP, Time & Life Building, 1 Bruton Street, London W1J 6TL (☎ 020 7518 7102)

COWAN, Paul Adrian Dallas; s of E Cowan (d 1988), and Peggy Dallas, *née* Johnston (d 2008); *b* 5 August 1951; *Educ* Oxted GS, London Coll of Printing and Design, Univ of Surrey (MSc), Metanoia/Middlesex Univ (MSc); *m* Jan 1979, Rosemary, *née* Nimmo; 3 da (Jo b 17 Sept 1980, Patty, Chrissy (twins) b 30 Nov 1983); *Career* tracing servs for detective agency 1970, messenger rising to account exec Ogilvy & Mather advtg agency 1971–73, sr account exec CPV Advertising 1973–74, account supr Ogilvy & Mather 1975–78; Saatchi & Saatchi: account supervisor 1978, account dir 1979–84, bd account dir 1984–86, gp account dir 1986–90; fndr md: Cowan Kemsley Taylor 1990–97, RPM3 (following merger with Butler Lutos Sutton Wilkinson) 1997–2000, fndr and md (e=) 2000–, fndr Client Relationship Consultancy; MIPA, MInstM; *Recreations* people watching; *Style—* Paul Cowan, Esq; ✉ 6 Valentines Place, London SE1 8QH (☎ 020 7401 9164)

COWAN, Robert Charles (Rob); s of Maurice Bernard Cowan, of Finchley, London, and Vera, *née* Zec; *b* 14 April 1948; *Educ* Leas House Sch London; *m* 30 July 1971, Georgina, *née* Gilmour; 2 da (Francesca Sara b 26 Dec 1977, Victoria Leah b 8 Nov 1980); *Career* archivist Boosey and Hawkes Music Publishers 1978–89; ed CD Review magazine 1990–92, ed Classics (published by Gramophone magazine) 1992–93, contributing ed Gramophone magazine 1999, classical record critic The Independent 1999–; presenter: Classic Verdict (Classic FM) 1993–96, CD Choice (Classic FM) 1999–2001, CD Masters (BBC Radio 3) 2001–07, The Cowan Collection (BBC Radio 3) 2003–07, Breakfast (BBC Radio 3) 2007–11, Sunday Morning (BBC Radio 3) 2011–16, Essential Classics (BBC Radio 3) 2011–, Rob's Gold Standards on Saturday Classics (BBC Radio 3) 2016–; memb Judging Panel: Gramophone Awards, Classical Brit Awards, Classic Record Collector Awards; Best Historical Album Grammy Award Heifetz Collection 1995; memb RSM 2014; *Publications* Guinness Classical 1000 (1998); *Recreations* reading, walking, studying the works of John Ruskin, Emily Dickinson and Wallace Stevens; *Style—* Rob Cowan, Esq

COWAN, Ronnie; MP; *Career* MP (SNP) Inverclyde 2015–; *Style—* Ronnie Cowan, Esq, MP; ✉ 20 Crawford Street, Greenock, Inverclyde PA15 1LJ (☎ 01475 721877, website www.ronniecowan.com); House of Commons, London SW1A 0AA

COWARD, Lt Gen Sir Gary Robert; KBE (2012, OBE 1996), CB (2008); s of Lt-Col R V Coward (d 2002), and Marion Avril Coward; *b* 26 August 1955, Hampstead, London; *Educ* Duke of York's Royal Mil Sch, RMA Sandhurst, RMCS Shrivenham; *m* 30 Dec 1978, Chrissie, *née* Hamerton; 1 s (Ben b 24 Sept 1982); *Career* Troop Cdr 2 Field Regt RA 1975–79, Flight Cdr 3 Regt AAC 1979–82, second-in-command and Flight Cdr 660 Sqdn AAC 1983–84, Adj 7 Regt AAC 1985–87, Div 2 ASC 1987–89, staff offr BAS Washington 1989–91, Cmd 656 Sqdn AAC 1991–93, SO1 HQ DAAVN 1993–94, UN mil spokesman Bosnia 1994–95, CO 1 Regt AAC 1996–98, Sec COS Ctee MOD 1998–2000, Dep Cdr JHC (Jt Helicopter Cmd) 2000–03, DEC (ALM) MOD 2003–05, Cmd JHC 2005–08, COS (jt warfare devpt) Perm Jt HQ 2008–09, Chief of Materiel (Land) and Quartermaster Gen 2009–12; chm Redline Aviation Security Ltd 2013–; Dep Col Comdt AAC 2012–; govr Duke of York's Royal Military Sch (DYRMS) 2009–, pres AOPOA 2012–, pres AAC Veterans Assoc 2013–, tstee Sandhurst Tst 2013–, chm Museum of Army Flying 2016–; CGIA; *Recreations* wine tasting, skiing; *Clubs* Army & Navy; *Style—* Lt Gen Sir Gary Coward, KBE, CB; ✉ e-mail cowardz@sky.com

COWARD, Nicholas Ian (Nic); s of John Coward, of Shrewsbury, Salop, and Jane, *née* Yaxley; *b* 13 February 1966, Shrewsbury, Salop; *Educ* Shrewsbury Sch, Univ of Bristol (LLB), Guildford Coll of Law; *m* Vivien, *née* Lyle; 1 da (Innes b 13 June 2000), 1 s (Lachlan b 3 June 2002); *Career* slr Freshfields 1990–96, dir of corporate and legal affrs then acting ceo FA 1996–2004, dep chm AS Biss & Co 2004–07, ceo Br Horseracing Authy 2007–11, gen sec Premier League 2011–; dir European Professional Football Leagues, non-exec dir FA 2014–; treas Sport and Recreation Alliance 2004–06, chm Sports Rights Owners Coalition 2005–10, exec Int Horseracing Fedn, memb Horse Race Betting Levy Bd 2007–09; dir Furrows Hldgs 2004–; *Recreations* cinema, cricket, gardening, golf, horse racing, music, skiing, travel; *Clubs* MCC, Royal Cinque Ports Golf, Ivy; *Style—* Nic Coward, Esq

COWDEN, Stephen (Steve); *b* 13 July 1952; *Educ* Allan Glen's Sch Glasgow, Univ of Edinburgh (LLB); *m* 1985; 1 s; *Career* slr Biggart Baillie & Gifford Glasgow 1974–77, Beecham Group plc 1977–90, Glaxo Wellcome plc 1991–2001, gen counsel and co sec Reed Elsevier plc 2001–; memb 100 Gp; memb Law Soc of Scotland 1976, memb Internatinal Bar Assoc; *Recreations* golf; *Style—* Stephen J Cowden, Esq; ✉ Reed Elsevier plc, 1–3 Strand, London WC2N 5JR (☎ 020 7166 5681, e-mail steve.cowden@reedelsevier.com)

COWDRAY, Christopher Charles Blanshard; s of Charles George Blanshard Cowdray, of Johannesburg, and Maureen, *née* Neil; *b* 4 November 1955; *Educ* Falcon Coll Essexvale Zimbabwe, Grad Sch of Business Columbia Univ NY, Tech Coll Bulawayo (HND); *m* 10 Jan 1981, Christine Anne, da of John Stewart Ian McIntosh; 1 s (Andrew Chris Blanshard b 17 Feb 1987), 1 da (Emma Rose b 8 Jan 1994); *Career* articled clerk Pulbrook, Wright & Underwood Harare 1977–79; asst front of house mange Selson Park Hotel S Croyden 1979–80; food and beverage mangr Oasis Motel Harare 1980, rooms div mangr then dep gen mangr Jameson Hotel Harare 1981–82, gen mangr Churchill Arms Hotel Bulawayo

1982–83, dep mangr Peterborough Moat House 1983–84; exec asst mangr: Eastern Province Palaces Saudi Arabia 1984–85, Riyadh Conf Palace 1985–86, Pavilion Inter-Continental Singapore 1986–88; resident mangr Hotel Inter-Continental Sydney 1988–91, gen mangr Al Bustan Palace Hotel Muscat Oman 1991–92, gen mangr Muscat Inter-Continental and regnl dir of ops Oman 1992–93, gen mangr Churchill Inter-Continental Hotel London 1993–98, md Claridge's London 1998–2004, gen mangr The Dorchester 2004–08, ceo The Dorchester Collection of Hotels 2007–; memb London Ctee Br Hospitality Assoc (chm 1999–2000); chm Bond St Assoc, memb West One Gen Mangrs' Assoc (chm 1998); govr Eng Nat Ballet; hon prof Thames Valley Univ; Master Innholder; Freeman City of London; FHCIMA; *Recreations* photography, sailing, travel, outdoor pursuits, sport (especially tennis and squash); *Style*— Christopher Cowdray, Esq; ✉ The Dorchester collection, 3 Tilney Street, London W1K 1BJ (☎ 020 7319 7501)

COWDRY, Sally; *b* 27 May 1968, Tenterden, Kent; *Educ* Highworth Sch for Girls Ashford Kent, Univ of Bath (BSc), CIM (DipM); *Career* Stena Line 1990–97, BAA Heathrow Express 1997–99, O2/Telefonica 1999–2013 (mktg and consumer dir 2006–13), mktg and consumer dir Camelot 2013–; memb Bd Mktg Acad; fell Mktg Soc, fell and vice-pres CIM, memb Mktg Gp of GB; *Recreations* cinema, music, reading, travel, walking; *Style*— Ms Sally Cowdry; ✉ Camelot Group of Companies, Tolpits Lane, Watford, Hertfordshire WD18 9RN (☎ 01923 425398, e-mail sally.cowdry@camelotgroup.co.uk, website www.national-lottery.co.uk)

COWELL, HE (Andrew John) Hamish; s of Barry Hulke Cowell, and of Anne Roberta *née* Menzies; *b* 31 January 1965; *Educ* Madras Coll St Andrews, Wadham Coll Oxford; *m* Shadi Akhtar Khankasmai; 3 da (Yasmineh b 2000, Leyli b 2002, Parissima b 2008); *Career* diplomat; ME Dept (Iran/Iraq) FCO 1987–88, second sec political and press Colombo 1989–92, dep head of mission Tehran 1992–94, EU Directorate FCO 1994–96, head Political and Economic Sections Cairo 1996–99, speechwriter to Foreign Sec FCO 1999–2000, 10 Downing St Press Office 2000, seconded to Int Inst for Strategic Studies 2000–01, first sec ME and N Africa UK Rep Brussels 2001–04, secondment to Quai d'Orsay 2004–05, first sec then head int policy Paris 2005–09, private sec to Min of State FCO 2010–11, head Libya Unit FCO 2011–12, head N Africa Dept FCO 2012–13, ambass to Tunisia 2013–; *Style*— HE Mr Hamish Cowell; ✉ BFPO 5304, Ruislip HA4 6EP

COWELL, Robert Douglas; s of Douglas Walter Cowell, of Newport, Gwent, and Gladys, *née* Williams; *b* 9 February 1947; *Educ* Newport GS Gwent, Balliol Coll Oxford (MA, DPhil); *m* 1, 18 Oct 1969 (m dis 1984), Janice Carol; 2 da (Elizabeth Sarah b 1978, Julia Mary b 1980); m 2, 24 July 1986, Elizabeth Henrietta, da of Timothy Patrick Neligan, of Petworth, West Sussex; *Career* night shift foreman Turner & Newall Ltd 1972, investment analyst Hoare Govett Ltd 1972–77, UK corporate devpt mangr Hanson Trust plc 1977–80, md Hoare Govett Securities (Hoare Govett) 1980–89, fndr ptnr Makinson Cowell (now KPMG Makinson Cowell) 1989–; *Recreations* horse racing, golf; *Style*— Robert Cowell, Esq; ✉ KPMG Makinson Cowell Ltd, 15 Canada Square, London E14 5GL (☎ 020 7670 2500, fax 020 7670 2501)

COWELL, Simon; s of Eric P Cowell (d 1999), and Julie Cowell; *b* 7 October 1959; *Educ* Dover Coll, St Columba's Coll St Albans; *Children* 1 s (Eric b 14 Feb 2014); *Career* with EMI Music Publishing 1977–82 (started as post boy), fndr and co-owner Fanfare Records 1982–89, joined as A&R conslt BMG Records (now Sony Music Entertainment) 1989, fndr Syco Entertainment, fndr Syco Music 2002 (No. 1 Label for A&R Music Week UK 2014; artists incl One Direction, Little Mix, Labrinth, Ella Henderson, Fifth Harmony, Susan Boyle, Collabro, Il Divo, artists have sold over 200 million records, more than 200 number 1 albums and 150 number 1 singles in UK and US); judge: Pop Idol (ITV) 2001–02, American Idol (Fox) 2002–10; exec prodr X-Factor (ITV) 2004– (judge 2004–10 and 2014; Best Entertainment Prog BAFTA Awards 2006 and 2007, Best Talent Show Nat TV Awards 2012 and 2015), creator and judge Britain's Got Talent (ITV) 2007–, creator and judge X-Factor USA 2011–13; creator and exec prodr: American Inventor 2006–07, America's Got Talent 2006–, Celebrity Duets 2006; appearances on numerous other TV shows; Record Exec of the Year 1998 and 1999, A&R Man of the Year 1999, included in Top Entertainers of the Year Entertainment Weekly 2004, UK Personality of the Year Variety 2006, ranked 29th Forbes Celebrity 100 Power List 2006, Special Recognition Award Nat Television Awards 2008, named no 1 Hollywood Reporter's Top 50 Most Powerful in Reality TV 2009, Entertainment Weekly's Top Entertainer of the Year 2009, Variety Int's Humanitarian Award 2010, Rose d'Or Golden Jubilee Award 2010, Special Award BAFTA Television Awards 2010, Int Emmy Fndrs Award 2010, MIPCOM Personality of the Year 2014, Outstanding Contribution to Entertainment Elle Style Awards 2015; patron Children's Hospices UK 2009–, vice-pres Shooting Star Chase 2015–; *Publications* I Don't Mean to Be Rude But... (2003); *Recreations* motor racing; *Style*— Simon Cowell, Esq

COWEN, (Alan) Geoffrey Yale (Geoff); s of Alan Cowen (d 1975), and Agnes, *née* Yale (d 1960); *b* 24 September 1937; *Educ* St Edward's Coll Liverpool; *m* 22 Sept 1962, Eileen Frances, da of Reginald Altoft Johnson (d 2002), of Henleaze, Bristol; 2 da (Sian b 18 March 1965, Sara b 17 May 1966); *Career* Nat Serv Sgt RAEC 1959–61; various appts in publishing 1962–, appointed md Phaidon Press 1987, chief exec Windsor Books 1991–2013, chm WRTH Publications Ltd 1998–, chm Meyer and Meyer Sport UK Ltd 2000–, chm Star Book Sales 2005–, pres Roundhouse Publishing Gp 2006–09; vice-pres World Sports Publishers Assoc 2003–; *Recreations* rugby; *Clubs* Maidenhead Rugby; *Style*— Geoff Cowen, Esq; ✉ Egerton Cottage, 31 Furze Platt Road, Maidenhead, Berkshire SL6 7NE (☎ 01628 29237); Windsor Books (☎ 01628 770542, fax 01628 770546)

COWING, Malcolm; s of Cyril Cowing (d 1992), of Doncaster, S Yorks, and Irene Cowing; *b* 7 August 1949; *m* 9 Sept 1988, Laura Madelaine, da of Henry Sutcliffe; 1 step da (Lucy Barwick-Ward b 12 Aug 1980); *Career* head of PR Union Carbide UK Ltd 1979–84, PR dir Borodin Communications 1984–89, managing ptnr Brahm Ltd 1989–2011; winner IPR Sword of Excellence 1994 and 1998; FCIM 2004 (MInstM 1979), MIPR 1979, MInstD 1984; *Recreations* horse racing, skiing, opera; *Style*— Malcolm Cowing, Esq; ✉ 19 Spofforth Hill, Wetherby, West Yorkshire LS22 6SF (☎ 01937 584901, mobile 07770 512266, e-mail m.cowing@mrc.uk.com)

COWLEY, Caroline; *b* 19 November 1967; *Educ* Kingston Univ (LLB), Coll of Law Guildford; *Career* admitted slr 1992; Owen White: joined as trainee slr 1990, ptnr 2000–, ldr social housing team; legal advsr Chartered Inst of Housing; founding memb Social Housing Law Assoc (SHLA); *Style*— Ms Caroline Cowley; ✉ Owen White, Senate House, 62–70 Bath Road, Slough SL1 3SR (☎ 01753 876800, fax 01753 876876, e-mail caroline.cowley@owenwhite.com)

COWLEY, 7 Earl (UK 1857); Garret Graham Wellesley; also Baron Cowley of Wellesley (UK 1828), Viscount Dangan (UK 1857); s of 4 Earl Cowley (d 1962), by his 2 w, Mary Elsie May; suc half n, 6 Earl, 1976; *b* 30 July 1934; *Educ* Univ of S Calif (BS), Harvard Univ (MBA); *m* 1, 1961 (m dis 1966), Elizabeth Susanne, da of late Haynes Lennon; 1 s, 1 da; m 2, 1968, Isabelle O'Bready; m 3, 1981, Paige Deming (d 2008); m 4, 2012, Carola Marion Stormonth Darling, da of late Sir Robert Erskine Hill, Bt; *Heir* s, Viscount Dangan, *qv*; *Career* gp vice-pres Bank of America NT and SA London; Int Investment Management Service 1980–85; dir Bank of America Int (London) 1978–85, dir various Bank of America Tst Cos; chm Cowley & Co financial and business consltss 1985–90, investment ptnr Thomas R Miller & Son (Bermuda) 1990–2000; dir: Duncan Laurie (Isle of Man) Ltd 1994–2002, Scottish Provident Int Ltd 1998–2009; chm L-R Global Fund 2003–09; dir Kazimir Russia, Ukraine and Caspian Funds 2006–; Lloyds Register: memb Investment Ctee 2004– (chm 2011–15), memb Gen Ctee 2006–12, memb Audit Ctee 2006–15; memb Assoc of Cons Peers; *Clubs* Brooks's, Philippics, The Pilgrims; *Style*— The Rt Hon the Earl Cowley

COWLEY, Lesley Ruth; OBE (2011); *b* 30 June, Bristol; *Educ* MBA; *Career* registrar/dir of corporate services New Coll Swindon 1990–99; Nominet: operations dir/dep md 1999–2002, ceo 2002–14; founding tstee Nominet Tst (memb Bd 2008–10); non-exec dir: aql 2014–, CERT-UK 2014–16; lead non-exec dir Nat Archives 2016–; chair DVLA 2014–; memb Panel RUSI Ind Review of Surveillance 2014–15; tstee Kennet Housing Soc 2005–09, tstee Jenner Hall 2009–13; councillor ccNSO 2007–16 (chair 2011–13); CBI First Woman Award for Technol 2007, IoD London and SE Chair's Award 2011, ICANN Leadership Award 2013, Debrett's 500 2014; Hon DTech UWE; FRSA, FCMI, FICM, FBCS, FIoD; *Recreations* stained glass, glass fusing, local history; *Style*— Mrs Lesley Cowley, OBE; ✉ website www.lesleycowley.com, Twitter @lesleycowley

COWLEY, HE Sarah; *b* 19 November 1977, King's Lynn, Norfolk; *m* Paul Boschi; 1 da; *Career* diplomat; FCO: nuclear energy policy offr 2005–06, internal communications advsr 2006–07, asst private sec to Min for the ME 2007–09; private sec to Special Rep for Afghanistan and Pakistan, Kabul and London 2009–10, seconded to Delgn of the EU in Afghanistan 2010–11, head of communications Islamabad 2011–12, head Olympic and Paralympic Coordination Centre FCO 2012, dep head Commercial and Economic Diplomacy Dept FCO 2012–13, ambass to Latvia 2013–; *Style*— HE Ms Sarah Cowley; ✉ c/o FCO (Riga), King Charles Street, London SW1A 2AH

COWPE, William Arthur; s of Allan Cowpe (d 1974), and Margery Cowpe (d 2004), of Worsley, Manchester; *b* 8 November 1945; *Educ* Hollings Coll Manchester (Dip Hotel & Catering); *m* 5 Aug 1972, Pauline Elizabeth, da of Frederick Trevor Holt; 2 da (Charlotte Elizabeth, Hannah Louise (twins) b 21 Feb 1976), 1 s (Richard William Allan b 12 May 1979); *Career* commis de cuisine: The Savoy London 1964–67, Hotel Chateau d'Ouchy Lausanne 1967–68, Hotel Baur au Lac Zurich 1968; chef de partie Kur Hotel Bad Neuenahr 1968–69; The Goring Hotel London: jr asst mangr 1969–70, sr asst mangr 1970–74, mangr 1974–78, gen mangr 1978–89, dir 1989–2002, md 2002–; chm Mgmnt Ctee St John's Church Waterloo; memb: Considerate Hoteliers City of Westminster, Union Soc of Westminster, Lord's Taverners; hon memb Acad of Food and Wine Service 1989, memb Euro Hotel Mangrs Assoc, memb Reunion des Gastronomes (memb Ctee 1981); Master Innholder 1995, Freeman City of London 1995; FHCIMA 1995; *Recreations* golf, cricket, tennis; *Clubs* Woking Golf, Wentworth Golf, MCC; *Style*— William Cowpe, Esq; ✉ The Goring, Beeston Place, Grosvenor Gardens, London SW1W 0JW (☎ 020 7396 9000, fax 020 7834 4393, e-mail wcowpe@goringhotel.co.uk)

COWPER-COLES, Sir Sherard Louis; KCMG (2004, CMG 1997), LVO (1991); s of Sherard Hamilton Cowper-Coles (d 1968), of Sevenoaks, Kent, and Dorothy, *née* Short; *b* 8 January 1955, London; *Educ* Freston Lodge, New Beacon, Tonbridge (scholar), Hertford Coll Oxford (scholar); *m* 1, 1982 (m dis 2011), Bridget Mary, da of Neil Emerson Elliott; 5 c (Henry Sherard b 27 Nov 1982, Rupert Neil b 16 Aug 1984, Minna Louise b 18 Feb 1986, Frederick Peter b 20 May 1987, Myles Philip b 21 March 1990); m 2, 2012, Jasmine Leila Myriam Zerinini; 1 c (Louise Elizabeth b 21 Jan 2012); *Career* Foreign Office London 1977–78, Arabic language trg 1978–80, third then second sec Cairo 1980–83, first sec Planning Staff FCO 1983–85, private sec to Perm Under Sec 1985–87, first sec Washington 1987–91, asst Security Policy Dept FCO 1991–93, efficiency scrutineer FCO 1993, res assoc Int Inst for Strategic Studies 1993–94, head Hong Kong Dept FCO 1994–97, political cnsllr Paris 1997–99, princ private sec to Sec of State for Foreign and Commonwealth Affairs 1999–2001, ambass to Israel 2001–03, ambass to Saudi Arabia 2003–07, ambass to Afghanistan 2007–09, Foreign Sec's special rep for Afghanistan and Pakistan 2009–10, buiness devpt dir int BAE Systems plc 2011–; chm: Saudi-Br Soc 2011, Pitzhanger Manor Tst 2012; hon prof of int relations Univ of Nottingham; Liveryman Worshipful Co of Skinners 1988; hon fell Hertford Coll Oxford, hon fell Univ of Exeter; *Publications* Cables from Kabul (2011), Ever the Diplomat (2012); *Clubs* Brooks's; *Style*— Sir Sherard Cowper-Coles, KCMG, LVO; ✉ BAE Systems plc, Stirling Square, 6 Carlton Gardens, London SW1Y 5AD (e-mail sherard.cowper-coles@baesystems.com)

COX, Alistair Richard; s of Gerald Cox, of Leeds, and Jean, *née* Townsend; *b* 25 February 1961, Leeds; *Educ* Univ of Salford (BSc, Dip), Stanford Grad Sch of Business (MBA); *m* 30 Jan 1988, Merete, *née* Oftedahl; 2 s (Henrik Thomas b 21 Oct 1995, Carl George b 30 July 1997); *Career* Br Aerospace 1978–82, Schlumberger 1983–90, McKinsey &Co 1990–94, Blue Circle Industries 1994–2002, chief exec Xansa plc 2002–07, chief exec Hays plc 2007–; *Recreations* skiing, scuba diving, wakeboarding, sailing; *Style*— Alistair Cox, Esq; ✉ Hays plc, Hays, 141 Moorgate, London EC2M 6TX

COX, Antonia Mary; *née* Feuchtwanger; da of Dr Edgar Joseph Feuchtwanger, of Sparsholt, Hants, and Primrose Mary, *née* Essame; *b* 12 November 1963; *Educ* St Swithun's Sch Winchester, Jesus Coll Cambridge (exhibitioner, MA, Fencing half blue); *m* 24 June 1989, Simon Cox, s of Prof Antony Dawson Cox; 3 s (George, Thomas, Peter); *Career* corporate fin analyst C J Lawrence Morgan Grenfell Inc (NY) 1987–89, banking corr Daily Telegraph 1989–94, freelance 1994–96, city columnist then capital markets corr Evening Standard 1997–2000, asst ed BreakingViews 2000–01, ldr writer Evening Standard 2001–10; policy advsr to Shadow Tport Sec 2009–10, Cons Parly candidate Islington S and Finsbury 2010, cncllr Hyde Park Ward Westminster City Cncl 2012–, GLA London-wide candidate 2016; non-exec dir Student Loan Co 2016–; proposer and govr Marylebone Boys' Sch 2012–; *Publications* The Best Kit: Why Britain's defence doesn't need an all-British defence industry (2004), More Bang for the Buck: How we can get better value from the defence budget (2010); *Style*— Mrs Antonia Cox; ✉ Westminster City Council, Westminster City Hall, 64 Victoria Street, London SW1E 6QP (e-mail acox@westminster.gov.uk)

COX, Barry Geoffrey; CBE (2013); *b* 25 May 1942, Guildford, Surrey; *Educ* Tiffin Sch Kingston upon Thames, Magdalen Coll Oxford (BA); *Children* 2 s, 2 da; *Career* journalist with: The Scotsman 1965–67, Sunday Telegraph 1967–70; reporter and prodr Granada TV 1970–74; London Weekend Television: ed 1974–77, head of current affrs 1977–81, controller of features and current affrs 1981–87, dir of corp affrs 1987–94, special advsr to chief exec 1994–95; dir ITV Assoc 1995–98, dep chm Channel 4 1999–2006; chm: Digital TV Stakeholders Gp 2002–04, Digital UK (formerly SwitchCo Ltd) 2005–12 (chm SwitchCo working gp 2004–05); conslt to: United Broadcasting & Entertainment (UBE) 1998–2001, ITN 1998–2009; memb Cncl Inst of Educn 2000–08, govr Euro Inst for the Media 1999–2001, chm Oval House 2001–07; visiting prof of broadcast media Univ of Oxford 2003; FRTS; *Books* Civil Liberties In Britain (1975), The Fall of Scotland Yard (jtly, 1977), Free for All? (2004); *Style*— Barry Cox, Esq, CBE; ✉ e-mail barry.cox3@btopenworld.com

COX, Brian Denis; CBE (2003); s of Charles Cox, and Mary Ann Guillerline McCann; *b* 1 June 1946; *Educ* London Acad of Music and Dramatic Arts; *m* 1, 1967 (m dis), Caroline Burt; 1 s (Alan), 1 da (Margaret); m 2, 2001, Nicole Elisabeth Ansari; 2 s (Orson, Torin); *Career* actor and director; elected rector Univ of Dundee 2010; LLD (hc) Univ of Dundee 1994; *Theatre* Orlando in As You Like It (Birmingham and Vaudeville (London debut)) 1967, title role in Peer Gynt (Birmingham Rep) 1967, Ulfhejm in When We Dead Awaken (Assembly Hall Edinburgh) 1968, Steven in In Celebration (Royal Court) 1969, Gregers Werle in The Wild Duck (Edinburgh Festival) 1969, Alan in The Big Romance (Royal Court) 1970, Norman in Don't Start Without Me (Garrick) 1971, Knight of Riprafatta in Mirandolina (Gardner Centre Brighton) 1971, Brian Lowther in Getting On (Queen's) 1971, Gustav in The Creditors (Open Space Theatre) 1972, Eilert Lovborg in Hedda

Gabler (Royal Court) 1972, Berowne in Love's Labour's Lost (Playhouse Nottingham) 1972, title role in Brand (Playhouse) 1972, Sergeant Match in What The Butler Saw (Playhouse) 1972, D'Artagnan in The Three Musketeers (Playhouse) 1972, Proctor in Cromwell (Royal Court) 1973, Sergius in Arms and the Man (Royal Exchange Manchester) 1974, Sir Henry Harcourt Reilly in The Cocktail Party (Royal Exchange) 1975, Emigres (Nat Theatre Co, Young Vic) 1976, Theridamas in Tamburlaine the Great (NT) 1976, Brutus in Julius Caesar (NT) 1977, De Flores in The Changeling (Riverside Studios) 1978, title role in Herod (NT) 1978, Ireton in The Putney Debates (NT) 1978, Mickey in On Top (Royal Court) 1979, Vicomte Robert de Trivelin in Have You Anything to Declare? (Royal Exchange then Round House) 1981, title role in Danton's Death (NT) 1982, Edmund Darrell in Strange Interlude (Duke of York 1984, Nederlander Theatre NY 1985), DI Nelson in Rat in the Skull (Royal Court 1984, Public Theatre NY 1985), Paul Cash in Fashion (RSC, The Pit) 1988, title role in Titus Andronicus (Swan Theatre Stratford-upon-Avon and on tour in Madrid, Paris and Copenhagen) 1988, The Taming of the Shrew (RSC, Theatre Royal), Johnny in Frankie and Johnny in the Clair-de-Lune (Comedy Theatre) 1989, title role in King Lear (NT, toured E and W Europe, Cairo and Tokyo) 1990–91, Richard III (RNT), Harold Hill in The Music Man (Open Air Theatre) 1995, Waiting for Godot (Royal Lyceum Theatre Edinburgh) 2015; as director prodns incl: The Man with a Flower in His Mouth (Edinburgh Festival) 1973, The Stronger (Edinburgh Festival) 1973, I Love My Love (Orange Tree) 1983, Mrs Warren's Profession (Orange Tree) 1989, The Crucible (Moscow Art Theatre, Riverside and Edinburgh) 1988–89, The Philanderer (Hampstead) 1991, The Master Builder (Royal Lyceum Edinburgh and Riverside) 1993–94, Richard III (Regent's Park) 1995, St Nicholas (London, Dublin, NY) 1997, St Nicholas off Broadway (Primary Stages, winner of The Lucille Lortel Award) 1998, Art (Broadway, The Royale Theatre) 1998, Dublin Carol (Royal Court) 1999, St Nicholas (Nice Drama Festival 1999), Uncle Varrick (Royal Lyceum Edinburgh) 2004, Ride Down Mount Morgan (LA) 2005, Rock'n'Roll (West End) 2006, Lolita (NT), That Championship Season (Broadway), The Weir (Donmar and West End) 2013; *Television* Laurent in Therese Raquin, Jemima Shore, Rat in the Skull, Alas Smith and Jones, Perfect Scoundrels, The Cloning of Joanna May, Lost Language of the Cranes, Van der Valk, Redfox, The Big Battalions, Six Characters in Search of an Author, Inspector Morse, Sharpe's, Grushko 1994, The Negotiator 1994, Food for Ravens 1997, Herman Goering in Nuremberg, Longitude, Morality Play, The Court, The Rookie, Frasier, Adaptation, Blue/Orange, The Strange Case of Sherlock Holmes and Arthur Conan Doyle, Deadwood 2006, The Outsiders 2006, The Secret of the Nutcracker 2007, The Take 2009, Kings 2009, Lost & Found 2009, Marple: They Do it With Mirrors 2009, Dr Who 2009, The Day of the Triffids 2009, On Expenses, The Big C 2010, The Sinking of the Laconia 2011, The Straits, A Touch of Cloth 2012, Gotham, Bob Servant (series, 2013–14), The Curse of Edgar 2013, An Adventure Through Space and Time 2013, Shetland 2014, The Game 2014, Scotland in a Day 2014, The Slap 2015, War & Peace 2015, Penny Dreadful (Series 3) 2016, Medici: Kingdom of Gold 2016; *Radio* James McLevy (series) 2001–14; *Film* Trotsky in Nicholas and Alexandra 1971, Steven Shaw in In Celebration 1975, Father Gora in Pope John Paul II (movie CBS) 1984, Dr McGrigor in Florence Nightingale (movie NBC) 1985, Dr Lektor in Manhunter 1986, Duffy in Shoot for the Sun 1986, Peter Kerrigan in Hidden Agenda 1990, Iron Will, Argyle in Braveheart 1994, Killearn in Rob Roy 1994, Chain Reaction 1996, The Glimmer Man 1996, Long Kiss Goodnight 1996, Kiss the Girl 1996, Desperate Measures 1996, Good Vibrations 1996, The Corruptor 1998, Mad About Mambo 1998, The Minus Man 1998, Rushmore 1998, For The Love of The Game 1999, Complicity 1999, Saltwater 1999, The Cup 1999, Nuremberg 1999, Strictly Sinatra 1999, Oz 2000, Supertroopers 2000, The Biographer 2000, L.I.E. 2000, Affair of the Necklace 2000, The Ring 2002, The 25th Hour 2002, The Bourne Identity 2002, X-Men 2 2003, Troy 2004, The Ringer 2004, The Bourne Supremacy 2004, The Reckoning 2004, Match Point 2005, A Woman in Winter 2005, Red Eye 2005, Running with Scissors 2005, The Ringer 2005, The Flying Scotsman 2006, Zodiac 2007, Shoot on Sight 2007, Red 2008, The Escapist 2008, The Good Heart 2009, Fantastic Mr Fox 2009, As Good as Dead 2010, Wide Blue Yonder 2010, Coriolanus 2011, Ironclad 2011, The Key Man 2011, The Veteran 2011, Rise of the Planet of the Apes 2011, Citizen Gangster 2011, I Missed My Mother's Funeral 2012, Believe 2013, Dog Fight, Blood 2012, The Campaign 2012, Red 2 2013, Anna 2013, The Jesuit 2014, The Anomaly 2014, Forsaken 2014, Pixels 2015, Killing Thyme 2015, The Carer 2015, The Autopsy of Jane Doe 2015, Morgan 2016, Road Trip 2016, Supertroopers 2016, The Etruscan Smile 2016; *Awards* Olivier Award Best Actor (for Rat in the Skull) 1985, Drama Magazine Best Actor Award (for Rat in the Skull) 1985, Olivier Award Best Actor in a Revival (for Titus Andronicus) 1988, Drama Magazine Award (for work in the RSC 1987–88 season) 1988, International Theatre Institute Award 1989, Emmy Award (for Nuremberg) 2001, Gemini Award (for Nuremberg) 2001, Boston Critics Award (for L.I.E.) 2002, Golden Satellite Award (for L.I.E.) 2002; *Publications* Salem to Moscow – An Actor's Odyssey (1991), The Lear Diaries (1993); *Recreations* keeping fit; *Style*— Brian Cox, Esq, CBE; ✉ c/o Conway van Gelder Grant, Third floor, 8/12 Broadwick Street, London W1F 8HW (e-mail vena@conwayvg.co.uk); PA Vanessa Green (vgreen@dsl.pipex.com)

COX, Prof Brian Edward; OBE (2010); *b* 3 March 1968; *Educ* Hulme GS Oldham, Univ of Manchester (BSc, MPhil, PhD); *m* 2004, Gia Milinovich; 1 s (George b 26 May 2009); *Career* early career as musician (bands incl Dare and D'Ream); prof of particle physics Univ of Manchester 2009–; contrib: New Statesman, The Telegraph, The Sun, The Times; Br Assoc Lord Kelvin Award 2006, Inst of Physics Kelvin Prize 2010, Royal Soc Michael Farraday Prize 2012; Hon DUniv Huddersfield 2012; int fell Explorers Club 2002; univ research fell Royal Soc; *Television* incl: Horizon: What Time Is It (BBC 2) 2008, Horizon: Can We Make A Star On Earth (BBC 2) 2009, Wonders of the Solar System (BBC 2) 2010 (Best Presenter RTS Award 2011, George Foster Peabody Award 2011), Wonders of the Universe (BBC 2) 2011, Wonders of Life (BBC 2) 2013; *Radio* incl The Infinite Monkey Cage (BBC Radio 4) 2009 (Sony Radio Gold Award 2011); *Books* Why Does E=mc2? (And Why Should We Care?) (jtly, 2010), Wonders of the Solar System (jtly, 2010), The Quantum Universe: everything that can happen does happens (jtly, 2011), Wonders of the Universe (jtly, 2011), Wonders of The Solar System (jtly, 2012), Wonders of Life (jtly, 2013); *Style*— Prof Brian Cox, OBE

COX, Baroness (Life Peer UK 1983), of Queensbury in Greater London; Caroline Anne Cox; da of Robert John McNeill Love, MS, FRCS (d 1974), and Dorothy Ida, *née* Borland; *b* 7 July 1937; *Educ* Channing Sch, Univ of London (BSc, MSc); *m* 1959, Murray Newell Cox, FRCPsych (d 1997), s of Rev Roland Lee Cox, of London (d 1988); 2 s (Hon Robin Michael b 1959, Hon Jonathan Murray b 1962), 1 da (Hon Philippa Ruth Dorothy b 1965); *Career* head Dept of Sociology N London Poly 1974–77, dir Nursing Educn Research Unit Chelsea Coll London 1977–83; sits as crossbench peer in House of Lords (dep speaker 1986–2005), baroness-in-waiting and Govt whip 1985; chllr: Bournemouth Univ 1991–2001, Liverpool Hope Univ 2006–13; vice-pres: RCN, Liverpool Sch of Tropical Med; chm Int Islamic Christian Orgn for Reconciliation and Reconstruction (IICORR); pres: Tushinskaya Children's Hosp Tst, Dean Close Sch Cheltenham until 2016, Humanitarian Aid Relief Tst (HART); patron: Med Aid for Poland Fund, Youth With a Mission, Physicians for Human Rights UK, Premier Radio; memb Trusthouse Charitable Fndn 1999–2009; William Wilberforce Award 1995, Medal from Fridtjof Nanen Int Fndn Moscow 2003; hon fell Univ of Westminster; Hon PhD Polish Univ in London 1988, Hon DH Univ of Utah, Hon LLD CNAA, Hon DSc City Univ, Hon DSc Univ of Wolverhampton, Hon DSS Queen's Univ Belfast, hon degree Eastern Coll USA, LLD (hc) Univ of Dundee; Hon Doctorate: Univ of Yerevan, Armenia, Univ of Nagorno Karabekh; Hon FRCS, Hon FCGI; Cdr Cross of the Order of Merit Republic of Poland 1990, Mkhitar Gosh Medal (Armenia) 2005; *Books* The Right to Learn (jtly, 1982), Sociology: An Introduction for Nurses, Midwives and Health Visitors (1983), Trajectories of Despair: Misdiagnosis and Maltreatment of Soviet Orphans (1991), Ethnic Cleansing in Progress: War in Nagorno Karabakh (jtly, 1993), Made to Care: The Case for Residential and Village Communities for People with a Mental Handicap (jtly, 1995), Remorse and Reparation (contrib, 1999), The 'West', Islam and Islamism: Is Ideological Islam Compatible with Liberal Democracy? (jtly, 2003, 2 edn 2006), Cox's Book of Modern Saints and Martyrs (jtly, 2006), This Immoral Trade: Slavery in the 21st Century (jtly, 2006, updated 2013), The Very Stones Cry Out: The Persecuted Church: Pain, Passion and Praise (jtly, 2011); *Recreations* campanology, hill walking; *Clubs* Royal Over-Seas League; *Style*— The Lady Cox; ✉ House of Lords, London SW1A 0PW (☎ 020 8204 7336, fax 020 8204 5661, e-mail caroline.cox@hart-uk.org)

C

COX, Charles; s of Harry Cox (d 1996), and Myra Emily, *née* Brooking; *b* 25 September 1949; *Educ* Stratford GS London; *m* 12 April 1975, Sandra Carol, da of Victor Anthony Willis Taylor (d 1974); 1 da (Helen b 1976), 1 s (Peter b 1978); *Career* CA; Turquands Barton Mayhew 1968–79, ptnr PKF (UK) LLP (Pannell Kerr Forster) 1984– (joined 1979); chm and non-exec dir HBV Enterprise; gp scout ldr 8 Horchurch Scout Gp, tstee Hornchurch Dist Scout Cncl; Liveryman Worshipful Co of Gardeners; FCA 1972, FRSA 1998; *Recreations* hill walking, reading, Scout leader; *Clubs* RAC, MCC; *Style*— Charles Cox, Esq; ✉ PKF (UK) LLP, Farringdon Place, 20 Farringdon Road, London EC1M 3AP (☎ 020 7065 0000, fax 020 7065 0650, e-mail charles.cox@uk.pkf.com)

COX, Christopher Charles Arthur; s of Col Harold Bernard Cox (d 1990), of Farnham, Surrey, and Ivie Vera, *née* Warren (d 1981); *b* 21 July 1944; *Educ* St Edward's Sch Oxford, Hertford Coll Oxford (MA, BCL); *m* 1, 5 May 1984, Kathleen Susan Anne May (d 2009), da of James Buist Mackenzie (d 1976), of Madrid, Spain; 2 da (Andrea b 1986, Georgina b 1987); m 2, 25 May 2015, Anne Elizabeth Wicks, da of Hector Sandells; *Career* admitted slr 1970; Coward Chance 1968–77, Spicer & Oppenheim 1981–84, ptnr Nabarro Nathanson 1986–97 (slr 1984–86), ptnr: Beachcroft Stanleys 1997–99, Beachcroft Wansbroughs 1999–2006, Beachcroft LLP (now DAC Beachcroft LLP) 2006–09 (conslt 2009–); memb: Int Fiscal Assoc, VAT Practitioners' Gp; Freeman City of London 1986; *Books* Capital Gains Tax on Businesses (jtly, 1992), Stamp Duty Land Tax (jtly, 2014); *Recreations* politics, mountain walking, music, theatre; *Style*— Christopher Cox, Esq; ✉ DAC Beachcroft LLP, 100 Fetter Lane, London EC4A 1BN (☎ 020 7242 1011, fax 020 7894 6550, e-mail ccox@dacbeachcroft.com)

COX, Daniel; s of Gerald Cox (d 1998), and Sylvia, *née* Cheeseman; *b* 2 February 1971, Greenwich, London; *Educ* UEA (DMS, MBA); *m* 2010, Katie, *née* Waghorn; *Career* Somerfield Stores 1988–2007; ldr Norfolk CC 2007–; *Recreations* golf, motor sport, sailing; *Clubs* Lions Int; *Style*— Councillor Daniel Cox; ✉ Thickthorn Hall, Norfolk NR9 3AT; Norfolk County Council, County Hall, Martineau Lane, Norwich, Norfolk NR1 2DH

COX, Dennis William; s of Albert Frederick Cox (d 1978), and Margot, *née* Auerbach; *b* 27 February 1957; *Educ* Hornchurch GS, Westfield Coll London (exhibitioner, BSc); *m* 31 Aug 1996, Lisette Mermod; 2 step da (Natalie b Nov 1981, Candace b Nov 1983); *Career* various positions rising to sr mangr banking and fin Arthur Young (now Ernst & Young) 1978–88, sr mangr banking and fin BDO Binder Hamlyn 1988–90, audit mangr Midland Bank rising to sr audit mangr (Compliance) HSBC Holdings plc 1991–97; dir: risk mgmnt Prudential Portfolio Managers 1997–2000, operational risk HSBC Operational Risk Consultantcy Div 2000–01; ceo: Risk Reward Ltd 2002–, Niven Capital Ltd 2013–; ICAEW: memb Cncl 1995–2013, memb Ctee Workplace 2000 1996–99, chm Quality and Practice Review Task Force 1998–2001, dep chm Fin Servs Authorisation Ctee 1998–2002 (memb 1996–2002), memb Remuneration Ctee 1998–2004, chm Pensions Task Force 1999–2000, chm Pensions Review Task Force 1999–2004, memb Professional Standards Bd 2001–07, memb AML Ctee 2001–, chm IMSIG 2004–, memb NEDSIG Ctee 2004–; fndr memb Chartered Investment and Securities Inst: Compliance Forum 1996–, Risk Forum 2002– (chairperson 2002–14); lectr on risk mgmnt for: ICAEW, Securities Inst, Inst of Internal Auditors and others; memb: Editorial Bd Securities and Investment Review 1998–2007, Working Gp on the Liberalization of Capital Markets Inst of Int Fin 1999–2001, Main Ctee LSCA 2001–13, Fin Planning Ctee LSCA 2001–11 (dep chm 2002–05, chm 2005–08), Professional Risk Mangrs' Int Assoc (PRMIA); ind memb Fin Authorisation Ctee Inst of Actuaries 1999–2007, ind memb Designated Professional Body Inst of Actuaries 2002–08, memb Technical Ctee Financial Accreditation Assoc (FAA) Malaysia 2015–; pres S Essex Soc of Chartered Accountants 1994–95 (memb Main Ctee 1983–2010, chm Educn and Trg 1983–93); Freeman City of London 2011, memb Worshipful Co of Chartered Accountants 2011–; MIB 1988, FCA 1991 (ACA 1981), FCSI 2006 (MSI 1992); *Publications* Banks: Accounts, Audit and Practice (1993), The Mathematics of Banking and Finance (2006), Frontiers of Risk Management (ed, 2007), Introduction to Money Laundering Deterrence (2010), International Handbook of Money Laundering Deterrence (2014); also author of various articles; *Recreations* hockey, travel, music, art; *Style*— Dennis Cox, Esq; ✉ Risk Reward Ltd, 60 Moorgate, London EC2R 6EH (☎ 020 7638 5558, mobile 07968 164793, e-mail dwc@riskrewardlimited.com, website www.riskrewardlimited.com)

COX, Geoffrey; QC (2003), MP; *b* 30 April 1960, Devon; *Educ* Kings Coll Taunton, Downing Coll Cambridge; *m* Jeanie; 1 da, 2 s; *Career* barrister, co-fndr Thomas More Chambers 1992, standing counsel Govt of Mauritius 1996; MP (Cons) Devon W and Torridge 2005– (also contested 2001); memb Criminal Bar Assoc, Br Inst International and Comparative Law; *Style*— Geoffrey Cox, Esq, QC, MP; ✉ House of Commons, London SW1A 0AA (e-mail tellgeoffrey@geoffreycox.co.uk, website www.geoffreycox.co.uk)

COX, Sir George Edwin; kt (2005); s of George Herbert Cox (d 1986), and Beatrice May, *née* Lillywhite (d 1981); *b* 28 May 1940; *Educ* QMC London (BSc); *m* 1, 1963 (m dis), Gillian Mary, *née* Mannings; 2 s (Russell Edwin b 24 Aug 1963, Paul Daniel James b 18 Aug 1966); m 2, 1996, Lorna Janet, *née* Moon; 2 da (Louise Beatrice b 3 Oct 1994, Eve Elizabeth b 29 Nov 1996); *Career* engr Flight Test Dept Vickers-Armstrong (later British Aircraft Corp) 1962–64, mgmnt trainee rising to mfrg admin mangr Molins Machine Co 1964–68, mgmnt conslt Urwick Orr & Ptnrs 1968–73, dir of UK ops Diebold 1973–77, md Butler Cox (later Butler Cox plc) 1977–92, chm and chief exec P-E International plc 1992–94; Unisys Corp: chief exec Unisys Ltd 1995, chief exec Information Services Europe 1996–98, chm Unisys Ltd 1996–99; DG IOD 1999–2004, chair Design Cncl 2004–07, pres Inst of Engrg Designers 2010–14; non-exec memb Mgmnt Bd Inland Revenue1996–99; memb Bd: LIFFE 1995–2002 (sr ind dir), Bradford & Bingley 2000–07 (sr ind dir and chm Renumeration Ctee 2003–), Shorts 2000–16; memb: Supervisory Bd Euronext 2002–07, Bd NYSE-Euronext 2007–13; author Cox Review for HM Govt 2005; pres Mgmnt Consultancies Assoc 1991; chair Bd Warwick Business Sch, pro-chllr Univ of Warwick 2010– (memb Cncl 2004–, chair Cncl 2011–); speaker at conferences on mgmnt-related topics worldwide; chm Bd of Tstees Merlin (Med Emergency Relief Int) 2001–07, tstee VSO 2005–08; pres Royal Coll of Speech and Language Therapists 2004–; chief coach Univ of London BC 1976–78 (pres 2015–), occasional coach OUBC, Br team coach and chm of selectors Br Men's Rowing 1978–80; Freeman City of London, memb Worshipful Co of Information Technologists, Master Guild of Mgmnt Conslts 1997; hon fell Queen Mary Univ of London, hon fell Instn of Engrg Designers (pres 2010–), hon fell Royal Coll of Speech and Language Therapists 2011; Hon Dr: Middx Univ, Univ of

Wolverhampton, Northumbria Univ, De Montfort Univ, Huddersfield Univ, Cranfield Univ; CRAeS, CIMgt, FInstD, FRSA; *Publications* Cox Review (of Overcoming Short-termism in UK Business) for HM Opposition (2013); *Recreations* rowing, gliding, theatre, history of aviation; *Clubs* Leander (pres 2008–13); *Style*— Sir George Cox

COX, John Colin Leslie; CBE (1994); s of Dr Leslie Reginald Cox, OBE, FRS (d 1965), and Hilda Cecilia Cox (d 1991); *b* 23 October 1933; *Educ* UCS London, Queens' Coll Cambridge (BA); *m* 16 April 1983, Avril Joyce, da of H A G Butt (d 1975), of Sibford Gower, Oxon; 1 da (Victoria b 13 Dec 1983), 1 s (Charles b 16 March 1987); *Career* Nat Serv 2 Lt 2/10 Princess Mary's Own Gurkha Rifles 1956–58, GSM Malaya 1958; Shell Gp: joined 1958, exec posts Shell Ghana 1962–65 and London 1966–67, personnel dir Shell Chemicals UK 1978–81; dir: business devpt and chm subsid companies 1981–86, Public Health Laboratory Service 1997–; DG Chem Ind Assoc 1987–95; chm: governing body Westminster Adult Educn Service 1998–, London Europe Gateway Ltd 1997–, UK Centre for Economic and Environmental Devpt 1999– (memb bd 1996–); chief exec: London First Centre 1995–96, Pensions Protection and Investment Accreditation Bd 2000–; memb: Public Standards Bd, Edexcel Fndn 1997–, Edexcel Cncl 2001–; elected memb for Knightsbridge Westminster City Cncl 1998–; FRSA 1989; *Recreations* sailing, antiques, country pursuits, photography; *Clubs* Army and Navy, Hurlingham, Leander, Royal Solent Yacht (IOW); *Style*— John C L Cox, Esq, CBE

COX, John Edward; OBE (1993); s of Edward Ralph Cox (d 2006), and Evelyn Lavinia Mary, *née* Pawley (d 2010); *b* 18 October 1946; *Educ* The GS Brigg, BNC Oxford (BA); *m* 17 Jan 1974, Diane, da of Bernard Sutcliffe (d 1985), of Hemingford Grey, Cambs; 1 da (Laura b 29 Jan 1976); *Career* called to the Bar Middle Temple; sales mangr: International Book Information Services Ltd 1968–71, The Open Univ 1971–76; md Open Univ Educational Enterprises Ltd 1976–81, mktg dir telepublishing Butterworth and Co Ltd 1981–83; md: Scholastic Publications Ltd 1983–90, B H Blackwell Ltd 1990–94, Carfax Publishing Ltd 1994–98; md John Cox Associates 2003–11 (ptnr 1998–2003), dir Portland Press Ltd 2011–; memb Air Travel Trust Ctee, chm Air Tport Users' Ctee until 1992; chm Air Travel Insolvency Protection Advsy Ctee 2000–; *Recreations* theatre, conversation, travel, walking, philately; *Style*— John Cox, Esq, OBE; ✉ Rookwood, Bradden, Towcester, Northamptonshire NN12 8ED (✆ 01327 861193, e-mail john.e.cox@btinternet.com); office tel 01327 861184

COX, Jonson; s of Peter Cox, and Bobbie, *née* Sutton; *b* 11 October 1956; *Educ* King Edward VI Sch Totnes, Clare Coll Cambridge (MA); *partner* Barbara Wight; 1 s, 2 da; *Career* Royal Dutch/Shell Gp 1979–92, md Kelda Gp plc 1992–2000, md Yorkshire Water 1996–2000, chief operating offr Railtrack plc 2000–01, chief exec Valpak 2002–03, ceo Anglian Water Gp plc 2004–10; chm: Morrisons plc 2004–10, UK Coal plc 2010–12, Harworth Gp plc 2012–, Ofwat 2012–, Cory Gp 2015–; non-exec dir Wincanton plc 2005–14; fndr dir: Right to Read, PoW Corporate Leaders Gp on Climate Change; *Recreations* outdoor activities; *Style*— Jonson Cox, Esq; ✉ e-mail jonson.cox@harworthgroup.com

COX, Josephine; da of Bernard Brindle, and Mary Jane Brindle; *b* 15 July 1940; *m* Kenneth George Cox; 2 s (Spencer John, Wayne Kenneth); *Career* writer; former jobs incl: clerk to Milton Keynes Devpt Cncl, various secretarial positions, ptnr family landscaping co, teacher for 14 years, sociology/history lectr Bletchley Coll Milton Keynes; 34 novels as Josephine Cox, 4 novels as Jane Brindle; Superwoman of GB 1980; *Books* Her Father's Sins, Let Loose the Tigers, Angels Cry Sometimes, Take This Woman, Outcast, Whistledown Woman, Alley Urchin, Vagabonds, Don't Cry Alone, Jessica's Girl, Nobody's Darling, Born to Serve, More Than Riches, A Little Badness, Living a Lie, The Devil You Know, A Time for Us, Cradle of Thorns, Bad Boy Jack, Lovers and Liars, Beachcomber, The Woman Who Left, Jonne, Live the Dream, The Journey, Journeys End, The Loner; as Jane Brindle: Scarlet, No Mercy, The Tallow Image, No Heaven No Hell, The Seeker; *Recreations* swimming, walking, reading, creating board games; *Style*— Mrs Josephine Cox

COX, Dr Julie; *b* Newcastle upon Tyne; *Educ* Univ of Newcastle (MB BS, Dip); *Career* former conslt radiologist Univ Hosp of North Durham, fndn prog dir County Durham and Darlington Fndn Tst, currently conslt radiologist and dep dir of med educn Sunderland Royal Hosp; hon sr clinical lectr Newcastle Univ; FRCS(Eng), FRCR, FAcadMEd; *Style*— Dr Julie Cox; ✉ Department of Radiology, Sunderland Royal Hospital, Sunderland SR4 7PT (e-mail julie.cox@chsft.nhs.uk)

COX, Hon Mrs Justice; Dame Laura Mary; DBE (2002); *née* Bryant; da of John Arthur Bryant (d 1972), of Wolverhampton, and Mary Eileen, *née* Clarke (d 2014); *b* 8 November 1951; *Educ* Wolverhampton HS for Girls, Queen Mary Coll London (LLB, LLM); *m* 1970, David John Cox, s of Harry Cox; 3 s (Jonathan James b 25 April 1980, Leo John b 7 June 1983, Benjamin David b 19 May 1993); *Career* called to the Bar Inner Temple 1975 (bencher 2000), QC 1994, recorder of the Crown Court 1995–2002, head of chambers 1996–2002, judge of the High Court of Justice (Queen's Bench Division) 2002–; judge Employment Appeal Tbnl 2000–; chm Sex Discrimination Ctee Bar Cncl 1996–2000, memb Cncl of Justice 1998–2002, chm Equal Opportunities Ctee Bar Cncl 2000–02; Br memb ILO Ctee of Experts 1998–2012, pres Assoc of Women Barrs 2005–, memb Ctee UK Assoc of Women Judges 2005– (vice-pres 2013–); hon fell Queen Mary Univ of London 2005; *Recreations* music, theatre, cinema, football, good food and wine; *Style*— The Hon Mrs Justice Cox, DBE; ✉ Royal Courts of Justice, Strand, London WC2A 2LL

COX, Neil Derek; s of Clifford Walter Ernest, and Meryl Rita, *née* Holland; *b* 1 August 1955; *Educ* King Edward VI GS Stafford, Glasgow Caledonian Univ (BSc); *m* 23 March 1981, Averin Moira, da of Philip Anthony Donovan; 2 da (Katy b 1984, Jocelyn b 1990), 1 s (Andrew b 1986); *Career* sr optometrist Moorfields and KCH London, private contact lens practice London; lectured widely and published papers on clinical applications of contact lenses; tstee London Corinthian Tst; vice-pres Warlingham RFC; Liveryman Worshipful Co of Spectaclemakers; FCOptom (FBCO 1978), FAAO 1991; *Recreations* wine, food, photography; *Style*— Neil D Cox, Esq; ✉ 11 Milford House, 7 Queen Anne Street, London W1G 9HN (✆ 020 7631 1046, fax 020 7436 0564)

COX, Patrick Lathbridge; s of Terry Brian Cox, of Victoria, BC, Canada, and Maureen Patricia, *née* Clarke; *b* 19 March 1963; *Educ* Cordwainer's Coll Hackney (DATech); *Career* footwear designer; work included in collections of: Vivienne Westwood, John Galliano, Richard James, Alistair Blair, Lanvin, John Flett & Katherine Hamnett London and Paris 1985–92; exhibited in: Aust Nat Gallery, V&A; Accessory Designer of the Year Br Fashion Awards 1994 and 1995; *Style*— Patrick Cox, Esq

COX, Paul William; s of Oliver Jasper Cox, CBE (d 2010), and Jean Denise, *née* Cooper; *b* 31 July 1957; *Educ* Port Regis Sch, Stanbridge Earls Sch, Camberwell Sch of Art And Crafts (BA), RCA (MA); *m* 28 Nov 1987, Julia Claire, da of Capt Peter Dale Nichol, RN, (d 1997), of Hayling Island, Hants; 1 da (Harriet Claire b 16 Aug 1991), 1 s (Jack William b 22 July 1994); *Career* freelance artist and illustrator 1982–; contrib: The Times, Telegraph, Independent, Spectator, Punch, Sunday Times, Observer, Sunday Express, Daily Express, Radio Times, The Guardian, New Yorker, Vanity Fair, Town and Country, Wall Street Jl, Traditional Home, Chatelaine, Business Week, House Beautiful, Country Life, Britain; visiting lectr in illustration Camberwell Sch of Art and Crafts 1982–90, sr tutor West Dean Coll 2009–11; reportage illustrations for Blueprint 1984–89 and Elle Decor; watercolour drawings exhibitions: Workshop Gallery 1984, Illustrators' Gallery 1985, Chris Beetle's Gallery 1989, 1993, 2001, 2006, 2009, 2010 and 2011, Scandinavian Contemporary Art Gallery 1993, Molesworth Gall (Dublin) 2001, Durrell Wildlife Conservation Tst 2006, major retrospective (Chris Beetle's Gallery) 2013; designed commemorative stamps for 600th anniversary of The Lord Mayor's Show 1989, historical images for Drama & Debate exhbn Hampton Ct Palace 2004, designed Mural for Eleanor Davies Colley Lecture Theatre Royal Coll of Surgns 2004, designed and painted sets for 50th anniversary prodn of Salad Days 2005 and 2006, 15 paintings for St Charles Hosp 2007, 65 covers for International Living 2010–15, 15 fashion illustrations for Taylors Anderson and Sheppard 2011, illustrated the Today Programme for opening of House of Illustration 2014; hon memb Soc of Architect Artists 1993; *Books* illustrated: Experiences of an Irish RM (1984), The Common Years (1984), A Varied Life (1984), The Outing (1985), The Character of Cricket (1986), Romantic Gardens (1988), Evacuee (1988), Rebuilding The Globe (1989), Dear Boy (1989), Leave it to Psmith (1989), Three Men in a Boat (1989), The Cricket Match (1991), Honourable Estates (1992), Favourite Songs of Denmark (1993), Wind in the Willows (1993), The Russian Tea Room (1993), Rumpole (1994), Look Out London (1995), Jeeves and Wooster (1996), The Plums of PG Wodehouse (1997), Three Men on the Bummel (1998), Tinkerbill (1999), Jeeves and Wooster II (2000), Best After-Dinner Stories (2003), The Giver (2003), The Train to Glasgow (2003), The Best of Blandings (2004), The Folio Book of Comic Short Stories (2005), My Family and other Animals (2006), The Elevator Man (2008), Absolute Corkers (2008), Jeeves and Wooster III (2010), Gay and Lesbian Etiquette (2011), Running is Flying (2012), Did I Mention the Free Wine (2012), Lord Peter Views the Body (2016); *Clubs* Chelsea Arts; *Style*— Paul Cox, Esq; ✉ 23 Bromwich Avenue, Highgate, London N6 6HQ (✆ 020 8347 9515, e-mail paulwcox@gmail.com)

COX, Philip Gotsall; CBE (2013); *b* 22 September 1951, Birmingham; *Educ* Bishop Vesey's GS, Queens' Coll Cambridge (MA); *m* Brenda Margaret; 1 da (Alexandra (Mrs McCavert), 1 s (Adam); *Career* audit sr Price Waterhouse 1973–76, divnl chief accountant Lucas Industries 1977–81, finance dir then md Private Engineering and Consumer Products 1981–89; Siebe plc: gp controller 1989–96, dep chief finance offr 1997–98, chief finance offr 1998–99; sr vice-pres operational planning Ivensys plc 1999–2000, chief finance offr Int Power plc 2000–03, ceo Int Power 2003–13; non-exec dir: Wincanton plc 2001–09, WM Morrisons plc 2009–, Meggitt plc 2-12–14, PPL Corporation 2013–; chm Drax plc 2015–; FCA; *Recreations* golf, football, running; *Style*— Philip Cox, Esq, CBE; ✉ e-mail philipgcox@gmail.com

COX, Simon Foster Trenchard; s of Foster Trenchard Cox (d 1996), and Madeleine Winifred Needham, *née* Cooper (d 1989); *b* 17 January 1956; *Educ* Eton, Trinity Coll Oxford (MA); *m* 1 Feb 1992, Hania Katherine, da of Jan and Sophie Mier Jedrzejowicz; *Career* HAC 1980–88, cmmnd 1985; admitted slr 1980; Norton Rose: articled clerk 1978–80, slr 1980–88, ptnr 1988–; chm and hon treas Br Polish Legal Assoc 2000–; tstee: Needham Cooper Charitable Tst 1990–, Peter Kirk Meml Fund 1997–; Freeman City of London Slrs Co; memb Law Soc 1980; MSI 1992; *Recreations* water sports, running; *Clubs* HAC, Ognisko Polskie; *Style*— Simon Cox, Esq; ✉ Norton Rose, 3 More London Riverside, London SE1 2AQ (✆ 020 7283 6000, fax 020 7283 6500, e-mail simon.ft.cox@nortonrose.com)

COX, Stephen James; CVO (1997); *b* 5 December 1946; *Educ* Univ of Birmingham (BA), Univ of Leeds (Dip ESL), Univ of Sussex (MA); *m* 1970, Pauline Victoria, *née* Greenwood; 1 s (David), 1 da (Rachel); *Career* English teacher Bolivia (VSO) 1965–66, Br Cncl 1969–84 (incl postings Warsaw, Accra and London), educn attaché Br Embassy Washington DC 1984–85, asst sec for int affrs Royal Soc 1985–91, DG Commonwealth Inst 1991–97, chief exec Westminster Fndn for Democracy 1995–97, exec sec Royal Soc 1997–; chair Br Cncl Whitley Cncl Trades Union Side 1981–84, chair Bd Cwlth Round Table 2002–06 (memb 1994–); memb: Exec Ctee GB-E Europe Centre 1988–91, educn and field work ctees Royal Geographical Soc 1995–; memb Cncl: Parly and Scientific Ctee 1997– (vice-pres 2004–2007), BAAS 1997–, Fndn for Sci and Technol 1997–; tstee: Cncl for Assisting Refugee Academics 1997–, Int Polar Fndn 2006–; Kingston Univ: memb Bd 2002–09, chair Audit Ctee 2004–08; chair Duke of Edinburgh Award Forum Richmond, chair of tstees Atlantic Coll S Wales 2010–; Hon DSc Lancaster Univ 2003; FRGS; *Recreations* cricket, visiting galleries; *Clubs* Royal Over-Seas League, Geographical; *Style*— Stephen Cox, Esq, CVO; ✉ Royal Society, 6 Carlton House Terrace, London SW1Y 5AG (✆ 020 7451 2506, fax 020 7451 2691, e-mail stephen.cox@royalsociety.org)

COX, Stephen Joseph; s of Leonard John Cox (d 1984), of Bristol, and Ethel Minnie May McGill (d 1980); *b* 16 September 1946; *Educ* St Mary Redcliffe Sch Bristol, Central Sch of Art and Design; *m* 1 June 1970, Judith, da of John Douglas Atkins, of Well Court Farm, Tyler Hill, nr Canterbury, Kent; 2 da (Pelé Delaney, Georgia Easterly); *Career* sculptor; Arts Cncl major awards 1978 and 1980, Br Cncl bursaries 1978 and 1979, Hakone Open Air Museum prize Japan 1985, Indian Triennale Gold medal 1986, Goldhill Sculpture prize Royal Acad 1988, Capital and Counties Art and Work award 1991; subject of book by Henry Moore Fndn, The Sculpture of Stephen Cox 1995; sr research fell Wimbledon Sch of Art 1995–96, Bryan Montgomery visiting fell in sculpture Lincoln Coll Oxford 2009; memb Royal Acad of Art 2010; RA; *Solo Exhibitions* Tate Gallery, Lisson Gallery, Nigel Greenwood Gallery, 25 Festival dei Due Mondi Spoleto 1982, Bath Festival Artsite 1988, Arnolfini Gallery Bristol 1985 (touring to MOMA Oxford, Midland Group Gallery Nottingham), also Amsterdam, Milan, Rome, Gothenberg, Bari, Florence, Geneva, Basle, Paris, New Delhi (Br rep Indian Triennale 1986)), Museum of Egyptian Modern Art Cairo 1995, Stephen Cox: Surfaces and Stones of Egypt Henry Moore Inst 1995, Sight of Kephren Michael Hue-Williams Fine Art 1995, Royal Botanic Gardens Kew 1995–96, An Indian Decade 3 exhibitions – Art Today Gallery, Indian Cncl for Cultural Rels (ICCR) Ajanta Gallery and Jamali Kamali Gardens, Michael Hugh-Williams Fine Art 1996, Dulwich Picture Gallery 1997, Glyndebourne Opera House 1998, Michael Hue-Williams Fine Art 1998–99, Interior Space (Santa Maria Della Scala) Siena 1999, Fasti (Museum Archeologico Aosta Italy) 2000, Organs of Action (Culture Gallery) NY 2001, Eyestorm Gallery London 2004, Mappa Mundi (Hereford Cathedral and Meadow Gallery Burford) 2004, Shrewsbury Museum 2005, San Fracesco Della Scarpa Bari 2005, Stephen Cox: Sculptor, Origins and Influences (Bristol City Museum and Art Gallery) 2006, Sculpture in the Quads (Lincoln Coll Oxford) 2009, Meaning in Drawing (Drawing Gallery), The Meaning of Stone (Ludlow Castle) 2011; *Group Exhibitions* Paris Biennale 1977, British Sculpture in the Twentieth Century (Whitechapel Art Gallery) 1981, Venice Biennale 1982 and 1984, New Art Tate Gallery 1983, Int Garden Festival Liverpool 1984, Int Survey of Painting and Sculpture (MOMA NY) 1984, 40 Years of Modern Art 1945–85 (Tate Gallery), British Art in the 1980s (Brussels) MOMA NY, New Displays (Tate Gallery) 1992, Sculptors Drawings (Tate Gallery) 1994, Time Machine (British Museum) 1994–95 (travelling to Museo Egizio Torino), Hathill Fndn Goodwood, Centenary Display (Tate Gallery) 1997, British Sculpture (Schloss Ambrass Innsbruck), Jesus Coll Cambridge 1999, Kamakura Mie Sapporo (Japanese tour), Encounters: New Art from Old (Nat Gallery), Sculpture and the Divine (Winchester Cathedral) 2000, Sculpture in the Park (Mile End Park) 2001, Thinking Big: Exhibition of British sculpture (Guggenheim Venice) 2002, Lingam of a 1000 Lingams (Cass Sculpture Fndn) 2002, BLOK: Festival of Sculpture (Canterbury) 2003, Sculpture: A Spectator Sport (Bryanston plc Dorset) 2003, Summer Exhibition (Burghley House Lince) 2003, Akeley Heads Art and Landscape Project (Durham) 2003, British Sculptor's Drawings (Br Museum) 2008–09, Meaning in Drawing (Drawing Gallery), The Meaning of Stone (Ludlow Castle) 2011; *Collections* Tate Gallery, V&A, Br Museum, Br Cncl, Arts Cncl, Walker Art Gallery Liverpool, Henry Moore Centre for Sculpture, Hunterian Art Gallery, Groningen Museum Netherlands, Peter Ludwig Collection FRG, Fogg Museum USA, Hakone Open Air Museum Japan, Gori Collection Celle Pistoia Italy, Uffizi Florence; *Commissions* Tondo: Ascension (Royal Festival Hall) 1983, Cairo Opera House (FCO cmmn) 1988–89, Ganapathi & Devi (Broadgate London) 1989, Osirisisis (Stockley Park London) 1991, Hymn (Univ of Kent

Canterbury) 1991, Mantra (Br Cncl building New Delhi) 1992, Echo (Fleet Place Ludgate), Reredos, altar, font and stations of the cross (Church of St Paul Haringey), Rajiv Gandhi Samadhi New Delhi (central feature) 1995–97, Adam and Eve vessels St Luke's Chelsea 1996, Eucharist Cathedral Church of St Nicholas Newcastle upon Tyne 1997, Br High Cmmn Canberra Aust (Tribute Sculpture, FCO cmmn) 1997, faceted column Finsbury pavement London 1999, altar St Anselm's Chapel Canterbury Cathedral consecrated 2006 (ACE Award for Art in a Religious Context 2007), Tribute to Saint Anselm Installation (Aosta Cathedral Italy) 2009, Peregrine Sculpture at Goodwood 2009, Virgin Mary and Saint Mildred (Tower Gateway Lincoln Coll Oxford) 2009, Holy Water Stoup (Canterbury Cathedral), St James's Gateway Jermyn St London, Figure Emerging – Inscribed Rail to E.L. (Apple Tree Yard 8 St James's Square) 2015; *Clubs* Chelsea Arts, Dover St Arts; *Style—* Stephen Cox, Esq, RA; ✉ Lower House Farm, Coreley, Ludlow, Shropshire SY8 3AS (☎ 01584 891532, e-mail coxstepstone@aol.com)

COX, Prof Timothy Martin; s of late William Neville Cox, of Leics, and late Joan Désirée, *née* Ward; *b* 10 May 1948, Leicester; *Educ* Oundle, London Hosp Med Coll (MSc, MD), Univ of Cambridge (MA, MD); *m* 1975, Susan Ruth, da of late Harry Phillips Mason, of Builth Wells, Powys; 3 s, 1 da; *Career* house physician and surgn Professorial Units The London Hosp 1971–72, jr lectr in morbid anatomy Bernard Baron Inst 1972–74, jr clinical posts United Oxford Hosp 1974–75, Wellcome Tst sr clinical fell 1979–85, Wellcome Tst sr lectr medical sci 1985–87; Imperial Coll of Med London (formerly Royal Post Grad Med Sch): jr clinical posts 1974, registrar, hon sr registrar and MRC res fell 1975–79, sr lectr 1985–87, sr lectr in haematology and conslt Dept of Med 1987–89; prof of med Univ of Cambridge and fell Sidney Sussex Coll 1989–2015 (professorial life fell 2010–); visiting scientist Dept of Biology MIT 1983–84, visiting prof Univ of Manchester 1994, Schorstein Meml lectr London Hosp Med Coll 1994, Bradshaw lectr RCP 1996, McFadzean Meml lectr Hong Kong Univ 1990, visiting prof Yale Univ 2005, Flynn lectr RCPath 2001 and 2009, orator Hunterian Soc 2012, Benoziyo lectr The Weizmann Inst Israel 2012, Mc Fadzean orator Coll of Physicians HK 2012, visiting prof Univ of Michigan Med Sch Ann Arbor USA 2015, lectr Cambridge Philosophical Soc 2016; external examiner in med: Hong Kong Univ 1990, Univ of London 1992–97, Royal Coll of Surgeons Ireland 1994–97, Chinese Univ Hong Kong 2001, Univ of Oxford 2001–05, Univ of Manchester 2006–09; memb Exec Ctee Assoc of Physicians of GB and Ireland 1995–97 (memb 1984, sr memb 2008–), pres Cambridge Philosophical Soc 2002–03 (memb Cncl 1994–, vice-pres 1998–2000), memb syndicate CUP 1998–, tstee Croucher Fndn Hong Kong 2001–, memb Cncl Galton Inst 2006–15 (vice-pres 2010–12), vice-chm Croucher Fndn 2013–, chm Evaluation Ctee Translational Research Prog Agence Nationale de la Recherche 2013–16, memb Strategic Devpt and Scientific Advsy Ctee Sanofi 2013–; Clé de la Compréhension Les Clés du Lysosome Awards 2013; FRCP 1984, FMedSci 1998, FRSA 2000; *Books* Molecular Biology in Medicine (co-ed, 1997, Spanish trans 1998, Chinese trans 2000, Serbo-croat trans 2001), Oxford Textbook of Medicine (co-ed, 6 edn 2017); *Publications* numerous articles on inborn errors and metabolic diseases; *Recreations* music; *Clubs* Medical Pilgrims, RSM; *Style—* Prof T M Cox, FMedSci; ✉ Department of Medicine, University of Cambridge School of Clinical Medicine, Addenbrooke's Hospital, Hills Road, Cambridge CB2 2QQ (☎ 01223 336864, fax 01233 336846, e-mail tmc12@medschl.cam.ac.uk, website www.cam.ac.uk)

COX, Dr Vivienne; CBE (2016); *Educ* Univ of Oxford (MA), INSEAD (MBA); *Career* BP plc: joined 1981, BP Chemicals 1981–85, BP Exploration 1985–87, BP Finance 1987, i/c commodity derivatives gp Oil Trading Dept 1991, Rotterdam refinery 1993, Central and Eastern Europe business devpt Vienna 1996, appointed ceo Air BP 1998, subsequently with BP Oil, exec vice-pres for integrated supply and trading and for gas, power and renewables 2004, chief exec BP Alternative Energy 2005–09; non-exec dir: Eurotunnel plc 2002–04, Rio Tinto plc and Rio Tinto Ltd 2005–, Climate Change Capital 2008–, BG Gp plc 2012–, Pearson plc 2012–; patron St Francis Hospice, Int Cncl INSEAD; Veuve Clicquot Businesswoman of the Year 2006; *Style—* Dr Vivienne Cox, CBE

COXON, Richard; *Educ* Royal Northern Coll of Music; *Career* tenor and composer; studies with John Mitchinson; princ Scottish Opera 1993–96, freelance 1996–; co-fndr Dean and Chadlington Summer Music Festival; performances with Scottish Opera incl: Alfredo in La Traviata, Trabuco in La Forza del Destino, Sailor in Tristan und Isolde, Jacquino in Fidelio, Nemorino in L'Elisir d'Amore, Narraboth in Salome, Flavio in Norma, Barbarigo in I due Foscari, Jiri in The Jacobin, Don Ottavio in Don Giovanni, Brighella in Ariadne, Alfred in Die Fledermaus, Kudrias in Katya Kabanova; other credits: Nemorino (Opera Northern Ireland and Opera Zuid Maastricht), Ralph Rackstraw in HMS Pinafore (National Operetta Company), Die Freunde von Salamanka (Edinburgh Int Festival and Aix-en-Provence Festival), Steuerman in Flying Dutchman (Opera Ireland), Messiah (Royal Albert Hall), Alfredo in La Traviata (Opera Northern Ireland), Brighella in Ariadne auf Naxos (ENO), Young Convict in House of the Dead (ENO), Fenton in Falstaff (ENO), Painter in Lulu (ENO), Peter Sample in Sir John in Love (ENO), Nick in Handmaiden's Tale (ENO), Mr By-Ends in The Pilgrims Progress (Royal Opera, also recorded for Chandos), Gaston in La Traviata (Royal Opera), Squeak in Billy Budd (Royal Opera, also recorded for Chandos), Iego in The Bird of Nigh (Royal Opera) Tom Rakewell in The Rake's Progress (New Israel Opera), Major Domo and Lieutenant Bonnet in War and Peace (Spoleto Festival, also recorded for Chandos), Bill in Flight (Nat Reiss Opera and Glyndebourne Festival Opera, recorded for Chandos), Italian singer in Der Rosenkavalier (Opera North, Spoleto Festival), Kudryash in Katya Kabanova (Florida Grand Opera and Opéra de Montréal), Eduardo in Un Giorno di Regno (Buxton Festival Opera), Piquillo in La Péricole (Buxton Festival Opera), Troilus in Troilus and Cressida, Gastone (Nat Reiss Opera and Opera North), Voice from the Forge (Opera North and Greek Nat Opera), Flute in Midsummer Night's Dream (La Monnaie Brussels and Opera Ireland), Monostatos in Magic Flute (Florida Grand Opera), Tisiphone in Hippolyte et Aricie (Nat Reiss Opera); oratorio and solo recitals with: Hallé Orchestra, Royal Scottish Nat Orchestra, Bergen Philharmonic Orchestra, Royal Liverpool Philharmonic, BBC Scottish Symphony Orchestra, London Pops Orchestra, London Musici (world premiere of A Live Flame), City of London Sinfonia, Scottish Chamber Orchestra, Scottish Opera Orchestra, Vara Radio Orchestra, BBC Symphony Orchestra, Israel Camerata, Philharmonica Orchestra, BBC Concert Orchestra; London Symphony Orch; recording Kurt Weill under Sir Andrew Davis Royal Place; filmed role of Edgardo at Toronto Festival, filmed role of Fox in The Cunning Little Vixen under Kent Nagano for DVD; Van Man in The Little Prince recorded for Sony Classical and DVD; Webster Booth/ Esso Award, Clonter Opera Prize, Ricordi Opera Prize, Peter Moores Foundation Award, Wolfson Tst Award; *Style—* Richard Coxon, Esq; ✉ c/o Helen Sykes Artists' Management, 100 Felsham Road, Putney, London SW15 1DQ (☎ 020 8780 0060, fax 020 8780 8772)

COYLE, Diane; OBE (2009); *b* 1961, Bury, Lancs; *Educ* BNC Oxford (exhibitioner, MA, Gibbs prize), Harvard Univ (MA, PhD); *m* 7 April 1990, Rory Cellan-Jones, *qv*; 2 s (Adam Joseph b 1990, Rufus Gareth b 1998); *Career* Sumner Slichter fell Harvard Univ and research asst Nat Bureau of Econ Research Cambridge MA 1981–85, sr econ asst HM Treasy 1985–86, sr economist DRI Europe 1986–88, intern The Economist 1988–89, Euro ed Investors Chronicle 1989–93 (actg features ed 1993), econ corr and reporter City and Business section then econ ed The Independent 1993–2001 (Wincott Award for Sr Financial Journalist 2000), currently md Enlightenment Economics, prof of economics Univ of Manchester 2014–; visiting research fell Smith Sch of Enterprise and the Environment Univ of Oxford; memb Competition Cmmn 2001–09; memb Advsy Bd EDF Energy; memb Migration Advsy Ctee 2007–12, memb Independent Review of HE Funding 2010, memb Cncl Nat Inst of Economic and Social Research 2013–, memb Nat Capital Ctee 2016–; tstee: Centre for Economic Policy Research, Pro Bono Economics; memb BBC Tst 2006–15 (vice-chair 2011–15); sometime broadcaster BBC Radio 4; memb: Royal Econ Soc, American Econ Assoc; FRSA, fell RSS, fell Soc of Business Economists; *Publications* incl: Governing the World Economy (2000), Understanding Economic Forecasts (contrib, 2001), Paradoxes of Prosperity (2001), Getting the Measure of the New Economy (jtly, 2002), Sex, Drugs and Economics (2002), Making Sense of Globalization: A Guide to the Economic Issues (jtly, 2002), The Consequences of Saying No (jtly, 2003), New Wealth for Old Nations: Scotland's Economic Prospects (jt ed, 2005), The Soulful Science (2007), Bailing Out the Banks (2010), The Economics of Enough (2011), What's the Use of Economics (2012), GDP: A Brief but Affectionate History (2014); *Style—* Ms Diane Coyle, OBE; ✉ e-mail diane@enlightenmenteconomics.com, website www.enlightenmenteconomics.com

COYLE, Michael Thomas Patrick; s of Michael Coyle (d 1985), and Mary Elizabeth, *née* Skelly; *b* 21 January 1955; *Educ* Finchley Catholic GS, UEA (BA), Lancaster Gate Coll of Law; *Career* advertising exec; trainee rising to account mangr Young & Rubicam 1979–83, account mangr rising to account dir Saatchi & Saatchi 1983–88, Ogilvy & Mather 1988–89 (dir (Australia), client service dir, dep md), int bd dir Bates (formerly BSB Dorland) 1989–; regnl dir and european client dir Bates Europe 1996–, vice-chm Bates Pan Gulf until 2000, exec vice-pres Bates Europe 2000–; *Recreations* reading, music, travelling, tennis, cricket, football, bobsleigh; *Clubs* Albanian Assoc, Queen's, Annabel's; *Style—* Michael Coyle, Esq; ✉ Bates Europe, 121–141 Westbourne Terrace, London W2 6JR (☎ 020 7262 5077, fax 020 7258 3757)

COYLE, Richard; s of Ronald Coyle (d 2000), of Sheffield, and Pearl, *née* Margereson; *b* Sheffield; *Educ* Birkdale Sch Sheffield, Univ of York (BA), Bristol Old Vic Theatre Sch; *m* 21 Aug 2004 (m dis 2010), Georgia Mackenzie; 1 da (Purdy b 9 Aug 2008); *Career* actor; supporter (fundraiser and involvement in campaigns) British Heart Fndn; *Film* Topsy Turvy 1999, Human Traffic 2000, The Libertine 2005, A Good Year 2006, Franklyn 2008, Prince of Persia 2010, WE 2012, Grabbers 2012, Pusher 2012, Food Guide to Love 2013, Dream On 2014; *Television* Coupling 2000–03, Lorna Doone 2000, Sword of Honour 2000, Othello 2001, Strange 2002, Whistleblowers 2007, Going Postal 2010, Crossbones (NBC TV) 2014, The Fall (BBC) 2016; *Theatre* The York Realist (Royal Court Theatre) 2001–02, Proof (Donmar Warehouse) 2002, After Miss Julie (Donmar Warehouse) 2004, Don Carlos (Gielgud Theatre) 2005, Look Back in Anger (Bath Theatre Royal) 2006, The Lover/The Collection (Comedy Theatre) 2008, Polar Bears (Donmar Warehouse) 2010, Macbeth (Park Avenue Armory NYC) 2014; *Style—* Richard Coyle, Esq; ✉ Troika, 74 Clerkenwell Road, London EC1M 5QA

CRABB, Stephen; MP; *b* 1973; *Educ* Tasker Milward Sch, Univ of Bristol, London Business Sch; *Career* Parly affrs offr Nat Cncl for Voluntary Youth Servs 1996–98, election monitor OSCE (Bosnia Herzegovina) 1998, policy mangr London C of C 1998–2002; MP (Cons) Preseli Pembrokeshire 2005– (Parly candidate (Cons) Preseli Pembrokeshire 2001); asst whip 2010–, parly under-sec of state for Wales 2012–14, sec of state for Wales 2014–16, Lord Cmmr of HM Treasy (Govt whip), sec of state for work and pensions 2016; chm N Southwark and Bermondsey Cons Assoc 1998–2000; *Style—* Stephen Crabb, Esq, MP; ✉ House of Commons, London SW1A 0AA (website www.stephencrabb.com)

CRABTREE, His Hon Judge Peter Dixon; OBE; s of Kenneth Crabtree (d 1997), and Ethel, *née* Dixon; *b* 2 March 1956, Burnley, Lancs; *Educ* Liverpool Coll, Manchester Polytechnic (BA), Bristol Univ (LLM); *m* 1981, Ann, *née* Cooper; 3 da (Charlotte b 19 Oct 1986, Catherine, Sophie b 4 June 1992 (twins)); *Career* RN: joined 1979 (served HMS Invincible, HMS Ark Royal, HMS Minerva, HMS Fearless), Captain, ret 2005; called to the Bar (Gray's Inn) 1985; dep dist judge (Magistrates' Cts) 2003, dist judge (Magistrates' Cts) 2005–13, recorder 2009, circuit judge (Western Circuit) 2014–; ACIS; *Recreations* golf, reading, hill walking/climbing; *Clubs* Royal Scots, High Post Golf; *Style—* His Hon Judge Crabtree, OBE; ✉ c/o Courts of Justice, Deansleigh Road, Bournemouth BH7 7DS

CRACKNELL, Carrie; *b* 1980; *Educ* Univ of Nottingham, RSAMD, Nat Theatre Studio; *Career* artistic dir Gate Theatre 2007–12, assoc dir Young Vic Theatre 2010–13, assoc dir Royal Court Theatre 2013–14; theatre credits incl: Blurred Lines (NT), Medea (NT), Pigeons (Royal Court), Birdland (Royal Court), Elektra (Young Vic), A Doll's House (Young Vic and Duke of York's Theatre, nomination Best Dir Evening Standard Award), Electra, Breathing Irregular, Hedda, Shoot/Get Treasure/Repeat, The Sexual Neuroses of Our Parents (all Gate Theatre), I Am Falling (Gate Theatre and Sadlers Wells, nomination Southbank Show Award in Dance), Dolls (Nat Theatre of Scotland), Stacy (The Tron Glasgow), A Mobile Thriller (nat tour and Harbourfront Toronto, winner Herald Angel Award), Broken Road (Br Cncl Showcase, winner Fringe First Award), Death and The City (The Tron Glasgow), The Hush (BAC and Ohio Theatre NY), Macbeth (Djanogly Theatre Nottingham); opera Wozzeck (ENO, nomination Best New Opera Production Olivier Award), film Nora (Young Vic and The Space); Bruce Millar Tst Award 2004; *Style—* Ms Carrie Cracknell; ✉ c/o Rose Cobbe, United Agents, 12–26 Lexington Street, London W1F 0LE

CRACKNELL, David John; s of David Lewis Cracknell, of Woodford Green, Essex, and Norma Rose, *née* Beasley; *Educ* Forest Sch, Univ of Southampton (LLB), Pembroke Coll Oxford (BCL); *m* 9 May 1998, Rachel Annie Laurent; 2 da (Poppy Natasha b 24 July 1999, Freya Sophie b 11 April 2001), 1 s (Laurent Patrick David b 18 Feb 2004); *Career* journalist; reporter Coventry Evening Telegraph 1993–95, political corr Press Assoc 1995–98, political ed Sunday Business 1998–99, dep political ed Sunday Telegraph 1999–2001, political ed Sunday Times 2001–08, chm FD-LLM Jan-Apr 2008, fndr Big Tent Communications 2008–; *Publications* The May Anthology of Oxford and Cambridge Short Stories (contrib, 1992); *Style—* David Cracknell, Esq; ✉ e-mail cracknelldavid@gmail.com

CRADDOCK, Malcolm Gordon; s of Gilbert Craddock, and Evelyn Marion, *née* Gordon; *b* 2 August 1938; *Educ* St Albans Sch, Queens' Coll Cambridge (MA); *m* 1, 29 May 1965, Jenni, da of David Maclay; 2 s (Sam, Ben), 1 da (Emily); m 2, 12 June 1999, Rachel, da of Peter and Jennifer Glaister; 1 s (Archie), 1 da (Lily); *Career* entered film industry 1962; asst dir to Joseph Losey 1964–66 (Accident, Modesty Blaise); dir: Mr Lewis 1965, The Beach 1967; film dir of TV commercials (Sunday Times awards) 1966–89, founding ptnr and dir Picture Palace Prodns Ltd 1970–; prodr TV drama 1984–: Tandoori Nights (Channel 4) 1985–87, Ping Pong (Venice Int Film Festival) 1986, twenty one short films, 4 Minutes (winner Gold Award for Drama NY 1986), Firing the Bullets, Hunting the Squirrel and Pushed (Channel 4 and ECA) 1989–90, When Love Dies (Channel 4) 1990, The Orchid House (series, Channel 4) 1991, Sharpe's Rifles and Sharpe's Eagle (ITV) 1993, Little Napoleons (Channel 4) 1994, Sharpe's Company, Sharpe's Enemy and Sharpe's Honour (ITV) 1994 (nominated BAFTA Award Best TV Drama Series), Karaoke Love Affair (NHK Tokyo) 1994, Sharpe's Sword, Sharpe's Gold and Sharpe's Battle (ITV) 1995, Sharpe's Regiment, Sharpe's Siege and Sharpe's Mission (ITV) 1996, Sharpe's Revenge, Sharpe's Justice and Sharpe's Waterloo (ITV) 1997, A Life for A Life – The True Story of Stefan Kiszko (ITV) 1998 (winner Royal TV Soc Best Writer and Best Newcomer, nominated BAFTA Award Best Single Drama), Extremely Dangerous (ITV) 1999, Rebel Heart (BBC1) 2001, Frances Tuesday (ITV) 2004, Sharpe's Challenge (ITV) 2006, Sharpe's Peril (ITV) 2008; *Recreations* tennis, watching Tottenham Hotspur FC; *Clubs* Groucho; *Style—* Malcolm Craddock, Esq;

✉ 13 Egbert Street, London NW1 8LJ (☎ 020 7722 2745); Picture Palace Films Ltd (☎ 020 7586 8763, website www.picturepalace.com)

CRAFT, Prof Sir Alan William; kt (2004); *b* 6 July 1946; *Educ* Rutherford GS Newcastle upon Tyne, Univ of Newcastle upon Tyne (MB BS, MD); *Career* postgrad trg in Newcastle upon Tyne Hosps, MRC trg fell Royal Marsden Hosp London 1976–77; conslt paediatrician: N Tyneside and Newcastle upon Tyne 1978–86, Royal Victoria Infirmary Newcastle upon Tyne 1986–91; James Spence prof of child health Univ of Newcastle upon Tyne 1993–2007 (prof of paediatric oncology 1991–93), dir Northern Inst for Cancer Research 2007–09; chm Scout Assoc 2009–15, pres Northumberland Scouts 2010– (chm 2015–); pres: Int Paediatric Oncology Soc (SIOP) 2001–04 (memb 1980, sec gen 1993–99), Together for Short Lives (formerly Assoc for Care of Terminally Ill Children (ACT)) 2002–, RCPCH 2003–06 (vice-pres 1998–2002); chm Acad of Medical Royal Colls 2004–07, memb Bd Medical Defence Union 2010–16; FMedSci, FRCPCH, FRCP, FRCPE, FRCA, FRCR, FRCPI, FAAP, FIAP, FRCN; *Clubs* Athenaeum; *Style*— Prof Sir Alan Craft; ✉ 1 The Villas, Embleton, Northumberland NE66 3XG (☎ 01665 576619); Department of Child Health, Royal Victoria Infirmary, Newcastle upon Tyne NE1 4LP (☎ 0191 282 1342, e-mail a.w.craft@ncl.ac.uk)

CRAFTS, Prof Nicholas Francis Robert; CBE (2014); s of Alfred Hedley Crafts, of Sutton-in-Ashfield, Notts, and Flora Geraldine Mary Crafts (d 1992); *b* 9 March 1949; *Educ* Brunts GS Mansfield, Trinity Coll Cambridge (Wrenbury scholar, MA); *m* 29 March 1969, Barbara, da of Arthur Daynes (d 1992); 2 da (Rachel b 22 Oct 1969, Helen b 13 Aug 1971), 1 s (Adam b 26 Sept 1973); *Career* lectr in economic history Univ of Exeter 1971–72, lectr in economics Univ of Warwick 1972–77, fell and praelector in economics UC Oxford 1977–86; prof of economic history: Univ of Leeds 1987–88, Univ of Warwick 1988–95, LSE 1995–2005, Univ of Warwick 2006–; visiting asst prof of economics Univ of Calif Berkeley 1974–76, visiting prof of economics Stanford Univ 1982–83; memb Cncl: Royal Econ Soc 1991–93, Econ History Soc 1992–; FBA 1992; *Books* British Economic Growth During the Industrial Revolution (1985), Britain's Relative Economic Performance 1870–1999 (2002); *Recreations* horse-racing; *Style*— Prof Nicholas Crafts, CBE, FBA; ✉ Department of Economics, University of Warwick, Coventry CV4 7AL

CRAGG, Anthony Douglas (Tony); CBE (2002); s of late Douglas Roland Cragg, and late Audrey May, *née* Rutter; *b* 9 April 1949, Liverpool; *Educ* Glos Coll of Art Cheltenham, Wimbledon Sch of Art (BA), RCA (MA); *m* 1 (m dis), Ute Oberste-Lehn; 2 s (Daniel Anthony b 1979, Thomas Douglas b 1981); m 2, Tatjana Verhasselt; 1 s (John Eric b 1987), 1 da (Catharina Eve May b 1989); *Career* sculptor; lab technician Nat Rubber Prodrs Research Assoc 1966–68, art college 1969–77, prof L'Ecole des Beaux Arts de Metz 1976; Düsseldorf Kunstakademie: tutor 1978–88, prof 1988–2001, vice-chllr 1988–2001; prof Universität der Künste Berlin 2001–06, prof Kunstakademie Düsseldorf 2006–; visiting prof Univ of the Arts London 2005; Von der Heydt prize 1988, Turner Prize 1988, Shakespeare Prize 2001, Piepenbrock Prize 2002, Best Sculpture Prize Beijing Biennale 2005, Praemium Imperiale for Sculpture 2007; memb Akademie der Künste Berlin 2001; hon prof Budapest Univ 1996, Hon Dr Univ of Surrey 2001, hon fell John Moores Univ Liverpool 2001, hon doctor RCA 2009; rector Kunstakademie Düsseldorf 2009; Chevalier de l'Ordre des Arts et des Lettres (France); RA 1994; *Solo Exhibitions* incl: Lisson Gallery London 1979, 1980, 1982, 1985, 1988, 1991, 1992, 1997, 1998, 2001 and 2006, Galerie Konrad Fischer Düsseldorf 1979, 1980, 1982, 1986, 1989, 1990 and 1999, Arnolfini Gallery Bristol 1980, Whitechapel Art Gallery London 1981, Nouveau Musée Lyon 1981 and 1982, Musée d'Art et d'Industrie St Etienne 1981, Schellmann & Klüser München 1981, 1982 and 1984, Rijksmuseum Kröller-Müller Otterloo 1982, Marian Goodman NYC 1982, 1983, 1984, 1986, 1987, 1989, 1991, 1994, 1998, 2000, 2003 and 2007, Badischer Kunstverein Karlsruhe 1982, Kanransha Gallery Tokyo 1982, 1984, 1987, 1989 and 1990, Kunsthalle Bern 1983, Thomas Cohn Rio de Janeiro 1983 and 1989 and Sao Paulo 1992, 2001, 2003 and 2006, Galerie Buchmann St Gallen 1983, Basel 1986, 1988, 1990, 1992, 1993 and 1995, Köln 1996, 1999, 2002 and 2004 and Berlin 2006, Louisiana MOMA 1984, Humlebaek Denmark 1984, Kölnischer Kunstverein Köln 1984, Galerie Bernd Klüser München 1985, 1988, 1990, 1991, 1994, 1997, 2000, 2003 and 2005, Palais des Beaux-Arts Brussels 1985, ARC Musée d'Art Moderne de la Ville de Paris 1985, Kestner-Gesellschaft Hannover 1985, Staatsgalerie Moderner Kunst Munich 1985, The Brooklyn Museum NYC 1986, Hayward Gallery London 1987, Corner House Manchester 1987, Gallerie Tucci Russo Turin 1987, 1990 and 1992, Venice Biennale 1988, Galerie Crousel-Robelin Paris 1988, 1991 and 1994, Stedelijk Van Abbemuseum Eindhoven 1989 and 1991, Kunstsammlung Nordrhein-Westfalen Düsseldorf 1989, Tate Gallery London 1989, Newport Harbour Art Museum Newport Beach Calif 1990, Corcoran Gallery of Art Washington DC 1991, Power Plant Toronto 1991, Houston Contemporary Art Museum 1991, IVAM Valencia 1992, Tramway Glasgow 1992, CCA Glasgow 1992, Mu?e des Beaux Arts Nantes 1994, Stadtgalerie Saarbrücken 1994, Museo Nacional Centro de Arte Reina Sofia Madrid 1995, Nationalgalerie Prag 1995, Centre Georges Pompidou Paris 1996, Henry Moore Fndn Halifax 1996, Galerie Karsten Greve Paris 1996, 1998 and 2000 and Milan 1996, Whitechapel Art Gallery 1997, Nationalgalerie Skopje 1997, Nationalgalerie Sofia 1997, Nationalgalerie Bratislava 1997, Nationalgalerie Warschau 1997, Gallerie Maeye-Ellinger Frankfurt 1997, National Museum of Contemporary Art Seoul 1997, Toyota Municipal Museum of Art 1997, Galerie Seitz Berlin 1998, 2001 and 2003, Kenji Taki Gallery Nagoya 1998, 1999, 2004 and 2006, Galerie Chantal Crousel Paris 1999 and 2003, Galerie Stefan Andersson Umea 1999, 2001 and 2006, Summer Exbhn (Royal Acad) 1999, Tate Gallery Liverpool 2000, Glyndebourne 2000, Malmö Konsthall 2001, Somerset House London 2001, Galerie Carles Taché Barcelona 2002 and 2005, Kunst und Auststellungshalle der Bundesrepublik Deutschland Bonn 2003, Macro Museum of Contemporary Art Rome 2003, Museu Serralves Porto 2004, Central House of Artists Moscow 2005, Neues Museum Nürnberg 2005, Galerie Catherine Putnam Paris 2005, Museum der Wahrnehmung Graz 2005, Galerie Thaddaeus Ropac Paris 2005, Cass Sculpture Fndn Goodwood 2005, Gow Langsford Gallery Auckland 2005, Jiri Svestka Gallery Prag 2006, Künstlerverein Malkasten Düsseldorf 2006, Krefelder Kunstverein 2006, Das Potential der Dinge (Akademie der Künste Berlin 2006 and (Lehmbruck Museum Duisburg) 2007, Tony Cragg Exposición (Argentina) 2006, Haunch of Venison Zürich 2007, Tony Cragg 1995–2006 (Museo de Arte de Lima Peru) 2007, Galleria Sculptor Helsinki 2007, Tony Cragg Exposición (MAVI Chile) 2007, Noteliska Akuarellmuseet 2008, TC vs Messerschmidt Belvedere Wien 2008, Second Nature Karksruke 2009, Lisson Gallery London 2010; *Group Exhibitions* incl: Aperto '80 Venice Biennale 1980, Venice Biennale 1986, Dokumenta 8 Kassel 1987, Venice Biennale 1993, Recent British Sculpture from the Arts Cncl Collection (South Bank Centre London) 1993, Museum of Contemporary Art Madrid 1994, Museum of Modern Art Dublin 1995, Museum Folkwang Essen 1996, Hayward Gallery London 1997, MAC Marseille 1998, Le Champs de la Skultur Paris 1999, Sprengel Museum Hannover 2000, Guggenheim Museum Venice 2002, Nasher Sculpture Center Dallas 2003, Tehran Museum of Contemporary Art Tehran 2004, 'Intersezoni' Catanzaro 2005, 'Contemporary Voices' at MOMA NY 2005, Kunstmuseum Wolfsburg 2006, Praemium Imperiale Art of Our Time Tokyo 2008, Glasstress 53 Biennale Venice 2009; *Major Projects and Commissions* 'World Events' High Museum of Modern Art Atlanta USA 1996, 'Wave Forms' Battery Park City Authy NYC 1996, 'Dancing Columns' Br Embassy Berlin 2000, 'Think Thing' Stockholm Univ 2001, 'Changing Minds' The Hobby Center for Performing Arts, Houston USA 2002, 'First Appearances, Second Thoughts' APO Bank Düsseldorf 2003, 'Constant Change' Barclay's Bank London 2005, 'Points of View' 2006 Winter Olympics Turin Italy 2005; *Style*— Tony Cragg, Esq, CBE, RA; ✉ website www.tony-cragg.com

CRAGG, Anthony John; CMG (2000), JP (2005); s of Samuel Arthur Leslie Cragg (d 2000), and Gwendolen Mary, *née* Pevler (d 1991); *b* 16 May 1943, Stockton on Tees, Co Durham; *Educ* Hastings GS, Lincoln Coll Oxford (open scholar); *m* 4 Sept 1971, Jeanette Ann, da of Alfred Richard Rix; 2 da (Alexandra Frances Helen b 14 Feb 1977, Susannah Rose b 14 April 1982); *Career* MOD: asst princ 1966, asst private sec to Perm Under Sec 1968–70, princ 1971, asst private sec to Sec of State for Defence 1974–76, seconded to FCO for service with NATO 1977–79, asst sec 1979, head of Naval Resource Planning Secretariat 1980–83, chief offr UK Sovereign Base Areas Cyprus 1983–85, RCDS 1988, under sec 1990, chm Defence Orgn Planning Team 1991–92; asst sec gen for Defence Planning & Operations NATO Brussels 1993–99, MOD 1999–2003, memb Jt Intelligence Ctee 1999–2003; sr assoc res fell Centre for Defence Studies KCL 2003–08, assoc fell RUSI 2003; lay memb Upper Tbnl and First Tier Tbnl (Immigration and Asylum Chamber) 2003–13; visiting lectr: NATO Defence Coll 2003–, Geneva Centre for Security Policy 2005–12; *Publications* Global Monitoring for Security and Stability (contrib), Remote Sensing from Space (contrib); articles and papers on int defence and security issues; *Recreations* swimming, walking, music, reading; *Style*— Anthony Cragg, Esq, CMG

CRAGG, Bernard Anthony; *Career* finance dir Carlton Communications plc 1987–2001 (co sec 1985–87); formerly non-exec chm: Datamonitor plc 2003–07, i-mate; non-exec dir: Mothercare plc 2003–, Workspace Group plc 2003–, Astro All Asia Networks plc, Bristol & West Investments plc; ACA; *Style*— Bernard Cragg, Esq

CRAIG, Amanda Pauline; da of Dennis Bathgate Craig, of Rome, and Zelda Rose Craig; *b* 22 September 1959; *Educ* Bedales, Clare Coll Cambridge (exhibitioner); *m* 1988, Robin John Cohen, s of L Jonathan Cohen; 1 da (Leonora Rose), 1 s (William Alexander); *Career* novelist, literary critic, columnist and children's critic; Young Journalist of the Year Award 1985, Catherine Pakenham Award 1987; memb: PEN, Soc of Authors; *Books* Foreign Bodies (1990), A Private Place (1991), A Vicious Circle (1996), In a Dark Wood (2000), Love in Idleness (2003), Hearts and Minds (2009); *Recreations* reading, gardening, music, children; *Clubs* Academy; *Style*— Ms Amanda Craig; ✉ c/o Antony Harwood Agency, 103 Walton Street, Oxford OX2 6EB (☎ 01865 559615); website www.amandacraig.com, Twitter @AmandaPCraig

CRAIG, Dr Brian George; s of Very Rev Dr William Magee Craig, of Moira Co Down, and Maud, *née* Macrory; *b* 6 September 1953; *Educ* Portadown Coll, Queen's Univ Belfast (MD, BCh, BAO); *m* Jennifer, da of Albert Mawhinney; 2 s (Adam b 1984, Matthew b 1986); *Career* sr registrar: cardiology Royal Victoria Hosp 1982–83, Hosp for Sick Children Toronto Canada (clinical fell in paediatric cardiology) 1983–85, paediatrics Royal Belfast Hosp for Sick Children 1985–86; conslt in paediatric cardiology Royal Belfast Hosp for Sick Children 1986–; author of numerous publications in learned jls; memb: Ulster Paediatric Soc 1979–, Br Paediatric Cardiac Assoc 1987–, Br Paediatric Assoc 1988–, Irish Cardiac Soc 1988–, Br Cardiac Soc 1990, Assoc of Euro Paediatric Cardiologists 1994, Boys Bde; elder Presbyterian Church; FRCP, FRCPCH; *Recreations* gardening, family, tennis; *Style*— Dr Brian Craig; ✉ 10 Plantation Avenue, Lisburn, Co Antrim BT27 5BL (☎ 028 9267 1587); Royal Belfast Hospital for Sick Children, 180–184 Falls Road, Belfast BT12 6BE (☎ 028 9063 2397, e-mail brian.craig@royalhospitals.n-i.nhs.uk)

CRAIG, Colin David; s of Joseph Craig, of Glasgow, and Phyllis, *née* Merrilees; *b* 15 January 1962; *Educ* Douglas Acad, Bell Coll Hamilton, Univ of Strathclyde (BSc); *Partner* Lesley Crosfield , *qv*; *Career* restaurateur; previous jobs incl: lumberjack, auxiliary nurse, lifeguard, electronic engr, itinerant folk singer, mountaineer, fish farmer; chef and co-prop Albannach Hotel 1990– (Michelin BIB Gourmand 1997, Award for McAllan Overall Excellence 1998, Award for McAllan Best Restaurant with Rooms 1998, Good Food Guide W Coast Newcomer of the Year 2000, Scotland the Best! Award for Excellence 2000, Which? Hotel Guide Hotels of the Year category 2002, 2 AA Rosettes 2002, Scottish Hotel Bedroom of the Year Hotel Review Scotland 2007, Michelin star 2009, runner-up Scottish Chef of the Year 2009), owner Caberfeidh Dining Pub Lochinver; tenant crofter; memb Assynt Mountain Rescue Team 1991–96, memb SNP (social convenor Milngavie); RYA, Br Motorcycle Fedn, Small Business Fedn; *Books* Scotland on a Plate (2001), Relish Scotland (2010); *Recreations* mountaineering, subaqua diving, sailing, motorcycling, Scotland, all things French (particularly those that can be eaten or drunk); *Clubs* Scottish SubAqua, Malt Whisky Soc, Triumph Owners Motorcycle, MG Owners; *Style*— Colin Craig, Esq; ✉ The Albannach, Baddidarroch, Lochinver, Sutherland IV27 4LP (☎ 01571 844407, fax 01571 844285, e-mail info@thealbannach.co.uk, website www.thealbannach.co.uk)

CRAIG, Dr David Crichton; s of William John Craig (d 1968), and Edith Blundell, *née* Kay (died 1994); *b* 2 June 1948, Southport, Lancs; *Educ* Victoria Univ of Manchester (Dental Surgery), Univ of Sheffield (Anaesthesia), Open Univ (Neurobiology), Univ of Oxford (Local History), Univ of Dundee (Heraldry); *m* 3 June 1972, Jill Barbara, *née* Preston; 2 da (Emma Jane Creighton b 1988, Elizabeth Creighton b 1993); *Career* sr systems analyst, asst mangr UCL Computer Centre 1967–79, resident house offr (oral surgery) Central Manchester Health Authy 1983–84, SHO (anaesthesia) Central Manchester Health Authy 1984–85, lectr (oral surgery) Univ of Manchester 1985–86, clinical asst (oral surgery) Queen Victoria Hosp East Grinstead 1986–91, gen dental practitioner Kent FPC 1986–91, lectr in dental sedation Guy's Hosp/United Medical and Dental Schs 1992–96, assoc specialist and head of sedation and special care dentistry KCL Dental Inst Guy's and St Thomas' NHS Fndn Tst 1996–2008, consultant, hon sr lectr and head of sedation and special care dentistry KCL Dental Inst Guy's and St Thomas' NHS Fdn Tst 2008–; Nat Examining Bd for Dental Nurses: Dental Anaesthetic Nursing Examination Ctee 1996–2000, chm Dental Sedation Nursing Examination Ctee 2001–06 (examiner and memb 1994–98), memb Cncl and Exec Ctee 2001–06, chm Dental Radiography Examination Ctee 2004–06, dep chm 2005–06, chm Qualifications Cncl and Bd of Tstees 2006–08, emeritus examiner 2011; memb: Cncl Assoc of Dental Anaesthetists 1993–96 (hon treas 1996–2000), Acad of Medical Royal Colls Safe Sedation Working Pty 2001, Standing Dental Advsy Ctee Expert Gp on Conscious Sedation 2003, Standing Ctee on Sedation for Dentistry Faculty of Dental Surgery RCS 2007, Dept of Health Sedation Working Pty 2007, Royal Coll of Anaesthetists Curriculum Working Gp on Conscious Sedation 2010; memb and chm Intercollegiate Advsy Ctee for Sedation in Dentistry 2010, hon life memb Soc for the Advancement of Anaesthesia in Dentistry 2011 (tstee and memb Cncl 1996, nat course dir 2000, pres 2003–06, founding memb and chm Dental Sedation Teachers Gp 2012–15); chm: Dept of Health/Faculty of Gen Dental Practice DwSI Working Gp on Conscious Sedation 2007, Ind Expert Gp on Trg and Standards for Sedation in Dentistry 2011, advsr on conscious sedation to RAF/Defence Dental Agency 1993; expert witness on conscious sedation: Gen Dental Cncl, Dental Defence Union, Dental Protection Ltd, NHS Dental Reference Service, Lambeth, Southwark and Lewisham Health Authy 1996; external examiner: UCL/Eastman Dental Hosp 2006–11, Trinity Coll Dublin 2012–15; author or co-author of approx 50 professional pubns incl 11 contrib chapters/books; Dr Charles H Preston Prize in Dental Surgery and Preston Medal 1983, SS White Prize in Dental Surgery 1983, BDA Prize for Vocational Trg 1983, Zyma (UK) Prize for Elective Study 1983, Farrar Prize in Dental Prosthetics 1983, Farrar Prize in Oral Surgery 1983, Zochonis Travel Award 1983; MMedSci 1992,

MFGDP (UK) 1992, MBCS 1993, FSA Scot 2012, FDSRCS(Ed) 2015; *Publications* Practical Conscious Sedation; chapters in: Anaesthesia for Oral and Maxillofacial Surgery (eds Shaw I, Kumar C, Dodds C), Safe Conscious Sedation (eds Skelly A M, Palmer D), Problems in Dentistry (ed Odell E); *Recreations* local history, genealogy, heraldry, photography, amateur radio (G2HIX); *Style—* Dr David Craig; ✉ Department of Sedation and Special Care Dentistry, Floor 26, Tower Wing, Guy's Hospital, Great Maze Pond, London, SE1 9RT (☎ 020 7188 6067, e-mail david.craig@kcl.ac.uk)

CRAIG, David Mark; QC (2015); s of Graham Harvey Craig, and Rosalind Louise Simmons, *née* Montague; *Educ* Univ Coll Sch, Univ of Manchester (BSc), Queen's Coll Cambridge (MPhil), City Univ (DipLaw); *m* 26 March 2000, Ruth Elana; 3 da (Jessica Sophie b 14 Feb 2002, Elliana Rachel b 11 Aug 2003, Eden Talia b 4 Feb 2006), 1 s (Benjamin Saul b 15 Aug 2007); *Career* called to the Bar 1997; Employment Junior of the Year Chambers and Partners 2011; *Style—* David Craig, Esq, QC; ✉ Essex Court Chambers, 24 Lincoln's Inn Fields, London WC2A 3EG

CRAIG, David N; *Educ* Selwyn Coll Cambridge (MA, MEd); *Career* dep headmaster Merchant Taylors' 2006–10, headmaster Queen Elizabeth GS Wakefield 2010–; memb HMC 2010–; *Recreations* cricket; *Style—* David Craig, Esq; ✉ Queen Elizabeth Grammar School, 154 Northgate, Wakefield WF1 3QX (e-mail dcraig@qegsss.org.uk)

CRAIG, Ian Alexander (Alec); s of Andrew Craig (d 1991), and Sarah Craig; *b* 28 September 1957; *Educ* Univ of Sheffield (BA); *m* 10 Feb 1992, Sally, *née* Bowen; 3 s (Alexander Richard b 17 Nov 1991, James William Blair b 27 Oct 1993, Thomas Patrick b 12 March 1995); *Career* admitted slr 1993; Halliwells: ptnr 1990–, sr ptnr 2001–10; chm Tepnel Life Sciences plc until 2009; dir of several public and private cos; memb Law Soc; sec Snowsport GB 2001–; MSI 1990; *Recreations* soccer, skiing, ornithology, shooting; *Clubs* RAC; *Style—* Alec Craig, Esq; ☎ 07802 364851, e-mail aleccraiguk@yahoo.co.uk

CRAIG, Prof Ian Watson; s of Gordon Craig, and Olive, *née* Watson; *b* 21 August 1943; *Educ* Univ of Liverpool (BSc, PhD); *m* 17 Sept 1966; 3 s (Robert James b 25 June 1972, Gavin Michael b 1 Sept 1973, Stuart Gordon b 28 Feb 1977 d 2002); *Career* NATO postdoctoral research fell Univ of Calif Santa Barbara 1968–1970 (sabbatical visitor 1979); Univ of Oxford: demonstrator 1970, lectr 1972, prof of genetics 1996–; St Catherine's Coll Oxford: fell 1972–, sr tutor 1983–87, domestic bursar; visiting fell Birth Defects Research Unit Melbourne 1986; head of Molecular Genetics Gp SGDP Research Centre Inst of Psychiatry London 1997–2015 (emeritus prof 2015–); Human Genome Organisation (HUGO): memb 1989–, sr genome database ed 1993–, elected to Cncl 1999; tstee HUGO London Ltd 2010–; co-chm Chromosome 12/13 Ctee Human Gene Mapping Genome Database (GDB) 1988–89, chm Chromosome 12 Human Gene Mapping 1989–, ed Chromosome 12 for GDB, sr genome database ed Chromosome Co-ordinating Ctee 1993–; co-author of numerous articles in learned jls; memb RSM; *Recreations* sailing, fishing, bell ringing, gardening; *Style—* Prof Ian Craig; ✉ 33 Standlake Road, Ducklington, Witney, Oxfordshire OX8 7UX; SGDP Centre, King's College London, Institute of Psychiatry, London SE5 8AF

CRAIG, Keren; da of Adam Craig (d 2001), and Bobbie Spargo; *b* 27 February 1976, Lucerne, Switzerland; *Educ* Brighton Art Coll (BA); *m* Piers North; *Career* textile designer; freelance designer creating one-off pieces for fashion houses 2001–04, co-fndr Marchesa (fashion house) 2004–; *Style—* Keren Craig

CRAIG, Rosalie; da of Raymond Craig, and Jane, *née* Shearer; *b* 30 May 1980, Nottingham; *Educ* Rose Bruford Coll of Speech and Drama; *m* 5 Oct 2014, Hadley Fraser; *Career* actress; *Theatre* incl: Aspects of Love (Menier Chocolate Factory), London Road (NT), Ragtime (Regents Park Open Air Theatre), Finding Neverland (Leicester Curve), Hitchcock Blonde (Hull Truck Theatre), Table (NT), Macbeth (Manchester Int Festival), The Light Princess (NT, nominated Olivier Awards) 2013 (Best Musical Performance Evening Standard Award 2013), Miss Julie/ Black Comedy (Chichester Festival Theatre) 2014, City of Angels (Donmar) 2014, Sweeney Todd (ENO) 2015, The Vote (Donmar) 2015, Wonder.land (NT) 2015, As You Like It (NT) 2016, The Threepenny Opera (NT) 2016; *Recreations* cinema, music, exercise, theatre, health, fashion, design; *Style—* Miss Rosalie Craig; ✉ c/o Mary FitzGerald and Lucy Johnson, Curtis Brown Group Ltd, Haymarket House, 28–29 Haymarket, London SW1Y 4SP

CRAIG, Stuart; OBE (2003); s of Norman Craig, and Kate, *née* Ralph; *b* 1942; *Educ* RCA; *Career* film prodn designer 1978–; *Films* credits incl: The Elephant Man (BAFTA Award), Gandhi (Acad Award 1981), Greystoke, Cal, The Mission, Cry Freedom, Memphis Belle, Chaplin, The Secret Garden (Evening Standard Film Award), Dangerous Liaisons (Acad Award 1988), Shadowlands, Mary Reilly, In Love and War, The English Patient (Acad Award 1996), The Avengers, The Legend of Bagger Vance, Harry Potter and the Philosopher's Stone (Evening Standard Film Award), Harry Potter and the Chamber of Secrets, Harry Potter and the Prisoner of Azkaban, Harry Potter and the Goblet of Fire, Harry Potter and the Order of the Phoenix (BAFTA Award), Harry Potter and the Half Blood Prince; *Style—* Stuart Craig, Esq, OBE; ✉ Steve Kenis & Co, Royalty House, 72–74 Dean Street, London W1D 3SG (☎ 020 7434 9055, fax 020 7287 6328); The Skouras Agency, 631 Wiltshire Boulevard, 2nd Floor Suite C, Santa Monica, CA 90401, USA (☎ 001 310 395 9550, fax 001 310 395 4295)

CRAIG, Ted; s of Hugh Hoad Craig, and Hazel Ethel Smith; *b* 20 April 1948, Melbourne; *Educ* Caulfield GS Melbourne; *Career* artistic dir Lyceum Theatre Crewe and Connaught Theatre Worthing 1969–73, assoc dir Old Tote Theatre Co Sydney 1973–75, dir of prods Drama Theatre Sydney Opera House 1977–78, freelance dir 1979–86, artistic dir and chief exec Warehouse Theatre Co 1986–2012, dir Warehouse Phoenix Ltd 2012–; MIOD, FRSA; *Recreations* wine appreciation, cinema, gardening; *Style—* Mr Ted Craig, MIOD, FRSA; ✉ 87 Great Titchfield Street, London W1W 6RL (☎ 020 7580 1000, mobile 07951 152002, e-mail tedcraig@live.co.uk); e-mail ted@warehousetheatre.co.uk, website www.warehousephoenix.co.uk or www.tedcraig.net

CRAIG, (Anne Gwendoline) Wendy; da of George Dixon Craig (d 1968), and Anne Lindsay (d 1998); *b* 20 June 1934; *Educ* Durham HS for Girls, Darlington HS, Yarm GS, Central Sch of Speech Training and Dramatic Art; *m* 30 Sept 1955, John Alexander (Jack) Bentley (d 1994), s of John Bentley (d 1944); 2 s (Alastair b 5 April 1957, Ross b 10 Nov 1961); *Career* actress; vice-pres The Leprosy Mission 1993–, pres Cookham Day Centre, patron Nat Osteoporosis Soc; Hon MA Teesside Univ 1994, Hon DArts Univ of Sunderland 2009; *Theatre* incl: Ipswich Repertory Theatre 1953, Epitaph For George Dillon (Royal Court and Broadway) 1957, The Wrong Side of the Park 1960, The Gingerman, Ride A Cock Horse, I Love You Mrs Patterson, Finishing Touches, Peter Pan 1968, Breezeblock Park 1975, Beyond Reasonable Doubt (Queen's) 1987, Matters Matrimonial 1996–98, Easy Virtue (Chichester Festival) 1999, The Rivals (RSC) 2000, The Circle 2002, The Importance of Being Earnest (tour) 2004; various pantomimes; *Television* incl: Not In Front Of The Children, And Mother Makes Three, And Mother Makes Five, Nanny, Butterflies, Laura and Disorder, Brighton Belles, The Forsyte Saga 2002, Midsomer Murders 2002 and 2013, The Royal 2002–08, Harley St 2008, Reginald Perrin 2009–10, Casualty 2013, Doctors 2014; *Films* incl: The Mindbenders, The Servant (British Academy nomination), The Nanny, Just Like A Woman, I'll Never Forget What's-Is-Name, Joseph Andrews; *Recordings* incl: Tales of Beatrix Potter (gold disc), Show Me The Way 1988, I'm Growing 1990; *Awards* incl: BAFTA Award Best Actress 1968, BBC Personality of the Year 1969 (ITV 1973); *Books* Happy Endings (1972), The Busy Mums Cook Book (1983), Busy Mums Baking Book (1986), Kid's Stuff (1988), Guideposts for Living (1999), Show Me the Way (2006); *Recreations* walking, gardening, classical music; *Style—* Miss Wendy Craig; ✉ c/o Daphne Waring, 1st and 2nd Floor, 17 South Molton Street, London W1K 5QT (☎ 020 7491 2666, fax 020 7409 7932)

CRAIG OF RADLEY, Marshal of the RAF Baron (Life Peer UK 1991), of Helhoughton in the County of Norfolk; Sir David Brownrigg Craig; GCB (1984, KCB 1981), OBE (1967); s of Maj Francis Brownrigg Craig (d 1943), of Dublin, and Olive Craig (d 1958); *b* 17 September 1929, Dublin; *Educ* Radley, Lincoln Coll Oxford; *m* 1955, Elisabeth June (d 2016), da of Charles James Derenburg (d 1976), of West Byfleet, Surrey; 1 s (Hon Christopher Charles Bronwrigg b 28 March 1957), 1 da (Hon Susan Elisabeth b 26 April 1960); *Career* cmmnd RAF 1951, AOC No 1 Gp RAF Strike Cmd 1978–80, VCAS 1980–82, AOC-in-C Strike Cmd and C-in-C UKAF 1982–85, CAS 1985–88, CDS 1988–91, Marshal of the RAF 1988; memb House of Lords Select Ctee on Science and Technology 1993–99, convenor of the Crossbench Peers 1999–2004; chm Cncl King Edward VII's Hosp Sister Agnes 1998–2004; FRAeS; *Clubs* RAF (pres 2002–12); *Style—* Marshal of the RAF the Lord Craig of Radley, GCB, OBE; ✉ House of Lords, London SW1A 0PW (e-mail craigd@parliament.uk)

C

CRAIG-COOPER, Sir (Frederick Howard) Michael; kt (1991), CBE (1982), TD (3 bars), DL (Gtr London 1986); s of Frederick William Valentine Craig-Cooper (d 1975), and Elizabeth Oliver-Thompson Craig-Cooper, *née* Macdonald (later Mrs Carroll-Leahy, d 2008); *b* 28 January 1936; *Educ* Horris Hill, Stowe, Coll of Law London; *m* 8 March 1968, Elizabeth Snagge, MVO, da of Leonard William Snagge (d 1971), and Eleanor Randolf Snagge (d 1983); 1 s (Peter William Howard b 3 March 1972); *Career* Nat Serv RA served combined ops UK Malta and Cyprus 1954–56, TA 1956–88 (cmd NGLO Unit 29 Commando Regt RA 1972–75); articled slr (to Sir Arthur Driver) Jaques & Co 1956–61, slr Allen & Overy 1962–64; Inco Ltd 1964–85: dir of cos in UK, Europe, Africa, ME and India 1972–84, conslt and non-exec dir UK and ME 1984–85; md: Craig Lloyd Ltd 1968–, Paul Ray International 1984–91 (also non-exec dir), Carré Orban & Partners Ltd 1989–93, Tichborne Enterprises Ltd 1993–, National Bank of Kuwait (International) plc 1993– (also non-exec dir), Whichford International Ltd 1994–96, Ely Place Holdings Ltd 1994–2010, Craigmyle and Company Ltd 1995–2009, Westminster Forum Ltd 1996–; memb Cncl Mining Assoc of UK 1977–82, chm Disciplinary Appeal Ctee Chartered Inst of Mgmnt Accountants 1994–2005; chm Employers' Support Ctee TAVRA Gtr London 1987–90; Cons Party: Parly candidate (Cons) Houghton-le-Spring 1966 and 1970, chm Chelsea Cons Assoc 1974–77 (pres 1983–95), pres Kensington and Chelsea Cons Assoc 1995–2005, treas Gtr London Area Nat Union of Cons and Unionist Assocs 1975–84 (memb 1975–91), chm Cons Nat Property Advsy Ctee 1986–93 (memb 1986–); Royal Borough of Kensington & Chelsea: cncllr 1968–74, memb Cncl 1968–78, Cons chief whip 1971–74, chm Fin Ctee 1972–74, memb Investment Ctee 1973–, Alderman 1974–78, Rep Lt Kensington and Chelsea 1987–2006, Hon Freeman 2011; chm Order of St John for London 1990–94 (memb Chapter-Gen 1993–99); tstee: Copper Devpt Tst Fund 1974–85, Order of Malta Homes Tst 1980–2003, The Orders of St John Care Tst 1988–2003, Thames Diamond Jubilee Fndn Ltd 2011–14; dir Diamond River Pageant Co Ltd 2011–14; founding tstee Lord Mayor's Scholarship Scheme (formerly Mansion House Scholarship Scheme) 1998; Cmmr Royal Hosp Chelsea 1998–2005, pres Friends of The Royal Hosp Chelsea 2008–; pres Boys' Bde (London Dist) 2002–05; Vice Lord-Lt Gtr London 2005–11; Freeman City of London 1964, master Worshipful Co of Drapers 1997–98 (Liveryman 1970, memb Ct of Assts 1987–); memb Law Soc 1962–; FCIArb 1992– (MCIArb 1983); Offr Order of Merit with Swords SMOM 1986, KStJ 1990 (OStJ 1978), Cdr of Merit in the Order Pro Merito Melitensi SMOM 2001; *Books* Management Audit: How to Create an Effective Management Team (with Philippe De Backer, 1993), Maw on Corporate Governance (with Prof N N Graham Maw and Lord Lane of Horsell, 1994), Maximum Leadership: The World's Top Business Leaders Discuss How They Add Value to Their Companies (with Charles Farkas, Philippe De Backer and Lord Sheppard of Didgemere, 1995, 2 edn 2000), Stepping Forward (with Field Marshal Sir John Chapple and the RFCA of Greater London, 2014); *Recreations* admiring wife's gardening, hill walking in the Scilly Isles; *Clubs* Beefsteak, Pratt's, White's; *Style—* Sir Michael Craig-Cooper, CBE, TD, DL

CRAIGAVON, 3 Viscount (UK 1927); Sir Janric Fraser Craig; 3 Bt (UK 1918); s of 2 Viscount Craigavon (d 1974); *b* 9 June 1944; *Educ* Eton, Univ of London (BA, BSc); *Heir* none; *Career* elected hereditary peer (crossbench) House of Lords 1999–, memb Hybrid Instruments Select Ctee 1993–97 and 1999–2005, vice-chair All Pty Population, Devpt and Reproductive Health Gp 1996–2010, sec All Pty Denmark Gp 1996–, treas All Pty Pro-Choice and Sexual Health Gp 1998–2010, sec All Pty Finland Gp 1999–, sec All Pty Sweden Gp 2000–, vice-chair All Pty Norway Gp 2000–, sec All Pty Iceland Gp 2001–; FCA; *Style—* The Rt Hon the Viscount Craigavon; ✉ House of Lords, London SW1A 0PW

CRAIGEN, Jeremy John; s of Desmond Craigen (d 2010), of Truro, Cornwall, and Elena Craigen (d 1995); *b* 7 May 1963, Tunbridge Wells; *Educ* Ludgrove Sch, Radley Coll; *Family* 1 da (Lily Elena b 28 Feb 1997), 2 s Crosby Peter Alfred (b 17 Dec 2011), Leopold Buster David (b 2 Apr 2014); partner, Candice Chubb; *Career* copywriter Ted Bates 1984–87, Dorlands 1987–90; BMP DDB Needham (now DDB): joined 1990, dir of creativity 1996, dep creative dir 2001, jt creative dir 2002, exec creative dir 2002–12, global creative offr VW/DDB 2012–15); Global Chief Creative Offr Innocean Worldwide 2015; chm BTAA 2007 (memb Bd 2006–), chm Clio Print 2008; 9 Cannes Lions, 10 Br TV Awards, 8 Campaign Press Awards, 5 D&AD nominations, DDB most awarded agency in the world Gunn Report 1999–2010; *Recreations* fine wine, food, golf, tennis, travel; *Clubs* BBR Wine; *Style—* Jeremy Craigen, Esq; ✉ e-mail jeremy.craigen@innocean.com

CRAKE, Paul Alexander; *b* 16 November 1962; *Educ* King Edward VII GS King's Lynn Norfolk, Univ of Southampton (BA), Dorset Business Sch Bournemouth Poly, Columbia Univ Grad Sch of Business NY (Sr Exec Prog); *Career* admin World Archaeological Congress 1985–86, Southampton City Cncl 1986–91 (latterly mktg mangr), head of mktg and communications Stirling District Cncl 1991–95, communication dir Design Cncl 1995–98; RSA: fellowship and communication dir 1998–2003, prog dir 2003–07, acting sec Faculty of Royal Designers for Industry 2004–07; sec Bd BFI 2007–11, co sec BFI Tst 2011, exec dir Int Psychoanalytical Assoc 2011–; memb: Ct Univ of Southampton 2000–10, Univ of Southampton Devpt Tst 2005–10; tstee Medact 2013–; FRSA 1996; *Recreations* archaeology, architecture, art, books, cinema; *Style—* Paul Crake; ✉ IPA, Broomhills, Woodside Lane, London N12 8UD

CRAM, Stephen (Steve); CBE (2015, MBE 1986); s of William Frank Cram, and Maria Helene, *née* Korte; *b* 14 October 1960; *Educ* Jarrow GS, Newcastle Poly (BA); *Family* 1 da (Josephine), 1 s (Marcus); *Career* middle distance runner; Cwlth Games: Gold medal 1500m 1982 and 1986, Gold medal 800m 1986; European Championships: Gold medal 1500m 1982 and 1986, Bronze medal 800m 1986; Gold medal 1500m World Championships 1983, Silver medal 1500m Olympic Games LA 1984, memb Br Olympic Squad 1980, 1984 and 1988; world mile record holder, former world record holder 1500m and 2000m; athletics presenter/commentator BBC TV; regular contributor to BBC Radio Live 5; motivational speaker and sports conslt; chm English Inst of Sport; chm and dir Comrades of Children Overseas (COCO); chm and tstee Northumberland Sport; pres London and Southern England Branch Sunderland AFC Supporters' Assoc; BBC Sports Personality of the Year 1983; hon fell and chllr Univ of Sunderland; Hon DUniv: Staffordshire, Sheffield Hallam; *Recreations* golf, football, snooker; *Clubs* Jarrow and

Hebburn AC, Sunderland AFC; *Style*— Steve Cram, Esq, CBE; ✉ Kiln Rigg, Wall, Hexham, Northumberland NE46 4EQ (e-mail allison@extramileme.com)

CRAMP, Prof Dame Rosemary Jean; DBE (2011, CBE 1987); da of Robert Raymond Kingston Cramp (d 1999), of Hallaton, Leics, and Vera Grace, *née* Ractliffe (d 1965); *b* 6 May 1929; *Educ* Market Harborough GS, St Anne's Coll Oxford (MA, BLitt); *Career* lectr St Anne's Coll Oxford 1950–55; Univ of Durham: lectr 1955–66, sr lectr 1966–71, prof 1971–90, prof emeritus 1990–; visiting fell All Souls Coll Oxford 1992; conslt archaeologist Durham Cathedral until 1997, memb Validation Panel Museum Trg Inst 1993–97, memb Review Ctee for Export of Works of Art 1994–2003; chm Archaeological Data Service 1997–2001; pres: Soc for Church Archaeology 1996–2000, Durham and Northumberland Architectural and Archaeological Soc 2000–02 (hon vice-pres 2005–), Soc of Antiquaries of London 2001–04; former pres: Cncl Br Archaeology (currently vice-pres), Cumberland and Westmorland Antiquarian and Archaeological Soc (hon vice-pres); vice-pres Royal Archaeological Inst 1992–97; cmmr: Royal Cmmn of Ancient and Historical Monuments for Scotland 1974–99, Cmmn Historic Buildings & Monuments 1984–89; tstee Br Museum 1978–98; Hon DSc: Univ of Durham 1995, Univ of Bradford 2002; Hon DLitt: UC Cork 2003, Univ of Leicester 2004, UCD 2015; FSA, FBA 2006 (now emeritus); *Books* Corpus of Anglo Saxon Stone Sculpture (vol 1 1984, vol 2 with R N Bailey 1988, vol 7 2006), Studies in Anglo Saxon Sculpture (1992), Wearmouth and Jarrow Monastic Sites (2 vols, 2006), The Hired Excavations (monograph, Soc for Medieval Archaeology, 2014); *Recreations* cooking, gardening, reading; *Clubs* Oxford and Cambridge; *Style*— Prof Dame Rosemary Cramp, DBE, FSA; ✉ 5 Leazes Place, Durham DH1 1RE (☎ and fax 0191 386 1843)

CRAMPIN, Peter; QC (1993); s of John Hames Crampin (d 2008), of Oundle, and Gwendoline Edith, *née* Richardson; *b* 7 July 1946; *Educ* St Albans Sch, UC Oxford (open exhibitioner, MA); *m* 2 Oct 1975, Frida Yvonne, eld da of late Henri Helmut Schoemann; 1 s (Joseph Charles b 11 July 1990); *Career* admitted slr 1973, called to the Bar Middle Temple 1976, second jr counsel to the Attorney-Gen in charity cases 1988–93, recorder 1995– (asst recorder 1990–95); *Style*— Peter Crampin, Esq, QC; ✉ Radcliffe Chambers, 11 New Square, Lincoln's Inn, London WC2A 3QB (☎ 020 7831 0081)

CRAMPIN, Dr Stuart; s of Sydney Crampin (d 1968), of Tiptree, Essex, and Kate, *née* Ireson (d 1984); *b* 22 October 1935; *Educ* Maldon GS, KCL (BSc, Jelf medal), Pembroke Coll Cambridge (PhD, ScD); *m* 15 June 1963, Roma Eluned, da of Lloyd Williams; 2 da (Liss-Carin b 7 Sept 1964, Amelia Catharine b 26 Aug 1966); *Career* Nat Serv RAF 1954–56; res fell Seismological Inst Univ of Uppsala 1963–65, Gassiot fell in seismology NERC 1965–67, dep chief scientific offr Br Geological Survey 1986–92 (princ scientific offr 1967–76, sr princ scientific offr 1976–86), prof of seismic anisotropy Sch of Geosciences Univ of Edinburgh 1992–97, hon prof of seismic anisotropy 1997–, hon res assoc Br Geological Survey 2008–; fndr dir Edinburgh Anisotropy Project 1988–92; pioneered dev seismic anisotropy and shear-wave splitting 1963–, fndr biennial Int Workshops on Seismic Anisotropy 1982–, currently pioneering the new geophysics of a crack-critical Earth 2006–; Mombusho visiting prof Hokkaido Univ 1985; chm Cmmn on Wave Propagation in Real Media Int Assoc of Seismology and Physics of the Earth's Interior 1984–90; first successful stress-forecast of earthquake time and magnitude; author of over 280 papers in int res jls; memb: Royal Astronomical Soc 1961, Seismological Soc of America 1963, American Geophysical Union 1981, Soc of Exploration Geophysicists 1982 (Virgil Kauffman Gold medal 1988), Euro Assoc of Geoscientists and Engineers 1982 (Conrad Schlumberger award 1986), Euro Geophysical Soc 1985; FRSE 1986, fell American Geophysical Union 2009; *Recreations* hill walking, travelling, gardening; *Style*— Dr Stuart Crampin, FRSE, FAGU; ✉ British Geological Survey, The Lyell Centre, Research Avenue South, Edinburgh EH14 4AP (☎ 0131 650 0362, fax 0131 668 2683, e-mail scrampin@ed.ac.uk, website www.geos.ed.ac.uk/homes/scrampin/opinion)

CRAMPTON, Prof Richard John; s of John Donald Crampton (d 1988), of Kidderminster, Worcs, and Norah, *née* Haden (d 2005); *b* 23 November 1940; *Educ* Queen Elizabeth's GS Hartlebury, Solihull Sch, Trinity Coll Dublin (MA), SSEES Univ of London (PhD); *m* 10 July 1965, Celia Primrose Mary, da of Dermot Marshall Harriss (d 1943), of Nyasaland; 2 s (Will b 1969, Ben b 1972); *Career* prof of E Euro history Univ of Kent at Canterbury 1988–90 (lectr in history 1967–78, sr lectr 1978–88), prof of E Euro history Univ of Oxford 1996–2006 (univ lectr 1990–96, fell St Edmund Hall 1990–2006, emeritus fell St Edmund Hall 2006–); visiting fell Woodrow Wilson Int Center for Scholars Washington DC 1998–99; Dr (hc) Kliment Ohridski Univ Sofia; *Books* The Hollow Detente (1981), Bulgaria 1878–1918: A History (1983), A Short History of Modern Bulgaria 1987, Bulgaria (1989), Eastern Europe in the Twentieth Century (1994), Concise History of Bulgaria (1997), Eastern Europe in the Twentieth Century – and After (1997), Atlas of Eastern Europe in the Twentieth Century (jtly, 1997), The Balkans since the Second World War (2002), Bulgaria (in Oxford History of Modern Europe series, 2007), Aleksandur Stamboliiski (2009); *Recreations* reading, cooking, bird watching, trying to teach myself further maths; *Style*— Prof RJ Crampton; ✉ St Edmund Hall, Oxford OX1 4AR (e-mail richard.crampton@retired.ox.ac.uk)

CRAMPTON SMITH, Prof Gillian; da of Alexander Crampton Smith (d 2010), and Rachel, *née* Lupton (d 1999); *b* 21 February 1946; *Educ* St Paul's Girls' Sch, Newnham Coll Cambridge (MA); *m* Philip, s of Owen Tabor; *Career* graphic designer: Sunday Times 1971–75, Times Literary Supplement 1975–78; freelance graphic designer 1978–84; lectr: Canterbury Coll of Art 1977–82, Central Sch of Art 1981–83, St Martin's Sch of Art 1982–88; prof of computer-related design RCA 1993–2000; dir Interaction Design Inst Ivrea 2000–05, IUAV Univ of Venice 2005–14 (Fondazione Venezia chair of design 2008–11); conslt: Apple Computer Cupertino 1992–94, Interval Research Palo Alto 1994–99; chm CONVIO EU Network of Excellence 2004; memb: Advsy Bd Wellcome Wing Science Museum 1999–2000, Art and Design Panel English AHRB 1999–2000, Advsy Panel EU Future and Emerging Technols 2000, Bd Grad Pioneer Scheme Nat Endowment for Science, Technol and the Arts (NESTA) 2003–07, Advsy Bd Copenhagen Interaction Design Inst 2007–10, Advsy Bd Senseable City Lab MIT 2007–; assessor Swedish Govt Research Fndn 1997–2000, distinguished advsr Special Interest Gp for Computer-Human Interaction American Computing Machinery (SIGCHI ACM) 2000–03; ACM SIGCHI Lifetime Achievement Award 2014; assoc fell and memb Governing Body Newnham Coll Cambridge 1993–96, sr fell RCA, hon prof Univ of Applied Sciences Potsdam 2014–; FRSA 1991; *Recreations* cooking, Venetian rowing and sailing; *Style*— Prof Gillian Crampton Smith; ✉ website www.interaction-venice.com

CRAN, Mark Dyson Gordon; QC (1988); s of Gordon Cran (d 1972), and Diana, *née* Mallinson (d 2010); *b* 18 May 1948; *Educ* Gordonstoun, Millfield, Univ of Bristol (LLB); *m* 29 July 1983 (m dis 1986), Prudence Elizabeth, *née* Hayles; *Career* called to the Bar Gray's Inn 1973; recorder 2000; in practice Bermuda; *Recreations* country sports, long walks, convivial disputation, wine and food, performing arts; *Clubs* Brooks's, MCC; *Style*— Mark Cran, Esq, QC; ✉ Brick Court Chambers, 7/8 Essex Street, London WC2R 3LD (☎ 020 7379 3550, e-mail mark.cran@brickcourt.co.uk)

CRANE, Prof Sir Peter Robert; kt (2004); s of Walter Robert Crane (d 1988), and Dorothy Mary, *née* Mills (d 2001); *b* 18 July 1954; *Educ* Univ of Reading (BSc, PhD); *m* 21 June 1986, Elinor Margaret Hamer-Crane, da of Paul Hamer Sr, of Chicago, IL; 1 da (Emily Elisabeth Mary b 9 August 1990), 1 s (Samuel Claire Robert b 26 July 1995); *Career* lectr Dept of Botany Univ of Reading 1978–81, postdoctoral scholar Dept of Biology Indiana Univ 1981–82, curator Field Museum of Natural History Chicago 1982–99 (vice-pres academic affrs 1994–99), dir Royal Botanic Gardens Kew 1999–2006, John and Marion Sullivan prof Univ of Chicago 2006–; pres: Palaeontological Soc, Palaeontological Assoc; author of more than 100 pubns in plant palaeontology and evolutionary biology; memb: Bd Nat Museum of Natural History Smithsonian Inst USA, Overseers Visiting Ctee Organic and Evolutionary Biology Harvard Univ, Bd Botanic Gardens Conservation Int, Bd WWF UK, Advsy Bd Royal Parks; Bicentenary Medal Linnean Soc 1984, Schuchert Award Paleontological Soc 1993, Henry Allan Gleason Award NY Botanical Garden 1998; patron Thomas Phillips Price Tst, memb Bd Lovaine Tst; Hon DDes Kingston Univ, Hon DSc Univ of Portsmouth, hon fell Royal Holloway Coll London; foreign assoc Nat Acad of Scis USA 2001, foreign memb Royal Swedish Acad of Scis 2002, memb Deutsche Akademie der Naturforscher Leopoldina; FRS 1998; *Recreations* travel, biographies; *Style*— Prof Sir Peter Crane, FRS; ✉ Department of Geophysical Science, University of Chicago, 5734 S Ellis Avenue, Chicago, IL 60637, USA

CRANE, Stephen John; s of Anthony Crane, and Lorraine, *née* Simmonds; *b* 29 October 1970, Wandsworth, London; *Educ* Warden Park Sch Cuckfield, Crawley Coll (Pastry Chef of the Year); *m* 22 Aug 2004, Jane, *née* Chapman; 2 s (Gareth b 10 June 1990, Andrew b 25 Nov 1994); *Career* chef; trainee Gatwick Penta 1987–90, demi chef Copthorne Hotel 1990–91, chef de partie Mollington Banastre Chester 1991–92, sous chef Old House Restaurant W Sussex 1992–93, chef tournant London Metropole 1993–94, sr sous chef Halcyon Hotel London 1994–98; head chef: Spread Eagle London 1998–2001, Ockenden Manor W Sussex 2001– (3 AA Rosettes 2002–, 1 Michelin Star 2003–, 1 Egon Ronay Star 2005–); *Recreations* manager first team Balcombe FC; *Style*— Stephen Crane, Esq; ✉ Ockenden Manor, Ockenden Lane, Cuckfield, West Sussex RH17 5LD (☎ 01444 416111, fax 01444 415549, e-mail kitchen@ockenden-manor.com)

CRANFIELD, Richard William Lionel; s of Lionel Sydney William Cranfield (d 1965), and Audrey Cecil Martin, *née* Pank; *b* 19 January 1956; *Educ* Winchester, Fitzwilliam Coll Cambridge (MA); *m* 26 Sept 1981, Gillian Isabel, da of Archibald Spence Fleming (d 1979), of Kelso, Roxburghshire; 2 s (Edward, George), 2 da (Sophie, Henrietta); *Career* admitted slr 1980; head corporate dept Allen & Overy 2000– (ptnr 1985); Freeman City of London 1985, memb Worshipful Co of Merchant Taylors; memb Law Soc; *Recreations* golf, field sports; *Style*— Richard Cranfield, Esq; ✉ Allen & Overy LLP, One Bishops Square, London E1 6AD (☎ 020 3088 0000, fax 020 3088 0088)

CRANHAM, Kenneth; s of Ronald Cranham (d 2009), and Margaret, *née* McKay Ferguson (d 2001); *b* 12 December 1944, Dunfermline; *Educ* Tulse Hill Sch, Royal Court Theatre, RADA (Christine Silver Meml prize, Bancroft gold medal, Herbert Tree prize, Fencing prize); *m* 25 July 1987, Fiona Victory; 2 da (Nancy Grace b 24 Oct 1982, Kathleen Mary Margaret b 24 Sept 1993); *Career* actor; *Television* Mayhew's London (BBC) 1966, Votzek (BBC) 1967, City '68 (Granada) 1968, Coronation Street (Granada) 1968, Sling Your Hook (BBC) 1969, Gangster Thirty Minute Theatre (BBC) 1969, The Samaritan (Granada) 1974, The Changeling (BBC) 1974, Peer Gynt (BBC) 1976, Butterflies Don't Count (BBC) 1978, The Sound of the Guns (Granada) 1979, Danger UXB 1979, The Merchant of Venice (BBC) 1980, 'Tis Pity She's a Whore (BBC) 1980, Thérèse Raquin (BBC) 1980, Cribb (Granada) 1980, The Sin Bin (BBC) 1981, Brideshead Revisited (Granada) 1981, Harvey Moon in Shine on Harvey Moon (ATV) 1982–85, Iris Murdoch's The Bell (BBC) 1982, Lenin in Reilly Ace of Spies (ITV) 1983, Heart of the High Country (ITV) 1985, Lady Windermere's Fan (BBC) 1985, The Birthday Party (BBC) 1985, The Dumb Waiter (BBC) 1985, The Caretaker (BBC) 1985, The Chauffeur and the Lady (BBC) 1985, A Sort of Innocence (BBC) 1986, Normal Service (BBC), The Black and Blue Lamp (BBC), Master of the Marionettes (BBC), The Vision Thing (BBC), Rules of Engagement (ITV), Dunrulin' (BBC), Oranges Are Not The Only Fruit (BBC), The Contractor (BBC), Chimera (ITV), A Little Bit of Lippy (BBC), El C.I.D. (Granada), The Party (BBC), Between the Lines (BBC), La Ronde (BBC), Royal Celebration (BBC), Requiem Apache (BBC), The Tenant of Wildfell Hall (BBC), Just Another Secret (ITV), Get Well Soon (BBC), Our Mutual Friend (BBC), The Murder of Stephen Lawrence (BBC), Without Motive (ITV), Justice in Wonderland (BBC), Lady Audley's Secret (ITV), The Sins (BBC), Night Flight (BBC), Dickens (BBC), The Sinking of the Lusitania (BBC), Pollyanna (ITV), Sparkling Cyanide (ITV), Leopold Mozart in The Genius of Mozart (BBC), Pompey in Rome (HBO), The Line of Beauty (BBC) 2005, Harold Wilson in The Lavender List (BBC) 2006, After Life (ITV) 2006, Lillies (ITV) 2006, W H Auden in The Addiction of Sin (BBC) 2007, Tess of the D'Urbervilles 2008, Merlin 2008, The People's Poetry, Thirty Years of Poetry Please, The Forgotten Fallen, Harold Pinter: A Celebration (BBC), Night Watch (BBC), Upstairs Downstairs, Falcoln, The Silent and the Damned, Private Lillywhite is Dead, 37 Days (BBC 2); *Films* incl: Prospero's Books, Stealing Heaven, A Good Year, Man Dancin', Trauma, Vampira, Layer Cake, The Rising: Ballad of Mangal Pandey, Joseph Andrews, Hellraiser II, Fratello Sole, Sorella Luna, The Clot, Chocolat, Under Suspicion, The Last Yellow, Women Talking Dirty, Gangster No 1, Shiner, Born Romantic, Two Men Went to War, A Man Sat Next to Me..., Hot Fuzz, Oliver, Tale of a Vampire, The Boxer, The Curry Club, Valkyrie, Made in Dagenham, Five Days of War, The Wedding Video, Suspension of Disbelief, Closed Circuit, Maleficent, Hercules, the Legend Begins; *Theatre* RSC: Ivanov, The Iceman Cometh, School for Scandal; RNT: The UN Inspector, Flight, An Inspector Calls (also Br tour, Aldwych, Broadway American tour, nomination Best Actor Olivier Awards 1994), Kick for Touch, Cardiff East, From Kipling to Vietnam, The Caretaker, Strawberry Fields, Love Letters on Blue Paper, The Passion, The Country Wife, Old Movies, Larkrise, Madras House; Royal Court Theatre: Narrow Road to the Deep North, Early Morning, Saved, Ruffian on the Stair, Samuel Beckett's Play, Cascando, The London Cuckolds, Tibetan Inroads, Magnificence, Cheek, Owners, Geography of a Horse Dreamer, Tooth of Crime, No One Was Saved, Their Very Own and Golden City, Ubu Roi; West End: Loot, Comedians, Entertaining Mr Sloane; other prodns incl: Long Day's Journey into Night, Subject to Fits, Early Morning (Bristol Old Vic) 1975, Doctor's Dilemma (Mermaid Theatre), Le Main Sal (Almeida), Paul Bunyan (ROH), The Entertainer (Greenwich), Gaslight (The Old Vic) 2007, Loot, End Game (Beckett Centenary Dublin) 2006, Scrawdyke in Little Malcolm and his Struggle Against the Eunuchs (European tour, Watford Palace and Traverse Theatre Edinburgh), A Midsummer Night's Dream (Manchester Royal Exchange), The Homecoming (Almeida) 2008, A Month in the Country (Chichester), The Cherry Orchard (NT), The Herd (Bush Theatre); *Radio* The Barchester Chronicles, New Grub St, Sons and Lovers, Hard Times, Answered Prayers, Earthly Powers, Barrack Room Ballads, The Call of the Dead, Boswell's Life of Johnson, The Pantomime Life of Joseph Grimaldi, The West End Front, The Interrogation (3 series); *Publications* The Royal Court Theatre – Inside Out (2007); *Recreations* home, family, music, art, dining, friends, walking in London, drinking and thinking on rail journeys; *Style*— Kenneth Cranham, Esq; ✉ c/o Markham & Froggatt, 4 Windmill Street, London W1T 2HZ (☎ 020 7636 4412)

CRANSTON, Hon Mr Justice; Sir Ross Frederick Cranston; kt (2007); s of Frederick Hugh Cranston (d 1999), of Brisbane, Aust, and Edna Elizabeth, *née* Davies; *b* 23 July 1948; *Educ* Nundah State Sch, Wavell HS Brisbane, Univ of Queensland (BA, LLB), Harvard Univ (LLM), Univ of Oxford (DPhil, DCL); *m* 1, 5 March 1976 (m dis 1985), Prof (Barbara) Jane Stapleton, da of Colin Arthur Stapleton, of Sydney, Aust; m 2, 25 Aug 1988 (m dis 1998), Elizabeth Anna, da of Leslie Victor Whyatt, of Kent; 1 da (Imogen Molly); m 3, 16 Nov 2007, Hazel Valerie, da of Douglas Howard Phillips, of Birmingham; *Career* called to the Bar Gray's Inn 1976 (bencher 1998), recorder 1997–2007 (asst recorder 1991–97), QC 1998; lectr in law Univ of Warwick 1975–77, ANU 1978–86, Lubbock prof of banking law Univ of London 1986–92, dir Centre for Commercial Law Studies Queen Mary & Westfield Coll London 1989–92 (dean Faculty of Laws 1988–91), Cassel prof of commercial law Univ of London 1993–97, MP (Lab) Dudley N 1997–2005 (Parly candidate (Lab) Richmond (Yorks) 1992), Slr-Gen for England and Wales 1998–2001, Centennial prof of law LSE 2005–07, judge of the High Court of Justice (Queen's Bench Div) 2007–, judge in charge Administration Court 2016–; visiting prof Law Dept LSE 1997–2005 and 2007–; assessor Lord Justice Jackson's Review of Civil Litigation Costs 2009; chair: All-Pty Parly Gp on Alcohol Misuse 2002–05, All-Pty Parly Gp for the Bar 2002–05; conslt Ctee of Inquiry Concerning Public Duty and Private Interest 1979, memb Legal Advsy Panel Nat Consumer Cncl 1976–77 and 1987–97; conslt: World Bank, IMF, UNCTAD, Cwlth Secretariat, European Cmmn, Lord Woolf's Inquiry into Access to Justice 1994–96; pres SPTL 1992–93 (vice-pres 1991–92), chm Bd of Tstees Public Concern at Work 1996–97 (dep chm 1993–96), chair Soc of Lab Lawyers 2003–06; memb American Law Inst; Hon LLD Univ of Greenwich 2016; fell Australian Acad of Law 2015; FBA 2007; *Books* Cranston's Consumers and the Law (1978, 3 edn (jtly) 2000), Regulating Business (1979), Law and Economics (jt ed, 1981), Delays and Efficiency in Civil Litigation (jtly, 1984), Legal Foundations of the Welfare State (1985), Law, Government and Public Policy (1987), European Banking Law (1993, 2 ed 1999), The Single Market and the Law of Banking (ed, 1991, 3 edn 1995), Reform of Civil Procedure (jt ed, 1995), Legal Ethics and Professional Responsibility (ed, 1995), Making Commercial Law (ed, 1997), Principles of Banking Law (1997, 2 edn 2002), Banks, Liability and Risk (ed, 1990, 3 edn 2000), How Law Works (2006); *Clubs* Reform; *Style*— The Hon Mr Justice Cranston; ✉ Royal Courts of Justice, Strand, London WC2A 2LL

CRASNOW, Rachel; QC (2015); *Educ* Univ of Oxford (BA); *Career* called to the Bar 1994, specialist in equality and employment law; chair Police Appeal Tbnl 2015–; chair Legislation and Guidance Ctee Bar Cncl; memb: Ctee Employment Law Bar Assoc, Equality and Diversity Ctee Bar Cncl, Human Rights Lawyers' Assoc; *Books* Employment Law and Human Rights (2007), Family Rights at Work (2012); *Recreations* travel, camping; *Style*— Ms Rachel Crasnow, QC; ✉ Cloisters, 1 Pump Court, Temple, London EC4Y 7AA

CRATHORNE, 2 Baron (UK 1959); Sir (Charles) James Dugdale; 2 Bt (UK 1945), KCVO (2013), JP (N Yorks 1999); s of 1 Baron, TD, PC (d 1977), and Nancy, OBE (d 1969), da of Sir Charles Tennant, 1 Bt; *b* 12 September 1939, Sutton, Surrey; *Educ* Eton, Trinity Coll Cambridge; *m* 1970, Sylvia Mary (d 2009), da of Brig Arthur Montgomery, OBE, TD; 2 da (Hon Charlotte b 1972, Hon Katharine b 1980), 1 s (Hon Thomas Arthur John b 1977); *Heir* s, Hon Thomas Dugdale; *Career* with Sotheby and Co 1963–66, asst to pres Parke-Bernet NY 1966–69, James Dugdale and Associates London (ind fine art consultancy serv) 1969–77, James Crathorne and Assocs 1977–; fine art lectr, annual lectr tours to USA 1970–99, lecture series Met Museum NY 1981, Aust Bicentennial Lectr Tour 1988; dir: Cliveden Hotel 1985–97, Woodhouse Securities 1989–99, Cliveden plc 1997–98, Hand Picked Hotels Ltd 2001–02; chm: Captain Cook Tst 1993–2015 (tstee 1978–2015), Jt Ctee of the Nat Amenity Socs 1996–99; contribs to Apollo and The Connoisseur; memb: Cncl RSA 1982–88, Editorial Bd House Magazine 1983–, Exec Ctee Georgian Gp 1985–99 (chm 1990–99, pres 1999–2015), Yorks Regnl Ctee Nat Tst 1974–84 and 1988–94; elected memb House of Lords 1999–; hon sec: All-Pty Parly Arts and Heritage Gp 1981– (chm 2010–, co-chm 2015), All-Pty Photography Gp 1997–; memb Works of Art Sub-Ctee 1983–2002, chm Works of Art Ctee 2004–07; pres: Cleveland Assoc of Nat Tst 1982–94, Yarm Civic Soc 1987–2014, Cleveland Family History Soc 1988–, Middlesbrough Sea Cadets (Cleveland and S Durham Branch) 1988–2015, Hambledon Dist CPRE 1988–, Cleveland and N Yorks Magistrates Assoc 1997–2003, St John Ambulance N Yorks-Teesside 1999–, Yorks and Humberside RFCA 2006–14 (vice-pres 1999–2006); vice-pres: Cleveland Wildlife Tst 1990–, Public Monuments and Sculpture Assoc 1997–, N Yorks Co Scouts 1998–2014, North of England RFCA 2001–14; govr Queen Margaret's Sch York 1986–99; memb Ct: Univ of Leeds 1985–97, Univ of York 1999–, Univ of Hull 1999–2014; tstee National Heritage Memorial Fund 1992–95; patron: Attingham Tst for the Study of the Br Country House 1991–, Cleveland Community Fndn 1990–, Friends of the Public Record Office 1998–, MIMA (Middlesbrough Inst of Modern Art) 2014–; church warden All Saints Crathorne 1977–, pres Yorks Agricultural Soc 2014–15; HM Lord-Lt N Yorks 1999–2014 (DL: Cleveland 1983–96, N Yorks 1996–99); Freedom of the Town of Richmond N Yorks 2014, Freedom of the City of York 2015; Hon LLD Teesside Univ 2013, Hon LLD Univ of York 2015; Queen's Golden Jubilee Medal 2002, Queen's Diamond Jubilee Medal 2012; FRSA 1972 (memb Cncl RSA 1982–88), FSA 2009; KStJ 1999; *Exhibitions* Photographs (Middlesbrough Art Gallery) 1980, All-Pty Photography Gp annual exhbn (Westminster and touring) 1992–, Georgian Theatre Royal Richmond N Yorks 2005; *Books* Edouard Vuillard (1967), Tennants Stalk (jtly 1973), A Present from Crathorne (jtly, 1989), Cliveden: The Place and the People (1995), The Royal Crescent Book of Bath (1998), Parliament in Pictures (co-photographer, 1999); *Recreations* photography, travel, family life in the country, jazz; *Clubs* Pratt's, Garrick; *Style*— The Lord Crathorne, KCVO; ✉ Crathorne House, Yarm, North Yorkshire TS15 0AT (✆ 01642 700431, e-mail james.crathorne@btconnect.com); House of Lords, London SW1A 0PW (✆ 020 7219 5224, e-mail crathornej@parliament.uk)

CRAUSBY, David Anthony; MP; s of Thomas Crausby (d 1993), and Kathleen, *née* Lavin (d 2002); *b* 17 June 1946; *Educ* Derby GS Bury, Bury Coll of FE; *m* 4 Sept 1965, Enid, da of William Noon; 2 s (David, Jason); *Career* skilled turner (former apprentice), former full time works convenor; MP (Lab) Bolton NE 1997–; Speech of the Year House Magazine Awards 2011; *Recreations* watching football, cinema, walking; *Style*— David Crausby, Esq, MP; ✉ c/o Bolton North East Labour Party, 426 Blackburn Road, Bolton BL1 8NL (✆ 01204 303340); House of Commons, London SW1A 0AA (✆ 020 7219 3000)

CRAVEN, Sir John Anthony; kt (1996); s of William Herbert Craven, and Hilda Lucy Craven; *b* 23 October 1940; *Educ* Michaelhouse SA, Jesus Coll Cambridge (BA), Queen's Univ Kingston Ontario; *m* 1, 1961, Gillian Margaret, *née* Murray; 1 s, 1 da; m 2, 1970, Jane Frances, *née* Stiles-Allen; 3 s; m 3, 5 Dec 2007, Ning Ning, *née* Chang (d 2009); *Career* Clarkson Gordon & Co 1961–64, Wood Gundy 1964–67, S G Warburg & Co 1967–73 (dir 1969–73), chief exec White Weld & Co Ltd 1973–78, vice-chm S G Warburg & Co 1979, fndr and chm Phoenix Securities Ltd 1981–89, chief exec Morgan Grenfell Gp plc 1987–89, chm Deutsche Morgan Grenfell Gp plc (formerly Morgan Grenfell Gp plc) 1989–97, memb Bd of MDs Deutsche Bank AG 1990–96; non-exec chm: Tootal Gp plc 1985–90, GEMS Funds Hong Kong 1998–, Fleming Family & Ptnrs 2003–07 (non-exec dir 2001–); chm: Lonmin plc (formerly Lonrho plc)1996–2009, Patagonia Gold plc 2004–13; non-exec dir: Société Generale de Surveillence SA 1986–95, Rothmans International BV 1991–99, Ducati SpA 1992–2001, Reuters Holdings plc 1997–2004; memb: Ontario Inst of CAs, Canadian Inst of CAs; *Style*— Sir John Craven

CRAVEN, Prof John Anthony George; CBE (2013); s of George Marriot Craven (d 1989), and Dorothy Maude, *née* Walford (d 2003); *b* 17 June 1949; *Educ* Pinner GS, King's Coll Cambridge (Kennedy Meml Scholar, Adam Smith Essay Prize, Stephenson Essay Prize, MA), MIT; *m* 1974, Laura Elizabeth, da of Prof John Loftis; 1 s (Matthew Thomas b 1978), 1 da (Rebecca Mary b 1981); *Career* Univ of Kent: lectr in economics 1971–76, sr lectr 1976–80, reader 1980–86, prof of economics 1986–96, dean Faculty of Social Scis 1987–91, pro-vice-chllr 1991–93, dep vice-chllr 1993–96; vice-chllr Univ of Portsmouth 1997–2013; visiting assoc prof Univ of Guelph Canada 1982–83; memb Archbishops' Cncl 2006–13; tstee Nat Museum of the Royal Navy 2009–; Hon DSc Univeristi Teknologi Malaysia 2000, Hon DSc Univ of Southampton 2013, Hon LLD Univ of Portsmouth 2013; memb Royal Economic Soc 1971, FRSA; *Books* Distribution of the Product (1979), Introduction to Economics (1984, 2 edn 1989), Social Choice (1992); *Recreations* choral singing, charity trustee; *Style*— Prof John Craven, CBE

CRAVEN, John Raymond; OBE (2000); s of Bill Craven (d 1990), and Marie, *née* Noble (d 1989); *Educ* Leeds Modern GS; *m* 27 March 1971, Jean Marilyn, da of Alfred (Blackie) Howe, CBE (d 1974); 2 da; *Career* journalist and television presenter; presenter and later ed John Craven's Newsround (BBC) 1972–89, currently presenter Countryfile (BBC1); other TV credits incl: Swap Shop, Saturday Superstore, Animal Sanctuary, Castle in the Country, Craven's Collectables, Britain's Heritage Heroes, The John Craven Years, Beat the Brain; columnist BBC Countryfile Magazine; winner: BAFTA Award (for best children's TV documentary) 1975, Pye TV Award (for distinguished services to TV) 1983, TV Times Award (for top children's personality) 1983, elected memb RTS Hall of Fame 1996, awarded The Baird Medal RTS 2002; patron: Whale and Dolphin Conservation Soc, The Soc for the Protection of Animals Abroad; fell Linnean Soc; *Recreations* walking in the countryside, swimming, aviation; *Style*— John Craven, Esq, OBE, FLS; ✉ c/o Talent4Media Ltd, Studio LG16, Shepherds Building Central, Charecroft Way, London W14 0EH (✆ 020 7183 4330, e-mail enquiries@talent4media.com)

CRAVEN, Michael Anthony (Mike); s of Henry Craven (d 1996), and Hilary, *née* Willcox (d 2008); *b* 1 February 1959; *Educ* Marist Coll Hull, Univ of Hull (BA); *Career* advsr to Rt Hon John Prescott, MP , *qv*, 1983–87; md Market Access 1995–97 (dir 1988–95), dir of communications Lab Pty 1998, founding ptnr Lexington Communications 1998–; Parly candidate (Lab) 1983; dir Tablet Publishing Co; chm of govrs Cardinal Vaughan Meml Sch; *Recreations* walking, reading; *Style*— Mike Craven, Esq; ✉ 198 High Holborn, London WC1V 7BD (✆ 020 7395 8949, e-mail michael.craven@lexcomm.co.uk)

CRAVEN, Sir Philip; kt (2005), MBE; *b* 4 July 1950, Bolton, Lancs; *Educ* Bolton Sch, Univ of Manchester (BA); *Career* former wheelchair basketball player; achievements incl: Gold medal Cwlth Games 1970, Gold medal European Championships 1971, Gold medal World Championships 1973, Gold medal European Championships 1974, Bronze medal World Championships 1975, Silver medal European Championships 1993, Gold medal European Champions Cup 1994; co sec Br Coal Corp 1986–91; ceo Int Wheelchair Basketball Fedn 1994–98, performance dir GB Wheelchair Basketball Assoc Men's Wheelchair Basketball Team 1998–2002; chm GB Wheelchair Basketball Assoc 1977–80, 1984–87 and 1989–94, pres Int Wheelchair Basketball Fedn 1998–2002, pres Int Paralympic Ctee 2001–, memb Int Olympic Ctee 2003–, memb Exec Bd Br Olympic Assoc 2003–; *Style*— Sir Philip Craven, MBE; ✉ International Paralympic Committee (IPC), Adenauerallee 212–214, 53113 Bonn, Germany

CRAWFORD, Prof Alistair; s of John Gardiner Crawford (d 1991), of Fraserburgh, Aberdeenshire, and Mary Ann, *née* Holiday (d 1993), of Hull; *b* 25 January 1945; *Educ* Fraserburgh Acad, Glasgow Sch of Art (DA), Aberdeen Coll of Educn (Art Teacher's Cert); *m* 5 Nov 1971, Joan, da of Clifford Martin; *Career* art teacher Woodfarm HS Glasgow 1966–67, lectr in textile design Dept of Textile Industries Univ of Leeds 1968–71, sr lectr in graphic design Coventry Poly 1971–73; UCW Aberystwyth: lectr in graphic art 1974–83, sr lectr 1983–87, actg head Dept of Visual Art and curator of coll collections 1986–90, reader 1987–90, prof of art and keeper of coll collections 1990–98, head Dept of Visual Art 1990–93, head School of Art 1993–95, research prof of art 1995–2010; painter, printmaker, photographer, art historian, performer, writer and ind curator; columnist Inscape jl of photography 1999–; memb Int Advsy Bd European Soc for the History of Photography 2004–16 (also co-ed Photoresearcher (Vienna) of soc jl 2004–08); Br School at Rome: Balsdon sr fell 1995–96, tstee 1996–2000, archive res fell 1997–2001, fndr The Picturemakers (exhibition gp) 2006–; fell Printmakers' Cncl of GB 1978–93, MSTD 1977–97, FRSA 1983–86, MSIAD 1977–86 (ASIAD 1973), FRPS 1991–98, RCA 1993–2010; Hon RE 2000–, Hon ESHPh 2009–; *Solo Exhibitions* incl: Curwen Gallery London 1981, Segno Grafico Venice 1981, Centro Iniziative Per l'Arte e la Cultura Palazzo Kechler Udine 1981, Cartesius Gallery Trieste 1982, Italian Journal (Curwen Gallery London) 1983, Printworks Gallery Chicago 1983, The Spirit of Place (Wales and Scot touring) 1986–88, Barcelona Tango (Printworks Gallery Chicago and Aberystwyth) 1994–97, Vedute d'Italia (Casa Cinus Sardinia) 1994, It is in the Nature of My Gaze (Univ of Wales Aberystwyth) 1995, A Return to Wales, retrospective (Nat Library of Wales) 2000, Pictures for an even smaller room (Univ of Wales Aberystwyth) 2004–05, Landscape Capriccios (Univ of Wales Aberystwyth) 2004–06, North by North West (Jersey Arts Centre) 2006, Pictures for a small room (Toko Gall Aberystwyth, Rowley Gall London) 2006–07, Made from Wales (Brecknock Museum Brecon) 2007–08, Some Thoughts and Feelings, Retrospective (Nat Library of Wales) 2009; *Group Exhibitions* incl: 4 times 20 (Oriel Theatre Clwyd Mold and touring, with Norman Ackroyd, David Hockney and Terry Willson) 1981–82, Vedute d'Italia (Univ of Wales Aberystwyth and Wales touring 1987–88 and Printworks Gallery Chicago 1988), National Print Exhibition (Mall Galleries London) 2000, 2001 and 2002, Off Cuts (Bankside Gallery London) 2001, Prima Luce Fotografia da Edward Weston a Mario Giacomelli (Universita' Politecnica delle Marche, Ancona and Palazzo del Monte di Pietà Padova and tour) 2005; *Work in Collections* incl: Glasgow Sch of Art, Nat Museum of Wales, Hunterian Museum and Art Gallery Glasgow, Welsh Arts Cncl, SW Thames HA, Continental Bank Chicago, Mazda Cars (UK), Br Sch at Rome, P&O London, Fleetwood, Newport, Leicester, Norwich, Hove, Arbroath, Buckie, Carmarthen, Grimsby, Haverfordwest and Peterhead Museums, Br Cncl, Nat Library of Wales, Imperial Coll London, Contemporary Art Soc of Wales, Frito-Lay Corporation Dallas, Eton Coll, The Getty Group Chicago, Town Docks Museum Hull, Univ of Illinois Champaign, The Scottish Fisheries Museum Anstruther, MOMA Wales, United Airlines, The Royal National Mission to Deep Sea Fishermen London, Maritime Museum Great Yarmouth, American Dairy Assoc Chicago, Seidman Jackson & Fisher Chicago, Greenberger & Kaufmann Chicago, Morse-Diesel Engineering Co Chicago, F I Torchia & Associates Chicago, International Minerals Corp Northbrook Illinois, Ashmolean Museum Oxford, Aberdeen Maritime Museum, Penlee House Museum Penzance, Univs of Aberystwyth, Bangor, Leeds, Liverpool, Northampton and Swansea, Leighton Park Sch Reading, London Oratory Sch, West Bromwich Coll, Walsall Educn Authy, Coates Inks UK, Moore Stephens Accountants Jersey, Nat Screen and Sound Archive of Wales, Denbighshire CC, Brecknock Museum Brecon, Dingwall Library, Br Museum, North Tyneside Cncl, Tate Gallery Archive, Alistair Crawford Archive Nat Library of Wales; *Touring Exhibitions* as designer and curator incl: Elio Ciol photographer 1977–81, John Thomas 1838–1905 photographer (UK tour) 1977–81, Mario Giacomelli – a retrospective 1955–83 (Fotogallery Cardiff and tour) 1983–86, Carlo Bevilacqua Il Maestro (UW Aberystwyth and tour) 1987–90, Mario Giacomelli (Printworks Gallery Chicago) 1994, The Welsh Lens (MOMA Wales, Zirpoli Gallery Switzerland, Museo Genna Maria Sardinia) 1997–99, Immagini del passato, the photography of Father Peter Paul Mackey 1851–1935 (Museo Nazionale Sassari, Exma Cagliari Sardinia) 2000, Eric Lessing. Vom Festhalten der Zeit. Reportage-Fotografie 1948–1973 (Kunsthistorisches Museum Vienna) 2002; *Performance* incl: An Evening with Eugénie Strong (Tabernacle Arts Centre Machynlleth, Br Sch at Rome, Lambeth Palace, Aberystwyth Arts Centre, Drovers Festival Lampeter, Girton Coll Cambridge) 1996–, Brief Exposure (Tabernacle Arts Centre Machynlleth, Aberystwyth Arts Centre, Drovers Festival Lampeter, Jersey Arts Centre, Steiner Theatre London, Shrewsbury Visual Art Festival, Nat Library of Wales) 2001–; *Awards* incl: Welsh Arts Cncl/Editions Alecto Major Printmaking Award 1977, W Wales Arts Assoc Cmmn Award 1977, Welsh Arts Cncl Travel Award 1978, Br Cncl 1981, Sir Winston Churchill travelling fellowship in

Photography 1982, Royal Nat Eisteddfod Gold Medal in Fine Art 1985, Krazna-Krausz Photograhy Award 1992, Printmaker of the Month Gainsborough's House Suffolk 2013; *Publications* incl: John Thomas 1838–1905 Photographer (with Hilary Woollen, 1977), Mario Giacomelli (1985), Elio Ciol – Italia Black & White (1986), Carlo Bevilacqua (1986), Elio Ciol – Assisi (1991, 1992), Will Roberts (1994), Kyffin Williams (1995), It is in the Nature of My Gaze, Alistair Crawford Collected Photographs 1989–94 (1995), Robert Macpherson 1814–1872, the foremost photographer of Rome (1999), Immagini del passato, the photography of Father Peter Paul Mackey 1851–1935 (2000), Mario Giacomelli (2001, 2002, 2005 and 2006), Erich Lessing, Reportage-Photography 1948–1973 (2002, 2003 and 2005), Encyclopedia of Nineteenth-Century Photography (contrib, 2008), Robert Mcpherson 1814–1872 The Final Proof, ESHPh Vienna (2009), Mario Giacomelli La Figura Nera Aspetta il Bianco (2009); *Recreations* collecting, gardening; *Style*— Prof Alistair Crawford; ✉ 64 Dove House Meadow, Sudbury, Suffolk CO10 0GF (website www.alistaircrawford.co.uk)

CRAWFORD, Charles Graham; CMG (1998); s of Graham Wellington James Crawford, of Hemel Hempstead, Herts, and Edith Ellen, *née* Orrah; *b* 22 May 1954; *Educ* St Albans Sch, St John's Coll Oxford (BA), Lincoln's Inn (Part II Bar Exams), Fletcher Sch of Law and Diplomacy USA (MA); *m* 1990, Helen Margaret, *née* Walsh; 2 s (James b 1991, Robert b 1993), 1 da (Ellen b 1999); *Career* HM Dip Serv: Indonesia Desk FCO 1979–81, second then first sec (press/info) Belgrade 1981–84, Civil Aviation Desk then speechwriter FCO 1984–87, first sec (political) Pretoria/Cape Town 1987–91, Soviet then Eastern Dept FCO 1991–93, political cnsllr Moscow 1993–96, ambass to Bosnia and Herzegovina 1996–98, Weatherhead Center for Int Affrs Harvard Univ 1998–99, dep political dir FCO 1999–2000, ambass to Fed Repub of Yugoslavia 2001–03, ambass to Poland 2003–07; currently speechwriter and exec communication conslt, writer and mediator; contrib: BBC, The Independent, The Guardian, National Review Online, DIPLOMAT magazine, PunditWire, Radio Free Europe/Radio Liberty; fndr ptnr Ambassador Partnership LLP 2010; *Books* Speeches for Leaders (2016); *Recreations* chess, music; *Clubs* Beefsteak; *Style*— Mr Charles Crawford, CMG; ✉ e-mail charlescrawf@gmail.com, website www.charlescrawford.biz

CRAWFORD, Prof Dorothy Hanson; OBE (2005); da of Sir Theo Crawford (d 1993, pres RCPath 1969–72), and Margaret, *née* Green (d 1973); *b* 13 April 1945, Glasgow; *Educ* Univ of London (MB BS, MD, DSc), Univ of Bristol (PhD); *m* 1968, Dr William Alexander; 2 s (Daniel b 1970, Theodore b 1973); *Career* sr lectr and reader Royal Postgrad Medical Sch 1985–90, prof of medical microbiology LSHTM 1990–97, prof of medical microbiology Univ of Edinburgh 1997–2010 (emeritus prof of medical microbiology 2011–); asst princ Public Understanding of Medicine 2007–; FRCPath 1993 (MRCPath 1981), FRSE 2001, FMedSci 2001, FRCPE 2010; *Publications* The Invisible Enemy (2000), Deadly Companions (2007), Bodysnatchers to Lifesavers (jtly, 2010); author of more than 200 scientific papers; *Style*— Prof Dorothy Crawford, OBE

CRAWFORD, Ilse; MBE (2014); *Career* launched Br Elle Decoration 1989, vice-pres Donna Karan Home, fndr, creative dir and designer StudioIlse; founding head Man and Wellbeing Dept Design Acad Eindhoven; hon doctorate London Coll of Communication Univ of the Arts London; *Style*— Ms Ilse Crawford, MBE; ✉ Studioilse, Studio 1 Neckinger Mills, 162–164 Abbey Street, London SE1 2AN

CRAWFORD, Prof James Richard; AC (2013); s of James Allen Crawford, of Hahndorf, S Australia, and Josephine Margaret, *née* Bond; *b* 14 November 1948; *Educ* Univ of Adelaide (BA, LLB, Stow scholar), Univ of Oxford (DPhil); *m* 1, Marisa Luigina, *née* Ballini; 2 da (Rebecca Jane b 5 Aug 1972, Emily Jessica Teresa b 17 Aug 1975); m 2 (m dis), Patricia Hyndman; 2 da (Alexandra Vijayalalitha b 26 Sept 1992, Natasha Mihiri b 3 Jan 1994); m 3, Joanna Gomula; 1 s (James Tadeusz b 26 April 1999); *Career* Univ of Adelaide: lectr 1974–77, sr lectr 1977–82, reader 1982–83, prof of law (personal chair) 1983–86; cmmr Australian Law Reform Cmmn 1982–84 (pt/t cmmr 1984–90), Challis prof of int law Univ of Sydney 1986–92 (dean Faculty of Law 1990–92), Whewell prof of int law Univ of Cambridge 1992–, professorial fell Jesus Coll Cambridge 1992–, dir Lauterpacht Research Centre for Int Law 1997–2003 and 2006–; barr of High Court of Australia and of the Supreme Court of NSW (SC NSW 1997), memb of Matrix Chambers London; dir of studies Int Law Assoc London 1991–98; memb: Advsy Ctee on the Australian Judicial System The Constitutional Cmmn 1985–87, Institut de Droit Int 1991 (assoc 1985), UN Int Law Cmmn 1992–2001; judge Admin Tbnl OECD 1993–; hon bencher Gray's Inn 1991; FBA 2000; *Publications* The Creation of States in International Law (1981, Creative Scholarship award American Soc of Int Law, 2 edn 2006), The Rights of Peoples (ed, 1988), Australian Courts of Law (3 edn 1993, 4 edn 2004), The ILC's Articles on State Responsibility (2002), Brownlie's Principles of International Law (8 edn 2012), state Responsibility: The General Part (2013); *Recreations* cricket, reading, walking; *Style*— Prof James Crawford, AC, SC, LLD, FBA; ✉ Lauterpacht Research Centre for International Law, Cambridge CB5 8BL (✆ 01223 335358, fax 01223 311668, e-mail jrc1000@hermes.cam.ac.uk)

CRAWFORD, Lincoln; OBE (1998); s of Norman Crawford (d 1983), and Ena Crawford (d 1972); *b* 1 November 1946; *Educ* Univ Tutorial Coll London, Brunel Univ (LLB); *m* 1, 26 July 1976 (m dis), Janet, da of John Clegg (d 1987); 3 s (Douglas Luke b 4 Dec 1978, Paul David b 26 Aug 1981, Jack Justin b 7 Sept 1988); m 2, 5 June 1999, Bronwen, da of Clive Jenkins (d 1999); 1 da (Ella Charlotte 7 Jan 1999), 1 s (Mostyn Clive b 5 March 2001); *Career* called to the Bar 1977, recorder 1997–; advsr to Lord Scarman following Brixton disorders 1981, exec memb Prison Reform Tst; pt/t chm Employment Tbnls Judicial Studies Bd; chm: Inquiry into the care and treatment of Martin Mursell, Inquiry into the employment practices of the London Borough of Hackney, Standards Panel London Borough of Camden (Sleezebuster), Bar Race Relations Ctee, Champion of the Community Legal Services; memb: Cmmn for Racial Equality 1984, Parole Bd 1985–88, Br Boxing Bd of Control, Black-Jewish Forum; chm: Prince's Tst Sports Ctee 1989, Ind Adoption Serv; S of England chm Special Needs Appeals Panel FEFC; vice-chm Charta Mede Tst; participant Duke of Edinburgh Study Conf 1989, govr Hampstead Comprehensive Sch; Hon LLD Brunel Univ; *Recreations* squash, swimming; *Clubs* Commonwealth; *Style*— Lincoln Crawford, Esq, OBE; ✉ 12 Kings Bench Walk, Temple, London EC4 (✆ 020 7583 0811, fax 020 7583 7228)

CRAWFORD, Michael; CBE (2014, OBE 1987); *b* 19 January 1942; *Educ* St Michael's Coll Bexley, Oakfield Sch Dulwich; *Career* actor 1955–; in original prodn of Britten's Noyes Fludde and of Let's Make an Opera; *Theatre* incl: Come Blow Your Horn (Prince of Wales) 1961, Travelling Light 1965, The Anniversary 1966, No Sex Please We're British (Strand) 1971, Billy (Drury Lane) 1974, Same Time Next Year (Prince of Wales) 1976, Flowers for Algernon (Queen's) 1979, Barnum (Palladium) 1981–83 and (Victoria Palace) 1985–86, The Phantom of the Opera (Her Majesty's) 1986 (also NY 1988, LA 1989, and tour of USA, Canada, Aust and UK), The Music of Andrew Lloyd Webber 1991–92, EFX (MGM Grand Las Vegas) 1995, Dance of the Vampires 2002–03, The Woman in White 2004, The Wizard of Oz 2011–12; *Television* incl: Some Mothers Do 'Ave 'Em, Chalk and Cheese; *Film* incl: Soap Box Derby, Blow Your Own Trumpet, Two Left Feet, The War Lover, Two Living One Dead, The Knack 1964, A Funny Thing Happened on the Way to the Forum 1965, The Jokers, How I Won the War 1966, Hello Dolly 1968, The Games 1969, Hello and Goodbye 1970, Alice in Wonderland 1972, The Condorman 1980; *Albums* Michael Crawford performs Andrew Lloyd Webber (1991), A Touch of Music in the Night (1993), With Love (1994), In Concert (1998), On Eagle's Wings (1998), Christmas (1999), The Disney Album (2001); cast albums incl: Alice in Wonderland, Billy, Flowers For Algernon, Barnum, The Phantom of the Opera, Songs from the Stage and Screen (1987) EFX (1995); *Awards* Variety Club Award for Most Promising Newcomer (for The Knack), TV Times Awards for Funniest Man on TV (for Some Mothers Do 'Ave 'Em), Sun Award for TV Actor of the Year (for Some Mothers Do 'Ave 'Em), Variety Club Show Business Personality of the Year and Silver Heart Award (for Billy), Variety Club Show Business Personality of the Year (for Barnum) , Oliver Award for Best Actor in a Musical (for Barnum), Broadways' Tony Award (for Phantom of the Opera), Olivier Award for Best Actor in a Musical (for Phantom of the Opera), Drama Desk and Outer Critics Circle Award, Los Angeles' Dramalogue Award and Drama Critics Award; *Books* Parcel Arrived Safely, Tied with String (autobiography, 2000); *Style*— Michael Crawford, Esq, CBE

CRAWFORD, Prof Michael Hewson; s of Brian Hewson Crawford, and Margarethe Bettina, *née* Nagel; *b* 7 December 1939; *Educ* St Paul's, Oriel Coll Oxford (MA), Br Sch at Rome (scholar); *Career* Jane Eliza Procter visiting fell Princeton Univ 1964–65; Christ's Coll Cambridge: res fell 1964–69, fell 1969–86, lectr 1969–86; prof of ancient history UCL 1986–; visiting prof: Univ of Pavia 1983, École Normale Supérieure Paris 1984, Univ of Padua 1986, Sorbonne Paris 1989, Univ of San Marino 1989, Univ Statale Milan 1990, Univ of L'Aquila 1990, Univ of Pavia 1992, École des Hautes Etudes Paris 1997, École des Hautes Etudes en Sciences Sociales Paris 1999, Univ of Trento 2007, Univ of Naples Federico II 2009; jt dir: Excavations of Fregellae 1980–86, Valpolcevera Project 1987–94, Veleia Project 1994–95, S Martino Project 1996–2003; chm Jt Assoc of Classical Teachers 1992–95 (chm Ancient History Ctee 1978–84), vice-pres Roman Soc 1981–; tstee Entente Cordiale Scholapships 2000, memb UK Research Reserve Bd 2010–; ed: Papers of the Br Sch at Rome 1975–79, Jl of Roman Studies 1980–84; Joseph Crabtree orator 2000; hon fell UCL 2009–10; foreign memb Istituto Lombardo 1990, memb Academia Europaea 1995, Reial Acadèmia de Bones Lletres 1998, corresponding memb Académie des Inscriptions et Belles-Lettres Paris 2006; FBA 1980; Officier de l'Ordre des Palmes Académiques de la République Française 2001; *Books* Roman Republican Coin Hoards (1969), Roman Republican Coinage (1974), Archaic and Classical Greece (with D Whitehead, 1982), Coinage and Money under the Roman Republic (1985), La Moneta in Grecia e a Roma (1986), L'impero romana e la struttura economica e sociale delle province (1986), The Coinage of the Roman World in the Late Republic (ed with A Burnett, 1987), Medals and Coins from Budé to Mommsen (ed with C Ligota and J B Trapp, 1991), Antonio Agustin between Renaissance and Counter-reform (ed, 1993), Roman Statutes (ed, 1996), Imagines Italicae (2011); contribs to Annales, Economic History Review, Jl of Roman Studies, Oxford DNB; *Style*— Prof Michael Crawford; ✉ Department of History, University College, Gower Street, London WC1E 6BT (✆ 020 7679 7396)

CRAWFORD, (Jeremy) Patrick Stewart; CB (2013); s of late Sir Stewart Crawford, GCMG, CVO, and late Mary Katherine Corbett; *b* 16 September 1952, London; *Educ* Eton, Worcester Coll Oxford (BA), Coll of Law; *m* Charlotte Elizabeth Cecily, *née* Burnaby-Atkins; 3 da, 1 s; *Career* formerly: md and global head of project and export finance Deutsche Bank, md Emerging Africa Advsrs Standard Bank London Ltd; chief exec Export Credits Guarantee Dept until 2012, chief exec The Charity Bank Ltd 2012–; non-exec dir: Crossrail Ltd, Emerging Africa Infrastructure Fund 2015–, Community Devpt Finance Assoc 2015–; tstee The Caxton Tst (operating as Catch Up) 2014–; *Style*— Patrick Crawford, Esq, CB; ✉ c/o The Charity Bank Ltd, Fosse House, 182 High Street, Tonbridge, Kent TN9 1BE

CRAWFORD, Prof Robert; s of Robert Alexander Nelson Crawford (d 1997), and Elizabeth Menzies Crawford; *b* 23 February 1959; *Educ* Hutchesons' GS Glasgow, Univ of Glasgow (MA), Univ of Oxford (DPhil); *m* 2 Sept 1988, Alice, *née* Wales; 1 s (Lewis Robert b 17 June 1994), 1 da (Blyth Iona b 14 Aug 1996); *Career* poet and critic; Elizabeth Wordsworth jr research fell St Hugh's Coll Oxford 1984–87, Br Acad post doctoral fell Univ of Glasgow 1987–89; Univ of St Andrews: lectr in modern Scottish literature 1989–95, prof 1995–, head Sch of English 2002–05; poetry ed Polygon 1992–99; pres: Classical Assoc 2015–16, Classical Assoc of Scotland 2016–17; FRSE 1998, fell English Assoc 1998, FBA 2011; *Awards* Scot Arts Cncl Book Award 1992 and 1999, selected as one of the best 20 UK New Generation Poets Arts Cncl of Eng 1994, recommendation Poetry Book Soc 1990, 1992, 1996, 2003 and 2005, Saltire Scottish Research Book of the Year Award 2007, Saltire Scottish Book of the Year Award 2009; *Poetry* major works: A Scottish Assembly (1990), Sharawaggi (with WN Herbert, 1990), Talkies (1992), Masculinity (1996), The Penguin Book of Poetry from Britain and Ireland since 1945 (ed with Simon Armitage, 1998), Spirit Machines (1999), The New Penguin Book of Scottish Verse (ed with Mick Imlah, 2000), The Tip of My Tongue (2003), Selected Poems (2005), Apollos of the North (2006), Full Volume (2008), Simonides (2011), Testament (2014), Chinese Makars (2016); *Prose* works incl: The Savage and the City in the Work of TS Eliot (1987), Devolving English Literature (1992, 2 edn 2000), Identifying Poets (1993), The Modern Poet (2001), Scotland's Books: The Penguin History of Scottish Literature (2007), Full Volume (2008), The Bard: Robert Burns – A Biography (2009), The Beginning and the End of the World (2011), On Glasgow and Edinburgh (2013), Bannockburns: Scottish Independence and Literary Imagination, 1314–2014 (2014), Young Eliot (2015); *Recreations* walking, painting; *Style*— Prof Robert Crawford; ✉ School of English, University of St Andrews, St Andrews, Fife KY16 9AL (✆ 01334 462666, fax 01334 462655, e-mail rc4@st-and.ac.uk)

CRAWFORD, Prof Robert James; *b* 6 April 1949; *Educ* Lisburn Tech Coll, Queen's Univ Belfast (BSc, PhD, DSc); *m* 1974, Isobel Catherine (Renee) Allen; 2 s, 1 da; *Career* tech serv engr Plastics Div ICI; Queen's Univ Belfast: lectr 1974–82, sr lectr 1982–84, reader 1984–88, actg head of dept 1988–89, prof 1989–2005, head Sch of Mech and Process Engrg 1989–2005, pro-vice-chllr 2001–05; prof of mech engrg Univ of Auckland 1999–2001, vice-chllr Univ of Waikato 2005–; dir: Rotosystems Ltd 1991–2005, Hughes and McLeod Ltd 1991–, University Bookshop Ltd 1993–99; memb Bd of Invest NI 2002–05; external examiner to univs throughout Ireland and UK; conslt to various bodies Ireland and abroad; former chm Plastics and Rubber Inst (PRI) NI, former memb Ctee NI Branch IMechE; winner: various awards of PRI 1979–92, Engrg Employers' Fedn Trophy 1992; memb: Soc of Plastics Engrs, Polymer Processing Soc; CEng, FIM, FIMechE, FREng 1997; *Books* Mechanics of Engineering Materials (jtly, 1987, latest edn 1996), Plastics and Rubber – Engineering Design and Applications (1985), The Packing of Particles (jtly, 1987), Mechanics of Engineering Materials (jtly, 1987), Mechanics of Engineering Materials – Solutions Manual (jtly, 1987), Rotational Moulding of Plastics (ed, 1992, 2 edn 1996), Plastics Engineering (3 edn, 1997), Rotational Moulding Technology (jtly, 2002), Practical guide to Rotational Moulding (jtly, 2012); also contrib various other books and author of numerous articles in professional and learned jls; *Style*— Prof Robert Crawford, FREng; ✉ The University of Waikato, Gate 1, Knighton Road, Private Bag 3105, Hamilton, New Zealand

CRAWFORD, Sir Robert William Kenneth; kt (2007), CBE (2002); s of Hugh Merrall Crawford (d 1982), of West Bergholt, Colchester, Essex, and Mary, *née* Percival (d 2001); *b* 3 July 1945, Colchester, Essex; *Educ* Culford Sch, Pembroke Coll Oxford (BA); *m* 9 Dec 1975, Vivienne Sylvia, da of Boghdan Andre Polakowski; 1 da (Helen b 1984), 1 s (Alistair b 1987); *Career* Imperial War Museum: research asst 1968–71, head research and info office 1971–89, keeper Dept of Photographs 1975–83, asst dir 1979–82, dep DG 1982–95, DG 1995–2008; chm: UK Nat Inventory of War Memls 1995–2008, Nat Museums Dirs Conf 2001–06; tstee: IWM Devpt Tst 1982–2008, Sir Winston Churchill Archives Tst 1995–2006, Holdsworth Tst 1995–, Florence Nightingale Museum 1999–2011, Royal

Logistic Corps Museum 2000–13, Fleet Air Arm Museum 2000–10, Horniman Museum & Public Park Tst 2001–13, Nat Maritime Museum 2008–16, Nat Museum of the Royal Navy 2008–; memb Bd: mda (Europe) 1998–2006, Nat Historic Ships Ctee 2000–06, Greenwich Fndn for the Old Royal Naval Coll 2007–14 (chm 2011–14), Chatham Historic Dockyard Tst 2008–; tstee Nat Museums Liverpool 2009–15, vice-patron Army Museums Ogilby Tst, vice-patron Evacuees Reunion Assoc, vice-pres Fedn of Merchant Mariners, tstee RN Submarine Museum 2014–; Freeman City of London 1998, Liveryman Worshipful Co of Glovers 1998; *Clubs* Special Forces, Royal Over-Seas League; *Style*— Sir Robert Crawford, CBE

CRAWFORD, Susan Louise (Mrs Jeremy Phipps); da of late Lt Cdr Wilfrid Hornby Crawford, RN, and late Patricia Mary, *née* McCosh; *b* 11 May 1941; *Educ* St Denis Sch Edinburgh, Prior's Field Godalming, Studio Simi Florence Italy; *m* 12 Oct 1974, Jeremy Joseph Julian Phipps, s of Lt Alan Phipps (ka 1943); 1 s (Jake Shimi Alan b 29 Aug 1975), 1 da (Jemma Louise Rose b 21 July 1977); *Career* artist and equestrian portrait painter; portrait cmmns incl: HM The Queen (mounted, twice), HRH The Prince of Wales, HM Queen Elizabeth the Queen Mother (for the Black Watch Regt), HRH The Princess Margaret, Countess of Snowdon (for The Royal Highland Fusiliers), HRH The Princess Royal (mounted), HH The Sultan of Brunei and HM Sultan Qaboos of Oman, 24 Epsom Derby winners, 4 of Frankel and steeplechasers incl Red Rum, Arkle and Desert Orchid; collections worldwide; work exhibited at: The Royal Scot Acad, The Nat Portrait Gallery, The Royal Acad of Arts, The Royal Soc of Portrait Painters, The Queen's Gallery, V&A, The National Gallery of Pahang Pinang Malaysia, Arthur Akermann & Son, The David Ker Gallery, The Tryon Gallery, Nat Horseracing Museum Newmarket, Royal Soc of Portrait Painters; *Style*— Susan Crawford; ✉ Heathfield House, Bonchester Bridge, Hawick, Roxburghshire TD9 8JB (✆ 01450 860668, website www.slcrawford.com)

CRAWLEY, Baroness (Life Peer UK 1998), of Edgbaston in the Co of West Midlands; Christine Crawley; *b* 9 January 1950; *Educ* Notre Dame Sch Plymouth, Digby Stuart Trg Coll Roehampton; *Career* former drama teacher and youth theatre leader, town and dist cncllr in Oxon, Parly candidate (Lab) SE Staffs 1983; MEP (Lab) Birmingham East 1984–99; European Parl: chair Women's Rights Ctee 1989–94, dep leader European PLP 1994–99, memb Civil Liberties Ctee and Women's Rights Ctee; Baroness in Waiting (Govt whip) House of Lords 2002–08; chm Women's Nat Cmmn 1999–2002, chm W Midlands Regnl Cultural Consortium 1999–2002; pres Trading Standards Inst; memb: Fabian Soc, Co-operative Party; *Recreations* grandchildren, reading, walking; *Style*— The Rt Hon Baroness Crawley; ✉ e-mail crawleyc@parliament.uk

CRAWSHAW, Gillian Anne (Jill); da of William Sumner Crawshaw (d 1983), and Trudy, *née* Riding; *Educ* West Kirby GS for Girls, St Anne's Coll Oxford (MA); *m* 1973, Stephen Rudolf Danos, s of Sir Laszlo Danos (d 1935); 2 s (Toby William Laszlo b 1974, Dominic Stephen Robert b 1977); *Career* freelance travel writer for numerous publications 1966–71; travel ed: Daily Mail 1971–82, Evening Standard 1982–87, Sunday Express and Sunday Express Magazine 1987–92, The European 1992–93; currently weekly travel columnist The Times; regular contrib to various magazines, radio and TV progs incl: The Observer, Landmark Travel TV; sole travel contrib The Doomsday Book project; three times Travel Writer of the Year, commended Br Press Awards, twice awarded French Govt Writers' Awards, Scottish Special Writer of the Year 1997, Travel Journalist of the Year 1997, Top Foreigners Prize Franciacorte 2000; memb Br Guild of Travel Writers; *Books* Holidays with Children at Home & Abroad (1982); *Recreations* Oriental carpets, Georgian architecture, skiing, obsessional travel, food, deserts; *Style*— Mrs Jill Crawshaw; ✉ Pond House, 54 Highgate West Hill, London N6 6DA (✆ 020 8340 0307, fax 020 8348 3782)

CRAY, Rt Rev Graham Alan; s of Alan Cray (d 1997), and Doris Mary Kathleen, *née* Hann (d 1963); *b* 21 April 1947, Croydon; *Educ* Trinity Sch of John Whitgift Croydon, Univ of Leeds (BA), St John's Coll Nottingham; *m* 14 July 1973, Jaqueline, *née* Webster; 2 da (Catherine Ann b 29 Sept 1979, Sarah Emma b 29 Dec 1982); *Career* curate St Mark's Gillingham 1971–75, Northern co-ordinator Youth Dept Church Pastoral Aid Soc 1975–78, vicar St Michael-le-Belfrey York 1978–92, princ Ridley Hall Cambridge 1992–2001, six-preacher Canterbury Cathedral 1997–2002, bishop of Maidstone 2001–09; asst bishop: Diocese of Canterbury 2009–14, Diocese of York 2009–, Diocese of Rochester 2011–14; York diocesan advocate for pioneer ministry and fresh expressions of church 2015–; visiting fell St John's Coll Durham 2016–; chm Soul Survivor Tst; *Publications* David Watson – A Portrait by his Friends (contrib, 1985), By My Spirit (contrib, 1988), In Spirit and Truth (contrib, 1989), The Gospel and Tomorrow's Culture (1994), To Proclaim Afresh (contrib, 1995), Building a Relational Society (contrib, 1996), The Post-Evangelical Debate (contrib, 1997), John Wimber – His Influence and Legacy (contrib, 1998), Postmodern Culture and Youth Discipleship (1998), Mass Culture (contrib, 1999), Christ and Consumerism (contrib, 2000), Being Culturally Relevant (2000), Youth Congregations and the Emerging Church (2002), Mission-Shaped Church (report, 2004), Scriptural Truth in a Postmodern Age (contrib, 2006), Making Sense of Generation Y (contrib, 2006), The Future of the Parish System (contrib, 2006), Mission Shaped Youth (contrib, 2007), Disciples and Citizens (2007), The Heart of Faith (contrib, 2008), Faith in the Future (contrib, 2008), The Art of Compassion (contrib, 2008), Discerning Leadership (2010), Who's Shaping You? (2010), New Monasticism As Fresh Expression of Church (ed and contrib, 2010), The Holy Spirit in the World Today (contrib, 2011), The Gospel After Christendom (contrib, 2012), Fresh Expressions of Church and the Kingdom of God (ed and contrib, 2012), Growing Disciples in Fresh Expressions of Church (2013), On Not Knowing the End at the Beginning (2013), Denominations and the Missional Church (2016), Discernment the Key to Planting Missional Churches (2016), The Journey Towards Missions (contrib, 2016); *Recreations* listening to rock music, reading theology, following sport; *Style*— The Rt Rev Graham Cray; ✉ The Dovecote, Main Street, Kirby Misperton, North Yorkshire YO17 6XL (✆ 01653 669365, e-mail grahamcray@me.com)

CRAYMER, Judy Sarah Jarman; MBE (2007); da of Leslie Craymer (d 2000), of London, and Betty, *née* Jarman (d 2002); *b* 26 October 1957, London; *Educ* Mount Sch Mill Hill, Guildhall Sch of Music and Drama; *Career* stage mangr: Leicester Haymarket Theatre 1979, Cats orig London prodn 1981; asst to Tim Rice 1982, exec prodr London prodn Chess 1984, film and TV prodr 1989–97, prodr (49 prodns worldwide) Mamma Mia! 1999–, prodr film Mamma Mia! 2008 (Women in Film ITV Achievement of the Year Award 2008), prodr Viva Forever! 2012; prodn sponsor Donmar Warehouse Theatre; Woman of the Year (arts) 2002, Humanitarian Award Breast Cancer Research Fndn (BCRF) NY 2010; ambass Br Showjumping; FGSM 2006; *Books* Mamma Mia!: How can I resist you? (co-author with Benny Andersson and Björn Ulvaeus); *Recreations* theatre, music, equestrian and National Hunt racing; *Style*— Miss Judy Craymer, MBE

CREAGH, Mary; MP; *b* 2 December 1967, Coventry; *Educ* Bishop Ullathorne Comp Coventry, Pembroke Coll Oxford, LSE; *Career* cncllr Islington BC 1998–2005, leader Lab Gp Islington BC 2000–04; MP (Lab) Wakefield 2005–; shadow sec for the environment, food and rural affrs 2010–13, shadow sec for transport 2013–14, shadow sec for int development 2014–; lectr Cranfield Sch of Mgmnt 1997–2005, tstee Rathbone Training 1998–2005; memb: Fabian Soc, Amnesty Int, RNID; *Recreations* yoga, reading, cycling; *Style*— Ms Mary Creagh, MP; ✉ House of Commons, London SW1A 0AA (e-mail mary@marycreagh.co.uk)

CREAMER, Brig Dr Ian Stephen; MC (1973); s of Joseph and Ruth Creamer; *b* 31 May 1942; *Educ* St Joseph's Coll Blackpool, Univ of Liverpool Med Sch, LSHTM (MSc), Army Staff Coll; *Children* 1 da (Dr Samantha Gardner); *Career* MO Southport Gen Infirmary 1966–67, locum neurosurgical houseman Mil Hosp Colchester 1967; army MO: NI 1968, Catterick Camp Yorks 1968–69, BAOR Minden 1969–71, Weeton Camp Lancs 1971–72; regtl MO 1 Bn The King's Regt 1972–74, second in cmd 19 Field Ambulance Colchester 1974–76, psc 1976, med staff offr HQ 1 Armoured Div BAOR 1978–80, CO 1 Armoured Field Ambulance 1980–83, sr lectr in preventive med Royal Army Med Coll 1984–85, Br liaison offr (med) to USA and Canada 1985–87, dep cdr med Br Army of the Rhine 1987–90, CO 33 Gen Surgical Hosp Al Jubayl Saudi Arabia 1990–91, CO Cambridge Mil Hosp Aldershot 1991–92, DACOS Med HQ UK Land Forces 1992–94, cdr med 3 UK Div 1994–97, cdr med 5 Div 1997–2000, dir Army Primary Health Care Project 2000–02, specialist advsr Care Quality Cmmn; vice-pres Three Ships Appeal Trinity Sailing Tst 2004–; MRCS, LRCP, memb Inst of Health Mgmnt 1993; FCIM 1992, FFPHM 1999; OStJ 2000; *Publications* numerous papers in med jls; *Recreations* offshore sailing, skiing, gliding, scuba diving, painting; *Clubs* Army and Navy, Royal Torbay Yacht; *Style*— Brig Dr Ian Creamer, MC; ✉ Owl Corner, 4 Parkhill Road, Torquay, Devon TQ1 2AL (e-mail owlman1@blueyonder.co.uk)

C

CREASEY, Richard John; s of John Creasey, MBE (d 1973), and (Evelyn) Jean, *née* Fudge; *b* 28 August 1944; *Educ* Malvern; *m* 1, 5 Jan 1968, Wendy; 2 s (Simon b 19 July 1972, Guy b 1 May 1974), 1 da (Sarah b 19 Jan 1980); m 2, 4 June 1999, Vera; *Career* Granada TV: researcher 1965–72, prodr 1972–74; ATV Network: prodr 1974–77, exec prodr 1977–78, head of documentaries 1978–81; Central TV: controller of features 1981–90, dir of special projects 1990–94; fndr Siguy Films 1987–; dir of factual progs Meridian Broadcasting 1992–94, ed-in-chief The Digital Village 1995–2001, exec prodr BBC New Media 2001–04, dir BUR Media Gp 2004–09, md BFC Media 2009–; expdn ldr Ford London-New York Overland Challenge 1993–94; chm Soviet Br Creative Assoc 1989–99, co fndr and emeritus chm Television Tst for the Environment (TVE); memb BAFTA; *Style*— Richard Creasey, Esq; ✉ 11 Regent's Park Road, London NW1 7TL (✆ 020 7482 6549, e-mail richard@richardcreasey.net)

CREBER, Frank Paul; s of Dr Geoffrey Tremain Creber and Hilda, *née* Lewey (d 1994); *b* 12 January 1959; *Educ* Dr Challoner's GS Amersham, Univ of Newcastle upon Tyne (BA), Chelsea Sch of Art (MA); *m* 1982, Marguerite Honor Blake, da of Rev Canon Peter Douglas Stuart Blake; 2 s (Theodore Sebastion Peter b 1983, Nicholas Tremaine b 1986); *Career* artist; notable works incl: White Light/Yellow Light 1987, Within One Flame go Two As One 1987, Open State 1988, Man with Bird 1989, Cliff Dance 1990, The Bather 1991, White Rock 1991, The Family 1993, The Planets 1995, Community Picnic 2004; exhibitions incl: Barclays Bank Young Painters Competition (Henry Moore Gallery, RCA London) 1987, Picker Fellowship Show (Kingston Poly) 1988, two man show Diorama Gallery London 1988, solo show Sue Williams Gallery Portobello Rd London 1988, 1989, 1991 and 1992, Picker Fellows at Kingston (Watermans Art Centre Brentford) 1989, Artist of The Day (Flowers East London) 1989, two person show Paton Gallery 1990, gp show ROI at Lloyd's London 1990, Painting Today (auction at Bonham's Knightsbridge) 1991, Where Art Meets Community (Tobacco Dock London) 1992, Bow's Arts (Sedgewick's Aldgate East London) 1992, Inner City Blues (gp show, Barbican Concourse Gallery) 1993, gp show (Great Banquet Exhibition Banqueting House Whitehall) 1995, gp show Homerton Hosp London 1996, solo show Mosaic Highgate London 1996, Travelling Light (Big Issue Clerkenwell Road London) 1997, Picker Fellows (Stanley Picker Gallery Kingston) 1997, Community Action Network London 1998, Arthur Anderson Group Show 1998, solo show Stanton Guildhouse 1999, gp show Community Action Network Haymarket London 2000, gp show Middlesex Hosp London 2000, solo show Art Space Gallery London 2004, 2006 and 2008; exhibitions organised and curated: Art Meets Community (Tobacco Dock London) 1992, gp show (Bow's Arts Gallery London) 1992, Inner City Blues (Barbican) 1993; works in collections: Unilever plc, Arthur Andersen & Co, Art for Hosps, Stanhope Construction Ltd, Leicestershire Collection, Int Business Machines; artist in residence The Bromley-by-Bow Centre London 1992–, artist in residence Water City E London 2005–12; awards: prizewinner Avon Open (Artsite Gallery Bath) 1984, prizewinner Brewhouse Open (Taunton) 1985, Herbert Read fellowship Chelsea Sch of Art 1986, jt winner Barclays Bank Young Painters award 1987, Picker fellowship Kingston Poly (now Kingston Univ) 1987–88; FRSA; *Recreations* sailing; *Style*— Frank Creber, Esq; ✉ 49 Darnley Road, Hackney, London E9 6QH (✆ 020 8533 5104, e-mail frankcreber@yahoo.co.uk); The Bromley-by-Bow Centre, 1 Bruce Road, London E3 3HN (✆ 020 8980 4618, fax 020 8880 6608, website www.bbbc.org.uk)

CREED, Martin; *b* 1968, Wakefield, W Yorks; *Educ* Slade Sch of Fine Art; *Career* artist; winner Turner Prize 2001; *Solo Exhibitions* incl: Mothers (Hauser & Wirth London) 2011, Martin Creed: Paintings (Johnen Galerie Berlin) 2011, 'Martin Creed: Work No. 200 (Musée d'Art Moderne et d'Art Contemporain (MAMAC) Nice) 2011, Martin Creed: Works (Museo dArte Contemporánea de Vigo (MARCO) Spain) 2011, Sightings: Martin Creed (Nasher Sculpture Center Dallas Texas) 2011, Martin Creed: Collected Works (Rennie Collection Vancouver) 2011, Things/Cosas (Sala Alcalá 31 Madrid) 2011, Work No. 1059 (Scotsman Steps Edinburgh) 2011, Tardis Projects: Martin Creed (Tardis House Truro) 2011, Martin Creed: Work No. 700 (Yorkshire Sculpture Park Wakefield) 2011, Martin Creed: Wanting to Say Hello (CAC Bukovje Landskrona Sweden) 2012, Work No. 965: Half the air in a given space (Cleveland Art Museum Ohio) 2012, House of Art (?eské Bud?jovice Czech Republic) 2012, Michael Lett (Auckland NZ) 2012, Martin Creed (Museo de Arte de Lima Peru) 2012, Martin Creed Plays Chicago (Museum of Contemporary Art Chicago) 2012, Work No. 268: Half the air in a given space (Pavement Gallery Manchester) 2012, Martin Creed at Sketch (Sketch London) 2012, Artist Rooms: Martin Creed (Tate Liverpool) 2012, Martin Creed: Scales (Aldrich Contemporary Art Museum Ridgefield CT) 2013, Artist Rooms: Martin Creed (Ferens Art Gallery Hull) 2013, Galleria Lorcan O'Neill Rome 2013, Hauser & Wirth NY 69th Street and Gavin Browns enterprise NY 2013, 'Work No. 1513: Half the air in a given space (THEMUSEUM Ontario, Canada) 2013, Work No. 1562: Half the Air in a Given Space (Museum De Paviljoens Almere Netherlands) 2013, Work No. 202 (Nat Gallery of Canada Ottawa) 2013, Artist Rooms: Martin Creed, Work No. 227: The lights going on and off (Tate Britain) 2013, The Warhol Pittsburgh Pennsylvania 2013, Work No. 1676: All the Bells – 3 minutes at 19:00 (Nuit Blanche Paris) 2013, Martin Creed: Whats the Point of It? (Hayward Gallery London) 2014, 'Martin Creed (Johnen Galerie Berlin) 2014, ARTIST ROOMS Martin Creed (Quay Arts Isle of Wight) England 2014; *Group Exhibitions* incl: Open House (Singapore Biennale) 2011, 8½ : a selection of works from the exhibitions organized by the Fondazione Nicola Trussardi from 2003 to the present (Stazione Leopolda Florence) 2011, 'Summer Collection Display (Tate St Ives Cornwall) 2011, ILLUMInations (Venice Biennale) 2011, Art and the City: Das Festival für Kunst im öffentlichen Raum in Zürich-West (Zurich) 2012, Art Returns to Art (Galleria dell'Accademia, Musei del Polo Florence) 2012, 2012–1 Building: Art in Relation to Architecture (Hiroshima MOCA City Museum of Contemporary Art Japan) 2012, Rhythm in it. On rhythm in contemporary art (Aargauer Kunsthaus Switzerland) 2013, The Universal Addressability of Dumb Things (Nottingham Contemporary) 2013, Simon Starling Commission at Tate Britain 2013, Optical Mix (Australian Centre for Contemporary Art Victoria Australia) 2014, Art or Sound (Fondazione Prada Venice) 2014, The Line (The Royal Docks London) 2014; *Recordings* incl: Thinking/Not Thinking (CD, 2011), Where You Go (CD, 2012), Die (CD, 2012), Fuck Off (CD, 2012), Love To You (CD and Vinyl, 2012), Youre The One For Me (Single Version) (CD, 2012), Chicago (CD, 2012), Mind Trap (CD, 2014); *Publications* Works (2010); *Style*— Martin Creed, Esq; ✉ c/o Hauser & Wirth, 23 Savile Row, London

W1S 2ET (☎ 020 7287 2300, fax 020 7287 6600, e-mail london@hauserwirth.com, website www.hauserwirth.com)

CREER, (Dahlis) Virginia; da of Cdre Bruce Loxton, RAN (ret), of Sydney, Aust, and Dahlis Ailsa, *née* Robertson; *b* 4 February 1948; *Educ* Ascham Sch Sydney Aust, Univ of Sydney (BA); *m* 1971, David Victor Charles Creer, s of Victor Charles Hamish Creer; 1 s (Benjamin Fulke Matthew b 7 Sept 1976), 1 da (Camilla Dahlis Elizabeth b 12 July 1979); *Career* Mktg Div Unilever Ltd 1969–72, asst brand mangr then brand mangr Schweppes Ltd 1972–77 (mktg mangr 1976), account dir Grey Advertising Ltd 1978–80; Davidson Pearce Ltd: sr planner 1980, Bd dir 1982, agency devpt dir 1985–87, exec planning and devpt dir 1987–88; asst md BMP Davidson Pearce Ltd 1988–89, managing ptnr BMP DDB Needham Ltd 1989, jt md BMP 4 1990–2000, ptnr The Yardley Creer Partnership 2000–; memb: Mktg Soc 1976, MRS 1980, IPA 1982, Forum 1992; *Recreations* running, riding, sailing; *Clubs* Women's Advertising Club of London, Royal Sydney Golf; *Style—* Mrs Virginia Creer

CREESE, Prof Sadie; *Career* dir of strategic progs Trusted Info Mgmnt Div QinetiQ until 2007, prof and dir of e-security Int Digital Lab Univ of Warwick 2007–11, dir Cyber Security Centre Univ of Oxford 2011–15, dir Global Centre for Cyber Security Capacity Building and co-dir Inst for the Future of Computing Oxford Martin Sch, currently prof of cybersecurity Dept of Computer Science Univ of Oxford; *Style—* Prof Sadie Creese; ✉ Department of Computer Science, Wolfson Building, Parks Road, Oxford OX1 3QD

CREGEEN, Peter Geoffrey; s of Geoffrey Hugh Stowell Cregeen (d 1980), and Viola Gertrude Dorothea, *née* Butler (d 2012); *b* 28 January 1940; *Educ* St Christopher's Sch Hove, Hove Coll, Guildhall Sch of Music and Drama; *m* Carole, da of Frederick Walker; 3 da (Lucy b 5 May 1969, Maria b 23 Aug 1971, Emma b 6 April 1974), 1 s (Tom (twin) b 6 April 1974); *Career* actor Palace Theatre Watford 1959–60, dir and actor Salisbury Playhouse 1960–63 (returned as assoc artistic dir 1969), television dir 1964–87 for BBC (also prodr), ATV, Yorkshire TV, LWT (also prodr) and Thames TV (also prodr), exec prodr The Bill (Thames) 1988, head of drama series BBC Television 1989–93, prodr BBC 1994–95, prodn dir Stoll Moss Theatres 1995–97 (conslt 1998–), TV dir Pearson Television and Cloudnine NZ 1998 (TV dir Pearson Television 1999 and 2000), TV prodr and dir Bentley Productions 1999, exec prodr LWT United Productions 2001–02, TV dir BBC Television 2003–, devpt exec prodr IA Prodns 2003–04, dir of play Finborough Theatre London 2011, co-dir of nat tour play Yvonne Arnaud Theatre Guildford 2012; conslt D L Tafner 1998; dir Ludlow Festival 1982–84, memb Bd Museum of Richmond 2011–; lectr: Guildhall Sch of Music and Drama 2004–, East 15 Acting Sch 2004–08, Guildford Sch of Acting 2004–11, Acad of Live and Recorded Arts 2005–15; drama and speech examiner Trinity Guildhall 2005–15, guest lectr The Drama Centre 2015; memb Cncl: Dirs' Guild of GB 1988, RTS 1989–92, BAFTA 1992–97; memb Bd: Actors Centre 1989– (chm 1995–2011), TAPS 1994–2007 (chm 1997–2007), Jerusalem Productions 1998– (chm 1999–), Tara Arts 2003–12, Arts Richmond 2016–; FGS; *Recreations* cinema, theatre, travel; *Style—* Peter Cregeen, Esq; ✉ Park Cottage, 237 Petersham Road, Petersham, Richmond, Surrey, TW10 7AW (☎ 020 8408 0800, e-mail petercregeen@aol.com)

CRERAR, Lorne Donald; s of Ronald Crerar, of Wester Ross, and Isobel Scott, *née* Pollock; *b* 29 July 1954, Renfrewshire; *Educ* Kelvinside Acad, Univ of Glasgow (LLB, Shaws Stewart Meml Prize and Bennet Miller Prize for Best Private Law Student); *m* 1, 29 Oct 1994 (m dis), Susan Mary, da Gerard Reilly; m 2, 14 June 2013 (m dis), Touzid Zahran; *Career* qualified slr 1978; ptnr Mackenzie Robertson & Co 1979–87, Harper Macleod: founding ptnr and chm 1987–, co-founding ptnr Business Law Div, head Commercial Property Dept and Banking Law Unit; non-exec chm InsureDirect.co.uk; chair Banking Law Univ of Glasgow 1997–2015; chm Scottish Rugby Union Discipline Ctee 1995–, judicial offr Int Rugby Bd 1995–, chm Discipline European Rugby Cup Ltd 1999–, chm Discipline 6 Nations Ltd 1999–; dep chm Scottish Enterprise Glasgow 2000–03, chm Sub-Gp Housing Improvement Task Force 2001–03; convenor Standards Cmmn for Scotland 2003–07, non-exec dir Justice Dept Scottish Govt until 2011, ind memb Purchasers Information Advsy Gp 2005–08, chm Ind Review of Audit, Regulation, Inspection and Complaints Handling in the Public Sector (The Crerar Review) 2006–08, ind reviewer of Lending Code 2010–11 (covering all aspects of personal and small business lending in the UK); memb Bd Highlands and Islands Enterprise 2007–11, chm Highlands and Islands Enterprise 2011–, chm Highlands and Islands Audit Ctee 2011–12, memb Advsy Bd Scottish Investment Bank 2011–; memb Editorial Bd World Sports Law Report; listed as sports law expert in Chambers Guide to the Legal Profession; memb Law Soc of Scotland; FCIB; *Publications* Stair Memorial Encyclopaedia for financial institutions, banking and currency (commissioned author, 2000), The Law of Banking in Scotland (2000, 2 edn 2007); *Recreations* hill walking, fishing, travel; *Clubs* Arlington Baths; *Style—* Prof Lorne Crerar; ✉ Harper Macleod, 45 Gordon Street, Glasgow G1 3PE (☎ 0141 221 8888, fax 0141 226 4198)

CRESSWELL, Jeremy Michael; CVO (1996); s of John Cresswell (d 1982), and Jean, *née* Lewis; *b* 1 October 1949, Windsor; *Educ* Sir William Borlase's Sch Marlow, Exeter Coll Oxford (BA), Johannes-Gutenberg Univ Mainz; *m* 1, 1974 (m dis 2006), Ursula Petra, *née* Forwick; 1 da (Julia b 1978), 1 s (David b 1985); m 2, 2009, Dr Barbara Munske; *Career* diplomat; entered HM Dip Serv 1972, desk offr West African Dept FCO 1972–73, third then second sec (Chancery) Brussels 1973–77, second then first sec (Chancery) Kuala Lumpur 1977–78; FCO: desk offr Trade Relations and Export Dept 1978–81, private sec Parly Under Sec's Office 1981, private sec Min of State's Office 1982; dep political advsr British Mil Govt Berlin 1982–86, dep head of dept Press Office FCO 1986–88, asst head of dept South America Dept FCO 1988–90, cnsllr and head of Chancery UK Delgn to NATO Brussels 1990–94, dep head of mission Prague 1995–98, sr dir RCDS 1998, head Western European Dept FCO 1998–99, head EU (Bilateral) Dept FCO 1999–2001, min and dep head of mission Berlin 2001–05, high cmmr to Jamaica and the Cwlth of the Bahamas 2005–09; dir Oxford Univ Foreign Service Prog 2010–; fell Kellogg Coll Oxford 2010; *Recreations* choral music, sport (especially tennis); *Style—* Mr Jeremy Cresswell; ✉ Oxford University Foreign Service Programme, Rewley House, 1 Wellington Square, Oxford OX1 2JA (☎ 01865 270366, e-mail jeremy.cresswell@conted.ox.ac.uk)

CRESSWELL, Dr Lyell Richard; s of Jack Cecil Cresswell (d 1986), and Muriel Minnie, *née* Sharp (d 1982); *b* 13 October 1944; *Educ* Victoria Univ of Wellington NZ (BMus), Univ of Toronto (MusM), Univ of Aberdeen (PhD); *m* 4 Jan 1972, Catherine Isabel, da of Keith James Mawson, of Otaki, NZ; *Career* composer; works incl: Concerto for Violin and Orchestra 1970, Salm 1977, Prayer for the Cure of a Sprained Back 1979, The Silver Pipes of Ur 1981, Le Sucre du Printemps 1982, O! 1982, Concerto for Cello and Orchestra 1984, The Fallen Dog 1984, Our Day Begins at Midnight 1985, To Aspro Pano Sto Aspro 1985, Speak For Us Great Sea 1985, A Modern Ecstasy 1986, The Pumpkin Massacre 1987, Sextet 1988, Passacagli 1988, Ixion 1988, Voices of Ocean Winds 1989, Ylur 1990, Il Suono di Enormi Distanze 1993, Dragspil 1995, Concerto for Orchestra and String Quartet 1997, KAEA (trombone concerto) 1997, Of Whirlwind Underground 1999, The Voice Inside (concerto for violin and soprano) 2001, Shadows Without Sun 2004, The Money Man (opera) 2009, Concerto for Piano and Orchestra 2010, The Clock Stops (song cycle for baritone and orchestra) 2013; memb: British Acad of Composers and Songwriters, Composers Assoc of NZ; various works recorded on Continuum label and Linn, NMC, Metier and Naxos Records; Inaugural Elgar Bursary 2002, SOUNZ Contemporary Award 2011; Hon DMus Victoria Univ of Wellington 2002; *Recreations* illustrating the book of Ezekiel; *Style—* Dr Lyell Cresswell; ✉ 4 Leslie Place, Edinburgh EH4 1NQ (☎ 0131 332 9181)

CRESWELL, Alexander Charles Justin; s of Sir Michael Justin Creswell, KCMG (d 1986), and Baroness Charlotte Mea thoe Schwartzenberg en Hohenlandsberg (d 2002); *b* 14 February 1957; *Educ* Winchester, W Surrey Coll of Art & Design, Byam Shaw Sch of Drawing & Painting; *m* 4 July 1992, Mary Curtis, da of John Green, of Calamansac, Cornwall; 1 s (Theodore b 1999), 2 da (Cicely b 2000, Constance b 2003); *Career* artist; tutor The Prince of Wales's Inst of Architecture London 1992–99; official artist HRH The Prince of Wales's tour of Central Europe 1998; memb: Inst of Classical Architecture, Int Network for Traditional Building Architecture and Urbanism; pres Ewhurst Village Soc; Arthur Ross Award for Excellence in the Classical Tradition (Fine Art) NY 2008; fell Royal Soc for Encouragement of Arts (RSA); Knight of the Order of Francis the First (KFO); *Exhibitions* contrib numerous gp exhbns 1982–; solo: White Horse Gallery London 1982, 1983 and 1984, Anima Gallery London 1983, Jonathan Poole Gallery London 1983, 1985 and 1987, Sally Le Gallais Gallery Jersey 1984, Addison Ross Gallery London 1984, 1985, 1986 and 1990, Crake Gallery Johannesburg 1984, Bulstrode Gallery London 1985, Brussels Europa Hotel 1985, Ritz Hotel London 1987, Fine Art Trade Guild Gallery London 1989, Arthur Andersen & Co London 1989, Spink & Son London 1991, 1994 and 1997, Atlantic Hotel Jersey 1991, Cadogan Gallery London 1992, China Club Hong Kong 1995, Grange Park Opera Hampshire 1998, New Academy Gallery 1999, Windsor Castle 2000, Br Cncl Touring Exhbn to Slovenia, Bulgaria and Romania 2000, John Martin of London 2000 and 2002, Hirschl & Adler NYC 2001, 2004, 2006, 2010, 2012 and 2015, ArtLondon 2007, Portland Gallery 2008, 2009 and 2010, Majlis Gallery Dubai 2008 and 2009, touring exhbn Summers Place Auctions Sussex and Grange Park Opera 2013, Watts Contemporary Gallery Compton 2015 and 2016; *Commissions* incl: HM The Queen, Duchy of Cornwall, The Royal Collection, The Duchess of Northumberland, English Heritage, Parliamentary Art Coll, Coutts Bank, Royal Bank of Scotland, HSBC, The BBC, London Capital Club, The Frick Collection NYC and significant private cmmns throughout Europe, ME, Far East and Russia; *Books* The Silent Houses of Britain (1991), Out of the Ashes – Watercolours of Windsor Castle (2000); *Television* 40-minute documentary for Central Television (1993); *Recreations* gardening, sailing, classic cars; *Clubs* Art Workers Guild, Port Navas Yacht, Vela al Terzo (Venice), Bentley Drivers, Royal Cornwall Yacht, Farmers (London); *Style—* Alexander Creswell, Esq; ✉ Copse Hill, Ewhurst, Surrey (☎ 01483 277311, e-mail info@alexandercreswell.com, website www.alexandercreswell.com)

CREWE, Candida Annabel; da of Quentin Hugh Crewe (d 1998), and Angela Maureen Huth, *qv*; *b* 6 June 1964; *Educ* The Manor Sch Great Durnford, St Mary's Sch Calne, Headington Sch Oxford; *m* Jan 1997; 2 s; *Career* bookshop asst 1983–86, jr ed Quartet Books Ltd London 1985–86, journalist weekly column London Evening Standard 1985–86; freelance journalist 1986–: The Spectator, The Guardian, The Independent, The Times, The Daily Telegraph, The Sunday Telegraph, The Observer, The Sunday Times, Tatler, Harpers & Queen, Marie-Claire, You Magazine, The Evening Standard; *Awards* runner-up for Catherine Pakenham meml award for Journalism 1987, winner Catherine Pakenham award for Journalism 1990, shortlisted for the John Llewellyn Ryhs meml award for Falling Away 1997; memb PEN Int; *Books* Focus (1985), Romantic Hero (1986), Accommodating Molly (1989), Mad About Bees (1991), Falling Away (1996), The Last to Know (1998); *Recreations* photography; *Clubs* Groucho; *Style—* Miss Candida Crewe

CREWE, Prof Sir Ivor Martin; kt (2006), DL (Essex 2002); s of late Francis Crewe, of West Didsbury, Gtr Manchester, and late Lilly Edith, *née* Neustadtl; *b* 15 December 1945; *Educ* Manchester Grammar, Exeter Coll Oxford (MA), LSE (MSc); *m* 3 July 1968, Jill Barbara, da of late Dr Theo Gadian, of Salford, Gtr Manchester; 1 da (Deborah b 1972), 2 s (Ben b 1974, Daniel b 1977); *Career* asst lectr Dept of Politics Lancaster Univ 1967–69, jr research fell Nuffield Coll Oxford 1969–71; Univ of Essex: lectr 1971, sr lectr 1974, dir ESRC data archive 1974–82, prof Dept of Govt 1982–2013, pro-vice-chllr (academic) 1992–95, vice-chllr 1995–2007; master Univ Coll Oxford 2008–; chair: 1994 Gp of Univs 1998–2001, Fndn Degree Gp DfES 2000–03; Eng and NI Cncl Universities UK 2001–03; pres Universities UK 2003–05, pres Acad of Social Sciences 2014–, chair of tstees HE Policy Inst 2015–; memb Governing Body: SOAS London, Univ of the Arts London, European Univ Inst Florence; co-dir British Election Study 1973–82, ed British Jl of Political Sci 1977–82 and 1984–92; commentator on elections and public opinion for Channel 4, The Guardian and The Observer; memb: Political Studies Assoc, American Political Studies Assoc; hon fell Exeter Coll Oxford 1998, hon fell Nuffield Coll 2008; Hon DLitt Univ of Salford, Hon D Univ Essex; High Steward Colchester 2003–; *Books* A Social Survey of Higher Civil Service (1969), Decade of Dealignment (1983), The British Electorate 1963–1987 (1991), SDP: The Birth, Life and Death of the Social Democratic Party (1995), The New British Politcs (1998, 3 edn 2004), The Blunders of our Government (2013); *Recreations* music, mountain walking, skiing; *Clubs* Oxford and Cambridge; *Style—* Prof Sir Ivor Crewe; ✉ University College, Oxford OX1 4BH (☎ 01865 276600)

CREWE, Susan Anne; da of late Richard Cavendish, and late Pamela Cavendish; *b* 31 August 1949; *Educ* St Mary's Sch Wantage, Cheshire Coll of Agric; *m* 1, 1970 (m dis), Quentin Crewe; 1 s (Nathaniel Richard b 1971), 1 da (Charity b 1972); m 2, 1984 (m dis), Nigel Ryan; *Career* journalist, freelance writer and broadcaster; contrib: The Times, Daily Telegraph, Evening Standard, Literary Review; social ed Harpers & Queen 1991–92, ed House & Garden 1994–2014 (currently conslt ed); fndr Friends of the Rehabilitation of Addictive Prisoners Tst (Rapt), tstee ASAP (African Solutions to African Problems); *Recreations* gardening, riding, travelling, theatre, music; *Clubs* The Academy; *Style—* Mrs Susan Crewe; ✉ House & Garden, Vogue House, Hanover Square, London W1S 1JU (☎ 020 7499 9080)

CRIBBENS, Dr Alan Hugh; MBE (1993); s of Eddie Victor Cribbens (d 2001), and Stella, *née* Penwill (d 2002); *b* 1 November 1942; *Educ* Aylesbury GS, UCL (BSc Eng, PhD); *m* 1, 1968 (m dis 2003), Christine Lesley, da of Leslie James Schofield; 2 da (Sarah Catherine b 1971, Emma Jane b 1974); m 2, 2003 (m dis 2010), Linda, da of Norman Domkowicz; m 3, Oct 2015, Stephanie Gay Taylor; *Career* engr; trained Marconi Wireless Telegraph Co 1961–62; BR: various appointments R&D Div 1970–76, team ldr Electronic Interlocking 1976–81, head Microelectronics Unit R&D Div (responsible for devpt of Solid State Interlocking, the standard railway signalling system in the UK) 1981–88, head Safety Critical Systems Unit BR Res 1988–94, technical strategist BR Res 1994–97; conslt to railway signalling industry 1997–; visiting prof in railway engrg ICSTM 2002–03; FIEE 1986 (MIEE 1972), FIRSE 1991 (Hon FIRSE 2008), FREng 2001; *Publications* Microwave polarisation measurements of four solar radio bursts (1969), High time resolution swept-frequency microwave polarimeter (1970), Microprocessors in Railway Signalling: The Solid State Interlocking (1987), Solid State Interlocking (SSI): an integrated electronic signalling system for main line railways (1987), Long distance transmission of safety information for the Solid State Interlocking (1989), The application of advanced computing techniques to the generation and checking of SSI data (1992), SSI – Ten Years of Electronic Interlocking (1995); *Recreations* walking, gardening, music, DIY; *Style—* Dr Alan Cribbens, MBE, FREng; ✉ High Barn, Hognaston, Ashbourne, Derbyshire DE6 1PR (e-mail alan.cribbens@btconnect.com)

CRICHTON, District Judge Nicholas; CBE (2012); s of late Charles Ainslie Crichton, and late Vera Pearl McCallum, *née* Harman-Mills; *b* 23 October 1943; *Educ* Haileybury, Queens Univ Belfast (LLB); *m* 29 March 1973 (m dis), Ann Valerie, da of late Col John Eliot Jackson, of Lopcombe Corner, Wilts; 2 s (Simon b 25 Feb 1975, Ian b 12 Jan 1977); m 2, 20 May 2014, Mrs Jane Maskell; *Career* admitted slr 1970; asst slr Currey & Co 1970–71 (articled 1968–70), ptnr Nicholls Christie & Crocker 1974–86 (asst slr 1972–74);

district judge (Magistrates' Court) 1987–2014, ret (dep district judge 2014–), recorder of the Crown Court 1995– (asst recorder 1991–95); memb Family Justice Cncl; *Recreations* cricket, golf, watching rugby, gardening, birdwatching, walking, grandparenting; *Style*— District Judge Crichton, CBE; ✉ c/o Inner London and City Family Proceedings Court, 59–65 Wells Street, London W1A 3AE

CRICK, Charles Anthony; s of Maurice Arthur Crick, TD (d 1979), of Peterborough, and Margaret Matilda, *née* Edney (d 2001); *b* 7 May 1949; *Educ* Oundle, UCL (LLB); *m* 1997, Jennifer Claire, *née* Luckham; 2 c; *Career* admitted slr 1974, articled clerk and asst slr Allen and Overy 1972–80, asst slr Middleton Potts and Co 1980–81, ptnr D J Freeman and Co 1981–96, dir Numis Corp plc 1996–2004, head of corp fin Numis Securities Ltd 1996–2004, ptnr Longbow Capital LLP 2005–; Freeman City of London Slrs' Co 1986; memb Law Soc; *Recreations* golf, music, painting; *Clubs* Hunstanton Golf, The Addington Golf, Royal Aberdeen; *Style*— Charles Crick, Esq

CRICKHOWELL, Baron (Life Peer UK 1987), of Pont Esgob in the Black Mountains and County of Powys; (Roger) Nicholas Edwards; PC (1979); s of (Herbert Cecil) Ralph Edwards, CBE, FSA (d 1977), and Marjorie Ingham Brooke; *b* 25 February 1934; *Educ* Westminster, Trinity Coll Cambridge (MA); *m* 1963, Ankaret, da of William James Healing, of Kinsham House, Glos; 1 s (Hon Rupert Timothy Guy b 1964), 2 da (Hon Sophie Elizabeth Ankaret b 1966, Hon Olivia Caroline b 1970); *Career* 2 Lt Royal Welch Fusiliers 1952–54; employed at Lloyd's by Wm Brandt's 1957–76 (memb Lloyd's 1968–2002), chief exec Insurance Gp; dir: Wm Brandt's Ltd 1974–76, R W Sturge (Holdings) Ltd 1970–76, PA International and Sturge Underwriting Agency Ltd 1977–79, Globtik Tankers Ltd 1976–79, Ryan International plc and subsids 1987–89, Associated British Ports Holdings plc 1987–99; dep chm Anglesey Mining plc 1988–2000; chm: ITNET plc 1996–2004, HTV Group Ltd 1997–2002 (dir 1987–97); MP (Cons) for Pembroke 1970–87 (ret), memb Shadow Cabinet and Cons Front Bench spokesman on Welsh Affairs 1977–79, sec of state of Wales 1979–87; chm: Advsy Ctee Nat Rivers Authy 1988–89, Nat Rivers Authy 1989–96; memb Ctee Automobile Assoc 1988–98; pres: Univ of Wales Cardiff 1988–98, Contemporary Art Soc for Wales 1988–93, SE Wales Arts Assoc 1987–94; Hon LLD Univ of Glamorgan; hon fell Cardiff Univ; *Books* Opera House Lottery: Zaha Hadid and the Cardiff Bay Opera House (1997), Westminster, Wales and Water (1999), The Conservative Party and Wales (2006), The Rivers Join (2009); *Recreations* fishing, gardening, collecting drawings and watercolours; *Clubs* Brooks's; *Style*— The Rt Hon Lord Crickhowell, PC; ✉ 4 Henning Street, London SW11 3DR; Y Cwt Mochyn, Manson Lane, Monmouth NP25 5RD

CRIDLAND, John; CBE (2006); *Educ* Christ's Coll Cambridge; *Career* DG CBI 2011–15 (joined 1982); *Style*— John Cridland, Esq, CBE; ✉ c/o CBI, Cannon Place, 78 Cannon Street, London EC4N 6HN

CRIGMAN, David Ian; QC (1989); s of Jack Crigman (d 1987), and Sylvia, *née* Rich; *b* 16 August 1945; *Educ* King Edward's Sch Birmingham, Univ of Leeds (LLB); *m* 20 Aug 1980, Judith Ann, da of Mark Penny; 1 s (Sam Mark b 7 April 1982); *Career* called to the Bar Gray's Inn 1969, recorder of the Crown Court 1985–; *Books* What's Truth Got To Do With It? (2006), The Molecule Man (2008), In Death We Trust (2009), The Hangman's Fracture (2011); *Recreations* writing, tennis, skiing; *Style*— David Crigman, Esq, QC; ✉ St Philips Chambers, 55 Temple Row, Birmingham B2 5LS (☎ 0121 246 7000, fax 0121 246 7001, e-mail dcrigman@st-philips.co.uk)

CRIPPS, Michael Frederick (Mike); s of late Maj Charles Philip Cripps, TD, and Betty Christine, *née* Flinn; *b* 22 October 1947, Brighton; *Educ* Felsted, Medway Coll (HNC); *m* 23 April 1982, Carolyn Louise, da of Elie Gabriel Farah; 3 s (Alexander Timothy James (step s) b 1974, Nicholas Frederick b 1985, Christopher Philip b 1988); *Career* exec search; dist mangr Johnson Group 1969–72, branch mangr Drake Conslts 1972–73; Cripps Sears & Partners Ltd: ptnr 1973–78, chm and md 1978–; memb Bd Transearch International 1997–99, memb Agilium Worldwide 2003–; memb Ctee Japan Assoc 1990–2001; MIPM, MEI; FInstD 1985; *Recreations* sport generally, rowing, cricket, golf, opera, reading, tennis, walking, rugby football, cycling, sailing, people, travel, contemporary and classical live music; *Clubs* City of London, MCC, Bembridge Sailing; *Style*— Mike Cripps; ✉ Cripps Sears & Partners, 1 Chancery Lane, London WC2A 1LF (☎ 020 7440 8999, e-mail london@crippssears.com, website www.cripssears.com)

CRISP, Dr Adrian James; s of Bertram William Crisp (d 1999), and Mary Louise Crisp (d 1999); *b* 21 November 1948; *Educ* Univ Coll Sch London, Magdalene Coll Cambridge (MA, MB BChir, MD), Univ Coll Hosp London (Filliter Exhibitioner in Pathology); *m* 1, 6 July 1974 (m dis 2005), Lesley Roberta; 1 s (Alasdair James Gavin b 1977 d 1990), 1 da (Alison Victoria b 1979); m 2, 25 Aug 2009, Ronia Julie, da of Emeritus Prof Robert Lovell Reid (d 1997), and Catherine Helen Macgregor (d 1980); *Career* house offr and SHO UCH and Northwick Park Hosp Harrow 1974–78, med registrar UCH 1978–80, sr registrar Guy's Hosp 1980–85, res fell Massachusetts Gen Hosp and Harvard Univ 1982–83; Addenbrooke's Hosp Cambridge: conslt rheumatologist 1985–2014, dir Bone Density Unit 1989–91, postgrad clinical tutor 1990–97; conslt rheumatologist: Newmarket Hosp 1985–2013, Princess of Wales Hosp Ely 1993–2013, Saffron Walden Hosp 2003–13; in private medical practice Spire Cambridge Lea Hosp 1988–; Univ of Cambridge: assoc lectr 1985–2014, dir of studies in clinical med 1992–2013, fell Churchill Coll 1993–, assoc dean Clinical Sch 1998–2003, chm Churchill Archives Ctee Churchill Coll 2014–; assoc postgrad dean (pre-registration house offrs) Eastern Deanery 2003–05; Woodward Scholar-elect in History Wadham Coll Oxford 1966; memb: Br Soc for Rheumatology (past chm Educn and Trg Ctee), Bone Research Soc, Nat Osteoporosis Soc; DRCOG 1977, FRCP 1991 (MRCP 1977); *Publications* Oxford Textbook of Rheumatology (contrib), Blackwell's Textbook of Diabetes (contrib), Management of Common Metabolic Bone Disorders (jtly); *Recreations* Twentieth Century history and politics, East Anglian and Scottish Borders gardening, British films; *Clubs* RSM; *Style*— Dr Adrian Crisp; ✉ Radfield, 4 Pound Farm Barns, Weston Colville, Cambridge CB21 5NZ (e-mail adrianjamescrisp@gmail.com)

CRISP, James; *b* 11 October 1982, Nottingham; *Career* Paralympic swimmer; achievements incl: 3 Gold medals (100m backstroke, 200m individual medley and 4x100m freestyle relay), 2 Silver medals (100m butterfly and 4x100m medley relay) and 2 Bronze medals (100m freestyle and 400m freestyle) Paralympic Games 2000, 3 Silver medals (400m freestyle, 100m backstroke and 100m breaststroke) and Bronze medal (200m individual medley) Paralympic Games 2004, Gold medal (400m freestyle), Silver medal (4x100m medley relay) and 2 Bronze medals (200m individual medley and 100m backstroke) World Championships 2006, Silver medal (100m backstroke) and Bronze medal (400m freestyle) Br Championships 2010, Silver medal (100m backstroke) and Bronze medal (400m freestyle) World Championships 2010, Silver medal (100m backstroke) Br Championships 2011, Gold medal (100m backstroke), Silver medal (200m individual medley) and 3 Bronze medals (400m freestyle, 4x100m freestyle relay and 4x100m medley relay) European Championships 2011, Silver medal (200m individual medley) and Bronze medal (100m backstroke) Br Championships 2012, Silver medal (100m backstroke) Paralympic Games 2012; *Style*— Mr James Crisp; ✉ Twitter @jcrispy24

CRISP, Baron (Life Peer UK 2006), of Eaglescliffe in the County of Durham; Sir (Edmund) Nigel Ramsay; KCB (2003); *b* 14 January 1952; *Educ* Uppingham, St John's Coll Cambridge (MA); *m* 1 May 1976; 1 s, 1 da; *Career* Halewood Community Cncl 1973–76, Trebor Ltd 1977–81, Cambridgeshire Community Cncl 1981–86, unit gen mangr East Berks HA 1986–92; chief exec: Heatherwood and Wexham Park Hosps NHS Tst 1992–93, Oxford John Radcliffe Hosp NHS Tst 1993–97; regnl dir NHS Exec: South Thames Region 1997–99, London Region 1999–2000; chief exec NHS 2000–06, perm sec Dept of Health 2000–06; chair SightSavers 2008–16; chair King's Advsy Bd on Global Health 2011–; hon fell St John's Coll Cambridge 2008, visiting fell Harvard Sch of Public Health 2010–15; fell Inst of Health Serv Mgmnt, Hon FRCP 2004, Hon FRCPath 2010, Hon FRCOG 2011, foreign assoc Inst of Medicine 2013, hon FRCPsych 2016, hon fell Faculty of Public Health 2016; *Books* Turning the World Upside Down (2010), 24 Hours to Save the NHS (2011), African Health Leaders (2014), One World Health (2016); *Style*— The Rt Hon the Lord Crisp, KCB

CRISPE, Simon Leslie Hare; *b* 31 July 1955, New Zealand; *Educ* BArch (NZ); *m* 28 April 1979, Marianne Denise; 2 c; *Career* assoc dir Lister Drew and Associates (before acquisition by W S Atkins) 1989–91, tech dir W S Atkins 1993–; projects incl: project mangr Chicago Beach Resort Dubai 1993–95 (project design dir 1997–99), project design dir BA World Cargo Centre UK 1995–97, commercial dir W S Atkins and Ptnrs Overseas Dubai 2000–; ARCUK, RIBA; *Recreations* motor sport, classic car restoration, wood carving and cabinet making; *Clubs* Daimler and Lanchester Owners', Porsche Club of GB, Ferrari Owners; *Style*— Simon Crispe, Esq; ✉ W S Atkins, Woodcote Grove, Ashley Road, Epsom, Surrey KT18 5BW (☎ 01372 726140, fax 01372 740055, e-mail scrispe@wsatkins-dxb.co.ae)

CRITCHLOW, His Hon Judge Christopher Allan; DL (Surrey 2009); s of Charles Brandon Critchlow (d 1996), and Eileen Marjorie, *née* Bowers (d 2014); *b* 8 July 1951; *Educ* Royal GS Lancaster, Univ of Exeter (LLB), Inns of Court Cncl of Legal Educn; *m* 7 Sept 1974, Wendy Anne, da of Anthony Lucey; 1 s (Samuel Brandon b 19 Nov 1979), 2 da (Abigail Lucey b 16 Sept 1981, Clementine Rose b 17 Aug 1984); *Career* called to the Bar Inner Temple 1973 (memb 1970, bencher 2003); appointed: asst recorder 1987, recorder 1991, circuit judge (SE Circuit) 2000–, resident judge Guildford Crown Court 2008–, hon recorder Guildford 2010–; vice-chm of govrs Royal GS Guildford; *Recreations* golf, bridge, reading history; *Clubs* Reform; *Style*— His Hon Judge Critchlow, DL; ✉ c/o Guildford Crown Court, Guildford, Surrey (☎ 01483 468500)

CRITCHLOW, Prof Keith Barry; s of Michael Bernard Critchlow (d 1972), and Rozalind Ruby, *née* Weston-Mann (d 1983); *b* 16 March 1933; *Educ* Summerhill Sch, St Martin's Sch of Art London (Inter NDD), RCA (ARCA); *m* Gail Susan, da of Geoffrey W Henebery; 1 s (Matthew Alexander), 3 da (Louise Penelope, Amanda Jane, Amelia Poppy); *Career* Nat Serv RAF 1951–53; lectr at most art and architecture schools in the UK; teaching appts at: Harrow, Sir John Cass, Hornsey, Watford, Wimbledon, The Slade, The Royal Coll; appts abroad incl: Ghana, Kuwait, Sweden, Aust, India, USA, Canada, Jordan, Iran, Saudi Arabia; formerly: tutor and res dir The Architectural Assoc, tutor in painting Sch of the Royal Coll of Art, tutor Slade Sch, dir Visual Islamic Arts Unit Royal Coll of Art; The Prince of Wales's Inst of Architecture: formerly actg dir Research, formerly actg dir of Visual Islamic and Traditional Arts (VITA); currently pt/t tutor (also emeritus prof); fndr of own architectural design office Keith Critchlow and Assocs; buildings designed in: USA, Kuwait, Saudi Arabia, Iran, UK (incl Krishnamurti Study Centre), India (incl SS Baba Inst of Higher Med Sciences Hosp Puttaparthi – second largest hosp in Asia); research dir KAIROS educnl charity; FRCA 1986 (Higher Dr 1989), FDIH (USA) 1987; *Books* Order in Space (1969, 2 edn 2000), Chartres Maze – A Model of the Universe?, Into the Hidden Environment (1972), Islamic Patterns – A Cosmological Approach (1976, 2 edn 1999), Time Stands Still (1979), The Sphere, Soul & Androgyne (1980), The Whole Question of Health (with Jon Allen, 1995); *Recreations* painting, writing, geometry, walking, photography, meditation; *Style*— Prof Keith Critchlow; ✉ VITA, Prince's Foundation, 19–22 Charlotte Road, London EC2A 3SG (☎ 020 7613 8500); KAIROS ☎ 01803 732135

CRITCHLOW, Stafford; s of Rex Critchlow (d 2010), and Jenifer Critchlow; *b* 1965, Lincs; *Educ* Uppingham, Univ of Newcastle (BA, William Bell meml scholar, BArch), Istituto Universitario di Architettura Venezia; *m* 1999, Harriet Lane (author), da of David Lane, CMG, of London, former ambass to the Holy See; 1 da (Poppy b 2001), 1 s (Barnaby b 2005); *Career* architect; Boilerhouse Project V&A Museum 1984–85, Gaul Assocs Chicago 1986, Skidmore Owings and Merrill Inc 1988–89, Chris Wilkinson Architects 1992–99, Wilkinson Eyre Architects: joined 1999, assoc 2000, dir 2005; projects incl: Explore@Bristol (RIBA Award 2001, Civic Tst Urban Design Award 2002), City & Islington Coll (AIA Excellence in Design Award 2006, Civi Tst Award 2006, Islington Soc Award 2006), Bristol Brunel Acad (RIBA Award 2008), Univ of Oxford Earth Sciences Building (Oxford Preservation Tst Cert 2011, ACE Award 2011), Queen Mary Univ of London Arts Two and Mathematical Sciences 2011, Univ of Exeter Forum 2012 (RIBA Nat Award 2013, HE Building of the Year World Architecture Festival 2013); exhbn 40 Under 40 (V&A) 2006; memb: Design Review Panel CABE 2007–10, Islington Design Review Panel 2009–11 and 2013–, Business Advsy Bd Creative Educn Tst 2010–; RIBA 1994 (memb Educn Ctee 2011–13), FRSA 1996; *Publications* Tectonics: a building for Earth Sciences in Oxford (2011), Wilkinson Eyre/ Works (2014); contrib articles to jls and govt pubns; *Recreations* Italy, hill walking, drawing, tennis; *Clubs* House of St Barnabas; *Style*— Stafford Critchlow, Esq; ✉ Wilkinson Eyre Architects, 33 Bowling Green Lane, London EC1R 0DA (☎ 020 7608 7900, fax 020 7608 7901, e-mail s.critchlow@wilkinsoneyre.com, website www.wilkinsoneyre.com)

CRITTENDEN, Eur Ing Prof Barry David; s of Henry John Crittenden (d 1990), and Rosina Katie, *née* Hedley (d 1969); *b* 23 May 1947; *Educ* Chislehurst and Sidcup GS (Hugh Oddy meml prize), Univ of Birmingham (BSc, PhD); *m* 30 Oct 1971, Janet Mary, da of Raymond Charles Pinches; 1 da (Lucy Rosina b 2 April 1979), 1 s (Daniel Charles b 4 Aug 1981); *Career* chemical engr UKAEA Aldermaston 1971–73; Univ of Bath: lectr 1973–88, sr lectr 1988–91, reader 1991, prof of chemical engrg 1991–, head of dept 2004–07; CEng, CSci, Eur Ing, FIChemE, FREng; *Books* Management of Hazardous and Toxic Wastes in the Process Industries (with S T Kolaczkowski, 1987), Waste Minimization: A Practical Guide (with S T Kolaczkowski, 1995), Adsorption Technology and Design (with WJ Thomas, 1998); *Recreations* photography, cycling; *Style*— Eur Ing Prof Barry Crittenden; ✉ Department of Chemical Engineering, University of Bath, Claverton Down, Bath BA2 7AY (☎ 01225 386501, fax 01225 385713)

CROCKARD, Emeritus Prof (Hugh) Alan; s of Hugh Crockard (d 1988), and Mary, *née* McKimm (d 1988); *b* 24 January 1943; *Educ* Royal Belfast Acad Instn, Queen's Univ Belfast (MB BCh, BOA, DSc, Sinclair Medal in Surgery); *m* 1978, Dr Caroline Orr; 2 s (Michael Charles b 30 Jan 1984, Thomas Hugh b 18 Jan 1987); *Career* Wellcome sr surgical fell 1973–74, Hunterian prof (treatment of head injury) RCS 1973–74, Fogarty int postdoctoral fell Chicago 1974–75, sr lectr in neurosurgery Queen's Univ Belfast 1974–78, conslt neurosurgn The Nat Hosp for Neurology and Neurosurgery 1978–2006, prof of surgical neurology Univ of WA and Inst of Neurology London; dir Raven Dept of Educn RCS 1998–2003, nat dir Modernising Medical Careers 2004–07; numerous visiting professorships; pres: Br Cervical Spine Soc 1998 (co-fndr 1986, sec), European Cervical Spine Research Soc 1999; Calvert medal 1972, Morrow lectr Belfast 1984, Jameson medal (Neurosurgical Soc of Australasia) 1989, Lund neurosurgical medal 1987, Olivacrona lectr 1995, Harrington medal 1995, Wylie McKissock medal 1996; memb: Soc of Br Neurological Surgns, American Acad of Neurological Surgery, American Assoc of Neurological Surgns, Soc of Neurological Surgns, Hungarian Spine Soc; FRCSEd 1970, FRCS 1971, FDSRCS 2001, FRCP 2003; *Books* Trauma Care (with W M Odling-Smee, 1981), Neurosurgery: The Scientific Basis of Clinical Practice (with R Hayward and J T Hoff, 3 edn 2000); also author of over 330 original articles; *Recreations* music, travel, sailing, photography; *Clubs* Athenaeum, Royal Ocean Racing; *Style*— Emeritus Prof Alan

Crockard; ✉ c/o Victor Horsely Department of Neurosurgery, National Hospital for Nervous Diseases, Queen Square, London WC1N 3BG

CROFT, 3 Baron (UK 1940); Sir Bernard William Henry Page Croft; 3 Bt (UK 1924); s of 2 Baron Croft (d 1997), by his w, Lady Antoinette Fredericka Hersey Cecilia Conyngham (d 1959), da of 6 Marquess Conyngham; *b* 28 August 1949; *Educ* Stowe, Univ of Wales (BSc Econ); *m* 1993, Mary Elizabeth, da of late James Richardson, of Co Tyrone; *Heir* none; *Career* publishing; *Recreations* shooting, fishing, skiing; *Clubs* Hurlingham, Naval and Military; *Style*— The Rt Hon the Lord Croft; ✉ Croft Castle, Leominster, Herefordshire HR6 9PW

CROFT, David Michael Bruce; s of Eric David Croft (d 2000), and Catherine Margaret, *née* Kelly; *b* 2 April 1955; *Educ* Epsom Coll, Magdalen Coll Oxford (MA, pres JCR); *m* 1 Sept 2001, Angela Jane, *née* Murray; *Career* began career with Ocean Transport & Trading 1976–82; various positions: Nat Freight Consortium 1982–87, Thames Television 1987–91, Channel Four Television 1992–96; currently dir: Anglia Television, Border Television, Granada Television, Meridian Broadcasting, Tyne Tees Television; *Recreations* horse racing, travel, golf; *Clubs* Royal Liverpool Golf; *Style*— David Croft, Esq; ✉ Flat 51, 5 Concordia Street, Leeds LS1 4ES

CROFT, Giles Laurance; s of John Rothschild Croft, of Perrymead, Somerset, and Nikki, *née* Geal; *b* 20 June 1957; *Educ* Monckton Combe Sch, City of Bath Tech Coll; *Career* artistic director; dir Bath Young People's Theatre Co 1978–80, regnl ed Bananas magazine 1979–80, admin Le Metro Theatre Co Bath 1980–82, artistic dir Gate Theatre 1985–89, series ed Absolute Classics 1988–90, literary mangr Royal Nat Theatre 1989–95; artistic dir: Palace Theatre Watford 1995–99, Nottingham Playhouse 1999–; vice-pres European Theatre Convention 2004–12; prodns incl: Conversations with a Cupboard Man (Lyric Hammersmith) 1983, Written in Sickness (Upstream) 1984, Orphee (Upstream) 1984, Elmer Gantry (Gate) 1986, The Boxer (Edinburgh Festival) 1986, Naomi (Gate) 1987, The Infant (Gate) 1989, The Secret Life (BBC Radio 4) 1993; Watford credits incl: Anna Karenina 1995, Foreign Lands 1996, Kind Hearts and Coronets 1997 (also adapted), The Talented Mr Ripley 1998; Nottingham Playhouse credits incl: Wonderful Tennessee 2000, Because It's There 2000, Polygraph 2001, Ratpack Confidential 2002–03, Chicken Soup with Barley 2005, All Quiet On The Western Front 2006, Vertigo 2008, Private Lives 2011, The Ashes, The Kite Runner 2013, Tony's Last Tape 2015, Any Means Necessary 2016; adapted for nat tour: The Ladykillers 1999, Passport to Pimlico 2000, Whisky Galore 2007, Loving April 2010; author of many short stories and articles (published and broadcast); FRSA; *Clubs* Blacks; *Style*— Giles Croft, Esq; ✉ Nottingham Playhouse, Wellington Circus, Nottingham NG1 5AF (☎ 0115 947 4361)

CROFT, Judith Mary; da of Thomas Edwin Hirst, of Wakefield, and Kathleen Mary, *née* Scholefield; *b* 16 August 1956; *Educ* Wakefield Girls HS, De Montfort Univ (BA), Bristol Old Vic Theatre Sch; *m* 28 Oct 1978, Robert Frank Croft; 1 da (Rosie Frances b 1 Aug 1986), 1 s (Lewis George b 13 Nov 1988); *Career* stage designer; assoc designer Gateway Theatre Chester 1981–83, head of design Oldham Coliseum Theatre 1983–86, freelance designer 1987–90, head of design Library Theatre Co Manchester 1991–; memb: Br Soc of Theatre Designers, Equity Designers Ctee; *Theatre* Gateway Theatre Chester: The Elephant Man, A Streetcar Named Desire, Tragical History Tour, Cider With Rosie, A Midsummer Night's Dream; Oldham Coliseum Theatre: Tartuffe, The Railway Children, Girlfriends; Library Theatre Co Manchester prodns incl: The Lion, the Witch and the Wardrobe, Assassins, Laughter on the 23rd Floor (also Guildford, Queen's Theatre West End and nat tour, nominated Olivier Award 1997), My Night with Reg, Neville's Island, Pygmalion, Perfect Days, The Borrowers (also nat tour with Watershed Prodns, nominated Best Design and Best Special Prodn Manchester Evening News Awards 2000), The Memory of Water, Beauty Queen of Lenanne (nominated Best Design Manchester Evening News Awards 2001), Falstaff (winner Best Prodn of an Opera Manchester Evening News); other credits incl: Top Girls (Lancaster Dukes), Falstaff (Royal Northern Coll of Music, winner Best Prodn of an Opera Manchester Evening News Awards 2001), Cinderella and Jack and the Beanstalk, Rock and Roll Pantos (Clwyd Theatr Cymru); *Style*— Mrs Judith Croft; ✉ 18 Lache Lane, Chester CH4 7LR (☎ 01244 676046); Head of Design, Library Theatre, St Peter's Square, Manchester M2 5PD

CROFT, Rodney John; s of late Ronald Croft, of Bolton, Lancs, and late Joan Constance, *née* Bolton; *b* 26 February 1944; *Educ* Bolton Sch, Selwyn Coll Cambridge and Middx Hosp Med Sch (Berkley fell, MA, MB BChir, MChir); *m* 28 July 1973, Hazel Ann, da of late Bernard Dudley Cattermole, and late Eva Cattermole; 2 s (Alexander James b 25 Nov 1974, Alistair Charles b 7 April 1977), 1 da (Antonia Jane b 9 April 1980); *Career* surgical registrar Ipswich Hosps 1971–73, surgical registrar in neurosurgery Maida Vale Hosp 1973; The Middx Hosps and Central Middx: surgical registrar 1973–75, sr surgical registrar 1975–80, research sr registrar 1976; North Middx Univ Hosp: conslt gen and vascular surgn 1980–2004, RCS surgical tutor 1983–89, undergrad tutor 1986–2001, co-clinical dir of surgery 2004–05, clinical governance lead Dept of Surgery and Anaesthetics 2005–06; Royal Free Hosp Med Sch: clinical sub dean 1988–2001, memb Sch Cncl 1991–98, School Medal 1993, hon conslt vascular surgn 2001–04; St George's Univ Sch of Med Grenada WI: assoc prof of surgery 1989–2000, prof of surgery 2000–, chm UK surgical faculty 2000–04, dean clinical studies UK 2003–; hon conslt vascular surgn Whittington Hosp 2001–04; hon sr lectr in surgery Univ of London 1994–; examiner in surgery (final MB BS) Univ of London 1989–2004; memb BSI Ctees for Cardio-Vascular Implants 1986–, princ UK expert ISO Ctees for cardio-vascular implants, princ UK expert CEN Ctee for cardio-vascular implants 1993–; pres Cambridge Univ Med Soc 1964–65; Capt RAMC TAVR 1972–74, Surgn Lt rising to Surgn Lt Cdr RNR 1974–83; Freeman City of London, Liveryman Worshipful Soc of Apothecaries, fell Guild of Freeman City of London 2015–; memb: BMA 1968–2007, Int Soc of Chirugie 1976–2007, Vascular Surgical Soc of GB and Ireland 1981–, Military Surgical Soc 1988–; FRSM 1975–2007, fell Assoc of Surgns of GB and Ireland 1980–, FRCS 1973, FACS 1984; *Books* Churchill's Final Farewell – The State and Private Funeral of Sir Winston Churchill (2014); *Recreations* music (classical, choral and jazz), cycling; *Clubs* Garrick, MCC, Lord's Taverners; *Style*— Rodney J Croft, Esq; ✉ 127 Queen's Road, Buckhurst Hill, Essex IG9 5BH (☎ 020 8505 7813); BMI The Cavell Hospital, Cavell Drive, Uplands Park Road, Enfield, Middlesex EN2 7PR (☎ 020 8366 2122)

CROFT, Thomas Richard (Tom); *b* 7 November 1985, Basingstoke, Hants; *Educ* Oakham Sch; *Career* rugby union player; with Leicester Tigers 2005–; England: 36 caps, debut v France 2008; memb British and Irish Lions touring squad S Africa 2009 (2 tries, played in all three test matches), memb British and Irish Lions touring squad Australia 2013; *Style*— Mr Tom Croft; ✉ c/o Leicester Tigers, Aylestone Road, Leicester LE2 7TR

CROFT, Sir Thomas Stephen Hutton; 6 Bt (UK 1818), of Cowling Hall, Yorks; s of Maj Sir John Archibald Radcliffe Croft, 5 Bt (d 1990), and Lucy Elizabeth, *née* Jupp; *b* 12 June 1959; *Educ* King's Sch Canterbury, UCL (BSc), RCA (MA); *m* 28 April 2001, Maxino Julia Benato; 1 da (Katharine Amelia Rosalind b 23 Nov 2003); *Career* architect; buildings incl Royal Yacht Squadron Pavilion Cowes 2000; RIBA; *Style*— Sir Thomas Croft, Bt; ✉ 9 Ivebury Court, 325 Latimer Road, London W10 6RA (☎ 020 8962 0066, e-mail tc@thomascroft.com, website www.thomascroft.com)

CROFT, Trevor Anthony; er s of late Kenneth Edward Croft, and late Gladys, *née* Bartle; *b* 9 June 1948; *Educ* Belle Vue Boys' GS Bradford, Univ of Hull (BSc), Univ of Sheffield (Dip Town and Regnl Planning); *m* 1980, Janet Frances Halley; 2 da (Hazel, Jennifer); *Career* with: Ministry of Development NI 1971–72, Countryside Cmmn for Scotland 1972–75, Govt of Malawi (Town and Country Planning Dept, Nat Parks and Wildlife Dept) 1976–81; National Trust for Scotland: planning offr 1982–84, head of policy research 1984–88, regnl dir for Central and Tayside 1988–95, dep dir and dir of countryside 1995–96, dir designate 1996–97, dir 1997–2001, conslt 2001–03; reporter Scot Govt Directorate for Planning and Environmental Appeals 2002–; memb S Scotland Advsy Ctee Forestry Cmmn 1988–90; memb Cncl Europa Nostra 1999–2001; property convenor and memb Congregational Bd St Fillan's Church Aberdour 1986–88; hon treas and memb Exec Ctee Euro Network of Nat Heritage Orgns 2000–01; chm Br Equestrian Vaulting Ltd 2002–03, memb Bd Br Equestrian Fedn 2002–03; assoc RSGS (memb Cncl 1998–2001 and 2002–05, memb Fin Ctee 2002–2008); chm Kinross Civic Tst Awards Ctee 2005–10; memb RTPI, FRSA; *Publications* Lake Malawi National Park: A Case Study in Conservation Planning (in Resident Peoples and National Parks by P C West and S R Brechin, 1991), What Price Access: Visitor Impact on Heritage in Trust (in Cultural Tourism by J M Fladmark, 1994); *Recreations* family, travel, motorcycling, restoring Series 1 Land Rover; *Clubs* Royal Scots (Edinburgh); *Style*— Trevor A Croft, Esq; ✉ Glenside, Tillyrie, Kinross KY13 0RW (☎ 01577 864105)

CROFTS, Prof Roger Stanley; CBE (1999); s of Stanley Crofts (d 1995), and Violet, *née* Dawson (d 2005); *b* 17 January 1944; *Educ* Hinckley GS, Univ of Liverpool (BA), Univ of Leicester (PGCE), Univ of Aberdeen (MLitt); *m* Lindsay Manson; 1 s (Tim), 1 da (Catharine); *Career* research asst Univ of Aberdeen 1966–72, research fell UCL 1972–74; Scottish Office: North Sea Oil Support Gp 1974–81, Central Research Unit 1981–84, Highlands and Tourism 1984–88, Rural Affrs 1988–91; chief exec Scottish Natural Heritage 1991–2002; hon prof of geography Univ of Aberdeen 1997–2007, visiting prof of environmental mgmnt Royal Holloway Coll London (later Royal Holloway Univ of London) 1997–2004, visiting prof of geoscience Univ of Edinburgh 2004–08 (hon prof of geoscience 2008–11), visiting prof of geography and environment Univ of Aberdeen 2007–12, hon prof of geography Univ of Dundee 2015–; The World Conservation Union (IUCN) Int Ecological Devpt plc 2004–, IUCN WCPA emeritus 2009; chair UK Ctee 1999–2002, chair WCPA Europe 2001–08; chair: The Sibthorp Tst, Plantlife until 2010; memb: Cncl and Bd National Tst for Scotland (also chm Conservation Ctee until 2009), Ctee Scottish Assoc of Marine Science until 2004, Bd Scot Agric Coll until 2010, Bd Fieldfare, Bd Crichton Carbon Centre 2009–, Bd Royal Scottish Geographical Soc 2013–; patron Scottish Assoc of Geography Teachers 2004–; Icelandic Soil Conservation Medal 2011, Chartered Inst of Ecology and Environmental Management 2016; Hon DSc Univ of St Andrews, Hon DSc Univ of Glasgow 2013; Knight's Cross fo the Icelandic Order of the Falcon 2014; FRSA 1996, FRSE 2001, FRSGS 2001 (chair 2014–), FRGS 2002, FIEEM 2008; *Publications* Scotland: The creation of its natural landscape (co-author, 1999), Scotland's Environment: The Future (co-author, 2000), Conserving Nature: Scotland and the Wider World (co-ed, 2005), Land of Mountain and Flood (co-author, 2007), Healing the Land (2011), Fair Isles and Fine Sailing: celebrating 60 years of cruising National Trust for Scotland; author of several articles and ed of books on environmental mgmnt, rural devpt, earth history and coastal processes; *Recreations* cooking without a book, garden design, singing in private, wildflower photography, hill walking, exploring English cathedrals and churches; *Style*— Prof Roger Crofts, CBE; ✉ 6 Eskside West, Fisherrow, Musselburgh EH21 6HZ (☎ 0131 665 0788)

CROISDALE-APPLEBY, Prof David; OBE (2008), JP (Thames Valley 2003); s of Mark Appleby (d 1980), of Bamburgh, Northumberland, and Florence Isabella, *née* White (d 2015); *Educ* Royal GS Newcastle upon Tyne, Univ of London (MA, MA, MA), Univ of Newcastle (BSc), Brunel Univ (MTech), Open Univ (MA) Univ of Lancaster (PhD); *m* 3 Aug 1968, Rev Carolynn Elizabeth, da of Maj Alan Cuthbert Croisdale, MBE (d 1974); 3 s (Mycroft Charles St John b 1971, Lindsay Redvers Mark Seymour b 1973, Rupert Merton David St Clair b 1976), 1 da (Catriona Juliette Carolynn Sophia b 1984); *Career* scientist O R Exec 1967–69, mktg mangr American Brands Inc 1969–72, account dir J Walter Thompson 1972–76, chief exec De Villiers & Schonfeldt SA Ltd 1976–78, election strategist Progressive Federal Party SA 1979, chief exec Allen Brady & Marsh Ltd 1979–82, worldwide ops dir SSC&B:Lintas Ltd 1982–84, chm and chief exec Creative Synergy Ltd 1984–99, dir of strategy, mktg and communications Univ for Industry (learndirect) 1999–2001; chm: The DCA Co Ltd 1985–99, Utilities Research Ltd 1986–99, Salmon Ventures 1988–92, NHS Ind Review Panels 1996–2002, Yarrow Housing Ltd 2001–12, Careplus 2002–04, Bucks Hosps NHS Tst 2002–06, Radian Gp 2006–10, Charities Evaluation Servs 2006–10, Prog Devpt Gp for Longterm Sickness and Incapacity NICE 2007–09, Cncl for the Registration of Forensic Practitioners 2007–12, Skills for Care 2008–14, English Fedn of Disability Sport 2008–10, Skills for Care and Devpt 2009–14, Hft (Home Farm Tst) 2009–15, Topic Expert Gp for Care of People with Dementia NICE 2011–13, Dementia UK 2013–, Public Health Advsy Ctee NICE 2015–, NICE Guidance on Prevention of Drug Misuse 2015–, NICE Guidance on Physical Exercise 2016–; exec chm Standing Cmmn on Carers 2014–; dep chm: Bucks Mental Health NHS Tst 2001–02, Cncl for the Registration of Forensic Practitioners 2002–07, Postwatch 2006–08; dir and chm Finance Ctee Centrex 2002–08, dir and chm Audit and Risk Ctee Food from Britain 2002–08, dir and chm Audit and Risk Ctee Turning Point 2003–08, dir NHS Confederation 2005–08; memb: Multi-Centre Medical Research Ethics Ctee 2000–09, Employment Tbnl Service 2000–10, Health Professions Cncl Regulatory Panels 2001–06, NHS Medical Research Ethics Ctee 2001–12, FHSAA and Primary Health Tbnl Service 2002–, Legal Services Cmmn 2002–06, Editorial Advsy Bd Jl of Mktg Intelligence and Planning 2003–, Medical Research Cncl Advsy Panels on Public Engagement, Stratified Medicine and Public Health Centres 2005–, Nat Social Care Research Ethics Ctee 2009–; nat memb for social care Assoc of Research Ethics Ctee 2011–14, dir and chm Audit and Risk Ctee Health Educn England 2014–; specialist race and discrimination advsr to HM Courts 2009–; inspr of medical educn GMC and PMETB 2004–; visiting prof of strategic mktg and communications Univ of Strathclyde 1990–2001, visiting prof Durham Business Sch 2002–, hon prof Wolfson Research Inst 2008–, hon prof Sch of Medicine and Health Univ of Durham 2008–; memb Cncl Univ of Durham 2000–10, chm Ustinov Coll Univ of Durham 2005–10, chm Life Sciences Ethical Review Ctee Univ of Durham 2005–10, chm Investment Ctee Univ of Durham 2006–10; tstee Colin Javens Spinal Injury Tst 2005–14; memb Strategic Advsy Gp Durham Cathedral 2006–13, county rep for Bucks and Milton Keynes St Johns Ambulance 2006–; hon ambass for the UK Nelson Mandela Children's Hosp Southern Africa; chapter memb The Priory of England and All the Islands of the Order of St John 2008–; Sunday Times NED of the Year 2016; Hon DCL Univ of Durham, Hon DSc Brunel Univ, Hon DBA Univ of Strathclyde, Hon DLitt Univ of Salford; FRSA 1988 (life fell), FRSH 2006, FRIPH 2006, fell Royal Soc of Public Health (FRSPH) 2008, FIoD 2010, hon fell Chartered Soc of Forensic Sciences (Hon FCSFS) 2015, FAcSS 2016; SBStJ 2011; *Publications* Re-visioning Social Work Education (ind review of social work education for Govt, 2014); *Recreations* 18th Century English literature, art history; *Clubs* Reform; *Style*— Prof David Croisdale-Appleby, OBE; ✉ Abbotsholme, Hervines Road, Amersham, Buckinghamshire HP6 5HS (☎ 07901 716136, e-mail croisdaleappleby@aol.com); Waren Lea Hall, Bamburgh, Northumberland NE70 7EE

CROISDALE-APPLEBY, HE Lindsay; *Educ* Eton, St Hugh's Coll Oxford; *m* Barbara Maria; 1 s (Edward), 1 da (Juliette); *Career* diplomat; desk offr Nigeria FCO 1996–97, UK Mission to UN Middle East Section 1997–98, second sec Caracas 1998–2001, desk offr Afghanistan Emergency Unit FCO 2001–02, DEFRA 2002, first sec UK Perm Rep to EU 2002–08; FCO: asst dir for recruitment and devpt HR Directorate 2008–10, princ private sec to Foreign Sec 2010–12; ambass to Colombia 2012–15; *Style*— HE Mr Lindsay

Croisdale-Appleby; ✉ c/o Foreign & Commonwealth Office (Bogota), King Charles Street, London SW1A 1AH (Twitter @lindsaycappleby)

CROLY, Colin Vernon; s of Dr Vernon Robert Arthur Croly (d 2006), and Martha Maria, *née* Albertyn (d 2003); *b* 9 October 1949; *Educ* St Andrew's Coll Grahamstown S Africa, Univ of Cape Town (BCom, LLB), UCL (LLM); *m* 24 Feb 1973, Clare Margaret, *née* Stroebel; *Career* admitted slr 1976; ptnr Barlow Lyde & Gilbert 1980–2009; sec gen Int Assoc of Insurance Lawyers 1994–, memb Bd Fedn of Defence and Corp Counsel 2004–08, govt appointee IBRC 1997–98, chm AIDA Europe 2008–; Who's Who Legal Int Insurance and Reinsurance Lawyer of the Year 2005, 2006, 2007, 2008 and 2009; memb Law Soc 1976; *Publications* Reinsurance Practice and the Law (jt ed, 1993); *Recreations* gardening, reading, opera, theatre; *Clubs* RAC; *Style*— Colin Croly, Esq; ✉ 99 Randolph Avenue, London W9 1DL

CROMARTIE, 5 Earl of (UK 1861); John Ruaridh Grant Mackenzie; also Viscount Tarbat (UK 1861), Baron Castlehaven (1861), Baron MacLeod of Castle Leod (UK 1861); Chief of the Clan Mackenzie; s of 4 Earl of Cromartie, MC, TD (d 1989), and his 2 w, Olga, *née* Laurance (d 1996); *b* 12 June 1948; *Educ* Rannoch Sch Perthshire, Univ of Strathclyde; *m* 1, 1973 (m dis 1983), Helen, da of John Murray; 1 s (decd); m 2, 1985, Janet Clare, da of Christopher James Harley, of Strathpeffer; 2 s (Colin Ruaridh, Viscount Tarbat b 7 Sept 1987, Hon Alasdair Kenelm Stuart b 6 Dec 1989); m 3, 8 Oct 2012, Jane Margaret Eve, *née* Austin; *Heir* s, Viscount Tarbat; *Career* sat as cross-bencher in House of Lords until 1999; explosives conslt, past editor Explosives Engineering; former tstee John Muir Tst; memb Inst of Explosive Engrs 1982, pres Mountaineering Cncl of Scotland 2003–07 (exec memb 1994); *Books* Rock and Ice Climbs in Skye (SMT); part author: Cold Climbs, Classic Rock, Wild Walks and many magazine articles both in the climbing and explosives press; *Recreations* mountaineering, geology, art; *Clubs* Scottish Mountaineering (pres 2012–14), Army and Navy, Pratt's; *Style*— The Rt Hon the Earl of Cromartie; ✉ Castle Leod, Strathpeffer, Ross-shire IV14 9AA

CROMER, 4 Earl of (UK 1901); Evelyn Rowland Esmond Baring; also Baron Cromer (UK 1892), Viscount Cromer (UK 1899), and Viscount Errington (UK 1901); s of 3 Earl of Cromer, KG, GCMG, MBE, PC (d 1991), and Hon Esme Mary Gabrielle Harmsworth, CVO, da of 2 Viscount Rothermere; *b* 3 June 1946; *Educ* Eton; *m* 1, 1971 (m dis 1992), Plern Isarankura na Ayudhya; m 2, 1993, Shelley Hu, da of Hu Guo-qin; 1 s (Alexander Rowland Hamsworth, Viscount Errington b 5 Jan 1994), 1 da (Lady Venetia Esme Mei b 22 Feb 1998); *Heir* s, Viscount Errington; *Career* md: Inchcape China Ltd 1979–94, Inchcape Vietnam Ltd 1987–94, Inchcape Special Markets Ltd 1990–94; chm: LGSC China Fund Ltd (Hong Kong) 1994–2001, Phillipine Discovery Investments Co Ltd 1995–2001, JF China Region Fund Inc (USA), Korea Asia Fund Ltd 1995–2001, Western Provident Assoc 2004–; dep chm: Land-Ocean Inchcape Int Container Transport Co Ltd (China) 1985–94, Motor Transport Co of Guangdong & Hong Kong Ltd (China) 1979–94; dir: Inchcape Pacific Ltd 1985–94, Schroder AsiaPacific Fund plc 1995–, Somerset TEC 1996–2001, Pacific Basin Shipping 2004–08, Cluff Oil China Ltd (Hong Kong), London Asia Capital plc 2009–; chm Business Link Somerset 1997–2008; memb St John's Cncl (Hong Kong) 1980–85; *Publications* The Son from the West (2008); *Recreations* mountain climbing, deep sea diving; *Clubs* White's, Oriental, Hong Kong (Hong Kong), Royal Yacht Squadron; *Style*— The Rt Hon the Earl of Cromer; ✉ 6 Sloane Terrace Mansions, London SW1X 9DG

CROMIE, Stephen John Henry; s of Dr Brian William Cromie, of Kings Cliffe, Northants, and Heather Anne Howie, *née* Wood; *b* 13 January 1957; *Educ* Abingdon Sch, Downing Coll Cambridge (MA); *m* 28 Aug 1982, Marianne Frances, da of John Edward Burton, East Ewell, Surrey; 1 s (Jonathan b 1989), 1 da (Charlotte b 1996); *Career* admitted slr 1981; ptnr Linklaters 1987–2001 (joined 1979), judicial asst to Royal Courts of Justice 2001–06, Treasy Slrs Dept 2006–08, HM Treasy 2008–12, Govt Legal Dept 2012–; FCIArb; *Books* International Commercial Litigation (jtly, 1990, 2 edn 1997), Merger Control in Europe (1991); *Recreations* wine, cooking, cycling; *Style*— S J H Cromie, Esq; ✉ 21 Regents Park Terrace, London NW1 7ED (☎ 020 7485 5328)

CROMPTON, David Andrew; QPM (2010); *Educ* Salford Univ (BA), Univ of Cambridge (Dip); *Career* Dep Chief Constable W Yorks Police 2008–12, Chief Constable S Yorks Police 2012–; *Style*— David Crompton, Esq, QPM; ✉ South Yorkshire Police Headquarters, Carbrook House, 5 Carbrook Hall Road, Sheffield S9 2EH

CROMPTON, Prof David William Thomasson; OBE (1999); s of Arthur Thomasson Crompton (d 1995), of Bolton, Lancs, and Gladys, *née* Mather (d 2003); *b* 5 December 1937; *Educ* Bolton Sch, Univ of Cambridge (MA, PhD, ScD); *m* 14 April 1962, Effie Mary, da of Robert Marshall (d 1989), Lancs; 1 s (John b 1963), 2 da (Tessa b 1964, Virginia b 1967); *Career* Nat Serv 2 Lt King's Own Royal Regt 1956–58; lectr Univ of Cambridge 1968–85 (asst in res 1963–68), vice-master Sidney Sussex Coll 1981–83 (res fell 1964–65, fell 1965–85), adjunct prof Div of Nutritional Sciences Cornell Univ NY 1981–2004; Univ of Glasgow: John Graham Kerr prof of zoology 1985–2000, vice-dean of science 1993–95; Scientific medal The Zoological Soc of London 1977; fndr memb Br Soc for Parasitology 1962, co ed Parasitology 1972–82; memb: Aquatic Life Sciences Ctee NERC 1981–84, WHO Expert Ctee for Parasitic Diseases 1985–; chm Co of Biologists Ltd 1994–2000, head of WHO Collaborating Centre for Soil-transmitted Helminthiases at Univ of Glasgow 1989–2004, dir St Andrew's Clinics for Children 1992–, chm WHO Strategic and Technical Advsy Gp for Neglected Tropical Diseases 2011–13; hon memb: The Slovak Parasitology Soc 1999, American Soc of Parasitologists 2001, The Helminthological Soc of Washington 2002; hon fell Univ of Glasgow 2005; fell Royal Soc of Tropical Med and Hygiene 1986–2000, FRSB, FRSE 1989; *Books* An Ecological Approach to Acanthocephalan Physiology (1970), Parasitic Worms (jtly, 1980), Parasites and People (1984), Biology of the Acanthocephala (jt ed), Ascariasis and its Public Health Significance (jt ed, 1985), Ascariasis and its Prevention and Control (jt ed, 1989), A Guide to Human Helminths (jtly, 1991), Helminth Control in School-Age Children (jtly, 2002), Controlling Disease due to Helminth Infections (jt ed, 2003), Handbook of Helminthiasis for Public Health (jtly), Afterthoughts of a Worm Hunter (2009); *Recreations* gardening, books, dogs; *Style*— Prof D W T Crompton, OBE, FRSE; ✉ 101A Clifton Hill, London NW8 0JR (e-mail dwtc@tyndrum.demon.co.uk)

CROMPTON, Richard Philip deJordan; QPM (2012); *Educ* Sunderland Poly (BA), Univ of Manchester (MA), Univ of Cambridge (Dip); *m* 2 c; *Career* Met Police 1976–79, subsequently various roles as inspr, chief inspr and supt Devon and Cornwall Constabulary, asst chief constable Cumbria Constabulary, dep chief constable rising to chief constable Lincs Police 2004–; *Style*— Richard Crompton, Esq, QPM; ✉ Lincolnshire Police, Deepdale Lane, Nettleham, Lincoln LN2 2LT

CROMPTON, Sarah Melanie; da of Donald Walker Crompton (d 1982), and Mary, *née* Barnes; *b* 30 August 1957; *Educ* Headington Sch Oxford, Hertford Coll Oxford (BA), UC Cardiff (Dip Journalism); *m* 1995, Icaro Kosak; 1 s (Augusto b 1997); *Career* features writer Coventry Evening Telegraph 1983–85 (reporter 1980–83), dep features ed Woman 1986–87 (researcher and features writer 1985–86), asst ed Woman's Own 1989–90 (features ed 1987–89), asst ed Telegraph Magazine 1990–94, arts ed The Daily Telegraph 1994–; *Recreations* watching Manchester United and other forms of armchair sport; *Style*— Ms Sarah Crompton; ✉ The Daily Telegraph, 111 Buckingham Palace Road, London SW1W 0DT

CROMWELL, 7 Baron (E 1375); Godfrey John Bewicke-Copley; s of 6 Baron Cromwell (d 1982; Barony abeyant 1497 to 1923, when abeyance terminated in favour of present Baron's gf, 5 Baron); *b* 4 March 1960; *m* 23 June 1990, Elizabeth A, da of John Hawksley; 1 da (Hon Helen Tatiana b 18 March 1995), 3 s (Hon David Godfrey b 21 Sept 1997, John William, Ralph Thomas (twins) b 14 Nov 2000); *Heir* s, Hon David Bewicke-Copley; *Career* dir: Britain-Russia Centre 2000–, British East-West Centre 2000–, Russo-British C of C 2004–07, British-Georgian C of C 2007–09; vice-pres Barclays Wealth 2007–16; memb House of Lords 2014–; *Style*— The Rt Hon the Lord Cromwell

CRONIN, Tacey Marguerite (Mrs David Bain); da of Flt Lt Anthony Arthur Cronin (d 1972), and Margaret Elizabeth, *née* Roberts (d 2003); *b* 28 June 1959; *Educ* Stamford HS, Bristol Univ (LLB); *m* 3 Jan 1987, David Ian Bain, s of Capt David Walter Bain (d 1972); 3 da (Athene Margaret b 1990, Esmé Rose b 1993, Cecily Mary b 1996); *Career* called to the Bar Middle Temple 1982; dep dist judge 2005; mediator; memb: Bar Cncl 1985–86, Gen Cncl of the Bar 1987; dir BMIF 1988–2002; govr Westbury Park Primary Sch 1996–2004 (chm 2001–03); *Recreations* theatre, motor sport, travel, Scottish country dancing; *Style*— Miss Tacey Cronin; ✉ Albion Chambers, Broad Street, Bristol BS1 1DR (☎ 0117 927 2144, fax 0117 926 2569)

CROOK, Prof Anthony Derek Howell (Tony); CBE (2014); s of Ernest Henry William Crook (d 1982), and Hilda Muriel, *née* Howell (d 1996); *b* 22 December 1944; *Educ* St Paul's, Univ of Bristol (BA), Univ of London (MPhil), Univ of Sheffield (PhD); *m* 1967, Jennifer Rose, *née* Miller; 2 da (Emily Jane b 1972, Hannah Louise b 1976); *Career* offr res branch GLC 1967–68; Dept of Town and Regional Planning Univ of Sheffield: lectr 1968–86, sr lectr 1986–95, reader 1990–94, personal chair 1994, head, prof 1994–; Univ of Sheffield: acting head Dept of Landscape, dep dean Faculty of Architectural Studies, pro-vice-chllr 1999–2008, prof emeritus 2010–; chm Conf of Heads of Planning Schs 1969–99; adsvr to Institute of Planning; also lectr, res and advsr overseas incl Canada, China, Hong Kong and Malaysia; chair: ConneXions S Yorks 2001–, Sheffield Homes; dir Orbit Housing Gp 2010–; memb Bd: S Yorks Housing Asoc 1973–, Nat Housing Fedn 1980–86, Nat Tenant Voice 2010; memb Cncl Acad of Social Sciences 2009–, chm Campaign for Social Science 2011–; tstee and chair Shelter; RTPI: memb Housing and Renewal Panel, memb Research Ctee, memb Accreditation Ctee 2004–, memb Tstee Bd 2013–, chair Educn Ctee 2015–; tstee UK Coalfields Regeneration Tst 2009–; Hon DLitt 2012; FRSA 1999, FRTPI 2001 (MRTPI 1977), FAcSS 2004; *Publications* author of various books, res reports, refereed journal articles and published conference papers on housing policy; *Clubs* Royal Overseas League; *Style*— Prof Tony Crook, CBE; ✉ University of Sheffield, Western Bank, Sheffield S10 2TN (☎ 0114 222 6303, fax 0114 272 2199, e-mail a.crook@sheffield.ac.uk)

CROOK, Frances Rachel; OBE (2010); da of Maurice Crook (d 1977), of London, and Sheila Sibson-Turnbull (d 1999); *b* 18 December 1952; *Educ* Camden Sch London, Univ of Liverpool (BA), Lancaster Univ (PGCE); 1 da (Sarah Rose Eleanor b 27 May 1988); *Career* campaign organiser Amnesty Int 1980–85, dir Howard League for Penal Reform 1986–; memb Bd Sch Food Tst 2005–, non-exec dir Barnet Primary Care Tst 2009–11; cncllr Barnet Borough 1982–90, govr Greenwich Univ (chair Staff and General Ctee) 1996–2002, sr visiting fell LSE 2011–; Freedom City of London 1997; *Style*— Ms Frances Crook, OBE; ✉ The Howard League, 1 Ardleigh Road, London N1 4HS (☎ 020 7249 7373)

CROOK, (Paul) Mackenzie; s of Michael Alan Crook, and Sheila Crook; *b* 29 September 1971, Maidstone, Kent; *m* Lindsay; 1 s (Jude Michael b 17 Jan 2003), 1 da (Scout Elizabeth b 24 Dec 2007); *Career* actor; *Television* incl: The Office 2001–03, Little Dorrit 2008, Skins 2009, North by Northamptonshire 2011, Game of Thrones 2013; *Film* incl: Pirates of the Caribbean: The Curse of the Black Pearl 2003, Sex Lives of the Potato Men 2004, The Merchant of Venice 2004, Finding Neverland 2004, Churchill: The Hollywood Years 2004, The Brothers Grimm 2005, Pirates of the Caribbean: Dean Man's Chest 2006, I Want Candy 2007, Pirates of the Caribbean: At World's End 2007, Three and Out 2008, Sex & Drugs & Rock & Roll 2010, The Adventures of Tintin: The Secret of the Unicorn 2011, Therese 2013, One Chance 2013; *Theatre* incl: The Seagull (Royal Court and Broadway) 2007–08, Jerusalem (Royal Court, Apollo and Broadway) 2009–11, The Recruiting Officer (Donmar Warehouse) 2012; *Books* The Windvale Sprites (children's fiction, 2011); *Style*— Mackenzie Crook; ✉ c/o Lisa Thomas Management Ltd, Unit 10, 7 Wenlock Road, London N1 7SL

CROOK, Paul; s of William Giles Crook, of Poole, Dorset, and Helen Margaret, *née* Swales; *b* 6 March 1952; *Educ* Ruzawi Sch Zimbabwe, Peterhouse Sch Zimbabwe, Jesus Coll Cambridge (MA, LLM); *m* 11 Sept 1976, Dr Susan Jill, da of Dr Andrew Ernest Dossetor, of Newmarket, Suffolk; 1 da (Anne b 1986), 2 s (John b 1988, Peter b 1990); *Career* admitted slr 1978, admitted Paris Bar 1994; Allen & Overy: ptnr 1984–2003, Global Head of Corp Know-How and Training 2003–2012, conslt 2012–; Freeman City of London Slrs Co 1984; memb Law Soc; *Recreations* golf, hockey, skiing, squash, tennis; *Style*— Paul Crook, Esq; ✉ Allen & Overy, One Bishops Square, London E1 6AD (☎ 020 3088 0000, fax 020 3088 0088)

CROOKENDEN, Simon Robert; QC (1996); s of late Maj Spencer Crookenden, CBE, MC, of Kendal, Cumbria, and late Jean, *née* Dewing; *b* 27 September 1946; *Educ* Winchester, Corpus Christi Coll Cambridge (MA); *m* 20 Aug 1983, Sarah Anne Georgina Margaret, da of late George Leonard Pragnell; 2 da (Rebecca Jean b 9 Nov 1985, Alice Lily b 5 Aug 1991), 1 s (Thomas Henry b 19 Sept 1987); *Career* called to the Bar Gray's Inn 1974; *Recreations* rowing; *Clubs* London Rowing; *Style*— Simon Crookenden, Esq, QC; ✉ Essex Court Chambers, 24 Lincoln's Inn Fields, London WC2A 3EG (☎ 020 7813 8000, fax 020 7813 8080)

CROOKSTON, Peter Christian; s of Robert Crookston (d 1969), and Nancy Hedley (d 2004); *b* 30 December 1936; *Educ* Clegwell Secondary Modern Sch Hebburn-on-Tyne, Newcastle upon Tyne Coll of Commerce; *m* 1 (m dis 1974), Julia Hampton; 1 s (James b 21 Feb 1970); m 2, 31 March 1988, Zoe Zenghelis, da of John Tsakiris (d 1985), and Anastasia Gabriel (d 1994), of Athens, Greece; *Career* trainee journalist Newcastle Journal and Evening Chronicle 1954–59, sub ed Daily Express 1959–61, picture ed The Observer 1961–64, asst ed/dep ed Sunday Times Magazine 1964–69, ed Nova magazine 1969–71; features ed: Sunday Times 1971–73, The Observer 1973–77; ed: The Observer Magazine 1977–82; freelance 1982–88, ed Geo International 1988–90, dep ed Departures 1990–91, ed WORLD Magazine 1991–93, contributing ed Telegraph Magazine 1993–94, ed English Heritage Magazine 1994–99, freelance contrib The Observer, The Guardian, Condé Nast Traveller, Saga Magazine, The Sunday Times and The Independent 1999–; *Books* Villain (1967), Village London (ed, 1978), Village England (ed, 1979), Island Britain (ed, 1981), The Ages of Britain (ed, 1982), The Pitmen's Requiem (2010); *Recreations* sailing, walking, reading; *Clubs* Chelsea Arts, Itchenor Sailing; *Style*— Peter Crookston, Esq; ✉ 84 Portland Road, London W11 4LQ (fax 020 7243 4280)

CROPPER, Sir James Anthony; KCVO (2011); s of Anthony Charles Cropper (d 1967), and Philippa Mary Gloria, *née* Clutterbuck (d 2009); *b* 22 December 1938; *Educ* Eton, Magdalene Coll Cambridge (BA); *m* 30 June 1967, Susan Rosemary, da of Col F J N Davis (d 1988), of Northwood, Middx; 2 s (Charles Michael Anthony b 1969, d 1974, Mark b 1974), 1 da (Sarah b 1972); *Career* dir: James Cropper plc papermakers 1966–2013 (chm 1971–2010, hon pres 2013–), East Lancs Paper Group plc 1982–84, NW Water Group plc 1989–90; pres Br Paper and Bd Industry Fedn 1987–89; dir Cumbria Rural Enterprise Agency 1987–2010, chm govrs of Abbot Hall Art Gallery and Museum 1983–88; memb: S Westmorland RDC 1967–74, Lancs River Authy 1968–74, NW Water Authy 1973–80 and 1987–89, S Lakeland Dist Cncl 1974–77; High Sheriff Westmorland 1971, HM Lord-Lt Cumbria 1994–2012 (Vice Lord-Lt 1991, DL 1986); Liveryman Worshipful Co of Stationers & Newspaper Makers; FCA; KStJ 1997; *Recreations* shooting, golf;

C

Style— Sir James Cropper, KCVO; ✉ Tolson Hall, Kendal, Cumbria (☎ 01539 722011); James Cropper plc, Burneside Mills, Kendal, Cumbria (☎ 01539 722002)

CROPPER, Peter John; s of Samuel Duncan Cropper (d 1961), and Anna Southwell, *née* Parkinson (d 1990); *b* 7 February 1940; *Educ* Salford GS, Univ of Manchester, RAC Cirencester (Postgrad Dip Advanced Farm Mgmnt); *m* 16 Sept 1963, Hilary Mary (d 2004), da of Arnold Trueman, of Bollington, Cheshire; 2 da (Elizabeth b Dec 1969, Charlotte b Feb 1973), 1 s (Carl b Oct 1971); *Career* various tech and mgmnt appts AEI and English Electric 1960–68, software devpt mangr ICL 1968–75, gen mangr Computer Gp CWS Ltd 1975–80; md: STC IDEC Ltd 1980–85, STC Technology Ltd 1985–87; dir corporate info systems STC plc 1987–91, vice-pres info systems Northern Telecom Ltd (following merger with STC plc) 1991–97, chm Consarc Consulting Architects Ltd 1997–, dir Zephen Ltd 1997–, dir Zephen Properties Ltd 2003–, dir Zephen Farms Ltd 2005–; dir and tstee Dame Hilary Cropper Charitable Fndn Ltd 2004–, dir Pinotage Youth Devpt Acad (South Africa) 2012–; Freeman City of London 1988, Liveryman Worshipful Co of Scientific Instrument Makers, Past Master Worshipful Co of Information Technologists; CEng, FBCS, CITP; *Recreations* bridge, theatre; *Clubs* Naval and Military, Farmers; *Style*— Peter Cropper, Esq; ✉ Zephen Ltd, Somerton Randle Farm, Somerton, Somerset TA11 7HW (☎ 01458 274900, fax 01458 274901, e-mail peter@zephen.com, website www.zephen.com)

CROSBY, Emma; *b* 1977; *Educ* Univ of Leeds, Univ of Cardiff; *Career* television broadcaster; formerly: prodr BBC News 24, Radio News Direct, LBC; The Money Channel 1999–2001, European Market Wrap (CNBC Europe) 2001–03, presenter Sky News 2003–08, London corr Fox Business Network 2007–, presenter GMTV 2009–10, presenter Channel 5 News 2011–; *Style*— Ms Emma Crosby; ✉ Five News, Grant Way, Isleworth, Middlesex TW7 5QD

CROSFIELD, Lesley; da of William Chapman Sharp (d 1965), and Joan Mary, *née* Wiltshire; *b* 27 July 1950; *Educ* Tal Handaq Malta, Bell Baxter HS, Duncan of Jordanstone Coll of Art Dundee; *Partner* Colin Craig, *qv*; *Career* ceramics and pottery art study: pottery sch Aarhus Denmark, Sir John Cass, Middx Poly 1970–77; ind travel 1977–80: 2-handed Atlantic crossing, one year spent in NY; hotelier Altskeith Hotel Trossachs 1980–87, organiser Altskeith Alefest 1983–86, co-chef and hotelier The Albannach 1990– (Michelin BIB Gourmand 1997, McAllan Award Overall Excellence 1998, McAllan Award Best Restaurant with Rooms 1998, Good Food Guide W Coast Newcomer of the Year 2000, Scotland the Best Award for Excellence 2000, Which? Hotel Guide Hotels of the Year category 2002, 2 AA Rosettes 2002, Scottish Hotel Bedroom of the Year Hotel Review Scotland 2007, Michelin star 2009), owner Caberfeidh Dining Pub Lochinver; runner up Scottish Chef of the Year 2009; *Books* Scotland on a Plate (2001), Celtic Cuisine (2008), Relish Scotland (2010); *Recreations* sailing, hill walking, the arts, food, wine, conversation; *Clubs* RYA; *Style*— Ms Lesley Crosfield; ✉ The Albannach, Lochinver, Sutherland IV27 4LP (☎ 01571 844407, e-mail info@thealbanach.co.uk, website www.thealbannach.co.uk)

CROSLAND, Neisha; da of C R H Crosland, and Felicity, *née* d'Abreu; *b* 11 December 1960; *Educ* Convent of the Sacred Heart Woldingham, Hatfield Girls Grammar Herts, Camberwell Schs of Arts and Crafts (BA), RCA (MA); *m* Stephane Perche; 2 s (Oscar Maurice b 1996, Samuel Alphonso b 1999); *Career* freelance textile designer; pt/t external teaching appts at Glasgow Sch of Art, Winchester Sch of Art, Northbroke College and Glasgow Sch of Art 1988–94; designed Romagna collection for Osborne & Little 1988, designed Carnaval Collection (wallpapers and furnishing fabrics) Harlequin Wallcoverings Ltd 1990–94, fndr Neisha Crosland own label 1994, launched Neisha at Debenhams 1998, fndr Ginka ready-to-wear 1999, first wallpaper collection 1999, launched home, decorative and stationery collection, opened own shop in London 2000–01, licensed collection for Hankyu Dept Stores Japan 2002, first home furnishings collection 2003, worldwide wallpaper and fabric distribution secured with Turnell & Gigon 2011; collaborations and licences: licensed collections and designs for Hankyu Dept Stores Japan 2002–, The Rug Co (rugs) 2006–, Reed Employment (ties and scarves) 2007, De Ferranti (tiles) 2008–, John Lewis Dept Stores (furnishing fabrics, wallpapers and bed linen) 2009, Chelsea Textiles (hand embroidered fabrics) 2010–, Harvey Maria (vinyl flooring) 2010–, Little Brown Book Group/Virago (designs used for book covers) 2010–, Make International (fine china) 2012–, Crate & Barrel (home accessories) 2014–, Fired Earth (tiles) 2014–, George Spencer (wallpapers) 2014–, Little Brown Book Group/Virago (fine china and notebooks) 2015–; judge RSA Bursary Awards 2006–08; MA external examiner RCA 2007–08; *Awards* nominated Peugeot Design Award 2000, nominated Homes & Gardens Awards 2000, Design and Decoration Award 2004, Elle Decoration Award 2005, Homes & Gardens Best Surface Designer 2013; RDI 2006; *Publications* featured in numerous books on textile design incl: The Victoria & Albert Museum's Textile Collection: British Textile Design from 1940 to the Present (by Ngozi Ikoku, 1999), Wallpaper, the Ultimate Guide (by Charlotte Abrahams, 2009), British Textiles 1700 to Present (by Linda Parry, 2010); *Clubs* Chelsea Arts; *Style*— Miss Neisha Crosland; ✉ 29 Oberstein Road, London SW11 2AE (☎ 020 7657 1150, e-mail info@neishacrosland.com, website www.neishacrosland.com)

CROSS, Andrew John; s of Colin Cross, and Mary, *née* McMurray; *Educ* St George's Sch Mayfair, Riverside Sch; *Career* RN 1979–84; prison offr: HMP Feltham 1985–87, HMP The Verne 1987–91; princ offr and govr HMP (level 5) Long Lartin 1991–93, govr (level 4) HMP The Mount 1994–97, dep govr HMP and YOI Bullwood Hall 1997–2000, govr HMP Bedford 2000–05, govr Feltham YOI 2005–; *Style*— Andrew Cross, Esq

CROSS, Prof Anthony Glenn; s of Walter Sidney Cross (d 1941), and Ada, *née* Lawson (d 2004); *b* 21 October 1936; *Educ* High Pavement Sch Nottingham, Trinity Hall Cambridge (Wootton Isaacson scholar, MA, PhD) Harvard Univ (AM), UEA (DLitt), Fitzwilliam Coll Cambridge (LittD); *m* 11 Aug 1960, Margaret, da of Eric Arthur Elson (d 1986); 2 da (Jane b 1964, Serena b 1967); *Career* Nat Serv 1955–57; Frank Knox meml fell Harvard Univ 1960–61, reader UEA 1972–81 (lectr 1964–69, sr lectr 1969–72); visiting fell: Centre for Advanced Study Univ of Illinois 1968–69, All Souls Coll Oxford 1977–78; dir Norwich Summer Russian Course 1969–81; Roberts prof of Russian Univ of Leeds 1981–85; Univ of Cambridge: prof of Slavonic studies 1985–2004, fell Fitzwilliam Coll 1986–2004; chm Br Academic Ctee for Liaison with Russian Archives 1981–95, memb Br Univs Assoc of Slavists (pres 1982–84), chm Academia Rossica 2001–05; gen ed: Russia through European Eyes 1968–75, Anglo-Russian Affinities 1989–95; reviews ed Jl of European Studies 1971–, ed Study Gp on Eighteenth-Century Russia Newsletter 1973–2009; Alec Nove Prize in Russia Studies 1997, Antsiferov Prize St Petersburg 1997, Dashkova Medal Moscow 2003; hon doctorate Inst of Russian Literature Russian Acad of Sciences 2008; Leverhulme emeritus fell 2008; fell Russian Acad for the Humanities 1996; FBA 1989; *Books* N M Karamzin (1971), Russia Under Western Eyes (ed, 1971), Russian Literature in the Age of Catherine the Great (ed, 1976), Anglo-Russian Relations in the Eighteenth Century (1977), By the Banks of The Thames – Russians in Eighteenth Century Britain (1980, Russian trans 1996), The 1780s: Russia under Western Eyes (1981), The Tale of the Russian Daughter and Her Suffocated Lover (1982), Eighteenth Century Russian Literature, Culture and Thought: A Bibliography of English-Language Scholarship and Translations (jtly, 1984), The Russian Theme in English Literature (1985), Russia and the World of the Eighteenth Century (ed jtly, 1986), An English Lady at the Court of Catherine the Great (ed, 1989), Anglophilia on the Throne – The British and Russians in the Age of Catherine the Great (1992), Anglo-Russica – Selected Essays on Anglo-Russian Cultural Relations (1993), Engraved in the Memory – James Walker and his Russian Anecdotes (ed, 1993), Literature, Lives and Legality in Catherine's Russia (jt ed, 1994), By the Banks of the Neva: Chapters from the Lives and Careers of the British in Eighteenth-Century Russia (1996, Russian trans 2005), Russia in the Reign of Peter the Great: Old and New Perspectives (ed, 1998), Britain and Russia in the Age of Peter the Great: Historical Documents (jt ed, 1998), Peter the Great through British Eyes: Perceptions and Representations of the Tsar since 1698 (2000, Russian trans 2013), Catherine the Great and the British: A Pot-Pourri of Essays (2001), St Petersburg, 1703–1825 (ed, 2003), Days from the Reigns of the Eighteenth-Century Russian Rulers (ed, 2007), St Petersburg and the British: The City through the Eyes of British Visitors and Residents (2008), A People Passing Rude: British Responses to Russian Culture (ed, 2012), In the Lands of the Romanovs: An Annotated Bibliography of First-hand English-language Accounts of the Russian Empire 1613–1917 (2014); *Recreations* food, travel, collecting books, watching cricket; *Style*— Prof Anthony Cross, FBA; ✉ Fitzwilliam College, Storey's Way, Cambridge CB3 0DG (☎ 01223 472121, fax 01223 477976, e-mail agc28@cam.ac.uk)

CROSS, Emma-Jane; da of Bryan Cross (d 1981), and Susan, *née* Surridge; *b* 7 October 1967, Harlow, Essex; *Educ* BA, MPhil; *partner* Sarah Dyer; *Career* academic and researcher 1997–99, fndr and ceo beatbullying 1999–2014 (Children's Charity of the Year 2005, UK Charity of the Year 2005 and 2006), currently md Digital Impacts; dir: Socialpreneurial Ltd, Primary Contact Solution; *Style*— Ms Emma-Jane Cross; ✉ beatbullying, Rochester House, 67–69 Belvedere Road, London SE19 2HP (☎ 020 8771 3888, e-mail emma-jane@beatbullying.org)

CROSS, Gillian Clare; da of James Eric Arnold (d 1988), and Joan Emma, *née* Manton (d 2007); *b* 24 December 1945; *Educ* N London Collegiate Sch for Girls, Somerville Coll Oxford (MA), Univ of Sussex (DPhil); *m* 1967, Martin Cross; 2 s (Jonathan b 1967, Anthony b 1984), 2 da (Elizabeth b 1970, Katherine b 1985); *Career* children's author; memb Soc of Authors; Liveryman Worshipful Co of Educators 2013; Hon DLitt Univ of Glamorgan 2008; *Books* The Runaway (1979), The Iron Way (1979), Revolt at Ratcliffe's Rags (1980), Save Our School (1981), A Whisper of Lace (1981), The Demon Headmaster (1982), The Dark Behind the Curtain (1982), The Mintyglo Kid (1983), Born of the Sun (1983), On the Edge (1984), The Prime Minister's Brain (1985), Swimathon (1986), Chartbreak (1986), Roscoe's Leap (1987), A Map of Nowhere (1988), Rescuing Gloria (1989), Wolf (1990, Carnegie medal Library Assoc), The Monster from Underground (1990), Twin and Super-Twin (1990), Gobbo the Great (1991), Rent-a-Genius (1991), The Great Elephant Chase (1992, winner first prize Smarties Awards, Whitbread children's book award), The Furry Maccaloo (1992), Beware Olga! (1993), The Tree House (1993), Hunky Parker is Watching You (1994), What Will Emily Do? (1994), New World (1994), The Crazy Shoe Shuffle (1995), Posh Watson (1995), The Roman Beanfeast (1996), The Demon Headmaster Strikes Again (1996), Pictures in the Dark (1996), The Demon Headmaster Takes Over (1997), The Goose Girl (1998), Tightrope (1999), Down With the Dirty Danes (2000), The Treasure in the Mud (2001), Calling a Dead Man (2001), Beware of the Demon Headmaster (2002), Facing the Demon Headmaster (2002), The Dark Ground (2004), The Black Room (2005), Sam Sorts it Out (2005), The Nightmare Game (2006), Brother Aelred's Feet (2007), Where I Belong (2010), Cave Wars (2011), The Monster Snowman (2012), The Odyssey (2012), After Tomorrow (2013, Little Rebels Book Award 2014), The Cupcake Wedding (2013), The Mystery of the Man with the Black Beard (2014), Mozart's Banana (2014), Shadow Cat (2015), The Iliad (2015), Amber's Song (2016), Changing Shape: Stories from Ovid's Metamorphoses (2016); *Recreations* orienteering, playing the piano; *Style*— Mrs Gillian Cross; ✉ c/o Philippa Milnes-Smith, Lucas, Alexander, Whitley Ltd, 14 Vernon Street, London W14 0RJ

CROSS, Dr Neil Earl; s of Sidney Cross (d 1993), and Winifred, *née* Earl (d 1980); *b* 17 March 1945; *Educ* Drayton Manor Co GS, Univ of Exeter (BSc), Univ of Edinburgh (PhD); *m* 7 Oct 1972, Carol Christian Buchan, *née* Gillan; 1 s (Alastair b 1976), 1 da (Georgina b 1980); *Career* various positions with 3i Group plc 1969–96 (incl main int bd dir 1988–96); chm: Albion Technol & Gen VCT plc, European Venture Capital Assoc 1986–87, BMT Gp Ltd 1997–2015, RSA 2001–03; dir: Business in the Environment 1994–96, Babraham Inst 1995–2003, Taylor Nelson Sofres plc 1996–2005, Perkins Foods plc 1997–2001, Alliance Unichem plc 1997–2006, Dawson Holdings plc 1997–2007; non-exec dir: Bernard Matthews Holdings Ltd 2005–08 (dep chm), Bayard Fund, Caliburn Absolute Strategies spc; advsr: Unilever UK Pension Fund 1997–2006, Baring European Private Equity Fund 1997–2007, Fifth Causeway Development Capital Fund 1997–2007; visiting prof Cranfield Business Sch 1992–93; memb Lottery Advsy Panel of the Arts Cncl of England 1996–99, memb Fundraising Campaign Bd Univ of Exeter 2007–11, memb Campaign Bd Univ of Edinburgh 2008–12; tstee The Mary Kinross Charitable Tst; Regent Univ of Edinburgh 2012–; FCIS 1981 (ACIS 1972), FRSA 1992; *Recreations* walking, theatre, reading; *Clubs* Savile; *Style*— Dr Neil Cross; ✉ Sycamore House, Bluntisham, Cambridgeshire PE28 3LA

CROSS, Nicholas John (Nick); s of John Cross, CBE, of Ixworth, Suffolk, and Janet, *née* Devitt; *b* 13 August 1962; *Educ* Uppingham, Univ of Cambridge (BA); *m* Non, da of Lord Morris of Aberavon, PC, QC, *qv*; 2 s (Henry John Caradog, Llewelyn John Edmund (twins) b 14 June 1996); *Career* dir SRU Ltd mgmnt consultancy 1992–93 (joined 1984), int planning dir Bartle Bogle Hegarty Ltd advtg agency 1993–96, mktg dir (i/c advtg, direct mail catalogues and storecard ops) Selfridges Ltd dept store 1996–2001, former chief mktg offr Egg (joined 2001), currently ptnr The Foundation LLP strategic innovation consulting; memb Mgmnt Ctee Nat Youth Agency (formerly Nat Youth Bureau) 1988–93; *Recreations* shooting, sailing; *Clubs* Farmers'; *Style*— Nick Cross, Esq; ✉ 206 Camberwell Grove, London SE5 8RJ

CROSS, Philippa Jane (Pippa); da of Robert Lionel Cross (d 1977), and Jill Patricia Abbott, MBE, of Ipswich, Suffolk; *b* 13 May 1956; *Educ* Ipswich HS GPDST, St Anne's Coll Oxford; *m* 1982, Graham Ronald Lee; 1 da (Maisie Victoria Kelda b 2 May 1983), 1 s (Pierrot Robert Alexander b 6 Aug 1991); *Career* entertainments mangr Wembley Conf Centre 1977–80; Granada Television Manchester mangr 1980–85; mangr factual progs TVS Television Maidstone 1985–88; Granada Television London 1988– (prodn exec My Left Foot, prodn exec The Field), head of devpt feature films and films for TV 1990–, head of film 1993–2002 (prodr: Jack & Sarah, August, Seeing Red, The Hole, The Gathering, Gifted, Summer in February, Desert Dancer; exec prodr: Heart, The Misadventures of Margaret, Girl's Night, Rogue Trader, Essex Boys, Longitude, Ghostworld, Bloody Sunday), dir CrossDay Productions Ltd 2002– (prodr: Gifted, Shooting Dogs, Knife Edge, Heartless, Chalet Girl, Summer in February, Desert Dancer, A Hundred Streets); *Books* Prepare Your Daughter for Boarding (additional material), Boarding Schools: All You Need To Know (ed, by Victoria Davies Jones and Jennifer Ma); *Recreations* cinema, theatre; *Style*— Ms Pippa Cross; ✉ e-mail info@crossdayproductions.com, website www.crossdayproductions.com, Twitter @pippacross13

CROSS, Stefan Tylney; Hon QC; s of Brian Cross, of Bournemouth, and Jackie, *née* Kirby; *b* 5 October 1960; *Educ* Univ of Southampton (LLB), Univ of Leicester (LLM); *m* 18 Jan 1986, Dr Alison Steele; 2 da (Anna b 22 Jan 1991, Rachael b 3 Feb 1993), 2 s (Michael b 31 July 1996, Daniel b 5 Sept 2004); *Career* slr; trainee slr G A Mooning Aldridge & Brownlee 1983–85, Thompsons Slrs 1986–2002 (equity ptnr 1990–2002), fndr Stefan Cross Solicitors 2002–; dir Action4Equality Scotland Ltd 2005–; Wig and Pen Award Bournemouth and Dist Law Soc 1983, TSB Articled Clerks Award 1984 and 1985; cncllr (Lab) Newcastle CC 1990–98; memb Law Soc 1985; *Recreations* politics, football, trashy crime thrillers, indie rock music, travel, art; *Clubs* Newcastle United FC; *Style—* Stefan Cross, QC; ✉ 23 Montagu Avenue, Newcastle upon Tyne NE3 4HY (☎ 0191 285 6110); Stefan Cross Solicitors Ltd, Buddle House, Buddle Road, Newcastle NE4 8AW (☎ 0191 226 6686, e-mail stc@stefancross.co.uk)

CROSS, Tom; *b* London; *Educ* Univ of Exeter (BSc); *m*; 3 c; *Career* early career as petroleum engr and economist with Conoco, Thomson and LL&E, research dir Petroleum Sci & Tech Inst, fndr and chief exec Dana Petroleum plc; currently non-exec chm AUPEC Ltd; currently chm Assoc of Br Ind Oil Cos (BRINDEX), former chm Soc of Petroleum Engrs, memb Governing Cncl UK Offshore Operators Assoc; advsr BBC Radio (on oil and gas affrs), editorial advsr Jl of Petroleum Technology, advsr Bd Trawlpac Seafoods (export and financing), currently non-exec dir Parkmead Gp plc; MEI, FInstD (chartered dir); *Recreations* outdoor sporting activities; *Style—* Tom Cross, Esq

CROSS, Dr Trevor Arthur; *b* 14 May 1960, Chelmsford, Essex; *Educ* Univ of Bath (BSc), Univ of Lancaster (PhD), Anglia Poly (Dip); 1 s; *Career* various roles rising to business unit mangr Space Solar Cell until 1999, business dir Communications Business Gp then business systems dir MTech (Marconi Applied Technologies) 1999–2001; e2v Gp: co-fndr and tech dir e2v technologies 2002 (following MBO of Marconi Applied Technologies), co listed on London Stock Exchange 2004, chief technol offr 2006–; memb Cncl PPARC 2005–; author of 30 tech papers and 4 patents; *Recreations* hill walking, travel, skiing, squash, theatre, cinema; *Style—* Dr Trevor Cross; ✉ e2v technologies Ltd, 106 Waterhouse Lane, Chelmsford, Essex CM1 2QU (☎ 01245 453417)

CROSS BROWN, Tom; s of Christopher James Cross Brown (d 1998), and Georgina, *née* Forrester (d 1999); *b* 22 December 1947; *Educ* Uppingham, BNC Oxford (MA), INSEAD (MBA); *m* 1972, Susan Rosemary, da of Col Mansel Halkett Jackson (d 1967); 1 s (Nicol b 1975 d 1998), 3 da (Gemma b 1977, Amelia, Claire (twins) b 1982); *Career* md Lazard Brothers & Co Ltd 1994–97 (dir 1985), chief exec Lazard Brothers Asset Management Ltd 1994–97; ABN AMRO Asset Management Ltd: chm 1997–2003, global chief exec 2000–03; non-exec chm: ABN AMRO Trustees Ltd 2001–04, ABN AMRO GSTS Ltd 2004–06, Pearl Assurance plc 2005–09, National Provident Life Ltd 2005–09, NPI Ltd 2005–09, London Life Ltd 2005–09, Just Retirement Gp plc 2006–16 (renamed JRP Gp plc, dep chm 2016–), Ignis Asset Mgmnt Ltd 2008–10, Axial Investment Mgmnt Ltd 2008–10; non-exec dir: Whitegate Leisure plc 1987–92, Artemis Investment Management Ltd 2002–06, Phoenix Gp Hldgs (formerly Pearl Gp Ltd) 2005–16, Quintain Estates and Development plc 2005–06, PAT (Pensions) Ltd 2005–08, Artemis Alpha Tst plc 2006–, Blue Bay Asset Management plc 2006–10, Artemis Investment Mgmnt LLP 2011–, Financial Planning Standards Bd Ltd 2011–15; tstee: Cancer Care and Haemotology Fund Stoke Mandeville Hosp 2004–14, Lazard Brothers Directors Pension Scheme 2007–14; hon sec The Benedict Soc 2005– (memb 2001–); chm Heathfield Sch 2005–14 and 2016– (govr 2000–); *Style—* Tom Cross Brown, Esq; ✉ Shipton Old Farm, Winslow, Buckinghamshire MK18 3JL

CROSSAN, Denis Gerard; s of Denis Crossan (d 1995), and Mary (d 2015), *née* McGinley; *Educ* St Mungo's Acad, Glasgow Sch of Art (BA), Nat Film Sch; *m* 1987, Gillian Louise, *née* Barclay; 1 s (Maxwell James b 1987), 2 da (Rachel Louise b 1990, Juliet Renée b 1997); *Career* cinematographer; working on various music videos, commercials and feature films 1983–; memb: Br Soc of Cinematographers 1993, BAFTA 2006; *Films* credits incl: The Real McCoy, I Know What You Did Last Summer, Clandestine Marriage (Newport Beach Film Festival Best Cinematography 2000), The Hole, Me Without You, Pink Panther 2, World Without End, Take Down, Urban Hymn, Outlander; *Awards* Best Cinematography D&AD, Creative Circle, Clio Gold Award; *Recreations* surfing; *Clubs* BAFTA; *Style—* Denis Crossan, Esq; ✉ c/o McKinney McCartney Management Ltd, 10 Barley Mow Passage, London W4 4PH (☎ 020 8995 4747, fax 020 8995 2414, e-mail mail@mckinneymacartney.com); c/o Grant, Savic, Kopaloff & Associates, 6399 Wilshire Boulevard, Suite 414, Los Angeles, CA 90048 USA (☎ 00 1 323 782 1854)

CROSSICK, Prof Geoffrey Joel; s of Louis Crossick (d 1989), of London, and Rebecca Naomi, *née* Backen (d 2001); *b* 13 June 1946, London; *Educ* Haberdashers' Aske's, Gonville & Caius Coll Cambridge (open scholar, MA), Birkbeck Coll Univ of London (PhD); *m* 1973, Rita Vaudrey; 2 s (Matthew Samuel b 10 Feb 1978, Joshua b 7 Nov 1980); *Career* research fell Emmanuel Coll Cambridge 1970–73, lectr in economic and social history Univ of Hull 1973–78; Univ of Essex: lectr in history 1979–83, sr lectr then reader in history 1983–91, prof of history 1991–2002, pro-vice-chllr (academic devpt) 1997–2002; chief exec AHRB 2002–05, warden Goldsmiths Univ of London 2005–10, vice-chllr Univ of London 2010–12, distinguished prof of the humanities Sch of Advanced Study Univ of London 2013–; dir AHRC Cultural Value Project 2012–16, chair Crafts Cncl 2014–; chair Governing Bd Trinity Long Room Hub Inst of Arts and Humanities Research Trinity Coll Dublin, memb Governing Bd Courtauld Inst; tstee: Samuel Courtauld Tst 2012–, Horniman Museum 2013– (also memb Governing Bd), Goldsmiths Centre 2014–; Freeman Goldsmiths Co 2010; hon fell Emmanuel Coll Cambridge 2004; FRHistS 1986, FRSA 2009; *Books* The Lower Middle Class in Britain 1870–1914 (ed, 1976), An Artisan Elite in Victorian Society (1978), Shopkeepers and Master Artisans in Nineteenth-Century Europe (ed with H G Haupt, 1984), The Petite Bourgeoisie in Europe 1780–1914 (with H G Haupt, 1995), The Artisan and the European Town (ed, 1997), Cathedrals of Consumption: The Department Store in European Society 1850–1940 (ed, 1999), Knowledge Transfer without Widgets: the Challenge of the Creative Economy (2007), The Future Is More Than Just Tomorrow: Higher Education, the Economy and the Longer-Term (2010), Monographs and Open Access (report to HE Funding Cncl for England 2015), Understanding the Value of Arts and Culture: the AHRC Cultural Value Project (with P Kaszynska, 2016); *Recreations* music, craft, Tottenham Hotspur FC; *Style—* Prof Geoffrey Crossick; ✉ e-mail geoffrey.crossick@london.ac.uk

CROSSLEY, Prof Michael; s of Kenneth Crossley (d 2015), and Kathleen, *née* Lumb (d 1975); *b* Halifax, Yorks; *Educ* Keele Univ (BEd), Univ of London (MA), La Trobe Univ Melbourne (PhD); *m* 1978, Anne, da of Dennis Morgan and Beryl Morgan; 2 s (Martin b 1987, Sam b 1990); *Career* Grad Sch of Educn Univ of Bristol: prof of comparative and int educn, founding dir Centre for Comparative and Int Research in Educn (CIRE), dir Educn in Small States Research Gp; adjunct prof Univ of the South Pacific; former assoc dean Faculty of Educn Univ of PNG, assoc memb and memb Editorial Advsy Bd Comparative Educn Research Centre Univ of Hong Kong; former chair and vice-chair British Assoc for Int and Comparative Educn (BAICE); memb: Br Educn Research Assoc (BERA), Comparative and Int Educn Soc (CIES) USA, Cncl for Educn for the Cwlth, Royal Cwlth Soc; founding series ed Bristol Papers in Educn, ed Comparative Educn 2004–10; memb Editorial Bd: Research in Post-compulsory Educn, Int Jl of Educnl Devpt, Int Review of Educn; FRSA 2001, FAcSS 2005; *Books* Pacific Perspectives on Non-Formal Education (jt ed, 1987), Research Training and Educational Management: International Perspectives (jt ed, 1994), Qualitative Educational Research in Developing Countries: Current Perspectives (jt ed, 1997), Learning and Teaching in an International Context: Research, Theory and Practice (jt ed, 1998), Educational Development in the Small States of the Commonwealth: Retrospect and Prospect (jtly, 1999), Globalisation, Educational Transformation and Societies in Transition (jt ed, 2000), Globalisation and Skills for Development in Rwanda and Tanzania (jtly, 2003), Comparative and International Research in Education: Globalisation, Context and Difference (jtly, 2003), Research and Evaluation for Educational Development (jtly, 2005), Changing Educational Contexts, Issues and Identities: 40 Years of Comparative Education (jt ed, 2007), Education in Small States (jtly, 2011), Education in Australia, New Zealand and the Pacific (jt ed, 2015), Revisiting Insider-Outsider Research in Comparative and International Education (jt ed, 2016); *Recreations* badminton, tennis, squash, surfing, windsurfing; *Style—* Prof Michael Crossley; ✉ The Graduate School of Education, University of Bristol, 35 Berkeley Square, Bristol BS8 1JA (website www.smallstates.net)

CROSSLEY, Paul Christopher Richard; CBE (1993); s of Lt Frank Crossley, RN (d 1948), and Myra, *née* Barrowcliffe (d 1979); *b* 17 May 1944; *Educ* Silcoates Sch Wakefield, Mansfield Coll Oxford; *Career* pianist; int concert career with world's leading orchs, ensembles, and conductors; solo recitalist and regular broadcaster; works specially written for him by leading composers incl: Adams, Berio, Gorecki, Henze, Takemitsu, Tippett; artistic dir London Sinfonietta 1988–94; sixteen TV progs on prominent composers; recordings incl: Janacek: Complete Piano Music 1979, Liszt: A Recital 1983, Ravel: Complete Piano Music 1983, Fauré: Complete Piano Music 1983–87, Tippett: Sonatas 1–4 1985, Messiaen: Turangalila-Symphonie 1986, Messiaen Des Canyons aux Etoiles Oiseaux Exotiques, Couleurs de la Cité Celeste 1988, Poulenc: Complete Piano Music 1989, Stravinsky: Complete Music for Piano and Orchestra 1990, Adams: Eros Piano 1991, Takemitsu: Riverrun 1991, Debussy: Complete Piano Music 1993, Franck: Symphonic Variations 1994 and Piano Music 1994, Lutoslawski: Piano Concerto 1995, Takemitsu: Quotation of Dream 1998, Takemitsu: Complete Piano Music 2000, Scriabin: Late Piano Works 2007, Grieg: Lyric Pieces 2007; hon fell Mansfield Coll Oxford 1991; *Recreations* crosswords, reading; *Style—* Paul Crossley, Esq, CBE; ✉ 39 Henry Tate Mews, London SW16 3HA (☎ 020 8769 4471, e-mail pcr.crossley@gmail.com, website www.paulcrossleypianist.com)

CROSSLEY-HOLLAND, Dr Kevin John William; s of Peter Charles Crossley-Holland (d 2001) of Dyfed, and Joan Mary Crossley-Holland, MBE, *née* Cowper (d 2005); *b* 7 February 1941; *Educ* Bryanston, St Edmund Hall Oxford (MA); *m* 19 March 1999; Linda Waslien; 2 s (Kieran b 1963, Dominic b 1967), 2 da (Oenone b 1982, Eleanor b 1986); *Career* ed Macmillan & Co 1962–69, Gregory fell in poetry Univ of Leeds 1969–71, talks prodr BBC 1972, editorial dir Victor Gollancz 1972–77, lectr in English Tufts in London program 1969–78, lektor Regensburg Univ 1979–80, Arts Cncl fellow in writing Winchester Sch of Art 1983 and 1984, visiting prof St Olaf Coll Minnesota 1987, 1988 and 1989, endowed chair in the humanities and fine arts Univ of St Thomas Minnesota 1991–95; editorial conslt Boydell and Brewer 1987–89; chm E Arts Assoc Literature Panel 1986–89; dir American Composers Forum 1991–96; chm Poetry next-the-Sea Festival 1999–2006; patron: Soc for Storytelling, Publishing House Me (The Young Gifted and Talented Learner Academy), European Storytelling Archive, The Story Museum; tstee Wingfield Coll 1986–99; hon fell St Edmund Hall Oxford 2001; Hon DLitt: Anglia Ruskin Univ 2011, Univ of Worcester 2013; FRSL, fell English Assoc; *Books* poetry: vols incl Waterslain (1986), The Language of Yes (1996), Poems from East Anglia (1997), Selected Poems (2001), Moored Man (2006), The Mountains of Norfolk: New and Selected Poems (2011, EDP Jarrold Poetry Award), The Breaking Hour (2015); memoir The Hidden Roads (2009); for children: The Green Children (1966, Arts Cncl Award), Storm (1985, Carnegie Medal), British Folk Tales (1987), Short! (1998), The King Who Was and Will Be (1998), Arthur: The Seeing Stone (2000, Guardian Children's Fiction Award, Tir na n-Og Award), At the Crossing-Places (2001), King of the Middle March (2003), How Many Miles to Bethlehem? (2004), Gatty's Tale (2006), Waterslain Angels (2008), Bracelet of Bones (2011), Scramasax (2012), Heartsong (2015), The Riddlemaster (2016); translations from Old English: Beowulf (1968), The Exeter Book of Riddles (revised edn, 1993); mythology: The Norse Myths (1981); travel and history: Pieces of Land (1972), The Stones Remain (1989); edited: The Anglo-Saxon World (1982), Folk-Tales of The British Isles (1985), The Oxford Book of Travel Verse (1986), Young Oxford Book of Folk-Tales (1998), Light Unlocked (with Lawrence Sail, 2005); opera: The Green Children (with Nicola LeFanu, 1990), The Wildman (with Nicola LeFanu, 1995), The Sailor's Tale (with Rupert Bawden, 2002); musical settings: A Knot of Riddles (with Sir Arthur Bliss), Riddles (with William Mathias), Pilgrim Jesus (with Stephen Paulus), The Nine Gifts (with Steve Heitzeg), The Death of Balder (with Bernard Hughes), Four Carols (with Bob Chilcott), Hubbub and Jesus Springing (with Giles Swayne), Sea Tongue, Gaudeamus Igitur (with Janet Wheeler), A Medieval Bestiary (with Bernard Hughes), A Time for All Seasons (with Cecilia McDowall, 2016); *Recreations* music, walking, wine, travel; *Clubs* Garrick; *Style—* Dr Kevin Crossley-Holland, FRSL; ✉ Chalk Hill, Burnham Market, Norfolk PE31 8JR (☎ 01328 730167, e-mail kevincrossleyholland@gmail.com, website www.kevincrossley-holland.com); literary agent: The Agency Ltd, 24 Pottery Lane, London W11 4LZ (☎ 020 7727 1346, e-mail hdelamere@theagency.co.uk)

CROSTHWAITE, Andrew Donald; s of Donald Rothery Crosthwaite, of Lytham, Lancs, and Jean Mary, *née* Cavill; *b* March 1957; *Educ* Manchester Grammar, Worcester Coll Oxford (BA); *Children* 2 s (Matthew Andrew, Sam Neil (twins) b 14 May 1990), 1 da (Katie Louisa b 19 Aug 1991); *Career* advtg exec; Ogilvy & Mather 1978–81, McCormick Publicis 1981–82, Doyle Dane Bernbach 1982–85; FCO Ltd: joined 1985, dir 1986, planning ptnr until 1993; dir of planning Euro RSCG London 1993–96, fndr Euro RSCG Upstream (Brand Consultancy) 1996–99, ptnr Futureshouse, fndr Core Values, planning dir BLAC Advertising; memb Marketing Soc; FIPA; *Recreations* trekking, surfing, swimming, snowshoeing, Land Rover Defender; *Style—* Andrew Crosthwaite; ✉ 2 Red Lion Cottages, Elm Road, Penn HP10 8LD (e-mail andrewcrosthwaite@yahoo.com)

CROSTHWAITE, Peregrine Kenneth Oughton (Perry); s of Kenneth Alan Crosthwaite, and Nora Elsie, *née* Oughton; *b* 24 March 1949; *Educ* St Paul's, Trinity Coll Oxford (MA); *m* 29 Oct 1982, Valerie Janet, yr da of Sir Albert Jonas Cahn, Bt, *qv*; 2 s (Nicholas Anthony b 22 Jan 1985, Thomas William b 23 Oct 1986), 1 da (Sally-Anne Claire b 8 May 1989); *Career* joined Fenn & Crosthwaite 1972 (merged with George Henderson to become Henderson Crosthwaite 1975), ptnr Henderson Crosthwaite 1979–86, chm Investec Investment Bank & Securities (formerly Investec Henderson Crosthwaite) 1997–2004, chm Jupiter Green Investment Tst; non-exec dir: Investec plc, Melrose plc; memb: Nordoff-Robbins Music Therapy Bd of Govrs, Trinity Coll Oxford Investment Ctee; memb: Worshipful Co of Merchant Taylors, Freeman City of London; memb London Stock Exchange 1975; *Recreations* cricket, tennis, skiing, music, books, theatre; *Style—* Perry Crosthwaite, Esq; ✉ 30 Larpent Avenue, London SW15 6UU (☎ 020 8789 7977)

CROTHERS, Bill; CB (2014); *Educ* Univ of Manchester; *Career* ptnr Accenture 1992–2007, gp commercial dir Home Office 2007–12, exec dir commercial relationships, DG commercial and govt chief procurement offr Cabinet Office 2012–14, chief commercial off HM's Govt 2014–; memb Bd Nat Citizenship Service; chair UK Youth; FCIPS, FICAEW, chartered FBCS; *Style—* Bill Crothers, Esq, CB; ✉ Cabinet Office, 70 Whitehall, London SW1A 2AS

CROUCH, Prof Colin John; s of Charles John Crouch (d 1990), of Charlbury, Oxon, and Doris Beatrice, *née* Baker (d 1990); *b* 1 March 1944; *Educ* Latymer Upper Sch, LSE (BA), Univ of Oxford (DPhil); *m* 10 June 1970, Joan Ann, da of David Freedman (d 1972), of London; 2 s (Daniel b 1974, Benjamin b 1978); *Career* lectr in sociology: LSE 1969–70, Univ of Bath 1972–73; reader LSE 1980–85 (lectr 1973–79, sr lectr 1979–80); Univ of Oxford: fell and tutor in politics Trinity Coll 1985–98, faculty lectr in sociology 1985–96, chm Sub-Faculty of Sociology 1987–89, proctor 1990–91, chm Social Studies Faculty Bd 1994, prof of sociology 1996–98; Euro Univ Inst Florence: prof of sociology 1995–2004, chm Dept of Political and Social Studies 2001–04; prof of governance and public mgmnt Univ of Warwick Business Sch 2005–11 (prof emeritus 2011–); research interests in the comparative sociology of Western Europe and economic sociology and in public servs mgmnt and policy; curator Bodleian Library 1990–95, delegate Oxford Univ Press 1992–98, vice-pres Br Acad 2012– (chm Sociology Section 2009–12); memb Standing Ctee of Ct of Govrs LSE 1980–84, jt ed The Political Quarterly 1985–95; chm: Fabian Soc 1976 (memb Exec Ctee 1969–78), Political Quarterly 2000–09; memb: Max Planck Soc Cologne 1997–, Regnl Policy Forum 2000–03; referee class 3 Oxfordshire Football Assoc; Friedrich Ebert Stiftung Prize 2012; FBA 2005, AcSS 2008; *Publications* The Student Revolt (1970), Class Conflict and the Industrial Relations Crisis (1977), The Politics of Industrial Relations (2 edn 1982), Trade Unions: the Logic of Collective Action (1982), Industrial Relations and European State Traditions (1993), Are Skills the Answer (jtly, 1999), Social Change in Western Europe (1999), Local Production Systems in Europe: Rise or Demise? (jtly, 2001), Postdemocrazia (2003), Changing Governance of Local Economics: Response of European Local Production Systems (jtly, 2004), Capitalist Diversity and Change: Recombinant Governance and Institutional Entrepreneurs (2005), Innovation in Local Economics: Germany in Comparative Context (jtly, 2009), The Strange Non-Death of Neoliberalism (2011), Making Capitalism Fit for Society (2013), Markt und Moral (with P Engelmann, 2014); ed: Stress and Contradiction in Modern Capitalism (with Lindberg et al, 1975), Br Political Sociology Yearbook Vol III Participation in Politics (1977), The Resurgence of Class Conflict in Western Europe since 1968 vol I Nat Studies vol II comparative Analyses (with A Pizzorno, 1978), State and Economics in Contemporary Capitalism (1979), Int Yearbook of Organizations Democracy vol I Organizational Democracy and Political Processes (with F Heller, 1983), The New Centralism (with D Marquand, 1989), Corporatism and Accountability Organised Interests in Br Public Life (with R P Dore, 1990), European Industrial Relations: the Challenge of Flexibility (with G Baglioni, 1990), The Politics of 1992 (with D Marquand, 1990), Towards Greater Europe? (with D Marquand, 1992), Social Research and Social Reform (with A Heath, 1992), Ethics and Markets (with D Marquand, 1993), Organized Industrial Relations in Europe (with F Traxler, 1995), Reinventing Collective Action (with D Marquand, 1995), Les capitalismes en Europe (with W Streeck, 1996), Political Economy of Modern Capitalism (with W Streeck, 1997), After the Euro (2000), Citizenship, Markets and the State (with C Eder and D Tambini, 2001), The Diversity of Democracy (with W Streeck, 2006), The Responsible Corporation (with C Maclean, 2011), Governing Social Risks in Post-Crisis Europe (2015), The Knowledge Corrupters: Hidden Consequences of the Financial Takeover of Public Life (2015), Society and Social Change in 21st Century Europe (2016); *Recreations* playing violin, listening to music, gardening; *Style—* Prof Colin Crouch; ✉ University of Warwick Business School, Coventry CV4 7AL (e-mail c.crouch@warwick.ac.uk)

CROUCH, Julian David; s of David James Frederick Crouch, and Barbara Victoria, *née* Heywood; *Educ* Ayr Acad, Univ of Edinburgh; *Career* theatre designer; maskmaker and designer Trickster Theatre Co, co-fndr Improbable Theatre (with Phelim McDermott and Lee Simpson) 1996, co-dir and co-designer Shockheaded Peter (Best Dir TMA Awards 1998, Best Designer Critics Soc Awards 1998, Best Entertainment Olivier Awards 2002), designer and assoc dir Jerry Springer The Opera (NT) 2003 (Best Musical Evening Standard Awards, Olivier Awards and Critics Soc Awards 2004); other prodns incl: 70 Hill Lane (Improbable, OBIE Best Prodn 1997), A Midsummer Nights Dream (English Shakespeare Co, Best Touring Prodn TMA Awards 1997); *Style—* Julian Crouch, Esq; ✉ Improbable, 4th Floor, 43 Aldwych, London WC24 4DN (☎ 020 7240 4556, e-mail crouch@dircon.co.uk)

CROUCH, Sunny; OBE (2006); da of Frederick Charles Moore, of London, and Edith Joyce, *née* Budd; *b* 11 February 1943; *Educ* Lancaster Univ (MA), Dip CIM, Dip MRS; *m*; *Career* mktg mgmnt Brocades (GB) Ltd 1966–72; course dir (honours degree in business studies) Univ of Portsmouth Business Sch 1972–83, visiting course dir (market research) Coll of Chartered Inst of Mktg 1977–83; mktg conslt 1972–83, chief mktg and tourism offr City of Portsmouth 1983–88 (Tourist Authy of the Year Award 1985, English Tourist Bd's first England for Excellence Award for Cities 1988), dir of mktg London Docklands Devpt Corp 1988–98 (nine years' winner Property Marketing Awards), md World Trade Centre London 1998–2010; chm Portsmouth Historic Dockyard 2013–; non-exec bd dir: Melody Radio 1989–92, Scottish Radio Holdings 1997–2005, London First 2002–08, Thurrock Urban Devpt Corp 2004–12, Places for People Gp plc 2005–12 (corporate tstee and dir Retirement Benefit Scheme 2014–), Island Health Tst 2009–11; chm: DOBRIC Publications 1990–98, TourEast London 1993–98, Centre of Excellence for Women Entrepreneurs 2010–; vice-pres Docklands Business Club 1989–98; memb: Tourism Soc 1983–2012 (Nat Cncl 1989–98, vice-chm 1994–97), ForumUK 1988–2012 (Nat Exec Ctee 1989–98), Industrial and Economic Affrs Ctee Gen Synod C of E 1991–98; govr: City of Portsmouth Girls' Sch 1977–88, Portsmouth Coll of Art, Design and FE 1984–88, Univ of East London 2000–09 and 2010–; memb Cncl Friends of the National Maritime Museum 1999–2006; London Borough of Tower Hamlets Civic Award 2004, SHINE Woman of the Year Award 2005, Lifetime Achievement Award Tourism Soc 2006; Freeman: City of London 1993, Worshipful Co of World Traders 1998; Hon DBA Univ of E London 2010; FCIM 1970, full memb MRS 1975, FTS 1985, MInstD 1990; *Publications* Mass Media and Cultural Relationship (jtly, 1975), Marketing Research for Managers (1984 and 1985, 3 edn 2003); *Style—* Sunny Crouch, OBE; ✉ 20 Centurion Gate, Southsea, Hampshire PO4 9TF (☎ 07775 603193, e-mail sunny.crouch20@gmail.com)

CROUCH, Tracey Elizabeth Anne; MP; *b* 24 July 1975, Ashford, Kent; *Educ* Folkestone Sch for Girls, Univ of Hull (BA); *Career* political consultancy 1998–2003, COS to Damian Green, MP, *qv* (as Shadow Sec of State for Educn) and Rt Hon David Davis, *qv* (as Shadow Home Sec) 2003–05; head of public affrs Aviva plc 2005–10; MP (Cons) Chatham and Aylesford 2010–; mangr Meridian Girls FC; *Style—* Ms Tracey Crouch, MP; ✉ House of Commons, London SW1A 0AA (☎ 020 7219 3000)

CROW, Bob; s of George Crow (d 1996), and Lillian Crow; *b* 13 June 1961; *Educ* Kingswood Secdy Modern Hainault; *m* Nicola, *née* Hoarau; 1 s (Anthony), 3 da (Kerrie, Natasha, Tanya); *Career* gen sec RMT 2002– (asst gen sec 1995–2002), memb Bd Transport for London 2002; *Recreations* football, boxing, darts; *Style—* Bob Crow, Esq; ✉ RMT, Unity House, 39 Chalton Street, London NW1 1JD (☎ 020 7387 4771, mobile 07799 893801)

CROW, Jonathan; QC (2006); s of Michael Frederick Crow, and Edith Mae, *née* Quayle; *Educ* Univ of Oxford (BA), City Univ (Dip); *m* 1998, Claudia Jane, *née* Turner; 1 da (Eleanor b 1999), 3 s (Frederick b 2001, Lucas b 2006, Felix b 2008); *Career* called to the Bar 1981; treasy counsel (chancery) 1994, first treasy counsel (chancery) 1998–2006, attorney-gen to HRH The Prince of Wales 2006–; dep judge High Court 2001–, judge Court of Appeal of Jersey and Guernsey 2011–; *Clubs* Athenaeum, RGS; *Style—* Jonathan Crow, Esq, QC; ✉ 4 Stone Buildings, Lincoln's Inn, London WC2A 3XT

CROWCROFT, Prof Jonathan Andrew (Jon); s of Prof Andrew Crowcroft, and Prof Kyla Greenbaum; *b* 23 November 1957; *Educ* Univ of Cambridge (BA), Univ of London (MSc, PhD); *m* 1988, Noreen, da of Leo McKeever; 1 da (Alice b 1989), 2 s (Daniel b 1996, Patrick b 1998); *Career* lectr rising to prof of networked systems Computer Science Dept UCL 1982–2001, Marconi prof of communications Univ of Cambridge 2001–; memb Internet Architecture Bd; FIEEE, FIET, FBCS, FREng, FACM; *Recreations* cycling; *Style—* Prof Jon Crowcroft; ☎ 01223 763 633

CROWE, Victoria Elizabeth; OBE (2004); da of Philip Farrands Crowe (d 1980), and Aziel, *née* Rowe; *b* 8 May 1945; *Educ* Kingston Sch of Art, RCA (MA); *Career* artist; pt/t lectr Edinburgh Coll of Art, sr visiting scholar St Catharine's Coll Cambridge 2004–07; hon doctorate Univ of Aberdeen 2009; RSW 1982, RSA 2004 (ARSA 1987), FRSE 2010; *Solo Exhibitions* incl: The Scottish Gallery Edinburgh 1970, 1973, 1977, 1982, 1995, 1998, 2001, 2004, 2006, 2008, 2010, 2012 and 2014, Thackeray Gallery London 1983, 1985, 1987, 1989, 1991, 1994, 1999, 2001, 2003, 2005 and 2007, Fine Art Society Glasgow and Edinburgh 1988, Scottish Nat Portrait Gallery 2000, A Shepherd's Life (touring Scotland, also at Hatton Gallery Newcastle upon Tyne and Mercer Art Gallery Harrogate) 2003 and (Fleming Collection London) 2009, Alchemy (Drumcroon and Wigan Educn Authy) 2003, RSA 2007, Fine Art Soc London 2009, Browse and Darby London 2012, From Fleece to Fibre: the Making of the Large Tree Tapestry (Dovecot Studios Edinburgh Festival) 2013 (touring Australian Tapestry Studio Melbourne, Inverness Museum and Art Gallery and Fleming Collection London) 2014–15; *Group Exhibitions* incl: Artist and Teacher (Fine Art Society Edinburgh and Glasgow), Contemporary Art from Scotland (touring exhbn), Light from the Window (Nat Gallery of Scotland), Portrait 84 (National Portrait Gallery London), Portraits on Paper (Scottish Arts Cncl touring exhbn) 1984–85, Sunday Times/Singer Friedlander Watercolour Exhbn 1988, 1990, 1991, 1992 and 1993, Scottish Art in the 20th Century (RWEA Bristol) 1991, Portrait of a Living Marsh (work from Artists for Nature Fndn Polish project, touring exhbn throughout Europe and USA with book) 1993, Artists for Nature in Extremadura (touring exhbn throughout Europe and USA with book, 1995), ANF Indian Project, Wild Tigers of Bhandhavgarh (Burrel Collection, Glasgow) 2000, Jesus 2000 (Glasgow Gall of Modern Art); regular exhibitor at Royal Acad of Arts London, RSA Edinburgh, Royal Scottish Watercolour Soc; *Public Collections* incl: RCA, Royal Acad of Arts, Scottish Nat Gallery of Modern Art, Univ of Edinburgh, Contemporary Art Soc, NT for Scotland, Scottish Nat Portrait Gallery, City Art Centre Edinburgh, Nat Portrait Gallery London; *Commissioned Portraits* incl: R D Laing (for SNPG), Tam Dalyell MP, Lord Wemyss (for Nat Tst Scotland), Kathleen Raine, Dame Janet Vaughn (Nat Portrait Gallery), Ole Lippmann (Danish Nat Portrait Collection), Thea Musgrave (Scottish Nat Portrait Gallery) 2005, Peter Higgs (cmmnd by RSE) 2013; *Awards* incl: Daler/Rowney Prize for Watercolour Royal Acad of Arts 1987, Hunting Gp major award 1988, Chris Beetles Prize RWS, Sir William Gillies Bequest RSA 1992 and 2004; *Publications* A Shepherd's Life (2000), Painted Insights (monograph, 2001), Victoria Crowe by Duncan Macmillan (monograph, 2012); *Style—* Ms Victoria Crowe, OBE; ✉ website www.victoriacrowe.com; c/o Scottish Gallery, 16 Dundas Street, Edinburgh EH3 6HZ

CROWLEY, Graham Neil; s of Victor Matthew Crowley, and Veronica Mary, *née* Lee; *b* 3 May 1950; *Educ* St Martin's Sch of Art (DipAD), RCA (MA); *m* 16 Dec 1978, Sally Ann, da of Warwick Arthur Townshend; 2 s (Robin Merrick 1 Aug 1982, Pearse Max Gary 20 July 1985); *Career* artist; artist in residence Univ of Oxford 1982–83, memb Fine Art Faculty British Sch at Rome 1982–88, sr fell in painting S Glamorgan Inst of HE Cardiff 1986–89, drawing residency Riverscape Int Cleveland 1991–92, head of fine art City & Guilds of London Art Sch 1997–98, prof of painting RCA 1998–2006; memb Advsy Bd ICA 1985–89, Fine Art Working Ctee Nat Advsy Bd DES 1987–88; *Solo Exhibitions* Air Gallery London 1982, Home Comforts (MOMA Oxford and touring) 1983, Reflections (Riverside Studios) 1984, Night Life (ICA) 1984, Table Manners (Edward Totah Gallery London) 1984, Forum Zurich Art Fair 1984, Domestic Crisis (Totah Gallery NYC) 1986, In Living Memory and Other Paintings (Edward Totah Gallery) 1987, Law and Order (Cleveland Gallery Middlesbrough) 1989, More Paintings About Speculating and Flower Arranging (Edward Totah Gallery) 1989, Ballads and Folk Songs – Paintings 1981–89 (Howard Gdns Gallery S Glamorgan Inst of HE) 1990, Somewhere Else (Edward Totah Gallery) 1991, Northern Seen (Northern Centre for Contemporary Art Sunderland) 1992, Lamont Gallery (London) 1995 and 1997, Lamont Gallery 1998, Familiar Ground (Beaux Arts London 2001), Beaux Arts London 2003 and 2005; *Group Exhibitions* incl: John Moores Exhbn (Walker Art Gallery Liverpool) 1976, 1980, 1982, 1983, 1985, 1987, 1993, 2004 and 2006 (prize winner 1983 and 2006), Drawing (Barbara Toll Gallery NYC) 1984, Venice Biennale (Anthony Reynolds Gallery) 1984, The Proper Study (Br Cncl New Delhi) 1985, Still Life – A New Life (Harris Museum and Art Gallery Preston and touring) 1985, Figuring Out the '80's (Laing Art Gallery Newcastle) 1988, The New British Painting (USA) 1988, Real Life Stories (Spacex Exeter) 1989–90, The New British Painting (Queen's Museum NYC) 1990, The Brew House Open Taunton (first prize) 1990, Riverscape (Middlesborough and Cleveland Galleries) 1993, John Jones/London Open (first prize), finalist Jerwood Painting Prize 2002; *Murals* Brompton Hosp London 1982, Chandler's Ford Library 1983; *Work in Public Collections* Imperial War Museum, Museum of Auckland NZ, Arts Cncl Collection, Ipswich Museum, Leicester Educn Authy, Leeds Educn Authy, V&A, Br Cncl Collection, Contemporary Arts Soc, Kettles Yard Cambridge, Castle Museum Nottingham, Univ of Northumbria at Newcastle; *Books* Gogol's Overcoat (1984, ICA for Nighlife Exhbn), subject of Graham Crowley (by Martin Holman, 2009), I Don't Like Art (2015); *Recreations* classic motor cycling, writing; *Style—* Graham Crowley; ✉ Greystone House, 87 High Street, Wickham Market, Suffolk IP13 0RA (website www.grahamcrowley.com)

CROWLEY, Jane Elizabeth Rosser; QC (1998); da of Robert Jenkyn Rosser (d 1967), and Marion, *née* Davies; *Educ* Howell's Sch Llandaff (head girl), King's Coll London (LLB), Inns of Court Sch of Law; *m* 1986, Mark Crowley; 1 s (Huw b 1988), 1 da (Sara b 1990); *Career* called to the Bar Gray's Inn 1976 (bencher 2006); recorder 1992, dep High Court judge 1999; pt/t pres Mental Health Review Tbnls Restricted Patients Panel 1999; assocs: Family Law Bar Assoc, Liberty; *Recreations* family, food and wine, countryside, music, sport; *Style—* Mrs Jane Crowley, QC; ✉ 30 Park Place, Cardiff CF10 3BS (☎ 029 2039 8421, fax 029 2039 8725); 1 Garden Court, Temple, London EC4Y 9BJ (☎ 020 7797 7900, fax 020 7797 7929, e-mail janecrowley@aol.com)

CROWLEY, John; QC (1982); s of John Joseph Crowley (d 1998), and Anne Marie, *née* Fallon (d 1987); *b* 25 June 1938; *Educ* St Edmund's Coll Ware, Christ's Coll Cambridge (MA, LLB); *m* 1977, Sarah Maria, da of Christopher Gage Jacobs (d 2004); 2 da (Rachel Maria b 1979, Rose Abigail b 1982); *Career* called to the Bar Inner Temple 1962 (bencher 1989), called to Irish Bar 1997; recorder 1980–2004, dep judge of the High Court 1991–2004; memb Criminal Injuries Compensation Bd 1985–2000, memb Criminal Injuries Compensation Appeals Panel 2000–02; chm Appeals Ctee ICAEW 2000–2004 (vice-chm 1998–2000); govr St Edmund's Coll Ware 1990–98; *Recreations* music, the turf, wine; *Style—* John Crowley, Esq, QC; ✉ 37 Viceroy Road, London SW8 2HA (☎ 020 7622 4742, fax 020 7622 7008)

CROWLEY, Robert (Bob); *Career* designer for theatre, opera and film; assoc artist: Royal Shakespeare Co, Nat Theatre; directing debut The Cure at Troy (Field Day Theatre Co); RDI; *Theatre* credits with the RSC: The Irish Play, Thirteenth Night, The Forest, The Taming of the Shrew, King Lear, Measure for Measure, The Time of Your Life, A New Way to Pay Old Debts, Henry V, Love's Labour's Lost, As You Like It, Les Liaisons Dangereuses (also West End, NY, Los Angeles and Tokyo), The Two Noble Kinsmen, Flight, Principia Scriptoriae, Macbeth, The Jew of Malta, The Plantaganets, Henry IV Parts I and II, tours of Romeo and Juliet, A Midsummer Night's Dream, The Winter's Tale, The Crucible, Othello and Hamlet; credits with the NT: A Midsummer's Night Dream, Ghetto, Hedda Gabler, Ma Rainey's Black Bottom, Racing Demon, White Chameleon, Richard III, Murmuring Judges, The Sea, Night of the Iguana, Carousel (also West End and Broadway), Macbeth, Absence of War, The Prince's Play, The Designated Mourner, The Cripple of Inishmaan, King Lear, Amy's View (also Broadway), His Girl Friday, Mourning Becomes Electra (Critics Circle Award), The History Boys, FRAM (designer and co dir), Phedra, Gethsemane, Every Good Boy Deserves Favour; other credits incl: Timon of Athens, A View from a Bridge and Destiny (all Bristol Old Vic),

A Midsummer Night's Dream (Bristol Old Vic and London), The Duchess of Malfi (Royal Exchange, Roundhouse and Paris), Dr Faustus (Royal Exchange), One of Us (Greenwich Theatre), After Aida (Welsh Nat Opera and The Old Vic), Two Way Mirror (The Young Vic), Saint Oscar (Field Day Theatre Co), Madame de Sade (Tokyo), The Three Sisters (Gate Theatre Dublin and The Royal Court London), When She Danced (with Vanessa Redgrave, The Globe Theatre), The Importance of Being Earnest (with Maggie Smith, The Aldwych), No Man's Land (with Harold Pinter, Almeida and Comedy Theatres), Moonlight (Almeida Theatre and West End), The Cryptogram (Ambassadors Theatre), Cunning Little Vixen (Chatelet Paris), Judas Kiss (transferred Broadway), The Iceman Cometh (The Old Vic and Broadway), Twelfth Night (with Helen Hunt, Lincoln Center Theater NY), Sweet Smell of Success (Broadway, 2002, Tony Award), Into the Woods (Donmar Warehouse), Elton John and Tim Rice's Aida for Disney (Chicago, Broadway and US tour, Tony Award), Cressida (Albery Theatre), Orpheus Descending (Donmar Warehouse), The Witches of Eastwick for Cameron Mackintoch (Drury Lane), Mary Poppins (Prince Edward Theatre, UK tour, Broadway and US tour), Tarzan (dir and designer, Broadway and The Netherlands), The Year of Magical Thinking (set designer, Broadway and Nat Theatre), The Coast of Utopia (set designer, Lincoln Center Theater); *Ballet* credits as designer of set and costumes (for Royal Ballet): Anastasia, Pavane; *Opera* Don Giovanni (Kent Opera), Alcina (Spitalfields Festival and Los Angeles), The King Goes Forth to France, The Knot Garden and La Traviata (all Royal Opera House), The Magic Flute (ENO), The Cunnning Little Vixen (Châtelet), Eugene Onegin (WNO, Opera North and the Lyric Opera Queensland), Don Giovanni (Bavarian State Opera), Don Carlos (ROH); *Film* Othello, Tales of Hollywood (with Jeremy Irons and Alec Guinness), Suddenly Last Summer (for BBC, dir Richard Eyre, with Maggie Smith), The Crucible (with Daniel Day-Lewis and Winona Ryder); *Awards* eleven Olivier Award nominations (incl two for Les Liaisons Dangereuses and two for Henry V), two Drama Desk Award nominations and two Tony Award nominations (for Les Liaisons Dangereuses on Broadway), Olivier Award for Designer of the Year 1990, Tony Award and Outer Critics Circle Award (for Carousel on Broadway) 1994, Tony Award nomination for Iceman Cometh and Twelfth Night 1999, Drama Desk Award for Twelfth Night 1999, RSA Royal Designer for Industry, Tony Award for Mary Poppins and The Coast of Utopia 2007; *Style*— Mr Bob Crowley; ✉ c/o David Watson, 6 Beauchamp Place, London SW3 1NG (☎ 020 7434 9167, fax 020 7494 2887, e-mail cary-parsons@simpson-fox.com)

CROWN, Giles Humphry; s of Sidney Crown, and June, *née* Downes; *b* 13 July 1969, London; *Educ* St Paul's, Jesus Coll Cambridge (MA), UCL (LLM), Inns of Court Sch of Law; *m* Nicola (Nicki), *née* Wilson; 1 da, 2 s; *Career* called to the Bar Middle Temple 1994 (Astbury scholar), admitted slr 2003; pupillage Blackstone Chambers and One Brick Court 1993–95, barr specialising in media law One Brick Court 1995–2000 (Inns of Court Pegasus scholar seconded to Potter Anderson & Corroon USA 1996), head of legal and business affrs TBWA UK Gp 2000–01; Lewis Silkin Slrs: joined 2001–, ptnr 2003–, head Media Brands and Technol Dept 2008– (dep head 2005–08), divnl managing ptnr 2016–; memb Secretariat: Royal Cmmn on Criminal Justice 1992, Court of Appeal (Civil Div) Review Ctee 1997; CEDR accredited mediator; memb: Advtg Lawyers Gp, Exec Ctee Branded Content Mktg Assoc, Law Soc Membership Bd (co-opted); chair and dir Westminster CAB 2005–08, Lib Dem candidate for Westminster's Hyde Park Ward 1998, membership sec Cities of London and Westminster Lib Dems 1998–2001; *Publications* Advertising Law and Regulation (1999, 2 edn 2004); regular commentator and contrib in legal jls, trade press and nat media; *Recreations* travel, theatre, running, amateur investor; *Clubs* Leander; *Style*— Giles Crown, Esq; ✉ Lewis Silkin LLP, 5 Chancery Lane, Clifford's Inn, London EC4A 1BL (☎ 020 7074 8090, e-mail giles.crown@lewissilkin.com)

CROWTHER, His Hon Judge Thomas Edward (Tom); QC (2013); s of His Hon Thomas Rowland Crowther, QC, and Gillian Jane, *née* Prince; *b* 25 May 1970, Newport; *Educ* Croesyceiliog Sch, Univ of Exeter (BSc, BA); *m* 20 Sept 2003, Molly Ratna, *née* Das; 2 da (Poppy b 13 April 2004, Leela b 10 July 2006); *Career* called to the Bar 1993; fee-paid judge First-Tier Tbnl Immigration and Asylum Chamber 2006, recorder 2009, circuit judge (Wales Circuit) 2013–, assoc judge Sovereign Base Areas Akrotiri and Dhekelia 2015–; fndr memb Apex Chambers 2007 (head of chambers 2012–13); memb Gen Cncl of the Bar 2006–08 and 2010–12; *Style*— His Hon Judge Crowther, QC; ✉ Cardiff Crown Court, The Law Courts, Cathays Park, Cardiff CF10 3PG

CROXALL, Prof John Patrick; CBE (2004); s of Harold Eli Croxall (d 1990), and Marjorie, *née* Jones (d 1996); *b* 19 January 1946, Birmingham; *Educ* King Edward's Sch Birmingham, The Queen's Coll Oxford (open scholar, MA), Univ of Auckland (Cwlth scholar, PhD); *Partner* Alison Jane Stattersfield, *née* Morris; *Career* dir Oiled Seabird Research Unit and sr research assoc in zoology Univ of Newcastle upon Tyne 1972–75; Br Antarctic Survey: PSO and head Birds and Mammals Section 1976–85, SPSO and head Higher Predators Section 1986–2000, DCSO and head Conservation Biology 2001–06; chair Global Seabird Prog Birdlife Int 2006–; pres Br Ornithologists' Union 1995–99 (memb Cncl 1974–78, vice-pres 1987–91), chm RSPB 1998–2003 (memb Cncl 1989–2003), memb Perm Exec Int Ornithological Ctee 1998–2006; author of 320 papers and books; Scientific Medal Zoological Soc of London 1984, Polar Medal 1992 and 2004, Pres's Medal Br Ecological Soc 1995, Murphy Prize and Medal Int Waterbird Soc 1997, Marsh Award Conservation Zoological Soc of London 2002, Godman-Salvin Medal Br Ornithologists' Union 2004, Lifetime Achievement Award Pacific Seabird Gp 2008, Union Medal Ornithologists' Union 2015, Premio Lobo Orensanz 2015; hon prof: Univ of Birmingham 1998–, Univ of Durham 1998–; memb Br Ornithologists' Union 1965–, memb Int Ornithological Ctee 1990–, hon fell American Ornithologists' Union 2004; FRS 2005; *Recreations* birdwatching, walking, rebuilding houses; *Style*— Prof John Croxall, CBE, FRS; ✉ 3 Oakington Road, Girton, Cambridge CB3 0QH (☎ 01223 234287); Birdlife International, The David Attenborough Building, Pembroke Street, Cambridge CB2 3QZ (☎ 01223 277318, fax 01223 277200, john.croxall@birdlife.org)

CROXFORD, Ian Lionel; QC (1993); s of Peter Patrick Croxford, BEM, Lloyds Medal, and Mary, *née* Richardson; *b* 23 July 1953; *Educ* Westcliff HS for Boys, Univ of Leicester (LLB); *m* Sandra; 1 da, 1 s; *Career* called to the Bar Gray's Inn 1976 (Bacon scholar, bencher 2001), ad eundem Lincoln's Inn 1977; practising barr specialising in professional liability, memb Wilberforce Chambers 1997–; dep High Court judge; memb Cncl Medical Protection Soc 2007–; memb: Commercial Bar Assoc, Chancery Bar Assoc, Criminal Bar Assoc; govr Westcliff HS for Boys 1990– (chm 1995–); *Recreations* watching sport; *Style*— Ian Croxford, Esq, QC; ✉ Wilberforce Chambers, 8 New Square, Lincoln's Inn, London WC2A 3QP (☎ 020 7306 0102, fax 020 7306 0095, website www.wilberforce.co.uk)

CROXSON, Andrew James; s of David Croxson, and Lucy, *née* Paterson; *b* 28 April 1973, Merton, Surrey; *Educ* King's Sch Chester, Mansfield Coll Oxford (exhibitioner, BA), Trinity Hall Cambridge (MPhil); *m* 25 Aug 2002, Siân, *née* Davies; 1 s (James Llewelyn Wilfred b 5 March 2005), 1 da (Marianne Bronwen b 12 March 2007); *Career* assoc rising to sr Tax Dept Finance and Real Estate Gp Arthur Andersen 1996–2000, assoc rising to ptnr Spectrum Strategy Consltts 2000–07 (roles incl head of strategy and innovation BBC account Siemens IT Solutions and Services 2004–07), currently chief financial offr and chief operating offr Phorms; ACA 1999; *Recreations* snowboarding, motor racing; *Style*— Andrew Croxson, Esq; ✉ 6A Woodland Grove, Weybridge, Surrey KT13 9EF (☎ 01932 848191, e-mail acroxson@msn.com)

CROYDON, Archdeacon of; *see:* Davies, Ven (Vincent) Anthony (Tony)

CROYDON, David John; s of John Farley Croydon, of Stourbridge, West Midlands, and Patricia Ethel, *née* Lloyd; *b* 26 February 1949; *Educ* King Edward VI GS Stourbridge, Univ of London (BA); *m* 29 July 1972, Catherine Mary (d 2005), da of James Goddard (d 2005), of Birmingham; 1 s (Luke James b 20 Jan 1981), 1 da (Madeleine Lucy b 26 June 1986); *Career* advertising exec 3M Corporation 1977–80, account mangr MSW Promotions 1980–81, account dir Counter Products Marketing 1981–86, fndr and md Marketing Principles Ltd (sales promotion consultancy) 1986–99, chief exec DraftWorldwide 1999–2000, fndr and md Hilltop Publishing Ltd and Force Majeure Records Ltd 2001–, fndr and dir M&A Team Ltd 2013; MInstD 2012; *Books* The Unprincipled (2012), The Little Green Business Growth Book (2014); *Recreations* rugby football; *Clubs* Chinnor, Saracens, Middx; *Style*— David Croydon, Esq; ✉ Monks Hill, South Hills, Brill, Aylesbury, Buckinghamshire (☎ 01844 237450, mobile 07836 334150, e-mail dave@hilltoppublishing.co.uk, website www.hilltopconsultancy.co.uk, Twitter @themandateam)

CROZIER, Adam; *b* Falkirk; *m* Annette; 2 da (Molly, Grace); *Career* Saatchi & Saatchi: joined 1988, bd dir 1990–94, jt chief exec 1994–2000; chief exec: Football Association 2000–02, Royal Mail Group plc 2003–10, ITV plc 2010–; non-exec dir G4S 2013–; *Style*— Adam Crozier, Esq; ✉ ITV plc, The London Television Centre, Upper Ground, London SE1 9LT

CRUDDAS, Jonathan (Jon); MP; s of John and Pat Cruddas; *Educ* Oaklands RC Comp Portsmouth, Univ of Warwick (BSc, MA, PhD); *m* Anna, *née* Healy; 1 s; *Career* policy offr Lab Pty 1989–94, chief asst to gen sec of Lab Pty 1994–97, dep political sec to the PM 1997–2001; MP (Lab) Dagenham 2001–; sec All-Party Olympics and Paralympics Gp 2003–; memb TGWU; *Recreations* golf, angling; *Clubs* Dagenham Working Men's, White Heart Angling, Dagenham Royal Naval Assoc; *Style*— Jon Cruddas, Esq, MP; ✉ House of Commons, London SW1A 0AA (☎ 020 7219 8161)

CRUDDAS, Dr Peter Andrew; s of John Cruddas, and Lilian Frances, *née* Grover; *b* 30 September 1953; *Educ* Shoreditch Comp Sch; *m* 4 June 1987, Fiona Jane, *née* French; 1 s (Stephen), 3 da (Sarah, Annabel, Lucinda); *Career* money markets trader at various banks 1970–88, fndr chm and ceo CMC Gp plc (pioneer of internet trading) 1989–; memb Mensa; London Entrepreneur of the Year 2004; *Recreations* golf (handicap 5), reading, chess; *Clubs* Royal Mougin Golf, Wentworth Golf, Oxford and Cambridge, Carlton, Arts; *Style*— Dr Peter Cruddas; ✉ CMC Markets UK plc, 133 Houndsditch, London EC3A 7BX (☎ 020 7170 8200, fax 020 7207 8499)

CRUICKSHANK, David John Ogilvie; s of Ogilvie Cruickshank (d 2004), of Scotland, and Rosemary Elizabeth, *née* Philip; *b* 20 February 1959; *Educ* Waid Acad Anstruther, Univ of Edinburgh (BCom); *m* 1984, Rona, da of Rowland Dalgliesh; 2 da (Lindsay Alexandra b 28 Aug 1990, Fiona Jacqueline b 4 June 1992); *Career* Deloitte: trainee chartered accountant Edinburgh 1979–82, tax mangr 1982–88, tax ptnr 1988–, ptnr i/c London Tax Practice 1995–99, managing ptnr Tax (UK) 1999–2006, chm UK Bd 2007–11, memb Global Bd Deloitte Touche Tohmatsu 2007–15, chm Global Bd Deloitte Touche Tohmatsu 2015–; chair Educn and Employers Taskforce, co-chair Partnering Against Corruption Initiative WEF; memb: Bd Social Progress Imperative, Cncl Int Integrated Reporting, World Business Cncl for Sustainable Devpt; MICAS 1982, MICAEW 1990; *Recreations* work, family, golf, tennis, travel, good company, current affairs; *Clubs* Caledonian, RSA, Coombe Hill Golf, Newtonmore Golf, Isle of Purbeck Golf; *Style*— David Cruickshank, Esq; ✉ Deloitte, 2 New Street Square, London EC4A 3BZ (direct ☎ 020 7007 1826, direct fax 020 7007 1066, e-mail dcruickshank@deloitte.co.uk)

CRUICKSHANK, Sir Donald Gordon (Don); kt (2006); s of Donald Campbell Cruickshank, of Moray, Scotland, and Margaret Buchan *née* Morrison; *b* 17 September 1942; *Educ* Fordyce Acad, Univ of Aberdeen (MA), Manchester Business Sch (MBA), Univ of Aberdeen (LLD); *m* 17 Oct 1964, Elizabeth Buchan, da of Alexander Watt Taylor, of Fraserburgh, Scotland; 1 s (Stewart b 1965), 1 da (Karen b 1969); *Career* McKinsey and Co Inc 1972–77, dir and gen mangr Sunday Times Times Newspapers Ltd 1977–80, dir Pearson Longman Ltd 1980–84, md Virgin Group plc 1984–89, chief exec NHS in Scotland 1989–93, DG of telecommunications Office of Telecommunications 1993–98, chm UK Banking Review 1998–2000, non-exec chm SMG plc 1999–2004, chm London Stock Exchange 2000–03, non-exec chm FormScape 2004–06, non-exec chm Clinovia 2005–06; non-exec dir Christian Salvesen plc 1993–95, T&F Informa plc 2004–05 (chm Taylor & Francis plc 2004), Qualcomm Inc 2005–; chm: Wandsworth DHA 1986–89, Action 2000 1997–2000; memb Financial Reporting Cncl 2002–; memb of Ct Univ of Aberdeen 2005–; *Recreations* opera, theatre, golf, sport; *Style*— Sir Don Cruickshank

CRUICKSHANK OF AUCHREOCH, Martin Melvin; s of Brig Martin Melvin Cruickshank, CIE (d 1964), and Florence Watson Cruickshank (d 1976); *b* 17 September 1933, Aberdeen; *Educ* Rugby, Eaton Hall, CCC Cambridge; *m* 1 March 1958, Rona, da of Mary Fenella Paton of Grandhome (d 1949), of Grandhome House, Aberdeen; 1 da (Fenella b 1959), 3 s (Martin b 1960, Nicholas b 1961 d 1973, Paul b 1963); *Career* cmmnd Gordon Highlanders 1952, serv Malaya 1952–53 (Despatches), Cyprus 1955–56, Germany 1960–61, Congo 1962 (Co cmd), Nigeria 1962–64 (chief instr Offr Cadet Sch, Bde Maj, Dep Cmdt Nigerian Military Coll), ret 1967; landowner; sec and past pres Strathfillan Golf Club; Order of St John in Scotland: memb Cncl 1970–75, memb Chapter 1970–96, Sword Bearer 1977–96; FRGS 1969; KStJ 1982 (OStJ 1965, CStJ 1974); *Recreations* travel (particularly deserts), bird watching, golf, music, oenology, rally driving (British Army Team 1961, 1965 and 1966); *Clubs* Army and Navy, Optimists', Pemaderoghs; *Style*— M M Cruickshank of Auchreoch; ✉ Auchreoch, Crianlarich, Perthshire (☎ 01838 400218, fax 01838 400217)

CRUISE, Prof (Adrian) Michael (Mike); s of Ambrose John Cruise (d 1972), and Ellen Florence Cruise (d 1997); *b* 12 May 1947, Rhwbina, Glamorgan; *Educ* Dorking Co GS, UCL (BSc, PhD); *m* 1971, Elizabeth Jennifer; 2 da (Becca b 1976, Rachel b 1978); *Career* UCL 1968–86 (lectr and dep dir Mullard Space Science Lab), Rutherford Appleton Lab 1986–95 (div head 1987, assoc dir and head Space Science Dept 1994–95), dep dir British Nat Space Centre 1994–95, prof of astrophysics and space research Univ of Birmingham 1995– (head Sch of Physics and Astronomy 1997–2002, pro-vice-chllr (research and knowledge transfer) 2002–08, now emeritus prof); visiting prof: Univ of Leicester, Cranfield Univ, Univ of Kent; UK delg Science Prog Ctee European Space Agency 1996–2000, chm European Space Agency Physical Sciences Working Gp; memb Cncl European Physical Soc, chm Scientific Ctee H CoSPAR, memb Cncl for the Central Lab of the Research Cncls (CCLRC); NASA Gp Achievement Award 1984, BMFT Award FRG 1984, ESA Hipparcos Science Team Award 1997, Geoffrey Pardoe Award RAeS 1998; CPhys, CSci, FRAS 1973, FInstP 1998; *Publications* Principles of Space Instrument Design (jtly, 1998); author of more than 120 scientific papers; *Recreations* music, cryptography; *Clubs* Royal Astronomical Soc Dining; *Style*— Prof Mike Cruise; ✉ University of Birmingham, Edgbaston, Birmingham B15 2TT (☎ 0121 414 6451, fax 0121 414 3722, e-mail a.m.cruise@bham.ac.uk)

CRUMP, Richard; *b* 6 September 1957; *Educ* St Paul's, Oriel Coll Oxford (BA); *Career* qualified slr 1981; ptnr Holman Fenwick Willan LLP 1987– (sr ptnr 2007–); Freeman Worshipful Co of Shipwrights; *Style*— Richard Crump, Esq; ✉ Holman Fenwick Willan LLP, Friary Court, 65 Crutched Friars, London EC3N 2AE

CRUSH, His Hon Harvey Michael; s of George Stanley Crush (d 1970), of Chislehurst, Kent, and Alison Isabel, *née* Lang (d 1992); *b* 12 April 1939; *Educ* Chigwell Sch Essex; *m* 1, 21 Aug 1965 (m dis 1982), Diana, da of Frederick Joseph Bassett (d 1965), of Coulsdon,

Surrey; 1 s (Nicholas b 1 Dec 1967), 1 da (Emily b 21 May 1971); m 2, 9 Dec 1982, Margaret (Maggie) Rose, da of Nicholas Dixson (d 1986); *Career* admitted slr 1963; ptnr Norton Rose 1968–91, dir TOSG Trust Fund Ltd 1970–95; memb Supreme Court Rule Ctee 1984–88, recorder of the Crown Court 1992–95 (asst recorder 1987–92); advocate Higher Courts 1994, circuit judge (SE Circuit) 1995–2001 (dep circuit judge 2001–04); called to the Bar 2001; vice-pres and chm City of London Law Soc 1989–91; memb: Law Soc, Swanley & Dist CAB Mgmnt Ctee 1991–2001 (chm 1991–93), Local then General Ctee London Legal Aid Area 1969–82 (memb Area Ctee 1982–95); memb Cncl Br Assoc of Aviation Conslts 1991–95 and 2001–14 (hon slr 1991–94, dep chm 2001–02 and 2004–05, chm 2002–04); hon life memb: Sevenoaks and Dist Motor Club (chm 1968–71), Slrs' Assoc of Higher Courts Advocates, London Slrs' Litigation Assoc; Liveryman Worshipful Co of Slrs 1982 (memb Ct of Assts 1987–, Master 1994–95), Liveryman Worshipful Co of Farriers 1984 (memb Ct of Assts 1997–2003); Honourable Co of Air Pilots: Freeman 1991, Liveryman 2000, memb Technical and Air Safety Ctee 2007–15, memb Technical Ctee 2015–; FRAeS 2004 (MRAeS 1980, memb Cncl 2011–14, tstee 2012–14); *Publications* British Manual of International Air Carriage (jtly, 2009); *Recreations* flying, travel; *Style*— His Hon Harvey Crush; ✉ Arbitrators at 10 Fleet Street, London EC4Y 1AU (☎ 845 262 0310, e-mail harvey.crush@quadrantchambers.com)

CRUTE, Prof Ian; CBE (2010); s of Walter Crute, and Rose Crute; *b* 3 June 1949, Sunderland; *Educ* Univ of Newcastle upon Tyne (BSc, PhD); *m* Elizabeth J, *née* Harden; 2 da (Catherine b 1977, Frances b 1979); *Career* research scientist Nat Vegetable Research Station 1973–87 (promoted princ scientific offr 1981), Fulbright fell Dept of Plant Pathology Univ of Wisconsin Madison 1986–87, head Crop and Environment Protection Dept Horticulture Research Int (HRI) East Malling 1987, head Plant Pathology and Weed Science Dept HRI Wellesbourne 1993–99 (site dir 1995–99), dir Rothamsted Research (formerly Inst of Arable Crops Research) 1999–2009, chief scientist Agriculture and Horticulture Devpt Bd 2009–14; visiting prof of plant pathology Univ of Oxford 1997; author of numerous scientific papers on plant pathology and genetics; pres British Soc for Plant Pathology 1995; tstee: John Innes Fndn, E Malling Tst; Research Medal RASE 1992, BCPC Medal 1995; Hon DSc Harper Adams UC 2010; Hon FRAgSoc 2010; *Recreations* golf, walking, gardening; *Style*— Prof Ian Crute, CBE; ✉ Agriculture and Horticulture Development Board, Stoneleigh Park, Kenilworth, Warwickshire

CRYAN, His Hon Judge Donald Michael; s of Thomas Cryan (d 1997), of Ireland, and Helen McBeath, *née* Munro (d 1974); *b* 18 January 1948; *Educ* Salvatorian Coll, UCL (LLB); *m* 1973, Pamela; 2 s; *Career* called to the Bar Inner Temple 1970 (bencher 1991); recorder 1993–96, circuit judge (SE Circuit) 1996–; designated family judge: Medway 2001–05, Kent 2005–08; chm Lord Chllr's Working Pty on Delay in Family Proceedings Courts (FPC) 2002–03; memb: Lord Chllr's Advsy Ctee on Judicial Case Mgmnt in Public Law Children Act Cases 2002–05, Unified Admin Judicial Ctee 2003–05, Family Ctee Judicial Studies Bd 2003–07; chair Family and Magisterial Sub-Ctee 2005–07, judicial memb Courts Bd for Kent-08, chm Advsy Bd City Univ Law Sch 2010–14, chair Advsy Ctee Inst of Family Law Arbitrators 2012–; memb Ctee: Centre for Child and Family Law Reform (chm 2012–15), Marshall Hall Tst 1992–2005; Freeman City of London 1978, Master Worshipful Co of Fruiterers 1999 (Liveryman 1978, Upper Warden 1998); Hon LLD City Univ; *Recreations* opera and walking; *Clubs* RAC, Garrick; *Style*— His Hon Judge Cryan; ✉ 4 Paper Buildings, Temple, London EC4Y 7EX (☎ 020 7583 0816, e-mail hhjudge.cryan@judiciary.gsi.gov.uk)

CRYER, John Robert; s of late Bob Cryer, MP, and Ann Cryer; *m* Narinder; 2 s, 1 da; *Career* MP (Lab): Hornchurch 1997–2005, Leyton and Wanstead 2010–; fndr: Labour Against the Euro, Unite Against Fascism, All-Pty Classic Car Gp; *Publications* Boldness Be My Friend: Remembering Bob Cryer MP; contrib to numerous newspaper and magazine articles; *Style*— John Cryer, Esq; ✉ House of Commons, London SW1A 0AA

CRYSTAL, Prof David; OBE (1995); s of Samuel Cyril Crystal, of London, and Mary Agnes, *née* Morris; *b* 6 July 1941; *Educ* St Mary's Coll Liverpool, UCL (BA), Univ of London (PhD); *m* 1, 1 April 1964, Molly Irene (d 1976), da of Capt Robert Stack (d 1965); 2 s (Steven David b 1964, Timothy Joseph b 1969 d 1972), 2 da (Susan Mary b 1966, Lucy Alexandra b 1973); m 2, Hilary Frances, da of Capt Kenneth Norman (d 1990), of Cuffley, Herts; 1 s (Benjamin Peter b 1977); *Career* res asst Survey of English Usage UCL 1962–63, asst lectr linguistics Univ Coll of North Wales 1963–65; Univ of Reading: lectr 1965–69, reader 1969–75, prof of linguistics 1975–85; hon prof of linguistics Univ of Wales (Bangor) 1985–; writer and ed of ref books 1985–2008; ed: Journal of Child Language 1974–85, The Language Library 1978–2009, Applied Language Studies 1980–84, Child Language Teaching and Therapy 1985–96, Linguistics Abstracts 1985–96; assoc ed Journal of Linguistics 1970–73, co-ed Studies in Language Disability 1974–2006, consulting ed English Today 1984–94, usage ed Great Illustrated Dictionary (Readers Digest, 1984), conslt AND Reference 1997–2001, chm Crystal Reference Systems 2001–06 (dir of research 2006–09); Sam Wanamaker fell Shakespeare's Globe 2003; author of numerous pubns connected with the English language and linguistics; dir The Ucheldre Centre Holyhead 1990–; memb Bd: Br Cncl 1996–2001, English Speaking Union 2001–06; vice-pres Inst of Linguistics 1998–, vice-pres Soc for Eds and Proofreaders 2004–16, pres Soc for Eds and Proofreaders 2016–; patron: Nat Assoc of Professionals Concerned with Language-Impaired Children 1986–2002, Int Assoc of Teachers of English as a Foreign Language 1993–, Assoc for Language Learning 2007–; fell Coll of Speech Therapists 1983, FRSA 1983, FBA 2000, FLSW 2010; *Books* incl: The Cambridge Encyclopedia of Language (1987, 3 edn 2010), The English Language (1988, 2 edn 2001), The Cambridge Encyclopedia (ed, 1990, 4 edn 2000), The Cambridge Encyclopedia of the English Language (1995, 2 edn 2003), Language Play (1998), Language Death (2000), Language and the Internet (2001, 2 edn 2006), The Penguin Encyclopedia (ed, 2002, 3 edn 2006), The Stories of English (2004), Shakespeare's Words (with Ben Crystal, 2002), The Language Revolution (2004), A Glossary of Netspeak and Textspeak (2004), Pronouncing Shakespeare (2005), The Shakespeare Miscellany (with Ben Crystal 2005), Dr Johnson's Dictionary (2005), How Language Works (2006), Words, Words, Words (2006), The Fight for English (2006), As They Say in Zanzibar (2006), By Hook or By Crook (2007), Think on my Words (2008), Txtng: the Gr8 Db8 (2008), Just a Phrase I'm Going Through: My Life in Language (2009), The Future of Language (2009), Fowler's Dictionary of Modern English Usage (ed, 2009), A Little Book of Language (2010), Evolving English (2010), Begat: the King James Bible and the English Language (2010), Internet Linguistics (2011), The Story of English in 100 Words (2011), Spell It Out (2012), Wordsmiths and Warriors: the English-language tourist's guide to Britain (with Hilary Crystal, 2013), Words In Time and Place: Exploring the Historical Thesaurus of the Oxford English Dictionary (2014), The Memors Glossary (2014), You Say Potato (with Ben Crystal, 2014), The Oxford Illustrated Shakespeare Dictionary (with Ben Crystal, 2015), The Disappearing Dictionary (2015), Making a Point (2015), The Oxford Dictionary of Shakespearean Pronunciation (2016), The Unbelievable Hamlet Discovery (2016), The Gift of the Gab: how eloquence works (2016); *Recreations* cinema, music, bibliophily, progressing the arts; *Style*— Prof David Crystal, OBE; ✉ Akaroa, Gors Avenue, Holyhead, Anglesey LL65 1PB (☎ 01407 762764, e-mail davidcrystal1@icloud.com)

CRYSTAL, Jonathan; s of Dr Samuel Cyril Crystal, OBE, of London, and Rachel Ethel, *née* Trewish; *b* 20 December 1949; *Educ* Leeds GS, QMC London (LLB); *m* Giselle Satya, *née* Jeremie; 2 s (Petros, Jeremie), 1 da (Sophie); *Career* called to the Bar Middle Temple 1972; practising barr; dir: Tottenham Hotspur FC 1991–93, Cardiff City FC 2000–07; memb Cncl RAH; *Recreations* sports, travel; *Style*— J Crystal, Esq; ✉ Goldsmith Chambers, Goldsmith Building, Temple, London EC4Y 7BL (☎ 020 7353 6802, e-mail j.crystal@goldsmithchambers.com)

CRYSTAL, Michael; QC (1984); s of late Dr Samuel Cyril Crystal, OBE, and late Rachel Ettel Crystal; *b* 5 March 1948; *Educ* Leeds GS, QMC London (LLB), Magdalen Coll Oxford (BCL); *m* 1972, Susan Felicia Sniderman; 1 s, 1 da; *Career* called to the Bar: Middle Temple 1970 (bencher 1993), Gray's Inn (ad eundem) 1989; dep judge of the High Court 1995–; lectr in law Pembroke Coll Oxford 1971–76; visiting prof Dept of Laws UCL 2002–; DTI inspr into: County NatWest Ltd and County NatWest Securities Ltd 1988–89, National Westminster Bank plc 1992; memb: Insolvency Rules Advsy Ctee 1993–97, Advsy Cncl Centre for Commercial Law Studies Queen Mary & Westfield Coll London 1996–, Fin Law Panel 1996–2002, FA Premier League Panel for Insolvency Matters 2004–; hon fell Queen Mary & Westfield Coll London 1996, hon fell Soc for Advanced Legal Studies 1997; govr RSC 1988–2006 (hon govr 2006–); memb Int Insolvency Inst 2005–, fell American Coll of Bankruptcy 2006–; fell Royal Instn of GB 2004–; *Publications* various legal textbooks; *Recreations* travel, music, theatre; *Clubs* RAC, MCC; *Style*— Michael Crystal, QC; ✉ 3–4 South Square, Gray's Inn, London WC1R 5HP (☎ 020 7696 9900, fax 020 7696 9911)

CRYSTAL, Peter Maurice; s of Boris Leonard Crystal, of Leeds, and Pauline Mary, *née* Fox; *b* 7 January 1948, Leeds; *Educ* Leeds GS, St Edmund Hall Oxford (MA), McGill Univ Montreal (LLM); *m* 1, 1978; 2 da (Emma, Anna); m 2, Jacqui, *née* Harper; 1 da (Carla), 1 s (Philip); *Career* sr ptnr Memery Crystal slrs; Parly candidate: Leeds NE (SDP) 1983 and 1987, Fulham (Lib Dem) 1992; currently chm and dir of various cos; memb Law Soc; *Recreations* sports, travel; *Clubs* Reform, Athenaeum, Vincent's (Oxford); *Style*— Peter Crystal, Esq; ✉ Memery Crystal, 44 Southampton Buildings, London WC2A 1AP (☎ 020 7242 5905, e-mail pmcrystal@memerycrystal.com)

CUCKNEY, Lady ; *see:* Newell, (Priscilla) Jane

CULL-CANDY, Prof Stuart Graham; s of late Stanley William Cull-Candy, and Margaret Cull-Candy; *b* 2 November 1946; *Educ* Univ of London (BSc), UCL (MSc), Univ of Glasgow (PhD); *m* Dr Barbara Paterson Fulton; 1 da (Sophie); *Career* postdoctoral fell Inst of Pharmacology Univ of Lund 1974–75; UCL: Beit meml research fell and assoc research staff Dept of Biophysics 1975–82, Wellcome Tst reader in pharmacology Dept of Pharmacology 1982–90, prof of neuroscience (personal chair) 1990–, Gaddum chair of pharmacology 2006–; int research scholar Howard Hughes Med Inst 1993–98; memb: Neuroscience Ctee MRC 1975–82, Int Interest Gp Grants Ctee Wellcome Tst 1991–97, Research Fellowship Ctee Royal Soc 2003–, Research Grants Ctee Royal Soc 2005–, Sr Research Fellowships Panel Leverhulme Tst 2006–; ed: Jl of Physiology 1987–95, European Jl of Neuroscience 1988–, Neuron 1994–98; external editorial advsr in neuroscience Nature 1993–97, reviewing ed Jl of Neuroscience 2000–, guest ed Current Opinions in Neurobiology 2007, Ed Bd Molecular Pharmacology 2011–; memb: American Neuroscience Soc, Physiological Soc, Br Neuroscience Soc, Int Brain Research Orgn (IBRO), Newton Int Fellowship Ctee Royal Soc 2016–19; memb panel Res Excellence Framework 2014 (HE Funding Cncl for Eng 2011–14); G L Brown Award Physiological Soc 1996, Wolfson Award Royal Soc 2003; FRS 2002, FMedSci 2004, fell British Pharmacological Soc 2005, Faculty of 1000 2006–, hon fell Physiological Soc 2015; *Publications* author of various book chapters and numerous articles on information transfer, synaptic transmission and glutamate receptors in the brain and peripheral nervous system in scientific jls incl Nature, Neuron and Nature Neuroscience and audio/video online publication; *Recreations* natural history, local history, antiquarian books relating to medicine and natural history, the Arts and Crafts movement, music; *Style*— Prof Stuart G Cull-Candy, FBPhS, FRS, FMedSci; ✉ Department of Neuroscience, Physiology and Pharmacology, University College London, Gower Street, London WC1E 6BT (☎ 020 7679 3766, fax 020 7679 7298, e-mail s.cull-candy@ucl.ac.uk)

CULLEN, Prof Michael Henry; s of Charles Gavin Cullen, and Olive, *née* Walker; *b* 29 March 1947, London; *Educ* Queen Elizabeth's Sch Barnet, Univ of Bristol (BSc, MB ChB, MD), Univ of Birmingham (MA); *m* 1, 2 July 1972 (m dis 1988), Rosemary Elizabeth; 3 s (Matthew Jacob b 13 March 1974, Alexander James b 11 Dec 1976, Thomas Oliver b 7 May 1980); m 2, 20 Aug 1989, Alison Helen, da of David Machin; 1 da (Flora Ruth b 28 March 1991); *Career* conslt med oncologist Queen Elizabeth Hosp Birmingham 1982–, clinical dir Oncology and Haematology Servs Univ Hosp Birmingham NHS Tst 1990–98, hon prof in medical oncology Univ of Birmingham 2008– (hon reader in med oncology 1997–2008); chm: Jt Collegiate Cncl for Oncology 1998–2002, RCP Ctee on Med Oncology 1998–, Highlights Working Gp European Soc of Medical Oncology 2008–; memb NCRI Working Pty on Testicular Tumours; author of pubns on: lung cancer, testicular cancer, lymphoma; memb: Int Assoc for the Study of Lung Cancer, Br Assoc for Cancer Res, Assoc of Cancer Physicians; UK nat rep Euro Soc of Med Oncology; memb Bd W Midlands Arts 1997–2002, memb W Midlands Regnl Arts Cncl 2002–04, co-curator Behind Closed Doors: Birmingham's Private Collections from Van Dyck to Cornelia Parker Barber Inst of Fine Arts Univ of Birmingham 2008; Br Thoracic Oncology Gp Lifetime Achievement Award 2010; FRCP 1988, FRCR 2001; *Publications* Behind Closed Doors: Birmingham's Private Collections from Van Dyck to Cornelia (exhbn catalogue); *Recreations* tennis, skiing, wine tasting, music, fine art; *Style*— Prof Michael Cullen; ✉ Priory Hospital, Edgbaston, Birmingham B5 7UG (☎ 0121 446 1670)

CULLEN, (Charles) Nigel; OBE (1987), TD (1976, and 2 Bars 1982 and 1990), DL (Notts 1991); s of Peter Carver Cullen (d 1990), and Dorothy, *née* Woodward (d 1992); *b* 26 September 1944; *Educ* Trent Coll; *m* 1, 15 April 1981 (m dis 2000), Brenda Suzanne, da of Flt Offr Franklin Paul Bowen, US Army, of Oklahoma, USA; 1 s (Stephen James b 1971), 1 da (Emily Josephine b 1979); m 2, 28 Dec 2009, Susan Elizabeth, da of Kenneth Coley, of Duffield, Derbys; *Career* TA: cmmnd 1964, platoon cdr 5/8 Bn Sherwood Foresters 1964–67, platoon cdr Mercian Vol 1967–72, co cdr 3 WFR 1972–78, GSO 2 V Notts 1978–81, 2 i/c 3 WFR 1981–83, SO 2 G3 V 54 Inf Bde 1984, CO 3 WFR 1984–87, SO 1 G3 V E Dist 1987–88, dep cdr 54 Inf Bde 1988–91, TA Col SPT DARC 1991–92, ADC (TA) 1991–93; admitted slr 1970, NP; memb Freeths plc; pres: Notts C of C and Indust 1991–92, Notts City Business Club 1989–90; chm: Assoc of E Midlands C of C and Industry 1994–96, Notts Business Venture Enterprise Agency 1996–2003; dir Business Link Greater Nottingham 1996–98; memb and sec E Midlands Branch STEP 1996–2000; Dep Under Sheriff of Derbyshire 1994–96; memb: Notts Law Soc, The Notaries' Soc, Law Soc; *Recreations* theatre, cinema; *Style*— Nigel Cullen, Esq, OBE, TD, DL; ✉ 2 William Close, Duffield, Belper, Derbyshire DE56 4HN (☎ 01332 842730); Freeths plc, Cumberland Court, 80 Mount Street, Nottingham NG1 6HH (☎ 01159 369385, fax 01158 599653, e-mail nigel.cullen@freeths.co.uk)

CULLEN, Timothy William Brian (Tim); MBE (2014); s of (James) Brian Cullen, CBE (d 1972), and (Sybil) Kathleen, *née* Jones (d 1991); *b* 23 March 1944; *Educ* King William's Coll IOM, Trinity Coll Dublin (MA); *m* 19 July 1980, Nora, da of Vytautas Meskauskas; 1 da (Jura b 1982), 1 s (Brian b 1986); *Career* English teacher St Edward's Sch FL 1967–69, press spokesman Ford Motor Co Ltd Warley England 1969–73, int press spokesman Ford Motor Co Dearborn MI 1973–75, int public affairs admin Continental Bank Chicago 1975–78, various external affairs posts World Bank Washington DC 1978–84, chief of external affairs Euro Office World Bank Paris 1984–90, dir Information and Public Affrs Div and chief spokesman World Bank Washington DC 1990–96, sr advsr external and UN affrs World Bank 1996–99, fndr and chm TCA Ltd 1999–; dir Oxford Programme on Negotiation Univ of Oxford 2004–, exec dir The Small Countries Financial Mgmnt Centre Isle of Man 2009–14; pres Bd of Dirs Int Sch of Paris 1988–89; memb: Jt UN

Information Ctee 1990–96, UNESCO Experts Gp on Information and Communication 2000–01; cmmr IOM Fin Supervision Cmmn 2001–15; tstee Inst of Business Ethics 2006–14, tstee Bishop Barrow's Charity King William's Coll IOM 2004–; sr memb St Antony's Coll Oxford 2000–15, assoc fell Saïd Business Sch Univ of Oxford 2005–, visiting prof Lingnan Univ Coll Sun Yat-sen Univ Guangzhou China 2015–; *Books* Yugoslavia and The World Bank (1979); *Recreations* writing, cooking, photography, fishing; *Clubs* East India; *Style*— Tim Cullen, Esq, MBE; ✉ TCA Ltd, Bridge Court, 10 Bridge Street, Castletown, Isle of Man IM9 1TX (☎ 01624 825948, fax 01624 825978, e-mail tim.cullen@tcalimited.co.uk, tim.cullen@sbs.ox.ac.uk, website www.tcalimited.co.uk)

CULLEN OF WHITEKIRK, Baron (Life Peer UK 2003), of Whitekirk in the County of East Lothian (William) Douglas Cullen; KT (2007), PC (1997); s of Sheriff Kenneth Douglas Cullen (d 1956), and Gladys Margaret, *née* Douglas-Wilson (d 1992); *b* 18 November 1935; *Educ* Dundee HS, Univ of St Andrews (MA), Univ of Edinburgh (LLB); *m* 1961, Rosamond Mary, da of William Henry Nassau Downer, OBE, of NI; 2 s, (Christopher, Adrian), 2 da (Sophia, Felicity); *Career* advocate 1960, standing jr counsel to HM Customs and Excise 1970–73, QC 1973, Advocate-Depute 1978–81, a senator Coll of Justice in Scotland (Lord of Session) 1986–2005, Lord Justice Clerk of Scotland 1997–2001, Lord Justice Gen of Scotland and Lord Pres of the Ct of Session 2001–05; memb Civil and Commercial Courts Qatar Financial Centre 2007–15; chm: Med Appeal Tbnl 1977–86, Ct of Inquiry into Piper Alpha Disaster 1988–90, Review of Business of the Outer House of the Ct of Session 1995, Tbnl of Inquiry into the shootings at Dunblane Primary Sch 1996, Ladbroke Grove Rail Inquiry 1999–2001, Review of Fatal Accident Inquiry Legislation 2008–09; memb Constitution Ctee House of Lords 2013–16; memb Royal Cmmn on Ancient and Historical Monuments of Scot 1987–97; pres SACRO 2000–15, Saltire Soc 2005–11; memb Ct Napier Univ 1996–2005, chllr Univ of Abertay Dundee 2009–; chm: Cncl The Cockburn Assoc (Edinburgh Civic Tst) 1984–86, Govrs St Margaret's Sch Edinburgh 1994–2001, Bd The Signet Accreditation Ltd 2007–15; Hon LLD: Univ of Aberdeen 1992, Univ of St Andrews 1997, Univ of Dundee 2000, Univ of Edinburgh 2000, Glasgow Caledonian Univ 2000; Hon DUniv Heriot-Watt Univ 1995; FRSE 1993, Hon FREng 1995, Hon FRCSEd 2006, FRCPE 2010; *Recreations* gardening, natural history; *Clubs* Caledonian, New (Edinburgh); *Style*— The Rt Hon the Lord Cullen of Whitekirk, KT; ✉ House of Lords, London SW1A OPW

CULLEY, Kenneth (Ken); CBE (1998); s of James Culley (d 1970), of Cheshire, and Lily Valentine, *née* Dale (d 1970); *b* 3 June 1942; *Educ* Kings Sch Macclesfield; *m* 1, 1964 (m dis 1984), Barbara May, da of Frank Hooley; 2 da (Alison Jane b 1966, Johanne Helen b 1968), 1 s (Nicholas James b 1971); m 2, 1985, Eleanor Pamela Broomhead, da of Dr David Alexander Whyte Fairweather; *Career* accountant Bradford & Bingley Building Society 1965–69, gen mangr Cheshire Building Society 1969–83, chief exec and dir Portman Building Society 1983–99; dir The Building Societies Trust Ltd 1995–97; chm: JPMorgan Fleming Elect plc 2004–08, 1st Credit (Funding) Ltd 2005–11, Marks and Spencer Financial Servs plc 2005–13 (non-exec dir 2000–05); non-exec dir: Fleming Managed Income plc 1999–2003, Fleming Managed Growth plc 1999–2004, BRIT Insurance Ltd 2000–11 (chm 2003–07), Football Licencing Authy 2000–04, Financial Markets Compensation Scheme Ltd 2000–05, BRIT Insurance (UK) Ltd 2003–11, BRIT Syndicates Ltd 2004–11, BRIT Insurance Hldgs plc 2007–10; memb Cncl: Building Socs Assoc 1986–99 (dep chm 1994–95, chm 1995–96), Int Union of Housing Fin Instns 1995–99 (dep pres 1997–99); memb Cncl of Mortgage Lenders 1994–97; FCIB; *Recreations* sport: fishing, horse riding, rugby football, soccer; *Style*— Ken Culley, Esq, CBE; ✉ Garden End, Cross Lane, Marlborough, Wiltshire SN8 1LA (☎ 01672 515420, mobile 07887 830001, e-mail kenculley@hotmail.com)

CULLINAN, Edward Horder; CBE; s of Dr Edward Revill Cullinan, CBE (d 1965), and Dorothea Joy, *née* Horder; *b* 17 July 1931; *Educ* Ampleforth, Univ of Cambridge (BA), AA Sch of Architecture (AADipl), Univ of Calif Berkeley; *m* Rosalind, *née* Yeates; 2 da (Emma Louise b 1962, Kate b 1963), 1 s (Thomas Edward b 1965); *Career* Nat Serv Lt RE 1949–51; architect in practice London 1959, fndr Edward Cullinan Architects 1968–; Bannister Fletcher prof Univ of London 1978–79; visiting critic 1973–85: Toronto, Cincinnati, MIT; Graham Willis prof Univ of Sheffield 1985–87, George Simpson prof Univ of Edinburgh 1987–89, visiting prof Univ of Nottingham 2004–; tstee: Academy Enterprises, Koestler Award Tst 1998–; Hon Dr Univ of Sheffield 2001–; Hon DUniv: Lincolnshire and Humberside, E London; FRSA 1981, RA 1991, Hon FRIAS 1995; *Books* Edward Cullinan Architects (1984 and 1995), Ends Middles Beginnings (2005); *Recreations* building, horticulture, silviculture, surfing; *Style*— Edward Cullinan, Esq, CBE, RA; ✉ Gib Tor, Quarnford, Buxton, Derbyshire SK17 0TA; Edward Cullinan Architects Ltd, 1 Baldwin Terrace, London N1 7RU (☎ 020 7704 1975, fax 020 7354 2739)

CULLINAN, Nicholas; *b* 1977; *Educ* Courtauld Inst of Art (BA, MA, PhD); *Career* curator of int modern art Tate Modern 2007–13, curator of modern and contemporary art Metropolitan Museum of Art New York 2013–15, dir Nat Portrait Gall 2015–; memb: Advsy Ctee Govt Art Collection 2015–, Faculty of Fine Arts Ctee Br Sch at Rome 2016–, Advsy Ctee Royal Mint 2016–, Advsy Ctee Palazzo Strozzi Fndn 2016–; vice-pres Malevich Soc, pres Romney Soc 2016–, patron The Art Room 2016–; *Style*— Nicholas Cullinan, Esq; ✉ National Portrait Gallery, St Martin's Place, London WC2H 0HE

CULLINANE, John Patrick; s of John Cullinane, of London, and Pauline Mary Elizabeth, *née* Rourke; *b* 4 March 1955; *Educ* St Benedict's Sch Ealing, Wadham Coll Oxford (MA); *m* 30 July 1983, Jane Margaret Dacre, *née* Spokes; 1 da (Laura Jane Elizabeth b 30 Aug 1985), 1 s (Ruairi John Spokes b 10 March 1987); *Career* Dept of Employment Gp 1977–86, Arthur Andersen 1986–2002 (ptnr 1995), ptnr Deloitte 2002–15; Chartered Inst of Taxation: dep pres 2005–06, pres 2006–07, tax policy dir Chartered Inst of Taxation 2015–; Freeman City of London; memb Worshipful Co of Tax Advsrs; Inst for Public Policy Res papers: Learning to live with the Demon Debt ('Promoting Growth and Shared Prosperity in the UK' series, Jan 2012), The Phantom of the Structural Deficit, The Economic Consequences of Mrs Merkel, The Not-So-New Politics; *Recreations* skiing; *Style*— John Cullinane, Esq; ✉ Chartered Institute of Taxation, Artillery House (2nd Floor), 1–19 Artillery Row, London SW1P 1RT (☎ 020 7340 2703, e-mail jcullinane@ciot.org.uk)

CULLIS, Prof Anthony George; s of George Thomas Cullis (d 1966), and Doris Mary, *née* Bowen (d 2003); *b* 16 January 1946, Worcester; *Educ* Univ of Oxford (MA, DPhil, DSc); *m* 6 Oct 1979, Ruth Edith; 1 s (Richard Anthony), 1 da (Elizabeth Ruth); *Career* memb tech staff Bell Labs Murray Hill NJ 1972–75; Defence Research Agency (Royal Signals and Radar Estab) Malvern: sr scientific offr 1975–78, princ scientific offr 1978–83), sr princ scientific offr 1983–95; Dept of Electronic and Electrical Engrg Univ of Sheffield: prof 1995–, head Semiconductor Materials and Devices Research Gp 1999–; dir Sheffield Field Emission Gun Transmission Electron Microscope Facility 1998–, dir Sheffield Focused Ion Beam Facility 2001–; pres Scientific Cncl TASC Italian Nat Lab Trieste 2001–03; chm: Microscopy of Semiconducting Materials Series of Int Confs 1977–, Electron Microscopy and Analysis Gp Inst of Physics 1980–82, Department of Industry Working Party on Transient Annealing 1981–84, SERC MSEC Instrumentation Panel 1988–93; memb Functional Materials Coll EPSRC 1997–; co-ordinating ed Materials Science and Engrg Reports 1994–; Holliday Award Inst of Materials Minerals and Mining 1984; FInstP, FRSC, FIMMM, FRS 2004; *Style*— Prof Anthony Cullis; ✉ 3 Dore Close, Dore, Sheffield S17 3PU (☎ 0114 235 3343); Department of Electronic and Electrical Engineering, University of Sheffield, Mappin Street, Sheffield S1 3JD (☎ 0114 222 5407, e-mail a.g.cullis@sheffield.ac.uk)

CULLUM, Jamie; s of John Cullum, of Bath, and Yvonne Cullum; *b* 20 August 1979, Rochford, Essex; *Educ* Grittleton House Sch Wilts, Sheldon Sch Wilts, Univ of Reading; *m* Jan 2009, Sophie Dahl; 1 da (Lyra b 2 March 2011); *Career* musician 2001–; albums: Pointless Nostalgic 2002, Twentysomething 2003, Catching Tales 2005; singles incl: All at Sea 2003, These are the Days 2004, Frontin 2004, Everlasting Love 2004, Get Your Way 2005, Mind Trick 2005, Photograph 2006; memb Judging Panel Must Be The Music (Sky 1) 2010; Br Jazz Awards Rising Star 2003; nominated: Br Breakthrough Act, Best Male and Best Live Act Brit Awards, Grammy Awards, Golden Globe (for soundtrack to Grace is Gone); radio show BBC Radio 2 2010–; memb Musicians Union; *Style*— Jamie Cullum, Esq; ✉ c/o Air Management, Unit 27 The Quadrangle, 49 Atalanta Street, London SW6 6TU (☎ 020 7386 1600, e-mail info@airmtm.com)

CULLUM, Peter Geoffrey; CBE (2010); s of Geoffrey Cullum (d 1994), and Doreen, *née* Cozens (d 2001); *b* 10 September 1950, Norwich; *Educ* City Business Sch (MBA), Cass Business Ch (PhD); *m* 7 May 2000, Ann, *née* Gray; 1 s (Simon b 22 Dec 1977), 2 da (Claire-Louise b 1 March 1981, Abigail b 8 Jan 1986); *Career* trainee Royal Insurance Group 1969–74, mktg exec Commercial Union 1975–82, mktg dir London & Edinburgh Insurance Co 1982–91, ceo Economic Insurance Co Ltd 1991–96, chm and fndr Towergate Partnership Ltd 1996–; chm Global Risk Partners Ltd, chm Minority Venture Partners Ltd; vice-pres Nat Autistic Soc; Ernst & Young UK Entrepreneur of the Year 2005; memb RSA; FCII 1971, ACIM 1999; *Publications* plethora of articles in the tech insurance trade press; *Recreations* golf, tennis, spectator of rugby and soccer; *Style*— Peter Cullum, Esq, CBE; ✉ Global Risk Partners, 50 Fenchurch Street, London EC3M 3JY (☎ 01622 809471, e-mail peter.cullum@grpgroup.co.uk)

CULSHAW, Jonathan Peter (Jon); s of James Culshaw, of Lancs, and Theresa Culshaw; *b* 2 June 1968; *Educ* St Bede's HS Ormskirk, St John Rigby Sixth Form Coll; *Career* comedian; voice artist Spitting Image 1994–96 (telephoned 10 Downing St using voice of William Hague, was put through to Tony Blair and the incident was reported in Hansard 1998), impersonator Dead Ringers BBC Radio 4 1999– and BBC2 2002–, voice artist 2DTV 2001–, impersonator The Impressions Show with Culshaw and Stephenson (BBC1) 2009–; Royal Variety Performance 2001 and 2002, Alter Ego ITV Specials 2001 and 2002, Meet The Dead Ringers (Arena documentary) BBC2 2001 and 2002, Secret Policeman's Ball 2006, The Sky at Night 50th Anniversary Edition 2007, Morecambe and Wise – The Garage Tapes (BBC Radio 4); *Awards* for Dead Ringers: Br Comedy Awards 2001, Gold Sony Radio Award 2001, Programme of Year Broadcasting Press Guild 2001, Best Comedy Spoken Word Awards 2001, Voice of the Listener Award 2002, Best Political Satire Award Political Studies Assoc; Montreux Rose D'Or Press Award 2002 (for 2DTV); *Style*— Jon Culshaw, Esq; ✉ Billy Marsh Associates, 76A Grove End Road, St John's Wood, London NW8 9ND

CULVERHOUSE, Lavinia Jane; da of Alan Frederick John Culverhouse, of Arizona, USA, and Mavis, *née* Budd; *b* 9 April 1965; *Educ* St Mary's Sch Gerrards Cross, Coll of Distributive Trades (Dip CAM); *m* 29 Sept 2000, Peter Thomas Dobie; 2 s (Lucas Christian b 2003, Fraser Alexander Fulton b 2006); *Career* media planner and buyer BBDO Ltd 1979–85, account dir Abbot Mead Vickers/BBDO 1989–92, gp account dir Doner Cardwell Hawkins 1992–94, md Design House Consultants Ltd 1994–; dir DBA 1999; FRSA 2000; *Recreations* literature, film, fashion; *Clubs* Groucho; *Style*— Ms Lavinia Culverhouse; ✉ Designhouse Consultants Ltd, 7–11 Herbrand Street, London WC1N 1EX (☎ 020 7202 2610, e-mail lavinia.culverhouse@designhouse.co.uk, website www.designhouse.co.uk)

CULYER, Prof Anthony John (Tony); CBE (1999); s of Thomas Reginald Culyer (d 1979), and Betty Ely, *née* Headland (d 2015); *b* 1 July 1942, Croydon, Gtr London; *Educ* Sir William Borlase's Sch Marlow, King's Sch Worcester, Univ of Exeter (BA), UCLA; *m* 26 Aug 1966, Sieglinde Birgit (d 2011), da of Kurt Kraut (d 1947); 1 s, 1 da; *Career* Fulbright scholar 1964–65, lectr Univ of Exeter 1965–69; Univ of York 1969–: lectr, sr lectr, reader, prof of economics; head Dept of Economics and Related Studies 1986–2001, pro-vice-chllr 1991–94, dep vice-chllr 1994–97, dir of health devpt 1997–2001; chief scientist Institute for Work and Health Toronto 2003–06; visiting prof: Queens Univ Canada 1976, Trent Univ Canada 1985–86, Medis Inst Munich 1990, Toronto Univ Canada 1991 (hon prof 1991–2007), Central Inst of Technol NZ 1997; adjunct prof Department of Health Policy Mgmnt and Evaluation Univ of Toronto 2003–07 (Ontario research chair in health policy and system design 2007–14), adjunct prof Inst of Health Policy Mgmnt and Evaluation Univ of Toronto 2014–; William Evans visiting prof Univ of Otago NZ 1979, Woodward lectr Univ of Br Columbia Canada 1986, Perey lectr McMaster Univ Canada 1991, Champlain lectr Trent Univ Canada 1991; chm: NHS Task Force on Funding of R&D 1993–94, Methodology Panel NHS Technology Assessment R&D Programme 1992–97, Central R&D Ctee Sub-Gp on Culyer Implementation 1997, Res Advsy Cncl Workplace Safety and Insurance Bd Ontario Canada 2006–10, Res and Devpt Ctee Nat Inst for Health & Clinical Excellence 2007–10; vice-chm: N Yorks HA 1995–99, Nat Inst for Clinical Excellence 1999–2003; memb: Central R&D Ctee for the NHS 1991–2001, Yorkshire Region R&D Ctee, Review Advsy Ctee on the London Special Health Authorities 1993, Subject Area Panel (Economics) ESRC, Br Cncl Health Advsy Ctee 1995–97, Central R&D Ctee Nat Working Gp on R&D in Primary Care 1996–97, Research Advsy Ctee Institute for Work and Health 1997–2002, Scientific Advsy Ctee Institute for Work and Health 1997–2003, memb Citizens' Cncl Ctee NICE 2007–, External Review Team for Cancer Care Ontario Research 2003–04, Ontario Health Technol Assessment Ctee 2005–07, Dept of Health Value Focus Gp on the Cost and Benefit Perspective of NICE 2008, Advsy Ctee NICE Int 2009–, Research Units Commissioning Panel Dept of Health Policy 2009; memb WHO two person mission to Kazakhstan on the privitisation and reform of health care services 1997; Ontario Miny of Health and Long Term Care: memb Career Scientist Relevance Review Panel 2007–, memb Citizen's Cncl Advsy Ctee 2007–, memb Health Research Advsy Cncl Ontario Miny of Health and Long Term Care 2007–, memb Health System Strategy Div External Advsy Gp 2009–; special advsr to: R&D Ctee High Security Psychiatric Services Commissioning Bd 1995–99, NHS Exec Comprehensive Spending Review Gp 1997–98, dir of R&D NHS 1997–99, Canada Health Cncl 2005–10; professional conslt to: UK Dept of Health, OECD, EEC, WHO, Govt of Canada, Govt of NZ; Office of Health Economics: chair Policy Ctee 1997–2015, chair Editorial Ctee 1997–2015, chair Mgmnt Ctee 1997–, chair 2001– (dep chair 1997–2001); co-ed Jl of Health Economics 1982–2013; memb Editorial Bd: Br Med Jl 1995–99, Med Law International, Clinical Effectiveness in Nursing, Jl of Medical Ethics; memb Conf of Heads of Univ Depts of Economics 1987–2001; memb Kenneth J Arrow Award Prize Ctee 1996–98, memb Canadian Institutes for Health Research Michael Smith Prize in Health Research Ctee 2005–06; memb and founding chm Health Economists Study Gp; memb: Royal EC Soc, Research Advsy Ctee Canadian Inst for Advanced Research, Acad Advsy Cncl Univ of Buckingham; tstee The Canadian Health Services Research Fndn Ottawa 2000–03; church organist and choirmaster, memb Liturgy and Music Advsy Gp Diocese of York 1995–2000, chm North East Yorkshire Area Royal Sch of Church Music 1995–2004, memb Advsy Cncl Royal Sch of Church Music 2002–04, tstee and memb Cncl Royal Sch of Church Music 2003–16, dir Royal Sch of Church Music Canada 2003–14; Emmett Hall Laureate and Hall Lectr 2015, William B Graham Prize for Health Services Research 2015, ISPOR Avedis Donabedian Outcomes Research Lifetime Achievement Award 2015; distinguished visiting fell Univ of the Witwatersrand SA 2015; Hon DEcon Stockholm Sch of Econs Sweden 1999; FMedSci 1999, FRSA 1999, Hon FRCP 2005; *Publications* incl: Health Economics (1973), Economics of Social Policy

(1973), Benham's Economics (1973), Economic Policies and Social Goals (1974), Need and the National Health Service (1976), Annotated Bibliography of Health Economics (1977), Human Resources and Public Finance (1977), Economic Aspects of Health Services (1978), Measuring Health (1978), Political Economy of Social Policy (1980 and 1991), Economic and Medical Evaluation of Health Care Technologies (1983), Health Indicators (1983), Economics (1985), Public Finance and Social Policy (1985), International Bibliography of Health Economics (1986), Public and Private Health Services (1986), Health Care Expenditures in Canada (1988), Perspectives on the Future of Health Care in Europe (1989), Standards for Socioeconomic Evaluation of Health Care Products and Services (1990), Competition in Health Care (1990), The Economics of Health (1991), International Review of the Swedish Health Care System (1991), Recent Developments in Health Economics (1992), Equity in Health Care Policy (1992), Supporting Research and Development in the NHS (1994), Reforming Health Care Systems: Experiments with the NHS (1996), Being Reasonable About the Economics of Health: Selected Essays by Alan Williams (1997), Handbook of Health Economics (2001), The Dictionary of Health Economics (2005, 3 edn 2014), Critical Perspectives on the World Economy 4 Vols, Economic Evaluation of Interventions for Occupational Health and Safety: Developing Good Practice (2008), The Humble Economist (2013), The Encyclopaedia of Health Economics (2014), Portrait of a Health Economist: essays by colleagues and friends of Bengt Jonsson (2014), A Star in the East: A Short History of HITAP (2016); also over 300 articles and pamphlets; *Recreations* music and gardening; *Style*— Prof Tony Culyer, CBE; ✉ The Laurels, Main Street, Barmby Moor, York YO42 4EJ; Institute of Health Policy, Management and Evaluation, University of Toronto, 155 College Street, Toronto, Ontario M5T 3M6, Canada (✆ +1 416 978 7340, fax +1 416 978 7350, e-mail tony.culyer@utoronto.ca, website www.hpme.utoronto.ca); Centre for Health Economics, University of York, Heslington, York, YO10 5DD (✆ 01904 32140, fax 01904 433759, e-mail tony.culyer@york.ac.uk, website www.york.ac.uk/economics/our-people/staff-profiles/anthony-culyer/)

CUMANI, Luca Matteo; s of Sergio Cumani (d 1980), and Elena, *née* Cardini; *b* 7 April 1949; *Educ* Milan; *m* 1979, Sara Doon, da of Simon Patrick Conyngham Plunket; 1 s (Matthew Sergio Simon b 1981), 1 da (Francesca Deepsea b 1983); *Career* racehorse trainer; rider of 85 winners in Italy, France and UK incl Moet and Chandon on Meissen and Prix Paul Noel de la Houtre on Harland 1972, champion amateur Italy 1972; formerly asst trainer to: S Cumani, H R A Cecil 1974–75; first held trainer's licence 1976; horses trained incl: Falbrav, Kahyasi, Freeze The Secret, Old Country, Tolomeo, Commanche Run, Free Guest, Bairn, Embla, Then Again, Celestial Storm, Presvis, Half a Year, Infamy, Markofdistinction, Barathea, Only Royale, High-Rise, One So Wonderful, Gossamer; Gp One races won incl: The English Derby (twice), Irish Derby, St Léger, Italian Derby, Premio Roma (twice), Arlington Million, Rothmans International, E P Taylor Stakes (twice), Juddmonte International Stakes (three times), Phoenix Champion Stakes, St James's Palace Stakes (twice), Cheveley Park Stakes, Prix Royal Oak, Queen Elizabeth II Stakes (twice), Sussex Stakes, Ascot Fillies Mile (three times), Irish 2000 Guineas, Yorkshire Oaks (twice), Breeders Cup Mile, Irish 1000 Guineas (twice), Singapore International Cup, Coral Eclipse, Hong Kong Cup, Prix Ispahan, Queen Elizabeth Hong Kong, Dubai Duty Free; *Style*— Luca Cumani; ✆ 01638 665432, fax 01638 667160, e-mail luca@lucacumani.com

CUMBERLEGE, Baroness (Life Peer UK 1990), of Newick in the County of East Sussex; Julia Frances Cumberlege; CBE (1985), DL (E Sussex 1986); da of Dr Lambert Ulrich Camm (d 1997), of Newick, E Sussex, and Mary Geraldine Gertrude, *née* Russell (d 1962); *b* 27 January 1943; *Educ* Convent of the Sacred Heart Kent; *m* 14 Jan 1961, Patrick Francis Howard Cumberlege, s of Geoffrey Fenwick Jocelyn Cumberlege, DSO, MC (d 1979); 3 s (Hon (Christopher) Mark b 1961, Hon Justin Francis b 1964, Hon Oliver Richard b 1968); *Career* memb: Lewes DC 1966–79 (ldr 1977–78), E Sussex CC 1974–85 (chm Social Servs Ctee 1979–82); JP 1973–85; memb E Sussex AHA 1977–81; chm: Brighton HA 1981–88, Nat Assoc of Health Authorities 1987–88, SW Thames RHA 1988–92; Parly under sec of state for health in House of Lords 1992–97, memb Jt Select Ctee on Draft Mental Health Bill 2004–05; exec dir MJM Healthcare Solutions 1997–2001, exec dir Cumberlege Connections Ltd 2001–; dir: Huntsworth plc 2001–03; memb: Cncl St George's Med Sch (chm 2000–06), Press Cncl 1977–83, Appts Cmmn 1984–90, NHS Policy Bd 1989–97, Cncl ICRF 1997–2001, Cncl Cancer Research UK 2001–07, Nat Advsy Cncl King's Fund; chm: Review of Community Nursing for England 1985, Review of Maternity Servs for England 1993, Tstees of Chailey Heritage 1998–, HR and Communications Cmmn Cancer Research UK, RCP Working Pty on Med Professionalism 2004–05, Assoc of Medical Research Charities 2007–11, Cumberlege Cmmn (report Safe Guarding with Confidence) 2007; vice-pres RCN 1988, vice-pres RCM 2001; chm and govr several schs, memb Cncl Brighton Poly 1987–89 (memb Formation Ctee 1988–89), memb Cncl Univ of Sussex 2001–09; tstee Leeds Castle Fndn 2005–; Vice Lord-Lt E Sussex 1991; hon degree: Univ of Surrey, Univ of Brighton, Univ of London, Northampton Univ, Univ of E Anglia; FRSA, Hon FRCP, Hon FRCGP, FRCN; Dame of the Order of St Gregory the Great; *Clubs* RSM; *Style*— The Rt Hon Baroness Cumberlege, CBE, DL; ✉ Snells Cottage, The Green, Newick, Lewes, East Sussex BN8 4LA (✆ 01825 722154, fax 01825 723873); House of Lords, London SW1A 0PW (e-mail cumberlegej@parliament.uk)

CUMING, Frederick George Rees; s of Harold Albert Cuming (d 1976), of Welling, Kent; and Grace Madeleine, *née* Rees; *b* 16 February 1930; *Educ* Sidcup Sch of Art, RCA; *m* Oct 1962, Audrey, da of Eric Lee, and Marie Lee, of Ashton-under-Lyme; 1 s (Daniel Lee b 5 Nov 1964), 1 da (Rachel Joanna b 25 Aug 1971); *Career* Nat Serv Sgt RAEC 1949–51; painter; artist in residence Christchurch Coll Canterbury 2015–; winner grand prix fine art Monaco Ingot Industrial Expo, Sir Brinsley Ford award New English Arts Club, House and Garden Prize RA 1994; advsr New Metropole Arts Centre Folkestone, tstee Rye Art Gallery and Eastern Rooms Gallery; memb Nat Tst; Hon DLitt Univ of Kent 2004; ARA 1964, RA 1974; *Solo Exhibitions* New Metropole Arts Centre Folkestone 1972–75, Jonleigh Guildford 1975, Thackeray London 1976, Chichester 1976, Grafton London 1983, 1985, 1987, 1988, 1990, 1992, 1994, 1996, and 1998, Drew Canterbury 1983–86, Easton Rooms Rye 1983, Nat Tst Fndn for Arts (Agnews), Salute to Turner (Agnews), Edinburgh Festival 1995, Johannesburg SA 1996–97, Dallas USA 1999, Greenwick Connecticut USA 1999, featured artist RA Summer Show 2001 (afforded solo exhbn Small Weston Room), portrait of Prof Stephen Hawking (Nat Portrait Gall London) 2007; *Group Exhibitions* incl: Royal Soc of Portrait Painters, John Moores Liverpool, Leicester Gallery, Pictures for Schools, 12 Royal Academicians Chichester, Little Studio NY, Artists of Fame and Promise (Brandler Galleries Brentwood) 1993; *Public Collections* incl: Royal Acad, Miny of Works, Monte Carlo Museum, Brighton and Hove Museum, St John's and Worcester Colls Oxford, New Metropole Arts Centre, Farringdon Tst, W H Smith, LWT, Southend Museum and Art Gallery, Canterbury Museum and Art Gallery, Scunthorpe Museum and Art Gallery, Preston Museum and Art Gallery, Kendall Museum and Art Gallery, Greenwich Conn USA, Dallas, San Francisco, Florida; *Private Collections* in countries incl: Argentina, Sicily, France, Germany, Singapore, Australia; *Publications* Figure in a Landscape (book), The Art of Fred Cuming, RA (video), Painters Progress Book; *Recreations* reading, music, travelling, walking; *Clubs* Chelsea Arts, Dover St Arts; *Style*— Frederick Cuming, RA, DLitt; ✉ The Gables, Wittersham Road, Iden, Rye, East Sussex TN31 7UY (✆ 01797 280882, e-mail gablesartfc@gmail.com, website www.fredcuming.com)

CUMMING, Maj-Gen Andrew Alexander John Rennie; CBE (1993); s of Donald Alexander Cumming (d 1995), and Evelyn Julia, *née* Rennie (d 1995); *b* 12 March 1948; *Educ* Bradfield Coll, Army Staff Coll, HCSC; *m* 1 Sept 1979, Gilly, *née* Thompson; 3 da (Camilla, Henrietta (twins) b 21 Sept 1982, Georgina b 7 Sept 1987); *Career* CO 17/21 Lancers 1988–90, Cdr 20 Armd Bde/11 Armd Bde 1992–93, ACOS (Ops) HQ Land 1993–95, Chief Jt Ops Intervention Force Sarajevo 1995–96, Cdr Initial Trg Gp 1996–99, Cdr Land Warfare Centre 1999–2002, co-ordinator Kosovo Protection Corps 2002–04, controller SSAFA Forces Help 2004–12; Hon Col Queen's Royal Lancers 2006–11; dir: Wincanton Race Course 2004–11, Southern Spinal Injuries Tst 2014–, Challenger Tst 2014–; *Recreations* field sports, skiing, sailing, walking, reading; *Clubs* Cavalry and Guards'; *Style*— Maj-Gen Andrew Cumming, CBE; ✉ HHQ The Royal Lancers, Prince William of Gloucester Barracks, Grantham NG31 7TJ

CUMMING, Prof Ian Roy; OBE (2003); s of late Roy Langdon Cumming, and Jean Evelyn, *née* Maxwell; *b* 10 September 1964, Manchester; *Educ* William Hulmes GS, Manchester Metropolitan Univ; *m* 1993, Gail Deborah, *née* Cox; *Career* healthcare scientist 1982–89, gen mangr Manchester Royal Infirmary 1990–93, asst chief exec NW RHA 1993–95; ceo: Lancaster Acute Hosp Tst 1995–98, Univ Hosps of Morecambe Bay NHS Tst 1998–2006, NHS North Lancs 2006–09, West Midlands SHA (NHS West Midlands) 2009–12, Health Educn England 2012–; hon prof Lancaster Univ Medical Sch 2008–; FIBMS, MHCM, FCMI, CSci, Hon FRCGP; *Books* The Little Black Book of Leadership: Hints and Tips for Healthcare Staff (2008); *Recreations* skiing, sailing, swimming coaching; *Style*— Prof Ian Cumming, OBE; ✉ e-mail ian.cumming@nhs.net; NHS West Midlands, St Chad's Court, 213 Hagley Road, Edgbaston, Birmingham B16 9RG

CUMMING, Prof Robert Alexander; s of Alexander Ian Cumming (d 1962), and Bery Mary Stevenson (d 2000); *b* 31 May 1945; *Educ* Trinity Hall Cambridge (MA); *m* 7 June 1975, Alison Carolyn, da of John George Jenkins, CBE; 2 da (Hester Chloe Mary b 2 June 1983, Phoebe Alice Elizabeth b 5 June 1988); *Career* author, art critic, broadcaster, curator; called to the Bar Middle Temple 1967 (Harmsworth scholar); practising barrister 1967–69, Hambros Bank 1970–71, lectr Tate Gallery 1974–78, dir Christie's Fine Arts Course 1978–88, chm Christie's Education 1988–2000, chm Christie's International Art Studies 1998–2000; pres: Christie's Education Inc (USA), Christie's Éducation (France); tstee: Christie's Educn Trust 1986–2000, Project Street Life 2004–06; memb: Exhbns Sub-Ctee Arts Cncl 1984–88, Cncl Friends of the Tate Gallery 1983–1995, Thames and Chiltern Regnl Ctee Nat Trust 1990–96; chm Contemporary Art Soc 1988–90; patron Royal Soc of Br Sculptors 1998–2006; ptnr Jenkins & Beckers Wine Merchants 1994–; external examiner: Univ of London 1976–80, Univ of Glasgow 1988–92; Buckingham Partnership 1998–2005, chm Exec Bd (British progs) Boston Univ London 2005–13, adjunct prof of art history Boston Univ 2008–; tstee Great Linford Art Centre Milton Keynes 2013–16, tstee Buckingham Library 2016–; writing awards: Silver Pencil Award Utrecht 1982, TES Sr Info Book Award 1983, Premio Europeo di Letteratura Giovainle Pier Paolo Vergerio Padua 1985; memb Gray's Inn 1969; Liveryman Worshipful Co of Painter-Stainers 2009; FRSA 1990; *Books* Macmillan Encyclopedia of Art (1977), Just Look (1979), Just Imagine (1982), Christie's Guide to Collecting (1984), Looking into Paintings (1985, with TV programme), Working with Colour (exhbn catalogue, 1985), The Colour Eye (1990), Discovering Turner (1990), Paolozzi Mythologies (exhbn catalogue, 1990), Annotated Art (1995), Great Artists (1998), ART a no nonsense guide to art and artists (2001), Art: Eyewitness Guide (2006), Treasures of MK (2014), My Dear BB – The Letters of Bernard Berenson and Kenneth Clark 1925–1959 (ed, 2015), Art – A Visual History (2015); *Recreations* all things European, family life, making and collecting, golf, wine, beekeeping; *Clubs* Arts, Anathema, Aula, Caledonian; *Style*— Prof Robert Cumming; ✉ The Old Mill House, Maids Moreton, Buckingham MK18 7AR (✆ 01280 816226, e-mail robertcumming@outlook.com, website www.robertcumming.net); Boston University, 43 Harrington Gardens, London SW7 4JU (✆ 020 7373 9430)

CUMMING-BRUCE, Edward Simon Hovell-Thurlow; s of late Rt Hon Sir Roualeyn Cumming-Bruce, and Lady Sarah Cumming-Bruce, *née* Savile (d 1991); *b* 7 June 1958; *Educ* Ampleforth, Magdalen Coll Oxford (MA); *m* 1984, Antonia, da of C S Gaisford-St Lawrence, of Howth Castle, Dublin, Eire; 2 s (Michael b 1985, William b 1987), 1 da (Isabelle b 1990); *Career* Laurence Prust & Co 1980–90, dir Schroder Securities Ltd 1990–91, dir Dresdner Kleinwort Benson Ltd 1992–2003 (positions incl co-head of global telecoms investment banking, co-head of UK invetment banking and global head of equity capital markets), md Gleacher Shacklock LLP 2003–; *Recreations* fishing, shooting; *Style*— Edward Cumming-Bruce, Esq; ✉ Gleacher Shacklock LLP, Cleveland House, 33 King Street, London SW1Y 6RJ (✆ 020 7484 1150, fax 020 7484 1160, website www.gleachershacklock.com)

CUMMINGS, His Hon Judge Brian; QC (2008); s of Wilbur Cummings (d 1998), and Shirley, *née* Drum; *b* 10 April 1965, Belfast; *Educ* Christ's Hosp Horsham, Trinity Coll Cambridge (MA); *Career* called to the Bar 1988; recorder 2005, circuit judge (Northern Circuit) 2015–; *Style*— His Hon Judge Cummings, QC

CUMMINGS, Jane; *Career* former chief nurse NHS North of England, currently chief nursing offr England; *Style*— Ms Jane Cummings; ✉ NHS England, PO Box 16738, Redditch B97 9PT (✆ 0113 825 1120, e-mail janecummings@nhs.net)

CUMMINS, Andrew Douglas; s of Douglas Charles Verdun Cummins, and Marjorie Pamela, *née* Sturrock; *b* 24 August 1949, Melbourne, Aust; *Educ* Stanford Univ (MBA); *m* 18 Feb 1972, Jennifer Muriel, *née* Knight; 1 da (Alexia), 1 s (Jonathan); *Career* BHP Ltd 1968–74, McKinsey & Company 1976–85, Elders IXL Ltd/Foster's Brewing Gp Ltd 1985–91, Inchcape plc 1992–97, CVC Capital Ptnrs and CVC Asia Pacific 1997–2015; chm: Cummins Gp 2006–, Helloworld Ltd (Aust) 2009–, Mantra Gp Ltd (Aust) 2009–; former directorships incl: Asia Bottles Hldgs (China), Rocla Concrete Tie Inc (USA), Nine Entertainment Gp (Aust), Affinity Health Ltd, Techpac Hldgs Ltd, Amatek Gp (Aust), Li & Fung (Distribution) Ltd (Hong Kong), Inchcape plc, ITT London & Edinburgh Ltd, Toyota (GB) Ltd, Bain Hogg Gp plc, Hudson Conway Ltd (Aust), Courage Ltd, Impulse Airlines Ltd, Samsonite Corp Inc (USA), Pacific Brands Ltd (Aust); memb Inst of Engrs Aust; *Clubs* Athenaeum (Melbourne), RAC (London); *Style*— Andrew Cummins, Esq; ✉ Prattendens, The Street, Bury, West Sussex RH20 1PA (✆ 01798 831573, e-mail adcummins@cumminsgroup.co.uk); 6 Academy Gardens, Duchess of Bedford's Walk, London W8 7QQ (✆ 020 7937 0339)

CUMMINS, Gus; s of Harold George Cummins (d 1986), of London, and Honor, *née* Bird (d 1978); *b* 28 January 1943; *Educ* Sutton Art Sch, Wimbledon Art Sch (NDD, sr drawing prize), RCA (MA); *m* 1968, Angela, da of Arthur C Braven; 2 s (Casper b 1968, Marcus b 1970), 1 da (Rosie b 1979); *Career* artist; taught pt/t 1969–: Hammersmith, Sutton, Croydon, Chelsea, Ravensbourne, Wimbledon, City & Guilds, RA Schs of Art; sculptural work for exhbn display during 1970s, exhibited paintings since 1970s; memb Rye Soc of Artists 1979–, memb London Gp 1982; memb Cncl Royal Acad of Arts 2002, memb Summer Exhibition Ctee Royal Acad 2014–15; RA 1992 (memb Cncl 2009–); *Solo Exhibitions* Gardner Art Centre Brighton 1991, Stormont Studios Rye 1991, Metropole Art Centre Folkestone 1992, Brian Sinfield Gallery Oxford 1993, Hastings Museum Gallery 1993, Lamont Gallery London 1995, St Mary-in-the-Castle Arts Centre Hastings 1999; two persons shows: Eastern Rooms Gallery Rye 1987, New Grafton Gallery London 1993, Star Gallery Lewes; exhibition with Fred Cuming, RA, and Mick Rooney, RA (Rye Art Gallery) 2011; *Group Exhibitions* incl: London Gp 1981–, RA 1982–, Hastings Museum 1979–, Eastern Rooms Gallery Rye 1984–, Spirit of London 1983 and 1984, Odette Gilbert Gallery 1984 and 1985, paintings and sculptural installations Dordrecht Festival 1986,

Lloyds of London Travelling 1986 and 1987, Gardner Art Centre Brighton Univ 1988, Hunting Group Mall Gallery 1989 and 1990, President's Choice RA and Arts Club 1989, Academicians Choice Mall Gallery and Eye Gallery Bristol 1990, Looking Glass Appeal (Riverside One London) 1990, Discerning Eye (Mall Gallery and tour) 1991–92, Barbican Centre 1992, New Grafton Gallery 1992, Singer Friedlander/Sunday Times Water Colour Competition Mall Gallery 1992, Woodlands Gallery London (with Anthony Green and Anthony Wishaw) 2002; also exhibited United Arab Emirates and USA; *Awards* Henry Moore Prize (London Gp) 1982, Second Prize Spirit of London 1983, Daler-Rowney Prize RA 1987, First Prize Hunting Gp Mall Gallery 1990, House & Garden Prize RA 1992, Blackstone Award RA 1992, First Prize Hunting Gp RCA 1999, Royal Watercolour Soc Prize 2001, Jack Goldhill Award for Sculpture RA 2005; *Recreations* music, poetry, swimming, snooker; *Clubs* Chelsea Arts, Dover St Arts; *Style*— Gus Cummins, Esq, RA; ✉ Harpsichord House, Cobourg Place, Hastings, East Sussex TN34 3HY (☎ 01424 426429, website www.guscummins.com); c/o Royal Academy of Arts, Piccadilly, London W1V 0DS

CUMMINS, Jack; s of Arthur Cummins (d 1987), and Jessie, *née* Milton (d 1981); *b* 17 June 1952, Irvine, Ayrshire; *Educ* Kilmarnock Acad, Univ of Glasgow (MA, LLB); *m* 17 March 1980, Josephine, *née* Donaldson; *Career* R & J M Hill Brown & Co: apprentice then asst 1976–80, ptnr 1980–2014, sr ptnr 2005–14, licensing dir 2014–; memb: Nicholson Ctee on liquor licensing law in Scotland 2001, expert Reference Gp on Licensing (Scotland) Bill 2003, Nat Licensing Forum; ed Scottish Licensing Law and Practice 1995–, columnist Scottish Licensed Trade News; contrib to radio and TV progs; regular speaker at confs; memb Law Soc of Scotland 1978; *Publications* Licensing Law in Scotland (1993, 2 edn 2000), Scottish Licensed Trade Handbook (contrib, 2003), Licensing Law Guide (contrib, 2003), Licensed Premises: Law and Practice (contrib, 2005), The Licensing (Scotland) Act 2005 (2006, 3 edn 2013); *Recreations* motoring; *Style*— Jack Cummins, Esq; ✉ Hill Brown Licensing, Miller Samuel Hill Brown, RWF House, 5 Renfield Street, Glasgow G2 5EZ (☎ 0141 221 1919, fax 0141 221 3796, e-mail jcc@mshblicensing.com)

CUNARD, Peter John; s of Basil Charles Henry Cunard (d 1962), and Christine May, *née* Tremer (d 1995); *b* 21 August 1945; *Educ* Latymer Fndn; *m* 1970, Susan Margaret Ethel, da of James Coleridge; 2 s (Nicholas Peter b 30 Oct 1971, Sebastian James b 29 Dec 1972), 1 da (Catherine Jane b 27 Nov 1976); *Career* press offr Assoc Television 1964–69, press and PR offr English Stage Co Royal Court Theatre 1969, PR advsr Duke of Bedford 1969–73, head of PR Trust House Forte 1973–76, dir Durden-Smith Communications 1976–80, fndr and md Granard Communications 1980–90, chief exec The Rowland Co (after merger of Granard Communications with Kingsway PR) 1990–92, memb Exec Ctee Rowland Worldwide Ltd, ptnr Tolman Cunard Ltd (strategic conslts) 1992–99, chm Cunard Communications Ltd 1983–2014, non-exec dir Creston Gp plc 2002–07, executive coach and mentor 2013–; chm Devpt Ctee Public Relations Consultants Assoc 1985; tstee Sick Children's Trust 1984–; chm Walled Gardens Gp Suffolk Gardens Tst; FInstD 1978 (memb 1980); *Books* Public Relations Case Book (1990); *Recreations* gardens, photography, wine, horse racing; *Clubs* Solus; *Style*— Peter Cunard, Esq; ✉ The Mill House, Stanningfield, Suffolk IP29 4RX

CUNDALL, Dr Peter Alan; s of Lester Alan Cundall (d 2011), and Emmie Pamela, *née* Johnson (d 2000); *b* 9 April 1944, Llandudno, Conwy; *Educ* Purley Co GS, Imperial Coll London (BSc, PhD); *m* 12 Nov 1966, Christine Ann, *née* Martin; 2 da (Alison Joyce b 6 Oct 1967, Anita Pamela b 26 Feb 1972); *Career* princ and sr engr Dames & Moore 1974–79, assoc prof Dept of Civil and Mineral Engrg Univ of Minnesota 1982–86 (asst prof 1972–74, adjunct prof 1990–), princ Itasca Consulting Gp Inc 2000–09 (sr conslt 1989–2000); author of 115 scientific papers; Award for Outstanding Contributions to Rock Mechanics American Rock Mechanics Assoc 2003, Rock Mechanics Award Soc for Mining, Metallurgy and Exploration 2003; FREng 2005, memb Nat Acad of Engrg USA 2008; *Recreations* sailing, oil painting; *Style*— Dr Peter Cundall; ✉ PO Box 120, Marine on St Croix, MN 55047, USA (☎ 00 1 651 433 3452, e-mail pacundall@aol.com)

CUNDEY, Angus Howard; MBE (2016); s of Samuel Howard Cundey (d 1982), and Eileen Florence, *née* Fitter; *b* 7 June 1937, London; *Educ* Downside, Framlingham Coll, Tailor and Cutter Acad London (Dip); *m* 1, 1968, Gudrun, *née* Munck; 1 s (Simon Howard b 29 Sept 1968), 1 da (Sarah Howard b 10 Dec 1971); m 2, 2002, Myranda, *née* Grainger Smith; *Career* apprentice Lanvin Paris 1955; Henry Poole & Co (Savile Row) Ltd: joined as cutter 1958, chm 1980–; dir Savile Row Bespoke Ltd; chm Milden Parish Meeting 2010–; Liveryman Merchant Taylors Co 1990; *Publications* Henry Poole: Founders of Savile Row (2003); *Recreations* motoring, gardening; *Clubs* Vintage Sports Car; *Style*— Angus Cundey, Esq, MBE; ✉ Old Well Cottage, Milden, Ipswich, Suffolk IP7 7AL (☎ 01787 247430); Henry Poole & Co (Savile Row) Limited, 15 Savile Row, London W1S 3PJ (☎ 020 7734 5985, fax 020 7287 2161, e-mail office@henrypoole.com)

CUNDY, Jody Alan; MBE (2009); s of Alan Cundy, and Ann Cundy; *b* 14 October 1978, Wisbech, Cambs; *Career* Paralympic cyclist and former swimmer; swimming achievements incl: Gold medal (100m butterfly) and Bronze medal (100m backstroke) World Championships 1994, Gold medal (100m butterfly) Paralympics 1996 (world record), Gold medal (100m butterfly) and Silver medal (4x100m medley relay) European Championships 1997, Silver medal (100m butterfly) World Championships 1998, 3 Gold medals (100m butterfly, 4x100m freestyle relay and 4x100m medley relay) European Championships 1999, 2 Gold medals (100m Butterfly and 4x100m freestyle relay (with Matthew Walker, Marc Woods and David Roberts)) and Bronze medal 100m backstroke Paralympics Sydney 2000, 3 Gold medals (100m butterfly (world record), 4x100m freestyle relay and 4x100m medly relay) and 2 Silver medals (100m backstrock and 50m freestyle) European Championships 2001, 2 Gold medals (100m butterfly (world record) and 4x100m medley relay) and Bronze medal (4x100m freestyle relay) World Championships 2002, Bronze medal (100m butterfly) Paralympics Athens 2004; cycling achievements incl: Gold medal (1km time trial) World Championships 2006 (world record), 2 Gold medals (1km time trial and team sprint) World Championships 2007 (two world records), 2 Gold medals (team sprint (with Darren Kenny and Mark Bristow, *qv*) and 1km time trial) Paralympics Beijing 2008 (two world records), 2 Gold medals (1km time trial (world record) and team sprint (with Darren Kenny and Mark Bristow, *qv*)) World Championships 2009, 2 Gold medals (1km time trial (world record) and team sprint (with Darren Kenny and Terry Byrne, world record)) and Silver medal (4km pursuit) World Championships 2011, Gold medal (1km time trial), Silver medal (team sprint (with Darren Kenny and Sarah Storey, OBE, *qv*)) and Bronze medal (4km pursuit) World Championships 2012, Bronze medal (individual pursuit) Paralympic Games 2012; Nationwide Achievement Award (Male Cycling) 2006, BBC East Disabled Sports Personality of the Year 2008 and 2011; *Style*— Jody Cundy, Esq, MBE; ✉ website www.jodycundy.com, Twitter @jodycundy; c/o JAC Sport Ltd, 81 The Vie, 189 Water Street, Manchester M3 4JE (☎ 07540 637542, e-mail (commercial requests) c-kelkel@jac-sport.com, e-mail (media requests) media@jac-sport.com, website www.jac-sport.com)

CUNINGHAME; *see:* Fairlie-Cuninghame, Montgomery Cuninghame

CUNLIFFE, Prof Sir Barrington Windsor (Barry); kt (2006), CBE (1994); s of George Percival Windsor (d 1942), and Beatrice Emma, *née* Mersh; *b* 10 December 1939; *Educ* Northern GS Portsmouth, St John's Coll Cambridge (BA, MA, PhD, LittD); *m* 1, 1962 (m dis 1978), Frances Ann, *née* Dunn; 1 s (Daniel b 1966), 1 da (Charlotte b 1969); m 2, 4 Jan 1979, Margaret, da of late Robert Herdman, of Brockworth, Glos; 1 s (Thomas b 1981), 1 da (Anna b 1984); *Career* asst lectr Univ of Bristol 1963–66, prof of archaeology Univ of Southampton 1966–72, prof of Euro archaeology Univ of Oxford 1972–; vice-pres: Soc of Antiquaries 1982–85 (pres 1991–95), Prehistoric Soc 1983–86; cmmr English Heritage 1986–92 and 2006–14, a govr Museum of London 1995–98, tstee British Museum 2000–09; memb: Roman Soc, Soc of Medieval Archaeology, Royal Archaeological Inst; Hon DLitt Univ of Sussex 1983, Hon DSc Univ of Bath 1984, Hon DUniv Open Univ 1995, Hon DLitt Univ of Southampton 2009, Hon DLitt Univ of Kent 2010, Hon DSc Univ of Bradford 2015; FSA 1964, FBA 1979, correspondent memb Deutschen Archaologischen Instituts, hon memb Royal Irish Acad, corresponding memb Real Academia de la Historia Spain, founding FLSW; *Books* incl: The Cradle of England (1972), Rome and the Barbarians (1975), Rome and her Empire (1978), The Celtic World (1979), Roman Bath Discovered (1984), The City of Bath (1986), Greeks, Romans and Barbarians (1988), Iron Age Communities in Britain (1991, 4 edn 2005), Wessex to AD 1000 (1993), The Oxford Illustrated Prehistory of Europe (1994), The Ancient Celts (1997), Facing the Ocean (2001), The Extraordinary Voyage of Pytheas the Greek (2001), The Celts: A Very Short Introduction (2003), Iron Age Britain (2005), Europe Between The Oceans (2007), The Druids: A Very Short Introduction (2010), Britain Begins (2012), By Steppe, Desert and Ocean (2016); *Clubs* Athenaeum; *Style*— Prof Sir Barry Cunliffe, CBE, FBA, FSA; ✉ Institute of Archaeology, 36 Beaumont Street, Oxford (☎ 01865 278240)

CUNLIFFE, Sir David Ellis; 9 Bt (GB 1759), of Liverpool, Lancashire; s of Sir Cyril Henley Cunliffe, 8 Bt (d 1969), and Eileen Mary, *née* Parkins; *b* 29 October 1957; *Educ* St Alban's GS for Boys; *m* 1983, Linda Carol, da of John Sidney Batchelor, of Harpenden; 3 da (Emma Mary b 1986, Katherine Alice b 1990, Bridget Carol b 1991); *Heir* bro, Andrew Cunliffe; *Career* business development manager; *Style*— Sir David Cunliffe, Bt; ✉ Sunnyside, Burnthouse Lane, Needham, Harleston, Norfolk IP20 9LN

CUNNINGHAM, Alexander (Alex); MP; s of John Cunningham, and Jean Cunningham; *b* 1 May 1955, Broxburn, W Lothian; *Educ* Branksome Comp Sch Darlington, Queen Elizabeth Sixth Form Coll Darlington, Coll of Techonol Darlington; *m* Evaline; 2 s (John, Andrew); *Career* journalist on NE newspapers and radio stations 1974–84, PR mangr Br Gas 1984–92, PR mangr Transco 1992–99, head of communications Transco 1999–2002, dir and prop Tees Valley Communicators Ltd 1992–2010; cncllr: Cleveland CC 1986–96 (vice-chair Educn Ctee 1990–96, chair Standing Advsy Cncl for Religious Educn 1989–96), Stockton Borough Cncl 1999–2010 (cabinet memb for children and young people 2000–10); MP (Lab) Stockton N 2010–, PPS to Rt Hon Sadiq Khan, MP, *qv* (as Shadow Justice Sec and Shadow Lord Chancellor) until 2015, PPS to Rt Hon the Lord Falconer of Thoroton, *qv* (as Shadow Justice Sec and Shadow Lord Chancellor) 2015, shadow min for the environment 2015–16; memb Bd One North East RDA 2007–10; non-exec dir N Tees and Hartlepool NHS Fndn Tst 2008–10; *Recreations* travel, reading; *Clubs* Stockton Rugby (patron); *Style*— Alex Cunningham, Esq, MP; ✉ c/o Robert Cook, Stockton Business Centre, 70 Brunswick Street, Stockton on Tees TS19 1DW (☎ 01642 345291); Westminster researcher Sam Reeve, (☎ 020 6219 7157); House of Commons, London SW1A 0AA

CUNNINGHAM, Allen; s of late Sir Graham Cunningham, KBE, and late Marjorie, *née* Harris; *Educ* Leighton Park Sch Reading, Univ of Liverpool (BArch, Sikorsky Prize); *m* 1958, late Sandra Lynne, da of late Edmund Bainbridge; 2 s (Graham b 1959, Neve b 1961), 1 da (Aldona b 1965); *Career* project architect: Sir Leslie Martin Cambridge 1957–60, Marcel Breuer & Associates NY 1960–63, Marcel Breuer Paris 1963–66; gp ldr City Architect's Office Nottingham 1966–68, princ architect Llewelyn-Davies, Weeks, Forestier-Walker & Bor London 1968–72, head of architecture Poly of Central London 1974–97; visiting prof Univ of Westminster 1997–2001; fndr The Jl of Architecture (chm Editorial Bd 1996–2012, exec ed 1997–2007, hon commissioning ed 2012–); memb Scientific Ctee DOCOMOMO Int 1992–2006; memb Bd of Architectural Educn ARCUK 1978–92; RIBA: memb Cncl RIBA Cities of London and Westminster Soc of Architects 1974–97, memb Educn and Professional Devpt Ctee 1980–84 and 1996–98, elected London regnl rep to RIBA Cncl 1996–99, fndr memb RIBA Reform Gp 1996–2007, juror RIBA Pres's Royal Gold Medal 1993, juror EAAE Prize 2005–07; co-fndr and vice-pres Terre Romane; registered ARCUK 1959, ARIBA 1959, FRSA 1993; *Publications* Modern Movement Heritage (ed, 1998); *Recreations* creating tableaux objets, paintings, sculptures; *Style*— Allen Cunningham; ✉ 38 Rue de l'Engin, 24500 Eymet, France (☎ 00 33 5 53 74 29 73, e-mail cunning@wanadoo.fr)

CUNNINGHAM, Andrew; s of Robert Cunningham (d 1998), and Lily, *née* McGalloway; *b* 22 July 1956, Fife; *Educ* King Edward VI GS Nuneaton, Christ's Coll Cambridge; *m* 29 Sept 1989, Deborah, *née* Moran; 3 s (James b 14 Feb 1992, Harry b 11 March 1994, Patrick b 21 June 1996), 1 da (Elspeth b 2 Aug 1999); *Career* ptnr Deloitte Haskins & Sells (latterly Coopers & Lybrand Deloitte) 1989–96 (joined 1978); Grainger Tst plc: finance dir 1996–2002, dep ceo 2002–; non-exec dir The Local Shopping REIT plc 2007–; FCA 1981; *Style*— Andrew Cunningham, Esq; ✉ Grainger plc, Citygate, St James Boulevard, Newcastle upon Tyne NE1 4JE

CUNNINGHAM, James Dolan (Jim); MP; s of Adam Cunningham, and Elizabeth, *née* Farrel; *b* 4 February 1941; *Educ* St Columbia HS, Tillicoultry Coll (Dip Industrial Law, Dip Social Sciences); *m* 1 March 1985, Marion, da of late Frank Muir Podmore; 1 s (Andrew), 1 da (Jeanette), 1 step s (Paul A Douglas), 1 step da (Jacqueline (Mrs Stevenson)); *Career* engr Rolls Royce until 1988; Coventry City Cncl: sometime vice-chm Fin Ctee, chm Leisure Ctee, vice-chm Tport and Highways Ctee, chief whip, dep ldr of the Cncl, and ldr 1988–92 (memb 1972–93); chief steward and shop steward MSF; sec then chm Coventry SE CLP; MP (Lab) Coventry S 1992–; *Recreations* walking, reading, music, football, politics, history, archaeology, political philosophy; *Style*— Jim Cunningham, Esq, MP; ✉ House of Commons, London SW1A 0AA

CUNNINGHAM, Prof Sir John; KCVO; *b* 27 June 1949, Oxford; *Educ* Magdalen Coll Sch Oxford, Trinity Hall Cambridge (BA), Oxford Univ Clinical Med Sch (BM BCh, DM); *Career* house physician and house surgn Radcliffe Infirmary Oxford 1974, SHO (rotating) Whittington Hosp London 1974–75, SHO (thoracic med) Brompton Hosp 1975, med registrar Cardiothoracic Dept Central Middx Hosp 1976–77, lectr in med Med Unit London Hosp Med Coll 1977–80, fell Div of Endocrinology and Metabolism Washington Univ Sch of Med St Louis Missouri USA 1980–82, conslt physician and nephrologist Royal London Hosp 1982–2003; St Bartholomew's and the Royal London Sch of Med & Dentistry (formerly London Hosp Med Coll): hon sr lectr in med 1986–2001, sub-dean for student admissions 1990–97, prof of renal and metabolic med 2001–03, prof of nephrology UCL 2003–, conslt nephrologist UCL Hosp and The Royal Free Hosp 2003–; physician to: The Royal Household 1993–2005, King Edward VII's Hosp for Officers 1993–, HM The Queen and Head of the Medical Household 2005–14; special tstee Royal London Hosp 1985–2000, recognised teacher Univ of London 1985–, Jan Brod Meml lectr Prague 1993; hon fell Trinity Hall Cambridge 2014; over 100 presentations to nat/int learned gps and societies; memb Editorial Bd: Nephrology Dialysis Transplantion 1993–, Int Procceedings Jl (Nephrology Section) 1993–; memb: RSM, American Soc of Nephrology, Renal Assoc, American Soc for Bone and Mineral Res, Euro Calcified Tissue Soc, Bone and Tooth Soc, Euro Dialysis and Transplant Assoc – Euro Renal Assoc, Int Soc of Nephrology; FRCP 1988; *Publications* author of chapters in med and scientific textbooks, invited reviews and over 100 original articles in scientific jls; *Recreations* music, various sports – active and passive; *Clubs* MCC; *Style*— Prof Sir John Cunningham, KCVO, FRCP; ✉ The Centre for Nephrology, The Royal Free and University College Medical School, The Royal Free Hospital, Rowland Hill Street, London NW3 2PF (e-mail drjohncunningham@gmail.com)

CUNNINGHAM, Mark James; QC (2001); s of James Arthur Cunningham, and late Carole Kathleen, *née* Wood; *b* 6 June 1956; *Educ* Stonyhurst, Magdalen Coll Oxford (BA), Poly of Central London (Dip Law); *m* 19 July 1980 (m dis 1995); 2 da (Clementine b 1981, Susannah b 1985), 2 s (Charles b 1984, Edward b 1989); *Career* called to the: Bar Inner Temple 1980, East Caribbean Bar 2005; jr counsel to the Crown Chancery 1992, inspr DTI 1998–99, jr counsel to the Crown A Panel 1999; *Recreations* tennis, cricket, horses, food; *Style*— Mark Cunningham, QC; ✉ Maitland Chambers, 7 Stone Buildings, Lincoln's Inn, London WC2A 3SZ (☏ 020 7406 1200, fax 020 7406 1300, e-mail mcunningham@maitlandchambers.com)

CUNNINGHAM, (Harold) Michael Clunie; s of Harold Cunningham, and Margaret Isabel, *née* McPherson; *b* 18 November 1947; *Educ* Rossall Sch, RMA Sandhurst; *m* 22 Dec 1970, Virginia Pamela Liege, da of Col Sir Thomas Butler, Bt, CVO, DSO, OBE (d 1994); 2 da (Sophia Louisa Caroline b 31 July 1973, Henrietta Maria Charlotte b 17 Dec 1975), 2 s (Charles Alexander Clunie b 9 Dec 1978, Rupert Jasper Clunie b 25 May 1984); *Career* cmmnd 2 Lt Queen's Own Hussars 1968, ret as Capt 1976; ptnr Neilson Hornby Crichton stockbrokers 1981–86 (joined 1976), dir Neilson Milnes 1986–91, dir Rathbone Neilson Cobbold (formerly Neilson Cobbold) 1991–99, chm Pennine Fund Managers Ltd 1994–98; dir: Rathbone Investment Management 1996–2007, Rathbone Unit Trust Managers Ltd 1997–2007, FirstCare Ltd 2006–12, Double Take Portraits Ltd 2006–10, Helios Underwriting plc 2007–, Downing Distribution VCT 1 plc 2009–13, Downing Absolute Income 3 plc (formerly Downing Distribution VCT 2 plc) 2009–13; chm: Nu Nu plc 2002–09, Equine Rescue Servs Ltd 2008–, Hazel Renewable Energy VCT plc 2010–; FSI (memb Stock Exchange 1981); *Recreations* field sports, fishing, sailing; *Clubs* Cavalry and Guards; *Style*— Michael Cunningham, Esq; ✉ Dolhyfryd, Lawnt, Denbigh, Denbighshire LL16 4SU (☏ 01745 814805, e-mail michael@dolhyfryd.com)

CUNNINGHAM, Roseanna; MSP; da of Hugh Cunningham (d 1993), and Catherine, *née* Dunlay; *b* 27 July 1951; *Educ* Univ of West Australia (BA), Univ of Edinburgh (LLB), Univ of Aberdeen (DipLP); *Career* asst research offr SNP 1977–79; slr: Dumbarton DC 1986 (trainee slr 1983–85), Glasgow DC 1986–89, Ross Harper & Murphy Glasgow 1989–90; admitted Faculty of Advocates 1990; MP (SNP): Perth and Kinross 1995–97, Perth 1997–2001; MSP (SNP): Perth 1999–2011, Perthshire S & Kinross-shire 2011–; shadow justice min 1999–2000, convener Scottish Parl Justice and Home Affrs Ctee 1999–2000, sr vice-convenor and dep leader SNP 2000–04, convener Scottish Parl Health and Community Care Ctee 2004–07, convener Rural Affrs and Environment Ctee 2007–09, min for environment 2009–11, min for community safety and legal affrs 2011–14, cabinet sec for fair work, skills and trg 2014–16, cabinet sec for environment, climate change and land reform 2016–; *Recreations* reading, arguing, music; *Style*— Ms Roseanna Cunningham, MSP; ✉ The Scottish Parliament, Edinburgh EH99 1SP (☏ 0131 348 6087, fax 0131 348 5563, e-mail roseanna.cunningham.msp@parliament.scot, website www.roseannacunningham.com); Constituency Office, 63 Glasgow Road, Perth PH2 0PE (☏ 01738 620540)

CUNNINGHAM, Sir Thomas Anthony (Tony); kt (2012); s of Daniel Cunningham (d 1987), and Bessie, *née* Lister; *Educ* Workington GS, Univ of Liverpool (BA), Didsbury Coll (PGCE), St John's Coll Manchester (RSA TESL); *m* 1985, Anne, da of Albert and Margaret Gilmore; 1 da (Angela b 1992), 1 s (Daniel b 2004), 1 step s (David b 1978), 1 step da (Marie b 1981); *Career* history teacher Alsager Comp Sch 1976–80, English teacher (VSO) Mikunguni Trade Sch Zanzibar 1980–82, history teacher Netherhall Sch Maryport 1983–93; MEP (Lab) Cumbria and Lancs N 1994–99, MP (Lab) Workington 2001–15; cncllr Allerdale BC 1987–94 (ldr 1992–94), Mayor of Workington 1990–91; govt whip 2005–; *Recreations* sports, reading; *Clubs* Station Road; *Style*— Sir Tony Cunningham

CUNNINGHAM, Prof Valentine David; s of Rev Valentine Cunningham, of Lutterworth, Leics, and Alma Lilian, *née* Alexander; *b* 28 October 1944; *Educ* Lawrence Sheriff Sch Rugby, Keble Coll Oxford (scholar, MA), St John's Coll Oxford (DPhil); *m* 6 August 1966, Carol Ann, da of Joseph Shaw; 2 s (Joseph Valentine Asa b 23 Dec 1970, Willoughby Buz Raphael Bunyan b 29 Jan 1975); *Career* jr res fell St John's Coll Oxford 1969–72; Univ of Oxford: lectr in English 1972–2015, chm English Faculty 1984–87, prof of English language and literature 1996–2015; CCC Oxford: fell and tutor in English 1972–2015, dean 1980–91, sr tutor 1991–94, vice-pres 2008–12; permanent visiting prof Univ of Konstanz Germany 1994–2001, prof (hc) Univ of Bucharest 2013, hon fell Grossbritannien-Zentrum Humboldt Univ Berlin; frequent broadcasts on BBC Radio; judge literary prizes incl: Booker Prize 1992 and 1998, Commonwealth Writers Prize 2000 and 2001; Int IMPAC Dublin Literary Award 2015; memb Labour Pty, memb St Margaret's Church N Oxford; *Publications* Everywhere Spoken Against: Dissent in the Victorian Novel (1975), The Penguin Book of Spanish Civil War Verse (ed, 1980), Spanish Front: Writers on the Civil War (ed, 1986), British Writers of the Thirties (1988), Cinco Escritores Britanicos/Five British Writers (ed, 1990), In the Reading Gaol: Postmodernity, Texts, and History (1994), George Eliot: Adam Bede (ed, 1996), The Victorians: An Anthology of Poetry and Poetics (ed, 2000), Reading After Theory (2002), Victorian Poetry Now: poets, poems, poetics (2011), The Connell Guide to Shakespeare's King Lear (2012), Victorian Poets: A Critical Reader (ed, 2014); numerous articles and introductions in books and learned jls; *Recreations* jazz trumpet and piano (ldr Dark Blues Jazz Band); *Clubs* London Library, Oxford & Cambridge; *Style*— Prof Valentine Cunningham; ✉ Corpus Christi College, Oxford OX1 4JF (☏ 01865 276700, fax 01865 276767, e-mail valentine.cunningham@ccc.ox.ac.uk)

CUNNINGHAM OF FELLING, Baron (Life Peer UK 2005), of Felling in the County of Tyne & Wear; Dr John Anderson (Jack) Cunningham; PC (1993), DL (Cumbria 1991); s of Andrew Cunningham; *b* 4 August 1939; *Educ* Jarrow GS, Bede Coll Univ of Durham (BSc, PhD); *m* 1964, Maureen; 1 s, 2 da; *Career* formerly research chemist Univ of Durham, then lectr and Trades Union official, cncllr Chester-Le-Street DC (chm Fin Ctee 1969–74); MP (Lab): Whitehaven 1970–83, Copeland 1983–2005; PPS to Rt Hon James Callaghan 1972–76, Parly under sec of state Dept of Energy 1976–79; front bench oppn spokesman on: Industry 1979–83, Environment 1983–92; memb Shadow Cabinet 1983–97, shadow ldr House of Commons and Lab campaign coordinator 1989–92; chief oppn spokesman on: foreign and Cwlth affrs (shadow foreign sec) 1992–94, trade and industry 1994–95, National Heritage 1995–97; min for: Agriculture, Fisheries and Food 1997–98, Cabinet Office 'enforcer' and chllr of the Duchy of Lancaster 1998–99; *Recreations* gardening, fell walking, fly fishing, music, books, ornithology, theatre; *Style*— The Rt Hon the Lord Cunningham of Felling, PC, DL

CUPITT, (Rev) Don; s of late Robert Cupitt, of Wendover, Bucks, and late Norah Cupitt; *b* 22 May 1934; *Educ* Charterhouse, Trinity Hall Cambridge (BA), Westcott House Cambridge; *m* 28 Dec 1963, Susan Marianne, da of Frank Cooper Day (d 1941); 1 s (John b 1965), 2 da (Caroline b 1966, Sally b 1970); *Career* Nat Serv 2 Lt Royal Signals 1956–57; curate St Philip's Salford 1959–62, vice-princ Westcott House Cambridge 1962–65; Emmanuel Coll Cambridge: dean 1965–91, asst univ lectr 1968–73, univ lectr 1973–96; ret 1996; Hon DLitt Univ of Bristol 1985; hon fell The Jesus Seminar 2001; *Books* Christ and the Hiddenness of God (1971), Crisis of Moral Authority (1972), The Leap of Reason (1976), The Worlds of Science and Religion (1976), Who Was Jesus? (with Peter Armstrong, 1977, BBC TV documentary, 1977), The Nature of Man (1979), Explorations in Theology (1979), The Debate about Christ (1979), Jesus and the Gospel of God (1979), Taking Leave of God (1980), The World to Come (1982), The Sea of Faith (1984, BBC TV series 1984), Only Human (1985), Life Lines (1986), The Long-Legged Fly (1987), The New Christian Ethics (1988), Radicals and the Future of the Church (1989), Creation out of Nothing (1990), What is a Story? (1991), The Time Being (1992), After All (1994), The Last Philosophy (1995), Solar Ethics (1995), After God (1997), Mysticism After Modernity (1998), The Religion of Being (1998), The Revelation of Being (1998), The New Religion of Life in Everyday Speech (1999), The Meaning of it All in Everyday Speech (1999), Kingdom Come in Everyday Speech (2000), Philosophy's Own Religion (2000), Reforming Christianity (2001), Emptiness and Brightness (2002), Is Nothing Sacred? (2002), Life, Life (2003), The Way to Happiness (2005), The Great Questions of Life (2006), The Old Creed and the New (2006), Radical Theology (2006), Impossible Loves (2007), Above Us Only Sky (2008), The Meaning of the West (2008), Jesus and Philosophy (2009), Theology's Strange Return (2010), A New Great Story (2010), The Fountain (2010), Turns of Phrase (2011), The Last Testament (2012), Creative Faith (2015), Ethics in the Last Days of Humanity (2016); *Recreations* family life; *Style*— Don Cupitt; ✉ Emmanuel College, Cambridge CB2 3AP (☏ 01223 334267, fax 01223 334426, website www.doncupitt.com)

CURIEL, Raúl Morris; s of Isaac Curiel Segura, of Montevideo, Uruguay, and Clara, *née* Margounato; *b* 31 March 1946; *Educ* Colegio Nacional Jose P Varela Scdy Sch Montevideo Uruguay, Univ de la Republica Montevideo Uruguay, Iowa State Univ USA (BArch), Univ of Minnesota USA (MArch); *m* 26 May 1976, Linda, da of Ronald Webb; 2 da (Alessandra Stephanie b 5 May 1985, Melanie Jane b 30 May 1989); *Career* formerly architect São Paulo; Fitzroy Robinson Ltd: architectural asst 1978–83, dir 1983–2005, chm 2002–05; dir of European ops Aukett Fitzroy Robinson 2005–; major architectural projects incl: The Standard Chartered Bank, Sedgwick House, HQ for the Moscow Narodny Bank, interiors for London HQ of Drexel Burnham Lambert, a mixed conservation/new office building at 75 King William St, numerous business parks; awarded: AIA merit award, selected design Sch of Architecture ISU 1971, selected design UNESCO's Int Design Competition 1972, Mason's award 1990 and Tiler's and Bricklayer's award 1990 for building at 75 King William St; memb: IAB 1977, RIBA 1979; *Recreations* theatre, reading, swimming, viewing buildings, sketching; *Style*— Raul Curiel, Esq; ✉ website www.aukettfitzroyrobinson.com

CURL, His Hon Judge Philip; s of Dr Oliver Curl, and Joan, *née* Crooks; *b* 31 October 1947; *Educ* Radley, Univ of Southampton (LLB); *m* 22 Oct 1983, Nicola Ruth, da of late Richard Quentin Gurney; 2 da (Olivia Elisabeth b 17 Jan 1986, Eleanor Rose b 16 May 1989); *Career* called to the Bar Gray's Inn 1970, recorder 1995–96 (asst recorder 1991), circuit judge (SE Circuit) 1996–, designated family judge Norwich Combined Court 1998–2007; memb Disciplinary Panel Br Horseracing Authy 2011–; *Recreations* playing and watching sport, art, travel; *Clubs* Boodle's, MCC, Norfolk (Norwich); *Style*— His Hon Judge Curl; ✉ Norwich Combined Courts Centre, Bishopgate, Norwich NR3 1UR

CURLEY, William; *m* Suzue; *Career* chocolatier; fndr William Curley Patissier Chocolatier; winner: gold medal Culinary Olympics 2004 (with wife Suzue), Best Br Chocolatier Acad of Chocolate 2007 and 2008; *Style*— William Curley, Esq; ✉ William Curley, 10 Paved Court, Richmond, Surrey TW9 1LZ

CURNOCK COOK, Jeremy Laurence; s of Colin Curnock Cook (d 2003), and Doris, *née* Wolsey (d 2002); *b* 3 September 1949, Bromley, Kent; *Educ* Westminster, TCD (MA); *m* 1, Elizabeth Joanna Badgett; m 2, Mary Elisabeth Thomasson; m 3, Sara Jane, *née* O'Donahue; 2 da (Jessica b 22 Aug 1989, Hannah b 12 Nov 1992), 1 s (Rory b 8 Feb 1991); *Career* md and fndr Int Biochem Gp 1975–87, md Rothschild Bioscience Unit 1987–2000, chm and fndr Int Bioscience Mangrs Ltd 2001–, md Bioscience Mangrs Pty Ltd (formerly IB Mangrs Pty Ltd) (Australia) 2003–, ceo Rex Bionics plc (formerly Union MedTech plc) 2012–14 (currently dep chm); chm: Ampliphi Biosciences Corp (USA) (formerly Targeted Genetics Inc) 1995–, Avena Therapeutics Ltd (Ireland) 2013–; dir: Biocompatibles Int plc 1992–2011 (former chm), Angiotech Pharmaceuticals Inc Canada 1995–2001, Sirna Therapeutics Inc USA 1995–2007, Silence Therapeutics plc 2005–10, Osteologix Inc USA 2006–10, EACOM Timber Co Inc 2008–13, Topigen Pharmaceuticals Inc (Canada) 2008–10, Excalibur Gp Hldgs Ltd 2009–, Bioxyne Ltd (formerly Hunter Immunology Ltd) (Australia) 2010–14, Virgin Health Bank QSTP-LLC (Qatar) 2011–13, SeaDragon Marine Oils Ltd (NZ) 2012–15, Adherium Ltd (formerly Nexus6 Ltd (Australia)) 2012–, Avita Medical Ltd (Australia) 2012–, Phylogica Ltd (Australia) 2012–, Smart Matrix Ltd 2013–, Arthurian Life Sciences Ltd 2013–16; memb Soc of Gen Microbiology 1971; FInstD 1983, FRSA 1995; *Recreations* theatre, music, skiing, keeping fit, Rolling Stones concerts; *Clubs* Univ and Kildare St (Dublin), RAC of Victoria (Melbourne); *Style*— Jeremy Curnock Cook, Esq; ✉ 56 Chiswick Green Studios, Evershed Walk, London W4 5BW (☏ 07802 268634, e-mail biojlcc@aol.com); Le Bourg, Flaugnac, Lot 46170, France (☏ 0033 9 7901 1335); Bioscience Managers Pty Ltd, Level 10, 330 Collins Street, Melbourne, VIC 3000, Australia (e-mail jlcc@biosciencemanagers.com, website www.biosciencemanagers.com)

CURNOCK COOK, Mary Elizabeth; OBE (2000); *née* Thomasson; da of Christopher Lucas Thomasson (d 2011), and Bryony, *née* Powell; *b* 10 October 1958, London; *Educ* London Business Sch (MSc); *m* (m dis 1997), Jeremy Curnock Cook; 2 da (Jessica b 22 Aug 1989, Hannah b 12 Nov 1992), 1 s (Rory b 8 Feb 1991); *Career* int sales and mktg dir Int Biochemicals 1980–88, mktg dir Food from Britain 1989–93, ceo BII 1994–2001, dir of qualifications and skills Qualifications and Curriculum Devpt Agency 2003–09, ceo UCAS 2010–; memb Cncl FEFC (Further Educn Funding Cncl) 1997–2001, dir Creative Learning Media 2002–05; dir Laurel Pub Co 2002–05; govr Swindon Acad, tstee The Access Project 2013–, tstee The Nat Star Fndn 2014–; *Recreations* tennis, sailing; *Clubs* Blacks, Gunnersbury Triangle Tennis; *Style*— Ms Mary Curnock Cook, OBE; ✉ The Warehouse, 6A Saville Road, London W4 5HQ (☏ 07774 901982, e-mail marycurnockcook@gmail.com); UCAS, Rosehill, New Barn Lane, Cheltenham, Gloucestershire GL52 3LZ (☏ 01242 544996, e-mail m.curnockcook@ucas.ac.uk, website www.ucas.com)

CURNOW, Barry John; s of Stuart John Curnow (d 1986), and Margaret Agnes (Daisy), *née* Parkhouse (d 2001); *b* 19 May 1948; *Educ* Sutton HS Plymouth, Univ of Exeter (BA), Univ of London (MA); *m* 1, 23 Oct 1971, Patricia Margaret, da of late Dr D R L Newton; m 2, 24 Dec 1987, Penelope Ann, da of Henry S J de Haas; *Career* certified mgmnt conslt and group analyst; personnel mangr GLC 1969–73, joined Hay-MSL 1974, gp md Hay-MSL Management Consultants 1984–86, chief exec Hay Management Consultants Asia Hong Kong 1986–87, worldwide dir Hay Group 1987–90, chm and chief exec MSL Group International 1987–91, fndr dir Future Perfect 1987 (exec chm 1991–), non-exec dir and advsr to several cos, chm Independent Counselling and Advsy Servs (ICAS) Ltd 1991–97, princ Maresfield Curnow Sch of Mgmnt Consulting 1991–; pres: UK Inst of Personnel Mgmnt 1989–91 (vice-pres pay and employment conditions 1984–86), Inst of Mgmnt Conslts 1996–97 (chm Int Ctee 2000–); chm Int Cncl Mgmnt Consulting Institutes 2003–05; tstee dir Tavistock Inst of Human Relations 1997–2008; hon psychotherapist Barts 1998–2000; res assoc Henley Mgmnt Coll 1974–83; visiting prof: Mgmnt Consltg CASS Business Sch City Univ 2001–, Univ of Durham 2003; former chair Educ Ctee and asst Worshipful Co of Mgmnt Conslts; memb Inst of Gp Analysis 2001–; Freeman City of London, Freeman Worshipful Co of Chartered Secs and Admins; CCIPD, FCMC, FIOD; *Publications* Managing Third Age Careers – The Corporate Challenge (with John McLean Fox, 1994), The Chance to Live More Than Once (companion vol to Third Age Careers – The Corporate Challenge, with John McLean Fox, 1996); International Guide to Management Consultancy (jt consltg ed 2001 and 2003); *Recreations* amateur radio licence G3UKI 1965; *Style*— Barry Curnow, Esq

CURRAN, Dr Edmund Russell; OBE (2006); s of William John Curran (d 1973), of Dungannon, NI, and Elizabeth, *née* Russell (d 1945); *b* 29 September 1944; *Educ* Royal

Sch Dungannon, Queen's Univ Belfast (BSc, DipEd); *m* 1, 1969 (m dis 1992), Romaine, da of William Carmichael; 2 s (Jonathan William b 18 Sept 1973, Andrew Edmund Simon b 13 Oct 1976), 2 da (Cathryn Ruth b 1 Sept 1975, Claire Susannah b 10 March 1978); m 2, 1994, Pauline Beckett, da of Jack Beckett; *Career* Belfast Telegraph: grad trainee journalist 1966–67, reporter, feature writer then ldr writer 1967–72, asst ed 1973–74, dep ed 1974–88; ed Sunday Life (Belfast) 1988–92 (seconded as ed Wales on Sunday 1991), ed Belfast Telegraph 1993–2005, ed-in-chief NI newspapers Independent News and Media 2005–09; columnist Belfast Telegraph 2009–; columnist Belfast Telegraph; pres UK Soc of Editors 2001, memb Bd Nat Cncl Trg of Journalists 2008–12; UK Regnl Newspaper Ed of the Year 1992; memb PCC 2002–06; Hon DLitt Univ of Ulster 2012; *Recreations* golf, tennis; *Clubs* Belvoir Park Golf, Royal Co Down Golf, Ulster Reform, Belfast Boat; *Style—* Dr Edmund Curran, OBE; ✉ e-mail edmund.curran@belfasttelegraph.co.uk

CURRAN, Margaret Patricia; da of James Curran (d 1991), of Glasgow, and Rose, *née* McConnellogue (d 2004); *b* 24 November 1958; *Educ* Our Lady & St Francis Sch (MA); *m* 1986, Rab Murray, s of George Murray; 2 s (Christopher b 16 March 1987, David b 3 May 1989); *Career* community worker 1982–87, sr community worker 1987–89, lectr Community Educn Univ of Strathclyde 1989–99, MSP (Labour) Glasgow Baillieston 1999–2011, MP (Lab) Glasgow E 2010–15; Scot Parl: convenor Social Inclusion Ctee 1999–2000, convenor Housing Ctee 1999–2000, min for social justice 2002–03 (dep min 2000–02), min for communities 2003–04, min for Parl 2004–11, shadow sec of state for Scotland 2011–15; donor: Oxfam, Amnesty Int; memb TGWU; *Recreations* reading, arts, cinema, family (especially children); *Style—* Ms Margaret Curran; ✉ 75 Langside Drive, Glasgow G43 2ST (tel 0141 637 3254, e-mail mag.curran@virgin.net); Constituency Office, Westwood Business Centre, Easterhouse, Glasgow (tel 0141 771 4844, fax 0141 771 4877)

CURRAN, His Hon Judge Patrick David; QC (1995); *b* 2 March 1948; *Educ* Ratcliffe Coll, The Queen's Coll Oxford (MA); *Career* called to the Bar Gray's Inn 1972 (bencher 2005), memb King's Inns and the Bar of Ireland 1994; asst recorder 1988–92, recorder 1992–2007, circuit judge (Wales Circuit) 2007–, dep judge of the High Court (Queen's Bench Div) 2008–; asst cmmr Parly Boundary Cmmn 1994–97, legal memb Mental Health Review Tbnls 1995–2008, legal assessor GMC 2000–07; *Publications* Personal Injuries and Quantum Reports (founding ed, 1992–04, conslt ed 2004–); Personal Injury Pleadings (1994, 5 edn 2014), Personal Injury Claims Manual (conslt-ed 2002–06); Criminal Law and Forensic Psychiatry (contrib, 1996); *Clubs* Athenaeum; *Style—* His Hon Judge Curran, QC; ✉ The Law Courts, Cathays Park, Cardiff CF10 3PG

CURRAN, Stephen William; s of Dr Richard Desmond Curran, CBE (d 1985, Capt RNVR), and Marguerite Claire, *née* Gothard; *b* 9 March 1943; *Educ* Marlborough House Sch, Wellington, RMA Sandhurst; *m* 21 June 1969, Anne Beatrice, da of late Harry Grumbar, of Rats Castle, Roughway, nr Tonbridge, Kent; 1 s (Charles b 1972), 1 da (Louise b 1979); *Career* Lt 1 The Queen's Dragoon Gds 1963–66; Permutit Co Ltd 1966–67, Bowater Co Ltd 1967–71, analyst Grumbar and Sée 1971–75, managing conslt Coopers and Lybrand Assocs 1975–79, project fin mangr NCB Pension Funds 1979–81; Candover Investments plc: dep chief exec 1981–90, chief exec 1991–99, chm 1999–2006, non-exec dir 2006–; non-exec dir: Jarvis Hotels plc, Greggs plc; FCCA 1973; *Recreations* skiing, swimming, tennis, riding; *Clubs* Cavalry and Guards', Hurlingham; *Style—* Stephen Curran, Esq

CURRAN, Susan; da of Norman Griffin, of Lincoln, and Maureen, *née* McGinnity; *b* 14 May 1952; *Educ* Abbeydale GS for Girls Sheffield, Univ of Sussex (BA), Univ of East Anglia (MBA); *m* 1, 1976 (m dis 1980), Timothy Curran; m 2, 1980 (m dis 1987), Raymond Curnow; 2 s (Rufus b 7 Nov 1980, Evan b 14 Dec 1982); m 3, 1997, Paul Simmonds; *Career* underwriter FM Insurance Co 1973–78, dir and sec Probit Consultancies Ltd 1979–87, freelance writer 1985–, md Rampant Horse Ltd 1993–95, md Curran Publishing Services Ltd 1999–, managing ed Lasse Press 2011–; *Books* fiction: The Mouse God (1987), The Heron's Catch (1989), Mrs Forster (1991), Mine (1994), Communion With Death (1995); non-fiction incl: How to Write a Book and Get it Published (1990), The Penguin Computing Book (with Ray Curnow, 1983), The Driver's Handbook (1997), The Environment Handbook (1999), The English Friend (2011), The Marriage of Margery Paston (2013), The Wife of Cobham (2016); *Recreations* politics, cooking, collecting contemporary art, other people; *Style—* Ms Susan Curran; ✉ 2 St Giles Terrace, Norwich NR2 1NS (☎ 01603 665843, e-mail susan@curranpublishing.com)

CURRIE, Andrew Buchanan; s of Buchanan Currie, of Loughborough, Leics, and Wilma, *née* Livingston; *b* 16 April 1954; *Educ* Loughborough GS, Univ of Birmingham (BA); *Career* employment research exec Inst of Dirs 1983–86, sr account exec Profile Public Relations 1986–88, dep dir and head of research Shopping Hours Reform Cncl 1988–94, ed Making Sense of Shopping 1988–94; BAA: asst dir of public affrs 1994–2000, dir of community relations 2000–03, dir of employee communications 2003–07, head CEO's Office 2007–08; freelance communications conslt 2008–10, press and PR mangr Bonhams 2010–11, dep press and pr dir Bonhams 2011–; FRSA; *Recreations* opera, reading, writing; *Style—* Andrew Currie, Esq; ✉ Flat 3, 52 Cumberland Street, London SW1V 4LZ (☎ 020 7821 7558, mobile 07710 331477, e-mail andrewbcurrie@hotmail.co.uk); 101 New Bond Street, London W1S 1SR (☎ 020 7468 5871, e-mail andrew.currie@bonhams.com, website www.bonhams.com)

CURRIE, Brian Murdoch; s of William Murdoch Currie (d 1984), and Dorothy, *née* Holloway (d 1995); *b* 20 December 1934; *Educ* Blundell's (open scholar), Oriel Coll Oxford (open scholar, MA); *m* 21 Oct 1961, Patricia Maria, da of Capt Frederick Eaton-Farr (d 1945); 3 s (Murdoch b 1964, Lachlan b 1967, Gregor b 1975), 1 da (Lucinda b 1966); *Career* Subaltern RTR 1957–59; Arthur Andersen and Andersen Consulting (now Accenture): ptnr 1970–90, managing ptnr London 1977–82, chm Partnership Cncl 1983–85; fin memb HMSO Bd 1972–74, inspr Dept of Trade 1978–81; memb: Restrictive Practices Court 1979–2004, Take-over Panel 1989–97; dep chm Fin Reporting Cncl 1996–98; ICAEW: vice-pres 1994–95, dep pres 1995–96, pres 1996–97; chm Public Sector Liaison Gp of Accounting Standards Ctee 1984–86, memb IFAC Compliance Ctee 2000–02; lay memb GDC 1994–99; tstee Oriel Coll Devpt Tst 1979–94; govr Blundell's Sch 2000–02, chm Peter Blundell Soc 1997–2002; hon treas The Glass Assoc 1999–2003 (jt ed The Glass Cone); Exmoor Soc Fndr's Award 2002 (treas 1993–2002); memb Ct of Assts Worshipful Co of Chartered Accountants 1994–97; fell Inst of Ops Mgmnt (memb Nat Cncl 1970–73); FIMC; *Publications* A Principle-based Framework for Professional Independence (1992); official public reports; papers and articles in professional and technical pubns; *Recreations* study of glass, Exmoor, church (lay assisting); *Clubs* Athenaeum; *Style—* Brian Currie, Esq; ✉ Westbrook House, Bampton, Devon EX16 9HU (☎ 01398 331418)

CURRIE, Ian Hamilton; s of John Currie (d 1984), and Vera Matilda Currie, *née* Lea; *b* 9 March 1948; *Educ* Portsmouth Northern GS; *m* 22 Feb 1972, Catherine Helen, da of Ernest William Pink (d 1983); 2 da (Victoria Catherine b 1979, Jacqueline Neoma b 1983); *Career* fin dir: Gieves Group plc 1981–97, Chivers Communications plc 2000–01; chm: Syrinx Securities Ltd, Cadmus Capital Ptnrs Ltd, Cadmus Property Hldgs Ltd; chm and chief exec Pullingers (Furnishers) Ltd, chm Roundabout Garages Ltd, chm Merlin Publishing plc; tstee and treas Fareham CAB; memb RYA Central Finance Ctee; FCA (England and Wales) 1970; *Recreations* cruiser sailing; *Clubs* Portchester Sailing (tstee); *Style—* Ian Currie, FCA; ✉ Clear Cottage, Manor Road, Hayling Island, Hampshire PO11 0QT (☎ 023 9263 6709, fax 023 9246 1123, car 07836 270166, e-mail ianhcurrie@gmail.com)

CURRIE, James McGill; s of late David Currie, of Kilmarnock, Scotland, and Mary, *née* Smith; *b* 17 November 1941; *Educ* St Joseph's Sch Kilmarnock, Blairs Coll Aberdeen, Royal Scots Coll, Valladolid Spain, Univ of Glasgow (MA); *m* 27 June 1968, Evelyn Barbara, da of Alexander Malcolm Macintyre, of Glasgow; 1 s (Alister John b 1971), 1 da (Jennifer b 1973); *Career* civil servant; asst princ Scot Home and Health Dept 1968–72, Scot Educn Dept 1972–75; asst sec: Tport Policy 1977–80, Industrial Devpt 1981–82; cnsllr for Social Affrs and Tport at UK Perm Representation to EEC in Brussels 1982–86, dir Euro Regnl Devpt Fund of Euro Cmmn (Brussels) 1987–89, chef de cabinet to Sir Leon Brittan 1989–92, dep ambass at EC Delgn to US in Washington 1993–96, DG Customs and Indirect Taxation 1996–97, DG Environment 1997–2001; non-exec dir: Bank of Scotland 2001–09, Total UK 2004–, Met Office 2007–12, Vimeteo NV 2007–; int advsr Eversheds LLP, sr advsr Burson-Marsteller; Hon DLitt Univ of Glasgow; *Recreations* guitar, tennis, golf, good food; *Clubs* New (Edinburgh); *Style—* James M Currie, Esq

CURRIE, Kenneth Alexander (Ken); s of Alexander Currie, of Barrhead, and Georgina, *née* Ruddie; *b* 9 March 1960; *Educ* Barrhead HS, John Nielson Sch Paisley, Paisley Coll of Technol, Glasgow Sch of Art (Elizabeth Greenshields Fndn scholar, Cargill scholar, BA, Dip Postgrad Studies, Newberry medal); *m* July 1992, Marie Barbour; 2 da (Eilidh Barbour b 27 Dec 1993, Kirsty Fraser b 26 Nov 1996), 1 s (Andrew Galloway (twin) b 26 Nov 1996); *Career* artist; visiting prof Glasgow Sch of Art 2002; *Selected Solo Exhibitions* New Work from Glasgow (Arnolfini Bristol) 1986, Third Eye Centre Glasgow 1988, Raab Galerie Berlin 1988, Story from Glasgow (Kelvingrove Museum Glasgow) 1990, Raab Gallery London 1991, Raab Gallery Berlin 1993, Galerie Christian Dam Copenhagen 1994, Raab Boukamel Gallery London 1995 and 1996, Galerie Christian Dam Oslo 1997, Boukamel Contemporary Art London 1999, BCA Gallery London 2001, Tullie House Museum and Art Gallery Carlisle 2002, Mackintosh Museum Glasgow Sch of Art 2002, Flowers East London 2003, Flowers NY 2004, Animals (Flowers East London) 2008, Immortality (Flowers NY) 2010, Ken Currie: New Work (Scottish National Portrait Gallery) 2013; *Group Exhibitions* incl: New Image Glasgow (Third Eye Centre and tour) 1985–86, The Vigorous Imagination (Scottish Nat Gallery of Modern Art) 1987, Art History (Hayward Gallery) 1987, The Lion Rampant: New Scottish Paintings & Photography (Artspace, San Francisco) 1988–89, Scottish Art since 1900 (Scottish Nat Gallery of Modern Art and Barbican Art Gallery) 1989–90, Mischaire le Carte Immague Speculare (Gian Ferrari Arte Contemporánea) 1990–91, Shocks to the System (Hayward Gallery) 1991, VI Biennale d'Arte (Sacra Teramo Italy) 1994, Bad Blood (Glasgow Print Studio) 1996, XXXVIII Premio Suzzara Italy 1998, Narcissus 20th Century Self-Portraits (Scottish Nat Portrait Gall) 2001, Goya, Köllowitz and Currie (Glasgow Print Studio/Sanctuary Gall of Modern Art Glasgow) 2003; *Works in Public Collections* Scottish Nat Gallery of Modern Art, Macmaster Univ Art Gallery Toronto, Br Cncl, Aberdeen Art Gallery, Nottingham Castle Museum, City of Manchester Art Gallery, Glasgow museums and art galleries, MOMA Copenhagen, Yale Center for British Art Connecticut, Gulbenkian Fndn Lisbon, Br Museum, Boston Museum of Fine Arts, Scot Nat Portrait Gallery, British Museum; *Style—* Ken Currie, Esq; ✉ 34 Riverside Road, Glasgow G43 2EF

CURRIE, Maj-Gen (Archibald) Peter Neil; CB (2001), CBE (2014); s of Dr Donald Currie, and Ysobel Marion, *née* Garland; *b* 30 June 1948, Dar es Salaam, Tanzania; *Educ* Monkton Combe, Univ of Nottingham (BA), RMA Sandhurst, Army Cmd and Staff Course, Higher Cmd and Staff Course; *m* 3 Aug 1974, Angela Margaret, *née* Howell; 2 s (Donald Jeremy James b 3 Sept 1977, Angus Peter Robert b 28 March 1979); *Career* CO 12 Regt RA 1987–90, instr Army Staff Coll 1990–91, Col Mil Ops 1 1991–93, Cdr Artillery Allied Rapid Reaction Corps 1994, Dep Cdr Multination Div Centre (Airmobile) 1995, Dir Personal Services (Army) 1996–98, mil advsr to high rep Bosnia-Herzegovina 1998–99, Dep Adj-Gen and DG Service Conditions (Army) 1999–2002; chm: Army Central Fund 1999–2002, Army Dependants' Tst 1999–2002, Army Sports Control Bd 1999–2002; conslt 2003–04; dir Blue Forces Group Ltd 2002–06, non-exec dir Close Brothers Military Services 2003–06; chm Combat Stress 2007–13 (vice-pres 2013–); memb: Bd Services Sound and Vision Corp 2002–10, dir Cncl Forces Pension Soc, Bd Race for Opportunity 1999–2002, Ctee Chelsea Arts Festival 2009; Col Cmdt RA 2002–08; Lt Govr Royal Hosp Chelsea 2005–14; Queen's Commendation for Valuable Service 1999; *Recreations* skiing, tennis, history, opera and jazz, oriental rugs, walking in wild places; *Style—* Maj-Gen Peter Currie, CB, CBE

CURRIE, Raymond Frank (Ray); s of William Murdoch Currie (d 1984), and Dorothy, *née* Holloway (d 1995), of South Molton, Devon; *b* 11 May 1945; *Educ* Blundell's, The Loomis Sch Windsor CT, CCC Cambridge (exhibitioner, BA); *m* 1, 1 July 1972 (m dis 2001), Edwina, da of Simon Cohen; 2 da (Deborah Josephine b 30 Oct 1974, Susannah Elizabeth b 19 May 1977); m 2, 27 May 2003, Sharon Frances Attwal, da of Anthony Munro; *Career* Arthur Andersen: articled clerk 1967–70, qualified 1970, London 1970–73, fndr memb Birmingham practice 1973–79, dir of training 1979–96; dir Tower House Training Ltd 1996–2014; memb Bd of Accreditation of Educn Courses CCAB 1985–95 (chm 1992–95); ICAEW: chm Dist Training Bd 1986–90, memb Educn and Training Directorate 1989–2001 (chm 1999–2000), chm Educn and Assessment Ctee 1995–99, memb Cncl 1994–2001; memb: Business and Mgmnt Studies Ctee CNAA 1986–91, Audit Ctee Qualifications and Curriculum Devpt Agency (QCDA) 1998–2012; pres Derby Soc of Chartered Accountants 1999–2000; FCA 1974 (ACA 1970), MITD 1983, MIPM 1987, MAAT 1998; *Recreations* all sports – playing some slowly, following all enthusiastically, reading, cinema; *Clubs* Le Beaujolais, MCC, N Devon CC; *Style—* Ray Currie, Esq; ✉ 160 Western Road, Mickleover, Derby DE3 9GT (☎ 01332 549486, e-mail ray@currie.co.uk)

CURRIE OF MARYLEBONE, Baron (Life Peer UK 1996), of Marylebone in the City of Westminster; David Anthony Currie; s of Kennedy Moir Currie (d 1972), of London, and Marjorie, *née* Thompson; *b* 9 December 1946; *Educ* Battersea GS, Univ of Manchester (BSc), Univ of Birmingham (M Soc Sci), Univ of London (PhD); *m* 9 July 1975 (m dis), Shaziye, da of Hussein Gazioglu, of Nicosia, Cyprus; 2 s (Hon James Mehmet b 9 April 1978, Hon Timothy Timur b 8 May 1982); m 2, 24 March 1995, Angela Mary Piers Dumas; *Career* Hoare and Govett Co 1971–72, Economic Models 1972; QMC London: lectr 1972–79, reader 1979–81, prof of economics 1981–88; London Business Sch: prof of economics 1988–2000, dir of Centre for Economic Forecasting 1988–95, dep princ 1992–95, dep dean external relations 1999–2000; dean Cass Business Sch City Univ 2001–08; chm Semperian Investment Ptnrs (formerly Trillium Investment Ptnrs) 2008–12, non-exec dir Abbey National plc 2001–02; memb Bd: BDO 2008–12, Royal Mail Gp 2009–12, IG Gp 2010–12; chm: Ofcom 2002–09, Int Centre for Financial Regulation 2009–12, Competition and Markets Authy 2012–; memb: HM Treasy Panel of Independent Forecasters 1992–95, Advsy Bd for the Research Cncls 1992–93, Advsy Cmmn RPI 1992–93, Mgmnt Bd Ofgem 1999–2002, Bd Dubai Financial Servs Authy 2004–, Bd London Philharmonic Orch 2007–12; chm Alacrity Fndn 2010–13; tstee Joseph Rowntree Reform Tst 1991–2002; hon fell Queen Mary Coll London 1997; Hon DLitt Univ of Glasgow 1998, Hon DSc City Univ London 2012, Hon PhD Univ of Essex 2014; *Books* Advances in Monetary Economics (ed, 1985), The Operation and Regulation of Financial Markets (ed, 1986), Macroeconomic Interactions between North and South (ed, 1988), Macroeconomic Policies in an Interdependent World (ed, 1989), Rules, Reputation and Macroeconomic Policy Coordination (1993), EMU: Problems in the Transition to a Single European Currency (ed, 1995), North-South Linkages and International Macroeconomic Policy (ed, 1995), The Pros and Cons of EMU (1997), Will the Euro Work? (1998); *Recreations* music, literature, swimming; *Style—* The Rt Hon Lord Currie of Marylebone

CURRY, Stephen Robert; s of Stanley Curry (d 1964), of Clitheroe, Lancashire, and Norah, *née* Rowlinson; *b* 17 October 1942; *Educ* Clitheroe Royal GS, Manchester Coll of Commerce (journalism course); *m* Angela, *née* Blackshaw; 1 s (Michael b 27 Jan 1970);

Career journalist; The Blackburn Times 1959–62, Lancashire Evening Post 1963, sports reporter Head Office United Newspapers London 1964–66, chief football writer Daily Express 1980–96 (football reporter 1966–80), former football columnist Sunday Telegraph, currently football columnist Daily Mail; *Style*— Stephen Curry, Esq

CURRY OF KIRKHARLE, Baron (Life Peer UK 2011), of Kirkharle in the County of Northumberland; Sir Donald Thomas Younger Curry; kt (2001), CBE (1997); *b* Rothbury, Northumberland; *m* 22 Sept 1966; 3 c; *Career* cmmr Crown Estate 2000–07; memb Bd NFU Mutual Insurance Co 1997–2011 (chm 2003–11); chair: Leckford Estate, Waitrose 2009–; chair Better Regulation Exec 2010–; fndr and chair At Home in the Community 1990–2014, chair Royal Veterinary Coll 2012–; Hon BSc Cranfield Univ 2004, hon doctorate Univ of Glos 2005, Hon DCL Newcastle Univ 2008; *Recreations* sports, gardening, photography; *Clubs* Farmers; *Style*— The Lord Curry of Kirkharle, CBE; ✉ House of Lords, London SW1A 0PW

CURTEIS, Ian Bayley; s of late John Richard Jones, of Lydd, Kent, and late Edith Marion Pomfret Cook, *née* Bayley; *b* 1 May 1935; *Educ* Slough GS, Univ of London; *m* 1, 8 July 1964, Mrs Joan MacDonald (d 2009); 2 s (Tobit b 1966, Mikol b 1968); m 2, 12 April 1985, Joanna Trollope, OBE, DL, *qv*, da of A G C Trollope, of Overton, Hants; 2 step da (Louise b 1969, Antonia b 1971); m 3, 20 Oct 2001, Lady Deirdre Freda Mary Hare, er da of 5 Earl of Listowel, GCMG, PC (d 1997) and wid of 7 Baron Grantley, MC (d 1995); 2 step s (Richard, 8 Baron Grantley , *qv*, b 1956, Francis Norton b 1960); *Career* TV playwright and dir; BBC TV script reader 1956–63, staff dir (drama) BBC and ATV 1963–67 (dir of plays by John Betjeman, John Hopkins, William Trevor and others); pres Writers' Guild of GB 1998–, chm Ctee on Censorship Writers' Guild of GB 1981–85, tstee Joanna Trollope Charitable Tst 1995–, pres Writers' Guild of Great Britain 1998–2001; author of numerous newspaper articles, speeches and lectures on the ethics and politics of British broadcasting; FSA 2011; *Television Plays* incl: Beethoven, Sir Alexander Fleming (BBC entry at Prague Festival 1973), Mr Rolls and Mr Royce, Long Voyage out of War (trilogy), The Folly, The Haunting, Second Time Round, A Distinct Chill, The Portland Millions, Philby, Burgess and Maclean (Br entry Monte Carlo Festival 1978, BAFTA nomination Best Play of the Year, performed RNT and BBC 4 2002), Hess, The Atom Spies, Churchill and the Generals (Grand Prize for Best Programme of 1981 New York Int Film and TV Festival and BAFTA nomination Best Play of the Year), Suez 1956 (BAFTA Nomination Best Play of the Year), Miss Morison's Ghosts (British entry Monte Carlo Festival), BB and Lord D, The Mitford Girls, The Falklands Play; *Radio Plays* Eroica, Love. The Falklands Play, After the Break, More Love, Yet More Love, Miss Morison's Ghosts, Boscobel, The Last Tsar; *Screenplays* Miss Morison's Ghosts, Andre Malraux's La condition humaine, Lost Empires (adapted from J B Priestley), Graham Greene's The Man Within (TV), The Nightmare Years (TV), The Zimmerman Telegram, Gorbachov, The Choir (BBC serial), Yalta (BBC); *Stageplays* A Personal Affair (Globe) 1982, The Bargain (nat tour) 2007, Lafayette (2015); *Published Plays* A Personal Affair, Long Voyage out of War (1971), Churchill and the Generals (1979), Suez 1956 (1980), The Falklands Play (1987); *Recreations* dissidence; *Clubs* Garrick, Beefsteak; *Style*— Ian Curteis, Esq; ✉ 2 Warwick Square, London SW1V 2AA; Markenfield Hall, Ripon, North Yorkshire HG4 3AD; c/o Alexander Cann Representation, Box 116, 4 Montpelier Street, London SW7 1EE (☎ 020 7584 9047, mobile 07796 954969)

CURTICE, Prof John Kevin; s of Thomas John Curtice (d 1978), and Mildred Winifred, *née* Menear (d 2006); *b* 10 December 1953, Redruth, Cornwall; *Educ* Magdalen Coll Oxford (MA), Nuffield Coll Oxford; *m* 1978, Lisa Joan; 1 da (Ruth Anne b 9 Aug 1984); *Career* research fell Nuffield Coll Oxford 1981–83, lectr in politics Univ of Liverpool 1983–88, successively lectr, sr lectr, reader and prof of politics Univ of Strathclyde 1988–; co-dir British General Election Study 1983–98, dep dir Centre for Research into Elections and Social Trends (CREST) 1994–2001, research conslt Soctcen Social Research 2001–15 (sr research fell 2015–); conslt British Social Attitudes series 1985–; conslt to BBC election progs 1979–, regular contrib to newspapers and broadcast media; pres British Polling Cncl 2008–; Political Communication Prize Political Studies Assoc 2004 and 2015, Market Research Soc Collaborative Research Award 2010; FRSA 1992, FRSE 2004, FAcSS 2013, FBA 2014; *Books* How Britain Votes (jtly, 1985), Understanding Political Change (jtly, 1991), Labour's Last Chance (co-ed, 1994), Labour's Last Chance (co-ed, 1994), British Social Attitudes Report (co-ed, annually 1994–), On Message (jtly, 1999), The Rise of New Labour (jtly, 2001), New Scotland, New Politics (jtly, 2001), New Scotland, New Society (co-ed, 2001), Devolution – Scottish Answers to Scottish Questions? (co-ed, 2003), Has Devolution Delivered? (co-ed, 2006), Has Devolution Worked? (co-ed, 2009), Revolution or Evolution? (jtly, 2009); *Recreations* music, gardening, theatre, walking; *Clubs* Nat Liberal; *Style*— Prof John Curtice; ✉ School of Government and Public Policy, University of Strathclyde, 16 Richmond Street, Glasgow G1 1XQ (☎ 0141 548 4223, mobile 07710 348755, fax 0141 552 5677, e-mail j.curtice@strath.ac.uk)

CURTIS, Prof Adam Sebastian Genevieve; s of Herbert Lewis Curtis, DSM (d 1974), of London, and Nora, *née* Stevens (d 1954); *b* 3 January 1934; *Educ* Aldenham, King's Coll Cambridge (MA), Univ of Edinburgh (PhD); *m* 3 May 1958, Ann, da of William Park (d 1993), of Berwick-upon-Tweed; 2 da (Penelope Jane b 1961, Susanna Clare b 1964); *Career* lectr in zoology UCL 1962–67 (hon res asst Dept of Anatomy 1957–62); Univ of Glasgow: prof of cell biology 1967–2004, head Molecular and Cellular Biology Div 1994–95, co-dir Centre for Cell Engrg 1997–2010; pres Scot Sub-Aqua Club 1972–75, memb Cncl RSE 1983–86, pres Soc for Experimental Biology 1991–93, pres Tissue of Cell Engrg Soc 2001–03; fell in Biomaterials Science and Engrg (FBSE) European Soc for Biomaterials 2004; Chapman Medal 2008; FIBiol 1968, FRSE 1969; *Books* The Cell Surface (1967), Cell-Cell Recognition (ed, 1978); *Recreations* gardening, sports diving, making mosaics; *Style*— Prof Adam Curtis, FRSE; ✉ 2 Kirklee Circus, Glasgow G12 0TW (☎ 0141 339 2152, e-mail a.curtis@atlas.co.uk); Centre for Cell Engineering, University of Glasgow, Glasgow G12 8QQ (☎ 0141 330 5147, fax 0141 330 3730, e-mail adam.curtis@glasgow.ac.uk)

CURTIS, Prof Charles David; OBE (2001); s of Flt Lt Charles Frederick Curtis (d 2008), and Kate Margaret, *née* Jackson (d 1988); *b* 11 November 1939; *Educ* High Storrs GS Sheffield, Imperial Coll London, Univ of Sheffield (BSc, PhD); *m* 24 Nov 1963, Diana Joy, da of Lionel Sidney Saxty (d 1990), of Sheffield; 2 da (Sarah b 1965, Kate b 1968); *Career* Univ of Sheffield 1965–88 (successively lectr, reader, prof); Univ of Manchester: head of Dept 1989–92, prof 1989–, research dean Faculty of Science and Engrg 1994–2000, dir Environment Centre 1996–2002, emeritus prof 2004–; head R&D strategy Radioactive Waste Mgmnt Div Nucelar Decommissioning Authy 2006–08, ind memb Repository Devpt Mgmnt Bd 2008–13; non-exec dir Dounreay Site Restoration Ltd 2008–12, ind non-exec dir Radioactive Waste Mgmnt Ltd 2013–; visiting prof UCLA 1970–71, industrial fell Marathon Oil Co Denver 1973, CSPG visiting prof Univ of Calgary 1981, visiting prof Tongji Univ Shanghai 1984, res assoc Br Petroleum Res Centre 1987–88, conslt BP Research International 1988–94, conslt ENRICERCHE Milan 1994–97; various pubns in jls; memb Cncl Natural Environment Research Cncl 1990–93; pres Geological Soc of London 1992–94; memb: Scientific and Educn Ctees Royal Soc 1977–89, CNAA 1980–89, Radioactive Waste Management Advsy Ctee 1994– (chm 2000–); Murchison Medal 1987; FGS 1977 (pres 1992–94); *Recreations* mountaineering, gardening, writing; *Style*— Prof Charles Curtis, OBE; ✉ Lodestone, 55 Eccles Close, Hope, Hope Valley S33 6RG (☎ 01433 620724, e-mail ccurtis355@aol.com)

CURTIS, James William Ockford; QC (1993); s of Eric William Curtis, MC (d 2005), of Bedford, and Margaret Joan, *née* Blunt (d 1998), of Bedford; *b* 2 September 1946; *Educ* Bedford Sch, Worcester Coll Oxford (MA); *m* 1985, Genevra Fiona Penelope Victoria Caws, QC (d 1997), da of Richard Byron Caws, CBE (d 1997); 1 da (Polly Joanna Sarah Clare b 26 Nov 1987); *Career* called to the Bar Inner Temple 1970, pupillages with William Gage (Hon Lord Justice Gage, ret), and Neil Denison (formerly The Common Serjeant of London), recorder of the Crown Court 1991–; *Recreations* farming, field sports, skiing, classics; *Clubs* Reform, Flyfishers'; *Style*— James Curtis, Esq, QC; ✉ 6 King's Bench Walk, Temple, London EC4Y 7DR (☎ 020 7583 0410, fax 020 7353 8791)

CURTIS, Oliver; s of Lionel Curtis, and Brenda Curtis; *Educ* London Coll of Printing (BA); *m* 15 Feb 2002 (sep), Andi Marie, *née* d'Sa; *Career* cinematographer; D&AD Gold Pencil for Poems on the Box; memb BSC 1998; *Film* dir of photography: Madagascar Skin 1993, Love and Death on Long Island 1995, Wisdom of Crocodiles 1997, Vanity Fair 1998 (BAFTA nomination), Saltwater 1999, Final Curtain 2000, Owning Mahowny 2001, Uncle Adolf 2004, The Wedding Date 2005, Death at a Funeral 2006, Unrelated 2007, American Virgin 2008; dir of documentaries incl: Trotsky's Home Movies 1990, Pontecorvo 1991, Affairs of the Heart 1992; dir of photography of commercials incl: Pantene, Wella, Rimmel, Guinness; *Recreations* tennis, squash, cycling; *Style*— Oliver Curtis, Esq; ✉ c/o Independent Talent Agency, Oxford House, 76 Oxford Street, London W1D 1BS (☎ 020 7636 6565, fax 01844 261740)

CURTIS, Dr Penelope; da of Adam S G Curtis, of Glasgow, and Ann, *née* Park; *b* 24 August 1961; *Educ* Westbourne Sch, CCC Oxford (BA), Courtauld Inst Univ of London (MA, PhD); *Career* Tate Gall Liverpool 1988–94, curator Henry Moore Inst 1994–2010, dir Tate Britain 2010–15, dir Calouste Gulbenkian Museum Lisbon 2015–; memb: musée Rodin advsy ctee, memb editorial bd perspective (INHA, Paris), advsy ctee Revuew de L'art (Paris); *Exhibitions* incl: Barbara Hepworth (Tate Gall Liverpool) 1994, Tate Britain 2015, Taking Positions: Figurative Sculpture and The Third Reich (Henry Moore Inst) 2001, Scultura Lingua Morta: Sculpture from Fascist Italy 2003, Figuring Space: Sculpture/Furniture from Mies to Moore 2007, Modern British Sculpture (Royal Acad) 2011; *Publications* Sculpture 1900–1945 (1999), Patio & Pavilion: the place of sculpture in modern architecture (2007); *Style*— Dr Penelope Curtis

CURTIS, Penelope Jane Hamilton (Mrs Christopher Crouch); da of late Thomas Curtis, of Buckland, Surrey, and Nancy Frances Mary, *née* Pearson; *b* 20 February 1957; *Educ* St Michael's Sch Oxted, Univ of Exeter (LLB, Lloyd Parry prize, Maxwell law prize); *m* 22 Aug 1987, Christopher Charles Crouch; 2 da (Alexandra b 1991, Serena b 1994); *Career* Freshfields: articled clerk 1979–81, slr 1981–87; N M Rothschild: head Compliance Dept 1987–97, dir 1989–97; dir UBS 1997–; memb City of London Slrs Co; govr St Catherine's Sch Bramley; Freeman City of London, hon ward clerk Coleman St Ward; memb Law Soc; *Recreations* theatre, opera, walking; *Style*— Ms Penelope Curtis; ✉ Church Woods, The Street, Wonersh, Surrey GU5 0PG; UBS, 1 Finsbury Avenue, London EC2M 2PP (☎ 020 7567 8000)

CURTIS, Richard Whalley Anthony; CBE (2000, MBE 1994); s of Anthony Curtis, and Glyness Curtis; *b* 8 November 1956, Wellington, New Zealand; *Educ* Harrow, ChCh Oxford; *Partner* Emma Freud, OBE, *qv*; 1 da (Scarlett b 1995), 3 s (Jake b 1997, Charlie b 2001, Spike b 2003); *Career* screenwriter; co-fndr and vice-chair of tstees Comic Relief 1985–; fell BAFTA 2007; *Television* incl: Not the Nine O'Clock News 1979, The Black Adder 1983, Spitting Image 1984, Blackadder II 1986, Blackadder the Third 1987, Blackadder Goes Forth 1989, Mr Bean 1990–95, Bernard and the Genie 1991, The Vicar of Dibley 1994–2007, Hooves of Fire 1999, The Girl in the Café 2005, The No 1 Ladies' Detective Agency 2008; prodr Night of Comic Relief 1988–; *Film* The Tall Guy 1989, Four Weddings and a Funeral 1994, Bean 1997, Notting Hill 1999, Bridget Jones's Diary 2001, Love Actually (also dir) 2003, Bridget Jones: The Edge of Reason 2004, The Boat That Rocked 2009 (also dir), War Horse 2011; *Awards* incl: Comedy Lifetime Achievement Award Writers Guild of GB 1993, Special Award BAFTA 1999; *Style*— Richard Curtis, Esq, CBE; ✉ c/o United Agents, 12–26 Lexington Stree, London W1F 0LE

CURTIS, Sarah; *née* Myers; da of Dr Carl Myers (d 1963), of Preston, Lancs, and Ruth, *née* Stross (d 1973); *b* 21 May 1936, Preston, Lancs; *Educ* Roedean (scholar), Sorbonne, St Hugh's Coll Oxford (exhibitioner, MA, pres OU Lib Club, jt chair Jt Action Ctee Against Racial Intolerance); *m* 3 Oct 1960, Anthony Curtis (d 2014); 3 s (Job b 1961, Charles b 1963, Quentin b 1965); *Career* Times Educnl Supplement 1958–59, The Times 1959–61, freelance journalist and reviewer (The Times, New Society, TES, TLS, Financial Times, Sunday Times, New Statesman & Society, BBC Radio 4 and World Service) 1961–, educn and info offr Family Planning Assoc SW London 1971–73, res project dir Wandsworth Cncl for Community Relations 1975–76, ed Adoption & Fostering (jl of British Agencies for Adoption & Fostering) 1976–87, ed RSA Jl and head of communications RSA 1989–95; Parly candidate (Lib) Enfield N Feb and Nov 1974; memb: Exec Bd UK Ctee for UNICEF 1971–84, Lord Chllr's Advsy Ctee on JPs for Inner London 1982–89; tstee Ind Adoption Serv 1988–2004; JP (Youth and Family Courts) Inner London 1978–2001; FRSA 1995; *Books* New Orbits (jt author, 1959), High Time for Radicals (jt author, 1960), Thinkstrip series (1976–79), Looking at Handicap (ed, 1982), It's Your Life series (jt author, 1983), From Asthma to Thalassaemia (ed, 1986), St Hugh's - 100 Years of Women's Education in Oxford (contrib, 1986), Juvenile Offending (1989); The Journals of Woodrow Wyatt: Vol I (ed, 1998), Vol II (ed, 1999), Vol III (ed, 2000); Children Who Break the Law or 'Everybody Does It' (1999), The Russell House Companion to Youth Justice (contrib, 2005); *Recreations* reading novels, gardening and cooking; *Clubs* Hurlingham; *Style*— Mrs Sarah Curtis; ✉ 9 Essex Villas, London W8 7BP (☎ 020 7937 7798, e-mail santicurtis@aol.com)

CURTIS, Simon; *b* 11 March 1960, London; *Career* stage and screen dir; *Television* The Student Prince 1998, David Copperfield 1999, Man and Boy 2002, Twenty Thousand Streets Under the Sky 2005, Five Days 2007, Cranford 2007–09, A Short Stay in Switzerland 2009; *Theatre* incl: Road (Royal Court and Steppenwolf Theatre Co), Serenading Louie (Donmar Warehouse) 2010; *Film* My Week With Marilyn 2011, Woman In Gold 2014; *Style*— Simon Curtis, Esq; ✉ website www.simoncurtis39.com; c/o Jago Irwin, Independent Talent Group, 40 Whitfield Street, London W1T 2RH

CURTIS, Stephen Russell; s of Barry Russell, and Joyce Muriel, *née* Smith; *b* 27 February 1948; *Educ* Forest Sch, Univ of Exeter (BA); *m* 1972, Gillian Mary, *née* Pitkin; 3 s, 1 da; *Career* asst statistician Business Statistics Office 1970–72; DTI: joined 1972, statistician Export Statistics 1975–78, statistician 1978–83, chief statistician 1983–85; Business Statistics Office: registrar of cos 1985–90, chief exec 1988–90; chief exec DVLA 1990–95, chief exec designate Employment Tbnl Serv 1996, md Professional Servs Div Jordans Ltd 1997–2004, statistician Office for Nat Statistics 2005–; chm Assoc of Co Registration Agents 2007–; *Recreations* walking, travel, photography; *Clubs* Civil Service; *Style*— Stephen Curtis, Esq; ✉ Jordans Ltd, 21 St Thomas Street, Bristol BS1 6JS

CURTIS, Prof Tony; s of Leslie Thomas Curtis (d 1978), and Doris Eileen, *née* Williams; *b* 26 December 1946, Carmarthen; *Educ* UC Swansea, Goddard Coll VT, Univ of Glamorgan (DLitt); *m* 1970, Margaret, *née* Blundell; 1 s (Gareth Wyn b 1973), 1 da (Bronwen Beatrice 1976); *Career* poet and writer; incl in The Oxford Companion to English Literature and The New Companion to the Literatures of Wales; chair Welsh Acad of Writers 1984–89; Univ of Glamorgan: dir MPhil in writing 1993–2009, prof of poetry 1994–2008, emeritus prof of poetry 2008–; poet in residence Nat Tst at Dyffryn Gardens Vale of Glamorgan 2015–16; Eric Gregory Award 1972, National Poetry Prize 1984, Dylan Thomas Award 1994, Cholmondeley Award 1997; FRSL 2000; *Books* 26 books of poetry, literary criticism and art criticism incl: The Art of Seamus Heaney (1982), How to Study Modern Poetry

(1990), Welsh Painters Talking to Tony Curtis (1997), Welsh Artists Talking to Tony Curtis (2001), Heaven's Gate (poems, 2001), Dal Confine: Selected Poems of Tony Curtis (2001), Related Twilights: Notes from an Artist's Diary (by Josef Herman, ed, 2002), Scelti Poesie: Dannie Abse (ed, 2003), Considering Cassandra (poems and a story, 2003), After the First Death (ed, 2007), Wales at War (ed, 2007), Crossing Over (2007), Following Petra (ed, 2008), Real South Pembrokeshire (2011), Alchemy of Water (with Grahame Davies, 2013), My Life With Dylan Thomas (2014), From the Fortunate Isles: New and Selected Poems (2016); *Recreations* golf, tennis; *Style—* Prof Tony Curtis

CURTIS-RALEIGH, His Hon Judge Giles; *Career* called to the Bar 1992; recorder 2009, circuit judge (SE Circuit) 2015–; *Style—* His Hon Judge Curtis-Raleigh

CURWIN, Nick; *Career* co-fndr Dragonfly 2004 (sold 2007), co-fndr and jt chief exec The Garden 2010 (sold 2013); exec prodr: 24 Hours in A&E (Best Documentary Series RTS Award, BAFTA nominated), Seven Dwarves, One Born Every Minute (Best Factual Series BAFTA), The Family (BAFTA nominated), Going Cold Turkey, Britain's Deadliest Addictions, Jamie's Fowl Dinners, Kill It Cook It Eat It, The Audience (BAFTA nominated); prodr: The Autopsy, Anatomy For Beginners (Best Science Programme RTS Award); *Style—* Nick Curwin, Esq; ✉ The Garden Productions, 1 America Street, London SE1 0NE

CURZON, Prof Martin Edward John; s of Stanley Arthur Curzon, of Selsdon, Surrey, and Antoinette Carmela, *née* Davies; *b* 11 May 1940; *Educ* Univ of London (BDS, PhD), Univ of Rochester (MS); *m* 1, 1964 (m dis 1992), Jennifer Anne; 3 s (Richard Martin b 1967, Thomas Paul b 1972, Neil Simon b 1974); m 2, 1994, Anne; *Career* extern Govt of BC 1965–66, lectr Univ of Bristol 1968–70, sr dental offr Govt of Canada 1970–73, chm Oral Biology Eastman Dental Center 1973–83 (fell 1966–68), prof Univ of Leeds 1983–2000 (emeritus 2000–); pres: Br Paedodontic Soc 1987–88, Euro Acad of Paediatric Dentistry 1990–94; memb: ORCA, EAPD, CAPD, AAPD, IADR; life hon memb: Belgian Acad of Paediatric Dentistry, Canadian Acad of Paediatric Dentistry; DSc (hc) Univ of Athens 2003; FDS 1993; *Books* Trace Elements and Dental Disease (1983), Paediatric Operative Dentistry (4 edn, 1996), Handbook of Dental Trauma (2001); *Recreations* gardening, opera, travel, walking; *Style—* Prof Martin Curzon; ✉ Golden Hill Farm, Thief Hole Lane, Thornton-le-Moor, North Yorkshire DL7 9DX (☎ 01609 778604)

CUSACK, Mark Paul John; s of Capt Robert Joseph Cusack, of Dublin, and Olive Mary, *née* Byrne; *b* 28 February 1958; *Educ* St Paul's Sch Dublin, Trinity Coll Dublin (BBS); *m* 1990, Susan Jane Williams; 2 da; *Career* Arthur Andersen & Co 1979–83; dir: Hoare Govett 1983–91 (head UK Research), BZW 1992–95, UBS 1995–98, Deutsche Bank 1998–2011, Seafield 2012–; FCA; *Recreations* squash, tennis, golf, cycling; *Clubs* Roehampton; *Style—* Mark P Cusack, Esq

CUSACK, Niamh; da of Cyril Cusack (d 1993), and Maureen (d 1977); *b* 20 October 1959; *Educ* Scoil Lorcan Dublin, Colaiste Iosagain, Royal Acad of Music, Guildhall Sch of Music and Drama; *Career* actress; *Theatre* Gate Theatre Dublin: Hester Worsley in A Woman of No Importance, Irina in Three Sisters, Nora in A Doll's House; RSC: Desdemona in Othello, Juliet in Romeo and Juliet, Jane Hogarth in The Art of Success, Rosalind in As You Like It; West Yorkshire Playhouse: Pegeen Mike in The Playboy of the Western World, Gemma in Captain Swing; Lady Mary in The Admirable Crichton (Theatre Royal Haymarket), Gustchen in The Tutor (Old Vic), Nora Clitheroe in The Plough and the Stars (Young Vic), Irina in Three Sisters (Royal Exchange Manchester), Helena in The Faerie Queen (Aix-en-Provence), The Maids (Donmar), Nabokov's Gloves, Molière's Learned Ladies, Portia in The Merchant of Venice (Chichester Festival Theatre), Serafina Pekkala in His Dark Materials, Ghosts (Gate London); *Television* Lucky Sunil, Poirot, Till We Meet Again, Jeeves and Wooster, Heartbeat, Angel Train, Shadow of the Sun, Colour Blind, Rhinoceros, Little Bird, A&E, Loving You, Too Good to be True, State of Mind; *Films* Paris By Night, Fools of Fortune, The Playboys, The Closer You Get; *Awards* Irish Life Award, Irish Post Award; *Recreations* walking, cooking, reading, dreaming; *Style—* Ms Niamh Cusack

CUSACK, Sinead Mary; da of the actor Cyril James Cusack (d 1993), and his 1 w, Maureen, *née* Kiely (d 1977); *m* 23 March 1977, Jeremy Irons, *qv*; 2 s (Samuel b 16 Sept 1978, Maximilian b 17 Oct 1985); *Career* actress; *Theatre* for RSC incl: Lady Amaranth in Wild Oats, Lisa in Children of the Sun, Isabella in Measure For Measure, Celia in As You Like It, Evadne in The Maid's Tragedy, Lady Anne in Richard III, Portia in The Merchant of Venice, Daisy in The Custom of the Country, Ingrid in Peer Gynt, Kate in Taming of the Shrew, Beatrice in Much Ado About Nothing, Roxanne in Cyrano de Bergerac, Lady Macbeth in Macbeth, Cleopatra in Antony and Cleopatra; other credits incl: Desdemona in Othello (Ludlow Festival), Raina in Arms And The Man (Oxford Festival), Alice in Aristocrats (Hampstead), Masha in The Three Sisters (Gate Dublin and Royal Court), Ruth in Map of the Heart (Globe), Grace in Faith Healer (Royal Court), Mai in Our Lady of Sligo (Nat Theatre), Abby in The Mercey Seat (Almeida); *Television* for BBC incl: Playboy of the Western World, Menace – The Solarium, Shadow of a Gunman, George Sand – Notorious Woman, Affairs of the Heart, Quiller, Love's Labour Lost, Trilby, Supernatural – Ghost in Venice, The Kitchen, The Henhouse, Twelfth Night, Tales From Hollywood, Oliver's Travels (also film), Have Your Cake and Eat It (winner of Best Actress RTS Awards 1998); other credits incl: The Eyes Have It (ATV), Romance: The Black Knight (Thames), Scoop (LWT), God on the Rocks (Channel 4); *Films* Alfred the Great, Tamlyn, David Copperfield, Hoffman, Revenge, Horowitz in Dublin Castle, The Last Remake of Beau Geste, Rocket Gibraltar, Venus Peter, Waterland, Bad Behaviour, Cement Garden, The Sparrow, Flemish Board, Stealing Beauty, Dream, I Capture the Castle, Matilde; *Style—* Ms Sinead Cusack

CUSCHIERI, Prof Sir Alfred; kt (1998); s of Saviour Cuschieri (d 1990), and Angela Galeá; *b* 30 September 1938, Sliema, Malta; *Educ* Malta (MD), Univ of Liverpool (ChM); *m* Marguerite, *née* Holley; *Career* Univ of Liverpool: lectr in surgery 1968–70, sr lectr 1970–74, reader 1974–76; prof of surgery and head Dept of Surgery Univ of Dundee 1976–2003, prof of surgery Savola Superiore Sant'Anna Pisa 2003–; chief scientific offr Inst for Medical Science and Technol Univ of Dundee 2007–; ed: Surgical Endoscopy, Seminars in Laparoscopic Surgery; pres: Br Soc of Surgical Oncology 1986–87, European Assoc of Endoscopic Surgery 1996–97; Gold medal Royal Soc 2000; Hon DM 2002, Hon DSc 2007, Hon LLD 2007; memb: Surgical Research Soc 1970, Br Soc of Gastroenterology 1970, BASO 1974, SAGES 1987, EAES 1991; FRSE, FRCS, FRCSEd, FRCSGlas, FMedSci, FIBiol, Hon FACS 2006; *Publications* author of 22 textbooks on surgery, and over 530 original pubns in peer-reviewed jls, 50 patents for medical devices/instruments; *Recreations* flyfishing, carving; *Clubs* Athenaeum; *Style—* Prof Sir Alfred Cuschieri; ✉ Institute for Medical Science and Technology, University of Dundee, Wilson House, 1 Wurzburg Loan, Dundee DD2 1FD (☎ 01382 381006, fax 01382 386588, e-mail a.cuschieri@dundee.ac.uk)

CUSHING, Her Hon Judge Penny; *Career* admitted slr 1974; district judge 1994 (dep district judge 1991), circuit judge (South Eastern Circuit) 2013–; *Style—* Her Hon Judge Cushing; ✉ Guildford County Court, The Law Courts, Mary Road, Guildford GU1 4PS

CUSHING, Philip Edward; *Educ* Highgate Sch, Christ's Coll Cambridge; *Career* formerly with Norcros plc then LEGO Group, chief exec international ops Norton Opax until 1990; Inchcape plc: joined as chief exec Inchcape Berhad 1990, main bd dir 1992–, dir i/c testing servs, shipping servs and buying servs 1992–95, also i/c mktg and distribution 1994–95, md 1995–99, gp chief exec 1996–99; gp chief exec Vitec Gp plc 2000–01; chm: Pelican Restaurants Ltd 2001–02, Paragon Print and Packaging Ltd 2002–, DCI Biologicals Inc 2002–, Tecmail Ltd 2003, Fosbel International Holdings Ltd 2003–05, Wrapfilm Systems Ltd 2007–, American Golf Ltd 2010–, Loyalty Street Ltd 2014–; non-exec dir Ikon Office Solutions Inc 1998–2008; *Style—* Philip Cushing, Esq

CUSINE, Sheriff Douglas James; s of James Fechney Cusine (d 1987), and Catherine, *née* McLean (d 1975); *b* 2 September 1946; *Educ* Hutchesons' Boys' GS Glasgow, Univ of Glasgow (LLB); *m* 21 July 1973, Marilyn Calvert, da of George Ramsay (d 1988), of Johnstone, Renfrewshire; 1 da (Jane b 19 Sept 1981), 1 s (Graeme b 2 Jan 1984); *Career* admitted slr 1971; lectr in private law Univ of Glasgow 1974–76; Dept of Conveyancing Univ of Aberdeen: lectr 1976–82, sr lectr 1982–90, head of dept 1987–98, prof 1990–2000; memb and examiner for Law Soc of Scotland 1988–96; memb: Cncl Law Soc 1988–2000, Lord President's Advsy Cncl for Messengers at Arms and Sheriff Offrs 1989–2000; chm Bd of Examiners Soc of Messengers at Arms and Sheriff Offrs 1990–92, rep Cncl Sheriff's Assoc 2006–09; Sheriff of Grampian, Highland and Islands at Aberdeen; *Books* The Impact of Marine Pollution (jt ed, 1980), Scottish Cases and Materials in Commercial Law (jt ed, 1987), A Scots Conveyancing Miscellany (ed, 1988), New Reproductive Techniques: A Legal Perspective (1988), Law and Practice of Diligence (jtly, 1990), Standard Securities (1991, 2 edn (jtly) 2002), Missives (jtly, 1993, 2 edn 1999), Requirements of Writing (jtly, 1995), McDonald's Conveyancing Manual (jt ed, 6 edn 1997), Servitudes and Rights of Way (jtly 1998); *Recreations* swimming, walking, bird watching, photography; *Style—* Sheriff Douglas Cusine

CUSITER, Christopher Peter (Chris); s of Stan Cusiter, of Aberdeen, and Ruth, *née* Gibson; *b* 13 June 1982, Aberdeen; *Educ* Robert Gordon's Coll Aberdeen, Univ of Edinburgh (LLB); *Career* rugby union player (scrum half); clubs: Boroughmuir, Watsonians, Border Reivers 2003–07 (provincial team, Player of the Year 2003–04), USAP (Perpignan) 2007–09, Glasgow Warriors 2009–; Scotland: 47 caps, debut v Wales 2004; memb British and Irish Lions touring squad NZ 2005; memb Scottish Inst of Sport; nominated Spirit of Scotland Awards 2004; *Recreations* guitar, languages, travel; *Style—* Mr Chris Cusiter; ✉ c/o Red Sky Management, 1 Colme Street, Edinburgh EH3 6AA (website www.redskymanagement.co.uk)

CUSK, Rachel Emma; da of Peter Cusk, of Bury St Edmunds, and Carolyn, *née* Woods; *b* 8 February 1967; *Educ* St Mary's Convent Cambridge, New Coll Oxford (BA); *Career* novelist; patron UN Year for Tolerance 1995, memb Bd London Arts Bd 1997–; *Books* Saving Agnes (1993, Whitbread First Novel Award 1993), The Temporary (1995), The Country Life (1997, Somerset Maugham Award 1998), A Life's Work: On Becoming a Mother (2001), The Lucky Ones (2003, shortlisted Whitbread Novel Award), In the Fold (2005), Arlington Park (2006, shortlisted Orange Prize for Fiction); various short stories; *Recreations* piano, walking; *Style—* Ms Rachel Cusk; ✉ c/o The Wylie Agency, 17 Bedford Square, London WC2B 3JA (website www.wylieagency.co.uk)

CUSSINS, Peter Ian; s of Philip Cussins (d 1976), of Newcastle upon Tyne, and Doreen Cussins; *b* 18 March 1949; *Educ* Bootham Sch York, Univ of London (BSc); *m* 18 Sept 1973, Vandra Jean (d 1998), da of Maynard Stubley, of Alnmouth, Northumberland; 3 da (Abigail b 1976, Alexandra b 1978, Lydia b 1983), 1 s (Jabin b 1980); m 2, 24 Oct 2000, Susan Deirdre, da of Kenneth Saxby (d 2001), and Gill Saxby, of Corbridge, Northumberland; 2 step da (Amy b 1979, Sophie b 1981); *Career* chm: Cussins Homes Ltd 1973–99, Cussins Investment Properties Ltd 1981–99, Cussins Commercial Developments Ltd 1981–99, Cussins Property Gp plc 1981–99, NBP Whitelam Homes Ltd 2000–, Cussins Ltd; dir: Hotspur Investments Ltd 2000–, Regent Homes Ltd 2001–; chm: Tyneside Foyer Appeal, Royal Victoria Infirmary Breast Cancer Appeal; *Recreations* golf, shooting, fishing; *Style—* Peter I Cussins, Esq; ✉ West Bitchfield Tower, Belsay, Newcastle upon Tyne NE20 0JP

CUTHBERT, Jeffrey Hambley (Jeff); AM; *b* 4 June 1948, Glasgow; *Educ* Whitchurch County Secdy Modern, UC Cardiff; *Career* memb Nat Assembly for Wales (Lab) Caerphilly 2003–, dep min for skills 2011–13, dep min for skills and technol 2013, min for communities and tackling poverty 2013–14; CIPD; *Recreations* reading, travel, walking; *Style—* Jeff Cuthbert, Esq, AM; ✉ National Assembly for Wales, Cardiff Bay, Cardiff CF99 1NA (☎ 0300 200 7154, e-mail jeff.cuthbert@assembly.wales, website www.jeffcuthbert.org.uk, Twitter @JeffCuthbert)

CUTHBERT, Michael William; s of Thomas Cuthbert (d 1977), of Coventry, Warks, and Thelma Josephine, *née* O'Hehir (d 2006); *b* 6 July 1956; *Educ* Archbishop Ullathorne RC Comp Sch, UCL (LLB); *m* 29 July 1989 (m dis 2001), Stephanie Edith, da of David Henry Tate (d 1994), of Leigh, Surrey; 1 da (Caroline Isabella Louise b 13 Aug 1991); *Career* slr; Slaughter and May: articled clerk 1978–80, asst slr 1980–82; Clifford-Turner: asst slr 1982–86, ptnr 1986–87; ptnr Clifford Chance London 1987–89 and 1993–99 (ptnr New York 1989–93), ptnr Clifford Chance LLP 2000–02, sr ptnr Clifford Chance Moscow 2002–04, regnl managing ptnr Central and Eastern Europe and Russian Fedn Clifford Chance 2004–09, princ Global Legal Search LLP and sr advsr Maitland & Co Monaco 2010–12, conslt Discreet Law LLP 2013–; exec chm Diamond Fields Int Ltd 2013, non-exec chm Movehut Ltd 2014–; dir: Reso Garantia 2011–, European Property Hldgs 2013–, World Titanium Resources Ltd 2013–; memb: Law Soc 1980, City of London Slrs' Co; Slr of the Supreme Court of: the Judicature of England and Wales 1980, Hong Kong 1986; licensed legal conslt State of NY 1990; *Recreations* opera, food and wine, the cinema; *Clubs* Yacht Club de Monaco, Ivy, Dover Street Arts; *Style—* Michael Cuthbert, Esq; ✉ mobile 00 377 643 915345, e-mail michael.cuthbert@mac.com

CUTHBERTSON, James Gordon (Jim); *b* 1942; *Educ* BArch; *m*; 2 da (Helen b 1970, Jacqueline b 1973); *Career* architect, arbiter and adjudicator; Keppie Henderson and Partners Glasgow 1966–78, liaison architect Bldg Div CSA, Cuthbertson Architects 1978–; mangr Ian Darby Partnerships Glasgow 2000–; memb Assoc of Planning Supervisors; memb Cncl: Glasgow Inst of Architects 1981–84 and 1985–88 (sr vice-pres 1985 and 1987), RIAS 1985–88 and 1995– (memb Practice Ctee and chm Insurance Ctee 1985–99), RIBA 1995– (memb Practice Bd 1995–97, chm Disciplinary Ctee 1995–2001); MCIArb 1984; *Recreations* sailing, photography, birdwatching, computers; *Style—* Jim Cuthbertson, Esq; ✉ 206 Nithsdale Road, Glasgow G41 5EU (☎ and fax 0141 423 6856, e-mail cuthj@aol.com)

CUTHBERTSON, District Judge; Peter; s of late Peter Brentley Cuthbertson, and late Edna, *née* Stockdale; *b* 3 March 1949; *Educ* Robert Richardson's GS Ryhope, Pembroke Coll Oxford (MA, chm Blackstone Soc); *m* 26 May 1971, Carole Margaret, da of late Sydney White and late Margaret Alice Humphrey White; 1 da (Caroline Helen b 7 Feb 1976), 1 s (Timothy Peter b 18 Aug 1979); *Career* admitted slr 1973; Latimer, Hinks, Marsham & Little (now Latimer Hinks): articled to late Eric Nelson Marsham 1971–73, ptnr 1975–92; district judge 1992–2014, ret; memb Law Soc; *Recreations* fishing, golf, sailing, theatre, tennis, walking; *Clubs* Oxford Union Society; *Style—* District Judge Cuthbertson; ✉ Teesside Combined Court Centre, Russell Street, Middlesbrough TS1 2AE

CUTLER, His Hon Judge Keith Charles; CBE (2010); s of Henry Walter Cutler, of Woburn Sands, Bucks, and Evelyn Constance, *née* Butcher; *b* 14 August 1950; *Educ* Rickmansworth GS, Cedars Sch, Univ of Bristol (LLB); *m* 30 Aug 1975, Judith Mary, da of Ronald Philip Haddy (d 1974); 1 s (James b 1982), 1 da (Anna b 1985); *Career* called to the Bar Lincoln's Inn 1972 (bencher 2005); recorder 1993–96 (asst recorder 1989–93), circuit judge (Western Circuit) 1996– (sr circuit judge 2009), resident judge Salisbury 2003–, liaison judge to Wilts magistrates 2006–12, hon recorder of Salisbury 2007–10, resident judge and recorder Winchester 2009–, additional judge Court of Appeal (Criminal Div) 2013–; memb: Cncl of HM Circuit Judges 2001– (asst sec 2003, hon sec 2005–09, sr vice-pres 2011, pres 2012), Parole Bd 2001–04, Judges' Cncl 2005–12; vice-pres Wiltshire Magistrates Assoc 2001–; chm Mediation (Salisbury & District) 2001–09,

C

dep chllr Dio of Portsmouth 2003–, lay canon Salisbury Cathedral 2009–14 (lay canon emeritus 2014–); *Style*— His Hon Judge Cutler, CBE; ⊠ The Law Courts, Winchester, Hampshire SO23 9EL

CUTT, Mike; s of Ronald Cutt (d 1998), and Margaret, *née* Langley; *b* 2 July 1958, Redhill; *Educ* Univ of Exeter (BA), Chartered Inst of Bankers, Thames Valley Univ (Dip); *Children* 2 s (Toby b 19 Aug 1995, Frasier b 16 March 1998); *Career* Nationwide Building Soc: head of gp mgmnt devpt 1979–91, head of gp profitability 1991–92, head of retail planning 1992–94, head of retail HR 1994–97; dir of resourcing and reward Kingfisher plc 1997–2000, HR dir B&Q plc 2000–05; gp HR dir: Boots Gp plc 2005–07, Thomas Cook Gp plc 2008–09; ind coach and conslt 2009–; non-exec dir: Land Registry 2005–09, Lincs Hosps 2009–11, Cooperative Specialist Businesses 2010–15, Svyaznoy NV 2011–; govr New Coll Swindon 1996–99; FCIB 1981, FCIPD 1989; *Recreations* following the England and British Lions rugby teams; *Clubs* RAC; *Style*— Mike Cutt, Esq

CUTTS, Her Hon Judge Johannah; QC (2008); *Career* called to the Bar 1986; recorder 2002, circuit judge (South Eastern Circuit) 2011–; *Style*— Her Hon Judge Cutts, QC; ⊠ Reading Crown Court, Old Shire Hall, The Forbury, Reading, Berkshire RG1 3EH

CUTTS, John William; s of William George Cutts (d 1951), and Ingeborg Ernestine, *née* Walter (d 2003); *b* 27 September 1950; *Educ* Dean Close Sch Cheltenham, Univ of Sussex (BSc), INSEAD Fontainebleau (MBA); *m* 1, 18 Sept 1976 (m dis); 4 da (Samantha Mady Nicola b 23 Feb 1985, Dominique Lara Elisabeth b 24 July 1986, Tatiana Rebecca Sara b 5 Feb 1988, Natasha Tara Josephine b 21 Jan 1991); m 2, 15 Sept 2001, Monika Christine Lipken; *Career* apprentice Rolls Royce Ltd 1968–72, technical export mangr Ansafone Ltd 1972–75, gen mangr H & B Real Gewerbebau GmbH 1976–79, gen mangr Eupic Services BV (property investment) 1979–81, md mergers and acquisitions Amsterdam Rotterdam Bank NV 1981–88, dir Euro mergers and acquisitions Corporate Fin Dept Samuel Montagu & Co Ltd 1988–92, md corporate fin WestLB Panmure Ltd (formerly West Merchant Bank Ltd 1992–2000), chief exec Pall Mall Capital Ltd 2000–; non-exec chm: BPL Holdings Ltd until 2008, DCM Holdings (Jersey) Ltd; *Recreations* opera, sailing; *Clubs* Royal Thames Yacht, Hurlingham; *Style*— John W Cutts, Esq; ⊠ Pall Mall Capital Ltd, 14 Charterhouse Square, London EC1M 6AX (✆ 020 7518 7301, e-mail john.cutts@pallmallcapital.com)

CYMERMAN, Dr Anthony; s of Alfred Cymerman, of Highgate, London, and Annette Cymerman; *b* 4 December 1944; *Educ* La Sainte Union Convent, Hargrave Park Sch, Dame Alice Owen's Sch, Univ of Leeds (BChD); *m* 28 March 1976, Cherry, da of Maj R Keal, MBE; 1 s (James Alexander b 9 June 1977), 1 da (Kate Elizabeth b 28 Dec 1981); *Career* qualified from Leeds Dental Sch 1970, assoc London 1970–72, started own private practice in Harley St 1971 (second practice in NW London 1974); conslt BUPA and Private Patients Plan 1982; former memb: Camden and Islington FPC (now Area Health Authy), Camden and Islington Local Dental Ctee, Camden and Islington Dental Serv Ctee, Dental Advsy Ctee UCH, Fedn London Area LDC's; hon tutor London Hosp Dental Sch 1986; memb: BDA 1970, RSM 1987; *Recreations* cricket, clay pigeon shooting; *Clubs* MCC; *Style*— Dr Anthony Cymerman; ⊠ Highpoint Dental Clinic, 82 North Road, Highgate, London N6 4AA (✆ 020 8340 4878, e-mail anthony@cymerman.co.uk)

CYPRUS AND THE GULF, Bishop in 2007–; Rt Rev Michael Augustine Owen Lewis; s of John Desmond Lewis, of Swaythling, Hants, and Jean Beryl, *née* Pope; *b* 8 June 1953; *Educ* King Edward VI Sch Southampton, Merton Coll Oxford (BA Oriental Studies, BA Theology, MA), Cuddesdon Theological Coll; *m* 1979, Julia Donneky, *née* Lennox; 2 s (Paul b 18 June 1969, George Isaac Andrew b 17 May 1983), 1 da (Eleanor Hannah Mary b 8 March 1982); *Career* ordained: deacon 1978, priest 1979; curate Christ the King (Salfords, Southwark) 1978–80, chaplain Thames Poly 1980–84, vicar St Mary the Virgin (Welling, Southwark) 1984–91, team rector Worcester SE 1991–99, rural dean Worcester East 1993–99, bishop of Middleton (Manchester) 1999–2007; chm House of Clergy (Worcester Diocesan Synod) 1997–99, chm Diocesan Advsy Ctee Worcester 1998–99, hon canon Worcester Cathedral 1998–99, chm Manchester Diocesan Bd of Educn 2000–07; chm: Jt Advsy Ctee Church Colls and Univs 2005–07, C of E Bd of Educn HE Panel 2006–07; memb: Bd Al-Amana Interfaith Centre Oman 2008–, Int Cmmn for Anglican-Orthodox Theological Dialogue 2009–, Anglican Consultative Cncl 2010–; governing tstee St Michael's Coll Llandaff 2006–07; warden of Readers and Lay Assts Diocese of Manchester 2001–07, visitor Community of the Sisters of the Love of God Fairacres 2006–; *Recreations* enjoying architecture, food and drink, Middle Eastern and Caucasian travel; *Style*— The Rt Rev the Bishop in Cyprus and the Gulf; ⊠ Bishop in Cyprus and the Gulf, PO Box 22075, 1517 Nicosia, CYPRUS (✆ +357 22 671220, fax +357 22 674553, e-mail bishop@spidernet.com.cy)

D

d'ANCONA, John Edward William; CB (1994); s of Adolph d'Ancona (d 1970), of Malta, and Margaret Simpson Gilbert, *née* Arnott (d 1977); *b* 28 May 1935; *Educ* St Edward's Coll Malta, St Cuthbert's GS Newcastle, King's Coll Durham (BA, DipEd); *m* 27 Dec 1958, (Mary) Helen (d 2014), da of Sqdn Ldr Ralph Taylor Hunter (d 1957), of Newcastle upon Tyne; 3 s (Matthew R, *qv*, b 1968, Patrick D b 1972, Michael P b 1974); *Career* teacher 1959–61; Civil Serv: asst princ Miny of Educn 1961–64, PPS to Min of State for Educn 1964–65; princ: Miny of Educn 1965–67, Miny of Technol 1967–70, DTI 1970–74; asst sec Dept of Energy 1974–81, under sec and dir gen Offshore Suppliers Office Dept of Energy 1981–94 (conslt 1994–); dir Spearhead Exhibitions Ltd 1996–99, chm and ceo Maris Int 2000–04; pres Soc for Underwater Technol 1997–99; *Recreations* cricket, philately, winebibbing; *Style*— John d'Ancona, Esq, CB

d'ANCONA, Matthew Robert Ralph; s of John d'Ancona, CB, *qv*, and Helen, *née* Hunter (d 2014); *b* 27 January 1968, London; *Educ* St Dunstan's Coll, Magdalen Coll Oxford (BA, Demy, HWC Davis History Prize); *m* 13 March 2002 (m dis 2011), Sarah Schaefer; 2 s (Zac b 2 April 2001, Teddy b 7 June 2003); *Career* asst ed The Times 1994–95 (joined 1991), dep ed The Sunday Telegraph 1998–2006 (dep ed Comment 1996–98, political columnist until 2014), contributing ed GQ 2006–, ed The Spectator 2006–09, political columnist Evening Standard 2009–, contributing opinion writer Int New York Times 2013–, political columnist and writer Guardian 2015–, political ed GQ 2015–; memb: Bd of Dirs Centre for Policy Studies 1998–2006, Advsy Cncl Demos 1998–2006, Br Exec Int Press Inst 1998–2006, Policy Advsy Bd Social Market Fndn 2002–06, Millennium Cmmn 2001–06, Hansard Soc Cmmn on Parliament in the Public Eye 2004–05, Steering Bd Digital Britain 2008–09; judge Man Booker Prize 2011; chair Bright Blue 2014–, tstee Bd Science Museum Gp 2015–, memb Bd Social Market Fndn 2015–; Charles Douglas-Home Meml Tst Prize 1995, Political Journalist of the Year Br Press Awards 2004, Political Journalist of the Year Political Studies Assoc 2006, Current Affrs Ed of the Year Br Soc of Magazine Editors 2007, Commentariat of the Year ei Comment Awards 2011; prize fell All Souls Coll Oxford 1989–96, visiting research fell Queen Mary Univ London 2014; FRSA 2004; *Books* The Jesus Papyrus (co-author, 1996), The Quest for the True Cross (co-author, 2000), Going East (novel, 2003), Tabatha's Code (2006), Nothing to Fear (2008), Magdalen College, A History (contrib, ed L W B Brockliss, 2008), Being British (ed, 2009), In It Together: The Inside Story of the Coalition Government (2013, updated 2014); *Recreations* cinema, Wagner's operas; *Clubs* Ivy; *Style*— Matthew d'Ancona, Esq; ✉ c/o Tessa David, Peters Fraser + Dunlop, Drury House, 34–43 Russell Street, London WC2B 5HA (☎ 020 7344 1084, e-mail tdavid@pfd.co.uk)

D'ARCY, Gordon; s of John D'Arcy, of Wexford, and Peggy, *née* Versey; *b* 10 February 1980, Wexford; *Educ* Clongowes Wood Coll, Dublin Inst of Technol; *Career* rugby union player (back); clubs: Lansdowne, Leinster (provincial team) 1998– (over 80 appearances); Ireland: 31 caps, debut v Romania 1999, memb squad World Cup 1999, winners Triple Crown 2006; memb British and Irish Lions touring squad NZ 2005; *Style*— Mr Gordon D'Arcy

D'ARCY, Robert John Bruce; s of Cecil Vivian Robert D'Arcy (d 1995), of Holbrook, Suffolk, and Margery Mary, *née* Bailey (d 1987); *b* 12 August 1942; *Educ* Marlborough, Univ of Munich, Coll of Estate Management; *m* 22 Nov 1969, Janet Maxwell, da of Maxwell Heron Matheson (d 1978), of Woodbridge, Suffolk; 2 s (Justin b 6 Sept 1971, Toby b 26 Jan 1977), 2 da (Annabel (twin) b 6 Sept 1971, Charlotte b 12 Jan 1973); *Career* chartered surveyor; Chestertons 1966–68, Donaldsons 1968–69, ptnr James Crichton and Co 1969–; FRICS; *Recreations* sailing, shooting, golf; *Clubs* Royal Thames Yacht; *Style*— Robert D'Arcy, Esq; ✉ The Old Rectory, Bredfield, Woodbridge, Suffolk IP13 6AX (☎ 01394 385223)

d'ASCOLI, Bernard; s of Georges d'Ascoli, of Aubagne, France, and Marcelle, *née* Thermes; *b* 18 November 1958; *Educ* Marseille Conservatoire; *Partner*, Eleanor Harris; 1 s (Stéphane b 1996); *Career* pianist; debuts: Queen Elizabeth Hall, Barbican and Royal Festival Hall 1982, Concertgebouw Amsterdam 1984, Houston TX 1985, The Proms Royal Albert Hall 1986, Tokyo 1988, Paris 1989; performed as soloist with: RPO, LPO, Philharmonia, BBC Symphony Orch, CBSO, Chamber Orch of Euro, English Chamber Orch, Montreal Symphony, Boston Symphony, Dresden Philharmonic; played under conductors incl: Paavo Berglund, Andrew Davis, Sergiu Comissiona, Kurt Sanderling, Sir Yehudi Menuhin, Andrew Litton, Yevgeny Svetlanov, Michel Plasson, Sir John Pritchard, Gunter Herbig, Ivan Fischer, Andrew Parrott; various int tours; artistic dir Piano Cantabile (training centre in Provence for advanced pianists, organising music camps throughout the year); *Awards* Best Young Talent in France 1976, First Prize Int Maria Canals Competition Barcelona 1978, Chopin Prize Santander 1980, Third Prize Leeds Int Piano Competition 1981; prize winner: Marguerite Long Competition Paris, Bach Competition Leipzig, Chopin Competition Warsaw; *Recordings* Liszt Sonata, La Legierezza; Franck: Prelude Chorale and Fugue (1982); Schumann: Carnaval, Papillons, Fantasie Stücke op 111 (1989), Piano Quintet with Schidlof Quartet (2001); Chopin: 4 Ballades, Nocturne in C Sharp Minor, Berceuse, Tarantelle, Andante Spianato and Grande Polonaise (1990), Chopin: Impromptus, Scherzi (2005), Complete Nocturnes (2005); *Recreations* philosophy, psychology, sport; *Style*— Bernard d'Ascoli, Esq; ✉ c/o Eleanor Harris, Piano Cantabile, 350 Impass du Baou, 13400 Aubagne, France (☎ 003 4 4284 0236, e-mail pianocantabile@orange.fr, website www.bernard-dascoli.com)

D'CRUZ, Prof David Pascal; s of Joseph C D'Cruz, of London, and Albertina, *née* De Sousa; *b* 22 June 1959; *Educ* Mount St Mary's Coll, St Mary's Hosp Med Sch London (MB BS, MD); *m* 9 March 1986, Dr Maria B Y Saldanha; 2 da (Rebecca b 1 May 1987, Olivia b 8 March 1990); *Career* pre-registration house offr St Mary's Hosp London 1983–84, SHO UCHL 1984–85, registrar in med Royal London Hosp 1986–88, registrar in rheumatology St Thomas' Hosp London 1988–93, sr registrar then conslt rheumatologist Bart's and Royal London Hosp 1993–2000, conslt rheumatologist Lupus Unit St Thomas' Hosp 2000–; reader in vascular rheumatology 2009–, prof of lupus biology KCL 2012; managing ed Lupus; tstee Hughes Syndrome Fndn, chm St Thomas Lupus Tst; FRCP 1998 (MRCP 1986); *Publications* author of 177 peer-reviewed pubns on systemic lupus erythematosus and systemic vasculitis, and 14 book chapters on autoimmune connective rheumatic diseases; *Recreations* fishing, cooking; *Style*— Prof David D'Cruz; ✉ The Louise Coote Lupus Unit, 4th Floor Tower Wing, Guy's Hospital, Great MAze Pond, London SE1 9RT (☎ 020 7188 9756, fax 020 7188 3574)

D'EYNCOURT; *see:* Tennyson-d'Eyncourt

d'INVERNO, Isobel Jane; da of Raymond Shaw, of Wembury, Devon, and Margaret, *née* Newall; *b* 1 September 1957, Withington, Manchester; *Educ* Cheadle Hulme Sch, Univ of St Andrews (MA); *m* 1983, Joseph d'Inverno; 3 s (Monty b 18 April 1988, Cospatric b 17 Sept 1990, Louis b 11 Sept 1995), 1 da (Lucia b 17 April 1994); *Career* CA 1983; Ernst & Whinney 1980–84, corporate tax supervisor and mangr Ernst & Young (formerly Arthur Young) 1984–90, head of corporate tax Brodies 1990–97, dir corporate tax MacRoberts 1997–2008 (head of charities gp 2005–08), dir of corp tax Brodies LLP 2008–; tstee Reform Scotland; convenor Tax Law Ctee Law Soc of Scotland, chair Tax Ctee Scottish Property Fedn; memb Cncl Stamp Taxes Practitioners Gp, memb Stamp Duty Land Tax Working Together Steering Gp (with HMRC), memb Cmmn on Local Tax Reform 2015; Deacon Incorporation of Fleshers of Glasgow 2015–16; memb ICAEW, CIOT 1984; *Recreations* reading novels, theatre; *Style*— Mrs Isobel d'Inverno; ✉ Brodies LLP, 15 Atholl Crescent, Edinburgh EH3 8HA (☎ 0131 228 3777, fax 0131 228 3878, e-mail isobel.dinverno@brodies.com, website www.brodies.com, Twitter @IsobeldInverno)

D'SOUZA, Baroness (Life Peer UK 2004), of Wychwood in the County of Oxfordshire; Rt Hon Dr Frances Gertrude Claire D'Souza; CMG (1998), PC (2009); da of Robert Anthony Gilbert Russell (d 1979), of Ardingly Farm, W Sussex, and Pauline, *née* Parmet (d 1988); *b* 18 April 1944; *Educ* St Mary's Princethorpe, UCL (BSc), Univ of Oxford (DPhil); *m* 1, 1959 (m dis 1974, remarried 2003), Stanislaus Joseph D'Souza (decd); 2 da (Hon Christa Claire b 1960, Hon Heloise b 1962); m 2, 1985 (m dis 1994), Martin John Griffiths; *Career* Ford Fndn research fell Wellcome Inst of Comparative Physiology 1973–77, pt/t lectr Dept of Anthropology LSE 1974–80, sr lectr in physical anthropology Dept of Humanities Oxford Poly (now Brookes Univ) 1977–79, res dir Relief and Development Inst 1983–86 (fndr dir 1979–83), dir Article 19 Int Centre against Censorship 1989–98; dir The Redress Tst 2003–05; Convenor of the Crossbench Peers House of Lords 2007–11, Lord Speaker 2011–16; govr Westminster Fndn for Democracy 1999–2007; memb Ind Monitoring Bd HMP Wormwood Scrubs 2006–07; Hon LLD Univ of Hull 2016; *Publications* author of numerous scientific papers, journalism and human rights pubns; regular broadcaster; *Recreations* music, especially opera, string quartets, serious walking; *Style*— The Rt Hon the Lady D'Souza, CMG; ✉ e-mail dsouzaf@parliament.uk

DABBOUS, Oliver; *b* Kuwait; *Career* chef-proprietor Dabbous (Michelin star 2013–); *Style*— Oliver Dabbous, Esq; ✉ Dabbous, 39 Whitfield Street, London W1T 2SF (☎ 020 7323 1544, e-mail info@dabbous.co.uk, website www.dabbous.co.uk)

DACRE, Prof Jane Elizabeth; da of Peter Verrill (d 2005), and Christine Verrill; *b* 11 November 1955, Halifax, Yorks; *Educ* UCL (BSc, MBBS), Univ of London (MD); *m* 1979, Nigel Dacre; 2 da (Claire b 24 July 1986, Anna b 5 Oct 1995), 1 s (Robert b 26 Jan 1989); *Career* trained and qualified as dr; clinical lead for devpt of first Clinical Skills Centre (St Barts Medical Coll), co-author GALS screen, instrumental in devpt, implementation and evaluation of undergrad and postgrad assessment systems in medicine; conslt physician and rheumatologist Whittington Hosp London 1995–; prof of med educn UCL 2000, dir UCL Med Sch 2008–14; pres RCP 2014–18 (academic vice-pres 2005–08, med dir 2009–13); memb GMC 2008–12, memb Medical Women's Fedn 2009; Women in the City Woman of Achievement (Medicine and Healthcare) 2012, Health Service Jl (HSJ) Inaugural 50 Influential Women in Healthcare 2013, HSJ Clinical Leaders 2014 and 2015, HSJ Top 100 2014, Debrett's 500 (Science and Medicine) 2015; FRCP 1994 (MRCP 1983), FRCPGlas 1999, FHEA 2006, FRCPEd 2010, hon FACP 2015, hon FAME 2015, hon FRCGP 2015, hon FRCPI 2015; *Publications* articles on women in medicine and medical education; Handbook of Clinical Skills (2002); *Style*— Prof Jane Dacre; ✉ Royal College of Physicians, 11 St Andrews Place, London NW1 4LE (☎ 020 3075 1233, e-mail jane.dacre@rcplondon.ac.uk, website www.rcplondon.ac.uk)

DACRE, Nigel; s of Peter Dacre (d 2003), and Joan, *née* Hill; *b* 3 September 1956; *Educ* UCS Hampstead, St John's Coll Oxford (MA); *m* Prof Jane Elizabeth Dacre, da of Peter Verrill; 2 da (Claire b 1986, Anna b 1995), 1 s (Robert b 1989); *Career* graduate trainee BBC 1978, BBC Bristol 1980, TV journalist News at Ten ITN 1982, prog ed World News ITN 1987, exec prodr News At One and News at 5:40 1990–92, head of prog output and exec prodr News at Ten 1992–93, ed ITV News 1995–2002, dean Media Sch London Coll of Printing 2002–03, chief exec Teachers' TV 2003–06, dir Ten Alps Digital 2006–07, chief exec Inclusive Digital TV 2007–; dir Notts TV 2012–; chair Local TV Network 2013–15; FRTS 2002; *Style*— Nigel Dacre, Esq

DACRE, Paul Michael; s of Peter Dacre (d 2003), and Joan, *née* Hill; *b* 14 November 1948; *Educ* UCS London, Univ of Leeds (BA); *m* Kathleen, da of Charles James Thomson; 2 s (James Charles b 21 May 1984, Alexander Peter b 6 Aug 1987); *Career* Daily Express: reporter Manchester 1970–71, reporter, feature writer and assoc features ed London 1971–76, NY corr 1976–79; Daily Mail: bureau chief NY 1980, dep news ed London 1981, news ed 1983, asst ed news and foreign 1986, asst ed features 1987, exec ed 1988, assoc ed 1989–91; ed: Evening Standard 1991–92, Daily Mail 1992–; ed-in-chief Associated Newspapers 1998–; dir: Associated Newspaper Holdings 1991–, DMGT 1998–, Teletext Holdings Ltd 2000–02; memb: Press Complaints Cmmn 1998–2008, Press Bd of Fin 2004–14; chm: Newspaper Industry's Code Ctee 2008–, Govt Review into Thirty Year Rule 2008; ambass Alzheimer's Soc 2007–, hon memb NSPCC 2009–; Cudlipp lectr 2007, delivered keynote speech to Soc of Eds 2008; FRSA 2007; *Clubs* Garrick; *Style*— Paul Dacre, Esq; ✉ The Daily Mail, Northcliffe House, 2 Derry Street, London W8 5TT (☎ 020 7938 6000)

DADA, Feroze Ahmad; s of Ahmad Valimohamed Dada, of Pakistan, and Halima; *b* 21 April 1952; *Educ* St Patrick's Sch Karachi, Univ of Karachi (BCom); *m* 4 Feb 1984, Farida, da of H L A Maung, of Burma; 1 da (Sumaya b 1986), 1 s (Nadir b 1990); *Career* md: Freeman & Partners Ltd Chartered Accountants 1981–2010, Crowe Clark Whitehill (London) Ltd 2010– (chm 2013–); dir: FSI Group plc 1986–2004, Brook Hotels plc 1994–2004, Reyker Investments Ltd 1995–, European Middleware Consulting Co Ltd 1997–, Tpoll Market Intelligence Ltd 2001–07, Chargebox (formerly BoxBrands) Ltd 2005–16, Aqua Botanica Ltd 2009–10; guest interviewer TVapex 2015–; memb Cncl ICAEW; CTA 1978, FCA 1983; *Books* Interest Relief for Companies (1981), Children of the Revolution (2014); *Recreations* cricket; *Clubs* Brondesbury Cricket; *Style*— F A Dada, Esq; ✉ Northfield, 158 Totteridge Lane, Totteridge, London N20 8JJ (☎ 020 8446 7846); Crowe Clark Whitehill (London) Ltd, 52 Jermyn Street, London SW1Y 6LX (☎ 020 7842 7100, e-mail feroze.dada@croweсw.co.uk)

DAGLISH, Simon; *b* 29 August 1965; *Educ* RMA Sandhurst; *Career* sales exec Express Newspapers 1987–88, gp head Daily Telegraph 1990–95; sales dir: Classic FM 1998–2005, GCap Media 2005–08, Channel 4 2008; vice-pres commercial dir Fox Interactive Media 2009–11, gp commercial dir ITV 2011–; co-fndr Walking with the Wounded; *Style—* Simon Daglish, Esq; ✉ ITV, 200 Gray's Inn Road, London WCX1 8HF

DAGWORTHY, Wendy; OBE (2011); *b* 4 March 1950; *Educ* Medway Coll of Art, Hornsey Coll of Art (DipAD); *Career* fashion designer with Radley (Quorum) 1971, designer/dir own label Wendy Dagworthy Ltd 1972–88 (outfit exhibited at V&A), freelance designer and conslt for Laura Ashley, Liberty and Betty Jackson; has exhibited internationally (London, Milan, NY, Paris), participating designer The Courtelle Awards, Fashion Aid and many other charity shows; dir London Designer Collections 1982–90, conslt to CNAA Fashion/Textiles Bd 1982, judge RSA Bd 1982; lectr at numerous colls since 1972 incl: Bristol, Kingston, Liverpool, Manchester, Newcastle and Lancashire Polys, Gloucester and Medway Colls of Art & Design, Salisbury Coll of Art, RCA; external assessor (fashion courses) for numerous colls incl: St Martin's Sch of Art 1986–88, Swire Coll of Design Hong Kong Poly 1989; judge of art and design projects, awards and competitions for various cos incl: Br Wool Textile Corp, Br Fashion Awards, Tissavel Fur, BP, Courtelle Awards, Lennard's Bursary Award, Fil d'Or Int Linen Award Monte Carlo 1985, Irish Designer Awards 1988, Smirnoff Awards 1989, Lloyd's Bank Fashion Challenge (chm) 1990–91, Nat Nescafe Design Competition 1991, ICI Fibres Tactel Awards Paris 1992, The Clothes Show Competition 1993; course dir (BA Hons Fashion) Central St Martin's Coll of Art and Design 1989–98, prof of Fashion RCA 1998–; course and document advsr Birmingham Poly 1991; has appeared regularly on TV and radio shows nationwide; hon memb Fashion Acts; *Style—* Prof Wendy Dagworthy, OBE; ✉ Royal College of Art, School of Material, Kensington Gore, London SW7 2EU (✆ 020 7590 4444)

DAINTITH, Prof Terence Charles; s of Edward Daintith (d 1942), and Irene, *née* Parsons; *b* 8 May 1942; *Educ* Wimbledon Coll, St Edmund Hall Oxford (MA), Univ of Nancy (Leverhulme Euro scholar); *m* 1965, Christine Anne, da of Sqdn Ldr Charles Edward Bulport; 1 s (Edward Charles b 1967), 1 da (Alexandra b 1968); *Career* called to the Bar 1966; assoc in law Univ of Calif 1963–64, lectr in constitutional law Univ of Edinburgh 1964–72, prof of public law and head Dept of Public Law Univ of Dundee 1972–83 (fndr and dir Centre for Petroleum and Mineral Law Studies 1977–83), prof of law Euro Univ Inst Florence 1981–87; Univ of London: prof of law 1988–2002, dir Inst of Advanced Legal Studies 1988–95, dean Insts of Advanced Study 1991–94, dean Sch of Advanced Study 1994–2002; prof of law Univ of WA Aust 2002–; bencher Lincoln's Inn 2000; Parsons scholar Univ of Sydney 1988; ed Jl of Energy and Nat Resources Law 1983–92; memb Academia Europaea 1989 (convenor legal ctee 1993–96, chm Soc Sciences Section 1996–98); Hon LLD De Montfort Univ 2001, Hon LLD Univ of Aberdeen 2013; *Publications* The Economic Law of the United Kingdom (1974), United Kingdom Oil and Gas Law (with G D M Willoughby, 1977, 3 edn 2000), The Legal Character of Petroleum Licences (ed and contrib, 1981), European Energy Strategy – The Legal Framework (with L Hancher, 1986), Contract and Organisation – Social Science Contributions to Legal Analysis (with G Teubner 1986), The Legal Integration of Energy Markets (with S Williams, 1987), Law as an Instrument of Economic Policy – Comparative and Critical Approaches (1988), Harmonization and Hazard – Regulating Workplace Health and Safety in the European Community (with G R Baldwin, 1992), Implementing EC Law in the United Kingdom: Structures for Indirect Rule (1995), The Executive in the Constitution (with A C Page, 1999), Discretion in the Administration of Offshore Oil and Gas (2006), Finders Keepers? How the Law of Capture Shaped the World Oil Industry (2010); *Recreations* cycling and carpentry; *Clubs* Scottish Arts; *Style—* Prof Terence Daintith; ✉ Institute of Advanced Legal Studies University of London, 17 Russell Square, London WC1B 5DR (✆ 020 7862 5800)

DAINTON, (Hon) Prof John Bourke; s of Baron Dainton, FRS (Life Peer, d 1997), and Barbara Hazlitt, *née* Wright (d 2009); *b* 10 September 1947, Cambridge; *Educ* Bradford GS, Merton Coll Oxford (MA, DPhil); *m* Josephine Zilberkweit (d 2010); *Career* SRC research student Dept of Nuclear Physics Univ of Oxford 1969–72, lectr in physics Merton Coll Oxford 1972–73, research assoc SRC Daresbury Lab 1973–77, research assoc Dept of Physics Univ of Sheffield 1977–78, lectr in physics Dept of Natural Philosophy Univ of Glasgow 1978–81 and 1982–85; Univ of Liverpool: lectr in physics 1986–88, sr lectr in physics 1988–91, reader in physics 1991–94, prof of physics 1994–2002, Sir James Chadwick chair of physics 2002–; founding dir Cockcroft Inst of Accelerator Science and technol 2005–07; Deutsches Elektronen-Synchrotron (DESY) Hamburg: visiting scientist 1981–82 and 1997–99, spokesman UK Insts in H1 experiment 1992–98, memb Exec Ctee H1 experiment 1993–95, physics co-ordinator H1 experiment 1995–97, spokesman H1 experiment 1997–99; author of over 250 papers in peer reviewed scientific jls incl Physics Letters, Nuclear Physics, Zeitschrift fuer Physik and European Jl of Physics; memb Editorial Bd Jl of High Energy Physics 1999–; referee: The Physical Review 1988–, Jl of Modern Physics 1991–, Physics Letters 1995–, European Jl of Physics 1999–, INTAS projects EU 2000–, DTI/Research Cncl Faraday Partnerships 2000; SERC: sr fell 1992–97, memb Particle Physics Experiments Selection Panel 1981–83, memb Particle Physics Ctee 1989–92; chair SPS Ctee CERN 2003–09, chair and memb STFC CMS Oversight Ctee 2006–; memb: High Energy and Particle Physics Sub-Ctee Inst of Physics 1985–88, High Energy and Particle Physics Bd European Physical Soc 1986–93, Gen Cncl and Gen Ctee BAAS 1989–91 (recorder Section A Physics 1988–91, sec 1987), LHC Detector Research Bd CERN 1995–96, LEP Ctee CERN 1996–98, Large Hadron Collider Ctee CERN 1999–2003, Science Ctee PPARC 2001–03, Wingate Fellowships Ctee 2005–11; external memb Scientific Advsy Ctee Helsinki Inst of Physics 2001; chair and memb Scientific Advsy Ctee Nat Inst for Nuclear Physics and High Energy Physics Amsterdam 2001–08, chair INFN review of SuperB proposal 2007–08; UK delg European Ctee for Future Accelerators 1989–92, external memb Helsinki Inst of Physics 2001; govr Stockport GS 2009–; Max Born Medal Inst of Physics and German Physical Soc 1999; Freeman City of London 1983, Liveryman Worshipful Co of Goldsmiths 1983; distinguished fell Alexander von Humboldt Stiftung Germany 2003; CPhys 1986, FInstP 1986, FRS 2002, FRSA 2003; *Recreations* travel, cycling, having time to think and understand; *Style—* Prof John Dainton; ✉ Department of Physics, Oliver Lodge Laboratory, University of Liverpool, Oxford Street, Liverpool L69 7ZE (✆ 0151 794 7769); Cockcroft Institute of Accelerator Science, Daresbury Science and Innovation Campus, Warrington WA4 4AD (✆ 01925 864229)

DAKIN, Nicholas (Nic); MP; *b* 1955; *Educ* Univ of Hull, KCL; *m* Audrey; 3 c; *Career* princ John Leggott Coll Scunthorpe until 2010; MP (Lab) Scunthorpe 2010–; *Style—* Nic Dakin, Esq, MP; ✉ 18a Ethel Court, Scunthorpe, North Lincolnshire DN15 6RP; House of Commons, London SW1A 0AA

DALDRY, Stephen David; CBE (2004); s of Patrick Daldry (d 1976), and Cherry, *née* Thompson; *b* 2 May 1961; *Educ* Huish GS Taunton, Univ of Sheffield (BA); *m* 2001, Lucy Sexton, the dancer and performance artist; 1 da (Annabel Clare b 2003); *Career* film and theatre director; appt incl: Metro Theatre 1984–86, artistic assoc Crucible Theatre Sheffield 1986–88 (trainee dir (Arts Cncl) 1985–86); artistic dir: Gate Theatre London 1989–92, Royal Court Theatre London 1992–97; prodns incl: Damned for Despair (Gate Theatre (winner best dir London Fringe Awards and Critics' Circle)), An Inspector Calls (NT) 1992 (winner best dir, Olivier Awards, Evening Standard Awards, Critics' Circle Awards, Drama Desk Awards, Tony Awards) and (Novello Theatre) 2009, Machinal (RNT (winner best dir Olivier Awards)), Judgement Day (Old Red Lion Theatre (winner best dir London Fringe Awards)), Ingolstadt (Gate Theatre (winner best dir London Fringe Awards and Time Out Awards)), Figaro gets Divorced (Gate Theatre (winner best dir Time Out Awards)), The Kitchen (Royal Court) 1995, Billy Elliot the Musical (Victoria Palace Theatre London) 2005; film prodn work incl: Eight 1998 (nominated for BAFTA Best Short Film Award), Billy Elliot 2000 (nominated Best Dir Academy Award, winner Alexander Korda Award BAFTA), The Hours 2001, The Reader 2009 (Best Dir Evening Standard Br Film Award 2009), Extremely Loud & Incredibly Close 2012 (nominated Best Picture Academy Award); exec dir of ceremonies London Olympics 2012; memb: Equity, Soc of Dirs (USA); *Style—* Stephen Daldry, Esq, CBE

DALE, Iain Campbell; s of Garry Dale, and Jane, *née* Orbell (d 2012); *b* 15 July 1962, Cambridge; *Educ* Saffron Walden County HS, UEA (BA); *m* 15 June 2008, John Simmons; *Career* publisher and broadcaster; public affrs mangr British Ports Assoc 1987–90, dep md The Waterfront Partnership 1990–96, fndr Politico's Bookstore 1997–2006, fndr Politico's Publishing 1998–2003, md Total Politics Magazine 2008–12, md Biteback Publishing 2009–; columnist Daily Telegraph 2007–09; contrib: Guardian, Independent, GQ, Spectator, New Statesman; presenter LBC Radio 2010–; visiting prof in politics and broadcasting UEA 2016–; Arqiva Radio Presenter of the Year 2013 and 2016; *Books* The NHS: Things That Need to be Said (2015), Prime Minister Corbyn and Other Things That Never Happened (2016); *Recreations* cinema, golf, reading, music, tennis, travel; *Clubs* West Ham United FC; *Style—* Iain Dale, Esq; ✉ Biteback Publishing, Westminster Tower, 3 Albert Embankment, London SE1 7SP

DALE, Laurence Vincent; s of George Robert Dale, of Keymer, W Sussex, and Thelma Jean, *née* Singleton; *b* 10 September 1957; *Educ* Brighton Hove & Sussex GS, Guildhall Sch of Music and Drama, Salzburg Mozarteum; *Career* tenor; memb Royal Opera Co Covent Garden 1980–81, professional debut as Camille in The Merry Widow (ENO) 1981; awarded Medaille de la Ville de Paris for contrib to French culture; stage dir 2000–; artistic dir: Opéra Théâtre de Metz 2002–04, Evian Festival 2001–; *Roles* incl: Don José in Peter Brook's La Tragedie de Carmen (cr role) 1981, title role in Orfeo (ENO 1983, Salzburg Festival 1993), Ulysses (ENO) 1989, Don Ottavio in Don Giovanni (Nice, Munich, Salzburg Festival, WNO, Berlin, Marseille, Genova), Ferrando in Cosi fan Tutte (WNO, Holland Festival, Frankfurt, Berlin), Alfredo in La Traviata (WNO), Fenton in Falstaff (Brussels, Aix-en-Provence, NY, Milano, Covent Garden, Buenos Aires), Eisenstein in Die Fledermaus (WNO), Tamino in The Magic Flute (Vienna Staatsoper, Salzburg, Zurich, Brussels, Toronto, Stuttgart, Berlin, Opera Bastille Paris), Romeo in Gounod's Romeo and Juliet (Basel, Zurich), Idamante in Idomeneo (Holland Festival), Ramino in La Cenerentola (Glyndebourne, Marseille), Pelléas et Mélisande (Bruxelles), Belfiore in La Finta Giardiniera (Salzburg Festival debut) 1992, title role in Werther (Lille and Paris) 1993, Debussy's Rodrigue et Chimene (world premiere Lyon Opera) 1993; *Recordings* incl: Recital of French Opera and Opera-Comique Arias (under Kenneth Montgomery, 1988), Gounod's St Cecilia Mass, Mozart's Mass in C Minor, Honegger's Le Roi David, Debussy's Rodrigue et Chimene, Purcell's The Fairy Queen, Cavalli's La Didone, Monteverdi's Orfeo, Chausson's La Tempete; *Productions* La Tragedie de Carmen (Opéra de Bordeaux) 2000, Der Zarewitsch (Bad Ischl Operetta Festival) 2000, L'Incontro Improvviso (HaydenTage Festival Eisenstadt and EXPO 2000 Hannover) 2000, Dido and Aeneas (NY) 2001, Les Malheurs d'Orphee (NY) 2001, Powder Her Face (French premiere, Nantes and Metz) 2002, Land des Lächelins (Salzburg, Bad Ischel, Metz) 2002, Graf von Luxemburg (Innsbruck, Bad Ischl) 2002, Turn of the Screw 2003, Gustave III (Metz) 2003, Gustavo III (French premiere, Metz) 2003, Les Huguenots 2004, Opera Seria (Dutch premiere, Reis Opera) 2005; *Style—* Laurence Dale, Esq

DALE, Peter David; s of David Howard Dale (d 2006), and Betty Marguerite, *née* Rosser (d 2013), of Cambs; *b* 25 July 1955; *Educ* King Henry VIII Sch Coventry, Univ of Liverpool (BA); *m* 1988, Victoria, *née* Pennington, 1 s (Christopher Leo b 1988), 2 da (Georgia Hope b 1997, Madeleine Grace b 1997); *Career* journalist; BBC Television: film ed 1979–80, research and traineeship 1980, dir/prodr BBC documentaries 1982–98; Channel 4: commissioning ed documentaries 1998–2000, head of documentaries 2000–05, head More4 2005–08, fndr and chief exec Rare Day Ltd 2008–; tstee The Grierson Tst 2008–11; *Awards* journalism prize Anglo-German Fndn 1992, best documentary award RTS 1994, best documentary series award RTS 1996, Prodr of the Year Award Broadcast Magazine 1997, BFI Grierson Award for best documentary 1997; *Recreations* family, sailing; *Style—* Peter Dale, Esq

DALE, Stephen Hugh; s of Frederick Francis George Dale, of Lewes, E Sussex, and Margaret Brenda Nancy, *née* Beales; *b* 12 July 1955, Ewell, Surrey; *Educ* Bolton Sch, Univ of Manchester (BA); *m* Corinne Jenny, *née* David; 1 da (Claire Jenny Margaret b Nov 1994); *Career* chartered accountant Deloitte Haskins & Sells Manchester 1976–80 (articled clerk 1976–79); PricewaterhouseCoopers (formerly Price Waterhouse before merger): joined Tax Dept Manchester 1980, specialised in VAT and transferred to London office 1983, ptnr 1989– (Paris office PwC Société d'Avocats 1991–); ICAEW: memb Tax Ctee, chm VAT Ctee 1988–96; pres Indirect Tax Ctee FEE 1993–2010, pres Int VAT Assoc 2014–; memb: VAT Practitioners Gp 1983–91 (memb Exec Ctee), Jt VAT Ctee 1990–93, Conseil de L'Association des Practiciens de la TVA Européenne, EU VAT Forum 2012–15, EU VAT Expert Gp 2014–16; FCA 1990; *Books* Advanced VAT Planning, Property and Financial Services (1989), Guide Pratique de la TVA (1999), VAT Yearbook (2010); *Recreations* music, walking, golf; *Style—* Stephen Dale, Esq

DALE-THOMAS, Philippa Mary; da of Peter Alan Dale Dale-Thomas, of Taunton, Somerset, and Thirle Wynette Alpha, *née* Tribe; *b* 5 March 1960; *Educ* Cheltenham Ladies' Coll, Cambridge Coll of Arts and Technol (HND); *Career* bd dir Edelman Public Relations 1989–93 (joined 1982); dep chm Fishburn Hedges until 2009 (bd dir 1993–, md 2000–03), dir Philippa Dale-Thomas Ltd 2010–; registered and approved growth coach for GrowthAccelerator 2014–; non-exec dir RIBA 2012–, non-exec dir Delta7 Ltd 2014–; CIPR Awards for: public affairs 1987 and 1991, commerce and industry 1989 and 1990, internal communications 1989, long-term PR programmes 1991; MIPR 1988, FCIPR 1999; *Recreations* horse riding, scuba diving, gardening, playing the piano, pottery; *Style—* Miss Philippa Dale-Thomas; ✉ website www.pdalethomas.co.uk

DALEY, Michael John William; s of late Desmond William Daley and late Alma Joan, *née* Bevan; *b* 23 September 1953; *Educ* Hatfield Sch; *m* 1993, Elizabeth Jane, *née* Hobson; 1 s, 1 da; *Career* S G Warburg & Co Ltd 1973–77, Credit Suisse First Boston Ltd 1977–86, vice-pres and head Fixed Income Group Morgan Stanley International 1986–91, exec dir Morgan Stanley Asset Management Ltd 1988–91; md Strategic Value Management Ltd 1992–, memb Gp Exec Ctee and dir various subsids Guinness Flight Hambro Asset Management Ltd 1994–99; pres Avebury Asset Management Ltd 2000–14; chm Avebury Soc 2011–; FInstD 1984, FCMI (MIMgt 1986), Chartered FCSI 2010; *Recreations* motoring, shooting; *Clubs* Carlton, RAC; *Style—* Michael Daley, Esq; ✉ Avebury Asset Management Ltd, PO Box 66100, London W4 9FF (✆ 020 8995 0724, e-mail michael.daley@globalfixedincome.com)

DALEY, Thomas Robert (Tom); s of Robert Daley (d 2011), and Debra, *née* Selvester; *b* 21 May 1994, Plymouth, Devon; *Educ* Plymouth Coll; *Career* diver; achievements incl: Under 18 Champion 2004 (aged 10), Sr Br Champion 2007, 2008 and 2009, 2 Silver medals Jr World Championships 2008, Gold medal European Championships 2008, Gold medal World Championships 2009, two Gold medals (10m platform synchro and 10m individual platform) Cwlth Games Delhi 2010, Bronze medal (10m individual platform) Olympic

Games 2012, Bronze medal (10m synchronised platform) Olympic Games 2016; BBC Young Sports Personality of the Year 2007, 2009 and 2010 (only person to win three times), youngest Br competitor at Beijing Olympics 2008, youngest ever Br World Champion in any sport, youngest ever European Champion; *Clubs* Plymouth Diving; *Style—* Tom Daley, Esq; ✉ c/o The Professional Sports Group, The Town House, 63 High Street, Chobham, Surrey GU24 8AF (☎ 01276 858930, e-mail charlotte@profsports.com)

DALGLEISH, Prof Angus George; s of Ronald Dalgleish, and Eileen Anna Dalgleish; *b* 14 May 1950; *Educ* Harrow Co GS for Boys, UCL (MRC scholar, BSc, MD), UCH (MB BS); *m* 28 Sept 1984, Judy Ann, da of Geoffrey Riley; 1 s (Tristan Amadeus b 7 Dec 1988); *Career* house surgn in gen surgery and orthopaedics and locum casualty offr St Stephen's Hosp 1975, house physician in gen med and oncology Poole District Hosp 1975, flying doctor serv Queensland 1976–77, gen med registrar Princess Alexandra Hosp Brisbane 1978–80 (resident MO 1977–78), gen med registrar Princess Alexandra Hosp and cardio-thoracic registrar Prince Charles Hosp 1980–81, registrar in radiotherapy Queensland Radium Inst Royal Brisbane Hosp 1981–82, sr registrar in oncology Royal Prince Alfred Hosp Sydney 1982–83, sr registrar in clinical immunology and haematology Clinical Immunological Research Centre Univ of Sydney and Kanematsu Inst Royal Prince Alfred Hosp 1983–84, clinical res fell Inst of Cancer Research and hon sr registrar Royal Marsden Hosp 1984–86, clinical scientist MRC/CRC and hon conslt physician, immunologist and oncologist Northwick Park Hosp 1986–88, head Retrovirus Research Gp CRC 1988–91, head of clinical virology, sr lectr and hon conslt physician Royal London Hosp Med Coll 1991–, prof and fndn chair of oncology St George's Hosp Med Sch (now St George's Univ of London) 1991–; fndr and research dir Onyvax Ltd 1997–2009, research dir Cancer Vaccine Inst, involved with major research progs; Celgene Corp Joshua Lederberg Prize 2011; FRCPath 1995, FRACP 1984, FRCP 1993, FMedSci 2001; *Publications* AIDS and the New Viruses, Tumour Immunology (co-ed), Inflamation and Cancer; author of numerous medical pubns and chapters in books; *Recreations* hiking, sailing, tennis, skiing, piano, opera; *Style—* Prof Angus Dalgleish; ✉ Division of Clinical Sciences, St George's University of London, Cranmer Terrace, Tooting, London SW17 0RE (☎ 020 8725 0809, e-mail dalgleis@sgul.ac.uk)

DALGLISH, Kenneth Mathieson (Kenny); MBE; *b* 4 March 1951; *Career* professional football manager; played for Celtic and Liverpool (mangr 1986–91 and 2011–12); honours with Celtic: Scottish League champions 1972–74 and 1977, Scottish Cup winners 1972, 1974, 1975 and 1977, Scottish League Cup winners 1975; with Liverpool: European Cup 1978, 1981 and 1984 (runners-up 1985), Div 1 champions 1979, 1980, 1982, 1983, 1984, 1986, 1988 and 1990, FA Cup 1986 and 1989, League Cup 1981–84; 102 full caps for Scotland; Blackburn Rovers FC: mangr 1991–95 (promoted Premier League 1992, Premier League Champions 1995), dir of football 1995–96; mangr Newcastle Utd FC 1997–98, dir of football ops Celtic FC 1999–2000, mangr Liverpool FC 2011–12 (non-exec dir 2013–); Football Writers' Footballer of the Year 1979, PFA Player of the Year 1983, Manager of the Year 1986 and 1988; Freeman City of Glasgow; *Style—* Kenny Dalglish, MBE

DALHOUSIE, 17 Earl of (S 1633); James Hubert Ramsay; DL (Angus 1993); s of 16 Earl of Dalhousie, KT, GCVO, GBE, MC, JP, DL (d 1999), by his w Margaret, da of late Brig-Gen Archibald Stirling of Keir (2 s of Sir John Stirling-Maxwell, 10 Bt, KT, DL, which Btcy has been dormant since 1956) and Hon Margaret Fraser, OBE, da of 13 Lord Lovat; suc f 1999; *b* 17 January 1948; *Educ* Ampleforth; *m* 1973, Marilyn, 2 da of Maj Sir David Henry Butter, KCVO, MC, and Myra Alice, da of Sir Harold Wernher, 3 and last Bt, GCVO, TD, by his w Lady Zia, *née* Countess Anastasia Mikhailovna; 2 da (Lady Lorna b 1975, Lady Alice b 1977), 1 s (Simon David, Lord Ramsay b 1981); *Heir* s, Lord Ramsay; *Career* cmmnd 2 Bn Coldstream Gds 1968–71; dir Hambros Bank 1981–82; exec dir Enskilda Securities 1982–87; dir: Central Capital Ltd 1987–91, Capel-Cure Myers 1987–91, Jamestown Investments Ltd 1987–, Edinburgh Japan Trust plc (formerly Dunedin Japan Investment Trust plc until 1996) 1993–99; chm: William Evans 1990–2000, Scottish Woodlands Ltd 1998–2005 (dir 1993–98), Dunedin Smaller Companies Investment plc 1998–2014; pres British Deer Soc 1987–2008, vice-chm Game and Wildlife Conservation Tst 1990–2010, cmmr Deer Cmmn Scotland 2005–10, pres Dundee and Angus branch Scots Guards Assoc 2007–, pres Royal Highland and Agricultural Soc of Scotland (RHASS) 2014–15; Capt Royal Co of Archers Queen's Bodyguard for Scotland, pres Cncl and Silver Stick for Scotland; chm of govrs Unicorn Preservation Soc 2002–14; Vice Lord-Lt Angus 2003, Lord Steward HM Household 2009–, Hon Capt RNR 2009–; CStJ; *Clubs* White's, Pratt's, Turf, Caledonian (pres 1990–); *Style—* The Rt Hon the Earl of Dalhousie; ✉ Brechin Castle, Brechin, Angus DD9 6SH (office ☎ 01356 624566, e-mail dalhousieestates@btinternet.com); Flat 15, 41 Courtfield Road, London SW7 4DB (☎ 020 7373 3724)

DALLAS, James Anthony; s of John Anthony Dallas (d 2003), and Joy, *née* Marriott (d 2002); *b* 21 April 1955; *Educ* Eton, St Edmund Hall Oxford (MA); *m* 7 Sept 1979, Annabel, *née* Hope; 1 s (Edward b 29 Nov 1984), 2 da (Katherine b 15 May 1986, Matilda b 15 Oct 1988); *Career* with City legal firm 1976–81, sr legal advsr Int Energy Devpt Corp 1981–84; Denton Hall: (then Denton Wilde Sapte, now Dentons) joined 1984, chm 1996–2009 (joined 1984), sr ptnr ME and Africa 2009–11; non-exec dir AMEC plc 1999–2007; exec dir Energy and Nat Resources Law Queen Mary Univ of London; memb Ctee Action for the River Kennet, tstee Thames Rivers Tst; *Recreations* fishing, tennis, ornithology; *Clubs* Whites; *Style—* James Dallas, Esq; ✉ Dentons, One Fleet Place, London EC4M 7WS (☎ 020 7246 7579, fax 020 7246 7794, e-mail james.dallas@dentons.com)

DALLAS, Michael John Linwood; s of Linwood Forbes Dallas (d 1982), and Helen, *née* Ralston (d 1990); *b* 2 February 1944; *Educ* Diocesan Coll Cape Town, Univ of Cape Town (BCom); *m* 28 April 1973, Elizabeth, da of John McGill Dick; 2 s (James Robert Linwood b 9 March 1976, Edward John McGill b 1 Aug 1979); *Career* PricewaterhouseCoopers (formerly Coopers & Lybrand before merger): trainee Cape Town, joined London office 1969, ptnr 1985–2001, ptnr i/c Public Services Assurance and Business Advsy Serv 1993–2001; memb: South African Inst of Chartered Accountants 1968, Public Sector Ctee Accounting Standards Bd 1991–2002, Dept of Health Audit Ctee 1999–2006 (chair 2002–06); chair Audit Cmmn Technical Advsy Gp 2002, Audit Ctee Gt Ormond St Hosp 2007–15; CIPFA 1992, FRSA 1996; *Recreations* walking, gardening, antiques, the Cotswolds, skiing, genealogy; *Style—* Michael Dallas, Esq; ✉ Ashley Manor Barn, Ashley, Tetbury, Gloucestershire GL8 8SX (☎ 01666 577336)

DALLEY, Janet Elizabeth (Jan); da of Christopher Mervyn Dalley (d 1999), and Elizabeth Alice, *née* Gammell (d 2001); *b* 2 January 1952; *Educ* Univ of Bristol (BA), Univ of Oxford (MSc); *m* 1985, Andrew Motion, FRSL, *qv*; 2 s (Andrew Jesse b 1986, Lucas Edward b 1988), 1 da (Sidonie Gillian Elizabeth (twin) b 1988); *Career* journalist; literary ed Independent on Sunday 1993–97, literary ed Financial Times 1999–2005, arts ed Financial Times 2005–; *Books* Diana Mosley: A Life (1999), The Black Hole: Money, Myth and Empire (2006); *Style—* Ms Jan Dalley; ✉ Financial Times, One Southwark Bridge, London SE1 9HL (☎ 020 7873 4782, fax 020 7873 3929, e-mail jan.dalley@ft.com)

DALLIMORE, Will; *Career* advtg sales mangr and editorial researcher Sight & Sound magazine 1996–97, mktg offr Inst of Contemporary Arts 1997–2000, publishing and mktg mangr Royal Coll of Art 2000–04, sr strategist Synergy Communications 2004–05, sr strategist and client dir Engage Gp 2005–09, travel and English teacher 2009–10, dir of communications Royal Academy of Arts 2011–14, dir of public engagement Royal Academy of Arts 2014–; *Style—* Will Dallimore, Esq

DALRYMPLE; *see also:* Hamilton-Dalrymple

DALRYMPLE, William Benedict (HAMILTON-); s of Major Sir Hew Hamilton-Dalrymple, Bt, KCVO, *qv*, and Lady Anne-Louise, *née* Keppel; *b* 20 March 1965, Edinburgh; *Educ* Ampleforth, Trinity Coll Cambridge (exhibitioner, sr history scholar, MA); *m* Olivia, da of Simon Fraser, of London; *Career* writer, broadcaster and historian; contrib to jls and newspapers incl: TLS, Granta, New Yorker, New York Review of Books, The Guardian; fndr and dir Jaipur Literature Festival 2004–; exhibition Princes and Painters in Mughal Delhi 1707–1857 (Asia Soc NY) 2012; patron: Sabeel, Palestinian Solidarity Gp; Mungo Park Medal RSGS 2002, Sir Percy Sykes Memorial Medal RSAA 2005, Col James Tod Meml Prize Maharana Mewar Fndn 2008, Media Citizen Puraskar Indian Confederation of NGOs 2011; Whitney J Oakes fell in South Asian studies Princeton Univ 2012; Hon DLitt: Univ of St Andrews 2006, Univ of Lucknow 2007, Univ of Aberdeen 2008, Univ of Bradford 2012, Univ of Edinburgh 2015; FRSL 1993, FRGS 1993, FRAS 1998; *Television* Stones of the Raj 1997, Indian Journeys 2000 (Grierson Award for Best Documentary Series 2000–01), Sufi Soul 2005, White Mughals 2015; *Radio* The Long Search 2002 (winner Sandford St Martin Prize for Religious Broadcasting 2003), Three Miles an Hour 2002, A History of Indian Art in Five Objects; *Books* In Xanadu (1989, Best First Work Award Yorkshire Post, Spring Book Award Scottish Arts Cncl 1990), City of Djinns (1993, Thomas Cook Travel Book Award, Young British Writer of the Year Award Sunday Times 1994), From the Holy Mountain (1997, Autumn Book Award Scottish Arts Cncl), The Age of Kali (collected journalism, 1998, Prix d'Astrolabe (France) 2005), The White Mughals: Love and Betrayal in 18th-Century India (2002; winner Wolfson History Prize 2003, Scottish Book of the Year 2003; shortlisted: Pen Hessel-Tiltman Prize 2003, Kiryama Prize 2004, James Tait Black Meml Prize 2004), The Last Mughal: The Fall of a Dynasty, Delhi 1857 (2006, Duff Cooper Memorial Prize 2006, Vodafone/Crossword Indian Book of the Year 2008), Nine Lives: In Search of the Sacred in Modern India (2009, Asia House Literary Award 2010), Princes and Painters in Mughal Delhi 1707–1857 (jtly), Return of a King: The Battle for Afghanistan 1839–42 (2013, Hemingway Prize, shortlisted Samuel Johnson Prize 2014, Duff Cooper Prize and PEN Hessel Tiltman History Prize); *CDs* The Rough Guide to Sufi Music (2011); *Recreations* walking, travelling, listening to music, reading, my children; *Style—* William Dalrymple, Esq; ✉ 1 Pages' Yard, Church Street, Chiswick, London W4 2PA (☎ 020 8994 4500, e-mail williamdalrymple@gmail.com, website www.williamdalrymple.com); c/o David Godwin, DGA, 55 Monmouth Street, London WC2H 9DG (☎ 020 7240 9992)

DALTON, Annie; da of late Cecil Henry James Dalton, and Audrey Beryl, *née* Harris; *b* 18 January 1948; *Educ* Felixstowe Secdy Modern, Ipswich Civic Coll, Univ of Warwick (BA); *m* (m dis); 1 da (Anna Rachel b 1 Jan 1971), 1 adopted s (Reuben Alexander 24 Nov 1973), 1 adopted da (Maria Jane b 5 Nov 1976); *Career* children's writer; formerly writer in residence HM Prison Wellingborough, writer's exchange in Jamaica; *Books* Nightmaze (shortlisted Carnegie Award 1990), The Alpha Box, Swan Sister, Naming the Dark, The Real Tilly Beany (commended for Carnegie Award 1992), The Afterdark Princess (winner Nottingham Oak Children's Book Award 1991), Angels Unlimited; *Style—* Ms Annie Dalton

DALTON, Ian Mark Marshall; CBE (2011); s of late Douglas Vivien Marshall Dalton, of Bournemouth, and Helgard, *née* Herzog; *b* 14 January 1964, Welwyn Garden City; *Educ* Verulam Sch St Albans, Univ of York (BA, MA), Univ of Durham (MBA); *m* 1 Aug 1992, Juliet, *née* Kearsley; 1 s (Max Joshua b 23 Sept 1998), 1 da (Alexandra Rachel Beth b 23 Sept 1998); *Career* residential care offr N Yorks CC Social Servs 1985–86, project offr then district offr Royal Soc for Mentally Handicapped Children and Adults 1986–90, devpt mangr community mental health Durham CC Social Servs 1990–91, various posts incl actg dir commissioning Northern RHA/Northern and Yorks RHA 1991–95; Northern and Yorks regnl office NHS Exec: head of primary and community care 1995–96, head of purchaser performance devpt 1996–97; dir of devpt and planning Hartlepool and E Durham NHS Tst 1997–99, dir of acute servs planning and devpt N Tees and Hartlepool NHS Tst 1999–2000; Dept of Health: regnl dir of performance mgmnt Northern and Yorks 2000–02, dir of performance North 2002–03; head of health Coalition Provisional Authy Southern Iraq (seconded to FCO) 2003; chief exec: N Cheshire Hosps NHS Tst 2003–05, N Tees and Hartlepool NHS Tst 2005–07, NE SHA 2007–09; seconded to Dept of Health as nat dir of NHS flu resilience 2009–10, seconded to Dept of Health as md of provider devpt 2010–11; chief exec NHS North of England 2011–12, chief operating offr and dep chief exec NHS England 2012–13, pres of global health BT Global Services/BT Business and Public Sector 2013–14, pres of global govt and health BT Global Services 2014–; non-exec dir Crown Agents Ltd 2016–; tstee Guy's and St Thomas's Charity; Hon Col B (250) Sqdn (V) 3 medical Regt RAMC until 2012; *Recreations* cinema, travel, walking; *Style—* Ian Dalton, Esq, CBE

DALTON, Timothy; *b* 21 March 1946; *Educ* RADA; *Career* actor; *Theatre* began career in regnl theatre: lead roles in The Merchant of Venice, Richard II, The Doctor's Dilemma, St Joan; London debut as Malcolm in Little Malcolm and His Struggle Against the Eunuchs (Royal Court); other credits incl: Arthur in A Game Called Arthur, Edgar in King Lear, Berowne in Love's Labour's Lost (Aldwych), Prince Hal in Henry IV (parts I and II), King Henry in Henry V (Roundhouse), Romeo in Romeo and Juliet, The Samaritan (Shaw), Black Comedy and White Liars, The Vortex (Greenwich), Lord Byron in Lunatic Lover and Poet (Old Vic), Mark Antony in The Romans (New Mermaid), Hotspur in Henry IV (part I (Barbican)), Antony & Cleopatra, The Taming of the Shrew (Haymarket), A Touch of the Poet (with Vanessa Redgrave, Young Vic), Lord Asriel in His Dark Materials (RNT); *Television* incl: Candida (BBC), Five Finger Exercise, Centennial (mini-series), Charlie's Angels, Mr Rochester in Jane Eyre (BBC), The Master of Ballantrae (HTV), Mistral's Daughter (US mini-series, with Lee Remick, Stephanie Powers & Stacey Keach), Florence Nightingale (US mini-series, with Jaclyn Smith, Timothy West), Sins (mini-series, with Joan Collins), Philip von Joel in Framed (mini-series, Anglia), In the Company of Wolves (Anglia), Rhett Butler in Scarlett (mini-series, Sky TV), Salt Water Moose (movie, USA/Canada), Chief Inspector Rennie in The Informant, Darrow in The Reef (CBS), Sheriff Dex in Made Men, Julius Caesar in Cleopatra, Father William Bowdern in Possessed (Showtime), Matt in Time Share (Fox Family Channel), Clive Trevelyan in Agatha Christie's The Sittaford Mystery 2006, Lord President Rassilon in Doctor Who 2009–10, Alexei Volkoff/Gregory Tuttle in Chuck 2010–11, Sir Malcolm Murray in Penny Dreadful 2014; *Film* incl: King of France in The Lion Winter (with Peter O'Toole and Katharine Hepburn), Prince Rupert in Cromwell (with Alec Guinness and Richard Harris), Heathcliffe in Wuthering Heights, Darnley in Mary, Queen of Scots (with Vanessa Redgrave and Glenda Jackson (Brit Film Award nomination)), Charles Lord in Permission to Kill (with Dirk Bogarde and Ava Gardner), Juan de Dios in The Man Who Knew Love, lead in Sextette (with Mae West, Tony Curtis and Ringo Starr), Col Christie in Agatha (with Dustin Hoffman and Vanessa Redgrave), Prince Barin in Flash Gordon, Chanel Solitaire (with Marie-France Pisier), Dr Rock in The Doctor and the Devils, Basil St John in Brenda Starr (with Brooke Shields), Bancroft in Hawks, James Bond in The Living Daylights and Licence to Kill, The King's Whore, Neville Sinclair in The Rocketeer, Boris in The Beautician and the Beast, Allan Pinkerton in American Outlaws, Looney Tunes – Back in Action, Amphitryon in Hercules 2004, Simon Skinner in Hot Fuzz 2007, Mr Pricklepants in Toy Story 3 2010, Chief Inspector Jones in The Tourist 2010, Lord Milori in Tinker Bell: Secret of the Wings 2012; *Style—* Timothy Dalton; ✉ c/o Independent Talent Group Limited, Oxford House, 40 Whitfield Street, London W1T 2RH

DALTREY, Roger Harry; CBE (2005); s of Harry Daltrey, and Irene Daltrey; *b* 1 March 1944, Hammersmith, London; *Educ* Acton Co GS; *Children* 5 c; *Career* fndr and lead singer The Who (formerly The Detours) 1963–; albums: My Generation 1965, A Quick One 1966, The Who Sell Out 1967, Tommy 1969, Who's Next 1971, Quadrophenia 1973, The Who By Numbers 1975, Who Are You 1978, Face Dances 1981, It's Hard 1982; solo albums: Daltrey 1973, Ride a Rock Horse 1975, One of the Boys 1977, McVicar 1980, Parting Should be Painless 1984, Under a Raging Moon 1985, Can't Wait to See the Movie 1987, Rocks in the Head 1992; actor on stage and TV and in more than thirty films incl Tommy 1975 (nominated Golden Globe Best Acting Debut in a Motion Picture) and McVicar 1980; *Recreations* history; *Style*— Roger Daltrey, Esq, CBE; ✉ c/o Jools Broom, Trinifold, 12 Oval Road, London NW1 7DH (☎ 020 7419 4300)

DALWOOD, Prof Dexter; *b* 1960, Bristol; *Educ* St Martin's Sch of Art (BA), RCA (MA); *Career* artist; artist tstee Nat Gallery London 2011; prof of art and design Bath Spa Univ 2012–; nominated Turner Prize 2010; *Solo Exhibitions* Clove Building London 1992, Galerie Unwahr Berlin 1995, Dexter Dalwood: New Paintings (Gagosian Gallery London) 2000, Dexter Dalwood: New Paintings (Gagosian Gallery LA) 2002, Dexter Dalwood: New Paintings (Gagosian Gallery NY) 2004, Recent History (Gagosian Gallery London) 2006, Endless Night (Gasosian Gallery LA) 2009, Tate St Ives 2010, Frac Champagne Ardenne Reims France 2010, CAC Malaga Spain 2010, Nolan Judin Berlin 2011, Orientalism (David Risley Gallery Copenhagen) 2012, Centre Pasquart Biel/Bienne Switzerland 2013, London Paintings (Simon Lee Gallery) 2014, Propaganda Paintaing (Simon Lee Gallery Hong Kong) 2016; *Group Exhibitions* incl: Whitechapel Open London 1992, 1994 and 1996, Wild (Ikon Gallery Birmingham and Harris Museum Preston) 1993, Base (Salama-Caro Gallery London) 1994, John Moores 19 (Walker Art Gallery Liverpool) 1995, Remaking Reality (Kettles Yard Cambridge) 1996, Thoughts (City Racing London) 1997, Humdrum (The Trade Apartment London) 1998, Die Young Stay Pretty (ICA London) 1998, Facts and Fictions (In Arco Turin) 1998, Dirty Realism (Robert Pearre Fine Art Tucson) 1999, Rebecca (Sali Gia London) 1999, Heart and Soul (60 Long Lane London and Sandroni Rey Venice LA) 1999, Young and Serious-Recycled Image (Ernst Museum Budapest) 1999, Caught (303 Gallery NY) 1999, Neurotic Realism: Part Two (Saatchi Gallery London) 1999, Sausages and Frankfurters: Recent British and German Paintings from the Ophiuchus Collection (The Hydra Workshop Hydra) 2000, Twisted: Urban and Visionary Landscapes in Contemporary Painting (van Abbe Museum Eindhoven) 2000, Arthur C Rose presents... (Vilma Gold London) 2001, Generator 3 (Baluardo di San Regalo Lucca) 2001, View Five: Westworld (Mary Boone Gallery NY) 2001, Remix (Tate Liverpool) 2002, Sydney Biennale 2002, Tate Triennial Exhibition of Contemporary British Art (Tate Britain) 2003, My Way Home (Galerie Thaddaeus Ropac Salzburg) 2003, Tate Turner Prize 2010, Dublin Contemporary Dublin 2011, Germany is your America (Broadway 1602 NY) 2011, Disaster Galerie Thaddeus Ropac Paris 2011, Paying No Attention I Notice Everything: Robert Walser and the Visual Arts Aargauer Kunsthaus Arau Switzerland 2014, Fighting History Tate Britain 2015, The Painting Show (CAC Vilnius Lithuania, British Council Touring Show) 2016; *Film* 1800; *Style*— Prof Dexter Dalwood; ✉ c/o Simon Lee Gallery, 12 Berkeley Street, London W1J 8DT (☎ 020 7491 0100, website www.dexterdalwood.com)

DALY, Francis D; s of Edward M Daly (d 1983), of Montenotte, Cork, and Clare, *née* Egan (d 1987); *b* 16 September 1943; *Educ* Glenstal Abbey, UC Cork (BCL); *m* 21 Feb 1970, Patricia Mary, da of late H P O'Connor, of Cork; 2 s (Teddy b 14 Nov 1970, Ken b 22 April 1972), 2 da (Aiveen b 14 Nov 1973, Alex b 6 Oct 1976); *Career* admitted slr 1966; ptnr Ronan Daly Jermyn 1970– (joined 1966); pres Law Soc of Ireland 1996–97, chm Slrs' Disciplinary Tbnl 2004–12; *Recreations* golf, Munster Rugby; *Clubs* Cork Golf, Cork Constution RFC; *Style*— Francis D Daly, Esq; ✉ Cleveland, Blackrock Road, Cork; Corthna, Schull, Co Cork (☎ 00 353 214 294 279, e-mail frank.daly@live.ie); Ronan Daly Jermyn, 12 South Mall, Cork (☎ 00 353 214 802700, e-mail frank.daly@rdj.ie)

DALY, James; CVO (1994); s of late Maurice Daly, and Christine Daly; *b* 8 September 1940; *Educ* St Thomas More Chelsea, UCL (BScEcon); *m* 1970, Dorothy Lillian, *née* Powell; 2 s; *Career* served RM 1958–67; HM Dip Serv: joined FO 1968, third sec Accra 1971–73, third sec Moscow 1973–76, second sec Karachi 1976–78, first sec FCO 1978–79, first sec Sofia 1979–86, consul-gen Paris 1986–92, cnsllr and consul-gen Moscow 1992–95, high cmmr to Vanuatu 1995–97, high cmmr to Mauritius 1997–2000, with FCO 2001–; memb Special Immigration Appeals Cmmn 2003–; Special Boat Service Assoc 2000–, tstee Charitable Fund St Francis Leprosy Guild 2003–08; *Recreations* reading, music, walking; *Clubs* In & Out; *Style*— James Daly, Esq, CVO; ✉ 44 Ashley Court, Morpeth Terrace, London SW1P 1EN

DALY, John; s of John Daly, and Emilie Daly; *b* 28 August 1955, London; *Educ* St Clement Danes GS; *m* 1978, Janet Westbury; 2 s (Scott, Lee); *Career* asst cameraman Film Dept BBC 1976–1987, dir of photography BBC 1987–98, freelance dir of photography 1998–; memb: BAFTA, BSC 1995 (memb Bd of Govrs 2008); *Television* credits incl: Persuasion (Photography and Lighting BAFTA 1995), Our Friends in the North (nomination Photography and Lighting BAFTA Awards 1996), Far From the Madding Crowd (Photography and Lighting BAFTA 1998), 20,000 Streets under the Sky 2005 (nomination Photography and Lighting BAFTA Awards 2005), Cape Wrath 2007; *Film* credits incl: Titanic Town 1998, Fanny & Elvis 1999, Essex Boys 2000, Dog Eat Dog 2000, The Parole Officer 2001, Greenfingers 2001, Johnny English 2003 (second unit), Lila Dit Câ 2003, Life and Lyrics 2006, Metamorphosis 2010; *Style*— John Daly, Esq, BSC; ✉ website www.johndalybsc.com; c/o Jessica Carney Associates, 4th Floor, 23 Golden Square, London W1F 9JP (☎ 020 7434 4143, website www.jessicacarneyassociates.co.uk)

DALY, Tess; *m* 2003, Vernon Kay *qv*; 2 da (Phoebe Elizabeth b 2004, Amber Isabella b 2009); *Career* former model Models One; TV presenter: Big Breakfast (Channel 4), Singled Out (Channel Five/MTV), Smash Hits TV (Sky One), SM:tv (ITV1), Dancestar Awards (MTV), Exclusive (Channel Five), LA Pool Party (BBC), Britain's Brainiest Kids (ITV1), Clothes Show (ITV1), National TV Awards (ITV2), Home on their Own (ITV1), The Christmas Show (ITV1), Back to Reality (Five), Strictly Come Dancing (BBC1), Children in Need (BBC1); fashion columnist The Mirror; beauty range Tess Daly Beauty; patron Great Ormond St Hosp; *Books* The Baby Diaries (2010), The Camera Never Lies (2011); *Style*— Ms Tess Daly

DALYELL, Hon Mrs (Kathleen Mary Agnes); OBE (2005), DL (W Lothian until 2012); da of Baron Wheatley (Life Peer, d 1988); *b* 17 November 1937; *Educ* Convent of Sacred Heart, Queens Cross Aberdeen, Univ of Edinburgh (MA); *m* 26 Dec 1963, Tam Dalyell, *qv*; 1 s, 1 da; *Career* teacher of history; NT Scot property mangr (vol) House of the Binns 1972–, memb Historic Buildings Cncl of Scotland 1975–87; dir: Heritage Education Tst 1987–2005, Weslo Housing Mgmnt 1994–2003, SCAN (Scottish Archive Network Ltd) 1998–2004; chm Bo'ness Heritage Tst 1988–95, memb Ancient Monuments Bd of Scotland 1989–2000, chm Royal Commission on Ancient and Historical Monuments of Scotland 2000–05; cmmr Royal Fine Art Cmmn for Scotland 1992–2000; tstee: Paxton Tst 1988–92, Carmont Tst 1997–2013, Hopetown Preservation Tst 2005–16, Museum of Scotland Charitable Tst 2005–; memb Ct Univ of Stirling 2003–08 (vice-chair 2008); Dr (hc) Univ of Edinburgh 2006, Hon Dr Univ of Stirling 2008; FSA Scot; *Recreations* reading, travel, hill walking, chess; *Style*— The Hon Mrs Dalyell, OBE, DL, FSA Scot; ✉ The Binns, Linlithgow EH49 7NA

DALYELL, (Sir) Tam; 11 Bt (NS 1685), of the Binns (but does not use title); s of Lt-Col Gordon Loch Dalyell, CIE, and (Dame) Eleanor Isabel Dalyell of The Binns, *de jure* Baronetess (d 1972); *b* 9 August 1932; *Educ* Eton, King's Coll Cambridge, Univ of Edinburgh; *m* 26 Dec 1963, Hon Kathleen Mary Agnes Dalyell, *qv*, da of Baron Wheatley (Life Peer, d 1988); 1 s (Gordon Wheatley b 26 Sept 1965), 1 da (Moira Eleanor b 25 May 1968); *Heir* s, Gordon Dalyell; *Career* Nat Serv Royal Scots Greys 1950–52; King's Coll Cambridge 1952–56, teacher Bo'ness Acad 1956–60, seconded to British India Steam Navigation Co as dir of studies on Ship Sch Dunera 1960–62, MP (Lab): West Lothian 1962–83, Linlithgow 1983–2005; Father of the House of Commons 2001–05; memb: Public Accounts Ctee, Select Ctee on Sci and Technol 1965–68, Nat Exec Ctee of Lab Pty 1986–87, Educn Inst of Scot; ldr Parly Union Delgn to: Brazil 1976, Zaïre 1990, Peru 1999, Bolivia 2000, Libya 2001; weekly columnist New Scientist 1967–2005; rector Univ of Edinburgh 2002–06; Hon DSc: Univ of Edinburgh 1994, City Univ 1998; Hon Dr: Univ of St Andrews 2001, Univ of Northumbria 2005, Univ of Stirling 2005, Napier Univ Edinburgh 2005, Open Univ 2006; FRSE 2003; *Books* Case for Ship Schools (1960), Ship School Dunera (1962), Devolution: the End of Britain? (1978), One Man's Falklands (1983), A Science Policy for Britain (1983), Misrule – How Mrs Thatcher Misled Parliament (1987), Dick Crossman: A Portrait (1989), The Importance of Being Awkward (2011), The Question of Scotland (2016); *Style*— Tam Dalyell, Esq; ✉ Binns, Linlithgow EH49 7NA

DALZIEL, Ian Martin; s of John Calvin Dalziel, FRCO (d 1983), and Elizabeth Roy, *née* Bain; *b* 21 June 1947; *Educ* Daniel Stewart's Coll Edinburgh, St John's Coll Cambridge, Université Libre de Bruxelles, London Business Sch; *m* 1972, Nadia Maria Iacovazzi; 4 s; *Career* Mullens & Co 1970–72, Manufacturers Hanover Ltd (London and NY) 1972–83, co fndr and dep md Adam & Co Group plc 1983–92; chm: Continental Assets Tst plc 1989–98, Invesco Continental Smaller Companies Tst plc 1998–; dir Lepercq-Amcur Fund NV 1988–; cncllr London Borough of Richmond upon Thames 1978–79; MEP (EDG) Lothians 1979–84; memb Queen's Body Guard for Scotland (Royal Co of Archers); *Recreations* golf, skiing, shooting; *Clubs* Brooks's, New (Edinburgh), Royal and Ancient Golf (St Andrews), Honourable Co of Edinburgh Golfers (Muirfield), Sunningdale Golf, Royal St George's; *Style*— Ian Dalziel, Esq; ✉ 45 route des Eaux-Belles, CH-1243 Presinge, Switzerland (☎ +41 22 759 1934, mobile +41 79 357 1837, e-mail imd4@mac.com)

DALZIEL, Dr Maureen; *née* Farrell; Peter P J Farrell, and Eileen Gavigan; *b* 7 April 1952, Glasgow; *Educ* Notre Dame HS Glasgow, Univ of Glasgow (MB ChB), Univ of London (MD); *m* Ian Dalziel; *Career* jr hosp doctor Glasgow and Lanarkshire Hosps 1976–79, GP E Kilbride Glasgow 1979–81, registrar then sr registrar in public health med Brent and SW Herts HAs 1981–85, assoc dir NW Thames RHA 1989 (conslt in public health med 1985–89); chief exec: SW Herts DHA 1990–93 (dir of public health 1989–90), Hillingdon Health Agency 1993–95; dir of public health N Thames Regional Office NHS Exec 1995–98, med dir NHS Litigation Authy 1999, dir Nat Co-Ordinating Centre for Serv Delivery and Orgn Research and Devpt 1999–2001, chief exec Human Fertilisation and Embryology Authy (HFEA) 2001–2002, md Health Consultancy 2004–, sr conslt Hoggett Bowers 2008–09; ptnr: Hill Coates, Solana Solutions, COC 2009–12; non-exec dir Barking Havering and Redbridge NHS Univ Hosps Tst 2013– (chair 2014–); hon sr lectr in public health med London Sch of Hygiene and Tropical Med 2000– (lectr 1981–85, sr lectr 1989–90); dir CSK 2002–05; memb: RHA 2005–07, Br Pregnancy Advsy Serv (BPAS) 2007–13; chair European Steering Gp 'Megapoles' Social Disadvantage in Capital Cities 1997–2001; memb Metropolitan Support Tst 2007– (vice-chair 2011), chair Migration Fndn 2009–11, chair CGC of BPAS 2009–13; memb ICN ARC; numerous articles in learned jls and papers presented at nat confs; MFCM 1985, FFPHM 1990, FRSA 1999; *Recreations* skiing, reading novels and biographies, golf (Par 3), watching old films; *Style*— Dr Maureen Dalziel; ✉ e-mail dalziel@btinternet.com

DAMAZER, Mark David; CBE (2011); s of Stanislau Damazer (d 1997), and Suzanne, *née* Buchs; *b* 15 April 1955; *Educ* Haberdashers' Aske's, Gonville & Caius Coll Cambridge (BA), Harvard Univ (Harkness fell); *m* Rosemary, *née* Morgan; *Career* trainee ITN 1979–81, BBC World Service 1981–82, TV-AM 1982–84; BBC: 6 O'Clock News 1984–86, output ed Newsnight 1986–88, ed 9 O'Clock News 1990–94 (dep ed 1988–90), ed TV News Progs 1994–96, head of Current Affrs 1996–98, head of Political Progs 1998–2000, dep dir BBC News 2000–04, controller Radio 4 and BBC 7 2004–10, head St Peter's Coll Oxford 2010–; vice-chm and Br exec Int Press Inst, memb Bd Inst for Contemporary History; Home News and News Programme of the Year RTS 1993, New York TV Festival (Gold) 1994; *Recreations* opera, poor tennis, gardening, Tottenham Hotspur; *Style*— Mark Damazer, Esq, CBE; ✉ 29 Killieser Avenue, London SW2 4NX (☎ 020 8674 9611, fax 020 8678 0636)

DAMTSA, Virginia; da of Spyros Damtsa, of Athens, Greece, and Voula Trikalinoy; *b* 15 May 1977, Paris, France; *Educ* Univ of Sussex (BA), London Coll of Printing Univ of the Arts London (MA), Sotheby's Univ (MA); *Career* working with creative team M&C Saatchi 1999–2000, dir Damtsattaberz Gall 2000–03, dir Riflemaker Gall 2003–; *Recreations* yoga, film, running, travelling somewhere hot; *Clubs* Groucho, Electric, Soho House; *Style*— Miss Virginia Damtsa; ✉ Riflemaker, 79 Beak Street, Regent Street, London W1F 9SU (☎ 020 7439 0000, e-mail virginia@riflemaker.org, website www.riflemaker.org)

DANAHER, Timothy (Tim); s of Anthony Danaher, and Madeleine, *née* Hewett; *b* 17 November 1975, London; *Educ* Alleyns Sch, Univ of York (BA); *Career* various roles Property Week Magazine 1999–2005, ed Retail Week 2005–; regular media commentator on retail issues, freelance writer for various nat newspapers; *Style*— Tim Danaher, Esq

DANCE, Charles Walter; OBE (2006); s of Walter Dance (d 1950), of Birmingham, and Eleanor, *née* Perks (d 1985); *b* 10 October 1946; *Educ* Widey Tech Sch Plymouth, Plymouth Sch of Art, Leicester Coll of Art and Design; *m* 18 July 1970, Joanna Elizabeth Nicola Daryl, da of Francis Harold Haythorn, of Plymstock, Devon; 1 s (Oliver b 1974), 1 da (Rebecca b 1980); *Career* actor 1970–; *Theatre* seasons at repertory theatres: Leeds, Oxford, Windsor, Swindon, Chichester, Greenwich; joined Royal Shakespeare Company 1975; leading roles in RSC prodns incl: Richard III, As You Like It, Henry IV Parts 1 and 2, Henry V, Henry VI Part 2, The Changeling, Perkin Warbeck, The Jail Diary of Albie Sachs, title roles in Henry V and Coriolanus, The Three Sisters, Good, Long Day's Journey into Night; Shadowlands (Wyndham's Theatre London) 2007 (Best Actor Critics' Circle Theatre Awards 2008); *Television* incl: The Fatal Spring, Rainy Day Women, The Secret Servant, The Jewel in the Crown (BAFTA Best Actor nomination), First Born, Out on a Limb, The Macguffin, Saigon – The Last Day, Rebecca, In the Presence of Mine Enemies, Randall & Hopkirk Deceased, Murder Rooms, Nicholas Nickleby, Foyle's War, Trial and Retribution, To the Ends of the Earth, Fingersmith, Last Rights, Bleak House (Best Actor Award Broadcasting Press Guild, Best Actor nomination Int Emmys), Fallen Angel, Consenting Adults, Dickens Secret Life, Trinity, Merlin, Jam & Jerusalem, Game of Thrones, This September, Neverland, Secret State, Strikeback 3, Would I Lie To You?, Floyd, Deadline Gallipoli, Childhood's End, And Then There Were None, The Great Fire; *Radio* Frederick Delius in The Paradise Garden Attained, Sydney Carton in A Tale of Two Cities, A Man For All Seasons; *Film* For Your Eyes Only, Plenty, The Golden Child, Good Morning Babylon, Hidden City, White Mischief, Pascali's Island, China Moon, Alien 3, La Valle de Pietra, Century, Last Action Hero, Kabloonak (Best Actor Paris Film festival 1996), Exquisite Tenderness, Shortcut to Paradise, Undertow, Michael Collins, Space Truckers, The Blood Oranges, Us Begins With You, What Rats Won't Do, Hilary and Jackie, Dark Blue World, Jurij, Gosford Park, Black and White, Ali G Inda House, Swimming Pool, Ladies in Lavender (writer and dir), Starter for Ten, The Perfect Disagreement, Your Highness, There Be Dragons, Ironclad, Winds of Change, Underworld 4, The Admiral, The Woman in Gold, Dracula Untold, Underworld

5, Ghostbusters, Me Before You, Fanny Lye Delivered, That Good Night; *Recreations* cycling, swimming; *Clubs* Chelsea Arts, Groucho, Union; *Style—* C W Dance, Esq, OBE; ✉ c/o Tavistock Wood, 45 Conduit Street, London W1S 2YN (☎ 020 7494 4767); c/o Susan Smith, 121 North San Vicente Boulevard, CA 90211 USA

DANCER, Sir Eric; KCVO (2013), CBE (1991), JP; s of Joseph and Mabel Dancer; *b* 17 April 1940; *Educ* King Edward VII Sch Sheffield, Sheffield Poly, Inst of Mgmnt, Chartered Inst of Purchasing and Supply; *m* Aug 1980, Carole Anne Moxon; *Career* surveying asst Fowler Standford & McNab Sheffield 1956–59, asst buyer Moorwood Vulcan Ltd 1959–63, buyer Balfour-Darwins Ltd 1963–67, asst purchasing offr Brightside Foundry & Engineering Co Ltd 1965–1967, chief buyer Metro Cammell Ltd Birmingham 1967–68, supplies mangr Jensen Motors Ltd 1969–72, dir Anglo Nordic Holdings plc London 1972–1980, tstee Dartington Hall Tst 1984–87, chm English Country Crystal 1983–87, md Dartington Hall Corp 1980–87, md Dartington Crystal Ltd 1987–2001; fndr chm: Devon and Cornwall TEC 1989–93, G10; chm Rural Devpt Cmmn Devon 1981–86; chm Magistracy Ctee; memb Bd: Prince's Youth Business Tst 1989–92, SW Regnl Devpt Bd 1984–91; TEC Nat Cncl memb SW Regnl Cncl CBI; memb Wedgwood plc Gp Mgmnt Ctee; memb Nat Cncl (CBI); tstee: Exeter Cathedral Music Fndn Tst, Exeter Cathedral Preservation Tst; govr Univ of Plymouth 1992–96; contrib Open Univ course material on effective mgmnt; HM Lord-Lt Devon 1998–2015; Hon Capt Royal Naval Reserve 2001; Freeman City of London 1992, Liveryman Worshipful Co of Glass Sellers 1992; Hon DUniv Sheffield Hallam 1999, Hon LLD Univ of Exeter 2010, Hon DBus Univ of Plymouth 2010; FRSA; KStJ 1998; *Recreations* sailing, reading, music; *Clubs* Royal Dart Yacht, Army and Navy; *Style—* Sir Eric Dancer, KCVO, CBE, JP; ✉ Lieutenancy Office, County Hall, Exeter EX2 4QD

DANCEY, His Hon Judge Martin Alan Gordon; *m* 5 June 1982, Hilary, *née* Davies; 2 da (Katie, Emily); *Career* admitted slr 1981; dep dist judge 1993, dist judge 1999, circuit judge (Western Circuit) 2015–; *Recreations* music, sailing; *Clubs* Christchurch Sailing; *Style—* His Hon Judge Dancey

DANCY, Hugh; *m* Claire Danes, the actress; 1 s (Cyrus Michael Christopher); *Career* actor; *Theatre* Billy and the Crab Lady (Soho Theatre), To the Green Fields Beyond (Donmar Warehouse); *Television* Kavanagh QC, Dangerfield, Trial & Retribution, Cold Feet, Madame Bovary, Relic Hunter, Daniel Deronda, Elizabeth I, The Big C, Hannibal; *Film* David Copperfield, Young Blades, The Sleeping Dictionary, Black Hawk Down, Tempo, Ella Enchanted, King Arthur, Shooting Dogs, Basic Instinct 2, Blood and Chocolate, Savage Grace, Evening, The Jane Austin Book Club, Adam, Confessions of a Shopaholic, Coach, Martha Marcy May Marlene, Hysteria; *Style—* Hugh Dancy, Esq; ✉ c/o Dallas Smith, United Agents Ltd, 12–26 Lexington Street, London W1F 0LE (☎ 020 3214 0800, fax 020 3214 080, website www.unitedagents.co.uk)

DANCZUK, Simon Christopher; MP; *b* 24 October 1966, Lancs; *Educ* Univ of Lancaster; *Career* co-fndr and dir Vision Twentyone; MP (Lab) Rochdale 2010–; *Style—* Simon Danczuk, Esq, MP; ✉ House of Commons, London SW1A 0AA

DAND, Dr Ian William; s of William Slight Dand (d 1988), and Mary Audrey Beryl, *née* Hepworth (d 1996); *b* 14 February 1941; *Educ* Bishop Vesey's GS Sutton Coldfield, Univ of Glasgow (BSc, PhD); *m* 7 April 1971 (m dis 2004), Rosemary Patterson (d 2009), da of late Lt Cdr Arthur Winter; 2 s (James Alexander b 1973, John Ross Patterson b 1977); *Career* tech apprentice John I Thornycroft & Co 1959–64; Ship Div National Physical Laboratory: sr scientific offr 1970–76, princ scientific offr 1976–81, sr princ scientific offr (IM) 1981; sr scientist NMI Ltd 1982–85, mangr Vessel Hydrodynamics Gp British Maritime Technology Ltd 1985–94, dir BMT SeaTech Ltd 1994–2007; vice-pres RNLI 2011– (memb Technical Ctee 1997–2011, memb Cncl 2003–11); Silver Medal RINA 1976 and 1982, Bronze Medal RINA 1999, Medal of Distinction RINA 2009 and 2012; FRINA 1993, FREng 1994, FRSA 1996, memb Nautical Inst 2010 (companion 1976); *Recreations* woodwork, model-making, sketching, DIY, playing the guitar, photography; *Style—* Dr Ian Dand, FREng; ✉ BMT Isis Ltd, Fareham, Hampshire PO15 5SU (☎ 01489 553100, fax 01489 553101)

DANDO, Stephen; *b* 13 February 1962, Scotland; *Educ* Univ of Strathclyde, Univ of Edinburgh (MBA); *Career* grad trainee Austin Rover 1984–85; various positions: Ferranti Int 1985–89, United Distillers 1989–97, Diageo 1997–99, UDV Europe 1999–2000; global HR dir Guinness Ltd 2000–01; BBC: dir HR and internal cmmns 2001–04, dir BBC People 2004–06, memb Exec Bd, dir BBC Pension Tst; gp HR dir Reuters plc 2006–08, exec vice-pres and chief HR offr Thomson Reuters 2008–12, operating ptnr Bain Capital 2013–; CCIPD, FRSA; *Style—* Stephen Dando, Esq

DANDRIDGE, Nicola; CBE (2015); *Career* chief exec: Equality Challenge Unit 2006–09, Univs UK 2009–; *Style—* Ms Nicola Dandridge, CBE; ✉ Universities UK, Woburn House, 20 Tavistock Square, London WC1H 9HQ

DANDY, David James; s of James Dandy (d 2000), and Margaret, *née* Coe (d 1984); *b* 30 May 1940, Southport, Lancs; *Educ* Forest Sch, Emmanuel Coll Cambridge, London Hosp Med Coll (MD, MA, MChir); *m* 17 Sept 1966, (Stephanie) Jane, da of Harold Vaughan Essex (d 1985), of Wellington, Somerset; 1 s (James b 1971), 1 da (Emma b 1973); *Career* sr fell Toronto Gen Hosp Canada 1972–73, conslt orthopaedic surgn Addenbrooke's Hosp Cambridge and Newmarket Gen Hosp 1975–2002, hon conslt Addenbrooke's Hosp Cambridge 2002–07; civilian advsr in knee surgery RN and RAF 1980–2006; Br Orthopaedic Assoc: fell 1975, Robert Jones prize 1991, Naughton Dunn meml lecture 1991, memb Cncl 1992–94, pres 1998–99; RCS: James Berry prize 1985, Hunterian prof 1994, memb Cncl 1994–2006, chm External Affairs Bd 1998–2002, hon treas 2002–06, vice-pres 2005–06, Cheselden Medal 2009; pres: Int Arthroscopy Assoc 1989–91, Br Orthopaedic Sports Trauma Assoc 1993–95, Br Assoc of Surgery of the Knee 1996–98, Combined Servs Orthopaedic Soc 2001–04; chm Granta Decorative and Fine Arts Soc 2007–11, tstee Gretton Court Ltd (formerly Barton Housing Assoc) 2009–; Freeman: City of London, Worshipful Soc of Apothecaries 1987; hon fell Br Orthopaedic Assoc 2011; FRCS; *Books* Arthroscopy of the Knee (1973), Arthroscopic Surgery of the Knee (1981), Arthroscopy of the Knee – A Diagnostic Atlas (1984), Essentials of Orthopaedics and Trauma (1989); *Recreations* gardening, writing; *Clubs* East India, RSM; *Style—* Mr David Dandy; ✉ Steeple View, Kings Mill Lane, Great Shelford, Cambridge CB22 5EN (☎ and fax 01223 840956)

DANDY, Gillian Margaret (Gill); da of George Thomas Dandy (d 2002), and Marjorie Walker Dandy (d 2014), of Heddington, Wilts; *b* 17 August 1957; *Educ* Ancaster House Sch Bexhill-on-Sea, Birmingham Coll of Food and Domestic Arts; *Career* Harrison Cowley Public Relations Ltd Birmingham 1980–83, assoc dir Leslie Bishop Company Ltd London 1983–90, bd dir Shandwick Communications Ltd London 1990–96, dir of devpt and PR London Bible Coll 1996–2002, communications dir Evangelical Alliance 2002–04, dir Vision Communications 2004–; sr conslt Centre for Strategy and Communications 2004–; non-exec dir Shared Interest Society Ltd 2004–12, tstee Shared Interest Fndn 2004–12, tstee Iprovision 2006–; FCIPR, FRSA; *Recreations* travel, skiing, theatre, opera, tennis, walking, active memb of St Barnabas Church Kensington; *Style—* Miss Gill Dandy; ✉ 56 Southerton Road, Hammersmith, London W6 0PH (☎ 020 8748 0809, e-mail gill.dandy@btinternet.com)

DANDY, Katherine; *b* 9 August 1960, Wigan, Gtr Manchester; *Educ* Wigan Girls HS, Univ of Sheffield; *Career* slr specialising in pensions litigation; slr Nabarro Nathanson 1993–96, head of dispute resolution Sackers LLP 1999–; lectures on pension law; memb: Assoc of Pension Lawyers, Law Soc; *Recreations* skiing, trekking, cooking, Wigan Athletic; *Style—* Ms Katherine Dandy; ✉ Sacker & Partners LLP, 29 Ludgate Hill, London EC4M 7NX (☎ 020 7615 9507, e-mail katherine.dandy@sackers.com)

DANG, Mohinder Singh; s of Mohan Singh, of Amritsar, India, and Shakuntal, *née* Kaur; *b* 2 April 1946; *Educ* Med Coll Amritsar (MB BS), Punjab Univ (MS Ophth), Univ of Dublin (DO), Univ of London (DO); *m* 5 Dec 1975, Swaran Sachdev, da of Aya Ram Sachdev (d 1989); 2 da (Neetika b 24 Jan 1977, Tarana b 11 May 1982); *Career* SHO: Charing Cross Hosp London 1973, Canterbury Hosp 1973–74; registrar in ophthalmology: Birkenhead Hosp 1974–78, Bournemouth Hosp 1978–80; sr registrar in ophthalmology Manchester Royal Eye Hosp 1980–83; conslt in ophthalmology: Darlington Meml NHS Tst 1983– (former memb Tst Mgmnt Bd, former chm Med Exec Ctee, chm Med Staff Ctee), Friarage NHS Tst Northallerton, SW Durham NHS Tst 1983–; currently conslt opthalmic surgn BMI Healthcare; examiner Royal Coll Ophthalmology; memb various working gps and ctees Darlington HA, memb UK, Euro and Int Intraocular Implant Socs; author of many pubns in int scientific jls and multiple presentations in nat and int academic conventions; Int Excellence Award NRI Inst UK 1992; memb Exec: Sikh Community Gp Darlington, Overseas Doctors Assoc UK, Indian Doctors of Cleveland; hon res fell Indian Cncl of Medical Res 1970–72; FRCSEd 1979, FCOphth 1988, FRCOphth 1993; *Recreations* walking, reading, travel, golf; *Clubs* Blackwell Golf Darlington; *Style—* Mohinder Singh Dang, Esq; ✉ Mussoorie House, 8 Compton Grove, Darlington, Durham DL3 9AZ (☎ 01325 486371, e-mail dangmohinder@gmail.com); BMI Woodlands Hospital, Morton Park, Darlington DL1 4PL

DANGAN, Viscount; Garret Graham Wellesley; s (by 1 m) and h of 7 Earl Cowley, *qv*; *b* 30 March 1965; *m* 30 June 1990, Claire L, da of Peter Brighton, of King's Lynn, Norfolk; 2 s (Hon Henry Arthur Peter b 3 Dec 1991, Hon Bertram Garret Graham b 12 April 1999), 1 da (Hon Natasha Rose b 28 June 1994); *Career* banker; traded options: Hoare Govett Ltd, money markets Banque Indosuez, ING (derivatives) Ltd, subsequently with Geldermann Ltd; chief exec IFX Ltd 1995–, gp chief exec IFX Group plc (formerly Zetters plc) 2000–03, chm ODL Gp Ltd 2004–; *Clubs* Brooks's; *Style—* Viscount Dangan; ✉ Ashbourne Manor, High Street, Widford, Hertfordshire SG12 8SZ

DANIEL, Barbara Mary; *née* Boote; da of Arthur Boote (d 1989), of Colehill, Dorset, and Joan, *née* West (d 1980); *b* 8 June 1954; *Educ* Bromley GS; *m* 19 Dec 2003, Tim Daniel; *Career* sec and editorial asst: Coronet Books 1973–77, Magnum Books 1977–80; Macdonald Sphere: editorial mangr 1981–86, editorial dir 1986–89, publishing dir 1989–92; editorial dir Little Brown and Co (UK)/Time Warner Books 1992–2005, gp administration dir Little, Brown Book Gp 2006–14, ret; *Style—* Barbara Daniel

DANIEL, Sir John Sagar; kt (1994); s of John Edward Daniel, and Winifred Sagar; *b* 31 May 1942, Banstead, Surrey; *Educ* Christ's Hosp, St Edmund Hall Oxford (open scholar, MA), Univ of Paris (NATO scholar, Joliot-Curie scholar, DSc), Thorneloe Coll (ATh), Concordia Univ (MA); *m* 1966, Kristin Anne Swanson (d 2011); 1 s, 2 da; *Career* assoc prof Dept of Metallurgical Engrg Univ of Montreal 1971–73 (asst prof 1969–71), dir of studies Télé-Université Univ of Quebec 1974–77 (co-ordinator 1973–74), vice-pres Learning Servs Athabasca Univ Alberta 1978–80, vice-rector academic affrs Concordia Univ Montreal 1980–84, pres Laurentian Univ Ontario 1984–90, vice-chllr The Open Univ 1990–2001, pres The US Open Univ 1998–2001; asst dir-gen for educn UNESCO 2001–04, pres Commonwealth of Learning Vancouver 2004–12, chair Int Bd United World Colleges 2013–, educn master Beijing DeTao Masters Acad China 2011–; pres: Canadian Soc for the Study of HE 1982–83 (vice-pres and prog chm 1981–82), Int Cncl for Distance Educn 1982–85 (prog chm 12th World Conf Vancouver 1978–82), Canadian Assoc for Distance Educn 1988–89; memb Editorial Bd: Distance Education 1980–90, Canadian Jl of Higher Education 1980–90, Jl of Distance Education 1988–90, Br Jl of Educational Technology 1988–90; numerous opening and keynote addresses at int conferences; vice-pres Organizing Ctee World Jr Athletics Championships Sudbury 1986–88, dir Milton Keynes and N Bucks Trg and Enterprise Cncl 1990–95; tstee Carnegie Fndn for the Advancement of Teaching 1993–2001; memb Cncl: Fndn International Baccalaureate 1992–99, Univ of Buckingham 1994–2001, Coll of St Mark and St John 1994–96, Central Sch of Speech and Drama 1994–96, Univ for Indust 1998–2001; memb: Nat Defence Coll Canada 1989–90, HE Quality Cncl 1992–94, Advsy Cncl Royal Naval Engrg Coll 1993–96, Defence Trg Review 2000–01, Conseil d'Administration Centre National d'Education à Distance 1994–97, Br North American Ctee 1995–2001 and 2006–10, Canadian Cncl on Learning 2005–, Steering Ctee Global Initiative for Quality Assurance Capacity 2008–; assoc cmmr Nat Cmmn on Educn 1992–93; reader C of E: Dio of St Albans 1991–2001, Dio in Europe 2003–05; hon chm Royal Overseas League Vancouver Branch; hon life memb: Canadian Assoc for Distance Educn 1990, Int Cncl for Distance Educn 1988; Distinguished Young Memb Award American Soc for Metals 1973, Frank Oppenheimer Award American Soc for Engrg Educn Annual Conf NY 1974, Cwlth of Learning Award of Excellence 1995, Morris D Keeton Award Cncl for Adult and Experiential Learning USA 1999, Symons Medal Assoc of Cwlth Univs 2008, Frank H Klassen Award Int Cncl on Educn for Teaching 2009; hon fell St Edmund Hall Oxford 1990, hon conslt prof TV Univ Shanghai 1998, hon fell Open Univ 2002; Hon DLitt: Deakin Univ Aust 1985, Univ of Lincolnshire and Humberside 1996, Athabasca Univ Alberta 1998, Sukhothai Thammathirat Open Univ Thailand 1999, Indira Gandhi Nat Open Univ India 2003, W Bengal Netaji Subhas Open Univ 2005, Thompson Rivers Univ BC 2005, Kota Open Univ India 2007, McGill Univ Canada 2007, Univ of Montreal Canada 2008, Univ of S Africa 2010, Empire State Coll SUNY 2011; Hon DSc: Royal Mil Coll St Jean Canada 1988, Open Univ of Sri Lanka 1994, Univ of Paris VI 2001, Univ of Educn Winneba Ghana 2006; Hon DEd: CNAA 1992, Open Univ Malaysia 2009; Hon LLD: Univ of Waterloo Canada 1993, Univ of Wales 2002, Laurentian Univ Canada 2006, Univ Canada West 2008, Univ of Ghana 2013; Hon DUniv: Universidade Aberta Portugal 1996, Anadolu Univ Turkey 1998, Univ du Québec Télé-université 1999, Univ of Derby 2000, New Bulgarian Univ 2000, Open Univ of Hong Kong 2001, Univ of Stirling 2003; Hon DHumLett: Thomas Edison State Coll New Jersey 1997, Richmond American International Univ London 1997; Hon DPhil Univ of S Africa 2010; Hon FCP 1997; Officier de l'Ordre des Palmes Académique (France) 1992 (Chevalier 1986), Queen's Jubilee Medal Canada 2003, Officer of the Order of Canada 2013; *Books* Mega-universities and Knowledge Media: Technology Strategies for Higher Education (1996), Mega-schools, Technology and Teachers: Achieving Education for All (2010); author of numerous articles in professional jls; *Recreations* walking, boating, reading; *Clubs* Royal Overseas League, Royal Cwlth Soc; *Style—* Sir John Daniel; ✉ 205–3133 Cambie Street, Vancouver, BC, V5Z 4N2, Canada (website www.sirjohn.ca)

DANIEL, Prof Nicholas; s of Jeremy Daniel (d 2006), and Margaret Louise (Billie) *née* Tomkins (d 1993); *b* 9 January 1962, Liss, Hants; *Educ* Salisbury Cathedral Sch, Purcell Sch, Royal Acad of Music; *m* 1, 1986 (m dis 2011), Joy, *née* Farrall; 2 s (Alastair William b 23 May 1994, Patrick Nicholas b 1 March 1996); m 2, Piotr Rudkowski; *Career* oboe soloist and conductor; prof Guildhall Sch 1985–97, prof Univ of Indiana USA 1997–99, Prince Consort prof Royal Coll of Music 1999–2002, artistic dir Osnabruck Festival Germany 2002–04, artistic dir Leicester Int Music Festival 2003–, co-fndr, princ oboe, artistic assoc Britten Sinfonia, fndr, oboist Haffner Wind Ensemble, oboist Britten Oboe Quartet; prof Guildhall Sch of Music and Drama 2014–; prof of Oboe Staatliche Hochschule für Musick Trossingen 2005–; duo with Julius Drake; many recordings, worldwide performances in festivals and with orchestras, hundreds of premieres over 30 years, regular performer at BBC Proms; major force in the commissioning of new works for oboe; winner BBC Young Musician of the Year 1980, Queen's Medal for Music 2012;

ARAM 1986, FGSM 1995, FRAM 1997; *Recreations* walking, cooking, wine, cinema, theatre, ballet, musical theatre; *Style—* Prof Nicholas Daniel; ✉ website www.nicholasdaniel.com, Twitter @ndanielmusic; c/o Sarah Bruce, Lomonaco Management

DANIEL, Paul Wilson; CBE (2000); s of Alfred Daniel, of Sutton Coldfield, Warks, and Margaret, *née* Poole; *b* 5 July 1958; *Educ* King Henry VIII Sch Coventry, King's Coll Cambridge, Guildhall Sch of Music and Drama; *m* 1, 1988 (m dis), Joan Rodgers, CBE, *qv*; 2 da (Eleanor Elizabeth b 4 Sept 1990, Rose Imogen b 14 May 1993); m 2, July 2008, Sarah Walley; *Career* conductor; music dir Opera Factory London 1987–90, music dir Opera North 1990–97, princ conductor English Northern Philharmonia (Opera North Orchestra) 1990–97, music dir ENO 1997–2005; studied with Sir Adrian Boult and Sir Edward Downes; conducted numerous major international orchs incl: London Symphony Orchestra, Philharmonia, London Philharmonic, Royal Philharmonic, BBC Symphony, London Sinfonietta, City of Birmingham Symphony Orchestra, Royal Liverpool Philharmonic, Scottish Chamber Orchestra, Hallé Orchestra, Royal Scottish Nat Orchestra, Bournemouth Symphony Orchestra, BBC Nat Orchestra of Wales, Orchestra of the Age of Enlightenment, Czech Philharmonic, National Orchestra of Belgium, Royal Flanders Philharmonic, Ensemble Intercontemporain, Ensemble Modern (Germany), Suisse Romande Orchestra, Orchestre de Paris, the Cleveland Orchestra, NY Philharmonic Orch, Gothenburg Symphony Orchestra, MDR Leipzig, Swedish Radio Symphony Orchestra; operas conducted with Opera North incl: Verdi's Jerusalem (Br stage première) and Attila, Dukas' Ariane et Barbe-Bleue, Tippett's King Priam, Boris Godunov (BBC Proms 1992), Don Carlos, Wozzeck, Schrecker's Der Ferne Klang, Britten's Gloriana, Janá?ek's Jenufa; operas conducted at ENO incl: The Flying Dutchman, Falstaff, From the House of the Dead, Manon, Otello, Boris Godunov, La Traviata, The Carmelites, Pelléas and Mélisande, Mark Anthony, Turnage's The Silver Tassie (world première), Nixon in China, War and Peace, Lulu, Peter Grimes, The Rape of Lucretia, A Midsummer Night's Dream, The Ring Cycle; other operas conducted incl: King Priam (for Nancy Opera, awarded French Critics' Prize), Mitridate (at Royal Opera House), Beatrice and Benedict and Khovanshchina (at La Monnaie Brussels), Erwartung and Duke Bluebeard's Castle (for Geneva Opera), La Clemenza di Tito (Aix Int Festival); has also conducted The Marriage of Figaro, Katya Kabanova and Hans-Jurgen von Bose's new opera Slaughterhouse 5 (with the Bayerische Staatsoper); recordings with various artists and orchestras incl: LSO and John Williams (Sony Classics), Scottish Chamber Orchestra and Evelyn Glennie (BMG), English Northern Philharmonia and Opera North companion to Harry Enfield's Guide to Opera (EMI), Boris Godunov (Chandos), Mendelssohn Elijah (Decca), Walton Series (Naxos), Bryn Terfel (Deutsche Grammophon), Elgar with LPO (BMG), Elgar 3rd Symphony (Naxos), Falstaff (Chandos), Belshazzar's Feast (Naxos); winner of Olivier Award for Outstanding Achievement in Opera; *Style—* Paul Daniel, CBE; ✉ c/o Ingpen & Williams Ltd, 7 St George's Court, 131 Putney Bridge Road, London SW15 2PA

DANIEL, Dr Reginald; s of Reginald Daniel (d 1988), and Alice, *née* Youell (d 1993); *b* 7 December 1939; *Educ* Palmers Sch Grays, Univ of London, Westminster Hosp Med Sch (MB BS, LRCP, DO, AKC, ECFMG); *m* Carol; 1 s (Lorne Piers b 23 July 1968), 1 da (Claire Suzanne b 2 Dec 1969); *Career* conslt ophthalmic surgn Guy's and St Thomas' Hosps, ophthalmic private practice Harley Street and London Bridge Hosp; lectr Univ of London; author of medical books and many ophthalmic papers in professional jls; memb: BMA, Euro Intraocular Implant Soc, American Academy of Ophthalmology, Contemporary Soc of Ophthalmologists in USA, Moorfield Hosp Surgns' Assoc; Freeman City of London, Liveryman Worshipful Co of Spectacle Makers; FRCS, FRCOpth; *Recreations* golf, tennis, skiing; *Clubs* City of London Livery; *Style—* Dr Reginald Daniel; ✉ 11 Stanmore Way, Loughton, Essex IG10 2SA (☎ 020 8281 4952, fax 020 8502 0728)

DANIELL, Gillian Mary; da of John Averell Daniell, of Lutterworth, Leicestershire, and Nancy Helen Law; *b* 23 February 1947, Mountsorrel, Leics; *Educ* The Sch of Sts Mary and Anne Abbots Bromley, Loughborough Coll of Art, Slade Sch of Fine Art (Dip Theatre Design), Goldsmiths Coll of Art (BA), RCA (MA); *m* 1972 (m dis 1987), Vaughan, s of Herman Grylls; 1 da (Sarah Hope (Mrs Pinny Grylls) b 22 June 1979); *Career* theatre designer, university lecturer and freelance practising artist; conslt John Csaky Assocs Museum and Exhibition Design 1996–98; memb: CNAA (examiner for fine art BA Hons) 1984–87, Soc of Br Theatre Designers 1989–; pt/t lectr variously at: Portsmouth Poly, Croydon Coll of Art, Homerton Coll Cambridge, International Agrarische Hoge Sch Larenstein Netherlands, The Chinese Univ of Hong Kong, Univ of Greenwich, Sch of Architecture and Construction (subject leader for Art and Design until 2011); visiting artist Millfields Community Sch Hackney 2015; co sec Invisible Films 2003–; contrib to a number of publications; FRSA 2002; *Exhibitions* incl: Young Contemporaries 1969, mixed show RCA 1970 and 1971, mixed show Trinity Coll Cambridge 1971, Art Spectrum Alexandra Palace London 1971, Past students of the Environmental Media Dept RCA 1972, mixed staff show Croydon Coll of Art 1973, Art Into Landscape exhbn Serpentine Gall 1974 (awarded second prize); Scaling Up Guild Hall Manchester 1986, From Wilson to Callaghan 1997, Whitstable Art Festival 2010, Bohemia Club St Leonards-on-Sea 2015; *Theatre* fndr Calliope Theatre Co Williamstown Mass; co-designer and dir: The Zoo Story (Royal Court) 1970, Fallen Woman 1985; designer credits incl: As Cuecas (The Bloomers 1975, German Inst Lisbon Portugal 1985), The Winter Dancers (Royal Court) 1977; freelance designer for Durham Theatre Co Darlington 1982–85; Liverpool Playhouse: Rat In The Skull 1987, Macbeth 1988, Second Lady 1988, Of Mice And Men (also UK tour) 1989; other prodns incl: Diary of A Somebody – The Orton Diaries (NT) 1987, Monopoly (The Old Red Lion) 1987, Two Acts Of Love (Prince of Wales Theatre) 1987, The Orton Diaries (The King's Head) 1987, Every Good Boy Deserves Favour (Queen Elizabeth Hall) 1987, A Slice of Saturday Night (The King's Head and The Arts Theatre) 1989; *Television* documentary prodr, formed own TV prodn co 1982; *Awards* Art into Landscape second prize (for the original concept and idea for the first urban farm, to be located in Kensington Gardens) 1974, nomination for Best Design in Charrington London Fringe Award (for Slice of Saturday Night) 1990; *Style—* Ms Gillian Daniell; ✉ 79 Mortimer Road, London N1 5AR (☎ 020 7254 4579, e-mail gillian@invisiblefilms.eclipse.co.uk)

DANIELLI, Simon Charles Jonathan; *b* 8 September 1979, Edinburgh; *Educ* Cheltenham Coll, Trinity Coll Oxford; *Career* rugby union player (winger); clubs: Bristol until 2001, Bath 2001–04, Border Reivers 2004–07, Ulster Rugby 2007–; Scotland: 24 caps, debut v Italy 2003, memb World Cup squad 2003 and 2007; *Style—* Mr Simon Danielli; ✉ c/o Ulster Rugby, Ravenhill Grounds, 85 Ravenhill Park, Belfast BT6 0DG

DANIELS, Ann; *b* 24 July 1964; *Children* 4 c (Joseph, Rachel, Lucy (triplets) b 23 March 1994, Sarah b 16 April 2003); *Career* key team memb in first all-women expedition to North Pole McVites Penguin North Pole Relay 1997, memb first all-Br women's team to ski to South Pole 2000, memb M&G Investments North Pole Expedition 2002 (becoming first all-women's team to ski to both poles); now motivational speaker and presenter and polar guide for the Arctic and Antarctic regions; memb James Caird Soc; involved with: Special Olympics, Expeditions Charity; judge and hon speaker for Avon in praise of women's awards; entry in: Guiness Book of Records, National Book of Statistics; Pride of Britain Award 2000; Freedom of Yeovil Town; Hon LLD; *Recreations* climbing, mountaineering, canoeing, outdoor activities; *Style—* Mrs Ann Daniels; ✉ SFX Entertainment, 35–36 Grosvenor Street, London W1X 9FG (☎ 020 7529 4300, fax 020 7529 4301, mobile 0797 1821122, e-mail rhesus@ukonline.co.uk)

DANIELS, Jack; s of David John Daniels (d 2002), of Swanage, Dorset, and Margaret Ann, *née* Owen; *b* 8 June 1963; *Educ* Lode Heath Comp Sch Solihull, Warblington Comp Sch Havant, Portsmouth Coll of Art (OND), Bournemouth Coll of Art (HND); *m* 1, (m dis 1999), Teresa Ann, da of Bernard Appleby; 2 s (Jake b 11 Jan 1989, Jaxon b 29 July 1991); m 2, 6 March 2000, Karla-Joy, da of Dr Neil Cherry, ONZM (d 2003); 1 da (Poppy-Joy Tokohana b 5 May 2005); *Career* former apprentice electrical engr; photographer (specialising in animal portraits) 1988–; editorial cmmns for: Sunday Times, Daily Telegraph, The Observer, Daily Mail, The Field, GQ, The New Scientist, Country Life, Elle, The Express Magazine, The Sunday Correspondent, Evening Standard, Esquire, BBC Wildlife, Loaded, The Guardian, Time Magazine etc; advtg cmmns for clients incl: Renault Kangoo, BSkyB, Ford Focus, Arthurs, MAFF Pet Passports, Cadbury's, Farleys, Citroën Austria, Birmingham Mint, Spillers Pet Foods, Winalot packaging and POS, Kitekat packaging, Bonio packaging, British Coal, Twickenham Rugby Club, Nationwide Building Society, National Westminster Bank, TSB/Our Price, Virgin Net, Jacobs Bakeries, Budget Car Hire, Nickelodeon TV, Pentax, NCDL, RSPCA, Prudential, IBM, Orange, London Zoo, British Telecom, Coca-Cola, Barclays Bank, The Prince's Youth Business Tst, British Gas, Nissan, Vicks, Logitech, British Airways/Airmiles, Chesterfield-Bieffe Helmets Milan, Conservative Pty Lion Campaign, Whiskas 1998 and 1999 Calendar, Yellow Pages, Bonjela; Anya Hindmarch handbag vending at Harrods/Liberty etc; other cmmns for book covers and record sleeves; work published throughout Europe, USA and Far East; contrib to Getty Images; lectr AoP @ Holborn Studios; tutor: Salisbury Coll, Bournemouth Arts Inst 2000–; exhibited at: AoP Gallery 'Urban Animals' 2000, Special Photographers Gallery, Hamilton's, Barbican, Royal Photographic and Smith's Galleries; memb Assoc of Photographers 1988; *Awards* Zig-Zag/Pentax Photographer of the Year 1988, Gold Medal Royal Photographic Soc 133rd Print Awards 1989, Merit Assoc of Photographers 11th Awards 1993; *Books* The Square and Compass (2007); *Recreations* sea fishing, target shooting, computing, frequenting The Square & Compass; *Clubs* Tennessee Squire, Victoria, Swanage Gun, Glastonbury '95 Vets, Square & Compass Hat (Worth Matravers, Dorset); *Style—* Jack Daniels, Esq; ✉ website www.jackdaniels.me.uk

DANIELS, Susan Tracy; OBE (2006); da of Sidney Daniels (d 2006), and Zena, *née* Deyong (d 1987); *b* 18 February 1959, London; *Educ* Keele Univ (BA), City Lit Adult Training Unit, Garnett Coll (Cert HE), Hatfield Poly (Cert for Teachers of Hearing Impaired Children); *Partner* Christopher; 2 da (Zoe, Nysa); *Career* lectr ILEA City Lit Centre for the Deaf 1984–88; RNID: HE devpt offr 1988–89, head of educn, employment and training 1989–91, head of policy, research and devpt 1991–92; chief exec National Deaf Children's Soc 1992–; cmmr Disability Rights; chair: UK Cncl of Deafness, Groundbreakers; memb ACEVO; Young Jewish Care Award 1992, Coverdale Training Bursary 1993; *Publications* Deaf with Honours: A Guide (1990), Cochlear Implants – Deaf People's Views (1993); *Style—* Ms Susan Daniels, OBE; ✉ The National Deaf Children's Society, Ground Floor South, Castle House, 37–45 Paul Street, London EC2A 4LS (☎ 020 7490 8656, fax 020 7251 5020, e-mail ndcs@ndcs.org.uk)

DANN, Trevor John; *b* 6 November 1951; *Educ* Nottingham HS, Univ of Cambridge (MA); *m* 5 Feb 1991, Maureen Patricia, *née* Gunn; 1 da (Celia b 22 Nov 1992), 1 s (Henry b 25 June 1994); *Career* writer, broadcaster and prodr; reporter and prodr Radio Nottingham 1974–79, prodr BBC Radio 1 1979–83, BBC TV progs incl Live Aid and Whistle Test 1983–88; freelance TV prodr 1988–91, managing ed BBC Greater London Radio 1991–93 (prog organiser 1988–91), md Confederate Broadcasting 1993–96, head of prodn BBC Radio 1 1995–96, head BBC Music Entertainment 1996–2000, md pop music Emap 2000–02, fndr ind prodn co 2002–, presenter breakfast show BBC Radio Cambridgeshire 2002–04; currently: creative dir TDC Ltd, prof of radio Univ of Lincoln, chair London Voiceover, hon prof of journalism Nottingham Trent Univ, visting lectr Univ of Salford, dir Cambridge 105 community radio station, sec Radio Independents Gp, contrib Newsweek; sometime contrib: The Times, Sunday Telegraph, The Guardian, The Independent, Evening Standard, Q, Music Week, Mojo; fell The Radio Acad, FRSA; *Publications* Darker Than The Deepest Sea (2006); *Clubs* Notts County Supporters; *Style—* Trevor Dann, Esq; ☎ 07831 505564, e-mail trevor@trevordann.com, website www.trevordann.com

DANNATT, Baron (Life Peer UK 2011), of Keswick in the County of Norfolk; Gen Sir (Francis) Richard Dannatt; GCB (2009, KCB 2004), CBE (1996), MC (1973), DL (Gtr London 2010 and Nofolk 2012); s of Anthony Richard Dannatt, and Mary Juliet, *née* Chilvers; *b* 23 December 1950; *Educ* Jr Sch Felsted, St Lawrence Coll, RMA Sandhurst, Univ of Durham (BA, pres Durham Union Soc); *m* 19 March 1977, Philippa Margaret, da of Archibald James Gurney; 3 s (Thomas Richard James b 25 Oct 1978, Edward Robert Samuel b 12 Jan 1981, Oliver William Jack 10 May 1984) 1 da (Richenda Juliet Rose b 5 Oct 1988); *Career* CO 1 Bn Green Howards 1989–91, Col Higher Cmd and Staff Course 1992–94, Col Green Howards 1994–2003, Cdr 4 Armd Bde 1994–96, dir Def Prog Staff (MOD) 1996–99, Cdr 3 UK Div 1999–2000, Dep Col Adj Gen's Corps (Provost) 1999–2005, Dep Cdr (ops) Stabilisation Force Bosnia 2000–01, Col Cmdt The King's Div 2001–05, ACGS 2001–02, Cdr Allied Rapid Reaction Corps 2003–05, Col Cmdt AAC 2004–09, C-in-C Land Cmd 2005–06, Chief of the Gen Staff 2006–09; vice-pres Armed Forces Christian Union 1998–2012; pres: Soldiers' and Airmen's Scripture Readers Assoc 1999–, Royal Norfolk Agric Assoc 2008, YMCA Norfolk 2010–, Norfolk Churches Tst 2011–, Help for Heroes 2011–, Veterans Norfolk 2013–; chm Advsy Bd Durham Global Security Inst; fell Hatfield Coll 2008; Hon DCL: Univ of Durham 2009, Univ of Kent 2010; Hon DTech Anglian Ruskin Univ 2010, Hon DLaws Univ of Buckingham 2013; Queen's Commendation for Valuable Service 2000; *Books* Leading from the Front (2010); *Recreations* tennis, cricket, skiing, fishing, shooting, reading; *Clubs* Army and Navy, Cavalry and Guards; *Style—* The Lord Dannatt, GCB, CBE, MC, DL

DANTZIC, Roy Matthew; s of David A Dantzic (d 2002), and Renee, *née* Cohen (d 2006); *b* 4 July 1944; *Educ* Brighton Coll Sussex; *m* 3 June 1969, Diane, da of Abraham Clapham (d 1984), and Pearl, *née* Shapiro; 1 da (Emma Lucy b 23 Sept 1973), 1 s (Toby Alexander b 15 Feb 1975); *Career* Coopers & Lybrand 1962–69, Kleinwort Benson Ltd 1970–72, Drayton Corporation Ltd 1972–73, Samuel Montagu & Co Ltd 1974–80 (dir 1975), fin dir Britoil plc (formerly Br National Oil Corporation) 1980–84; dir: Pallas SA 1984–85, Wood Mackenzie & Co 1985–89, Stanhope Properties plc 1989–95, Merrill Lynch International Ltd 1995–96; md: Port Greenwich Ltd 1996–97, British Gas Properties 1997–2003 (non-exec dir 2003–04); non-exec chm: Premier Portfolio Gp plc 1985–92, ABC Cinemas 1998–2000, Development Securities plc 2003–07, ISG plc 2004–; non-exec dir: Moor Park (1958) Ltd 1980–90, Saxon Oil plc 1984–85, British Nuclear Fuels plc 1987–91, Total Oil Holdings Ltd 1995–96, Airplanes Ltd 1996–, AeroUSA Inc 1996–, Architectural Heritage Fund 2003– (dep chm 2014–), Blenheim Bishop Ltd 2004–07; tstee Portman Estate 2005–; govr Brighton Coll 1990–98, pt/t memb CEGB 1984–87; FICAS 1968; *Recreations* golf, theatre, sitting in the shade; *Clubs* MCC, Moor Park Golf; *Style—* Roy Dantzic, Esq

DANZIGER, Daniel Guggenheim (Danny); s of Edward Danziger (decd), of Palm Beach, Los Angeles, and Gigi, *née* Guggenheim; *b* 1 February 1953; *Educ* Harrow, Rollins Coll Florida (BA); *m* (m dis 1991), Victoria Constance Baillieu; *Career* author and journalist; formerly with family businesses, writer Sunday Times; columnist: The Independent 1990–95, Daily Mail 1996–97, Sunday Times Magazine 1999–; co-fndr Cover magazine 1997; nominated Columnist of the Year 1991, nominated Ed of the Year BSME 1999; *Books* The Happiness Book (1980), All in a Day's Work (1987), Eton Voices (1988), The Cathedral (1989), The Noble Tradition (1990), Lost Hearts (1992), The Orchestra (1995),

Year 1000 (1999), 1215: The Year of Magna Carta (2003), Hadrian: When Rome Ruled the World (2005), Museum: Behind the Scenes at the Metropolitan Museum of Art (2007), The Thingummy (2008), We Are Soldiers (2010), Submarine (2011), Goldfish Club (2012); *Recreations* swimming, golf, running; *Clubs* Wentworth, RAC, Epicurean Soc, Hillcrest CC; *Style—* Danny Danziger, Esq; ✉ c/o Georgina Capel (☎ 020 7734 2414, e-mail georgina@capelland.co.uk)

DANZIGER, Nicholas; s of Harry Lee Danziger, and Angela, *née* King; *b* 22 April 1958; *Educ* Switzerland, Chelsea Art Sch (BA, MA); *m* 24 May 2003, Anne Delforge; 2 da (May b 30 Aug 2003, Freya b 2 Nov 2005 (twin)), 1 s (Samuel b 2 Nov 2005 (twin)); 1 adopted s (Satar), 2 adopted da (Khadija, Farishta); *Career* painter, photographer, author and documentary filmmaker; visiting lectr various arts schs and univs 1980–; numerous solo exhbns USA, Japan, Europe, features in nat and int newspapers and magazines; works in public collections incl: The Royal Photographic Soc, Nat Museum of Photography Film and Television, Julia Margaret Cameron Tst, The Gallery of Modern Art Glasgow, Hillsborough Castle NI, Nat Media Museum Bradford, Primary Collection and Photographic Collection Nat Portrait Gallery, Théatre de la Photographie et de l'Image Nice; fndr orphanage Kabul Afghanistan; memb Cncl Winston Churchill Memorial Tst 1998–, memb Mission Enfance 2001–, vice-pres Action Innocence Monaco 2002–, patron PhotoVoice 2007; Hon DUniv Birmingham City Univ 2004; FRGS 1982, Hon FRPS 2007; Officier de l'Ordre du Mérite Culturel Monaco 2012; *Television* incl: War Lives & Videotape (BBC) 1991, Adventures in the Land of SPLAJ (Channel 4) 1993, Down & Out in Paris and London (Channel 4) 1993, French Letters (Channel 4) 1994, Postcards from the Edge (Channel 4) 1996, The Fight for Hearts and Minds (Channel 4), Orphans of War (Channel 4) 1998, The Establishment (Channel 4) 1999, Out of Kosovo (Channel 4) 1999, Mongolia (Discovery Channel), Afghanistan (Discovery Channel) 2000, Niger/Mali (Discovery Channel), Nomads of the Sahara (Discovery Channel) 2000, Aids The Global Killer (Channel 4) 2000, The Unquiet Peace (BBC) 2001, To the Roof of the World (NMO), Women Facing War (ICRC/Channel 4/BBC) 2002, Jacques Henri Lanfigue: The Boy Who Never Grew Up (BBC) 2004, Digital Picture of Britain (BBC) 2005; *Radio* Desert Island Discs (BBC Radio 4), Great Lives – Tintin (BBC Radio 4); *Awards* Winston Churchill Memorial Tst Fellowship 1982, winner Prix Italia (best tv documentary for War Lives & Videotape) 1992, fell in photography Nat Museum of Photography Film & Television 1994, Prix Italia 1992, Special Award The World Television Festival Japan 1993, Broadcast Award Best Single Documentary UK 1999, Journalist of the Year AMADE 1999, Ness Award RGS 2000, Photography of the Year Face Value geographical magazine 2001, Special Award Festival Nord-Sud Geneva 2002, Journalist of the Year Premio Russo Italy 2002, runner-up Best Short Documentary IFCT NY 2003, first prize Single Portrait Award World Press Photo 2004, Nikon Photo Essay of the Year Special Award 2004, Silver Award China Int Press Photo Contest on Peace and Development 2005, Neville Shulman Challenge Award 2010, Prix de la Commission Nationale pour l'UNESCO 2014; Officier de l'Ordre du Mérite Culturel Monaco 2012; *Books* Danziger's Travels (1987), Danziger's Adventures (1992), Danziger's Britain (1996), The British (2001), Femmes Face à la Guerre (2008), Missing Lives (2010), Mana (2010), Onze Femmes (2011), Above The Line: People and Places in the DPRK (2014), Back in the USSR (2014), Eleven Women Facing War (2015), Beneath the Carob Trees (2015); *Style—* Nicholas Danziger; ✉ website www.nickdanziger.com; c/o United Agents Limited, 12–26 Lexington Street, London W1F 0LE (☎ 020 3214 0800, fax 020 3214 0801, website www.unitedagents.co.uk); photography agent: c/o Neil Burgess, NB Pictures, 32 Clarence Mews, London E5 2HL (☎ 020 8985 8765, fax 020 8525 5530, e-mail neil@nbpictures.com)

DARBY, Adrian Marten George; OBE (1996); s of Col C G Darby, MC (d 1971), of Kemerton Court, Tewkesbury, Glos, and Monica, *née* Dunne (d 1958); *b* 25 September 1937, London; *Educ* Eton (Oppidan scholar), ChCh Oxford (MA); *m* 30 March 1964, Lady Meriel Kathleen, *née* Douglas-Home; 1 da (Catherine Monica b 1964), 1 s (Matthew George b 1967); *Career* lectr ChCh Oxford 1962–63, fell and tutor in economics Keble Coll Oxford 1963–85 (bursar 1968–82), owner Kemerton Estate 1971–; chm: RSPB 1986–93 (vice-pres 1996–), Kemerton Conservation Tst 1989–, Plantlife Int 1994–2002, UK Ctee World Conservation Union 1996–99, Planta Europa 1998–2004, Jt Nature Conservation Ctee (JNCC) 2004–07; Plantlife Award for Outstanding Contrib to Plant Conservation 2002; memb Wychavon DC 1998–; fell Eton Coll 1979–94, hon fell Keble Coll Oxford 1998; *Recreations* bibliophilia, botany; *Style—* Adrian Darby, Esq, OBE; ✉ Kemerton Court, Kemerton, Tewkesbury, Gloucestershire GL20 7HY (☎ 01386 725254)

DARBY, George; s of late Norman Darby, and Joanna Eleanor, *née* Willock; *b* 20 July 1942; *Educ* Bolton Sch, Univ of Nottingham (BA); *m* 1, Constance Smith; 2 da (Susanne b 28 Sept 1966, Amanda b 21 Nov 1975), 2 s (Antony b 9 Feb 1969, Christopher b 31 May 1978); m 2, Helene Feger; 1 da (Stephanie b 22 April 1996), 1 s (Benjamin b 29 Aug 1999); *Career* Westminster Press grad trainee Keighley News 1964–65; sub-ed: Northern Echo 1965–67, Daily Mirror 1967–68; The Sunday Times 1968–85: personal asst to Harold Evans (ed), editorial mangr, asst ed, assoc managing ed features, assoc magazine ed, chief asst to Frank Giles (ed), exec features ed, ed The Times Royal Wedding Magazine 1981 and The Times Bicentenary Magazine 1984; managing ed then ed Sunday Today 1985–86, dep ed Today 1987, exec ed The Observer Magazine 1987–88, conslt ed The Independent Magazine 1988, dep ed The Telegraph Magazine 1988–96, editorial projects dir The Telegraph Group Ltd 1996–; adjunct prof Univ of Missouri Sch of Journalism 1985–86, proprietor Jigsaw Productions design consultancy 1970–; *Books* various ghosted autobiographies; ed: The Sunday Times Bedside Book (1983 and 1984), Thalidomide Children and the Law (1977); contrib Pictures on a Page (by Harold Evans, 1978); *Clubs* Garrick; *Style—* George Darby, Esq

DARBYSHIRE, (John) Anthony Charles; s of (Leslie) Noel Darbyshire (d 1981), of S Normanton, Derbys, and Marjorie Darbyshire (d 1947); *b* 7 May 1939; *Educ* Uppingham, Keble Coll Oxford (MA), McGill Univ Montreal; *m* 1, 3 June 1967 (m dis 1982), (Faith) Lorraine, da of Noel William Hempsall, of Walesby, Notts; 1 s (Markham Noel Charles b 10 June 1968 d 2009); m 2, 28 Aug 1982, Sheena Nanette Mabel, da of Capt Thomas Wilson Taylor, of Barnby Moor, Retford, Notts; 1 s ((John) Hamish McGregor b 26 Sept 1984), 1 da (Keturah Mona Ellen b 8 Dec 1986); *Career* prodn mangr John Darbyshire & Co Ltd 1964–66, conslt Urwick Orr & Ptnrs 1966–67, chm AH Turner Gp Ltd 1967–90, md AD Securities Ltd 1981–, princ ADA Communications 1990–2001, md ADA Assessment Solutions Ltd 2001–12; memb: Mgmnt Ctee Br Vehicle Rental and Leasing Assoc 1980–90, Cncl CBI 1982–90 (Smaller Firms Cncl 1979–89, E Midlands Regnl Cncl 1980–90); chm Bassetlaw Industry Assoc 1986–89, memb Nat Exec Bd Young Enterprise 1989–90 (chm Notts area Bd 1986–90), chm N Notts Trg and Enterprise Cncl 1989–90, dir N Notts Bus Link 1995–96; tstee Comino Fndn 1993–2007, environment fell 2007–11, administrator 2012–; chm Pilgrim Fathers Origins Assoc 2006–15; FInstD 1976, FRSA 1988, CCMI (CIMgt 1989, MIMgt 1971, FIMgt 1983); *Publications* Demetrius Comino OBE – a life and legacy of achievement; *Recreations* investment mgmnt, improving the quality of life; *Style—* Anthony Darbyshire, Esq; ✉ Firs Farm House, Bilby, Retford, Nottinghamshire DN22 8JB (☎ 01777 711141, e-mail ad@improver.co.uk, websites www.cominofoundation.org.uk and www.pilgrimfathersorigins.org)

DARBYSHIRE, David Glen; s of Thomas Leslie Darbyshire (d 1979), and Alice, *née* Moss; *b* 20 May 1944; *Educ* Wigan GS, Liverpool Coll of Art, Univ of Newcastle upon Tyne (BA, BArch); *m* 7 July 1973 (m dis 1990), Jane Helen; 1 da (Kate); *Career* architect Ryder and Yates Ptnrs 1972–75, princ architect Washington Devpt Corp 1975–79, ptnr Jane and David Darbyshire 1979–87, princ Darbyshire Architects 1987–; Civic Tst Award for Dukes Cottages Backworth; Civic Tst Commendation for: Church St Cramlington, St John's Green Percy Main; winner of: St Oswald's Hospice Special Category Regnl Ltd Competition and Civic Tst Award, RIBA Nat Award Building of the Year 1988, The Times/RIBA Community Enterprise Scheme Commendation, Housing Design Award for Collingwood Ct Morpeth 1989; RIBA; *Recreations* music, mechanical engineering, fine art; *Clubs* Bristol Owners'; *Style—* David Darbyshire, Esq; ✉ Darbyshire Architects, Hawthorn Cottage, Hawthorn Road, Gosforth, Newcastle upon Tyne NE3 4DE (☎ 0191 284 2813)

DARBYSHIRE, Jane Helen; OBE (1994); da of Gordon Desmond Wroe (d 1994), of Brixham, Devon, and Patricia, *née* Keough; *b* 5 June 1948; *Educ* Dorking GS, Univ of Newcastle upon Tyne (BA, BArch); *m* 1, 7 July 1973 (m dis), David Glen Darbyshire, s of Thomas Darbyshire (d 1980), of Wigan, Lancs; 1 da (Kate b 1979); m 2, 25 July 1993, Michael Murray Walker; *Career* chartered architect in private practice; ptnr Jane and David Darbyshire 1979–87, princ Jane Darbyshire Associates 1987–94, dir Jane Darbyshire and David Kendall Ltd 1995–2000 (conslt 2000–); memb Cncl RIBA 1998–2001; exhibitor Women in Architecture (RIBA) 1983, winner St Oswalds Hospice Design Competition 1981, exhibitor DLI Museum Durham 1981; Civic Tst: award for restoration 1982, commendation for Cramlington Housing 1983, commendation for flat refurbishment Percy Main 1986, award for St Oswalds Hospice Gosforth Newcastle upon Tyne 1987; award for housing design Morpeth 1988, Nat RIBA award 1988, Building of the Year Award 1988, Nat Housing Design award 1989, 2 housing design awards 1991, RIBA award for St Cuthbert's Church Durham 1991, Civic Tst Award 1992 and 1993; features: Channel 4 Design Matters, BBC Townscape; Civic Tst assessor, RIBA Awards assessor 1984–90, memb Bd Tyne & Wear Urban Devpt Corp 1993–98, external examiner Univ of Newcastle upon Tyne 1992–2000, memb Bd Culture North East 2000–01; *Recreations* music, art, history of architecture, horses; *Style—* Ms Jane Darbyshire-Walker, OBE; ✉ Little Hallgarth, 18 Brundholme Gardens, Keswick, Cumbria CA12 4NZ; Jane Darbyshire and David Kendall Ltd, Millmount, Ponteland Road, Newcastle upon Tyne NE5 3AL

DARCEY, Mike; *Educ* Victoria Univ Wellington NZ, LSE (MSc); *m* Julie; 1 s (Jonathan), 1 da (Laura); *Career* chief operating offr BSkyB 2008–13, ceo News UK 2013–15; non-exec dir Press Assoc Gp Bd, chm News Media Assoc 2015–; non-exec dir and sr ind dir Home Retail Gp; *Style—* Mike Darcey, Esq

DARESBURY, 4 Baron (UK 1927), of Walton, Co Chester; Sir Peter Gilbert Greenall; 5 Bt (UK 1876), DL (Cheshire 1994); eldest s of 3 Baron Daresbury (d 1996), and his 1 w, Margaret Ada, *née* Crawford; *b* 18 July 1953; *Educ* Eton, Magdalene Coll Cambridge (MA), London Business Sch (Sloan fellowship); *m* 11 Sept 1982, Clare Alison, da of Christopher Nicholas Weatherby, MC, of Whaddon House, Whaddon, Bucks; 4 s (Hon Thomas Edward b 1984, Hon Oliver Christopher b 1986, Hon Toby Peter b 1988, Hon Jonathan James (Jake) b 1992); *Heir* s, Hon Thomas Greenall; *Career* chm: Aintree Racecourse Co Ltd 1988–2014, Nasstar plc 2005–, Sumatra Copper & Gold 2007–11, Mallett plc 2007–, Stellar Diamonds plc 2008–, Haydock Park Racecourse 2013–, Timico Technology Gp 2014–; High Sheriff Cheshire 1992; *Clubs* Jockey, MCC, Royal & Ancient Golf (St Andrews); *Style—* The Lord Daresbury, DL; ☎ 01948 860963, e-mail peter.daresbury@daresburyltd.co.uk

DARKE, Christopher; s of late Derek Herbert Darke, and Helen Navina, *née* Davies; *b* 5 August 1949; *m* 1, Marian; 1 s (Cerith James), 1 da (Joanna Siân); m 2, Lorraine Julie; 2 da (Ellen Cordelia, Anna Madeleine); *Career* engrg draughtsman 1970–77, TU offr AUEW-TASS 1977–82, nat offr AUEW-TASS/MSF 1982–92, gen sec Br Air Line Pilots' Assoc (BALPA) 1992–2002, currently dir of memb relations BMA; memb Competition Cmmn 1998–; *Recreations* flying, travel, reading, gardening; *Style—* Christopher Darke, Esq

DARLEY, Kevin Paul; s of Clifford Darley, of Wolverhampton, W Midlands, and Dorothy Thelma, *née* Newby; *b* 5 August 1960; *Educ* Colton Hills Comp Sch; *m* 22 Nov 1982, Debby, da of Donald Ford; 2 da (Lianne Kerry b 1983, Gemma Louise b 1988); *Career* flat race jockey; apprenticed to Reg Hollinshead 1976, rode out claim 1978, Champion apprentice 1978 (70 winners); first winner Dust-Up Haydock 1977, first group winner Borushka Gp 2 Park Hill Stakes 1983, Cock of the North (champion northern jockey) 1990, 1992, 1993, 1995, 1997, 1999, 2000, 2001, 2002 and 2003, champion jockey 2000; 158 winners Best Season 2001 (155 winners in 2000), first Gp 1 winner River North Aral Pokal Gp 1 1994, winner first Classic French Derby Chantilly (riding Celtic Swing) 1995, winner first British Classic St Leger (riding Bollin Eric) 2002, 2000 domestic winners as at Oct 2002 (2000th winner Heir to Be), winner 55 Gp races in Britain, winner 17 Gp 1 races; jt pres Jockeys' Assoc 2001–07, ceo Professional Jockeys Assoc 2009–12; int rep Qatar/Pearl Bloodstock Ltd 2013–; *Recreations* gardening, listening to music, DIY, shooting, fishing, skiing; *Style—* Kevin Darley, Esq; ✉ The Ord Granary, Gale Road, Alne, York YO61 1TH (☎ 01347 833015, e-mail kpdracing@hotmail.co.uk)

DARLING, His Hon Judge Ian Galen; s of William Darling, CBE, of South Shields, Tyne and Wear, and Ann, *née* Allen; *Educ* Winchester, KCL (LLB); *m* 27 July 2002, Emma Darling; 1 s (Alfie George b 3 May 2004), 1 da (Athena Sophia b 26 June 2006); *Career* called to the Bar 1985; recorder Crown Court 2003, circuit judge (South Eastern Circuit) 2009–; *Style—* His Hon Judge Darling; ✉ c/o The South Eastern Circuit, 289–293 High Holborn, London WC1V 7HZ

DARLING, 3 Baron (UK 1924); (Robert) Julian Henry Darling; s of 2 Baron Darling (d 2003), and Rosemary, *née* Dickson (d 1997); *b* 29 April 1944, Lyndhurst, Hants; *Educ* Wellington, RAC Cirencester; *m* 1 Oct 1970, Janet Rachel, *née* Mallinson; 2 s (Hon (Robert) James Cyprian b 6 March 1972, Hon (Henry) Thomas Unthank b 27 Aug 1978), 1 da (Hon (Rachel) Pollyanna Margaret (Hon Mrs Colin) b 4 March 1974); *Heir* s, Hon James Darling; *Career* chartered surveyor; ptnr Smith-Woolley 1971–89, sole princ Julian Darling 1990–; md Intwood Farms 1972–2010; chm Rural Enterprise Panel Nat Trust 2007–13; G R Judd Prize for Estate Economy 1965, Nuffield scholar 1984 (tstee 2010–); memb: Bath RFC first XV 1962–64, Hants first XV 1965; FRICS 1975; *Recreations* fishing, gardening; *Clubs* Norfolk; *Style—* The Lord Darling; ✉ Wood, Bishopsteignton, Nr Teignmouth, Devon TQ14 9TN (e-mail jdarling@paston.co.uk)

DARLING, Paul Antony; OBE (2015), QC (1999); *b* 15 March 1960; *Educ* Tonstall Sch Sunderland, Winchester, St Edmund Hall Oxford (BA, BCL); *Career* called to the Bar 1983, in private practice Keating Chambers 1985– (head of chambers 2010–15), bencher Middle Temple 2004; chm Football Licensing Authy 2009–11, chm Sports Grounds Safety Authy 2011–15, Govt appointed memb Horseracing Betting Levy Bd 2008–14; ed Construction Law Letter 1991–95, memb editorial team Keating on Building Contracts (edn 5, 6, 7 and 8); lectr on construction and engineering law; chm TECBAR 2003–07; tstee Free Representation Unit 2004–12; non-exec dir Horseracing Totalisator Bd 2006–08, chm Assoc of Br Bookmakers 2014–; *Recreations* horse racing, Newcastle United; *Clubs* Garrick; *Style—* Paul Darling, Esq, OBE, QC; ✉ Keating Chambers, 15 Essex Street, Outer Temple, London WC2R 3AA (☎ 020 7544 2600, fax 020 7544 2700, e-mail pdarling@keatingchambers.com)

DARLING OF ROULANISH, Baron (Life Peer UK 2015), of Roulanish, of Great Bernera in the County of Ross and Cromarty; Rt Hon Alistair Maclean Darling; PC (1997); s of Thomas Young Darling (d 1995), and Anna Darling; *b* 28 November 1953; *Educ* Loretto, Univ of Aberdeen (LLB); *m* 12 Nov 1986, Margaret McQueen Vaughan; 1 s (Calum), 1 da (Anna); *Career* slr 1978–82, admitted advocate 1984; memb Lothian Regnl Cncl 1982–

87; MP (Lab): Edinburgh Central 1987–2005, Edinburgh SW 2005–15; oppn front bench spokesman on: home affairs 1988–92, Treasy and economic affrs 1992–96; chief sec to the Treasy 1997–98 (shadow chief sec 1996–97), sec of state for Social Security 1998–2001, sec of state for Work and Pensions 2001–02, sec of state for Tport 2002–06, sec of state for Scotland 2003–06, sec of state for trade and industry 2006–07, chllr of the Exchequer 2007–10; memb Lab Pty's Economic Cmmn 1994–97, chair Better Together campaign 2012–14; govr Napier Coll Edinburgh 1985–87; *Style—* The Rt Hon the Lord Darling of Roulanish; ✉ House of Commons, London SW1A 0AA (☎ 020 7219 4584)

DARLINGTON, Gavin Leslie Brook; s of Arthur Brook Darlington, and Pamela Leslie, *née* Roberts; *b* 27 June 1949; *Educ* Rugby, Downing Coll Cambridge (LLB); *m* 11 April 1977, Pavla Ann, da of Karel Kucek; 1 s (Nicholas James b 7 Jan 1986), 1 da (Georgina Ruth b 19 Nov 1989); *Career* Freshfields: articled clerk 1972–74, asst slr 1974–80, ptnr 1980–2005, head of corp law London 1996–99 and Paris 1999–2002, global head of corp law 2003–05; memb Law Soc; *Recreations* gardening, golf, swimming, theatre, cinema; *Style—* Gavin Darlington, Esq

DARLINGTON, Jonathan Philip; s of John Oliver Darlington, of Kidderminster, and Bernice Constance Elizabeth, *née* Murphy; *b* 1 February 1956; *Educ* King's Sch Worcester, Univ of Durham, Royal Acad of Music; *m* 1, 8 Dec 1979 (m dis 1999), Katherine Theresa, da of Lt Col Anthony Wynter Lister; 2 s (William John Anthony b 8 Aug 1988, Edmund Harry b 2 April 1992); m 2, 1 June 2003, Clotilde Vayer; 1 s (Max Virgil Louis David b 19 April 2003); *Career* conductor and pianist; has conducted various major orchs and opera cos, particularly in France, given numerous concerts as pianist and chamber musician; dep music dir Paris Opera 1992–94, music dir Vancouver Opera and Duisburg Philharmonic 2002–; first res conductor Düsseldorf Opera 1997–, princ guest conductor Deutsche Oper am Rhein 1998–; conductor: The Marriage of Figaro (Paris Opera debut) 1991, A Midsummer Night's Dream (Paris Opera, also tour to Bolshoi) 1991, The Barber of Seville (Paris Opera), Swan Lake (Paris Opera, also video recording) 1992, The Nutcracker (Paris Opera) 1993, The Magic Flute (Paris Opera) 1994, Das Lied von der Erde (Paris Opera) 1994, Marriage of Figaro (Lausanne) 1995, Metropolitan Opera NY (with Paris Opera Ballet) 1996, Barber of Seville (Lausanne) 1997, Katya Kabanova (Deutsche Oper am Rhein) 1997, La Cerentola (Deutsche Oper) 1997, Tosca (Deutsche Oper), Der Freischutz (Deutsche Oper), Madame Butterfly (Deutsche Oper) 1997, Tamerlano (Deutsche Oper) 1997, L'Elisir d'Amore (Lausanne Opera) 1998, Matrimonio Segreto (Lausanne Opera) 1998, Le Finta Giardiniera (Deutsche Oper am Rhein) 1998, Jenufa (Deutsche Oper) 1998, Cosi fan Tutte (Lausanne Opera) 1998, The Rake's Progress (Lausanne Opera) 1999, Cosi fan Tutte (Naples Opera) 1999, Haydn's Orfeo (Lausanne Opera) 1999, Alcina (Deutsche Oper am Rhein) 1999, Romeo et Juliette (Bordeaux Opera) 2000, Freischutz (Lausanne Opera) 2000, Cenerentola (Lausanne Opera) 2001, The Marriage of Figaro (Vancouver Opera) 2001, Macbeth (Bordeaux Opera) 2002, Cunning Little Vixen (TCE Paris) 2002, La Boheme (Vancouver Opera) 2003, Eugene Onegin (ENO) 2005, Traviata (ENO) 2006, La Clemenzia di Tito (Opera Australia) 2006, La Grande Magia (world premiere, Dresden Semper Oper); Chevalier de l'Ordre des Arts et des Lettres (France) 1992; FRAM; *Recreations* mountaineering, skiing, wind-surfing, reading, chamber music; *Style—* Jonathan Darlington, Esq; ✉ c/o Vancouver Opera (website www.vancouveropera.ca)

DARLOW, Annabel; QC (2015); *Educ* Univ of Cambridge (MA); *Career* called to the Bar 1993; recorder of the Crown Ct 2009; *Style—* Ms Annabel Darlow, QC; ✉ 6 King's Bench Walk, 21 College Hill, London EC4R 2RP

DARNELL, Jennie; da of John Darnell, and Jean, *née* Martin; *Educ* Richmond-upon-Thames Coll, Royal Holloway and Bedford New Coll London (BA), Univ of Sheffield (MA); *Family* 1 da; *Career* freelance theatre and television dir; previously assoc dir: West Yorkshire Playhouse 1995–96, Hampstead Theatre 2001–04, Ambassadors Theatre Gp 2004–06; assoc dir Plymouth Theatre Royal 1996–; participant BB Dirs Acad 2006; winner Regnl Theatre Young Dirs Scheme Central TV 1993; patron Scene and Heard; *Recreations* travel, cinema; *Style—* Ms Jennie Darnell; ✉ c/o Clare Vidal-Hall Agency, 57 Carthew Road, London W6 0DU

DARNTON, Phillip L; OBE (2010); s of Neil Darnton (d 1993), and Kaye, *née* Gummer; *b* 7 January 1943, London; *Educ* Univ of Oxford (BA); *m* 1966 (m dis 1991, remarried 2007), Angela B, *née* Joyce; 1 da (Catharine b 3 Aug 1970), 1 s (Andrew b 4 Sept 1973); *Career* Unilever plc 1966–96, dir Reckitt and Colman plc 1996–2000, chief exec and chm Raleigh Industries 2000–03; chm Cycling England 2005–11, pres Bicycle Assoc of GB 2004–08 (currently exec dir); Freeman City of London, Freeman Merchant Taylors' Co 1969; *Style—* Phillip Darnton, Esq, OBE; ✉ 75 Limerston Street, London SW10 0BL (☎ 020 7352 4265, e-mail phillipdarnton@talktalk.net)

DARROCH, His Hon Alasdair; s of Ronald George Darroch (d 1957), and Diana Graburn Smith (d 1992); *b* 18 February 1947; *Educ* Harrow, Trinity Coll Cambridge; *m* 15 July 1972, Elizabeth Lesley, *née* Humphrey; 1 s (Gordon b 30 July 1974); *Career* admitted slr 1971; ptnr Mills & Reeve 1974 (articles 1969–71), recorder 1998, circuit judge (SE Circuit) 2000–12; past pres Norwich and Norfolk Law Soc; *Recreations* gardening, antique collecting, real ale, cider making; *Style—* His Hon Alasdair Darroch

DARROCH, (Nigel) Kim; KCMG (2008); s of Alastair Macphee Darroch, and Enid Thompson; step s of Monica, *née* Davis; *b* 30 April 1954, S Stanley, Co Durham; *Educ* Abingdon Sch, Univ of Durham (BSc); *m* 25 March 1978, Vanessa Claire, *née* Jackson; 1 s (Simon Alastair b 25 June 1983), 1 da (Georgina b 17 April 1986); *Career* joined FCO 1976, news dept and planning staff FCO 1976–80, third, second then first sec Tokyo 1980–84, FCO 1985, private sec to Min of State FCO 1986–88, first sec Rome 1989–92, dep head European Integration Dept FCO 1993–95, head E Adriatic Dept FCO 1995–97, cnsllr UK rep to EU 1997–98, head News Dept FCO 1998–2000, dir EU Cmd FCO 2000–02, DG Europe FCO 2003–04, EU advsr to PM and head European Secretariat Cabinet Office 2004–007, UK perm rep to the EU 2007–11, nat security advsr 2012–15; ambass to the USA 2016–; *Recreations* sailing, cinema, skiing, squash; *Style—* Sir Kim Darroch, KCMG

DART, Geoffrey Stanley; s of Wilfrid Stanley Dart, of Torquay, and Irene Jean, *née* Crews; *b* 2 October 1952; *Educ* Devonport HS, Torquay Boys' GS, St Peter's Coll Oxford (scholar, MA); *m* 17 Aug 1974, Rosemary Penelope, da of late Gordon Frederick Hinton; 1 s (Thomas James b 15 Nov 1978), 1 da (Rebecca Clare b 17 Oct 1980); *Career* civil servant; researcher Electricity Cncl 1974–77, various positions Dept of Energy 1977–84, cabinet sec Cabinet Office 1984–85, princ private sec to Sec of State for Energy 1985–87; Dept of Energy: asst sec Electricity Div 1987–89, asst sec Offshore Safety Div 1989–91, head Finance Branch 1991–92; DTI: asst sec Competitiveness Div 1992–94, dir De-Regulation Unit 1994, head Regnl Devpt Div 1995–96, dir Simplification Project 1996–97, dir Insurance Directorate 1997–98, dir Oil and Gas 1998–2002, head Strategy Unit 2003–05, dir Corporate Law and Governance 2005–09, dir Advanced Manufacturing Industries 2009–10, dir Office of Manpower Economics 2010–; non-exec dir Laing Engineering Ltd 1991–95, dir European Investment Bank 1994–96; tstee Public Concern at Work 2012–; FRSA; *Recreations* reading, listening to music, films, football, cricket; *Style—* Geoffrey Dart, Esq; ✉ Office of Manpower Economics, Victoria House, Southampton Row, London WC1B 4AD (☎ 020 7271 0482, fax 020 7271 0499, e-mail geoff.dart@bis.gsi.gov.uk, website www.gov.uk)

DARTFORD, Peter Andrew; QFSM (2014); s of William Alfred Eric Dartford (d 1992), and Maureen Margaret, *née* Mattey; *b* 21 June 1963, London; *Educ* Knights Templar Sch Baldock, London South Bank Univ (BEng), Univ of Coventry Business Sch (MA); *m* 8 May 2007, Natalie Rebecca, *née* Handforth; 3 s (Myles William b 6 April 1994, Isaac Luca Daniel b 13 Aug 2006, Reuben Luis Joseph b 14 July 2009), 1 da (Sophie Rebecca b 23 Sept 1995); *Career* firefighter rising to divnl offr grade I Herts Fire and Rescue Serv 1982–99; Staffs Fire and Rescue Serv: sr divnl offr 1999–2000, asst chief fire offr 2001–05, dep chief fire offr 2005–08, chief fire offr 2008–; memb Chief Fire Offrs Assoc; Fire Brigade Long Serv and Good Conduct Medal 2002, Queen's Jubilee Medal 2005; FIFireE; *Recreations* golf, football, cricket, spending time with family; *Style—* Peter Dartford, Esq, QFSM; ✉ Staffordshire Fire and Rescue Service, Pirehill, Stone, Staffordshire ST15 0BS (☎ 01785 898669)

DARTMOUTH, 10 Earl of (GB 1711); William Legge; MEP; also Baron Dartmouth (E 1682) and Viscount Lewisham (GB 1711); s of 9 Earl of Dartmouth (d 1997), and his 1 w (now Raine, Countess Spencer, *qv*); *b* 23 September 1949; *Educ* Eton, ChCh Oxford, Harvard Business Sch (MBA); *Heir* bro, Hon Rupert Legge; *Career* chm and fndr Kirklees Cable; contested (Cons): Leigh Lancs 1974, Stockport South 1974, European Parl Yorkshire Region 1999; MEP (UKIP) South West 2009–; FCA; *Style—* The Rt Hon the Earl of Dartmouth, MEP

DARTON, Prof Richard Charles; OBE (2011); s of Allan John Darton, and Beryl Clare, *née* Davies; *b* 1 July 1948; *Educ* King's Sch Rochester (King's scholar), Univ of Birmingham (BSc), Downing Coll Cambridge (PhD); *m* 27 April 1974, Diana Mildred, da of Alan Theophilus Warrell; 2 s (Nicholas John b 3 Aug 1976, Thomas Charles b 15 Jan 1978), 1 da (Frances Clare b 27 Feb 1982); *Career* ICI postdoctoral res fell Univ of Cambridge 1973–75; various appointments Shell Int Petroleum The Netherlands 1975–91, on secondment Shell UK 1991; prof Dept of Engrg Science Univ of Oxford 2000–14 (head of dept 2004–09, emeritus prof 2014–), reader in chemical engrg, sr research fell and tutor Keble Coll Oxford 2001–14 (emeritus fell 2014–); Stephen Anderman visiting lectr: Mendelev Univ 1999, Kurnakov Inst Moscow 1999, Univ of St Petersburg 2000; Cncl Medal IChemE 2005 (dep pres 2007–08, pres 2008–09); pres European Fedn of Chemical Engrg 2010–13; hon memb Czech Soc of Chemical Engrg 2000; FIChemE 1987, FREng 2000; *Recreations* Scottish country dancing, reading history; *Style—* Prof Richard Darton, OBE; ✉ 3 Cameron Avenue, Abingdon, Oxfordshire OX14 3SR; University of Oxford, Department of Engineering Science, Parks Road, Oxford OX1 3PJ (e-mail richard.darton@eng.ox.ac.uk)

DARVILL, Keith Ernest; s of Ernest Darvill (d 1989), and Ellen, *née* Clark (d 1992); *b* 28 May 1948, London; *Educ* Norlington Secdy Modern Leytonstone, East Ham Tech Coll, Thurrock Coll of FE, Poly of Central London, Coll of Law Chester; *m* 1971, Julia; 1 da (Nicole b 1974), 2 s (Andrew b 1977, Simon b 1988); *Career* Port of London Authy: various clerical positions 1963–73, asst slr 1973–84; ptnr Duthie Hart and Duthie Solicitors 1984–93, sole practitioner 1993–99, ptnr Kenneth Elliott & Rowe Solicitors 1999–; MP (Lab) Upminster 1997–2001 (Parly candidate 2001 and 2005), memb Select Ctee on Procedure 1997–2001; cncllr Heaton Ward London Borough of Havering 2002– (ldr Lab Gp Havering Cncl 2006–); govr Gaynes Sch Upminster 1985–, memb Havering Sixth Form Coll Corporation 1990– (chair 2002–), govr Kings Wood Sch 1998–; memb: Law Soc 1981–, T&GWU, Fabian Soc, Hornchurch and Upminster Rotary Club 1994–; *Recreations* tennis, badminton, gardening; *Clubs* Cranston Park Lawn Tennis (Upminster); *Style—* Keith Darvill, Esq; ✉ 54 Park Drive, Upminster RM14 3AR (☎ 01708 225715); Kenneth Elliott & Rowe, Enterprise House, 18 Eastern Road, Romford, Essex RM1 3PJ (☎ 01708 707806, fax 01708 766674, e-mail keith.darvill@ker.co.uk, website www.ker.co.uk)

DARWALL-SMITH, Lucy Ellen; da of Herbert Francis Eade, and Anne Barbara, *née* Forbes; *b* 1 June 1955; *Educ* Micklefield Sch for Girls; *m* (m dis); 1 da (Daisy b 26 Nov 1985); *Career* assoc dir Lopex 1979–81, chm Darwall Smith Associates Ltd 1981–2012; MInstD, MRCA; *Recreations* theatre, ballet, food, friends; *Clubs* Commonwealth, Sloane; *Style—* Ms Lucy Darwall-Smith; ✉ 44 Delves Way, Ringmer, Nr Lewes, East Sussex BN8 5JU (☎ 01273 813503)

DARZI OF DENHAM, Baron (Life Peer UK 2007), of Denham in the County of Buckinghamshire; Prof Sir Ara Warkes Darzi; OM (2016), KBE (2002), PC (2009); *b* 7 May 1960; *Educ* RCSI (MB, BCh, BAO, LRCPI, LRCSI), TCD (MD); *m* Wendy; 2 c (Freddie, Nina); *Career* conslt surgn Central Middlesex Hosp London 1994–95; currently hon conslt surgn St Mary's Hosp NHS Tst, conslt Royal Marsden Hosp NHS Tst, Paul Hamlyn chair of surgery Imperial Coll London 2005–, head Div of Surgery Imperial Coll London 2009–12, dir Inst of Global Health Innovation 2010–, chair Imperial Coll Healthcare Partners 2012–; hon prof Inst of Cancer Research, visiting prof London Sch of Economics and Political Science 2013–; Parly under-sec of state for health 2007–09, UK business ambass Dept of Business, Innovation and Skills 2009–13; sec and memb Cncl Soc of Minimal Invasive Therapy 1998–99; chm London Modernisation Bd 2000–03; memb: Policy and Evaluation Advsy Gp The Nuffield Tst 1997–2001, Educn Bd Raven Dept of Educn RCS 1998–, Steering Ctee of New and Emerging Application of Technologies NHS Exec Health, Tech R&D 1999–, Modernisation Action Gp NHS Exec Dept of Health (Profession and NHS Force) 2000–03, External Advsy Bd MD Anderson Cancer Center Univ of Texas 2003–07; EPSRC memb Integrated Healthcare Technologies Sector Programme Ctee, Parly advsr to Health Select Ctee, memb MRC Research Panel; career has spanned across the domains of cutting-edge surgical robotics through to researching and implementing low-cost, high-impact technological and frugal innovations; patron: Beating Bowel Cancer 2005–, Meningitis Tst 2009–, Barrett's Oesophagus Campaign 2011–, Chordoma UK 2013–; vice-patron The Cyberbullying Fndn 2014–; hon fell Nat Inst of Clinical Excellence 2010; Hon DSc Cranfield Univ 2009, Hon MD Newcastle Univ 2009, Hon DSc De Montfort Univ 2011, Hon LLD Trinity Coll Dublin 2011; FMedSci 2003, FRCPGlas 2003, FCGI 2004, Hon FRCSEd 2005, Hon FREng 2006, FRCPEd 2008, Hon FRCR 2009, Hon FRCPI 2010, FRCP 2010, Hon FACS 2011, hon memb Japan Soc for Endoscopic Surgery 2012, FRS 2013, hon fell American Soc for Colon and Rectal Surgeons 2013, hon fell College of Surgns of Hong Kong (FHKAM (Surgery)) 2014, HonFASA 2014, foreign assoc memb Inst of Medicine 2014; Sash of Independence Qatar 2014; *Publications* author of over 950 papers and author/ed of over 10 books; reviewer for: Br Jl of Surgery, Annals of Surgery, Surgery; *Clubs* Athenaeum, Mossimans; *Style—* Prof the Lord Darzi of Denham, OM, KBE, PC, FRS; ✉ Imperial College London, St Mary's Hospital, South Wharf Road, London W2 1NY (☎ 020 3312 1310, fax 020 3312 6950, e-mail a.darzi@imperial.ac.uk)

DAS, Dr Sankar Kumar; s of D Das (d 1974), of Calcutta, India, and late Nilima, *née* Roy Chondbury; *b* 1 December 1933; *Educ* Univ of Calcutta (MB BS); *m* 26 Nov 1977, Enakshi, da of P K Roy (d 1976); 1 s (Shumit b 1 June 1979), 1 da (Priya b 27 Feb 1984); *Career* med registrar Victoria Hosp Blackpool 1964–66, fell of internal, chest and nuclear med and asst instr in med VA Hosp Milwaukee 1966–69, sr med registrar King's Coll Hosp and St Francis Hosp London 1970–74; conslt physician in geriatric med: Manor Hosp Derby and Derby City Hosp 1974–77, St Helier Gp Hosp and London Borough of Sutton 1977–; hon sr lectr Univ of London 1977–, recognised teacher St George's Hosp Tooting 1977–; conslt Specialists' Assoc; inventor of: hind paddle walker Mark I, II and III, exercising machine, DAK mobile Mark I and II walking frames, disc computer for analytical prog on geriatric med, clinical audi urinary incontinence gadgets (male and female); memb Panel on Residential Accommodation Sutton Borough; Mother India Int Award for servs to the elderly and disabled people in the UK 1989, Man of the Year (American Biographical Assoc) for servs to the elderly 1990; memb: Br Geriatric Soc 1966, NY Acad of Sciences 1992, Royal Inst of GB, Br Geriatric Soc, American Coll of

Chest Physicians; fell: Int Biographical Assoc 1980, Int Youth in Achievement 1980; FRSH 1966, FRCP 1974 (MRCP), FCCP (USA) 1974; *Publications* Lecture Notes on Medical Infirmities, Europe (1981), Fits, Faints and Falls (1985), contrib to med jls and author of papers on computers in medicine; *Recreations* flying, polo, horse riding, cricket; *Style*— Dr Sankar Das; ✉ 62 Rose Hill, Sutton, Surrey SM1 3EX (☎ 020 8644 1639); St Helier Hospital, Wrythe Lane, Carshalton, Surrey SM5 1AA (e-mail sankardas@aol.com)

DASGUPTA, Prof Sir Partha Sarathi; kt (2002); s of Prof Amiya Dasgupta (d 1992), of Santiniketan, India, and Shanti, *née* Dasgupta (d 2001); *b* 17 November 1942; *Educ* Univ of Delhi (BSc), Univ of Cambridge (BA, Stevenson prize, PhD); *m* 29 June 1968, Carol Margaret, da of Prof James Edward Meade (d 1995); 2 da (Zubeida b 11 Jan 1974, Aisha b 3 July 1983), 1 s (Shamik b 13 Aug 1977); *Career* supernumery fell Trinity Hall Cambridge 1971–74 (research fell 1968–71); LSE: lectr 1971–75, reader 1975–78, prof of economics 1978–84; Univ of Cambridge: prof of economics 1985–, fell St John's Coll Cambridge 1985–, Frank Ramsay prof of economics 1994–; prof of economics, prof of philosophy and dir Programme in Ethics in Society Stanford Univ 1989–92; visiting asst prof Carnegie-Mellon Univ 1968–69, visiting fell Delhi Sch of Economics 1970–71, Ford visiting prof Inst of Economic Growth Univ of Delhi 1981; visiting prof: Jawaharlal Nehru Univ 1978, Stanford Univ 1983–84 (visiting assoc prof 1974–75), Harvard Univ 1987, Princeton Univ 1988; Royal Economic Soc: memb Cncl 1988–93, pres 1998–2001; European Economic Assoc: memb Cncl 1989–93, pres 1999; memb Cncl: Econometric Soc 1984–90, European Soc for Populaton Economics 1987–91; assoc ed: Jl of Development Economics 1972–76, Social Choice and Welfare 1984–96, Jl of Environmental Economics and Management 1985–89; memb Advsy Bd Environment and Development Economics 1996–; memb Panel of Experts of Environmental Health WHO 1975–85, prog dir for applied economic theory and econometrics Centre for Public Policy Research London 1984–86 (research fell 1983–93), research advsr UNU/World Inst for Devpt Economics 1991–94, memb Scientific Bd Santa Fe Inst 1991–96, chm Beijer Int Inst of Ecological Economics Royal Swedish Acad of Sciences 1991–97, sr research fell Inst for Policy Reform Washington DC 1992–94; foreign hon memb American Acad of Arts and Sciences 1991, foreign memb Royal Swedish Acad of Sciences 1991, hon fell LSE 1994, hon memb American Economic Assoc 1997, memb Pontifical Acad of Soc Scis 1998, foreign assoc US Nat Acad of Scis 2001, fell Third World Acad of Sci 2002, foreign memb American Philosophical Soc 2005; fell Econometric Soc 1975; Volvo Environment Prize (jtly with K G Mäler) 2002, John Kenneth Galbraith Award American Agricultural Economics Assoc 2007; Dr (hc): Wageningen Univ 2000, Catholic Univ of Louvain 2007; FBA 1989, FRS 2004; *Books* Guidelines for Project Evaluation (with S A Marglin and A K Sen, 1972), Economic Theory and Exhaustible Resources (with G M Heal, 1979), The Control of Resources (1982), Environmental Decision-Making (jt ed, 1984), Economic Organizations as Games (jt ed, 1986), The Economics of Bargainning (jt ed, 1987), An Inquiry into Well-Being and Destitution (1993), The Environment and Emerging Development Issues (jt ed with K-G Maler, 1997), Human Well-Being and the Natural Environment (2001), Economics: A Very Short Introduction (2007); author of numerous articles in jls, lectrs and reviews; *Clubs* MCC; *Style*— Prof Sir Partha Dasgupta, FBA, FRS; ✉ 1 Dean Drive, Holbrook Road, Cambridge CB1 7SW (☎ 01223 212179); University of Cambridge, Sidgwick Avenue, Faculty of Economics, Cambridge CB3 9DD (☎ 01223 335207)

DASHWOOD, Sir Edward John Francis; 12 Bt (Premier Bt of GB, cr 1707), of West Wycombe, Buckinghamshire; s (by 1 m) of Sir Francis John Vernon Hereward Dashwood, 11 Bt (d 2000); *b* 25 September 1964; *Educ* Eton, Univ of Reading (BSc); *m* 10 April 1989, Lucinda Nell, o da of Gerrard Herman Francis Miesegaes and Mrs D Parker; 1 da (Victoria Lucinda b 21 March 1991), 2 s (George Francis b 17 June 1992, Robert Edward b 15 Nov 1993); *Heir* s, George Dashwood; *Career* land agent, landowner; ARICS; *Recreations* shooting, fishing, tennis; *Style*— Sir E J F Dashwood, Bt; ✉ West Wycombe Park, Buckinghamshire (☎ 01494 524412, fax 01494 471617)

DATTA, Dr Shreelata; da of T Datta, and M Datta; *b* London; *Educ* St Albans HS for Girls (scholar), Imperial Coll Sch of Medicine London (BSc, MB BS, Arthur Macey scholar, travelling scholar), Cardiff Law Sch; *Career* house offr Hemel Hempstead Gen Hosp and Queen Mary's Hosp 2003–04, SHO Queen Charlotte's and Chelsea Hosp and Hillingdon Hosp 2004–; sr registrar: Queen Mary's Hosp 2009–11, St Thomas' Hosp 2011; conslt obstetrician and gynaecologist KCH 2013–; memb Exec Ctee Medical Women's Fedn 2003–, dir BMA (jr drs rep Obstetrics and Gynaecology Central Conslts and Specialists Ctee and Medico-Legal Ctee, memb Cncl 2004–14, chair Jr Doctors Ctee 2009–11, fell 2014), memb Cncl GMC 2012; advsr: Elsevier Sciences 1999–, Oxford Univ Press 1999–, Blackwell Sciences 1999–, Unimed Sciences Publishing 2003–; Arthur Macey Scholarship 2000, RCOG Travel Award 2009, BMA Helen Lawson Award 2011; fell BMA 2014; *Publications* Crash Course Renal and Urinary Systems (2001), Oxford Handbook of the Foundation Programme (co-author, 2005), Crash Course Obstetrics and Gynaecology (2015); *Recreations* travel, mystery shopping, yoga; *Style*— Dr Shreelata Datta; ✉ 4th Floor, Golden Jubilee Wing, King's College Hospital, Denmark Hill, London SE4 (e-mail statta@doctors.org.uk)

DATTA, Soumendra Nath; *b* Chertsey; *Educ* Merchant Taylors Sch, UCL; *m* 9 Aug 2008, Hema Datta; 1 da (Karishma Datta); *Career* house offr Univ Coll and The Middlesex Hosp 2000–01, SHO Royal Brompton Hosp 2001, surgical rotation Hammersmith Hosp 2002–04, RCS research fell Inst of Neurology 2004–07, Urology Higher Surgery Trg Prog 2007–12, sr registrar Guy's Hosp 2011–12, locum urologist Royal Free Hosp 2013–14, conslt urological surgn Colchester Hosp Univ 2014–; hon sr lectr Univ of London; Duke of Edinburgh Gold Award 1994, Lord Liston Prize in Surgery UCL 2000, Section Prize RSM 2004 and 2013, Int Continence Soc Award 2006, American Urological Assoc Award 2007, European Assoc of Urology Award 2008, Br Assoc of Urological Surgeons Award 2016; memb: BMA 1994, RCS 2003, RSM 2004, Br Assoc of Urological Surgeons 2006, European Assoc of Urology 2007; *Publications* numerous articles and chapters in pubns incl: BJU International, Jl of Urology and European Urology; *Recreations* cricket, sailing, skiing; *Style*— Dr Soumendra Datta; ✉ Department of Urology, Colchester Hospital, University Foundation Trust, Turner Road, Colchester CO4 5JL (Twitter @dattasn)

DAUBENEY, Philip Edward Giles; s of Cyril Walter Philip Daubeney (d 1969), and Emily Margaret, *née* Gleed; *b* 27 March 1938; *Educ* Hardye's Sch Dorchester, Balliol Coll Oxford (MA); *m* 12 Aug 1961, Heather Margaret; 1 s (Piers Edward Francis b 25 March 1964), 1 da (Clare Elizabeth b 19 April 1966); *Career* served: Parachute Regt 1956–58 (Nat Serv 2 Lt), TA (Maj); ICI 1961–93 (ceo ICI India 1983–90, regnl chief exec ICI African and Eastern Region 1990–93), chief exec Electricity Assoc 1993–2002, chm JP Morgan Fleming Indian Investment Tst 2002–, chm AFNOR Ltd 2002–; chm: South Africa Business Assoc 1993–95, South Africa Area Advsy Gp BOTB 1993–95, Int Air Compressor Mfrs Assoc 2002–, New Forest West Cons Assoc; *Recreations* gardening, shooting, watercolours; *Clubs* Oxford and Cambridge; *Style*— Philip Daubeney, Esq; ✉ Durmast House, Burley, Hampshire BH24 4AT

DAUBENEY, Dr Piers Edward Francis; s of Philip Daubeney, of Durmast House, Burley, Hants, and Margaret, *née* Pidgeon; *b* 25 March 1964, London; *Educ* Manchester Grammar (Cheshire Co Scholarship), Balliol College Oxford (Periam Prize, MA, DM), St Thomas's Hosp Medical Sch (MBBS, Grainger Prize); *m* 19 June 2004, Dr Nara, *née* Orban; 2 s (Henry b 9 Nov 2005, Hugo b 18 June 2012), 2 da (Beatrice b 6 May 2008, Daphne b 21 July 2010); *Career* Southampton Gen Hosp: paediatric and neonatal registrar 1993, paediatric cardiology registrar 1993–94, res fell in paediatric cardiology 1994–95, sr registrar in paediatric cardiology 1995–96 and 1997–99; sr clinical fell in cardiology Royal Children's Hosp Melbourne 1996–97, clinical fell in echocardiography and fetal echo Hospital for Sick Children Toronto 1997, conslt paediatric and fetal cardiologist Royal Brompton Hosp and Chelsea Westminster Hosp 1999– (lead clinician for paediatric cardiology 2002–08); hon sr lectr Nat Heart and Lung Inst Imperial Coll 1999– (reader in paediatric cardiology 2009–); fndr Children's Heart Res Assoc (CHUKRA) 2008; jt fndr and tstee: Harrison Heart Res Fndn 2003–, Brompton Fountain Parents Gp 2005–; memb: Med Bd Chain of Hope 2000–, Br Paediatric Surveillance Unit; paediatric cardiology rep UK Medicines for Children Clinical Research Network; memb: Br Paediatric Cardiac Assoc 1995–, RCPCH, BMA; FRCP; *Books* Diagnosis and Management of Adult Congenital Heart Disease (jt ed, 2003, 2 edn 2010), Pediatric cardiology: A practical guide (jt ed, 2012); author of multiple articles and editorials in medical jls; *Recreations* oenology, rowing, sailing, bridge; *Clubs* Cresta, Phoenix Boat (pres), United Hosps Boat (vice-pres), Old Bromptonians (treas); *Style*— Dr Piers Daubeney; ✉ c/o Mrs Gardenia Matley, Suite 5a, London House, 266 Fulham Road, London SW10 9EL (☎ 020 7351 3121, fax 020 7376 5536, e-mail paedcare@btconnect.com, websites www.childrensheartcentre.com and www.imperial.ac.uk/medicine/people/p.daubeney)

DAUNTON, Prof Martin James; s of Ronald James Daunton, and Dorothy May, *née* Bellett; *b* 7 February 1949; *Educ* Barry GS for Boys, Univ of Nottingham (BA), Univ of Kent (PhD), Univ of Cambridge (LittD); *m* 1984, Claire Hilda Gabriel, da of Philip Gobbi; *Career* lectr in economic history Univ of Durham 1973–79, successively lectr, reader and then Astor prof of Br history UCL 1979–97; Univ of Cambridge: prof of economic history 1997–2015, fell Churchill Coll 1997–2004 and 2014–15, chm Faculty of History 2001–2003, chm Sch of Humanities and Social Sciences 2003–05, master Trinity Hall 2004–14 (hon fell 2015–), head Sch of Humanities and Social Sciences 2012–15; visiting fell ANU 1985 and 1994, visiting prof Nihon Univ 2000; chm Inst of Historical Research 1994–98; Royal Historical Soc: hon treas 1986–91, vice-pres 1996–2000, pres 2004–08; convenor Editorial Bd Studies in History 1994–2000, conslt ed Oxford DNB 1993–98; tstee Nat Maritime Museum 2002–10, chm Syndics of Fitzwilliam Museum 2008–14, memb Advsy Ctee Leverhulme Tst 2009– (chair 2012–), tstee Baring Archive Tst 2009–15, tstee Maritime Fndn 2012–, cmmr English Heritage 2014–; FRHistS 1980, FBA 1997; *Books* Coal Metropolis: Cardiff 1870–1914 (1977), House and Home in the Victorian City (1983), Royal Mail: The Post Office Since 1840 (1985), A Property Owning Democracy? (1987), Progress and Poverty: An Economic & Social History of Britain 1700–1850 (1995), Trusting Leviathan: The Politics of Taxation in Britain, 1799–1914 (2001), Just Taxes: The Politics of Taxation in Britain 1914–79 (2002), Wealth and Welfare: An Economic and Social History of Britain 1851–1951 (2007), State and Market in Victorian Britain (2008); *Recreations* architectural tourism, collecting modern ceramics, walking; *Clubs* Reform; *Style*— Prof Martin Daunton, FBA; ✉ Primrose Farm, Primrose Farm Road, Little Wilbraham, Cambridge CB21 5JZ (☎ 01223 811207, e-mail mjd42@cam.ac.uk)

DAURIS, (HE) James; s of Colin James Dauris, and Prudence Ann, *née* Butterworth; *b* 15 January 1966, Harlow, Essex; *Educ* Haileybury, Downing Coll Cambridge (MA), Coll of Law London; *m* 1995, Helen Claire, *née* Parker; 3 da; *Career* diplomat; admitted slr 1991; slr Ashurst Morris Crisp 1991–95, head Maritime Section Aviation and Maritime Dept FCO 1995–97, head Commercial Section Moscow 1998–2002, dep head EU (External) Dept FCO 2002–03, dep head then acting head South Asia Gp FCO 2003–05, dep head of mission Bogota 2005–09, ambass to Peru 2010–14, high cmmr to Sri Lanka and Maldives 2015–; *Recreations* travel, bird watching, choral singing; *Style*— Mr James Dauris; ✉ c/o FCO, King Charles Street, London SW1A 2AH

DAVAN WETTON, Hilary John; s of Eric Davan Wetton, CBE (d 1986), and Valerie, *née* Edwards (d 1970); *b* 23 December 1943; *Educ* Westminster, Royal Coll of Music, BNC Oxford; *m* 1, 19 Sept 1964, Elizabeth Jane Tayler; 3 da (Charlotte, b 1966, Venetia b 1969, Fenella b 1972); m 2, 5 Jan 1989, Alison Mary Moncrieff; 1 s (Alexander b 1991), 1 da (Camilla b 1995); m 3, 18 Oct 2003, Dr Tonia Vincent; 1 da (Eleanor b 2004); *Career* dir of music: St Albans Sch 1965–67, Cranleigh Sch 1967–74, Stantonbury Educn Campus and Music Centre 1974–79, St Paul's Girls Sch 1979–94, Tonbridge Sch 1994–2006; sr music assoc Somerville Coll Oxford 2015–; conductor: St Albans Choral Soc 1965–67, Guildford Choral Soc 1968–2008 (now conductor emeritus), Milton Keynes Chorale 1974–79, Milton Keynes City Orch (formerly Chamber Orch) 1975–2007 (now conductor emeritus), The Holst Singers of London 1978–91, Birmingham Schs' Symphony Orch 1983–85, Scottish Schs' Orch 1984–95, Buckinghamshire Youth Orch 1985–89, City of London Choir 1989–, Wren Orch 1989–96, Canticum 1992–94, Edinburgh Youth Orch 1994–97, Wellington Coll Orch 2007–14; artistic dir Leicester Philharmonic Choir 2012–; assoc conductor London Mozart Players 2010–; guest conductor with orchs in Australia, Bulgaria, Denmark, Iceland, Norway, Singapore and USA; performances on Radio 3 (with Ulster Orch and BBC Concert Orch), Classic FM, BBC 1, BBC 2 and Thames Television; conslt for Classic FM Masterclass 1994–97, conslt for Play It Again (BBC 1) 2009; author of articles in Daily Telegraph, The Guardian, Music and Musicians, Musical Times, Choir and Organ and Classic FM Magazine; Hon MA Open Univ 1983, Hon DMus De Montfort Univ 1994; hon fell Birmingham Conservatoire 2011; memb RCO; *Recordings* with LPO 1988: Mozart Jupiter Symphony, Holst Planets, Elgar Enigma Variations; other recordings incl: Vaughan Williams 5 Tudor Portraits, Holst Golden Goose (with Philharmonia and Guildford Choral Soc), Holst Choral Symphony (winner of Diapason D'Or 1994), Vaughan Williams's Hodie (RPO and Guildford Choral Soc), In Terra Pax (RPO and CLC), Bliss Pastoral, Vaughan Williams G Minor mass (Holst singers), 5 CDs of 19th century British symphonists (with Milton Keynes City Orch), Beethoven Glorreiche Augenblick (RPO and CLC); *Recreations* tennis; *Clubs* Garrick, Pepys; *Style*— Hilary Davan Wetton, Esq; ✉ c/o Richard Haigh, Performing Arts Management, 6 Windmill Street, London W1P 1HF (☎ 020 7255 1362, fax 020 7631 4631, website www.hilarydavanwetton.co.uk, Twitter@HilaryConductor)

DAVENPORT; *see also:* Bromley-Davenport

DAVENPORT, Hugo Benedick; s of (Arthur) Nigel Davenport (d 2013), and Helena Margaret, *née* White (d 1979); *b* 6 June 1953; *Educ* Westminster, Univ of Sussex (BA); *m* 10 Aug 1988, Sarah, da of Hugh Mollison; 1 s, 1 da; *Career* The Observer 1981–85, Mail on Sunday 1985–87, features and film critic Daily Telegraph 1989–96, ed FT New Media Markets 1998–2000, Broadband Media 2001–02; writer on culture, communications and business; mktg and communications Caseworks Customer Interaction (CCI) 2005–16; memb Hon Devpt Bd Booktrust 2003; prize Population Inst Washington 1988; FRSA 2003; *Books* Days that Shook the World (2003); *Style*— Hugo Davenport, Esq; ✉ 33 Swan Island, Strawberry Vale, Twickenham TW1 4RP (☎ 020 8892 7402, e-mail hugodavenport1@gmail.com)

DAVENPORT, Ian Richard; s of Ellis Davenport, of Cheshire, and Shirley, *née* Silk; *b* 8 July 1966; *Educ* King's GS Macclesfield, Goldsmiths Coll London (BA), Northwich Coll of Art and Design; *m* 6 July 2004, Sue Arrowsmith; *Career* artist; exhibited Freeze (Surrey Docks London) 1988, retrospective (Ikon Birmingham) 2004; Contemporary Art Soc cmmn for wall painting at Univ of Warwick 2004, Western Bridge Southwark St cmmn; *Awards* prizewinner John Moores 21 Liverpool Exhibition 1999, prizewinner Primo del Golfo La Spezia Italy 2000, winner Prospects Essor Project Space London 2002; nominated Turner Prize 1991; *Recreations* arts, music, walking, cooking; *Style*— Ian Davenport, Esq; ✉ Waddington Galleries, 11 Cork Street, London W1S 3LT

D

DAVENPORT, Ian Richard; s of Martin Robert Davenport, of Cannes, France, and Ann Maxwell, *née* Fyfe (d 2000); *b* 27 May 1960, Chicoutimi, Canada; *Educ* Bloxham Sch, Univ of Durham (BA); *m* 1987, Katherine, *née* Bates; 1 s (Samuel b 1995), 1 da (Ella b 1999); *Career* Arthur Andersen & Co 1983–85, Morgan Stanley Int Ltd 1985–87, Kleinwort Benson 1987–88, St George's Coll Weybridge 1988–92, Radley Coll 1992–2004, headmaster Blundell's Sch 2004–12; memb HMC 2004; author of articles in Politics Assoc jls; *Recreations* American political biographies, fell running, skiing, opera, contemporary music; *Clubs* East India, Lansdowne, Jesters; *Style*— Ian Davenport, Esq

DAVENPORT, Jack; s of Nigel Davenport (d 2013), and Maria Aitken; *b* 1 March 1973, Wimbledon; *Educ* Cheltenham Coll, UEA; *m* 2000, Michelle Gomez; *Career* actor; *Theatre* incl: The Tempest, Hamlet, The Servant, Lady Windermere's Fan, How to Lose Friends and Alienate People, Enemies; *Radio* A Clockwork Orange 1998; *Television* incl: This Life 1996, The Moth 1997, Macbeth 1998, Ultraviolet 1998, The Wyvern Mystery 2000, Coupling 2000–02, Swingtown 2008, FlashForward 2009–10, Smash 2012; *Film* incl: Fierce Creatures 1997, Talos the Mummy 1998, The Wisdom of Crocodiles 1998, The Talented Mr Ripley 1999, The Cookie Thief 1999, Not Afraid Not Afraid 2001, The Bunker 2001, The Pirates of the Caribbean: The Curse of the Black Pearl 2003, The Pirates of the Caribbean: Dead Man's Chest 2006, Pirates of the Caribbean: At World's End 2007, The Key Man 2007, The Boat That Rocked 2008; *Style*— Jack Davenport, Esq; ✉ c/o Hamilton Hodell, Fifth Floor, 66–68 Margaret Street, London W1W 8SR

DAVENPORT, Prof John; s of William Kenneth Davenport, of Coventry, and Eda Bessie, *née* Taylor; *b* 12 February 1946; *Educ* Bablake Sch Coventry, St Mary's Hosp Med Sch, Univ of London (BSc, DSc), Univ of Southampton (MSc), UC Wales (PhD); *m* 1970, Julia Lesley, *née* Ladner; 2 da (Emma b 9 Nov 1973, Kate b 19 April 1976); *Career* demonstrator Dept of Marine Biology UC Wales 1970–72; Unit of Marine Invertebrate Biology NERC: higher scientific offr 1972–74, sr scientific offr 1974–80, princ scientific offr 1980–83; UCNW: sr lectr Sch of Animal Biology 1987–88 (lectr 1983–87), reader Sch of Ocean Sciences 1989–91 (sr lectr 1988–89); dir Univ Marine Biological Station and chair Marine Biology Univ of London 1991–99; UC Cork: prof and head Dept of Zoology and Animal Ecology 1999–, prof and head Dept of Zoology, Ecology and Plant Science 2002–, emeritus prof of zoology 2011–; dir Environmental Res Inst UC Cork 2000–02; MRIA 2001; FIBiol 1987, FRSE 1995; *Books* Animal Osmoregulation (with J C Rankin, 1981), Environmental Stress and Behavioural Adaptation (1985), Animal Life at Low Temperature (1992), Aquaculture: The Ecological Issues (jtly, 2003); author of numerous articles in scientific jls; *Recreations* skiing, sailboarding, walking, birding; *Style*— Prof John Davenport, FRSE; ✉ e-mail jdavenport@zoology.ucc.ie

DAVENPORT, Juliet Sarah Lovedy; OBE (2013); da of John Douglas Frank Davenport, of Lyneham, Wilts, and Alexa Pauline Lovedy, *née* Smith; *b* 5 February 1968, Haslemere, Surrey; *Educ* Merton Coll Oxford (MA), Birkbeck Coll London (MSc); *m* 8 Aug 2008, Mark Christopher Shorrock; *Career* joined Energy for Sustainable Devpt (ESD) 1995, exec dir ESD (now CAMCO) and ESD Ventures Ltd 1996; Good Energy Gp plc (formerly Unit[e]): fndr, commercial dir 1999–2002, chief exec 2002–; prof of practice Univ of Wales; hon doctorate Plymouth Univ; *Recreations* gardening, music, skiing, polo, running, yoga, cooking; *Style*— Ms Juliet Davenport, OBE; ✉ Good Energy Group plc, Monkton Reach, Monkton Hill, Avon Reach, Chippenham SN15 1EE

DAVENPORT, HE Michael Hayward; MBE; s of Montague Davenport (d 2011), and Olive, *née* Brabner (d 2008); *b* 25 September 1961, London; *Educ* Univ of Cambridge (MA); *m* 13 June 1992, Dr Lavinia, *née* Braun; 1 s (Sam b 1994), 2 da (Jessica b 1996, Gwendoline b 2002); *Career* diplomat; admitted slr Supreme Court 1988; desk offr E Africa Dept FCO 1988–89, second sec Know-How Fund Warsaw 1990–93, head UN Peacekeeping Section UN Dept FCO 1993–96, first sec political (external) Moscow 1996–99, consul-gen and dir for trade promotion Warsaw 2000–03, dep head of mission Cairo 2004–07, dir Russia, S Caucasus and Central Asia Directorate FCO 2007–10, ambass to Serbia 2010–13, EU ambass to Serbia 2013–; memb Law Soc 1988; *Style*— HE Mr Michael Davenport, MBE; ✉ EU Residence, Uicka 21A, Belgrade, Serbia (e-mail michael.davenport@eeas.europa.eu)

DAVENPORT-HINES, Dr Richard Peter Treadwell; s of John Hines (d 2003), and June Pearson, *née* Treadwell; *b* 21 June 1953, London; *Educ* St Paul's, Selwyn Coll Cambridge (exhibitioner, MA, PhD); *m* 20 May 1978, Frances Jane, *née* Davenport; 2 s (Hugo Denzil Rufus b 11 Oct 1983, Cosmo Rory Hector Albertyn b 14 June 1986); *Career* historian; res fell LSE 1982–86, freelance historian and reviewer 1986–; res assoc Oxford DNB 1995–2004, tstee London Library 1996–2005, tstee Royal Literary Fund 2007–, tstee J R Ackerley Tst 2011–; visiting fell All Souls Coll Oxford 2016; Wolfson Prize for History and Biography 1985, Wadsworth Prize for History 1986; FRHistS 1984, FRSL 2003; *Publications* Dudley Docker (1984), Speculators and Patriots (ed, 1986), Business in the Age of Reason (ed, 1987), British Business in Asia since 1860 (ed, 1989), Sex, Death and Punishment (1990), The Macmillans (1992), Glaxo (1992), Vice (1993), Auden (1995), Gothic (1998), The Pursuit of Oblivion (2001), A Night at the Majestic (2006), Hugh Trevor-Roper's Letters from Oxford (ed, 2006), Ettie: The Intimate Life of Lady Desborough (2008), Hugh Trevor-Roper's Wartime Journals (ed, 2011), Titanic Lives (2012), An English Affair: Sex, Class and Power in the Age of Profumo (2013), One Hundred Letters from Hugh Trevor-Roper (ed, 2014), Seven Lives of Maynard Keynes (2015), Edward VII: The Cosmopolitan King (2016); *Recreations* élitism, Europhilia; *Clubs* Athenaeum, Brooks's; *Style*— Richard Davenport-Hines, Esq; ✉ 51 Elsham Road, London W14 8HD; Le Meygris, 07200 Ailhon, France

DAVENTRY, 4 Viscount (UK 1943) James Edward FitzRoy Newdegate; s of 3 Viscount Daventry, JP, DL (d 2000); gf assumed the additional surname of Newdegate by Royal Licence 1936; *b* 27 July 1960; *Educ* Milton Abbey, Univ of Cirencester; *m* 10 Sept 1994, Georgia, yr da of John Stuart Lodge, of Daglingworth Place, Cirencester, Glos; 1 s (Humphrey John b 23 Nov 1995), 2 da (Hester Anne b 31 Dec 1997, Sophia Hebe b 8 March 2001); *Career* dir R K Harrison Gp Ltd; *Recreations* shooting, fishing, racing, golf, farming, occasional gardening; *Clubs* White's, Turf, MCC, Saints and Sinners; *Style*— The Rt Hon the Viscount Daventry; ✉ Arbury, Nuneaton, Warwickshire CV10 7PT

DAVEY, Andrew Paul (Andy); s of Peter Anthony Cecil Davey, of Bristol, and Joan Venville, of Alverstoke, Hants; *b* 12 July 1962; *Educ* W Sussex Coll of Design, RCA (MDes); *Children* 1 s (Joseph Stephen b 4 Feb 2002), 1 da (Eleanor Grace b 18 Jan 2005); *Career* product designer fndr princ TKO Product Design Consultants London 1990–; clients incl: Seiko,Yamaha, Tomy, Olympus, Honda; lectr on design issues at various venues incl Japan; featured in various articles and pubns incl: AXIS (int design magazine Japan), The I.D. 40 (int design magazine NY) 1996 and Terence Conran on Design 1996, The Design Museum Directory of 20th Century Design 1997, The International Design Yearbook 1998, 2000 and 2001, The Product Book (D&AD) 1999, Design Report (int design magazine South Korea) 2000, Power of Ten 2001, Design Directory – Great Britain 2001, Designing the 21st Century 2002, Designers on Design 2005, British Design 2007/8 2007; work in the perm collection of Design Museum London; various appearances on TV incl: Rough Guide to Design (BBC2) 1992, BBC Design Awards (BBC2) 1996, Style Tribes 'Design' (FCO) 2000; memb D&AD; *Exhibitions* incl: 'thinkteck!' (Tokyo Design Network Design Museum London) 1995, Baygen Clockwork Radio 1996 (selected by Design Museum as one of 25 top designs in museum's 25th Year 2007), Design of the Times – One Hundred Years of the Royal College of Art (RCA) 1996, Shiny and New: Contemporary British Design in Metal (San Francisco) 1997, Design for Creative Britain (FCO London) 1998, Powerhous::uk (DTI London) 1998, Millennium Products (Design Cncl Millennium Dome) 1999, creativebritain (stilverk Berlin) 2000, Great Expectations (Design Cncl Exhbn NY) 2001, Designed for Use (Design Cncl-Br Cncl Europe) 2002–03; *Awards* Red Dot Award for High Design Quality (Germany) 1999, G-Mark Good Design Award (Japan) 2001, IF Design Award (Germany) 2002; Detail, Exceptional Japanese Design (2003); *Recreations* sailing, multimedia; *Style*— Andy Davey, Esq; ✉ TKO Design (e-mail mail@tkodesign.co.uk, website www.tkodesign.co.uk)

DAVEY, Christopher Stephen (Chris); s of John James Murrell Davey, and Nan W Pattison; *b* 22 March 1967, Rochford, Essex; *Educ* Guildhall Sch of Music and Drama; *Career* lighting designer; memb Assoc of Lighting Designers; *Theatre* for RSC: Twelfth Night, The Winter's Tale, Pericles, Cymbeline, Alice in Wonderland, Night of the Soul, Romeo and Juliet, A Midsummer Night's Dream (also NY), Everyman (also NY), A Month in the Country, Troilus and Cressida, The Comedy of Errors (world tour), Mysteria, Easter; for Shared Experience Theatre: Madame Bovary, After Mrs Rochester, A Passage to India, Mill on the Floss, Jane Eyre, Anna Karenina, The Tempest, War and Peace, Desire Under the Elms, The Danube; for RNT: Harper Regan, The Seagull, The Pillars of the Community, A Dream Play, Iphiginia at Aulis, War and Peace, Baby Doll, The Colour of Justice; extensive designs for: Shared Experience Theatre, Royal Court, Hampstead Theatre, Lyric Hammersmith, Royal Exchange Manchester, West Yorkhire Playhouse, Royal Lyceum Edinburgh, Birmingham Rep; other designs incl: War and Peace (Shared Experience and Hampstead Theatre), Mattnew Bourne's The Car Man (Sadler's Wells, Old Vic and nat tour), The Pianist (Manchester Int Festival), Peer Gynt (Scottish Nat Theatre), One Flew Over The Cuckoo's Nest (Garrick, Geilgud Theatres and nat tour), Don't Look Now (Sheffield Lyceum and Lyric Hammersmith), Catch, The Sugar Syndrome, Crazyblackmuthaf***inself, The Force of Change (Royal Court), Three Thousand Troubled Threads (Edinburgh Int Festival), Watership Down, The Odyssey, The Magic Carpet, Then Again, Cause Celebre (Lyric Hammersmith), The Earthly Paradise (Almeida Theatre), Yellowman (Liverpool and Hampstead), The Odyssey, Beasts and Beauties (Bristol Old Vic), 21 (Rambert Dance Company), Jekyll and Hyde (Northern Ballet Theatre), Shining Souls (Old Vic), In a Little World of Our Own, Endgame (Donmar Warehouse), Blood Wedding, Grimm Tales (Young Vic); opera incl: l'Arbore de Diana Palau de les ARts Reina Sofia, Valencia, I Capuleti E I Montecchi (Opera North), Skellig (The Sage Gateshead), Aida (Houston Grand Opera), Bird of Night (ROH), Bluebeard Bregenz Festpsiele, St Polten, Jephtha (ENO, Welsh Nat Opera), The Magic Flute (Welsh Nat Opera), eight seasons for Grange Park Opera, The Rake's Progress (Aldeburgh Festival), The Picture of Dorian Gray (Opera de Monte Carlo), Le Recontre Imprevu (Guildhall), A Night at the Chines Opera (RAM), La Traviata (Castleward Opera Belfast), Gli Equivoci Nel Sebiant (Batignano Opera Tuscany); *Recreations* gym, theatre, dance; *Style*— Chris Davey, Esq; ✉ website http://web.mac.com/chrisdaveylx

DAVEY, Rt Hon Sir Edward Jonathan; kt (2016), PC (2012); s of John George Davey (d 1970), and Nina Joan, *née* Stanbrook (d 1981); *b* 25 December 1965; *Educ* Nottingham HS, Jesus Coll Oxford (BA, pres JCR), Birkbeck Coll London (MSc); *m* July 2005, Emily Gasson; *Career* sr econs advsr to Lib Dem MPs (primarily Paddy Ashdown and Alan Beith) 1989–93, conslt Omega Partners 1993–97, MP (Lib Dem) Kingston and Surbiton 1997–2015; Lib Dem econ affrs and London economy spokesman 1997–2001, Lib Dem shadow chief secretary to the Treasy 2001–02, Lib Dem shadow to the Office of the Dep PM 2002–05, Lib Dem shadow educn and skills spokesman 2005–06, Lib Dem shadow trade and industry spokesman 2006, Lib Dem COS and chair Campaign and Communications 2006–10, Parly under-sec of state Dept for Business, Innovation and Skills 2010–12, sec of state for energy and climate change 2012–15; memb: Fin Bill Standing Ctee 1997, 1998, 1999, 2000 and 2001, Bank of England Standing Ctee 1997, Procedure Select Ctee 1997–99, Greater London Authy Standing Ctee 1999, Treasy Select Ctee 2000–01; awarded Hon Testimonial of the Royal Humane Soc and Certificate of Commendation by the Chief Constable of the Br Tport Police 1994; FRSA 2001; *Publications* Making MPs Work for Our Money (2000); *Recreations* walking, hiking, tennis; *Clubs* National Liberal; *Style*— The Rt Hon Sir Edward Davey; ✉ House of Commons, London SW1A 0AA (☎ 020 7219 3512, fax 020 7219 0250, e-mail edward.davey.mp@parliament.uk, website www.edwarddavey.co.uk)

DAVEY, Prof Grenville; s of Clifford Davey, and Joyce Davey; *b* 28 April 1961, Launceston, Cornwall; *Educ* Exeter Coll of Art and Design, Goldsmiths Coll London; *m* 22 May 2006, Victoria Alice Davey; 1 s (Sennen b 25 Dec 2005); *Career* sculptor; numerous exhbns incl No1 Canada Square London and Chelsea Space London 2014, cmmn Cambridge Linear Park 2014; visiting prof in fine art Univ of the Arts London 1997; artist in residence Dept of Tehoretical Physics and Astronomy Queen Mary Univ of London 2010, artist in residence Isaac Newton Inst for Mathematical Science Cambridge 2011; Turner Prize winner 1992; *Publications* Objectives The New Sculpture (1990), Sculpture at Goodwood: A Vision for 21st Century British Sculpture (2002); *Recreations* walking; *Style*— Prof Grenville Davey; ✉ e-mail grenvillecdavey@yahoo.co.uk

DAVEY, Prof Kenneth Jackson; OBE (1997); s of Reginald Alfred Davey (d 1962), and Vera Elizabeth, *née* Jackson (d 1973); *b* 7 December 1932; *Educ* Silcoates Sch, Merton Coll Oxford (MA), Univ of Birmingham (MSocSc); *m* 18 Aug 1962, Beryl Joyce, da of John Iliff Herbert (d 1975); 2 s (Guy b 1964, Julian b 1966), 1 da (Stephanie b 1971); *Career* RA 1954–56: 2 Lt 1955, Lt 1956; HM Overseas Admin Serv in Uganda 1957–69, dir of studies E African Staff Coll 1970–72; Inst of Local Govt Studies Univ of Birmingham 1972–: assoc dir 1974–83, prof of devpt admin 1981– 2000, dir 1983–89, emeritus prof 2000–; conslt to govts of: Kenya 1975–76, Indonesia 1978–98, Pakistan 1981–82, Georgia 2000–01, Ukraine 2000–02; conslt to World Bank on urban fin 1982– (in Bangladesh, Brazil, China, Jordan, Kenya, Mexico, Poland, Russia, South Africa, Tanzania, Turkey and Uganda); co-ordinator British assistance to local govt reform in Czech Republic, Slovakia and Hungary 1991–2003, chm Steering Ctee Local Govt Initiative Open Soc Inst 2005–07; memb Cncl Malvern Coll 1986– (vice-chm 1994–2007); FRSA 1988; Offr's Cross Order of Merit of the Repub of Hungary 2004; *Books* Taxing a Peasant Society (1974), Financing Regional Government (1983), Strengthening Municipal Government (1989), Urban Management (1996), Balancing National and Local Responsibilities: Education Finance and Management in four Central European Countries (ed, 2002), The Impact of the Economic Down Turn on Local Government in Europe (ed, 2010), Local Government in Critical Times (ed, 2012); *Recreations* choral singing, walking; *Style*— Prof Kenneth Davey, OBE; ✉ Haymesbrook, Haymes Drive, Cleeve Hill, Cheltenham, Gloucestershire GL52 3QQ (☎ 01242 526232, e-mail k.j.davey@bham.ac.uk)

DAVEY, Richard H; s of Hubert H Davey, and May, *née* Harding; *b* 22 July 1948; *Educ* Lancing, Lincoln Coll Oxford (BA); *m*; 5 c (Anna b 17 Jan 1974, Edward b 30 July 1981, Nicholas b 10 Feb 1984, Benedict b 31 Aug 1989, Thomas b 14 Sept 1991); *Career* Slater Walker 1970–76, NM Rothschild & Sons 1976–83, dir Exco International plc 1983–87; md Merrill Lynch International 1987–89, exec vice-chm N M Rothschild & Sons 1989–99; non-exec chm London Capital Group Holdings plc 2007–12; non-exec dir: Scottish Widows Life Insurance 1996–2000, Freeserve plc 1999–2001, Yorkshire Building Soc 2005–12, Amlin plc 2005–, Severn Trent plc 2006–14; *Style*— Richard Davey, Esq

DAVEY SMITH, Prof George; *b* 9 May 1959; *Educ* Univ of Oxford (MA, DSc), Univ of Cambridge (MB BChir), London Sch of Hygiene and Tropical Med (MSc), Univ of Cambridge (MD); *Career* clinical research fell and hon clinical med offr Welsh Heart Prog 1985–86, Wellcome research fell in clinical epidemiology Univ Coll and Middx Sch of Med Dept of Community Med 1986–89, lectr in epidemiology London Sch of Hygiene and Tropical Med 1989–92, sr lectr in public health and epidemiology and hon sr registrar then conslt in public health med Dept of Public Health Univ of Glasgow 1992–94, prof of clinical epidemiology Univ of Bristol and hon conslt in public health med Avon Health 1994–; dir MRC Integrative Epidemiology Unit 2013–; hon prof Dept of Public Health Univ of Glasgow, visiting prof LSHTM; conslt ODA/Govt of India Nat AIDS Control Prog; memb Steering Ctee Nat Fitness Survey 1987–91; memb Editorial Bd: Jl of Health Psychology, Critical Public Health; ed Int Jl Epidemiology; author of numerous pubns in academic jls and book chapters; memb: Int Epidemiological Assoc, Soc for Social Med; FFPHM 1996 (MFPHM 1992), FRCP 2005, FMedSci 2006, FRSE 2014; *Style*— Prof George Davey Smith; ✉ School of Social and Community Medicine, University of Bristol, Oakfield House, Oakfield Grove, Bristol BS8 2BN (e-mail julia.mackay@bristol.ac.uk)

DAVID, Jo Roy Hill; s of Gerald Hill David (d 2004), of Bradenham, Bucks, and Deen Millicent, *née* Pashley (d 2007); *b* 7 December 1959, Amersham, Bucks; *Educ* Bucks Coll of FE, Camberwell Sch of Art; *Partner* Rachael House, *qv*; *Career* artist and curator; various art projects including: Outlinks Lesbian, Gay, Bisexual and Trangender (LGBT) Youth Project 1993–2001, Venus Project Islington 1994–2001, Consent 1997–2002, Community Art (S London) 1990–94, various work with people with learning disabilities 1990–2001; fndr and co-dir (with Rachael House) Space Station Sixty-Five 2002–, fndr JRHD & RLH Partnership; exhibiting artist Art Caucasus 2007; dir Mgmnt Ctee Metro Centre Ltd 1994–99, tstee David Family Foundation, David Family Tsts; artist and curator; various art projects including: Outlinks Lesbian, Gay, Bisexual and Trangender (LGBT) Youth Project 1993–2001, Venus Project Islington 1994–2001, Consent 1997–2002, Community Art (S London) 1990–94, various work with people with learning disabilities 1990–2001; fndr and co-dir (with Rachael House) Space Station Sixty-Five 2002– (publisher Space Station Sixty-Five Imprint), fndr JRHD & RLH Partnership; exhibiting artist Art Caucasus 2007; dir Mgmnt Ctee Metro Centre Ltd 1994–99, tstee David Family Foundation, David Family Tsts; *Recreations* contemporary art, mid 20th Century design, collecting, robots, British coast; *Style*— Jo David, Esq; ✉ Space Station Sixty-Five, 65 North Cross Road, London SE22 9ET (☎ 020 8299 5036, e-mail info@spacestationsixtyfive.com)

DAVID, Joanna; da of Maj John Almond Hacking, and Davida Elizabeth, *née* Nesbitt; *b* 17 January 1947; *Educ* Altrincham GS, Elmhurst Ballet Sch, Royal Acad of Dancing, Webber Douglas Acad of Dramatic Art; *Partner* (since 1972), Edward Charles Morice Fox, *qv*; 1 da (Emilia Rose Elizabeth Fox, *qv*, b 31 July 1974), 1 s (Frederick Samson Robert Morice b 5 April 1989); *Career* actress and broadcaster for radio and audio books; vice-pres Theatrical Guild, patron Unicorn Theatre for Children; patron and chair Grants Ctee Ralph and Meriel Richardson Fndn, memb Cncl King George V Fund, tstee Nat Hosp for Neurology and Neurosurgery Devpt Fndn 2009, patron Pancreatic Cancer Awareness, tstee Denville Hall; *Theatre* incl: Chichester Festival Theatre 1971, The Family Reunion 1973 and Uncle Vanya (Royal Exchange Manchester) 1977, The Cherry Orchard 1983 and Breaking the Code (Theatre Royal Haymarket) 1986, Stages (RNT) 1992, The Deep Blue Sea (Royal Theatre Northampton) 1997, Ghost Train Tattoo (Royal Exchange) 2000, Copenhagen (Salisbury Playhouse) 2003, The Importance of Being Earnest (Royal Exchange) 2004, A Voyage Round My Father (Donmar Warehouse and Wyndhams Theatre) 2006, Woman In Mind (Stephen Joseph Theatre Scarborough) 2008, Ring Round the Moon (Playhouse Theatre London) 2008, Woman in Mind (Vaudeville Theatre) 2009, Hobson's Choice (Regent's Park) 2014, HomeChat (Finborough Theatre) 2016; *Television* incl: War and Peace, Sense and Sensibility, Last of the Mohicans, Duchess of Duke Street, Rebecca, Carrington and Strachey, Fame is the Spur, First Among Equals, Paying Guests, Unexplained Laughter, Hannay, Children of the North, Secret Friends, Inspector Morse, Maigret, Rumpole of the Bailey, Darling Buds of May, The Good Guys, Sherlock Holmes – The Cardboard Box, Pride and Prejudice, A Touch of Frost, Bramwell, A Dance to the Music of Time, Midsummer Murders, Dalziel and Pascoe, Blind Date, Heartbeat, The Mill on the Floss, The Dark Room, The Glass, The Way We Live Now, The Forsyte Saga, He Knew He Was Right, Brides in the Bath, Monarch of the Glen 2004, Falling 2004, Heartbeat 2004, Bleak House 2005, Never Better 2007, Mutual Friends 2008, Doctors 2011, Miss Marple 2012, Downton Abbey 2013, Holby City 2013, Death In Paradise 2013, Doctors 2014, Casualty 2015, Letters from Baghdad 2015, The Living and the Dead (BBC) 2016; *Films* In the Name of the Pharoah 1998, Cotton Mary 1999, Soulkeeper 2002, The Tulse Hill Suitcase 2003, These Foolish Things 2004, One of Those Days 2008, Another Mother's Son 2016; *Radio* Homefront (series, BBC Radio 4) 2016; *Style*— Miss Joanna David; ✉ c/o Angharad Wood, Tavistock Wood Management Limited, 45 Conduit Street, London W1S 2YN (☎ 020 7494 4767, fax 020 7434 2017, e-mail wood@tavistockwood.com)

DAVID, Peter Howard; s of George Maurice David (d 1969), and Ruth, *née* Bloch; *b* 7 September 1951; *Educ* Liverpool Coll, Univ of London (BA); *m* 1 July 1978, Celia, da of Norman Binns; 1 s (Ian George b 8 Jan 1980), 1 da (Tessa b 12 Feb 1982); *Career* formerly on staff The Teacher Newspaper; The Times Higher Education Supplement until 1983, Washington ed Nature 1983–84; The Economist: joined 1984, foreign ed 2002–09, Washington bureau chief and author Lexington column 2009–; *Books* Star Wars and Arms Control (1984), Triumph in the Desert (1990); *Clubs* RAC; *Style*— Peter David, Esq; ✉ The Economist, 1730 Rhode Island Avenue NW, Suite 1210, Washington, DC 20036, USA (☎ 00 1 202 429 0893)

DAVID, Prof Timothy J; *Educ* Clifton Coll, Univ of Bristol (MB ChB, PhD, MD), DCH; *Family* 2 s; *Career* prof of child health and paediatrics Univ of Manchester and hon conslt paediatrician Booth Hall Children's Hosp Manchester and Royal Manchester Children's Hosp 1991–; proceedings ed Jl of Royal Soc of Medicine 1995–2011; memb Manchester Family Justice Cncl 2005–11; FRCP 1986 (MRCP 1976), FRCPCH 1997; *Publications* Recent Advances in Paediatrics (vols 9–25, 1991–2009), Food and Food Additive Intolerance in Childhood (1993), Symptoms of Disease in Childhood (1995), Problem-Based Learning in Medicine (jtly, 1999); author or ed of more than 400 pubns; *Recreations* classical music, opera; *Style*— Prof Timothy J David; ✉ Medical School, University of Manchester, Oxford Road, Manchester M13 9PL

DAVID, Wayne; MP; s of David Haydn David, of Bridgend, Mid Glamorgan, and Edna Amelia, *née* Jones; *b* 1 July 1957, Bridgend, Wales; *Educ* Cynffig Comp Sch, UC Cardiff (BA, PGCE FE, Charles Morgan prize in Welsh history), UC Swansea; *m* 8 June 1991 (m dis 2007), Catherine Thomas; *Career* teacher of history Brynteg Comp Sch 1983–85, tutor organiser Workers' Educn Assoc Mid Glamorgan 1985–89, MEP (Lab) South Wales 1989–94 and South Wales Central 1994–99, Lab candidate Nat Assembly for Wales election 1999, advsr Youth Serv 1999–2001, MP (Lab) Caerphilly 2001–; European Parl: treas European PLP 1989–91, first vice-pres Regnl Policy Ctee 1992–94, vice-pres Socialist Gp 1994–98, ldr European PLP 1994–98; House of Commons: memb EU Scrutiny Select Ctee 2001–07, chair All-Pty Poland Gp 2003–07 (sec 2001–03), PPS to Min of State MOD 2005–06, chair All-Pty EU Gp 2006–07; sec: Dept for Work and Pensions Ctee PLP 2002–07, Welsh Gp PLP 2003–07, asst Govt whip 2007–08, parly under-sec of state for Wales 2008–10, shadow min for Europe 2010–11, shadow min for Constitutional and political reform 2011–13, PPS to Ed Miliband 2013–15, PPS to Harriet Harman 2015–; pres: Labour Heritage, Cncl for Wales of Vol Youth Services, Aber Valley Male Voice Choir, Caerphilly Local History Soc; memb: Bd European Movement 2002–06 (pres Wales Cncl), Fabian Soc; fell Univ of Cardiff 1995; *Books* Remaining True: A Biography of Ness Edwards (2006); *Recreations* music, reading; *Clubs* Bargoed Labour; *Style*— Wayne David, Esq, MP; ✉ Constituency Office, The Community Council Offices, Newport Road, Bedwas, Caerphilly CF83 8YB (☎ 029 2088 1061, fax 029 2088 1954, e-mail wayne.david.mp@parliament.uk); House of Commons, London SW1A 0AA (☎ 020 7219 8152)

DAVID-WEILL, Michel Alexandre; s of Pierre David-Weill, and Berthe, *née* Haardt; *b* 23 November 1932; *Educ* Institut de Sciences Politiques Paris, Lycée Français New York; *m* 1956, Helene Lehideux; 4 da; *Career* Brown Brothers Harriman 1954–55, Lehman Brothers NY 1955–56; Lazard Frères & Co NY: joined 1956, ptnr 1961–2005, sr ptnr 1977–2005; Lazard Brothers & Co London: dir 1965–2005, chm 1990–91, dep chm 1992–2005; ptnr Lazard Frères et Cie Paris 1965–2005, vice-chm Lazard Frères & Co LLC 1995–2005; pres Monitoring Ctee Eurazeo; non-exec dir Pearson plc 1970–; tstee Met Museum of Art NY, govr Presbyterian NY Hosp; pres Conseil Artistique des Musées Nationaux 1988–, memb Acad des Beaux-Arts France; Grand Croix de la Légion d'Honneur (France) – Commandeur des Arts det des Lettres; *Books* L'Esprit en Fête (2007); *Clubs* Knickerbocker (NY), Brook (NY), Creek (Locust Valley); *Style*— Mr Michel David-Weill; ✉ 45 Peacock Lane, Locust Valley NY 11560, USA (☎ 00 1 576 671 7111, fax 00 1 516 674 4076); office 820 Fifth Avenue, New York, NY 10065, USA (☎ 00 1 212 355 6125, fax 00 1 242 355 6126, e-mail staff@md-w.com); Eurazeo, 32, rue de Monceau, Paris 75008, France (☎ 00 33 1 44 15 89 34, fax 00 33 1 47 66 43 72, e-mail ncipres@eurazeo.com)

DAVIDGE, Christopher Guy Vere; OBE (1982), DL (1994); s of (Cecil) Vere Davidge (d 1981), of Little Houghton, Northants, and his 1 w, (Ursula) Catherine (d 1948), yr da and co-heir of Christopher Smyth, JP, DL (d 1934); *see* Burke's Landed Gentry, 18 edn, vol II, 1969; *b* 5 November 1929; *Educ* Eton, Trinity Coll Oxford (MA); *m* 1, 1 Feb 1963, Winifred Marian (d 2000), da of John Stanley Crome; m 2, 1 June 1993, Jill Annette, da of Ewart William Girdler (d 1990); *Career* dir Mixconcrete (Holdings) plc 1964–82 (md 1964–69), chm various private cos 1960–; underwriting memb Lloyd's 1957–, memb Cncl Lloyd's 1982–88, dir Lloyd's of London Press Ltd 1985–91 (chm 1989–91); High Sheriff of Northants 1988–89; rowed for: Eton 1947–48, Oxford 1949–52 (pres OUBC 1950–51), GB 1952–63; winner of 9 Henley medals, steward Henley Royal Regatta 1967– (memb Ctee of Mgmnt 1973–2004), tstee Leander Club 1968– (chm 1968–78), tstee Henley Stewards Charitable Tst 1988–; rowed at Olympic Games 1952, 1956 and 1960, rowed at Cwlth Games 1962 (Gold medal); chef de mission GB team Olympic Games 1976; vice-pres: Br Olympic Assoc 1976– (vice-chm 1972–76), Cwlth Games Cncl 1990– (hon treas 1969–74, gen team mangr England 1974, vice-chm 1974–90); pres Amateur Rowing Assoc 1977–85 (hon life vice-pres 1985–); memb Cncl FISA (Medal of Honour 1973, chm Regattas Cmmn 1976–90), FISA technical delegate Olympic Games 1976, 1980, 1984 and 1988; vice-pres St Andrew's Hosp Northampton 2004– (govr 1969–, vice-chm 1991–94, chm of tstees 1991–2004, chm 1994–2004); chm of govrs and tstees Three Shires Hosp Northampton 1981–2004, tstee Maidwell Hall Sch Northampton 1969– (chm of govrs and tste 1979–94, govr 1969–2001), chm of tstees Univ of Northampton 2007–; pres Northamptonshire Branch Britsh Red Cross 1992–94; chm Northamptonshire Record Soc 1989–, chm River Nene Rgnl Park CIC 2007–, pres South Northants Constituency Cons Assoc 2007–14; Hon Fell Univ of Northampton 2002– (memb Ct 1995–); Freeman: City of London, Worshipful Co of Watermen; *Recreations* rowing, gardening, restoration of old houses; *Clubs* Leander, Vincent's (Oxford); *Style*— Christopher Davidge, Esq, OBE, DL; ✉ Little Houghton House, Northampton (☎ 01604 890204)

DAVIDOVITZ, (Robert Hyman) Colin; BEM (1954); s of Lambert Samuel Davidson, and Rose-Marie Davidson; *b* 18 August 1930; *Educ* Tynecastle Secdy Sch Edinburgh; *m* 20 Sept 1958, Catherine, da of Archibald Callaghan; 2 da (Judith b 1959, Theresa b 1963), 2 s (Philip b 1961, Robert b 1964); *Career* RN: boy telegraphist 1946, telegraphist 1948, leading telegraphist (special) 1951, PO telegraphist (PROV) 1954; Assoc-Rediffusion telerecordist 1955, sr engr Scottish TV 1957; Southern TV: sr engr 1958, prodn mangr 1964, prodn controller 1975; West Midland studio controller ATV/Central 1981, dir ops TV-am 1987–92, dir Kingsway Production Services Ltd 1992–; cncllr: Eastleigh BC 1996–2009, Hants CC 2001– (chm 2014–15, appointed hon alderman 2016); pres Catenians Southampton 1976; memb Rotary Club of Itchen Valley 2001–; *Recreations* photography, painting, yachting; *Style*— Colin Davidovitz, Esq, BEM; ✉ 55 Kingsway, Chandlers Ford, Hampshire SO5 1FH (☎ 023 8025 1342, e-mail colin.dav@hants.gov.uk)

DAVIDSON, HE Brian John; s of John Burton Davidson, and Joan Margaret Stevenson; *b* 28 April 1964, Kingston, Jamaica; *Educ* Trinity Coll Cambridge (BA); *m* 6 Sept 2014, Scott Kelly Chang; 1 s (Eliot Byron Davidson-Chang b 4 April 2016); *Career* diplomat; desk offr Czechoslovakia/Bulgaria East European Dept FCO 1985–86, Mandarin Chinese language trg 1986–88, second sec Beijing 1988–92, desk offr Assessments Staff Cabinet Office 1992–94, head China Section FCO 1994–96, first sec Canberra 1996–2000, Hajj Pilgrimage ctee reviewer Consular Directorate 2001, Lithuanian language trg 2001, dep head of mission Vilnius 2001–04, dep chief exec Int Financial Servs London 2005–06, consul-gen Guangzhou 2006–10, consul-gen Shanghai 2011–15, ambass to Thailand 2015–; *Style*— HE Mr Brian Davidson

DAVIDSON, Prof Donald Allen; s of John Forsyth Davidson (d 1976), and Jean, *née* Cole Morton (d 1984); *b* 27 April 1945, Lumphanan, Scotland; *Educ* Robert Gordon's Coll Aberdeen, Univ of Aberdeen (MacFarlane Prize in geography, BSc), Univ of Sheffield (PhD); *m* 3 April 1969, Caroline Elizabeth, *née* Brown; 2 da (Caroline Louise b 29 May 1971, Lorna Elizabeth b 5 Dec 1973), 1 s (Alan John MacDonald b 9 Feb 1986); *Career* jr research fell and temp lectr Dept of Geography Univ of Sheffield 1967–71, lectr Dept of Geography St David's UC Univ of Wales at Lampeter 1971–76; Dept of Geography Univ of Strathclyde: lectr, sr lectr then reader 1976–86; Dept of Environmental Science Univ of Stirling: reader 1986–91, prof 1991–2008, head of dept 1993–99, emeritus prof 2008–; managing ed Progress in Environmental Science jl; chm: Geography Panel Scottish Exam Bd 1986–90, Geography Panel Higher Skill Prog 1995–97, Advsy Ctee on Sites of Special Scientific Interest (SSSI) 2004–; memb: science-based archaeology ctee SERC 1992–95, Terrestrial Sciences Ctee NERC 1995–98; memb Editorial Bd: Geoarchaeology 1988–95, Soil Use and Management 1995–2013 (formerly ed-in-chief), NERC Coll 2003–06; currently ed Earth and Environmental Science Transactions of the Royal Society of Edinburgh; hon pres Scottish Assoc of Geography Teachers 1990–92; FRSE 1997; *Books* Geoarchaeology: Earth Science and the Past (ed jtly with M L Shackley, 1976), Science for Physical Geographers (1978), Timescales in Geomorphology (ed jtly with R Cullingford and J Lewin, 1980), Principles and Applications of Soil Geography (ed jtly with E M Bridges, 1982), Landscape Ecology and Land Use (ed jtly with A Vink, 1983), Land Evaluation (ed, 1986), Soil Erosion (ed jtly with R P C Morgan, 1986), Conceptual Issues in Environmental Archaeology (ed jtly with J Bintliff and E G Grant, 1988), The Evaluation of Land Resources (1992); also author of numerous articles and papers in academic jls incl Journal of Archaeological Science, Geoarchaeology, Int Journal of Geographical Information Systems, Applied Soil Ecology, Environment Int; *Recreations* maintaining large garden, hillwalking; *Style*— Prof Donald Davidson, FRSE; ✉ 26 Ochlochy Park, Dunblane, Perthshire FK15 0DU (☎ 01786 823599, e-mail d.a.davidson@stir.ac.uk)

DAVIDSON, Duncan Henry; s of Col Colin Keppel Davidson, CIE, OBE (ka 1943), and Lady (Mary) Rachel Davidson (later Lady (Mary) Rachel Pepys DCVO); *b* 29 March 1941; *Educ* Ampleforth; *m* 22 Sept 1965, Sarah Katherine, *née* Wilson; 4 da (Camilla b 7 Feb 1968, Natasha b 10 Oct 1969, Flora b 11 Aug 1975, Rose b 12 April 1979); *Career* Lt Royal Scots Greys 1959–63; mangr George Wimpey plc 1963–65, fndr and chm Ryedale Homes

D

Ltd 1965–72, fndr and chm Persimmon plc 1972–; non-exec dir Wm Morrison Supermarkets plc 2004–05; memb Ct Univ of Newcastle upon Tyne; *Recreations* country pursuits; *Clubs* White's, Turf, Northern Counties; *Style*— Duncan Davidson, Esq; ✉ Lilburn Tower, Alnwick, Northumberland NE66 4PQ (☎ 01668 217291, fax 01668 217371); Persimmon plc, Persimmon House, Fulford, York YO19 4FE (☎ 01904 642199, fax 01904 630924)

DAVIDSON, Edward Alan; QC (1994); s of Alan Thomas Davidson (d 1977), of Sheffield, and Helen Muriel, *née* Johnston (d 1952); *b* 12 July 1943; *Educ* King's Sch Canterbury, Gonville & Caius Coll Cambridge (scholar, Tapp Postgrad scholar, MA, LLB); *m* 19 May 1973, Hilary Jill, da of Norman S Fairman; 2 s (Mark b 14 June 1976, Philip b 27 Aug 1978); *Career* called to the Bar Gray's Inn 1966 (Atkin & Birkenhead scholar, bencher 2002); in practice Chancery Bar 1968–2007; sec The Institute 2001–06 (pres 2006–07); govr Summer Fields Sch Tst Ltd 1998– (chm 2007–13); *Recreations* tennis, bridge, gardening; *Style*— Edward Davidson, Esq, QC; ✉ Radcliffe Chambers, 11 New Square, London WC2A 3QB (☎ 020 7831 0081, fax 020 7405 2560, e-mail clerks@radcliffechambers.com)

DAVIDSON, Ian; *Educ* Jedburgh GS, Galashiels Acad, Univ of Edinburgh (MA), Jordanhill Coll Glasgow; *m*; 1 s, 1 da; *Career* MP (Lab/Co-op): Glasgow Govan 1992–97, Glasgow Pollok 1997–2005, Glasgow SW 2005–15; memb Public Accounts and Scottish Affrs Select Ctees, chair Scottish Affrs Select Ctee 2010–; memb Backbench: Overseas Aid Ctee, Trade & Industry Ctee, Defence Ctee; former chm: MSF Gp, Co-op Gp; chair Br Bermuda Gp, vice-chair Construction Gp; sec: Tribune Gp, Parly Rugby Team, Br-Japan Gp, German Gp, Trade Union Gp, Shipbuilding and Ship Repair Gp, New Europe All-Pty Gp, Aerospace Gp; memb All-Pty Royal Marines Gp, memb All-Pty Br Russia Gp; memb All-Pty Country Gps: America, Canada, ANZAC, Zimbabwe, South Africa, Japan, China, Germany (vice-chair), Gibraltar, Cayman Islands, Falkland Islands, Nigeria (chair 2001), India, UK and Arab Repub of Egypt; chair: Lab Against the Euro 2002, Lab Against European Superstate, Centre for a Social Europe; treas British Cncl; capt Parl rugby team; *Recreations* running, swimming, rugby union; *Style*— Ian Davidson, Esq; ✉ House of Commons, London SW1A 0AA (☎ 020 7219 3000)

DAVIDSON, Kenneth Muir (Ken); *b* 11 November 1948; *m* 1973, Judy, *née* Dick; *Career* dir Bain Dawes (Scotland) Ltd 1977–80, chief devpt exec Bowring (UK) Ltd 1980–83, chm and md Frizzell Insurance Brokers Ltd 1983–92, chief exec FirstCity Insurance Gp Ltd 1992–94 (non-exec dir 1994–99); chm: Harel (UK) Ltd 1987–, Davidson Partnership Ltd 1994–, Netquote Ltd 1995–97, Kingsmead Underwriting Agency Ltd 1995–2003, Crispin Speers and Partners Ltd 1999–, Associated Insurance Experts 2001–, CSP Holding Ltd 2005–, Ascent Insurance Brokers Ltd 2006–; dir: CII Enterprises Ltd 1992–97, Simplemethod Ltd 1992–99, Educn and Trg Tst Chartered Inst Ltd 1993–, Insurance Solutions Ltd 1995–97, Soc of Fin Advsrs Ltd 1997–98, B F Caudle Agencies Ltd 2001–03; pres Insurance Charities Ltd 2007– (dep pres 2006–07); conslt Barlow Lyde & Gilbert 1995–2003; pres CII 1997–98, vice-pres Insurance Inst of London 1999–; Liveryman: Worshipful Co of Insurers, Worshipful Co of Wheelwrights (Master 2007–08); chm Br Insurance Law Assoc 2002–04; ACIArb, ACII; *Books* Insuring Environmental Risks (1987); *Style*— Ken Davidson, Esq

DAVIDSON, Prof Marilyn Joy; da of Wallace Eyre, and Joyce Mary, *née* Robinson, of Queniborough, Leics; *b* 22 November 1951; *Educ* Melton Mowbray Upper Sch, Bolton Inst of Technol (external BA Univ of London), Barnet Coll London (CertEd), Univ of Queensland (MA), UMIST (PhD); *m* (m dis); 1 da (Fern Eyre-Morgan b 8 Oct 1986), 1 s (Lloyd Eyre-Morgan b 16 Aug 1988); *Career* lectr Dept of Community Studies Barnet Coll of Further Educn 1974–75, tutor in psychology Univ of Queensland 1975–79, guest psychology lectr and supervisor Dept of Mgmnt Sciences UMIST 1980–83, guest lectr Univ of Manchester and Manchester Business Sch 1980–84, prof in work psychology and co-dir Centre for Equality and Diversity at Work Manchester Business Sch Univ of Manchester (formerly Manchester Sch of Mgmnt UMIST) 1998– (lectr 1984–89, sr lectr 1989–98); ed Women in Management Review 1991–96, former assoc ed Occupational and Organizational Psychology; assoc editorial memb: Gender, Work and Organisations, The International Review of Women and Leadership, The International Journal of Police Science and Management; British Psychological Soc Award for Promoting Equality of Opportunity 2008; CPsychol, FBPsS (memb Div of Occupational Psychology, memb Div of Psychology Women Section), FRSA; *Books* with C L Cooper: High Pressure: The Working Lives of Women Managers (1982), Stress and the Woman Manager (1983), Working Women – An International Survey (1984), Women in Management (1984), Women and Information Technology (ed, 1987), The Stress Survivors (1991), Shattering the Glass Ceiling – The Woman Manager (1992), European Women in Business and Management Europe 1992 (ed, 1993); others: Reach for the Top: A Woman's Guide to Success in Business and Management (1985), Vulnerable Workers – Psychological and Legal Issues (jt ed, 1991), Women in Management – Current Research Issues (jt ed, 1994), The Black and Ethnic Minority Woman Manager – Cracking the Concrete Ceiling (1997), Women in Management – Current Research Issues Vol II (jt ed, 2000), Individual Diversity and Psychology in Organizations (jt ed, 2003), International Handbook of Women and Small Business Entrepreneurship (jt ed, 2005), Managing Diversity and Equality in Construction (ed with A Gale, 2006), Gender and Communication at Work (jt ed, 2006), International Research Handbook on Successful Women Entrepreneurs (jt ed, 2010); author of numerous articles and chapters in jls and pubns; *Recreations* playing cello, horse riding, theatre, cinema; *Style*— Prof Marilyn Davidson; ✉ Manchester Business School, The University of Manchester, Booth Street West, Manchester M15 6PB (☎ 0161 306 3449, fax 0161 306 3450, e-mail marilyn.davidson@mbs.ac.uk)

DAVIDSON, Sir Martin Stuart; KCMG (2014, CMG 2007); s of Westland Davidson (d 2002), and Freda, *née* Hill (d 2008); *b* 14 October 1955, Lowestoft, Suffolk; *Educ* Royal GS Guildford, Univ of St Andrews (MA), Henley Mgmnt Coll (Dip); *m* 1980, Elizabeth, *née* Fanner; 2 s (Thomas b 1985, William b 1988), 1 da (Charlotte b 1991); *Career* admin offr Hong Kong Govt 1979–83; Br Cncl: Peking 1984–87, regnl offr China 1987–89, dir S China 1989–93, asst regnl dir E and S Europe 1993–95, cultural cnsllr and dir China 1995–2000, regnl dir E Asia and Americas 2000–03, regnl dir Europe 2003–06, dep DG 2006–07, ceo 2007–14; chm GB China Centre; vice-chm Leonard Cheshire Disability; FRSA 2008; *Recreations* hill walking, flying, gliding, beekeeping; *Clubs* Royal Cwlth Soc; *Style*— Sir Martin Davidson, KCMG; ✉ Great Britain China Centre, 15 Belgrave Square, London SW1X 8PS (e-mail martin.davidson@gbbc.org.uk)

DAVIDSON, Nicholas Ranking; QC (1993); s of Brian Davidson, CBE (d 1995), and Priscilla Margaret, *née* Chilver (d 1981); *b* 2 March 1951; *Educ* Winchester (scholar), Trinity Coll Cambridge (exhibitioner, MA, vice-pres Cambridge Union); *m* 7 Sept 1978, Gillian Frances, da of Michael Leslie Watts; 2 da (Alexandra Frances Priscilla b 20 July 1983, Elizabeth Frances Hermione b 9 April 1989); *Career* called to the Bar Inner Temple 1974 (Inner Temple scholar, Cert of Honour, Treasurer's prize, Hughes Parry prize, bencher 1998); dep judge of the High Court 2000–; chm Professional Negligence Bar Assoc 1998–99 (treas 1990–95, dep chm 1996–97); govr St Mary's Sch Ascot 1996–2006 (tstee 2012–); MCIArb; *Publications* contrib Professional Negligence and Liability (ed Simpson, 2000); *Recreations* bridge, music, skiing; *Style*— Nicholas Davidson, Esq, QC; ✉ 4 New Square, Lincoln's Inn, London WC2A 3RJ (☎ 020 7822 2000, fax 020 7822 2001, e-mail n.davidson@4newsquare.com)

DAVIDSON, Peter John; s of John Frank Davidson, and Susanne, *née* Ostberg; *b* 25 July 1954; *Educ* Perse Sch, Trinity Coll Cambridge (sr scholar, MA), IMD, INSEAD; *m* Ann; 1 da (Katherine); *Career* process engr; ICI Agricultural Division Billingham: process engr Projects & Engrg Dept 1977–81, NITRAM plants mangr 1981–83, ammonia section mangr res 1983–86, res mangr 1986–89; process engrg mangr ICI Engineering 1989–94, gp research and technol mangr Tioxide plc 1994–98, vice-pres R & T Quest Foods 1998–2005, non-exec dir D1 Oils plc 2005–07, sr innovation advsr Dept for Business, Enterprise and Regulatory Reform and Dept for Innovation, Univs and Skills 2007–09; corporate memb Inst of Chemical Engrs and Chartered Engrs 1983, FIChemE, MEng, FREng 1992, FRSA 1995; *Recreations* hill walking, planning gardens, skiing, sailing, watercolours, cooking; *Style*— Peter Davidson, Esq, FREng

DAVIDSON, Philomena Mary; da of Thomas Oliver Grant Davidson, violinist (d 1985), and Mary Bridget Bourke; *b* 24 March 1949; *Educ* City & Guilds of London Art Sch (Edward Stott travel scholarship, Dip Sculpture), Royal Acad Schs London (RAS Dip Sculpture, Gold Medal for sculpture, Bronze Medal for work from the figure); *m* 7 Dec 1974, Michael Frank Davis; 2 da (Lucy Victoria b 3 June 1977, Ruth Alexandra b 18 Jan 1982); *Career* sculptor; studied Japanese language arts and architecture Japan 1973–76, opened Bronze Foundry Milton Keynes 1980; tstee Forest of Dean Sculpture Park 2013–; exhibitions: Royal Acad Summer Exhibition, Royal West of England Acad Annual Show, Westminster City Gallery, Bircham Gallery, Margam Sculpture Park, Woodlands Gallery, Well Hung Gallery, Artspace 2000, Study Gallery 2002, Jerram Gallery 2013; dir Chelsea Harbour Sculpture 1993 and 1996, md The Sculpture Co Ltd 1994–98, md Davidson Arts Partnership 1999–; first one woman show Coopers & Lybrand Atrium Gallery 1997, one woman show Kube Gallery Poole 2004; first woman pres Royal Soc of Br Sculptors 1990–96; FRSBS 1990 (assoc fell 1984), FRSA 1990, RWA 1996; *Publications* Chelsea Harbour Sculpture 93; *Recreations* swimming, reading biographies; *Style*— Ms Philomena Davidson; ✉ 4 Church Walk, Bletchingley, Surrey RH1 4PD (☎ 01883 741928, e-mail phil@davidsonarts.com)

DAVIDSON, Rt Hon Ruth; PC (2016), MSP; da of Douglas Davidson, and Elizabeth, *née* Ritchie; *Educ* Univ of Edinburgh (MA); *Career* former journalist BBC; MSP (Cons): Glasgow 2011–16, Edinburgh Central 2016–; ldr Scottish Cons Pty 2011–; *Style*— The Rt Hon Ruth Davidson, MSP; ✉ The Scottish Parliament, Edinburgh EH99 1SP

DAVIDSON, Stephen Robert; DL (W Yorks 2002); s of Cecil Robert Davidson, of Tynemouth, and Joan, *née* Robinson (d 2003); *b* 20 October 1950; *Educ* Tynemouth GS, UMIST (BSc), Univ of Newcastle upon Tyne (PGCE); *m* 1983, Carol Anne, da of Ralston Smith; 1 s (Jamie b 1993); *Career* grad trainee Tube Investments Gp 1972–73; former sch appts: Lord Wandsworth Coll 1974–83, middle sch master Manchester GS 1983–96; headmaster Bradford GS 1996–2011; High Sheriff in nomination W Yorks 2012; *Recreations* sport, travel, civil aviation; *Clubs* East India, MCC, Bradford, Ilkley Golf; *Style*— Stephen Davidson, Esq, DL

DAVIDSON OF GLEN CLOVA, Baron (Life Peer UK 2006), of Glen Clova in Angus; Neil Forbes Davidson; QC (Scot 1993); *b* 13 September 1950; *Educ* Univ of Stirling (BA), Univ of Bradford Mgmnt Centre (MSc), Univ of Edinburgh (LLB, LLM); *m* 1980, Regina Anne, *née* Sprissler; *Career* analyst J & A Scrimgeour 1972; admitted to Faculty of Advocates 1979; slr-gen for Scotland 2000–01, advocate-gen for Scotland 2006–10; dir: Scot Cncl for Int Arbitration 1990–2006, City Disputes Panel 1994–2000; ICJ chef de mission Egypt 1997 and 1998; pres Clan Davidson Assoc 2002–; Hon 5th Dan Int Taekwondo Fedn; Hon DUniv Stirling; *Books* Judicial Review in Scotland (1986), The Davidson Review – UK Implementation of EU Regluation (2007); *Style*— The Lord Davidson of Glen Clova, QC

DAVIE, Jonathan Richard; s of Richard Davie, of Wimbledon, and Anne Christine Margaret, *née* Wilmot; *b* 21 September 1946; *Educ* Tonbridge, Univ of Neuchâtel; *m* 13 Sept 1986, Belinda Mary, da of Wing Cdr M V Blake; 2 da (Samantha Jane b 4 Jan 1991, Francesca Louise b 23 Aug 1995); *Career* articled to J Dix Lewis Caesar Duncan & Co (now Robson Rhodes) CAs 1965–69; Wedd Durlacher Mordaunt & Co: joined 1969, memb Stock Exchange 1974, ptnr 1976–86, sr dealing ptnr 1986; main bd dir Barclays de Zoete Wedd Holdings 1986–97 (md Fixed Income 1986–91), chief exec BZW Global Equities 1991–96, dep chm BZW 1996–97, vice-chm Credit Suisse First Boston 1997–2007, chm First Avenue Ptnrs LLP 2007–; non-exec chm IG Gp plc 2004–14; non-exec dir: Credit Suisse (UK) Ltd 2003–09, Persimmon plc 2010–, Hansa Investment Tst 2013–, Gabelli Value Plus Tst plc; govr Heathfield Sch for Girls 2006–13; FCA (ACA 1970); *Recreations* golf, tennis, skiing; *Clubs* City of London, Queen's, Royal and Ancient, Royal St George's Golf, Prestwick Golf, Berkshire Golf, Sunningdale Golf, Rye Golf, White's, Golfe de Morfontaine; *Style*— Jonathan Davie, Esq; ✉ First Avenue LLP, Swan House, 17–19 Stratford Place, London W1C 1BQ

DAVIE, Sue; *b* 22 July 1964, Balloch, Scotland; *Educ* BA, MBA; *Career* formerly with: International Computers, Dixons Stores Gp, Freeserve; Meningitis Tst: dir of finance 2002–07, chief exec 2007–; fell CIMA 2001 (memb 1994); *Style*— Ms Sue Davie; ✉ Meningitis Trust, Fern House, Bath Road, Stroud, Gloucestershire GL5 3TJ (☎ 01453 768000)

DAVIE, Tim Douglas; s of Douglas Davie, of Herstmonceux, Sussex, and Alicia, *née* Higson; *b* 25 April 1967, Croydon; *Educ* Whitgift Sch Croydon, Univ of Cambridge (MA); *m* 1997, Anne, *née* Shotbolt; 3 s (James b 18 Feb 2000, William b 16 Sept 2002, Edward b 14 Jan 2006); *Career* brand mangr Proctor and Gamble 1989–93; PepsiCo: UK mktg dir 1993–2000, vice-pres int mktg 2000–05; dir Mktg, Cmmns and Audiences BBC 2005–08, dir Audio and Music BBC 2008–, acting DG BBC 2012, ceo BBC Worldwide 2013–; chm Comic Relief; *Recreations* running, skiing, reading; *Clubs* Soho House; *Style*— Tim Davie, Esq; ✉ BBC Worldwide, Television Centre, 101 Wood Lane, London W12 7FA (☎ 020 8433 2000, e-mail tim.davie@bbc.com)

DAVIES, Alan; *m* 13 Jan 2007, Katie, *née* Maskell; 1 da (b 2009); *Career* comedian and actor; Hon DLitt Univ of Kent at Canterbury 2003; *Television* for BBC incl: Jonathan Creek (winner of Best Drama BAFTA Awards 1997, winner of Most Popular Drama Series National Television Awards 1998), QI (Comedy Panel Show Nat Television Award 2013), Urban Trauma, A Many Splintered Thing; other credits incl: The Clive James Show (ITV), Bob and Rose (ITV), The Brief (ITV); *Radio* shows for BBC incl: Sick as a Parrot (Radio 5), Alan's Big One FM (Radio 1), The Alan Davies Show 1998; *Tours* UK Tour, Melbourne Comedy Festival, Auckland Comedy Festival, Montreal Comedy Festival; *Video* Live From the Lyric Theatre (1995), Urban Trauma (1998); *Awards* Best Young Comic Time Out Awards 1991, Festival Critics Award Edinburgh Festival 1994, Best Actor Monte Carlo TV Festival 2002; *Recreations* supporter of Arsenal FC, motor cycling; *Style*— Alan Davies, Esq

DAVIES, Prof Alun Huw; *b* 16 January 1960; *Educ* Bishop Gore GS Swansea, Emmanuel Coll Cambridge (Windsor scholar, BA), Magdalen Coll Oxford and Univ of Oxford Med Sch (BM BCh), Univ of Oxford (MA, DM, DSc); *Children* 2 c; *Career* house surgn Nuffield Dept of Surgery Univ of Oxford and John Radcliffe Hosp 1984–85, house physician Northampton Gen Hosp 1985, demonstrator in anatomy Univ of Cambridge and supervisor in anatomy Downing, Girton and Wolfson Colls 1985–86, hon research worker Dept of Anatomy RCS 1986; SHO: John Radcliffe Hosp 1986–87, Bristol Royal Infirmary 1987–88; surgical registrar Churchill and John Radcliffe Hosps Oxford and Milton Keynes Hosp 1988–90, research fell, hon registrar and tutor in surgery Bristol Royal Infirmary and Univ of Bristol 1990–92, research fell and hon registrar Royal United Hosp Bath 1992, lectr Univ of Bristol 1992–95, sr registrar Derriford Hosp Plymouth 1992–93, sr registrar Bristol Royal Infirmary 1993–95, sr lectr and hon conslt in surgery Charing Cross and Westminster Med Sch 1995–97; Imperial Coll of Med and Charing Cross Hosp:

sr lectr and hon conslt in surgery 1997–99, dir of undergraduate trg and dep head Div of Surgery, Anaethesia and Intensive Care 1998–2002, reader in surgery 1999–2008, prof of vascular surgery 2008–, head of undergrad medicine (year 3); head Academic Section Vascular Surgery Imperial Coll London 2010–; currently hon conslt surgn: Imperial Coll NHS Tst, Chelsea and Westminster NHS Tst; regnl advsr in vascular surgery 2003–07; dir European Coll of Phlebology; ed: Phlebology 2003–, Venous News 2008; reviewer: Br Jl of Surgery, Annals of RCS, BMJ, Br Jl of Radiology, European Jl of Vascular & Endovascular Surgery, Br Jl of Neurology & Psychiatry, Lancet, Cochrane Database, European Jl of Cardiology, Jl of Vascular Surgery; sometime examiner: Univ of Bristol, Univ of London, Univ of Leicester; chm Nice Guidelines Ctee 2011–; memb NHS Panel of Experts Dept of Health; Sir Jules Thorn research fell 1991, Hunterian prof RCS 1993, Abdol Islami int guest scholar American Coll of Surgns 2000–01; RSM: memb Cncl Quality and Mgmnt Section 1998–, memb Cncl Venous Forum 1999– (pres 2008–10), memb Cncl Section of Surgery 2000–; memb: BMA, European Soc of Vascular Surgery, European Venous Forum (memb Bd 2000–, pres 2006–07), Surgical Research Soc, Soc of Academic Surgns, American Inst of Ultrasound in Med, Int Soc of Cardiovascular Surgery (UK rep European Chapter), Vascular Surgery Soc of GB and I (memb Cncl 1994–96), Br Assoc of Atherosclerosis, Vascular Soc of GB and I (memb Cncl 2002–07); fell: Assoc of Surgns of GB and I, Soc of Vascular Med and Biology, American Venous Forum, American Coll of Phlebology (Order of Merit in Phlebology 2011 and 2012, Order for Lifetime Achievement 2014), Australian Coll of Phlebology; FRCS 1988, FRSM, FHEA 2007; *Publications* incl: Fast Facts: Vascular Surgery Highlights (published annually 1999–), Essential Vascular Surgery (co-author, 1999), Essential Postgraduate Surgery (co-ed, 2000), An Atlas of Endovascular and Vascular Surgery (co-author, 2001), Renal Access (co-ed, 2003) Leg Ulcers (co-author, 2003); numerous chapters in books, papers and articles in learned jls; *Style*— Prof Alun Davies; ✉ Department of Surgery, Charing Cross Hospital, Imperial College, London W6 8RF (☎ 020 3311 7309, fax 020 3311 7362, e-mail a.h.davies@imperial.ac.uk)

DAVIES, (Thomas) Alun Rhys; AM; s of Rhys Davies, and Mair, *née* Williams; *b* 12 February 1964, Tredegar, Wales; *Educ* Tredegar Comp Sch, Univ of Wales Aberystwyth (BA); *Partner* Megan Mathias; 1 da (Beca b 9 April 1998); *Career* pres NUS Wales 1987–89, regnl organiser WWF UK 1990–94, public affrs mangr Oxfam Wales 1994–98, PR mangr Hyder 1998–99, head of public affrs UK Atomic Energy Authy (UKAEA) 1999–2000, dir of corporate affrs S4C 2000–04, dir Bute Cmmns 2004–07, memb Nat Assembly for Wales (Lab): Mid and West Wales 2007–11, Blaenau Gwent 2011–; memb: NUJ, UNISON; *Recreations* rugby, cycling, hill walking, France; *Clubs* Groucho, Cameo; *Style*— Alun Davies, Esq, AM; ✉ National Assembly for Wales, Cardiff Bay, Cardiff CF99 1NA

DAVIES, Prof Alwyn George; s of Rev John Lewis Davies (d 1986), of Hunstanton, Norfolk, and Victoria May, *née* Rowe (d 1996); *b* 1926; *Educ* Hamonds GS Swaffham Norfolk, UCL (BSc, PhD, DSc); *m* 11 Aug 1956, Margaret, da of Geoffrey Drake (d 1980), of Menai Bridge, Anglesey; 1 da (Sarah b 1958), 1 s (Stephen b 1960); *Career* lectr Battersea Poly 1949, prof of chemistry UCL 1969– (lectr 1953, reader 1964); fell UCL 1991; FRSC; FRS 1989; *Books* Organic Peroxides (1961), Organotin Chemistry (1997, 2 edn 2004), Tin Chemistry (jt ed, 2008), UCL Chemistry Department 1828–1974 (with P J Garratt, 2013); *Style*— Prof Alwyn Davies, FRS; ✉ 26 South Approach, Moor Park, Northwood, Middlesex HA6 2ET (☎ 01923 823528, e-mail a.g.davies@talktalk.net); Chemistry Department, UCL, 20 Gordon Street, London WC1H 0AJ (☎ 020 7679 4701, fax 020 7679 7463, e-mail a.g.davies@ucl.ac.uk)

DAVIES, Andrew Robert Tudor; AM; s of Tudor John Davies, of Cowbridge, Vale of Glamorgan, and Margaret Elizabeth Davies (d 1983); *b* 8 April 1968, Cowbridge, Vale of Glamorgan; *Educ* Wycliffe Coll Stroud, Balfour House Sch St Athan; *m* 1 June 1991, Julia Mary; 2 da (Sophie b 7 May 1993, Sarah b 13 March 2002), 2 s (Mathew b 9 Oct 1995, James b 20 April 1998); *Career* farmer, ptnr T F Davies & Sons; memb Nat Assembly for Wales (Cons) S Wales Central 2007–, ldr Cons Pty Nat Assembly for Wales 2011–; memb: NFU, Young Farmers Clubs, Royal Welsh Agricultural Soc (Oxford scholarship) 2002; *Recreations* rugby, family, countryside; *Style*— Andrew R T Davies, Esq, AM; ✉ National Assembly for Wales, Cardiff Bay, Cardiff CF99 1NA (☎ 029 2089 8747, e-mail andrewrt.davies@wales.gov.uk)

DAVIES, Andrew Wynford; *b* 20 September 1936; *Educ* Whitchurch GS Cardiff, UCL; *m* 1960; *Career* author, screenwriter and playwright; Hon DLitt: Coventry Univ 1994, Univ of Warwick 2004, Open Univ 2004, UCL 2006; Hon Dr Arts De Montfort Univ 2003; hon fell Univ of Wales 1997; fell BAFTA 2003, FRSL 1996; *Awards* Guardian Children's Fiction Award 1979, Boston Globe Horn Award 1979, Broadcasting Press Guild Award 1980, 1990, 1998, 1999 and 2002, Pye Colour TV Award Best Children's Writer 1981, RTS Writer's Award 1986,1987 and 2006, BAFTA Writer's Award 1989, BAFTA Award 1989, 1993, 1999, 2002 and 2006, Primetime Emmy Award 1991, Writers' Guild Award 1991, 1993, 1994, 1996, 1998 and 2006, Samuelson Award (Lifetime Achievement) 2004; *Television* scripts/adaptations: To Serve Them All My Days 1979 (from R F Delderfield novel, BBC1), A Very Peculiar Practice 1986–87, Mother Love 1989, House of Cards (from Michael Dobbs novel) 1990, Filipina Dreamers 1991, The Old Devils (from Kingsley Amis novel) 1992, Anglo-Saxon Attitudes 1992, A Very Polish Practice 1992, To Play the King (Michael Dobbs, BBC1) 1993, Middlemarch (from George Eliot novel, BBC1) 1994, Pride and Prejudice (Jane Austen, BBC1) 1995, Game On (with Bernadette Davis) 1995, The Final Cut (Michael Dobbs, BBC1) 1995, Emma (Jane Austen, ITV) 1996, Wilderness (with Bernadette Davis) 1996, Moll Flanders (Defoe, ITV) 1996, Bill's New Frock (Channel 4) 1997, Getting Hurt (BBC) 1998, Vanity Fair (BBC) 1998, A Rather English Marriage (BBC) 1998, Wives and Daughters (BBC) 1999, Take a Girl Like You 2000, The Way We Live Now (Anthony Trollope, BBC) 2001, Othello (ITV) 2001, Daniel Deronda (from George Eliot novel, BBC) 2002, Tipping the Velevet (BBC) 2002, Dr Zhivago (ITV) 2002, Boudica (ITV) 2002, He Knew He Was Right 2004, Falling (ITV) 2005, Bleak House (BBC) 2005, The Chatterley Affair (BBC) 2006, The Line of Beauty (BBC) 2006, Diary of a Nobody 2007, Northanger Abbey 2007, A Room with a View 2007, Sense and Sensibility 2008, Little Dorrit 2008, Affinity 2008, Sleep With Me 2008, South Riding 2011, Mr Selfridge 2013, A Poet In New York 2014, Quirke 2014; *Stage Plays* Rose 1981, Prin 1990; *Films* Circle of Friends 1995, Bridget Jones's Diary 2001, The Tailor of Panama 2001, Bridget Jones: The Edge of Reason 2004; *Fiction* A Very Peculiar Practice (1986), The New Frontier (1987), Getting Hurt (1989), Dirty Faxes (1990); *Children's books* The Fantastic Feats of Dr Boox (1972), Conrad's War (1978), Marmalade and Rufus (1981), Marmalade Atkins in Space (1981), Educating Marmalade (1982), Danger Marmalade at Work (1983), Marmalade Hits the Big Time (1984), Alfonso Bonzo (1987), Poonam's Pets (with Diana Davies, 1990), Marmalade on the Ball (1995); *Recreations* tennis, food, alcohol; *Style*— Andrew Davies, Esq, FRSL; ✉ c/o The Agency, 24 Pottery Lane, London W11 4LZ (☎ 020 7727 1346, fax 020 7727 9037)

DAVIES, Anna Elbina; *see:* Morpurgo Davies, Prof Anna

DAVIES, Betty Alicia; JP (Nottingham 1971); da of Charles William Pearl, of Nottingham, and Alice, *née* Stevenson; *Educ* Haywood Sch Nottingham, Guildhall Sch of Music and Drama (LGSM); *Career* fashion and textile designer; fndr and chief exec Campus Gp Oxford, Edinburgh, Glasgow, Nottingham and Aberdeen 1966–89, designer Harris Tweed Acad Collections 1989–93, chief exec and design dir Betty Davies SFI (design and mgmnt consits, corp and ceremonial dress) 1993–, princ Perform PR Scotland 2003; designer: Royal Bank of Scotland 1993–, Royal Collections 1993–, choir robes St Giles Cathedral Bank of Scotland 1997–2003, Levee dress for first woman Herald Ct of the Lord Lyon, Royal Scot Acad robes 2002–03, ceremonial robes Moderator of the General Assembly of the Church of Scotland 2004, academic robes Edinburgh Coll of Art; public memb Press Cncl 1983–90; memb Ct Univ of Nottingham, memb Bd of Govrs Nottingham Girls' HS 1987–94, govr Edinburgh Coll of Art 1989–2002 (hon fell 2003); vice-chm Edinburgh Coll of Art Alumni Assoc 2003–11, conslt dir of alumni and ed Decades Edinburgh Coll of Art 2003–11; chm Nottingham Cncl for Voluntary Serv 1981–84; fndr chm Edinburgh Theatre Workshop; organiser Lunch-time Proms Nottingham Playhouse 1966–89 and Royal Scottish Acad 1989–94, chair Friends of David Talbot Rice Gallery Univ of Edinburgh 2011–; MIMgt 1982; *Recreations* visual and performing arts; *Style*— Mrs Betty Davies; ✉ 5 Blackie House, Lady Stair's Close, Edinburgh EH1 2NY (☎ 0131 225 6065, mobile 07720 441363, e-mail betty.davies2@btopenworld.com)

DAVIES, Bob; *b* 12 October 1948; *Educ* Univ of Edinburgh (LLB); *m* 1971, Eileen; 1 s (Christopher b 1978); *Career* Ford Motor Co: joined 1970, mangr treasy analysis Ford Motor Credit 1982–83, dir of fin Ford Spain 1983–85; dir Coopers & Lybrand Assoc 1985–87, chief fin offr Waterford Wedgewood plc 1987–91, fin dir Ferranti International plc 1991–93, chief exec East Midlands Electricity plc 1997–98 (fin dir 1994–97), chief exec Arriva plc 1998–2006, chm Biffa plc 2006–08, chm Eurosports Hldgs Sarl 2010–13, chm Home Gp 2012–, chm Countrywide plc 2013; non-exec dir: Geest plc 1998–2004, Barratt Devpts 2004–12, British Energy Group plc 2006–09, Northern Rock plc 2008–10, Kelda Hldgs Ltd 2012–; chm NE Regnl Cncl CBI 2007–08, dir Sunderland Urban Regeneration Co 2002–07; chm Bd of Govrs Univ of Sunderland 2003–09; Hon LLD Univ of Sunderland; FCMA; *Recreations* golf, vintage cars; *Style*— Bob Davies, Esq

DAVIES, (Henry) Byron; AM; *b* Swansea; *Educ* LLB; *Career* former police offr Met Police Service and Nat Crime Squad; memb Nat Assembly for Wales (Cons) S Wales W 2011–15, MP (Cons) Gower 2015–; *Recreations* rugby, general aviation; *Clubs* RAF, Gowerton Conservatives and Unionist, Carlton; *Style*— Byron Davies, Esq, MP; ✉ 98 Sterry Road, Gowerton, Swansea SA4 3BW (☎ 01792 650555, e-mail byron.davies.mp@parliament.uk, website www.byrondavies.org.uk)

DAVIES, Charles Simon Hartley; s of Graham Hartley Davies, and Carolyn, *née* Murrell; *b* 2 April 1970; *Educ* Shrewsbury, Univ of Durham (BA); *Career* Cargill 1992–93, Sunrise Asset Co Ltd 1993–98, fndr and ceo The Link Asset & Securities Co Ltd 1998–, fndr Linkbrokers Inc (NY) 2003, fndr Link Securities (HK) 2005; sold Link to ICAP Gp 2008 (continues to run Link within ICAP Gp); Deloitte 5th Fastest Gp Company in UK 2004; *Recreations* fly fishing, rock climbing; *Clubs* Soho House, Quo Vadis; *Style*— Charles Davies, Esq; ✉ The Link Asset and Securities Co Ltd, The Courtyard, 12 Sutton Row, London W1D 4AD (☎ 020 7663 4300, fax 020 7851 6630, e-mail charlie@linkbrokers.co.uk)

DAVIES, Chris; MEP (Lib Dem) NW England; *b* 7 July 1954; *Educ* Cheadle Hulme Sch Stockport, Gonville & Caius Coll Cambridge (MA), Univ of Kent at Canterbury; *m* 27 Oct 1979, Carol; 1 da; *Career* chm Housing Liverpool City Cncl 1982–83, marketing and communications conslt 1983–95 and 1997–99; MP (Lib Dem) Littleborough and Saddleworth 1995–97, MEP (Lib Dem) NW England 1999–, environment spokesman European Parl; *Recreations* fell running; *Style*— Chris Davies, Esq, MEP; ✉ 87A Castle Street, Stockport SK3 9AR (☎ 0161 477 7070); European Parliament, Rue Wiertz, B-1047, Brussels (☎ 0032 2284 5353/7353, e-mail chris.davies@europarl.europa.eu)

DAVIES, Christopher Paul (Chris); MP; s of Terrence Stephen Davies, and Mary, *née* Morgan; *b* 18 August 1967, Swansea; *Educ* Morriston Sch Swansea; *m* 20 Oct 2006, Elizabeth Mary, *née* Dwyer; 2 da (Sophie, Charlotte); *Career* former auctioneer; former cncllr Powys CC, MP (Cons) Brecon and Radnorshire 2015–; memb Brecon Beacons Nat Park Authy; asst hon dir Royal Welsh Show; *Recreations* shooting, skiing, countryside activities; *Style*— Chris Davies, Esq, MP; ✉ 4a Lion Yard, Brecon, Powys LD3 7BA (☎ 01874 624796, e-mail chris.davies.mp@parliament.uk, website www.chrisdavies.org.uk); House of Commons, London SW1A 0AA

DAVIES, David; s of Paul Davies, and Susan, *née* Stark; *b* 3 March 1985, Cardiff; *Educ* St Cyres Comp Sch Penarth; *Career* swimmer; achievements incl: Silver medal 200m freestyle and Silver medal mixed 4 x 200m freestyle relay European Youth Olympics 2001, Silver medal 400m freestyle and Bronze medal 4 x 200m freestyle relay European Jr Long-Course Championships 2002, Silver medal 1500m freestyle European Short-Course Championships 2002, Gold medal 1500m freestyle, Silver medal 200m freestyle and Bronze medal 400m freestyle European Jr Long-Course Championships 2003, Bronze medal 1500m freestyle Olympic Games Athens 2004, Bronze medal 1500m freestyle World Championships Montreal 2005, Gold medal 1500m freestyle and Bronze medal 400m freestyle Cwlth Games Melbourne 2006, Bronze medal 1500m freestyle World Championships Melbourne 2007, Silver medal 1500m freestyle European Championships Eindhoven 2008, Silver medal 1500m freestyle World Short Course Championships Manchester 2008, Silver medal 10k Open Water World Championships Seville 2008, Silver medal 10km marathon Olympic Games Beijing 2008; hon druid Gorsedd of the Bards 2013; *Style*— David Davies, Esq

DAVIES, Prof Sir David Evan Naunton; kt (1994), CBE (1986); s of David Evan Davies (d 1935), and Sarah, *née* Samuel (d 1982); *b* 28 October 1935; *Educ* West Monmouth Sch, Univ of Birmingham (MSc, PhD, DSc); *m* 1, 21 July 1962, Enid (d 1990), da of James Edwin Patilla; 2 s (Christopher James b 1965, Michael Evan b 1967); m 2, 19 Nov 1992, Jennifer Eason Rayner; *Career* lectr and sr lectr Univ of Birmingham 1961–67, hon sr princ sci offr Royal Radar Estab Malvern 1966–67, asst dir Res Dept BR Derby 1967–71, prof of electrical engrg UCL 1971–86 (vice-provost 1986–88), vice-chllr Loughborough Univ of Technol 1988–1993, chief scientific advsr MOD 1993–99; pres Royal Acad of Engrg 1996–2001; pro-chllr Univ of Sussex 1998–2001; chm: Railway Safety 2001–03, Hazard Forum 2003–10; memb Bd: ERA Technology Ltd 1994–2003, Lattice plc 2001–02, ERA Fndn 2001–07, Parly Office of Science and Technology 2001–2016; memb and chm of numerous ctees of: MOD, DES, Cabinet Office; Rank Prize for Optoelectronics 1984, Callendar Medal (Inst of Measurement and Control) 1984, Centennial Medal (Inst of Electrical and Electronic Engrs USA) 1984, Faraday Medal (IEE) 1987, President's Medal Royal Acad of Engrg; Master Worshipful Co of Engineers 2003–04; Hon DSc: Loughborough Univ 1994, Univ of Bradford 1995, Univ of Warwick 1997, Univ of Wales 2002; Hon DEng: Univ of Birmingham 1994, South Bank Univ 1994, Herriot Watt Univ 1999, UMIST 2000; Hon DUniv Surrey 1996; hon fell UCL 2006; FIEE 1967, FREng 1979, FRS 1984; *Publications* author of publications on radar and fibre optics; *Style*— Prof Sir David Davies, CBE, FRS, FREng; ✉ Church Hill House, Church Lane, Danehill, East Sussex RH17 7EY; 29 Victoria House, 25 Tudor Street, London EC4Y 0DD (☎ 01825 790321, e-mail david.e.n.davies@gmail.com)

DAVIES, David Johnston; OBE (2007); s of John Edwardes Davies, MBE (d 1948), and Margaret Frances, *née* Morrison (d 1999); *b* 28 May 1948; *Educ* Royal Masonic Sch for Boys, Univ of Sheffield (BA(Econ)), Univ of Oxford (CertEd); *m* July 1977, Susan Anne, *née* Cuff; 2 da (Amanda Jane b March 1980, Caroline Frances b April 1983); *Career* Thomson Regional Newspapers (Belfast Telegraph) 1970–71, BBC corr and presenter 1971–94 (variously BBC TV News political corr, BBC TV News educn corr, presenter/corr Grandstand and Match of the Day, assignments incl General Elections and World Cups); The FA: dir public affrs 1994–98, exec dir 1998–2000, dir int strategy and exec dir 2000–06; sports/media conslt 2006–, regnl chm (London) Coutts Bank 2006–13; panels/ctees UEFA/FIFA 2000–06; Govt Football Task Force 1997–99, BOA 1999–2006;

chair DCMS Panel on Listed Events 2008–09; advsr to: Chief Exec FIFA World Cup 2010 Organising Ctee, Leaders in Football Conferences 2007–12, Hong Kong FA Reform Prog 2010–11, Confedn of North, Soccerex Football Conferences 2013–, Central American and Caribbean Assoc Football 2013–15; memb Bd Int Inspiration 2012 Olympic Legacy, tstee Level Playing Field 2014–; Duke of Edinburgh's Gold Award 1965, Clear Speaking Award Birmingham Inst for the Deaf 1993; memb Cncl Univ of Birmingham 2012–, visiting sr memb St Peter's Coll Oxford 2016–; *Recreations* family, watching cricket, tennis, theatre; *Clubs* Lancashire CCC, Ivy; *Style*— David Davies, Esq, OBE; ✉ Tregaron Associates, West Meadows, Grange Lane, Alvechurch, Birmingham B48 7DJ (e-mail david@daviestregaron.co.uk)

DAVIES, David Thomas Charles; MP; s of Peter Hugh Charles Davies, and Kathleen Diane, *née* Elton, of Newport; *b* 27 July 1970; *Educ* Bassaleg Comp Sch Newport; *m* 2003, Aliz, *née* Harnisföger; *Career* Br Steel Corp 1988–89, seasonal jobs in Australia 1989–91, gen mangr tea importing and shipping co 1991–99, memb Nat Assembly for Wales (Cons) Monmouth 1999–2007; Parly candidate (Cons) Bridgend 1997, MP (Cons) Monmouth 2005–; led NO campaign Newport 1997; memb: Inst of Traffic Admin, Inst of Freight Forwarding; MILog; *Recreations* surfing, long distance running, keeping fit; *Clubs* Abergavenny Constitutional, Chepstow Cons, Monmouth Cons, Usk Cons; *Style*— David Davies, Esq, MP; ✉ The Grange, 16 Maryport Street, Usk, Monmouthshire (☎ 01291 672780)

DAVIES, Dr Edwin; CBE (2012, OBE 2000); Lord of the Manor of Farnworth; s of Edwin Davies (d 1983), and Hannah, *née* Kelly (d 1979); *b* 18 June 1946, Salford; *Educ* Farnworth GS, Univ of Durham (BA); *m* 1, 22 Aug 1969 (m dis 1987), Jean, *née* Ellison; 1 da (Sarah Jane b 22 March 1971), 1 s (Roger John b 14 Feb 1974); m 2, 30 June 1989, Susan Chinn, *née* Crellin; *Career* various positions rising to asst gp md Scapa Group plc 1968–84, chm STRIX Group Ltd 1984–2006; dir Bolton Wanderers FC 1999–; chm Advsy Bd Manchester Business Sch 2015–; tstee: V&A 2007–, Kew Gardens 2014–; DSocSc (hc) Univ of Manchester 2008; CMI 1996; FCMA 1985; *Recreations* soccer, shooting, travel; *Style*— Dr Edwin Davies, CBE; ✉ Moorecroft, Crossag Road, Ballasalla, Isle of Man IM9 3EF (☎ 01624 828730, fax 01624 824578, e-mail gilly@fildraw.com)

DAVIES, Elsa Myfanwy; LVO (2004); da of Mary, *née* Williams, and John Rees; *Educ* Univ of Wales (Teacher's Cert), Open Univ (BA), Univ of London (DipEd, MA); *Career* teacher Glamorgan CC 1965–70, dep head London Borough of Hillingdon 1970–74; head teacher: Surrey CC 1974–83, London Borough of Hillingdon 1983–87; mangr Chartered Mgmnt Inst 1988–91, dir National Playing Fields Assoc (NPFA) 1991–2004, chief exec NPFA Services Ltd 1991–2004, chief exec Millenium Centres Devpt Co Ltd 1997–2004, chief exec Mackworth Ltd 2004–07; conslt to various bodies incl: Univ of London, Moorhead State Univ MN, Univ of Ulster, Univ of Leicester, Manchester Poly, Brighton Poly, BBC Enterprises, Welsh Consumer Cncl, The Spastics Soc (now Scope), National Foundation for Educn and Research, Commission of the European Communities; lectr to various orgns, local authorities and colleges incl: Capita Training, The Engineering Cncl, The Industrial Soc, Surrey, Hants, Essex and Sheffield Local Authorities, Univ of Antwerp, Univ of Birmingham, Kingston Poly, Poly of Wales, Mid Kent Coll of HE; govr Royal Welsh Coll of Music and Drama 2001–06; memb: Central Cncl of Physical Recreation (CCPR), Cncl for Nat Academic Awards Educnl Orgn, Mgmnt Bd and Initial Teacher Educn Bd 1985–91, Nat Curriculum Working Gp on Design and Technol 1989–91, Cncl Advsy Centre for Educn 1977–90 (former chm), Cncl British Educnl Mgmnt and Admin Soc 1980–92, ESU 1980–2000 (Page scholar 1981), UK/US Teacher Exchange Ctee Central Bureau for Educnl Visits and Exchanges 1981–92 (former vice-chm), Euro Forum for Educn Mgmnt 1981–92, Commonwealth Cncl for Educnl Admin 1981–92, Educn 2000 1983, Court Univ of Wales Coll of Cardiff 1989–92, Ct Nat Library of Wales 2002–06, Organising Ctee Educn Mgmnt Int Intervisitation Prog 1990, Cncl Action for Govrs Info and Trg Sponsorship Ctee 1990–91, Working Gp Human Resource Devpt Partnership 1990–91, Belgravia Breakfast Club 1991–2000, Lady Taverners 1992–97, London Businesswomen's Network 1992–97, City of London Sport and Recreation Cncl 1992–94, Shadow Sec of State's Nat Lottery Gp 1996, Glas Cymru 2001–12, Cncl Univ of Wales 2006– (chair Univ of Wales Audit Ctee), Cncl Swansea Univ 2007–11 (memb Audit and HR Ctees); hon advsr World Educn Fellowship (GB) 1977– (former chm); external examiner Wales Poly 1985–91; author of several chapters and articles in educnl pubns; mayoress St Clears 2009–10; FCMI 1987, FRSA 1989 (memb Examinations Bd Educnl Policy Ctee and chm Advsy Ctee on Initial Educn 1990), MILAM 1997–2001; *Style*— Mrs Elsa Davies, LVO

DAVIES, Gavyn; OBE (1979); s of W J F Davies, of Southampton, and M G Watkins; *b* 27 November 1950; *Educ* Taunton's Sch Southampton, St John's Coll Cambridge (BA), Balliol Coll Oxford; *m* 1989, Susan Jane Nye (The Baroness Nye); 1 da (Rosie b 31 Jan 1990), 2 s (Ben b 14 March 1995, Matthew b 2 July 1998); *Career* econ advsr Policy Unit 10 Downing St 1974–79, UK economist Phillips and Drew 1979–81, chief UK economist Simon and Coates 1981–86, chief int economist Goldman Sachs 1986–2001 (ptnr 1988–2001, advsy dir 2001–), chm BBC 2001–04 (vice-chm 2001), currently co-fndr Prisma Capital Ptnrs; memb HM Treasy independent panel of economic forecasting advisers 1992–97; chm UK govt inquiry into The Future Funding of the BBC 1999; visiting prof LSE 1988–98; fell Univ of Wales Aberyswyth 2002–; Hon DSc Univ of Southampton 1998, Hon LLD Univ of Nottingham 2002; *Recreations* sport; *Style*— Gavyn Davies, Esq, OBE

DAVIES, George William; s of George Davies (d 1987), and Mary, *née* Wright (d 2006); *b* 29 October 1941; *Educ* Bootle GS, Univ of Birmingham, Northumbria Univ (DCL); *m* 1, 25 Sept 1965 (m dis 1985), Anne Margaret, da of Maj Donald Dyson Allan; 3 da (Melanie b 8 Aug 1966, Emma b 23 Sept 1968, Alexandra b 7 Sept 1973); m 2, 7 Dec 1985 (m dis 1992), Mrs Elzbieta Krystyna (Liz) Devereux-Batchelor, da of Stanislaw Ryszard Szadbey; 2 da (Lucia b 22 May 1988, Jessica b 2 June 1989), m 3, 16 Oct 1992 (m dis 2008), Fiona Teresa, da of Donovan Karl Shead; 2 s (George Jeremy b 19 Feb 1992, Barnaby Charles b 9 Dec 1993); *Career* buyer and designer Littlewoods Stores 1967–72, School Care (own business) 1972–75, Party Plan and Pippadee Lingerie 1975–81; J Hepworth & Son: joined 1981, responsible for launch of Next Feb 1982, jt gp md 1984, chief exec 1985, chm and chief exec 1987–88; chm and md The George Davies Partnership plc 1989, md George Clothing (part of Asda Group plc) 1995–2000, fndr S'porter (themed designer clothing for football clubs) 1995; launched Per Una into Marks and Spencer stores 2001, launched George Davies postgrad course in Retail in Mktg Heriot-Watt Univ 2005, launched GD25 collection to celebrate 25 years in fashion 2007, launched fourth womenswear brand GIVe 2009, lauched FG4 (new women's and childrenswear brand) with over 78 stores in the Middle East and other countries; hon prof Sch of Mgmnt and Languages Heriot-Watt Univ 2006–; Guardian Young Businessman of the Year 1985, Wood MacKenzie Retailer of the Year 1987, Marketing Personality of the Year 1988, Drapers Lifetime Achievement Award 2003, Prima Designer of the Decade 2004 (also High Street Designer of the Decade), TextilWirtschaft Magazine Forum Award 2004, voted tenth most influential person in fashion Drapers Record 2010; Hon DBA Liverpool Poly 1989, Hon DDes Nottingham Trent Univ 1996, Hon DDes Middlesex Univ 2002, Hon DLitt Heriot-Watt Univ 2003, Hon DCL Northumbria Univ 2005, Hon DDes De Montfort Univ 2006, Hon DUniv Birmingham 2009, Hon DBA Edge-hill Univ 2012; estab George Davies Charitable Tst 1995; FRSA 1987, sr fell RCA 1988, hon fell Soc of Dyers and Colourists 2004, memb Vascular Soc 2008; *Books* What Next (1989); *Recreations* golf, tennis, cycling; *Clubs* Formby Golf, Blackwell Golf, Naunton Downs Golf, St Enodoc Golf; *Style*— George Davies, Esq; ✉ PO Box 19, Gloucestershire GL56 9TL (☎ 01386 852862, fax 01386 852180, website www.georgedavies.com)

DAVIES, Geraint Richard; MP; s of Thomas Morgan Davies, and Betty Ferrer Davies; *b* 3 May 1960; *Educ* Llanishen Comprehensive Cardiff, Jesus Coll Oxford; *m* Dr Vanessa Fry; 3 da (Angharad b July 1994, Meirian b May 1997, Eluned b Oct 2000); *Career* formerly: gp product mangr Unilever, mktg mangr Colgate Palmolive Ltd, dir Pure Crete Ltd; MP (Lab) Croydon Central 1997–2005, MP (Lab and Co-op) Swansea W 2010– (Parly candidate Croydon South 1987 and Croydon Central 1992 and 2005); PPS Dept for Constitutional Affrs 2003–05; memb: Public Accounts Select Ctee House of Commons 1997–2003, Welsh Affrs Ctee 2010–, European Scrutiny Ctee 2010–, Cncl for Europe 2010–; chair PLP Environment Tport and the Regions Ctee 1997–2003; cncllr New Addington London Borough of Croydon 1986–94, chair of housing and chair London Borough's Housing Ctee 1994–96, ldr Cncl London Borough of Croydon 1996–97; memb Labour Finance & Industry Gp, Co-op Pty, GMB; *Recreations* spending time with the family; *Clubs* Ruskin House (Croydon); *Style*— Geraint Davies, Esq, MP; ✉ House of Commons, London SW1A 0AA

DAVIES, Geraint Talfan; OBE (2014); s of Aneirin Talfan Davies, OBE (d 1980), of Cardiff, and Mary Anne, *née* Evans (d 1971); *b* 30 December 1943; *Educ* Cardiff HS for Boys, Jesus Coll Oxford (MA); *m* 9 Sept 1967, Elizabeth Shan, da of Thomas Vaughan Yorath, of Cardiff; 3 s (Matthew b 1969, Rhodri b 1971, Edward b 1974); *Career* asst ed Western Mail 1974–78, head of news and current affairs HTV Wales 1978–82, asst controller of programmes HTV Wales 1982–87, dir of programmes Tyne Tees TV 1987–90, controller BBC Wales 1990–2000; chm: Inst of Welsh Affrs 1992–, CBAT The Arts and Regeneration Agency 1996–2003, Int Film Festival of Wales 1998–2001, WNO 2000–03 and 2006–, Arts Cncl of Wales 2003–06; dir Screen Wales 1994–2000; non-exec dir: Wales Millennium Centre 2000–03 and 2006–09, Glas Cymru Cyf 2000–11; memb: Mgmnt Ctee Northern Sinfonia 1989–90, Mgmnt Ctee Northern Stage 1989–90, Prince of Wales Ctee on the Environment 1993–96, NCVQ 1996–97, Radio Authy 2001–03, BT Wales Advsy Forum 2001–09; govr: Welsh Coll of Music and Drama 1993–97, Univ of Wales Inst Cardiff (UWIC) 2001–06; chm Newydd Housing Assoc 1975–78; tstee: Tenovus Cancer Appeal 1984–87, Br Bone Marrow Donor Appeal 1987–95, Media Standards Tst 2006–; Hon FRIBA; *Books* At Arm's Length (2008); *Style*— Geraint Talfan Davies, Esq, OBE; ✉ 15 The Parade, Whitchurch, Cardiff CF14 2EF (☎ 029 2062 6571, e-mail geraint.talfan@btopenworld.com)

DAVIES, (Edward) Glyn; MP; *b* 16 February 1944; *Educ* Llanfair Caereinion HS, Aberystwyth Univ; *Career* dist cncllr Montgomeryshire Cncl 1976–88 (chm 1985–88), memb Nat Assembly for Wales (Cons) Mid and West Wales 1999–2007, MP (Cons) Montgomeryshire 2010–; *Style*— Glyn Davies, Esq, MP; ✉ House of Commons, London SW1A 0AA

DAVIES, Prof Graham Arthur; s of Evan Henry Davies (d 1978), and Esther Alice, *née* Powell (d 1979); *b* 2 July 1938; *Educ* Wolverhampton Municipal GS, Univ of Birmingham (BSc, PhD), Victoria Univ of Manchester (DSc, Sir John Cadman Medal, Moulton Medal IChemE); *m* July 1963, Christine Pamela, da of Frederick Charles Harris; 1 s (Andrew Simon Craig), 1 da (Joanna Elizabeth); *Career* Procter & Gamble Ltd Newcastle upon Tyne 1963–65; UMIST (now Univ of Manchester): lectr in chemical engrg 1965–70, sr lectr 1970–76, reader 1976–88, prof 1988–, head Dept of Chemical Engrg 1993–; FIChemE, CEng, FREng 1995; *Books* Recent Advances in Liquid-Liquid Extraction (co-author, 1970), Science & Practice of Liquid-Liquid Extraction (1993); *Recreations* golf; *Style*— Prof Graham Davies, FREng; ✉ Chemical Engineering Department, University of Manchester, PO Box 88, Manchester M60 1QD (☎ 0161 200 4342)

DAVIES, Prof Graham James; s of William Thomas Davies (d 1992), and Amy, *née* Lewis (d 1995); *b* 2 July 1946, Swansea; *Educ* Univ of Wales Aberystwyth (BSc, PhD), Univ of Wales (DSc); *m* 1975 (m dis 2010), Frances Vivienne, *née* Martin; 2 s (Steffan James b 22 Nov 1976, Timothy Martin b 28 Nov 1982); *Career* research offr King's Coll London 1971–72; BT Research Labs: jr research fell and exec engr 1972–79, head Surface Science and Epitaxy Gp 1979–84, head Advanced Materials Section 1984–90, mangr Technol Analysis Unit 1991–93, mangr Corporate Research Prog 1993–98, gen mangr (vice-pres) Technol Acquisition and Int Devpt 1998–2001; Sir James Timmins Chance prof of engrg and exec head (dean) Sch of Engrg Univ of Birmingham 2001–08, dean Faculty of Engrg Univ of NSW 2008–; dir: Birmingham Research and Development Ltd, Diamond Light Source, CRC Advanced Manufacturing 2009–, New South Innovations 2009–; chm Mining Educn Australia 2013–; cncl memb Cncl for the Central Lab of the Research Cncls (CCLRC); author of over 160 pubns and four patents, contrib to seven books; Duddell Premium IEE 1974; Platinum Medal IMMM 2008, named as one of the top 100 Most Influential Engrs in Australia 2008, 2009, 2013 and 2014; Liveryman Worshipful Co of Engrs; MRSC, FIEE, FInstP, FIMMM, FREng, FIE(Aust), fell Australian Acad of Technological Sciences and Engrg (FTSE) 2013, FLSW 2015; *Publications* Semiconductor Growth, Surfaces and Interfaces (jtly, 1994), Chemical Beam Epitaxy and Related Techniques (jtly, 1997); *Recreations* golf, walking, reading; *Style*— Prof Graham Davies

DAVIES, (Andrew) Gregory Simon (Gregg); s of Jack Coppenhall (d 1979), and Joan Davies (d 2006); *b* 1 December 1960, Wales; *Educ* Shrewsbury, Kent Sch CT USA, Univ of St Andrews (BSc), Open Univ (Cert of Mgmnt); *m* 20 April 1987, Alison Margaret Elizabeth, *née* McVeigh; 1 da (Anna Alice Elizabeth b 12 Feb 1998); *Career* Haberdashers' Aske's Sch 1984–89; Fettes Coll: appointed 1989, housemaster 1993–99, dep headmaster 1999–2004, actg headmaster Fettes Coll Prep Sch 2000–03; headmaster Shiplake Coll 2004–; memb: Boarding Schs Assoc, HMC, Soc of Heads; *Recreations* rugby refereeing, loud singing, log chopping, cabinet making; *Clubs* Leander, Stewards; *Style*— Gregg Davies, Esq; ✉ Shiplake College, Henley-on-Thames, Oxfordshire RG9 4BW (☎ 0118 940 5254, e-mail headspa@shiplake.org.uk, Twitter @ShiplakeHM, website www.shiplake.org.uk)

DAVIES, (Stephen) Howard; CBE (2011); s of Thomas Emrys Davies, and (Eileen) Hilda, *née* Bevan (d 1991); *b* 26 April 1945; *Educ* Christ's Hosp, Univ of Durham (BA), Univ of Bristol; *m* Susan, da of Rt Rev Eric St Q Wall (former Bishop of Huntingdon); 2 da (Hannah Clare b 1973, Katherine Sian (Kate) b 1978); *Career* theatre dir; assoc dir Bristol Old Vic 1971–73 (prodns incl: Troilus and Cressida, Candida, Spring Awakening), fndr memb Avon Touring Co, asst dir RSC 1974; freelance dir 1974–76: The Caucasian Chalk Circle (Birmingham Rep), The Threepenny Opera (York Rep), The Iceman Cometh (RSC Aldwych), Man is Man (RSC); assoc dir RSC 1976–86, fndr and dir The Warehouse RSC 1977–82 (prodns incl: Piaf, Good, Les Liaisons Dangereuses), visiting dir RNT 1987–88 (prodns incl: The Shaughraun, Cat on a Hot Tin Roof, The Secret Rapture), assoc dir RNT 1989– (prodns incl: Hedda Gabler, The Crucible, Piano, A Long Day's Journey into Night, Mary Stuart, Chips with Everything), former assoc dir Almeida, currently assoc dir RNT (prodns incl Mourning Becomes Electra); dir: The Iceman Cometh (Almeida, Old Vic and Broadway) 1999 (Evening Standard and Olivier Awards for Best Dir 1999), All My Sons (Cottesloe, Olivier Award for Best Dir 2001), Private Lives (Albery Theatre) 2001 (nomination Olivier Award for Best Dir 2002), The White Guard (Lyttelton) 2010 (Best Dir Laurence Olivier Award 2011); opera dir: Idomeneo, Eugene Onegin; TV dir: Tales from Hollywood, Armadillo, Copenhagen, Blue Orange; dir film The Secret Rapture; *Recreations* travel, hill walking, watching rugby, drawing and painting; *Style*— Howard Davies, Esq, CBE, FRSA; ✉ c/o Royal National Theatre, South Bank, London SE1 9PX (☎ 020 7928 2033, fax 020 7620 1197)

DAVIES, (Sir) Howard John; kt (2000); s of Leslie Powell Davies (d 1989), of Rochdale, Lancs, and Marjorie, *née* Magowan (d 2014); *b* 12 February 1951; *Educ* Manchester Grammar, Memorial Univ of Newfoundland, Merton Coll Oxford (MA), Stanford Univ (MS); *m* 30 June 1984, Prudence Mary, da of Eric Phillipps Keely, CBE (d 1988), of Findon; 2 s (George b 1984, Archibald b 1987); *Career* FO 1973–74, private sec to HM Ambass Paris 1974–76, HM Treasy 1976–82, McKinsey and Co 1982–85, special advsr to Chllr of the Exchequer 1985–86, re-joined McKinsey and Co 1986–87, controller Audit Cmmn for Local Authorities and the NHS (formerly for Local Authorities) 1987–92, DG CBI 1992–95, dep govr Bank of England 1995–97 (non-exec dir Bank of England 1998–2003), chm FSA (formerly SIB) 1997–2003, dir LSE 2003–11, chm Phoenix Gp plc 2012–15, chm Royal Bank of Scotland 2015–; non-exec dir: GKN plc until 1995, Morgan Stanley 2004–15, Paternoster Ltd 2006–10, Prudential plc 2010–; prof Institut d'etudes Politiques 2011–; chm: Airports Cmmn 2012–15, London Library 2015–; tstee: Tate Gallery 2002–10, RNT 2011–15; *Recreations* cricket, writing; *Clubs* Barnes Common Cricket; *Style—* Mr Howard Davies

DAVIES, Hugh Llewelyn; CMG (1994); s of Vincent Ellis Davies, OBE (d 2002), and Rose Trench, *née* Temple (d 1993); *b* 8 November 1941; *Educ* Rugby, Churchill Coll Cambridge (BA); *m* 21 Sept 1968, Virginia Ann, da of Hugh Lucius; 1 da (Charlotte b 1970), 1 s (Jonathan b 1973); *Career* HM Dip Serv: FO 1965, Chinese language studies Hong Kong 1966–68, second sec and HM consul Peking 1969–71, China Desk FCO 1971–74, first sec (econ) Br Embassy Bonn 1974–77, head of Chancery Br High Cmmn Singapore 1977–79, asst head Far Eastern Dept FCO 1979–82, secondment Barclays Bank Int 1982–83, commercial cnsllr Br Embassy Peking 1984–87, dep perm UK rep OECD Paris 1987–90, head Far East Dept FCO 1990–93, sr Br trade cmmr Hong Kong 1993, Br sr rep (ambass) on the Sino-British Jt Liaison Gp Hong Kong 1993–97, special co-ordinator for China, Hong Kong FCO 1998–99; exec dir Prudential Corporation Asia 1999–2005, conslt on Asia 2002–, sr China business advsr Old Mutual plc 2005–06, sr ptnr Orient Asian Ptnrs 2005–; non-exec dir Sinophi Healthcare Ltd 2013–; chm China Assoc 2002–15, vice-chm GB China Centre 2005–16, memb Bd China Britain Business Cncl 2000–13, memb Advsy Bd China Policy Inst Univ of Nottingham 2010–; govr Bruton Sch for Girls 2008, chm Cucklington Parish Meeting 2016–; *Recreations* travel, sports, art, gardens; *Clubs* Hong Kong; *Style—* Hugh Davies, Esq, CMG

DAVIES, (Edward) Hunter; OBE (2014); s of John Davies (d 1958), of Cambuslang, and Marion, *née* Brechin (d 1987); *b* 7 January 1936; *Educ* Creighton Sch Carlisle, Carlisle GS, Univ of Durham; *m* 1960, Margaret Forster, *qv*; 1 s, 2 da; *Career* author, broadcaster, publisher; journalist Sunday Times 1960–84 (ed Sunday Times Magazine 1975–77); columnist: Punch 1979–89, Stamp News 1981–86, Evening Standard 1987, The Independent 1989–95, New Statesman 1996–; presenter BBC Radio Four's Bookshelf 1983–86; memb: Br Library Consultative Gp on Newspapers 1987–89, Bd Edinburgh Book Festival 1990–95; pres Cumbria Wildlife Tst 1994–; *Books* fiction incl: Here We Go Round the Mulberry Bush (1965, filmed 1968), A Very Loving Couple (1971), Flossie Teacake's Fur Coat (1982), Come on Ossie! (1985), Saturday Night (1989), Striker (1992); non-fiction incl: The Other Half (1966), The Beatles (1968, 3 edn 2002), The Glory Game (1972, 2 edn 1985), A Walk Around the Lakes (1979), William Wordsworth (1980), Father's Day (1981, TV series 1983), The Joy of Stamps (1983), The Good Guide to the Lakes (also publisher, 1984, 4 edn 1993), In Search of Columbus (1991), Hunting People (1994), Teller of Tales (1994), Wainwright (1995), Living on the Lottery (1996), Born 1900 (1998), A Walk Around the West Indies (2000), The Quarrymen (2001), The Eddie Stobart Story (2001), Boots, Balls and Haircuts (2003), Relative Strangers (2003), The Fan (2003), My Story So Far (with Wayne Rooney, 2006), The Beatles, Football and Me (2006), The Bumper Book of Football (2007), Cold Meat and How to Disguise It (2009), Confessions of a Collection (2009), Behind the Scenes of the Museum of Baked Beans (2010), Postcards from the Edge of Football (2010), The Lennon Letters (2012), The Beatles Lyrics (2014), The Biscuit Girls (2014); *Recreations* collecting footbal memorabilia, Lakeland books; *Style—* Hunter Davies, Esq, OBE; ✉ 11 Boscastle Road, London NW5; Grasmoor House, Loweswater, Cockermouth, Cumbria

DAVIES, Prof Huw Cathan; OBE; *b* 5 February 1944, Wales; *Educ* Univ of Wales (BSc), Imperial Coll London (DIC), Univ of London (PhD); *m* 20 Aug 1966, Marian, *née* Williams; 1 s, 1 da; *Career* lectr Univ of Reading 1968–82, prof ETH Zürich 1982–2009 (head Dept of Environmental Science 2002–04); pres Int Assoc for Meteorology and Atmospheric Science 1999–2003, memb Cncl NERC 2005–11; memb Academia Europaea 1990; Hon DSc Aberystwyth Univ; FRMetS, fell Int Union of Geodesy and Geophysics (IUGG); *Style—* Prof Huw Davies, OBE; ✉ Institute for Atmospheric and Climate Science, ETH, Universitätsstrasse 16, CH-8092 Zürich, Switzerland (☎ 00 41 44 633 3506, fax 00 41 44 633 1058, e-mail huw.davies@env.ethz.ch)

DAVIES, Huw Humphreys; s of William Davies (d 1984), of Llangynog, and Harriet Jane, *née* Humphreys (d 1991); *b* 4 August 1940; *Educ* Llandovery Coll, Pembroke Coll Oxford (MA); *m* 1966, Elizabeth Shân, da of William Harries; 2 da (Elin Mari b 25 April 1969, Catrin Humphreys b 23 Sept 1971); *Career* prog dir and prodr TWW 1964–68; HTV Wales: programme dir and prodr 1968–78, asst controller of programmes 1978–79, controller of programmes 1979–81, dir of programmes 1981–89, chief exec 1987; gp dir of TV HTV Group 1989–94, pres HTV International 1994–96; fndr independent TV prodn co Square Circle 1996–2002, dir Winchester Entertainment plc 1996–2004; chief exec Channel Television Ltd 2000–06; chm Winchester Entertainment plc 2003–04, dir Content Film plc 2004–10, chm Content Media Corporation 2010–14; memb Gorsedd of Bards; FRSA 1989; *Recreations* walking, reading, driving around America; *Style—* Huw Davies, Esq

DAVIES, James Baumann; s of Anthony Baumann Davies, of Farndon, Cheshire, and Anne, *née* Richardson; *b* 26 February 1962, Corbridge, Northumberland; *Educ* Ysgol Gyfun David Hughes Menai Bridge, Univ of Leicester (LLB, LLM), Univ of Strasbourg (Dip); *m* 30 Dec 1989, Priska Carel, *née* Johnston; *Career* slr; Denton Hall 1986–90, Lewis Silkin 1992– (currently ptnr and jt head Employment Reward and Immigration Dept); memb Bd Ius Laboris, tstee and memb Advsy Bd Advice on Individual Rights in Europe; contrib to various employment law pubns; memb: Employment Lawyers Assoc (sometime treas), European Employment Lawyers Assoc; *Publications* Age Discrimination; *Recreations* sports, travel, France; *Style—* James Davies; ✉ Lewis Silkin LLP, 5 Chancery Lane, Clifford's Inn, London EC4A 1BL (☎ 020 7074 8035, fax 020 7864 1737, e-mail james.davies@lewissilkin.com)

DAVIES, James Michael; MP; s of Michael Davies, of Higher Wych, near Malpas, and Belinda, *née* Brookes-Parry; *b* 27 February 1980, St Asaph, Wales; *Educ* King's Sch Chester, Christ's Coll Cambridge (MA, MB BChir); *m* 25 Aug 2012, Nina, *née* Jones; 2 s (Wilfred b 4 Nov 2013, Ralph b 3 June 2016); *Career* pre-registration house offr Glan Clwyd Hosp 2004–05, SHO Countess of Chester Hosp 2005–07, GP registrar City Walls Med Centre Chester 2007–08, GP Boughton Med Gp Chester 2008–15 (ptnr 2010–15); cncllr Denbighshire County 2004–15; MP (Cons) Vale of Clwyd 2015–; MRCGP 2008; *Recreations* cinema, skiing, travel, walking, languages, local community, regeneration, real ale, dining out, DIY; *Clubs* Carlton; *Style—* Dr James Davies, MP; ✉ House of Commons, London SW1A 0AA (020 7219 4627, e-mail james.davies.mp@parliament.uk, website www.jamesdaviesmp.co.uk, Twitter @JamesDaviesMP)

DAVIES, James Selwyn (Joe); s of John Selwyn Davies (d 2000), of Cardiff, and Joan, *née* Williams (d 2002); *b* 29 June 1956; *Educ* Christ Coll Brecon, St John's Coll Cambridge (MA, Sir Joseph Lamour prize, Rugby blue), UC Cardiff (PGCE); *m* 28 March 1981, Virginia Felicity, da of Jeffrey Graham; 3 s (Edward Selwyn b 22 Sept 1982, Charles Alan b 13 June 1984, James Peter b 24 Nov 1986), 1 da (Rebecca Helen b 11 Dec 1989); *Career* housemaster Tonbridge Sch 1980–94, exchange teacher Anglican Church GS Brisbane Aust 1988, dep head St John's Sch Leatherhead 1994–2000, headmaster Sutton Valence Sch 2000–09, master Haileybury 2009–; govr: Yardley Court Sch, Heath Mount, Lochinver, Orwell Park, Tudor Hall; chm ISTIP 2014; memb: HMC 2001 (chair South East Div 2007–08), SHA 2001, Nat Tst; *Recreations* rugby (played for Cardiff, Penarth, Bedford and London Welsh), cricket, squash, reading, cycling, camping, marathon running; *Clubs* Hawks', East India, Landsdowne; *Style—* Joe Davies, Esq; ✉ Master's Lodge, Haileybury, Hertford SG13 7NU

DAVIES, Jocelyn Ann; AM; da of Thomas Davies, and Majorie, *née* Smith, of Newbridge, Gwent; *b* 18 June 1959; *Children* 1 s (Lewis b 5 May 1980), 2 da (Anna b 4 Nov 1989, Katie b 29 Dec 1990); *Career* borough cncllr 1987–91, Pty by-election candidate Islwyn 1995, memb Nat Assembly for Wales (Plaid Cymru) South Wales East 1999–; *Recreations* drawing, walking, people watching; *Style—* Ms Jocelyn Davies, AM; ✉ National Assembly for Wales, Cardiff Bay, Cardiff CF99 1NA (☎ 029 2089 5289); Constituency Office, 1 Griffiths Building, Victoria Terrace, Newbridge, Gwent NP11 4ET (☎ 01495 241100, fax 01495 241104)

DAVIES, John; s of John Charles Davies (d 1987), of Birmingham, and Kathleen Anne, *née* Snipe (d 2004); *b* 12 July 1946; *Educ* Bournville Boys' Tech Sch Birmingham; *m* 6 Nov 1971, Jacqueline, da of William Springall Wheeler; 1 s (Charles William b 26 Nov 1974), 3 da (Alison Jane b 29 April 1976, Nicola Kate b 23 March 1978, Lucy Anne b 25 June 1980); *Career* trainee investment analyst Midland Assurance Ltd Birmingham 1964–67; investment analyst: J M Finn & Co (Stockbrokers) 1968–71, Nat Coal Bd Pension Fund 1971–73; Confederation Life Insurance Co: asst mangr equity investment 1973–74, mangr pension investment 1974–76, mangr segregated funds investment 1976–79, dep investment mangr 1979–82; investment mangr 3i Group plc 1982–84, md 3i Asset Management 1984–2002; dir: BlackRock Smaller Companies Tst plc 1999–2011, Baronsmead VCT 5 plc 2006– (chm 2010), Gardens Pension Trustees Ltd 2011–; tstee St Michael Sch Sunninghill; ASIP, FCSI; *Recreations* music, reading, hill walking; *Clubs* Girt Clog Climbing; *Style—* John Davies, Esq; ✉ c/o Livingbridge EP LLP, 100 Wood Street, London EC2V 7AN (☎ 020 7506 5600, e-mail john.davies1@btinternet.com)

DAVIES, John Booth; s of Harry Davies, and Nora, *née* Booth; *Educ* Haslingden GS, Univ of Leeds (BA); *Career* managing ed Phoebus Publishing (later Macdonald Phoebus) 1976–81, estab Grub Street Book Packagers 1982, estab Grub Street Publishing Ltd 1992 (International Cookbook Publisher of the Year World Cookbook Awards 2000); father of chapel NUJ 1980–81, memb Guild of Aviation Artists; *Books* Octopus Book of Aircraft and Aviation (1977); *Recreations* cricket, chess, watching Blackburn Rovers, travel, reading; *Style—* John Booth, Esq; ✉ Grub Street, 4 Rainham Close, London SW11 6SS (☎ 020 7924 3966, fax 020 7738 1009, e-mail john@grubstreet.co.uk)

DAVIES, Rt Rev John David Edward; *see:* Swansea and Brecon, Bishop of

DAVIES, John Hywel; s of Bruce Davies, and Mary Davies; *b* Aberdare, Mid Glamorgan; *Educ* Cathedral Sch Llandaff, Christ Coll Brecon, Univ of Swansea (BSc, PGDip), Univ of the West of England (PGDip, legal practice course); *m* Tracey; 2 s (Jack, Oliver); *Career* slr; full equity ptnr and head SW Corporate Team (Bath, Bristol and Swindon), head Swindon Office, memb Mgmnt Bd and chair Bank Gp Thrings LLP; sector specialist FMCG defence and aerospace and bank refinance; ranked in first tier in region for corporate law by Chambers & Partners Guide to the Legal Profession, recommended by Legal 500, Client Partner of the Year Lawyer Awards 2014, Insider SW Corporate Deal of the Year Insider Dealmaker Awards 2014; memb: Cncl Swindon C of C 2007–11, Bd Swindon Strategic Economic Partnership 2007–11, Bd of Influence 2011–; memb Law Soc 2000–; *Recreations* family, sports, travel, food, wine, music, the outdoors; *Clubs* Old Llandavians Soc, Old Breconians Soc, Law Soc, Business West; *Style—* John Davies, Esq; ✉ Thrings LLP, 6 Drakes Meadow, Penny Lane, Swindon, Wiltshire SN3 3LL (☎ 01793 412634, mobile 07799 338382, e-mail jdavies@thrings.com, website www.thrings.com)

DAVIES, Prof John Kenyon; s of Harold Edward Davies (d 1990), and Clarice Theresa, *née* Woodburn (d 1989); *b* 19 September 1937; *Educ* Manchester Grammar, Wadham Coll Oxford (BA), Merton Coll Oxford (MA), Balliol Coll Oxford (DPhil); *m* 1, 8 Sept 1962 (m dis 1978), Anna Elbina Laura Margherita (d 2014), da of A Morpurgo (d 1939), of Rome; m 2, 5 Aug 1978, Nicola Jane, da of Dr R M S Perrin; 1 s (Martin b 1979), 1 da (Penelope b 1981); *Career* Harmsworth scholar Merton Coll Oxford 1960–63, jr fell Center for Hellenic Studies Washington DC 1961–62, Dyson jr fell Balliol Coll Oxford 1963–65, lectr Univ of St Andrews 1965–68, fell in ancient history Oriel Coll Oxford 1968–77; Univ of Liverpool: Rathbone prof of ancient history and classical archaeology 1977–2003, pro-vice-chllr 1986–90, head Sch of Archeology, Classics and Oriental Studies 1990–95 and 2000–02; Leverhulme research prof 1995–2000; dir Post-Grad Residential Course Br Sch of Archeology Athens 2004, 2006 and 2008, chair Advsy Ctee Inst of Classical Studies Univ of London 2005–; expert advsr Europe Science Fndn 2006–; ed: Jl of Hellenic Studies 1973–77, Archaeological Reports 1972–74; chm: St Patrick's Isle (IOM) Archaeological Tst 1982–85, NW Archaeological Tst 1982–91; auditor CVCP Academic Audit Unit 1990–93; corresponding memb Deutsche Archäologische Institut 2000, visiting sr fell Istituto di Studi Avanzati Unv of Bologna 2006, Onassis Fndn visiting fell KERA Athens 2010, hon fell Inst of Classical Studies Univ of London; FBA 1985, FSA 1986, FRSA 1988; *Books* Athenian Propertied Families 600–300 BC (1971), Democracy and Classical Greece (1978, 2 edn 1993), Wealth and the Power of Wealth in Classical Athens (1981), The Trojan War: Its Historicity and Context (ed with L Foxhall, 1984), Hellenistic Economies (ed jtly, 2000), Making, Moving and Managing: The New World of Ancient Economies 323–31 BC (ed jtly, 2005), The Economics of Hellenistic Societies, Third to First Centuries BC (ed jtly, 2011), Epigraphy and the Historical Sciences (ed jtly, 2012); *Recreations* canal walking, hill walking; *Clubs* Royal Over-Seas League; *Style—* Prof John K Davies; ✉ 20 North Road, Grassendale Park, Liverpool L19 0LR (☎ 0151 427 2126, e-mail jkdavies@liv.ac.uk)

DAVIES, Prof Dame Kay Elizabeth; DBE (2008, CBE 1995); *née* Partridge; da of Harry Partridge and Florence, *née* Farmer; *b* 1 April 1951; *Educ* Stourbridge Girls' HS, Somerville Coll Oxford (Kirkaldy Prize, MA, DPhil); *m* 1973 (m dis 2000), Stephen Graham Davies; 1 s; *Career* Guy Newton jr research fell Wolfson Coll Oxford 1976–78, Royal Soc Euro post-doctoral fell Service de Biochimie Centre d'Études Nucleaires de Saclay Gif-sur-Yvette France 1978–80; St Mary's Hosp Med Sch Dept of Biochemistry: Cystic Fibrosis research fell 1980–82, MRC sr research fell 1982–84; Nuffield Dept of Clinical Med John Radcliffe Hosp Oxford: MRC sr research fell 1984–86, MRC external staff 1986–89, univ research lectr 1990; MRC research dir MRC Clinical Scis Centre Royal Post Graduate Med Sch Hammersmith and prof of molecular genetics Univ of London 1992–94, MRC external staff head Molecular Genetics Gp Inst of Molecular Med Oxford 1994–95 (MRC external staff 1989–92); Univ of Oxford: prof of genetics 1995–98, assoc head for external rels Dept of Biochemistry 1996–, Dr Lee's prof of anatomy 1998–, co-dir Oxford Centre for Gene Function 2001–, head Physiology, Anatomy and Genetics Dept 2008–, assoc head (devpt, impact and equality) Medical Sciences Div 2011–; hon dir MRC Functional Genetics Unit 1999–; dep chm Wellcome Tst 2013–; fell: Green Coll Oxford 1989–92 and 1994–95, Keble Coll Oxford 1995–98, Hertford Coll Oxford 1998–; memb MRC 2002–; Bristol-Myers visiting prof USA 1986, James and Jean Davis Prestige visitorship Univ of Otago NZ 1996; memb: Advsy Ctee Euro Cell and Tissue Bank 1989–,

Med Ethics Advsy Gp Lambeth Palace 1994–, Scientific Advsy Panel CIBA Fndn 1994–, Genetics Interest Gp Wellcome Tst 1996–; founding ed Human Molecular Genetics 1992–; memb numerous Editorial Bds incl: Jl of Biotherapeutics and Gene Therapy 1994–, Gene Therapy 1994–, Molecular Medicine Society 1994–, Molecular Medicine Today 1994–; memb: Academia Europaea, EMBO, Biochemical Soc, Genetics Soc, Euro Human Genetics Soc; govr Wellcome Tst 2008–; 7th Annual Colleen Giblin distinguished lectr Columbia Univ USA 1992, distinguished lectr Mayo Clinic 1994; Annual Medal Int Inst of Biotechnology 1993, Wellcome Tst Award 1996, SCI Medal 1999; hon fell Somerville Coll Oxford 1995; Hon DSc Univ of Victoria BC 1990, Hon DUniv Open 1999; Hon FRCP 1994, FRCPath 1997 (MRCPath 1990), FMedSci 1998, FRS 2003; *Books* Molecular Analysis of Inherited Diseases (with A P Read, 1988, revised edn 1992), Human Genetics Diseases. A Practical Approach (ed, 1988), Genome Analysis. A Practical Approach (ed, 1988), The Fragile X Syndrome (ed, 1989), Application of Molecular Genetics to the Diagnosis of Inherited Disease (ed, 1989), Genome Analysis Review (ed with S Tilghman, 1990–); also author of numerous articles for learned jls; *Recreations* music, walking; *Clubs* Athenaeum; *Style*— Prof Dame Kay Davies, DBE; ✉ Department of Physiology, Anatomy and Genetics, University of Oxford, Parks Road, Oxford OX1 3PT (☎ 01865 285880, fax 01865 285878, e-mail kay.davies@dpag.ox.ac.uk)

DAVIES, Keith; AM; s of Glyn Davies (d 1999), and Iris, *née* Thomas (d 2002); *b* 25 May 1940, Gwaun-Cae-Gurwen, Wales; *Educ* Ystalyfera GS, Swansea Univ (BSc, MSc), Cardiff Univ (PGCE); *m* 1, 1963, Margaret, *née* Legge; 2 s (Huw b 1964, Berian b 1972), 1 da (Rhiannon b 1966); m 2, 1992, Heddyr Gregory; 2 s (Ifan b 1993, Iolo b 1996); *Career* teacher 1963–65, lectr 1965–72, educn advsr 1972–94, dir of educn Mid Glamorgan 1994–96, dir of educn Carmarthenshire 1996–2000, acting chief exec CEBP Birmingham 2001, dir Welsh Baccalaureate Qualification Project 2003–07, cncllr Carmarthenshire CC 2004–08, memb Nat Assembly for Wales (Lab) Llanelli 2011–; memb: Nat Assoc of Inspectors and Educnl Advsrs (NAIEA) 1979–2003, UNISON 2011–; *Recreations* rugby, sport in general, reading; *Style*— Keith Davies, Esq, AM; ✉ Caedelyn, 2 Pen y-Fai Lane, Llanelli SA15 4EN (☎ 01554 754687); National Assembly for Wales, Cardiff Bay, Cardiff CF99 1NA (☎ 02920 898378, e-mail keith.davies@cymru.gov.uk)

DAVIES, Dame Laura Jane; DBE (2014, CBE 2000, MBE 1988); da of David Thomas Davies, and Rita Ann, *née* Foskett; *b* 5 October 1963; *Educ* Fullbrook Co Secdy Sch; *Career* golfer; memb Curtis Cup Team 1984, turned professional 1985, Br Open Ladies Golf champion 1986, US Open champion 1987, memb winning European Solheim Cup team 1992, 2000, 2003 and 2011; ranked world No 1 in 1995 and 1996; 77 tournament wins in professional career incl 4 Majors; *Recreations* all sport, cars, music; *Style*— Dame Laura Davies, DBE; ✉ c/o Vicky Cuming, IMG Golf Client Division, McCormack House, Burlington Lane, London W4 2TH (☎ 020 233 5300)

DAVIES, (Robert) Leighton; QC (1994); s of Robert Brinley Davies (d 1978), of Cwm-parc, Mid Glamorgan, and Elizabeth Nesta, *née* Jones; *b* 7 September 1949; *Educ* Rhondda County GS Porth, CCC Oxford (BA, BCL, Boxing blue); *m* 25 Aug 1979, Linda Davies, da of David Fox, of Cwm-parc, Mid Glamorgan; 2 s (Rhoss b 30 May 1980, Greg b 9 Jan 1991), 1 da (Rhia b 12 Nov 1985); *Career* called to the Bar Gray's Inn 1975 (bencher 2002); practising barr: Cardiff 1975–97, Farrar's Building Temple 1997–; recorder of the Crown Court 1994– (asst recorder 1990); memb Criminal Bar Assoc 1988; memb Greenpeace; *Recreations* fly fishing, gardening, watching rugby football; *Style*— Leighton Davies, Esq, QC; ✉ Bryn Corun, Glyncoli Road, Treorchy, Rhondda, Mid-Glamorgan CF42 6SB (☎ 01443 774559, fax 01443 774573, e-mail leightondaviesqc@msn.com); Farrar's Building, Temple, London EC4Y 7BD (☎ 020 75839241, fax 020 7583 0090)

DAVIES, Dr Lindsey Margaret; CBE (2004); da of Dr Frank Newby, of Horsham, W Sussex, and Margaret, *née* Thomsett; *b* 21 May 1953; *Educ* Univ of Nottingham (BMedSci, BM BS); *m* 21 Sept 1974 (m dis 1994), Dr Peter Davies; 2 s (James b 11 July 1979, Adam b 30 Sept 1980); *Career* house surgn Mansfield Gen Hosp 1975, house physician Nottingham City Hosp 1976, clinical med offr (child health and occupational med) Nottingham HA 1977–80, sr clinical med offr (community child health) Nottingham DHA 1981–83, registrar then sr registrar in community med Trent RHA 1983–85, dir of public health Southern Derbyshire HA 1985–90 (seconded as visiting scholar Georgetown Univ 1988), dir of public health Nottingham HA 1990–93; NHS Exec: head Public Health Div 1993–94, regnl dir of public health (Trent and E Midlands) 1994–2006, nat dir of pandemic influenza preparedness 2006–10; pres UK Faculty of Public Health 2010–13; hon prof Univ of Nottingham Med Sch 2000– (special lectr 1991–2000); chair/memb various nat and int ctees; memb Cncl and Cncl Exec BMA 1991–93 (chm Ctee for Public Health Med and Community Health 1992–93); author of various articles in learned jls; govr Henry Mellish Sch Bulwell 2001–06; Hon DM Sheffield Univ 2013; MHSM, FFPH, FRCP, FRCPEd, FRCPI; *Style*— Dr Lindsey Davies, CBE; ✉ e-mail lindseydavies@doctors.org.uk

DAVIES, Mark Edward Trehearne; s of late Denis Norman Davies, of Slinfold, W Sussex, and late Patricia Helen, *née* Trehearne; *b* 20 May 1948; *Educ* Stowe; *m* 1, 8 June 1974 (m dis 1984), Serena Barbara, *née* Palmer; m 2, 20 Nov 1987, Antonia Catharine, da of Jeremy Barrow Chittenden, of Lytes Cary Manor, Somerset; 2 da (Sophia b 13 May 1988, Mollie b 18 March 1993), 2 s (Hugo b 5 Oct 1989, Harry b 24 Sept 1996); *Career* commodity broker Ralli International 1969, fndr Inter Commodities 1972 (awarded Queen's Award for Export Achievement 1981); chm and chief exec Inter Commodities 1972–84, chm and chief exec GNI Ltd 1984–94 (chm 1994–2001), dir Gerrard Group plc 1986–2001 (chief exec 1995–2001); chm: Admington Hall Farms Ltd 1995–, Greig Middleton Holdings 1999–2001, Thornhill Holdings Ltd 2001–10, FF&P Asset Mgmnt Ltd 2003–10, FF&P Capital Management Ltd 2004–09; dir: The Rank Fndn Ltd 1991–, Thornhill Investment Management Ltd 2001–10, Racing Welfare 2001–10, Thornhill Nominees Ltd 2001–10, Thornhill Unit Tst Managers Ltd 2001–10, Ascot Authority (Holdings) Ltd 2002–, Caledonia Investments plc 2002–12, Stonehage Fleming Family & Partners Ltd 2003– (chief exec 2008–15), Racing Welfare (Enterprises) Ltd 2006–10; chm: Stonehage Fleming Advsy 2015–, Stonehage Fleming Private Equity 2015–, Stonehage Fleming (UK) Ltd 2015; *Books* Trading in Commodities (co-author, 1974); *Recreations* hunting, racing; *Clubs* White's; *Style*— Mark Davies, Esq; ✉ 26 Chester Street, London SW1X 7BL; Stonehage Fleming Family & Partners Ltd, 15 Suffolk Street, London SW1Y 4HG (☎ 020 7036 5678, fax 020 7036 5791)

DAVIES, Mefin; *b* 2 September 1972, Nantgaredig, Carmarthen; *Career* rugby union coach and former player (hooker); clubs: Carmarthen Quins, Dunvant, Neath, Pontypridd (winners Principality Cup 2002, finalists Parken Pen Trophy 2002), Celtic Warriors 2003–04, Neath-Swansea Ospreys 2004–05, Gloucester 2005–07, Leicester Tigers 2007–10, Neath-Swansea Ospreys 2010–12; Wales: 39 caps (1 as capt), debut v South Africa 2002, memb squad World Cup 2003, winners Six Nations Championship and Grand Slam 2005; head coach Swansea RFC 2012–; control systems engr and ptnr Process and General Technology Bridgend; *Style*— Mr Mefin Davies

DAVIES, Michael; CBE (2000); s of Leonard Gwerfyl Davies (d 1996), of London, and Nancy Hannah, *née* Jones; *b* 23 January 1942; *Educ* Architectural Assoc (Dipl, M Arch), UD (UCLA), RIBA; *m* 1, 3 March 1966, Isabel Christina, *née* Hogg; 1 s (Oliver Joanne Pascal Schafer b 5 July 1972), 1 da (Dio Andromeda Mistral b 4 June 1977); m 2, 8 Dec 1977, Elizabeth Renee Yvonne, da of Marius Escalmel; *Career* architect; Airstructures Design 1967–69, Chrysalis USA 1969–72, Piano + Rogers 1972–77, Chrysalis Architects (London) 1979–83; Richard Rogers Partnership: fndr ptnr 1977, River CADS Ltd; projects incl: Pompidou Centre, IRCAM, Lloyd's Bldg, Inmos, terminal 1 and Europier at London Heathrow Airport, London Royal Docks masterplan, City of Dunkirk masterplan, Greenwich Peninsula masterplan, Millennium Dome; currently dir T5 Project London Heathrow; lectr: Architectural Assoc, Univ of Calif, Univ of Texas, Calif Poly; memb: Cncl Architectural Assoc Sch of Architecture, advsy panel Sunday Times 'A Future for London' 1990, Docklands Urban Design Panel, Millennium Experience Litmus gp; tstee Camden Arts Centre; FICPD, FRGS, FRSA; *Style*— Michael Davies, Esq, CBE, FRSA; ✉ Rogers Stirk Harbour & Partners, Thames Wharf, Rainville Road, London W6 9HA

DAVIES, Prof (John) Michael; s of Alfred Ernest Davies (d 1975), of Walsall, and Mavis Muriel, *née* Wildgoose (d 1979); *Educ* Queen Mary's GS Walsall, Victoria Univ of Manchester (BSc, PhD, DSc); *m* 24 June 1967, Anthea Dorothy, da of Rex Henry Percy, MBE, DL, of Guildford; 1 s (Peter b 18 Nov 1972), 1 da (Claire b 16 Oct 1974); *Career* lectr Victoria Univ of Manchester 1962–65, engr Ove Arup & Partners Edinburgh 1965–70, visiting prof Univ of Karlsruhe 1980–81; Univ of Salford: reader 1971–80, prof of civil engrg 1981–95, chm Civil Engrg Dept 1988–91; prof of structural engrg Victoria Univ of Manchester 1995–2002, prof of structural engrg UMIST (latterly Univ of Manchester) 2002–05, emeritus prof Univ of Manchester 2005–; memb: Br Standards Ctees, Ctee Euro Convention for Constructional Steelwork (chm 1991–99); ctee coordinator Int Bldg Cncl 1985–89; FIStructE 1976, FICE 1977, FREng 1997; *Books* Manual of Stressed Skin Diaphragm Design (with E R Bryan, 1982), Plastic Design to BS 5950 (with B A Brown, 1996), Lightweight Sandwich Construction (2001); *Recreations* tennis, skiing, walking; *Style*— Prof Michael Davies, FREng; ✉ 83 Park Road, Hale, Altrincham, Cheshire WA15 9LQ (☎ 0161 980 2838)

DAVIES, Miriam; MP; *b* 1975; *m* ; 2 c; *Career* MP (Cons) Eastleigh 2015–; *Style*— Mrs Mims Davies, MP; ✉ House of Commons, London SW1A 0AA

DAVIES, Neil Llewellyn; s of Thomas Davies (d 1988), and Beatrice, *née* Croker; *b* 19 March 1961, Aberdare; *Educ* Aberdare Boys GS, Univ of Kent (BA); *Partner* Benjamin Marc Powis; *Career* slr, collaborative lawyer and mediator specialising in family law; Morgan Bruce Slrs Cardiff 1986–94, ptnr and head Private Client Div Paris Smith Southampton 1994–; chair: Hampshire Resolution, Skills and Support Ctee Resolution; memb UK Coll of Family Mediators; *Recreations* art and philosophy, boot camps; *Clubs* Royal Motor Yacht; *Style*— Neil Davies, Esq; ✉ Paris Smith LLP, 1 London Road, Southampton SO15 2AE (☎ 023 8048 2482, fax 023 8048 2230)

DAVIES, Neil Valentine; s of late Isadore Edward Davies, and late Carmel, *née* Greenberg; *b* 14 February 1957; *Educ* Harrow Co Boys' GS, King's Coll Cambridge (MA), QMC London (MSc); *Partner* Suzanne Farrell; *Career* econ asst rising to econ advsr Dept of Employment Gp 1978–86; HSE: econ advsr 1986–89, head Econ Advsrs Unit 1989–94, head Mgmnt, Small Firms and Trg Unit 1994–96; chief economist MOD 1996–2012, chief economist Defence Economics Ltd and md Davies Economic Consultancy Ltd 2012–; memb Soc of Business Economists 1996; contrib various articles to learned jls; chair of govrs Geoffrey Chaucer Sch Southwark 1982–83; *Publications* Costs of Workplace Accidents and Work Related Ill Health to the British Economy (jtly, 1994), Cost Benefit Analysis in Safety Policy Making (1989), The Economic Costs and Benefits of UK Defence Exports (contrib, 2002); author of articles in learned jls; *Recreations* swimming, walking, gardening; *Style*— Neil Davies, Esq; ✉ Davies Economic Consultancy Ltd, 9 Hazelbury Close, Merton Park, London SW19 3JL (☎ 020 8545 0634, e-mail neil.davies@davieseconconsultancy.co.uk)

DAVIES, Nick; *b* 28 March 1953; *Educ* Royal Latin GS Buckingham, Stowe, UC Oxford (BA); *Career* BR guard Cambridge 1974–75; messenger boy The Guardian 1975–76, trainee Mirror Gp 1976–78, with Evening Standard Diary 1978–79, news reporter The Guardian 1979–84, home affrs corr The Observer 1984–86, chief feature writer London Daily News 1986–87, Washington columnist The Scotsman 1987–88; freelance writer 1988–: The Guardian, World in Action; writer My Kingdom (film) 2002; *Awards* Crime Reporter of the Year 1980, Br Press Awards Commendations 1981, 1982, 1983, 1991, 1993, Feature Writer of the Year 1997, Journalist of the Year 1998, Reporter of the Year 1999, Martha Gellhorn Award 1999, European Journalism Prize 2003; *Books* White Lies (1991), Murder on Ward Four (1993), Dark Heart, The Shocking Truth About Hidden Britain (1997), The School Report (2000), Flat Earth News (2008, Bristol Festival of Ideas Book Award 2009); *Style*— Nick Davies, Esq; ✉ The Guardian, c/o News Desk, Kings Place, 90 York Way, London N1 9GU (☎ 020 3353 2000, e-mail mail@nickdavies.net)

DAVIES, Hon Mrs Justice; Dame Nicola Velfor Davies; DBE (2010), QC (1992); *b* 13 March 1953; *Educ* Bridgend Girls' GS, Univ of Birmingham (LLB); *Career* called to the Bar Gray's Inn 1976 (bencher 2001), recorder 1998–, dep judge of the High Court 2003–10, judge of the High Court 2010–, presiding judge Wales Circuit 2014–; hon fell Univ of Cardiff 2012, Hon LLD Univ of South Wales 2014; *Style*— The Hon Mrs Justice Nicola Davies; ✉ The Royal Courts of Justice, Strand, London WC2A 2LL

DAVIES, His Hon Judge Owen Handel; QC (1999); s of David Trevor Davies, and Mary Davies; *b* 22 September 1949; *Educ* Hazelwick Comp, Magdalene Coll Cambridge; *m* Caroline Jane Davies; 1 s (Jack Andrew Bowen 30 May 1982), 1 da (Mary Laura Caroline b 22 Feb 1988); *Career* called to the Bar Inner Temple 1973 (bencher 2001); recorder of the Crown Court 2000–, head Garden Court Chambers, judge South Eastern Circuit 2011–; tutor Judicial Coll; *Publications* articles and pamphlets on law and disarmament and human rights; *Recreations* narrowboating; *Clubs* India; *Style*— His Hon Judge Owen Davies, QC

DAVIES, Prof Paul Charles William; s of Hugh Augustus Robert Davies, of London, and Pearl Vera, *née* Birrell; *b* 22 April 1946; *Educ* Woodhouse GS Finchley, UCL (BSc, PhD); *Children* 1 s (Charles Hugh Aidan b 1981), 1 da (Annabel Rebecca Eleanor b 1977); *Career* formerly: lectr in applied mathematics King's Coll London, prof Dept of Physics Univ of Newcastle upon Tyne; currently dir Beyond Center Arizona State Univ; ABC Eureka Prize for the Promotion of Science 1991; Advance Australia Award 1993, Templeton Prize for Progress in Religion 1995, Kelvin Medal InstP 2001, Faraday Prize Royal Soc 2002; memb Order of Australia 2007; FInstP 1984, FAIP 1990, FRSL 1999; *Books* non-fiction: The Physics of Time Asymmetry (1974 and 1977), Space and Time in the Modern Universe (1977), The Forces of Nature (1979, 2 edn 1986), The Search for Gravity Waves (1980), The Runaway Universe (1978), The Edge of Infinity (1981), The Accidental Universe (1982), Quantum Fields in Curved Space (with N D Birrell, 1982), God and the New Physics (1983), Quantum Mechanics (1984), Superforce (1984), The Ghost in the Atom (with J R Brown, 1986), The Cosmic Blueprint (1987), Superstrings (with J R Brown, 1988), The New Physics (ed, 1989), The Matter Myth (1991), The Mind of God (1992), The Last Three Minutes (1994), Are We Alone? (1995), About Time (1995), More Big Questions (1998), The Fifth Miracle (1998), How to Build a Time Machine (2001), The Goldilocks Enigma (2006); fiction: Fireball (1987); numerous tech papers; *Recreations* running; *Style*— Prof Paul Davies

DAVIES, Paul Windsor; AM; *b* 1969; *Educ* Llandysul GS, Newcastle Emlyn Comp Sch; *Career* Lloyds TSB 1987–2007; memb Nat Assembly for Wales (Cons) Preseli Pembrokeshire 2007–, shadow min for culture, Welsh language and sport 2007–09, shadow min for educn and the Welsh language 2009–11, interim ldr Welsh Cons Assembly Gp 2011, dep ldr Welsh Cons Assembly Gp 2011–, shadow min for finance 2011–14, chief whip 2014–; *Style*— Paul Davies, Esq, AM; ✉ National Assembly for Wales, Cardiff Bay, Cardiff CF99 1NA

DAVIES, His Hon Judge (Francis) Peter; *Career* called to the Bar 1986; recorder 2002, circuit judge (Northern Circuit) 2012–; legal chair First Tier Health and Social Educn Chamber

(Mental Health) 2012; *Style*— His Hon Judge Peter Davies; ✉ Bolton Crown Court, The Law Courts, Blackhorse Street, Bolton BL1 1SU

DAVIES, Prof Peter David Owen; s of Herbert Lewis Owen Davies (d 2000), of Caldy, Wirral, and Mary Ann Lockerbie, *née* Curry (d 1983); *b* 30 April 1949; *Educ* Marlborough, UC Oxford, St Thomas' Hosp London (MA, BM BCh, DM); *m* 1975, Eleanor Mary Baskerville, da of David Mynors (d 1999); 3 s (Richard b 1976, Edward b 1978, Michael b 1985), 1 da (Mary b 1982); *Career* various jr posts London Hosps until 1978, clinical offr MRC Tuberculosis and Chest Diseases Unit Brompton Hosp 1978–80, subsequently various posts Cardiff 1980–88, conslt respiratory physician Aintree Hosps and Cardiothoracic Centre Liverpool 1988–; licenced reader (Anglican Church) Dio of Chester; memb: BMA 1973, Br Thoracic Soc 1979, American Thoracic Soc 1987; sec TB Alert 1999; FRCP, RSM 1996; *Books* Clinical Tuberculosis (ed), Cases in Clinical Tuberculosis (co-author); also author of papers on many aspects of tuberculosis particularly epidemiological; *Style*— Prof Peter Davies; ✉ Tuberculosis Research Unit, Cardiothoracic Centre, Thomas Drive, Liverpool L14 3PE (☎ 0151 228 1616, fax 0151 293 2254, e-mail p.d.o.davies@liverpool.ac.uk)

DAVIES, Peter Donald; s of Stanley Davies (d 1991), of Aberystwyth, Dyfed, and Dorothy Margaret, *née* Addicott (d 1987); *b* 14 May 1940; *Educ* Ardwyn Sch Aberystwyth, Guy's Hosp Univ of London (MB BS); *m* 23 May 1965 (m dis 1989), Penelope Anne, da of Wilfred Reginald Dawes; 2 da (Lucy Bronwen b 1969, Emma Sian b 1971); m 2, 24 Dec 1993, Margaret Ruth, da of Horace Gallant; *Career* lectr in experimental ophthalmology Inst of Ophthalmology London 1967–70, resident Moorfields Eye Hosp 1970–74, sr registrar Middx Hosp and Moorfields Eye Hosp 1974–78, conslt ophthalmic surgn Norwich Health Dist 1978–2001, initiated the devpt of out-patient cataract surgery in the UK 1983–, fndr and dir East Anglian Eye Bank 1993–2001; author of pubns on ophthalmology and corneal surgery; FRCS 1973, FRCOphth 1989, hon reader Biological Sciences UEA 1998; *Recreations* equestrian pursuits, ornithology, model engineering; *Style*— Peter Davies, Esq

DAVIES, Rear Adm Peter Roland; CB (2005), CBE (1996, MBE 1984); s of Roland Davies (d 1982), and Winifred, *née* Stephen; *b* 2 April 1950; *Educ* Thornleigh GS Bolton, KCL (BSc), RMCS Shrivenham (MSc); *m* 13 July 1974, Dianne Helen, *née* Whittaker; 1 s (Malcolm b 1977), 1 da (Louise b 1979); *Career* univ cadet entry RN 1969; submarine weapon engr offr HMS Opportune, HMS Narwhal and HMS Courageous, staff posts Faslane, Devonport and Northwood, staff course NATO Defence Coll Rome; MOD and Procurement posts incl: RN SUB Harpoon project, Directorate of Operational Requirements, project mangr TOMAHAWK prog, Directorate of Naval Communication and Info Systems; Cdre HMS Collingwood 1998–2001, Flag Offr Trg and Recruiting and chief exec Naval Recruiting and Trg Agency 2001–04; princ and chief exec City Lit 2004–11; chair of govrs Morley Coll London 2014–; *Recreations* swimming, sailing (RYA offshore skipper); *Clubs* RNSA; *Style*— Rear Adm Peter Davies; ✉ 39 Granary, Royal Clarence Marina, Weevil Lane, Gosport, Hampshire PO12 1FX

DAVIES, Maj-Gen Peter Ronald; CB (1991); s of Lt-Col Charles Henry Davies (d 2004), and Joy, *née* Moore (d 2012); *b* 10 May 1938, Gibraltar; *Educ* Llandovery Coll, Welbeck Coll, RMA Sandhurst; *m* 12 Sept 1960, (Rosemary) Julia, da of David Felice (d 1961), of Douglas, IOM; 1 s (Tristan David Henry b 1961), 1 da (Dr Cecilia d'Felice b 1963); *Career* cmmnd Royal Signals 1958, served BAOR Berlin, Cyprus, Borneo and UK 1958–72, Bde Maj 20 Armd Bde 1973–74, Instr Staff Coll Camberley 1975–76, CO 1 Armd Div Signal Regt 1976–79, Col GS SD HQ UKLF 1979–82, Bde Cdr 12 Armd Bde 1982–84, RCDS 1985, Dep Cmdt and Dir of Studies Army Staff Coll 1985–86, Cdr Communications BAOR 1987–90, GOC Wales 1990–91; Col King's Regt (8th, 63rd, 96th) 1986–94, Chm Regtl Cncl and King's Liverpool and Manchester Regts' Assoc 1986–94, Col Cmdt Royal Signals 1991–96, life pres Jullundur Bde Assoc 1989; DG RSPCA 1991–2002, DG World SPA 2003–09 (vice-pres 1998–99, pres 2000–02), dir Flora for Fauna Soc 2001–08, chm Freedom Food Ltd 1994–2002, pres Euro Gp for Animal Welfare 2012– (exec dir 1992–2002); conslt Int Strategic Planning Advsy Bd Andrew Corporation USA 1991–92; memb Exec Ctee: Forces Help Soc and Lord Robert's Workshops 1994–96, Addaction 1997–99, Wildlife Information Network 2002–04; chm Animals in War Meml Fund 1997–2009, chm Bd of Tstees The Brooke 2009–13, chm Marjin Centre for Study of Conflict and Conservation KCL 2010–, tstee Four Paws UK 2012–, patron Sikh1914 2013–; govr Welbeck Coll 1980–81, tstee Llandovery Coll 1992–2004; Queen Victoria Silver Medal RSPCA 2003, Massachusetts SPA George T Angell Meritorious Award 2003, NZ Assisi Medal 2007; CIMgt 1994 (FIMgt 1991), FIPD 1991, FRSA 2002; *Recreations* rugby football, Welsh nostalgia; *Clubs* Army and Navy, Fadeaways (fndr and chm 1992); *Style*— Maj-Gen Peter Davies, CB; ✉ e-mail pdavies@fastmail.fm

DAVIES, Dr Peter Thomas; CBE (2003); s of Thomas Henry Davies (d 1980), and Molly Rose, *née* Gardner; *b* 24 February 1948; *Educ* Sweyne Sch Rayleigh, Univ of Reading (BSc), Univ of London (PhD); *m* 1972, Phyllis, *née* Campbell; 2 s (Alan b 1975, Bryan b 1976); *Career* postdoctoral res fell Physics Dept QMC London 1972–73; SERC: memb Engrg Div 1973–78, private sec to chm Prof Sir Geoffrey Allen 1978–80, memb Astronomy Div 1980–82; memb Central Policy Review Staff and princ advsr to Chief Scientist at Cabinet Office 1982–84, ops dir and sec Royal Greenwich Observatory 1984–85, fndr dir Rover Advanced Technol Centre Univ of Warwick 1985–96, chief exec Pera International 1999–2008 (md 1996–99), fndr Pera Fndn 2008; Royal Acad of Engrg visiting prof Univ of Loughborough 2009–; memb Design Cncl 1999–2005; *Style*— Dr Peter Davies, CBE; ✉ Pera, Innovation Park, Melton Mowbray, Leicestershire LE13 0PB (☎ 01664 501501)

DAVIES, Philip; MP; *b* 5 January 1972, Doncaster; *Educ* Old Swinford Hosp Sch, Univ of Huddersfield; *Career* Asda: cashier 1993–95, trainee customer servs mangr 1995–97, customer rels supervisor 1997–99, customer servs project mangr 1999–2004, sr mktg mangr 2004–05; MP (Cons) Shipley 2005– (Parly candidate (Cons) Colne Valley 2001); memb: Culture Media and Sport Select Ctee 2006–15, Exec 1922 Ctee 2006–12, Modernisation Select Ctee 2007–10, Backbench Business Ctee 2010–12, Panel of Chairs 2010–, Justice Select Ctee 2015–; memb Cons Pty 1988–; *Style*— Philip Davies, Esq, MP; ✉ House of Commons, London SW1A 0AA (☎ 020 7219 8264, e-mail daviesp@parliament.uk); Constituency Office ☎ 01274 592248, website www.philip-davies.org.uk

DAVIES, Philip John; CB (2001); s of Glynn Davies (d 1997), and Catherine Mary, *née* Adams (d 2013); *b* 19 September 1954; *Educ* St Julian's HS Newport, Hertford Coll Oxford (BA, BCL); *m* 5 Sept 1981, Jacqueline Sara, da of George Boutcher; 1 da (Helen Louise Amanda b 5 June 1989); *Career* barr; lectr Univ of Manchester 1977–1982; Parly Counsel Office: successively asst, sr asst then dep counsel 1982–1994, Parly counsel 1994–2011; dep counsel House of Commons and conslt legislative drafter 2011–; memb Editorial Bd Statute Law Review; author of articles and notes in various legal periodicals; *Recreations* family, Welsh terriers, the garden; *Style*— Philip Davies, Esq, CB; ✉ Pinecroft, The Downs, Givons Grove, Leatherhead, Surrey KT22 8JY (☎ 01372 373915, e-mail davies.pinecroft@hotmail.co.uk); 5 Glendower House, The Guildhall, The Norton, Tenby SA70 8AH

DAVIES, (William) Rhodri; QC (1999); s of His Hon Judge (Lewis) John Davies, QC, and Janet Mary, *née* Morris; *b* 29 January 1957; *Educ* Winchester, Downing Coll Cambridge (BA); *m* 28 July 1984, Hon Victoria Catherine (Vicky), da of Stewart Platt, of Writtle, Essex; 3 da (Rachael b 1985, Joanna b 1987, Jessica b 1990); *Career* called to the Bar Middle Temple 1979, practising in London 1980–; *Recreations* running, sailing, swimming, family; *Clubs* Thames Hare & Hounds; *Style*— Rhodri Davies, Esq, QC; ✉ 1 Essex Court, Temple, London EC4Y 9AR (☎ 020 7583 2000)

DAVIES, Richard James Guy; s of George Glyn Davies, MBE, of Frinton-on-Sea, Essex, and Cynthia Joan, *née* Franklin; *b* 7 December 1953; *Educ* Felsted, St Catharine's Coll Cambridge (MA); *m* 19 July 1980 (m dis 1992); 2 s (Michael b 1985, Christopher b 1987); *Career* with Lazard Bros & Co Ltd 1976–93, chief exec LET Ventures Ltd 1993–95; British Linen Bank Ltd: joined as dir 1995, head of corp fin 1995–99; dir British Linen Advisers 1999–2008; non-exec dir: Kiplun Ltd 2006–, Snoozebox Hldgs plc 2012–; *Recreations* sailing, music, literature; *Clubs* Royal Thames Yacht, Royal Corinthian Yacht; *Style*— Richard Davies, Esq; ✉ Highfield Farm, Fordham Road, West Bergholt, Colchester C06 3DP

D

DAVIES, Richard John; s of Sydney John Davies, and Valerie Reynolds Davies; *Educ* King's Coll Taunton, Univ of Liverpool (BA, MA); *m* Margaret Mary, *née* Goddard; 1 s (John), 1 da (Emelye); *Career* teaching asst Dept of Political Theory and Institutions Univ of Liverpool 1972–73; entered Civil Serv 1973, served MOD, FCO, MPO etc 1973–84, asst sec Welsh Office 1985; head of div Welsh Office: Health Mgmnt, Systems and Personnel 1985–87, Health and Social Servs Policy 1987–89, Housing 1989–94, School Performance 1994–97; dir Welsh Office Dept of Educn; Welsh Assembly Govt: dir Dept for Trg and Educn 1997–2006, dir Mgmnt Bd 2000–09, head Dept for Public Servs and Performance 2006–09; registered cmmr Infrastructure Planning Cmmn 2010–12; non-exec dir: HM Court Service Wales 2005–10, SRA Panel of Adjudicators 2009–13, Bds RICS 2010–; lay memb: Bar Standards Bd Educn and Trg Ctee 2012–15, Advsy Ctee Medical Practitioners Tribunal Service (MPTS) 2013–; assoc GMC and Gen Pharmaceutical Cncl 2010–, a CCC chair Nursing and Midwifery Cncl 2012–, a PCC chair Gen Osteopathic Cncl 2013–; visiting prof Univ of Glamorgan 2006–11; tstee: Nationwide Fndn 2008–13, Carnegie (UK) 2009–, Regent's Coll London 2009–10; Nuffield-Leverhulme fell 1990, Doctoral Fellowship Coll of Teachers 2016; FCMI, FRSA; *Recreations* family, walking, swimming, music; *Style*— Richard Davies, Esq

DAVIES, Dr Robert James; s of Canon Dilwyn Morgan Davies (d 2000), of Ilmington, Warks, and Kate, *née* Maltby (d 1987); *b* 24 February 1943; *Educ* St John's Sch Leatherhead, St Catharine's Coll Cambridge (MA, MB BS, MD), Univ of Greenwich (MSc, PGCE, Cert CMT); *m* 1, 1969 (m dis 1979); 2 s (Mark b 10 Oct 1972, James b 27 May 1975); m 2, 1981, Karen, da of Dennis Stanley Seymour Henley, of Bexley, London; *Career* res fell Brompton Hosp London 1971–73, lectr in med St Thomas' Hosp London 1973–76, med res Univ of Tulane New Orleans 1976–77; Bart's: conslt physician 1977–99, dir Asthma and Allergy Res Dept 1981–99, conslt in charge Dept of Respiratory Med 1987–99, prof of respiratory med 1991–99 (reader 1983–90); dir Gen and Emergency Med Royal Hosps Tst 1994–96, dir of R&D Royal Hosps NHS Tst 1996–97; pres: Br Soc for Allergy and Clinical Immunology 1987–90, Br Allergy Fndn 1996–2000; second vice-pres Int Assoc for Allergy and Immunology 1997–99 (treas 1985–94); md Masters-in-Science 2004–; lectr in computing NW Kent Coll 2004–11; Medal of Faculty of Med Univ of Montpellier France 1981; FRCP 1982, fell American Acad of Allergy and Immunology 1984, hon memb Argentinian Soc for Allergy and Immunology 1997; MBCS 2004; *Publications* Respiratory Medicine (ed, 1988–94), Allergy – The Facts (ed, 1989), Understanding Hay Fever and Other Allergies (1995); *Recreations* hill walking, mountain and moorland ponies; *Style*— Dr Robert J Davies; ✉ 96 Vanbrugh Park, Blackheath, London SE3 7AL (☎ 020 8858 9215, e-mail drrobertdavies@gmail.com)

DAVIES, (Robert) Russell; s of John Gwilym Davies, of Llanbedr, Merioneth, and Gladys, *née* Davies; *b* 5 April 1946; *Educ* Manchester Grammar, St John's Coll Cambridge (scholar, BA, Tiarks German award); *m* 23 March 1972 (m dis), Judith Anne, da of Noel Stephen Slater; 1 s (Steffan John b 5 Feb 1979); m 2, Emma Jane, da of Gerald Kingsley; 3 s (Joseph Philip b 14 July 2000, Matthew Gwilym, Oliver Nathaniel (twins) b 14 Nov 2003); *Career* freelance journalist and broadcaster; TV actor and presenter 1970–71, cartoonist Liberal News 1971, caricaturist Times Literary Supplement 1972–74; The Observer: football reporter 1973–76, film critic 1973–78, contracted writer 1983–88; sports columnist New Statesman 1978–79, TV critic Sunday Times 1979–83 (columnist 1978–), dep ed Punch 1988 (contrib 1976–92); sports columnist: Sunday Telegraph 1989–94, Daily Express 1996–; radio critic Sunday Telegraph 1996–97; radio incl: documentaries on American culture for Radio 3, biographies of jazz and blues singers, plays for radio, sports documentaries, Midweek 1979–81, Jazz Century, Beethoven or Bust, Russell Davies Song Show, Friday Night Is Music Night, Just Before Goonrise, Spike Milligan: 21 Goon Salute, Oh What A Beautiful Evening, Living In Harmony, The Guv'nor: The Rober Farnon Story, Radio Roots, Pick of the Week, Opening Nights, The Bix Beiderbecke Story, Brain of Britain 2004, The Archive Hour: Charles Chilton, George on George (Radio 4), biographical series (Cole Porter, Irving Berlin, George Gershwin, Harry Warren, Johnny Mercer, Richard Rogers, Louis Armstrong, Nat King Cole, Fats Waller, Bing Crosby, Ella Fitzgerald), radio series (When Housewives had the Choice, Radio Fun, Seven Deadly Singsongs, What An Institution, Quad Wrangles, Turns of the Century, Word of Mouth (Ondas Prize Barcelona 1996)); script editor Frank Sinatra: Voice of the Century (Radio 2), author of radio scripts for Denis Norden, David Jacobs, Harry Connick Jr, Al Jarreau, Pat Boone, Stewart Copeland, Henry Goodman, Ruthie Henshall; television incl: What The Papers Say, What The Papers Say Annual Awards 1989–97, presenter Saturday Review, presenter Jazz Week and Jazz On a Summer's Day weekend BBC2, music documentaries BBC2 (Laughing Louie, Duke Ellington and his Famous Orchestra, Le Jazz Hot, The Lowest of the Low, Buddy Bolden's Children, A Musical Nation?, The Honky Tonk Professor), Statements (arts series BBC Wales), Knowing My Place (HTV), Dudley Moore: After the Laughter (BBC 4), Artie Shaw: Quest for Perfection (BBC 4), University Challenge (BBC 2), script editor Private Life of a Masterpiece (BBC 2); formerly: librettist Love And The Ice Cream Vendor (Roundhouse and South Bank Show LWT), actor Charles Charming's Challenges (Apollo Theatre); recorded The World of Buddy Bolden (with Humphrey Lyttelton) 1986; *Books* Peregrine Prykke's Pilgrimage (illustrator, 1976), Vicky (with Liz Ottaway, 1987), Ronald Searle (1990), The Diaries of Kenneth Williams (ed), The Kenneth Williams Letters (ed), Foreign Body: The Secret Life of Robert Maxwell (1996); *Recreations* jazz and jazz history, trombone, tuba, bass saxophone and piano playing, comic art, cartooning, tidying up; *Style*— Russell Davies, Esq

DAVIES, Ryland; s of late Gethin Davies, and Joan Davies; *b* 9 February 1943; *Educ* Royal Manchester Coll of Music (studied with Frederic R Cox, OBE); *m* 1, 1966 (m dis 1981), Anne Elizabeth Howells; m 2, 1983, Deborah Rees; 1 da (Emily); *Career* tenor, operatic prodr and voice teacher; debut as Almaviva in The Barber of Seville WNO 1964, debut as prodr L'Elisir d'Amore 1991; pt/t prof of singing RNCM 1987–94, teacher RCM 1995–2005, prof of singing RAM 2007–; performed at venues incl Covent Garden, Glyndebourne, NY Met, La Scala Milan, Paris, Vienna, Salzburg, Berlin, Hamburg, Stuttgart, Buenos Aires, Bonn, Geneva, Nice, Madrid, Barcelona, Palermo, Rome, Edinburgh Festival; worked with orchs incl: London Symphony, London Philharmonic, English Chamber Orch, Chicago Symphony, Philadelphia Orch, Vienna Symphony, Boston Symphony, Cleveland Symphony, Bavarian Radio Orch; worked under conductors incl: Sir John Pritchard, Sir Colin Davis, Sir Charles Mackerras, Daniel Barenboim, Sir Georg Solti, Richard Bonynge, Simon Rattle, Andrew Davis, Erich Leinsdorf, Karl Böhm, Zubin Mehta, Claudio Abbado, Herbert von Karajan, Bernard Haitink, James Levine, John Eliot Gardiner; made numerous recordings, given performances on radio (incl RAI Radio), TV and film; Boyce and Mendelssohn Fndn scholarship 1964, John Christie award 1965; fell Royal Manchester Coll of Music 1971, fell Welsh Coll of Music and Drama 1996, hon RAM 2012; *Roles* incl: Belmonte in Die Entführung aus dem Serail (Glyndebourne, Paris, Amsterdam and Lyons), Fenton in Falstaff (Scottish Opera and Covent Garden), Ferrando in Cosi Fan Tutte (Covent Garden, Met Opera NY), Flamand in Capriccio (Glyndebourne), Tamino in The Magic Flute (Glyndebourne, WNO, Scottish Opera), Essex in Britten's Gloriana (Sadler's Wells), Hylas in The Trojans, Don Ottavio in Don Giovanni (Covent Garden), Cassio in Otello, Ernesto in Don Pasquale (Covent Garden), Lysander in A Midsummer Night's Dream (Covent Garden, Glyndebourne), The Prince in The Love for Three Oranges (Glyndebourne), Eisenstein in Die Fledermaus (ENO), Nemorino in L'Elisir d'Amore (Covent Garden), Le Duc, Chérubin and Basilio in Le Nozze di Figaro (Covent Garden), Arbace in Idomeneo (Met Opera NY), Don Basilio in Le Nozze di Figaro (New Israeli Opera), Don Basilio in Figaro's Wedding (ENO 1999), Rev Horace Adams in Peter Grimes (ENO 1999, Saito Kinen Festival Japan 2002, Florence 2002), Don Basilio in Le Nozze Di Figaro (Glyndebourne) 2001; other productions incl: Dialogue of the Carmelites (Netherlands Opera) 1997 and 2002, Le Nozze di Figaro (Chicago Lyric Opera 1998), Die Zauberflöte (Santa Fe Opera 1998), Carmen (Netherlands Opera 1999), Dialogue of the Carmelites (ENO, Santa Fe Opera 1999), Turk in Italy LA Boheme (ENO) 2000, Monostatos-Zauberelöte (Met Opera NY) 2001, The Makropulos Case (Houston Grand Opera) 2002, Arbace in Idomeno (Opera North) 2003, Monostatos (Amsterdam and Covent Garden) 2003, Francis Flute in A Midsummer Night's Dream (La Fenice Venice) 2004, Rev Horace Adams in Peter Grimes (Salzburg Easter Festival and Berlin Philharmonie) 2005, The Makropulos Case (Lyon) 2005, Dialogue of the Carmelites (ENO) 2005, Monsieur Triquet in Eugene Onegin (ROH) 2006, (Canadian Opera) 2007 and (Salzburg Festival) 2007, Tristan und Isolde (La Scala) 2007 and 2009 and (Covent Garden) 2009, The Makropoulos Case (Paris Opera) 2007 and (Madrid Opera) 2008, Theodora (Salzburg) 2009, The Makropulos Case (ENO) 2010, (Salzburg) 2011 and (Paris) 2013, Monsieur Taupé/ Capriccio (Paris Opera) 2012, Emperor Altoum in Turandot (Scottish Opera) 2014; *Style*— Ryland Davies, Esq; ✉ Elm Cottage, Loseberry Road, Claygate, Surrey KT10 9DQ

DAVIES, Prof Dame Sally Claire; DBE (2009); da of Prof J G Davies (d 1990), and E M Davies, *née* Tordoff; *b* 24 November 1949, Birmingham; *Educ* Edgbaston High Sch for Girls, Manchester Univ MB ChB; *m* 7 Oct 1989, Dr Willem H Ouwehand; 2 da (Olivia b 26 Nov 1991, Isa b 3 Feb 1995); *Career* conslt haematologist Central Middx Hosp 1995–2011, prof of haemoglobinopathies Faculty of Med Imperial Coll London 1997–2011 (emeritus prof 2011–), dir of R&D NHS London Region 1999–2004, DG of R&D and chief scientific advsr Dept of Health 2004–11, chief medical offr and chief scientific advsr Dept of Health 2011–16, chief medical offr 2016–; ed Int Cochrane Collaboration 1999–; chair UK Clinical Research Collaboration 2004–, memb Advsy Ctee on Health Research WHO 2006–; govr Ashridge Mgmnt Sch 2006–13, tstee Cumberland Lodge 2012–; prof fell Inst of Mental Health Nottingham; hon visiting fell Trinity Coll Oxford 2013–; hon fell: Harris Manchester Coll 2012, Queen Mary Univ London 2015, Homerton Coll 2016, Univ of Cambridge 2016; Hon DM: Univ of Southampton 2007, Univ of Birmingham 2008, Univ of Leeds 2011, KCL 2011, Univ of York; Hon DSc: Univ of Sheffield 2008, Cranfield Univ 2008, Univ of Liverpool 2009, Univ of Lincoln 2010, Univ of Exeter 2010, Keele Univ 2011, Univ of Lancaster 2011, Aston Univ 2012, Univ of Manchester, Brunel Univ 2013, Nottingham Trent Univ 2014, Univ of Leicester 2014, Surrey Univ 2014, Loughborough Univ 2014, Univ of Warwick 2015, Univ of Bradford 2015, Hon DSc UCL 2016; Hon DCL Newcastle Univ; FRCP 1992, FRCPath 1997, FRCPCH 1997, FFPH 1999, FMedSci 2002, Hon FRCPCH 2012, hon fell Royal Soc for Public Health, Hon FRCS, hon fell Br Pharmacological Soc, Hon FRCOG 2016, Hon FRS 2014, Hon FRSM 2014, hon fell Assoc of Anaethetists of GB and Ireland 2015; *Publications* The Drugs Don't Work – A Global Threat (jtly, 2013); author of more than 50 peer-reviewed pubns, 19 chapters in books and more than 80 other articles in the fields of sickle cell disease and R&D strategies for health; *Recreations* opera, cooking, skiing; *Clubs* RSM, Royal Soc, RCP; *Style*— Prof Dame Sally C Davies, DBE, FRS, FMedSci; ✉ Department of Health, Richmond House, 79 Whitehall, London SW1A 2NL (☎ 020 7210 5151, e-mail sally.davies@dh.gsi.gov.uk)

DAVIES, (Hilary) Sarah Ellis; da of Michael E Davies, of Bungay, Suffolk, and Maureen Davies; *b* 11 January 1962; *Educ* Cheltenham Ladies' Coll, Wimbledon Sch of Art (fndn course), Kingston Poly; *m* 26 July 1997, Jeremy F Bourke, s of Ben Bourke; 1 da (Natasha Ellis b 15 July 2000), 1 s (Samuel Ellis b 25 Feb 2004); *Career* Lambie-Nairn & Co Ltd: runner 1982–84, TV commercials prodr 1984–85, head of TV (responsible for commercials prodn, brand identity for TV Cos and TV graphics) 1985–93, md Lambie-Nairn & Co Ltd 1993–97; commercial dir The Brand Union Ltd (incorporating Lambie-Nairn and Tutssels) 1997–99; corp branding and business devpt conslt 1999– (clients incl: Royal Acad of Arts, Music Choice, 3i, Pearson Television, Thames Television, Red Bee Media Ltd, Framestore, Shell, Ipulse, ASK US FOR IDEAS, ITV); produced Marketing for Television Companies Promax Europe 1999; memb: Commissioning Design Panel Promax UK 1997, Promax Europe 1998 (seminar ctee Promax UK 1998, 1999, 2000 and 2001), Marketing Soc 1997, Women in Marketing and Design 1997, RTS 1997 (Multichannel Ctee 1999, 2000 and 2001); tstee Media Tst 1994–2008, tstee ONE20 (TimeBank) until 2013; Lambie-Nairn & Co recipient of Queen's Award for Export Achievement 1995; co-chair Newton Prep PTA 2010–12 (treas 2009–10), tstee Newton Scholarship Fund 2010–; Fell Liveryman Worshipful Co of Glaziers and Painters of Glass; *Publications* Building the Brand (Spectrum magazine, 1995); *Recreations* skiing, scuba diving, fly fishing, travel; *Clubs* Chelsea Arts, RTS, Hospital; *Style*— Ms Sarah Davies; ☎ and fax 020 8623 9129, e-mail sarah@sarahdavies.biz

DAVIES, Dr Sheilagh; da of Arthur Brython Davies (d 1967), and Rachel Edith, *née* Penn (d 1965); *b* 4 March 1946; *Educ* Moreton Hall Oswestry, Royal Free Hosp Sch of Med Univ of London (LRCP MRCS, MB BS, DObstRCOG, DPsycholM, Laughlin prize); *m* (m dis); 1 da (Gwenllian Catherine Mary b 25 Dec 1985); *Career* SHO/registrar in psychiatry Nat Hosp for Nervous Diseases UCH and the Maudsley and Bethlem Hosps 1972–76, sr registrar in gen adult psychiatry then in psychotherapy Maudsley and Bethlem Hosps 1976–80, conslt psychiatrist in psychotherapy, head Psychotherapy Unit and hon sr lectr Royal Free Hosp 1981– (divnl med dir and chm Psychiatric Specialty Gp 1994–97), clinical tutor Inst of Psychiatry 1981–87, hon conslt psychiatrist in psychotherapy Tavistock Clinic 1994–; Br Psychoanalytical Soc: memb Cncl 1987–89, hon sec 1989–92, memb Scientific Ctee 1995– (chm 1999–), memb Ct of Electors 1999–; chm Psychotherapy Faculty Royal Coll of Psychiatrists 1994–99; fndr memb: Assoc for Psychoanalytical Psychotherapy in the NHS (memb Cncl 1982–86 and 1994–), Int Assoc for Forensic Psychotherapy (memb Steering and Advsy Ctee 1992–), NI Inst of Human Rels; FRCPsych 1990 (MRCPsych 1975); *Recreations* walking, dogs, Wales, opera, classical music, theatre; *Clubs* Groucho, RSM; *Style*— Dr Sheilagh Davies; ✉ Royal Free Hospital, Psychotherapy Unit, Second Floor, Pond Street, London NW3 2QG (☎ 020 7830 2046, fax 020 7830 2139)

DAVIES, Simon James; *Educ* Emmanuel Coll Cambridge (BA); *Career* Linklaters: trainee slr London 1990–92, asst slr London 1992–95, asst slr Hong Kong 1995–99, ptnr Hong Kong 1999, ptnr Tokyo 1999–2003, Asia managing ptnr 2003–07, firmwide managing ptnr 2008–15; chief people, legal and strategy offr and memb Exec Ctee Lloyds Banking Gp 2016–; *Style*— Simon James Davies, Esq; ✉ Lloyds Banking Group, 25 Gresham Street, London EC2V 7HN

DAVIES, Simon Philip; s of The Ven Philip Davies (d 2005), and Jane, *née* Richardson; *b* 27 July 1964, Bolton, Lancs; *Educ* Radley, Lady Margaret Hall Oxford (MA), Inst of Educn (PGCE); *m* 1 June 1991, Robina Pelham Burn; 2 s (Patrick b 15 Sept 1994, Tom b 18 April 1996), 1 da (Celia b 5 April 1998); *Career* Chase Manhattan Bank 1986–87, broker and dealer, conslt and freelance lectr in derivative products James Capel Stockbrokers 1987–92, form teacher Hereward House Prep Sch 1992–93, asst biology teacher, head Biology Dept, boarding housemaster and sr housemaster Abingdon Sch 1994–2002, vice-master and usher Bedford Sch 2002–05, headmaster Eastbourne Coll 2005–; govr: St Andrew's Sch, Holmewood House, St Ronan's Sch; RFU coach and referee; *Recreations* fly fishing, gardening, walking, reading; *Style*— Simon Davies, Esq; ✉ Eastbourne College, Old Wish Road, Eastbourne, East Sussex BN21 4JX

DAVIES, Siobhan; CBE (2002, MBE 1995); *b* 18 September 1950; *Educ* London Contemporary Dance Studio; *Career* choreographer; lead dancer and choreographer London Contemporary Dance Theatre (cr 17 works) 1972–87, assoc choreographer Rambert Dance Co 1988–93; fndr (with Richard Alston and Ian Spink) Second Stride, fndr Siobhan Davies Dance Co 1988; composers worked with incl: Steve Reich, Kevin Volans, Gerald Barry, Max Eastley, Matteo Fargion; others worked with incl: David Buckland (set designer), Peter Mumford (lighting designer), Sasha Keir (costume designer), Antony McDonald (costume designer), Caryl Churchill (text), David Ward (artist), David Hinton (film); Hon DUniv Surrey 1999, Hon Dr Univ of Leicester 2003; *Works created* for Rambert Dance Co: Embarque 1988, Sounding 1989, Signature 1990, Winnsboro Cotton Mill Blues 1992, remounted Carnival 2009, remounted Art of Touch 2010; for Siobhan Davies Dance Co: White Man Sleeps 1988, Wyoming 1988, Cover Him With Grass 1989, Drawn Breath 1989, Different Trains 1990, Arctic Heart 1991, White Bird Featherless 1992, Make-Make 1992, Wanting to Tell Stories 1993, The Glass Blew In 1994, Wild Translations 1995, The Art of Touch 1995, Trespass 1996, Affections 1996, Bank 1997, Eighty Eight 1998, Wild Air 1999, Of Oil and Water 2000, Plants and Ghosts 2002, Bird Song 2004, In Plain Clothes 2006, Two Quartets 2007, Endangered Species 2007, The Collection 2009, ROTOR 2010, To hand 2011, Siobhan Davies Commissions 2011, All This Can Happen 2012, Manual 2013, Table of Contents 2014, The Running Tongue 2015; for Royal Ballet: A Stranger's Taste 1999, 13 Different Keys 1999 (cmmnd by Artangel, dancers from Royal Ballet and Siobhan Davies Dance Co); other credits: Dancing Ledge (for Eng Nat Ballet) 1990; *Awards* Fulbright Arts Fellowship 1986–87, Digital Dance Award 1988, 1989, 1990 and 1992, Prudential Award for the Arts (commendation) 1991, 1992, 1993 and 1995, Laurence Olivier Award for Outstanding Achievement in Dance 1993, Prudential Award for the Arts 1996, Time Out Award 1998 and 1999, South Bank Award for Dance 2000, Creative Briton Award 2000; *Style*— Ms Siobhan Davies, CBE; ✉ Siobhan Davies Dance, Siobhan Davies Studios, 85 St Georges Road, London SE1 6ER (☎ 020 7091 9650, e-mail info@siobhandavies.com, website www.siobhandavies.com)

DAVIES, Stephanie; da of Phillip John Davies, of Aberdare, and Elaine, *née* Powell; *b* 21 October 1987, Aberdare, Wales; *Educ* Ysgol Gyfun Rhydywaun, Univ of Wales; *Career* cricketer; with clubs: Bath CC and Somerset WCCC; memb Ashes-winning side 2008, memb England touring squad Aust and NZ 2008; *Style*— Ms Stephanie Davies; ✉ 2 Glasfryn, Cwmdare, Aberdare, Wales CF44 8SB (☎ 01685 883401, e-mail stephdavies21@aol.com); The England and Wales Cricket Board, Lord's Cricket Ground, London NW8 8QZ

DAVIES, His Hon Judge Stephen; *b* 7 February 1963, Kent; *Educ* Baines Sch Poulton-le-Fylde, Downing Coll Cambridge; *m* 1996; 2 c; *Career* barr 8 King St Chambers Manchester 1986–2007, circuit judge (Northern Circuit) and judge Technol and Construction Court 2007–; *Style*— His Hon Judge Stephen Davies; ✉ Manchester Civil Justice Centre, 1 Bridge Street West, Manchester M60 9DJ (☎ 0161 240 5000, e-mail hhjudge.davies3@judiciary.gsi.gov.uk)

DAVIES, Dr Stevie; da of Henry James Davies (d 1974), of Swansea, and Mona Joan Davies; *b* 2 December 1946; *Educ* Priory Girls' GS Shrewsbury, Univ of Manchester (BA, MA, PhD); *m* 1; 2 da (Emily Jane b 1977, Grace Hannah b 1980), 1 s (Robin Harry (twin) b 1980); m 2, 1990, Frank Regan; *Career* lectr in English lit Univ of Manchester 1971–84, author and pt tutor 1984–2001, sr res fell Roehampton Inst 1994–2001, Royal Literary Fund writing fell Univ of Wales Swansea 2001–03; dir of writing Univ of Wales Swansea 2004–; memb Greenpeace, involved in the peace movement and feminism; Arts Cncl Writer's Award 1996; FRSL 1998, fell Academi Cymreig 2000 (memb 1999); *Books* literary criticism: Emily Brontë: The Artist as a Free Woman (1983), Images of Kingship in 'Paradise Lost' (1983), The Idea of Woman in Renaissance Literature (1986), Emily Brontë (1988), Virginia Woolf's 'To the Lighthouse' (1989), John Milton (1991), Shakespeare's 'Twelfth Night' (1993), John Donne (1994), Emily Brontë: Heretic (1994), Shakespeare's Taming of the Shrew (1995), Henry Vaughan (1995); novels: Boy Blue (1987, Fawcett Soc Book Prize 1989), Primavera (1990), Arms and the Girl (1992), Closing the Book (1994, shortlisted Fawcett Soc Prize 1994), Four Dreamers and Emily (1996), The Web of Belonging (1997, shortlisted Arts Cncl of Wales Book of the Year 1998), Unbridled Spirits: Women of the English Revolution (1998), Impassioned Clay (1999, shortlisted Arts Cncl of Wales Book of the Year 2000), The Element of Water (2001, winner Arts Cncl of Wales Book of the Year 2002), Kith & Kin (2004); *Recreations* playing piano, listening to music, reading; *Style*— Dr Stevie Davies, FRSL

DAVIES, Suzy; AM; *b* Swansea; *Educ* Aberdare Girls' GS, Llanishen HS, Brecon HS, Univ of Exeter, Univ of Glamorgan; *Career* memb Nat Assembly for Wales (Cons) S Wales W 2011–; *Style*— Mrs Suzy Davies, AM; ✉ National Assembly for Wales, Cardiff Bay, Cardiff CF99 1NA

DAVIES, Terence; s of Thomas Davies (d 1952), of Liverpool, and Helen, *née* O'Brien (d 1997); *b* 10 November 1945; *Educ* Sacred Heart RC Boys' Sch, Coventry Drama Sch, Nat Film and TV Sch; *Career* writer and director (film) 1973–; shipping office clerk 1960–61, unqualified book-keeper and accountant 1961–73; dir: The Terence Davies Trilogy (7 int prizes), Distant Voices Still Lives (17 int prizes), The Long Day Closes (2 int prizes), The Neon Bible, The House of Mirth (1 prize), Of Time and The City (documentary film) 2008, The Deep Blue Sea 2010, Sunset Song 2014; radio plays: The Walk to the Paradise Garden, Virginia Woolf's The Waves (adaptation), Intensive Care (BBC Radio 3) 2010; professorship Univ of Liverpool 2010; hon degree Univ of Liverpool 2010; *Books* Hallelujah Now (novel, 1983), A Modest Pageant (1992); subject of Terence Davies: A Critical Study (by Wendy Everett); *Recreations* reading, listening to music, dining, humour; *Clubs* Soho House; *Style*— Mr Terence Davies; ✉ e-mail terencedavies@aol.com, website www.terencedavies.com

DAVIES, Prof Trevor; *b* 1946; *Educ* Univ of Sheffield (BSc, PhD); *Career* UEA: lectr, reader in atmospheric sciences 1988, dir Climatic Research Unit 1993–98, prof of environmental sciences 1998–, dean Sch of Environmental Sciences 1998–2004, pro-vice-chllr (research, enterprise and engagement) 2004–11, pro-vice-cllr 2011–; special prof and dir Fudan Tyndall Centre Fudan Univ Shanghai 2011–; fndr Carbon Reduction Prog (CRed) 2003, memb NERC 2004–10; *Style*— Prof Trevor Davies; ✉ Vice-Chancellor's Office, University of East Anglia, Norwich NR4 7TJ

DAVIES, Tristan David Henry; s of Maj-Gen Peter Ronald Davies, and Julia Rosemary, *née* Felice; *b* 26 October 1961; *Educ* Douai Sch, Univ of Bristol; *Children* 2 s (Thomas Charles Brook, Guy Robert Brook), 1 da (Harriet Rosemary Brook); *Career* journalist; ed Covent Garden Courier 1983–86, Piazza magazine 1986–87; The Independent: joined 1987, listings ed 1988–90, arts and weekend ed 1990–95, dep features ed 1993–96; asst ed Night and Day magazine Mail on Sunday 1996–98, exec ed (features) The Independent 1998–2001, ed Independent on Sunday 2001–08, exec ed Sunday Times 2008–;

Recreations singing, football; *Clubs* Groucho; *Style—* Tristan Davies, Esq; ✉ The Sunday Times, 3 Thomas More Square, London E98 1XY

DAVIES, (William) Vivian; s of late Walter Percival Davies, and late Gwenllian, *née* Evans; *b* 14 October 1947; *Educ* Llanelli GS, Jesus Coll Oxford (MA), The Queen's Coll Oxford (Randall-MacIver student in archaeology); *m* 1, 30 Oct 1970 (m dis 1994), Janet Olwen May, da of late Laurie Frederick Foat, DFM, of Llanelli, Carmarthenshire; 1 da (Elen Mai b 24 May 1971), 1 s (Thomas Dafydd Robert b 30 June 1974); m 2, 11 Aug 1996, Renée Frances, da of Lester Friedman, of LA, USA; *Career* Egyptologist; dep keeper Dept of Egyptian Antiquities Br Museum 1981–88 (asst keeper 1974–81), keeper of Egyptian Antiquities Br Museum 1988–2011; visiting prof of Egyptology Univ of Heidelberg 1984–85; hon librarian Egypt Exploration Soc 1975–85, reviews ed Jl of Egyptian Archaeology 1975–85, gen ed EES Publications 1989–99; chm Sudan Archaeological Research Soc 1991–2012; memb: Governing Cncl Br Inst in Eastern Africa 1989–2005, German Archaeological Inst 1992–; FSA 1980; *Books* Egyptian Sculpture (with T G H James, 1983), Saqqara Tombs (with A B Lloyd and A J Spencer, 1984), Problems and Priorities in Egyptian Archaeology (ed with J Assmann and G Burkard, 1987), Egyptian Hieroglyphs (1987), Catalogue of Egyptian Antiquities in the British Museum VII Axes (1987), Egypt and Africa Nubia from Prehistory to Islam (ed, 1991), Biological Anthropology and the Study of Ancient Egypt (ed with Roxie Walker, 1993), Time Machine, Ancient Egypt and Contemporary Art (ed with James Putnam, 1994), Egypt, the Aegean and the Levant (ed with Louise Schofield, 1995), Egypt (with Renée Friedman, 1998), Studies in Egyptian Antiquities: A Tribute to T G H James (ed, 1999), Colour and Painting in Ancient Egypt (ed, 2001), Uncovering Ancient Sudan: A Decade of Discovery by the Sudan Archaeological Research Soc (ed with Derek Welsby, 2002); *Style—* Vivian Davies, Esq, FSA; ✉ Department of Ancient Egypt and Sudan, British Museum, London WC1B 3DG (☎ 020 7323 8306, fax 020 7323 8303, e-mail wdavies@thebritishmuseum.ac.uk)

DAVIES, Dr (David) Wyn; s of David Neville Morgan Davies (d 1991), and Meudwen, *née* Smith; *b* 20 August 1953, Aberdare, S Wales; *Educ* Univ of London (MB, BS, MD); *Career* sr registrar St Bartholomew's Hosp 1986–90, consIt cardiologist St Mary's Hosp 1991–; memb Med Advsy Panel Civil Aviation Authy, past pres Euro Cardiac Arrhythmia Soc; author of over 100 published peer reviewed scientific papers; memb Br Cardiac Soc 1988 (hon treas 2001–06); FRCP 1994, FHRS 2006; *Recreations* flyfishing, skiing, reading; *Clubs* Flyfishers, RAC, Athanaeum; *Style—* Dr Wyn Davies; ✉ Cardiology Department, St Mary's Hospital, Praed Street, London W2 1NY

DAVIES OF ABERSOCH, Baron (Life Peer UK 2009), of Abersoch in the County of Gwynedd; (Evan) Mervyn Davies; CBE (2002), JP (Hong Kong 2000); s of Richard Aled Davies, and Margaret Davies; *b* 21 November 1952; *Educ* Rydal Sch, Harvard Business Sch (PMD); *m* 979, Jeanne Marie, *née* Gammie; 1 s (Thomas Gwyn), 1 da (Laura Jane); *Career* md (UK banking) and sr credit offr Citibank 1983–93; Standard Chartered plc: joined 1993, dir 1997–2009, gp chief exec 2001–06, chm 2006–09; min of state for trade, investment and business DBIS and FCO 2009–10; currently: ptnr and chair Corsair Capital, non-exec dir Diageo plc, chm Jack Wills 2014–, dep chair LetterOne Holdings 2015–; chair of tstees Royal Acad of Arts, dir Glyndebourne, chm Garden Bridge Tst 2013–; FCIB 1990; *Recreations* soccer, cricket, golf, rugby, Welsh art; *Clubs* Hong Kong, Shek O (Hong Kong), Arts, Alfred's; *Style—* The Lord Davies of Abersoch, CBE; ✉ House of Lords, London SW1A 0PW

DAVIES OF COITY, Baron (Life Peer UK 1997), of Penybont in the County of Mid Glamorgan (David) Garfield Davies; CBE (1996); s of David John Davies (d 1976), of Bridgend, Glamorgan, and Lizzie Ann, *née* Evans (d 1993); *b* 24 June 1935; *Educ* Heolgam Secdy Modern Bridgend, Bridgend Tech Coll, Port Talbot Sch of Further Educn; *m* 12 March 1960, Marian, da of Raymond Jones, of Trelewis, nr Treharris, Glamorgan; 4 da (Hon Helen Claire b 16 Jan 1961, Hon Susan Karen b 22 May 1962, Hon Karen Jayne b 16 June 1965, Hon Rachel Louise b 24 Jan 1969); *Career* Nat Service Sr Aircraftsman RAF 1956–58; British Steel Corp: jr operative Corp 1950–51, apprentice electrician 1951–56, electrician 1958–69; Union of Shop Distributive and Allied Workers (USDAW): area organiser 1969–73, dep divnl offr 1973–78, nat offr 1978–86, gen sec 1986–97; TUC: memb Gen Cncl 1986–97, memb Employment Appeal Tbnl 1991–2006, chm Int Ctee TUC 1992–97; cncllr Penybont RDC 1966–69; JP Ipswich 1972–78; *Style—* The Lord Davies of Coity, CBE; ✉ 64 Dairyground Road, Bramhall, Stockport, Cheshire SK7 2QW (☎ 0161 439 9548)

DAVIES OF OLDHAM, Baron (Life Peer UK 1997), of Broxbourne in the County of Hertfordshire; Bryan Davies; PC (2006); s of George William Davies (d 1989), and Beryl Davies (d 1989); *b* 9 November 1939; *Educ* Redditch Co HS, UCL (BA), Inst of Educn Univ of London, LSE (BSc); *m* 1963, Monica Rosemary Mildred, da of Jack Shearing (d 1980), and Doris Shearing; 2 s (Hon Roderick Gareth b 1964, Hon Gordon Huw b 1966), 1 da (Hon Amanda Jane b 1969); *Career* teacher Latymer Sch 1962–65, lectr Middx Poly 1965–74; Parly candidate (Lab) Norfolk Central 1966, MP (Lab) Enfield North Feb 1974–1979, Parly candidate (Lab) Newport West 1983, MP (Lab) Oldham Central and Royton 1992–97; sec Parly Lab Pty 1979–92; PPS: to dep PM 1975–76, Dept of Educn 1976, Treasy 1977; Govt whip 1979, Lord in Waiting (Govt whip) 2000–03, Capt HM's Body Guard of Yeomen of the Guard (dep govt chief whip in Lords) 2003–10, oppn spokesperson on tport 2010–, spokesperson on treasy 2013–; memb Select Ctee on: Overseas Devpt 1975–78, Public Expenditure 1975–78, Nat Heritage 1992–93; shadow higher educn min 1993–97; memb MRC 1977–79; chair FE Funding Cncl 1998–2000, pres RoSPA 1999–2001; *Recreations* literature, sport; *Style—* The Rt Hon the Lord Davies of Oldham

DAVIES OF STAMFORD, Baron (Life Peer UK 2010), of Stamford in the County of Lincolnshire; (John) Quentin Davies; s of late Dr Michael Ivor Davies, and late Thelma Davies; *b* 29 May 1944; *Educ* Leighton Park Sch Reading, Gonville & Caius Coll Cambridge (MA), Harvard Univ (Frank Knox fell); *m* 1983, Chantal, da of late Lt-Col R L C Tamplin, Military Knight of Windsor, and late Claudine Tamplin; 2 s (Alexander, Nicholas); *Career* HM Dip Serv: third sec FCO 1967–69, second sec Moscow 1969–72, first sec FCO 1973–74; Morgan Grenfell & Co Ltd: asst dir 1974–78, DG and pres Morgan Grenfell France SA 1978–81, dir Main Bd and head of Euro Corp Fin 1981–87, consIt 1987–93; MP (Cons until 2007, then Lab): Stamford and Spalding 1987–97, Grantham and Stamford 1997–2010; oppn spokesman on pensions 1998–99, shadow Paymaster General 1999–2000, oppn spokesman on defence 2000–01, shadow sec of state for NI 2001–03, min of defence equipment and support 2008–10; tstee and memb Exec Ctee Centre for Economic Policy Research 1993–2008; memb: Euro Standing Ctee 1990–97, Treasy Select Ctee 1992–98, Standards and Privileges Ctee 1996–98, Euro Legislation Ctee 1997–98, Int Devpt Select Ctee 2003–07; chair Inquiry into Nat Recognition of the Armed Forces 2007–08; dir: Dewe Rogerson International 1987–96, SGE 1999–2000, Vinci SA and Vinci plc 2003–08; advsr: Chartered Inst of Taxation 1993–2008, NatWest Markets 1993–2000, Royal Bank of Scotland Global Markets 2000–03; memb Cncl Lloyd's of London 2004–08; assoc RCDS 2014–; Freeman City of London, Liveryman Worshipful Co of Goldsmiths; *Recreations* reading, walking, riding, skiing, travel; *Clubs* Beefsteak, Brooks's, Travellers; *Style—* The Lord Davies of Stamford; ✉ House of Lords, London SW1A 0PW

DAVIS; *see also:* Hart-Davis

DAVIS, Albert Edward; s of Albert Ellerd Davis (d 1954), of Luton, Beds, and Kate Elizabeth, *née* Sell (d 1962); *b* 15 July 1928; *Educ* Luton GS, Metropolitan Coll St Albans; *m* 1 March 1952, Rhona, da of Walter Maurice Temple-Smith (d 1980), of Harpenden, Herts; 1 s (Andrew Albert b 1956); *Career* sr ptnr Davis & Co LLP (chartered certified accountants) 1964– (joined 1945, jr ptnr 1950–64); dir Beacon Private Tst 1960–; retired chartered arbitrator; memb: City of London Branch Royal Soc of St George, United Wards Club City of London, Farringdon Ward Club; past pres Ward of Cheap Club; Freeman City of London 1984, Liveryman Worshipful Co of Arbitrators 1984; CTA (Fell) 1951, FCCA 1952, FCIArb 1968–2015 (ret), fell Fedn of Tax Advsrs 2014, FFA/FIPA 2015; *Recreations* music, walking, travel, horticulture, theatre; *Clubs* City Livery (past chm Music Section, past chm Motoring Section, memb History and Antiques Soc, memb Aero Section), Queenhithe Ward; *Style—* Albert Davis, Esq; ✉ Davis & Co LLP; ☎ 0333 123 5521, e-mail oak.hurst@hotmail.com, website www.davis-co.co.uk

DAVIS, Andrew; s of Brendon G F Davis, and Catharine Agnes, *née* Smyth; *b* 22 February 1964; *Children* 1 s (Joscelyn Andrew b 24 June 1992); *Career* property devpt and investment, art consulting; fndr and exec chm von Essen gp of companies 1997–, exec chm PremiAir Aviation Services Ltd 2007–; *Style—* Andrew Davis, Esq; ✉ Von Essen Group, Ston Easton Park, Ston Easton, Bath BA3 4DF (e-mail andrew.davis@andrew-davis.co.uk)

D

DAVIS, Sir Andrew Frank; kt (1999), CBE (1992); *b* 2 February 1944; *Educ* Watford GS, Royal Acad of Music, King's Coll Cambridge (organ scholar); *m* 26 April 2014, Dr Rehanwant Singh Gomez; *Career* conductor; continuo player for Eng Chamber Orch and Acad of St Martin-in-the-Fields, studied conducting with Franco Ferrara in Rome; Festival Hall debut 1970 conducting BBC Symphony Orch; asst conductor BBC Scottish Symphony Orch 1970–72, assoc conductor The Philharmonia Orch 1973–77, princ guest conductor Royal Liverpool Philharmonic Orch 1974–77, music dir Toronto Symphony Orch 1975–88 (conductor laureate 1988–), music dir Glyndebourne Festival Opera 1988–2000, chief conductor BBC Symphony Orch 1989–2000 (incl tours to Hong Kong, Europe and Japan, conductor laureate 2000–), princ guest conductor Royal Stockholm Philharmonic Orch 1995–98, music dir and princ conductor Lyric Opera of Chicago 2000–; has worked with other orchs incl: Berlin Philharmonic, Frankfurt Radio Symphony, Tonhalle, Stockholm Philharmonic, Israel Philharmonic, NY Philharmonic, Boston, Chicago and Philadelphia Orchs, LA Philharmonic; appeared at venues incl: Bayreuth Festival, Paris Opera, Royal Opera House Covent Garden, Met Opera NY, Chicago Lyric Opera, La Scala Milan, BBC Proms (conductor Last Night 1993–), All Saints' Day Concert Musikverein Vienna, various Br and Euro festivals, numerous other venues in N America, Europe and Far East; work for Glyndebourne Festival Opera incl: Eugene Onegin, Falstaff, Ariadne auf Naxos, Don Giovanni, Katya Kabanova 1988, Jenufa 1989, Tippett's New Year 1990, The Marriage of Figaro 1991, La Clemenza di Tito 1991, The Magic Flute 1991, Peter Grimes 1992, Pique Dame 1992, Onegin 1994, Makropulos Case, Ermione 1995, Lulu 1996 (Gramophone Award for Best Video 1997), Conte Ory 1997; other operatic work incl: The Marriage of Figaro (Chicago Lyric Opera), La Clemenza di Tito (Chicago Lyric Opera), Peter Grimes (Bavarian Staatsoper) 1991; awarded Royal Philharmonic Soc/Charles Heidsieck Conductor's Award 1990; *Recordings* incl: all Dvorák Symphonies (with The Philharmonia), Mendelssohn Symphonies (with Bavarian Radio Symphony Orch), Tippett The Mask of Time (with BBC Symphony Orch, following Euro premiere BBC Proms 1984, winner Gramophone Record of the Year 1987, Grand Prix du Disque 1988), Birtwistle Mask of Orpheus (with BBC Symphony Orch, Gramophone Award for Best Contemporary Recording 1998), Shostakovich Violin Concertos, Brahms Piano Concertos, Nielsen Symphonies 4 and 5, various by Elgar, Vaughan Williams, Britten, Delius and Tippett; over 25 recordings with Toronto Symphony Orch incl: Strauss Four Last Songs and Salome final scene, Holsts Planets Suite, Handel Messiah; *Recreations* cinema, golf, walking; *Style—* Sir Andrew Davis, CBE; ✉ c/o Askonas Holt, Lincoln House, 300 High Holborn, London WC1V 7JH (☎ 020 7400 1700, fax 020 7400 1799, e-mail info@askonasholt.co.uk)

DAVIS, Prof Bryn Derby; s of William Derby Davis (d 1995), and Joan, *née* Stansfield (d 1994); *b* 22 March 1938, Thurnscoe, Yorks; *Educ* Archbishop Holgate's GS York, Univ of London (Sister Tutor's Dip/RNT, BSc, PhD); *m* 1, 1962 (m dis 1979), Valerie; 2 s (Timothy, Jonathan); m 2, 1979, Catherine; 1 s (Robert), 1 da (Sarah); *Career* princ tutor (mental health) Holloway Sanatorium NW Surrey Gp of Hosps 1970–73, DHSS nursing research fell 1973–76, dep dir Nursing Research Unit Univ of Edinburgh 1976–84 (univ fell 1983–84), princ lectr and dir of nursing research Brighton Poly 1984–89, prof of nursing educn, head dept and dean Sch of Nursing Univ of Wales Coll of Med Cardiff 1989–99, emeritus prof Univ of Wales Coll of Med 1999–; visiting prof of psychology Univ of Wales Bangor, visiting prof of nursing NE Wales Inst Wrexham; ed Jl of Psychiatric and Mental Health Nursing 1997–2004; non-exec dir Pontypridd and Rhondda NHS Tst 2000–04; memb: UKCC 1998–2002, Royal Coll of Nursing Pain Forum (chm 1991–97), UK Pain Soc; Lifetime Achievement Award Jl of Psychiatric and Mental Health Nursing 2008; Cdre Brading Haven Yacht Club Isle of Wight 2008–10; chm: Amnesty Int Isle of Wight 2007–, Isle of Wight Art Club 2012–, Vectis Astronomical Soc 2012–; *Books* Research into Nurse Education (ed, 1983), Transcultural Psychiatry (contrib, 1986), Psychiatric Nursing Research (contrib, 1986), Nursing Education: research and developments (ed, 1987), Empathy in the Helping Relationship (contrib, 1990), Perspectives on Pain: mapping the territory (contrib, 1998), Caring for People in Pain (1999); *Recreations* sailing, amateur astronomy, reading, writing, painting, music, theatre, walking; *Style—* Prof Bryn Davis

DAVIS, Calum; s of Roy Albert George Davis (d 2002), of Rockford, Hants, and Catherine Jessie Davis (d 2010), of Oban, Scotland; *b* 18 June 1951, Christchurch, Dorset; *Educ* Taunton Sch, Canterbury Sch of Architecture (DipArch); *m* 1, 20 Aug 1977 (m dis 1996); 1 s (Jamie b 1981), 1 da (Josie b 1984); m 2, 9 April 2004, Hayley Ann Tasmin Bebb; 1 da (Rosy Catherine Bebb-Davis b 1998); *Career* architect; sr ptnr Architon LLP architects, interior designers, video animations and building information modelling; dir: Architon Developments Ltd 1986–, Architon Services Ltd 1986–, Architon Media Graphics Ltd 1995–; ARB 1979, RIBA 1979; Eng trialist under 19 rugby 1969; rep: SW Eng Schs rugby 1969, S Eng under 19 rugby 1969; *Recreations* golf, skiing, reading, conservation of historic buildings; *Clubs* RAC; *Style—* Calum Davis, Esq; ✉ Architon LLP, Regency House, 17 West Street, Epsom, Surrey KT18 7RL (☎ 01372 745600, fax 01372 745016, mobile 07831 837908, e-mail calum@architon.com)

DAVIS, Carl; Hon CBE (2005); *b* 28 October 1936; *m* Jean Boht, *qv*; 2 da (Hannah b 1 Jan 1972, Jessie b 3 May 1974); *Career* composer and conductor; studied with: Paul Nordoff and Hugo Kauder NY, Per Norgaad Copenhagen; asst conductor New York City Opera 1958, artistic dir and princ conductor Royal Liverpool Philharmonic Orch Summer Pops 1992–2000; launched Carl Davis Collection (record label) 2009; BAFTA Lifetime Achievement Award 2003; hon fell Liverpool John Moores Univ 1992, Hon DMus Univ of Liverpool 2002; Chevalier de l'Ordre des Arts et des Lettres (France) 1983; *Musical Theatre* Diversions (Obie Prize Best Review) 1958, Twists (Arts Theatre London) 1962, The Projector and Cranford (Theatre Royal Stanford East), Pilgrim (Edinburgh Festival), The Wind in the Willows (Haymarket) 1985, Alice in Wonderland (Hammersmith) 1987, The Vackees (Haymarket) 1987; *Incidental Music for Theatre* incl: The Prospect Theatre Co, The National Theatre, The Royal Shakespeare Co; *Ballet* A Simple Man 1987, Lipizzaner 1988, Liaison Amoureuses (Northern Ballet Theatre) 1988, Madly, Badly, Sadly, Gladly, David and Goliath, Dances of Love and Death (London Contemporary Dance Theatre), The Picture of Dorian Gray (Sadler's Wells Royal Ballet), A Christmas Carol (Northern Theatre Ballet) 1992, The Savoy Suite (English Nat Ballet) 1993, Alice in Wonderland (English Nat Ballet) 1995, Aladdin (Scottish Ballet) 2000, Pride and Prejudice (Ballet Central) 2002, Cyrano (Birmingham Hippdrome) 2007, Cyrano 2008; *Music for Television* incl: The Snow Goose (BBC TV) 1971, The World at War (Thames TV, Emmy Award) 1972, The Naked Civil Servant (Thames TV) 1975, Our Mutual Friend (BBC TV) 1978, Hollywood (Thames TV) 1980, Churchill – The Wilderness Years (Southern TV) 1981, Silas Marner (BBC TV) 1985, Hotel du Lac (BBC TV) 1986, The Accountant 1989 (BAFTA Award), The Secret Life of Ian Fleming 1989, Separate but Equal 1991, The Royal Collection 1991, A Year in Provence 1992, Fame in the 20th Century – Clive James 1992, Ghengis Cohn 1993, Thatcher – The Downing Street Years 1993, Message for Posterity (Dennis Potter) 1994, Pride and Prejudice 1995, Oliver's Travels 1995, British Film Music (BBC TV) 1995, European Cinema 1995, Anne Frank Remembered (BBC TV) 1995, Celtic Symphony 1996, Real Women (BBC TV) 1997, A Dance to the Music of Time (Channel 4) 1997, The Cold War (Turner), Seasaw (ITV), Coming Home (ITV), Good Night Mr Tom (Carlton), The Queen's Nose (five series, BBC), The Great Gatsby 2000, Back Home (film) 2001, The Cranford Chronicles (BBC) 2007 and 2009; *Music for Radio* Carl Davis Classics (Radio 2) 1997–; *Operas for Television* The Arrangement, Who Takes You to The Party, Orpheus in the Underground, Peace; *Film Music* The Bofors Gun 1969, The French Lieutenant's Woman 1981 (BAFTA award), Champions 1984, The Girl in a Swing 1988, Rainbow 1988, Scandal 1988, Frankenstein Unbound 1989, The Raft of the Medusa 1991, The Trial 1992, The Voyage 1993, Widow's Peak 1994, Topsy Turvy 2000; series of Thames Silents incl Napoleon (revised and enlarged score 2000), The Wind, The Big Parade, Greed, The General, Ben Hur, Intolerance, Safety Last, The Four Horsemen of Apocalypse 1992, Wings 1993, Waterloo 1995, Phantom of the Opera (Channel 4) 1996, Wedding March, Topsy Turvey, Book of Eve 2002, An Angel for May 2001 (Best Score Ale Kino Film Festival Poland 2003), Promoted to Glory 2003, Mothers & Daughters 2004, The Understudy 2009; *Silent Film Music* The Wedding March 1998, Old Heidelberg 1999, Iron Mask 1999, The Adventurer 2000; several Chaplin Mutuals incl: Behind the Screen, The Rink, The Cure, The Immigrant, The Adventurer, The Crowd, Easy Street 2002, Charlie Chaplin The Mutual Films Vol 1 DVD 2003, The Mutual Films Vol 2 2005, The Godless Girl 2007; *Concert Works* Music for the Royal Wedding, Variations on a Bus Route, Overture on Australian Themes, Clarinet Concerto 1984, Lines on London Symphony 1984, Fantasy for Flute and Harpsichord 1985, The Searle Suite for Wind Ensemble, Fanfare for Jerusalem 1987, The Glenlivet Fireworks Music 1988, Norwegian Brass Music 1988, Variations for a Polish Beggar's Theme 1988, Pigeons Progress 1988, Jazz Age Fanfare 1989, Everest 1989, Landscapes 1990, Paul McCartney's Liverpool Oratorio (with Paul McCartney) 1991, the BBC Proms 1999; *Recordings* incl: Christmas with Kiri (with Kiri Te Kanawa) 1986, Beautiful Dreamer (with Marilyn Horne) 1986, The Silents 1987, Ben Hur 1989, A Simple Man 1989, The Town Fox and Other Musical Tales (text by Carla Lane) 1990, Paul McCartney's Liverpool Oratorio 1991, Liverpool Pops At Home 1995, Pride and Prejudice 1995, The World at War, Pride and Prejudice and other Great Themes 1996, Phantom of the Opera 1997, Carl Davis 1997, Classics for a Summer Evening from Leeds Castle 1997, A Classical Celebration from Leeds Castle 1999, The Silents 2000, The World at War 2003, Christmas Album with Halle 2003, CD with Willard White and BBC Concert Orch 2005; *DVDs* A Simple Man, A Christmas Carol, Unknown Chaplin, Mutuals – Chaplin Vols 1, 4 and 11; *Composition* On the Beach At Night Alone (premièred at Leeds Castle) 1999; *CDs* Aladdin 2006, Show Music 2007; *Style*— Carl Davis, Esq, CBE; ✉ website www.carldaviscollection.com; c/o Threefold Music, 2 The Court Yard, London SW3 4EE (☎ 020 7730 9477, fax 020 7730 9199, e-mail admin@threefoldmusic.co.uk)

DAVIS, Clive Timothy; s of Sherman Alexander Davis, of Bath, and Betty Mavis, *née* Savery; *b* 8 October 1959; *Educ* Culverhay Comp Sch, St Catherine's Coll Oxford (BA); *m* 2 May 1986, Mohini, da of Mohanbhai Patel; 3 s (Shivan Clive b 7 Sept 1990, Krishan Alexander b 11 March 1993, Anand Anthony b 20 June 1997); *Career* journalist; books ed West Indian World newspaper 1981–85 (gen reporter and arts ed 1981–82), BBC News trainee 1982–84, sub ed BBC Radio News 1984–86, freelance feature writer and gen reporter The Guardian 1985–86, feature writer London Daily News 1986–87, writer The Times 1987–, feature writer Sunday Times 1994–; based New York 1994; contrib Wilson Quarterly (Woodrow Wilson Center for Int Scholars Washington DC) 1997–; politics/culture blogger The Spectator 2007–09, book reviewer The Independent 2014–; writer and presenter: Richard Wright – A Native Son (Radio 4 documentary), Eyewitness – William L Shirer (Radio 4 documentary); media fell Hoover Instn Stanford Univ; *Recreations* piano; *Style*— Clive Davis, Esq; ✉ e-mail clivedav@aol.com, website www.clivedavis.net (Twitter @CliveDavisUK, Facebook www.facebook.com/clive.davis.10)

DAVIS, Rt Hon David Michael; PC (1997), MP; s of Ronald Alexander Davis, and Elizabeth, *née* Brown; *b* 23 December 1948; *Educ* Bec GS, Univ of Warwick (BSc), London Business Sch (MSc), Harvard Univ (AMP); *m* 28 July 1973, Doreen, da of Alfred John Cook; 2 da (Rebecca b 1974, Sarah b 1977), 1 s (Alexander b 1987); *Career* strategic planning dir Tate & Lyle plc 1984–87 (non-exec dir 1987–90); MP (Cons): Boothferry 1987–97, Haltemprice and Howden 1997–; Govt whip 1989–93, Parly sec Office of Public Service and Science 1993–94, min of state for Europe FCO 1994–97; chm Cons Pty 2001–02, shadow sec of state for the Office of the Dep PM 2002–03, shadow sec of state for home, constitutional and legal affrs and shadow home sec 2003–08, candidate Cons Pty leadership election 2005, sec of state for exiting the EU 2016–; chm Public Accounts Ctee 1997–2001; memb Cons Pty Policy Bd 2001–; dir Globe Investment Trust plc 1989–90; *Recreations* flying, mountaineering, writing; *Style*— The Rt Hon David Davis, MP

DAVIS, David William; s of George Henry Davis (d 1999), of Beaconsfield, and Lucy Ada, *née* Tylee (d 1959); *b* 29 October 1942; *Educ* Emanuel Sch; *m* 25 Nov 1967, Jennifer, da of Wilfred Snell; 1 da (Jacqueline b 25 Feb 1970), 1 s (Kenneth b 28 May 1971); *Career* CA 1966; ptnr: Fryer Sutton Morris & Co 1967–, Fryer Whitehill & Co 1971–, Clark Whitehill 1982– (now Crowe Clark Whitehill); FCA 1975; *Recreations* bridge; *Clubs* Phyllis Court; *Style*— David Davis, Esq; ✉ Blue Hills, Ibstone, Buckinghamshire HP14 3XT (☎ 01491 638245)

DAVIS, Prof Edward Arthur; s of Edward Davis (d 1988), and Elizabeth, *née* Smith (d 2000); *b* 26 November 1936; *Educ* Univ of Birmingham (BSc), Univ of Reading (PhD), Univ of Cambridge (MA); *m* 30 Oct 1960, Christine Elizabeth, da of Philip Edwyn Riley (d 1987); 2 s (Philip b 1962, Andrew b 1964); *Career* res asst prof Physics Dept Univ of Illinois 1963–64, scientist Xerox Corp Rochester NY 1964–67, lectr Physics Dept Univ of Cambridge 1973–80 (Royal Soc Mr and Mrs John Jaffé Donation res fell Cavendish Laboratory 1968–73), prof of experimental physics Univ of Leicester 1980–2002 (dean Faculty of Science 1987–90), distinguished research fell Dept of Materials Science and Metallurgy Univ of Cambridge 2002–; ed/conslt ed Philosophical Magazine; chm History of Physics Gp Inst of Physics 2012–; CPhys, FInstP, fell American Physical Soc; *Books* Electronic Properties of Non-Crystalline Materials (with N F Mott, 1971, 2 edn 1979), Science in the Making (Vol I 1995, Vol II 1997, Vol III 1998, Vol IV 1999), JJ Thomson and the Discovery of the Electron (with I Falconer, 1997), Nevill Mott: Reminiscences and Appreciations (1998); *Recreations* tennis, golf; *Style*— Prof Edward Davis; ✉ Department of Materials Science and Metallurgy, University of Cambridge, Pembroke Street, Cambridge CB2 3QZ

DAVIS, Lt-Gen Edward Grant Martin (Ed); CB (2014), CBE (2012, OBE 2006, MBE 1996); *Career* cmmnd Royal Marines 1981; chief of staff Combat Service Support Gp HQ 1996, chief of staff to the Commander UK's Amphibious Forces, chief Jt Effects ISAF (deployed to Afghanistan), cdr 3 Commando Bde 2010 (deployed to Afghanistan as cdr Task Force Helmand) 2010, commandant gen Royal Marines 2011–14, dep cdr NATO Allied Land Command Izmir 2014–16, govr Gibraltar 2016–; KStJ 2016; *Style*— Lt-Gen Edward Davis, CB, CBE, KStJ

DAVIS, Emma; da of P K B Davis, and Jennifer Davis; *Educ* Univ of York (MA), Université Catholique Lyon, Slade Sch of Fine Art (MA, bursary), Chelsea Coll of Art; *Career* designer and artist; freelance ed: Routledge 1996–2011, Bloomsbury 2012–13; artist in residence Vallauris Cote d'Azur France 2008; memb: BECTU, Soc of Br Theatre Designers; *Theatre* costume designer Macbeth: False Memory (Lyric Hammersmith and UK tour) 2000, asst designer Whose Life is it Anyway? (Comedy Theatre London) 2005, asst designer Peter Hall Season (prodns Much Ado About Nothing, Waiting for Godot, Private Lives and You Never Can Tell; Theatre Royal Bath and nat tour) 2005, designer Edinburgh's Christmas festival 2013; *Film, Television and Video* art dept Dirty Pretty Things (film) 2001–02, asst art dir Mrs Henderson Presents (feature) 2004, prodn buyer United 93 (feature) 2005–06, prodn buyer Celebration (TV) 2006, set designer Man on the Moon, set designer This Life +10 2006, set designer Somers Town (feature) 2007, art dir King Lear (feature) 2008, prodn and costume designer Satie & Friends (feature) 2008, set designer Four Seasons (TV) 2008, set designer Secret Diary of a Call Girl (TV) 2009, prodn and costume designer A Palace for Us (short film) 2010, set decorator Sinbad (TV) 2011, prodn designer Benjamin Britten: Peace and Conflict (feature) 2012, set decorator Warner Hotels (commercial), set decorator Mapp and Lucia (TV) 2014; *Art Exhibitions* RCA Secret 1999–2013, The Discerning Eye (Mall Galleries London) 2007–08 and 2010–12, Originals (Mall Galleries London) 2009, group show Gallery Highwaymans Suffolk 2012, RCA Summer Exhibition 2013, The Other Art Fair 2014 and 2015, RCA Secret Stuart's Law 2015, RCA Secret Dubai 2015, group show Limited Editions (Lubomirov Easton London) 2015; *Publications* VISIBLE supplement in STATE/F22 Magazine; *Recreations* painting, drawing, photography, reading, writing; *Style*— Ms Emma Davis; ✉ website www.emmadavisartist.com

DAVIS, Evan Harold; s of Quintin Visser Davis, of Leatherhead, Surrey, and Hazel Noreen, *née* Groves; *b* 8 April 1962; *Educ* The Ashcombe Sch Dorking, St John's Coll Oxford (MA, ed Cherwell), Kennedy Sch of Govt Harvard Univ (MPA); *Career* research offr Inst for Fiscal Studies 1984–86, Harvard Univ 1986–88, research fell Centre for Business Strategy London Business Sch 1988–92, co-ordinator corporate policy research Inst for Fiscal Studies 1992–93, economics ed BBC 2001–08 (corr 1993–2001); presenter: Dragons' Den (BBC) 2005–, Today Programme (BBC Radio 4) 2008–14; host Newsnight (BBC) 2014–; Speech Broadcaster of the Year Sony Radio Acad Bronze Award 2012; *Books* The Penguin Dictionary of Economics (with G Bannock and R Baxter, 1987), Public Spending (1998), The New Penguin Dictionary of Business (with G Bannock, P Trott and M Uncles, 2003), Made in Britain (2011); *Style*— Evan Davis; ✉ BBC Broadcasting House, Portland Place, London W1A 1AA (e-mail evan.davis@bbc.co.uk)

DAVIS, Gareth; *b* 13 May 1950; *Educ* Univ of Sheffield; *Career* Imperial Tobacco plc: joined W D & H O Wills as mgmnt trainee1972, manufacturing dir 1987, md Imperial Tobacco Int 1987, chief exec 1996–; non-exec dir Wolseley plc 2003–; *Style*— Gareth Davis, Esq; ✉ Imperial Tobacco Group plc, Upton Road, Southville, Bristol BS99 7UJ

DAVIS, Ian Edward Lamert; s of (Walter) Patrick Carless Davis (d 1996), of Roehampton, and Jane, *née* Lamert (d 1987); bro of James Patrick Lamert Davis, *qv*, Sir Crispin Henry Lamert Davis, and Sir Nigel Anthony Lamert Davis (Hon Mr Justice Davis), *qv*; *b* 10 March 1951; *Educ* Charterhouse, Balliol Coll Oxford (MA); *m* 1, 1977, Sally Fuller; 1 s, 1 da; m 2, 1994, Penny Thring; *Career* with Bowater 1972–79; McKinsey & Co: assoc 1979–85, princ 1985–90, dir 1990–, UK md 1996–2003, worldwide md 2003–09; chm Rolls-Royce plc; non-exec dir: BP plc, Johnson & Johnson Inc, Teach for All; *Recreations* sport, opera, the Alps; *Style*— Mr Ian Davis; ✉ Rolls-Royce Group plc, 65 Buckingham Gate, London SW1E 6AT

DAVIS, Ian Paul; *b* 26 December 1954; *Educ* Univ of Liverpool (BEng), Open Univ (MBA); *Career* site engr Head Wrightson Process Engrg 1976–78, design engr Simpson Coulson and Partners 1978–80, design and project engr Davy International 1980–83; National House Building Cncl (NHBC): regnl engr 1983–90, dir of Technical Services 1990–94, dep chief exec (ops) 1994–97, dir 1994–97; DG Fedn of Master Builders 1997–2006, ops dir and memb Bd NHBC 2006–; chm NHBC Services Ltd 1995–97; dir: PRC Homes Ltd 1990–97, NHBC Building Control Services Ltd 1994–99, Soha Housing 1996–2004 (chm 1999–2003), Builders Information Services Ltd 1997–98, Trade Debt Recovery Services Ltd 1997–99, National Register of Warranted Builders Ltd 1997–2006, Building Industry Certification Scheme Ltd 1997–2006, Constructing Better Health Ltd 2004–06, Trustmark (2005) Ltd 2005–06; advsr Joseph Rowntree Fndn Housing Standards Inquiry 1993–94; memb Cncl: Confedn of Registered Gas Installers 1990–94, National Inspection Cncl for the Electrical Contracting Industry 1990–94, CIC 1990–94; memb: BSI Tech Ctees 1987–97, Examination Bd National Energy Fndn 1992–96; tech sec European Union of Promoters and Contractors; govr John Hampden Sch 1996–2000; CEng 1981, MICE; *Style*— Ian Davis, Esq

DAVIS, James Gresham; CBE (1988); s of Col Robert Davis, OBE, JP (d 1963), and Josephine, *née* Edwards (d 1976); *b* 20 July 1928; *Educ* Bradfield Coll, Clare Coll Cambridge (MA); *m* 24 Nov 1973, Adriana Johanna (Hanny), da of Evert Verhoef (d 1978), and Petronella Verhoef-Stuy, of Rhoon, Holland; 3 da (Mariske b 1974, Katrina b 1978, Charlotte b 1980); *Career* RN 1946–49; P&O Steam Navigation Co: joined 1952, Calcutta 1953–54, Kobe (Japan) 1954–56, Hong Kong 1956–57, dir P&O Lines 1967–72; chm: British Rail Anglian Bd 1988–92, Bromley Shipping plc 1989–94, TIP Europe plc 1990–93, P Wigham Richardson 2003–; dep chm Hanjin Eurobulk 2003–07; dir: Kleinwort Benson Ltd 1973–88, DFDS Ltd 1975–96 (chm 1984–95), DFDS Travel Ltd 1975–96, Pearl Cruises of Scandinavia Inc 1982–86, Rodskog Shipbrokers (Hong Kong) Ltd 1983–88, Associated British Ports Holdings plc 1983–97, Transport Development Group plc 1984–91, Sedgwick Marine Energy & Cargo Ltd 1988–2000, Global Ocean Carriers Ltd 1988– (chm 1996–), British International Freight Assoc 1989–, Hempel Paints Ltd 1992–2000, Trinitas Services Ltd 1993–99, Tsavliris Salvage (International) Ltd 1994–99, 2M Invest Copenhagen 1996–99; dir Catenas Ltd 2000–02; memb Advsy Bd: J Lauritzen A/S Copenhagen 1981–85, DFDS A/S Copenhagen 1981–85; advsr Tjaereborg (UK) Ltd 1985–87; pres: Chartered Inst of Tport 1981–82, World Ship Soc 1969, 1971, 1984, 1985, 1986 and 2003–08, Harwich Lifeboat (RNLI) 1984–, Inst of Freight Forwarders Ltd 1984–86, National Waterways Tport Assoc 1986–92, Inst of Supervisory Mgmnt 1989–93, Inst of Chartered Shipbrokers 1990–92 (vice-pres 1988–90), Inst of Export 1995–2002 and 2008– (vice-pres 1991–95), Danish-UK C of C 1992– (chm 1992–2000); vice-pres: Br Maritime League 1984–89, The Marine Soc 1986– (chm Cncl 1987–93); chm: Int Maritime Industries Forum 1981–, Simpler Trade Procedures Bd (SITPRO) 1987–98, Marine Risk Mgmnt Services Ltd 1995–99, Liberia Maritime Advsy Bd 1998–2000, Br Ctee Nippon Kaiji Kyokai 2003–; memb: Cncl Mission to Seafarers 1981–, Int and Br Ctee Bureau Veritas 1989–, Gen Ctee Lloyd's Register 1989–; pt/t memb Br Transport Docks Bd 1981–83; tstee National Maritime Museum 1993–98, govr World Maritime Univ 1985– (chm Friends of the World Maritime Univ 1985–); memb: Baltic Exchange 1973–, Greenwich Forum 1982–; delivered: Thomas More Meml Lecture 1983, Reginald Grout Lecture 1989, Wakeford Meml Lecture 1989; Seatrade Personality of the Year 2002–03, Lifetime Achievement Award Lloyds List 2011; Freeman City of London 1973, Liveryman and Asst to the Ct Worshipful Co of Shipwrights, Master Worshipful Co of World Traders

1996–97, Younger Br Trinity House; FCIT 1969, Hon FNI 1985, Hon FInstFF 1986, FRSA 1986, FISM 1989, FICS 1990; Knight Cdr Order of Dannebrog (Denmark) 1995; *Recreations* golf, family, ships, reading, tennis, travel, drawing and painting; *Clubs* Brooks's, Hurlingham, Golfers, Harwich and Dovercourt Golf, Royal Calcutta Golf, Fanlingerers, Holland Park Lawn Tennis; *Style*— James Davis, Esq, CBE, K(DK); ✉ 115 Woodsford Square, London W14 8DT (☎ 020 7602 0675); Summer Lawn, Dovercourt, Essex CO12 4EF (☎ 01255 502981); c/o Baltic Exchange, 38 St Mary Axe, London EC3A 8BH (☎ 020 7929 6429, fax 020 7929 6430, e-mail imif@btconnect.com)

DAVIS, James Patrick Lamert; s of (Walter) Patrick Carless Davis (d 1996), of Roehampton, and Jane, *née* Lamert (d 1987); er bro of Sir Nigel Anthony Lamert Davis (Hon Mr Justice Davis), and Ian Edward Lamert Davis, *qqv*; *b* 23 September 1946; *Educ* Charterhouse, Balliol Coll Oxford; *m* 18 May 1974, Sally Anne, da of Noel Kemball, and Margaret Kemball; 1 s (Andrew b 23 March 1978), 3 da (Nicola b 23 March 1980, Sarah b 9 June 1982, Clare b 30 June 1986); *Career* Freshfields (now Freshfields Bruckhaus Deringer): articled clerk 1969, ptnr 1976–, ptnr i/c Singapore Office 1980–84; *Recreations* fishing, golf; *Clubs* MCC, Singapore Cricket, Berkshire Golf; *Style*— James Davis, Esq; ✉ Freshfields Bruckhaus Deringer, 65 Fleet Street, London EC4Y 1HS (☎ 020 7936 4000, fax 020 7832 7001)

DAVIS, Prof John Patrick; s of Ralph Patrick Davis, formerly of Chaldon, Surrey, and Vivian Hilda, *née* Braund; *b* 12 June 1944; *Educ* Tonbridge, Univ of Nottingham (BSc); *m* 5 Aug 1972, Fenella Irene, da of Guy Charles Madoc, CBE, KPM, of Ramsey, Isle of Man; 1 s (Michael b 23 Jan 1975), 1 da (Rosemary b 11 June 1976); *Career* gen mangr mech engrg Redpath Dorman Long Ltd 1979–83; chm: Intelek plc 1990–99 (chief exec and gp md 1985–90), 3s Group Ltd 2000, Drew Scientific Group plc 2003–; special prof Sch of Electrical and Electronic Engrg Univ of Nottingham 2007; govr and chm of finance Rossall Sch 2013–, chm Industrial Advsy Bd Univ of Nottingham 2015–; CEng 1971, MIWeldE 1983, FIEE 1986, FIMechE 1992, FInstD 1997; *Recreations* mountain rescue, bee keeping, sailing; *Style*— Prof John Davis; ✉ Craiglands, Joss Lane, Sedbergh, Cumbria LA10 5AS (☎ 01539 622136, e-mail john@davisj.com)

DAVIS, Lindsey Margaret; da of late William Alfred Davis, and late Joan Margaret Davis; *Educ* King Edward VI HS for Girls Birmingham, Lady Margaret Hall Oxford (MA); *Career* civil servant Property Services Agency 1972–85, full time writer 1986–; memb: Soc of Authors (chair 2011–12), The Detection Club; chair Crimewriters' Assoc 2002–03, hon pres The Classical Assoc 1997–98; shortlisted Georgette Heyer Historical Novel prize 1985, 1986 and 1988; winner Crimewriters' Assoc (CWA) Dagger in the Library award 1995, winner CWA Ellis Peters Historical Dagger 1999, Premio de Honor de Novela Histórica Cuidad de Zaragoza 2009, Premio Colosseo for Enhancing the Image of Rome 2010, CWA Cartier Diamond Dagger 2011; author of various romantic serials for Woman's Realm; pres Birmingham and Midland Inst 2015; *Books* The Course of Honour (1997), Rebels and Traitors (2009); incl The Falco series: The Silver Pigs (1989, Authors' Club Best First Novel award 1990), Shadows in Bronze (1990), Venus in Copper (1991), The Iron Hand of Mars (1992), Poseidon's Gold (1993), Last Act in Palmyra (1994), Time to Depart (1995), A Dying Light in Corduba (1996), Three Hands in the Fountain (1997), Two for the Lions (1998), One Virgin Too Many (1999), Ode to a Banker (2000), A Body in the Bath House (2001), The Jupiter Myth (2002), The Accusers (2003), Scandal Takes a Holiday (2004), See Delphi and Die (2005), Saturnalia (2007), Alexandria (2009), Nemesis (2010), Falco: The Official Companion (2010), Master and God (2012), The Albia Series (The Ides of April 2013, Enemies at Home 2014, The Spook Who Spoke Again 2015, Deadly Election 2015), A Cruel Fate (2014); contrib author: No Alibi (1995), Perfectly Criminal (1997), Past Poisons (1998), Great Stories of Crime and Detection (2002), Mysterious Pleasures (2003), A Midlands Odyssey (2014), The Graveyard of the Hesperides (2016); *Recreations* gardening, travel, theatre; *Style*— Ms Lindsey Davis; ✉ c/o Euan Thorneycroft, A M Heath & Co Ltd, 6 Warwick Court, Holborn, London WC1R 5DJ (☎ 020 7242 2811); e-mail pt@lindseydavis.co.uk, website www.lindseydavis.co.uk

DAVIS, Margaret Ann McLeod Leo (Meg); da of John Alexander Bede McLeod Davis (d 1976), of Montréal, Canada, and Barbara Ann Lusby; *b* 26 September 1957; *Educ* École Classique Sécondaire Villa Maria, McGill Univ Montreal (BA); *m* 19 March 2006, J Pimblett; *Career* dir MBA Literary Agents 1988–2011 (joined 1984), md Ki Agency 2011–; sec Assoc of Authors' Agents 1998–2001 (treas 2015–); co-chair: Dramatists' section Personal Mangrs Assoc 2004–09, Public Lending Right Advsy Bd 2008–15; *Style*— Ms Meg Davis; ☎ 020 3214 8287, e-mail meg@ki-agency.co.uk, website www.ki-agency.co.uk

DAVIS, Prof Mark Herbert Ainsworth; s of Christopher Ainsworth Davis (d 1951), and Frances Emily Davis, JP, *née* Marsden (d 2007); *b* 1 May 1945, Colne, Lancs; *Educ* Oundle, Clare Coll Cambridge (MA, ScD), Univ of Calif Berkeley (MS, PhD); *m* 15 Oct 1988, Jessica Isabella Caroline, da of Robert Sinclair Smith, of Broadstairs, Kent; *Career* research asst Electronics Research Laboratory Univ of Calif Berkeley 1969–71; Imperial Coll London: lectr 1971–79, reader 1979–84, prof of system theory 1984–95; dir and head of research and product devpt Tokyo-Mitsubishi International plc 1995–99; Imperial Coll London: prof of mathematics 2000–09, research fell 2010–; sometime visiting prof: Harvard Univ, MIT, Univ of Oslo, TU Vienna; FSS 1985, FIMS 1994, Hon FIA 2001; *Books* Linear Estimation and Stochastic Control (1977), Stochastic Modelling and Control (jtly, 1985), Markov Models and Optimization (1993), Louis Bachelier's Theory of Speculation (jtly, 2006), Risk-Sensitive Investment Management (jtly, 2014); *Recreations* classical music (violin and viola); *Style*— Prof Mark Davis; ✉ Department of Mathematics, Imperial College, London SW7 2AZ (☎ 020 7594 8486, e-mail mark.davis@imperial.ac.uk)

DAVIS, Rt Hon Lord Justice; Sir Nigel Anthony Lamert Davis; kt (2001), PC (2011); s of (Walter) Patrick Carless Davis (d 1996), of Roehampton, and Jane, *née* Lamert (d 1987); bro of James Patrick Lamert Davis, and Ian Edward Lamert Davis, *qqv*; *b* 10 March 1951; *Educ* Charterhouse, UC Oxford (MA); *m* 1, (m dis 1992), Sheila Ann Gillies Nickel; 3 da (Louisa Mary, Katherine Elizabeth (twins) b 6 Dec 1980, Marianna Jane b 10 July 1984); m 2, 2001, Emma Douglas; *Career* called to the Bar Lincoln's Inn (Hardwicke scholar, Kennedy scholar) 1975 (bencher 2000), jr Treasy counsel 1985–92, QC 1992, recorder of the Crown Court 1995–2001, judge of the High Court of Justice (Queen's Bench Div) 2001–11, presiding judge on Wales Circuit 2006–10, a Lord Justice of Appeal 2011–; *Clubs* MCC, Vincent's (Oxford); *Style*— The Rt Hon Lord Justice Davis; ✉ Royal Courts of Justice, Strand, London WC2A 2LL

DAVIS, Nigel Ruscoe; s of John Haydn Davis (d 2008), of Lichfield, Staffs, and Marion, *née* Ruscoe (d 2012); *b* 30 November 1949, Solihull, Warks; *Educ* Tudor Grange GS Solihull, Fitzwilliam Coll Cambridge (MA); *m* 24 Feb 1973, Susan Mary, *née* Porter; 3 s (Edwin Thomas Ruscoe b 18 Aug 1975, Ancel Philip Ruscoe b 28 March 1978 d 1979, Benjamin William Ruscoe b 21 Feb 1981), 2 da (Sophie Agnetha Klara b 7 Feb 1982, Stephanie Ruth Emily b 2 Sept 1985); *Career* slr specialising in agric law; articled clerk then asst slr Wedlake Bell 1972–76, ptnr Holland Rigby & Williams 1977–85 (asst slr 1976–77); ptnr and head Agric Law Unit: Flint Bishop & Barnett 1985–94, Shakespeares 1994–96, Roythorne & Co 1996–2000; princ Nigel Davis slrs 2000–12, princ The Rural Law Practice (formerly Felldale Law) 2012–16, conslt Thomas Hayton Winkley (formerly The Rural Law Practice) 2016–; past chm Agric Law Assoc; various agric and livestock breed socs; memb: Law Soc, CLA, NFU; fndr memb AgriLaw Gp of Legal Practices; contrib to Legal Network TV on agric matters, legal advsr to livestock and agric show socs, conslt ed on agric law Amicus Curiae (Soc for Advanced Legal Studies jl); livestock panel judge (sheep); govr Derbyshire Agric & Hort Soc; accredited mediator 1997, fell Soc of Advanced Legal Studies 1998; *Publications* Agricultural Precedents Handbook (co-author, 2001, 2 edn 2009), CLA handbook on farm business tenancy agreements (co-author, 2006), Agric Law Assoc compilation of European Regulations on the Sheepmeat and Goatmeat regime and Beef and Suckler Cow regimes (ed); various articles in jls and farming press; *Recreations* agric history, farming (sheep and beef), exhibiting and judging sheep, emergence and devpt of Central and Eastern Europe and the Baltic states, watching most sports especially rugby and cricket; *Style*— Nigel Davis, Esq; ✉ Carr Hall Farmhouse, Turnditch, Belper, Derbyshire DE56 2LW (☎ 01335 370227, e-mail nrdavis@btinternet.com)

DAVIS, Peter Anthony; *b* 10 October 1941; *Educ* Winchester, Lincoln Coll Oxford (MA); *m*; 2 s (b 1975 and 1977); *Career* gen audit ptnr Price Waterhouse 1974–80 (joined 1963), exec dep chm Harris Queensway 1980–87; Sturge Holdings plc: gp fin dir 1988–93, dep chm 1991–93; DG National Lottery (OFLOT) 1993–98; non-exec dir: Symphony Group plc 1984–87, Horne Brothers plc 1984–89, Avis Europe plc 1987–89, Abbey National Building Society then Abbey National plc 1982–94 (dep chm 1988–94), Provident Financial plc 1994–2000, Equitable Life Assurance Society 1995–2001, Boosey & Hawkes plc 1998–2003 (chm 2002–03), Ascent Gp (chm 2001–); memb Cncl ICAEW 1989–95 (chm Bd for Chartered Accountants in Business 1990–93); Liveryman Worshipful Co of Chartered Accountants; FCA (ACA 1967); *Recreations* fishing, football, theatre; *Clubs* Hurlingham; *Style*— Peter Davis, Esq; ☎ 07771 710200

DAVIS, Richard Charles; s of Joseph Arthur Davis, of Fairford, Glos, and Dorothy Ellen, *née* Head; *b* 15 May 1949; *Educ* Queen's Coll Taunton, Univ of Leeds (LLB); *m* 21 Sept 1974, Margaret Jane, da of William Dixon, OBE; 1 da (Sarah Margaret b 8 Sept 1981), 1 s (James William Richard b 14 March 1984); *Career* admitted slr 1974; ptnr LCF Barber Titleys; memb Law Soc; *Recreations* art, music, travel, sailing; *Clubs* Morgan Sports Car, The Ripon, Assoc Nautique de Port la Forêt; *Style*— Richard C Davis, Esq; ✉ The Gables, Bishop Thornton, Harrogate, North Yorkshire HG3 3JR (☎ 01423 770172); LCF Barber Titleys, 6 North Park Road, Harrogate, North Yorkshire HG1 5PA (☎ 01423 502211, fax 01243 503835, e-mail richard.davis@lcf.co.uk)

DAVIS, Cncllr Robert Jonathan; MBE (2015), DL (Gtr London); s of Gerald Davis (d 2000), and Pamela, *née* Lee (d 1997); *b* 27 September 1957, London; *Educ* Christ's Coll Finchley, Gonville & Caius Coll Cambridge, Wolfson Coll Cambridge, Coll of Law Lancaster Gate; *Partner* Sir Simon Milton (civil partnership 2007, d 2011); *Career* slr; ptnr Freeman Box 1985–2015; Westminster City Cncl: cncllr 1982–, Lord Mayor 1996–97, Lord Mayor of Westminster Locum Tenens 2001–, dep ldr, cabinet memb for the built environment, chair Planning Applications Sub-Ctee, memb Standards Ctee; Conservative Councillor of the Year Asian Voice 2014; chm Lord Mayors' Assoc 1998–, prodr and fndr West End Live, founding tstee Sir Simon Milton Fndn, chm Westminster World Heritage Site, int goodwill ambass London Parade; chm Bd of Dirs Open Air Theatre Regent's Park; tstee: Savoy Educational Tst, Heritage of London Tst (vice-pres), Mousetrap projects 2011–; pres City of Westminster Guild Lectrs Assoc; Liveryman Fan Maker's Co, Freeman Waterman's Co; *Books* Civic Ceremonial – Advice on Protocol for the Mayoralty in London (2009); *Style*— Councillor Robert Davis, MBE, DL; ✉ Westminster City Council, 64 Victoria Street, London SW1E 6QP (☎ 020 7641 3255)

DAVIS, Roger O'Byrne; s of Paul Patterson Davis (d 1984), of Burnham Market, Norfolk, and Mabel Beryl Davis (d 2009); *b* 1 August 1943; *Educ* Wrekin Coll; *m* 11 March 2006, Dr Jutta Maria Huesmann, da of Dr Josef Huesmann, of Meppen, Germany; *Career* CA; articled clerk Chantrey Button & Co 1960–66; Cooper Brothers & Co (now PricewaterhouseCoopers): joined 1966, ptnr 1975–2003, seconded to HM Treasy 1975–77, head of audit Coopers & Lybrand 1992–98, head of professional affrs 1999–2003; dep chm Turnbull Ctee on Corporate Governance 1999; memb Company Law Consultative Ctee DTI 2000–01, European Services Forum 2001–03, memb Professional Oversight Bd for Accountancy and Actuaries 2004–09, panel memb Competition and Markets Authy (formerly Competition Cmmn) 2005–; memb RSA; FCA; *Recreations* English countryside, boating, music, adventure travel; *Clubs* Carlton; *Style*— Roger Davis, Esq; ✉ Crafers Barn, North Street, Langham, Holt, Norfolk NR25 7DG (☎ 01328 830677, e-mail rogerobdavis@aol.com)

DAVIS, Sandra Sharon; da of Josef Martin Davis, and Milly Edith Davis; *b* 3 July 1956; *Educ* South Hampstead HS, Univ of Sussex (BA), Univ of Aix-en-Provence, Coll of Law; *m* 6 Sept 1987, Avron Woolf Smith, of South Africa; 2 s (Zakari Louis Smith b 5 Sept 1989, Elliott Nathan Smith b 8 Dec 1991); *Career* Mishcon de Reya (formerly Victor Mishcon & Co): articled clerk 1979–81, ptnr 1984–, head of Family Dept; memb: Slrs' Family Law Assoc, Lord Chllr's Child Abduction Panel, Int Bar Assoc; fell Int Acad of Matrimonial Lawyers; *Books* International Child Abduction (1993); *Recreations* photography, travel, theatre, art, family; *Style*— Ms Sandra Davis; ✉ Mishcon de Reya, Summit House, 12 Red Lion Square, London WC1R 4QD (☎ 020 7440 7000, e-mail sandra.davis@mischon.co.uk)

DAVIS, His Hon Judge (Richard) Simon; s of Peter Richard Davis, of Amersham, Bucks, and Evelyn, *née* Richmond; *b* 29 July 1956, Frome, Somerset; *Educ* Wellington Sch, Univ of Leicester (LLB); *m* 26 July 1980, Caroline Jane, *née* Neal; 2 s (Toby William Neal b 15 Feb 1987, Guy Hugo Hobson b 1 April 1989), 1 da (Imogen Caroline b 24 Dec 1990); *Career* called to the Bar Inner Temple 1978 (bencher 2007), recorder 2000–04 (asst recorder 1998–2000), circuit judge (South Eastern Circuit) 2004–; *Recreations* tennis, swimming, skiing, cycling; *Clubs* Roehampton, Rye Golf; *Style*— His Hon Judge Simon Davis; ✉ Isleworth Crown Court, 36 Ridgeway Road, Middlesex TW7 5LP

DAVIS, Simon Ward; s of Anthony Davis, of Glos, and Susan, *née* Hames; *b* 26 June 1959, Mauritius; *Educ* Wellington, Magdalen Coll Oxford (Kitchener scholar, Underhill exhibitioner); *m* 13 Dec 1997, Jane, *née* Ray; 1 s (Gabriel b 23 Feb 1999), 1 da (Lara b 13 April 2001); *Career* slr; ptnr Clifford Chance (formerly Clifford Turner) 1994– (joined 1982); former pres London Slrs Litigation Assoc, memb Law Soc 1982 (memb Cncl), memb City of London Law Soc Ctee; *Recreations* family and friends; *Style*— Simon Davis, Esq

DAVIS, Prof Stanley Stewart; s of William Stanley Davis, of Warwick, and Joan, *née* Lawson; *b* 17 December 1942; *Educ* Warwick Sch, Univ of London (BPharm, PhD, DSc); *m* 24 Nov 1984, Lisbeth, da of Erik Illum (d 1986), of Denmark; 3 s (Benjamin b 1970, Nathaniel b 1974, Daniel b 1984); *Career* lectr Univ of London 1967–70, sr lectr Aston Univ 1970–75, Lord Trent prof of pharmacy Univ of Nottingham 1975–2003; fndr chm: Pharmaceutical Profiles Ltd, Danbiosyst (UK) Ltd; FRSC, FRPharmS; *Books* Imaging in Drug Research (1982), Microspheres in Drug Therapy (1984), Site Specific Drug Delivery (1986), Delivery Systems for Peptides (1987), Polymers for Controlled Drug Delivery (1987), Pharmaceutical Applications of Cell and Tissue Culture in Drug Transport (1991); *Recreations* skiing, tennis, painting; *Style*— Prof Stanley Davis; ✉ 19 Cavendish Crescent North, The Park, Nottingham NG7 1BA (e-mail bobdavis@illumdavis.com)

DAVIS-WHITE, Malcolm; QC (2003); s of Bret Davis-White, and Valerie, *née* Bates; *b* 18 September 1960, Ongar, Essex; *Educ* St Edmund's Coll Ware, Hertford Coll Oxford (MA, BCL); *m* Sarah Louise, *née* O'Hara; 1 da (Harriet b 27 May 1994), 2 s (Alexander b 14 Sept 1995, Edmund b 7 May 1998); *Career* called to the Bar; jr counsel to the Crown (Chancery) 1994–2003, recorder 2009, dep judge of the High Court of Justice 2013–; chm Chancery Bar Assoc 2010–12; *Publications* Atkins Court Forms (Companies Insolvency 2006, Companies General 2010), Directors Disqualification and Insolvency Restrictions (jtly, 3 edn 2010), Kerr & Hunter on Receivers and Administrators (jtly, 19 edn 2010); conslt Annotated Companies Acts (2010); *Clubs* Norfolk; *Style*— Malcolm Davis-White, Esq, QC; ✉ website www.xxiv.co.uk

DAVISON, Clive Phillip; s of Maj Laurence Napier Davison (d 1966), and Rosa Rachel Louisa, *née* Parker (d 1994); *b* 14 March 1944; *Educ* Grange Sch Christchurch, South Bank Poly, Thames Poly; *m* 1, 1968 (m dis 1982), Sandra, da of Thomas Keith Lord, of Billericay, Essex; m 2, 1993, Jane Elise, da of Roger Howorth, of West Moors, Dorset; 1 s (Alexander Napier b 2 Oct 1988), 1 da (Hannah Louise b 26 Jan 1990); *Career* chartered architect; assoc Trehearne & Norman Preston & Partners 1974–77, ptnr Trehearnes 1977–79, design and site supervisor of Min of P T T Riyadh 1977–83, co sec and dir I M Coleridge Ltd 1987, princ Davison Associates, md Davison Partnering Ltd, md Davison Mondon Associates Ltd; designer of various hosp and healthcare projects for NHS trusts; RIBA; *Recreations* squash, guitar, reading, skiing; *Style*— Clive Davison, Esq; ✉ 157 Bure Lane, Christchurch, Dorset BH23 4HB (☎ 01425 280 749); Davison Mondon Associates, 87 Southbourne Road, Bournemouth, Dorset BH6 3QL (☎ and fax 01202 434453, e-mail clive.davison@btconnect.com)

DAVOUD, Nicole Matilde; OBE (1994, MBE 1982); *b* 6 October 1939; *Educ* Lyceo Nacional No 1 Buenos Aires, Univ of Buenos Aires; *m* 31 March 1960, Raymond Davoud (decd); 1 s (Alexander Joseph b 5 April 1966); *Career* fndr and dir Nicole Davoud Associates (qualitative research conslts) 1963–74, ind researcher and advsr disability policy issues 1974–; fndr Crack MS (young arm of Multiple Sclerosis Soc) 1974–76; memb: MRS 1970–95, Cncl Multiple Sclerosis Soc 1976–80, Ctee Int Year of Disabled 1979–82, N London Ctee for Employment of People with Disabilities 1991–97, Presidential Working Party Disability Appeal Tbnl 1991–92, Disability Living Allowance Advsy Bd 1995–2000, Disability Benefits Forum 1998–, Innovative Schemes Tender Bd 1998–99; *Publications* Turning Objectives into Realities – the Challenge of 1981 (1979), Multiple Sclerosis and Its Effect on Employment (1980), Part Time Employment – Time For Recognition, Organisation and Legal Reform (1980), Where Do I Go From Here? (autobiography, 1985), Disability Employment Credit – The Way Ahead (1990), Employing People With Disabilities – Employers' Perspective (1992), Welfare to Work: Disability Perspective (1996), Disability Living Allowance – An Alternative Approach (1998), Disability in the Millennium (1999); *Recreations* meditation, friends and the arts; *Style*— Mrs Nicole Davoud, OBE

DAWE, Howard C; *b* 7 April 1944; *Career* Bellway plc: joined 1961, dir 1977–, gp chief exec 1985–99, acting chm 1997–99, chm 1999–2004, non-exec chm 2004–; *Style*— Howard Dawe, Esq; ✉ Bellway plc, Seaton Burn House, Dudley Lane, Seaton Burn, Newcastle upon Tyne NE13 6BE

DAWES, Howard Anthony Leigh; s of George Roland Dawes (d 1965), and (Phyllis) Kathleen, *née* Reeves; *b* 4 August 1936; *Educ* Uppingham; *m* 1 (m dis); 1 s, 3 da; m 2, Aug 1991, Judith Ann, *née* Bolton; *Career* chm and chief exec: Neville Industrial Securities 1965–88, Dawes Trust Ltd 1965–; dir Velcourt Group plc 1968–99, chm Wine & Dine plc 1997–2000; chm Nuffield Hosp 1984–89; past chm Ctee of Friends of Birmingham Museums and Galleries, hon treas Birmingham Cons Assoc 1968–76, memb Midland Industrial Cncl 1977–97, pres Scientific Instrument Soc 2001– (chm 1994–97, vice-pres 1997–2001); chm Pershore Abbey Appeal 1991–2007, memb Visitors Ctee Museum of the History of Science Oxford 2004–14; Freeman City of London, Liveryman Worshipful Co of Glaziers; FCA, FRAS 1960, FRSA 1975; *Books* Ideas in Brass (2002), Making Things from New Ideas (2005), Instruments of the Imagination (2009); *Recreations* history of science, trees; *Clubs* 20 Portman Square; *Style*— Howard Dawes, Esq; ✉ Craycombe House, Fladbury, Worcestershire WR10 2QS (☎ 01386 860692, e-mail daweshal@aol.com)

DAWES, Dr Peter Terence; s of John Geoffrey Dawes, of Stone, Staffs, and Lorna Graham, *née* Wholey; *b* 1 May 1953; *Educ* Herbert Strutt GS Belper (Rugby capt), Univ of Liverpool (MB ChB, Rugby capt); *m* 1, 1974 (m dis 1992), Barbara, da of Frank Charnley; 2 da (Georgina Martell b 21 Feb 1981, Hannah Elisabeth b 27 July 1982), 2 s (John Mansfield b 13 Jan 1984, Samuel Edward b 25 May 1987); m 2, 1998, Carol Anne Stanton, da of late Norman Loweth; 2 step da (Claire Louise Stanton b 4 Sept 1980, Gemma Victoria Stanton b 27 Nov 1982); *Career* house offr Whiston Hosp Merseyside 1976–77, SHO then registrar (med) St Helens Hosp and Whiston Hosp Merseyside 1977–80, registrar (rheumatology) Middlesbrough Gen Hosp 1981–82, conslt rheumatologist Staffs Rheumatology Centre Haywood Hosp Stoke-on-Trent 1987– (sr registrar (rheumatology) 1982–87), clinical sr lectr in postgrad med Keele Univ 1987–, head of div Locomotor Directorate N Staffs Hosp Tst 1987–; memb: MSSC Audit Advsy Gp 1989–90, N Staffs Audit Res Gp 1989–91, N Staffs MRCP Course Working Pty 1989–, Awards Ctee N Staffs Med Inst 1990–92, Drugs and Therapeutics Ctee 1994–97, N Staffs Rehabilitation Strategy Gp 1997–99, Discretionary Points Ctee 1997–, N Staffs Estates Strategy Gp 1997–, N Staffs Musculoskeletal Bd 1997–, Devpt of Integrated Care Packages Serv Devpt Bd 1998–, Waiting List Task Force 1999–, Benchmarking Gp 1999–; BSR: memb Educn Ctee 1988–90, Advsy Gp for Read coding in Rheumatology 1990–96, rep on BSR/Br Orthopaedic Assoc/Arthritis and Rheumatism Cncl (ARC)/Primary Care Rheumatology Soc/RCGP/Br League Against Rheumatism Working Pty devising a Musculoskeletal Undergrad Curriculum, sec 2002–; conslt advsr Primary Care Rheumatology Soc 1990–92, chm Fastrak Users Gp 1995–98, clinical assessor Jt Conslts Ctee Ind Review, exec memb Midlands Rheumatology Soc 1996–99; memb: BSR/Res Unit RCP Jt Working Gp 1990–, Int League of Assocs for Rheumatology/Outcome Measures in Rheumatoid Arthritis Clinical Trials Gp developing outcome measures in Rheumatoid Arthritis 1993–, People to People Prog 1993–, Cochrane Musculoskeletal Advsy Gp 1994–97, ARC Educn Working Gp 1995–, Br Rheumatology Outcome Study Gp (BROSG), Rheumatology Regnl Specialists Gp; chair, convenor and rapporteur at numerous confs and symposia; memb: Assoc of Liverpool Med Sch, Nat Ankylosing Spondylitis Soc, N Staffs Med Inst, NW Rheumatology Club, Nat Osteoporosis Soc (local chm 1995–97), W Midlands Physicians; assoc ed Rheumatology in Practice 1988–90, memb Editorial Bd Br Jl of Rheumatology (now Rheumatology) 1989– (guest ed 1988), editorial advsr Medicom Excel Newsletter, book assessor OUP; external reviewer for jls incl: The Lancet, Jl of Rheumatology, Annals of Rheumatic Diseases, Arthritis and Rheumatism, Drugs & Therapeutics Bulletin, Prescribers Jl; grant reviewer: ARC, Med Inst, Haywood Fndn; memb: American Coll of Rheumatology, Br Health Professionals in Rheumatology, BMA, Br Soc of Immunology, BSR, Br Soc of Inflammation; supporter Haywood Rheumatism R&D Fndn; Sr Registrar Prize in Rheumatology Annual Sr Registrar Meeting 1983 and 1985 (runner-up 1984), Syntex Award Midland Rheumatology Soc 1984, BSR UK Travelling Fellowship 1986; FRCP 1994 (MRCP 1980); *Publications* author of over 350 pubns in books and med jls; *Recreations* hill walking, fishing, music, campanology; *Style*— Dr Peter Dawes; ✉ Staffordshire Rheumatology Centre, The Haywood, High Lane, Burslem, Stoke-on-Trent ST6 7AG (☎ 01782 556302, fax 01782 813419, e-mail pt.dawes@whns.nhs.uk)

DAWES, Richard; s of Ronald Dawes, and Margaret Dawes; *b* 13 July 1975, Isleworth, London; *Educ* BA; *m* Tanya; *Career* press asst A&M Records 1996–98; Polydor Records: jr PR 1998–99, PR 1999–2003, sr PR 2003–07, head of press 2007–09; co-fndr (with Stuart Bell) Dawbell Ltd 2009– (clients incl: Sir Paul McCartney, Jamie Cullum *qqv*, James Corden, Razorlight, Black Sabbath, Bombay Bicycle Club, Two Door Cinema Club, The Wanted, Sex Pistols, Nordoff Robbins, Soundgarden, Laura Wright, Oberhofer, Take That, Leona Lewis, The BRIT Awards, Queens Of The Stone Age, The Kills, Ronan Keating, Kelly Rowland, Eels, Children in Need); Ind PR Co of the Year Record of the Day Award 2010, PR Campaign of the Year Music Week Award 2011 (for Take That's Progress album), Re-issue Campaign of the Year Record of the Day Award 2011 (for Nirvana's Nevermind album), listed in Evening Standard's Most Influential Londoners 2010 and 2011; *Recreations* golf, wine, cooking, FIFA 2012, documentaries, books by Seth Godin and Malcolm Gladwell, eating out; *Clubs* Ivy; *Style*— Richard Dawes, Esq; ✉ Twitter @splashaddict; DawBell Ltd, 1st Floor, 1–11 Carteret Street, London SW1H 9DJ (☎ 020 3327 7151, e-mail richard.dawes@dawbell.com, website www.dawbell.com, Twitter @dawbell)

DAWID, Prof (Alexander) Philip; s of Israel Dawid, and Rita, *née* Abel; *b* 1 February 1946, Blackburn, Lancs; *Educ* City of London Sch, Trinity Hall and Darwin Coll Cambridge (MA, Dip Math Statistics, ScD); *m* 18 March 1974, (Fatemeh) Elahe, da of Mohamed Ali Madjd; 1 s (Jonathan b 10 May 1975), 1 da (Julie b 29 July 1979); *Career* prof of statistics City Univ 1978–81, prof UCL 1982–2007 (lectr 1969–78, reader 1981–82), prof Univ of Cambridge 2007–13 (emeritus prof 2013–); medicines cmmr 1988–91; ed Biometrika 1992–96; pres Int Soc for Bayesian Analysis 2000; memb ISI 1978, FIMS 1979, Chartered Statistician 1993; fell Darwin Coll Cambridge 2007–13 (emeritus fell 2013–); *Publications* Probabilistic Networks and Expert Systems (1999), Simplicity, Complexity and Modelling (ed, 2011), Evidence, Inference and Enquiry (ed, 2011), Causality: Statistical Perspectives and Applications (ed, 2012), Beauty (ed, 2013); *Recreations* music; *Style*— Prof Philip Dawid; ✉ Department of Pure Mathematics and Mathematical Statistics, Wilberforce Road, Cambridge CB3 0WL

DAWKINS, Prof Marian Ellina Stamp; CBE (2014); *née* Stamp; da of Hon A Maxwell Stamp (d 1984), and Alice Mary, *née* Richards (d 2000); *b* 13 February 1945, Hereford; *Educ* Queen's Coll Sch London (E E Florence scholar), Somerville Coll Oxford (BA, Nuffield exhibitioner), Univ of Oxford (DPhil); *m* 1967 (m dis 1984); *Career* res offr Animal Behaviour Res Gp Dept of Zoology Univ of Oxford 1969–74, jr res fell Wolfson Coll Oxford 1974–78, departmental demonstrator in animal behaviour Dept of Zoology Univ of Oxford 1974–80; Somerville Coll Oxford: lectr in zoology 1977–80, fell and tutor in biological sciences 1980–, vice-princ 2005–; Univ of Oxford: res lectr 1991–96, reader 1996–97, prof of animal behaviour 1998–, head Animal Behaviour Res Gp Dept of Zoology; dir John Krebs Field Lab; memb: Standing Advsy Ctee on Standards for Psychological Res and Teaching Involving Animals Br Psychological Soc 1981–84, Farm Animal Welfare Cncl 1983–89, Farm Livestock Advsy Cncl RSPCA 1980–89, Animal Experiments Ctee Royal Soc 1982–97; sec Ethical Ctee Assoc for the Study of Animal Behaviour 1986–90, chm of tstees Farm Animal Care Tst 2009–; ed: Animal Behaviour 1994–96, Animal Welfare 1996–; sec gen Int Ethological Congress 1995–99; RSPCA/Br Soc for Animal Protection prize 1991, Assoc for the Study of Animal Behaviour Niko Tinbergen Medal 2009, World Poultry Science Assoc Robert Fraser Gordon Medal 2011, Sir Patrick Moore Award RSPCA 2014; memb: Int Soc for Applied Ethology, Assoc for the Study of Animal Behaviour; Hon DSc Univ of Guelph Canada 2000; FRS 2014; *Publications* Animal Suffering: The Science of Animal Welfare (1980), Unravelling Animal Behaviour (1986, 2 edn 1995), The Tinbergen Legacy (ed with T R Halliday and R Dawkins, 1991), Through Our Eyes Only? The Search for Animal Consciousness (1993), Observing Animal Behaviour: Design and Analysis of Quantitative Data (2007), The Future of Animal Farming: Renewing an Ancient Contract (2008), An Introduction to Animal Behaviour (with A Manning, 6 edn 2012), Why Animals Matter: Animal Walfare, Animal Consciousness and Human Well-being (2012); *Recreations* windsurfing, photography, music, natural history; *Style*— Prof Marian Dawkins, CBE, FRS; ✉ Dept of Zoology, University of Oxford, South Parks Road, Oxford OX1 3PS (☎ 01865 271215, fax 01865 310447, e-mail marian.dawkins@zoo.ox.ac.uk)

DAWKINS, Mark; *Career* admitted slr 1985; Simmons & Simmons: joined as articled clerk 1983, ptnr 1990–, managing ptnr Litigation Dept 1997–2000, head Financial Markets Dept 2000–05, managing ptnr 2005–; *Style*— Mark Dawkins, Esq; ✉ Simmons & Simmons, CityPoint, One Ropemaker Street, London EC2Y 9SS

DAWKINS, Prof (Clinton) Richard; s of Clinton John Dawkins, and Jean Mary Vyvyan, *née* Ladner; *b* 26 March 1941, Nairobi, Kenya; *Educ* Oundle, Balliol Coll Oxford (MA, DPhil, DSc); *m* 1; m 2; 1 da (Juliet Emma); m 3, 1992, Hon Sarah Ward (the actress Lalla Ward), only da of 7 Viscount Bangor (d 1993); *Career* asst prof of zoology Univ of Calif Berkeley 1967–69; Univ of Oxford: univ lectr in zoology and fell New Coll 1970–90, univ reader in zoology 1990–95, Charles Simonyi prof in public understanding of sci 1995–2008; estab charity Richard Dawkins Fndn for Reason and Science; RSL Award 1987, Los Angeles Times Literary Prize 1987, Silver Medal Zoological Soc of London 1989, Michael Faraday Award Royal Soc of London 1990, Royal Instn Christmas Lectures 1991, Nakayama Prize 1994, Int Cosmos Prize 1997, Kistler Prize 2001, Shakespeare Prize 2005, Lewis Thomas Prize 2007, Karl Deschner Prize 2007, Deschner Prize Johann-Wolfgang-Goethe Univ Frankfurt 2007; Time Life 100 Most Influential People list NY 2007; Hon DLitt: Univ of St Andrews 1995, ANU 1996; Hon DSc: Westminster Coll 1997, Univ of Hull 2001, Univ of Sussex 2005, Univ of Durham 2005, Free Univ of Brussels 2005, Univ of Huddersfield 2008; Hon DUniv Open Univ 2003; hon fell Regent's Coll London 1988; FRSL 1997, FRS 2001; *Books* The Selfish Gene (1976, 2 edn 1989), The Extended Phenotype (1982), The Blind Watchmaker (1986), River Out of Eden (1995), Climbing Mount Improbable (1996), Unweaving the Rainbow (1998), A Devil's Chaplain (2003), The Ancestor's Tale (2004), The God Delusion (2006, Book of the Year Galaxy Book Awards 2007), The Oxford Book of Modern Science Writing (ed, 2008), The Greatest Show on Earth (2009), The Magic of Reality (2011), An Appetite for Wonder (autobiography, 2013); *Style*— Prof Richard Dawkins, FRS; ✉ New College, Oxford OX1 3BN (☎ 01865 514103, website www.richarddawkins.net); The Richard Dawkins Foundation for Reason and Science (www.richarddawkinsfoundation.org)

DAWNAY, Caroline Margaret; da of Capt Oliver Payan Dawnay, CVO (d 1988), of Longparish and Wexcombe, and Lady Margaret Boyle, da of 8 Earl of Glasgow; *b* 22 January 1950; *Children* 1 s (Hugo Ronald Alexander MacPherson b 28 Jan 1980); *Career* dir A D Peters & Co Ltd Writers' Agents 1981–94 (joined 1977, merger to form Peters Fraser & Dunlop 1988), dir June Hall Agency 1989–93, dir Peters Fraser & Dunlop 1993–2007, dir United Agents plc 2008–12, ptnr United Agents LLD 2012–; pres Assoc of Authors' Agents 1994–97 (treas 1991–94); Agent of the Year 2014; *Books* An Alphabet of Aunts (jtly, 2007); *Style*— Ms Caroline Dawnay; ✉ 14 Sterndale Road, London W14 0HS

DAWNAY, (Charles) James Payan; DL (Lanarkshire 2012); s of Capt Oliver Payan Dawnay, CVO (d 1988), and Lady Margaret Stirling-Aird, *née* Boyle; *b* 7 November 1946; *Educ* Eton, Trinity Hall Cambridge (MA); *m* 10 June 1978, Sarah, da of late Edgar David Stogdon, MBE, of Balavoulin, Pitlochry; 3 da (Alice b 1979, Olivia b 1981, Fenella b 1988), 1 s (David b 1985); *Career* dir S G Warburg 1984–85, dir Mercury Asset Management Group plc 1985–91, chm Mercury Fund Managers Ltd 1987–91, dir Martin Currie Ltd 1992–2000, dep chm Martin Currie Ltd 1999–2000; chm: China Heartland Fund Ltd 1997–2004, Northern AIM VCT plc 2000–, Investec High Income Tst plc 2001–09, Gurr Johns Ltd 2001–06, Penicuik House Preservation Tst 2003–, CCLA Investment Mgmnt Ltd 2004–, Resources Investment Tst plc 2005–08, Biggar Museum Tst 2005–; dir: Taiwan Opportunities Tst plc 2001–, AON Alexander & Alexander UK Pension Tstees Ltd 2007–11; tstee Nat Galleries of Scotland 2004–11; *Recreations* fishing, collecting; *Clubs* Brooks's, Garrick, Pratt's, New (Edinburgh), Biggar; *Style*— James

Dawnay, Esq, DL; ✉ Symington House, by Biggar, Lanarkshire ML12 6LW (✆ 01899 308211, fax 01899 308727, e-mail jdawnay@yahoo.co.uk)

DAWSON, (Ian) Grant; s of Stanley Dawson, and Marian, *née* Haswell; *b* 17 March 1959; *Educ* Holmemead Secdy Modern Sch, Bedford Coll of FE, Univ of Leicester (BA), Inns of Court Sch of Law; *Children* 2 da (Faye b 12 April 1991, Eve b 21 Jan 1997), 1 s (Elliot b 30 Oct 1994); *Career* general counsel and co sec Centrica plc 1996–; previously with: Racal Gp 1984–86, STC plc 1986–91, Northern Telecom Europe Ltd 1991–96; called to the Bar Lincoln's Inn; *Recreations* golf, scuba diving, sailing, opera; *Style*— Grant Dawson, Esq; ✉ Centrica plc, Millstream, Maidenhead Road, Windsor, Berkshire SL4 5GD (✆ 01753 494000, fax 01753 494001)

DAWSON, John A L; *b* 1950; *Educ* Mill Hill Sch, Univ of Southampton; *m* Frances; 2 da; *Career* dir of tport London Regnl Office Dept of Tport 1985–88, chief road engr Scottish Devpt Dept 1988, dir of roads Industry Dept Scottish Office 1989–95; AA: gp public affrs dir 1995–2002, policy and int dir 2003–04; chm EuroRAP AISBL 2002–16, chm Int Road Assessment Prog (iRAP) 2005–; dir Nat Assoc of Air Ambulance Services 1999–2002, currently vice-chm FIA Fndn for the Automobile and Soc 2001–; FIHT 1987, FICE 1996 (MICE 1976); *Recreations* touring; *Style*— John Dawson, Esq; ✉ EuroRAP AISBL, Worting House, Basingstoke, Hampshire RG23 8PX (✆ 01256 345598)

DAWSON, Prof John; *b* 19 August 1944, Hyde, Greater Manchester; *Educ* UCL (BSc, MPhil), Univ of Nottingham (PhD); *Career* various posts Univ of Wales, chair in distributive studies Univ of Stirling until 1990, prof of mktg and head Mktg Gp Univ of Edinburgh 1990–2005 (head Dept of Business Studies 1993–98), prof of retail studies Univ of Stirling 2005–; distinguished prof Univ of Mktg Kobe 2002–; founding ed: Cambria, Int Jl of Retailing 1984, Int Review of Retail, Distribution and Consumer Research (currently co-ed); author of several books on the retail industry in Europe and Asia; Hon DBA Abertay Univ; FRSE 2004; *Style*— Prof John Dawson

DAWSON, Lynne; da of Francis Lewis Dawson, of Newton-on-Ouse, N Yorks, and Rita, *née* Slater; *Educ* Easingwold Sch, Guildhall Sch of Music and Drama London, Britten-Pears Sch Snape; *Career* soprano; initially worked as French translator; currently head Sch of Vocal Studies and Opera RNCM Manchester; has performed with orchs incl: Berlin Philharmonic, Vienna Philharmonic, Boston Symphony, San Francisco Symphony, all major Br orchs; concert venues incl: Lincoln Center NY, La Scala Milan, Colon Buenos Aires, Aix-en-Provence Festival, Salzburg Festival, Edinburgh Festival, Royal Albert Hall, Wigmore Hall, South Bank; *Operatic performances* incl: Constanze in Mozart's Die Entführung aus dem Serail (La Monnaie Brussels) 1990, Teresa in Berlioz' Benvenuto Cellini (Amsterdam Opera) 1991, Countess in the Marriage of Figaro (Strasbourg Festival) 1991, Fiordiligi Cosi Fan Tutte (Naples) 1992, Amenaide in Rossini's Tancredi (Berlin State Opera) 1994, Cleopatra in Handel's Julius Caesar (Berlin Staatsopera) 1996, Pamina in The Magic Flute (Berlin Staatsoper) 1997, Dido in Dido Aeneas (De Vlaamse Opera) 1998; *Recordings* over 80 recordings incl: Bach's B Minor Mass, Beethoven Choral Symphony, Gluck's Iphigenie en Aulide, Handel's Messiah, Haydn's Creation, Mozart's C Minor Mass, Requiem, Don Giovanni and Die Entführung aus dem Serail, Orff's Carmina Burana; sang Verdi Requiem Libera Me At Funeral of Diana, Princess of Wales 1997; *Style*— Miss Lynne Dawson; ✉ School of Vocal Studies, Royal Northern College of Music, 124 Oxford Road, Manchester M13 9RD

DAWSON, Mark Patrick; s of Douglas George Damer Dawson; *b* 19 October 1941; *Educ* Wellington; *m* 1, 1970 (m dis 1983), Carol Anne, da of late John Dudley Groves; 2 s; m 2, 1987 (Constance) Clare Power, *née* Mumford; *Career* Lt Essex Yeo; chm and md Pickford Dawson & Holland Ltd 1970–78; md: Jardine Matheson Insurance Brokers UK Ltd 1978–79, Jardine Matheson Underwriting Agencies Ltd 1979; dep chm: Jardine Lloyd's Underwriting Agencies Ltd (formerly Jardine Glanvill Underwriting Agencies Ltd) 1991–95 (md until 1990), Jardine Lloyd's Advisers Ltd 1994–95 (conslt 1995–97); qualified Cert in Teaching English as a Foreign Language to Adults (CTEFLA) 1996; fndr The Friends of Holy Innocents Church Lamarsh 2001 (treas and tstee 2001–), memb Ctee Colne-Stour Countryside Assoc 2006– (ed Colne Stour Countryside Assoc Magazine 2008–); *Style*— Mark Dawson, Esq; ✉ Black Swan House, 4 Benton Street, Hadleigh, Suffolk IP7 5AT (✆ 01473 824550, e-mail mark@markpadawson.co.uk)

DAWSON, Matthew James Sutherland (Matt); MBE (2004); s of Ronald Sutherland Dawson, and Lois, *née* Thompson; *b* 31 October 1972; *Educ* Royal GS High Wycombe; *Career* former rugby union player; clubs: Northampton Saints RFC 1991–2003 (over 240 appearances, winners European Cup 2000), London Wasps RFC 2003–06 (winners Zurich Premiership 2005); England: 77 caps (9 as capt), winners 6 Nations Championship 2000, 2001 and 2003 (winners Grand Slam 2003), winners World Cup Aust 2003; memb squad Br & I Lions tour South Africa 1997, Aust 2001 and NZ 2005 (5 test caps); RFU Player of the Year 2000; ret from rugby 2006; resident capt A Question of Sport (BBC TV); supporter NSPCC, supporter and patron Beating Bowel Cancer; *Recreations* golf, football, cricket, theatre, exhibitions; *Style*— Matt Dawson, Esq, MBE; ✉ c/o M&C Saatchi Merlin, 36 Golden Square, London W1F 9EE (✆ 020 8834 8900, e-mail brea.welch@merlinelite.co.uk)

DAWSON, Prof Peter; s of Frederick Dawson, of Sheffield, S Yorks, and May, *née* Pierrepoint; *b* 17 May 1945; *Educ* Firth Park Sch Sheffield, KCL (BSc, PhD), Westminster Med Sch (MB BS); *m* 20 July 1968, Hilary Avril, da of Kenneth Reginald Sturley, of Amersham, Bucks; 1 da (Kate b 1976), 1 s (James b 1978); *Career* SHO in: gen and renal med Hammersmith Hosp 1979–80, med oncology Royal Marsden Hosp 1980; registrar in radiology Guy's Hosp 1980–82, sr registrar in radiology Middx Hosp 1982–85, prof of diagnostic radiology Royal Postgrad Med Sch and Hammersmith Hosp 1996– (reader and hon conslt 1985–96); conslt UCL Hosps London 1999–2009, chm and clinical dir UCL Hosps 2002–09; prof of radiology Univ of London 1999–2009; author of various scientific med res papers; pres British Inst of Radiology, Roentgen prof RCR; Barclay Medal Br Inst of Radiology 2000; FRCR 1984 (registrar 2006–08), FRCP 1997 (MRCP 1980), FInstP 2007 (MInstP 1966), memb RSM; *Books* A Textbook of Contrast Media, Contrast Media in Practice, Protocols for Multi-slice Helical Computed Tomography, Functional Computed Tomography; *Recreations* grand opera, wine, snooker; *Style*— Prof Peter Dawson; ✉ Beechers, Green Lane, Chesham Bois, Amersham, Buckinghamshire HP6 5LQ (✆ 01494 728222, e-mail peterxdawson@gmail.com)

DAWSON, Prof Dame Sandra June Noble; DBE (2004); da of Wilfred Denyer (d 1996), and Joy Victoria Jeanne, *née* Noble (d 2009); *b* 4 June 1946; *Educ* Dr Challoner's Sch Amersham, Keele Univ (BA); *m* 23 Aug 1969, Henry Richards Currey Dawson, s of Horace Dawson (d 1952), of Sotik, Kenya; 2 da (Hannah Louise Joy b 1976, Rebecca Annie Brenda b 1978), 1 s (Tom Stephen John b 1983); *Career* Imperial Coll London: res offr 1969–70, lectr then sr lectr 1971–90, prof of organisational behaviour 1990–95; KPMG prof of mgmnt studies 1995–2013 (prof emeritus 2013–), dir Judge Business Sch Univ of Cambridge 1995–2006, fell Jesus Coll Cambridge 1995–99, master Sidney Sussex Coll Cambridge 1999–2009 (fell 2009–), dep vice-chllr Univ of Cambridge 2008–12; chm Riverside Mental Health Tst 1992–95; non-exec dir: Public Health Lab Serv 1996–99 (memb Strategic Review Gp 1994–96), Fleming Claverhouse Investment Tst 1996–2003, Cambridge Econometrics 1996–2007, Barclays plc 2003–09, FSA 2010–13, DRS plc 2012–, Winton Capital Gp 2013–, TSB 2014–; chair: Exec Steering Ctee ESRC Advanced Inst of Mgmnt 2007–11; Cambridge India Partnership 2008–12; memb: Res Strategy Bd Offshore Safety Div HSE 1990–95, N Thames NHS Regnl R&D Ctee 1994–95, HEFCE Business and Mgmnt Research Assessment Panel 1995–97 and 2000–01, Sr Salaries Review Bd 1997–2003, DTI Futures and Innovation Bd 1998–2001, ESRC Research Priorities Bd 2000–03, DTI Taskforce Accounting for People 2003, UK India Roundtable 2006–, UK Indian Business Cncl 2007–12, PM's Cncl for Science and Technol 2011–13; tstee RAND Europe (UK) 2001–04, non-exec dir and tstee: Oxfam GB 2006–12, Social Science Research Cncl (USA) 2009–, Inst of Govt 2012–, American Univ of Sharjah 2014–; *Books* Analysing Organisations (1986, 3 edn 1996), Safety at Work: The Limits of Self Regulation (1988), Managing in the NHS: a Study of Senior Executives (1995), Future Health Organisations and Systems (ed, 2005), Policy Futures for UK Health (jt ed, 2006), Engaging with Care: A vision for the health and care workforces of England (jtly, 2007), Future Public Health (jt ed, 2009); *Recreations* music, walking; *Style*— Prof Dame Sandra Dawson, DBE; ✉ Judge Business School, University of Cambridge, Trumpington Street, Cambridge CB2 1AG (✆ 01223 765277)

DAWSON, William Strachan; s of John Oliver Hanbury Dawson, of South Cadbury, Somerset, and Elizabeth Sutherland, *née* Strachan; *b* 10 September 1955; *Educ* Winchester, Selwyn Coll Cambridge (MA); *m* 1, 8 Sept 1984 (m dis), Alison Jill, da of John Eric Aldridge, of Halland, E Sussex; 1 da (Lucinda b 1986), 2 s (Henry b 1988, Archie William b 1994); *Career* admitted slr 1980, ptnr Simmons & Simmons 1986–2007 (head of int employment law 2001–07), ptnr Farrer & Co 2007– (head Professional Practices Gp 2010–13, memb Mgmnt Bd 2013–16); *Books* Tolley's Company Acquisitions Handbook (contrib, 1989, 10 edn 2011); *Recreations* piano, cooking, classical music, cycling; *Clubs* WACA Australia, Surrey and England UK; *Style*— William Dawson, Esq; ✉ Farrer & Co, 66 Lincoln's Inn Fields, London WC2A 3LH

D

DAY, Anneliese Mary; QC (2012); da of Alan Frederick Day, and Katherine Julie, *née* Spencer; *b* 6 March 1973, Edinburgh; *Educ* Clare Coll Cambridge; *Children* 1 da (Cecilia Ruth Lindsay b 20 Nov 2009), 1 s (Alexander Frederick Lindsay b 21 April 2012); *Career* called to the Bar 1996; memb Legal Services Bd 2013–16; Construction Silk of the Year Chambers Bar Awards 2014, The Lawyer Hot 100 2014, Barrister of the Year The Lawyer Awards 2014; *Publications* Jackson & Powell on Professional Liability (ed, 2002–); *Recreations* running, hot yoga; *Style*— Ms Anneliese Day, QC; ✉ 4 New Square, Lincoln's Inn, London WC2A 3RJ

DAY, Elinor Jane; da of Barry Day, and Jean, *née* Walker; *b* 9 November 1962, London; *Educ* St Stephen's Coll Broadstairs, Malvern Boys Coll, Emmanuel Coll Cambridge (MA); *Career* ind theatre dir (Sadlers Wells, fringe, tours) 1985–88, BBC: script ed 1988–90, drama prodr 1990–98; dep head prodn FilmFour 1998–2002, launched The Light Club (ind prodn co) 2002; memb BAFTA; *Film* produced BBC: Loved Up (BAFTA Best Schools Drama 1995), Killing Me Softly, In Your Dreams, The Perfect Blue, Face; exec prodr FilmFour: Some Voices, Jump Tomorrow (Sundance Film Festival 2000), Late Night Shopping, Lucky Break, Miranda, Gangster No 1, Crush, The Warrior (winner Sutherland Trophy London Film Festival 2001), East is East, Charlotte Gray; *Recreations* theatre, cinema, travel; *Style*— Ms Elinor Day; ✉ 57 Elms Cresent, London SW4 8QE (✆ 020 7622 5933, e-mail elinor@thelightclub.fsnet.co.uk)

DAY, Prof John; s of Horace John Ernest Day (d 1996), and Violet Augusta, *née* Liggitt (d 1993); *b* 13 September 1948, London; *Educ* Bexley GS, Christ's Coll Cambridge (scholar, MA, PhD, Sr Hebrew Prize), Univ of Oxford (DD); *m* 20 June 1981, Jane Mary, *née* Osborn; 1 adopted da (Lisa Marie b 11 Dec 1982), 1 adopted s (Sebastian John b 26 June 1984); *Career* John Goodenday fell Hebrew Univ of Jerusalem 1972–73, res fell in arts Univ of Durham 1977–80, fell and tutor in theology Lady Margaret Hall Oxford 1980–2013 (emeritus fell 2013–); Univ of Oxford: lectr in Old Testament 1980–96, reader in biblical studies 1996–2004, prof of Old Testament studies 2004–13 (emeritus prof 2013–); sr res fell Br Acad/Leverhulme Tst 1995–96, visiting prof Univ of Malta 2011; memb: Soc for Old Testament Study (pres 2014), Soc of Biblical Lit (USA); Dahood Meml Prize Soc of Biblical Lit 1984; *Publications* Oxford Bible Atlas (ed, 3 edn 1984), God's Conflict with the Dragon and the Sea: Echoes of a Canaanite Myth in the Old Testament (1985), Molech: A God of Human Sacrifice in the Old Testament (1989), Psalms (1990), Wisdom in Ancient Israel: Essays in Honour of J A Emerton (ed with R P Gordon and H G M Williamson, 1995), William Robertson Smith's Lectures on the Religion of the Semites (ed 2 and 3 series, 1995), King and Messiah in Israel and the Ancient Near East: Proceedings of the Oxford Old Testament Seminar (ed, 1998), Yahweh and the Gods and Goddesses of Canaan (2000), In Search of Pre-Exilic Israel: Proceedings of the Oxford Old Testament Seminar (ed, 2004), Temple and Worship in Biblical Israel: Proceedings of the Oxford Old Testament Seminar (ed, 2005), Society for Old Testament Study Book List (ed, annually 2007–009), Prophecy and the Prophets in Ancient Israel: Proceedings of the Oxford Old Testament Seminar (ed, 2010), The Recovery of the Ancient Hebrew Language: The Lexicographical Writings of D Winton Thomas (2013), From Creation to Babel: Studies in Genesis 1–11 (2013); author of 70 articles and 200 reviews; *Recreations* travel in the Near East, attending congresses, collecting books; *Style*— Prof John Day; ✉ Lady Margaret Hall, Oxford OX2 6QA (e-mail john.day@theology.ox.ac.uk)

DAY, Air Chief Marshal Sir John Romney; KCB (1999), OBE (1985); s of John George Day (d 1987), and Daphne Myrtle, *née* Kelly (d 1979); *b* 15 July 1947; *Educ* King's Sch Canterbury, Imperial Coll London (BSc(Eng)); *m* April 1969, Jane Richards; 2 s (Mark John b 19 Sept 1970, Jonathan Philip b 18 Aug 1974); *Career* flying trg RAF 1968–70, pilot Wessex helicopters 72 Sqdn 1970–73, flying instr Jet Provosts RAF Linton-on-Ouse 1973–76, OC Oxford Univ Air Sqdn 1976–79, Flt Cdr 18 Sqdn 1979–80, RAF Staff Coll Bracknell 1981, PSO to Air Member for Personnel 1982–83, OC 72 Sqdn 1983–85, Gp Capt Support Helicopters HQ No 1 Gp 1986–87, OC RAF Odiham 1987–89, RCDS 1990, Dir Air Force Plans and Progs MOD 1991–94, AOC No 1 Gp 1994–97, DCDS (Commitments) MOD 1997–2000, Air Memb for Personnel and C-in-C Personnel and Trg Command 2000–01, C-in-C Strike Command 2001–03, sr military advsr BAE Systems 2003–; FCGI 2002 (ACGI 1968), FRAeS 2003; *Clubs* RAF; *Style*— Air Chief Marshal Sir John Day, KCB, OBE; ✉ Lloyds Bank, 81 High Street, Ashford, Kent TN24 8SS

DAY, Sir Jonathan Stephen (Jon); kt (2016), CBE; *b* 23 April 1954; *Educ* Univ of Nottingham; *m* Sandra; 1 da (Catherine); *Career* MOD: policy and operations posts 1979–88, seconded as first sec Europe UK Delgn to NATO FCO 1988–92, seconded to NATO 1992–95, dep command sec land 1995–97, dir of defence policy 1997–99, seconded as chief Jt Intelligence Ctee Assessments Staff Cabinet Office 2000–01, seconded as dir Sec Gen's Private Office Cabinet Office 2001–03, command sec fleet 2004–07, head Streamlining Project 2007, DG operational policy 2007–08, DG security policy (formerly policy dir) 2008–11, second perm under sec 2011–12; chair Jt Intelligence Ctee Cabinet Office 2012–15; *Style*— Sir Jon Day, CBE

DAY, Martin James; s of Clifford Day (d 1961), and Molly, *née* Dale (d 2002); *b* 12 April 1944; *Educ* City of London Sch, Univ of Durham (BA), Christ's Coll Cambridge (LLM), London Guildhall Univ (MSc), Heythrop Coll London (Postgrad Cert); *m* 1 (m dis 1976), Elizabeth Mary, da of Thomas H Sykes (d 1999); m 2 (m dis 1995), Loraine Frances, da of Frank Leslie Hodkinson (d 1984); 1 s (James b 1978), 1 da (Philippa b 1983), m 3, Reiko Ishibashi, da of Yoichi Inaba (d 1975); *Career* articled clerk Austin Wright & Co 1966–68, admitted slr 1969, ptnr Linklaters & Paines 1976–94 (asst slr 1969–76); memb Disciplinary and Appeal Tbnls IMRO 1994–99, gp legal and compliance advsr Guinness Flight Hambro Asset Management Ltd 1995–98, conslt Arnheim & Co Slrs 1997–98, dir PricewaterhouseCoopers 1997–98, ind legal conslt 1999–2003, slr Herbert Smith 2003–05, conslt Farrer & Co 2005–12, slr Dechert LLP 2010–12; memb Law Soc Standing Ctee on EU Law 2012–16; visiting lectr in law Daito Bunka Univ Tokyo Japan 2013–15; chm: Hampton Music Festival 1969–71, Tstees of the Hampton Arts Tst 1969–72, Thameside Arts Tst 1973–74, Westminster Children's Charitable Fndn 1976–90, Kibogora Hosp Tst

1989–91; memb: Ct of Common Cncl (Ward of Aldersgate) 1977–79 and 1986–87 and (Bishsgate Ward) 1997–2012, Governing Body SOAS Univ of London 1978–79; dir Slrs' Benevolent Assoc 1988–96, chm Br Korean Law Assoc 2004–09 (vice-pres 2012–16); govr: Christ's Hosp 2006–13, Lady Eleanor Holles Sch 2006–07, City of London Sch for Girls 2013; memb: Tst Law Ctee, Ctee City of London Law Soc 2005–07, Bd of Dirs Japan Soc 2009–15, Editorial Bd Beijing Univ Law Review 2010–12; tstee Soc for the Relief of Homeless Poor 2011–12; Liveryman City of London Slrs' Co 1976; FRGS 1965; *Books* Unit Trusts: The Law and Practice (with P I Harris, 1974), Tolley's Trust Law International (memb Editorial Bd 1989–99), A Practical Guide to Conflicts of Interest in the Financial Services Industry (with R Frase and R Helm, 2012); *Recreations* music, reading; *Style*— Martin J Day, Esq; ✉ c/o Messrs C Hoare & Co, 37 Fleet Street, London EC4P 4DQ

DAY, Martyn; s of Brian Day (d 1983), and Hazel Mules Berry, *née* Abraham; *b* Ossett, Yorks; *m* Carol, *née* Hatton; 2 s (Harry b 19 Oct 1990, Jack b 28 March 1992), 3 da (Martha b 10 Oct 1993, Sally b 29 April 1996, Evie b 20 Dec 2004); *Career* admitted slr 1981; Colombotti & Ptnrs until 1981, Clifford & Co 1981, Bindman & Ptnrs 1981–87, sr ptnr Leigh Day & Co 1987–; memb Exec Ctee Soc of Labour Lawyers; dir Greenpeace Environmental Tst; memb Assoc of Professional Injury Lawyers; *Books* Toxic Torts, Personal Injury Handbook, Multi-Party Actions, Environmental Action: A Citizen's Guide; *Style*— Martyn Day, Esq; ✉ Leigh Day & Co, Priory House, 25 St John's Lane, London EC1M 4LB (☎ 020 7650 1234, fax 020 7253 4433, e-mail mday@leighday.co.uk)

DAY, Martyn; MP; s of Ronald Day, and Margaret, *née* Grant, of Linlithgow; *b* 26 March 1971, Falkirk; *Educ* Linlithgow Acad; *Career* Bank of Scotland 1989–98; cnclr West Lothian 1999–2015; MP (SNP) Linlithgow and E Falkirk 2015–; memb SNP 1988–; memb Chartered Inst of Bankers; *Recreations* cinema, music, reading; *Style*— Martyn Day, Esq, MP; ✉ 6 Preston Crescent, Linlithgow EH49 6HW (☎ 01506 846056, Twitter @MartynDaySNP); 62 Hopetoun Street, Bathgate EH48 4PD (☎ 01506 654415, e-mail martyn.day.mp@parliament.uk, website www.martynday.scot)

DAY, Michael Patrick; CVO (2015); s of Harry Day (d 2010), and Anne Day (d 2002); *b* 20 February 1953, Nottingham; *Educ* Nottingham HS, Univ of Leeds (BA); *m* Anne Murch; 1 s (Daniel b 30 Sept 1985), 1 da (Felicity b 29 Nov 1988); *Career* grad trainee and asst keeper Norfolk Museums Serv 1974–83, curator of social history Ironbridge Gorge Museum 1983–87, dir Jersey Heritage Tst 1987–2003, chief exec Historic Royal Palaces 2003–; chair Battersea Arts Centre 2012–; tstee Alnwick Garden Tst 2010–13, vice-pres Assoc of Ind Museums 2015–; Hon DArts Kingston Univ 2010; fell Museums Assoc 1994, FRSA 1995, CIMgt 2007; *Recreations* real tennis, skiing, sailing, cycling; *Clubs* Royal Tennis Court, Ski Club of GB; *Style*— Michael Day, Esq, CVO; ✉ Historic Royal Palaces, Apartment 39A, Hampton Court Palace, Surrey KT8 9AU (e-mail michael.day@hrp.org.uk)

DAY, Prof Peter; s of Edgar Day, and Ethel Hilda, *née* Russell; *b* 20 August 1938, Wrotham, Kent; *Educ* Maidstone GS, Wadham Coll Oxford (Gibbs prize in chemistry, MA, DPhil); *m* 1964, Frances Mary Elizabeth, *née* Anderson; 1 da (Alison b 1968), 1 s (Christopher b 1971); *Career* jr res fell St John's Coll Oxford 1963–65, departmental demonstrator Inorganic Chemistry Laboratory Oxford 1965–68, fell and tutor in inorganic chemistry St John's Coll Oxford (jr dean 1967–70, vice-pres 1974), lectr in inorganic chemistry Univ of Oxford 1965–88, dir Institut Laue-Langevin Grenoble 1989–91, (Br assoc dir 1988–89), dir and resident prof of chemistry Royal Instn of GB 1991–94, Fullerian prof Royal Instn of GB 1994–2008 (emeritus prof 2008–); ad hominem prof of solid state chemistry Univ of Oxford 1988–91, visiting prof UCL 1991–2008, emeritus prof of chemistry Univ of London 2008–; professeur associé Faculté des Sciences Université de Paris-Sud Orsay 1975, guest prof H C Ørsted Inst Univ of Copenhagen 1978, visiting fell Res Sch of Chemistry ANU Canberra 1980, visiting prof Univ of Valencia 2002–06; visiting appts at res laboratories: Cyanamid Euro Res Inst Geneva 1962, Bell Laboratories Murray Hill NJ 1966, IBM Res Laboratories San José CA 1974, Xerox Corp Webster Res Center Rochester NY 1978; counsellor Inst of Molecular Science Okazaki Japan 1994–98, memb Advsy Cncl RIKEN Advsy Science Inst Tokyo 2005–10; memb Cncl: Parly and Scientific Ctee 1991–98, COPUS 1991–98; memb Medicines Cmmn 1999–2005; chm Royal Soc Res Grant Bd for Chemistry 1992–95 (memb 1983–85 and 1991–95); Br Cncl: memb Science Advsy Ctee 1991–98, chm Anglo-French Advsy Ctee 1992–97; Royal Soc of Chemistry: memb Dalton Div Cncl 1983–88, memb Books and Review Ctee 1984–85, vice-pres 1986–88, memb Pubn and Information Bd 1997–2003; memb numerous ctees SERC 1976–92; memb: Nat Ctee on Superconductivity 1987–89, Univ of Oxford Superconductivity Gp 1988–91 (chm Steering Ctee 1987), ISIS Science Advsy Cncl 1988–91 (chm Experimental Selection Panel (Structures) 1988); memb Physics and Engrg Sci Ctee Europe Euro Sci Fndn 1994–2000; memb Editorial Advsy Bds: Nouveau Journal de Chimie, Synthetic Metals, Review of Solid State Sciences, Dictionary of Inorganic Compounds, Journal of Materials Chemistry (scientific advsy ed 1999–2003), Chemistry of Materials; rep govr Sevenoaks Sch 1977–88, govr Birkbeck Coll London 1994–2001; hon fell: Wadham Coll Oxford 1991, Indian Acad Sci 1994, St John's Coll Oxford 1996, UCL 2003; Hon DSc: Univ of Newcastle 1994, Univ of Kent 1999; memb Academia Europaea 1992– (treas Cncl 2000–10, tstee 2002–10); FRS 1986; *Publications* The Philosopher's Tree (1999), Nature Not Mocked (2005), Molecules in Materials (2007), On the Cucumber Tree (2012); ed seven chemistry books; many articles in sci jls; *Recreations* gazing at the European landscape; *Style*— Prof Peter Day, FRS; ✉ Department of Chemistry, University College London, 20 Gordon Street, London WC1H 0AJ (☎ 020 7679 7499, e-mail pday@ri.ac.uk)

DAY, Rosemary; da of Albert Rich (d 1985), and Alice, *née* Wren (d 2000); *b* 20 September 1942; *Educ* Christ's Hosp, Bedford Coll London (BA), Birkbeck Coll London (MA); *m* (m dis); *Career* asst dir gen GLC 1979–82 (joined 1964), dir of admin London Tport 1983–87, chief exec Data Networks plc 1986–88, ops dir Allied Dunbar Assurance plc 1988–94; non-exec dir: Nationwide Anglia Building Society 1983–88, London Buses Ltd 1988–93, London Transport 1993–98, Milk Marketing Bd 1993–94, Legal Aid Advsy Ctee 1993–94, Senior Salaries Review Body 1994–2000, UKAEA 1999–2006, NI Dept of Regnl Devpt 2007–08; dir Picker Inst Europe 2002–05; chm: London Ambulance Serv Trust 1996–99, Govt Offices Mgmnt Bd 1996–98, National Air Traffic Servs 1997–2001; chm Joyful Co of Singers 1987–2001 (Gran Premio Citta D'Arezzo 1994), tstee Railway Children 1999–2015, tstee Chiswick House and Gardens 2005–; ATII 1980, FRSA 1983, CIMgt 1988; *Recreations* the arts, gardening, study; *Style*— Mrs Rosemary Day; ✉ 63A Barrowgate Road, London W4 4QT (☎ and fax 020 8995 4390, e-mail rosemaryday@btinternet.com)

DAY, William Michael; s of Sir Derek Day, KCMG (d 2015), and Sheila, *née* Nott; *b* 26 June 1956; *Educ* Tonbridge, Univ of Exeter (BA); *m* 1986, Kate Susanna, da of Bill Gardener; 1 s (Rupert b 7 Sept 1987), 2 da (Eleanor b 21 April 1989, Susanna b 6 Dec 1991); *Career* Save the Children Fund: Uganda 1983, Ethiopia 1983–84, Sudan 1984; BBC World Serv for Africa 1985–87, Oxfam Ethiopia 1987–88, grants dir for Africa Charity Projects/Comic Relief 1988–94, dir Opportunity Tst 1994–96, chief exec CARE International UK 1996–2004; sr assoc Cambridge Prog for Sustainability Leadership 2003–12 (fell 2013–), special advsr UN Devpt Prog 2004–11, sustainability advsr PricewaterhouseCooper UK 2008–; non-exec dir South Kent Hosps NHS Tst 1994–96; chm: Central Appeals Ctee BBC 1997–2003 (memb 1992–2003), Water and Sanitation for the Urban Poor (WSUP) 2006–, Sustainable Devpt Cmmn 2009–11; memb: Grants Cncl Charities Aid Fndn 1990–94, Globalisation and Global Poverty Cmmn 2006, Ramphal Centre Cmmn on Migration and Devpt 2010–11, Cncl of Ambassadors WWF (UK) 2010–, Corp Responsibility Advy Gp ICAEW 2012–14, Corp Responsibility Panel Br Land 2012–14, Advsy Cncl SEEChange Network 2014–; tstee: Disasters Emergency Ctee 1998–2004, BBC Children in Need 1998–2008 (chm 2006–08); memb Cncl ODI 2000–12 (chm 2012), co-chair Kent Nature Partnership 2014–; ind assessor Public Appointments DCMS 1999–2008; fell Cambridge Institute for Sustainability Leadership (formerly CPSL) 2014–; *Style*— William Day, Esq

DAY-LEWIS, Sir Daniel; kt (2014); s of Cecil Day-Lewis, CBE (Poet Laureate, d 1972), by his 2 w, Jill Balcon, actress, da of late Sir Michael Balcon, film prodr; *Educ* Bristol Old Vic Theatre Sch; *Family* 1 s (Gabriel b 1995); m, 1996, Rebecca Miller, da of Arthur Miller, of USA; *Career* actor; *Theatre* Bristol Old Vic Co: The Recruiting Officer, Troilus and Cressida, Funny Peculiar, Old King Cole, A Midsummer Night's Dream (transferred to Old Vic), Class Enemy, Edward II, Oh! What A Lovely War; Little Theatre Co: Look Back in Anger, Dracula; other roles incl: Guy Bennet in Another Country (Queen's) 1982, Romeo in Romeo and Juliet (RSC tour) 1983–84, Mayakovsky in The Futurists (NT) 1986, title role in Hamlet (NT) 1989; *Television* Shoestring, Artemis II, The Lost Traveller, The Sugar House, Beyond the Glass, How Many Miles to Babylon, Thank You PG Woodhouse, Dangerous Corner, My Brother Jonathan, Insurance Man; *Films* Gandhi 1981, The Saga of HMS Bounty 1983, My Beautiful Launderette 1985, A Room With A View 1985, Nanou 1985, The Unbearable Lightness of Being 1986, Stars and Bars 1987, My Left Foot 1988, Ever Smile New Jersey 1988, Last of the Mohicans 1991, Age of Innocence 1992, In the Name of the Father 1993, The Crucible 1995, The Boxer 1998, The Gangs of New York 2001, The Ballad of Jack and Rose 2005, There Will Be Blood 2007, Nine 2009, Lincoln 2012; *Awards* Best Supporting Actor NY Critics' Awards for My Beautiful Launderette and A Room With A View 1986; Best Actor Awards for My Left Foot incl: Evening Standard Film Awards 1989, Rehab Entertainment Awards 1989, Boston Soc of Film Critics 1989, Oscar 1990, BAFTA 1990, NY Critics' 1990, LA Critics'1990, Nat Soc of Film Critics' 1990, London Critics' Film Circle 1990, Montreal Critics' 1990, Dublin Independent 1990; Variety Club Best Film Actor Award for Last of the Mohicans 1992; for There Will Be Blood: Best Actor LA Film Critics Assoc 2007, Best Performance by an Actor in a Motion Picture (Drama) Golden Globe 2008, Best Actor Screen Actors Guild 2008, Best Leading Actor BAFTA 2008, Best Actor Oscar 2008; for Lincoln: Best Performance by an Actor in a Motion Picture (Drama) Golden Globe 2013, Best Actor Screen Actors Guild 2013, Best Actor BAFTA 2013, Best Actor Acad Award 2013; *Style*— Sir Daniel Day-Lewis; ✉ c/o Julian Belfrage Associates, 46 Albemarle Street, London W1X 4PP (☎ 020 7491 4400, fax 020 7493 5460)

DAYKIN, Christopher David; CB (1993); s of John Francis (d 1983), and Mona, *née* Carey (d 2012); *b* 18 July 1948; *Educ* Merchant Taylors', Pembroke Coll Cambridge (MA); *m* 1977, Kathryn Ruth, da of Harold William Tingey; 1 da (Rachel b 1981), 2 s (Jonathan b 1982, Jeremy b 1984); *Career* Govt Actuary's Dept: 1970, 1972–78 and 1980–2007, princ actuary 1982–84, directing actuary 1985–89, govt actuary 1989–2007; princ (Health and Social Servs) HM Treasy 1978–80, dir Civil Service Insurance Soc (CSIS) 1991–; dir NOW Pension Trustees Ltd 2012–; VSO Brunei 1971; FIA 1973 (pres 1994–96); *Publications* Practical Risk Theory for Actuaries (1993); *Recreations* travel, photography, language; *Style*— Christopher Daykin, Esq, CB

de BERNIÈRES, Louis Henry Piers; s of Maj Reginald Piers Alexander de Bernière-Smart; *b* 8 December 1954, London; *Educ* Bradfield Coll, Victoria Univ of Manchester (BA), Leicester Poly (PGCE), Inst of Educn Univ of London (MA); *Career* novelist, poet and musician; former jobs incl teacher, landscape gardener, car mechanic and bookshop asst; patron: Families House; named Granta Best of Young British Novelists list 1993, Author of the Year British Book Awards 1997; *Publications* as Louis de Bernières: The War of Don Emmanuel's Nether Parts (1990, Best First Book Eurasia Region Cwlth Writers' Prize 1991), Señor Vivo and the Coca Lord (1991, Best Book Eurasia Region Cwlth Writers' Prize 1992), The Troublesome Offspring of Cardinal Guzman (1992), Captain Corelli's Mandolin (1994, shortlisted Book of the Year Sunday Express 1994, Best Book Cwlth Writers' Prize 1995, stage adaptation 1999, film adaptation 2001), Labels (1997), The Book of Job (introduction, 1998), Red Dog (2001), Sunday Morning at the Centre of the World (radio play, 2001, broadcast BBC Radio 4 1999), Birds Without Wings (2004, shortlisted Whitbread Novel Award 2004), A Partisan's Daughter (2008, shortlisted Costa Prize), Notwithstanding (2009), Imagining Alexandria (poetry, 2013), The Dust That Falls From Dreams (2015), Of Love and Desire (poetry, 2016), Blue Dog (2016); regular contrib of short stories to newspapers and magazines; *Recreations* golf, music, reading, shooting, travel; *Style*— Louis de Bernières, Esq; ✉ c/o Publicity, Random House, 20 Vauxhall Bridge Road, London SW1V 2SA (☎ 020 7840 8617, fax 020 7932 0761)

de BLOCQ van KUFFELER, John Philip; s of Capt F de Blocq van Kuffeler (d 2005), of Royal Netherlands Navy, and Stella, *née* Hall; *b* 9 January 1949; *Educ* Atlantic Coll, Clare Coll Cambridge (MA); *m* 3 April 1971, Lesley, da of Dr E M Callander; 2 s (Hugo b 1974, Alexander b 1979), 1 da (Venetia b 1977); *Career* Peat Marwick Mitchell & Co 1970–77, head of corp fin Grindlay Brandts Ltd 1980–82 (mangr 1977–80); Brown Shipley & Co Ltd: dir 1983–91, head of corp fin 1983–88, memb Exec Ctee 1985–91, head of investment banking UK and USA 1986–88; gp chief exec Brown Shipley Holdings plc 1988–91; chm: Finsbury Smaller Companies Tst plc 1992–2003, Provident Financial plc 1997– (chief exec 1991–97), JP Morgan Fleming Technol Tst plc 1998–2003, Huveaux plc 2001–08, Eidos plc 2002–05, Hyperion Insurance Gp Ltd 2009–, Marlin Financial Gp Ltd 2010–; dir: Medical Defence Union Ltd 2001–04, TV Eye Ltd 2003–05; memb Ctee Issuing Houses Assoc 1984–88; FCA 1979 (ACA 1973); *Recreations* fishing, shooting; *Clubs* City; *Style*— John de Blocq van Kuffeler, Esq; ✉ Hyperion Insurance Group Limited, 16 Eastcheap, London EC3M 1BD (☎ 020 7398 4888)

de BOER-KRUYT, Dien; da of Henk Kruyt (d 1991), and Fiet Ferman (d 1998); *b* 18 August 1944, Netherlands; *Educ* Groningen Univ, Harvard Univ (MA); *m* 15 June 1985, Hans de Boer; 6 s (Ivan b 22 April 1973, Andreas b 21 Sept 1975 d 1998, Dimitri b 4 Oct 1976, Hugo b 24 May 1978, Michael b 4 Dec 1987), 2 da (Naomi b 1 Sept 1977, Sarah b 18 Jan 1989), 1 adopted s (Alexander b 29 May 1978); *Career* teacher Harvard Univ 1974, researcher MIT 1974–75, strategy and policy conslt Bosboon and Hegener (KPMG) 1975–80, dir Inst for Strategy and Policy 1980–87, coach (in Asia and Europe) 1985–; advsr to Min of Economic Affrs 2010–; non-exec dir: Sara Lee Int 1994–, HBG Construction 1994–2001, Imtech Installation 1999–, Reed Elsevier 2000–, Allianz NL 2002–; involved with Dutch Peace Corps and Inst for Home Care; *Recreations* coaching, sailing, reading, travelling, Chinese Chi Kung, dancing, singing; *Style*— Mrs Dien de Boer-Kruyt; ✉ Hoofdgracht 65, 1411 LB Naarden, The Netherlands (☎ 00 31 35 69 44455, e-mail dien@diendeboer.com, website www.diendeboer.com); c/o Reed Elsevier Group plc, 1–3 Strand, London WC2N 5JR

de BOINVILLE, Simon Murdoch Chastel; s of Charles Alfred Chastel de Boinville (d 1985), of Farnham, Surrey, and Frances Anne, *née* Morrison (d 1984); *b* 16 March 1955, Kilmacolm, Scotland; *Educ* Radley, RAC Cirencester; *m* 4 Oct 1980, late Shaunagh Elisabeth, da of Dermott Bibby Magill, of Baughurst, Hants; 3 s (Reuben b 1986 d 1988, Nicolai b 1989, Lucian b 1991), 1 da (Cornelia b 1988); *Career* ptnr Cluttons Chartered Surveyors 1989–91 (joined 1979); dir: John D Wood & Co (Residential and Agricultural) Ltd 1991–96, INIGO Business Centres Ltd 1997–2002, Lonsdale Insurance Brokers (Lloyd's brokers); FRICS; *Clubs* Farmers'; *Style*— Simon de Boinville, Esq; ✉ Grantham Farm, Baughurst, Tadley, Hampshire RG26 5JS (☎ 0118 981 1364, e-mail simon@granthamfarm.org)

de BONO, Edward Francis Charles Publius; s of late Prof Joseph Edward de Bono, CBE, of St Julian's Bay, Malta, and Josephine, *née* Burns; *b* 19 May 1933; *Educ* St Edward's

Coll Malta, Royal Univ of Malta (BSc, MD), ChCh Oxford (Rhodes scholar, DPhil), Univ of Cambridge (PhD); *m* 1971 (m dis 2006), Josephine, da of Major Francis Hall-White; 2 s; *Career* Univ of Cambridge: asst dir of res Dept of Investigative Med 1963–76, lectr in med 1976–83; fndr and dir Cognitive Research Trust Cambridge 1971–83, sec gen Supranational Independent Thinking Orgn (SITO) 1983–, fndr Int Creative Forum 1990–, prof of thinking Univ of Pretoria 2002–, fndr The World Centre for New Thinking 2004, Da Vinci prof of thinking Univ of Advancing Technol Arizona 2006; chm Cncl Young Enterprise Europe 1998–; invited to be king: Geraldton WA 2000, Margaret River WA 2000, Launceston Tasmania 2002; the planet formerly known as DE 73 named Edebono by the Naming Ctee of the Int Astronomic Union; TV series: de Bono's Course in Thinking (BBC), The Greatest Thinkers (WDR Germany); lectured extensively worldwide; Carl Sloane Award Int Assoc of Mgmnt Consulting Firms 2006; Hon LLD Univ of Dundee 2005; *Books* incl: The Use of Lateral Thinking (1967), Lateral Thinking: A Textbook of Creativity (1970), Wordpower (1977), de Bono's Thinking Course (1982), Six Thinking Hats (1985), Letters to Thinkers (1987), I am Right, You are Wrong (1990), Handbook for the Positive Revolution (1991), Six Action Shoes (1991), Teach Your Child to Think (1992), Serpetition (1992), Serious Creativity (1992), Textbook of Wisdom (1993), Teach Yourself to Think (1994), Water Logic (1995), Parallel Thinking (1996), How to be More Interesting (1997), Mind Pack (1997), Simplicity (1998), Super Mind Pack (1998), Why I Want to be King of Australia (1999), New Thinking for the New Millennium (1999), Textbook of Wisdom (2000), The de Bono Code (2000), Why So Stupid: How the Human Race has Never Learned to Think (2003), How to Have a Beautiful Mind (2004), Six Value Medals (2005), H+ a new religion? (2006), How to Have Creative Ideas: 62 exercises to develop the mind (2007), Are Americans Really Free? (2007), Six Frames for Looking at Information (2008), Think: before it is too late (2009); *Recreations* travel, toys, thinking; *Clubs* Athenaeum; *Style*— Dr Edward de Bono; ✉ L2 Albany, Piccadilly, London W1V 9RR (website www.edwdebono.com, www.edwarddebono.com, www.debonosociety.com, www.debonopost.com and www.debono.org)

de BORMAN, (Chevalier) Jean-Marc (John); s of Alexandre de Borman (d 1999), and Genevieve de Borman (d 1966); Arnold Ferdinand Jacques de Borman granted the title of Chevalier on 6 May 1857; *b* 1954; *Educ* Stowe, Chelsea Sch of Art (BA); *m* 6 May 1982, Julia, *née* Murray; 2 c (Arthur Alexandre David, Rosie Genevieve Ann (twins) b 19 Feb 1983); *Career* cinematographer; memb: BSC 1996–, BAFTA 1997–; *Film* Small Faces 1995, Trojan Eddie 1995, The Full Monty 1996, Photographing Fairies 1996, The Mighty 1997, Hideous Kinky 1997 (Evening Standard Award for Technical Achievement 1999), Gregory's 2 Girls 1998, Hamlet 1998 (nominee Best Cinematography Independent Spirit Awards 2001), New Year's Day 1999, Saving Grace 1999, There's Only One Jimmy Grimble 1999, Serendipity 2000, The Guru 2001, Pure 2002, Ella Enchanted 2002, Shall We Dance 2003, A Lot Like Love 2004, Tara Road 2005, Fade to Black 2005, Tsunami the Aftermath 2007, Miss Pettigrew Lives for a Day 2007, Last Chance Harvey 2008, An Education 2008 (Best Cinematography Sundance Film Festival 2009, Best Foreign Film Spirit Awards 2010), Made In Dagenham 2009, Quartet 2011, Half of a Yellow Sun 2012, If I Stay (also camera operator) 2014, Coalition (TV movie, also camera operator) 2015, Indian Summers 2015, The Bull (screenwriter) 2016; *Recreations* watching rugby, tennis; *Clubs* Soho House, Chelsea Arts, Electric Cinema; *Style*— John de Borman, Esq; ✉ c/o Linda Mamy, United Agents, 12–26 Lexington Street, London W1F 0LE (☎ 020 3214 0896)

de BOTTON, Hon Dame Janet Frances; DBE (2013, CBE 2006); *née* Wolfson; da of Baron Wolfson (Life Peer, d 2010) and Ruth, *née* Sterling; *b* 31 March 1952, London; *Educ* St Paul's Girls Sch; *m* 1, 1972 (m dis 1989), Michael Philip Green; 2 da (Rebecca Sarah b 27 April 1974, Catherine Victoria b 1 Sept 1976); m 2, 1990, Gilbert de Botton (d 2000); *Career* dir Christie's Int 1994–98, chair Tate Modern 1999–2002; chm Wolfson Fndn 2010–; tstee: Tate Gallery 1992–2002, Tate Fndn 2006–; *Recreations* bridge; *Style*— The Hon Dame Janet de Botton, CBE; ✉ The Wolfson Foundation, 8 Queen Anne Street, London W1G 9LD

de BRAUX, John Andrew; s of Cecil Hubert de Braux (d 2008), of Watford, Herts, and Vera Nellie, *née* Ford (d 2001); *b* 5 July 1950; *Educ* Watford Boys' GS, St Albans Coll (HNC), Univ of Westminster (MBA); *m* 21 Aug 1971, Judith Gwendoline, *née* Stanton; 2 da (Anna Katherine b 1 Jan 1975, Alexandra Claire b 24 Feb 1978); *Career* British Railways: tech offr/IT project asst 1968–82, permanent way engr 1982–88; infrastructure mangr British Rail Network SouthEast 1988–90; chief exec: Hillingdon Community Health NHS Tst 1990–93, W Middx Univ Hosp NHS Tst 1994–2001, Epsom and St Helier NHS Tst 2001–03, Beds and Herts SHA 2003–06; md debraux consulting limited 2006–; dir Frontrunner Recruitment Ltd 2011–; sometime chair W London Orthopaedic Network and Cancer Collaborative, memb Action on Orthopaedics Steering Bd, estab Learning Partnership for Acute Tsts (in partnership with NW London Hosp's Tst); chair of govrs Rickmansworth Sch 2013–; MInstD 1998; *Recreations* choral singing, walking, canal boating, golf; *Clubs* Old Fullerians Assoc; *Style*— John de Braux, Esq; ✉ debraux consulting limited, 71 Kenilworth Drive, Croxley Green, Rickmansworth, Hertfordshire WD3 3NN (☎ 01923 231173, fax 01923 237067, mobile 07831 559269, e-mail john@debraux.com)

de CANDOLE, (Mark) Andrew Vully; s of Eric Armar Vully de Candole, CMG, CBE (d 1989), and Elizabeth Marion, *née* Constable-Roberts (d 1997); *b* 15 April 1953; *Educ* Marlborough; *Career* md City Gate Estates plc 1985–90, md Pathfinder Group 1991–2000, co-fndr Private Equity Investor plc 2000–05; fndr Einstein Fund 2004; non-exec dir Queen Victoria Hospital NHS Trust 1994–96; *Recreations* garden design, skiing, sailing; *Style*— Andrew de Candole, Esq; ✉ Villa 1, Montgomerie Maisonettes, Emirates Hills, PO Box 282, 489 Dubai, UAE

de CHASSIRON, Charles Richard Lucien; CVO (2000); s of Brig H E C de Chassiron (d 1974), and Deane, *née* Richardson (d 1996); *b* 27 April 1948; *Educ* Rugby, Jesus Coll Cambridge (MA), Kennedy Sch of Govt Harvard Univ (MPA); *m* 28 Sept 1974, Britt-Marie Sonja, da of Nils G Medhammar; 1 da (Anna b 1975), 1 s (Hugo b 1976); *Career* HM Dip Serv: joined FCO 1971, Stockholm 1972–75, Maputo 1975–78, memb UK Delgn at Lancaster House Rhodesia Conf 1979, Salisbury 1980, Brasilia 1982–85, head of S American Dept 1988–89, cnsllr (econ and commercial) Rome 1989–94, ambass Estonia 1994–97, DG for trade and investment in Italy and consul-general Milan 1997–2001, protocol dir FCO 2002–06, Vice Marshal of the Diplomatic Corps 2002–06, chm Spencer House 2006–11; chm Br-Italian Soc 2006–15, govr Br Inst of Florence; *Publications* chapter on the Baltic states in The Fall of the Iron Curtain and the Culture of Europe (Prof Peter Barta ed, 2013), numerous magazine articles on Italian topics; *Recreations* walking, history of art; *Clubs* RAC; *Style*— Charles de Chassiron, Esq, CVO; ✉ e-mail cdechassiron@virginmedia.com

de COURCY, Anne Grey; da of Maj John Lionel Mackenzie Barrett (d 1940), of Tendring, Essex, and Evelyn Kathleen Frances, *née* Ellison-Macartney; *Educ* Wroxall Abbey Leamington Spa; *m* 1, 1951, Michael Charles Cameron Claremont Constantine de Courcy (d 1953), elder son of Lt Cdr Hon Michael John Rancé de Courcy, RN (d 1940); m 2, 24 Jan 1959, Robert Armitage, 2 s of Gen Sir (Charles) Clement Armitage, KCB, CMG, DSO, DL, of Downington House, Glos; 1 s (John b Dec 1959), 2 da (Sophy b June 1961, Rose b March 1964); *Career* Evening News: writer, columnist, woman's ed 1972–80; Evening Standard: writer, columnist, section ed 1982–92; Daily Mail 1993–2003; *Books* Kitchens (1973), Starting From Scratch (1975), Making Room at the Top (1976), A Guide to Modern Manners (1985), The English in Love (1986), 1939 – The Last Season (1989, new edn 2003), Circe – The Life of Edith, Marchioness of Londonderry (1992, new edn (as Society's Queen) 2004), The Viceroy's Daughters (2000), Diana Mosley (2003), Debs at War (2005), Snowdon: The Biography (2008), The Fishing Fleet: Husband-Hunting in the Raj (2012), Margot at War: Love and Betrayal in Downing Street 1912–16 (2014); *Recreations* reading, writing, walking, gardening; *Style*— Ms Anne de Courcy; ✉ website www.annedecourcy.com

DE FEO, Joseph; s of Ralph and Jean De Feo; *b* 31 May 1947; *Educ* Adelphi Univ New York (BA, MBA, MS); *m* Anna Julie; 1 s (Christian Joseph), 1 da (Danielle Julie); *Career* asst mangr Computer Ops Interstate Stores Inc 1969–71, systems programmer Chemical Bank New York 1971–72, mangr Systems Software Blyth & Co Inc 1972, sr systems programmer Federal Reserve Bank of New York 1972–74, vice-pres Info Servs Smith Barney, Harris Upham 1974–77, vice-pres Int Bank Servs Chase Manhattan Bank 1982–84 (vice-pres Bank Support Servs 1977–82), vice-pres Systems Devpt and User Support Gp Goldman Sachs & Co 1984–87, dir Gp Systems and Ops Morgan Grenfell & Co Ltd 1988–89, dir Gp Ops and Technol Barclays Bank plc 1989–96, chief exec Open Gp 1996–98 (former non-exec dir), chief exec CLS Gp Hldgs 2000–, pres and ceo CLS Bank International; author of numerous articles in indust and mgmnt pubns and nat newspapers, frequent lectr and speaker; memb Cncl APACS, fndr memb Group of 20, chm CHAPS Clearing Co (formerly Cheque and Credit Clearing Co); non-exec dir Dept of Social Security, sr rep for Barclays Gp in SWIFT, memb Advsy Bd Cross Border Exchange Inc; Freeman Worshipful Co of Information Technologists; *Style*— Joseph De Feo, Esq; ✉ CLS Group Holdings, Exchange Tower, 1 Harbour Exchange Square, London E14 9GE; CLS Bank International, 39 Broadway, New York, NY 1006, USA (e-mail jdefeo@cis-bank.com)

de GREY, Lady; *see:* Irwin, Flavia

de GREY, Spencer Thomas; CBE (1997); s of Sir Roger de Grey, KCVO, PPRA (d 1995), and Flavia Irwin, RA (d 2009); *b* 7 June 1944; *Educ* Eton, Churchill Coll Cambridge (MA, DipArch); *m* 3 Sept 1977, Hon (Amanda) Lucy, da of Baron Annan, OBE (Life Peer, d 2000); 1 da (b 22 Aug 1988), 1 s (b 29 Aug 1992); *Career* architect London Borough of Merton 1969–73; Foster + Partners (formerly Foster Associates): joined 1973, estab Hong Kong office 1979, dir 1981 (responsible for Third London Airport at Stansted and Sackler Galleries Royal Acad), design ptnr 1991–, head of design 2007–; projects as design ptnr incl: Commerzbank HQ Frankfurt, Lycée Albert Camus Fréjus, EDF regional operational centre Bordeaux, Law Faculty Univ of Cambridge, Great Court British Museum, Alexander Fleming Bldg and Business Sch Imperial Coll London, Nat Botanical Gardens for Wales, World Squares for All, Sage music centre Gateshead, Boston Museum of Fine Arts, Opera House Dallas, Dresden Railway Station, HM Treasy Whitehall London, Smithsonian Inst Washington DC, Slussen masterplan Stockholm, W Kowloon Cultural District masterplan, Museum of Roman Antiquities Narbonne, Ombriere Vieux Port Marseille; visiting prof of design Sch of Architecture Univ of Cambridge 2010–; architectural advsr Royal Botanic Gardens Kew 2016–; tstee Building Centre Tst; ARCUK 1969, RIBA 1993, FRSA 2006, RA 2008; *Recreations* music, theatre, travel; *Style*— Spencer de Grey, Esq, CBE, RA; ✉ Foster & Partners, Riverside 3, 22 Hester Road, London SW11 4AN (☎ 020 7738 0455, fax 020 7738 1107)

DE GROOSE, Tracy; da of Colin Darwen, of Cadiz, Spain, and Pauline Darwen; *b* 11 March 1968, Darwen, Lancs; *Educ* West Kirby GS, Brunel Univ (LLB); *m* Andrew De Groose; *Career* various positions rising to mktg controller Stella Artois Interbrew UK 1992–98, business dir Starcom Motive 1998–2002, md Naked Communications 2002–; Mktg Soc Award for work on Stella Artois brand 1997; memb Mktg Soc; *Style*— Mrs Tracey De Groose; ✉ Naked Communications, 159–173 St John Street, London EC1V 4QJ (☎ 020 7663 1774, e-mail tracy@nakedcomms.com)

de GUINGAND, Anthony Paul; s of Paul Emile de Guingand (d 1976), and Olwen Doreen, *née* Witts (d 1999); *b* 7 August 1947; *Educ* Ampleforth; *m* 24 Nov 1973, Diana Mary, da of John Harrington Parr (d 1998); 2 s (Marcus b 1977, Peter b 1982), 1 da (Emily b 1979); *Career* exec dir International Commodities Clearing House Ltd 1973–86; md London Traded Options Market 1986–92, dir fin LIFFE 1992–2002, md Paul E de Guingand Ltd 2002–, dir fin Metronaps (UK) Ltd 2006–; FCA; *Recreations* rugby, golf; *Style*— Anthony de Guingand; ✉ Playfoots, Bramble Reed Lane, Matfield, Kent TN12 7ET

de HAAN, Kevin Charles; QC (2000); s of Michael James de Haan (d 1988), and Barbara Ada, *née* Wood; *b* 30 October 1952; *Educ* Davenant Fndn GS, QMC London (LLB), Univ of Brussels; *m* 1983, Katy Monica, da of Kenneth Martin Foster; *Career* barrister; called to the Bar Inner Temple 1976 (bencher 1997); recorder; *Books* Food Safety Law (contrib, 1995), Pollution in the UK (contrib, 1995), The Law of Betting, Gaming and Lotteries (ed, 2001); *Recreations* skiing, flying light aircraft, aerobatics, cycling, walking, music; *Clubs* Ski Club of GB; *Style*— Kevin de Haan, Esq, QC; ✉ Francis Taylor Building, Temple, London EC4Y 7BY (☎ 020 7353 8415, fax 020 7353 7622, e-mail mgoba@mgoba.demon.co.uk)

de HAAS, Her Hon Judge Margaret Ruth; QC (1998); da of Joseph de Haas, of London, and Lisalotte Herte, *née* Meyer; *b* 21 May 1954; *Educ* Townsend Girls' Sch Bulawayo, Univ of Bristol (LLB); *m* 18 May 1980, Iain Saville Goldrein, s of Neville Clive Goldrein; 1 s (Alastair Philip b 1 Oct 1982), 1 da (Alexandra Ann b 22 Feb 1985); *Career* called to the Bar Middle Temple 1977; practised Northern Circuit, recorder 1999–2004 (asst recorder 1995–99), dep judge of the High Court 2000, circuit judge (Northern Circuit) 2004–; memb: Personal Injury Bar Assoc, Professional Negligence Bar Assoc, Family Law Bar Assoc; FRSA; *Books* Property Distribution on Divorce (2 edn with Iain S Goldrein, 1985), Personal Injury Litigation (with Iain S Goldrein, 1985), Domestic Injunctions (1987 and co-author 1998), Butterworths Personal Injury Litigation Service (with Iain S Goldrein), Family Court Practice (contrib, 1993), Structured Settlements (jt ed-in-chief with Iain S Goldrein, 1993), Medical Negligence: Cost Effective Case Management (with Iain S Goldrein, 1996), Civil Court Practice (co-ed, 2000); *Recreations* family, swimming, theatre; *Style*— Her Hon Judge de Haas, QC

de HAMEL, Dr Christopher Francis Rivers; s of Dr Francis Alexander de Hamel, and Joan Littledale, *née* Pollock; *b* 20 November 1950; *Educ* Univ of Otago (BA), Univ of Oxford (DPhil); *m* 1, 1978 (m dis 1989); 2 s; m 2, 1993, Mette Tang Simpson, *née* Svendsen; *Career* Sotheby's: cataloguer of medieval manuscripts 1975–77, asst dir 1977–82, dir western manuscripts 1982–2000, Donnelley fell librarian CCC Cambridge 2000–16; visiting fell All Souls Coll Oxford 1999–2000, Sandars reader in bibliography Univ of Cambridge 2003–04, J P R Lyell reader in bibliography Univ of Oxford 2008–09; memb Comité international de paléographie latine 2004; Hon LittD St John's Univ Minnesota 1994, Hon DLitt Univ of Otago 2002, PhD Univ of Cambridge 2005; FSA 1981, FRHistS 1986; *Books* incl: Glossed Books of the Bible and the Origins of the Paris Booktrade (1984), A History of Illuminated Manuscripts (1986, 2 edn 1994), Medieval & Renaissance Manuscripts in New Zealand (with M Manion and V Vines, 1989), Syon Abbey, the Library of the Bridgettine Nuns and their Peregrinations after the Reformation (1991), Scribes and Illuminators (1992), The Book: A History of the Bible (2001), The Rothschilds and their Collections of Illuminated Manuscripts (2005), Gilding the Lilly (2010); various reviews, articles and catalogues; Festschrift: The Medieval Book, Glosses from Friends and Colleagues of Christopher de Hamel (ed J H Marrow, R A Linenthal and W Noel, 2010), Meetings with Remarkable Manuscripts (2016); *Clubs* Roxburghe, Grolier (NY), Association Internationale de Bibliophilie (Paris), Athenaeum; *Style*— Dr Christopher de Hamel, FSA; ✉ Corpus Christi College, Trumpington Street, Cambridge CB2 1RH

de JONQUIERES, Guy; s of Maurice de Fauque de Jonquières (d 2001), of London, and late Pauline de Jonquières; *b* 14 May 1945; *Educ* Lancing, Exeter Coll Oxford; *m* 1977, Diana Elizabeth, da of T V N Fortescue; 2 s (Alexander b 1981, Julian b 1983); *Career* graduate trainee Reuters 1966–68; Financial Times: staff corr 1968–80 (Paris, Washington, Saigon, NY, Brussels), electronics industry corr 1980–86, int business ed 1986–90, consumer industries ed 1990–94, world trade ed 1994–2004, Asia columnist and commentator 2005–07; currently sr fell European Centre for Int Political Economy; *Recreations* reading, travel; *Style*— Guy de Jonquières, Esq

DE L'ISLE, 2 Viscount (UK 1956), of Penshurst, Co Kent; Maj Philip John Algernon Sidney; 10 Bt (UK 1806), of Castle Goring, Co Sussex, and 8 Bt (UK 1818), of Penshurst Place, Co Kent; MBE (1977), DL (Kent 1996); also Baron De L'Isle and Dudley (UK 1835); o s of 1 Viscount De L'Isle, VC, KG, GCMG, GCVO, PC (d 1991), and his 1 w, Hon Jacqueline Corinne Yvonne, *née* Vereker (d 1962), da of FM 6 Viscount Gort, VC, GCB, CBE, DSO, MVO, MC; *b* 21 April 1945; *Educ* Tabley House Cheshire; *m* 15 Nov 1980, Isobel Tresyllian, da of Sir Edmund Gerald Compton, GCB, KBE; 1 da (Hon Sophia Jacqueline Mary (Hon Mrs Maybanks) b 25 March 1983), 1 s (Dr Hon Philip William Edmund b 2 April 1985); *Heir* s, Dr Hon Philip Sidney; *Career* cmmnd Grenadier Gds 1966, served BAOR, NI and Belize, GSO3 Ops/SD HQ 3 Inf Bde NI 1974–76, ret 1979; Hon Col 5 Bn Princess of Wales Royal Regt (Queen's and Royal Hampshires) 1992–99; farmer and landowner; Lord-Lt Kent 2012– (Vice Lord-Lt 2002–11); memb Lord Chllr's Advsy Cncl on Nat Records and Archives 2004–09; pres: W Kent Branch Grenadier Guards Assoc 1989–2015, Royal Br Legion Industries 2011, Kent Branch SSAFA Forces Help 2011, Assoc of Men of Kent and Kentish Men 2012; vice-pres: SE Reserve Forces and Cadet Assoc 2011, Royal Engrs Museum Fndn 2011–13; chm Canterbury Cathedral Tst Fund 2008–; patron: Lord Leycester Hosp at Warwick 1991, Action with Communities in Rural Kent 2011, Kent Branch Army Benevolent Fund 2011, City of Canterbury Shrievalty Assoc 2011, Friends of Kent Churches 2011, Kent Community Fndn 2011, Safer Kent (formerly Kent People's Tst) 2011, Kent Churches – Ride and Stride 2011, Royal Br Legion Kent 2011, St John Kent Priory Gp; vice-patron South of England Agricultural Soc 2007, tstee Rochester Cathedral Tst 2011; visitor Sidney Sussex Coll Cambridge 1991; Hon Col Kent Army Cadet Force (KACF) 2006–12; Freeman City of London, Liveryman Worshipful Co of Goldsmiths; Cdr Order of St John 2013; *Clubs* White's, Pratt's; *Style*— The Viscount De L'Isle, MBE; ✉ The Lieutenancy Office, Penshurst Place, Penshurst, Tonbridge, Kent TN11 8DG (☎ 01892 870343, e-mail kentll343@penshurstplace.com, website www.kent-lieutenancy.org.uk and www.penshurstplace.com)

de la BÉDOYÈRE, Guy Martyn Thorold Huchet; s of Count de la Bédoyère , *qv*, and Countess Irene T P de la Bédoyère; *b* 28 November 1957, Wimbledon, London; *Educ* KCS Wimbledon, Wimbledon Coll, Univ of Durham (BA), Univ of London (BA), UCL (MA); *m* 4 July 1981, Rosemary Anne, da of Canon R C A Carey; 4 s (Hugh b 27 Jan 1985, Thomas b 19 Nov 1986, Robert b 16 Oct 1988, William b 16 Aug 1990); *Career* freelance historian, archaeologist, writer and broadcaster; presenter: The Romans in Britain (BBC Radio 4) 1997, The Romans in Britain (BBC 2/Open Univ); co-presenter My Famous Family (UKTV History) 2006; regular guest Time Team (Channel 4) 1998–, Chm of the War Cabinet in The 1940s House (Channel 4); history and classical civilisation teacher Kesteven and Sleaford HS 2007–; memb Soc for Promotion of Roman Studies 1997–; FSA 2007, fell Historical Assoc 2008; *Publications* Samian Ware (1988), Finds of Roman Britain (1989), Buildings of Roman Britain (1991, reprinted 2001), Towns of Roman Britain (1992, revised edn 2003), Roman Villas and the Countryside (1993), The Writings of John Evelyn (1995), The Diary of John Evelyn (1995), Particular Friends. The Correspondence of Samuel Pepys and John Evelyn (1997, 2 edn 2005), Hadrian's Wall. A History and Guide (1998), The Golden Age of Roman Britain (1999, shortlisted Br Archaeological Book of the Year 2000), Companion to Roman Britain (1999), Battles over Britain. The Archaeology of the Air War (2000), Voices of Imperial Rome (2000), Pottery in Roman Britain (2000), Aviation Archaeology in Britain (2001), Eagles over Britannia. The Roman Army in Britain (2001), The Home Front (2002), Architecture in Roman Britain (2002), Gods with Thunderbolts. Religion in Roman Britain (2002), Defying Rome. The Rebels of Roman Britain (2003), A New History of Roman Britain (2006, 2 edn 2013), The Letters of Samuel Pepys (2006), The Romans for Dummies (2006), Cities of Roman Italy (2010), Real Lives of Roman Britain (2015); *Recreations* coin collector, piano, travelling in the USA, photography, aviation (private pilot's licence 2000), genealogy; *Style*— Guy de la Bédoyère, Esq; ✉ The Old Post House, Welby, Grantham, Lincolnshire NG32 3LN (☎ 01400 231190, e-mail guydelabed@yahoo.co.uk)

de la BÉDOYÈRE, Count Quentin Michael Algar; s of Count Michael de la Bédoyère (d 1973), and Catherine, *née* Thorold (d 1959); *b* 23 November 1934; *Educ* Beaumont Coll, LAMDA; *m* 28 July 1956, Irene Therese Philippa, da of late Martyn Gough; 2 s (Guy Martyn Thorold Huchet de la Bédoyère , *qv*, b 28 Nov 1957, Raoul Maurice Greville Huchet de la Bédoyère, *qv* b 20 Aug 1959), 3 da (Catherine Christina Mansel b 20 April 1961, Camilla Louise Nugent b 27 Sept 1963, Christina Sibyl Montagu b 15 April 1966); *Career* Nat Serv 2 Lt RASC 1953–55; Jacqmar Ltd 1956–57; Sun Life of Canada: sales rep 1957, field mgmnt 1960, London Head Office 1972, field trg offr 1972–76, mktg offr 1976–79, dir mktg devpt and PR 1980, vice-pres individual product mktg 1984, vice-pres planning and devpt 1987–90, vice-pres product mgmnt 1990–94, md Sun Life of Canada Unit Managers Ltd 1994–96 (dir 1990–96), ptnr IQ Productions 1997–; The Catholic Herald: columnist and ldr writer 2001–, science ed 2008–; *Books* The Doctrinal Teaching of the Church (1963), The Family (1975), Barriers and Communication (1976), The Remaking of Marriages (1978), Managing People and Problems (1988), How to Get Your Own Way in Business (1990), Getting What You Want (1994), Autonomy and Obedience in the Catholic Church (2003), Drawing Techniques (2008); *Recreations* freelance writing, public speaking, painting, motorscootering; *Style*— Count de la Bédoyère; ✉ 10 Edge Hill, Wimbledon, London SW19 4LP (e-mail quentin@blueyonder.co.uk, websites www.quentindelabedoyere.com and (discussion blog) www.secondsightblog.net)

de la BÉDOYÈRE, (Count) Raoul Maurice Greville Huchet; s of Count Quentin de la Bedoyere, *qv*, of London, and Irene, *née* Gough; *b* 20 August 1959; *Educ* KCS Wimbledon, Wimbledon Coll, Univ of Birmingham (BA); *m* 24 Nov 1989, Sally Jean, da of Frank Carswell; 1 da (Eléonore Frances Kallisto b 2 April 1993), 1 s (Zacharie Adam Kronos b 28 Jan 1996); *Career* media sales VNU Publications 1982–84, media buyer Foote Cone and Belding advtg 1984–86, media planner Davidson Pearce 1986–87, bd account planner Gold Greenlees Trott 1991–92 (media planner 1987–91); planning dir: Woollams Moira Gaskin O'Malley 1994–95 (account planner 1992–94), Burkitt Edwards Martin 1995; account planner rising to bd planning dir Bates Dorland 1995; *Style*— Raoul de la Bédoyère, Esq

de la CRUZ, Angela; *b* 1965, La Coruna, Spain; *Educ* Santiago de Compostela (BA), Chelsea Coll of Art, Goldsmiths Coll London (BA), Slade Sch of Fine Art (MA); *Career* artist; commissions incl At Any Time – New Work (stage set) for Ballet Rambert 2001; *Solo Exhibitions* Untitled (Premises London) 1993, Galerie In Situ (Aalst Belgium) 1997, Everyday Painting (John Weber Gallery NY) 1998, 4xSolo (De Markten Brussels) 1998, Larger Than Life (commission, Royal Festival Hall London) 1998, Everyday Painting (Anthony Wilkinson Gallery London 1998) and (Galerie Krinzinger Vienna) 1999, One Painting (Lift Gallery London) 1999, John Weber Gallery NY 2000, Anthony Wilkinson Gallery London 2001, Perth Int Arts Festival 2002, Galleri Bouhlou Norway, Weterling Gallery Stockholm, Anna Schwarz Gallery Melbourne; *Group Exhibitions* Rubber Works Installation (Spitalfields Market Project London) 1993, Surface Tension (Curwen Gallery London) 1994, Making Mischief (St James's St London) 1994, Memory (Riverside Studios London) 1995, Abstract Eroticism (MOCA London) 1996, Art and Design (Academy Editions London) 1996, Wasted (Hyena Co website) 1996, Stepping Out (33 Gt Sutton St London) 1996, Lineart (Galerie in Situ Aalst) 1997, Shuttle (Anthony Wilkinson Fine Art London) 1997, Fasten Seatbelt (Galerie Krinzinger Vienna) 1997, Dissolution (Laurent Delaye Gallery London) 1997, Take Off (Benger Fabrik Bregenz Hamburg) 1997, Destroyer/Creator (John Weber Gallery NY) 1998, Speed (New Langton Arts Centre San Francisco) 1998, Contemporary Women Painters (Hillwood Art Museum NY) 1998, UK Maximum Diversity (Benger Fabrik Bregenz Hamburg and Atelierhaus der Akademie der bildenden Kunste Wien) 1998, 54x54 (MOCA London) 1999, Peinture sur PEINTURE (Salle de Bal Vienna) 1999, Fundacion Lazaro Guadiano Madrid 1999, French Inst Vienna 1999, I'm a Virgin (The Waiting Room Wolverhampton) 1999, Links – Schilderkunst in extremis? (Provincehuis Maastricht) 1999, Europe on a Shoestring (John Weber Gallery NY) 1999, Transgressions and Transformations (Yale Univ) 1999, Getting the Corners (Or Gallery Vancouver) 1999, John Moores 21 (prizewinner, Walker Museum & Art Gallery Liverpool) 1999, White Out (Gallery Fine London) 1999, Aktuelle Kunst (The Water Tower Vlissingen) 1999, My Old Man Said Follow the Van (Rosemary Branch London) 1999, Art for the 21st Century (John Weber Gallery NY) 2000, Point of View I/II (Richard Salmon Gallery London) 2000, The Wreck of Hope (The Nunnery London) 2000, 3 Rooms (Anthony Wilkinson Gallery London) 2000, Landscape (Barbara Gillman Gallery Miami) 2000, Makeshift (Univ of Brighton Gallery) 2001, Nothing: Exploring Invisibilities (Northern Gallery Contemporary Art) 2001, Record Collection (VTO Gallery London) 2001, Ingenting (Rooseum Malmo) 2001, Melancholy (Sunderland) 2001, Sitting Tenants (Lotta Hammer Projects London) 2002, Beauty (Laing Art Gallery Newcastle) 2002; *Work in Public Collections* Br Cncl Collection, Contemporary Art Soc; *Style*— Ms Angela de la Cruz; ✉ c/o Lisson Gallery, 52–54 Bell Street, London NW1 5DA (☎ 020 7724 2739)

de la MARE, (Walter) Giles Ingpen; s of Richard Herbert Ingpen de la Mare (d 1986), of Much Hadham, Herts, and Amy Catherine, *née* Donaldson (d 1968); *b* 21 October 1934; *Educ* Eton, Trinity Coll Oxford (MA); *m* 10 Aug 1968, Ursula Alice, da of Nigel Oliver Willoughby Steward, OBE (d 1991), of Cullompton, Devon; 1 s (Joshua b 1969), 1 da (Catherine b 1971); *Career* Nat Serv RN 1953–55, Midshipman RNVR 1954 (Sub Lt 1955); dir: Faber and Faber Ltd 1969–98, Faber Music Ltd 1977–87, Geoffrey Faber Holdings Ltd 1990–, Giles de la Mare Publishers 1995–; Publishers Assoc: chm Univ Coll and Professional Publishers Cncl 1982–84, memb Cncl 1982–85, chm Copyright Ctee 1988, chm Freedom to Publish Ctee 1992–95 and 1998–2000; memb: Stefan Zweig Ctee Br Library 1986–95, Freedom to Publish Ctee Int Publishers Assoc 1993–96, Translation Advsy Gp Arts Cncl of England 1995–98, Exec Ctee Patrons of Br Art Tate Gallery 1998–2001; literary tstee Walter de la Mare 1982–, fndr Walter de la Mare Soc 1997; *Books* The Complete Poems of Walter de la Mare (ed, 1969), Publishing Now (contrib gen chapter, 1993), Short Stories 1895–1926 by Walter de la Mare (ed, 1996), Short Stories 1927–1956 by Walter de la Mare (ed, 2001), Short Stories for Children by Walter de la Mare (ed, 2006), The Walter de la Mare Library (2008), Exploring the World of Walter de la Mare's The Listeners (2009), Senate House Library University of London: Treasures (contrib, 2012); lectures incl: Publishing in the Blood (St Catharine's Coll Cambridge 2011), Walter de la Mare and his Family in London, 1730–1925 (Huguenot Soc, 2015); *Recreations* music (performance and listening), art and architecture, photography, exploring remote places; *Clubs* Garrick; *Style*— Giles de la Mare, Esq; ✉ PO Box 25351, London NW5 1ZT (e-mail gilesdelamare@dial.pipex.com, website www.gilesdelamare.co.uk)

de la TOUR, Frances; da of Charles de la Tour (d 1983), and Moyra Silberman, *née* Fessas (d 2010); family of the painter Georges de la Tour (d 1652); *b* 30 July 1945; *Educ* Lycée Français de Londres, Drama Centre London; *Children* 1 da (Tamasin Kempinski b 12 Nov 1973), 1 s (Josh Kempinski b 7 Feb 1977); *Career* actress; hon fell Goldsmiths Coll London 1999 *Theatre* RSC 1965–71: various roles incl Hoyden in Trevor Nunn's prodn of The Relapse, Helena in Peter Brook's prodn of A Midsummer Night's Dream; other credits incl: Violet in Small Craft Warnings (Hampstead and Comedy) 1973 (Best Supporting Actress Plays and Players Awards), Ruth Jones in The Banana Box (Apollo) 1973, Rosalind in As You Like It (Oxford Playhouse) 1974, Isabella in The White Devil (Old Vic) 1976, Eleanor Marx in Landscape of Exiles (Half Moon) 1978, title role in Hamlet (Half Moon) 1979, Stephanie in Duet for One (Bush and Duke of York's) 1980 (Standard Best Actress, Critics' Best Actress, SWET Best Actress in a New Play Awards), Jean in Skirmishes (Hampstead) 1982, Sonya in Chekhov's Uncle Vanya (Haymarket) 1982, Josie in A Moon for the Misbegotten (Riverside and Mermaid) 1983 (SWET Best Actress in a Revival Award), title role in St Joan (RNT) 1984, Dance of Death (Riverside) 1985, Sonya and Masha in Chekhov's Women (Lyric) 1985, Brighton Beach Memoirs (NT) 1986, Lillian (Lyric and Fortune) 1986, Façades (Lyric Hammersmith) 1988, Regan in King Lear (Old Vic) 1989, Olga Knipper in Chekhov's Women (Moscow Lytcée Theatre and a special performance at Moscow Arts Theatre) 1990, When She Danced (Globe) 1991 (Best Supporting Actress Olivier Awards 1992), The Pope and the Witch (Comedy) 1992, Greasepaint (Lyric Hammersmith) 1993, Les Parents Terribles (RNT) 1994 (nominated Olivier Award for Best Actress), Three Tall Women (Wyndham's) 1995, The Fire Raisers (Riverside Studios) 1995, Blinded by the Sun (RNT) 1996, The Play About the Baby (Almeida) 1998, The Forest (RNT) 1998–99, Antony and Cleopatra (RSC) 1999–2000, Fallen Angels (Apollo) 2001 (Variety Club Best Actress Award), The Good Hope (RNT) 2001–02, Dance of Death by Strindberg (Lyric) 2003, The History Boys (RNT) 2004 and (Broadway NY) 2006 (Best Featured Actress Tony Awards), The Habit of Art (NT) 2009, People (NT) 2012–13; *Television* incl: Play for Today 1973 and 1975, Rising Damp (series) 1974–76, Flickers (series) 1980, Duet for One 1985 (BAFTA Best Actress nomination), Clem by Andy de la Tour, Ghengis Cohn (TV film) 1994, Dennis Potter's Cold Lazarus (TV Film) 1996, Tom Jones (series) 1997, The Egg by Partrick Arber 2002, Death on the Nile 2003, Vicious (series, ITV) 2013, 2015 and 2016 (BAFTA Best Actress nomination 2013), Big School (series, BBC) 2013 and 2014, Outlander (USA) 2015; *Film* incl: Rising Damp 1979 (Standard Best Film Actress Award 1980), The Cherry Orchard 1998, Harry Potter and the Goblet of Fire 2004, The History Boys 2006 (BAFTA Best Actress nomination), The Book of Eli 2008, Alice in Wonderland 2009, Hugo 2010, Private Peaceful 2011, Alice Through the Looking Glass 2013, Survivor 2014, Mr Holmes 2015; *Style*— Ms Frances de la Tour; ✉ c/o Claire Maroussas, ICM, Oxford House, 76 Oxford Street, London W1N 0AX (☎ 020 7636 6565, fax 020 7323 0101)

DE LA WARR, 11 Earl (GB 1761); William Herbrand Sackville; DL (E Sussex); also Baron De La Warr (E 1299 and 1570), Viscount Cantelupe (GB 1761), and Baron Buckhurst (UK 1864); er s of 10 Earl De La Warr, DL (d 1988); *b* 10 April 1948; *Educ* Eton; *m* 1978, Anne, *née* Leveson, former w of Earl of Hopetoun (s of 3 Marq of Linlithgow); 2 s (William Herbrand Thomas, Lord Buckhurst b 1979, Hon Edward b 1980); *Heir* s, Lord Buckhurst; *Career* farmer and investment banker; Mullens & Co 1976–81, Credit Lyonnais Securities 1981–2004, dir Shore Capital Stockbrokers 2004–16, dir Cluff Natural Resources plc 2012–, ptnr Toscafund 2016–; jt pres Youth Clubs Sussex, pres Bowles Outdoor Centre; patron De La Warr Pavilion Tst, tstee Moorcroft Racehorse Welfare Centre; *Recreations* country pursuits, sausages; *Clubs* White's, Turf, Pratts; *Style*— The Rt Hon the Earl De La Warr, DL; ✉ Buckhurst Park, Withyham, East Sussex TN7 4BL; Toscafund Asset Management LLP, 7th Floor, 90 Long Acre, London WC2E 9RA

de LACY, Richard Michael; QC (2000); *b* 4 December 1954; *Educ* Hymers Coll Hull, Clare Coll Cambridge (open scholar, MA); *m* 1980 (m dis 2003), Sybil, *née* del Strother; 1s, 2 da; *Career* called to the Bar Middle Temple 1976 (Harmsworth scholar), bencher 2001; in practice Chancery Bar 1978–, admitted to Cayman Islands Bar 2012, ptnr Ogier LLP Cayman Islands 2012–, admitted to Eastern Caribbean Supreme Ct (Territory of the Virgin Islands) 2013, head of litigation Br Virgin Islands and Cayman Islands Ogier 2014–; practising arbitrator 1991–; visiting prof Queen Mary Univ of London 2009–; memb: Panel Practice Regulation Review Ctee ICAEW 1997–2003, Tbnl Panel Accountancy and Actuarial Disciplinary Bd 2005–14; hon treas Barristers' Benevolent Assoc 1989–99 (memb Ctee 1984–89); chm Endeavour Trg 2004–11 (hon treas 2001–04), memb Cncl Royal Br Legion Poppy Factory 2005–12; accredited mediator CEDR 1997; FCIArb 1991–2011; *Publications* Precedents of Pleadings (specialist ed, 15–18 (2013) edns); articles on company law, trusts, property law and arbitration; *Recreations* music, history; *Clubs* Travellers, Garrick; *Style*— Richard de Lacy, Esq, QC; ✉ 89 Nexus Way, Camana Bay, Grand Cayman KY1-9007, Cayman Islands (e-mail Richard.deLacy@ogier.com)

DE LAIRE STAINES, Paul (Guido Fawkes); s of Terril De Laire Staines, and Mary, *née* Cronin; *b* 11 February 1967, London; *Educ* Salvatorian Coll Harrow; *m* 2003, Orla, *née* Murphy; 2 da (Saoirse b 10 April 2005, Caoimhe b 6 July 2007); *Career* futures broking ticket clerk Cargill Investor Servs 1993, futures broker Yasuda Tst Europe 1993–95, fund mangr Orbitex Fund Mgmnt 1995, broker (capital markets) Yamaichi Europe 1996–97, fund mangr Mondial Global Investors LLC 1997–2001, trader Westminster Investors (Bahamas) Ltd 2002–03, investment advsr United Growth Opportunities LLC 2004–05, investment advsr Global & General Nominees Ltd 2007–11 (dir 2009–), md MessageSpace Ltd 2011–13; fndr Guido Fawkes 2004–; *Recreations* tennis, wine; *Clubs* St Anne's Waterford Tennis; *Style*— Paul Staines, Esq; ✉ e-mail sales@messagespace.co.uk, websites www.messagespace.co.uk, www.order-order.com, Twitter @GuidoFawkes

de LANDTSHEER, Jan; s of Karel de Landtsheer (d 1971), of Antwerp, and Virginia, *née* Petre; *b* 27 December 1950; *Educ* KA Antwerp, RUC Antwerp (BA), Vrije Universiteit Brussel (MSc); *m* Christine, *née* Schaeken; *Career* Vrije Universiteit Brussel: res asst 1973, teaching asst 1979; publisher De Sikkel 1979, publishing ed Wiley Europe 1992, sr publishing ed Wiley 1997–; memb: Int Assoc of Computational Mechanics 1992, Euromech 1997; *Recreations* long distance swimming and running, sea sailing, saxophone-playing in concert bands; *Clubs* Trinity Triathlon (Littlehampton), Bognor Regis Concert Band, Harmonie Sainte Jeanne-d'Arc (France); *Style*— Jan de Landtsheer, Esq; ✉ John Wiley & Sons, Baffins Lane, Chichester, West Sussex PO19 1UD (☎ 01243 70 147, e-mail jdelandt@wiley.co.uk)

de LANGE, (Rabbi) Prof Nicholas Robert Michael; s of George Douglas de Lange, of London, and Elaine, *née* Jacobus; *b* 7 August 1944; *Educ* ChCh Oxford (MA, DPhil, James Mew Rabbinic Hebrew prize), Leo Baeck Coll London (Rabbinic Dip); *Career* Parkes Library fell Univ of Southampton 1969–71; Univ of Cambridge: lectr in Rabbinics 1971–95, fell Wolfson Coll 1984–, reader in Hebrew and Jewish studies 1995–2001, prof of Hebrew and Jewish Studies 2001–11; memb: Br Assoc for Jewish Studies 1974– (past pres), Cncl Jewish Historical Soc of England 1975–2015, Ctee The Translators Assoc 1990–93, 1998–2001 and 2007–08 (chm 2001), Soc of Authors; founding ed (with Judith Humphrey) Bulletin of Judeo-Greek Studies 1987–; FBA 2011; memb Academia Europaea 2013; *Books* Origen and the Jews (1976), Apocrypha – Jewish Literature of the Hellenistic Age (1978), Origène – Philocalie 1–20 (with Marguerite Harl, 1983), Atlas of the Jewish World (1984), Judaism (1986, 2 edn 2003), Greek Jewish Texts from the Cairo Genizah (1996), Illustrated History of the Jewish People (ed, 1997), An Introduction to Judaism (2000, 2 edn 2010), Hebrew Scholarship and the Medieval World (ed, 2001), The Penguin Dictionary of Judaism (2008); many literary translations; author of numerous articles in jls and pubns; Japheth in the Tents of Shem (2015); *Style*— Prof Nicholas de Lange, FBA; ✉ Wolfson College, Cambridge CB3 9BB (☎ 01223 740561)

de LISI, Benedetto (Ben); s of Vincent Michael de Lisi, of Long Island, NY, and Palma Aida, *née* Afflitto; *b* 31 May 1955; *Educ* Hauppauge HS Long Island NY, Suffolk Community Coll Long Island NY, Pratt Inst of Fine Arts Brooklyn NY; *Career* fashion designer; fndr: Benedetto Inc menswear 1980–82, Ci Boure restaurant Belgravia (with ptnr J L Journade) 1982, Benedetto Ltd producing Ben de Lisi label 1982–91; fndr dir BDL (Design) Ltd 1991–; first London shop opened 1998; IWS Freestyle Awards 1987, nominated Most Innovative Designer of the Year 1990, winner Glamour category British Fashion Awards 1994 and 1995 (nominated 1992), nominated Glamour Awards in 1996, 1997 and 1998; *Style*— Ben de Lisi, Esq; ✉ 40 Elizabeth Street, London SW1W 9NZ (☎ 020 7730 2994, e-mail feedback@bendelisi.com)

de LISLE, Timothy John March Phillipps (Tim); s of Everard de Lisle, DL (d 2003), of Stockerston, Leics, and Hon Mary Rose, *née* Peake, da of 1 Viscount Ingleby (d 1966); *b* 25 June 1962; *Educ* Eton, Worcester Coll Oxford (exhibitioner, BA); *m* 1991, Amanda, da of Clive Barford, of Aldworth, Berks; 1 s (Daniel b 24 Jan 1994), 1 da (Laura b 20 April 1998); *Career* freelance journalist 1979–86, fndr Undergraduate Tutors 1983–87; The Daily Telegraph: diary reporter 1986–87, chief rock critic 1986–89, gen reporter 1987, news feature writer 1987–89, ed Weekend Section 1989–90; arts ed The Times 1989; The Independent on Sunday: cricket corr 1990–91, arts ed 1991–95; freelance arts and sports writer 1995– (cricket columnist The Independent 1995–96 and 1999–2000, and Evening Standard 1997–98, arts feature writer The Daily Telegraph, rock critic The Mail on Sunday 1999–); ed Wisden Cricket Monthly 1996–2000, ed Wisden.com website 1999–, ed Wisden Cricketers' Almanack 2003; Editor of The Year (Special Interest Magazines) Br Society of Magazine Editors 1999; memb NUJ 1983–; *Publications* Lives of the Great Songs (ed, 1994, revised and expanded edn 1995); *Recreations* swimming, television, books, photography; *Clubs* Cricket Writers', Eton Ramblers; *Style*— Tim de Lisle, Esq; ✉ c/o Wisden, 136 Bramley Road, London W10 6SR (☎ 020 7565 3114, fax 020 7565 3051)

DE LYON, Rev Hilary Barbara; da of Leonard John De Lyon (d 1984), and Margaret Vera De Lyon (d 2011); *b* 8 April 1956, Epsom, Surrey; *Educ* Rosebery GS Epsom, Univ of Liverpool (BA, MPhil), St Mellitus Coll London (BA); *m* 1, 5 Aug 1978 (m dis), Stephen Williams; m 2, 3 May 1997, Martin Webster; *Career* lectr in English and drama Milton Keynes Coll 1980–83, educn/equal opportunities policy offr NUT 1983–86, princ policy offr (educn) Assoc of Metropolitan Authorities 1986–94, asst educn offr London Borough of Sutton (secondment) 1992–93, sec (conduct and admin) Lord Chllr's Advsy Ctee on Legal Educn and Conduct 1994–99; chief exec: Soc of Chiropodists and Podiatrists 1999–2002, RCGP 2002–11; non-exec dir NHS Norfolk and Waveney 2011–13, dep chair and chair Audit Ctee NHS W Norfolk Clinical Commissioning Gp 2013–; tstee RGCP Superannuation Fund Tst Co Ltd 2013–, memb Cncl and tstee RSM 2014–; co-fndr: Labour Women's Network, Emily's List UK; ind chair Nominations Ctee Coll of Social Work 2011–15; memb ACEVO 1999–2010; former memb: First Division Assoc Equal Opportunities Ctee, Soc of Educn Offrs Equal Opportunities Cttee, Fawcett Soc Educn Ctee; former chair Friends of Castle Acre Church; govr Swaffham CE Jr Acad 2013–; asst curate Parishes of Swaffham and Sporle 2013–; fell RSM 2001 (memb RSM 1999), Hon FRCGP 2011; *Publications* Women Teachers: Issues and Experiences (co-ed, 1989), The Good Employers' Guide: An essential guide for school governors (1998), Production Values: Futures for Professionalism (contrib, 2006); columnist Podiatry Now 1999–2002; contrib: The New Generalist, British Journal of General Practice 2002–11; various pubns on educn and equal opportunities 1984–; *Recreations* theatre, opera, chamber music, gardens and gardening; *Clubs* RSM; *Style*— The Rev Hilary De Lyon; ✉ Flat 14, The Courtyard, 154 Goswell Road, London EC1V 7DX (☎ 020 7250 0120)

de MAULEY, 7 Baron (UK 1838); Rupert Charles; TD (1988); s of Hon Thomas Maurice Ponsonby, TD (d 2001), and Maxine Henrietta, *née* Thellusson; suc unc, 6 Baron de Mauley, 2002; *b* 30 June 1957, Oxford; *Educ* Eton; *m* 2002, Hon Lucinda Katherine Fanshawe Royle, da of Baron Fanshawe of Richmond, KCMG (Life Peer, d 2001); *Heir* bro, Hon George Ponsonby; *Career* dir: Samuel Montagu & Co Ltd 1990–93, Standard Chartered Merchant Bank Asia Ltd Singapore 1994–99 (md 1996–99), FixIT Worldwide Ltd 1999–2006; CO Royal Wessex Yeo (TA) 2003–04 (cmmnd 1976); oppn whip and BERR (formerly DTI) spokesman House of Lords and shadow min Dept for Innovation, Univ and Skills until 2010, Home Office 2010–11, Lord in Waiting (Govt whip) and spokesman for Treasy, BIS and DEFRA 2010–12, DWP 2011–12, Parly under sec of state for resource mgmnt, the local environment and environmental science DEFRA 2012–13, Parly under sec of state for the natural environment and science 2013–15; pres Soc for Protection of Animals Abroad (SPANA) 2010–, pres UK Cncl of the Reserve Forces and Cadets Assocs 2010–; Col Commandant The Yeomanry 2011–. Hon Col Royal Wessex Yeomanry 2015–; FCA 1990 (ACA 1980); *Style*— The Rt Hon the Lord de Mauley, TD

D

de MOLLER, June Frances; DL; *b* 25 June 1947; *Educ* Roedean, Hastings Coll, Sorbonne; *m* 1967 (m dis 1980); m 2, 1996, J R Giles Crisp; *Career* md Carlton Communications plc 1993–99 (dir 1983–99); non-exec dir: Anglian Water plc 1992–99, Riverside Mental Health NHS Trust 1992–96, Lynx Gp plc1999–2002, Cookson Gp plc 1999–2004, British Telecommunications plc 1999–2002, J Sainsbury plc 1999–2005, Archant Ltd 2002–11 (non-exec dir Eastern Counties Newspapers Gp 1999–2002), London Merchant Securities plc 2002–07, Temple Bar Investment Tst plc 2005–, Derwent London plc 2007–; memb: Advsy Bd Judge Inst Mgmnt Studies 1996–2003, Home of Rest for Horses 1999–2005, Cncl Aldeburgh Productions 2000–11, Cncl UEA 2002–11; *Recreations* reading, tennis, the arts, breeding Red Poll Cattle; *Style*— Mrs June de Moller, DL

DE NARDIS DI PRATA, Mainardo; s of Balduccio de Nardis di Prata, of London, and Simonetta Vallarino Gancia; *b* 24 November 1960; *Educ* Aiglon Coll Switzerland, Bedales, Univ Bocconi Milan (Economics); *m* 2 July 1988, Cristiana Clerici di Cavenago; 2 s (Alberico b 14 Feb 1992, Gherardo b 14 March 1994); *Career* McCann Erickson Rome 1980–81, Young and Rubicam Milan 1981–85, fndr ptnr of advtg agency Alberto Cremona 1985–87, vice-chm Medianetwork Group Italy 1987–93 (merged with CIA Group plc 1993), chm MNI (Assoc of Euro Media Independents) 1988–93, ceo CIA Medianetwork Europe Holdings and chm various gp cos in Europe 1993–; exec dir F.lli Gancia & C SpA Canelli Italy; *Books* La Mappa dei Media in Europa (The Map of European Media) (1994); *Recreations* ski, sailing, classic cars; *Clubs* Il Clubino Milan Italy (affiliated to Boodle's London); *Style*— Mainardo de Nardis di Prata, Esq; ✉ 111 Old Church Street, London SW3 6DX (☎ 020 7352 6340, fax 020 7352 1287); Mediaedge:cia, 1 Paris Garden, London SE1 8NU (☎ 020 7803 2254, fax 020 7803 2094, mobile 077 1017 1623, e-mail mdenardi@cia-group.com)

de NAVARRO, Michael Antony; QC (1990); s of Alma José Maria de Navarro (d 1979), of Broadway, Worcs, and Agnes Dorothy McKenzie, *née* Hoare (d 1987); *b* 1 May 1944; *Educ* Downside, Trinity Coll Cambridge (BA); *m* 20 Dec 1975, Jill Margaret, da of Charles Walker, of Southwell, Notts (d 2013); 1 s (Antony Charles b 1980), 2 da (Katharine Mary b 1978, Frances Anne b 1982); *Career* called to the Bar Inner Temple 1968 (bencher 2000), recorder Western Circuit 1990–2015; chm Personal Injury Bar Assoc 1997–99; tstee Longborough Festival Opera 2001–15, tstee Broadway Arts Festival 2010–; *Recreations* opera, cricket, gardening; *Clubs* MCC; *Style*— Michael de Navarro, QC; ✉ 2 Temple Gardens, Temple, London EC4Y 9AY (☎ 020 7822 1200, fax 020 7822 1300, e-mail mdenavarro@2templegardens.co.uk)

de PASS, David Vincent Guy; s of Lt Cdr John Gerald Irvine de Pass, RN (d 1981), and Marie Elizabeth, *née* Eberhardt (d 1988); *b* 27 August 1949; *Educ* Harrow, Coll of Law, Nat Law Center, George Washington Univ (MCL), LSE (LLM), KCL; *m* Violet Elizabeth, *née* Jacobsen; *Career* admitted slr 1973; admitted to the Bar of Dist of Columbia 1978, ptnr and head of private client dept Holman Fenwick & Willan 1986–2002, dir Specialist Advice Dept Coutts & Co 2002–; pubns in law jls and magazines, contrib to legal precedents book; memb Phi Delta Phi Legal Fraternity; *Recreations* cricket, philately, music; *Clubs* Harrovian Rifle Assoc, Harrow Wanderers, Hurlingham; *Style*— David de Pass, Esq

DE PEAR, Ben; s of John Andrew de Pear, and Susan Elizabeth Kerr *née* Everall; *b* 5 December 1970, London; *Educ* St Gabriel's Sch Barbados, Oakham Sch Rutland, Univ of Leeds; *m* 13 Sep 2008, Leila Theresa Amanpour; 2 s (Cassius George b 11 Jan 2005, Thomas Firouz b 27 Jul 2009), 1 da (Eva Homa b 9 Sept 2007); *Career* trainee Staines and Ashford News 1994; Sky News: runner 1994–95, foreign prodr 1996–2000; Africa ed Sky News Johannesburg 2000–05; Channel 4 News: sr foreign prodr 2005–08, foreign ed 2008–12, ed 2012–; memb NUJ, Soc of Eds; tstee: Rory Peck Tst, Duchenne's Children's Tst, Diabetes UK; 4 RTS Foreign Awards, 4 Amnesty Int Awards, 2 BAFTAs, Emmy Award, 6 FPA Awards; nominee Nobel Prize; *Recreations* cinema, cricket, music, reading, tennis, travel, football, literature, reggae; *Clubs* QPR, Frontline, Serpentine Swimming, Wolverhampton Wanderers, Surrey County Cricket, Turks Cricket; *Style*— Ben de Pear, Esq; ✉ Channel 4 News, 200 Gray's Inn Road, London WC1X 8XZ

de PURY, Christopher Mark (Chris); s of Andrew de Pury, and Lois, *née* Costen; *b* 11 February 1968, London; *Educ* Aylesbury GS, ChCh Oxford (MA); *m* 5 Feb 2000, Carolyn, *née* Rice-Oxley; 2 s (Sebastian, Theo), 1 da (Olivia); *Career* slr specialising in property law; ptnr Herbert Smith until 2007, with Three Delta LLP 2007, ptnr Berwin Leighton Paisner LLP 2008–; tstee Stock Exchange Drama Soc; *Recreations* family, theatre, drama; *Style*— Chris de Pury, Esq; ✉ Berwin Leighton Paisner LLP, Adelaide House, London EC4R 9HA (☎ 020 7760 4089, e-mail chris.de.pury@blplaw.com)

de PUYFONTAINE, Arnaud; *Educ* Harvard Business Sch; *Career* Le Figaro 1990–95, Emap France Gp 1995–2006 (ceo 1998–2006), pres Mondadori France 2006–07, pres Gp Mondadori France and ceo of digital operations 2007–08, special advsr to Vice-Chm and CEO 2008–09, chief exec Hearst Magazines UK and exec vice-pres Hearst Magazines Int 2009–; *Style*— Arnaud de Puyfontaine, Esq; ✉ Hearst Magazines UK, 72 Broadwick Street, London W1F 9EP

de QUINCEY, Paul Morrison; s of Ronald Anthony de Quincey, and Margaret Winifred Claire, *née* Dingley (d 1990); *b* 23 June 1954; *Educ* Sutton HS Plymouth, Univ of Leeds (MA, PGCE); *m* 1 May 1976, Teresa Elizabeth Patricia, *née* Casabayo; 1 da (Lara Claire b 8 April 1983), 1 s (Thomas Anthony b 16 Oct 1985); *Career* English teacher Esan Teacher Trg Coll Nigeria 1976–78, English master Wakefield Girls' HS 1979–81; British Council: asst rep Korea 1981–84, conslt 1984–87, asst rep Algeria 1987–91, dep dir Czechoslovakia 1991–93, dir Venezuela 1993–98, dir Americas 1998–2000, dir UK 2000–02, dir GFS and memb Sr Mgmnt Team 2002–04, dir France 2004–; *Recreations* fishing, shooting, theatre, skiing; *Style*— Paul de Quincey, Esq; ✉ The British Council, 9 Rue de Constantine, 75340 Paris cedex 07, France

de RIVAZ, Vincent; CBE (2012); s of François de Rivaz, and Isabelle de Buttet; *b* 4 October 1953; *Educ* Ecole Nationale Superieure d'Hydraulique de Grenoble; *m* 10 May 1980, Anne, *née* de Valence de Minardière; 3 c (Ailred b 5 June 1981, Albéric b 29 Oct 1982, Amaury b 22 April 1987); *Career* hydroelectric engr; EDF: joined External Engrg Centre 1977–, mangr Far East Div 1985–91, md Hydro Power Dept 1991–94, dep head Int Div and mangr New Projects Dept 1995–98, dep chief fin offr 1999–2000, head of strategy and fin 2000–03, chief exec London Electricity Gp (now EDF Energy) 2003– (memb Exec Ctee 2004–); Melchett Medal 2006; Chevalier de la Légiòn d'Honneur; *Style*— Vincent de Rivaz, Esq, CBE; ✉ EDF Energy, 40 Grosvenor Place, London SW1X 7EN (☎ 020 7752 2101, fax 020 7752 2104, e-mail vincent.de-rivaz@edfenergy.com)

de ROTHSCHILD, Baron Eric Alain Robert David; s of Baron Alain James Gustave Jules de Rothschild (d 1982), and Mary Germaine, *née* Chauvin du Treuil; *b* 3 October 1940; *Educ* Lycée Janson de Sailly Paris, Polytechnicum of Zürich; *m* 21 Dec 1983, (Donna) Maria Beatrice, da of Don Alfonso Caracciolo di Forino (d 1990); 2 s (James Alain Robert Alexandro b 7 Dec 1985, Pietro Noé Genaro b 21 March 1991), 1 da (Anna Saskia Esther b 29 April 1987); *Career* managing ptnr Chateau Lafite Rothschild 1974–; chm: Paris Orleans SA 1975–, Rothschild Continuation Ltd London 1977–, N M Rothschild Asset Management Ltd London 1997– (dir 1989–), Rothschild Bank AG 2000–, N M Rothschild & Sons Ltd London 2004– (dir 1978–); ptnr Rothschild et Compagnie Banque 1987–; dir Chalone Inc San Francisco 1989–; *Style*— Baron Eric de Rothschild; ✉ Rothschild & Co Banque, 3 rue de Messine, 75008 Paris, France (☎ 00 33 1 40 74 40 06, fax 00 33 1 40 74 98 16)

de SAVARY, Peter John; *Educ* Charterhouse; *m* 1 (m dis), Marcia (now Hon Lady (John) Astor); 2 da (Lisa, Nicola); m 2 (m dis), Alice, *née* Simms; m 3, (Lucille Lana), *née* Paton; 3 da (Tara, Amber, Savannah); *Career* int entrepreneur (petroleum, property, maritime interests, hotels and resorts); diplomatic ambass for the Govt of Grenada, W Indies, with responsibilites for int relations and inward investment; America's Cup challenger 1983 and 1987; Tourism Personality of the Year (English Tourist Bd) 1988; *Recreations* sailing, riding, carriage driving; *Clubs* Royal Thames Yacht, Royal Burnham Yacht, Royal Torbay Yacht, Royal Corinthian Yacht, New York Yacht; *Style*— Peter de Savary Esq

de SEGUNDO, Karen Maria Alida; da of Gerard Jacobus Platerink (d 1995), and Hendrika Alida, *née* Bolk (d 2008); *b* 12 December 1946, The Hague; *Educ* Leiden Univ (LLM), Michigan State Univ (MBA); *m* 29 Nov 1975, William Nigel de Segundo; 3 s (Charles Sempill b 15 Dec 1977, Robert Daniell b 23 April 1980, Julian William Alexander b 8 May 1986); *Career* Royal Dutch Shell 1971–2005; memb Supervisory Bd Koninklijke Ahold 2004–11, dir Poÿry Oyj 2005–, non-exec dir Lonmin plc 2005–, non-exec dir British American Tobacco plc 2007–, memb Supervisory Bd E.On AG; memb Advsy Cncl Anglo Netherlands Soc; *Style*— Mrs Karen de Segundo; ✉ Lonmin plc, 4 Grosvenor Place, London SW1X 7YL

de SILVA, Rt Hon Sir (George) Desmond Lorenz; kt (2007), PC (2011), QC (1984); s of Edmund Frederick Lorenz de Silva, MBE (d 1994), and Esme Norah Gregg de Silva (d 1982); *b* 13 December 1939; *Educ* privately; *m* 5 Dec 1987, HRH Princess Katarina of Yugoslavia, o da of HRH Prince Tomislav of Yugoslavia, and HGDH Princess Margarita of Baden, and ggggda of Queen Victoria; 1 da (Victoria Marie Esme Margarita b 6 Sept 1991); *Career* int lawyer; called to the Bar: Middle Temple 1964 (bencher 2008), Sierra Leone 1968, Gambia 1981, Gibraltar 1992, Botswana 2001; dep circuit judge 1976–80, head of chambers 1987–; dep chief prosecutor UN War Crimes Tbnl Sierra Leone 2002 (at level of asst sec-gen of UN), prosecutor (at level of under sec-gen of UN) 2005, UNDP envoy to Belgrade 2005; memb: Home Affrs Standing Ctee Bow Gp 1982, Editorial Advsy Bd Crossbow 1984; one of three int experts who provided the Gaza Flotilla Report for the UNHRC 2010, appointed by Govt in 2011 to review and report on state involvement in the assassination of Patrick Finucane in Belfast in 1989; vice-pres St John Ambulance London (Prince of Wales Dist) 1984–; councilman City of London (Ward of Farringdon Without) 1980–95; landowner (Taprobane Island in the Indian Ocean); memb Racehorse Owners Assoc; patron Memorial Gates Tst; Freeman City of London, Liveryman Worshipful Co of Gunmakers; KStJ 1994 (CStJ 1985, OStJ 1980); *Recreations* politics, shooting, travel; *Clubs* Brooks's, Carlton, Naval and Military, Orient (Colombo); *Style*— The Rt Hon Sir Desmond de Silva, QC; ✉ 5 Bell Yard, London WC2A 2JR (☎ 020 7556 5500, e-mail ddsqc@yahoo.co.uk, website www.sirdesmonddesilvaqc.com)

de SILVA, Harendra Aneurin Domingo; QC (1995); s of Annesley de Silva (d 1978), of Colombo, Sri Lanka, and Maharani of Porbandar (d 1989); *b* 29 September 1945; *Educ* Millfield, Queens' Coll Cambridge (MA, LLM); *m* 10 June 1972, Indira; 1 da (Ayesha Annette b 30 July 1975), 1 s (Nihal Ceri b 17 Jan 1979); *Career* called to the Bar Middle Temple 1970 (bencher); recorder of the Crown Court; *Recreations* golf, bridge, tennis; *Clubs* Roehampton; *Style*— Harendra de Silva, Esq, QC; ✉ Goldsmiths Chambers Goldsmith Building London EC4Y 7BL

de SOUZA, Christopher Edward; s of Denis Walter de Souza (d 2002), and Dorothy Edna, *née* Woodman (d 1984); *b* 6 June 1943; *Educ* Prior Park Coll Bath, Univ of Bristol, Old Vic Theatre Sch Bristol; *m* 1971 (m dis 1981), Robyn Ann Williams; partner, Elinor Ann Kelly; 2 s (Tristan Edward b 17 June 1987, Sebastian Denis b 19 April 1993); *Career* broadcaster, also composer, opera producer and director; head of music St Bernadette's Sch Bristol 1966–70, staff prodr Sadler's Wells/ENO 1971–75, arts prodr BBC Radio London 1975–79, music prodr BBC Radio 3 1980–86, prodr BBC Promenade Concerts 1987–88, presenter BBC Radio 3 1988–, own prog Tuning Up focusing on young musicians 1990–92, awarded NY Radio Show Silver Medal 1992), artistic dir Southern Sinfonia 1998–; fndr dir Liszt Festival of London 1977; prodr of over 100 operas for BBC Radio, Abbey Opera, Northern Ireland Opera, Handel Opera, Opera East, Royal Coll of Music, Aldeburgh Festival, Bologna Festival, Kraków Festival and Miami Festival; dir Br stage premières of: Liszt's Don Sanche 1977, Virgil Thompson's The Mother of Us All 1979, Pfitzner's Palestrina 1983, Gretry's William Tell 1984; regular competition adjudicator, contributed articles to The Listener, Music and Musicians, Musical Times, The Strad, BBC Proms Guides; chm: SE Branch Composers' Guild of GB 1974–76, AVANTI (agency for young musicians) 1985–91; memb: Park Lane Group 1984–92, Redcliffe Concerts 1985–90, British Youth Opera 1986–99; memb: Equity, BASCA, Performing Rights Soc (PRS), Royal Soc of Musicians, Royal Phiharmonic Soc, Liszt Soc; *Compositions* incl: 8 Epithalamia for Organ (1966–71), Sonata for Flute and Piano (1974), Maharajahs (music for BBC2 series), Four Brecht Songs (1991), Six-foot Cinderella (music for BBC2), Symphonic Suite from Britten's music for The Rescue, The Ides of March (a capella, 1993), Children of the Light (with Adrian Morris, 2001), Missa Douensis (2003), Bottom's Dream (BBC commission, 2008), Combe Gibbett (2009), Trombone Concerto (2010); *Recordings* incl first modern prodn of Liszt's opera Don Sanche (BBC Studio Recording with BBC Scottish Symphony Orch); *Books* A Child's Guide to Looking at Music (1980); *Recreations* entertaining, travel, languages, painting, drawing; *Clubs* Royal Over-Seas League; *Style*— Christopher de Souza, Esq; ✉ Westbrook Farm Cottage, Boxford, Newbury, Berkshire RG20 8DL (☎ 01488 608503, mobile 07884 056135, e-mail chris@chrisdesouza.co.uk)

de SOUZA, Howard Gareth; s of Joseph Anthony de Souza, and Rose de Souza; *b* 1 October 1956; *Educ* Watford Boys' GS, Lancaster Univ (BSc); *m* 1995, Nicole, *née* Stalker; 1 s (Joseph), 1 da (Kitty); *Career* State of the Art London 1982–85, Burson Marsteller London 1985–89, Bell Pottinger Communications 1989–2000, Ogilvy Public Relations Worldwide 2000–02, with The PR Office then exec dir TAG (Transforming a Generation); *Recreations* enjoying myself; *Style*— Howard de Souza, Esq

DE STEMPEL, Sophie Christina; da of Baron Michael De Stempel, of Crosfield Road, Hampstead, and Cristina MacDonald; *b* 31 December 1960; *Educ* Lady Eden's Sch London, Convent of the Sacred Heart Woldingham, City and Guilds Sch of Art Kennington; *m* 2003, Sir Ian Holm, *qv*; *Career* artist; exhibitions incl: Gallery 24 Powis Terrace 1985, Conway Hall 1986, Albemarle Gallery 1987, The Mall Galleries 1988, Rebecca Hossack Gallery, Houldsworth Gallery, Freud Musuem, Royal Acad, and many mixed shows; most important works: The Unmade Bed 1986 (Saatchi collection), Profile of Gillian Melling 1988 (Catherine Parma collection), interior 1989 (Berry collection), Interior Bathroom 1989 (Saatchi collection), India Jane Birley 1990 (Pigoztsi collection), India Jane in an Interior 1990–91 (Saatchi collection); currently prof The Prince's Drawing Sch; *Style*— Sophie De Stempel

de SWIET, Prof Michael; s of John de Swiet (d 2001), of Trewen Pentrych, Cardiff, and Mary Marguerite, *née* Smith (d 2002); *b* 15 August 1941; *Educ* Cheltenham Coll, Univ of Cambridge (MD); *m* 12 Sept 1964, (Eleanor) Jane de Swiet, da of Richard Miles Hawkins, of Broadwas-on-Teme, Worcs; 1 da (Harriet Kate b Aug 1968), 2 s (Thomas Michael b 12 May 1970, Charles Richard John b 12 Dec 1972); *Career* SHO Nat Hosp for Nervous Diseases 1968; UCH: house physician 1966–67, SHO 1967–68, res fell 1968–70; res fell Univ of Calif San Francisco 1970–71, registrar Radcliffe Infirmary Oxford 1971–73; conslt physician Queen Charlotte's Hosp, UCH and Whittington Hosp 1973–; prof of obstetric medicine Imperial Coll Sch of Med London until 2006 (emeritus prof 2006–); *Books* Basic Science in Obstetrics Gynaecology (co-ed, 3 edn 2002), Medical Disorders in Obstetric Practice (4 edn, 2002); *Recreations* the arts, gardening, woodwork, walking; *Style*— Prof Michael de Swiet; ✉ 15 Wren View, 75 Hornsey Lane, London N6 5LH (☎ 020 8347 9014)

de THAME, Rachel; da of Michael Cohen, and Ghita Cohen, of Hadley Wood, Herts; *Educ* Royal Ballet Sch, City Lit Inst, English Gardening Sch; *m* 1, 1986, Stephen Colover; 1 da (Lauren Lucy b 1989), 1 s (Joseph David Simon b 1991); m 2, 1999, Gerard de Thame; 1 da (Emma Grace b 2004); *Career* TV presenter and writer; previously fashion model and actress, film credits incl Merlin and Bodywork; contrib: Daily Telegraph, The Guardian, Gardeners' World Magazine, Garden News, New Eden; *Television* for BBC: Gardeners' World 1999–, Small Town Gardens 2001, Going for a Song 2001, Call My Bluff 2002, Gardening with the Experts 2003; Heart of the Country (ITV) 1999; *Books* Small Town Gardens (2001), Rachel de Thame's Top 100 Star Plants (2002), Gardening with the Experts (jtly, 2003); *Recreations* reading, theatre, antiques, country walks; *Style*— Mrs Rachel de Thame; ✉ c/o Hilary Murray-Watts, Arlington Enterprises Ltd, 1–3 Charlotte Street, London W1T 1RD (☎ 020 7580 0702, fax 020 7580 4994, website www.arlingtonenterprises.co.uk); c/o Luigi Bonomi, Sheil Land Associates Ltd, 43 Doughty Street, London WC1N 2LH (☎ 020 7405 9351, fax 020 7831 2127, e-mail info@sheilland.co.uk)

de TRAFFORD, Sir John Humphrey; 7 Bt (UK 1841), of Trafford Park, Lancs; MBE (2010); *b* 12 September 1950; *Educ* Ampleforth, Univ of Bristol (BSc); *m* 1975, Anne, da of Jacques Faure de Pebeyre; 1 s (Alexander Humphrey b 28 June 1978), 1 da (Isabel June b 1980); *Career* American Express Europe Ltd 1987–2005 (regnl pres Northern Europe 2000–04); non-exec dir NS&I 2010– (chair 2012–); chair Pension, Disabilities and Carers Serv DWP 2008–10; tstee Nat Benevolent Fund for the Aged; *Clubs* Royal Ocean Racing, Royal Cruising; *Style*— Sir John de Trafford, Bt

de VESCI, 7 Viscount (I 1776); Thomas Eustace Vesey; 9 Bt (I 1698); also Baron Knapton (I 1750); s of 6 Viscount de Vesci (d 1983), by his w Susan Anne (d 1986), da of late Ronald Owen Lloyd Armstrong-Jones, MBE (and sis of Earl of Snowdon, *qv*); *b* 8 October 1955, Dublin, Ireland; *Educ* Eton, St Benet's Hall Oxford; *m* 5 Sept 1987 (m dis 2011), Sita-Maria Arabella, o da of Brian de Breffny (d 1989), and Maharaj Kumari Jyotsna Devi, da of late Sir Uday Chand Mahtab KCIE Maharajadhiraja Bahadur, of Burdwan; 2 s (Hon Damian John b 1985, Hon Oliver Ivo b 16 July 1991), 1 da (Hon Cosima Frances b 1988); *Heir* s, Hon Oliver Vesey; *Career* md Horticultural Coir Ltd; *Style*— The Rt Hon the Viscount de Vesci; ✉ Knapton, Abbeyleix, Co Laois, Ireland

de VINK, Peter Henry John; s of Dr Ludovicus Petrus Hendricus Josephus de Vink (d 1987), and Catharina Louisa Maria, *née* Van Iersel (d 1993); *b* 9 October 1940; *Educ* Univ of Edinburgh (BCom); *m* 1, 27 May 1967 (m dis 1993), Jenipher Jean, da of Ronald Malcolm Murray-Lyon, MD (d 1969); 1 da (Natalie b 1970), 1 s (Patrick b 1971); m 2, 23 Sept 1994, Julia Christine Quarles van Ufford (d 2007); *Career* Nat Serv 1961–63, cmmnd Dutch Army; dir Ivory & Sime 1975 (joined 1966, ptnr 1969), fndr dir Edinburgh Financial & General Holdings Ltd 1978–; dir: Viking Resources Oil & Gas Ltd 1972–88, Viking Resources Tst plc 1972–88, Wereldhave NY 1973–90, Benline Offshore Contractors Ltd 1974–96, Albany Oil & Gas Ltd 1987–91, Capital Copiers (Edinburgh) Ltd 1989–90, Screen Consultants NV 1994–2002, Oxford Philanthropic 1994–96; cncllr former People's Repub of Midlothian 2012–; former memb: Exec Scot Cncl (Devpt and Ind) Ct Heriot Watt Univ, Bd of Govrs Edinburgh Napier Univ, Scottish Industrial Development Advsy Bd, Scottish Ctee Game Conservancy Cncl, Scottish Cons Bd of Fin; *Recreations* shooting, golf, farming and local political hustings; *Clubs* New (Edinburgh), Tuesday; *Style*— Peter H J de Vink, Esq; ✉ Edinburgh Financial & General Holdings Ltd, Huntly Cot, Temple, Midlothian EH23 4TF (☎ 0131 225 6661, mobile 07836 702335, e-mail pdev@efgh.co.uk)

de WILDE, (Alan) Robin; QC (1993); s of Capt Ronald Cedric de Wilde (d 1985), and Dorothea Elizabeth Mary, *née* Fenningworth (d 2005); *b* 12 July 1945; *Educ* Dean Close Sch Cheltenham, RAF Coll Cranwell; *m* 16 April 1977, Patricia Teresa, da of Gerald Ivan Bearcroft (d 1980), and Kathleen Mary, *née* O'Toole (d 1975); 3 s; *Career* called to the Bar Inner Temple 1971 (bencher 1996); chm Professional Negligence Bar Assoc 1995–97; Liveryman Worshipful Co of Bowyers; *Style*— Robin de Wilde, Esq, QC; ✉ 218 Strand Chambers, Third Floor, 218 Strand, London WC2R 1AT (☎ 0845 083 3000)

de WINTER, Louise Margaret; *née* Fergusson; da of Alec Crowther Fergusson (d 2000), and Margaret Ewing, *née* Humphries; *b* 6 February 1964, Singapore; *Educ* Westonbirt Sch, Univ of E Anglia (BA); *m* 1993, Richard Mark de Winter; 1 d (b 1996), 1 s (b 1998); *Career* dir Citigate Public Affrs 2000–04, external relations dir Museums, Libraries and Archives Cncl 2004–06, dir Nat Campaign for the Arts 2006–, chief exec Urology Fndn 2011–; FRSA 2004; *Recreations* reading, cycling, walking, baking, embarrassing my children; *Style*— Louise de Winter; ✉ The Urology Foundation, Unit 3 Pride Court, 80–82 White Lion Street, London N1 9PF (☎ 020 7713 9538, e-mail ldewinter@theurologyfoundation.org)

DE WITT, Sir Ronald Wayne; kt (2002); s of James Goldwyn De Witt, of Saskatoon, Canada, and Una Doreen, *née* Lane; *b* 31 March 1948; *Educ* Sch of Advanced Nursing Wellington NZ (Dip Nursing), Univ of Humberside (BA, MA); *Career* student nurse Misericordia Hosp 1967–70, staff nurse Winnipeg Children's Hosp 1970, charge nurse Stoke Mandeville Hosp 1971–73 (staff nurse 1971), nursing offr Queen Mary Hosp Roehampton 1973–75, asst princ nurse Auckland Hosp 1980–83 (supervisor 1975, sr supervisor 1976–80), dir of nursing Green Lane Hosp Auckland 1983–86, chief nurse Auckland Health 1988–90 (dep chief nurse 1986–88), dist mangr Auckland City 1989–90, gen mangr Auckland Hosp 1990–91; chief exec: Royal Hull Hosp NHS Tst 1991–96, Leeds HA 1996–99, King's Healthcare NHS Tst 1999–2002, NW London SHA 2002–04, Her Majesty's Courts Service (HMCS) 2004–08; princ conslt Agencia Consulting Ltd; visiting prof of health and educn commissioning Sheffield Hallam Univ 1997–2005; chm Eng Nat Bd for Nursing, Midwifery and Health Visiting 1997–2002 (now emeritus prof), chm and tstee LEPRA UK 2007–15, chm Thera East 2016–; regency patron Brighton Royal Pavilion, chm Brunswick Town Assoc 2016–; Dow Corning Int Award for Plastic Surgery 1973; hon fell Univ of Humberside and Lincolnshire; DCL (hc) UEA 2004; *Style*— Sir Ronald De Witt

de ZULUETA, Dr Felicity Ines Soledad (Mrs Kahya); da of Dr Julian de Zulueta, and Gillian Owtram de Zulueta; *b* 26 March 1948; *Educ* UEA (BSc), Univ of Cambridge (MA), Univ of Sheffield (MB ChB); *m* 30 Sept 1977, Sedat Kahya, s of late Samuel Kahya, of Istanbul,

Turkey; 1 s (Damian Samuel Hakan b 10 Nov 1979); *Career* private psychotherapist, qualified gp analyst, systemic therapist and EMDR therapist; SHO, registrar and sr registrar Maudsley Hosp where trained in psychotherapy, trained at Tavistock Clinic in family therapy, hon sr lectr Inst of Psychiatry, conslt psychiatrist in psychotherapy and lead clinicain Traumatic Stress Serv Maudsley Hosp; currently: emeritus conslt psychiatrist and hon sr lectr in traumatic studies S London and Maudsley Fndn Tst, freelance conslt and lectr; memb: Med Section Amnesty Int, Inst of Group Analysis, European Soc for Traumatic Stress Studies; fndr memb Int Attachment Network; FRCPsych (MRCPsych), memb RSM; *Books* From Pain to Violence: The Traumatic Roots of Destructiveness (1993, 2 edn 2006); also contrib chapters to various books; *Recreations* travelling, photography, walking, scuba diving; *Style—* Dr Felicity de Zulueta

DE ZULUETA, Paul Gerald; *see:* Torre Diaz, Count of

DEACON, Richard; CBE, RA (1999); s of Gp Capt Edward William Deacon (d 2004), of Somerset, and Dr Joan Bullivant Winstanley (d 1973); *b* 15 August 1949; *Educ* Plymouth Coll, Somerset Coll of Art, St Martin's Sch of Art (DipAD), RCA (MA), Chelsea Sch of Art; *m* 1977 (m dis 2000), Jacqueline Poncelet; 1 s (Alexis b 1978), 1 da (Alice b 1982); *Career* artist; prof Ecole Nationale Supérieure des Beaux Arts 1998–2009, prof Kunst Akademie Dusseldorf 2009–15; tstee Tate Gallery 1992–97, vice-chm Baltic Centre for Contemporary Art Tst 1999–2005, tstee The Art Fund 2015–; Turner Prize 1987; hon fell London Univ of the Arts 2013; Chevalier de l'Ordre des Arts et des Lettres (France) 1998; *Exhibitions* incl: Tate Gallery 1985, Bonnefanten Museum 1987, Whitechapel Art Gallery 1989, Hannover Kunstverein 1993, British Cncl touring exhibition S America 1996–97, Tate Gallery Liverpool 1999, DCA Dundee 2001, Ludwig Museum Cologne 2003, Atelier Brancusi Paris 2004, Tate Gallery St Ives 2005, Museo Artium Vitonia-Gasteiz 2005, Sara Hilden Art Museum Tampere 2005–06, Arp Museum Germany 2006, Ikon Gallery Birmingham 2007, Wales at the Venice Biennale of Art 2007, Musée d'Art Contemporain Strasbourg 2010, STPI Singapore 2012, CAC Malaga Spain 2012, Tate Britain 2014, Kunstmuseum Winterthur 2015, Heydar Alyev Centre Baku; *Commissions* Toronto, Plymouth, Gateshead, Krefeld, Villeneuve d'Ascq, Auckland, Tokyo, Beijing, Haarlem, San Francisco, Niigata, Assen, Logrono, Zaragosa, Winterthur, Piccadilly London, Gjøvik; *Publications* Richard Deacon – Monograph (1995, 2000 and 2014), Por Escrito RD Collected Writings (2012), So, And, If, But – selected writings (2014); *Recreations* walking; *Style—* Prof Richard Deacon, CBE, RA; ✉ website www.richarddeacon.net; Lisson Gallery, London (website www.lissongallery.com), Marian Goodman Gallery, New York (website www.mariangoodman.com)

DEACON, Prof Susan Catherine; da of James Deacon (d 1980), and Barbara, *née* Timmins (d 2003); *b* 2 February 1964, Musselburgh, E Lothian; *Educ* Musselburgh GS, Univ of Edinburgh (MA, MBA); *partner* John Boothman; 1 da (Clare b 10 Aug 1997), 1 s (James b 9 June 2002); *Career* research asst W Lothian DC 1987–89, corp servs mangr East Lothian DC 1990–94, sr conslt Eglinton Mgmnt Centre Edinburgh 1994, MBA dir of progs Edinburgh Business Sch Heriot-Watt Univ 1994–98, business and mktg conslt 1998–99, MSP (Scottish Lab Party) Edinburgh East and Musselburgh 1999–2007; min for health and community care Scottish Govt 1999–2001, early years champion Scottish Govt 2010–11; policy and strategy conslt 2007–; prof of social change Queen Margaret Univ 2007–10, hon prof Univ of Edinburgh 2010–12, asst princ external relations and professorial fell Univ of Edinburgh 2012–; memb: RSA Cmmn on Illegal Drugs, Communities and Public Policy 2005–07, Nat Tst for Scotland Strategic Review 2009–10, Scotland Ctee IOD 2012–; chair IOD Scotland 2015–; chm ScottishPower Renewables 2009–12 (dir 2009–10), non-exec dir ScottishPower 2012–, non-exec dir Lothian Buses Ltd 2015–; chair: Hibernian Community Fndn 2008–12, Edinburgh Festivals Forum 2016–; memb: Bd Pfizer UK Fndn 2007–13, Bd Traverse Theatre 2007–10, Advsy Bd Scottish Power 2007–09, Bd and govr Inst of Occupational Medicine 2013–, Bd Edinburgh Coll Devpt Tst 2014–15; tstee Dewar Arts Awards 2008–10, tstee Iberdrola Fndn 2009–14; Frontbencher of the Year Scottish Politician of the Year Awards 2000; CIPD 1993, FRSA 2007; *Recreations* music, reading, creative arts, historic buildings; *Style—* Prof Susan Deacon; ✉ University of Edinburgh, Charles Stewart House, 9–16 Chambers Street, Edinburgh EH1 1HT (e-mail susan.deacon@ed.ac.uk)

DEAKIN, Michael; s of Sir William Deakin, DSO (d 2005), and Margaret, *née* Beatson Bell; bro of Prof Nicholas Deakin, CBE, *qv*; *b* 21 February 1939; *Educ* Bryanston, Universite d'Aix Marseilles, Emmanuel Coll Cambridge (MA); *Career* writer, documentary and film maker; fndr ptnr Editions Alecto (fine art publishers) 1960–64, prodr BBC Radio Current Affairs Dept 1964–68, prodr then editor Documentary Unit Yorkshire TV 1968–81; prodns incl: Out of Shadow into the Sun – The Eiger, Struggle for China, Whicker's World – Way Out West, Johnny Go Home (Br Acad award, 1976), David Frost's Global Village, The Frost Interview – The Shah, Act of Betrayal 1987, Not a Penny More, Not a Penny Less 1989, Secret Weapon 1990, Doomsday Gun 1993, The Good King 1994; fndr memb TV-am Breakfast Time Consortium 1980; TV-am: dir of progs 1982–84, memb Bd 1984–85, conslt 1984–87; dir Griffin Productions Ltd 1985–, sr vice-pres Paramount/Revcom 1987–93; *Books* Restif de la Bretonne – Les Nuits de Paris (translated with Nicholas Deakin, 1968), Gaetano Donizetti (1968), Tom Grattan's War (1970), The Children on the Hill (1972, 9 edn 1982), Johnny Go Home (with John Willis, 1976), The Arab Experience (with Antony Thomas, 1975, 2 edn 1976), Flame in the Desert (1976), I Could Have Kicked Myself (with David Frost, 1982), Who Wants to be Millionaire (with David Frost, 1983), If You'll Believe That You'll Believe Anything... (1986); *Recreations* motorcycling, eating, music, dalmatians; *Clubs* BAFTA; *Style—* Michael Deakin, Esq

DEAKIN, Prof Nicholas Dampier; CBE (1997); s of Sir William Deakin, DSO (d 2005), and Margaret, *née* Beatson Bell; bro of Michael Deakin, *qv*; *b* 5 June 1936; *Educ* Westminster, Milton Acad USA, ChCh Oxford (MA), Univ of Sussex (DPhil); *m*; 3 c, 3 step c; *Career* civil servant (admin class) 1959–63: asst princ Home Office, private sec to Minister of State 1962–63; asst dir Nuffield Survey of Race Rels 1963–68, res fell Centre for Multi-Racial Studies Univ of Sussex 1969–71, lectr Sch of African and Asian Studies Univ of Sussex 1971–72, head Social Studies then Central Policy Unit GLC 1972–80; Univ of Birmingham: prof of social policy and admin 1980–98, head Dept Social Admin 1980–91, dean Faculty of Commerce and Social Science 1986–89 (dep dean 1984–86), hon prof 1998–2001, emeritus prof 2001–, fndn fell 2006; public orator 1992–95; visiting fell Adlai Stevenson Inst of Int Affrs Univ of Chicago 1972, visitor Centre for Environmental Studies 1971–72 (then memb Res Advsy Ctee), visiting prof Local Government Centre Univ of Warwick 1997–2000, visiting prof Dept of Social Policy and Administration, Centre for Civil Soc LSE 1999–2005; held European Union Chair of Social Policy Eötvös Lorant Univ Budapest 1998; memb Social Affrs Ctee Econ and Social Res Cncl 1982–86 (vice-chm 1984–86), scientific advsr Personal Servs DHSS 1986–91; chm: Birmingham Standing Conf for the Single Homeless 1983–86, Cncl for Voluntary Service Nat Assoc 1982–85, Nat Cncl for Vol Orgns Cmmn on Future of Vol Sector in England 1995–96 (report published as Meeting the Challenge of Change 1996), Birmingham City Pride 1999–2001, ESRC Centre for Charitable Giving and Philantropy 2007–09; memb Exec Ctee Nat Cncl for Voluntary Orgns 1982–85 and 1988–91; govr: Royal Inst of Public Admin 1981–88, Family Policy Studies Centre 1984–2001; memb Ctee W Midlands Low Pay Unit 1983–84; regular lectr for Civil Serv; external examiner: UCL, Univ of Glasgow, Brunel Univ, Southampton Univ, Univ of Edinburgh, Univ of Exeter, Univ of Bath, LSE, Univ of Nottingham, Loughborough Univ; FAcSS 2015; *Publications* incl: Colour and Citizenship (co-author, 1969), Colour and the British Electorate (ed, 1965), Policy Change in Government (ed, 1986), The Politics of Welfare (1987, 2 edn 1994), The Enterprise Culture and the Inner Cities (co-author, 1993), Contracting for Change (co-author, 1997), The Treasury and Social Policy (with Richard Parry, 2000), In Search of Civil Society (2001); contrib: The Yearbook of Social Policy in Britain (eds Catherine Jones and June Stevenson, 1984), Party Ideology in Britain (eds L J Tivey and A W Wright, 1989), Consuming Public Services (with A W Wright, 1990), The Costs of Welfare (jt ed and contrib, 1993), Transforming British Governments (ed with R A W Rhodes, 2000), The Student's Companion to Social Policy (eds A Erskine, P Alcock, M May, 2001, 2 edn 2004), Welfare and the State (jt ed, 2003), A Companion to Contemporary Britain (eds P Addison and H Jones, 2005, 2 edn 2007), Angleterre ou Albion, entre Fascination et Répulsion (ed G Millat, 2006), Beveridge and Voluntary Action in Britain and the Wider British World (ed and contrib, 2011); also author of numerous articles in various learned publications; *Style—* Prof Nicholas Deakin, CBE; ✉ Chedington, Lynmouth Road, London N2 9LR (☎ 020 8883 8659)

DEAKIN-STEPHENSON, Pippa Caroline; da of (Iver) Tim Deakin, of Botesdale, Suffolk, and (Elizabeth) Joyce, *née* Knuckey; *b* 30 October 1965, Reading, Berks; *Educ* The Manor House Great Durnford, Princess Helena Coll Temple Dinsley; *Career* hotelier; teacher Hill House prep sch 1982, nursery sch teacher 1983–86, governess and nursery sch teacher abroad 1986–91, fndr proprietor Pippa Popins (first children's nursery hotel) 1992–, childcare and educnl conslt 1997–, second Pippa Popins opened Oct 1999, third Pippa Popins opened Feb 2008; public speaker and lectr on childcare and education; nat and Euro schs interior design and mktg conslt Le Rosey Swizerland 2001–; England Tourist Bd England for Excellence award 1992, Which? Hotel Guide London Hotel of the Year 1994, Entrepreneur of the Year BAWE 1996, Most Original New Business for GB and Europe 1996, represented GB as the most original new business in the FCEM World Awards 1996; Focus on Food RSA advsr Children's Act 1989, govr Princess Helena Coll Herts 1993–96, tstee St Nicholas Montessori Centre London/Int 1996–2001; memb RSA Millennium Educnl Ctee for under 8s 1997–98, memb Br Assoc of Women Entrepreneurs; FRGS, Hon FRSA 1995; *Recreations* riding, skiing, sailing, the Arts, charity fund-raising and illustration for children; *Style—* Mrs Pippa Deakin-Stephenson; ✉ 52 New Kings Road, London SW6 4LS (☎ 020 7736 1712, e-mail pippa@homedon.co.uk)

DEALTRY, Prof (Thomas) Richard; s of George Raymond Dealtry (d 1966), and Edith, *née* Gardiner (d 1990); *b* 24 November 1936; *Educ* Cranfield Univ (MBA); *m* 17 Sept 1963 (m dis 1982), Pauline Sedgwick; 1 s (Roger Paul b 5 June 1968), 1 da (Claire Elizabeth b 1 Nov 1972); *Career* Nat Serv 1959–61, Capt RAEC 1960; under sec Scottish Office and Industrial Advsr for Scotland 1977–78, regnl dir and conslt industrial advsr Gulf Orgn for Industrial Consulting Arabian Gulf Territories Orgn 1978–82, business and mgmnt devpt conslt 1982–, md Intellectual Partnerships Consultancy Ltd 1996–; dir: BAA plc, Corp Mgmnt Progs Univ of Surrey 1999–; company broker regnl dir Diverco Ltd 1982–; fndr and co-ordinating ptnr EC Leonardo Da Vinci ECUANET multistate corp univ devpt projects 2005–07; fndr and chm Global Assoc of Corporate Univs and Enterprise Acads (G-ACUA); CEng, MIMechE, MCIM, Master Teacher; *Publications* Dynamic SWOT Analysis (1994), The Corporate University Blueprint (2000), A Chronology of Corporate University Thinking (2000), Quantum Management (2012); *Recreations* golf, rugby union, walking; *Style—* Prof Richard Dealtry; ✉ 43 Hunstanton Avenue, Harborne, Birmingham B17 8SX (☎ 0121 429 8995, mobile 07815 651830, e-mail richarddealtry@btconnect.com, website www.g-acua.org and www.corporateuniversity.org.uk)

DEAN, Andy; s of late John Dean, and late Esme Dean; *b* 15 July 1963, Congleton, Cheshire; *m* Stevie, *née* White; 1 s (Jagger John), 1 da (Mimi); *Career* songwriter, prodr and DJ; memb (with Ben Wolff, *qv*) The Boilerhouse Boys 1985–; written, produced and remixed for artists incl Paul Weller, Donna Summer, Gabrielle, Texas, Shaznay Lewis, Chaka Khan, The Stereophonics, Sarah McLachlan, A Tribe Called Quest, Pop Will Eat Itself and Joss Stone; worked in A&R (incl for Arista) and released albums on own label; involved in the discovery and signing of artists incl Bush, Lily Allen and Joss Stone; over 20 million credited sales to date, writer of numerous soundtracks for TV and cinema campaigns, numerous awards and nominations incl Grammy, Brits, Mobo and Ivor Novello; co-fndr (with Ben Wolff, *qv*) Society Supper Club, ambass Krug; *Style—* Andy Dean, Esq

DEAN, Rev Mark; s of Robert M Dean, and Barbara L Dean; *b* 1958; *Educ* Brighton Poly (BA), Goldsmiths Coll London (MA); *Career* artist; BT New Contemporaries Award 1993, awarded Imaginaria Cmmn ICA 1999, Paul Hamlyn Award for Artists 2009; ordained priest C of E 2011, chaplain Univ of Arts London 2013; *Solo Exhibitions* City Racing London 1996, Heavier Than Air with Mark Fairnington (Imperial War Museum) 1998, Dust (Laurent Delaye Gallery London) 1999, Casa de las Conchas (IMAGO Univ of Salamanca) 2000, Ascension (Laurent Delaye Gallery London) 2000, Video Works (Evolution Millennium Square Leeds) 2001, Video Screenings by Mark Dean (IKON Gallery Birmingham) 2001, Volker Diehl Gallery Berlin 2002, The Return of Jackie & Judy (+ Joey) (Laurent Delaye Gallery London) 2002, Disco Maquette (Sketch London) 2004, (Version) for Lightsilver (Beaconsfield London) 2005, Masochistic Opposite (Matthew Bown Gallery London) 2006, The Beginning of the End (Beaconsfield London) 2010, My Mum (V2-Sensitive) (Beaconsfield London) 2011, Christian Disco (Museum Boijmans van Beuningen Rotterdam) 2014; *Selected Group Exhibitions* A Simple Twist of Fate (Riverside Studios London) 1992, Mark Dean/Sera Furneaux/Richard Wright (City Racing London) 1992, BT New Contemporaries 93 (UK tour) 1993, Lost Property (W139 Amsterdam) 1995, I Beg to Differ (Milch London) 1996, Flag (Clink Wharf London) 1996, BONGO (Bricks & Kicks Vienna) 1997, Ne me quitte pas (GlassBox Paris) 1997, Instantaneous (Beaconsfield London) 1998, Host (Tramway Glasgow) 1998, Imaginaria (ICA London) 1999, Version_2000 (Centre pour l'Image Contemporaine/Attitudes Geneva) 2000, Realm of the Senses (Turku Art Museum) 2000, Mommy Dearest (Gimpel Fils London) 2000, Video Vibe (Gallery of the Br Sch in Rome) 2000, Black Box Recorder (Br Cncl Int Touring Show Museum Ludwig Cologne) 2000, Exit: Art and Cinema at the end of the century (Chisenhale Gallery London) 2000, VideoROM (Valencia Biennial) 2001, WR001 (WRO Centre Wroclaw) 2001, Invitation (Galerie Anton Weller Paris) 2001, Video in the City (HEDAH film festival Centrum voor Hedendaagse Kunst Maastricht) 2001, New Acquisitions: Video Works by Mark Dean & Mark Wallinger (Leeds City Art Gallery) 2001, Century City: Art and Culture in the Modern Metropolis (Tate Modern London) 2001, City Racing 1988–98: A Partial Account (ICA London) 2001, Game On (Barbican Gallery London) 2002, About Belief (South London Gallery) 2002, ThugLife (Smart Project Space Amsterdam) 2002, So Jackie! (Galerie P Brussells) 2002, Independence (South London Gallery) 2003, Love Story (Danielle Arnaud Gallery London) 2004, Planet B (Palais Thurn und Taxis and Magazin 4 Bregenz) 2004, Artfutures (Bloomberg Space London) 2005, Dance on Screen (The Place London) 2006, Eldorado (Musee d'Art Moderne Grand Duc Jean Luxembourg) 2006, Play Yourself (Gimpel Fils London) 2007, Forest (Temple Bar Gallery Dublin) 2007, Film on Film (Berwick Film & Media Arts Festival, Berwick Upon Tweed) 2007, The Enigma of Arrival (Leeds Art Gallery) 2009, A Fire In The Master's House Is Set (Chapter Cardiff) 2010, Vortex Revisions (Tate Britain) 2011, Let's Twist Again: Song and Sound in Artists' Film Installations (WOMAD Festival) 2012, Brittle Crazie Glass (Islington Mill Salford) 2012, After/Hours/Drop/Box (Andor Gallery London and Istanbul) 2013, On the (im)possibility of a pure praise poem (Man&Eve London) 2013, Nothing Compares 2 U (SIC Helsinki) 2013, Bad Copy (Cardiff Story Museum) 2014; *Work in Public Collections* Arts Cncl of England, Leeds City Art Gallery, Musée d'Art Moderne Grand-Duc Jean Luxembourg,

London Transport Museum, Espoo Museum of Modern Art Finland; *Style*— Rev Mark Dean; ✉ website www.tailbiter.com/art

DEAN, Peter Henry; CBE (1993); s of Alan Walduck Dean, and Gertrude, *née* Bürger; *b* 24 July 1939; *Educ* Rugby, Univ of London (LLB); *m* 31 July 1965, Linda Louise, da of Rev William Edward Keating; 1 da (Amanda b 1967); *Career* admitted slr 1962; RTZ Corporation plc: joined 1966, sec 1972–74, dir 1974–85; freelance business conslt 1985–96; dep chm Monopolies and Mergers Cmmn 1990–97 (memb 1982–97), Investment Ombudsman 1996–2001, chm Gaming Bd for GB 1998–2005, chm Gambling Cmmn 2005–07; dir G H Dean & Co Ltd 1999–2014 (chm 2002–14); non-exec dir: Associated British Ports Holdings plc 1980–2001, Liberty Life Assurance Co Ltd 1986–95, Seeboard plc 1993–96; chm: English Baroque Choir 1985–89 and 1999–2000, City Chamber Choir 2003–07; chm Cncl of Mgmnt Highgate Counselling Centre 1991–2002 (memb 1985–2002); memb Law Soc; *Recreations* music (especially choral singing), skiing, tennis; *Clubs* Ski Club of GB; *Style*— Peter Dean, Esq, CBE; ✉ 52 Lanchester Road, Highgate, London N6 4TA (☎ 020 8883 5417, mobile 07850 583576, e-mail phdean@blueyonder.co.uk)

DEAN, Raymond Frank; s of Mario Frank Dean (d 1957), and late Leah Marsh Shannon; *b* 29 July 1936; *Educ* Britannia HS Vancouver, Guildford Coll of Art; *m* 26 Oct 1971, Anne Elisabeth, *née* Young; *Career* engine room apprentice RCN 1953–56; draughtsman Alcan Canada 1956–59 (chief shop steward United Steelworkers of America); photographer 1961–; assignments incl: still photography for Oscar winning documentary Dylan Thomas by Jack Howells, first exhbn Wig & Pen Club, work published by Br Jl of Photography and Photography Magazine; theatre and ballet photography incl: The Royal Opera House, Nureyev, Fonteyn, Marcel Marceau, Le Coq Mime, Comedie Française; design work for Derek Jarman incl: The Devils, Jazz Calendar; jt fndr Job Magazine 1973–84; int industrial photographer; clients incl: Shell International, Elf Oil, Buitoni, Honeywell, Design Magazine, British Steel, Coutts Bank, Hill Samuel, Lloyd's, Alcan, Michelin, ICI; *Recreations* France and NY, eating, drinking, taking pictures; *Style*— Raymond Dean, Esq; ✉ e-mail macdean.zinphotog@btinternet.com, website Raymond-dean-photography.com

DEAN, Her Hon Judge Rosa Mary; *Career* called to the Bar 1993; dep district judge 2006, recorder 2009, circuit judge (South Eastern Circuit) 2011–; *Style*— Her Hon Judge Dean; ✉ Wood Green Crown Court, Woodall House, Lordship Lane, London N22 5LF

DEAN, Stafford Roderick; s of Eric Edwin Dean, and Vera Standish, *née* Bathurst; *b* 20 June 1937; *Educ* Epsom Coll, Royal Coll of Music (opera scholar); *m* 1, 1963, Carolyn Joan, *née* Lambourne; 4 s (Russell Edwin b 9 Feb 1966, Mark Roderick b 24 Aug 1967, Warwick Ashcroft b 19 March 1969, Ashley Jameson b 15 Aug 1974); m 2, 1981, Anne Elizabeth, *née* Howells; 1 s (Matthew Stafford Howells b 12 May 1981), 1 da (Laura Elizabeth Howells b 27 April 1983); *Career* bass; with: Glyndebourne Chorus and Opera For All 1962–64, Sadler's Wells Opera 1964–69, Covent Garden Opera 1969–2002 (guest singer); Sadler's Wells Opera debut as Zuniga in Carmen 1964, Royal Opera House debut as Masetto in Don Giovanni 1969, int debut as Leporello in Don Giovanni Stuttgart 1971, performed with all major Euro and American opera cos (especially in prodns of Mozart repertoire); *Performances* operatic roles incl: Figaro in Le Nozze di Figaro (Scottish Opera, Munich, Hamburg, Cologne, Bonn, Covent Garden, Chicago, Met NY and Vienna), Leporello in Don Giovanni (ENO, Scottish Opera, Stuttgart, Munich, Hamburg, Cologne, Bonn, San Francisco, Chicago, Covent Garden, Glyndebourne, Paris, Tokyo, Osaka, Prague and Berlin), Alfonso d'Este in Lucrezia Borgia (Covent Garden), Osmin in Die Entführung aus dem Serail (Scot Opera, Hamburg, Geneva and Madrid), Bottom in A Midsummer Night's Dream (Covent Garden), Rangoni in Boris Godunov (Covent Garden, Orange, Florence), Rocco in Fidelio (Scottish Opera, ENO and WNO), The Count in Jacobin (Scottish Opera), The King of Portugal in Ines de Castro (Scottish Opera), Waldner in Arabella, Dr Bartolo in Le Nozze di Figaro (Covent Garden, Paris), Don Alfonso in Cosi fan tutte (Madrid, Barcelona, Covent Garden, Glyndebourne, Athens Cologne and Zurich), Swallow in Peter Grimes (Covent Garden, San Francisco, Paris, Genoa, Nancy, Tours, Toulouse, Glyndebourne, Florence, Saito Kinen Fest Japan, recording with Haitink), Prof Bieganski in Sophie's Choice (Covent Garden), King Philip (WNO), Seneca (Scottish Opera, WNO), Sarastro (Scottish Opera, WNO); recital repertoire incl: Beethoven 9th Symphony and Missa Solemnis, Mozart, Verdi and Penderecki Requiems, Shostakovich 14th Symphony; *Style*— Stafford Dean, Esq; ✉ Kingswood House, Mark Way, Godalming, Surrey GU7 2BW (e-mail stafford.dean@sky.com)

DEAN, Tacita Charlotte; OBE (2013); *b* 1965, Canterbury, Kent; *Educ* Kent Coll Canterbury, Canterbury Coll of Art, Falmouth Sch of Art (BA), Slade Sch of Fine Art (Dip); *Career* artist; Greek govt scholar Supreme Sch of Fine Art Athens 1989–90, artist in residence Ecole Nationale des Beaux-Arts Bourges 1995, Screenwriters' Lab Sundance Inst 1997, artist in residence Wexner Center for the Arts Columbus 1999, scholarship Deutscher Akademischer Austauschdienst Berlin 2000–01; creator Berlin Project: Between the Ears (Radio 3) 2002; Barclays Young Artist Award 1999, shortlisted Turner Prize 1998; *Solo Exhibitions* incl: Marian Goodman Gallery NY 2000, Museum für Gegenwartskunst Basel 2000, Art Gallery of York Univ Toronto 2000, Banewl (Berkeley Art Museum Univ of Calif Berkeley) 2000, Museu d'Art Contemporani de Barcelona 2001, Tate Britain 2001, Hirshhorn Museum Washington 2001; *Group Exhibitions* incl: Landscape (ACC Galerie Weimar and int tour organised by Br Cncl) 2000, The Sea and the Sky (Beaver Coll Art Gallery Philadelphia and Royal Hibernian Gallery Dublin) 2000, L'ombra della ragione (La Galleria d'Arte Moderna Bologna) 2000, Intelligence: New British Art 2000 (Tate Britain) 2000, On the Edge of the Western World (Yerba Buena Center for the Arts San Francisco) 2000, Amateur/Liebhaber (Kunstmuseum, Kunsthallen & Hasselblad Gothenburg) 2000, Mixing Memory and Desire (Neues Kunstmuseum Luzerne) 2000, Artifice (Deste Fndn Museum and Br Cncl int tour) 2000, Somewhere Near Vada (Project Art Center Dublin) 2000, Another Place (Tramway Glasgow) 2000, media_city Seoul 2000 (Seoul Metropolitan Museum) 2000, Tout le Temps (La Biennale de Montréal) 2000, Vision and Reality (Louisiana Museum of Art) 2000, Arcadia (Nat Gallery of Canada Ottawa) 2001, Humid (Spike Island Bristol) 2001, Nothing: Exploring Invisibilities (Northern Gallery of Contemporary Art Sunderland) 2001, Double Vision (Galerie für Zeitgenoessische Kunst Leipzig) 2001, AUBETTE – The Longing for a(nother) place (Museum Dhont Dhaenens Belgium) 2001, Under/Above (Melbourne Festival Australia) 2001, Yokohama International Triennial of Contemporary Art (Yokohama Japan) 2001, Elusive Paradise: The Millenium Prize (National Gallery of Canada Ontario) 2001, At Sea (Tate Liverpool) 2001, A pause for breath (Frith Street Gallery London) 2001, Futureland2001.com (Städisches Museum Abteiberg Mönchengladbach Germany) 2001, Tacita Dean, Ingar Dragset, Michael Elmgreen, Maria Eichhorn, Daniel Richter (Preis der nationalgalerie für junge Kunst Hamburger Bahnhof Berlin) 2002, Arte allArte: Arte Architettura Paesaggio (Arte Continua Cultural Association San Gimignano Italy) 2002, Frequencies (Frith Street Gallery) 2003, The Moderns (Castello di Rivoli Museo dArt Contemporanea Rivoli-Turin Italy) 2003, Trauer (Zentrum für zeitgenössische Kunst der Österreichischen Galerie Belvedere, Vienna) 2003, Ritardi e Rivoluzioni and Utopia Station (The 50th Venice Biennale) 2003, Fotografie, Video, Mixed Media (organized by Daimler Chrysler Contemporary, Galerie der Stadt Sindelfingern Germany) 2003, Utopia Station Poster Project (Haus der Kunst Munich Germany) 2003, Image Stream (Wexner Center for the Arts Ohio) 2003, Fast Forward: Media Art from the Goetz Collection (ZKM Center for Art and Media Germany) 2003, Remind (Kunsthaus Bregenz Austria) 2003, Summer Show (Frith Street Gallery) 2004, Aligned (Frith Street Gallery) 2004, Premiers (MOMA Film Dept NY) 2004, TIME CLASH (Fundação de Serralves Porto Portugal) 2004, Colecção (Museu Serralves Portugal) 2004, Memory and Landscape (La Casa Encendida Madrid) 2004, Fade In, New Film and Video (Contemporary Arts Museum Houston Texas) 2004, Reflecting the Mirror (Marian Goodman Gallery NY) 2004, Universal Experience: Art, Life, and the Tourists Eye (Museum of Contemporary Art Chicago) 2005, Hayward Gallery London 2005, Truth Universally Acknowledged (Australian Centre for Contemporary Art Victoria) 2005, The Experience of Art (Italian Pavilion 51st Venice Biennial) 2005, New British Art (Vancouver Art Gallery) 2005, Likeness: Portraits of Artists by Other Artists (ICA Boston) 2005, Universal Experience: Art, Life and the Tourists Eye (MCA Chicago) 2005, Hayward Gallery London 2005, Daumenkino: The Flip Book Show (Kunsthalle Düsseldorf) 2005, An Aside, (curator, Fruitmarket Gallery Einburgh) 2005, Bidibidobidiboo (Fondazione Sandretto Re Rebaudengo, Turin) 2005, Elements of Nature (National Gallery of Canada) 2005, Soul (Museum Voor Moderne Kunst Oostende) 2005, Documentary Creations (Kunst Museum Lucerne Switzerland) 2005, Very Early Drawings (Luckman Gallery California State Univ) 2005, Arcadia (Univ Art Gallery Glenside Pennsylvania) 2005, Berlin Works (Tate St Ives) 2005, Resonance: The Final Exhibition at 59–60 Frith Street, London 2006, Print Run (Frith Street Gallery) 2006, Constructing New Berlin (Phoenix Art Museum and Bass Museum of Art Miami) 2006, Grey Flags (Sculpture Center Long Island City NY) 2006, Universal Experience: Art, Life, and the Tourists Eye (MART Roverto Italy) 2006, 4th Berlin Biennial for Contemporary Art Berlin 2006, Sydney Biennale 2006, On History (Fundacion Santander Central Hispano Madrid) 2007, Il Tempo del Postino Group Show (Manchester International Festival) 2007, Marking Time (York Art Gallery) 2007, Sea Pieces (Hamburger Kunshalle Germany) 2007, Scenes and Sequences (Aargauer Kunsthaus Germany) 2007, Waterlog (Castle Museum Norwich) 2007, Archive Fever (International Center of Photography NY) 2008, The Cinema Effect: Illusion, Reality and the Moving Image (Hirshhorn Museum and Sculpture Garden Washington DC) 2008, Tales of Time and Space (Folkestone Triennial) 2008, Order. Desire. Light. (Irish Museum of Modern Art Dublin) 2008, PerformA (NY) 2008, Utopia (Museu Berardo Lisbon) 2008, Photoespana Festival Madrid 2008, Porzadki Urojone so ist es und Andres (Muzeum Sztuki Poland) 2008, Mark Wallinger Curates The Russian Linesman (Hayward Gallery) 2009, The Quick and the Dead (Walker Art Center Minneapolis) 2009, The Times of a Place (CDAN Spain) Sonic Youth etc: Sensational Fix (Kunsthalle Düsseldorf, Museum of Malmö Sweden) 2009, Altermodern (Tate Triennial Tate Britain) 2009, Pequeña historia de la fotografía (CGAC Spain) 2009, Santiago de Compostela 2009, A mancha humana / the human stain (CGAC Spain) 2009, aus/gezeichnet/zeichnen (Akademie der Künste Germany) 2009, elles@centrepompidou (Centre Pompidou Paris) 2009, Il Tempo del Postino (Theater Basel Switzerland) 2009, Paisagens Oblicas Exposition (Museu Municipal de Faro Portugal) 2009, As Long As It Lasts (Marian Goodman Gallery NY) 2009, Moby Dick (CCA Wattis Institute for Contemporary Arts, San Francisco) 2009, After the Volcano (Frith Street Gallery) 2010, The Cinema Effect: Illusion, Reality and the Moving Image (Hirshhorn Museum and Sculpture Garden) 2010, Festival dAutomne, Paris, elles@centrepompidou (Centre Pompidou) 2010, Production Site: The Artists Studio Inside-Out (Museum of Contemporary Art Chicago) 2010, En presence (Centre Européen dActions Artistiques Contemporaines Strasbourg) 2010, Haunted: Contemporary Photography/ Video/ Performance (Guggenheim NY) 2010, Les Promesses du passé (Centre Pompidou) France 2010, PhotoEspaña Festival (Teatro Fernán Gómez Arts Center Madrid) MAN (Museo DArte Della Provincia Di Nuoro Sardinia, La Regenta Arts Centre, Las Palmas de Gran Canarias) 2010, ATLAS. How to Carry the World on Ones Back? (Zentrum für Kunst und Medientechnologie Karlsruhe Germany) 2011, Neue Realitäten. Von Warhol bis Havekost: Fotografie im Medium der Druckgrafik (Kupferstichkabinett Berlin) 2011, BLOCKBUSTER: Cinema for Exhibitions (Museo de Arte Contemporaneo de Monterrey Mexico) 2011, Staging the Archive (MACE Portugal) 2011, The Art of Deceleration, Motion and Rest in Modern Art (Kunstmuseum Wolfsburg Germany, Hamburger Kunsthalle Germany) 2011, The Cinema Effect: Illusion, Reality and the Moving Image (La Caixa Barcelona Ostalgia, New Museum NY) Drawing 2011 (Biennial Fundraiser The Drawing Room London) 2011, The Smithson Effect (Utah Museum of Fine Arts) 2011, Project Europa: Imagining the (Im)Possible (Miriam and Ira D Wallach Art Gallery Columbia Univ NY) 2011, Dance with Camera (SMoCA Arizona) 2011, Twombly and Poussin: Arcadian Painters (Dulwich Picture Gallery London) 2011, First Act (Museo Tamayo Mexico City) 2012, Motion Capture: Drawing and the Moving Image (Lewis Glucksman Gallery Cork) 2012, Gravity and Disgrace Ep. 2 (CGAC) 2012, Malerei in Fotografie – Strategien der Aneignung (Städel Museum Frankfurt, Documenta Kassel) 2012, Time out of Mind (Irish Museum of Modern Art) 2012, In the Spirit of Walser (Donald Young Gallery Chicago) 2012, Klang und Stille Sammlung Goetz im Haus der Kunst (Haus der Kunst Munich) 2012, The Artists Postcard Show (Spike Island Bristol) 2012, Lugares en pérdida (Centro Huarte de Arte Contemporáneo) 2012, fotoGRAFISK (Fotografisk Center, Copenhagen) 2012, Beyond Memory (Museum on the Seam Jerusalem) 2012, Unfinished Journeys (Museum of Contemporary Art Oslo) 2012, Tacita Dean, William Kentridge (Galerie Marian Goodman Paris) 2012, Revolution vs. Revolution (Beirut Art Center) 2012, Mirages d'Orient, grenades et figures de barbarie/ Chassé-croisé en Méditerranée (La Collection Lambert Avignon) 2012–13, The Way of the Shovel: Art as Archaeology (Museum of Contemporary Art Chicago) 2013, Looking at the View (Tate Britain) 2013, Besser scheitern (Hamburger Kunsthalle Germany) 2013, Limage Papillon (MUDAM Musee dArt Moderne Luxembourg) 2013, Paisaje. Revision de un genero (Museo del Palacio de Bellas Artes Mexico City) 2013, Ulysse(s) Lautre mer (Fonds Regional dArt Contemporain Bretagne France) 2013, Il Palazzo Enciclopedico (55th Venice Biennale) 2013, Tacita Dean Workshop (Foundation Botin Spain) 2013, Mirages d'Orient, grenades et figures de barbarie/ Chassé-croisé en Méditerranée (La Collection Lambert en Avignon) 2013, Unattained Landscape (CCA Kitakyushu Japan) 2013, Ruin Lust (Tate Britain) 2014, The Eye on Time: Works from Adrastus Collection (Museo de Arte de Sonora Mexico) 2014, Ship to Shore: Art and the Lure of the Sea (John Hansard Gallery Southampton) 2014, You Imagine What You Desire (19th Biennale of Sydney) 2014, The Dying of the Light: Film as Medium and Metaphor (Massachusetts Museum of Contemporary Art) 2014; *Publications* Teignmouth Electron (1999), Floh (2001) Tacita Dean: Seven Books (2003), Tacita Dean: Berlin Works (2005), Tacita Dean (2006), Tacita Dean: Die Regimentstochter (2006), Tacita Dean: Analogue (2006), Tacita Dean: Film Works with Merce Cunningham (2009), Tacita Dean (introduction by Juliana Engberg, 2009), Tacita Dean: Film (2011), Tacita Dean: De Mar en Mar (2013), Tacita Dean: Michael Hamburger (2013), Tacita Dean: JG, Key Stroke (collaboration with Will Self, 2013), Tacita Dean: c/o Jolyon Special Edition (2013), Tacita Dean: Hans Ulrich Obrist, The Conversation Series (2013); *Style*— Ms Tacita Dean, OBE; ✉ c/o Frith Street Gallery, 17–18 Golden Square, London W1F 9JJ (☎ 020 7494 1550, fax 020 7287 3733, e-mail info@frithstreetgallery.com)

DEAN, Timothy Nicholas; s of Geoffrey Dean, of Penzance, Cornwall, and Hilda, *née* Floyd; *b* 23 April 1956; *Educ* Dr Challoner's GS, Guildhall Sch of Music and Drama (ATCL), Univ of Reading (BA), Royal Coll of Music (ARCM); *m* 1981, Ruth Mary, da of Dr Peter Reid Duncan; 3 s (Jonathan Andrew b 26 Sept 1983, Thomas Carey b 28 Dec 1986, Duncan Matthew b 26 Dec 1992); *Career* head of music/chorus master Kent Opera 1983–90, asst music dir D'Oyly Carte Opera Co 1990–91, music dir The Opera Co Tunbridge Wells 1991–94, head of opera RSAMD 1994–, artistic dir British Youth Opera 2002–07 (music dir 1987–2001), chorus dir Royal Scottish Nat Orchestra 2006–; conductor London Bach Soc 1988–90; conducting debuts: ENO 1991, Scottish Opera 1991; festival appearances incl: City of London, Bath, Spitalfields, Aldeburgh, Covent Garden, Stour, Cheltenham, Brighton, Canterbury; conductor: Queen Elizabeth Hall, Purcell Room, Sadler's Wells, Theatre Royal Drury Lane, Royal Opera House, St John's Smith Square, Wigmore Hall, St Martin-in-the-Fields, St James's Palace, Chequers, 10 Downing St; FRSA, fell Royal Conservatoire of Scotland; *Recreations* walking, reading, theatre, racquet sports; *Clubs* Bearsden Tennis (second team capt); *Style—* Timothy Dean, Esq; ✉ Braeval, 4 Ellergreen Road, Bearsden, Glasgow G61 2RJ (☎ 0141 942 8121); Royal Scottish Academy of Music and Drama, 100 Renfrew Street, Glasgow G2 3BD (☎ 0141 270 8318, fax 0141 270 8352, e-mail t.dean@rsamd.ac.uk); British Youth Opera, c/o South Bank University, 103 Borough Road, London SE1 0AA (☎ 020 7815 6090/1/2/3, fax 020 7815 6094)

DEAN OF THORNTON-LE-FYLDE, Baroness (Life Peer UK 1993), of Eccles in the County of Greater Manchester; Brenda Dean; PC (1998); da of Hugh Dean, of Thornton, Lancs; *b* 29 April 1943; *Educ* St Andrews Sch Eccles, Stretford GS; *m* 30 April 1988, Keith Desmond McDowall, CBE; *Career* admin sec Manchester Branch SOGAT 1959–71 (asst branch sec 1971, sec 1976), gen sec SOGAT 1985–91 (pres 1983–85), dep gen sec GPMU 1991–92; chm Ind Ctee for the Supervision of Standards of Telephone Information Servs 1993–99; non-exec Bd memb Univ Coll Hosps London 1993–98; memb: Women's Nat Cmmn (co-chm 1975–78), NEDC 1985–92, BBC Gen Advsy Cncl 1985–89, TUC Gen Cncl 1985–92, TUC Econ Ctee 1987–92, Cncl Assoc of Business Sponsorship of the Arts 1989–95, Cncl City Univ 1991–95, Advsy Ctee Carnegie 3rd Age Enquiry, Press Complaints Cmmn 1993–98, Broadcasting Complaints Cmmn 1993–94, Armed Forces Pay Review Body 1993–94 (chm 1999–2005), LSE Governing Body 1994–98, Cncl Open Univ 1995–97, Dearing Ctee 1996–97, Regulated Bd Places for People 2013–, Cncl Univ of Nottingham 2013–, Places for People Gp Bd 2015–, Business Oversight Bd Law Soc 2015–; govr Ditchley Fndn 1992–; non-exec dir: Inveresk plc 1993–97, Chamberlain Phipps plc 1994–96, Care First plc (formerly Takare plc) 1995–98, Assured British Meat 1997–2001, Sr Salaries Review Body 1999–2005, Gen Insurance Standards Cncl 1999–2005, Dawson Holdings 2004–11; partnership dir Nat Air Traffic Servs (NATS) 2006–; non-exec chm Empiric Student Property plc 2014–; pres Coll of Occupational Therapists 1995–2005; chm: Housing Corporation 1997–2003, Covent Garden Market Authy 2005–13, Advsy Bd Runways UK 2013–; House of Lords: jr spokesman on employment 1994–96, jr spokesman on culture 1996–97, Lab whip 1995–97; memb: Ctee on reform of House of Lords 1999, House of Lords Appointments Cmmn 2000–10, House of Lords Constitution Ctee 2014–; tstee: Pension Scheme of Inveresk plc 1994–97, Prince's Youth Business Tst 1994–2000, Industry & Parliament Tst 1997–2009; Hon MA Univ of Salford 1986, Hon BA City Univ 1993, Hon MA South Bank Univ 1995, Hon LLD Univ of North London 1996, Hon LLD De Montfort Univ 1998, Hon MA Univ of Nottingham 2002, Hon LLD Univ of Warwick 2010; hon fell Univ of Central Lancashire 1991; FRSA; *Recreations* family, cooking, theatre; *Clubs* Reform, Royal Cornwall Yacht; *Style—* The Rt Hon Baroness Dean of Thornton-le-Fylde, PC; ✉ House of Lords, London SW1A 0PW

DEANE, Michael; s of Ted Deane, and Ellen Deane (d 1998); *b* 19 March 1961; *m* Kate, *née* Smith; 1 s (Marco Chokdee b March 2000); *Career* chef prop: Restaurant Michael Deane, Deane's Brasserie, Deane's Deli; *Awards* Northern Ireland Chef of the Year 1993, 1 Michelin Star 1997–2011, 3 AA Rosettes 1997–2004, Restaurant of the Year Jameson Guide 2000, Chef of the Year Jameson Guide 2001, AA Restaurant of the Year 2001, Craft Guild of Chefs UK Restaurant Chef of the Year 2002, 2 Stars Jameson Guide to Ireland; *Style—* Michael Deane, Esq; ✉ Restaurant Michael Deane, 38–40 Howard Street, Belfast BT1 6PD (☎ 028 9033 1134, fax 028 9056 0001)

DEAR, Alan Ferguson; s of Frank McKenzie Rae Dear, and Kathleen Ferguson Dear, *née* Ferguson; *b* 16 January 1965, Forfar, Scotland; *Educ* Forfar Acad, Royal Scottish Acad of Music and Drama (BA), UC Cardiff (Post Grad Dip Theatre); *Career* dir Sherman Youth Project Sherman Theatre Cardiff 1985–87, dir Dundee City Festival 1987–89, arts offr City of Westminster 1989–91, dir Roadmender Arts Centre Roadmender Tst Northampton 1991–92, head of educn and community WNO Cardiff 1992–97, chief exec Royal Coll of Organists 1997–2005; tstee Hackney Music Devpt Tst 1998–2002, advsr: Bird Coll 2005–07, NoFit State Circus 2006–08, Centre for Creative Writing Wales 2008–09; head of performing arts and sport Dundee Coll 2009–10, dir Gardyne Theatre Dundee 2010–; prodr Jackie the Musical 2015; *Recreations* theatre, travel, the visual arts, singing; *Style—* Alan Dear, Esq; ✉ 81 Gray Street, Broughty Ferry, Dundee DD5 2BP (e-mail findalandear@gmail.com)

DEAR, Baron (Life Peer UK 2006), of Willersey in the County of Gloucestershire; Sir Geoffrey James Dear; kt (1997), QPM (1982), DL (1985); s of Cecil William Dear, and Violet Mildred, *née* Mackney; *b* 20 September 1937; *Educ* Fletton GS, UCL (LLB); *m* 1, 1958, Judith Ann (d 1996), da of J W Stocker (d 1972), of Peterborough; 2 da (Catherine b 1961, Fiona b 1966), 1 s (Simon b 1963); m 2, 1998, Alison Jean Martin; *Career* joined Peterborough Combined Police after cadet serv 1956, various posts rising to supt Mid Anglia Constabulary 1970–72, asst chief constable Nottinghamshire Constabulary 1972, dep asst cmmnr Met Police 1980–81, asst cmmr Met Police 1981–85, chief constable West Midlands Police 1985–90, HM inspr of constabulary 1990–97; non-exec chm: Skyguard Technologies Ltd 2001–10, Image Metrics plc 2001–03, Assoc for Business Crime Partnerships Ltd (formerly Action Against Business Crime) 2004–12, Key Forensic Services Ltd 2005–11, Omniperception Ltd 2005–12, Blue Star Capital plc 2009–; non-exec dir: Reliance Security 1997–2005, Reliance Secure Task Management 2001–05; Vice Lord-Lt Worcs 1998–2002; Queen's Commendation for Bravery 1979; hon bencher Gray's Inn 2008; fell UCL 1990; FRSA 1989; *Recreations* field sports, rugby football, fell walking, music, reading, gardening; *Clubs* East India, Special Forces; *Style—* The Lord Dear, QPM, DL

DEAR, Jeremy; s of John Dear, of Bruges, Belgium, and Jan Dear; *b* 6 December 1966; *Educ* Br Sch Brussels, Coventry Poly (BA), Univ of Wales Cardiff (Dip Journalism); *m* 16 Oct 1999, Paula, *née* Jolly; *Career* former Midlands ed Big Issue; NUJ: former nat organiser Newspapers and Agencies, pres 1997–98, gen sec 2001–; memb: Gen Cncl TUC 2002–, NCTJ, Int Fedn of Journalists (IFJ) European Labour Rights Expert Gp; *Style—* Jeremy Dear, Esq

DEARDEN, Dr Andrew Richard; s of Philip Dearden (d 2000), and Wendy Saville, *née* Protheroe; *b* 7 November 1962, Wales; *Educ* Laverton HS Aust, Church Coll of NZ, Tonyrefail Comp Sch Porth, Welsh Nat Coll of Med (MB, BCh); *m* 24 Aug 1985, Ann, *née* Evans; 3 da (Eleanor b 25 March 1988, Melissa b 8 Nov 1990, Lois b 26 March 1995); *Career* princ GP Cardiff practice 1994–; chm Welsh Assoc of GP Trainees 1991–93, chm GP Ctee Wales 2002– (memb 1996–, dep chm 1999–2002), memb Bro Taf Local Med Ctee 1994–, memb UK GP Ctee 1997–, exec memb Cardiff Local Health Gp 1999–2003, chm BMA Ctee on Community Care 2000–04, chm Pensions Ctee BMA 2004–; asst registrar of marriages 1987–2000; DCCH (Dip in Community Child Health) 1992, DGM (Dip in Geriatric Med) 1992, DFFP 1994; MRCGP 1993, FRSA 2004, fell BMA 2006; *Publications* Successful Negotiation in the New Contract (2004), The Insider's Guide to the New GMS Contract (2004), The A-Z Reference Book of the New GMS Contract (2005), The Enhanced Service Handbook (2006); author author of articles in med jls; *Recreations* science fiction, eating out, collecting ancient Egyptian amulets and antiquities, owned classic motor car 1999–2004; *Style—* Dr Andrew Dearden; ✉ 116 Newport Road, Cardiff CF24 1YT (☎ 02920 494537, fax 02920 498086)

DEARDEN, Dr (Norman) Mark; s of Norman Gerald Dearden, of Leeds, and Mary Isobel Emily, *née* Mosby; *b* 30 June 1953; *Educ* Lord William's GS, Univ of Leeds (BSc, MB ChB); *m* 6 Sept 1986, Margaret Ruth, da of Eric Burkinshaw; 2 s (Paul b 1988, Richard b 1989); *Career* jr doctor Leeds 1977–81, lectr in anaesthetics Univ of Leeds 1981–84, conslt neuro anaesthetist and pt/t sr lectr in anaesthetics Edinburgh 1985–92, conslt anaesthetist and clinical sr lectr in anaesthesia Leeds 1992–; contrib to: Lancet, BMJ, Br Jl of Anaesthesia, Br Jl of Hospital Medicine, Jl of Neurosurgery, Jl of Neurosurgical Anaesthesiology, Anaesthesia, Current Opinion in Anaesthesiology, Current Anaesthesia and Critical Care, Jl of Physiology, Br Jl of Intensive Care, Jl of Neurotrauma, Behavioural Brain Res, Clinical and Laboratory Haematology, Care of the Critically Ill, Jl of Anatomy, Jl of Neurology Neurosurgery and Psychiatry; Br rep Intensive Care Gp of The World Fedn of Neurology; memb: Yorks Soc of Anaesthetists 1980, Intensive Care Soc 1983, Scottish Soc of Anaesthetists 1985, E of Scotland Soc of Anaesthetists 1985, World Fedn of Neurologists 1988, Euro Intensive Care Soc 1989, Exec Euro Brain Injury Consortium (EBIC, also sec), Neuroanaesthesia Soc of GB and Ireland 2000; *Books* Brain Protection (1983), The Clinical Use of Hypnotic Drugs in Head Injury (contrib), Advances in Brain Resuscitation (1991), Management of Brain Edema in Head Injury (contrib), Réanimation et Neurologie (contrib, 1995), Neurochemical Monitoring in the Intensive Care Unit (contrib, 1995), Management of Cerebral Oedema and Raised Intracranial Pressure – Principles and Practice of Critical Care (contrib,1997), Diagnosis of Raised Intracranial Pressure, Medical Management of Head Injury, Oxford Textbook of Critical Care (contrib, 1999); *Recreations* horticulture, DIY, swimming, fishing; *Style—* Dr Mark Dearden; ✉ Nan Tan House, Dixon Lane, Wortley, Leeds LS12 4AD; Department of Anaesthesia, Leeds General Infirmary, Great George Street, Leeds LS1 3EX (☎ 0113 243 2799, fax 0113 231 6821, mobile 07885 211717, e-mail nmarkdearden@aol.com)

DEARDEN, Michael Bailey (Mike); s of John Skelton Dearden (d 1962), and Doris Dearden (d 1969); *b* 15 September 1942; *Educ* Manchester Grammar, Merton Coll Oxford (MA); *m* 1, 16 July 1964, Monica Tatiana (d 2002), da of Gordon Hewlett Johnson; 1 s (Jonathan Michael b 31 Jan 1965), 1 da (Kathryn Tatiana b 2 Feb 1969); m 2, 25 June 2015, Mary Bartholomew (*née* Slater); *Career* Castrol Ltd: mktg mangr 1980–84, chief exec Castrol Malaysia 1984–86, gen mangr New Ventures Castrol Ltd 1986–88, regnl dir Castrol Ltd 1988–91; chief exec Foseco International 1991–95; Burmah Castrol plc: chemicals dir (main bd) 1995–98, lubricants dir 1998–2000; chm: The Brick Business 2003–04, Minova International Ltd 2003–06, Mondo Minerals Int 2007–11; non-exec dir: Johnson Mathey plc 1999–2008, Travis Perkins plc 2000–08, The Weir Gp 2003–12; Liveryman Worshipful Co of Coachmakers and Coach Harness Makers; ACIM 1965, MIMC 1975; *Recreations* gardening, bridge, rugby, opera, scuba diving, shooting, wine; *Clubs* Oxford and Cambridge; *Style—* Mike Dearden, Esq

DEARDEN, Neville; s of Maj Issac Samuel Dearden (d 1979), and Lilian Anne, *née* Claxton (d 1983); *b* 1 March 1940; *Educ* Rowlinson Tech Sch Sheffield, King Alfred Coll Winchester, Univ of Southampton (Student of the Year); *m* 1, 4 April 1963, Jean Rosemary, da of Walter Francis Garratt, of Sheffield; 1 da (Karen b 1966), 2 s (Adrian b 1968, David b 1970); m 2, 3 May 1980, Eileen Bernadette, da of Dr William John Sheehan; 4 s (Michael b 1981, Patrick b 1984, Ciaran b 1987, Liam b 1990); *Career* head of Science Dept Lafford Sch Lincs 1961–67; md: W Garratt & Son Ltd 1972–78, M & H Fabrications Ltd 1972–77; chief exec S W Fabrications Ltd 1980–84, md Sheffield Brick Group plc 1982–87, chief exec Pan Computer Systems Ltd 1982–85; chm: Parker Winder and Achurch Ltd 1983–85, C H Wood Security Ltd 1983, Mylnhurst Limited 1996–; Smith Widdowson Eadem Ltd: chm 1983, md 1986; md F G Machin Ltd 1983; chief exec: JCL Engineering Services Ltd, Crompton Engineering (Lancs) Ltd 1989, Doncaster C of C and Enterprise 1997–2007, Doncaster Business Link Ltd 1997–; Comyn Ching Ltd: gp manufacturing dir 1990, gp sales and mktg dir 1995; independent dir Marshall Bros (Bury) Ltd 1993; dir: SRC Advanced Systems Ltd 1996–, Yorks and Humber C of C 1997–, South Yorks Small Business Serv, DBIC Ltd, Donbac Ltd, Newcastle Sports Injury Clinic Ltd; business devpt dir Company of Cutlers in Hallamshire 2008–10; sr conslt Quantum Enterprise Development 1996, internal strategic conslt Keeble Hawson Solicitors 2008–10, vol horticulture, viticulture and bee-keeping advsr Whirlow Hall Farm Tst Ltd 2010–; BBKA Bee-Keeping Award, BBKA Certificate for 50 years of bee-keeping; FIMgt, FIIM, FICM, FinstD, DMS; *Recreations* practical craft work, horticulture, computing, bee-keeping; *Style—* Neville Dearden, Esq; ✉ home ☎ 0114 236 4386, fax 0114 235 4382, e-mail nevilledearden@outlook.com

DEARLOVE, Sir Richard Billing; KCMG (2001), OBE (1984); *b* 23 January 1945; *Educ* Monkton Combe Sch, Kent Sch CT, Queens' Coll Cambridge (MA); *m* 1968, Rosalind, *née* McKenzie; 2 s, 1 da; *Career* joined FCO 1966; served: Nairobi 1968–71, FCO 1971–73, 1976–80 and 1984–87, Prague 1973–76, Paris 1980–84, UKMIS Geneva 1987–91, Washington 1991–93; Secret Intelligence Service: dir personnel and admin 1993–94, dir ops 1994–98, asst chief 1998–99, chief 1999–2004; master Pembroke Coll Cambridge 2004–15, dep vice-chllr Univ of Cambridge 2005–10, chm of tstees Cambridge Union Soc 2007–15, chm of tstees Univ of London 2014–; chm Ascot Underwriting 2006–; memb Advsy Bd American Int Gp 2005–10, advsr to Monitor Gp 2005–11, dir Kosmos Energy 2013–; tstee Kent Sch CT 2001–; hon fell Queens' Coll Cambridge 2004, emeritus fell Pembroke Coll Cambridge 2016; Hon LLD Univ of Exeter 2011, hon doctorate Nat Intelligence Univ Washington DC 2016; *Style—* Sir Richard Dearlove, KCMG, OBE; ✉ Pembroke College, Cambridge CB2 1RF

DEARY, Prof Ian J; s of Hugh McCulloch Deary, of Carluke, Lanarkshire, and Isobelle Ferguson, *née* Higgins; *b* 17 May 1954, Carluke, Lanarkshire; *Educ* Hamilton Acad, David Dale Coll Glasgow (ONC), Glasgow Coll of Technol (HNC), Univ of Edinburgh (BSc, MB ChB, PhD); *m* 26 June 1978, Ann Marie, *née* Barclay; 2 da (Elayne b 1 April 1979, Joanna Frances Halla b 5 Aug 1982), 1 s (Matthew John Hugh b 5 May 1988); *Career* house physician, house surgn, locum sr house surgn and SHO in psychiatry Edinburgh and London 1983–85, registrar in psychiatry Royal Edinburgh Hosp 1989–90; Univ of Edinburgh: lectr A 1985–90, sr lectr 1990–92, reader 1992–95, prof of differential psychology (personal chair) 1995–, dir MRC Centre for Cognitive Ageing and Cognitive Epidemiology 2008–; fndr memb Int Soc for Intelligence Research (memb Advsy Ctee); Int Soc for the Study of Individual Differences: memb, memb Bd of Dirs 1993–2003, pres 1999–2001, past pres 2001–03; Chllr's Award Univ of Edinburgh 2003, Royal Soc-Wolfson Research Merit Award 2003–07, Margaret McLellan Award Tenovus Scotland 2006, European Assoc of Personality Psychology Distinguished European Personality Psychologist Award 2010, Lifetime Achievement Award Int Soc for Intelligence Research 2014, James McKeen Cattell Fell Award Assoc for Psychological Science 2015, Distinguished Contribution Award Int Soc for the Study of Individual Differences 2015; FRCPE 1996, FRSE 2003, FBA 2003, FMedSci 2007, FRCPsych 2008 (MRCPsych 1991); *Publications* Foundations of Personality (jt ed, 1993), Personality Psychology in Europe, volume 4 (jt ed, 1993), Personality Traits (jtly, 1998, 3 edn 2009), Personality Psychology in Europe, volume 7 (jt ed, 1999), Looking Down on Human Intelligence: From Psychometrics to the Brain (2000, Br Psychology Soc Book Award 2002), Intelligence: A Very Short Introduction (2001), A Lifetime of Intelligence (jtly, 2009); also author of over 600 book chapters and refereed jl articles; *Recreations* cycling, saxophone, lyric writing, English romantic composers, late Victorian novelists, Motherwell FC; *Style—* Prof Ian J Deary; ✉ Department of Psychology, University of Edinburgh, 7 George Square, Edinburgh EH8 9JZ (☎ 0131 650 3452, fax 0131 651 1771, e-mail i.deary@ed.ac.uk)

DEAS, Roger Stewart; s of George Stewart (d 1983), of Motherwell, and Winifred Mary, *née* Ogden (d 1996); *b* 1 August 1943; *Educ* The HS of Glasgow, Univ of Glasgow (BSc); *m* 27 June 1970, Carole, da of Percy Woodward, of Nottingham; 2 da (Angela Elizabeth b 1972, Wendy Jane b 1974); *Career* fin dir: Brown Bros Ltd 1974–81, Currys Group plc 1981–85, Heron Corporation plc 1985–86; nat fin ptnr Coopers & Lybrand 1986–95; md Bridewell Group plc 1995–; FCMA 1986 (ACMA 1974); *Recreations* sailing; *Clubs* Royal Motor Yacht; *Style—* Roger Deas, Esq; ✉ Sunset House, 10 Chaddesley Glen, Canford Cliffs, Poole, Dorset BH13 7PF (✆ 01202 709394); The Bridewell Group plc, Bridewell House, Reading, Berkshire RG1 1JG (✆ 0118 960 7550)

DEATHRIDGE, Prof John William; s of Leslie Deathridge (d 1984), and Iris, *née* Jones (d 2011); *b* 21 October 1944, Birmingham; *Educ* King Edward's Sch Birmingham, Lincoln Coll Oxford (MA, DPhil); *m* 15 Dec 1985, Victoria, *née* Cooper; 1 da (Julia b 13 Feb 1992); *Career* lectr in music Univ of Cambridge 1983–96 (reader 1995), dir of musical studies King's Coll Cambridge (fell 1983–96), King Edward VII prof of music KCL 1996–2013 (head Dept of Music 2005–09, now emeritus King Edward VII prof of music); memb: RMA 1971 (pres 2005–08), American Musicological Soc 1982; FRCO; Wagner's Rienzi (1977), New Grove Wagner (1984), Wagner Handbook (ed, 1992), Wagner Beyond Good and Evil (2008); *Recreations* fitness; *Clubs* Athenaeum; *Style—* Prof John Deathridge; ✉ King's College London, Strand, London WC2R 2LS

DEAYTON, (Gordon) Angus; s of Roger Davall Deayton, of Caterham, Surrey, and Susan Agnes, *née* Weir; *b* 6 January 1956; *Educ* Caterham Sch Surrey, New Coll Oxford (BA); *Career* writer and broadcaster; with Oxford Revue at Edinburgh Festival 1978 and 1979, memb Hee Bee Gee Bees pop parody gp 1979–85, writer and performer Radio Active (BBC Radio 4) 1980–87 (various awards incl from BPG and Sony); writer/performer: Brunch (Capital Radio) 1985–88, Uncyclopaedia of Rock (Capital Radio) 1986–87 (Monaco Radio award 1986), Rowan Atkinson Stage Show (UK, Aust and NY) 1986–90, Alexei Sayle's Stuff (BBC2) 1988–91, One Foot in the Grave (BBC1) 1989–2000, Waterloo Road (BBC 1) 2013–15; writer/presenter: KYTV (BBC2) 1989–93 (Grand Prix and Silver Rose of Montreux 1992), TV Hell (BBC2) 1992, Have I Got News For You 1990–2002, In Search of Happiness 1995, End of the Year Show 1995, 1996, 1997, 1998 and 2000, The Lying Game 1997, Before They Were Famous 1997–2005, The Temptation Game 1998, History of Alternative Comedy 1999, Not Another Awards Show 1999, Millenium Sketch Show 1999, Not Another Gameshow, News Bulletin, Eurovision Song Contest 2002, Posh'n'Becks: The Reign in Spain 2003–05, Nighty Night 2003–05; presenter: BAFTA Awards 1996 and 2001, Hell's Kitchen 2004–07, Bognor or Bust 2004, New Year's Dishonours List 2005, Heartless 2005, Comic Relief Does University Challenge 2003 and 2005, Absolute Power 2005–07, Stick to What You Know 2005, Help Your Self 2006, Only Fools on Horses 2006, Would I Lie to You? 2007 and 2008, Comedy Sketchbook 2008, British Comedy Awards 2008, Pete'n Dud – The Lost Sketches 2010, It's Your Round (Radio 4) 2011 and 2012, Pramface 2012–13, World's Most Dangerous Roads 2013, World Cup Epic Fails 2014, Christmas Epic Fails 2014; appeared on Drive (ITV) 2016; *Film* appearances incl: Elizabeth 1998, Swinging with the Finkels 2011, The Great European Disaster Movie 2015; other awards incl: Newcomer of the Year TV Comedy Awards 1991, Best TV Performance in a non-acting role BPG Awards 1992, New Talent of the Year TV and Radio Industry Club Awards 1992, BBC TV Personality of the Year TV and Radio Industry Club Awards 1995; *Books* Radio Active Times (1986), The Uncyclopaedia of Rock (1987), In Search of Happiness (1995); *Recreations* soccer (former Crystal Palace FC triallist), tennis, skiing; *Clubs* Groucho, Soho House, Home House, Garrick; *Style—* Angus Deayton; ✉ c/o Independent Talent, Oxford House, 76 Oxford Street, London W1D 1BS (✆ 020 7636 6565, e-mail nickforgacs@icmlondon.co.uk)

DEBEN, Baron (Life Peer UK 2010), of Winston in the County of Suffolk; Rt Hon John Selwyn Gummer; PC (1985); s of Rev Canon Selwyn Gummer (d 1999), and (Margaret) Sybille Vera, *née* Mason (d 1993); bro of Baron Chadlington, *qv*; *b* 26 November 1939; *Educ* King's Sch Rochester, Selwyn Coll Cambridge; *m* 1977, Penelope Jane, yr da of John P Gardner; 2 s, 2 da; *Career* md EP Group of Companies 1975–80; chm: Selwyn Sancroft International 1976–81, Siemssen Hunter Ltd 1980 (dir 1973), Sancroft International 1997–, Valpak Ltd 1998–, Veolia Water UK (formerly Vivendi UK) 2004–13; non-exec dir: Kidde 2000–05, Sovereign Reversions 2004–10, Sistema-Hals 2007–09, Castle Tst 2011–; MP (Cons): Lewisham W 1970–74, Eye Suffolk 1979–83, Suffolk Coastal 1983–2010; vice-chm Cons Pty 1972–74, PPS to Min of Agric 1972, govt whip 1981–83, under sec of state Employment 1983, chm Cons Pty 1983–85, min of state Employment 1983–84, paymaster gen 1984–85, min of state Agric Fisheries and Food 1985–88, min for Local Govt 1988–89, min Agric Fisheries and Food 1989–93, sec of state for the Environment 1993–97; memb Parly Ecclesiastical Ctee 1993–2010; chm: Marine Stewardship Cncl 1998–2005, International Cmmn on Sustainable Consumption 1999–2005, Assoc of Professional Fin Advsrs 2003–, Quality of Life Cmmn 2007–08, Ctee on Climate Change 2012–; memb Gen Synod C of E 1978–92, guardian of the Shrine of Our Lady of Walsingham 1983–2002; *Books* To Church with Enthusiasm (1969), The Permissive Society (1971), The Christian Calendar (1973), Faith in Politics (1987), Christianity and Conservatism (1990); *Recreations* reading, gardening, Victorian buildings; *Style—* The Rt Hon the Lord Deben; ✉ 46 Queen Anne's Gate, London SW1H 9AP (✆ 020 7960 7900)

DECIES, 7 Baron (I 1812); Marcus Hugh Tristam de la Poer Beresford; only s of 6 Baron Decies (d 1992), and his 2 w, Diana, *née* Turner Cain; *b* 5 August 1948; *Educ* St Columba's Coll, Univ of Dublin (MLitt); *m* 1, 1970 (m dis 1974), Sarah Jane, only da of Col Basil Gunnell; m 2, 1981, Edel Jeanette, da of late Vincent Ambrose Hendron, of Dublin; 2 da (Hon Louisa Katherine de la Poer b 23 Oct 1984, Hon Jessica Laragh Marion de la Poer b 16 Nov 1996), 2 s (Hon Robert Marcus Duncan de la Poer b 14 July 1988, Hon David George Morley Hugh de la Poer b 4 May 1991); *Heir* s, Hon Robert Beresford; *Career* lawyer and historian; FCIArb; *Clubs* MCC, Kildare St and Univ (Dublin); *Style—* The Rt Hon Lord Decies; ✉ Straffan Lodge, Straffan, Co Kildare, Ireland

DEDMAN, Dr Paul Anthony; *b* 5 September 1955; *Educ* Shenfield HS, Brentwood Sch, Univ of Cardiff (MB BCh); *Career* sr house offr/registrar in psychiatry Royal Free and Gt Ormond St Hosps London 1981–85, vocational trainee in gen practice N London 1986–89, consult psychiatrist Melbourne Aust 1989–91, sr registrar Academic Unit Keele Univ 1991–93, conslt psychiatrist United Bristol Healthcare Tst and hon sr clinical lectr Univ of Bristol 1993–97, conslt psychiatrist Priory Hosp Bristol 1997–; author of articles in medical jls on a variety of topics including eating disorders, community-based psychiatry and cognitive behaviour therapy; MRCGP 1987, memb BMA 1991, memb Br Assoc of Behavioural and Cognitive Psychotherapists 1991, FRCPsych 2005 (MRCPsych 1985); *Style—* Dr Paul Dedman; ✉ Litfield House, 1 Litfield Place, Clifton, Bristol BS8 3LS (✆ 0117 317 1461, e-mail dedmansec@gmail.com); Priory Hospital Bristol, Heath House Lane, Bristol BS16 1EQ (✆ 0117 952 5255)

DEDRING, Isabel; *Educ* Harvard Univ (JD, BA); *m* 21 May 2005, Roland Sinker; 2 s (Jacob b 21 July 2007, Conrad b 8 July 2010); *Career* Ernst and Young 1993–95, Mckinsey 1998–2002, COS to Tport Cmmr TfL 2003–04, dir Policy Unit TfL 2004–08, environmental advsr to Mayor of London GLA 2008–10, dep mayor for transport GLA 2010–; memb NY Bar, memb Bd IFS; *Style—* Ms Isabel Dedring; ✉ Greater London Authority, City Hall, The Queen's Walk, More London, London SE1 2AA

DEE, Michael James Damian; s of Kenneth William Dee (d 1977), of Bath, and Dorothy Josephine, *née* Whittern-Carter (d 1999); *b* 12 June 1946; *Educ* Douai Coll, Univ of Edinburgh (BSc); *m* m 1, 28 April 1973 (m dis 1997), Pamela Sarah, da of Cecil George Moore, of Jersey; 5 da (Samantha b 1974, Joanna b 1976, Nicola b 1977, Belinda b 1980, Emily b 1991); m 2, 16 June 2007 (m dis 2010), Jane Elizabeth, da of Thomas John Baker, of Droitwich, Worcs; *Career* dir Damian Investment Tst 1972–73, chm Europlan Financial Services 1976–2012 (merged with Volaw Gp Hldgs Ltd 2012), chm Europlan Continuation Ltd 1984–; dir Volaw Gp Hldgs Ltd 2012–14; FInstD; *Recreations* sailing, golf, motor racing, shooting; *Clubs* Royal Channel Islands Yacht, La Moye Golf; *Style—* Michael Dee, Esq; ✉ Le Fromentel, La Grande Route de la Cote, St Clement, Jersey JE2 6SD (✆ 01534 858135, fax 01534 858134, e-mail michael@chateaudevialer.com)

DEECH, Baroness (Life Peer UK 2005), of Cumnor in the County of Oxfordshire; Dame Ruth Lynn Deech; DBE (2002), Hon QC (2013); *née* Fraenkel; da of Josef Asher Fraenkel (d 1987), of London, and Dora, *née* Rosenfeld (d 1989); *b* 29 April 1943; *Educ* Christ's Hosp, St Anne's Coll Oxford (BA), Brandeis Univ USA (Fulbright award, MA); *m* 23 July 1967, Dr John Stewart Deech, s of Max Deech; 1 da (Hon Sarah Rosalind Phyllis b 13 Nov 1974); *Career* legal asst Law Cmmn 1966–67, called to the Bar 1967, research asst to Leslie Scarman (later Rt Hon Lord Scarman) 1967–68, asst prof of law Univ of Windsor Canada 1968–70, fell and tutor in law St Anne's Coll Oxford 1970–91, princ St Anne's Coll Oxford 1991–2004; visiting prof Osgoode Hall Law Sch York Univ Canada 1978; Univ of Oxford: sr proctor 1985–86, memb Hebdomadal Cncl 1986–2000, chm Admissions Ctee 1993–97 and 2000–03, pro-vice-chllr 2001–04; visiting lectr Faculty of Law Univ of Cape Town 1994, Gresham prof of law 2008–11; memb Ctee of Inquiry into Equal Opportunities on the Bar Vocational Course 1993–94, memb Exec Cncl of Int Soc of Family Law, chm Human Fertilisation and Embryology Authy 1994–2002, chair Nat Working Gp on Women in Medicine 2008–09, chair Bar Standards Bd 2009–15; ind adjudicator for HE 2004–08; chm House of Lords Ctee on Equality and Disability 2015–16; govr: Carmel Coll Wallingford 1980–90, Oxford Centre for Hebrew and Jewish Studies 1994–2000, UCS 1997–2002; chm Stuart Young Awards 1988–, Rhodes tstee 1996–2006; Liveryman Worshipful Co of Drapers 2003; bencher Inner Temple 1996; Hon LLD: Univ of Strathclyde 2003, Richmond the American Int Univ 2006, Ben Gurion Univ 2012; hon fell Soc for Advanced Legal Studies 1997–; FRSM 2001; *Books* From IVF to Immortality (2007); *Recreations* after dinner speaking, music, entertaining; *Clubs* RSM; *Style—* The Lady Deech, DBE; ✉ House of Lords, London SW1A 0PW (✆ 020 7219 3000, e-mail deechr@parliament.uk)

DEEDES, Hon Jeremy Wyndham; s of Baron Deedes, MC, PC, DL (Life Peer, d 2007), and Evelyn Hilary, *née* Branfoot (d 2004); *b* 24 November 1943; *Educ* Eton; *m* 1973, Anna Rosemary, da of late Maj Elwin Gray; 2 s (George William b 28 Feb 1976, Henry Julius b 8 June 1978); *Career* reporter: Kent & Sussex Courier 1963–66, Daily Sketch 1966–69; dep ed Daily Express 1976–79, managing ed Evening Standard 1979–85 (ed Londoner's Diary 1970–76), managing ed Today 1985–86; Daily and Sunday Telegraph: exec ed 1986–92, editorial dir 1992–96; Telegraph Group: md 1996–2003, chief exec 2004, vice-chm 2004; exec chm The Sportsman 2006, non-exec chm Pelham PR 2007–09 (currently dir Pelham Bell Pottinger), memb Advsy Bd Bell Pottinger Private; chm Newspaper Publishers Assoc 1998; dir Warwick Racecourse 2002–14, memb Horserace Totalisator Bd 1992–98; *Recreations* cricket, racing, golf, cabinet making; *Clubs* Boodle's, Royal Cape Golf, Sunningdale Golf, Huntercombe Golf, MCC; *Style—* The Hon Jeremy Deedes; ✉ Hamilton House, Compton, Newbury, Berkshire RG16 0QJ (✆ 01635 578 695); Pelham Bell Pottinger, 5th Floor, Holborn Gate, 330 High Holborn, London WC1V 7QD

DEELEY, Catherine Elizabeth (Cat); *b* 23 October 1976, Birmingham; *Educ* Sutton Coldfield GS for Girls, Bishop Vesey's GS Sixth Form Birmingham; *Career* television presenter, actress, prodr and former model; presenter: MTV UK 1997, SMTV Live (ITV) 1998–2002, CD:UK (ITV) 1998–2005, So You Think You Can Dance (Fox) 2006– and (BBC) 2010–, American Idol (ITV2) 2007; entertainment reporter ABC News; *Style—* Ms Cat Deeley; ✉ c/o Curtis Brown Group Ltd, Haymarket House, 5th Floor, 28–29 Haymarket, London SW1Y 4SP

DEELEY, Her Hon Patricia Anne; da of Walter Edgar Jones (d 1983), and Ellen Elizabeth, *née* Goddard (d 1973); *b* 30 September 1944; *Educ* St Joseph's Convent Kenilworth, Univ of Bristol (LLB); *m* 9 July 1966, Peter Anthony William Deeley, *qv*, s of William Deeley; 3 da (Eleanor Elizabeth Jude b 28 Sept 1976, Anna Shahida Jude b 10 Aug 1982, Rosemary Lucy Jude b 27 Nov 1984); *Career* called to the Bar Lincoln's Inn 1970, head of chambers 1992–98, recorder of the Crown Ct 1993–98, circuit judge (Midland Circuit) 1998–2015, ret; memb Ct Univ of Warwick; *Recreations* food, friends, flowers; *Style—* Her Hon Patricia Deeley; ✉ Midland Circuit Office, The Priory Courts, 33 Bull Street, Birmingham B4 6DW

DEELEY, Peter Anthony William; s of George William Deeley (d 1985), of Warks, and Bridie Deeley, of Balsall Common, nr Coventry; *b* 30 August 1942; *Educ* Ratcliffe Coll, Coventry Poly; *m* 9 July 1966, Patricia Ann, *qv* (Her Hon Judge Deeley), da of Walter Edgar Jones (d 1983), of Coventry; 3 da (Eleanor Elizabeth Jude b 28 Sept 1976, Anna Shahida Jude b 10 Aug 1982, Rosemary Lucy Jude b 27 Nov 1984); *Career* dep md GW Deeley Ltd 1968 (joined 1958); chm Deeley Group Ltd 1985; pres Builder Employers' Confedn (Coventry) 1970–; vice-chm: Coventry Hosps Tst (chm 1992–), Coventry Tech Coll (chm 1991–95); Freeman City of Coventry 1963; memb Inst of Bldg; *Recreations* golf, walking; *Style—* Peter Deeley, Esq; ✉ Pemberley,Longbourn Farm, Pittern Hill, Kineton, Warwickshire CV35 0JF (✆ 01926 632755); Deeley Group Ltd, George House, Herald Avenue, Coventry, Warwickshire CV5 6UB (✆ 024 7671 8718)

DEEM, Prof Rosemary; OBE (2013); da of Lesley George Deem (d 1986), of Liff, Dundee, and Peggy, *née* Stoyle, of Liff, Dundee (d 2008); *b* 18 January 1949, Plymouth, Devon; *Educ* Queen Eleanor's GS Dunstable, Univ of Leicester (BA, MPhil), Open Univ (PhD); *m* 12 March 1985, Prof Kevin Joseph Brehony (d 2013), s of Eddie Joseph Brehony (d 1984), of Birmingham; *Career* tutorial asst in sociology Univ of Leicester 1972–73; temp lectr in sociology: Loughborough Univ 1973–74, Univ of York 1974–75; lectr in sociology N Staffs Poly 1975–79; Open Univ: lectr in sociology of educn 1980–87, sr lectr in sociology of educn 1987–91, sub dean (research) Faculty of Educn 1986–91; Lancaster Univ: prof of educnl research 1991–2000, dean of social sciences 1994–97, founding dir Grad Sch 1998–2000; prof of educn Univ of Bristol 2001–09; Royal Holloway Univ of London: dean Faculty of History and Social Sciences 2009–11, vice-princ (educn) 2011–; dir ESCalate (UK Learning and Teaching Support Network Educn Subject Centre) 2001–04; chair: Research Ctee Univs Cncl on the Educn of Teachers 1991–93, Pubns Ctee Soc for Research in HE 2003–07; memb: HE Funding Bodies Research Assessment Panel for Educn 1996, 2001 and 2008, Grants Bd ESRC 1999–2003; elected memb Cncl BERA 1993–97; jt managing ed The Sociological Review 2001–05, co-ed Higher Education 2013–; chair Br Sociological Assoc 1986–87 and 1994–96 (treas 1985–86), chair R&D Ctee 2007–09, vice-chair Soc for Res into HE 2007–09, exec memb UK Cncl for Graduate Educn 2012–; *Publications* Women and Schooling (1978), Schooling for Women's Work (ed, 1980), Co-education Reconsidered (ed, 1984), All Work and No Play (1986), Work, Unemployment and Leisure (1988), Active Citizenship and the Governing of Schools (with K J Brehony and S J Heath, 1995), Knowledge, Higher Education and the New Managerialism (with M Reed and S Hillyard, 2007); also author of over 110 academic articles and chapters in social science jls and books; *Recreations* hill walking, cycling, photography, caravanning, reading, theatre, visiting art galleries, travel; *Style—* Prof Rosemary Deem, OBE; ✉ Principal's Office, Royal Holloway, University of London, Egham, Surrey TW20 0EX (✆ 01784 443944, e-mail r.deem@rhul.ac.uk, PA Christine Brown tel 01784 276171, e-mail christine.brown@rhul.ac.uk)

DEENY, Hon Mr Justice; Sir Donnell Justin Patrick Deeny; kt (2005), DL (Belfast, 2003), JP (Co Down); *b* 25 April 1950; *Educ* Clongowes Wood Coll, TCD, Queen's Univ Belfast (BL); *m* 1998, Alison Jane, *née* Scott; 2 da (Grace b 1999, Elessa b 2006), 1 s (Alexander b 2001), 2 da from previous m (Maeve, Rebecca); *Career* called to the Bar NI 1974, bencher Middle Temple and NI, QC (NI) 1989, SC Repub of Ireland 1996, judge of the High Court of Justice in NI 2004–; chm: Opera NI 1988–92, Arts Cncl of NI 1993–98 (memb 1991–98); pres Ulster Architectural Heritage Soc 2006–; pro-chllr Univ of Dublin 2014–; tstee Ulster Museum 1983–85; chm UK Spoliation Panel; memb (Alliance) Belfast City Cncl 1981–85; High Sheriff Belfast 1983; Hon MRTPI; *Recreations* books, the arts, skiing; *Style*— The Hon Mr Justice Deeny, DL, JP; ✉ c/o Royal Courts of Justice, Chichester Street, Belfast BT1 3JF

DEER, John; *Career* Rolls-Royce plc 1960–74; Renishaw plc: md 1974–89, currently dep chm; *Style*— John Deer, Esq; ✉ Renishaw plc, New Mills, Wotton-Under-Edge, Gloucestershire GL12 8JR

DEERY, Dr Alastair Robin Stewart; s of late Sgt-Major Michael John Stewart Deery, MM, and Isabella Stout, *née* Murray; *b* 5 October 1953; *Educ* Alleynes Sch, Univ of London (BSc, MB BS); *m* 1, 24 Dec 1981 (m dis 1993), Dr Clare Constantine Davey, da of Dr Charles James Constantine Davey; m 2, April 1994, Dr Valerie Thomas, da of David Thomas; 2 s (Andrew, Michael), 1 da (Charlotte); *Career* house offr UCH London 1979, SHO Manchester 1980, registrar in histopathology Western Infirmary Glasgow 1981–83, sr registrar in histopathology and cytopathology Charing Cross Hosp London 1984–86, conslt, hon sr lectr in histopathology and cytopathology and dir cytopathology unit Royal Free Hosp London 1986– (chm of pathology 1994–96, unit trg dir 1996–); med lab head London Regnl QAT; memb: Br Soc of Clinical Cytology, Pathological Soc of UK, London Regnl Cncl, NHSCSP, RCPath 2001–; chm LNC 2000–; FRCPath 1996; *Recreations* collecting writing instruments, skiing; *Style*— Dr Alastair Deery

DEFRIES, Jeffrey; *b* 14 February 1948; *Educ* Univ of Birmingham (BCom); *m* Dr Elizabeth Defries; 2 s; *Career* asst to fin sec Imperial Coll of Science and Technol London 1972–73, asst sec Inst of Devpt Studies Univ of Sussex 1974–76, sec Inst of Cancer Research 1982–88 (dep sec 1977–82), asst dir The Science Museum 1988–98, dep dean and sec London Business Sch 1998–2001, sec and head of corp affrs NHSU 2002–05, latterly chief exec Careers Research and Advsy Centre (CRAC); sr advr European Fndn for Mgmnt Devpt; lectr Civil Service Coll; creator icould; leading conference facilitator; various voluntary positions; CPFA; *Clubs* RSA, Nat Lib; *Style*— Jeffrey Defries, Esq

DeGALE, James Frederick; MBE (2009); s of Leroy Frederick DeGale, and Diane DeGale; *b* 3 February 1986, Hammersmith, London; *Career* professional boxer; memb Dale Youth Amateur Boxing Club; amateur career: Gold medal Cwlth Youth Games Bendigo 2004, Gold medal middleweight ABA Championships March and Dec 2005, Bronze medal middleweight Cwlth Games Melbourne 2006, Gold medal middleweight European Olympic qualifying tournament Pescara 2008, Gold medal middleweight Olympic Games Beijing 2008; turned professional 2008, 12 wins to date, Supermiddleweight Br Champion 2010, reigning European Champion; *Style*— James DeGale, Esq, MBE; ✉ website www.jamesdegale.com

DEGHY, Julian; s of Guy Deghy (d 1992), of London, and Mari, *née* Hooper; *b* 16 October 1960; *Educ* St Clement Danes GS for Boys; *Career* freelance photographic asst 1980–82, photographic asst to James Cotier, *qv* 1983–86, freelance photographer 1987–; various exhbns incl Assoc of Photographers Awards exhbns 1993 and 1999; solo exhbn of the art bronze foundry Museum of London 1999, photographic exhbn of Elizabeth Frink's work River and Rowing Museum Henley 2000–01; memb Assoc of Photographers 1987; *Recreations* racing, theatre, music, travel, food and wine; *Clubs* Chelsea Arts, Groucho; *Style*— Julian Deghy; ✉ 69A Greenside Road, London W12 9JQ (☎ 07702 974767, website www.deghy.com)

DEHN, Thomas Clark Bruce; s of Harold Bruce Dehn, and Jean Margaret Henderson, *née* Ewing; *b* 6 March 1949; *Educ* Harrow, RAF Coll Cranwell, Bart's Med Coll London (MB BS, MS, LRCP); *m* 15 Sept 1984, (Dorothea) Lorraine, da of Gilbert Maurice Baird, of Dunbartonshire; 2 da (Henrietta b 1986, Emily b 1988); *Career* gen surgn; conslt gen surgn Royal Berks Hosp Reading, clinical lectr in surgery Nuffield Dept of Surgery John Radcliffe Hosp Oxford 1984–88, lectr in surgery Bart's Med Coll London 1980–84; conslt surgn Royal Berks Hosp Reading 1990–; examiner in surgery Faculty of Dental Surgeons RCS 1990–95, examiner Intercollegiate Bd in Gen Surgery 2001–; chm Oxford Deanery Gen Surgery Higher Surgical Trg Ctee 1995–2001, chm Oesophageal Section Br Soc of Gastroenterology 2006– (sec 2000–05); memb: Hosp Jr Staff Ctee 1987–88, Cncl Section of Surgery RSM 1993–96, RCS Comparative Audit Serv Ctee 1992–98, MRC Working Pty on Oesophageal Cancer 1994–96, Grey Turner Surgical Club 1994–, Br Oesophageal Gp 1994–, Cncl Assoc of Surgeons of GB and I 2005–, Br Soc of Gastroenterologists, Cncl Assoc of Laparoscopic Surgns of GB and I; Freeman City of London, Liveryman and Steward Worshipful Co of Distillers; FRCS; *Publications* author of research publications on oesophageal cancer, surgery and physiology of hiatus hernia, and laparoscopic (key-hole) surgery; *Recreations* flying, rowing, shooting, sailing; *Style*— Thomas Dehn, Esq; ✉ Department of Surgery, Royal Berkshire Hospital, Reading, Berkshire RG1 5AN (☎ 0118 322 8623); Capio Hospital, Reading, Berkshire RG1 6UZ (☎ 0118 902 8012, website www.lapsurg.info)

DEIGHTON, Gary; s of Eric Deighton, and Joan Margaret, *née* Brittle; *b* 2 August 1961, Nottingham; *Educ* Glaisdale Sch Nottingham, Bilborough Coll Nottingham, Univ of Dundee (MA), Humberside Coll (PGCE), Univ of Nottingham (MA), Henley Coll (Dip), Br Assoc for Counselling and Psychotherapy (Dip); *m* 1 July 1989, Alison, *née* Davies; 1 s (Alexander Huw b 8 March 1998), 1 da (Anastasia Helen b 8 Aug 2000); *Career* teacher 1984–86, asst govr HM Prison Serv 1986–96, auditor HM Prison Serv 1995–97, govr HMP Swansea 1997–99, govr HMP Exeter 1999–2002, HM inspr of prisons 2002–05, govr HMP Pentonville 2005–07, head Professional Standards Unit Prison Serv 2007–;Queen's Golden Jubilee Medal 2002; *Recreations* the sea; *Style*— Gary Deighton, Esq; ✉ Corporate Security Group, HM Prison Service Headquarters, Cleland House, Page Street, London SW1P 4LN (☎ 020 7217 3000, e-mail gary.deighton01@hmps.gsi.gov.uk)

DEIGHTON, Jane Elizabeth; da of Herbert Stanley Deighton (d 1976), and Mary Elizabeth Anne, *née* Duncan; *b* 18 March 1952; *Educ* Univ of Sussex (BA), Coll of Law; *Career* admitted slr 1985; slr Seifert Sedley Williams 1983–90, ptnr Deighton Guedalla 1990–2012, ptnr Deighton Pierce Glynn 2012–; memb Law Soc; *Publications* Human Rights in Malawi (1992), Emergency Powers in Northern Ireland (1998); *Style*— Ms Jane Deighton; ✉ Deighton Pierce Glynn, 382 City Road, London EC1V 2QA (☎ 020 7407 0007, fax 020 7837 7473, e-mail jdeighton@dpglaw.co.uk)

DEIGHTON, Baron (Life Peer UK 2012), of Carshalton in the County of Surrey; Paul Clive Deighton; KBE (2013); *b* 18 January 1956, Carshalton, Surrey; *Educ* Wallington County GS, Trinity Coll Cambridge (BA); *m* Alison Zoë, *née* Klebanoff; 2 s (Daniel William b 13 Feb 1988, Thomas Benjamin b 20 June 1990); *Career* Goldman Sachs: London 1983–94, jt head of controllers NY 1994–96, ptnr and head of European operations, technology and fin 1996–2000, chief operating offr Europe 2000–05; ceo London Organising Ctee of the Games (LOCOG) 2005–12; commercial sec to HM Treasy 2013–15, chm Heathrow Airport (Hldgs) Ltd 2016–; non-exec dir: Holdingham Gp Ltd 2016–, Square Inc 2016–; *Style*— The Lord Deighton, KBE; ✉ House of Lords, London SW1A 0PW

DELANEY, Francis James Joseph (Frank); 5 s of Edward Joseph Delaney (d 1968), of Tipperary, Ireland, and Elizabeth Josephine, *née* O'Sullivan (d 1990); *b* 24 October 1942, Tipperary, Ireland; *Educ* Abbey Schs Tipperary, Rosse Coll Dublin; *m* 1, 1966 (m dis 1980), Eilish, *née* Kelliher; 3 s (Edward b 1968, Bryan b 1971, Owen b 1976); m 2, 1988 (m dis 1997), Susan, *née* Collier; m 3, 1999 (m dis 2000), Salley, *née* Vickers; m 4, 2002, Diane Meier; *Career* writer, broadcaster and journalist in news, current affrs and arts; work incl: RTE News Dublin, BBC N Ireland, BBC TV, BBC Radio 4 and BSkyB News; *Non-Fiction* James Joyce's Odyssey (1981), Betjeman Country (1983), The Celts (1986), A Walk in the Dark Ages (1988), Legends of the Celts (1989), A Walk to the Western Isles (1993), Simple Courage (2007); *Fiction* My Dark Rosaleen (novella, 1989), The Sins of the Mothers (1992), Telling the Pictures (1993), A Stranger in their Midst (1995), The Amethysts (1997), Desire and Pursuit (1998), Pearl (novel, 1999), At Ruby's (2001), Jim Hawkins and the Curse of Treasure Island (2002), Ireland, A Novel (2005), Tipperary (2008), Shannon (2009), Venetia Kelly's Traveling Show (2010), The Matchmaker of Kenmare (2011), Undead (e-book, 2011), The Last Storyteller (2012); *Clubs* Athenaeum, Chelsea Arts; *Style*— Frank Delaney, Esq; ✉ e-mail frankdelaney@frankdelaney.com, website www.frankdelaney.com; c/o Meier & Partners, 907 Broadway, New York, NY 10010, USA (☎ 001 212 460 5655, fax 001 212 460 5957)

D

DELANEY, Theo John Samuel; s of Barry John Samuel Delaney, of Hamilton Terrace, London, and Brenda Jean, *née* Darby; *b* 31 December 1965; *Educ* Shene Sch, Richmond Coll; *m* Sally Delaney *née* Leadbetter; 2 da (Daisy, Agnes); *Career* prodn runner John Clive & Co 1984–86, prodn asst Berkofsky Barrett Productions 1986–87, news ed Direction Magazine (Haymarket Publishing) 1988–89; film dir: Tony Kaye Films 1990–91 (film prodr 1989–90), Spots Film Services 1991–96, Tomboy Films 1996–2002, Hotspur and Argyle 2002–; ptnr and creative dir Watchable 2015–; *Awards* Bronze (NY Advtg Festival) 1990, Gold (Creative Circle Awards) 1990, Silver Lion (Int Advtg Festival Cannes) 1990 and 1991, work accepted for D&AD Annual 1992 and 1997, Best New Director (Saatchi and Saatchi New Directors Showcase/Int Advtg Festival Cannes) 1993; memb D&AD 1992; *Recreations* Tottenham Hotspur FC; *Clubs* Groucho; *Style*— Theo Delaney, Esq; ✉ e-mail theo@watchablefilms.com

DELANY, Oliver; OBE (1990); *b* 12 October 1949, Dublin, Ireland; *Educ* BA, MBA; *m* 17 Dec 1971, Dr Ros Delany; 1 s (Simon b 30 April 1976), 1 da (Helen b 31 Dec 1977); *Career* RAF 1969–1998 (ret as Air Cdre); bursar Clifton Coll Bristol 1998–2006, dir of central services Bar Cncl 2006–13, rotational post as acting ceo Bar Cncl 2011–13; dir QC Appts 2011–13; co-fndr Petoli Assoc 2015–; chair 1625 Ind People; treas and tstee Flying Sch for Disabled People, tstee Combat Stress; coach Warrior Programme; Master Coach, master and trainer of hypnotherapy; FCIPD, FCMI, FBIFM; *Recreations* road cycling, travel, theatre, gym; *Clubs* RAF; *Style*— Oliver Delany, Esq, OBE; ✉ Pendle House, 57A Church Road, Abbots Leigh, Bristol BS8 3QU (☎ e-mail odldelany@gmail.com)

DELBRIDGE, Richard; s of Tom Delbridge, and Vera, *née* Lancashire; *b* 21 May 1942, Ipswich; *Educ* LSE (BSc), Univ of Calif Berkeley (MBA); *m* 19 March 1966, Diana Genevra Rose, da of H W Bowers-Broadbent; 2 da (Roseanna b 1970, Cressida b 1982), 1 s (Mark b 1973); *Career* CA 1966; Arthur Andersen: articled clerk 1963–66, mgmnt conslt 1968–, ptnr 1974–76; md and gen mangr London office J P Morgan & Co Inc 1987–89 (int operations 1976–79, comptroller 1979–85, asst gen mangr 1985–87), gp fin dir Midland Bank plc 1989–92, gp fin dir HSBC Holdings plc (following takeover of Midland Bank) 1993–95, dir and chief fin offr Nat Westminster Bank plc 1996–2000; non-exec dir: Innogy plc 2000–2002, Egg plc 2000–2003, Tate & Lyle plc 2000–10 (sr non-exec dr 2003–10), Gallaher Gp plc 2001–07, Balfour Beatty plc 2002–05, Cazenove Group plc 2002–05, Fortis Gp 2004–09, JP Morgan Cazenove 2005–10, Standard Chartered plc 2010–13, UCL Hospitals Fndn Tst 2010–13; memb: Bd Securities Assoc 1988–89, Financial Reporting Review Panel 1999–2007; dir City Arts Tst 1997–2001, tstee Wordsworth Tst 2000–07, memb Cncl and treas Open Univ 2001–09; FCA 1972; *Recreations* hill walking, swimming, books; *Style*— Richard Delbridge, Esq

DELEVINGNE, Charles Hamar; s of (Edward) Dudley Delevingne (d 1974), and Hon Angela Margo Hamar, *née* Greenwood; *b* 25 June 1949; *Educ* Embley Park; *m* 18 June 1983, Pandora Anne, da of Sir Jocelyn Stevens, CVO, *qv*, of Testbourne, Hants; 3 da (Chloe b 1984, Poppy b 1986, Cara Jocelyn b 1992); *Career* chm Property Investment Co; *Recreations* shooting, fishing; *Clubs* Buck's; *Style*— Charles Delevingne, Esq; ✉ 95 Albert Bridge Road, London SW11 (☎ 071 585 0301); Testbourne Lodge, Hampshire (☎ 026 472 569); Kimbolton Lodge, Fulham Road, SW3 (☎ 071 589 1126)

DELLA SALA, Prof Sergio; *b* 23 September 1955; *Educ* Univ of Calif Berkeley (pre-med), Univ of Milan Medical Sch (MD, PhD); *Career* Univ of Milan: registrar in neurology 1980–84, conslt in neurology 1987–93, head of Neuropsychology Unit 1989–93; Univ of Aberdeen: prof of psychology 1994–2004, hon conslt in neurology; Univ of Edinburgh: prof of human cognitive neuroscience 2004–, hon conslt in neurology; *Style*— Prof Sergio Della Sala; ✉ Department of Psychology, University of Edinburgh, 7 George Square, Edinburgh EH8 9JZ (☎ 0131 651 3242, fax 0131 651 3230, e-mail sergio@ed.ac.uk)

DELLER, Jeremy; *b* 1966, London; *Educ* Courtauld Inst of Art London, Univ of Sussex (MA); *Career* artist, winter Turner Prize 2004; *Solo Exhibitions* incl: Centre 181 Gallery London 1993, The Search for Bez (Art Cologne London) 1994, Ten Day Weekend (The Arches Glasgow) 1995, The Uses of Literacy (Norwich Art Gallery) 1997, Art:Concept Paris 1998 and 2002, Unconvention (Centre for Visual Arts Cardiff) 1999, Intelligence (Tate Triennalle London) 2000, Low Gallery LA 2002, Memory Bucket (Art Pace San Antonio Texas) 2003, New Works 03.3 (Art Pace San Antonio Texas) 2003, Carnegie Museum Pittsburgh 2004; *Group Exhibitions* incl: The Love Show (Daniel Bucholz Gallery Cologne) 1993, Lost Paradise (The Kunstraum Vienna) 1994, Sex, Drugs and Rock and Roll (Phoenix Hotel San Francisco) 1995, The Butterfly Ball (Stringfellows Night Club London) 1995, Life/Live (Musee de Belem Portugal) 1997, Bring Your Own Walkman (W139 Amsterdam) 1997, Transfert: Fifth Swiss Exhibition of Sculpture (Bienne) 2000, Democracy! (RCA London) 2000, Protest and Survive (Whitechapel Gallery London) 2000, Pyramids of Mars (Barbican Centre London) 2001, Century City (Tate Modern London) 2001, City Racing (ICA London) 2001, Happy Outside (British Cncl Warsaw) 2002, Rock My World (Calif Coll of Arts and Crafts) 2002, This Is Us (music project, Bard Coll NY) 2003, We'll Meet You in the Lobby (Buyuk Londra Oteli Istanbul) 2003, Utopia Station (Venice Biennale) 2003, Micro/Macro: British Art 1996–2002 (Kunsthalle Mucsarknok Budapest) 2003, Shh!!! (V&A Museum London) 2004, This Much is Certain (RCA London) 2004, Britannia Works (Br Cncl show, Ileana Tounta Contemporary Art Centre Athens) 2004, Turner Prize (Tate Britian London) 2004; *Project Works* incl: Acid Brass (ongoing project and collaboration with the Williams Fairey Brass Band) 1997, Folk Archive (ongoing project with Alan Kane investigating UK folk and vernacular art) 2000, Battle of Orgreave (co-production Artangel, Orgreave South Yorkshire) 2001, After The Goldrush (guidebook and treasure hunt around California, cmmnd Wattis Inst San Fransisco) 2002, This is US (CD produced in assoc with the Centre for Curatorial Studies Red Hook NY) 2003; *Style*— Jeremy Deller; ✉ c/o The Modern Institute, Suite 6, Floor 1, 73 Robertson Street, Glasgow G2 8QD (☎ 0141 248 3711)

DELLOW, Jeffrey (Jeff); s of Ernest Dellow (d 1966), of Heworth, Co Durham, and Edith, *née* Greenwell; *b* 19 January 1949, Newcastle; *Educ* Bill Quay Sch, St Martin's Sch of Art, Maidstone Coll of Art, Slade Sch of Fine Art (Cheltenham Fellowship); *m* June 1976, Paula Jean Alison, da of Lt Col Roy Cleasby, MBE; 1 da (Bryony Grace b 27 Jan 1987); *Career* artist; lectr: Hull Coll of Art 1977–86, Roehampton Inst London 1978–80, NE London Poly 1978–86, Slade Sch of Fine Art (postgrad painters) 1980–82, Winchester Sch of Art 1982–86, Central Sch of Art 1982–84; head of painting and print lectr Hull of Coll of Art 1986–88, princ lectr in fine art Kingston Univ 1988–2013; visiting artist: RAF Brüggen 1974–75, Hull Coll of Art 1977, NE London Poly 1978, Roehampton Inst London 1978, Maidstone Coll of Art 1979, Slade Sch of Fine Art 1979, Manchester Poly Fine Art 1980, Norwich Sch of Art 1981, Winchester Sch of Art 1981; artis painter Art in Perpetuity Tst 1995–; work in collections incl: Arts Cncl of GB, Unilever, James Capel, Coopers & Lybrand, Arthur Andersen & Co, BASF UK, Grand Valley State Univ Michigan; Boise travelling scholarship, Arts Cncl of GB minor bursary, prizewinner Athena Art Awards Barbican 1988; *Solo Exhibitions* solo show New Paintings Castlefield Gallery 1987, Recent Paintings (Cafe Gallery London) 1995, paintings and works on paper Grand State Univ Michigan 1996, eff Dellow Recent Paintings (Standort Ausstellungshalle) 2000, Recent Small Paintings (Deli Art) 2001, Beyond Surface (APT Gallery) 2004; *Group Exhibitions* incl: John Moores 10 Liverpool 1976, Drawing in Action (Arts Cncl Touring Show) 1978–79, Open Attitudes (MOMA Oxford) 1979, Small Works by Younger Br Artists 1980, Small Works (Roehampton Inst) 1980, Sculpture and Painting from the Greenwich Studios (Woodlands Gallery Blackheath) 1981, Opening Show (Hull Artists Assoc) 1982, Small Works (Newcastle upon Tyne Poly Gallery) 1982, Marseille Art Present (Artis Gallery Marseille and Maison du Peuple Gardance) 1983, Whitechapel Open 1983–91, 100 Artists (The Showroom Gallery London) 1984, Drawings and Watercolours (Hull Coll of Art) 1984, Greenwich Festival Studio Open 1985–93, Summer in the City (Ikon Gallery Birmingham) 1985, Three Painters (Arteast Gallery collective) 1986, Three Abstract Painters (Todd Gallery) 1987, Art for Sale (Minories Gallery) 1988, Idylls (Todd Gallery Summer Show) 1989, Bath Art Fair 1989, John Moores 16 Liverpool 1989, Art 90 Islington Art Fair 1990, Todd Soho Gallery 1990, Olympia Art Fair 1990, Creative Assets (Harris Museum Preston) 1990, Works on Paper (Todd Gallery) 1990, Pachipamwe III (Nat Gallery of Zimbabwe Harare) 1990, Broadgate Art Week 1990, John Moores 17 (prizewinner) 1991, Whitechapel Studio Open 1992, Greenwich Studios Painting and Sculpture (Woodlands Gallery Blackheath) 1992, Leeds Poly Artists Symposium/Workshop 1992, Watercolour Curwen Gallery (Windmill St London), Sunday Times Singer & Friedlander Watercolour Competition (Mall Galleries London), Sans Frontiers (Waterman Art Centre) 1993, Delight (Manchester Metropolitan Univ) 1996, Delight (Stanley Picker Gallery Kingston Univ) 1997, Art in Perpetuity (Trust Studio Open Deptford) 1997, Cheltenham Fellows Tricentennial Exhbn Cheltenham 1997, Critical Faculty (Stanley Picker Gallery) 1998, Critical Faculty (Grand Valley State Univ Michigan) 1998, Forks and Hope (Sun and Doves Gallery London), Deptford X open studios at Art in Perpetuity Tst, Open Studios APT 2001, Open Studios Brockley Artists London 2002, Ten Days in Deptford Brockley Artists Woodlands Gallery London 2002, Open Studios APT On Show Art in Perpetuity Tst 2003, Nues aus den Ateliers de Kunstler Frankfurt 2003, London Gp Menhier (guest exhibitor), Present APT Gallery, Open Studios APT, Deptford X Open APT, thewalk gallery London Gp Jeff Dellow, Mark Ainsworth, Tricia Gillman, Marcelle Hanselaar, Deptford X Open, Open Studios APT 2005, Deptford X Open, Open Studios APT 2007, London Group at Deutsche Bank 2007, Deptford X Open selected by Matthew Collings 2007, META 2008, Anglia Univ Cambridge 2008, Mini META Beardsmore Gallery London 2009, Mix APT Gallery London 2010, Uncaught Hares 1 Painting and Sculpture at Greenwich Studios 1974–1994 (Stephen Lawrence Gallery London) 2011, Uncaught Hares 2 (Clifford Chance) 2011, Uncaught Hares 3 (Stephen Lawrence Gallery London) 2011, Artists Open House Dulwich Festival 2011, Invaluable (APT Gallery London and Open Studios APT London) 2011, Affordable Art Fair Battersea London Bischa Gallery 2011, Art Toronto Int Art Fair 2011, Affordable Art Fair Singapore 2011 and 2012, Perfect Nude (Wimbledon Sch of Art) 2012, Pheonix Gallery Exeter 2012, Charlie Smith Gallery London 2012, Dulwich Open House Dulwich Festival 2012, Brockley Open Studios 2012, APT Open Studios 2012, Delineation APT Gallery 2012, invited artist Summer Show Royal Acad 2012, Affordable Art Fair Stockholm 2012, Islington Art Fair BDC with Bischa Gallery 2013, Brussels Art Fair 2013, Hong Kong Art Fair 2013, NY Art Fair 2013, Clarendon Rise Studio Gallery 2013, APT Open Studios 2014, Switch Pulchri Studios Gallery The Hague 2014, Drawing to Making Part 1 (Clarendon Studios Gallery) 2014, Colour and Otherness (Grace Teshima Gallery Paris) 2014, Sale of Work (Berloni Gallery London) 2015, Sol-space (APT) 2015, Conference of the Birds (Iklektic London) 2015, Twentieth (APT) 2015, Stockwell Depot 1967–79 (Stephen Lawrence Gallery) 2015; *Books* Jeff Dellow Recent Paintings 2000; *Recreations* playing mandolin and violin music, walking, motorcycling; *Style*— Jeff Dellow, Esq; ✉ Art in Perpetuity Trust, Harold Wharf, 6 Creekside, Deptford, London SE8 4SA (e-mail jeffdellow@talktalk.net, websites www.jeffdellow.com and https://jeffdellow.wordpress.com)

DELPY, Prof David Thomas; CBE (2014); *b* 11 August 1948, Newcastle upon Tyne; *Educ* Brunel Univ (BSc), Univ of London (DSc); *m* Margaret Elizabeth; *Career* Dept of Med Physics and Bioengineering UCL: sr physicist 1976–82, princ physicist 1982–86, sr lectr 1986–91, Hamamatsu prof of med photonics 1991–2007, head of dept 1992–99, emeritus prof of biomedical optics 2014–; vice-provost UCL 1999–2007; ceo Engrg and Physical Sciences Research Cncl 2007–14, chm Defence Scientific Advsy Cncl 2014–; FRS; *Recreations* music, SF stories; *Style*— Prof David Delpy, CBE; ✉ Defence Scientific Advisory Council, First floor, Zone K, MOD Main Building, Whitehall, London SW1A 2HB

DEMIDENKO, Nikolai; s of Anatoli Antonovich Demidenko; *b* 1 July 1955; *Educ* Moscow Conservatoire; *m* Julya Borisovna Dovgiallo; *Career* pianist; visiting prof: Univ of Surrey, Yehudi Menuhin Sch; medallist: Concours International de Montreal 1976, Tchaikovsky Int Competition 1978; performances incl: Br debut with Moscow Radio Symphony Orch 1990, Piano Masterworks series Wigmore Hall 1993; 1994–95 appearances incl: Hollywood Bowl, Berlin with Berliner Symphoniker, Royal Festival Hall with RPO and Yuri Temirkanov, various Scottish venues with Scottish Chamber Orch, Toronto, Haskil-Kempff Festival Luxembourg, St John's Smith Square for BBC, Belfast, Chester and Ribble Valley Festivals, complete Mussorgsky song cycles with Anatoli Safiulin St John's Smith Square, Rouen and Verbier Festival, Int Piano Series Royal Festival Hall, Gramophone Award Winners Festival Wigmore Hall; 1995–96 season incl: Celebrity Recital Series Barbican, Scriabin Concerto with Netherlands Radio Philharmonic, Prokofiev Second Concerto with LPO, Gershwin Rhapsody in Blue with BBC Philharmonic Orch, series with Israel Philharmonic, tour of Australia for ABC, Int Piano Festival Singapore, Gramophone Award Winners Festival Wigmore Hall; 1996–97 season incl: recitals in Amsterdam, Istanbul, Munich, Prague, Toronto, Warsaw, Bristol, Windsor Festival, Barbican Great Orchs of the World Series (with Moscow Philharmonic), Polish Radio Symphony Orch, Orchestre Philharmonique de Luxembourg; 1997–98 season incl: A Romantic Voyage (3 part recital series) Wigmore Hall, recitals in Brisbane, Melbourne, Perth and Sydney; 1998–99 season incl: Barbican Celebrity Recital Series, Beethoven's Diabelli Variations with Twyla Tharp Dance Co in Paris and London; 1999–2000 season incl: Int Piano Series recital at Royal Festival Hall; *Recordings* for Hyperion Records incl: works by Bach-Busoni, Chopin, Liszt, Medtner Second and Third Piano Concertos with BBC Scottish Symphony Orch (winner Gramophone Award 1992), Rachmaninov Music for Two Pianos with Dmitri Alexeev (nominated Classic CD Instrumental Award 1995), Live at Wigmore double album, Tchaikovsky First Piano Concerto, Scriabin Piano Concerto (winner Classic CD Award 1994), Weber Concertos, Clementi Sonatas, Mussorgsky Song Cycles, Schubert Impromptus, Prokofiev Piano Concerto cycle (with London Philharmonic and Alexander Lazarev); *Style*— Nikolai Demidenko, Esq

DEMPSEY, Michael Bernard (Mike); s of John Patrick Dempsey (d 1993), latterly of Ramsgate, Kent, and Britannia May, *née* Thompson (d 1993); *b* 25 July 1944; *Educ* Bishop Ward RC Secdy Modern Dagenham; *m* 1, 21 Oct 1967 (m dis 1988), Sonja, da of George Mathew Green; 1 da (Polly b 15 Oct 1969), 2 s (Joe, Ben (twins) b 2 Jan 1972); m 2, 15 Aug 1989 (m dis 2008), Charlotte Antonia, da of David Elliot Richardson; 3 da (Daisy b 2 May 1990, Fleur May b 15 July 1994, Jemima b 20 May 1998); *Career* asst designer Chevron Studio 1963–64, in-house designer Bryan Colmer Artist Agents 1964–65, freelance designer 1965–66, designer Cato Peters O'Brien 1966–68, art dir William Heinemann Publishers 1968–74, art dir William Collins/Fontana Publishers 1974–79, fndr ptnr Carroll & Dempsey 1979–85, chm and creative dir CDT Design (formerly Carroll Dempsey & Thirkell) 1985–2007, Studio Dempsey 2008–; conslt designer Dept for Culture, Media and Sport 1997–98, art dir RSA Jl 1997–2002, conslt art dir Royal Mail 1999 Millennium Stamp Prog 1998–99, designer Royal Mail Definitive Stamps 2006, designer Royal Mail special issue stamps Sounds of Britain 2006 and Endangered Plants 2009, designer Royal Mail stamps Classic Album Covers 2010; external design advsr Design Cncl 2009–; feature film title designer for: The Duellists 1977, Weatherby 1985, Comrades 1986, Strapless 1989, Paris by Night 1989, Call It Night 1990, Heading Home 1991, Damage 1992, The Secret Rapture 1993, Look Me in the Eye 1994, Blue Juice 1995, The Designated Mourner 1996, Last Dance 1996; feature writer: Design Week 2001–, Blueprint magazine, Varoom, Creative Review, V&A Magazine, Eye Magazine; presenter RDInsight recordings; memb: D&AD 1968 (memb Exec 1996–98, pres 1997–98), Design Cncl Millennium Products Selection Panel 1998–99, BAFTA 2003–; FCSD 1980, RDI 1994 (master 2005–07), AGI 1998, FRSA 2005 (memb Cncl 2005–); *Awards* D&AD Silver 1981 (most outstanding technical lit) and 1984 (most outstanding book jacket), D&AD Gold and Silver 1985 (most outstanding book design), 2 D&AD Silvers 1989 (most outstanding annual report and album covers), 2 D&AD Silvers 1992 (most outstanding corp ID and logo), CSD Minerva Award 1993 (most outstanding corp ID), D&AD Silver 2000 (most outstanding use of illustration), D&AD Silver 2001 (most outstanding use of photography), nomination D&AD 2008 (writing for design), Royal Mail Reginald M Phillips Medal 2011 (for contribution to Br stamp design), Art Directors Club NYC Silver Award 2011 (stamp design), D&AD Special Award for Most Awarded Designer in their 50 Year History 2012; *Books* Bubbles – Early Advertising Art of A & F Pears (1978), The Magical Paintings of Justin Todd (1978), Pipe Dreams – Early Advertising Art of The Imperial Tobacco Company (1982); *Recreations* living; *Clubs* Groucho, BAFTA; *Style*— Mike Dempsey, Esq; ✉ The Hayloft, Church Lane, Osmington, Dorset DT3 6EW (☎ 01305 832520); Studio Dempsey, 1 The Warehouse, 19 Bowling Green Lane, London EC1R 0BD (e-mail mike@studiodempsey.co.uk, website www.studiodempsey.co.uk, blog www.mikedempsey.typepad.com)

DEMPSEY, Nick; *b* 13 August 1980, Norwich; *m* Oct 2008, Sarah Ayton; 2 s; *Career* windsurfer; achievements in Mistral class incl: Bronze medal Volvo Youth Sailing ISAF World Championships 1998, sixteenth place Olympic Games 2000, Bronze medal Olympic Games 2004; achievements in RS:X class incl: Gold medal RS:X European Championships 2006, fourth place Olympic Games 2008, Gold medal RS:X World Championships 2009, Silver medal RS:X Olympic Games 2012, Silver medal RS:X Olympic Games 2016; *Style*— Mr Nick Dempsey; ✉ c/o Three60 Sports Management, The Studio, Hudson Street, Deddington, Oxfordshire OX15 0SW; website www.nickdempsey.com

DEMPSTER, Prof Michael Alan Howarth; s of late Cedric William Dempster, and late Honor Fitz Simmons, *née* Gowan; *b* 10 April 1938; *Educ* Univ of Toronto (BA), Carnegie Inst of Technology (MS, PhD), Univ of Oxford (MA), Univ of Cambridge (MA); *m* 1 (m dis), Ann Laura, *née* Lazier; 1 da (Trinity Catherine Laura Fitz Simmons); m 2, Elena Anatolievna, *née* Medova; 1 da (Anna Medova); *Career* jr research fell Nuffield Coll Oxford 1966; Balliol Coll Oxford: fell and tutor in mathematics 1967–79, sr research fell 1979–81, lectr in mathematics 1981–87; univ lectr in industrial mathematics Univ of Oxford 1967–81, fell Center for Advanced Study in Behavioural Sciences Stanford Calif 1974–75, sr research scholar System and Decision Sciences International Inst for Applied Systems Analysis Laxenburg Austria 1979–81, prof of mathematics, statistics and computing science/R A Jodrey research prof of mgmnt and information sciences Dalhousie Univ 1981–93, prof of mathematics Univ of Essex 1990–95 (dir Inst for Studies in Fin 1993–95); Judge Business Sch Univ of Cambridge: dir Centre for Financial Research 1996–2008, dir of research 1997–2001, dir PhD prog 1997–2002, currently emeritus prof of finance and mgmnt sciences and emeritus prof Statistical Lab Centre for Mathematical Sciences; fell Hughes Hall Cambridge 2003–; resident participant progs on financial mathematics and devpt in quantitative finance Isaac Newton Inst for Mathematical Sciences Cambridge 1995, 2005 and 2014; Oxford Systems Associates Ltd: md 1974–79, chm 1974–80; chm and md Cambridge Systems Assocs Ltd 1996–; conslt to various cos incl: Eni, BT, Citigroup, CSFB, Swiss Re, HSBC, Fujitsu, Frank Russell Co, Morgan Stanley, Anglo American, Rio Tinto; founding co-ed-in-chief Quantitative Finance 2000–; visiting prof: Univ of Rome, Univ of Toronto, Univ of Melbourne, Univ of Calif Berkeley; visiting sr fell Manchester Business Sch, visiting fell Princeton Univ; memb: London Mathematical Soc, American Mathematical Soc, Canadian Mathematical Soc, Mathematical Programming Soc, Operational Research Soc, Inst for Operations Research and Mgmnt Sciences, Assoc for Computing Machinery, Inst of Mathematical Statistics, American Statistical Assoc, Econometric Soc, Oxford Political Economy Club, American Inst of Decision Science, Public Choice Soc, Sigma Xi Hon Scientific Fraternity, Linceo; FIMA, Hon FIA; *Publications* Introduction to Optimization Methods (with P R Adby, 1974), Stochastic Programming (contrib and ed, 1980), Analysis and Optimization of Stochastic Systems (co-ed with M H A Davis, C J Harris, O L R Jacobs, P C Parks, 1980), Large-Scale Linear Programming (co-ed with G B Dantzig and M Kallio, 1981), Deterministic and Stochastic Scheduling (contrib and co-ed with J K Lenstra and A H G Rinnooy Kan, 1982), Proceedings of the IIASA Task Force Meeting on Stochastic Optimization (guest ed, 1983), Mathematical Models in Economics (contrib and co-ed with M O L Bacharach and J L Enos, 1990), Mathematics of Derivative Securities (contrib and co-ed with S R Pliska, 1997), Risk Management: Value at Risk and Beyond (contrib and ed, 2002), Quantitative Fund Management (contrib and co-ed with G Mitra and G Pflug, 2009), Stochastic Optimization Methods in Finance and Energy (contrib and co-ed with M Bertocchi and G Consigli, 2011), The Euro in Danger: Reform and Reset (with J S Chadha and D E Pickford, 2012), Commodities (contrib and co-ed with K Tang, 2015); also ed translations and author of numerous articles in learned jls; *Recreations* reading, gardening, tennis, sailing, skiing; *Style*— Prof M A H Dempster; ✉ Statistical Laboratory, Centre for Mathematical Sciences, University of Cambridge, Wilberforce Road, Cambridge CB3 0WB (☎ 01223 557643, fax 01223 557641, e-mail mahd2@cam.ac.uk, website www-cfr.statslab.cam.ac.uk)

DENARO, Maj-Gen Arthur George; CBE (1996, OBE 1991), DL (Herefords); s of late Brig George Tancred Denaro, CBE, DSO, and Francesca Violet Denaro; *Educ* Downside, RMA Sandhurst; *m* 1980, Margaret Roney, *née* Acworth, wid of Maj M J Kealy, DSO (d 1979); 1 da (b 1982), 1 s (b 1985), 2 step da, 1 step s; *Career* cmmnd QRIH 1968; Staff Coll 1979–80; CO QRIH 1989–91, Cdr 33 (later 20) Armd Brigade 1992–94, RCDS 1994, COS HQ UNPROFOR Former Yugoslavia 1994–95, COS HQ Br Forces Cyprus 1995–96, Chief Combat Support HQ ARRC 1996–97, Cmdt RMA Sandhurst 1997–2000, GOC 5th Div 2001–03; Middle East advsr to the Sec of State for Defence 1997–2002, Extra Equerry to HRH The Prince of Wales 2000–, sr advsr Olive Gp 2003–07, advsr The Court of HH The Crown Prince of Bahrain 2003–07, Middle East and military advsr JCB 2004–08; memb Cncl Prince's Tst 2000–08, Hon Col The Royal Wessex Yeomanry 2003–09, Hon Col The Royal Glos Hussars 2003–13, Col The Queen's Royal Hussars (Queen's Own and Royal Irish) 2004–09; chm Army Benevolent Fund (Hereford) 2003–13, steward Hurlingham Polo Assoc (HPA) 2005–10, pres Hereford St John Ambulance 2011–15, chm

Bd of Govrs Moor Park Sch; *Recreations* field sports, polo, skiing; *Clubs* Cavalry and Guards', Pratts; *Style—* Maj-Gen Arthur Denaro, CBE, DL

DENBIGH AND DESMOND, 12 and 11 Earl of (E1622 and I 1622); Alexander Stephen Rudolph Feilding; also Baron Feilding, Viscount Feilding (both E 1620), Baron Feilding, Viscount Callan (both I 1622), and Baron St Liz (E 1663); o s of 11 Earl of Denbigh and 10 Earl of Desmond (d 1995), and Caroline Judith Vivienne, *née* Cooke; *b* 4 November 1970; *Educ* Stowe; *m* 27 Jan 1996, Suzanne Jane, yr da of Gregory R Allen, of Brixham, Devon; 2 s (Peregrine Rudolph Henry, Viscount Feilding b 19 Feb 2005, Orlando Gregory Danger b 12 Jan 2009), 1 da (Hester Imelda Florence b 5 July 2006); *Heir* s, Viscount Feilding; *Style—* The Rt Hon the Earl of Denbigh and Desmond; ✉ Newnham Paddox House, Monks Kirby, Warwickshire CV23 0RX (☎ 01788 833291, e-mail info@newnhampaddox.com, website www.newnhampaddox.com)

DENBY, Georgia; da of Raymond Ridgwell, and Joyce Ridgwell; *Educ* N Devon Art Coll; *Career* photographer; travelling exhibitions: worldwide BIPP 2000, 2001, 2002, 2003 and 2004, worldwide Master Photographers Assoc (MPA) 2001, GB and I Photographic Alliance of GB (PAGB) 2001 and 2002, Euro Qualification of the Euro Photographer (QEP) 2001–02; cmmns incl: Amber Books, Advision Advtg, Turton Advtg, Visual Language Prodns, Safetylite Ltd, Napthans Photography, Seven Security Servs, A&C Black; work sold at Bonhams London 2005; patron Stiff Upper Lip (NY drama co); supporter: Norfolk Deaf Assoc (NDA), VLM (sign language channel); BIPP Photographer of the Year Central Region 2000, 2001, and 2003, 4 MPA Awards of Excellence 2001, QEP 2001, credit Photographic Alliance of GB 2001, Br Professional Photography Awards Oskar 2004; also numerous Gold, Silver and Bronze BIPP awards; ARPS 2000, FBIPP (ABIPP 2000), assoc MPA (AMPA) 2000; *Publications* Psychic Detectives (2001), Image 26 (2002), Tudor Flashbacks (series, 2002); *Recreations* art in all forms, computer software, jazz and classical music; *Style—* Mrs Georgia Denby; ✉ Orchard Farmhouse, Saxlingham Green, Norwich, Norfolk NR15 1TG (☎ 01508 498431, e-mail georgia@safetylite.com, website www.georgiadenby.co.uk)

DENCH, Dame Judith Olivia (Judi); CH (2005), DBE (1988, OBE 1970); da of Dr Reginald Arthur Dench (d 1964), of York, and Eleanora Olave Dench; *b* 9 December 1934; *Educ* The Mount Sch York, Central Sch of Speech and Drama; *m* 5 Feb 1971, Michael Williams (d 2001); 1 da (Finty b 24 Sept 1972); *Career* actress and director; assoc memb RSC 1969–; fndr memb Surrey Soc CPRE; The Patricia Rothermere Award for Outstanding Service to Theatre 1997, Lifetime Achievement Award Women in Film and Television Awards 1997, Special Award for Services to British Theatre Olivier Awards 2004, Lifetime Achievement Award European Film Acad 2008; Hon DLitt: Univ of York 1978, Univ of Warwick 1980, Univ of Birmingham 1989, Loughborough Univ 1991, Open Univ 1992, Univ of London 1994, St Andrews Univ 2008; hon degree Royal Scottish Acad of Music and Drama; fell BAFTA; *Theatre* stage roles for RSC incl: The Gift of the Gorgon, The Cherry Orchard, Measure for Measure, A Midsummer Night's Dream, Penny for a Song, Twelfth Night, The Winter's Tale, The Comedy of Errors, Macbeth (SWET Best Actress Award), Pillars of the Community, Juno and the Paycock (SWET, Standard, Plays and Players and Variety Club Awards), Waste, All's Well That Ends Well, Merry Wives the Musical 2006–07; roles in the West End incl: The Promise, Cabaret, The Wolf, The Good Companions, The Gay Lord Quex, Pack of Lies (SWET and Plays & Players Best Actress Award), Mr and Mrs Nobody, The Plough and the Stars, Filumena, The Royal Family, The Breath of Life, The Breath Of Life (Haymarket Theatre Royal), Peter and Alice 2013; roles at RNT incl: The Importance of Being Earnest (Evening Standard Best Actress Award), Other Places (Standard, Plays & Players and Drama Awards), Antony and Cleopatra (Olivier, Drama Magazine, and Evening Standard Best Actress Awards), Entertaining Strangers, Hamlet, The Sea, The Seagull, Absolute Hell (Olivier Award for Best Actress 1996), A Little Night Music (Olivier Award for Best Actress in a Musical 1996), Esme Allen in Amy's View (also Broadway, Tony Award 1999); as dir: Much Ado About Nothing, Look Back in Anger (Renaissance Theatre Co), Macbeth (Central School), The Boys from Syracuse (Regent's Park, Best Revival of a Musical Olivier Awards 1992), Romeo and Juliet (Regent's Park) 1993; *Television* incl: Marching Song, Hilda Lessways, Pink String and Sealing Wax, An Age of Kings, Major Barbara, Talking to a Stranger (BAFTA Best TV Actress Award), A Fine Romance (BAFTA Best TV Actress Award), Going Gently (BAFTA Best TV Actress Award), Saigon Year of the Cat, The Browning Version, Mrs & Mrs Edgehill (ACE Award for Best Actress), Absolute Hell, As Time Goes By, Last of the Blonde Bombshells, Cranford; *Film* incl: Four in the Morning (BAFTA Award for Most Promising Newcomer), Wetherby, A Room With a View (BAFTA Award for Best Supporting Actress), 84 Charing Cross Road, A Handful of Dust (BAFTA Award for Best Supporting Actress), Henry V, Jack & Sarah, Hamlet, Mrs Brown (winner of Best Actress Golden Globe Awards 1997, Oscar nomination for Best Actress 1997, BAFTA Award for Best Leading Actress 1997), M in GoldenEye, Tomorrow Never Dies, The World is Not Enough, Die Another Day, Casino Royale, Quantum of Solace and Skyfall, Shakespeare in Love (Oscar winner for Best Supporting Actress 1999, BAFTA Award for Best Supporting Actress 1999), Tea with Mussolini, Chocolat (Oscar nomination for Best Supporting Actress 2001, winner Best Supporting Actress Screen Actors Guild Awards 2001), Iris (Oscar nomination for Best Actress 2002, BAFTA Award for Best Actress, Variety Club Award), The Shipping News 2002, The Importance of Being Ernest 2002, The Chronicles of Riddick 2003, Ladies in Lavender 2003, Mrs Henderson Presents 2005, Notes on a Scandal 2006 (Best Actress Evening Standard British Film Award 2007, nomination Best Actress Oscars 2007, Best Actress Br Ind Film Award 2007), Nine 2009, Jane Eyre 2011, Pirates of the Caribbean: On Stranger Tides 2011, My Week with Marilyn 2011, The Best Exotic Marigold Hotel 2011, J Edgar 2011, Skyfall 2012, Philomena 2013, The Second Best Exotic Marigold Hotel 2014; *Books* Behind the Scenes (2014); *Style—* Dame Judi Dench, CH, DBE; ✉ c/o Julian Belfrage Associates, 3rd Floor, 9 Argyll Street, London W1F 7TG (☎ 020 7287 8544, fax 020 7287 8832, e-mail email@julianbelfrage.co.uk)

DENCH, Robert Graham (Bob); BEM (1972); s of Eric Leslie Dench (d 2007), and Gladys May, *née* Knowles (d 1980); *b* 14 February 1950, Surrey; *Educ* John Ruskin GS Shirley; *m* 9 Sept 1972, Christina Mary, *née* Norman; 2 da (Anna Elizabeth b 1974, Melanie Louise b 1976); *Career* Metropolitan Police 1969–76, Barclays Bank 1976–2004 (memb Bd: Barclays Retail Bank, Barclays Wealth); chm: Axa (Ireland) 2006–, Paragon Gp plc 2007– (non-exec dir 2004–); non-exec dir AXA plc 2004–; *Recreations* sailing, golf, reading; *Clubs* Carlton, Addington Palace Golf; *Style—* Bob Dench, Esq, BEM; ✉ e-mail bob.dench@paragon-group.co.uk

DENHAM, Gary George; s of Maurice Denham (d 2011), and late Patricia Denham; *b* 4 July 1951; *Educ* Bennets End Secdy Sch; *m* 6 May 1972, Vivienne, da of Roy Howlett; 4 s (Nathan b 10 Dec 1975, Jacob b 3 Oct 1979, Joshua b 31 Aug 1983, Elijah b 13 June 1986), 1 da (Krsna b 14 June 1977); *Career* art dir The Kirkwood Company advtg agency 1971–73, head of art Maisey Mukerjee Russell 1973–74; art dir: French Gold Abbott 1974–76, Greys Sydney 1976–77; freelance art dir/photographer 1977–83; art dir: Bartle Bogle Hegarty 1983–84, Boase Massimi Pollitt 1984–86; head of art Holmes Knight Ritchie 1986–87, jt creative dir Aspect Hill Holliday 1987–89, art dir/gp head Bartle Bogle Hegarty 1989–92, head of art CME KHBB 1992–95, sr creative Leagas Delaney 1995, freelance art dir/photographer/painter 1995–; awards incl: Bronze Irish Int Advtg Awards, Silver Campaign Press Awards, Gold Pegasus (Readers Digest) Awards, Gold NY Art Dirs Show; photography exhibited: New Australian Photography 1977, Venezia 1979, Pompidou Centre 1980; work in The Polaroid Collection Boston USA; memb D&AD 1975; *Recreations* gardening, painting, photography; *Style—* Gary Denham, Esq

DENHAM, (John Martin) Giles; CBE (2004); s of E W Denham, and late P A Denham, *née* Gregory; *b* 13 February 1959, Hertford; *Educ* Merchant Taylors', ChCh Oxford; *m* 1986, Gill, *née* Yarker; 3 da (Harriet b 1989, Beth b 1991, Olivia b 1993); *Career* civil servant 1981–2016; gen mangr Eastman Dental Hosp 1990–95, head of policy, children, older people and social care Dept of Health 2001–03, dir of civil affrs Coalition Provisional Authy Iraq 2004, dir Policy Gp Health and Safety Exec 2005–09, dir Medicines, Pharmacy and Industry Gp Dept of Health 2009–14, dir Workforce Dept of Health 2014–16, dir Strategic Relationships Health Educn Eng 2016–; tstee: Marie Curie Cancer Care 1991–2000, Kepplewray Tst 2001–; *Recreations* family, squash, tennis; *Clubs* Athenaeum, Eastcote Lawn Tennis; *Style—* Giles Denham, Esq, CBE

DENHAM, Grey; *b* 11 February 1949; *Educ* Handsworth GS, Brooklyn Tech Coll, Bristol Coll of Commerce, Univ of London (LLB), Inns of Court Sch of Law, Columbia Univ Grad Sch of Business (CSEP); *m* 3 July 1976, Janet Miranda, *née* Lea; 1 s (Matthew Giles b 8 Aug 1982); *Career* called to the Bar Inner Temple 1972; lectr in law Leicester Poly 1972–74, sr lectr in law Nottingham Law Sch 1974–76 and 1977–78; co legal offr Alfred Herbert Ltd 1978–80; GKN plc: co lawyer 1980–83, dep head of legal 1983–86, head of legal 1986–95, chm GKN Gp Services Ltd 1995–97 (exec dir 1997–2009), pres GKN North America Inc 1996–2001, exec dir GKN (UK) plc 1996–2009, chm GKN Charitable Appeals Ctee 1998–2009, co sec and gp dir legal and compliance 1996–2009, pres GKN America Corp 2001–09, exec dir GKN Hldgs plc 2001–09, exec dir Westland Group plc 2001–09; non-exec dir Charter plc 2005–08, non-exec dir Charter Int plc 2008–12 (sr ind dr and chm Remuneration Ctee 2009–12); regnl chm W Midlands CBI 2005–07 (regnl vice-chm 2004–05 and 2007–08); non-exec dir and tstee Young Enterprise 2006– (chm Remuneration Ctee 2011–15, chm 2015–); non-exec memb Cncl Competition Cmmn 2009–14 (chm Remuneration Ctee 2011–14); memb: Legal Ctee SMMT 1985–95, Regnl Advsy Gp London Stock Exchange 1996–2000, Cncl Birmingham C of C and Industry 1996–2009, W Midlands Cncl CBI 1998–2009, Exchange Markets Gp London Stock Exchange 2000–04, Primary Markets Gp London Stock Exchange 2000–05 (chm 2000–04), Young Enterprise Business Leadership Cncl 2003–05, Chairman's Ctee CBI 2005–07, Hon Soc of the Inner Temple, Inst of European Law, Alumni Soc of Univ of London, Alumni Soc of Columbia Univ; govr memb RNLI; FRSA 1992; *Recreations* watching and playing cricket, watching Wasps and England Rugby Union, watching ballet, ornithology; *Clubs* Warwickshire CCC, Knowle and Dorridge LTC; *Style—* Grey Denham, Esq; ✉ e-mail greydenham@aol.com

DENHAM, Rt Hon John; PC (2000); *b* 15 July 1953; *Educ* Woodroffe Comp Lyme Regis, Univ of Southampton (BSc); *m* (m dis), Ruth Dixon; 1 s, 1 da; partner, Sue Littlemore; 1 s; *Career* voluntary sector work; MP (Lab) Southampton Itchen 1992–2015 (contested Southampton Itchen 1983 and 1987); Parly under-sec of state DSS 1997–98 (min of state 1998), min of state Dept of Health 1998–2001, min of state for Crime Reduction, Policing and Community Safety Home Office 2001–03, sec of state for Innovation, Univs and Skills 2007–09, sec of state for the community and local govt 2009–10, shadow sec for business 2010–11; chm Home Affrs Select Ctee; elected memb: Hampshire CC 1981–89 (dep ldr and spokesperson on educn), Southampton City Cncl 1989–93 (chair Housing Ctee); memb MSF; *Style—* The Rt Hon John Denham; ✉ House of Commons, London SW1A 0AA (☎ 020 7219 3000)

DENHAM, Hon Mrs Justice Susan Gageby Denham; *née* Gageby; da of R J D Gageby (d 2004), and Dorothy Mary, *née* Lester (d 2002); *b* 22 August 1945, Dublin; *Educ* Alexandra Coll Dublin, TCD, Columbia Univ NY; *m* 18 July 1970, Dr Brian Denham; 1 da (Niamh b 1979), 3 s (Niall b 1980, Colm, Cian b 1984 (twins)); *Career* called to the Bar King's Inns Dublin (bencher 1991); jr counsel 1971–87, sr counsel 1987–, judge of the High Court of Ireland 1991–92, judge of the Supreme Court of Ireland 1992–2011, Chief Justice of Ireland 2011–; vice-pres Network of Presidents of Supreme Judicial Courts of the EU 2011–15, pres Network of Presidents of Supreme Judicial Courts of the EU 2015–; chair: Working Gp on a Courts Cmmn 1995–98, Family Law Devpt Ctee 1999–2001, Finance Ctee 2001–04, Courts Service Bd 2001–04 and 2011–, ISC Steering Ctee on Sentencing Info 2005–, Working Gp on a Court of Appeal 2007–09, Interim Judicial Cncl 2011–, Ctee for Judicial Studies 2011–, Superior Court Rules Ctee 2011–, Judicial Appointments Advsy Bd 2011–; pro-chllr TCD 1996–2010; tstee Holocaust Education Tst Ireland; hon bencher Middle Temple 2005; Distinguished Fellowship Award Griffith Coll Dublin 2013; Hon LLD: Queen's Univ Belfast 2002, Univ of Ulster 2013, Univ Coll Dublin 2014; Hon DPhil Dublin City Univ 2014; *Recreations* horses, gardening, reading; *Style—* The Hon Mrs Justice Susan Denham; ✉ The Supreme Court, The Four Courts, Dublin 7, Ireland (☎ 00 353 1 888 6540)

DENHOLM, John Clark; s of Robert Denholm (d 1986), of Lower Largo, Fife, and Ann King, *née* Clark; *b* 10 September 1950; *Educ* Buckhaven HS, Univ of St Andrews (MA); *m* 16 Dec 1978, Julia Margaret, da of Ben Gregory; 1 da (Katy b 16 April 1986), 1 s (Michael b 19 Sept 1988); *Career* product mangr The Boots Co Nottingham 1972–76, brand mangr Scottish & Newcastle Breweries 1976–80, account dir Hall Advertising 1980–84, chm The Leith Agency Edinburgh 1995– (md 1984–95), gp md Silvermills (holding co) 1995–; MIPA 1986; *Recreations* golf; *Style—* John Denholm, Esq; ✉ The Leith Agency, 37 The Shore, Leith, Edinburgh EH6 6QU (☎ 0131 561 8600)

DENIS, Germain; s of Joseph Denis, and Elizabeth, *née* Veilleux; *Educ* Laval Univ Canada; *Career* public serv int trade and domestic econ devpt issues Canadian Govt 1965–95, served GATT, WTO and NAFTA panels, memb team for free trade with USA; exec dir Int Grains Cncl and Food Aid Ctee 1995–; memb: Int Food and Agribusiness Mgmnt Assoc (IAMA), RIIA, World Trade Law Assoc, Canning House, Hong Kong Assoc; MInstD; Medal Alimentos Argentinos Secretario de Agricultura 1997, Medal Ordre du Mérite Agricole de France 1998, Medal Mérite Professionnel Bourse de Commerce de Paris 1998; *Publications* author of a broad range of articles related to global food markets, globalisation and int trade, int devpt issues, and domestic trade matters; *Recreations* gardening, golfing, reading; *Style—* Germain Denis, Esq; ✉ International Grains Council, 1 Canada Square, Canary Wharf, London E14 5AE (☎ 020 7513 1122, fax 020 7513 0630)

DENNIS, Caspian Michael; s of John Peter Leslie Dennis, of the Isle of Bute, and Veronica Helen, *née* Demoore; *b* 11 September 1977, Margate, Kent; *Educ* Stantonbury Campus Milton Keynes, Univ of Manchester (BA), Birkbeck Coll London (MA); *m* Tara Louise Hiatt; 1 da (Manon b 12 Aug 2005), 1 s (Theo b 21 April 2008); *Career* rights asst rising to rights exec Faber and Faber Ltd 1999–2002, literary agent Abner Stein 2002–; *Style—* Caspian Dennis, Esq; ✉ Abner Stein, 10 Roland Gardens, London SW7 3PH (☎ 020 7373 0456, fax 020 7370 6316, e-mail caspian@abnerstein.co.uk)

DENNIS, Geoffrey; *Career* early career as dir Economics and Fin Div Ewbank Preece Consltg and md Travers Morgan Environmental Consultancy; formerly: int dir Br Red Cross, head S Asia Int Fedn of the Red Cross (IFRC); chief exec: Friends of the Elderly 2000–04, CARE Int UK 2004–; *Style—* Geoffrey Dennis, Esq; ✉ CARE International UK, 9th Floor, 89 Albert Embankment, London SE1 7TP (☎ 020 7091 6000, fax 020 7582 0728)

DENNIS, (Peter) Hugh; s of The Rt Rev John Dennis, and Dorothy Mary, *née* Hinnels; *b* 1962, Kettering, Northants; *Educ* Univ Coll Sch Hampstead, St John's Coll Cambridge; *m* 1996, Catherine (Kate) Abbot-Anderson; 1 s, 1 da; *Career* comedian and actor; hon fell Univ of Northampton 2008; *Television* incl: Spitting Image, The Mary Whitehouse Experience, regular panelist Mock the Week, The Imaginatively Titled Punt and Dennis

D

Show, Me, You and Him, My Hero (BBC 1), guest host Have I Got News For You, Outnumbered (BBC) 2007–14; *Radio* incl: The Mary Whitehouse Experience (BBC Radio 1), Punt and Dennis, It's Been a Bad Week, The Now Show; *Style*— Hugh Dennis; ✉ c/o Independent Talent Group Ltd, 40 Whitfield Street, London W1T 2RH

DENNIS, Prof Ian Howard; s of Flt Lt Bernard Cecil Dennis (d 1982), of Altrincham, Cheshire, and Jean Harrison, *née* Dennis; *b* 17 September 1948; *Educ* Manchester Grammar, Queens' Coll Cambridge (MA, PhD); *m* 17 July 1982, Dr Susan Mary Bower, da of Ivan William Bower (d 1989), of Southsea, Hants; 1 s (Robert William b 1984), 1 da (Katherine Mary b 1986); *Career* called to the Bar Gray's Inn 1971; lectr in law Cncl of Legal Educn 1971–73; UCL: lectr 1974–82, reader 1982–87, prof 1987–2013, head of dept 2002–07; Allen, Allen and Hemsley visiting professorial fell Univ of Sydney 1995; special conslt Law Cmmn 1986–87 (memb criminal codification team 1981–89); ed Criminal Law Review 1999–2011; *Books* Codification of the Criminal Law, a Report to the Law Commission (with J C Smith and E J Griew, 1985), The Law of Evidence (5 edn 2013); author of numerous articles and essays on criminal law and the law of evidence; *Recreations* chess, cycling, wine, mountain walking; *Style*— Prof Ian Dennis; ✉ Faculty of Laws, University College London, Bentham House, Endsleigh Gardens, London WC1H 0EG (✆ 020 7679 1431)

DENNIS, HE John David; *m* Jillian Margaret; 2 s; *Career* diplomat; desk offr Tanzania and Uganda FCO 1981–82, Mandarin Chinese language trg 1982–84, second sec (political) Beijing 1985–87, head Malaysia, Singapore and Brunei Section FCO 1987–89, head Recruitment Section FCO 1989–92, head Political Section Kuala Lumpur 1992–96, special advsr to Chm Standard Chartered Bank 1997–98, dir motor vehicles Dept of Trade and Industry 1998–2001, dir for trade and investment New Delhi 2001–03, min and dep head of mission Beijing 2003–06, additional dir Asia FCO 2007–08, head Zimbabwe Unit Africa Directorate FCO 2009–10, head Africa Dept (Central and Southern) FCO 2010–13, ambass to Angola and to São Tomé and Principe 2014–; *Style*— HE Mr John Dennis; ✉ c/o FCO (Luanda), King Charles Street, London SW1A 2AH

DENNIS, Dr John Stephen; s of Patrick John Dennis (d 1990), and Audrey, *née* Martin (d 1971); *b* 26 September 1955; *Educ* Churchfields Sch Swindon, Selwyn Coll Cambridge (nat engrg scholar, BA, N Carolina State Univ prize, Coll Book prize, res scholar, PhD); *m* 5 Sept 1981, Ruth Dennis, MRCVS, da of Rev Dr John Wall; *Career* lectr Dept of Chemical Engrg Univ of Cambridge 1984–88, self employed conslt chem engr 1989–, mangr LINK Biochemical Engrg Prog 1989–, biochemical engrg co-ordinator SERC 1991–; visiting prof UCL 1996–; Steetley Award Inst of Energy 1989; memb Ctee Biotechnology Gp SCI; corporate memb IChemE 1986, CEng 1986; *Publications* author of numerous articles and symposia on combustion, heat transfer, fluidisation and biochemical engrg; *Recreations* rowing (formerly memb Cambridge Univ 2nd VIII), sculling, running, reading; *Style*— Dr John Dennis; ✉ 20 High Street, Stetchworth, Newmarket, Suffolk CB8 9TJ (✆ 01638 508171, fax 01638 508344)

DENNIS, His Hon Judge Mark Jonathan; QC (2006); s of Edward John Dennis, and Patricia Edna, *née* Roberts; *b* 15 March 1955; *Educ* Battersea GS, Peterhouse Cambridge (BA, MA); *m* 26 July 1985, Christabel Harriet, *née* Birbeck; 1 s, 1 da; *Career* called to the Bar Middle Temple 1977; jr Treasury counsel 1993–98, sr Treasury counsel 1998–2006, recorder of the Crown Court 2000–, circuit judge (SE Circuit) 2016–; memb Criminal Bar Assoc; *Clubs* Reform; *Style*— His Hon Judge Dennis, QC; ✉ 6KBW, 21 College Hill, London EC4R 2RP (✆ 020 3301 0910, fax 020 3301 0911, e-mail clerks@6kbw.com, website www.6kbw.com)

DENNIS, Rodney John; s of William Gordon Dennis, and Shiela Dennis; *b* 7 November 1952; *Educ* Univ of Cape Town (BBusSci); *m* 27 Aug 1979, Pamela Mary, *née* Hartnady; *Career* chief investment offr Prudential Portfolio Managers Ltd March 1996–, chm Gartmore European Investment Tst plc 2006–; *Recreations* flying, sailing, skiing, reading, music; *Style*— Rodney Dennis, Esq

DENNIS, Ronald (Ron); CBE; s of Norman Stanley Dennis (d 1986), of Woking, Surrey, and Evelyn, *née* Reader; *b* 1 June 1947, Woking; *Educ* Guildford Tech Coll (Vehicle Technol Course); *m* 31 Dec 1985, Lisa Ann, da of Gary K Shelton; 2 da (Charlotte Victoria b 25 Aug 1987, Francesca Olivia b 11 Nov 1993), 1 s (Christian Shelton b 27 Oct 1990); *Career* apprentice Thomson & Taylor, owner/mangr Project Four team (winning ProCar Championship 1979 and Formula 3 Championship 1979–80), merged with McLaren team 1980; McLaren Formula One racing team: winners Constructors' Cup 1984–85 and 1988, 1989, 1990, 1991 and 1998, nine driving championships; McLaren F1 winner Le Mans 24 hour race 1995 (first attempt); chm and ceo McLaren Gp (incl: McLaren Racing Ltd, McLaren Marketing Ltd, McLaren Electronic Systems Ltd, McLaren Composites Ltd, McLaren Applied Technologies Ltd) until 2009; memb Formula One Cmmn; chm Tommy's Campaign; Gold Medal BRDC 2001, Colin Chapman Award BRDC 2007, Prince Philip Medal Royal Acad of Engrg 2008; Hon DTech De Montfort Univ 1996, Hon DSci City Univ 1997, Hon DUniv Surrey 2000; *Recreations* golf, shooting, snow and water skiing; *Clubs* The Arts, BRDC, Annabel's, Harry's Bar, George; *Style*— Ron Dennis, Esq, CBE

DENNISS, His Hon Judge John Annear; *b* 7 October 1951; *Educ* Winchester, Univ of Bristol (LLB); *m* Angela, *née* Raisman; 2 da (Frances, Charlotte), 1 s (Michael); *Career* called to the Bar Inner Temple 1974; recorder 2000, circuit judge (South Eastern Circuit) 2009–; *Recreations* fishing, skiing; *Clubs* Lansdown, Royal Cornwall Yacht; *Style*— His Hon Judge Denniss; ✉ Isleworth Crown Court, 36 Ridgeway Road, Isleworth, London TW7 5LP

DENNY, John Ingram; CMG (1997); s of Thomas Ingram Denny, of Macclesfield, Cheshire, and Claire Dorothy, *née* Lewis; *b* 28 May 1941; *Educ* Normain Coll Chester, Poly of N London (DipArch), Univ of Reading (MSc); *m* 2 June 1967, Carol Ann Frances, da of Walter James Hughes, of St Leonards, Bournemouth, Hants; 1 s (Paul b 7 Oct 1969), 2 da (Louise (Mrs Adrian Myers) b 23 July 1971, Sarah b 31 Jan 1974); *Career* md Cecil Denny Highton Partnership, jt md HOK International Ltd 1995–2001 (joined 1970, ptnr 1971, sr ptnr 1990, incorporated 1995), md Property Consulting Ltd 2002–04; conslt architect to: FCO, Home Office, Parly Works Office, Royal Household, HM Treasy, Cabinet Office, PACE, Crown Estate and Natural History Museum; memb RIBA; *Recreations* golf, photography; *Style*— John Denny, Esq, CMG

DENNY, (Edward) Michael Patrick; s of Edward Maynard Donald Denny, of Cowfold, W Sussex, and Patricia, *née* Musprett-Williams; *b* 8 April 1943, Sussex; *Educ* Eton; *m* March 1968, Gay Amanda Louise, *née* Hobrow; 1 s (Charles Henry b 1973), 1 da (Joanna Elizabeth Louise b 1975); *Career* fndr Northern Investors Co 1984, chm NVM Private Equity 1988–2008, chm Macklays Inns Ltd 2010–; chm Br Venture Capital Assoc 1990; govr Univ of Durham 1989–96, chm of tstees Hopetoun House Preservation Tst 2002–14; MSI; *Recreations* golf, shooting, skiing; *Clubs* New (Edinburgh); *Style*— Michael Denny, Esq; ✉ Westsidewood House, Carnwath, South Lanarkshire ML11 8LJ (✆ 01501 785236, fax 01501 785444); Northern Venture Managers Limited, Northumberland House, Princess Square, Newcastle upon Tyne NE1 8ER (e-mail michael.denny@nvm.co.uk)

DENNY, Neill Quentin William; s of Alfred Christopher Denny, of Alresford, Hants, and Alison Mary, *née* McLellan; *b* 31 July 1966, Cheam, Surrey; *Educ* Dulwich Coll (scholar), Hounslow Borough Coll (HND, pres Student Union); *m* 2 June 2001, Anne, *née* Whitaker; 2 da (Alexandra Kathleen Elizabeth b 11 March 2003, Susannah Rachel Alison b 6 Nov 2008), 1 s (Jack Alfred Charles b 18 Sept 2005); *Career* reporter Direct Response 1989, reporter then news ed Precision Marketing 1990–94, dep ed Promotions & Incentives 1994–95, reporter Marketing magazine 1995, launch ed Marketing Direct 1995–98, dep

ed Marketing magazine 1998–99, ed Retail Week 1999–2004, ed-in-chief The Bookseller 2004–12, jt ed BookBrunch 2016–; memb Soc of Bookmen; Freeman City of London 2001; highly commended PPA Ed of the Year 2002; *Recreations* reading, wine, football, cycling; *Style*— Neill Denny, Esq; ✉ e-mail neill.denny@btinternet.com

DENNY, HE Ross Patrick; s of Clifford Denny, of Hedge End, Hants, and Doreen, *née* Ramsden; *b* 13 September 1955, Southampton, Hants; *m* Claudenise, *née* Pinto de Lima; 2 da (Ceri b 17 April 1979, Amanda Rebecca b 3 Jan 2005), 2 s (Marc b 24 Nov 1981, José Victor b 17 July 1997); *Career* diplomat; West Indies and Atlantic Dept FCO 1979–80, Santiago 1980–83, Doha 1983–85, vice consul Warsaw 1985–88, Research Unit Personnel Services Dept FCO 1988–89, South Pacific Dept FCO 1989–92, second sec political/EU affrs The Hague 1992–97, vice consul (commercial/press and public affrs) Sao Paulo 1998–2001, dep head of mission HM Consul, dir of trade devpt Luanda 2002–05, Research Analysts FCO 2005–08, administrator Ascension Island 2008–11, ambass to Bolivia 2011–15, ambass to Costa Rica and non-resident ambass to Nicaragua 2015–; memb MENSA Int; *Recreations* aviation, sailing, travel, independent cinema; *Style*— HE Mr Ross Denny; ✉ c/o FCO (San José), King Charles Street, London SW1A 2AH

DENNYS, Nicholas Charles Jonathan; QC (1991); s of John Edward Dennys, MC (d 1973), and Hon Lavinia Mary Yolande Lyttelton; *b* 14 July 1951; *Educ* Eton, BNC Oxford (BA); *m* 19 Feb 1977 (m dis 2000), Frances Winifred, da of Rev Canon Gervase William Markham, of Morland, Cumbria; 4 da (Harriet b 5 Feb 1979, Sophie b 2 Feb 1981, Romilly Mary b 31 March 1984, Katharine b 14 July 1986); *Career* called to the Bar Middle Temple 1975 (bencher 2007); recorder 1999–2011 (asst recorder 1997–99); chair China Oxford Scholarship Fund 2003–; *Publications* Hudson's Building and Engineering Contracts (gen ed 12 edn); *Recreations* golf, windsurfing, reading; *Style*— Nicholas Dennys, Esq, QC; ✉ 1 Atkin Buildings, Gray's Inn, London WC1R 5AT (✆ 020 7404 0102)

DENT, Grace; *Career* writer and broadcaster; television critic The Guardian 2000–12, columnist Independent 2012–, restaurant critic Evening Standard; contrib: Tatler, Marie Claire; judge Baileys Prize for Fiction 2015; Stonewall Journalist of the Year; *Television* incl: The Culture Show (as presenter, BBC 2), Screenwipe (as writer, BBC 4), Big Brother: A Decade In The Headlines (as writer and presenter, Channel 4); *Radio* as presenter incl: Blood, Sage and Grace (BBC Radio 4), The Frequency of Laughter (BBC Radio 4), Epic Fail (BBC Radio 4); *Books* incl: It's A Girl Thing (2003), How To Leave Twitter (My Time As Queen of the Universe and Why This Must Stop) (2011); *Style*— Ms Grace Dent; ✉ c/o Jacquie Drewe, Curtis Brown, Haymarket House, 28 -29 Haymarket, London SW1Y 4SP

DENT, Helen Anne; CBE (2010); da of Frederick Dent, of Grays, Essex, and Muriel, *née* Antcliffe; *b* 29 June 1951; *Educ* Grays Convent Thurrock, Lancaster Univ (BEd), South Bank Univ (MSc), Salford Univ; *Career* various social work posts London 1974–78, lectr in social work and social policy 1978–81, with London Borough of Enfield 1981–86, asst dir Cambs CC 1986–90, dir of external affrs Action for Children 1990–96, latterly chief exec Family Action; formerly: non-exec dir Gt Ormond St Hosp for Children NHS Tst, memb Cncl ESRC; tstee Internet Watch Fndn; *Recreations* opera, choral music (London Welsh Choral), gardening, reading; *Style*— Ms Helen Dent, CBE; ✉ 14 Cloudsley Place, London N1 0JA (✆ 020 7837 6065)

DENT, Prof Jeremy Francis; s of Cdr Adrian James Dent, of Sway, Hants, and Diana Elizabeth, *née* Buxton; *b* 24 January 1952; *Educ* Bradfield Coll, Univ of Southampton (BSc); *Career* trainee accountant KPMG 1974–77; lectr in accounting: Univ of Southampton 1977–82, London Business Sch 1982–88; prof of accounting: Manchester Business Sch 1988–90, London Business Sch 2009–; fell in accounting: London Business Sch 1999–2009, LSE 1999–2007 (reader in accounting 1991–99); visiting prof: Stockholm, Copenhagen, Turku, Paris, Sydney; FCA 1977; *Style*— Prof Jeremy Dent; ✉ 560 Hamilton House, 6 St George Wharf, London SW8 2JE (✆ 020 7582 4598, e-mail jdent@jeremydent.com)

DENT, Julie Elizabeth; CBE (2006); da of Thomas Michael Patrick Delaney (d 1985), and Kathleen Rose, *née* Stratford; *b* 3 April 1956; *Educ* Rosebury GS Epsom, Lanchester Poly (BA), Brunel Univ (MA), Cornell Univ (Exec Devpt Prog); *m* 25 March 1978, Anthony Middleton Dent, s of Montague Middleton Dent (d 2000); 1 s (Thomas Isambard Middleton b 22 Oct 1979), 1 da (Emily Elizabeth Middleton b 8 April 1982); *Career* ceo Ealing, Hammersmith and Hounslow Family Health Services Authy 1991–95, dir Ealing, Hammersmith and Hounslow HA 1995–2000, dir performance mgmnt Dept of Health 2000–02, ceo SW London SHA 2002–06; mgmnt conslt 2007–; chm: Secure Healthcare 2007–, London Probation Bd 2007–; visiting prof Royal Holloway Univ of London; tstee Elemental; *Recreations* travelling, reading, music, gardening; *Style*— Mrs Julie Dent, CBE

DENT-BROCKLEHURST, Henry; s of Mark Dent-Brocklehurst, and Mary Elizabeth Chipps; *b* 6 May 1966; *Educ* Stowe, Univ of Southern Calif; *m* 9 May 1998, Lili Maltese; 3 s (Mark b 27 April 2001, Lucas b 10 Feb 2002, Jake b 26 Oct 2006); *Career* landowner; owner Sudeley Castle; film and documentary maker; *Recreations* surfing, tennis, golf; *Clubs* Annabel's; *Style*— Henry Dent-Brocklehurst, Esq

DENT-BROCKLEHURST, Mollie; da of late Geoffrey Mark Dent-Brocklehurst, and Mary Elizabeth, *née* Chipps (now Lady Ashcombe, 3 wife of 4 Baron Ashcombe, *qv*); *Career* int dir and prog co-ordinator The Garage Moscow 2008–10, pres Pace Gallery 2010–; *Style*— Ms Mollie Dent-Brocklehurst; ✉ Pace Gallery, 6 Burlington Gardens, London W15 3ET

DENTON, Nicholas John (Nick); s of John Richard Denton, and Jennifer Jane, *née* Forbes; *b* 18 October 1955; *Educ* Winchester, Magdalene Coll Cambridge (MA); *m* 23 March 1991, Katie, da of Michael Benzecry; 1 s (Toby John b 19 May 1993), 2 da (Rebecca Louisa b 2 June 1995, Eliza Lucy b 30 Oct 1998); *Career* Dewe Rogerson Ltd: account dir London 1981–86, dir Australia 1986–87; corp affrs mangr Eurotunnel plc 1987–88, dir Shandwick Consultants Ltd 1988–97, fndr ptnr The Hogarth Partnership 1997 (now MPH Communications following merger, currently md and head of pensions advisory and investor services); *Recreations* tennis, history, reading, opera, walking; *Style*— Nick Denton, Esq

DENTON, Prof Richard Michael (Dick); s of Arthur Benjamin Denton (d 1968), of Chippenham, Wilts, and Eileen Mary, *née* Evans (d 2002); *b* 16 October 1941; *Educ* Wycliffe Coll, Christ's Coll Cambridge (MA, PhD), Univ of Bristol (DSc); *m* 1965, Janet Mary, *née* Jones; 2 da (Sally Catherine b 1967, Hannah Rachel b 1972), 1 s (Stephen Richard b 1969); *Career* Dept of Biochemistry Univ of Bristol: MRC Metabolism Control Gp 1966–72, lectr 1973–78, reader 1978–87, prof of biochemistry (personal chair) 1987–2010, head of dept 1995–2000, chm of med sciences 2000–04, dean of med and veterinary science 2003–04, emeritus prof of biochemistry 2010–; MRC sr research leave fellowship 1984–88; memb: MRC Grants Ctee and Physiological Systems Bd 1977–85, MRC Cncl 1999–04, Research Ctee Br Diabetic Assoc 1986–92 (chm 1990–92), Molecular and Cell Biology Panel Wellcome Tst Research Ctee 1993–96; R D Lawrence lecture Br Diabetic Assoc 1981; memb Biochemical Soc 1965; FMedSci 1998, FRS 1998; *Publications* over 220 research papers in Nature, Biochemical Jl and other int research jls on topics incl molecular basis of the control of metabolism by insulin and other hormones; *Recreations* family, fell walking, keeping fit, cooking, reading; *Style*— Prof Dick Denton, FRS; ✉ School of Biochemistry, Medical Sciences Building, University of Bristol, Bristol BS8 1TD (✆ 0117 331 2117, e-mail r.denton@bristol.ac.uk)

DENYER, Roderick Lawrence; QC (1990); s of Oliver James Denyer (d 1982), and Olive Mabel, *née* Jones; *b* 1 March 1948; *Educ* Grove Park GS for Boys Wrexham, LSE (LLM);

m 21 April 1973, Pauline; 2 da (Hannah b 4 March 1978, Alexandra b 10 Feb 1981); *Career* called to the Bar Inner Temple 1970 (bencher 1996); lectr in law Univ of Bristol 1971–73, practising barr 1973–2002, former head of chambers, recorder of the Crown Court 1990–2002, circuit judge (Wales & Chester Circuit) 2002–; Personal Injury Litigation and Children (1993, 2 edn 2002), various pubns in legal jls; *Recreations* cricket, 1960s pop music; *Style*— His Hon Judge Denyer, QC

DENYER, Stephen Robert Noble; s of Wilfred Denyer, of Sherborne, Dorset, and Joy Victoria Jeanne, *née* Noble; *b* 27 December 1955; *Educ* Fosters GS Sherborne, Univ of Durham (BA); *m* 3 Sept 1988, Monika Maria, da of Heinrich Christoph Wolf, of Lübeck, Germany; 3 s (Martin, Timothy, Frank), 1 da (Helen); *Career* admitted slr 1980; ptnr Allen & Overy 1987–2014, regnl managing ptnr for Europe 1998–2014, global markets ptnr 2009–14; head City and Int Law Soc 2014–; Freeman Worshipful Co of Slrs 1986; memb Law Soc 1980; memb Int Bar Assoc 1987; *Recreations* walking, travel, gardening; *Style*— Stephen Denyer, Esq; ✉ The Law Society, The Law Society's Hall, 113 Chancery Lane, London WC2A 1PL

DENZ, Silvio Werner; s of Werner Josef Denz, and Doris, *née* Steiger; *b* 14 September 1956, Basle, Switzerland; *Educ* Basler Kantonalbank Basel, Swiss Business Sch Basel; *Family* 1 s (Claudio Werner b 31 Jan 1988); *Career* Swiss Army 1976, finance dept André & Cie Lausanne 1977–79, mktg dept Miller Brewing Milwaukee WI 1979–80, creator chain of perfumeries (120 stores) Switzerland 1980–2000, fndr Art and Fragrance Ltd Zurich 2000, fndr Jaguar Fragrance Ltd London 2001, owner Lalique SA; prop vineyards: Clos d'Agon Spain 1998, Château Faugeres Saint-Emilion 2005, Château Rocheyron Saint-Emilion, Château de Chambrun Lalande-de-Pomerol 2007, Tenuta Montepeloso Suvereto Italy, Château Lafaurie-Peyraguey 2014 (first growth Sauternes); property buying and renovating London 2002–; *Recreations* skiing, diving, flying, biking, tennis, collecting art; *Style*— Silvio Denz, Esq; ✉ 130 Wigmore Street, London W1U 3SB (☎ 020 3230 2005, fax 020 3230 2004)

DERBY, Bishop of 2005–; Rt Rev Dr Alastair Llewellyn John Redfern; s of Victor Redfern (d 1995), and Audrey, *née* Musty; *b* 1 September 1948; *Educ* ChCh Oxford, Trinity Coll Cambridge, Univ of Bristol; *m* 1, 21 Dec 1974, Jane Valerie (d 2004), da of Kenneth Straw; 2 da (Elizabeth Jane b 3 April 1978, Zoë Louise 30 June 1980); m 2, 6 May 2006, Caroline Elizabeth, da of David Gamgee Boddington; *Career* curate Tettenhall Wolverhampton 1976–79, lectr and vice-princ Ripon Coll Cuddesdon 1979–87, curate All Saints Cuddesdon 1983–87, canon theologian Bristol Cathedral 1987–97, bishop of Grantham and dean of Stamford 1997–2005; *Books* Ministry and Priesthood (1999), Being Anglican (2000), Growing the Kingdom (2009), Thomas Hobbes and the Limits of Democracy (2009), Public Space and Private Faith (2009), Community and Conflict (2011), Out of the Depths (2012), The Leadership of the People of God (2013), Discipleship (2013), Mission in Action (2014), Living in Love (2014), Word on the Street (2015), Peace that Passes Understanding (2015), The Church (2016); *Recreations* reading, walking; *Style*— The Rt Rev the Bishop of Derby; ✉ The Bishop's House, 6 King Street, Duffield, Belper, Derbyshire DE56 4EU (☎ 01332 840132, e-mail bishop@bishopofderby.org)

DERBY, 19 Earl of (E 1485); Edward Richard William Stanley; 12 Bt (E 1627), DL (Merseyside 1999); also Baron Stanley of Bickerstaffe (UK 1832) and Baron Stanley of Preston (UK 1886); s of Hon Hugh Henry Montagu Stanley (d 1971, gs of 17 Earl of Derby), and Mary Rose (who m 2, William Spiegelberg) da of late Charles Francis Birch, of Rhodesia; suc uncle, 18 Earl of Derby, MC, DL (d 1994); *b* 10 October 1962; *Educ* Eton, RAC Cirencester; *m* 21 Oct 1995, Hon Caroline Emma Neville, da of 10 Baron Braybrooke, *qv*; 1 da (Lady Henrietta Mary Rose b 6 February 1997), 2 s (Edward John Robin, Baron Stanley of Bickerstaffe b 21 April 1998, Hon Oliver Hugh Henry b 26 April 2002); *Heir* s, Baron Stanley of Bickerstaffe; *Career* cmmnd Grenadier Gds 1982–85; dir incl: Fleming Private Asset Management Ltd 1992–2000, Robert Fleming & Co Ltd 1996–98, Robert Fleming Int Ltd 1998–2001, Haydock Park Racecourse Co Ltd 1994–2013, Fleming Family and Ptnrs 2001–15, Stonehage Fleming 2015–; pres: Liverpool C of C 1995–, Royal Liverpool Philharmonic Soc 1995–, Royal Lytham & St Annes Golf Club 1995–, Formby Golf Club 1995–, Royal Botanical and Horticultural Soc of Manchester and the Northern Counties 1995–, Henshaw's Soc for the Blind 1996–2007, Sefton C of C 1998–, Knowsley C of C 1995–; vice-pres PGA 2001–; chm: Knowsley Ltd 1998–, FF&P Tstee Co Ltd 2004–; hon pres: Liverpool Cncl of Social Services, Boys Brigade Liverpool Battalion 1995–; tstee: Nat Museums and Galleries on Merseyside 1995–2005, Aintree Racecourse Charitable Appeal Tst 1995–; tstee and memb Regimental Cncl Grenadier Guards 2007; memb Cncl Univ of Liverpool 1998–2004 and 2011– (vice-pres 2012–14, pres 2015–); patron: Friends of Liverpool Cathedral 1995–, Liverpool Branch RNLI 1995–, Liverpool Area Prince's Tst, numerous other charities; life pres Rugby Football League 1996–; Hon Cdr RNR 2015–; LLD (hc) Univ of Liverpool 2008, DBA (hc) Univ of Chester 2009; *Publications* Ouija Board: A Mare in a Million (2007); *Clubs* White's, Jockey Club Rooms; *Style*— The Rt Hon the Earl of Derby, DL; ✉ Knowsley, Prescot, Merseyside L34 4AF (☎ 0151 489 6147, office fax 0151 482 1988, e-mail private.office@knowsley.com, website www.knowsley.com)

DERBYSHIRE, Benjamin Charles Edward; s of Sir Andrew George Derbyshire, and Lily, *née* Binns; *b* 15 May 1953; *Educ* Bryanston, Hatfield GS, Sch of Architecture Birmingham Poly, Sch of Architecture Univ of Cambridge (DipArch); *m* 1, 14 April 1979 (m dis 2003), Annie Anoja Sapumali, da of I D S Weerawardina; 1 s (Albert Guy Devakumara b 24 April 1987), 1 da (Millicent Grace Ranjani b 15 Jan 1990); m 2, 2 April 2011, Jane, *née* McNeill; 2 step-s (Archie Hollway b 4 May 1988, Angus McNeill b 21 July 1996), 1 step-da (Louisa Hollway b 3 Jan 1990); *Career* architect; HTA Design: joined 1976, assoc 1979–, ptnr 1986–, managing ptnr 2013–; chm USER Research 1991–95 (fndr dir 1989); memb: RIBA Community Architecture Gp 1983–87, Business in the Community Professional Firms Gp 1990–93, Ctee Nat Tenants' Resource Centre 1991–95, Bd Prince's Trust 1992–95, New London Sounding Board 2011–, Cncl RIBA 2014, Ctee London Soc 2014; chm Housing Forum 2013; winner of numerous architectural and building construction awards; contrib to architectural pubns; chair of Govrs Columbia Primary Sch 1995–98; RIBA 1977, FRSA 1993; *Recreations* walking, cycling, music; *Style*— Benjamin Derbyshire, Esq; ✉ HTA Design LLP, 106–110 Kentish Town Road, London NW1 9PX (e-mail ben.derbyshire@hta.co.uk, website www.hta.co.uk, Twitter @ben_derbyshire)

DERBYSHIRE, Prof Edward; s of late Edward Derbyshire, of Timonium, Maryland, and late Kathleen, *née* Wall; *b* 18 August 1932; *Educ* Alleyne's GS Stone, Keele Univ (BA, DipEd), McGill Univ Montreal (MSc), Monash Univ (PhD); *m* 2 June 1956, Maryon Joyce, da of late Arthur John Lloyd, of Keele, Staffs; 3 s (Edmund Lloyd b 20 Jan 1959, Edward Arthur b 13 April 1965, Dominic Giles b 17 Nov 1968); *Career* RAEC 1954–56; lectr in geography Univ of NSW 1960–62, sr lectr in geography Monash Univ 1965–66 (lectr 1963–65); Keele Univ: lectr in physical geography 1967–70, sr lectr 1970–74, reader 1974–84, prof of geomorphology 1984; Univ of Leicester: prof of physical geography 1985–90, res prof 1990–92, prof emeritus 1991–; res prof of physical geography Royal Holloway Coll London (now Royal Holloway Univ of London) 1991–, hon res prof Gansu Acad of Sciences PRC 1991–, Belle Van Zuylen prof Univ of Utrecht 1992; pres Br Geomorphological Res Gp 1982–83 (hon sec 1971–75), pres Section E BAAS 1989–90, sec-gen Int Union for Quaternary Res (INQUA) 1991–95, chm Int Geological Correlation Prog (UNESCO/IUGS) 1996–2001, chm Ctee for Research Directions Int Union of Geological Sciences (IUGS) 2002–06, chm Science Prog Ctee Int Year of Planet Earth (UNESCO/IUGS) 2002–08; Geological Soc London: sec foreign and external affrs 2007–10, chm External Rels Ctee 2007–10 (memb 1999–2006); Antarctic Serv Medal USA 1974, Varnes Medal Int Consort Landslides UNESCO 2008, J M Harrison Outstanding Achievement Award Int Union of Geological Sciences 2012; hon life memb: INQUA 1999, Quaternary Res Assoc 1999; FGS 1974, FRGS 1980, FBSG 2013 (inaugural fell); *Books* The Topographical Map (1966), Climatic Geomorphology (ed, 1973), Geomorphology and Climate (ed, 1976), Geomorphological Processes (with J R Hails and K J Gregory, 1980), Genesis and Properties of Collapsible Soils (ed with I J Smalley and T A Dijkstra, 1995), Landslides in the Thick Loess Terrain of Northwest China (ed with X M Meng and T A Dijkstra, 2000), Palaeoenvironmental Reconstruction in Quaternary Arid Lands (ed with A K Singhi, 1999), Planet Earth (ed, 2008, 2 edn 2009), Tales Set in Stone: 40 Years of the International Geoscience Programme (ed, 2012); also 280 Earth Science research articles published in int scientific jls 1958–; *Style*— Prof Edward Derbyshire; ✉ Department of Geography, Royal Holloway, University of London, Egham, Surrey TW20 0EX (☎ 01242 461348, e-mail ed4gsl@sky.com)

D

DERBYSHIRE, Eileen; MBE (2010); da of Frank Derbyshire (d 1976), of Manchester, and Mary Edna, *née* Taylor (d 1993); *b* 6 October 1931; *Educ* Manchester HS for Girls, Northern Sch of Music; *m* 1 April 1965, Thomas Wilfrid Holt, s of George Wrangham Holt; 1 s (Oliver Charles Thomas b 22 May 1966); *Career* actress; first broadcast in 1948, has taken part in numerous radio prodns; first appeared in rep 1952 (toured with Century Theatre and others); plays role of Emily Bishop in Coronation Street (joined in first year 1961); LRAM; *Style*— Miss Eileen Derbyshire, MBE; ✉ c/o Granada Television Ltd, Granada TV Centre, Quay Street, Manchester M60 9EA

DERBYSHIRE, Victoria A; da of Pauline Derbyshire, *née* Mulrooney; *b* 2 October 1968, Bury, Gtr Manchester; *Educ* Univ of Liverpool, Lancashire Poly (Dip); *Career* journalist and broadcaster; BRMB Birmingham 1991–92, BBC Coventry and Warks Radio 1992–95, co-host breakfast show BBC GMR Manchester 1995–98, co-host Breakfast Show then Victoria Derbyshire Show BBC Radio Five Live 1998– (Radio Show of the Year TRIC Award 1999, Best Breakfast Show Sony Gold Radio Award 1999 and 2002); Radio Personality of the Year Variety Club of GB 2006, Speech Broadcaster of the Year Sony Radio Acad Gold Award 2012; *Style*— Miss Victoria Derbyshire; ✉ c/o BBC Radio Five Live, TV Centre, MediaCityUK, Salford M50 2EQ (☎ 020 8624 9502)

DERCON, Prof Stefan; s of Rene Dercon of Bevel, Belgium, and Maria, *née* Nelen (d 1981); *b* 4 December 1964, Ekeren, Belgium; *Educ* K U Leuven Belgium (BPhil, Licence in Economics), Univ of Oxford (MPhil, DPhil); *m* 21 July 1996, Pramila, *née* Krishnan; 1 s (Quentin b 11 Aug 1998); *Career* visiting prof Econs Dept Addis Ababa Univ Ethiopia 1992–93, res fell Nuffield Coll Oxford 1993–97, prof (devpt econ) Katholieke Univsersiteit Leuven Belgium 1993–2000, prog dir World Inst of Devpt Economics (WIDER) UN Univ Helsinki 2000–02; Univ of Oxford: fell and tutor in econ Jesus Coll and univ lectr 2001–04, prof of devpt econ (statutory) and fell Wolfson Coll 2004–; sr fell Bureau for Res in Econ and Devpt (BREAD) 2007–, res fell Centre for Economic Policy Res (CEPR), fell European Devpt Network (EUDN); chief economist Dept for Int Devpt 2011–; Insurance against Poverty (2004); author of various articles published in numerous learned jls on Africa and devpt problems; *Recreations* hiking, family travel, music, the company of my son Quentin; *Style*— Prof Stefan Dercon; ✉ Department of International Development, 3 Mansfield Road, Oxford, OX1 3TB (☎ 0185 281822, fax 01865 281801)

DEREGOWSKI, Prof Jan Bronisław; s of Jan Deregowski (d 1964), and Szczestawa Helena, *née* Enskajt (d 1987); *b* 1 March 1933; *Educ* schooling abroad and N Copernicus Polish Coll, Univ of London (BSc, BA, PhD), Univ of Aberdeen (DSc); *m* 14 August 1958, Eva Loft, da of Eiler Gudmund Nielsen; 2 s (Sven Marek b 2 Dec 1966, Niels Tadeusz b 12 Feb 1969), 1 da (Anna Halina b 16 Nov 1976); *Career* various engrg appts 1960–65, Miny of Overseas Devpt research fell Univ of Zambia 1965–69; Univ of Aberdeen: lectr 1969–77, sr lectr 1977–81, reader 1981–88, prof 1988–; memb Soc Polonaise des Sciences et des Lettres a l'Etranger 1990; fell Netherlands Inst for Advanced Studies; FBPsS, FRSE 1994; *Books* Illusions, Patterns and Pictures (1980), Distortion in Art: The Eye and the Mind (1984), Perception and Artistic Style (co-author, 1990); *Recreations* reading, history of the Grand Duchy of Lithuania, Polish language; *Style*— Prof Jan Deregowski, FRSE; ✉ Department of Psychology, University of Aberdeen, King's College, Old Aberdeen, Aberdeen AB9 2UB (☎ 01224 272246 and 01224 272228, fax 01224 273426, e-mail psy022@abdn.ac.uk)

DERHAM, Katie; *Educ* Magdalene Coll Cambridge; *m* 1999; 2 da (Natasha, Eleanor); *Career* broadcaster; *Radio* researcher Moneybox BBC Radio 4 1993–94, presenter Moneycheck BBC Radio 5 Live 1995–96 (Bradford and Bingley Personal Fin Broadcaster Award), ed Financial World Tonight BBC Radio 4, presenter Classic FM 2002–09, presenter LBC 2003, presenter Traveller's Tree (BBC Radio 4) 2008–, presenter BBC Radio 3 2010–; *Television* BBC: reporter Film 96 and Film 97, consumer affairs corr 1996–97, reporter Here and Now 1997, presenter BBC 2 2010– (incl Proms); ITV: presenter Wide Angle ITV2 1998–99, media and arts corr 1998–2001, media and arts ed 2001–03, newscaster ITV News, presenter ITV Lunchtime News and London Tonight 2004–10; The People's Review 2006, Tour de France 2007; presenter Classical Brit Awards 2001, 2002, 2003 and 2004; contestant Maestro (BBC2) 2008; New TV Talent of the Year TRIC Awards 1999; *Style*— Ms Katie Derham; ✉ BBC Broadcasting House, Portland Place, London W1A 1AA

DERHAM, Dr Kenneth Walter; s of Kenneth Reginald Derham, of Southampton, Hants, and Edith Sybil, *née* Harden; *b* 16 May 1949, Southampton; *Educ* Univ of Bath (BSc), Univ of Essex (PhD); *m* 16 April 1977, Janet Mary, da of Edgar Victor Garton (d 1984), of Enfield, Middx; 1 da (Anna Rose b 1980); *Career* commissioning ed Elsevier Applied Science Publishers 1974–77, sr ed Plenum Publishing Co 1977–99, md Plenum UK & Euro 1978–91, md Plenum Publishing Co Ltd 1991–98, publishing dir Kluwer Academic/Plenum Publishers 1998–2003, editorial dir Springer 2004–14, freelance publishing conslt 2014–; gamesmaker London Olympics 2012; *Recreations* environmental conservation at NT Dunwich Heath and Halesworth Millennium Green Suffolk, volunteer steward at Snape Maltings Concert Hall; *Clubs* Science Study Gp Halesworth U3A (chair); *Style*— Dr Kenneth Derham; ✉ e-mail ken-jan@live.co.uk

DERHAM, Patrick; s of John Joseph Sibley Derham, and Helena Petronella Timby, *née* Verhagen; *b* 23 August 1959; *Educ* training ship Arethusa, Pangbourne Coll, Pembroke Coll Cambridge (MA); *m* 1982, Alison Jane, *née* Sheardown; 1 s (Rupert), 1 da (Emma); *Career* asst master Cheam Sch 1982–84, history teacher and housemaster Radley Coll 1984–96; headmaster: Solihull Sch 1996–2001, Rugby Sch 2001–14, Westminster Sch 2014–; dep chm IntoUniversity; memb Advsy Bd New Coll of Humanities; tstee Gladstone Library; *Publications* The Irish Question 1868–1886, Liberating Learning Widening Participation (jt ed, 2010), Cultural Olympians (jt ed, 2013), Loyal Dissent (ed, 2016); *Recreations* quizzes, reading, running, family; *Style*— Patrick Derham, Esq; ✉ Westminster School, 17 Dean's Yard, London SW1P 3PB

DERING, Christopher John; s of Dr John Charles Dering, of Southampton, and late Annette Joan, *née* Green; *b* 21 September 1964; *Educ* Weymouth GS, Exeter Coll Oxford (scholar, Maxwell Law Prize, Slaughter & May Contract Prize, proxime accessit Martin Wronker Prize, BA, MA); *m* 18 July 1987, Julie Ann, da of late Harry Alfred Killick; 1 da (Lucy Ann b 18 May 1993), 1 s (James Christopher b 11 Nov 1999); *Career* lectr in law Exeter Coll Oxford 1986–88, called to the Bar Middle Temple 1989, admitted slr 1992, admitted slr (Hong Kong) 1999, ptnr Pinsent Masons 1992–2005 (joined 1989, memb Partnership Bd 1998–2001, head Int and Energy Div 2002–03), princ vice-pres Bechtel 2006–14 (sr vice-pres 2014–); Bechtel Ltd: princ counsel 2005, dir 2006–12, asst gen counsel 2012, md Aviation 2013–15, gen mangr ME and N Africa 2015–; visiting lectr KCL Centre of Construction Law 2005–; memb Cncl Soc of Construction Law 2004–06; govr Canadian Int Sch of Hong Kong 2000–02; *Books* Jersey Law Reports (ed, 1987–88), Service Level Agreements (contrib, 1993), Eco-Management and Eco-Auditing (contrib and co-ed, 1993), Health and Safety Law for the Construction Industry (consulting ed, 1997, 2 edn 2004), Environmental Law for the Construction Industry (consulting ed, 1998, 2 edn 2002), Facilities Management Legal Update (memb ed bd, 1997–98), Employment Law for the Construction Industry (consulting ed, 2000); *Style*— Christopher Dering, Esq; ✉ 11 Pilgrim Street, London EC4V 6RN (✆ 020 7651 7878, e-mail cdering@bechtel.com)

DERRICK, Robin James; s of Ivor Charles Derrick (d 1998), and Jean Mary Derrick (d 2001); *b* 29 May 1962, Bristol; *Educ* Clerk GS Bristol, Filton Tech Coll, St Martin's Sch of Art London (BA); *Children* 1 s (Luke William b 1995); *Career* creative dir and photographer; art dir: The Face 1986–87 (designer 1984–86), Elle (Italy) 1987–89, Glamour (France) 1989–91, Arena 1991–93 (contrib ed 1986); Vogue: art dir 1993–2001, creative dir 2001–11, conslt on numerous int edns; former guest art dir: Per Lui (Milan), Actuel (Paris); co-fndr Studio Box 1988; photographer for various magazines incl: British, German, Spanish, Russian and Japanese Vogue, Nylon (USA), Dolce Vita, i-D; co-curator Unseen Vogue Design Museum 2003, Big Head (solo exhbn, Galerie Gordon Pym & Fils Paris) 2004; *Books* The Impossible Image (co-ed, 2000), Unseen Vogue (co-ed, 2002), People in Vogue (co-ed, 2003); *Style*— Robin Derrick, Esq

DERWENT, Henry Clifford Sydney; CB (2006); s of Clifford Sydney Derwent (d 1995), and Joan Kathleen, *née* Craft (d 2004); *b* 19 November 1951; *Educ* Berkhamsted Sch, Worcester Coll Oxford; *m* 26 Nov 1988, Rosemary Patricia Jesse, da of Reginald Meaker (d 1980); 3 da (Rachel Patricia Alice (Mrs Edmonds), Olivia Christiana Maud, Romola Henrietta Rose b); *Career* DOE and PSA 1974–85 (seconded to Midland Bank 1984), Dept of Tport 1986–96 (various posts 1986–92, dir Nat Roads Policy 1992–96, seconded to SBC Warburg Dillon Read 1996), dir Environment Risks and Atmosphere DETR 1999–2002, dir Climate, Energy and Environmental Risks DEFRA 2002, PM's special rep on climate change 2005, pres and ceo Int Emissions Trading Assoc (IETA) 2008–12 (vice-pres 2012–), climate change conslt 2012–, ceo Climate Strategies 2013–; *Recreations* riding, watercolours, playing music (flute, trombone, saxophone); *Style*— Henry Derwent, Esq, CB; ✉ e-mail derwent@ieta.org

DESAI, Anita; da of Toni Nimé, of Berlin, and D N Mazumdar, of Dhaka, Bangladesh; *b* 24 June 1937; *Educ* Queen Mary's Sch for Girls Delhi, Univ of Delhi (BA); *Career* writer; Helen Cam fell Girton Coll Cambridge 1986–87, Purington prof of English Mount Holyoke Coll US 1988–93, John E Burchard prof of writing MIT 1993–; visting prof: Elizabeth Drew prof Smith Coll USA 1987–88, Gildersleeves prof Barnard Coll NY 1989, American Univ of Cairo Egypt 1992; visiting fell Clare Hall Cambridge 1989, visiting scholar Rockefeller Foundation Bellagio Itlay 1992; author of several reports for UN and UNICEF; book reviewer for numerous litereray jls and newspapers; hon fell: Girton Coll Cambridge, Clare Hall Cambridge; hon memb American Acad of Arts and Letters; FRSL; *Books* Cry, The Peacock (1963), Voices in the City (1965), Bye-Bye, Blackbird (1971), Where Shall We Go This Summer? (1975), Fire on the Mountain (Winnifred Holtby Prize, National Acad of Letters Award India, 1978), Games At Twilight And Other Stories (short stories, 1979), Clear Light of Day (1980), In Custody (1984, filmed by Merchant Ivory Productions 1994), Journey To Ithaca (1995), The Peacock Garden (for children), Cat On A Houseboat (for children), The Village By The Sea (for children, Guardian Award for children's fiction 1984, filmed by BBC 1992), Fasting Feasting (1999, Shortlisted for Booker Prize), Diamond Dust and Others Stories (2000), The Zig Zag Way (2004); *Style*— Ms Anita Desai, FRSL; ✉ c/o David Miller, Rogers, Coleridge & White Ltd, 20 Powis Mews, London W11 1JN

DESAI, Baron (Life Peer UK 1991), of St Clement Danes in the City of Westminster; Meghnad Jagdishchandra Desai; s of Jagdishchandra Chandulal Desai (d 1984), of Baroda, India, and Mandakini, *née* Majmundar (d 1989); *b* 10 July 1940; *Educ* Univ of Bombay (BA, MA), Univ of Pennsylvania (PhD); *m* 1 (m dis 2004), Gail Graham, da of George Ambler Wilson, CBE (d 1978), of London; 2 da (Hon Tanvi b 1972, Hon Nuala b 1974), 1 s (Hon Sven b 1975); m 2, Kishwar Ahluwalia, *née* Rosha; 1 step s (Gaurav b 1981), 1 step da (Mallika b 1982); *Career* assoc specialist Dept of Agric Econ Univ of Calif 1963–65; LSE: lectr 1965–77, sr lectr 1977–80, reader 1980–83, prof 1983–2003 (emeritus prof 2003–), head Devpt Studies Inst 1990–95, dir Centre for the Study of Global Governance 1992–2003; memb: Exec Ctee Fabian Soc 1991–92, Cncl Royal Econ Soc 1991–94; chm Islington South and Finsbury Constituency Lab Pty 1986–92; pres Assoc of Univ Teachers in Economics 1987–90; Hon DSc Kingston Univ 1992, Hon DPhil London Guildhall Univ 1996, Hon LLD Monash Univ 2005; Hon DUniv: Middx 1993, E London 1994; FRSA 1991; *Books* Marxian Economic Theory (1974), Applied Econometrics (1976), Marxian Economics (1979), Testing Monetarism (1981), Cambridge Economic History of India vol 2 (co-ed, 1983), Agrarian Power and Agricultural Productivity in South Asia (co-ed, 1984), Lectures on Advanced Econometric Theory (ed, 1988), Lenin's Economic Writings (ed, 1989), Marx's Revenge: The Resurgence of Capitalism and the Death of Statist Socialism (2002), Nehru's Hero: Dilip Kumar in the Life of India 1944–1964 (2004), Development and Nationhood: Essays in the Political Economy of South Asia (2004), Why is India a Democracy (2005), The Route of All Evil: The Political Economy of Ezra Pound (2006), Rethinking Islamism, The Rediscovery of India (2009), Dead on Time (2009), Pakeeza (2013), Who Wrote the Bhagavad Gita (2014), Hubris: Why Economists Failed to Predict the Crisis and How to Avoid the Next One (2015); *Recreations* reading, politics; *Style*— The Rt Hon Lord Desai; ✉ 3 Deepdene Road, London SE5 8EG (e-mail m.desai@lse.ac.uk); House of Lords, London SW1A 0AA (✆ 020 7219 5066)

DESLANDES, Joan; da of Melbourne Elicio Deslandes, and Olive Joyce Deslandes; *b* Coventry; *Educ* Pres Kennedy Comp Sch Coventry, Univ of London Inst of Educn (BEd, MA); *Children* 2 s (Antonio b 31 July 1994, Howard Floyd b 5 Dec 1997), 1 da (Belinda Joanne b 6 Sept 2003); *Career* headteacher Kingsford Community Sch 2002–; memb: Dept for Educn Teachers'/Master Standards Review Gp, 100 Gp of Head Teachers (co-chair with Richard Cairns, *qv*), 48 Gp Club, Univ of London Inst of Educn Steering Gp for Chinese, HSBC Family of Schs, Dept for Educn Ind/State Sch Partnerships Forum, Cabinet Office Third Sector Forum; govr Brighton Coll; twice listed in Evening Standard's 1000 Most Influential Londoners, head teacher of first UK sch to gain Best Confucius Classroom in the World status from Chinese Govt; *Publications* Chinese Learning and Teaching (contrib, 2007), China Now (contrib, 2008); *Recreations* travel, reading; *Clubs* 48 Gp; *Style*— Ms Joan Deslandes; ✉ Kingsford Community School, Kingsford Way, Beckton, London E6 5JG (✆ 020 7476 4700 extn 205, e-mail jdeslandes@kingsford.newham.sch.uk)

DESMET, Anne Julie; da of Louis Desmet (d 1973), and Irene, *née* Irving, of Liverpool; *b* 14 June 1964, Liverpool; *Educ* Seafield GS (became Sacred Heart HS), Worcester Coll Oxford (BA), Central Sch of Art and Design (Postgrad Dip), Br School at Rome (scholarship), Univ of Oxford (MA); *m* 2 June 1994, Roy Willingham; 1 s (Thomas b 25 Sept 1997), 1 da (Marion b 11 June 2001); *Career* artist and printmaker 1987– (specialising in wood engraved prints and collages of architectural and metamorphosing subjects); ed Printmaking Today magazine 1998–2013; visiting lectr various art schs and print workshops 1987–, external examiner Aberystwyth Univ Sch of Art 2003–07 external examiner Kingston Coll of Art 2010–13; hon fell Aberystwyth Univ 2010–15 (creative associate 2015–19); elected memb Royal Soc of Painter-Printmakers 1988, elected memb Soc of Wood Engravers 1991, memb Royal W of Eng Acad (RWA) 2008, RA 2011; *Solo Exhibitions* over 40 incl: 17 in London, 2 major museum retrospectives (Ashmolean Oxford and touring UK 1998–99 and Whitworth Art Gallery Manchester and touring UK 2008–10); *Work in Collections* 37 nat and int collections incl: Ashmolean, V&A, British Museum, Whitworth, Fitzwilliam, Ex Libris Museum Moscow, Lodz Museum Poland, Ostrobothnian Art Museum Finland, Lahti Art Museum Finland, Museo Civico Cremona Italy, Guanlan Print Museum China; *Commissions* engravings incl: V&A, British Museum, Nat Gallery, British Library, Sotheby's, Oxford Univ Press, The Times; *Awards* 35 awards and prizes incl: Elizabeth Greenshields Fndn Awards 1989, 1996 and 2007, Pollock-Krasner Fndn Award NY 1998, RA Summer Exhibition Print Prize 2010, V&A Purchase Prize 2011; *Books* Anne Desmet – Towers and Transformations (1998), Handmade Prints (co-author, 2000), Printmakers – The Directory (co-ed, 2006), Anne Desmet – Urban Evolution (2008), Primary Prints (2010), Anne Desmet – Olympic Metamorphoses (2010), Fragments of Time (2012), Time Sequences (2015); *Recreations* cinema, reading, vegetarian cooking; *Style*— Ms Anne Desmet, RA; ✉ website www.annedesmet.com

DESMOND, Daniel Frank (Danny); s of Frank Albert Desmond (d 1973), and Beatrice Ena, *née* Mitchison (d 1998); *b* 10 January 1940, Feltham Middlesex; *Educ* St Mary's Sch Northampton; *m* 1; 2 s (Nicholas b 24 Aug 1963, Nigel 14 Aug 1967), 1 da (Louise b 26 Nov 1970); m 2, 8 Nov 1980, Diana Chalkley, *née* Mayne; 1 da (Lara 19 Nov 1981), 1 s (Charles b 22 Sept 1983); *Career* gp md Hunting Gate Gp 1969–83; fndr Bride Hall Gp 1983 (currently chm and chief exec); dir: GL Portland Estates 1987–92; *Recreations* family, golf; *Clubs* Mark's, Harry's Bar, Annabel's, George, Mosimann's, 5 Hertford Street; *Style*— Danny Desmond, Esq

DESMOND, Denis Fitzgerald; CBE (1989); s of Maj James Fitzgerald Desmond, JP, DL, of Killaloo, Londonderry, and Harriet Ivy, *née* Evans (d 1972); *b* 11 May 1943; *Educ* Castle Park Dublin, Trinity Coll Glenalmond; *m* 25 July 1965, Annick Marie Marguerite Francoise, da of M Jean Faussemagne, of Nancy, France; 1 da (Stephanie b 1970); *Career* 2 Lt and Lt RCT (TA) 1964–69; Hon Col 1 Bt (NI) ACF 2005–, Hon Col 152 (U) Tpt Regt RLC (V) 2010–; chm and md Desmond & Sons Ltd Londonderry 1970–2004 (dir 1966–70), chm Adria Ltd Strabane 1976–81, dir Ulster Development Capital Ltd Belfast 1985–90, regnl dir Nationwide Anglia Building Society 1986–90, dir Ulster Bank Ltd 1990–97; chm Altnagelvin Hosps Health Tst 1996–2004; High Sheriff Co Londonderry 1974; HM Lord-Lt County Londonderry 2000– (DL 1992–2000); ADC to Govr NI 1967–69; Hon DSc: Queen's Univ Belfast 1987, Univ of Ulster 1991; *Recreations* fishing, tennis; *Style*— Denis Desmond, Esq, CBE; ✉ Bellarena, Limavady, Co Londonderry BT49 0HZ

DESMOND, Dermot; *b* 1950, Cork, Republic of Ireland; *Educ* Scoil Mhuire Marino, Good Counsel Coll New Ross; *Career* stockbroker; early career with Citibank, Investment Bank of Ireland and Price Waterhouse Coopers (banking conslt Afghanistan); fndr and chm NCB 1981–94, fndr International Investment and Underwriting Ltd (IIU) 1995 (cos incl Daon, GBE Technologies, Intuition Publishing, eSpatial, Sporting Emporium); owner London City Airport until 2006, dir and shareholding in Celtic FC 1995–, other investments incl Sandy Lane Hotel Barbados, Rietumu Bank Latvia, Kennady Diamonds, Barchester and Acision, investor in numerous other cos; chm Respect; tstee Chester Beatty Library; *Recreations* golf; *Style*— Mr Dermot Desmond; ✉ International Investment and Underwriting, IFSC House, Custom House Quay, Dublin 1, Ireland

DESMOND, Richard Clive; s of Cyril Desmond (d 1987), and Millie, *née* Harris; *b* 8 December 1951, London; *Educ* Christ's Coll Finchley; *m* 1, 4 Aug 1983 (m dis), Janet, *née* Robertson; 1 s (Robert b 10 June 1989); m 2, 27 July 2012, Joy, *née* Canfield; 1 da (Angel-Millie b 9 March 2011); *Career* publisher; early career: advtg exec Thomson Newspapers, advtg mangr Beat Pubns Ltd, publisher Int Musician & Recording World magazine, De Monde Advtg Ltd; prop: Northern and Shell plc 1982– (pubns incl OK! magazine (launched 1993)), Express Newspapers 2000– (pubns incl Daily Express, Sunday Express, Daily Star and Daly Star Sunday), Portland TV, Channel Five 2010–, YouView 2010– (ptnr), The Health Lottery 2011–; charitable involvement incl: Richard Desmond Charitable Tst, Disability Fndn, Richard Desmond Children's Eye Centre, pres Norwood, RD Crusaders Supergroup (with Roger Daltrey) for Teenage Cancer Tst, Bomber Command Meml, World Jewish Relief, Jewish Care, Niger Appeal, Elton John's AIDS Fndn, Darfur – Not on Our Watch; supporter: Jewish Care, Niger Appeal, Elton John's AIDS Fndn, Darfur- Not on Our Watch; *Recreations* fitness, drumming; *Style*— Mr Richard Desmond; ✉ Northern & Shell plc, The Northern & Shell Building, 10 Lower Thames Street, London EC3R 6EN

DETMER, Prof Don Eugene; s of Lawrence O Detmer (d 1962), of Great Bend, KS, and Esther B, *née* McCormick (d 1997); *b* 2 February 1939; *Educ* Univ of Durham, Univ of Kansas, Univ of Cambridge; *m* 26 Aug 1961, Mary Helen McFerson; 2 da (Mary Catherine b 28 June 1963, Emily Anne b 28 Oct 1966); *Career* surgical educn: Johns Hopkins Univ 1965–67, NIH 1967–69, Duke Med Center 1969–72; health policy trg: Inst of Med Nat Acads 1972, Harvard Business Sch 1973; asst and assoc prof of surgery and preventive med Univ of Wisconsin Madison 1973–74, vice-pres for health sciences and prof of surgery and med informatics Univ of Utah 1984–88, vice-pres and provost for health sciences, sr vice-pres and prof of surgery, business admin and health evaluation sciences Univ of Virginia 1988–99 (prof emeritus and prof of med educn 1999–), Dennis Gillings prof of health mgmnt and dir Cambridge Univ Health Univ of Cambridge 1999–2003 (sr associate 2004–); fell Clare Hall Cambridge; chm Nat Ctee on Vital and Health Statistics Dept of Health and Human Servs Washington DC (also chair Bd of Regents), chair Bd on Health Care Servs Inst of Med, co-chair Blue Ridge Academic Health Gp; memb Bd: Assoc of Academic Health Centers, China Med Bd of NY Inc, Nuffield Tst; memb Editorial Bd Quality and Safety in Healthcare; Chancellor's Award for Distinguished Teaching Univ of Wisconsin Madison, President's Award American Med Informatics Assoc 1996 and 1998, Medal Mongolian State Univ 2001; Distinguished Med Alumnus Duke Univ Med Center Alumni Assoc 1993; nat assoc Nat Academies Washington DC; fell: AAAS 1998, American Coll of Med Informatics, Acad of Health, American Coll of Sports Med; memb: Inst of Med, RSM, Soc of Med Administrators; FACS; *Publications* author of numerous papers in learned jls; *Recreations* fly fishing, crafts, wilderness canoeing, horse riding; *Clubs* Cosmos (Washington DC); *Style*— Prof Don Detmer; ✉ Judge Institute of Management, University of Cambridge, Trumpington Street, Cambridge CB2 1AG (✆ 01223 339700, fax 01223 339701, e-mail d.detmer@jims.cam.ac.uk)

DETSINY, (Anthony) Michael; s of Rudolph Detsiny, JP (d 1987), and Edith, *née* Scheff (d 1993); *b* 25 July 1941; *Educ* Highgate Sch; *m* 2 Dec 1967, Angela Hazel, da of Francis Charles Cornell (d 1977); 2 s (Warren Rodney b 1969, Stephen Charles b 1978), 1 da (Hazel Karen b 1972); *Career* dir: Cadbury Ltd 1977–83, Allied Breweries 1983–86; md The Creative Business Ltd 1986–91, chm and chief exec Foote Cone and Belding (London) 1991–96, dir The Marketing and Communications Business 1996–97, DG The Marketing Soc 1997–; MInstD; *Recreations* gardening, reading; *Style*— Michael Detsiny, Esq; ✉ The Willows, Moor End Common, Frieth, Henley-on-Thames, Oxfordshire RG9 6PU (✆ 01494 881176); The Marketing Society, St George's House, 3–5 Pepys Road, London SW20 8NJ (✆ 020 8879 3464, fax 020 8879 0362)

DEUCHAR, Dr Stephen John; CBE (2010); s of late Rev John Deuchar, and Nancy Dorothea, *née* Jenkyns; *b* 11 March 1957; *Educ* Dulwich Coll (scholar), Univ of Southampton (BA), Westfield Coll London (PhD); *m* 1982, Prof Katie Scott; 1 s, 3 da; *Career* Andrew W Mellon fell in Br art Yale Univ 1981–82; Nat Maritime Museum: curator of paintings

1985–87, curator Armada exhbn 1987–88, corp planning mangr 1988–89, organiser of exhbns and display projects 1990–95, dir Neptune Court Project 1995–97; dir Tate Britain 1998–2010, dir Art Fund 2010–; tstee Creative Fndn 2008–; *Books* Noble Exericse: the sporting ideal in 18th century British art (1982), Paintings, Politics and Porter: Samuel Whitbread and British Art (1984), Concise Catalogue of Oil Paintings in the National Maritime Museum (jtly, 1988), Sporting Art in 18th Century England: a social and political history (1988), Nelson: an illustrated history (jtly, 1995); *Style*— Dr Stephen Deuchar, CBE

DEUTSCH, Antonia Sara; da of Ronald Leopold Deutsch, of Ilmington, Warks, and Jill Patricia, *née* Davis; *b* 24 June 1957; *Educ* The Abbey Sch, Sorbonne; *m* 31 May 1980, Colin David Guy Robinson, s of Guy Martyn Robinson; 1 s (Oscar Charles Thomas b 4 Nov 1989), 1 da (Eliza Alice Louise b 10 Aug 1991); *Career* photographic asst 1981–84, freelance photographer specialising in people, landscapes and black and white images 1984–; solo exhibition Grey Coll Univ of Durham 2010, solo online exhibition Assoc of Photographers 2012; awards incl: Assoc of Photographers Silver Award 1989, Gold and Merit Awards 1991 and Judges' Choice 1996, Ilford Print of the Year 1989; memb Assoc of Photographers (formerly AFAEP) 1988; *Books* Portrait of Home; *Recreations* photography, independent rough travel, family; *Style*— Ms Antonia Deutsch; ☎ mobile 07836 344972, e-mail ad@antoniadeutsch.co.uk, website www.antoniadeutsch.co.uk and www.portraitofhome.co.uk

DEVA, Niranjan Joseph (Nirj); DL (Greater London) 1985, MEP (Cons) SE England; s of late Thakur Dr Kingley de Silva Deva Aditya, and Zita de Silva Deva, da of Sen Dr M G Perera, MVO; *b* 11 May 1948; *Educ* St Joseph's Coll Colombo, Loughborough Univ; *m* Indra, da of late Romy Govindia; 1 step s; *Career* company dir and scientific advsr, memb Cncl RCS 1977–79, chm Bow Gp 1981 (sec Foreign Affrs Ctee 1985–87), former advsr to Viscount Whitelaw and Rt Hon David Howell, MP, memb Nat Consumer Cncl 1985–88, chm DTI/NCC Ctee on deregulation of Euro air tport 1985–87; MP (Cons) Brentford and Isleworth 1992–97 (first Asian Cons MP elected this century, Parly candidate (Cons) Hammersmith 1987); memb: Euro Standing Ctee B 1992–97, All-Pty Mfrg Gp 1993–97; memb Standing Ctee on: Immigration Bill 1992–97, Parly Admin (Ombudsman) 1993–97; jt sec Cons Pty Aviation Ctee 1992–97; PPS Scottish Office 1996–97, Select Ctee on Educn 1994–96; MEP (Cons) South East England 1999–; Euro Parl: front bench spokesman Devpt and Co-operation Ctee 1999–, memb Environment Ctee 1999–, memb UK Cons Delgn, delg EU-ACP Jt Parly Assembly 1999–, rapporteur Trade, WTO and Devpt 2000–, delg to Asean countries 2002–, memb Regnl Economy Tport and Tourism Ctee 2002–, delg to UN Gen Assembly 2003, delg to SAARC countries 2004–, coordinator EPP-ED Gp Devpt Cmmn 2004–, first vice-chm S Asia Delgn 2004–09, rapporteur on Financial Perspectives 2005–, memb Foreign Affrs Ctee 2005, chm delgn to World Summit UN Gen Assembly 2005, rapporteur EU Devpt Budget 2006, chm Working Gp A Devpt Ctee 2007–, chm Right Approach Gp, vice-pres Working Gp on Human Dignity, fndr Friends of Sri Lanka, chm von Mises Circle; nominated as candidate to succeed Kofi Annan as Sec Gen of the UN 2006, runner up as Speaker of the European Parliament 2012; Cons Pty special advsr on ethnic affrs 2001–03; currently DG Policy Research Centre for Business; hon life pres EU India Chamber of Commerce; chm: EU-China Friendship Gp, EU Indonesia Gp, EUAfghanistan Gp; memb Int Cmmn on Human Dignity; hon ambass at large Govt of Sri Lanka 2003–, hon advsr to PM of Sri Lanka 2003–; candidate for UN Sec Gen 2006, candidate and runner-up for pres European Parl 2012; chm Symphony Plastics Ltd; dir: Erabodagama Estates Ltd 1990–, Waulngalle Distilleries Ltd 1990–, Distilleries Co of Sri Lanka Ltd 2004–, Aitken Spence Ltd Sri Lanka 2005, Deva Hldgs Sri Lanka (Pvt) L:td 2008–; patron CHASE (Childrens Hospice Service); author of various articles and pamphlets on Chile, Zimbabwe, Rhodesia, enterprise zones, air tport, deregulation; FRSA; Vishwa Kirthi Sri Lanka Abhimani 2006, Knight Cdr Constantinian Mil Order of St George 2008; *Recreations* tennis, riding, reading; *Clubs* Carlton, Hownslow Conservative; *Style*— Nirj Joseph Deva, Esq, DL, FRSA, MEP; ✉ Policy Research Centre for Business, 169B Kennington Road, London SE11 6SF (☎ 01784 432070, fax +32 22 849245, e-mail office@nirjdeva.com, website www.nirjdeva.com)

DEVANE, Sir Ciarán; kt (2015); s o f Michael Devane and Eibhlín Moriarty; *Educ* UC Dublin, George Washington Univ; *m* 1998, Katy Ashburner (d 2003); *Career* engineer and mgmnt conslt, chief exec Macmillan Cancer Support 2007–14, chief exec Br Cncl 2015–; non-exec dir NHS Eng 2011–15; *Style*— Sir Ciarán Devane; ✉ British Council, 10 Spring Gardens, London, SW1A 2BN

DEVANEY, John F; *b* 1946; *Educ* BEng, Harvard Univ (Advanced Mgmnt Prog); *Career* Perkins Engines: grad trainee 1968–76, project mangr Canton Ohio 1976–78, dir quality control then dir mfrg UK 1978–82, dir sales and business devpt Engines Div 1982–83, pres Engines Div 1983–88, gp vice-pres European Components Gp (now Perkins Gp) Peterborough 1988; gp vice-pres Kelsey-Hayes Corporation Romulus Michigan 1989–92; Eastern Group plc (formerly Eastern Electricity plc): md 1992–95, chief exec 1993–95, exec chm 1995–98, dir subsids EA Technology Ltd; chm: Exel plc 2000–02, Liberata until 2002, Telent plc (formerly Marconi Corp plc) 2002–07, National Express 2009–; fndr and chm BizzEnergy; non-exec dir: Midland Bank plc 1994–, NFC plc 1996–, Norwich Capital Investments Ltd 1996–, MEL Ltd 1997–, British Steel plc 1998–; pres Electricity Assoc 1994–95; CEng, FIEE, FIMechE; *Clubs* Reform; *Style*— John Devaney, Esq

DEVAUX, His Hon Judge John Edward; DL (Suffolk 2013); s of Henry Edward Devaux (d 1988), and Anne Elizabeth Devaux (d 1984); *b* 1947; *Educ* Beaumont Coll, Univ of Bristol (LLB); *m* 1979, Fiona Mary, *née* O'Conor; 2 da; *Career* called to the Bar Lincoln's Inn 1970; recorder of the Crown Court 1989–93, circuit judge (SE Circuit) 1993–, resident judge Ipswich 1998–2006, hon recorder of Ipswich 2000–; *Style*— His Hon Judge Devaux, DL; ✉ Ipswich Crown Court, The Courthouse, 1 Russell Road, Ipswich, Suffolk IP1 2AG (☎ 01473 228585)

DEVERELL, Brig John Duncan; CBE (2007, OBE 1998); s of John Christopher Byron Deverell (d 1998), and Elizabeth Letitia, *née* Duncan (d 2013); *b* 1 May 1955; *Educ* Eton, RMA Sandhurst, Christ's Coll Cambridge (MPhil); *m* 1993, Susanne Christiane, *née* Kampert; 1 s (John Conrad Christopher b 1993), 2 da (Georgina Elisabeth Mary b 1994, Flora Sophia b 1996); *Career* cmmnd Royal Scots Dragoon Guards 1975; served: UK, Germany, Belize, former Yugoslavia, Kuwait, Saudi Arabia, Yemen, Iraq, Occupied Palestinian Territories; Royal Irish Regt 1995–2008; with Invensys plc 2009–11, with Keyhaven 2011–13; *Recreations* horses, hunting, music, art; *Clubs* Cavalry; *Style*— Brigadier John Deverell, CBE; ✉ website www.deverellassociates.com

DEVERELL, Gen Sir John Freegard (Jack); KCB (1999), OBE (1987, MBE 1979); s of Harold James Frank Deverell (d 1986), of Bath, and Joan Beatrice, *née* Carter (d 2006); *b* 27 April 1945, Birmingham; *Educ* King Edward's Sch Bath, RMA Sandhurst, RNC Greenwich; *m* 15 Dec 1973, Jane Ellen, da of Gerald Tankerville Norris Solomon, of Hindon, Wilts; 1 da (Emma b 23 Nov 1976), 1 s (Simon b 21 Oct 1978); *Career* RMA Sandhurst 1964–65, cmmnd Somerset and Cornwall Light Infantry 1965, Cmd 3 Bn Light Infantry 1984–86, Dir of Studies Royal Mil Coll of Sci 1986–88, Cdr UK Mobile Force 1988–90, DG Army Manning and Recruiting 1993–95, Cmdt Royal Mil Acad Sandhurst 1995–97, Dep C-in-C Land 1997–, Dep Commander Mil Ops SFOR 1998–99, Dep C-in-C Land 1999–2001, C-in-C Allied Forces N Europe 2001–04; chm Nat Army Museum 2005–14; *Recreations* cricket, golf, horses; *Clubs* Cavalry and Guards, Free Foresters Cricket (2013–); *Style*— Gen Sir Jack Deverell, KCB, OBE

DEVEREUX, Richard; s of Austin Augustus Devereux (d 1970), of Lincoln, and Vera Evelyn, *née* Whylde (d 2005); *b* 3 April 1956; *Educ* Bishop King Sch Lincoln, Portsmouth Coll of Art (scholar, DipAD); *m* 20 Aug 1977, Christine Anne, da of Stanley Holmes; 1 da (Hannah Galadriel b 22 March 1988); *Career* artist; *Solo Exhibitions* Recent Works (Axis Gallery Brighton) 1979, Recent Works (Hiscock Gallery Portsmouth) 1980, Circles (Usher Art Gallery Lincoln) 1984, Assembled Rites (Artsite Bath) 1987, On Sacred Ground (Cairn Gallery Glos) 1988, Beyond the Hall of Dreams (New Art Centre London) 1989, In Stillness and In Silence (Usher Art Gallery Lincoln then The Gallery Cork Street London) 1994, Primordium (Cairn Gallery Glos) 1994–95, Casting Visions (Angel Row Gallery Nottingham) 1997, Source (Hart Gallery London) 1998, Thresholds (Hart Gallery London) 2000, Silent Portals (Yorkshire Sculpture Park) 2002, Seeing Silence (Atrium Gallery Bournemouth Univ) 2003, Works: 1999–2005 (Bend in the River, Gainsborough) 2005, This is Our Intense Desire (Bend in the River Gainsborough) 2007, Encounters Take Precedence (The Collection Lincoln) 2012, Works by Richard Devereux (Showing Space Lincoln) 2013/14, Encounters (Roselidden Centre for Reflection and Creativity Cornwall) 2014, New Works by Richard Devereux (Galleri Mjøsva?gen Hosanger Norway) 2015; *Group Exhibitions* incl: Rufford Arts Centre 1982, Sculpture to Touch (Usher Gallery Lincoln, Ferens Gallery Hull and Normanby Hall Scunthorpe) 1986, 20th Century Br Sculpture (Roche Court Wilts) 1988–2006, New Art Centre London 1989 and 1990, The Journey (Lincoln) 1990, Southampton City Art Gallery 1990, Shared Earth (Peterborough Art Gallery and 6 venue tour) 1991–92, 20th Century Br Sculpture (Millfield Sch) 1992, The Solstice (Cairn Gallery Glos) 1992, Painting the Earth (The Gallery at John Jones London) 1993, ARCO (Madrid) 1994, Art 25! (Basel) 1994, Art 26! (Basel) 1995, Alchemy (Bury St Edmunds Art Gallery and Ickworth House) 1995, Art 27 (Basel) 1996, Peter Bartlow Gallery (Chicago) 1999, Art 99 (Miami) 1999, Gathering Light (Maltby Contemporary Art Winchester) 2001, Lacerta (Dorset) 2006 and 2007, London Art Fair 2011; *Collections* incl: Bodleian Library Oxford, Nat Library of Scotland, Tate Gallery Library London, Trinity Coll Dublin, The Nat Tst, Vancouver Art Gallery and various private collections UK and abroad; *Published Limited Edition Books* Quiet Flame (1986), Assembled Rites (1987), The Bowl of Grain (1989–90), In Stillness and In Silence (1991), From the Angel's Palm (1992), Marked by Ritual (1992), Travaux Publics (1996), Silent Umbra (2003), Within Voids (2003), Iren/Iron (2003), Ferrum Portal (2003), Intervention 1 (2003), Guide to Thresholds (2005); subject of several articles in various pubns; *Books* Encounters Take Precedence (2013); *Style*— Richard Devereux, Esq; ✉ e-mail richard@richarddevereux.org, website www.richarddevereux.com

DEVEREUX, Sir Robert John; KCB (2016); s of Roy Devereux, and Mary Margaret Devereux; *b* 15 January 1957; *Educ* St John's Coll Oxford (MA), Univ of Edinburgh (MSc); *m* 1980, Margaret Alexandra Johnson; 2 da; *Career* ODA 1979–83, HM Treasy 1984–94 (head of defence expenditure 1992–94), seconded to Guinness Brewing Worldwide 1995–96; Dept for Social Security 1996–2001, DWP 2001–02; Dept for Transport: DG road transport, aviation and shipping 2003–07, perm sec 2007–10; perm sec Dept for Work and Pensions 2011–; *Style*— Sir Robert Devereux, KCB; ✉ Department for Work and Pensions, Caxton House, Tothill Street, London SW1H 9DA

DEVEY, Hilary Lorraine; CBE (2013); *b* 10 March 1957; *Career* fndr, chm and chief exec Pall-Ex Gp; panel memb Dragon's Den (BBC 2) 2011–12; patron: Princess Royal Tst for Carers 2007–, Stroke Assoc 2010–; Midlands Business Woman Award 2004, Business Woman of the Year Women of Acheivement Award 2005, Business Personality of the Year Leics Business Award 2005, Inspirational Woman Prowess Award 2008, Business of the Year Leics Business Award 2007, UK Entrepreneur (Business Services) and Southern Regnl Entrepreneur of the Year Ernst & Young Awards 2007, Business of the Year (regnl winner) Chamber Award 2007, Entrepreneur of the Year (regnl winner) Nat Business Award 2007, NatWest everywoman Award 2008, Woman of the Year Vitalise Business Woman of the Year Award 2008, Regnl Entrepreneur of the Year Chamber Award 2008, Businesswoman of the Year E Midlands Devpt Agency Women of Worth Award 2009, Inspirational Woman of the Year Derbys and Notts Chamber Enterprising Women Excellence Award 2009, Sir Robert Lawrence Award for Lifetime Achievement CILT 2009, Personality of the Year Int Freight Weekly Award 2010; Hon LLD Univ of Leicester 2010; *Style*— Ms Hilary Devey, CBE

DEVINE, David Patrick; s of Brendan Devine, of Liverpool, and Karen, *née* Sweatman; *b* 13 February 1992, Liverpool; *Educ* St Margaret's C of E HS Liverpool; *Career* Paralympic athlete; achievements incl: Bronze medal (800m) Athletics World Championships 2011, 2 Bronze medals (800m and 1500m) Paralympic Games 2012; patron Vision 4 Children; Citizenship Award; *Style*— Mr David Devine; ✉ Twitter @devine800_1500m

DEVINE, Prof Fiona; OBE (2010); da of Patrick Noel Devine (d 1990), and Martha, *née* Daly; *b* 6 June 1962, London; *Educ* Univ of Essex (BA, MA, PhD); *m* 2008, James B Husband; *Career* research offr Social Science Branch Dept of Employment 1988, research offr Policy Studies Inst 1988–89, lectr in sociology Univ of Liverpool 1989–94; Univ of Manchester (formerly Victoria Univ of Manchester): lectr in sociology 1994–97, sr lectr in sociology 1997–99, reader in sociology 1999–2001, prof of sociology 2001–, head of sociology Sch of Social Sciences 2004–07, head Sch of Social Sciences 2009–13, head Alliance Manchester Business Sch 2013–; visiting prof Univ of Queensland 2007–08; memb Cncl and chair Int Advsy Ctee ESRC 2003–07; visiting scholar Kennedy Sch of Govt Harvard Univ (Leverhulme Tst grant) 1999; memb: British Sociological Assoc 1985, American Sociological Soc 1995; FAcSS 2011, FRSA; *Books* Affluent Workers Revisited: Privatism and the Working Class (1992), Social Class in America and Britain (1997), Sociological Research Methods in Context (with Sue Heath, 1999), Class Practices: How Parents Help their Children get Good Jobs (2004), Doing Social Science (ed with Sue Heath, 2009), Social Class in the 21st Century (with Mike Savage et al, 2015); *Recreations* swimming, walking, classical and world music, travel; *Style*— Prof Fiona Devine, OBE, FAcSS, FRSA; ✉ Room 2.15, Alliance Manchester Business School, Booth Street West, Manchester M15 6PB (☎ 0161 306 1322, e-mail fiona.devine@manchester.ac.uk)

DEVINE, Rt Rev Joseph; s of Joseph Devine (d 1989), and Christina, *née* Murphy (d 1981); *b* 7 August 1937; *Educ* Blairs Coll Aberdeen, St Peter's Coll Dumbarton, Pontificial Scots Coll Rome, Gregorian Univ Rome (PhD); *Career* personal sec to Archbishop of Glasgow 1964–66, lectr in philosophy St Peter's Coll Dumbarton 1966–74, chaplain Univ of Glasgow 1974–77, auxiliary bishop Glasgow 1977–83, bishop of Motherwell 1983–2013, bishop emeritus 2013–; Papal Bene Merenti 1962; *Recreations* reading, music, soccer; *Style*— The Rt Rev Joseph Devine

DEVINE, Prof Sir Thomas Martin; kt (2014), OBE (2005); *b* 30 July 1945; *Educ* Univ of Strathclyde (BA, PhD, DLitt); *m*; 2 s (twins), 3 da; *Career* Univ of Strathclyde: asst lectr in econ history 1969–70, lectr in history 1970–78, sr lectr 1978–83, reader in Scottish history 1983–88, prof of Scottish history 1988–98, chm Dept of History 1989–92, dean Faculty of Arts and Social Sciences 1993–94, dir Research Centre in Scottish History 1993–98, dep princ 1994–97; Univ of Aberdeen: dir Research Inst of Irish and Scottish Studies 1998–2003, research prof of Scottish history 1998–2004, Louis and Loretta B Glucksmann research prof in Irish and Scottish studies 2004–06; dir AHRB (now AHRC) Centre for Irish and Scottish Studies 2001–06; Univ of Edinburgh: Sir William Fraser prof of Scottish history and palaeography 2006–11, head Sch of History, Classics and Archaeology 2008–10, personal seminar research prof in history 2012–; dir Scottish Centre for Diaspora Studies 2008–; Univ of Guelph Canada: visiting prof of Scottish history 1983 and 1988, adjunct prof of Scottish history Faculty of Graduate Studies 1989–; adjunct prof of history Univ of N Carolina 1997–; British Acad/Leverhulme Tst

D

sr research fell 1992–93; chm Cncl of Economic and Social History Soc of Scotland 1984–88 (memb Cncl 1989–90); ed Scottish Economic and Social History 1981–86; convener Section Ctee Archaeology and Historical Studies RSE 1994–98 (memb 1993–98); memb: Cncl Scottish History Soc 1976–79, Cncl Scottish Catholic Historical Soc 1977–82 (convenor of Cncl 1991–95), Company of Scottish History 1981–, Bd of Govrs St Andrew's Coll of Educn 1990–95, Cncl British Acad 1998–2001, Research Advsy Ctee Leverhulme Tst, Advsy Ctee ESRC Devolution Research Prog 2001–09; tstee: Nat Museums of Scotland 1995–2002, Edinburgh UNESCO World City of Literature; chair Euro Ethnological Research Centre 1998–2002; Sr Hume Brown Prize in Scottish History Univ of Edinburgh 1976, Royal Gold Medal RSE 2001, Beltane Senior Prize for Excellence in Public Engagement RSE 2012, Sir Walter Scott Senior Prize for Excellence in the Humanities and Creative Arts RSE 2012; Hon DLitt Queen's Univ Belfast, Hon DLitt Abertay Univ Dundee, Hon DUniv Univ of Strathclyde 2006; hon fell Univ of West Scotland 2005; FRHistS 1980, FRSE 1992 (Henry Duncan Prize and lectr 1993), FBA 1994, Hon MRIA 2001; *Books* The Tobacco Lords: A Study of the Tobacco Merchants of Glasgow and their Trading Activities 1740–1790 (1975), Lairds and Improvement in the Scotland of the Enlightenment (ed, 1979), Ireland and Scotland 1600–1850: Parallels and Contrasts in Economic and Social Development (ed with D Dickson, 1983), Farm Servants and Labour in Lowland Scotland 1770–1914 (1984), A Scottish Firm in Virginia: William Cunninghame and Co 1767–1777 (1984), People and Society in Scotland 1760–1830 (ed with R Mitchison, 1988), The Great Highland Famine: Hunger, Emigration and the Scottish Highlands in the Nineteenth Century (1988, Agnes Muir MacKenzie Prize Saltire Soc 1991), Improvement and Enlightenment (ed, 1989), Conflict and Stability in Scottish Society 1700–1850 (ed, 1990), Irish Immigrants and Scottish Society in the Eighteenth and Nineteenth Centuries (ed, 1991), Scottish Emigration & Scottish Society (ed, 1992), The Transformation of Rural Scotland: Social Change and Agrarian Development 1660–1815 (1994), Clanship to Crofters' War: The Social Transformation of the Scottish Highlands (1994), Scottish Elites (ed, 1994), Industry, Business and Society in Scotland since 1700 (ed with A J G Cummings, 1994), Glasgow, Vol I, Beginnings to 1830 (ed with G Jackson, 1995), Exploring the Scottish Past: Themes in History of Scottish Society (1995), Scotland in the Twentieth Century (ed with R J Finlay, 1996), Eighteenth Century Scotland: New Perspectives (ed with J R Young, 1998), Celebrating Columba: Irish-Scottish Connections 597–1997 (ed with J F McMillan, 1998), The Scottish Nation 1700–2000 (1999), Scotland's Shame? Bigotry and Sectarianism in Modern Scotland (ed, 2000), Being Scottish: Personal Reflections on Scottish Identity Today (ed, 2002), Scotland's Empire, 1600–1815 (2003), Scotland's Empire and the Shaping of the Americas (2004), The Transformation of Scotland (jt ed, 2005), Clearance and Improvement: Land, Power and People in Scotland 1700–1900 (2006), The Scottish Nation 1700–2007 (2006), Scotland and the Union 1707–2007 (ed, 2008), To the Ends of the Earth: Scotland's Global Diaspora (2011), Scotland and the British Empire (ed with John Mackenzie, 2011), Scotland and Poland: Historical Encounters (ed with David Hesse, 2011), The Oxford Handbook of Modern Scottish History 1500–2010 (ed with Jenny Wormald, 2012); also author of over 100 book chapters and contribs to learned jls; *Recreations* grandchildren, watching skilful football, exploring the Hebrides, visiting Italy; *Style*— Prof Sir Thomas M Devine, OBE, FRSE, Hon MRIA, FBA; ✉ School of History, Classics and Archaeology, University of Edinburgh, William Robertson Wing, Old Medical Building, Edinburgh EH8 9LN (☎ 0131 650 1000, e-mail t.m.devine@ed.ac.uk)

DEVITT, Sir James Hugh Thomas; 3 Bt (UK 1916), of Chelsea, Co London; s of Lt-Col Sir Thomas Gordon Devitt, 2 Bt (d 1995), and his 3 w, Janet Lilian, da of late Col Hugh Sidney Ellis, CBE, MC; *b* 18 September 1956; *Educ* Sherborne, Corpus Christi Coll Cambridge (MA); *m* 20 April 1985, Susan Carol, er da of Dr (Adrian) Michael Campbell Duffus, of Woodhouse Farm, Thelbridge, Crediton, Devon; 1 da (Gemma Florence b 1987), 2 s (Jack Thomas Michael b 1988, William James Alexander b 1990); *Heir* s, Jack Devitt; *Career* chartered surveyor CB Richard Ellis Hotels; MRICS; *Clubs* Ipswich Town FC; *Style*— Sir James Devitt, Bt

DEVLIN, Es; OBE (2015); da of Timothy Devlin, and Angela, *née* Laramy; *b* 24 September 1971; *Educ* Cranbrook Sch, Univ of Bristol, Central St Martins, Motley Design Sch; *Career* set and costume designer; teacher: Wimbledon Sch of Art 2000, Br Cncl Bangladesh 2001, Anglo American Educn 2002; costume designer opening ceremony London Olympics 2012; *Theatre* Edward II (Bolton Octagon) 1996, Piano (TPT Tokyo) 1997, Love and Understanding (Bush Theatre) 1997, Snake in the Grass (Peter Hall Co at the Old Vic) 1997, Yard Gal (Royal Court Theatre) 1997, Love You Too (Bush Theatre) 1998, Betrayal (RNT) 1998, Howie the Rookie (Bush Theatre) 1999, The Death of Cool (Hampstead Theatre) 1999, Drink, Dance, Laugh, Lie (Bush Theatre) 1999, Hamlet (Young Vic) 1999, Perapalas (Gate Theatre) 2000, Rita, Sue and Bob Too/A State Affair (Soho Theatre and Out of Joint) 2000, Henry IV (RSC) 2000, Meat (Plymouth Theatre Royal) 2000, Credible Witness (Royal Court Theatre) 2000, Closer to Heaven – the Pet Shop Boys Musical (Arts Theatre) 2001, The Prisoner's Dilemma (RSC) 2001, A Day in the Death of Joe Egg (Comedy Theatre) 2001 (Broadway 2003), Hinterland (RNT and Out of Joint) 2001, That was Then (Abbey Theatre Dublin) 2002, Arabian Night (Soho Theatre and ATC) 2002, Antony and Cleopatra (RSC) 2002, Five Gold Rings (Almeida) 2003, Wire/Dinos and Jake Chapman/Es Devlin (Only Connect Festival Barbican) 2003, Chimerica (Almeida Theatre and Harold Pinter Theatre) 2013, American Psycho (Almeida) 2013, The Nether (Royal Court) 2014; *Opera* The Cunning Peasant (Guildhall Sch of Music and Drama) 1997, Live Culture (ENO Works) 1998, Don Giovanni (Br Youth Opera) 1999, Fidelio (English Touring Opera) 1998, Powder Her Face (Ystad Festival) 1999, National Opera Studio Showcase (Queen Elizabeth Hall) 1999, Hansel and Gretel (Scottish Opera Go Round) 2001, Macbeth (Klangbogen Festival Vienna) 2003; *Dance* Four Scenes (Rambert Dance Co) 1998, Gods Plenty (Rambert Dance Co) 2000, A Streetcar Named Desire (Northern Ballet Theatre) 2002, I Remember Red (Cullberg Ballet Sweden) 2002; *Film* A Tale of Two Heads 1998, Beggar's Belief 1999, Brilliant 2000, Snow on Saturday 2001, Victoria Station 2002; *Exhibitions* work included in: Prague Quadrennial 1999, Make Space (SBTD) 1998, 2D>3D (SBTD) 2002; *Awards* Linbury Prize for Stage Design 1995–96, TMA Award for Best Design 1999 (nominated 2000), XL Video Award for Best Set Design Olivier Award 2014 (for Chimerica); *Recreations* travel; *Style*— Miss Es Devlin, OBE; ✉ c/o Sally Hope Associates, 108 Leonard Street, London EC2A 4RH (☎ 020 7613 5353, fax 020 7613 4848, e-mail sally@sallyhope.biz); website www.esdevlin.com

DEVLIN, Roger William; s of William Devlin, of Lancs, and Edna, *née* Cross; *b* 22 August 1957; *Educ* Manchester Grammar, Wadham Coll Oxford (MA); *m* 1983, Louise Alice Temlett, da of John Frost Tucker, of Somerset; 2 da (Sophie Victoria Temlett b 29 Nov 1989, Grace Katherine b 4 March 1993); *Career* dir: Hill Samuel & Co Ltd 1978–91, Corning Europe 1991–94, Henry Ansbacher & Co Ltd (head of corp fin) 1994–96; corp devpt dir: Hilton Group 1996–, Ladbroke Worldwide Betting 1996–; non-exec chm: First Residential Properties 1991–03, The Monitor Group Ltd 1994–2000, Baydrive Group 2003–; non-exec dir: PGA European Tour 2000–03, RPS Group 2002–; advsr Phoenix Private Equity 2002–; *Recreations* golf, horse racing, Blackburn Rovers; *Clubs* Racehorse Owners Assoc, Worplesdon, Royal St George's Golf, Royal & Ancient; *Style*— Roger Devlin, Esq; ✉ Hilton Group, Maple Court, Central Park, Reeds Crescent, Watford, Hertfordshire WD1 1HZ (☎ 020 7856 8788, fax 020 7856 8409)

DEVLIN, Stuart Leslie; AO (1988), CMG (1980); *b* 9 October 1931; *Educ* Gordon Inst of Technol Geelong, Royal Melbourne Inst of Technol, RCA; *m* 1986, Carole; *Career* goldsmith, silversmith and designer; designed set of four UK £1 coins 2010; postgrad dir Goldsmiths' Inst 2012–; Royal Warrant as Goldsmith Jeweller to HM The Queen 1982; Goldsmiths' Crafted Design Cncl's Lifetime Achievement Award 2009, Australia Day Fndn Australian of the Year in the UK 2011, Hall of Fame Design Inst of Australia 2016; Freeman City of London 1966, Prime Warden Worshipful Co of Goldsmiths 1996–97; Dr (hc) RMIT Univ Melbourne; DesRCA (Silversmith), DesRCA (Industrial Design-Engrg); *Style*— Dr Stuart Devlin, AO, CMG; ✉ 72 Shippam Street, Chichester, West Sussex PO19 1AG (☎ 01243 778007, e-mail stuart@stuart-devlin.co.uk)

DEVLIN, Timothy Robert (Tim); s of (Hugh) Brendan Devlin, CBE (d 1998), and Ann Elizabeth, *née* Heatley; gs of Maj John Joseph Devlin, OBE; *b* 13 June 1959; *m* 1, 1987 (m dis 1989); m 2, 1991 (m dis 2002); m 3, 2011, Donna, *née* Kusman; *Career* with Cons Res Dept 1981, accountant 1981–84, called to the Bar Lincoln's Inn 1985; MP (Cons) Stockton S 1987–97; PPS: to Sir Nicholas Lyell, QC, MP as Attorney Gen 1992–94, to Anthony Nelson, MP as Min of Trade 1995–97; in practice as barr 1997–, Attorney Gen's list of approved prosecutors 1998–; conslt Stanbrook & Hooper Brussels, sr expert TACIS Legislative Early Warning System Kiev Ukraine 1997–99, dep chm NHS Tbnl 2002–; memb Bar Cncl 2007–10 and 2012–; memb: Soc of Cons Lawyers, Bow Gp; former chm LSE Cons, chm Islington N Cons Assoc 1986 (sec 1985), former chm Northern Gp of Cons MPs, pres Northern Cons Trade Unions; memb Bd of Tstees NSPCC 1994–96; *Recreations* sailing, opera, travel; *Clubs* Royal Ocean Racing, Island Sailing; *Style*— Tim Devlin, Esq; ✉ 32 Furnival Street, London EC4A 1JQ

DEVON, Natasha; MBE (2014); *Educ* Univ of Wales Aberystwyth (BA); *Career* social entrepreneur, campaigner, writer and television presenter; contrib: Independent, Telegraph, Cosmopolitan, Guardian; columnist Cosmopolitan 2013–16; mental health champion Dept for Educn 2015–16, fndr education prog for Body Gossip (arts charity); qualified trainer B-EAT and Mental Health First Aid England; Ultimate Woman of the Year Cosmopolitan 2012, Top 50 Social Entrepreneurs Ernst & Young 2013; fell Univ of Wales Aberystwyth; *Publications* Fundamentals (2015), Self-Esteem Team's Guide to Sex, Drugs and WTFs?! (2015); *Recreations* music, reading, walking; *Style*— Ms Natasha Devon, MBE; ✉ website www.selfesteemteam.org, Twitter @NatashaDevonMBE

DEVONPORT, 3 Viscount (UK 1917); Sir Terence Kearley; 3 Bt (UK 1908); also Baron Devonport (UK 1910); s of 2 Viscount Devonport (d 1973); *b* 29 August 1944; *Educ* Aiglon Coll Switzerland, Selwyn Coll Cambridge (BA, DipArch, MA), Univ of Newcastle upon Tyne (BPhil); *m* 1, 7 Dec 1968 (m dis 1979), Elizabeth Rosemary, 2 da of late John G Hopton, of Chute Manor, Andover; 2 da (Hon Velvet b 1975, Hon Idonia b 1977); m 2, 7 May 2000, Dr Meiyi Pu, da of Prof Wan Jan Pu, of Beijing; 1 da (Hon Minya Dandie, b 24 Nov 2000); *Heir* kinsman, Chester Kearley; *Career* architect: David Brody NY 1967–68, London Borough of Lambeth 1971–72, Barnett Winskill Newcastle upon Tyne 1972–75; landscape architect Ralph Erskine Newcastle upon Tyne 1977–78, in private practice 1979–84; forestry mangr 1973–, farmer 1978–; md Tweedswood Enterprises 1979; dir various other cos 1984–; chm Millhouse Developments Ltd 1989–; memb: Lloyd's 1976–90, Int Dendrology Soc 1978–, TGEW Northern Advsy Ctee 1978–92, TGUK Nat Land Use and Environment Ctee 1984–87, CLA Northern Advsy Ctee 1980–85; pres: Arboricultural Assoc 1995–98, Forestry Cmmn Ref Panel 1987–93; House of Lords: vice-chm All-Pty Parly Forestry Ctee, memb Parly Select Ctee on Public Bldgs and Architecture; chair Genesis (Charitable) Tst Co Durham, tstee Friends of the Elderly London; RIBA, ALI, FRSA 1996, memb IOD; *Recreations* nature, travel, the arts, good food, trees, music, country sports; *Clubs* Beefsteak, Farmers', RAC, Royal Over-Seas League, Northern Counties (Newcastle upon Tyne); *Style*— The Rt Hon the Viscount Devonport; ✉ Ray Demesne, Kirkwhelpington, Newcastle upon Tyne NE19 2RG

DEVONSHIRE, 12 Duke of (E 1694); Sir Peregrine Andrew Morny Cavendish; KCVO (2009), CBE (1997), DL (Derbys 2008); also Baron Cavendish of Hardwicke (E 1605), Earl of Devonshire (E 1618), Marquess of Hartington (E 1694), Earl of Burlington and Baron Cavendish of Keighley (both UK 1831); s of 11 Duke of Devonshire, KG, MC, PC (d 2004), and Hon Deborah Mitford (Dowager Duchess of Devonshire, DCVO) (d 2014), da of 2 Baron Redesdale; *b* 27 April 1944; *Educ* Eton, Exeter Coll Oxford; *m* 28 June 1967, Amanda Carmen, da of late Cdr Edward Gavin Heywood-Lonsdale, RN; 1 s (William, Earl of Burlington b 1969), 2 da (Lady Celina Imogen (Lady Celina Carter) b 1971, Lady Jasmine Nancy (Lady Jasmine Dunne) b 1973); *Heir* s, Earl of Burlington; *Career* sr steward The Jockey Club 1989–94, chm British Horseracing Board 1994–97, HM's representative at Ascot Racecourse 1997–2011 (chm 1997–2008); dep chm Sotheby's 1996–; tstee: Museums Sheffield (formerly Sheffield Galleries and Museums Tst) 2006–12, Wallace Collection 2007–, Storm King Art Centre USA 2007–, Derby Museums 2012–; chllr Univ of Derby 2008–; memb D2N2 Local Enterprise Partnership 2010–12; Hon FBA 2016–; *Style*— The Duke of Devonshire, KCVO, CBE, DL; ✉ Chatsworth, Bakewell, Derbyshire DE45 1PP (☎ 01246 565300, fax 01246 565436, e-mail beamsley2@me.com, website www.chatsworth.org)

DEWAR; *see:* Beauclerk-Dewar

DEWAR, Hamish Richard John; s of Richard John Gresley Dewar (d 1991), of Hay Hedge, Bisley, nr Stroud, Glos, and Andrena Victoria Dewar; *b* 15 January 1956; *Educ* Sherborne, Downing Coll Cambridge (MA); *m* 21 May 1983, Anna Maria, da of Patrick Cloonan, of Sawbridgeworth, Herts; 2 s (Lachlan b 18 July 1987, Woody b 25 Feb 1991), 1 da (India b 3 Jan 1989); *Career* specialist in conservation and restoration of paintings; studied under Richard Maelzer at Edward Speelman Ltd 1977–81, own practice 1982–; main restoration works incl: David with Head of Goliath by Guido Reni, Seed of David (altar piece from Llandaff Cathedral) by D G Rossetti, Angel di Soto by Picasso, The Light of the World by Holman Hunt (for St Paul's Cathedral); *Recreations* golf, football; *Clubs* Sunningdale Golf; *Style*— Hamish Dewar, Esq; ✉ 14 Mason's Yard, Duke Street, St James's, London SW1Y 6BU (☎ 020 7930 4004, fax 020 7930 4100, e-mail hamish@hamishdewar.co.uk)

DEWHIRST, Timothy Charles; DL (E Yorks); s of Alistair Jowitt Dewhirst, CBE, of Driffield, E Yorks, and Hazel Eleanor, *née* Reed; *b* 19 August 1953; *Educ* Worksop Coll; *m* 1, 15 July 1978 (m dis 1997), Prudence Rosalind, née Horsell; 1 s (Charles Alistair Geoffrey b 4 June 1980), 1 da (Samantha Prudence b 26 June 1983); m 2, 28 April 1999, Charlotte Edwina Mary, née Birkett; 1 da (Matilda Charlotte b 2 May 2001); *Career* chm Dewhirst Group plc (clothing and toiletry mfrs) 1993– (chief exec 1986–93); vice-chm BCIA 1990–; memb Cncl BATC 1993–; *Recreations* shooting, golf, fishing, sailing; *Style*— Timothy C Dewhirst, Esq, DL; ✉ Nafferton Heights, Nafferton, Driffield, East Yorkshire YO25 0LD; Dewhirst Group Ltd, Dewhirst House, Westgate, Driffield, East Yorkshire YO25 6TH (☎ 01377 252561, fax 01377 252030)

DEWHURST, Philip Anthony; s of Alfred John Dewhurst, and Rosalind Georgina Dewhurst; *b* 25 September 1949; *Educ* Mark Hall Sch; *m* Joan Catherine; 1 da (Grace b 14 June 1983), 1 s (Tom b 27 March 1987); *Career* mgmnt trainee then copywriter Longman Group Ltd 1968–71, int publicity controller Evans Publishing Ltd 1971–73; PRO: Havering London BC 1973–76, Hackney London BC 1976–77; head of PR and publicity City of Canterbury 1977–80, PRO Surrey CC 1980–84; dir of public affrs: Chemical Industries Assoc 1984–88, Sterling Public Relations 1988–92; md public affrs GCI Group 1992–94, gen mangr GCI Europe 1993–94; chief exec The Rowland Company (Saatchi & Saatchi PR) 1994–95, dir of corp affrs Railtrack plc 1995–99, UK chief exec Shandwick Int 1999–2001, gp dir Corp Affrs BNFL Gp 2001–07, head of PR Gazprom Mktg and

Trading 2007–; pres IPR (now CIPR) 1999– (chm CIPR Excellence Awards 2004–05), chm Nuclear Industry Assoc 2004–, hon sec NATPRO 2003–; visiting fell Bournemouth Univ 2004–; FCIPR (FIPR 1989), FRSA 1989; *Recreations* art, travel; *Style—* Philip Dewhurst, Esq

DEWS, Vivienne Margaret; da of late Albert Dews, and Eva Margaret, *née* Hayman; *b* 29 December 1952; *Educ* Northampton HS for Girls, Univ of Cambridge (BA), Univ of Warwick (Dip); *m* 1, 1972 (m dis), Stephen Ladner; m 2, 1979, Alan Cogbill; 1 s, 1 da (and 2 da decd); *Career* civil servant; joined Home Office 1974, private sec to Min for Police and Prisons 1979, dep dir Top Mgmnt Prog 1987, head immigration policy 1989, head after entry casework and appeals 1991, head consulting efficiency and market testing Home Office 1994, dir fin and services Immigration and Nationality Directorate 1995, chief exec Police IT Org (PITO) 1999, dir (modernising corp support) Inland Revenue 2002, dir Resources and Planning Health and Safety Exec 2002–08, ceo Office of Fair Trading 2008–14, ret; tstee: Charity for Civil Servants, Henry Smith Charity, Young Epilepsy; tstee Ind Age; chair of govrs Winterbourne Nursery and Infant Sch, vice-chair Fedn of St Elphege's and Regina Coeli Catholic Schs; memb CIPFA; *Recreations* family, home, garden; *Clubs* Oxford and Cambridge; *Style—* Miss Vivienne Dews; ✉ e-mail vivienne.cogbill@virginmedia.com

DEXTER, Emma; da of Colin Hall Dexter, of London, and Carteret, France, and Mercia, *née* Ife; *b* 25 June 1959, London; *Educ* Croydon HS for Girls, Somerville Coll Oxford (MA), Courtauld Inst (MPhil); *m* 19 March 2003, Adrian Jackson; 2 s (Silas b 7 May 1992, Zachary b 12 Feb 1997); *Career* asst curator Stoke-on-Trent City Museum and Art Gallery 1985–87, dir Chisenhale Gallery London 1987–90; Inst of Contemporary Arts (ICA) London: dep dir of exhbns 1990–92, dir of exhbns 1992–99; sr curator Tate Modern 2000–, dir of exhbns Timothy Taylor Gallery London 2007–; visiting lectr: Goldsmiths Coll, Christies Contemporary Art, De Montfort Univ, Essex Univ; memb Critical Curating (London Univ); mentor RCA Curating Course 2005–06, Nesta mentor for artist Joy Gregory 2004–06, mentor for Inspire Fell at Tate Modern 2005–; jury memb and chair Becks Futures Awards ICA 2000; memb jury: Present Future section Artissima Fair Turin 2002–05, Deutsche Börse Photography Prize London 2006, Spectrum Int Prize for Photography Germany 2008; *Exhibitions* prog at ICA introducing: Marlene Dumas, Charles Ray, Luc Tuymans, John Currin, Thomas Schiebitz, Steve McQueen, Jake and Dinos Chapman, Mark Leckey; at Tate: Cruel and Tender 2003 (Tate's first photography show), Luc Tuymans and Bruce Nauman 2004, Frida Kahlo 2005; at Timothy Taylor Gallery: Enter the Path 2007, Ballet Mecanique 2007, Armen Eloyan Bookstore Cure 2008, mai-Thu Perret 2008, Ventriloquist 2009, Armen Eloyan 2009; *Publications* Cruel and Tender (ed and contrib, 2003), Luc Tuymans (ed and contrib, 2004), Raw Materials (ed and contrib, 2004), Frida Kahlo (ed and contrib, 2005), Vitamin D: New Perspectives in Drawing (contrib, 2005); *Recreations* cooking, foreign languages; *Style—* Ms Emma Dexter; ✉ Timothy Taylor Gallery, 15 Carlos Place, London W1K 2EX (☎ 020 7409 3344)

DEXTER, Julietta; *Career* fndr and co-dir The Communications Store 1995–; clients incl: John Frieda Hare Care, Versace, Liz Earle Beauty Company, Erdem, Charlotte Tilbury, Electrolux Grand Cuisine; *Style—* Ms Julietta Dexter; ✉ The Communications Store, 2 Kensington Square, London W8 5EP

DEXTER, Emeritus Prof (Thomas) Michael; s of Thomas Richard Dexter (d 1976), and (Gertrude) Agnes, *née* Depledge (d 1991); *b* 15 May 1945; *Educ* Manchester Central GS, Univ of Salford (BSc, DSc), Univ of Manchester (PhD); *m* 1, 10 Aug 1966 (m dis 1978), (Frances) Ann, da of John Sutton, of Hurdsfield, Cheshire; 2 s (Alexander Michael b 1972, Thomas b 1987), 2 da (Katrina Ann (twin) b 1972, Rachel b 1985); m 2, 14 Nov 2009, Dr Clare Mercia Heyworth; 2 step-da (Kate Whetton b 18 May 1988, Dr Beth Whetton b 16 Aug 1986); *Career* visiting fell Sloan Kettering Inst NY 1976–77, sr scientist Paterson Laboratories Manchester 1977–87 (scientist 1973), life fell Cancer Research Campaign 1978–98, head of Dept of Experimental Haematology Paterson Inst for Cancer Research Manchester 1982–98, prof of haematology (personal chair) Univ of Manchester 1985–98, dir Paterson Inst 1997–98 (dep dir 1994–97), dir Wellcome Trust 1998–2003, chm Stem Cell Sciences Holdings 2003–08, scientific advsr Rothschild Asset Management 2003–08; Gibb research fell 1992–98; author of 300 papers in jls; pres Int Soc for Experimental Haematology 1988–89; memb: Scientific Ctee Leukaemia Research Fund 1985–88, Grants Ctee Cancer Research Campaign 1986–93, Scientific Advsy Bd Biomedical Research Center Univ of Br Columbia 1988–91, Ctee on Effects of Ionising Radiation 1988–93, Steering Ctee Electro-Magnetic Fields National Grid 1989–98, Scientifc Ctee Gunnar Nilsson Research Tst Fund 1991–97; memb Editorial Bd of 10 scientific jls; memb: Ctee SERC 1991–94, Ctee AFRC (now BBSRC) 1991–94, Cncl MRC 1993–96 (chm MCMB 1994–96, chm Human Genome Co-ordinating Ctee 1996–98), Ctee on Med Affects of Radiations in the Environment (COMARE) 1993–98, World Ctee IACRLD 1994–99, Cncl Royal Soc 1995–96 and 2002–04, Ctee SEBCC 1998–2000, NW Science Cncl 2003–09; chm Int Centre for Life Newcastle 2003–07, chair Cockroft Inst 2004–09; emeritus prof Univ of Manchester 2012; Hon DSc: UMIST 1999, Univ of Salford 2000, Mahidol Univ Thailand 2001, Imperial Coll London 2002, Univ of Lancaster 2006, Manchester Met Univ 2014; FRS 1991, FRCPath 1997 (MRCPath 1987), FIBiol 1997 (CIBiol), FMedSci 1997 (founding fell), Hon FRCP 1998 (Hon MRCP 1994); *Recreations* folk singing, poetry, gardening; *Style—* Emeritus Prof Michael Dexter, FRS; ✉ 11 Broughton Road, Adlington, Macclesfield, Cheshire SK10 4ND (☎ 07747 814326, e-mail tmdexter@btinternet.com)

DEY, Graeme; MSP; *b* Aberdeen; *Educ* Harlaw Acad Aberdeen; *m* Linda; 1 da (Caroline), 1 s (Lewis); *Career* sports reporter 1980–90, sports ed Dundee Courier 1991–2010; MSP (SNP) Angus S 2011–; *Recreations* golf, music, stand up comedy, swimming; *Style—* Graeme Dey, Esq, MSP; ✉ The Scottish Parliament, Edinburgh EH99 1SP

DEY, Rajeeb; MBE (2016); *b* 6 December 1985; *Educ* Jesus Coll Univ of Oxford (MA); *Career* fndr and ceo Enternships.com 2009–; co-fndr StartUp Britain 2011–; tstee UNLtd; O2 X Young Entrepreneur of the Year 2009, World Economic Forum Young Global Leader 2012, Queen's Award for Enterprise Promotion 2013, Evening Standard's 1000 Most Influential People in London; *Style—* Rajeeb Dey, Esq, MBE; ✉ Enternships.com, 2nd Floor, 38–40 Commercial Road, London E1 1LN (☎ 020 3397 3216, e-mail questions@enternships.com, website www.enternships.com, Twitter @rajdey)

DHARGALKAR, Suresh Dinkar; LVO (1994); s of Dinkar Laxman Dhargalkar (d 1979), of Bombay, India, and Sushila, *née* Belwalkar (d 1993); *b* 16 December 1934; *Educ* Hind Vidhylaya HS Bombay, Sch of Architecture Sir J J Sch of Art Bombay, Sch of Architecture Regent Street Poly London, Poly Coll of Architecture and Advance Building Technol London; *m* 3 Aug 1962, Hildegard (d 1991), da of Oswald Bente (d 1964); 2 s (Hans b 1963, Martin b 1967 d 1985); *Career* architectural asst in private architectural practice: Bombay 1952–55, London 1955–70; architect in private practice London 1970–74, princ architect with PSA/DOE for Royal Palaces 1979–90 (architect 1975–79), actg conslt architect project mangr with Royal Household 1995– (superintending architect 1990–95); dep keeper of the Royal Philatelic Collection 2003–06; special interest in environmental control for preservation of historic artefacts, lighting and precaution against fire and theft in historic bldgs, palaces and museums; works undertaken in restoration and new works at: Windsor Castle, St James's Palace, Hampton Court Palace, British Museum, National Maritime Museum; active participant in organising seminars for conservation of cultural historic properties for ICCROM until 1989 (Cert 1984); conservation architect: Egypt Exploration Soc 1997–, Amarna Tst 2008–; Freeman City of London 1965; corp memb RIBA 1970, memb ARCUK 1970; FRPSL 2002; *Recreations* travel, cooking; *Style—* Suresh Dhargalkar, Esq, LVO, RIBA, FRPSL; ✉ 3 Elmer Gardens, Edgware, Middlesex HA8 9AR (☎ 020 8952 3075)

DHINSA, Jojar Singh; s of Joginder Singh Dhinsa (d 2002), and Gurmej Kaur Dhillon; *b* 12 February 1977, Coventry, Warks; *Educ* Sidney Stringer Sch and Community Coll Coventry, UCE (BSc); *Children* 1 da (Olivia Kaur Dhinsa); *Career* fndr and prop JK Trading 1989–96, chm and ceo Athlone Gp 2000–; pres Alchamist Assoc; Newcomer of the Year Asian Business Awards 2004 (nomination Businessman of the Year); ambass Coventry City; *Recreations* reading, classical music, extreme sports; *Style—* Jojar S Dhinsa, Esq; ✉ Athlone Group, 200 Brook Drive, Green Park, Reading RG2 6UB (e-mail PA Charles E Bird cbird@athlonegroup.com)

DHIR, Her Hon Judge Anuja Ravindra; QC (2010); da of Prof Ravindra Dhir, OBE, and Bharti, *née* Trikam; *b* 19 January 1968, Dundee, Scotland; *Educ* Univ of Dundee (LLB); *m* 2002, Nicholas Lavender, QC; 1 d (Nikita b 2003), 2 s (Sachin b 2004, Arjun b 2006); *Career* called to the Bar Gray's Inn 1989 (bencher 2009); recorder 2009, circuit judge (South Eastern Circuit) 2012–; *Recreations* tennis, walking, theatre; *Style—* Her Hon Judge Dhir, QC; ✉ Woolwich Crown Court, 2 Belmarsh Road, London SE28 0EY

DHOLAKIA, Baron (Life Peer UK 1997), of Waltham Brooks in the County of West Sussex; Rt Hon Navnit; OBE (1994), PC (2010), DL (W Sussex 1999); s of Permananddas Mulji Dholakia, of Bhavnagar, India; *b* 4 March 1937; *Educ* Home Sch and Inst of Science Bhavnagar Gujarat, Brighton Tech Coll; *m* 1967, Ann, da of Harold McLuskie, of London; 2 da (Hon Anjali, Hon Alene); *Career* med lab technician 1960–66, devpt offr Nat Ctee for Commonwealth Immigrants 1966–68 (sr devpt offr 1968–74, princ offr and sec 1974–76), with Cmmn for Racial Equality 1976–94; previous appts with: Police Complaints Cmmn, Ethnic Minority Advsy Ctee of the Judicial Studies Bd, Lord Carlisle's Ctee of the Parole Ststems Review; chm Brighton Young Liberals 1959–62, chm Brighton Liberal Assoc 1962–64, memb (Lib) Brighton CBC 1961–64; sits as Lib Dem peer House of Lords, communities spokesman, pres Lib Dems 2000–04; pres: NACRO 2003– (chm 1998–2003, chm Race Issues Advsy Ctee), Friends Circle Int; vice-pres The Family Welfare Assoc; memb Cncl: Save the Children Fund 1992–98, Howard League for Penal Reform 1992–2002, Indian Jewish Assoc UK, Cmmn on the Future of Multi-Ethnic Britain, The Caine Prize for African Writing; memb: Editorial Bd Howard Jl, Mannheim Centre for Criminology and Criminal Justice LSE, Home Sec's Race Forum; memb Advsy Bd: Centre for Reform, Human Rights Act Research Unit, Centre for Ethnic Minority Studies Royal Holloway Univ of London, Int Trade & Law Inst; tstee: The Ghandi Tst, Dr L M Singhvi Fndn, Police Fndn, The Apex Tst, Pallant House Gallery Chichester; patron and vice-patron of numerous charities; govr Commonwealth Inst 1998–2005; assoc RPS Rainer; former magistrate and memb Bd of Visitors HM Prison Lewes; Asian Who's Who Int Asian of the Year Award 2000, Pravasi Bharatiya Sanman Award 2003; Hon LLD: Univ of Herts 2009, Univ of York 2010, E London Univ 2010; *Style—* The Rt Hon the Lord Dholakia, OBE, DL; ✉ House of Lords, London SW1A 0PW (☎ 020 7219 5203, fax 020 7219 3423, e-mail dholakian@parliament.uk)

DHOLAKIA, Uday Kumar; OBE (2009); s of Dhiru Bhagwandas Dholakia, of Oadby, Leicester, and Chandrika Dhiru, *née* Bhatti; *b* 2 January 1958; *Educ* Westlain GS Brighton, Sunderland Poly; *m* 9 July 1989, Hardika, da of late Rangitlal Modi; 2 da (Saffron Banita b 25 Aug 1997, Serene Devashree b 19 Nov 1999); *Career* small business advsr Dept of Planning and Transportation Leics CC 1984–86, princ business conslt Chief Exec's Dept Leicester City Cncl 1986–88, dep dir Leics Business Venture (DTI) 1990–91, ptnr planning and corp affrs Global Consulting IJK Ltd 1991–; chm Pharmaoptica Ltd 2011; non-exec dir: Leicester Boiler Engineers Ltd 1990–93, Watford Electronics Ltd 1993–95; vice-pres Small Business Bureau 1998–, fndr dir Westminster African Caribbean Business Initiative 1997–2000, cmmr Broadcasting Standards Cmmn 1999–2003, tstee Nat Employment Policy Inst 1995–2000, fndr memb Euro Ethnic Minority Business Network 1999, chm Leics Asian Business Assoc 2010, chm Nat Asian Business Assoc 2011–; memb: Ctee Leicester Family Services Unit 1985–87, Leicester and Co C of C and Industry 1987–88 (fndr chm Leics Business Awards), Advsy Bd Central Television plc (later Carlton Television plc) 1993–95, Bd Leics and Rutland Probation Bd 1994– (chm Complaints and Appeals Ctee), E Midlands Electricity Consumer Ctee 1997–2000, Oftel Small Business Taskforce 2001–, Minority Media and Telecommunications Cncl of USA 2003–, Leics Police Authy 2006–, Bd Local Better Regulation Office Cabinet Office 2007–12; hon vice-pres Leics Asian Business Assoc; tstee: Leics Orgn for the Relief of Suffering (LOROS) 2001, Leics and Rutland Community Fndn 2005–; memb Equality, Diversity and Inclusion Ctee Slrs Regulatory Authy 2015–, memb Charter Ctee HMRC 2016; memb Advsy Bd Twycross Zoo, memb Ctee Leics and Rutland ABF Soldiers Charity Fund, chair Mktg and Commercial Ctee Twycross Zoo 2016; brand ambass Birmingham Airport 2010; assoc Inst of Export, MIMC, MBCS, MCIM, MIMgt, FRSA, FIBC; hon citizen Haskovo City Bulgaria 2005; *Awards* Young Stockbroker of the Year 1978, Young Entrepreneur of the Year 1979, NE Enterprise Tst Award 1983, Cmmn for Racial Equality Bursary to US 1986, Asian Times/Caribbean Times Community Award 1989, Leicester Common Purpose grad 1991–92, E Midlands Ethnic Minority Business Award 1998; *Recreations* wine, marine antiques, travelling, cricket, television; *Clubs* Royal British Club of Portugal; *Style—* Uday Dholakia, Esq, OBE; ✉ Birmingham Airport, 5th Floor, Diamond House, Birmingham B26 3QJ

di VITA, Dr Charlotte; MBE (1998); *b* 5 September 1966; *Educ* Univ of Edinburgh (MA); *Career* early career as voluntary research, mktg and fundraising conslt for environmental, human rights and medical orgns, co-ordinator Anglo-Brazilian Conference on the Environment 1990, founder Trade plus Aid 1997–; launched: Charlotte di Vita Collections 1998–2007, Trade plus Aid Design Studio South Africa; memb Business Gp Co-ordinating Ctee Amnesty Int 1990–92, environmental conslt 1990–92; goodwill ambass Nelson Mandela Children Fund 2003–, launched 21st Century Leaders project 2004–; Pilkington Window to the World Award Woman of the Year Awards 2003, Honorary Acheivement Award UK Gift Industry Awards 2004; Hon DBA Huddersfield Univ; *Style—* Dr Charlotte di Vita, MBE; ✉ Trade plus Aid, PO Box 920011, Dubai, UAE

DIAMOND, Prof Sir Ian; kt (2013); s of Harold Frederick Diamond (d 1985), of Torquay, Devon, and Sylvia Betty Diamond; *b* 14 March 1954, Kingskerswell, Devon; *Educ* LSE (BSc, MSc), Univ of St Andrews (PhD); *m* 1997, Jane; 1 s (Tom b 8 Sept 1999), 1 step da (Alexandra b 20 March 1991), 1 step s (Mark b 3 Sept 1992); *Career* lectr Heriot-Watt Univ 1979–80; Univ of Southampton: lectr 1980–88, sr lectr 1988–92, prof 1992–2003; chief exec ESRC 2003–10; princ and vice-chllr Univ of Aberdeen; chair Exec Gp Research Cncls UK 2004–08 author of 120 articles in learned jls; Clifford C Clogg Prize Population Assoc of America 2000; FAcSS 2000, FBA 2005, FRSE 2009; *Recreations* swimming, running, football referee, Southampton FC, Torquay United FC; *Clubs* Gordonians Cricket; *Style—* Prof Sir Ian Diamond; ✉ University of Aberdeen, Kings College, Aberdeen AB24 (☎ 01224 272135, e-mail ian.diamond@abdn.ac.uk)

DIAMOND, Yasmin; CB (2011); *Career* asst press offr Nat Museum of Photography, Film and Television 1989–91, press and pubns mangr Axis 1991–92, mktg mangr Bradford Health Authy 1992–95, sr communications mangr NHS Exec 1995–99, publicity cmmr BBC Broadcast 1999–2000, head of mktg Welfare to Work Dept for Educn and Employment 2000–01, head of corp communications Dept for Educn and Skills 2001–05, dir of communications DEFRA 2005–08, dir of communications Home Office 2008–; *Style—* Ms Yasmin Diamond, CB; ✉ Home Office, Peel Building, 2 Marsham Street, London SW1P 4DF

D

DICK, Frank William; OBE (1989); s of Frank Dick, of Edinburgh, and Diana May, *née* Sinclair; *b* 1 May 1941; *Educ* Royal HS Edinburgh, Loughborough Coll (DLC), Univ of Oregon (BSc); *m* 1, 1970 (m dis 1977), Margaret Fish; 1 s (Frank Sinclair Shacklock b 3 Oct 1972); m 2, 1980, Linda Elizabeth, da of Frank Brady; 2 da (Erin Emma Louise b 18 July 1981, Cara Charlotte Elizabeth b 18 May 1985); *Career* dep dir of physical educn Worksop Coll 1965–69, nat athletics coach for Scotland 1970–79, dir of coaching Br Athletics Fedn 1979–94 (resigned), coaching conslt 1995–, conslt performance dir SA Olympic and Paralympic Teams 2015–16; athletics coach: European Cup 1979–93, Olympic Games 1980–92, European Championships 1982–90, World Championships 1983–93; coach to: Daley Thompson (athletics) 1983–92, Boris Becker (conditioning tennis) 1986–89, Jeff Thompson (conditioning karate) 1986–88, Mark MacLean (conditioning squash) 1987–90, Gerhard Berger (conditioning Formula One) 1990–98, Katarina Witt (conditioning skating) 1991–, Ronnie Irani (cricket) 1998–, Denise Lewis (athletics) 2002–03, Justin Rose (golf) 2003–; chm Br Assoc of Nat Coaches 1985–86; pres: Euro Athletics Coaches Assoc 1985–, Br Inst of Sports Coaching 1990–91; memb Bd of Dirs Scottish Inst of Sport 1998–2006, chair Scottish Athletics Ltd 2009–; winner Geoffrey Dyson Award and memb UK Coaches' Hall of Fame 1998, Golden Pin European Athletics Assoc 2003, Loughborough Hall of Fame 2015; Hon DTech Loughborough Univ 2003, professorship (hc) Nat Sports Acad Bulgaria 2011; FBISC 1989; *Books* Sports Training Principles (1980, 1989, 1995, 2002, 2007 and 2014), Winning (1992), Winning Lines (2004), Winning Matters (2010); *Recreations* music, public speaking, jogging; *Style*— Frank Dick, Esq, OBE; ✉ Selwood, Zeals Row, Zeals, Wiltshire BA12 6PE (☎ 01747 841334, e-mail fwd.coaching@btinternet.com); 120 Pall Mall, London SW1Y 5EA (☎ 020 3603 0115, e-mail office@fwd.uk.com, Twitter @FrankDickCoach)

DICK, Dr Jeremy Peter Rose; s of Peter Dick (d 2001), and Diana, *née* George (d 1983); *b* 29 September 1953; *Educ* Marlborough (exhibitioner), King's Coll Cambridge (exhibitioner, MA), KCH (MB BChir, PhD); *m* 21 Sept 1985, Bridget Mary, da of Roger Gates (d 2010); 1 s (Andrew b 1988), 2 da (Madeleine b 1989, Catherine b 1994); *Career* SHO Douera Hosp Algeria and house physician St Luke's Guildford 1977–78, house surgn KCH and SHO St Nicholas Plumstead 1978–79, SHO Maudsley, KCH and Brompton Hosp 1979–80, registrar in cardiology Papworth and in nephrology Addenbrooke's 1980–82, SHO in neurology Nat Hosp 1982–83, res registrar in neurology Maudsley and KCH 1983–86, registrar in neurology N Manchester Gen and Manchester Royal Infirmary 1987–89, sr registrar in neurology Charing Cross Hosp 1989–91; conslt in neurology: Royal London, Newham Gen and St Andrew's Hosps 1991–97, Bart's 1994–97, Manchester Royal Infirmary 1997–2001, Withington and Wythenshaw Hosps 1997–, Hope Hosp 2001–; dir Gtr Manchester Neurosciences Centre 2008–11; Pfizer prize for res in clinical med Manchester Med Soc 1989; chm NW Regional Training Ctee in neurology 1999–2006, memb RCP: Part II Question Gp 1992– (examiner 1999–, memb Bd 2003–); memb: Assoc of Br Neurologists, American Acad of Neurology, RSM (memb Cncl Neurology Section 1994–96); FRCP 1996; *Recreations* squash, golf, skiing, cycling; *Clubs* Jesters; *Style*— Dr Jeremy Dick; ✉ Department of Neurology, University Hospital of South Manchester, Southmoor Road, Manchester M23 9LT; Department of Neurology, Greater Manchester Neurosciences Centre, Hope Hospital, Stott Lane, Manchester M6 8HD

DICK, Katherine (Daisy); da of Dave Dick (the jockey, winner of the Cheltenham Gold Cup and 1956 Grand National (beating Devon Loch), d 2001), and Caroline Dick (the three day eventer); *b* 29 March 1972, Oxford; *Educ* Univ of Oxford (MA); *Partner* Charles Berkeley; *Career* three-day eventer; winner Blenheim Horse Trials CCI*** 2006, Silver medal team World Equestrian Games Aachen 2006, winner Gatcombe Horse Trials CIC*** 2007, Gold medal team European Championships 2007, Bronze medal team Olympic Games Beijing 2008; *Style*— Miss Daisy Dick

DICK, Stewart John Cunningham; s of John David Cunningham Dick (d 1990), of Edinburgh, and Jessie Anderson Calder (d 1985); *b* 14 January 1946; *Educ* George Watson's Coll Edinburgh, Univ of Edinburgh (MA, LLB); *m* 12 April 1974, Alison Aileen Mackintosh Dickson; *Career* Wallace and Sommerville (became Whinney Murray) 1968–72, dir of banking Brown, Shipley and Co Ltd 1980–92 (joined 1972), dir and head of banking Ansbacher & Co Ltd 1993–2001, head of int private banking Singer & Friedlander Ltd 2001–06, dir private client finance Arbuthnot Latham & Co Ltd 2006–13; non-exec dir Hampshire Trust plc 1993–2001; MICAS 1972; *Recreations* gardening, golf; *Clubs* RAC, MCC; *Style*— Stewart Dick, Esq; ✉ Dunvegan, 2 Oak Park, Old Avenue, West Byfleet, Surrey KT14 6AG

DICKENS, Barnaby John; s of Archie Bernard Dickens, and June Mary McNeile; *b* 9 June 1954; *Educ* Dulwich Coll, Trinity Coll Cambridge (scholar, MA); *m* 13 Oct 1983, Lucy Anne, da of Sir Oliver Nicholas Millar, GCVO, FBA (d 2007); 3 s (Roland Oliver Porter b 9 April 1979, Max John Porter b 27 Aug 1981, Archie Dickens b 2 March 1994), 1 da (Marnie Dickens b 13 Nov 1985); *Career* account exec: The Creative Business 1977–78, WS Crawford 1978–79; Public Advertising Cncl LA 1980, account dir Marsteller 1984 (account mangr 1981), Bd account dir GGK London 1986–92, md Crammond Dickens Lerner 1993–; *Style*— Barnaby Dickens, Esq; ✉ Crammond Dickens Lerner & Partners Ltd, 1 Earlham Street, London WC2H 9LL (☎ 020 7240 8100)

DICKETTS, Simon Charles Hedley; s of Brian John Dicketts, of Glastonbury, Somerset, and Daphne Francis, *née* Little; *b* 13 September 1954; *Educ* Corchester Sch Corbridge Northumberland, St Edward's Sch Oxford; *m* Nicola Jane, da of Hamish Hedley; *Career* porter Christie's auctioneers 1975, employed at J Walter Thompson 1976–80; Saatchi & Saatchi: joined as copywriter 1985, creative gp head 1985–92, jt creative dir 1992–95 (resigned); M&C Saatchi: founding memb and creative dir 1995–2002, exec creative dir 2002–09, worldwide creative dir 2009–; awards incl: 4 Gold Lions Cannes Film Advtg Awards, 15 Campaign Press Silver Awards, 3 times winner Best Written Advertisement of the Year; memb D&AD; *Publications* Brutal Simplicity of Thought (contrib), The Copy Book; *Recreations* wine, bridge, tennis, shooting, mushroom and truffle hunting, cooking, golf; *Clubs* Soho House; *Style*— Simon Dicketts, Esq; ✉ M&C Saatchi Ltd, 34–36 Golden Square, London W1R 4EE (☎ 020 7543 4500, fax 020 7543 4501, e-mail simond@mcsaatchi.com)

DICKIE, John; s of John Dickie (d 1977), and Gladys, *née* O'Neil (d 2000); *b* 31 August 1965, Glasgow; *Educ* Morecambe HS, Worcester Coll Oxford (BA), London Business Sch (MBA); *m* July 1991, Sue, *née* Grunstein; 1 s (Jack b 1998), 1 da (Eve b 2000); *Career* Swiss Bank Corp 1987–88, public policy conslt Prima Europe 1988–98 (md 1997–98), md GPC Market Access London 1997–98, head Int Regulatory Practice GPC Int 1998–2000, regulatory affrs dir European Competitive Telecommunications Assoc (ECTA) 2000–03, head Political and Parly Affrs BBC 2003–, head corporate affrs BBC 2006–08, dir of strategy and policy London First 2008–; cncllr Camden BC 1994–2003 (dep leader 2000–03); chair Go Neighbourhood Mgmnt Pathfinder; *Recreations* reading, keeping fit, cinema, opera; *Clubs* Reform; *Style*— John Dickie, Esq; ✉ London First, 3 Whitcomb Street, London WC2H 7HA

DICKIE, Dr Nigel Hugh; s of John Dickie, OBE, of Cobham, Surrey, and Inez Campbell, *née* White; *b* 4 October 1956, Bromley, Kent; *Educ* KCS Wimbledon, Queen Elizabeth Coll Univ of London (BSc, The Copping Prize in Nutrition, PhD); *m* 24 Aug 1986, Alison Susan May, da of John Michael Duffin; 2 s (Andrew James John b 27 Feb 1988, Alexander Stuart b 8 Oct 1990); *Career* nutritionist Van den Berghs and Jurgens Ltd 1982–83, conslt nutritionist Slimming Magazine, Slimming Magazine Clubs and various leading food companies 1983–85, md Counsel PR co (formerly Holmes & Marchant Counsel Gp) 1992–2005 (dir 1985), exec dir Huntsworth Gp Ltd 2001–05, dir corp and govt affrs H J Heinz Co Ltd 2005–; Freeman City of London 1989; FRSH 1991, MCIPR (MIPR 1991); *Recreations* good food and wine, family and home; *Style*— Nigel Dickie; ✉ H J Heinz Foods UK Limited, South Building, Hayes Park, Hayes, Middlesex UB4 8AL (☎ 020 8573 7757)

DICKIE, Robert Stewart; s of Robert Dickie, of Hamilton, Strathclyde, and Helen, *née* Hutton; *b* 31 October 1959, Glasgow; *Educ* Hamilton GS, Strathclyde Grad Business Sch Glasgow (MBA); *m* 20 Aug 1982, Karen; 4 s (Cameron b 23 Feb 1986, Jonathan b 3 Dec 1987, Matthew b 23 May 1990, Gregor b 1 June 1995); *Career* various retail banking roles Clydesdale Bank plc 1976–93, Nat Australia Bank Gp Melbourne 1993–97, head of ops and customer services and head of direct and channel mgmnt Nat Australia Gp (Europe) 1997–2000, md (UK enterprise) Zurich Financial Services (UKISA) Ltd 2000–02, gp ops dir Braford & Bingley plc 2003–08; AIG: sr vice-pres ops and systems and chief ops offr 2008–09, corp vice-pres and chief operations and systems offr 2009–14; chief operations and technol offr Zurich Insurance Gp Ltd Zurich 2014–; memb Bd Farmers Insurance Inc LA 2015–; Scottish Young Banker of the Year 1991; FCIBS 1994 (memb Cncl), FRSA 2004; *Recreations* rugby union, reading, American football, blues music; *Style*— Robert S Dickie, Esq; ✉ Zurich Insurance Company Ltd, Austrasse 46, 8045 Zurich, Switzerland (☎ 00 41 44 625 3300, fax 00 41 44 625 0202, e-mail robert.dickie@zurich.com)

DICKINS, Julian Grahame; s of Grahame John Dickins, of Newbury, Berks, and Claire Daisy, *née* Myers; *b* 31 December 1957; *Educ* St Bartholomew's Sch Newbury, Univ of Southampton (LLB), Coll of Law Guildford; *m* 1997, Ellie, da of Ian and Lesley Hickling; *Career* admitted slr 1983; ptnr: Penningtons 1986–96 (joined 1983), Dickins Hopgood Chidley LLP 1996–; church warden PCC St Michael's and All Angels Church Enborne Berks, memb Law Soc 1983; *Recreations* travelling, skiing, piano; *Clubs* Kintbury Players; *Style*— Julian Dickins, Esq; ✉ Dickins Hopgood Chidley LLP, The Old School House, 42 High Street, Hungerford RG17 0NF (☎ 01488 683555, fax 01488 681919, e-mail jdickins@dhc-solicitors.co.uk, website www.dhc-solicitors.co.uk)

DICKINSON, His Hon Judge Gregory David; QC (2002); *b* 26 August 1959, Sheffield, Yorkshire; *Educ* Poole GS Dorset, Univ of Leicester (LLB); *m* 1989, Frances Judith, *née* Betts; *Career* called to the Bar Gray's Inn 1981; asst recorder 1998, recorder 2000, bencher (Gray's Inn) 2008–, circuit judge (Midland Circuit) 2012–, sr circuit judge and resident judge Nottingham Crown Court 2016–; Midland Circuit rep Bar Cncl 2004–09; memb Ct Univ of Leicester 2011–; *Style*— His Hon Judge Dickinson, QC; ✉ Nottingham Crown Court, 60 Canal Street, Nottingham NG1 7EL

DICKINSON, Prof Harry Thomas; s of Joseph Dickinson (d 1979), and Elizabeth Stearman, *née* Warriner (d 1979); *b* 9 March 1939; *Educ* Gateshead GS, Univ of Durham (BA, DipEd, MA), Univ of Newcastle upon Tyne (PhD), Univ of Edinburgh (DLitt); *m* 26 Aug 1961, Jennifer Elizabeth, da of Albert Galtry, of Kilham, E Yorks; 1 s (Mark James b 1967), 1 da (Anna Elizabeth b 1972); *Career* Earl Grey fell Univ of Newcastle upon Tyne 1964–66; Univ of Edinburgh: asst lectr 1966–68, lectr 1968–73, reader 1973–80, prof of Br history 1980–06, emeritus prof 2006–; concurrent prof of history Nanjing Univ China 1987–, Douglas Southall Freeman prof Richmond Univ USA 1997, visiting prof Peking Univ 2011; author of many historical essays and articles, ed History 1993–2000; FRHistS, FRSE 1998, fell Historical Assoc 2006, FHEA 2007; *Books* The Correspondence of Sir James Clavering (1967), Bolingbroke (1970), Walpole and the Whig Supremacy (1973), Politics and Literature in the Eighteenth Century (1974), Liberty and Property (1977), Political Works of Thomas Spence (1982), British Radicalism and the French Revolution (1985), Caricatures and the Constitution (1986), Britain and the French Revolution (1989), The Politics of the People in Eighteenth-Century Britain (1995), Britain and the American Revolution (1998), The Challenge to Westminster (with M Lynch, 2000), The Blackwell Companion to Eighteenth-Century Britain (2002), Constitutional Documents of the United Kingdom 1782–1835 (2005), Reactions to Revolutions (jtly, 2007), British Pamphlets on the American Revolution (8 vols, 2007–08), Ireland in the Age of Revolution 1760–1805 (6 vols, 2013); *Recreations* watching sports, theatre, cinema; *Style*— Prof Harry Dickinson, FRSE; ✉ 44 Viewforth Terrace, Edinburgh EH10 4LJ (☎ 0131 229 1379); History, Classics and Archaeology, University of Edinburgh, Edinburgh EH8 9AG (☎ 0131 650 4140, e-mail harry.dickinson@ed.ac.uk)

DICKINSON, Prof John Philip; s of George Snowden Dickinson (d 1974), of Morecambe, and Evelyn, *née* Stobbart (d 1999); *b* 29 April 1945; *Educ* Univ of Cambridge (MA), Univ of Leeds (MSc, PhD); *m* 17 Feb 1968, Christine, da of Maurice Houghton (d 1980), of Morecambe; 1 s (Anthony), 2 da (Rachel, Vanessa); *Career* lectr: Univ of Leeds 1968–71, Lancaster Univ 1971–75; sr lectr: Univ of Western Aust 1975–80, Univ of Dundee 1980–81; prof of accounting Univ of Stirling 1981–85; Univ of Glasgow: prof of accounting and fin 1985, head Dept of Accounting and Fin 1987–91, dir Glasgow Business Sch 1987–89, dean Faculty of Law and Fin Studies 1989–92; princ Univ Coll Winchester 1992–2001, hon prof Univ of Southampton 2000–; chm Br Accounting Assoc 1994–95; dir and tstee National Autistic Soc 2002–11 (nat cncllr 2000–11, vice-chm 2010–11, lifetime vice-pres 2011–), gen sec Autism Europe 2004–08, tstee Research Autism 2005–12; dist organiser Christian Aid 1989–92; FASA CPA 1976, FIMgt 1980, FRSA 1980, FCIS 1992 (ACIS 1976); *Books* Portfolio Analysis (1974), Risk and Uncertainty in Accounting and Finance (1974), Statistics for Business Finance and Accounting (1976), Portfolio Analysis and Capital Markets (1976), Management Accounting: An Introduction (1988), Statistical Analysis in Accounting and Finance (1990); *Recreations* photography, travel, languages, poetry; *Style*— Prof John Dickinson; ✉ Swans Mead, Haverbreaks Road, Lancaster LA1 5BJ (☎ 01524 68792, e-mail swansmead@hotmail.com)

DICKINSON, Lorna; MVO (2002); da of Michael Eugene Dickinson, and Barbara, *née* Benfield; *b* 20 December 1958; *Educ* Univ of Warwick (BA); *m* 4 June 1983, Michael Ingham, BBC football corr; 1 s (Marshall Quincy Ingham b 7 Aug 1993); *Career* TV prodr; credits incl: A Royal Celebration in Honour of HRH the Prince of Wales 50th Birthday, An Audience with Elton John, An Audience with Rod Stewart, An Audience with Ken Dodd, An Audience with Billy Connolly, Robin Williams in the Wild with Dolphins, Goldie Hawn in the Wild with Elephants, The Trouble with Michael Caine, 30 Years of James Bond, The Full Wax, Page Three, Aspel and Company, Schofield in Hawaii, Two Rooms – A Celebration of the Songs of Elton John and Bernie Taupin, The World According to Smith and Jones, Clive James meets Katharine Hepburn, The Dame Edna Experience; *Awards* BAFTA Awards 1994 and 1996, Gold Award NY Int Film Festival & TV Festival; *Style*— Ms Lorna Dickinson, MVO; ✉ Original Productions (☎ 079 6636 2792)

DICKINSON, Mark; s of Stanley Park Dickinson, and Beatrice Joan Dickinson; *b* 20 January 1951; *Educ* Dame Alice Owen Sch, Univ of Manchester (BA); *m* Pauline; 2 da (Emily b 1982, Megan b 1985), 2 s (Samuel (twin) b 1985, Josiah b 1990); *Career* trainee Macmillan Journals 1974–76, ed New Manchester Review 1976–81, sub ed and TV writer Daily Telegraph 1976–86, author 1986–88, asst chief sub ed Evening Leader (Wrexham) 1988–89, chief sub ed Tonight (Chester) 1989–90, chief sub ed Evening Express (Aberdeen) 1991–92, asst ed The Journal (Newcastle) 1992–93, dep ed-in-chief Chronicle Newspapers 1993–96, ed The Journal (Newcastle) 1996–2000, ed Liverpool Echo 2000–05, ed-in-chief Trinity Mirror NW and N Wales, editorial dir Trinity Mirror Midlands 2005–07, business devpt dir Trinity Mirror NW and Wales 2007–10, business devpt dir Trinity Mirror Regnls Trinity Mirror Gp plc 2010–; memb Guild of Eds; *Publications* The Manchester

Book, Goodbye Piccadilly; *Recreations* football, rugby, golf, tennis, wine and food, countryside; *Style*— Mark Dickinson, Esq

DICKINSON, Patric Laurence; LVO (2006); s of John Laurence Dickinson (d 2003), and April Katherine, *née* Forgan (d 1998); *b* 24 November 1950; *Educ* Marling Sch, Exeter Coll Oxford (MA, pres Oxford Union); *Career* res asst Coll of Arms 1968–78, Rouge Dragon Pursuivant of Arms 1978–89, Richmond Herald 1989–2010, treas Coll of Arms 1995–, Earl Marshal's sec 1996–2012, sec Order of the Garter 2004–, Norroy and Ulster King of Arms 2010, Clarenceux King of Arms 2010–; called to the Bar Middle Temple 1979; hon treas: English Genealogical Congress 1975–91, Bar Theatrical Soc 1978–; hon sec and registrar Br Record Soc 1979–2010; pres: Bristol and Glos Archaeological Soc 1998–99, Soc of Genealogists 2005– (vice-pres 1997–2005); pres Assoc of Genealogists and Researchers in Archives (AGRA) 2011– (vice-pres 1988–2011); chm Anthony Powell Soc 2003–07 (vice-pres 2008–); FSG 2000; *Recreations* music, cycling, swimming, walking, talking, attending memorial services; *Clubs* Brooks's; *Style*— P L Dickinson, Esq, LVO; ✉ College of Arms, Queen Victoria Street, London EC4V 4BT (☎ 020 7236 9612); 13 Old Square, Lincoln's Inn, London WC2A 3UA

DICKINSON, Prof Peter; s of Frank Dickinson (d 1978), and Muriel, *née* Porter (d 2003); *b* 15 November 1934, Lytham St Annes, Lancs; *Educ* The Leys Sch Cambridge, Queens' Coll Cambridge (MA), Juilliard Sch of Music NY, Univ of London (DMus); *m* 29 July 1964, Bridget Jane, da of Lt Cdr Edward Philip Tomkinson, DSO (ka 1942); 2 s (Jasper b 1968, Francis b 1971); *Career* composer, writer and pianist; recorded works incl: organ concerto, piano concerto, violin concerto, Merseyside Echoes, Outcry, Mass of the Apocalypse, The Unicorns, Rags, Blues and Parodies, Songcycles, Surrealist Landscape, American Trio, Sonatas, complete solo organ works, piano music, clavichord pieces; pianist; recorded works largely with sister Meriel Dickinson (mezzo); academic posts incl: prof Keele Univ 1974–84 (now emeritus), prof of music Goldsmiths Coll London 1991–97, head of music Inst of US Studies Univ of London 1997–2004, currently emeritus prof Univ of London; numerous contribs to books periodicals and BBC radio; memb Bd Trinity Coll of Music 1984–98; tstee: Bernarr Rainbow Tst, Berners Tst; RSM; Hon DMus Keele Univ 1999; LRAM, ARCM, FRCO, Hon FTCL (1999); *Books* Twenty British Composers (ed, 1975), The Music of Lennox Berkeley (1989, 2 edn 2003), Marigold: the Music of Billy Mayerl (1999), Copland Connotations: Studies and Interviews (ed, 2002), CageTalk: Dialogues with and about John Cage (2006, 2 edn 2014), Lord Berners: Composer, Writer, Painter (2008), Samuel Barber Remembered (2010), Lennox Berkeley and Friends: Writings, Letters and Interviews (2012), Music Education in Crisis: the Bernarr Rainbow Lectures and Other Assessements (ed, 2013), Peter Dickinson: Words and Music (2016); many CDs of compositions and performances; *Recreations* rare books; *Clubs* Garrick; *Style*— Prof Peter Dickinson; ✉ c/o Novello and Co Ltd, 14–15 Berners Street, London W1T 3LJ (website www.foxborough.co.uk)

DICKINSON, Simon Clervaux; s of Peter Dickinson, of Northumberland, and Anne, *née* Chayter; *b* 26 October 1948; *Educ* Aysgarth Sch, Harrow (art scholar, first cricket and football XIs); *m* Hon Jessica, da of 2 Baron Mancroft (d 1987); 2 da (Phoebe Victoria b 27 Sept 1984, Octavia Jessica b 18 Feb 1986), 1 s (Milo Clervaux Mancroft b 28 June 1989); *Career* art dealer; Christies: joined 1968, dir 1974–93, sr picture dir 1990–93; chm Simon C Dickinson Ltd and Simon Dickinson Inc 1993–; paintings discovered/re-discovered incl: Titian's Portrait of Giacomo Delfino 1977 (last previously recorded in 16th century), Watteau's Allegory of Spring 1983, Van Dyck's Portrait of Ann Carr 1983, Constable sketch for The Young Waltonians 1984, Guido Reni's Portrait of St James the Greater 1988, Claude Landscape 1989, Titian's Venus and Adonis 1991 (subsequently sold to Getty Museum for £7.5m), Hendrick Goltzius' The Crucifixion 1991 (missing since 1604), Guido Reni self-portrait 1992, Botticelli's Virgin Adoring The Christ Child 1999 (subsequently sold to the National Galleries of Scotland); *Recreations* gardening, shooting, fishing, tennis, golf; *Clubs* White's; *Style*— Simon Dickinson, Esq; ✉ Simon C Dickinson Ltd, 58 Jermyn Street, London SW1Y 6LX (☎ 020 7493 0340, fax 020 7493 0796, e-mail simon@simondickinson.com)

DICKSON, Michael Douglas (Mike); s of Dr (William) Powell Greenlie Dickson (d 1986), of Lancaster, and Muriel Constance, *née* MacKinnon; *b* 25 January 1948; *Educ* Sedbergh, Coll for Distributive Trades London (HNC Business Studies); *m* 30 Aug 1986, Elizabeth Anne, da of Graham George Giles; 2 s (Edward Alexander Dickson b 4 Sept 1987, William George Dickson b 20 June 1989); *Career* KMP Partnership advtg agency London 1967–71, broadcaster Radio Hong Kong 1971, Lintas London 1972–76, TBWA 1976–80, dep md Astral Advertising 1980–82, dir Aspect Advertising 1982–85, ptnr Edwards Martin Thornton 1985–88, mgmnt bd dir D'Arcy 1988–; memb Mktg Soc 1980; *Publications* Marketing: Communicating with the Consumer (contrib, 1992); *Recreations* sailing (former vice-chm Sigma Class Assoc); *Clubs* Royal Ocean Racing; *Style*— Mike Dickson, Esq; ✉ D'Arcy, Warwick Building, Kensington Village, Avonmore Road, London W14 8HQ (☎ 020 7071 2052, fax 020 7071 1024, mobile 07768 448443, e-mail mike.dickson@darcyww.co.uk)

DICKSON, Niall Forbes Ross; s of Sheriff Ian Anderson Dickson (d 1982), and Margaret Forbes, *née* Ross (d 1981); *b* 5 November 1953; *Educ* Glasgow Acad, Edinburgh Acad, Univ of Edinburgh (MA, DipEd), Moray House Coll (CertEd); *m* 1979, Elizabeth Selina, da of James Mercer Taggart, of Lisburn, Co Antrim; 2 da (Jennifer Margaret b 1982, Julia Amy Victoria b 1987), 1 s (Andrew James Ross b 1984); *Career* teacher Broughton HS Edinburgh 1976–78, publicity offr National Corporation for the Care of Old People 1978–79, head of publishing Age Concern England 1980–82 (press offr 1979–80); ed: Therapy Weekly 1982–83, Nursing Times 1983–88; BBC: health corr 1988–90, chief social affairs corr 1990–95, social affrs ed 1995–2004; chief exec The King's Fund 2004–09, chief exec and registrar GMC 2010–16; chm: Dept of Health Direct Payments Steering Gp 2004–06, Dept of Health Individual Budgets Reference Gp, Local Govt Assoc Health Cmmn 2007–08, Dept of Health Working Gp on Enhancing Professional Regulation 2007; chair Int Assoc of Medical Regulatory Authorities 2014–16; memb: NHS Modernisation Bd 2004–05, NHS Leadership Network 2004–, Sec of State for Health's Sounding Bd 2006–07, Cabinet Office Honours Ctee (Health) 2006–12, Ministerial Sounding Bd on Social Care 2008–09, NHS Nat Quality Bd 2012–; tstee Consumers Assoc (Which?) 2006–09, chm Leeds Castle Fndn 2012–; visiting fell Office for Public Mgmnt 1994–2004; winner Business and Professional Periodical of the Year Award 1985 and 1988, Charles Fletcher Medical Broadcaster of the Year Award 1997; hon fell: Univ of Cardiff 2006, Inst of Educn Univ of London 2007, Queen's Nursing Inst 2009; Hon Dr Oxford Brookes Univ 2007; Hon FRCP 2007, Hon FRCGP 2008; *Books* Ageing in the 80's – What Prospects for the Elderly? (1981), Who's Accountable for Health (2008); *Recreations* tennis, golf; *Clubs* Reform,Golf House (Elie), Hever Castle Golf, Isle of Harris Golf; *Style*— Niall Dickson, Esq; ✉ General Medical Council, Regents Place, 350 Euston Road, London NW1 3JN (e-mail ndickson@gmc-uk.org, website www.gmc-uk.org)

DICKSON, Sheriff Robert Hamish; DL (Lanarkshire 2012), WS (1969); s of Sheriff Ian Anderson Dickson, WS (d 1982), of Glasgow, and Margaret Forbes, *née* Ross (d 1981); *b* 19 October 1945; *Educ* Glasgow Acad, Drumtochty Castle, Glenalmond Coll, Univ of Glasgow (LLB); *m* 12 Aug 1976, Janet Laird (d 2004), da of Alexander Campbell (d 1987), of Port of Menteith; 1 s (Graeme Ross Campbell b 13 Nov 1977); *Career* legal asst Edinburgh 1969–71, ptnr Brown Mair Gemmill & Hislop Solicitors 1973–86 (joined 1971), Sheriff of S Strathclyde, Dumfries and Galloway at Airdrie 1988–2015 (floating Sheriff 1986–88); pres Sheriffs Assoc 2006–09; *Books* Medical and Dental Negligence (1997); also author of various articles on med legal matters; *Recreations* golf, music, reading; *Clubs* Royal & Ancient, Elie Golf (capt 1997–99), Harris Golf; *Style*— Sheriff Robert Dickson, DL, WS; ✉ Airdrie Sheriff Court, Graham Street, Airdrie ML6 6EE (☎ 01236 751121, fax 01236 747497)

DICKSON, HE Sarah Margaret; *m* Philip Antony; 2 da (b 2008 and 2012); *Career* diplomat; desk offr health and social affrs FCO 1995–96, third sec Br Embassy Belgrade 1996–97, second sec political Br Embassy Buenos Aires 1997–2000, head Int Secuity Section Security Policy Dept FCO 2000–02, first sec political/military Br Embassy Madrid 2002–03, head Migration and Justice and Home Affrs Section FCO 2003–04, head Consular and Africa Section Press Office FCO 2004, communications dir and internal political offr Br Embassy Madrid 2005–08, project mangr for Embassy and Consulate Gen relocation Br Embassy Madrid 2008–09, COS during Spanish presidency of the EU Br Embassy Madrid 2009–10, ambass to Guatemala and non-resident ambass to Honduras 2012–; *Style*— HE Mrs Sarah Dickson; ✉ BFPO 5532, HA4 6EP; c/o FCO (Guatemala City), King Charles Street, London SW1A 2AH

D

DICKSON, Stewart; MLA; *b* 8 December 1950, Carrickfergus, Co Antrim; *Career* MLA (Alliance) E Antrim 2011–; *Style*— Stewart Dickson, Esq, MLA; ✉ Northern Ireland Assembly, Parliament Buildings, Stormont, Belfast BT4 3XX

DIGBY-BELL, Christopher Harvey; s of Lt-Col Horatio Arthur Digby-Bell (d 1997), and Elizabeth Margaret Ann, *née* Cochrane; *b* 21 June 1948; *Educ* Marlborough; *m* 7 Sept 1974 (m dis 2007), Claire, da of Stephen Sutherland Pilch, of Finchampstead, Berks; 1 da (Melissa b 1980), 2 s (Timothy b 1981, William b 1984); *Career* admitted slr 1972; Taylor & Humbert 1966–82, managing ptnr Taylor Garrett 1987–89 (joined 1982); Frere Cholmeley Bischoff: joined as ptnr 1989, sometime mktg and business devpt ptnr, int managing ptnr until 1998; dep chm and gen counsel Palmer Capital Partners 1998–2015, conslt 2015–; hon legal advsr Down's Syndrome Assoc 1990, fndr William's Way 2001–, dir Jerwood Gallery 2013–, tstee Contact A Family 2014–; memb Law Soc 1972 (memb Ruling Cncl for City of London); *Recreations* cricket, golf, writing, collecting cricket prints, photography, cooking, cinema, pop music, American football; *Clubs* MCC, Naval; *Style*— Christopher Digby-Bell, Esq; ✉ Palmer Capital, Time & Life Building, 1 Bruton Street, Mayfair, London W1J 6TL (☎ 020 7409 5500, fax 020 7409 5501, e-mail chdb@palmercapital.co.uk)

DIGGLE, Prof James; s of James Diggle, and Elizabeth Alice, *née* Buckley; *b* 29 March 1944; *Educ* Rochdale GS, St John's Coll Cambridge (Henry Arthur Thomas scholar, Pitt scholar, Browne scholar, Allen scholar, BA, MA, PhD, LittD, Hallam prize, Montagu Butler prize, 2 Browne medals, Porson prize, Members' Latin essay prize, Chllr's classical medal); *m* 8 June 1974, Sedwell Mary, da of Preb Frederick Alexander Routley Chapman (d 1988); 3 s (Charles James b 1975, Julian Alexander b 1977, Nicholas Marcel b 1978); *Career* Univ of Cambridge: fell Queens' Coll 1966–, librarian Queens' Coll 1969–77, asst lectr in classics 1970–75, praelector Queens' Coll 1971–73 and 1978–2015, lectr in classics 1975–89, univ orator 1982–93, chm Faculty of Classics 1989–90 (librarian 1975–81), reader in Greek and Latin 1989–95, prof of Greek and Latin 1995–2011; pres Cambridge Philological Soc 1996–98 (hon sec 1970–74, jt ed Proceedings 1970–82), jt ed Cambridge Classical Texts and Commentaries 1977–, chm Classical Jls Bd 1990–97 (treas 1979–90); Corresponding memb Acad of Athens 2001–; FBA 1985; *Books* The Phaethon of Euripides (1970), Flavii Cresconii Corippi Iohannidos... Libri VIII (jt ed, 1970), The Classical Papers of A E Housman (jt ed, 1972), Studies on the text of Euripides (1981), The Textual Tradition of Euripides' Orestes (1991), Euripidis Fabulae (vol 2 1981, vol 1 1984, vol 3 1994), Cambridge Orations 1982–93: A Selection (1994), Euripidea: Collected Essays (1994), Tragicorum Graecorum Fragmenta Selecta (1998), The Characters of Theophrastus (2004), Odysseus Unbound: The Search for Homer's Ithaca (jtly, 2005); *Style*— Prof James Diggle; ✉ Queens' College, Cambridge CB3 9ET (e-mail jd10000@cam.ac.uk)

DIGGORY, Dr Colin; s of John Harold Diggory (d 2002), of Redcar, Cleveland, and Olga, *née* Midcalf (d 1985); *b* 22 July 1954; *Educ* Sir William Turner's Sch Redcar, Grey Coll Durham (BSc, PGCE), Open Univ (MA, EdD); *m* 10 Aug 1976, Susan Janet, da of R A Robinson; 2 da (Sarah b 24 Sept 1979, Ruth b 13 Sept 1981), 1 s (Mark b 11 Nov 1982); *Career* asst master Manchester Grammar 1976–83, asst master St Paul's Sch 1983–87, head of maths Merchant Taylors' Sch 1987–90, headmaster Latymer Upper Sch 1991–2002 (second master 1990–91), headmaster Alleyn's Sch 2002–10; sr educn conslt C F Appointments Ltd 2011–13, sr advsr RSAcademics Ltd 2013–; chief examiner A Level maths Univ of London 1989–91; chm: London Div HMC 1999, Jr Schs Sub-Ctee HMC 1999–2001; govr Highgate Sch 2003–08, vice-pres Soc of Schoolmasters and Schoolmistresses 2011– (tstee 2004–08), chm Bd Radnor House Gp of Schs 2010–; tstee Dulwich Picture Gallery 2005–08; Open Univ vice chancellor Sir John Daniel Award 2005; CMath 1994, FIMA 1994, FRSA 1994; *Recreations* theatre, walking, reading; *Clubs* East India, Devonshire, Sports and Public Schs, Edward Alleyn (pres 2012–13); *Style*— Dr Colin Diggory; ✉ c/o Radnor House School, Pope's Villa, Cross Deep, Twickenham, Middlesex TW1 4QG

DILBERT, Jennifer Pearl; MBE (2005); da of Vernon L Jackson, OBE, and Francine Jackson; *Educ* Brock Univ Ontario, Univ of Western Ontario; *m* Leonard Dilbert; 2 da (Rita, Juliette); *Career* Dept of Fin and Devpt Cayman Islands Govt: higher exec offr 1980, higher exec offr and admin offr 1981–84, mangr Cayman Islands Currency Bd 1984–86, inspr of banks and trust companies 1991–93 (dep inspr 1987–91), inspr of fin servs Fin Servs Supervision Div 1993–96; exec dir Deutsche Bank (Cayman) Ltd 1996–99, Cayman Islands Govt rep UK 2000–08; analyst Banking Supervision Div Bank of England 1986–87; Cayman Islands Monetary Authy: memb Bd 2000–02, md (on secondment) 2002; vice-pres Cayman Islands Bankers' Assoc 1999–2002, memb Cncl Cayman Islands Stock Exchange 1997–99; treas Nat Ctee Duke of Edinburgh's Award 1996–99 (Gold Award 1983), head Fin Ctee and memb Bd of Elders John Gray Meml Church 1996–99; Miss Cayman Islands 1979; *Style*— Mrs Jennifer Dilbert, MBE

DILLON, Sir Andrew Patrick; kt (2010), CBE (2003); *b* 9 May 1954; *Educ* Univ of Manchester (BSc); *Career* unit gen mangr The Royal Free Hosp London 1986–91, chief exec St George's Healthcare NHS Tst London 1991–99, chief exec Nat Inst for Health and Clinical Excellence (NICE) 1999–; *Recreations* family; *Style*— Sir Andrew Dillon, CBE; ✉ National Institute for Health & Care Excellence, 10 Spring Gardens, London SW1A 2BU

DILLWYN-VENABLES-LLEWELYN; *see also:* Venables-Llewelyn

DILNOT, Sir Andrew William; kt (2013), CBE (2000); s of A W J Dilnot, and P J Dilnot, *née* Ozmond; *b* 19 June 1960; *m* Catherine, *née* Morrish; 2 da (Rosemary b 29 Sept 1990, Julia b 30 March 1993); *Career* Inst for Fiscal Studies: research asst rising to sr research offr 1981–86, dir of personal sector research 1987–90, dep dir 1990–91, dir 1991–2002; coll lectr in economics LMH Oxford 1987–88, dir of studies and coll lectr in economics Exeter Coll Oxford 1988–89; princ St Hugh's Coll Oxford 2002–12, warden Nuffield Coll Oxford 2012–; hon research fell UCL 1985–91, visiting fell ANU Canberra 1986, visiting prof of social economics (Downing meml fell) Univ of Melbourne 1989; pt/t presenter Analysis (BBC Radio 4), presenter More or Less (BBC Radio 4); regular contrib to TV and radio news and current affrs progs, also articles in national broadsheets; special advsr to House of Lords Select Ctee enquiries into harmonisation of European social security systems and withholding tax on investment income; memb: Social Security Advsy Ctee 1992–2002, Cncl Royal Economic Soc 1993–98, Fiscal Studies Task Force of the Effect of the Tax System on Innovative Activity Office of Science and Technol 1993–94, Retirement Income Enquiry (Anson Ctee) 1994, Costs of Continuing Care Enquiry (Barclay Ctee)

1995; *Books* The Reform of Social Security (1984), The Economics of Social Security (1989), Pensions Policy in the UK: An Economic Analysis (1994), The Tiger That Isn't (2007); also author of numerous book chapters, articles, reports and other papers; *Style*— Sir Andrew Dilnot, CBE

DILNOT, Peter George; s of Richard John Dilnot, of Warminster, and Elizabeth Mary, *née* Dickens; *b* 26 August 1969, Basingstoke, Hants; *Educ* Univ of Bristol (BEng), RMA Sandhurst; *m* 1 July 2000, Alice Louise Cecilia, *née* Holden; *Career* offr Army Air Corps 1990–99; Boston Consulting Gp London/Chicago 1999–2006, md EMEA Gilbarco Veeder-Root 2006–10, pres ME Danaher Corp 2010–12, ceo Shanks Gp plc 2012–; *Recreations* skiing, windsurfing, motorsport; *Style*— Peter Dilnot, Esq; ✉ Shanks Group plc, Dunedin House, Auckland Park, Mount Farm, Milton Keynes MK1 1BU

DILWORTH, Richard John; MVO (2006); s of John Eric Dilworth, of Hackforth N Yorks, and Kathleen Anne, *née* Tootill; *b* 24 April 1971; *Educ* Scarisbrick Hall Sch Lancs, Welbeck Coll Notts, RMA Sandhurst, Cranfield Univ (BEng), De Montfort Univ (LLM); *m* 12 April 2008, Susan Margaret, *née* Harper; *Career* served as Troop Cdr and Squadron 2 in Cmd 1995–97, instructor RSME 1997–98, adj Royal Engrs 1998–2000; equerry to HRH The Duke of York 2000–02, dir Royal Lodge Project 2002–05; dir In and Out Ltd 2001–10, sr advsr to chm and Bd Foster & Partners 2005–, advsy ptnr Catalyst Corporate Finance 2010–, dir Malex Ltd 2010–, founding ptnr Expression Ptnrs LLP 2011–, dir DH Investments Ltd 2013–, equity ptnr Foster & Ptnrs 2015–, sr ptnr (ME) Mergers Alliance 2016–; tstee Royal Aero Club Tst 2009–, tstee: Nat Byway Tst 2011–, Development Bd Bowel Cancer UK 2012–; FCMI 2012; *Recreations* rugby, road and cross country running, cycling; *Clubs* In and Out; *Style*— Richard Dilworth, Esq, MVO; ✉ 7 Home Farm, Bagshot Park, Surrey GU19 5PJ (e-mail rdilworth@mal-ex.com, website www.mal-ex.com, Twitter @richdilworth)

DILWORTH, Stephen Patrick Dominic; s of Patrick Dilworth, of Cork, and Ida Dilworth, of London; *b* 20 October 1951; *Educ* St Joseph's Acad Blackheath, Open Univ (BA), UMIST (BSc); *m* Siobhan, da of Brendan and Marie Anglin; 2 da (Louise b 1972, Laura b 1982), 1 s (Nicholas b 1981); *Career* regnl mangr Leeds Permanent Building Soc: Thames Valley 1982–86, London 1986–88; asst gen mangr of mktg Town and Country Building Soc 1988–92, Stephen Dilworth Marketing Consultancy 1992–94, head of corp affrs Bank of Ireland (GB) 1994–99; Foresters UK: head of gp mktg and communications 1999–2002, UK membership dir 2002–12, md Foresters Member Network 2012–15; chief exec SD Assocs 2015–; chair Soho Ltd 2012–16, dir Yamada International plc; dir and audit chair Oxleas NHS Tst; chm: Soho Housing Assoc, Bromley Police Panel 2008–; pres Chartered Inst of Bankers (London Centre); Building Soc Marketing Award 1990, Manchester Univ Volunteer of the Year Award 2008, Inst of Financial Servs Innovation in Communications and PR 2009, Bromley Community Champion 2013, Bromley Commitment to the Community 2014; Freeman Worshipful Co of Marketers 2008–; FCBSI 1977, MCIM 1992, AIPR 1992, FCIB 1993, FCIM 2007; *Books* More Than A Building Society (1987); *Recreations* Shakespeare, theatre, golf, films, football, history, economics, scuba diving; *Clubs* RAC, House of St Barnabas; *Style*— Stephen Dilworth, Esq; ✉ 35 Palace Road, Bromley, Kent BR1 3JT (✆ 020 8460 9012, e-mail the.dilworths@ntlworld.com, Twitter @steviepdd)

DIMBLEBY, David; s of Richard Dimbleby, CBE (d 1965), and Dilys, *née* Thomas; *b* 28 October 1938; *Educ* Charterhouse, ChCh Oxford, Paris Univ, Perugia Univ; *m* 1, 1967 (m dis 2000), Josceline Rose, *qv*, da of late Thomas Gaskell; 1 s, 2 da; m 2, 2000, Belinda Giles; 1 s; *Career* broadcaster; news reporter BBC Bristol 1960–61; presenter and interviewer on network programmes incl: Quest (religion), What's New (science for children), In My Opinion (politics), Top of the Form 1961–63; documentary films incl: Ku-Klux-Klan, The Forgotten Million, Cyprus – The Thin Blue Line 1964–65, South Africa – The White Tribe 1979 (RTS supreme documentary award), The Struggle for South Africa 1990 (US Emmy award, Monte Carlo Golden Nymph award), US-UK Relations – An Ocean Apart (7 films) 1988, David Dimbleby's India 1997, Rebellion 1999; special corr CBS News New York, film reports (and documentary film Texas-England) for 60 minutes 1966–68, commentator Current Events 1969, presenter 24 Hours (BBC1) 1969–72, chm The Dimbleby Talk-In 1971–74, films for Reporter at Large 1973, Election Campaign Report 1974; presenter: Panorama (BBC1) 1974–77 and 1980–82 (reporter 1967–69), People and Power 1982–83, BBC General Election Results programmes 1979, 1983, 1987, 1992, 1997 and 2001, This Week Next Week 1984–86, Question Time 1994–, A Picture of Britain (BBC) 2005; live commentary on public occasions incl: State Opening of Parliament, Trooping the Colour, wedding of Prince Andrew and Sarah Ferguson, Queen Mother's 90th birthday parade (RTS outstanding documentary award), meml services incl Sir Laurence Olivier (RTS outstanding documentary award); chm Dimbleby and Sons Ltd 1986–2001 (md 1966–86); winner of Richard Dimbleby Award for Personal Contribution in Factual TV BAFTA 1998; *Books* An Ocean Apart (with David Reynolds, 1988); *Style*— David Dimbleby, Esq

DIMBLEBY, Henry; MBE (2015); s of David Dimbleby, *qv*, and Josceline Dimbleby, *qv*; *Career* co-fndr Leon Restaurants 2005–, co-fndr London Union; co-author The School Food Plan; *Style*— Henry Dimbleby, MBE; ✉ Leon, 18–20 Southwark Street, London SE1 1TJ

DIMBLEBY, Jonathan; s of Richard Dimbleby, CBE (d 1965), and Dilys, *née* Thomas (d 2009); *b* 31 July 1944; *Educ* UCL (BA); *m* 1, 1968 (m dis 2006), Bel Mooney, *qv*; 1 s (Daniel Richard b 1974), 1 da (Katherine Rose b 1980); m 2, 2007, Jessica Ray; 2 da (Daisy b 2007, Gwendolen b 2009); *Career* freelance journalist, broadcaster and author; TV and radio reporter BBC Bristol 1969–70, World at One (BBC Radio) 1970–71, This Week (Thames TV) 1972–78 and 1986–88, presenter Jonathan Dimbleby in South America (Thames) 1979, Jonathan Dimbleby in Evidence (YTV) 1980–82, assoc ed and presenter First Tuesday series (YTV) 1982–85, presenter Jonathan Dimbleby on Sunday (TV-am) 1985–86, presenter On the Record (BBC TV) 1988–93, chm Any Questions? (BBC Radio) 1987–, presenter Any Answers? (BBC Radio) 1988–2012, THe BBC at War (VSO) 1999–2013, writer and presenter Charles – The Private Man, The Public Role (Central) 1994, presenter political series (LWT) 1995–2006, Index on Censorship 2008–13, writer and presenter The Last Governor (BBC TV) 1997, presenter The General Election '97, 2001 and 2005 (ITV); writer and presenter: An Ethiopian Journey (LWT) 1998, A Kosovo Journey (LWT) 2000, Russia, A Journey with Jonathan Dimbleby (BBC TV) 2008, An African Journey with Jonathan Dimbleby (BBC TV) 2010, presenter A South American Journey with Jonathan Dimbleby (BBC TV) 2012, Churchill's Desert War: The Road to El Alamein (BBC TV) 2013; awards incl Soc of Film and TV Arts Richard Dimbleby Award (for most outstanding contrib to factual TV) 1974; pres: Soil Assoc 1998–2008, VSO 1999–2011; vice-pres Cncl for Protection of Rural England 1997– (pres 1992–97), pres RSPB 2002–04, chair Index on Censorship 2008–13, tstee Dimbleby Cancer Care (chair 2013–); hon fell Bath Spa Univ 2006, Hon LLD Univ of Exeter 2008; *Books* Richard Dimbleby (1975), The Palestinians (1979), The Prince of Wales: A Biography (1994), The Last Governor: Chris Patten and the Handover of Hong Kong (1997), Russia, A Journey to the Heart of a Land and its People (2008), Destiny in the Desert: the Road to El Alamein (2012); *Recreations* music, sailing, tennis; *Style*— Jonathan Dimbleby, Esq

DIMBLEBY, Josceline Rose; da of late Thomas Josceline Gaskell, and Barbara, *née* Jowett; *b* 1 February 1943; *Educ* Cranborne Chase Sch, Guildhall Sch of Music; *m* 1967 (m dis 2000), David Dimbleby, *qv*; 2 da (Liza b 1968, Kate b 1973), 1 s (Henry b 1970); *Career* cookery writer for Sainsbury's 1978–92, cookery ed Sunday Telegraph 1982–97; regular contrib: BBC Good Food Magazine 1993–94, Ideal Home Magazine 1999–2000; regular demonstrator annual BBC Cooking & Kitchen shows, House & Garden Show, Country Living Show and others, after dinner speaker, literary festival talks and occasional TV incl Masterchef and Good Food Prog (both BBC), Carlton Food Network; André Simon Award 1979, Glenfiddich Cookery Writer of the Year Award 1993; contrib travel articles: Condé Nast Traveller, Mail on Sunday; *Books* A Taste of Dreams (1976), Party Pieces (1977), Josceline Dimbleby's Book of Puddings, Desserts and Savouries (1979), Favourite Food (1983), The Essential Josceline Dimbleby (1989), The Practically Vegetarian Book (USA edn, 1995), The Cooking Enthusiast (USA edn, 2000), A Profound Secret (2004, 2 edn 2005), May and Amy (USA edn, 2005); for Sainsbury's: Cooking for Christmas (1978), Family Meat and Fish Cookery (1979), Cooking with Herbs and Spices (1979), Curries and Oriental Cookery (1980), Salads for all Seasons (1981), Marvellous Meals with Mince (1982, 3 edn, revised edn 2012), Festive Food (1982), Sweet Dreams (1983), First Impressions (1984), The Josceline Dimbleby Collection (1984), Main Attractions (1985), A Traveller's Tastes (1986), The Josceline Dimbleby Christmas Book (1987), The Josceline Dimbleby Book of Entertaining (1988), The Cook's Companion (1991), The Almost Vegetarian Cookbook (1994), The Christmas Book (1994), Josceline Dimbleby's Complete Cookbook (1997), Josceline Dimbleby's Cooking Course (1999), Josceline Dimbleby's Almost Vegetarian Cookbook (2000), Orchards in the Oasis – Food, Travels and Memories (2010, Kate Whiteman Award for Work in Food and Travel 2011); *Recreations* singing, travel, cinema, gardening, music, opera, walking; *Style*— Josceline Dimbleby; ✉ 18 Ashchurch Park Villas, London W12 9SP (✆ 020 8743 1216, e-mail jossydimbleby@gmail.com, website www.joscelinedimbleby.com)

DIMSDALE, Oliver; s of Robert Edward Dimsdale, of Barkway House, Herts, and Françoise, *née* Gerber; *b* 28 October 1972, Aylesbury, Bucks; *Educ* Eton, Univ of Reading (BA), Guildhall School of Music and Drama (BA); *Career* actor; fndr and co-artistic dir with Ferdy Roberts, *qv* and Tim Phillips, Filter Theatre; *Theatre* Beautiful Thing (Salisbury Playhouse Theatre) 1999, The Changeling (Salisbury Playhouse Theatre) 1999, A Midsummer Night's Dream 2000, Workers Writes (Royal Court Theatre) 2001, The Tempest (RSC nat and world tour) 2001, Faster (Filter Theatre at BAC) 2001, Five Finger Exercise (Salisbury Playhouse Theatre) 2002, The Dead Wait (Manchester Royal Exchange) 2002 (Manchester Evening News award for Best Fringe Performer), Great Expectations (Manchester Royal Exchange) 2004, Body Stories (Filter Theatre at Nat Theatre Studio) 2004, The Comedy of Errors (Sheffield Crucible) 2005, The Creeper (West End and tour) 2006, Pravda (Birmingham Rep and Chichester Festival Theatre) 2006, Twelfth Night (Filter Theatre, Tricycle and tour) 2006, Caucasian Chalk Circle (Nat Theatre and Filter Theatre) 2007, Water (Filter Theatre at Lyric Hammersmith) 2007; *Television* Byron 2003, He Knew Was Right 2003, Dalziel and Pascoe 2004, Fallen Angel 2006, Harley Street 2008, Lark Rise to Candleford 2008; *Film* Nostradamus 2006, RocknRolla 2007; *Recreations* writing, skiing, art; *Style*— Oliver Dimsdale, Esq; ✉ website www.filtertheatre.com

DIMSON, Prof Elroy; s of David Dimson, of London, and Phyllis, *née* Heilpern; *b* 17 January 1947; *Educ* Univ of Newcastle upon Tyne (BA), Univ of Birmingham (MCom), Univ of London (PhD); *m* 1 July 1969, Dr Helen Patricia Dimson, da of Max Sonn, of Whitley Bay, Tyne & Wear; 3 s (Jonathan Ashley b 1971, Benjamin Simon b 1979, Daniel Marc b 1986), 1 da (Susanna Rachel b 1973); *Career* Tube Investments 1969–70, Unilever Ltd 1970–72; London Business Sch: joined 1972, dean MBA Progs 1986–90, chair Fin Faculty 1992–94, chair Accounting Faculty 1999–2002, govr 2000–03 and 2007–09, currently prof emeritus of finance; Univ of Cambridge: joined 2009, prof of finance Judge Business Sch 2009–, chm Newton Centre for Endowment Asset Mgmnt 2013–; chm The German Investment Trust plc 1995–97; dir: Mobil Trustee Co Ltd 1984–2003, Hoare Govett Indices Ltd 1992–2012, TP70 2010 Venture Capital Tst 2011–16, FTSE Int 2016–; chm Strategy Cncl Norwegian Govt Pension Fund 2007–, chm Advsy Bd FTSE Gp 2013–; former visiting prof: Univ of Chicago, Univ of Calif Berkeley, Univ of Hawaii, Euro Inst Brussels, Bank of England; author of numerous published papers; Hon FIA, hon fell Soc of Investment Professionals, FRHistS; *Books* Risk Measurement Service (jtly, 1979, and subsequent edns to 2016), Cases in Corporate Finance (jtly, 1988), Stock Market Anomalies (1988), The Millennium Book: A Century of Investment Returns (jtly, 2000), Global Investment Returns Yearbook (jtly, 2001, and subsequent edns to 2016), Triumph of the Optimists: 101 Years of Global Investment Returns (jtly, 2002), Endowment Asset Management (jtly, 2007), Global Investment Returns Sourcebook (jtly, 2008, and subsequent edns to 2016); *Style*— Prof Elroy Dimson; ✉ e-mail edimson@london.edu and e.dimson@jbs.cam.ac.uk, Skype elroydimson

DIN, Russhied Ali; s of Matab Ali Din, of Rawalpindi, Pakistan, and Hilda Rose, *née* Dring (d 1985); *b* 8 April 1956; *Educ* Ordsall Secdy Modern, Salford Coll of Technol, Birmingham Poly (BA); *Career* designer: City Industrial Shopfitters 1978, Fitch & Co 1979, Italy Studios Giardi Rome 1980, Thomas Saunders Architects 1981, Peter Glynn Smith Assoc 1982–84 (BAA Gatwick refurbishment 1983), Allied Int Designers 1984–86; formed DIN Associates 1986– (became Ltd Co 1988); design conslt to: Next Retail plc 1987, French Connection, Nicole Farhi, Escada, Joop!; other projects incl: Polo Ralph Lauren Paris 1991, Tommy Hilfiger, Selfridges, Habitat, Diana, Princess of Wales Museum & Visitors Centre Althorp 1998; external assessor Kingston Poly and École Superiure D'Arts Graphiques & D'Architecture Interiure (ESAG), judge Student Design Awards 1998; Young Business Person of the Year (Observer and Harvey Nichols) 1991; MCSD 1991, FRSA; *Recreations* equestrian pursuits, tennis; *Style*— Russhied Din, Esq; ✉ DIN Associates Ltd, 32 St Oswalds Place, London SE11 5JE (✆ 020 7582 0777)

DINARDO, Carlo; s of Nicandro Dinardo (1987), and Rosaria, *née* Iannacone; *b* 5 July 1939; *Educ* St Patrick's HS Coatbridge Scotland, Paddington Tech Coll, Tech Coll Coatbridge Scotland, Univ of Strathclyde; *m* 30 Aug 1962, Irene Rutherford, da of William James Niven (d 1977), of Helensburgh; 2 da (Karen b 24 Oct 1965, Lorraine b 7 Aug 1973), 1 s (Mark b 27 April 1967); *Career* fndr ptnr own practice of consulting engrs 1969; princ: Dinardo & Ptnrs 1978–, Dinardo Partnership 1990–; dir Scottish Conslts Int 1987–90; estab DP Gp of cos (investments) in mid 1980s and continues as chm; memb Ctee: Educn Task Gp Inst of Structural Engrs 1987–89, Industrial Trg Advsy Bd Paisley Coll of Technol, Inst of Engs and Shipbuilders Scotland 1994– (elected as pres 1999–2001); memb Bd of Govrs of Westbourne Sch for Girls Glasgow 1984–91, memb Bd Renfrewshire Learning Bus Partnership; CEng 1965, MIStructE 1965, MICE 1967, FIStructE 1976, FICE 1976, MIHT 1979, FInstPet 1979, MCIA 1980, FGS 1982, FIHT 1982, MConsE 1984, MASCE 1991, FEANI, FHKIE 1992, FIES 1994; *Publications* author of papers published in learned jls; *Recreations* golf, spectator rugby and sport, historical travels, curling, ancient history; *Clubs* Royal Northern & Univ (Aberdeen), Buchanan Castle Golf (Drymen), Glasgow Golf; *Style*— Carlo Dinardo, Esq; ✉ Cleveden, Main Street, Killearn, Glasgow G63 9NE (✆ 01360 550459); Dinardo Partnership Ltd, Mirren Court, 119 Renfrew Road, Paisley, Renfrewshire PA3 4EA (✆ 0141 889 1212, fax 0141 889 5446, mobile 07860 836757, email paisley@dinardo.co.uk)

DINENAGE, Caroline Julia; MP; da of Fred Dinenage, MBE; *b* 1971, Portsmouth, Hants; *Educ* Univ of Wales Swansea; *m* 14 Feb 2014, Mark Lancaster, TD, MP, *qv*; *Career* MP (Cons) Gosport 2010–; *Style*— Ms Caroline Dinenage, MP; ✉ House of Commons, London SW1A 0AA

DINGEMANS, Hon Mr Justice; Sir James Michael Dingemans; kt (2013), QC (2002); s of Rear Adm P G V Dingemans, CB, DSO, of Sussex, and Faith, *née* Bristow; *b* 25 June 1964; *Educ* Mansfield Coll Oxford (BA, Rugby Union blue), Inns of Court Sch of Law;

m 20 April 1991, Janet Elizabeth, *née* Griffiths; 2 da (Phoebe b 10 Aug 1992, Freya b 29 Jan 1997), 1 s (Alexander b 16 April 1994); *Career* called to the Bar Inner Temple 1987; recorder 2002–, dep High Court judge 2010–13, judge of the High Court of Justice (Queen's Bench Div) 2013–, presiding judge Western Circuit 2014–; leading counsel Hutton Inquiry 2003; chm Int Ctee Bar of Eng and Wales 2008–10; memb: Organising Ctee Cwlth Law Conf London 2005, Advsy Panel Rugby Football League; judicial offr RFU 2013–; FCIArb 2007; *Books* Employers Liability Cases (2003), Settlement of Investment Disputes under the Energy Charter Treaty (conslt ed, 2011), Public Inquiries (conslt ed, 2011), The Protections for Religious Rights (2013); *Recreations* rugby, sailing, cricket; *Clubs* Broadhalfpenny Brigands Cricket, Bar Yacht; *Style—* The Hon Mr Justice Dingemans; ✉ Royal Courts of Justice, Strand, London WC2A 2LL

DINHAM, Martin John; CBE (1997); s of John Archibald Dinham, and Gwenyth, *née* Jones; *b* 9 July 1950, London; *Educ* Haberdashers' Aske's, Christ's Coll Cambridge (BA); *m* 11 Sept 1980, Jannie, *née* Sanderson; 1 s (Nathaniel John b 22 July 1985), 1 da (Rachel Louise b 4 Oct 1988); *Career* Miny of Overseas Devpt (later Overseas Devpt Admin, now Dept for Int Devpt): joined as exec offr 1974, private sec to successive Mins for Overseas Devpt 1978–79, desk offr Malawi and Zambia 1979–81, asst to UK Exec Dir World Bank 1981–83 (secondment), head Personnel Branch 1983–85, private sec to successive Mins of Overseas Devpt 1985–87, head SE Asia Devpt Div Bangkok 1988–92, advsr to Govr Hong Kong Govt 1992–97 (secondment), head of personnel and princ establishment offr 1997–2000, dir Asia 2000–04, dir Europe, ME, Americas and E Asia 2005–07, dir UN Conflict and Humanitarian 2007, DG int 2008–10; tstee Bd: Sightsavers 2010– (vice-chm 2012–15, chm 2015–), Int HIV/AIDS Alliance 2010– (chair Finance and Audit Ctee 2011–15, chm of Bd 2015–), BBC Media Action 2013– (vice-chair 2016–); chm Bd Global Fund to Fight AIDS, Tuberculosis and Malaria 2011; *Recreations* tennis, cinema, planning holidays, rock concerts for the over 50s; *Style—* Martin Dinham, Esq, CBE; ✉ e-mail martin.dinham@btinternet.com

DINKEL, Philip Charles Christian; s of Prof Ernest Michael Dinkel (d 1983), and Emmy Dinkel (d 2003); *b* 1946; *Educ* Ampleforth, AA Sch of Architecture; *m* 1981, Lucia, *née* Stevens; 1 da, 2 s; *Career* architect; project architect Hobhouse Ct Trafalgar Square 1973–77 (Civic Tst Award 1981), in private practice specialising in conservation work, commercial and residential projects in UK, Albania, Sweden and Far East 1977–; AA Prize 1970; RIBA; *Recreations* the arts, cello, conservation matters; *Style—* Philip Dinkel, Esq; ✉ Aycote House, Rendcomb, Gloucestershire GL7 7EP (☎ 01285 831866); 3 Montpelier Mews, London SW7 1HB

DINKIN, Anthony David; QC (1991); s of Hyman Dinkin (d 2004), of London, and Mary, *née* Hine (d 1992); *b* 2 August 1944; *Educ* Henry Thornton GS Clapham, Coll of Estate Mgmnt London (BSc); *m* 20 Oct 1968, Derina Tanya, MBE, da of Benjamin Green (d 1994); *Career* called to the Bar Lincoln's Inn 1968 (bencher 2003, master of the moots 2008); recorder of the Crown Court 1989–, tbnl judge Health, Educn and Social Care Chamber 2008–; memb: Lands Tbnl 1997–98, Mental Health Review Tbnl 1999–; examiner in law Univ of Reading 1985–92, external examiner in law City Univ 2003–; former memb Anglo-American Real Property Inst; pres Estate Mgmnt Club 1998; *Recreations* gardening, theatre, music, travel; *Style—* Anthony Dinkin, Esq, QC; ✉ Cornerstone Barristers, 2–3 Gray's Inn Square, London WC1R 5JH (☎ 020 7242 4986, fax 020 7405 1166, e-mail ad.qc@cornerstonebarristers.com)

DINSDALE, Owen Malcolm; s of Malcolm George Frank Dinsdale, and Suzanne, *née* van Rooyen; *b* 15 January 1947; *Educ* King Edward VII Sch Johannesburg, Univ of Witwatersrand; *m* 9 July 1972, Bernice, da of William Greenblatt; 3 s (Tarquin Ian b 24 April 1974, Ryan Stuart b 22 Nov 1976, Ewan Anthony b 5 May 1980); *Career* md Telerama Redifussion 1979–81; md: Barlow Manufacturing Co 1984–86 (gen mangr 1981–84), Imperial Cold Storage 1986–87, Gerber Foods Holdings 1987–88; chief exec Acsis Group plc until 1994, dir Premier Health Group plc, chm Didata Ltd 1998–2010; *Recreations* fly fishing, hockey, tennis, golf; *Clubs* Country (Johannesburg), Wanderers, Woburn Golf and Country; *Style—* Owen Dinsdale, Esq; ✉ Ridge End, 82 West Hill, Aspley, Guise, Bedfordshire MK17 8DX (☎ 01908 583318)

DINWIDDIE, Ian Maitland; s of Lauderdale Maitland Dinwiddie (d 1978), and Frances Lilian Pedrick; *b* 8 February 1952; *Educ* Sherborne, Univ Exeter (BA); *m* 1978, Sally Jane, da of Leslie Ronald Croydon; 2 da (Laura b 1981, Lucy b 1991), 1 s (Andrew b 1984); *Career* audit mangr Ernst & Young 1972–82, fin controller Arbuthnot Savory Milln Holdings Ltd 1982–86, gen mangr Savory Milln Ltd 1986; fin dir: Arbuthnot Latham Bank Ltd 1987, gp fin dir Guinness Mahon Holdings plc until 1990; currently fin dir Allen & Overy LLP; *Recreations* sailing, golf; *Style—* Ian Dinwiddie; ✉ Allen & Overy LLP, One Bishops Square, London E1 6AD (☎ 020 3088 0000, fax 020 3088 0088)

DINWIDDY, Bruce Harry; CMG (2003); s of Thomas Lutwyche Dinwiddy (d 1992), and Ruth, *née* Abbott (d 1996); *b* 1 February 1946; *Educ* Winchester, New Coll Oxford (MA); *m* 29 June 1974, Emma Victoria, da of Sir David Llewellyn (d 1992), and Lady Joan Llewellyn, OBE, *née* Williams (d 2013); 1 da (Celia Rose (Mrs James Stone) b 22 Sept 1976), 1 s (Thomas Rhidian b 13 May 1979); *Career* economist Govt of Swaziland (ODI Nuffield fell) 1967–69, reseach offr ODI 1970–73; HM Dip Serv: entered 1973, first sec UK delgn to MBFR talks Vienna 1975–77, FCO 1977–81, head of Chancery Cairo 1981–83, FCO 1983–86, asst sec Cabinet Office 1986–88, cnsllr Bonn 1989–91, dep high cmmr Ottawa 1992–95, head African Dept (Southern) FCO 1995–98, cmmr (non-resident) Br Indian Ocean Territory 1996–98, high cmmr to Tanzania 1998–2001, seconded to Standard Chartered Bank 2001–02, govr Cayman Is 2002–05; memb Cncl and chm Wider Caribbean Working Gp UK Overseas Territories Conservation Forum 2006–15, conslt UK Trade and Investment 2007–09; *Publications* Promoting African Enterprise (1974); *Recreations* golf, swimming, music (piano), travel; *Clubs* Vincent's (Oxford), Royal Wimbledon Golf; *Style—* Bruce Dinwiddy, Esq, CMG; ✉ 8 Connaught Avenue, London SW14 7RH

DIPPLE, Joanna Shannon (Jo); *b* 5 June 1968, London; *Educ* Benenden Sch, Univ of East Anglia; *Career* columnist Dear Jo column Daily Mirror 1995–2000, head of public affrs Trinity Mirror plc 2000–06, special advsr HM Treasy 2006–07, special advsr Strategic Communications Unit Downing St 2007–08; UK Music: sr political advsr 2008–12, ceo 2012–; *Recreations* music, swimming, cycling; *Clubs* Soho House, Shoreditch House; *Style—* Ms Jo Dipple; ✉ UK Music, 4th Floor, 49 Whitehall, London SW1A 2BX (Twitter @uk_music)

DISMORE, Andrew; AM; s of Ian Dismore (d 1965), and Brenda Hartley; *b* 2 September 1954; *Educ* Bridlington GS, Univ of Warwick (LLB), LSE (LLM), Coll of Law Guildford; *Career* slr: Robin Thompson and Partners 1978–95, Russell Jones and Walker 1995–97; cncllr Westminster City Cncl 1982–97 (ldr Lab Gp 1990–97), MP (Lab) Hendon 1997–2010, memb London Assembly (Lab) Barnet and Camden 2012–; *Recreations* gardening, opera, Greece, Greek culture; *Style—* Andrew Dismore, Esq, AM; ✉ London Assembly, City Hall, The Queen's Walk, London SE1 2AA

DISNEY, Patrick William Wynn; s of Hugh Disney (d 2009), and Eira, *née* Wynn-Williams (d 1974); *b* 21 September 1956, London; *Educ* Winchester, BNC Oxford (MA); *m* 28 Jan 1995, Melissa, *née* Colston; 1 da (Laura Elizabeth b 6 Nov 1996); *Career* Morgan Grenfell and Co Ltd 1978, chief exec Morgan Grenfell Investment Services 1988–99 (dir 1987), dir Morgan Grenfell Asset Mgmnt 1991–99, md SEI Investments (Europe) Ltd 1999–; chm: Anita Goulden Tst 1996–2002, Guy's and St Thomas' Charity 2006–10, Investment Ctee KCL 2010–14; memb: Governing Cncl KCL 2001–10, Investment Ctee Winchester Coll 2013–, Investment Ctee CW+ (Chelsea and Westminster Hosp charity) 2015–; vice-chm Audit Ctee KCL 2005–10; dir Crown and Manor 1995–2010, tstee Wykeham Crown and Manor Tst 1995–2014; Liveryman Worshipful Co of Fishmongers 2006–; FKC 2010; *Recreations* sailing, skiing, opera, shooting; *Clubs* Royal Yacht Squadron, Boodle's, Hurlingham, Bosham Sailing; *Style—* Patrick Disney, Esq; ✉ c/o SEI Investments (Europe) Ltd, 14–18 Finsbury Square, London EC2A 1BR (☎ 020 3810 7764, e-mail pdisney@seic.com)

DISPENZA, Adriano; s of late Mario Dispenza, of France, and Lina, *née* Inzirillo; *b* 24 September 1948; *Educ* QMC (BSc), Paris (Dip Faculté de Droit et Sciences Economiques); *m* 12 March 1979, Rallia Jean, da of John Adam Hadjipateras, of Greece; 1 da (Carolina b 5 March 1981); *Career* Morgan Grenfell & Co Ltd 1973–77, Amex Bank Ltd 1977–79, md First Chicago Ltd 1979–88, md Merrill Lynch Int Ltd 1988–95, md Folio Corp Fin Ltd, ret; *Recreations* reading, travel, crosswords; *Style—* Adriano Dispenza, Esq

D

DITTMAR, Henry (Hank); *Educ* Northwestern Univ (BS), Univ of Texas Sch of Architecture (MCRP); *m*; *Career* pres Reconnecting America 2000–04, chief exec Prince's Fndn for the Built Environment 2005–13; special advsr for global urbanisation to HRH The Prince of Wales 2013–; princ Hank Dittmar Assocs 2013–; chair Congress for the New Urbanism America 2001–07; Seaside Prize 2008, Outstanding Graduate Alumnus Univ of Texas 2008; *Publications* New Transit Town (co-ed and co-author, 2004), Transport and Neighbourhoods (2008); *Style—* Hank Dittmar, Esq; ✉ Prince's Foundation for the Built Environment, 19–22 Charlotte Road, London EC2A 3SG (website www.hankdittmar.com)

DIX, Wing Cdr Kenneth John Weeks; OBE (1975), AFC (1958), QCVSA (1967); adopted s of Eric John Dix (d 1982), of Dorset, and Kate, *née* Weeks (d 1986); *b* 12 September 1930, Pontllanfraith, Wales; *Educ* HMC Canford, RAF Colls Cranwell, Bracknell, Manby (PSC, AWC), Univ of Oxford, Univ of Bristol; *m* 1, 1953 (m dis); 1 da (Linda b 1954), 1 s (Michael b 1956); m 2, 1969 (m dis); *Career* RAF 1948–83 (Europe, ME, Far E, USA), ret with rank of Wing Cdr; conslt for electronic defence systems and mil advsr (Eldecon), specialist in avionics, navigation, weapons and reconnaissance systems; dir Electronic Defence Assoc; represented various counties and clubs, RAF, Combined Servs and Oxbridge combined XV at rugby 1953; Queen's Commendation 1967; MRAeS, MIMgt, MIEE, memb BHS; *Recreations* fly fishing, equestrian events, shooting, car events, cinema, cricket, golf, motorsport, opera, ballet; *Clubs* RAF, Victory Services, SFC; *Style—* Wing Cdr Kenneth J W Dix, OBE, AFC, QCVSA, RAF; ✉ c/o Lloyds Bank, Bournemouth BH1 1ED (☎ 01202 538002)

DIXEY, Judy; da of John Dixey, and Jane, *née* Dobson; *Educ* St Hilda's Coll Oxford (MA); *Career* charity dir; qualified as CA with Peat Marwick Mitchell 1975–78; asst dir Eastern Arts Assoc 1985–89, dir Bankside Gallery 1993–2004; exec dir VocalEyes 2004–; tstee Gemini, tstee Opera Up Close; govr St Patrick's Primary Sch; CA 1979; *Recreations* singing, walking, writing; *Style—* Ms Judy Dixey; ✉ e-mail judydixey@blueyonder.co.uk

DIXON, Prof Adrian Kendal; s of Kendal Dixon, and Annette, *née* Darley; *b* 5 February 1948; *Educ* Uppingham, King's Coll Cambridge (MA, MB BChir, MD), Bart's Med Coll London (Golf purple); *m* 1979, Anne Hazel, *née* Lucas; 2 s (Charles Kendal b 21 Jan 1981, Thomas Christopher b 12 March 1987), 1 da (Emily Louise b 3 Feb 1983); *Career* jr hosp posts Bart's, Nottingham Gen Hosp and Hosp for Sick Children Great Ormond St 1972–79, lectr in radiology and hon conslt radiologist Addenbrooke's Hosp Cambridge 1979–94, prof of radiology Univ of Cambridge 1994–2009 (emeritus prof 2009–), Master Peterhouse Cambridge 2008–16 (fell 1986–); conslt radiologist Addenbrooke's Hosp Cambridge 2009–14; ed-in-chief European Radiology 2008–13; Hon MD UC Cork 2011, Hon MD Univ of Munich 2013; FRCR 1978, FRCP 1991, FMedSci 1998, Hon FFRRCSI 1999, Hon FRANZCR 2001, FRCS 2003, Hon FRACR 2009; *Books* Body CT (1983), Human Cross Sectional Anatomy (1991 and 2007), Diagnostic Radiology (2007, 2014); *Recreations* family, golf; *Clubs* Cambridge Univ Golf (pres); *Style—* Prof Adrian Dixon

DIXON, Andrew Gareth; s of Geoff Dixon, and Maureen, *née* Young; *b* 5 December 1958, Manchester; *Educ* Univ of Bradford Mgmnt Centre (BSc); *m* 16 July 1988, Charlotte, da of Richard Kendall; 1 s (Elliott b 8 July 1996), 1 da (Lilly b 6 January 1998); *Career* sec social and cultural affrs Univ of Bradford 1979–80, administrator and youth projects dir Major Road Theatre Company 1981–84, county arts offr Humberside CC 1984–89; Northern Arts: asst dir 1989–92, dep chief exec and head regnl devpt 1992–97, chief exec 1997–2002; exec dir Arts Cncl 2002–05, chief exec Newcastle Gateshead Initiative 2005–, exec dir Tourism Tyne & Wear 2006–; Hon DCL Univ of Northumbria; *Recreations* arts, skiing, photography, vegetarian cookery; *Style—* Andrew Dixon, Esq

DIXON, Anthony (Tony); s of John Dixon (d 1997), of Burnley, and Eva, *née* Jackson; *b* 12 September 1946, Burnley, Lancs; *Educ* Whitefield Secdy Modern, Univ of Hull (MBA), Univ of Central Lancs (LLM), Ambulance Serv Inst (grad); *m* 12 Sept 1970, Marjorie Anne, *née* Lund; 2 da (Karen b 16 April 1973, Claire b 23 May 1975), 1 s (David b 12 July 1979); *Career* Lancs Ambulance Serv 1972–2003 (latterly dep dir ops), commercial dir Daisy Communications Ltd 2003–09; md Results Ltd; dir Your Mobile Co Ltd; gp head of security Daisy Gp plc 2012–; memb: Bd Office of the Telecommunications Ombudsman, Fin Bd The Ombudsman Serv Ltd; past pres Ambulance Serv Inst; *Recreations* sailing; *Clubs* Rotary Int (Burnley Pendleside, past pres); *Style—* Tony Dixon, Esq

DIXON, Baron (Life Peer UK 1997), of Jarrow in the County of Tyne & Wear; Donald (Don) Dixon; PC (1996), DL (Tyne & Wear 1997); s of late Christopher Albert Dixon, and Jane Dixon; *b* 6 March 1929; *Educ* Ellison Street Elementary Sch Jarrow; *m* Doreen Morad; 1 s, 1 da; *Career* shipyard worker 1947–74, branch sec GMWU 1974–79, cncllr S Tyneside MDC 1963–; MP (Lab) Jarrow 1979–97, formerly Lab dep chief whip until 1996; Freeman: Borough of Jarrow 1972, Metropolitan Borough of South Tyneside 1997; *Recreations* football, boxing, reading; *Clubs* Jarrow Labour, Ex Servicemen's (Jarrow), Hastings (Hebburn); *Style—* The Rt Hon Lord Dixon, PC; ✉ 1 Hillcrest, Jarrow, Tyne & Wear NE32 4DP (☎ 0191 897635); House of Lords, London SW1A 0PW

DIXON, Isobel; *b* Umtata, South Africa; *Educ* Univ of Stellenbosch, Univ of Edinburgh; *Career* poet and literary agent; agent Blake Friedmann Literary Agency Ltd; contrib to numerous poetry jls and anthologies, trans South African novels into English; Sanlam Literary Award 2000, Olive Schreiner Award 2004; *Books* Weather Eye (2000), A Fold in the Map (2007), The Tempest Prognosticator (2011), The Debris Field (co-writer, 2014), Bearings (2016), The Leonids (2016); *Style—* Ms Isobel Dixon; ✉ Blake Friedmann Literary Agency Ltd, Selous House, 5–12 Mandela Street, London NW1 0DU

DIXON, Sir (David) Jeremy; kt (2000); s of Joseph Lawrence Dixon, and Beryl Margaret, *née* Braund; *b* 31 May 1939; *Educ* Merchant Taylors', AA Sch of Architecture (AADipl); *m* 1 (sep); 1 s, 2 da; partner, Julia Somerville; *Career* architect: in private practice since 1973: princ Jeremy Dixon 1975–90 (with Fenella Dixon), Jeremy Dixon BDP 1983–90, Dixon Jones Ltd 1991–; int competition-winning work: Northampton Co offices 1973, Royal Opera House 1983, Piazzale Roma Venice 1990; other competition-winning work: Tate Gallery coffee shop and restaurant 1984, study centre Darwin Coll Cambridge 1988, Robert Gordon Univ residence Aberdeen 1991, Univ of Portsmouth science building 1993, Nat Portrait Gallery extension 1994, Saïd Business Sch Univ of Oxford 1996, Magna Carta Bldg Salisbury Cathedral 2001, Panopticon UCL 2001, Kings Place devpt 2002, Oxford Castle Hotel Oxford 2003, Exhibition Rd project 2004; other works incl: reconstruction of the Tatlin Tower 1971 and at Royal Acad 2012, housing in St Mark's Road London 1975, Henry Moore Sculpture Inst Leeds 1988, Compass Point Docklands 1989, Plymouth Superstore for J Sainsbury 1991, quadrant 3 Regents Palace Hotel 2005,

St Peter's Arcade Liverpool 2006, Chelsea Barracks London 2009; chm RIBA Regnl Awards Gp 1991–; tutor AA Sch 1972–82, external examiner President's Gold Medal Ctee RIBA; tstee Midsummer Music 2012–, patron London Chamber Music Soc 2012–; RIBA; *Exhibitions* Venice Biennale 1980, Paris 1981, Bordeaux Chateau Paris 1998; Jeremy Dixon and Edward Jones: Buildings & Projects 1959–2002 (2002); *Recreations* walking, cooking, playing the piano badly; *Style*— Sir Jeremy Dixon; ✉ Dixon Jones Ltd, 2–3 Hanover Yard, Noel Road, London N1 8YA (☎ 020 7483 8888, e-mail jeremydixon@dixonjones.co.uk)

DIXON, Josie; da of Brian Hugh Dixon, and Ailsa Mary Pauline, *née* Harrison; *Educ* Lord Williams's Sch Thame, UC Oxford (open scholarship, Violet Vaughan Morgan Prize, BA), Wolfson Coll Oxford (MPhil); *m* 2002, Dr Bryan Wells; 2 s (Marcus Julian b 2003, Orlando Lucian b 2005); *Career* A-level examiner Oxford and Cambridge Examinations Bd 1986–89; CUP: ed 1989–91, commissioning ed 1992–94, sr commissioning ed for literature 1995–98, assoc editorial manager for humanities 1998–99; publishing dir Academic Div Palgrave Macmillan 1999–2003, publishing and research training conslt 2003–; fndr Lucian Consulting 2007; over 80 univ clients in UK, Europe and USA, publishing clients in UK and Europe; vol work with tuberculosis patients Hosp del Niño Lima 1983, lifelong Oxfam supporter, tstee The Magdalena Consort 2010–, fndr Cambridge Renaissance Voices 2013; Sir Stanley Unwin Travelling Scholar 1993; *Publications* essays published in Revolution and English Romanticism: Politics and Rhetoric (ed Hanley and Selden, 1990) and The Cambridge Companion to Coleridge (ed Newlyn, 2002); reviews in The Times Higher Education Supplement and Early Music Review, feature articles and reviews in Oxford Today and The Reader magazine; *Recreations* music (recordings of Renaissance polyphony made with the Cambridge Taverner Choir), Italy; *Style*— Ms Josie Dixon; ✉ e-mail josiedixon@lucianconsulting.com, website www.lucianconsulting.com

DIXON, Dr Sir Michael; kt (2014); s of Walter Dixon (d 2010), and Sonia Ivy, *née* Doidge (d 1997); *b* 16 March 1956, Plymouth; *Educ* Tiffin Boys' Sch Kingston upon Thames, Imperial Coll London (BSc, ARCS), Univ of York (DPhil); *m* 1, 1988; 1 da (Isabel Richenda b 4 June 1990), 1 s (Samuel John b 20 Jan 1992); m 2, 29 Dec 2001, Deborah Mary, *née* McMahon; 1 s (Noah b 10 Sept 1999); *Career* sponsoring ed Pitman Publishing Ltd 1980–83, publisher then publishing dir John Wiley & Sons Ltd 1983–96, md Thomson Science Europe 1996–98, gp md Sweet & Maxwell Ltd 1998–99, DG Zoological Soc of London 2000–04, dir Natural History Museum 2004–; chief scientific advsr Dept for Culture Media and Sport 2006–07, memb Cncl Royal Albert Hall 2004–, memb Bd Ecsite 2005–07, chair Science Advsy Cncl Dept for Culture Media and Sport 2009–15 (now memb), chair Nat Museum Dir's Cncl 2009–13; tstee Int Tst for Zoological Nomenclature 2004–15 (chair 2008–); memb Ct: Imperial Coll 2006–, Univ of Reading 2008–; govr Powell-Cotton Museum 2008–; Hon DSc Imperial Coll London 2015; *Recreations* natural history, photography, music; *Clubs* Chelsea Arts; *Style*— Dr Sir Michael Dixon; ✉ The Natural History Museum, Cromwell Road, London SW7 5BD (☎ 020 7942 5471, e-mail m.dixon@nhm.ac.uk)

DIXON, Peter John; s of George Edward Dixon, and Violet Jose, *née* Bell; *b* 4 February 1949; *Educ* King Edward VI GS, Wellingborough GS, LSE (BSc), London Inst of Educn (postgrad CertEd), Brunel Univ (MEd); *m* 28 July 1973, (Elizabeth) Susan, da of Joseph Arthur Butterworth; 2 s (Simon Peter b 29 Sept 1979, Nicholas Jonathan b 8 Nov 1981); *Career* head of history and integrated studies Hayes Co GS 1972–80, chef and proprietor White Moss House Cumbria 1980–; winner of food and wine awards in all leading guide books; Master Chef of GB (memb Exec Ctee); *Recreations* walking, tennis, wine tasting, bridge, chess; *Style*— Peter Dixon, Esq; ✉ White Moss House, Rydal Water, Grasmere, Cumbria LA22 9SE (☎ 01539 435295, fax 01539 435516, e-mail dixon@whitemoss.com)

DIXON, Sir Peter John Bellett; kt (2009); *Educ* CCC Cambridge (MA, open exhibitioner), London Business Sch (MSc); *Career* arbitrage trader Vickers da Costa stockbrokers 1967–73, asst dir Edward Bates and Sons Ltd merchant bankers 1973–77, dir then md Turner Curzon Ltd 1977–86, dir and head of capital markets Den norske Bank plc 1986–90, non-exec dir and business conslt 1990–, former dir Quintain Estates and Devpts plc; former chm: Union Discount Ltd (also non-exec dir Union plc), Optoplast plc, Megamode Ltd, Manifest Voting Agency Ltd, Ketlon (UK) Ltd, Welpac plc, Enfield and Haringey HA, UCL Hosps NHS Fndn Tst; former memb Cncl and tstee NHS Confedn, joined E Coast Ambulance Service NHS Fndn Tst; current chm: Diabetes UK, Imperial Coll Health Partners, Anglia Ruskin Health Partnership; former chm: The Housing Corporation, Pharmaceutical Services Negotiating Ctee, Office for Public Mgmnt, N Thames region London & Quadrant Housing Tst and New Islington and Hackney Housing Assoc; former cnclIr London Borough of Islington (chm Planning Application Ctee 1973–74); lay memb Info Tbnl Lord Chllr's Dept 2004–12; current memb Broads Authy; *Clubs* Athenaeum, Alpine; *Style*— Sir Peter Dixon; ☎ 020 7226 2011, e-mail peterjbdixon@hotmail.com

DIXON, Prof Richard Newland; s of Robert Thomas Dixon (d 1985), of Borough Green, Kent, and Lilian, *née* Newland (d 1973); *b* 25 December 1930, Borough Green, Kent; *Educ* Judd Sch Tonbridge, KCL (BSc), St Catharine's Coll Cambridge (PhD, ScD); *m* 18 Sept 1954, Alison Mary, da of Gilbert Arnold Birks (d 1966), of Horsforth, Leeds; 1 s (Paul b 1959), 2 da (Joan b 1961, Sheila b 1962); *Career* scientific off UKAEA 1954–56, post doctoral fell Univ W Ontario 1956–57, post doctoral fell Nat Res Cncl of Canada 1957–59, ICI fell lectr in chem Univ of Sheffield 1959–69, Sorby research fell Royal Soc 1964–69; Univ of Bristol: prof of chemistry 1969–96, dean of sci 1979–82, pro-vice-chllr 1989–92, Alfred Capper Pass prof of chemistry 1990–96, prof emeritus 1996, sr research fell 1996–; Leverhulme emeritus fell 1996–98; visiting scholar Stanford Univ USA 1982–83; non-exec dir United Bristol Healthcare NHS Tst 1994–2003 (vice-chm 1995–2003), tstee Charitable Tsts for United Bristol Hosps 2003–11 (chm 2006–11); memb: Faraday Cncl RSC (vice-pres 1989–98), SERC Ctees; Hallam lectr Univ of Wales 1988, Liversidge lectr RSC 1993, Harkins lectr Univ of Chicago 1993; Corday-Morgan Medal Chem Soc 1968, Spectroscopy Medal RSC 1985, Rumford Medal Royal Soc 2004; CChem 1976, FRSC 1976, FRS 1986; *Books* Spectroscopy and Structure (1965), Theoretical Chemistry (Vol 1 1971, Vol 2 1973, Vol 3 1975); author of 225 papers in research jls; *Recreations* mountain walking, travel, theatre, concerts, photography; *Clubs* Royal Soc of London; *Style*— Prof Richard Dixon, FRS; ✉ 22 Westbury Lane, Bristol BS9 2PE (☎ 0117 968 1691); School of Chemistry, University of Bristol, Cantock's Close, Bristol BS8 1TS (☎ 0117 928 7661 fax 0117 925 1295, e-mail r.n.dixon@bris.ac.uk)

DIXON, Tom; OBE (2000); *b* 21 May 1959; *Educ* Holland Park Comp; *Career* designer; professional musician Funkopolitans 1980–82, nightclub promotion and event organisation 1981–84; inauguration of Creative Salvage 1984; launched: Space and Space Studio (manufacturing and retail venture) 1991, Eurolounge 1994; creative dir: Habitat 2001– (head of design 1998–2001), Art & Technology 2004–; launched Tom Dixon design shop 2001; Hon Dr UCE Birmingham 2004; *Publications* International Design Yearbook, One Hundred Chairs (1987), The Modern Chair (1988), Tom Dixon (1989), New British Designers (1990), The Modern Chair (1993), 100 Designs/100 Years (1999), Rethink (2000), Design Directory Great Britain (2001), The Eco-design Handbook (2002), 30–30 Vision (2003), The International Design Year Book (2003), 100 Future Products 2004 (2003), The Official Point of View Milan 03 (2003), Who's Who in Design Vol 2 (2004), The International Design Year Book (ed, 2004), Designers on Design (2004), Love Your Home (2004), The Lighthouse Book; featured in various catalogues and exhbn papers; *Style*— Tom Dixon, Esq, OBE; ✉ Tom Dixon, 28 All Saints Road, London W11 1HG (☎ 020 7792 5335, fax 020 7792 2156, e-mail info@tomdixon.net, website www.tomdixon.net)

DIXON-SMITH, Baron (Life Peer UK 1993), of Bocking in the County of Essex; Robert William (Bill) Dixon-Smith; DL (Essex 1986); 2 s of Dixon Smith (d 1995) of Braintree, Essex, and his 1 w, (Alice) Winifred, *née* Stratton (d 1976); *b* 30 September 1934; *Educ* Oundle, Writtle Agric Coll; *m* 13 Feb 1960, Georgina Janet, da of George Cook, of Halstead, Essex; 1 da (Hon Sarah Jane (*see* Christopher Henry St John Hoare) b 16 Dec 1960), 1 s (Hon Adam William George b 11 Jan 1963); *Career* Nat Serv 2 Lt King's Dragoon Gds 1955–57; farmer; memb Essex CC 1965–93 (chm 1986–89), memb Assoc of CCs 1983–93 (chm 1992–93), memb Local Govt Mgmnt Bd 1991–93, chm Anglia Poly Univ 1992–93 (Hon Dr 1994), memb Cncl Essex Univ 1991–94, govr Writtle Coll 1967–94 (chm of govrs 1973–85, fell 1993); memb: Select Ctee for European Communities, Sub-ctee 4 1994–96, Select Ctee for Science and Technology House of Lords 1994–98; oppn House of Lords spokesman on: environment, tport and the regions 1998–2001, home affrs 2001–02, environment 2003–08, communities and local govt 2008–09; Freeman City of London 1988, Liveryman Worshipful Co of Farmers 1991; *Recreations* shooting, fishing, golf; *Style*— The Rt Hon Lord Dixon-Smith, DL; ✉ Sun House, Hall Lane, Long Melford, Suffolk CO10 9HZ

DIXSON, Maurice Christopher Scott; s of H G (George) Dixson (d 1992), and E E (Lilla) Dixson, *née* McCartney (d 1999); *b* 5 November 1941; *Educ* Palmers GS , UC Swansea (BA), Carleton Univ Ottawa (MA), Pembroke Coll Oxford (DPhil); *m* Anne Beverley, da of late Wilfred Morris; *Career* mgmnt trainee and commercial exec Hawker Siddeley Aviation 1969–74; BAC (British Aerospace): dir Al Yamamah Defence Project and commercial dir Military Aircraft Div 1983–86, chief exec Royal Ordnance 1986–88, md Commercial Aircraft Co 1988–90; exec dir and md Smaller Companies Gp GEC 1990–93, chief exec Simon Gp plc 1993–2002, non-exec dir Swan Hill plc 1994–2003, exec chm Cranfield Aerospace Ltd 2003–, chm Southside Thermal Sciences (STS) Ltd 2004–; memb Econ Policy Ctee Engrg Employers Assoc 1994–2002; memb Cons Pty; FRAeS 1986, FInstPS 1989; *Recreations* shooting, fishing, soccer (played for Br Universities), watching rugby, fine arts; *Clubs* RAC; *Style*— Dr Maurice Dixson; ✉ Pound House, Middle Common, Kington Langley, Wiltshire SN15 5NW (☎ 01249 758171, fax 01249 758880)

DJALILI, Omid; s of Ahmad Djalili, and Parvaneh Samii Djalili; *b* 1965, London; *Educ* Holland Park Sch London, Univ of Ulster Coleraine; *Career* comedian and actor; Edinburgh Festival shows: Short Fat Kebab Shop Owner's Son 1995, Arab and the Jew 1996, Omid Djalili is Ethnic 1997, The Iranian Ceilidh 1999, Warm to My Winning Smile 2000, Behind Enemy Lines 2002 (Perrier Award nominee); Freedom City of Montreal 1986; *Television* Bloody Foreigners (Best Documentary One World Media Awards 2001), Small Potatoes, Whoopi (US), Casanova, HBO half hour stand-up special, The Omid Djalili Show (BBC 1) 2007; *Film* The Calcium Kid, Anita and Me, The Mummy, The World is Not Enough, Gladiator, Spy Game, Modigliani, Sky Captain and the World of Tomorrow, Casanova, Alien Autopsy, Over The Hedge (voice), Pirates of the Caribbean: At World's End, Deadlines, The Love Guru, Mr Nice, The Infidel, Sex and the City 2; *Theatre* Fagin in Oliver! 2009, What the Butler Saw (Vaudeville) 2012; *Awards* Time Out Comedy Award 2001, Best Stand-Up EMMA Awards 2002, nominee Best Comedy South Bank Awards 2002, nominee Canadian Gemini Award; *Recreations* tennis, football; *Style*— Omid Djalili, Esq; ✉ c/o Scott Marshall, 54 Poland Street, London W1V 7NR; c/o Bound & Gagged Comedy, 25 Melrose Avenue, Willesden Green, London NW2 4LH

DJANOGLY, Jonathan; MP; *Educ* Oxford Brookes Univ (BA), Guildford Law Sch, ICAEW (Corp Finance); *Career* slr 1990–98, ptnr SJ Berwin LLP 1998–2009; cncllr Regent's Park Westminster London BC 1994–2001; Parly candidate (Cons) Oxford E 1997, MP (Cons) Huntingdon 2001–, shadow min for home, constitutional and legal affrs 2004–05, shadow slr-gen 2005–10, shadow min for business, enterprise and regulatory reform 2005–10, Parly under-sec of state for justice 2010–12; memb Trade and Industry Select Ctee 2001–05; memb Law Soc 1991; chm Pembroke VCT plc 2012–; *Style*— Jonathan Djanogly, Esq, MP; ✉ House of Commons, London SW1A 0AA (☎ 020 7219 2367)

DJURKOVIC, Maria; *Career* production designer; *Television* incl Doctor Zhivago 2002; *Film* incl: The Young Poisoner's Handbook 1994, Sweet Angel Mine 1995, Wilde 1996, Sliding Doors 1997, Fanny & Elvis 1998, Billy Elliot 1999, The Grey Zone 2000, The Hours 2001, Sylvia 2002, Vanity Fair 2003, Man to Man 2004, Scoop 2005, Cassandra's Dream 2006, Mamma Mia 2007, The Special Relationship 2009, Tinker, Tailor, Soldier, Spy 2011, The Invisible Woman 2012; *Style*— Ms Maria Djurkovic; ✉ c/oIndependent Talent Group, 40 Whitfield Street, London W1T 2RH

DOBASH, Prof Rebecca Emerson; da of I M Emerson, and Helen, *née* Cooper; *b* 3 February 1943; *Educ* Arizona State Univ (BA, MS), Washington State Univ (PhD); *m* 5 June 1965, Russell P Dobash, s of Paul Dobash; *Career* social research Faculty of Law Univ of Manchester; memb: American Criminology Soc, Br Criminology Assoc, European Criminology Soc; awards for outstanding research and pubns Int Soc of Victimology and American Soc of Criminology, August Vollmer Award; fell: Rockefeller Centre Bellagio 1981 and 1992, Univ of Melbourne 1996; *Books* Violence Against Wives (1979), The Imprisonment of Women (1986), Women, Violence and Social Change (1992), Women Viewing Violence (1992), Gender and Crime (1995), The Simulated Client (1996), Research Evaluation and Programmes for Violent Men (1996), Rethinking Violence Against Women (1998), Changing Violent Men (2000); *Recreations* travel, food, gardening; *Style*— Prof Rebecca Emerson Dobash; ✉ School of Law (Criminology), University of Manchester, Oxford Road, Manchester M13 9PL (☎ 0161 275 4490, fax 0161 275 4922)

DOBBIE, Scott Jamieson; CBE (1998); s of Scott Dobbie (d 1943), and Isobel, *née* Jamieson (d 1969); *b* 24 July 1939; *Educ* Dollar Acad, Univ of Edinburgh (BSc); *m* 1962, Brenda; 2 da; *Career* with Unilever 1961–66, with ICI 1966–72; Wood Mackenzie & Co Stockbrokers: ptnr 1975–82, manging ptnr 1982–88; NatWest Securities: md 1988–93, chm 1993–98; chm: CRESTCo Ltd 1996–2001, Securities and Investment Inst 2000–09, Pre-Emption Gp 2000–10, Standard Life European Private Equity Tst 2001–13, The Edinburgh Investment Tst plc 2003–11 (dir 1998); vice-chm Bankers Tst Int 1998–99; dir: SFA 1993–2001, Murray VCT4 plc 2000–03, Premier Oil plc 2000–08, Scottish Fin Enterprise 2001–06; sr advsr Deutsche Bank AG 1999–; cmmr Jersey Fin Servs Cmmn 2000–08; assessor Irish Regulatory Authy 2007–12; memb: Regulatory Decisions Ctee FSA 2001–06; chm Standards Ctee Corp of London 2008–09, dir Qualifications and Curriculum Authy 2008–12; Liveryman Clockmakers; Co; Hon DSc City Univ 2009; Hon FCSI 1996; *Recreations* mechanical objects, buildings, books; *Style*— Scott J Dobbie, Esq, CBE; ✉ Deutsche Bank AG, Winchester House, 1 Great Winchester Street, London EC2M 2DB (e-mail scott.dobbie@db.com)

DOBBIN, Jim; MP; s of William Dobbin, and Catherine Dobbin; *b* 26 May 1941; *Educ* St Columba's RC HS Cowdenbeath, St Andrew's RC HS Kirkcaldy, Napier Coll Edinburgh; *m* 1964, Pat; 2 s (Barry, Patrick), 2 da (Mary, Kerry); *Career* microbiologist Royal Oldham Hosp 1973–94 (with NHS for 30 years), MP (Lab/Co-op) Heywood and Middleton 1997–; chair All-Pty Pro-Life Gp NI 1997–; memb: Standing Ctee C for Euro Legislation 1997–, European Scrutiny Ctee 1998–, Dep Speaker's Panel of Chairs 2010–, Consolidation Bills Ctee 2010–, Transport Select Ctee 2011–; rep Cncl of Europe 2010–; Rochdale MBC: cncllr 1983–97, chm Housing 1986, chm Neighbourhood Servs 1989, dep ldr 1990–92, ldr 1996–97; contested Bury N 1992; memb AMICUS; *Recreations* walking, gardening, theatre, cinema, football (Glasgow Celtic FC); *Style*— Jim Dobbin, MP; ✉ House of Commons, London SW1A 0AA (☎ 020 7219 3000)

DOBBS, Hon Dame Linda Penelope; DBE (2004); *b* 3 January 1951; *Educ* Moreton Hall, Univ of Surrey (BSc), LSE (LLM, PhD); *Career* called to the Bar Gray's Inn 1981 (bencher 2002); QC 1998, dep judge of the High Court 2003–04, judge of the High Court of Justice (Queen's Bench Div) 2004–13, ret; ind assessor for miscarriages of justice compensation; vice-pres NACRO, pres ILFA; memb: Cwlth Magistrates and Judges Assoc, Advsy Cncl Protimos, Advsy Cncl IProBono, Br South Africa Lawyers Assoc; tstee Oxford Sch of Drama; patron: African Prisons Project, Masiphumelele Tst, Lottie Betts-Priddy Educn Tst, Pinotage Youth Devpt Acad, Make It Happen In Sierra Leone BLD Fndn, LexLead Gp, Int Law Book Facility; memb Ct of Govrs LSE 2006–15; hon doctorate: Sheffield Hallam Univ 2006, City Univ 2008, Univ of Law 2009, Univ of Surrey 2010, BPP UC 2010; *Publications* incl: Road Traffic Law and Practice, Archbold (contrib ed), Fraud: Law, Practice and Procedure (conslt ed); *Recreations* reading, music, theatre, travel, food and wine; *Style—* The Hon Dame Linda Dobbs, DBE

DOBBS, Baron (Life Peer UK 2010), of Wylye in the County of Wiltshire; Dr Michael John Dobbs; s of Eric William Dobbs (d 1990), and Eileen Dobbs (d 1974); *b* Nov 1948; *Educ* Hertford GS, ChCh Oxford (MA), Fletcher Sch of Law and Diplomacy USA (PhD, MALD); *Career* novelist, playwright, broadcaster; advsr to Margaret Thatcher, MP as ldr of the Oppn 1977–79, govt special advsr 1981–87, chief of staff Cons Pty 1986–87, jt dep chm Cons Pty 1994–95; dep chm Saatchi & Saatchi 1983–91; presenter Despatch Box (BBC2) 1999–2001, exec prodr House of Cards (Netflix) 2012–; columnist Mail on Sunday 2000–02; judge Whitbread Book Awards 2003; Lifetime Achievement Award for Political Literature 2014, PT Barnum Award for Excellence in Literature 2014, Lifetime Achievement Award Tufts Univ 2014, Huw Weldon Meml Lecture 2015; *Books* Salt on the Dragon's Tail (PhD thesis, 1975), House of Cards (1989, televised 1990, 2013 in the US), To Play the King (1992, televised 1993), The Final Cut (1995), Goodfellowe MP (1997), The Buddha of Brewer Street (1998), Whispers of Betrayal (2000), Winston's War (2002), Never Surrender (2003), Churchill's Hour (2004), Churchill's Triumph (2005), First Lady (2006), The Lords' Day (2007), Edge of Madness (2008), The Reluctant Hero (2010), Old Enemies (2011), A Sentimental Traitor (2012), A Ghost at the Door (2013); *Plays* The Turning Point (Sky Arts, 2009), A Family Affair (BBC Radio 4, 2009); *Recreations* recreational slimmer, genealogy; *Style—* The Lord Dobbs; ✉ website www.michaeldobbs.com, Twitter @dobbs_michael

DOBBY, John Michael; s of Herbert Charles Dobby (d 1982), of Dover, and Gwendoline Dobby; *b* 21 November 1941; *Educ* Nautical Sch Mercury, City of London Coll; *m* 23 July 1966, Janet Constance, da of Albert Victor Williams; 3 s (Timothy James b 2 Jan 1968, Simon John b 30 March 1970, Martin Jason b 5 June 1972); *Career* apprentice timber importer 1959; Meyer International plc: md subsid Gabriel Wade (Southern) Ltd 1976–80 (dir 1972–80), gen mangr Meyer Merchants 1980–82, jt md Jewson Ltd 1983 (sometime chm), dir MI Nederland 1984–97, dir Van Hoorebeke et Fils 1985–99, chm Pont Meyer NV 1993–97 (dir 1986–97), also former chm Meyer Forest Products Ltd, chief exec Meyer International plc 1993–97 (dir 1983–97); supervisory dir: Jongeneel Holding BV 2000–06, NV Deli Maatschappij 2006–12; FIWSc; *Recreations* swimming, gardening, sailing; *Style—* John Dobby, Esq; ✉ Hill Rise, High Street, Meonstoke, Hampshire SO32 3NH (☎ 01489 878657, e-mail j.dobby@virgin.net)

DOBKIN, His Hon Judge Ian James; s of Morris Dobkin (d 1979), and Rhoda, *née* Saipe (d 2006); *b* 8 June 1948; *Educ* Leeds GS, The Queen's Coll Oxford (Hastings exhibitioner, MA); *m* Oct 1980, Andrea Ruth, da of Jack Dante, and Rose Dante; 2 s (Matthew Jacob b 6 July 1983, Jonathan Edward b 4 Aug 1985); *Career* called to the Bar Gray's Inn 1971; in practice NE Circuit 1971–95, recorder of the Crown Court 1990–95 (asst recorder 1986–90), circuit judge (NE Circuit) 1995–; judicial memb W Yorks Probation Bd 2001–08; liaison judge Leeds Area Magistrates Courts 2002–05; Parly candidate (Cons) Penistone 1978 and 1979; United Hebrew Congregation Leeds: vice-pres 1981–84 and 1992–96, pres 1984–88, 1996–99 and 2005–06, hon life vice-pres 2003; vice-chm Leeds Hillel Fndn, memb Advsy Ctee Leeds Centre for Criminal Justice Studies Univ of Leeds 1987–; *Recreations* crosswords, music, theatre, reading; *Clubs* Moor Allerton Golf (Leeds), Yorks CCC; *Style—* His Hon Judge Dobkin; ✉ Leeds Crown Court, Oxford Row, Leeds LS1 3BG

DOBLE, Michael John; s of Brian Sinclair Doble (d 1979), and Margaret Ingham, *née* Eastwood; *b* 31 October 1951; *Educ* St George's Sch Harpenden, Coll of Law; *m* 8 Sept 1984, Nandika Shankari, da of Dr Victor Thevathasan; 2 s (George Michael b 28 Aug 1985, Edward Oliver b 8 Nov 1987), 2 da (Harriett Victoria Rose b 27 April 1993, Anna Elizabeth b 26 Nov 1994); *Career* slr; articled clerk Denton Hall & Burgin, ptnr Denton Hall 1981, ptnr Denton Wilde Sapte 2000–04 (head Energy and Infrastructure Dept 2000–04), dir (energy) Denton Wilde Sapte 2004–; *Recreations* golf, cricket, country sports; *Clubs* MCC, Tanglin, Dulwich and Sydenham Golf, Sherborne Golf; *Style—* Michael Doble, Esq; ✉ Denton Wilde Sapte, One Fleet Place, London EC4M 7WS (☎ 020 7246 7000, fax 020 7246 7777)

DOBRES, Charlie; *m* Karen; 1 da (Millicent-Muriel), 1 s (Alfie); *Career* account mangr Lowe Howard-Spink 1995, fndr Lowe Digital 1996, co-fndr (with Andrew Walmsley, *qv*) i-level 1998 (ceo 1998–2007, non-exec advsr 2007–10); fndr gen sec Interactive Advtg Bureau 1998, fndr memb Digital Mktg Gp; *Style—* Charlie Dobres, Esq

DOBSON, Andrew Charles; s of Raymond Dobson, FRICS, of Rowlands Gill, Tyne & Wear, and Dr Mary Dobson, *née* Meikle; *b* 20 February 1956; *Educ* Oundle, St Catharine's Coll Cambridge (MA), Coll of Law Guildford; *m* 10 Aug 1985, Janet Margaret, da of Eric Shiells (decd); 1 s (Patrick Archie Shiells b 18 Jan 1988), 2 da (Alexandra Emma b 30 Dec 1989, Laura Poppy b 19 Nov 1991); *Career* litigation slr Macfarlanes 1980–86 (joined 1978), litigation ptnr Knapp Fishers 1986–87; Wragge Lawrence Graham & Co (formerly Lawrence Graham): ptnr 1987–, head Commercial Litigation 1987–92, head Dispute Resolution 1995–2008, head Singapore Office 2014–; memb: Law Soc 1980, Int Bar Assoc 1990; *Style—* Andrew Dobson, Esq; ✉ Wragge Lawrence Graham & Co, 133 Cecil Street, #17.02 Keck Seng Tower Singapore 069535 (☎ 0065 6521 3556, fax 0065 6521 3566)

DOBSON, Carolan; da of Thomas Michael Geekie, of Glasgow, and June, *née* Lusk; *b* 4 December 1954, Glasgow; *Educ* Univ of St Andrews (BSc); *m* 19 Dec 1981, James Kenneth Dobson; 2 da (Charlotte Isobel b 5 June 1986, Anna Elizabeth 5 Dec 1989); *Career* dir: Murray Johnstone Ltd 1987–93, Abbey Asset Mangrs Ltd 1997–2003, Shires Smaller Companies plc 2004–; non-exec dir: British Waterways plc 1998–2001, Securities and Investment Inst 1997–2003, Sport Scotland and Scottish Sports Cncl Tst Cos; chm: JP Morgan European Smaller Cos plc, Aberdeen Smaller Cos High Incomes plc; ind investment advsr to pension funds of: Environment Agency 2004–, London Borough of Enfield, Rhondda Cynon Taf BC; memb Competition Cmmn 2005–; chm Lomond Sch 2002–, tstee Nest; MSI 1993; *Recreations* skiing, tennis; *Style—* Mrs Carolan Dobson; ✉ Competition Commission, Victoria House, Southampton Row, London WC1B 4AD

DOBSON, Prof Christopher Martin; s of Arthur Dobson (d 1973), and Mabel, *née* Pollard; *b* 8 October 1949; *Educ* Abingdon Sch, Keble Coll Oxford (scholar, BSc, MA, Gibbs award), Merton Coll Oxford (sr scholar, DPhil), Univ of Cambridge (ScD); *m* 1977, Dr Mary Janet Dobson, da of Dr Derek Justin Schove; 2 s (Richard James b 16 Aug 1982, William Thomas b 11 March 1986); *Career* research fell Univ of Oxford 1975–77, asst prof of chemistry Harvard Univ and visiting scientist MIT 1977–80; Univ of Oxford: lectr BNC 1980–2001, fell LMH 1980–2001, univ lectr in chemistry 1980–95, reader 1995–96, prof (Aldrichian praelector) of chemistry 1996–2001, dir Oxford Centre for Molecular Sciences 1998–2001 (dep dir 1989–98); John Humphrey Plummer prof of chemical and structural biology Univ of Cambridge 2001–; St John's Coll Cambridge: fell 2001–, master 2007–; pres Protein Soc 1999–2001 (memb 1995–); nat lectr Biophysical Soc 1998; named lectureships incl: Sackler Distinguished Lecture Univ of Cambridge 2002, Bakerian Lecture Royal Soc 2003, Wills Lecture Univ of London 2003, Bayer Distinguished Lecture Univ of Washington 2003, Anfinsen Meml Lecture Johns Hopkins Univ 2003, Joseph Black Lecture Univ of Glasgow 2003, Centenary Lecture Andersonian Chemical Soc Univ of Strathclyde 2004, EMBO Lecture Biochemical Soc 2004, Presidential Lecture Scripps Research Inst La Jolla 2005, Burroughs Wellcome Lectures Univ of E Carolina 2005, Fiftieth Anniversary Lecture Int Union of Biochemistry and Molecular Biology 2005, Sir John Kendrew Lecture Weizmann Inst 2005, William H Stein Meml Lecture Rockefeller Univ 2006, John D Ferry Lectures Univ of Wisconsin 2006, Linus Pauling Lecture and Medal Stanford Univ 2006, Distinguished Lecture Rutgers Univ 2007, Class of 1942 James B Sumner Lecture Cornell Univ 2008, Ada Doisy Meml Lecture Univ of Illinois 2008, Weaver Meml Lecture Univ of Calif Davis 2008, Linus Pauling Lecture Calif Inst of Technol 2008, Roy E Moon Distinguished Lectures Angelo State Univ 2009, Hans Neurath Lecture Univ of Washington 2009, Brian Bent Meml Lecture Columbia Univ 2010, Alumni Lecture Univ of Queensland 2010, Linacre Lecture St John's Coll Cambridge 2011, TY Shen Lectures Massachusetts Inst of Technol 2012, Heron-Allen Lecture Lady Margaret Hall Oxford 2012, GN Ramachandran Meml Lecture Indian Biophysical Soc 2012, Evans Lectures Ohio State Univ 2012, Antonini Meml Lecture Univ of Rome 2013, Frontiers in Biological Sciences Annual Lecture Case Western Reserve Univ 2014, Searle Distinguished Lecture Northwestern Univ 2014, Philippe Wiener Lecture Fondation Wiener Anspach Brussels 2014; Corday Morgan Medal and Prize Royal Soc of Chemistry 1983, Brunauer Award American Ceramic Soc 1996, Dewey and Kelly Award Univ of Nebraska 1997, Interdisciplinary Award Royal Soc of Chemistry 1999, Bijovet Medal Univ of Utrecht 2002, Silver Medal Italian Soc of Biochemistry 2002, Stein and Moore Award Protein Soc 2003, Davy Medal Royal Soc 2005, Hans Neurath Award Protein Soc 2006, Royal Medal Royal Soc 2009, Khorana Award RSC 2010, Heineken Prize for Biophysics and Biochemistry Royal Netherlands Acad 2014, Feltrinelli Int Prize for Medicine Accademia Nazionale dei Lincei 2014; int research scholar Howard Hughes Med Inst USA 1992, Leverhulme Tst sr research fell Royal Soc 1993; fell Eton Coll 2001, Presidential visiting prof Univ of Calif San Francisco 2001–02, Sammet guest prof Johann Wolfgang Goethe Univ Frankfurt 2007, hon fell Linacre Coll Oxford 2008, hon fell Lady Margaret Hall Oxford 2008, hon fell Merton Coll Oxford 2009, hon fell Keble Coll Oxford 2009, hon fell TCD 2013, visiting prof Vallee Fndn 2013, hon fell Darwin Coll Univ of Cambridge 2014; Dr (hc) Univ of Leuven 2001, Hon MD Umea Univ 2005, Hon MD Univ of Florence 2006, Dr (hc) Univ of Liège 2007, Hon DSc KCL 2012; memb: Biochemical Soc 1988, Biophysical Soc 1998, EMBO 1999; hon memb National Magnetic Resonance Soc India 2004, hon foreign memb American Acad of Arts and Sciences 2007, fell Int Soc of Magnetic Resonance 2008, hon fell Chemical Cncl of India 2010, memb Academia Europaea 2011, hon fell Indian Biophysical Soc 2012, foreign assoc US Nat Acad of Sciences 2013; CChem, FRSC 1996 (MRSC 1973), FRS 1996, FMedSci 2005; *Publications* author of over 650 papers in learned jls; *Recreations* family, friends, travel; *Clubs* Oxford and Cambridge; *Style—* Prof Christopher Dobson, FRS; ✉ Department of Chemistry, University of Cambridge, Lensfield Road, Cambridge CB2 1EW (☎ 01223 763070, fax 01223 763418, e-mail cmd44@cam.ac.uk); The Master's Lodge, St John's College, Cambridge CB2 1TP

DOBSON, Rt Hon Frank Gordon; PC (1997); s of James William Dobson, and Irene Shortland, *née* Laley; *b* 15 March 1940; *Educ* Archbishop Holgate's GS York, LSE; *m* 1967, Janet Mary, da of Henry Alker, and Edith Alker; 3 c; *Career* former administrator CEGB and Electricity Cncl; asst sec Cmmn for Local Admin 1975–79; MP (Lab, RMT sponsored): Holborn and St Pancras South 1979–83, Holborn and St Pancras 1983–2015; oppn front bench spokesman on: educn 1981–83, health 1983–87, energy 1989–92; shadow leader of the House and Lab Pty campaign co-ordinator 1987–89; chief oppn spokesman on: employment 1992–93, transport and London 1993–94, environment and London 1994–97; sec of state for health 1997–99; mayoral candidate (Lab) London 2000; *Style—* The Rt Hon Frank Dobson; ✉ 22 Great Russell Mansions, Great Russell Street, London WC1B 3BE; House of Commons, London SW1A 0AA

DOBSON, Jo-Anne; MLA; *Career* MLA (UUP) Upper Bann 2011–; memb NI Kidney Patients Assoc (NIKPA), organ donation campaigner and fundraiser; *Style—* Mrs Jo-Anne Dobson, MLA; ✉ Northern Ireland Assembly, Parliament Buildings, Belfast BT4 3XX

DOBSON, Michael William Romsey; s of Sir Denis Dobson, KCB, OBE, QC (d 1995), of London, and Lady Mary Elizabeth, *née* Allen; *b* 13 May 1952; *Educ* Eton, Trinity Coll Cambridge (MA); *m* 1998, Frances Mary Josephine, *née* de Salis; 2 da (Olivia Carolyn Romsey, Hannah Rainbow Romsey); *Career* Morgan Grenfell Group plc: joined 1973, chief exec Morgan Grenfell Asset Mgmnt 1987–88, gp chief exec Morgan Grenfell Gp plc 1989–93, chief exec Deutsche Morgan Grenfell 1993–96; memb Bd of MDs Deutsche Bank AG 1996–2000 (responsible for: investment banking 1996–98, asset mgmnt 1998–2000), chief exec Schroders plc 2001–; *Style—* Michael Dobson, Esq

DOBSON, Dr Nicholas; s of Martin Dobson (d 2004), of Ellesmere Park, Manchester, and Mary Frances, *née* Ormonde; *b* Southport; *Educ* De La Salle Coll Pendleton, Univ of Leeds (BA, CertEd), Univ of Manchester (Dip), Coll of Law (Dip), Univ of Sheffield (PhD); *m* 16 April 1977, Jennifer Ruth Elizabeth, *née* Mercer; 1 da (Victoria Jane b 15 April 1986), 2 s (Matthew James b 20 Aug 1988, Benjamin Joseph b 10 Oct 1992); *Career* admitted slr 1984; early career as teacher (incl at St Bede's Coll Manchester) and social worker, articled clerk Leak, Almond and Parkinson, lawyer Bolton MBC, Tameside MBC, Bradford MBC then Calderdale MBC, asst head of legal servs Leicester City Cncl, chief slr Doncaster Cncl, ptnr and head of local govt law then sr conslt Pinsent Masons (formerly Pinsent Curtis) 1999–2009, freelance conslt 2009–10, sr conslt Pannone LLP 2010–13, conslt Freeths LLP 2013–; a memb Exec Bd and communications offr Assoc of Cncl Secretaries 2009–13 and Lawyers in Local Govt 2013–16, memb Editorial Advsy Bd Law Soc Gazette 2010–13; memb Law Soc; *Publications* TUPE, Contracting Out and Best Value (1998), Best Value, Law and Management (2000); regular contrib to Law Gazette and New Law Journal; *Recreations* walking, outdoor swimming, reading, writing, music (eclectic), opera, Friend of Opera North, art, digital photography, playing blues guitar and for church music group; *Style—* Dr Nicholas Dobson; ✉ e-mail nicholasdobson@btinternet.com

DOBSON, Nigel Hewitt; s of George Hewitt Dobson (d 1984), of Beckenham, Kent, and Ethel Grace, *née* Boxshall (d 2004); *b* 13 August 1949; *Educ* St Dunstan's Coll; *m* 19 Aug 2007, Penelope Johan, *née* Richardson; *Career* Whinney Murray & Co (now Ernst & Young LLP) 1968–2001: Ernst & Ernst St Louis Missouri 1974–75, seconded Corporate Fin Dept Midland Bank 1978–80, ptnr 1981–2001; FCA (ACA 1972), MCSI 1993; *Recreations* sailing, gardening, reading, travel; *Style—* Nigel Dobson, Esq; ✉ Red Lodge, The Parade, Minnis Bay, Birchington, Kent CT7 9LX; Port St Charles, St Peter, Barbados, West Indies

DOBSON, Prof Peter James; OBE (2013); s of Cyril James Dobson (d 1991), and Mary, *née* Bright (d 2011); *b* 24 October 1942; *Educ* Newquay GS, Univ of Southampton (BSc, PhD); *m* 6 Nov 1965, Catherine, *née* Roberts; 2 da (Laura b 22 Sept 1969, Emma b 25 Jan 1973); *Career* sr lectr in physics Imperial Coll London 1980–84 (lectr 1968–80), sr princ scientist Philips Research Labs 1984–88; Univ of Oxford: lectr Dept of Engrg Science 1988–96, prof of engrg science 1996–2002, academic dir Begbroke Science Park 2002–13, princ fell Warwick Manufacturing Gp Univ of Warwick 2013–; fell The Queen's Coll Oxford 1988;

holder of over 30 patents, author of over 185 papers in refereed jls; MA (by incorporation) Univ of Oxford 1988; memb American Chemical Soc 2001; FInstP 2003 (MInstP 1966), FRSC; *Recreations* gardening, jazz, cooking; *Style*— Prof Peter Dobson, OBE; ✉ 92 Lonsdale Road, Oxford OX2 7ER (☎ 01865 515436, e-mail peter.dobson@queens.ox.ac.uk)

DOBSON, Ron; CBE (2011), QFSM; *Career* London Fire Brigade: joined 1979, asst divisional offr 1988–92, divisional offr 1992–96, divisional cdr 1996–2000, asst cmmr 2000–07, chief fire offr 2007– (concurrently cmmr for fire and emergency planning London Fire and Emergency Planning Authy); FIFireE; *Clubs* London Golf; *Style*— Ron Dobson, Esq, CBE, QFSM, FIFireE; ✉ London Fire Brigade, 169 Union Street, Southwark, London SE1 0LL (☎ 020 8555 1200, website www.london-fire.gov.uk)

DOBSON, Susan Angela (Sue); da of Arthur George Henshaw (d 1994), and Nellie Henshaw (d 1978); *Educ* Holy Family Convent, Assumption Convent Ramsgate, Ursuline Convent Westgate-on-Sea, NE London Poly (BA, Dip HE); *m* 1966 (m dis 1974), Michael Dobson; *Career* fashion, cookery and beauty ed Femina 1965–69, contributing ed Fair Lady 1969–71; ed: SA Inst of Race Rels 1972, Wedding Day and First Home 1978–81, Successful Slimming 1981, Woman & Home 1982–94; ed-in-chief Choice 1994–2002, freelance travel writer and ed 2002–; memb: Br Guild of Travel Writers, www.travelwriters.co.uk, Bd Plan International UK 1993–2004; FRGS; *Books* The Wedding Day Book (1981, 2 edn 1989), Travellers Cape Verde (2008, 2 edn 2010), Travellers Namibia (2008, 2 edn 2010); revised: CityPack Dublin (2011), Spiral Egypt (2011), CityPack London (2012), CityPack Budapest (2015), TwinPack Malta & Gozo (2015), London 25 Best (2015), Sydney 25 Best (2015), Guide to Norfolk & Suffolk (2016); *Recreations* travel, books, photography, theatre, music, exploring Britain; *Style*— Ms Sue Dobson; ✉ e-mail dobsonsue@btinternet.com

DOCHERTY, Dr David; s of David Docherty (d 1972); *b* 10 December 1956; *Educ* St Mungo's Acad Glasgow, Univ of Strathclyde (BA), LSE (PhD, MSc); *m* 1992, Kate, da of Rt Hon Sir Murray Stuart-Smith, *qv*; 2 da (Flora b 17 Oct 1993, Polly b 9 July 1997); *Career* fell Broadcasting Research Unit 1984–89, research dir Broadcasting Standards Cncl 1989–91; BBC 1990–2000 (roles incl: dir of strategy, dep dir of TV, dir of new services, BBC Bd of Mgmnt); md broadband content Telewest Communications, chief exec Yoo Media 2003–05, ceo CSC Media 2006–09, chief exec Nat Centre for Univs and Business 2009–; chm Digital Television Gp 2009–; chm Bd of Govrs: Univ of Luton 2001–06, Univ of Bedfordshire 2006–; *Books* The Last Picture Show (1989), Keeping Faith? Channel 4 and its Audience (1989), Running the Show: 21 Years of London Weekend Television (1990), Violence in Television Fiction (1991), The Spirit Death (2000), The Killing Jar (2002), The Fifth Season (2002), Growing Value: Business-University Collaboration for the 21st Century (2014); *Recreations* writing; *Style*— Dr David Docherty; ✉ Serge Hill, Abbots Langley, Hertfordshire WD5 0RY

DOCHERTY, Paul; s of Joseph Docherty (d 1997), and Elizabeth Eileen, *née* Waters (d 2012); *b* 17 September 1951, Fayid, Egypt; *Educ* Queen Victoria Sch Dunblane, Univ of Strathclyde (BA, MLitt); *Children* 4 s (Thomas b 13 April 1989, Edward b 6 Dec 1992, Harry b 23 Sept 1994, Benjamin b 20 Dec 2008); *Career* lectr in English Univ of Moscow 1983–84; British Cncl: posted London and Helsinki 1985–93, dep dir Moscow 1993–96 (concurrently cultural attaché British Embassy Moscow), sec 1996–2000, dir Czech Repub 2000–03 (concurrently cultural cnsllr British Embassy), dir Italy 2003–09 (concurrently cultural cnsllr British Embassy), dir Scotland 2009–11, dir UK 2012, dir France 2013; FRSA 2008; *Recreations* playing the guitar (blues), music (especially opera), film, books; *Style*— Paul Docherty, Esq; ✉ c/o British Council, 10 Spring Gardens, London SW1A 2BN

DOCKERY, Michelle; *b* 15 December 1981, Essex; *Educ* GSM; *Career* actress; *Theatre* incl: His Dark Marterials (RNT) 2004, Pillars of the Community (RNT) 2006, Eliza Doolittle in Pygmalion (Theatre Royal Bath, nat tour, Old Vic) 2008 (second prize Ian Charleson Awards), Burnt By the Sun (RNT) 2009, Hamlet (Crucible); *Television* incl: Hogfather 2006, Poppy Shakespeare 2008, Red Riding: 1974 2009, Red Riding: 1983 2009, Waking the Dead 2009, Cranford 2009, The Turn of the Screw 2009, Downton Abbey 2010–, Good Behaviour 2016; *Film* Hanna 2011, Anna Karenina 2012, Non-stop 2014, Self/less 2015; *Style*— Ms Michelle Dockery; ✉ c/o Hamilton Hodell, 20 Golden Square, London W1F 9JL

DOD, Bernard Geoffrey; s of Arthur Edwin Ashton Dod, and Hilda Edith, *née* Crammond; *Educ* Collyers Sch Horsham, Downing Coll Cambridge, Lincoln Coll Oxford (BLitt); *Career* copy-ed OUP 1969–76, ed Elsevier Int Projects 1976–79, sr ed Phaidon Press 1997–2004; cncllr Charlbury Town Cncl; *Books* Aristoteles Latinus: Analytica Posteriora (ed with L Minio-Paluello, 1968), Aristoteles Latinus: De Sophisticis Elenchis (1975), The Cambridge History of Later Medieval Philosophy (contrib chapter, 1982); *Recreations* walking, gardening, reading, music; *Style*— Bernard Dod, Esq

DOD MANTLE, Anthony; s of Charles Ian Mantle, and Dorothy Ruth Mantle; *b* 1955, Oxon; *Educ* BA, BSc, Royal Danish Filmschool; *m* Susanne; 1 s (Clemens); *Career* cinematographer; memb: Dansk Filmfotograf Forbund, BSC, European and American Acad; hon dr Univ of the Arts London; *Film* incl: Festen/Celebration 1998, Julien Donkey-Boy 1999, 28 Days Later 2002, It's All About Love 2003, Dogville 2003, Millions 2004, Dear Wendy 2005, Manderlay 2005, The Last King of Scotland 2006, Slumdog Millionaire 2008, Antichrist 2009, 127 Hours 2010, The Eagle of the Ninth 2011, Dredd 3D 2012, Trance 2013, Rush 2013, In the Heart of the Sea 2015, Our Kind of Traitor 2015, Snowden 2015; *Television* Wallander; *Awards* incl European Cinematographer of the Year 2005 (for 28 Days Later and Dogville); for Slumdog Millionaire: Best Cinematography NY Film Critics Circle Award 2008, Golden Frog Camerimage 2008, European Cinematographer of the Year 2008, Best Cinematography Acad Award 2009, Best Cinematography BAFTA 2009, ASC Cinematography Award 2009; Cinematography BAFTA 2009 (for Wallander), Lumiere Award Royal Photographic Soc 2011; *Style*— Anthony Dod Mantle, Esq; ✉ website www.dodmantle.com; c/o Vanessa Jones, Independent Talent Group Ltd, 40 Whitfield Street, London W1T 2RH

DODD, Barry John; CBE (2014, OBE 2006); *b* Manchester; *Educ* BSc; *Career* chm GSM Gp; chm and pro-chllr Univ of Hull 2013–, chm Hull York Medical Sch, chm York and N Yorks Local Enterprise Partnership, memb UK Automotive Cncl; HM Lord-Lt N Yorkshire 2014; *Recreations* classic vehicle collector; *Clubs* Merchant Adventurers of York; *Style*— Barry Dodd, Esq, CBE; ✉ HM Lord-Lieutenant of North Yorkshire, GSM Group Ltd, Sandbeck Way, Sandbeck Industrial Estate, Wetherby LS22 7DN

DODD, His Hon Judge John Stanislaus; QC (2006); *Career* called to the Bar 1979; asst recorder then recorder 2000, circuit judge South Eastern Circuit 2012–; *Style*— His Hon Judge Dodd, QC; ✉ Harrow Crown Court, Hailsham Drive, off Headstone Drive, Harrow, London HA1 4TU

DODDS, John Allan; s of John Dodds (d 1966), and Violet, *née* Allen (d 1989); *b* 24 October 1942, Redcar, N Yorks; *Educ* St Mary's Coll Middlesbrough, Loughborough Univ (BTech, PhD); *m* 16 Sept 1965, Kate, *née* Moscrop; 2 da (Ellen b 1966, Jennifer b 1973), 1 s (John Michael b 1967 d 1989); *Career* contract researcher Nancy France 1968–72, Centre Nationale de la Recherche Scientifique (CNRS) researcher Laboratoire des Sciences du Genie Chimique (LSGC) Nancy 1972–96, prof Ecole des Mines Albi France 1996–2008; dir: Centre Poudres et Procedes 1996–2004, UMR CNRS Albi 2005–08; conslt Chemical Engrg Particle Technol; visiting prof Univ of NSW; author of 160 pubns in scientific jls and 200 presentations at symposia; pres Science en Tarn; town cncllr Graulhet France; Sr Moulton Medal IChemE 2003, Palmes Academiques 2009; CEng 1978, FIChemE 2002, FREng 2005; *Books* The Physics of Granular Media (jtly, 1991); *Recreations* history, music; *Style*— John Dodds; ✉ 43 Rue Gambetta, 81300 Graulhet, France

DODDS, Rt Hon Nigel Alexander; OBE (1997), PC (2010), MP; s of Joseph Alexander Dodds, of Enniskillen, Co Fermanagh, and Doreen Elizabeth, *née* McMahon; *b* 20 August 1958; *Educ* Portora Royal Sch, St John's Coll Cambridge (univ scholarship, McMahan studentship, BA, Winfield prize for law), Inst of Professional Legal Studies Belfast; *m* 17 Aug 1985, Diana Jean Dodds, MEP, da of James Harris, of Loughbrickland, Banbridge, Co Down; 2 s ((Nigel Andrew) Mark b 5 Aug 1986, Andrew James Joseph b 5 Jan 1990), 1 da (Robyn Elizabeth Helen b 17 Aug 1996); *Career* called to the Bar NI 1981; elected memb Belfast City Cncl 1985–, Lord Mayor of Belfast 1988–89 and 1991–92; MLA (DUP) Belfast N 1998–2010, MP (DUP) Belfast N 2001–; NI Assembly: min for social devpt 1999–2000 and 2001–02, min for enterprise, trade and investment 2007–08, min for finance 2008–09; dep ldr DUP 2008–; delg NI Forum 1996–98; vice-pres Assoc of Local Authorities of NI 1988–89; memb Senate Queen's Univ Belfast 1988–93; *Style*— The Rt Hon Nigel Dodds, OBE, MP; ✉ House of Commons, London SW1A 0AA; Constituency Office, 39 Shore Road, Belfast BT15 3PG (☎ 028 9077 4774, e-mail ndodds@dup-belfast.co.uk, website www.dup.org.uk)

DODDS, (John) Nigel William; *b* 18 June 1949; *Educ* Barnard Castle Sch, Univ of Nottingham (LLB), Coll of Law; *Career* admitted slr 1973; memb Cncl Law Soc 1994–, chm Law Soc Tstees Ltd (Law Soc charity) 2000–, reviewer of complaints Market Research Soc 2003–; memb Law Soc 1973; *Style*— Nigel Dodds, Esq; ☎ 07810 881735

DODDS-SMITH, Ian Charles; *b* 1951; *Educ* Solihull Sch, Downing Coll Cambridge (MA); *Career* admitted slr 1976; specialises in product liability and the law relating to pharmaceuticals and healthcare; Cameron McKenna (formerly McKenna & Co): asst slr 1976–83, seconded to Schering Health Care Ltd 1978–83, ptnr 1984–2002; ptnr Arnold & Porter LLP 2002– (currently co-head of food, drug and medical devices gp and head of European product liability gp); memb: Legal Ctee Assoc of the Br Pharmaceutical Industry, various Royal Coll and MRC working parties on research and liability issues, Defence Research Inst; FRSM, hon fell Orgn of Professionals in Regulatory Affrs; *Publications* contrib to pubns incl: Medical Negligence, Early Phase Human Drug Evaluation in Man, Pharmaceutical Medicine; *Style*— Ian Dodds-Smith, Esq; ✉ Arnold & Porter (UK) LLP, Tower 42, 25 Old Broad Street, London EC2N 1HQ (☎ 020 7786 6216, fax 020 7786 6299, e-mail ian.dodds-smith@aporter.com)

DODGSHON, Prof Robert Andrew; s of Robert Dodgshon (d 1964), and Dorothy, *née* Owens; *b* 8 December 1941, Bangor, Wales; *Educ* Univ of Liverpool (BA, PhD); *m* 1969, Katherine, *née* Simmonds; 2 da (Clare b 1971, Lucy b 1973); *Career* Univ of Wales Aberystwyth: lectr 1970, sr lectr 1980, reader 1984, prof 1988–2007, dir Inst of Geography and Earth Sciences 1998–2003, Gregynog prof 2000–07, emeritus prof 2007–; pres Soc for Landscape Studies 1998–2008; memb Cncl: Countryside Cncl for Wales 1999–2006, Nat Tst 2001–08, Joint Nature Conservation Ctee (JNCC) 2005–06; Murchison Award RGS 1996, Scottish Geographical Medal RSGS 2003; FBA 2002, founding FLSW 2010; *Books* Land and Society in Early Scotland (1981), The European Past (1987), From Chiefs to Landlords (1998), Society in Time and Space (1998), No Stone Unturned: A History of Farming, Landscape and Environment in the Scottish Highlands and Islands (2015); *Recreations* music, walking, landscape, travel; *Style*— Prof Robert Dodgshon; ✉ 4 Stratton Audley Manor, Mill Road, Stratton Audley, Oxfordshire OX27 9AF (☎ 01869 278258, e-mail rad@aber.ac.uk)

DODGSON, Clare; da of William Baxter, and Ann, *née* Mattimoe; *b* 10 September 1962, Durham; *Educ* Newcastle Business Sch; *m* 1988, Gerard Dodgson; *Career* administrative posts NHS Newcastle upon Tyne 1980–90, dir of planning and service devpt 1990–92, chief exec Sunderland HA 1993–99, chief operating offr Employment Serv 2001–02 (dir jobcentre servs 1999–2001), chief operating offr Jobcentre Plus 2002–03 (actg chief exec 2003), chief exec Legal Services Cmmn 2003–07, dir CD Consulting 2007–; external complaints reviewer Parly and Health Services Ombudsman (PHSO) 2011–; non-exec dir: Prescription Pricing Authority 1993–97, Contributions Agency 1997–99, Child Support Agency 1999–2001, NW London SHA 2002–05, Agric and Horticulture Devpt Bd (AHDB, formerly Levy Board) UK 2007–, Seafish Industry Authy DEFRA 2012–; memb: Bd of Cmmrs Healthcare Cmmn 2007–09, Bd Revenue and Customs Prosecution Office (RCPO) 2008–09; public interest memb Regulation and Compliance Bd ICAS AHDB 2011–2012, panel memb Judicial Conduct Investigation Office Miny of Justice 2012–15, ind memb Service Complaints Panels MOD 2012–, chair Strategic Advsy Bd Bar Tbnls and Adjudication Service 2014–; public appointments ambass Govt Equalities Office Home Office (previously with Cabinet Office) 2009–13; *Recreations* Ariel Atom, travel, good food; *Style*— Ms Clare Dodgson; ✉ e-mail clare.dodgson@btinternet.com

DODGSON, Elyse Anne; MBE (2010); *née* Kramer; da of Samuel Kramer (d 1991), and Mildred, *née* Seltzer (d 2007); *b* 26 August 1945; *Educ* Abraham Lincoln HS NY, Northwestern Univ (BSc), Guildhall Sch of Music and Drama, Univ of Essex; *Family* 1 da (Tamsin Rebecca Dodgson b 8 July 1970), 1 s (Matthew Jesse William Dodgson b 18 April 1972); m, 2 July 1988 (m dis), Prof Gerd R Hoff; *Career* actor and theatre dir and prodr; actor with Brighton Combination 1968–69, head of drama Vauxhall Manor Sch 1979–82 (dir Motherland 1981–82), ILEA advsy teacher for equal opportunities 1984–85; Royal Court Theatre: dir Young People's Theatre 1985–91, prodr Young Writers' Festival 1986–91, fndr and dir int residency 1989–, assoc dir (educn) 1992–95, assoc dir (int) 1996–, prodr Int Seasons 1997–, Int Playwrights Season 2007 and Bliss 2008; prodn credits for Royal Court Int Dept incl: Via Dolorosa 1998, Mr Kolpert 2000, Alive from Palestine (Al Kasaba Theatre) 2001 and 2002, Plasticine 2002, Black Milk 2003, Terrorism 2003, Ladybird 2004, At the Table/Almost Nothing 2004, New Cuban Playwrights 2004, Way to Heaven 2005, On Insomnia and Midnight 2006, int season 2007, The Ugly One 2007, Free Outgoing 2007, Bliss 2008, The Stone 2009, Disconnect 2010, Our Private Life 2011, Remembrance Day 2011, Feast 2013, A Time to Reap 2013, The Djinns of Eidgah 2013, Fireworks 2015; memb Bd Out of Joint 1999–2014; tstee Nat Life Story Collection 1990–2000; Int Theatre Inst Award for Excellence in Int Theatre 1999, Young Vic Award 2004; *Books* Motherland: West Indian Women to Britain (1984, The Other Award 1984), First Lines (ed, 1988), New German Plays (ed, vol 1 1997, vol 2 1998), New Spanish Plays (co-ed, 1999), Mexican Plays (ed, 2007), Voices from the Arab World (2010); *Style*— Ms Elyse Dodgson, MBE; ✉ Royal Court Theatre, Sloane Square, London SW1W 8AS (☎ 020 7565 5050, fax 020 7565 5001, e-mail international@royalcourttheatre.com, Twitter @ElyseDodgson)

DODGSON, His Hon Judge Paul; s of late Reginald Dodgson, and Kathleen Slyvia, *née* Jay; *b* 14 August 1951; *Educ* Tiffin Sch Kingston upon Thames, Univ of Birmingham; *m* 20 Feb 1982, Jan, da of Geoffrey Hemingway (d 1966); 2 da (Eleanor b 17 Sept 1984, Laura b 22 July 1986), 1 s (William Geoffrey b 1 Feb 1991); *Career* called to the Bar Inner Temple 1975, in practice criminal law, recorder of the Crown Ct 1996–2001 (asst recorder 1992–96), circuit judge 2001–; judicial memb Parole Bd 2003–; *Recreations* sailing; *Style*— His Hon Judge Dodgson; ✉ c/o Kingston Crown Court, 6 Penrhyn Road, Kingston on Thames, Surrey KT1 2BB

DODSON, Joanna; QC (1993); da of Jack Herbert Dodson, and Joan Muriel, *née* Webb; *b* 5 September 1945; *Educ* James Allen's Girls' Sch, Newnham Coll Cambridge (entrance exhibitioner, MA); *m* 1974 (m dis 1981); *Career* called to the Bar Middle Temple 1971 (bencher 2000); memb: SE Circuit, Family Law Bar Assoc; govr James Allen's Girls' Sch 1999–2009; *Style*— Miss Joanna Dodson, QC; ✉ Thomas Bingham Chambers, 33

Bedford Row, London WC1R 4JH (✆ 020 7242 6476, fax 020 7831 6065, e-mail clerks@tbchambers.co.uk)

DODSON, (Peter) Mark Loveys; s of Peter Sidney Dodson, OBE (d 2011), and Elizabeth Katherine Loveys, *née* Davis; *b* 6 October 1957; *Educ* St Helena Sch Colchester, Colchester Inst of HE (Dip); *m* 28 Dec 1991, Sarah Margaret McGregor, da of Derek Charles Ralph Burn (d 2003); 3 da (Alexandra Grace b 12 April 1997, Charlotte Rosemary b 21 May 1999, Louisa Mae b 31 Jan 2003); *Career* chef; Portman Hotel London 1978–79 and 1980–81, Old Court House Hotel Jersey 1979–80, sous chef Le Talbooth Dedham 1981–83, head chef The Waterside Inn Bray 1988–2001 (joined 1983, sous chef 1986–88), exec head chef Cliveden 2001–05, chef and prop The Masons Arms Knowstone 2005– (Michelin Star 2006–, Egon Ronay Star 2006, 6/10 Good Food Guide 2007–10, named 90th in Restaurant Magazine Top UK Restaurants 2008, named Best Restaurant in the North Devon Food & Drink Awards 2008, Michelin Guide Pub of the Year 2010), Best Pub N Devon Food and Drink Award 2011, named 15th in Morning Advertiser Top 30 Gastro Pubs 2012; memb Académie Culinaire de France (now Royal Acad of Culinary Arts) 1988–; second prize Mouton Rothschild Menu Competition 1986, Domaines Drouhin Prix des Deux Cartes 1993; *Books* Advanced Practical Cookery (contrib, 1995), Desert Island Dishes (contrib, 2012), Recreate (contrib, 2012); *Recreations* record collecting, sport; *Style*— Mark Dodson, Esq; ✉ The Masons Arms, Knowstone, Devon EX36 4RY (e-mail enqs@masonsarmsdevon.co.uk, website www.markdodson.co.uk)

DODSON, Richard Charles; s of John Summerville Dodson, of Woodford Green, Essex, and Muriel Edith, *née* Bunce; *b* 2 January 1951; *Educ* Buckhurst Hill County HS, UCL (BSc); *m* 14 April 1979, Barbara, da of Allan Carrington, of Kenilworth, Warks; 1 s (Lee b 1968); *Career* media res dir Foote Cone and Belding Ltd 1984–87 (media res mangr 1972), md Telmar Communications Ltd 1988–, pres Telmar Group Inc NY 1989–; treas Woodford Green CC; FIPA 1987; *Recreations* racing horses, cricket, bridge; *Style*— Richard Dodson, Esq; ✉ Warren House, The Warren, Polperro, Cornwall PL13 2RB; Telmar Communications Ltd, 46 Chagford Street, London NW1 6EB (✆ 020 7569 7500, fax 020 7569 7501, mobile 07710 355777)

DODSWORTH; *see also:* Smith-Dodsworth

DODWELL, Christina; da of Christopher Bradford Dodwell, of Sussex, and Evelyn, *née* Beddow; *b* 1 February 1951; *Educ* Southover Manor Lewes, Beechlawn Coll Oxford; *m* 1991, Stephen Hobbs; *Career* explorer and author; 3 year journey through Africa by horse 1975–78; 2 year journey through Papua New Guinea by horse and canoe 1980–81, presenter BBC film River Journey-Waghi 1984 (winner BAFTA award); sr attaché Madagascar Consulate, chm Dodwell Tst; Freedom Sepik River region of Papua New Guinea 1984, winner Mungo Park medal Royal Scottish Geographical Soc 1989, winnter Int Award for Contrib to Geographical Knowledge and Cultural Understanding Spanish Geographical Soc 2011; FRGS 1982, FRSA 1985; *Books* Travels with Fortune (1979), In Papua New Guinea (1982), An Explorers Handbook (1984), A Traveller in China (1986), A Traveller on Horseback (1987), Travels with Pegasus (1989), Beyond Siberia (1993), Madagascar Travels (1995); *Recreations* fossil hunting, walking; *Style*— Ms Christina Dodwell; ✉ e-mail dodwellandhobbs@gmail.com, website www.dodwell-trust.org

DODWORTH, Air Vice Marshal Peter; CB (1994), OBE (1982), AFC (1971), DL (Lincs 2004); s of Eric Albert Dodworth (d 1988), of Southport, and Edna, *née* Barker (d 1988); *b* 12 September 1940; *Educ* Southport GS, Univ of Leeds (BSc); *m* 1963, Kay (d 2016), da of Hugh Parry; 4 s (Antony b 18 March 1965, Christopher b and d 1965, Bruce b 6 Aug 1967, Jonathan b 6 Feb 1976); *Career* cmmnd RAF 1961, flying trg (Jet Provosts and Vampires) 1961–63, No 54 Sqdn (Hunters) 1963–65, No 4 Flying Trg Sch (Gnats) 1965–67, advanced instr Central Flying Sch (Gnats) 1967–69, Harrier Conversion Team 1969–72, Air Staff HQ RAF Germany 1972–76, OC Ops Wing RAF Wittering (Harriers) 1976–79, Nat Defence Coll 1980, Air Cdr Belize 1980–82, Directing Staff RAF Staff Coll 1982–83, Station Cdr RAF Wittering 1983–85, Cmd Gp Exec HQ Allied Air Forces Central Europe Ramstein Germany 1985–87, RCDS 1987, Dir of Personnel MOD 1988–91, Defence Attaché and head of Br Defence Staff Br Embassy Washington DC 1991–94, head Operations Branch Implementation Team 1994, Sr Directing Staff (Air) RCDS 1994–96, ret; mil advsr Bombardier Services Defence 1997–2000, def advsr Vosper Thorneycroft Aerospace 2000–02; chm of govrs Stamford Endowed Schs 2005–09; Liveryman GAPAN 2004; FRAeS 1996; *Recreations* golf, DIY, reading, gardening; *Clubs* RAF (chm 1994–96); *Style*— Air Vice Marshal Peter Dodworth, CB, OBE, AFC, DL; ✆ 01780 740340, fax 01780 740598, e-mail peterdodworth@btinternet.com

DOE, Prof William Fairbank; s of Asa Garfield Doe (d 1985), and Hazel Thelma, *née* Young (d 2002); *b* 6 May 1941; *Educ* Newington Coll, Univ of Sydney (MB BS), Univ of London (MSc); *m* 20 March 1982, Ms Dallas Elizabeth Ariotti, da of James D McIntosh; 2 s (Jamie b 28 April 1985, Thomas b 6 July 1986); *Career* MRC fell 1970–71, lectr in med RPMS 1973–74, conslt Hammersmith Hosp 1973–74, Lilly int fell 1974–75, Nat Inst for Health Research fell Scripps Clinic and Research Fndn 1975–77, assoc prof Univ of Sydney and hon physician Royal N Shore Hosp 1978–81; John Curtin Sch of Med Research ANU: prof 1982–98, head Dept of Med and Clinical Science 1982–88, head Div of Molecular Med 1988–98; dir of gastroenterolgy Canberra Hosp 1991–97, prof of med Univ of Sydney 1995–98, prof of med and dean Sch of Med Univ of Birmingham 1998–2007 (memb Univ Senate 1998–2007, memb Cncl 2002–07), hon conslt physician Univ Hosp Birmingham NHS Tst and City Hosp NHS Tst 1998–2007, provost Aga Khan Univ Pakistan 2008–; distinguished visiting fell Christ's Coll Cambridge 1988–89; non-exec dir Birmingham and Black Country Strategic HA 1998–2007; sr ed Jl of Gastroenterology and Hepatology 1993–2002 (memb Editorial Bd 1987–2006, tstee 2002–06), assoc ed Inflammatory Bowel Disease 1994–98; memb Editorial Bd Australian Prescriber 1987–90; author of numerous scientific papers on molecular cell biology of mucosal inflammation and colon cancer; WHO conslt Beijing 1987; memb: Advsy Ctee Social Psychiatry Research Unit Nat Health and Med Research Ctee Aust 1982–95, Cncl Nat Centre for Epidemiology Population Health 1987–98, Aust Drug Evaluation Ctee 1988–95, Cncl RACP 1993–98, Research Strategy Ctee Nat Health and Med Research Ctee Aust 1997–98, Cncl of Heads of Med Schs 1998– (memb Exec 2000–); memb: Gastroenterological Soc of Aust (pres 1989–91), Br Soc of Gastroenterology, American Gastroenterology Assoc, BMA, Aust Coeliac Soc; tstee Canberra Arts Patrons Orgn 1983–86, involved with Canberra Cancerians 1990–98, govr Univ of Worcester 2005–07; Distinguished Research Prize and Medal Gastroenterolgy Soc of Australia 1997; FRACP 1978, FRCP 1993 (MRCP 1969), FMedSci 1999; *Recreations* opera, reading, oriental rugs, walking; *Clubs* Cwlth, Athenaeum; *Style*— Prof William Doe; ✉ The Aga Khan University, Stadium Road, PO Box 3500, Karachi – 74800, Pakistan (✆ 00 92 21 3486 2600, e-mail william.doe@aku.edu)

DOEH, Doran; *b* 14 May 1948; *Educ* Dartmouth Coll USA (Reynolds scholar, BA), Univ of Oxford (MA), Univ of London (LLB); *Career* barrister 1973; legal advsr: Burmah Oil North Sea Limited 1975–76, The British National Oil Corporation 1977–82, Britoil plc 1982–86; admitted slr 1987; Allen & Overy: joined 1986, ptnr Moscow 1995–98, ptnr London 1998–99; ptnr Dentons (and predecessor firms) 1999–; memb: Law Soc, Int Bar Assoc; FSALS, MCIArb; *Recreations* cooking, wine, opera; *Clubs* United Oxford and Cambridge Univ; *Style*— Doran Doeh, Esq; ✉ Dentons, 1 Fleet Place, London EC4M 7WS (✆ 020 7242 1212, fax 020 7246 7777); White Gardens Business Centre, Lesnaya ulitsa 7, Moscow 125047, Russia (✆ 00 7 495 644 0500, fax 00 7 495 644 0599)

DOEL, District Judge John Michael; s of Harry and Edith Doel; *Educ* Brockley CGS London, UC Cardiff (BSc, Welsh vest in rowing), Washington State Univ; *m*; 2 s (Owen, Lewis); *Career* articled A C Hepburn Slr, admitted slr 1974; district judge (Wales & Chester Circuit) 2000– (dep district judge 1991–2000); govr Barry Comp Sch; *Recreations* opera, gardening, walking, yoga; *Style*— District Judge Doel; ✉ c/o Wales & Chester Circuit Secretariat, 2nd Floor, Churchill House, Churchill Way, Cardiff CF1 4HH (e-mail jdoel@lix.compulink.co.uk)

DOEL, Air Cdre Martin Terry; CBE (2016, OBE 1998); s of Terry Doel, of Hythe, Hants, and Brenda Doel; *b* 21 November 1956, Romsey, Hants; *Educ* Totton GS, King Alfred's Coll Winchester (BEd), KCL (MA), RAF Coll Cranwell, RAF Staff Coll, Jt Servs Cmd and Staff Coll; *m* 9 Aug 1980, Angela, *née* Ransom; 2 s (Matthew b 14 Nov 1985, Andrew b 12 Sep 1989); *Career* various appts RAF 1980–2004, dir Personnel & Trg Strategy RAF 2004–07, dir Trg and Educn MOD 2001–08; chm RAF FA 2006–08; ret RAF 2008; chief exec Assoc of Colls 2008–; memb Advsy Bd and Audit Ctee Skills Funding Agency 2014–, memb Apprenticeship Stakeholder Bd BIS/DfE 2015–; tstee Inspire and Achieve Fndn, memb Cncl Career Academies UK, hon treas World Congress of Colleges and Polytechnics; Alistair Black Meml Trophy for War Studies 1981; FRAeS, FRSA; *Publications* Humanitarian Intervention (RUSI jl, 1995, Trench Gasgoigne Essay Prize), Perspectives on Enterprise (2010), Rethinking Apprenticeships (2011); *Recreations* football (UEFA grade B coach), cricket; *Clubs* RAF; *Style*— Air Commodore M T Doel, CBE; ✉ Association of Colleges, 3–5 Stedham Place, London WC1A 1HU

D

DOERRIES, Chantal-Aimée; QC (2008); da of Prof Reinhard R Doerries, and Elaine Sulli Doerries; *Educ* Univ of Pennsylvania, New Hall Cambridge (pres Cambridge Union Soc); *Career* called to the Bar 1992; memb: Int Bar Assoc (co-chair Forum for Barristers and Advocates 2009–11, Cncl rep Bar of Eng and Wales 2009–14 and 2016); Bar Cncl of Eng and Wales: memb Int Business Devpt Gp (chair 2009–13), memb Int Ctee (chm 2011–13), memb Bar Branded Arbitration Working Gp (chair 2008–09), Technol and Construction Bar Assoc (chm 2010–13), chm 2016; fell American Bar Fndn; *Style*— Ms Chantal-Aimée Doerries, QC; ✉ Atkin Chambers, 1 Atkin Building, Gray's Inn, London WC1R 5AT

DOHERTY, Dr Ciaran Conor; s of John Doherty, and Kathleen, *née* Hunter; *b* 29 March 1948; *Educ* St Mary's CBS GS Belfast, Queen's Univ Belfast (MB, MD); *m* Kathleen Mary, da of John Michael Collins, of Belfast; 2 da (Karen b 1978, Catherine b 1981), 1 s (Conor b 1981); *Career* NI kidney res fell 1976–78, clinical fell in nephrology Univ of S Calif 1979–81, conslt renal physician Belfast City Hosp and Royal Victoria Hosp 1981–, special lectr Dept of Med Queen's Univ Belfast 1983– (jr tutor 1973–75, clinical teacher in nephrology 1981–), postgrad clinical tutor Belfast Postgrad Med Centre 1985–90, clinical dir of nephrology Belfast City Hosp 1996–2001; author and co-author of 65 papers on kidney disease, contrib to 10 nephrology textbooks; pres Irish Nephrology Soc 1986–88, NI rep and memb Cncl Nat Assoc of Clinical Tutors 1986; memb Assoc of Physicians of GB and NI 1988, fell Royal Acad of Med in Ireland 1990, censor RCPI 1999–2002, hon sr lectr Dept of Med Queen's Univ Belfast 1999–; FRCP 1992 (MRCP), FRCPI 1992; *Recreations* boating, golf, gardening; *Clubs* Corrigan; *Style*— Dr Ciaran Doherty; ✉ Regional Nephrology Unit, Belfast City Hospital Tower, Lisburn Road, Belfast BT9 5JY (✆ 028 9032 9241, e-mail cc.doherty@belfasttrust.hscni.net)

DOHERTY, Daniel; *b* 15 April 1984; *Career* exec chef Duck & Waffle 2012–; *Books* Duck & Waffle: Recipes and Stories (2014); *Style*— Daniel Doherty, Esq

DOHERTY, Prof Michael; s of Donald Doherty (d 2006), of Upton, Devon, and Eileen May, *née* Fairchild (d 1980); *b* 7 March 1951; *Educ* City of London Freemen's Sch, St John's Coll Cambridge (MA, MB BChir, MD); *m* 27 Sept 1980, Sally Anne; 2 da (Emma b 1982, Jill b 1983); *Career* prof of rheumatology Univ of Nottingham; ed Annals of Rheumatic Diseases 1992–99; Freeman City of London 1984; fell Higher Educn Acad (FHEA), FRCP; *Books* Rheumatological Medicine (1985), Pyrophosphate Arthropathy – A Clinical Study (1988), Clinical Examination in Rheumatology (1992), Rheumatology Examination and Injection Techniques (1992); *Recreations* cinema, opera, osteology, art; *Style*— Prof Michael Doherty; ✉ Academic Rheumatology, City Hospital, Nottingham NG5 1PB (✆ 0115 823 1756)

DOHERTY, Pat; MP; *b* 18 July 1945, Glasgow; *Educ* St Joseph's Coll Lochwinnoch; *Career* vice-pres Sinn Féin 1988–2008, memb NI Assembly (Sinn Féin) Tyrone W 1998–2012, MP (Sinn Féin) Tyrone W 2001– (Parly candidate (Sinn Féin) Tyrone W 1997); *Style*— Pat Doherty, MP; ✉ e-mail patsf.doherty@gmail.com; House of Commons, London SW1A 0AA

DOHERTY, Hon Lord; (Joseph) Raymond Doherty; QC (1997); *b* 30 January 1958, Stirling; *Educ* St Joseph's Coll Dumfries, Univ of Edinburgh (LLB), Hertford Coll Oxford (BCL), Harvard Law Sch (LLM); *m* 23 July 1994, Arlene Elizabeth Donaghy; 2 da, 1 s; *Career* admitted as advocate 1984 (Lord Reid scholarship 1983–85); standing jr counsel to: MOD in Scotland 1990–91, Scottish Office Industry Dept 1992–97; clerk of Faculty of Advocates 1990–95, advocate depute 1998–2001, senator Coll of Justice 2010–; *Publications* Armour on Valuation for Rating (jt ed, 1990–), Stair Memorial Encyclopaedia of the Laws of Scotland (contrib); *Style*— The Hon Lord Doherty; ✉ Court of Session, Parliament House, Parliament Square, Edinburgh EH1 1RQ

DOHMANN, Barbara; QC (1987); *Educ* Univ of Erlangen, Univ of Mainz, Univ of Paris; *Career* called to the Bar 1971, memb Bar Br Virgin Islands; bencher Gray's Inn; recorder 1990–2002, dep judge of the High Court (Commercial Court Queen's Bench and Chancery Div) 1994–2002, judge of the Civil and Commercial Court Doha Qatar; arbitrator and mediator; memb Ctee: Commercial Bar Assoc (chm 1999–2001), ldr European Circuit, London Common Law & Commercial Bar Assoc (LCLCBA), German Bar Assoc (DVA); memb: Gen Cncl of the Bar (memb Legal Services Ctee 1999–2001), Special Ctee Appeal Panel and Arbitration Panel LME, Lord Chllr's Standing Ctee of Int Law, Learned Soc for Int Procedure Law; founding memb Chllr's Forum of the Univ of the Arts London; former memb Court of Govrs London Inst HE Corp; *Clubs* Athenaeum; *Style*— Miss Barbara Dohmann, QC; ✉ Blackstone Chambers, Blackstone House, Temple, London EC4Y 9BW

DOIG, Alan David; CBE (2006), QFSM (2004); s of Alexander Doig (d 1997), and Myra Bisset, *née* Reid; *b* 11 May 1957, Kirkcaldy, Fife; *Educ* Kirkcaldy HS, Kirkcaldy Tech Coll (HNC), Inst of Industrial Mangrs (Cert), Open Univ (BSc); *m* 7 June 1975, Senga, *née* Somerville; 2 da (Maxine b 9 March 1976, Rachael b 27 Sept 1988), 1 s (Christopher b 24 June 1992); *Career* Fife Fire Brigade 1976–88 (seconded: Scottish Fire Serv Trg Sch 1979–81, Fire Servs Coll 1985–87); Staffs Fire and Rescue Serv: joined 1988, asst chief fire offr 1993–95, dep chief fire offr 1995–99, chief fire offr and chief exec 1999–2008; dep ceo East of England Ambulance Service 2009–10; non-exec dir Govt Decontamination Serv Defra; author of numerous articles in fire specialist media; FIFireE 1997; *Recreations* golf, reading; *Style*— Alan Doig, Esq, CBE, QFSM; ✉ Cramond House, 57 West Road, Buxton Spa (✆ 07710 982886, e-mail thedoigs@btopenworld.com)

DOIG, John; s of David Doig (d 1994), and Mary (Mamie), *née* Maguire (d 1991); *b* 2 August 1958, Helensburgh, Scotland; *Educ* Holyrod Sch Glasgow, St Mary's Music Sch Edinburgh (first pupil enrolled at request of Lord Menuhin); *Career* violinist; BBC Symphony Orch 1975–78, princ first violin BBC Philharmonic Orch 1979–81; Scottish Chamber Orch: co ldr 1986–88, guest ldr and dir 1988–90; ldr Scottish Opera Orch 1990–97; fndr and dir Scottish Bach Consort 1994–99 (memb Bd of Dirs), fndr and artistic dir Killearn Series 1994; performances with Scottish Chamber Orch incl: Flanders Festival, Edinburgh Int Festival, BBC Proms, Carnegie Hall NY; *Recordings* with Scottish Chamber Orch: Bach Brandenburg Concerto No 2, Stravinsky Apollon Musagète, Tchaikovsky/Stravinsky Entr'Acte From The Sleeping Beauty (world premiere), Tchaikovsky Mozartiana, Britten Young Apollo and Les Illuminations; *Recreations* horse riding, dogs, water sports, country walks; *Style*— John Doig, Esq; ✉ Endrick Mews, Killearn, Stirlingshire G63 9ND

DOIG, Maxwell Kirkcaldy; s of David Thomas Doig, and June Doig; *b* 21 February 1966; *Educ* Manchester Sch of Art (BA), Slade Sch of Art (scholar); *Partner* Nicola Rose; *Career* artist in residence Hochshule Der Künst Berlin 1991–92; travelled extensively through USA, Mexico and Aust 1997; over 20 solo exhbns since 1990 at Hart Gallery, Albemarle Gallery and Messum's Gallery and over 60 national and international group exhbns since 1990; *Public Collections* Univ of Manchester, Univ of London, Mercer Gallery Harrogate, Provident Financial Group, Huddersfield Art Gallery, Prudential plc, Holman Fenwick and Willan, Jersey Arts Centre (New Light Prize); *Awards* Landscape Drawing Award Manchester Acad Open Exhibition 1986, Joseph Webb Prize for Draughtsman under 35 1990, Villiers David Prize 1997 (shortlisted 1995); *Recreations* cinema, walking; *Style*— Maxwell Doig, Esq; ✉ c/o Messum's, 28 Cork Street, London W1S 3NG (☎ 020 7437 5545, e-mail info@maxwelldoig.com, website www.messums.com)

DOIG, Peter; *b* 1959; *Educ* Wimbledon Sch of Art, St Martin's Sch of Art (BA), Chelsea Sch of Art (MA); *Career* artist; tstee Tate Gallery 1996–; *Solo Exhibitions* Metropolitan Gallery 1984, The Naked City (Air Gallery) 1986, Articule (Montreal) 1990, Whitechapel Artist Award (Whitechapel Gallery) 1991, Victoria Miro Gallery 1994, Enterprise (NY) 1994; *Group Exhibitions* New Contemporaries (ICA) 1982 and 1983, Things as They Are (Riverside Studios) 1985, Into the Nineties (Mall Galleries) 1990, Barclays Young Artist Award (Serpentine Gallery) 1991, Inside a Microcosm (Laure Genillard Gallery) 1992, New Voices (Centre Albert Borschette) 1992, Moving into View (Royal Festival Hall) 1993, Twelve Stars (Barbican Centre) 1993, Projet Unite Firminy (Firminy Vert) 1993, John Moores Liverpool Exhbn 18 (1st prize) 1993, Prix Eliette von Karajan (tour, 1st prize) 1994, Unbound: Possibilities in Painting (Hayward Gallery) 1994, New Voices (Br Cncl tour to Spain) 1994, Enterprise 1994, Imprint '93 (Cabinet Gallery) 1994, Here and Now (Serpentine Gallery) 1994, Turner Prize (Tate Gallery) 1994; *Work in Collections* Contemporary Arts Soc, John Moores, Br Cncl, Arts Cncl, Euro Parliament; *Style*— Peter Doig, Esq

DOLBY, Trevor John; s of Kenneth Douglas Dolby (d 1999), of Ellastone, Derbys, and Elsie Dolby; *b* 24 April 1957; *Educ* King Edward VI Sch Lichfield, Lanchester Poly (BSc); *m*; 2 c; *Career* writer and ed New Leaf Books 1979–82, science ed John Murray Publisher 1982–84, publishing manager Reed Illustrated Div 1990–92, ed Natural History div rising to publishing manager Illustrated div Hamlyn/Reed 1984–92, publishing dir Pavilion Books 1992–96, publishing dir Orion Non-Fiction and Orion Audio 1996–2003, md and publisher HarperEntertainment 2003–06, publisher Preface Publishing 2007–; opinion columist BookBrunch 2009–, occasional columnist Br GQ magazine; non-exec dir Maverick Television 2000–04; Ed of the Year Br Book Awards 2003 (shortlisted 2002); *Recreations* collecting modern first editions; *Clubs* Mornington Crescent (offr and memb), Academy, Soho House, Groucho, Cafe Royal; *Style*— Trevor Dolby, Esq; ✉ Penguin Random House Publishers, 20 Vauxhall Bridge Road, London SW1V 2SA

DOLMAN, Edward James; s of James William Dolman, and Jean, *née* Angles (d 2006); *b* 24 February 1960, Wimbledon; *Educ* Dulwich Coll, Univ of Southampton (BA); *Children* 1 da (Esther Maria b 15 Nov 1988), 1 s (Alexander William b 17 Aug 1990); *Career* joined Christie's 1984, dir and head of furniture Christie's South Kensington 1990–96, md Christie's Amsterdam 1996–97, dir Christie Manson & Woods 1997, md Christie's Europe 1998–99 (commercial dir 1997–98), md Christie's America 1999–2000, ceo Christie's International plc 1999–2011; memb Governing Bd Courtauld 2015–; Qatar Museums Authy: dir Office of HE Sheikha Al Mayassa bint Hamad bin Khalifa Al-Thani 2011–14, actg ceo 2012–14; chm and ceo Phillips 2014–; Officier de la Légion d'Honneur 2011 (Chevalier 2007); *Recreations* art history, rugby, sailing, Chelsea FC; *Clubs* RAC, Old Alleynians, Royal Thames Yacht, NY Yacht; *Style*— Edward Dolman, Esq; ✉ Phillips, 30 Berkeley Square, London W1J 6EX

DOMINICZAK, Professor Marek Henryk; s of Dr Tadeusz Dominiczak, of Gdansk, Poland, and Dr Aleksandra Dominiczak; *b* 1951, Gda?sk, Poland; *Educ* Copernicus HS Gdansk, Med Acad of Gdansk (MB, PhD), Univ of Cambridge (Cert English Language Teaching to Adults (CELTA)); *m* 1976, Professor Dame Anna Felicja Dominiczak, da of Prof Jakub Penson (d 1971); 1 s (Peter b 1985); *Career* conslt pathologist St Luke's Hosp Malta 1979–82, registrar and sr registrar Glasgow Royal Infirmary 1982–85, conslt biochemist West Glasgow Hosps Univ NHS Tst 1985– (head Biochemistry Dept 1996–2000); Univ of Glasgow: hon lectr 1986–90, hon sr lectr 1990–2006, hon prof 2007–; dir Med Humanities Unit Gartnavel Gen Hosp Glasgow 2002–; fndr ArtScience Lab Inst for Art History Univ of Glasgow 2001; special prof: Univ of Oslo 1974, Rockefeller Univ NY 1989; co-ordinator EC TEMPUS: Jt Euro Project Poland 1991–93, Jt Euro Network 1994–, Structural Jt Euro Project Estonia 1994–97; ed Clinical Chemistry and Laboratory Med 1998–2003; memb Assoc of Clinical Biochemists; pres Royal Medico-Chirurgical Soc of Glasgow 2010–11 (vice-pres 2009–10); FRCPath, FRCPGlas, dr hab med (Gdansk); *Books* Joint European Project Management Handbook (1994), Handbook of Lipoprotein Testing (ed, 1997 and 2000), International Collaboration in Laboratory Medicine: a model programme (ed, 1998), Medical Biochemistry (ed, 1999, 4 edn 2014), Flesh and Bones of Metab and Nutrition (2007), Medical Biochem Flash Cards (2011); monthly Science in the Arts series in the Clinical Chemistry Jl USA (2011–); *Recreations* painting, drawing, photography (representing gallery Art Forum Milngavie Glasgow); *Clubs* Athenaeum; *Style*— Professor Marek Dominiczak; ✉ Department of Biochemistry, Gartnavel General Hospital, Glasgow G12 0YN (☎ 0141 211 2788, fax 0141 211 3452, e-mail marek.dominiczak@gla.ac.uk)

DON, Nigel Anderson; s of Derek Don (d 1975), and Margaret Don (d 2002); *b* 16 April 1954, Sutton, Surrey; *Educ* KCS Wimbledon, Pembroke Coll Cambridge (MA, MEng), Univ of London (LLB); *m* 1977, Wendy; 1 s (Laurence b 1982), 1 da (Karen b 1983); *Career* various tech posts in the detergents industry Unilever plc 1976–89, self-employed music publisher and teacher 1989–2007, cncllr Dundee City Cncl 2003–07; MSP (SNP): NE Scotland 2007–11, Angus N & Mearns 2011–16; self-employed composer 2016–; MIChemE 1982; *Recreations* music, walking; *Style*— Nigel Don, Esq

DON, Robert Seymour; s of Air Vice-Marshal Francis Percival Don, OBE, DL (d 1964), of North Elmham, Norfolk, and Angela Jane, *née* Birkbeck (d 1995); *b* 5 April 1932, Cambridge; *Educ* Eton, Trinity Coll Cambridge (MA); *m* 2 July 1955, Judith Henrietta, da of Geoffrey Nicholas Holmes, of Shotesham All Saints, Norfolk; 4 da Charlotte (Mrs Timothy Laing) b 1956, Joanna Mary (Mrs Thomas Fitzalan Howard) b 1958, Fiona (Mrs James Gibson Fleming) b 1962, Henrietta (Mrs Mark Burdon) b 1965); *Career* Nat Serv 1 The Royal Dragoons 1950–52, TA Fife and Forfar Yeomanry 1953–54; John Harvey & Sons Ltd 1957–65, dir Hicks & Don Ltd Wine Merchants (formerly RS Don Ltd) 1965–2002, dir Elmham Wines Ltd 1967–; former chm: E Counties Wine and Spirit Assoc, English Vineyards Assoc, Norfolk Fruit Growers Assoc; gen cmmr of Income Tax 1975–2007; MW 1965; memb Inst of Masters of Wine; *Books* Off the Shelf (1967), Teach Yourself Wine (1968); *Recreations* shooting, fishing, deer stalking, skiing, photography; *Clubs* Cavalry and Guards'; *Style*— Robert Don, Esq; ✉ Garden Cottage, Elmham House, North Elmham, Dereham, Norfolk NR20 5JY (☎ 01362 668363, mobile 07711 565952, e-mail r.s.don@zen.co.uk)

DON, Robin Cameron; s of John Buttercase Don (d 1970), of Newport-on-Tay, Fife, Scotland, and Elizabeth Seath, *née* Fairbairn (d 1986); *b* 9 June 1941; *Educ* Bell Baxter HS Cupar; *Career* theatre designer; trained at Dundee Art Coll and studied engrg in Edinburgh; apprentice to theatre designer Ralph Koltai 1967–71; designs for Open Space Theatre 1971–77: Four Little Girls, Othello, Tooth of Crime, How Beautiful with Badges, The Taming of the Shrew, And They Put Handcuffs on the Flowers, Sherlock's Last Case, Measure for Measure, Hamlet, The Merchant of Venice; designs for other prodns: Mary Queen of Scots (Scot Opera) 1977, Bartholomew Fair (Round House) 1978, Les Mamelles de Tiresias (RAM/Opera North 1978, ENO 1979), Eugene Onegin (Aldeburgh 1979, Ottawa 1982, San Francisco Opera 1986), The Marriage of Figaro (Opera North) 1979, A Midsummer Night's Dream (Aldeburgh 1980, Royal Opera House Covent Garden 1986), The Flying Dutchman (Opera North) 1980, The Ticket of Leave Man (NT) 1981, Shakespeare's Rome (Mermaid) 1981, Hotel Paradiso (NT of Iceland) 1981, The Trumpet Major (RNCM and WNO) 1981, The Last Elephant (Bush) 1981, Cosi Fan Tutti (NIOT Belfast) 1981, The Birthday Party (Pitlochry) 1981–82, Song and Dance (Palace London) 1982, Madame Butterfly (Opera North) 1982, L'Elisir d' Amore (NIOT Belfast) 1982, The Midsummer Marriage (San Francisco Opera) 1983, Peter Grimes (WNO 1983, Aust Opera Sydney 1986), Twelfth Night (RSC Stratford 1983 and RSC Barbican 1984), The Boyfriend (Old Vic) 1984, Tamerlano (Opera de Lyon) 1984, When I Was a Girl I Used to Scream and Shout (Bush 1984, Edinburgh Festival 1985, Sydney and Whitehall 1986), Giasone (Buxton Festival) 1984, Kiss of the Spiderwoman (Bush) 1985, On The Edge (Hampstead) 1985, Chicago (NT of Iceland) 1985, Man of Two Worlds (Westminster) 1985, Don Quixote (NY City Opera) 1986, More Light (Bush) 1987, Norma (Covent Garden) 1987, Carmen (Sydney) 1987, La Forza del Destino (Toronto) 1987, Fat Pig (Haymarket Leicester) 1987, Spookhouse (Hampstead) 1987, The Brave (Bush) 1988, Ziegfeld (London Palladium) 1988, A Walk in the Woods (Comedy) 1988, Cavalleria Rusticana (Sydney) 1989, Hidden Laughter (Vaudeville) 1990, The Rocky Horror Show (Piccadilly) 1990, Macbeth (Santiago Ballet) 1991, The Magic Flute (Iceland) 1991, (Sweden) 1992, Someone Who'll Watch Over Me (Hampstead Theatre 1992, Broadway 1992, Dublin 1993), Beautiful Thing (Bush) 1993, Eugene Onegin (Iceland) 1993, Black Comedy (Zurich) 1993, The Rocky Horror Show (Minneapolis) 1993, Il Pagliacci (Sydney) 1994, Darwin's Flood (Bush) 1994, The Knocky (Royal Court) 1995, The Winter Guest 1995 (Almeida, West Yorkshire Playhouse (TMA Regional Theatre Awards for Best Design)), The Maiden Stone (Hampstead) 1995, Boom Bang A Bang (Bush) 1995, Hamlet (Royal Lyceum Theatre Co Edinburgh) 1995, Les Enfants du Paradis (RSC) 1996, A Perfect Ganesh (West Yorkshire Playhouse) 1996, Fool for Love (Donmar) 1996, Steaming (Picadilly) 1997, Cracked (Hampstead) 1997, Of Mice and Men (West Yorkshire Playhouse) 1997, The Rocky Horror Show (Wolfsburg and Euro tour) 1997, The Winter Guest (Venice Film Festival) 1997, The Weeping of Angels (Dublin Festival) 1997, Romeo and Juliet (Royal Ballet of Flanders) 1998, Hey Persephone! (Aldeburgh Festival and Almeida Festival) 1998, A Long Day's Journey into Night (Gate Theatre Dublin) 1999, The Gin Game (Savoy and nat tour) 1999, The Storm (Almeida Theatre, Br entry at Prague Quadriennale 1999) 1999, Carmen (Chicago) 2000, Arms and the Man (Gate Theatre Dublin) 2000, Il Corsaro (Athens Megaron) 2001, Turandot (ballet, China) 2001, The Girl with Red Hair (Royal Lyceum Theatre Co Edinburgh, Hampstead Theatre London) 2005, The Flint Street nativity (Liverpool Playhouse) 2006, Bent (Trafalgar Studios) 2006, Salome (Nuffield Theatre) 2006, The Emperor Jones (RNT) 2007 (nominated Best Design Evening Standard Awards 2007), The Winter's Tale (Royal Lyceum Edinburgh) 2007, Tuesdays at Tesco's (with Simon Callow, Edinburgh Festival) 2012 and (59E59 Theatre NY) 2015, Hamlet – The Rest is Silence (Dreamthinkspeak nat tour) 2012, Twelfth Night (Fort Canning Park Singapore) 2012, Othello (Singapore) 2013, Juvenalia (with Simon Callow, Assembly Hall Edinburgh) 2014, Simon Boccanegra (NCPA Beijing (cancelled)), 2015, The Barber of Seville, The Marriage of Figaro and Figaro Gets A Divorce (all Welsh Nat Opera) 2016; dir Int Scenography Course Central St Martin's Sch of Art and Design London 1990–95, dir 1st term project at Motley Theatre Design Course 1999; memb: Exec Ctee Soc of Br Theatre Designers 1975–91, British Theatre Design 1979–1983, British Theatre Design 1983–87; winner Golden Troika (for Eugene Onegin) at Prague Quadriennale 1979, Best Designer Award (Critics' Circle) 1996, first prize Garden of Islington competition 1999–2000; *Recreations* exploration of natural phenomena; *Style*— Robin Don, Esq; ✉ e-mail robin@robindon.com, website www.robindon.com

DONAGHY, Baroness (Life Peer UK 2010), of Peckham in the London Borough of Southwark; Rita Margaret Donaghy; CBE (2005, OBE 1998); *née* Willis; da of William Scott Willis (d 1963), of Leamington Spa, and Margaret Brenda, *née* Howard (later Mrs Bryan, d 2006); *b* 9 October 1944, Bristol; *Educ* Univ of Durham (BA); *m* Feb 2000, Edward Easen-Thomas; *Career* perm sec to Students' Union Inst of Educn Univ of London 1984–2000 (joined registry 1968), chair ACAS 2000–07; memb: NALGO/UNISON Nat Exec Cncl 1973–2000 (pres NALGO 1989–90), Gen Cncl TUC 1987–2000 (pres 1999–2000), Advsy Ctee on Employment of People with Disabilities 1995–97, Low Pay Cmmn 1997–2000, Ctee on Standards in Public Life 2001– (interim chair 2007), House of Lords Select Ctee on Personal Services 2014, House of Lords Information Ctee 2014–; chair: Dept for Work and Pensions Inquiry into Underlying Causes of Construction Fatal Accidents 2009, Diffuse Mesothelioma Fund Oversight Ctee; Hon DUniv: Open Univ 2003, Keele 2004; Hon DBA Univ of Greenwich 2005; FCIPD 2003, FRSA 2004; *Recreations* theatre, gardening, watching cricket; *Clubs* Surrey CCC; *Style*— The Baroness Donaghy, CBE; ✉ e-mail r.donaghy@btinternet.com

DONALD, Prof Dame Athene Margaret; DBE (2010); *née* Griffith; da of Walter Griffith, of London, and Annette Marian, *née* Tylor; *b* 15 May 1953; *Educ* Camden Sch for Girls, Univ of Cambridge (BA, PhD); *m* 3 July 1976, Dr Matthew J Donald; 1 s (James George b 19 May 1986), 1 da (Margaret Frances b 27 July 1988); *Career* postdoctoral assoc Dept of Materials Sci and Engrg Cornell Univ 1977–81, SERC fell Dept of Metallurgy and Materials Sci Univ of Cambridge 1981–83, res fell Cavendish Lab Cambridge 1983–85, prof of experimental physics Dept of Physics Univ of Cambridge 1998– (lectr 1985–95, reader in experimental physics 1995–98); memb: OST Foresight Technol Panel on Food/Drink 1994–97, Biology Neutron Advsy Panel 1995–99, EPSRC Coll 1995–, Large Scale Structures Instr Beam Scheduling Panel 1996–99, Prog Mgmnt Ctee for LINK Prog on Competitive Industrial Materials from Non-Food Crops 1997, Editorial Bd Polymer Int 1998–, BBSRC Agrifood Ctee 1999–2002, Governing Cncl and Science Sub-Ctee IFR 1999–2003, Advsy Bd Jl Macromolecular Sci 1999–, Editorial Advsy Bd Int Jl of Biological Macromolecules 1999–, Steering Advsy Ctee ISIS 2nd Target Station 2002–, EPSRC Physics SAT 2002–04, BBSRC Strategy Bd 2003–04, 2008 RAE Physics Sub Panel, Int Scientific Ctee ESPCI Paris 2006–, Steering Ctee UKRC4SetWomen 2007–08, REF Physics Pilot Panel 2010, Scientific Cncl European Research Cncl 2013–; chm BBSRC JREI Ctee 1999–2000, chair BBSRC Ctee C 2010–11, chair Educn Ctee Royal Soc 2011–14, pres Br Science Assoc 2015–16, memb Scientific Cncl European Research Cncl 2013–; ed-in-chief European Physics Jl E 1999–2004, symposium organiser on Materials Sci of Food MRS Boston 1998–99; chair Athena Forum 2009– (dep chair 2008–09), CaSE Advsy Cncl 2011–; tstee Science Museum 2011–; Charles Vernon Boys Prize Inst of Physics 1989, Samuel Locker Award in Physics 1989, Rosenhain Medal and Prize Inst of Materials 1995, William Hopkins Prize Cambridge Philosophical Soc 2003, Mott Medal and Prize Inst of Physics 2005, Bakerian Prize lectr Royal Soc 2006, Laureate for Europe L'Oreal/UNESCO for Women for Science Awards 2009, Faraday Medal Inst of Physics 2010, Rideal Award SCI 2014, Global Achievement Award Bradford Univ 2016; fell Robinson Coll Cambridge 1981–2014, memb Cncl Univ of Cambridge 2009–14, master Churchill Coll Cambridge; hon degrees: Univ of East Anglia 2012, Univ of Exeter 2012, Univ of Sheffield 2013, Swansea Univ 2014, UCL 2014, Heriot Watt Univ 2015, Univ of

Manchester 2015, Univ of Liverpool 2015, Univ of Leeds 2016; fell APS, FInstP, FRS 1999 (memb Cncl 2004–06 and 2012–, tstee 2012–); *Publications* Liquid Crystalline Polymers (with A H Windle, 1992, 2 edn 2006), Starch: Structure and Function (1997 and 2001); also author of over 300 papers in learned jls and numerous book chapters and reviews; *Style*— Prof Dame Athene Donald, DBE, FRS; ✉ Cavendish Laboratory, J J Thomson Avenue, Cambridge CB3 0HE (☎ 01223 337382, fax 01223 337000, e-mail amd3@cam.ac.uk); Churchill College Cambridge CB3 0DS

DONALD, Chris Mark; s of Hugh Ernest James Donald, of Newcastle upon Tyne, and late Kathleen Evelyn, *née* Rickard; *b* 25 April 1960; *Educ* Heaton Comp Newcastle, Newcastle Coll of Arts; *m* 15 May 1988, Dolores Clare, da of Charles Doherty; 1 s (Dale Thomas b 30 Sept 1989), 1 da (Jamie Clare b 15 Sept 1991); *Career* clerical offr DHSS Central Office Newcastle 1978–80, founded Viz Magazine 1979, ed Viz 1979–99, student Newcastle Coll of Arts 1981–82, set up House of Viz to publish Viz full time 1984 (signed publishing agreement Virgin Books 1985 then John Brown Publishing Ltd 1987); Br Magazine Publishing Awards Youth Magazine Ed of the Year 1989; *Books* Viz: The Big Hard One (1986), Viz: The Big Hard Number Two (1987), Viz: The Big Pink Stiff One (1988), Viz: Holiday Special (1988), Viz: The Dog's Bollocks (1989), The Viz Book of Crap Jokes (1989), The Billy the Fish Football Yearbook (1989), Viz: The Spunky Parts (1990), Viz: The Sausage Sandwich (1991), Viz: The Fish Supper (1992), Viz: The Pork Chopper (1993), The Viz Book of Absolute Shite for Boys and Girls (1993), Viz: The Pan Handle (1994), The Viz Book of Top Tips (1994), Viz: The Bell End (1995), Top Tips Two (1995), Viz: The Turtle's Head (1996), Viz Letterbocks (1996), Viz: The Joy of Sexism (1996), The Full Toss (1997), Rude Kids (2004); *Recreations* railway station restoration, Newcastle United supporter, signwriting; *Style*— Chris Donald, Esq

DONALD, George Malcolm; s of George Donald (d 2000), of Bieldside, Aberdeen, and Margaret, *née* Tait (d 1947); *b* 12 September 1943, Ootacamund, Tamil Nadu, India; *Educ* Robert Gordon's Coll Aberdeen, Aberdeen Acad, Edinburgh Coll of Art (Andrew Grant scholar, postgrad scholar, DA), Benares Hindu Univ (travelling scholar), Hornsey Coll of Art (ATC), Univ of Edinburgh (MEd); *m* 1969 (m dis 1986); 1 da (Saskia b 1971), 1 s (Ninian Fraser b 1973 d 2007); *Career* artist and printmaker; dir Centre for Continuing Studies Edinburgh Coll of Art until 2001, dir Edinburgh Coll of Art Summer Sch until 2004; former keeper RSA; adjunct prof: Univ of Central Florida 1981–, Chinese Acad of Fine Art 1993 and 1994, Kyoto Saga Univ of Arts 2002, Univ of Sharjah 2003, American Coll of Dubai 2004; hon prof Almaktoum Inst 2009–; memb Printmaker's Workshop; RSA 1992; *Solo Exhibitions* 57 Gall 1971, Pool Theatre Gall 1972, Shed 50 Gall 1974, Edinburgh Scottish Gall 1981, Bohun Gall 1984, Chine Collé 1984 and 1987, Peacock Printmakers' Gall 1985, Glasgow Print Workshops Gall 1985, Helsinki Festival 1985, Finnish Assoc of Printmakers' Gall 1985, New Paintings (Open Eye Gall) 1985, 1995, 1998, 2002 and 2003, Galerija Fakulteta Likovnih Umetnosti 1987, From the Edge (tour) 1990, New Paintings from China (Open Eye Gall) 1991, Christopher Hull Gall 1992, Far East – New Paintings from China and Japan (Open Eye Gall) 1993, 9 Translations from the Chinese 1994, Open Eye Gall 2000, 2003, 2005, 2007 and 2012, Bohun Gallery Henley on Thames 2009 and 2011, Open Eye Gall 2015, Scottish Arts Club 2015; *Group Exhibitions* Marjorie Parr Gall 1968 and 1971, Edinburgh Int Festival 1968, Pernod Exhbn 1968, Scottish Graphics (57 Gall) 1971, Int Graphics (Carnegie Festival) 1971, Richard Demarco Gall 1972, Goosewell Gall 1972, McLellan Galls 1974, Mall Gall 1974, Among the Quiet Weavers (Weavers' Workshop) 1974, 20 x 57 Exhbn (57 Gall) 1975, Compass Gall 1975 and 1981, Young Scottish Artists (Scottish Gall) 1976, Scottish Print Open (Scottish Arts Cncl) 1976, New Prints (Printmakers' Workshop) 1976, Alamo Gall 1978, Scottish Gall 1978, Photo-Graphic (Printmakers' Workshop) 1979, Contemporary Papermakers (City Art Centre Edinburgh) 1980, UCF Gall 1981, Print Annual 2 (PMW) 1981, NY Festival City Gall 1983, Open Eye Gall 1983 and 1986, Mercury Gall 1983, 1984 and 1986, Sue Rankin Gall 1984 and 1987, Fine Art Soc 1984 and 1985, Nicholson Gall 1986, Charter House Gall 1986, Christopher Hull Gall 1987 and 1990, Smiths Galls 1987, Sarajevo Winter Festival 1988, Graphica Creativa 90 (Alvar Aalto Museum) 1990, One Hundred Years of Scottish Printmakers (Hunterian Museum) 1990, Bohun Gall 1990, Images of the Orient (Kingfisher Gall) 1990, Cormund Gall 1990, Gall 41 1992, RSW (annually) 1992–, RSA (annually) 1992–, Open Eye Gall (annually) 1992–, Loomshop Gall 1993, Thompsons Gall 2003, Bohun Gall Henley 2009, 2010 and 2016, Billcliffe Gall Glasgow 2016; *Works in Collections* V&A, Nat Library of Scotland, Hunterian Museum, Scottish Arts Cncl, BBC, Nuffield Fndn, Miro Fndn Mallorca, Sharjah Gall of Fine Art UAE, Univ of Central Florida, Dubai Racing Club, Univ of Edinburgh; *Awards* Latimer Award RSA 1970, Guthrie Award RSA 1973, Gillies prize RSA 1982, May Marshall Brown Award RSW 1983, Gillies Award RSA 2003, RSW/Scottish Arts Club 2007 and 2013, Charles Rennie Mackintosh Residency 2014; *Recreations* fiddling, pottering, travelling; *Style*— George Donald, Esq, RSA; ✉ e-mail g.donald@surfree.co.uk, website www.georgedonald.com

DONALD, Howard Paul; *b* 28 April 1968, Droylsden, Manchester; *Children* 2 da (Grace b 1999, Lola b 2005); *Career* singer and songwriter; memb Take That 1990–96 and 2006–; *Albums* Take That and Party 1992, Everything Changes 1993, Nobody Else 1995, Greatest Hits 1996, Never Forget: The Ultimate Collection 2005, Beautiful World 2006, The Circus 2008, Progress 2010; *Singles* Do What You Like 1991, Promises 1991, Once You've Tasted Love 1992, It Only Takes a Minute 1992, I Found Heaven 1992, A Million Love Songs 1992, Could It Be Magic 1992, Why Can't I Wake Up With You 1993, Pray 1993 (UK no 1), Relight My Fire 1993 (with Lulu, UK no 1), Babe 1993 (UK no 1), Everything Changes 1994 (UK no 1), Love Ain't Here Anymore 1994, Sure 1994 (UK no 1), Back For Good 1995 (UK no 1), Never Forget 1995 (UK no 1), How Deep Is Your Love 1996 (UK no 1), Patience 2006 (UK no 1), Shine 2007 (UK no 1), I'd Wait For Life 2007, Rule The World 2007, Greatest Day 2008 (UK no 1), Up All Night 2009, Said It All 2009, The Flood 2010, Kidz 2011; *Awards* BRIT Awards: Best Br Single 1993 (for Could It Be Magic), 1994 (for Pray), 1996 (for Back For Good), 2007 (for Patience) and 2008 (for Shine), Best Br Video 1994 (for Pray), Best Br Live Act 2008; MTV Europe Music Awards: Best Group 1994, Best Live Act 1995, Best Br Band 2011; Most Performed Work Ivor Novello Awards 2008 (for Shine), PRS For Music Outstanding Contribution to British Music Ivor Novello Award 2012; *Style*— Mr Howard Donald

DONALD, Hugh Robertson; OBE (1999); s of Robert Donald, of Edinburgh, and Anne Mary, *née* Watt (d 1994); *b* 5 November 1951; *Educ* Melville Coll Edinburgh, Univ of Edinburgh (LLB); *m* 16 Aug 1975, Margaret Grace; 1 s (Euan Christopher b 6 July 1979), 1 da (Morag Elizabeth b 21 July 1981); *Career* slr and mediator; Shepherd & Wedderburn: apprentice 1973–75, slr 1975–77, ptnr 1977–, managing ptnr 1994, chief exec 1995–99, chm 2005–; chm Family Mediation Scotland; WS 1979; *Recreations* walking, gardening, family, church; *Style*— Hugh Donald, Esq; ✉ Shepherd & Wedderburn WS, 1 Exchange Crescent, Conference Square, Edinburgh EH3 8UL (☎ 0131 228 9900, fax 0131 228 1222)

DONALDSON, Craig Francis; s of Frank Donaldson, and Lisa Donaldson, of Sunderland; *b* 25 December 1971, Sunderland; *Educ* Newcastle Royal GS, Univ of Bradford (BSc); *m* 12 Dec 2007, Elizabeth, *née* Gale; 1 s (Bryn b 6 Feb 2008), 1 da (Megan b 25 Jan 2010); *Career* Barclays 1995–2001, HBOS 2001–05, RBS 2005–09, ceo Metro Bank 2009–; dir: The City UK, Banking Standards Bd; *Recreations* football, rugby; *Style*— Craig Donaldson, Esq; ✉ Metro Bank plc, One Southampton Row, London WC1B 5HA (☎ 020 3402 8331, e-mail craig.donaldson@metrobank.plc.uk)

DONALDSON, Prof Iain Malcolm Lane; s of Archibald Thomson Donaldson (d 1981), of Edinburgh, and Milly, *née* Bailey (d 1986); *b* 22 October 1937; *Educ* Fettes, Univ of Edinburgh (MB ChB, BSc), Univ of Oxford (MA, by special resolution); *m* 18 July 1961, Jean Patricia, da of John Patrick Maule, OBE (d 2002), of Edinburgh; 1 s (David b 1971); *Career* jr med and res posts Univ of Edinburgh 1962–69, Anglo-French res scholar Université de Paris 1969–70, res offr Laboratory of Physiology Univ of Oxford 1970–79 (MRC clinical res fell 1970–73), fell and tutor in med St Edmund Hall Oxford 1973–79 (emeritus fell 1979–), prof of zoology Univ of Hull 1979–87, prof of neurophysiology Univ of Edinburgh 1987–2003 (prof emeritus 2003–); hon librarian RCP Edinburgh 2000–; author of papers on physiology of the central nervous system and on the history of medicine; MRCP 1965, FRCPEd 1981 (MRCPEd 1965); *Recreations* studying the past; *Style*— Prof I M L Donaldson; ✉ Royal College of Physicians, 9 Queen Street, Edinburgh EH2 1JQ (e-mail i.m.l.d@ed.ac.uk)

D

DONALDSON, Prof (Charles) Ian Edward; s of Dr William Edward Donaldson, and Elizabeth, *née* Weigall; *b* 6 May 1935, Melbourne; *Educ* Melbourne GS, Univ of Melbourne (BA), Magdalen Coll Oxford (MA); *m* 1, 1962 (m dis 1990), Tamsin Jane Procter; 1 s, 1 da; m 2, 1991, Grazia Maria Therese Gunn; *Career* sr tutor in English Univ of Melbourne 1958; Univ of Oxford: Harmsworth sr scholar Merton Coll 1960–62, fell and lectr in English Wadham Coll 1962–69; CUF lectr in English 1963–69, prof of English ANU Canberra 1969–91, fndn dir Humanities Res Centre ANU 1974–90, regius prof of rhetoric and English literature Univ of Edinburgh 1991–95; Univ of Cambridge: Grace I prof of English 1995–2002, fell King's Coll 1995–2005, chm English Faculty 1999–2001, dir Centre for Research in the Arts, Social Sciences and Humanities 2001–03; dir Humanities Research Centre ANU Canberra 2003–07 (emeritus prof 2007–); visiting appts: Univ of Calif Santa Barbara, Gonville & Caius Coll Cambridge, Cornell Univ, Univ of Melbourne; Syndicate, CUP 1997–2001; professorial fell Sch of Culture and Communication Univ of Melbourne 2007–, fell Trinity Coll Melbourne 2012–; fell Aust Acad of the Humanities (FAHA) 1975 (pres 2008–09), FBA 1987, FRSE 1993; *Books* The World Upside-Down: Comedy from Jonson to Fielding (1970), Ben Jonson: Poems (ed, 1975), The Rapes of Lucretia (1982), Jonson and Shakespeare (ed, 1983), Transformations in Modern European Drama (ed, 1983), Seeing the First Australians (ed with Tamsin Donaldson, 1985), Ben Jonson (ed, 1985), Shaping Lives: Reflections on Biography (jt ed, 1992), Ben Jonson: Selected Poems (ed, 1995), Jonson's Magic Houses (1997), Ben Jonson: A Life (2011), The Cambridge Edition of the Works of Ben Jonson (7 vols, jt gen ed, 2012, enlarged online edns 2014 and 2015), Taking Stock: The Humanities in Australian Life since 1968 (ed with Mark Finnane, 2012); *Clubs* Oxford and Cambridge; *Style*— Emeritus Prof Ian Donaldson, FAHA, FBA, FRSE; ✉ School of Culture and Communication, University of Melbourne, VIC 3010, Australia

DONALDSON, Rt Hon Sir Jeffrey Mark; kt (2016), PC (2007), MP; s of James Alexander Donaldson, and Sarah Anne, *née* Charleton; *b* 7 December 1962; *Educ* Kilkeel HS, Castlereagh Coll Belfast (Dip Electrical Engrg); *m* 26 June 1987, Eleanor Mary Elizabeth, da of late Gilbert Cousins; 2 da (Claire Victoria b 21 Nov 1990, Laura Alexandra b 13 April 1992); *Career* agent to Rt Hon J Enoch Powell, MBE, MP 1983–84, personal asst to Rt Hon James Molyneaux, MP 1984–85, memb NI Assembly 1985–86, ptnr in fin servs/estate agency practice 1986–; MP (UUP until 2003, now DUP) Lagan Valley 1997–, MLA (DUP (elected as UUP)) Lagan Valley 2003–10; Parly spokesman (UUP) trade and industry and defence 1997–2003, currently Parly spokesman (DUP) def and Home Office; memb Select Ctees on: NI 1997–2000, Tport 2000–01 and 2005–, Statutory Instruments and Regulatory Reform 2001–05, Defence 2010–; PM's trade envoy to Egypt 2015–; hon sec Ulster Unionist Cncl 1988–2000 (vice-pres 2000–03), memb Northern Ireland Forum 1996–98; asst grand master Loyal Orange Order 1994–97; alderman Lisburn City Cncl 2005–10; *Recreations* military history, Presbyterian Church, walking, reading, travelling; *Clubs* Ulster Reform; *Style*— The Rt Hon Sir Jeffrey Donaldson, MP; ✉ House of Commons, London SW1A 0AA (☎ 020 7219 3407, fax 020 7219 0696, e-mail jeffrey.donaldson.mp@parliament.uk, Twitter @j_donaldson_mp)

DONALDSON, Prof John Dallas; s of John Donaldson (d 1988), of Elgin, Moray, and Alexandrina Murray Ross, *née* Dallas (d 1985); *b* 11 November 1935; *Educ* Elgin Acad, Univ of Aberdeen (BSc, PhD), Univ of London (DSc); *m* 22 March 1961, Elisabeth Ann, da of George Edmond Forrest, of Eastbourne, E Sussex; 2 da (Claire b 1962, Sarah b 1965), 1 s (Richard b 1969); *Career* asst lectr Univ of Aberdeen 1958–61, chemistry lectr Chelsea Coll London 1961–72, reader in inorganic chemistry Univ of London 1972–80; City Univ: prof of industrial chemistry 1980–90, dir Industrial & Biological Chemistry Res Centre 1988–91; Brunel Univ: head Dept of Chemistry 1990–97, dir Centre for Environmental Research 1991–2005; visiting prof Imperial Coll London 2006–; chm: J D Donaldson Research Ltd 1984–2013, Hopeman Associates Ltd 1991–; dir Cause Action Ltd 2012–; pres WAMITAB 2015–; memb Nat Ctee for Chemistry 1985–89; tstee Zimbabwe Tech Mgmnt Trg Tst 1983–94; Freeman (by redemption) City of London 1982, Master Worshipful Co of Pewterers 2010–11 (Liveryman 1983, memb Ct of Assts 2005); fell Soc of Industrial Chemistry, FRSC 1959, CChem, FRSA 1986, hon fell Chartered Inst of Wastes Mgmnt 2002; *Books* Symmetry & Sterochemistry (with S D Ross, 1972), Cobalt in Batteries (with S J Clark and S M Grimes, 1986), Cobalt in Electronic Technology (with S J Clark and S M Grimes, 1988), Cobalt in Medicine Agriculture and the Environment (with S J Clark and S M Grimes, 2000), Report on the Environmental Benefits of Recycling (with S M Grimes and M G Cebrian-Gomez, 2008); *Clubs* Roehampton; *Style*— Prof John Donaldson; ✉ 21 Orchard Rise, Richmond, Surrey TW10 5BX (☎ 020 8876 6534, e-mail jd.donaldson@btinternet.com); Hopeman Associates Limited, Parknasilla, Farnham, Hampshire GU10 5HH (☎ 07973 148921, fax 01932 411024)

DONALDSON, Julia Catherine; MBE (2011); *b* 1948, London; *Educ* Univ of Bristol; *m* Malcolm; 3 s; *Career* writer; Children's Laureate 2011–13; patron ArtLink Central; *Books* A Squash and a Squeeze (1993), The Gruffalo (1999), Monkey Puzzle (2000), Room on the Broom (2002), The Smartest Giant in Town (2002), Night Monkey, Day Monkey (2002), The Snail and the Whale (2003), Tales from Acorn Wood (2003), The Gruffalo's Child (2004), Wriggle and Roar (2004), The Giants and the Joneses (2004), The Magic Paintbrush (2004), Charlie Cook's Favourite Book (2005), Sharing a Shell (2005), Princess Mirror-Belle (2005), Chocolate Mousse for Greedy Goose (2005), Hippo Has a Hat (2006), The Princess and the Wizard (2006), Rosie's Hat (2006), Follow the Swallow (2007), Tiddler (2007), Tyrannosaurus Drip (2007), One Mole Digging a Hole (2008), Stick Man (2008), Taby McTat (2009), Toddle Waddle (2009), What the Ladybird Heard (2009), The Troll (2009), Zog (2010), Cave Baby (2010), The Highway Rat (2011), Freddie and the Fairy (2011), Jack and the Flumflum Tree (2011), The Rhyming Rabbit (2011), The Singing Mermaid (2012); *Style*— Mrs Julia Donaldson, MBE; ✉ c/o Caroline Sheldon Literary Agency Ltd, 71 Hillgate Place, London W8 7SS

DONALDSON, Hon Michael John Francis; o s of Baron Donaldson of Lymington, PC (Life Peer, d 2005), and Dame (Dorothy) Mary Donaldson, GBE (d 2003); bro of Jenny Williams, *qv*; *b* 16 November 1950, London; *Educ* Stanbridge Earls Sch; *m* 11 Nov 1972, Judith Margaret, da of late Edgar William Somerville, of Garsington, Oxon; 2 s (William Michael Somerville, James John Francis (twins) b 29 Aug 1977); *Career* negotiator Knight Frank & Rutley London 1969–71; dir: Edwood Property Co Ltd 1972–75, Nab Properties Ltd 1972–80, Marquis & Co Chartered Surveyors 1975–; chm Figaro PMA 2006–; Incorporated Soc of Valuers and Auctioneers: chm SW London branch 1982–85, memb Nat Cncl 1985–96; Freeman City of London 1972, memb Ct of Assts Worshipful Co of Cutlers 2001– (Liveryman 1975–2001, Master 2005–06); ASVA, ARVA, FSVA, IRRV 1981–99, MAE 1995, MCIArb 1999 (ACIArb 1973), FRICS 2000; *Recreations* sailing, skiing; *Clubs* Royal Lymington Yacht, City Livery Yacht; *Style*— The Hon Michael Donaldson; ✉ Windlesham, Surrey GU20 6LT (☎ 01344 626909, e-mail donaldson.westwood@btinternet.com); Marquis & Co, Marquis House, 54 Richmond Road, Twickenham, Middlesex TW1 3BE (☎ 020 8891 0222, fax 020 8892 6215, e-mail mjfd@marquisandco.com)

DONALDSON, Prof Sir Simon Kirwan; kt (2012); s of Peter Eden Kirwan Donaldson, and Edith Jane, *née* Stirland; *b* 20 August 1957; *Educ* St Faith's Sch Cambridge, Sevenoaks Sch, Pembroke Coll Cambridge (Sailing blue), Worcester Coll Oxford; *m* (Ana) Nora, *née* Hurtado; 2 s (Andres b 1984, Nicholas b 1993), 1 da (Jane b 1987); *Career* Univ of Oxford: jr res fell All Souls Coll 1983–85, Wallis prof of mathematics 1985–97, prof Stanford Univ 1997–98, prof Imperial Coll London 1998–; Royal Soc research prof 2001–12; Jr Whitehead Prize London Mathematical Soc 1985, Fields Medal Int Congress of Mathematicians 1986, Sir William Hopkins Prize Cambridge Philosophical Soc 1991, Royal Medal Royal Soc 1992, Crafoord Prize Royal Swedish Academy of Sciences 1994, Nemmers Prize Northwestern Univ 2008, Shaw Prize 2009; FRS 1986; *Books* The Geometry of 4-Manifolds (with P B Kronheimer, 1990); *Recreations* sailing; *Style*— Prof Sir Simon Donaldson, FRS; ✉ Department of Mathematics, Imperial College, 180 Queen's Gate, London SW7 2BZ (☎ 020 7594 8559, fax 020 7594 8517, e-mail s.donaldson@imperial.ac.uk)

DONALDSON, Stuart; MP; *b* 1991; *Career* MP (SNP) W Aberdeenshire and Kincardine 2015–; *Style*— Stuart Donaldson, Esq, MP; ✉ House of Commons, London SW1A 0AA

DONCASTER, Archdeacon of; *see:* Fitzharris, Ven Robert Aidan

DONEGAN, Kathleen (Kate); OBE (2014); *b* 1953, Fife; *Educ* Univ of Stirling (BA); *m* Dr Chris Donegan; 2 s; *Career* former memb Scottish Office Home Dept; joined Prison Serv 1977, asst govr HMP Cornton Vale 1977–84, asst govr HMP Barlinnie 1984–87, dep govr HMP Reading 1987–89, govr (resources and services) HMP Glenochil 1989, dep govr HMP Perth 1989–91, head Operational Manpower Planning Unit Scottish Prison Serv HQ 1991–93, dep project mangr Staffing Structure Review (SSR) 1993–94, dep govr HMP Barlinnie 1994–95, HM inspr then dep chief inspr of prisons for Scot 1995–96, govr HMP & YOI Cornton Vale 1996–2001, govr HMP Glenochil 2001–06, govr HMP Perth 2006–10, dep chief inspr of prisons HM Prisons Inspectorate Scotland 2010–; *Recreations* computing, reading; *Style*— Mrs Kate Donegan, OBE

DONNACHIE, Ian Louis; s of late Louis Donnachie, and Dorothy Donnachie; *b* 4 June 1947; *Educ* DLit, DBA, MMS, MHSM, DipHSM, Graduate Prog Hosp Mgmnt Chicago; *m* (m dis); 2 da (Samantha, Elspeth); *Career* chief exec St James's Univ Hosp NHS Tst Leeds 1981–90, chief exec Chelsea and Westminster, Charing Cross and Hammersmith Hosps 1990–94, chief exec Bradford HA 1994–2002, sr vice-pres Nations Healthcare Inc 2003–07; memb HRH The Duke of Edinburgh's Sixth Cwlth Study Conf Australia; dir and memb Bd Martin House Children's Hospice; Hon DLit Univ of Bradford; *Recreations* sculpture, theatre, walking, reading; *Clubs* East India; *Style*— Ian Donnachie, Esq; ✉ Pen-y-Ghent, The Maltings, Langthorpe, York YO51 9GY (☎ 01423 325665, e-mail ianldonnachie@aol.com)

DONNE, His Hon Judge Jeremy Nigel; RD (1994), QC (2003); s of Tom Bevan Donne, of Cardiff, and Shirley Rogers, *née* Pateman; *b* 22 January 1954, Barry, Glamorgan; *Educ* Merthyr County GS, Cyfarthfa HS, Inns of Court Sch of Law; *m* 3 Nov 1984, Caroline Susan, *née* O'Brien-Gore; 2 da (Emma b 1998, Rebecca b 2000); *Career* RNR 1977–94; called to the Bar Middle Temple 1978 (bencher 2011); in practice Queen Elizabeth Building Hollis Whiteman 1980–2012, asst recorder 1998, recorder 2000, circuit judge (South Eastern Circuit) 2012–; govr All Saints Primary Sch Putney 2005–10 (chair 2008–10); memb: Justice, Br Acad for Forensic Science (Exec Cncl 2013–, treas 2015–); *Recreations* sailing, skiing, cycling; *Clubs* RNVR Yacht (Cdre 2006–08), Royal Thames Yacht; *Style*— His Hon Judge Donne, RD, QC; ✉ Inner London Sessions House, Newington Causeway, London SE1 6AZ (e-mail hhj.jeremy.donne.qc@ejudiciary.net)

DONNELLAN, Declan Michael Dominic Martin; *b* 4 August 1953; *Career* called to the Bar Middle Temple 1978; artistic dir Cheek By Jowl Theatre Co 1981–, assoc dir RNT 1989–97, first dir RSC Acad Stratford-upon-Avon; awards in Paris, London, Moscow and NY; Chevalier de l'Ordre des Arts et des Lettres; *Productions* for Cheek By Jowl Theatre Co incl: Twelfth Night 1987, Lady Betty 1989, As You Like It 1992 and 1995, Measure for Measure 1994, The Duchess of Malfi 1996, Much Ado About Nothing 1998, Othello 2004, The Changeling 2006, Cymbeline 2007, Troilus and Cressida 2008, Macbeth 2009 and 2011, 'Tis Pity She's A Whore 2011, 2012 and 2014, Ubu Roi 2013, Measure For Measure 2014; for RNT: Fuente Ovejuna 1989, Peer Gynt 1990, Angels in America Part 1 Millennium 1991 and Part 2 Perestroika 1993, Sweeney Todd 1992, The Mandate 2004; for RSC: The School for Scandal 1998, King Lear 2002, Great Expectations 2005; for Russian Theatre Confedn: Boris Godunov 2000, Twelfth Night 2003, Three Sisters 2005, The Tempest 2010; other prodns incl: The Winter's Tale (Maly Theatre St Petersburg) 1997, Le Cid (Avignon Festival) 1998, Falstaff (Salzburg Festival) 2001, Homebody/Kabul (NY Theatre Workshop) 2001, Romeo and Juliet (Bolshoi Ballet Moscow) 2003, Andromaque (Bouffes du Nord) 2007; *Film* Bel Ami 2012; *Publications* incl The Actor and the Target (2000, 2 edn 2005, translated into 15 languages); *Style*— Declan Donnellan, Esq; ✉ c/o Cheek by Jowl Theatre Company, Stage Door, The Barbican, Silk Street, London EC2Y 8DS

DONNELLY, Sir (Joseph) Brian; KBE (2003), CMG (1998); s of Joseph Donnelly (d 1986), and Ada Agnes, *née* Bowness (d 1971); *b* Workington, Cumbria; *Educ* Workington GS, The Queen's Coll Oxford (Wyndham scholar, MA, ed Cherwell), Univ of Wisconsin (MA); *m* 1, 20 Aug 1966 (m dis 1994), Susanne Gibb; 1 da (Kathryn Charlotte b 27 Oct 1970); m 2, 6 Nov 1997, Julia Mary Newsome; 1 step da (Alexandra Petch b 5 Sept 1977), 1 step s (Andrew Petch b 23 July 1980); *Career* GCHQ 1970–73; joined HM Dip Serv 1973, second sec FCO 1973–75, first sec (Economic and Social Cncl (ECOSOC)) UKMIS NY 1975–79, first sec and head of Chancery Singapore 1979–82, asst head Personnel Policy Dept FCO 1982–84, dep to chief scientific advsr Cabinet Office 1984–87, cnsllr and consul-gen Athens 1988–90, RCDS 1991, head Non-Proliferation Dept FCO 1992–95, min and dep perm rep UK Delgn to NATO and WEU Brussels 1995–97, ambass to Serbia and Montenegro 1997–99, dir FCO 1999–2000, on secondment to Standard Chartered Bank and BP (Southern Africa) 2000–01, high cmmr to Zimbabwe 2001–03, ambass to Zimbabwe 2003–04, ret; special advsr to Sec of State for Foreign and Cwlth Affrs 2005–06, visiting dir staff Royal Coll of Defence Studies 2006–08; memb Cwlth Scholarships Cmmn 2006–12; Evelyn Wrench lectr English Speaking Union USA 2008–; memb Shadow Bd Roman Maryport Ltd 2011–13, memb Special Immigrtion Appeals Commission 2012–15; tstee: Keswick Sch 2010–11, Cumberland Community Fndn 2010–13; hon fell Queen's Coll Oxford 2015–; *Recreations* golf, reading, kite flying, watching sport; *Clubs* Royal Cwlth Soc, Maryport Golf; *Style*— Sir Brian Donnelly, KBE, CMG

DONNELLY, Declan; OBE (2016); *b* 25 September 1975, Newcastle upon Tyne; *m* 2015, Alison Astall; *Career* actor and presenter; performed with Ant McPartlin, *qv*, as 'Ant & Dec' since 1993; jt winner (with Ant McPartlin): Best Double Act Carling Loaded Awards 2000, People's Choice Comedy Awards 2000, Entertainment Personality of the Year Nat TV Awards 2001, TV Personality of the Year Variety Club Awards 2002, TV Personality of the Year TRIC Awards 2002, 2013, 2014, Special Recognition Award Nat TV Awards 2002, Best Entertainment Presenter Nat TV Awards 2001–08 and 2010–15, Most Popular Entertainment Presenter TV Choice Awards 2003, TV Personality Award GQ 2003 and 2004, Best Comedy Duo Loaded Awards 2003, Outstanding Contribution Award TV Choice Awards 2009, Most Popular Entertainment Presenters BAFTA 2010, Best Entertainment Performance RTS Award 2005 & 2011, Landmark Award: 25 Years in TV Nat TV Awards 2014, Best Entertainment Presenters Nat TV Awards 2014, Personality of the Year FreeSat Free TV Award 2012–14, UK TV Legends Nickelodeon Kid's Choice Award 2015; *Television* as actor incl: Byker Grove (as Duncan) 1989–93, A Tribute to the Likely Lads 2002; as presenter incl: The Ant & Dec Show 1995 (BAFTA, RTS Award), Ant and Dec Unzipped 1997 (BAFTA), SM:TV Live 1998–2001 (Best Entertainment Prog Children's BAFTAs 2000, Best Children's Show TV Quick Awards 2000 and 2001, Best Children's Entertainment Prog RTS Awards 2000, Best Children's Prog Broadcast Awards 2001, Best Children's Prog Indie Awards 2001, Best Presenters RTS Awards 2001, Kids Award Disney Channel 2001, TV Presenters of the Year RTS Awards 2002), CD:UK 1998–2001 (Best Teen Show TV Hits Awards 2000), Ant and Dec's Secret Camera Show 2000, Friends Like These 2000 (Bronze Rose Montreux Awards 2000), Slap Bang with Ant and Dec 2001, Pop Idol 2001 (Entertainment Prog of the Year TRIC Awards 2002, Best Entertainment Prog BAFTA Awards 2002, Golden Rose Montreaux Awards 2002, Best Entertainment Prog Nat TV Awards 2002), Brit Awards 2001, Party in the Park 2001, Comic Relief: Say Pants to Poverty 2001, Record of the Year 2001 and 2002, Ant & Dec's Saturday Night Takeaway 2002– (Best Entertainment Prog TV Choice Awards 2003, 2004, 2007, 2008, 2009, 2010, 2013, 2014, Best Entertainment Prog Nat TV Awards 2003 and 2004, People's Choice and Best Comedy Entertainment Performance Comedy Awards 2003, Best Comedy Entertainment Performance and Best Comedy Entertainment Prog Comedy Awards 2004, Best Entertainment Presenter RTS Awards 2005, Best Entertainment Prog Broadcast Awards 2006, Best Prog Nat TV Awards 2010, Best Entertainment Prog Broadcast Awards 2006, 2014, 2015, Entertainment Prog Br Acad TV Award 2014, Entertainment Performance Br Acad TV Award 2014, BAFTA TV Craft Award Entertainment Craft Awards 2014, Best Live TV Prog or Series FreeSat Free TV Award 2014), Best Entertainment Performance 2014 & 2015 and Best Entertainment Programme BAFTA Television Awards 2010, 2014, 2015, I'm a Celebrity, Get Me Out of Here! 2002– (Best Reality Prog TV Choice Awards 2003, 2004, 2012, 2013, 2014, Lew Grade Award for Entertainment Prog or Series BAFTA Television Award 2005, Best Entertainment Performance BAFTA Television Award 2010, Best Entertainment Performance RTS Award 2011 and 2013, Best Reality TV Nat TV Award 2007 & 2012, TRIC Special Award, Tric Awards 2013, Best Entertainment Prog Nat TV Award 2011–2015), Pride of Britain Awards 2003, Comic Relief: The Big Hair Do 2003, World Idol 2003, British Comedy Awards 2003 and 2004, Comic Relief: Red Nose Night Live 2005, Game Show Marathon 2005 (Most Popular Quiz Prog NTA Awards 2006), Soccer Aid 2006, All-Star Cup 2006, Pokerface 2006–07, Britain's Got Talent 2007– (Favourite Funny Person, Favourite TV Presenter and Favourite Family TV Show Nickelodeon Kids Choice Awards UK 2008), Best Talent Show TV Choice Awards 2009, 2011, 2013, 2014, Wanna Bet 2008, Push The Button 2010 & 2011, Red or Black 2011 & 2012; *Films* incl Love Actually 2003, Alien Autopsy 2006; *Albums* with Ant McPartlin: Psyche 1994, Top Katz 1995, The Cult of Ant & Dec 1997; *Style*— Declan Donnelly, OBE; ✉ c/o James Grant Media Ltd, 94 Strand On The Green, Chiswick, London W4 3NN

DONNELLY, Sir Martin Eugene; KCB (2016), CMG (2002); s of Eugene Donnelly, and Mary Ormsby; *b* 4 June 1958, Newbury; *Educ* St Ignatius Coll, Campion Hall Oxford (BA), Coll of Europe Bruges (Dip Euro Studies), Ecole Nationale d'Administration Paris; *Children* 3 da; *Career* HM Treasury: admin trainee Public Enterprises Div 1980–81, External Fin Div 1981–82, private sec to Fin Sec to the Treasury 1982–83, seconded to Ecole Nationale d'Administration Paris 1983–84, princ European Community Gp 1984–87, private sec to Sec of State on secondment to NI Office (London) 1988–89, at Cabinet of Cmmn EC Brussels 1989–92, head of Defence Team 1993–95, seconded to French Trésor Monetary Affrs and Govt Debt Bureau 1995–96, head of Treasury Econ and Monetary Union Div 1997–98; dep head Cabinet Office European Secretariat 1998–2003, dep DG (policy) Immigration and Nationality Dept Home Office 2003–04, DG (europe and globalisation) FCO 2004–10, sr ptnr Ofcom 2008–09 (on secondment), acting perm sec FCO 2010, perm sec Dept for Business, Innovation and Skills 2010–; *Recreations* family, reading, hill walking, music; *Clubs* Athenaeum; *Style*— Sir Martin Donnelly, KCB, CMG

DONNELLY, Prof Peter Duncan; s of Dr James Duncan Donnelly, and Gwyneth Donnelly; *b* 27 January 1963; *Educ* Univ of Edinburgh (MB ChB, MD), DA (RCS Eng), Univ of Stirling (MBA), Univ of Wales Coll of Med (MPH), Harvard Univ (PMD); *m* Joan; 3 s; *Career* jr hosp dr positions 1985–88, NHS MDG scholar Stirling MBA Prog 1988–89; South Glamorgan HA: registrar 1989–90, sr registrar 1990–92, conslt in public health med 1992–93, actg dir of planning and procurement 1993–94, dep chief admin MO/dep dir of public health med 1994–96; dir of public health and exec memb Bd Morgannwg HA 1996–2000; dir Public Health and Health Policy Lothian Health Bd 2000–04, dep chief medical offr Scottish Government 2004–08, hon conslt PHM NHS Fife 2008–; sr lectr in public health med Univ of Wales Coll of Med 1992–96 (lectr 1989–92), prof of public health medicine Univ of St Andrews 2008–14, pres and ceo Public Health Ontario 2014–; pres Assoc of Dirs of Public Health 1999–2001, vice-pres Faculty of Public Health Med RCP 2001–04 (treas 1999–2001); hon sr lectr in public health med Univ of Wales Coll of Med and Univ of Wales Swansea 1996–2000, hon prof of public health Univ of Edinburgh 2002–11, hon prof Med Sch Univ of St Andrews 2014–, status prof Dalla Lana Sch of Public Health Univ of Toronto 2015–, adjunct prof Queen's Univ 2015–; Hon DSc Napier Univ; FFPH, FRCP, FRCPE; *Publications* The Oxford Textbook of Violence Prevention (co-ed), author of scientific articles on public health; *Recreations* skiing, keeping fit, cooking, reading; *Style*— Prof Peter D Donnelly, MD; ✉ Public Health Ontario, 480 University Avenue, Suite 300, Toronto ON M5G1V2

DONNELLY, Prof Peter James; s of Augustine Stanislaus Donnelly, of Brisbane, Aust, and Sheila Bernadette, *née* O'Hagan; *b* 15 May 1959; *Educ* St Joseph's Coll Brisbane, Univ of Queensland (BSc), Balliol Coll Oxford (Rhodes scholar, DPhil); *m* 28 June 1986 (m dis 2006), Sarah Helen, da of Robert John Harper; 2 da (Imogen Clare b 1990, Caroline Emma b 1996), 1 s (Giles James b 1993); 1 da (Keira b 2007) by Kerstin Sallows; *Career* research fell UC Swansea 1984–85, lectr UCL 1985–88, prof of mathematical statistics and operational research Queen Mary & Westfield Coll London 1988–94, prof of statistics and ecology and evolution Univ of Chicago 1994–96; Univ of Oxford: head Dept of Statistics 1996–2001, prof of statistical science 1996–, fell St Anne's Coll, hon fell Balliol Coll 2013; visiting asst prof Univ of Michigan 1983–84; dir Wellcome Tst Centre for Human Genetics 2007–; Mitchell Prize 2002, Guy Medal in Silver RSS 2004, Weldon Memorial Prize 2009; memb: Int Statistical Inst, RSS, EMBO 2014; FIMS, Hon FIA, FRS 2006, fell Acad of Medical Sciences 2008; FRS, FMed Sci; *Publications* author of many articles in academic jls; *Recreations* sport, music, children; *Clubs* Tattersall's; *Style*— Prof Peter Donnelly, FRS, FMedSci; ✉ Wellcome Trust Centre for Human Genetics, Roosevelt Drive, Oxford OX3 7BN (☎ 01865 287725, e-mail directorpa@well.ox.ac.uk)

DONNELLY, Roisin Jane Catherine; da of Thomas John Donnelly, of Glasgow, and Catherine Joyce, *née* Doherty; *b* 17 June 1961, Paisley; *Educ* Notre Dame HS Glasgow, Univ of Glasgow (MA); *m* 29 April 1995, Robert George Hughes; 3 da (Lorna Catherine b 22 Oct 1996, Cordelia Georgia b 18 May 1999, Juliet Aurora b 13 Feb 2001), 1 s (Angus John b 24 March 1998 d 1998); *Career* Procter & Gamble: mktg dir cosmetics and fragrances UK 1992–94, mktg dir cosmetics and male toiletries Western Europe, Eastern Europe, ME and Africa 1994–96, mktg dir fine fragrance Western Hemisphere (USA and S America) 1996–98, corp mktg dir and head of mktg UK and Ireland 1998–; chm Cosmetic Exec Women, memb Marketing Gp of GB, memb WACL, memb Cncl ASA;

fell Marketing Soc; *Style—* Ms Roisin Donnelly; ✉ Procter & Gamble, The Heights, Brooklands, Surrey KT13 0XP (☎ 01932 896500, fax 01932 896554, mobile 07787 105607, e-mail donnelly.rj@pg.com)

DONOGHUE, Barbara Joan; *b* 16 July 1951, Canada; *Educ* McGill Univ Canada (Ontario scholar, Univ scholar, Govt of Canada fell, BCom, MBA); *m* 1976, late Stefanos Vavalidis; 2 s (Alexander Charles b 27 Nov 1984, Philip Zacharias b 8 May 1989); *Career* Canadian Pacific Ltd 1973–77, Bank of Nova Scotia 1977–79, vice-pres int and corporate banking Bankers Tst Co 1979–93, md Hawkpoint Ptnrs and Natwest Markets 1994–98; ptnr Manzanita Capital 2007–; non-exec dir and chm Audit Ctee Eniro AB 2003–11; chair Co-regulatory Design Gp Office of Communications 2005; chm Byredo AB 2013–; memb: ITC 1999–2003, London Business Sch 1999– (teaching fell Strategic and Int Mgmnt Faculty 1999–2004), Competition Cmmn 2005–14, Competition and Markets Authy 2014–15; tstee Refuge 2008–; *Recreations* learning Greek; *Clubs* Hurlingham; *Style—* Barbara Donoghue; ✉ e-mail barbara.donoghue@btinternet.com

DONOGHUE, Dr Emma; da of Denis Donoghue, and Frances, *née* Rutledge; *b* 1969, Dublin; *Educ* Muckross Park Convent Sch Dublin, UCD (BA), Univ of Cambridge (PhD); *Partner* Dr Chris Roulston; 1 s (Finn Roulston b 2003), 1 da (Una Roulston b 2007); *Career* writer; *Publications* Passions Between Women: British Lesbian Culture 1668–1801 (1993), What Sappho Would Have Said: Four Centuries of Love Poems between Women (ed, 1997), We Are Michael Field (1998), The Mammoth Book of Lesbian Short Stories (ed, 1999), Inseparable: Desire Between Women In Literature (2010); fiction: Stir-Fry (1994), Hood (1995, winner American Library Assoc Gay, Lesbian and Bisexual Book Award 1997), Kissing the Witch (linked fairytales, 1997), Slammerkin (2000, Ferro-Grumley Award for Lesbian Fiction 2002), The Woman Who Gave Birth to Rabbits (stories, 2002), Life Mask (2004), Touchy Subjects (stories, 2006), Landing (2007), The Sealed Letter (2008, jt winner Lambda Award for Lesbian Fiction 2009), Room (2010, Cwlth Fiction Prize (Canada/Caribbean), Rogers Writers' Tst Fiction Prize, Hughes & Hughes Irish Novel of the Year, W H Smith Paperback of the Year), Astray (stories, 2012), Frog Music (2014); stage plays: I Know My Own Heart (Dublin, Glasshouse, 1993), Ladies and Gentlemen (Dublin, Glasshouse, 1996), Kissing the Witch (San Francisco Magic Theatre, 2000), The Talk of the Town (Dublin Theatre Festival, Hatch, Landmark) 2012; screenplays: Room (2015, Film Independent Spirit Award for First Screenplay, Evening Standard British Film Award for Best Screenplay, Canadian Screen Award for Best Adapted Screenplay); radio plays: Trespasses (RTE Radio, 1996), Don't Die Wondering (BBC Radio 4, 2000), Exes (BBC Radio 4, 2001), Humans and Other Animals (BBC Radio 4, 2003), Mix (BBC Radio 3, 2003); *Style—* Emma Donoghue; ✉ c/o Caroline Davidson Literary Agency, 5 Queen Anne's Gardens, London W4 1TU (☎ 020 8995 5768, 020 8994 2770, e-mail emma@emmadonoghue.com, website www.emmadonoghue.com)

DONOHOE, Brian; s of George Donohoe, and Catherine Donohoe; *b* 10 September 1948; *Educ* Irvine Royal Acad, Kilmarnock Tech Coll; *m* 16 July 1973, Christine, da of Raymond Pawson; 2 s; *Career* draughtsman Ailsa Shipyard 1970–77 (engrg apprentice 1965–70), Hunterston Nuclear Power Station 1977, draughtsman ICI Organics Div 1977–81; convener Political and Educn Ctee TASS 1969–81, sec Irvine Trades Cncl 1973–82, chm Cunninghame Industrial Devpt Ctee 1975–85, dist offr NALGO 1981–92, treas Cunninghame S Constituency Lab Pty 1983–91; MP (Lab) Cunninghame S 1992–2015; sec All-Pty Parly Gardening & Horticultural Gp 1994–, sec All-Pty Parly Scotch Whisky Gp 1996–, hon sec Br-American Parly Gp 2002–, chm PLP Transport Ctee 2004–, jt chm All-Pty Parly Gp against Fluoridation 2005– (vice-chm 1996–2005), PPS to Lord Adonis (as Sec of State for Transport), chm All Party Aviation Gp 2009–; memb: Tport Select Ctee 1993–97 and 2002–05, Environment, Tport and the Regions Select Ctee 1997–2002; tstee Thrive 2003–12 (chm 2010–12); *Recreations* gardening; *Style—* Brian H Donohoe, Esq; ✉ House of Commons, London SW1A 0AA (☎ 020 7219 6230, constituency 01294 276844, mobile 07774 646 600, pager 07644 066 100)

DONOUGHUE, Baron (Life Peer UK 1985), of Ashton in the County of Northamptonshire; Bernard Donoughue; s of Thomas Joseph Donoughue and Maud Violet, *née* Andrews; *b* 8 September 1934; *Educ* Northampton GS, Lincoln Coll Oxford (BA), Harvard Univ, Nuffield Coll Oxford (MA, DPhil); *m* 1, 1959 (m dis 1990), Carol Ruth, da of late Abraham Goodman; 2 da (Hon Rachel Anne b 1965, Hon Kate Miriam b 1967), 2 s (Hon Paul Michael David b 1969, Hon Stephen Joel b 1969); m 2, 2009, Hon Sarah Ann, w of Hon Sir Anthony George Berry, MP; *Career* lectr, sr lectr, reader LSE 1963–74, sr policy advsr to PM 1974–79, devpt dir Economist Intelligence Unit 1979–81, asst ed The Times 1981–82, head of res and investment policy Grieveson Grant & Co 1984–86 (ptnr 1983), dir Kleinwort Benson Securities 1986–88, exec vice-chm LBI 1988–91; oppn House of Lords spokesman on Treasy matters and energy 1991–92, on National Heritage 1993–97; Parly sec MAFF (min for Farming and Food) 1997–99; visiting prof in govt LSE 2003–04; sec All Pty Parly Gp on Racing and Bloodstock, chm Starting Price Regulatory Cmmn 2004–, chm Future Funding of Horseracing Gp 2005–06, chm Review of Regulation of Greyhound Racing 2007; memb: Advsy Bd Wissenschaftszentrum Berlin 1978–90, London Arts Bd 1991–97, Cncl LSE, Cncl LSO, Int League for the Protection of Horses (ILPH); hon fell: Lincoln Coll Oxford, LSE, Northampton Univ; Hon LLD Univ of Leicester; FRHistS; *Books* Trade Unions in a Changing Society (1963), British Politics and the American Revolution (1964), The People into Parliament (with W T Rogers, 1966), Herbert Morrison: Portrait of a Politician (with G W Jones, 1973), Prime Minister (1987), The Heat of the Kitchen (2003), Downing Street Diaries Vol 1 (2005) and Vol 2 (2008), Westminster Diaries, Reluctant Ministers Under Blair (2016); *Clubs* Pratt's; *Style—* The Rt Hon the Lord Donoughue; ✉ House of Lords, London SW1A 0PW

DONOVAN, Ian Alexander; s of Ivar Kirkwood Donovan (d 1983), and Marion Sutherland, *née* Esslemont (d 1995); *b* 19 December 1945; *Educ* Malvern Coll, Univ of Birmingham (MB ChB, MD); *m* 3 May 1975, Rosamund Mary, da of Reginald Vickors, of Worcs; 2 da (Amy b 1980, Lorna b 1982), 1 s (Robert b 1985); *Career* sr lectr in surgery Univ of Birmingham 1979–87, conslt surgn W Midlands RHA 1987–; memb: Cncl Assoc of Surgns GB and Ireland, Advsy Ctee Admin of Radioactive Substances DHSS, Ct of Examiners Royal Coll of Surgns of Eng, Intercollegiate Bd of Examiners in Gen Surgery; hon sec and pres W Midland Surgns Soc, RCS regnl advsr W Midlands Region; FRCS; *Recreations* photography, family, painting; *Clubs* East India; *Style—* Ian Donovan, Esq; ✉ 57 Birmingham Road, Hagley, Worcestershire DY9 9JY (☎ 01562 884625)

DONOVAN, Judith; CBE (1997); da of Ernest Nicholson, of Bradford, W Yorks, and Joyce, *née* Finding; *b* 5 July 1951; *Educ* St Joseph's Coll Bradford, Woking Girls' GS, Univ of Hull (BA); *m* 12 Nov 1977, John Patrick Donovan, s of William Donovan, of Darlington; *Career* mktg trainee Ford Motor Co 1973–75, account mangr J Walter Thomson 1976, advertising mangr Grattan 1977–82, chm JDA (formerly Judith Donovan Associates) 1982–2000, chm DIY Direct Marketing 2001–; pres Bradford Jr C of C 1980, pres Bradford C of C 1999–2001 (memb Cncl 1998–2003); chm: Bradford Business Club 1985, Bradford TEC 1990–98, Millennium Cmmn 2000–06, Direct Mktg Assoc 1999–2001 (dir 1991–), Health and Safety Cmmn 2000–08 (non-exec dir HSE 2008–10), Northern Postwatch 2001–08, Yorks Tourist Bd 2005–08, Ripon City Partnership 2009–13; chair Eden Project Ltd 2013–; non-exec dir Br Wool Mktg Bd 2009–15, non-exec dir YM Gp 2013–15; chair Project Bd York Minster Revealed 2009–11, chair Ripon Cathedral Cncl 2016–26; memb: Fin Bd Ripon Cathedral 2006–16, UK Bd Big Lottery Fund 2007–11; public memb Network Rail 2011–15, lay memb Lord Chllr Advsy Ctee N Yorks 2012–18, sec of state memb Yorks Dales Nat Park Authy 2012–20; ambass Diversity in Public Appointments 2010; ed-in-chief Direct Marketing Strategies 1999–2001; dir: Northern Ballet Theatre 1990–2008, Business Link W Yorks 2000–03; pres Bradford Samaritans 1999–2002, govr Friends of Bradford Art Galleries & Museums 1984–89, govr Legacy Tst, tstee Yorkshire Dales Millennium Tst 2003–05, fndr patron Women Mean Business, patron Small Business Bureau, memb Int Women's Forum (IWF, formerly Forum), chair Keep Me Posted Campaign, tstee Univ of Hull Union; Freeman City of London, Liveryman Worshipful Co of Marketors 1999, Liveryman Worshipful Co of Woolmen 2010, Fndr Freeman Guild of Entrepreneurs; Hon DUniv Leeds Met Univ 2003, Hon DLitt Univ of Hull 2009; MInstM 1977, MCIM 1978, MCAM 1979, memb Mktg Soc 1987, CIMgt, FRSA 1995, FCAM, FCIM, FInstD (MInstD 1983), FIDM 2001; *Recreations* reading, the Western Front, pets; *Clubs* Reform; *Style—* Mrs Judith Donovan, CBE; ✉ Biggin Grange, Kirkby Malzeard, Ripon, North Yorkshire HG4 3QG; DIY Direct Marketing, Biggin Barns, Ringbeck, Kirkby Malzeard, Ripon, North Yorkshire HG4 3TT (☎ 01765 650000, fax 01765 650153, e-mail judith@diydirectmarketing.co.uk)

D

DONOVAN, Michael John (Mike); *b* 11 May 1953; *m* Helen; 2 s (Adam, Ross); *Career* product validation engr rising to project ops manager Land Rover Ltd 1976–87, project dir Land Rover Discovery 1988–89, dir mfrg planning Rover Gp 1989–90, regnl dir Rover Cars 1990–91, dir of strategic planning and new progs then md (commercial) Rolls-Royce Motor Cars 1991, with Vickers plc 1991–94; British Aerospace plc: chief exec Avro Int Aerospace 1994–96, chief exec BAe Regnl Aircraft 1996–97, pres Aero Int Asia 1997, gp md defence systems 1997–98; chief exec Marconi Systems and Marconi Capital 1998–2001, chief operating offr Marconi Gp plc 2001–04 (dir 2000); non-exec dir Balfour Beatty plc 2006–; *Style—* Mike Donovan, Esq

DONOVAN, Paul James Kingsley; s of Brian Donovan (d 1992), of Croydon, Surrey, and Enid Constance, *née* Shaylor (d 1992); *b* 8 April 1949; *Educ* Queen Elizabeth's GS Barnet, Oriel Coll Oxford (MA); *m* 27 Oct 1979, Hazel Margaret, da of William Hubert Case (d 1987), of Kenya; 1 s (Toby b 1981), 2 da (Emily b 1987, Mary b 1989); *Career* journalist and writer; trainee Mirror Group Newspapers 1970–73, night news ed and reporter Sunday Mirror 1973–78, reporter, showbusiness writer and critic Daily Mail 1978–85, showbusiness ed, TV critic and media corr Today 1986–88; self-employed 1988–; TV previewer Hello! 1988–2001; radio columnist Sunday Times 1988–, community corr North Devon Jl 2011–, contrib Oxford Dictionary of National Biography; memb: Devonshire Assoc, Devon Wildlife Trust, Oxford Alumni; *Books* Roger Moore (1983), Dudley (1988), The Radio Companion (1991), All Our Todays (1997); *Recreations* wildlife, Devon, walking; *Style—* Paul Donovan, Esq; ✉ Courtiford, Dolton, Winkleigh, Devon EX19 8RE (☎ 01805 804402, e-mail pauldon@scribbler.freeserve.co.uk)

DONOVAN, Prof Emeritus Robert John; OBE (2007); s of Francis Alexander Donovan (d 1991), of Sandbach, Cheshire, and Ida, *née* Brooks (d 2002); *b* 13 July 1941; *Educ* Sandbach Sch, UCW (BSc), Univ of Cambridge (PhD); *Children* 1 da (Jane Frances); *Career* res fell Gonville & Caius Coll Cambridge 1966–70; Univ of Edinburgh: lectr in physical chemistry 1970, reader 1974, appointed to personal chair of physical chemistry 1979, head Dept of Chemistry 1984–87 and 1995–97, chair of chemistry 1986–2006, sr hon professorial fell 2006–; visiting scientist Max-Planck Inst für Strömungsforshung Göttingen 1975, JSPS sr visiting fell Inst of Molecular Sci Okazaki Japan 1982 (visiting fell 1983 and 1989), visiting fell Aust Nat Univ Canberra 1993, Erskine fell Univ of Christchurch NZ 2001, visiting prof Tokyo Inst of Technol Japan 2005; SERC: chm Laser Facility Ctee 1988–92, chm Facilities Cmmn 1993–95; memb CCLRC (Cncl for the Central Lab of the Research Cncls) 2004–07, dir of synchotrons and free-electron laser science CCLRC/STFC 2006–09, memb Cncl European Synchotron Radiation Facility 2006–13; Hon DSc Univ of Edinburgh; FRSE 1976 (vice-pres 1998–2001), FRSC 1980; *Publications* incl Laser Chemistry (2007); *Recreations* skiing, hill walking, travel, reading, gardening; *Style—* Prof Emeritus Robert Donovan,OBE, FRSE; ✉ School of Chemistry, The University of Edinburgh, West Mains Road, Edinburgh EH9 3FJ

DORAN, Frank; s of Francis Doran, and Betty, *née* Hedges; *b* 13 April 1949; *Educ* Leith Acad, Univ of Dundee (LLB); *m* 1, 1967 (m dis), Patricia Ann (Pat), *née* Govan; 2 s (Frank, Adrian); m 2, 18 Sept 2010, Rt Hon Joan Ruddock, MP, *qv*; *Career* admitted slr 1977; MP (Lab): Aberdeen S 1987–92, Aberdeen Central 1997–2005, Aberdeen N 2005–15; shadow spokesman on oil and gas 1988–92, chm House of Commons Admin Ctee 2005–, chm Speaker's Advsy Ctee on Art 2010–, memb House of Commons Cmmn 2010–, sec Trade Union Gp of Lab MPs; fndr memb Scottish Legal Action Gp, fndr memb and former chm Dundee Assoc for Mental Health; *Recreations* cinema, football, art, sport; *Style—* Frank Doran, Esq; ✉ House of Commons, London SW1A 0AA (☎ 020 7219 3000)

DORAN, Gregory; s of John Doran, and Margaret, *née* Freeman; *b* 24 November 1958; *Educ* Univ of Bristol (BA), Bristol Old Vic Theatre Sch; *m* Dec 2005, Sir Antony Sher, KBE, *qv* (civil partnership converted Dec 2015); *Career* theatre dir; RSC: chief assoc dir 1997–2012, artistic dir 2012–; humanitas visiting prof in drama Univ of Oxford 2012–13; hon fell Shakespeare Birthplace Tst, hon sr research fell Shakespeare Inst; Sam Wanamaker Award 2012; delivered Richard Dimbleby Lecture 2016; Hon DLitt: Univ of Nottingham 2011, Univ of Bristol 2011, Univ of Warwick 2013, Univ of Birmingham 2015; *Theatre* RSC prodns incl: The Odyssey 1992, Henry VIII 1996, Cyrano de Bergerac 1997, The Merchant of Venice 1997, The Winter's Tale 1998, Oroonoko 1999 (Best Prodn Emma Awards 2000), Timon of Athens 1999, Macbeth 1999, As You Like It 2000, Jubilee 2001, King John 2001, Much Ado About Nothing 2002, The Island Princess 2002, The Jacobean Season 2003 (Olivier Award for Outstanding Achievement of the Year 2003), The Taming of the Shrew 2003, The Tamer Tamed 2003, All's Well That Ends Well 2003, Othello 2004, Venus and Adonis 2004, A Midsummer Night's Dream 2005 and 2008, Sejanus 2005, The Canterbury Tales 2005, Antony and Cleopatra 2006, Merry Wives: the Musical 2006, Coriolanus 2007, Hamlet 2008, Love's Labours Lost 2008, Morte d'Arthur 2010, Cardenio 2011, Written on the Heart 2011, Julius Caesar 2012, The Orphan of Zhao 2012, Richard II 2013, Henry IV Parts One and Two 2014, The Witch of Edmonton 2014, Death of a Salesman 2015, Henry V 2015, King Lear 2016 (incl Live from Stratford-upon-Avon RSC broadcast), The Tempest 2016; Live from Stratford-upon-Avon RSC broadcasts incl: Richard II 2013, Henry IV Parts One and Two 2014, Henry V 2015, King Lear 2016; other credits incl: Titus Andronicus (Market Theatre Johannesburg and RNT) 1995, The Real Inspector Hound/Black Comedy (Donmar Warehouse Prodns Comedy Theatre) 1998, The York Mystery Plays (York Minster) 2000 (Best Prodn TMA Awards), Merchant of Venice (Tokyo) 2007, The Giant (Hampstead Theatre) 2007, Anjin: The Shogun and the English Samurai (Tokyo and Sadlers Wells) 2012; *Film* Macbeth, Hamlet, Julius Caesar; *Television* A Midsummer Night's Dreaming (BBC4 documentary), Shakespeare Live! from the RSC 2016; *Books* Woza Shakespeare! (with Antony Sher, 1996), The Shakespeare Almanac (2009), Shakespeare's Lost Play: in Search of Cardenio (2011); *Style—* Gregory Doran, Esq; ✉ Royal Shakespeare Company, Royal Shakespeare Theatre, Stratford-upon-Avon, Warwickshire CV37 6BB (☎ 01789 412600, website www.rsc.org.uk)

DORCHESTER, Bishop of 2000–; Rt Rev Colin William Fletcher; OBE (2000); s of Alan Philip Fletcher, and Annette Grace Fletcher; *b* 17 November 1950, London; *Educ* Marlborough, Trinity Coll Oxford, Wycliffe Hall Oxford; *m* 1980, Sarah; 1 s (b 1982), 2 da (b 1984, 1986); *Career* asst curate St Peter Shipley 1975–79, asst curate St Andrew Oxford and tutor Wycliffe Hall Oxford 1979–84, vicar Holy Trinity Margate 1984–93, rural dean Thanet 1988–93, domestic chaplain to the Archbishop of Canterbury 1993–2000; Cross of St Augustine 2009; *Recreations* ornithology, walking, sport; *Style—* The Rt Rev the Bishop of Dorchester; ✉ Church House Oxford, Langford Locks, Kidlington

OX5 1GF (tel 01865 208218, e-mail bishop.dorchester@oxford.anglican.org, website www.oxford.anglican.org)

DORE, Simon Peter George Taylor; s of Peter George Dore, of Hants, and Gillian Helena Read, *née* Martin; *b* 10 October 1961; *m* 4 May 1996, Kate, da of John Ayers; 3 s (William b 14 June 1990, George b 10 Jan 1992, Thomas b 12 Aug 1997), 1 da (Bethany b 14 July 1994); *Career* studio mangr BBC Radio 1987–88, prodr/presenter BBC World Service Radio for Europe 1988–90, sr presentation dir British Satellite Broadcasting Ltd (BSB) 1990–91 (presentation dir 1990), freelance promotions prodr 1991; BBC: asst ed World Service TV 1991–92, ed Worldwide TV 1992–93, managing ed Worldwide TV 1993–95; managing dir BTAS Advsy Ltd 1995–96, dir of broadcasting Granada Sky Broadcasting 1996–98, dir of channel devpt Granada Media 1998–99, chief technol offr ITV Digital 1999–2003, chief technol offr ITV 2001–03, sr vice-pres Technol and Ops Showtime 2003–, chief technol offr Top UpTV 2006–12, chief exec MediaPaedia 2011–12 (chm 2012–), chief technol offr WPSChallenger 2012–14, chief operations offr GoMedia 2015–; chm MediaPaedia Broadcast 2015–; FRSA, FIET; *Clubs* Frontline; *Style—* Simon Dore, Esq; ✉ MediaPaedia Ltd, 11 Castle Hill, Maidenhead, Berkshire SL6 4AA (☎ 0844 854 1376, e-mail simon.dore@mediapaedia.co.uk)

DOREY, HE Gregory John (Greg); CVO (1997); s of Michael Dorey, of Bristol, and Avril, *née* Gregory; *b* 1 May 1956, Stroud, Glos; *Educ* Rendcomb Coll, Exeter Coll Oxford (MA), Open Univ (Cert); *m* 1981, Alison Patricia, *née* Taylor; 2 s (Christopher Guy (Kit) b 7 May 1988, Gabriel Simon b 24 May 1994), 1 da (Johanna Caroline Alice b 14 April 1990); *Career* diplomat; NatWest Bank 1974–77, MoD 1977–81, second sec UK Delgn to NATO 1982–84, MoD 1984–86, FCO 1986–89, first sec Br Embassy Budapest 1989–92, FCO 1992–96, counsellor then dep head of mission Br High Cmmn Islamabad 1996–99, secondment to HSBC 2000, dep head of mission Br Consulate Gen Hong Kong 2000–04, FCO 2005–07, ambass to Hungary 2007–11, ambass to Ethiopia and Djibouti and perm rep to the African Union and UN Economic Cmmn for Africa 2011–15, sr policy coordinator Africa Directorate FCO 2016–; *Recreations* tennis, walking, gardening, literature, theatre, cinema, travel; *Clubs* Athenaeum; *Style—* HE Mr Greg Dorey, CVO; ✉ FCO, King Charles Street, London SW1A 2AH

DORKEN, (Anthony) John; s of Oscar Roy Dorken (d 1996), and Margaret, *née* Barker (d 2011); *b* 24 April 1944; *Educ* Mill Hill Sch, King's Coll Cambridge (MA); *m* 1972, Satanay, da of Fawzi Mufti; 1 da (Marina Charlotte b 1976), 1 s (Adam Alexander b 1981); *Career* VSO Libya 1965–66, asst princ Bd of Trade 1967–71, private sec to Parly under sec of state for Industry 1971–72, princ Dept of Trade and latterly Dept of Energy 1972–77, seconded to Cabinet Office 1977–79, asst sec Dept of Energy 1980–86, seconded to Shell UK Exploration and Production 1986–89, dir of resource mgmnt Dept of Energy 1989–92, dep DG Office of Gas Supply 1992–93, head Consumer Affairs Div DTI 1993–96; dir Br Rubber Manufacturers' Assoc 1997–2005 (dep dir 1996–97), ceo Br Tyre Manufacturers' Assoc 2006–09, dir Br Rubber and Polyurethane Products Assoc 2008–; sec and treas Medical Aid and Relief for the Children of Chechnya; *Recreations* reading, walking, music, squash; *Clubs* Stormont Lawn Tennis and Squash Rackets; *Style—* Mr John Dorken; ✉ 10 Connaught Gardens, London N10 3LB (☎ 020 8372 6213, e-mail dorken24@aol.com)

DORMAN, Sir Philip Henry Keppel; 4 Bt (UK 1923), of Nunthorpe, Co York; s of Richard Dorman (d 1976), and Diana Keppel, *née* Barrett; suc kinsman, Sir Charles Geoffrey Dorman, 3 Bt, MC (d 1996); *b* 19 May 1954; *Educ* Marlborough, Univ of St Andrews; *m* 1, 12 April 1982 (m dis 1992); 1 da (Megan Bay Keppel b 1984); m 2, 15 June 1996 (m dis 2004); m 3, 4 April 2011, Sarah Ann Crawford; *Heir* none; *Career* tax accountant; life protector Dorman Museum Middlesbrough; *Recreations* golf; *Clubs* MCC, Lewes Golf; *Style—* Sir Philip Dorman, Bt

DORMENT, Richard; CBE (2014); s of James Dorment, and Marguerite, *née* O'Callaghan; *b* 15 November 1946; *Educ* Georgetown Prep Sch MD, Princeton Univ (BA), Columbia Univ NYC (MA, MPhil, PhD); *m* 1, 1970 (m dis 1981), Kate Ganz; 1 s (Anthony Ganz b 1975), 1 da (Lily Sophia b 1977); m 2, 1985, Harriet Waugh; *Career* faculty fell Columbia Univ NYC 1968–72, asst curator of paintings Philadelphia Museum of Art 1973–76; guest curator for the exhbn Alfred Gilbert – Sculptor and Goldsmith (Royal Acad of Arts London) 1985–86; art critic: Country Life 1986, Daily Telegraph 1986–2015; frequent contrib NY Review of Books; guest curator: Alfred Gilbert: Sculptor and Goldsmith Exhbn (Royal Acad) 1986, James McNeill Whistler Exhbn (Tate Gallery, Musée d'Orsay, Nat Gallery of Art Washington DC) 1994–95; memb: Reviewing Ctee on the Export of Works of Art 1995–2002, Advsy Ctee Govt Art Collection 1995–2005; tstee: Watts Gallery 1996–, Wallace Collection 2003–13, Wallace Fndn Tst 2014–; winner Hawthornden Prize for art criticism 1992, Critic of the Year Br Press Awards 2000; FSA 2014; *Books* Alfred Gilbert (1985), British Painting in the Philadelphia Museum of Art (1986), James McNeill Whistler (with Margaret MacDonald, 1994), Exhibitionist: Writing about Art in a Daily Newspaper (2016); *Publications* essays for exhibition catalogues incl Victorian High Renaissance (1978), Pre-Raphaelite and Other Masters: The Andrew Lloyd Webber Collection (2003), Manet and the Sea (2003); *Clubs* Brooks's; *Style—* Richard Dorment, Esq, CBE; ✉ e-mail richard@rdorment.com

DORMER, Ian; CBE (2016); *Educ* Univ of Essex (BA); *m* 1996, Prof Julia Newton; 1 da (Emily b 1998), 1 s (Mark b 2002); *Career* md Rosh Engineering Ltd 1989–; chm IOD 2012–15; CDir; *Style—* Ian Dormer, Esq, CBE; ✉ ROSH Engineering Ltd, Durham Road, Birtley, Durham DH3 2QW

DORMER, Natalie; *b* 11 February 1982, Reading, Berks; *Educ* Webber Douglas Acad of Dramatic Art; *Career* actress; *Film* incl: Casanova 2005, Flawless 2007, City of Life 2009, Captain America: The First Avenger 2011, WE 2011, Rush 2013, The Counselor 2013, A Long Way From Home 2013, The Riot Club 2014, The Hunger Games: Mockingjay Part I 2014, The Hunger Games: Mockingjay Part II 2015, Patient Zero 2016, The Forest 2016; *Television* incl: The Tudors 2007–10, Masterwork 2009, Marple: Why Didn't They Ask Evans? 2009, Poe 2011, Silk 2011, The Fades 2011, Game of Thrones 2012–, Elementary 2013–, The Scandalous Lady W 2015; *Theatre* incl: Sweet Nothings (Young Vic) 2010, .45 (Hampstead Theatre) 2010, After Miss Julie (Young Vic) 2012; *Style—* Ms Natalie Dormer; ✉ c/o Dallas Smith, United Agents, 12–26 Lexington Street, London W1F 0LE

DORRELL, Rt Hon Stephen James; PC (1994); s of Philip George Dorrell (d 1994) and Christine Dorrell; *b* 25 March 1952; *Educ* Uppingham, BNC Oxford; *m* 1980, Penelope Anne (Annette) Wears Taylor, da of Maurice James Taylor, of Windsor, Berks; 1 da (Alexandra Elizabeth Nancy b 11 July 1988), 3 s (Philip James Andrew b 13 Nov 1992, William Edward Charles b 27 March 1997, Christopher George Robert b 11 March 1999); *Career* PA to Rt Hon Peter Walker MP 1974; Parly candidate (Cons) Kingston upon Hull E Oct 1974; MP (Cons): Loughborough 1979–97, Charnwood 1997–2015; PPS to Rt Hon Peter Walker MP (sec of state for Energy) 1983–87, asst Govt whip 1987–88, a Lord Cmmr of HM Treasy (govt whip) 1988–90, Parly under sec of state Dept of Health 1990–92, financial sec to Treasy 1992–94, sec of state for Nat Heritage 1994–95, sec of state for Health 1995–97, shadow sec for Educn and Employment 1997–98; chair Health Select Ctee 2010–14; *Recreations* walking, reading; *Style—* The Rt Hon Stephen Dorrell; ✉ House of Commons, London SW1A 0AA (☎ 020 7219 4472, fax 020 7219 5838, e-mail stephen.dorrell.mp@parliament.uk)

DORRIAN, Hon Lady; Leeona June Dorrian; da of Thomas Michael Dorrian (d 1975), of Edinburgh, and June Sylvia, *née* Neill; *b* 16 June 1957; *Educ* Cranley Sch Edinburgh, Univ of Aberdeen (LLB); *Career* admitted to Faculty of Advocates 1981, standing jr counsel to Health & Safety Exec in Scotland 1987–94, advocate depute 1988–91, standing jr counsel to Dept of Energy 1991–94, QC (Scot) 1994, temporary judge 2002–05, senator Coll of Justice in Scot and Lord of Session 2005–; memb Criminal Injuries Compensation Bd 1997–2002; *Clubs* RAC, Scottish Arts (Edinburgh), Royal Forth Yacht (Edinburgh), Royal Highland Yacht; *Style—* The Hon Lady Dorrian; ✉ 23 Dundas Street, Edinburgh EH3 6QQ (☎ 0131 556 2256, fax 0131 556 8398, e-mail ljdorrian@lineone.net); Court of Session, Parliament Square, Edinburgh EH1 1RF (☎ 0131 225 2595)

DORRIES, Nadine; MP; *b* Liverpool; *Career* early career as nurse; advsr to Dr Oliver Letwin, MP, *qv*, memb shadow Treasy team steering ctee; memb Kirkhope Cmmn for Asylum; MP (Cons) Bedfordshire Mid 2005–; *Style—* Ms Nadine Dorries, MP; ✉ House of Commons, London SW1A 0AA

DOUBLE, Stephen Daniel (Steve); MP; s of Donald Double, of Tregony, Cornwall, and Heather, *née* Martin (d 2007); *b* 19 December 1966, St Blazey, Cornwall; *Educ* Poltair Sch St Austell; *m* 1986, Anne Double; 2 s (Joshua b 29 Sept 1990, Jacob b 16 Oct 1994); *Career* with Barclays Bank 1983–92, church pastor 1992–2002, company dir 2001–; MP (Cons) St Austell and Newquay 2015–; *Recreations* travel, walking, boating; *Style—* Steve Double, Esq, MP; ✉ House of Commons, London SW1A 0AA (☎ 020 7219 4408, e-mail steve.double.mp@parliament.uk, website www.stevedouble.org.uk, Twitter @SteveDouble)

DOUBLEDAY, John Vincent; s of Gordon Vincent Doubleday (d 1993), and Margaret, *née* Harris (d 1992); *b* 9 October 1947; *Educ* Stowe, Goldsmiths' Coll Sch of Art; *m* 1969, Isobel Jean Campbell, da of Maj Frederick Robert Edwin Durie (d 1995), of Argyll; 3 s (Robert b 1974, Edwin b 1976 d 2000, James b 1978); *Career* artist; *Exhibitions* incl: Waterhouse Gallery 1968–69 and 1970–71, Richard Demarco Gallery Edinburgh 1973, Laing Art Gallery Newcastle, Bowes Barnard Castle 1974, Pandion Gallery NY, Aldeborough Festival 1983, Municipal Museum Meiringen Switzerland 2012, Firstsite and the Minories Colchester 2015; *Portraits/Portrait Sculpture* incl: Prince Philip Duke of Edinburgh, Golda Meir 1976, Lord Olivier, Mary and Child Christ (Rochester Cathedral), Caduceus (Harvard Mass), Isambard Kingdom Brunel (two works in Paddington and Bristol), Charlie Chaplin (Vevey and London) 1982, Beatles (Liverpool), Dylan Thomas (Swansea) 1984, Commando Memorial 1986, Sherlock Holmes (Meiringen) 1991, Johann Pflug (Biberach) 1994, Nelson Mandela (United World Colls) 1996, Gerald Durrell (Jersey) 1999, Sherlock Holmes (Baker St Station London) 1999, The Dorset Shepherd (Dorchester) 2000, Col Jabara (USAF Acad Colorado Springs) 2004, Nelson (Gibraltar) 2005, Working with Tribal Bronze Casters (Chhattisgarh) 2011, HM The Queen (Gibraltar) 2013 and (Southend-on-Sea) 2014, Herbert Columbine VC (Walton-on-the-Naze) 2014; *Work in Public Collections* Ashmolean, Br Museum, Herbert F Johnson NY, Tate Gallery, V&A, Nat Museum of Wales; *Books* John Doubleday: Work (ed Katherine Wood, 2016); *Recreations* impractical projects; *Style—* John Doubleday, Esq; ✉ Goat Lodge, Goat Lodge Road, Great Totham, Maldon, Essex CM9 8BX (☎ 01621 891329, e-mail jd@johndoubleday.co.uk, www.johndoubleday.co.uk)

DOUETIL, Dane Jonathan; CBE (2007); *b* 28 July 1960; *Educ* Univ of Birmingham; *m* Antonia Clare; 3 da (Grace Caroline b 18 Nov 1991, Abigail Nicola b 12 Dec 1993, Kate Isobel b 8 June 1997); *Career* Willis Faber Group: joined 1982, exec dir Political and Risk Div 1988; founding shareholder and dir Special Risk Servs 1989–94, conslt for various financial instns 1994–98, conslt Benfield Gp 1997; Brit Insurance Holdings plc: chief exec Brit Insurance Ltd 1998, memb Bd 1999, chief exec Brit Syndicates Ltd 2002, dep chief exec 2004, gp chief exec 2005–; former chm Lloyd's Market Assoc, former chm Market Reform Gp, memb Bd ABI 2009–; *Recreations* shooting, fishing; *Clubs* Boodles; *Style—* Dane Douetil, Esq, CBE; ✉ Brit Insurance, 55 Bishopsgate, London EC2N 3AS (☎ 020 7984 8803, fax 020 7984 8801)

DOUGAL, Andrew James Harrower; s of Andrew J H Dougal (d 1987), and Muriel, *née* Macdonald; *b* 2 September 1951, Glasgow; *Educ* Greenock Academy, Paisley GS, Univ of Glasgow (BAcc); *m* 21 July 1978, Margaret, *née* Carmichael; 1 da (Alison b 28 Dec 1979), 2 s (Gavin b 21 July 1982, Calum b 2 June 1992); *Career* CA 1975; successively articled clerk and asst mangr Ernst & Young 1972–77, chief accountant Scottish & Universal Investments Ltd 1977–86; Hanson plc: finance comptroller 1986–89, finance dir ARC Ltd (subsid) 1989–92, md ARC Southern (subsid) 1992–93, dep finance dir 1993–95, finance dir 1995–97, chief exec 1997–2002; dir: Taylor Woodrow plc 2002–07, BPB plc 2003–05, Celtel Int BV 2004–05, Premier Farnell plc 2006–15, Taylor Wimpey plc 2007–11, Creston plc 2006–15, Carillion plc 2011–, Victrex plc 2015–; MICAS 1975 (memb Cncl 2012–, chair Tech Policy Bd 2012–), CCMI 1999, FRSA 2005; *Recreations* family, sports, travel, history; *Style—* Andrew Dougal, Esq; ✉ Carillion Plc, 84 Salop Street, Wolverhampton WV3 0SR

DOUGLAS, Alasdair Ferguson; s of George Douglas, of Perth, Scotland, and Christina, *née* Ferguson; *b* 16 March 1953; *Educ* Perth Acad, Univ of Edinburgh (LLB), Univ of London (LLM); *m* Kathryn Veronica Cecile, da of Cecil Kennard, OBE (d 1971); 1 s (Robert Ferguson), 1 da (Alice Jane); *Career* admitted slr 1981; conslt Travers Smith (ptnr 1985–2010, managing ptnr 1995–2001, latterly sr ptnr); memb City of London Slrs' Co; memb: Law Soc, Law Soc of Scotland; fell Soc for Advanced Legal Studies; *Books* contrib: Tolley's Tax Planning, Tolley's Company Law; *Recreations* family, bagpiping; *Clubs* City of London, Royal Scottish Pipers' Soc, Scottish Piping Soc of London, MCC; *Style—* Alasdair Douglas, Esq

DOUGLAS, Barry; OBE (2002); s of Barry Douglas (d 1988), and Sarah Jane, *née* Henry; *b* 23 April 1960; *Educ* RCM (with John Barstow, further study with Maria Curcio); *Career* concert pianist and conductor; debut London 1981, Gold medal Tchaikovsky Int Piano Competition Moscow 1986; worldwide concert career; tours: USA, Japan, Far East, USSR, Europe; worked with conductors incl: Ashkenazy, Davis, Masur, Jansons, Maazel, Temirkanov, Tilson Thomas, Janowski, Mackerras, McFerrin; subject of TV documentary After The Gold, appeared in Dudley Moore's TV series Concerto; former visiting fell Oriel Coll Oxford, Prince Consort prof Royal Coll of Music; music dir Camerata Ireland; Hon DMus Queen's Univ Belfast; FRCM 1988; *Recordings* Tchaikovsky Piano Concerto Nos 1, 2 and 3, Mussorgsky Pictures at an Exhibition, Brahms Piano Quintet in F Minor, Beethoven Hammerklavier, Brahms Piano Concerto No 1, Tchaikovsky Sonata in G, Liszt Piano Concertos, Prokofiev Sonatas 2 and 7, Berg Sonata, Liszt Sonata in B Minor, Beethoven Sonata Op 53, 57, 90, Rachmaninov Piano Concerto No 2, Corigliano Piano Concerto, Britten Piano Concerto, Reger Piano Concerto Op 114, Strauss Burleske, Britten Piano Concerto Op 13, Debussy Fantasie for piano and orchestra, Debussy Pour le piano; *Recreations* driving, reading, food and wine; *Style—* Barry Douglas, Esq, OBE; ✉ c/o IMG Artists, IMG Artists, The Light Box, 111 Power Road, London W4 5PY (☎ 020 8233 5800, fax 020 8233 5801)

DOUGLAS, Colin; s of Kendric Douglas (d 1974), and Adassa, *née* Thompson; *b* 10 September 1963, London; *Educ* Tulse Hill Comp Sch, Univ of Oxford (BA), Oxford Brookes Univ (MBA); *m* Aug 1992, Petrina Douglas-Hall; 2 s (Nile b 1998, Luke b 2001); *Career* various communications roles in local govt rising to head of communications Hammersmith and Fulham Cncl 1985–94, dep md PR Citigate Communications 1994–99, dir of communications Sport England 1999–2001, dir of communications and public affrs Transport for London 2001–02; dir of communications: Audit Cmmn 2002–04, HSE 2004–08, NHS Dept of Health 2008–13, NHS England 2012–13; dir Southside Communications Ltd 2013–; FCIPR, FCIM; *Publications* West Indian Women at War: British Racism in World War 2 (1991); *Style—* Colin Douglas, Esq; ✉ e-mail colin.douglas@southsidecomms.co.uk

DOUGLAS, Dr (John) Graham; s of Dr Keith Douglas, of Menston, nr Ilkley, and Mavis Douglas; *b* 20 October 1949; *Educ* Bradford GS, Univ of Edinburgh (BSc, MB ChB); *Children* 1 s (Jamie b 5 Oct 1980), 1 da (Catriona Douglas b 7 June 1983); *Career* jr med and surgical house offr Edinburgh Royal Infirmary 1974–75, SHO and registrar in gen medicine, gastroenterology and renal medicine Eastern Gen Hosp and Edinburgh Royal Infirmary 1975–81, sr registrar in chest med and infection Edinburgh Royal Infirmary and Northern Gen Hosp 1981–86, conslt physician with an interest in thoracic med and infection Aberdeen 1986–, reader in med 2002–; FRCP, FSA Scot, FRSPEd; *Publications* Macleod's Clinical Examination (co-ed, 11, 12 and 13 edns), Clinician's Desk Reference: Asthma (co-ed), Flesh & Bones: Medicine (co-ed); author of 160 scientific publications on gen and thoracic med and infection; *Recreations* hill walking, cycling, golf, DIY, history; *Style—* Dr Graham Douglas; ✉ Respiratory Unit, Chest Clinic, Aberdeen Royal Infirmary, Aberdeen AB25 2ZN (☎ 0845 456 6000 ext 51212, e-mail graham.douglas@nhs.net)

DOUGLAS, Hilary; CB (2002); da of James Robert Keith Black (d 1992), and Joan Margaret, *née* Boxall; *b* 27 July 1950; *Educ* Wimbledon HS, New Hall Cambridge (BA); *m* 1972, Robert Harold Douglas, s of Robert Francis Douglas; 2 s (Robert b 5 Oct 1979, Andrew b 11 July 1982); *Career* press librarian RIIA 1971–73; DES: joined 1973, worked on educn policy 1973–89, freelance work Netherlands 1989–91, fndr FEFC 1991–92, fndr Sch Curriculum and Assessment Authy 1992–93, head Personnel Dept 1993–94, dir Admin and Finance Office For Standards of Educn 1994–96; dir Civil Service Employer Gp and Top Mgmnt Prog Cabinet Office 1996–97, dir Personnel and Support Services DfES 1997–2000; md Corp Services and Devpt HM Treasy 2000–04, chief operating offr National Statistics 2004–06, chief operating offr Dept for Business 2006–; FRSA 1999; *Recreations* travel, European languages, singing, family; *Style—* Mrs Hilary Douglas, CB; ✉ Department for Business, Enterprise and Regulatory Reform, 1 Victoria Street, London SW1H 0ET

DOUGLAS, Prof Ian; s of Prof Ronald Walter Douglas (d 2000), and Edna Maud, *née* Cadle (d 1995); *b* 2 December 1936; *Educ* Merchant Taylors', Balliol Coll Oxford (MA, BLitt), Aust Nat Univ (PhD); *m* 16 Nov 1963, Maureen Ann, da of Frank Bowler (d 1988); 2 s (David b 1965 d 1981, Aidan b 1967), 1 da (Fiona b 1972); *Career* Nat Serv Bombardier RA 1956–58; lectr Univ of Hull 1966–71, prof of geography Univ of New England Armidale NSW 1971–78, prof of physical geography Univ of Manchester 1979–97 (research prof 1997–2006, emeritus prof 1997–); sci co-ordinator NERC Lowland Permeable Catchment Directed Research Programme (LOCAR) 2000–06; dir Salford and Trafford Groundwork Tst 1993–2002; pres Inst of Aust Geographers 1978, pres Soc for Human Ecology 2009–11; chm: Br Geomorphological Res Gp 1980–81, UK/MAB Urban Forum 1993–97 and 2010–12; organiser first Int Conf On Geomorphology Manchester 1985, treas Scientific Ctee on Problems of the Environment (SCOPE) 2001–09; Australia Int Medal Inst of Australian Geographers 2006; *Books* Humid Landforms (1977), The Urban Environment (1983), Environmental Change and Tropical Geomorphology (co-ed, 1985), Encyclopaedia of Global Environmental Change Vol 3 (ed, 2002), Companion Encyclopaedia of Geography (co-ed, 2 edn 2007), Routledge Handbook of Urban Ecology (co-ed, 2011), Cities: an environmental history (2013), Urban Ecology: an introduction (with Philip James, 2014), Urban Ecology: Critical Concepts in Geography (ed, 2015); *Recreations* walking in rainforests, music, travel, gardening; *Style—* Prof Ian Douglas; ✉ 21 Taunton Road, Sale, Cheshire M33 5DD (☎ 0161 973 1708); School of Environment and Development, University of Manchester M13 9PL (e-mail ian.douglas@manchester.ac.uk)

DOUGLAS, James; s of James Douglas (d 1936), of Edinburgh, and Mary Helen Douglas (d 1933); *b* 4 July 1932; *Educ* Heriot-Watt Coll, Paris Conservatoire, Mozarteum Salzburg, Hochschule Munich, Royal Coll of Music London (LRAM, ARCM); *m* 1, 1959, Mary Henderson Irving (d 1967); 2 s (Stephen James b 1961, Gavin John b 1962); m 2, 1968, Helen Torrance Fairweather; 1 da (Katharine Helen b 1971); *Career* pianist, composer, accompanist, organist and conductor; asst organist St Thomas' Church Edinburgh 1948–50; dir of music: Nicolson Square Church Edinburgh 1953–63, Mayfield Church Edinburgh 1963–69, Reid Meml Church Edinburgh 1969–73; music staff Edinburgh Acad 1967–79, dir of music Christ Church Edinburgh 1986–91, hon prof l'Académie des Sciences Universelles Paris 1992; fndr: Eschenbach Editions 1986–, Caritas Records 1989–; compositions incl: 15 symphonies (Sky Canticles, Musica della Passione, Symphony for Organ: Clouds of Mystery, From the Deeps, Majestas Divini, Musica dalla Serenissima, Rituals in Transformed Time, Meditation on the Divine, Fire and Love, A Time for Singing, Torridon, Canti Spirituali, Le Mystere de Noel, La Corona, Metamorphosis), String Quartet I (Missa), String Quartet II (Metrum), orchestral works, cello music, music for brass (Formations, Emblems & Sonnets for Orpheus 2011 (brass quintet)), The Christ Church Sequence (75 chamber works 2001–06), The Glorious Sequence (instrumental works 2006–), The Highlands and Islands Sequence (66 works 1968–2007), Music for the 21st Century 1–5 (2008), Lindisfarne Music (words by David Adam), A Tide That Sings (words by G R D Maclean), piano music, organ music (Advent Meditations, From the Deeps, Symphony for Organ: Clouds of Mystery, Praise Sion Switzerland, Concerto for Organ, Trilogia, A Vision, Nativity Recessional, Le Soleil Dansant, High Mountains I, Glory to Glory, Inverness Cathedral and To the Cairngorms), and choral music; stage works: Mask (7 Deadly Sins, premiered Stirling Festival 1973 and Edinburgh Int Festival 1974), Cuthbert; recordings: Visions of Glory (1990 and 2001, words by David Adam), Cry of the Deer (1991 and 2001, words by David Adam), A Vision (2000), Cloud of Unknowing (2001), Caritas Live series 12 CDs 2001–, incl Vigil of the Ascension, Into the Forest, Music for the Fallen, Doors of Perception, Cranes Dancing, Threnody for Lost Time, The Feast of his Joy, Summertime Song, The City Never Sleeps, Nocturnal, Peace of the Highlands and Land of the Lochans, A Musical Journey (DVD with Helen Douglas, 2010); memb: Performing Right Soc, Br Acad of Composers and Songwriters 2001–09; LRAM, ARCM; *Books* The Music of Hermann Reutter (1966); *Recreations* reading, cultural activities; *Style—* James Douglas, Esq; ✉ c/o Eschenbach Editions (publisher), Achmore, Moss Road, Ullapool, Ross-shire IV26 2TF (☎ and fax 01854 612236, e-mail eschenbach@caritas-music.co.uk, website www.caritas-music.co.uk/james_douglas.html)

DOUGLAS, Dr James Frederick; s of Capt Rev James Douglas, CF (ka 1944), and Annie Hildegarde, *née* Harte; *b* 22 September 1938; *Educ* Portora Royal Sch Enniskillen, Wadham Coll Oxford (MA, BM BCh, BCL), Queen's Univ Belfast (MB BCh); *m* 27 April 1973, Giselle Sook An Lim; 3 s (Jeremy b 1975, Timothy b 1978, Andrew b 1981); *Career* lectr Coll of Law 1963–64, called to the Bar Middle Temple 1964; houseman Royal Victoria Hosp Belfast 1969–70, tutor in pharmacology Queen's Univ Belfast 1970–71, casualty posts Oxford and Belfast 1971–72, nephrologist 1972, conslt Belfast City and Royal Victoria Hosps 1975, sr nephrologist Belfast City Hosp 1988–2003 (dir 1990–96), lectr Dept of Clinical Pharmacology Queen's Univ Belfast 2003–, conslt Antrim Area Hosp 2004–07, visiting physician St Helena 2008; med advsr NI Kidney Research Fund 1988–2003 (patron 2003–); memb: UK Transplant Support Assoc 1996–2002, ULTRA (Unrelated Living Transplant Regulatory Authy) 1996–2006; author of various pubns on: renal transplantation, renal failure, renal toxicology, the law and renal failure; memb: Renal Assoc, Euro Dialysis and Transplantation Assoc, Br Transplant Soc (memb Cncl 2002–), Transplantation Soc, Int Soc of Nephrology, American Soc of Nephrology; FRCP 1987 (MRCP 1973); *Recreations* astronomy, chess, cricket, country pursuits; *Style—* Dr James Douglas; ✉ e-mail jamesfdouglas38@hotmail.com

DOUGLAS, Prof Kenneth Thomas (Ken); s of Thomas William Douglas, and Irene, *née* Cluney; *b* 10 January 1948, Folkestone, Kent; *Educ* Belfast Royal Acad (Sir Hans Sloane Medal, Royal Inst of Chem Prize), Balliol Coll Oxford (MA), Univ of Kent at Canterbury (PhD); *m* 29 July 1972, (Sylvia) Claire, *née* Shrigley; 1 da (Rosalind Kate b 10 July 1979), 1 s (Jeremy Shrigley b 29 May 1982); *Career* postdoctoral res fell Univ of Chicago 1973–75, asst prof of chemistry and biochemistry Duquesne Univ Pittsburgh 1975–78 (assoc prof 1978), lectr in biological chemistry Univ of Essex 1978–87; Univ of Manchester: prof of medicinal chemistry and ldr Drug Design and Action Gp 1987–, head Dept of Pharmacy 1991–94, fndr Discovery To Medicines Ltd 2007; dir and fndr Wolfson Centre for Structure-Based Rational Design of Molecular Diagnostics 2003–09; exchange prof Univ de Paris-Sud 1978, hon prof Univ of Nagasaki 1983, visiting prof Univ Paul-Sabatier Toulouse 1991–92, hon prof Sch of Pharmacy Univ of Manchester 2009–; ed Biochimica et Biophysica Acta 1985–95 and 2002–09; Matsumae Medal and int fell Japan 1983, RSC Silver Medal and Prize 2002; ed and editorial advisor on numerous professional jls, author of over 240 articles and 4 patents; memb panel Res Assessment Exercise 2008 2004; served on numerous nat and int grants ctees and panels; refereed grants and funding proposals to various instns; *Recreations* painting, listening to others sing but never singing myself; *Style—* Prof Ken Douglas; ✉ School of Pharmacy & Pharmaceutical Sciences, University of Manchester, Oxford Road, Manchester M13 9PL (e-mail ken.douglas@manchester.ac.uk)

DOUGLAS, Michael John; QC (1997); s of James Murray Douglas, and Julie Friederike Douglas; *b* 7 August 1952; *Educ* Westminster, Balliol Coll Oxford (MA); *Career* called to the Bar Gray's Inn 1974, recorder 2000; *Recreations* theatre, cinema, eating out, football, travel; *Style—* Michael Douglas, Esq, QC; ✉ 4 Pump Court, Temple, London EC4Y 7AN (☎ 020 7842 5555, fax 020 7583 2036)

DOUGLAS, Prof Sir Neil James; kt (2009); s of Prof Sir Donald Douglas (d 1993), and Margaret Diana, *née* Whitley; *b* 28 May 1949; *Educ* Glenalmond Coll, Univ of St Andrews (scholar), Univ of Edinburgh (MB ChB, MD, DSc); *m* 16 July 1977, Dr Susan McLaren Galloway, da of Dr Thomas McLaren Galloway; 1 s (Sandy Donald b 6 Jan 1983), 1 da (Kirsty McLaren b 21 Feb 1985); *Career* lectr in med Univ of Edinburgh 1974–83, MRC fell Univ of Colorado 1980–81; Univ of Edinburgh: sr lectr in med 1983–91, reader in med/respiratory med 1991–95, prof of respiratory and sleep med 1995–2012, emeritus prof 2012–; physician Royal Infirmary Edinburgh 1983–2012, dir Scottish Nat Sleep Labs 1983–2004; pres Royal Coll of Physicians Edinburgh 2004–10 (vice-pres 2000–04), chm UK Acad of Medical Royal Colls 2009–12, chm Faculty of Medical Leadership and Mgmnt 2011–17; formerly: chm Editorial Bd Clinical Sci, hon sec Br Thoracic Soc, chm Br Sleep Soc; Hon MD Univ of St Andrews; *Publications* 400 pubns, mainly on breathing during sleep; *Recreations* hill walking, fly fishing, skiing, sailing; *Style—* Prof Sir Neil Douglas

DOUGLAS, Sue; *see:* Douglas Ferguson, Susan Margaret

DOUGLAS, Torin Stuart; MBE (2013); s of Stuart Douglas (d 1994), of Reigate, and Hazel Joyce, *née* Smith (d 1989); *b* 24 September 1950; *Educ* Eastbourne Coll, Univ of Warwick (BA); *m* 6 Oct 1973, Carol Sheila, da of Kenneth Douglas Winstanley; 2 s (Richard Torin Winstanley b 18 Oct 1981, Michael Stuart b 6 March 1985), 1 da (Eleanor Frances b 20 April 1991); *Career* trainee journalist D C Thomson 1972–73, media writer/features ed Campaign 1973–76, information offr IBA 1976–78, assoc ed Marketing Week 1978–82, ed Creative Review 1980–82, advtg and mktg writer The Times and The Economist 1982–84, presenter Advertising World LBC Radio 1984–89, media page columnist The Independent 1988–89, media corr BBC News 1989–2013; columnist Marketing Week 1979–2006, also contrib to Sunday Times, The Observer, The Guardian, Radio Times, Punch and The Listener; Mktg Soc Journalism Award 1983, Magazine Publishing Awards Best Business Columnist 1987; chm Broadcasting Press Guild 1996–98, advsr Media Tst 2013–; memb NUJ; fell CAM Fndn; co-ordinator Bedford Park Festival 2003–12, dir Chiswick Book Festival 2009–, tstee Sandford St Martins Tst 2013–; visiting prof in communications and media Univ of Beds 2013–; Hon DLitt Univ of W London 2013; *Publications* The Complete Guide to Advertising (1985), Is the BBC In Crisis? (contrib, 2014), Children's Media Yearbook (2014); lectures: 40 Years of Business Journalism (Warwick Business Sch) 2012, The Wonder of Wireless – Why Video Didn't Kill the Radio Star (Univ of W London) 2013; *Recreations* promoting community events in Chiswick; *Clubs* High Road House, Hogarth Health; *Style—* Torin Douglas, Esq, MBE; ✉ 70 Ramillies Road, Chiswick, London W4 1JA ☎ 07860 422992, e-mail torindouglas@aol.com, website www.chiswickbookfestival.net/contact, Twitter @torindouglas)

DOUGLAS FERGUSON, Susan Margaret; da of Kenneth Frank Douglas, of London, and Vivienne Mary, *née* Harris; *b* 29 January 1957; *Educ* Tiffin Girls' Sch Kingston upon Thames, Univ of Southampton (BSc); *m* 26 July 1994; 2 s (Felix b 1994, Lachlan b 1999), 1 da (Freya b 1995); *Career* Arthur Andersen & Co Mgmnt Consultancy 1978–79, Mims Magazine Haymarket Publishing 1979–80; reporter: Sunday Express Johannesburg 1980–81; Mail on Sunday 1982–87: med corr, features ed, asst ed, assoc ed; asst ed Daily Mail 1987–91, dep ed Sunday Times 1992–95, ed Sunday Express 1996, conslt ed The European, The Scotsman, Scotland on Sunday and Gear Magazine NY 1997–2001, pres of new business Condé Nast 2001–; *Recreations* riding; *Style—* Ms Susan Douglas Ferguson

DOUGLAS MILLER, Robert Alexander Gavin; s of Maj Francis Gavin Douglas Miller (d 1950), and Mary Morison, *née* Kennedy (d 2002); *b* 11 February 1937; *Educ* Harrow, Univ of Oxford (MA); *m* 9 March 1963, Judith Madeleine Smith, da of Richard Michael Desmond Dunstan, OBE, of Firbeck, nr Worksop, Notts; 3 s (Andrew Gavin b 30 Sept 1963, Robert Peter b 15 Jan 1965, Edward James b 20 May 1966), 1 da (Emma Lucy Jane b 8 Jan 1969); *Career* served in 9 Lancers 1955–57; joined Jenners Edinburgh 1962: md 1972–96, chm 1982–; chm and md Kennington Leasing; dir: First Scottish American Investment Tst, Northern American Tst; memb Kyle of Sutherland Fishery Bd; landowner (5850 acres); *Recreations* fishing, shooting, gardening; *Clubs* New (Edinburgh); *Style—* Robert Douglas Miller, Esq; ✉ Bavelaw Castle, Balerno, Midlothian (☎ 0131 449 3972); Jenners, 48 Princes Street, Edinburgh EH2 2YJ (☎ 0131 260 2324)

DOUGLAS-HAMILTON, The Rt Hon Lord James Alexander; *see:* Selkirk of Douglas, The Rt Hon Lord

DOUGLAS-HOME, (Alexander) Sholto; s of Robin Douglas-Home (d 1968), and Sandra Howard, *née* Paul; step s of Rt Hon Michael Howard, QC, MP, *qv*; *b* Sept 1962; *Educ* Bradfield Coll, Warwick Business Sch (BSc); *m* 1992, Alexandra Jane, da of Ben Miller; 1 s (Louis Robin b 1999), 1 da (Tallula Elizabeth b 2001); *Career* account mangr Euro RSCG 1983–87, business mangr Chiat Day Mojo 1987–89, business dir Still Price Lintas 1989–93, head of advtg and PR BT plc 1993–98, on secondment from BT as dir of mktg and sales New Millennium Experience Co 1998–2001, mktg dir (Kalends) Reuters plc 2001–02, publisher Reuters Magazine 2001–04, global head Mktg Communications Reuters plc 2001–08, chief mktg offr and memb Mgmnt Bd Hays plc 2008–; chm NABS Charity Ctee 2001–02; chm Mktg Gp GB (MGGB) 2006–07 (memb Cncl 1999–), chm Existing Betting Areas Ctee Dept of Culture Media and Sport 2008–09; memb Cncl ISBA 2006– (memb Exec Ctee 1997–2006); Grand Prix and Gold Award IPA Advtg Effectiveness Awards (for BT's 'It's Good to Talk' campaign) 1996; FCIM 2002; *Publications* London Zagat Survey (ed, 1997–); *Recreations* restaurants, international masters athletics competitor (60m and 100m); *Clubs* Morton's, George; *Style—* Sholto

D

Douglas-Home, Esq; ✉ Hays plc, 250 Euston Road, London NW1 2AF (✆ 020 7383 2266, Twitter @sholtodh)

DOUKAS, Sarah; da of Dr John Chambers, and Noelle, *née* Strange; *b* 21 December 1952; *m* 1; 1 da (Noelle *b* 10 Nov 1979); *m* 2, 14 Feb 1994, Tim Garner; 2 da (Genevieve *b* 30 Sept 1991, Poppy *b* 2 Oct 1997); *Career* formerly model, punk band mangr and antiques business prop Clignancourt Market Paris, jr booker Laraine Ashton Model Agency (now IMG) 1980–87, fndr and md Storm Model Mgmnt 1987–; *Style—* Ms Sarah Doukas; ✉ Storm Model Management, 1st Floor, 5 Jubilee Place, London SW3 3TD (✆ 020 7376 7764, fax 020 7376 5145, e-mail sarah@stormmodels.co.uk)

DOUST, Tim Charles; s of Peter Michael Doust, of Marden, Kent, and Linda, *née* Page; *b* 20 June 1963, London; *Educ* Sutton Valence Sch; *m* 16 June 1990, Alison, *née* Ruck; 1 s (Freddie *b* 16 Nov 1992), 1 da (Romilly *b* 7 April 1995); *Career* vice-chm and founding ptnr Inferno 2000– (merged 2013); *MIPA; Publications* articles in Campaign Magazine; *Recreations* cinema, cricket, gardening, golf, opera, tennis; *Clubs* Ivy; *Style—* Tim Doust, Esq; ✉ FCB Inferno, 31 Great Queen Street, London WC2B 5AE (✆ 020 7092 0302, e-mail antonia.c@inferno-group.com)

DOVE, Hon Mr Justice Ian William Dove; QC (2003); s of Jack Richard Dove, of Northampton, and Janet Yvonne, *née* Clarke; *b* 31 December 1963, Northampton; *Educ* Northampton Sch for Boys, St Catherine's Coll Oxford (MA), Inns of Court Sch of Law; *m* 4 June 1988, Juliet Caroline, *née* Gladston; 2 s (Tobias John *b* 3 Sept 1993, Wilfred Henry *b* 30 Jan 1996); *Career* called to Bar Inner Temple 1986 (master of the bench 2010), pt/t immigration judge 2000, recorder 2003, dep judge High Court 2008, judge of the High Court of Justice (Queen's Bench Div) 2014–; *Style—* Hon Mr Justice Dove, QC; ✉ Royal Courts of Justice, Strand, London WC2A 2LL

DOVE, John; s of Anthony Dove, and Betty Margaret, *née* Curran; *b* 24 July 1944; *Educ* Ampleforth, Univ of Durham (BA), Univ of Manchester (Dip Drama); *Career* theatre director; Arts Cncl trainee dir under Philip Hedley Birmingham 1971–72, assoc dir to Jane Howell Northcott Theatre Exeter 1973–74 (co dir Bingo), freelance dir 1974–84 (worked with Richard Eyre at Nottingham, Richard Cotterell at Bristol Old Vic, Toby Robertson at Old Vic), assoc dir Hampstead Theatre 1984–; *Productions* for Hampstead Theatre incl: A Little Like Drowning (Plays and Players Award), Ask for the Moon, The Daughter in Law, The Awakening, Hedda Gabler, Bold Girls (Evening Standard Award), A Colliers Friday Night, Flight into Egypt, My Boy Jack 1997; other prodns incl: Rafts and Dreams (Royal Court), Goodnight Siobhan (Royal Court), A Muse of Fire (Edinburgh Festival), adaptation of Angelic Avengers for Denmark, Backstroke in a Crowded Pool (Bush Theatre, Susan Smith Blackburn Award), Democracy (Bush Theatre), Someone Who'll Watch Over Me (West Yorkshire Playhouse), Morning and Evening (Hampstead), Crossing the Equator (Bush), The Soldiers Song (Theatre Royal Stratford East), Prayers of Sherkin (Peter Hall Co, Old Vic) 1997, The Airman Who Would Not Die (Radio 4) 1997, Man and Boy (Radio 3) 1998, Saigon – Year of the Cat (Radio 4) 1998, wrote Mother Teresa in Kilburn (Radio 4) 1998, Falling (Hampstead) 1999, The Good Samaritan (Hampstead) 2000, La Grande Terese (Radio 4), Be Not Afraid – A Life of Handel (Radio 4) 2001, Vita Virginia (Stuttgart State Theater Germany), Darwin in Malibu (Birmingham Theatre), Death of a Salesman (Royal Lyceum Edinburgh), Measure for Measure (Globe Theatre London and USA tour), The Winter's Tale (Globe Theatre), In Extremis (Globe Theatre) 2006, All My Sons (Royal Lyceum) 2006 (Scottish Critics Award), Living Quarters (Royal Lyceum) 2007, I am Shakespeare (Chichester Theatre) 2007, The Clean House (UK tour) 2008, A Winter's Tale (Globe Theatre and UK tour) 2008, The Man Who Had All the Luck (Royal Lyceum) 2009, Red White and Blacklisted (UK tour) 2009, Observe the Sons of Ulster Marching Towards the Somme (Hampstead Theatre) 2009, The Price (Royal Lyceum) 2010, Anne Boleyn (Globe Theatre) 2010, View from the Bridge (Royal Lyceum) 2011, All's Well That Ends Well (Globe Theatre) 2011, Anne Boleyn (Globe Theatre and tour) 2011 and (nat tour) 2012, Of Mice and Men (Royal Lyceum Theatre) 2012, Mrs Updike (BBC Radio 3) 2012, Bluestockings (Globe Theatre) 2013, Eternal Love (English Touring Theatre) 2013, Pressure (Chichester Festival Theatre) 2014, Dr Scroggy's War (Globe Theatre) 2014, Faith Healer (Royal Lyceum Edinburgh) 2015, Farinelli and The King (Globe Theatre, Duke of York's Theatre) 2015, Heresy of Love (Globe Theatre) 2015, Crucible (Royal Lyceum Edinburgh) 2016, Lawrence After Arabia (Hampstead Theatre) 2016; *Recreations* painting, music, athletics, writing; *Style—* John Dove, Esq; ✉ c/o Simpson Fox Associates, 6 Beauchamp Place, London SW3 1NG

DOVE, Jonathan; s of Myles Harrison Dove, of Blackheath, London, and Deirdre Cecily, *née* Downer (d 1979); *b* 18 July 1959, London; *Educ* St Joseph's Acad Blackheath, ILEA Centre for Young Musicians, Trinity Coll Cambridge (MA), Goldsmiths' Coll London (MMus); *Career* composer; freelance pianist, arranger and composer 1980–88, freelance composer 1988–; asst chorus master Glyndebourne 1987–88, music advsr Almeida Theatre 1990–2009, artistic dir Spitalfields Festival 2001–06 (now hon life patron); tstee Oliver Tst 1997–2006, tstee Michael Tippett Fndn 1999–, assoc Nat Theatre 2003–, patron London Festival of Contemporary Church Music 2007–, patron Durham Opera Ensemble 2007–; Hon DMus Univ of East London 2006–; BASCA 1998; Ivor Novello Classical Music Award 2008; Hon RAM 2013; *Compositions* incl: Figures in the Garden 1991, Seaside Postcards 1995, Tuning In 1995, The Ringing Isle 1997, The Magic Flute Dances 1999, The Passing of the Year 2000, Stargazer 2001, Out of Time 2001, Moonlight Revels 2002, Koethener Messe 2002, The Middleham Jewel 2003, The Far Theatricals of Day 2003, Run to the Edge 2003, The Crocodiamond 2003, Out of Winter 2003, Across The Walls 2004, All The Future Days 2004, On Spital Fields 2004 (Royal Philharmonic Soc Award 2006, Br Composer Award 2006), Airport Scenes 2005, Hojoki 2006, It sounded as if the Streets were running 2007, Minterne 2007, There Was a Child 2009, Missa Brevis 2009, Piano Quintet 2009, A Song of Joys 2010, River Songs 2010, Cut My Shadow 2011, Three Tennyson Songs 2011, Two Sonnets 2011, The Pied Piper 2011, Diana and Actaeon 2012, The Immortal Ship 2012, A Portrait of Aung San Suu Kyi 2012, The Wells Service 2012, The Portsmouth Service 2013, Out of the Whirlwind 2013, Who Wrote the Book of Love? 2013, Gaia Theory 2014, Psalms for Leo 2014, For an Unknown Soldier 2014, The Dancing Pipes 2014, Arion and the Dolphin 2015, Nights Not Spent Alone 2015; *Operas* Pig 1992, L'augellino Belverde 1994, Siren Song 1994, Flight 1998, Tobias and the Angel 1999, The Palace in the Sky 2000, The Hackney Chronicles 2001, L'Altra Euridice 2001, When She Died 2002, La Dama ed il Pulitore di Damasco 2003, Le Porte di Bagdad 2003, Kwasi & Kwame 2005, The Enchanted Pig 2006, Man on the Moon 2006 (Rose D'Or 2007, Gold Medal Park City Film Festival 2008), An Old Way to Pay New Debts 2006, The Adventures of Pinocchio 2007 (Br Composers Award 2008), Swanhunter 2009, Seven Angels 2009, Mansfield Park 2010, Life is a Dream 2011, The Walk from the Garden 2011, The Day After 2012, The Monster in the Maze 2015; *Books* A Brief History of Creation (2016), In Damascus (2016), Seasons & Charms (2016); *Recreations* photography; *Style—* Jonathan Dove, Esq; ✉ c/o Katie Tearle, Peters Edition Ltd, 10–12 Baches Street, London N1 6DN (✆ 020 7553 4000, e-mail katie.tearle@editionpeters.com)

DOVER, Michael Grehan; s of Maj E J Dover (d 1983), and Ida, *née* Grehan (d 2001); *b* 22 October 1948; *Educ* The King's Sch Canterbury, Trinity Coll Dublin (BA); *m* 1972, Ruth, da of Capt T A Pearson (d 1972); 2 s (Alexander *b* 1975, Linden *b* 1983), 1 da (Katherine *b* 1979); *Career* Penguin Books 1972–83, publisher Weidenfeld Publishers Ltd 1987 (editorial dir 1983), dir Orion Publishing Group Ltd 1992–99, publisher and dir Cassell & Co 1999–2001, ed-in-chief and dir Weidenfeld & Nicolson 2002–11, writer 2011–; *Clubs*

Chelsea Arts, London Rowing, Hurlingham; *Style—* Michael Dover, Esq; ✉ Jasmine House, 190 New King's Road, London SW6 4NF (✆ 020 7731 8065, e-mail michaeldover@mailforce.net); c/o Luigi Bonomi, LBA Associates, 91 Great Russell Street, London WC1B 3PS (✆ 020 7637 1234, e-mail info@bonomiassociates.co.uk, website www.bonomiassociates.co.uk)

DOVER, Bishop of 2010–; Rt Rev Trevor Willmott; *b* 29 March 1950; *Educ* Plymouth Coll for Boys, St Peter's Coll Oxford (MA), Univ of Thessaloniki (Philip Usher scholar), Fitzwilliam Coll Cambridge (DipTh), Westcott House Cambridge, Dept of Continuing Educn Virginia Theological Seminary; *m* 1973, Margaret; 1 da (Elizabeth); *Career* ordained: deacon 1974, priest 1975; asst curate St George's Norton 1974–77 (actg ecumenical offr Dio of St Albans 1976–77), asst chaplain of Oslo with Trondheim 1978–79, chaplain of Naples with Capri, Bari and Sorrento and officiating chaplain to HM and American Armed Forces serving in Southern Europe 1979–83, rector of Ecton and warden Peterborough Diocesan Retreat House 1983–89, diocesan dir of ordinands and of post-ordination trg 1986–97, sec Diocesan Bd for the Devpt of Miny 1989–97, canon residentiary and precentor Peterborough Cathedral 1989–97, archdeacon of Durham and canon treas Durham Cathedral 1997–2002, bishop of Basingstoke 2002–10; memb Gen Synod C of E 2000–; sr selector Advsy Bd of Miny, chm Bd of Mgmnt Edward King Inst for Miny Devpt, chm Durham Diocesan Bd for Mission and Unity; govr Queen's Fndn Birmingham; *Recreations* travel, cooking, gardening, wine, sport (as spectator), music, opera, reading; *Clubs* Nikaean; *Style—* The Rt Rev the Bishop of Dover; ✉ The Bishop's Office, Old Palace, Canterbury, Kent CT1 2EE (✆ 01227 459382, e-mail trevor.willmott@bishcant.org)

DOVER, Prof William Duncan; s of Joseph Dover (d 1940), and Sarah Jane Graham, *née* Wilson (d 1989); *Educ* Bishopshalt Sch, Univ of Surrey (DipTech), UCL (PhD); *m* 27 July 1968, Dilys, da of John Richard Edwards (d 1989); 1 s (James William *b* 1973), 1 da (Elizabeth Mary *b* 1976); *Career* asst Faculté Polytechnique De Mons Belgium 1966–67, lectr City Univ London 1967–69, Shell prof of mechanical engrg UCL 1987– (lectr 1969–78, reader 1978–83, prof of mechanical engrg 1983–87); chm Dover & Partners Ltd 1979–86; dir: UCL NDE Centre 1985–, TSC Ltd 1985–, NDE Technology Ltd 1994–; visiting prof City Univ 1985–; CEng, FIMechE, fell Br Inst of Nondestructive Testing (FInstNDT); *Books* Fatigue and Crack Growth in Offshore Structures (ed, 1986), Fatigue of Offshore Structures (ed, 1989), Fatigue of Large Scale Threaded Connections (ed, 1989), Non Destructive Testing of Materials (ed 1995); 250 tech and sci papers; *Recreations* golf, swimming, skiing; *Clubs* Gerrards Cross Golf; *Style—* Prof William Dover; ✉ Coniston House, Orchehill Avenue, Gerrards Cross, Buckinghamshire SL9 8QH (✆ 01753 886097); NDE Centre, Department of Mechanical Engineering, University College London, Torrington Place, London WC1E 7JE (✆ 020 7380 7184, fax 020 7383 0831, e-mail wddover@btinternet.com)

DOW, Rt Rev (Geoffrey) Graham; s of Ronald Graham Dow (d 1983), of Harpenden, Herts, and Dorothy May, *née* Christie (d 1995); *b* 4 July 1942, Southgate, London; *Educ* St Albans Sch, The Queen's Coll Oxford (BA, BSc, MA), Univ of Birmingham (Dip Pastoral Studies), Univ of Nottingham (MPhil); *m* 23 July 1966, Molly Patricia, da of Roland Eric Sturges; 3 s (Alastair Graham *b* 8 Dec 1968, James Peter Graham (Jamie) *b* 12 Dec 1970, Michael Graham *b* 10 Jan 1975), 1 da (Lindsay Patricia *b* 26 April 1972); *Career* ordained (Rochester): deacon 1967, priest 1968; asst curate Tonbridge Parish Church 1967–72, chaplain student St John's Coll Oxford 1972–75 (acting chaplain 1974–75), lectr in Christian doctrine St John's Coll Nottingham 1975–81, supr Univ of Nottingham 1975–81, vicar Holy Trinity Coventry 1981–92, canon theologian Coventry Cathedral 1988, bishop of Willesden 1992–2000, bishop of Carlisle 2000–09, asst bishop Chester 2009–asst bishop Manchester 2011; memb House of Lords 2007–09; Coventry Dio: memb Bishop's Cncl for Miny 1981–87, memb Bishop's Cncl 1982–85, memb Deanery and Diocesan Synods 1982–, chm Coventry Christian Trg Project 1982–88 (dir Christian Trg Prog 1988–92), tstee Church Patronage Tst 1985; chm Bd of Social Responsibility London Dio 1992–97; chaplain Coventry Branch Owen Owen plc 1981–92, govr Blue Coat Sch Coventry 1981–92 (tstee 1981–87), tstee Settle & Carlisle Railway Tst 2009 (chair 2015); *Publications* incl: The Local Church's Political Responsibility (1980), Whose Hand on the Tiller? (1983), Those Tiresome Intruders (1990), Christian Renewal in Europe (1992), Explaining Deliverance (1991), A Christian Understanding of Daily Work (1994), Pathways of Prayer (1996), When He Comes (2010), Leading Rural Churches for Growth (2015); *Recreations* steam and model railways, travel, music; *Style—* The Rt Rev Graham Dow; ✉ 34 Kimberley Avenue, Romiley, Stockport SK6 4AB (mobile 07774 421678, e-mail graham@gdow.co.uk)

DOW, Prof Julian Alexander Thomas; s of William Alexander Nicholas Dow, of Glos, and Eirona Elizabeth Dow; *b* 1957; *Educ* King's Sch Gloucester, St Catharine's Coll Cambridge (scholar, MA, PhD, ScD, Athletics blue); *m* 2001, Shireen-Anne Davies; 2 s (Nicholas, Jamie), 1 step s (Benjamin), 2 step da (Sofya, Clara); *Career* Harkness fell 1981–83, research fell St Catharine's Coll Cambridge 1983–84; Univ of Glasgow: lectr in cell biology 1984–94, sr lectr in cell biology 1994–97, reader in genetics 1997–99, prof of molecular and integrative physiology 1999–, head Div of Molecular Genetics 2001–05; BBSRC: memb Investigating Gene Function Panel 1998, memb Genomics in Animal Function Panel 1999, memb Animal Sciences Panel 1999–2002, memb Research Equipment Initative Panel 1999–2001; chair UK Drosophila Genomics Steering Ctee 2000–02; memb: Soc for Experimental Biology 1981–, Royal Entomological Soc of London 1985–, Physiological Soc 1998–; President's Medal Soc for Experimental Biology 1992, Bidder lectr Soc for Experimental Biology; FRSE 2010; *Books* Dictionary of Cell and Molecular Biology (3 edn, 1999); *Recreations* skiing, diving; *Clubs* Achilles, Hawks' (Cambridge); *Style—* Prof Julian Dow; ✉ Institute of Molecular, Cell and Systems Biology, University of Glasgow, Glasgow G12 8QQ (e-mail julian.dow@glasgow.ac.uk)

DOWD, George Simon Edmund; s of George Francis Edmund Dowd, of Scarborough, N Yorks, and Lily, *née* Clay; *b* 9 November 1946, Halifax, Yorks; *Educ* Scarborough HS for Boys, Univ of Liverpool Med Sch (MB ChB, FRCS, MCh (Orth), MD); *m* Angela Christine, da of John Anthony Sedman; 3 da (Olivia Jayne *b* 13 Oct 1975, Caroline Suzanne *b* 19 Oct 1977, Charlotte Louise *b* 12 Nov 1980); *Career* house surgn and physician David Lewis Northern Hosp Liverpool 1971–72, lectr in orthopaedics Univ of Liverpool 1978–81; sr lectr and conslt orthopaedic surgn: Royal Liverpool Hosp and Royal Liverpool Children's Hosp 1981–82, Univ of London and Royal Nat Orthopaedic Hosp 1982–87; conslt orthopaedic surgn St Bartholomew's Hosp and sr lectr Univ of London 1987–96; currently: hon conslt orthopaedic surgn Royal Free Hosp, hon sr lectr Royal Free Med Sch, dir Knee Surgery Unit Wellington Hosp London; Hunterian prof RCS 1985; ABC travelling fell, Heritage visiting prof Calgary Canada 1986; Norman Roberts medal 1978, President's medal BR Orthopaedic Res Soc 1986; memb: BMA, Br Orthopaedic Assoc, Br Orthopaedic Res Soc, Br Assoc for Surgery of the Knee; hon memb Arthroscopy of N America; *Publications* Multiple Choice Questions In Orthopaedics and Trauma (1987), Self-assessment on Trauma and Orthopaedics (co-author); also nine book chapters and papers on trauma, arthritis and knee disorders in leading med jls; *Recreations* sailing, tennis, travel, photography; *Style—* George Dowd, Esq; ✉ Royal Free Hospital, Pond Street, London NW3 2QG (✆ 020 7794 0500, e-mail dowd007@aol.com); Wellington Knee Surgery Unit, Wellington Hospital, Wellington Place, London NW8 9LR (✆ 020 7586 5959)

DOWD, James (Jim); MP; s of late James Dowd, and Elfriede Dowd; *b* 5 March 1951; *Educ* Sedgehill Comp Sch London, London Nautical Sch; *Career* apprentice Post Office telephone engr 1967–72, station mangr Heron Petrol Stations 1972–73, telecommunications engr Plessey 1973–92; London Borough of Lewisham: cncllr 1974–94, sometime chm Fin Ctee, dep mayor 1987 and 1991, mayor 1992; former memb Lewisham and N Southwark DHA; Parly candidate (Lab) Beckenham 1983, MP (Lab): Lewisham W 1992–2010 (also contested 1987), Lewisham W and Penge 2010–; London whip 1993–95, memb Shadow NI Team 1995–97, a Lord Cmmr of HM Treasy (Govt whip) 1997–2001, memb Health Select Ctee 2001–10, chair All Pty Parly Small Shops 2002–06, memb Science and Technol Select Ctee 2012–; memb: Lab Pty 1970–, Int Fund for Animal Welfare, GMB; *Style—* Jim Dowd, Esq, MP; ✉ House of Commons, London SW1A 0AA (☎ 020 7219 4617, fax 020 7219 2686, e-mail dowdj@parliament.uk)

DOWD, Peter; MP; *Career* MP (Lab) Bootle 2015–; *Style—* Peter Dowd, Esq, MP; ✉ House of Commons, London SW1A 0AA

DOWD, Prof Peter Alan; s of Andrew James Dowd, of NSW, Aust, and Lorna May, *née* Harris; *b* 21 July 1946; *Educ* Marist Brothers' Coll Broken Hill Aust, Univ of New England (BSc), Ecole Polytechnique de l'Université de Montréal Canada (MSc), Univ of Leeds (PhD); *m* 1978, Ingrid Elizabeth, da of Stanley Crystal Gittings; 1 s (Dylan Benjamin b 15 June 1979); *Career* operational research offr Zinc Corp/New Broken Hill Consolidated Ltd NSW 1967–71, res fell Ecole Poly Montréal 1971–75; Dept of Mining and Mineral Engrg Univ of Leeds: BP research fell 1975–78, lectr 1978–86, sr lectr 1986–90, reader in mining geostatistics and operational research 1990–92, prof of mine design and geostatistics 1992, prof of mining engrg 1993–2004, head Mining Engrg Dept 1995–2001, acting head Dept of Chem Engrg 1997–2000, head Sch of Process Environmental and Materials Engrg 1997–2003; Univ of Adelaide Aust: exec dean Faculty of Engrg, Computer and Mathematical Sciences 2004–12, prof of mining engrg and exec dir Mining Educn Australia 2013–15, prof of mining engrg 2016–; visiting prof: Ecole Nationale Supérieure des Mines de Paris 1981–83, Dept of Mine Planning and Mineral Processing Tech Univ of Lisbon 1977–91, Dept of Chem, Materials, Mining and Metallurgical Engrg Univ of Rome 1985–86; visiting lectr: Dept of Mining Engrg Univ of Queensland 1982, Otago Sch of Mines Univ of Dunedin 1983, China Univ of Mining and Technol 1986–87; Inst of Mining and Metallurgy: sec North of England Section 1983–98, Exec Ctee 1993, vice-pres 1996–98, pres 1998–99; chm: Int Assoc for Mathematical Geology Geostatics Ctee 1990–95, Nat Mining Industry Conference Organising Ctee 1992–95, IMM Serial Pubs Ctee 1992–2000, Univ of Leeds Mining Assoc; chair Gp of Eight Engrg Deans and Assocs 2007–12, pres Australian Cncl of Engrg Deans 2009–10; UK ed De Geostatisticus 1987–2002, chair Editorial Bd Mining Technology 2003–, memb Editorial Bd Mathematical Geosciences 2007–; memb: Soc of Mining Professors 1993–, Leeds GS Bd of Governors 1997–2004, Canadian Inst of Mining and Metallurgy (fell 1973–), Int Assoc for Mathematical Geology, Int Geostatistics Assoc; fell Australasian Inst of Mining and Metallurgy 1983; FREng 1998, FTSE 2006, FRSA, FIMMM, FIChemE, FIQ; *Publications* author of numerous papers and parts of books and articles in learned jls; *Recreations* cross country running, cinema, theatre, opera, cricket; *Style—* Prof Peter Dowd, FREng, FRSA, FTSE; ✉ Faculty of Engineering, Computer and Mathematical Sciences, University of Adelaide, Adelaide, SA 5005, Australia (☎ 00 61 8 8313 4543, e-mail peter.dowd@adelaide.edu.au)

DOWDEN, Richard George; s of Peter John Dowden (d 2003), of Fairford, Glos, and Eleanor Isabella, *née* Hepple (d 2005); *b* 20 March 1949; *Educ* St George's Coll, Bedford Coll London (BA); *m* 3 July 1976, (Mary Catherine) Penny Mansfield, CBE, da of Stanley William Mansfield (d 1977); 2 da (Isabella Catherine b 1981, Sophie Elizabeth b 1983); *Career* sec Cmmn for Int Justice and Peace RC Bishops Conf 1972–75, ed Catholic Herald 1976–79, journalist The Times 1980–86, Africa ed The Independent 1986–94, dip ed The Independent 1994, Africa ed The Economist 1995–2001, exec dir Royal African Soc 2002–; *Books* Africa: Altered States, Ordinary Miracles (2008); *Style—* Richard Dowden, Esq; ✉ The Royal African Society, 36 Gordon Square, London WC1H 0PD

DOWDESWELL, Prof Julian Andrew; s of Robert Dowdeswell, of Oxford, and Joan Marion, *née* Longshaw; *b* 18 November 1957; *Educ* Magdalen Coll Sch Oxford, Jesus Coll Cambridge (scholar, BA, PhD, ScD), Univ of Colorado (MA); *m* 20 Aug 1983, Evelyn Kae, *née* Lind; 1 da (Victoria Marie b 16 June 1988), 1 s (Adam Robert b 26 Feb 1992); *Career* research assoc Scott Polar Research Inst Univ of Cambridge 1985, lectr Univ of Wales Aberystwyth 1986–89, sr asst in research then asst dir of research Scott Polar Research Inst Univ of Cambridge 1989–94, prof of glaciology and dir Centre for Glaciology Univ of Wales Aberystwyth 1994–98, prof of physical geography and dir Bristol Glaciology Centre Univ of Bristol 1998–2001, prof of physical geography and dir Scott Polar Research Inst Univ of Cambridge 2001–, fell Jesus Coll Cambridge 2002–; head Glaciers and Ice Sheets Div Int Cmmn for Snow and Ice 1999–; memb Cncl Int Glaciology Soc 1993–96, UK memb Cncl of Int Arctic Science Ctee 2001–, chair UK Nat Antarctic Research Ctee 2002–06, UK alternate delg Cncl of Scientific Ctee on Antarctic Research 2002–06 and 2012–; govr Plascrug Sch Aberystwyth 1996–98; hon fell Aberystwyth Univ 2016; Polar Medal 1995, Gill Meml Award RGS 1998, Fndr's Medal RGS 2008, Louis Agassiz Medal European Geosciences Union 2011, IASC Medal Int Arctic Science Ctee 2014; fell Br Soc for Geomorphology 2014, hon memb American Polar Soc 2015; FRGS 1985; *Publications* Glacimarine Environments: Processes and Sediments (jt ed, 1990), The Arctic and Environmental Change (jt ed, 1996), Glacial and Oceanic History of the Polar North Atlantic Margins (jt ed, 1998), Glacially Influenced Sedimentation on High Latitude Continental Margins (jt ed, 2002), Islands of the Arctic (2002), The Antarctic Paintings of Edward Seago (2006), Scott of the Antractic (2012), Ernest Shackleton – Polar Explorer (2015); author of more than 275 articles on glaciology, glacier-marine interactions, cryosphere and climate change, and satellite sensing of ice; *Recreations* hill and coastal walking, skiing, travel, watching Oxford United FC; *Clubs* Arctic, Antarctic; *Style—* Prof Julian Dowdeswell; ✉ Scott Polar Research Institute, University of Cambridge, Cambridge CB2 1ER (☎ 01223 336541, fax 01223 336549, e-mail jd16@cam.ac.uk, website www.spri.cam.ac.uk/people/dowdeswell); Jesus College, Jesus Lane, Cambridge CB5 8BL

DOWDING, Prof Keith Martin; s of Jeffrey William Dowding, and Sheila Leanora, *née* Patton; *b* 6 May 1960, Swindon, Wilts; *Educ* Noel-Baker Comp Sch, Keele Univ (BA), Nuffield Coll Oxford (DPhil); *m* Anne Vivienne Gelling; 2 s (Jonathon, Christopher); *Career* lectr in politics: St Catherine's Coll Oxford 1984–88, Univ Coll Oxford 1986–87, Brunel Univ 1988–93; lectr in political theory Poly of N London 1987, Hallsworth fell Univ of Manchester 1993–94; LSE: lectr in public choice and public policy 1993–96, reader in public choice and public admin 1996–2000, prof of political science 2000–07; visiting fell: ANU 2000–02, Netherlands Inst for Advanced Study 2006; Br Acad research readership 2005–07, assoc memb Nuffield Coll Oxford 2005–, prof of political sci ANU 2007–; Rational Choice and Political Power (1991), Preferences, Institutions and Rational Choice (ed with Desmond King, 1995), The Civil Service (1995), Power (1996), Challenges to Democracy (ed with James Hughes and Helen Margetts, 2001), The Ethics of Stakeholding (ed with Jurgen De Wispelaere and Stuart White, 2003), Justice and Democracy (ed with Robert E Goodin and Carole Pateman, 2004); numerous chapters, articles and reviews in jls and books; *Style—* Prof Keith Dowding; ✉ Department of Government, London School of Economics and Political Science, Houghton Street, London WC2A 2AE (☎ 020 7955 7176, fax 020 7831 1707, e-mail k.m.dowding@lse.ac.uk)

DOWDING, Nicholas Alan Tatham; QC (1997); s of Alan Lorimer Dowding, of Witney, Oxon, and Jennifer Mary, *née* Hughes; *b* 24 February 1956; *m* 23 March 2007, Alison Denise Oakes; 3 da (Eleanor Clare b 24 Aug 1985, Rebecca Judith b 9 Sept 1987, Katherine Sarah b 14 May 1989); *Career* called to the Bar Inner Temple 1979; past chm Property Bar Assoc; memb: Chancery Bar Assoc, London and Common Law Bar Assoc; Hon MRICS; *Publications* ed Handbook of Rent Review (jtly, 1980–85), ed Woodfall on Landlord and Tenant (jtly, 1994), Dilapidations: The Modern Law and Practice (jtly, 1994, 5 edn 2014), ed Landlord and Tenant Reports; *Recreations* sailing, riding, juggling, limericks; *Style—* Nicholas Dowding, Esq, QC; ✉ Falcon Chambers, Falcon Court, Temple, London EC4Y 1AA (☎ 020 7353 2484, fax 020 7353 1261, e-mail dowding@falcon-chambers.com)

DOWDING, 3 Baron (UK 1943); Piers Hugh Tremenheere Dowding; s of 2 Baron Dowding (d 1992), and his 2 w, Alison Margaret, *née* Bannerman; *b* 18 February 1948; *Educ* Fettes, Amherst Coll Mass (BA); *m* 1973, Noriko Shiho; 2 da (Hon Rosemary June b 25 Sept 1975, Hon Elizabeth Yuki b 16 Feb 1989); *Heir* bro, Hon Mark Dowding; *Career* prof of English Okayama Shoka Univ 1999– (assoc prof 1977–); life pres Dumfries and Galloway Branch Aircrew Assoc; *Style—* The Rt Hon Lord Dowding

DOWDING, Her Hon Judge Sally; da of Edward Charles Wisnom Dowding, and Grace Evelyn, *née* Ridley; *b* Hereford; *Educ* Univ of Manchester (LLB), Keele Univ (MA); *m*; 2 da; *Career* admitted slr 1979; dep district judge 2000, district judge 2007, circuit judge (Midland Circuit) 2013–; *Style—* Her Hon Judge Dowding; ✉ Wolverhampton Combined Court Centre, Pipers Row, Wolverhampton WV1 3LQ

DOWDS, Donal Joseph; s of William James Dowds (d 1992), and Mary, *née* Noone (d 2002); *b* 3 May 1953, Burnfoot, Co Donegal; *Educ* Paisley Coll of Tech (BSc), Univ of Glasgow (MBA); *m* 29 July 1978, Jane Marie; 3 c (Mark b 2 May 1981, Ruari b 27 Nov 1982, Grainne b 8 Jan 1985); *Career* BAA plc: joined 1979, ops dir Glasgow Airport 1988–92, md Glasgow Airport Ltd 1992–96, dep md BAA Scottish Airports 1995, md Edinburgh Airport Ltd 1996–99, md BAA Scotland 1999–2003, divnl md BAA Scotland & USA 2003–07, chm and pres BAA USA Hldgs Inc 2003–07, chm and pres BAA USA Inc 2003–07; former chm: Scottish Airports Ltd, Aberdeen Airport Ltd, Edinburgh Airport Ltd, Glasgow Airport Ltd; former dir: BAA Int Ltd, BAA (Int Hldgs) Ltd; non-exec dir BAA Naples Airport; memb Bd Airport Operators' Assoc (chm until 2004); former vice-chm Scottish Tourism Forum, dir Glasgow C of C until 2000, vice-chm Edinburgh Lothians and Borders Tourist Bd until 2000, memb Bd VisitScotland 2000–06, memb Bd Scottish Cncl for Devpt and Industry 2001–; CEng, MICE; *Recreations* reading, music, shooting, golf, fishing; *Style—* Donal Dowds, Esq

DOWELL, Prof John Derek; s of William Ernest Dowell, of Ellistown, Leics, and Elsie Dorothy, *née* Jarvis; *b* 6 January 1935; *Educ* Coalville GS, Univ of Birmingham (BSc, PhD); *m* 19 Aug 1959, Patricia, da of Lesley Clarkson, of Maltby, S Yorks; 1 da (Laura b 1962), 1 s (Simon Jeremy b 1964); *Career* research fell Univ of Birmingham 1958–60, research assoc CERN Geneva 1960–62, lectr in physics Univ of Birmingham 1962–68, visiting scientist Argonne Nat Laboratory 1968–69, sr lectr Univ of Birmingham 1970–73 (lectr 1969–70), scientific assoc CERN Geneva 1973–74 and 1985–87; Univ of Birmingham: sr lectr 1974–75, reader 1975–80, prof of elementary particle physics 1980–, Poynting prof of physics 1997–2002, emeritus prof 2002–; co-spokesman UA1 experiment CERN 1985–88; chm SERC Particle Physics Ctee 1981–85 (memb Nuclear Physics Bd 1974–77 and 1981–85), chm CERN LEP Ctee 1993–96, chm Rutherford Appleton Laboratory Users Advsy Ctee 1993–98, chm ATLAS Collaboration Bd (CERN) 1996–98, memb CERN Scientific Policy Ctee 1982–90 and 1993–96, UK memb Euro Ctee for Future Accelerators 1989–93; memb: BBC Sci Consultative Gp 1992–94, DESY Extended Scientific Cncl 1992–98, Ct Univ of Warwick 1992–2001, Particle Physics and Astronomy Research Cncl 1994–97, Cncl Royal Soc 1997–98 (vice-pres 1998), HEFCE RAE Panel (Physics) 1999–2001; lay chair Birmingham Children's Hosp NHS Tst 2004–; author of over 200 papers in scientific jls; fell American Physical Soc 2004; FRS 1986, FInstP 1987 (Rutherford medal and prize 1988), CPhys 1987; *Recreations* piano, amateur theatre, golf; *Style—* Prof John Dowell, FRS; ✉ 57 Oxford Road, Moseley, Birmingham B13 9ES (☎ 0121 449 3332); School of Physics and Astronomy, The University of Birmingham, Birmingham B15 2TT (☎ 0121 414 4658, fax 0121 414 6709, e-mail j.d.dowell@bham.ac.uk)

DOWER, Robert Charles Philips (Robin); s of John Gordon Dower (d 1947), and Pauline Dower, CBE, JP, *née* Trevelyan; *b* 27 October 1938; *Educ* The Leys Sch Cambridge, St John's Coll Cambridge (MA), Univ of Edinburgh (BArch), Univ of Newcastle upon Tyne (DipLD); *m* 4 Nov 1967, Frances Helen, da of Henry Edmeades Baker, of Owletts, Kent; 1 s (Thomas b 1971), 2 da (Beatrice b 1974, Caroline b 1976); *Career* architect, historic buildings conslt; Yorke Rosenberg Mardall London 1964–71, in private practice as princ Spence & Dower (chartered architects) Newcastle upon Tyne 1974–; memb: Northumberland and Newcastle Soc 1971– (chm 1997–2008), Northern Cncl for Sport and Recreation 1976–86, Countryside Cmmn for England and Wales 1982–91, Diocesan Advsy Ctee (Newcastle Dio) 1995–; minister's nominee to Northumberland Nat Park 1978–81, Cathedrals Fabric Cmmn for England nominee to Fabric Ctee Durham Cathedral 1991– (chm 1997–); ARIBA 1965; *Recreations* wood engraving, lettering inscriptions, walking, gardening; *Style—* Robin Dower, Esq; ✉ Cambo House, Cambo, Morpeth, Northumberland NE61 4AY (☎ 01670 774297); c/o Spence & Dower, 25 Main Street, Ponteland, Newcastle-upon-Tyne NE20 9NH (☎ 01661 820071)

DOWLEY, (Laurence) Justin; s of Laurence Edward Dowley, of Great Bowden, Leics, and Virginia, *née* Jorgensen; *b* 9 June 1955; *Educ* Ampleforth, Balliol Coll Oxford (MA); *m* 2, 11 Oct 1986, Emma, da of Martin and Felice Lampard, of Theberton, Suffolk; 2 da (Laura b 1987, Florrie b 1994), 2 s (Myles b 1989, Finn b 1992); *Career* Price Waterhouse 1977–80, Morgan Grenfell & Co Ltd 1981–96 (dir 1988–96); Merrill Lynch: md 1996–, co-head M&A Europe 1997–99, co-head investment banking Europe 1999–2001; fndr ptnr Tricorn Partners LLP 2003–09, vice-chm Nomura Int 2010–11; non-exec dir: Intermediate Capital Gp plc 2006–10 (chm 2010–16), Ascot Authy (Hldgs) Ltd 2008–, Melrose plc 2011–, Novae Gp plc 2015–; non-exec Nat Crime Agency 2013–; ACA 1980; *Clubs* MCC (memb Fin Ctee 1997–, treas 2006–12), Boodle's, Garrick, Jockey; *Style—* Justin Dowley, Esq; ✉ e-mail justin@dowley.me

DOWLING, Prof Dame Ann Patricia; OM (2016), DBE (2007, CBE 2002); da of Mortimer Joseph Patrick Dowling, of Birchington, Kent, and Joyce, *née* Barnes; *Educ* Ursuline Convent Sch Westgate, Girton Coll Cambridge (MA, PhD), Univ of Cambridge (ScD); *m* 31 Aug 1974, Dr Thomas Paul Hynes, s of Thomas Hynes; *Career* Sidney Sussex Coll Cambridge: research fell 1977–78, dir of studies in engrg 1979–90, fell 1979–; Univ of Cambridge: asst lectr in engrg 1979–82, lectr 1982–86, reader in acoustics 1986–93, dep head Engrg Dept 1990–93 and 1996–99, prof of mechanical engrg 1993–, chm Univ Gas Turbine Partnership 2009– (dir 2001–09), head Engrg Dept 2009–14; Jerome C Hunsaker visiting prof MIT 1999–2000, Moore distinguished scholar Caltech 2001; non-exec dir DRA 1995–97, non-exec dir BP plc 2012–, non-exec Bd memb Dept of Business Innovation and Skills 2014–; chm: EPSRC Technical Opportunities Panel 2002–06 (memb 1998–2002), Rolls-Royce Propulsion and Power Advsy Bd 2003–08; Royal Acad of Engrg: memb Cncl 1998–2002, vice-pres 1999–2002, pres 2014–; memb Cncl EPSRC 2001–06; ind memb Defence Science Advsy Cncl 1998–2001, memb PM's Cncl for Science and Technol 2014–; tstee: Ford of Britain Tst 1993–2002, Nat Museum of Science and Industry 1999–2008, Fndn of the Queen Elizabeth II Prize for Engrg 2014–, Cambridge Tsts 2015–; govr Felsted Sch 1994–99; winner A B Wood Medal Inst of Acoustics 1990, ASME Kate Gleason Award 2013; ScD (hc) Univ of Dublin 2008, Hon DSc Imperial Coll London 2013, Hon DSc KTH Royal Inst of Technol Stockholm 2013, DSc (hc) Univ of

Oxford 2015, DSc (hc) Univ of Leeds 2015, Hon DScEng Queen's Univ Belfast 2015, Hon DEng London South Bank Univ 2015, Hon DEng Heriot-Watt Univ 2015; fell: Inst of Acoustics 1989, Cambridge Philosophical Soc 1993, AIAA 2012 (memb 1990); foreign assoc: French Acad of Science 2002, US Nat Acad of Engrg 2008–; CEng 1990, FIMechE 1990 (hon FIMechE 2011), FREng 1996, FRS 2003 (memb Cncl 2009–), FRAeS, hon fell Instn of Engrg Designers 2011; *Books* Sound and Sources of Sound (with J E Ffowcs Williams, 1983), Modern Methods in Analytical Acoustics (with D G Crighton et al, 1992), contribs to various scientific jls; *Recreations* opera, walking; *Style*— Prof Dame Ann Dowling, OM, DBE, FRS, FREng; ✉ Engineering Department, University of Cambridge, Trumpington Street, Cambridge CB2 1PZ (✆ 01223 332739, e-mail apd1@cam.ac.uk)

DOWN, Lesley-Anne; da of P J Down, of London, and Isabella, *née* Gordon-Young; *b* 17 March 1955; *Educ* Professional Children's Sch; *m* 1, 1982 (m dis 1985), William Friedkin; 1 s (Jack b 1982); *m* 2, 1986, Don E FauntLeRoy, s of Donald FauntLeRoy; *Career* actress 1967–; *Theatre* incl: The Marquise, Hamlet, Great Expectations, Pygmalion; *Television* incl: The Snow Queen, Upstairs Downstairs, The One and Only Phyliss Dixie, Heartbreak House, Unity Mitford, The Hunchback of Notre Dame, The Last Days of Pompeii, Arch of Triumph, North And South (books 1, 2 and 3), Indiscreet, Ladykillers, Nightwalk, Frog Girl, The Brewery, Sunset Beach, The Bold and the Beautiful; *Film* incl: The Smashing Bird I Used to Know, All the Right Noises, Countess Dracula, Assault, Scalawag, Tales from Beyond The Grave, Brannigan, The Pink Panther Strikes Again, A Little Night Music, The Betsy, Hanover Street, The Great Train Robbery, Rough Cut, Sphinx, Scenes from A Goldmine, Nomads, Munchie Strikes Back, The Unfaithful, Meet Wally Sparks; *Awards* nominee Golden Globe Best Actress for North And South; winner: Evening Standard Award Best New Actress for The Pink Panther Strikes Again, Bravo Award Best Actress for North And South; *Style*— Ms Lesley-Anne Down

DOWN AND DROMORE, Bishop of 1997–; Rt Rev Harold Creeth Miller; s of Harold Miller (d 1984), of Belfast, and Violet, *née* McGinley (d 1991); *b* 23 February 1950; *Educ* Belfast HS, Trinity Coll Dublin (BA, MA), Univ of Nottingham (BA), St John's Coll Nottingham (DPS); *m* 2 Jan 1978, Elizabeth Adelaide, *née* Harper; 2 s (Kevin Samuel b 18 July 1981, Niall Matthew Harold b 21 Sept 1988), 2 da (Ciara Elizabeth Maeve b 17 Feb 1983, Laura Ruth b 27 Sept 1985); *Career* ordained: deacon 1976, priest 1977; curate St Nicholas' Carrickfergus 1976–79, chaplain and dir of extension studies St John's Coll Nottingham 1979–84, chaplain Queen's Univ Belfast 1984–89, rector Carrigrohane Union of Parishes 1989–97; canon: St Fin Barre's Cathedral, Cork and Cloyne Cathedral, St Patrick's Cathedral Dublin; co-chair AMICUM (Anglican-Methodist Int Communion for Unity in Mission); memb Bd TEAR Fund; memb Mensa; DD (hc) Nashotah House; *Recreations* travel, music, phillumeny; *Style*— The Rt Rev the Bishop of Down and Dromore; ✉ The See House, 32 Knockdene Park South, Belfast BT5 7AB (✆ 028 9047 1973, fax 028 9065 0584, e-mail bishop@down.anglican.org)

DOWNER, Philip John; s of John Downer, and Judith, *née* Brentnall; *b* 29 September 1960; *Educ* Uppingham; *m* 21 Sept 1991, Julia, *née* Watson; 1 da; *Career* personnel and trg dir Our Price Records 1990–94 (retail ops 1980–90), vice-pres Waterstone's Inc 1994–96, ops dir Thomas Pink 1996–97; Borders (UK) Ltd: ops dir Superstores 1997–2000, md Superstores 2000–03, md 2003–06, retail dir 2006–07, ceo 2008–09; retail conslt Front of Store 2010–, md Calliope Gifts Ltd 2012–; chm World Book Day 2007; memb Cncl Booksellers' Assoc 2003; *Publications* A Year at Front of Store (e-book), articles in The Bookseller, Retail Week and Publishing Perspectives; *Recreations* books, music, travel; *Style*— Philip Downer, Esq; ✉ e-mail philipdowner@btinternet.com

DOWNES, Justin; s of Patrick Downes (d 1978), and late Eileen Marie, *née* Mackie; *b* 26 September 1950, Warks; *Educ* The Oratory Sch Reading; *Career* dir: Financial Strategy 1980–85, Streets Financial Strategy 1985–86, Embradoc UK 2013, Yemanja Ventures Ltd 2013; fndr Financial Dynamics Ltd 1986–87; dir London Financial News 1996–97; former dir: Corporate Dynamics Ltd, Rizwan Nash Ltd; non-exec dir Hansard Group plc 1999–2002; various private cos; patron Cncl Family Holidays Assoc 1990; memb Somerset CC 1976–78; *Style*— Justin Downes, Esq; ✉ e-mail jd@downes.com

DOWNES, Prof Sir Pete; kt (2015), OBE (2004); *Career* Univ of Dundee: joined 1989, head Dept of Biochemistry 1994–2002, head Sch of Life Sciences 2002–04, dean Faculty of Life Sciences 2004–06, vice-princ and head Coll of Life Sciences 2006–09, princ and vice-chllr 2009–; chm Exec Ctee Biochemical Soc 2001–04, memb Cncl Soc of Biology; convener Univs Scotland 2012–16; tstee The Saltire Fndn; Colworth Medal Br Biochemical Soc 1987; FRSE 1991, FMedSci 2010; *Style*— Prof Sir Pete Downes, OBE; ✉ University of Dundee, Nethergate, Dundee DD1 4HN

DOWNEY, Her Hon Judge Aileen Patricia; *Career* called to the Bar 1991; recorder 2009, circuit judge (South Eastern Circuit) 2014–; *Style*— Her Hon Judge Downey; ✉ c/o Croydon County Court and Family Court, The Law Courts, Altyre Road, Croydon, Surrey CR9 5AB

DOWNHILL, Ronald Edward; s of John Edward Downhill (d 1986), of Burghfield Common, Berks and Lily, *née* Darraugh (d 2008); *b* 11 August 1943; *Educ* Hyde Co GS; *m* 1969, Olwen Elizabeth, da of Ronald Siddle; 3 da (Helen Louise b 1972, Rebecca Clare Elizabeth b 1975, Victoria Ruth b 1984); *Career* called to the Bar 1968, admitted slr 1974; Inland Revenue: Chief Inspector's Branch 1960–64, Estate Duty Office 1964–69, Slr's Office 1969–74; self employed tax conslt in partnership 1977–82, tax specialist and conslt Berwin Leighton Paisner (joined 1974, ptnr 1976–77 and 1982–2013); advsr to Inland Revenue Tax Rewrite Project 1996; chm Revenue Law Ctee of Law Soc 1997–2000 (memb 1989–2009); memb: Law Soc 1974, STEP 1993; ATII 1978; *Recreations* watching soccer, theatre; *Style*— Ronald Downhill, Esq; ✉ Berwin Leighton Paisner Solicitors, Adelaide House, London Bridge, London EC4R 9HA (✆ 020 3400 1000, fax 020 3400 1111, e-mail ron.downhill@blplaw.com)

DOWNIE, Prof Robert Silcock; s of Capt Robert Mackie Downie (d 1980), of Glasgow, and Margaret Barlas, *née* Brown (d 1974); *b* 19 April 1933; *Educ* HS of Glasgow, Univ of Glasgow (MA), The Queen's Coll Oxford (BPhil); *m* 15 Sept 1958, Eileen Dorothea, da of Capt Wilson Ashley Flynn (d 1942), of Glasgow; 3 da (Alison, Catherine, Barbara); *Career* Russian linguist Intelligence Corps 1955–57; Univ of Glasgow: lectr in philosophy 1959–69, prof of moral philosophy 1969–2002, professorial research fell 2002–; visiting prof of philosophy Syracuse Univ NY 1963–64; Stevenson lectr in medical ethics 1986–88; FRSE 1986, FRSA 1999; *Books* Government Action and Morality (1964), Respect for Persons (1969), Roles and Values (1971), Education and Personal Relationships (1974), Caring and Curing (1980), Healthy Respect (1987), Health Promotion (1990), The Making of a Doctor (1992), Francis Hutcheson (1994), The Healing Arts: An Illustrated Oxford Anthology (1994), Palliative Care Ethics (1995), Medical Ethics (1996), Clinical Judgement Evidence in Practice (2000), Palliative Care Philosophy: Critique and Reconstruction (2006), Bioethics and the Humanities (2007), End of Life Choices: Consensus and Controversy (2009); *Recreations* music; *Style*— Prof Robert Downie, FRSE, FRSA; ✉ 17 Hamilton Drive, Glasgow G12 8DN; Kilnaish, by Tarbert, Argyll PA29 6XZ (✆ 0141 339 1345); Department of Philosophy, University of Glasgow, Glasgow G12 8QQ (e-mail robert.downie@glasgow.ac.uk)

DOWNING, John; MBE (1992); *b* 17 April 1940; *m* 2007, Anita D'Attelis; *Career* photographer; apprentice photographic printer Daily Mail 1956–61; The Express: perm freelance photographer 1962–64, staff photographer 1964–2001, chief photographer 1985–2001; freelance photographer 2001–; maj news events covered incl: Vietnam, Beirut, The Falklands, Nicaragua, Afghanistan, The Gulf, Bosnia, Somalia and Rwanda; fndr Press Photographers' Assoc (now Br Press Photographers' Assoc) 1984 (pres until 1986); memb

judging panel: Ian Parry Scholarship 2002, Picture Editor Awards (student section) 2002; patron Ian Parry Scholarship 2006; life memb NUJ; memb London Welsh Male Voice Choir 1998; tstee Jubilee Campaign 2009; Hon FRPS 2011; *Awards* Rothman's Br Press Pictures of the Year (human interest) 1971, runner up (news feature) World Press Photo Competition 1972 and 1978, Ilford Br Press Phtographer of the Year 1977, 1979, 1980, 1981, 1984, 1988 and 1989, IPC Br Press Photographer of the Year 1977 and 1980 (runner-up 1991), UN Photography Gold Medal 1978, Photokina Gold Medal 1978, Martini Royal Newspaper Photographer of the Year 1990, Kodak Feature Photographer of the Year 1992/93, runner up Photographer of the Year Br Picture Editors' Awards 1994, 1995 and 1999, La Nacion (Argentina) Int Photographer of the Year 1994–95, overall winner Br Airways London Eye Photography Competition 2001, Br Picture Editors' Guild Lifetime Achievement Award 2001; *Style*— John Downing, Esq, MBE; ✉ 9 Norman House, Norman Avenue, Henley on Thames, Oxfordshire RG9 1ER (✆ 01491 578260, e-mail jd@johndowning.co.uk)

DOWNING, Prof Richard; s of John Clifford Downing, of Stourbridge, W Midlands, and Greta Irene, *née* Kelley; *b* 8 February 1951, Stourbridge, W Midlands; *Educ* King Edward VI Sch Stourbridge, Univ of Birmingham (BSc, MB ChB, MD); *m* 24 July 1976, Stella Elizabeth, da of Stefan Kolada, of Chaddesley Corbett, Worcs; 2 s (Benjamin Louis b 1978, Thomas Kolada b 1982), 2 da (Alice Elizabeth Gwendoline b 1984, Lily Anastazia b 1991); *Career* lectr in anatomy Univ of Birmingham 1976–77, res assoc Washington Univ St Louis MO 1977–78; surgical registrar: Birmingham AHA 1979–80, Worcester Royal Infirmary 1980–83; sr lectr and hon conslt in surgery Univ of Birmingham 1986–90 (lectr 1983–86), conslt vascular surgn and dir Islet Res Lab Worcestershire Royal Hosp 1990–, clinical lead for vascular surgery 2012–14; hon sr clinical lectr Univ of Birmingham 2009–, hon prof Sch of Life and Health Sciences Aston Univ Birmingham 2012; author of pubns on vascular surgery and pancreatic islet transplantation, memb Editorial Bd Br Jl of Diabetes and Vascular Disease (jl discontinued); examiner Faculty of Dental Surgery RCS, advsr in surgery Int Hosps Gp 1987–90; memb: BMA, Diabetes UK (also fndr memb Islet Transplant Consortium), Br Transplantation Soc, European Soc Vascular Surgery, Pancreatic Soc GB and Ireland, Vascular Soc GB and Ireland, Int Pancreas Soc, Islet Transplant Soc; FRCS 1980; *Recreations* antiquarian books, the countryside; *Style*— Prof Richard Downing; ✉ Department of Vascular Surgery, Worcestershire Royal Hospital, Worcester WR5 1DD (✆ 01905 760725, fax 01905 760681, e-mail r_downing@btinternet.com)

DOWNING, Stewart; *b* 22 July 1984, Middlesbrough; *Career* professional footballer; Middlesbrough FC: joined as apprentice, first team debut 2002, winners League Cup 2004, runners-up UEFA Cup 2006; Aston Villa FC 2009–11, Liverpool 2011–13, West Ham United 2013–; England: 33 caps, debut v Holland 2005, memb squad World Cup 2006; *Style*— Stewart Downing, Esq; ✉ c/o West Ham United, Boleyn Ground, Green Street, Upton Park, London E13 9AZ

DOWNS, Carolyn Grace; CB (2011); da of Eric Downs, of Hyde, Gtr Manchester, and Mildred, *née* Thomasson (d 2003); *b* 25 February 1960, Hyde, Manchester; *Educ* Kingston Univ (BA), UCL (MA); *m* 5 Nov 1988, Prof Jonathan Michie; 2 s (Alex b 7 Dec 1989, Duncan b 11 Dec 1995); *Career* Salops CC 1999–2009 (latterly chief exec); Miny of Justice: dep perm sec 2009–10, chief exec Legal Servs Cmmn 2010–11, chief exec Local Govt Assoc 2011–; *Recreations* skiing, tennis; *Style*— Ms Carolyn Downs, CB; ✉ 11 Norham Road, Oxford OX2 6SF (✆ 07581 730090); Local Government Association, Local Government House, Smith Square, London SW1P 3HZ (e-mail carolyn.downs@local.gov.uk)

DOWNSHIRE, 9 Marquess of (I 1789); (Arthur Francis) Nicholas Wills Hill; also Earl of Hillsborough (I 1751 and GB 1772), Viscount Hillsborough (I 1717), Viscount Fairford (GB 1772), Viscount Kilwarlin (I 1771), Baron Harwich (GB 1756), Baron Hill (I 1717) and Baron Sandys (UK 1802); Hereditary Constable of Hillsborough Fort; s of 8 Marquess of Downshire (d 2003), and Hon Juliet Mary, *née* Weld Forester (d 1986); *b* 4 February 1959; *Educ* Eton, RAC Cirencester, Poly of Central London; *m* 28 April 1990, Diana Jane (Janey), o da of Gerald Leeson Bunting, DL, of Northallerton, N Yorks; 3 da (Lady Isabella Diana Juliet b 3 April 1991, Lady Beatrice Hannah Georgina b 10 Feb 1994, Lady Claudia Lucy Helena b 15 March 1998), 1 s (Edmund Robin Arthur, Earl of Hillsborough b 21 May 1996); *Heir* s, Earl of Hillsborough; *Career* with Touche Ross & Co 1981–87, gp fin dir and co sec Scheduling Technology Gp (STG) Ltd 1988–2000, actg fin dir STG as subsid of Manugistics Inc 2001–02, co dir 2002–; co-dir: Animalcare Gp plc (formerly Ritchey plc), Identify UK Ltd until 2013, base2stay Ltd until 2012, Farmway Ltd until 2014, MFB Ltd; dir: Secure Tag Ltd 2012–, Willey Estates Ltd 2014–, Spices Galore Ltd 2015–, Moorland Assoc 2014–; memb: Woodard Fndn until 2012, Historic Houses Assoc, CLA, Game & Wildlife Conservation Tst; *Recreations* shooting and country pursuits, skiing, keen player of many sports; *Clubs* Whites; *Style*— The Most Hon the Marquess of Downshire

DOWSE, His Hon Judge John; s of Douglas Richard Maurice Dowse (d 1995), and Lilian Maude, *née* Cade; *b* 12 November 1946, Grayford, Kent; *Educ* Chatham House GS Ramsgate, Univ of Leeds (LLB), Cardiff Law Sch Univ of Wales (LLM); *m* 27 Dec 2000, Elaine, *née* McLean; 2 da (Phillippa Catherine Chaplin b 20 Oct 1977, Francesca Joanne b 27 May 1979), 1 s (Jonathan Douglas b 31 Oct 1981), 2 step-s (Mark Elliott Winstanley b 5 Oct 1978, Jonathan Scott Winstanley b 12 June 1980), 1 step-da (Chloe Louise Winstanley b 21 July 1983); *Career* various firms of slrs 1964–69, called to the Bar Lincoln's Inn 1973 (Sir Thomas More Bursar), barr 9 St John Street Manchester 1976–2001 (also dep head of chambers), asst recorder 1990, recorder 1994, circuit judge (North Eastern Circuit) 2001–, designated family judge Humberside 2007–; chm Humber Family Justice Cncl; Law Soc Prize to the Inst of Legal Execs 1969; *Recreations* tennis, golf driving ranges, dining out; *Style*— His Hon Judge Dowse; ✉ c/o The North Eastern Circuit, Brunswick House, Pocklington, York YO42 2QJ

DOWSON, Antony Peter; s of John Robert Dowson, and Sheila Margret, *née* Horstead; *b* 27 January 1958; *Educ* Royal Ballet Sch White Lodge, ARAD, PDTC; *m* 1, 17 March 1990 (m dis), Fiona Jane Chadwick; 1 da (Emily b 23 April 1991); *m* 2, 28 Aug 1997, Ruth Spivak; 1 da (Sophie b 24 Nov 1998), 1 s (Jacob b 1 March 2002); *Career* currently princ teacher English National Ballet Sch, former princ dancer Royal Ballet Co; leading roles with Royal Ballet incl: Mayerling, Manon, Sleeping Beauty, La Fille Mal Gardée, Prince of the Pagodas; *Recreations* watching football, Chelsea FC, listening to music, cooking; *Style*— Antony Dowson, Esq; ✉ c/o English National Ballet School, Carlyle Building, Hortensia Road, London SW10 0QS

DOWSON, Dr Jonathan Hudson; s of John Heaton Dowson (d 1994), and Margot Blanche, *née* Hudson (d 1992); *b* 19 March 1942; *Educ* The Leys Sch Cambridge, Queens' Coll Cambridge (MA, MB BChir, MD), St Thomas' Hosp, Univ of Edinburgh (DPM, PhD); *m* 29 Dec 1965, Lynn Susan, *née* Dothie; 1 da (Emma b 1967), 2 s (James b 1968, Jonathan b 1972); *Career* lectr in psychiatry Univ of Edinburgh 1973–75 (lectr in anatomy 1969–72), conslt psychiatrist Addenbrooke's Hosp Cambridge 1977–2009, lectr in psychiatry Univ of Cambridge 1977–2009, dir Studies in Clinical Med Queens' Coll Cambridge 1999–2009; visiting prof Univ of Florida 1983; examiner: RCPsych 1981–90 (regnl advsr 1990–95), Univ of Cambridge 1988–2009; papers on ageing, brain lipopigment, personality disorders and adult attention-deficit disorder; fell commoner Queens' Coll Cambridge 1985; FRCPsych; *Books* Personality Disorders: Recognition and Clinical Management (with A T Grounds, CUP, 1995); *Recreations* theatre; *Clubs* Oxford and Cambridge;

Style— Dr Jonathan Dowson; ✉ Old Vicarage, Church Lane, Sawston, Cambridge CB22 3JR

DOYLE, Prof Anthony (Tony); s of John Francis Doyle, of Leeds, and Eileen, *née* Simpson; *b* 28 January 1963, Leeds; *Educ* Cardinal Heenan HS Leeds, Univ of Manchester (BSc, PhD); *m* 15 July 1989, Jacqueline Ann, *née* Halliday; 3 s (Liam Matthew b 9 Jan 1990, Craig Robert b 11 Aug 1991, Adam Russell b 4 Oct 1994); *Career* SERC res assoc Univ of Manchester 1987–90; Univ of Glasgow: lectr 1990–99, reader 1999–2002, GridPP project ldr 2001–, prof 2002–; DESY visiting research scientist 1994–97, Alexander von Humboldt fell Univ of Hamburg 1998, PPARC sr res fell 2000, scientific assoc CERN 2011–12; author of more than 700 pubns on particle physics and grid computing; EPS Hepp Prize (ATLAS Collaboration) 2013, RSE Lord Kelvin Prize 2016; FInstP 2001, FRSE 2005; *Style*— Prof Tony Doyle; ✉ Dept of Physics and Astronomy, Kelvin Building, Univ of Glasgow G12 8QQ

DOYLE, Avril; da of Dr Richard Belton (d 1974), and Dr Freda Belton, *née* Ryan (d 2004); *b* 18 April 1949, Dublin; *Educ* Holy Child Convent Killiney, UCD (BSc); *m* Dec 1971, Frederick Doyle (d 2014); 3 da (Christina b 1972, Elizabeth b 1973, Kate b 1979); *Career* memb (Fine Gael) Wexford Corp and CC 1974–95 (mayor of Wexford 1976), TD (Fine Gael) Wexford 1982–89 and 1992–97, memb (senator) Seanad Éireann (Fine Gael) Agric Panel 1989–92 and 1997–2002, MEP (Fine Gael) Leinster 1999–2009; min of state Depts of Finance and Environment Ireland 1986–87, memb shadow cabinet 1992, min of state Taoiseach's Dept, Dept of Finance and Dept of Tport Energy and Communications Ireland 1995–97, ldr Irish Delgn European People's Party and European Dems 1999–2009, pres Equestrian Fedn of Ireland 2001–05; memb Royal Dublin Soc; hon assoc Br Veterinary Assoc; *Style*— Mrs Avril Doyle; ✉ Kitestown House, Wexford, Ireland (✆ 00 353 53 914 2873, e-mail office@avrildoyle.ie)

DOYLE, Craig; s of Sean Doyle, of Dublin, and Eithne, *née* Hannigan; *b* 17 December 1970; *Educ* Blackrock Coll Dublin, Nat Univ of Ireland Maynooth (BA), London Coll of Printing (Dip Broadcast Journalism); *m* 2001, Doon, *née* Hutson; 2 s (Quin, Milo), 2 da (Muireann, Elsa); *Career* formerly staff reporter then staff prodr News and Current Affairs BBC Radio; with BBC until 2008; presenter/host: Tomorrow's World and Tomorrow's World Live (BBC1), Midweek (BBC Radio 4), Holiday on a Shoestring (BBC1), 50 Places to See Before You Die (BBC1), Holiday Prog (BBC1), Innovation Nation (BBC1); reporter: Grandstand (BBC TV), Wimbledon (BBC TV); presenter ITV Sport 2008– (Aviva Partnership and Heineken Cup Show (ITV) 2009–, 2011 Rugby World Cup (ITV) 2009–); host of own chat show RTE (Ireland) 2010–, currently presenter Lorraine Show (ITV); dir Boxer Prodns Belfast; New TV Talent of the Year TRIC Awards 2001; *Publications* Where to Go When (2007), The Americas (2008); *Recreations* a range of badly played sports incl running (ran NY marathon 2001 and Dublin marathon 2002), golf, football, canoeing and triathlon (rep Ireland in Triathlon World Championships Hamburg 2007); nappy changing; *Clubs* Grange Golf (Dublin), Druids Glen Gold (Co Wicklow), Wicklow Triathlon; *Style*— Craig Doyle, Esq; ✉ c/o Diane Evans, Noel Gay Management, Shepperton Studios, Studios Road, Shepperton, Middlesex TW17 0QD (✆ 01932 572569, fax 01932 572712)

DOYLE, Dr David; RD (1973, and bar 1983); s of Edward Doyle, of Edinburgh, and Mary Stevenson, *née* Shand; *b* 28 September 1937; *Educ* George Heriot's Sch Edinburgh, Univ of Edinburgh (MD); *m* 1, 24 Oct 1964, Janet Caryl (d 1984), da of late Phyllis and late Stanley Maurice Gresham Potter, of Nottingham; 5 s (Michael b 1966, Stanley b 1968, Edward b 1970, Arthur b 1972, Quintin b 1977); m 2, 28 Sept 1996, Catherine Ford Whitley, wife of late John Whitley, da of late Dr A G and Anna Cruikshank, of Edinburgh; *Career* RAFVR 1958–61, Univ of Edinburgh Air Sqdn, RAuxAF 1962–67, RNR 1967–; house offr in med and surgery Edinburgh Royal Infirmary 1961–62, anatomy demonstrator Univ of Edinburgh 1962–63, SHO in surgical neurology Edinburgh 1963; appts in academic pathology and neuropathology 1963–71: Edinburgh, KCH London; conslt neuropathologist Glasgow 1971–; Dip in Forensic Med, Cert in Aviation Med; CBiol, FIBiol, FRAeS, FFPathRCPI, FRCPEd 1996; *Recreations* Highland bagpiping, flying, climbing with Kate; *Clubs* RSM, Royal Scottish Piping Soc, Glasgow Highland; *Style*— Dr David Doyle, RD; ✉ Neuropathology, 35 Thorn Road, Bearsden, Glasgow G61 4BS

DOYLE, Gemma; *b* 1981; *Educ* Univ of Glasgow; *Career* MP (Lab Co-op) Dumbartonshire W 2010–15, shadow defence min for defence personnel, welfare and veterans 2010–; *Style*— Ms Gemma Doyle; ✉ House of Commons, London SW1A 0AA (Twitter @Gemmawdmp)

DOYLE, Prof William; s of Stanley Joseph Doyle (d 1973), of Scarborough, N Yorks, and Mary Alice, *née* Bielby (d 2003); *b* 4 March 1942; *Educ* Bridlington Sch, Oriel Coll Oxford (MA, DPhil); *m* 2 Aug 1968, Christine, da of William Joseph Thomas (d 1969), of Aberdare, Glamorgan; *Career* sr lectr in history Univ of York 1978–81 (asst lectr 1967–69, lectr 1969–78), prof of modern history Univ of Nottingham 1981–85, prof of history Univ of Bristol 1986–2008 (emeritus prof and sr research fell 2008–); visiting prof: Columbia SC 1969–70, Bordeaux 1976, Paris 1988; visiting fell All Souls Coll Oxford 1991–92, Hans Kohn memb Inst for Advanced Study Princeton 2004; Douglas Southall Freeman prof of history Univ of Richmond VA 2010; pres Soc for the Study of French History 1992–95; Hon DUniv Bordeaux III France; Jubilee fell Historical Assoc 2016; FRHistS, FBA 1998; *Books* The Parlement of Bordeaux and the End of the Old Regime 1771–90 (1974), The Old European Order 1660–1800 (1978), Origins of the French Revolution (1980), The Ancien Regime (1986), The Oxford History of the French Revolution (1989), Officers, Nobles and Revolutionaries (1995), Venality. The Sale of Offices in Eighteenth Century France (1996), Jansenism (1999), Robespierre (jt ed with Colin Haydon, 1999), La Vénalité (2000), Old Regime France (ed, 2001), The French Revolution: A Very Short Introduction (2001), Aristocracy and its Enemies in the Age of Revolution (2009), Aristocracy: A Very Short Introduction (2010), The Oxford Handbook of the Ancien Regime (ed, 2011), France and the Age of Revolution, Regimes Old and New from Louis XIV to Napoleon Bonaparte (2013), Napoleon Bonaparte (2015), Louis XIV (2016); *Recreations* books, decorating, travelling about, historical memorabilia; *Clubs* Athenaeum, Oxford and Cambridge; *Style*— Prof W Doyle, FBA; ✉ Linden House, College Road, Lansdown, Bath, Somerset BA1 5RR (✆ 01225 314341, e-mail william.doyle@bristol.ac.uk)

DOYLE-PRICE, Jacqueline (Jackie); MP; da of Brian Doyle-Price, and Kathleen, *née* Coyle; *b* 5 August 1969, Sheffield, S Yorks; *Educ* Univ of Durham (BA); *Career* asst parly offr 1993–2000, asst private sec to Lord Mayor of London 2000–05, assoc FSA 2005–10, MP (Cons) Thurrock 2010–; asst govt whip 2015–; *Recreations* theatre, reading; *Style*— Miss Jackie Doyle-Price, MP; ✉ House of Commons, London SW1A 0AA (✆ 020 7219 7171, e-mail jackie.doyleprice.mp@parliament.uk)

DRABBLE, Jane; OBE (2000); da of late Walter Drabble, of Hilton, Dorset, and Molly, *née* Boreham; *b* 15 January 1947; *Educ* Clayton Hall GS Newcastle-under-Lyme, Plympton GS Plymouth, Univ of Bristol (BA); *m* Bill Nemtin; 3 step-c; *Career* BBC: studio mangr BBC Radio 1968–73, prodr Radio Current Affrs 1973–75, asst prodr, prodr, then sr prodr TV Current Affrs 1975–86, ed London Plus 1986–87, ed Everyman 1987–91, asst md Network TV 1991–94, concurrently head of factual progs Network TV 1993–94, dir of educn and memb Bd of Mgmnt 1994–99; cmmr for judicial appointments 2001–06; chair Mental Health Media 2002–06, vice-chair Basic Skills Agency 2001–04, memb Nat LSC 2000–06; dir Birmingham Royal Ballet 2002–10, govr RSC 2002– (memb Bd 2002–12), govr Royal Ballet Cos 2004–10, chair Bath Festivals 2009–14, memb South West Regnl Arts Cncl 2011–13, dir Bournemouth Symphony Orchestra 2013–; *Recreations* music, theatre, ballet, walking; *Style*— Ms Jane Drabble, OBE

DRABBLE, Dame Margaret; DBE (2008); da of His Hon John Frederick Drabble, QC (d 1982), by his w Kathleen, *née* Bloor; *b* 5 June 1939; *Educ* The Mount Sch York, Newnham Coll Cambridge; *m* 1, 1960 (m dis 1975), Clive Walter Swift, *qv*; 2 s, 1 da; m 2, 1982, Michael Holroyd, CBE, FRSL, *qv*; *Career* author; Hon DLitt: Univ of Sheffield, UEA 1994; FRSL 1973; *Books* A Summer Birdcage (1962), The Garrick Year (1964), The Millstone (1966), Wordsworth (1966), Jerusalem the Golden (1967), The Waterfall (1969), The Needle's Eye (1972), London Consequences (ed with B S Johnson, 1972), Arnold Bennett – A Biography (1974), The Realms of Gold (1975), The Genius of Thomas Hardy (ed, 1976), New Stories 1 (co-ed, 1976), The Ice Age (1977), For Queen and Country (1978), A Writer's Britain (1979), The Middle Ground (1980), The Oxford Companion to English Literature (ed 5 edn, 1985), The Radiant Way (1987), The Concise Oxford Companion to English Literature (with Jenny Stringer, 1987), A Natural Curiosity (1989), Safe As Houses (1989), The Gates of Ivory (1991), Angus Wilson: A Biography (1995), The Witch of Exmoor (1996), The Oxford Companion to English Literature (ed 6 edn, 2000), The Peppered Moth (2001), The Seven Sisters (2002), The Red Queen (2004), The Sea Lady (2006), The Pattern in the Carpet (2009), The Pure Gold Baby (2013); *Style*— Dame Margaret Drabble, DBE; ✉ c/o United Agents, 12–26 Lexington Street, London W1F 0LE

DRABBLE, Richard John Bloor; QC (1995); s of His Hon Frederick John Drabble, QC (d 1982), and Kathleen Marie, *née* Bloor (d 1984); *b* 23 May 1950; *Educ* Leighton Park Sch Reading, Downing Coll Cambridge (BA); *m* 31 May 1980, Sarah Madeleine Hope, da of Lt Cdr John David Walter Thomas Lewis (d 1966); 3 s (William b and d 1981, Frederick b 1982, Samuel b 1985); *Career* called to the Bar Inner Temple 1975 (bencher 2002); jr counsel to the Crown Common Law 1992–95; chm Administrative Law Bar Assoc 1998–2000; fell Inst of Advanced Legal Studies 1998; *Publications* Halsburys Laws Social Security (contrib), Goudie & Supperstone Judicial Review (contrib), Local Authorities and Human Rights (jt edn); numerous articles; *Recreations* reading, walking, dogs; *Style*— Richard Drabble, Esq, QC; ✉ Landwark Chambers, 180 Fleet Street, London EC4A 2HG (✆ 020 7430 1221, fax 020 7421 6060)

DRABBLE, William Alexander; s of William Alan Drabble, and Gladys Edith, *née* Johnson; *b* 10 August 1971; *Educ* Reepham HS, Norwich City Coll (Dip Catering, Outstanding Student of the Year 1990); *m* 21 Oct 2006, Claudine Erica, *née* Barbour; 1 da (Valentina Josephine b 14 Feb 2008); *Career* chef; Mirabelle restaurant Grand Hotel Eastbourne 1990–93, Capital Hotel Knightsbridge 1993–94, Nico Central London 1994, jr sous chef Nico Park Lane London 1994–96, sous chef Pied à Terre London 1996–97, head chef Michaels Nook Grasmere 1997–98 (1 Michelin Star, 4 AA Rosettes), head chef Aubergine Restaurant London 1998–2009 (1 Michelin Star, 4 AA Rosettes, French Restaurant of the Year 2000), exec head chef Seven Park Place 2009– (1 Michelin Star, 4 AA Rosettes); winner Nat Final Assoc Culinaire Française Coupe Emile Fêtu 1991, memb GB jr nat team Culinary Olympics Frankfurt 1992 (winners Silver and Bronze medals); *Publications* London on a Plate: Recipes from London's Finest Chefs (contrib, 2002); *Recreations* walking, reading, relaxing with friends and family; *Style*— William Drabble, Esq; ✉ Seven Park Place, St James's Hotel and Club, 7–8 Park Place, St James's, London, SW1A 1LS (e-mail william@stjameshotelandclub.com)

DRABU, Dr Yasmin Jeelani (Mrs Naqushbandi); da of Dr Ghulam Jeelani Drabu, of Hale, Cheshire, and Ayesha Jeelani, *née* Ashai; *b* 21 June 1950; *Educ* N Manchester GS, Univ of Manchester Med Sch (MB ChB); *m* 17 Aug 1975, Dr Khalid Naqushbandi, s of Ghulam Nabi Naqushbandi, of Srinagar Kashmir; 3 da (Lara Hennah b 3 Feb 1981, Shama, Sabah (twins) b 10 Oct 1983); *Career* sr registrar UCH 1980–82, conslt microbiologist N Middx Hosp 1982–; Royal Free Hosp: hon sr lectr 1989–, clinical dir of pathology 1993–95, clinical dir of diagnostic and therapy servs 1995–97, chm Supplies Evaluation Ctee 1997–2000, med dir 2000–; memb GMC working gp for medical microbiology performance procedures 1999–; dep ed Jl of Clinical Pathology 2000– (med exec dir 2001–); memb Kashmiri Assoc of GB; DCH, FRCPath; *Style*— Dr Yasmin Drabu; ✉ Department of Microbiology, North Middlesex Hospital, Sterling Way, London N18 1QX (✆ 020 8887 2892, fax 020 8887 4227)

DRAGUN, Richard Eugenjusz; s of Jan Dragun (d 1996), of Anlaby, nr Hull, and Genowefa, *née* Hulnicka (d 1990); *b* 13 May 1951; *Educ* Marist Coll Hull, London Coll of Printing (DipAD); *Career* dir Design Research Unit Ltd 1980–89 (designer 1974–80); conslt designer: Baghdad Metro project 1981–84, Br Mass Transit Consltss Taipei Metro project 1986–87; head of graphic design BDP Design 1993– (ptnr 1989–93); recognised expertise in strategic wayfinding and design with an emphasis on healthcare environments; recent and current projects incl: Alder Hey Children's Hosp Liverpool, Southmead Hosp Bristol, Brighton & Hove Univ Hosps, New Children's Hosp Dublin, Br Museum World Exhbns and Conservation Centre; dir Sign Design Soc 1997–2016 (memb Steering Gp 1996–2016, co sec 2000–16); memb Expert Panel Wayfinding book NHS Estates; memb Governing Body Southwark Coll, chm Art and Design Consultative Ctee 1988–92; FCSD 1998; *Recreations* fine art, modern prints, books; *Style*— Richard Dragun, Esq; ✉ BDP, 16 Brewhouse House, Clerkenwell, London EC1V 4LJ

DRAKE, (HE) Howard Ronald; OBE; *b* 13 August 1956; *m* Gillian; 1s, 1 da; *Career* diplomat; vice-consul (commercial) LA 1981–83, 2 sec (chancery) Santiago 1985–88, European Community Dept (Internal) FCO 1998–90, Southern European Dept FCO 1990–92, head of chancery Singapore 1992–95, dep head Counter-Proliferation Dept FCO 1995–97, dep consul-gen and head of inward investment NY 1997–2002, asst dir HR Directorate FCO 2002–05, ambass to Chile 2005–10, high cmmr to Jamaica 2010–13 (also non-resident high-cmmr to the Bahamas), high cmmr to Canada 2013–; *Style*— Mr Howard Drake, OBE; ✉ British High Commission, 80 Elgin Street, Ottawa, ON K1P5K7, Canada

DRAKE, Steve; *Educ* Southend Technical Coll; *Career* chef prop Drake's Restaurant Ripley 2004– (Michelin star 2005–); *Style*— Steve Drake, Esq; ✉ Drake's Restaurant, The Clock House, High Street, Ripley, Surrey GU23 6AQ

DRAKES, Paul William Foster; s of Donald Frank Drakes (d 1986), and Kathleen, *née* Caldicott; *b* 6 November 1950; *Educ* Wyggeston GS; *m* 1, 1973 (m dis 1980), Janet Bell; 2 s (Oliver b 30 Dec 1975, William b 3 Jan 1979); m 2, 1981, Stephanie Anne, da of Melvyn Moffatt; 2 s (Jonathan b 18 Dec 1986, Harry b 4 July 1989); *Career* trainee Sun Life Co Leicester 1967, mgmnt trainee Dunlop Leicester 1967, trainee media planner and buyer Gee Advertising Leicester 1968, media planner and buyer C R Cassons London 1969, media gp head Allardyce Hampshire 1970, appointed media gp head The Media Department Ltd 1973; Primary Contact Ltd: media mangr 1973, media dir and Bd dir 1976, account gp head 1986, dir of client servs 1988; client servs dir ACGB Nottingham 1991; ptnr CHCchoir 1992–2006 (following merger 2002, formerly Drakes Jardine Ltd (fndr ptnr), then choir), ptnr 23red Central 2006–; MIPA; *Recreations* four sons, a love for Leicester City FC and a successful company; *Style*— Paul Drakes, Esq; ✉ 2 Huntingdon Drive, The Park, Nottingham NG7 1BW (✆ 0115 941 8776); 23red Central, 32A Stoney Street, Nottingham NG1 1AA (✆ 0115 9247157)

DRANSFIELD, Graham; s of Gordon Dransfield, of Linthwaite, W Yorks, and Barbara, *née* Booth; *b* 5 March 1951; *Educ* Colne Valley HS Huddersfield, St Catherine's Coll Oxford (coll scholar, BA, Soccer blue); *m* 21 June 1980, Helen Frances, da of Lawrence Demchy; 1 da (Louise Jane b 14 Feb 1981), 1 s (Mark Lucas b 21 Dec 1984); *Career* articled clerk then asst slr Slaughter & May 1974–82; Hanson plc: slr 1982–86, co sec 1986, assoc dir 1989, dir 1992–2007, currently chm pension scheme; govr Eltham Coll; memb Law Soc

1976–2007; *Recreations* squash, tennis, running, cycling, golf; *Clubs* Beckenham CC, The Addington Golf; *Style*— Graham Dransfield, Esq

DRAPER, Christopher (Chris); s of Lawrie Draper, of Landford, Wilts, and Susan, *née* Davey; *b* 20 March 1978, Sheffield; *Educ* Univ of Portsmouth (Dip); *m* 27 Oct 2007, Helen Claire Laura, *née* Brown; 1 s (Harry Finn b 27 April 2010), 1 da (Lily Belle b 17 Jan 2013); *Career* yachtsman; achievements in 49er class incl: Gold medal World Championships 2003 (Silver medal 2002 and 2004), Gold medal European Championships 2004 (Silver medal 2002 and 2003), Bronze medal Olympic Games Athens 2004, helmsman Ishares Cup Extreme 40 World Series champion 2009, helmsman 34th Americas Cup Luna Rossa 2013; nominated World Sailor of the Year 2003; *Recreations* surfing, mountain biking; *Style*— Chris Draper, Esq; ✉ Woodlands, Pear Tree Drive, Landford, Salisbury SP5 2AY (e-mail c.draper2@ukonline.co.uk, Twitter @draperchris)

DRAPER, Prof Paul Richard; s of James Krishen Draper, of York, and Dorothy Jean Draper; *b* 28 December 1946; *Educ* Univ of Exeter (BA), Univ of Reading (MA), Univ of Stirling (PhD); *m* Janet Margaret, *née* Grant; 1 s (Timothy James Jonathan b 29 Sept 1977), 1 da (Lucy Jane Jessica b 30 April 1980); *Career* research fell Univ of Stirling 1972–73, lectr Univ of St Andrews 1973–75, lectr Univ of Edinburgh 1976–78; Univ of Strathclyde: Esmée Fairbairn sr lectr 1978–86, prof 1986–97, head Dept of Accounting & Finance 1990–95, vice-dean Strathclyde Business Sch 1993–97; Walter Scott and Partners prof of fin Univ of Edinburgh 1997–2001, head Sch of Business and Economics and prof of fin Univ of Exeter 2002–08, emeritus prof Univ of Exeter 2009–; prof of finance Univ of Leeds 2009–14, ret; hon prof Herriot Watt Univ 2012–15, visiting prof Univ of Portsmouth 2013–15; dir China Eagle Hedge Fund 2014– (chm 2015); Research Prize Inst for Quantitative Investment (with G Brown and E McKenzie) 1992; *Books* The Scottish Financial Sector (with I Smith, W Stewart and N Hood, 1988), The Investment Trust Industry in the UK (1989); author of numerous pubns in academic jls; *Recreations* urban walking, houses; *Style*— Prof Paul Draper; ✉ 58 Lynch Road, Farnham, Surrey GU9 8BX (☎ 01252 710175)

DRAPER, Roger; *Educ* Bolton Sch, Winstanley Coll, Loughborough Univ (BSc); *Career* ceo: Sport England 2002–06, Lawn Tennis Assoc 2006–14, chief exec Warrington Wolves 2015–; *Style*— Roger Draper, Esq; ✉ c/o Warrington Wolves, The Halliwell Jones Stadium, Mike Gregory Way, Warrington, Cheshire WA2 7NE

DRAX, Richard; né Richard Grosvenor Plunkett-Ernle-Erle-Drax; MP; s of Walter Plunkett-Ernle-Erle-Drax, and Hon Pamela Weeks; *b* 29 January 1958; *Educ* Harrow, RAC, RMA Sandhurst; *Career* offr Coldstream Guards 1978–87, journalist 1990–2006; MP (Cons) Dorset S 2010–; *Style*— Richard Drax, Esq, MP; ✉ House of Commons, London SW1A 0AA

DRAYSON, Baron (Life Peer UK 2004), of Kensington in the Royal Borough of Kensington and Chelsea; Paul Rudd Drayson; s of Michael Rudd Drayson, of Lymington, Hants; *b* 5 March 1960; *Educ* Aston Univ (BSc, PhD); *m* 1994, Elspeth Jane, da of Prof Brian John Bellhouse, of Islip, Oxon; 2 da (Hon Olivia Grace Georgina b 1996, Hon Francesca Alice Celina b 2003), 3 s (Hon James Alexander b 1997, Hon George Edward b 1999, Hon Charles Frederick b 2001); *Career* fndr and md Lambourn Food Co 1986–91, fndr and dir Genisys Development Ltd 1991–95, fndr and chief exec Powderject Pharmaceuticals plc 1993–2003, entrepreneur in residence Saïd Business Sch Univ of Oxford 2003–05; chm UK Bioindustry Assoc 2001–02; memb Investment Advsy Ctee Isis Coll Venture Fund 1999–2004; sits as Lab peer in House of Lords, min for defence procurement 2005–07, min of state for defence equipment and support 2007–08, min of state for science 2008–09, min of state for science and innovation 2009–10; racing driver: British GT Championships 2007 (runner-up), American Le Mans series 2008; fndr: Drayson Racing Technologies LLP 2007–, Drayson-Barwell racing team 2007–08; chm and ceo Drayson Technols Ltd 2014–; memb Advsy Bd Oxford Univ Challenge Seed Fund 1999–2004, chm fundraising campaign Oxford Children's Hosp 2002–05, memb Cncl Univ of Oxford 2014–, non-exec dir and memb Bd RN 2014–; Hon DSc Aston Univ 2007; FRSA 1998, FREng 2011, hon FIMechE, FIET; *Recreations* motor racing, fencing; *Clubs* British Racing Drivers, RAC, Lansdowne; *Style*— The Lord Drayson

DRECHSLER, Paul Joseph; CBE (2015); *b* 16 April 1956; *Educ* TCD (BA BAI), INSEAD (IEP); *m* Jan 1981, Wendy Isobel, *née* Hackett; 2 s (Mark, Jonathan), 1 da (Sophie); *Career* Imperial Chemical Industries plc: various positions 1978–92, chm and pres ICI Brasil SA 1992–93, chief exec ICI Acrylics Inc (USA) 1993–96, chief exec ICI Polyester 1996–98, chm and chief exec Quest Int 1998–, exec dir ICI plc 1999–2003, exec chm Wates Gp Ltd 2006–14 (ceo 2004), chm Bibby Line gp 2015 (dir 2014); sr ind dir Filtrona plc 2005–15; dir Business in the Community 2011–, chm Skills Funding Agency 2013–15, chm Teach First 2014–; dir CBI 2012, pres CBI 2015–; memb Business Sch Advsy Bd Trinity Coll Dublin 2005–; memb Advsy Cncl Step Up to Serve 2014–; FRICS; *Recreations* family, music, skiing, political science; *Clubs* Dulwich and Sydenham Golf; *Style*— Paul Drechsler, CBE; ✉ 17 Ardbeg Road, Dulwich, London SE24 9JL (e-mail wdrechsler@aol.com)

DRESCHER, Derek Peter; s of Clifford Drescher (d 1966), and Joan Ringrose, *née* Jackson (d 2001); *b* 13 March 1940; *Educ* Pocklington Sch, Univ of Birmingham; *m* 11 April 1966, Gillian Mary, da of Ronald Harry Eden, of Oxford; 2 da (Lucy, Alison); *Career* lighting designer Lincoln and Oldham Repertory Theatre Cos 1961–63; BBC Radio: studio mangr 1963–71, music prodr 1971–89, sr prodr (jazz) 1989–99; freelance prodr and photographer 1999–, dir New Vortex Jazz Club 2003–; memb Ctee Cheltenham Jazz Festival 1996–2006; documentaries incl: Constant Lambert, Jelly Roll Morton, Charlie Parker, Little Titch, Shostakovich, Miles Davis (The Phoenix, nominated Sony award 1991), George Russell (The Invisible Guru), Billy Mayerl (A Formula for Success); series incl: Man-Woman of Action, Desert Island Discs 1976–86, Jazz Today, Concerto, Highway to Heaven, Before the Blues (Sony award for best specialist music prog 1988), This Week's Composer (Duke Ellington), Play as I Please (Humphrey Lyttelton), Touch of Genius (George Shearing), Impressions, A Man for All Music (André Previn), Misterioso (Thelonious Monk), Kiri (Dame Kiri Te Kanawa), Saxophone Colossus (Sonny Rollins), Bright Size Life (Pat Metheny); exhbn of photographs of jazz musicians at Vortex Jazz Club and Bloomsbury Theatre 1999, enlarged exhbn at Cheltenham International Jazz Festival 2000, exhbn of photgraphs at Laine Dankworth Centre Wavendon 2002–03; jt first prize winners exhbn Lauderdale House Highgate 2001; *Books* Desert Islands Lists (with Roy Plomley, 1984); *Recreations* theatre, music, travel, books; *Style*— Derek Drescher, Esq; ✉ 10 Fortismere Avenue, Muswell Hill, London N10 3BL (☎ 020 8883 8081)

DREW, Dan Hamilton; s of Daniel Edward Drew (d 1974), of Petworth, W Sussex, and Rena Frayer, *née* Hamilton (d 1990); *b* 31 January 1938; *Educ* Stubbington House, Tonbridge Sch; *m* 1, 1963 (m dis), Carol Ann, da of Dr Robert Gibson Miller, of Helston, Cornwall; 1 da (Xanthe b 1966) 1 s (Angus b 1967); m 2, 1976, Beverley, da of Alan Lestocq Roberts (d 1981), of Graffham, W Sussex; 1 da (Frances b 1979); *Career* chartered accountant; gp fin dir Interlink Express plc 1982–92; chm Bath and Wessex Opera Ltd 1992–97; *Recreations* fishing, beekeeping; *Style*— D H Drew, Esq; ✉ Lower Poswick, Whitbourne, Worcester WR6 5SS (☎ 01886 821275, fax 01886 822027, e-mail danhdrew@msn.com)

DREW, Prof John Sydney Neville; s of John William Henry Drew (d 1989), and Kathleen Marjorie, *née* Wright (d 1991); *b* 7 October 1936; *Educ* King Edward's Sch Birmingham, St John's Coll Oxford (MA), Fletcher Sch of Law and Diplomacy, Tufts Univ (AM), Middle East Centre for Arabic Studies; *m* 22 Dec 1962, Rebecca Margaret Amanda, *née* Usher; 2 s (Jason b 1965, David b 1972), 1 da (Emma b 1967); *Career* Lt Somerset LI 1955–57; HM Dip Serv 1960–73: third sec Paris 1962–64, second sec Kuwait 1965–67, first sec Bucharest 1968–70; dir of mktg and exec programmes London Business Sch 1973–79, dir of corp affairs Rank Xerox 1979–84, dir of European affrs Touche Ross Int 1984–86, head of UK Offices European Cmmn 1987–93; visiting prof of European mgmnt: Imperial Coll of Sci and Technol London 1987–90, Open Univ 1992–99; visiting prof of European business mgmnt Univ of Durham 1995–2003; sr advsr European Business Sch 2006–07, Jean Monnet prof of European business and mgmnt Regent's Coll London 2007–; dir: Europa Times 1993–94, The Change Group International plc 1996–2003; pres Inst of Linguists 1993–99, pres EUROTAS 1998–2003, chm Durham Inst 1995–2003, dep chm Enterprise Support Group 1993–95, tstee Thomson Fndn 1994–2007, dir Inst of Contemporary European Studies Regent's Coll 2012–; Sloan fell London Business Sch 1970, assoc fell Templeton Coll Oxford 1982–87, chllr Regent's Univ London 2013–; Hon MBA Univ of Northumbria 1991; *Books* Doing Business in the European Community (1979, 3 edn 1991), Networking in Organisations (1986), Europe 1992 – Developing an Active Company Approach to the European Market (1988), Readings in International Enterprise (1994, 2 edn 1999), Ways through the Wall (2005), The UK and Europe: Costs, Benefits and Options (ed, 2013), Transatlantic Relations: A European Perspective (ed, 2014), Europe and its Neighbours; From Morocco to Moscow (ed, 2016); *Recreations* travel, golf, personal development, values; *Clubs* Oxford and Cambridge; *Style*— Prof John Drew; ✉ 49 The Ridgeway, London NW11 8PQ (☎ 020 8455 5054)

DREW, His Hon Judge Simon Patrick; QC (2011); *Career* called to the Bar 1987; recorder 2005, circuit judge Midland Circuit 2012–; *Style*— His Hon Judge Drew, QC; ✉ Birmingham Crown Court, Queen Elizabeth II Law Courts, 1 Newton Street, Birmingham B4 7NA

DREWRY, Prof David John; s of Norman Tidman Drewry (d 1984), of Grimsby, Lincs, and Mary Edwina, *née* Wray (d 1993); *b* 22 September 1947; *Educ* Havelock Sch Grimsby, QMC London (BSc), Emmanuel Coll Cambridge (PhD); *m* 10 July 1971, Gillian Elizabeth, da of Clifford Francis Holbrook (d 1979); *Career* Univ of Cambridge: Sir Henry Strakosh fell 1972, sr asst in res 1978–83, asst dir of res 1983, sr visiting scholar 1999; dir Scott Polar Res Inst 1984–87, dir Br Antarctic Survey 1987–94, dir of science and technology and dep chief exec NERC 1994–98, DG British Cncl 1998; visiting fell Green Coll Oxford 1995–96, visiting prof Univ of London 1996–, vice-chllr Univ of Hull 1999–2009, guest prof Xiamen Univ China 2006–, hon prof Krakow Acad 2010–; pres Int Arctic Sci Ctee 1997–2002; chm Yorkshire Univs 2002–04; memb: Int Glaciological Soc 1969– (vice-pres 1991–96), Royal Geographical Soc (vice-pres 1990–93, Cuthbert Peek Award 1979, Patron's Medal 1998), Cncl of Mangrs of Nat Antarctic Programmes (chm 1989–91), European Science Fndn 1989–98; vice-pres European Univ Assoc 2009–, chm S Georgia Assoc 2010–; tstee: Antarctic Heritage Tst, Natural History Museum London 2008–16, chm Hull Maritime History Tst 2014–; memb: Univs UK 1999–2009, Bd Yorkshire Science 2005–09; US Antarctic Serv Medal 1979, Polar Medal 1986, Gold Medal (Prix de la Belgica) Royal Acad of Belgium 1995; Hon DSc: Robert Gordon Univ 1993, Univ of Lincoln 1994, Anglia Poly Univ 1998, Univ of Hull 2010; hon fell: Queen Mary Univ of London 1991, Emmanuel Coll Cambridge 2007–; FRGS 1972, CGeog, MInstD 2000, CCMI 2002; *Books* Antarctica: Glaciological and Geophysical Folio (1983), Glacial Geologic Processes (1986), Antarctica and Environmental Change (1993); *Recreations* hill walking, skiing, classical music, theatre, gastronomy; *Clubs* Athenaeum; *Style*— Prof David J Drewry; ✉ University of Hull, Hull HU6 7RX (e-mail david.drewry@hull.ac.uk)

DREYFUS, James; *Career* actor; patron of Kairos, Lesbian and Gay Bereavement Centre; *Theatre* Russell Paxton in Lady in the Dark (RNT), Medvedenko in The Seagull (Thelma Holt Productions), Grimald in King Arthur (Centro Cultural de Belém); with Birmingham Repetory: Cassius in Julius Caesar, Gentlemen Prefer Blondes, Al in The Grapes of Wrath, Sean in Playing by the Rules; Gary in Eurovision (Vaudeville), Christopher/Patrick in Elegies for Angels, Punks and Raging Queens (Criterion), Ned Lowenscroft in Elizabeth Rex 2002, Billy, Rupert, Michael and Pierre Hickory-Wood in One for the Pot 2002–03, Carmen Ghia in The Producers (Theatre Royal) 2004–05, Donkey Years 2006, Cabaret 2006, The Common Persuit 2008, Amongst Friends 2009; *Television* Paris 1994, Thin Blue Line 1995, Absolutely Fabulous 1996, Gimme, Gimme, Gimme 1999, Gormenghast 2000, Oscar in Bette 2000, Waking the Dead 2004, Willo the Wisp (voice for animation) 2004, The Lenny Henry Show 2005, The Man and the Mouse 2005, My Hero 2005, The All New Alexei Sayle Show, The Complete and Utter History of Everything, Frontiers, Dame Edna Nurses it Better; *Radio* Robbie Ross in Friends of Oscar, The Short Straw; *Film* Thin Ice 1995, Richard III 1995, Boyfriends 1996, Notting Hill 1999, Being Considered 2000, Cody Banks II: Destination London 2003, Churchill: The Hollywood Years 2004, Fat Slags 2004, Colour Me Kubrick 2004; *Awards* Television Comedy Newcomer Award 1996, second prize Ian Charleson Award 1997 (for Julius Caesar), Olivier Award 1998 (for Lady in the Dark); *Recreations* lounging, loafing, napping and writing; *Style*— James Dreyfus, Esq; ✉ c/o Cassie Mayer Ltd, 5 Old Garden House, The Lanterns, Bridge Lane, London SW11 3AD

DRISCOLL, Fiona Elizabeth Lawrence; da of James Patrick Driscoll, and Jeanne Lawrence Williams; *b* 27 April 1958; *Educ* Sorbonne (Dip), Somerville Coll Oxford (MA); *Career* mktg advsr Republican Campaign NY 1976, fin servs broker FPC 1976–80, mgmnt conslt Deloitte Haskins and Sells 1980–84, account dir Collett Dickenson Pearce 1984–87, sr conslt Bell Pottinger Communications 1987–94, jt md The Rowland Company 1994–95, chief exec Ogilvy Adams Rinehart 1995–97, princ Driscoll Communications 1997–, mktg dir QinetiQ 1999–2001, strategy dir Hedra plc 2003–06; non-exec chair: 300 Gp 1994–96, City Women's Network 1996–98, Non Executive Directors Forum Alumni Cncl 2000–01, Health Lottery Ltd 2007–10, EnterMedia Ltd 2009–10; chair Wessex Academic Science Health Network 2013–, memb Cncl Univ of Bradford; non-exec dir: Inst of Leadership 1998–2000, Horserace Totalisator Bd 1999–2006, Fleming Managed Growth plc 1999–2004, Ebquity plc (formerly Thomson Intermedia plc) 2000–09, HM Treasy Public Services Productivity Panel 2000–06, DEFRA Waste Implementation Prog (WIP) Steering Ctee 2003–05, HM Treasy Efficiency Prog Bd 2006–08, Nat Police Improvement Agency IMPACT Bd 2006–07, Home Office Bichard Bd 2006–09; govr Nuffield Health 2010–; memb Nat Youth Cncl 1975; librarian (vice-pres) Oxford Union 1979; A Millennium Woman of the Year 2000; *Style*— Ms Fiona Driscoll; ✉ e-mail fiona@driscoll.org.uk

DRISCOLL, Helen Deborah; da of John Cupitt, and Doris, *née* Jones; *b* 22 November 1956, Bromley, Kent; *Educ* Univ of Leicester (LLB); *Children* 2 s (James b 14 April 1977, Rory b 5 May 1979), 1 da (Sophie b 3 Nov 1982); *Career* slr; Eversheds 1991–97, Freeth Cartwright 1997–2001, Martineau Johnson 2001–; memb Law Soc 1993, MENSA; *Style*— Ms Helen Driscoll; ✉ Martineau Johnson, 1 Colmore Square, Birmingham B4 6AA (☎ 0870 763 1635, fax 0870 763 2035, e-mail helen.driscoll@martjohn.com)

DRISCOLL, Lindsay Jane; *née* Woodburn; da of Clement Milligan Woodburn (d 2005), and Evelyn Miriam Woodburn (d 1978); *b* 17 April 1947, Lowestoft, Suffolk; *Educ* The Queen's Sch Chester, St Hugh's Coll Oxford (MA); *m* 29 Dec 1978, Rev Canon David Driscoll; 2 s (Richard Woodburn b 7 July 1980, Jonathan Peter b 13 May 1983); *Career* slr Biddle & Co 1971–73 (articled clerk 1969–71), asst registrar gen Kenya 1973–78, lectr Kenya Sch of Law 1973–78, charity law conslt 1980–87, legal advsr NCVO 1987–95, ptnr Sinclair Taylor and Martin 1995–2003, legal cmmr Charity Cmmn for England and Wales 2003–08, conslt Bates Wells & Braithwaite LLP 2008–; memb Bd Int Centre for Not for Profit Law 1995–2003 and 2007–13, memb Exec Ctee Charity Law Assoc 1996–2003, chair Steering Gp Code of Good Governance 2009–, memb Bd Pemsel Case Fndn (Canada) 2012–; memb Bd Dance United 2006–11, dir St Laurence Sch Acad Tst 2014–;

tstee: Womankind Worldwide 1998–2006, Widows Rights Int 2002–05, Balkans Community Initiatives Fund 2002–06, Historia Theatre Co, Rosa Fund, St Katherine's and Shadwell Tst 2005–10; memb Law Soc 1971; *Publications* Modernising Charity Law (contrib, 2010); *Recreations* walking, travel, theatre; *Style—* Mrs Lindsay Driscoll; ✉ Bates Wells & Braithwaite, 10 Queen Street Place, London EC4R 1BE (☎ 020 7551 7620, e-mail l.driscoll@bwbllp.com)

DRISCOLL, Prof Michael John; s of Michael Driscoll (d 1987), and Catherine, *née* Nash; *b* 27 October 1950; *Educ* Boteler GS Warrington, Trent Poly (Lord Kings Norton Prize, BA); *Children* 1 da (Alice b 2 June 1981), 1 s (Jack b 10 Aug 1984); *Career* research asst Univ of Sheffield 1973–77, lectr Univ of Birmingham 1977–89; head Sch of Economics Middlesex Poly 1989–91; Middlesex Univ: dean and pro-vice-chllr 1991–95, dep vice-chllr 1995–96, vice-chllr 1996–; economist OECD Paris 1985–88; chair: Standing Conf of Princs (SCOP)/Univs UK (UUK) Sector Gp on Sustainability 2000, Million+ 2003–; memb: Bd Coll of NE London 1997, Steering Gp London Higher Bd UUK 2001–; patron N London Hospice 2001; FRSA, CCIM; *Publications* author of numerous articles and books on monetary policy and macroeconomics; *Recreations* walking, cinema, theatre, watching Aston Villa FC; *Clubs* IOD; *Style—* Prof Michael Driscoll; ✉ Middlesex University, The Burroughs, London NW4 4BT (☎ 020 8411 5606, fax 020 8411 5465, e-mail m.driscoll@mdx.ac.uk)

DRISSELL, Air Cdre Peter James; s of Anthony Drissell (d 1978), of Bristol, and Alicia, *née* Miller; *b* 24 November 1955, Bristol; *Educ* Hartcliffe Sch Bristol, City Univ (BSc), RAF Coll Cranwell, KCL (MA), JSDC Greenwich (Advanced Staff Course), RCDS; *m* 2 Aug 2008, Tatiana, *née* Averyanova; 2 da (Diva b 1996, Alina b 2010), 1 s (Dominic b 2012); *Career* cmmnd RAF Regt 1974, Sqdn Ldr 1988 OC 48 Sqdn RAF Regt 1989–91, Wing Cdr 1994, OC Ops Wing RAF Honington 1996–97, personal staff offr CAS 1997–98, RCDS 2003, Provost Marshal RAF 2004–05, Cmdt Gen RAF Regt and AO RAF Police 2005–07, dir of security Home Office 2008–13, dir of aviation security CAA 2013–, dir Transformation Prog, memb ExCo and Board CAA; chair RAF Regt Assoc 2010–13; dir Plan UK 2004–, tstee Chilterns Multiple Sclerosis Centre 2005–07, tstee City and Guilds 2012– (memb Cncl 2011–); FInstD 2006 (MInstD 1997), FCGI 2007; *Recreations* horse riding, fly fishing, walking, music; *Style—* Air Cdre Peter Drissell; ✉ 5 Oldbury Grove, Beaconsfield, Buckinghamshire HP9 2AJ (☎ 07789 542982, e-mail peterdrissell@aol.com)

DRIVER, David John; s of Denis Alan Driver (d 1968), and Mona Eileen, *née* Scott (d 2003); *b* 4 August 1942; *Educ* Perse Sch Cambridge, Cambridge Sch of Art; *m* 27 Nov 1976, Sara Penelope, da of Ashley Rock; 1 s (Paul Robert Thomas b 28 Dec 1979), 1 da (Helen Rachel b 5 April 1984); *Career* freelance illustrator and designer for various publications since 1963 incl: Town, Queen, Vogue, Penguin Books, Observer Magazine, Sunday Times, Harpers Bazaar (re-design 1969), The Listener (re-design 1980); art ed Farm and Country (Thomson Organisation) 1963–67, asst art ed Woman's Mirror (IPC) 1967–68, art dir Cornmarket Press 1968–69, art ed and dep ed Radio Times 1969–81, freelance art dir Francis Kyle Gallery 1979–2014, head of design and asst ed The Times (News International) 1981–2008, ret; designer: Royal Mail Christmas stamps 1991, Queen's Golden Wedding stamps 1997; winner various awards incl: Gold & Silver awards for Radio Times D&AD 1976, Editorial Award of Excellence Soc of Newspaper Design Awards (USA) 1987, 1989 and 1997, Newspaper Design Awards 1989 and 1994, Colour Newspaper of the Year and Features Design Awards 1992, Hon DLitt Anglia Poly Univ (now Anglia Ruskin Univ) 2001; *Books* The Art of Radio Times (ed, compiler and designer, 1981); designer: Graham Greene Country (by Paul Hogarth and Graham Greene), The Windsor Style (by Suzy Menkes), The Mediterranean Shore (by Paul Hogarth and Lawrence Durrell); design conslt Salt Yard Food and Wine from Spain and Italy (by Morris, Tish and Mullins, 2012); *Recreations* cricket; *Style—* David Driver, Esq; ✉ 56 Milton Park, London N6 5QA (☎ 020 8341 0761, e-mail daviddriver@hotmail.co.uk)

DRIVER, Olga Lindholm; *see:* Aikin, Olga Lindholm

DROGHEDA, 12 Earl of (I 1661); Henry Dermot Ponsonby Moore; also Baron Moore (I 1616 and UK 1954, by which latter title he sat in House of Lords) and Viscount Moore (I 1621); s of 11 Earl of Drogheda, KG, KBE (d 1989), and Joan Eleanor, *née* Carr (d 1989); *b* 14 January 1937; *Educ* Eton, Trinity Coll Cambridge (BA); *m* 1, 15 May 1968 (m dis 1972), Eliza, da of Stacy Barcroft Lloyd, Jr, of Philadelphia; m 2, 1978, Alexandra, da of Sir Nicholas Henderson, GCMG; 2 s (Benjamin Garrett Henderson, Viscount Moore b 1983, Hon Garrett Alexander b 1986), 1 da (Lady Marina Alice b 1988); *Heir* s, Viscount Moore; *Career* Lt Life Gds 1957; photographer (professional name Derry Moore); *Books* The Dream Come True, Great Houses of Los Angeles (with Brendan Gill, 1980), Royal Gardens (with George Plumptre, 1982), Stately Homes of Britain (with Sybilla Jane Flower, 1982), Washington, Houses of the Capital (with Henry Mitchell, 1982), The English Room (with Michael Pick, 1984), The Englishwoman's House (with Alvilde Lees-Milne, 1984), The Englishman's Room (with Alvilde Lees-Milne, 1986), The Gardens of Queen Elizabeth The Queen Mother (with the Marchioness of Salisbury, 1988), Evening Ragas, a photographer in India (1997), Inside the House of Lords (with Clive Aslet, 1998), Rooms (with Joseph Hotzman, 2007), Notting Hill (2007), In House (with Mitchell Owen, 2009), Great Gardens of Italy (with Monty Don, 2011), An English Room (2013); *Clubs* Brooks's, Garrick; *Style—* The Earl of Drogheda; ✉ 40 Ledbury Road, London W11 2AB (☎ 020 7229 5950, fax 020 7221 8135, e-mail moorederry@aol.com)

DROMEY, Jack; MP; *b* 21 September 1948, London; *m* The Rt Hon Harriet Harman, QC, MP, *qv*; 2 s, 1 da; *Career* MP (Lab) Birmingham Erdington 2010–, shadow min for communities and local govt 2010–13, shadow min for policing 2013–; *Style—* Jack Dromey, Esq, MP; ✉ House of Commons, London SW1A 0AA

DROMGOOLE, Dominic; *b* 1963; *Educ* Univ of Cambridge; *Career* prodr and dir; artistic dir Bush Theatre London 1990–96 (nat tour 1994), new plays dir Old Vic (working alongside Sir Peter Hall) 1997, artistic dir Oxford Stage Co 1998–2005 (prodr and dir of numerous prodns, plays directed incl Troilus and Cressida and Hay Fever), artistic dir Shakespeare's Globe Theatre 2005–; regular contributor to The Guardian and The Sunday Times; *Books* The Full Room (2001), Will and Me: How Shakespeare Took Over My Life (2006); *Style—* Dominic Dromgoole, Esq; ✉ Shakespeare's Globe, 21 New Globe Walk, Bankside, London SE1 9DT (☎ 020 7902 1400, fax 020 7902 1401)

DROMORE, Bishop of 1999–; Most Rev John (Thomas) McAreavey; s of John McAreavey (d 1980) and Mary Elisabeth (May); *b* 2 February 1949; *Educ* St Colman's Coll Newry, Nat Univ of Ireland Maynooth (BA), Pontifical Univ Maynooth (BD, STL), Pontifical Gregorian Univ Rome (JCD); *Career* ordained priest Maynooth 1973; prof of canon law Pontifical Univ Maynooth 1988–99, memb Armagh Regnl Marriage Tbnl 1979–92; sec Exec Ctee Int Cmmn on English in the Liturgy (ICEL) 2002; *Recreations* hill walking, swimming, reading; *Style—* The Most Rev the Bishop of Dromore; ✉ Bishop's House, 44 Armagh Road, Newry, Co Down BT35 6PN (☎ 028 302 62444, fax 028 302 60496, e-mail bishopofdromore@btinternet.com)

DRONKE, Prof (Ernst) Peter Michael; s of A H R Dronke, and M M Dronke, *née* Kronfeld; *b* 30 May 1934; *Educ* Victoria Univ NZ (MA), Magdalen Coll Oxford (MA), Univ of Cambridge (MA); *m* 1960, Ursula Miriam, *née* Brown; 1 da; *Career* res fell Merton Coll Oxford 1958–61; Univ of Cambridge: lectr in medieval Latin 1961–79, fell Clare Hall 1964–, reader 1979–89, prof of medieval Latin lit 1989– (emeritus 2001–); guest lectr Univ of Munich 1960, guest prof Centre d'Études Médiévales Poitiers 1969, Leverhulme fell 1973, W P Ker lectr Univ of Glasgow 1976, guest prof Univ Autònoma Barcelona 1977, visiting fell Humanities Res Centre Canberra 1978, visiting prof of medieval studies Westfield Coll London 1981–86, Matthews lectr Birkbeck Coll London 1983, Carl Newell Jackson lectr Harvard Univ 1992, O'Donnell lectr Univ of Toronto 1993, Barlow lectr UCL 1995; co ed: Mittellateinisches Jahrbuch 1977–, Premio Internazionale Ascoli Piceno 1988; author of essays in learned jls and symposia; hon pres Int Courtly Literature Soc 1974, corresponding fell Real Academia de Buenas Letras 1976; FBA 1984; *Books* Medieval Latin and the Rise of the European Love-Lyric (2 volumes, 1965–66), The Medieval Lyric (1968), Poetic Individuality in the Middle Ages (1970), Fabula (1974), Abelard and Heloise in Medieval Testimonies (1976), Barbara et Antiquissima Carmina (with Ursula Dronke, 1977), Bernardus Silvestris Cosmographia (ed, 1978), Introduction to Francesco Colonna Hypnerotomachia (1981), Women Writers of the Middle Ages (1984), The Medieval Poet and his World (1984), Dante and Medieval Latin Traditions (1986), Introduction to Rosvita, Dialoghi Drammatici (1986), A History of Twelfth Century Western Philosophy (1988), Hermes and the Sibyls (1990), Latin and Vernacular Poets of the Middle Ages (1991), Intellectuals and Poets in Medieval Europe (1992), Verse with Prose from Petronius to Dante (1994), Nine Medieval Latin Plays (1994), Hildegard of Bingen Liber divinorum operum (co-ed, 1996), Sources of Inspiration (1997), Dante's Second Love (lectures, 1997), Introduction to Alessandro nel medioevo occidentale (1997), Growth of Literature: the Sea and the God of the Sea (jtly, 1998), Etienne Gilson's Letters to Bruno Nardi (ed, 1998), Hildegard of Bingen: The Context of Her Thought and Art (co-ed, 1998), Imagination in the Late Pagan and Early Christian World (2003), Forms and Imaginings (2007), The Spell of Calcidius (2008), Giovanni Scoto Eriugena Periphyseon I (ed, 2012, II 2013, III 2014); essays in learned jls and symposia; *Recreations* music, film, Brittany; *Style—* Prof Peter Dronke, FBA; ✉ 6 Parker Street, Cambridge CB1 1JL

DROWNE, Steve John; s of Michael Drowne (d 2002), and Tina, *née* Viggers; *b* 10 December 1971, Launceston, Cornwall; *Educ* Shebbear Coll Devon; *m* 21 Nov 1999, Clare, *née* Hartfall; 2 da (Emily, Alice b 31 July 2007 (twins)); *Career* jockey 1997–; pres Professional Jockeys' Assoc; winner: Chively Park CPI, Molyglare Stakes, Prix D'Abbaye 2003 and 2005; Flat Race Ride of the Year 2002; *Recreations* shooting, skiing; *Style—* Stephen Drowne, Esq; ✉ Moat Cottage, West Grafton, Marlborough, Wiltshire SN8 3BY (e-mail stevedrowne@btinternet.com)

DRUCKMAN, Paul Bryan; s of Leonard Druckman, of Eastbourne, E Sussex, and Phoebe, *née* Hodes; *b* 23 December 1954, Bulawayo, Zimbabwe; *Educ* KCS Wimbledon, Univ of Warwick (PGCE); *m* 1983, Angela, *née* Samuel; 1 s (Alan b 9 Feb 1985), 1 da (Emma 21 Feb 1988); *Career* dir Orchard Business Systems 1985–90, fndr and md Dit 1991–2001, md Orange Consulting 2001–04; chm: Access Technol Gp 2004–11, Clear Gp 2005–; non-exec dir: Business Links for London 2004–07, Allen & Allen Gp 2006–08; pres ICAEW 2004–05, chm Consultative Ctees of Accounting Bodies (CCAB) 2004–05, dir Fin Reporting Cncl 2004–08, memb Takeover Panel 2004–05; chm: Mgmnt Inst 2006–, Prince of Wales' Accounting for Sustainability Project 2007–11, Federation des Experts Compables Europeans Sustainability Policy Gp 2007–11; ceo Int Integrated Reporting Cncl 2011–; FCA 1979, assoc memb Inst of Environmental Mgmnt 2002, FBCS, CITP 2007; *Recreations* golf, tennis; *Clubs* Royal Wimbledon Golf, RSA; *Style—* Paul Druckman, Esq; ✉ IIRC, The Helicon, 1 South Place, London EC2M 2RB (☎ 020 7504 2577, e-mail paul.druckman@theiirc.org)

DRUMMOND, Colin Irwin John Hamilton; OBE (2012); s of Rev William Balfour Drummond (d 1983), and Annie Rebecca, *née* Roy (d 1996); *b* 22 February 1951, Belfast; *Educ* Trinity Coll of Music (LCTL, Colman Prize), Wadham Coll Oxford (MA), Harvard Grad Sch of Business Admin (Harkness fell, MBA); *m* 28 June 1975, Georgina, *née* Lloyd; 2 s (Colin Hugh Lloyd b 27 Nov 1981, Alexander George Balfour b 10 July 1984); *Career* official Economic Intelligence Dept Bank of England 1973–78, conslt Boston Consulting Gp 1978–84, exec dir Renold plc 1984–86, chief exec Yarns Div Coats Viyella plc 1986–92, chief exec Viridor and exec dir Pennon Gp plc 1992–13, chm Viridor 2013–14, ret; memb Advsy Ctee on Business and the Environment 2003–05, chm Govt's Environmental Sector Advsy Gp 2005–12, chm Environmental Sustainability Knowledge Transfer Network 2007–14, chm Govt's Living With Environmental Change Business Advsy Bd 2009–15, chm Taunton and Somerset NHS Fndn Tst 2014–; chm WET 10 City Livery Companies 2008–13; sr visiting fell Dept of Earth Sciences Univ of Oxford 2005–12; organist and choirmaster St John the Baptist Church Wellington 1993–2006; Master Worshipful Co of Water Conservators 2007–08; Liveryman: Worshipful Co of Musicians 2011, Worshipful Co of Gardeners 2011; Hon DBA Edge Hill Univ 2014; CCMI 2002, Hon FSE 2013; *Recreations* sport, music, gardening; *Clubs* Oxford and Cambridge; *Style—* Colin Drummond, Esq, OBE; ✉ Taunton and Somerset NHS Foundation Trust, Musgrove Park Hospital, Taunton TA1 5DA (☎ 01823 342512, e-mail colin.drummond@tst.nhs.uk)

DRUMMOND, David James; s of James Drummond, of Edinburgh, and Audrey Joan, *née* Morrison; *b* 4 August 1956; *Educ* George Watson's Coll Edinburgh, Univ of Edinburgh (BMus), RNCM Manchester; *m* 1, 25 June 1983 (m dis 1988), Jane Caroline, da of Derek Tregilges, of Perranporth, Cornwall; m 2, 9 April 1994, Elizabeth Kate, da of Tom Hutchinson; 2 da (Imogen Mary b 9 July 1997, Katherine Phyllis b 5 March 2004), 1 s (William Tavis b 26 Nov 2000); *Career* staff conductor and chorus master Stora Teatern Gothenburg 1982–84 (conducted Katerina Ismailova, The Turn of the Screw, Don Giovanni, Spöket på Canterville, Lo Sposo Senza Moglie), asst chorus master ENO 1984–88 (conducted Die Fledermaus, The Mikado, The Magic Flute), chorus master Scottish Opera 1988–90 (conducted Street Scene), musical dir London Oriana Choir 1996–2013 (recordings incl: Everyman (by Walford Davies) 2004, If Love could say God's Name (DVD with Beth Nielsen Chapman) 2006, Armstrong-Gibbs' Odysseus (with BBC Concert Orch) 2007); dir Music and Opera UCL 1990–2001: conducted Le Roi d'Ys 1992, Ruslan & Ludmilla 1993, César Franck's opera Hulda 1994 (world première), La Wally 1995, Ballad of Baby Doe 1996 and Heise's Drot og Marsk 1997 (both Br premières), Mignon 1998 Mazeppa 1999, Jewels of the Madonna 2000, Aulis Sallinen's Kullervo 2001 (Br première); conducted Boris Godunov (Kharkov Opera House, 1998); made arrangements for Robert Plant for Sound & Vision at Abbey Road and for Robert Plant and The Band of Joy in BBC Electric Proms 2010; Dream of Gerontius (Barbican) 2011; orchestras conducted include: Kharhov Philharmonic, London Mozart Players, BBC Concert Orch (recorded music for BBC Olympics 2000), Royal Philharmonic; currently: freelance conductor and vocal coach, opera coach Royal Coll of Music and Royal Acad of Music; speaker TEDxHousesofParliament 2013; *Recreations* squash, golf, hill walking, tai-kwon-do, football, languages, travel, sailing; *Style—* David Drummond, Esq; ✉ 540 Las Lomas Way, Walnut Creek, San Francisco, CA 94598, USA

DRUMMOND, Felicia (Flick); MP; da of George Anthony Shepherd, CMG (d 1996), and Sarah Shepherd; *b* 16 June 1962, Aden, Yemen; *Educ* Roedean, Godalming Sixth Form Coll, Univ of Hull (BA), Univ of Southampton (MSc); *m* 7 Aug 1987, Hereward Drummond; 2 s, 2 da; *Career* Porchester Gp 1983–87, lay inspector Ofsted 1994–99, city cncllr Winchester CC 1996–99; MP (Cons) Portsmouth S 2015–; memb Cons ME Cncl 2011; memb TA Intelligence Corps 1984–87; tstee: Portsmouth Citizens Advice Bureau, Int Boatbuilding Trg Coll (ITBC) Portsmouth; govr Milton Park Primary Sch; *Recreations* cinema, cricket, music, opera, reading, sailing, tennis, travel, walking; *Style—* Mrs Flick Drummond, MP; ✉ House of Commons, London SW1A 0AA (e-mail flick.drummond.mp@parliament.uk, website www.flickdrummond.com, Twitter @FlickD)

DRUMMOND, Gillian Vera (Gilly); OBE (2008), DL (Hants 1994); *née* Clark; da of Gavin Clark (d 1997), of Fawley, Hants, and Vera, *née* Royden (d 1998); *b* 15 September 1939, Clatterbridge, Cheshire; *Educ* Roedean, Poggio Imperiale Florence; *m* 1, 1958 (m dis 1978), Graham Turner Laing; 3 da (Sophie, *qv*, b 1960, Ariane (Mrs Koopman) b 1963, Laura b 1969); *m* 2, 1978, Maldwin Andrew Cyril Drummond; 1 s (Aldred b 1978); *Career* cmmr English Heritage 2002–10 (memb Historic Parks and Gardens Advsy Ctee 1988–2001, chm Historic Parks and Gardens Panel 2001–07); pres: Waterside Charities 1981–95, Blackfield Gardening Soc 1993–, Assoc of Gardens Tsts 1995– (fndr chm 1992–95), Hampshire Gardens Tst 2011– (fndr chm 1984–96); vice-pres Royal Southampton Horticultural Soc 1986–; chm SW Region Historic Houses Assoc 2000–05, chm Urban Green Spaces Taskforce ODPM 2001–04; memb: Gardens and Parks Ctee RZS 1986–88, Gardens Ctee Historic Houses Assoc 1986–2000, Jt Mgmnt Ctee Sir George Staunton Country Park Havant 1988–96, Cncl of Mgmnt Sir Harold Hillier Gardens and Arboretum 1989–, Advsy Gp Educn and Historic Built Environment Survey Attingham Tst 2001–03; tstee: Solent Rescue 1988–98, Learning through Landscapes Tst 1991–2009, Gilbert White's House and the Oates Museum 1992–2013, Chawton House Library 1993–, Countryside Educn Tst 1999–2013, Nat Maritime Museum 2005–12, Chiswick House and Gardens Tst 2006–12, Llanthony Priory Tst 2007–10; advsr St Martin-in-the-Fields Appeal 2005–09; sr judge Southern Region in Bloom 1986–2001; county pres St John Ambulance Hants 1990–2003; govr Millbrook Community Sch Southampton 1988–2005; Gold Veitch Meml Medal RHS 1996; *Recreations* gardening, sailing, art, architecture; *Clubs* Royal Yacht Squadron (lay assoc memb), Royal Cruising; *Style—* Mrs Gilly Drummond, OBE, DL, VMH; ✉ Stanswood Farm House, Fawley, Southampton SO45 1AB (✆ 023 8089 1543); Wester Kames Castle, Port Bannatyne, Isle of Bute PA20 0QW

DRUMMOND, Greg; s of Alan Drummond, and Carol, *née* Ross; *b* 3 February 1989, Dundee; *Career* curler; achievements incl: Silver medals World Championships 2011 and 2012, Bronze medal World Championships 2013, Bronze medal European Championships 2013, Silver medal Winter Olympic Games 2014; *Recreations* cinema, golf, horse racing, motorsport, music, travel, football; *Style—* Greg Drummond, Esq; ✉ c/o British Curling, The Royal Caledonian Curling Club, Cairnie House, Ingleston, Newbridge, Midlothian EH28 8NB; e-mail alan@hamiltonmanagement.co.uk, website www.hamiltonmanagement.co.uk

DRUMMOND, Maldwin Andrew Cyril; OBE (1990), JP (1963), DL (Hants 1976); s of Maj Cyril Augustus Drummond, JP, DL (d 1945), of Cadland House, and Mildred Joan, *née* Humphreys (d 1976); *b* 30 April 1932; *Educ* Eton, RAC Cirencester, Univ of Southampton; *m* 1, 1955 (m dis 1977), Susan, da of Sir Kenelm Cayley; 2 da (Frederica (Mrs Templer) b 1957, Annabella (Mrs Villers) b 1959); *m* 2, 18 Jan 1978, Gillian Vera (Gilly), da of Gavin Clark, of Fawley, Hampshire; 1 s (Aldred b 1978); *Career* Nat Serv The Rifle Bde 1950–52, Capt Queen Victoria's Rifles TA 1952–65; farmer, tstee Manor of Cadland; dir: Southampton Harbour Bd and Br Tports Docks Bd 1965–75, Rothesay Seafoods 1968–92, Southern Water Authy 1983–86, Ocean Sound Ltd 1985–91; chm: Bldg Ctee STS Sir Winston Churchill 1964–66, Sail Trg Assoc 1967–72, Warrior (formerly Ships) Preservation Tst 1979–91, Maritime Tst 1980–89, Boat Ctee RNLI 1984–92, New Forest 9th Centenary Tst 1987–94, Heritage Coast Forum 1988–96, New Forest Ctee 1990–96; past pres Hampshire Field Club and Archaeological Soc, pres Shellfish Assoc of GB and NI 1987–2008; tstee: Mary Rose Tst 1976–91, Royal Naval Museum 1986–96; memb Ctee of Mgmnt RNLI 1971–2005; memb: New Forest DC 1957–65, Hampshire CC 1965–75; High Sheriff Hants 1980–81, Countryside Cmmr 1980–86; Verderer of the New Forest 1961–90, Official Verderer 1999–2002; Freeman City of London 1986, Prime Warden Worshipful Co of Fishmongers 1996–97 (memb Ct 1986); younger bro Trinity House 1991–; Hon DSc: Bournemouth Univ 1994, Nottingham Trent Univ 1996; FRGS, FRSA, FSA 2003; *Books* Conflicts in an Estuary (1973), Secrets of George Smith Fisherman (ed and illustrator, 1973), Tall Ships (1976), Salt-Water Palaces (1979), The Yachtsman's Naturalist (with Paul Rodhouse, 1980), The New Forest (with Philip Allison, 1980), The Riddle (1985), West Highland Shores (1990), John Bute, An Informal Portrait (ed, 1996), The Book of the Solent (ed with Robin McInnis, 2001), After You Mr Lear (2007); *Recreations* sailing; *Clubs* Royal Yacht Squadron (cdre 1991–96), Royal Cruising, White's, Pratt's, Leander; *Style—* Maldwin Drummond, Esq, OBE, DL, DSc, FSA; ✉ Stanswood Farm House, Fawley, Southampton SO45 1AB (home ✆ 023 8089 1543, office ✆ 023 8089 2039, fax 023 8024 3040, e-mail office@cadland.co.uk); Wester Kames Castle, Isle of Bute PA20 0QW (✆ 01700 503983)

DRUMMOND, Prof Michael Frank; s of Kenneth John Drummond (d 1973), and Ethel Irene, *née* Spencer; *b* 30 April 1948; *Educ* Atherstone GS, Univ of Birmingham (BSc, MCom), Univ of York (DPhil); *m* 8 June 1973, Margaret, da of James Brennan, of Tamworth, Staffs, 1 s (Thomas b 1980), 1 da (Kate b 1987); *Career* Univ of Birmingham: lectr 1978–84, sr lectr 1984–86, prof of health services management 1986–90; Univ of York: prof of economics 1990–, dir Centre for Health Economics 1995–; memb: North Warwickshire Health Authy 1982–90, Med Comm 1988–91; *Books* Principles of Economic Appraisal in Health Care (1980), Studies in Economic Appraisal in Health Care (1981), Economic Appraisal of Health Technology in the European Community (1987), Methods for the Economic Evaluation of Health Care Programmes (1987, 3 edn 2005); *Recreations* walking, travel; *Style—* Prof Michael Drummond; ✉ Centre for Health Economics, University of York, Heslington, York YO10 5DD (✆ 01904 213409, fax 01904 213402)

DRUMMOND, Rev Prof Norman Walker; CBE (2014); s of Edwin Payne Drummond (d 1971), of Greenock, and Jean Drummond, *née* Walker (d 1992); *b* 1 April 1952; *Educ* Merchiston Castle Sch Edinburgh, Fitzwilliam Coll Cambridge (MA), New Coll Edinburgh (BD); *m* 1976, Lady Elizabeth Kennedy, da of 7 Marquess of Ailsa (d 1994); 3 s (Andrew b 1977, Christian b 1986, Ruaraidh b 1993), 2 da (Margaret b 1980, Marie Clare b 1981); *Career* ordained as minister Church of Scot, cmmnd to serv as Chaplain to HM Servs Army 1976; chaplain: Depot Parachute Regt and Airborne Forces 1977–78, 1 Bn The Black Watch (Royal Highland Regt) 1978–82, Fettes Coll 1982–84, to Moderator of Gen Assembly of Church of Scot 1980, to Govr Edinburgh Castle 1990–92; headmaster Loretto Sch 1984–95, min of Kilmuir and Stenscholl Isle of Skye 1996–98; prof of leadership in educn Univ of Edinburgh 2009–; BBC nat govr and chm Broadcasting Cncl for Scot 1994–99, chm BBC Children in Need 1997–99; chaplain to HM The Queen in Scotland, memb Queen's Body Guard for Scotland (Royal Co of Archers); fndr and chm Columba 1400, Community and Int Leadership Centre Isle of Skye 1997–; chm: Drummond International 1999–, Community Action Network Scotland 2001–03, Lloyds TSB Fndn for Scotland 2003–09; chair Scottish Commemorations Panel 2012–; non-exec chm dir The Change Partnership Scotland 1999–2003, non-exec dir J & J Denholm Ltd 2002–; pres: Edinburgh Battalion The Boys' Brigade 1993–98, Victoria League for Overseas Students in Scot 1995–98; govr Gordonstoun Sch 1995–2000, chm Aiglon Coll Switzerland 1999–2005; memb Scottish Ctee ICRF 1995–98, former tstee Fndn for Skin Research; former memb: Scottish Ctee Duke of Edinburgh's Award Scheme, Ct Heriot-Watt Univ; former chm Musselburgh and District Social Services; special rep for Scotland UK Advsy Gp World War I Commemorations 2012–; Hon Col The Black Watch ACF 2015–; Hon DUniv Glasgow Caledonian Univ 2010; FRSE 2008; *Books* The First 25 Years – the Official History of the Kirk Session of The Black Watch (Royal Highland Regiment), Mother's Hands, The Spirit of Success – How to Connect Your Heart to Your Head in Work and Life, The Power of Three – discovering what really matters in life, Step Back – Finding the Way Forward in Life; *Recreations* rugby football, cricket, golf, curling,

traditional jazz; *Clubs* MCC, New (Edinburgh), Hawks' (Cambridge); *Style—* The Rev Prof Norman Drummond, CBE, FRSE; ✉ 35 Drummond Place, Edinburgh EH3 6PW

DRUMMOND YOUNG, Hon Lord; James Edward Drummond Young; s of the late Duncan Drummond Young, MBE, DL, of Edinburgh, and Annette, *née* Mackay; *b* 17 February 1950; *Educ* John Watson's Sch Edinburgh, Sidney Sussex Coll Cambridge (BA), Harvard Law Sch (Joseph Hodges Choate Meml fell, LLM), Univ of Edinburgh (LLB); *m* 1991, Elizabeth Mary, da of John Campbell-Kease; 1 da; *Career* admitted to Faculty of Advocates 1976, standing jr counsel Bd of Inland Revenue 1986–88, QC 1988, advocate depute 1999–2001, senator Coll of Justice 2001–, chm Scottish Law Cmmn 2007–; *Books* The Law of Corporate Insolvency in Scotland (with J B St Clair, 3 edn 2004), Stair Memorial Encyclopaedia of the Laws of Scotland (contrib, 1989); *Recreations* music, travel; *Style—* The Hon Lord Drummond Young; ✉ Parliament House, Edinburgh EH1 1RQ (✆ 0131 225 2595, fax 0131 240 6711)

DRURY, David Robert; s of Albert Drury (d 1970), of Leeds, and Anne, *née* Crewe (d 1970); *Educ* Temple Moor GS Leeds, Leeds Coll of Art (BA); *m* 1, 1970 (m dis), Pamela Mary, da of George Ratcliffe; 1 s (Benjamin b 4 Sept 1975), 1 da (Rebecca b 8 Jan 1977); *m* 2, 1984 (m dis), Janet Elizabeth, da of Reginald Carter; 1 s (Samuel b 23 Sept 1984); 2 da by Judith Anne Hayes (Bethan b 29 July 1991, Rhiannon b 8 Dec 1993); *Career* film and television director and producer; dir: Forever Young 1984, Intrigue 1988, Children of the North 1990 (winner RTS Award for best series), The Secret Agent 1992, Bad Company 1993 (winner Samuelson Int Film and TV Award for best series), Prime Suspect III 1993 (winner BAFTA Award for best drama series, American Critics Award and Banff TV Festival Award for best series, Emmy for best mini-series), Runway One 1995, Rhodes (series) 1995, Hostile Waters 1997, The Unknown Soldier 1998, Trust 1999, Tough Love 2000, Bomber 2000, The Swap 2002, The Cry 2002, Family (series) 2003, The Crooked Man 2003, Messiah: The Promise 2004, Marian, Again 2005, The Brief 2005, Love Lies Bleeding 2006, Fallen Angel 2006, The Midnight Man 2007, The Take 2008, Ashes to Ashes 2009–10, Come Rain or Come Shine 2010; film dir: Defence of the Realm 1986 (selected for dirs' fortnight Cannes Film Festival, winner Rimini Film Festival Award for best dir, Madrid Film Festival Award best film); *Clubs* Groucho, Century; *Style—* David Drury, Esq; ✉ c/o United Agents Limited, 12–26 Lexington Street, London W1F 0LE (✆ 020 3214 0800, fax 020 3214 0801, website www.unitedagents.co.uk)

DRURY, Ian Charles; s of Arthur Drury, of Winchester, and Mary Drury; *b* 13 February 1961, Hemel Hempstead, Herts; *Educ* Peter Symonds' GS Winchester, New Coll Oxford (MA); *m* 20 May 2005, Joanna, *née* Abercrombie-Gould-Fletcher; 1 s (James Edward Browning b 20 Dec 1991), 1 da (Sophie Anne Marie b 20 May 1994); *Career* ed Aerospace Publishing 1984–94, editorial dir HarperCollins Publishers 1994–2001, publishing dir Cassell & Co 2001–03, publishing dir Weidenfeld & Nicholson 2003–07, literary agent Sheil Land Assocs 2007–; memb: Br Cmmn for Military Hist 1996–, RUSI 2001–; *Publications* The Russo-Turkish War (1990), Verdun (1992), Jutland (1994), Hitler's War on Russia (2007); *Recreations* freemasonry, long distance running, film and theatre; *Style—* Ian Drury, Esq; ✉ Sheil Land Associates, 52 Doughty Street, London WC1N 2LS

DRURY, John Kenneth; s of John Kenneth Drury, of Paisley and Elizabeth Laird McNeil, *née* Pattison; *b* 23 January 1947; *Educ* Paisley GS, Univ of Glasgow (MB ChB, PhD); *m* 16 July 1974, Gillian Ruth Alexandra, da of Dr Thomas Gilmore, of Paisley; 1 da (Sarah b 1978), 1 s (Colin b 1981); *Career* res fell Inst of Physiology Univ of Glasgow, conslt gen surgn with interest in peripheral vascular surgery and clinical dir of gen surgery Victoria Infirmary NHS Tst Glasgow 1987–2010, hon clinical sr lectr Univ of Glasgow 1987– (memb Faculty of Med 1992–95, memb Univ Senate 1993–2000); RCPS Glasgow: hon registrar for surgical examinations 2001–04, dir of surgical examinations 2004–10; RCS Glasgow: examiner in fellowship, memb Intercollegiate Ctee for Basic Surgical Examinations 2003–06; Scottish Audit Surgical Mortality: memb Mgmnt Ctee 2003–10, coordinator for vascular surgery 2004–10; memb Bd of Gen Surgery Jt Surgical Colls Fellowship Examination 2011–, chair Intercollegiate Report on Jt Ctee for Surgical Training 2011; author of 65 papers on gen and vascular surgery (new vascular graft, vascular trauma, redo vascular surgery, laparoscopic cholecystectomy, blood transfusion, Legionnaires Disease); memb Ctee Paisley RNLI; memb: Cncl Southern Med Soc, Vascular Soc GB 1987, European Soc of Vascular Surgery; FRCS 1978; *Recreations* yachting, squash, golf, skiing, local art; *Clubs* Western Gailes Golf, Western Medical, Ranfurly Castle Golf; *Style—* John Drury, Esq; ✉ 10 Main Road, Castlehead, Paisley, Renfrewshire PA2 6AJ (✆ 0141 8894512, e-mail jkdalba@btinternet.com); Ross Hall Hospital, Crookston Road, Glasgow G52 3NQ

DRURY, Jolyon Victor Paul; s of Alfred Paul Dalou Drury (d 1987), and Enid Marie, *née* Solomon (d 1996); *b* 19 November 1946; *Educ* Tonbridge, Pembroke Coll Cambridge (exhibitioner, DipArch, MA); *m* 25 April 1975, Christine Evelyn Cary, da of Dr John Gilson, CBE; 2 s (Adrian John Jolyon b 24 Nov 1977, Charles Worthington Paul b 26 May 1981); *Career* Arup Assocs 1971–75, fndr Jolyon Drury Consultancy 1975–2000, Arup JDC 2000–03, dir Surge Logistics Conslts 2005–; chm Public Policies Ctee CILT 2006–; Col Engr and Logistics Staff Corps 2004–; tstee Public Monuments and Sculpture Assoc 2007–15; Freeman City of London 2005, Liveryman Worshipful Co of Carmen 2005; RIBA 1972, FIMH 1984, FILog 1993, FILT 2000, FCIT 2000, FCILT 2004, MInstRE 2010; *Publications* Building and Planning for Industrial Storage and Distribution (with Peter Falconer, 1975, updated 2003), Factories, Planning, Design and Modernisation (1981), Automated Warehouses (1988), Revelation to Revolution: The Legacy of Samuel Palmer (2005); *Recreations* small holding, France, etchings; *Clubs* City Univ; *Style—* Jolyon Drury, Esq; ✉ Woodside, Potters Corner, Ashford, Kent TN26 1AE (e-mail jolyon.drury@btinternet.com)

DRURY, Martin Dru; CBE (2001); s of Walter Neville Dru Drury, TD (d 1999), of Edenbridge, Kent, and Rae, *née* Sandiland (d 2002); *b* 22 April 1938; *Educ* Rugby; *m* 5 Jan 1971, Elizabeth Caroline, da of Hon Sir Maurice Bridgeman, KBE (d 1980), of Selham, W Sussex; 2 s (Matthew b 8 Aug 1972, Joseph b 18 June 1977), 1 da (Daisy b 6 Sept 1974); *Career* 2 Lt 3 Hussars 1957, Capt Army Emergency Reserve 1967; broker at Lloyd's 1959–65, Mallett & Son (Antiques) Ltd 1965–73; National Tst: historic bldgs rep and advsr on furniture 1973–81, historic bldgs sec 1981–95, dep DG 1992–96, DG 1996–2001, memb Arts Panel 2004–; chm Landmark Tst 1992–95 and 2001–11, chm Stowe Advsy Panel 2005, dir Arundel Castle Tst Ltd 1987–95, vice-chm Attingham Tst 1982–2013; memb: Fabric Advsy Ctee St Paul's Cathedral 1991–, Cncl Georgian Gp 1994–, Cncl UK Overseas Territories Conservation Forum 2000–06, Exec Ctee Soc for the Protection of Ancient Buildings 2006–14; tstee: Heritage of London Tst 1996– 2008 (chm 2007–08, vice-pres 2008–15, pres 2015–), The Wallace Collection 2001–11; chm of tstees Goldsmith's Centre 2007–12, Project Hougoumount Appeal Ctee 2012–; cmmr Royal Hosp Chelsea 2002–08; vice-pres Nat Assoc of Decorative and Fine Arts Socs 2008–; Esher Award for services to the protection of ancient buildings 2002, Europa Nostra Award for Lifetime Service 2013; memb Ct of Assts Worshipful Co of Goldsmiths (Prime Warden 2005–06); Hon Dr Arts Univ of Greenwich 2000; FSA 1992; *Clubs* Brooks's, Pratt's, Seaview Yacht; *Style—* Martin Drury, Esq, CBE, FSA; ✉ 3 Victoria Rise, London SW4 0PB (✆ 020 7622 9688, e-mail martindrury@btinternet.com)

DRURY, Stephen Patrick; s of late Patrick Keith Drury, and Anne Rosemary, *née* Major-Lucas; *b* 20 May 1954; *Educ* Charterhouse, Oriel Coll Oxford (MA); *m* 25 June 1983, Deborah Ann, da of late Wilfred McBrien Swain, OBE; 2 s (Patrick b 1984, Benjamin b 1993), 1 da (Frances b 1987); *Career* called to the Bar 1977, admitted slr 1980, admitted slr Hong Kong 1984, ptnr Holman Fenwick Willan LLP 1985– (joined 1978); visiting lectr in ship fin law Business Sch City Univ 1990–; memb Cncl: Amateur Rowing Assoc 1980–84, Hong Kong Amateur Rowing Assoc 1984–87; licensed umpire Br Rowing 1999; Freeman City of London, Liveryman Worshipful Co of Merchant Taylors 1988; *Books* Arrest of Ships (vol 6, 1987); *Recreations* rowing, golf; *Clubs* Kingston Rowing, Royal Hong Kong Yacht, Effingham Golf, Lansdowne; *Style—* Stephen Drury, Esq; ✉ Holman Fenwick Willan LLP, Friary Court, 65 Crutched Friars, London EC3N 2AE (☎ 020 7264 8000, fax 020 7264 8888, e-mail stephen.drury@hfw.com)

DRYSDALE, Prof David Douglas (Dougal); s of David Drysdale (d 1979), of Dunfermline, Fife, and Christina Campbell, *née* Rae (d 1988); *b* 30 September 1939; *Educ* Edinburgh Acad, Univ of Edinburgh (BSc), Univ of Cambridge (PhD); *m* 8 Aug 1964, Judyth, *née* McIntyre; 3 s (David John b 22 July 1965, Andrew James b 8 July 1967, Peter Robert b 4 May 1971); *Career* post doctoral research fell Dept of Chemistry Univ of Toronto 1966–67, research lectureship Dept of Physical Chemistry Univ of Leeds 1971–74 (post doctoral research fell 1967–71); Univ of Edinburgh: lectr Dept of Fire Engrg 1974–90, reader in fire safety engrg Dept of Civil and Environmental Engrg 1990–98, prof of fire safety engrg 1998–2004 (prof emeritus 2004–); visiting prof Centre for Firesafety Studies Worcester Poly Inst MA 1982, visiting prof Tianjin Inst of Technol 2001; co-ordinator ODA China Fire Science Trg Project 1993–98; chm Int Assoc for Fire Safety Science 2002–05; memb: Soc of Fire Protection Engrs (USA), Combustion Inst, Forensic Science Soc, Int Assoc of Fire Safety Science; ed Fire Safety Jl 1989–2009, memb Editorial Bd Soc of Fire Protection Engrs Handbook of Fire Protection Engrg (fourth edn); author of numerous papers in learned jls; Fire Research lectr Fire Research Station Building Research Estab 1995, Howard W Emmons lectr Worcester Poly Inst MA 1995; Man of the Year Soc of Fire Protection Engrs (USA) 1983, Arthur B Guise Medal Soc of Fire Protection Engrs (USA) 1995, Kawagoe Medal Int Assoc for Fire Safety Science 2002, Rasbash Medal Inst of Fire Engrs 2005, Sjolin Award Int Forum of Fire Research Dirs 2005; CEng 1999, FRSE 2002, FSFPE 2004, MRSC, FIFireE; *Books* Introduction to Fire Dynamics (1985, 3 edn 2011); *Recreations* music, hill walking, golf, curling; *Style—* Prof Dougal Drysdale; ✉ School of Engineering, University of Edinburgh, King's Buildings, Edinburgh EH9 3JL (☎ 0131 650 5724, e-mail d.drysdale@ed.ac.uk, website www.see.ed.ac.uk/fire)

DU NOYER, Paul Anthony; s of Anthony George Du Noyer, of Liverpool, and Jean, *née* Moran; *b* 21 May 1954, Liverpool; *Educ* Bootle Salesian Coll, Wigan Tech Coll, LSE (BScEcon); *m* 25 June 1977, Una Mary O'Farrell, da of Edward Farrell; 2 s (Edward Paul b 22 Feb 1984, Daniel Paul b 25 June 1992); *Career* freelance journalist 1978–80, asst ed New Musical Express 1983–85 (staff writer 1980–83), ed Q magazine 1990–92 (asst ed 1986–90), ed Mojo magazine 1993–95, ed dir Emap Digital Music 1999–2001, assoc ed Word magazine 2002–11; *Books* The Story of Rock'n'Roll (1995), We All Shine On: John Lennon's Solo Songs (1997), Liverpool: Wondrous Place (2002), In The City: A Celebration of London Music (2009), Deaf School (2013), Conversations With McCartney (2015); *Style—* Paul Du Noyer, Esq; ✉ c/o Edwards Fuglewicz, 49 Great Ormond Street, London WC1N 3HZ (☎ 020 7405 6725, e-mail info@etla.co.uk, website www.pauldunoyer.com)

du PLESSIS, Jan Petrus; *b* 22 January 1954; *Educ* Univ of Stellenbosch SA; *Career* with International Div Rembrandt Group Ltd 1981–88, fin dir Compagnie Financière Richemont AG Switzerland (ultimate parent co of Rothmans International) 1988–2004, dir Richemont International Ltd 1990–2004; non-exec chm: British American Tobacco plc 2004– (non-exec dir 1999–), RHM plc 2005–07; non-exec dir Lloyds TSB 2005–; *Style—* Jan du Plessis, Esq

DU SAUTOY, Prof Marcus Peter Francis; OBE (2010); *b* 26 August 1965, London; *Career* Charles Simonyi prof for the public understanding of science Univ of Oxford, prof of mathematics Univ of Oxford, fell New Coll Oxford; EPSRC sr media fell; memb: Science and Society Ctee Royal Soc 1999–2005, Dialogue in Med Science and Society Assoc of Med Research Charities 2003–; judge: Crighton Medal London Mathematical Soc 2003 and 2006, Aventis Science Book Prize 2003, BBC 4 Samuel Johnson Non-Fiction Book Prize 2005, Art Fund Prize for Museums 2009, Grierson Prize for TV Documentaries 2009 and 2011; pres Mathematical Assoc 2012–13; Royal Instn Christmas lectr 2006; presenter: Mindgames (BBC 4), The Music of the Primes (BBC 4) 2005, The Story of Maths (BBC 4) 2008, Horizon (BBC 2) 2009, 2010, 2011 and 2012, The Beauty of Diagrams (BBC 4) 2010, The Code (BBC 2) 2011, The School of Hard Sums (Dave) 2012–13, Maestro at the Opera (BBC 2) 2012, Precision (BBC 4) 2013, The Secret Rules of Modern Living: Algorithms (BBC 4) 2015; Berwick Prize London Mathematical Soc 2001, Faraday Prize Royal Soc 2009, Jt Policy for Mathematics Bd Communications Award 2010, IMA-LMS Christopher Zeeman Medal 2014; Hon Dr: Open Univ 2008, Univ of Bath 2010, Queen Mary Coll London 2013, Univ of Liverpool 2013, Univ of S Wales; FRS 2016; *Books* The Music of the Primes: Why an Unsolved Problem in Mathematics Matters (2003), Finding Moonshine: A Mathematician's Journey Through Symmetry (2008), The Number Mysteries (2010), What We Cannot Know (2016); *Recreations* number 17 for Recreativo Hackney FC, theatre, music; *Clubs* Arts; *Style—* Prof Marcus du Sautoy, OBE, FRS; ✉ Mathematical Institute, University of Oxford, 24–29 St Giles', Oxford OX1 3LB

du VIVIER, Dr Anthony Wilfred Paul; s of Maj Paul Edward du Vivier (d 1967), and Joan Beryl, *née* Swann; *b* 16 June 1944; *Educ* Ampleforth, Bart's Med Sch (MD); *m* 13 Aug 1977, Judith Vivienne, da of late Cdr Reginald Sidney Brett, RN; *Career* conslt dermatologist KCH London 1978–; FRCP; *Publications* Clinical Dermatology (4 edn); *Clubs* RSM; *Style—* Dr Anthony du Vivier; ✉ Department of Dermatology, King's College Hospital, London SE5 9RS (☎ 020 3299 3258); 62 Wimpole Street, London W1G 8AJ (☎ 020 7935 6465, fax 020 7935 5014, e-mail anthonyduvivier@aol.com)

DU-FEU, Vivian John; *Educ* Univ of Cardiff; *Career* admitted slr 1979, early career in Employment Law, joined Eversheds Phillips & Buck (now Eversheds) 1983, currently chm Eversheds Human Resources Gp; pt/t lectr in labour law Univ of Cardiff 1983–87 (pt/t tutor 1981–83); dir Principle Training Ltd; memb Croner Editorial Advsy Bd; FIPD; *Books* The Conduct of Proceedings Before Industrial Tribunals, Protecting Your Business and Confidential Information (co-author 1992), Collective Labour Law (co-author 1992), Procedure in Industrial Tribunal Cases (co-author 1992), Flexible Working Practices (contrib 1996), Employment Law in the NHS (co-author 1996), EU Comparative Labour Law (co-ed, 2001); *Style—* Vivian Du-Feu, Esq; ✉ Eversheds, 1 Callaghan Square, Cardiff CF10 5BT (☎ 029 2047 1147, fax 029 2046 4347, DX 33016 Cardiff, e-mail vivdufeu@eversheds.com)

DUBERLY, Sir (Archibald) Hugh; KCVO (2015), CBE (1996); s of Cdr Archibald Gray, RN, DSO, DL (d 1991), and Grey Cunliffe, *née* Duberly (d 2012); name changed by deed poll 1963; *b* 4 April 1942, Huntingdon; *Educ* Winchester; *m* 4 Nov 1967, Sarah Elizabeth Duberly, DL, da of Maj-Gen I A Robertson, CB, MBE, DL; 2 s (James Gray b 24 Sept 1968, Harry Grey b 9 Oct 1975), 1 da (Kate Saffron b 2 April 1971); *Career* cncllr Hunts DC 1979–2004; High Sheriff Cambs 1991–92, HM Lord-Lt Cambs 2003– (DL 1989); cmmr Crown Estate 2002–09; dir Agricultural Mortgage Corp plc 1995–2002; pres CLA 1993–95; chm: Kimbolton Sch 1992–2000, Ely Diocesan Bd of Fin 1992–, Papworth Tst 1995–2012, Shuttleworth Tst 2001–13; Hon MA Univ of Cambridge 2016; *Clubs* Boodle's, Nairn Golf; *Style—* Sir Hugh Duberly, KCVO, CBE

DUBLIN, Archbishop of 2011–; Most Rev Dr Michael Geoffrey St Aubyn Jackson; s of Robert Stewart Jackson (d 2001), and Margaret Jane Frances, *née* Sloan; *b* 24 May 1956; *Educ* Portora Royal Sch Enniskillen, TCD (BA, Gold medal, MA), St John's Coll Cambridge (fndn scholar, MA, Nowell-Rostron prize, Bishop Lightfoot prize, Wordsworth scholar, PhD), Church of Ireland Theol Coll (Downes essay prize, Moncrieff-Cox sermon prize, Elrington theol prize); *m* 2 May 1987, Inez Elizabeth, *née* Cooke; 1 da (Camilla Elizabeth St Aubyn b 21 March 1990); *Career* ordained: deacon 1986, priest 1987; curate asst Zion parish Rathgar 1986–89, minor canon, treas's vicar and chllr's vicar St Patrick's Cathedral Dublin 1987–89, asst lectr Dept of Hebrew, Biblical and Theol Studies TCD and Church of Ireland Theol Coll 1987–89; Univ of Oxford: MA and DPhil (by incorporation) 1989, coll chaplain ChCh 1989–97 (student 1993–97), asst lectr Theology Faculty 1991–97, dir of studies in theology St Anne's Coll 1995–97; incumbent St Fin Barre's Union Cork and dean of Cork 1997–2002, chaplain UC Cork and Cork Inst of Technol 1997–2002, asst lectr Schs of Classics and Educn UC Cork 1997–2002, examining chaplain to bishop of Cork, Cloyne and Ross 1999–2002, bishop of Clogher 2002–11; chaplain: Vincents' Club 1992–97, Oxford Diocesan Branch C of E Guild of Vergers 1996–97; Travers Smith lectr St Bartholomew's Church 1997; author of articles and reviews published in: Classica et Mediaevalia, Studia Patristica, The Church Times, Search, Jl of Theol Studies, Hermathena, The Furrow, The Irish Theol Quarterly, Doctrine and Life, The Ecumenical Review; chm: Oxford Univ Chaplains' Mission Ctee 1991–92, St Fin Barre's Beyond 2000 1998–2002; chairperson Network for Inter-Faith Concerns in the Anglican Communion (NIFCON) 2004–; memb: Ethics Ctee Cork Univ Hosp 1999–2002, Int Anglican-Oriental Orthodox Cmmn 2002–; *Clubs* Kildare St and Univ (Dublin); *Style—* The Most Rev the Archbishop of Dublin; ✉ Archbishop's House, Drumcondra, Dublin, Ireland

D

DUBOWITZ, Prof Victor; s of Charley Dubowitz, and Olga, *née* Schattel; *b* 6 August 1931; *Educ* Beaufort West Central HS, Univ of Cape Town (BSc, MB ChB, MD), Univ of Sheffield (PhD); *m* 10 July 1960, Lilly Magdalena Suzanne, *née* Sebok; 4 s (David b 1963, Michael b 1964, Gerald b 1965, Daniel b 1969); *Career* res assoc (histochemistry) Royal Postgrad Med Sch 1958–60, clinical asst Queen Mary's Hosp for Children Carshalton 1958–60, lectr in clinical pathology Nat Hosp for Nervous Diseases 1960–61, lectr in child health Univ of Sheffield 1961–65 (sr lectr 1965–67), reader in child health and developmental neurology Univ of Sheffield 1967–72, prof of paediatrics Univ of London 1972–96 (prof emeritus 1996–), hon conslt paediatrician Hammersmith Hosp 1972–; dir Muscle Res Centre 1972–96, dir Therapeutic Studies European Neuromuscular Centre (ENMC) Holland 1999–2003; pres: Br Paediatric Neurology Assoc 1992–1994, European Paediatric Neurology Soc 1993–97, World Muscle Soc 1995–, Med Art Soc 1997–2000; Jean Hunter Prize RCP 1987; FRCP 1972, Hon FRCPCH 2000; Cdr Order Constantine the Great 1980, Arvo Ylppo Gold Medal Finland 1982, Gaetano Conte Gold Medal Italy 1991, Cornelia de Lange Medal The Netherlands 1997, James Spence Gold Medal RCPCH 2007, Jennifer Tst for Spinal Muscular Atrophy Inaugural Gold Medal 2009, Peter Emil Becker Prize German Speaking Paediatric Neurology Socs 2011; *Books* Developing and Diseased Muscle A Histochemical Study (1968), The Floppy Infant (2 edn, 1980), Muscle Biopsy – A Modern Approach (2 edn, 1985, 4 edn 2012), Gestational Age of the Newborn – A Clinical Manual (1977), Muscle Disorders in Childhood (2 edn, 1995), Neurological Assessment of the Preterm and Full-term Infant (1981, 2 edn 1999), A Colour Atlas of Muscle Disorders in Childhood (1989), A Colour Atlas of Brain Disorders in the Newborn (1990), Ramblings of a Peripatetic Paediatrician (2005); *Recreations* sculpting, hiking, photography; *Style—* Prof Victor Dubowitz; ✉ Dubowitz Neuromuscular Unit, 1st Floor, UCL Institute of Child Health, 30 Guilford Street, London WC1N 1EH (☎ 020 7905 2221, fax 020 7905 2832)

DUBS, Baron (Life Peer UK 1994), of Battersea in the London Borough of Wandsworth; Alfred (Alf) Dubs; *Educ* LSE (BSc); *Career* MP (Lab) Battersea S (later Battersea) 1979–87, Parly under sec NI Office 1997–99; dir Refugee Cncl 1988–95, dep chm ITC 2000–01, chm Broadcasting Standards Cmmn 2001–04; sits as Lab peer in House of Lords, chair Lab Pty in House of Lords 2000–05, memb Jt Ctee on Communications, memb Parly Assembly of OSCE, memb Br-Irish Inter-Parly Assembly; *Recreations* walking in the Lake District; *Style—* The Lord Dubs; ✉ House of Lords, London SW1P 0PW (☎ 020 7219 3590)

DUCAS, Annoushka; MBE (2012); *m* John Ayton, MBE, *qv*; *Career* fndr and creative dir Links of London 1990–2007, fndr and creative dir Annoushka Ltd 2009–; *Style—* Ms Annoushka Ducas, MBE; ✉ Annoushka, 41 Cadogan Gardens, London SW3 2TB

DUCKWORTH, Simon D'Olier; OBE (2014), DL (Gtr London, 2008); s of John Alexander D'Olier Duckworth (d 1988), of Wimbledon, and Anne Judith (d 2010), o c of Brig P M Medill, DSO; *b* 16 November 1964; *Educ* KCS, Girton Coll Cambridge (organ exhibitioner, MA); *m* 20 Oct 2012, Lady Caroline Sara Frances Primrose, yr da of 7 Earl of Rosebery, DL; *Career* Coll of Arms 1993–2001, clerk Gunmakers' Co 2001–03; dir: Fidelity European Values plc 2003–13, Barings Targeted Return Fund 2004– (chm 2011–), Assoc of Police Authorities 2008–12 (dep chm 2012), Gresham Coll 2009–, Accumuli plc 2010–15, Bann System Ltd 2010–12, Assoc of Police and Crime Cmmrs 2012– (chm Transitional Bd 2012–13), Broca plc (now MXC Capital plc) 2013–14, Pinnacle Technology plc (now Adept4 plc) 2015–; non-exec dir Serious Fraud Office (SFO) 2011–; memb: Ct of Common Cncl City of London 2000– (Fin and Investment Ctees 2002–, Policy and Resources Ctee 2008–, Gresham Ctee 2008– (dep chm 2012–14, chm 2014–)), City of London Police Authy 2002– (dep chm 2006–08 and 2012–13, chm 2008–12, chm Economic Crime Bd 2012–), Assoc of London Govt Crime and Public Protection Forum 2006–12, Advsy Bd London First Security & Policing 2009–; Assoc of Police Authorities: memb Strategic Policing Policy Gp 2006–12, memb Police Authy Reform Gp 2006–08, Nat Olympics Security Oversight Gp 2007–12 (chm 2009–12); Home Office: memb Olympic Security and Safety Strategy Gp 2007–09, memb Olympic Security Bd 2009–12, memb NCA Steering Gp 2010–12, memb Economic Crime Coordination Bd 2011–14, memb NCA Prog Bd 2012–14, memb Fraud Oversight Bd 2014–; memb Advsy Bd City Univ 2006–12 (memb Cncl 2001–06), memb Cncl Gresham Coll 2009– (vice chm 2014–); clerk Queen's Chapel of the Savoy 1999–; tstee: Lord Mayor's 800th Anniversary Awards Tst 2003–; memb RFCA 2002– (exec memb City Assoc 2006–, vice chm 2013–), memb Ct of Assts Hon The Irish Soc 2002– (dep govr 2013–15), patron City of London Crime Prevention Assoc 2008–12 (hon memb 2012); one of HM's Lieutenants City of London 2010– (memb Standing Ctee 2012–, vice chm 2015–), Lt Col Engineer and Logistic Staff Corps (E&LSC) Royal Engineers (Army Reserve), Hon Col Royal Military Police 2015– (Dep Hon Col 2012–15); Liveryman Skinners' Co 1998 (Ct of Assts 2012–15), memb Parish Clerks' Co 2000–; OStJ 2005 (SBStJ 2001); *Recreations* cooking, claret, and sampling both with friends, country sports; *Clubs* Brooks's, University Pitt (hon sec 1989), Guildhall, Newmarket and Suffolk Real Tennis; *Style—* Simon Duckworth, Esq, OBE, DL; ✉ 11 Gladstone Street, Southwark, London SE1 6EY (e-mail ciduc@yahoo.co.uk)

DUCKWORTH-CHAD, Anthony Nicholas George; OBE (1999), DL (Norfolk 1994); s of A J S Duckworth (d 1993), of Southacre House, King's Lynn, Norfolk; *b* 20 November 1942; *Educ* Eton, RAC Cirencester; *m* 6 May 1970, Elizabeth Sarah, da of Capt C B H Wake-Walker (d 1998), of East Bergholt Lodge, Suffolk; 2 s (James b 1972, William b 1975), 1 da (Davina b 1978); *Career* farmer and landowner; memb: Walsingham RDC 1963–74, North Norfolk DC 1974–95 (chm 1987–89); pres: Norfolk branch CLA 1997–2002 (chm 1977–78), Royal Norfolk Agricultural Assoc 2006; govr Greshams Sch 1974–2011 (chm 2005–11); High Sheriff Norfolk 1992; Prime Warden Worshipful Co of Fishmongers 2004; *Recreations* country sports; *Clubs* White's, Pratt's; *Style—* Anthony Duckworth-Chad, Esq, OBE, DL; ✉ 178 Cambridge Street, London SW1V 4QE; Pynkney Hall, East Rudham, King's Lynn, Norfolk PE31 6TF

DUDDRIDGE, James; MP; *Educ* Crestwood Sch, Huddersfield New Coll, Wells Blue Sch, Univ of Essex; *m* Katy; 2 s (Tom b 2006, Henry b 2008), 1 da (Mary b 2011); *Career*

retail and merchant banker Barclays Bank 1993–95 (joined as grad trainee), Barclays Bank of Swaziland 1995–96, sales dir Banque Belgolaise Ivory Coast 1997–98, nat sales mangr Barclays Bank 1998, former service delivery dir Barclays Bank Botswana; conslt YouGov 2000–05; dir Okavango Ltd 2002–05; MP (Cons) Rochford and Southend E 2005– (Parly candidate (Cons) Rother Valley 2001), oppn whip 2008–10, lord cmmr (whip) 2010–, FCO Min for Africa, Overseas Territories and Carribean 2014–; *Style*— James Duddridge, Esq, MP; ✉ House of Commons, London SW1A 0AA (☎ 020 7219 4830, e-mail james@jamesduddridge.com, website www.jamesduddridge.com)

DUDLEY, Anne Jennifer; da of late William James Beckingham, of Brighton, and Dorothy Thelma Beckingham; *Educ* Eltham Hill GS, Royal Coll of Music (Performer's Dip, BMus), KCL (MMus); *m* 1978, Roger Dudley, s of Leonard William Dudley; 1 da (Angela b 7 April 1992); *Career* musician, composer, arranger, prodr; composer in assoc with the BBC Concert Orch 2002–05; keyboard player and arranger with: ABC (Lexicon of Love album), Wham! (Young Guns, Bad Boys and Everything She Wants), Malcolm McLaren (co-wrote Buffalo Gals and other tracks on Duck Rock), Frankie Goes to Hollywood (Two Tribes and The Power of Love); fndr memb Art of Noise (performed, wrote and co-produced all six albums); freelance arranger and musician with: Paul McCartney, Wham, Liza Minelli, Lloyd Cole, Rod Stewart, Marc Almond, Robbie Williams, Seal, Tina Turner, Cher, Elton John, Pulp, Boyzone, Will Young, Pet Shop Boys, Jaz Coleman of Killing Joke (songs From the Victorious City 1990); solo albums: Ancient and Modern 1995, A Different Light 2002, Seriously Chilled 2004; composer of soundtracks for cinematic feature films incl: Hiding Out, Buster, Wilt, Silence Like Glass, Say Anything, Mighty Quinn, The Pope Must Die, Disorderlies, The Miracle, The Crying Game, Knight Moves, When Saturday Comes, The Grotesque, Hollow Reed, The Full Monty, Pushing Tin, American History, The Miracle Maker, Monkeybone, Lucky Break, The Gathering, Bright Young Things, Perfect creature, Tristan and Isolde, Black Book, The Walker; composer of soundtrack music for TV: Jeeves and Wooster 1990–93, Krypton Factor, Down to Earth, Anna Lee, Kavanagh QC, Crime Traveller, The Perfect Blue, The Tenth Kingdom, The Key, Trial and Retribution, Above Suspicious; composer of music for TV and cinema commercials incl: Volvo, World Wildlife Fund, Commercial Union, Reebok, Guinness, Stella Artois; concert music: Music and Silence, Winter Solstice, Northern Lights; music for theatre prodn Cinderella (Old Vic) 2008, opera The Doctor's Take (ROH) 2011; Grammy Award for Peter Gunn 1988, Midsummer Award for Volvo (Twister) 1996, Academy Award (Oscar) for The Full Monty 1997; memb: BAFTA, Academy of Motion Picture Arts and Sciences; FRCM 2004; *Style*— Anne Dudley; ✉ c/o Darrell Alexander, Cool Music, 1a Fishers Lane, London W4 1RX (☎ 020 8995 7766, fax 020 8987 8996, e-mail enquiries@coolmusicltd.com, website www.annedudley.co.uk)

DUDLEY, Rev Dr Martin Raymond; s of Ronald Frank Dudley, and Joyce Mary, *née* Gardiner, of Birmingham; *b* 31 May 1953; *Educ* King Edward's Sch Birmingham, RMA Sandhurst, KCL (BD, MTh, PhD, AKC), St Michael's Coll Llandaff and UC Cardiff, Cass Business Sch City Univ (MSc); *m* Paula, *née* Jones; 2 s (Thomas Edward b 1989, Joseph Nicholas b 1994); *Career* ordained: deacon 1979, priest 1980; asst curate Whitchurch Cardiff 1979–83; vicar Weston 1983–88; priest-in-charge Ardeley 1986–88; vicar Owlsmoor Sandhurst 1988–95, rector St Bartholomew the Great Smithfield 1995–, priest in charge Bartholomew the Less 2013–15; lectr Simon of Cyrene Theological Inst 1992–94; vice-chm St Bartholomew the Great Heritage Tst 1999–2015; vice-pres American Friends of St Bartholomew the Great 2000–15; non-exec dir Whitehall Consultants 2001–03; memb: Bar Cncl Professional Conduct and Complaints Ctee 2000–06, London Diocesan Synod 2003–06, Bishop's Cncl 2003–06; tstee: Butchers and Drovers Charitable Inst 1997–2004, Field Lane Fndn 2000–01, The London Library 2003–07, City Parochial Fndn (now Tst for London) 2005–15; govr: The City Literary Inst 2001–03, City of London Sch for Girls 2002–, City of London Acad (Southwark) 2003–13, Museum of London 2007–15 (chm Audit Ctee 2009–15); memb: City of London Libraries Archives and Guildhall Art Gallery Ctee 2002–07, Hampstead Heath Mgmnt Ctee 2003–04 and 2012–, Ct Bridewell Royal Fndn 2003–13, City of London Licensing Ctee 2004–, City of London Planning and Transportation Ctee 2005–, City of London City Bridge Tst 2007–11, Standards Ctee 2007–14; chair City of London Health Scrutiny Ctee 2010–13, chair City of London Health and Wellbeing Bd 2013–; chm City of London Community and Children's Services Ctee 2011–14 (dep chm 2010); chm Resource Centre (London) Ltd 2007–11; Common Councilman City of London (Aldersgate Ward) 2002–; chaplain to: Master Butcher 1995–2009, 2013–14 and 2015–16, Imperial Soc of Knights Bachelor 1995–2005, Chartered Secretaries and Administrators 1995–2000, Hackney Carriage Drivers 1998–, Master Farmer 1999–2000 and 2002–03, Information Technologists 2001–, Master Fletcher 2001–02, 2004–09 and 2010–11, PR Practitioners 2001–, Tax Advsrs 2002–, Royal Soc of St George (City of London branch) 2003– (vice chm 2014–15, chm 2015–16, vice-pres 2016), Alderman & Sheriff Anstee 2003–04; pres Farringdon Ward Club 2008–09 (jr vice-pres 2006–07, sr vice-pres 2007–08); memb: ctee City of London Archeological Tst 2006–12, Corporation of London Community & Children's Servs Ctee 2006–, Professional Conduct & Complaints Ctee CIArb 2005–15, Ct City Univ 2009–; Dr of Arts (hc) City Univ London 2014, Dr of Arts (hc) Univ of Helsinki; Limborough Lecturer Worshipful Co of Weavers 2005; Freeman City of London 1996, Liveryman Worshipful Co of Farriers 2000, Hon Freeman Worshipful Co of Farmers 2000, Master City of London Guild of Public Relations Practioners 2012–13 (Hon Freeman 2005, Middle Warden 2010–11), Hon Liveryman Hackney Carriage Drivers 2014; FRHistS 1995, FSA 1997; SBStJ 1998; *Publications* Confession and Absolution (jt ed, 1990), The Oil of Gladness (jt ed, 1993), The Collect in Anglican Liturgy (ed, 1994), Like a Two-Edged Sword (ed, 1995), A Manual of Ministry to the Sick (1997), Humanity and Healing (1998), Ashes to Glory (1999), A Herald Voice (2000), Risen, Ascended, Glorified (2002), Crowning the Year (2003), Churchwardens: A Survival Guide (jtly, 2003, 2 edn 2009), The Parish Survival Guide (jtly, 2004), Serving the Parish (jtly, 2006); contrib: Studies in Church History, Anglican Theological Review, Heythrop Jl, Contemporary Review, Church Times and numerous dictionaries and encyclopaedias; *Clubs* Athenaeum, Guildhall, Aldersgate Ward (pres 2015); *Style*— The Rev Dr Martin Dudley, FSA, FRHistS; ✉ SBG Parish Office, Church House, Cloth Fair, London EC1A 7JQ (☎ 020 7600 0440, e-mail martin.dudley@btinternet.com, rector@greatstbarts.com (office) or martin.dudley@cityoflondon.gov.uk (for City matters), website www.greatstbarts.com)

DUDLEY, His Hon Michael John; s of John Kenneth Dudley (d 1982), and Ruby Marguerite, *née* Curtis (d 1991); *b* 24 January 1947, Bristol; *Educ* Magdalen Coll Sch Brackley, Univ of Birmingham (LLB), Univ of Leeds (GCertEd); *m* 27 April 1968, Barbara, *née* Taranienko; 1 s (Robert Michael b 28 Dec 1968), 1 da (Kate b 16 Sept 1972); *Career* called to the Bar Lincoln's Inn 1972; practising barr Birmingham 1972–2003, recorder until 2003, circuit judge 2003–15, ret; *Recreations* music, golf, rugby, walking, photography; *Clubs* Sutton Coldfield Rugby, Sutton Coldfield Golf; *Style*— His Hon Michael Dudley

DUDLEY, William Stuart; s of William Stuart Dudley, and Dorothy Irene, *née* Stacey; *b* 4 March 1947; *Educ* Highbury GS, St Martin's Sch Art (BA), Slade Sch of Art UCL (Post Grad Dip Fine Art); *Career* theatre designer; assoc designer RNT 1981– (res stage designer 1970–81); hon pres Tower Theatre 1988, hon dir Irish Theatre Co London; fndr memb folk band Morris Minor and the Austin Seven 1980; memb Soc of Br Theatre Designers, RDI 1989; *Theatre* RNT incl: Lavender Blue, Larkrise to Candleford, Lost Worlds, The World Turned Upside Down, Undiscovered Country (SWET Award), Dispatches, Don Quixote, Schweyk in the Second World War, Cinderella, The Mysteries, The Real Inspector Hound, The Critic (Olivier Award for Best Costume Design 1993), Entertaining Strangers, Waiting for Godot, Cat on a Hot Tin Roof, The Shaughraun, The Changeling, Bartholomew Fair, The Voysey Inheritance, The Crucible, The Coup, Pygmalion, The Rise and Fall of Little Voice, On The Ledge, Johnny on a Spot, Under Milk Wood 1995, Wild Oats 1995, Mary Stuart 1996, The Homecoming 1997, All My Sons 2000 (Olivier Award for Best Set Design 2001); RSC incl: Ivanov, That Good Between Us, Richard III, A Midsummer Night's Dream, The General from America; Royal Court incl: Small Change, The Fool, Hamlet, Edmund, Kafka's Dick, Etta Jenks; other prodns incl: Hamlet (Neue Schauspielhaus Hamburg), The Ship, I Claudius, Mutiny!, Kiss me Kate, Girlfriends, Matador, Heartbreak House, My Night with Reg, A Street Car Named Desire; *Opera* WNO incl: Anna Christie, The Barber of Seville, Indomeneo; Royal Opera House incl: Don Giovanni, Tales of Hoffman, Der Rosenkavalier, The Cunning Little Vixen; other opera incl: Billy Budd (Metropolitan Opera), The Ring (Bayreuth) 1983, Un Ballo in Maschera (Salzburg Festival) 1989, Lucia di Lammermoor (Lyric Opera of Chicago), The Big Picnic (Harland and Wolff, Glasgow), Lucia di Lammermoor (Opera National de Paris); *Television* Persuasion (BBC (BAFTA Award for Production Design 1996)); *Recreations* playing the concertina and the cajun accordion; *Style*— William Dudley, Esq

DUDMAN, Graham Michael; s of Andrew Alistair Dudman, and Elaine Mary, *née* Brown; *b* 2 October 1963; *Educ* Whitehaven GS, Preston Poly; *Career* reporter: Stockport Express 1983–85, Middlesbrough Evening Gazette 1985–87, Daily Mail 1987–89 (freelance), Daily Express 1989–90; The Sun 1990–: reporter, News Editor, Head of News, Associate Editor, Asst Ed (Features); *Recreations* tennis, watching cricket; *Style*— Graham Dudman, Esq; ✉ Head of News, The Sun, 1 Virginia Street, London E1 9XP (☎ 020 7782 4000, fax 020 7782 4108)

DUERDEN, Prof Brian Ion; CBE (2008); s of late Cyril Duerden, and Mildred, *née* Ion; *b* 21 June 1948, Nelson, Lancs; *Educ* Nelson GS, Univ of Edinburgh (BSc, MB ChB, MD); *m* 5 Aug 1972, Marjorie, da of late Thomas Blakey Hudson, and late Letitia Margaret, *née* Kenyon; *Career* house offr thoracic surgery and infectious diseases City Hosp Edinburgh 1972–73, lectr and hon registrar in bacteriology Univ of Edinburgh Med Sch 1973–76; Univ of Sheffield Med Sch: lectr and hon sr registrar in med microbiology 1976–79, sr lectr and hon conslt in med microbiology 1979–83; prof and hon conslt microbiologist and infection control dr Children's Hosp Sheffield 1983–90; Univ of Wales Coll of Med/Cardiff Univ: prof of med microbiology 1991–2008, dir Cardiff Public Health Laboratory 1991–95, dir of med microbiology S Glamorgan 1991–95, emeritus prof of med microbiology 2009–; dep dir Public Health Laboratory Service Bd 1995–2002 (med dir 2000–03, actg dir 2002–03), dir of clinical quality Health Protection Agency 2003, inspr of microbiology and infection control Dept of Health 2004–10; memb Editorial Bd Jl of Med Microbiology 1977–2006 (ed-in-chief 1982–2002, chm 1987–2002); memb Editorial Ctee: Reviews Med Microbiology 1989–2002, Anaerobe 1989–2012, Jl of Hospital Infection 2011–15; chm Assoc of Profs of Med Microbiology 1994–2000 (hon sec 1989–94), chm Jt Working Pty on Infection in Renal Units 1995–2002 and 2009–10; memb: Nat Quality Assurance Advsy Panel 1986–91, Microbiology Advsy Ctee 1988–94 and 2004–09, Advsy Ctee on Dangerous Pathogens 1991–94 and 2004–10, Jt Dental Ctee MRC 1989–93, SMAC Sub-Gp on Antimicrobial Resistance 1997–98, Int Gp on Antimicrobial Resistance Clinical Prescribing and Research Sub-Gps 1999–2002, CMO UK Zoonoses Gp 1999–2009, CVO Gp on Surveillance of Diseases and Infections in Animals 1999–2009, Healthcare Assoc Infections Surveillance Steering Gp 2000–02, Specialist Advsy Ctee on Antimicrobial Resistance 2002–07, Nat Expert Panel on New and Emerging Infections 2004–10, Advsy Ctee on Antimicrobial Resistance and Healthcare Associated Infections 2007–10, UK Zoonoses Animal Diseases and Infections Gp 2009–10; RCPath: memb Cncl 1986–89 and 1990–93, examiner 1981–2005, memb Specialist Advsy Ctee on Medical Microbiology 1982–99 and 2004–10, memb Exec Ctee 1990–93, memb Examiners Sub-Ctee 1994–2004, chm microbiology examiners 1994–99, membership by published works 1999–2004; memb: Pathological Soc of GB and I 1974–2002 (memb Ctee 1981–2002), Soc for Anaerobic Microbiology 1976– (chm 1989–93), Assoc of Med Microbiologists 1983–2010 (hon sec 1984–87, memb Exec Ctee 1984–94), Soc for Gen Microbiology 2000–12, Br Infection Assoc 2010–, Anaerobe Soc of the Americas; hon life memb: Hungarian Soc for Clinical Pathology 1998, Soc for Applied Microbiology 2006, Assoc of Clinical Pathologists 2008; fell Infectious Diseases Soc of America, FRCPath 1990 (MRCPath 1978), FRCPEd 2005; *Books* Short Textbook of Medical Microbiology (5 edn, 1983), A New Short Textbook of Microbial and Parasitic Infection (1987), Topley and Wilson's Principles of Bacteriology, Virology and Immunity (contrib 7 edn, 1983–84, ed and contrib 8 edn, 1990 and 9 edn, 1998), Anaerobes in Human Disease (1991), Medical and Environmental Aspects of Anaerobes (1992), Microbial and Parasitic Infection (1993), Medical and Dental Aspects of Anaerobes (1995); *Recreations* cricket, photography, travel, music, Burnley FC, wildlife; *Style*— Prof Brian Duerden, CBE; ✉ Pendle, Welsh Street, Chepstow, Monmouthshire NP16 5LU (e-mail bduerden@doctors.org.uk)

DUFF, Andrew Nicholas; OBE (1997); s of Norman Bruce Duff (d 1997), and Diana, *née* Wilcoxson (d 2010); *b* 25 December 1950, Birkenhead; *Educ* Sherborne, St John's Coll Cambridge (MA, MLitt); *Career* res offr Hansard Soc 1974–76, res fell Joseph Rowntree Reform Tst 1989–92, dir Federal Tst for Educn and Res 1993–99; cncllr Cambridge City 1982–90, vice-pres Liberal Democrat Pty 1994–97; MEP (Lib Dem) Eastern England 1999–2014, ldr Lib Dems in European Parl 2007–09, spokesman on constitutional affrs Alliance of Liberals and Democrats for Europe 1999–2014; visiting fell European Policy Centre 2015–; *Publications* Treaty of Amsterdam (1997), Reforming the European Union (1997), Understanding the Euro (1999), The Struggle for Europe's Constitution (2005), Saving the European Union (2009), Making the Difference (2010), A Fundamental Law of the EU (2013), Pandora, Penelope, Polity: How to Change the European Union (2015), The Protocol of Frankfurt: a new treaty for the eurozone (2016); *Recreations* music; *Clubs* Nat Liberal; *Style*— Andrew Duff, Esq, OBE; ✉ e-mail andrewduff@andrewduff.eu

DUFF, Anne-Marie; *m* James McAvoy, *qv*; 1 s (Andrew b 2010); *Career* actress; *Theatre* Mill on the Floss 1994, La Grande Magia 1995, St Joan (Nat Theatre) 2007 (Best Actress Evening Standard Award 2007); *Television* The Way We Live Now 2001, Shameless 2004–05, Elizabeth – The Virgin Queen 2005, The History of Mr Polly 2007 (Best Actress BAFTA CYMRU 2008), Margot 2009; *Film* Enigma 2001, Notes on a Scandal 2006, Garage 2007, The Waiting Room 2007, Is Anybody There? 2008, French Film 2008, The Last Station 2009, Nowhere Boy 2009 (Best Actress London Evening Standard Br Film Award 2010); *Style*— Ms Anne-Marie Duff; ✉ Gordon & French, Noland House, 12–13 Poland Street, London W1F 8QB (☎ 020 7734 4818)

DUFF, Prof (Robin) Antony; s of The Rt Hon Sir Antony Duff, GCMG, CVO, DSO, DSC (d 2000), of Dorset, and Lady Duff, *née* Pauline Bevan (d2014); *b* 9 March 1945; *Educ* Sedbergh, ChCh Oxford (BA); *Career* visiting lectr Univ of Washington Seattle 1968–69, Dept of Philosophy Univ of Stirling 1970–2009, prof Univ of Minnesota Law Sch 2010–; research readership British Acad 1989–91, Leverhulme major research fellowship 2002–05; FRSE 1996, FBA 2004; *Books* Trials and Punishments (1986), Intention, Agency and Criminal Liability (1990), Criminal Attempts (1996), Punishment, Communication and Community (2001), Answering for Crime (2007), The Trial on Trial (3): Towards a Normative Theory of the Criminal Trial (jtly, 2007); *Style*— Prof R A Duff, FRSE, FBA; ✉ 9A Rutland Square, Edinburgh EH1 2AS (e-mail r.a.duff@stir.ac.uk)

DUFF, Dr Keith Leslie; s of Leslie Alexander George Duff (d 2001), of London, and Elsie Muriel Janet, *née* Evans (d 1990); *b* 16 July 1949, London; *Educ* Haberdashers' Aske's, UC Cardiff (BSc), Univ of Leicester (PhD); *m* 21 June 1975, Janet, da of Dr William Smith Russell, of Leicester; 2 da (Katy b 1977, Elizabeth b 1979); *Career* Geology and Physiography Section Nature Conservancy Cncl: joined 1975, dep head 1978–85, head Earth Sci Conservation 1985–87; asst chief scientist Nature Conservancy Cncl 1987–91, chief scientist English Nature 1991–2006, environmental conslt 2006–; Geologists' Association: memb Cncl 1976–85 and 2009–12, sec Field Meetings 1978–82, vice-pres 1982–85, hon memb 1996; Inst of Geologists: memb Cncl 1987–90, sec External Rels Ctee 1987–90; chm UK Minerals Forum 2009–12; memb: Geological Soc (memb Conservation Ctee 1977–89, memb Cncl 1994–97), Palaeontographical Soc (memb Cncl 1979–82), Environmental Advsy Bd Shanks plc 1989–2004, Euro Working Gp on Earth Science Conservation 1988– (fndr memb), Science and Innovation Strategy Bd NERC 2003–07, Br Geological Survey Univ Funding Initiative Ctee 2005–12, Cncl Scottish Assoc for Marine Sciences 2006–12 (memb Audit Ctee 2012–15), Research Policy Ctee RICS 2006–08; pres Earth Sci Teachers' Assoc 1997–99; hon res fell Dept Geology Univ of Leicester; ldr several geological study tours to Western USA for Centre for Extra-Mural Studies Univ of London and GA 1981–92, assessor Marine Sciences Ctee NERC 1988–91, external examiner for MSc in Earth Sci and the Environment Kingston Univ 1998–2002; dir Nat Stone Centre 1985–88; memb Editorial Bd Geology Today 1985–2000; judge BIGGA (Br and Int Golf Greenkeepers' Assoc) Golf Environment Competition 1997–2002, advsy memb R&A Golf Course Ctee 2004–11, course dir Raising the Standard of Sustainable Golf Course Devpt (continuing professional devpt course) European Inst of Golf Architects 2012–; recipient Foulerton Award; Hon DSc Univ of Plymouth 2007; CGeol 1990; *Books* Bivalvia of the Lower Oxford Clay of Southern England (1978), New Sites for Old (ed, 1985), Fossils of the Oxford Clay (contrib, 1991), Birds and Golf Courses (2009); author of numerous papers and articles in jnls; *Recreations* golf, travel; *Clubs* Burghley Park Golf (capt 2011), Askernish Golf (life memb); *Style—* Dr Keith Duff

DUFF, Michael John; s of Geoffrey William Hugh Duff (d 1996), and Carol Jean, *née* Ritchie; *b* 16 February 1973, Kent; *Educ* Judd GS Tonbridge, Univ of Reading (BA); *Career* dir Lou Coulson Assocs Ltd 1997–2005, co-fndr (with Melanie Rockcliffe and Conor McCaughan, *qqv*) and agent TROIKA 2005–; co-chair Personal Mangrs Assoc (PMA); *Style—* Michael Duff, Esq; ✉ TROIKA, Cosmopolitan House, 10a Christina Street, London EC2A 4PA

DUFF, Rev Timothy Cameron; s of Timothy Duff (d 1974) of Tynemouth, and Marjory Magdalene, *née* Cameron (d 2004); *b* 2 February 1940; *Educ* Royal GS Newcastle upon Tyne, Gonville & Caius Coll Cambridge (MA, LLM); *m* 23 June 1966, Patricia, da of Capt John Munby Walker DLI (d 1955), of North Shields; 2 s (John b 1968, James b 1970), 1 da (Rev Emma b 1973); *Career* admitted slr 1965, sr ptnr Hadaway & Hadaway 1988–2000; Tyne Mariners Benevolent Instn: sec and clerk to tstees 1983–2006, tstee 2006–13; dir: Tynemouth Building Society 1985–94, Universal Building Society 1994–2005; ordained 1993; hon asst priest St John the Evangelist Wallsend; grand offr United Grand Lodge of England 1998–; *Books* Old Salt (2009), More Old Salt (2012); *Recreations* sailing, sea swimming, wine, real ale; *Clubs* Northern Counties, Green Wyvern Yacht; *Style—* The Rev Timothy Duff; ✉ 24A Percy Gardens, Tynemouth, North Shields NE30 4HQ (☏ 0191 2571463, e-mail timothy@timothyduff.co.uk)

DUFFELL, Lt Gen Sir Peter Royson; KCB (1992), CBE (1988, OBE 1981), MC (1966); s of Roy John Duffell (d 1979), of Lenham, Kent, and Ruth Doris, *née* Gustaffson; *b* 19 June 1939; *Educ* Dulwich Coll; *m* 9 Oct 1982, Ann Murray, da of Col Basil Bethune Neville Woodd (d 1975), of Rolvenden, Kent; 1 da (Rachel Leonie Sylvia b 9 April 1985), 1 s (Charles Basil Royson b 20 Oct 1986); *Career* cmmnd 2 KEO Gurkha Rifles 1960, Staff Coll Camberley 1971, Brigade Maj 5 Brigade 1972–74, MA to C in C UKLF 1976–78, Cmdt 1 Bn 2 KEO Gurkha Rifles 1978–81, Col GS MOD 1981–83, Cdr Gurkha Field Force 1984–85; COS 1 (BR) Corps 1986–87, RCDS 1988, Cabinet Office 1989, Cdr Br Forces Hong Kong 1989–92, Inspr Gen of Doctrine and Trg 1992–95; Col Royal Gurkha Rifles 1994–99; chief exec Dechert LLP 1995–2006 (dir Special Projects 2006–14); tstee Foyle Fndn 2006–; govr Sandroyd Sch 1995–2009, memb Advsy Bd SOAS 2006–; pres: Alleyn Club 2006–07, Sirmoor Rifles Assoc 2006–15; Freeman City of London; FRGS 1975; *Recreations* collecting pictures, wine, country and armchair pursuits; *Clubs* Travellers, Pratt's, MCC, Pilgrims, Tripehounds; *Style—* Sir Peter Duffell; ✉ e-mail peterduffell@gmail.com

DUFFETT, Christopher Charles Biddulph; s of Capt Charles Henry Duffett, CBE, DSO, RN (d 1981), and Leonora Biddulph; *b* 23 August 1943; *Educ* Bryanston, Peterhouse Cambridge (MA), Wharton Sch Univ of Pennsylvania (MBA); *m* 1973, Jennifer Edwards; 2 s (Samuel Owen Salisbury b 1975, Daniel Charles William Biddulph b 1977); *Career* Nat Devpt Office 1965–67, S G Warburg and Co Ltd 1969–71, Inco Ltd NY 1971–74, treas Inco Europe Ltd 1974–77, gp treas Rank Organization Ltd 1977–79, gp fin dir The Economist Newspaper Ltd 1979–88, ceo The Law Debenture Corp plc 1988–, chm Assoc of Investment Tst Cos 1999–; dir City Disputes Panel Panel Ltd 2000–; FCT; *Recreations* gardening, sailing, walking; *Clubs* Royal Ocean Racing, City of London; *Style—* Christopher Duffett, Esq

DUFFIELD, Linda Joy; CMG (2002); da of late Bryan Charles Duffield, of Northwood, Middx, and Joyce Eileen, *née* Barr; *b* 18 April 1953; *Educ* St Mary's GS Northwood Hills, Univ of Exeter (BA), Ecole Nationale d'Administration Paris; *Career* grad trainee DHSS 1976; entered HM Dip Serv 1987, EU Dept FCO 1987–88, language trg 1988, first sec (commercial) Moscow 1989–92, dep head Eastern Dept FCO 1993–94, head Transcaucasus and Central Asia Dept FCO 1994–95, dep high cmmr Ottawa 1995–99, high cmmr to Sri Lanka 1999–2002 (concurrently non-resident high cmmr to the Maldives), dir wider Europe FCO 2002–04, ambass to Czech Repub 2004–09; *Recreations* skiing, skating, classical music, reading; *Style—* Miss Linda Duffield, CMG

DUFFIELD, Dame Vivien Louise; DBE (2000, CBE 1989); da of Sir Charles Clore (d 1978), and Francine, *née* Halphen (d 1993); *b* 26 March 1946; *Educ* French Lycée London, Cours Victor Hugo Paris, Heathfield Sch Ascot, LMH Oxford (MA); *m* 1969 (m dis 1976), John Duffield; 1 da (Arabella Elizabeth b 1971), 1 s (George Lincoln b 1973); *Career* chm Clore Fndn UK and Israel 1978–; NSPCC: memb Centenary Appeal Ctee 1983, memb Fin Devpt Ctee 1985, vice-chm National Appeal Bd 1998–2002; vice-chm: Wishing Well Appeal Great Ormond St Hosp 1987–90, Cancer Appeal Royal Marsden Hosp 1990–95; dir Royal Ballet 1990–97 (govr 2002–), dir Royal Opera House 1990–2002 (dep chm 1998–), dir ROH Tst 1985– (dep chm 1988–95, chm 1995–2002, chm Devpt Appeal 1996), chm ROH Endowment Fund 2005–; chm Campaign for the Univ of Oxford 2007–10; chm Eureka children's museum Halifax 1986–96; govr South Bank Bd 2002–; tstee Dulwich Picture Gallery 2002; benefactor of the year NACF; Hon DPhil Weizmann Inst 1985, Hon DLitt Univ of Buckingham 1990, hon degree Imperial Coll London 2007; FKC, Hon RCM 1987, Hon FRAM 2003; *Recreations* skiing, shooting, opera, ballet; *Style—* Dame Vivien Duffield, DBE; ✉ c/o The Clore Foundation, Unit 3, Chelsea Manor Studios, Flood Street, London SW3 5SR

DUFFIN, John Charles Henry; s of Greg Duffin, and Marilyn Duffin; *b* 2 July 1985, Leicester; *Career* chef; Fischer's Baslow Hall (1 Michelin Star), Rhodes W1 London (1 Michelin Star), Hibiscus (2 Michelin Stars), The Berkeley (2 Michelin Stars), Texture London (1 Michelin Star), Roganic London, head chef and owner John's House 2014– (1 Michelin Star 2015–); *Recreations* motorsport, shooting, racing vintage cars, fishing; *Clubs* Woodhouse Eaves Gun, Vintage Sports Car (VSCC); *Style—* John Duffin, Esq; ✉ John's House Restaurant, 139–141 Loughborough Road, Mountsorrel, Loughborough, Leicestershire LE12 7AA (☏ 01509 415569, e-mail dine@johns.house.co.uk, website www.JohnsHouseRestaurant.com)

DUFFIN, Stuart; s of Ian Duffin (d 1984), of Glasgow, and Isobel Wands; *b* 13 June 1959; *Educ* Gray's Sch of Art Aberdeen; *Career* artist; Scottish Arts Cncl Award (to study and travel in Italy) 1987, exchange artist to Moscow 1992, exchange artist to Jerusalem Printmakers Workshop 1996, artist in residence Belfast Print Workshop 2004; visiting lectr Whanganui Sch of Fine Arts NZ 2002, 2007 and 2008; Royal Scottish Acad Gillies Bequest Award 2006 (for research in Belfast), Br Cncl Award 2012 (for research in Jerusalem); RE 1995, RSA 2005 (ARSA 1996); *Solo Exhibitions* Laughter and Forgetting (Edinburgh) 1989, Nostalgia (Glasgow Print Studio) 1989, Colour of Ashes (Glasgow Print Studio) 1995, Dreaming of Jerusalem (Gallery of Jerusalem Printmakers Workshop) 1998, Sacred Science (Glasgow Print Studio) 2001, Tabula Rasa (Open Eye Gallery Edinburgh) 2007, Reason or Revelation (Glasgow Print Studio) 2013; *Group Exhibitions* incl: etching and intaglio techniques (Scottish Arts Cncl tour) 1983, Int Contemporary Art Fair LA 1988, Ka De We (exhbn of Scottish printmaking, Berlin) 1988, Royal Festival Hall London 1990, Int Miniature Prints (NY and tour of USA) 1991, Scottish Contemporary Printmaking (Moscow) 1991, Int Exhbn of Graphic Art (Kharkov Museum Ukraine) 1993, Nat Print Open (Mall Galleries London) 1995, Out of Darkness (Glasgow Print Studio) 2004; *Recreations* reading, music; *Style—* Stuart Duffin, Esq; ✉ Jackdaw Cottage, 20 Kinnear Square, Laurencekirk, AB30 1UL (e-mail info@stuartduffin.com, website www.stuartduffin.com)

DUFFY, Dame Carol Ann; DBE (2015, CBE 2002, OBE 1995); da of Francis Duffy, and Mary, *née* Black; *b* 23 December 1955; *Educ* St Joseph's Convent Stafford, Stafford Girls' HS, Univ of Liverpool (BA); *Career* freelance writer and poet; Poet Laureate 2009–; FRSL; *Awards* Eric Gregory Award 1984, C Day Lewis fellowship 1982–84, Somerset Maugham Award 1988, Dylan Thomas Award 1990, Scottish Arts Cncl Book Award of Merit 1985 and 1990, Whitbread Award for Poetry 1993, T S Eliot Prize, Costa Poetry Prize 2012, Pen Pinter Prize 2012; *Books* Standing Female Nude (1985), Selling Manhattan (1987, 4 edn 1994), The Other Country (1990), Mean Time (1993), Selected Poems (1994), Anvil New Poets (ed, 1994), The World's Wife (2000), Feminine Gospels (2002), Rapture (2005), Love Poems (2009), The Bees (2011); *Style—* Dame Carol Ann Duffy, DBE; ✉ c/o Picador Books, Pan Macmillan Publishers, 20 New Wharf Road, London N1 9RR

DUFFY, Dr Francis Cuthbert (Frank); CBE (1997); s of John Austin Duffy (d 1944), and Annie Margaret, *née* Reed (d 2000); *b* 3 September 1940, Berwick upon Tweed, Northumberland; *Educ* St Cuthbert's GS Newcastle upon Tyne, Architectural Assoc Sch London (Leverhulme scholar, AADipl), Univ of Calif (MArch), Princeton Univ (MA, PhD); *m* 4 Sept 1965, Jessica Mary, da of Philip Bear, of Chiddingstone, Kent; 3 da (Sibylla b 1966, Eleanor b 1969, Katya b 1970); *Career* asst architect Nat Bldg Agency 1964–67, ed AA Jl 1965–67, Cwlth Fund Harkness fell USA 1967–70, estab and head of London Office JFN Associates 1971–73, fndr ptnr DEGW plc architects 1973–2011; fndr and chm Bldg Use Studies 1980–88, fndr and chief ed Facilities (newsletter) 1984–90, conslt on the working environment to many cos and instns; chair: Design Review Panel Stratford City 2006–13, Architecture Design and Workplace Advsy Cncl BBC 2006–09; visiting prof: MIT 2001–04, UCL 2005–, Univ of Reading 2007–, Univ of Lancs 2009–; memb Advsy Cncl Dept of Architecture Princeton Univ 2008–; pres: Architects' Cncl of Europe 1994, RIBA 1993–95 (memb Cncl 1989–99); vice-pres Architectural Assoc 2013–; tstee Architecture Fndn 2000–09; memb Architects Registration Bd (ARB) 1997–2003; Br Cncl of Offices (BCO) Pres's Award 2004, Br Inst of Facilities Mgmnt (BIFM) Lifetime Achievement Award 2013; *Books* Planning Office Space (jtly, 1976), The Orbit Study (princ author, 1984), Orbit 2 (jtly, 1985), The Changing City (jtly, 1989), The Changing Workplace (1992), The Responsible Workplace (jtly, 1993), The New Office (1997), New Environments for Working (jtly, 1998), Architectural Knowledge (jtly, 1998), Work and the City (2008); *Recreations* reading, walking; *Clubs* Architectural Association, Reform; *Style—* Dr Francis Duffy, CBE; ✉ Threeways, The Street, Walberswick, Suffolk IP18 6UE (☏ 01502 723814, e-mail frank@duffydesign.com)

DUFFY, James Bernard; s of Bernard Duffy, and Teresa Duffy; *b* 10 September 1955; *Educ* St Mary's Coll Middlesbrough, Univ of Newcastle Sch of Architecture (BA, BArch); *m* 1, 27 May 1985, Fiona (d 1996); 1 da (Sarah Catherine b 26 Oct 1986); m 2, 29 June 2002, Susie; *Career* architect; assoc dir Fitch & Co London 1984–86, assoc dir McColl London 1986–88, princ James Duffy Associates 1988–95 (sold practice to BDG McColl London 1995), dir of architecture BDG McColl London 1995–2000, architect dir Building Design Partnership (BDP) 2000–; sr competitions assessor RIBA 1994, memb Br Cncl of Shopping Centres (BCSC) 1995–; author of conference papers and occasional magazine articles; regular conference speaker incl 66 airport conferences worldwide; Bunz Travelling Studentship 1980, Urban Infill Award Irish Planning Inst 1992, Civic Tst Award 1995; memb Parish Cncl St Theodore's RC Church; ARB 1982, RIBA 1982; *Recreations* gym, singing and guitar, running, walking, skiing; *Clubs* Cannons (Surbiton), Stragglers, Ramblers, Ski Club of GB, Nat Tst; *Style—* James Duffy, Esq

DUFFY, Most Rev Joseph Augustine; *see:* Clogher, Bishop of (RC)

DUFFY, Maureen; da of late Hugh Andrew Duffy, and Mary, *née* McAtamney; *b* 4 May 1959; *Educ* Kingston Univ (BA, MBA), Univ of London (Dip Mgmnt); *Career* J Walter Thompson Co Ltd: grad to sr media exec 1982–87, assoc media dir 1987–89, gp media dir 1989–95, world ptnr 1996–98, strategic communication dir 1996–98; controller of mktg BBC TV 1998–2000, controller of daytime ITV 2000–02, ceo Newspaper Marketing Agency 2003–11, ceo TNS UK Ltd 2012–; *Recreations* keeping fit, squash, film, theatre, reading, antiques, travel; *Style—* Ms Maureen Duffy

DUFFY, Maureen Patricia; da of Grace Wright; *b* 1933; *Educ* Trowbridge HS, Sarah Bonnell HS for Girls, KCL (BA); *Career* author, playwright and poet; co fndr Writers' Action Gp; chm: Authors Licensing and Collecting Soc 1980–95, Copyright Licensing Agency 1996–99; pres Writers' Guild of GB 1986–89 (jt chm 1977–88), hon pres Br Copyright Cncl 2003– (chm 1989–98, vice-pres 1998–2003); hon pres Authors Licensing and Collecting Soc 2002–, pres European Writers Congress 2003–05 (vice-pres 1991–2003); Int Confedn of Socs of Authors and Composers (CISAC) Gold Medal for Literature 2002, Benson Medal for Literature RSL 2004, Portuguese Soc of Authors Medal of Honour 2009; Hon DLitt Univ of Loughborough 2011, Hon DLitt Univ of Kent 2013; FKC 2002, FRSL, FEA 2015; *Books* incl: Illuminations (1991), Occam's Razor (1993), Henry Purcell (1994), Restitution (1998), England: the making of the myth (2001), Alchemy (2004), Family Values (2008), The Orpheus Trail (2009), Environmental Studies (poems, 2013), In Times Like These (novel, 2013); *Recreations* gardening, music; *Style—* Ms Maureen Duffy; ✉ 18 Fabian Road, London SW6 7TZ (e-mail 113714.1610@compuserve.com)

DUFFY, Patrick G; s of Dr J B Duffy, and Mrs E C Duffy; *b* 8 January 1949; *Educ* MB, BCh, BAO; *m* 13 July 1987, Dr Zara Anne, *née* McClenahan; 2 s (Frederick b 16 July 1989, Peter b 12 July 1991), 2 da (Emmylene b 28 Oct 1993, Sarah-Jane b 24 Aug 1995); *Career* conslt paediatric urologist London, hon sr lectr in paediatric urology Inst of Child Health Gt Ormond St Hosp for Children London; memb: European Soc of Paediatric Urology (ESPU), Br Assoc of Urological Surgeons (BAUS); FRCS; *Recreations* sailing, squash, music; *Style—* Patrick Duffy, Esq; ✉ Old Willow Farm, Wickhambreaux, Canterbury, Kent CT3 1RQ (☏ 01227 728390)

DUFFY, Peter; *Educ* MBA; *Career* former mktg services dir Barclays, mktg dir Audi UK until 2011, gp commercial dir customer, product and mktg easyJet (joined as mktg dir

D

2011); *Style—* Peter Duffy, Esq; ✉ easyJet Airline Company Ltd, Hangar 89, London Luton Airport, Luton LU2 9PF

DUFFY, Philip Edmund; s of Walter Duffy (d 1991), and Ellen Dalton (d 1995); *b* 21 January 1943; *Educ* St Edward's Coll W Derby, Royal Manchester Coll of Music (GRSM, ARMCM), Univ of London; *Career* master of the music Liverpool Metropolitan Cathedral 1966–96; Liverpool Hope Univ: princ lectr 2000–06, dir of performance 2006–12; assoc dir Schola Gregoriana of Cambridge 2008–, dir Liverpool Bach Collective 2013–; hon fell Guild of Church Musicians 1994, FRSCM 2009; ISM 1966; KSG 1981; *Recreations* reading, theatre, walking; *Style—* Philip Duffy, Esq; ✉ 2 South Court, Wexford Road, Oxton CH43 9TD (e-mail pipduf@me.com)

DUFFY, Terence John; s of John Edward Duffy (d 1989), of Birkenhead, Cheshire, and Theresa, *née* Williamson (d 1961); *b* 24 August 1947; *Educ* St Anselm's Coll Cheshire, Jesus Coll Cambridge (BA, MA), New Coll Oxford (BM BCh); *m* 6 Aug 1971, Rowena Siriol, da of Henry Vaughan-Roberts, BM, of Conwy, N Wales; 1 s (Elliot Edward Vaughan b 1977), 1 da (Alexandra Margaret Theresa (Sasha) b 1983); *Career* house appts Bedford and Oxford 1972–73, demonstrator in anatomy Univ of Cambridge 1973–74 (supervisor Jesus Coll 1973–74), SHO and registrar Bedford and Cambridge Hosp 1974–78, registrar Swansea 1978–79, Wellcome res fell Cambridge 1979–80, lectr in surgery Univ of Cambridge and fell Jesus Coll 1980–84, sr lectr in surgery Keele Univ 1984–89, conslt in gen and breast surgery N Staffs Hosp 1984–; author of numerous pubns on gen and transplant surgery 1978–; memb: W Midlands Surgical Soc, BMA 1969, BTS 1980, BASO 1990; FRCS 1977, FRSM 1989; *Recreations* music, sport; *Style—* Terence Duffy, Esq; ✉ University Hospital North Staffordshire, City General Hospital, Newcastle Road, Stoke-on-Trent, Staffordshire ST4 6QG (☎ 01782 552741, fax 01782 680199, e-mail tjduffy@merrytree.net)

DUFTON, Robert; s of Maj Felix Dufton, RE, and Rosemary, *née* Orpin; *b* 20 March 1962; *Educ* Sevenoaks Sch, Univ of Bristol (LLB), Coll of Law, Ashridge Mgmnt Coll (Dip Gen Mgmnt); *Career* slr Lovells 1984–90, conslt AEA 1991, prog dir and co sec Arts and Business 1992–94, dep dir of ops Heritage Lottery Fund 1995–2002, dir Rayne Fndn 2002–04, dir Paul Hamlyn Fndn 2004–13, dir of campaigns Univ of Sheffield 2014–; patron Nat Funding Scheme DONATE; sr fell Cass Business Sch 2013–; memb Ct Univ of Bristol, memb Arts & Humanities Research Cncl; Hon LLD Univ of Bristol 2014; memb Law Soc 1986; *Style—* Robert Dufton; ✉ 55 Thomas More House, Barbican, London EC2Y 8BT (☎ 07986 544410)

DUGDALE, Hon David John; DL (N Yorks 1998); s of 1 Baron Crathorne, PC, TD (d 1977), and Nancy, OBE (d 1969), da of Sir Charles Tennant, 1 Bt; *b* 4 May 1942; *Educ* Eton, Trinity Coll Cambridge; *m* 1972, Susan Louise, da of Maj L A Powell (d 1972); 1 da (Clare Nancy Louise b 1978), 1 s (Jonathan William Sean b 1980); *Career* farmer and engr; dir: United Oilseeds Marketing Ltd 1996–2012, Dairy Crest Gp plc 2002–07; High Sheriff for Co of Cleveland 1995; CEng, MIMechE; *Recreations* building, photography, shooting; *Style—* The Hon David Dugdale, DL; ✉ Park House, Crathorne, Yarm, North Yorkshire TS15 0BD (☎ 01642 700225, work 01642 700295)

DUGDALE, Kezia; MSP; *Career* MSP (Lab) Lothians 2011–; *Style—* Ms Kezia Dugdale, MSP; ✉ The Scottish Parliament, Edinburgh EH99 1SP (website www.keziadugdale.com)

DUGDALE, His Hon Judge Paul Damian Norwood; *Educ* Canford Sch Wimborne, KCL (LLB); *Career* called to the Bar 1990; 2 King's Bench Walk 1991–2011, recorder 2005, circuit judge (South Eastern Circuit) 2011–; memb: Western Circuit 1991–, Criminal Bar Assoc; *Style—* His Hon Judge Dugdale; ✉ Reading Crown Court, The Old Shire Hall, The Forbury, Reading RG1 3EH

DUGGAN, His Hon Judge (James) Ross; s of Leonard Heaton Duggan (d 2006), and Dr Mona Leslie Duggan (d 2014); *b* 14 July 1956, Ormskirk, Lancs; *Educ* Merchant Taylors' Sch Crosby, Univ of Liverpool; *m* 1983, Fiona Elsbeth Robb Duggan, JP, *née* Fowlie; *Career* barr Liverpool 1978–2006, circuit judge: Midland Circuit 2006–14, Northern Circuit Family Court 2014–; designated family judge (Staffs) 2007–14, dep High Court judge 2007–; tstee Lancs Wildlife Tst 2015–; *Recreations* cricket, travel, theatre, music; *Clubs* Lancs CCC; *Style—* His Hon Judge Duggan; ✉ Sessions House, Lancaster Road, Preston PR1 2PD

DUGHER, Michael Vincent; MP; s of Robert Dugher, of Doncaster, and Isobel, *née* Archer; *b* Doncaster, S Yorks; *Educ* Mcauley RC Sch Doncaster, Univ of Nottingham (BA, Univ Prize); *m* 6 Nov 2004, Joanna, *née* Nunney; 2 da (Isabella b 20 Sept 2005, Mia b 15 May 2007), 1 s (Sean b 11 July 2012); *Career* convenor Notts and Derbys NUS 1995–96, nat chair Lab Students Lab Pty 1997–98; AEEU (now UNITE): research offr 1998–2000, head of policy 2000–01, special advsr to Min for Tport 2001–02, special advsr to Sec of State for Defence 2002–05, special advsr to Ldr of the House of Commons 2005–06, UK dir of govt rels EDS 2006–07, special advsr to Govt Chief Whip 2007–08, chief political spokesman to PM 2008–10, MP (Lab) Barnsley E 2010–, shadow min for defence 2010–11, PPS to Rt Hon Ed Miliband (as Ldr of the Oppn) 2011, shadow min without portfolio (Cabinet Office) 2011–13, shadow min for the Cabinet Office 2013–14, shadow sec of state for transport 2014–15, shadow sec of state for culture, media and sport 2015–; vice-chair Lab Pty 2012–14; memb: MSF 1997, AEEU 1998, UNITE, UNISON 2009, Public Administration 2010–12; *Publications* Fools Gold: Dispelling the Myth of the Tory Economic Legacy (with John Spellar, 1999), Dictionary of Labour Biography (contrib, 2001); *Recreations* football (watching), music (playing and listening); *Style—* Michael Dugher, Esq, MP; ✉ West Bank House, West Street, Hoyland, Barnsley S74 9EE (☎ 01226 743483); House of Commons, London SW1A 0AA (e-mail michael.dugher.mp@parliament.uk)

DUKE, Prof Christopher (Chris); s of Frederick Alexander Duke, of London, and Edith, *née* Page; *b* 4 October 1938; *Educ* Eltham Coll, Jesus Coll Cambridge (BA, CertEd, MA), KCL (PhD); *m* 1, (m dis 1981), Audrey Ann, *née* Solomon; 1 s (Stephen b 1968), 2 da (Annie b 1970, Cathy b 1972); m 2, Jan 1982, Elizabeth Ann, da of E Lloyd Sommerlad, of Sydney, Aust; 2 s (Alex b 1978, Paul b 1981 d 2007); *Career* lectr: Woolwich Poly 1961–66, Univ of Leeds 1966–69; fndn dir of continuing educn ANU 1969–85, fndn prof, chm of continuing educn and dir of open studies Univ of Warwick 1985–96 (pro-vice-chllr 1991–95), dep vice-chllr Univ of Western City and pres Univ of Western Sydney Nepean 1996–2000, prof and chm of continuing educn Univ of Auckland 2001–02, prof of regnl partnerships and learning RMIT Univ Melbourne 2002–08 (dir of community and regnl partnerships 2002–04); dir of HE NIACE 2002–05, assoc dir of adult learning Action on Access 2003–05, ceo Pascal Int Observatory 2003–08, dir Pascal PURE Project 2009–12, chair Pascal Advsy Cncl 2013–; ed Int Jl of Univ Adult Educn 1971–96; vice-chm Univs Assoc for Continuing Educn 1994–96 (sec 1989–94), various other int and local continuing educn positions; hon prof of lifelong learning: Stirling Univ, Univ of Scotland, Univ of Leicester, Univ of Glasgow 2009–; visiting prof of lifelong learning RMIT Univ 2009–; Hon DLitt Keimyung Univ Korea; FACE, FRSA; *Books* incl: The Learning University (1992), The Adult University (1999), Managing the Learning University (2002), A New Imperative: Regions and Higher Education in Difficult Times (2013); *Recreations* gardening, bird-watching, reading, conversation, learning French, France; *Style—* Prof Chris Duke; ☎ 01926 420864 or 0033 3 8532 5064, mobile 07788 564057, e-mail chris.duke@rmit.edu.au

DUKE, Timothy Hugh Stewart; s of William Falcon Duke (d 1954), of Sway, Hants, and Mary Cecile, *née* Jackson (d 2003); *b* 12 June 1953; *Educ* Uppingham, Fitzwilliam Coll Cambridge (MA); *Career* Peat Marwick Mitchell & Co 1974–81; College of Arms: research asst 1981–89, Rouge Dragon Pursuivant of Arms 1989–95, Chester Herald of Arms 1995–2014, Norroy and Ulster King of Arms 2014–; Registrar Coll of Arms 2001–07; hon sec Harleian Soc 1994–, hon genealogist Order of St Michael and St George 2010–; Liveryman Worshipful Co of Broderers 1987; *Clubs* Travellers; *Style—* Timothy Duke, Esq, Norroy and Ulster King of Arms; ✉ College of Arms, Queen Victoria Street, London EC4V 4BT (☎ 020 7236 7728, e-mail norroy&ulster@college-of-arms.gov.uk)

DULVERTON, 3 Baron (UK 1929); Sir (Gilbert) Michael Hamilton Wills; 4 Bt (UK) 1897; s of 2 Baron Dulverton, CBE, TD, DL (d 1992), and his 1 w Judith Betty, *née* Leslie Melville (d 1983); *b* 2 May 1944; *Educ* Gordonstoun; *m* 1, 1980 (m dis 1999), Rosalind van der Velde; 1 da (Hon Charlotte Alexandra Hamilton b 1981), 1 s (Hon Robert Anthony Hamilton b 20 Oct 1983); m 2, 2000, Mrs Mary Vicary; *Heir* s, Hon Robert Wills; *Career* farmer, forester and industrialist; chm Thwaites Ltd 1995–; dir: West Highland Woodlands Ltd, Batsford Estate Co (1983) Ltd; tstee Dulverton Tst; *Style—* The Rt Hon the Lord Dulverton

DUMA, Alexander Agim; s of Dervish Duma (d 1998), and Naftali, *née* Andoni (d 1966); *b* 30 March 1946; *Educ* St John's Sch Leatherhead, UCL (LLB); *m* 1980 (m dis 1983), Mary Gertrude, da of Surgn-Col E W Hayward; *Career* called to the Bar Gray's Inn 1969; Parly candidate (Cons) 1979, GLC candidate (Cons) Bermondsey 1977; Barton Mayhew & Co 1968–72, Philips Industries 1973–75, Barclays Merchant Bank 1975–87; dir: Blackfriars Settlement 1977–84 and 1986–89, Barclays de Zoete Wedd Ltd 1983–87, Chase Investment Bank Ltd 1987–89, Equity & General plc 1987–90, Torday & Carlisle plc 1988–92, The London & Northumberland Estates Co Ltd 1988–, Smith New Court Corporate Finance Ltd 1989–92 (conslt 1992–94), The New Plastics Co Ltd 1990–94, Lady Clare Ltd 1994–99, Headgear Investments Ltd 1997–, Richmond Theatre Prodns Ltd 2006–14, Willerby Estates Ltd 2016–; chm: Pickett Ltd 1988–, Poundfloat Ltd 1992–95, EC-1 Ltd 1999–2001, The Plain English Gp Ltd 2000–03, Opera Players Ltd 2000–03 (dir 1995), Room Service Gp plc 2001–03, Sky Capital Holdings plc 2002–03 and 2005–07, Sky Capital Enterprises plc 2005–07; conslt Granville & Co Ltd 1992–94, UK rep Deloitte & Touche Albania 1993–95; memb Cncl Newcomen Collett Fndn 1977–94, tstee Devas Club 1996–2000, tstee Denys Holland Scholarship 1996–, memb Finance Ctee Terrence Higgins Tst 1997–2003, chm of tstees Terrence Higgins Pension Fund 2002–08, pres Crabtree Fndn 2004, govr St John's Sch Leatherhead 2015–; pres Bermondsey Cons Assoc 1979–83; hon consul and chargé d'affaires Republic of Albania 1992–94; chm: The Centre for Albanian Studies 1998–, Br-Albanian Cncl 1998–2008, Anglo-Albanian Assoc 2005–12 (memb Cncl 1966–2005); pres Friends of UCL 2001–07; Crabtree Orator 2017; Order of the Honour of the Nation (Albania) 2014; fell UCL 2005; FCA; *Recreations* reading; *Clubs* Brooks's; *Style—* Alexander Duma, Esq; ✉ 39 Donne Place, London SW3 2NH (☎ 020 7823 7422); Le Grès, 82110 Lauzerte, France (☎ 00 33 563 95 70 23); e-mail alexander.duma@le-gres.com

DUMFRIES, Johnny; *see:* Bute, 7 Marquess of

DUMVILLE, Prof David Norman; s of Norman Dumville (d 1958), and Eileen Florence Lillie, *née* Gibbs (d 1996); *b* 5 May 1949; *Educ* St Nicholas GS Northwood, Emmanuel Coll Cambridge (open entrance exhibitioner, sr scholar, MA), Univ of Edinburgh (PhD, Jeremiah Dalziel Prize); *m* 23 Nov 1974, Sally Lois, *née* Hannay (d 1989); 1 s (Elliott Thomas b 19 July 1978); partner, Dr Clare Downham; 1 da (Jennifer Elisabeth Brighid b 1 Feb 2006); *Career* Univ of Wales fell Dept of Welsh UC Swansea 1976–77, asst prof Dept of English Univ of Pennsylvania 1977–78; Univ of Cambridge: univ lectr Dept of Anglo-Saxon, Norse and Celtic 1978–91, reader in early mediaeval history and culture of the British Isles 1991–95, prof of palaeography and cultural history 1995–2004; Girton Coll Cambridge: fell 1978–2004 (life fell 2005–), dir of studies in Anglo-Saxon, Norse and Celtic 1978–2004, coll lectr 1978–99, (moral) tutor 1980–82, memb Cncl 1981–82, memb various Coll ctees; external dir of studies in Anglo-Saxon, Norse and Celtic: Emmanuel Coll and St Catharine's Coll Cambridge 1978–85, Fitzwilliam Coll Cambridge 1991–2003; sixth-century prof in history, palaeography and Celtic Univ of Aberdeen 2005–; visiting prof and Pepys lectr Center for Medieval and Renaissance Studies UCLA 1995, visiting prof Sch of Celtic Studies Dublin Inst for Advanced Studies 1996–97, distinguished visiting prof of mediaeval studies Univ of Calif Berkeley 1997, visiting fell Huntington Library San Marino CA 1984, hon prof of Irish studies Univ of Liverpool 2009–12; vice-pres Centre Int de Recherche et de Documentation sur le Monachisme Celtique (Daoulas) 1986–; Br Acad research reader in the humanities 1985–87, research assoc Sch of Celtic Studies Dublin Inst for Advanced Studies 1989–2010; managing ed: Mediaeval Scandinavia and Jl of Celtic Studies 2002–, Anglo-Saxon Studies in Archaeology and History 2007–; memb Editorial Advsy Bd: Anglo-Saxon Studies in Archaeology and History 1978–85, Toronto Medieval Texts and Translations 1978–, Cambridge Medieval Celtic Studies 1980–93, Cambrian Medieval Celtic Studies 1993–, Innes Review 1997–; author of numerous reviews and articles in learned jls; memb jt Br Acad and Royal Historical Soc Ctee on Anglo-Saxon Charters 1986–90 and 1993–2003; O'Donnell lectr in Celtic Studies: Univ of Oxford 1977/78, Univ of Edinburgh 1980/81, Univ of Wales 1982/83; Proinsias Mac Cana meml lectures (series of 40 on Gaelic Literature from Late Antiquity to Early Modernity) Royal Irish Acad and Dublin Inst for Advanced Studies 2013, T J Brown meml lectures in palaeography (series of 12 on Insular Script in Context: a 1500-year History) KCL and Univ of London 2013; hon memb Royal Irish Acad 2009; FRHistS 1976, FSA 1983, FRSAIre 1989, FSA Scot 1999; *Books* Chronicles and Annals of Mediaeval Ireland and Wales: The Clonmacnoise-group Texts (with K Grabowski, 1984), The Historia Brittonum: The 'Vatican' Recension (1985), Britain's Literary Heritage: The Early and Central Middle Ages c650-c1200 AD (1986), Histories and Pseudo-histories of the Insular Middle Ages (1990), Wessex and England from Alfred to Edgar: Six Essays on Political, Cultural, and Ecclesiastical Revival (1992), Liturgy and the Ecclesiastical History of Late Anglo-Saxon England: Four Studies (1992), English Caroline Script and Monastic History: Studies in Benedictinism AD 950–1030 (1993), Saint Patrick AD 493–1993 (jtly, 1993), Britons and Anglo-Saxons in the Early Middle Ages (1993), The Churches of North Britain in the First Viking-Age (1997), Three Men in a Boat: Scribe, Language, and Culture in the Church of Viking-Age Europe (1997), Councils and Synods of the Gaelic Early and Central Middle Ages (1997), A Palaeographer's Review: The Insular System of Scripts in the Early Middle Ages (2 vols, 1999–2007), Saint David of Wales (2001), Annales Cambriae (2002–), The Annals of Ulster (2002–), Cáin Adomnáin and Canones Adomnani (with P P Ó Néill, 2003), Abbreviations used in Insular Script (2004), The Early Mediaeval Insular Churches and the Preservation of Roman Literature (2004), Brenhinoedd y Saeson, 'The Kings of the English' (2005–), The Mediaeval Foundations of England? (2006), Anglo-Saxon Essays 2001–07 (2007), Celtic Essays 2001–07 (2 vols, 2007), Vikings in Britain and Ireland: A Question of Sources (2014); *Recreations* travel in North America, politics and other arguments; *Style—* Professor David Dumville; ✉ Department of History, University of Aberdeen, Old Aberdeen AB24 3FX (☎ 01224 272455)

DUNANT, Sarah; da of David Dunant, and Estelle, *née* Joseph; *Educ* Godolphin & Latymer Sch, Newnham Coll Cambridge (BA); *m*; 2 da (Zoe b 12 March 1987, Georgia b 30 Dec 1990); *Career* prodr BBC Radio 3 and 4 1974–76; freelance journalist, writer and broadcaster 1976–; presenter The Late Show (BBC2), co-writer Thin Air (BBC1), presenter Nightwaves (BBC Radio 3); also appeared on other Radio 4 and Radio 3 progs, BBC World Service and Capital Radio; critic and writer: The Guardian, The Times and The Observer; *Books* Exterminating Angels (jtly, 1983), Intensive Care (jtly, 1986), Snow Storms In A Hot Climate (1988), Birth Marks (1991), Fatlands (1993), War of the Words (ed, 1994), Under My Skin (1995), The Age of Anxiety (ed, 1996), Transgressions (1997), Mapping The Edge (1999), Birth of Venus (2003), In the Company of the Courtesan (2006); *Recreations* travel; *Style*— Ms Sarah Dunant; ✉ c/o Aitken & Stone Ltd, 18–21 Cavaye Place, London SW10 9PT (☎ 020 7373 6002)

DUNBAR; *see also:* Hope-Dunbar

DUNBAR, Sir James Michael; 14 Bt (NS 1694), of Mochrum, Wigtownshire; er s of Sir Jean Ivor Dunbar, 13 Bt (d 1993), and his 1 w, Rose Jeanne, *née* Hertsch; *b* 17 January 1950; *m* 1, 1978 (m dis 1989), Margaret Marie, da of Albert Jacobs; 2 s (Michael Joseph b 5 July 1980, David Scott b 22 May 1983), 1 da (Stacy Beth b 29 July 1985); m 2, 1989, Margaret Elizabeth, da of Gordon Talbot; 1 da (Cassandra Talbot b 23 July 1991); *Heir* s, Michael Dunbar; *Career* Col USAF, ret; *Style*— Sir James Dunbar, Bt; ✉ fax 00 1 704 321 5966, e-mail dunbar1989@hotmail.com

DUNBAR, Prof Lennox Robert; *b* 17 May 1952; *Career* Peacock Printmakers Aberdeen: etching technician 1978–81, educn offr 1981–86; Grays Sch of Art Aberdeen: lectr in painting and printmaking 1986–87, head of printmaking 1987–97, acting head of fine art 1997–; visiting artist/tutor Louisiana State Univ and Univ of Kansas 1986; visiting lectr: Duncan of Jordanstone Coll of Art Dundee 1987, Coll of Santa Fe New Mexico 1999–, Acad of Fine Art Prague; prof Robert Gordon Univ 2008; RSA 2006 (ARSA 1990); *Exhibitions* Scottish Print Open 2 (tour Scotland and Australia) 1980, Peacock Printmakers (Finland) 1980, RSA Award Winners 1945–79 (Artspace Gallery Aberdeen) 1980, Five Artists from Aberdeen (Third Eye Centre Glasgow) 1982, Printmakers Drawings (Printmakers Workshop Edinburgh) 1982, New Scottish Prints (City Gallery NY then tour of USA and Canada 1983–84) 1983, Printmaking in Scotland (Festival Exhibition) 1983, RSA Galleries (Edinburgh) 1983, Etching (Scottish Arts Cncl touring exhbn) 1983, Scottish Print Open 3 (tour of Scotland) 1983, Four North East Artists (Fruitmarket Gallery Edinburgh & Aberdeen Art Gallery) 1983, Eight Br Print Biennale (Bradford) 1984, Lennox Dunbar and Ian Howard (Glasgow Arts Centre) 1984, Contemporary Scottish Drawings (Fine Art Soc) 1984, Double Elephant – Br Prints (Barbican Arts Centre) 1985, Peacock Printmakers (Talbot Rice Gallery Edinburgh and Aberdeen Art Gallery) 1986, Scottish Print Open 4 (tour of Scotland) 1987, Humberside Print Open 1987, Art of the Print – A Century of Scottish Printmaking (Fine Art Soc) 1987, Premio Biella Per L'Inlusione (Italy) 1987, Printmakers Drawings (Mercury Gallery Edinburgh) 1987, Six North East Artists (369 Gallery Edinburgh, Pier Arts Centre Orkney and Artspace Gallery Aberdeen) 1988, Scottish Art (Collegium Artisticum Sarajevo) 1988, Cleveland Drawing Biennale (Middlesbrough) 1989, Humberside Print Open (tour of USSR) 1989, Intergrafik 90 (Berlin) 1990, Fruitmarket Open (Fruitmarket Gallery Edinburgh) 1990, Guthrie Award Winners (RSA, Fine Art Soc) 1990, RGI (Mall Galleries London) 1990, Inverclyde Biennial 1990, Paperworks IV (Seagate Gallery Dundee) 1993, Five Printmakers (RSA) 1995, New Work on Paper (Hatton Gallery Newcastle upon Tyne and Peacock Printmakers Aberdeen) 1995, Cheltenham Drawing Open 1996, Peacock 21 (Aberdeen Art Gallery) 1996, Int Print Triennal (Cracow) 1997, The Large Edition (Quicksilver Gallery London and Malvern Gallery) 1997, Contemporary Scottish Painters & Printmakers (Beatrice Royal Contemporary Art Gallery Hants) 1997, 36 Units (Compass Gallery Glasgow) 1999, Peacock Printmakers Aberdeen 1999, Bonhoga Gallery Shetland 1999, Trondheim Biennale (Norway and Touring USA) 1999; *Awards* RSA Meyer Oppenheim Award for Painting 1976, RSA Latimer Award for Painting 1978, Scottish Arts Cncl Bursary 1981, Scottish Arts Cncl Travel Award (to NY) 1983, RSA Guthrie Award for Painting 1984, winner Paisley Art Inst Drawing Competition 1987 (2nd prize 1985), maj prizewinner Cleveland Drawing Biennale 1989, Shell Expro Premier Award 1991, 1993 and 2006, RSA Highland Soc of London Award 1992, SSA Whyte and Mackay Award 1995, RSA Gillies Award 1999, prizewinner Int Print Biennale Varna 2001; *Style*— Prof Lennox Dunbar

DUNBAR, Prof Robin Ian MacDonald; s of George MacDonald Dunbar (d 1998), and Betty Lilian, *née* Toon (d 1998); *b* 28 June 1947; *Educ* Magdalen Coll Sch Brackley, Magdalen Coll Oxford (BA), Univ of Bristol (PhD); *m* 1971, Eva Patricia, *née* Melvin; 2 s (Jared Ian MacDonald b 1975, Arran Joseph William b 1982), 1 da (Zaila Yvette b 1979); *Career* SERC research fell King's Coll and Dept of Zoology Univ of Cambridge 1977–82, lectr Zoological Inst Univ of Stockholm 1983, research fell Zoology Dept Univ of Liverpool 1985–87, successively lectr, reader and prof Anthropology Dept UCL 1987–94, prof of psychology Psychology Dept Univ of Liverpool, prof of evolutionary psychology Sch of Biological Sciences Univ of Liverpool 1997–2007; Univ of Oxford: fell Magdelen Coll 2007–, prof of evolutionary anthropology 2007–12, prof of evolutionary psychology 2012–; memb Home Office Animal Procedures Ctee 1997–2004, memb Scientific Advsy Ctee Fondacion J-M Delwast 2000–04; Hon DSc Aalto Univ Finland; govr Magdalen Coll Sch Brackley 2009–; memb: Assoc for Study of Animal Behaviour, Primate Soc of GB, International Behavioural Ecology Soc, American Psychological Assoc, Br Ecological Soc, Br Assoc for Advancement of Sci, American Assoc for the Advancement of Science, Save British Science, Galton Inst, Human Behaviour and Evolution Soc; FRAI 1989 (Huxley Medal 2015), FBA 1998, fell Assoc for Psychological Science 2010; *Books* Social Dynamics of Gelada Baboons (jtly, 1975), Current Problems in Sociobiology (jt ed, 1982), Reproductive Decisions: An Economic Analysis of Gelada Baboon Social Strategies (1984), The World of Nature (1986), Primate Social Systems (1988), The Trouble with Science (1995), Human Reproductive Decisions: Biological and Social Perspectives (ed, 1995), Grooming, Gossip and the Evolution of Language (1996), Evolution of Culture and Language in Primates and Humans (jt ed, 1996), The Evolution of Culture (jt ed, 1999), Primate Conservation Biology (jtly, 2000), Cousins (jtly, 2000), Human Evolutionary Psychology (jtly, 2001), The Human Story (2004), Evolutionary Psychology (jtly, 2005), Oxford Handbook of Evolutionary Psychology (jt ed, 2007), How Many Friends Does One Person Need? (2010), Science of Love and Betrayal (2012), Lucy to Language (2014), Thinking Big (2014), Human Evolution (2014), Online Social Networks (2015); *Recreations* hill walking, medieval, Renaissance and Baroque music, ecclesiastical architecture, archaeology; *Clubs* Chester Caledonian Assoc, Nat Tst; *Style*— Prof Robin Dunbar; ✉ Department of Experimental Psychology, University of Oxford, 64 Banbury Road, Oxford OX1 3UD

DUNCAN, Rt Hon Sir Alan J C; KCMG (2014), PC (2010), MP; *b* 31 March 1957; *Educ* Merchant Taylors', St John's Coll Oxford (pres Oxford Union, cox coll 1st VIII), Harvard Univ (Kennedy Scholar); *Career* with Shell International Petroleum 1979–81, oil trader and conslt on oil supply and refining industries 1982–92 (in Singapore 1984–86), MP (Cons) Rutland and Melton 1992– (Parly candidate (Cons) Barnsley W and Penistone 1987); PPS to: min of state for Health 1993–94 (resigned), Dr Brian Mawhinney as chm Cons Pty 1995–97; Parly political sec to Rt Hon William Hague MP, Leader of the Oppn 1997–98, vice-chm Cons Pty until 1998, oppn front bench spokesman on health 1998–99, oppn front bench spokesman on trade and industry 1999–2001, shadow min for foreign and Cwlth affrs 2001–03, shadow sec of state for constitutional affrs 2003–04, shadow int devpt sec 2004–05, shadow sec of state for tport 2005, shadow sec of state for trade and industry 2005–07, shadow sec of state for business, enterprise and regulatory reform 2007–09, shadow ldr House of Commons 2009, shadow min for prisons 2009–10, min of state for int devpt 2010–14, PM's special envoy to Yemen 2014–; Freeman City of London, Liveryman Worshipful Co of Merchant Taylors; *Books* Saturn's Children, How the State Devours Liberty, Prosperity and Virtue (with Dominic Hobson, 1995); An End to Illusions (1993); *Recreations* skiing, shooting; *Clubs* Beefsteak; *Style*— The Rt Hon Sir Alan Duncan, MP; ✉ House of Commons, London SW1A 0AA (e-mail alan.duncan.mp@parliament.uk)

DUNCAN, Rev Canon Bruce; MBE (1993); s of Andrew Allan Duncan (d 1984), and Dora, *née* Young; *b* 28 January 1938, London; *Educ* St Albans Sch, Univ of Leeds (BA), Cuddesdon Theol Coll; *m* 17 Dec 1966, Margaret Holmes, da of late Ralph Lister Smith; 3 da (Sarah (Mrs Julian Bush) b 17 Sept 1967, Kate (Mrs Linus McCloskey) b 27 June 1969, Helen b 24 Jan 1971); *Career* fndr dir: Children's Relief Int 1960–65, Northorpe Hall Tst 1960–65; asst curate St Bartholomew's and i/c St Mary of Bethany Armley Leeds (concurrently asst chaplain Armley Prison) 1967–69, hon curate St Mary the Less Cambridge 1969–70, chaplain Order of the Holy Paraclete and St Hilda's Sch Whitby 1970–71, chaplain to HM Ambassadors in Austria, Hungary and Czechoslovakia (based Vienna) 1971–75, vicar Collegiate Church of the Holy Cross and the Mother of Him Who Hung Thereon Crediton 1975–86, rural dean Cadbury 1976–81, rector Crediton and Shobrooke 1982–86, residentiary canon Manchester Cathedral and fell Coll of Christ Manchester 1986–95, princ Sarum Coll (formerly Salisbury and Wells Theol Coll) 1995–2002, canon Salisbury Cathedral and prebendary Chesenbury with Chute 1995–2002, canon emeritus Salisbury Cathedral 2002–, Lazenby chaplain Univ of Exeter 2003–04; archbishops' advsr for foreign rels 1971–75, chm Diocesan Bd for Mission and Unity 1975–86, hon asst priest Sarum St Martin Salisbury 2009–15; devpt consit: Scargill Movement 2009–14, Lee Abbey Movement 2009–; chm Cathedral Fabric Ctee Manchester 1988–91; memb: Exeter Diocesan Synod 1975–86, Bishop's Cncl 1975–86, Diocesan Advsy Ctee Manchester 1987–93, Cathedral Fabric Advsy Ctee Bradford 1997–2002, Salisbury Diocesan Synod 1997–2002; The Northorpe Hall Tst: tstee 1965–97, chm 1977–97, pres 1997–; memb Int Ctee of Vol Agencies Working for Refugees Geneva 1960–65, govr Hayward's Sch 1975–86, lectr S Manchester Coll Dip in Counselling 1986–95, dir Manchester Cathedral Devpt Tst 1986–95; memb Int Conslts Bd and memb Devpt Gp Awareness Fndn 2004–14; memb Br Assoc of Psychological Type 1989 (memb Bd 1990–93); chm of tstees: St Luke's Coll Fndn 2006–09 (tstee 2005–09), Families for Children Adoption Agency 2006–10; Commissary in the UK for the Bishop of the North Eastern Caribbean & Aruba 2006; awarded Archbishop of Canterbury's Cross of St Augustine 2004; Hon DD Grad Theol Fndn Indiana 2002, hon fell Sarum Coll 2006–; FRSA 1989; *Books* Children at Risk (ed A H Denny, 1968), Sich Selbst Verstehen (1993), Pray Your Way: Your Personality and God (1993); articles and chapters in numerous jls; *Recreations* travel, six grandchildren, music, cookery, Jungian psychology, growing clematis, learning to play the clarinet; *Clubs* Athenaeum; *Style*— The Rev Canon Bruce Duncan, MBE; ✉ 92 Harnham Road, Salisbury, Wiltshire SP2 8JW (☎ 01722 502227, mobile 07851 737230, e-mail canon.duncan@gmail.com)

DUNCAN, Clive; John Charles Duncan (d 1973), of Dublin, and Irene Florence, *née* Boys (d 1973); *b* 5 September 1944; *Educ* John Colet Sch Wendover, High Wycombe Coll of Art, Camberwell Sch of Art (NDD), City & Guilds Sch of Art; *m* Jan 1970, Janet, *née* McQueen (d 2010); 1 da (Catharine), 1 s (Alexander); *Career* sculptor and teacher; head of sch Heatherley Wilson Sch of Art 1969–71, head of sculpture and princ lectr Sir John Cass Faculty of Art and Design London Guildhall Univ 1973–93, pres Thomas Heatherley Educational Tst 1973–93; visiting lectr City & Guilds Sculpture Sch, UCL, Slade Summer Sch; exhibitions design conslt Sothebys London; gall lectr on bronze casting V&A; FRBS 1984, RBA 1984, memb Soc of Portrait Sculptors 2005; *Selected Exhibitions* Royal Acad Summer Show 1968, 1969, 1971, 1975, 1979, 1981, 1982, 1987, 1988, 1993 and 1996, Glasgow Inst of Fine Art 1968, The Guildhall London 1974 and 1978, Nicholas Treadwell Gall London 1978, Portland Sculpture Park Dorset 1981, RBA 1983, Playhouse Gall Harlow 1983, Henley Mgmnt Coll 1993, Oxfordshire Artists Culham 1994 and 1995, Henley Arts Festival 1996, Soc of Portrait Sculptors; Trafalgar Crown and fifty pence piece both commissioned by Royal Mint, other commissions incl portraits, head studies, sculptures and inscriptions; work featured in Museum of Reading and in sculpture collections in US, Spain, England and Scotland; *Awards* Bucks Art Scholarship 1963, Leon Underwood Drawing Prize 1965, Surdival Meml Award for Sculpture 1998; *Publications* From Lost Wax to Found Bronze (booklet and video); *Style*— Clive Duncan, Esq; ✉ Holme Cottage, Station Road, Shiplake, Henley-on-Thames, Oxfordshire RG9 3JS (☎ 01189 402563)

DUNCAN, Grant Stuart; s of Stuart Duncan, of London, and Pat, *née* Wollen; *b* 15 April 1958, Singapore; *Educ* Dulwich Coll, Univ of St Andrews (MA), INSEAD; *m* 1, 1989 (m dis), Penny, *née* Marson; 1 s (Louis b 2 June 1995), 1 da (Nina b 3 July 1998); m 2, 2008, Sarah, *née* McAvoy; *Career* grad trainee rising to client services dir Collett Dickenson Pearce 1982–93, md Gold Greenlees Trott/TBWA 1993–99, md rising to chief exec Publicis 1999–2007, ptnr Grace Blue Worldwide 2007–; bd dir Mktg Soc, non-exec dir World Archipelago; tstee Prostate Cancer Charity; FIPA 2004; *Recreations* watching Chelsea, collecting art, loving my children; *Clubs* Soho House, The Hospital; *Style*— Grant Duncan, Esq; ✉ mobile 07770 271068

DUNCAN, Very Rev Dr Gregor Duthie; *see:* Glasgow and Galloway, Bishop of

DUNCAN, Ian Alexander; s of Kenneth George Duncan (d 1979), and Peggy Pauline, *née* Stuchbury (d 2004); *b* 21 April 1946, Smethwick, W Midlands; *Educ* Central GS Birmingham, Coll of Commerce Birmingham; *m* Carol Hammond, da of William Wilford Smith (d 1991), of Watnall, Notts; 2 s (Adam Harvey b 1966, Alexander James b 1975), 1 da (Tavira Caroline b 1975); *Career* certified CA; European controller Otis Elevator 1970–72, dir treasy ops Europe Rockwell Int 1972–75, treas int ops Avis Rent a Car 1975–79, vice-pres Leasco and Reliance World Trade Co 1979–80, fin dir Pentos plc 1980–84; Tomkins plc: fin dir 1984–92, md fin 1992–99, dep chm 1995–99; ptnr: Compass Partners Int 2000–02; chm: Darchem Holdings 2002–04, Volution Holdings 2003–06; currently chm various private equity interests incl Eddie Stobart Logistics Ltd 2014–; Freeman City of London, Liveryman Worshipful Co of Glaziers; CCMI, Fndn FCT, FCCA, FRSA; *Recreations* field sports, the Arts, travel, flying helicopters, scuba diving; *Style*— Ian A Duncan, Esq; ✉ C2102 NEO Bankside, 70 Holland Street, London SE1 9NX (e-mail ianaduncan@email1000.fsnet.co.uk); Kildermorie Estate, Ardross, Easter Ross IV17 0YH (☎ 01349 880654)

DUNCAN, Jacqueline Ann; OBE (2013); *née* Bromley; da of late Sonia Whitaker, *née* Pentney; *b* 16 December 1931, London; *Educ* Convent of the Sacred Heart Brighton, House of Citizenship London; *m* 1, 1955 (m dis 1963), Michael Inchbald; 1 s (Courtenay Charles b 1958), 1 da (Charlotte Amanda b 1960); m 2, 5 June 1974, Brig Peter Trevenen Thwaites (d 1991); m 3, 10 Feb 1994, Col Andrew Duncan, LVO, OBE; *Career* fndr and princ: Inchbald Sch of Design 1960–, Inchbald Sch of Fine Arts 1970–, Inchbald Sch of Garden Design 1972–; memb: Monopolies Cmmn 1972–75, Whitfield Ctee on Copyright and Design 1974–76, London Electricity Conservation Cncl 1973–76, Visiting Ctee RCA 1986–90; tstee St Peter's Res Tst 1987–90; cncllr Westminster City Cncl (Warwick Ward) 1974–78; acting pres Int Soc of Interior Designers (London Chapter) 1987–90; fndr Inchbald Online 2006; govr Oaklands Primary Sch Welwyn Herts 2003–06; JP South Westminster 1976–94; fell Int Soc of Interior Designers 1994 (chm 1990–92), memb Br Inst of Interior Designers 1996; *Books* Directory of Interior Designers (1966), Bedrooms (1968), Design & Decoration (1971); *Recreations* arboriculture, fishing, historical research; *Clubs* Cavalry and Guards', Guards Polo; *Style*— Mrs Andrew Duncan, OBE; ✉ Inchbald School of Design, 32 Eccleston Square, London SW1V 1PB (☎ 020 7630 9011, fax 020 7976 5979, e-mail principal@inchbald.co.uk)

DUNCAN, Jane Elsa; da of Leonard Julian Michaels, of London, and Ruth Gertrude, *née* Sugar; *b* 7 July 1953, London; *Educ* Bartlett Sch of Architecture UCL (BSc, DipArch); *m*

D

23 July 1976, Ian Martin Duncan; 1 da (Alice Rachel b 16 Oct 1984), 1 s (William John b 11 Sept 1987); *Career* architect; formerly ptnr Adrem Architectural Servs and princ Abraxas Architects, dir Jane Duncan Architects Ltd 1992–; memb Amersham on the Hill Revitalisation Ctee; Newark Civil Tst Award, Chiltern Design Award, Architect Inspirational Ldr Atkins Inspire Award 2007; RIBA (equality and diversity champion 2013–15, pres-elect 2014–15, pres 2015–17); *Style*— Mrs Jane Duncan; ✉ Jane Duncan Architects Ltd, The Old Warehouse, Chalfont Station Road, Little Chalfont, Amersham, Buckinghamshire HP7 9PN (☎ 01494 766999, fax 01494 766789, e-mail jane@janeduncanarchitects.co.uk)

DUNCAN, Lindsay Vere; CBE (2009); *b* 7 November 1950; *m* Hilton McRae; 1 s (Cal); *Career* actress; *Theatre* incl: Progress (Bush Theatre), Hedda Gabler (Hampstead Theatre), Top Girls (Royal Court London and Joe Papps Public Theatre NY, awarded NY Obie), The Merry Wives of Windsor, Les Liaisons Dangereuses (West End and Broadway, Olivier Award, Theatre World Award and Tony nomination for Best Actress) and Troilus & Cressida (all RSC), Berenice, Cat on a Hot Tin Roof (Evening Standard Best Actress Award), Plenty, The Provok'd Wife, The Homecoming and The Prince of Homburg (all NT), Three Hotels (Tricycle Theatre), The Cryptogram (Ambassadors Theatre), A Midsummer Night's Dream (RSC, US tour and Broadway), Ashes to Ashes (Royal Court and Gramercy Theatre NYC), Celebration and The Room (both Almeida and Pinter Festival NYC), Mouth to Mouth (Royal Court and Albery Theatre, won Critics Circle Best Actress Award), Private Lives (Albery Theatre, winner of Critics Circle, Olivier, Variety Club, Tony and Drama Desk (NY) Awards for Best Actress), That Face (Royal Court) 2007 and (Duke of York) 2008, John Gabriel Borkman (Abbey Theatre Dublin and Brooklyn Acad of Music) 2010–11, Hay Fever (Noel Coward Theatre) 2012; also performed in the opening season at Royal Exchange Theatre; *Television* incl: Rainy Day Women (BBC), Grown Ups (BBC), GBH (Channel 4, Bafta nomination for Best Actress), Traffik (Channel 4, FIPA D'Or (Cannes)), Redemption (BBC), A Year in Provence (BBC), The Rector's Wife (Channel 4, Best Actress Monte Carlo TV Festival), Jake's Progress (Channel 4), Tom Jones (BBC), Shooting the Past (BBC), Oliver Twist (ITV), Perfect Strangers (BBC, Bafta nomination for Best Actress), Rome (HBO, series 1 and 2), Poirot: The Mystery of the Blue Train, Spooks, Longford, Criminal Justice, Lost in Austen, Margaret, Dr Who, The Sinking of the Laconia, Cristopher and His Kind, Richard II, Merlin, The Mirror Crack'd, White Heat, Black Mirror – The National Anthem, Absolutely Fabulous, Wallander, Spy, Count Arthur Strong; *Film* incl: Loose Connections, Prick Up Your Ears, The Reflecting Skin, City Hall, A Midsummer Night's Dream, An Ideal Husband, Mansfield Park, Under the Tuscan Sun, Afterlife (Best Actress Bratislava Film Festival and Bowmore Scottish Screen Award), Starter for Ten, Tim Burton's Alice in Wonderland, About Time, Le Weekend; *Style*— Lindsay Duncan, CBE; ✉ c/o Dalzell and Beresford, 26 Astwood Mews, London SW7 4DE (☎ 020 7341 9411)

DUNCAN, Mary (Mrs Adrian White); da of Kenneth Playfair Duncan (d 1999), and Gillian Duncan; *b* 1958; *Educ* Bicester Comp, Univ of Exeter (LLB), Coll of Law; *m* Sept 1985, Adrian White; 2 s (Alexander b 1991, Thomas b 1994); *Career* admitted slr 1983; articled clerk then asst slr Henmans 1981–85, asst slr Greenwoods 1985–86, asst slr then ptnr Henmans LLP 1986–2011; accredited Law Society personal injury specialist until 2012; accredited mediator; currently slr (non practising), part time Ct of Protection visitor and Citizens Advice volunteer; *Books* Fatal Accident Claims (1993), Trauma Care: A Team Approach (contrib, 2000), Health and Safety at Work Essentials (co-author, 2003); *Recreations* family, music, tennis, gardening; *Style*— Ms Mary Duncan; ✉ Westfield, Fenway, Steeple Aston, Bicester OX25 4SS

DUNCAN, Michael Greig; s of Alec Greig Duncan (d 1979), and Betty, *née* Shaw; *b* 9 September 1957; *Educ* King Williams Coll IOM, Downing Coll Cambridge (MA); *m* 2 July 1983, Fiona Helen, da of Michael John Carlisle Glaze, CMG; 2 s (Rory b 8 March 1985, Adam b 12 June 1989), 1 da (Chloe b 14 Oct 1986); *Career* admitted slr 1981, ptnr Allen & Overy 1987– (asst slr 1981–86, currently chm Global Banking Practice); memb City of London Law Soc; *Style*— Michael Duncan, Esq; ✉ Allen & Overy LLP, One Bishops Square, London E1 6AD

DUNCAN, Dr Peter Watson; s of Arthur Alexander Watson Duncan, of Edinburgh, and Catherine Bowes, *née* Williamson; *b* 14 April 1954, Edinburgh; *Educ* George Heriot's Sch, Univ of Edinburgh (MB ChB); *m* 16 April 1983, Fiona Margaret, da of Arthur Murray Grierson, of Tetbury, Glos; 2 da (Meg b 3 April 1985, Jane b 18 Aug 1989), 1 s (Ian b 27 Feb 1987); *Career* registrar in anaesthetics Royal Infirmary of Edinburgh 1979–82; sr registrar in anaesthetics: Newcastle upon Tyne 1982–85, Univ of Natal Durban 1983–84; Royal Preston Hosp: conslt in anaesthetics and intensive care 1985–14 (ret), clinical dir (anaesthetics) 1991–97; chm Assoc of NW Intensive Care Units 1996–2000, memb Guidelines Advsy Gp Nat Inst for Clinical Excellence (NICE) 2003–06; former memb Intensive Care Soc; hon sr lectr Univ of Manchester 2011–14; FRCA 1981, FFICM 2011; *Recreations* photography, music, watching football; *Style*— Dr Peter Duncan; ✉ e-mail duncans@fellbrow.fsnet.co.uk

DUNCAN, Richard; *see:* Rudin, Richard Duncan

DUNCAN SMITH, Rt Hon (George) Iain; PC (2001), MP; s of late Gp Capt Wilfred George Gerald Duncan Smith, DSO (and bar), DFC (and 2 bars), and Pamela Duncan Smith; *b* 9 April 1954; *Educ* Conway, Univ per Stranieri di Perugia, RMA Sandhurst, Dunchurch Coll; *m* 1982, Hon Elizabeth Wynne, da of 5 Baron Cottesloe, *qv*; 2 s, 2 da; *Career* cmmnd Scots Gds 1975, ADC to Gen Sir John Acland and Cdr of Cwlth Monitoring Force in Zimbabwe 1979; with GEC Marconi 1981–88; dir: Bellwinch Property Ltd 1988–89, Jane's Information Group 1989–92; Parly candidate (Cons) Bradford W 1987; MP (Cons): Chingford 1992–97, Chingford and Woodford Green 1997–; shadow sec of state for Social Security 1997–99, shadow sec of state for Defence 1999–2001, ldr Cons Pty and ldr HM Opposition 2001–03, sec of state for work and pensions 2010–; fndr Centre for Social Justice 2004– (chm 2004–10, patron 2010–); jt sec: Cons Back Bench Foreign and Cwlth Affrs Ctee 1992–97, Cons Back Bench Def Ctee 1995–96; chm Cons Back Bench Social Security Ctee 1997–99, chm Cons Back Bench Defence Ctee 1999–; memb Select Ctee: Health 1993–95, Administration 1993–97, Standards in Public Life (Standards and Privileges Ctee) 1995–97; chm: Cons Pty Policy Bd 2001–03, Cons Pty Social Justice Policy Gp 2005–; vice-chm Fulham Cons Assoc 1991; Freeman City of London 1993; The Devil's Tune (novel), Who Benefits (Social Security), Game, Set and Match? (Maastricht), Facing the Future (Defence and Foreign and Commonwealth Affairs), 1994 and Beyond, A European Germany or A German Europe?, Five Years and Counting ... Britain and Europe's Growing Vulnerability to Missile Attack, A Race Against Time, Britain's conservative Majority: Good for Me Good for My Neighbour; *Recreations* family, football, rugby, cricket, painting, shooting, fishing; *Style*— The Rt Hon Iain Duncan Smith, MP; ✉ House of Commons, London SW1A 0AA (☎ 020 7219 2667, fax 020 7219 4867, e-mail nashj@parliament.uk)

DUNCAN-JONES, Prof Katherine Dorothea; da of Prof Austin Duncan-Jones (d 1964), and Elsie Elizabeth, *née* Phare (d 2003); *b* 13 May 1941; *Educ* King Edward VI HS for Girls Birmingham, St Hilda's Coll Oxford (Violet Vaughan Morgan scholarship, Charles Oldham Shakespeare Prize, Matthew Arnold Prize); *m* 1971 (m dis 1989), A N Wilson, *qv*; 2 da (Emily b 20 Nov 1971, Beatrice b 7 March 1974); *Career* fell: New Hall Cambridge 1964–65, Somerville Coll Oxford 1965–2001 (sr res fell 2001–); author numerous articles on Renaissance literature and theatre reviews; memb Cncl: Malone Soc, Mgmnt of the Friends of the Bodleian Library; first recipient Ben Jonson Discoveries Prize 1997, awarded prof as title of distinction Univ of Oxford 1998; fell Folger Shakespeare Library 1998, memb Shakespeare Birthplace Tst 2000, hon res fell UCL; FRSL 1991; *Books* Sir Philip Sidney: Courtier Poet (1991), Shakespeare's Sonnets (1997), Ungentle Shakespeare: Scenes from His Life (2001), Shakespeare's Life and World (2004), Shakespeare's Poems (jtly, 2007), Shakespeare: Upstart Crow to Sweet Swan 1592–1623 (2011); *Recreations* swimming, theatre-going; *Clubs* Summerfields Sch Pool (Oxford); *Style*— Prof Katherine Duncan-Jones, FRSL; ✉ Somerville College, Oxford OX2 6HD (☎ 01865 511024, e-mail katherine.duncan-jones@some.ox.ac.uk)

DUNCAN-JONES, Dr Richard Phare; s of Austin Ernest Duncan-Jones, and Elsie Elizabeth Duncan-Jones (d 2003); *b* 14 September 1937; *Educ* King Edward's Sch Birmingham, King's Coll Cambridge (MA, PhD); *m* 1986, Julia Elizabeth, *née* Poole; *Career* Gonville & Caius Coll Cambridge: W M Tapp research fell 1963–67, domestic bursar 1967–84, official fell 1967–, coll lectr and dir of studies in classics 1984–; memb Inst for Advanced Study Princeton 1971–72; FBA 1992, FSA 2000; *Books* The Economy of the Roman Empire (1974, 2 edn 1982), Structure and Scale in the Roman Economy (1990), Money and Government in the Roman Empire (1994); also author of articles in learned jls; *Recreations* walking, wine tasting, continental cinema; *Style*— Dr Richard Duncan-Jones, FBA, FSA; ✉ Gonville & Caius College, Cambridge CB2 1TA (☎ 01223 332394)

DUNCANSON, Neil; s of Jack Duncanson (d 1994), and Olive, *née* Smith, of Saxmundham, Suffolk; *b* 14 February 1960; *Educ* Coopers' Co and Coborn Sch Upminster Essex, Harlow Tech Coll Essex, NCTJ (full cert), Nat Film and TV Sch (directors' course); *m* 1980, Julie, da of Reginald Green; 1 s (Sam b 7 Dec 1988), 1 da (Jessica b 12 Aug 1993); *Career* chief reporter Newham Recorder 1978–84, news journalist (on and off screen) Thames TV 1984–86, deviser/prodr Men on Earth series and others for Thames TV Sport 1986–88 (news ed ITV Olympic Games Seoul 1988), prodr/dir 2 Eyewitness series and 7-Sport for LWT 1988–90, freelance prodr 1990–91, with Chrysalis Television 1991–92, md Chrysalis Television 1992–; credits incl: Italian Football (Channel 4), Rugby Special/ Bowls (BBC), NBA (Channel 4), Graham Taylor: Cutting Edge (Channel 4), Formula One (ITV), Spanish Soccer, Baseball, Angling (BSkyB), Gazza's Coming Home (Channel 4 and ITV), Nick Hancock videos, Arsenal videos, Inside Rugby (Channel 4), It's Only A Game (Channel 4), No Balls Allowed (Channel 4), Reg and Harry's Classic Fight Night (ITV 2), Top Ten Series (Channel 4); awards incl: Silver Shot (for The Fastest Men on Earth) Euro Film and TV Festival 1989, Gold Medal (for 7-Sport) NY Film and TV Festival 1990, Indie Award for Best Sports Programming (for Italian Football 1993 and Formula One 1999, Sports Video of the Year Award 1994 and 1995, RTS Sports Journalism Award (for Graham Taylor: Cutting Edge) 1995, RTS Best Live Sports Coverage (for Formula One) 1998; dir: Queen's Park Rangers FC, Wasps RUFC; memb RTS 1994; *Books* The Fastest Men on Earth (1988), Sports Technology (1991), The Olympic Games (1992), Tales of Gold (with Patrick Collins, 1992), Crown of Thorns (with Norman Giller, 1992); *Recreations* soccer, tennis, movies, writing, Egyptology, sports history, collecting sports memorabilia; *Style*— Neil Duncanson, Esq; ✉ Chrysalis TV Building, 46–52 Pentonville Road, London N1 9HF (☎ 020 7502 6000, fax 020 7502 5600)

DUNCOMBE; *see:* Pauncefort-Duncombe

DUNDAS, James Frederick Trevor (Jamie); s of Sir Hugh Dundas, CBE, DSO, DFC (d 1995), and Hon Lady Dundas; *b* 4 November 1950; *Educ* Eton, New Coll Oxford, Inns of Court Sch of Law; *m* 27 June 1979, Jennifer Ann, da of John Daukes; 1 s, 2 da; *Career* called to the Bar Inner Temple 1972; dir Morgan Grenfell & Co Ltd 1981–91, fin dir Hong Kong Airport Authy 1992–96; MEPC Ltd: fin dir 1997–99, chief exec 1999–2003; chm Jupiter Fund Mgmnt plc 2008–14; non-exec dir: J Sainsbury plc 2000–07, Standard Chartered plc 2004–14, Drax Gp plc 2005–10; chm Macmillan Cancer Support 2001–10, dir Francis Crick Inst 2011–14; *Style*— Jamie Dundas, Esq; ✉ Jupiter Fund Management plc, 1 Grosvenor Place, London SW1X 7JJ

DUNDAS, Kevin John; s of A M Dundas, of Mid Glamorgan, and D V Dundas; *b* 6 October 1961; *Educ* King Edward VI Sch Bury St Edmunds, Trinity & All Saints' Coll Leeds (BSc); *m* 29 Oct 1994, Elizabeth, *née* Ede; 2 s (Hamish James b 24 Jan 1997, Oliver William b 5 Oct 1998), 1 da (Isabella Daisy b 3 Nov 2002); *Career* account planner Publicis 1986–89, bd dir Young & Rubicam London 1989–93, sr vice-pres and dir of planning Saatchi & Saatchi San Francisco 1993–95, exec vice-pres and dir of planning FCB Advtg San Francisco 1995–99; Saatchi & Saatchi London: exec planning dir 1999–2002, md 2002–03, ceo 2003–05; worldwide strategy dir Saatchi & Saatchi 2005–07, conslt Droga5/Honeyshed NY 2008, pres and ceo Sapient Nitro 2009, ceo and managing ptnr 180 Amsterdam 2009–13, ceo Droga5 Europe 2013–; *Recreations* flying (PPL); *Clubs* White Waltham Aero, Century, Soho House, Wentworth Golf; *Style*— Kevin Dundas, Esq

DUNDERDALE, Sue; da of John Mason Dunderdale (d 1988), and Dorothy, *née* Alderson (d 1997); *Educ* Morecambe GS, Univ of Manchester; *Career* dir; fndr and first artistic dir Pentbus Theatre Co; artistic dir: Soho Poly Theatre 1984–88, Greenwich Theatre 1988–89; BBC drama dirs course 1989; TV drama dir 1991–; writer and dir Last Laugh (short film, selected Brisbane, LA and Chicago Film Festivals) 2004; co-chair Dirs' Guild of GB 1986–87, chair Dir's Guild 2001–03; *Style*— Ms Sue Dunderdale; ✉ c/o Peter MacFarlane, MacFarlane Chard Associates, 3 Percy Street, London W1T 1DF (☎ 020 7636 7750)

DUNDONALD, 15 Earl of (S 1669); (Iain Alexander) Douglas Blair; also Lord Cochrane of Dundonald (S 1647), Lord Cochrane of Dundonald, Paisley and Ochiltree (S 1669), and Marquis of Maranhão (Empire of Brazil 1823 by Dom Pedro I for 10 Earl); s (by 1 m) of 14 Earl of Dundonald (d 1986); *b* 17 February 1961; *Educ* Wellington, RAC Cirencester (DipAg); *m* 4 July 1987 (m dis 2011), (M) Beatrice (L), da of Adolphus Russo, of Gibraltar; 2 s (Archie Iain Thomas, Lord Cochrane b 14 March 1991, Hon James Douglas Richard b 10 May 1995), 1 da (Lady Marina Aphra Mariola b 26 Nov 1992); *Heir* s, Lord Cochrane; *Career* investment and technology start ups; hon Chilean consul to Scotland; *Recreations* skiing, sailing, country pursuits; *Style*— The Rt Hon the Earl of Dundonald; ✉ Lochnell Castle, Ledaig, Argyll PA37 1QT

DUNFORD, Sir John Ernest; kt (2014), OBE (1994); s of Leslie Dunford (d 1990), and Mary, *née* Ravenscroft (d 2001); *b* 10 November 1946, Burnham-on-Sea, Somerset; *Educ* Univ of Nottingham (BSc, PGCE, pres Union), Univ of Durham (MEd, PhD); *m* Sue, *née* Rust D'Eye; 1 s (Alastair Michael), 1 da (Ashley Elizabeth), 2 step da (Rachel Emily, Rebecca Lucy); *Career* maths teacher Nottingham 1970–72, maths teacher Sunderland 1972–73, head of maths Durham 1973–78, dep head Bede Sch Sunderland 1978–82, head Durham Johnston Comp Sch 1982–98, gen sec ASCL 1998–2010, educn conslt 2010–; chair: Step Together Volunteering (formerly Worldwide Volunteering), Whole Educn, South Glos Educn Partnership, Chartered Inst of Educnl Assessors 2011–14; Nat Pupil Premium Champion 2013–15; Hon LLD Univ of Nottingham 2014; *Publications* HM Inspectorate of Schools Since 1944 (1998), New Labour and the Conservative Legacy (ed, 2000), School Leadership: National and International Perspectives (ed, 2001); *Recreations* cooking, opera, gardening, family, golf; *Style*— Sir John Dunford, OBE; ✉ Cobblestones, Church Street, North Kilworth, Leicestershire LE17 6EZ (Twitter @johndunford)

DUNFORD, Martin; s of Stan Dunford, of Hants, and Margaret, *née* Lines; *b* 7 June 1959, London; *Educ* Roan Sch Blackheath, Univ of Kent at Canterbury (BA); *m* 31 May 2003, Caroline Osborne; 2 da (Daisy b 14 Oct 2003, Lucy b 10 April 2007); *Career* co-fndr and publisher Rough Guides, now freelance writer and publishing and digital conslt; *Publications* Rough Guides to: Amsterdam, The Netherlands, Brussels, Belgium and Luxembourg, New York, Italy, Rome, Norfolk and Suffolk; *Style*— Martin Dunford; ✉ e-mail mdunford@bigcat.co.uk

DUNHILL, Richard; s of Vernon Dunhill (d 1938), and Helen, *née* Field Moser (d 1984); Co Alfred Dunhill formed by gf 1907; *b* 27 October 1926; *Educ* Beaumont Coll; *m* 5 April

1952, Patricia Susannah, da of Henry B Rump (d 1965); 1 da (Susan Mary b 1953), 3 s (Christopher John b 1954, (Alfred) Mark b 1961, Jonathan Henry b 1962); *Career* army conscript 1944–48; Alfred Dunhill Ltd: joined 1948, dir 1961, dep chm 1967, chm 1977, pres 2000, life pres 2007; chm Dunhill Holdings plc 1981–89 (pres 1989–93); former Barker Variety Club of GB; Master Worshipful Co of Pipemakers and Tobacco Blenders 1987–88; *Recreations* gardening, backgammon; *Style*— Richard Dunhill, Esq

DUNKELS, Paul Renton; QC (1993); s of George Antony Dunkels (d 1985), and Mollie, *née* Renton (d 1991); *b* 26 November 1947; *Educ* Harrow; *m* 2 Sept 1972, Melanie Gail, da of Lawrence Taverner; 2 da (Cynthia Leigh b 7 March 1975, Eleanor Claire b 6 Sept 1982), 1 s (Antony Lawrence Renton b 31 May 1977); *Career* called to the Bar Inner Temple 1972, in practice Western Circuit 1974–, recorder of the Crown Court 1988–; *Style*— Paul Dunkels, Esq, QC; ✉ Walnut House, 63 St David's Hill, Exeter, Devon EX4 4DW (☎ 01392 279751, fax 01392 412080, e-mail paul.dunkels@walnuthouse.co.uk)

DUNKERLEY, Christopher; s of George William Dunkerley (d 1994), of Smallfield, Surrey, and Diana Margaret, *née* Lang (d 2009); *b* 12 December 1951; *Educ* Charterhouse, Pembroke Coll Oxford (MA); *m* 16 Sept 1983, Kathleen Jane, *née* Hansen; 1 s (Jonathan b 18 Oct 1986), 1 da (Laura b 8 Sept 1988); *Career* graduate trainee William Brandts 1973–75, mangr Orion Bank 1975–76, asst gen mangr Saudi International Bank 1977–87, asst dir James Capel & Co 1987–89, chief exec Dartington & Co Gp plc 1989–92, md Glen House Associates 1992–96, chief exec Swire Fraser Financial Management 1993–95, ptnr Coutts & Co 1996–2000, dir Dunkerley Financial Planning Ltd 2000–; non-exec dir Henderson High Income Tst plc 1989–2008; govr Clifton Coll 2002–; *Recreations* ocean racing, golf; *Clubs* Royal Ocean Racing, Lansdowne; *Style*— Christopher Dunkerley, Esq; ✉ Glen House, Sandy Lane, Abbots Leigh, Bristol BS8 3SE (☎ 01275 375200, fax 01275 375047)

DUNKERTON, Julian; *b* 1 March 1965, London; *Career* co-fndr Cult Clothing (subsequently SuperGroup plc) 1985, created Superdry brand with James Holder 2003, currently ceo SuperGroup plc (listed on London stock exchange 2010); Entrepreneur of the Year Ernst & Young 2010, CEO of the Year UK Stock Market Awards 2011, Entrepreneur of the Year PLC Awards 2013; *Style*— Julian Dunkerton, Esq; ✉ SuperGroup plc, Unit 60, The Runnings, Cheltenham, Gloucestershire GL51 9NW

DUNLEATH, 6 Baron (UK 1892); Brian Henry Mulholland; 3 Bt (UK) 1945), DL (Co Down 2009); o s of 5 Baron Dunleath (d 1997), and his 2 w, Elizabeth M, *née* Hyde (d 1989); *b* 25 September 1950, Belfast; *Educ* Eton, Royal Agricultural Coll Cirencester; *m* 1, 1976 (m dis 2004), Mary Joan, yst da of late Maj Robert John Fuller Whistler; 1 da (Hon Tara Miranda b 15 April 1980), 2 s (Hon Andrew Henry b 15 Dec 1981, Hon William Alexander b 15 Feb 1986); m 2, 2006, Vibeke Lunn, yr da of late Col Jens Christian Lunn, of Knabstrup Hovedgaard Denmark; *Heir* s, Hon Andrew Mulholland; *Career* landowner and co dir; production mangr Finsbury Distillery Co Ltd 1972–82, brands mangr Matthew Clark Gp plc with responsibility for Irish Distillers 1982–85, dir Lanyon Developments Ltd 1985–91, admin Belle Isle Estate 1991–94, chm Dunleath Estates Ltd 1997– (dir 1994–97), dir Downpatrick Race Club Ltd 1999–; memb Business Tourism Steering Gp NI Tourist Bd 2005–; *Recreations* shooting, fishing, gardening; *Clubs* MCC, Kildare Street and Univ (Dublin); *Style*— The Rt Hon the Lord Dunleath; ✉ Ballywalter Park, Ballywalter, Newtownards BT22 2PP; Dunleath Estates Ltd, Ballywalter Park Estate Office, Newtownards BT22 2PA (☎ 028 4275 8264, fax 028 4275 8818, e-mail bd@dunleath-estates.co.uk)

DUNLOP, Andrew Alexander; s of Andrew Roberts Jeffrey Dunlop, of Renfrewshire, and Merope Jane, *née* Haggart, of Perthshire; *b* 22 June 1964, Perthshire; *Educ* HS of Glasgow, Univ of Aberdeen; *m* 16 Feb 1991, Jusna; 2 da (Octavia Taqiyah b 4 Nov 1999, Alyssa Kamilah b 25 May 2003), 1 s (Matthias Daniyal Andrew Alexander b 1 Oct 2007); *Career* slr; Arthur Andersen 1991, Freshfields 1993, ptnr Shaw Pittman Potts and Trowbridge 1998, ptnr Burges Salmon 2001–; dir: Nat Outsourcing Assoc 1998–2012, European Outsourcing Assoc 2005–12; memb Law Soc 1991; *Recreations* flyfishing, golf, skiing; *Style*— Andrew Dunlop, Esq; ✉ Burges Salmon, Narrow Quay House, Bristol BS1 4AH (☎ 0117 939 2000)

DUNLOP, Baron (Life Peer UK 2015), of Helensburgh in the County of Dunbarton; Andrew James Dunlop; *b* 21 June 1959; *Educ* Trinity Coll Glenalmond, Glasgow Acad, Univ of Edinburgh (MA); *Career* Midland Bank Int 1981–82, Cons Res Dept 1982–86; special advsr: to Rt Hon George Younger as sec of state for defence 1986–88, to PM's Policy Unit 1988–90; md Politics International 1991–2008, md Interel UK 2008–10, exec chm Interel UK 2010–11; chief advsr to Rt Hon David Cameron 2012–15, Parly under-sec of state for Scotland 2015–16, Parly under-sec of state for Scotland and NI 2016–; *Clubs* Reform; *Style*— The Lord Dunlop

DUNLOP, Eileen Rhona; da of James Dunlop (d 1982), and Grace, *née* Love (d 1977); *b* 13 October 1938; *Educ* Alloa Acad, Moray House Coll of Educn Edinburgh (Dip, Steele Prize); *m* 1979, Antony Kamm (d 2011), s of George Kamm, and Josephine Kamm; *Career* author; teacher Eastfield Sch Penicuik 1959–61, teacher Abercromby Sch Alloa 1961–63, dep head Sunnyside Sch Alloa 1963–79, headmistress Prep Sch of Dollar Acad 1980–90; *Books* Robinsheugh (1975), A Flute in Mayferry Street (1976), Fox Farm (1978), The Maze Stone (1982), A Book of Old Edinburgh (jt ed with Antony Kamm, 1983), Scottish Verse to 1800 (jt ed with Antony Kamm, 1985), Scottish Traditional Rhymes (jt ed with Antony Kamm, 1985), Clementina (1985), The House on the Hill (1987), The Valley of Deer (1989), Finn's Island (1991), Green Willow's Secret (1993), Finn's Roman Fort (1994), Stones of Destiny (1994), Castle Gryffe (1995), The Ghost by the Sea (1996), Waters of Life (1996), Warrior's Bride (1998), A Royal Ring of Gold (1999), Ghoul's Den (1999), The Haunting of Alice Fairlie (2001), Nicholas Moonlight (2002), Weerdwood (2003), Queen Margaret of Scotland (2005), Robert Louis Stevenson: The Travelling Mind (2008), Supernatural Scotland (2011), Sir Walter Scott: A Life in Story (2016); *Recreations* reading, theatre, gardening; *Clubs* Royal Over-Seas League; *Style*— Miss Eileen Dunlop; ✉ 46 Tarmangie Drive, Dollar, Clackmannanshire FK14 7BP (☎ 01259 742007)

DUNLOP, Graeme Dermott Stuart; OBE (2006); *b* 1942; *Educ* Charterhouse, Magdalene Coll Cambridge; *Career* P&O SNCO: joined as mgmnt trainee 1964, (attached to Mackinnon Mackenzie Bombay until 1967), asst mangr Personnel Container Fleets Ltd 1967–70, asst to the sec Australia 1970, devpt asst General Cargo Div (GCD) 1971–72, asst devpt mangr GCD 1972–74, devpt mangr 1974–75, dir P&O Strath Services Ltd 1975–77, general mangr Arabian Peninsular Container Line 1977–79, md North Sea Ferries Rotterdam 1979–87, md P&O European Ferries Ltd 1987–2003, memb Bd 1991–2003, chm P&O European Ferries Ltd 1993–2003, chm P&O Trans European (Holdings) Ltd (formerly P&O European Transport Services) 1996–2003; pres: Chamber of Shipping 1999–2000, EC Shipowners Assoc 2003–; chm: Standard Steamship Owners' P&I Assoc (Bermuda) Ltd 1997–, AWSR Shipping Ltd 2003–; *Style*— Graeme Dunlop, Esq, OBE

DUNLOP, Sir Thomas; 4 Bt (UK 1916), of Woodbourne, Co Renfrew; s of Sir Thomas Dunlop, 3 Bt (d 1999); *b* 22 April 1951; *Educ* Rugby, Univ of Aberdeen (BSc); *m* 1984, Eileen, er da of Alexander Henry Stevenson (d 1990); 1 da (Nicola Mary b 1987), 1 s (Thomas b 11 March 1990); *Heir* s, Thomas Dunlop; *Career* ptnr Abbey Forestry Pershore; memb Inst of Chartered Foresters; *Style*— Sir Thomas Dunlop, Bt; ✉ Bredon Croft, Bredon's Norton, Tewkesbury, Gloucestershire GL20 7HB

DUNLOP, Prof William; CBE (2005); s of Alexander Morton Dunlop, and Annie Denholm Rennie, *née* Ingram; *b* 18 August 1944; *Educ* Kilmarnock Acad, Univ of Glasgow (MB ChB), Univ of Newcastle upon Tyne (PhD); *m* 25 March 1968, Sylvia Louise, da of Dr Irwin Krauthamer; 1 s (Keith b 1972), 1 da (Emma b 1973); *Career* various jr posts in Obstetrics and Gynaecology Dept, regius prof Univ of Glasgow 1969–74, seconded as lectr Univ of Nairobi 1972–73, MRC scientific staff Newcastle 1974–75, visiting assoc prof Med Univ of S Carolina 1980, prof and head of Dept Obstetrics and Gynaecology Univ of Newcastle upon Tyne 1982–99 (sr lectr 1975–82), head Sch of Surgical and Reproductive Sciences 1999–2001; pres RCOG 2001–04 (hon sec 1992–98); chm: Blair-Bell Res Soc 1989–92, Assoc of Profs of Obstetrics and Gynaecology 1999–2001, Jt Conslts Ctee 2003–05; vice-chm: Specialist Trg Authy 2002–04, Acad of Med Royal Colls 2002–04; treas: Section of Obstetrics and Gynaecology Union Européenne de Médecins Spécialistes 2001–05 (pres 2006–08), European Bd and Coll of Obstetrics and Gynaecology 2002–05 (pres 2005–07); chair Scientific Prog Ctee XX FIGO World Congress of Gynecology and Obstetrics 2009–12; ed-in-chief Fetal and Maternal Med Review 1989–99; ed Recent Advances in Obstetrics and Gynaecology 2003–07; memb South African Soc of Obstetricians and Gynaecologists 2003; fell Acad of Med Singapore 2002, hon fell American Coll of Obstetricians and Gynaecologists 2003; FRCSEd 1971, FRCOG 1984 (MRCOG 1971), FRCPSGlas 2003; *Recreations* music, drama, literature; *Style*— Prof William Dunlop, CBE

D

DUNLUCE, Viscount Randal Alexander St John McDonnell; DL (Co Antrim 2014); s and h of 9 Earl of Antrim, *qv*, and Sarah Elizabeth Anne, *née* Harmsworth (Mrs Gates); *b* 2 July 1967, London; *Educ* Gresham's, Worcester Coll Oxford (MA); *m* 1 Oct 2004, Aurora, *née* Gunn; 1 s (Hon Alexander David Somerled b 30 June 2006), 1 da (Hon Helena Maeve Aurora b 19 Feb 2008); *Heir* s, Hon Alexander McDonnell; *Career* investment mangr: NCL Investments Ltd 1993–97, Sarasin & Ptnrs LLP 1998– (ptnr); dir: Antrim Estates Co, Northern Salmon Co, Aberdeen Asian Smaller Companies Investment Tst 2013; tstee: Irish Landmark Tst until 2008, Glenarm Buildings Preservation Tst until 2010, Irish Grouse Conservation Tst; *Recreations* country pursuits, conservation, vintage cars; *Clubs* White's, Pratt's; *Style*— Viscount Dunluce, DL; ✉ Glenarm Castle, Glenarm, Ballymena, Co Antrim BT44 0AL (☎ 02828 841229, e-mail randal@glenarmcastle.com); Juxon House, 100 St Paul's Churchyard, London EC4M 8BU (☎ 0207 038 7000)

DUNMORE, Helen; da of Maurice Ronald Dunmore, and Betty, *née* Smith; *b* 12 December 1952; *Educ* Nottingham HS for Girls, Univ of York (BA); *m* 24 Oct 1980, Francis Benedict Charnley; 1 s (Patrick Maurice b 28 July 1981), 1 da (Teresa Mary Benedicta b 11 Feb 1994), 1 step s (Oliver Benjamin b 13 Feb 1977); *Career* poet and novelist; FRSL; *Poetry* incl: The Apple Fall (1983), The Sea Skater (1986, winner Poetry Soc's Alice Hunt Bartlett Award 1987), The Raw Garden (1988, Poetry Book Soc Choice winter 1988–89), Short Days, Long Nights, New and Selected Poems (1991), Recovering a Body (1994), Secrets (1994, The Signal Poetry Award 1995), Bestiary (1997), Out of the Blue (2001), Glad of These Times (2007); *Children's Novels* Going to Egypt (1992), In the Money (1993), Amina's Blanket (1996), Go Fox (1996), Fatal Error (1996), Brother Brother Sister Sister (1999), Zillah and Me (2000), The Zillah Rebellion (2001), Ingo (2005), The Tide Knot (2006), The Deep (2007), The Crossing of Ingo (2008); *Fiction* Zennor in Darkness (1993, The McKitterick Prize 1994), Burning Bright (1994), A Spell of Winter (1995, winner inaugural Orange Prize for fiction 1996), Talking to the Dead (1996), Love of Fat Men (1997), Your Blue-Eyed Boy (1998), With Your Crooked Heart (1999), Ice Cream (2000), The Siege (2001), Mourning Ruby (2003), House of Orphans (2006), Counting the Stars (2008), The Betrayal (2010); *Recreations* family life and friendships; *Style*— Ms Helen Dunmore, FRSL; ✉ c/o Caradoc King, A P Watt Ltd, 20 John Street, London WC1N 2DR (☎ 020 7405 6774, fax 020 7831 2154)

DUNMORE, 12 Earl of (S 1686); Malcolm Kenneth Murray; also Viscount of Fincastle, Lord Murray of Blair, Moulin and Tillimet (Tullimet; both S 1686); er s of 11 Earl of Dunmore (d 1995), and Margaret Joy, *née* Cousins (d 1976); *b* 17 September 1946, Launceston, Tasmania; *Educ* Queechy HS, Launceston, Schs' Bd 'A' certificate and various other technical qualifications; *m* 1970, Joy Anne (d 2015), da of Arthur Partridge (d 1987), of Launceston, Tasmania; 1 s (Hon Leigh Kenneth b 1978), 1 da (Lady Elisa Anne b 1981) (both adopted); *Heir* bro, Hon Geoffrey Murray; *Career* electrical tech offr Air Services Australia 1968–99, licensed aircraft maintenance engr, ret; pte pilot; patron: Armorial & Heraldry Soc of Australasia, Co of Armigers Inc (Australian chapter), Scottish Australian Heritage Cncl, Murray Clan Socs of Edinburgh, New Zealand Soc, Victoria and Queensland, St Andrew Soc Tasmania, Tasmanian Caledonian Cncl, Launceston Caledonian Soc; co-patron (with Countess): Crown Int Dance Assoc Australia, Australia Day Cncl (Victoria) Inc, St Andrew's First Aid Australia; patron: Sunny Bank RSL Sub-Branch Inc, Lodge Amalthea No 914 Victorian Consitution (master 2011 and 2012); past master Concord Masonic Lodge: No 10 Tasmanian Constitution, Clan Murray high cmmr for Australia and NZ; sat in House of Lords 1998; Cyfail y Celtaid Celtic Cncl of Australia; Knight of Justice Orthodox Order of St John, Knight Imperial and Royal Order of St Stanislaw; *Recreations* flying, astronomy, fly fishing, music (saxophone and piano); *Clubs* Soaring Club of Tasmania, Devonport Fly Fishing, Burns Club of Launceston (Tasmania); *Style*— The Rt Hon the Earl of Dunmore; ✉ PO Box 100E, East Devonport, Tasmania 7310, Australia (e-mail malc5@bigpond.com)

DUNN, David; *Career* CA; early career with: BPB Industries plc, Lex Service Gp plc, Newman Industries plc; non-exec chm: Scapa Gp plc until 2002 (formerly fin dir and chief exec), Brammer plc 2001–12; *Style*— David Dunn, Esq

DUNN, David Hedley; s of Francis Hedley Dunn, of Charlestown, Cornwall, and Jean Mary, *née* Osborne; *b* 21 September 1968; *Educ* Penrice Comp Sch, St Austell Coll; *Career* political offr Br Embassy Oslo 1992–94, political offr Br Embassy Suva 1996–97, UK Mission to the UN 1997–98, special advsr on secondment to UN 1998–2000, Br Embassy Stockholm 2000–01, private sec to Min for Europe 2001–03, dep high cmmr to Sierra Leone 2004–06, high cmmr to Papua New Guinea 2006–10; *Recreations* rugby, squash, sea fishing; *Clubs* Papuan; *Style*— Mr David Dunn; ✉ c/o FCO, King Charles Street, London SW1A 2AH (e-mail david.dunn2@fco.gov.uk)

DUNN, Prof Douglas Eaglesham; OBE (2003); s of William Douglas Dunn (d 1980), and Margaret, *née* McGowan; *b* 23 October 1942; *Educ* Renfrew HS, Camphill Sch Paisley, Scottish Sch of Librarianship, Univ of Hull (BA); *m* 1, Lesley Balfour, *née* Wallace (d 1981); m 2, 10 Aug 1985, Lesley Jane, da of Robert Bathgate (d 1979); 1 s (William Robert Bathgate b 5 Jan 1987), 1 da (Lillias Ella Bathgate b 18 June 1990); *Career* writer; head Sch of English Univ of St Andrews 1995–99 (prof 1991–), St Andrews Scottish Studies Inst 1993– (fell in creative writing 1989–91); Somerset Maugham Award 1972, Geoffrey Faber Meml Prize 1975, Hawthornden Prize 1982, Whitbread Book of the Year Award for 1985 (1986), Cholmondeley Award 1989; Hon LLD Univ of Dundee 1987, Hon DLitt Univ of Hull 1995, Hon DLitt Univ of St Andrews 2009; hon prof Univ of Dundee 1987, hon fell Humberside Coll; FRSL 1981, FRSE 2009; *Books* books of poetry incl: Terry Street (1969), The Happier Life (1972), Love or Nothing (1974), Barbarians (1979), St Kilda's Parliament (1982), Elegies (1985), Selected Poems (1986), Northlight (1988), Dante's Drum-kit (1993), The Donkey's Ears (2000), The Year's Afternoon (2000), Selected Poems 1964–2000 (2003), A Line in the Water (with Norman Ackroyd, 2009); other books: Secret Villages (short stories, 1985), Andromache (translation, 1990), Poll Tax: The Fiscal Fake (1990), The Essential Browning (ed, 1990), Scotland: An Anthology (ed, 1991), Faber Book of Twentieth Century Scottish Poetry (ed, 1992), Boyfriends and Girlfriends (short stories, 1995), Oxford Book of Scottish Short Stories (ed, 1995), 20th Century Scottish Poems (ed, 2000); *Recreations* music, philately; *Style*— Prof Douglas Dunn, OBE, FRSL; ✉ School of English, Castle House, University of St Andrews, St Andrews, Fife KY16 9AL (☎ 01334 462666, fax 01334 462655, e-mail ded@st-andrews.ac.uk)

DUNN, Geoffrey Richard; s of late K G Dunn, of W Sussex, and Nila Jane, *née* Griffiths; *b* 10 July 1949; *Educ* Ifield GS, Univ of Manchester (BSc, MSc), Manchester Business Sch (Dip); *m* 12-Sep-03; *Career* investment controller ICFC Ltd 1975–78, corp fin exec SG Warburg & Co Ltd 1978–80; asst gp treas GKN plc 1980–83, head of fin and planning Midland Bank plc 1984–87, gp fin dir Exco International plc 1987–92, conslt 1993–94; chief fin offr: SWIFT SC Brussels 1994–97, GlobalOne Telecommunications SA Brussels 1997–98; gp fin dir Xansa plc 1999–2002, interim fin dir Bank of England 2004–05, Co-op Financial Servs 2008, chief fin offr for reconstruction Northern Rock 2009–10, non-exec dir Citadele Banka SA 2010– (dep chm 2010–15), non-exec dir Datamonitor plc 2001–02, chm and non-exec dir Saffron BS 2011–; FCT 1997; *Recreations* mountaineering, skiing, opera and music; *Clubs* Alpine, London Mountaineering, Manchester United; *Style*— Geoffrey Dunn, Esq; ✉ Sandlings, Leiston Road, Aldeburgh, Suffolk IP15 5QE

DUNN, Jane Ellinor; *née* Thesen; da of David Rolf Thesen (d 2002), and Ellinor Hodder Thesen, *née* Wilson (d 2015); *b* Durban, South Africa; *Educ* Bentley GS, Clifton HS Bristol, UCL; *m* 1, (m dis 1985), Philip Martin Dunn; 1 s (Benjamin David Harald b 19 Oct 1971), 1 da (Lily Caroline b 19 Oct 1973); m 2, 22 Feb 1996, Nicholas David MacLachlan Ostler; *Career* author; formerly with Copy Dept Vogue magazine, co-fndr and editorial dir Pierrot Publishing; freelance journalist: Vogue, Brides, Sunday Times, Guardian, Observer, Literary Review, Sunday Telegraph; FRSL 1999; *Publications* Moon In Eclipse: A Life of Mary Shelley (1978), A Very Close Conspiracy: Vanessa Bell and Virginia Woolf (1990), Virginia Woolf: An Illustrated Anthology (1994), Antonia White: A Life (1998), Elizabeth and Mary: Cousins, Rivals, Queens (2003), Read My Heart: Dorothy Osborne and Sir William Temple – A Love Story in the Age of Revolution (2008), Daphne du Maurier and her Sisters: The Hidden Lives of Pifty, Bird and Bing (2013); *Style*— Ms Jane Dunn; ✉ c/o Natasha Faireweather, United Agents, 12–26 Lexington Street, London W1F 0LE (☎ 020 3214 0800, e-mail nfairweather@unitedagents.co.uk)

DUNN, Prof John Montfort; s of Col Henry George Montfort Dunn (d 1970), and Catherine Mary, *née* Kinloch (d 1986); *b* 9 September 1940; *Educ* Winchester, Millfield, King's Coll Cambridge (BA), Harvard Univ (Harkness fell); *m* 1, 1965 (m dis 1971), Susan Deborah, *née* Fyvel; m 2, 1973 (m dis 1987), Judith Frances Bernal; 2 s (Thomas William b 8 Dec 1989 d 1990, Charles Montfort b 11 Jan 1991); m 3 (m dis 2013), 1997, Ruth Ginette Scurr; 2 da (Polly Anna Montfort b 15 May 1998, Rosalind Jean Montfort b 23 April 2003); m 4, 2014, Anastasia Piliavsky; *Career* Univ of Cambridge: fell Jesus Coll 1965–66, fell King's Coll 1966–, lectr in political science 1972–77, reader in politics 1977–87, prof of political theory 1987–2007; visiting prof: Univ of Ghana, Univ of Br Columbia, Univ of Bombay, Tokyo Met Univ, Tulane Univ, Univ of Minnesota, Chiba Univ; Olmsted visiting prof Yale Univ 1991, Leitner visiting prof in int affrs and political science Yale Univ 2008, Simson lectr and visiting prof Yale Univ 2011; Br Acad: chm Political Studies Section 1994–97, memb Cncl 2004–07; foreign hon memb: American Acad of Arts and Sciences 1991, Bd of Conslts Kim Dae-Jung Fndn for the Asia-Pacific Region 1994; Sir Isaiah Berlin Prize Political Studies Assoc 2007, Ad Portas Winchester Coll 2011; FBA 1989, FSA 1993, Academician Acad of the Social Sciences 2010; *Books* The Political Thought of John Locke (1969), Modern Revolutions (1972), Dependence and Opportunity (with A F Robertson, 1973), West African States: Failure and Promise (ed, 1978), Western Political Theory in the Face of the Future (1979), Political Obligation in its Historical Context (1980), The Politics of Socialism (1984), Rethinking Modern Political Theory (1985), Contemporary West Africa Studies (jt ed, 1989), Interpreting Political Responsibility (1990), Democracy: the unfinished journey 508 BC – 1993 AD (ed, 1992), Contemporary Crisis of the Nation State? (ed, 1995), The History of Political Theory and Other Essays (1996), Great Political Thinkers (ed with Ian Harris, 1997), The Cunning of Unreason (2000), Pensare la Politica (2002), Locke: A Very Short Introduction (2003), Setting the People Free: The Story of Democracy (2005), Exploring Utopian Futures of Politics (with Inwon Choue and John Ikenberry, 2008), Breaking Democracy's Spell (2014); *Recreations* birdwatching; *Style*— Prof John Dunn, FBA, FSA; ✉ King's College, Cambridge CB2 1ST; Department of Politics, University of Cambridge, Alison Richard Building, West Road, Cambridge (☎ 01223 529223, e-mail jmd24@cam.ac.uk)

DUNN, Baroness (Life Peer UK 1990), of Hong Kong Island in Hong Kong and of Knightsbridge in the Royal Borough of Kensington and Chelsea; Lydia Selina Dunn; DBE (1989, CBE 1983, OBE 1978), JP (1976); da of Yen Chuen Yeh Dunn (d 1965), and Chen Yin-chu (d 1990); *b* 29 February 1940; *Educ* St Paul's Convent Sch Hong Kong, Univ of Calif Berkeley; *m* 1988, Michael David Thomas, CMG, QC, *qv*; *Career* dir: John Swire & Sons (Hong Kong) Ltd 1978–2003, Swire Pacific Ltd 1981–2015, Cathay Pacific Airways Ltd 1985–97 (Bd advsr 1997–2002), Christie's International plc 1996–98, John Swire & Sons Ltd 1996–, Marconi plc (formerly GEC plc) 1997–2002, Christie's Fine Art Ltd 1998–2000; dep chm: Hongkong and Shanghai Banking Corp 1992–96 (dir 1981–96), HSBC Holdings plc 1992–2008 (dir 1990–2008); pres Hong Kong LEP Tst 1993–; memb: Hong Kong Exec Cncl 1982–88 (sr memb 1988–95), Hong Kong Legislative Cncl 1976–85 (sr memb 1985–88), Advsy Cncl Cunfucius Inst for Business London 2006–, Christies Gtr China Advsy Bd 2009–; chm: Hong Kong Trade Devpt Cncl 1983–91, Hong Kong/Japan Business Co-operation Ctee 1988–95 (memb 1983–88), Lord Wilson Heritage Tst 1993–95; dir Volvo AB 1991–93 (memb Int Advsy Bd 1985–91), memb Hong Kong/US Econ Co-operation Ctee 1984–93; Prime Minister of Japan's Trade Award 1987, US Sec of Commerce's Peace and Commerce Award 1988; Hon LLD: Chinese Univ of Hong Kong 1984, Univ of Hong Kong 1991, Univ of Br Columbia 1991, Univ of Leeds 1994; Hon DSc Univ of Buckingham 1995, hon fell London Business Sch; *Books* In the Kingdom of the Blind (1983); *Recreations* art, music, opera; *Style*— The Baroness Dunn, DBE; ✉ John Swire & Sons Ltd, Swire House, 59 Buckingham Gate, London SW1E 6AJ

DUNN, Sam; s of Nicholas Dunn, and Jennifer, *née* Hazelwood-Randall; *b* 28 December 1972, Bristol; *Educ* Univ of Birmingham (BA), Univ of Wales Cardiff (Dip); *m* 12 Jan 2008, Hana, *née* Irani; 2 s (Louis Irani Dunn b 17 July 2009, Rafi Irani Dunn b 26 Feb 2012), 1 da (Imani Elizabeth Rose Irani Dunn b 11 March 2016); *Career* journalist; reporter Evening Herald Plymouth 1998–99, sr business corr Western Daily Press 1999–2002, sr reporter Financial Adviser/Investment Adviser 2002–03; Independent on Sunday: dep personal fin ed 2003–04, personal fin ed 2004–07; freelance The Guardian, The Independent, Moneysavingexpert.com, The Observer and Sunday Express 2007–, dep personal finance ed Daily Mail 2011–15, asst ed Moneysavingexpert.com 2016–; Personal Fin Journalist of the Year Harold Wincott Award 2005, Journalist of the Year Headlinemoney Awards 2006, Freelance Financial Journalist of the Year Assoc of Br Insurers 2008; *Recreations* long-distance running, guitar, disco; *Style*— Sam Dunn, Esq; ✉ 23 Elmbank Way, Ealing, London W7 3DE (☎ 07967 229343)

DUNN OSTLER, Jane; *see:* Dunn, Jane

DUNNE, Gordon; MBE (2016), MLA (2011); *Career* MLA (DUP) N Down 2011–; *Style*— Gordon Dunne, Esq, MBE, MLA; ✉ Northern Ireland Assembly, Parliament Buildings, Belfast BT4 3XX (e-mail gordon.dunne@mla.niassembly.gov.uk)

DUNNE, Philip Martin; MP; s of Sir Thomas Dunne, KG, KCVO, *qv*, and Henrietta Rose, *née* Crawley; *b* 14 August 1958, Oxford; *Educ* Univ of Oxford; *m* 1989, Domenica Margaret Anne, *née* Fraser; *Career* SG Warburg 1981–88, ptnr Phoenix Securities 1991–97, md DLJ Int 1997–2000; chm Ottakar's plc 1998–2006 (co-fndr 1987); chm Baronsmead 4 VCT plc 2001–10, dir Ruffer LLP 2002–09; MP (Cons) Ludlow 2005–; cncllr (Cons) South Shropshire DC 2001–07; memb: Work and Pensions Ctee 2005–06, Public Accounts Ctee 2006–08, Treasy Select Ctee 2007–08; dep chm Int Office Cons Pty 2008–10; opposition asst whip 2008–10, asst Govt whip 2010–12, min for defence equipment, support and technol 2012–15, min of state for defence procurement 2015–; dir Juvenile Diabetes Research Fndn 1999–2005; *Style*— Philip Dunne, MP; ✉ website www.philipdunne.com; House of Commons, London SW1A 0AA

DUNNE, Sir Thomas Raymond; KG (2008), KCVO (1995), JP (Hereford and Worcester 1977); s of Philip Dunne, MC (d 1965), of East Clandon, Surrey, and his 1 wife Margaret Ann Willis, CBE, *née* Walker; *b* 24 October 1933; *Educ* Eton; *m* 17 July 1957, Henrietta Rose, da of Cosmo Stafford Crawley (d 1989); 2 s (Philip Dunne, MP, *qv*, b 1958, Nicholas b 1970), 2 da (Camilla (Hon Mrs Rupert Soames) b 1960, Letitia b 1965); *Career* RMA Sandhurst 1951–53, cmmnd RHG 1953–58, farmer; Hon Col: 2 (volunteer) Bn Mercian Volunteers 1985–87, 4 (volunteer) Bn The Worcestershire and Sherwood Foresters Regt 1987–93 (formerly 2 Bn Mercian Volunteers), 5 (Shropshire and Herefordshire) Bn The Light Infantry (Volunteers) 1993–98; memb Hereford CC 1962–68; High Sheriff Herefordshire 1970, DL Hereford and Worcester 1974 (Herefordshire 1973), HM Lord-Lt and Custos Rotulorum Hereford and Worcester 1977–98, HM Lord-Lt for the separate counties of Herefordshire and Worcestershire on the formation of those counties April 1998–2001, HM Lord-Lt of Herefordshire 2001–08, chm Lord-Lts Assoc 2001–08; pres Three Counties Agricultural show 1977 and 1997; memb W Mercia Police Authy 1979–99, dir W Midland Regnl Bd Central TV, chm of tstees Worcester Museum of Porcelain 1985–2000, chm Hereford Cathedral Cncl 2001–; pres W Midlands TAVRA 1989–98, dir Hereford Race Club Ltd 1989–98; hon fell Univ of Worcester 2008; KStJ 1977; *Style*— Sir Thomas Dunne, KG, KCVO; ✉ Trippleton House, Leintwardine, Craven Arms SY7 0LZ

DUNNETT, Anthony Gordon; CBE (2004); s of Peter Sydney Dunnett (d 1988), and Margaret Eileen, *née* Johnson, of Wadhurst, East Sussex; *b* 17 June 1953, Bromley, Kent; *Educ* St Dunstan's Coll London, McGill Univ Montreal (Dip CS, BCom), Univ of Exeter (MA); *m* 1975, Ruth Elizabeth, da of Dennis Henry Barker; 1 s (Timothy b 1978), 2 da (Penelope b 1980, Emily b 1982); *Career* Nat Westminster Bank plc 1975–77; Royal Bank of Canada: Montreal 1977–80, Curacao 1980–82, Montreal 1982–86; corp banking dir Midland Bank 1986–88, corp dir Samuel Montagu 1988–89, corp dir Midland Bank 1990–91, fin dir Corp & Institutional Banking HSBC Bank plc London 1991–94, on secondment as dir Industrial Devpt Unit DTI 1994–96; chief exec: English Partnerships 1996–98, South East England Devpt Agency 1998–2003; pres International Health Partners UK 2004–15, chm Two-Five-Four-O LLP 2004–07, pres IHP Inc 2009–15; dir: Kingsmead Homes 1997–99, Countryside Maritime 1997–2003, City Life 2002–03, Berkshire Learning and Skills Cncl 2002–04, Esteem Resource Network 2011–14 (tstee 2011–14, chm 2012–), Health Ptnrs Int of Canada 2010–15, Mercy Ships 2012–; chair EURMED 2013–15; cncllr Wadhurst Parish Cncl 2013–15; memb Urban Task Force 1998–2008; memb Advsy Bd: Insolvency Agency 1994–96, Relationships Fndn 2000–09; tstee AIDS Care & Educn Tst 2014–15; memb local church; FCIB 1981, FRSA 1997, MInstD 1999, hon FRCOG 2012; *Recreations* gardening, theatre, opera, music; *Style*— Anthony Dunnett, Esq, CBE; ✉ The Fold, Beech Hill, Wadhurst, East Sussex TN5 6JR (e-mail a.dunnett@me.com)

DUNNIGAN, David; s of Walter Dunnigan, and Jean, *née* Johnston; *b* 10 December 1961; *Educ* Univ of Nottingham (LLB), Chester Coll of Law; *m* 23 Jan 1993, Lavinia, *née* Buswell; 2 da (Anna b 31 March 1993, Clara b 10 July 1998), 1 s (William b 16 Nov 1994); *Career* admitted slr; articled clerk Turner Kenneth Brown 1984–86; Clifford Chance: joined 1987, ptnr 1992–, memb World Firm Mgmnt Ctee, global practice ldr capital markets; *Recreations* opera, fine wine, family; *Style*— David Dunnigan, Esq; ✉ Clifford Chance LLP, 10 Upper Bank Street, London E14 5JJ

DUNNING, Graham; QC (2001); s of Maj James Edwin Dunning, of Romsey, Hants, and Jane Priscilla, *née* Hunt; *b* 13 March 1958, Aldershot, Hants; *Educ* King Edward VI Sch Southampton, RMA Sandhurst, Emmanuel Coll Cambridge (entrance scholar, Squire law scholar, MA), Harvard Law Sch (Kennedy scholar, LLM); *m* 26 July 1986, Claire Abigael, da of Dr W S C Williams, of Oxford; 3 s (William, Thomas, Samuel), 1 da (Sophie); *Career* short serv ltd cmmn 3 RTR 1977; called to the Bar Lincoln's Inn 1982; practising barr specialising in commercial law and arbitration, memb Essex Court Chambers (formerly 4 Essex Court) 1983– (co-head of chambers 2013–); memb: Br Insur Law Assoc, Br Maritime Law Assoc, Commercial Bar Assoc (COMBAR), London Law and Commercial Bar Assoc, London Court of Int Arbitration, London Maritime Arbitrators Assoc; *Recreations* golf, skiing, family; *Clubs* Woking Golf, Rye Golf; *Style*— Graham Dunning, Esq, QC; ✉ Essex Court Chambers, 24 Lincoln's Inn Fields, London WC2A 3EG (☎ 020 7813 8000, fax 020 7813 8080, e-mail gdunning@essexcourt.net)

DUNSTER, Bill; *Educ* MA; *Career* fndr Bill Dunster architects ZEDfactory Ltd 1998–; RIBA; *Style*— Bill Dunster, Esq; ✉ ZEDfactory, 21 Sandmartin Way, Wallington, Surrey SM6 7DF

DUNSTON, John Herbert; *b* 10 July 1952, London; *Educ* The John Lyon Sch Harrow, Lyceé St Maixent l'École, Selwyn Coll Cambridge, Univ of York; *m* Aug 1988, Susie; 1 s (Matthew b 1990), 1 da (Naomi b 1992); *Career* Eng language asst Gymnasium Eppendorf Hamburg 1973–74, teacher and housemaster Cheltenham GS 1975–79, teacher Bancroft's Sch Woodford Green 1979–90 (head of modern languages 1983–90), head Sibford Sch Banbury 1990–96, head Leighton Park Sch Reading 1996–2010; inspector Ind Schs Jt Cncl 1995–1999, reporting inspector Ind Schs Inspectorate 1999–; chm: Quaker Schs Heads Conference 2001–03, Soc of Heads of Ind Schs 1999, Assoc for the Educn and Guardianship of Int Students 2004–06; memb Trg Team Independent Schs Inspectorate 2008; govr: John Lyon Sch Harrow, Crosfields Prep Sch Reading; Farmington Fellowship 2009, visiting fell Harris Manchester Coll Oxford 2009; author of numerous articles; tstee: Macular Disease Soc, Amaka Beautiful Child; Liveryman Worshipful Co of Musicians; Winston Churchill travelling fell 1990; ACIL 1977, FRSA 1994; *Recreations* music, piano, choral conducting, Paris, modern history, Reading FC, theatre, photography, hill-walking, travel, genealogy; *Clubs* East India; *Style*— John Dunston

DUNSTONE, Sir Charles William; kt (2012); *b* 21 November 1964; *Educ* Uppingham; *Career* former computer salesman NEC; estab Carphone Warehouse 1989 (currently chief exec); non-exec dir: HBOS plc, Daily Mail General Tst; chm Prince's Tst Trading Bd; *Recreations* sailing; *Style*— Sir Charles Dunstone; ✉ Carphone Warehouse, 1 Portal Way, London W3 6RS (☎ 020 8896 5000, fax 020 8896 5160)

DUNT, Vice Adm Peter; CB (2002), DL (Surrey 2011); s of Hugh Dunt, of Prestatyn, N Wales, and Margaret, *née* Morgan; *b* 23 June 1947; *Educ* Duke of York Sch Nairobi, Merchant Taylors'; *m* 3 Aug 1974, Lesley Rae, *née* Gilchrist; 2 da (Rebecca b 21 Nov 1979, Sarah b 6 Aug 1981); *Career* Supply and Secretariat Offr RNC 1965, various RN sea and shore appointments incl Sec to Adm Woodward and Gp Logistics Offr (Falklands conflict) HMS Hermes 1982; subsequent MOD appointments incl: Dep Dir New Mgmnt Strategy (Directorate of Naval Staff Duties) and Sec to Second Sea Lord, Cmd HMS Raleigh (Navy's Ratings' New Entry Trg Estab) 1992, Dir Naval Personnel Corp Programming until 1997; RCDS 1997, appointed Rear Adm 1998, COS and DG Naval Personnel Strategy and Plans to the Second Sea Lord and C-in-C Naval Home Cmd 1998–2000, Chief Naval Supply Offr 2000–02, sr directing staff RCDS 2001–02, promoted Vice Adm 2002, chief exec Defence Estates 2002–07, Chief Naval Logistics Offr 2005; Cncl White Ensign Assoc 2007–, pres Guildford Sea Cadets 2009–; tstee Grey Coat Fndn 2007–, chm of govrs Queen Anne's Sch Caversham 2007–, chair Royal Surrey County Hospital NHS Fndn Tst 2010–; FCIPD 2001; *Recreations* all sport, gardening, DIY; *Clubs* I Zingari, Free Foresters, Incogniti, The Mount; *Style*— Vice Adm Peter Dunt, CB, DL

DUNTHORNE, John William Bayne; s of Philip Bayne Dunthorne (d 2003), of Alton, Hants, and Ruth Mabelle, *née* Sturch (d 2007); *b* 26 August 1946, Meopham, Kent; *Educ* Abingdon Sch, Oxford Sch of Architecture (DipArch); *m* 16 Aug 1974, Maggie Alice, da of John Edgar Taylor (d 1988), of Blofield, Norfolk; 1 da (Joanna b 1981), 1 s (Oliver b 1983); *Career* assoc ptnr Chapman Lisle Assocs 1972–74, jt sr ptnr Dunthorne Parker Architects 1978–, dir DPSL 1985–; RIBA 1973; *Projects* incl: offices for BUPA, Brooke Bond and Swiss Life, industrial parks, historic shopping schemes in Oxford, Colchester, High Wycombe and Bury St Edmunds, restoration of Grade I listed buildings Golden Cross in Oxford, Red Lion in Colchester, Grade II offices in Clifton, residential schemes in Whitehall and Featherstone St London, masterplanning and phase 1 of Kendrew Quadrangle for St John's Coll Oxford 2001–08; *Awards* incl: Robertson Award, Ideas in Architecture Award, Oxford Preservation Tst Award, Royal Tunbridge Wells Civic Soc Conservation Award, Civic Tst Award; *Books* An Airport Interface (with M P Parker, 1971); *Recreations* cricket, golf, skiing; *Clubs* MCC, Chelsea Arts, Forty, Lord Gnome's CC; *Style*— J W B Dunthorne, Esq; ✉ 5 Aspley Road, London SW18 2DB; Dunthorne Parker, Architects, 16 Hampton Gurney Street, London W1H 5AL (☎ 020 7258 0411)

DUNWICH, Bishop of 2016–; Rt Rev Michael Robert (Mike) Harrison; *b* 7 March 1963, Bolton; *m* 8 Aug 1992, Rachel Anne, *née* Bentley; 3 da (Susannah b 21 Oct 1994, Sarah b 15 Oct 2002, Rebekah b 27 April 2009), 1 s (Nathaniel b 24 March 1997); *Career* ordained: deacon 1990, priest 1991; curate St Anne and All Saints Dio of Southwark 1990–94, chaplain Univ of Bradford and Bradford and Ilkley Community Coll, vicar Holy Trinity Eltham 1998–2006 (rural dean Eltham and Mottingham 2005–06), dir Ministry and Mission Dio of Leicester 2006–16; *Recreations* live comedy; *Style*— The Rt Rev the Bishop of Dunwich; ✉ Bishop's House, 4 Park Road, Ipswich IP1 3ST (☎ 0173 252829, e-mail bishop.mike@cofesuffolk.org)

DUPLEIX, Jillian Edith; da of Edward Anzac Dupleix, of Victoria, Aust, and Rosemary Ann, *née* Campbell; *Educ* Hermitage C of E Girls' GS Geelong; *m* 26 June 1981, Terry Peter Durack; *Career* food writer, cookery editor, author and photographer; food columnist Melbourne Age 1981–87 and 1990–95, restaurant critic Melbourne Herald 1987–90; food ed: New Woman 1991–94, Elle Australia 1994–98, Sunday Age 1994–98, Sydney Morning Herald 1994–2000; The Times Cook and cookery ed The Times 2000–07; ed (with Terry Durack) Sydney Morning Herald Good Food Guide 1994–2001, ed Sydney Morning Herald Good Cafe Guide 2009–, ed Hot Food SMH 2012–, food and wine publishing conslt Murdoch Books 2013–, food ed Australian Financial Review Magazine 2015–, co-dir Australia's Top Restaurants 2015–; creative dir Melbourne Food & Wine Festival 2009–10, food curator TEDxSydney 2013–; Cookery Journalist of the Year Br Guild of Food Writers 2002; *Books* incl: Hot Food Cool Jazz (1993), New Food (1994), Allegro Al Dente (1995), Old Food (1998), Simple Food (2002), Very Simple Food (2003), Good Cooking (2005), Lighten Up (2007), Sydney Morning Herald Good Cafe Guide (2010, 2011, 2013); *Recreations* eating and drinking; *Style*— Ms Jill Dupleix; ✉ e-mail jill@jilldupleix.com

DURANTE, Nicandro; *Career* British American Tobacco plc: joined Souza Cruz Brazil 1981, fin dir Hong Kong 1998–2000, fin dir then pres Souza Cruz Brazil 2000–06, memb Bd 2006–, regnl dir Africa and ME then chief operating offr until 2010, chief exec designate 2010–11, chief exec 2011–; *Style*— Mr Nicandro Durante; ✉ British American Tobacco plc, Globe House, 4 Temple Place, London WC2R 2PG

DURBIN, Dr Richard Michael; *Educ* Univ of Cambridge; *m* Julie; 1 da (Zoe b 26 Dec 1997), 1 s (Benjamin b 19 Feb 2000); *Career* research posts: Lab of Molecular Biology Univ of Cambridge, Harvard Univ, Stanford Univ; sr gp ldr and acting head Computational Genomics Wellcome Tst Sanger Inst; FRS 2004; *Books* The Computing Neuron (jt ed, 1989), Biological Sequence Analysis: Probabilistic Models of Proteins and Nucleic Acids (jtly, 1998); *Style*— Dr Richard Durbin; ✉ Wellcome Trust Sanger Institute, Wellcome Trust Genome Campus, Hinxton, Cambridge CB10 1SA

DURCAN, Paul; s of John James Durcan (d 1988), and Sheila MacBride (d 2004); *b* 16 October 1944; *Educ* Gonzaga Coll Dublin, UC Cork (BA); *m* 1 Aug 1967 (sep), Nessa, *née* O'Neill; 2 da (Sarah O'Neill b 22 June 1969, Siabhra O'Neill b 20 July 1970); *Career* poet; Patrick Kavanagh Award 1974, Irish American Cultural Institute Poetry Award 1989, Whitbread Poetry Award 1990, Heinemann Bequest Royal Soc of Literature 1995, Cholmondley Award for Poetry 2001; Ireland prof of poetry 2004–07; memb Aosdána 1981; Hon DLitt Trinity Coll Dublin 2009, Hon DLitt UC Dublin 2011; *Poetry* O Westport In The Light of Asia Minor (1975), Teresa's Bar (1976), Sam's Cross (1978), Selected Poems (1982), The Berlin Wall Café (1985, Poetry Book Soc Choice 1985), Going Home To Russia (1987), Jesus and Angela (1988), Daddy, Daddy (1990), Crazy About Women (1991), A Snail In My Prime (1993), Give Me Your Hand (1994), Christmas Day (1996, Poetry Book Soc Recommendation 1996), Greetings to Our Friends in Brazil (1999, Poetry Book Soc Recommendation 1999), Cries of an Irish Caveman (2001), Paul Durcan's Diary (2003), The Art of Life (2004), The Laughter of Mothers (2007), Life Is A Dream (2009), Praise In Which I Live and Move and Have My Being (2012); *Recreations* walking; *Style*— Paul Durcan, Esq; ✉ 14 Cambridge Avenue, Ringsend, Dublin 4 (☎ 00 353 01 668 2276)

DURDEN-SMITH, Neil; OBE (1997); s of Anthony James Durden-Smith MB, BS, FRCS (d 1963), of Middx, and Grace Elizabeth, *née* Neill (d 1938); *b* 18 August 1933; *Educ* Aldenham, BRNC Dartmouth; *m* 3 Jan 1964, Judith Chalmers, OBE, *qv*, da of David Norman Chalmers, FRICS (d 1952), of Cheshire; 1 da (Emma (Mrs Gordon Dawson) b 1967), 1 s (Mark b 1968); *Career* RN 1952–63 (Capt HMS Rampart 1961–62); ADC to Govr-Gen of NZ 1957–59; played cricket and hockey for RN, Combined Services and Herts; prodr BBC Outside Broadcasts Dept (special responsibility 1966 World Cup) 1963–66; radio and TV broadcasting incl: Test Match and Co Cricket, Olympic Games 1968 and 1972, Trooping the Colour, Royal Tournament, Money Matters, Sports Special; chm and md Durden-Smith Communications 1974–81, dir Ruben Sedgwick 1987–95, dir Tangible Securities; chm: Sports Sponsorship Int 1982–87, The Altro Group 1982–94, Woodside Communications 1992–; conslt AON 1995–; dir: BCM Grandstand 1993–, Children in Crisis 1993–95, The Anglo-American Sporting Clubs 1969–74; chm Lord's Taverners 1980–82 (pres Middx Region 1993–), pres Lord's Taverners Buccaneers; vice-pres: Eng Schools Cricket Assoc, Northwood Cricket Club, Eng Indoor Hockey Assoc, The Peter May Meml Appeal; chm The Brian Johnston Meml Tst 1994–99; patron: Motor Neurone Disease Assoc, Aspire, Westminster Soc for People with Hearing Difficulties; tstee: ISIS Assoc, Charlie Waller Meml Tst, The Martin Lawrence Meml Tst; pres Vale do Lobo Property Owners' Assoc; Freeman City of London; *Books* Forward for England (1967), World Cup '66 (1967); *Recreations* theatre, current affairs, cricket, rugby, golf, reading the newspapers; *Clubs* MCC, Lord's Taverners, Saints & Sinners, I Zingari, Free Foresters, Lords & Commons Cricket, RN Cricket, County Cricketers Golf, Cricket Writers, Home House, Castaways, Highgate Golf, Vale do Lobo Golf, Archerfield Golf, Ladykillers, Surbiton Hockey, Forty; *Style*— Neil Durden-Smith, Esq, OBE; ✉ 28 Hillway, Highgate, London N6 6HH (☎ 020 8348 2340, fax 020 8348 8224)

DURGAN, Graham Richard; *b* 7 January 1957; *Educ* BSc; *m* Jane; 2 s, 1 da; *Career* Deloitte & Co 1977–82, fin trg 1982–85, md BPP Accountancy Courses Ltd 1985–88, dir Esprit Ltd 1988–90; chief exec: Business Training Network 1990–92, Accountancy Tuition Centres 1992–99, BNB Resources plc 1997–2000, Durgan Monstein plc 2001–; chm: Emile Woolf International 2002–, Foulks Lynch plc 2002–04, TPMA 2006–, Non-Exec Dirs Assoc 2007–, Thomas Murray 2007–, Int Financial Publishing 2007–; memb Cncl ICAEW 1995–2010 and 2011–; FCA; *Books* Essential Strategy; *Recreations* sailing, skiing, tennis; *Clubs* Travellers; *Style*— Graham Durgan, Esq

DURHAM, Archdeacon of; *see:* Jagger, Ven Ian

DURHAM, Dean of; *see:* Sadgrove, Very Rev Michael

DURHAM, Bishop of 2014–; Rt Rev Paul Roger Butler; s of Denys Michael Butler, and Jean Florence, *née* Giddy; *b* 18 September 1955, Kingston upon Thames; *Educ* Kingston GS, Univ of Nottingham (BA), Wycliffe Hall Oxford (BA, CertTheol); *m* 11 Sept 1982, Rosemary Jean, *née* Johnson; 2 da (Caroline Mary b 17 Aug 1985, Sarah Bethany b 22 Feb 1994), 2 s (David Peter b 27 March 1987, Andrew Paul b 28 May 1989); *Career* travelling sec UCCF 1978–80, curate All Saints with Holy Trinity Wandsworth 1983–87, dep head of missions Scripture Union 1992–94 (inner London evangelist 1987–92), team rector Walthamstow 1994–2004, area dean Waltham Forest 2001–04, bishop of Southampton 2004–10, bishop of Southwell and Nottingham 2010–14; canon Byumba Cathedral Rwanda 2001–; chair Friends of Byumba Tst, chair Church Mission Soc 2007–10, pres Scripture Union; hon doctorate Univ of Nottingham 2016; Reaching Children (1992), Following Jesus (1993), Friends of God (1993), Want to be in God's Family? (1994), Growing Up in God's Family (1994), Reaching Families (1995), Temptation and Testing (2007), Through the Eyes of a Child (contrib, 2009), Offering the Best in Children's Ministry (2011), Living Your Confirmation (2012), Being a Curate (contrib, 2014), Clergy in a Complex Age (contrib, 2016); *Recreations* gardening, walking, reading; *Style*— The Rt Rev the Bishop of Durham

DURHAM, Vivienne Mary; da of Donald Johnson, of Chichester, W Sussex, and Patricia, *née* Wiltshire; *b* 12 July 1961, Rustington, W Sussex; *Educ* St Hilda's Coll Oxford (MA), PGCE; *m* 1984, Kenneth Durham, *qv*; *Career* teacher; Haberdashers' Aske's Sch for Girls 1983–87, Godolphin & Latymer Sch 1987–91, head of Eng Guildford HS 1991–93, head of Eng Haberdashers' Aske's 1993–97, dep head South Hampstead HS 1997–2004, headmistress Francis Holland Sch 2004–15; accredited inspr Ind Schs Inspectorate 2000–15; dir Schs Advsy Service Enjoy Education 2016–; memb Exec Ctee Ind Schs Examinations Bd (ISEB), GSA rep HMC/GSA Univs Ctee; govr Sarum Hall Sch London; Best Head of a Public School: Tatler Head of Year 2015; memb: GSA 2004, SHA, HMC, RSA; *Recreations* reading, theatre, cinema, opera, riding, tennis, skiing, travel; *Clubs* Univ Women's, Lansdowne; *Style*— Mrs Vivienne Durham; ✉ Enjoy Education, 1 Relton Mews, Knightsbridge, London SW7 1ET (☎ 020 7352 8800, website www.enjoyeducation.co.uk)

DURHAM HALL, His Hon Judge Jonathan David; QC (1995); *b* 2 June 1952; *Educ* King Edward VII Sch Sheffield, Univ of Nottingham (LLB); *m* 1, Patricia Helen Bychowska; 1 da (Antonia b 14 July 1977), 1 s (Christian b 29 Oct 1980); m 2, Hilary Hart; *Career* called to the Bar Gray's Inn 1975; in practice NE Circuit, recorder 1995–2003 (asst recorder 1991–95), head of chambers 1995–2003, circuit judge (Wales & Chester Circuit) 2003–; memb Gen Cncl of the Bar 1994–95, chm Mental Health Review Tbnl, legal assessor GMC; memb Gray's Inn Barristers' Ctee; former memb Parochial Deanery and Diocesan Synod; served TA The Hallamshire Regt 1969–72; *Recreations* walking, all things countryside especially creation of rural woodland, plays of Shakespeare, all things Portuguese; *Style*— His Hon Judge Durham Hall, QC; ✉ Bradford Law Courts, Exchange Square, Bradford BD 1 1JA

DURKAN, (John) Mark; MP; s of Brendan Durkan, and Isobel, *née* Tinney; *b* 26 June 1960; *Educ* St Columb's Coll Derry, Queen's Univ Belfast; *m* 10 Sept 1993, Jackie, *née* Green; 1 c (Dearbhàil b 10 Jan 2005); *Career* asst to John Hume MP 1984–98; memb Derry City Cncl 1993–2000; chairperson SDLP 1990–95, Multi-Party Talks Negotiator SDLP 1996–98, MLA (SDLP) Foyle 1998–2010; min of finance and personnel 1999–2001, dep first min 2001–02; ldr SDLP 2001–10; MP (SDLP) Foyle 2005–; *Style*— Mark Durkan, Esq, MP; ✉ 23 Bishop Street, Derry BT48 6PR (☎ 02871 360700, fax 02871 360808, e-mail m.durkan@sdlp.ie); House of Commons, London SW1A 0AA (☎ 020 7219 5096, e-mail mark.durkan.mp@parliament.uk)

DURKIN, Dr Michael Anthony Patrick; s of John Durkin (d 1986), of Cheltenham and Wimbledon, and Philomena, *née* O'Shea (d 1999); *b* 26 July 1950; *Educ* Whitefriars Sch Cheltenham, Middx Hosp Med Sch London (MB BS); *m* 19 July 1978, Susan Claire, da of Lawrence Paul Cotterell, of Cheltenham; 3 s (Luke b 1979, Jack b 1981, James b 1983), 1 da (Ellen b 1990); *Career* registrar in anaesthesia St Thomas' Hosp London 1976–79, res registrar Middx Hosp London 1980–81, sr registrar S Western RHA 1981–85; Gloucestershire Royal Hosp: conslt in anaesthesia and intensive care 1985–, clinical dir and chm Med Staff Ctee; med dir Gloucestershire Royal NHS Tst 1993–2002, med dir and dir of clinical quality Avon, Gloucestershire and Wiltshire Strategic HA 2003–06 (exec dir of clinical performance 2002–03), medical dir South West Strategic Health Authority 2006–, currently nat dir of patient safety NHS England; visiting prof Yale Univ Sch of Med (asst prof 1982–84, visiting assoc faculty 1989); lectr Keele Univ 1996–, med dir tutor NHS Leadership Prog 2001–; chapters in books and articles in jls on anaesthesia, intensive care and monitoring, ed Anaesthesia Points West; referee: BMJ, Intensive Care Med, Critical Care Med, Br Jl of Hosp Med; chair: Quality Taskforce NHS Exec SW, Clinical Governance Taskforce for South West, Genetics Steering Bd for South; memb Ctee: Soc of Anaesthetists of S Western Region, Gloucestershire Clinical Advsy Gp, Medical Workforce Advsy Gp, Cancer Strategy Gp, Research and Devpt Gp Gloucestershire HA; memb Cncl: Inst of Medical Sciences Cranfield Univ, Gloucestershire Royal Hosp, Univ for Gloucester Steering Gp; memb: Regnl Modernisation Bd NHS Exec SW, Emergency Planning Steering Gp DH; co-leader Clinical Governance and Leadership Review Team Ethiopia; tstee Intensive Care Charity; memb: Euro Intensive Care Soc, Int Anaesthesia Res Soc, Intensive Care Soc, Assoc of Anaesthetists GB, Assoc of Trust Medical Dirs, Br Assoc of Medical Mangrs, BMA; FRCA 1981, FCAnaes; *Books* Post Anaesthetic Recovery (3 edn, 1996); *Recreations* skiing, tennis, watching rugby; *Clubs* Lilleybrook; *Style*— Dr Michael Durkin

DURLACHER, Nicholas John; CBE (1995); s of John Sydney Durlacher, MC; *b* 20 March 1946; *Educ* Stowe, Magdalene Coll Cambridge; *m* 1971, Mary Caroline, da of Maj Guy Lewis Ian McLaren (d 1978); 1 s (David Michael b 1976); *Career* memb London Stock Exchange 1971–86; chm: LIFFE 1992–95, Securities and Futures Authy 1995–2001, Ennismore Smaller Cos 1999–, EMX Co 2000–07, Elexon Ltd 2000–, Electricity Balancing and Settlement Code Panel 2000–, Quilter Global Enhanced Income Tst plc 2000–05, FFastFill plc 2000–02; *Recreations* skiing, tennis, golf, shooting; *Clubs* White's; *Style*— Nicholas Durlacher, Esq, CBE; ✉ Elexon Ltd, 350 Euston Road, London NW1 3AW (☎ 020 7380 4252, e-mail nick.durlacher@elexon.co.uk)

DURLING, Prof David; *b* 15 October 1946; *Educ* Sir Philip Magnus Secdy Tech Sch London, Barnet Coll of FE (fndn course), Buckinghamshire Inst High Wycombe (BA), RCA (MA), Open Univ (PhD 1996); *m* Aug 2008, Prof Kristina Niedderer; 1 c (b 1987); *Career* industrial and furniture designer; design asst then sr designer and assoc i/c industrial design team Graphics + Industrial Design Ltd Richmond Surrey 1971–75 (clients incl Royal Navy, Vickers Ship Engineering, ICI), freelance designer London 1975–76, sr designer Architect's Dept Notts CC 1976–83 (i/c interiors, furniture design and building graphics), sr lectr in industrial design Sheffield City Poly 1983–84, fndr dir EDGE Ltd design and R&D conslts 1984–96 (pt/t dir 1984–89), course ldr and sr lectr in 3D design (furniture) Sch of Industrial Design Leicester Poly 1986–89, md Lab Systems Ltd mfrs of laboratory furniture and equipment in UK 1991–93, dir Advanced Research Inst Sch of Art and Design Staffs Univ 1996, prof of design Sch of Arts and Educn Middlesex Univ 2004–09, assoc dean (research) Birmingham Inst of Art and Design 2009–12, prof

D

of design research Coventry Univ 2012–; various visiting lectureships, visiting prof in design Univ of Central Lancashire, external examiner for industrial design Nat Univ of Singapore; registered inspr FE Funding Cncl 1993–96; Chartered Soc of Designers: memb Nat Cncl 1987–91, local organiser Sheffield Area 1987–91, chm NE Regnl Cncl 1987–91; memb Nat Cncl Design Res Soc 1993–2006 (ed DR News 1996–, chm 1998–2006, fell), sec gen Int Assoc of Socs of Design Research 2011–, memb various tech ctees BSI; appointed memb panel for Art and Design Res Assessment Exercise 2001 HEFCE 2001 and 2008, FRSA, hon fell Design Research Soc 2016; *Recreations* yacht cruising, sea fishing, cycling, reading and cyberspace; *Style*— Prof David Durling; ✉ website http://durling.tel

DURRANI, Prof Tariq Salim; OBE (2003); s of Mohammed Salim Khan Durrani (d 1980), of London, and Bilquis Jamal; *b* 27 October 1943; *Educ* EPUET Dacca Bangladesh (BEng), Univ of Southampton (MSc, PhD); *m* 6 Aug 1972, Clare Elizabeth, da of late Howard Kellas; 2 da (Monise Nadia b 1977, Sophia Jasmine b 1981), 1 s (Jamiel Tariq b 1986); *Career* res fell Univ of Southampton 1970–76; Univ of Strathclyde: lectr 1976–79, sr lectr 1979–82, prof of signal processing 1982–, chm Dept of Electronic and Electrical Engrg 1986–90, dep princ (IT) 1990–91, dep princ 2000–06, sr advsr 2006–; IEEE: pres Signal Processing Soc 1994–96, chm Periodicals Cncl 1996–97, former chm Professional Gps on Signal Processing and Image Processing, vice-chair Technical Activities Region 8, pres Engrg Mgmnt Soc 2006–07, vice-pres (educnl activities) 2010–11; RSE: memb Cncl 2003–06, vice-convenor Int Ctee 2006–, vice-pres (int) 2008–15; chm: Centre for Parallel Signal Processing, Scottish Electronics Technol Gp; dir Inst of System Level Integration 2000–18; vice-chair UNESCO UK Nat Cmmn Science Ctee 2010–; memb: Scottish Science Advsy Ctee 2002–04, Scottish Funding Cncl 2006–; GG2 Leadership and Diversity Award as Asian Man of the Year 1999, IEEE Millennium Medal 2000, IEEE Signal Processing Soc Meritorious Service Award 2000; dir: Scottish Inst for Enterprise 2001–04, Glasgow C of C 2002–13, Leadership Foundation for Higher Educn 2004–09; FIEE 1983, FIEEE 1989, FRSE 1994, FREng 1996; *Books* Laser Systems in Flow Measurements (with C Greated, 1977), Geophysical Signal Processing (with E A Robinson, 1986), Signal Processing (co-ed with J L Lacoume and R Stora, 1987), Mathematics and Signal Processing (ed, 1987), Transputer Applications 3 (ed, 1991); *Recreations* swimming; *Clubs* Ross Priory, Western (Glasgow); *Style*— Prof Tariq Durrani, OBE, FRSE, FREng; ✉ 14 Duchess Park, Helensburgh, Dunbartonshire G84 9PY (☎ 01436 676590); University of Strathclyde, Department of Electronic and Electrical Engineering, 204 George Street, Glasgow G1 1XW (☎ 0141 548 2540, fax 0141 552 2487, e-mail durrani@strath.ac.uk)

DURRANT, Hugh Russell; s of Derek Walter Durrant (d 1990), and Elsie Violet, *née* Russell (d 1980); *b* 12 July 1947; *Educ* Latymer Upper Sch, Magdalene Coll Cambridge (MA); *Career* costume, set and fashion designer; head of design: Birmingham Repertory 1973–76, Theatre Royal York 1976–78, Northcott Theatre Exeter 1979–81; assoc dir Nottingham Playhouse 1982–85; fashion posts held incl: Emanuel couture 1985, head of design Cojana Ltd London 1985–90, couture designer Rafa Abu Dhabi 1991–92; estab own couture label 1988; design conslt (scenery) Holland America Westours Ltd 1993–2012; exhibition design The Triumph of Pleasure (Foundling Museum) 2012; visiting prof: Nat Theater Inst Eugene O'Neill Center USA 1996–98, London Acad of Theatre 1999–2001; memb Acad of Television Arts and Sciences USA; *Theatre* designed over 14 prodns Regent's Park Open Air Theatre, 12 pantomimes for Paul Elliott; costume design credits incl: Mystery of Irma Vep (Ambassadors) 1990, Seven Brides for Seven Brothers (Old Vic and Prince of Wales, London and Canada), The Mikado (Cambridge and Prince of Wales), Barry Manilow's Copacabana (Prince of Wales) 1994–95 (also UK tour 1995–96, Holland and America 1998, Australia 1999), Cher Farewell Tour and NBC special (USA) 2002 (Emmy Award Best Costume Design 2003); set and costume credits incl: Sister Mary Ignatius (Ambassadors) 1984, The Hot Shoe Show (Palladium) 1984, Cinderella (Palladium) 1985, Babes in the Wood (Palladium) 1986–87, Lock Up Your Daughters (Chichester and Savoy Theatre London) 1996, Lady Windermere's Fan (Chichester) 1997, Sandy Wilson's Divorce Me Darling (Chichester) 1997 (TMA Award for Best Musical), Jerry Herman's The Best of Times (Vaudeville) 1998, Nymph Errant (Chichester) 1999, Midnight Fantasy (Luxor Las Vegas) 2000, Dreamcatcher (UK) 2001, Ann-Margret...Here, Now! (USA tour) 2003, The Boyfriend (UK tour, 50th anniversary prodn) 2003, Jack and the Beanstalk (Nelson Mandela Theatre Johannesburg) 2003, Full Circle with Joan Collins (Triumph Prodns) 2004, The Merry Widow (Carl Rosa Opera) 2004, Wonderland (Harrah's Casino Reno) 2004, New Fantasies (Luxor Las Vegas) 2005, Manilow: Music and Passion (Las Vegas and USA tour), Babes in Arms (Chichester and West End) 2007, Cher (Caesar's Palace Las Vegas) 2008, Spamalot (Pinter and Playhouse Theatres West End) 2012–13, Cher: Dressed to Kill (all costumes, USA tour) 2015, Nell Gwynn (Globe Playhouse) 2015 and (Apollo Theatre) 2016 (Best Costume Design Olivier Award nomination); UK tours incl: Amadeus, A Little Night Music, Company, Naked Justice, Hot Flush, Monty Python's Spamalot 2010–11, Rocky Horror Show: 40th Anniversary Production 2013–16 (also Australia tour 2014); Br premieres incl: Mack and Mabel, Lady in the Dark; *Dance* credits incl: Symphony in Waves (Dutch Nat Ballet), Frankenstein (Royal Ballet, La Scala Milan, Dutch Nat Ballet (sets only)), Footnotes (Nederland Dans), Window & Sleeping Birds (Rambert), Dash and Hot Shoe Show (for Wayne Sleep, *qv*); *Other Credits* incl: Thomas Hardy's The Dynasts (Exeter Cathedral 900th anniversary (adapted and designed)), Voices from the Great War (Nottingham Playhouse (adapted, designed and directed)); concert costumes for: Sarah Brightman 1985–97, Cher, Ruthie Henshall, Gloria Hunniford, Barry Manilow; photographic styling for Cher 2002; new safety curtain design Wimbledon Theatre 2009, designer of new uniforms for entire Holland America Westours fleet 2015; *Television* and film incl: Ivanhoe (costumes), Boadicea (prodn designer), Young Alexander (costume designer), Telephone Detectives (prodn and costume designer); videos: Sarah Brightman, Andrea Bocelli, The Hey-Makers; *Style*— Hugh Durrant, Esq; ✉ website www.hughdurrant.co.uk; c/o Jean Diamond, Diamond Management, 31 Percy Street, London W1T 2DD (☎ 020 7631 0400, e-mail setsquare1@me.com)

DURRANT, John; s of Edward Henry Samual Stokes Durrant (d 1972), and Phyllis, *née* Howard-Spink (d 1988); *b* 6 July 1949; *Educ* N Paddington Sch, Oxford Poly (now Oxford Brooks Univ) (DMS); *m* June 1974, Susan, da of Thomas Clark, of Cliftonville, Kent; 3 s (Oliver Jon b 20 Nov 1975, Thomas Edward b 22 Sept 1978, William Jack b 3 Dec 1981); *Career* promotion mangr W B Saunders medical publishers London 1969–73, mktg dir European Bibliographical Centre Oxford 1973–78; Clio Press Ltd Oxford: jt md 1978–81, chm and md 1981–94, currently dir; chm and md: Isis Publishing Ltd Oxford and Orlando USA 1994–, Soundings Ltd Newcastle upon Tyne; *Books* Microcomputer Software Guide (1982), Microcomputer Software Guide Vol II (1982); *Style*— John Durrant, Esq; ✉ Isis Publishing Ltd, 7 Centremead, Osney Mead, Oxford OX2 0ES (☎ 01865 250333, fax 01865 790358)

DURRELL, Prof Martin; s of Leslie Hay Durrell (d 1972), of Coltishall, Norfolk, and Audrey Lillian, *née* Easton; *b* 6 November 1943, Norwich; *Educ* Manchester Grammar, Jesus Coll Cambridge (MA), Univ of Manchester (DipLing), Univ of Marburg (Dr Phil); *m* 30 Aug 1969, Ruth, da of Geoffrey Loy Barlow (d 1977), of Bury, Lancs; 1 s (John b 1975), 1 da (Ann b 1978); *Career* sr lectr (formerly lectr) Univ of Manchester 1967–86, guest prof Univ of Alberta 1983–84; prof of German: Univ of London 1986–90, Univ of Manchester 1990–2008 (prof emeritus 2008–); vice-pres Int Assoc of Germanists 2004–05, corresponding memb Int Academic Cncl Institut für Deutsche Sprache 1984–2012; Philological Soc: memb Cncl 1989–, hon treas 1994–2008; Cross Order of Merit of the Federal Repub of Germany 2002; *Publications* Hammer's German Grammar and Usage (5 edn, 2011); *Recreations* music, theatre, ornithology; *Style*— Prof Martin Durrell; ✉ School of Arts, Languages and Cultures, University of Manchester, Manchester M13 9PL (☎ 0161 275 3185, e-mail martin.durrell@manchester.ac.uk)

DURRINGTON, Prof Paul Nelson; s of late Alec Edward Durrington, of Wilmslow, Cheshire, and late May Ena, *née* Nelson; *b* 24 July 1947; *Educ* Chislehurst and Sidcup GS, Univ of Bristol (BSc, MB, ChB, MD); *m* 13 Dec 1969, Patricia Joyce, da of late Capt Alfred Newton Gibbs, MBE, MC, of Barming, Kent; 2 da (Hannah Jane b 1975, Charlotte Lucy b 1987), 1 s (Mark Christopher Newton b 1977); *Career* house offr and sr house offr appts 1972–76 (Bristol Royal Infirmary, Bristol Royal Hosp for Sick Children, Frenchay Hosp Bristol); travelling fell: Br Heart Fndn, American Heart Assoc Univ of Calif San Diego 1979–80; Univ of Manchester: lectr in med 1976–82, sr lectr in med 1982–92, reader in med 1992–95, prof of med 1995–; hon conslt physician Manchester Royal Infirmary 1982–2012; med dir Family Heart Assoc 1995–2005, dir of R&D Central Manchester Healthcare Tst 1997–2001; chm Br Hyperlipidaemia Assoc 1992–95; memb Editorial Bd Atherosclerosis; FRCP 1987, FRCPath 1994, FMedSci 2001, fell American Heart Assoc (FAHA) 2001; *Books* Hyperlipidaemia Diagnosis and Management (1989, 3 edn 2007), Hyperlipidaemia (with Allan Sniderman 2000, 5 edn 2010); *Recreations* angling, hill-walking, wine; *Clubs* Prince Albert Angling Soc, Old Boys' and Park Green, Ramblers' Assoc; *Style*— Prof Paul Durrington; ✉ Cardiovascular Research Group, School of Biomedicine, University of Manchester, Core Technology Facility (3rd Floor), 46 Grafton Street, Manchester M13 9NT (☎ 0161 275 1201, fax 0161 275 1183, e-mail pdurrington@manchester.ac.uk)

DUTHIE, Sir Robert Grieve (Robin); kt (1987), CBE (1978); s of George Duthie, and Mary, *née* Lyle; *b* 2 October 1928; *Educ* Greenock Acad; *m* 5 April 1955, (Violetta) Noel, da of Harry Maclean; 2 s (David b 1956, Peter b 1959), 1 da (Susan b 1962); *Career* Nat Serv 1946–49; apprentice CA Thomson Jackson Gourlay & Taylor 1946–51, qualified CA 1952; chm: Black & Edgington plc 1972–83 (md 1962–80), R G Duthie and Company Ltd 1983–, Bruntons (Musselburgh) plc 1984–86, Britoil plc 1988–90, Capital House plc 1988–92, Tay Residential Investments plc 1989–96, Neill Clerk Group plc 1994–98; dir: British Asset Trust plc 1977–98, Royal Bank of Scotland plc 1978–99, Insight Gp plc 1983–90 (formerly Black and Edgington), Investors Capital Tst plc 1985–95, Carclo Engineering Gp plc 1986–98, Royal Bank of Scotland Gp plc 1986–99, Sea Catch plc 1987–93, British Polythene Industries plc 1988–99, Charterhouse plc 1991–93, Devol Engineering Ltd 1994–2003; chm: Made Up Textiles Assoc of Great Britain 1972, Clyde Port Authy 1978–81, Scottish Development Agency 1979–88; vice-chm BP Advsy Bd Scotland 1990–2002; treas Greenock West United Reform Church Greenock 1970–; memb: Scottish Telecommunications Bd 1972–78, Scottish Econ Cncl 1980–95, Ct Univ of Strathclyde 1988–94; Hon LLD Univ of Strathclyde 1984, Hon DTech Napier Univ 1989; CIMgt 1975, FRSA 1983, FScotvec 1988, FRIAS 1989; *Recreations* curling, golf; *Style*— Sir Robin Duthie, CBE; ✉ Fairhaven, 181 Finnart Street, Greenock, Strathclyde (☎ 01475 722642)

DUTTON, Maj-Gen Bryan Hawkins; CB (1997), CBE (1990, OBE 1984, MBE 1978); s of George Ralph Neale Dutton (d 1983), and Honor Badcoe, *née* Morris (d 2007); *b* 1 March 1943, Chester; *Educ* Lord Weymouth Sch, RMA Sandhurst, RMCS Shrivenham, Staff Coll Camberley; *m* 15 July 1972, Angela Margaret, da of Harold Keith Wilson (d 1970); 1 s (Charles b 1974), 1 da (Sophie b 1977); *Career* cmmnd Devonshire and Dorset Regt 1963, Regtl serv 1963–73 (NI, Germany, Libya, Br Guiana, UK, Belize); C-in-C's Mission to Soviet forces in E Germany 1976–78, Regtl duty NI and BAOR 1978–79 (despatches 1979), staff security co-ordinator NI 1979–81, instr Staff Coll Camberley 1981–82, mil asst to Adj-Gen 1982–84, CO 1 Bn Devonshire and Dorset Regt NI and Berlin 1984–87, UKLF overseas ops 1987, cmd 39 Infantry Brigade Ulster 1987–89, Dir Public Relations (Army) 1990–92, Dir of Infantry 1992–94, Cdr Br Forces Hong Kong 1994–97 (Handover to PLA/PRC); Col Cmdt The Prince of Wales's Div 1996–99, Col The Devonshire and Dorset Regt 1998–2003; DG Leonard Cheshire Disability 1998–2008; govr Holidaycare 1999–2003, tstee and govr E Hayes Dashwood Housing Assoc 1999–, tstee Hong Kong LEP Tst 1994–2010; chair Voluntary Organisations Disability Gp 2004–08, chair Military Museum of Devon and Dorset 2008–, chair Action for Stammering Children (formerly Assoc for Research into Stammering in Childhood) 2009–14; CCIM 2003, FRSA 2003; *Recreations* country pursuits, wildlife, music, history, learning golf; *Style*— Maj-Gen Bryan Dutton, CB, CBE; ✉ Highwood, Bugmore Lane, East Grimstead, Wiltshire SP5 3SA

DUTTON, His Hon Judge Roger Thomas Dutton; DL; s of late Donald Roger Dutton, JP, and late Doreen May, *née* Ankers; *b* 24 March 1952; *Educ* Grove Park GS Wrexham, Univ of Kent at Canterbury (BA), Inns of Court Sch of Law; *m* 9 July 1977, Elaine Alison, *née* Dixon (d 2014); 2 da (Katie Joanna b 23 Dec 1980, Sarah Louise b 5 Aug 1983), 1 s (James Roger George b 3 April 1991); *Career* called to the Bar Middle Temple 1974; in practice King St Chambers Chester 1974–96, asst recorder 1988–92, recorder 1992–96; circuit judge: (Wales & Chester Circuit) 1996–, (Northern Circuit) 2007–; liaison judge N Wales Magistrates 1999–2003, currently liaison judge Crewe, Nantwich and Macclesfield Justices and temp resident judge Chester Crown Court 2016–; memb: Cncl of Circuit Judges 1996–, memb Judicial Appt Cmmn's panel for interviewing for circuit judge and recorder applicants 1999, Judicial Studies Tutor Judge Panel 2007–, Lord Chief Justice's Disciplinary Panel for Judges 2007–; pres Cncl of HM's Circuit Judges 2014 (circuit rep Ctee 2004–05, hon treas 2005–12); memb Judges' Cncl 2014–15; occasional contrib New Law Jl; govr NE Wales Inst of HE 2001–07, co-opted memb Nominations Ctee Glynd?r Univ 2009–14; hon fell Glynd?r Univ 2009; *Recreations* walking, golf, gardening, soccer, rugby and cricket spectating; *Clubs* Chester City (pres 2011–12), Lansdowne, Wrexham Golf; *Style*— His Hon Judge Dutton, DL; ✉ The Crown Court, The Castle, Chester CH1 2AN (☎ 01244 317606)

DUTTON, Timothy James; CBE (2016), QC (1998); s of late James Derek Dutton, JP, and late Joan Rosemary, *née* Parsons; *b* 25 February 1957; *Educ* Repton, Keble Coll Oxford (BA); *m* 1 April 1987, Sappho, da of B Raschid, of Washington DC, USA; 1 da (Pia Leila b 4 June 1988); *Career* called to the Bar Middle Temple 1979; recorder South Eastern Circuit 2000–, ldr South Eastern Circuit 2004–06, dep judge of the High Court of Justice 2009–; appeared in many leading commercial, public law and regulatory cases; chm Bar Cncl 2008 (vice-chm 2007), chair Working Pty into Advocacy Trg, chm Inns of Ct Advocacy Trg Ctee 2000–03, chm Inquiry into World Class Payments Bureau 2009; memb: Commercial Bar Assoc, Admin Law Bar Assoc, London Common Law and Commercial Bar Assoc, Liberty, Assoc of Regulatory and Disciplinary Lawyers (chm 2009–15); tstee Legal Educn Fndn 2013–; *Publications* author of various articles and lectures on the law; *Recreations* French horn, sailing; *Clubs* Harbour; *Style*— Timothy J Dutton, Esq, CBE, QC; ✉ Fountain Court Chambers, Temple, London EC4Y 9DH (☎ 020 7583 3335, fax 020 7353 0329, e-mail tdutton@fountaincourt.co.uk)

DUVALL, Len; OBE (1998), AM; *b* 26 September 1961; *Educ* Hawthorn Sch London; *Career* memb Greenwich Cncl 1990–2001 (ldr 1992–2000); GLA: memb London Assembly (Lab) Greenwich and Lewisham 2000–, vice-chair London Devpt Agency 2000–03, chair London Health Cmmn 2002–04, ldr Lab Gp 2004–, chair Met Police Authy 2004–08; former memb London Fire Authy; vice-chair Local Govt Info Unit 1994–96, chair London Thames Gateway Partnership 1997–2000, former dep chair Assoc of London Govt, fndr memb New Local Govt Network, chair Cwlth Local Govt Forum 1998–2005; former non-exec dir New Millennium Experience Ltd; chair Gtr London Lab Pty 2002–; non-exec dir

Royal Artillery Museums Tst 1997–2014, chair Royal Greenwich Heritage Tst 2015–; *Style*— Len Duvall, Esq, OBE, AM; ✉ Greater London Authority, City Hall, The Queen's Walk, Southwark, London SE1 2AA (☎ 020 7983 4517, e-mail len.duvall@london.gov.uk)

DUXBURY, Prof Geoffrey; s of John Heap Duxbury (d 1972), and Nora, *née* Lightbown (d 1989); *b* 6 November 1942; *Educ* Cheadle Hulme Sch Cheshire, Univ of Sheffield (BSc, PhD, Turner Prize); *m* 8 Nov 1969, Mary Rose, da of Thomas John Tarrant; 1 s (Neil b 11 May 1973), 1 da (Elspeth b 9 Dec 1975); *Career* jr research fell Div of Electrical Sci Nat Physical Lab 1967–69, lectr in chemical physics Univ of Bristol 1970–80; Univ of Strathclyde: sr lectr in physics 1981–85, reader 1985–87, prof 1987–2006, emeritus prof 2006–, chm of Dept 1988–90; various visiting appts incl: Nat Research Cncl of Canada 1972, 1974 and 1980, Kitt Peak Nat Observatory USA 1980 and 1981, Univ of Nottingham (Kipping fell) 1983, Univ of Lille 1984, Univ of Colorado 1996, Univ de Paris Süd 1998 and 2005; memb: RSC, Optical Soc of America, IOP; awarded Marlow Medal Faraday Div RSC 1975, Royal Soc of Chemistry 50 Years of Membership 2013; FInstP 1991, FRSE 1997; *Books* Infrared Vibration-Rotation Spectroscopy, From Free Radicals to the Infrared Sky (2000); author of numerous scientific papers in learned jls; *Style*— Prof Geoffrey Duxbury, FRSE; ✉ Department of Physics, University of Strathclyde, John Anderson Building, Glasgow G4 0NG (e-mail g.duxbury@strath.ac.uk)

DWEK, Dr Joseph Claude (Joe); CBE; *b* 1 May 1940; *Educ* Carmel Coll, Univ of Manchester (BSc, BA); *m*; 2 c; *Career* chm: Bodycote International plc 1972–98, Penmarric Ltd; exec chm Worthington Group 1999–2010; past dir Mercury Recycling Ltd; dir: Gaynor plc, Panelflex plc, Branon Oil; dir NWIDB DTI 1980–90, chm CBI NW 1994–96 (vice-chm 1994 and 1997), memb Bd NW Devpt Agency 2004–12 (chm Environmental Ctee, vice-chm Business and Innovations Ctee); past chm: Enworks, Mersey Basin Campaign DETR 1999–2004, Healthy Waterways Tst; chm Envirolink, past memb Cncl of Environmental Campaigns (ENCAMS), past memb Environmental Innovations Advsy Gp DTI/DEFRA; former dir: Royal Exchange Theatre, NORWIDA/INWARD, North West Broadcasting Ltd; dir NW Regnl Advsy Ctee Forestry Cmmn, memb Forestry and Woodlands Advsy Ctee; past memb Gen Assembly Univ of Manchester; past memb: Ct Victoria Univ of Manchester, Cncl UMIST, Manchester Business Sch; pres UMIST Assoc 1992–94; govr Manchester HS for Girls; Hon DSc UMIST; FTI, AMCT; *Recreations* golf; *Style*— Dr Joe Dwek, CBE; ✉ Penmarric plc, Suite One, Courthill House, 66 Water Lane, Wilmslow SK9 5AP (☎ 01625 549081/2, fax 01625 530791, e-mail penjcdwek@aol.com)

DWEK, Prof Raymond Allen; CBE (2013); s of Victor Joseph Dwek (d 1988), of Manchester, and Alice, *née* Liniado; *b* 10 November 1941; *Educ* Carmel Coll, Univ of Manchester (BSc, MSc), Lincoln Coll Oxford (DPhil), Exeter Coll Oxford (DSc); *m* 21 June 1964, Sandra, da of Dr David I Livingstone, of Manchester; 2 da (Juliet b 19 Dec 1965, Deborah b 3 Oct 1974), 2 s (Robert b 14 July 1967, Joshua b 23 March 1978); *Career* Univ of Oxford: res lectr in physical chemistry ChCh 1966–68, lectr in inorganic chemistry ChCh 1968–75, departmental demonstrator Dept of Biochemistry 1969–74, res lectr in biochemistry ChCh 1975–76, lectr in biochemistry Trinity Coll 1976–84, fell Exeter Coll 1976–, prof of glycobiology and dir Glycobiology Inst Dept of Biochemistry 1988–, assoc head Dept of Biochemistry (with special responsibilities for postgrad and post doctoral trg) 1996–2000, head Dept of Biochemistry 2000–06; visiting Royal Soc Res fell at Weizmann Inst Rehovot Israel 1969, Royal Soc Locke res fell 1974–76; visiting prof: Duke Univ NC 1968 (seconded to Inst of Exploratory Res Fort Monmouth NJ), Univ of Trieste 1974, Univ of Lund 1977, Inst of Enzymology Budapest 1980; prof Scripps Research Inst La Jolla 2008; author various articles in books and jls on physical chemistry, biochemistry and med; memb of various scientific ctees incl: Oxford Enzyme Gp 1971–88, Oxford Oligosaccharide Gp 1983–88, MRC AIDS Antiviral Steering Ctee 1987–92; dir and founding memb scientist Oxford GlycoScience Ltd (formerly Oxford GlycoSystems) 1988–, dir and memb Scientific Advsy Bd United Therapeutics Corp (USA) 2002–, dir Isis Innovation Univ of Oxford 2003–; special advsr to pres of Ben Gurion Univ of the Negev Israel 2000–; inst prof Scripps Research Inst La Jolla 2008–; memb EMBO 1998–; holder 70 patents; Wellcome Tst Award 1994, award for research in biochemistry related to med 1996, Boyce Thompson Distinguished Lectr Series Cornell Univ 1997, Centennial Award Delaware Valley Coll Pennsylvania USA 1997, First Scientific Leadership Award Hepatitis B Fndn Philadelphia 1997, Fndn of Med Sciences Lectureship McGill Univ Montreal 2001, Lemieux Lecture Alberta 2003, Kluge Chair of Science and Society Library of Congress USA 2007, Huxley Medal 2007; foreign memb American Philosophical Soc 2006–; Dr (hc): Katholieke Universitat Leuven 1996, Ben Gurion Univ 2001, Scripps Research Inst La Jolla CA 2004; CChem, CBiol, FRSC 1993, FRS 1998, FRSA 1998, FIBiol 1999 (pres 2008–), Hon FRCP 2007; Cdr Order of Merit (Romania) 2000; *Books* Nuclear Magnetic Resonance in Biochemistry (1973), Principles and Problems in Physical Chemistry for Biochemists (jtly, 1975), Nuclear Magnetic Resonance in Biology (jtly 1977), Biological Spectroscopy (jtly, 1984); author over 450 scientific papers; *Style*— Prof Raymond Dwek, CBE, FRS; ✉ Glycobiology Institute, Department of Biochemistry, University of Oxford, South Parks Road, Oxford OX1 3QU (☎ 01865 275344, fax 01865 275771, e-mail kathryn.scott@bioch.ox.ac.uk)

DWYER, Jenny; *Educ* Univ of Cambridge (BEd); *Career* headmistress: Prior's Field Sch Godalming 1999–2006, Sherborne Sch for Girls 2006–; *Style*— Mrs Jenny Dwyer; ✉ Sherborne School for Girls, Bradford Road, Sherborne, Dorset DT9 3QN

DYER, Dr James A T; OBE (2003); s of Rev T J Dyer (d 1994), and Mary Watt, *née* Thomson (d 2007); *b* 31 December 1946; *Educ* Robert Gordon's Coll, Univ of Aberdeen (MB, ChB, Ogston prize in surgery, Keith gold medal, Anderson gold medal and prize); *m* 1, 1969 (m dis 1994), Lorna, *née* Townson; 2 s (Paul b 1 Sept 1971, Euan b 22 Sept 1976), 1 da (Rowan b 11 Aug 1978); m 2, 1994 (m dis 2012), Suzanne, *née* Whitaker; 1 step s (Christopher b 4 April 1984 d 2009), 2 step da (Sophie b 1 Sept 1989, Emily b 7 Nov 1990); *Career* various house jobs in Aberdeen Hosps 1970–71, trainee GP 1971–72; Royal Edinburgh Hosp: SHO and registrar posts in psychiatry 1972–75, sr registrar in psychiatry 1975–77; scientific offr MRC Unit for Epidemiological Studies in Psychiatry Edinburgh 1977–80, conslt in general and rehabilitation psychiatry Royal Edinburgh Hosp 1981–91, dir Mental Welfare Cmmn for Scotland 1993–2003 (HM med cmmr 1991–2003); hon sr lectr in psychiatry Univ of Edinburgh 1981–91; chm Section for social community and rehabilitation RCPsych 1994–97; author of papers on parasuicide, schizophrenia, care of long term mentally ill, mental health legislation and psychological aspects of nuclear war; Scottish Parly Standards Cmmr 2003–09, medical memb Mental Health Tbnl Scotland 2005–, memb Scottish Social Services Cncl Registration and Conduct Ctees 2010–13; FRCPsych, FRSA; *Recreations* current affairs, photography, reading, opera; *Style*— Dr James Dyer, OBE; ☎ 07702 682515, e-mail jdyer@dyer2.plus.com

DYKE; *see also:* Hart Dyke

DYKE, Gregory (Greg); *b* 20 May 1947; *Educ* Hayes GS, Univ of York; *Career* journalist LWT 1977, ed-in-chief TV-am 1983–84, dir of progs TVS 1984–87; London Weekend Television: dir of progs 1987–90, md 1990, gp chief exec LWT (Holdings) plc 1991–94; chm Independent Television Association 1992–94, exec chm GMTV 1993–94, chief exec Pearson Television 1995–99, main bd dir Pearson plc 1996–99, chm Channel 5 Broadcasting Ltd 1997–99 (non-exec dir 1996–99), DG BBC 2000–04, chm HIT Entertainment 2005–; memb Media Advsy Bd Apax Partners 2004–, chm BFI 2008–, chm Brentford FC 2006–13; chm FA 2013–; non-exec dir: Channel Four Television 1988–90, ITN Ltd until 1992; chllr Univ of York 2004–15; FRTS 1998; *Recreations* football, riding, skiing; *Style*— Greg Dyke

DYKE-COOMES, Martin; s of Ernest Thomas Dyke-Coomes (d 2005), and Gladys Dorothy, *née* Bignell (d 1995); *b* 14 August 1948; *Educ* Sarah Robinson Secdy Modern, Ifield GS, Architectural Assoc; *m* 24 June 1978, Maggie Pinhorn, *qv*, da of George Herbert Pinhorn (d 1996); 1 s (Ned Alexander b 1981), 1 da (Amy Elizabeth b 1983); 2 adopted s (Anthony b 1967, Claude b 1973); *Career* architect ARCUK 1973; fndr CGHP Architects in 1979; fndr Dyke Coomes Architects 1989; princ works: Hoxton St London N1 Regeneration (Times/RIBA award 1985), Jubilee Hall Redevelopment Covent Garden 1984–87 (Times/RIBA award 1988), Holland and Thurstan Dwellings 1982–86; participant in 1986 RIBA 40 under 40's exhibition; other works incl Stoke Newington Theatre and projects for Housing Assocs in Islington and Hackney; RIBA; *Recreations* thinking, fishing, wishing, eating, sleeping, dreaming, loving; *Clubs* Manchester United; *Style*— Martin Dyke-Coomes, Esq; ✉ Dyke Coomes Architects Ltd, 530 Commerical Road, London E1 0HY (☎ 020 7265 9102, mobile 07914 010252, e-mail martin@dykecoomes.co.uk)

DYKES, Dr David Wilmer; s of Capt David Dykes, OBE (d 1978), and Jenny, *née* Thomas (d 1971); *b* 18 December 1933; *Educ* Swansea GS, CCC Oxford (MA), Univ of Wales (PhD); *m* 22 Sept 1967, Margaret Anne, da of Harvey Clifford George (d 1969); 2 da (Elizabeth Anne b 28 July 1972, Rosemary Louise b 29 July 1978); *Career* cmmnd RN and RNR 1955–62; civil servant Bd of Inland Revenue 1958–59, admin appts Univ of Bristol and UC Swansea 1959–63, dep registrar UC Swansea 1963–69, registrar Univ of Warwick 1969–72; Nat Museum of Wales: sec 1972–86, actg dir 1985–86, dir 1986–89; memb Treasure Valuation Ctee DCMS 2010–14; hon lectr in history UC Cardiff (later Univ of Wales Coll of Cardiff) 1975–95; vice-pres Br Numismatic Soc 2009– (memb Cncl 1966–70 and 1997–, pres 1999–2003); chllr Order of St John Priory for Wales 1991–98, bailiff of St Davids 1999–2002; awarded Parkes-Weber prize and medal RNS 1954; fndn memb Welsh Livery Guild 1993; Freeman City of London 1985, Liveryman Worshipful Co of Tin Plate Workers 1985; FRNS 1958, FRHistS 1965, FRSAI 1963, FSA 1973; KStJ 1993; *Books* Anglo-Saxon Coins in the National Museum of Wales (1977), Alan Sorrell: Early Wales Recreated (1980), Wales in Vanity Fair (1989), The University Coll of Swansea (1992), Coinage and Currency in Eighteenth-Century Britain (2011, North Book Prize Br Numismatic Soc 2012), Medieval Anglo-Irish Coinage (forthcoming); author of articles and reviews in numismatic, historical and other jls; *Recreations* numismatics, writing; *Clubs* Athenaeum, Cardiff & County (Cardiff); *Style*— Dr David Dykes, FSA; ✉ e-mail davwd@btinternet.com

DYKES, Baron (Life Peer UK 2004), of Harrow Weald in the London Borough of Harrow; Hugh John Maxwell Dykes; s of Richard Dykes, of Weston-super-Mare, Somerset; *b* 17 May 1939; *Educ* Weston-super-Mare GS, Pembroke Coll Cambridge; *m* 1965, Susan Margaret, da of Elwand Smith of Wakefield, W Yorks; 3 s; *Career* investment analyst and stockbroker; ptnr Simon & Coates 1968–78, assoc memb Quilter Goodison & Co, dir Dixons plc Far Eastern Div 1985–; MP (Cons) Harrow E 1970–97 (Parly candidate (Cons) Tottenham 1966); PPS to: Parly under secs for Defence 1970–73, Parly under sec Civil Service Dept 1973; UK memb Euro Parl 1974, chm: Cons Parly European Ctee 1979–80 (former sec, vice-chm), Cons Gp for Europe 1979–80 (vice-pres 1982), UK European Movement 1990–95; joined Lib Dem Pty 1997, Lib Dem front bench EU spokesman House of Lords; pres European Atlantic Gp 2007– (chm 2005–07); chm Mid-Atlantic Club 2003–; *Clubs* Beefsteak, Garrick, English Speaking Union; *Style*— The Rt Hon the Lord Dykes

DYKES, Richard Thornton Booth; s of Alan Thornton Dykes (d 1979), and Myra McFie Booth (d 1991); *b* 7 April 1945, Bolton, Lancs; *Educ* Rossall Sch; *m* 1970 (m dis), Janet Rosemary, da of Cdr R J R Cundall; 1 s (Nicholas Thornton b 27 Oct 1972); *Career* articled clerk Dehn and Lauderdale slrs 1965–67, exec offr then higher exec offr Miny of Labour 1967–73, private sec to Sec of State for Employment 1973–76, princ Econ Policy Div Dept of Employment 1976–77, dir of industrial relations British Shipbuilders 1977–80, non-exec dir Austin & Pickersgill Ltd Sunderland 1979–80; Dept of Employment: princ private sec to Sec of State for Employment 1980–82, head Unemployment Benefit Serv 1982–85, sec Sr Mgmnt Gp 1985–86, head Inner Cities Central Unit 1986; Post Office Counters Ltd: gen mangr Gtr London 1986–87, dir of ops 1987–92, md 1992–96; md Royal Mail 1996–2001, currently chm Carrenza Ltd; chm DETR/HSC Work-related Road Safety Task Gp 2000–01; memb: Design Cncl 1976–2001, Forensic Sci Serv Advsy Bd 1993–98, Economic Devpt Ctee Business in the Community 1992–2003; non-exec dir Employment Serv 1998–2002; *Style*— Richard Dykes, Esq; ✉ 513 Gilbert House, Barbican, London EC2Y 8BD (☎ 020 7638 3756)

DYMOCK, Vice Adm Sir Anthony Knox; KBE (2008), CB (2003); s of Richard Challis Dymock (d 1987), and Irene Mary, *née* Knox; *b* 18 July 1949, Liverpool; *Educ* Brighton Hove and Sussex GS, UEA (BA), BRNC, RNC Greenwich; *m* 1 Jan 1977, Elizabeth Mary, *née* Frewer (d 2015); 1 da (Amy b 1980), 1 s (Charles b 1983); *Career* served: HMS Falmouth 1971–72, HMS Yarmouth 1972–73, HMS Kirkliston 1974, HMS Britannia 1974–75, HMS Brighton 1975, HMS Rothesay 1976–77, HMS Alacrity 1978–80, HMS Antrim 1981–83 (Falklands); cmd: HMS Plymouth 1985–88, HMS Campbeltown 1992–93, HMS Cornwall 1996–98; MOD Naval Central Staffs 1988–90 and 1993–96, dir Tactical Sch 1992; Gulf War: USS Midway, HMS London, HMS Brave 1990–91; Dep Cdr UK Task Gp 1991–92, Strike Force South NATO 2000–02, Def Attaché Washington US 2002–05, UK Mil Rep to NATO and the EU 2006–08, maritime security advsr European Defence Agency; dir Wise Pens Int Ltd; MNI 1992; *Recreations* sailing; *Clubs* Naval and Military, RNSA, RYS, Pilgrims, RCC; *Style*— Vice Adm Sir Anthony Dymock, KBE, CB

DYMOND, Dr Duncan Simon; s of Dr Sydney Cyril Dymond (d 1978), and Adele, *née* Spector (d 1977); *b* 25 February 1950; *Educ* St Paul's, Bart's Med Sch Univ of London (MB BS, MD); *Family* 1 da (Francesca b 1979), 1 s (Daniel b 1982); *Career* asst prof of med and cardiology Mount Sinai Med Sch Univ of Wisconsin 1980–81, sr registrar in cardiology 1981–86, conslt cardiologist Bart's 1987–; fndr Br Nuclear Cardiology Gp, memb Cncl Br Cardiovascular Intervention Soc Scientific Ctee, hon sec Br Cardiac Soc 1990–94; memb: Br Nuclear Med Soc 1979, Br Cardiology Soc 1980, MRS 1981; fell American Coll of Cardiology 1983, fndr fell Euro Soc of Cardiology 1989; *Books* An Atlas of Myocardial Infarction (1994), The Jargon-Busters Guide to Heart Disease (1996), How to Cope with High Blood Pressure (2003); *Recreations* cricket, tennis, skiing, pianoforte, Italian opera, watercolours; *Clubs* MCC; *Style*— Dr Duncan Dymond; ✉ 84 Harley Street, London W1G 7HW (☎ 020 7079 4260, e-mail dymondheart@hotmail.co.uk)

DYSART, Earl of (13 holder of title, S 1643); John Peter Grant of Rothiemurchus; DL (Inverness-shire 1986); 16 of Rothiemurchus; s of Lt-Col John Grant of Rothiemurchus, MBE (d 1987), and s of Countess of Dysart (d 2011); *b* 22 October 1946; *Educ* Gordonstoun; *m* 1971, Philippa, da of John Chance, of Llanvapley Court, Abergavenny; 1 s, 2 da; *Career* dir and chm Scottish Trout Ltd 1989–95; memb: Bd NE River Purification Bd 1990–96, Cairngorms Working Party 1991–92, Tourism Trg Scotland 1993–95, Native Woodlands Advsy Panel to the Forestry Cmmn 1993–96, Aviemore Partnership 1994–98, Cairngorm Partnership 1995–2003; dir Aviemore, Badenoch and Stratlspey Mktg Co 2003–; Nat Tst for Scotland: memb Cncl 1990–95, memb Countryside and Nature Conservation Ctee 1992–96, memb Exec Ctee 1994–98; vice-pres Scottish Landowners' Fedn 1991–2004, chm Tourism and Environment Task Force 1995–98; pres Royal Zoological Soc of Scotland 1996–2006; memb The Access Forum 1994–99; FRSGS; *Style*— The Earl of Dysart, DL; ✉ The Doune of Rothiemurchus, by Aviemore, Inverness-shire PH22 1QP

D

DYSON, Sir James; OM (2016), kt (2007), CBE (1998); s of Alec Dyson (d 1956), of Holt, Norfolk, and Mary, *née* Bolton (d 1978); *b* 2 May 1947; *Educ* Gresham's, RCA (MDesRCA); *m* 1967, Deirdre, *née* Hindmarsh; 1 da (Emily b 26 Feb 1971), 2 s (Jacob b 21 Oct 1972, Sam b 26 Jan 1978); *Career* dir Rotork Marine 1970–74 (design and manufacture of Sea Truck high speed landing craft), md Kirk-Dyson 1974–79 (design and manufacture of Ballbarrow wheelbarrow), founded Dyson Research Ltd 1979 (developed and designed: Dyson Dual Cyclone vacuum cleaner 1979–93, Contrarotator washing machine 2000, Dyson Airblade hand dryer 2006, DC24 Dyson Ball vacuum cleaner 2008, Dyson digital motor V2 2009), chm Dyson Ltd 1992–; memb Design Cncl 1997–, fndr James Dyson Fndn 2002, chm Design Museum 1999–2004, chm Design London, memb Cncl RCA (external examiner 1993–96), memb Advsy Bd MAK Vienna, cmmr for Royal Cmmn for the Exhbn of 1851; exhbn Doing a Dyson (Design Museum) 1996–97, other Dyson exhbns at Glasgow and Arnhem Holland; Dyson vacuum cleaners on perm display at: Sci Museum, Design Museum London, V&A, Boyman's Museum Rotterdam, San Francisco MOMA, Design Museum Zurich, Design Museum Lisbon, Museum fur Angewandte Kunst Cologne, Danish Design Centre Copenhagen, Centre Georges Pompidou Paris, Museum für Angewandte Kunst (MAK) Vienna; patron Nat Assoc of Inspectors and Advsrs in Design and Technol; memb Ct Univ of Bath, dir Imperial Coll London; tstee The Roundhouse Theatre London 1998; hon fell Liverpool John Moores Univ 1997; Hon DLitt Staffs Univ 1990, Hon MIED Inst of Design 1997, Hon DSc Oxford Brookes Univ; Hon Dr: Univ of Bradford 1998, UWE, Univ of Middx, Brunel Univ, Bath Spa Univ, RCA, Univ of Bath, Huddersfield Univ Business Sch, Liverpool John Moores Univ, Imperial Coll; FCSD 1996, FREng 2005; *Awards* for Dyson designs numerous incl since 2009: Australia's Favourite Cleaning Product Australian Women's Weekly Product of the Year Awards 2009 (for DC24 Ball), Adding Value to Small Domestic Appliance Award Australia 2009, Gold for Energy Management IIDEX Awards Canada 2009 (for Airblade), Silver in the Bath and Plumbing category IIDEX Awards Canada 2009 (for Airblade), Bronze for Booth Design IIDEX Awards Canada 2009 (for Airblade), HACCP Accreditation Canada 2009 (for Airblade), Red Dot Awards Germany 2009 (for DC22 and DC23), Best of the Red Dot Award Germany 2009 (for Airblade), iF Product Design Award Germany 2009, IFA Preview Award Germany 2009 (for DC30 and DC31), Best in Category Floor Care Electrics Home World Business Housewares Design Awards USA (for DC24) 2009, Good Design Award Best Domestic Appliance Category Australia 2014, winner Heater Category New Zealand's Consumer and Australia's Choice Magazine (for AM05 Hot+Cool fan heater) 2014, Vacuum Cleaner of the Year Product of the Year Awards Russia 2014 (for DC52 Animal Compete), Most Innovative Gadget Digital Home Section Spain 2014 (for Dyson 360 Eye Robot Vacuum), Best Idea of the Year Tu Experto Spain 2014 (for Dyson Humidifier), Excellent Prize China Red Start Design Awards 2014 (for DC62), Gold prize China Red Star Design Awards 2014 (for Dyson Cool), Product of the Year Consumer Awards 2014 (for DC52); awards for Dyson R&D Centre incl: Civic Tst Award Commendation 1999, Royal Fine Art Cmmn Tst/BSB Building of the Year Award Commendation 1999, The Carbon Trust Standard (for Dyson HQ) 2009; other awards incl, since 2009–: Best of the Best for highest design quality Red Dot Award Germany (for DC24) 2009, Small Appliances Award Harvey Norman Supplier of the Year Australia 2009, ERA Floorcare Supplier of the Year Australia, Innovator of the Year Stuff Magazine 2014; *Publications* Doing a Dyson (1996), Against the Odds (1997), History of Great Inventions (2001); *Recreations* running, garden design, bassoon and opera, tennis; *Clubs* Chelsea Arts, Bluebird; *Style*— Sir James Dyson, OM, CBE; ✉ Dyson Ltd, Tetbury Hill, Malmesbury, Wiltshire SN16 0RP

DYSON, Jeremy Robert; s of Melvyn Dyson, and Elaine, *née* Saville; *b* 14 June 1966; *Educ* Leeds GS, Jacob Kramer Coll of Art and Design, Univ of Leeds (BA), Northern Sch of Film and TV (MA); *m* 20 April 2002, Nicola, *née* Clarke; 1 da (Eve b 2005); *Career* writer, memb The League of Gentlemen comedy gp (with Mark Gatiss, *qv*); performed oratorio The Same Dog (with Joby Talbot) Barbican 2000; Hon DLitt Univ of Huddersfield 2003; *Television* The League of Gentlemen (BBC 2) 1999, 2000 and 2002, The League of Gentlemen Christmas Special (BBC 2) 2000, 'Two Can Play at That Game' Randall and Hopkirk (Deceased) 2001, Funland (with Simon Ashdown, BBC 3 and BBC 2) 2005, Billy Goat (BBC 1) 2007; *Radio* On the Town with the League of Gentlemen (Radio 4) 1997, Ringing the Changes (Radio 4) 2000, Never Trust a Rabbit (Radio 4) 2001; *Awards* Perrier Award 1997, Sony Silver Award for Radio Comedy 1998, Golden Rose of Montreux 1999, BAFTA Award for Best Comedy 2000, RTS Award for Best Entertainment 2000, NME Award for Best TV Prog 2001, South Bank Show Award for Best Comedy 2003; *Books* The Essex Files (with Mark Gatiss, 1997), Bright Darkness: The Lost Art of the Supernatural Horror Film (1997), Never Trust a Rabbit (2000), A Local Book for Local People (2000), What Happens Now (2006); *Recreations* conjuring, music; *Style*— Jeremy Dyson, Esq; ✉ c/o PBJ Management, 7 Soho Street, London W1D 3DQ (✆ 020 7287 1112)

DYSON, Rt Hon Lord John Anthony Dyson; kt (1993), PC (2001); s of Richard Dyson (d 1988), and Gisella Elizabeth, *née* Kremsier (d 2005); *b* 31 July 1943; *Educ* Leeds GS (fndn scholar), Wadham Coll Oxford (open classical scholar, MA); *m* 5 July 1970, Jacqueline Carmel, *née* Levy; 1 da (Michelle b 25 June 1971), 1 s (Steven b 21 May 1973); *Career* called to the Bar Middle Temple 1968 (Harmsworth scholar); QC 1982, recorder of the Crown Court 1986–93, judge of the High Court of Justice (Queen's Bench Div) 1993–2000, a Lord Jusice of Appeal 2001–10, dep head of civil justice 2003–06, Justice of the Supreme Court 2010–12, master of the rolls 2012; judge in charge of Technology and Construction Court 1998–2000; memb: Cncl of Legal Educn 1992–96, Judicial Studies Bd 1994–98 (chm Ethnic Minorities Advsy Ctee 1994–98); hon fell Wadham Coll Oxford, Hon LLD Univ of Essex, Hon LLD UCL, Hon LLD Univ of Leeds; *Recreations* music, walking, skiing, tennis; *Style*— The Rt Hon Lord Dyson, PC; ✉ Master of the Rolls Private Office, Room E214, Royal Courts of Justice, Strand, London WC2A 2LL

DYSON, Prof Robert Graham; s of Jack Dyson (d 1970), and Sylvia, *née* Schofield (d 1992); *b* 6 September 1942; *Educ* Hulme GS Oldham, Univ of Liverpool (BSc), Lancaster Univ (PhD); *m* 31 July 1965, Dorothy, da of Daniel Prestwich (d 1987), of Oldham, Lancs; 1 s (Michael), 1 da (Joanne); *Career* sr systems technologist Pilkington Bros plc 1968–70 (res mathematician 1964–68); Univ of Warwick: lectr 1970–77, sr lectr 1977–84, prof of operational res and systems 1984–, pro-vice-chllr 1989–95 and 1999–2005; chm Warwick Business Sch 1978–81 (dean 1998–2000); memb OR Panel SERC 1985–89, memb Maths Coll EPSRC 1997–; pres Operational Res Soc 1998–99; chm Ctee of Professors of Operational Research 1995–97; ed European Jl of Operational Research; President's Medal Operational Res Soc, Pergamon Prize for articles in Jl of Operational Res Soc; chm of govrs Kenilworth Sch 1993–97; *Books* Strategic Planning: Models and Analytical Techniques (1989), Strategic Development: Methods and Models (1998), Supporting Strategy (2007); *Recreations* cricket (played for Uppermill, Southport & Birkdale and Leamington CCs), theatre; *Clubs* Warwickshire CCC, Coventry RFC; *Style*— Prof Robert Dyson; ✉ Warwick Business School, University of Warwick, Coventry CV4 7AL (✆ 024 7652 3775, e-mail r.g.dyson@warwick.ac.uk)

DYSON, Prof Tim; s of Geoffrey Harry George Dyson (d 1981), and Maureen Angela Jane, *née* Gardner (d 1974); *b* 1 August 1949; *Educ* Queens Univ Canada, LSE (BSc, MSc); *m* 17 May 1978, Susan Ann, da of Frank Borman (d 2002); 2 s (Tristram Simon b 25 Dec 1978, Nicholas Adam b 19 Oct 1983); *Career* res offr in demography Inst of Devpt Studies Univ of Sussex 1973–75, res fell Centre for Population Studies LSHTM 1975–80; LSE: lectr 1980–88, reader 1988–92, prof of population studies 1992–, chair Population Studies Gp 1995–99, convenor Dept of Social Policy 1997–99; memb numerous ctees at LSE incl: Social Res Div, Collegiate Ctee for the BSc (Econ), Res Ctee, Mgmnt Ctee Asia Res Centre, Mgmnt Ctee Centre for Global Governance, Standing Sub-Ctee Appointments Ctee; visiting fell Dept of Demography ANU 1986, visiting prof Inst for Developing Economies Tokyo 1996, visiting prof Faculty of Health Sciences American Univ of Beirut 1996–98; external examiner: LSHTM 1983–86, Univ of Surrey 1997–99, Univ of Southampton 1997–99, Univ of Liverpool 1998–2000; UN conslt: Int Inst for Population Studies Bombay 1981, Int Trg Prog on Population and Devpt Centre for Devpt Studies Trivandrum 1990; conslt Int African Inst and UNHCR Somalia 1985, demographic conslt USAID New Delhi 1986; advsr: FAO (on food prodn and population growth) 1996, UN Population Div (on population, devpt and the environment) 2000; various assignments: Health Statistics Div WHO, ODA, Office of Registrar Gen New Delhi; pres Br Soc for Population Studies 1994–96 (memb Cncl 1981–85, vice-pres 1991–93), vice-pres Population Investigation Ctee 1996– (memb 1991–); memb: US Nat Acad of Sciences Panel on India's Demography 1978–84, Ctee on Anthropological Demography Int Union for the Scientific Study of Population 1986–91, Population Studies Science Panel Wellcome Tst 1996–2001, Monitoring Panel on Food World Fedn of Scientists 2000; tstee Simon Population Tst 1992–2002; organiser of confs and seminars worldwide; co-ed Population Studies 1990–95; memb Editorial/Advsy Bd: Int Jl of Population Geography 1998–, Jl of Health and Population in Developing Countries 1998–; dir Options Consultancy Services (formerly Marie Stopes Consultancy) 1993–99; memb: Int Union for the Scientific Study of Population, Br Assoc of S Asian Studies, Soc for S Asian Studies, Indian Assoc for the Study of Population; FBA 2001; *Publications* incl: India's Historical Demography (ed, 1989), Population and Food: Global Trends and Future Prospects (1996), Famine Demography (jt ed, 2002), Twenty-first Century India (jt ed, 2004), Population and Development: The Demographic Transition (2010); author of numerous articles and papers in learned jls; *Style*— Prof Tim Dyson; ✉ 56 Beechwood Road, Sanderstead, London CR2 0AA (✆ 020 8657 6834); Department of International Development, London School of Economics and Political Science, Houghton Street, London WC2A 2AE (✆ 020 7955 7662, e-mail t.dyson@lse.ac.uk)

DYSON, Timothy John Bruce; s of Michael Bruce Dyson (d 1965), and Joyce Mary, *née* Simpson; *b* 3 December 1960; *Educ* Mirfield HS, Greenhead Coll, Loughborough Univ (BSc); *Career* Text 100: joined as graduate trainee 1984, account mangr 1986–87, assoc dir 1987–89, co dir 1989–90, gp md Text 100 International 1991– (dir 1990–); MIPR, MInstD; *Recreations* skiing, windsurfing, sailing; *Style*— Timothy Dyson, Esq

DYTOR, Clive Idris; MC (1982); s of Cecil Frederick Dytor (d 1976), of Milford Haven, Pembs, and Maureen Margaret, *née* Owen; *b* 29 October 1956; *Educ* Christ Coll Brecon, Trinity Coll Cambridge (MA), Wycliffe Hall Oxford (MA); *m* 17 Aug 1985, Sarah Louise, da of David Kingsley Payler; 1 s (Benjamin b 14 June 1989), 1 da (Francesca b 5 May 1995); *Career* Royal Marines: offr 1980–86, Commando Trg Centre 1980–81, troop cdre 45 Commando RM, staff instr Officers' Trg Unit 1982–83, trg instr Persian Gulf 1983–84, chief recruiting offr 1984–86; Commando medal 1981, Commandant's prize 1981; curate St Michael's Walsall 1989–92, chaplain Tonbridge Sch 1992–94, housemaster St Edward's Sch Oxford 1994–2000, head master The Oratory Sch 2000–15; memb HMC; *Recreations* Hispanic studies, sport, music; *Clubs* Pitt (Cambridge), Leander, East India; *Style*— Clive Dytor, Esq, MC; ✉ The Oratory School, Woodcote, South Oxfordshire RG8 0PJ (website www.oratory.co.uk)

E

EADE, Robert Francis; s of Stanley Robert Eade (d 1994), and Kathleen Eade (d 1998); *b* 17 August 1937, Rugby; *Educ* Bromsgrove Sch, Univ of London (external BSc); *m* 1965, Mary Lindsay, da of Sidney John Coulson (d 1993), of Stratton-on-the-Fosse, Somerset; 2 s (Simon, James), 1 da (Jane); *Career* AEI (became GEC Group): sr design engr Industrial Electronics Div 1963–65 (engr 1960–63), asst chief engr Devpt 1965–68; Thorn EMI plc: gen mangr then md Avo Ltd 1972–76 (tech dir 1970–72), md Measurement and Components Div 1976–79, md Thorn EMI Technology 1979–83, dir Commercial Technology 1983–85, md Int 1985–87; non-exec dir: Lloyd's Register Quality Assurance Ltd 1985–98 (chm Tech Ctee until 2015), Northern Engineering Centre 1992–95, Engineering Centre for Wales 1993–95, Sussex Careers Ltd 1995–2009 (chm 1998–2009), Lloyds Register Gen Ctee 1998–2015; dir Hurst Associates Ltd 1996–99; Crystalate Holdings plc: divnl dir 1987–88, gp chief exec 1988–90; conslt 1990–; dir Industry and Regions The Engrg Cncl 1992–95; memb Cncl: British Electrical and Allied Mfrs' Assoc (BEAMA) 1980–87, Standing Conf on Schs Science and Technol (SCSST) 1993–95; pres: Scientific Instrument Mfrs' Assoc (SIMA) 1981–82, Assoc for the Instrumentation, Control and Automation Industry (GAMBICA) 1982–84; formerly memb: Cncl ERA Technol, Sec of State for Industry Advsy Cncl on Calibration and Measurement, Sino Br Trade Cncl (and chm Electronics Ctee); chm Sussex Advice and Skills 2004–09; CEng, FIEE, CCMI, FRSA; *Style—* Robert Eade, Esq; ✉ Furnace Lodge, Furnace Farm Road, Felbridge, East Grinstead, West Sussex RH19 2PU (☎ 01342 713278, e-mail bob@eade.uk.com)

EADES, His Hon Judge Robert Mark; s of John Robert Eades (d 1982), of Staffs, and Margaret Ursula, *née* Megginson; *b* 6 May 1951; *Educ* Moffats Sch Bewdley, Leighton Park Sch Reading, Univ of Bristol; *m* 1982, Afsaneh (Sunny), da of Mohammed Atri; 2 da (Alexandra b 1984, Jessica b 1988); *Career* called to the Bar 1974; in practice 1975–2001, circuit judge (Midland Circuit) 2001–; *Recreations* gardening, historic buildings, local history; *Style—* His Hon Judge Eades

EADIE, Alastair Gordon; s of Col James Alister Eadie, DSO, TD, DL (d 1961), of Sudbury, Derbys; *b* 25 June 1940; *Educ* Eton; *m* 1, 14 April 1966, Hon Jacqueline (d 2002), da of 5 Baron Ashtown (d 1979); 3 s (James b 1967, Christopher b 1969, Edward b 1972); m 2, 31 Oct 2003, Caroline, da of Col John Conyers O'Dwyer (d 1986), of Ballinamallard, Co Fermanagh; *Career* trainee Crowleys Brewery 1958, trainee Labatts Brewery Canada 1959, clerk Shuttleworth & Howerth CAs 1960–61, trainee Watney Mann Breweries 1962–64, PA to md Watney Mann Breweries 1964–65, distribution dir Phipps Brewery 1965–66, dir Phipps Brewery Lankaster Wells Off-Licenses and Brown & Pank Wine and Spirit Merchants 1966–69, md Westminster Wine 1969–72, md IDV Retail Ltd, md W & A Gilbey/Mogan Furze Wine and Spirit Wholesalers 1977–87, dir External Affairs IDV UK Ltd 1987–98, dir External Affairs UDV UK Ltd 1998–2001; Ext Wine & Spirit Assoc of GB and NI (chm 1989–91, pres 1998–2000), Wine & Spirit Benevolent Soc (chm 1987–88), The Benevolent Soc of the Licensed Trade of Scotland (pres 1998–99); pres Licensed Victuallers Schools 1991–92, pres FIVS (int wine and spirit fedn) 1997–99; tstee: Wine and Spirit Educn Tst 2001–05, Licensed Trade Charities Tst 1997–2007, Hospitality Action 2000–07; memb Alcohol Educn & Research Cncl 1995–2001; Liveryman Worshipful Co of Distillers; *Recreations* gardening, shooting and stalking; *Clubs* Cavalry and Guards; *Style—* Alastair Eadie, Esq; ✉ Becket Barn, South Cadbury, Yeovil, Somerset BA22 7HA

EADIE, Craig Farquhar; *b* 22 April 1955; *Educ* Canford, Worcester Coll Oxford, Aix-Marseilles Univ France; *m* 3 Oct 1987, Deborah Ann, da of Leslie Burnett, of W Wycombe, Bucks; *Career* admitted slr 1980; ptnr Frere Cholmeley Bischoff 1986–98, founding ptnr Forsters 1998–2009, sr ptnr PCP Capital Ptnrs LLP 2009–13, dir Kernow and Mayfair 2013–; *Style—* Craig Eadie

EADIE, Jim; MSP; s of James Eadie (d 2001), and Helen, *née* Norwood; *b* 10 February 1968, Glasgow; *Educ* Waverley Secndy Sch Glasgow, Univ of Strathclyde; *Career* Assoc of the Br Pharmaceutical Industry (ABPI): head of Parly affrs 2001–02, dir 2002–07; dir Jim Eadie Consulting Ltd 2008–11; MSP (SNP) Edinburgh Southern 2011– (Convenor Scottish Parl Infrastructure and Capital Investment Cttee 2014–, Parl Liason Office to the First Min 2014–, Parl Liason Offr to dep First Min 2011–); *Style—* Jim Eadie, Esq, MSP; ✉ The Scottish Parliament, Edinburgh EH99 1SP

EADY, Her Hon Judge Jennifer Jane; QC (2006); da of Gordon Eady (d 2008), and Theresa Eady (d 2004); *Children* 1 s; *Career* called to the Bar Inner Temple 1989, called to the Bar of NI 1994; fee-paid chm Employment Tbnls (England and Wales) 2001–08, recorder 2004, circuit judge (Employment Appeal Tbnl) 2013–; ind memb ACAS Cncl 2008–14; tstee Wallace Collection 2013–; *Style—* Her Hon Judge Eady, QC; ✉ Employment Appeal Tribunal, Fleetbank House, 2–6 Salisbury Square, London EC4Y 8AE

EAGLE, Angela; MP; da of André Eagle, and late Shirley Eagle; sis of Maria Eagle, MP, *qv*; *b* 17 February 1961; *Educ* Formby HS, St John's Coll Oxford (BA); *Career* various posts Crosby CLP 1978–80; COHSE: joined as researcher 1984, later nat press offr, Parly liaison offr until 1992; MP (Lab, UNISON sponsored) Wallasey 1992–; former memb: Backbench Health Ctee and Treasy Ctee, Select Ctee on Members Interests, Select Ctee on Employment 1992–96; memb PAC 1995–96, former oppn whip; Parly under sec of state: Tport 1997–98, DSS 1998–2001, Home Office 2001–02; Exchequer sec to the Treasy 2007–09, min of state for pensions and ageing society 2009–10, shadow chief sec to the Treasy 2010–11, shadow ldr of the House of Commons 2011–15 shadow business sec & first secretary of state 2015–; chm Nat Conf of Lab Women 1991, chair Lab Backbench Employment Ctee; chm Oxford Univ Fabian Club 1980–83, sec Peckham CLP 1989–91; memb Lab Pty NEC Women's Ctee 1989–92; memb Exec Ctee: Socialist Health Assoc, Co-op Pty; memb NUJ, memb Br Film Inst; *Recreations* chess, cricket, cinema; *Style—* Ms Angela Eagle, MP; ✉ House of Commons, London SW1A 0AA

EAGLE, Maria; MP; da of André Eagle, and late Shirley Eagle; sis of Angela Eagle, MP, *qv*; *Career* MP (Lab): Liverpool Garston 1997–2010, Garston and Halewood 2010–; Parly under-sec of state Dept of Work and Pensions 2001–06, Parly under-sec of state NI Office 2006–07, Miny of Justice 2007–10 (min of state for justice 2009–10), shadow sec for transport 2010–15, shadow defence sec 2015–; *Style—* Ms Maria Eagle, MP; ✉ House of Commons, London SW1A 0AA (☎ 020 7219 4019, e-mail maria.eagle.mp@parliament.uk)

EAGLEN, Jane; da of Ronald Eaglen (d 1970), and Kathleen, *née* Kent; *Educ* South Park GS Lincoln, RNCM; *Career* soprano; princ memb ENO 1983–90; Peter Moores Fndn scholarship, Carl Rosa Tst award, Countess of Munster scholarship; *Performances* incl: Leonora in Il Trovatore (ENO), Elizabeth I in Mary Stuart (ENO), Eva in Die Meistersinger (ENO), Tosca (ENO, Perth Opera Aust, Buenos Aires, Cleveland Symphony Orch), Donna Anna in Don Giovanni (ENO, Scottish Opera, Vienna State Opera, Bologna Opera, Metropolitan Opera NY), Turandot (at the Met and Bologna), Mimi in La Bohème (Scottish Opera), Fiordiligi in Cosi fan Tutte (Scottish Opera), Brünnhilde in Die Walküre (Scottish Opera, Costa Mesa USA, La Scala Milan and Vienna), Brünnhilde in Siegried (Chicago), complete Ring Cycle (Chicago, Met, Seattle, La Scala), Madam Butterfly (Brisbane Opera Aust), Amelia in Un Ballo in Maschera (Bologna Opera, Opera Bastille Paris 1995), Mathilde in William Tell (Geneva Opera, Royal Opera House), Norma (Scottish Opera, Seattle Opera, Ravenna Festival), La Gioconda (Chicago), Tristan und Isolde (Seattle), recitals for Wagner Socs in London, NY and Argentina, Verdi's Requiem (gave performance for Lockerbie Disaster Appeal), Mahler's Eighth Symphony (broadcast live by Channel 4), Turandot (Royal Opera House); exclusive recording contract with Sony Classical; *Recordings* incl: Norma, Third Norn in Götterdämmerung, Die Flammen, Medea in Corinto, Tosca, soundtrack for Sense and Sensibility, Bellini & Wagner, Mozart & Strauss; *Style—* Miss Jane Eaglen; ✉ c/o AOR Management Ltd (Personal Management), Westwood, Lorraine Park, Harrow Weald, Middlesex HA3 6BX (☎ 020 8954 7646, fax 020 8420 7499)

EAGLES, Brian; s of David Eagles (d 1982), of London, and Anne, *née* Estrin (d 1994); *b* 4 February 1937; *Educ* Kilburn GS, Univ of London (LLB); *m* 30 May 1961, Marjorie, da of Leopold Weiss (d 1983), of London; 1 da (Karen b 1963), 2 s (Simon b 1965, Paul b 1967); *Career* slr; ptnr: J Sanson & Co 1960–67, Herbert Oppenheimer Nathan & Vandyk 1967–88, SJ Berwin & Co 1988–94, Hammond Suddards 1994–99, Howard Kennedy 1999–2013, HowardKennedyFsi 2013–14, Howard Kennedy 2015–16, Burlingtons Legal LLP 2016–; arbitrator and mediator; panel memb: World Intellectual Property Orgn (WIPO), American Arbitration Assoc, Law Soc, Ind Film and Television Alliance, Sports Dispute Resolution; accredited CEDR mediator; Consensus Mediation, Intermediation; hon slr Celebrities Guild of GB 1983–; memb: Int Bar Assoc, Br Assoc of Lawyer Mediators (BALM), Int Assoc of Entertainment Lawyers, Law Soc 1960; regular contributor of articles to legal and entertainment industry publications; ACIArb; *Recreations* music, film, theatre, skiing, walking; *Style—* Brian Eagles, Esq; ✉ Montague House, 107 Frognal, Hampstead, London NW3 6XR; Burlingtons Legal LLP, 38 Hertford Street, Mayfair, London W1J 7SG (☎ 020 7529 5420, e-mail brian.eagles@burlingtonsllp.com, website www.burlingtonsllp.com)

EAGLETON, Prof Terry; s of Francis Eagleton (d 1961), and Rosaleen, *née* Riley (d 2001); *b* 22 February 1943, Salford, Lancs; *Educ* De La Salle Coll Salford, Trinity Coll Cambridge (sr scholar, MA, PhD); *m* 1994, Willa Murphy; 4 s (Dominic b 1971, Daniel b 1974, Oliver b 1997, Owen b 2007), 1 da (Alice b 2004); *Career* fell Jesus Coll Cambridge 1964–69, fell and tutor in English Wadham Coll Oxford 1969–89, fell Linacre Coll Oxford 1989–93, Thomas Warton prof of English lit Univ of Oxford 1993–2001, John Edward Taylor prof of English Univ of Manchester 2001–08, chair in English lit Dept of English and Creative Writing Univ of Lancaster 2008–; Hon DLitt: Univ of Salford, Nat Univ of Ireland, Univ of Dalien China, Univ of Santiago di Compestela Spain, Univ of Central Lancs; FBA 2002; *Publications* Criticism and Ideology (1976), The Rape of Clarissa (1982), Literary Theory (1983), Saint Oscar (play, Irish Sunday Tribune Award 1989), Sweet Violence (2001), Holy Terror (2005), On Evil (2010), Why Marx Was Right (2011); *Recreations* Irish music; *Style—* Prof Terry Eagleton, FBA; ✉ Lancaster University, Lancaster LA1 4YW

EAGLING, Wayne John; s of Eddie Eagling, and Thelma, *née* Dunsmore; *b* 27 November 1950, Montreal, Canada; *Educ* Robert Louis Stevenson Sch Pebble Beach CA, Royal Ballet Sch London; *Career* ballet dancer; Royal Ballet Co: joined 1969, soloist 1972–75, princ 1975–91; artistic dir: Dutch Nat Ballet 1991–2005, English Nat Ballet 2005–; created/choreographed new works incl: R B Sque (for Amnesty Int Gala 1983, Sadler's Wells Theatre 1984), Frankenstein – The Modern Prometheus (one act, for Royal Ballet 1985, La Scala Milan 1987, Dutch Nat Ballet 1993), Beauty and the Beast (one act, for Royal Ballet 1986), Manfred (two acts), Senso (three acts), Nijinsky (two acts), Pas de Deuxs (Naples, Mantova, on RAI TV), The Queen of Spades (opera at La Scala Milan), The Wall Concert (with Roger Waters, Berlin), I Want to Break Free (video for pop group Queen), Alma (two act ballet on life of Alma Mahler, La Scala Milan) 1994; for Dutch National Ballet: Ruins of Times 1993, Symphony in Waves 1994, Duet 1995; co-choreographed: Nutcracker and Mouseking 1996 (with Toer van Schayk), Lost Touch (for Dancing for Duchenne, a Charity Gala Amsterdam) 1995, Holding a Balance (for opening of Vermeer exhbn, Mauritshuis The Hague) 1996, The Last Emperor (for The Hong Kong Ballet) 1997, Toverfluit (with Toer van Schayle) 1999, La Sacre du Printemps 2000, Frozen (for opening of Mintus von Weleer exbn Vermeer-Mauritshuis The Hague; *Roles* incl: Prince Siegfried in Swan Lake, Prince Florimund in The Sleeping Beauty, The Prince in The Nutcracker, The Poet in Les Sylphides, Solor in La Bayadère, Albrecht in Giselle; by Sir Frederick Ashton incl: Colas in La Fille Mal Gardée, Tirrenio in Ondine, The Prince in Cinderella, The Young Man in The Two Pigeons, Tuesday and Friday's Child in Jazz Calendar; by Sir Kenneth MacMillan incl: The Brother in Triad (first created role), des Grieux in Manon Lescaut, Prince Rudolf in Mayerling, Edward Gordon Craig and Oskar Beregi in Isadora, Romeo and Mercutio in Romeo and Mercutio, The Messenger of Death in Song of the Earth, The Chosen One in The Rite of Spring, title role in Orpheus; by Jerome Robbins incl: Requiem Canticles, In the Night, Dances at a Gathering; by Balanchine incl: The Four Temperaments, Violin Concerto, Agon, Apollo, The Prodigal Son, Bugaku, Serenade; others incl: The Boy with Matted Hair in Tudor's Shadowplay, title role in Robert Helpmann's Hamlet, Jean de Brienne in Rudolf Nureyev's Raymonda Act III, created role of Ariel in Rudolph Nureyev's The Tempest; *Recreations* scuba diving, golf; *Style—* Wayne Eagling, Esq

EALES, Darryl Charles; s of Barrie George Eales, of Birmingham, and Janet May, *née* Lewis; *b* 4 October 1960, Birmingham; *Educ* King Edward VI Camp Hill Sch for Boys, Univ of Exeter (BA); *m* 4 July 1987, Joanne, *née* Stevenson; 2 da (Harriet Caroline Victoria b 28 March 1990, Caroline Georgina Grace b 4 Oct 1992); *Career* Price Waterhouse 1983–87; Lloyds TSB Development Capital: joined 1987, dir 1994, regnl md 1997, chief exec 2003–14, advsy chm 2014–; chm Oxford United FC 2014–; involved with: Acorns Children's Hospice, The Great Generation, Dept of Military Studies Univ of Birmingham; CA 1986

(Tattersal Walker Prize ICAEW 1985); *Recreations* military and political history, sport, marathon running, wine collecting, supporting Birmingham FC; *Clubs* Copt Heath Golf; *Style*— Darryl Eales, Esq; ✉ Pinfield House, 27 Cherry Hill Road, Barnt Green, Birmingham B45 8LN (☎ 0121 445 5754)

EAMES, Baron (Life Peer UK 1995), of Armagh in the County of Armagh; Most Rev Robert Henry Alexander Eames; OM (2007); s of William Edward Eames, of Belfast, and Mary Eleanor Thompson, *née* Alexander; *b* 27 April 1937; *Educ* Belfast Royal Acad, Methodist Coll Belfast, Queen's Univ Belfast (LLB, PhD), Trinity Coll Dublin (LLD); *m* 1966, (Ann) Christine, OBE, da of Capt William Adrian Reynolds Daly (d 1943), and Olive Margaret Daly; 2 s (Hon Niall b 1967, Hon Michael b 1969); *Career* researcher and lectr Faculty of Laws Queen's Univ Belfast 1960–63, curate of Bangor Co Down 1963–66; incumbent of: Gilnahirk Down 1966–74, Dundela Down 1974–75; bishop of: Derry and Raphoe 1975–80, Down and Dromore 1980–86; archbishop of Armagh and Primate of All Ireland 1986–2006, Sr Primate of the Anglican Church 2006; chm: Archbishop of Canterbury's Int Cmmn on Communion and Women in the Episcopate 1988, Archbishop of Canterbury's Lambeth Int Cmmn on Anglican Structures 2004; govr Church Army 1985–, co-chair Br Govt Consultative Panel on the Past in NI 2007–08; memb: House of Lords Privileges Ctee 2008–, House of Lords Sub-Ctee on EU 2008–12, Scrutiny of Statutory Instruments Ctee 2010–; chair House of Lords Leaders Gp on Code of Conduct 2009; chair: Mgmnt Ctee Armagh Planetarium and Observatory 1986–2006, Govrs Armagh Royal Sch 1986–2006; memb Royal Yachting Assoc, memb Inst of Advanced Motorists; select preacher: Cambridge, Trinity Coll Dublin; Archbishop of Canterbury's Award for Outstanding Serv to the Anglican Communion 2006, Tipperary Peace Int Prize 2007; hon bencher Lincoln's Inn 1998; Hon LLD: Queen's Univ Belfast 1989, Univ of London 2008; Hon DLitt Univ of Greenwich Univ; Hon DD: Univ of Cambridge 1994, Univ of Aberdeen 1997, Virginia Theological Seminary USA 2005, Yale Univ USA 2005; Hon Doctorate Open Univ 2008; *Books* A Form of Worship for Teenagers (1965), The Quiet Revolution: Irish Disestablishment (1970), Through Suffering (1973), Thinking Through Lent (1978), Through Lent (1984), Chains to be Broken (1992), Nobody's Fool (biography by Alf McCreary, 1993); *Recreations* sailing, reading; *Clubs* Strangford Yacht, Ringhaddy Yacht, Carrickfergus Marina (Co Antrim), Kildare St and Univ (Dublin), Athenaeum; *Style*— The Most Rev the Rt Hon Lord Eames, OM; ✉ 3 Downshire Crescent, Hillsborough BT26 6DD; House of Lords, London SW1A 0PW

EARL, Belinda Jane; *b* 20 December 1961, Plymouth, Devon; *Educ* Univ of Wales Aberystwyth; *Career* grad trainee Harrods 1983–85; Debenhams: joined as menswear merchandiser 1985, memb Bd 1997–, chief exec 2000–03; chief exec Jaeger 2004–11, style dir Marks & Spencer 2012–; *Style*— Ms Belinda Earl; ✉ Marks & Spencer, Waterside House, 35 North Wharf Road, London W2 1NW

EARL, Kimble David; s of late Leonard Arthur Earl, of Surrey, and late Margaret Lucy, *née* Pulker; *b* 29 November 1951, Ross on Wye, Herefordshire; *Educ* Caterham Sch; *m* 1996, Susanne, *née* Gill; 2 da (Rosemary b 1998, Joanna b 2001); *Career* former dep chief exec Argus Press Gp, chief exec Newspaper Div and Consumer Publishing Div Argus Press Ltd 1988–1993, mktg dir Oak Craft Traditional Buildings/Holmsley Mill Ltd, mktg conslt Field Seymour Parkes Slrs 1994–2003, mktg conslt Personal Injury Med Services 1996–2007, mktg dir Theodore Goddard Slrs 1998–2001, chief exec The Bull Nelson Ltd 2000–, fndr and dir Wherecanwego.com 2004–, fndr and ed Ind Schs Magazine 2007–; former chm: Reading Newspaper Co Ltd, Windsor Newspaper Co Ltd, London and North Surrey Newspapers Ltd, West London and Surrey Newspapers Ltd, Surrey and South London Newspapers Ltd, South London Press Ltd, Argus Specialist Publications, Trident Press, Reading Newspaper Printing Co Ltd, Thames Valley Publishing, Argus Consumer Magazines Ltd, Argus Books, Argus Specialist Exhibitions, West London and Surrey Newspapers; former dir: SM Distribution Ltd, Argus Press Holdings Inc, Team Argus Inc, Argus Business Publications Ltd, Argus Retail Services Ltd; *Recreations* walking, travel, heritage railways; *Style*— Kimble Earl, Esq; ✉ The Bull Nelson Ltd, PO Box 4136, Upper Basildon, Reading RG8 6BS (☎ 01491 671998, e-mail mail@bullnelson.co.uk)

EARL, Prof Michael John; s of Vincent Earl (d 1975), and Marjorie Earl (d 1990); *b* 11 January 1944, Cheadle, Cheshire; *Educ* Univ of Newcastle upon Tyne (BA), Univ of Warwick (MSc), Univ of Oxford (MA); *m* 1969, Alison Jennifer, *née* Eades; 1 s (Jonathan Christopher b 24 May 1983), 1 da (Justine Elizabeth b 17 June 1985); *Career* gp systems mangr GEC Telecommunications 1972–74, lectr in mgmnt control Manchester Business Sch 1974–76, fell in info mgmnt Templeton Coll Oxford 1976–90, prof of info mgmnt London Business Sch 1990–2002 (dep princ and actg princ 1998–2000), emeritus prof of info mgmnt Univ of Oxford, dean Templeton Coll Oxford 2002–08, pro-vice-chlr (devpt and external rels) Univ of Oxford 2008–10; chm Oxford Centre for the Study of Philanthropy; tstee Oxford Philomusica Orch; hon fell: Green Templeton Coll Oxford, Harris Manchester Coll Oxford; FBCS 1992; *Books* Information Management: The Strategic Dimension (1988), Management Strategies for Information Technology (1989), Information Management: The Organisation Dimension (1996); *Recreations* golf, tennis, travel, music; *Clubs* Oxford and Cambridge, Frilford Heath Golf, Burford Golf, Frewen (Oxford); *Style*— Prof Michael Earl; ✉ Green Templeton College, Oxford OX2 6HG (☎ 01865 274797, e-mail michael.earl@gtc.ox.ac.uk)

EARL, Peter Richard Stephen; s of late Peter Richard Walter Earl, and late Patricia Earl; *b* 20 January 1955; *Educ* City of London Sch, Worcester Coll Oxford (open exhibitioner, MA, rowed for Univ of Oxford), Harvard Univ Graduate Sch of Arts and Sciences (Kennedy scholar, rowed for Harvard third heavyweight crew); *m* 1 (m dis), Emma Elizabeth, *née* Saunders; 1 da (Amelia Rose Elizabeth b 8 July 1985), 1 s (Peter Richard William John b 10 March 1987); m 2, Anastasia Protasova; 1 da (Tatiana Annabel Catherine b 10 Nov 2009), 1 s (Alexander Michael Nicholas b 9 Sept 2012); *Career* conslt Boston Consulting Group 1978–79, assoc Blyth Eastman Dillon Inc 1979–80, mangr Orion Bank 1980–82, dir ABC International Ltd 1982–85, vice-pres Arab Banking Corporation 1982–85, chm Tranwood Earl & Co Ltd (formerly Ifincorp Earl & Co Ltd) 1985–91, chief exec Tranwood plc 1988–91, chm and chief exec Carter Organization Inc NYC 1990–, head of European corp fin Fieldstone Private Capital Group 1994–96, chief exec The Independent Power Corporation plc 1995–, ceo Rurelec plc 2004–15, chief exec IPSA Gp plc 2005–15; tstee: Everest Meml Tst, City of London Sch Bursary Tst; chm of tstees Oxford Philharmonic Tst; *Books* International Mergers & Acquisitions (1986); *Recreations* mountaineering (joint leader British 40th Anniversary Everest Expedition 1993), marathons, skiing; *Clubs* Vincent's (Oxford), Brooks's; *Style*— Peter Earl, Esq; ✉ 17th Floor IPC, Millbank Tower, 21–24 Millbank, London SW1P 4AP (☎ 020 7793 7676, fax 020 7793 7654, e-mail pearl@indpow.com)

EARL, Roger Lawrence; s of Lawrence William Earl (d 1994), of Hove, E Sussex, and Doris Florence, *née* Copelin (d 1997); *b* 4 October 1940, Greenwich, London; *Educ* St Christopher's Sch Kingswood, Hollingbury Ct Brighton, St Paul's; *m* 22 June 1968, Lynda Marion, da of late Harold Frederick Waldock, of Enfield, Middx; 2 da (Meredith Louise b 12 July 1970, Alexandra Kirsten b 20 June 1972); *Career* Arbon Langrish & Co (Lloyd's brokers) 1957–65; Bland Welch & Co/Bland Payne & Co (Lloyd's brokers): asst dir 1966–70, exec dir 1970–73, bd dir and md N American Div 1973–79; md and chief exec Fenchurch plc (Lloyd's brokers) 1979–96 (dep chm 1996–98); dir GPG plc 1987–89 (md 1989), dir Lambert Fenchurch Insurance Brokers Ltd 1998–2000, dir Heath Lambert Insurance Brokers Ltd 2000–04, chm and ceo Carabela Consits Ltd 2005–; dir and tstee Charles Letts Meml Tst 2002–, hon ambass Fly Navy Heritage Tst; memb Kew Soc; memb Lloyd's 1970–96; Liveryman Hon Co of Coachmakers and Coach Harness Makers; *Recreations* motor sport, tennis; *Clubs* Hurlingham, City of London, Maserati Owners, Automobile Club de Monaco (ACM), Automobile Club de l'Ouest (ACO), Lloyd's Motor (chm), LTA; *Style*— Roger Earl, Esq; ✉ 4 Cumberland Road, Kew, Surrey TW9 3HQ (☎ 020 8948 1714, mobile 07774 120614); Flouquet, Lacour de Visa, Tarn et Garonne, France; La Carabela 2, 27 Via Del Bosque, Canyamel, Mallorca, Spain

EARL, His Hon Judge Stephen; TD; s of Leslie Earl (d 2013), and Anne, *née* Mortimer; *b* 16 April 1958, Leeds; *Educ* Beverley GS, Manchester Polytechnic (BA), Guildford Coll of Law; *m* 25 March 2002, Gillian Douglass-Earl, *née* Douglass; 1 s (Matthew James Leslie b 2002), 1 da (Aimee Jayne Maria b 2004); *Career* admitted slr 1982; dep dist judge Magistrates' Courts 2000, dist judge Magistrates' Courts 2004, circuit judge (NE Circuit) 2015–; memb Criminal Procedure Rule Ctee 2011–16; *Recreations* reading, travel, walking; *Style*— His Hon Judge Earl, TD; ✉ Newcastle upon Tyne Combined Court Centre, The Law Courts, Quayside, Newcastle upon Tyne NE1 3LA (☎ 0191 201 2000, e-mail hhj.stephen.earl@ejudiciary.net)

EARLE, Joel Vincent (Joe); s of James Basil Foster Earle (d 1989), of Kyle of Lochalsh, Ross-shire, and Mary Isabel Jessie, *née* Weeks (d 1992); *b* 1 September 1952; *Educ* Westminster, New Coll Oxford (MA); *m* 10 May 1980, Sophia Charlotte, da of Oliver Arbuthnot Knox, of London; 2 s (Leo b 1981, Martin b 1984); *Career* V&A: keeper Far Eastern Dept 1983–87 (res asst 1974–77, asst keeper 1977–83), head of public servs 1987–89; exhibitions co-ordinator and head of public affairs Japan Festival 1991, chair Dept of Art of Asia, Oceania, and Africa Museum of Fine Arts Boston 2003–07, vice-pres Japan Soc and dir Japan Soc Gallery 2007–12, currently sr conslt for Japanese art Bonhams 1793; ind arts conslt 1991–2003; major exhbns: Japan Style 1980, Great Japan Exhibition 1981, Toshiba Gallery of Japanese Art 1986, Visions of Japan 1991, Songs of My People 1992, Shibata Zeshin 1997, Splendors of Meiji 1999, Netsuke: Fantasy and Reality in Japanese Miniature Sculpture 2001, Serizawa: Master of Japanese Textile Design 2001, Contemporary Clay: Japanese Ceramics for the New Century 2005, Beyond Basketry: Japanese Bamboo Art 2006, The Genius of Japanese Laquer: Masterworks by Shibata Zeshin 2008, New Bamboo: Contemporary Japanese Masters 2008, KRAZY! The Delirious World of Manga + Anime + Video Games 2009, Japanese Tin Toys from the Golden Age of the American Automobile 2009, Serizawa: Master of Japanese Textile Design 2009, Bye Bye Kitty!!! Between Heaven and Hell in Contemporary Japanese Art 2011, Fiber Futures: Japan's Textile Pioneers 2011, Silver Wind: The Arts of Sakai Hoitsu 2012; tstee The Design Museum 1988–2002; *Books* The Great Japan Exhibition (contrib, 1981), The Japanese Sword (translator, 1983), Japanese Art and Design (ed, 1987), Masterpieces by Shibata Zeshin (1995), The Index of Inro Artists (ed, 1995), The Khalili Collection of Japanese Art: Lacquer (ed, 1995), Flower Bronzes of Japan (1995), Splendors of Meiji (1999), Infinite Spaces: The Art and Wisdom of the Japanese Garden (2000), Japanese Lacquer: The Chiddingstone Castle Collection (2000), The Robert S Huthart Collection of Iwami Netsuke (2000), Netsuke: Fantasy and Reality in Japanese Miniature Sculpture (2001), Splendors of Imperial Japan (2001), Lethal Elegance: Samurai Sword Fittings (2004), Contemporary Clay: Japanese Ceramics for the New Century (2005), New Bamboo: Contemporary Japanese Masters (2008), Buriki: Japanese Tin Toys from the Golden Age of the American Automobile (2009), Serizawa: Master of Japanese Textile Design (2009), Melk's Golden Acres (translator, 2010), Fiber Futures: Japan's Textile Pioneers (2011), A White Camellia in a Vase (trans, 2012), The Misumi Collection: Important Works of Lacquer Art and Paintings Part 1 (2014), Transformation Summation Creation: Masterpieces of Japanese Meiji-Era Craft from a Private Collection (2015), The Misumi Collection: Important Works of Lacquer Art and Paintings Part 2 (2015), From Edo to Tokyo: A Special Exhibition of Masterpieces of Japanese Art from a Private Collection (2016); catalogues for Christie's, Spink, Eskenazi, Barry Davies Oriental Art Ltd, Erik Thomsen Gallery, Malcolm Fairley Japanese Art, Grace Tsumugi Fine Art; *Recreations* reading Japanese fiction; *Style*— Mr Joe Earle; ✉ Bonhams, 580 Madison Avenue, New York NY 10022 (☎ 00 1 917 206 1620 or 00 1 646 596 2939, e-mail joe.earle@bonhams.com or joevearle@gmail.com)

EARLE, Laurence Foster; s of Robert Foster Earle, of London, and Joy, *née* Cartwright; *b* 11 July 1965; *Educ* Westminster, Univ of Sussex (BA); *m* 20 Sept 1997, Maria Christina, da of Robert Johnston Arnold; 1 s (Gabriel Harry Foster b 13 Oct 2001), 1 da (Eliza Constance b 13 Aug 2003); *Career* film ed iD Magazine 1989–91; Time Out Pubns: dep ed 1990–92; Independent on Sunday: arts ed 1995–96, ed Independent on Sunday Review 1996–98; The Independent: features ed 1999–2002, exec ed (features) 2002–03, ed The Independent Magazine 2003–10, exec ed Independent on Sunday 2010–13; team dir SHM prodns Ltd 2014–; *Recreations* football, skiing, hill walking; *Style*— Laurence Earle, Esq; ✉ SHM Productions Ltd, 20–22 Bedford Row, London WC1R 4EB (☎ 020 7242 5504, e-mail laurence@shm-ltd.co.uk)

EARLS, Mark Benedict; s of Gerard Warmington Earls, of Harrow, Middx, and Kathleen Mary, *née* Orchard; *b* 12 July 1961; *Educ* John Lyon Sch Harrow, St Edmund Hall Oxford (BA); *Career* trainee Grey London (advtg agency) 1984–86, planner/sr planner Boase Massimi Pollit 1986–89, actg head of planning CDP Financial 1989–90; Ammirati and Puris/Lintas (formerly S P Lintas): sr planner/bd dir 1990–95, dir of planning Europe 1994–95; former bd planning dir Bates Dorland and St Luke's; exec planning offr Ogilvy & Mather 2001–; memb Ctee Account Planning Gp 1994–; memb Market Research Soc 1986; *Recreations* cricket (chm Wandsworth Gods CC), travel, walking, Italian cuisine, oysters; *Clubs* Vincent's (Oxford); *Style*— Mark Earls, Esq

EARNSHAW, Christopher Martin (Chris); OBE (2015); *b* 4 May 1954; *Educ* Wellington GS, Adams GS Newport, Univ of Sheffield (BSc); *m* 25 Aug 1979, Moira May, da of Donald Turner; 2 s (Nicholas b 4 Nov 1984, Matthew b 27 Sept 1992), 1 da (Rachel b 1 May 1987); *Career* British Telecommunications plc: dir Network BTUK 1989–91, md Worldwide Networks 1991–93, pres and ceo Concert Communications Inc 1993–95, md Networks and Systems/Info Servs 1995–99, gp engrg dir and chief technol offr 1999–2002, dir Oakleigh Ventures Ltd 2002–16; non-exec chm: Cranfield Ventures Ltd 2008–, Cranfield Aerospace Ltd 2010–; sr non-exec dir BRE Gp 2010–13 (non-exec chm 2014–); pres IET 2008–09; dir Engrg and Technol Bd (ETB) 2002–05, non-exec chm Police IT Orgn (PITO) 2004–07; fell Int Engrg Consortium; CEng, FREng, FIET, FRSA; *Clubs* Athenaeum; *Style*— Chris Earnshaw, Esq, OBE, FREng; ☎ 01582 712573, e-mail chris@oakleighassociates.com

EARWICKER, Prof Martin John; s of George Allen Earwicker (d 1983), and Joan Mary, *née* West (d 2008); *b* 11 May 1948, Farnborough, Hants; *Educ* Farnborough GS, Univ of Surrey (BSc); *m* 1970, Pauline Ann Josey; 2 s (Simon Paul b 1970, Alexander b 1977); *Career* various research posts ARE Portland 1970–86, dir Science (SEA) MOD 1986–89, head Attack Weapons Dept RAE 1989–90, head Flight Systems Dept DRA 1990–92, dir Op Studies DRA 1992–93, dir Air Systems Def Evaluation Res Agency (DERA) 1993–96, dep chief scientist Scrutiny and Analysis MOD 1996–98, DG Scrutiny and Analysis MOD 1998–99, md Analysis DERA 1998–99, head Science and Technology Base Office of Science and Technology DTI 1999–2001, chief exec Defence Science and Technol Lab 2001–06, dir Nat Museum of Science & Industry 2006–09, vice-chllr and chief exec London South Bank Univ 2009–13; vice-chm Dorset County Hosp NHS Fndn Tst 2013–; pres: Assoc of European Research Establishments in Aeronautics (AEREA) 1995–96, Assoc for Science Educn 2008; vice-pres Royal Acad of Engrg 2009–12; chair: Corporation Farnborough Coll of Technol 2004–11 and 2015–, Tower Hamlets Coll 2010–16; tstee Hart CAB 2013–, tstee Regent's Univ London 2014; awarded AB Wood Silver Medal Inst of Acoustics 1984; Hon DUniv Surrey 2009, prof emeritus London South

Bank Univ 2014; FREng 2000; *Recreations* cycling, walking, woodwork, music; *Style*— Prof Martin J Earwicker, FREng; ✉ 21 Basingbourne Road, Fleet, Hants GU52 6TE

EASSIE, Rt Hon Lord; Ronald David Mackay; PC (2006); *Educ* Univ of St Andrews (MA), Univ of Edinburgh (LLB); *Career* admitted Faculty of Advocates 1972; official at Court of Justice of the European Communities Luxembourg 1979–82, QC (Scot) 1986, advocate depute 1986–90, senator Coll of Justice 1997–2015; chm Scottish Law Cmmn 2002–04; *Style*— The Rt Hon Lord Eassie; ✉ Parliament House, Edinburgh EH1 1RQ

EASSON, Prof Angus; s of William Coleridge Easson (d 1987), and Olive Mary, *née* Hornfeck (d 1962); *b* 18 July 1940; *Educ* William Ellis GS, Univ of Nottingham (BA), Univ of Oxford (DPhil); *Career* lectr in English: Univ of Newcastle upon Tyne 1965–71, Royal Holloway Coll London 1971–77; Univ of Salford: prof of English 1977–2000, dean Faculty of Social Sciences and Arts 1986–89 and 1992–95, chm Modern Languages Dept 1989–92, chm English Dept 1992–99, research prof of English 2000–05, hon visiting fell 2005–10, emeritus prof 2010–; *Books* Elizabeth Gaskell (1979), Elizabeth Gaskell - Critical Heritage (1991), Gerard Manley Hopkins (2011); *Recreations* opera; *Style*— Prof Angus Easson; ✉ 17 Dawlish Road, Manchester M21 8XR

EASSON, Gillian; da of Stanley Oakley (d 2001), and Joan, *née* Blackburn (d 1995); *b* 2 December 1950, Stockport, Cheshire; *Educ* Marple Hall GS for Girls, Girton Coll Cambridge (BA, MA); *m* 6 July 1972, Malcolm Cameron Greig Easson (d 2010); 1 s (James Thomas Greig b 22 Oct 1979), 1 da (Helen Antonia Oakley b 25 March 1982); *Career* prosecuting slr Greater Manchester Cncl 1977–86, crown prosecutor 1986–87, sole practitioner and agent for the CPS 1987–2000; Christie Hospital NHS Tst: non-exec dir 2000–06, chair Charitable Funds Ctee 2001–02, chair Audit Ctee 2001–03, chair Fin Ctee 2003–06; chm Stockport NHS Fndn Tst 2012– (non-exec dir 2007–12, dep chm 2007–12), dir and tstee NHS Providers 2014–; memb: Law Soc 1975–, Manchester Medico Legal Soc 2010–; Nat Steering Ctee Int Health Promoting Hosps Conference 2010, NW Leadership Academy 2012 (non-exec dir Devpt Gp 2012); Univ of Manchester: memb Cncl and Ct Inst of Science and Technol 2001–04, memb Bd of Govrs 2004–12 (dep chm 2008–12), chair Risk Ctee 2004–08, non-exec dir and chair Audit Ctee Intellectual Property 2005–07, chair Staffing Ctee 2011–12, pro-chllr and chm Nominations Ctee 2012–, memb Global Leadership Bd 2012–; chm Manchester Univ Press 2010–13; OFQUAL: memb Bd 2010–12, chair external Advsy Gp for Equality & Diversity, head GCSE 2010, head AS & A-Level Marking Inquiry (for 3 exam regulators for England, Wales and NI OFQUAL, DCELLS and CCEA) 2011, memb Audit & Risk Ctee; cncllr Prestbury Parish 1999–2000, volunteer East Cheshire Hospice 2000; *Recreations* light aviation; *Style*— Mrs Gillian Easson; ✉ Stockport NHS Foundation Trust, Poplar Grove, Hazel Grove, Stockport, Cheshire SK10 7JE (☎ 0161 419 5030, fax 0161 487 3341, e-mail gillian.easson@stockport.nhs.uk)

EAST, John Richard Alan; s of Bertram David (Barry) East (d 1996), of Eaton Square, London, and Gladys, *née* Stone (d 1957); *b* 14 May 1949; *Educ* Westminster Sch; *m* 1, 14 May 1971 (m dis 1986), Judith Adrienne, da of Clive Hill, of Horshall, Surrey; 2 s (Robin b 1974, Christopher b 1978); m 2, 12 July 1986 (m dis 2001), Charlotte Sylvia, da of Lt Cdr Peter Gordon Merriman, DSC, RN (d 1965), and Alison Grace Merriman, *née* Williams (d 1997); m 3, 17 Jan 2007, Frances Ruth, da of Christopher John Ollard (d 1974) and Rachel Ollard MBE, *née* Swain, of Wold Newton, Lincs; *Career* Speechly Bircham (Slrs) 1967–70, Mitton Butler Priest & Co Ltd 1971–73, Panmure Gordon & Co 1973–77; Margetts & Addenbrooke (formerly Margetts & Addenbrooke East Newton, Kent East Newton & Co) 1977–86: sr ptnr 1977–80, managing ptnr 1980–86, sr ptnr 1983–86; dir: Barwood Securities Ltd 1977–, National Investment Group plc 1986–87, Guidehouse Group plc and subsids 1987–91; chm and chief exec John East & Partners Ltd (formerly Guidehouse Securities Ltd) 1987–2009, dep ceo and chm on corporate fin Merchant Securities Ltd 2009–13 (dir Merchant Securities plc 2007–12); Sanlam Securities UK Ltd: dir and chm of corp fin 2013–14 (following mergers and name changes), conslt 2014–; non-exec dir Sanlam Private Wealth (UK) Holdings Ltd 2014–; co-fndr CISCO (now Quoted Cos Alliance); non-exec dir County Broadband Holdings Ltd, non-exec memb 606 Club LLP, chm of tstees Project Motorhouse; memb and memb Conseil La Commanderie de Bordeaux à Londres; jt pres Dagenham and Redbridge FC; memb Stock Exchange 1974, FCSI 2000 (MSI (dip) 1992), FRSA 2005; *Recreations* music predominantly jazz (listening, recording, playing and singing at live venues), non-league football (and now Football League football following promotion), fine wine, travel; *Clubs* Carlton (dep chm 2003–12, tstee 2012–), United and Cecil, Arts; *Style*— John East, Esq; ✉ e-mail john.east@sanlamsecuritiesuk.com

EAST, Prof Robin Alexander; s of Percy Alexander East (d 1981), of Romsey, Hants, and Winifred May, *née* Southwell (d 1993); *b* 11 December 1935; *Educ* Barton Peveril GS, Univ of Southampton (BSc, PhD); *m* 6 Oct 1962, June, da of George Henry Slingsby (d 1977), of Sheffield; 1 da (Jennifer Lynn b 1963); *Career* apprentice Vickers Supermarine 1953–57, visiting res fell Aust Nat Univ at Canberra 1973; Univ of Southampton: Sir Alan Cobham res fell 1960–63, lectr, sr lectr and reader in aeronautics 1963–85, head of Aeronautics Dept 1985–90, prof of aeronautics 1985–96 (emeritus prof 1996); memb various ctees and former chm Southampton Branch RAeS, chm Accreditation Ctee RAeS 1991–2004, chm Aerodynamics Gp Ctee 1997–2001; memb Aviation Ctee DTI 1995–99; assoc fell American Inst of Aeronautics and Astronautics 1991; CEng 1983, FRAeS 1985; *Books* Forty Years of the Spitfire (jt ed with I C Cheeseman, 1976), Spacecraft Systems Engineering (contrib, 1991), Encyclopedia of Aerospace Engineering (contrib, 2010); around 100 pubns on hypersonic aerodynamics and experimental facilities in int jls and conf proceedings; *Recreations* gardening, photography, ornithology, walking; *Style*— Prof Robin East; ✉ East Croft, North Common, Sherfield English, Romsey, Hampshire SO51 6JT (☎ 01794 340444); School of Engineering Sciences, Aeronautics and Astronautics, University of Southampton, Southampton, Hampshire SO17 1BJ (e-mail rae@soton.ac.uk)

EAST ANGLIA, Bishop of (RC) 2013–; Rt Rev Alan Stephen Hopes; s of William Hopes, and Beatrice, *née* Tate; *b* 17 March 1944, Oxford; *Educ* Oxford HS, Enfield GS, KCL (BD, AKC), St Boniface Coll Warminster; *Career* ordained: C of E deacon 1967, C of E priest 1968; asst curate East Finchley 1967–73, priest in charge St Augustine's Grahame Park 1973–78, vicar St Paul's Tottenham 1978–94, ordained RC priest 1995, asst priest Our Lady of Victories Kensington 1995–97, parish priest Our Most Holy Redeemer and St Thomas More Chelsea 1997–2001, vicar gen Dio of Westminster 2001, ordained bishop (titular see Cuncacestre) 2003, auxiliary bishop (RC) of Westminster 2003–13; *Style*— The Rt Rev the Bishop of East Anglia; ✉ The White House, 21 Upgate, Poringland, Norwich NR14 7SH

EASTAWAY, Nigel Antony; OBE (2012); s of Kenneth George Eastaway, and Muriel, *née* Angus; *b* 17 November 1943, Woodford, Essex; *Educ* Chigwell Sch; *m* 17 Aug 1968, Ann, da of Cecil Douglas Geddes; 1 da (Suzanne Emma Louise b 4 July 1980), 1 s (James Nigel Andrew b 18 May 1983); *Career* chartered accountant; ptnr Moores Rowland (formerly F Rowland & Co) 1969–98 (articles 1960), joined NCS Conslts Ltd and Tax Services for Professionals Ltd (latterly part of Chiltern plc and Moores Rowland Int) 1998; ptnr: BDO LLP (following takeover) 2008–13, MHA MacIntyre Hudson 2013–, dir MacIntyre Hudson Corp Fin Ltd 2013–; memb: Cncl Chartered Inst of Taxation 1985–99 and 2003– (chm Tech Ctee 1997–99 and 2003–05, past chm Personal Taxes, Capital Taxes, Tax Policy Sub-Ctees and EU and Human Rights Ctee and memb Tech Ctee, Audit Ctee and Grants and Management of Taxes Sub-Ctees), Tech Ctee Tax Faculty ICAEW; former memb Exec Ctee and chm European branch Offshore Inst, former memb Taxation Ctee London C of C and Industry; editorial conslt Asia Pacific Jl of Taxation, author of numerous articles in professional jls; Tax Writer of the Year Lexis Nexis UK Tax Awards 2003; tstee Russian Aviation Res Tst, fell Br Interplanetary Soc, affiliate RAeS; fndr memb: Worshipful Co of Tax Advsrs, Acad of Experts, Expert Witness Inst; memb: Soc of Share and Business Valuers, Int Tax Planning Assoc Int Fiscal Assoc; AIIT, MEWI, MBAE, FCInstT 1965 (Fellowship Examination prize), FCIS 1965 (J F Clark Prize, Sir Ernest Clark Prize, A W Goodbody Prize), FCA 1966 (Sendell Prize, Walter Knox scholar, Plender Prize), FCCA 1967, FCMA 1967 (Lewton Coronation Prize), CGMA 2011, MRICS, FRSA, FBIS, CTA, fell Offshore Inst, hon fell Hong Kong Inst of Taxation, fell Hong Kong Inst of Certified Public Accountants; *Books* MHA MacIntyre Hudson's Yellow Tax Guide (formerly: BDO's, Chiltern's, Moores Rowland's), MHA MacIntyre Hudson's Orange Tax Guide (formerly: BDO's, Chiltern's, Moores Rowland's), Moores Rowland's Taxation of Farmers and Farming, Moores Rowland's A to Z of Tax Planning, Moores Rowland's Tax Planning for Recording Stars, The Tax Advisers Guide to Trusts, Visiting Entertainers and Sportsmen, Handbook on the Capital Gains Tax 1979, Tax and Financial Planning for Medical Practitioners, Tax and Financial Planning for Professional Partnerships, Practical Share Valuation, Share Valuation Cases, Utilising Personal Tax Losses and Reliefs, Tax Aspects of Company Reorganisations, Utilising Company Tax Losses and Reliefs, Intellectual Property Law and Taxation, Zurich Expatriate Tax and Investment Handbook, Taxation of Lloyd's Underwriters, Principles of Capital Transfer Tax, Hong Kong Stamp Duty, Tottel's Self-Assessment (formerly Tolley's), Tottel's Corporation Tax Self-Assessment (formerly Tolley's), Tolley's Partnership Taxation, Simons Taxes (contrib), ICAEW Taxation Service (contrib); Soviet Aircraft Since 1918 (ed), Aircraft of the Soviet Union (contrib), Encyclopaedia of Russian Aircraft (contrib), Mikoyan MiG-21 (contrib), The Soviet Air Force (contrib), Janes All the World's Aircraft (contrib); *Recreations* Russian aircraft history, playing with old cars; *Clubs* Bentley Drivers', Vintage Sports Car, Morgan Sports Car, Ferrari Owners', Club Lotus, Jaguar Drivers', Air Britain; *Style*— Nigel Eastaway, Esq, OBE; ✉ Wood Farm, Pledgdon Green, Henham, Bishop's Stortford CM22 6BN (☎ 01279 850338, fax 01279 851979, e-mail neastaway@aol.com); MHA MacIntyre Hudson (part of Baker Tilley International), 30–34 New Bridge Street, London EC4V 6BJ (☎ 020 7429 0529, e-mail nigel.eastaway@mhllp.co.uk, website www.macintyrehudson.co.uk)

EASTELL, Prof Richard; *b* 12 February 1953, Shipley, W Yorks; *Educ* Univ of Edinburgh (BSc, MB ChB, MD); *m*; 3 c; *Career* Western Gen Hosp Edinburgh: house offr 1977–78 (also at Royal Infirmary Edinburgh), MRC research fell 1978–80, registrar 1980–82; registrar Northwick Park Hosp Harrow 1982–84, research assoc and sr clinical fell Mayo Clinic Rochester MN 1984–89; Dept Human Metabolism Clinical Biochemistry Univ of Sheffield: sr research fell and hon conslt 1989–92, sr lectr 1992–95, hon conslt physician 1992–, prof 1995–; Univ of Sheffield: research dean Sch of Med and Biomedical Sciences 2002–, dep dir Div of Clinical Sciences (N) 2003–, head Bone Metabolism Gp; dir of R&D Sheffield Teaching Hosps Tst; FRCP 1996 (MRCP 1981), Hon FRCPI 1998, FRCPath 2000, FMedSci 2000, FRCPEd 2000; *Publications* author and co-author of numerous research papers in learned jls; *Style*— Prof Richard Eastell; ✉ Division of Clinical Sciences (North), University of Sheffield, Clinical Sciences Centre, Northern General Hospital, Sheffield S5 7AU

EASTER, Nick; s of John Easter, and Glynis Easter; *b* 15 August 1978, Epsom, Surrey; *Educ* Dulwich Coll, Nottingham Trent Univ; *Career* rugby union player; clubs: Orrell 2001–04, Harlequins 2004– (234 caps (record), Harlequins Player of the Year 2005, 2006 and 2013), Aviva Premiership Forward of the Year 2014; International: England player 2007–11 (47 caps), memb World Cup squad 2007 and 2011, England Player of the Year 2008; *Style*— Mr Nick Easter; ✉ c/o Harlequins, Twickenham Stoop Stadium, Langhorn Drive, Twickenham TW2 7SX

EASTERMAN, Nicholas Barrie; s of Cyril Saul Herman Easterman (d 2003), of Lausanne, Switzerland, and Sheila, *née* Cope (d 1983); *b* 11 April 1950; *Educ* Millfield, UCL (LLB), Cncl of Legal Educn; *Partner* civil partnership 2008; *Career* called to the Bar Lincoln's Inn 1975 (bencher 1998); acting stipendiary magistrate 1995–2001, dep district judge (crime) 2001–; immigration judge 2003–10, judge of the First-tier Tbnl (Immigration and Asylum Chamber) 2010– diversity and community relations judge 2013–; *Recreations* photography, driving, good wine and cognac; *Clubs* Bentham; *Style*— Nicholas Easterman, Esq; ✉ c/o AIT Hatton Cross, 2–4 Dukes Green Avenue, Feltham TW14 0LR (e-mail nick.easterman@londonweb.net)

EASTMOND, Dr Clifford John; s of Charles John Henry Eastmond (d 1980), and Hilda, *née* Horrocks; *b* 19 January 1945; *Educ* Audenshaw GS, Univ of Edinburgh Med Sch (BSc, MB ChB, MD); *m* 25 March 1967, Margaret, da of Stanley Wadsworth (d 1976); 2 s (Nigel b 1970, Timothy b 1972), 1 da (Heather b 1975); *Career* house physician Northern Gen Hosp Edinburgh 1969, house surgn Royal Infirmary Edinburgh 1970, sr house offr Sefton Gen Hosp Liverpool 1970, registrar Liverpool Hosps 1971–74, res fell Univ of Liverpool Med Sch 1974–76, sr registrar Rheumatism Res Unit Leeds Univ and Gen Infirmary 1976–79, consl t rheumatologist Grampian Health Bd 1979–95; Grampian Univ Hosps Tst (formerly Aberdeen Royal Hosps NHS Tst): consl t rheumatologist 1995–2007, clinical dir of med 1995–99, assoc med dir 1999–2007; clinical sr lectr Univ of Aberdeen 1979–2007, rheumatologist in private practice Albyn Hosp Aberdeen 1997–2013; memb Scottish Soc of Rheumatology, memb Br Soc of Rheumatology (memb Cncl 1987–90), memb Scottish Soc of Physicians, memb Aberdeen Medico-Chirurgical Soc; elder Skene Parish Church, memb Westhill and Dist Rotary Club 1984– (pres 1989–90, Paul Harris fell 2012), memb Cairngorm Mountaineering Club, dir Seabank House, memb Ctee St John Scotland Aberdeen and North East Area; FRCPEd 1984, FRCP 1990; MStJ; *Recreations* Scottish mountaineering, skiing, game shooting, music, curling, golf; *Clubs* Royal Northern and Univ; *Style*— Dr Clifford Eastmond; ✉ The Rowans, Skene, Aberdeenshire AB32 6YP (☎ 01224 790370)

EASTON, Antony Miles; *née* Miles; s of Peter Easton (d 2010), and Bobbie Easton (d 1987); *b* 3 October 1963; *Educ* St Paul's, Chelsea Sch of Art, St Martin's Sch of Art; *m* Anna Claire, da of Richard Curtis; *Career* graphic designer and TV prog maker 1983–87, bd dir Saatchi & Saatchi Advertising 1989–92 (art dir 1987–89), Chiat/Day 1992–93, commercials dir, screenwriter and dir; *Recreations* art, politics, media, sport, Chelsea FC; *Style*— Antony Easton, Esq; ✉ website www.anteaston.com

EASTON, Dr Carole; *Educ* PhD; *Career* child and family psychotherapist 1980–92, counselling mangr ChildLine 1992–96, head of clinical servs Place to Be 1996–98, exec dir Cruse Bereavement Care 1998–2001, chief exec ChildLine 2001–; *Style*— Dr Carole Easton

EASTON, Ewan Reid; s of Norman Kidston Easton (d 1987), of Dumgoyne, Stirlingshire, and Alison Gray Easton (d 2014); *b* 10 May 1958; *Educ* Kelvinside Acad Glasgow, Sedbergh, Univ of Glasgow; *Career* Maclay Murray & Spens LLP: 1980–84, seconded to Herbert Smith Slrs London 1984–85, ptnr 1985–, head Commercial Litigation Dept 1992–2000, head of mediation 2001–; CORE accredited mediator 2001, CEDR mediator 2002; legal advsr to Edinburgh Int Festival 1990–, memb Bd Edinburgh Book Festival 2001–; Writer to the Signet 1987–; *Recreations* architecture, building restoration, Scottish paintings; *Style*— Ewan Easton, Esq; ✉ Maclay Murray & Spens LLP, Quartermile One, 15 Lauriston Place, Edinburgh EH3 9EP (☎ 0131 228 7000)

EASTON, Mark Richard Erskine; *b* 12 March 1959, Glasgow; *Educ* Peter Symonds GS Winchester; *Career* Southern Evening Echo 1979–80, Radio Victory 1980–81, Radio Aire 1981–82, LBC 1982–86, reporter London Plus, BBC Breakfast News, Newsnight and Here and Now 1986–96, political ed Five News 1996–98, home and social affrs ed Channel 4 News 1998–2004, home ed BBC News 2004–; RSS Award for Statistical Excellence 2009 and 2010; *Books* Britain etc (2012); *Style*— Mark Easton, Esq; ✉ BBC News, BBC Broadcasting House, Portland Place, London W1A 1AA

EASTWELL, Nicholas Wakefield (Nick); s of Thomas William Eastwell, and Zena Diane, *née* Wakefield; *Educ* Westcliff HS, Trinity Hall Cambridge (Cooper scholar, MA); *m* 1988, Sally Jane Geddes; 2 da (Alexandra b 1993, Charlotte b 1996), 1 s (Frederick b 1994); *Career* slr; Linklaters: articled clerk 1980–82, Hong Kong office 1983–89, ptnr (capital markets) 1989–2009, managing ptnr Central and Eastern Europe 1999–2005, global head Capital Markets 2003–08, regnl managing ptnr Emerging Europe, Middle East and North Africa 2008–09; London conslt Kinstellar 2009–, special advsr SR Search 2009–16, chief advsr City Law Firms Slrs Regulation Authy 2010–; memb Listing Advsy Ctee UK Law Assoc (UKLA) 2000–02, memb City Corporation EU Advsy Gp 2008–09; hon lawyer and founding memb Hong Kong Capital Markets Assoc 1986–89; regular conf speaker; author of articles in various legal jls; co-chair Securities Law Ctee Int Bar Assoc 2014–15; memb: Trinity Hall Assoc (Year Rep 1975), Univ of Greenwich Law Advsy Forum 2007–, Ct Univ of Greenwich 2008– (currently dep chair and chair Finance Ctee and Remuneration Ctee); chm of tstees Beyond Sports Fndn 2013–; memb Law Soc 1982; *Recreations* family, history and archaeology, watching rugby and soccer, skiing, walking, travel; *Clubs* Aula (Trinity Hall), Hawks' (Cambridge); *Style*— Nick Eastwell, Esq; ✉ 5 Dartmouth Grove, London SE10 8AR (mobile 07768 345683, e-mail nick.eastwell@kinstellar.com or nick@eastwell.me.uk)

EASTWOOD, Prof Sir David Stephen; kt (2014), DL (W Midlands 2012); s of Colin Eastwood, of Sandbach, Cheshire, and Elaine Clara, *née* Hunt; *b* 5 January 1959, Oldham, Lancs; *Educ* Sandbach Sch, St Peter's Coll Oxford (open scholar, coll prize, MA, coll grad award), Univ of Oxford (DPhil); *m* 26 July 1980, Jan, *née* Page; 2 da (Miriam b 20 April 1984, Lydia b 21 Oct 1986), 1 s (Jonathan b 1 March 1989); *Career* stipendiary lectr in modern history St Peter's Coll Oxford 1984–85, research fell Keble Coll Oxford 1986–87 (jr research fell 1983–86), Br Acad postdoctoral fell 1986–87, fell and tutor in modern history Pembroke Coll Oxford 1988–95 (dean of grads 1989–92, sr tutor 1992–95); Univ of Wales Swansea: prof of history 1995–2000, head Dept of History 1996–2000, dean Faculty of Arts and Social Studies 1997–99, pro-vice-chllr 1999–2000; chief exec AHRB 2000–02 (memb Postgrad History Panel 1999–2000), vice-chllr UEA 2002–06, chief exec HE Funding Cncl 2006–09, vice-chllr Univ of Birmingham 2009–; visiting lectr: Cornell Univ, Univ of Virginia; delg Univ of Oxford Delegacy of Local Examinations 1991–95; chair and co-fndr Nat Centre for Public Policy 1998–2000; chair: Benchmarking Gp Quality Assurance Agency (QAA) 2003–06, Assoc of Univs of E of England 2003–06, 1994 Gp of Univs 2005–06, City of Westminster Educn Cmmn 2009, UCAS 2011–12, Russell Gp of Univs 2012–15, Universitas 21 2015–; memb: Jt Funding Cncls Working Gp on Interdisciplinary Research 1998–99, History Benchmarking Gp 1998–99, Steering Gp for DfES Review of Research Funding in the Arts and Humanities 2001–02, Science and Engrg Base Co-ordinating Ctee Office of Science and Technol (OST) 2001–02, DCMS Creative Industries/HE Forum 2001–04, Research Libraries Support Gp 2002–03, Research Assessment Exercise Review Gp 2002–03, Cncl John Innes Centre Norwich 2002– (also dep chair Cncl), Governing Cncl Sainsbury Lab John Innes Centre Norwich 2002–06, DfES Working Gp on 14–19 Reform 2003–04, Bd HE Policy Inst 2003–, Bd QAA 2004–06, Bd HEFCE 2005–09 (memb Research Ctee 2003–06), Ind Review of HE Fees and Funding 2009–10, Hong Kong Univ Grants Ctee 2011–, Gtr Birmingham and Solihull LEP 2011–13, Bd Univs W Midlands, Arts and Humanities Research Cncl (AHRC); dir Univs UK; dir INTO Univ Ptnrshps 2015–; tstee Univs Superannuation Scheme 2007– (chair 2015); cmmr Marshall Aid Meml Cmmn 2003–10 (dep chair 2005–); literary dir Royal Historical Soc 1994–2000; chair Editorial Bd Studies in History 2000–04 (memb 1994–2000); regular broadcaster for radio and TV; govr Bishopston Comp Sch 1996–2000; hon fell: St Peter's Coll Oxford 2002, Keble Coll Oxford 2006; Hon DLitt: UWE 2002, UEA 2006; FRHistS 1991; *Publications* Governing Rural England: Tradition and Transformation in Local Government 1780–1840 (1994, shortlisted History Today Prize), Government and Community in the English Provinces 1700–1870 (1997), A Union of Multiple Identities: The British Isles c1750-c1850 (ed with L Brockliss, 1997), The Social and Political Writings of William Cobbett (ed with N Thompson, 16 vols 1998); also author of more than 30 scholarly articles and book chapters; *Recreations* music, collecting CDs and books, current affairs, watching sport, walking, wine; *Clubs* Athenaeum; *Style*— Prof Sir David Eastwood, DL; ✉ The Vice-Chancellor's Office, University of Birmingham, Edgbaston, Birmingham B15 2TT (✆ 0121 414 4536)

EASTWOOD, (Anne) Mairi; da of John Waddington (d 1979), and Helen Cowan, *née* MacPherson (d 2009); *b* 11 July 1951; *Educ* St Leonards Sch, Imperial Coll London (BSc); *m* 1, 10 Aug 1974 (m dis 1987), James William Eastwood, s of late Donald Smith Eastwood; 1 da (Joanna Elizabeth Irene b 1980), 1 s (Donald James b 1983); m 2, 7 July 2001, Richard Napier Findlater, s of George Richard Park Findlater (d 2009); *Career* Arthur Young: chartered accountant 1976, ptnr in charge computer servs consultancy 1985–87, recruitment ptnr 1985–87, nat staff ptnr 1988–89; chief exec Eastwood Consulting Ltd 1989–99, ptnr Whitehead Mann 2000–05; Praesta Partners LLP: managing ptnr 2005–09, 2009–13; dir AME Resources Ltd 2013–; non-exec dir Kaisen Ltd 1992–95; memb Central Tport Consultative Ctee 1992–95; dir Royal Exchange Theatre Manchester 2002–04, govr Dragon Sch Oxford 1995–2007; FCA 1981; *Clubs* Lansdowne; *Style*— Mrs Mairi Eastwood; ✉ Flexney's House, Stanton Harcourt, Oxfordshire OX29 5RP; 90 Harley Street, London W1G 7HS (e-mail mairi@mairieastwood.com)

EASUN, William John; s of Michael John Easun, of Surrey, and Mary Patricia, *née* McKinstry; *b* 19 April 1955; *Educ* Haileybury, Guildford Coll of Law, Aix en Provence Univ (scholar); *m* 28 Sept 1991, Irene Ann, da of Bryce Luke; *Career* articled clerk Dale & Newbery Middx 1974–78, admitted slr 1979, Aix en Provence Univ 1979–80, asst slr Frere Cholmeley Paris and Monaco 1980–83, ptnr Frere Cholmeley Monaco 1983–89, ptnr i/c Monaco office Frere Cholmeley Bischoff 1989–98, ptnr i/c Lawrence Graham (formerly Eversheds (Monaco)) 2003–12, founding ptnr Tempest Legal Services Monaco SARL 2012–; memb: Law Soc (England and Wales), STEP, Outward Bound Monaco (vice-chm), Conseil Stratégique pour L'Attractivité (Monaco), Monaco Air League; Chevalier de l'Ordre Saint Charles, Chevalier du Tastevin Clos de Vougeot; *Recreations* wine and food, educating three wonderful but expensive daughters, mowing; *Clubs* Automobile (Monaco), The Monte Carlo, IOD (Monaco (chm)); *Style*— William Easun, Esq; ✉ Monte Carlo Palace, 7 Boulevard des Moulins, MC 98000, Monaco (✆ 00377 9798 1255, e-mail easun.william@tempestlegal.com, website www.tempestlegal.com)

EATON, Andrew; *b* 7 December 1959, Londonderry; *Educ* Campbell Coll Belfast, Churchill Coll Cambridge (BA); *m* Linda Eaton; 3 da (Anna, Rebecca, Olivia); *Career* film prodr; Prodr of the Year Br Ind Film Award 2000; *Films* incl: 24 Hour Party People 2002, In This World 2002 (Best Foreign Film BAFTA 2004), 9 Songs 2004, A Cock and Bull Story 2005, A Mighty Heart 2007, The Killer Inside Me 2010, Rush 2013; *Television* incl: Red Riding 2009, The Unloved 2009 (Best Single Drama BAFTA 2010), The Trip 2010, Doll & Em 2013; *Style*— Andrew Eaton, Esq; ✉ Revolution Films, 9A Dallington Street, London EC1V 0BQ

EATON, Baroness (Life Peer UK 2010), of Cottingley in the County of West Yorkshire; Dame (Ellen) Margaret Eaton; DBE (2010, OBE 2003), DL; da of John Midgley (d 2001), and Evelyn, *née* Smith; *b* Bradford; *m* 16 Aug 1969, John Eaton; 1 da (Gretchen b 1972), 1 s (Yorke Joseph John b 1976); *Career* teacher Bradford 1960–72; Bradford Metropolitan Borough Cncl: cncllr 1986–, ldr Cons Gp 1995–, ldr Cncl 2000–06; chm Local Govt Assoc until 2011; chm Near Neighbours (charity of church urban fund); fell Bradford Coll; Hon DEd Univ of Bradford; FRSA 2007; *Recreations* theatre, music, cooking; *Style*— The Baroness Eaton, DBE, DL; ✉ House of Lords, London SW1A 0PW (✆ 020 7219 6380, e-mail eatonm@parliament.uk)

EATWELL, Baron (Life Peer UK 1992), of Stratton St Margaret in the County of Wiltshire; John Leonard Eatwell; s of Harold Jack Eatwell (d 1998), and Mary, *née* Tucker (d 1987); *b* 2 February 1945; *Educ* Headlands GS Swindon, Queens' Coll Cambridge (BA, MA), Harvard Univ (AM, PhD); *m* 1, 24 April 1970 (m dis), Hélène, da of Georges Seppain, of Marly-le-Roi, France; 2 s (Hon Nikolai b 1971, Hon Vladimir b 1973), 1 da (Hon Tatyana b 1978); m 2, 1 July 2006, Hon Mrs Susan Digby, OBE; *Career* teaching fell Harvard Univ 1968–69; Univ of Cambridge: research fell Queens' Coll 1969–70, fell and dir of studies in economics Trinity Coll 1970–96, univ lectr in economics 1977–2002 (asst lectr 1975–77), pres Queens' Coll 1997–, prof of fin policy 2002–; visiting prof of economics New School for Social Research NY 1980–96; econ advsr to Rt Hon Neil Kinnock MP 1985–92, princ oppn spokesman (treasy and econ affairs) House of Lords 1993–97; cmmr Jersey Financial Services Cmmn 2010–; chm British Screen Finance Ltd 1997–2000, dir Anglia Television Group Ltd 1994–2001, advsr EM Warburg Pincus & Co International Ltd 1996–, non-exec dir Cambridge Econometrics Ltd 1996–2007, dir and ind Bd memb SFA 1997–2002, non-exec dir Rontech Ltd 2003–08, non-exec dir SAV Credit Ltd 2007–; memb Regulatory Decisions Ctee FSA 1997–2001; dir: Royal Opera House 1998–2002 (chm Pension Fund 2007–), Cambridge Endowment for Research in Fin 2002–; chm: Commercial Radio Companies Assoc 2000–04, Br Library Bd 2001–06, Consumer Panel Classic fm 2007–; memb: Cambridge Constituency Lab Pty, Royal Econ Soc, American Econ Assoc; *Books* An Introduction to Modern Economics (with Joan Robinson, 1973), Keynes's Economics and the Theory of Value and Distribution (with Murray Milgate, 1982), Whatever Happened to Britain? (1982), The New Palgrave Dictionary of Economics (with Murray Milgate and Peter Newman, 1987), The New Palgrave Dictionary of Money and Finance (with Murray Milgate and Peter Newman, 1992), Transformation and Integration: Shaping the Future of Central and Eastern Europe (1995), Global Unemployment (1996), Not 'Just Another Accession': The Political Economy of EU Enlargement to the East (1997), Global Finance at Risk (with Lance Taylor, 2000), Hard Budgets, Soft States: Social Policy Choices in Central and Eastern Europe (2000), International Capital Markets (with L Taylor, 2002); *Recreations* watching ballet, modern dance and rugby union football; *Clubs* Harvard (NY); *Style*— The Rt Hon Lord Eatwell; ✉ Queens' College, Cambridge CB3 9ET (✆ 01223 335556, e-mail president@queens.cam.ac.uk)

EAVES, Prof Laurence; CBE (2003); s of Raymond Eaves, of Rhondda, Glamorgan, and Margaret, *née* Howells; *b* 13 May 1948; *Educ* Rhondda County GS, CCC Oxford (fndn scholar, MA), St John's Coll Oxford (sr scholar, DPhil); *m* Dr Ffiona Gilmore Eaves; *Career* research lectr ChCh Oxford and research fell Clarendon Laboratory Oxford 1972–74, Miller fell Univ of Calif Berkeley 1974–75; Univ of Nottingham: lectr in physics 1976–84, reader 1984–86, prof of physics 1986–2000, Lancashire-Spencer prof of physics 2000–11, research prof 2011–; prof of physics Univ of Manchester 2012–; visiting fell Univ of Wollongong 1982, Leverhulme sr research fell Royal Soc 1993–94, EPSRC sr fell 1994–99, visiting prof Univ of Tokyo 1995; hon fell CCC Oxford 2013–; memb Cncl Royal Soc 2002–04, memb HEFCE RAE Physics Sub-Panel 2004–08 and 2011–14, memb Research Awards Advsy Ctee Leverhulme Tst 2008–15, memb Scientific Advsy Cncl for Wales 2015–; Guthrie medal and prize Inst of Physics 2001; FInstP 1996, FRS 1997, FLSW 2011; *Publications* author of research articles in scientific jls; *Style*— Prof Laurence Eaves, CBE, FRS; ✉ School of Physics and Astronomy, University of Nottingham, Nottingham NG7 2RD (e-mail laurence.eaves@nottingham.ac.uk)

EBDON, Prof Leslie Colin (Les); CBE (2009); s of Harold Arthur Reid Ebdon (d 1989), and Doris, *née* Hasler (d 1979); *b* 26 January 1947, Edmonton, Middx; *Educ* Imperial Coll London (BSc, DIC, PhD); *m* 6 June 1970, Judith Margaret, da of Rev Dr Stanley Thomas; 3 s (Benjamin Thomas b 1973 d 1982, Daniel Mark b 1975, Matthew Samuel b 1978), 1 da (Hannah Joy b 1983); *Career* lectr in chemistry Makerere Univ Uganda 1971–73, lectr rising to sr lectr in analytical chemistry Sheffield City Poly 1973–80; Plymouth Poly (later Poly SW then Univ of Plymouth): reader rising to prof of analytical chemistry 1981–89, head Dept of Environmental Science 1989, VG prof of analytical chemistry 1989–2003, dep vice-chllr (academic) 1989–2003; vice-chllr and chief exec: Univ of Luton 2003–06, Univ of Bedfordshire 2006–12; dir Fair Access to HE 2012–; dir Univ of Luton Enterprises Ltd 2003–; chair: Masters Courses in Chemistry Review Panel EPSRC 1997, Mass Spectrometry Serv Review Gp EPSRC 1998, Assoc of Univs in the E of England 2006–, Million + 2007–; memb: Central Science Lab Review Gp 1995, Structure and Bonding Coll EPSRC 1995–2006, Certification Evaluation Panel European Cmmn 1997, Research Proposal Evaluation Panel European Cmmn 1998, Nat Cncl for Educnl Excellence 2007–, Measurement Bd Dept of Innovation, Univs and Skills 2007–; RSC: chair Pubns Bd 1991–97, memb Cncl 1991–2008, chair Strategy and Resources Bd 2003–05; Universities UK: memb Strategy Gp on Leadership, Mgmnt and Governance 2003–06, memb Health Ctee 2003–, chair Policy Ctee on Student Experience 2006–, memb Bd 2006–; DTI: memb Prog Mgmnt Ctee DTI/SERC LINK Prog on Techniques of Analytical and Physical Measurement 1990–95, SQMAC (Measurement Advsy Ctee) Steering Gp and Working Pty 1990–2007, memb Measurement Advsy Ctee 1999–2007, chair Valid Analytical Measurement Working Gp 1999–2007; memb Mgmnt Bd BIS 2007–; chair Editorial Bd Chemistry World 2002–08, author of over 250 papers in refereed jls and over 300 conf presentations; Schools lectr Analytical Div RSC 1986, 13th SAC Silver Medal for Analytical Chemistry RSC, Benedetti-Pichler Meml Award American Microchemical Soc 1995; dir: Centre for Competitiveness Ltd 2003–08, Luton Dunstable Partnership 2004–07, Beds and Luton Economic Devpt Partnership 2004–09; tstee Nat Marine Aquarium 1998–2007; memb Beds and Luton LSC 2004–08; Hon DSc Univ of Plymouth 2008; ARCS, FRSC 1971, CChem 1971, MCIWEM 1975, FRSA 2008; *Publications* An Introduction to Analytical Atomic Spectrometry (1982, 2 edn 1988); *Recreations* vegetable gardening, Baptist lay preacher; *Style*— Prof Les Ebdon, CBE; ✉ Office for Fair Access, Nicholson House, Lime Kiln Close, Stoke Gifford, Bristol BS34 8SR

EBDON, Peter David; s of Michael George Ebdon, and Barbara, *née* Cheeseman; *b* 27 August 1970; *Educ* Highbury Grove Secdy Sch; *m* 18 July 1992, Deborah Karen, da of Garry Baldrey; *Career* professional snooker player 1991–; winner Skoda Grand Prix 1993, runner-up Dubai Duty Free 1994, winner Benson & Hedges Irish Masters 1995, winner Regal Masters 1996, runner-up UK Championship 1996, runner-up World Championship 1996, winner Thailand Open 1997, winner British Open 2001, winner Regal Scottish Masters 2001, winner World Championship 2002; England rep at jr and sr level, world under 21 jr champion 1990; world record holder for most century breaks (4) in a 9-frame match Euro Open 1992 (also jt world record holder with 3 successive century breaks in same match); WPBSA Young Playerof the Year 1991; *Recreations* swimming, golf, cricket, chess, reading; *Style*— Peter Ebdon, Esq

EBSWORTH, Prof Evelyn Algernon Valentine; CBE (1996); s of Brig Wilfred Algernon Ebsworth, CB, CBE, (d 1978) of Cambridge, and Cynthia, *née* Blech (d 1975); *b* 14 February 1933; *Educ* Marlborough, Univ of Cambridge (MA, PhD, ScD); *m* 1, 1955, Mary (d 1987), da of Frank Reyner Salter, OBE; 3 da (Nicolette b 1958, Rachel b 1960, Lucy b 1964), 1 s (Jonathan b 1962); m 2, 1990, Rose, *née* Stinson, wid of Prof J J Zuckerman; *Career* Univ of Cambridge: fell King's Coll 1957–59, fell Christ's Coll 1959–67, demonstrator 1959–64, lectr 1964–67, tutor Christ's Coll 1964–67; Crum Brown prof of chemistry Univ of Edinburgh 1967–90, vice-chllr and warden Univ of Durham 1990–98; chm Cncl for the Registration of Forensic Practitioners 1998–2005; chm of govrs The Leys and St Faith's Schs Cambridge 2002–10; author of numerous papers published in learned jls; former memb Scot Examinations Bd, corresponding memb Acad of Sciences Göttingen; DCL (hc) Univ of Durham 2002, DSc (hc) Univ of Edinburgh 2013; FRSC, FRSE 1969; *Books* Volatile Silicon Compounds (1963), Structural Methods in Inorganic Chemistry (jtly, 1987); *Recreations* opera, gardening; *Style*— Prof E A V Ebsworth, CBE, FRSE; ✉ c/o Royal Society of Chemistry, Burlington House, Piccadilly House, London W1V 0BN (☎ 020 7437 8656)

ECCLES, George William; s of George Dunluce Eccles (d 1951), and Eileen Margaret Smith, *née* O'Neale (d 2003); *b* 26 December 1950, London; *Educ* Downside, LSE (LLB); *m* 1986, Eve, *née* Wooler; 1 s (Dunluce b 1988), 1 da (Tabitha b 1991); *Career* PricewaterhouseCoopers (formerly Coopers & Lybrand, Deloitte Haskins & Sells): trainee accountant 1974–77, worked in tech dept 1978–80, audit mangr 1980–87, ptnr UK 1987–94, ptnr Russia 1995–97; md Deloitte & Touche CIS 1997–99, chief operating offr Central Asian-American Enterprise Fund 2002–04 (dep chief operating offr 2000–01); chm: Media Group 1982–94, Hambleton Mining plc 2004–12; dir Amur Minerals Corp 2005–08; author 2012–; memb: RTS, Ctee Media Soc 1993–94, Standards Ctee EC Club Moscow 1996, St George's Soc Moscow 1997–99, Br Isles Club Moscow 1997–99, St George's Soc Kazakhstan 2001; Silver Medal Ind Publishers Award 2013, Silver Medal Global Ebook Award 2013; FCA (ICAEW); *Books* Corruption of Power (2015); *Publications* Accounting for Research and Development (1978), EEC Fourth Directive: Company Accounts (1978), EEC Third Directive: Mergers (1979), EEC Sixth Directive: Prospectuses (1979), Unfair Dismissal (1979), The Seventh Directive: Group Accounts (1980), Employment Act 1980 (1980), Company's Act 1980 (1980), Company's Act 1981 (1982), Climate for Cable: Legislation, SMATV and Marketing (1983), Television in Focus: Broadcasting in Europe (1990), Investing in UK Television (1991), The Oligarch: A Thriller (2012); *Recreations* horse racing, opera, Russian icons, Central Asia, France, bridge; *Clubs* Special Forces, Cwlth, Monte Carlo, Air Force League of Monaco; *Style*— George Eccles, Esq; ✉ 27 Old Gloucester Street, London WC1N 3XX (e-mail gweccles@yahoo.co.uk); 93 Chemin de la Carraire, 83600 Les Adrets, France

ECCLES, 2 Viscount (UK 1964); John Dawson Eccles; CBE (1985); s of 1 Viscount Eccles, CH, KCVO, PC (d 1999), and his 1 w Hon Sybil Frances Dawson (d 1977), da of 1 Viscount Dawson of Penn; *b* 20 April 1931; *Educ* Winchester, Magdalen Coll Oxford (BA); *m* 29 Jan 1955, Diana Catherine (Baroness Eccles of Moulton (Life Peer), *qv*), 2 da of late Raymond Wilson Sturge, of Ashmore, Wilts; 3 da (Hon Alice Belinda (Hon Mrs Ward) b 1958, Hon Catherine Sara (Hon Mrs Gannon) b 1963, Hon Emily Frances (Hon Mrs Irwin) b 1970), 1 s (Hon William David b 1960); *Heir* s, Hon William Eccles; *Career* Capt TA; Head Wrightson & Co Ltd 1955–77; dir: Glynwed International plc 1972–96, Investors in Industry plc 1974–88, Davy International plc 1977–81, Courtaulds Textiles plc 1992–2000 (non-exec chm 1995–2000); chm Chamberlin & Hill plc 1982–2005; memb: Monopolies & Mergers Cmmn 1976–85 (dep chm 1981–85), Cwlth Devpt Corp 1982–85 (chief exec 1985–94); sits as Cons peer in House of Lords, elected hereditary peer 2005; chm: Bd of Tstees Royal Botanic Gdns Kew 1983–91, The Georgian Theatre Royal Richmond Yorks until 2000, Bowes Museum Barnard Castle 2000–08; Hon DSc Silsoe Coll Cranfield Inst of Technol 1989; *Recreations* gardening, theatre; *Clubs* Brooks's; *Style*— The Rt Hon Viscount Eccles, CBE; ✉ Moulton Hall, Richmond, North Yorkshire DL10 6QH (☎ 01325 377227); No 5, 30 Smith Square, London SW1P 3HF (☎ 020 7222 4040, e-mail ecclesj@parliament.uk)

ECCLES, Terence; *Career* vice chm investment banking JP Morgan 1970–2006, vice chm JP Morgan Cazenove 2006–07, sr ind non-exec dir Paragon Gp plc, sr ind non-exec dir BlueBay Asset Mgmnt plc, non-exec dir Horizon plc; dir Royal Parks Fndn; *Style*— Terence Eccles, Esq; ✉ BlueBay Asset Management plc, 77 Grosvenor Street, London W1K 3JR (☎ 020 7389 3700, fax 020 7389 3499)

ECCLES OF MOULTON, Baroness (Life Peer UK 1990), of Moulton in the County of North Yorkshire; Diana Catherine Eccles (Viscountess Eccles); DL (N Yorks); 2 da of late Raymond Wilson Sturge, of Ashmore, Wilts, and late Margaret Sturge; *b* 4 October 1933; *Educ* St James's Sch West Malvern, Open Univ (BA); *m* 29 Jan 1955, 2 Viscount Eccles, CBE, *qv*, er s of 1 Viscount Eccles, CH, KCVO, PC (d 1999); 3 da (Hon Alice Belinda (Hon Mrs Ward) b 1958, Hon Catherine Sara (Hon Mrs Gannon) b 1963, Hon Emily Frances (Hon Mrs Irwin) b 1970), 1 s (Hon William David b 1960); *Career* chm: Ealing Dist HA 1988–93, Ealing, Hammersmith & Hounslow HA 1993–2000; dir: Tyne Tees Television 1986–94, J Sainsbury plc 1986–95, Yorkshire Electricity Group plc 1990–97; ind nat dir Times Newspapers Holdings Ltd 1998–2015; memb: North Eastern Electricity Bd 1974–85, British Railways Eastern Bd 1986–92, Yorkshire Electricity Bd 1989–90, National & Provincial Building Society 1991–96, Advsy Cncl for Energy Conservation 1982–84, Widdicombe Enquiry into Local Govt 1985–86, Home Office Advsy Panel on Licences for Experimental Community Radio 1985–86, Cncl Br Heart Fndn 1989–98, Unrelated Live Transplant Regulatory Authy 1990–99; vice-chm: NCVO 1981–87, Durham Univ Cncl 1985–2004 (lay memb 1981–85); chm Tyne Tees Television Programme Consultative Cncl 1982–84; dir Opera North 1998–2011; tstee: Charities Aid Fndn 1982–89, The London Clinic 2003–08; Hon DCL 1995; *Style*— The Rt Hon Lady Eccles of Moulton, DL; ✉ Moulton Hall, Moulton, Richmond, North Yorkshire DL10 6QH; 5/30 Smith Square, London SW1P 3HF

ECCLESHARE, (Christopher) William; s of Colin Forster Eccleshare (d 1989), and Elizabeth, *née* Bennett; *b* 26 October 1955, London; *Educ* William Ellis Sch Highgate, Trinity Coll Cambridge (MA); *m* 1980, Carol Ann, da of Arnold W Seigel; 2 s (Thomas Christopher b 2 Jan 1984, Charles David (Charlie) b 10 Dec 1986), 1 da (Rose Judith b 9 May 1989); *Career* J Walter Thompson Company Ltd advtg agency: joined as graduate trainee 1978, assoc dir 1983, sr assoc dir 1985, main bd dir 1986, head of account mgmnt 1988, md London 1990–92, ceo PPGH/JWT Amsterdam 1992–95, dir of worldwide strategic planning 1995–96; chm and ceo Northern Europe Ammirati Puris Lintas Ltd 1997–99, ptnr and ldr mktg practice McKinsey & Co 1999–2002, EMEA chm and ceo Young & Rubicam 2002–05 (also chm and ceo Wunderman Europe 2003–05), EMEA chm and ceo BBDO 2006–09, pres and ceo Clear Channel Int 2009–; non-exec dir Hays plc 2004–14, sr ind dir Centaur Media plc 2016–; memb Cncl Univ Coll Sch 2002–12, memb Bd Donmar Warehouse Theatre 2013–; FIPA 1994; *Recreations* British politics, the music of Bruce Springsteen, theatre, running; *Clubs* Thirty Club of London; *Style*— William Eccleshare, Esq; ✉ CCI, 33 Golden Square, London W1F 9JT (☎ 020 7478 2200 or 020 7478 2334, mobile 07710 574976, fax 020 7287 9155, e-mail williameccleshaire@clearchannel.com, website www.clearchannelinternational.com)

ECCLESTON, Prof William (Bill); s of Henry Eccleston (d 1996), and Bertha Eccleston (d 1997); *b* 3 March 1941; *Educ* Harris Coll Preston, Univ of London (BSc, MSc, PhD); *m* 12 April 1966, Catherine Yvonne, *née* Daley; 2 s (John b 25 Jan 1967, Daniel b 13 July 1969); *Career* sr princ sci Plessey Res Laboratories 1966–71; Univ of Liverpool: lectr 1971–81, sr lectr 1981–85, prof of electronics 1985–86, Robert Rankin prof of electronic engrg 1986–, head Dept of Electrical Engrg and Electronics 1986–91, dean of Faculty of Engrg 1992–95; by-fell Churchill Coll Cambridge 1996–; numerous pubns in learned jls; chm: SERC/DTI VLSI Technology Sub-Ctee 1992–95, SERC/DTI IT Advsy Bd 1992–95; chm: EPSRC Microelectronics Centre Steering Ctee 1996–2001, Int Electron Devices Meeting Washington 1999–01; co-ord EPSRC Carbon Based Electronics Consortium 2000–06, memb Bd EC Integrated Project Poly Apply 2004–; Freeman Borough of Preston; FIEE 1985, CEng 1985, FREng 1997; *Recreations* music, football, walking, cricket; *Clubs* Lancashire Cricket, Preston North End; *Style*— Prof Bill Eccleston, FREng; ✉ Department of Electrical Engineering & Electronics, University of Liverpool, Liverpool L69 3BX (☎ 0151 794 4502, e-mail beccle@liverpool.ac.uk)

ECHENIQUE, Emeritus Prof Marcial Hernan; OBE (2009); s of Marcial Echenique (d 1995), of Santiago, Chile, and Rosa, *née* Talavera (d 2012); *b* 23 February 1943; *Educ* Catholic Univ Santiago, Univ of Barcelona (DipArch, DArch), Univ of Cambridge (MA, ScD); *m* 23 Nov 1963, Maria Louisa, da of Ernesto Holzmann (d 1978), of Santiago, Chile; 2 s (Marcial Antonio b 16 July 1964, Martin Jose b 25 Nov 1965 d 1994), 1 da (Alejandra b 1 Aug 1969); *Career* asst lectr in urbanism Univ of Barcelona 1963–65; Univ of Cambridge: lectr in architecture 1970–80, fell Churchill Coll 1972–, reader in architecture and urban studies 1980–93, prof of land use and tport studies 1993–2013 (emeritus prof 2014–), head Dept of Architecture 2004–08; chm Marcial Echenique & Partners Ltd (architectural and planning conslts) 1990–2001; memb Bd: Banco de Bilbao y Vizcaya (BBVA) Spain 1988–94, Autopista Vasco-Aragonesa Spain 1994–99, Tecnologica SA Spain 1994–95, Ferrovial-Agroman Constructora Spain 1995–2000, Dockways Ltd Jersey 1996–99; memb Civic Soc Huntingdon and Godmanchester 1979; MRTPI 1991, RIBA 1997; *Books* Urban Development Models (jtly, 1975), Modelos de la Estructura Espacial Urbana (1975), La Estructura Del Espacio Urbano (jtly, 1975), Cambridge Futures (jtly, 1999), Cities for the New Millennium (jtly, 2001); *Recreations* music; *Style*— Emeritus Prof Marcial Echenique, OBE; ✉ Farm Hall, Godmanchester, Cambridgeshire; Churchill College, Storey's Way, Cambridge CB3 0DS

EDDINGTON, Sir Roderick Ian (Rod); kt (2005); s of Gilbert Eddington, and April Eddington; *b* 2 January 1950; *Educ* Christ Church GS Perth WA, Univ of WA (BEng, MEngSci), Lincoln Coll Oxford (DPhil); *m* 1994, Young Sook; 1 s (James), 1 da (Michelle); *Career* md Cathay Pacific Airways 1992–96 (dir 1988–96), dir Swire Pacific (HK) 1992–1996, exec chm Ansett Holdings 1997–2000, chief exec British Airways plc 2000–05, non-exec chm Aust and NZ JPMorgan 2006–; chm: EU/Hong Kong Business Corp Ctee 2002–06, Assoc of European Airlines 2003, Lion (formerly Lion Nathan Nat Foods Pty Ltd) 2011–; memb Bd: John Swire & Sons Pty Ltd 1997–, News Corp 1999–2014, Qantas 2001–02, Rio Tinto 2005–11, CLP Holdings 2006–, 21st Century Fox 2014–; memb APEC Business Advsy Cncl (ABAC) 2014–; hon fell Lincoln Coll Oxford, hon fell Pembroke Coll Oxford (res lectr 1978–79); Hon LLD Univ of WA; FRAeS 1993, FILT 2000; AO 2012, Grand Cordon of the Order of the Rising Sun 2015; *Recreations* cricket, Australian rules football, rugby, bridge; *Clubs* Vincent's (Oxford), Shek-O (Hong Kong), Hong Kong CC, Lord's Taverners, Melbourne (Australia); *Style*— Sir Rod Eddington, AO; ✉ JPMorgan, 31st Floor, 101 Collins Street, Melbourne, Victoria, 3000, Australia (☎ 0061 3 9633 4079, e-mail rod.i.eddington@jpmorgan.com)

EDE, Maurice Gordon; s of William Gordon Ede, of Ashburton, Devon, and Phyllis Maud; *b* 12 December 1946; *Educ* Weymouth GS; *m* 1969, Margaret Anne, da of Robert Lockhart; 1 s (Simon Maurice b 1973), 1 da (Catherine Jane b 1976); *Career* articled clerk Butterworth Jones & Co Weymouth Dorset, CA Coopers & Lybrand, ptnr Finn-Kelcey and Chapman 1976–92, sole practitioner and co sec Hearn Engineering 1992–98, chief exec Assoc of Br Independent Accounting Firms (ABIAF) 1992–2013, currently dir Network 4m Ltd; memb: Ctee S Eastern Soc of CAs 1980–2009 (pres 1987–88), Cncl ICAEW 1988–2009; FICE 1969; *Style*— Maurice Ede, Esq; ✉ Suite One, Park Farm Barn, Brabourne, Kent TN25 6RG (☎ 01303 812811, fax 01303 814707, e-mail maurice@network4m.com)

EDELMAN, Colin Neil; QC (1995); s of Gerald Bertram Edelman (d 1955), and Lynn Queenie, *née* Tropp; *b* 2 March 1954; *Educ* Haberdashers' Aske's, Clare Coll Cambridge (MA); *m* 26 Oct 1978, Jacqueline Claire, da of Hardy Wolfgang Seidel, of London; 1 da (Rachel Laura b 17 Sept 1982), 1 s (James Simon b 14 Jan 1984); *Career* called to the Bar Middle Temple 1977 (bencher 2003); recorder 1996–2016 (asst recorder 1993), head of chambers 2002–11, dep High Court judge 2008–16; chm Bar Mutual Indemnity Fund Ltd 2013– (dir 2007–, dep chm 2009–13); *Recreations* supporting Luton Town FC, walking, badminton, skiing; *Style*— Colin Edelman, Esq, QC; ✉ Devereux Chambers, Devereux Court, London WC2R 3JH (☎ 020 7353 7534)

EDELMAN, Keith Graeme; *b* 10 July 1950; *Educ* Haberdashers' Aske's, UMIST (BSc); *m* 29 June 1974, Susan Margaret; 2 s (Daniel b 3 April 1978, Nicholas b 1 July 1980); *Career* dir Ladbroke Group plc and chm Texas Homecare subsid 1986–91, md Carlton Communications plc 1991–93, group chief exec Storehouse plc (and subsid BhS Ltd) 1993–99, md Arsenal FC 2000–08; chm Glenmorangie plc 2002–03 (formerly non-exec dir), non-exec chm Metrobet 2006–; non-exec dir: Eurotunnel until 2004, Qualceram Shires plc 2005–; *Recreations* skiing, tennis, collecting antiques, cooking; *Style*— Keith Edelman, Esq; ✉ Arsenal Football Club, Highbury Stadium, Highbury, London N5 1BU

EDELMANN, Anton; *b* 2 July 1952, Bubesheim, W Germany; *Educ* Volkschule; *m*; 3 da; *Career* apprentice chef Ulm Bundesbahn Hotel W Germany, commis saucier The Savoy London 1969–70, first commis saucier and gardemanger Hotel de la Paix Geneva 1970–71, chef de partie, chef gardemanger and chef de partie saucier Franziskauer Düsseldorf 1971–72; Mil Serv German Air Force 1972–74; chef saucier Bayrischer-Hof Munich 1974–75, successively chef de partie saucier, poissonier chaud, gardemanger then sr sous chef the Dorchester London 1975–79, premier sous chef and actg head chef Portman Intercontinental Hotel 1979–80, head chef Grosvenor House Hotel 1980–82 (oversaw opening of Ninety Park Lane), maître chef des cuisines and dir The Savoy London 1982–2003 (recipient AA Rosette and The Ackerman Guide's Black Clover Award), chef/patron Allium (Dolphin Square Hotel) 2003, chef princ Directors Table 2003–07; Caterer & Hotelkeeper Chef of the Year Award 1985 and 1991; Christmas Cook (LBC Radio) since 1985, subject of profile in series The Real McCoy (Thames TV) 1990, regular appearances on Masterchef (BBC TV) since 1991, participant in Hot Chefs (BBC TV) 1992, subject of BBC Radio 4's Desert Island Discs prog 1993; memb British Branch Académie Culinaire; *Books* The Savoy Food and Drink Book (1989), Canapes and Frivolities (1991), Creative Cuisine (1993), Fast Feasts (1995), Christmas Feast (1996), Perfect Pastries (1996), Music and Food for Romance (1999), Tea at the Savoy (2000); *Style*— Anton Edelmann, Esq

EDEN, Christopher James (Chris); s of Robert Christopher Eden, and Jacqueline, *née* Ede; *b* 18 August 1978; *Educ* Penrice Sch St Austell, St Austell Coll; *m* Sam, *née* Forsdick; 1 s (Lucas b 10 May 2012); *Career* Marco Pierre White Restaurants 1999–2001, The Square London 2001–04, The Wolseley London 2005–07, head chef Driftwood Hotel Portscatho 2007– (Michelin star 2012–); *Recreations* euchre, surfing; *Style*— Chris Eden, Esq; ✉ Driftwood Hotel, Rosevine, Portscatho, South Cornwall TR2 5EW (Twitter @chrisedendrifty)

EDER, Prof Andrew Howard Eric; s of Hans Eder (d 1998), and Helga, *née* Fall (d 2001); bro of Hon Mr Justice Eder, *qv*; *b* 21 April 1964; *Educ* St Paul's, King's Coll Sch of Med and Dentistry London, UCL Eastman Dental Inst London (BDS, MSc, LDS RCS, MRD RCS RCPS, MFGDP, FDS RCS, FHEA); *m* 31 July 1988, Rosina Jayne, da of Seymour Saideman, and Shirley Saideman; 2 s (David Philip b 16 Dec 1990, Daniel Lewis b 12 Aug 1993), 1 da (Deborah Ann b 11 Dec 1996); *Career* specialist in restorative dentistry and prosthodontics 1998–; clinical dir Specialist Dental Care and London Tooth Wear Centre Wimple St 1998–; hon conslt in restorative dentistry Eastman Dental Hosp UCLH Fndn Tst 2002–; UCL Eastman Dental Inst: teacher in conservative dentistry 1993–, examiner in conservative dentistry 1999–, dir of continuing professional devpt 2002–12, dir of educn 2006–12, prof of restorative dentistry and dental educn 2008–; UCL: visiting prof 2003–08, assoc dean Sch of Life and Medical Sciences 2008–12, pro-vice-provost (Life Learning) 2013–; visiting prof: Univ of Middlesex 2003–08, Tel Aviv Univ Sch of Dental Medicine 2008–; Alpha Omega: memb 1984–, memb Cncl 1988–, tstee 1989–, treas 1989–93, chm 1994–95, chm of tstees 2003–; Odontological Section RSM: memb 1991–, jr fell 1991, Pres's award 1992, memb Cncl 1992–2003, hon sec 1993–96, hon treas 1996–98, vice-pres 1998–2001, pres 2001–02; Br Soc for Restorative Dentistry: memb 1987–, memb Cncl 1994–2007, hon fell 1997, pres-elect 2004–05, pres 2005–06; memb Cncl Br Prosthodontic Conf 1998–2005; memb Editorial Advsy Bd Euro Jl of Prosthodontics and Restorative Dentistry 1996–2014, memb Editorial Bd Private Dentistry 1997–, memb Bd of Advsrs British Dental Jl 2005–13, academic CPD lead British Dental Jl 2005–, chm Editorial Advsy Bd Premium Practice Dentistry 2010–14, memb Editorial Bd Dental Tribune 2011–14; memb SAC in Restorative Dentistry 2000–05; memb: BDA 1984–, Med Defence Union 1987–, Faculty of Gen Dental Practitioners 1992–; Hon MFGDP, Hon FDS RCSEd, Hon FHEA; *Publications* Tooth Surface Loss Book Br Dental Jl (co-ed, 2000); published chapters in textbooks and articles in academic jls; *Recreations* tennis, swimming, skiing; *Style*— Prof Andrew Eder, MRD FDS; ✉ 57A Wimpole Street, London W1G 8YP (☎ 020 7486 7180, e-mail andreweder@restorative-dentistry.co.uk, website www.restorative-dentistry.co.uk); UCL Life Learning, The Network Building, 97 Tottenham Court Road, London W1T 4TP (☎ 020 7679 9358, e-mail a.eder@ucl.ac.uk, website www.ucl.ac.uk/lifelearning)

EDER, Hon Mr Justice; Sir (Henry) Bernard Eder; kt (2011), QC (1990); s of Hans Eder (d 1998), and Helga Eder (d 2001); bro of Prof Andrew H Eder, MRD FDS, *qv*; *b* 16 October 1952; *Educ* Haberdashers' Aske's, Downing Coll Cambridge (BA); *Children* 4 s (Simon b 1979, Michael b 1981, James b 1983, Benjamin b 1991), 1 da (Hannah b 1988); *Career* called to the Bar Inner Temple 1975 (bencher 2007), judge of the High Court of Justice (Queen's Bench Division) 2010–; visiting prof Faculty of Laws UCL 1999–2003; *Publications* Scrutton on Charterparties (jt ed, 22 edn 2011); *Recreations* tennis, skiing; *Style*— The Hon Mr Justice Eder; ✉ Royal Courts of Justice, Rolls Building, Fetter Lane, London EC4A 1NL

EDEY, Russell Philip; s of Lt-Col Anthony Russell Edey (d 1994), and Barbara Stephanie Ann, *née* Rees-Jones (d 2011); *b* 2 August 1942; *Educ* St Andrew's Coll Grahamstown; *m* 8 June 1968, Celia Ann Malcolm, da of James Bisdee Malcolm Green, FRCS, of Colchester, Essex; 2 s (Philip b 1971, Anthony b 1975), 1 da (Kate b 1973); *Career* chartered accountant; N M Rothschild & Sons Ltd: dir 1981–, an md and head of corp fin 1990–96, non-exec dep chm N M Rothschild Corporate Finance 1996–2008; chm: Anglogold Ashanti Ltd 2002–10, Avocet Mining plc 2010–; non-exec dir: English China Clays plc 1995–99, FKI plc 1996–2006, Wassall plc 1997–2000, Express Dairies plc 1998–2002, Old Mutual plc 2004–13, Paris Orleans SA 2004–12, Associated British Ports Holdings plc 2006, BlackRock World Mining Tst plc 2014–, Genesis Emerging MArkets Fund Ltd 2015–; dir The New Shakespeare Company Ltd 1990–2004; *Recreations* golf, opera, tennis, current affairs, wine, country pursuits; *Clubs* City of London; *Style*— Russell Edey, Esq; ✉ Starling Leeze, 65 East Street, Coggeshall, Essex CO6 1SL

EDGAR, David Burman; *b* 26 February 1948; *Educ* Univ of Manchester (BA); *m* 1979, Eve Brook (d 1998); *Career* author and playwright; Univ of Birmingham: dir of playwriting studies 1989–99, hon sr res fell 1988–, hon prof 1992–, prof of playwriting studies 1995–99; hon assoc artist RSC 1989, hon fell Birmingham Poly 1991, Hon MA Univ of Bradford 1984, Hon DUniv of Surrey 1993, Hon DLitt Univ of Birmingham 2002; FRSL; *Plays* The National Interest 1971, Excuses Excuses (Coventry) 1972, Death, Story (Birmingham Rep) 1972, Baby Love 1973, The Dunkirk Spirit 1974, Dick Deterred (Bush) 1974, O Fair Jerusalem (Birmingham Rep) 1975, Saigon Rose (Edinburgh) 1976, Blood Sports (Bush) 1976, Destiny (Aldwych) 1976 (John Whiting Award 1976), Wreckers 1977, Our Own People 1977, The Jail Diary of Albie Sachs (adaptation, Warehouse Theatre) 1978, Mary Barnes (adaptation, Birmingham Rep then Royal Court) 1978–79, Teendreams (with Susan Todd) 1979, Nicholas Nickleby (adaptation, Aldwych then Plymouth Theatre NY) 1980–81 (Soc of West End Theatres Best Play Award 1980, Tony Best Play Award (NY) 1981), Maydays (Barbican) 1983, Entertaining Strangers (NT 1987) 1985, That Summer (Hampstead) 1987, Heartlanders (with Stephen Bill and Anne Devlin, Birmingham Rep) 1989, The Shape of the Table (NT) 1990, The Strange Case of Dr Jekyll and Mr Hyde (Barbican) 1991, Pentecost (RSC Other Place, then Young Vic) 1994 (Evening Standard Best Play Award 1995, Olivier nomination for Best Play 1996), Albert Speer (adaptation, NT) 2000, The Prisoner's Dilemma (RSC) 2001, Daughters of the Revolution and Mothers Against (Continental Divide, Oregon Shakespeare Festival and Berkeley Rep Co) 2003, Playing with Fire (NT) 2005; *TV and Radio* The Eagle Has Landed 1973, Sanctuary 1973, I Know What I Meant 1974, Ecclesiastes 1977, Vote For Them (with Neil Grant) 1989, A Movie Starring Me 1991, Buying A Landslide 1992, Citizen Locke 1994, Talking to Mars (play, BBC) 1996, The Secret Parts (BBC) 2000; *Film* Lady Jane 1986; *Books* Destiny (1976), Wreckers (1977), The Jail Diary of Albie Sachs (1978), Teendreams (1979), Mary Barnes (1979), Maydays (1983), Entertaining Strangers (1985), Plays One (1987), That Summer (1987), The Second Time as Farce (1988), Vote For Them (1989), Heartlanders (1989), Edgar Shorts (1990), Plays Two (1990), The Shape of the Table (1990), Plays Three (1991), The Strange Case of Dr Jekyll and Mr Hyde (1992), Pentecost (1995), State of Play (ed, 1999), Albert Speer (2000), The Prisoner's Dilemma (2001), Continental Divide (2004); *Style*— David Edgar, Esq

EDGAR, (Christopher) George; OBE (2011); s of Drs William M and F E Edgar, of Baildon, W Yorks; *b* 21 April 1960; *Educ* Univ of Cambridge (MA), Open Univ (MA); *m* 1994, Elena Ryurikovna, *née* Nagornichnykh; 2 da (Anna Laura b 1994, Katerina Maria b 1998); *Career* HM Dip Serv; FCO 1981–92 (resigned 1992, reinstated 1995), ambass to Cambodia 1997–2000, ambass to Repub of Macedonia 2001–04, consul gen St Petersburg 2004–06, FCO envoy for climate security in Africa 2006–07, head Consular Assistance Gp FCO 2007–10, head Papal Visit Team FCO 2010, chargé d'affaires Holy See 2011, additional dir (protocol) 2011–12, ambass to Uzbekistan 2012–15; *Recreations* music; *Style*— Mr George Edgar, OBE

EDGAR, Pauline Claire; da of Peter George Brown, of Kempsey, Worcs, and Christine Daisy, *née* Denley; *b* 13 March 1956, Birmingham; *Educ* Dudley Girls' HS, Bedford Coll Univ of London (BA), Inst of Educn Univ of London (PGCE); *m* 14 Aug 1982, James Patrick Hamish Edgar; 2 s (James Peter Campbell b 4 March 1984, Hamish Andrew b 7 Oct 1986), 1 da (Jessie Ann b 7 June 1990); *Career* history teacher Copthall Sch 1981–87, head of history and politics, head of sixth form and teaching and learning co-ordinator Francis Holland Sch 1987–2006, princ Queenswood Sch 2006–; memb: GSA 2006, Assoc of Sch and Coll Ldrs 2006; *Recreations* singing, running, swimming, sailing, travel; *Style*— Mrs Pauline Edgar; ✉ Queenswood School, Shepherd's Way, Brookmans Park, Hatfield, Hertfordshire AL9 6NS (☎ 01707 602500, fax 01707 602597, e-mail principal@queenswood.herts.sch.uk)

EDGAR, Ross; *b* 3 January 1983, Newmarket, Suffolk; *Career* cyclist; Bronze medal team sprint Cwlth Games Manchester 2002, Gold medal individual sprint European Track Championships (Under 23s) 2004 (Silver medal 2005), Gold medal team sprint, Silver medal individual sprint and Bronze medal keirin Cwlth Games Melbourne 2006, Silver medal team sprint World Track Championships 2007 and 2008 (Bronze medal keirin 2007), Silver medal keirin Olympic Games Beijing 2008; *Style*— Ross Edgar, Esq

EDGAR-JONES, Philip; s of Edward Jones, of Prestbury, Cheshire, and Isabella Jones; *b* 13 July 1966, Leeds; *Educ* Royal HS Edinburgh, Queen Margaret Coll Edinburgh (BA); *m* 14 July 1990, Wendy, *née* Edgar; 1 da (Daisy b 24 May 1998); *Career* co-presenter Moviewatch, journalist Sky magazine; series prodr The Big Breakfast 1994–97, series ed The Jack Docherty Show 1997–99, exec prodr The Priory 1999–2001, head of factual entertainment Endemol UK 2001–11 (exec prodr Big Brother, The Salon and Shattered), head of entertainment BSkyB 2012–13, dir Sky Arts 2013–; Nat Television Award for Big Brother 3 2002, Indie Award for Big Brother 3 2002; *Recreations* cinema, gardening, golf, music, opera, reading, skiing, tennis; *Style*— Philip Edgar-Jones, Esq; ✉ Sky UK, Grant Way, Isleworth, Middlesex (e-mail philip.edgar-jones@sky.uk, Twitter @PEdgarJones)

EDGE, Geoffrey; s of John Edge (d 1977), of Tividale, Warley, W Midlands, and Alice Edith, *née* Rimell (d 1986); *b* 26 May 1943; *Educ* Rowley Regis GS, LSE (BA), Univ of Birmingham; *Career* asst lectr in geography Univ of Leicester 1967–70, lectr in geography Open Univ 1970–74, res fell Birmingham Poly 1979–80, sr res fell Preston and NE London Polys 1980–84; chm W Midlands Enterprise 1982–2007 (also chief exec 2000–07), md Geonomics Ltd 2007–; New Initiatives co-ordinator Copec Housing Tst 1984–87, sr assoc PE International 1987–97, assoc dir W S Atkins 1997–1999; chm Planning Ctee Bletchley UDC 1972–74, vice-chm Planning Ctee Milton Keynes BC 1973–76, MP (Lab) Aldridge Brownhills 1974–79 (Parly private sec, Dept Educn Science and Privy Cncl Office), chm Econ Devpt Ctee W Midlands CC 1981–86, leader Walsall MBC 1988–90 (chm Policy and Resources Ctee) 1988–90; FRGS; *Books* Regional Analysis & Development (jt ed, 1973); *Recreations* gardening, walking, travel, reading, listening to classical music; *Style*— Geoffrey Edge, Esq; ✉ 5 Sedgefield Close, Dudley, West Midlands DY1 2UU (☎ 01384 259308, mobile 07970 817374, e-mail geoff@geonomics.co.uk)

EDGE, Prof Kevin Anthony; s of George Edge (d 2008), and Marion, *née* Leonard (d 1993); *b* 1 July 1949, Bristol; *Educ* Kingswood GS Bristol, Univ of Bath (BSc, PhD, DSc); *m* Delyth Ann, *née* Jones; *Career* sr control systems engr Rolls Royce Ltd 1972–76 (engrg apprentice 1967–71); Univ of Bath: research offr 1976, lectr 1976–87, sr lectr 1987–91, reader 1991, prof 1991–2015, dep dir Centre for Power Transmission and Motion Control 1993–2008, head Dept of Mechanical Engrg 1997–2003, pro-vice-chllr (Research) 2003–08, dep vice-chllr 2008–15, prof emeritus 2015–; Bramah Medal IMechE 1990 (and various awards for proceedings papers 1986, 1987, 1990 and 1998); FIMechE 1990, FREng 2003; *Publications* contrib to numerous pubns and jls; co-ed of 17 conf proceedings; *Recreations* classical music, photography; *Style*— Prof Kevin Edge; ✉ University of Bath, Claverton Down, Bath BA2 7AY (e-mail k.a.edge@bath.ac.uk)

EDGE, Stephen Martin; s of Harry Hurst Edge (d 2003), and Mary, *née* Rigg (d 2010); *b* 29 November 1950, Farnworth, Lancs; *Educ* Canon Slade GS Bolton, Univ of Exeter (LLB); *m* 6 Sept 1975, Melanie, da of Eric Stanley Lawler (d 1995), of Hassocks, W Sussex; 2 da (Charlotte Louise (Mrs Kertesz) b 1982, Katharine Imogen b 1987); *Career* admitted slr 1975; ptnr (specialising in corp tax) Slaughter and May 1973–; memb Practice Cncl Int Tax Prog NYU; various contribs to pubns and articles on tax; patron: TaxAid, Bridge the Gap appeal; vice-pres Lancs CCC, vice-pres Lancs Cricket Fedn, pres Amberley Cricket Club, chm Exeter Univ Alumni Network Bd, non-exec dir Bournemouth Symphony Orch; Hon LLD Univ of Exeter 2012; *Clubs* MCC; *Style*— Stephen Edge, Esq; ✉ Slaughter and May, 1 Bunhill Row, London EC1Y 8YY (☎ 020 7600 1200, fax 020 7090 5000)

EDGE, The; *see:* Evans, David

EDINGTON, (George) Gordon; CBE (2007); s of George Adam Edington (d 1994), and Phyllis Mary, *née* Allan (d 1971); *b* 7 September 1945, London; *Educ* St Mary's Sch Kenya, St Lawrence Coll Kent; *m* 23 June 1973 (m dis), Jane Mary, da of Jack Jesson Adie, CMG; 4 s (Daniel Jesson b 18 Jan 1975, Joel Adam b 7 Oct 1976, Sam Gordon b 31 July 1980, Jack Jesson b 1 June 1985); m 2, Sep 2013, Paula Carrington Edmunds; *Career* with Knight Frank & Rutley 1964–68, ptnr Anthony Lipton & Co 1968–72, dir Sterling Land Co Ltd 1972–73, dir Westwood Commercial Holdings Ltd 1973–75, conslt Amalgamated Investment and Property Co Ltd and Deloitte Haskins & Sells/Price Waterhouse 1975–76, jt md Summerbridge Investments Ltd 1976–81, md Lynton plc 1981–94; BAA plc: joined following takeover of Lynton plc 1988, gp property dir (main bd appt) 1991–99 (resigned), chm BAA International 1992–99, chm Airports UK Ltd 1991–92, Scottish Express International 1991–93, BAA Hotels Ltd 1991–92 and Skycare Cargo Ltd 1991–94, BAA Art Prog 1994–99, chm BAA Lynton plc 1994–99 (resigned); non-exec chm: Greycoat Estates Ltd 1999–, Earls Court and Olympia Gp Ltd 2000–01 (resigned); non-exec dir Lend Lease Corp 1999–2013; past pres Br Property Fedn; chm: Michael Stuckey Tst (supporting young musicians) 1988–98, Public Art Devpt Tst 1992–98, Land and City Families Tst 1994–98; dep chm Fulham Palace Tst 2011–; dir Snowshill Securities Ltd; memb: Bd of Govrs The Wilson Centre Fitzwilliam Coll Cambridge 1993–98, Lord Mayor of London's 1997/98 Charity Appeal Steering Ctee; chair of tstees Action For Children (formerly NCH) 2001–07 (ambass 1998–2016), chm Tennis First Charitable Tst, tstee Fulham Palace Tst 2011– (dep chm), tstee Chobham Acad Stratford 2013–, fndr annual John O'Halloran Symposium (supporting those in the property industry with mental illness) 2016; Liveryman Worshipful Co of Chartered Surveyors; FRICS 1970, FRSA 1992; *Books* The Clowes Family of Chester Sporting Artists (Grosvenor Museum Chester, 1985), Property Management: A Customer Focused Approach (1997), Gordon McLean Allan 1912 – 1944 (2014); *Recreations* tennis, fly fishing, golf, family, photography, historic Thames rivercraft, hill walking; *Clubs* Riverside Racquet, Royal Wimbledon Golf, Henley Royal Regatta, Leander; *Style*— Gordon Edington, Esq, CBE

EDIS, Hon Mr Justice Andrew Jeremy Coulter Edis; QC (1997); s of late Dr Peter Edis, of Liverpool, and late Barbara, *née* Creer; *b* 9 June 1957; *Educ* Liverpool Coll, UC Oxford (MA); *m* 16 Dec 1984, Sandy, da of Albert Wilkinson; 3 c (Sam b 6 July 1987, Philippa b 19 Oct 1989, Eleanor b 3 July 1996); *Career* called to the Bar Middle Temple 1980 (bencher 2004); jr of Northern Circuit 1983–84, hon sec Northern Circuit 1994–97, recorder of the Crown Court 1999 (asst recorder 1994), dep High Court judge 2001–14, judge of the High Court of Justice (Queen's Bench Div) 2014–, head of chambers 2000–06; sr treasy cnsl to the Crown Central Criminal Court 2008; memb Bar Cncl 1989–91; *Recreations* cricket, food and wine, history; *Clubs* Oxford and Cambridge, Liverpool Bar Cricket; *Style*— The Hon Mr Justice Edis, QC; ✉ Royal Courts of Justice, Strand, London WC2A 2LL

EDMANS, Laurence Michael (Laurie); CBE (2006); s of Edmund Lionel Edmans, of Maidstone, Kent, and May Florence, *née* Paul; *b* 20 February 1948, London; *Educ* Chistlehurst and Sidcup GS, William Penn Comp Sch London, East London Coll of Commerce (Cert); *m* 6 Nov 1971, Linda Rose, *née* Spencer; 5 c (Jacqueline b 1965, Kirstie b 1974, Alexandra b 1976, Timothy b 1981, Robin b 1984); *Career* gen mangr employee benefits Crusader Insurance/CIGNA Corp 1964–89, mktg dir then dep chief exec National Provident Inst 1989–2000, dir of corp devpt AEGON UK plc 2000–06; dep chm CPA Hldgs Ltd until 2010; chm: MGM Assurance until 2015, BDifferent Ltd, Trinity Mirror Pension Tstees Ltd, Independent Governance Ctee Zurich UK 2014–; memb Bd The Pensions Regulator until 2010, chm Safe Home Income Plans until 2012, treas Family and Parenting Inst until 2012, govr and cncl memb Pensions Policy Inst, memb Bd Money Advice Service, tstee memb NEST Corp until 2014, cmmr Financial Inclusion Cmmn 2014–; jt prop La Tour de Chollet Bordeaux; Tstee Quest Sch for Autistic

Children; FCII 1982, FPMI 1990; *Recreations* winemaking, opera, ballet, golf, soccer (West Ham United season ticket holder); *Clubs* RAC, Royal Over-Seas League, Hever Castle Golf; *Style—* Laurie Edmans, Esq, CBE; ✉ Allens Oast, Old Road, East Peckham, Kent TN12 5ER (☎ 01622 871603, e-mail laurie_edmans@hotmail.com)

EDMISTON, Baron (Life Peer UK 2011), of Lapworth in the County of Warwickshire; Robert Norman Edmiston; s of Vivian Randolph Edmiston, and Norma Margaret Edmiston; *b* 6 October 1946; *Educ* Abbs Cross Tech Sch, Barking Regnl Coll of Technol; *m* 1; 1 s (Andrew b 1969), 2 da (Deborah b 1971, Angela b 1975); m 2, 1998, Tracie Jacqueline, da of Donald Spicer; *Career* fin analyst Ford Motor Co, capital planning mangr Chrysler (mangr fin analysis), fin dir Jensen Motor Co, chm IM Group Ltd; *Recreations* Christian activities, swimming, scuba, guitar-playing, shooting, skiing; *Style—* The Lord Edmiston; ✉ IM Group Ltd, IM House, South Drive, Coleshill B46 1DF

EDMONDS, David Albert; CBE (2003); s of Albert Edmonds, of Kingsley, Cheshire, and Gladys Edmonds; *b* 6 March 1944; *Educ* Helsby GS, Keele Univ (BA); *m* 1966, Ruth, da of Eric Beech, of Christleton, Chester; 2 s (Jonathan, Benedict), 2 da (Jane, Elizabeth); *Career* asst princ Miny of Housing and Local Govt 1966–69 (private sec/Parly sec 1969–71), princ DOE 1971–73, observer Civil Serv Selection Bd 1973–74, visiting fell Johns Hopkins Univ Baltimore 1974–75; DOE: private sec/permanent sec 1975–77, asst sec 1977–79, private sec to sec of state 1979–83, under-sec Inner Cities Directorate 1983–84; chief exec The Housing Corp 1984–91, dep chm New Statesman and Society 1988–90; pres Int New Towns Assoc 1988–91, dir The Housing Fin Corp 1988–91, md Group Central Servs NatWest Group 1991–98, DG Oftel 1998–2003 (memb Bd Ofcom 2002–05); chm NHS Direct Special HA 2004–09, chm NHS Shared Business Services Ltd 2005–; memb Bd: Hammerson plc 2003–11, Wincanton 2004–11 (chm 2009–11), William Hill plc 2005–, Olympic Park Legacy Company 2009–; memb Bd and chm Property Planning and Project Ctee English Partnerships 2000–01, memb Bd and chm Remco Barchester Healthcare 2012–, chm Swanton Care and Community 2012–; tstee CRISIS 1994– (chm of tstees 1996–), memb Cncl Keele Univ 1996–2004 (treas 1997–2004), govr Kingston Univ 2012– (chm 2013–); Hon DLitt Keele Univ 2004; *Recreations* opera, golf, walking; *Clubs* Wimbledon Park Golf (captain 1997–98, currently vice-pres), Wimbledon Wanderers CC, Savile, MCC; *Style—* David Edmonds, Esq, CBE

EDMONDS, John; *b* 8 May 1950, Middx; *Educ* Eliots Green GS Middx, Birmingham Sch of Architecture (DipArch), Univ of Aston (BSc); *Children* 1 da (Poppy b 11 Dec 1981), 1 s (Lawrence b 22 June 1985); *Career* chartered architect and asst prof; project architect Weedon Partnership 1973–75, res fell Univ of York 1976–81, ptnr David Crease & Ptnrs 1982–86, ptnr and dir Crease Edmonds Strickland 1987–97; project co-ordinator Hull Truck Theatre 2000–03; RIBA: chm Yorks 2001–03, memb Nat Cncl 2003–07, chm Professional Educn Task Force London 2005–08; course dir Leeds Beckett Univ 2001–07; external examiner 2005–: Univ of Wales, Univ of Lincoln, Univ of Cardiff, UWE, Westminster Univ, Univ of Portsmouth, Univ of Malaga; course dir Univ of Nottingham 2007–; chm of tstees Yorks Air Museum 1995–; RIBA 1976, FRAeS; *Recreations* architecture, aviation, conservation; *Clubs* RAF; *Style—* John Edmonds, Esq, RIBA, FRAeS; ✉ University of Nottingham, University Park, Nottingham NG7 2RD (☎ 0115 951 4884, e-mail john.edmonds@nottingham.ac.uk)

EDMONDS, John Walter; s of Walter Edgar Edmonds (d 1986), and Maude Rose, *née* Edwards (d 1995); *b* 28 January 1944; *Educ* Christ's Hosp, Oriel Coll Oxford (MA); *m* 30 Sept 1967, (Janet) Linden, da of Franklin Arthur Callaby (d 1978); 2 da (Lucinda Jane b 1969, Nanette Sally b 1972); *Career* GMB (formerly GMWU): res asst 1965–67, dep res offr 1967–68, regnl organiser 1968–72, nat offr 1972–85, gen sec 1986–2003; pres TUC 1997–98; visiting fell Nuffield Coll Oxford 1986–94; sr research fell KCL 2003–, visiting prof Durham Univ Business Sch 2015–; formerly: dir Nat Building Agency, memb Royal Cmmn on Environmental Pollution; govr: LSE, Nat Inst of Economic and Social Research 1999–; pres Unity Bank 2000–03, memb Nat Economic Devpt Cncl 1986–88; chair Inland Waterways Advsy Cncl (IWAC) 2006–12, chair River Thames Alliance 2011–; non-exec dir: Carbon Tst 2001–12, Environment Agency 2002–09, Salix Finance 2003–; tstee: Inst of Public Policy Res 1990–2000, NSPCC 1997–2001; memb: Cncl ACAS 1990–2001, Cncl Consumers' Assoc 1993–96, Gen Cncl TUC, Forestry Cmmn 1995–2001; Hon LLD Univ of Sussex 1993; FRSA 1989–91, hon fell Soc for the Environment; *Books* Man-Made (with Eva Tutchell, 2015); *Recreations* cricket, carpentry; *Clubs* Wibbandune CC, Thorpe Manhattans CC; *Style—* Mr John Edmonds; ✉ 50 Graham Road, Mitcham, Surrey CR4 2HA (☎ 07793 746814, e-mail johnedmonds1@hotmail.com)

EDMONDS, Prof (Douglas) Keith; s of (Maxwell) John Edmonds, of Duffield, Derbys, and Margaret Agnes, *née* Morrison (d 1977); *b* 23 July 1949; *Educ* Ecclesbourne Sch, Univ of Sheffield Med Sch (MB ChB, capt Rugby Club); *m* 13 Oct 1990, Gillian Linda, da of Cyril Rose; 3 s (Alastair b 1991, Nicholas b 1992, Timothy b 1995); *Career* lectr Dept of Anatomy Univ of Sheffield 1975, SHO (obstetrics and gynaecology) Jessop Hosp for Women Sheffield 1975–77, registrar in obstetrics and gynaecology Southampton Hosp 1977–78; sr registrar in obstetrics and gynaecology: Queen Elizabeth Hosp Aust 1979–80, Southampton and Winchester Hosps 1980–82; conslt obstetrician and gynaecologist to Queen Charlotte and Chelsea Hosp and dir Nat Centre for Surgery of Congenital Malformations of Genital Tract 1982–, dir Inst of Obstetrics and Gynaecology Imperial Coll Sch of Med 2005–07, clinical prog dir Imperial Coll Healthcare 2008–13; author of many scientific pubns; pres Nat Endometriosis Soc 2000–04; memb: Blair-Bell Research Soc, Ovarian Club, Br Fertility Soc (and American), World Cncl of Paediatric and Adolescent Gynaecology; FRSM, FRANZCOG (Aust) 1982 (MRACOG 1979), FRCOG 1990 (MRCOG 1979); *Books* Paediatric and Adolescent Gynaecology (1989, 2 edn 2009), Textbook of Post-graduate Obstetrics and Gynaecology (1999, 3 edn 2012); 70 peer-reviewed sci pubns; *Recreations* tennis, golf, rugby; *Clubs* Gynaecological Club of GB, Roehampton; *Style—* Prof Keith Edmonds; ✉ Queen Charlotte's and Chelsea Hospital, DuCane Road, London W12 0HS (☎ 020 8383 3586)

EDMONDSON, Rt Rev Christopher Paul; s of Rev Jack Edmondson (d 1986), and Margaret, *née* O'Connell (d 1996); *b* 25 June 1950, Carlisle, Cumbria; *Educ* Blandford GS Dorset, Univ of Durham (Wallis organ scholar, Van Mildert exhibitioner, BA, DipTh, MA), Cranmer Hall Theological Coll Durham; *m* 18 Aug 1973, Susan Margaret; 2 s (Martin Christopher b 13 April 1978, Timothy Peter b 20 May 1981); *Career* Kirkheaton Parish Church 1973–79, vicar Ovenden St George 1979–86, dio offr for Evangilism and priest in charge Bampton Carlisle 1986–92, vicar Shipley St Peter Bradford 1992–2002, warden Lee Abbey 2002–08, bishop of Bolton 2008–16 (ret); memb Bishop's Cncl Carlisle 1989–92, memb Bishop's Cncl Manchester 2008–, chair Scargill House Cncl 2009–; chair Southern NW Trg Partnership 2008–14, chair Gtr Manchester Fresh Expressions Area Strategy Team 2009–; pres Archway 2010–, tstee Credit Union Fndn 2015–; former memb Rotary; memb Br Inst of Innkeepers 2004; *Publications* Fit to Lead (2002, 3 edn 2009), Celebrating Community (jtly, 2006), Leaders Learning to Listen (2010); *Recreations* music, sport (cricket and football); *Style—* The Rt Rev Christopher Edmondson; ✉ 16 Cavalier Drive, Apperley Bridge, Bradford BD10 0UF (☎ 07817 511118, e-mail chris.edmondson@me.com)

EDMONDSON, Prof Hugh Dunstan Christopher; s of Dr Dunstan Hugh Edmondson (d 1990), and Audrey Mary, *née* Burdon (d 1989); *b* 13 April 1936; *Educ* Stonyhurst, Univ of Birmingham (DDS, BDS, DA, MB ChB); *m* 13 May 1961, Eileen Margaret, da of William Burley; 2 da (Rowena Mary b 1962, Caroline Audrey b 1963), 1 s (Christopher Hugh b 1964); *Career* prof of oral surgery and oral med and head of dept Univ of Birmingham 1983–97 (lectr 1971–75, sr lectr 1975–83, emeritus prof 1997); conslt maxillofacial surgeon 1975–2003, service lead maxillofacial surgery 1997–2003; chm Dental Formulary Sub-Ctee 1987–2006; former memb: Medicines Control Agency, Ctee on Safety of Medicines Advsy Panel, Advsy Cncl on the Misuse of Drugs, Ctee on Dental and Surgical Materials, Advsy Ctee on NHS Drugs, Formulary Ctee BDA; chm Worcs branch Game Conservancy Tst; BDA Roll of Distinction 2007; fell BAOMS, MRCS, LRCP, LDS RCS, FDS RCS; *Books* A Radiological Atlas of Diseases of the Teeth and Jaws (with R M Browne and P G J Rout, 1983), Atlas of Dental and Maxillofacial Radiology and Imaging (with R M Browne and P G J Rout, 1995); *Recreations* country pursuits, woodland management, gardening; *Style—* Prof Hugh Edmondson; ✉ Huddington Court, Huddington, Droitwich, Worcestershire WR9 7LJ (☎ 01905 391247, e-mail hughedmondson@btinternet.com)

EDMONDSON, Mark Andrew; s of Lambert Edmondson (d 1967), of Carlisle and Derby, and (Ethel) Lally, *née* Atkins (d 2002); *b* 2 February 1963, Derby; *Educ* Noel Baker GS Derby, Nottingham Trent Univ (LLB), Anglia Ruskin Univ (LLM); *m* 15 June 1991, Judy, *née* Cooke; 2 da (Olivia Alyss b 11 Nov 1991, Francesca Elizabeth Grace b 4 March 1996); *Career* Smith Partnership Slrs until 1994, co-fndr Edmondson Hall Slrs 1994–, accredited mediator 2013; fndr Equine Professionals Conference 2010; dir: Rectory House Stud Ltd, Mark Edmondson Ltd; lectr in sports law and equine law; author of various articles in Int Sports Law Jl; chm Newmarket Festival CIC, chair Newmarket Business Day since 2008, memb YEP Sports and Media LLP 2013; memb: Law Soc, Employment Lawyers Assoc 2013; *Recreations* football, horse racing and breeding, walking, gardening, Derby County season ticket holder; *Clubs* The Felons (chm), Jockey Club Rooms; *Style—* Mark Edmondson, Esq; ✉ Edmondson Hall Solicitors, 25 Exeter Road, Newmarket, Suffolk CB8 8AR (☎ 01638 560556, fax 01638 561656, e-mail solicitors@edmondsonhall.com, website www.edmondsonhall.com, Twitter @MarkEdmondson63)

EDMONDSON, Dr Philip Charles; s of Dr Reginald Edmondson (d 1964), of Dunchurch, Rugby, and Phyllis Mary, *née* Elam (d 1996); *b* 30 April 1938; *Educ* Uppingham, Christ's Coll Cambridge (MA, MD, MB BChir), St Bartholomew's Hosp London; *m* 7 Sept 1968, Margaret Lysbeth, da of Stanley Bayston, of Saxton, N Yorks; 3 da (Camilla b 25 April 1970, Claire b 12 May 1972, Cordelia b 5 Jan 1980); *Career* physician to: Westminster Abbey 1979, KLM (Royal Dutch Airlines) London, Australian High Cmmn London; conslt physician to many major industrial cos; visiting med offr King Edward VII Hosp for Offrs London; Freeman City of London, Liveryman Worshipful Soc of Apothecaries; fell Med Soc of London, MRCP; *Recreations* fishing, country pursuits; *Clubs* Boodle's; *Style—* Dr Philip Edmondson; ✉ The Corderries, Abnash, Chalford Hill, Stroud, Gloucestershire GL6 8QL (☎ 01453 883176)

EDMONDSON, Stephen John; s of George Edmondson, of Scunthorpe, and Jean Mary, *née* Stanton; *b* 21 August 1950; *Educ* Scunthorpe GS, Middx Hosp Med Sch, Univ of London (BSc, MB BS); *m* 17 July 1976 (dis 1992), Barbara Bridget Alison, da of Dr Malcolm Nugent Samuel Duncan, TD; 2 c (Adam George b 1984, John David b 1989); m 2, 5 Feb 1994, Yolande Monique Laret; 3 c (Augustus b 1995, Sienna b 1998, Luca b 2000); *Career* conslt cardiothoracic surgn: Bart's 1984–, Heart Hosp 1997–; registrar: Hammersmith Hosp 1980–, Royal Post Grad Medical Sch 1980–, North Middlesex Hosp 1982–; memb: Soc of Cardiothoracic Surgns of GB and Ireland 1982, Br Cardiac Soc 1984, Euro Assoc of Cardiothoracic Surgery 1989; FRCS 1979, FRCP 1991 (MRCP 1980); *Recreations* tennis, football, skiing; *Clubs* Vanderbilt Racquet, Ealing Golf, Ulysses FC; *Style—* Stephen Edmondson, Esq; ✉ 50 Wimpole Street, London W1M 7DG (☎ 020 7935 6375, fax 020 7224 3823, e-mail sedmondson@uk-consultants.co.uk)

EDMONTON, Bishop of 2015–; Rt Rev Robert James (Rob) Wickham; *b* 3 May 1972, Kingston upon Thames; *Educ* Hampton Sch, Grey Coll Durham Univ (BA), Ridley Hall Cambridge, KCL (MA); *m* 19 Aug 2000, Helen, *née* Parker; 2 s (Joseph b 14 Dec 2004, Harry b 24 Dec 2014), 1 da (Susannah b 22 July 2008); *Career* curate Parish Church of Willesden, team vicar Parish of Old St Pancras, rector St John at Hackney (area dean Hackney); *Style—* The Rt Rev the Bishop of Edmonton; ✉ Twitter @bpedmonton

EDMUNDS, Wayne; *m* Roxanne; 1 da (Amanda); *Career* Invensys: chief fin offr 2009–11, chief exec 2011–14; non-exec dir BBA Aviation; *Style—* Wayne Edmunds, Esq; ✉ BBA Aviation plc, 105 Wigmore Street, London W1U 1QY

EDNEY, Dr Andrew Thomas Bailey; s of Sydney George Edney (d 1986), and Dorothy Mary, *née* Smith (d 1990); *b* 1 August 1932; *Educ* Borden Sch, Univ of London, RVC (BVetMed, DVetMed), Open Univ (BA, MA); *Career* Nat Serv 201 Sqdn RAF 1950–52; gen practice Odiham Hants 1958–65, MAFF 1966–67, vet advsr in industry Waltham Centre Leics 1968–85, vet conslt, author and ed 1985–, vet ed Butterworth Heinemann plc 1985–2000; chm Round Table; BSAVA: sec 1976–77, nat pres 1979–80; WSAVA: sec 1982–86, vice-pres 1986–90, pres 1990–92, sr vice-pres 1992–94, hon memb 2000; vice-pres Blue Cross Animal Charity 2011–13 (memb Bd of Govrs 1994–2011, vice-chm 1998–99, chm 1999–2001, hon memb 2013–), hon memb Feline Advsy Bureau (FAB), membre d'honneur French Veterinary Soc (AFVAC) 2000–, pres Section of Comparative Med RSM 2001–03, govr Soc for Companion Animal Studies (SCAS) 2002– (chm 1986–88), memb Cncl Harveian Soc of London 2005–06 and 2010–12, pres Central Veterinary Soc 2007–09 (jr vice-pres 2006–07); Int Award for Service to the Veterinary Profession 1996; DVetMed Univ of London 1997; MRCVS 1958, FRSM 1970, fell Medical Soc of London 2012–; *Books* Dog and Cat Nutrition (1982, 1988), Pet Care (1984), Dog and Puppy Care (1985), Practical Animal Handling (with R S Anderson, 1990), Manual of Cat Care (1992 and 2006), Cat (1999), The Complete Cat Handbook (with C Bessant, 2001), And While You're Here, Episodes in a Vet's Life (2011); *Recreations* fine art related to animals, vintage aircraft, gardening; *Clubs* RSM, Kennel, Harveian Soc of London, Medical Soc of London; *Style—* Dr Andrew Edney; ✉ Olde Dangstones, 147 Lower Street, Pulborough, West Sussex RH20 2DP

EDRIC, Robert; s of E H Armitage, of Sheffield; *b* 14 April 1956; *Educ* Firth Park GS Sheffield, Univ of Hull (BA, PhD); *m* Helen Sara, *née* Jones; 1 s (Bruce Copley Jones); *Career* novelist; *Awards* James Tait Black Fiction Prize 1985, runner up Guardian Fiction Prize 1986, Arts Cncl Bursary 1995; *Books* Winter Garden (1985), A New Ice Age (1986), A Lunar Eclipse (1989), In The Days of The American Museum (1990), The Broken Lands (1992), The Earth Made of Glass (1994), Elysium (1995), In Desolate Heaven (1997), The Sword Cabinet (1999), The Book of the Heathen (2000), Peacetime (2002), Cradle Song (2003), Siren Song (2004), Swan Song (2005), Gathering the Water (2006), In the Kingdom of Ashes (2007), In Zodiac Light (2008), Salvage (2009), The London Satyr (2010), The Devil's Beat (2011), The Monster's Lament (2012), Sanctuary (2013), Field Service (2014); *Style—* Robert Edric, Esq; ✉ Glenfinnan, Springbank Avenue, Hornsea HU18 1ED (☎ 01914 532069)

EDRIDGE, Olga; JP (2008); da of Col Bernard Alfred Edridge, OBE, and Erica, *née* Mavrommati; *b* 22 March 1951; *Educ* Makris HS for Girls Athens Greece, London Film Sch (Dip Film Making), Univ of Reading (BA); *m* 2014, Clare Lawrence Moody (civil partnership converted 12 Jan 2015); *Career* BBC: asst film ed and acting ed 1975–79, grad prodn trainee 1979–81, asst prodr and dir 1981–83, prodr of religious progs 1983–86, series ed Heart of the Matter 1986–91, exec prodr BBC Corporate Prodr Choice 1992–93, project mangr BBC Corporate Performance Review 1993–94, project dir BBC World Services Prodr Choice 1994–95, dir Special Projects BBC Worldwide TV 1995–97, launch dir BBC/Telewest (jt venture UK TV channels) 1997–98, dir Joint Ventures and New Channels Devpt BBC Worldwide (DCI/Discovery, Telewest UKTV, Alliance Antlantis Canada, Jupiter Japan) 1998–2005, global strategic conslt Discovery Int Channels 2006–07, sr ptnr Int Media & Entertainment Ptnrs 2008–, co-fndr and ptnr Ymediate LLP

E

2011–; non-exec memb Bd Shared Experience Theatre Co 2010–; ADR accredited mediator; JP appointed to Family Court 2011–; visiting prof of media arts St Mary's UC Univ of Surrey 1997–; Sandford St Martin Tst Award 1985, One World Broadcast Tst Award 1987; *Recreations* the cottage in Dartmoor, cooking for friends; *Style*— Olga Edridge, JP; ✉ 33 Aldensley Road, London W6 0DH (e-mail oedridge@aol.com)

EDUR, Thomas; CBE (2010); s of Enn Edur, of Estonia, and Liuda, *née* Mishustina, of Estonia; *b* 20 January 1969; *Educ* Tallinn Ballet Sch; *m* 1990, Agnes Oaks, CBE, *qv*, da of Juhan Oaks; *Career* ballet dancer; Estonia Ballet Theatre: Coppelia 1987, Giselle 1988, Paquita 1988, Sleeping Beauty 1989, Nostalgia 1989, Romeo and Juliet 1990, Swan Lake 1990, Estonian Ballads; English National Ballet: Coppélia 1990, The Nutcracker, Les Sylphides, Sphinx, 3 Preludes 1991–, Lucensio in The Taming of the Shrew, Lenski in Eugene Onegin, Études, Four Last Songs, Apollo, Stranger I Came, Cinderella 1992, Swan Lake, La Bayadère 1992, Spectre de la Rose, Ashton Romeo and Juliet, Sphinx 1993–, Impromptu, Sleeping Beauty, Don Quixote (pas de deux), Seven Silences of Salome (winner Time Out Award), D Deane's Paquita 1994, D Deane's Giselle 1994, Romeo and Mercutio in Nureyev Romeo and Juliet 1995, Alice in Wonderland 1995, Christopher Dean's Encounters 1996, Corda's Cinderella 1996, Our Waltzes 1997, Sanguine Fan 1997; joined Birmingham Royal Ballet 1996: Swan Lake 1996, Nutcracker Sweeties 1996, Peter Wright's Nutcracker 1996, Peter Wright's Sleeping Beauty 1997; freelance 1997–: Sleeping Beauty (Estonian Opera), Nutcracker (Sao Paolo Brazil and Tokyo Japan), Swan Lake 1998, Giselle (Balet de Nancy) 1998, D Deane's Romeo and Juliet (Albert Hall) 1998, D Deane's Swan Lake (Albert Hall and Hong Kong and Australia tour) 1998, Nureyev's Don Quixote (La Scala Milan) 1999, P Bart's Giselle (La Scala Milan) 1999, Cinderella (Zurich Ballet) 2000, Romeo and Juliet (Zurich Ballet) 2000, D Deane's Sleeping Beauty (Albert Hall) 2000, P Bart's Giselle (Berlin Staatsoper) 2000, Rest of the Cavalery (Tokyo) 2000, P Bart's Swan Lake (Berlin Staatsoper) 2001, Grand Pas Classique 2001, Romeo and Juliet (Estonian Nat Opera) 2001, Wedding Journey (Estonian Nat Opera) 2001, Swan Lake (Cape Town City Ballet) 2001, Romeo and Juliet (Albert Hall and Australian Tour) 2001; *Awards*: Best Couple (with Agnes Oaks) Int Ballet Competition Jackson Mississippi 1990, London Evening Standard Outstanding Performance in Ballet Award 1994, nominated for Laurence Olivier Award for Outstanding Achievement in Dance 1995 and 1997; Third Class Order of the White Star Estonia 2001; *Recreations* nature lover, scuba diving; *Style*— Thomas Edur, Esq, CBE; ✉ Continental Classics, 49 Tierney Road, London SW2 4QL

EDWARDS, Prof Anthony William Fairbank; s of Harold Clifford Edwards (d 1989), of Cambridge, and Ida Margaret Atkinson, *née* Phillips (d 1981); *b* 4 October 1935, London; *Educ* Uppingham, Trinity Hall Cambridge (MA, PhD, ScD, LittD); *m* 9 Aug 1958, (Elsa Helny) Catharina, da of Nils-Jonas Edlund, ADC to HM Gustav VI Adolf of Sweden; 2 da (Ann Ruth b 1959, Alice Margaret Charlotte b 1964), 1 s (David Thomas b 1960); *Career* Eugenics Soc Leonard Darwin research fell Dept of Genetics Univ of Cambridge 1960, research assoc Int Lab of Genetics and Biophysics Inst of Genetics Univ of Pavia 1961, actg asst prof Depts of Genetics and Mathematics Stanford Univ 1964, sr lectr Dept of Statistics Univ of Aberdeen 1965; Univ of Cambridge: asst dir of research Dept of Human Ecology (later Dept of Community Med) 1970, reader in mathematical biology (later biometry) 1978, sr proctor 1978–79, prof of biometry 2000–03 (ret), sometime memb Cncl of Senate and Gen Bd; fell Gonville & Caius Coll Cambridge 1970– (Berkeley bye-fell in med 1968, sometime memb Cncl); visiting prof of mathematics Dept of Theoretical Statistics Univ of Aarhus 1973; pres Br Regn Int Biometric Soc 1992–94, chm Cambridge Univ Library Syndicate 1993–98, chm Christiaan Huygens Ctee for the History of Statistics Int Statistical Inst 1999–2003, former memb Cncl Int Biometric Soc; Buehler lectr Univ of Minnesota 1992, II Fisher Meml lectr Univ of Adelaide 1992, XVIII Fisher Meml lectr GB 1994, Snedecor lectr Iowa State Univ 1996, Galton lectr Galton Inst 1997, VII Adriano Buzzati-Traverso lectr Univ of Pavia 1999, Zyskind lectr Iowa State Univ 1999; pres Cambridge Univ Gliding Tst Ltd 1978–96, chm Cambridge Univ Gliding Club 1968–77; fell Linnean Soc 1994, tstee and treas Sir Ronald Fisher Meml Tst 1969–2009, sometime memb Cambridge Dist HA; hon prof Univ of Pavia 1999; Gold Medal Telesio-Galilei Acad of Science 2011; hon memb Genetics Soc; FRSS 1962, memb Int Statistical Inst 1976, CMath 1991, FIMA 1991, FRS 2015; *Books* Likelihood (1972, 2 edn 1992), Foundations of Mathematical Genetics (1977, 2 edn 2000), Pascal's Arithmetical Triangle (1987, 2 edn 2002), Annotated Readings in the History of Statistics (with H A David, 2001), Cogwheels of the Mind (2004), Ending the Mendel-Fisher Controversy (with A Franklin, D J Fairbanks, D L Hartl and T Seidenfeld, 2008); *Recreations* gliding, skiing; *Style*— Prof A W F Edwards; ✉ Gonville and Caius College, Cambridge CB2 1TA (e-mail awfe@cam.ac.uk)

EDWARDS, Arthur John; MBE (2003); s of late Arthur James Edwards, and late Dorothy May, *née* Ward; *b* 12 August 1940; *Educ* St Bernard's RC GS Stepney London; *m* 16 Sept 1961, Ann Patricia, *née* Heaphy; 2 s (John Gerard b 7 April 1964, Paul Patrick b 26 Feb 1966), 1 da (Annmarie b 26 March 1971); *Career* press photographer; formerly freelance, with The Sun 1975–; *Recreations* walking, watching West Ham Utd; *Style*— Arthur Edwards, Esq, MBE; ✉ c/o The Picture Desk, The Sun, 1 Virginia Street, London E1 9XP (☎ 020 7782 4110)

EDWARDS, Prof Brian; CBE (1988); s of John Albert Edwards (d 1979), of Bebington, and (Ethel) Pat, *née* Davis (d 1980); *b* 19 February 1942; *Educ* Wirral GS; *m* 7 Nov 1964, Jean, da of William Cannon, of Neston; 2 da (Penny Adrienne b 27 May 1967, Paula Michelle b 14 Nov 1968), 2 s (Christopher, Jonathan (twins) b 28 April 1973); *Career* various hosp posts 1958–69, lectr in health serv studies Univ of Leeds 1969–71, dep gp sec Hull Hosp Mgmnt Ctee 1971–73, dist admin Leeds Dist Health Authy 1973–76, area admin Cheshire AHA 1976–81, regnl gen mangr Trent RHA 1984–93 (regnl admin 1981–83), chief exec W Midlands RHA 1993–96, regnl dir NHS Exec (West Midlands) 1994–96, prof of health care devpt Sch of Health and Related Research Univ of Sheffield 1996–2002 (fndn dean 1996–98, emeritus prof 2002); visiting prof Keele Univ 1989–2000, leader Patient's Charter Team 1992–93; pres: Inst of Health Servs Mgmnt 1983, Health Supplies Assoc 2001–02, European Hospitals Fedn (HOPE) 2005–08; chm: Manpower Advsy Gp NHS 1983–85, Regnl Gen Mangrs Gp England 1986 and 1990–93, CPA (Ltd) 1992–2000, Health on the Box Ltd 2000–02, Cncl for the Professions Supplementary to Med 1997–2002, ATM Ltd 2000–09, Notts Health NHS Tst 2001–06, Pain Mgmnt Solutions Ltd 2009–10; memb: Fallon Judicial Inquiry 1997–98, Standing Advsy Ctee on Audit RCP, Hayes Review of Acute Health Services in NI 2000–01; conslt WHO in: India, Russia, Guyana, Czechoslovakia; ed: Health Servs Manpower Review, NHS 50th Anniversary Lectures 1999; Queen Elizabeth the Queen Mother Nuffield fell 1992; Hon DUniv Univ of Central England 1998; FHSA, CIMgt, FRSPH; Hon FRCPath 1996, Hon ACP; *Books* Si Vis Pacem (1973), Planning the Child Health Services (1975), Manager and Industrial Relations (1979), Merit Awards for Doctors (1987), Controlling Doctors (1991), Managing the NHS (1992), A Manager's Tale (1993, 2 edn 1995), The Executive Years (2005), The Stafford Inquiries (2013), Social History of the Devonshire Graveyard (2016); ed: HOPE European Year Book (1998, 1999, 2000 and 2001), An Independent NHS (2007); many contributions to professional jls; *Recreations* golf; *Clubs* Bakewell Golf (capt 1991, pres 2015), Athenaeum, La Manga; *Style*— Prof Brian Edwards, CBE; ✉ 3 Royal Croft Drive, Baslow, Derbyshire DE45 1SN (☎ 01246 583459)

EDWARDS, (David) Cenwyn; s of Alwyn John Edwards (d 1986), of Pontarddulais, and Edwina Jane, *née* Thomas; *b* 27 October 1945; *Educ* Llanelli Boys GS, Univ of N Wales Bangor (BA); *m* 1, 17 April 1971 (m dis 1990), Margaret Eluned, da of Thomas Owen Davies (d 1977); 1 da (Lowri b 1977), 1 s (Gruffudd b 1979); m 2, 12 Oct 1993 (m dis 2005), Meri Huws, da of Val Hughes, and Gwynne Hughes; *Career* joined HTV 1969, asst head of news and current affrs 1978–82, head of current affrs 1982–85, asst prog controller and N Wales exec 1985–89, controller of factual and general progs 1989–91, commissioning ed of factual progs S4C 1991, head of co-prodns S4C until 2005, dir of TV Tinopolis Gp 2005–07, media conslt 2007–; memb S4C Authy 2007–12; memb Nat Eisteddfod Court; *Recreations* drama, rugby, cricket; *Clubs* Llanelli RFC, Llangennech RFC, Groucho, Scarlets Rugby; *Style*— Cenwyn Edwards, Esq

EDWARDS, Charles; *b* 1 October 1969; *Educ* Winchester Coll, GSMD; *Career* actor; *Theatre* incl: Waste, This House, Strange Interlude, Twelfth Night (National Theatre); Richard II, Much Ado About Nothing (Shakespeare's Globe), The 39 Steps (West End and Broadway), The King's Speech (West End), Blithe Spirit (West End and Los Angeles); *Television* incl: Sherlock, Arthur and George, Downton Abbey, Trying Again, Holy Flying Circus, A Young Doctor's Notebook; *Film* incl: Dunkirk, Florence Foster Jenkins, Philomena, Batman Begins, Mansfield Park; *Style*— Charles Edwards, Esq; ✉ c/o Conway van Gelder Grant, 3rd Floor, 8–12 Broadwick Street, London W1F 8HW

EDWARDS, Chris; s of Francis Edwards (d 1992), and Frances, *née* Kennedy; *b* 28 March 1964; *Educ* Merton Coll Oxford (MA); *m* 1996, Karen, *née* Butler; *Career* Merchant Taylors 1990–94, St Paul's Sch São Paulo 1994–98, Stowe 1998–2004, headmaster Bromsgrove Sch 2004–; vice-pres Housman Soc; govr Winterford Sch; *Recreations* music; *Clubs* East India; *Style*— Chris Edwards, Esq; ✉ Bromsgrove School, Worcester Road, Bromsgrove, Worcestershire B61 7DU (☎ 01527 577336, e-mail head@bromsgrove-school.co.uk, website www.bromsgrove-school.co.uk)

EDWARDS, Prof Sir Christopher Richard Watkin; kt 2008; s of Wing Cdr Thomas Archibald Watkin Edwards (d 1986), and Beatrice Elizabeth Ruby, *née* Telfer (d 1993); *b* 12 February 1942; *Educ* Marlborough, Univ of Cambridge (MB BChir, MD); *m* 6 April 1968, Sally Amanda Le Blount, da of Wing Cdr Gerald Le Blount Kidd, OBE, of Westerham, Kent; 2 s (Adam b 1969, Crispin b 1974), 1 da (Kate b 1971); *Career* sr lectr in medicine and hon conslt physician Bart's 1975, prof of clinical med Univ of Edinburgh and hon conslt physician to the Lothian Health Bd 1980–95, chm Dept of Med Western Gen Hosp Edinburgh 1981–91, dean Faculty of Med 1991–95, provost Faculty Gp of Med and Vet Med 1992–95, princ Imperial Coll Sch of Med 1995–2001 (fell 2003); vice-chllr Univ of Newcastle upon Tyne 2001–07; memb MRC Cncl 1992–95, govr Wellcome Tst 1994–2005; chm: Chelsea & Westminster NHS Fndn Tst 2007–14, Medical Educn England 2009–12, Cncl Br Heart Fndn 2009–16, Med Advsy Bd Buckingham Univ 2015–; chm Cluff Geothermal 2015–, chm icappic 2015–; tstee The Planet Earth Institute, patron Tom's Tst; hon fell City & Guilds Inst London 2007; Hon DSc Univ of Aberdeen 2000, Hon DCL Univ of Newcastle 2008; FRCP 1979, FRCPE 1981, FRSE 1990, FMedSci 1998; *Books* Essential Hypertension as an Endocrine Disease (co ed, 1985), Recent Advances in Endocrinology and Metabolism (co ed, 1992), Davidson's Principles and Practice of Medicine (co ed, 1995); *Recreations* golf, painting; *Clubs* Athenaeum; *Style*— Prof Sir Christopher Edwards, FRSE

EDWARDS, Prof David John; s of late Percy Oliver Edwards, of Cwmbran, Gwent, and late Ceinwen Elizabeth, *née* Salter; *b* 20 February 1951; *Educ* Croesyceiliog GS Gwent, Univ of Bristol (BSc, MSc, PhD), Univ of Oxford (MA); *m* 1973, Georgina Elizabeth, da of late R V Janson; 2 da (Eleanor Georgina b 24 Feb 1978, Charlotte Elizabeth b 15 Dec 1981); *Career* various positions in computer systems and satellite communications British Telecom 1973–85, New Blood lectr Univ of Bristol 1985–89; Univ of Oxford: fell Wadham Coll 1989–14, lectr 1989–96, admissions tutor Wadham Coll 1993–98, reader 1996–98, prof of engrg sci 1998–2014, sr pro-proctor 2006–07, faculty chm 2010–11, sub-warden Wadham Coll 2011–14, emeritus fell Wadham Coll 2014–; dir Oxford Electromagnetic Solutions Ltd, dir Oxford Enhanced Medical Ltd; IEE Prize for Innovation 1986, NPL Metrology Award 1990, IEE Mountbatten Premium 1990, IEEE Neal Shepherd Meml Award 1990; approx 300 publications in scientific and technical jls and patents; curator Sheldonian Theatre; CEng 1985, FIEE 1997 (MIEE 1985), FRAS 1985; *Recreations* music, astronomy, clocks, classic/vintage motor cars, architecture; *Style*— Prof David Edwards; ✉ e-mail david.edwards@eng.ox.ac.uk

EDWARDS, David Michael; CMG (1989); s of Ernest William Edwards (d 1991), and Thelma Irene, *née* Foxley (d 1998); *b* 28 February 1940; *Educ* King's Sch Canterbury, Univ of Bristol (LLB); *m* 1 (m dis), Veronica Margaret, da of Robert Postgate, of Cannes, France (d 1997); 1 da (Vanessa Louise b 1967), 1 s (Capt Adrian David b 1969); m 2, Rain Ren; 1 s (Charles Ren b 1997), 1 da (Chloe Ren b 1999); *Career* admitted slr 1964, asst legal advsr FO 1967; legal advsr: Br Mil Govt Berlin 1972, Br Embassy Bonn 1974; legal cnsllr 1977, gen counsel and dir legal div IAEA Vienna 1977–79, legal cnsllr FCO 1979, agent of the UK Govt in cases before Euro Cmmn and Court of Human Rights 1979–82, cnsllr and legal advsr UK Mission to UN NY and HM Embassy Washington 1985–88, dep legal advsr FCO 1989–90, law offr (International Law) Hong Kong Govt 1990–95, sr counsel Bechtel Ltd 1995–97, vice-pres and region counsel Bechtel Asia Pacific (Singapore) 1997–2002, chief legal counsel Shell Petrochemicals Co Ltd and CNOOC's Petrochemical Complex Guangdong Province China 2002–, memb Panel of Mediators Singapore Mediation Centre 2002–; *Recreations* reading, travel, antique clocks; *Style*— David Edwards, Esq, CMG; ☎ 00 86 752 556 4132, e-mail edwards.david@cspc.net.cn

EDWARDS, (John) Duncan; s of Dr Vernon Edwards, OBE, JP (d 1991), and Jean, *née* Macgregor; *b* 28 March 1964, Watford; *Educ* Merchant Taylors', Univ of Sheffield (BA); *m* 2 Oct 1993, Sarah; 2 s (Freddie b 8 Oct 1994, Findlay b 7 Aug 1996); *Career* currently pres and ceo Hearst Magazines Int and dir Bd Hearst Corp; vice-chm The National Magazine Co Ltd (former ceo); memb Advsy Bd: Br American Business Assoc, Foreign Policy Assoc; Freeman City of London, memb Worshipful Co of Merchant Taylors; *Recreations* running, triathlon, rugby union, chopping firewood; *Clubs* OMT FC, Soho House, George, New York Athletic; *Style*— J Duncan Edwards, Esq; ✉ Hearst, 300 West 57th Street, New York, NY 10019, USA

EDWARDS, Guy Richard Goronwy; QGM (1977), Austrian AC Gold Medal 1977; s of Sqdn Ldr Goronwy Edwards, DFC, RAF, of Liverpool, and Mary Christine Edwards; *b* 30 December 1942; *Educ* Liverpool Coll, Univ of Durham (BSc); *m* 26 April 1986, Daphne Caroline, da of William George McKinley, MRCVS, of Co Meath, Ireland; 1 s (Sean), 2 da (Natasha, Jade); *Career* professional racing driver 1965–85, winner 40 int races, drove as team mate to Graham Hill; Grand Prix Formula One: Lola 1974, Lord Hesketh 1976, BRM 1977; drove Le Mans Twenty Four Hour 9 times for Porsche, BMW and Lola (fourth 1985); awarded QGM for helping rescue Niki Lauda from burning Ferrari at German Grand Prix 1976; chm Guy Edwards Racing Ltd (organising sponsorship for motor racing) 1985–, responsible for Jaguar Car Co's commercial sponsorship prog (resulted in their winning World Championship 1987, 1988 and 1991, and Le Mans 1988 and 1990), dir of mktg Lotus Formula One Team; Freeman: City of London, Worshipful Co of Coachmakers and Coach Harness Makers; *Books* Sponsorship and the World of Motor Racing; *Recreations* country pursuits, reading, water sports, fishing; *Clubs* British Racing Drivers, Club International des Anciens Pilotes de Grand Prix F1 BARC; *Style*— Guy Edwards, Esq, QGM

EDWARDS, Prof Gwynne; s of William Edwards (d 1964), of Clydach Vale, Mid Glamorgan, S Wales, and Rachel Mary Lamb (d 1986); *b* 14 April 1937; *Educ* Porth Co GS, UC Cardiff, KCL (BA, PhD); *m* 1 Aug 1964, Gillian Marilyn Davies; 1 da (Eleri b 1968), 1 s (Gareth b 1971); *Career* lectr in Spanish Univ of Liverpool 1962–67; Dept of Euro Languages Univ of Wales Aberystwyth: lectr 1967–73, sr lectr 1973–80, reader 1980–83, prof 1983–2005, head of dept 1984–87, emeritus prof 2005–; *Theatre Productions* Lorca's Blood Wedding 1987, 1992, 2001, 2004 and 2013, Lorca's Women 1987–88, Mario Vargas Llosa's La Chunga 1988, Lorca's Dona Rosita 1989 and 2004, Lorca's When Five Years Pass 1989 (Scotsman Fringe First) and 2006, Lorca's The Shoemaker's Wonderful Wife 1990 and 1991, Carlos Muñiz's The Ink-Well 1990, Lope de Vega's Punishment Without Revenge 1991, Calderón's Three Judgements in One 1991, Life is a Dream 1992, Egon Wolff's Paper Flowers 1993, 2003 and 2014, José Triana's Medea in the Mirror 1996, Calderón's The Surgeon of Honour 1998, Sophocles' Antigone 1998, Poet in New York 1998, Francisco Ors' Contradance 1999, Garcia Márquez's Diatribe of Love 2001 and 2008, Puccini's Edgar 2001, Lorca's Mariana Pineda 2002 and 2006, Lorca's The House of Bernarda Alba 2003 and 2009, Dylan Thomas in America 2003–09 (adaptation), Dylan Thomas in London 2006–07 (adaptation), Three Dylan Thomas Short Stories 2008 and 2013(adaptations), Dylan and Caitlin 2008 (opera), Burton 2009–11, 2013 and 2014, Dylan Thomas: the Clown in the Moon 2011, 2013 and 2014, Cut My Shadow (three Lorca poems set to music by Jonathan Dove) 2011; *Books* The Prison and the Labyrinth: Studies in Calderonian Tragedy (1978), Lorca: The Theatre Beneath the Sand (1980), The Discreet Art of Luis Bunuel (1982), Dramatists in Perspective: Spanish Theatre in the Twentieth Century (1985), Lorca: Three Plays (1987), Lorca Plays: Two (1990), Calderón Plays: One (1991), Indecent Exposures: Buñuel, Saura, Erice, Almodóvar (1994), Lorca Plays: Three (1994), Burning the Curtain: Four Revolutionary Spanish Plays (1995), Lorca's Blood Wedding, student edn (1997), The House of Bernarda Alba, student edn (1998), Lope de Vega, Three Major Plays (1999), Flamenco (2000), Almodóvar: Labyrinths of Passion (2001), Lorca: Living in the Theatre (2003 and 2013), Contemporary South American Plays (2004), Three Spanish Golden Age Plays (2005), A Companion to Luis Buñuel (2005), Lorca's Yerma (2007), Lorca's Doña Rosita the Spinster (2008), A Cultural Journey Through Andalusia (2009), Lorca, Bunuel and Dali: Forbidden Pleasures, Connected Lives (2009); *Recreations* theatre, opera, music, sport, cinema, travel; *Style*— Prof Gwynne Edwards; ✉ 66 Maeshendre, Waun Fawr, Aberystwyth

EDWARDS, Huw; s of late Prof Hywel Teifi Edwards, and Aerona Protheroe; *b* 18 August 1961, Bridgend, Wales; *Educ* Llanelli Boys' GS, UC Cardiff (BA); *m* Victoria Flind; 5 c; *Career* BBC: joined as trainee journalist 1984, parly corr BBC Wales 1986–88, political corr then chief political corr BBC TV News and BBC News 24 1988–99, presenter News at Six 1999–2002, presenter News at Ten 2003–, presenter News at Five BBC News channel 2006–, presenter of BBC TV and radio progs incl the wedding of Prince William and Catherine Middleton, Trooping the Colour, Festival of Remembrance, State Opening of Parliament, D-Day 60, The Story of Wales, Songs of Praise, Lloyd George, Gladstone and Disraeli, coverage of The Queen's Diamond Jubilee and progs on classical music incl BBC Cardiff Singer of the World, commentator London 2012 Olympic Opening and Closing Ceremonies, D-Day 70; hon prof of journalism Cardiff Univ 2007; Presenter of the Year BAFTA Cymru 2001, 2002, 2003, 2004 and 2009, Best News Coverage BAFTA 2004 (for coverage of the Madrid bombings), Best Live Event Coverage BAFTA 2012 (for the Royal Wedding), Presenter of the Year BAFTA Cymru 2012, Best Live Programme RTS Award (for DDAY70 The Heroes' Return) 2014, Best Live Event Coverage BAFTA (for WW1 Remembered) 2014; pres London Welsh Tst 2008–; pres: Gwalia Male Choir 2006–, London Welsh Male Voice Choir 2012–, vice-pres Cardiff Univ 2009 (pro-chllr 2013); patron: Nat Coll of Music 2005–, George Thomas Hospice 2007–, Bridgend Male Choir 2008, Trinity Hospice 2011–, Ty Bryngwyn Hospice Llanelli 2012–, Cancer Research Wales; ambass Prince's Tst; hon fell: Univ of Cardiff 2003, Univ of Wales Lampeter 2006, Univ of Wales Swansea 2007, Univ of Wales Newport 2007, Swansea Inst of HE 2007, Bangor Univ 2014; Hon DUniv Glamorgan 2007; *Books* Capeli Llanelli: Our Rich Heritage (2009), City Mission: The Story of London's Welsh Chapels (2014); *Clubs* Garrick, London Welsh Club (Pres. 2008–); *Style*— Huw Edwards, Esq; ✉ BBC News, New Broadcasting House, London W1A 1AA

EDWARDS, Jennifer; CBE (2011); da of William Terence Edwards (d 1982), and Cora Marion Milton (d 1987); *b* 26 December 1954; *Educ* Torquay Girls' GS, Girton Coll Cambridge (BA); *m* Jean Pierre Ferraroli; 1 s (Jovan b 25 March 1995); *Career* civil servant 1976–81, local govt offr 1983–93; dep ldr of the oppn Westminster City Cncl 1990–94, nat campaigns organiser CND 1991–93, dir Nat Campaign for the Arts 1993–98, dir of external rels and devpt Arts Council England (formerly London Arts) 1998–2004, ceo Homeless Link until 2011, chief exec Mental Health Fndn 2013–; dir Taproot Consultancy 2012–15; FRSA; *Recreations* opera, family history, song, gardening; *Style*— Ms Jenny Edwards, CBE

EDWARDS, Jeremy Paul; s of Peter Edwards, of Deli, N Cornwall, and Philippa, *née* Fielding; *b* 12 September 1962, Stroud; *Educ* Allhallows Sch Lyme Regis, Keele Univ (LLB), Coll of Law Guildford; *m* 29 July 1989, Kay, *née* Rawson; 1 da (Sophie), 2 s (Thomas, Rory); *Career* admitted slr 1989; Norton Rose: articled clerk 1987–89, Paris office 1992–95, ptnr 1997–, head of aviation 2002–09, memb Bd 2005–09, gp head of banking 2009–, global head of banking and finance Norton Rose Fulbright 2013–; memb: Law Soc 1987, City of London Slrs Co 1989; *Recreations* fishing, sailing (yachts), golf, tennis, shooting; *Style*— Jeremy Edwards, Esq; ✉ Norton Rose Fulbright, 3 More London Riverside, London SE1 2AQ (☎ 020 7283 6000, e-mail jeremy.edwards@nortonrosefulbright.com)

EDWARDS, Rev Dr Joel Nigel Patrick; *b* Kingston, Jamaica; *Educ* London Bible Coll (BA), St John's Coll Univ of Durham (DThM); *Career* probation offr 1978–88; min New Testament Church of God 1985–2003; gen sec African Caribbean Evangelical Alliance 1988–92, dir UK Evangelical Alliance 1992–97, gen dir Evangelical Alliance 1997–2008, int dir Micah Challenge Int 2009–2014; memb Equality and Human Rights Cmmn 2007–10, advsr Tony Blair Faith Fndn 2008–, advsr Foreign Sec's Advsy Gp on Human Rights 2010–; visiting fell St John's Coll Durham; hon canon St Paul's Cathedral; Hon DD: Caribbean Grad Sch of Theology Jamaica 2006, St Andrews Univ 2007; PM's Medal of Appreciation (Jamaica); *Publications* Lord Make Us One – But Not All The Same! (1999), The Cradle, The Cross and The Empty Tomb (2000), Hope, Respect and Trust: Valuing These Three (2004), An Agenda for Change: A global call for spiritual and social transformation (2008), The Jesus Agenda (2012); *Recreations* swimming, reading, the occasional jog; *Style*— The Rev Dr Joel Edwards; ✉ website www.micahchallenge.org

EDWARDS, John Thomas; s of Jack Edwards (d 1953), and Gwendoline, *née* Davies (d 1982); *b* 16 November 1935; *Educ* Haverfordwest GS; *m* Iris Mary; *Career* reporter: West Wales Guardian 1953–54, Liverpool Daily Post 1955–57; US corr Daily Mirror 1961–63 (staff corr London 1958–61); Daily Mail: feature writer 1969–71, SE Asia corr 1971–75, sr writer 1975–84, columnist 1984–; British Press Awards: Reporter of the Year 1975, commended feature writer 1977, commended foreign corr 1981; Reporter of the Year Granada TV Awards 1976; *Recreations* sailing, gardening; *Clubs* Cardiff and County, Hong Kong Press; *Style*— John Edwards, Esq; ✉ The Daily Mail, Northcliffe House, 2 Derry Street, Kensington, London W8 5TT (☎ 020 7938 6210)

EDWARDS, Prof Kevin John; s of John Cyril William Edwards, of Northfleet, Kent, and Elsie May, *née* Clark; *b* 18 September 1949; *Educ* Northfleet Boys' Sch, Gravesend GS, Univ of St Andrews (MA, DSc), Univ of Aberdeen (PhD); *Children* 2 s (Fraser John Alf Regan b 17 Aug 1989, Calum Tom Regan b 6 Aug 1993); *Career* tutorial fell Dept of Geography Univ of Aberdeen 1972–75, lectr in environmental reconstruction Queen's Univ Belfast 1975–80; Univ of Birmingham: lectr in biogeography 1980–90, sr lectr in geography 1990–92, reader in palaeoecology 1992–94; Univ of Sheffield: prof of palaeoecology 1994–2000, head Dept of Archaeology and Prehistory 1996–99; Univ of Aberdeen: prof of physical geography 2000–, adjunct prof in archaeology 2007–; hon research assoc Limnological Research Center Univ of Minnesota 1983, adjunct prof Grad Sch City Univ of NY 2002–, research assoc Macaulay Land Use Research Inst 2002–, visiting researcher Dept of Geography and Geology Univ of Copenhagen 2007–09, visiting fell Clare Hall Cambridge 2011–12 (life memb 2012), visiting scholar McDonald Inst for Archaeologicial Research Univ of Cambridge 2011–12, Christensen fell St Catherine's Coll Oxford 2012; chm Users' Ctee Univ of Oxford Radiocarbon Accelerator Unit 1995–2000, dep chm Scottish Coastal Archaeology and Palaeoenvironment Tst 2001–04; convenor Earth Sciences and Chemistry Ctee RSE 2006–10; memb: Radiocarbon Ctees Natural Environment Research Cncl 1995–2000, Research Ctee Soc of Antiquaries of Scotland 2000–10 (memb Cncl 2006–09), Earth and Environmental Sciences Ctee RSE 2003–06, Geography and Environmental Studies UK Nat Panel for the Research Assessment Exercise 2008, Geography, Environmental Studies and Archaeology UK Nat Panel for the Research Excellence Framework 2014; memb Editorial Bd: Jl of Archaeological Science 1983–, Transactions of the Institute of British Geographers 1994–98, Environmental Archaeology 1997–2012, Landscapes 2003–11, Transactions of the Royal Society of Edinburgh 2005–08, Mediaeval Scandinavia 2005–, Proceedings of the Society of Antiquaries of Scotland 2007–, Jl of the North Atlantic 2011–, Biodiversity and Conservation 2014–; Univs Medal RSGS 1972, 133rd Rhind lectr Soc of Antiquaries of Scotland 2012; FRGS 1972, FSA Scot 1972, FSA 1999, FRSE 2002, CGeog RGS 2003, MAE 2012; *Publications* Quaternary History of Ireland (1985), Scotland: Environment and Archaeology 8000 BC-AD 1000 (1997), Holocene Environments of Prehistoric Britain (1999); author of approximately 270 articles in geography, archaeology, botany and quaternary science; *Recreations* reading, family history; *Style*— Prof Kevin Edwards, FRSE; ✉ Department of Geography and Environment, University of Aberdeen, Elphinstone Road, Aberdeen AB24 3UF (☎ 01224 272346, e-mail kevin.edwards@abdn.ac.uk)

E

EDWARDS, Lionel Antony (Tony); *b* 4 November 1944; *Educ* Univ of Birmingham (BSc), Harvard Business Sch (MBA with Distinction); *Career* apprenticeship and later sr mgmnt positions with Rolls-Royce, General Electric (USA), Motorola and Canadair 1962–89, md Lucas Aerospace (subsequently gp md) Lucas Industries plc 1989–92, chm Dowty Group and Main Bd dir TI Group plc 1992–98, chm and chief exec Messier-Dowty International 1994–98; head of Defence Export Services Organisation MOD 1998–2001; chm The Air League 2003–; former pres Soc of Br Aerospace Cos; past chm Def & Aerospace Sector Panel UK Technol Foresight Prog; past pres Royal Aeronautical Soc; tstee: RAF Museum Hendon, The Swordfish Heritage Tst, Battle of Britain Meml Tst; former memb Nat Def Industries Cncl, former memb Aviation Ctee DTI; CEng, FRAeS; *Recreations* farming, classic car restoration, historic aircraft preservation; *Style*— Tony Edwards, Esq; ✉ Wincotts Hill Farm, Whichford, Warwickshire CV36 5PQ

EDWARDS, Lyn; s of William David Edwards (d 1972), and Gwenllian, *née* Cox; *b* 28 August 1947, Bridgend, Glamorgan; *Educ* Ogmore GS, Birmingham Sch of Architecture (DipArch), Aston Univ (BSc), Univ of Reading (MSc); *Children* 1 s (Nicholas Lloyd b 1978); 2 da (Philippa Louise b 1982, Rebecca Kathryn b 1985); *Career* asst: Malcolm H Peck & Partners 1969–70, Oxfordshire Co Architect's Dept 1971–72; GMW Architects: project architect 1972, resident ptnr GMW International 1978, sr ptnr 1991–2014 (ptnr 1980), chm GMW Architects International 1998–2014, dir Lyn Edwards Associates 2014–; projects incl: Royal Opera House master plan and extension, King Saud Univ Riyadh, bomb damage refurbishment NatWest Tower and 99 Bishopsgate London 1988–; dir Wren Insurance Ltd; chm European Architects' Alliance, former chm Br Expertise; RIBA 1972 (client advsr 2013), FRSA; *Recreations* rugby football, reading, music, family; *Clubs* East India; *Style*— Lyn Edwards, Esq; ✉ e-mail lyn@lynedwards.com

EDWARDS, Mark John; s of Eric Edwards, of Penarth, and Mary O'Flynn; *b* 10 July 1954, Nairobi, Kenya; *Educ* St Mary's Sch Nairobi, Clongowes Wood Coll Kildare, Univ of Bristol (BSc); *m* 8 Sept 1979, Micheline; 2 s (Richard b 26 Aug 1981, Michael b 26 Nov 1985), 1 da (Georgina b 3 March 1983); *Career* accountant PricewaterhouseCoopers 1975–79, auditor Warner Lambert 1979–81, accountant Grant Thornton 1981–82, subsidiary finance dir Whitbread plc 1982–89, divnl finance dir Williams plc 1989–96; Baxi Gp: finance dir 1997–2003, gp ceo 2003–08; ceo AIM Altitude 2010–; chm Atlas Fine Wines Ltd 2010–, non-exec dir Marshalls plc 2010–; FCA 1979; *Recreations* golf, skiing, theatre; *Clubs* RAC, Kedleston Park Golf, Loch Lomond Golf; *Style*— Mark Edwards, Esq; ✉ The Glen, 35 Hazelwood Road, Duffield, Derbyshire DE56 4DP (☎ 07785 355128, e-mail mje.edwards@btinternet.com)

EDWARDS, (Kenneth) Martin; s of late Kenneth Reginald Edwards, and late Joan Isabel, *née* Bradley; *b* 7 July 1955; *Educ* Sir John Deane's GS Northwich, Balliol Coll Oxford (MA, Jenkyns Prize, Keasbey bursary, David Paton studentship, Winter Williams Award, Martin Wronker Award), Chester Coll of Law; *m* 30 April 1988, Helena Mary Caroline, da of late Michael James Shanks; 1 s (Jonathan Michael b 28 Dec 1990), 1 da (Catherine Juliet Ruth b 5 June 1993); *Career* writer and slr; articled clerk Booth and Co Solicitors Leeds 1978–80, admitted slr 1980, ptnr Mace and Jones Liverpool 1984–2011 (slr 1980–84), ptnr Weightmans Liverpool 2011–; memb editorial bd Business Law Review; memb: Standing Ctee on Employment Law Law Soc 1987–97, Working Pty on Alternative Dispute Resolution Law Soc 1997–2001, Crime Writers' Assoc, Soc of Authors, Detection Club (pres 2011–); *Books* Understanding Computer Contracts (1983), Understanding Dismissal Law (1984, 2 edn 1991), Managing Redundancies (1986), Executive Survival (1987, 2 edn 1991), Northern Blood (ed, 1992), Careers in the Law (1995, 6 edns), Anglian Blood (co-ed, 1995), Northern Blood 2 (ed, 1995), Know-How for Employment Lawyers (jtly, 1995), Perfectly Criminal (ed, 1996), Whydunit? (ed, 1997), Past Crimes (ed, 1998), Northern Blood 3 (ed, 1998), Missing Persons (ed, 1999), Scenes of Crime (ed, 2000), Tolley's Equal Opportunities Handbook (2000, 4 edns), Murder Squad (ed, 2001), Crime in the City (ed, 2002), Urge To Kill (2002), Green for Danger (ed, 2003), Mysterious Pleasures (ed, 2003), Crime on the Move (ed, 2004), ID (ed, 2006), MO (ed, 2008), Original Sins (2010), Best Eaten Cold (2011), Guilty Consciences (2011), Deadly Pleasures (2013), Guilty Parties (2014), Capital Crimes (2015), Resorting to Murder (2015), Truly Criminal (2015), The Golden Age of Murder (2015), Silent Nights (2015); *Novels* All The Lonely People (1991), Suspicious Minds (1992), I Remember You (1993), Yesterday's Papers (1994), Eve of Destruction (1996), The Devil in Disguise (1998), First Cut is the Deepest (1999), The Lazarus Widow (jtly, 1999), Take My Breath Away (2002), The Coffin Trail (2004), The Cipher Garden (2005), The Arsenic Labyrinth (2006), Waterloo Sunset (2008), Dancing for the Hangman (2008), The Serpent Pool (2010), The Hanging Wood (2011), The Frozen Shroud (2013), The Dungeon House (2015), Murder at the Manor (2015), Serpents in Eden (2015); *Recreations* writing, music, cricket, travel, films; *Clubs* Athenaeum (Liverpool); *Style*— Martin Edwards, Esq; ✉ Watson Little Ltd, 48–56 Bayham Place, London (e-mail martinedwards10@btconnect.com, website www.martinedwardsbooks.com)

EDWARDS, Prof Sir Michael; kt (2014), OBE (2005); s of Frank Ernest Walter Edwards (d 1995), and Irene Louise Dalliston (d 1985); *b* 29 April 1938; *Educ* Kingston GS, Christ's Coll Cambridge (BA, MA, PhD); *m* 7 July 1964, Danielle, da of Jacques Bourdin, of Lamotte-Beuvron, France; 1 s (Paul), 1 da (Catherine); *Career* lectr in French Univ of Warwick 1965–73, sr lectr then reader in lit Univ of Essex 1973–87, prof of English Univ of Warwick 1987–2002, prof of English Collège de France 2002–; visiting prof: Univ of Paris 1989–90, Collège de France and Univ of Witwatersrand 1997, Ecole Normale

Supérieure 1998, European chair Collège de France 2000–01; memb Cncl Institut Collégial Européen; memb Editorial Advsy Bd: Literature and Theology, Christianity and Literature; Dagnan-Bouveret Prize Académie des Sciences Morales et Politiques 2008; hon fell Christ's Coll Cambridge 2013–; memb Académie Fraçaise 2013, Commandeur des Arts et des Lettres (France) 2013, Chevalier de la Légion d'Honneur (France) 2015; *Books* La Tragédie Racinienne (1972), To Kindle The Starling (poems, 1972), Eliot/Language (1975), Where (poems, 1975), The Ballad of Mobb Conroy (poems, 1977), Towards a Christian Poetics (1984), The Magic, Unquiet Body (poems, 1985), Poetry and Possibility (1988), Of Making Many Books (1990), Raymond Mason (1994), Eloge de l'Attente (1996), De Poetica Christiana (1997), Beckett ou le don des Langues (1998), Leçons de Poésie (2001), Sur un vers d'Hamlet (2001), Ombres de Lune (2001), Un Monde Même et Autre (2002), Shakespeare et la Comédie de l'émerveillement (2003), Terre de Poésie (2003), Rivage Mobile (poems, 2003), Etude de la Création Littéraire en Langue Anglaise (2004), Racine et Shakespeare (2004), Shakespeare et L'Oeuvre de la Tragédie (2005), Le Genie de la Poesie Anglaise (2006), De l'émerveillement (2008), Paris Demeure (poetry, 2008), A la Racine du Feu (poetry, 2009), Shakespeare: le Poete au Theatre (2009), Ce Que Dit La Lumière (poetry, 2010), Trilogie (playlet, 2010), Le Bonheur d'être ici (2011), Le Rire de Molière (2012), Paris Aubaine (poetry, 2012), Discours de Réception à l'Académie Française (2014), Bible et Poésie (2016), L'Infiniment Proche (poems, 2016); *CD* L'Etrangèreté (2010); *Recreations* walking; *Clubs* Cambridge Union; *Style—* Prof Sir Michael Edwards, OBE; ✉ 22 rue de Rivoli, 75004 Paris, France; Académie Française, 23 Quai de Conti, 75006 Paris, France (e-mail michael.edwards@college-de-france.fr)

EDWARDS, Paul David Thomas; s of Robert Thomas Edwards, and Ailsa Edith, *née* Brown; *Educ* Toowoomba GS, Queensland Univ of Technol (Dip Educn Art and Drama), RADA (Dip Scene Design); *Career* designer; assoc memb RADA, memb Soc of Br Theatre Designers; *Theatre* designs incl: Trojan Women (La Boite), Did You Say Love (La Boite), One Flew Over the Cuckoo's Nest (Brisbane Arts Theatre), Time and Time Again (Sydney Ensemble Theatre), The Young Idea (Chester Gateway), The Last Yankee (Leicester Haymarket), The Pleasure Principle (The Young Vic), No Flies On Mr Hunter (Chelsea Arts Theatre), Birdbath (Etc Theatre), Post of the Cosmos (Etc Theatre), Vita and Virginia (Sphinx Theatre Co), The Servant of Two Masters (Wolsey Theatre Ipswich), Brighton Beach Memories (Stephen Joseph Theatre), Little Women (Sheffield Crucible Theatre), Fair Game (Theatre Royal Plymouth), Kiss Me Kate (Norwich Playhouse), The Importance of Being Earnest (Nat Theatre of Israel), Boutique (London Studio Centre), Jyroscape (Sadlers Wells), The Taming of the Shrew (New Shakespeare Co), Is That All There Is? (Almeida and NY), Viva Espana, Trelawney of the Wells; designs for Harrogate Theatre: The Odd Couple, The Importance of Being Earnest, Private Lives, Jack and the Beanstalk, Gasping, On the Piste, Cat on a Hot Tin Roof, The Barber of Seville, Romeo and Juliet; designs for Queens Theatre Hornchurch: Noises Off, Great Expectations, The Sound of Music, The Turn of the Screw, Dames at Sea; designs for Theatre Clwyd: Pygmalion, Hamlet, The Seagull, School for Scandal; *Opera* designs incl: The Bartered Bride (Tel Aviv), Orfeo et Euridice (Tel Aviv), Little Magic Flute (Tel Aviv), L'Egoiste (RAM), La Finta Semplice (Nice, Vichy and Paris), The Marriage of Figaro (Dublin), The Secret Marriage (Paris), L'Italiana in Algeri (Garsington), Il Mondo Della Luna (Garsington), The Mikado (Cardiff), Orfeo et Euridice (Strasbourg, Valladolid and La Coruna), Jakobin (Wexford), Die Walküre (Caracas), The Pearl Fishers (Russia and Holland); *Recreations* skiing, sailing; *Style—* Paul Edwards, Esq; ✉ c/o Cassie Mayer Ltd, 5 Old Garden House, The Lanterns, Bridge Lane, London SW11 3AD

EDWARDS, Prof Paul Kerr; s of Ernest Edwards (d 1979), and Ida Vivienne, *née* Kerr; *b* 18 March 1952; *Educ* King Edward VI Sch Stratford-on-Avon, Magdalene Coll Cambridge (BA), Nuffield Coll Oxford (BPhil, DPhil); *m* 1975, Susan Jane, da of John Geeson Martin; 1 s (William John b 1980), 1 da (Rebecca Jane b 1983); *Career* Univ of Warwick: various research positions Industrial Relations Research Unit (IRRU) 1977–88, prof of industrial relations 1992–2011, dir IRRU 1998–2002 (dep dir 1988–98); prof of employment relations and head Dept of Mgmnt Univ of Birmingham 2011–14 (emeritus prof 2014–); sr fell Advanced Inst of Mgmnt Research 2004–07; chm Social Science Gp Br Acad 2006–10, memb Business and Mgmnt Sub-Panel for Research Assessment Exercise 2008, memb Business and Mgmnt Sub-Panel for Research Excellence Framework 2014; ed-in-chief Human Relations 2012–; memb Br Sociological Assoc (1980); FBA 1998, academician Academy of Social Sciences 2008; *Books* Strikes in the United States (1981), The Social Organization of Industrial Conflict (co-author, 1982), Conflict at Work (1986), Managing the Factory (1987), Attending to Work (co-author, 1993), Managers in the Making (co-author, 1997), Industrial Relations (ed, 2003), The Politics of Working Life (co-author, 2005), Social Theory at Work (co-ed, 2006), Studying Organizations Using Critical Realism (co-ed, 2014); *Recreations* cycling; *Style—* Prof Paul Edwards, FBA; ✉ Birmingham Business School, Edgbaston Park Road, Birmingham B15 2TT

EDWARDS, Prof Peter Philip; s of late Ronald Goodlass, and Ethel Mary, who later m Arthur Edwards; *b* 30 June 1949; *Educ* Univ of Salford (Chemistry Prize, BSc, PhD); *m* 4 Sept 1970, Patricia Anne, da of John and Mary Clancy; 1 da (Kerrie b 13 Dec 1971), 2 s (Peter John b 23 April 1973, Karl b 17 March 1980); *Career* Fulbright scholar and Nat Science fell Baker Lab of Chemistry Cornell Univ 1975–77, SERC/NATO fell and Ramsay Meml fell Inorganic Chemistry Lab Univ of Oxford 1977–79; Univ of Cambridge: lectr and dir of studies in chemistry 1979–90, dir of studies in natural scis and fell Jesus Coll 1979–90, Nuffield Science Research fell 1986–87, co-fndr and co-dir first Interdisciplinary Research Centre in Superconductivity 1988, British Petroleum Venture Research fell 1988–90; Univ of Birmingham: prof of inorganic chemistry 1991–99, head Sch of Chemistry 1997–99, prof of chemistry and of materials 1999–2003; head and prof of inorganic chemistry Univ of Oxford 2003–; co-ordinator EPSRC UK Sustainable Hydrogen Energy Consortium 2003–; visiting prof Cornell Univ 1983–86, F S Kipping visitor Univ of Nottingham 1987, Royal Soc Leverhulme Tst sr research fell 1996–97; memb HEFCE: Research Assessment Exercise Panels 1996 and 2001, Non-Formula Funding Panel 1997; Royal Soc of Chemistry: Corday-Morgan Medal 1987, Tilden Medal 1992, vice-pres Dalton Div 1995; memb: Materials Research Soc of India, German Acad of Sciences 2009; Liversidge Medal 1999, Hughes Medal Royal Soc 2003; FRS 1996; *Books* The Metallic and Nonmetallic States of Matter (ed with C N R Rao, 1985), Metal-Insulator Transitions Revisited (ed with C N R Rao, 1995), Gold in a Metallic Divided State – From Faraday to the Present Day Nanoscience (with J M Thomas, 2007); *Style—* Prof Peter P Edwards, FRS; ✉ Inorganic Chemistry Laboratory, University of Oxford, South Parks Road, Oxford OX1 3QR (☎ 01865 272646, fax 01865 272690)

EDWARDS, Peter Robert; s of Robert Edwards, of Worthing, West Sussex, and Doris Edith, *née* Cooper; *b* 30 October 1937; *Educ* Christ's Hosp; *m* 1, 1967, Jennefer Ann, da of Frederick Boys; m 2, 1970, Elizabeth Janet, da of Maitland Barrett; 1 s (Simon b 1970), 1 da (Sarah b 1971); *Career* Arthur Young 1955–90 (managing ptnr 1986–90), md Secretan plc 1990–92, ind memb Cncl FIMBRA 1990–94, currently public interest dir Personal Investment Authy; non-exec dir Blackwall Green Ltd 1993–96; Freeman City of London 1956, memb Worshipful Co of Merchant Taylors; ICAS 1960; *Recreations* ornithology; *Style—* Peter Edwards, Esq; ✉ The Personal Investment Authority, 25 The North Colonnade, Canary Wharf, London E14 5HS (☎ 020 7676 1000, fax 020 7676 1099)

EDWARDS, Robert Charlton (Rob); s of Lawrence Edwin Edwards (d 1977), and Muriel Eugénie, *née* Peel (d 1989); *b* 24 May 1949; *Educ* Worcester Royal GS, Pembroke Coll Oxford, Bristol Old Vic Theatre Sch; *m* 1 Nov 1997, Markéta; 2 s (Oskar b 28 May 2001, Lukas b 16 Feb 2004); *Career* actor; *Theatre* RSC Stratford and the Aldwych 1980–81: Amintor in The Maid's Tragedy, Young Gobbo in The Merchant of Venice, Khomich in Lovegirl and the Innocent by Solzhenitsin, Charles Lamb in The Fool by Edward Bond; Young Vic 1986, 1989 and 1990: Lucio and The Duke in Measure for Measure, Mercutio in Romeo and Juliet; RSC Stratford and Barbican 1990–91: title role in Pericles (Barbican only), Pritikin in Barbarians by Maxim Gorky (Barbican only), First Citizen in Coriolanus; Apoo in Topakano's Martyrs' Day (Bush), Hamlet in Hamlet with the London Shakespeare Group (Far Eastern Tours for Br Cncl) 1985 and 1986, Max and Singer in Definitely the Bahamas by Martin Crimp and Angus in No More a-Roving by John Whiting (Orange Tree) 1987, Polynices in The Thebans (RSC) 1991, Poins in Henry IV (RSC) 1991, Horatio in Hamlet (RSC) 1992, Cassius in Julius Caesar (RSC) 1993, Quarlous in Bartholomew Fair (RSC) 1997, Walt Disney in Talk of the City (RSC) 1998, Scar in The Lion King (West End) 1999, Hippolito in Women Beware Women (RSC) 2006, Page in Merry Wives, the Musical (RSC) 2006–07, Theseus/Oberon in Midsummer Night's Dream (Bolton Octogon) 2010, Ralph Messenger in Secret Thoughts (Bolton Octogon) 2011; *Television* incl: Stephen Lovell in The Fourth Arm (BBC) 1981–82, John Fletcher in By the Sword Divided (BBC) 1983–84, Dr Chris Clarke in The Practice (Granada) 1985, Gilbert Whippet in Campion (BBC) 1988, Prince John in Henry IV Parts I & II and Henry V (BBC), Arthur Goslett in In Suspicious Circumstances 1993, John Drewe in Trail of Guilt (BBC) 1999, Richard Florian in Midsomer Murders (ITV) 2006, Geoff Holhurst in The Thick of It (BBC) 2007; *Recreations* scrambling, mountain walking; *Style—* Rob Edwards, Esq

EDWARDS, Robert Philip (Rob); s of Robert Aelwyn Edwards, of Abbots Langley, Herts, and Kathleen Isobel, *née* Brockbank; *b* 13 October 1953; *Educ* Watford Boys' GS, Jesus Coll Cambridge (MA); *m* 8 June 1977, Dr Fiona Grant Riddoch, da of Thomas Grant Riddoch; 2 da (Robyn Edwards Riddoch b 20 Feb 1990, Lindsay Edwards Riddoch b 1 Jan 1993); *Career* journalist, television prodr and writer; organiser Scottish Campaign to Resist the Atomic Menace 1977–78, campaigns organiser Shelter (Scotland) 1978–80; work as Scottish corr Social Work Today 1981–83, res asst to Robin Cook MP 1980–83, co-ordinator of CND's case at Sizewell Inquiry 1982–85; Scottish corr: New Statesman 1983–89, The Guardian 1989–93; columnist Edinburgh Evening News 1989–94, environment ed Scotland on Sunday 1989–94, German corr New Scientist, Scotland on Sunday and The Scotsman 1994–96, conslt with New Scientist 1996–, environment ed Sunday Herald 1999–, contrib The Guardian 2010–; co-fndr The Ferret (https://theferret.scot) 2015; prodr: documentary Children Under Fire (Channel 4) 1993, CCTV (Channel 4) 1999; Media Natura Regnl Journalist of the Year Br Environment and Media Awards 1989 (specially commended 1992), commended Industrial Soc Environment Award 1993, commended UK Press Gazette Regnl Awards 1993, Sunday Herald Br Environment and Media Award Newspaper of the Year 2001, shortlisted Journalist of the Year Br Environment and Media Awards 2006; memb NUJ, shortlisted Scoop of the Year Scottish Press Awards 2016; *Books* Fuelling the Nuclear Arms Race: the Links Between Nuclear Power and Nuclear Weapons (with Sheila Durie, 1982), Britain's Nuclear Nightmare (with James Cutler, 1988), Still Fighting for Gemma (with Susan D'Arcy, 1995); *Recreations* walking, opera, theatre, films and rock music; *Style—* Rob Edwards, Esq; ✉ 53 Nile Grove, Edinburgh EH10 4RE (☎ 0131 447 2796, e-mail rob.edwards@blueyonder.co.uk, website www.robedwards.com, Twitter @robedwards53)

EDWARDS, Roger John; s of late Flt Lt John Alfred Edwards, of Ewhurst, Surrey, and Melva Joyce, *née* Burrell; *b* 30 November 1941; *Educ* Isleworth GS, Univ of Hull; *m* 4 July 1964, Janet Amelia, da of Stanley Victor Holmes (d 1971); 2 s (Nicholas St John b 29 July 1966, Barnaby James b 20 Aug 1969); *Career* McCann Erickson 1964–67, Chesebrough Ponds 1967–70, Davidson Pearce Ltd 1970–77, ceo Leo Burnett 1979–81, Grey Communications Group 1982– (formerly chm and chief exec, now md); FIPA 1983, FInstD; *Recreations* theatre, travel, walking, books, golf; *Clubs* Wisley Golf (dep chm); *Style—* Roger Edwards, Esq

EDWARDS, Ruth Dudley; da of Robert Walter Dudley Edwards (d 1988), and Sheila, *née* O'Sullivan (d 1985); *b* 24 May 1944; *Educ* Sacred Heart Convent Dublin, Sandymount HS Dublin, UCD (BA, MA, DLitt), Girton Coll and Univ (now Wolfson) Coll Cambridge, City of London Poly (Dip Business Studies); *m* 1, 31 July 1965 (m dis 1975), Patrick John Cosgrave (d 2001), s of Patrick Joseph Cosgrave (d 1952); m 2, 10 Jan 1976 (m dis 1991), John Robert Mattock, s of John Leonard Mattock (d 1986); *Career* teacher 1965–67, mktg exec Post Office 1970–74, principal DOI 1975–79, freelance writer 1979–, company historian The Economist 1982–2000, freelance journalist and broadcaster 1994–; memb Exec Ctee: Br Irish Assoc 1981–93, Crime Writers' Assoc 1995–98 and 2015–, Soc of Authors 1996–99; chm Br Assoc for Irish Studies 1986–93; Hon DLitt Queen's Univ Belfast; *Books* An Atlas of Irish History (1973), Patrick Pearse: the triumph of failure (1977, Nat Univ of Ireland Historical Research Prize), James Connolly (1981), Corridors of Death (1981), Harold Macmillan: a life in pictures (1983), The Saint Valentine's Day Murders (1984), Victor Gollancz: a biography (1987, James Tait Black Memorial Prize), The School of English Murder (1990), Clubbed to Death (1992), The Pursuit of Reason: The Economist 1843–1993 (1993), The Best of Bagehot (1993), True Brits (1994), Matricide at St Martha's (1994), Ten Lords A-Leaping (1995), Murder in a Cathedral (1996), Publish and be Murdered (1998), The Faithful Tribe: an intimate portrait of the loyal institutions (1999), The Anglo-Irish Murders (2000), Newspapermen: Hugh Cudlipp, Cecil Harmsworth King and the glory days of Fleet Street (2003), Carnage on the Committee (2004), Murdering Americans (2007, CrimeFest Last Laugh Award 2008), Aftermath: the Omagh Bombing and the Families' Pursuit of Justice (2009, Crime Writers' Assoc Gold Dagger Award for Non-Fiction), Killing the Emperors (2012, CrimeFest Last Laugh Award 2013),The Seven: the lives and legacies of the founding fathers of the Irish Republic (2016); *Recreations* friends, books, politics, laughter; *Clubs* Academy, Reform; *Style—* Miss Ruth Dudley Edwards; ✉ Flat 47, Charing Cross Mansions, 26 Charing Cross Road, London WC2H 0DH (☎ 07768 838344, e-mail ruthdudleyedwards@rdemail.co.uk, website www.ruthdudleyedwards.com, Twitter @ruthde)

EDWARDS, Dr Victoria Mary; OBE (2004); da of George Wade Brown Edwards, of Sway, Hants, and Betty Kathlene, *née* Mack (d 2000); *b* 14 August 1963, Wallasey, Merseyside; *Educ* Univ of Reading (Strutt and Parker Award, BSc, PhD), Univ of Canterbury NZ (Cwlth scholar, MSc); *m* 15 May 1999, Richard Taylor; 1 step da (Stephanie Rose), 1 step s (Michael James); *Career* chartered surveyor Rural Dept Dreweatt-Neate 1984–87, conslt strategic devpt and mgmnt QEII Nat Tst Wellington NZ 1987–89; Univ of Portsmouth: sr lectr and dir of research 1989–94, princ lectr and dir of research Sch of Environmental Design and Mgmnt 1994–2010 (head of sch 2006–07); assoc prof Henley Business Sch Univ of Reading 2010–16; chief exec Ernest Cook Tst 2016–; non-exec dir: Countryside Agency 1998–2004, Forestry Cmmn 1999–2006 (chair Research Strategy Mgmnt Bd), Macaulay Land Use Research Inst 2001–04, Forest Holidays LLP 2006–12; memb: Academic Advsy Cncl Environment Unit Inst of Economic Affrs 1990–95, Survey Courses Bd RICS 1991–96, Educn and Membership Ctee RICS 1992–96, Academic Ctee Cambridge Int Land Inst Fitzwilliam Coll Cambridge 1995–98, Advsy Ctee Sch of Rural Economy and Land Mgmnt RAC Cirencester 1996–2001, Burns Ctee (Inquiry into Hunting) 1999–2000; tstee: Countryside Educn Tst 1998–2001, Ernest Cook Tst 2007–16, Habitat Research Tst; Carthage fell USA 1991, Winston Churchill travelling fell 1991, RICS teaching fell 1993–95, Jones Lang Wootton scholar 1995–96; fell Central Assoc of Agricultural Valuers 1985, FRICS 1986; *Books* Dealing in Diversity: America's Market for Nature Conservation (1995), Corporate Property Management: Aligning Real Estate with Business Strategy (jtly, 2004); *Recreations* local community interests in New Forest, walking, golf, skiing, fundraising for hospice movement (250km sponsored dog sled Arctic Circle 2006), wildlife filmmaking, cooking for friends; *Style—* Dr Victoria Edwards, OBE; ✉ Ernest Cook Trust, The Estate Office, Fairford Park, Fairford, Gloucestershire GL7 4JH (☎ 01285 712492, e-mail victoria@ernestcooktrust.org.uk, website www.ernestcooktrust.org.uk)

EDWARDS-STUART, Hon Mr Justice; Sir Antony James Cobham Edwards-Stuart; kt (2009), QC (1991); s of Lt-Col Ivor Arthur James Edwards-Stuart (decd), and Elizabeth Aileen Le Mesurier, *née* Deck (d 2003); *b* 2 November 1946; *Educ* Sherborne, RMA Sandhurst (RAC Young Officers Prize), St Catharine's Coll Cambridge (MA); *m* 11 May 1973, Fiona Ann, da of (Albert) Paul Weaver, OBE (d 1993), of London; 2 s (Luke b 29 Sept 1973, Thomas b 4 Sept 1980), 2 da (Anna b 26 March 1976, Rachel b 25 Feb 1982); *Career* cmmnd 1 Royal Tank Regt 1966, Adj 1973–75, Adj Kent & Sharpshooters Yeo 1975–77; called to the Bar Gray's Inn 1976, recorder 1997– (asst recorder 1991–97), dep judge of the High Court 2003–09, head of chambers 2005–09, judge of the High Court 2009–, judge in charge Technology and Construction Court 2013–; chm Home Office Advsy Ctee on Service Candidates 1995–98; MCIArb 2001; *Recreations* theatre, restoring listed property in France; *Style—* The Hon Mr Justice Edwards-Stuart; ✉ Royal Courts of Justice, Rolls Building, London EC4A 1NL (☎ 020 7947 7205, fax 0870 761 7694)

EFFORD, Clive; MP; *Career* MP (Lab) Eltham 1997–; *Style—* Clive Efford, Esq, MP; ✉ House of Commons, London SW1A 0AA (☎ 020 7219 3000)

EFSTATHIOU, Prof George Petros; s of Petros Efstathiou, of London, and Christina, *née* Parperis; *b* 2 September 1955; *Educ* The Somerset Sch London, Keble Coll Oxford (BA), Univ of Durham (PhD); *m* 27 July 1976 (m dis 1997), Helena Jane (Janet), da of James Lewis Smart, of Poyntzpass, Newry, NI; 1 da (Zoe b 1986), 1 s (Peter b 1988); m 2, 23 May 1998, Yvonne, da of Gianfranco Nobis of Bournemouth, Dorset; 2 s (Francesco b 2002, Alexander b 2005); *Career* res asst Univ of Calif Berkley 1979–80, sr res fell King's Coll Cambridge 1984–88 (jr res fell 1980–84, fell 1997–), asst dir of res Inst of Astronomy Cambridge 1984–88 (SERC res fell 1980–84), Savilian prof of astronomy Univ of Oxford 1988–97 (head of astrophysics 1988–94), fell New Coll Oxford 1988–97, prof of astrophysics Univ of Cambridge 1997–; sr research fell PPARC 1994–99, dir Inst of Astronomy 2004–08, dir Kuuli Inst for Cosmology Cambridge 2008–; memb: various ctees SERC, IAU 1980, PPARC; Maxwell Medal and Prize Inst of Physics 1990, Vainu Bappu Award Astronomical Soc of India 1988, Sherman Fairchild Distinguished Scholar Caltech 1991, Bodassaki Prize for astrophysics 1994, Robinson Prize in cosmology Univ of Newcastle upon Tyne 1997, Dannie Heineman Prize American Inst of Physics 2005, Gruber Cosmology Prize; FRAS 1983, FRS 1994, FInstP 1995; *Recreations* running, guitar music; *Style—* Prof George Efstathiou, FRS; ✉ Institute of Astronomy, Madingley Road, Cambridge CB3 0HA (e-mail gpe@ast.cam.ac.uk)

EGAN, Penny; CBE (2013); da of Derek Morris (d 1994), and June, *née* Vorst; *b* 18 July 1951; *Educ* St Paul's Girls' Sch (dep head girl), Univ of Leicester (BA); *m* 1975, David Egan (d 2016), s of Henry Lawrence Egan; 2 s (Oliver b 1980, Henry b 1982); *Career* museum asst Circulation Dept rising to press offr V&A 1972–75, press offr 10 Downing St 1975–77, press and publicity offr Crafts Advsy Ctee Crafts Cncl 1977–82, conference organiser Glass in the Environment 1984–86; RSA: lecture sec 1986–95, prog devpt dir 1995–97, exec dir 1998–2006; exec dir US-UK Fulbright Cmmn 2007–; memb Bd Design Cncl 1999–2008, cmmr Mayor's Cmmn on the Creative Industries 2003–05; non-exe dir Wardour Publishing and Design 2007–09; tstee: Campaign for Learning 1998–2005, Geffrye Museum 2007–14 (chair 2010–14), DEMOS 2009–13; memb Cncl Univ of Warwick 2007–15, memb Cncl Univ of Reading 2016–; Hon FRSA, Hon Fell RCA; *Recreations* tennis, cooking, the Arts; *Clubs* Roehampton; *Style—* Mrs Penny Egan, CBE; ☎ 07885 398050, e-mail penny@pennyegan.com

EGAN, Peter; *Educ* RADA; *m* Myra Frances, actress; 1 da (Rebecca); *Career* actor; *Theatre* roles with RSC incl: Valentine in Two Gentlemen of Verona, Osric in Hamlet, Richmond in Richard II, Sergei Nikolayich Tsyganov in Barbarians 1990; most recently Casanova in Camino Real 1996–97; Chichester Festival Theatre roles incl: Apollodorus in Caesar and Cleopatra (with Sir John Gielgud), Jack Absolute in The Rivals (with Sir John Clements), Alexander in Dear Antoine; other stage credits incl: Stanhope in Journey's End (Cambridge, won Best Actor London Theatre Critics award) 1972, John Shand in What Every Woman Knows (Albery) 1973, Cheviot Hills in Engaged (NT) 1975, Charles Rolls in Rolls Hyphen Royce (Shaftesbury) 1977, Valentine in You Never Can Tell (Royal Gala opening Lyric) 1979, Sergius in Arms and the Man (Lyric) 1981, Rene Gallimard in M Butterfly (Shaftesbury) 1989, Astrov in Uncle Vanya (also dir, with Renaissance Theatre Co, Manchester Evening News Best Actor Award) 1991, Jimmy Porter in Déjà Vu (Comedy Theatre) 1992, Three Hotels (Tricycle and West End) 1993, Casanova in Camino Real (RSC) 1997, Serge in Art (Wyndhams) 1999, Lloyd Dallas in Noises Off (NT) 2000 and (Picadilly Theatre) 2001, Tom in Secret Rapture (Lyric) 2003, Claudius and Ghost in Hamlet (Barbican) 2004, Sherlock Holmes in The Hound of the Baskervilles (nat tour), Sir Hugo Latymer: A Song at Twilight (nat tour) 2008, The Secret of Sherlock Holmes (West End and nat tour) 2010, People (Nat Theatre Lyttleton) 2012–13, First Love (Gate Theatre Dublin at the Lyceum for Edinburgh Festival) 2013; has also directed numerous plays at the Lyric and Savoy Theatres and at Mills Coll Oakland San Francisco; *Television* incl: Seth in Cold Comfort Farm 1967, the Earl of Southampton in Elizabeth R 1971, Millais in The Love School 1974, Oscar Wilde in Lillie Langtry 1978, title role in The Prince Regent 1978, Fothergill in Reilly Ace of Spies 1982, The Dark Side of the Sun 1983, Ever Decreasing Circles 1984, 1986, 1987 and 1989, A Woman of Substance, Pym in The Perfect Spy 1986, Joint Account 1988 and 1990, A Day in Summer 1988, The Price of the Bride 1989, Ruth Rendell's A New Lease Of Death 1991, MacGyver 1992, Vanity Dies Hard 1992, The Chief 1993, Chiller 1994, The Peacock Spring 1995, Edward Ellisson in Cater St Hangman 1998, A Touch of Frost 1998, Michael Cochrane in The Ambassador 1998, Dr Hook in Cry Wolf, Inspector Lynley Mysteries 2002, The Family 2004, Jericho (Granada) 2005, Whatever Love Means 2005, Home Again (BBC1) 2005, Midsomer Murders 2010, Downton Abbey 2012; *Film* incl: The Hireling (BAFTA Best Actor Award) 1972, Hennessy 1973, Callan 1974, Chariots of Fire 1980, Henry Simcox in Paradise Postponed (Euston Films, winner TV Times Award 1986) 1985, Gobble 1996, Bean 1996, 2001: A Space Travesty 1999, Eye Inside 2002, Something Borrowed 2003, Man to Man 2004, Death at a Funeral 2006; *Style—* Peter Egan, Esq; ✉ c/o Simon Beresford, Dalzell and Beresford, 26 Astwood Mews, London SW7 4DE (☎ 020 7341 9411)

EGBUNA, His Hon Judge Robert Obiora; s of Dr Robert Egbuna, and Dr Phyllis Wakile, *née* Onwuagba; *b* 30 November 1963, London; *Educ* Sibford Sch Banbury, Polytechnic Central London (LLB), Cncl of Legal Educn; *m* 29 Feb 1992, Maite Gloria Egbuna-Ruiz, *née* Ruiz-Guerro; 1 da (Ebele Edurne Egbuna-Ruiz), 1 s (Pablo José Egbuna-Ruiz); *Career* called to the Bar (Gray's Inn) 1988; recorder 2009, circuit judge (Midland Circuit) 2015–; *Recreations* golf, music, reading, travel; *Clubs* Nottingham Golf (Hollinwell); *Style—* His Hon Judge Egbuna; ✉ Derby Combined Court Centre, Morledge, Derby DE1 2XE (☎ 01332 622572)

EGDELL, Dr (John) Duncan; s of John William Egdell (d 1990), of Bristol, and Nellie Egdell (d 1996); *b* 5 March 1938; *Educ* Clifton, Univ of Bristol (MB ChB), Univ of Edinburgh (DipSocMed); *m* 9 Aug 1963, Dr Linda Mary Flint, da of Edmund Harold Flint (d 1974), of Barnehurst, Kent; 2 s (Brian, Robin), 1 da (Ann); *Career* house physician and surgn United Bristol Hosps 1961–62, in gen practice 1962–65, asst sr med offr Newcastle Regnl Hosp Bd 1968–69 (admin med offr 1966–67), regnl specialist in community med SW RHA 1974–76 (asst sr med offr 1969–72, princ asst sr med offr 1972–74), regnl med offr Mersey RHA 1977–86, community physician and conslt in public health med Clwyd Health Authy 1986–93 (hon conslt 1993–96), hon conslt in public health med N Wales Health Authy 1996–; FFPHM (1990, FFCM 1979); *Recreations* nature conservation, delving into the past; *Style—* Dr Duncan Egdell; ✉ Ravenswood, Glen Auldyn, Lezayre, Isle of Man IM7 2AQ (☎ 01624 818012)

EGERTON-WARBURTON, Peter; o s of Col Geoffrey Egerton-Warburton, DSO, TD, JP, DL (d 1961; ggs of Rowland Egerton, bro of Sir John Grey-Egerton, 8 Bt, and Rev Sir Philip Grey-Egerton, 9 Bt), and Hon Georgiana Mary Dormer, MBE (d 1955), eldest da of 14 Baron Dormer, CBE, DL; *b* 17 January 1933; *Educ* Eton, RMA Sandhurst; *m* 1, 29 Jan 1955 (m dis 1958), Belinda Vera, da of James R A Young; m 2, 10 Nov 1960 (m dis 1967), Sarah Jessica, er da of Maj Willoughby Rollo Norman; 2 s; m 3, 6 June 1969, Hon Marya Anne, 2 da of Baron Glenkinglas, PC; 1 s, 1 da (twins); *Career* cmmnd Coldstream Gds 1953, ret 1962 with rank of Capt; Maj Cheshire Yeo 1963; ptnr John D Wood Estate Agents 1966–86, fndr and chm Egerton Ltd Estate Agents 1986–; landowner; Lord of the Manor of Grafton, patron of the livings of Plemstall and Guilden Sutton; Companion Order of St John; *Clubs* White's, Beefsteak, Turf; *Style—* Peter Egerton-Warburton, Esq; ✉ 54 Prince's Gate Mews, London SW7 2PR (☎ 020 7589 9254); Mulberry House, Bentworth, Alton, Hampshire GU34 5RB (☎ 01420 562360)

EGGAR, Timothy John Crommelin (Tim); PC (1995); s of John Drennan Eggar (d 1983), and Pamela Rosemary Eggar; *b* 19 December 1951; *Educ* Winchester, Magdalene Coll Cambridge, London Coll of Law; *m* 1977, Charmian Diana, da of Peter William Vincent Minoprio, CBE; 1 s, 1 da; *Career* barr, banker; PA to Rt Hon William Whitelaw 1974, MP (Cons) Enfield N 1979–97, PPS to min for Overseas Devpt 1982–85, Parly under-sec of state FCO 1985–89; min of state: Dept of Employment 1989–90, DES 1990–92, DTI 1992–96; dir Charterhouse Petroleum 1983–85; chm: M W Kellogg Group Ltd 1996–98, chm AGIP (UK) Ltd 1997–98, chief exec Monument Oil and Gas plc 1998–99 (non-exec dir 1997–98), vice-chm ABN AMRO Corp Finance 2000–03, vice-chm ABN AMRO UK 2004–, chm Harrison Lovegrove & Co 2005–; non-exec dir: LASMO plc 1999–2000, Expro plc 2004–07; sr advsr Int Gas Union; chm Anglo-Azeri Soc 1997–2001, pres Russo-British C of C 2003–; *Style—* The Rt Hon Tim Eggar

EGINGTON, Richard; s of Phillip Egington, and Barbara Egington; *b* 26 February 1979, Warrington, Cheshire; *Educ* Warrington Sch; *Career* rower; Silver medal (fours) World Championships 2003, Bronze medal (eights) World Championships 2007, Silver medal (eights) Olympic Games 2008, Gold medal (coxless fours) World Championships 2009, Gold medal (coxless fours) World Championships 2011, Bronze medal (eights) Olympic Games 2012; *Clubs* Leander (capt 2010–); *Style—* Richard Egington, Esq

EGLIN, Philip; s of Jack Eglin, and Mary, *née* Whitaker; *b* 29 November 1959, Gibraltar; *Educ* Harlow Tech Coll, Staffs Poly, RCA; *Career* ceramicist; various teaching posts: Brighton Poly, Univ of Wolverhampton, Dundee Coll of Art, Crewe and Alsager Coll, Camberwell Sch of Art, Loughborough Coll of Art, Staffs Univ, Falmouth Coll of Art, W Glamorgan Inst, RCA, Harbourfront Centre Toronto; *Solo Exhibitions* Stafford Art Gallery 1990, Oxford Gallery 1991, Philip Eglin – A Staffordshire Tradition? (South Bank Centre London) 1991, Crafts Cncl Shop at the V&A 1993, Scottish Gallery Edinburgh 1994, 1997, 2000 and 2004, Garth Clark Gallery NY 1995, 1999, 2000 and 2003, Barrett Marsden Gallery London 2001, 2003, 2006 and 2008, V&A 2001, Philip Eglin – Ceramics (Franklin Parrasch Gallery NY) 2005 and (Scottish Gallery Edinburgh) 2009, Borrowings (Nottingham Museum and Art Gallery) 2007, Dean Project Sofa NY 2008, Hands Off Berbatov 2008, Spiritual Heroes (Glynn Vivian Art Gallery Swansea) 2008; *Group Exhibitions* RCA Exhibition (Japan and Korea) 1987, Contemporary Applied Arts London 1988, Garden Pots (Gainsborough's House Suffolk) 1989, A Summer Picnic (City Gallery Leicester) 1989, Clay Bodies (Contemporary Applied Arts London) 1989, The Decade Ahead (Scottish Gallery Edinburgh) 1990, Great Br Design Exhibition (Tokyo) 1990, EC Exhibition (Avignon) 1990, The Abstract Vessel (Oriel Cardiff) 1991, Aspects of Sculpture (Galerie für Englishe Keramik Sandhausen) 1991, Favourite Things (Crafts Cncl Gallery London) 1991, Colours of the Earth – 20th century British Ceramics (Br Cncl touring exhibition India) 1991, 25th Anniversary Exhibition (Contemporary Applied Arts London) 1992, 25th Anniversary Exhibition (Oxford Gallery) 1993, The Raw and the Cooked (MOMA Oxford and tour), One From the Heart (Aberystwyth Arts Centre and tour) 1995, The Nude in Clay (Perimeter Gallery Chicago) 1995, Hot off the Press (Tullie House Carlisle and tour) 1996, Living at Belsay Hall (Belsay Hall Northumberland) 1996, 10 Years Crafts (Scottish Gallery Edinburgh) 1996, Jerwood Prize Exhibition (Crafts Cncl Gallery London and German tour) 1996, Philip Eglin and Claire Curneen (Contemporary Applied Arts London) 1996, Objects of Our Time (Crafts Cncl Gallery London and tour) 1996, Selection from the Collection (Ipswich Museum and Art Gallery) 1997, European Ceramics Workcentre s'Hertogenbosch 1998, A View of Clay (Contemporary Applied Arts London) 1998, Freighted with Wonders (Wolsey Art Gallery Ipswich) 1998, 541 Vases, Pots, Sculptures and Services (Stedelijk Museum Amsterdam) 1999, Only Human (Crafts Cncl Gallery London) 1999, 25th Anniversary Exhibition (Crafts Cncl Shop at the V&A) 1999, An Inaugural Gift: The Founders' Circle Collecton (Mint Museum N Carolina) 2000, British Ceramics.2000.dk (Grimmerhus Ceramics Museum Middelfart) 2000, Br Cncl touring show of Br Ceramics (Brazil and other venues in S America) 2000, Poetics of Clay: An International Perspective (Philadelphia Art Alliance and tour to Museum of Art and Design Helsinki) 2001–02, BLUR (Stedelijk Museum) 2002, Fragile, Think with Care (Univ of Essex) 2004, Celebrating 30 Years (Crafts Cncl Shop at V&A) 2005, Collect (V&A) 2006, European Ceramic Context (Art Museum of Bornholm) 2006, Barrett Marsden Gallery London 2008, Hell Fire (Niewe Kerke Amsterdam) 2008, Galerie Handwerk Munich 2009; *Work in Public Collections* V&A, Crafts Cncl London, Contemporary Art Soc London, Br Cncl, Stedelijk Museum Amsterdam, Mint Museum N Carolina, Auckland Museum, Fitzwilliam Museum Cambridge, Brighton and Hove Museum and Art Gallery, Portsmouth Museum and Art Gallery, Shipley Museum and Art Gallery Gateshead, Liverpool Museum and Art Gallery, Hants CC, Potteries Museum Stoke-on-Trent, Norwich City Museum and Art Gallery, Nat Museum of Scotland, Aberystwyth Arts Centre, York Museum and Art Gallery; *Awards* Crafts Cncl setting-up grant 1987, Crafts Cncl Selected Index 1991, Arts Fndn Fellowship 1993, Jerwood Prize for Applied Arts 1996; *Publications* Philip Eglin (1997), Borrowings (2007), Eglin's Etchings (2008); *Recreations* mangr Shamblers FC (under 13s) in Potteries Jr Youth League; *Style—* Philip Eglin, Esq; ✉ c/o Barrett Marsden Gallery, 17–18 Great Sutton Street, London EC1 0DN (☎ 020 7336 6396, fax 020 7336 6391)

EGLIN, Roger David; s of George Eglin (d 1968), of West Kirby, and Evelyn, *née* Sharrocks; *b* 29 June 1940, Bolton, Lancs; *Educ* Preston GS, Calday Grange GS, LSE (BSc Econ); *m* 5 Sept 1964, Judith Ann, da of Frederick Albert Kay; 2 da (Cordelia Jane b 26 Feb 1968, Penelope Lydia b 28 Jan 1970); *Career* journalist; res asst Financial Times 1960–61, economics corr Business Magazine 1962–66, business corr The Observer 1966–72; The Sunday Times: successively industrial and business ed, then managing ed, assoc business ed, currently supplements ed; *Books* Fly Me I'm Freddie (1980); *Recreations* sailing, walking dog, reading; *Clubs* Island Sailing, Royal Corinthian Yacht; *Style—* Roger Eglin, Esq; ✉ The Sunday Times, 1 Pennington Street, London E1 9XW (☎ 020 7782 5752, fax 020 7782 5100)

EGREMONT, 2 Baron (UK 1963) and 7 Baron Leconfield (UK 1859); (John) Max Henry Scawen Wyndham; DL (W Sussex); s of 6 Baron Leconfield and 1 Baron Egremont,

E

MBE (d 1972; as John Wyndham was private sec to Rt Hon Harold Macmillan, when PM); *b* 21 April 1948; *Educ* Eton, ChCh Oxford; *m* 15 April 1978, Caroline, da of Alexander Ronan Nelson, and Hon Audrey Paget (da of 1 and last Baron Queenborough, s of Lord Alfred Paget, 5 s of 1 Marquess of Anglesey); 3 da (Hon Jessica Mary b 27 April 1979, Hon Constance Rose b 20 Dec 1980, Hon Mary Christian b 4 Oct 1985), 1 s (Hon George Ronan Valentine b 31 July 1983); *Heir* s, Hon George Wyndham; *Career* farmer and writer; chm The Friends of the Nat Libraries 1985–, memb Royal Cmmn on Historical Manuscripts 1989–2001, memb National Manuscripts Conservation Tst 1995– (chm 2000–); pres South of England Show 2013–14; tstee: The Wallace Collection, Br Museum 1990–2000; Liveryman Worshipful Co of Drapers; FRSL 2001, FSA 2005; *Books* The Cousins (1977), Balfour (1980), The Ladies Man (1983), Dear Shadows (1986), Painted Lives (1989), Second Spring (1993), Under Two Flags: The Life of Major General Sir Edward Spears (1997), Siegfried Sassoon (2005), Forgotten Land: Journeys Among the Ghosts of East Prussia (2011), Some Desperate Glory: The First World War The Poets Knew (2014); *Style*— The Rt Hon Lord Egremont, DL, FRSL; ✉ Petworth House, Petworth, West Sussex GU28 0AE (☎ 01798 342447, fax 01798 344331, e-mail egremont@leconfield.net)

EHRET, Thomas (Tom); s of F X Ehret (d 2001), and J Ehret, *née* Giethlen; *b* 10 March 1952, Mulhouse, France; *Educ* Ecole Nationale Supérieure des Arts et Métiers Paris; *m* 6 July 1974, G Ehret, *née* Boisson; 2 s (Xavier b 21 July 1976, Charles b 5 Aug 1983); *Career* md Comex Houlder Diving Ltd 1983–88, ceo Stena Offshore BV 1989–95, chief operating offr Coflexip Stena Offshore SA 1996–2001, vice-chm Technip SA and pres Technip Offshore 2001–03, ceo Acergy Gp 2003–08 (non-exec dir 2008–), operating ptnr Advent Int 2009–11; non-exec dir: Dockwise 2007–, SBM Offshore 2008–, Huisman Equipt BV 2011–; sr advsr Oak Tree Capital Mgt 2011–; *Recreations* music, reading; *Style*— Tom Ehret, Esq; ✉ 31 Rue de Verneuil, 75007 Paris, France (☎ 0033 6 0897 1485, e-mail tomehret@gmail.com)

EILBECK, Prof (John) Christopher; *b* 8 April 1945; *Educ* The Queen's Coll Oxford (BSc), Lancaster Univ (PhD); *Career* Royal Soc European fell ICTP Trieste 1969–70, research fell UMIST 1970–73; Heriot-Watt Univ 1973–: head Dept of Mathematics 1984–89, prof of scientific computing 1986–2010, dean of sci 1998–2001, prof emeritus 2010–; visiting fell: Los Alamos Nat Lab New Mexico 1983–84, CCC Cambridge 2001; FRSE 1987; *Books* Solitons and Nonlinear Wave Equations (jtly, 1982); also author of over 130 papers in learned jls; *Style*— Prof Chris Eilbeck, FRSE; ✉ Department of Mathematics, Heriot-Watt University, Edinburgh EH14 4AS (☎ 0131 451 3220, fax 0131 451 3249, e-mail j.c.eilbeck@hw.ac.uk)

EISENBERG, Neville; s of Dr Benjamin Eisenberg (d 2006), of Pretoria, South Africa, and Masha, *née* Weinberg; *b* 12 April 1962, Cape Town, South Africa; *Educ* Pretoria Boys' HS, Univ of the Witwatersrand (BCom, LLB), LSE (LLM); *Career* admitted slr 1991; Werksmans Attorneys 1985–87; Berwin Leighton Paisner Slrs: slr 1989–95, ptnr 1996–, managing ptnr 1999–2015; memb London Cncl CBI; chm Br Israel Law Assoc, assoc govr Hebrew Univ of Jerusalem; chm South African Union of Jewish Students 1982–84, comptroller World Union of Jewish Students 1986–89; *Recreations* theatre, music, travel; *Clubs* Home House; *Style*— Neville Eisenberg, Esq; ✉ Berwin Leighton Paisner, Adelaide House, London Bridge, London EC4R 9HA (☎ 020 3400 1000, fax 020 3400 1111, e-mail neville.eisenberg@blplaw.com)

EISERMANN, Richard; *b* 2 August 1959, Santiago, Chile; *Educ* Int Sch of The Hague (Dip), Rhode Island Sch of Design (BFA); *Career* designer Chicago and Milan 1983–88, sr designer Sottsass Associati Milan 1988–94, asst prof of industrial design Rhode Island Sch of Design 1994–95, design team leader IDEO Lexington MA 1995–99, design dir Whirlpool Europe 1999–2003, dir design and innovation Design Cncl 2003–06, fndr and strategic dir Prospect 2006–13, fndr Instill 2013–, vice-pres of integrated experience design and devpt Lowe's 2014–; work exhibited: Axis Gallery Tokyo 1991, Municipal Museum Rotterdam 1991, Design Museum London (perm collection) 1992–; *Awards* Design Selection Award Austrian Design Cncl 1994, Good Design Award Industrie Forum Design Hannover 1994, Design Distinction Award ID Magazine Annual Design Review 1994, Bronze and Gold Industrial Design Excellence Awards (IDEA) Industrial Designers Soc of America (IDSA)/Business Week 2001, Nat Design Award Smithsonian Inst 2002, Gold IDEA IDSA/Business Week 2003 and 2004; *Style*— Richard Eisermann, Esq; ✉ Lowe's Corporation, 1000 Lowe's Boulevard, Mooresville, NC 28117 USA (website www.lowes.com)

EKERT, Prof Artur Konrad; *Educ* Jagiellonian Univ Kraków (MSc), Univ of Oxford (Soros scholar, Pirie-Reid scholar, DPhil); *Career* Merton Coll Oxford: jr res fell 1991–94, memb Governing Body 1991–98, jr dean 1992–93, res fell 1994–98, memb JRF Ctee 1995–96, tutor for grad admissions 1997–98, dean of graduates 1997–98; Keble Coll Oxford: fell and tutor in physics 1998–2002, memb Governing Body 1998–2002, head IT Ctee 2000–2002; prof of physics Univ of Oxford 1998–2002; prof of quantum physics Univ of Cambridge 2002–; fell King's Coll Cambridge 2002–; head Quantum Computation & Cryptography Gp (renamed The Oxford Centre for Quantum Computation 1999, acting dir 1999–) 1993–, memb Publicity Ctee Dept of Physics Univ of Oxford 1996; visiting posts: prof Univ of Innsbruck Austria 1993 and 1998, prof Univ of Camerino Italy 1999, prof NTT Atsugi Japan 2000, distinguished prof Nat Univ of Singapore; delivered over 100 invited lectures on quantum information science and public understanding of science incl: Roger Penrose 65th birthday conf, Br Assoc for the Advancement of Science at Festivals of Science 1994, 1996, and 2000, Nobel Symposium on the Foundations of Quantum Mechanics 1997, Dept of Continuing Educn Univ of Oxford 1993, 1995, and 2000; author of several articles on quantum cryptography and science, organized scientific conferences and programme committees, conslt for companies and govt agencies incl US Army and DRA/DERA; memb editorial bd The Proceedings of the Royal Society A, memb editorial bd New Jl of Physics; memb: European Science Fndn Steering Ctee for the Quantum Info Theory Prog, EPSRC Physics Coll, EPSRC fellowship panels, Euro Cmmn Pathfinder Ctee; *Style*— Prof Artur Ekert

EL BANNA, Dr Hany Abdel Gawad; OBE (2004); s of Abdel Gawad El Banna, of Mansoura, Egypt, and Nafisa Ahmed Al Jrisis, of Cairo, Egypt; *b* 9 December 1950, Egypt; *Educ* Al Azhar Univ Cairo (MbBCh), Medical Sch Univ of Birmingham (MD); *Partner* Youseria Labib; 3 da (Asmaa b 14 Aug 1984, Fatima Al Zahra b 10 Oct 1985, Maryam b 21 July 1989), 2 s (Al Hassan b 21 Nov 1986, Omar b 15 March 1994); *Career* doctor NHS 1977–94: radiotherapy Royal Berks Hosp, radiotherapy Belvedere Hosp, ENT Hosp Glasgow, gen surgery Stophill Gen Hosp, gen pathology Dudley Road Hosp, foetal pathology Maternity Hosp Queen Elizabeth Medical Centre Birmingham; co-fndr and pres Islamic Relief Worldwide 1984–, tstee's fndr Muslim Aid 1985–99; memb: Advsy Bd Three Faiths Forum, World Economic Forum West-Islamic World Dialogue Cncl of 100 Leaders, Advsy to the Int Prog Charity Cmmn; MInstD; *Awards* Hamilton Bailey Prize Dudley Road (City) Hosp 1981, Award for Service to Medicine and Humanity Egyptian Medical Syndicate 2004, Muslim News Award for Excellence Ibn Khaldun Award (for execellence in promoting peace and understanding between global cultures and faiths) 2004, Kashmiri and Pakistani Professional Assoc Award 2005, Asian Jewel Awards (for lifetime achievements) 2006, Muslim Power 100 Award (for lifetime achievements) 2007; *Style*— Dr Hany El Banna, OBE; ✉ Islamic Relief, 19 Rea Street South, Birmingham B5 6LB (☎ 0121 622 0628, fax 0121 622 5003)

EL NAHAS, Prof (Abdel) Meguid; s of Hassan Khalil El Nahas (d 1978), of Cairo, Egypt, and Fatma Galal Selim, *née* El Hegazy; *b* 1 December 1949; *Educ* Jesuits' Coll Cairo, Univ of Geneva Med Sch, Univ of London (PhD); *m* 30 April 1983, Penelope Anne, da of Henry Denys Hanan, DSC, of Shrewsbury; 2 da (Gemma b 1983, Holly b 1985); *Career* res Mass Gen Hosp Boston USA 1977–78; res fell in nephrology: Paris 1978–79, Royal Postgrad Med Sch London 1979–82; renal registrar Royal Free Hospital London 1982–84, lectr in nephrology Univ of Wales Coll of Med Cardiff 1984–86, conslt renal physician Sheffield Kidney Inst Northern Gen Hosp Sheffield 1986–, prof of nephrology Sheffield Kidney Inst Univ of Sheffield 1996–; memb: Nat and Int Socs of Nephrology, Assoc of Physicians, Assoc of Clinical Professors of Medicine; FRCP; *Recreations* sports, history, travelling; *Style*— Prof A Meguid El Nahas; ✉ Sheffield Kidney Institute, Northern General Hospital, Herries Road, Sheffield S5 7AU (☎ 0114 271 4018, fax 0114 256 2514, e-mail m.el-nahas@sheffield.ac.uk)

ELAND, Michael John; CB (2006); s of George Eland, and Betty Eland; *b* 26 September 1952; *Educ* Worksop Coll, Trinity Coll Oxford (MA); *m* Luned Rhiannon, *née* Wynn Jones; 1 da (Charlotte Sophie Fairbairn b 1986), 1 s (Thomas George Benjamin b 1988); *Career* called to the Bar Middle Temple 1975; HM Customs and Excise: admin trainee 1975, private sec to Chm 1979–81; Cabinet Office 1982–87, private sec to Lord Pres of the Cncl (Viscount Whitelaw) 1987–88; HM Customs and Excise: asst sec 1988–92, cmmr 1992–97; dep DG (policy) Immigration and Nationality Directorate Home Office 1997–2000; HM Revenue and Customs (formerly Customs and Excise): cmmr 2000–, DG Business Servs and Taxes 2000–03, actg chm 2003–04, DG Law Enforcement and Compliance 2004–; *Style*— Michael Eland, Esq, CB

ELBA, Idris; OBE (2016); *b* 6 September 1972, London; *Career* actor; *Television* incl: Dangerfield 1999, The Wire 2002–04, The No 1 Ladies' Detective Agency 2008, The Office (NBC) 2009, Luther (BBC 1) 2010–15 (Best Actor – Miniseries or Television Film Golden Globe 2012), The Big C 2010, Idris Elba: King of Speed 2013, Idris Elba: No Limits 2015; *Film* incl: Buffalo Soldiers 2001, One Love 2003, 28 Weeks Later 2007, American Gangster 2007, RocknRolla 2008, The Human Contract 2008, The Unborn 2009, Obsessed 2009, Takers 2010, Thor 2011, Ghost Rider – Spirit of Vengeance 2011, Prometheus 2012, Pacific Rim 2013, No Good Deed 2013, Thor 2 2013, Long Walk to Freedom 2014, Second Coming 2015, Avengers: Age of Ultron 2015, Beasts of No Nation 2015 (Outstanding Performance by a Male Actor in a Supporting Role Screen Actors Guild Award 2015), The Jungle Book 2016, Bastille Day 2016; *Style*— Mr Idris Elba, OBE; ✉ c/o The Artists Partnership, 101 Finsbury Pavement, London EC2A 1RS

ELCOMB, Brig Christopher Mark George; OBE (1993); s of Lt-Col Michael Elcomb, of Codford St Mary, Wilts, and late Elizabeth May, *née* Armour; *b* 2 July 1951, Windlesham, Surrey; *Educ* Marlborough, RMA Sandhurst, Univ of Exeter (BA); *m* 26 May 1984, Nicola Gillian Branford, da of Maj Euan Hutchings; *Career* CO 2 Bn Light Infantry 1991–92, Cmdt Jr Div Staff Coll 1994–96, Cmd 24 Airmobile Bde and Colchester Garrison 1997–98, Dep Mil Sec 1999–2002, Asst Div Cmd 3 (UK) Div 2002–03, Cmd 1 Recce Bde/Chief ISTAR 2004–05, Cmd Multinational Task Force NW Bosnia 2005–06; Dep Col (Yorks) Light Infantry 1994–2005; chapter clerk Salisbury Cathedral 2006–11, chm Light Infantry Club 2012–, chm Fovant Badges Soc 2012–; *Style*— Brig C M G Elcomb, OBE; ✉ Pembroke Cottage, Stapleford, Salisbury SP3 4LT (e-mail melcomb@btinternet.com)

ELDER, Prof James Brown; s of David Elder (d 1988), of Linwood, Renfrewshire, and Margaret Helen, *née* Cowan (d 1982); *b* 20 May 1938; *Educ* Shawlands Acad Glasgow, Univ of Glasgow (MB ChB, MD); *m* 12 Dec 1964, Sheena Jean Reid Fyfe, da of Colin McLay, of Paisley (d 1996); 3 da (Jacqueline b 1966, Karen b 1967, Alison b 1969); *Career* sr registrar in gen surgery Glasgow Western Infirmary 1968–71 (registrar 1965–68), reader in surgery Manchester Royal Infirmary Univ of Manchester 1976–83 (sr lectr and conslt surgn 1971–76), prof of surgery Keele Univ Sch of Postgraduate Med 1983–2004 (now emeritus prof), conslt surgn to N Staffs Hosp Centre 1983–2003, hon conslt surgn Univ Hosp of N Staffs 2004–; examiner in surgery Univs of: Manchester 1976–83, Glasgow 1981–83, Sheffield 1986–89, Nottingham 1985–89, Hong Kong 1994–; examiner: RCPS Glasgow, Univ of Manchester 1992–96, Univ of Birmingham 1994–96 and 1999–2002, UCH London 1997–99, Univ of Malta 2003, Univ of Warwick 2006–08; pt/t lectr in human anatomy Keele Undergrad Med Sch 2004–; chm W Midlands Regnl Research Awards Ctee 1994–2000; tstee N Staffs Medical Inst 2010–; past pres: W Midlands Surgical Soc, Midlands Gastroenterology Soc; author of numerous papers and contrib and/or ed of 11 books; FRCSEd 1966, FRCS 1966, FRCS Glasgow 1981; *Recreations* hill walking, classical music, reading, photography, home cooking, French wine; *Clubs* British Pottery Manufacturers' Fedn (Stoke-on-Trent); *Style*— Prof James B Elder; ✉ Keele University, School of Medicine, Thornburrow Drive, Hartshill, Stoke-on-Trent ST4 7QB (☎ 01782 554047, fax 01782 747319, e-mail j.b.elder@ntlworld.com)

ELDER, Sir Mark Philip; kt (2008), CBE (1989); *b* 2 June 1947; *Educ* Bryanston, CCC Cambridge (music scholar, choral scholar, BA, MA); *m* 30 May 1980, Amanda Jane, *née* Stein; 1 da (Katherine Olivia b 13 April 1986); *Career* music dir: English National Opera 1979–93, Rochester Philharmonic Orchestra NY 1989–94; princ guest conductor City of Birmingham Orchestra 1992–95, music dir Hallé Orch 2000–, artistic dir Opera Rara 2010–; reg work with orchs worldwide incl Royal Concertgebouw Amsterdam, Chicago Symphony, Boston Symphony and London Philharmonic; freq appearances at int opera houses incl: ROH, Met Opera NY, Opéra National de Paris, Lyric Opera Chicago, Glyndebourne Festival; annual appearances at Proms, first Br conductor to conduct new prodn at Bayreuth Festival, involved in several TV projects; *Recordings* with orchs incl: Hallé, LPO, CBSO, BBC Symphony Orch, Orch of Age of Enlightenment, ROH, ENO; *Style*— Sir Mark Elder, CBE; ✉ c/o Ingpen & Williams Ltd, 7 St George's Court, 131 Putney Bridge Road, London SW15 2PA (☎ 020 8874 3222, fax 020 8877 3113)

ELDER, Prof Murdoch George; s of Archibald James Elder (d 1992), and Lotta Annie Catherine, *née* Craig (d 1998); *b* 4 January 1938; *Educ* Edinburgh Acad, Univ of Edinburgh (MB ChB, MD), Univ of London (DSc); *m* 3 Oct 1964, Margaret Adelaide, da of Dr James McVicker (d 1985), of Portrush, Co Antrim; 2 s (James b 1968, Andrew b 1970); *Career* Nat Serv Captain RAMC (TA&VR) 1964; lectr Univ of Malta 1969–71, sr lectr and reader Univ of London (Charing Cross Hosp Med Sch) 1971–78, res fell WHO 1976, travelling fell RCOG 1977, prof and head Dept of Obstetrics & Gynaecology Royal Postgraduate Med Sch Univ of London 1978–96, prof of obstetrics & gynaecology and chm Academic Div of Paediatrics and Obstetrics & Gynaecology Imperial Coll Sch of Med London (following merger) 1996–98, fell Imperial Coll Sch of Med London 2001–; dir: Obstetrics and Gynaecology Service Hammersmith, Queen Charlotte's Special Health Authy, WHO Clinical Res Centre 1980–92; visiting prof Univs of: Calif (LA), Singapore, Natal; examiner Univs of: London, Oxford, Cambridge, Edinburgh, Glasgow, Leeds, Liverpool, Birmingham, Bristol, Dundee, Malta, Malaya, Malaysia, Cape Town, Singapore, Rotterdam, Helsinki; memb Hammersmith and Queen Charlotte's Special HA 1982–90, chm Hosp Med Ctee 1980–85, sec Assoc of Profs (O and G) 1984–86; memb: WHO Steering Ctee on Contraception 1980–86, WHO Research and Ethics Group 1994–2004; author of over 200 scientific pubns; Silver Medal Hellenic Obstetrical Soc 1983, Bronze Medal Helsinki Univ 1995; FRCSEd 1968, FRCOG 1979; *Books* Current Fertility Control (1978), Pre Term Labour (1982), Reproduction, Obstetrics and Gynaecology (1988), Pre Term Labour (1997), Obstetrics and Gynaecology (2001); *Recreations* golf, travel; *Clubs* 1942; *Style*— Prof Murdoch Elder; ✉ Burnholm, Broughton, By Biggar, Lanarkshire ML12 6HQ (☎ 01899 830359, e-mail meldereastercalzeat@btinternet.com)

ELDERFIELD, Prof Henry; *b* 25 April 1943; *Educ* Univ of Liverpool (BSc, PhD), Imperial Coll London (DIC), Univ of Cambridge (MA, ScD); *Career* res fell Dept of Geology Imperial Coll London 1968–69, lectr Dept of Earth Sciences Univ of Leeds 1969–82; Univ of

Cambridge: asst dir in res Dept of Earth Sciences 1982–89, fell and dir of studies St Catharine's Coll 1984–, reader in geochemistry 1989–99, prof of ocean geochemistry and palaeochemistry 1999–, exec sec Ctee for Interdisciplinary Environmental Studies (CIES) 2001–; visiting prof Univ of RI 1977–78, visiting scholar Woods Hole Oceanographic Instn 1982, Fulbright scholar 1988, visiting prof MIT 1988–89, Lady Davis visiting prof Hebrew Univ Jerusalem 1992; examiner for various univs incl: Liverpool, Reading, Amsterdam, Caen, Edinburgh, London, Newcastle upon Tyne, Oxford, Paris, Sheffield, Southampton, Utrecht, Toulouse, Lyon, Bergen; chm: Steering Ctee Biogeochemical Ocean Flux Study (BOFS), Int Steering Ctee Jt Global Ocean Flux Study (JGOFS) 1987–90, Ocean Drilling Project Sedimentary and Geochemical Processes Panel (SGPP) 1989–93, Scientific Ctee Prog Flux Oceaniques (PFO) 1989–94, French component JGOFS, Steering Ctee Br Mid Ocean Ridge Initiative (BRIDGE) NERC Community Res Assoc 1992–95, Scientific Gp on Decommissioning of Offshore Structures (NERC/DTI) 1996, Swedish Res Cncl Gp on Exogenic Geochemistry 1998, Internal Lithosphere Prog Project: Hydrogeology of the Oceanic Lithosphere 1998–, CEREGE (CNRS/ Univ of Aix-Marsailles) review of environmental research 1999; advsr on chairs and other academic posts and research profiles for various academic instns incl Harvard Univ, Univs of Wales, Southampton, Stockholm and Edinburgh and Woods Hole Oceanographic Instn; ed Geochemistry, Geophysics, Geosystems (G3) 1999–2004; ed: Earth and Planetary Science Letters 2005–08, Geochimica et Cosmochimica Aca, Geology; author of 250 articles and papers in learned jls; NOAA Outstanding Scientific Paper for 1996, Newth lectr Scottish Inst for Marine Sciences 1997, Plymouth Marine Medal Marine Biological Assoc of the UK, Plymouth Marine Lab and Univ of Plymouth 1998, Prestwich Medal Geological Soc of London 2000, Patterson Medal Geochemical Soc 2002, Lyell Medal Geological Soc of London 2003, Urey Medal European Assoc of Geochemistry 2007, Goldschmidt Medal of Geochemical Soc 2013; vice-pres Euro Fedn for Marine Sciences 1998–99, memb Challenger Soc for Marine Science (pres 1998–2000); fell: Geochemical Soc 2000, Euro Assoc for Geochemistry 2000, American Geophysical Union; hon fell Euro Union of Geosciences 2001; FRS 2001; *Style*— Prof Henry Elderfield; ✉ Department of Earth Sciences, Cambridge University, Downing Street, Cambridge CB2 3EQ (☎ 01233 333400, fax 01233 333450, e-mail he101@cam.ac.uk); St Catharine's College, Trumpington Street, Cambridge CB2 1RL

ELDON, David Gordon; CBE (2005), JP; s of Leslie Gordon Eldon (d 1945), and Mary Forbes, *née* Smith (d 2015); *b* 14 October 1945, Inverness, Scotland; *Educ* Duke of York's Royal Military Sch Dover; *m* 14 May 1975, Maria Margarita, *née* Gaus; 2 s (Andrew Gordon b 1977, Paul Román b 1979), 1 da (Cristina Margarita b 1982); *Career* HSBC Gp 1968–2005, retired chm Asia Pacific and exec dir HSBC Holdings plc; HSBC: chm Bank Middle East 2011–, chm Global Commercial Bank Risk Ctee 2012–, chm Bank Oman SAOG 2013–; sr advsr PricewaterhouseCoopers 2005–14; chm Dubai Int Financial Centre Authy 2006–11, vice-chm Noble Gp 2010–; dir: Dubai Int Financial Centre Higher Bd 2011–, K C Maritime Ltd; chm Octopus Hldgs Ltd 2016–, chm Octopus Cards Ltd 2016–; advsr: Hong Kong Acad of Performing Arts, Southern Capital Gp, New Lily Int Ltd 2013–; vice-patron The Community Chest; Hong Kong Businessman of the Year 2003, Asian Banker Lifetime Achievement Award 2005; Hon DBA Hong Kong City Univ 2003, Hon Dr Hong Kong Acad for Performing Arts 2011; FCIB 1986 (ACIB 1972), fell Inst of Bankers Hong Kong (FIBHK) 1999; Gold Bauhinia Star (GBS, Hong Kong) 2004; *Recreations* music, sports, reading, travel; *Clubs* Hong Kong, China, Hong Kong Jockey (hon steward); *Style*— David Eldon, GBS, CBE, JP; ✉ 16th Floor, The Hong Kong Club Building, 3A Chater Road, Central, Hong kong (☎ 00 852 3974 8715, e-mail davideldon@eldon-online.com)

ELDON, Sir Stewart Graham; KCMG (2009, CMG 1998), OBE (1991); s of John Hodgson Eldon (d 2012), and Rose Helen, *née* Stinton (d 2002); *b* 18 September 1953, Accra, Ghana; *Educ* Pocklington Sch, Christ's Coll Cambridge (MA, MSc); *m* Jan 1978, Christine Mary, *née* Mason; 1 da (Laura Madeleine b 24 Jan 1982), 1 s (Thomas Henry b 16 Aug 1985); *Career* diplomat; first sec Repub of Ireland Dept FCO 1982–83, private sec to min of state FCO 1983–86, first sec UK Mission to the UN NY 1986–90, asst head Middle Eastern Dept FCO 1990–91 (dep crisis mangr during Gulf War), cnsllr European Secretariat Cabinet Office 1991–93, cnsllr (political) UK Delgn to NATO and WEU Brussels 1994–97, dir (confs) FCO 1997–98, UK dep perm rep to UN NY (with personal rank of ambass) 1998–2002, ambass to Ireland 2003–06, UK perm rep to NATO (with personal rank of ambass) 2006–10, sr advsr on defence and security Transparency Int 2010–; NATO subject matter expert on building integrity 2010–; sr civil advsr UK Higher Command and Staff Course 2012–; ind memb Parole Bd for England and Wales 2010–; fell Center for Int Affrs Harvard Univ 1993–94, visiting fell Yale Univ 2002; MIEE 2002; *Books* From Quill Pen to Satellite: Foreign Ministries in the Information Age (1994); *Recreations* travel, good food, reading science fiction, breaking computers; *Clubs* Athenaeum; *Style*— Sir Stewart Eldon, KCMG, OBE; ✉ website www.stewarteldon.com

ELDRIDGE, David Albert; s of John Anthony Eldridge, of Hackney, London, and Linda Irene, *née* Benton; *b* 20 September 1973; *Educ* Brentwood Sch, Univ of Exeter (BA); *Career* playwright; playwright in residence: RNT 1997, Soho Theatre at TBWA-GGT (advtg agency) 2002; extensive work as dramaturg play-reader in London and Essex; stage plays: Serving It Up 1996, A Week With Tony 1996, Summer Begins 1997, Falling 1999, Under The Blue Sky 2000 (Time Out Live Award for Best New Play in the West End 2001), MAD 2004, Incomplete and Random Acts of Kindness 2005, Market Boy 2006; other work: Killers (BBC) 2000, Michael and Me (BBC Radio 4) 2001, The Nugget Run (short film) 2002; Hon DLitt Univ of Exeter 2007; *Publications* Serving It Up & A Week With Tony (1997), Under the Blue Sky (2001); *Recreations* friends, family, books, football; *Style*— David Eldridge, Esq; ✉ c/o ICM, Oxford House, 76 Oxford Street, London W1N 0AX (☎ 020 7636 6565, fax 020 7323 0101)

ELDRIDGE, David John; s of Lt-Col Frederick George Eldridge (ret), of Haslemere, Surrey, and Irene Mary, *née* Buston; *b* 12 January 1935; *Educ* KCS Wimbledon; *m* 1, 14 May 1960, Diana Mary (d 1981), da of Eric Copp, of Hartlepool, Cleveland; 1 s (Charles b 1962), 2 da (Catherine b 1964, Victoria b 1966); *m* 2, 15 Dec 1984, Anna Maria, da of Jerzy Kowalski, of Warsaw, Poland; *Career* admitted slr 1956; ptnr: Stanley Attenborough & Co 1958–74, Martin & Nicholson 1975–77, Amhurst Brown Colombotti 1977–2003, Howard Kennedy 2003–13; tstee (since inception 1974) Museum of Islamic Art Jerusalem; donation govr Christ's Hosp Horsham; Freeman City of London, Liveryman and memb Ct of Assts Worshipful Co of Fletchers (Master 1984–86), memb Ct of Assts Guild of Freemen (Master 1983–84); memb Law Soc 1957; *Recreations* fine arts, sport; *Clubs* City Livery; *Style*— David Eldridge, Esq; ✉ 50A Howards Lane, London SW15 5QF (☎ 020 8780 9084)

ELDRIDGE, Mark; s of Bernard Derrick Eldridge, of Toronto, Canada (foster f George Hoare (d 2014)), and Anne May, *née* Murphy (foster mother Eileen Violet, *née* Luff, d 2008); *b* 9 August 1954; *Educ* Churcher's Coll Petersfield, Lancaster Univ (BA), City Univ (Dip Law), Inns of Court Sch of Law; *m* 3 July 1982, Alexandra Catherine, da of John Watling Illingworth (d 2010); 3 da (Charlotte b 27 March 1983, Elizabeth b 27 Sept 1984, Catherine b 31 Jan 1986), 1 s (Joseph b 10 July 1987); *Career* practising barr; called to the Bar Gray's Inn 1982, memb Inner Temple 1985, elected memb Gen Cncl of the Bar 1986–91, chm Young Bar of England and Wales 1989; memb Western Circuit; memb Criminal Bar Assoc; memb Bar European Gp; govr Thornhill Primary Sch 1986–88, chm Bd of Govrs Clerkenwell Parochial Sch 1993–96; Islington South and Finsbury Cons Assoc: vice-chm 1986–89, chm 1989–92, vice-pres 1992–2006; vice-pres Islington Cons Assoc 2006–07; *Recreations* swimming, golf, tennis; *Clubs* Carlton; *Style*— Mark Eldridge, Esq; ✉ 114 Liverpool Road, Islington, London N1 0RE (☎ 020 7226 9863, fax 020 7704 1111, e-mail mark.eldridge3@btinternet.com); 5 Pump Court, Temple, London EC4Y 7AD (☎ 020 7353 2532, fax 020 7253 5321, e-mail clerks@5pumpcourt.com or markeldridge@5pumpcourt.com)

ELGAR, Edward James; s of Frank Elgar, and Mary, *née* Dee; *Educ* Tonbridge, Univ of Bristol (BA); *Career* publisher; coll sales rep George Allen & Unwin 1972–74; Martin Robertson Ltd: field ed 1974–76, editorial dir 1977–79; fndr memb and md Wheatsheaf Books 1979–86, fndr memb and chm Edward Elgar Publishing Ltd 1986–; *Recreations* reading, rugby, cricket, wine, renovating house in France; *Style*— Edward Elgar, Esq; ✉ Edward Elgar Publishing Ltd, The Lypiatts, 15 Lansdown Road, Cheltenham, Gloucestershire GL50 2JA (☎ 01242 226939, fax 01242 262111)

ELIAS, Brian David; s of Albert Murad Elias, and Julie Sophie, *née* Ephraim; *b* 30 August 1948; *Educ* St Christopher Sch, RCM, and with Elisabeth Lutyens; *Career* composer: La Chevelure 1969, Peroration 1973, Somnia 1979, L'Eylah (cmmnd for BBC Promenade Concerts) 1984, Geranos (cmmnd by Fires of London) 1985, Variations (for solo piano) 1987, Five Songs to Poems by Irina Ratushinskaya (cmmnd by the BBC) 1989, The Judas Tree (cmmnd by Royal Opera House) 1992, Laments (cmmnd by the BBC) 1998, The House that Jack Built (cmmnd by the BBC) 2002, A Talisman (cmmnd by Cheltenham Festival) 2004, Doubles (cmmnd by the BBC) 2009, Electra Mourns (premiered BBC Promenade Concerts) 2012, String Quartet (cmmnd by Jerusalem String Quartet) 2013; *Recreations* reading, gardening, theatre, art; *Style*— Brian Elias, Esq; ✉ Chester Music, 14–15 Berners Street, London W1T 3LJ (☎ 020 7612 7400, fax 020 7612 7545)

ELIAS, Gerard; QC (1984); bro of Patrick Elias (The Hon Mr Justice Elias), *qv*; *b* 19 November 1944; *Educ* Cardiff HS, Univ of Exeter (LLB, capt cricket XI); *m* 14 March 1970, Elisabeth, da of Sir George Henry Kenyon, JP, DL, of Hyde, Cheshire; 3 s (David b 7 May 1971, Robert b 24 Feb 1973, James b 1 May 1976); *Career* called to the Bar Inner Temple 1968 (bencher 1993); recorder of the Crown Court 1984–, dep judge of the High Court 1996–; asst boundary cmmr for Wales 1984–, ldr Wales & Chester Circuit 1993–95 (treas 1990–92); leading counsel to N Wales Tbnl of Inquiry into Child Abuse 1996–98; memb Bar Cncl 1986–89, dir Bar Mutual Insurance Fund 1987–97, govr and memb Cncl Malvern Coll 1988–96; Glamorgan CCC: memb Exec Ctee 1985–93, dep chm 1993–98, chm 1998–2003; ECB: memb Registration Ctee 1993–96, chm Disciplinary Standing-Ctee 1996–; chllr Diocese of Swansea & Brecon 1999–; *Recreations* sailing, cricket, music; *Clubs* Cardiff & County; *Style*— Gerard Elias, Esq, QC

ELIAS, Rt Hon Lord Justice; Sir Patrick Elias; kt (1999); s of Leonard Elias, and Patricia Mary, *née* O'Neill; bro of Gerard Elias, QC, *qv*; *b* 28 March 1947, Cardiff; *Educ* Cardiff HS, Univ of Exeter (LLB), King's Coll Cambridge (MA, PhD); *m* 15 Aug 1970, Wendy, *née* Kinnersley-Haddock; 3 s (James, Thomas, Edward), 1 da (Emily); *Career* called to the Bar Inner Temple 1973 (bencher 1995); fell Pembroke Coll Cambridge 1973–84 (hon fell 2010), lectr Univ of Cambridge 1975–84, QC 1990, judge of the High Court of Justice (Queen's Bench Div) 1999–2009, Lord Justice of Appeal 2009–; pres Employment Appeal Tbnl 2006–08; Hon LLD: Univ of Exeter 2001, City Univ London 2003; *Recreations* reading, music, cricket, rugby; *Style*— The Rt Hon Lord Justice Elias; ✉ Royal Courts of Justice (☎ 020 7947 6774)

ELIAS, Robin Pieter; s of Carel George Elias (d 2001), and Nancy Elizabeth, *née* Harvey (d 2010); *b* 11 December 1953; *Educ* Therfield Comp Leatherhead; *m* 24 June 1978, Sally Anne, da of Malcolm Alfred Henry Holder; 1 s (Samuel Jeremy b 19 March 1987), 1 da (Amy Grace b 10 Aug 1990); *Career* reporter Surrey Advertiser Guildford 1971–77, sub ed Press Association 1977–79, sub ed London Evening News 1979–80; ITN: joined as prodr 1980, prog ed Lunchtime News 1990–92, prog ed News at Ten 1992–99, prog ed Evening News 1999–2000, head of Output 1996–99, dep ed ITV News 1999–2002, managing ed ITV News 2002–; *Style*— Robin Elias, Esq; ✉ ITN Ltd, 200 Gray's Inn Road, London WC1X 8XZ (☎ 020 7833 3000, e-mail robin.elias@itn.co.uk)

ELIASCH, Johan Carl; *b* 15 February 1962, Sweden; *Educ* Royal Inst of Technol Sweden (MSc), Stockholm Univ (BA); *m*; 2 c; *Career* chm and ceo Head 1995–, chm Investment Gp Equity Ptnrs Gp, chm London Films; sr dep party treas Cons Party until 2007, special rep of the PM on deforestation and clean energy 2007–; memb Pres of the Repub of Austria's Trade Delegation; chm Young Cons Party Sweden 1979–82; memb: Bd Special Olympics Ctee, Int Advisory Bd Brasilinvest, Bd Sports on Addiction, Resources for Autism (founding memb), Advsy Bd Centre for Social Justice, World Econ Forum (also govr Retail and Consumer Goods Industry); chm The Duke of York NSPCC Challenge; patron Univ of Stockholm; exec prodr: Best of Friends 1991, Lady Chatterley 1993, Resort to Murder 1995, The Scarlet Pimpernel 1998 and 2000; *Recreations* golf (scratch handicap, played in British Open), curling (Swedish regnl champion), skiing (forerunner downhill, super giant slalom and giant slalom, skied at World Cup and World Championships); *Style*— Mr Johan Eliasch

ELIS-THOMAS, Baron (Life Peer UK 1992), of Nant Conwy in the County of Conwy; Dafydd Elis-Thomas; PC (2004), AM; *b* 18 October 1946; *Educ* Ysgol Dyffryn Conwy, UCNW (PhD); *m* 1 (m dis), 1970, Elen M Williams; 3 s; *m* 2, 29 Dec 1993, Mair Parry Jones; *Career* tutor in Welsh studies Coleg Harlech 1971, subsequently taught at UCNW Bangor, Aberystwyth, Cardiff and Open Univ, former visiting fell Univ of St Andrews; MP (Plaid Cymru): Merionnydd Feb 1974–83, Meirionnydd Nant Conwy 1983–92 (Parly candidate (Plaid Cymru) Conway 1970); Plaid Cymru spokesman on agric and rural devpt 1974 and on educn and social policy 1975, memb Parly Select Ctee on Educn, Science and Arts 1979–83, served as memb of various other select ctees and standing ctees of House of Commons; memb Nat Assembly for Wales (Plaid Cymru): Merionnydd Nant Conwy 1999–2007, Dwyfor Meironnydd 2007–; presiding offr Nat Assembly for Wales 1999–2011, chair Assembly Cmmn, chair Environment and Sustainability Ctee Nat Assembly for Wales 2011–14, memb Constitutional and Legislative Affrs Ctee and Enterprise and Business Ctee 2011–; chair Future Landscapes Working Gp Welsh Govt; pres Plaid Cymru 1984–91 (vice-pres 1979–81); writer, journalist and columnist, former broadcaster and prog presenter BBC Wales, HTV, S4C and Radio Wales; first chm Welsh Language Bd 1993–99; former memb: Welsh Arts Cncl, Wales Film Cncl, Welsh Film Bd, Gen Consultative Cncl BBC, BFI; Univ of Wales Bangor: pres 2001–12, chllr 2012–; hon sec: All-Pty Mental Health Gp, Mind, Inst for Workers Control and Shelter; *Recreations* environmental issues, hill walking, theatre, film, arts, music, active member Church in Wales; *Style*— The Rt Hon Lord Elis-Thomas, AM; ✉ Constituency Office, 7 Bank Place, Porthmadog, Gwynedd LL49 9AA

ELKELES, Prof Robert Samuel; s of Dr Arthur Elkeles (d 1978), of London, and Margaret, *née* Stein (d 1970); *b* 1 June 1942; *Educ* Highgate Sch, Middx Hosp Med Sch London (Ken Clifford scholar, Boldero scholar in med, MB BS, LRCP, MD); *m* Jan 1971, Arran, *née* Miller; 1 s (Daniel Alexander b 4 May 1973), 1 da (Jennifer Margaret b 17 March 1976); *Career* house surgn in gen surgery Chase Farm Hosp Enfield 1965; house physician: Middx then Brompton Hosp 1966, Hammersmith Hosp 1967; asst to Sir George Pickering Radcliffe Infirmary Oxford 1967–68, registrar in endocrinology Hammersmith Hosp 1968–70, lectr in med Univ Hosp of Wales 1973–74 (registrar 1970–72), conslt physician Northwick Park Hosp and Clinical Research Centre Harrow 1974–78, conslt physician and sr lectr in med St Mary's Hosp Med Sch London 1978–2014, prof of diabetic medicine Imperial Coll London 2006–14, clinical lead NW London Diabetes Local Research Network 2006–13; chm: Div of Med Paddington and N Kensington Health Dist

E

1982–85, NW Thames Regnl Physicians in Diabetes and Endocrinology 1990–96, N Thames Specialist Trg Ctee in Diabetes and Endocrinology 1996–2000, St Mary's Hospital Tst Med Advsy Ctee 2000–06; Br Diabetic Assoc: past memb Professional Advsy Ctee, chm Nutrition Sub-Ctee, memb Med and Scientific Assoc Ctee 1992–95, governing bd memb secdy care Enfield Clinical Commissioning Gp 2012–; tstee Peace Hospice Care Watford 2009–15 (dep chm 2012–15), tstee St Luke's Hospice Harrow 2015–; memb: Ctee Br Hyperlipidaemia Assoc 1993–96, Cncl RCP London 1998–2001 and 2003–06; FRCP; *Books* Biochemical Aspects of Human Disease (with A S Tavill, 1983); *Recreations* music, cycling, walking; *Style*— Prof Robert Elkeles; ✉ 11 Askew Road, Moor Park, Northwood, Middlesex HA6 2JE (☎ 01923 827341, e-mail robert.elkeles@kelear.co.uk)

ELL, Prof Peter Josef; s of Josef Ell (d 1957), of Lisbon, Portugal, and Maria Karola Ell (d 1990); *b* 7 May 1944; *Educ* Univ of Lisbon (MD), Univ of London (MSc), Univ of Bern (PD); *m* 1980, Yvonne, da of Jan Brink; 2 s (Georg Mischa b 2 March 1981, Patrick Sascha b 8 Dec 1983); *Career* conslt physician Landes Unfallkrankenhaus Feldkirch 1974–76, conslt physician i/c nuclear med Middx Hosp 1976–, dir Inst of Nuclear Med UC Med Sch London 1986–, prof of nuclear med and established chair Univ of London 1987–; dep dir Inst of Nuclear Med 1984–, hon conslt physician Middx Hosp 1976–; tstee UCLH Charity; visiting prof: Univ of Saskatchewan 1982, Kuwait 1983, Islamabad 1983, Cairo 1984, Univ of Lisbon 1986; UK del: European Nuclear Med Soc 1981–82, World Fedn of Nuclear Med and Biology 1984, 1988 and 1990; annual prize Soc of Med Sciences Portugal 1976, annual prize Soc of Medical Sciences Vorarlberg Austria 1979, first and third prize for best scientific oral presentation Br Nuclear Med Soc 1990, Gold Medal Univ of Ghent 2004, Georg Hevesy Pioneer Award Soc of Nuclear Med USA 2008; Freeman City of Montpellier 1991; Dr (hc) Univ of Barcelona 2004; fndr memb European Assoc of Nuclear Med 1985 (sec 1987–91 and 1991–93, pres 1994–); corresponding memb: Finnish Soc of Nuclear Med 1984, Swiss Soc of Nuclear Med 1993, German Soc Nuclear Med 2000; memb: American Soc of Nuclear Med 1974, Br Nuclear Med Soc 1974 (memb Cncl 1991–93, sec 1992–94), Br Inst of Radiology 1974 (memb Cncl 1984–87), NY Acad of Sciences 1976, Hosp Physicists Assoc 1977, RSM 1978, Br Cardiac Soc 1983, Assoc of Physicians of Great Br and Ireland 1984; FRCR 1984, FRCP 1990 (MRCP 1984), FMedSci 2004; *Recreations* the study of languages, the arts in general, photography and cinema; *Style*— Prof Peter Ell; ✉ Institute of Nuclear Medicine, University College London Hospitals NHS Trust, 235 Euston Road, London NW1 2BU (☎ 020 7631 1066, fax 020 7436 0603, e-mail peter.ell@uclh.nhs.uk)

ELLAM, Michael James; CB (2014); s of Brian Alfred Ellam, and Kathleen Mary Ellam; *b* London; *Educ* Forest Hill Sch for Boys, Peterhouse Cambridge (MA), LSE (MSc); *m* 1995, Karina Saroukhanian; 1 da (Maria Rose b 2004), 1 s (Edward Alexander b 2007); *Career* various positions HM Treasy 1993–2009, dir of communications PM's Office until 2009, md int and Europe HM Treasy 2009–13, md public sector banking HSBC 2013–; *Style*— Michael Ellam, Esq, CB; ✉ HSBC, 8 Canada Square, London E14 5HQ

ELLARD, John Francis; s of (John) Edward Ellard (d 1999), and Marie, *née* Topping; *b* 5 April 1953; *Educ* John Fisher Sch Purley Surrey, King's Sch Chester, Trinity Hall Cambridge (MA); *m* 4 April 1987, Nicola Marigo, da of John David Pugh (d 1973); 2 s ((John) David b 12 Sept 1988, Robert Edward b 8 May 1990), 2 da (Caroline Francesca b 13 June 1992, (Sarah) Jane b 26 Dec 1993); *Career* admitted slr 1977; Linklaters & Paines: articled clerk 1975–77, asst slr 1977–83, ptnr 1983–2004, resident ptnr NY office 1986–89; of counsel Shearman & Sterling LLP 2004–10, Nat Audit Office: dir capital markets and banking 2010–13, sr corp fin advsr 2013–; tstee Retrospect Ensemble (formerly The King's Consort) 1998–2009; memb Trinity Hall Devpt Bd 1998–2009, memb St Luke's and Christ Church Chelsea PCC 2006–, memb Law Soc; *Recreations* music, reading, mountain walking, photography; *Clubs* Oxford and Cambridge; *Style*— John Ellard, Esq; ✉ 38 Shawfield Street, London SW3 4BD; National Audit Office, 157–197 Buckingham Palace Road, London SW1W 9SP (☎ 020 7798 7000, e-mail john.ellard@nao.gsi.gov.uk)

ELLEN, Eric Frank; QPM (1980); s of Robert Frank Ellen (d 1969), and Jane Lydia Ellen (d 1982); *b* 30 August 1930; *Educ* Univ of London (LLB); *m* 1, 1949 (m dis 2010), Gwendoline Dorothy, da of John Thomas Perkins (d 1937); 1 s (Stephen), 1 da (Susan); *m* 2, 24 Dec 2010, S Lin Kuo-Ellen; 1 da (Elizabeth Jane b 11 Nov 1982); *Career* Nat Serv; joined Port of London Police 1950, Chief Constable 1975, ret 1980; first dir ICC: Int Maritime Bureau 1981–99, Counterfeiting Intelligence Bureau 1985–99, Commercial Crime Bureau 1992–99; chief exec ICC Commercial Crime Services (incorporating Int Maritime Bureau, Counterfeiting Intelligence Bureau and Commercial Crime Bureau) 1990–99; conslt Commercial Crime Unit, special advsr on port security matters and maritime crime Int Assoc of Ports and Harbours, pres Int Assoc of Airport and Seaport Police 1977–79, chm Euro Assoc of Airport and Seaport Police 1975–78 (now life memb, exec sec 1980–88); chm: PEBs 1985, Electronic Intelligence Ltd 1985–86, Task Force on Commercial Crime 1996, ICC Commercial Crime Services; memb Bd ICC Commercial Crime Service 1999–2000, conslt on fraud to ICC 1999–2000; chm First Approach Ltd 2003–; memb: Hon Soc of the Middle Temple, Br Acad of Forensic Sciences, Ctee of Cons Lawyers Examining Maritime Fraud, Inst of Shipbrokers Ctee on Maritime Fraud; presented or chaired seminars on int commercial fraud and product counterfeiting in over 50 countries, advised Barbados Govt on formation of a new police force for the Barbados Port Authy 1983, reviewed security at ports of Jeddah and Dammam in Saudi Arabia, chm Cambridge Symposia on Commercial Crime 1985–, memb Anti-Corruption Working Gp Soc for Advanced Legal Studies 2000; frequent TV and radio appearances on the subject of marine fraud, terrorism, piracy and product counterfeiting; Freeman City of London; Police Long Serv and Good Conduct medal 1 class 1973, Repub of China Police medal 1 class 1979; CIMgt; *Publications* International Maritime Fraud (co-author), Air and Seaport Security International Reference Book (conslt ed, 1987–89), Violence at Sea (ed, 1987), Piracy at Sea (ed, 1989), Ports at Risk (ed, 1994), Shipping at Risk (ed 1997), A Guide to the Prevention of Money Laundering (1998), A Banker's Guide for the Prevention of Fraud and Money Laundering in Documentary Credits (co-ed, 1999), published many articles on varied subjects including specialist policemen, marine sabotage, piracy and terrorism, product counterfeiting and fraud; *Recreations* golf; *Style*— Eric Ellen, Esq, QPM; ✉ First Approach Ltd, 38 Tyle Green, Hornchurch, Essex RM11 2TB (☎ 01708 442538, e-mail ericellen@btinternet.com)

ELLEN, Emeritus Prof Roy Frank; s of Gerald Frank Ellen, of Mill Hill, London, and Nancy Eileen, *née* Childs; *b* 30 January 1947, London; *Educ* LSE (BSc, PhD), Univ of Leiden; *m* 18 Feb 1978, Nicola Jane, da of F Stanley Goward; 2 da (Philippa Louise b 23 Aug 1986, Olivia Grace b 6 Dec 1990); *Career* temp lectr LSE 1972–73; Univ of Kent (formerly Univ of Kent at Canterbury): lectr in social anthropology 1973–80, sr lectr in social anthropology 1980–86, reader in social anthropology 1986–88, prof of anthropology and human ecology 1988–, head Dept of Anthropology 1996–99, dir Centre for Biocultural Diversity 2007–12, emeritus prof of anthropology and human ecology 2012–; visiting fell: Research Sch of Pacific Studies ANU 1981, Netherlands Inst for Advanced Study Wassenaar 1984; visiting prof Indonesian Environmental History Prog Univ of Leiden 1994; referee: ESRC, Leverhulme Tst, Nuffield Fndn, Carnegie Tst, Wenner-Gren Fndn, Nat Inst for Mental Health USA, Nat Science Fndn USA; pres Anthropology and Archaeology Section BAAS 2005; memb: Exec Ctee Cwlth Human Ecology Cncl 1978–81, Ctee Radcliffe-Brown Fund RAI 1982–85, Ctee Horniman Tst RAI 1982–85, Section H Ctee Br Assoc 1984, Bd Int Soc of Ethnobiology 2002–07, Cncl RAI 2003–, Cncl Br

Acad 2010–13; managing ed Assoc of Social Anthropologists Research Methods Series 1980–85, ed Studies in Environmental Anthropology and Ethnobiology 1994–; memb Editorial Bd: Reviews in Anthropology, Cakalele: Maluku Research Jl; organiser of numerous confs, speaker at confs and symposia worldwide; memb: Assoc of Social Anthropologists of the Cwlth (memb Ctee 1981–85, hon sec 1982–85), Assoc of SE Asianists in the UK, European Assoc of Social Anthropologists, Koninklijk Instituut voor Taal, Land- en Volkenkunde; Munro Lectureship Univ of Edinburgh 1984, Nuffield Social Science Research Fellowship 1985–86, Royal Anthropological Inst Curl Lectureship 1987; Hayter Travel Award 1973, Firth Award 1973; govr Powell-Cotton Museum Birchington 1983–2003; FRAI 1966 (vice-pres 2003–06 and 2011–, pres 2007–11), FLS 2001, FBA 2003; *Publications* Nuaulu Settlement and Ecology: the environmental relations of an eastern Indonesian community (1978), Social and Ecological Systems (ed with P H Burnham, 1979), Classifications in their Social Context (ed with D Reason, 1979), Environment, Subsistence and System: the ecology of small-scale social formations (1982), Ethnographic Research: a guide to general conduct (ed, 1984), Malinowski between Two Worlds: the Polish roots of an anthropological tradition (with E Gellner, G Kubica and J Mucha, 1988), The Cultural Relations of Classification: an analysis of Nuaulu animal categories from central Seram (1993), Nuaulu Ethnozoology: a systematic inventory (1993), Understanding Witchcraft and Sorcery in Southeast Asia (ed with C W Watson, 1993), Redefining Nature: ecology, culture and domestication (ed with K Fukui, 1996), Indigenous Environmental Knowledge and its Transformations: critical anthropological perspectives (ed with P Parkes and A Bicker, 2000), On the Edge of the Banda Zone: past and present in the social organization of a Moluccan trading network (2003), The Categorical Impulse: Essays in the anthropology of classifying behaviour (2006), Ethnobiology and the Science of Humankind (ed, 2006), Modern Crises and Traditional Strategies: Local Ecological Knowledge in Island Southeast Asia (ed, 2007), Nuaulu Religious Practices: The Frequency and Reproduction of Rituals in a Moluccan Society (2012), Understanding Cultural Transmission in Anthropology: A Critical Synthesis (ed, with S Lycett and S Johns, 2013); also author of articles in refereed professional jls; *Style*— Emeritus Prof Roy Ellen; ✉ School of Anthropology and Conservation, Marlowe Building, University of Kent, Canterbury CT2 7NR (☎ 01227 823421, e-mail r.f.ellen@kent.ac.uk)

ELLEN, Susan Caroline; *née* Davies; da of Albert John Davies, and Winifred Ivy Caroline, *née* Emberton; *b* 15 December 1948; *Educ* Cardiff HS for Girls, Malvern Girls' Coll, Univ of Bristol (BSc); *m* 2 March 1974, Simon Tudor Ellen, s of Wing Cdr R A G Ellen, Rtd, OBE; 2 da (Katie Louise b 14 Feb 1980, Joanna Caroline b 14 April 1982); *Career* BUPA Hosps: exec dir 1977–80, devpt dir 1980–82, op dir 1982–87; BUPA Health Services: business devpt dir 1987–90, md 1990–95; govr BUPA 1990–95; chm West Middx Univ Hosp Tst 2002–10; md United Racecourses (Holdings) Ltd 1996–2002; non-exec dir: Asda Group plc 1992–98, Birmingham Midshires Building Society 1996–2000, Portman Building Soc 2001–07, Pru Health 2006–, Vitality Life 2006–, Vitality Health 2006–, Nationwide Building Soc 2007–09; dep chm Independent Health Care Assoc 1990–95; memb: Fin Review Panel 1992–98, Fin Reporting Cncl 1995–97; MHSM 1972; *Recreations* national hunt racing, theatre, opera; *Style*— Mrs Susan Ellen; ✉ 47 Ennerdale Road, Kew, Richmond, Surrey TW9 3DN (☎ 020 8948 0858)

ELLERAY, Anthony John; QC (1993); s of late Alexander John Elleray, of Waddington, Lancs, and Sheila Mary, *née* Perkins; *b* 19 August 1954; *Educ* Bishop's Stortford Coll, Trinity Coll Cambridge (MA); *m* 17 July 1982, Alison Elizabeth, da of William Goring Potter, DFC, of Bollington, Cheshire; 1 da (Harriet b 29 Aug 1985), 1 s (Adam b 22 Sept 1989); *Career* called to the Bar Inner Temple 1977, barr Chancery Div Northern Circuit, dep judge of the High Ct 1997–, recorder 1999; memb: Chancery Bar Assoc, Northern Chancery Bar Assoc (chm); *Recreations* bridge, theatre, pictures, wine; *Clubs* Oxford and Cambridge, Manchester Tennis and Racquets; *Style*— Anthony Elleray, Esq, QC; ✉ Exchange Chambers, 201 Deansgate, Manchester M3 3NW (☎ 0161 833 2722, fax 0161 833 2789, e-mail ellerayqc@exchangechambers.co.uk)

ELLES, (Hon) James Edmund Moncrieff; MEP; s of Neil Elles, of London, and Baroness Elles, *qv*; *b* 3 September 1949; *Educ* Eton, Univ of Edinburgh; *m* 1977 (m dis), Françoise, da of François Le Bail; 1 da (Victoria b 27 July 1980), 1 s (Nicholas b 22 Aug 1982); *Career* admin external rels EC 1977–80, asst to Dep DG of Agric EC 1980–84; MEP (EPP-ED): Oxford and Bucks 1984–94, Bucks and Oxon E 1994–99, SE England 1999–2014; Euro Parl: vice-pres EPP-ED Gp 1994–2004, EPP-ED Gp Budget spokesman 1994–99; rapporteur for EU budget 1996 and 2007; co-fndr Euro Internet Fndn (EIF), fndr Transatlantic Policy Network (TPN), fndr European Ideas Network (EIN); *Recreations* music, skiing, golf; *Clubs* Royal and Ancient Golf (St Andrews), Carlton; *Style*— James Elles, Esq; ✉ jamselles1@gmail.com

ELLICOTT, Russel; *Educ* Univ of London; *Career* asst head teacher Marling Sch Stroud until 2008, dep head Pate's GS 2008–12, head Pate's GS 2012–; *Style*— Russel Ellicott, Esq

ELLINGTON, Marc Floyd; DL (Aberdeenshire 1984); Baron of Towie Barclay, Laird of Gardenstown and Crovie; s of Homer Frank Ellington (d 1984), of Memsie, Aberdeenshire, and Vancouver, and Harriette Hannah Kellas; *b* 16 December 1945; *m* 21 Dec 1967, Karen Leigh, da of Capt Warren Sydney Streater; 2 da (Iona Angeline Barclay of Gardenstown b 1979, Kirstie Naomi Barclay b 1983); *Career* memb Historic Houses Assoc; vice-pres Buchan Heritage Soc, chm Heritage Press (Scot); dir: Grampian Enterprise Ltd 1992–96, Aberdeen Univ Research Ltd 1999–2004, Gardenstown Estates Ltd, Soundcraft Audio Guides, The Scottish Traditional Skills Training Centre; ptnr Heritage Sound Recordings; Saltire Award 1973, Euro Architectural Heritage Award 1975, Civic Tst Award 1975 and 1993; contrib various architectural and historical jls and periodicals, composer and recording artiste, communications, marketing conslt, prodr of documentary films and TV progs; non-exec dir Historic Scotland, chm Grampian Region Tourism Task Force, tstee Nat Galleries of Scot; memb: Historic Building Cncl for Scotland 1980–98, Heritage Lottery Fund Ctee for Scotland 1998–2004, Br Heritage Ctee, Performing Rights Soc; Convention of Baronage of Scotland; patron Banffshire Wildlife Rehabilitation Tst; Doctorem et Magistrum (hc) Univ of Aberdeen 2015; Hon Fell Royal Inc Architects of Scot 2015; FSA; OStJ; *Recreations* sailing, historic architecture, art collecting, music; *Style*— Marc Ellington of Towie Barclay, DL; ✉ Towie Barclay Castle, Auchterless, Turriff, Aberdeenshire AB53 8EP (☎ 01888 511347)

ELLINGWORTH, Charles Vincent; s of William Ellingworth, and Shirley *née* Roach; *b* 7 February 1957, Leicester; *Educ* Ampleforth, Univ of Oxford (BA); *m* 1987 Amanda, *née* Knatchbull; 3 s (Luke b Jan 1991, Joseph b Dec 1992, Louis b Oct 1995); *Career* fndr Property Vision; dir and tstee Cadogan Estate, chm Londonwide Properties; *Books* Silent Night (2012); *Recreations* sailing, skiing, travel; *Clubs* Chelsea Arts; *Style*— Charles Ellingworth, Esq; ✉ Property Vision, 8 Cromwell Place, London SW7 2JN

ELLIOT, Ben; *Educ* Univ of Bristol; *Career* co-fndr Quintessentially Gp 2000–; *Style*— Ben Elliot, Esq; ✉ Quintessentially, 29 Portland Place, London W1B 1QB (☎ 020 3073 6600, website www.quintessentially.com)

ELLIOTT, Prof Alexander Thomas; *b* 1 February 1949; *Educ* Trinity Acad Edinburgh, Univ of Stirling (BA), Univ of Glasgow (PhD, DSc); *m* Barbara, *née* Idle; 2 da (Fiona b 6 Jan 1979, Elspeth b 1 July 1980); *Career* temporary lectr Nuclear Med Unit Univ of Strathclyde 1974–75, lectr Dept of Nuclear Med Middlesex Hosp Med Sch and hon sr physicist Middlesex Hosp 1975–77, princ physicist Dept of Nuclear Med Bart's and hon lectr Bart's Med Coll 1977–81, top grade physicist Western Infirmary/Gartnavel General

Unit, West of Scotland Health Bds, Dept of Clinical Physics and Bioengineering Univ of Glasgow 1981–90, dir West of Scotland Health Bds Dept of Clinical Physics and Bioengrg and prof of clinical physics Univ of Glasgow 1990–, clinical dir Laboratory Med and Clinical Physics West Glasgow Hosps Univ NHS Tst 1997–2000; chm: Nat Consultative Ctee of Scientists in Med 1989– (memb 1982–), Clinical Services Div North Glasgow Univ Hosps NHS Tst 2000–; memb: Hosp Physicists' Assoc 1975 (memb Cncl 1984–86), American Soc of Nuclear Med 1978, British Nuclear Med Soc 1983 (memb Cncl 1987–90), Admin of Radioactive Substances Advsy Ctee 1988–98, Editorial Bd Euro Jl of Nuclear Med 1989–, Acute Healthcare Res Ctee Scottish Office 1993–99, American Soc of Nuclear Cardiology 1993, Ctee on Med Aspects of Radiation in the Environment 2000–; ed Nuclear Med Communications 1999–, author of over 200 papers, book chapters and presentations; FInstP 1983 (MInstP 1978), ARCP 2002; *Style—* Prof Alexander Elliott; ✉ Department of Clinical Physics and Bioengineering, Western Infirmary, Glasgow G11 6NT (☎ 0141 211 2948, fax 0141 211 1920)

ELLIOTT, Ann Margaret; da of John Frederick Hildred (d 1976), and Evelyn Rose Collier (d 2003); *b* 23 February 1945; *Educ* Shurnhold Sch Melksham (now George Ward Sch), Chippenham GS, Bath Acad of Art (Dip Art and Design Graphics), Dept of Educn Univ of Bath (DipEd); *m* 1972, Robert Anthony Elliott; 2 s (b 1978 and 1983), 1 da (b 1980); *Career* art asst Cammell Hudson & Brownjohn Ltd (Films) 1967–68, curatorial asst Sheffield City Art Galleries 1969–72, gallery organiser Gardner Centre Gallery Univ of Sussex 1972–73, exhibition offr Fine Arts Dept Br Cncl 1973–77 and 1985–94 (temp offr 1972), head of sculpture The Hat Hill Sculpture Fndn (Sculpture at Goodwood) 1994–97, currently ind curator and exhbn and visual arts projects organiser, assoc curator Sculpture at Goodwood 1997–; pt/t res asst Aust Crafts Cncl 1977–78, advsr for SE Arts Visual Arts Bd; memb: Bd Gardner Arts Centre Univ of Sussex, Fabric Ctee of Portsmouth Cathedral 2006–16, Gallery Advsy Ctee The Lightbox Woking 2008–11; tstee: Ironbridge Open Air Museum of Steel Sculpture 1998–2012, Gabo Tst for Sculpture Conservation 1999– (chair 2011–), Artpoint 2004–05; projects incl: Rodin in Lewes 1999, Bronze: contemporary Br Sculpture (Holland Park) 2000, A Sculptor's Development: Anthony Caro 2001, Sculpture in the Workplace series (Canary Wharf) 2001–, Henry Moore: Land and Sea (Lewes and Dieppe) 2004, With the Grain: Wood Sculpture by David Nash (Lewes) 2007; *Books* Sculpture at Goodwood, 6 vols (1995–2001), Sculpture at Goodwood Drawings and Models (1994–98), The Art of Prior's Court School (2002), Bleep: The Eric and Jean Cass Collection (2004), The Sculpture and Drawings of Bridget McCrum (2005), Out of China: Monumental Ceramics by Felicity Aylieff (ed, 2008), Sculpture at Canary Wharf: A Decade of Exhibitions (2012), Emily Ball Painting (2013), Sculpture at Canary Wharf: A Permanent Collection (contrib), Kenneth Armitage Sculptor: a Centenary Celebration (commissioning ed and contrib); *Recreations* art, making ceramics, King Charles Cavaliers; *Style—* Mrs Ann Elliott; ✉ Burton Hill Court, Burton Park Road, Petworth, West Sussex GU28 0JS (☎ 01798 342432, e-mail amelliott@btinternet.com)

ELLIOTT, Anthony Michael Manton (Tony); s of Alan Elliott, and Katherine Elliott; *b* 7 January 1947; *Educ* Stowe, Keele Univ; *m* 1, Nov 1976 (m dis 1978), Janet Street-Porter, *qv*; m 2, June 1989, Jane Laetitia, *née* Coke; 3 s (Rufus George b 19 April 1988, Bruce Roland, Lawrence John (twins) b 17 Oct 1990); *Career* fndr and chm Time Out Group 1968–, dir various Time Out cos; govr BFI 1997–2003 (chm Prodn Bd 1998–2000); dir: The Roundhouse Tst 1998–, Somerset House Tst 1999–, The Photographers Gallery 1999–, Soho Theatre Co 2000–04 (resigned); chair London Ctee Human Rights Watch 2003–; *Recreations* travel, watching TV, cinema going, eating out with friends, newspapers and magazines, being with family in time left from working; *Style—* Tony Elliott, Esq; ✉ Time Out Group, Universal House, 251 Tottenham Court Road, London W1T 7AB (☎ 020 7813 3000, fax 020 7813 6001)

ELLIOTT, Maj-Gen Christopher Leslie; CB (1999), MBE (1969); s of Peter Archibald Elliott, and Evelyn Sarah, *née* Wallace; *b* 18 March 1947; *Educ* Pocklington Sch York, RMAS, RMCS (BSc(Eng)), Cranfield Inst of Technol (MPhil), Staff Coll Camberley; *m* 1970, Margaret Bennett; 2 da (Naomi Sarah (d 2005), Georgina Nancy); *Career* cmmnd RE, OC 48 Field Sqdn RE 1980, CO 21 Engr Regt 1986–88, ACOS 1 (Br) Corps 1988–90, Cdr 6th Armoured Bde 1990–91, Dir of Studies Staff Coll Camberley 1991–92, Dir Mil Ops 1993–95, UK Mil Advsr to Chm Int Conf on former Yugoslavia 1995–96, DG Army Trg and Recruiting Agency 1996–99, COS HQ Quartermaster General 1999–2000, DG Doctrine and Devpt 2000–02; Col Cmdt Corps of Royal Engrs 2000–07; chm Purple Secure Systems Ltd 2006–09, dir Doctrine and Strategic Analysis General Dynamics UK Ltd 2002–12, conslt Ove Arup and Ptnrs; visiting prof Cranfield Univ; visiting fell: Faculty of History Univ of Oxford, Sch of Politics and Int Relations Univ of Reading; memb Senate Cranfield Univ 1996–99, memb Advsy Cncl RMCS 2000–02; pres Jt Services Paragliding and Hang Gliding Assoc 1993–2002, Cdre Royal Engr Yacht Club 1995–96, Cdre Army Sailing Assoc 2000– (Vice-Cdre 1993–94); cmmr The Royal Hosp Chelsea 1996–2002, tstee The Army Central Fund 1998–2000; pres Victim Support Wiltshire 2003–09, parish cncllr Easton Royal 2003– (chair Parish Cncl 2014); fell Instn of Royal Engrs (FInstRE) 2007 (pres 2001–07), assoc fell Royal United Services Inst 2012–; *Publications* Blast Damage to Buildings (contrib, 1995), High Command: British Military Leadership in the Iraq and Afghan Wars (2015); *Recreations* human nature; *Clubs* Royal Ocean Racing, Royal Cruising (main ctee memb 2000–), Royal Engineers Yacht, Royal Lymington Yacht; *Style—* Maj-Gen Christopher Elliott, CB, MBE; ✉ e-mail cle@clelliott24.freeserve.co.uk

ELLIOTT, David Stuart; s of Arthur Elliott (d 1979), of East Leake, Notts, and May, *née* Wright (d 1989); *b* 29 April 1949; *Educ* Loughborough GS, Univ of Durham (BA), Courtauld Inst of Art London (MA); *m* 23 Feb 1974 (m dis 2005), Julia Alison, da of Lt-Col John Debenham, MC, of Shrivenham, Wilts; 2 da (Joanna b 10 July 1977, Kate b 3 May 1979); *Career* regnl art offr Arts Cncl 1973–76, dir MOMA Oxford 1976–96, dir Moderna Museet Stockholm 1996–2001, dir Mori Art Museum Tokyo 2001–06, dir Istanbul Modern 2007; artistic dir: 17th Biennale of Sydney The Beauty of Distance: Songs of Survival in a Precarious Age 2008–10, 1st Kiev Int Biennale The Best of Times, The Worst of Times: Rebirth and Apocalypse in Contemporary Art 2010–12, IV Int Moscow Biennale of Young Art: A Time For Dreams 2013–14, Belgrade Salon of Contemporary Art 2015–16; museum winner Sotheby's prize for excellence in the visual arts, Museum of the Year award 1983, winner Nat Art Collections Fund Collect award 1988; advsr VAAC Br Cncl 1979–96, Centre for Int Contemporary Arts NY 1986–92; memb: Cncl Great Britain-Russia Soc, London Cncl Central Sch of Speech and Drama 1994–96, Art Panel of Arts Cncl of GB 1992–95; visitor Ashmolean Museum 1994–2001, memb Advsy Bd Mori Art Museum 2007–, memb Asia Advsy Bd Guggenheim Museum NY 2008–14; exec and pres CIMAM (ICOM) 1998–2004; pres Int Jury Dakar Biennale des Arts Africains et Contemporains Senegal 2000, chm Bd Triangle Network 2010–, chm Bd MOMENTUM Worldwide Berlin 2012–; Rudolf Arnheim Prof in art history Humboldt Univ Berlin 2008, visiting prof Chinese Univ of Hong Kong 2008– (visiting prof in curatorship 2010–); Hon Dr Arts Oxford Brookes Univ 1998; Orden de Mayo Argentina 2000; *Books* Alexander Rodchenko (ed 1979), José Clemente Orozco (1981), Tradition and Renewal – Art in the GDR (1984), New Worlds – Art and Society in Russia (1986), Eisenstein at Ninety (ed 1988), 100 Years of Russian Art (1989), Alexander Rodchenko – Works on Paper 1914–1920 (1991), Photography in Russia 1840–1940 (1992), Art in Argentina 1920–1994 (ed 1994), After the Wall: art and culture in Post-Communist Europe (ed with B Peji?, 1999), Organising Freedom: Nordic Art in the Nineties (2000), Happiness: A Survival Guide for Art and Life (2003), Hiroshi Sugimoto (2005), Tokyo-Berlin/Berlin-Tokyo (2006), Bill Viola: Hatsu-yume (First Dream) (2006), Anonymous: Contemporary Art in Tibet (2013), Art From Elsewhere (2014); also author of numerous reviews, catalogues and articles; *Recreations* collecting art books; *Clubs* Blacks; *Style—* David Elliott; ✉ e-mail david@elliott.as

ELLIOTT, Edward Charles; s of (Charles) Richard Elliott, of Tenbury Wells, Worcs, and Janet Elizabeth, *née* Cooper (d 1981); *b* 27 May 1970, Worcester; *Educ* St Anne's Coll Oxford (MA); *m* 10 Aug 2002, Susan Claire, *née* Broster; 2 da (Isobel b 20 Nov 2003, Evie b 19 Oct 2006), 1 s (Harry b 3 Nov 2008); *Career* headmaster The Perse Sch 2008– (joined 1997); *Publications* University Applications (2004); *Recreations* cricket, horticulture, political history; *Style—* Edward Elliott, Esq; ✉ The Perse School, Hills Road, Cambridge CB2 8QF (☎ 01223 403800, e-mail office@perse.co.uk, website www.perse.co.uk)

ELLIOTT, Giles Roderick McGregor; s of James McGregor Elliott (d 1996), and Drusilla Lucy Christine, *née* Juniper; *b* 6 February 1953; *Educ* Gresham's, Magdalene Coll Cambridge; *m* 1978, Charlotte Mary; 5 da (Alexandra, Laura, Orlanda, Victoria, Matilda), 1 s (Dominic); *Career* dir: J Henry Schroder & Co Ltd 1989–96, Guinness Mahon & Co Ltd 1996–97, HM Publishers Holdings Ltd 1996–, Singer & Friedlander Ltd 1997–2000, Bridgewell Gp Ltd 2000–06; FCA, FRSA; *Recreations* golf, fishing, farming, shooting; *Clubs* Rye, Neville, Hong Kong; *Style—* Giles Elliott, Esq; ✉ Barelands Farm, Bells Yew Green, Tunbridge Wells TN3 9BD (☎ 01892 750495, fax 01892 750010)

ELLIOTT, Guy Robert; s of Robert George Ian Elliott (d 2012), and Susan Mary Jane, *née* de Wend Fenton (d 2012); *b* 1955, London; *Educ* Harrow, Exeter Coll Oxford, INSEAD; *m* 1988, Hon Sophia Sackville West; da of 6 Baron Sackville (d 2004); 1 s (Lucius Adam Robert b 2002); *Career* Kleinwort Benson 1977–79, Rio Tinto plc 1980–2013 (chief fin offr Rio Tinto 2002–13); non-exec dir: Cadbury plc 2007–10, Royal Dutch Shell plc 2010–, SAB Miller plc 2013– (also deputy chm 2013–); memb Takeover Panel 2012–; memb Int Advsy Cncl Fundacao Dom Cabral 2010–; chm Sir John Soane's Museum 2013– (tstee 2012–); *Clubs* Beefsteak; *Style—* Guy Elliott, Esq; ✉ 13 Lincoln's Inn Fields, London WC2A 3BP (e-mail guy.elliott55@gmail.com)

ELLIOTT, John; s of Leonard John Elliott (d 2001), and Elsie, *née* Maule; *b* 13 January 1949, London; *Educ* London Business Sch (MBA); *m* 1, April 1972; 1 s (Richard b Feb 1978); m 2, March 2005, Gillian, *née* Blythe; 3 da (Carrie b Oct 1985, Samantha b Nov 1987, Rebecca b Oct 1989); *Career* md Millwood Homes 1981–; FNAEA 1970; *Recreations* boats; *Style—* John Elliott, Esq; ✉ Millwood Designer Homes, Bordyke End, East Street, Tonbridge, Kent TN9 1HA (☎ 01732 770991, fax 01732 770997, e-mail johne@mdh.uk.com)

ELLIOTT, Prof John; s of Alfred George Lewis Elliott (d 1989), and Mary Dorothy, *née* Greason (d 1992); *b* 20 June 1938; *Educ* Ashford GS, Univ of London (MPhil, Dip Philosophy of Educn), UEA (DLitt); *m* 20 June 1998, Dr Christine, *née* O'Hanlon; 3 da from previous m (Dominique, Katherine, Jessica); *Career* sch teacher 1962–67, res offr Schs Cncl Humanities Project 1967–72, tutor Cambridge Inst of Educn 1976–84; UEA: prof of educn 1987–, lectr 1972–76, reader in educn 1984–86, dean Sch of Educn 1992–95, dir Centre for Applied Res in Educn 1996–99, professorial fell 2002–04, emeritus prof 2004–; advsy prof Hong Kong Inst of Educn 2000–06; conslt on res devpt Hong Kong Curriculum Devpt Inst 2001–06; chief ed Int Jl of Lesson and Learning Studies 2011–; tstee Keswick Hall Tst 1987–93, pres Br Educnl Res Assoc 1989–90 (memb Cncl 1987–92, vice-pres 1988–89), pres World Assoc of Lesson Studies 2009–10 (memb Cncl and Exec Ctee 2010–); memb: Norfolk LSC 2001–06, Norfolk 14–19 Educn Strategy Gp 2005–09; govr Sewell Park Coll Norwich 2008–12; Hon Dr: (in Education) Hong Kong Inst of Educn 2002, Autonomous Univ of Barcelona 2003, Univ of Jönköping Sweden 2014; FRSA, FAcSS 2011; *Books* Issues in Teaching for Understanding (ed with D Ebbutt, 1985), Case Studies in Teaching for Understanding (ed with D Ebbutt, 1986), Rethinking Assessment and Appraisal (ed with H Simons, 1989), La Investigacion-Accion en Educacion (1989), Action-Research for Educational Change (1991), Reconstructing Teacher Education (ed, 1993), The Curriculum Experiment (1998), Images of Educational Change (ed with H Altrichter, 2000), Reflecting Where the Action Is: The Selected Works of John Elliott (2007), Curriculum, Pedagogy and Educational Research (ed with Nigel Norris, 2012); *Recreations* walking, golf, reading, travel; *Clubs* Royal Norwich Golf, Narin and Portnoo Golf Donegal; *Style—* Prof John Elliott; ✉ School of Education and Lifelong, University of East Anglia, Norwich NR4 7TJ (e-mail john.elliott@uea.ac.uk)

ELLIOTT, Prof Sir John Huxtable; kt (1994); s of Thomas Charles Elliott (d 1969), and Janet Mary, *née* Payne (d 1991); *b* 23 June 1930; *Educ* Eton, Univ of Cambridge (MA, PhD); *m* 1958, Oonah Sophia, da of Sir Nevile Butler; *Career* lectr in history Univ of Cambridge 1962–67 (asst lectr 1957–62), prof of history KCL 1968–73 (hon fell 1998), prof of history Inst for Advanced Study Princeton 1973–90, regius prof of modern history Univ of Oxford 1990–97; fell: Trinity Coll Cambridge 1954–67 (hon fell 1991), Oriel Coll Oxford 1990–98 (hon fell 1998); King Juan Carlos visiting prof NYU 1988, visiting hon prof Univ of Warwick 2003–06; memb American Philosophical Soc 1982; corr memb: Hispanic Soc of America 1975, Real Academia Sevillana de Buenas Letras 1976 (Académico de Honor 2009), Accademia delle Scienze di Torino 2009; foreign memb Academia Nazionale dei Lincei 2003; hon tstee Prado Museum 2015; Wolfson Prize for History 1986, Gold Medal for the Fine Arts Spain 1990, Eloy Antonio de Nebrija Prize Spain 1993, Prince of Asturias Prize for Social Sciences Spain 1996, Balzan Prize for History 1500–1800 1999, Francis Parkman Prize 2007; Visitante Ilustre de Madrid 1983; Medal of Honour Universidad Internacional Menéndez y Pelayo 1987; Hon Dr: Universidad Autónoma de Madrid 1983, Univ of Genoa 1992, Univ of Portsmouth 1993, Univ of Barcelona 1994, Univ of Warwick 1995, Brown Univ RI 1996, Univ of Valencia 1998, Univ of Lleida 1999, Universidad Complutense Madrid 2003, Coll of William and Mary Williamsburg VA 2005, Univ of London 2007, Universidad Carlos III Madrid 2008, Univ of Seville 2011, Univ of Alcalá 2012, Univ of Cambridge 2013, Univ of Cantabria 2015; FBA 1972, FAAAS 1977; Cdr Order of Isabel la Católica 1987 (Grand Cross 1996), Grand Cross Order of Alfonso X El Sabio 1988, Cross of St George (Catalonia) 1999; *Books* The Revolt of the Catalans (1963), Imperial Spain 1469–1716 (1963), Europe Divided 1559–1598 (1968), The Old World and the New 1492–1650 (1970), Memoriales y Cartas del Conde Duque de Olivares Vol I (1978), Memoriales y Cartas del Conde Duque de Olivares Vol II (1980), A Palace for King (with Jonathan Brown, 1980), Richelieu and Olivares (1984), The Count-Duke of Olivares (1986), Spain and Its World 1500–1700 (1989), The World of the Favourite (ed with L W B Brockliss, 1999), Sale of the Century (Prado exhibition catalogue, ed with Jonathan Brown, 2002), Empires of the Atlantic World (2006), Spain, Europe and the Wider World 1500–1800 (2009), History in the Making (2012); *Recreations* looking at paintings; *Style—* Prof Sir John Elliott, FBA; ✉ 122 Church Way, Iffley, Oxford OX4 4EG (☎ 01865 716703); Oriel College, Oxford OX1 4EW

ELLIOTT, Julie; MP; *b* 1963, Whitburn, Sunderland; *Educ* Seaham Northlea Comp, Newcastle Poly; *Career* MP (Lab) Sunderland Central 2010–; *Style—* Ms Julie Elliott, MP; ✉ House of Commons, London SW1A 0AA

ELLIOTT, Marianne; da of Michael Elliott, and Rosalind, *née* Knight; *Educ* St Hilary's Sch Alderley Edge, Stockport GS, Univ of Hull; *Career* artistic dir Royal Exchange Theatre Manchester, assoc dir Royal Court Theatre London, currently assoc dir NT; *Theatre* Royal Exchange Theatre Manchester: Coyote Ugly 1996, I Have Been Here Before 1996, Poor Superman 1997, Mad For It 1997, The Deep Blue Sea 1997, Martin Yesterday 1998–99, Fast Food 1999, Nude With Violin 1999, A Woman of no Importance 2000, As You Like It 2000, Les Blancs 2001; other prodns incl: Terracotta (Hampstead Theatre and

E

Birmingham Rep) 2000, Local (Royal Court Upstairs) 2000, The Little Foxes (Donmar Warehouse) 2001, The Sugar Syndrome (Royal Court) 2004, Notes on Falling Leaves (Royal Court) 2004, Pillars of the Community (RNT) 2005, Much Ado About Nothing (RSC) 2006, Therese Raquin (RNT) 2006, St Joan (RNT) 2007, War Horse (RNT) 2007 and (NY) 2011, Harper Regan (2008), All's Well That Ends Well 2009, Women Beware Women 2010, Season's Greetings 2010, The Curious Incident of the Dog in the Night-Time 2012 (Best Director Olivier 2013); *Style*— Ms Marianne Elliott; ✉ National Theatre, South Bank, London SE1 (☎ 020 7452 3333)

ELLIOTT, Prof Marianne; OBE (2000); da of Terence J Burns (d 1982), and Sheila, *née* O'Neill; *b* 25 May 1948; *Educ* Dominican Coll Fortwilliam Belfast, Queen's Univ Belfast (BA), Lady Margaret Hall Oxford (DPhil); *m* 19 July 1975, Trevor Elliott, s of Clifford Elliott; 1 s (Marc b 11 Jan 1989); *Career* lectr II W London Inst of HE 1975–77, univ research fell UC Swansea 1977–79, temp lectr UC Swansea 1981–82, visiting prof Iowa State Univ 1983, visiting prof Univ of S Carolina 1984; Univ of Liverpool: univ research fell Dept of History 1984–87, hon fell Dept of History 1987–93, Andrew Geddes and John Rankin prof of modern history 1993–, dir of research 1995–, dir Inst of Irish Studies 1997–, dir of grad studies Dept of History, dir Humanities Grad Sch, chair Arts Faculty Res Ctee, first holder of Blain chair in Irish studies 2009– ; pt/t course tutor Open Univ 1979–85, pt/t tutor Univ of Warwick 1980–81, Simon sr research fell Univ of Manchester 1988–89, lectr in history Birkbeck Coll London 1991–93, visiting prof history/Irish studies Boston Coll MA 1998; Leverhume Research Fell 1988–89, Nuffield Fndn Research Readership 1996–97, Br Acad Res Readership 2001–03, Royal Historical Soc Colin Matthew meml lectr 2002, Univ of Oxford Ford Lectures 2004–05; HE offr Br Assoc for Irish Studies 1985–88; external assessor for history chairs: Nat Univ of Ireland (UCD), Univ of Limerick, Nat Univ Maynooth; memb: Opsahl Cmmn on NI 1992–93, History and Archaeology Res Panel Br Acad/HRB 1995–98 (chair 1997–98), Bd Anglo-Irish Encounter 1997–2007, Br Acad Res Ctee 2002–05 (memb Cncl 2006–09); FRHistS 1985, FBA 2002; *Publications* Partners in Revolution. The United Irishmen and France (1982, Leo Gershov Award American Historical Assoc 1983), The People's Armies (trans, 1987), Wolfe Tone. Prophet of Irish Independence (1989, Irish Independent/Irish Life Award for Biography 1990, American Conf for Irish Studies James R Donnelly Sr Prize for History 1992), A Citizens' Inquiry. The Opsahl Report on Northern Ireland (jtly, 1992), The Catholics of Ulster, A History (2000, runner-up Ewart-Biggs Meml Prize 2001), The Long Road to Peace in Northern Ireland (ed, 2001), Robert Emmet. The Making of a Legend (2003), When God Took Sides: Religion and Identity in Ireland – Unfinished History (2009); author of numerous articles and contributions to edited collections; *Recreations* running, reading, music; *Style*— Prof Marianne Elliott, OBE, FBA; ✉ Institute of Irish Studies, The University of Liverpool, 1 Abercromby Square, Liverpool L69 7WY (☎ 0151 794 3831, fax 0151 794 3836, e-mail melliott@liv.ac.uk)

ELLIOTT, Prof Martin John; s of John Elliott, MBE, of Sheffield, S Yorks, and Muriel, *née* Dyson; *b* 8 March 1951; *Educ* King Edward VII GS, Univ of Newcastle upon Tyne (MB BS, MD); *m* 15 Jan 1977, Lesley Rickard, da of Alan Rickard (d 1989), of Puddletown, Dorset; 2 s (Becan b 3 June 1981, Toby b 12 May 1983 d 2009); *Career* sr registrar and first asst in cardiothoracic surgery Freeman Hosp Newcastle upon Tyne 1978–83; Gt Ormond St Hosp: sr registrar 1984–85, conslt paediatric cardiothoracic surgeon 1985–, med dir 2010–, clinical ambass Children's Charity 2015–; prof of cardiothoracic surgery UCL 2004–, prof of physic Gresham Coll London 2014–; hon conslt cardiothoracic surgeon: UCH London, Royal Brompton Hosp London; chm Int Nomenclature Gp, dir Nat Service for Severe Tracheal Disease in Children 2006–; 37th Prof of Physic Gresham Coll London 2014; FRCS 1978 (Hunterian Orator 2015), FRSA 2016; *Publications* author of pubns relating to outcomes of treatment, pathophysiology of cardiopulmonary bypass, management of tracheal problems in children and information management in children (280 peer-reviewed pubns and 35 chapters in books, Gresham Coll lecture series at http://www.gresham.ac.uk/gresham-professor-of-physic); *Recreations* cycling, reading, cinema, music, the allotment; *Style*— Prof Martin Elliott; ✉ The Cardiothoracic Unit, MNH Level 7, The Great Ormond Street Hospital for Children NHS Foundation Trust, Great Ormond Street, London WC1N 3JH (☎ 020 7405 9200 (ext 8853), e-mail martin.elliott@gosh.nhs.uk, website www.gosh.nhs.uk)

ELLIOTT, Martin John Henry; s of Patrick James Lawrence Elliott, of Boars Hill, Oxford, and Beryl Olivia Catherine, *née* Carroll; *b* 26 August 1955; *Educ* St Benedict's Sch Ealing, ChCh Oxford (BA); *m* 4 Aug 1984, Rosanna Lina, da of late Capt William James Gorard, of Ealing, London; 3 s (Benedict Edward Henry b 29 Nov 1988, Oliver James Ambrose b 16 Jan 1990, Edmund Giles Augustus b 4 Aug 1991), 3 da (Alice Clare Ianthe b 1 Aug 1993, Josephine Eleanor Naomi b 1 Sept 1995, Genevieve Elizabeth Cecilia b 24 Feb 1997); *Career* admitted slr 1979; Linklaters: articled clerk 1977–79, slr 1979–85, ptnr 1985–; memb Law Soc; *Recreations* rugby, cricket, tennis, cycling, gardening; *Clubs* MCC; *Style*— Martin Elliott, Esq; ✉ Linklaters, One Silk Street, London EC2Y 8HQ (☎ 020 7456 2000, fax 020 7456 2222)

ELLIOTT, Matthew; s of Geoffrey Elliott, and Kathryn, *née* Collins; *b* 12 February 1978, Leeds; *Educ* LSE (BSc); *m* 29 Aug 2014, Sarah, *née* Smith; *Career* lobbyist and campaigner; press offr European Fndn 2000, political sec to Timothy Kirkhope MEP 2001, co-fndr and chief exec TaxPayers' Alliance 2004, fndr Big Brother Watch 2009; campaign dir NOtoAV Campaign 2011, currently chief exec Business for Britain, chief exec Vote Leave 2015–16; tstee Social Affrs Unit; FRSA 2008; *Recreations* music, reading, travel; *Clubs* Arts, Boisdale, 5 Hertford Street; *Style*— Matthew Elliott, Esq; ✉ Flat 702, Courtenay House, 9 New Park Road, London SW2 4DP; Business for Britain, Westminster Tower, 3 Albert Embankment, London SE1 7SP (e-mail mjelliott78@gmail.com, Twitter @Matthew_Elliott)

ELLIOTT, Michael John; *b* 22 August 1953; *Educ* Manor Park GS Nuneaton, Sheffield City Coll of Educn (Univ of Sheffield Cert in Educn), Sheffield City Poly (Univ of Sheffield BEd); *Career* pt/t lectr Dept of Gen Studies Rotherham Coll of Technol 1978, res asst Dept of Educn Mgmnt Sheffield City Poly 1978–79, political advsr and res asst R G Caborn MEP 1979–82; Sheffield City Poly: gen mangr Union of Students 1982–84, asst to the princ 1984–86, head Publicity and Information Servs 1986; asst dir (resources) Yorkshire Arts Assoc 1987–88, dir West Midlands Arts Assoc 1989–91; chief exec: West Midlands Regnl Arts Bd 1992–96, Heart of England Tourist Bd 1996–2000, Royal Liverpool Philharmonic Soc 2001–08, dir of culture Dept of Culture, Media and Sport 2008–11, ceo Royal Scottish Nat Orchestra 2011–; chair: Regnl Arts Bd Chief Execs' Gp 1990–94, RAB Services Ltd 1992, Aston Arts Advsy Bd 1995–98; chm Regnl Tourist Bd Director's Gp 1999–2000; chm Tourism Working Gp for English Heritage's Review of the Historic Environment 2000; treas Euro Forum for Arts and Heritage 1995–96, advsr Dept Culture Media and Sport on implementation of English tourism 1999; memb: Cncl Univ of Birmingham 1990–96, Arts Liaison Ctee 1990–96, Governing Body Herefordshire Coll of Arts and Design 1990–97, Governing Body Handsworth Coll 1995–98, Governing Body Clarendon Coll Nottingham 1997–98, Chief Offrs' Gp 1991–96, Information Mgmnt Policy Gp Arts Funding System 1991–95, Mgmnt Ctee English Regnl Arts Bds 1993–95, Exec of the Chief Offrs' Gp Integrated Arts Funding System 1993–95, Convocation Tst for the Arts Univ of Sheffield 1994–96, Sec of State for Culture's Strategic Planning Working Gp on Tourism 1997–2000, Sheffield City Hall Capital Devpt Advsy Bd 2001, Artworks Steering Gp Paul Hamlyn Fndn 2010–; chm Belgrade Theatre (Coventry) Tst ltd 1998–2001, dir Assoc of Br Orchestras 2011–; govr Univ of Wolverhampton 2000–, memb Cncl Liverpool Inst of Performing Arts 2002–08, chair Governing Body Univ of Wolverhampton 2009–; Hon DUniv Sheffield Hallam Univ; fell Tourism Soc 1998, FRSA; *Publications* The Development of Consortia for Post 16 Provision in the Face of Falling Enrolments (with J A Mundy, 1978); *Recreations* walking, cycling, swimming, watching theatre, dance and football, listening to music, reading contemporary literature and keeping up to date with current affairs and good management practice, travel and continued learning through experience and practice; *Style*— Michael Elliott, Esq

ELLIOTT, Nicholas Blethyn; QC (1995); s of late Col B W T Elliott, of Wilts, and Zara, *née* Codrington; *b* 11 December 1949; *Educ* Kelly Coll Tavistock, Univ of Bristol (LLB); *m* Penelope Margaret Longbourne (Nemmy), da of Brig Hugh Browne; 2 s (Max Blethyn b 14 Aug 1982, George Hugh b 10 Feb 1984); *Career* pupillage chambers of Andrew Leggatt QC (now Sir Andrew Leggatt), called to the Bar Gray's Inn 1972 (bencher), currently in practice Gray's Inn; asst boundary cmmr 2000; *Publications* Banking Litigation (co-ed), Byles on Bills of Exchange and Cheques, Butterworths Money Laundering; *Recreations* tennis, bridge, bicycling, swimming, rock and roll dancing; *Style*— Nicholas Elliott, Esq, QC; ✉ 3 Verulam Buildings, Gray's Inn, London WC1R 5NT (☎ 020 7831 8441, fax 020 7831 8479)

ELLIOTT, Robert James; s of Robert Alfred Elliott (d 1994), and Dorothy, *née* Pullar; *b* 3 July 1952, Newcastle upon Tyne; *Educ* Leeds GS, Univ of London (LLB), Coll of Law Lancaster Gate; *m* 1 April 1978, Sara Elizabeth, *née* Scott; 2 s (Robert Arthur John b 27 Oct 1981, James Henry Percival b 1 May 1988), 1 da (Katharine Frances b 24 Jan 1984); *Career* Wilde Sapte: slr 1976–79, ptnr 1979–90; chm and sr ptnr Linklaters 2011– (joined 1990, ptnr 1991, global head of banking 2006–11; memb: Law Soc, City of London Solicitors' Co; govr Tonbridge Sch; dir and tstee Surrey County Cricket Club, dir Ben Ainslie Racing Holdings Ltd; Freeman Co of Watermen & Lightermen of the River Thames, Liveryman Worshipful Co of Skinners; *Recreations* golf, sailing, theatre; *Clubs* Hurlingham, Royal Ocean Racing, New York Yacht, Royal Yacht Squadron; *Style*— Robert Elliott, Esq; ✉ Linklaters, One Silk Street, London EC2Y 8HQ (☎ 020 7456 4478, fax 020 7456 2222, e-mail robert.elliott@linklaters.com)

ELLIOTT, Prof Stephen Richard; s of Cyril Albert Elliott, and Mavis Mary, *née* Lumb; *b* 30 September 1952; *Educ* Trinity Coll and Cavendish Lab Cambridge (MA, PhD); *m* 3 Sept 1983, Penelope Ann Hylton, *née* Johnson; *Career* Trinity Coll Cambridge: prize (res) fell 1977–81, teaching fell 1981–; Univ of Cambridge: lectr 1979–94, reader in solid-state chemical physics 1994–99, prof of chemical physics 1999–; prof of physics Ecole Polytechnique France 1998–2000; ed Philosophical Magazine Letters; memb Editorial Bd: Philosophical Magazine, Jl of Non-Crystalline Solids, Current Opinion in Solid State and Materials Science, Jl of Optoelectronics and Advanced Materials; Zachariasen Prize 1992; *Books* Physics of Amorphous Materials (1983), Physics and Chemistry of Solids (1998); *Recreations* wine, 18th and 19th century caricatures, Italian life and culture; *Style*— Prof Stephen Elliott; ✉ Trinity College, Cambridge CB2 1TQ (☎ 01223 336525/338512, fax 01223 336362, e-mail srel@cam.ac.uk)

ELLIOTT, Prof (Charles) Thomas; CBE (1994); s of Charles Thomas Elliott (d 1970), and Mary Jane, *née* Higgins (d 1991); *b* 16 January 1939; *Educ* Washington Alderman Smith GS, Univ of Manchester (BSc, PhD); *m* Brenda; 1 s (David b 1962), 2 da (Catherine Ann b 1963, Elizabeth Mary b 1966); *Career* asst lectr and lectr Electrical Engrg Dept Univ of Manchester 1963–67, visiting scientist MIT Lincoln Laboratory 1970–71; Royal Signals and Radar Establishment (later DERA, now QinetiQ): sr scientific offr 1967–73, princ scientific offr 1973–79, sr princ scientific offr (individual merit) 1979–86, dep chief scientific offr (individual merit) 1986–91, chief scientific offr (individual merit) 1991–, chief scientist Electronics Sector 1995–99, conslt 1999–2006; distinguished visiting scientist Jet Propulsion Laboratory Calif 1987, visiting prof of physics Heriot-Watt Univ 1992–99 (hon prof of physics 1999–); Rank Prize for Optoelectronics 1982, The Churchill Medal for Engrg (Soc of Engrs) 1986, MacRobert Award for Engrg (Royal Acad of Engrs) 1991, Patterson Medal (Inst of Physics) 1997, J J Thompson Medal (Instn of Electrical Engrs) 1998, Progress Medal RPS 2001; Hon FRPS 2001, FRS 1988, FInstP 1990; *Publications* author of numerous papers in scientific jls; *Recreations* reading, music, travel; *Style*— Prof Thomas Elliott, CBE, FRS; ☎ 01684 562474, e-mail ctomelliott@sky.com

ELLIOTT, Timothy Stanley; QC (1992); *b* 2 April 1950; *Educ* Marlborough, Trinity Coll Oxford (exhibitioner, MA); *m* 1973, late Katharine Barbara, *née* Lawrance; 1 s (b 1980), 1 da (b 1983); *Career* called to the Bar Middle Temple 1975; *Style*— Timothy Elliott, Esq, QC; ✉ 15 Essex Street, London WC2R 3AA (☎ 020 7544 2600, fax 020 7240 7722)

ELLIOTT-KELLY, Prof Anthony Le Poer fFrench; s of Colm Le Poer-Kelly, and Dr Patricia Elliott; *b* 29 November 1957, Ireland; *Educ* Univ of Cambridge (BA, MSc, PhD, MPhil); *m* 1 Aug 1985, Ann, *née* Cleary; 1 da (Jane b 20 May 1986), 1 s (Colum b 17 Oct 1987); *Career* formerly headmaster Ireland, research fell Cambridge 1998–; prof of education Univ of Southampton 2004–, dean Sch of Educn Univ of Southampton 2011–15; advsr to several govts, memb Panel (Education) Research Excellence Framework 2011–14, memb Advsy Bd Education Foundation; FIMA 1994, FInstP 2006, FAcSS 2012; *Publications* approx 100 papers and books, presentations in over 30 countries incl: Decision Making Using Game Theory (2003), Intellectual Capital (2004), School Choice and Well-being (2007), Using Effectiveness Data (2011), Developing Metrics for Equity (2016); *Recreations* cricket, golf, shooting, skiing, football, rugby; *Clubs* Oxford and Cambridge, Hawks Cambridge; *Style*— Professor Tony Kelly; ✉ School of Education, Building 32, University of Southampton, Highfield, Southampton SO17 1BJ

ELLIS, HE Alexander Wykeham; CMG (2013); s of Roger Ellis, and Margaret, *née* Stevenson; *b* 5 June 1967, London; *Educ* Winchester, Magdalene Coll Cambridge (MA); *m* 21 Sept 1996, Teresa Adegas; 1 s (Tomas b 23 Sept 1997); *Career* diplomat; teacher St Edward's Sch Oxford 1989–90; FCO: joined 1990, Lisbon 1992–96, UK rep to EU 1996–2001, cnsllr 2001–03, Madrid 2003–05, seconded as advsr to Pres of EC 2005–07, ambass to Portugal 2007–11, dir of strategy 2011–13, ambass to Brazil 2013–; *Recreations* sport, theatre, history, travel; *Style*— HE Mr Alexander Ellis, CMG

ELLIS, Anthony John; s of Jack Ellis, of Scunthorpe, S Humberside, and Nancy Doreen, *née* Reed; *b* 15 June 1945; *Educ* Univ of London (BD, MA); *m* 1, 1966 (m dis), Maureen Jane Anne Twomey; 2 da (Kate b 14 Feb 1973, Seònaid b 19 May 1975); m 2, 4 Sept 1980, Alice Anne, da of late James Stanley Stewart Findlay, of Helmsdale, Sutherland; 1 da (Bridget b 7 May 1985); *Career* sr lectr Dept of Moral Philosophy Univ of St Andrews 1987–90 (lectr 1971–1987, chm 1985–89), prof of philosophy Virginia Cwlth Univ Richmond VA 1990– (visiting prof 1987–88); univ fell Univ of Wollongong 1989; ed and author of various pubns and books; *Recreations* music, hill walking; *Style*— Anthony Ellis, Esq; ✉ Department of Philosophy, Virginia Commonwealth University, 915 W Franklin Street, Richmond, Virginia 23284, USA (☎ 00 1 804 827 2188)

ELLIS, Prof Brian William; s of Frank Albert Ernest Ellis (d 1988), and Beryl Christine, *née* Holdsworth (d 1955); *b* 28 November 1947, Hove, E Sussex; *Educ* Harrow, St Mary's Hosp Med Sch London (MB BS); *m* 10 July 1976, Loveday Ann, da of David Ernest Pusey (d 1952), of Coleshill, Bucks; 1 da (Rebecca b 1978), 1 s (David b 1981); *Career* conslt urological surgn Ashford & St Peter's NHS Tst 1983–2007 (dir of surgery 1999–2003), conslt urological surgeon Cobham Hosp 2008–12; hon sr clinical res fell Academic Surgical Unit St Mary's Hosp Med Sch London, hon clinical tutor Charing Cross Med Sch London, visiting prof Middx Univ, dir Film Unit Rila Inst of Health Sciences, advsr in urology Swinfen Telemedicine Tst, dir Medical Software Ltd, clinical lead for NHS modernisation agency project 'Ultrasound in Urology'; former memb Cncl Br Assoc of Urological Surgns, former clinical advsr in surgery to British Airways; hon sec

Travelling Surgical Soc; ed Jl of Integrated Care, referee for submissions to Br Jl of Surgery and BMJ, author of various papers on clinical audit, computing, prostate surgery; Best Videotape Prize Br Assoc of Urological Surgns 1997 and 1999, Hosp Doctor Urology Team of the Year Award 1998; FRCS 1977; *Books* Hamilton Bailey's Emergency Surgery (ed, 13 edn); *Recreations* photography, wine, music, roses; *Style*— Prof Brian W Ellis, FRCS; ✉ Tangley Mount, Tangley, Andover, Hampshire SP11 0SH (☎ 01264 730453, e-mail brian@tangleymount.co.uk)

ELLIS, Christopher Matthew (Chris); s of Dr John Matthew Ellis, and Mary Evelyn, *née* Ford; *Educ* Dean Close Sch Cheltenham; *m* Georgina, *née* Tilley; 2 s (Timothy, Benjamin); *Career* lighting designer; theatre dir and ceo Leicester Haymarket Theatre 1990–92, lighting advsr Leics Dio, theatre conslt Singapore Rep Theatre; memb Bd Derby Playhouse, memb Drama Panel E Midlands Arts; Lighting Designer of the Year Live 2000 Silver Award 2000; memb: Soc of Br Theatre Lighting Designers (now Assoc of Lighting Designers) 1972, Assoc of Br Theatre Technicians 1974; *Theatre* Chichester Festival Theatre: 42nd Street, Pravda, 5/11, Government Inspector, How to Succeed in Business, Merchant of Venice, Blunt Speaking; RNT: St Joan, Lorenzaccio, The Ancient Mariner, Uncle Vanya, Hiawatha, The Mayor of Zalamea, Sir Gawain and the Green Knight, The Wonder of Sex, The Hypochondriac, Romans in Britain; RSC: The Venetian Twins, Romeo and Juliet, Hamlet, Love's Labour's Lost, Maysdays, A Midsummer Night's Dream, The Winter's Tale, The Knight of the Burning Pestle, They Shoot Horses Don't They, The Taming of the Shrew, Breaking the Silence, Faust Parts I and II; Savoy Theatre: Ute Lemper, HMS Pinafore, Lloyd George Knew My Father, Lady Harry; Old Vic: Hair, Henry IV Parts I and II, Henry V, Masterclass, The Importance of Being Earnest; Victoria Palace Theatre: High Society, Brigadoon, Soul Train; Deutsches Schauspielhaus Hamburg: Maria Stuart, Hamlet, Regie von Zalamea, Guys and Dolls; other credits incl: Rat Pack (Sands Hotel), Rent (Prince of Wales Theatre), Annie Get Your Gun (Prince of Wales Theatre), Taboo (The Venue), La Cava (Piccadilly Theatre), Mac and Mabel (Piccadilly Theatre), Boyband (Gielgud Theatre), All You Need is Love (Queen's Theatre), The Pirates of Penzance (Queen's Theatre), Brief Encounter (Lyric Theatre), Hotstuff (Cambridge Theatre), West Side Story (Her Majesty's Theatre), Me and My Girl (Adelphi Theatre, Broadway and LA), Irma Vep (Duke of York's Theatre), Upon the Throne (Comedy Theatre), Signs of the Times (Vaudeville Theatre), Pygmalion (Shaftesbury Theatre), On Your Toes (Royal Festival Hall), The Mikado (Royal Festival Hall), Dance of the Vampires (Budapest), They're Playing Our Song (Singapore Rep Theatre), Sing to the Dawn (Singapore Rep Theatre), The Big Picnic (Glasgow Promenade Prodns/BBC), Telstar (New Ambassador's), Singing in the Rain (Sadlers' Wells), Sweet Charity and Pinocchio (Teatro della Luna Milan and Teatro Sistina Rome), Great Expectations (Walnut Street Theatre Philadelphia), Blood Money (Walnut Street Theatre Philadelphia), On Your Toes (Japan), Forbidden City (Esplanade Singapore), Hello Dolly (Sweden), My Fair Lady (Copenhagen), Amazing Grace (Cardiff Music Festival), Man of La Mancha (Edinburgh Lyceum), Jerry Springer the Opera (nat tour), Simply Cinderella (Curve Leicester), Chester Mystery Plays 2013, Dans der Vampiren (Antwerp), 3 Minute Heroes (Coventry Belgrade); *Opera* ENO: The Gambler, La Traviata, Christmas Eve, Hansel and Gretel (also Netherlands, La Fenice and BBC); Scottish Opera: La Traviata, The Magic Flute, The Jacobin, Peter Grimes, Ariadne Auf Naxos (also Den Nortske Opera), From the House of the Dead (also WNO and Vancouver), Julius Caesar (also Ludwigshaven and Montpellier), From the House of the Dead (Savolinna Opera Festival) 2016; other credits incl: Benzin (Chemnitz Oper), The Nightingale's To Blame (Opera North), Wozzeck (Netherlands), A Midsummer Night's Dream (Netherlands and Tel Aviv), Donnerstag Aus Licht (ROH), The Chinese Conjuror (Almeida Opera), From the House of the Dead (Teatro Massimo Sicily), Don Giovanni (New Vic), Rigaletto, Carmen (Clonter Opera), Noye's Fludde (Aldeburgh Opera); *Ballet* The Dancing Room (Dance Umbrella/BBC), Petrushka (Hong Kong Acad), Maxwell's Demons (Hong Kong Acad); *Lighting Architecture* works incl: stage lighting Haymarket Theatre Leics 1973, The Nat Centre of Popular Music Sheffield 1998, Loft Apartment Nether Hall Leics 1999, St John the Baptist Church Cold Overton Leics 1999, Glenfield Methodist Church Leics 1999, St Andrew's Church Aylestone Leics 1999, The Printworks Centre Manchester 2000, DBS Arts Centre Singapore Repertory Theatre 2001, St Peter's Church Church Langton Leics 2003, St Remigius Church Long Clawson Leics 2005, Stamford Methodist Church Leics 2005, Old Rectory Church Langton Leics 2006, All Saints Church Slawston Leics 2006, St Mary The Virgin Church Harby Leics 2006, St Michael and All Angels Church Aylsham Norfolk 2007, Curve Theatre Leicester Stage Lighting 2008, Harrogate Sch 2009, St James Church West Malvern 2011, Derby Art Gallery 2011, Much Wenlock Lady Chapel 2012, Derby Museum Enlightenment Gallery 2013; *Recreations* sailing, photography, church organist; *Style*— Chris Ellis, Esq; ✉ Kiplings, Seworgan, Constantine, Falmouth TR11 5QN (☎ 01326 340846, mobile 07885 581311, e-mail chrisellislighting@me.com); Performing Arts, 6 Windmill Street, London W1P 1HF (☎ 020 7255 1362, fax 020 7631 4631, e-mail info@performing-arts.co.uk)

ELLIS, His Hon David Raymond; s of Raymond Ellis (d 1986), and Ethel, *née* Gordon (d 2012); *b* 4 September 1946; *Educ* St Edward's Sch Oxford, ChCh Oxford (MA); *m* 18 December 1974, Cathleen Margaret, da of late Dr Albert Joseph Hawe, CBE, of Accra, Ghana; 1 s (Thomas b 1978), 1 da (Caroline b 1979); *Career* called to the Bar Inner Temple 1970, recorder of the Crown Court 1991–95 (asst recorder 1986), circuit judge (SE Circuit) 1995–2014; *Clubs* Leander; *Style*— His Hon David Ellis; ✉ The Law Courts, Altyre Road, Croydon CR9 5AB

ELLIS, Diana; QC (2001); da of Evan Henry Ellis (d 1970), and Irene Sarah Jeanette Ellis (d 1998); *Educ* Highbury Hill HS, LSE (Dip Social Admin), Univ of London (LLB); *m* 14 Jan 2001, Geoffrey Keith Watts, s of late Geoffrey Watts; *Career* former teacher; barr practising in criminal law (international and domestic jurisdictions), recorder SE Circuit 1998–; *Recreations* theatre and concerts, reading, walking, enjoying Italy; *Style*— Ms Diana Ellis, QC; ✉ 25 Bedford Row, London WC1R 4HD

ELLIS, Dame Diana Margaret; DBE (2013, CBE 2004); da of Robert Hall (d 1981), of Twickenham, Middx, and Mabel Helen, *née* Steadman (d 1990); *b* 11 April 1938; *Educ* Perivale Girls' Sch, Guildford Coll of Technol (MRSH); *m* 3 Sept 1966, John David Ellis, s of Frederick Henry Ellis (d 1994); 1 da (Claire Suzanne b 24 Aug 1969); *Career* dist mangr Surrey CC; competitive career: Middx 1954–57, coxed winning crew Women's Eights Head of River Race 1969, 1971, 1972 and 1973 (stroked 1966–68), stroked GB eight European Championships 1966, coxed England 1972, Gold medal Nat Championships 1972 (Silver medal 1973); memb: Nat Championship Ctee 1977 (chm 1987–89), Women's Rowing Ctee 1977–, World Rowing Championship 1996 (vice-pres), Ctee Women's Eights Head of River Race 1980–93; chm: Women's Rowing Cmmn 1984–87, Serpentine Regatta 1987–89, Amateur Rowing Assoc 2000–13 (Exec Ctee 1989–2000); hon pres Br Rowing 2013–; GB team mangr 1988; qualified umpire 1978–, elected Henley steward 1997; exec BOA 1997–2013, exec CCPR 2000–13 (dep chm 2005–11), life vice-pres BOA; FRSA; *Recreations* rowing; *Clubs* Leander, Twickenham Rowing, St George's Ladies Rowing; *Style*— Dame Diana Ellis, DBE; ✉ British Rowing, 6 Lower Mall, Hammersmith, London W6 9DJ (☎ 020 8237 6703, fax 020 8237 6749)

ELLIS, Ian David; s of John D V Ellis (d 1998), and Heather, *née* Gosnell (d 1987); *b* 4 December 1955; *Educ* Sir Charles Lucas Sch; *m* 27 Oct 1998, Clare, *née* Poyner; 3 s (Stuart David b 17 Aug 1985, Adam John b 8 Sept 2000, Harry Alexander b 17 Nov 2003), 2 da (Sophie Louise b 27 Feb 1989, Lauren Daniel b 2 Oct 1992); *Career* Dist Valuers Office Ipswich 1974–83, Richard Ellis (now CBRE) 1983–98 (equity ptnr 1991, ceo Investment Mgmnt), md Corp Real Estate Gp Trillium 1998–2000, ceo Land Securities Trillium 2002–09 (dep ceo 2000–02), dir Land Securities plc 2002–09, chm Telereal Trillium 2009–14 (non-exec dir 2014–); non-exec chm Arcus Solutions Ltd 2011–; ind dir Portman Settled Estates 2006–, chair NHS Property Servs 2016–; memb Estates Bd KCL 2010–16; FRICS 1991; *Recreations* garden, history, family, team sports; *Style*— Ian Ellis, Esq; ✉ Telereal Trillium, 140 London Wall, London EC2Y 5DN (☎ 020 7796 5553, fax 020 7796 2900, e-mail ian.ellis@telerealtrillium.com)

ELLIS, Prof Ian Ogilvie; s of Philip Senior Ellis, of Cranford, Manchester, and Anna *née* Ure; *b* 24 August 1955; *Educ* Stockport GS, Univ of Nottingham Med Sch (BMed Sci, BM BS); *m* 1, 20 Oct 1979 (m dis 1997), Jane Elisabeth, da of Dudley John Stevens, of Westbere, Kent; 1 s (James Ogilvie b 1987), 1 da (Sophie Hannah b 1989); m 2, Eileen Jane, da of John Barrett (decd); 1 s (Tristan Alistair Malcolm b 1997); *Career* lectr pathology Univ of Nottingham 1980–87, conslt histopathologist specialising in breast disease City Hosp Nottingham 1987–, prof of cancer pathology Univ of Nottingham 2004– (reader in pathology 1997–2004); author of numerous pubns on breast cancer pathology and prognostic factors; chm National Coordinating Ctee for Breast Screening Pathology; lectr UK Breast Screening Prog Nottingham Trg Centre; MRCPath 1985; *Recreations* game fishing, wine tasting; *Style*— Prof Ian Ellis; ✉ Yew Tree House, 2 Kenilworth Road, The Park, Nottingham NG7 1DD (☎ 0115 947 2186); Department of Histopathology, City Hospital, Hucknall Road, Nottingham NG5 1PB (☎ 0115 969 1169, ext 46875, e-mail ian.ellis@nottingham.ac.uk)

ELLIS, Prof Jonathan Richard (John); CBE (2012); s of Richard Ellis, of Potters Bar, Herts, and Beryl Lilian, *née* Ranger (d 1985); *b* 1946; *Educ* Lochinver House Sch, Highgate Sch, King's Coll Cambridge (BA, PhD); *m* 11 July 1985, Maria Mercedes, da of Alfonso Martinez (d 1982), of Cali, Colombia and Miami Beach, Florida; 1 s (Sebastian b 1990), 1 da (Jennifer b 1988); *Career* research assoc Stanford Linear Accelerator Centre 1971–72, Richard Chase Tolman fell Caltech 1972–73, ldr Theoretical Studies Div Euro Orgn for Nuclear Research (CERN) Geneva 1988–94; Miller prof Univ of Calif Berkeley 1988, Clerk Maxwell prof of theoretical physics KCL 2010–; memb Cncl PPARC; FRS 1984, FIOP 1991; *Recreations* reading, listening to music, hiking in mountains; *Style*— Prof John Ellis, CBE, FRS; ✉ Tannay, 1295 Mies, Switzerland; Theoretical Studies Division, CERN, 1211-Geneva 23, Switzerland (☎ 00 41 22 767 4142, fax 00 41 22 767 3850)

ELLIS, Kevin; *Career* PricewaterhouseCoopers: joined 1984, ptnr 1996–, memb Exec Bd 2008–, managing ptnr 2012–, chm and sr ptnr 2016–; *Style*— Kevin Ellis, Esq

ELLIS, Michael Henry (Mike); OBE (2007); s of John Ellis (d 1988), of Sheffield, S Yorks, and Joan, *née* Lawton (d 2003); *b* 4 August 1951; *Educ* High Storrs GS Sheffield, Open Univ (BA); *m* 9 June 1973, Jeanette, *née* Booth; 2 da (Elizabeth Anne b 13 Oct 1978, Catherine Jane b 9 March 1980); *Career* worked in local govt sector 1967–87; Halifax Building Soc: gp treas 1987–92, gen mangr treasy and European ops 1992–95, md treasy and overseas ops 1995–96, banking and savings dir 1996–97; Halifax plc: banking and savings dir 1997–99, retail fin servs dir 1999, chief operating offr 1999–2001; gp fin dir HBOS plc 2001–04 and 2008–09; chm Skipton Building Soc 2011–; memb CIPFA 1973; *Recreations* travel, reading, music, football; *Clubs* RAC; *Style*— Mike Ellis, Esq, OBE

ELLIS, Michael Tyrone; MP; s of Jack Ellis, and Margaret, *née* Surgenor; *b* 13 October 1967, Northampton; *Educ* Wellingborough Sch, Univ of Buckingham (LLB), Inns of Court Sch of Law; *Career* called to the Bar Middle Temple 1993; MP (Cons) Northampton N 2010–, memb Home Affrs Select Ctee 2011–15, chm All Party Parly Gp on the Queen's Diamond Jubilee 2010–13, Parly advsr to Rt Hon Lord Feldman of Elstree (Cons Pty chm) 2012–15, PPS to the Home Secretary 2015–16, dep ldr House of Commons and asst govt whip 2016–; pres Cwlth Jewish Cncl 2012–14; *Clubs* Carlton; *Style*— Michael Ellis, Esq, MP; ✉ House of Commons, London SW1A 0AA

ELLIS, Dr Paul Anthony; s of Kevin Royce Ellis (d 1995), and Kathleen Margaret, *née* Gallagher; *b* 29 April 1963; *Educ* Christchurch Boys' HS NZ, Univ of Otago (MB ChB, MD); *m* 27 April 1996, Dr Isis Dove-Edwin, da of George Dove-Edwin, KCVO; 3 s (Alexander b 3 Aug 1998, Zachary b 6 Jan 2000, Cameron b 22 Sept 2004), 1 da (Georgia b 6 Oct 2001); *Career* registrar in oncology Christchurch Hosp NZ 1990–92; Royal Marsden Hosp: sr registrar in med oncology 1992–94, clinical res fell Royal Marsden Hosp 1994–96; conslt med oncologist Guy's and St Thomas' Hosps NHS Tst 1997–, hon sr lectr in med oncology KCL 1997–; co-chair CRUK Nat Adjuvant Breast Cancer Trial (TACT) 1999–; med advsr: UK Breast Cancer Care 1997–; memb various pharmaceutical industry advsy gps; memb: Assoc of Cancer Physicians 1993–, Br Breast Gp 1996–, American Soc of Clinical Oncology (ASCO) 1997–; memb Editorial Bd Jl of Clinical Oncology 2001–; delivered numerous presentations and invited lectures to int confs and learned socs; NZ Soc for Oncology Young Investigator of the Year 1992, 6th Odlin Res Fellowship 1994, Inaugural ASCO Fellowship Award Best Young Ivestigator ASCO annual meeting 1996; FRACP 1992; *Publications* author of peer reviewed articles, invited reviews, published abstracts and book chapters; *Recreations* golf, skiing, football, cricket; *Style*— Dr Paul Ellis; ✉ Department of Medical Oncology, Guy's Hospital, London SE1 9RT (☎ 020 7188 4253, mobile 07775 783852, e-mail paul.ellis@gstt.nhs.uk); London Oncology Clinic, 95 Harley Street London (☎ 020 7317 2535)

ELLIS, Prof Richard Salisbury; CBE (2008); s of late Capt Arthur Ellis, MBE, of Colwyn Bay, Wales, and Marion, *née* Davies; *b* 25 May 1950; *Educ* Ysgol Emrys ap Iwan, UCL (BSc), Wolfson Coll Oxford (DPhil); *m* 28 July 1972, Barbara; 1 da (Hilary Rhona b 1976), 1 s (Thomas Marc b 1978); *Career* princ res fell Royal Greenwich Observatory 1983–85, prof of astronomy Univ of Durham 1985–93 (lectr 1981–83), sr res fell SERC 1989–94 (chm Large Telescope Panel), Plumian prof of astronomy and experimental philosophy Univ of Cambridge 1993–99, dir Inst of Astronomy Cambridge 1994–99, professorial fell Magdalene Coll Cambridge 1994–99, prof of obs astrophysics Univ of Cambridge 2000–03, Steele prof of astronomy Caltech 2002– (prof of astronomy 1999–2002), dir Palomar Observatory 2000–02, dir Caltech Optical Observatories 2002–05, Royal Soc research prof Univ of Oxford and professorial fell Merton Coll Oxford 2008–09; memb American Astronomical Soc; Hon DSc Univ of Durham 2002; fell UCL 1999; FRAS 1974, FRS 1995, FInstP 1998, fell AAAS 2003; *Books* The Epoch of Galaxy Formation (with C S Frenk, 1988), Observational Tests of Inflation (with T Shanks, 1991), The Development of Large Scale Structure (1999); *Recreations* travel; *Style*— Prof Richard Ellis, CBE, FRS; ✉ Astronomy MS 249–17, California Institute of Technology, Pasadena, CA 91125, USA (☎ 00 1 626 395 4970, fax 00 1 626 568 9352, e-mail rse@astro.caltech.edu)

ELLIS, Simon Edgar Hargreaves; s of John Edgar Hargreaves Ellis, of Cheshire, and Yvonne Valerie Ellis (d 2008); *b* Tidworth, Hants; *Educ* Pauline Meml Sch Colorado Springs USA, Abbey Gate Coll Chester, Univ of Hull (BA), RMA Sandhurst, Coll of Law Chester; *m* 2 Jan 1992, Susan Carey, *née* Watt; 2 s (James Edgar Hargreaves b 6 Dec 1992, Michael Edgar Hargreaves b 22 Jan 1997); *Career* served Army Cheshire Regt 1986–93; slr specialising in ecclesiastical and charity law particularly relating to property (especially utilities), currently ptnr Aaron & Ptnrs LLP Slrs; Cheshire/Mercian Regt TA 1993–2013; memb: Charity Law Assoc, Law Soc 1997; tstee King's Sch Bursary Tst Fund, memb Fell Running Assoc; *Recreations* fell and mountain running especially over longer distances, skiing; *Clubs* Tattenhall Running, City of Chester Triathlon; *Style*— Simon Ellis, Esq; ✉ Aaron & Partners LLP, 5–7 Grosvenor Court, Foregate Street, Chester CH1 1HG (☎ 01244 405555, fax 01244 405566, e-mail enquiries@aaronandpartners.com)

ELLIS, Susan Jacqueline; da of Michael John Irving Ellis, of Bridgwater, Somerset, and Juliette Wendy Scott, *née* Smith; *b* 30 April 1963; *Educ* Leamington Coll for Girls, City Univ Business Sch (BSc); *m*; 1 s; *Career* Midland Bank International 1981–85, National

Opinion Polls 1985–86, PR mangr Broad Street Associates 1987–88, md Square Mile Communications 1992–2000 (jt fndr 1988); Weber Shandwick Square Mile (formerly Square Mile Communications): gp chief exec 2000–04, chm 2000–09; sr communications advsr: Ultra Electronics plc 2009–, Cobham plc 2009–; non-exec dir Ideal Shopping Direct 2006–09, dir Phoenix Home Trading 2009–; *Recreations* sport, cinema, theatre, literature; *Style*— Miss Susan Ellis

ELLIS, Sir Vernon James; kt (2011); *b* 1 July 1947, Oxford; *Educ* Magdalen Coll Sch, Magdalen Coll Oxford (MA); *m* 1972, Hazel Marilyn Ellis, *née* Lucas; 1 da (Katie Cousins b 10 Sept 1974), 1 s (Andrew Ellis b 3 Dec 1976); *Career* Andersen Consulting (later Accenture): joined 1969, ptnr 1979, managing ptnr UK 1986–89, managing ptnr Europe ME Africa and India 1989–99, int chm 1999–2008 (sr advsr 2008–10), chm Martin Randall Travel Ltd 2008–; non-exec dir FTI Consulting Inc 2012–, chm One Medical Gp 2014–; tstee RCM 2004–10, chm ENO 2005–12 (pres 2012–), pres Classical Opera 2009–, chair Br Cncl 2010–16, chair Arts and Media Honours Ctee 2012–15, chm Stop MS Appeal 2014–, chm Leeds Int Piano Competition 2015–; FCA 1982, FRCM 2012; *Recreations* gardening, music, opera, theatre, wine, cooking, photography; *Clubs* Athenaeum, Garrick; *Style*— Sir Vernon Ellis; ✉ British Council, 10 Spring Gardens, London SW1A 2BN

ELLISON, Jane Elizabeth; MP; da of Philip Ellison, of Bradford, W Yorks, and Patricia Ellison; *b* 15 August 1964, Bradford, W Yorks; *Educ* St Joseph's Coll Bradford, St Hilda's Coll Oxford; *m* John Samiotis; *Career* John Lewis Partnership 1986–2010 (mangr customer magazine 2005–10); MP (Cons) Battersea 2010–; memb Backbench Business Ctee 2010–13, Parly under-sec of state for public health 2013–; tstee Sing For Pleasure; *Style*— Ms Jane Ellison, MP; ✉ House of Commons, London SW1A 0AA (☎ 020 8944 2065, e-mail jane.ellison.mp@parliament.uk)

ELLISON, Mark Christopher; QC (2008); s of Anthony Ellison (d 1959), and Arlette Maguire, *née* Blundell; *b* 8 October 1957, Sutton, Surrey; *Educ* Pocklington Sch, Skinners Sch, Univ of Wales (LLB), Inns of Court Sch of Law; *m* 21 Nov 1981, Kate Augusta, da of Michael Humphrey Middleton, CBE; 2 s (Ned, Rollo), 2 da (Flora, Maudie); *Career* called to the Bar Gray's Inn 1979; first sr treasy counsel Central Criminal Court 2006–08; recorder 2006–15, dep High Court judge 2010–15; *Publications* Fraud Law Practice and Procedure; *Recreations* sailing; *Clubs* Goodwood Road Racing; *Style*— Mark Ellison, Esq, QC; ✉ QEB HollisWhiteman, 1–2 Laurence Pountney Hill, London EC4R 0EU (☎ 020 7933 8855, e-mail clerks@qebhw.co.uk)

ELLMAN, Louise Joyce; MP; *b* 14 November 1945; *Educ* Manchester HS for Girls, Univ of Hull (BA), Univ of York (MPhil); *m* Geoffrey David Ellman; 1 s, 1 da; *Career* vice-chm Lancashire Enterprises 1982–97; chm: Lancashire's Environment Forum 1989–97, NW Regnl Assoc 1992–97; memb: Lancashire Co-op Devpt Agency and Co-op Enterprise NW 1981–97, NW Partnership 1992–97; MP (Lab/Co-op) Liverpool Riverside 1997–; memb Environment, Tport and Regnl Affrs Select Ctee 1997–, memb Tport Select Ctee (chair 2008–), pres Jewish Lab Movement, chair All Pty Bahais Gp, chair All Pty Br-Israel Gp; vice-chair Lab Friends of Israel, memb Bd of Deputies of Br Jews 2008–; memb Lancs CC 1970–97, memb W Lancs DC 1974–87, ldr Lancs CC 1981–97, ldr Lab Gp Lancs CC 1977–97; chm NW Regnl Exec Lab Pty 1993–98 (memb 1985–); *Style*— Mrs Louise Ellman, MP; ✉ House of Commons, London SW1A 0AA (☎ 020 7219 3000)

ELLMANN, Dr Maud; da of Richard David Ellmann (d 1987), of Oxford, and Mary Joan Donahue Ellmann (d 1989); *b* 16 January 1954; *Educ* Oxford HS, Université de Paris Sorbonne, King's Coll Cambridge (MA, Rylands prize), St Anne's Coll Oxford (DPhil); *m* 2000, John Wilkinson; *Career* lectr Dept of English Univ of Southampton 1979–89, Andrew W Mellon faculty fell in humanities Harvard Univ 1989–90; Univ of Cambridge: reader in modern literature Faculty of English 1989–2005, fell and dir of studies King's Coll 1989–2005; Notre Dame prof of English Univ of Notre Dame 2005; visiting prof: of Irish literature Northwestern Univ 2002, Universidade de Santiago de Compostela Spain; visiting asst prof: Smith Coll 1984–85, Amherst Coll 1985–86; Rose Mary Crawshay Award Br Acad 2004; fell American Cncl of Learned Socs, Bernhard fell Williams Coll Williamstown 1997–98, Guggenheim fell 1998–99, Knopf fell Harry Ransom Center Univ of Texas 2002, Margaret Bundy Scott visiting prof of English Williams Coll 2003, Keough distinguished prof of Irish studies Univ of Notre Dame 2004, founding fell English Assoc (FEA), FRSA; *Books* The Poetics of Impersonality: T S Eliot and Ezra Pound (1987), The Hunger Artists: Starving, Writing and Imprisonment (1993), Psychoanalytic Literary Criticism (1994), Elizabeth Bowen: The Shadow Across the Page (2003); *Style*— Dr Maud Ellmann; ✉ Keough Institute for Irish Studies, University of Notre Dame, Notre Dame, IN 46556, USA

ELLWOOD, Peter David Roger; s of John Hassall George Stanley Ellwood (d 1984), and Eileen Eleanor, *née* Kenny (d 1990); *b* 17 October 1948; *Educ* Watford GS, Calday Grange GS, Univ of Cambridge (MA); *m* 1976, Susan Dianne, *née* Chester; 2 da (Emily b 1977, Katie b 1979), 1 s (Christian b 1985); *Career* various positions with Shell Mex and BP Ltd 1970–75; British Council: asst rep Nepal 1975–79, London 1979–83, dep dir Indonesia 1983–86, dir Cameroon 1986–89, dep dir France 1989–94, dir Sri Lanka 1994–95, dir Pakistan 1998–2002, regnl dir ME 2002–04, regnl dir North and Central Europe 2004–; *Recreations* travel, theatre-going, music, birdwatching; *Style*— Peter Ellwood, Esq; ✉ British Council, c/o British Embassy, Skarpögatan 6–8, PO Box 27819, S-115 93 Stockholm

ELLWOOD, Tobias; MP; *b* 12 August 1966, NY; *Educ* Vienna Int Sch, Loughbrough Univ, City Univ (MBA); *Career* Offr Royal Green Jackets 1991–96, served NI, Cyprus, Kuwait, Germany, Gibraltar, Bosnia; researcher to Rt Hon Tom King, MP 1996–97, sr business devpt mangr London Stock Exchange 1999; cncllr (Cons) Dacorum BC 1999; Parly candidate (Cons) Worsley 2001, MP (Cons) Bournemouth E 2005–; shadow min for tourism, licensing and gambling 2007–10, PPS to Sec of State for Defence 2010–11, PPS to Min for Europe 2011–13, PPS to Sec of State for Health 2013–; parly advsr to the PM for the 2014 NATO Summit; govr Queen's Park Infant Sch; *Publications* Post Conflict Reconstruction (2009), Time to Change the Clocks (2010), An Introduction to the Conservative Party (5 edn), Upgrading UK Influence in the European Union (2012), Stabilising Afghanistan (2013), Improving Efficiency, Interoperability and Resiliance of our Blue Light Services (2013); *Style*— Tobias Ellwood, Esq, MP; ✉ House of Commons, London SW1A 0AA

ELMS-ELEY, (Elizabeth) Susan (Sue); da of Ernest Frederick Butler, and Renée, *née* Dale; *b* 2 April 1962; *Educ* Brynteg Comp Sch, Bridgend Tech Coll, Kingston Poly (BA, Postgrad Mktg Dip); *m* (m dis); m 2, 1996; *Career* student Kingston Poly 1981–85, research exec Leo Burnett advtg 1985–87, research mangr Lintas advtg 1987–89, bd dir Initiative Media London 1989–90, md Initiative Technologies Paris 1990–94, chief exec SP Consultants Worldwide 1994–95, int head of research Initiative Media Worldwide 1995–98, md Futures Worldwide Research Gp 1998–2001, md Carat Insight Ltd 2001–; former chm Media Research Group; memb: European Society for Opinion Surveys and Mkt Research (ESOMAR), IOD, MRS, IDM; *Recreations* cinema, travel; *Style*— Mrs Sue Elms-Eley; ✉ Carat Insight Ltd, Parker Tower, Parker Street, London (☎ 020 7430 7000)

ELPHICKE, (Brett) Charles Anthony (Charlie); MP; *b* 14 March 1971, Cambs; *Educ* Felsted, Univ of Nottingham; *m* Natalie Elphicke, *qv*; 2 c; *Career* slr specialising in tax, latterly ptnr and head of European tax Hunter and Williams 1996–2010; MP (Cons) Dover and Deal 2010–; PPS to Min for Europe, Rt Hon David Lidington, MP, *qv* 2013–, PPS to Sec of State for Work and Pensions 2014–15; Govt whip (Lord Cmmr of HM Treasy) 2015–; *Publications* many papers for Centre for Policy Studies; *Recreations* sailing, cooking, travel; *Style*— Charlie Elphicke, Esq, MP; ✉ House of Commons, London SW1A 0AA

ELPHICKE, Natalie; OBE (2015); *b* 5 November 1970; *Educ* Univ of Kent (LLB), Inns of Court Sch of Law; *m* 1 June 1996, Charlie Elphicke, MP, *qv*; 1 da, 1 s; *Career* called to the Bar Lincoln's Inn 1994 (Hardwicke scholar), admitted slr 1999; law firm ptnr 2003–12, fndr and chm Million Homes Million Lives 2013, chief exec The Housing and Finance Institute; nat dir Cons Policy Forum 2010–12, co-chair Ind Housing Review HM Treasy and Dept for Communities and Local Govt 2014, ind advsr UK Govt 2014; non-exec dir Principality Building Soc 2012–; memb Norwood Advice Centre 1995–99, cmmr Westminster Housing Cmmn 2005–06; memb Law Soc, Cons Party; Freeman City of London; *Publications* Housing People: Financing Housing (2010), Nation Rent (2014), A Better Deal for Nation Rent (2014), The Elphicke-House Report for UK Government (with Keith House, 2015); *Recreations* housing and finance policy, regeneration and social welfare, song writing, writing children's books, sea sports; *Style*— Mrs Natalie Elphicke, OBE; ✉ e-mail n.c.elphicke@gmail.com, website www.millionhomes.org

ELSE, Martin Thomas; s of Richard Else (d 1992), and Lilian Margaret, *née* Stickells; *b* 21 May 1953; *Educ* Farnborough GS, Univ of Salford (BScEcon), Southampton Coll of Technol (qualified accountant IPFA), London Business Sch (Sloan fell with distinction); *m* 1 July 1978, Jennifer Louise, da of Timothy George Bridges; 1 s (David Thomas b 20 May 1980), 1 da (Sharon Louise b 29 Jan 1982); *Career* fin trainee City and Hackney HA and City and E London AHA 1975–79; NE Thames RHA: princ fin planning mangr 1979–82, princ asst treas 1982–83; Hampstead HA: dep treas 1983–86, dir of fin 1986–90, dep dist gen mangr 1986–90, memb Tavistock Special Mgmnt Ctee; Royal Free Hampstead NHS Tst: dir of fin, planning and supplies 1990–94, dep chief exec 1990–94, chief exec 1994–2005; sr policy advsr Dept of Health 2005, chief exec RCP 2005–13, ret; dir RCP Regent's Park Ltd 2005–13; cmmr Liverpool Healthcare Cmmn 2013–14; hon sec, treas and special tstee Royal Free Hosp 1986–2005, tstee Appeal Tst for the Royal Free Hosp 1988–92, chm Mgmnt Ctee Cancerkin charity 1990–94; variously memb nat NHS ctees incl: Costing for Contracting Steering Gp (chm 1994–97), Nat Steering Gp on Costing (chm 1997–2001), Estate Info Review Ctee 1994–97, Review of Financial Regime for NHS Tsts 1995–96, Nat Programme Co-ordination Bd 1996–98, Fin Issues Gp 1997–98, Regnl Advsy Ctee on Distinction Awards 1998–2001, Chief Executive's Information Mgmnt and Technol Forum 1998–2001; variously memb NHS nat influence gps incl: NAHAT (now NHS Confedn) Contracting and Resource Gp 1991–97, Tst Fedn Fin and Capital Standing Ctee 1994–97 (chm of Fin Dirs), Main Universities Teaching Hosps Tsts 1991–94 (fndr memb and former chm of Fin Dirs); CIPFA/Healthcare Fin Mangrs Assoc: memb Provider Mgmnt Gp 1993–94, memb Risk Mgmnt Review 1994; lectr to various orgns incl London Business Sch, Royal Free Sch of Med, City Univ, King's Fund, Audit Cmmn, Dept of Health Mgmnt Exec and CIPFA Conf and to professional health gps incl Coll of Radiographers and RCN; chair London Agency Project 1999–, tstee Hampstead Wells and Camden Tst 1996–2005, dir and treas Alzheimer's Disease Int (ADI) 2005–13, tstee Friends of ADI 2005–, dir and tstee Confidential Reporting System for Surgery (CORESS) 2006–; memb CIPFA 1979, MHSM 1994, Hon FRCP 2013; *Recreations* football, cricket, golf, horse racing; *Style*— Martin Else, Esq; ✉ Chief Executive's Office, Royal College of Physicians, 11 St Andrew's Place, Regent's Park, London NW1 4LE (☎ 020 7935 1174)

ELSON, Andrew Charles (Andy); s of Donald Frederick Elson (d 1995), and Phyllis Elson (d 2015); *b* 9 June 1953; *m* (m dis); 2 da (Victoria, Emily); *Career* aeronautical engr and balloonist; apprentice Rolls Royce Technical Coll, estab own engrg co, currently researcher, designer and pilot of hot air balloons; pilot world's first hot air balloon flight over Mt Everest 1991, designer and co-pilot Brietling Orbiter II balloon flight Switzerland to Burma 1998 (9 days 17 hours, 55 mins), co-pilot Cable and Wireless balloon flight Spain to Japan 1999 (17 days, 18 hours, 25 mins, a record for non-stop sub-orbital flight), designed and constructed Solo Spirit gondola for Steve Fossett's solo around the world balloon attempt 2001, pilot, designer and project dir QinetiQ 1 project 2002–; Royal Aero Club: Salomons Trophy 1991, Gold Medal 1999; *Recreations* extreme sports, mountain biking, cave-diving, heliskiing, mountain climbing; *Style*— Andy Elson, Esq

ELSTEIN, David Keith; s of Albert Elstein (d 1983), and Millie Cohen (d 1985); *b* 14 November 1944; *Educ* Haberdashers' Aske's, Gonville & Caius Coll Cambridge (MA); *m* 16 July 1978, Jenny, da of Alfred Conway; 1 s (Daniel b 1981); *Career* prodr: BBC 1964–68, Thames Television 1968–72, LWT 1972–73; ed This Week and exec prodr documentaries Thames Television 1973–82, exec prodr Goldcrest TV 1982–83, md and exec prodr Brook Productions 1982–86, md and exec prodr Primetime TV 1983–86, dir of progs Thames Television 1986–93, head of programming Sky TV 1993–96, chief exec Channel 5 1996–2000; chm: Br Screen Advsy Cncl 1997–, Really Useful Theatres Ltd 2001–, Screen Digest Ltd 2003–, Broadcasting Policy Gp 2003–, Sports Network plc 2004–, Commercial Radio Companies Assoc 2004–, Sparrowhawk Investments Ltd 2004–, Digital Classics 2005–, Luther Pendragon Hldgs 2006–, openDemocracy; vice-chm Kingsbridge Capital Ltd 2003–; non-exec dir NTL Inc 2003–; visiting prof: Univ of Stirling 1995–, Univ of Oxford 1998–99, Univ of Westminster 2001–04; James McTaggart meml lectr Edinburgh Int Television Festival 1991, Forman lectr 1995, Raymond Williams lectr 1997, Goodman lectr 1998, Bernard Simons lectr 1999; Media Achiever of the Year Campaign Media Awards 1998; *Publications* Beyond the Charter: The Future of the BBC (2004); *Recreations* cinema, theatre, bridge, reading; *Style*— David Elstein, Esq

ELSTON, John Scorgie; s of Charles Henry Elston, of West Kirby, Merseyside, and Hilda Constance Mary Elston (d 1986); *b* 22 March 1949; *Educ* St Bees Sch Cumberland, St Thomas' Hosp Med Sch (BSc, MB BS); *Partner* Frederika Estelle Smith; 1 da (Charlotte Rose Scorgie b 10 June 1990), 1 s (Guy Scorgie b 11 March 1993); *Career* med practitioner; house appts in gen med and surgery before specialising in ophthalmology; trg in ophthalmology: St Thomas' Hosp 1975–78, Moorfields Eye Hosp 1979–87, Hosp for Sick Children 1983–87; conslt ophthalmologist: Nat Hosp for Neurology and Neurosurgery 1987–91, St Mary's Hosp London 1987–91, Western Ophthalmic Hosp London 1987–91, Radcliffe Infirmary Oxford 1991–; FRCS 1982, FRSM 1988, FRCOphth 1989, MD 1990; *Books* Dystonia II (jtly, 1987), Pediatric Ophthalmology (jtly, 1990, 3 edn 2005), Scientific Basis of Neurosurgery (jtly, 1991, 2 edn 1999), Community Paediatrics (jtly, 1991), Clinical Uses of Botulinum Toxin (jtly, 2007), Training in Ophthalmology (jtly, 2009); *Recreations* golf, tennis, walking, English literature; *Clubs* RSM; *Style*— John Elston, Esq; ✉ Oxford Eye Hospital, John Radcliffe Hospital, Oxford OX3 9DU (☎ 01865 234151, e-mail jselston@hotmail.com)

ELSTOW, Clare Marie Michelle; da of Geoffrey Charles Elstow, and Marie Patricia, *née* Ferriday; *Educ* Notre Dame HS Northampton, UCL (BA); *m*; 2 c; *Career* studio mangr BBC Radio 1977–82, studio mangr and composer BBC Radiophonic Workshop 1979, asst prodr rising to exec prodr BBC Educn 1983–2000, head of pre-school/CBeebies prodn BBC Children's 2000–06 (creative conslt 2006–); Hosa Bunka Award for Pre-School Excellence (Japan Prize) for Words and Pictures series 1992, RTS Educn Award for Numbertime 1994, RTS Educn Razzledazzle Award 2006, Bafta Award for (Boogie Beebies) 2006; govr Dr Challoner's HS for Girls; memb: Nat Childbirth Tst, NSPCC, Fawcett Soc, Friends of UCL, Amnesty Int, Friends of the Earth, Intermediate Technol; supporter Medical Fndn; *Recreations* music, creative writing, gardening, reading; *Style*— Ms Clare Elstow

ELSY, Richard (Dick); *b* 4 November 1959, South Shields, Tyne and Wear; *Educ* Durham Sch, Loughborough Univ; *m* Margaret; 1 da (Hannah); *Career* Land Rover: devpt engr rising to chief engr for vehicle engrg 1983–91, product dir Discover 1991–93, project dir Freelander and dir Rover Australia 1993–98; project dir BMW AG 1999; Jaguar Cars Ltd: dir of product engrg 1999–2002, product devpt dir 2002–03; ceo Torotrak plc 2003–12, ceo High Value Manufacturing Catapult 2012–; dir Rotrex AS 2010–12, dir AIRTO 2015–; former dir and tstee Engrg UK; Royal Acad of Engrg Silver Medal 1998; CEng, FIMechE, FIET; *Style*— Dick Elsy, Esq; ✉ HVM Catapult, The Oracle Building, Blythe Valley Business Park, Solihull B90 8AD

ELTON, 2 Baron (UK 1934); Rodney Elton; TD (1970); s of 1 Baron Elton (d 1973), and Dedi (d 1977), da of Gustav Hartmann, of Oslo, Norway; *b* 2 March 1930; *Educ* Eton, New Coll Oxford, Northants Inst of Agriculture Moulton; *m* 1, 18 Sept 1958 (sep 1973, m dis 1979), Anne Frances, da of late Brig Robert Adolphus George Tilney, CBE, DSO, TD, DL; 1 s, 3 da; m 2, 24 Aug 1979, (Susan) Richenda (The Lady Elton, DCVO), yst da of late Sir Hugh Gurney, KCMG, MVO; *Heir* s, Hon Edward Paget Elton; *Career* formerly: farmer, teacher and lectr; contested (Cons) Loughborough 1966 and 1970; oppn spokesman Educn and Welsh Affrs 1974–79, dep sec Int Affrs Ctee of Gen Synod of C of E 1976–78, dep chm Andry Montgomery Ltd 1977–79 and 1987–2003; memb Boyd Cmmn (Southern Rhodesia elections 1979); Parly under sec of state: NI Office 1979–81, DHSS 1981–82, Home Office 1982–84; min of state Home Office 1984–85, DOE 1985–86; vice-chm Parly All Party Norwegian Gp 1996–; memb: Select Ctee on the Scrutiny of Delegated Powers 1992–96, Select Ctee on the Constitution 2003–08; a dep chm of Ctees House of Lords 1997–2008 (dep speaker 1999–2008), elected hereditary peer House of Lords 1999–; dep chm Assoc of Cons Peers 1988–93; memb Panel on Takeovers and Mergers 1987–90; chm: FIMBRA 1987–90, Enquiry into Discipline in Schs 1988, Intermediate Treatment Fund 1990–93, Divert Tst 1993–99 (pres 1999–2002); pres Bldg Conservation Tst 1990–95, tstee City Parochial Fndn & Tst for London 1991–97; chm Quality and Standards Ctee C&G 1999–2005; hon vice-pres Inst of Trading Standards Admin; licensed lay min C of E 1998–; Hon FCGI; *Clubs* Cavalry and Guards', Beefsteak, Pratt's; *Style*— The Rt Hon the Lord Elton, TD; ✉ House of Lords, London SW1A 0PW

ELVIDGE, Sir John William; KCB (2006); s of late Herbert William Elvidge, and late Irene Teresa, *née* Reynolds; *b* 9 February 1951; *Educ* Sir George Monoux Sch Walthamstow, St Catherine's Coll Oxford (BA); *m* Maureen Margaret Ann, *née* McGinn; *Career* Scottish Office: joined as admin trainee 1973, various posts in educn, housing and tport, higher exec offr (A) 1976–78, princ 1978–84, asst sec and fin offr Scottish Economic Planning and Devpt Depts 1984, seconded as dir of implementation Scottish Homes 1988–89, asst sec 1989–93, under sec Industry and Devpt Depts 1993–98; dep head Economic and Domestic Secretariat Cabinet Office 1998–99; sec and head Scottish Exec Educn Dept 1999–2002, sec and head Scottish Exec Fin and Central Services Dept 2002–03; permanent sec Scottish Executive 2003–07, perm sec Scottish Govt 2007–10; chm Edinburgh Airport 2012–; adjunct prof Overseas Educn Coll Shanghai Jiao Tong Univ 2013–; FRSE; *Publications* Northen Exposure: Lessons from the first 12 years of devolution (2011), The Enabling State: a discussion document (2012), Scotland's Future: the economics of constitutional change (contrib, 2013), Remembering Sam (contrib, 2016); *Recreations* painting, film, theatre, modern novels, music, swimming, walking, food and drink; *Style*— Sir John Elvidge, KCB; ✉ 6 Sciennes Gardens, Edinburgh EH9 1NR (☎ 0131 668 3501, e-mail sirjohn.elvidge@btinternet.com)

ELVIN, Andy; *b* 3 January 1970, London; *Educ* Liverpool John Moores Univ (BA), Univ of Kent at Canterbury (MA); *Career* former children and families social worker, dir Soho Family Centre 2001–06, project mangr Children's Centres and Extended Schs London Borough of Richmond 2006–09, chief exec Children and Families Across Borders 2009–; *Recreations* theatre, Luton Town FC; *Style*— Andy Elvin, Esq; ✉ CFAB, Canterbury Court, Unit 1.03, 1–3 Brixton Road, London SW9 6DE (website www.cfab.uk.net)

ELVIN, Jo; da of Harry Elvin, of Sydney, Aust, and Leonie, *née* Burgess; *b* 21 February 1970; *Educ* Cambridge Park HS, Univ of Western Sydney; *m* 29 Jan 2000, Ross Jones; 1 da (Evie); *Career* dep ed TV Hits magazine 1993–94; ed: Sugar magazine 1994–96, B magazine 1996–98, New Woman magazine 1998–2000, Glamour magazine 2000–; contrib of articles to The Independent, Evening Standard, The Observer and Media Week; featured in TV series Model Behaviour (Channel 4), also numerous TV, radio and public speaking appearances; memb: BSME, Women in Journalism; Ed of the Year BSME 1995, 1996 and 2002, Launch Ed of the Year BSME 2001, Editors' Ed of the Year BSME 2002; *Clubs* Groucho, Adam Street; *Style*— Ms Jo Elvin; ✉ Glamour Magazine, 6–8 Old Bond Street, London W1S 4PH (☎ 020 7499 9080, fax 020 7491 2597, e-mail editor@glamourmagazine.co.uk)

ELWES, Sir Henry William George; KCVO (2009), JP; s of Maj John Hargreaves Elwes, MC, Scots Gds (ka N Africa 1943), and Isabel Pamela Ivy, *née* Beckwith (later Mrs John Talbot, d 1993), gda of 7 Duke of Richmond and Gordon; *b* 24 October 1935; *Educ* Eton, RAC Cirencester; *m* 8 Sept 1962, Carolyn Dawn, da of Joseph William Wykeham Cripps (d 1958), of Ampney Crucis, Glos (3 cous of the post war chllr Sir Stafford Cripps); 3 s (John b 1964, Frederick b 1966, George b 1971 d 1993); *Career* late Lt Scots Gds; farmer and forester; chm Western Woodland Owners Ltd 1971–86 (pres 1986–2003), regnl dir Lloyds Bank plc 1985–91, dir Colebourne Estate Co; former patron, pres or memb of many Glos tsts and socs; memb: Cirencester Rural Dist Cncl 1959–74, Glos CC 1971–91 (vice-chm 1976–83 and 1991, chm 1983–85); hon lay canon Gloucester Cathedral 2001–; pro-chllr Univ of Glos 2012–; High Sheriff Glos 1979–80; Hon Alderman Glos 1992; HM Lord-Lt Glos 1992–2010 (DL 1982); hon fell Royal Agricultural Univ 2010; Liveryman Worshipful Co of Gardeners, Fndr and Warden Emeritus Honourable Co of Glos; Hon DPhil Univ of Glos 2002, Hon LLD UWE 2006; *Clubs* Confrerie des Chevaliers du Tastevin; *Style*— Sir Henry Elwes, KCVO; ✉ Colesbourne Park, Gloucestershire GL53 9NP (☎ 01242 870262, e-mail hwg@globalnet.co.uk)

ELWES, Nigel Robert; CBE (2008); s of late Maj Robert Philip Henry Elwes, MBE, MC, of Ballinafad, Ireland, and his 1 wife, late Vivien Elizabeth Fripp, *née* Martin-Smith; *b* 8 August 1941, Hitchin, Herts; *Educ* Eton; *m* 22 June 1965, Carolyn Peta, da of late Sir Robin McAlpine, CBE; 2 da (Serena (Mrs Jeremy Bradbeer) b 1967, Melisa (Mrs Nicholas Aikenhead) b 1973), 1 s (Andrew b 1969); *Career* CA, stockbroker, farmer and bloodstock breeder; ptnr Rowe & Pitman 1970–86, fin dir S G Warburg Securities 1986–91, chm Reyker Securities Ltd 1991–94; Stock Exchange: joined 1970, memb Cncl 1983–86 and 1988–91, chm Domestic Equity Market Ctee 1988–91, chm Special Ctee on Market Devpt (Elwes Ctee); ptnr: Aylesfield Farms 1991–, Aylesfield Farms Stud 1993–; dir Kempton Park Racecourse Co Ltd 2003–; chm: Cncl Thoroughbred Breeders' Assoc 1997–2003 (memb 2006–11), Racing Welfare 2000–08 (vice-chm 1992–2000), Stable Lads Welfare Tst 2000–01 (vice-chm 1993–2000), Br Racing Sch 2004–11 (tstee 1992–2003); dir Br Horseracing Bd 1999–2003 (memb Race Planning Ctee 1996–99); dir Dorchester Hotel 1974–76, dir Jeddah Blookstock Ltd 2009–; govr Lord Mayor Treloar Sch 1992–2000; MSI; *Recreations* hunting, shooting, racing; *Clubs* White's (chm House Ctee 1997–2000), Jockey; *Style*— Nigel Elwes, Esq, CBE; ✉ Mulberry House, Dummer, Basingstoke, RG25 2AF (☎ 01256 541 535)

ELWORTHY, Air Cdre the Hon Sir Timothy Charles; KCVO (2001, CVO 1995), CBE (1986); eldest s of Marshal of the RAF Baron Elworthy, KG, GCB, CBE, DSO, LVO, DFC, AFC (Life Peer, d 1993), and Audrey, *née* Hutchinson (d 1986); *b* 27 January 1938; *Educ* Radley, RAF Coll Cranwell; *m* 1, 1961 (m dis 1969), Victoria Ann, eldest da of late Lt-Col H C W Bowring; 2 da (Katharine Emma Victoria b 1963, Lucinda Rose b 1965); m 2, 1971, Anabel, da of late Reginald Ernest Harding, OBE; 1 s (Edward Charles b 1974); *Career* RAF; Capt of The Queen's Flight 1989–94, Extra Equerry to HM The Queen 1991–, HM's Sr Air Equerry 1995–2001, dir of Royal Travel 1997–2001; QCVSA 1968; *Recreations* country pursuits, wine, travel; *Clubs* Boodle's; *Style*— Air Cdre the Hon Sir Timothy Elworthy, KCVO, CBE; ✉ Coates House, Swyncombe, Henley-on-Thames, Oxfordshire RG9 6EG

ELY, Bishop of 2010–; Rt Rev Stephen Conway; *Career* ordained: deacon 1986, priest 1987; in ministry dio of Durham, archdeacon of Durham and canon treasurer Durham Cathedral 2002–06, bishop of Ramsbury 2006–10; *Style*— The Rt Rev the Bishop of Ely

ELYAN, David Asher Gremson; s of Max Elyan (d 2002), and Freda, *née* Gremson (d 2006); *b* 4 October 1940; *Educ* Cork GS, TCD (BA, BCom, MA); *Career* co sec Gordon & Gotch Hldgs plc 1970–74, assoc dir AGB Research plc 1980–87 (co sec 1974–87); dir: Attwood Research of Ireland Ltd 1981–90, Irish TAM Ltd 1981–90, Corporate Lease Mgmnt Ltd 1984–93, Elyan Estates Ltd 1987–93, Communication Investments Ltd 1987–2006, Langton Software Ltd 1987–2002, Bankside Gallery Ltd 1992–2003 (sec 1992–2009), CLM Fleet Mgmnt plc 1993–96, Wigmore Investments Ltd 1994–, Royal Albert Hall Devpts Ltd 2000–, Manx Public Art 2001–07, Mediterranean Inst Malta 2003–13; hon treas: TCD Dining Club 1968–94 (vice-chm 1994–), Friends of Royal Watercolour Soc 1990–1994; memb: Senate Univ of Dublin 1966–, Corp of Lloyds 1983–, Post Office Advsy Ctee (POAC) 1991–98, Cncl Royal Albert Hall 1996–, Isle of Man Arts Cncl (visual arts panel) 2000–02, Cncl Music Club of London 2003–06; chm Friends of Royal Acad of Music 1993–2000, tstee: Fenton Arts Tst 2004–12, Santander Charitable Fndn 2009–11, Manx Nat Heritage 2012–; Freeman City of London, Liveryman Worshipful Co of Chartered Secs 1978; hon fell: Univ of Malta 2000, Univ of Glos 2008; ACCS 1967, FRSA 1972, FCIS 1976 (ACIS 1969), Hon ARAM 1999, Hon RWS 2012; *Recreations* collecting first editions, tennis, art, music, bridge; *Clubs* MCC, Casino Maltese, Union (Malta); *Style*— David Elyan, Esq; ✉ 49 Chester Court, Regent's Park, London NW1 4BU; 31 Woodbourne Road, Douglas, Isle of Man IM2 3AB

ELYSTAN-MORGAN, Baron (Life Peer UK 1981), of Aberteifi in the County of Dyfed; (Dafydd) Elystan Elystan-Morgan; s of Dewi Morgan (d 1971), of Llandre, Aberystwyth, and Olwen Morgan (d 1947); *b* 7 December 1932; *Educ* Ardwyn GS Aberystwyth, UCW Aberystwyth (LLB); *m* 1959, Alwen (d 2006), *née* Roberts; 1 da (Hon Eleri (Hon Mrs Hurt) b 1960), 1 s (Hon Owain b 1962); *Career* sat as Lab Peer in House of Lords 1981–87, MP (Lab) Cardiganshire 1966–74, Parly under sec of state Home Office 1968–70, pres Welsh Local Authorities Assoc 1967–73, chm Welsh Parly Party 1967–68; called to the Bar Gray's Inn 1971; recorder (Wales & Chester Circuit) 1983–87, circuit judge (Wales & Chester Circuit) 1987–2003; dep High Court judge 1989–2003; hon fell UCW Aberystwyth 1991 (vice-pres 1992–97, pres and chm Cncl 1997–2007), pres Sch of Welsh Legal Affrs 2001–; DCL (hc) Univ of Wales 2015; *Style*— His Hon Lord Elystan-Morgan; ✉ House of Lords, London SW1A 0PW

EMANUEL, David Leslie; s of John Lawrence Morris Emanuel, and Elizabeth Emanuel (decd); *b* 17 November 1952, Wales; *Educ* Cardiff Coll of Art (dip), Harrow Sch of Art (dip), RCA (MA); *m* 1975 (sep), Elizabeth Emanuel, *qv*; 1 s (Oliver), 1 da (Eloise); *Career* fashion designer; early career experience at Hardy Amies, Cojana and Marcel Fenez (with Roland Klein); fndr ptnr (with wife) Emanuel 1977–90 (designers of HRH The Princess of Wales' wedding dress), fndr David Emanuel Couture 1990–; TV work incl: co-presenter Swank (ITV) 1994, Frock Doctor (ABC, USA) 1995, Designed by Emanuel (own series for HTV), The David Emanuel Fashion Show (GSB), co-hosted Afternoon Live (ITV) 1997; finale spot: Night of 100 Stars Gala Fashion Show (Radio City Hall NY) 1984, Fashion Aid (with Bob Geldof, Royal Albert Hall) 1985, Fashion Aid Japan (Tokyo) 1986, 150th Anniversary Celebration of RCA Art Gala Fashion Show 1987; designs for ballet prodns incl Frankenstein, the Modern Prometheus (Royal Opera House Covent Garden 1985 and La Scala Milan 1987); FCSD; *Books* Style for All Seasons (1983); *Recreations* sport (horse riding, tennis, jet/water skiing), the arts; *Clubs* Royal Ascot Tennis, White Elephant; *Style*— David Emanuel, Esq

EMANUEL, Elizabeth Florence; da of Samuel Charles Weiner (Croix de Guerre), of Warfield, Berks, and Brahna Betty, *née* Charkham; *b* 5 July 1953; *Educ* City of London Sch for Girls, Harrow Coll of Art, Royal Coll of Art (MA); *m* 12 July 1975 (sep 1990), David Leslie Emanuel, *qv*, s of John Lawrence Morris Emanuel; 1 s (Oliver b 21 March 1978), 1 da (Eloise b 25 Dec 1979); *Career* fashion designer; opened London Salon 1978, designed wedding dress for HRH Princess of Wales 1981, launched new shop and design studio 1996, launched own brand label (with backer Richard Thompson) 1999; theatre designs incl: costumes for Andrew Lloyd Webber's Song and Dance 1982, sets and costumes for ballet Frankenstein – The Modern Prometheus (Royal Opera House Covent Garden, La Scala Milan) 1985, costumes for Stoll Moss prodn of Cinderella 1985; designed uniforms for: Virgin Atlantic Airlines 1990, Britannia Airways 1996; launched international fashion label under own name 1992, costumes for film The Changeling 1995, designed new range for Berkertex Brides 1994, launched new wedding lifestyle range in Japan 1994, designed Elizabeth Hurley's dress for Esteé Lauder Beautiful campaign 1996–98 and Pleasures campaign 1999, costume design for short film Ros Beef 2003; active involvement with charities: Born Free Fndn, WWF, WSPA, London Lighthouse, IFAW; FCSD 1984; *Books* Style For All Seasons (with David Emanuel, 1983); *Recreations* music, ballet, cinema; *Clubs* Chelsea Arts; *Style*— Mrs Elizabeth Emanuel

EMBERSON, Eleanor; *Educ* Arran HS, Univ of St Andrews; *Career* former chief exec Scottish Ct Service, dir of financial strategy and head Revenue Scotland 2012–15, CE of Revenue Scotland 2015–; *Style*— Ms Eleanor Emberson; ✉ Scottish Government, Victoria Quay, Edinburgh EH6 6QQ

EMBERY, Prof Graham; s of Joseph Henry Embery (d 1987), and Elizabeth Jane; *b* 20 August 1939; *Educ* King Edward VI GS Stourbridge; *m* 14 Jan 1967, Vivienne Lacey, da of William Horace Powell (d 1973); 1 da (Philippa Jane b 24 June 1970), 2 s (Russell Geraint b 25 Nov 1971, James Toby William b 30 Dec 1973); *Career* lectr Queen's Univ Belfast 1968–70, lectr Royal Dental Hosp 1970–73, reader Univ of Liverpool 1984–87 (lectr 1973–77, sr lectr 1977–84), prof of basic dental sci Univ of Wales Coll of Med Cardiff 1987–2001, prof of dental sci and dean Univ of Liverpool Dental Sch 2001–; sec-gen Cncl of Euro Study Gp for Res on Surface and Colloidal Phenomena in the Oral Cavity; memb: Int Assoc for Dental Res, Br Connective Tissue Soc, Biochemical Soc, Jt Dental Ctee MRC 1991–95, Sci and Engrg Res Cncl and Health Authorities 1991–, Res Assessment Panel in Clinical Dentistry 1999–; pres: Br Soc for Dental Res 1994–96, Int Assoc for Dental Res 1999–; treas European Orgn for Caries Res 1994–96, Welsh Devpt Scheme for Health and Social Res 1995–99, Welsh NHS R&D Forum 1995–98; Colgate Prize 1973, IADR Distinguished Scientist Prize in Oral Biology; Hon DSc Univ of Wales; memb (fell) RSM; *Books* Clinical and Biological Aspects Dentifrizes (trans Japanese 2003); author of over 250 publications and articles; *Recreations* golf, oil painting, classic cars; *Style*— Prof Graham Embery; ✉ 16 Townfield Road, West Kirby, Wirral, Merseyside L48 7EZ (☎ 0151 625 5954); Department of Clinical Dental Sciences, University of Liverpool Dental School, Edwards Research Building, Liverpool L69 3GN (☎ 0151 706 5252/5275, fax 0151 706 5809, e-mail g.embery@liverpool.ac.uk)

EMBIRICOS, Epaminondas George; s of George Epaminondas Embiricos (d 1980), of Athens, and Sophie, *née* Douma (d 1999); *b* 15 July 1943; *Educ* Philips Exeter Acad New Hampshire USA, MIT (BSc, MSc); *m* 19 March 1977, Angela, da of Nicholas Pittas, of London; 2 s (George Epaminondas b 8 May 1978, Nicholas Epaminondas b 8 June 1980); *Career* chm: Embiricos Shipping Agency Ltd 1969–91, Embiricos Shipbrokers Ltd 1991–, Chartering Brokers Mutual Insurance Assoc 1999–2002; dir: Liberian Shipowners Cncl 1979–84, Baltic Exchange Ltd 1985–90; chm Greek Ctee Det Norske Veritas 1997–2001

E

(memb 1986–2001, vice-chm 1987–97), vice-chm Greek Shipping Co-op Ctee 1986–99; chm UK Freight Demurrage and Def Assoc 1993–96 (dir 1984–99), chm Greek Shipping Co-op Ctee 1999–2010; memb: American Bureau of Shipping 1990–, Br Ctee American Bureau of Shipping 1994–, Cncl of the Union of Greek Shipowners 1996–2009, Det Norske Veritas Classification Ctee 1997–2000, Visiting Ctee of the Dept of Ocean Engrg of MIT 1998–2002; ex officio memb Lloyd's Register Gen Ctee 2000–04; Freeman City of London 1984, memb Ct of Assts Worshipful Co of Shipwrights 1994 (Liveryman 1985); *Recreations* sailing, reading; *Clubs* Royal Thames Yacht, Royal Yacht Club of Greece; *Style*— Epaminondas Embiricos, Esq; ✉ 6th Floor, 100 New Oxford Street, London WC1A 1HB (✆ 020 7404 0420, fax 020 7400 0887)

EMBLEY, Lloyd; *b* 16 March 1966; *Educ* Malvern Coll; *Career* Daily Mirror: asst night ed 1999–2001, night ed 2001–04, asst ed 2004–08; ed: The People 2008–12, Daily Mirror 2012–, Sunday Mirror 2012–; *Style*— Lloyd Embley, Esq; ✉ Daily Mirror, 1 Canada Square, Canary Wharf, London E14 5AP

EMERSON, Michael Ronald; s of late James Emerson, of Wilmslow, Cheshire, and Priscilla Emerson; *b* 12 May 1940; *Educ* Hurstpierpoint Coll and Balliol Coll Oxford (MA); *m* 1966, Barbara Christine, da of late Harold Brierley; 1 s, 2 da; *Career* Price Waterhouse & Co London 1962–65; Orgn for Economic Cooperation and Devpt Paris: posts Devpt and Econs Depts, laterally head of General Economics Div 1966–73; EEC Brussels: head of Div for Budgetary Policy Directorate-Gen II 1973–76, econ advsr to President of the Commission 1977, dir for Nat Econs and Econ Trends 1978–81, dir Macroeconomic Analyses and Policy 1981–87, dir Econ Evaluation of Community Policies Directorate-Gen II EC Cmmn Brussels 1987–90, ambass and head of delgn of the EC to the USSR and Russia 1991–96; fell Centre for Int Affairs Harvard Univ 1985–86; sr research fell: LSE 1996–98, Centre for European Policy Studies Brussels 1998–; *Publications* Europe's Stagflation (ed, 1984), What Model for Europe (1987), The Economics of 1992 (1988), One Money, One Market (1990), The ECU Report (1991); contrib to various economic jls and ed of volumes on int and Euro economics; *Style*— Michael Emerson, Esq

EMERSON, Ronald Victor; s of Albert Victor Emerson, and Doris, *née* Hird; *b* 22 February 1947; *Educ* W Hartlepool GS, Univ of Manchester (BSc), Univ of Durham (MSc), Univ of Oxford (MLitt, MA); *m* 1, 21 June 1969, Joan Margaret (d 1988), da of James Hubery Willis; 2 s (Christopher Mark b 28 May 1971, Simon Nicholas b 5 March 1975); m 2, 13 July 1996, Angela Jane, da of Dr K Stephenson; 2 s (Thomas Harry b 29 Nov 1996, William Alexander b 11 June 1998); *Career* De La Rue Gp 1970–75, commercial devpt controller Formica International; Bank of America: joined 1975, head of London corp office and UK country mangr 1985–89, head of payment servs and fin insts Europe Middle East and Africa 1989; dir and gen mangr Nomura Bank International 1989–91, regnl gen mangr UK/Europe Standard Chartered Bank 1991–94, ceo Standard Chartered Malaysia Berhad 1994–95, gp head corp banking Standard Chartered Bank 1995–96, sr advsr Bank of England 1997–98, sr advsr Fin Services Authy 1998–2000; non-exec dir: Premier Oil plc 2001–08, Ace European Gp Ltd 2005–12, Noventa Ltd 2007–09, Habib Gp 2008–14; chm Fairfield Energy Ltd 2010–16, chm Br Business Bank plc 2013–; assoc fell: Templeton Coll Oxford 2001–12, Said Business Sch Univ of Oxford 2005–16; Barclay fell Green Templeton Coll Univ of Oxford 2014–; FRSA, FIoD; *Recreations* flying, sport, reading; *Clubs* Oxford and Cambridge; *Style*— Ronald Emerson, Esq

EMERTON, Baroness (Life Peer UK 1997), of Tunbridge Wells, in the County of Kent and of Clerkenwell in the London Borough of Islington; Dame Audrey Caroline Emerton; DBE (1989), DL (Kent 1992); da of George William Emerton (d 1971), of Tunbridge Wells, Kent, and Lily Harriet, *née* Squirrell; *b* 10 September 1935; *Educ* Tunbridge Wells GS, Battersea Coll of Technol; *Career* SRN 1956; sr tutor St George's Hosp London 1968, princ nursing offr teaching Bromley HMC 1968–70, chief nursing offr Tunbridge Wells and Leybourne HMC 1970–73, regnl nursing offr SE Thames RHA 1973–91; chief nursing offr St John Ambulance 1988–96 (co nursing offr 1970–84, Kent co cmmr 1984–88), chief offr Care in the Community 1996–98 (chief cdr 1998–2002); chm: Eng Nat Bd for Nurses Midwives and Health Visitors 1983–85, UK Central Cncl Nursing Midwives and Health Visitors 1985–93, Nurses Welfare Service 1992–98, Brighton Health Care NHS Trust 1994–2000, Nat Assoc of Hosp and Community Friends 2003–06; tstee: Kent Community Housing Tst 1992–98, Defence Med Welfare Serv 2001–, Burdett Nursing Tst 2002–04; lay memb GMC 1996–2001; pres Florence Nightingale Fndn 2004–; Hon DCL Univ of Kent 1989, Hon DUniv Central England 1997, Hon DSc Univ of Brighton 1997, Hon DSc Kingston Univ; hon fell Christ Church UC Canterbury 2003, Hon FKC 2009; FRCN 2009, FRSA; DGCStJ 2004 (DStJ 1993); *Style*— The Rt Hon Baroness Emerton, DBE, DL; ✉ House of Lords, London SW1A 0PW

EMERTON, Mark Simon; s of Rev Prof John Emerton (d 2015), and Dr Norma Emerton, *née* Bennington, of Cambridge; *b* 26 February 1961; *Educ* Perse Sch Cambridge, BRNC Dartmouth, St Peter's Coll Oxford (MA), City Univ (Dip), Univ of Portsmouth (LLM, Sherwin Oliver Prize), Cardiff Univ (LLM); *m* 16 July 1994, Hannah Kate, da of Martin Buckley (d 2014); 3 da (Rebecca b 23 Sept 1997, Susanna b 24 Aug 1999, Martha b 7 April 2001); *Career* RN: joined 1979, various appts as supply offr and naval barr incl Supply Offr HMS Brilliant 1992–93, judge advocate at Naval Courts-Martial 1997–2002, dep chief naval judge advocate 1997–98, judge advocate Summary Appeal Court 2000–02, ret as Cdr; called to the Bar Gray's Inn 1991; cmmr Criminal Cases Review Cmmn 2002–09, salaried employment judge London S Region 2009–16 and SW Region 2016–; pt/t appts: parking adjudicator 2000–10, immigration judge 2000–, employment judge 2000–09, legal assessor to GMC 2002–11, chm Investigating Ctee GDC 2009–14; memb: Barrs Ctee Gray's Inn 2001–, Remuneration Ctee Bar Cncl 2003, Employed Barrs Ctee Bar Cncl 2004–09 (vice-chm 2009), Public Affrs Ctee Bar Cncl 2009, Srs-in-Hall Panel Gray's Inn 2012–; ind bd memb Office of the Ind Adjudicator for HE 2004–10, ind scrutiny panel memb UK Sport Nat Anti-Doping Organisation 2005–09; govr RNLI 1994–2013 (branch ctee memb 1996–2007); govr Solent Infant Sch 2003–07, medico-legal advsr St John Ambulance 2008–12, memb Ctee Ecclesiastical Law Soc 2012–, memb Portsmouth Deanery Synod 2012–, memb Portsmouth Diocesan Synod 2012–, memb Gen Synod C of E 2015– (memb Appeal Panel 2015–), memb Remuneration and Conditions of Service Ctee Archbishops' Cncl 2016–; assoc memb Centre for Law and Religion Cardiff Univ; FRGS 1984, FCMI 2004 (MIMgt 1995), FRSM 2009; *Publications* Manual of Naval Law (ed, 1997), Halsbury's Laws of England (contrib, 4 edn 2003), contrib to Ecclesiastical Law Jl; *Recreations* family, theatre and the arts, conservation of the natural and built environment, travel, the sea; *Clubs* Naval and Military; *Style*— Mark Emerton, Esq; ✉ Employment Tribunals, 100 The Avenue, Southampton, Hants SO17 1EY (✆ 023 8038 4200)

EMERY, Prof Alan Eglin Heathcote; s of Harold Heathcote-Emery (d 1977), and Alice, *née* Eglin (d 1972); *b* 21 August 1928; *Educ* Chester Coll, Univ of Manchester (BSc, MSc, MB ChB, MD, DSc), Johns Hopkins Univ USA (PhD); *m* 13 Oct 1988, Marcia Lynn, da of John Miller (d 1986), of Cleveland, USA; *Career* Nat Serv 14/20 Kings Hussars 1947–49; conslt physician 1966–; emeritus prof and hon fell Univ of Edinburgh 1983– (prof of human genetics 1968–83), hon visiting fell Green Coll Oxford 1986–2006 (hon fell 2006–), res dir and chm Euro Neuromuscular Center 1990–99 (chief scientific advsr 1999–), hon prof Peninsula Med Sch Exeter 2006–; foreign assoc RSS Africa; vice-pres Muscular Dystrophy Gp of GB 1999–; memb: Exec Ctee World Fedn Neurology 1994–2002, RSL; advsr Asian Myology Centre Tokyo 2000–; pres Medical Genetics section RSM 2002–04; author of various articles in learned scientific and medical jls; various professorships, lectureships and awards incl Nat Fndn Int Award (USA), Pro Finlandiae Gold Medal, Conte Prize (Italy) 2000, Association Francaise Contre Les Myopathies Prize 2001, Lifetime Achievement Award World Fedn of Neurology 2002, Alumnus of the Year and Cockcroft Medal Univ of Manchester 2006, Double Day Award 2007, American Soc of Human Genetics Int Award for Excellence in Human Genetics Educn 2012, Lifetime Achievement Award Muscular Dystrophy Campaign UK 2012; Hon MD: Univ of Naples, Univ of Würzburg, Univ of Athens; Hon DSc Univ of Chester; hon memb Gaetano Conte Acad (Italy); emeritus fell American Coll of Med Genetics; hon fell: Assoc Br Neurology, Netherlands Genetic Soc, Brazilian Muscular Dystrophy Assoc; FRCPEd 1970, FRSE 1972, FLS 1985, FRCP, FRSA, Hon FRS, Hon FRSM; *Books* 20 books incl: Duchenne Muscular Dystrophy (4 edn 2015), Muscular Dystrophy – The Facts (3 edn 2008), The History of a History of a Genetic Disease (1995, 2 edn 2011), Diagnostic Criteria for Neuromuscular Disorders (2 edn 1997), Neuromuscular Disorders: Clinical and Molecular Genetics (1998), The Muscular Dystrophies (2001), Medicine and Art (2003), Surgical and Medical Treatment in Art (2006), Mother and Child Care in Art (2007), Poems (2007), Questioning Days (2010), Haiku (2 edn 2013); *Recreations* oil painting, writing poetry; *Style*— Prof Alan Emery, FRSE; ✉ 2 Ingleside Court, Budleigh Salterton, Devon EX9 6NZ (✆ 01395 445847); Green Templeton College, Oxford OX2 6HG (✆ 01865 514974, e-mail alan.emery@gtc.ox.ac.uk)

EMERY, Prof Paul; s of Lt Cdr Dr Leonard Lesley Emery RNVR, of Cardiff, and Beryl Olive, *née* Davis; *b* 30 November 1952, London; *Educ* Cardiff HS, Churchill Coll Cambridge (MB BChir, MA, MD), Guy's Hosp; *m* 19 July 1980, Shirley Macdonald, da of Sub Lt David Morton Bayne RNVR; 2 da (Lorna Megan b 25 Oct 1987, Joanna Louise b 17 March 1989); *Career* SHO Guy's Hosp Brompton, subsequently med registrar Guy's Hosp Lewisham 1980–83, sr registrar Guy's Hosp 1983–85, head of rheumatology Walter Eliza Hall and asst physician Royal Melbourne Hosp 1985–88, conslt and sr lectr Dept of Rheumatology Univ of Birmingham 1988–95, ARC prof of rheumatology Univ of Leeds 1995– (dir Leeds Inst of Rheumatic and Musculoskeletal Med), dir Leeds Musculoskeletal Biomedical Research Unit 2008–; pres European League Against Rheumatism (EULAR) 2009–11; Roche Prize 1992, Carol Nachman Prize 2012; memb: Br Soc of Rheumatology, Br Soc of Immunology, BMA; FRCP 1992 (MRCP 1979), FMedSci 2015; *Books* incl: The Role of Cytokines in Rheumatological Inflammation Autoimmunregation and Autoimmune Disease (jtly, 1987), Local Injection Therapy in Rheumatic Diseases (jtly, 1992), Management of Early Inflammatory Arthritis (ed, 1992), Clinical Rheumatology International Practice and Research (ed and contrib, 1992), Visual Diagnosis Self-Tests in Rheumatology (jtly, 1996, 2 edn 2001), What is Early Rheumatoid Arthritis? Definition and Diagnosis (jtly, 1997), Treatment of Rheumatoid Arthritis: New Drugs, New Hopes (1999), Rheumatology Highlights 1998–99 (jtly, 1999), How to Manage Rheumatoid Arthritis – A Quick Reference Guide (1999, 3 edn 2001), Lupus and the Joints – A GP Guide to Diagnosis (jtly, 2000), The Future of Cox-2 Inhibitors (jtly, 2001), Clinician's Manual on Cox-2 Inhibition and Arthritis (jtly, 2001), Rheumatology and the Kidney (jtly, 2001), Atlas of Rheumatology Arthritis 2015; also contrib numerous chapters to medical textbooks, author of more than 100 peer-reviewed papers; *Recreations* golf; *Clubs* Oakdale Golf; *Style*— Prof Paul Emery; ✉ Leeds Institute of Rheumatic and Musculoskeletal Medicine, University of Leeds, Chapel Allerton Hospital, Chapeltown Road, Leeds LS7 4SA (✆ 0113 392 4884)

EMERY, Prof Vincent Clive; s of Ronald Emery (d 1985), and Doreen, *née* Tarr; *b* 9 May 1960, Hemel Hempstead, Herts; *Educ* Surbiton GS, Univ of Southampton (BSc, PhD); *m* 14 Sept 1991, Sarah Ann, *née* Stephens; 1 s (Timothy Simon b 16 Feb 1995); *Career* post-doctoral fell NERC Inst of Virology Univ of Oxford 1985–88; Royal Free Hosp Sch of Med: lectr in virology 1988–92, sr lectr in virology 1992–96, reader in virology 1996–2000; UCL: prof of virology 2000–, vice-head Grad Sch 2004–, pro-provost (S Asia and the Middle East) 2005–; memb Biochemistry and Cell Biology Ctee BBSRC, memb Advsy Panel Assoc of Cwlth Univs; Nat Physical Lab Prize for Measurement 1992; over 170 peer-reviewed pubns in jls and text books on virology; *Recreations* playing the piano and organ, bell ringing; *Clubs* Medical Research Club (sec 1997–2001), City Glee Club (pres 2003–05); *Style*— Prof Vincent Emery; ✉ Department of Infection, University College London, Rowland Hill Street, London NW3 2QG (✆ 020 7830 2997, fax 020 7830 2854, e-mail v.emery@ucl.ac.uk)

EMIÉ, HE Bernard; s of Pierre Emié, and Jacqueline Bernard; *b* 6 September 1958; *Educ* Paris Institut d'Etudes Politiques, Ecole Nationale d'Administration; *m* 30 Sept 1989, Isabelle, *née* de Chabannes La Palice Tournon; 2 da (Constance b 1991, Pauline b 1994), 1 s (Louis b 1999); *Career* French diplomat; joined Foreign Miny 1983, Asia-Oceania Dept Miny of Foreign Affrs 1983–84, second then first sec New Delhi 1984–86, advsr Foreign Min Jean-Bernard Raimond's private office 1986–88, first sec then second counsellor Washington DC 1988–92, dep dir N Africa ME and N Africa Dept Miny of Foreign Affrs 1992–93, advsr Foreign Min Alain Juppé's private office 1993–95, counsellor and dep diplomatic advsr Pres Jacques Chirac's office 1995–98, ambass to Jordan 1998–2002, dir ME and N Africa Dept Miny of Foreign Affrs 2002–04, ambass to Lebanon 2004–07, ambass to Turkey 2007–11, ambass to the Ct of St James's 2011–; Chevalier de la Légion d'Honneur 2005, Officier de l'Ordre National du Mérite 2009; *Style*— HE Mr Bernard Emié; ✉ Embassy of France, 58 Knightsbridge, London SW1X 7JT (✆ 020 7073 1000, fax 020 7073 1003)

EMILSON, Lars; *Career* chm Charter plc 2007–12; non-exec dir: Filtrona plc 2007–, East Capital Explorer AB 2007–; *Style*— Lars Emilson, Esq

EMIN, Tracey; CBE (2013); *Educ* Maidstone Coll of Art (BA), Royal Coll of Art; *Career* artist; set designer Les Parents Terribles (Jermyn Street Theatre) 2004; prof of drawing Royal Acad 2011–; *Solo Exhibitions* incl: The Shop (103 Bethnal Green Road London, with Sarah Lucas) 1993, My Major Retrospective (Jay Jopling/White Cube London) 1993, Exploration of the Soul – Journey Across America (tour) 1994, Tracey Emin Museum (221 Waterloo Road London) 1995–1998, Exorcism of the Last Painting I Ever Made (Galleri Andreas Brändström Stockholm) 1996, Istanbul Biennial (performance at Pera Palace Hotel Turkey) 1997, I Need Art Like I Need God (South London Gallery London, Gestellschaft für Aktuelle Kunst Bremen) 1997–1998, Sobasex (My Cunt is Wet With Fear) (Sagacho Exhibition Space Tokyo) 1998, Tracey Emin Every Part of Me is Bleeding (Lehmann Maupin NY) 1999, What do you Know About Love (Galerie Gebauer Berlin) 2000, Tracey Emin You Forgot To Kiss My Soul (White Cube London) 2001, I Think it's in my head (Lehmann Maupin Gall NY) 2002, Ten Years Tracey Emin (Stedelijk Muesum Amsterdam) 2002, Tracey Emin (Art Gall of NSW Aust) 2003, Menphis (Counter Gallery London) 2003, I'll Meet You in Heaven (Lorcan O'Neill Rome) 2004, Can't See Past My Own Eyes (Sketch London) 2004, Fear, War And The Scream (Roslyn Oxley Sydney/ City Gallery Wellington) 2004, Tracey Emin (BP British Art Displays Tate Britain) 2004, Tracey Istanbulda (Platform Garanti Contemporary Art Center Istanbul) 2004, Tracey Emin Monoprints (Museo de Ballas Artes Santiago) 2004, Death Mask (Nat Portrait Gallery) 2005, When I Think About Sex... (White Cube) 2005, More Flow (Galleria Lorcan O'Neill Rome) 2006, Tracey Emin: You Left Me Breathing (Gagosian Gallery Beverly Hills) 2007, Tracey Emin: Borrowed Light (British Pavilion Venice Biennale) 2007, Tracey Emin 20 Years (Centro de Arte Contemporáneo Málaga and Scottish Nat Gallery of Modern Art) 2008 and (Kunstmuseum Bern) 2009, Those who Suffer Love (White Cube) 2009, Only God Knows I'm Good (Lehmann Maupin New York) 2009, Why Be Afraid? (Galleria Lorcan O'Neill Rome) 2010, Walking with Tears (RA London) 2010, Do Not Abandon Me (with Louise Bourgeois, Carolina Nitsch New York) 2010 and (Hauser & Wirth London) 2011, Praying to a Different God (Amanda

Love Art Sydney) 2010, Love is What You Want (Maison Louis Vuitton and Hayward Gallery London) 2011, Walking Around My World (Selfridges Concept Store London) 2011, The Vanishing Lake (White Cube Fitzroy Square London) 2011, You Saved Me (Galleria Lorcan O'Neill Rome) 2012, You Don't Believe in Love But I Believe in You (White Cube São Paulo) 2012, How it Feels (MALBA Buenos Aires) 2012, She Lay Deep Beneath the Sea (Turner Contemporary Margate) 2012, Self Portrait (Château La Coste Aix-en-Provence) 2013, Roman Standard (Petrosino Park New York) 2013, I Followed You to the Sun (Lehmann Maupin New York) 2013, Angel Without You (Miaim MoCA Florida) 2013, The Last Great Adventure is You (White Cube) 2014, Waiting to Love (Galleria Lorcan O'Neill Rome) 2015, Tracey Emin – Egon Schiele: Where I Want to Go (Leopold Museum Vienna) 2015; *Group Exhibitions* incl: Sensation (Royal Acad of Arts London) 1997, Art from the UK: Angela Bulloch, Willie Doherty, Tracey Emin, Sarah Lucas, Sam Taylor-Wood (Sammlung Goetz, Munich) 1998, Turner Prize (Tate Gallery London) 1999, Art in Sacred Spaces (St. Mary's Church Islington London) 2000, Out There (White Cube Hoxton Square London) 2000, Peter Blake: About Collage (Tate Gallery London) 2000, Summer Exhibition (Royal Acad of Arts London) 2001, and 2004, A Bigger Splash: British Art from the Tate 1960–2003 (Pavilhão Lucas Nogueira Garcez São Paulo) 2003, Einleuchten (Museum der Moderne Salzburg) 2004, Critic's Choice (FACT Liverpool) 2005, 25 Twenty Five Years of the Deutsche Bank Collection (Duetsche Guggenheim Berlin) 2005, Body: New Art from the UK (Vancouver Art Gallery) 2005, Youth of Today (Schim Kunsthalle Frankfurt) 2006, Hot/Cold – Summer Loving (Zacheta Nat Gallery of Art Warsaw) 2006, In the darkest hour there may be light: works from Damien Hirst's murderme collection (Serpentine Gallery London) 2006, Aftershock: Contemporary British Art 1990–2006 (Guandong Museum of Art Guangzhou) 2006, Lights, Camera, Action: Artists' Films for the Camera (Whitney Mseum of American Art Whitney) 2007, The Naked Portrait (Scottish Nat Gallery Edinburgh) 2007, Fourth Plinth (Nat Gallery London) 2008, Summer Exhbn (curator, RA London) 2008, Fokestone Triennial: Tales of Time and Space 2008, Making of Art (Schirn Kunsthalle Frankfurt) 2009, Once Upon a Time... Artists and Storytelling (Courtauld Inst of Art Somerset House London) 2009, Emporte-moi/Sweep me of my feet (Musée National des Beaux-Arts de Québec) 2009, Pop Life (Tate Modern London) 2009, In Stitches (Leila Taghinia-Milani Heller Gallery New York) 2009, Performa 09 Biennial New York 2009, Earth: Art of a Changing World (GSK Contemporary RA London) 2009, Matt Collishaw, Tracey Emin and Paula Rego: At the Foundling (Foundling Museum London) 2010, Cream (KIASMA Helsinki) 2010, Move: Choreographing You (Hayward Gallery London) 2010 and (K20 Dusseldorf) 2011, No New Thing Under the Sun (RA London) 2010, This is Sculpture (Tate Liverpool) 2010, Quilts 1700–2010 (V&A London) 2010, Five in Istanbul (Borusan Muzik Evi Istanbul) 2010, At Work, the Government Art Collection (Whitechapel Art Gallery London) 2011, Watercolour (Tate Britain London) 2011, Text/Video/Female: Art after 60s (PKM Trinity Gallery Seoul) 2011, Newspeak (Gallery of S Australia Adelaide) 2011, Dance/Draw (ICA Boston) 2011, Fourth Plinth: Contemporary Monument (ICA London), Privacy (Schirn Kunsthalle Frankfurt) 2012, The Perfect Place to Grow: 175 Years of the Royal College of Art (RCA London) 2012, All You Need is Love: From Chagall to Kusama and Hatsune Miku (Mori Art Museum Tokyo) 2013, do it (Manchester Art Gallery) 2013, Mad, Bad & Sad: Women and the Mind Doctors (Freud Museum London) 2013, Art from Britain and Poland from 1990 (Centre for Contemporary Art Ujazdowski Castle Warsaw) 2013, White Light/White Heat: Contemporary Artists and Glass (Wallace Collection London) 2013, One Foot in the Real World (Irish Museum of Modern Art Dublin) 2013, Set in Motion (Petach Tivka Museum of Art Israel) 2014, Private Utopia: Contemporary Works from the British Council Collection (touring) 2014, REALLY? Overview of the Arario Collection (Arario Museum in Space Seoul) 2014, Self: Image and Identity – from Van Dyck to Louise Bourgeois (Turner Contemporary Margate) 2015, Lust for Life – Bourgeois/Emin/Kneebone (Galleri Andersson/Sandström Stockholm) 2015, Sleepless: The Bed in History and Contemporary Art (21er Haus Vienna) 2015; *Works in Collections* incl: Arts Cncl of Br, Br Museum London, Museum of Contemporary Art San Diego, Pompidou Centre Paris, Saatchi Collection London, Tate Gallery London, Scottish Nat Gallery Edinburgh, Art Gall of NSW Sydney, Deutsche Bank, National Portrait Gall London, San Francisco MOMA, Guggenheim Museum NY, an Francisco MOMA, Stedelijk Museum Amsterdam; *Awards* Int Award for Video Art Baden-Baden 1997, Video Art Prize Südwest Bank Stuttgart 1997, Turner Prize nominee 1997, The Jury Prize Cairo Biennale Award 2001; RA 2007; *Publications* Strangeland (2005); *Style—* Ms Tracey Emin, CBE, RA; ✉ Tracey Emin Studio, 1 Tenter Ground, London E1 7NH (✆ 020 7375 1358, fax 020 7247 6978, e-mail office@traceyeminstudio.com)

EMLY, John Richard Keith; s of Charles Richard Lewis Emly (d 1975), and Lillian Villette Emly (d 1971); *b* 15 September 1941; *Educ* St Dunstan's Coll Catford; *m* 26 July 1969, Maria Joan, da of Frederic Jozef Jan Gumosz (d 1964), of Catford; 2 da (Gillian b 1972, Sarah b 1974), 2 s (Timothy b 1978, Benjamin b 1980); *Career* jt investment mangr The Law Debenture Corp Ltd 1971–75 (joined 1960), dir Robert Fleming Investment Management Ltd 1978–88, main bd dir Robert Fleming Holdings Ltd 1985–98 (joined 1975); dir: Fleming Investment Management Ltd 1988–2000, Fleming Income and Capital Investment Trust plc 1993–98, JP Morgan Mid-Cap Investment Trust plc 1996–2014, Robert Fleming Asset Management Ltd 1998–2000, F&C Income Growth Investment Trust plc 2001–05, F&C Capital and Income Investment Trust plc 2005–16; investment dir CAA Pension Scheme 2000–; non-exec dir: Hemingway Properties plc 1995–99, Shaftesbury plc 2000–12; memb Investment Ctee: P&O Pension Scheme 2003–14, Balfour Beatty Pension Scheme 2003–10; tstee St Paul's Cathedral (1972) Pension and Life Insurance Scheme 2006–; hon treas Scout Assoc 1996–2003; FRICS 1972, ASIP, MSI; *Recreations* family life; *Style—* John Emly, Esq; ✉ The Civil Aviation Authority Pension Scheme, CAA House, London WC2B 6TE (✆ 020 7453 6742)

EMMERSON, Ian Robert; OBE (1994); s of late Robert Leslie Emmerson, of Lincoln, and late Ida Kathleen, *née* Marshall; *b* 18 February 1944; *Educ* City GS Lincoln; *m* 23 Nov 1968, Sheila Margaret, da of Ernest Raymond (Dick) Barber (d 1968); 2 s (Nathan Robert b 1972, Richard Ian b 1974); *Career* GPO 1960–83 (asst exec engr BT), dir Impsport 1983–2003; chm Cwlth Games Cncl for Eng 1999–2007, vice-pres Europe Cwlth Games Fedn 2000–11, dir Glasgow 2014 Cwlth Games 2007–11; pres Br Cycling Fedn 1985–95, vice-pres Union Cycliste Internationale 1993–97; pres UCI Masters Cmmn 1993–2005; chm Velo Club Lincoln 1964–95, pres Lincolnshire Sport, organiser Lincoln Grand Prix Cycle Race 1983–2015; tstee/dir Magna Vitae Tst East Lindsey; Sheriff of Lincoln 1990–91; Hon DSc Univ of Lincoln 2009; *Recreations* cycling, photography, travel; *Style—* Ian Emmerson, Esq, OBE; ✉ 5 Larkin Avenue, Cherry Willingham, Lincoln LN3 4AZ (✆ 01522 750000, mobile 07785 347174, e-mail ian.emmerson@ntlworld.com)

EMMERSON, Robert Frank; s of Harold Claude Emmerson (d 1993), and Gladys Amy, *née* Gautrey (d 1991); *b* 5 October 1938; *Educ* Perse Sch Cambridge, Trinity Coll Cambridge (MA); *m* 26 April 1962, Anne, *née* Crabtree; 1 da (Nancy Victoria b 11 June 1970), 1 s (John Philip b 23 Feb 1972); *Career* project engr W J Lemessurier Cambridge MA 1965–67; Ove Arup & Partners: project and gp engr 1960–65 and 1967–77, dir 1977; Arup Gp: gp bd dir 1984, tstee dir 1995–2008, dep chm 1995–2000, chm 2000–04; projects supervised as design gp ldr incl: Bracken House London, Royal Mint Devpt London, HQ for Trustees Savings Bank Edinburgh, Fitzwilliam Coll Cambridge, John Lewis Dept Store Kingston, Patscenter Princeton, Derngate Theatre Northampton, Dental Teaching Hosp Hong Kong, ROH London, Glyndebourne Theatre, Millennium Bridge London, Lords Media Centre, Portcullis House London; projects supervised as project engr incl: Inst of Educn and Law Univ of London, SOAS Univ of London, Christ's Coll Cambridge, Colby Coll ME, Newport Jazz Festival RI, Adult Educn Centre NH; projects as structual engr incl: Queen Elizabeth Hall London (as project engr), Hayward Gall London (as project engr), Sydney Opera House; tstee Architectural Assoc Fndn; author of numerous articles in professional pubns and jls; FREng, MCIBSE, FICE; *Recreations* skiing, golf, art; *Clubs* Coombe Hill Golf; *Style—* Robert Emmerson, Esq; ✉ Arup Group Ltd, 13 Fitzroy Street, London W1T 4BQ (✆ 020 7755 3373, fax 020 7755 3666, e-mail bob.emmerson@arup.com)

EMMETT, Robert; *Educ* UK and Switzerland; *Career* fashion designer; clothes and material design Geneva, moulage and further design Paris, opened London shop 1992; *Style—* Robert Emmett, Esq

EMMOTT, William (Bill); *b* 1956; *Educ* Magdalen Coll Oxford; *Career* The Economist: Brussels corr 1980–82, dep economics writer 1982–83, Tokyo corr 1983–86, fin ed 1986–89, business affairs ed 1989–93, ed 1993–2006; memb Exec Ctee Trilateral Cmmn 1998–; Hon LLD Univ of Warwick 1999, Hon DLitt City Univ 2001; hon fell Magdalen Coll Oxford; *Books* The Pocket Economist (1983), The Sun Also Sets (1989), Japan's Global Reach (1993), 20:21 Vision (2003); *Style—* Bill Emmott, Esq; ✉ The Economist, 25 St James's Street, London SW1A 1HG

E

EMMS, Gail Elizabeth; MBE (2009); da of Anthony Charles Emms, of Bedford, and Janice Dorothy Barnes, *née* Barton; *b* 23 July 1977, Hitchin, Herts; *Educ* Dame Alice Harpur Sch Bedford, Kingston Univ (BSc); *Career* badminton player; achievements incl: winner women's doubles USA Open 2000, winner mixed doubles Dutch Open 2001, winner BMW Open 2001, winner mixed doubles Malaysia Open 2002, team Gold medal and Bronze medal women's doubles Cwlth Games 2002, Gold medal mixed doubles European Championships 2004, winner mixed doubles Thailand Open 2004, Silver medal mixed doubles Olympic Games Athens 2004, winner mixed doubles All-England Championships 2005, winner mixed doubles China Open 2005, Gold medal ladies doubles European Championships 2006, Gold medal mixed doubles, Silver medal team event and Bronze medal ladies doubles Cwlth Games Melbourne 2006, winner mixed doubles World Championships Madrid 2006; ret 2008; *Style—* Miss Gail Emms, MBE; ✉ c/o Professional Sports Group, The Town House, 63 High Street, Chobham, Surrey GU24 8AF (✆ 01276 858930, fax 01276 856974); website www.gailemms.com

EMPEY, Baron (Life Peer UK 2011), of Shandon in the City and County Borough of Belfast; Sir Reginald Norman Morgan Empey; kt (1999), OBE (1994); s of Samuel Frederick Empey, and Emily Winifred, *née* Morgan; *b* 26 October 1947, Belfast; *Educ* Royal Sch Armagh, Queens Univ Belfast; *m* 1977, Stella Ethna Donnan; 1 s, 1 da; *Career* Lord Mayor Belfast City Cncl 1989–90 and 1993–94, MLA (UUP) Belfast E 1998–2011, dep ldr UUP 2003–05, ldr UUP 2005–10, chm UUP 2012–; NI Exec: min of enterprise, trade and investment 1999–2002, acting first min 2001, min for employment and learning 2007–10; vice-pres Inst of Export; *Recreations* walking, gardening; *Clubs* Army and Navy; *Style—* The Lord Empey, kt, OBE; ✉ House of Lords, London SW1A 0PW

EMSLEY, Paul; *b* 25 August 1947, Glasgow; *Educ* Rondebosch Boys HS S Africa, Cape Tech Coll S Africa, Univ of Stellenbosch S Africa; *Career* artist; teacher of drawing and painting Dept of Creative Art Univ of Stellenbosch S Africa 1983–95; chosen to paint first portrait of HRH The Duchess of Cambridge 2012; further portrait subjects incl: Nelson Mandela, William Kentridge, Lord Tanlaw, Sir Vidia Naipaul, *qqv* (for Nat Portrait Gallery); *Public Collections* Nat Portait Gallery, Br Museum, S African Nat Gallery, Northwestern Univ Chicago, Johannesburg Art Gallery, Univ of the Witwatersrand, Univ of Stellenbosch, Univ of the Orange Free State, William Humphreys Art Gallery Kimberley, Sasol Collection, Sanlam Collection; *Selected Exhibitions* solo exhibition Redfern Gallery 2011, Masterpiece London (Redfern Gallery) 2011 and 2012, Joburg Art Fair Brundyn and Gonsalves 2011, retrospective exhibition Wordfest Artist (Sasol Art Museum Stellenbosch S Africa) 2012, Sunday Times Watercolour Competition 2012; *Style—* Paul Emsley, Esq; ✉ c/o The Redfern Gallery, 20 Cork Street, London W1S 3HL

EMSLIE, Donald; *m* 1; 2 da (Sarah, Jenny); m 2, Sarah; *Career* Scottish TV (now part of SMG plc): joined 1985, commercial dir 1994, md Broadcasting Div 1997, chief exec SMG Television 1999–2007, memb Bd SMG plc 1999–2007; chm: Cncl ITV, Bd GMTV 2002–04; memb Bd: Scottish Screen, Skillset UK (chm Scottish Industry Skills Panel Skillset Scotland), Film Acad Scotland (chm Advsy Bd); chm Royal Lyceum Theatre Co; FRTS (vice-pres); *Recreations* golf; *Style—* Donald Emslie, Esq

EMSLIE, Rt Hon Lord; (George) Nigel Hannington Emslie; PC (2011); eldest s of Baron Emslie, MBE, PC (Life Peer, d 2002); bro of Rt Hon Lord Kingarth, and Dr the Hon Richard Emslie, *qqv*; *b* 1947; *Educ* Edinburgh Acad, Trinity Coll Glenalmond, Gonville & Caius Coll Cambridge (BA), Univ of Edinburgh (LLB); *m* 1973, Heather Ann, da of late Arthur Frank Davis, of Bristol; 1 s, 2 da; *Career* advocate; admitted Faculty of Advocates 1972, QC (Scot) 1986, Dean of the Faculty of Advocates 1997–2001, senator Coll of Justice (Lord of Session) 2001–12; *Style—* The Rt Hon Lord Emslie; ✉ Parliament House, Edinburgh EH1 1RQ

EMSLIE, Dr the Hon Richard Hannington; 3 and yst s of The Rt Hon Lord Emslie, MBE, PC, FRSE (d 2002); bro of Hon George Nigel Hannington Emslie (Rt Hon Lord Emslie) and Hon Derek Robert Alexander Emslie (Rt Hon Lord Kingarth), *qqv*; *b* 28 July 1957; *Educ* Edinburgh Acad, Trinity Coll Glenalmond, Gonville & Caius Coll Cambridge (MA), Univ of Stellenbosch (PhD), Coll of Business Administration Univ of Nebraska (Cert of Business Excellence in Lifelong Learning); *Partner* Keryn Adcock; *Career* wildlife biologist, res into applied white rhino grazing ecology and black rhino browsing ecology and mgmnt in Hluhluwe-iMfolozi Park Zululand South Africa; conslt ecologist incl conservation of the black and white rhino; author and developer of Bayesian Mark-Recapture population estimation statistical software package (Rhino); scientific/prog offr IUCN/Species Survival Cmmn African Rhino Specialist Gp; memb: IUCN SSC Asian Rhino Specialist Gp, SADC Rhino and Elephant Security Gp/ Interpol Environmental Crime Working Gp, IUCN SSC Species Conservation Action Planning Task Force, CITES Rhino Working Gp, IUCN Delgn to 6 CITES Conf of the Parties, Advsy Bd RhoDIS (rhino DNA); elected expert Southern African Rhino Mgmnt Gp, consortium memb Southern African Devpt Community (SADC) regnl rhino conservation prog 1999–2006, patron SAB Boucher Conservation, friend of Kaziranga; sole prop Ecoscot Consultancy Services; memb SA Statistical Assoc; Harry Messel Award for Conservation Leadership IUCN Species Survival Cmmn; fell Darwin Initiative 2003–06; *Publications* African Rhino – IUCN Status Survey & Action Plan (with PM Brooks, 1999), Guidelines for Implementing SADC Rhino Conservation Strategiessee (RF du Toit with RH Emslie, M Brooks, G Daconto and L Mungwashu, 2006), IUCN Guidelines for the In-situ Re-introduction and Translocation of African and Asian Rhinoceros (with R Amin and R Kock, 2009); *Recreations* watching sport (especially football), running, cooking, listening to music, enjoying nature, reading, golf, value investing; *Clubs* Isle of Colonsay (golf), Hilton Harriers (running); *Style—* Dr the Hon Richard Emslie; ✉ PO Box 1212 Hilton, Kwa-Zulu Natal 3245, South Africa (✆ 00 27 33 3434065, e-mail emslieafrsg@telkomsa.net)

EMSON, Colin Jack; s of Alfred Jack Emson (d 2002), of Ashford, Kent, and Rose Florence Jobson (d 1987); *b* 25 July 1941; *Educ* Maidstone GS; *m* 14 Sept 1974, Jennifer Claire, da of Lt-Col James Lynch, of Vancouver, Canada; 2 da (Annabel Christina b 1975, Camilla Rose b 1985), 2 s (Alexander Chase b 1976, Henry James b 1980); *Career* fndr ptnr

Emson & Dudley 1966–79; chm: Robert Fraser & Partners Ltd (investment and finance gp) 1979–, Sterling Trust Ltd (investment holding company) 1988–, Ellenborough Park Ltd 2008–, Independent Power Corporation plc 2010, Rurelec plc 2013–; *Recreations* polo, skiing, tennis, tobogganing; *Clubs* Turf, Cowdray Park Polo, St Moritz Toboggan, Corviglia Ski; *Style*— Colin Emson, Esq; ✉ Shotters Farm, Newton Valence, nr Alton, Hampshire GU34 3RJ

ENDACOTT, Charles George; s of John Kinsman Endacott, of London, and Rita, *née* Ellul; *b* 24 September 1950; *Educ* St John's Coll Southsea; *m* 1973 (m dis 1983), Hazel, *née* Short; 1 da (Natalie b 1 Aug 1979); *Career* messenger E Allan Cooper Advertising 1967–68, studio jr J L Lakings Studio 1968–69, jr designer SF & Partner Advertising 1969–70, freelance designer and visualiser 1970–71, sole proprietor RJB Associates (design and promotions conslts) 1976–83 (fndr ptnr 1971–76), chm RJB Manpower Ltd 1979–83, md Endacott RJB Ltd 1983–89; chm RJB Group Ltd (chm/md various subsids) 1989–; mktg dir Digital United; dir: Pristine Products Ltd 1991–, Computer Professionals (UK) Ltd 1992–, Endacott Corner Ltd 2001–, Green Media Ltd 2003–; charity tstee Marketing Services UK – 'Promoting for Children' 1995; memb Inst of Sales Promotion; Liveryman Worshipful Co of Marketors; *Recreations* tennis, classic cars, riding, scuba, golf; *Clubs* David Lloyd, Hazelwood Golf; *Style*— Charles Endacott, Esq

ENDERBY, (Samuel) Charles; LVO (2010), JP (1991); s of Col Samuel Enderby, CVO, DSO, MC (d 1997) and Pamela Innocence Enderby; *b* 18 September 1939; *Educ* Sandroyd Sch, Wellington Coll, RMA Sandhurst; *m* 1973 Mary Justina, da of PW Compton, DSC; 2 da (Amelia b 1974, Verena b 1977); *Career* cmmnd 12 Royal Lancers 1959, served with 9/12 Royal Lancers 1960–84; HM The Queen's Body Guard of Yeoman of the Guard: Exon 1987, Ensign 2002, Clerk of the Cheque 2005, Lt 2006, ret 2009; chm Hexham Steeplechase Co Ltd 1997–2016 (dir 1985–2016); High Sheriff Northumberland 2000–; *Recreations* shooting, ornithology, gardening, reading; *Clubs* Army and Navy, Pratt's; *Style*— Charles Enderby, Esq, LVO

ENDERS, Claire; da of Hon Thomas Enders; *b* 6 February 1958, USA; *Educ* Yale Univ (BA), London Business Sch (MBA); *m* 1983 (m dis), Sir Ronald Cohen, *qv*; m 2, 1987, Christopher Thomson; 1 da (Heloise b 28 May 1989), 1 s (Thomas b 8 July 1994); *Career* Thorn EMI 1984–85, Virgin Gp 1985–87, Superchannel 1987–89, TVS Entertainment 1989–92, EMI 1992–97, fndr Enders Analysis Ltd 1997–; memb Bd NSPCC; patron: Nat History Museum, Royal Scottish Nat Orch, Nat Museums of Scotland; tstee Glyndebourne Prodns; *Recreations* bridge, classical music; *Style*— Ms Claire Enders; ✉ Enders Analysis Ltd, 46A Great Marlborough Street, London W1F 7JW (☎ 01273 611140, fax 01273 611677, e-mail info@endersanalysis.com, website www.endersanalysis.com)

ENFIELD, Henry Richard (Harry); s of Edward Enfield and Deirdre Enfield, of Billingshurst, W Sussex; *b* 30 May 1961; *Educ* Worth Abbey, Univ of York; *m* 22 Feb 1997, Lucy Caroline, yr da of Rae Lyster, of Layer de la Haye, Essex; *Career* writer, actor and comedian; began performing whilst at York Univ, toured UK (incl London and Edinburgh Festival) with fringe show Dusty and Dick 1983, reg appearances on Spitting Image (Channel 4) 1984 and Saturday Night Live (Channel 4, creating characters incl Stavros and Loadsamoney) 1986, writer and actor Sir Norbert Smith... A Life? (Channel 4) 1989 (Gold Rockie Banff Awards 1989, Silver Rose of Montreux 1990, Int Emmy for Popular Arts Progs 1991), own series Harry Enfield's Television Programme (BBC 2) 1990 and 1992, Men Behaving Badly (Thames) 1992, Gone to the Dogs (Central) 1993, Harry Enfield's Guide to Opera (Channel 4) 1993, Harry Enfield and Chums (BBC 1) 1994 and 1996 (Best Entertainment Series Writers Guild Awards 1995, Best Entertainment Prog RTS Awards 1997, Silver Rose of Montreux 1998), Smashie and Nicey... The End of an Era (BBC 2) 1994 (Silver Rose of Montreux 1995), Harry Enfield & Chums Christmas Special 1997, Norman Ormal (BBC) 1998, Harry Enfield's Yule Log Chums (BBC) 1998, Sermon from St Albions (Granada) 1999, Sermon from St Albions (Granada) 1999, Harry Enfield Presents Kevin's Guide to Being a Teenager (Tiger Aspect) 1999, Harry Enfield's Real Kevins (Tiger Aspect) 2000, Harry Enfield's Brand Spanking New Show (Sky One) 2000 (Satellite and Digital TV Programme of the Year TRIC Awards 2001), Harry Enfield Presents Tim-Nice-But-Dim's Guide to Being a Bloody Nice Bloke (BBC 1) 2001, Harry Enfield Presents Wayne & Waynetta's Guide to Wedded Bliss (BBC1) 2001, We Know Where You Live (Channel 4) 2001, Celeb (BBC 1) 2002, Peter Cook Foundation Benefit Show (BBC 2) 2002, Harry Enfield's Excellent Adventure (Sky One) 2005, Ruddy Hell! It's Harry and Paul (BBC 1) 2007, Harry and Paul (BBC 1) 2008– (Best Comedy Prog BAFTA 2009 and 2011); film: Kevin & Perry Go Large 1999 (Best Comedy Film Quality Street Awards 2001), Churchill: The Hollywood Years 2003, Tooth 2004; video: Harry Enfield Undressed (1997), The New Harry Enfield & Chums Video (1998), More Harry Enfield and Chums (2000); guest Desert Island Discs (BBC Radio 4) 1997; *Books* Harry Enfield and His Humorous Chums (1997), Kevin & Perry Go Large (novel based on a screenplay written with Dave Cummings, 2000), Havin' it Large – Kevin & Perry's Guide to Looking Cool and Getting Girls (2000); *Style*— Harry Enfield, Esq; ✉ c/o PBJ Management Ltd, PBJ and JBJ Management, 22 Rathbone Street, London W1T 1LA (☎ 020 7287 1112, fax 020 7287 1191, e-mail general@pbjmgt.co.uk, website www.pbjmgt.co.uk)

ENGEL, Matthew Lewis; s of Max David Engel, of Northampton (d 2005), and Betty Ruth, *née* Lesser (d 1998); *b* 11 June 1951; *Educ* Carmel Coll, Univ of Manchester (BA); *m* 27 Oct 1990, Hilary, da of late Laurence Davies; 1 s (Laurence Gabriel b 28 May 1992 d 2005), 1 da (Victoria Betty b 26 May 1998); *Career* reporter: Northampton Chronicle and Echo 1972–75, Reuters 1977–79; The Guardian: joined 1979, cricket corr 1982–87, feature writer, sports columnist and occasional political, foreign and war corr 1987–98, columnist 1998–2003, Washington corr 2001–03; columnist Financial Times 2004–; ed Wisden Cricketers' Almanack 1993–2000 and 2004–07; NI visiting prof of media Univ of Oxford 2010–11; Granada Sportswriter of the Year 1985, Sports Journalist of the Year Br Press Awards 1992, shortlisted Reporter of the Year Br Press Awards 1998; *Books include* Ashes '85 (1985), The Guardian Book of Cricket (ed, 1986), Sportswriter's Eye (1989), The Sportspages Almanac (ed, 1989, 1990, 1991), Tickle The Public: a hundred years of popular newspapers (1996), Extracts from the Red Notebooks (2007), Eleven Minutes Late (2009), Engel's England (2014); *Recreations* wishful thinking; *Clubs* Northamptonshire CCC (vice-pres), Garrick; *Style*— Matthew Engel, Esq; ✉ Fair Oak, Bacton, Herefordshire HR2 0AT (website www.matthewengel.co.uk)

ENGEL, Natascha; MP; *b* 9 April 1967; *Career* MP (Lab) NE Derbyshire 2005–; political fund ballot co-ordinator Trade Union Co-ordinating Ctee 2005; memb: GMB, UCATT; *Style*— Natascha Engel, MP; ✉ House of Commons, London SW1A 0AA

ENGLAND, Neil Martin; s of Brian England, and Jean England; *b* 10 May 1954, Birmingham; *Educ* Univ of Reading (BSc); *m* 26 July 1980, Debra; 1 s (Samuel b 10 Jan 1990), 2 da (Nadya b 17 July 1993, Anastasia b 26 April 1996); *Career* vice-pres Mars Inc 1993–96, gp chief exec The Albert Fisher Gp plc 1996–98, chief exec Mindweavers Ltd 2000–02, gp commercial dir Gallaher Gp plc 2002–07; non-exec chm: Blackrock Emerging Europe plc 2003–, Silverstone Hldgs 2006–14, Angel Springs Ltd 2011–14, Luchford APM Ltd 2013–14; sr ind dir Wincanton plc 2007–11, non-exec dir ITE Gp plc 2007–, non-exec chm Prolog Ltd 2015–, non-exec chm TPN Ltd 2016–; FInstM; *Recreations* motor sport, golf; *Style*— Neil England, Esq; ✉ 124 Waterman Quay, London SW6 2UW

ENGLANDER, Dr Peter David; s of Geoffrey Englander (d 1993), and Doris Ruth, *née* Levy (d 2009); *b* 29 November 1951; *Educ* St Paul's, Univ of Manchester (BSc), MIT (Kennedy scholar, SM), Univ of London (PhD); *m* 1985, Leanda Abigail, *née* Kroll; 3 s; *Career* conslt Boston Consulting Gp 1977–80, Apax Partners 1981–2011, ceo Apax Fndn 2005–, chm Bridges Ventures 2012–; tstee Kennedy Meml Tst 2007–; *Recreations* walking, cinema; *Style*— Dr Peter Englander; ✉ Apax Partners, 33 Jermyn Street, London SW1Y 6DN (☎ 020 7872 6331)

ENGLEHART, Robert Michael; QC (1986); s of G A F Englehart (d 1969), of London, and of K P Englehart, *née* Harvey (d 1973); *b* 1 October 1943; *Educ* St Edward's Sch Oxford, Trinity Coll Oxford (MA), Harvard Law Sch (LLM), Bologna Centre; *m* 2 Jan 1971, Rosalind Mary Foster, *qv*, da of Ludovic Anthony Foster (d 1990); 2 da (Alice b 1976, Lucinda b 1978), 1 s (Oliver b 1982); *Career* assistente Univ of Florence 1967–68, called to the Bar Middle Temple 1969 (bencher 1995), recorder of the Crown Court 1987–, dep judge of the High Court 1994–; chm London Common Law and Commercial Bar Assoc 1989–91, chm Jt Regulations Ctee of Inns of Court 2000–07; *Books* Il Controllo Giudiziario: a Comparative Study in Civil Procedure (contrib 1968); *Recreations* shooting, cricket; *Clubs* Garrick, MCC; *Style*— Robert Englehart, Esq, QC; ✉ Blackstone House, Temple, London EC4Y 9BW (☎ 020 7583 1770, fax 020 7822 7350, e-mail robertenglehart@blackstonechambers.com)

ENGLISH, Her Hon Judge Caroline Frances; da of Maureen Frances Streight, *née* English; *Educ* Nottingham Trent Univ (LLB); *m* 16 Sept 1996, Floyd Ramsey Porter; *Career* called to the Bar 1989; fee-paid legal memb Mental Health Review Tbnl (England) 2003, recorder 2007, circuit judge (SE Circuit) 2015–; *Recreations* travel, equestrianism, wildlife, photography; *Style*— Her Hon Judge English

ENNINFUL, Edward; OBE (2016); s of Crosby Enninful, and Grace, *née* Aboah; *b* 22 February 1972, Ghana; *Partner* Alec Maxwell; *Career* stylist; formerly: contrib fashion ed Italian Vogue, fashion ed at large Japanese Vogue, American Vogue; fashion dir iD magazine 1991, fashion and style dir W magazine 2011–; campaigns incl: Commes des Garcons, Jil Sander, Armani, Calvin Klein, Fendi, Alessandro Dell'Acqua, Strenesse, Gap, Levis, Hugo Boss, Missoni, Lancôme, Cover Girl, Blumarine, H&M, Gucci, Etro, Bally, Mulberry; *Style*— Edward Enninful, Esq, OBE; ✉ Maximfma, Unit 34, 249 Kensal Road, London W10 5DB (☎ 020 8968 0047, e-mail akua@maximfma.com, website www.maximfma.com)

ENNIS, Catherine; da of Séamus Ennis (d 1982), of Dublin, and Margaret, *née* Glynn; *b* 20 January 1955; *Educ* Christ's Hosp Hertford, St Hugh's Coll Oxford; *m* 10 Dec 1988, John Arthur Higham, QC, *qv*, s of Frank Higham (d 1988); 2 s (Patrick b 14 Sept 1989, Edmund b 24 March 1992), 1 da (Cecily b 17 Jan 1994), 2 step da (Miranda, Charlotte), 1 step s (Christian); *Career* organist; organ scholar St Hugh's Coll Oxford 1973–76, dir of music St Marylebone Parish Church London NW1 1979–81, asst organist ChCh Cathedral Oxford 1984–86, organist St Lawrence-Jewry-next-Guildhall London EC2 1985–; prof: RAM 1982–90, Guildhall Sch of Music 1986–88; fndr ed London Organ Concerts Guide 1995–; has given numerous concerts throughout UK and I, solo recitals at Royal Festival Hall/South Bank Centre 1985, 1988 and 2006, concert tours of USA, Scandinavia and Eastern Europe, given numerous recitals and concerto performances and presented various progs BBC Radio 3 1982–, performed at Proms; various recordings (EMI); tstee Nicholas Danby Tst 2001–, pres Incorporated Assoc of Organists 2005–07, pres Royal Coll of Organists 2013–15; dir John Hill Memorial Recitals 2006–, memb Bd Benevolent Soc of Blues 2008; *Publications* fndr ed London Organ Concerts Guide 1994–2016; *Recreations* family, opera, cricket, gardening; *Style*— Ms Catherine Ennis; ✉ e-mail cmennis@aol.com

ENNIS-HILL, Jessica; CBE (2013, MBE 2011); da of Vinnie Ennis, and Alison Powell; *b* 28 January 1986, Sheffield; *m* 2013, Andrew Hill; 1 s (Reggie Ennis-Hill b 2014); *Career* athlete; achievements incl: Bronze medal heptathlon Commonwealth Games 2006, Gold medal heptathlon World Championships 2009, Gold medal haptathlon European Championships 2010, Gold medal pentathlon World Indoor Championships 2010, Silver medal heptathlon World Championships 2011, Silver medal pentathlon World Indoor Championships 2012, Gold medal heptathlon Olympic Games 2012, Gold medal heptathlon World Championships 2015, Silver medal heptathlon Olympic Games 2016; third place BBC Sports Personality of the Year 2010; *Style*— Mrs Jessica Ennis-Hill, CBE; ✉ c/o JCCM Ltd, 12 Whiteladies Road, Bristol BS8 1PD

ENO, Brian Peter George St John Baptiste de la Salle; s of William Arnold Eno (d 1988), of Woodbridge, Suffolk, and Maria Alphonsine, *née* Buslot; *b* 15 May 1948; *Educ* St Mary's Convent, St Joseph's Coll, Ipswich Sch of Art, Winchester Coll of Art; *m* 1, 11 March 1967, Sarah Grenville; 1 c (Hannah b 25 July 1967); m 2, 11 Jan 1988, Anthea Norman-Taylor; 2 c (Irial b 25 Jan 1990, Darla b 5 Aug 1991); *Career* musician and prodr; visiting prof RCA 1995–; numerous lectures worldwide on matters of culture; memb Global Business Network; hon prof of new media Berlin Univ of Art; Hon DTech Univ of Plymouth; *Music* The Maxwell Demon 1969, The Scratch Orchestra 1970, The Portsmouth Sinfonia 1971–73, Roxy Music 1971–73; solo records: Here Come The Warm Jets 1974, Taking Tiger Mountain (by Strategy) 1974, Another Green World 1975, Discreet Music 1975, Before and After Science 1977, Music For Films 1978, Music for Airports 1978, On Land 1981, Thursday Afternoon 1984, Nerve Net 1992, The Shutov Assembly 1992, Neroli 1993, The Drop 1997, Another Day on Earth 2005; collaborations: No Pussyfooting (with Robert Fripp) 1972, Evening Star (with Robert Fripp) 1975, Possible Musics (with Jon Hassell) 1980, Low, Heroes and Lodger (all with David Bowie) 1978–80, The Plateaux of Mirror (with Harold Budd) 1980, My Life in The Bush of Ghosts (with David Byrne) 1980, Apollo (with Daniel Lanois and Roger Eno) 1983, The Pearl (with Harold Budd) 1984, Wrong Way Up (with John Cale) 1990, Spinner (with Jan Wobble) 1995, Drawn from Life (with J Peter Schwalm) 2001, Equatorial Stars (with Robert Fripp) 2004, Beyond Even (with Robert Fripp) 2007, Everything That Happens Will Happen Today (with David Byrne) 2008; selected prodns: Lucky Lief and the Longships (Bob Calvert) 1975, Are we not men? (Devo) 1978, More songs about buildings and food, Fear of Music and Remain in Light (all with Talking Heads) 1978–80, Unforgettable Fire, The Joshua Tree, Achtung Baby, Zooropa, All That You Can't Leave Behind and No Line On The Horizon (all with U2) 1984–2009, Bright Red (Laurie Anderson) 1995, Outside (David Bowie) 1995, Surprise (Paul Simon) 2006, Viva la Vida (Coldplay) 2008; *Visual* over 70 exhibitions of video artworks in museums and galleries worldwide incl: La Forêt Museum (Tokyo) 1983, Stedelijk Museum (Amsterdam) 1984, Venice Biennale 1986, Centre D'Art (Barcelona) 1992, Circulo de Bellas Artes (Madrid) 1993, Permanent Inst Swarovski (nr Innsbruck, Austria) 1995, Russian Museum (St Petersburg) 1997, Kunsthalle (Bonn) 1998, Kiasma (Helsinki) 1999, Hayward Gallery (London) 2000, SFMOMA (San Francisco) 2001, Lyon Biennial 2005, Museum für Abgüsse Klassicher Bildwerke Munich 2005, Venice Biennale 2006, Selfridges (London) 2007, Baltic Exchange (Newcastle) 2007, Ara Pacis (Rome) 2008, Madre (Naples) 2008; *DVD* 77 Million Paintings 2006; *Awards* Best Producer BRIT Awards 1994, Record of the Year Grammy Awards 2001 and 2002, The Joe Meek Award for Innovation in Production Music Prodrs' Guild Award 2009; *Publications* Oblique Strategies (with Peter Schmidt, 1975), A Year With Swollen Appendices (1996); *Recreations* perfumery, thinking, futurology, Long Now Fndn; *Style*— Brian Eno, Esq; ✉ Opal Ltd, 4 Pembridge Mews, London W11 3EQ (☎ 020 7221 4933, fax 020 7727 5404, e-mail opal@opaloffice.com)

ENTWISTLE, George; s of Philip Richardson Entwistle, and Wendy Patricia, *née* Firth; *b* 8 July 1962; *Educ* Silcoates Sch Wakefield, Univ of Durham (BA), St Catherine's Coll Oxford (MSt); *Career* magazine journalist Haymarket Publishing 1984–89; BBC: prodr On the Record 1993–94, prodr Newsnight 1994–97, asst ed Newsnight 1997–99, dep ed

Tomorrow's World 1999–2000, dep ed Newsnight 2000–01, ed Newsnight 2002–04, ed The Culture Show 2004–05, head of TV current affrs 2005–07, acting controller BBC Four 2007, controller of knowledge commissioning 2008–11, dir BBC TV 2011–12, DG BBC 2012; tstee Public Catalogue Fndn 2013–, tstee Art UK 2013–; memb Exec Ctee Georgian Gp 2016–; *Recreations* architectural and design history, reading, music, fell walking, watching rugby union; *Style*— George Entwistle, Esq

ENTWISTLE, John Nicholas McAlpine; OBE (2005); s of Sir (John Nuttall) Maxwell Entwistle (d 1994), and Jean Cunliffe McAlpine, *née* Penman (d 1993); *b* 1941; *Educ* Uppingham; *m* 6 Sept 1968, Phillida Entwistle, *qv*; 1 s (Nicholas b 1970), 1 da (Louise b 1971); *Career* admitted slr 1963; asst attorney Shearman & Sterling New York 1963–64, UK rep Salzburg Seminar Scholarship 1966, ptnr Maxwell Entwistle & Byrne (solicitors) 1966–91, conslt slr Davies Wallis Foyster 1992–2002, dir Rathbone Brothers plc 1992–98; underwriting memb Lloyd's 1971–2000, gen cmmr for Income Tax 1978–83, pt/t chm Social Security Appeal Tbnls 1992–2006, memb Parole Bd 1994–2000, pt/t immigration judge 2000–10; Merseyside regnl chm NW Industrial Cncl 1981–87, dir Merseyside TEC 1990–91; chm: Liverpool Chamber of Commerce and Industry 1992–94, NW Chambers of Commerce Assoc 1993–97; pres British Chambers of Commerce 1998–2000 (a dep pres 1996–98), memb Chllr of the Exchequer's Standing Ctee on Preparation for EMU 1998–2000; Home Sec's representative for appointment to the Merseyside Police Authy 1994–2000; nat vice-chm Bow Gp 1967–68, memb Liverpool City Cncl 1968–71, Parly candidate Huyton (opposed by Harold Wilson) 1970; memb Cncl Nat Fedn of Housing Assocs 1972–75, govr and dep treas Blue Coat Sch Liverpool 1971–85, pres Friends of the Nat Museums & Galleries on Merseyside 1987–90 (chm and tstee 1984–87), Merseyside rep Nat Art-Collections Fund 1985–89, memb NW Regnl Ctee Nat Tst 1992–98, tstee Nat Museums & Galleries on Merseyside 1990–97 (chm Devpt Tst 1991–96), tstee Royal Acad Tst 2006–11 (emeritus tstee 2011–), chm Romney Soc 2012–16, tstee Friends of the Lake District 2014 (chm 2016–); memb: Disciplinary Ctee Mortgage Compliance Bd 1999–2004, Cncl for Britain in Europe 1999–2004, Criminal Injuries Compensation Appeals Panel 2000–12, Advsy Cncl Migration Watch UK 2010–16; hon fell Liverpool John Moores Univ 2010; DL Merseyside 1992–2002; *Recreations* collecting and painting pictures, gardening and fishing; *Clubs* Carlton (memb Political Ctee 2004–08), Lansdowne; *Style*— John Entwistle, Esq, OBE; ✉ 6 Nutwood Manor, Windermere Road, Grange-Over-Sands, Cumbria LA11 6EY (☎ 015395 83726, e-mail entwistlej@mail.com)

ENTWISTLE, Raymond Marvin; *b* 12 June 1944; *Educ* John Ruskin GS Surrey; *m* 23 March 1965, Barbara, *née* Hennessy; 2 s, 1 da; *Career* Lloyds Bank 1960–84 (latterly mangr Edinburgh); Adam & Co Gp plc: joined 1984, md Adam & Co plc 1991–2004, gp md 1993–2004, chm 2004–09, Adam & Co Investment Management Ltd; chm Scoban plc 2010–13; dir: John Davidson Holdings and John Davidson (Pipes) Ltd 1990–96, I & H Brown Ltd 2002–; chm The FruitMarket Gallery 1990–2000, govr Edinburgh Coll of Art 1989–99, dir J W International plc 1995–96, dir Dunedin Smaller Companies Investment Tst plc 1998–2014, chm Hampden & Co plc 2013–, chm Bonhams Scotland 2016–; chm Scottish Civic Tst 2003–13, memb Ctee Royal Botanic Gardens 2003–08, tstee Fundraising Bd Victim Support Scotland 2007–15, tstee Royal High Sch Preservation Tst 2015–; FCIB 1992, FCIBS 2001; *Recreations* antiques, fishing, golfing, shooting, walking; *Clubs* New (Edinburgh), Lauder Golf; *Style*— Raymond Entwistle, Esq; ✉ The Glebe, Lauder, Berwickshire TD2 6RW (☎ 01578 718751)

EPHSON, Martin Frederick Emmanuel; s of HE Anthony W C G Ephson, and Pamela, *née* May; *b* 17 August 1956, London; *Educ* Charterhouse, Univ of Westminster (BA); *m* 9 August 1985, Eugenia, da of Dr B Collins; 1 da (Ciara b 10 July 1988), 2 s (Patrick b 3 May 1990, Ludo b 8 June 1993); *Career* in corp fin 1988–92, fndr dir Farrow & Ball paint and wallpaper mfrs 1992–2006 (with Tom Helme, *qv*), fndr and dir Fermoie (fabric mfrs) 2010–; winner Queen's Award for Enterprise 2004; *Publications* Paint and Colour in Decoration (2003); *Recreations* playing polo, sailing, contemporary art collecting; *Clubs* Royal Cork Yacht, Cirencester Park Polo; *Style*— Martin Ephson, Esq; ✉ Poulton House, Marlborough, Wilts SN8 2LN (☎ 01672 514663)

EPSTEIN, Dr Owen; s of Dr Morris Epstein, and Nancy, *née* Frysh; *b* 12 May 1950; *Educ* Univ of the Witwatersrand (MB BCh); *m* 10 Dec 1972, June, da of D David Armist; 2 s (Daniel b 4 Aug 1976, Marc b 14 June 1979); *Career* med registrar 1977–79, clinical res fell 1979–82, lectr in medicine 1982–85, conslt and clinical postgrad tutor Royal Free Hosp London 1985–; author of several scientific publications; chm gastroenterology Royal Free Hosp; FRCP 1989, (MRCP 1976); *Style*— Dr Owen Epstein; ✉ Royal Free Hampstead NHS Trust, Pond Street, Hampstead, London NW3 2QG (☎ 020 7794 0500, fax 020 7794 6614, website www.epsteingastro.demon.co.uk)

ERAUT, Prof Michael Ruarc; s of Lt-Col Ruarc Bertram Sorel Eraut (d 1987), and Frances Hurst (d 1972); *b* 15 November 1940; *Educ* Winchester, Trinity Hall Cambridge (BA, PhD); *m* 7 Aug 1964, (Mary) Cynthia, da of Michael William Wynne (d 2005), of Great Shelford; 2 s (Patrick b 10 May 1968, Christopher b 27 Aug 1971); *Career* Univ of Sussex Centre for Educnl Technol: fell 1967, sr fell 1971, dir 1973–76, reader in educn 1976–86, prof of educn 1986–2006, dir Inst of Continuing and Professional Educn 1986–91, prof emeritus 2006–; visiting prof of evaluation Univ of Illinois 1980–81 (educnl technol 1965–67); jl ed Learning in Health and Social Care 2000–05; *Books* incl: Teaching and Learning: New Methods and Resources in Higher Education (1970), Analysis of Curriculum Materials (1975), Curriculum Development in Further Education (1985), Improving the Quality of YTS (1986), International Encyclopedia of Educational Technology (1989), Education and the Information Society (1991), Flexible Learning in Schools (1991), Developing Professional Knowledge and Competence (1994), Learning to Use Scientific Knowledge in Education and Practice Settings (1995), Development of Knowledge and Skill in Employment (1998), Developing the Attributes of Medical Professional Judgement and Competence (2000), Evaluation of Higher Level S/NVQs (2001), The Significance of Workplace Learning for Individuals, Groups and Organisations (jtly, 2007), Evaluation of the Introduction of the Intercollegiate Surgical Curriculum Programme (contrib, 2008), Learning Trajectories, Innovation and Identity for Professional Development (contrib and co-ed, 2011, Professional Outstanding Publication Award American Educnl Research Assoc 2013); *Style*— Prof Michael Eraut; ✉ 49 St Annes Crescent, Lewes, East Sussex BN7 1SD (☎ 01273 475955, e-mail michael@eraut.eclipse.co.uk)

EREMIN, Prof Oleg; s of Theodore Eremin (d 1995), of Melbourne, Aust, and Maria, *née* Avramenko (d 1978); *b* 12 November 1938; *Educ* Christian Brothers Coll Melbourne, Univ of Melbourne (MB BS, MD); *m* 23 Feb 1963, Jennifer Mary, da of Ellis Charles Ching (d 1972), of Melbourne, Aust; 1 da (Katherine b 1968), 2 s (Andrew b 1972, Nicholas b 1973); *Career* asst surgn Royal Melbourne Hosp Aust 1971–72 (house offr, sr house offr, registrar 1965–71), sr registrar Combined Norwich Hosps 1972–74, sr res assoc in immunology Dept of Pathology Univ of Cambridge 1977–80 (res asst 1974–77), sr lectr and conslt surgn Edinburgh Royal Infirmary 1981–85, prof of surgery and conslt surgn Aberdeen Royal Infirmary 1985–98, conslt surgeon United Lincolnshire Hosps NHS Tst 1999–2011, dir of research and devpt ULH Tst 2001–14; hon professorial fell Rowett Research Inst Aberdeen 1992–98, hon prof Univ of Nottingham 1998–; clinical dir Trent Comp Local Research Network 2007–14; ed Jl of RCS(Ed) 1997–2002, ed-in-chief The Surgeon 2003–07; tstee Thalidomide Tst 2003–15; memb: Assoc of Surgns of GB and I, Surgical Research Soc until 2015, Br Assoc of Surgical Oncology until 2015, James IV Assoc of Surgns, Int Surgical Gp; hon fell Royal Coll of Surgns of Thailand 2003; Hon DSc Univ of Lincoln 2006; FRACS, FRCSEd (memb Cncl 1994–98 and 2000–05, examiner and chm Research Bd 1996–2006), FMedSci 2000; *Recreations* classical music, literature, sport; *Style*— Prof Oleg Eremin; ✉ Orchard House, 51A Washdyke Lane, Nettleham, Lincoln LN2 2PX (☎ 01522 750669)

ERGATOUDIS, George; *m*; 2 s; *Career* Kiss FM 1991–97, prodr BBC Radio 1 1997–2000, mangr of music policy BBC 1Xtra 2000–04, head of music BBC Radio 1 2005–16 (and 1Xtra 2009–16), head of content programming Spotify UK/Aust/New Zealand 2016–; *Style*— George Ergatoudis, Esq; ✉ Spotify UK Ltd, 4th Floor, 25 Argyll Street, London W1F 7TU (Twitter @GeorgErgatoudis)

ERIAN, Prof John; s of Dr Habib Erian (d 1976), of Cairo, and Aida, *née* Mitry; *b* 12 August 1948; *Educ* St George's Coll, Ain-Shams Med Univ Cairo (MB BCh); *m* 1, 7 July 1973, Jennifer, da of Norman Frank Felton, of Hanworth, Middx; 1 s (Michael b 1974), 2 da (Gehanne b 1976, Simonne b 1977); m 2; m 3, 25 Nov 1995, Hilary, da of George Walter Hutchings, of Leigh-on-Sea, Southend; *Career* conslt obstetrician and gynaecologist: W Cumberland Hosp 1975–79, St George's Hosp 1979–82, Queen Charlotte's Hosp and Chelsea Hosp for Women 1982–83, St Thomas' Hosp 1983, Guy's Hosp 1983–85, Farnborough Hosp Kent 1985–; clinical dir Dept of Obstetrics and Gynaecology Bromley NHS Tst 1997–, divnl dir of surgery Bromley NHS Tst 1998, medical dir Bromley Hosps NHS Tst 2003–05; chm Endoscopic Laser Fndn 1998; fndr of Bromley Dist Colposcopy Serv and Endocrine Unit and Gift Treatment, pioneered YAG laser surgery in UK as an alternative to hysterectomy, preceptor in endoscopic surgery, pioneered laparoscopic subtotal hysterectomy as day case procedure 2002; author of various papers on endoscopic and laser surgery in gynaecology; prof of gynaecology Univ of Athens 2006; memb: Br Endoscopy Soc (memb Cncl 1997–), SE Gynaecological Soc, Egyptian Med Soc; MRCOG 1981, FRCOG 1993 (Merit Award 1995); *Recreations* tennis, table tennis, swimming, skiing, horse riding, travelling, theatre, music, food and wine; *Style*— Prof John Erian; ✉ Briar Porch, Sevenoaks Road, Chelsfield Park, Orpington, Kent BR6 15E (☎ 01689 851192); Farnborough Hospital, Farnborough Common, Locksbottom, Orpington, Kent (☎ 01689 814094)

E

ERITH, Robert Felix; TD (1977), DL (Essex 1998); eld s of Felix Henry Erith, FSA (d 1991), of Ardleigh, Essex, and Barbara Penelope, *née* Hawken (d 2004); *b* 8 August 1938, Ardleigh, Essex; *Educ* Ipswich Sch, Writtle Agric Coll; *m* 7 May 1966, Sara Kingsford Joan, da of Dr Christopher Muller (d 1990); 3 s (Charles b 1967, James, Edward (twins) b 1970); *Career* 10 Hussars: 2 Lt Serv in Aqaba Jordan and Tidworth Hants 1957–58, AVR serv in Aden, Oman, Cyprus, Hong Kong, Germany, UK 1962–79, Maj 1973; builders merchants' salesman and mgmnt trainee 1960–64: London, Washington DC, Oakland California, Perth W Aust; EB Savory Milln & Co (Milln & Robinson until 1967): bldg specialist 1966, ptnr 1969–83, sr ptnr 1983–87; chm: SBCI Savory Milln Ltd 1987–89, Swiss Bank Corporation Equities Group 1989–93; conslt UBS Warburg 1993–2002; dir Central Capital Hldgs 1996–2009; farmer; current roles incl: memb Ctee Colne Stour Countryside Assoc 1988–, vice-pres CPRE (Essex) 1998–, pres Dedham Vale Soc 2003–, chm Dedham Vale AONB and Stour Valley Partnership 2009–, vice-pres Essex Community Fndn 2012–; past roles incl: tstee Shakespeare Globe Tst 1993–2008, chm Essex Environment Tst 1998–2004, pres Essex Agicultural Soc 1999–2000, memb Ctee Essex CLA 2009–16; churchwarden Holy Innocents Lamarsh 1969–2009; Parly candidate (Cons) Ipswich 1976–79; High Sheriff Essex 1997–98; Liveryman Worshipful Co of Builders Merchants 1987, Freeman City of London 1987; FRPSL 1994, FRSA 1995; *Books* Britain into Europe (jtly, 1962), The Role of the Monarchy (jtly, 1965), Savory Milln's Building Book (annual edns 1968–83); *Recreations* environmental pursuits, stamp collecting, golf; *Clubs* Cavalry and Guards', Pratt's, MCC, Royal Philatelic Soc; *Style*— Robert Erith, Esq, TD, DL; ✉ Shrubs Farm, Lamarsh, Bures, Essex C08 5EA (☎ 01787 227520, mobile 078 3624 5536, e-mail bob@shrubsfarm.co.uk, website www.shrubsfarm.co.uk)

ERMISCH, Prof John; s of Elmer Ermisch (d 1986), and Frances, *née* Bertrand; *b* 1 July 1947; *Educ* Univ of Wisconsin (BS), Univ of Kansas (MA, PhD); *m* 7 May 1977, Dianne Monti; *Career* research economist US Dept of Housing and Urban Devpt 1974–76, sr research fell PSI 1976–86, sr research offr NIESR 1986–91, Bonar-McFie prof Univ of Glasgow 1991–94, prof Univ of Essex 1994–2011, prof of family demography Univ of Oxford 2011–; FBA 1995; *Books* The Political Economy of Demographic Change (1983), Lone Parenthood: An Economic Analysis (1991), An Economic Analysis of the Family (2003); *Recreations* film, opera, theatre; *Style*— Prof John Ermisch; ✉ Department of Sociology, Manor Road Building, Manor Road, Oxford OX1 3UQ (☎ 01865 286175, e-mail john.ermisch@sociology.ox.ac.uk)

ERNE, 6 Earl of (I 1798); Sir Henry George Victor John Crichton; KCVO, JP; sat as Baron Fermanagh (UK 1876); also Baron Erne (I 1768) and Viscount Erne (I 1781); s of 5 Earl of Erne (ka 1940), and Lady Davidema (d 1995), da of 2 Earl of Lytton, KG, GCSI, GCIE, PC; *b* 9 July 1937; *Educ* Eton; *m* 1, 5 Nov 1958 (m dis 1980), Camilla Marguerite, da of late Wing Cdr Owen George Endicott Roberts; 1 s, 4 da; m 2, 1980, Mrs Anna Carin Hitchcock (*née* Bjorck); *Heir* s, Viscount Crichton; *Career* page of honour to HM King George VI 1952 and to HM The Queen 1952–54; Lt N Irish Horse 1960–68; HM Lord-Lt Co Fermanagh; *Clubs* White's, Lough Erne Yacht; *Style*— The Rt Hon the Earl of Erne, KCVO; ✉ Crom Castle, Newtown Butler, Co Fermanagh (☎ 028 6773 8208)

ERROLL, 24 Earl of (S 1452); Sir Merlin Sereld Victor Gilbert Hay of Erroll; 12 Bt (Baronetcy originally Moncreiffe of that Ilk, Perthshire, NS 1685); also 28 Hereditary Lord High Constable of Scotland (conferred as Great Constable of Scotland *ante* 1309 and made hereditary by charter of Robert I 1314), Lord Hay (S 1429) and Lord Slains (S 1452); Chief of the Hays; as Lord High Constable, has precedence in Scotland before all other hereditary honours after the Blood Royal; also maintains private officer-at-arms (Slains Pursuivant); s of Countess of Erroll (d 1978) by her 1 husb, Sir Iain Moncreiffe of that Ilk, 11 Bt (d 1985); his gggggf (the 18 Earl)'s w, Elizabeth FitzClarence, natural da of King William IV, whose arms he quarters debruised by a baton sinister; *b* 20 April 1948; *Educ* Eton, Trinty Coll Cambridge; *m* 8 May 1982, Isabelle, o da of Thomas Sidney Astell Hohler (*né* Hohler, assumed name and arms of Astell by Royal licence 1978, d 1989), of Wolverton Park, Basingstoke; 2 s (Harry Thomas William, Lord Hay b 8 Aug 1984, Hon Richard b 14 Dec 1990), 2 da (Lady Amelia b 23 Nov 1986, Lady Laline b 21 Dec 1987); *Heir* s, Lord Hay; *Career* mktg and trg conslt; chm: CRC Ltd, Fonem Ltd; ICT advsr; elected hereditary peer House of Lords 1999–, memb Bd Parly Office of Sci and Technol; memb Cncl: EURIM, PITCOM; memb Queen's Body Guard for Scotland (Royal Co of Archers); Lt Atholl Highlanders; Prime Warden Worshipful Co of Fishmongers 2000–01; Hon Col RMPTA 1992–97; OStJ, TEM; *Recreations* country pursuits; *Clubs* White's, Pratt's, Puffins; *Style*— The Rt Hon the Earl of Erroll; ✉ Woodbury Hall, Sandy, Bedfordshire SG19 2HR (☎ 01767 650251, fax 01767 651553)

ERSKINE, Barbara; da of Stuart Nigel Rose, of Hay-on-Wye, and Pamela Yvonne, *née* Anding (d 1988); *b* 10 August 1944; *Educ* St George's Harpenden, Univ of Edinburgh (MA); *m*; 2 s (Adrian James Earl, Jonathan Erskine Alexander); *Career* freelance editor and journalist, short story writer, novelist; memb: Soc of Authors, Scientific and Medical Network, Academi (The Welsh Acad); *Books* Lady of Hay (1986), Kingdom of Shadows (1988), Encounters (1990), Child of the Phoenix (1992), Midnight is a Lonely Place (1994), House of Echoes (1996), Distant Voices (1996), On the Edge of Darkness (1998), Whispers in the Sand (2000), Hiding from the Light (2002), Sands of Time (2003), Daughters of Fire (2006), The Warrior's Princess (2008), Time's Legacy (2010), River of Destiny (2012), The Darkest Hour (2014), Sleeper's Castle (2016); *Recreations* reading, growing and using herbs, exploring the past; *Style*— Mrs Barbara Erskine; ✉ c/o Blake Friedmann, Literary

Agents, Frst Floor, Selous House, 5–12 Mandela Street, London NW1 0DU (✆ 020 7387 0842)

ERSKINE, Robert Simon; s of Dr Maurice Erskine (d 2007), and Victoria, *née* Travers (d 2008); *b* 24 April 1954; *Educ* JFS Comp Sch, Ealing Tech Coll, Kingston Poly (BA), UCL, Slade Sch of Fine Art (Higher Dip Fine Art); *m* 1984, Jo, *née* Singer; 3 s (Liam Sasher b 1989, Wyatt Lloyd b 1992, Asher Aiden b 1995); *Career* sculptor and designer specialising in direct working of bronze and stainless steel; design co-ordinator Dale Keller Design Corp USA 1978–84, numerous worldwide architectural projects in Hong Kong, Switzerland, India, Greece and England 1978–84, numerous landmark sculptures sited UK, full time professional architectural sculptor 1984–, design conslt Marks & Spencer London and Nestle UK Ltd 1998–, design co-ordinator for Sultan of Brunei's Palace (world's largest palace); sculptor in residence: Caterpillar and Perkins Diesel Engine facility, Peterborough Sculpture Tst, Peterborough Green Wheel 2000; cmmnd sculptor Chartered Inst of Personnel and Devpt; holder of design patents for advanced lifting system; visiting lectr Frink Sch of Figurative Sculpture Stoke-on-Trent; contrib: The Times, BBC Cambridge, BBC Radio 4, Tyne Tees TV, Netherlands TV, AutoLab (radio, USA), radio and national press; memb Inst of Advanced Motorists, memb Int Motor Press Assoc (sr European corr); ARBS 1993, FRBS 1997; *Exhibitions* Nat Soc Painters and Sculptors Mall Gallery London 1977–79, Ben Uri Gallery London 1985, Int Yorkshire Sculpture Park 1986–88, Andrew Usiskin Gallery London 1989–92, Hakone Open Air Museum 1992, World Wildlife Fund Exhibition London 1992, Hannah Peschar Sculpture Garden Sussex 1994, Trade Indemnity Centre London 1994, Int Welding and Metal Working Exhibition Birmingham NEC 1994, Osterly Park London 1995, Cultural Village of Europe Holland 1999, world HQ of Pfizer Inc NY 1999 (solo exhbn), Art For Art's Sake Show (Cork St Gallery London) 2012; *Awards* winner maquette of excellence Hakone Int Open-Air Museum of Sculpture 1992, winner Sir Otto Beit Bronze Award RBS 1993–94, White Rhythm named most outstanding sculpture at Cultural Village of Europe in Holland 1999, public and landmark sculptures awarded status of perm public monuments by Courtauld Inst in assoc with Public Monuments and Sculptures Assoc, Nat Competition Winner for Landmark Sculpture for City of Peterborough 2000; *Publications* The Building of SS Oriana (1995), European Village of Culture, Sculpture Symposium (1999), Public Art in Coventry (2001), Public Sculpture of Staffordshire and the Black Country (by George Thomas Noszlopy and Fiona Waterhouse, 2005), British Industrial History in Sculpture (online, 2016); People Management publication 1995–2004; *Recreations* playing jazz (trumpet), swimming every day, cycling, photography, cooking, theatre, sci and technol (reading about and going to see), fixing broken things (at home and family), reading, listening to jazz and classical music, drawing, going to the cinema, concerts, playing with the children, being on the beach, flying my big and powerful kite, looking at the clouds and sunsets, climbing hills, thinking and designing my next sculptures, watching any TV documentary about sci, archeology and design, long walks with open eyes; *Clubs* East Anglia Historic AutoCycle and Moped; *Style*— Robert Erskine, Esq; ✉ website www.roberterskine.com

ERSKINE-HILL, Sir (Alexander) Roger; 3 Bt (UK 1945), of Quothquhan, Co Lanark; er s of Sir Robert Erskine-Hill, 2 Bt (d 1989), and Christine Alison, *née* Johnstone; *b* 15 August 1949, Biggar, Scotland; *Educ* Eton, Univ of Aberdeen (LLB); *m* 1 (m dis 1994), Sarah Anne Sydenham, da of Dr Richard John Sydenham Clarke (d 1970); 1 da (Kirsty Rose b 1985), 1 s (Robert Benjamin b 1986); m 2, Gillian Elizabeth Borlase Mitchell, da of Mr and Mrs David Surgey; *Heir* s, Robert Erskine-Hill; *Career* dir: The Hillbrooke Partnership Ltd, Map Marketing Ltd; *Style*— Sir Roger Erskine-Hill, Bt; ✉ The Old Malthouse, Briton Street, Bampton, Devon EX16 9LN (e-mail roger@hillbrooke.co.uk)

ESHUN, Ekow; *b* 27 May 1968; *Educ* Kingsbury HS, LSE (BSc); *Career* with Kiss FM 1987–88, freelance contrib 1990–93 (The Guardian, The Observer, The Face, BBC Radio 4, BBC Radio 5, BBC World Service), asst ed The Face 1993–96, ed Arena 1996, founding dir Bug Consultancy, editorial dir Tank magazine, artistic dir ICA 2005–11; writer and presenter of numerous TV and radio documentaries; currently contrib to: Late Review/Newsnight Review (BBC 2), The Daily Politics, Front Row (BBC Radio 4), The Guardian, The Observer, New Statesman, Sunday Times, Wallpaper; memb: Cncl ICA 1999–2003, Bd London Arts Board 1999–, Bd Tate Members 2003–; govr Univ of Arts London 2001–; *Books* Black Gold of the Sun (2005); *Recreations* fashion design, contemporary art; *Style*— Ekow Eshun, Esq

ESIRI, Prof Margaret Miriam; da of William Evans (d 1974), and Doreen, *née* Bates (d 1994); *b* 5 October 1941; *Educ* Croydon HS GDST, St Hugh's Coll Oxford (BA, BSc, BM BCh, DM, Hilary Howarth Science Prize, Martin Wronker Prize in Med); *m* 1963, Frederick Esiri; 1 da (Henrietta b 1963), 2 s (Mark b 1964, Frederick b 1967); *Career* trainee pathologist/neuropathologist United Oxford Hosps 1973–79; Univ of Oxford: jr research fell in neuropathology 1970–73, MRC sr clinical fell 1980–85, reader 1985–96, prof of neuropathology 1996–2007, emeritus prof 2008–; former vice-princ St Hugh's Coll Oxford; author of over 300 peer-reviewed research papers; former dir Thomas Willis Oxford Brain Collection and the Brain Bank for Autism and related developmental research; memb British Neuropathology Soc, former sponsor Oxford branch Alzheimers Soc; FRCPath 1988 (MRCPath 1976); *Books* Viral Encephalitis: Pathology, Diagnosis and Management (with John Booss, 1986), Diagnostic Neuropathology (with D R Oppenheimer, 1989, 3 edn with Daniel Perl, 2006), The Neuropathology of Dementia (ed with James H Morris, 1997, 2 edn 2004), Viral Encephalitis in Humans (with John Booss, 2003); *Recreations* family, reading, theatre, walking, gardening, visiting Nigeria; *Style*— Prof Margaret Esiri; ✉ Nuffield Dept of Clinical Neurosciences, West Wing, John Radcliffe Hospital, Oxford OX3 9DU (✆ 01865 234403, fax 01865 231157, e-mail margaret.esiri@ndcn.ox.ac.uk)

ESLER, Gavin William James; s of William John Esler, and Georgena, *née* Knight; *b* 27 February 1953; *Educ* George Heriot's Sch Edinburgh, Univ of Kent at Canterbury (BA, DCL), Univ of Leeds (MA); *Career* Thompson Newspapers grad trainee then journalist Belfast Telegraph 1975–77, reporter/presenter Spotlight BBC Northern Ireland current affrs prog 1977–81; BBC: reporter/presenter Newsnight and TV News 1982–89, Washington corr 1989–, chief N America corr 1990–97, presenter BBC News 1997–2002, presenter Newsnight and Panorama 2003–; columnist The Scotsman 1998–2005, freelance magazine and newspaper journalist; chllr Univ of Kent 2014–; RTS Journalism Award for Newsnight Report 1987; memb White House Corrs' Assoc; Hon MA Univ of Kent at Canterbury 1995, DCL Univ of Kent 2005; Sony Gold Award for Radio 4 documentary Letters from Guantanamo 2007; FRSA; *Books* Loyalties (novel, 1990), Deep Blue (novel, 1992), The Bloodbrother (novel, 1995), The United States of Anger (non-fiction, 1997), A Scandalous Man (novel, 2008), Powerplay (novel, 2009), Lessons from the Top (non-fiction, 2012); *Recreations* skiing, squash, hill walking, backwoods camping; *Style*— Gavin Esler, Esq; ✉ BBC Broadcasting House, Portland Place, London W1A 1AA (e-mail gavin.esler@bbc.co.uk)

ESPENHAHN, Peter Ian; s of Edward William Espenhahn, of E Molesey, and Barbara Mary, *née* Winmill; *b* 14 March 1944; *Educ* Westminster, Sidney Sussex Coll Cambridge (MA); *m* 10 Feb 1968, Fiona Elizabeth, da of Air Vice Marshal Brian Pashley Young, of Didmarton, Glos; 2 d (Sarah b 1971, Caroline b 1975); *Career* Deloitte Plender Griffiths London 1965–72, dir Corp Fin Dept Morgan Grenfell & Co Ltd 1983– (joined 1973); FCA; *Recreations* sailing, rugby, opera; *Style*— Peter Espenhahn, Esq; ✉ 79 Mount Ararat Road, Richmond, Surrey TW10 6PL

ESPEY, James S; OBE (2013); s of Joseph Espey (d 2003), and Joan Bond, *née* Nightingale; *b* 11 May 1943, Livingstone, Zambia; *Educ* BCom, MBA, PhD; *m* 6 Nov 1981, Celia, *née* Freeman; 2 da (Caroline b 3 May 1982, Jessica b 3 Oct 1984); *Career* gp mktg dir IDV Gp 1977–82, exec chm IDV UK Ltd 1982–86, United Distillers 1986–92 (pres United Distillers North America 1989–92), chm Seagram Distillers plc until 1998, pres Chivas and Glenlivet Gp until 1998; fndr James Espey and Assocs, co-fndr and chm The Last Drop Distillers Ltd 2007; non-exec dir: Fuller Smith and Turner plc 1998–2010, A G Barr plc 1999–2011, Whyte and Mackay Ltd 2003–10; sr conslt APU Ltd Mongolia 2012–15; *Books* Making Your Marque – 100 tips to build your personal brand and succeed in business (2014); *Recreations* int travel, sport (active golf); *Clubs* Richmond RFC (vice-pres), Oxford Rugby Football Union (vice-pres), Royal Wimbledon Golf; *Style*— James Espey, Esq, OBE; ✉ James Espey and Associates, 17 Somerset Road, Wimbledon, London SW19 5JZ

ESSER, Robin Charles; s of Charles Esser (d 1982), and Winifred Eileen Esser (d 1972); *b* 6 May 1935; *Educ* Wheelwright GS Dewsbury, Wadham Coll Oxford (MA); *m* 1, 5 Jan 1959, Irene Shirley, *née* Clough (d 1973); 2 s (Daniel b 1962, Toby b 1963), 2 da (Sarah Jane b 1961, Rebecca b 1965); m 2, 30 May 1981, Tui, *née* France; 2 s (Jacob b 1986, Samuel b 1990); *Career* cmmnd 2 Lt KOYLI 1955, transferred General Corps 1956, Capt acting ADPR BAOR 1957, awarded GSM; Daily Express: staff reporter 1957–60, ed William Hickey Column 1962, features ed 1963, NY Bureau 1965, northern ed 1969, exec ed 1970; conslt ed Evening News 1977, exec ed Daily Express 1984–86, ed Sunday Express 1986–89, ind editorial conslt 1990–, exec managing ed Daily Mail 1998– (conslt 1997); fell Soc of Eds; Freeman of the City of London 2015; *Books* The Hot Potato (1969), The Paper Chase (1971), Crusaders in Chains (2015); *Recreations* lunching, reading, tennis; *Clubs* Garrick, Hurlingham; *Style*— Robin Esser, Esq; ✉ 35 Elthiron Road, London SW6 4BW

ESSWOOD, Paul Lawrence Vincent; s of Alfred Walter Esswood, and Freda, *née* Garratt; *b* 6 June 1942; *Educ* West Bridgford GS Nottingham, Royal Coll of Music (Henry Blower singing prize); *m* 1, (m dis 1990); 2 s (Gabriel Peter b 1968, Michael William b 1971); m 2, 4 Aug 1990, Aimée Desirée; 1 da (Stella Jane b 1992), 1 s (Lawrence Galahad b 1993); *Career* opera, concert and recital singer (counter-tenor) specializing in Baroque period and conductor; operatic debut Univ of Calif Berkeley 1966, conducting debut Chichester Festival 2000; given performances (as singer) at venues incl: Zürich, Cologne, Stuttgart, Chicago, La Scala Milan; regular conducting work with Capella Cracovienis and Capella Bydgostiensis (both Poland) and The Concert of Twelve (orch and choir), conducted the modern world première of Pompeo Magno by Cavalli in Varazdin Croatioa; prof of singing RCM 1977–80, prof of Baroque vocal interpretation RAM 1985–; lay vicar Westminster Abbey 1964–71; ARCM 1964, Hon RAM 1990; *Performances* as singer incl: Monteverdi operas (Zürich), Britten's A Midsummer Night's Dream (Cologne), Penderecki's Paradise Lost (La Scala), Glass's Akhnaten (Stuttgart); solo recitals incl: Purcell's Music for a While, Schumann's Dichterliebe and Liederkreis Op39, English lute songs from Songs to My Lady; counter-tenor vocalist in The Musicre Companye; *Recordings* as singer incl: all Bach Cantatas, St Matthew Passion, Christmas Oratorio, Purcell's Dido and Aeneas; recordings of Handel works incl: Brockes Passion, Jephte, Saul, Belshazzar, Rinaldo, Xerxes, Messiah, Il Pastor Fido, Britten Folk Songs and Canticle II, Abraham & Isaac; *Recreations* gardening (organic); *Style*— Paul Esswood, Esq; ✉ Jasmine Cottage, 42 Ferring Lane, Ferring, West Sussex BN12 6QT (✆ and fax 01903 504480)

ESTEVE-COLL, Dame Elizabeth Anne Loosemore; DBE (1995); da of P W Kingdon, and Nora Kingdon; *b* 14 October 1938; *Educ* Darlington Girls HS, Birkbeck Coll London (BA); *m* 1960, Jose Alexander Timothy Esteve-Coll; *Career* head of learning resources Kingston Poly 1977, univ librarian Univ of Surrey 1982, keeper Nat Art Library V&A 1985, dir V&A 1988–95, vice-chllr UEA 1995–97, chllr Univ of Lincoln 2001–09; tstee Sainsbury Inst for the Study of Japanese Arts and Cultures (SISJAC); freelance cultural consultancy; *Recreations* reading, music, foreign travel; *Style*— Dame Elizabeth Esteve-Coll, DBE; ✉ The Tabernacle, Millgate, Aylsham, Norfolk NR11 6HR

ESTORICK, Michael Jacob; s of Eric Estorick (d 1993), and Salome, *née* Dessau (d 1989); *b* 24 June 1951; *Educ* Haberdashers' Aske's, Magdalene Coll Cambridge, City & Guilds of London Art Sch; *Children*; 1 s (Alexander b 1988); *Career* chm Estorick Collection of Modern Italian Art London; formerly jt chm Gerald Duckworth and Co Publishers; book reviewer The Tablet, obiturist The Independent; vice-pres Hazlitt Soc; hon memb 56 Group Wales; *Publications* Heirs and Graces (1981), Can't Buy Me Love (1986), What are Friends For (1990), Just Business (1996), Fortune (2001), Brief Wives (2010); *Recreations* real tennis (Harbour Club champion 1996), golf, reading, drawing, over-reacting; *Clubs* Savile, MCC, Buck's, Beefsteak, far too many golf clubs; *Style*— Michael Estorick, Esq; ✉ c/o Estorick Collection, 39A Canonbury Square, London N1 2AN

ETCHINGHAM, Julie; *b* 1969, Leicester; *Educ* English Martyrs RC Comp Leicester, Newnham Coll Cambridge (BA); *m* 1997, Nick Gardner; 2 s (Leo Francis, James Joseph); *Career* reporter BBC 1992–94, presenter Newsround (BBC) 1994–97, reporter BBC News 1997–2001, presenter Sky News 2002–08, presenter ITV News At Ten 2008–; Presenter of the Year RTS Award 2010; Hon LLD Univ of Leicester 2012; *Style*— Ms Julie Etchingham; ✉ ITV Network Centre, 200 Gray's Inn Road, London WC1X 8HF

ETHERIDGE, Hugh Charles; s of Fredan Etheridge (d 1989), and Monica, *née* Bird; *b* 1 July 1950, Weybridge, Surrey; *Educ* Bradfield College; *m* 26 Jan 1974, Jacqueline, *née* Parnell; 2 s (Tobias b 1 July 1976, Oliver b 9 Sept 1981); *Career* articled clerk Herbert Parnell 1969–73, asst mangr Peat Marwick Mitchell 1974–77, gp chief accountant Fitch Lovell plc 1977–87, finance dir Strong & Fisher Holdings plc 1987–91, finance dir Matthew Clark plc 1991–2001, finance dir Waste Recycling Group plc 2001–03, chief finance offr WRAP 2004–10; non-exec dir: Ashtead Group plc 2004–14, William Sinclair Hldgs plc 2011–14; mentor Prince's Tst; FCA 1974, ACT 1981; *Style*— Hugh Etheridge, Esq; ✉ 5 Springfield Place, Bath BA1 5RA

ETHERINGTON, Sir Stuart James; kt (2010); s of Ronald George Etherington, of Mudeford, Dorset, and Dorothy Lillian, *née* West; *b* 26 February 1955; *Educ* Sondes Place Sch Dorking, Brunel Univ (BSc), Univ of Essex (MA), London Business Sch (MBA), SOAS Univ of London (MA); *m* 18 May 2013, Rosamund McCarthy; *Career* social worker 1977–79, researcher employed by housing tst 1980–83, policy advsr Br Assoc of Social Workers 1983–85, dir Good Practices in Mental Health 1985–87, chief exec RNID 1991–94 (dir of public affrs 1987–91), chief exec NCVO 1994–; cmmr Cmmn on Living Wage 2013–14; chair London United 2014–; visiting prof: South Bank Univ, City Univ; chm: Heritage Care 1996–2002, Civicus in Europe 1992–2000; tstee: Charity Aid Fndn (CAF) 1995–2004, English Churches Housing Tst 1999–2002, Civicus 2000–07 (treas 2004–07), Actors of Dionysus 2003–06; chair Patrons Fund 2015–; memb: New Deal Advsy Ctee 1997–2001, ESRC 1998–2003 (chm External Relations Ctee 1999–2003), RIIA; memb Cncl Open Univ 2002–06, memb Ct Greenwich Univ 2004–13 (pro-chllr 2008–13); Hon DSc Brunel Univ, HonDUniv Univ of Greenwich 2014; FRSA, hon fell Inst of Environmental Sciences (IES) 2015–; *Books* Mental Health and Housing (1984), Emergency Duty Teams (1985), Social Work and Citizenship (1987), The Sensitive Bureaucracy (1986), Worlds Apart (1990), The Essential Manager (1993); *Recreations* watching cricket, Charlton Athletic FC and Blackheath Rugby, reading, watching opera, film and theatre, Italian foodie; *Clubs* Reform, Surrey CCC, Blacks, Le Beaujolais; *Style*— Sir Stuart Etherington; ✉ 49 King George Street, London SE10 8QB; National Council for Voluntary Organisations, Society

Building, 8 All Saints Street, London N1 9RL (☎ 020 7520 2456, e-mail stuart.etherington@ncvo.org.uk)

ETTINGER, Robert Gerard Louis; s of Gerard Ettinger (d 2002), and Elizabeth, *née* Martinek (d 2004); *b* 17 August 1955, London; *Educ* Saint Nicolas Sch Northwood, Theresianische Acad Vienna, Coll St Benoit Ardouane; *m* 11 Aug 1993, Jane, *née* Gale; *Career* Mappins Jewellers Canada 1974–75, Zimmermann Co Frankfurt 1975–76, G Ettinger Ltd London 1977–; chm British Travelgoods and Accessories Assoc 2001–04; *Recreations* skiing. cycling, tennis, travel; *Clubs* Hurlingham, Ski Club of GB (memb Cncl 1981–84, chm Home Ctee 1983–86); *Style—* Robert Ettinger, Esq; ✉ G Ettinger Ltd, 215 Putney Bridge Road, London SW15 2NY (☎ 020 8877 1616, fax 020 8877 1146, e-mail robert@ettinger.co.uk)

EUSTACE, Dudley Graham; s of Albert Eustace, MBE (d 1992), of Bristol, and Mary, *née* Manning (d 2004); *b* 3 July 1936; *Educ* The Cathedral Sch Bristol, Univ of Bristol (BA Econ); *m* 30 May 1964, Diane, da of Karl Zakrajsek (d 1974), of Nova Racek, Yugoslavia; 2 da (Gabriella b 1965, Chantal b 1967); *Career* actg PO RAFVR 1955–58; various appts (incl treas Canada and dir of fin UK) Alcan Aluminium Ltd of Canada 1964–87, dir of fin British Aerospace plc 1987–92, exec vice-pres Philips Electronics NV Netherlands 1992–99 (dir of fin 1992–97, vice-chm 1997–99), chm Smith & Nephew 2000–06 (dep chm 1999), non-exec chm Aegon NV, chm Providence Capital NV Netherlands 2011–; non-exec dir: Hagemeyer NV, Royal KPN NV KLM, Stork NV; memb Advsy Cncl Rothchilds 2011–13; vice-chm Univ of Surrey; dr (hc) Univ of Surrey 2015; Freeman: City of London, Worshipful Co of Chartered Accountants; FCA 1962; Offr Order of Oranje Nassau Netherlands 2013; *Recreations* philately, gardening, reading; *Style—* Dudley Eustace, Esq; ✉ Avalon, Old Barn Lane, Churt, Surrey GU10 2NA

EUSTICE, (Charles) George; MP; s of (George) Paul Eustice, and Adele Eustice; *b* 28 September 1971, Cornwall; *Educ* Truro Sch, Cornwall Coll; *m* Katy Taylor-Richards; *Career* campaign dir No Campaign 1999–2003, head of press Cons Pty 2003–05, press sec to Rt Hon David Cameron, MP, *qv*, 2005–07, MP (Cons) Camborne and Redruth 2010–, min for farming, food and marine environment 2013–; *Style—* George Eustice, Esq, MP; ✉ House of Commons, London SW1A 0AA

EVAN, Prof Gerard Ian; s of Robert Evan (*né* Robert Ekstein; d 1971), and Gwendoline, *née* Groom (d 1963); *b* 17 August 1955, London; *Educ* Forest Sch, St Peter's Coll Oxford (MA, Gibb Prize), King's Coll Cambridge (PhD, Max Perutz Prize); *Children* 1 da (Tamara Jane b 19 Jan 1990), 1 s (Theodore Robert William b 26 July 1991); *Career* SERC postdoctoral research fell Dept of Microbiology and Immunology Univ of Calif San Francisco 1982–84 (MRC travelling fell 1982–83), asst memb Ludwig Inst for Cancer Research Cambridge 1984–88, fell Downing Coll Cambridge 1987–88 (research fell 1984–87), princ scientist ICRF 1988–99, Royal Soc Napier research prof UCL 1996–99, Gerson and Barbara Bass Bakar distinguished prof of cancer biology Univ of Calif San Francisco 1999–, Sir William Dunn prof of biochemistry Univ of Cambridge 2009; author of 250 pubns in learned jls; fndr memb European Life Sciences Orgn 1999; memb: Biochemical Soc 1988, British Soc for Developmental Biology 1990, EMBO 1996, American Soc for Cell Biology 1999, American Assoc for Cancer Research (AACR) 2000, AAAS 2000; Pfizer Prize in Biology 1996, Joseph Steiner Prize in Cancer Research Swiss Oncological Soc 1996, Neal P Levitan chair of research Brain Tumor Soc 2004; FMedSci 1999, FRS 2004, fell European Acad of Scis 2010, fell European Acad of Cancer Scis 2015; *Recreations* hiking, music, biking; *Style—* Prof Gerard Evan; ✉ Sanger Building, Department of Biochemistry, University of Cambridge, 80 Tennis Court Road, Old Addenbrookes Site, Cambridge CB2 1GA (☎ 01223 765944, e-mail giesec@bioc.cam.ac.uk)

EVANS, Alan William; s of Harold Evans (d 1980), and Dorothy, *née* Surry (d 1999); *b* 21 February 1938; *Educ* Charterhouse, UCL (BA, PhD), Univ of Michigan; *m* 10 Aug 1964, Jill Alexandra (d 2011), da of George Otto Brightwell (d 1961); 2 s (Christopher b 1969, Stephen b 1971); *Career* lectr Univ of Glasgow 1967–71, res offr Centre for Environmental Studies 1971–76, lectr LSE 1976–77; Univ of Reading: reader 1977–81, prof 1981–, pro-vice-chllr 1990–94, dep vice-chllr 1994–96; visiting res fell: Univ of Melbourne 1983, Australian Nat Univ 1998; Denman Lecture Univ of Cambridge 1990; other public lectures at: Tokyo 1994, Santiago de Chile 1996 and 2002, Seoul 2001, RSA 2001; socio corrispondente Societa Geographica Italiana 1994; Int Real Estate Soc Achievement Award 2012; FCA 1961, AcSS 2001; *Publications* The Economics of Residential Location (1973), Urban Economics (1985), No Room! No Room! (1988), Economics, Real Estate and the Supply of Land (2004), Economics and Land Use Planning (2004), Unaffordable Housing (jtly, 2005, Prospect Think Tank Awards Pubn of the Year), Bigger Better Faster More (jtly, 2005), Better Homes, Greener Cities (jtly, 2006), The Best Laid Plans (jtly, 2007); also author of Rabbit Hutches on Postage Stamps (1991) and numerous other articles on the economics of cities, land and land use planning in academic and other jls; *Recreations* theatre, cinema, reading, travel; *Style—* Alan Evans, Esq; ✉ Lianda, Hill Close, Harrow on the Hill, Middlesex HA1 3PQ (☎ 020 8423 0767); Department of Economics, University of Reading, Whiteknights, Reading, Berkshire RG6 6AA (☎ 0118 378 8208, e-mail a.w.evans@reading.ac.uk)

EVANS, Dr Alexander; OBE (2010); *Educ* SOAS (PhD); *Career* Adam Smith Int Ltd 1997–98, GMC 1999–2000, dir of studies Centre for the Study of Financial Innovation 2000–02, research dir Policy Exchange 2002–03; entered HM Diplomatic Service 2003, first sec New Delhi 2005, FCO policy planning staff 2005–07, first sec Islamabad 2007–09, sr advsr to US Special Rep for Afghanistan and Pakistan 2009–11, Henry Kissinger chair in foreign policy Library of Congress 2011, sr fell Yale Univ 2011–13, coordinator Al Qaida/Taliban Monitoring Team UN Security Cncl 2013–; memb Cncl Royal Soc for Asian Affrs 2004–07; Gwilym Gibbon fell Nuffield Coll Oxford 2006–10, Yale world fell 2009, sr research fell KCL 2010–; fell Asia Soc 2012; *Publications* The United States and South Asia After Afghanistan (2012), various contributions to books and jls; *Style—* Dr Alexander Evans, OBE

EVANS, Dame Anne Elizabeth Jane; DBE (2000); da of David Evans (d 1965), of London, and Eleanor, *née* Lewis (d 1988); *b* 20 August 1941; *Educ* RCM, Conservatoire de Genève (Thomas Beecham operatic scholarship, Countess of Munster scholarship, Boise Fndn award); *m* 1, 1962 (m dis 1981), John Heulyn Jones; m 2, 1981, John Philip Lucas; *Career* soprano; Geneva debut as Annina in La Traviata 1967, UK debut as Mimi in La Bohème 1968; subseq roles incl: Brünnhilde in Der Ring (Bayreuth Festival 1989–92, Vienna Staatsoper, Deutsche Oper Berlin, Covent Garden, etc), Isolde in Tristan und Isolde (WNO, Brussels, Berlin, Dresden), Elisabeth in Tannhäuser (Metropolitan Opera NYC, Berlin), Elsa in Lohengrin (San Francisco, Buenos Aires), Leonore in Fidelio (Metropolitan Opera NYC), Chrysothemis in Elektra (Rome, Marseilles, Geneva), Ariadne in Ariadne auf Naxos (Edinburgh Festival, 1997); also numerous roles with English National Opera and Welsh National Opera incl: Marschallin in Der Rosenkavalier, Kundry in Parsifal, Donna Anna in Don Giovanni, Empress and Dyer's Wife in Die Frau ohne Schatten; Edinburgh Festival recital 1993, soloist last night of the Proms 1997; tstee Countess of Munster Musical Scholarships; Hon DMus Univ of Kent 2005; *Recordings* Brünnhilde in Der Ring 1991–92 (also DVD), Immolation Scene 1987, The Turn of the Screw 1998, Chrysothemis in Elektra 2005; *Recreations* cooking, gardening; *Style—* Dame Anne Evans, DBE; ✉ c/o Ingpen & Williams Ltd, 7 St George's Court, 131 Putney Bridge Road, London SW15 2PA (☎ 020 8874 3222, fax 020 8877 3113)

EVANS, Prof Barry George; s of William Arthur Evans (d 1984), of Dartford, Kent, and Jean Ida, *née* Lipscombe; *b* 15 October 1944; *Educ* Univ of Leeds (BSc, PhD); *m* 1 (m dis 1983), Carol Ann, *née* Gillis; 1 da (Lisa Jane b 1969), 1 s (Robert Iain Lawrie b 1971); m 2, 10 March 1984, Rhian Elizabeth Marilyn, da of Russell Lewis Jones (d 1974), of Camarthen; 1 s (Rhys David Russell b 1984), 1 da (Cerian Elizabeth Lucy b 1985); *Career* lectr, sr lectr and reader in telecommunications Univ of Essex 1968–83, Satellite Systems Consits C&W Ltd 1976–80; Univ of Surrey: Alec Harley Reeves prof of info systems engrg 1983–, dean of Engrg Res 1999–2001, pro-vice-chllr Res and Enterprise 2001–09; dir: Centre for Satellite Engineering 1990–96, Centre for Communications Systems Research 1996–2009, Satconsult Ltd, Mulsys Ltd; technical advsr to DG OFTEL 1997–2000; memb Bd: BNSC TNAB 2002–, Ofcom OSAB 2003–10; ed International Jl of Satellite Communications; author of over 500 papers on telecommunications and satellite systems published; memb: UK Foresight ITEC Panel, UK CCIR Ctees 5 and 8, DTI and EPSRC Link Mgmnt and SAT Ctee, Ofcom Spectrum Advsy Bd 2004; finalist McRobert award 1997; CEng, FIEE, FREng 1991, FRSA; *Books* Telecommunications Systems Design (1974), Satellite Systems Design (1988, 3 edn 1998); *Recreations* travel, wine, sport; *Style—* Prof Barry Evans, FREng; ✉ Centre for Communications Systems, University of Surrey, Guildford GU2 7XH (☎ 01483 689131, fax 01483 686011, e-mail b.evans@surrey.ac.uk)

E

EVANS, Cerith Wyn; *b* 1958, Wales; *Educ* St Martin's Sch of Art London, RCA (MA); *Career* artist and film maker; selector Bloomberg New Contemporaries 2003; *Solo Exhibitions* incl: And Then I 'Woke Up' (London Film Makers Co-op) 1980, A Certain Sensibility (ICA Cinematheque London) 1981, Solo Project (London Film Makers Co-op) 1981 and 1983, Solo Exhibition (ICA Cinemateque London) 1989, Sense and Influence (Kijkhuis The Hague) 1990, Crossoverworkshop (HFAK Vienna) 1992, Les Visiteurs du Soir (London Film Festival) 1993, Studio Casa Grande Rome 1996, Inverse Reverse Perverse (White Cube London) 1996, Deitch Projects New York 1997, Br Sch of Rome (in collaboration with Asprey Jacques Contemporary Art Exhibitions Rome) 1998, Asprey Jacques Contemporary Art Exhibitions London 1999, 'Has the film already started?' (Galerie Neu Berlin) 2000, fig-1 London 2000, Cleave.00 Art Now (Tate Britain London) 2000, Galerie Neu Berlin 2000 and 2003, Cerith Wyn Evans The Art Newspaper Project (Venice Biennale) 2001, Georg Kargl Gallery Vienna 2001, Kunsthaus Glarus 2001, Galerie Daniel Buchholz Cologne 2001, Cerith Wyn Evans Screening (Galerie Daniel Buchholz Cologne) 2002, mini MATRIX Berkeley Art Museum San Francisco 2003, Look at that picture...How does it appear to you now? Does it seem to be Persisting (White Cube London) 2003, Rabbit's Moon (Camden Arts Centre) 2004, Meanwhile Across Town (Centre Point London) 2004, The Sky is Thin as Paper Here... (Galerie Daniel Buchholz Cologne) 2004, Kunstverein Frankfurt 2004, film screening Centre Pompidou Paris 2004, Museum of Fine Arts Boston 2004, Thoughts unsaid, not forgotten... (MIT Visual Arts Center Boston) 2004, 299792458m/s (BAWAG Fndn Vienna) 2005, Once a Noun, Now a Verb (Galerie Neu Berlin) 2005; *Group Exhibitions* incl: The New Art (Tate Gallery London) 1983, Artist as Film Maker (Nat Film Theatre London) 1984, The Salon of 1984 (ICA Gallery London) 1984, The New Pluralism (Tate Gallery London) 1985, Syncronisation of the Senses (ICA Cinematheque London) 1985, The Elusive Sign (Tate Gallery London) 1987, The Melancholy Imaginary (in collaboration with Jean Mathee, London Film Makers Co-op) 1988, Degrees of Blindness (Edinburgh Film Festival) 1988, Image and Object in Current British Art (Centre Georges Pompidou Paris) 1990, Sign of the Times (MOMA Oxford) 1990, Cerith Wyn Evans and Gaylen Gerber (Wooster Gardens Gallery NY) 1992, 240 Minutes (Galerie Esther Schipper Cologne) 1992, 5th Oriel Mostyn Open Exhibition (Oriel Mostyn Llandudno) 1993, Liar (Hoxton Sq London) 1994, Flux (film screening, Minema Cinema London) 1994, Superstore Boutique (Laure Genillard Gallery London) 1994, Potato (IAS London) 1994, Future Anterior (Eigen + Art's/IIAS – Young British Artists London) 1995, Faction Video (Royal Danish Acad of Fine Arts Copenhagen) 1995, General Release: Young British Artists (Scuola di San Pasquale Venice) 1995, Stoppage (FRAC Tours) 1995, Sick (152 Brick Lane London) 1995, Kiss This (Focal Point Gallery Southend) 1996, British Artists in Rome (Studio Casagrande Rome) 1996, Against (Anthony d'Offay London) 1996, Life/Live (Musée d'Art Moderne de la Ville de Paris and Centro de Exposições do Centro Cultural de Belém Lisbon) 1996, Material Culture (Hayward Gallery London) 1997, Falseimpressions (The British Sch at Rome) 1997, Gothic (ICA Boston) 1997, A Print Portfolio from London (Atle Gehardsen Oslo) 1997, Sensation (Royal Acad of Arts London) 1997 (also at Hamburger Bahnhof Berlin 1998–99), Ray Rapp (Tz'Art & Co New York) 1998, View Four (Mary Boone New York) 1998, From the Corner of the Eye (Stedelijk Museum Amsterdam) 1998, How will we behave? (Robert Prime London) 1998, Retrace your steps: Remember Tomorrow (Sir John Soane's Museum London) 1999, Neu Gallery Berlin 1999, 54x54 (Financial Times Building London) 1999, Lost (Ikon Gallery London) 2000, The Greenhouse Effect (Serpentine Gallery London in collaboration with The Natural History Museum) 2000, The British Art Show 5 (The Scottish Nat Gallery of Modern Art Edinburgh) 2000, Out There (White Cube 2 London) 2000, There is something you should know (Die EVN Sammlung im Belvedere Vienna) 2000, Ever get the feeling you've been... (A22 Projects London) 2000, Rumours (Arc en Reve Centre d'Architecture Bordeaux) 2000, Sensitive (Le Printemps de Cahors Saint-Cloud) 2000, Diesseits und jenseits des Traums (Sigmund Freud Museum Vienna) 2001, What's Wrong (Trade Apartment London) 2001, Zusammenhänge in Biotop Kunst (Kunsthaus Muertz) 2001, Dedalic Convention (Stefan Kalmár-MAK Vienna) 2001, How do you change... (Inst of Visual Culture Cambridge) 2001, Wales – Unauthorised Versions (House of Croatian Artists Zagreb) 2001, Wir, Comawoche Film Screening (Metropolis Cinema Hamburg) 2001, My Generation 24 Hours of Video Art (Atlantis Gallery London) 2001, Gymnasion (Bregenzer Kunstverein Bregenz) 2001, There is something you should know. Die EVN Sammlung in Belvedere (Österreichische Galerie Belvedere Vienna) 2001, Yokohama 2001 International Triennale of Contemporary Art 2001, In the Freud Museum (Freud Museum London) 2002, ForwArt (Palais des Beaux-Arts Brussels) 2002, It's Only Words (Mirror Gallery London Inst) 2002, Void Archive (CCA Kitakyushu) 2002, Iconoclash. Image Wars in Science, Religion and Art (Center for Art and Media Karlsruhe) 2002, Screen Memories (Contemporary Art Centre Art Tower Mito Tokyo) 2002, My Head is on Fire but My Heart is Full of Love (Charlottenborg Museum Copenhagen) 2002, Shine (The Lowry Centre Manchester) 2002, Mirror: It's Only Words (London Coll of Printing) 2002, Edén (La Colección Jumex Mexico City) 2003, Cardinales (MARCO Vigo) 2003, The Straight or the Crooked Way (Royal Coll of Art Galleries London) 2003, Someone to Share My Life With (The Approach London) 2003, Light Works (Taka Ishii Gallery Tokyo) 2003, Utopia Station (50th International Venice Biennale) 2003, Addiction (15 Micawber Street London) 2003, Independence (South London Gallery London) 2003, Galleria Lorcan O'Neill Rome 2003, Adorno (Frankfurter Kunstverein Frankfurt am Main) 2003, St Sebastian. A Splendid Readiness For Death (Kunsthalle Vienna) 2003, Wittgenstein Family Likeness (Inst of Visual Culture Cambridge) 2003, Take a Bowery: The Art and (larger than) Life of Leigh Bowery (MCA Sydney) 2003, Sans Soleil (Galerie Neu Berlin) 2004, Ulysses (Galerie Belvedere Vienna) 2004, Hidden Histories (New Art Gallery Walsall) 2004, Doubtful Dans Les Plis Du Reel (Galerie Art & Essai Rennes) 2004, Marc Camille Chaimowicz (Angel Row Gallery Nottingham) 2004, Making Visible (Galleri Faurschou Copenhagen) 2004, Drunken Masters (Galeria Fortes Vilaça São Paulo) 2004, The Ten Commandments (Deutsches Hygiene-Museum Dresden) 2004, Black Friday: Exercise in Hermetics (Revolver Frankfurt) 2004, Eclipse (White Cube) 2004, Einleuchten (Museum der Moderne Salzburg) 2004, The Future Has a Silver Lining (Migros Museum Zurich) 2004, Trafic d'influences (Tri Postal Lille) 2004, Quodlibet (Galerie Daniel Buchholz Cologne) 2004, Utopia Station (Hans der Kunst Munich) 2004,

Prince Charles Cinema London 2004, E-Flux Video Rental Store (KW Inst for Contemporary Art Berlin) 2005, I'd Rather Jack (Edinburgh) 2005, Ice Storm (Kunstverein Munich) 2005, Can Buildings Curate (AA Sch of Architecture London) 2005, Light Lab (Museoin Bolzano) 2005; *Work in Public Collections* Br Cncl London, Caldic Collection Rotterdam, ReRebaudengo, EVN Vienna, Museo de Arte Acarigua-Araure Caracas, Saatchi Collection London, Tate Gallery London, La Coleccion Jumex Mexico City, Frankfurter Kunstverein Frankfurt, Pompidou Centre Paris; *Style*— Cerith Wyn Evans, Esq; ✉ c/o White Cube, 144 152 Bermondsey Street, London, SE1 3TQ

EVANS, Charlotte; MBE (2014); da of Keith Evans, and Siobhan, *née* Urech, of Kent; *b* 29 March 1991, Kent; *Educ* BSc; *Career* skier and sighted guide; with Kelly Gallagher: Silver medal (slalom) and Bronze medal (giant slalom) IPC World Championships 2011, Gold medal (slalom) Europa Cup Finals 2011, Gold medal (Super-G competition) Winter Paralympic Games Sochi 2014; Hon Dr Queen's Univ; *Recreations* cinema, fashion, music, skiing; *Style*— Ms Charlotte Evans, MBE; ✉ c/o Sports Sphere, CILIP building, 7 Ridgemount Street, London WC1E 7AE (☎ 07585 707659, e-mail hugo@sport-sphere.com, website www.sports-sphere.com, Twitter @CharEvans1)

EVANS, Chris; *Career* ed Daily Telegraph 2014–; *Style*— Chris Evans, Esq; ✉ Daily Telegraph, 111 Buckingham Palace Road, London SW1 0DT

EVANS, Dr Christopher Charles; s of Robert Percy (d 1974), and Nora Carson, *née* Crowther (d 1992); *b* 2 October 1941; *Educ* Wade Deacon GS Widnes, Univ of Liverpool (MB ChB, MD); *m* 5 Feb 1966, Dr Susan Evans, da of Dr Heinz Fuld (d 2008), of Llanarmon-yn-Ial, Denbighshire; 2 da (Joanne b 1971, Sophie b 1975), 1 s (Matthew b 1973); *Career* sr lectr in med and hon conslt physician Univ of Liverpool 1974–78, conslt physician in gen and thoracic med Royal Liverpool Univ Hosp and Cardio-Thoracic Centre Liverpool 1978–2003 (now emeritus), clinical sub-dean Royal Liverpool Hosp 1978–88; chief MO Swiss Life, conslt MO Royal Sun Alliance plc 1978–2005, chm and pres Med Def Union 2006–12; pres Liverpool Med Inst 1991–92; memb: Assoc of Physicians, Br Thoracic Soc; examiner, censor and academic vice-pres RCP London; FRCP 1979 (MRCP 1968), FRCPI (1997); *Books* Chamberlain's Symptoms and Signs in Clinical Medicine (with C M Ogilvie, 1987, 12 edn 1997); *Recreations* skiing, tennis, bird watching, fell walking, watching theatre and Liverpool FC; *Clubs* XX, Artists (Liverpool), Liverpool Cricket Club (pres 2014/16); *Style*— Dr Christopher Evans; ✉ Lagom, Glendyke Road, Liverpool L18 6JR (☎ 0151 724 5386, e-mail christoffe58@hotmail.com)

EVANS, Christopher James (Chris); MP; s of Michael Alan Evans (d 2003), and Lynne Evans; *b* Llywnipia, Wales; *Educ* Porth County Comp, Pontypridd Coll, Trinity Coll Carmarthen; *m* 23 Dec 2013, Julia Teresa Ockenden; *Career* office mangr Jack Brown Bookmaker 1998–2001, personal account mangr Lloyds TSB 2001–04, area sec Union of Finance Staff 2004–06, Parly researcher to Rt Hon Don Touhig, *qv* 2006–10, MP (Lab/Co-op) Islwyn 2010–; pres Twmbarlwm Soc, pres Blackwood Musical Theatre Soc; *Recreations* golf, horse racing, music, reading, running; *Style*— Chris Evans, Esq, MP; ✉ 6 Woodfieldside Business Park, Penmaen Road, Pontllanfraith, Blackwood, Gwent NP12 2FW (☎ 01495 231990, fax 01495 222484); House of Commons, London SW1A 0AA

EVANS, Prof Sir Christopher Thomas (Chris); kt (2001), OBE (1995); s of Cyril Evans, and Jean Evans; *b* 29 November 1957; *Educ* Imperial Coll London (BSc, ARCS), Univ of Hull (PhD), DSc; *m* 1985, Judith Anne; 2 s, 2 da; *Career* postdoctoral res Univ of Michigan 1983, Alleix Inc 1984–86, Genzyme Biochemicals Ltd 1986–87, fndr and chm Excalibur Gp Hldgs Ltd; fndr and dir: Enzymatix Ltd 1987–, Chiroscience plc 1992–, Celsis International plc 1992– (chm 1998–), Cerebrus Ltd 1995–; fndr, dir and chm: Toad Innovations plc 1993–, Merlin Scientific Services Ltd 1995–, Enviros Ltd 1995–, Cyclacel Ltd 1996–; chair: Bushcraft Co 2009–11, Excalibur Medical Ventures 2011–; dir: Microscience Ltd 1997, GEO plc; fndr: Merlin Fund 1996, British Growth Tst (formerly FLIT) 1997, Vectura plc 1997, Merlin Biosciences Fund, Stem Cell Fndn 2004, AV22 Ltd 2013; founding investor and chm Biovex 1998, founding investor and chm Piramed 2004, fndr and chm Arthurian Life Sciences Ltd 2012–, fndr and dep chm Arix Bioscience Ltd 2016–; memb PM's Cncl for Science and Technology, tstee Nat Endowment for Sci, Technol and the Arts, memb Competitiveness Cncl, ambass Nat Enterprise Campaign; former: dir BioIndustry Assoc, chm BEST Ctee EC; BVCA Cartier Vetiver Award, Henderson Meml Medal Porton Down 1997, SCI Centenary Medal 1998, RSC Interdiciplinary Medal 1999; hon prof: Univ of Manchester, Univ of Liverpool, Univ of Exeter, Univ of Bath (also fell), Imperial Coll London; hon fell: Univ of Wales Coll Cardiff 1996, Univ of Wales Swansea 1996; Hon DSc: Univ of Hull 1995, Univ of Nottingham 1995, UEA 1998, Cranfield Univ 1998; CBiol 1994, FIBiol 1994, CChem 1995, FRSC 1995, FRSA 1995, fell Acad of Med 2003, Hon FREng 2005; *Publications* author of numerous scientific papers and patents; *Recreations* rugby, gym, fly fishing, shooting, electric guitar, song writing; *Style*— Prof Sir Chris Evans, OBE; ✉ Arix Bioscience Ltd, Berkeley Square House, Berkeley Square, Mayfair, London W1J 6BD

EVANS, Prof David Emrys; s of Evan Emrys Evans (d 1985), of Cross Hands, Carmarthenshire, and Gwynneth Mair Eurfron, *née* Owen (d 1969); *b* 14 October 1950; *Educ* Ysgol Ramadeg Dyffrun Gwendraeth, Univ of Oxford (BA, MSc, DPhil); *m* 20 Oct 1984, Pornsawan; 2 s (Emrys Wyn b 12 June 1990, Arwyn Dafydd b 15 March 1993); *Career* Dublin Inst for Advanced Studies 1975–76, Oslo Univ 1976–77, Royal Soc exchange fell Copenhagen Univ 1978, SERC res fell Univ of Newcastle upon Tyne 1979, reader Univ of Warwick 1986–87 (lectr 1979–86), prof Univ of Wales Swansea 1987–98, prof Cardiff Univ (formerly Univ of Wales Cardiff) 1998–, visiting prof Kyoto Univ Japan 1990–91; Jr Whitehead prize London Mathematical Soc 1989; memb: London Mathematical Soc, American Mathematical Soc; FLSW 2011; *Books* Dilations of Irreversible Evolutions in Algebraic Quantum Theory (with J T Lewis, 1977), Quantum Symmetries on Operator algebras (with Y Kawahigashi, 1998); *Style*— Prof David Evans; ✉ School of Mathematics, Cardiff University, Senghennydd Road, Cardiff CF24 4AG (☎ 029 2087 4522, fax 029 2087 4199, e-mail evansDE@cf.ac.uk)

EVANS, Prof (John) David Gemmill; s of John Desmond Evans (d 1977), and Babette Evans (d 1985); *b* 27 August 1942; *Educ* St Edward's Sch Oxford, Queens' Coll Cambridge (BA, MA, PhD); *m* 14 Sept 1974, Rosemary, da of Gweirydd Ellis, of Chippenham; *Career* fell Sidney Sussex Coll Cambridge 1964–78, prof of logic and metaphysics Queen's Univ Belfast 1978– (dean Faculty of Arts 1986–89); memb Exec Ctee Int Fedn of Philosophical Socs, memb Exec Ctee Aristotelian Soc, memb Cncl Royal Inst of Philosophy, chm UK Nat Ctee for Philosophy, memb Conseil d'Administration AIPPh (Assoc Internationale des Professeurs de Philosophie); MRIA 1983; *Books* Aristotle's Concept of Dialectic (1977), Truth and Proof (1979), Aristotle (1987), Moral Philosophy and Contemporary Problems (1987), Teaching Philosophy on the Eve of the Twenty-First Century (1997), Proceedings of the 21st World Conference of Philosophy: Vol 4, Philosophy of Education (2006); *Recreations* mountaineering, astronomy, poker; *Style*— Prof David Evans; ✉ Philosophy Department, Queen's University, Belfast BT7 1NN (☎ 028 9097 3848, fax 028 9024 7895, e-mail jdg.evans@qub.ac.uk)

EVANS, David Howard; QC (1991); s of David Hopkin Evans, of Stoneleigh, Warwicks, and Phoebe Dora, *née* Reading; *b* 27 July 1944; *Educ* The Woodlands Sch Coventry, LSE (BSc, MSc), Wadham Coll Oxford (MA); *m* 20 June 1973, Anne Celia, da of John Segall, of W London; 2 s (Oliver Anthony b 1977, Edward Alexander b 1980); *Career* called to the Bar Middle Temple 1972 (bencher 2004), practising barrister 1972–, recorder of the Crown Court 1992–2010; Freeman City of London, memb Worshipful Co of Pattenmakers; *Recreations* tennis, golf, reading, listening to music; *Style*— David Evans, Esq, QC; ✉ 33 Chancery Lane, London WC2A 1EN (☎ 020 7440 9950, fax 020 7430 2818, website www.33cllaw.com)

EVANS, David Pugh; s of John David Charles Evans (d 1972), and Katherine Pugh (d 1947); *b* 20 November 1942; *Educ* Newbridge GS, Newport Coll of Art, Royal Coll of Art (RCA Silver Medal for Painting); *m* 1971 (m dis 1977), Patricia Ann, da of Kenneth Keay; *Career* artist; lectr Edinburgh Coll of Art 1965–68 and 1969–98; Granada arts fell Univ of York 1968–69; ARCA 1965, RSW 1974, RSA 1985 (ARSA 1974); *Solo Exhibitions* Univ of York 1969, Goosewell Gallery 1969, Marjorie Parr Gallery 1970, 1972 and 1974, Gilbert Parr Gallery 1977 and 1980, Fruitmarket Gallery (retrospective) 1982, Mercury Gallery 1985, Open Eye Gallery 1991 and 2005, Scottish Arts Club Edinburgh (retrospective) 2006, Open Eye Gallery 2009; *Group Exhibitions* Royal Acad, Royal Scottish Acad, Soc of Scottish Artists, Univ of Stirling, Univ of York, Aberdeen Art Gallery, Dundee Art Gallery, Fine Art Soc, Royal Glasgow Inst, Richard Demarco Gallery, The Scottish Gallery, Middlesbrough Art Gallery, Kirkcaldy Art Gallery, Mercury Gallery, Galerija Fakulteta Belgrade, Compass Gallery, Royal West of England Gallery, Bath Festival of Contemporary Arts, Basle Arts Fair, British Airways Exec Lounge Edinburgh Airport (2 man) 1997, Open Eye Gallery (3 man) 1997, Thompson's Gallery London, Blythswood Gallery Glasgow 2006 and 2007, Scottish Gallery Edinburgh 2006; *Work in Collections* RA, City of Edinburgh, Royal Burgh of Arbroath, Hunterian Museum, Glasgow Art Galleries and Museums, Carlisle Art Gallery, Scottish Arts Cncl, Contemporary Arts Soc, Aberdeen Art Gallery, St Catherine's Coll Oxford, Imperial Coll London, Scottish Television, Royal Bank of Scotland, Scottish and Newcastle Breweries; *Awards* Royal Burgh of Arbroath painting prize 1971, May Marshall Brown Award RSW 1978, W G Gillies Award RSW 1983, 1986 and 1989, W J Macaulay Award RSA 1984 and 2004, Scottish Arts Club Award RSW 1993, Scottish Post Office Bd Award RSA 1994, RSW Cncl Prize RSW 1997, Scottish Arts Club Award at annual RSA Exhibition 2015; *Books* work featured in: Scottish Watercolour Painting (Jack Firth 1979), David Evans (Paul Stirton 1982), Contemporary Painting in Scotland (Bill Hare), The Eye in the Wind, Scottish Painting Since 1945 (Edward Gage 1997); *Style*— David Evans, Esq, RSA; ✉ 17 Inverleith Gardens, Edinburgh EH3 5PS (☎ 0131 552 2329)

EVANS, David Robert Howard; s of Rev Denys Roberts Evans (d 1988), of Oxford, and Beryl Mary, *née* Toye; *b* 27 February 1950; *Educ* Magdalen Coll Sch Oxford, Univ of Exeter (LLB), King's Coll and LSE Univ of London (LLM), Brasenose Coll Oxford (DipLaw); *m* 1, 6 Jan 1979 (m dis 1988), Gillian Mary; 1 s (Matthew Charles b 1985); m 2, 7 May 1989, Janet Lea, formerly w of Amos Kollek, of Jerusalem, da of Nat T Kanarek, of New York; 1 da (Cordelia Moses Roberts b 1991); *Career* admitted slr 1976; slr: Freshfields 1975–77, British Railways Bd 1977–79, Linklaters & Paines 1980–82; ptnr: Berwin Leighton 1984–87 (slr 1982–83), D J Freeman & Co 1987–91; sr ptnr David Evans Slrs 1991–2002; md: Lox, Stock and Bagel Ltd 1992–2002, Anglo International Education Consultants Ltd 1992–, Janet's Bar 1996–2002; tstee Statute Law Tst; Freeman City of London 1981, Liveryman Worshipful Co of Slrs 1988; memb Law Soc 1976; *Recreations* playing clarinet and piano, tennis, squash; *Clubs* Reform; *Style*— David Evans, Esq; ✉ 51 Drayton Gardens, London SW10 9RX (☎ 07768 683109)

EVANS, David; aka The Edge; s of Garvin Evans, of Dublin, and Gwenda Evans; *b* 8 August 1961; *Educ* Mount Temple Sch; *Career* guitarist and fndr memb U2 1978– (with Bono, Adam Clayton, and Larry Mullen, Jr, *qqv*); first U2 release U23 (EP) 1979; *Albums* Boy 1980, October 1981, War 1983 (entered UK chart at no 1), Under A Blood Red Sky 1983 (live album), The Unforgettable Fire 1984 (entered UK charts at no 1), Wide Awake in America 1985, The Joshua Tree 1987 (entered UK charts at no 1, fastest selling album ever in UK, Album of the Year Grammy Awards 1987), The Joshua Tree Singles 1988, Rattle & Hum 1988 (entered UK charts at no 1), Achtung Baby 1991, Zooropa 1993 (no 1 in 18 countries, Best Alternative Album Grammy Awards 1993), Pop 1997 (no 1), The Best of 1980–1990 1998, All That You Can't Leave Behind 2000 (no 1, Best Rock Album Grammy Awards 2002), The Best of 1990–2000 2002, How To Dismantle An Atomic Bomb 2004 (Album of the Year and Best Rock Album Grammy Awards 2006), U218 Singles 2006, No Line on the Horizon 2009; *Singles* incl: Fire 1981, New Year's Day (first UK Top Ten hit) 1983, Pride (In the Name of Love) 1984, Unforgettable Fire 1985, With or Without You 1987, I Still Haven't Found What I'm Looking For 1987, Where The Streets Have No Name 1987 (Best Video Grammy Awards 1989), Desire (first UK no 1 single) 1988 (Best Rock Performance Grammy Awards 1989), Angel of Harlem 1988, When Love Comes to Town 1989, All I Want Is You 1989, Night & Day (for AIDS benefit LP Red Hot & Blue) 1990, The Fly (UK no 1) 1991, Stay 1993, Discotheque (UK no 1) 1997, Staring at the Sun 1997, Sweetest Thing 1998, Beautiful Day (UK no 1) 2000 (Record of the Year, Song of the Year and Best Rock Performance by a Duo or Group with Vocal Grammy Awards 2001), Stuck in a Moment You Can't Get Out Of 2001 (Best Song by a Pop Duo or Group Grammy Awards 2002), Elevation 2001 (Best Rock Performance by a Duo or Group with Vocal Grammy Awards 2002), Walk On 2001 (Record of the Year Grammy Awards 2002), Electrical Storm 2002, Vertigo (UK no 1) 2004 (Best Rock Performance by a Duo or Group with Vocal, Best Rock Song and Best Short Form Music Video Grammy Awards 2004), Sometimes You Can't Make It On Your Own (UK no 1) 2005 (Song of the Year, Best Rock Duo or Group Vocal and Best Rock Song Grammy Awards 2006), City of Blinding Lights 2005 (Best Rock Song Grammy Awards 2006), All Because of You 2005, the Saints are Coming 2006, Window in the Skies 2007, Get on Your Boots 2009, Magnificent 2009, I'll Go Crazy If I Don't Go Crazy Tonight 2009, Ordinary Love 2013 (Best Original Song – Motion Picture Golden Globe Award 2014); *Film* Rattle & Hum 1988, U2 3D 2008; *Tours* incl: UK, US, Belgium and Holland 1980, UK, US, Ireland and Europe 1981–83, Aust, NZ and Europe 1984, A Conspiracy of Hope (Amnesty International Tour) 1986, Joshua Tree tour 1987, Rattle & Hum tour 1988, Zoo TV tour (played to 5 million people) 1992–93, Popmart tour 1997–98, Elevation 2001 tour 2001, Vertigo tour 2005; also appeared at: Live Aid 1985 (Best Live Aid Performance Rolling Stone Readers' Poll 1986), Self Aid Dublin, Smile Jamaica (Dominion Theatre, in aid of hurricane disaster relief) 1988, New Year's Eve concert Dublin (broadcast live to Europe and USSR) 1989; performed at venues incl: Wembley Stadium, Madison Square Garden NY, Longest Day Festival Milton Keynes Bowl, Croke Park Dublin, Sun Devil Stadium AZ; *Awards* Best Band Rolling Stone Readers' Poll 1986 (also jt winner Critics' Poll), Band of the Year Rolling Stone Writers' Poll 1984, Best International Act BPI Awards 1989 and 1990, Best Live Act BPI Awards 1993, Best International Group Brit Awards 2001, Outstanding Contribution to the Music Industry Brit Awards 2001, Outstanding Song Collection Ivor Novello Awards 2003, Golden Globe Award (for Hands that Built America) 2003, Oscar nomination (for Hands that Built America) 2003; *Publications* U2 by U2 (2006); *Style*— The Edge; ✉ c/o Regine Moylett Publicity, 2C Woodstock Studios, Woodstock Grove, London W12 8LE (☎ 020 8749 7999)

EVANS, Prof (William) Desmond; s of Bryn Gwyn Evans (d 1993), and Evelyn Evans (d 1974); *b* 7 March 1940; *Educ* Ystalyfera GS, Univ of Swansea (BSc), Univ of Oxford (DPhil); *m* 27 Aug 1966, Mari, da of Murray Richards (d 1953); 2 s (Dyfed b 1969, Owain b 1973); *Career* UC Cardiff: lectr 1964–73, sr lectr 1973–75, reader 1975–77, prof 1977–; London Maths Soc: memb 1964, editorial advsr 1977–86, ed Proceedings 1986–92, memb Cncl 1989–91; memb Editorial Bd: Jl of Inequalities and Applications 1995–, Proceedings of the Georgian Academy of Sciences 1999–, Revista Complutense Mathematica 1999–; elected fell Learned Soc of Wales (FLSW) 2011; *Publications* Spectral Theory and Differential Equations (with D E Edmunds, 1987), Hardy Operators, Function Spaces and Embeddings (with D E Edmunds, 2004), Spectral Analysis of Relativistic Operators (with A A Balinsky, 2010), Representations of Linnear Operators Between Banach Spaces (with D E Edmunds, 2013), The Analysis and Geometry of Hardy's Inequality (with A A Balinsky and R T Lewis, 2015); over 150 articles on differential equations and related topics in academic jls; *Recreations* walking, music; *Clubs* Dinas Powys Probus; *Style*— Prof Desmond Evans; ✉ School of Mathematics, Cardiff University, Senghennydd Road, Cardiff CF24 4AG (☎ 029 2087 4206, fax 029 2087 4199, e-mail evanswd@cf.ac.uk)

EVANS, Gareth Robert William; QC (1994); s of David Morris John Evans (d 2006), of Pontllanfraith, Gwent, and Megan, *née* Hughes (d 1964); *b* 19 January 1947; *Educ* Caerfilli GS, Univ of London (external LLB); *m* 1971, Marion, *née* Green; 1 da (Judith Ann b 1 Nov 1978), 1 s (David Glyn b 18 April 1982); *Career* called to the Bar Gray's Inn 1973 (bencher 2007); jr Midland & Oxford Circuit 1983, recorder of the Crown Court 1993–, head of chambers 2002–07, ldr Midland Circuit 2008–11; *Recreations* watching rugby, reading poetry, cooking, travelling, golf; *Clubs* Cardiff and County; *Style*— Gareth Evans, QC; ✉ No 5 Chambers, Steelhouse Lane, Birmingham B4 6DR (☎ 0121 606 0500, fax 0121 606 1501, e-mail ge@no5.com)

EVANS, Garry Owen; s of Derek Alwyn Evans (d 1984), and Pamela, *née* Sladden; *b* 13 February 1961; *Educ* King's Sch Canterbury, Corpus Christi Coll Cambridge (MA), Kyoto Univ; *m* 15 Dec 1985, Michiko, da of Hisami Matsuda, of Miyazaki, Japan; 2 da (Anna Sian b 1 March 1991, Maya Emily b 16 April 1994); *Career* Euromoney Publications plc: joined 1986, ed Euromoney (Japanese edn) 1987–90, ed Euromoney 1990–98; HSBC: strategist HSBC Securities (Japan) Ltd until 2003 (latterly chief strategist), head of pan-Asian equity research Corporate, Investment Banking and Markets Division 2003–; *Books* Memories of Silk and Straw (trans, by Junichi Saga, 1987); *Recreations* classical music, flying; *Style*— Garry Evans, Esq

EVANS, Garth; *Educ* Slade Sch of Art, UCL (Dip Fine Art), Manchester Regnl Coll of Art, Manchester Jr Coll of Art; *Career* artist and sculptor; visiting lectr: Central Sch of Art London 1960–65, Camberwell Sch of Art London 1960–69, St Martin's Sch of Art London 1965–79, Chelsea Sch of Art London 1978–79, Yale Sch of Art Yale Univ 1983, 1985 and 1986; visiting prof Minneapolis Coll of Art and Design 1973; visiting tutor Slade Sch of Fine Art UCL 1970–81, Goldsmiths Coll London 1978–81; visiting artist: Sculpture Dept RCA London 1970–81, Mount Holyoke Coll 1979–81, Manchester Poly 1978–83, NY Studio Sch 1988–; assoc lectr in sculpture Camberwell Sch of Art London 1971–83, lectr Faculty of Sculpture Br Sch at Rome 1978–83; memb: Fine Art Advsy Panel S Glamorgan Inst of Higher Educn 1977–79, Fine Arts Award Policy Ctee Arts Cncl of GB 1977–79, Fine Art Bd Photography Bd CNAA 1976–79, Ctee for Art and Design CNAA 1976–79; *Solo Exhibitions* Rowan Gallery London 1962, 1964, 1966, 1968, 1969, 1972, 1974, 1976, 1978 and 1980, Sch of Art and Design Gallery Sheffield 1971, Ferens Art Gallery Hull 1971, Faculty of Art and Design Gallery Leeds Poly 1971, Oriel Gallery of the Welsh Arts Cncl Cardiff 1976, Mount Holyoke Coll Art Museum S Hadley Mass 1980, Robert Elkon Gallery NY 1983, Tibor de Nagy Gallery NY 1984, HF Manes Gallery NY 1984, John Davis Gallery Akron Ohio 1986, Garth Evans Sculptures and Drawings 1979–87 (Yale Center for Br Art New Haven CT) 1988, Charles Cowles Gallery NY 1988, Compass Rose Gallery Chicago 1989, Hill Gallery Birmingham Michigan 1990, Mayor Gallery London 1991, Wrexham Museum and Art Centre Wales 1991, Sheffield Poly Art Gallery 1991, Echoes: Sculpture from 1970 and Recent Works (Paul Mellon Gallery Choate Rosemary Hall Sch Wallingford CT) 1993, Sculptural Metamorphosis (Freedman Gallery Reading PA), Watercolours (Dana Arts Centre Colgate Univ USA) 1995, Phoenix Sculptures (Opera House Gallery Earlville USA) 1995, Sculptures and Works on Paper (Korn Gallery Drew Univ USA) 1996, Watercolours (Claudia Carr Gallery NY) 1997, The 1982 (YADDO) Drawings (Marist College NY, NY Studio School, Halsey Gallery Charleston) 1997–98; *Group Exhibitions* incl: John Moores Exhibition (Liverpool) 1960, Reliefs Collages and Drawings (V&A) 1967, Drawings (MOMA NY) 1969, British Sculpture '72 (Royal Acad) 1972, The Condition of Sculpture (Hayward Gallery) 1975, David Leverett Garth Evans and Dicter Rot (Tate Gallery) 1978, Sculpture Now 1 (Gallery Wintersburger Cologne) 1983, Three Sculptors (Wolff Gallery NY) 1984, Quest – Drawings by Faculty (NY Studio Sch) 1989, Before Sculpture – British Sculptors Drawings (NY Studio Sch) 1990, Evans Saunders Tribe Tucker Turnbull (Phillips Staib Gallery NY) 1990, Newer Sculpture (Charles Cowles Gallery NY) 1990, Discourse (NY Studio Sch) 1990, Physicality (Hunter Coll City Univ NY) 1990, Summer Group (Charles Cowles Gallery NY) 1991, Sculpture in the Yard (PMW Gallery Stamford) 1992, Set A/B (Tribeca 148 Gallery NY) 1992, Millfield British 20th Century Sculpture Exhbn (Millfield Sch Somerset) 1992, Form, Shape and Vision (Schick Art Gallery NY) 1993, Summer Salon Show (Robert Morrison Gallery NY) 1993, French Ideals: French Idylls (NY Studio Sch of Drawing, Painting and Sculpture) 1993, American Academy Invitational Exhibition of Painting and Sculpture (American Acad of Arts and Letters NY) 1996, Watercolours (with Andrew Forge, Kendall Art & Design Hudson NY) 1998; *Public collections* incl: Brooklyn Museum NY, Gulbenkian Fndn Lisbon, Joseph H Hirshhorn Museum and Sculpture Garden Washington DC, Met Museum of Art NY, MOMA NY, Nat MOMA Brazil, Power Gallery of Contemporary Art Sydney, Tate Gallery London, V&A; *Awards* Newcastle Cruddas Park Sculpture Competition 1961, Gulbenkian purchase award 1964, Arts Cncl of GB sabbatical 1966, BSC fellowship 1969, Oxford Gallery purchase prize 1972, Welsh Arts Cncl purchase prize 1974, Arts Cncl of GB maj award 1975, Gtr London Arts Assoc bursary 1978, Arts Cncl of GB film bursary 1979, Br Cncl exhbns abroad grant 1979, Mount Holyoke Coll faculty award 1980, residency Yaddo Saratoga Springs NY 1982 and 1991, fell John Simon Guggenheim Meml Fndn 1986, The Marie Walsh Sharpe Art Fndn The Space Program 1992–93, Pollock-Krasner Fndn Award 1996; *Style*— Garth Evans; ✉ 287 Pulpit Rock Road, Woodstock, CT 06281, USA; c/o Lori Bookstein Fine Art, 138 Tenth Avenue, New York, NY 10011, USA (website www.loribooksteinfineart.com)

EVANS, Geraint; s of David Lynn Evans, and Elvira Evans; *Educ* Olchfa Sch Swansea, W Glamorgan Inst of HE, Manchester Poly (BA), Royal Acad Sch of Art (Dip Fine Art); *Career* artist; new media projects for: Jibby Beane London (Through The Looking Glass) 1997, Containership (internet project) 1998, ICA 1998, Canary Wharf 1998, LEA London 1998; work in collections: The Prudential, Br Embassy Berlin, Ferens Art Gall Hull; resident Banff Centre for the Arts Alberta 1994; visiting lectr: Univ of Tennessee 1994, Manchester Met Univ 1994–98, Liverpool John Moores Univ 1999, Univ of Lincoln 2000–01, RCA 2001, Norwich Sch of Art and Design 2002, De Montfort Univ 2002, London Coll of Fashion 2002; Br Inst Prize (printmaking) 1992 and 1993, Tooth Travel Scholarship 1993, Woo Charitable Fndn Award 2001, Berwick Gymnasium Fellowship 2002–03; *Solo Exhibitions* Univ of Tennessee 1994, Jason and Rhodes London 1998, Soho House London 1999, Anthony Wilkinson London 2000, Where Happiness Happens (Chapter Cardiff) 2001, Where Happiness Happens (Glynn Vivian Art Gallery Swansea) 2002, Centro de Arte de Salamanca Spain 2003, Berwick Gymnasium Gall 2003; *Group Exhibitions* incl: Western Exposure (Waterman's Art Centre London) 1993, London/Leipzig (Grassimuseum Leipzig) 1993, Pet Show (63 Union Street London) 1993, Whitechapel Open (Atlantis London) 1994, Oriel Mostyn Open (Mostyn Art Gallery Llandudno) 1994, Grin and Bear It (Gasworks London) 1995, John Moores 19 (Walker Art Gallery Liverpool) 1995, Wishful Thinking (Art House Lewisham) 1996, Six Monkeys (RAW London) 1996, Whitechapel Open (Whitechapel Art Gallery London) 1996, Sad (Gasworks London) 1996, Intimate (Jason and Rhodes London) 1997, Bittersweet (Whitworth Art Gallery Manchester) 1997, Sickly Sweet (Battersea Arts Centre London) 1998, Whitechapel Open (The Tannery London) 1998, London Now (Saks Fifth Avenue Arts Project NY) 1998, Asylum (Milch London) 1999, Idlewild (The Approach London) 1999, Fresh Paint (MOMA Glasgow) 1999, British Art part 2 (Diehl Vorderwuelbecke Berlin) 2000, Landscape (Barbara Gilman Miami) 2000, Record Collection (VTO London) 2001, Wales, Unauthorized Versions (The House of Croatian Artists Zagreb) 2001, On Home Ground (Oriel Mostyn, Llandudno) 2002, Art and Mountains (The Alpine Club) 2002, Dirty Pictures (The Approach London), Yes! I am a Long Way From Home (NGCA Sunderland and touring); *Style*— Geraint Evans, Esq

EVANS, Prof Gillian Rosemary; da of Arthur Raymond Evans (d 1987), of Huntley, Glos, and Gertrude Elizabeth, *née* Goodfellow (d 1980); *b* 26 October 1944, Birmingham; *Educ* King Edward VI HS for Girls Birmingham, St Anne's Coll Oxford (MA, DipEd), Univ of Reading (PhD), Univ of Oxford (DLitt), Univ of Cambridge (LittD), Middx Univ (Dip Law), Inns of Court Sch of Law; *Career* asst mistress Queen Anne's Sch Caversham 1967–72, research asst Univ of Reading 1974–78, lectr Univ of Bristol 1978–80, asst lectr rising to prof of medieval theology and intellectual history Univ of Cambridge 1980–2005; memb Cncl Univ of Cambridge 1997–2000; public policy sec Cncl for Academic Freedom and Academic Standards 1996–2003, co-fndr Oxcheps HE Mediation Serv 2004; memb Faith and Order Advsy Gp Gen Synod C of E 1985–95; ldr HEFCE-funded project improving dispute resolution in HE 2007–09, chief exec improving dispute resolution Advsy Service for Further and Higher Educn 2010–; called to the Bar Gray's Inn 2002; Liveryman Worshipful Co of Educators; Hon DLitt Southampton Inst of HE 2001; FRHistS 1976, FRSA 1996, FCollT 2011; *Books* History of Western Monasticism (2015); *Publications* incl: Anselm and Talking About God (1978), Anselm and a New Generation (1980), Old Arts and New Theology (1980), The Mind of St Bernard of Clairvaux (1983), Alan of Lille (1983), Augustine on Evil (1983), The Anselm Concordance (1984), The Logic and Language of the Bible (2 vols, 1984 and 1985), The Thought of Gregory the Great (1986), Christian Authority (ed, 1988), Problems of Authority in the Reformation Debates (1992), Philosophy and Theology in the Middle Ages (1994), The Church and the Churches (1994), Method in Ecumenical Theology (1996), The Reception of the Faith (1997), Calling Academia to Account (1998), The Medieval Epistemology of Error (1998), Discipline and Justice in the Church of England (1999), Bernard of Clairvaux (2000), Managing the Church (ed, 2000), A History of Pastoral Care (ed, 2000), The Medieval Theologians (ed, 2001), Universities and Students (jtly, 2001), Law and Theology in the Middle Ages (2002), Academics and the Real World (2002), Faith in the Medieval World (2003), A Brief History of Heresy (2003), The Medieval Theologians (ed, 2004), Inside the University of Cambridge (2004), Wyclif (2005), Belief (2006), The Church in the Early Middle Ages (2007), The Good, the Bad and the Moral Dilemma (2007), An illustrated history of Christian Europe (2007), Cambridge: A New History (2009), The Effort to Create a National System of Higher Education in Britain (2009), Oxford: A New History (2010), Roots of the Reformation (2012), First Light (2013), Edward Hicks (2014); I B Tauris History of the Christian Church (gen ed); also author of articles published in learned jls; *Recreations* painting; *Clubs* Royal Over-Seas League; *Style*— Prof G R Evans; ✉ e-mail gre1001@cam.ac.uk, website www.idras.ac.uk

EVANS, Graham Thomas; MP; s of Gordon Thomas Evans (d 1983), and Violet, *née* Payne; *b* 10 November 1963, Poynton, Cheshire; *Educ* Poynton HS, Manchester Met Univ (BA, MA), Royal Coll of Defence Studies; *m* 18 Aug 1995, Cheryl, *née* Browne; 2 s (George b 27 Oct 1996, Tom b 3 May 2003), 1 da (Sophie b 13 March 2007); *Career* technical asst BAE Systems 1982–88, sales mgmnt Sun Chemical 1988–98, sales mgmnt Hewlett Packard 1999–2003, md Durst AG 2004–08; cncllr Macclesfield Borough Cncl 2000–09, MP (Cons) Weaver Vale 2010–; PPS to Rt Hon Sir Michael Fallon, KCB, MP (sec of state for defence) 2012–; memb Work and Pensions Select Ctee 2012–15, sec All Pty Parly Gp for the Armed Forces, chm All Pty Parly Gp for Chemicals, vice-chair All Pty Parly Gp for Energy Intensive Industries; memb: Lords and Commons Cricket Club, Lords and Commons Rugby Club, UK Parl FC; MInstD 2004; *Recreations* football, cricket, rugby history, British history, running; *Clubs* RAF; *Style*— Graham Evans, Esq, MP; ✉ House of Commons, London SW1A 0AA (☎ 020 7219 7183, e-mail mail@grahamevansmp.com, website www.grahamevansmp.com and www.linkedin.com/in/grahamtevans, Twitter @grahamevansmp)

EVANS, HE (David) Hugh; *b* Santa Elena, Ecuador; *Educ* Univ of London (BA), Univ of Chicago (MA, Fulbright-Hays Scholarship); 1988, Nirmala Evans, née Vinodhini; 2 da; *Career* diplomat; research analyst for S and SE Asia FCO 1985–94, second sec Islamabad 1989–90, assessments staff offr Cabinet Office 1991, regional analyst US State Dept 1995–98, dep head N American Dept FCO 1999, sr policy offr Confedn of Br Industry 1999–2000, political offr Kabul 2002, head Political Section Nairobi 2001–05, mgmnt cnsllr and consul gen Moscow 2008–12, HM's consul gen Erbil 2012–14, ambass to Laos 2015–; *Recreations* reading, travel, walking; *Style*— HE Mr Hugh Evans; ✉ c/o Foreign & Commonwealth Office, (Vientiane), King Charles Street, London SW1A 1AH

EVANS, Iain Richard; CBE (2013); *b* 17 May 1951; *Educ* Univ of Bristol (BSc), Harvard Business Sch (MBA); *Career* sr accountant Arthur Young McClelland Moores & Co 1975–76 (joined 1972); Bain & Co: conslt 1978–80, mangr 1980–82, ptnr 1982–83; Hyder plc (formerly Welsh Water plc): non-exec dir 1989–93, exec chm 1993–96, non-exec chm 1996–98; fndr LEK Consulting 1983– (chm 1991–2015); FCA 1981 (ACA 1975); *Recreations* golf, fishing, tennis; *Style*— Iain Evans, Esq, CBE

EVANS, Ian Robert; s of Ellwyn Evans, and Violet, *née* Ashbridge; *b* 10 May 1950, Yorks; *Educ* Keswick Sch, Univ of Liverpool (LLB); *m* 22 Sept 1989, Victoria; 2 s (James b 13 March 1978, David b 23 Dec 1992), 4 da (Sian b 13 May 1980, Jane b 28 Feb 1986, Sally b 31 July 1994, Beth b 9 Jan 1997); *Career* admitted slr 1975; Weightmans: ptnr 1978–, sr ptnr 2000–; *Recreations* all sports, particularly rugby, soccer, cricket and sailing; *Style*— Ian Evans, Esq; ✉ Weightmans, India Buildings, Water Street, Liverpool L2 0GA (☎ 0151 227 2601, fax 0151 242 7986, e-mail ian.evans@weightmans.com)

EVANS, Capt James; MBE (1992), RD (1975), DL (1978); s of Thomas Evans (d 1966), and Hilda Margaret, *née* Atkinson (d 1976); *b* 9 May 1933; *Educ* Merchiston Castle Sch Edinburgh, Univ of Newcastle upon Tyne (BSc); *m* 12 July 1958, Patricia Alexena (Pat), da of Harry Kerr (d 1973); 1 s (Ian b 1963), 2 da (Lynn b 1961, Gwen b 1967); *Career* RNR 1956–80, Hon ADC 1979–80, ret 1980; apprenticeship: Wm Weatherhead & Sons 1950–52, Swan Hunter and Whigham Richardson 1952–56; engr Yarrow-Admiralty Res Dept 1958–63, nuclear engrg certificate 1960, engr UK Atomic Energy Authy 1963–68, md Eyemouth Boat Building Co Ltd 1968–90, conslt Naval Architect 1990–2006; tech advsr Scottish Fishermen's Fedn 1993–2009; chm Fishing Boat Builders' Assoc 1979–90, pres Anglo Scottish Fishermen's Assoc 2006– (sec/treas 1993–2006); chm: Freemen Housing Tst, Thomas Evans Properties Ltd; dir South of Scotland Seafish Trg Assoc Ltd; chm Berwickshire Dist Co Cncl 1980–96; Freeman of Berwick-upon-Tweed (chm Tstees Freemen of England and Wales 1975–2015); Lord Pres Court of Deans of Guilds of Scotland 1994–95, 2003–04 and 2014–15; Merchant Navy Medal (MNM) 2009; Gold Cross of Merit (Poland) 1999; *Publications* Features of Interest in Small Pressurised Water Reactors (1963, Nuclear Engrg Soc Silver Medal Award), East Coast Fishing Boat Building (1990); *Clubs* Eyemouth and Dist Rotary; *Style*— Capt James Evans, MBE, RD, DL; ✉ Makore, Northburn View, Eyemouth, Berwickshire TD14 5BG (☎ 01890 750701, e-mail captjamesevans@gmail.com); Dundee House, Harbour Road, Eyemouth, Berwickshire TD14 5JB

EVANS, Janet Charmian Christabel; da of Dr Joseph Evans (d 1981), of Bishop's Stortford, Herts, and Eileen Betty Evans-Booker, *née* Moulding (d 1989); *b* 14 December 1951; *Educ*

Herts & Essex HS for Girls, Somerville Coll Oxford (MA), Birkbeck Coll London (MSc); *m* 1, 1976, Robin Aaronson; m 2, 2000, Andy McLellan; *Career* civil servant; admin trainee rising to princ Dept of Employment 1975–92, head of div Dept for Culture, Media and Sport 1992–, currently head Museums, Libraries and Archives Div; *Recreations* visiting cities, food, friends, cats; *Style—* Ms Janet Evans; ✉ Department for Culture, Media and Sport, 2–4 Cockspur Street, London SW1Y 5DH (☎ 020 7211 6132, fax 020 7211 6130, e-mail janet.evans@culture.gov.uk)

EVANS, Jill; MEP; da of Horace Burge, of Llwynypia, Rhondda, and Valma, *née* Yeates; *b* 8 May 1959; *Educ* Tonypandy GS, UCW Aberystwyth (BA), Poly of Wales (MPhil); *m* June 1992, Syd Morgan; *Career* res asst Poly of Wales Treforest 1981–86, admin and public affairs offr NFWI 1989–94, Wales organiser for CHILD the Nat Infertility Support Network 1997–99; cncllr: Rhonda BC 1992–95, Mid Glamorgan CC 1993–95, Rhondda Cynon Taff CBC 1995–99; memb Nat Exec Ctee Plaid Cymru; MEP (Plaid Cymru) Wales 1999–, substitute memb Ctee on Agric and Rural Devpt, memb Ctee on the Environment, Public Health and Food Safety; memb CND; *Style—* Ms Jill Evans, MEP; ✉ European Parliament ASP, 4F374, Rue Wiertz, Brussels 1040, Belgium

EVANS, His Hon Judge (Maldwn) John; s of David Anthony Evans (d 1996), and Margaret, *née* Reid; *b* 11 July 1950; *Educ* Royal Hosp Sch Holbrook, Univ of Northumbria (BA); *m* 1, 17 Aug 1974, Miriam Dorothy, *née* Beaumont; 2 s (Matthew Richard b 6 Jan 1977, Daniel John b 29 Nov 1978), 1 da (Louisa Kate b 9 Aug 1980); m 2, 29 May 1989, Angela Louise, *née* Swaddle; 2 step da (Charlotte Amy b 19 May 1988, Emily Josephine b 10 April 1991), 1 step s (Lawrence Henry b 17 Sept 1989); *Career* called to the Bar 1973, barr in practice Criminal Bar Newcastle upon Tyne 1973–2005, recorder 1989–2005, head New Court Chambers Newcastle 1999–2005, circuit judge (NE Circuit) 2005–; govr Kings Sch Tynemouth, fell Woodard Corp; *Recreations* sport, rugby, cricket, squash, sailing, walking, holidays, cinema; *Clubs* Tynemouth Squash; *Style—* His Hon Judge Evans; ✉ Newcastle upon Tyne Combined Court Centre, Quayside, Newcastle upon Tyne NE1 3LA (☎ 0191 201 2000)

EVANS, Dr (Daniel) John Owen; s of John Leslie Evans (d 1971), and Avis *née* Jones (d 2009); *b* 17 November 1953, Morriston, Swansea; *Educ* Gowerton Boys' GS, Univ of Wales Cardiff (BMus, MA, PhD), ATCL; *Career* artistic dir Welsh Chamber Ensemble 1975–78, administrator Britten-Pears Sch 1978–80, research scholar Britten-Pears Library & Archive 1980–85, prodr Radio 3 Music Dept BBC 1985–89; artistic dir: Covent Garden Chamber Orchestra 1985–93, Volte Face Opera 1986–89; sr prodr BBC Singers 1989–92; BBC Radio: chief prodr Music Dept Radio 3 1992–93, head of Music Dept Radio 3 1993–96, head of classical music 1996–2000, head of music programming Radio 3 2000–06; pres and gen dir Oregon Bach Festival 2007–15; juror: Int Conductors' Competition Lisbon 1995, Kondrashin Conduction Competiton 1998, BBC Cardiff Singer of the World Competition 2003 and 2005, Tost: Int Singing Competition 2004, BBC Choir of the Year 2005; chair Opera Jury Royal Philharmonic Society Awards 2000–05; chair: Concentric Circles Theatre Co 2000–05, DreamArts Theatre of the Possible 2005–07; memb Bd: Chorus America, All Classical Portland; dir The Britten Estate; tstee: Peter Pears Award 1989–92, Masterprize Composers' Competition 1997–2001, Britten-Pears Fndn 2000–07, Britten-Pears Will Tst; vice-pres Welsh Music Guild; *Awards* Prix Italia 1989, Charles Heidsieck Royal Philharmonic Award for Duke Bluebeard's Castle 1989, Royal Philharmonic Award for The Art of Conducting 1994, Gold Sony Radio Award for Live from Tanglewood 1997; *Books* Benjamin Britten: Pictures from a Life 1913–76 (1978), Benjamin Britten: His Life and Operas (ed, 1982), The Britten Companion (contrib, 1984), A Britten Source Book (1987), Journeying Boy: The Diaries of the Young Benjamin Britten 1928–1938 (2009); *Recreations* architecture, contemporary art, theatre, musicals, travel, food and wine; *Style—* Dr John Evans; ✉ Apartment 2, 1 Adelaide Crescent, Hove, East Sussex BN3 2JD (☎ 01273 777089, mobile 07850 287712, e-mail djoevans@mac.com)

EVANS, Sir John Stanley; kt (2000), QPM (1990), DL (Devon, 2000); s of William Stanley Evans (d 1970), and Doris, *née* Wooldridge (d 1994); *b* 6 August 1943; *Educ* Wade Deacon GS, Univ of Liverpool (LLB); *m* 25 Sept 1965, Beryl, da of Albert Smith (d 1976); 1 s (Mark 1967), 1 da (Lindsey 1971); *Career* Liverpool City then Merseyside Police 1960–80, asst chief constable Gtr Manchester Police 1980–84, dep chief constable Surrey Constabulary 1984–88, chief constable Devon & Cornwall Constabulary 1989–2002; pres ACPO 1999–2000, chm Police Athletic Assoc 1989–2002; ret; special security advsr to FA 2004–09, security advsr to ECB 2008– (head of security ICC World Twenty20 England 2009 and ICC World Champions Trophy England 2013); memb public enquiry into 1997 murder of Robert Hamill in Portadown 2005–11; patron Dream-a-Way 1990–, vice-patron Exeter Leukaemia Fund (ELF) 2003–, Devon county patron Wooden Spoon 2002–, pres Life Educn Wessex (LEW) 2010–; OStJ; *Recreations* most sports (ran London Marathon in 1988 and 1989), service and charitable activities; *Clubs* Woodbury Park Golf and Country (pres 2001–), Rotary (Otter Valley 2004–, pres 2012–13), Musgrove; *Style—* Sir John S Evans, QPM, DL, LLB; ✉ Woodbury Park Golf and Country Club, Woodbury Castle, Woodbury, Exeter, Devon EX5 1JJ (☎ 01395 233 352, sirjohn.s.evans@gmail.com)

EVANS, Jonathan Peter; s of David Evans, and Harriet Evans; *b* 2 June 1950; *Educ* Lewis Sch Pengam, Howardian HS Cardiff, Coll of Law Guildford and Lancaster Gate; *m* 24 Aug 1975, Margaret, *née* Thomas; 1 s, 2 da; *Career* slr, managing ptnr Leo Abse and Cohen slrs until 1992; MP (Cons): Brecon and Radnor 1992–97, Cardiff N 2010–15 (Parly candidate (Cons): Ebbw Vale 1974 (both gen elections), Wolverhampton NE 1979, Brecon and Radnor 1987); MEP (Cons) Wales 1999–2009; House of Commons: PPS to Michael Mates, MP, Min of State NI Office 1992–93, PPS to Rt Hon Sir John Wheeler, MP, Min of State 1993–94, Parly under sec DTI 1994–95 (min for corp affrs 1994–95, min for competition and consumer affrs 1995), Parly sec Lord Chancellor's Department 1995–96, Parly under sec of state Welsh Office 1996–97, former memb Welsh Affrs Select Ctee and Health Select Ctee, chm All-Pty Parly Gp for Insurance and Financial Services 2010–; ldr Conservatives in European Parl 2001–05; chm: Welsh Cons Parly Candidates 1985–90, Welsh Cons Policy Gp 1987–91; memb Bd Cons Pty 2002–05; dir of insurance Eversheds 1997–99, conslt 1999–2009; dir: NFU Mutual 2000–10, Country Mutual Insurance Brokers Ltd 2003–05; chm Pearl Gp 2005–09, chm Phoenix Life Hldgs 2009–; dep chm Tai Cymru (Housing Wales) 1988–92, dep chm Wales Cncl NSPCC 1991–1994; *Recreations* rugby, music, family, reading; *Clubs* Farmers', Cardiff and County; *Style—* Jonathan Evans, Esq

EVANS, Julian Marcus; s of Gillian Goddard; *b* 25 October 1972, Melton Mowbray, Leics; *Educ* Oakham Sch, Nottingham Trent Univ, Sheffield Hallam Univ, Univ of Cambridge; *m* 13 Sept 2008, Victoria, née Bates; 1 da (Grace b 25 Oct 2012), 1 s (Jasper b 23 June 2015); *Career* chartered surveyor and explorer; proprietary partner and head of healthcare Knight Frank LLP; expeditions incl: Mount Kilimanjaro 2004, Marathon Des Sables 2008, North Pole 2009, Land's End to John O'Groats 2010, South Pole 2011, Mont Blanc 2012, Mount Aconcagua 2013, Mount Kosciuszko 2014, Mount Vinson 2016; tstee: PSP Assoc, Matt Hampson Fndn; FRICS, FRGS; *Recreations* cricket, golf, motorsport, music, skiing, tennis, travel, walking, rugby; *Clubs* East India, Leicester Tigers RFC, Explorers Club, The Alpine Club; *Style—* Julian Evans, Esq; ✉ Knight Frank, 55 Baker Street, London W1V 8AN (☎ 020 7861 1147, e-mail julian.evans@knightfrank.com, website www.knightfrank.com)

EVANS, Kim; OBE (2007); da of Jon Evans, and Gwendolen, *née* McLeod; *b* 3 January 1951; *Educ* Putney HS, Univ of Warwick (BA), Univ of Leicester (MA); *m* David Hucker; *Career* asst ed Crafts magazine 1974–76, sub-ed and restaurant critic Harpers & Queen magazine 1976–78, researcher The South Bank Show (LWT) 1978–82; prodr/dir: Hey Good Looking (Channel 4) 1982–83, The South Bank Show (LWT) 1983–88; BBC TV: prodr 1989–92, asst head of music and arts 1992–93, head of arts and music 1993–99; exec dir arts Arts Cncl England 1999–2007; chair Clean Break Theatre Co 2012–; memb: Parole Bd 2006–, Bd London Artists Projects 2007–10, Bd Akademi 2010–13; tstee: Heritage Lottery Fund 2008–14, Chelsea & Westminster Health Charity 2008–12, Nat Portrait Gallery 2010–; Huw Wheldon (BAFTA) Award for Best Arts Documentary (for 'Angela Carter's Curious Room') 1993; hon fell RCA; FRTS; *Recreations* travelling (particularly in Africa), reading, dreaming; *Style—* Kim Evans; ✉ c/o Clean Break, 2 Patshull Road, London NW5 2LB

EVANS, Laurie; s of Hugh Evans (d 1997), and Greta, *née* Bryden (d 1989); *b* 10 July 1955; *Educ* Royal HS Edinburgh, Newcastle Poly, Bournemouth and Poole Coll of Art (DipAD); *m* March 1982, Lesley, da of Stanley Richardson, of Edinburgh; 2 s (James Ewan b 30 May 1983, Calum Thomas b 21 Sept 1986); *Career* photographer; Arts in Fife, freelance reportage photographer for Rock and Roll press (NME, Melody Maker), asst to Bryce Attwell, proprietor Laurie Evans Photographer 1982– (specialising in food and still life); clients incl: Heinz, Morrisons, Asda, Tesco, Waitrose; winner various awards incl: Silver award Assoc of Photographers 1986, 4 Clio awards USA 1986, 1988, 1989 and 1993, Award of Excellence Communication Arts Magazine, Silver award D&AD 1990; columnist Image Magazine, contrib to over 30 cookery books; *Recreations* very keen sailor, blues and jazz guitar, cycling, gardening, landscape photography; *Style—* Laurie Evans, Esq; ✉ e-mail laurieevans@btconnect.com

EVANS, Leslie Douglas; s of Leslie Edward Evans, of St Albans, Herts, and Violet Rosina, *née* Rogerson; *b* 24 June 1945; *Educ* St Albans GS for Boys, St Albans Sch of Art, Leeds Coll of Art (DipAD), Hornsey Coll of Art (Art Teachers' Certificate); *m* 4 Sept 1965, Fionnuala Boyd, *qv*, da of Joseph Douglas Allen Boyd (d 1990); 1 s (Jack Luis b 12 Sept 1969), 1 da (Ruby Rose b 2 Dec 1971); *Career* artist; began working with Fionnuala Boyd 1968, Bi-Centennial fell USA 1977–78; artist in residence: Milton Keynes Devpt Corp 1982–84, RGS 1991, Brunei Rainforest Project 1991–92; *Exhibitions* with Fionnuala Boyd: Angela Flowers Gallery 1972, 1974, 1977, 1979, 1980, 1982, 1984, 1986, 1988, 1990, 1992, 1994, 1996, 1998, 2000, 2002 and 2003, Park Square Gallery Leeds 1972, Boyd and Evans 1970–75 (Turnpike Gallery, Leigh) 1976, Fendrick Gallery Washington DC 1978, Graves Art Gallery Sheffield 1979, Spectro Arts Workshop Newcastle 1980, Ton Peek Utrecht 1981, A Decade of Paintings (Milton Keynes Exhibition Gallery) 1982–83, Drumcroon Art Centre Wigan 1985, Bird (Flowers East, London) 1990, English Paintings (Brendan Walter Gallery, Santa Monica) 1990, Angela Flowers (Ireland) 1990, Flowers East London 1991, Brunei Rainforest (Milton Keynes, Brunei, Malaysia & Singapore) 1993, New Rain Forest Paintings (Flowers East) 1994, Portrayal (Flowers East) 1996, Western Photographs (Flowers East) 1999, Natural Wonder (Flowers West Santa Monica) 1999 and 2001, solo show (Flowers West Santa Monica), solo show (Flowers East London) 2000, Colour in Black & White (Flowers Graphics London and Keller & Greene LA) 2003, Landmarks (Milton Keynes Gallery and Flowers Central London) 2005, Color in Black & White (Flowers NY) 2006, Boyd & Evans (Galerie d'Art Int Solana Beach CA) 2006, Looking Differently (Flowers East London) 2007, Black & White (Flowers East London) 2009, Portrait of a Landscape (LewAllen Gallery Santa Fe) 2011, Views (Ikon Gallery Birmingham) 2012, New Photographs (Flowers Central London) 2012, Collecting (Flowers Central London) 2012, Paintings (Flowers Central London) 2013, Photographs (Leeds Coll of Art) 2013, A Big Tree and Other Photographs (Milton Keynes Coll) 2014; *Group Exhibitions* incl: Postcards (Angela Flowers Gallery) 1970, British Drawing 1952–72 (Angela Flowers Gallery) 1972, British Realist Show (Ikon Gallery) 1976, Aspects of Realism (Rothmans of Pall Mall, Canada) 1976–78, The Real British (Fischer Fine Art) 1981, Black and White Show (Angela Flowers Gallery) 1985, Sixteen (Angela Flowers Gallery) 1986, State of the Nation (Herbert Gallery, Coventry) 1987, Contemporary Portraits (Flowers East) 1988, The Thatcher Years (Flowers East) 1989, Picturing People – British Figurative Art since 1945 (touring exhibition Far East) 1989–90, Art '90 London (Business Design Centre) 1990, 25th Anniversary Exhibition (Flowers East) 1995, Wheels on Fire (Wolverhampton Stoke-on-Trent) 1996, Sight Lines (Honiton Festival) 1996, Contemporary British Landscape (Flowers East) 1999, Double Signature (Fermyn Woods Northants) 2009, This Could Happen to You (Ikon Gallery Birmingham) 2010; *Work in Public Collections* incl: Arts Cncl of GB, Br Cncl, MOMA NY, Sheffield City Art Gallery, Wolverhampton City Art Gallery, Leeds City Art Gallery, Contemporary Art Soc, Leicester Educn Authy, Manchester City Art Gallery, Unilever plc, Tate Gallery, Williamson Art Gallery, Metropolitan Museum NY, Borough of Milton Keynes; *Awards* prizewinner Bradford Print Biennale, first prize 6 Festival Int de la Peinture Cagnes-sur-Mer, Visitors Choice Threadneedle Prize 2010; *Recreations* films, friends, music, hill walking; *Style—* Leslie Evans; ✉ website www.boydandevans.com

EVANS, Liz; *Career* Coast: retail dir 2006–07, md 2007–10; md Oasis 2010–13, ceo Oasis and Warehouse 2013–; *Style—* Ms Liz Evans; ✉ Oasis & Warehouse, 1st floor, 69–77 Paul Street, London EC2A 4PN

EVANS, Dr Mark Lewis; s of Rev Frank Owen Evans (d 2008), and Joan, *née* Lewis (d 1978); *b* 24 March 1954; *Educ* Llanelli Boys' GS, Westfield Coll London (BA), UEA (Thomas and Elizabeth Williams scholar, PhD); *m* 27 March 1985, Reinhild, da of Helmut Weiss (d 1996), of Bückeburg, Germany; *Career* res asst Dept of Western Manuscripts Br Library 1977, lectr in history of art Univ of St Andrews 1978, asst keeper of foreign art Walker Art Gallery Liverpool 1979–84, asst keeper of fine art Nat Museum of Wales 1984–99 (actg keeper 1986–87 and 1994), curator of numerous art exhibns 1988–, sr curator of paintings V&A 2000–; dir Inventory of Public Sculpture in Wales 1998–99, expert advsr on pastels and miniatures Reviewing Ctee on the Export of Works of Art 2002–; memb: Assoc of Art Historians 1976–2003 (exec memb 1993–96, chm Museums and Galleries Sub-Ctee 2000–03), Soc of Renaissance Studies 1984– (memb Cncl 2004–09), Hon Soc of Cymmrodorion 1985–, Cncl for Curators of Dutch and Flemish Art 2002–; FSA; *Publications* Catalogue of Foreign Paintings: Lady Lever Art Gallery (with E Morris, 1983), Supplementary Foreign Catalogue: Walker Art Gallery (with E Morris, 1984), Augustus John Portraits (1988), The Derek Williams Collection (1989), Twentieth Century Art in Wales (1989), Paintings from Windsor Castle (1990), Impressions of Venice from Turner to Monet (1992), The Sforza Hours (1992), The Art Gallery of the National Museum of Wales (with O Fairclough, 1993, 2 edn 1997), Das Stundenbuch der Sforza (with B Brinkmann, 1995), The Drawings of Augustus John (ed, 1996), Princes as Patrons (ed, 1998), The Romantic Tradition in British Painting 1800–1950 (2002), A Masterpiece Reconstructed: The Hours of Louis XII (ed with Thomas Kren, 2005), The Painted World: from Illumination to Abstraction (2005), Art Collecting and Lineage in the Elizabethan Age: The Lumley Inventory and Pedigree (ed, 2010), Raphael: Cartoons and Tapestries for the Sistine Chapel (ed with C Browne and A Nesselrath, 2010), John Constable: Oil Sketches from the Victoria and Albert Museum (2011, German, French and Flemish edns 2011), Dutch and Flemish Drawings in the Victoria and Albert Museum (introduction and ed, with J S Turner and C White, 2014), John Constable: The Making of a Master (2014), Botticelli Reimagined (ed, with S Weppelmann, 2016, German edn 2015); numerous articles and reviews in learned jls, volumes of essays and other jt pubns; *Recreations* travel, cooking; *Style—* Dr Mark Evans; ✉ Word and Image Department, Victoria and Albert Museum, South Kensington, London SW7 2RL (☎ 020 7942 2553, e-mail m.evans@vam.ac.uk)

EVANS, Michael (Mike); *b* 25 May 1961, Tonbridge, Kent; *Educ* Skinners Tunbridge Wells, Univ of Bristol (BSc); *Career* chief operating offr Skandia UK Ltd 2004–06; non-exec dir:

CBRE Global Investors UK 2011–14, esure Gp plc 2013–15; currently non-exec chm Hargreaves Lansdown plc (non-exec dir 2006–); sr ind dir Chesnara plc 2013–, non-exec chm Zoopla Property Gp plc 2014–; FIA 1988; *Style—* Mike Evans, Esq; ✉ Hargreaves Lansdown, One College Square South, Anchor Road, Bristol BS1 5HL

EVANS, Michael Stephen James; s of William Henry Reginald Evans, of Seaford, E Sussex, and Beatrix Catherine, *née* Mottram; *b* 5 January 1945, Worthing; *Educ* Christ's Hosp, QMC London (BA); *m* 1971, Robyn Nicola, da of Samuel John Wilson Coles, MBE; 3 s (Samuel b 29 Nov 1974, Christopher b 6 July 1978, James b 1 July 1980); *Career* news ed Express & Independent Loughton Essex 1969–70 (reporter E London Office 1968); Daily Express: reporter Action Line consumer column 1970–72, gen news reporter 1972–77, home affairs corr 1977–82, def and dip corr 1982–86; The Times: Whitehall corr 1986–87, def corr The Times 1987–98, def ed 1998–2010, Pentagon corr 2010–13; freelance security writer 2013–; vice-pres and acting pres Dip and Cwlth Writers Assoc 1985–86; memb: Defence Correspondents Assoc, Assoc of Foreign Affrs Journalists; winner of Desmond Wettern Maritime Media Award 1998; *Books* A Crack in the Dam (1978), False Arrest (1979), Great Disasters (1981), South Africa (1987), The Gulf Crisis (1988), Double Lives (2011); *Recreations* cricket, tennis, golf, playing piano; *Style—* Michael Evans, Esq; ✉ 1 Percival Road, East Sheen, London SW14 7QE (☏ 07768 081797, e-mail michael.evans@thetimes.co.uk, Twitter @MikeEvansTimes)

EVANS, Nicholas; s of Anthony B Evans (d 1984), and Eileen, *née* Whitehouse (d 2005); *b* 26 July 1950; *Educ* Bromsgrove Sch, St Edmund Hall Oxford (BA); *m* 1, (m dis), Jennifer, da of Ian Lyon; 1 s (Max b 3 Feb 1981), 1 da (Lauren b 31 March 1982); m 2, Charlotte Gordon Cumming; 1 s (Finlay b 11 Feb 2002); 1 s from a previous relationship (Harry Hewland b 9 Jan 1980); *Career* reporter Evening Chronicle Newcastle 1972–75, reporter then prodr Weekend World (LWT) 1975–79, ed The London Programme (LWT) 1979–82, exec prodr The South Bank Show (LWT) 1982–84, ind prodr and screenplay writer 1985–93 (winner US ACE Award for best int movie on cable (Murder by the Book) 1991), currently author; *Books* The Horse Whisperer (1995), The Loop (1998), The Smoke Jumper (2001), The Divide (2005), The Brave (2010); *Recreations* tennis, skiing, running, movies; *Style—* Nicholas Evans, Esq

EVANS, Nicholas; s of Steven Evans, and Kathleen Ann Pidgeon, *née* Nicholas; *b* 2 December 1972; *Educ* Crosskeys Coll Gwent; *m* October 2011, Charlotte Ann Priestley; *Career* chef; commis chef Middlethorpe Hall Hotel York 1991–92, commis to sr chef de partie Royal Crescent Hotel Bath 1992–96, chef tournant rising to jr sous chef Harvey's Restaurant Bristol 1996–96, sous chef 36 on The Quay Emsworth 1996–99, sr chef de partie Lettoine Bath 1999, sous chef Llangoed Hall Llyswen 2000, head chef Newbury Manor Hotel 2000–03, head chef Thornbury Castle 2003–04, chef Owens Restaurant The Celtic Manor Resort S Wales 2004–06, head chef Middlethorpe Hall & Spa York 2006–15, exec chef The Royal York Hotel 2015–; Hotel Employee of the Year 1995, Caterer and Hotelkeeper Acorn Award 2002, S Wales Chef of the Year 2005, Nat Chef of Wales 2006, 3rd Brit culinary fedn chef of the year 2014; *Style—* Nicholas Evans, Esq; ✉ The Refectory Kitchen, The Royal York Hotel, Station Road, York YO24 1AA

EVANS, Nick; *b* July 1950; *Educ* Reading Sch, St John's Coll Oxford; *m*; 2 s; *Career* with MOD: joined 1971, asst private sec to Sec of State for Def 1981–84, head Naval Manpower and Training Div 1984–86, head Management Consultancy Div 1986–89, head Framework Team 1989–91, head Resources and Programmes (Air) 1991–95, asst under sec (Quartermaster) 1995–99, exec dir Defence Procurement Agency 1999–2000, DG (Resources) Defence Logistics Orgn 2000–02, DG Mgmnt and Orgn 2003–06, DG Resources Land Forces 2006; *Style—* Nick Evans, Esq

EVANS, Nigel Martin; MP; s of late Albert Evans, and late Betty Evans; *b* 10 November 1957; *Educ* Dynevor Sch Swansea, UC Swansea (BA); *Career* family newsagent business 1979–90; Parly candidate (Cons): Swansea W 1987, Pontypridd (by-election) 1989; MP (Cons) Ribble Valley 1992– (also contested by-election 1991); PPS to: Rt Hon David Hunt as Chllr of Duchy of Lancaster and sec of state at Office of Public Serv and Sci 1993–95, Tony Baldry, MP, *qv*, 1995–96, Rt Hon William Hague, MP, *qv*, 1996–97; oppn front bench spokesman on constitutional affrs (Wales) 1997–2001, shadow sec of state for Wales 2001–05, first dep chm of ways and means, dep speaker House of Commons 2010–13; memb: Trade and Industry Select Ctee 2003–05, Welsh Select Ctee 2003–05, Quadrapartite Select Ctee 2003–, Culture, Media and Sport Select Ctee 2005–; chm All-Pty Music Gp 1992–, sec All-Pty Tourism Gp 1992–, sec 1922 Ctee 2015–; memb UK delgn to: Parly Assembly Cncl of Europe 2005–, Assembly of WEU 2005–; former chm Swansea W Young Conservatives, former pres Swansea W Cons Assoc, chm Cons Welsh Parly Candidates Policy Gp 1990, pres Cons North West Parly Candidates Gp 1991, sec NW Cons MPs 1992– (chair 2015–), chair Inter Parly Union 2015–; cncllr (Cons) Sketty Ward W Glamorgan CC 1985–91; chm Central Lancs Marie Curie Cancer Centre; campaigned for Republican Pty in NY, Florida and California US presidential elections 1980, 1984 and 1988; *Recreations* tennis, swimming, all spectator sports; *Clubs* Carlton, RAC, Groucho; *Style—* Nigel Evans, Esq, MP; ✉ House of Commons, London SW1A 0AA (☏ 020 7219 6939, e-mail evansn@parliament.uk, website www.nigelmp.com)

EVANS, Peter Michael; s of Michael Evans (d 1976), of Chesterfield, and Fiona Mary, *née* Cassidy (d 1999); *b* 21 September 1952; *Educ* Uppingham, Univ of Oxford (MA); *m* 1, 1975 (m dis 1989), Mary-Ann, da of George Vere Howell; 1 s (Simon Michael b 9 May 1980), 1 da (Eloise Mary b 21 Sept 1981); m 2, 1992, Carol, da of Frank Longridge; 2 da (Holly Susannah, Sacha Fiona (twins) b 18 March 1995); *Career* IMI plc 1975–80 (personnel trainee, grad recruitment offr, export mktg exec), regnl mangr W Africa Wellcome plc 1980–83, int personnel exec Booker plc 1983–85, MSL International (formerly Hay-MSL) 1985–91 (conslt, regnl dir, dir), dir Whitehead Mann Ltd 1991–99, md Russell Reynolds Associates 1999–; *Style—* Peter Evans, Esq; ✉ Russell Reynolds Associates, 12 Marina View, Asia Square Tower 2, Singapore 018961 (☏ 0065 6496 0602, fax 0065 6224 4058, e-mail peter.evans@russellreynolds.com)

EVANS, Dr Philip Rhys; s of James Howard Evans, and Ruby Gertrude, *née* Crouch; *b* 25 January 1946; *Educ* Shene Co GS, Guy's Hosp London (MB BS), Open Univ (BA); *m* 1, 1971 (m dis 1992), Wendy Sunderland; 3 da (Rachael b 1973, Katy b 1974, Suzanne b 1977), 1 s (Ralph b 1979); m 2, 1996, Christine Mary Stone Haywood; 2 step-s (Karl b 1960, Mark b 1962); *Career* VSO Fiji Islands 1965–66; in gen practice: Dargaville NZ 1976–77, Leaf Rapids Canada 1977–78; princ in gen practice Bury St Edmunds 1979–2011; postgrad trainer in gen practice 1981–89; RCGP: memb Cncl 1985–88 and 1991–2010, memb Int Ctee 1987–2000, sec 1991–94, chm 1994–2000, chm UK Euro Forum 1994–96, chm Royal Coll Int Forum 1999–2001; advsr to WHO in Romania, Hungary, Czech Repub and Turkey 1991–94, external advsr Health Service Ombudsman 2000–05; memb UK Delgn to Euro Union of Gen Practitioners (UEMO) 1988–2001, UK delg Standing Ctee of Euro Doctors (CP) 1988–2001, medical memb HM Courts and Tbnl Service 2011–; UK rep: Int Soc of Gen Practice (SIMG) 1991–95, World Orgn of Family Doctors (WONCA) 1993–2002; hon sec Euro Soc of Gen Practice/Family Med 1995–2001, pres Euro Soc of Gen Practice/Family Med 2001–04; author of pubns on int gen practice and family med, jt ed Euro Jl of Gen Practice 1995–96; academic referee: Br Med Jl, Br Jl of Gen Practice; memb VSO; DipObst RCOG, FRCGP, MRCS, LRCP; *Recreations* cricket, golf, history, travel, growing sweet peas, oenology; *Clubs* East India, Surrey CCC, Flempton Golf, Suffolk Hares Cricket, The Straw Boater; *Style—* Dr Philip R Evans; ✉ Michaelmas Cottage, Bury Road, Hengrave, Bury St Edmunds, Suffolk IP28 6LS (e-mail nx44@dial.pipex.com)

EVANS, Philip Wyn; CBE (2005); s of Wyndham Hubert Evans, of Tenby, Pembs, and Enid Caroline Evans; *b* 27 November 1948; *Educ* Greenhill GS Tenby, London Sch of Marine Engrg; *m* 17 Oct 1970, Jacqueline Jean, da of Malcolm C Herbert; 2 s (Mathew Giles Wyn b 1972, Daniel Charles Wyn b 1974), 3 da (Louise Elizabeth b 1982, Claire Emma Jane b 1983, Polly Anne b 1984); *Career* chm: Vox Leisure Services Ltd 1975–90, The Vox Group plc 1990–2013, Coastal Cottages Ltd 1992–2001, Activity Wales Ltd 1994–2001, Wales Tourist Bd 1999–2006, Tourism UK, Tst Port of Saundersfoot 2011–; ceo: The Vox Wine Co Ltd 1980–84, Shopper Direct Ltd 1984–88; memb Bd Br Tourism Authy; WTB/Schroeders Bank Tourism Award 1995; memb Lord Chllr's Advsy Panel 2008–; govr Univ of Wales; tstee Springboard Charitable Tst, ordained elder United Reform Church; FIMgt 1985; *Books* Man Management and Motivation (1974); *Recreations* ocean cruising and navigation, rugby, wildlife conservation, travel, walking; *Style—* Philip Evans, Esq, CBE; ✉ The Admiral's Mews Partnership, 3 Paddock Way, Heath House, Portsmouth Road, London SW15 3TN (☏ 01834 814000, e-mail philip@admiralsmews.com)

EVANS, Rebecca Mary; AM; da of Ven Rev Alun Wyn Evans, and Evelyn Mary, *née* Hughes; *b* 2 August 1976, Bridgend, Glamorgan; *Educ* Bishop of Llandaff Church in Wales HS, Univ of Leeds (BA), Sidney Sussex Coll Cambridge (MPhil), Sheffield Hallam Univ (PG Cert); *m* 25 July 2010, Paul Michael Evans; *Career* Welsh Lab regnl organiser for Mid and W Wales 2004–06, research and communications offr for Carl Sargeant, AM, Nat Assembly for Wales 2006–09, policy and public affrs offr Nat Autistic Soc 2009–11, memb Nat Assembly for Wales (Lab) Mid and W Wales 2011–, dep min for Agriculture and Fisheries 2014, dep min for Farming and Food 2014–; *Style—* Mrs Rebecca Evans, AM; ✉ National Assembly for Wales, Cardiff Bay, Cardiff CF99 1NA (☏ 02920 898288, e-mail rebecca.evans@wales.gov.uk)

EVANS, Prof Sir Richard John; kt (2012); s of Ieuan Trefor Evans, and Evelyn, *née* Jones; *b* 29 September 1947, Woodford, London; *Educ* Jesus Coll Oxford (MA), St Antony's Coll Oxford (DPhil), UEA (LittD), Univ of Cambridge (DLitt); *m* 1, 2 March 1976 (m dis 1993), Elin Hjaltadóttir, da of Hjalti Arnason; 1 step da (Sigridur Jónsdóttir b 1964); m 2, 17 April 2004, Christine L, da of Alec Corton; 2 s (Mathew b 1995, Nicholas b 1998); *Career* lectr in history Univ of Stirling 1972–76, prof of European history UEA 1983–89 (lectr 1976–83), prof of history Birkbeck Coll London 1989–98 (vice-master 1993–98, acting master 1997); Univ of Cambridge: prof of modern history 1998–2008, fell Gonville & Caius Coll 1998–2010 (hon fell 2010–), Regius prof of modern history 2008–10, Gresham prof of rhetoric Gresham Coll 2009–13, Regius prof of history 2010–14, pres Wolfson Coll 2010–17, provost Gresham Coll 2014–; visiting assoc prof of European history Columbia Univ NY 1980; chair German History Soc 1989–92; Wolfson Literary Award for History 1988, William H Welch Medal of the American Assoc for the History of Med 1989, Hamburger Medaille für Kunst und Wissenschaft 1993, Fraenkel Prize for Contemporary History 1994, Norton Medlicott Medal Historical Assoc 2014, Leverhulme Medal and Prize Br Acad 2015; hon fell Jesus Coll Oxford 1998, hon fell Birkbeck Coll London 1999; hon LitD Univ of London 2012, hon DLitt Oxon 2015; FRHistS 1978, FBA 1993, FRSL 1999, FLSW 2010; *Books* The Feminist Movement in Germany 1894–1933 (1976), The Feminists (1977), Society and Politics in Wilhelmine Germany (ed, 1978), Sozialdemokratie und Frauenemanzipation im Deutschen Kaiserreich (1979), The German Family (ed with W R Lee, 1981), The German Working Class (ed, 1982), The German Peasantry (ed with W R Lee, 1986), Rethinking German History (1987), Death in Hamburg (1987), Comrades and Sisters (1987), The German Unemployed (ed with D Geary, 1987), The German Underworld (ed, 1988), Kneipengespräche im Kaiserreich (1989), In Hitler's Shadow (1989), Proletarians and Politics (1990), The German Bourgeoisie (ed with D Blackbourn, 1991), Rituals of Retribution (1996), In Defence of History (1997), Rereading German History (1997), Tales from the German Underworld (1998), Lying About Hitler (2001), The Coming of the Third Reich (2003), The Third Reich in Power (2005), The Third Reich at War (2008), Cosmopolitan Islanders (2009), Altered Pasts (2014), The Third Reich in History and Memory (2015); *Recreations* music (piano), cooking, reading fiction; *Clubs* Athenaeum, Oxford and Cambridge; *Style—* Prof Sir Richard J Evans, FBA; ✉ President's Lodge, Wolfson College, Barton Road, Cambridge CB3 9BB (☏ 01223 335938, fax 01223 335937, e-mail rje36@cam.ac.uk, website www.wolfson.cam.ac.uk)

EVANS, Roderick Michael; s of Michael White Evans, of Monaco, and Helga Ingeborg, *née* Schneider; *b* 19 April 1962; *Educ* Millfield; *m* 7 April 1995, Ms Dawn Silver, er da of Geoffrey Richmond, of Alwoodley, Leeds; 1 s (Oliver William Roderick b 6 Nov 1996), 1 d (Isabella Daisy Florence b 27 July 1999); *Career* dir of numerous companies incl: Evans Management Ltd (md), Evans Property Gp Ltd, Deehurst Ltd; *Recreations* motorcycling, shooting, flying; *Clubs* RAC; *Style—* Roderick Evans, Esq; ✉ Evans Management Ltd, 70 Jermyn Street, London SW1Y 6NY (☏ 020 7024 9730)

EVANS, Roger; s of Eric Evans (d 1947), of Bristol, and Celia Mavis, *née* Roe (d 1988); *b* 28 October 1945, Bristol; *Educ* Lord Wandsworth Coll; *m* (m dis) Julia Margaret, da of Arthur Horace Moore Household (d 1998); 2 c (Rupert Alexander, Rebecca Grace (twins) b 14 June 1981); *Career* gen mangr St George's Hosp 1985–90, gen mangr SW Thames RHA 1991–92, chief exec Mid Kent Healthcare Tst 1992–2000, md Roger Evans & Assocs 2000–, md Roger Evans Mgmnt Conslts Ltd 2006–, chief exec Neurosciences Research Fndn 2005–; chm Macfarlane Tst 2012–16, tstee London City Mission 2013; memb Inst of Health Care Mgmnt 1971; FRSA, FRSM 2007; *Recreations* cricket, rugby union, fine arts, 18th century music, jazz, theatre, soccer (dir AFC Wimbledon); *Clubs* RSM, MCC, National, Gloucestershire CCC, London Wasps RFC; *Style—* Roger Evans, Esq; ✉ 36 Pepys Road, Wimbledon, London SW20 8PF (☏ 020 8879 0729, mobile 07702 250844, e-mail rogerevans4@hotmail.com)

EVANS, (Jeremy) Roger; AM; s of Ronald Evans, of Rochdale, Lancs, and Doris Valentine, *née* Stanley; *b* 23 June 1964; *Educ* Laurence Jackson Sch Guisborough, Univ of Sheffield (BSc), Univ of Westminster, Inns of Court Sch of Law; *Career* various managerial roles Royal Mail 1985–95; called to the Bar Middle Temple 1997; memb Waltham Forest BC 1990–2000 (ldr Cons Gp Waltham Forest 1994–98), memb London Assembly GLA (Cons) Havering and Redbridge 2000– (ldr Cons Gp 2008–), memb Havering London BC 2006–; project mangr The Spring Gp 1998–2000; memb London Fire and Emergency Planning Authy; *Recreations* swimming, badminton; *Style—* Mr Roger Evans, Esq, AM; ✉ London Assembly, City Hall, Queens Walk, Southwark, London SE1 2AA (☏ 020 7983 4359, fax 020 7983 4419, e-mail roger.evans@london.gov.uk)

EVANS, Roger Kenneth; s of late Gerald Raymond Evans, and late Dr Annie Margaret Evans; *b* 18 March 1947; *Educ* Bristol GS, Trinity Hall Cambridge (MA, pres Cambridge Union); *m* 6 Oct 1973, Worshipful (Doris) June Rodgers, *qv*, da of late James Rodgers, of Co Down, NI; 2 s (Edward Arthur, Henry William); *Career* Parly candidate (Cons): Warley West Oct 1974 and 1979, Ynys Môn (Anglesey) 1987, Monmouth by-election May 1991; MP (Cons) Monmouth 1992–97, PPS to Jonathan Aitken 1994, Parly under-sec of state Dept of Social Security 1994–97; memb: Ecclesiastical Ctee of Parliament 1992–97, Welsh Affairs Select Ctee 1992–94; called to the Bar Middle Temple 1970 (ad eundum Inner Temple 1979); barr Midland Circuit 1997–, asst recorder 1998, recorder 2000–; pres Cambridge Georgian Gp 1969, chm Cambridge Univ Cons Assoc 1969, pres Cambridge Union Soc 1970; chm Prayer Book Soc 2001–06 (vice-pres 1994–2001), memb Exec Ctee Friends of Friendless Churches 1983– (chm 1998–); Freeman City of London 1976; *Recreations* architectural and garden history, building and gardening; *Clubs* Carlton, Coningsby (chm 1976–77, treas 1983–87); *Style—* Roger Evans, Esq; ✉ 2

Harcourt Buildings, Temple, London EC4Y 9DB (☎ 020 7353 6961, fax 020 7353 6968, e-mail revans@harcourtchambers.co.uk)

EVANS, Ruth Elizabeth; *b* 12 October 1957; *Educ* Camden Sch for Girls, Girton Coll Cambridge (MA); *Children* 1 da; *Career* vol Liberty 1980, first dir Maternity Alliance 1981–86, dep dir then actg dir MIND 1986–89 (bd dir Minds Matter Ltd 1986–90), gen sec War on Want 1990, mgmnt conslt Dept of Health 1990–91, ceo and chief accounting offr Nat Consumer Cncl 1992–99 (3 terms of office); non-exec dir: Fin Ombudsman Services 1999–2002, Liverpool Victoria Gp 1999–2002, Nationwide Bldg Soc 2002–05, Phonepay Plus 2008–11, Serious Fraud Office 2014–; sr ind dir and chair Remuneration Bd CCP Gp plc 2013–16; cmmr Ind Police Complaints Cmmn 2009–; memb Advsy Bd ING Direct UK 2007–10; chair: Standing Advsy Gp on Consumer Involvement in NHS 1995–99, Ind Inquiry into Paediatric Cardiac Services Royal Brompton and Harefield Hospitals 1999–2001, Ind Inquiry into Drug Testing at Work 2002–04, Authy for Television on Demand 2009–15, Payments Strategy Forum 2015–, Ind Parly Standards Authy (IPSA) 2016–; chm Bar Standards Bd 2005–08; dep chair Ofcom Consumer Panel 2004–08; non-exec cmmr and chair Remuneration Bd Ind Police Complaints Cmmn 2009–15, chair Remuneration Bd and non-exec dir Nat Audit Office 2009–12, founding dir Bd Alacrity Entrepreneurship Fndn 2010–; memb: Bd Nat Perinatal Epidemiology Unit 1983–86, Brook Advsy Centres 1984–87, Good Practices in Mental Health 1986–89, Ctee of Mgmnt UK Cochrane Centre 1993–95, Prevention of Professional Abuse Network 1994–97, Central Research and Devpt Ctee for the NHS 1995–99, UK Round Table on Sustainable Devpt 1995–99, Acting on Complaints Advsy Bd Dept of Health 1996–97, NHS Charter Advsy Gp 1998, Expert Panel on Sustainable Devpt 1998–99, (lay memb) GMC 1999–2008 (chm Standards Ctee 2003–05), Fabian Soc Cmmn on Taxation and Citizenship 1999–2000, Panel of Ind Assessors Office of the Cmmr for Public Appts 1999–2005, Ind Review Panel on the Future Funding of the BBC 1999–2000, Cncl Britain in Europe 1999–2002 (chair Shoppers in Europe), Human Genetics Cmmn 1999–2002, Ind Review Panel for the Advertising of Medicines 1999–2005, Medicines Cmmn 2002–03, Audit Cmmn Ind Complaints Panel 2002–06, Tbnls for Users Prog Interdepartmental Steering Gp Lord Chllr's Dept 2003–05, Governance Review Gp Law Soc 2003–05, Customer Impact Panel Assoc of Br Insurers 2005–11; lay memb QC Selection Panel 2004–08; tstee Money Advice Tst 1994–2000 (chair Advsy Gp of UK money advice agencies); govr Camden Sch for Girls 1985–89; *Recreations* swimming, opera, writing; *Style*— Ms Ruth Evans; ☎ 020 7482 0420, e-mail ruth@ruthevans.org

EVANS, Sarah Hauldys; OBE (2014); da of Wyndham Bowen Evans, and Nancy Sarah, *née* Mills; *b* 4 March 1953; *Educ* King James' GS Knaresborough, Univ of Sussex (BA), Univ of Leicester (MA), Univ of Leeds (PGCE); *m* 1989, Andrew Romanis Fowler; 1 s (Kit Wyndam Romanis b 1993); *Career* asst teacher then head of English Leeds Girls' HS 1976–84, dep head Fulneck Girls' Sch Pudsey 1986–89; head: Friends' Sch Saffron Walden 1989–96, King Edward VI High Sch for Girls Birmingham 1996–2013; pres Guild of Friends in Educn 1991–92, co-chair HMC/GSA Educn Ctee 2001–03, memb Exec Ctee Boarding Schs' Assoc 1990–96 (vice-chm 1995–96); SHMIS: memb Educn Ctee 1991–96, chair Educn Ctee 1992–96; non-exec dir Essex Ambulance Tst 1991–96, chair ISC teacher induction panel (ISCtip) 2007–13, memb Teachers' Professional Conduct Panels 2013–; govr: Queenswood Sch 2004–08, Elmhurst 2008–, West House Sch 2008–; tstee: Acad of Youth 2002–, Westhill Endowment Tst 2002–, Nishkam Schools Tst 2013–; *Recreations* the arts; *Style*— Ms Sarah Evans, OBE; ✉ 38 Amesbury Road, Moseley, Birmingham B13 8LE (☎ 0121 449 4536)

EVANS, Stephen Nicholas; CMG (2002), OBE (1994); s of Vincent Morris Evans, of Poole, Dorset, and Doris Mary Evans (d 1977); *b* 29 June 1950, Harrow, Middx; *Educ* King's Coll Taunton, Univ of Bristol (BA), Univ of Cambridge (MPhil); *m* 29 Dec 1975, Sharon Ann, *née* Holdcroft; 2 da (Juliette b 14 April 1981, Olivia b 1 Feb 1984), 1 s (Nicholas b 20 Feb 1986); *Career* 1 Royal Tank Regt 1971–74; HM Dip Serv: FCO 1974–78, head of Chancery Hanoi 1978–80, FCO 1980–82, first sec Bangkok 1982–88, FCO 1988–90, head Political Section Ankara 1990–93, cnsllr Islamabad 1993–96, UN Special Mission to Afghanistan 1996–97, head S Asian Dept FCO 1998–2001, chargé d'affaires Kabul 2001–02, high cmmr to Sri Lanka 2002–06 (concurrently non-resident high cmmr to the Maldives), ambass to Afghanistan 2006–07, dir of Afghanistan Information Strategy FCO 2007, high cmmr to Bangladesh 2008–11; *Recreations* naval and military history, golf, cycling; *Clubs* Athenaeum, Royal Colombo Golf (Sri Lanka); *Style*— Mr Stephen Evans, CMG, OBE

EVANS, Dr Stephen Nicholas (Steve); s of William Raymond Evans, of Llanelli, and Carole Dalling, *née* White; *b* 1 December 1964; *Educ* Penyrheol Comp Sch Gorseinon, Univ of Bristol Med Sch (MB ChB), postgrad dip; *m* 5 Sept 1992, Lysette Emma, da of Michael Newman; 1 s (Joel Ieuan b 12 Sept 1999); *Career* house physician Royal Cornwall Hosp (Treliske) Truro 1988–89, house surgn Bristol Royal Infirmary 1989, MO Br Antarctic Survey 1989–91, med SHO Birmingham Heartlands Hosp 1991–94, registrar (gen and geriatric med) Jersey Gen Hosp and Southampton Gen Hosp 1995, registrar Napier Public Hosp NZ 1995–96, sr registrar (gen and geriatric med) Glenfield Gen Hosp NHS Tst and Leicester Gen Hosp NHS Tst 1997–99, locum Withybush Gen Hosp Haverfordwest 1999; Leicester Gen Hosp: conslt physician Dept of Cerebrovascular Med 1999–2002, lead clinician for emergency med 2001–02; currently conslt physician Med Specialist Gp Guernsey; memb: BMA, Br Geriatric Soc, Br Assoc of Stroke Physicians; MRCP 1994; *Publications* author of numerous papers and articles in learned jls; *Recreations* rugby, snowboarding, power kites; *Clubs* Oakham RFC; *Style*— Dr Steve Evans; ✉ c/o Medical Specialist Group, Alexandra House, Les Frieteaux, St Martin's, Guernsey GY1 3EX (☎ 01481 238565, fax 01481 237782, e-mail snevans@doctors.net)

EVANS, Stuart John; s of John Redshaw Evans (d 1992), and Mabel Elizabeth, *née* Brown (d 1974); *b* 31 December 1947; *Educ* Royal GS Newcastle upon Tyne, Univ of Leeds (LLB); *m* 2 Jan 1971, Margaret Elizabeth, da of Edgar John Evans (d 1966), and Kathleen Gerardine, *née* Goulding (d 2006); 2 s (John Daniel b 1976, Thomas b 1977), 1 da (Elizabeth b 1983); *Career* articled clerk Stanley Brent & Co 1970–72, asst slr Slaughter and May 1972–79, head of corp fin Simmons & Simmons 2001–05 (asst slr 1979–80, ptnr 1981–2008, conslt 2009–); chair Tate Patrons of New Art 1997–2000, juror Turner Prize 2001; fndr (with s, John Daniel Evans): Lodeveans Collection of Contemporary Art, Balon (promoters of art from Latin America); reader St Stephen's Church Canonbury; *Books* A Practitioner's Guide to The FSA Regulation of Investment Banking (contrib), Global Corporate Governance Guide 2004: Best Practice in the Boardroom (contrib), A Practitioner's Guide to The Financial Services Authority Listing Rules 2006/2007 (contrib); *Recreations* contemporary art; *Clubs* Arts; *Style*— Stuart Evans, Esq; ✉ Simmons & Simmons, CityPoint, One Ropemaker Street, London EC2Y 9SS (☎ 020 7628 2020, fax 020 7628 2070); Lodeveans Limited, 13 Camden Passage, London N1 8EA

EVANS, Her Hon Judge Susan Louise; QC (2010); *b* 16 June 1966, Arbroath, Scotland; *Career* called to the Bar 1989; recorder 2005, circuit judge (Western Circuit) 2011–; *Style*— Her Hon Judge Susan Evans, QC; ✉ Winchester Law Courts, Winchester, SO23 9EL

EVANS, Suzanne Elizabeth; *b* 2 February 1965, Shrewsbury; *Educ* The Corbet Sch Shropshire, Univ of Lancaster (BA); *Children* 1 da (Lucinda b 28 Feb 1993); *Career* reporter and presenter BBC Radio 1987–99, freelance PR and mktg conslt 2000–15, communications dir Aquarius PR 2006–15; cncllr London Borough of Merton Cons Pty 2010–13, memb UKIP 2013– (head of policy 2014–15, dep chm 2014–16, currently Parly spokesperson); fndr and tstee Lipoedema UK; listed in Debrett's 500 2016; *Publications* Why Vote UKIP (2015), UKIP Gen Election Manifesto (2015); *Style*— Miss Suzanne Evans; ✉ Twitter @suzanneevans1

EVANS, Timothy James (Tim); s of David Evans (d 2006), and Janet Monica Handley; *b* 22 August 1962, Dartford, Kent; *Educ* South Bank Poly, Oxford Poly (BA Arch, DipArch); *m* 5 Dec 1992, Elizabeth Lane; 2 da (Jasmine Isobella b 21 May 1993, Scarlett Amelia b 28 July 1995); *Career* architect; Burns Guthrie and Partners 1983–84, Terry Farrell & Co 1986–89; vol work Managua Nicaragua 1989; Daryl Jackson (Aust) 1989–90; Sheppard Robson: joined 1990, ptnr 1998–, equity ptnr and creative dir i/c design direction London, Manchester, Glasgow and Abu Dhabi offices 2003–; *Style*— Tim Evans, Esq; ✉ 77 Agar Grove, London NW1 9UE (☎ 020 7504 1700); Sheppard Robson, 77 Parkway, London NW1 7PU (☎ 020 7504 1700, fax 020 7504 1701, e-mail tim.evans@sheppardrobson.com)

EVANS, Prof Timothy William; s of Philip Charles Evans, of Endcliffe, Sheffield, and Mary Elizabeth, *née* Else; *b* 29 May 1954; *Educ* High Storrs GS Sheffield, Univ of Manchester (BSc, MB ChB, MD), Univ of Sheffield (PhD, DSc), Univ of Calif San Francisco; *m* Dr Josephine Emir MacSweeney, da of Prof James MacSweeney (d 1972); 3 s (Charles James b 1990, Freddie William b 1992, Edward Christopher George b 1998), 1 da (Verity Sarah Mary b 1995); *Career* Manchester Royal Infirmary 1980, Univ of Sheffield 1981, Royal Postgraduate Med Sch 1982, Nat Heart and Lung Inst 1982, Univ of Sheffield 1982–84, Univ of Calif San Francisco 1984–85, prof of intensive care med Imperial Coll Sch of Med London, vice dean Faculty of Intensive Care Medicine 2012–14, tstee and memb Bd Faculty of Pharmaceutical Medicine 2013–; conslt in intensive care/thoracic med: Royal Brompton Hosp 1987–, Westminster London 1987–2010, civilian conslt to HM Forces 1998–, hon conslt Royal Hosp Chelsea 2004–, academic registrar RCP 2005–09 (vice-pres 2009–12), med dir Royal Brompton and Harefield NHS Tst 2005–15 (dep ceo 2006–, dir R&D 2008–), sr clinical investigator NIHR 2010–13, nat dir for clinical productivity Dept of Health 2015–; chair Nat Cardiac Benchmarking Collaborative 2014–16; tstee and memb Bd Nuffield Tst 2014–; FRCP, Hon FRCA, FMedSci; *Publications* author of 5 books and over 200 chapters, invited articles and peer reviewed papers, memb Editorial Bds of 2 scientific jls; *Recreations* flying and sailing; *Clubs* RSM; *Style*— Prof Timothy Evans; ✉ Department of Anaesthesia and Intensive Care, Royal Brompton Hospital NHS Trust, Sydney Street, London SW3 6NP (☎ 020 7351 8523, fax 020 7351 8524, e-mail t.evans@rbht.nhs.uk)

EVANS, Dr Trevor John; o s of late Evan Alban (John) Evans, and late Margaret Alice, *née* Hilton; *b* 14 February 1947; *Educ* King's Sch Rochester, UCL (BSc, PhD), Univ of Liverpool (MA); *m* 1973, Margaret Elizabeth, da of late Felix Whitham; 3 s (Thomas b 1979, Owen b 1984, Jacob b 1988), 1 da (Jessica b 1981); *Career* chem engr; chief exec Inst of Chem Engrs 1976–2006, chief exec Ergonomics Soc 2007, ceo Australian Acad of Technological Sciences and Engrg Melbourne 2007–08; conslt on governance to not-for-profit sector 2010–; visiting prof UCL 2011–; formerly: jt sec-gen Euro Fedn of Chem Engrg, dep chm Bd Engrg Cncl (UK), dir Engrg and Technol Bd (ETB), memb Bd Science Cncl; Kurnakov Meml Medal, Titanium ACHEMA Plaque; hon fell UCL 1997; CEng, Hon FIChemE, FRSA, hon memb Czech Soc of Chemical Engrg 2006, hon memb European Fedn of Chemical Engrg 2007; *Recreations* the complexities of family life, historical research into slavery and technology; *Style*— Dr T J Evans; ✉ e-mail tevansj@aol.com

EVANS, Rt Rev (John) Wyn; *see:* St Davids, Bishop of

EVANS OF BOWES PARK, Baroness (Life Peer UK 2014), of Bowes Park in the London Borough of Haringey; Natalie Jessica Evans; PC (2016); *b* 29 November 1975, London; *m* 18 Dec 2010, James Wild; *Career* formerly dep dir Policy Exchange; New Schools Network: chief operating offr 2011–13, dir 2013–15; govt whip 2015–, ldr House of Lords and Lord Privy Seal 2016–; *Style*— The Baroness Evans of Bowes Park, PC; ✉ House of Lords, London SW1A 0PW

EVANS OF PARKSIDE, Baron (Life Peer UK 1997), of St Helens in the County of Merseyside; John Evans; s of James Evans (d 1937), and Margaret, *née* Robson (d 1987); *b* 19 October 1930; *Educ* Jarrow Central Sch; *m* 1959, Joan, da of Thomas Slater; 2 s, 1 da; *Career* former marine fitter and engr, memb Hebburn UDC 1962–74 (chm 1972–73, ldr 1969–74), memb S Tyneside MDC 1973–74, memb Euro Parl 1975–78 (chm Regnl Policy and Tport Ctee 1976–78); MP (Lab): Newton Feb 1974–83, St Helens N 1983–97; asst govt whip 1978–79, oppn whip 1979–80, PPS to Rt Hon Michael Foot as ldr of oppn 1980–83, memb Lab Pty NEC 1982–96, oppn front bench spokesman on employment 1983–87, chm National Lab Pty 1991–92; *Style*— The Rt Hon Lord Evans of Parkside; ✉ House of Lords, London SW1A 0PW

EVANS OF TEMPLE GUITING, Baron (Life Peer UK 2000), of Temple Guiting in the County of Gloucestershire; Matthew Evans; CBE (1999); s of George Ewart Evans; *b* 7 August 1941; *Educ* Friends' Sch Saffron Walden, LSE (BSc); *m* 1, 1966 (m dis 1990), Elizabeth, da of Alan P Mead, MC; 2 s (Hon Theodore Julian b 1972, Hon Daniel Michael b 1974); m 2, 1991, Caroline, da of Wolfgang Richard Max Michel; 2 s (Hon Tomas Wolf Ewart b 1992, Hon Merlin Finnian Seamus b 1994), 1 da (Hon Mabel Marie b 1995); *Career* Faber & Faber Ltd: md 1972–98, chm 1981–2002; Lord in Waiting (government whip) 2002–07, chm EFG Private Bank 2008–; pres Br Antique Dealers Assoc 2013–; FRSA 1990, Hon FRCA 1999; *Clubs* Groucho; *Style*— The Lord Evans of Temple Guiting, CBE; ✉ House of Lords, London SW1A 0PW

EVANS OF WATFORD, Baron (Life Peer UK 1998), of Chipperfield in the County of Hertfordshire; David Charles Evans; *b* 30 November 1942; *Educ* Watford Coll of Technology (City and Guilds, Edward Hunter Medal); *m* (m dis); 3 c; *Career* apprentice printer 1957, fndr and chm Centurion Press Gp 1971–2002; co-fndr Senate Consulting Ltd 2003–, fndr Evans Mitchell Books; chm: Senate Consulting Ltd, TU ink Ltd, Evans Mitchell Books, Ace Funding Ltd, Forum Print Mgmnt Ltd, Kennedy Scott Ltd, Stormount Energy, Senate Publishing; former chm: Redactive Media Gp, Centurion Press Gp, Ace Consortium Ltd, Newsdesk Media Ltd; chm Advanced Oncotherapy plc; former dir KISS 100 FM; memb House of Lords Select Ctee for Small and Medium Enterprises; dep chm Int Medical Educn Tst, chm Inst of Collaborative Working, former memb Bd UCL Hosps Charitable Tst, former tstee Royal Air Force Museum, dir Royal Air Force Trading Co; patron: Watford Peace Hospice, VITAL, Alma Hosp Tst, Eliminating Domestic Violence; dir Watford Community Events; hon fell Cancer Research UK; memb Worshipful Co of Marketors; FCIM, FCGI; *Recreations* family and friends, theatre, travelling, meeting new people and tea; *Style*— The Lord Evans of Watford; ✉ House of Lords, London SW1A 0PW; Senate Consulting Ltd, 4th Floor, 184–192 Drummond Street, London NW1 3HP (☎ 020 7650 1600, e-mail lordevans@senateconsulting.co.uk)

EVANS-GORDON, Her Hon Judge Jane-Anne Mary; da of Dr D G O'Hagan (d 1971), and Mrs P J O'Hagan (d 1969); *b* 18 November 1956, Northampton; *Educ* Our Lady's Grove Dublin, Univ of Reading (LLB), Inns of Court Sch of Law; *m* 10 Sept 1982, Alastair James Kenmure Evans-Gordon; 1 s (Christopher James Kenmure b 27 July 1992); *Career* called to the Bar Inner Temple 1992, barr New Square Chambers 1993–2014, recorder 2009, circuit judge (Midland Circuit) 2014–; *Publications* contrib: Cohabitation: Law & Precedents 1999–, Williams Mortimer and Sunnucks Executors Administrators & Probate (20 edn 2013), Theobald on Wills (18 edn 2015); *Clubs* LDC (dining), LEGS (golf); *Style*— Her Hon Judge Evans-Gordon; ✉ Birmingham Civil and Family Justice Centre, 33 Bull Street, Birmingham, West Midlands B4 6DS

EVARISTO, Bernardine; MBE (2009); *Career* writer; Nat Endowment for Science, Technol and the Arts Award 2003; FRSA, FRSL; *Books* Lara (1997, Best Book/Novel BT Ethnic and Multicultural Media Award 1999), The Emperor's Babe (2001, Arts Cncl Writers' Award 2000), Soul Tourists (2005), Blonde Roots (2008); *Style*— Ms Bernardine Evaristo, MBE; ✉ c/o Curtis Brown Group Ltd, Haymarket House, 28–29 Haymarket, London SW1Y 4SP

EVE, Trevor John; s of Stewart Frederick Eve, of Staffordshire, and Elsie, *née* Hamer; *b* 1 July 1951; *Educ* Bromsgrove Sch, Kingston Art Coll, RADA; *m* 1 March 1980, Sharon Patricia, da of Francis Maughan, of Holland Park, London; 1 da (Alice b 6 Feb 1982), 2 s (James Jonathan (Jack) b 23 Sept 1985, George Francis b 7 March 1994); *Career* actor, producer; patron Childhope Int; prodr Projector Productions; *Theatre* incl: Children of a Lesser God (Olivier Award for best actor) 1981, The Genius (Royal Court) 1983, High Society (NT) 1986, Man Beast and Virtue (NT) 1989, The Winter's Tale (Young Vic) 1991, Inadmissible Evidence (RNT) 1993, Uncle Vanya (Albery, Olivier Award for Best Supporting Actor 1997) 1996; *Television* incl: Shoestring 1980, Jamaica Inn, A Sense of Guilt 1990, Parnell and the Englishwoman 1991, A Doll's House 1991, The Politician's Wife (Channel 4) 1995, Black Easter (Screen Two) 1995, Heat of the Sun (Carlton) 1997, Evilstreak (LWT) 1999, David Copperfield (BBC) 1999, Waking The Dead (9 series, BBC) 2004–10, Lawless (ITV) 2004, The Family Man (BBC) 2006, Hughie Green, Most Sincerely 2008, Framed 2009, Bouquet of Barbed Wire 2010, The Other Woman (Sky Arts) 2012; as prodr: Alice Through the Looking Glass (Projector/Channel 4) 1998, Cinderella (Projector/Channel 4) 1999, Twefth Night (Projector/Channel 4), Body Farm 2011; as actor and prodr: Kidnap and Ransom 2010, Kidnap and Ransom II 2011; *Film* incl: Hindle Wakes, Dracula, A Wreath of Roses, The Corsican Brothers, Aspen Extreme, Psychotherapy, The Knight's Tale, The Tribe, Appetite, Possession, Troy, The Farmer 2012; *Recreations* golf, tennis; *Clubs* Queen's, Hurlingham, Chelsea Arts, Wentworth; *Style*— Trevor Eve, Esq; ✉ c/o ARG Ltd, 4 Great Portland Street, London W1W 8PA (☎ 020 7436 6400)

EVENNETT, Rt Hon David Anthony; PC (2015), MP; s of late Norman Thomas Evennett, and late Irene Evennett; *b* 3 June 1949; *Educ* Buckhurst Hill Co HS for Boys, LSE (MSc Econ); *m* 1975, Marilyn Anne, da of late Ronald Stanley Smith; 2 s (Mark, Thomas); *Career* sch teacher 1972–74; Lloyds: broker 1974–81, memb 1976–92, dir Underwriting Agency 1982–91; Parly candidate (Cons): Hackney S and Shoreditch 1979, Bexleyheath and Crayford 1997 and 2001; MP (Cons): Erith and Crayford 1983–97, Bexleyheath and Crayford 2005–; memb Select Ctee on Educn, Sci and the Arts House of Commons 1986–92; PPS: to Lady Blatch (Min of State at Dept of Educn) 1992–93, to John Redwood (Sec of State for Wales) 1993–95, to David Maclean and Lady Blatch (Mins of State at Home Office) 1995–96, to Rt Hon Gillian Shepherd (Sec of State for Educn and Employment) 1996–97; memb Select Ctee for Educn and Skills 2005, oppn whip 2005–09, shadow min for innovation, univ and skills 2009–10, PPS to Michael Gove (Sec of State for Educn) 2010, Lord Cmmr of HM Treasy (Govt whip) 2012–; commercial liaison mangr for Bexley Coll 1997–2001, conslt Marsh McLennan 1998–2000, mgmnt conslt and lectr 2001–05; cncllr Redbridge BC 1974–78; *Recreations* family, reading novels and biographies, cinema, travel; *Clubs* Bexleyheath Cons; *Style*— The Rt Hon David Evennett, MP; ✉ House of Commons, London SW1A 0AA

EVERALL, His Hon Judge Mark Andrew; QC (1994); s of John Dudley Everall (d 1997), of London, and Pamela, *née* Odone; *b* 30 June 1950; *Educ* Ampleforth, Lincoln Coll Oxford (MA); *m* 16 Dec 1978, (Elizabeth) Anne, da of Thomas Hugh Richard Perkins; 2 da; *Career* called to the Bar Inner Temple 1975; circuit judge (SE Circuit) 2006–; *Style*— His Hon Judge Everall, QC; ✉ 1 Hare Court, Temple, London EC4 (☎ 020 7797 7070, fax 020 7797 7435, e-mail clerks@1hc.com)

EVERARD, James Rupert; KCB (2016), CBE (2005, OBE 2000); *b* 23 September 1962, Tilton, Leicestershire; *Career* cmmnd 17th/21st Lancers 1983; COS 4 Armoured Bde 1995, military asst to the Cdr of the Kosovo Force 1999, CO Queen's Royal Lancers 2000, Cdr 20 Armoured Bde 2005, Dir Commitments Land Command 2007, Gen Offr Commanding 3 Div 2009, Asst Chief of the Gen Staff 2011, Dep Chief of the Defence Staff Military Strategy and Operations 2013, Cdr Field Army (formerly Cdr Land Forces) 2014–; *Style*— Lt-Gen Sir James Everard, KCB, CBE

EVERARD, Richard Anthony Spencer; OBE (2011), DL (Leics 1997); s of Maj Richard Peter Michael Spencer (d 1990), of Melton Mowbray, Leics, and Bettyne Ione, formerly Lady Newtown Butler (d 1989); *b* 31 March 1954; *Educ* Eton, RMA Sandhurst; *m* 9 May 1981, Caroline Anne, da of Reginald J Tower Hill, of Coggeshall, Essex; 1 da (Charlotte b 1985), 1 s (Julian b 1988); *Career* Royal Horse Gds 1st Dragoons (Blues and Royals) 1973–77, cmmnd 1973, Lt 1975; hon Col Leics Northants and Rutland Army Cadet Force 2007–; chm Everards Brewery Ltd 1988– (dir 1983–); pres Age Concern Leics; tstee: Leics Police Charitable Tst, County Air Ambulance; Dip in Company Direction IOD; High Sheriff Leics 2002–03, Vice Lord-Lt Leics 2003–13; Master Worshipful Co of Brewers 2004; Hon LLD Univ of Leicester 2009; *Recreations* shooting, skiing, tennis, flying helicopters, motorcycling, golf; *Clubs* MCC, Eton Ramblers, Luffenham Heath Golf; *Style*— Richard Everard, Esq, OBE, DL; ✉ East Farndon Hall, Market Harborough, Leicestershire LE16 9SE; Everards Brewery Ltd, Castle Acres, Narborough, Leicestershire LE19 1BY (☎ 0116 201 4307)

EVEREST, Timothy; MBE (2010); *Career* tailor; clients incl Tom Cruise and David Beckham, costumes created for films incl Mission Impossible, Eyes Wide Shut, Atonement and Mamma Mia, designed Br Olympic Team uniforms 2000; creative conslt Marks & Spencer; *Style*— Timothy Everest, Esq, MBE; ✉ 32 Elder Street, London E1 6BT (☎ 020 7426 4880, mobile 07801 399777, e-mail timothy@timothyeverest.co.uk)

EVERETT, Charles William Vogt; s of Dr Thomas Everett (d 1976), and Ingeborg, *née* Vogt (d 1971); *b* 15 October 1949; *Educ* Bryanston, Univ of Reading; *m* 1978, Elizabeth Vanessa, *née* Ellis; 3 s; *Career* Lord Chancellor's Dept: joined 1971, asst private sec to the Lord Chancellor 1974–76, seconded to Dept of Tport 1982–84, Legal Aid Bill Div 1987–88, sec to Legal Aid Bd 1988–89, Central Unit 1990–91, head Policy and Legal Services Gp 1991–95, dir of fin and admin The Court Service 1995–99, dir of fire and emergency planning Home Office 1999–2002, dir of corp devpt and services Home Office 2002–06; chair Hastings and Rother PCT 2007–11, vice-chair NHS Sussex 2011–13, vice-chair Hastings and Rother Clinical Commissioning Gp 2013–15; memb Sussex Probation Bd 2007–10, memb Bd Surrey and Sussex Probation Tst 2010–14; *Style*— Charles Everett, Esq

EVERETT, Oliver William; CVO (1991, LVO 1980); s of Walter George Charles Everett, MC, DSO (d 1979), of Bognor Regis, W Sussex, and Gertrude Florence Rothwell, *née* Hellicar (d 1997); *b* 28 February 1943; *Educ* Felsted, Western Res Acad OH, Christ's Coll Cambridge (MA), Fletcher Sch of Law & Diplomacy Tufts Univ (MA), LSE; *m* 28 Aug 1965 (sep 2004), Theffania, da of Lt Robert Vesey Stoney (d 1944), of Rosturk Castle, Co Mayo; 2 da (Kathleen b 1966, Grania b 1969), 2 s (Toby b 1979, William b 1982); partner, Diana Jervis-Read; *Career* Dip Serv: first sec Br High Cmmn New Delhi 1969–73, first sec FCO 1973–78, asst private sec to HRH The Prince of Wales 1978–80, head Chancery Br Embassy Madrid 1980–81, private sec to HRH The Princess of Wales 1981–83, asst librarian Windsor Castle 1984, librarian and asst keeper of the Queen's Archives Windsor Castle 1985–2002, librarian emeritus Royal Library Windsor Castle 2002–; NADFAS lectr 2005–; *Recreations* lecturing, film, baseball; *Clubs* Roxburghe, Chelsea Arts; *Style*— Oliver Everett, Esq, CVO; ✉ Cawdles Barn, Keeres Green, Great Dunmow, Essex CM6 1PQ (☎ 01245 231364, e-mail o.everett05@tiscali.co.uk)

EVERETT, Rupert; *b* Norfolk; *Educ* Ampleforth, Central Sch of Speech and Drama; *Career* actor; *Theatre* incl: Waste of Time (Citizens Theatre Glasgow), Don Juan (Glasgow and London), Chinchilla (Glasgow and London), Another Country (Greenwich Theatre and Queen's Theatre), Mass Appeal (Lyric Hammersmith), Heartbreak House (Citizens Theatre Glasgow), The Vortex (Citizens Theatre Glasgow and Garrick), The Milk Train Doesn't Stop Here Anymore (Glasgow and London), Some Sunny Day (London), Pygmalion (London), The Judas Kiss (Hampstead Theatre), Pygmalion (Chichester Festival Theatre and West End); *Television* incl: The Far Pavilions 1994, Sherlock Holmes and the Case of the Silk Stocking 2004, Parade's End 2012, The Other Wife 2012; *Films* incl: A Shocking Accident 1982, Princess Daisy 1983, Another Country 1984, Dance with a Stranger 1985, Arthur the King 1985, Duet for One 1986, The Gold Rimmed Glasses 1987, Hearts of Fire 1987, Chronicle of a Death Foretold 1987, The Right Hand Man 1987, Tolérance 1989, The Comfort of Strangers 1990, Inside Monkey Zetterland 1992, Remembrance of Things Fast: True Stories Visual Lies 1994, Pret-à-Porter 1994, Of Death and Love 1994, The Madness of King George 1995, Dunston Checks In 1996, My Best Friend's Wedding 1997, Shakespeare in Love 1998, B. Monkey 1998, The Next Best Thing 1999, A Midsummer Night's Dream 1999, Inspector Gadget 1999, An Ideal Husband 1999, Unconditional Love 2001, The Importance of Being Earnest 2002, To Kill a King 2003, Stage Beauty 2004, Shrek 2 2004, People 2004, A Different Loyalty 2004, Separate Lies 2005, The Chronicles of Narnia: The Lion, the Witch and the Wardrobe 2005, Quiet Flows the Don 2006, Shrek the Third 2007, Stardust 2007, St Trinian's 2007, St Trinian's 2: The Legend of Fritton's Gold 2009, Hysteria 2011; *Books* Hello Darling Are You Working? (1992); *Style*— Rupert Everett, Esq

EVERETT, His Hon Judge Steven George; *Educ* Lanchester Poly; *m* Melinda; 2 s (William, Edward); *Career* admitted slr 1981, called to the Bar 1989; asst recorder then recorder 2000, circuit judge (Northern Circuit) 2007–; *Style*— His Hon Judge Everett; ✉ c/o Northern Circuit Office, Young Street Chambers, 76 Quay Street, Manchester M3 4PR

EVERINGTON, Dr Sir Anthony Herbert (Sam); kt (2015), OBE (1999); s of Geoffrey Everington, QC (d 1982), and Laila Everington; *b* Limpsfield, Surrey; *Educ* Inns of Court Sch of Law, Royal Free Hosp Sch of Med (MB BS); *m* Linda Aldous; 3 s (Raoul, Jordan, Oliver), 2 da (Song-Lian, Kirsty); *Career* called to the Bar Gray's Inn 1978; cadet pilot RAF 1980–81; GP Tower Hamlets 1989–, memb Bd and chm of clinical governance Tower Hamlets PCT 2001–04; advsr to membs of shadow cabinet 1991–97; med dir and fndr GP out of hours co-op 1996–99, GP trainer 1996–2006; dep chm BMA 2004–07, vice pres 2015–; memb Bd Coll of Health 1998–2000, founding cmmr Cmmn for Health Improvement 1999–2004, dir Community Health Partnerships 2002–; GP trainer 1996–2002; chair Tower Hamlets CCG 2012–; tstee: Parents Against Tobacco 1990–93, Quit 1990–94, Community Action Network 1998–2004, Stanton Guildhouse art and enterprise centre 1998–; ambass Social Enterprise 2007–10; memb Bd Young Fndn Innovation Fund 2008–12; contrib to BMJ on racism and racial discrimination; nat award from Campaign for Freedom of Information for res on racial discrimination 1995, Int Award of Excellence in Health Care The 5 Star Doctor World Family Doctors Europe 2006; memb Cncl BMA 1989– (actg chair 2007, vice-pres 2015–), nat advsr New Models of Care NHS Eng 2015–; MRCGP 1989, memb Cncl GMC 2009–13, memb Bd NHS Clinical Cmmrs 2012–; tstee King's Fund 2015–; fell Queen Mary Univ 2015–; *Recreations* boating, Norway; *Clubs* RSA; *Style*— Dr Sir Sam Everington, OBE; ✉ Bromley by Bow Health Centre, St Leonards Street, London E3 3BT (☎ 020 8983 7082, e-mail sam.everington@nhs.net)

EVERITT, Prof Barry John; s of Frederick Everitt, and Winifred, *née* Tibble; *b* 19 February 1946; *Educ* SE Essex Co Technical HS, Univ of Hull (BSc), Univ of Birmingham (PhD), Univ of Cambridge (ScD); *m* 1, 1966 (m dis 1978), Valerie Sowter; 1 s (Alex Daniel b 23 Dec 1966); m 2, 1979, Jane Sterling; 1 da (Jessica Chloë b 6 May 1988); *Career* research fell Dept of Anatomy Univ of Birmingham Med Sch 1970–73, MRC travellng research fell Karolinska Institutet 1973–74; Univ of Cambridge: demonstrator Dept of Anatomy 1974–79, lectr 1979–91, reader in neuroscience Dept of Anatomy 1991–94, reader in neuroscience Dept of Experimental Psychology 1994–97, prof of behavioural neuroscience Dept of Experimental Psychology 1997–2013 (dir of research 2013–); Downing Coll Cambridge: fell 1976–2003, dir of studies in med 1978–98, master 2003–13; Ciba-Geigy sr research fell Karolinska Institutet 1982–83, Soc for Neuroscience Grass lectr Univ of Texas 1997; visiting prof Univ of Calif San Francisco 2000, Sterling visiting prof Albany Medical Coll NY 2005, Swammerdam lectr Amsterdam 1999, Matarazzo lectr Univ of Oregon Portland 2005, Int Distinguished Scientist lectr Riken Inst Tokyo 2006, Dalbir Bindra lectr McGill Univ Montreal 2006, Grass Fndn Int Distinguished Scientist lectr UCLA 2006, Elsevier Lecture European Brain and Behaviour Soc 2007, lecture Int Basal Ganglia Soc 2007, Pres's Lecture Fedn of European Neurosciences Forum 2008, Thomas James Okey Memorial Lecture Psychiatry Research Tst 2008, Stephan Apáthy Lecture Hungarian Acad of Sciences 2009, NIDA Research Lecture 2009, Karolinska Research Lecture Stockholm 2009, John Flynn Meml Lecture Yale Univ 2010, Bryan Kolb Lecture Univ of Calgary 2011, Plenary Lecture French Neurosci Soc (2013), FENS/EJN Lecture Barcelona (2012), Fondation Ipsen Prize Lecture FENS Milan 2014, Camb Neurosci Public Lecture 2015, Karolinska Institutet Nobel Forum 2015; pres: Br Assoc for Psychopharmacology 1992–94, Euro Brain and Behaviour Soc 1998–2000, Euro Behavioural Pharmacology Soc 2003–05, pres-elect Federation of European Neuroscience Societies 2014–16 (pres 2016–18); chm: Fellowships Ctee Human Frontier Sci Program Orgn 1993–95, MRC Research Studentships and Trg Awards Panel 1995–97, MRC, Neurosciences and Mental Health Bd 2001–, Nat Inst on Drug Abuse, Scientific Cnsllr 2001–; memb Scientific Advsy Bd: Astra-Zeneca 2001–04, Helsinki Neuroscience Centre 2000–, Neurogenetics & Behavior Center, John Hopkins Univ 2002–, Brain-Mind Inst 2008–, Écoles des Neurosciences Paris Ile-de-France 2008–, Brain-Mind Inst Lausanne 2008–, Portland Alcohol Research Center 2012–, EMBO 2014–; memb: Ind Scientific Ctee on Drugs 2010–, Soc for Neuroscience Ctee on Ctees 2010–13, Video Standards Cncl Appeals Ctee 2012–, Int Scientific Advsy Bd Wellcome Tst Centre for Neuroimaging 2012–16; cncllr Soc for Neuroscience 2014–18, cncllr American Coll for Neuropsychopharmacology 2013–16; pres Fedn of European Neuroscience Socs 2016–18; ed-in-chief: Physiology and Behaviour 1994–98, Euro Jl of Neuroscience 1997–2008; reviewing ed Science 2003–; highly cited author Inst for Scientific Information (ISI); American Psychological Assoc Distinguished Scientific Contribution Award 2011, European Behavioural Pharmacology Soc Distinguished Scientific Achievement Award 2011, Federation of European Neuroscience Societies European Jl of Neuroscience Award 2012, Br Assoc for Psychopharmacology Lifetime Achievement Award 2012, Fndn Ipsen Neuronal Plasticity Prize 2014; Hon DSc Univ of Hull 2009, Hon DSc Univ of Birmingham 2010; Hon MD Karolinska Institutet Stockholm 2015–; memb: Soc for Neuroscience, Euro Brain and Behaviour Soc, Br Assoc for Psychopharmacology, Euro Behavioural Pharmacological Soc, Br Neuroscience Assoc, EMBO 2014; provost Cambridge Gates Tst 2013–; fell American Coll of Neuropsychopharmacology (Cncl 2013–); FRS 2007, FMedSci 2008; *Books* Essential Reproduction (5 edn, 2000); author of over 400 publications in scientific jls incl: Nature, Science, Nature Neuroscience, Jl of Neuroscience, Neuron; *Recreations* opera, cricket, wine; *Clubs* Oxford and Cambridge; *Style*— Prof Barry Everitt, FRS, FMedSci; ✉ Downing College, Cambridge CB2 1DQ (☎ 01223 333583, e-mail bje10@cam.ac.uk)

EVERITT, Richard Leslie; CBE (2014); *b* 22 December 1948; *Educ* Univ of Southampton; *Career* BAA plc: slr 1978, dir of legal services 1988, memb bd 1990, gp strategy and compliance dir 1991; chief exec: National Air Traffic Services (NATS) 2001–04, Port of London Authy 2004–; non-exec chm Air Partner 2012; *Style*— Richard Everitt, Esq, CBE

E

EVERITT-MATTHIAS, David Richard; s of Ronald Joseph Matthias (d 1996), and Kathleen Betty Matthias (d 1994); *b* 29 October 1960; *Educ* Sir Walter St Johns GS London, Ealing Coll of HE (City and Guilds); *m* 1 June 1985, Helen Mary Everitt-Matthias, *qv*, da of Peter Kingston Everitt; *Career* chef Inn on the Park London 1978–83, head chef Grand Cafe 1983–85, head chef Steamers Fish Restaurant 1985–86, head chef Fingals Restaurant Putney 1986–87, chef/co-prop (with wife, Helen) Le Champignon Sauvage Cheltenham 1987–; taken part in: The Restaurant Show London 1994–96, Hotel Olympia 1994 and 1996, Nat Restaurateurs Dinner 1995, Nat Chef of the Year Dinner 1996; TV appearances: Junior Masterchef 1996, Suprise Chefs 1996, This Morning TV 1996, Central TV 1996, Saturday Kitchen 2013 and 2014, Hairy Bikers 2014; monthly columnist Gloucestershire Echo 2014–; memb Académie Culinaire de France; memb Sir Walter St Johns Old Boys Assoc; Hon DPhil Univ of Gloucestershire 2009; *Awards* Acorn Award, Midland Chef of the Year 1995 and 1996, Egon Ronay Dessert Chef of the Year 1996, Nat Chef of the Year 1996 and 1997, Michelin Star 1995, 1996, 1997, 1998 and 1999, 2 Michelin Stars 2000–08, AA Guide 4 Rosettes 1997–2008, Roy Ackerman Guide Clover Leaf, Good Food Guide County Restaurant of the Year 2000, Egon Ronay Star and Upward Arrow, Decanter Restaurant of the Year 2001, Birmingham Plus Restaurant of the Year 2004, 2 Egon Ronay Stars 2005, Good Food Guide Restaurant of the Year 2005, Chef of the Year Cotswold Life 2005, Restaurant of the Year Square Meal 2006, Chef of the Year Catey Award 2007, number 5 in UK Good Food Guide 2007, Gourmet Britain Restaurant of the Year 2010, Observer Outstanding Achievement Award 2013, Good Food Guide Chef of the Year 2014; *Publications* Essence: Recipes from Le Champignon Sauvage (2006), Dessert: Dessert Recipes from Le Champignon Sauvage (2009, runner-up Best Cookbook in the World Gourmand Book Award 2010), Beyond Essence (2014, Best Photography Award 2014); *Recreations* cricket, squash, art, jazz, reading; *Style*— David Everitt-Matthias, Esq; ✉ Le Champignon Sauvage, 24–26 Suffolk Road, Cheltenham, Gloucestershire GL50 2AQ (☎ 01242 573449, fax 01242 254365, website www.lechampignonsauvage.com)

EVERITT-MATTHIAS, Helen Mary; da of Peter Everitt, of Loxwood, W Sussex, and Cynthia, *née* Frisby; *b* 25 March 1962, Sheffield; *Educ* Horsham HS for Girls, Guildford Co Coll of Technol; *m* 1 June 1985, David Everitt Matthias, *qv*, s of Ronald Joseph Matthias (d 1996); *Career* restaurateur; receptionist: Center Hotels London 1980–82, Inn on the Park London 1982–84, Cromwell Hosp London 1984–86; sec IBM Ltd 1986–87; prop (with husband, David) Le Champignon Sauvage Cheltenham 1987– (1 Michelin Star 1995, 2 Michelin Stars 2000, number 5 in UK Good Food Guide 2007); *Style*— Mrs Helen Everitt-Matthias; ✉ Le Champignon Sauvage, 24–28 Suffolk Road, Cheltenham, Gloucestershire GL50 2AQ (☎ 01242 573449, fax 01242 254365, website www.lechampignonsauvage.com)

EVERS, Peter Lawson; s of John Henry Evers (d 1982), and Evelyn Jessica, *née* Hill (d 1997); *b* 4 January 1938; *Educ* King Edward VI GS; *m* 5 Oct 1963, Margaret Elaine, da of William Edwin Homer; 2 da (Elaine Louise b 14 Sept 1965, Alison Jane b 4 June 1967), 2 s (Jonathan, Philip Alexander (twins) b 21 March 1971); *Career* press offr J Lucas Industries 1965–67 (press and publicity asst 1959–67), publicity mangr Fafnir Bearing Co Ltd 1967–68, gp press offr John Thompson Group 1968–71, conslt John Fowler Public Relations 1971–72, ptnr and co fndr Edson Evers Public Relations 1972–99, dir and chief exec Edson Evers Communications Ltd 1980–95, UK dir PR Organisation International Ltd 1973–99 (pres 1985, 1991, 1992, 1993 and 1994), freelance PR conslt 1999–; BAIE (renamed British Assoc of Communicators in Business 1995) newspaper award winner: 1985, 1988, 1989, 1990, 1991, 1992; FIPR 1993–99 (MIPR 1969–93), memb BAIE (BACB) 1974–99, MRHS 1980; *Recreations* golf, gardening; *Style*— Peter Evers, Esq; ✉ Peter L Evers, Freshfield House, Lower Way, Upper Longdon, Staffordshire WS15 1QG

EVERSHED, Ralph Jocelyn; s of Norman William Evershed (d 1983), and Jocelyn Slade, *née* Lyons (d 2005); *b* 16 November 1944; *Educ* St Albans Boys GS, Univ of Strathclyde (BA); *m* 6 Sept 1968, Carol Ann, da of Jerry Esmond Cullum (d 1987); 3 s (Timothy b 1973, David b 1974, John b 1982 d 1994), 2 da (Ruth b 1977, Susannah b 1980); *Career* chm Inter Varsity Press 2004–13; dir Eversheds Group Ltd 1987–2005, Woodsilk Properties Ltd 1988–; *Style*— Ralph Evershed, Esq

EVERSON, Noel Williams; s of Mervyn Cyril George Everson (d 1981), and Beryl Irene, *née* Williams; *b* 8 December 1944; *Educ* W Monmouth Sch, Middx Hosp Med Sch (MB BS), Univ of London (MS); *m* 1, 1969 (m dis 1982), Caroline Juliet Adams; 2 da (Juliet Claire b 1971, Katherine Frances Vivien b 1974); *m* 2, 27 June 1987, Elizabeth Mary, da of Donald Sellen; 2 da (Francesca Victoria Louise b 1990, Lucy Helen Jane b 1992); *Career* conslt surgn Leicester Royal Infirmary 1981–; memb: Assoc of Coloproctology, Assoc of Surgns; FRSM 1972, FRCS 1972; *Recreations* fly fishing; *Style*— Noel Everson, Esq; ✉ 6 Meadowcourt Road, Oadby, Leicester LE2 2PB (☎ 0116 271 2512); Glenfield General Hospital, University Hospitals of Leicester NHS Trust (☎ 0116 287 1471)

EVERTON, Clive Harold; s of Harold Brimley Everton (d 1996), and Alma, *née* Pugh (d 1980); *b* 7 September 1937; *Educ* Kings's Sch Worcester, UCW Cardiff (BA); *m* Valerie, *née* Teasdale; 4 da (Jane b 7 Aug 1963, Julie b 2 Sept 1965, Kate b 22 Dec 1966, Lucy b 7 Oct 1969), 1 s (Daniel b 10 April 1974); *Career* journalist, author and broadcaster; freelance broadcaster and sports writer for various pubns 1962–, specialist in snooker and billiards 1973–; ed: Billiards and Snooker magazine 1966–70, Snooker Scene 1971–; billiards and snooker corr The Guardian 1976–2011; snooker commentator BBC TV 1978–2011; billiards player; Br under 16 champion 1952, Br under 19 champion 1955, Welsh amateur champion 5 times, semi-finalist World Amateur Billiards Championship 1975 and 1977, ranked 10 in world professional ratings 1991; 6 Welsh amateur snooker caps; *Publications* Embassy Book of World Snooker (1993), Black Farce and Cueball Wizards (2007), A History of Billiards (2013); author of various snooker compendiums and instructional books, co-author various biographies; *Recreations* books, films, theatre; *Style*— Clive Everton, Esq; ✉ Snooker Scene, Hayley Green Court, 130 Hagley Road, Halesowen, West Midlands B63 1DY (☎ 0121 585 9188, fax 0121 585 7117, e-mail clive.everton@talk21.com)

EVERY, Sir Henry John Michael; 13 Bt (E 1641), of Egginton, Derbyshire; DL (Derbys 2007); o s of Sir John Simon Every, 12 Bt (d 1988), and his 2 w Janet Marion, *née* Page (d 2010); *b* 6 April 1947; *Educ* Malvern Coll; *m* 1974, Susan Mary, eldest da of late Kenneth Beaton, JP, of Eastshotte, Hartford, Cambs; 3 s (Edward James Henry b 1975, Jonathan Charles Hugo b 1977, Nicholas John Simon b 1981); *Heir* s, Edward Every; *Career* ptnr Deloitte & Touche CAs Birmingham until 2001, dir Angelbourse Group plc 2001–03; chm Tala PR 2010–14; pres Birmingham and W Midlands Dist Soc of CAs 1995–96 (chm Dist Trg Bd 1989–92), chm Burton Hosps NHS Tst 2003–04, memb Consumer Advsy Bd McCarthy & Stone 2012–14; tstee Eginton Meml Hall 1987– (chm 2014–) memb Ctee The Birmingham Lunar Soc 1991–2003, tstee Nat Meml Arboretum 1996–2003 (conslt 2003–14), patron Derby Heritage Devpt Tst 1998–2006, tstee Repton Fndn 2001–04 and 2009–, govr Repton Sch 2003– (chm of govrs 2012–), chm Derby Cathedral Cncl 2003–12, patron Derbys Children's Holiday Centre 2012–; High Sheriff Derbys 2009–10; parish cncllr 1987–2007 and 2011–; freedom City of London; memb Worshipful Co of Chartered Accountants 1998–; FCA 1970, FRSA; *Recreations* family, travel, gardening, theatre, The National Trust, supporting Nottingham Forest FC; *Style*— Sir Henry Every, Bt; ✉ Cothay, 26 Fishpond Lane, Egginton, Derby DE65 6HJ

EWAN, Dr Pamela Wilson; CBE (2007); da of Norman Wilson Ewan (d 1997), of Cambridge, and Frances Patterson, *née* Sellars (d 1984); *b* 23 September 1945; *Educ* Forfar Acad, Royal Free Hosp Sch of Med (MA, MB BS, DObstRCOG); *m* 15 Sept 1979, Prof Sir (David) Keith Peters, s of Lionel Herbert Peters; 2 s (James b 1980, William b 1989), 1 da (Hannah b 1982); *Career* sr lectr in clinical immunology and dir Allergy Clinic St Mary's Hosp 1980–88; Addenbrooke's Hosp 1988–: MRC clinical scientist and hon conslt in clinical immunology and allergy Univ of Cambridge Clinical Sch 1988–97, conslt allergist 1997–, dir Allergy Dept; dir of med studies Clare Hall Cambridge 1988–, assoc lectr Univ of Cambridge 1988–; pres Br Soc for Allergy and Clinical Immunology 1999–2002, chair Nat Allergy Strategy Gp 2005–, hon sec RCP Ctee in Allergy and Clinical Immunology; memb Ctee Euro Acad of Allergy and Clinical Immunology; author of various chapters and papers in med books and scientific jls; William Frankland Award 2000; memb: Assoc of Physicians, BSACI, BSI, MRS; FRCP, FRCPath; *Style*— Dr Pamela Ewan, CBE; ✉ 7 Chaucer Road, Cambridge CB2 7EB; Addenbrooke's Hospital, Hills Road, Cambridge CB2 2QQ (☎ 01223 217777, fax 01223 216953, e-mail pamela.ewan@addenbrookes.nhs.uk)

EWARD, Paul Anthony; s of Rev Harvey Kennedy Eward (d 1969), and Delphine Eugenie Louise, *née* Pain (d 2007); *b* 22 December 1942, Colchester, Essex; *Educ* Radley; *m* 6 Sept 1966, Dene Kathleen, da of Geoffrey Louis Bartrip (d 1991), of Ross-on-Wye; 2 da (Sarah b 1969, Lucy b 1971 d 2010); *Career* admitted slr 1967; ptnr: Slades (Newent), Orme Dykes & Yates (Ledbury) 1970–2002 (conslt 2002–09), conslt Orme & Slade 2009–; chm Newent Business & Professional Assoc 1981–83, sec PCC Ross-on-Wye 1972–88 and 2008–09, lay co chm Ross and Archenfield Deanery Synod 1988–96 (hon treas (1980–88); memb Hereford Diocesan Synod 1988–96; memb Hereford Diocesan: Bd of Fin 1990–2010 (and its Exec Ctee 1995–2010), Revenue Ctee 1985–98, Vacancy in See Ctee 1985–97, Patronage Ctee 1988–95, Benefice Buildings Ctee 1998–2002; hon jt treas Hereford DBF 1999–2002; tstee: Holts Health Centre Fund 1996– (chm 2010–), Bishop Mascall Centre 2007–; memb: Transport Users Consultative Ctee for W England 1990–94, Rail Users' Consultative Ctee for W England 1994–2000, Rail Passenger Ctee for W England 2000–02 (vice-chm 2001–02); chm: Other Train Operating Companies sub-ctee 1999–2000, Thames Trains Jt Sub-Ctee 2000–02; Ctee Gloucestershire & Wiltshire Law Soc 1990–96; signalman Dean Forest Railway; *Clubs* Gloucester Model Railway, EM Gauge Soc, Scalefour Soc; *Style*— Paul Eward, Esq; ✉ 1 The Walled Garden, Ross-on-Wye, Herefordshire HR9 7GX (☎ 01989 563845); Orme & Slade, NatWest Bank Chambers, 12 The Homend, Ledbury, Herefordshire HR8 2AB (☎ 01531 532226)

EWART, Mike; *Career* chief exec Scottish Ct Service 1994–99, Educn Dept Scottish Exec 1999, chief exec Scottish Prison Service 2007–; *Style*— Mike Ewart, Esq; ✉ Education Scotland, Denholm House, Almondvale Business Park, Almondvale Way, Livingston EH54 6GA

EWART, Timothy John Pelham (Tim); s of John Terence Pelham Ewart (d 2003), of Woodbridge, Suffolk, and Nancy, *née* Girling (d 1990); *b* 6 February 1949; *Educ* Gresham's, Ipswich Civic Coll; *m* 3, 8 Aug 1991, Penny, da of Alan Marshall; 3 c (Jessica b 4 June 1993, Georgia b 24 Jan 1995, Holly b 4 Oct 1996); 2 c from previous m (Ben b 16 July 1977, Alice b 30 Nov 1980); *Career* newspapers 1967–74 (Bury Free Press, Leicester Mercury, Bermuda Sun), Radio 1974–77 (BBC World Service, Radio Orwell); reporter/presenter: BBC TV North (Leeds) 1977–80, Thames TV News 1980–81; ITN 1981–92: Warsaw correspondent 1983–85, Washington correspondent 1986–90, Moscow correspondent 1990–92; chief correspondent GMTV 1992 (prior to start of franchise), rejoined ITN as weekend news presenter and reporter News at Ten Focus on Britain 1992, main presenter BBC Newsroom South East Sept 1993–96; ITN: rejoined as sr reporter 1996, Africa correspondent 1998–2003, sports ed 2003–05, sr news corr 2005–08, royal corr 2008–; *Recreations* golf, running; *Clubs* Royal Mid Surrey Golf, Woodbridge Golf; *Style*— Tim Ewart, Esq; ✉ Independent Television News Ltd, 200 Gray's Inn Road, London WC1X 8XZ (☎ 020 7833 3000)

EWING, Annabelle; MSP; da of Stewart Martin Ewing (d 2003), and Dr Winifred Margaret, *née* Woodburn; *b* 20 August 1960; *Educ* Craigholme Sch Glasgow, Univ of Glasgow (LLB), Johns Hopkins Univ (Dip Int Rels), Univ of Amsterdam (Dip European Integration); *Career* apprentice lawyer Ruth Anderson and Co 1984–86, admitted slr 1986, stagiaire European Cmmn Legal Service 1987, assoc Lebrun de Smedt and Dassesse Brussels 1987–89, contract ptnr Akin Gump Brussels 1993–96 (assoc 1989–92), special counsel McKenna and Cuneo Brussels 1996, freelance EC lawyer 1997, ptnr Ewing and Co Slrs Glasgow 1999–2001 (assoc 1998–99), conslt Leslie Wolfson and Co Slrs Glasgow 2001–2003; MP (SNP) Perth 2001–05, MSP (SNP): Mid Scotland and Fife 2011–16, Cowdenbeath 2016–; min for youth and women's employment Scottish Govt 2014–16, min for community safety and legal affrs Scottish Govt 2016–; memb Law Soc of Scot 1986; *Recreations* walking, reading, travel; *Style*— Miss Annabelle Ewing, MSP; ✉ The Scottish Parliament, Edinburgh EH99 1SP

EWING, Fergus; MSP; s of Stewart Martin Ewing, and Dr Winifred Ewing; bro of Annabelle Ewing, MSP, *qqv*; *b* 23 September 1957, Glasgow; *Educ* Loretto Sch Edinburgh, Univ of Glasgow (LLB); *m* Margaret Ewing (d 2006, former MSP for Moray); partner Dr Fiona Pearsall, *qv*; 1 da (Natasha); *Career* apprentice slr 1979–81, slr Leslie Wolfson & Co 1981–1985, ptnr Ewing & Co 1985–1999; MSP (SNP): Inverness E Nairn and Lochaber 1999–2011, Inverness & Nairn 2011–; pty spokesperson on telecommunications, transport and tourism, min for community safety 2007–11, min for energy, enterprise and tourism 2011–, memb Local Govt and Transport Ctee; memb Law Soc of Scotland; *Recreations* running, jazz, playing piano; *Style*— Fergus Ewing, Esq, MSP; ✉ Highland Railhouse, Station Square, Inverness IV1 1LE (☎ 01463 713004); The Scottish Parliament, Edinburgh EH99 1SP (☎ 0131 348 5731, e-mail fergus.ewing.msp@scottish.parliament.uk or fergus@fergusewing.com, website www.fergusewing.com, Twitter @fergusewingmsp)

EWINS, Prof David John; s of late Wilfred James Ewins, of Hemyock, Devon, and Patricia, *née* Goacher; *b* 25 March 1942; *Educ* Kingswood GS Bristol, Imperial Coll London (BSc, DSc), Trinity Coll Cambridge (PhD); *m* 1964 (m dis 1997), Brenda Rene, *née* Chalk; 3 da (Sally Ann b 1966, Sarah b 1968, Caroline Helene b 1971); *Career* research asst for Rolls-Royce Ltd at Univ of Cambridge 1966–67; Imperial Coll London: lectr then reader in mechanical engrg 1967–83, prof of vibration engrg 1983–, fndr Modal Testing Unit 1981, dir Centre of Vibration Engrg 1990–, pro-rector (int rels) 2001–05; Temasek prof and dir Centre for Mechanics of Microsystems Nanyang Technological Univ Singapore 1999–2001; sr lectr Chulalongkorn Univ Bangkok 1968–69, maitre de conf INSA Lyon 1974–75; visiting prof: Virginia Poly and State Univ 1981, ETH Zurich 1986, Institut Nationale Polytechnique de Grenoble 1990, Nanyang Tech Univ Singapore 1994, Univ of Rome 1998; Dynamic Testing Agency: fndr 1990, chm 1990–94, pres 1995–; ptnr ICATS; conslt to: Rolls-Royce 1969–, MOD 1977–, Boeing, Ford, NASA, Intevep, Bosch, BMW, Mercedes, GM; MSEE 1970, MASME 1983, FIMechE 1982, FREng 1995, FCGI 2002, FRS 2006; *Books* Modal Testing: Theory and Practice (1984, 9 edn 1996), Modal Testing: Theory, Practice and Application (2000), Structural Dynamics @ 2000 (ed with D J Inman, 2000); *Recreations* music, hill walking, travel, good food, French; *Style*— Prof David Ewins, FRS, FREng; ✉ Imperial College of Science, Technology and Medicine, Exhibition Road, London SW7 2AZ

EXELL, Richard Daniel; OBE (1999); s of Donald William Exell (d 1983), and Olwen Madeleine, *née* Anderson (d 1992); *b* 21 July 1956, Liverpool; *Educ* Friars Sch Bangor, Univ of Bristol (BA); *m* 16 Oct 1991, Penny Zea, *née* Bromfield; 1 da (Madeleine Zena Florence Thomasina Frederica b 22 May 1993); *Career* policy offr TUC 1990–; memb: Social Security Advsy Ctee 1997–2009, Disability Rights Cmmn 2000–07, Industial Injuries Advsy Cncl 2009–; *Recreations* politics, the arts; *Style*— Richard Exell,

Esq, OBE; ✉ Trades Union Congress, Great Russell Street, London WC1B 3LS (☎ 020 7467 1319, fax 020 7467 1317, e-mail rexell@tuc.org.uk)

EXMOUTH, 10 Viscount (UK 1816); Sir Paul Edward Pellew; 10 Bt (GB 1796); also Baron Exmouth (UK 1814), Marques de Olias (Spain 1625); patron of one living; s of 9 Viscount (d 1970) and Maria Luisa, Marquesa de Olias (d 1994), da of late Luis de Urquijo, Marques de Amurrio, of Madrid; *b* 8 October 1940; *Educ* Downside; *m* 1, 10 Dec 1964 (m dis 1974), Maria Krystina Garay-Marques; 1 da (Hon Patricia Sofia b 1966); m 2, 1975 (m dis 2000), Rosemary Frances, formerly w of Earl of Burford (now 14 Duke of St Albans, *qv*); 2 s (Hon Edward, Hon Alexander (twins) b 30 Oct 1978); *Heir* s, Hon Edward Pellew; *Career* former Cross Bench Peer in House of Lords; *Books* A Prisoner of Fortune (2014); *Style*— The Rt Hon Viscount Exmouth; ✉ e-mail paulexmouth@aol.com

EYRE, Prof Brian Leonard; CBE (1993); s of Leonard George Eyre (d 1988), and Mabel, *née* Rumsey (d 1984); *b* 29 November 1933, London; *Educ* Greenford GS, Univ of Surrey (BSc, DSc); *m* 5 June 1965, Elizabeth Caroline, da of Arthur Rackham (d 1954); 2 s (Peter John b 5 March 1966, Stephen Andrew b 22 Oct 1967); *Career* research offr CEGB 1959–62, prof of materials sci Univ of Liverpool 1979–84; UKAEA: various posts 1962–79, dir of fuel and engrg technol 1984–87, memb Bd 1987–96, dep chm 1989–96, chief exec 1990–94; dep chm AEA Technology plc 1996–97; visiting prof: Univ of Liverpool 1984–, UCL 1995–, Univ of Oxford 1997–2002; industrial fell Wolfson Coll Oxford 1996–2001, sr visiting fell Materials Dept Univ of Oxford 2002–; memb Cncl: Univ of Salford 1986–97, Fndn for Sci and Technol 1994–2001, Particle Physics and Astronomy Research Cncl 1996–2000, Cncl of the Central Research Labs 1998–2001 (chm 2000–2001), Royal Acad of Engrg 1996–99, Inst of Materials 1996–2000; chm Hants Neurological Alliance; author of over 150 scientific papers, former chm Editorial Bd Jl of Nuclear Materials; foreign assoc US Nat Acad of Engrg 2009; FREng 1992, FRS 2001, FIM, CEng, FInstP, CPhys; *Recreations* walking, sailing, reading; *Style*— Prof Brian Eyre, CBE, FREng, FRS; ✉ 2 Thameside Mansion, Castle Lane, Wallingford, Oxfordshire OX10 0BY; Department of Materials, University of Oxford, Parks Road, Oxford OX1 3PH (☎ 01865 273708, fax 01865 273764, e-mail brian.eyre@materials.ox.ac.uk)

EYRE, Richard Anthony; CBE (2014); *b* 3 May 1954; *Educ* KCS Wimbledon, Lincoln Coll Oxford (MA), Harvard Business Sch (AMP); *Career* airtime buyer Benton & Bowles 1975–78, sales gp head Scottish Television 1978–79, head of media planning Benton & Bowles 1980–84 (media planner 1979–80), media dir Aspect 1984–86, media dir Bartle Bogle Hegarty 1986–91 (Media Week Agency of the Year 1990 and 1991), chief exec Capital Radio plc 1991–97, chief exec ITV 1997–99, chm and chief exec Pearson Television Ltd 2000, dir of strategy and content RTL (following merger with Pearson TV) 2000–01; fndr Radio Crimson 2014–; ind non-exec Grant Thornton UK LLP 2010–16, chm Next15 plc 2011–; chm: Interactive Advertising Bureau 2003–, Media Tst 2013–; Mackintosh Medal for Outstanding Personal and Public Service to Advertising 2013; *Books* The Club (2005); *Style*— Richard Eyre, Esq, CBE

EYRE, Sir Richard Charles Hastings; kt (1997), CBE (1992); s of Cdr Richard Galfridus Hastings Giles Eyre, RN (d 1990), and Minna Mary Jessica (d 1992), o child of Vice Adm Sir Charles William Rawson Royds, KBE, CMG, antarctic explorer Scott's 1st Lt; *b* 28 March 1943; *Educ* Sherborne, Univ of Cambridge (BA); *m* 1973, Sue Elizabeth Birtwistle, *qv*; 1 da (Lucy b 1974); *Career* theatre, television and film director; assoc dir Lyceum Theatre Edinburgh 1968–71, dir Nottingham Playhouse 1973–78, prodr Play For Today BBC TV 1978–80, dir Royal Nat Theatre 1988–97 (assoc dir 1980–86); Cameron Mackintosh visiting prof of contemporary theatre Univ of Oxford and fell St Catherine's Coll 1997; pres Rose Bruford Coll 2010–; Hon DLitt: Nottingham Trent Univ 1992, South Bank Univ 1994, Univ of Liverpool 2003, Univ of E Anglia 2011; Hon Dr Oxford Brookes Univ, Hon Degree Univ of Surrey 1998, Hon DLitt Univ of Nottingham 2008; hon fell: Goldsmiths Coll London 1993, KCL 1995; hon memb Guildhall 1996; FRSL 2011; Officier de l'Ordre des Arts et des Lettres (France) 1998; *Theatre* incl: Comedians 1974, Hamlet 1989, Guys and Dolls 1982 (revived 1996–97), Futurists 1986, The Changling 1988, Bartholomew Fair 1988, Voysey Inheritance 1989, Richard III 1990, Napoli Milionaria 1991, White Cameleon 1991, Night of the Iguana 1992, David Hare Trilogy 1993, Macbeth 1993, Sweet Bird of Youth 1994, Skylight (also Broadway, Wyndham's, Vaudeville 1996) 1995, La Grande Magia 1995, The Prince's Play 1996, John Gabriel Borkman 1996, Amy's View 1997 (also Broadway, Aldwych), King Lear 1997, The Invention of Love 1997, The Judas Kiss 1998, The Novice 2000, The Crucible 2002, Vincent in Brixton 2002, Mary Poppins 2005, Hedda Gabler 2006, The Reporter 2007, The Observer 2009, Private Lives 2010, Welcome to Thebes 2010, Flea in the Ear 2010, Betty Blue Eyes 2011, The Last of the Duchess 2011, The Dark Earth and the Light Sky 2012, Quartermaine's Terms 2013, The Pajama Game 2013 and 2014, Ghosts 2013, (West End 2014 and Brooklyn Acad of Music 2015), Liolà 2013, Stephen Ward 2013; *Opera* incl: La Traviata (Royal Opera House) 1994, Le Nozze di Figaro (Aix-en-Provence), Carmen (Met Opera) 2009, Werther (Met Opera) 2014, Manon Lescaut (Baden-Baden Festspielhaus) 2014, Le Nozze di Figaro (Met Opera) 2014; *Television* films incl: Suddenly Last Summer 1992, The Imitation Game, Pasmore 1980, Country 1981, The Insurance Man 1986 (Tokyo Prize), Past Caring 1986, v 1988 (RTS Award), Tumbledown 1988 (Italia RAI Prize, BAFTA Award), Absence of War 1995, King Lear 1998, Henry IV Parts 1 and 2 2012; *Film* The Ploughman's Lunch 1983 (Evening Standard Award for Best Film), Laughterhouse 1984 (TV Prize Venice Film Festival), Iris 2001 (Humanitas Award), Stage Beauty 2003, Notes on a Scandal 2007, The Other Man 2009; *Awards* incl: SWET Dir of the Year 1982, Evening Standard Best Dir 1982, STV Awards for Best Production 1969, 1970 and 1971, Sorrento Film Festival De Sica Award 1986, The Patricia Rothermere Award 1995, Olivier Award for Outstanding Achievement 1997, Critics' Circle Awards for Lifetime Achievement and Best Dir 1997, South Bank Show Award for Outstanding Achievement 1997, Dirs' Guild Award for Lifetime Achievement 1997, Evening Standard Awards for King Lear, The Invention of Love and Special Award for running the RNT 1997, Olivier Award for Best Dir 2006 (for Hedda Gabler), Best Dir Evening Standard Awards 2013, Best Revival Olivier Award 2014 (for Ghosts); for King Lear: Olivier Award for Best Dir 1998, Peabody Award 1999, Eebo d'Oro Award 1998; *Books* Utopia and Other Places (autobiography, 1993), The Eyre Review: the future of lyric theatre in London (1998), Changing Stages: A Personal View of 20th Century Theatre (with Nicholas Wright, 2000), Iris (screenplay, 2002), National Service (2003), Hedda Gabler (2006), Talking Theatre (2009), Ghosts (2013), What Do I Know? (2014); *Style*— Sir Richard Eyre, CBE; ✉ c/o Judy Daish Associates, 2 St Charles Place, London W10 6EG (☎ 020 8964 8811, fax 020 8964 8966)

EYRE, Stephen John Arthur; QC (2015); s of Leslie James Eyre, of Solihull, and Joyce Mary, *née* Whitehouse; *b* 17 October 1957; *Educ* Solihull Sch, New Coll Oxford (MA, BCL), Cardiff Univ (LLM); *m* 1 July 1989, Margaret Lynn, da of William John Goodman, of Coalville; *Career* called to the Bar Inner Temple 1981; lectr in law New Coll Oxford 1980–84, recorder 2005–; memb BSB Complaints Ctee 2006–11, legal memb Mental Health Review Tbnl 2007–, dep chllr Southwell and Nottingham 2007–12, chllr Coventry 2009–, chllr Lichfield 2012–; memb Solihull MBC 1983–91 and 1992–96; Parly candidate (Cons): Birmingham (Hodge Hill) 1987, Strangford 1992, Stourbridge 2001, Birmingham (Hodge Hill) by-election 2004; *Recreations* gardening, reading, theatre; *Style*— Stephen Eyre, Esq; ✉ St Philips Chambers, 55 Temple Row, Birmingham B2 5LS (☎ 0121 246 7000)

EYRE-TANNER, Peter Giles; *see:* Squire, Giles

EYSENCK, Prof Michael William; s of Hans Jürgen Eysenck (d 1997), of London, and Margaret Malcolm, *née* Davies (d 1986); *b* 8 February 1944; *Educ* Dulwich Coll, UCL (BA, Rosa Morison Prize for Outstanding Arts Graduate), Birkbeck Univ of London (PhD); *m* 22 March 1975, (Mary) Christine, da of Waldemar Kabyn, of London; 2 da (Fleur Davina Ruth b 1979, Juliet Margaret Maria Alexandra b 1985), 1 s (William James Thomas b 1983); *Career* reader in psychology Birkbeck Coll London 1981–87 (lectr 1965–80); Royal Holloway and Bedford New Coll London (now Royal Holloway Univ of London): prof of psychology 1987–2009, head of dept 1987–2005, emeritus prof 2009–, professorial fell 2013–; hon fell Roehampton Univ 2010–; pres Stress and Anxiety Research Soc 2006–08, chm Cognitive Psychology Section Br Psychological Soc 1982–87, memb Advsy Bd Euro Soc for Cognitive Psychology; MBPsS 1965; *Books* Human Memory – Theory, Research and Individual Differences (1977), Mindwatching (with H J Eysenck, 1981), Attention and Arousal – Cognition and Performance (1982), A Handbook of Cognitive Psychology (1984), Personality and Individual Differences (with H J Eysenck, 1985), Memory – A Cognitive Approach (with G Cohen and M E Levoi, 1986), Student Learning – Research in Education and Cognitive Psychology (with J T E Richardson and D W Piper, 1987), Mindwatching – Why We Behave the Way We Do (with H J Eysenck, 1989), Happiness – Facts and Myths (1990), Cognitive Psychology – An International Review (1990), Cognitive Psychology – A Student's Handbook (with M T Keane, 1990, 6 edn 2010), Blackwell's Dictionary of Cognitive Psychology (1990), Anxiety – The Cognitive Perspective (1992), Principles of Cognitive Psychology (1994), Perspectives on Psychology (1994), Individual Differences – Normal and Abnormal (1994), Simply Psychology (1996, 2 edn 2001), Anxiety and Cognition: A Unified Theory (1997), Psychology: An Integrated Approach (1998), Cognitive Psychology: A Student's Handbook (2000, 6 edn 2010), Psychology for AS Level (with C.Flanagan, 2000), Psychology for A2 Level (with C.Flanagan, 2001, 2 edn 2009), Key Topics in A2 Psychology (2003), Psychology: An International Perspective (2004), Fundamentals of Cognition (2007, 2 edn 2011), AS Level Psychology (4 edn, 2008), Fundamentals of Psychology (2008), Memory (with A Baddeley and M Anderson, 2009), Handbook of Managerial Behaviour and Occupational Health (jtly, 2009), Warsaw Lectures on Personality and Social Psychology Vol 1: Personality from Biological, Cognitive and Social Perspectives (jtly, 2009), Warsaw Lectures on Personality and Social Psychology Vol 2: Personality, Cognition and Emotion (jtly, 2012), Warsaw Lectures on Personality and Social Psychology Vol 3: Personality Dynamics: Meaning Construction, the Social World and the Embodied Mind (jtly, 2013), Cognitive Psychology: Classic Studies Revisited (with D Groome, 2015), Introduction to Applied Cognitive Psychology (with D Groome, 2016); *Recreations* tennis, travel, walking, golf, bridge, croquet, theatre; *Clubs* Campden Hill Lawn Tennis, Surbiton Croquet, Wimbledon Bridge; *Style*— Prof Michael Eysenck; ✉ Royal Holloway, University of London, Department of Psychology, Egham Hill, Egham, Surrey TW20 0EX (☎ 01784 443530, fax 01784 434347, e-mail m.eysenck@rhul.ac.uk); Roehampton University, Whitelands College, Holybourne Avenue, London SW15 4JD (☎ 020 8392 3510, e-mail michael.eysenck@roehampton.ac.uk)

EYTON, Anthony John Plowden; s of Capt John Seymour Eyton (d 1979), and Phyllis Annie, *née* Tyser (d 1929); *b* 17 May 1923; *Educ* Canford Sch, Univ of Reading, Camberwell Sch of Art (NDD); *m* 20 Aug 1960 (m dis 1986), (Frances) Mary Capell (decd); 3 da (Jane, Clare, Sarah); *Career* served Army 1942–47; artist; resident artist Eden Project 1999–2009; Abbey Maj scholarship 1951–53, John Moores prizewinner Liverpool 1972, Worshipful Co of Grocers fellowship 1973, first prize Second Br Int Drawing Biennale 1975, retrospective S London Art Gallery 1980, Charles Woolaston award Royal Acad 1981; exhibitions: Browse and Darby 1975, 1978, 1981, 1985, 1987, 1990, 1993, 1996, 2000, 2005, 2009 and 2013, Hong Kong Imperial War Museum 1983, Austin/Desmond Fine Art 1990, A T Kearney 1997, The Prince of Wales Inst of Architecture 1998, King's Road Gallery 2002, Woodlands Art Gallery 2003, Eden Project 2009, Eleven Spitalfields Gallery 2011, Built (Male Galleries) 2012; subject of book Eyton's Eye: Anthony Eyton – A Life in Painting (by Jenny Pery, 2005); hon fell London Univ of the Arts 2011; RA 1986 (ARA 1976), RWS 1987, Royal Cambrian Acad 1993, memb RWA, hon memb Pastel Soc, Hon ROI; *Recreations* gardening; *Clubs* Arts; *Style*— Anthony Eyton, Esq, RA

EZZAMEL, Prof Mahmoud Azmy; s of Mahmoud Mahmoud Ezzamel (d 1975), of Egypt, and Fatima, *née* El-Shirbini (d 1992); *b* 24 October 1942; *Educ* Univ of Alexandria (BCom, MCom), Univ of Southampton (PhD); *m* 31 March 1979, Ann, da of Herbert Edgar Jackman, of Coventry; 1 s (Adam b 29 March 1983), 2 da (Nadia b 29 Jan 1985, Samia b 6 July 1988); *Career* lectr and sr lectr Univ of Southampton 1975–88, visiting assoc prof Queen's Univ Kingston Ontario Canada 1986–87, Ernst & Young prof of accounting Univ Coll Wales Aberystwyth 1988–90, Price Waterhouse prof of accounting and fin UMIST 1990–96, prof of accounting and fin Univ of Manchester 1996–99, Cardiff professorial fell Univ of Cardiff 2000–; hon prof Univ Coll Wales Aberystwyth 1991–, visiting prof Massey Univ New Zealand March 1993, visiting Scholar Queen's Univ Canada July-Aug 1994, distinguished visiting prof Instituto de Empresa Madrid 2003–; ed Accounting and Business Research; *Books* Advanced Management Accounting: An Organisational Emphasis (1987), Perspectives on Financial Control (1992), Business Unit and Divisional Performance Measurement (1992, Italian edn 1996), Changing Managers and Managing Change (1996), Local Management of Schools Iniative: The Implementation of Formula Funding in Three English LEAs (1997), New Public Sector Reforms and Institutional Change: The Local Management of Schools Initiative (1999), The Challenge of Management Accounting Change (2003), The Future Direction of UK Management Accounting Practice (2003), Governance, Directors and Boards (2005), Regulating Accounting in Foreign Invested Firms in China: From Mao to Deng (2007), Accounting in Politics (2008); *Recreations* volleyball, tennis; *Style*— Prof Mahmoud Ezzamel; ✉ Cardiff Business School, Cardiff University, Aberconway Building, Colum Drive, Cardiff CF10 3EU (e-mail ezzamel@cardiff.ac.uk)

E

F

FABIANI, Linda; MSP; da of Giovanni Fabiani (d 1998), and Claire Smith; *b* 14 December 1956, Glasgow; *Educ* Hyndland Sch Glasgow, Napier Coll Edinburgh, Univ of Glasgow (Dip Housing Studies); *Career* admin asst Yoker Housing Assoc Glasgow 1982–85, housing offr Clydebank Housing Assoc 1985–88, devpt mangr Bute Housing Assoc 1988–94, dir East Kilbride Housing Assoc 1994–99; MSP (SNP): Scotland Central 1999–2011, E Kilbride 2011–; min for Europe, external affrs and culture 2007–09, dep presiding offr 2016–; FCIH (MCIH 1988), Hon FRIAS 2009; Cavaliere dell'Ordine della Stella della Solidarieta' Italiana; *Recreations* reading, folk music, culture; *Style*— Linda Fabiani, MSP

FABRICANT, Michael Louis David; MP; s of late Isaac Nathan Fabricant, and Helen, *née* Freed; *b* 12 June 1950; *Educ* state schs, Loughborough Univ (BA), Univ of Sussex (MSc), Univs of London, Oxford and Southern Calif (DPhil); *Career* former broadcaster BBC News and Current Affrs, co-fndr and dir int broadcast and communications gp until 1992, economist and advsr on broadcasting to Home Office and various foreign govts; MP (Cons): Staffs Mid 1992–97, Lichfield 1997– (Parly candidate (Cons) South Shields 1987); PPS to Michael Jack as Fin Sec to the Treasy 1996–97; memb Nat Heritage Select Ctee 1993–96, memb Euro Scrutiny Ctee B (Trade and Industry) 1993–97, memb Culture Media & Sport Select Ctee 1997–99, memb Home Affairs Select Ctee 1999–2001, chm Info Select Ctee 2001–03, memb Culture Media and Sport Select Ctee 2001–, memb Fin and Servs Select Ctee 2001–03, memb Liaison Select Ctee 2001–03, shadow min for DTI 2002–03, shadow min for economic affrs 2003–05, sr oppn whip 2005–10, lord cmmr (whip) 2010–, memb Administration Ctee 2013–; jt chm: Royal Marines All-Pty Gp, Cable & Satellite Gp; lawyer and chartered electronics engr; elected to Senate Engrg Cncl 1999–, dir Engrg and Technol Bd 2002–; memb Cncl IEE; CEng, FIEE 1994; *Recreations* reading, music, fell walking, skiing, listening to the Archers; *Clubs* Rottingdean; *Style*— Michael Fabricant, Esq, MP; ✉ House of Commons, London SW1A 0AA (☎ 020 7219 5022, website www.michael.fabricant.mp.co.uk)

FACHIE, Neil; MBE (2013); *b* 12 March 1984; *Career* Paralympic cyclist; achievements incl: 2 Gold medals (1km time trial and sprint, both with Barney Storey, MBE, *qv*) Para-Cycling Track World Championships 2009, 2 Gold medals (1km time trial and sprint, both with Craig Maclean) Para-Cycling Track World Championships 2011, Silver medal (1km time trial, with Barney Storey, MBE) Para-Cycling Track World Championships 2012, Gold medal (1km time trial) and Silver medal (individual sprint, both with Barney Storey, MBE) Paralmypic Games 2012; *Style*— Mr Neil Fachie, MBE

FAGAN, Elizabeth; *Career* formerly with DSG Int and The Link; Boots: md Opticians Div 2006–07, UK exec mktg dir 2007–13, mktg dir of health and beauty int and brands Alliance Boots 2013–14, sr vice-pres and md Int Retail Walgreens Boots Alliance 2014–16, sr vice-pres and md Boots UK and ROI 2016–; memb and past pres Women in Advertisng and Communications Club, past memb ASA Cncl; Achiever Award Cosmetic Exec Women UK 2013; fell Mktg Soc; *Style*— Ms Elizabeth Fagan; ✉ Walgreens Boots Alliance, Nottingham NG2 3AA

FAGAN, Neil John; s of Lt Cdr C H Fagan, of Bucks Horn Oak, Hants, and Majorie Sadie-Jane, *née* Campbell-Bannerman; *b* 5 June 1947; *Educ* Charterhouse, Univ of Southampton (LLB); *m* 21 June 1975, Catherine, da of R J Hewitt, of Hurtmore, Surrey; 3 da (Caroline Louise b 31 Oct 1977, Felicity Clare b 1 May 1980, Emily Catherine b 20 June 1983); *Career* Lovells (formerly Lovell White Durrant and Durrant Piesse, originally Durrant Cooper and Hambling): articled clerk 1969–71, ptnr 1975–; memb Worshipful Co of Slrs; memb: Law Soc, Int Bar Assoc; *Books* Contracts of Employment (1990); *Recreations* family, swimming, sailing, gardening; *Clubs* Royal Lymington Yacht, MCC, Travellers; *Style*— Neil Fagan, Esq; ✉ Little Orchard, Farm Lane, Crondall, Farnham, Surrey GU10 5QE; Lovells, 65 Holborn Viaduct, London EC1A 2DY (☎ 020 7296 2000, e-mail neilfagan@lovells.com)

FAHY, Kristof; *Educ* Univ of Leeds; *Career* global brand communication dir Orange 2003–06, brand dir EMEA BlackBerry 2006–07, vice-pres mktg Yahoo! 2007–09, chief mktg offr William Hill 2010–15, chief mktg offr Telegraph Media Gp 2015–16, chief mktg offr Ladbrokes plc 2016–; *Recreations* reading, walking; *Style*— Kristof Fahy, Esq; ✉ Ladbrokes plc, Imperial House, Imperial Drive, Harrow HA2 7JW

FAIRBAIRN, Carolyn Julie; da of David Ritchie Fairbairn, and Hon Susan Fairbairn, *née* Hill; *b* 13 December 1960; *Educ* Wycombe HS for Girls, Bryanston (scholar), Gonville & Caius Coll Cambridge (hon sr scholarship, BA), Univ of Pennsylvania (Thouron scholar, MA), INSEAD Fontainebleau (MBA); *m* 29 June 1991, Peter Harrison Chittick, s of Robert Chittick; 2 da (Emily b 25 Nov 1994, Anna b 4 May 1996), 1 s (Thomas b 18 Jan 1999); *Career* economist World Bank Washington 1984–85, fin writer The Economist 1985–87, mgmnt conslt McKinsey & Co London and Paris 1988–94, memb PM's Policy Unit 1995–97, dir of strategy BBC Worldwide 1997–99, dir of strategy BBC 2000–04, ptnr McKinsey & Co 2006–07, dir of gp devpt and strategy ITV plc 2007–11; non-exec dir FSA 2008–15, vice-chair Royal TV Soc 2008–15, non-exec dir competition and markets authy 2013–15; dir-gen CBI 2015–; tstee marie curie cancer care; *Recreations* tennis, travel; *Style*— Carolyn Fairbairn; ✉ 24 St Thomas Street, Winchester, Hampshire SO23 9HJ

FAIRBAIRNS, Zoë Ann; da of John Fairbairns, and Isabel Catherine Fairbairns; *b* 20 December 1948; *Educ* St Catherine's Convent Sch Twickenham, Univ of St Andrews (MA), Coll of William and Mary Williamsburg VA (exchange scholarship); *Career* writer; journalist; ed Sanity 1973–74, freelance journalist 1975–; contrib: The Guardian, TES, Times Higher Educational Supplement, The Leveller, Women's Studies International Quarterly, New African, New Scientist, New Society, New Behaviour, New Statesman, Spare Rib, Time Out; poetry ed Spare Rib 1978–82; occasional contrib 1982–: Women's Review, New Internationalist, New Statesman and New Society; fiction reviewer Everywoman 1990–, contrib Sunday Times and Independent 1991–; C Day Lewis Fellowship Rutherford Sch London 1977–78; creative writing tutor: City Lit Inst London 1978–82 and 2004–, Holloway Prison 1978–82, Wandsworth Prison 1987, Silver Moon Women's Bookshop London 1987–89, Morley Coll London 1988–89; various appts London Borough of Bromley under Writers in Schs Scheme 1981–; writer in residence: Deakin Univ Geelong 1983, Sunderland Poly 1983–85, Surrey CC (working in schs and Brooklands Tech Coll) 1989; subtitler: BBC Television London 1992–93, Independent Television Facilities Centre London 1993–2010; Br Cncl travel grant to attend and give paper Women's Worlds – Realities and Choices Congress NY, visiting writer Dept of Creative Writing Univ of Minnesota 2003, lectr City Lit London 2004–; memb Women's Equality Party; memb Writers' Guild of GB 1985; *Publications* incl: Live as Family (1968), Down (1969), Benefits (1979, shortlisted Hawthornden prize 1980, adapted for stage 1980), Stand We At Last (1983), Here Today (1984, Fawcett Book Prize 1985), Closing (1987), Daddy's Girls (1991), Other Names (1998, shortlisted Romantic Novelists' Assoc Award 1999); Tales I Tell My Mother (contrib, 1978), Despatches From the Frontiers of the Female Mind (contrib, 1985), Voices from Arts for Labour (contrib, 1985), More Tales I Tell My Mother (contrib, 1987), The Seven Deadly Sins (contrib, 1988), Finding Courage (contrib, 1989), The Seven Cardinal Virtues (contrib, 1990), Dialogue and Difference: English into the Nineties (contrib, 1989), By The Light of The Silvery Moon (contrib, 1994), Brilliant Careers: The Virago Book of 20th Century Fiction (contrib, 2000), The Road from George Orwell – His Achievement and Legacy (contrib, 2001), Endangering Realism and Postmodernism (contrib, 2001), Saying What We Want: Women's Demands in the Feminist Seventies and Now (contrib, 2002), How Do You Pronounce Nulliparous? (2004), The Belgian Nurse (radio play, BBC Radio 4, 2007), Write Short Stories and Get Them Published: Teach Yourself (2011), London Fictions (contrib, 2013); interviews with Mary Lawson, Sue Townsend, Gyles Brandreth, Marina Lewycka, Jonathan Coe, Pat Barker, Edna O'Brien, Karen Slaughter Xinran, Carol Ann Duffy, Fay Weldon and Katharine McMahon New Books magazine (2007–10); *Recreations* walking, reading; *Clubs* Writers Guild of GB; *Style*— Ms Zoë Fairbairns; ✉ e-mail zoe@zoefairbairns.co.uk, website www.zoefairbairns.co.uk

FAIRBURN, Prof Christopher Granville; s of Ernest Alfred Fairburn, and Margaret Isabel, *née* Nicholson; *b* 20 September 1950, Belfast; *Educ* Malvern Coll, Worcester Coll Oxford (BA, BM, BCh), Univ of Edinburgh (MPhil), Univ of Oxford (DM); *m* 1, 1979 (m dis 2006), Susan Margaret, *née* Russam; 1 s (Guy Granville b 16 Sept 1989), 1 da (Sarah Granville b 24 Jan 1992); m 2, 2009, Kristin Sonja, *née* Bohn; 2 s (George Henrik b 4 Oct 2010, Henry Niclas b 20 July 2013); *Career* registrar in psychiatry Royal Edinburgh Hosp 1975–78, lectr in psychiatry Univ of Edinburgh 1978–80, sr registrar in psychiatry Oxfordshire AHA 1980–81; Univ of Oxford: research psychiatrist 1981–84, Wellcome Tst sr lectr 1984–96, Wellcome princ research fell and prof of psychiatry 1996–; govr Wellcome Tst 2008–11; 9 books on eating disorders and cognitive behaviour therapy and over 300 scientific pubns; FRCPsych 1992, FMedSci 2001; *Recreations* travelling off the beaten track; *Style*— Prof Christopher Fairburn; ✉ University Department, Warneford Hospital, Oxford OX3 7JX (website www.credo-oxford.com)

FAIRCLOUGH, Geoffrey Charles; s of late John Holden Fairclough, and Kay, *née* Kear; *b* 16 October 1955, Leigh, Lancs; *Educ* Mount St Mary's Coll, Univ of London (BSc(Econ), external); *m* Sylvia, da of late Thomas Marshall Bird; 2 s (Alistair John b 20 April 1982, Richard Anthony b 6 Aug 1983); *Career* chartered accountant: Herring Conn Manchester 1976–80, Harry L Price Manchester 1980–83, Haines Watts Gp 1983–, Haines Watts Ltd 1992–2010 and 2012–13 (chm 2006–10), H W Group Services Ltd 1992–2010, H W Financial Services Ltd 1992–2010 (chm 2004–10), HWCA Ltd 2005–09, Trust Technology Investments Ltd 2010–15, Trust Investments Ltd 2010–; tstee Bath Recreation Ground Tst 2013–; FCA 1990 (ACA 1980); *Recreations* watching football, walking, cycling; *Style*— Geoffrey Fairclough, Esq; ✉ 28 Carriage Court, Circus Mews, Bath BA1 2PW (e-mail gcfairclough@hwca.com); Haines Watts, Advantage, 87 Castle Street, Reading, Berks, RG1 7SN (☎ 01189 584111)

FAIRCLOUGH, Oliver Noel Francis; s of late Arthur Basil Rowland Fairclough, and late Jean McKenzie, *née* Fraser; *Educ* Bryanston, Trinity Coll Oxford (BA), Keele Univ (MA); *Career* asst Liverpool Museum 1971–74; Birmingham Museum and Art Gallery: asst keeper of art 1975–79, dep keeper of applied art 1979–86; asst keeper of applied art Nat Museum of Wales 1986–98, keeper of art Amgueddfa Cymru – National Museum Wales 1998–2015; chm French Porcelain Soc, memb various arts and heritage advsy bodies and learned socs; assoc Museums Assoc 1978; FSA; *Publications* Textiles by William Morris (with E Leary, 1981), The Grand Old Mansion (1984), Companion Guide to the National Art Gallery (1993 and 1997); *Recreations* walking, travel, architectural history; *Style*— Oliver Fairclough, Esq; ✉ Tyn y Llwyn, Partishow, Crickhowell, Breconshire NP7 7LT (☎ 01873 890540, e-mail oliverfairclough@yahoo.co.uk)

FAIREY, Dr Anne; *b* 6 November 1961; *Educ* Univ of Southampton (BM); *Career* medical dir Novartis Pharmaceuticals UK Ltd 2001–03, dir Fairey Medical Ltd 2003–12, medical dir Ipsen Ltd 2012–; ind non-exec dir Biocompatibles Int plc 2008–; MFPM 2004, FRCP 2006; *Style*— Dr Anne Fairey; ✉ Biocompatibles International plc, Chapman House, Farnham Business Park, Weydon Lane, Farnham, Surrey GU9 8QL

FAIRFAX OF CAMERON, 14 Lord (S 1627); Nicholas John Albert Fairfax; s of 13 Lord (d 1964); ninth in descent from the bro of the 2 Lord who defeated Prince Rupert at Marston Moor, and unc of the 3 Lord who, as C-in-C of the Parliamentarians, was the victor at Naseby, and who hired the poet, Andrew Marvell, as a tutor for his da Mary who m another poet, the 2 Duke of Buckingham); *b* 4 January 1956; *Educ* Eton, Downing Coll Cambridge; *m* 24 April 1982, Annabel, er da of late Nicholas Morriss, of Newmarket, Suffolk; 3 s (Hon Edward Nicholas Thomas b 20 Sept 1984, Hon John Frederick Anthony b 27 June 1986, Hon Rory Henry Francis b 21 May 1991); *Heir* s, Hon Edward Fairfax; *Career* dir: Sedgwick Marine & Cargo Ltd 1995–96, Aquatask Ltd 1997–2005, Sovcomflot (UK) Ltd (SCF) 2005– (memb Exec Bd 2007–12), chm SCF Overses Hldg Ltd 2012–; Cons memb House of Lords 2015–; *Recreations* sailing, astronomy; *Clubs* Royal Yacht Squadron; *Style*— The Rt Hon the Lord Fairfax of Cameron; ✉ 10 Orlando Road, London SW4 0LF

FAIRGRIEVE, James; s of Andrew Davidson Fairgrieve, and Helen Dunn Hanratty; *b* 17 June 1944, Prestonpans; *Educ* Edinburgh Coll of Art (Andrew Grant jr open scholarship, DA, post-grad scholarship, Andrew Grant travelling scholarship to Italy); *m* Margaret Duncan Ross; 3 c; *Career* artist (full-time 1999–); sr lectr Sch of Drawing and Painting Edinburgh Coll of Art (ret 1998); memb 57 Gallery Assoc; RSA (ARSA 2004), RSW, SSA (past pres); *Solo Exhibitions* New 57 Gallery Edinburgh 1969 and 1971, Scottish Arts Club Edinburgh 1973, Scottish Gallery Edinburgh 1974, 1978 and 2007, Univ of Edinburgh 1975, Mercury Gallery London 1980, 1982, 1984 and 1987, Macaulay Gallery Stenton E Lothian 1983, Belgrade Acad Yugoslavia 1989, Stichill Gallery Roxburghshire 1990, London Art Fair (McLean Fine Art) 2002, Randolph Gallery Edinburgh 2004, 2007 and 2008, New Grafton Gallery London 2006, Art Fair (Olympia) Maclean Fine Art 2007, Randolf Gallery Edinburgh 2007, E.Gallery Glasgow 2007, Open Eye Gallery Edinburgh 2008, 2010 and 2014, RGI 2008, Scottish Arts Club 2013; *Group Exhibitions* incl: Reeves Bi-centenary (Edinburgh Festival) 1966, Drawing and Prints Strasbourg 1967, Glasgow

Inst of Fine Art 1968, Marjorie Parr Gallery London 1968, 20x57 Festival Exhibition Edinburgh 1969–72, The Edinburgh Sch (Edinburgh Festival) 1971, Richard Demarco Gallery Edinburgh 1973 and 1976, Triad Arts Centre (Bishop's Stortford) 1974, Howarth Art Gallery Accrington 1974, Howden Park Centre Livingston 1975, The Mall Galleries London 1975, Talbot Rice Art Centre Edinburgh 1975, City Art Centre Edinburgh 1975, N B Gallery 1976, Stirling Gallery 1976, Alamo Gallery London 1978, Mercury Gallery London 1978, Fine Art Soc Glasgow 1978, Gracefield Art Gallery Dumfries 1978, Basle Art Fair 1981, Pictures of Ourselves (Scottish Arts Cncl travelling exhbn) 1982, Compass Gallery Glasgow 1984 and 1996, ESU Gallery 1986, Royal Glasgow Inst 1987, Edinburgh Sch (Kingfisher Gallery) 1988, Artists Choice (Open Eye Gallery) 1989, Mercury/Scotland 1964–89 (London) 1989, State of the Art (Fine Art Soc) 1989, Scottish Painters (Fosse Gallery) 1989 and 1992, Scottish Painters (Beaux Arts Gallery, Bath Tolquhon Gallery) 1990, Arts Club Edinburgh 1990, RSW 1991, 1993, 1995 and 1996, Gillies Travel Award Exhibition (RSA annual exhbn) 1992, CD Exhibition (The Collective Gallery) 1992, Roger Billcliffe Fine Art 1993, Scottish Arts Club 1994, Fosse Gallery 1994 and 1995, Pontevedra Spain 1995, Burns Bi-centenary (Compass Gallery touring exhbn) 1996, Postcard Exhibition (Roger Billcliffe Gallery) 1996, 3 Man Show (Open Eye Gallery) 1997, Christmas Exhibition (Stenton Gallery) 1997, My Patch (Compass Gallery touring exhbn) 1997, The Big Picture Show (City Art Centre Edinburgh) 1998, Art 99 (Portland Gallery London) 1999, Frank T Sabin Gallery 2000, Fosse Gallery 2000, Compass Gallery 2000, RSW Exhbn Newport 2001, Noble-Grossart Prize Exhbn 2001, 20th Century and Modern Masters 2001, Cabinet Paintings (Compass Gallery) 2001, Art London (McLean Fine Art) 2002, Artists of Today and Tomorrow (New Grafton Gallery London) 2002, Christmas Exhibition (New Grafton Gallery London) 2002, Christmas Exhbition (McLean Fine Art) 2002, South Street Gallery St Andrews 2003, Artists of Today and Tomorrow (New Grafton Gallery London) 2003, Christmas Exhibition (Medici Gallery London) 2003, Visual Feast (Leith Gallery Edinburgh) 2004, Valentine Exhibition (Randolph Gallery Edinburgh) 2004, Affordable Art Fair (Maclean Fine Art London) 2005; *Work in Collections* HRH Prince Philip, Edinburgh City Art Centre, Scottish Arts Cncl, Lothian Regnl Schs Collection, Argyll Educn Dept, First Nat Bank of Chicago, Lillie Art Gallery, Ridderick Municipal Collection, RCP, Perth Art Gallery, Perth Art Gallery, Robert Fleming & Co, Leeds Sch Collection, I Rankin Esq, J K Rowling; *Awards* RA David Murray Landscape Award 1968, Andrew Grant travelling scholarship 1968, RSW Gillies Award 1987 and 1997, RSA Gillies Travel Award 1991, RSA Maude Gemell Hutchinson Prize 1993, RSA Macauly Award 2002; *Books* Eye In The Wind, Contemporary Scottish Painting Since 1945 (Edward Gage), Scottish Watercolour Painting (Jack Firth), A Picture of Flemings (B Smith), Dictionary of Scottish Art and Architecture (P McEwan); *Recreations* competitive fly-fishing (most capped Scottish angler); *Clubs* Edinburgh Breadalbane Angling; *Style—* James Fairgrieve, Esq

FAIRHAVEN, 3 Baron (UK 1961); Ailwyn Henry George Broughton; JP (S Cambridgeshire 1975), DL (Cambridgeshire and Isle of Ely 1977); s of 2 Baron (d 1973), and Hon Diana (d 1937), da of Capt Hon Coulson Fellowes (s of 2 Baron De Ramsey, JP, DL, and Lady Rosamond Spencer-Churchill, da of 7 Duke of Marlborough, KG); *b* 16 November 1936; *Educ* Eton, RMA Sandhurst; *m* 23 Sept 1960, Kathleen Patricia, er da of late Col James Henry Magill, OBE; 4 s (Hon James, Hon Huttleston Rupert (decd), Hon Charles Leander, Hon Henry Robert), 2 da (Hon Diana Cara, Hon Melanie Frances); *Heir* s, Hon James Broughton; *Career* RHG 1957–71, Maj; Vice Lord-Lt Cambridgeshire 1977–85; vice-pres: The Animal Health Tst, The Kennel Club; Kt of the White Rose (Finland) 1970, KStJ 1992 (CStJ 1983); *Recreations* gardening, cooking; *Clubs* Jockey (sr steward 1985–89), White's; *Style—* The Rt Hon the Lord Fairhaven, DL; ✉ Kirtling Tower, Cambridgeshire CB8 9PA

FAIRHEAD, Rona A; CBE (2012); da of Douglas Andrew Haig, of Oxon, and Isabella Somerville, *née* Farmer; *b* 28 August 1961; *Educ* Yarm GS, St Catharine's Coll Cambridge (LLB, Jacobson Law Prize, Addersley Law Prize, pres Univ Law Soc), Harvard Business Sch (MBA); *m* 5 Dec 1992, Thomas Edwin, s of John Edwin Fairhead; 2 s (James Douglas Edwin b 1996, Alexander Edward Haig b 1998), 1 da (Iona Charlotte Haig b 2000); *Career* assoc conslt Bain & Co 1983–87, analyst Morgan Stanley Int 1988, mangr Bain & Co 1989–90, ind conslt British Aerospace plc 1991; Bombardier Inc/Shorts Brothers plc: joined 1991, vice-pres corp strategy and public affrs 1994–95, vice-pres UK Aerospace Servs 1995–96; ICI plc: dir of planning & acquisitions 1996–97, exec vice-pres for planning and communications 1997–98, exec vice-pres strategy and control 1998–2001 (also memb Exec Mgmnt Team); chief financial offr Pearson plc 2002–06 (dep finance dir 2001–02), chief exec FT Gp 2006–13, chair BBC Tst 2014–16; non-exec dir: Laganside Corp Belfast 1994–2000, Harvard Business School Publishing 2002–, HSBC Holdings plc 2004–16, PepsiCo Inc 2014–; Hon Doctorate: Teeside Univ, Queen's Univ Belfast; *Recreations* skiing, flying, scuba diving, family; *Clubs* Bournemouth Flying; *Style—* Mrs Rona Fairhead, CBE

FAIRLEY, Ross; *b* 11 October 1968, Epsom, Surrey; *Educ* City of London Freemen's Sch, Univ of Leicester (LLB), Guildford Coll of Law; *Children* 3 da; *Career* slr; ptnr: Allen & Overy 2001–04 (joined as trainee), Burges Salmon LLP 2004– (co-head Environmental Law Unit and head of renewable energy 2004–); memb: Law Soc, UK Environmental Law Assoc; assoc Inst of Environmental Mgmnt and Assessment (IEMA); Tolley's Environmental Law and Procedures Management (ed), Sweet & Maxwell's Commercial Environmental Law and Liability (contrib); *Recreations* hockey, all sport, driving an old Austin Healey Frogeye; *Style—* Ross Fairley, Esq; ✉ Burges Salmon LLP, One Glass Wharf, Bristol BS2 0ZX

FAIRLIE, Andrew; s of James McGregor Fairlie, and Kay, *née* Sweeny; *b* 21 November 1963; *Educ* Perth Acad, Westminster Hotel Sch; *m* Ashley Gillian, da of William Laird; 2 da (Iiona b 15 Aug 1989, Leah b 1 Oct 1996); *Career* apprentice Station Hotel Perth 1980–82, commis de cuisine Charing Cross Hotel 1982–84, chef de partie Boodles Restaurant 1984–85, stagiaire Chez Michel Guerard France June-Nov 1985, commis de cuisine tournant Hotel de Crillon Paris 1985–86, sous chef Chez Nanos Megeve 1986–87, chef de cuisine Royal Scotsman Edinburgh April-Nov 1987, stage sous chef Intercontinental Hotel Sydney 1987–88, chef de cuisine Royal Scotsman Edinburgh April-Nov 1988, chef conslt A & K Travel Kenya 1988–89, sous chef Ritz Club London 1989–90, sr sous chef Adare Manor Co Limerick 1990–91, chef de cuisine Disneyland Paris 1991–94, chef de cuisine One Devonshire Gardens Glasgow 1994–, opened own restaurant Andrew Fairlie at Gleneagles 2001; team capt Ritz Club Olympia 1990 (9 silver medals, 8 bronze medals, 4 best exhibits); memb Académie Culinaire de France 1995; *Awards* third place Robert Carrier Nat Competition 1982, winner Michel Roux scholarship 1984, Scottish Chef of the Year 1996, Michelin Star 1996, 2 Michelin Stars 2006, Hospitality Industry Trg, Lifetime Achievement Award 2006, Scottish Chef of the Year Scottish Restaurant Awards 2008; *Recreations* hill walking, football; *Style—* Andrew Fairlie, Esq; ✉ Gleneagles Hotel, Auchterarder, Perthshire PH3 1NF (☎ 01764 694267, fax 01764 694163, e-mail andrew.fairlie@gleneagles.com)

FAIRMAN, Dr Martin John; s of Henry Douglas Fairman, FRCS, of Bristol, and Stella Margaret, *née* Sheath; *b* 8 May 1945; *Educ* Monkton Combe Sch, London Hosp Med Coll (MB BS); *m* 12 Aug 1967, Marianne Alison Louis, da of Sqdn Ldr Roland Ernest Burton, of Limousin, France; 2 s (James b 1969, Jack b 1978), 2 da (Jocelyn b 1971, Lydia b 1980); *Career* conslt physician Pilgrim Hosp (United Lincs Hosps NHS Tst) 1979–, hon sr lectr med Leicester Univ 1979–, fell in gastroenterology Cincinnati 1976–77, med dir Pilgrim Health NHS Tst 1993–2000, med dir United Lincs Hosps NHS Tst 2000–02; FRCP; *Recreations* golf; *Style—* Dr Martin J Fairman; ✉ Skirbeck Grange, Sibsey Road, Boston, Lincolnshire (☎ 01205 360743); Pilgrim Hospital, Boston, Lincolnshire (☎ 01205 364801)

FAIRWEATHER, George Rollo; s of Rollo Fairweather (d 1970), and Edith, *née* Patterson; *b* 11 October 1957; *Educ* Montrose Acad, Univ of Edinburgh (BCom); *m* 1993, Victoria, *née* Lanfear; 2 da (Natasha b 1995, Emily b 1996); *Career* Thomson McLintock & Co 1978–82, Procter & Gamble 1982–86, Dixons Gp plc 1986–94; gp fin dir: Dawson Int plc 1994–97, Elementis plc (formerly Harrisons & Crosfield plc) 1997–2002, Alliance UniChem plc 2002–2006, Alliance Boots 2006–14, Walgreens Boots Alliance Inc 2015–; non-exec dir Mitchell & Butlers plc 2003–08; MICAS 1981; *Recreations* sailing, golf, music; *Clubs* West Surrey Golf; *Style—* George Fairweather, Esq; ✉ Walgreens Boots Alliance, Sedley Place, 361 Oxford Street, London W1C 2JL (e-mail george.fairweather@allianceboots.com)

FAITH, Dr Lesley; da of Norman Faith (d 1970), of Belfast, and Estelle, *née* Sharp; *b* 30 August 1955; *Educ* Methodist Coll Belfast, Univ of St Andrews (BSc), Univ of Manchester (MB ChB); *m* 1 (m dis); 2 da (Natasha b 1988, Nicole b 1989), 1 s (Aaron b 1991); m 2, Howard Young; *Career* conslt psychiatrist: Bermuda 1986, Sydney Aust 1986–87, Stepping Hill Hosp Stockport 1987–98, Cheadle Royal Hosp Stockport 1998–; special interest in intensive care psychiatry; MRCPsych 1984; *Recreations* travel, reading; *Style—* Dr Lesley Faith; ✉ Faith & Young LLP, Broomy Bank, Hampton Green, Malpas, Cheshire (☎ 01948 820011)

FALCONBRIDGE, Prof Brian William; s of James Henry Falconbridge (d 1994), of Cromer, Norfolk, and Joyce Vera Lucy Spong (d 1995); *b* 1 May 1950; *Educ* Fakenham GS, Canterbury Coll of Art, Goldsmiths Coll Sch of Art London, Slade Sch of Fine Art; *m* 1970 (m dis 1989), Elizabeth Margaret, *née* Green; 1 da (Camilla Elizabeth Vita b 9 Sept 1982), 1 s (Oliver William Merton b 9 Aug 1985); *Career* sculptor; academic: Eton 1977–81, Goldsmiths Coll London 1978–2004 (head Visual Arts Dept 1997–2002), Slade Sch of Fine Art 1979–86, Blackheath Sch of Art 1985–89, London Metropolitan Univ 2005–11 (dean Sir John Cass Faculty of Art, Media and Design 2006–11, emeritus prof 2011); visitor The Royal Acad Schs 2006–10; memb Visual Art Panel Eastern Arts Assoc 1983–88, memb Exec Ctee Tolly Cobbold/Eastern Arts 5th Nat Exhibition 1984–86, curator and selector A Spiritual Dimension 1986–90, Academic and Mgmnt Bds Blackheath Sch of Art 1987–89; advsr Chinese Acad of Sculpture 2008; vice-pres Int Sculpture Conf Beijing Chinese Acad of Sculpture 2010; RBS: assoc memb 1994, memb Cncl 1995–98, 2001–03 and 2011–14, elected fell (FRBS) 2001, elected treas 2003, elected pres (PRBS) 2004–09; memb: City of Westminster Public Arts Advsy Panel 2006–10, Taiwan Panel Br Cncl 2003–13 (chair 2003–13), Bd Cultural Industries Devpt Agency 2006–08; external assessor Heatherley's Sch of Art 2009–, external academic advsr Royal Acad Schs Ctee 2011–, external advsr Panel Brian Marsh Award for Public Sculpture 2011–, external examiner PhD Brunel Univ 2012, visiting lectr UEA 2013–, external advsr on sculpture to All England Lawn Tennis Club 2014; tstee Blackheath Conservatoire 2011–12; work in several public collections; vice-patron Project Vernon Portsmouth 2008–; keynote speaker 4th Annual Int ACSA Conf Assumption Univ Bangkok 2010; *Solo Exhibitions* House Gallery London 1977, Angela Flowers Gallery 1983, The Minories Colchester 1984, Newcastle Poly Art Gallery 1984, Arcade Gallery Harrogate 1984, Drawing Schs Gallery Eton Coll 1984, The Fermoy Centre Art Gallery King's Lynn 1986, Artist in Residence Kings' Lynn Festival (All Saints' Church with The Fermoy Centre) 1986, Artist in Residence Gaywood Park HS King's Lynn 1987, Great St Mary's Cambridge 1989, Jill George Gallery London 1990, Masterpiece Art Gallery Taipei Int Convention Centre 1996, Chappel Galleries 2002, The Fermoy Gallery King's Lynn Arts Centre 2003, Place Arte Contemporanea Caravagnolo Turin (jt exhibition) 2003, Massmaanska Kvarnen Kultucentrum Ronneby 2004, The Constantine Gallery Teesside Univ 2013; *Group Exhibitions* incl: Goldsmiths (South London Art Gallery) 1972, Royal Acad Summer Exhibition 1977, 1988, 1990, 1991, 1992, 1993, 1994, 1996, 1997, 1998, 1999, 2000, 2001, 2002, 2003, 2004 and 2005, Art for Today (Portsmouth Festival) 1979, Tolly Cobbold/Eastern Arts 3rd Nat Exhibition, Small is Beautiful (Angela Flowers Gallery) 1983, The Falconbridge Cross Highgate URC 1984, Art for Everywhere (Peterborough Museum and Art Gallery) 1985, A Spiritual Dimension (touring exhibition) 1989 and 1990, LA Art Fair (Thumb Gallery) 1989, New Icons touring exhibition 1989–90, Academicians' Choice (London Contemporary Arts and the Eye Gallery Bristol) 1990, London to Atlanta (Atlanta Thumb Gallery) 1990, Los Angeles Art Fair (Thumb Gallery) 1990, Drawing Show II (Thumb Gallery) 1990, Art 91 London (Thumb Gallery) 1990, Decouvertes – Grand Palais Paris (Jill George Gallery) 1991, Goldsmiths Coll Centenary Exhibition 1991, Los Angeles Art Fair (Jill George Gallery) 1991, 1992 and 1993, ART 92 Business Design Centre (Jill George Gallery) 1992, ARCO 1992 Madrid (Jill George Gallery) 1992, Sumida Riverside Hall Gallery Tokyo 1993, Chelsea Harbour Sculpture 1993, Artists for Romanian Orphans at Bonhams 1994, The Language of Sculpture (Collyer-Bristow Gallery London) 1995, Absolut Secret (RCA) 1996, 1997, 1998 and 1999, Secret (RCA) 2000, 2001 and 2002, London Underground (Sungkok Art Museum Seoul) 2001, Blue (Place Arte Contemporanea Cavagnolo Turin) 2002, London Underground/Taipei (Taipei Fine Arts Museum Taipei) 2002, Manufactured in the UK (Villa Boriglionne Parco Culturale 'Le Serra' Grugliasco Torino) 2003, Scultura Internazionale ad Agliè (Castle d'Agliè Associazione Piemontese Arte Torino) 2004, Salthouse 05 2005, Bronze (Greyfriars Art Space King's Lynn) 2008, 10th Anniversary Exhibition Martin Arte Internazionale Torino 2011, The Room (Korean Cultural Centre London) 2011, International Exhibition of Wood Sculpture (San Yi Wood Sculpture Museum Taiwan) 2012, Heatherley's Sch of Art 170th Anniversary Drawing Exhbn 2015; *Awards* Walter Newrath Art History award 1972, Arts Cncl minor award 1976, Eastern Arts Assoc award 1977, Tolly Cobbold E Arts regnl prize 1981, E Vincent Harris award for mural decoration 1984, prizewinner 3 Int Exhibition of Miniature Art (Del Bello Gallery Toronto) 1988, Blackstone award Royal Acad Summer Exhibition 1991; *Clubs* Chelsea Arts; *Style—* Prof Brian Falconbridge, PPRBS; ✉ Royal British Society of Sculptors, 108 Old Brompton Road, South Kensington, London SW7 3RA (☎ 020 7373 5554, e-mail brian.falconbridge@gmail.com)

FALCONER, Colin; s of James Falconer, and Winnifred Falconer; *Educ* Forres Acad Moray, Duncan of Jordanstone Coll Univ of Dundee, Nottingham Trent Univ; *Career* theatre designer; prodns incl: Aladdin (costume, Scottish Ballet) 2000, The Blue Room (Minerva Theatre Chichester and West End) 2000, Hysteria (Minerva Theatre Chichester) 2000, The Merchant of Venice (RSC, London, Stratford and tour) 2001, Three Sisters (Chichester Festival Theatre) 2001, The Secret Rapture (Minerva Theatre Chichester) 2001, Twelfth Night (Liverpool Playhouse) 2001, Romeo and Juliet (Chichester Festival Theatre) 2002, The Misanthrope (Minerva Theatre Chichester) 2002, Acis and Galatea, Dido and Aeneas (RSAMD Glasgow) 2004, Madam T (Meridien Theatre Co Cork) 2005, Dominos (Theatr Genedlaethol Cymru) 2006, Endgame (Theatr Genedlaethol Cymru) 2006, plunder (Watermill Theatre) 2006, Cariad Mr Bustl (Theatr Genedlaethol Cymru) 2007, Blithe Spirit (Watford Palace) 2007, Northanger Abbey (Salisbury Playhouse) 2007, Maes Terfyn (Sherman Cymru) 2007, Anasi Trades Places (Talawa) 2007, Siwan (Theatr Genedlaethol Cymru) 2008, Barabas (Hall for Cornwall) 2008, The Winslow Boy (Salisbury Playhouse) 2009, Restoration (Salisbury Playhouse) 2009, The House of Bernarda Alba (Theatr Genedlaethol Cymru) 2009, Private Lives (Salisbury Playhouse) 2010, The Rime of the Ancient Mariner (Southbank Centre) 2010, The Picture (Salisbury Playhouse) 2010, The Constant Wife (Salisbury Playhouse) 2011, The Graft (Theatre Royal Stratford East) 2011, Hansel Und Gretel (RSAMD Glasgow) 2011, The Importance

F

of Being Earnest, Travesties (Birmingham Rep Theatre) 2011, Mustafa (Soho Theatre) 2012, There We Have Been/Everything and Nothing (Sadlers Wells) 2012, Blue/Orange (Theatre Royal Brighton and tour) 2012, Travels with my Aunt (Menier Chocolate Factory) 2013 and (Chichester Festival Theatre) 2016, The Other School (NYMT) 2013, The Three Lions (Pleasance) 2013 and (St James Theatre) 2015, Happy Birthday Sunita (RIFCO/ Watford Palace Theatre) 2014, The Realness (The Big House) 2014, Rumpelstiltskin (Theatre Royal Bath) 2014 and (The MAC Belfast) 2015, Urinetown (Arts Ed) 2016, Workshop Negative (Gate Theatre) 2016, La Traviata and Cosi Fan Tutte (West Green House Opera) 2016; *Style*— Colin Falconer, Esq; ✉ e-mail colin.falconer@mac.com

FALCONER, Prof Roger Alexander; s of Cyril Thomas Falconer (d 2000), of Bridgend, and Winnifred Matilda Mary, *née* Rudge (d 2004); *b* 12 December 1951, Carmarthen, Dyfed; *Educ* KCL (BSc), Univ of Washington USA (MSCE), Imperial Coll London (PhD, DIC), Univ of Birmingham (DEng), Univ of London (DSc(Eng)); *m* April 1977, Nicola Jane, da of Kenneth Hayward Wonson (d 1967); 2 s (James b 30 July 1980, Simon b 19 March 1983), 1 da (Sarah b 23 June 1988); *Career* lectr Dept of Civil Engrg Univ of Birmingham 1977–86; Univ of Bradford: prof of water engrg 1987–97, head Dept of Civil and Environmental Engrg 1994–97; prof of water mgmnt (part-time) Sch of Engrg Cardiff Univ 1997–, dir Roger Falconer Water Consultancy Ltd 2016–; visiting prof: Tongji Univ Shanghai 1987–, Tianjin Univ China 2004–, IWHR China 2012–; memb Cncl: CIWEM 1997–2003, IAHR 2000– (pres 2011–15), ICE 2000–03, Welsh Govt Flood Risk Mgmnt Ctee 2006–, Expert Panel for Severn Tidal Power Studies 2008–10; advsr to: Nat Environment Protection Agency China 1987–92, Wetland Mgmnt Project Southern California Edison USA 1992–93, BNFL 1993–94, BP Chemicals 1993–94, US Navy 1995–96, Tianjin Municipal Government China 2000–, Hafren Power Ltd 2010–13; expert Malaysia v Singapore Land Reclamation Study 2004–05; supplier of computer models for water quality predictions to water indust cos for over 100 EIA projects worldwide; recipient: Ippen Award Int Assoc for Hydraulic Research 1991, Telford Premium ICE 1994, Royal Acad of Engrg Silver Medal 1999–, Robert Carr Prize ICE 2003 and 2007, Hai He Award China 2004; FCIWEM 1990, FICE 1992, FASCE 1993, FCGI 1997, FREng 1997, FLSW 2011; *Publications* author of over 400 published papers in jls and conf proceedings; also lectr to over 450 instns in 19 countries on environmental water mgmnt; *Recreations* walking, music, sport, travel; *Clubs* Welsh Livery Guild; *Style*— Prof Roger Falconer, FREng; ✉ School of Engineering, Cardiff University, The Parade, Cardiff CF24 3AA (☎ 029 2087 4280, e-mail falconerra@cardiff.ac.uk)

FALCONER OF THOROTON, Baron (Life Peer UK 1997), of Thoroton in the County of Nottinghamshire; Charles Leslie Falconer; PC (2003), QC (1991); s of late John Leslie Falconer, and late Anne Mansel Falconer; *b* 19 November 1951; *Educ* Trinity Coll Glenalmond, Queens' Coll Cambridge; *m* 1985, Marianna Catherine Thoroton, da of Sir David Hildyard KCMG, DFC (d 1997); 3 s, 1 da; *Career* called to the Bar Inner Temple 1974; slr-gen 1997–98, min of state Cabinet Office 1998–2001, min of state for housing and planning 2001–02, min of state Home Office 2002–03, sec of state for constitutional affrs and Lord Chllr 2003–07, shadow Lord Chllr and shadow sec of state for justice 2015–; sole shareholder New Millennium Experience Co with responsibility for Millennium Dome 1999–; *Style*— The Rt Hon the Lord Falconer of Thoroton

FALDO, Sir Nicholas Alexander (Nick); kt (2009), MBE (1988); s of George Arthur Faldo, of Welwyn Garden City, Herts, and Joyce, *née* Smalley; *b* 18 July 1957; *Educ* Sir Fredric Osborne Sch Welwyn Garden City; *m* (m dis); 1 s (Matthew Alexander b 17 March 1989), 3 da (Natalie Lauren b 18 Sept 1986, Georgia Kate b 20 March 1993, Emma Scarlett b 28 July 2003); *Career* professional golfer, golf course designer, televised sports commentator; amateur victories: Br Youths' Open 1975, English Championship 1975; tournament victories since turning professional 1976: Skol Lager 1977, Br PGA Championship 1978, 1980 and 1981, ICL Tournament SA 1979, Haig Tournament Players' Championship 1982, French Open 1983, 1988 and 1989, Martini Int 1983, Car Care Plan Int 1983 and 1984, Lawrence Batley Int 1983, Ebel Swiss Masters 1983, Sea Pines Heritage Classic USA 1984, Spanish Open 1987, Br Open 1987, 1990 and 1992 (runner up 1993), Volvo Masters 1988, US Masters 1989, 1990 and 1996, Volvo PGA Championship 1989, Dunhill British Masters 1989, World Match-Play 1989 and 1992, Irish Open 1991, 1992 and 1993, Johnnie Walker Classic 1990 and 1993, Scandinavian Masters 1992, Euro Open 1992, Johnnie Walker World Championship 1992, Alfred Dunhill Open 1994, Million Dollar Challenge 1994, Doral-Ryder open 1995, Nissan Open 1997, World Cup 1998; England Boys rep 1974, England int 1975–, with Br team 1975; memb Ryder Cup team: 1977, 1979, 1981, 1983, 1985 (winners), 1987 (winners), 1989 (winners), 1991, 1993, 1995 (winners), and 1997 (winners), capt 2008, holds record as leading points scorer for Europe in Ryder Cup history and most appearances in the Ryder Cup; memb England team Dunhill Cup 1985, 1986, 1987 (winners), 1988, 1991 and 1993; memb Hennessy Cup team: 1978 (winners), 1980 (winners), 1982 (winners) and 1984 (capt, winners), UBS Cup 2001, 2002 and 2003; world number one for 97 weeks between 1990 and 1994; Rookie of the Year 1977, finished top Order of Merit 1983 and 1992, BBC Sports Personality of the Year 1989; *Recreations* cars, flying helicopters, photography, fishing; *Style*— Sir Nick Faldo, MBE; ✉ e-mail info@nickfaldo.com, website www.nickfaldo.com

FALK, Sarah Valerie (Mrs Marcus Flint); da of John Falk, of Radlett, Herts, and Annette Falk; *b* 1 June 1962, London; *Educ* St Albans HS, Univ of Cambridge (David Gottlieb Prize, Slaughter and May Prize, MA); *m* 23 March 1985, Marcus Flint; 1 s (Thomas b 27 Sept 1989), 1 da (Rachel b 11 Sept 1995); *Career* admitted slr 1986; Freshfields (now Freshfields Bruckhaus Deringer LLP): joined 1984, ptnr 1994–2013, conslt 2013–; dep judge Upper Tbunl (Tax and Chancery Chamber) 2015–; *Recreations* horse riding, classical music (flautist), charitable work, walking, gardening, cookery; *Style*— Ms Sarah Falk; ✉ Freshfields Bruckhaus Deringer LLP, 65 Fleet Street, London EC4Y 1HS (☎ 020 7936 4000, e-mail sarah.falk@freshfields.com)

FALKENDER, Baroness (Life Peer UK 1974), of West Haddon in the County of Northamptonshire; Marcia Matilda Falkender; CBE (1970); da of Harry Field; assumed by deed poll 1974 surname Falkender in lieu of Williams; *b* 10 March 1932; *Educ* Queen Mary Coll London (BA); *m* 1955 (m dis 1961), George Edmund Charles Williams; *Career* private sec Morgan Phillips (gen sec of Lab Pty) 1954–56, private and political sec to Rt Hon Lord Wilson of Rievaulx, formerly Rt Hon Sir Harold Wilson, KG, OBE, MP 1956–83, political columnist Mail on Sunday 1983–88; memb: BSAC 1976–, BSAC Charitable Tst 1997–; dir Peckham Building Soc 1986–91, chm Canvasback Productions 1989–91; lay govr Queen Mary & Westfield Coll London 1988–93 (lay memb External Relations Ctee 1993–96), tstee The Silver Tst 1986–; FRSA; *Books* Inside No 10 (1972), Perspective on Downing Street (1983); *Recreations* reading, film; *Style*— The Lady Falkender, CBE; ✉ House of Lords, London SW1A 0PW (☎ 020 7219 3156)

FALKINER, Sir Benjamin Simon Patrick; 10 Bt (I 1778), of Annemount, Cork; s of Sir Edmond Charles Falkiner, 9 Bt (d 1997), and Janet Iris, *née* Darby; *b* 16 January 1962; *Educ* Queen Elizabeth's Boys' Sch Barnet; *m* 1998, Linda Louise, *née* Mason (d 2006); 1 s (Samuel James Matthew b 30 Aug 1993), 1 da (Alice Katharine Sally b 19 Oct 1996); *Heir* bro, Matthew Falkiner; *Career* master parts technician; *Recreations* rugby, cricket, music (drummer); *Clubs* Old Elizabethans Rugby Football, Old Elizabethans Cricket; *Style*— Sir Benjamin Falkiner, Bt; ✉ 29 Glebeland, Hatfield, Hertfordshire AL10 8AA (☎ 01707 274921, e-mail benfalkiner@hotmail.com); Quickco, Stirling Way, Stirling Corner, Borehamwood, Hertfordshire WD6 2AX (☎ 020 8207 3100)

FALKLAND, 15 Viscount of (S 1620); Premier Viscount of Scotland on the Roll; Lucius Edward William Plantagenet Cary; also 15 Lord Cary (S 1620); s of 14 Viscount (d 1984), and his 2 w Constance Mary, *née* Berry (d 1995); *b* 8 May 1935; *Educ* Wellington; *m* 1, 26 April 1962 (m dis 1990), Caroline Anne, da of late Lt Cdr Gerald Butler, DSC, RN; 1 s (Lucius Alexander Plantagenet, Master of Falkland b 1963), 2 da (Hon Samantha b 1973, Hon Lucinda b 1974) (and 1 da decd); *m* 2, 12 Sept 1990, Nicole, da of late Milburn Mackey; 1 s (Hon Charles b 1992); *Heir* s, Master of Falkland; *Career* 2 Lt 8 King's Royal Irish Hussars; journalist, theatrical agent, chartered shipbroker and former chief exec C T Bowring Trading (Hldgs) Ltd; memb: House of Lords Select Ctee on Overseas Trade 1984–85, Jt Select Ctee on Gambling 2003–04; chm House of Lords Works of Art Ctee 2008–10; dep chief whip Lib Democrats House of Lords 1988–2002, spokesman on culture, media, sport and tourism 1995–2006; elected hereditary peer under provisions of House of Lords Bill 1999, joined Ind Cross Benches 2011; *Recreations* golf, racing, motorcycling, cinema, reading; *Clubs* Brooks's; *Style*— The Rt Hon the Viscount Falkland; ✉ House of Lords, London SW1

FALL, Baroness (Life Peer UK 2015), of Ladbrooke Grove in the Royal Borough of Kensington and Chelsea Catherine Fall; da of Sir Brian Fall, GCVO, KCMG, and Delmar Alexandra Roos; *Educ* St Hilda's Coll Oxford; *Family* 2 c; *Career* former dir Atlantic Partnership; currently dep COS to The Rt Hon David Cameron, MP, qv; *Style*— The Baroness Fall

FALLA, David; s of Horace Waldron Falla (d 2007), of Guernsey, and Eileen Angela Falla; *b* 30 May 1949, Guernsey; *Educ* Kingston upon Thames Sch of Architecture; *m* 9 March 1973, Jane, *née* Dale; 2 s (Matthew James b 6 Dec 1980, Nicholas Edward b 1 March 1987), 1 da (Kathryn Margaret b 20 May 1985); *Career* architect; assoc Andrews Downie & Kelly 1973–79 (designer and team ldr construction of Royal Mint Square London, Cartier refurbishment Bond Street), fndr Falla Assocs 1979–; RIBA: main pres Guernsey Soc of Architects 2001–04, chm RIBA S E Region 2003–06, memb Cncl 2004–10, bd dir 2005–10, vice-pres int rels 2005–10, ldr UK Delgn at Architects Cncl of Europe 2005–10 and 2011–12, chm Int Rels Ctee and Int Membership Ctee 2005–10, chm EU Affairs Ctee, memb Competition Sub-Ctee; pres Guernsey Soc of Architects; memb London Borough of Wandsworth Conservation Area Advsy Ctee, tstee St Peter Port Town Centre Partnership 2004–, memb Cncl Friends of St James Guernsey 2004–, memb Cncl Friends of the Priaulx Library 2005–, memb Cncl Guernsey C of C; memb Ct of Assts Worshipful Co of Chartered Architects (Freeman 2003), Freeman City of London; RIBA 1975; *Projects* incl: Battersea Arts Centre studios and facilities, Ibstock Sch Science and Technology Centre Roehampton, Grand Hotel Le Touquet France, Marylebone High Street renewal master plan, Thames Edge apartments Staines, Links Halt residential devpt St Brelade Jersey, Lion Plaza project City of London, 7–12 Grace Church Street London, sports and educn facility St Sampsons and Le Murier Schs Guernsey, numerous projects in UK, France, Netherlands, Germany, Austria, Sweden and Luxembourg; *Recreations* photography, art, travelling; *Style*— David Falla, Esq; ✉ Falla Associates International Ltd, Newlands Lodge, Prince Albert Road, St Peter Port, Guernsey GY1 1EZ (☎ 01481 728020, e-mail dfalla@falla.com, website www.falla.com)

FALLEN, Malcolm James; *b* 26 October 1959, Wilts; *Educ* Queen's Coll Cambridge (MA); *Career* chief financial offr eircom until 2000; KCOM Gp plc: chief financial offr 2001–03, ceo 2003–08; ceo Candover Investments plc 2009–; memb ICAEW 1986; *Style*— Malcolm Fallen, Esq; ✉ Candover Investments plc, 34–36 Lime Street, London EC3M 7AT

FALLON, Ivan Gregory; s of Padraic Joseph Fallon (d 1974), and Dorothea, *née* Maher (d 1985); *b* 26 June 1944; *Educ* St Peter's Coll Wexford, TCD (BBS); *m* 14 Jan 1967 (m dis 1997), Susan Mary, da of Dr Robert Francis Lurring, of Kidderminster; 2 da (Tania Helen b 1967, Lara Catherine b 1970), 1 s (Padraic Robert b 1974); *m* 2, 1997, Elizabeth, *née* Rees-Jones; *Career* Irish Times 1964–66, Thomson Provincial Newspapers 1966–67, Daily Mirror 1967–68, Sunday Telegraph 1968–84, city ed Sunday Telegraph 1979–84, dep ed Sunday Times 1984–94, gp editorial dir Independent Group Newspapers Ltd 1994–, memb Bd Independent News & Media plc 1995–2009, ceo Independent News & Media (South Africa) (Pty) Ltd 1997–2002, ceo Independent News & Media (UK) Ltd 2002–; non-exec chm iTouch plc 2000–, non-exec dir N Brown Gp plc 1994–; FRSA 1989; *Books* DeLorean: The Rise and Fall of a Dream Maker (with James Srodes, 1983), Takeovers (with James Srodes, 1987), The Brothers: The Rise of Saatchi and Saatchi (1988), Billionaire: The Life and Times of Sir James Goldsmith (1991), Paperchase (1993), The Player: The Life of Tony O'Reilly (1994); *Recreations* cycling, tennis; *Clubs* Beefsteak, The Rand (Johannesburg); *Style*— Ivan Fallon, Esq

FALLON, Jane; *Career* prodr: Eastenders (BBC1) 1994, This Life (BBC) 1995 and 1996–97, Undercover Heart (BBC1), Massive Landmarks of the 20th Century (Channel 4 with Nat Theatre of Brent) 1999; exec prodr: Teachers (Channel 4) 2000–01, 2001–02, 2002–03 and 2004, 20 Things to do Before You're 30 (Channel 4) 2002–03, Single (ITV) 2002–03; *Awards* nominations for This Life (Series 1) incl: Best Drama Series BAFTA Awards, Best Drama RTS Awards, Best Drama Indie Awards; for This Life (Series 2) incl: Best Drama RTS Awards, Best Drama Indie Awards, The Indie Indie Awards, Best Drama South Bank Show Awards, Best Original Drama Serial Writers Guild, nominated Best Drama Serial BAFTA Awards; nominations for Undercover Heart incl: Best Drama Serial BAFTA Awards, Best Drama Birmingham Film & TV Festival; nominations for Teachers (Series 1) incl: Best New Drama TV Quick Awards, Best Drama Birmingham Film & TV Festival, Best Drama Series and Best New Programme Broadcast Awards; nominations for Teachers (Series 2) incl: Best Drama Series BAFTA Awards, Best Drama Series RTS Awards, Best Drama Series Monte Carlo TV Festival, Best Drama Series or Serial Broadcast Awards, Best Drama Indie Awards, Best Drama Series Banff Television Festival; for Teachers (Series 3) incl: Best TV Show Emma Awards, nomination Best Drama Series RTS Awards, nomination Best Drama Indie Awards; *Books* Getting Rid of Matthew (2007), Got You Back (2008), Foursome (2010), The Ugly Sister (2011), Skeletons (2014), Strictly Between Us (2016); *Style*— Ms Jane Fallon; ✉ c/o Curtis Brown, Haymarket House, 28–29 Haymarket, London SW1Y 4SP (☎ 020 7393 4400)

FALLON, John Joseph; *b* 25 August 1962, Blackpool; *Educ* Cardinal Langley Sch Manchester, Univ of Hull; *Career* Pearson: joined as dir of communications 1997, pres 2000–03, ceo educational publishing EMEA 2003, chief exec Pearson plc 2013–; *Style*— John Fallon, Esq; ✉ Pearson plc, 80 Strand, London WC2R 0RL

FALLON, Rt Hon Sir Michael Cathel; KCB (2016), PC (2012), MP; s of Martin Fallon, OBE (d 1994), and Hazel Fallon; *b* 14 May 1952; *Educ* Univ of St Andrews (MA); *m* 1986, Wendy Elisabeth; 2 s; *Career* advsr to Rt Hon Lord Carrington 1975–77, EEC desk offr CRD 1977–79; MP (Cons): Darlington 1983–92, Sevenoaks 1997–; PPS to Rt Hon Cecil Parkinson as sec of state for energy 1987–88, asst govt whip 1988–90, parliamentary under sec Dept of Educn and Science 1990–92, oppn spokesman on trade and industry 1997–98, oppn spokesman treasy 1998–99, memb Treas Select Ctee 1999– (chm Sub-Ctee 2001–10), vice-chm Cons Pty 2010–12, min for business and enterprise 2012–14, min of state for energy 2013–14, sec of state for defence 2014–; co dir Quality Care Homes plc Darlington 1992–97; dir: Just Learning Ltd 1996–, International Care and Relief 1998–2003, Bannatyne Fitness Ltd 1999–2000, Just Learning Holdings 2001–09, Learning Just Ltd 2001–09, Just Learning Developments Ltd 2001–09, Careshare Ltd 2003–09, Collins Stewart Tullett plc 2004–06, Tullett Prebon plc 2006–, Attendo AB 2008–; *Style*— The Rt Hon Sir Michael Fallon, KCB, MP; ✉ House of Commons, London SW1A 0AA (☎ 020 7219 6482)

FALLOWELL, Duncan Richard; s of Thomas Edgar Fallowell, of Finchampstead, Berks, and La Croix Valmer, France, and Celia, *née* Waller; *b* 26 September 1948, London; *Educ* St Paul's, Magdalen Coll Oxford; *Career* author; FRSL 2015; *Books* Drug Tales (1979), April Ashley's Odyssey (1982), Satyrday (1986), The Underbelly (1987), To Noto (1989), One Hot Summer In St Petersburg (1994), 20th Century Characters (1994), A History Of Facelifting (2003), Going As Far As I Can (2008), How To Disappear (memoir, 2011, PEN Ackerley Prize 2012), Three Romes (2014), The Rise and Fall of the Celebrity Interview (2014); *Opera Libretto* Gormenghast (1998); *Recreations* swimming; *Clubs* Groucho; *Style—* Duncan Fallowell, Esq; ✉ c/o Aitken Alexander Associates Ltd, London; website www.duncanfallowell.com

FALLOWFIELD, Prof Dame Lesley; DBE (2016); da of William Mason, and Jean, *née* Paull; *b* 31 October 1949, Southampton; *Educ* Parkstone Girls GS Poole, Univ of Sussex (BSc, DPhil); *m* 1972 (m dis 1983) Anthony Fallowfield; 1 s (Dr Jonathan Fallowfield b 5 April 1973), 1 da (Mrs Caroline Reeve b 10 Oct 1975); *Career* SRN Guy's Hosp London 1968–71, research fell Univ of Cambridge 1982–84, research fell CRC Trials Unit KCH 1984–87, sr lectr in health psychology The Royal London Hosp 1987–94, dir Psychosocial Oncology UCL Med Sch 1994–2001, prof of psycho-oncology and dir Sussex Health Outcomes Research and Educn in Cancer Brighton & Sussex Med Sch Univ of Sussex 2001–; tstee/ memb Scientific Advsy Ctee numerous cancer charities incl Cancer Backup and Maggie's Centres; Pfizer/BOA Excellence in Oncology Lifetime Achievement Award 2010; memb: Br Psychological Soc, American Soc for Clinical Oncology; FMedSci, FRSM; *Publications* more than 350 learned academic papers and 3 text books; *Recreations* cinema, golf, music, reading, walking; *Style—* Prof Dame Lesley Fallowfield; ✉ 64 Wayland Avenue, Brighton, East Sussex BN1 5JN; Sussex Health Outcomes Research and Education in Cancer (SHORE-C), Room 1, University of Sussex, Brighton BN1 9RX (☎ 01273 873015, e-mail l.j.fallowfield@sussex.ac.uk, Twitter @FallowfieldLJ, website http://shore-c.sussex.ac.uk)

FANCOURT, Timothy Miles; QC (2003); s of Philip Fancourt, of Thakeham, W Sussex, and Georgina Mary, *née* Brown; *b* 30 August 1964, London; *Educ* Whitgift Sch Croydon, Gonville & Caius Coll Cambridge (MA), Inns of Court Sch of Law; *m* 9 Dec 2000, Emily May Windsor; 1 da (Agatha b 23 April 2007); *Career* called to the Bar Lincoln's Inn 1987 (bencher); recorder 2009–, dep High Court judge 2013–; memb Bar Cncl 1996–2001, vice-chm Standards Ctee Bar Standards Bd 2006–10, chm Chancery Bar Assoc 2012–14, dep High Court judge 2013–; *Books* Enforceability of Landlord and Tenant Covenants (1997, 3 edn 2014), Megarry's Assured Tenancies (1999); *Recreations* cricket, classical music; *Style—* Timothy Fancourt, Esq, QC; ✉ Falcon Chambers, Falcon Court, London EC4Y 1AA (☎ 020 7353 2484, fax 020 7353 1261, e-mail fancourt@falcon-chambers.com)

FANE, Andrew William Mildmay; s of Robert Fane, and Valerie Fane; *b* 9 August 1949, London; *Educ* Radley Coll, Emmanuel Coll Cambridge (MA); *m* 1989, Clare Marx, CBE, DL, PRCS, *qv*; *Career* chief exec Whitburgh Investments Ltd 1982–92, dir and dep chm Borthwicks plc 1988–92; dep chm English Heritage 2001–04 (cmmr 1995–2004, chm Historic Buildings and Areas Advsy Ctee 1995–2001, chm London Advsy Ctee 1999–2004, chm Audit Ctee 2002–11), memb Royal Cmmn on Historical Monuments of England 1999–2003; cncllr Royal Borough of Kensington and Chelsea 1987–94 (chm Planning Ctee); memb E Anglia Regnl Ctee Nat Tst 1994–2002; hon fell Emmanuel Coll Cambridge 2013; non-exec dir Gt Ormond St Hosp for Children NHS Tst 2001–11, chm Special Tstees Great Ormond St Hosp Children's Charity 1999–2007, chm of govrs Children's Hosp Sch at Gt Ormond St and UCH 2000–12, chm of govrs Framlingham Coll 2001–, memb Cncl Radley Coll 2003–11 (tstee Fndn 2002–14), chm of tstees Child Health Research CIO UCL Inst of Child Health 2006– (hon fell 2001), tstee Foundling Museum 2007– (chm of tstees 2009–12), chm Stowe House Preservation Tst 2007–, pres Emmanuel Soc 2009–, tstee Britten Pears Fndn 2009– (chm Building Ctee2009–), chm Chiswick House and Gardens Tst 2011–, chm Suffolk Preservation Soc 2013–; Suffolk farmer; FCA 1974; *Recreations* conservation; *Style—* Andrew W Fane, Esq; ✉ Hoo House, Hoo, Woodbridge, Suffolk; 64 Ladbroke Road, London W11 3NR (☎ and fax 020 7221 2748)

FANNING, Aengus Aquinas; s of Arnold P Fanning, of Birr, Co Offaly, and Clara, *née* Connell; gggs of Charles Connell, shipbuilder who launched in 1838 the first passenger steamship built in Belfast, the SS Aurora; descendant of Dominic Fanning, Mayor of Limerick, executed by Oliver Cromwell's forces in 1651; *b* 22 April 1947, Tralee, Co Kerry; *Educ* Tralee Christian Bros Sch, UC Cork; *m* 1, 1969, Mary, *née* O'Brien (d 1999); 3 s (Dion b 1972, Evan b 1979, Stephen b 1985); m 2, 2006, Anne Harris, *née* O'Sullivan; *Career* began career as journalist Midland Tribune (co-founded by g-gf 1882), ed Sunday Independent (Ireland) 1984–; *Recreations* playing cricket, playing the clarinet; *Style—* Aengus Fanning, Esq; ✉ Independent House, 27–32 Talbot Street, Dublin 1 (☎ 00 353 705 5333, fax 00 353 705 5770)

FANNING, Phil; s of James Anthony Fanning, and Janet Fanning; *b* 19 June 1982, High Wycombe, Bucks; *m* Claire; 1 da (Ella); *Career* John Lewis High Wycombe 2001–03, The Vanilla Pod Marlow 2003–05, jr chef de partie rising to sous chef L'Ortolan 2007–10, owner and head chef Paris House Woburn 2014– (head chef 2010–, Michelin star 2011–, Acorn Award 2011, High Life Dinners Chef of the Year 2012); memb Canadian Assoc of Snowboard Instructors (Level 1 snowboard instructor); *Recreations* cinema, gardening, skiing, travel; *Style—* Phil Fanning, Esq; ✉ Paris House, Woburn Park, Woburn, Bedfordshire MK17 9QP

FANSON, David Jonathan; s of Gordon Samuel Fanson (d 1995), and Pamela Alleyne, *née* Thomas (d 2006); *b* 18 December 1954, Bristol; *Educ* Queen Elizabeth Hosp Sch Bristol, Avonhurst Sch Bristol, S Bristol Tech Coll, Bristol Poly (BA); *m* 2 March 1996, Heidi Louise, *née* Gould; 2 da (Lauren b 6 Oct 1991, Maia b 6 March 2001), 2 s (Sam b 23 Dec 1996, Josh b 3 Sept 1998); *Career* admitted slr 1985, court and police station duty slr 1987, higher court advocate (criminal) 2006; slr's clerk Trump & Ptnrs 1981–85, asst slr Rodney King 1985–86, asst slr Trump & Ptnrs 1986–87, slr then ptnr Douglas & Ptnrs 1987–09, ptnr Sansbury Douglas Slrs 2009–; advocate Higher Court; memb Cncl Bristol Law Soc 1988–96 (memb and past chm Criminal Law Ctee), slr rep Bristol Magistrates Court User Gp; past chair: Duke of Edinburgh's Award Scheme, Bristol Support and Liaison Gp; memb Law Soc 1985; *Recreations* Clifton RFC (asst coach jrs), taekwon-do (Clifton and Henleaze Club, 4th Kup), playing bridge, family and child related activities; *Style—* David Fanson, Esq; ✉ Sansbury Douglas Solicitors, 6 Unity Street, Bristol BS1 5HH (☎ 0117 926 5341, fax 0117 922 5621)

FARAGE, Nigel Paul; MEP; s of Guy Farage, and Barbara Stevens; *b* 3 April 1964; *Educ* Dulwich Coll; *m* 1, July 1988 (m dis 1997), Grainne Clare Hayes; m 2, Nov 1999, Kirsten Mehr; 2 s (Samuel b 21 Jan 1989, Thomas b 28 Nov 1991), 2 da (Victoria b 28 March 2000, Isabelle b 8 Sept 2005); *Career* commodity broker: Drexel Burnham Lambert 1982–86, Credit Lyonnais Rouse Ltd 1986–93, REFCO Overseas Ltd 1994–2003, Natexis Metals Ltd 2003–04; MEP (UKIP) SE England 1999–, ldr UKIP 2006–09 and 2010–16, co-pres Independence and Democracy Gp; candidate UK Parl: Eastleigh (by-election) 1994, Salisbury 1997, Bexhill and Battle 2001; candidate European Parl Itchen, Test and Avon 1994; *Publications* Fighting Bull (2009), Flying Free (2011); *Recreations* sea angling, 1914–18 military history, proper English pubs; *Clubs* East India; *Style—* Nigel Farage, Esq, MEP; ✉ The Old Grain Store, Church Lane, Lyminster, Littlehampton, West Sussex BN17 7QJ (☎ 01903 885573, fax 01903 885574, e-mail nigel.farage@europarl.europa.eu)

FARAH, Mohammed (Mo); CBE (2013); *b* 23 March 1983, Mogadishu, Somalia; *Career* athlete; career highlights incl: European jr 5000m champion 2001, European jr cross country champion 2001, silver medal 5000m European U23 Championships 2003, silver medal 5000m European T&F Championships 2006, Europan cross country champion 2006, 11th IAAF World Cross Country Championships 2007, 6th 5000m IAAF World T&F Championships 2007, silver medal European Cross Country 2008, European indoor 3000m champion 2009, silver medal European Cross Country Championships 2009, European 5000m and 10000m champion 2010, European indoor 3000m champion 2011, world 5000m champion 2011, silver medal world 10000m 2011, 2 Gold medals 5000m and 10000m Olympic Games 2012, world 5000m and 10000m champion 2013, European 5000m and 10000m champion 2015, world 5000m and 10000m champion 2015, 2 Gold medals 5000m and 10000m Olympic Games 2016; *Books* Twin Ambitions – My Autobiography (2013); *Style—* Mr Mo Farah, CBE

FARAJ, Mohammed; s of Faiq Faraj (d 2006), of Baghadad, Iraq, and Hassiba Amin (d 1978); *b* 21 July 1947; *Educ* Coll of Engrg Univ of Baghdad Iraq (BSc), Inst of Planning Studies Univ of Nottingham (MA); *Children* 1 da (Lara Elianor Hogan); *Career* architect; conslt firm Iraq 1968–70, James Cubitt & Ptnrs London 1973–80, conslt Design Works London 1980–, dir Designworks Ltd 1998–2009, project dir Saudi Arabian Nat Guard Housing Project 2009–; memb: ARB, RIBA 1982, RTPI 1984; *Recreations* tennis, keep fit, photography; *Style—* Mohammed Faraj, Esq; ✉ 75 Christchurch Road, Southend on Sea, Essex SS2 4JW

FARHI, (Musa) Moris; MBE (2001); *b* 5 July 1935, Ankara, Turkey; *Educ* American Coll Istanbul (BA), RADA; *m* Nina, *née* Gould (d 2009); 1 step da (Rachel Sievers); *Career* author; chair Writers in Prison Ctee English PEN 1994–97, chair Writers in Prison Ctee Int PEN 1997–2000; vice-pres Int PEN 2001–; Amico Rom Associazione Them Romano Italy 2002, Special Prize Roma Acad of Culture and Sciences Germany 2003, Alberto Benveniste Prize France 2007; FRGS, FRSL; *Publications* author of numerous TV scripts, The Primitives (film script), From the Ashes of Thebes (stage play); novels: The Pleasure of Your Death (1972), The Last of Days (1983), Journey Through the Wilderness (1989), Children of the Rainbow (1999), Young Turk (2004), A Designated Man (2009), Songs From Two Continents – Collected Poems (2011); poems and short stories published in numerous anthologies and periodicals; *Recreations* sport; *Style—* Moris Farhi, Esq, MBE; ✉ c/o The Marsh Agency, 50 Albemarle Street, London W15 4BD (☎ 020 7493 4361, website www.marsh-agency.co.uk)

FARINGDON, 3 Baron (UK 1916); Sir Charles Michael Henderson; 3 Bt (UK 1902), KCVO (2008); s of Lt-Col Hon Michael Thomas Henderson (16/5 Lancers, d 1953), 2 gs of 1 Baron; suc unc 1977; *b* 3 July 1937; *Educ* Eton, Trinity Coll Cambridge (BA); *m* 30 June 1959, Sarah Caroline, o da of Maj John Marjoribanks Eskdale Askew, CBE (d 1996), and Lady Susan Alice, *née* Egerton (d 2010), da of 4 Earl of Ellesmere; 3 s (Hon James b 1961, Hon Thomas b 1966, Hon Angus b 1969), 1 da (Hon Susannah b 1963); *Heir* s, Hon James Henderson; *Career* ptnr Cazenove & Co 1968–96; chm Witan Investment plc 1980–2003; a Lord-in-Waiting to HM The Queen 1998–2008; chm Bd of Govrs Royal Marsden Hosp 1980–85 (memb 1971–85), hon treas Nat Art-Collections Fund 1985–92, chm Royal Cmmn on the Historical Monuments of England 1994–98, cmmr English Heritage 1998–2001, chm Bd of Mgmnt Inst of Cancer Res 2001–05 (memb 1980–2000), pro-chllr Univ of W London 2014–; fell Inst of Cancer Res 2000–; *Style—* The Rt Hon the Lord Faringdon, KCVO; ✉ 28 Brompton Square, London SW3 2AD (fax 020 7589 0724); Plantation House, Buscot Park, Faringdon, Oxfordshire SN7 8BU (e-mail farbuscot@aol.com, website www.buscotpark.com)

FARLEY, Alastair Hugh; s of George Walker Farley (d 1970), of Bovinger, Essex, and Phyllis Mary, *née* Davies (d 1978); *b* 2 January 1946; *Educ* Felsted, Jesus Coll Cambridge (MA); *m* 1, 1971; 2 da (Claire Katharine b 26 Nov 1974, Joanna Helen b 22 June 1980), 1 s (Edward McMurdo b 20 Jan 1976); m 2, 1995; 2 step s (Michael Reid Winn b 23 April 1975, Peter Matthew Baumann-Winn b 30 June 1978); *Career* Norton Rose: articled clerk 1968–71, admitted slr 1971, asst slr 1971–73, ptnr 1974–82; fndr ptnr Watson, Farley & Williams 1982–2001 (sr advsr 2001–14); sr advsr Chandris Gp 2001–; non-exec dir: Close Brothers Gp plc 1993–2004, Opus Portfolio Ltd 2001–13, Nautilus Hldgs Ltd 2006–15, Braemar Shipping Services plc 2011–; memb Cncl White Ensign Assoc; memb Law Soc 1971; Liveryman: City of London Slrs' Co, Worshipful Co of Gunmakers; Prime Warden Worshipful Co of Shipwrights 2003–04 (Warden 1999–2005); *Recreations* country pursuits; *Clubs* Boodle's; *Style—* Alastair Farley, Esq; ✉ (☎ 07818 412652, e-mail afarley@wardleyfarm.com)

FARLEY, Michael (Mike); *Educ* BSc; *Career* Persimmon plc: joined 1983, memb Bd 1989–, gp chief exec 2006–; MCIOB, FRICS 2011; *Style—* Mike Farley, Esq; ✉ Persimmon plc, Persimmon House, Fulford, York YO19 4FE

FARLEY, Paul James; s of James Matthew Farley (d 1986), of Liverpool, and Thelma Irene, *née* Harris; *b* 5 June 1965; *Educ* Mabel Fletcher Tech Coll Liverpool, Chelsea Sch of Art (Christopher Head drawing scholar, BA); *m* 2006, Carole Freda Romaya; *Career* poet; writer in residence The Wordsworth Tst 2000–02, reader in poetry Lancaster Univ 2005– (lectr 2002–05); fell Royal Literary Fund 2000–02; winner Arvon/Observer Int Poetry Competition 1995, Geoffrey Dearmer Meml Prize 1997, Forward Prize for Best First Collection 1998, Sunday Times Young Writer of the Year 1999, Somerset Maugham Award 1999, Writer's Award Arts Cncl of Eng and Wales 2000, Whitbread Poetry Award 2002, Next Generation Poets 2004, Forward Prize for Best Individual Poem 2005, American Acad of Arts and Letters E M Forster Award 2009, RSL Jerwood Prize 2009, travelling scholarship Soc of Authors 2009, Foyles Best Book of Ideas 2012, Cholmondeley Prize 2013; FRSL 2012; *Publications* The Boy from the Chemist is Here to See You (1998), The Ice Age (2002), Tramp in Flames (2006), Distant Voices, Still Lives (2006), John Clare: Poet to Poet (ed, 2007), Field Recordings (2009), The Atlantic Tunnel (2010), Edgelands (2011), The Dark Film (2012), Selected Poems (2014); *Recreations* photography, birding, supporting Liverpool FC; *Style—* Paul Farley, FRSL; ✉ c/o Peter Straus, Rogers, Coleridge & White, 20 Powis Mews, London W11 1JN (☎ 020 7221 3717)

FARMER, Dr (Edwin) Bruce; CBE (1997); s of Edwin Bruce Farmer, and Doris Farmer; *b* 18 September 1936; *Educ* King Edward's Birmingham, Univ of Birmingham (BSc, PhD); *m* 1962, Beryl Ann; 1 da (Amanda b 1969), 1 s (Andrew b 1967); *Career* dir and gen mangr Brico Metals 1967–69; md: Brico Engineering 1970–76 (tech dir 1969–70), Wellworthy Ltd 1976–81; The Morgan Crucible Co plc: dir 1981–, gp md and chief exec 1983–97, chm 1998–2003; chm: Allied Colloids plc 1996–98, Southern Electric plc 1998, Devro plc 1998–2001, Bodycote Int plc 1999–2002, Scottish and Southern Energy plc 2000–05 (dep chm 1998–2000); dir: Scapa Gp plc 1993–99, Foreign & Colonial Smaller Companies plc 1999–2007; pres Inst of Materials 1999–2002, chm Mgmnt Bd IMMM 2002–04, chm Communications Bd IMMM 2006–15; memb Fin Ctee Cancer Research UK 1997–2008; Platinum Medal IMMM 2004; Freeman City of London, Liveryman Worshipful Co of Scientific Instrument Makers; FREng, FIMMM, FRSA, CIMgt, CEng; *Recreations* music, hill walking, cricket; *Clubs* Athenaeum; *Style—* Dr Bruce Farmer, CBE, FREng; ✉ Weston House, Bracken Close, Wonersh, Surrey GU5 0QS (☎ 01483 898182)

FARMER, Ian Peter; s of Brian John Farmer, and Alice Kathleen, *née* Tatchell; *b* 25 March 1962; *Educ* Univ of South Africa; *m* 1, 7 Sept 1985; 2 s (Chase Patrick b 31 Oct 1986, Kyle Leonard b 9 Aug 1989); m 2, 7 May 1994, Diane, *née* Chilangwa; 1 da (Alice Chilangwa b 24 Feb 1995), 1 s (Hugh Mutale b 12 June 1997); *Career* CA S Africa 1985; audit sr Campbell Bude Brown & Stewart South Africa 1980–85, audit sr Coopers & Lybrand London 1985–86, treasy accountant Lonrho plc 1988–89 (asst gp accountant 1986–87), regnl fin controller Lonrho Zambia Ltd 1990–95, fin dir Lonmin Platinum 1995–2000; Lonmin plc: exec dir and chief strategic offr 2001–08, ceo 2008–; pres Int

F

Platinum Assoc 2005–06; Gleasons Deal of the Year South Africa 2004; *Style*— Ian Farmer, Esq; ✉ Lonmin plc, 4 Grosvenor Place, London SW1X 7YL (✆ 020 7201 6029, fax 020 7201 6100, e-mail ian.farmer@lonmin.com)

FARMER, Paul David Charles; CBE (2016); s of David Farmer, and Ann Farmer (d 1998); *b* 8 October 1966, Oxford; *Educ* The Oratory Reading, St Peter's Coll Oxford; *m* 1994, Claire Dwyer; 2 s (Benedict b 10 Sept 1998, Thomas b 4 Jan 2003); *Career* asst dir Clerkenwell Heritage Centre 1989–90, communications mangr The Samaritans 1992–97 (press offr 1990–92), dir of public affrs Rethink 1997–2006, chief exec Mind 2006–; chair Mental Health Alliance 1999–2006, chair NHS 5-Year Forward View for Mental Health 2015–16; tstee: Directory of Social Change 1998–2010, Assoc of Chief Execs of Voluntary Orgns (chair 2015–), Lloyds Bank Fndn; memb:; *Recreations* cricket, football, film; *Style*— Paul Farmer, Esq, CBE; ✉ Mind, 15–19 Broadway, Stratford, London E15 4BQ (✆ 020 8215 2295, fax 020 8522 1745, e-mail p.farmer@mind.org.uk)

FARMER, Peter; s of Kenneth Carl Farmer, and Phylis Marie Farmer (d 1973); *Career* artist and theatre designer; Prix Benois de la Danse for Lifetime Achievement 2010; *Exhibitions* Redfern Gallery London 1961, Mercury Gallery London 1964, 1965, 1970 and 1973, Wright Hepburn Gallery London 1969, Lasson Gallery London 1974, 1975 and 1977, Cat Gallery Copenhagen 1975, Meredith Long Galleries Houston 1980, Royal Festival Hall 1983; *Theatre* designs incl: On a Clear Day you can see Canterbury (Stratford East) 1962, Anyone for England? (Lyric Theatre Hammersmith) 1964, The Night of the Iguana (Savoy Theatre London) 1965, The Physicists (Crest Theatre Toronto) 1965, Hayfever (Crest Theatre Toronto) 1965, Man and Superman (Vaudeville Theatre London) 1966, Kean (Globe Theatre London) 1971, Dame Edith Evans and Friends (Haymarket Theatre London) 1974, What Every Woman Knows (Albery Theatre London) 1976, A Woman of No Importance (Chichester Festival) 1981; *Ballet* Sadlers Wells Royal Ballet: The Dream 1966, Giselle 1968, Arpege 1975, Pandora 1976, Paquitta 1981, Theme & Variations 1988; London Festival Ballet: Night Shadow 1967, Les Sylphides 1967, Meadowlark 1968, Three Preludes 1972, Cinderella 1974, Bourrée Fantastique 1978, The Storm 1981, Verdi Variations 1981, That Certain Feeling 1984; London Contemporary Dance Theatre: Conversation Piece 1970, Eclipse 1970, Stages 1971, Cantabille 1971, Sky 1971, Consolations of the Rising Moon 1971, Troy Games 1974, Dressed to Kill 1974, No-Mans Land 1974, Meetings and Partings 1975, Stone Garden 1989, In Memory 1989, Metamorphoses 1989, Crescendo 1989; Washington Nat Ballet: Sleeping Beauty 1971, Graduation Ball 1973, Raymonda 1974; Houston Ballet: The Nutcracker 1972 and 1977, Coppélia 1973, Cupiditas 1981, Peer Gynt 1981, Bartok Concerto 1987, Manon 1993; New London Ballet: Othello 1974, Intimate Voices 1974, Simorge 1975, Months 1975, Soft Blue Shadows 1976, Tristan & Isolde 1979; Australian Ballet: Anna Karenina 1977, Three Musketeers 1980, Manon 1993, Butterfly 1995; Inouie Ballet Tokyo: Sleeping Beauty 1977, Coppélia 1990, Swan Lake 1995; Northern Ballet Theatre: Les Sylphides 1978, Cinderella 1979 and 1982, Faust Divertimento 1982, Brahms Love Songs 1983; Rome Opera House: Soft Blue Shadows 1979, Daydreams 1979, Faust 1979, The Nutcracker 1991; London City Ballet: Romeo & Juliet 1985, La Sylphides 1987, La Traviata 1989, Giselle 1994; Birmingham Royal Ballet: Divertimento No 15 1989, Les Sylphides 1991, Street 1994, Coppélia 1995, Birthday Offering 1995; Hong Kong Ballet: Tales of Hoffman 1991, Graduation Ball 1991, Swan Lake 1996; other credits incl: Agrionia (London Dance Theatre) 1964, Giselle (Ballet Rambert), Giselle (Stuttgart Ballet) 1966, Giselle (Cologne Opera House) 1967, Beauty and the Beast (Western Theatre Ballet) 1967, Giselle/Danse Macabre (Western Theatre Ballet) 1968, Sleeping Beauty (Cologne Opera House) 1968, Chopiana (Royal Danish Ballet) 1972, Mendelssohn Symphony (American Ballet Theatre) 1973, Sleeping Beauty (Royal Ballet) 1973, Giselle (Munich Opera House) 1974, Othello (Scottish Ballet Theatre) 1974, Running Figures (Ballet Rambert) 1975, Sleeping Beauty (Ballet Int) 1976, The Nutcracker (Ballet Int) 1976, Namoua (Stuttgart Ballet) 1976, Sleeping Beauty (Munich Staatsoper) 1976, Giselle (Dutch Nat Ballet) 1977, Giselle (Frankfurt Opera House) 1980, Konigsmark (NZ Ballet) 1980, Giselle (Rio de Janeiro) 1982, The Nutcracker (Cincinnati Ballet) 1987, The Great Gatsby (Pittsburgh Ballet Theatre) 1987 and 1996, Coppélia (Nat Ballet of Portugal) 1989, Swan Lake (Royal Winnipeg Ballet) 1989, The Nutcracker (Pittsburgh Ballet Theatre) 1990 and 1991, Winter Dreams (Royal Ballet) 1991, Manon (Vienna Ballet) 1993, Raymonde Act III (Eng Nat Ballet) 1993, The Nutcracker (Hong Kong Ballet) 1997, Swan Lake (Eng Nat Ballet) 1999, Manon (Marinsky Theatre St Petersburg) 2000, Giselle (K Ballet Japan) 2001, Giselle (Berlin Staatsoper) 2001, Swan Lake (Rio Opera House) 2001; *Style*— Peter Farmer, Esq; ✉ 8 River Road, Littlehampton, West Sussex BN17 5BN

FARNES, Richard; *Educ* Eton, Royal Acad of Music, GSM, Nat Opera Studio; *Career* conducted operas at: ROH, ENO, Scottish Opera, English Touring Opera, Glyndebourne Festival Opera, Glyndebourne on Tour; also conductor: Royal Scottish Nat Orch, Scottish Chamber Orch; musical dir Opera North 2004–16; *Style*— Richard Farnes, Esq; ✉ c/o Maestro Arts, One Eastfields Avenue, London SW18 1FQ (✆ 020 3637 2789)

FARNISH, Christine; CBE (2013); da of Harry Farnish, of Ipswich, and Agnes Monica, *née* Smith; *b* 21 April 1950, Ipswich; *Educ* Ipswich HS, Univ of Manchester (BSc), UCL (MSc); *m* 1, Jan 1976 (m diss); 3 s (Sam b 10 June 1976, Jack b 25 March 1978, Harry b 27 Jan 1981); m 2, March 1992, John Hayes; 1 da (Hannah b 6 Dec 1986); *Career* asst chief exec Cambridge City Cncl 1988–94, consumer affrs dir then dep DG Oftel 1994–98, consumer affrs dir FSA 1998–2002, ceo Nat Assoc of Pension Funds 2002–06, md public policy Barclays 2006–11, cmmr Civil Service 2012–14; chair Family and Parenting Inst 2010–13, chair Peer to Peer Finance Assoc 2012–, ind reviewer Money Advice Service HM Treasy 2014; non-exec dir: ASA 2002–08, OFT 2002–06, Consumer Focus 2008– (chair 2010–14), ABTA 2010–16, Aggregate Industries 2012–14, Brighton and Sussex Univ Hosps 2013–16, OFWAT 2014–, OFGEM 2016–; memb Advsy Bd ING Direct 2004–06; former non-exec dir Papworth NHS Tst; *Recreations* mountain walking, swimming, family; *Style*— Ms Christine Farnish, CBE; ✉ 173 Artillery Mansions, 75 Victoria Street, London SW1H 0HU

FARNWORTH, HE Judith Margaret; da of Roy Farnworth (d 1992), and Kathleen Mary, *née* Hulme; *b* 25 April 1966, Sutton Coldfield, W Midlands; *Educ* Univ of Durham (BA), Univ of E Anglia (MA); *m* Christopher Anthony Cooke; *Career* diplomat; sr research analyst Research and Analysis Dept FCO 1991–95, second sec political/press public affrs Kyiv 1996–2000, head Political Section Prague 2000–04, dep head of mission and HM consul Riga 2005–08, dep head of mission and HM consul Kyiv 2008–12, ambass to the Kyrgyz Repub 2012–15, ambass to the Repub of Armenia 2015–; *Style*— HE Ms Judith Farnworth; ✉ c/o FCO (Yerevan), King Charles Street, London SW1A 2AH (e-mail judith.farnworth@fco.gov.uk)

FAROOKHI, Imtiaz; s of Mumtaz Farookhi (d 1968), and Anwar, *née* Razvi; *b* 17 January 1951, Washington DC; *Educ* Univ of Kent (BA), London Univ (MSc), Univ of London (Dip); *m* (m dis 2005); 1 da (Mariam Eleanor b 16 Jan 1986), 2 s (Luke David Liaquat b 28 Jan 1988, Eden Anwar b 18 Oct 2005); *Career* CEGB 1976–79: parly branch graduate trainee then admin offr; London Borough of Camden 1979–83: sr admin offr then princ admin offr; asst chief exec London Borough of Hackney 1983–88, head of co-ordination City of Wakefield MDC 1988–89, dir of policy and admin London Borough of Southwark 1989–91, chief exec Leicester City Cncl 1991–96, chief exec National House Building Cncl 1997–2012; chm: Strategic Forum for Construction Skills 2004–06, Land Data CIC 2004–; Bd memb: Leicestershire TEC 1992–97, East Midlands Devpt 1994–96, Environment Agency 1995–97, Leicestershire Businesslink 1995–97, British Urban Regeneration Assoc 1999–2004, Construction Skills Cncl 2004–, SE England Devpt Agency 2004–, London Thames Gateway Urban Devpt Corp 2004–; tstee Common Purpose 2000–04; memb: FEFC 1998–2001 (memb Widening Participation Ctee 1994–97), BBA 1999–, Learning and Skills Cncl 2001–05, SEEDA 2004–; FRSA 1993; *Publications* author of various learned articles in Political Quarterly, Local Government Chronicle and Municipal Journal; *Recreations* supporting QPR, fitness, food and wine, parenting; *Style*— Imtiaz Farookhi, Esq

FARQUHARSON, Alex; *Educ* Univ of Exeter (BA), City Univ London (MA); *Career* dir Nottingham Contemporary 2007–15, dir Tate Britain 2015–; *Style*— Alex Farquharson, Esq

FARQUHARSON-ROBERTS, Surgn Rear Adm Michael Atholl (Mike); CBE (2001); s of Rev Donald Arthur Farquharson-Roberts (d 2000), and Violet, *née* Crooks (d 1984); *b* 23 September 1947, Belfast; *Educ* Dorking GS, Westminster Hosp Sch of Med Univ of London (MB BS), KCL (MA), Univ of Exeter (PhD); *m* 1974, Jean Neilsen, *née* Harding; 2 s (Guy b 1977, David b 1979), 2 da (Katherine b 1983, Megan b 1986), guardian to bro's c (Stuart b 1975, Charlotte b 1978); *Career* registrar in orthopaedic surgery Royal Naval Hosps Plymouth and Haslar then sr registrar in orthopaedics Nuffield Orthopaedic Centre Oxford, Addenbrookes Hosp Cambridge and Royal Nat Orthopaedic Hosp 1973–83, conslt in orthopaedic surgery RNH Haslar 1983, conslt advsr in orthopaedic surgery to Med DG (Naval) 1989, def conslt advsr in orthopaedic surgery to Surgn Gen 1996–2000, Queen's Hon Surgn 1998–2007, RCDS 2001, dir med ops (Navy) 2002–03, Surgn Rear Adm 2003, med DG (Naval) 2003–07; memb Intercollegiate Specialist Advsy Ctee in Orthopaedics 1996–2000; govr Royal Star and Garter Home; Errol Eldridge Prize 1982; accredited Jt Ctee of Higher Surgical Trg 1983; Liveryman Soc of Apothecaries 2006; FRCS 1976, FBOA 1983, OStJ; *Publications* Ballistic Trauma (contrib, 1997), Naval Leadership and Management 1650–1950 (contrib, 2012), A History of the Royal Navy: World War I (2014), Royal Naval Officers from War to War, 1918–1939 (2015); author of articles in learned journals; *Recreations* model-making (ships), golf (badly), sailing (RYA Day Skipper); *Clubs* Army and Navy, Hornet Services Sailing; *Style*— Surgn Rear Adm Mike Farquharson-Roberts, CBE; ✉ 45 Bury Road, Gosport, Hampshire PO12 3UE (e-mail mfr@globalnet.co.uk)

FARR, Clarissa Mary; da of Alan Farr (d 2001), and Wendy, *née* Reynard (d 2010); *b* 30 June 1958, Woking, Surrey; *Educ* Bruton Sch for Girls, Univ of Exeter (BA, MA), Univ of Bristol (PGCE); *m* 16 July 1993, John Goodbody; 1 da (Isobel Frances Mary b 6 Aug 1995), 1 s (Adam John Reynard b 20 May 1997); *Career* teacher of English Farnborough Sixth Form Coll 1981–83, teacher of English Filton HS Bristol 1983–86, head of sixth form Sha Tin Coll Hong Kong 1986–89, sr mistress Leicester GS 1990–92, princ Queenswood Sch 1996–2006 (dep head 1992–96), high mistress St Paul's Girls' Sch 2006–; chm Boarding Schs Assoc 2001–02, pres GSA 2005–06; govr: Royal Ballet Sch 2009; fell Winchester Coll 2013; *Style*— Ms Clarissa Farr; ✉ St Paul's Girls' School, Brook Green, London W6 7BS (✆ 020 7605 4801, fax 020 7605 4870, e-mail clarissa.farr@spgs.org)

FARR, David; *b* 29 October 1969, Guildford, Surrey; *Career* dir and writer; artistic dir Gate Theatre 1995–98 (directed productions incl: Danton's Death, Leonce and Lena, Candide, The Barbarous Comedies, The Boat Plays, The Great Highway and Seven Doors), jt artistic dir Bristol Old Vic 2003–05 (directed productions incl: A Midsummer Night's Dream (TMA Award Best Dir 2003), Comedy of Errors, Paradise Lost (also writer), Loot, Twelfth Night, The Odyssey (also West Yorkshire Playhouse)), artistic dir Lyric Hammersmith 2005–09 (directed productions incl: The Magic Carpet, The Odyssey, Metamorphosis, Water, The Resistible Rise of Arturo Uir Ramayana, The Birthday Party), assoc dir RSC 2009– (prodns incl Winters Tale, Silence, King Lear, The Homecoming, Twefth Night and The Tempest); *Theatre* incl: Slight Possesion (writer and dir) 1991, Max Klapper – A Life in Pictures (writer and dir, The Electric Cinema) 1995, Powder Her Face (dir, The Almeida) 1995, Snatched By the Gods (dir, The Almeida) 1996, Elton John's Glasses (writer, Watford Palace Theatre and nat tour) 1997, The Winter's Tale (dir, Gavella Theatre Zagreb) 1998, Night of the Soul (writer, RSC) 1999, The Nativity (writer and dir, Young Vic Theatre) 2000, The Danny Crowe Show (writer, Bush Theatre) 2001, Joan of Arc's Thoughts on the English as she Burns at the Stake (writer and dir, RSC at the Young Vic Theatre) 2001, Crime and Punishment in Dalston (writer and dir, Arcola Theatre) 2002 (broadcast on BBC Radio 3), Night of the Soul (writer and dir, RSC at the Pit) 2002, The Taming of the Shrew (dir, Nottingham Playhouse) 2002, Coriolanus (dir, Swan Theatre RSC and Old Vic) 2002, The Queen Must Die, Ruckus in the Garden (writer, Shell Connections), Great Expectations (writer, Bristol Old Vic) 2003, Julius Caesar (dir, Swan Theatre RSC and regnl tour) 2004, Tamburlaine (Barbican, 2005), The UN Inspector (dir, NT) 2005; *Television* writer Spooks (several episodes, BBC) 2005–08; *Film* writer Hanna 2011; *Plays* The Odyssey, Crime and Punishment in Dalston, Great Expectations, Elton John's Glasses, The Nativity, Night of the Soul, The Danny Crowe Show, The UN Inspector, The Heart of Robin Hood; *Recreations* guitar, banjo, folk music, football; *Style*— David Farr, Esq; ✉ c/o Curtis Brown, Haymarket House, 28–29 Haymarket, London SW1Y 4SP (✆ 020 7939 4401, website www.curtisbrown.co.uk)

FARR, John Robert; s of Lt Col John E D Farr, MBE (d 1993), and Ank J W M, *née* Bol (d 2000); *b* 16 March 1949, Kuala Lumpur, Malaya; *Educ* Beaumont Coll, Univ of London (LLB); *m* 1, 975 (m dis 1987), Caroline, *née* Masefield; 1 da (Sarah b 1977), 2 s (Richard b 1979, Timothy b 1982); m 2, 1994, Katherine, *née* Ferris; 1 s (Henry b 1996), 1 da (Emily b 1998); *Career* admitted slr 1974; slr specialising in employment law, particularly disputes and employment aspects of corporate matters; Herbert Smith: joined 1972, Litigation Dept 1974–91, ptnr 1982–2009, Employment Gp 1991–2012, conslt 2009–; memb: Law Soc, Employment Lawyers Assoc, European Employment Lawyers Assoc, City of London Law Soc; tstee Royal Medical Benevolent Fund 2006–; Freeman City of London; *Recreations* hill walking, gardening, travel, skiing, cultural and sporting events; *Clubs* Reform, Richmond FC; *Style*— John Farr, Esq; ✉ Herbert Smith, Exchange House, Primrose Street, London EC2A 2HS (✆ 020 7374 8000, e-mail john.farr@herbertsmith.com)

FARR, Nigel Jonathan; s of Julian Farr, and Helen Patricia, *née* Owen; *b* 27 May 1962, London; *Educ* Wimbledon Coll, Gonville & Caius Coll Cambridge (MA); *m* 17 Aug 2012, Patricia Francisca; 1 da (Valentina); *Career* admitted slr 1987; specialises in investment funds and the asset management sector; ptnr Herbert Smith Freehills LLP 1994– (joined 1985); *Recreations* wine, food, cinema, sport, music, reading; *Style*— Nigel Farr; ✉ Herbert Smith Freehills LLP, Exchange House, Primrose Street, London EC2A 2EG (✆ 020 7466 2360, fax 020 7374 0888, e-mail nigel.farr@hsf.com)

FARR, Richard Peter; s of Peter James Farr (d 1987), and Josephine Farr; *b* 8 July 1954; *Educ* Bedford Sch, Ecole de Commerce Neuchâtel, Univ of Reading (BSc); *m* 1, 1979 (m dis 2003), Susan Jane, *née* Fairburn; m 2, 14 June 2014, Christine Leist; *Career* surveyor Knight Frank and Rutley 1977–80, sr surveyor Richard Ellis 1980–83, assoc dir Greycoat Gp plc 1983–88, chief exec New Cavendish Estates plc 1988–90, chief exec Park Square Estates 1990–2008; dir Adam Estates 1994–; Freeman City of London; FRICS; *Recreations* skiing, vintage Bentleys; *Style*— Richard Farr, Esq; ✉ Adams Estates Limited, 8 Oak Hill Park Mews, London NW3 7LH (✆ 07776 187735, e-mail richard.farr@virgin.net)

FARR, Sue; *née* Fairburn; da of Mr and Mrs D Fairburn; *b* 29 February 1956; *Educ* Sheffield HS for Girls GPDST, Univ of Reading (BA); *m* 1 (m dis); m 2, Anthony Christopher Mair; *Career* graduate trainee Northern Foods plc 1977–79, sr conslt Kraushar And Eassie (KAE) Ltd (mktg consultancy) 1979–83, account dir BSB Dorland (advtg agency) 1983–85, new business devpt dir Wight Collins Rutherford Scott 1986–90, dir of corp communications Thames Television plc 1990–93 (seconded as launch mktg dir UK Gold 1992–93); BBC: head of mktg BBC Network Radio 1993–96, dir of mktg and communications BBC Broadcast 1997–99, dir of public service mktg 1999–2001; md Golin/Harris Int (London office and EMEA) 2001–02, chm Advtg and Mktg Servs Div Chime Communications plc 2003–; non-exec dir: New Look plc 1994–96, Motivcom plc 2007–, Dairy Crest plc 2011–, Accsys Technologies 2011–, Millennium and Copthorne Hotels plc 2013–, British American Tobacco 2015–; tstee Historic Royal Palaces 2007–13; memb Business in the Community; Mktg Soc: fell 1987, first woman chair 1991–93; memb Mktg Gp of GB (chm 1990–92), Forum UK, Women's Advtg Club of London; Advertising Woman of the Year 1998; Hon Dr Univ of Bedfordshire 2010; FRSA; *Recreations* riding, reading, travel; *Style—* Mrs Sue Farr; ✉ Chime Communications, 3rd Floor, 62 Buckingham Gate, London SW1E 6AJ

FARRAR, Dr Jeremy James; OBE (2005); *Educ* UCL (BSc, MBBS), Univ of Oxford (DPhil); m; 3 c; *Career* dir Univ of Oxford Clinical Research Unit Vietnam, dir Wellcome Tst; estab (with Christiane Dolecek) Farrar Fndn 2011–; Frederick Murgatroyd Prize for Tropical Med RCP, Bailey Ashford Award American Soc for Tropical Med; Memorial Medal Vietnam, Ho Chi Minh City Medal Vietnam; FRCP, FMedSci, FRS 2015; *Style—* Dr Jeremy Farrar, OBE; ✉ Wellcome Trust, Gibbs Building, 215 Euston Road, London NW1 2BE

FARRAR, Mark; s of Ronald Farrar, and Doreen Farrar; *b* 14 August 1961, Dublin, Repub of Ireland; *Educ* BSc; *m* 2005, Francesca, *née* Beckerleg; 3 s (Peter b 1990, Thomas b 1994, Joseph b 1997), 1 da (Catherine b 1991); *Career* qualified chartered accountant; former chief exec Centre for Environment, Fisheries and Aquaculture Sci; ConstructionSkills: corp servs dir until 2008, chief exec 2008–13, ceo Assoc of Accounting Technicians (AAT) 2014–; memb Advsy Bd Skills Funding Agency; FCA 1988, AMCT 1994; *Recreations* saling (RYA yachtsmaster: ocean); *Clubs* Royal Ocean Racing; *Style—* Mark Farrar, Esq; ✉ Association of Accounting Technicians, 140 Aldersgate, London EC1A 4HY

FARRELL, His Hon Judge David Anthony; QC (2000); *Career* called to the Bar 1978; asst recorder 1996, recorder 2000, circuit judge (South Eastern Circuit) 2011–, hon recorder of Cambridge and Peterborough; *Style—* His Hon Judge Farrell, QC; ✉ Cambridge Crown Court, 83 East Road, Cambridge CB1 1BT

FARRELL, Gavin; *Career* slr; ptnr Ozannes; memb Bd AXA Property Tst; *Style—* Gavin Farrell, Esq; ✉ AXA Property Trust, Trafalgar Court, Les Banques, St Peter Port, Guernsey GY1 3QL

FARRELL, Sir Terence (Terry); kt (2001), CBE (1996, OBE 1978); s of Thomas Farrell, and Molly, *née* Maguire; *b* 12 May 1938; *Educ* St Cuthbert's GS, Univ of Newcastle Sch of Architecture (BArch), Univ of Pennsylvania Sch of Fine Arts (MArch, Master of City Planning); *m* 1, 1960, Angela Rosemarie Mallam; 2 da; m 2, 1973, Susan Hilary Aplin; 2 s, 1 da; m 3, 2007, Mei Xin Wang; 1 step-s; *Career* Planning Dept: Camden New Jersey USA, Colin Buchanan & Partners 1964–65; fndr ptnr Farrell Grimshaw Partnership 1965–80; currently princ Terry Farrell & Partners; former teaching positions: Univ of Cambridge, UCL, AA London, Univ of Strathclyde, Univ of Sheffield, Univ of Pennsylvania; visiting prof Univ of Westminster 1998–; English Heritage: cmmr 1990–96, memb London Advsy Ctee, memb Royal Parks Review Group 1991–96; memb Cncl RIBA 1997–, memb Bd London First 1998–, memb Advsy Bd Royal Parks 2003, chm Central London Partnerships Walking Co-Ordination Gp 2003, memb City of Westminster Housing Cmmn; former memb: RIBA Clients Advsy Bd, RIBA Visiting Bd, RIBA Awards Panel, Historic Areas Advsy Ctee; past pres Urban Design Gp, architectural assessor for Financial Times Architectural Awards 1983, external examiner RCA; representative projects: HQ Henley Regatta, Charing Cross devpt complex London, Edinburgh int fin and conf centre, Govt HQ bldg for MI6 at Vauxhall Cross, redevelopment of The Peak Hong Kong, new Br Consulate-Gen bldg Hong Kong, Kowloon Station and Masterplan Hong Kong, Dean Art Gall Edinburgh, Int Centre for Life Newcastle upon Tyne, The Deep aquarium Hull, Greenwich Peninsular Masterplan, Home Office HQ London, Regeneration of Marylebone Euston Road London, Transportation Centre Inchon Int Airport Seoul, Univ of Newcastle Masterplan, Manchester Southern Gateway Masterplan, Univ of Manchester Masterplan, Regent's Place London, The Great North Museum Newcastle, The Royal Inst London, Peninsula Central Greenwich, Beijing South Station, Dameisha Hotel, Shenzen & China Nat Petroleum HQ Beijing; appointed Design Champion: City of Edinburgh 2004–09, Medway 2006, Thames Gateway Parklands 2007–; numerous lectures in UK and abroad; Hon DCL Univ of Newcastle, Hon Dr Arts Univ of Lincoln 2003; Hon FAIA 1998; MCP, ARIBA 1963, memb RTPI 1970, FCSD (formerly FSIAD) 1981, FRSA 1989, FRIAS 1996; *Publications* Urban Design Monograph (1993), The Master Architect Series: Terry Farrell (1994), Sketchbook (1998), Ten Years: Ten Cities The Work of Terry Farrell & Partners 1991–2001 (2002), Place: A Story of Modelmaking Menageries and Paper Rounds (Life and Work: Early Years to 1981, 2004), Shaping London: The patterns and forms that make the metropolis (2009), Interiors and the Legacy of Postmodernism (2011), Continuum: Farrells 2001–2011: Work of the Hong Kong and London Offices (2012), The City as a Tangled Bank: Urban Design vs Urban Evolution (2014), The Farrell Review of Architecture and the Built Environment (2014); articles in: Architectural Review, Architects' Journal, L'Architecture d'Aujourd'hui, Domus, Progressive Architecture, Bauen und Wohnen, Abitare, Cree, Architectural Record, RIBA Journal, Architectural Design; *Style—* Sir Terry Farrell, CBE; ✉ Farrells, 7 Hatton Street, London NW8 8PL (☎ 020 7258 3433, fax 020 7723 7059, e-mail enquiries@terryfarrell.co.uk, website www.terryfarrell.co.uk)

FARRELLY, (Christopher) Paul; MP; s of Thomas Farrelly (d 1997), and Anne, *née* King; *b* 2 March 1962; *Educ* Wolstanton GS Newcastle-under-Lyme, Marshlands Comp Sch Newcastle-under-Lyme, St Edmund Hall Oxford (BA); *m* 19 Sept 1998, Victoria, da of David Perry; 1 s (Joe b 2 Feb 1999), 2 da (Aneira Kate b 21 Sept 2001, Octavia b 1 April 2006); *Career* mangr Corp Fin Div Barclays de Zoete Wedd Ltd 1984–90, corr Reuters 1990–95, dep city and business ed Independent on Sunday 1995–97, city ed The Observer 1997–2001; MP (Lab) Newcastle-under-Lyme 2001–, memb Culture, Media and Sport Select Ctee 2005–, chair All Pty Parly Br-German Gp; vice-chair: Br-Japanese Gp, Br-Icelandic Gp, Br-Norwegian Gp, Rugby Union Gp; sec Br-Italian Gp; memb: Unite, Unity, Amnesty Int, Greenpeace, Socialist Educn Assoc, Lab Pty Irish Soc; registered rep London Stock Exchange 1986; *Recreations* rugby, football, writing; *Clubs* Finchley RFC, Newcastle (Staffs) RUFC, Commons & Lords RUFC, Holy Trinity Catholic, Newcastle Working Men's; *Style—* Paul Farrelly, Esq, MP; ✉ House of Commons, London SW1A 0AA (☎ 020 7219 8391, fax 020 7219 1986, e-mail farrellyp@parliament.uk)

FARRER, David John; QC (1986); s of John Hall Farrer (d 1993), and Mary, *née* Stubbs (d 1996); *b* 15 March 1943; *Educ* Queen Elizabeth GS Barnet, Downing Coll Cambridge; *m* 29 March 1969, Hilary Jean, da of John Conway Bryson; 1 da (Emma Catherine b 22 May 1971), 2 s (Robert Edward b 20 March 1974, Thomas Andrew b 10 February 1977); *Career* called to the Bar Middle Temple 1967, recorder 1981; memb Bar Council 1987–93, chm Bar Services Ctee; chm: Parish Cncl, Rutland and Melton Liberal Soc (Parly candidate 1979 and 1983, regnl foreign affrs spokesman 1979–86); *Publications* Advice to a Suspected Abuser – Family Law Review (jtly with Rachel Langdale, 1997); *Recreations* tennis, watching rugby, listening to Sir Simon Rattle conducting Mahler, 19th century political history; *Clubs* Hamilton Tennis; *Style—* David Farrer, Esq, QC

FARRINGTON, Colin; s of Joseph Farrington, and Doris Farrington; *b* 12 March 1951; *Educ* Ellesmere Port Co GS for Boys, Christ's Coll Cambridge; *Partner* Paul Knott; *Career* civil servant Home Office 1972–88 (private sec to Home Sec 1974–77, on secondment HM Treasy 1980–83), dir IRRV 1988–98, DG IPR (now CIPR) 1998–2010; chair Global Alliance for Public Relations 2007 and 2009; chm of judges Cream Awards 2000–02, chm Membership Ctee City PR Guild, tstee CAM Fndn 1998–2001; chm: Cambridge Univ English Club 1970, Cambridge Univ Lab Club 1971; Freeman City of London 2011; FRSA; *Publications* Council Tax: Your Guide (1992), Business Rates: Your Guide (1993); author of numerous articles and speeches on public sector mgmnt, local govt, and PR and communications issues; *Recreations* travel, opera, whippets; *Style—* Colin Farrington, Esq; ✉ The Paladins, Innhams Wood, Crowborough, East Sussex TN6 1TE

FARRINGTON, Prof David Philip; OBE (2004); s of William Farrington (d 1967), of Ormskirk, Lancs, and Gladys Holden, *née* Spurr (d 1980); *b* 7 March 1944; *Educ* Ormskirk GS (state scholar), Clare Coll Cambridge (MA, PhD); *m* 30 July 1966, Sally, da of Frank Chamberlain (d 1977); 3 da (Lucy Clare b 14 April 1970, Katie Ruth b 28 March 1972, Alice Charlotte b 21 Feb 1975); *Career* research student Univ of Cambridge Psychological Lab 1966–69; Inst of Criminology Univ of Cambridge: research offr 1969–70, sr research offr 1970–74, asst dir of research 1974–76, lectr in criminology 1976–88, reader in psychological criminology 1988–92, prof of psychological criminology 1992–2012 (emeritus prof 2012–); visiting prof Dept of Sociology Univ of Akron 1977, visiting research worker Miny of the Solicitor Gen Ottawa 1978–79, visiting fell US Nat Inst of Justice Washington 1981, visiting scholar Nat Centre for Juvenile Justice Pittsburgh 1986, visiting fell US Bureau of Justice Statistics Washington 1995–98; memb Parole Bd for England and Wales 1984–87; memb Advsy Bd: Nat Archive of Criminal Justice Data USA 1983–93, Nat Juvenile Court Data Archive USA 1987–2000, UK Nat Prog on Forensic Mental Health 1999–2003 (chair 2000–03); memb Scientific Advsy Gp Nat Acad for Parenting Practitioners 2008–12, memb Evidence Panel Early Intervention Fndn 2013–15; co-chair: US Office of Juvenile Justice and Delinquency Prevention Study Gp on Serious and Violent Juvenile Offenders 1995–97, UK Dept of Health (High Security Psychiatric Servs Commissioning Bd) Network on Primary Prevention of Adult Antisocial Behaviour 1997, US Office of Juvenile Justice and Delinquency Prevention Study Gp on Very Young Offenders 1998–2000, US Centre for Disease Control Expert Panel on Protective Factors Against Youth Violence 2007–12, US Nat Inst of Justice Study Gp on Transitions from Juvenile Delinquency to Adult Crime 2008–11; Nat Acad of Sciences: memb Ctee on Law and Justice 1986–93, vice-chair Panel on Violence 1989–92; Br Psychological Soc: memb 1974, hon life memb Div of Forensic Psychology (chm 1983–85), memb Scientific Affairs Bd 1977–78, memb Professional Affairs Bd 1983–85, memb Cncl 1983–85, chair Bd of Examiners in Forensic Psychology 2000–03, Sr Prize 2007; Br Soc of Criminology: memb 1975, memb Organising Ctee 1978 and 1980–83, memb Cncl 1990–93, pres 1990–93, hon life memb 1996; American Soc of Criminology: fell 1983, Sellin-Glueck Award for int contribs to criminology 1984, memb Awards Ctee 1988–89, 1991–92 and 1993–94, memb Fells Ctee 1992–93, pres 1998–99, chair Nominations Ctee 2001–02, Sutherland Award for outstanding contribs to criminology 2002, chair Sellin-Glueck Award Ctee 2002–03, Inaugural Jerry Lee Award American Soc of Criminology Div of Experimental Criminology for Life-time Achievements in Experimental Criminology 2010, chair Div of Developmental and Life-Course Criminology 2012–16; memb Bd of Dirs Int Soc of Criminology 2000–08; Euro Assoc of Psychology and Law: memb 1991–, memb Exec Bd 1991–, pres 1997–99; memb Scientific Ctee Netherlands Inst for Study of Criminality and Law Enforcement 1995–99; pres Acad of Experimental Criminology 2001–03; Joan McCord Award Acad of Experimental Criminology 2005, Beccaria Gold Medal Criminology Soc of German-Speaking Countries 2005, European Assoc of Psychology and Law Award for Outstanding Career-Long Contributions to the Scientific Study of Law and Human Behaviour 2009, Robert Boruch Award of the Campbell Collaboration for Contributions to Research that Informs Public Policy 2012, Stockholm Prize in Criminology 2013, Freda Adler Distinguished Scholar Award Div of Int Criminology American Soc of Criminology 2013, Juvenile Justice Without Borders Int Award Int Juvenile Justice Observatory Brussels Belgium 2014, August Vollmer Award for outstanding contributions to justice or to the treatment or prevention of criminal or delinquent behaviour American Soc of Criminology 2014; Hon ScD Trinity Coll Dublin 2008; FBPsS, CPsychol, FBA 1997, FMedSci 2000, hon fell Br Psychological Soc 2012; *Books* Who Becomes Delinquent? (co-author, 1973), The Delinquent Way of Life (co-author, 1977), Behaviour Modification with Offenders: A Criminological Symposium (co-ed, 1979), Psychology, Law and Legal Processes (co-ed, 1979), Abnormal Offenders, Delinquency and the Criminal Justice System (co-ed, 1982), Aggression and Dangerousness (co-ed, 1985), Reactions to Crime: The Public, The Police, Courts, and Prisons (co-ed, 1985), Prediction in Criminology (co-ed, 1985), Understanding and Controlling Crime: Toward a New Research Strategy (co-author, 1986, Prize for Distinguished Scholarship Criminology Section American Sociological Assoc 1988), Human Development and Criminal Behaviour: New Ways of Advancing Knowledge (co-author, 1991), Offenders and Victims: Theory and Policy (co-ed, 1992), Integrating Individual and Ecological Aspects of Crime (co-ed, 1993), Psychological Explanations of Crime (ed, 1994), Building a Safer Society: Strategic Approaches to Crime Prevention (co-ed, 1995), Biosocial Bases of Violence (co-ed, 1997), Serious and Violent Juvenile Offenders: Risk Factors and Successful Interventions (co-ed, 1998), Antisocial Behaviour and Mental Health Problems: Explanatory Factors in Childhood and Adolescence (co-author, 1998), Evaluating Criminology and Criminal Justice (co-author, 1998), Costs and Benefits of Preventing Crime (co-ed, 2001), Child Delinquents (co-ed, 2001), Sex and Violence (co-ed, 2001), Offender Rehabilitation in Practice (co-ed, 2001), Evidence-Based Crime Prevention (co-ed, 2002), Early Prevention of Adult Antisocial Behaviour (co-ed, 2003), Integrated Developmental and Life-Course Theories of Offending (ed, 2005), Crime and Punishment in Western Countries (co-ed, 2005), Reducing Crime: The Effectiveness of Criminal Justice Interventions (co-ed, 2006), Preventing Crime: What Works for Children, Offenders, Victims and Places (co-ed, 2006), Key Issues in Criminal Career Research (co-author, 2007), Saving Children from a Life of Crime (co-author, 2007), Violence and Serious Theft (co-author, 2008), Dictionary of Forensic Psychology (co-ed, 2008), Making Public Places Safer (co-author, 2009), Young Homicide Offenders and Victims (co-author, 2011), Explaining Criminal Careers (co-author, 2012), Scholarly Influence in Criminology and Criminal Justice (co-author, 2012), Young Adult Offenders (co-ed, 2012), From Juvenile Delinquency to Adult Crime (co-ed, 2012), The Oxford Handbook of Crime Prevention (co-ed, 2012), Offending from Childhood to Late Middle Age (co-author, 2013), Most-Cited Scholars in Criminology and Criminal Justice 1986–2010 (co-author, 2014), Labelling Theory: Empirical Tests (co-author, 2014), Effects of Parental Incarceration on Children (co-author, 2014), Criminal Recidivism: Explanation, Prediction and Prevention (co-author, 2016); *Style—* Prof David P Farrington, OBE, FBA, FMedSci; ✉ Institute of Criminology, Sidgwick Avenue, Cambridge CB3 9DA (☎ 01223 335360, fax 01223 335356)

FARRON, Tim; MP; *b* 27 May 1970; *Educ* Runshaw Tertiary Coll, Univ of Newcastle; *Career* sr mangr St Martin's Coll Ambleside, Lancaster and Carlisle; cnclr (Lib Dem): S Ribble BC 1995–99, S Lakeland DC 2004–; MP (Lib Dem) Westmoreland and Lonsdale 2005– (Parly candidate (Lib Dem) Westmorland and Lonsdale 2001); *Style—* Tim Farron, Esq, MP; ✉ House of Commons, London SW1A 0AA

FARROW, Gary; OBE (2011); s of Leslie Bertram Farrow, and Evelyn Joyce, *née* Young; *b* 25 August 1955, Orpington, Kent; *Educ* Walsingham Sch for Boys, St Martin's Sch of Art London; *m* 4 July 2002, Jane Moore, qv; 3 da (Lauren, Ellie, Grace); *Career* shop asst One Stop Records 1973, runner Rocket Records 1974, worked with record prodr Mickie Most and Rod Stewart EMI Records 1976, Chinnichap (with Nicky Chinn and Mike Chapman) 1978, estab Gary Farrow Enterprises Media Mgmnt 1980 (worked with artists incl Elton John, Wham!, George Michael, David Bowie, Paul Young, Blondie, Duran Duran, Frankie Goes to Hollywood, Bob Geldof and Heaven 17, and managed Jonathan Ross and Paula Yates), vice-pres communications Sony Music Entertainment 1995–2004 (worked with artists incl Michael Jackson, Bruce Springsteen and Jamiroquai), estab The Corporation Gp 2005 (clients incl Sir Elton John, Sharon Osbourne, Gordon Ramsay, Jeremy Clarkson, Kelly Osbourne, Michael McIntyre, Jack Dee, Alan Carr, Lloyd Grossman, Matt Lucas, Jimmy Carr, Ozzy Osbourne and Jonathan Ross); patron: Elton John Aids Fndn, Music Therapy Nordoff-Robbins; dep chm Music Industry Tst (MITS); Music Therapy Award for Outstanding Achievement 2006, Scott Piering Media Award 2006, PR Week Most Powerful PR in Entertainment; fell Radio Acad; *Recreations* football, boxing, movies, music, art, reading, photography, cooking, cricket; *Clubs* Soho House, Groucho; *Style*— Gary Farrow, Esq, OBE

FARROW, Nigel Alexander Emery; s of Arthur Hemsworth Farrow, of Bentley, Hants, and Estelle Frances, *née* Emery; *b* 24 March 1939; *Educ* Cheltenham Coll, Queens' Coll Cambridge (MA); *m* 2 Dec 1961, Susan, da of Thomas Bertram Daltry (d 1974); 3 da (Miranda b 1965, Sarah b 1967, Imogen b 1970); *Career* publisher; ed Business Mgmnt 1964–67; chm: Xerox Publishing Group Ltd 1972–82, Ginn & Co Ltd 1972–78, University Microfilms Ltd 1972–82, Information Publications International Ltd 1982–99, Scolar Fine Art Ltd; dir and chm: Ashgate Publishing Ltd, Dartmouth Publishing Co Ltd, Gower Publishing Co Ltd 1982–2015, Lund Humphries Ltd, CDY Ltd; pres: Cheltonian Soc 1988–91, Cncl Cheltenham Coll 1992–96; chm of tstees The Estelle Tst; Hon DBA, Hon DLitt; FRSA; *Books* Gower Handbook of Management (ed), The English Library (ed); *Recreations* enjoying and supporting the arts, collecting 20th century British paintings; *Style*— Nigel Farrow, Esq; ✉ Dippenhall Gate, Dippenhall, Farnham, Surrey GU10 5DP

FARRY, Dr Stephen Anthony; MLA; s of Vincent Farry, of Bangor, and Margaret, *née* Greer; *b* 22 April 1971, Newtownards, Co Down; *Educ* Our Lady and St Patrick's Coll Belfast, Queen's Univ Belfast (BSocSc, PhD); *m* 25 July 2005, Wendy, *née* Watt; *Career* tutor Queen's Univ Belfast 1992–95, self-employed research conslt 1996–99; Alliance Pty: pty organiser 1997–2000, policy offr 2000, gen sec 2000–07 (leave of absence as sr fell US Inst of Peace 2005–06); MLA (Alliance) N Down 2007– (Assembly candidate 1998 and 2003), min for employment and learning 2011–; cncllr N Down BC 1993–, mayor N Down 2007–08 (dep mayor 2002–03); memb NI Community Rels Cncl 2007–; non-exec dir N Down Development Organisation Ltd 1996–2005, co sec Lagan Properties (1970) Ltd 2000–, non-exec dir Bangor and Holywood Town Centre Mgmnt Ltd 2001–; memb N Down Dist Police Partnership 2003–05, trainer/conslt Nat Democratic Inst for Int Affairs, author of articles in several jls, newspapers and magazines; *Recreations* quizzes, football, cricket, snooker, reading, travel, international affairs; *Style*— Dr Stephen Farry, MLA; ✉ Northern Ireland Assembly, Parliament Buildings, Stormont Estate, Belfast BT4 3XX (☎ 07775 687152, e-mail stephen.farry@allianceparty.org)

FARTHING, Ramon; s of Clifford Ramon George Farthing (d 1983), and Patricia Carter, of Harwich, Essex; *b* 9 February 1961; *Educ* Sir Anthony Deane Secdy Sch, Colchester Inst of HE; *m* Karen Elaine, da of John Arundel; 1 s (Kai Ramon b 6 Dec 1990), 1 da (Leila Patricia b 20 June 1995); *Career* apprentice under Chris Oakley at The Pier Restaurant 1978–80, commis chef under Sam Chalmers at Le Talbooth Restaurant Dedham 1980–83, personal chef to Earl and Countess Spencer Althorp House 1983–84, second chef to Chris Oakes The Castle Hotel Taunton 1984–86, first head chef Calcot Manor 1986–92 (Michelin Star Rating 1986–92, 1 AA Rosette for cooking 1987 rising to 3 AA Rosettes 1992, Akermann Guide Clover Leaf 1990–91, Catey Function Menu of the Year 1991), head chef and mgr Harveys Restaurant Bristol 1994–96 (head chef 1992–96) (3 AA Rosettes, Ackermann Guide Clover Leaf, County Restaurant of the Year, 1 Michelin star 1994), currently chef/patron 36 The Quay Emsworth (1 Michelin Star 1997, 3 AA Rosettes); rep chef of Br Food Festival Mandarin Hotel Jakarta Indonesia 1989; entries in Egon Ronay and The Good Food Guide; *Books* Great Fish Book (contrib), Great Pasta Book (contrib); *Recreations* music, reading cookery books; *Clubs* Caterer Acorn; *Style*— Ramon Farthing, Esq

FARTHING, Stephen Frederick Godfrey; s of Dennis Jack Farthing (d 1985), of London, and Joan Margaret, *née* Godfrey (d 2006); *b* 16 September 1950; *Educ* St Martin's Sch of Art, Royal Coll of Art, Br Sch Rome (Abbey Major scholar); *m* 1 (m dis 2005), Joan Elizabeth, *née* Jackson; 1 da (Constance Beatrice); m 2, 2010, Ami Abou-Bakr; 1 s (Jackson Joseph); *Career* lectr in painting Canterbury Coll of Art 1977–79, tutor in painting Royal Coll of Art 1979–85, head Dept of Fine Art W Surrey Coll of Art and Design Farnham 1987–88 (head of painting 1985–87), artist in residence Hayward Gallery 1989; elected Ruskin master and professorial fell St Edmund Hall Oxford, exec dir NY Acad of Art 2000–04, Rootstein Hopkins prof of drawing Univ of the Arts London 2004–; tstee Br Sch at Rome 2002–; RA 1998 (hon curator RA collections 1999, chm Exhibitions Ctee 2013–); *Selected One Man Exhibitions* Town and Country (Edward Totah Gallery London) 1986, Mute Accomplices (MOMA Oxford (touring)) 1988, Stephen Farthing and the Leonardo Exhibition (Queen Elizabeth Hall London) 1989, Stephen Farthing at the Paco Imperial Rio De Janeiro, National Museum of Art Montevideo Uruguay, Museo de Monterray Mexico 1990, Museo de Gil Mexico 1990, The Knowledge (Nat MOMAt Kyoto) 1993, The Knowledge SE1 (The Cut Gallery London) 1995, Absolute Monarchy (Anne Berthoud Gallery London) 1996, L'Alchemie du portrait (Hôtel de la Monnaie Paris) 1997, Stephen Farthing Paintings 2000–2003 (Amagansett Applied Arts NY) 2003, The Back Story (Royal Acad of Arts) 2010; *Group Exhibitions* Now for the Future (Hayward Gallery London) 1990, RA Summer Exhibition 1995–2013; *Work in Collections* Leicester City Museum, Nat Museum of Wales, Bradford Art Galleries and Museums, Government Art Collection Fund, Br Cncl, Nat Portrait Gallery; *Publications* An Intelligent Person's Guide to Modern Art (2000), 1001 Paintings You Should See Before You Die (2006), 501 Great Artists (2008), Art: the whole story (2011), The Sketch Books of Derek Jarman (2013); *Style*— Stephen Farthing, Esq; ✉ The Royal Academy of Arts, Burlington House, Piccadilly, London W1J 0BD (☎ 020 7300 8000)

FARWELL, Prof Ruth; CBE (2015); *b* 22 February 1954; *Educ* PhD, BSc; *m* 10 April 2001, Dr Martin Daniels; *Career* St Mary's UC: lectr in maths 1982–86, head Dept of Maths 1986–90; Univ of Brighton: dir of studies 1990–93, head of strategic planning 1994–98; pro vice-chllr London South Bank Univ 1998–2006, vice-chllr and chief exec Bucks New Univ 2006–; memb Bd: HEFCE 2009–, Bucks Business First 2011–, Bucks Thames Valley Local Enterprise Partnership 2012–, Bucks Univ Technical Coll 2012–, Aylesbury Coll 2012–, Bucks Educn Skills and Trg 2012–; chair GuildHE 2009–13; hon degree Univ of Kent 2010; *Recreations* gardening, beekeeping; *Style*— Prof Ruth Farwell, CBE; ✉ Buckinghamshire New University, High Wycombe Campus, Queen Alexandra Road, High Wycombe, Buckinghamshire HP11 2JZ

FARZANEH, Prof Farzin; *b* 19 August 1953, Teheran, Iran; *Educ* Univ of Aberdeen (BSc, MSc), Univ of Sussex (SERC studentship, DPhil); *m* Lindsay Claire, *née* Stockley; 1 da (Leili Claire b 5 July 1987), 1 s (Benjamin Bijan b 18 Dec 1993); *Career* Beit meml fell Univ of Sussex 1979–82, EMBO fell Univ of Amsterdam 1982–83, MRC fell Univ of Sussex 1983–84; KCL: 'new blood' lectr Dept of Obstetrics and Gynaecology 1985–87, sr lectr Molecular Genetics Unit Dept of Obstetrics and Gynaecology 1987–90, dir Molecular Med Unit 1990–93, head Dept of Molecular Med 1993–, awarded personal chair in Molecular Med 1996; jt holder of patents on the prevention of retroviral infection and devpt of vectors for gene therapy; recognised teacher Univ of London; co-fndr and pres Int Soc for Cell and Gene Therapy of Cancer 2007–08; European ed Experimental Biology and Medicine; memb Editorial Bd: Cancer Gene Therapy, Gene Therapy, Cancer Immunology Immunotherapy; elected memb Cncl US Soc for Experimental Biology and Med 2015–; SEBM Distinguished Scientist Award 2016; FRCPath, FRSA 1997, FRSB 2011; *Publications* author of numerous original res papers in peer reviewed jls and of review articles and conf proceedings, also author of published books; *Recreations* badminton; *Style*— Prof Farzin Farzaneh; ✉ King's College London, Department of Haematological Medicine, 123 Cold Harbour Lane, London SE5 9NU (☎ and fax 020 7848 5902, e-mail farzin.farzaneh@kcl.ac.uk)

FAULKNER, Amanda Jane; da of Richard George Butler Faulkner (d 1976), and Gillian Mary Josephine Hopkinson, *née* Park; *b* 5 December 1953; *Educ* St Anthony's Leweston, Canford Sch, Bournemouth Coll of Art, Ravensbourne Coll of Art, Chelsea Sch of Art; 1 s (Joseph b 21 March 1993); *Career* artist; Sch of Fine Art Chelsea Coll of Art and Design London: princ lectr in printmaking 1991–93, sr lectr in fine art 1993–; work in various public collections, selector for various awards; *Solo Exhibitions* incl: Woodlands Art Gallery Blackheath London 1983, Angela Flowers Gallery 1985–86, Big Women (Metropole Arts Centre Folkestone) 1987, Seven Deadly Sins and Recent Drawings and Prints (Flowers East London) 1988, Breaking Water (Drumcroon Arts and Educn Centre Wigan) 1989, Flowers East London 1990 and 1992, Amanda Faulkner – Recent Drawings (Manchester City Art Galleries) 1992, Amanda Faulkner – Mares' Tails Flowers East at London Fields, London 1995, Plymouth Arts Centre 1996, Amanda Faulkner – Small Mysteries (Abbot Hall Art Gallery and Museum Kendal) 1998, Amanda Faulkner – Small Mysteries (Flowers East London) 1999, Amanda Faulkner (Flowers East London) 2001, Amanda Faulkner: New Work (Flowers East London) 2002; *Group Exhibitions* incl: The Print Show (Angela Flowers Gallery London) 1983; What's New in the Arts Council Collection (touring) 1984, Double Elephant (Concourse Gallery Barbican London) 1985, The Print Show – Woodcuts and Linocuts (Angela Flowers Gallery London) 1985, Identity/Desire – Representing the Body (Scot Arts Cncl touring) 1986, Print Biennale of Liège (Musée d'Art Moderne Belgium) 1987, Mother and Child (Lefevre Gallery London) 1988, Excavations (Galerie Hubert Winter Vienna and John Hansard Gallery Southampton) 1988, New Contemporary British Painting (The Contemporary Arts Centre Cincinnati Ohio and touring) 1988, Ljubljana Print Biennale (Yugoslavia) 1989, Barbican Concourse Gallery London 1989, Angela Flowers Gallery 1990, Flowers at Moos (Gallery Moos NY) 1990, Inaugural Exhibition (Cannon Cole Gallery Chicago) 1991, European Large Formant Printmaking (Guinness Hopstore Dublin) 1991, Postmodern Prints (V&A) 1991, Images of Hope and Disquiet – Expressionism in Britain in the Nineties (Castlefield Gallery Manchester) 1992, Myth, Dream and fable (Angel Row Gallery Nottingham) 1992, New MonoPrints Amanda Faulkner and Alison Watt (Flowers East London) 1996, From the Interior (Ferens Art Gallery, Stanley Picker Gallery, Kingston Univ, Oldham Art Gallery, Univ of Brighton, Hot Bath Gallery) 1997 and also Aberystwyth Arts Centre 1998, The Body Politic (Wolverhampton Art Gallery, Derby Art Gallery) 1997, Works of Artifice: Make-Up Uncovered (Grundy Art Gallery Blackpool) 2000 and (Williamson Gallery Birkenhead) 2001, Spiritus Mundi (Flowers East London) 2004, Drawing Inspiration (Abbot Hall Museum and Gallery Kendal) 2005, After Hiroshima: Nuclear Imaginaries (Brunei Gallery SOAS and Millais Gallery Southampton Inst) 2005; *Style*— Ms Amanda Faulkner; ✉ c/o Flowers East, 82 Kingsland Road, London E2 8DP (☎ 020 7920 7777, fax 020 7920 7770)

FAULKNER, David Edwart Riley; CB (1985); s of Harold Ewart Faulkner (d 1968), and Mabel, *née* Riley (d 1960); *b* 23 October 1934; *Educ* Manchester Grammar, Merchant Taylors', St John's Coll Oxford (MA); *m* 16 Sept 1961, Sheila Jean, da of James Stevenson (d 1985), of Bucks; 1 s (Martin b 1962), 1 da (Rosemary b 1965); *Career* Nat Serv RA and Intelligence Corps, 2 Lt 1957–59; Home Office: asst princ 1959, princ 1963, asst sec 1969, private sec to the Home Sec 1969, Prison Dept 1970, Police Dept 1975, asst under sec of state 1976, seconded to the Cabinet Office 1978–79, dir of operational policy Prison Dept 1980, dep under sec of state Criminal and Res and Statistical Depts 1982, princ establishment offr 1990–92; fell St John's Coll Oxford 1992–99, sr res assoc Centre for Criminological Res Univ of Oxford 1992–; memb: UN Ctee on Crime Prevention and Control 1984–91, Advsy Bd of Helsinki Inst for Crime Prevention and Control 1984–92; chm Howard League for Penal Reform 1999–2002, tstee Gilbert Murray Tst, tstee Thames Valley Partnership; *Books* Crime, State and Citizen: A Field Full of Folk (2001, 2 edn 2006), Where Next for Criminal Justice? (jtly, 2011), Servant of the Crown: A civil servant's story of criminal justice and public service reform (2014); *Style*— David Faulkner, Esq, CB; ✉ 99 Blacketts Wood Drive, Chorleywood, Rickmansworth, Hertfordshire WD3 5PS (e-mail david.faulkner57@ntlworld.com)

FAULKNER OF WORCESTER, Baron (Life Peer UK 1999), of Wimbledon in the London Borough of Merton; Richard Oliver Faulkner; s of Harold Ewart Faulkner (d 1968), and Mabel, *née* Riley (d 1960); *b* 22 March 1946, Manchester; *Educ* Merchant Taylors', Worcester Coll Oxford (MA); *m* 5 July 1968, Susan, da of Donald James Heyes (d 1978); 2 da (Julia b 1969, Tamsin b 1970); *Career* dep chm Citigate Westminster (formerly Westminster Communications Group) until 1999; communications advsr: Railway Trade Unions 1976–77, Bd BR 1977–98, Littlewoods 1977–2009, Lloyds TSB Group (formerly TSB Group) 1987–99, Interparly Union 1988–90, The Bishop at Lambeth 1990, FSA 1997–2000; acting head of communications SIB 1997; vice-chm Campaign for Better Transport (formerly Transport 2000 Ltd) 1986–99 (vice-pres 2000–); dir Westminster Europe Ltd 1994–99, vice chm Cardiff Millennium Stadium plc 2004–08 (dir 1997–2004); Parly candidate (Lab): Devizes 1970 and Feb 1974, Monmouth Oct 1974, Huddersfield West 1979; departmental liaison peer DETR 2000–01, departmental liaison peer Cabinet Office 2001–05; memb Euro Community Select Ctee Sub-Ctee B 1999–2002; sec Br-Norwegian Parly Gp 2000–09 and 2010–15, (vice-chm 2015–), vice-chm Br-Caribbean Gp 2000–09, treas Railways Parly Gp 2000–09 and 2010–15, co-chm Br Taiwan Gp 2005–09 and 2010–15 (vice-chm 2001–05), sec Br-Argentine Parly Gp 2001–09 and 2010–15 (vice-chm 2015–), jt treas Br-Danish Parly Gp 2001–09, jt treas Br-Swedish Parly Gp 2001–09, chm War Heritage Parly Gp 2002–09 and 2010–15 (jt chm 2015–), memb Jt Scrutiny Ctee Draft Gambling Bill 2003–04, chm All-Parly Inquiry on Betting in Sport 2005–06, chm Sustainable Aviation Gp 2004–09, a Lord in Waiting House of Lords 2009–10 (dep chm Ctees 2007–09, dep speaker 2009 and 2010–), chm Opposed Private Bill Ctee on London Local Authorities and Transport for London Bill 2009, memb Sub-Ctee F EU Select Ctee 2009–10, memb Select Ctee on Olympic Legacy 2013, HM's Govt trade envoy to Taiwan 2016–; memb Merton Borough Cncl 1971–78, communications advsr to oppn ldr and Lab Pty gen elections 1987 and 1992 (memb John Prescott's campaign team at 1997 gen election), co fndr Parly jl The House Magazine (memb Editorial Bd 2003–); Football Tst: fndr tstee 1979–83, sec 1983–86, dep chm 1986–90, first dep chm 1990–98; chm: Women's FA 1988–91, Sports Grounds Initiative 1995–2000; vice-chm Football Task Force 1997–99; vice-pres Level Playing Field (formerly Nat Assoc of Disabled Supporters) 2007–09 and 2011–, Football Conference 2007–09 and 2010–; dir Football Assoc of Wales 2007–09; memb: Sports Cncl 1986–88, Fndn for Sport and the Arts 2000–12; tstee Nat Football Museum 2007–09 and 2010–; chm Worcester Coll Oxford UK Appeal 1996–2003, memb Ct Univ of Beds 1999–2009, pres Worcester Coll Soc 2013–;

patron Roy Castle Fndn 1999– (tstee 2003–07), pres Royal Soc for the Prevention of Accidents 2001–04 (vice-pres 2004–), chm Railway Heritage Committee 2004–09 (memb 2002–04), tstee Gamcare 2005–09, tstee Science Museum 2007–09 and 2011– (dep chm 2015–), pres Cotswold Line Promotion Gp 2007–09 and 2010–, pres Heritage Railway Assoc 2011–, chm SMG Railway Heritage Designation Advsy Bd 2013–, chm Alderney Gambling Control Cmmn 2014– (cmmr 2013–), chm Worcester Live 2014– (dir 2011–); tstee ASH 2007–09, vice-pres Old Merchant Taylors' Soc (pres 2011–12); Friendship Medal of Diplomacy Min of Foreign Affairs Rep of China (Taiwan) 2004; hon fell Worcester Coll Oxford 2002, fell Univ of Worcester 2008; Hon Dr of Laws Univ of Beds 2003; Order of the Brilliant Star with Grand Cordon Repub of China (Taiwan) 2008; *Publications* Holding the Line – How Britain's Railways Were Saved (2012, winner Popular Transport Book of the Year Award Railway & Canal Historical Soc), Disconnected! Broken Links in Britain's Rail Policy (2015); *Recreations* collecting Lloyd George memorabilia, tinplate trains, watching association football, travelling by railway; *Style—* The Rt Hon the Lord Faulkner of Worcester; ✉ House of Lords, London SW1A 0PW (☎ 020 7219 8503, fax 020 7219 1460, e-mail faulknerro@parliament.uk, website www.lordfaulkner.net)

FAULKS, Baron (Life Peer UK 2010), of Donnington in the Royal County of Berkshire; Edward Peter Lawless Faulks; QC (1996); s of His Hon Peter Faulks, MC (d 1998), and Pamela, *née* Lawless (d 2003); bro of Sebastian Charles Faulks, CBE, FRSL, *qv*; *b* 19 August 1950; *Educ* Wellington, Jesus Coll Oxford (MA); *m* 1990, Catherine Frances Turner; 2 s (Leo Alexander Lawless b 8 Aug 1992, Archie Dominic b 11 Nov 1994); *Career* called to the Bar Middle Temple 1973; recorder of the Crown Court 2000–06, special advsr to DCA 2005–06, min of state Miny of Justice 2014–; chm Professional Negligence Bar Assoc 2002–04; cmmr Cmmn on a Bill of Rights 2012–13; hon fell Jesus Coll Oxford; FCIArb; *Publications* Local Authority Liability (contributing ed 1–5 edns); *Recreations* sports, the Arts; *Clubs* Garrick; *Style—* The Lord Faulks; ✉ 33 Ladbroke Grove, London W11 3AY; 1 Chancery Lane, London W2A 1LF (☎ 0845 634 6666, e-mail efaulks@1chancerylane.com)

FAULKS, Sebastian Charles; CBE (2002); s of His Hon Peter Ronald Faulks, MC (d 1998), and Pamela, *née* Lawless (d 2003); bro of Edward Peter Lawless Faulks, QC (The Lord Faulks), *qv*; *b* 20 April 1953; *Educ* Wellington (scholar), Emmanuel Coll Cambridge (exhibitioner, MA); *m* 1989, Veronica, *née* Youlten; 2 s (William b 1990, Arthur b 1996), 1 da (Holly b 1992); *Career* writer; ed New Fiction Soc 1978–81, reporter Daily Telegraph 1978–82, feature writer Sunday Telegraph 1983–86, literary ed The Independent 1986–89; Independent on Sunday: dep ed 1989–90, assoc ed 1990–91; columnist: The Guardian 1992–98, Evening Standard 1997–99, Mail on Sunday 1999–2000; wrote and presented Churchill's Secret Army (Channel 4) 2000, panelist The Write Stuff (BBC Radio 4) 1998–, Faulks on Fiction (BBC 2) 2011; Author of the Year British Book Awards 1995; Hon DLitt Tavistock Clinic/Univ of E London 2007, Hon DLitt Univ of Herts 2012; hon fell Emmanuel Coll Cambridge 2007; FRSL 1995; *Books* A Trick of the Light (1984), The Girl at the Lion d'Or (1989), A Fool's Alphabet (1992), Birdsong (1993), The Fatal Englishman: Three Short Lives (1996), Charlotte Gray (1998), The Vintage Book of War Stories (ed, 1999), On Green Dolphin Street (2001), Human Traces (2005), Pistache (2006), Engleby (2007), Devil May Care (2008), A Week in December (2009), Faulks on Fiction (2011), A Possible Life (2012), Jeeves and the Wedding Bells (2013); *Recreations* tennis, wine; *Style—* Sebastian Faulks, Esq, CBE, FRSL; ✉ c/o Aitken and Stone, 18–21 Cavaye Place, London SW10 9PT; e-mail scf35@btconnect.com, website www.sebastianfaulks.com

FAULL, Dr Margaret Lindsay; OBE (2009); da of Norman Augustus Faull (d 1956), of Sydney, Aust, and Myra Beryl, *née* Smith (d 2006); *b* 4 April 1946; *Educ* Fort St Girls' HS, Univ of Sydney (BA), Univ of Macquarie (MA), Univ of Sheffield (MA), Univ of Leeds (PhD); *Career* secdy sch teacher NSW Dept of Educn 1970–71, dep co archaeologist W Yorks CC 1984–85 (field archaeologist 1975–84), project mangr Thwaite Mills Industrial Museum 1985–86, dir National Coal Mining Museum for England (formerly Yorkshire Mining Museum) Caphouse Colliery 1986–2015; ed Soc for Landscape Studies 1979–86, chm Yorkshire Cncl for Br Archaeology 1982–84, chm and sec Thwaite Mills Soc 1986–2011, vice-pres Cncl for Br Archaeology 2001–08, chm Soc for Church Archaeology 2005–10; non-exec dir: Wakefield HA 2000–02, Wakefield and Dist Housing 2003–13, Local Care Direct 2005–13, Mid Yorks Hosps NHS Tst 2008–12; chm: Wakefield Dist Med Res Ethics Ctee 2000–06, Leeds Central Med Res Ethics Ctee 2007–13, Network of European Coal Mining Museums 2016–; Hon Dr Univ of Bradford, Hon Dr Univ of Huddersfield; FILAM 1986–2011, FInstD 1990–2015, FRSA 1996, fell Inst of Materials, Minerals and Mining 2009–15 (affiliate 1988); *Books* Domesday Book: Yorkshire Chichester (jt ed, 1986); *Recreations* collecting African carvings, opera, cricket; *Style—* Dr Margaret Faull, OBE; ✉ 39 Eldon Terrace, Leeds Road, Wakefield, West Yorkshire WF1 3JW (☎ 01924 379690)

FAUX, (James) Christopher; s of Dr Francis Reginald Faux (d 1974), of Bolton, Lancs, and Alison Mungo, *née* Park (d 1981); *b* 11 March 1940; *Educ* Fettes, Univ of Liverpool, Univ of Glasgow; *m* 29 July 1967, Patricia Anne Lyon, da of Hugh Lyon Denson (d 1991), of Chester; 1 s (James), 2 da (Rachel, Charlotte); *Career* Liverpool Scottish TA 1960–65; conslt orthopaedic surgn Preston HA 1977–99, conslt orthopaedic surgn Wrightington Hosp Centre for Hip Surgery 1999–2003, lower limb tutor 2003–; memb: Br Hip Soc, Charnley Low Friction Soc, Liverpool Orthopaedic Circle, Sir John Charnley Tst (chm of tstees 1999–), Liverpool Med Inst; Gold Medal BOA Sydney 2004, Charnley Gold Medal 2004; LRCP, FBOA, FRCSGlas 1973, FRCS (ad eundum) 1997; *Publications* After Charnley (ed, 2002), The Closed Treatment of Common Fractures (ed Centenary Edn, 2010); *Recreations* boating, rugby; *Style—* Christopher Faux, Esq; ✉ Foxfield, Alston Lane, Longridge, Preston, Lancashire PR3 3BN (☎ 01772 782333); 7 Moor Park Avenue, Preston, Lancashire PR1 6AS (☎ 07761 238470, e-mail chrisandpattifaux@btinternet.com)

FAWCETT, Dame Amelia Chilcott; DBE (2010, CBE 2002); da of Frederick J Fawcett II (d 2008), and Betsey Chilcott Fawcett (d 2009); *b* 16 September 1956, Boston, Mass; *Educ* Pingree Sch South Hamilton Mass, Wellesley Coll Mass (BA), Univ of Virginia Sch of Law (JD); *Career* called to the Bar NY 1984; Sullivan & Cromwell NY 1983–85 and Paris 1986–87; Morgan Stanley London: joined 1987, vice-pres 1990, exec dir 1992, memb European Mgmnt Ctee 1996–2006, md and chief administrative offr 1996–2002, vice-chm and chief operating offr 2002–06, sr advsr 2006–07; chair Pensions First LLP 2007–10; memb Bd of Dirs: State Street Corp Boston 2006– (chm Risk and Capital Ctee 2010–), Guardian Media Gp 2007–13 (chm 2009–13), Investment AB Kinnevik Stockholm 2011– (dep chm 2013–), Millicom Int Cellular SA Luxembourg 2014–16; cmmr UK-US Fulbright Cmmn 2011; chm Hedge Fund Standards Bd 2011–; memb Ct Bank of England 2004–09 (chm Audit Ctee 2005–09); chm London Int Festival of Theatre 2002–10, memb Cncl Univ of London 2002–08 (chm Audit Ctee 2005–08), tstee Nat Portrait Gallery 2003–11 (dep chm 2005–11), tstee Nat Maritime Museum Cornwall 2004–06; memb Bd: Business in the Community 2005–09, HM Treasy 2012–; govr London Business Sch 2009–, tstee Project HOPE (UK) 2011, pres American Friends of the Nat Portrait Gallery 2011–12, chm of tstees Bd Prince of Wales's Charitable Fndn 2012–; Prince of Wales Ambass Award 2004; Hon DIB American Univ in London 2006; Lady Usher of the Purple Rod (first Lady Usher) 2013; memb: American Bar Assoc 1984, Guild of Int Bankers 2004; *Publications* Pendragon Diaries; *Recreations* fly fishing, hill walking, sailing; *Clubs* Reform, Cradoc Golf, St Mawes Sailing, Manchester Yacht (USA), 5 Hertford Street; *Style—* Dame Amelia Fawcett, DBE; ✉ e-mail amelia@acfawcett.com

FAWCETT, Prof James; s of Edward Fawcett, and Jane Fawcett; *b* 13 March 1950; *Educ* Westminster, Balliol Coll Oxford (BA), St Thomas' Hosp Med Sch London (MB BS); *m* 1979, Prof Kay-Tee Khaw; 1 da (Nicola b 1981), 1 s (Andrew b 1984); *Career* house physician St Thomas' Hosp London and Addenbrooke's Hosp Cambridge 1975–76, SHO St Thomas' Hosp London 1976–77, SHO Northwick Park Hosp 1977–79, scientist Nat Inst for Med Research 1979–82, asst prof Salk Inst La Jolla 1982–86, lectr Dept of Physiology Univ of Cambridge 1986–2001, prof of experimental neurology Univ of Cambridge 2001–, chm Cambridge Centre for Brain Repair 2001–; chm Scientific Ctee Int Spinal Research Tst; FRCP 2000, FMedSci 2003; *Publications* Brain Damage, Brain Repair (with Rosser and Dunnett, 2001); author of other scientific pubns on brain devpt and repair; *Recreations* sailing, bagpiping; *Clubs* Pinstriped Highlanders Pipe Band, Brancaster Staithe Sailing; *Style—* Prof James Fawcett; ✉ Cambridge University Centre for Brain Repair, Robinson Way, Cambridge CB2 2PY (☎ 01223 331160, fax 01223 331174, e-mail jf108@cam.ac.uk)

FAWZI, Ahmad; *Career* lectr Cairo Univ and Inst of Strategic Studies 1968–76; ed and anchor nightly news (Egyptian television), Reuters Television: news ed, reporter, prodr, reg news ops mngr (London, Prague, Cairo and NY); press sec and chef de cabinet for wife of pres of Egypt, Jehan Sedat 1974–84; dep spokesman for sec-gen UNHQ NY 1992–96, dir UNIC 1997–; *Style—* Ahmad Fawzi, Esq

F

FAY, Anthony William (Tony); s of Francis Joseph Fay (d 1970), and Mary Monica, *née* Brennan (d 1986); *b* 24 August 1938; *Educ* Xaverian Coll, Univ of Birmingham (BCom, capt Br Univs Assoc Football, memb Br Olympic Squad Assoc Football); *m* 9 Oct 1963, Dr Mary Patricia Fay, da of Dr John Patrick McGovern; 3 s (Michael John b 26 Sept 1964, Paul Antony b 17 April 1966, Christopher Damian b 9 Jan 1968); *Career* Coopers and Lybrand: articled 1960–63, qualified CA 1963–64; successively mktg mangr, div md Alcan Booth Industries 1965–71, corp vice-pres Europe Data 100 Corp 1972–80, dir and chief exec trading Crest Nicholson plc 1981–88; chm: SPC International 1998–, BSS Gp plc 1999–2003 (non-exec dir 1994–99); non-exec chm: Hugh Fay Ltd 1970–88, Reynolds Med Gp Ltd 1992–2001; non-exec dir Ferraris Gp 2001–08; govr St Columba's Coll 1994–2005; Liveryman Worshipful Co of Spectacle Makers; memb ICA 1963, MInstM 1970; *Recreations* golf, cricket, soccer, skiing, sailing, reading, theatre, travel; *Clubs* Ashridge Golf (capt 1992, pres 2007–10), Royal Thames Yacht, MCC, Middlesex Wanderers AFC (chm); *Style—* Tony Fay, Esq; ✉ Gatesdene House, Little Gaddesden, Hertfordshire HP4 1PB (☎ 01442 842585)

FAY, Dr Christopher Ernest; CBE (1999); *b* 4 April 1945; *Educ* Univ of Leeds (BSc, PhD); *m* 1971, Jennifer; 2 da, 1 s; *Career* Royal Dutch/Shell Group: joined 1970, various appts in Holland, Nigeria, Malaysia and Scandinavia 1971–78, devpt mangr Dansk Undergrunds Consortium Copenhagen 1978–81, tech mangr Norske Shell Exploration and Prodn Stavanger 1981–84, dir of exploration and prodn Norway 1984–86, gen mangr and chief exec Shell cos in Turkey 1986–89, md Shell UK Exploration and Prodn and an md Shell UK Ltd 1989–93, chm and chief exec Shell UK Ltd 1993–98; non-exec chm: STENA Int 1999–, EXPRO Int Gp 1999–2008, Tuscan Energy Gp 2002–05, Brightside plc 2008–; non-exec chm Iofina plc 2008–; non-exec dir: BAA plc 1998–2006, Anglo-American plc 1999–2010, The Weir Gp 2001–03, Conister Financial Gp 2006–08; chm Advsy Ctee on Business and the Environment 1999–2003; pres UK Offshore Operators' Assoc 1992; CEng 1974, FRSE 1996, FREng 1996, Hon FICE 1998 (MICE 1973, FICE 1994), FEI (FInstPet 1994); *Recreations* gardening, golf, travel; *Clubs* Sunningdale Golf, Bramley Golf; *Style—* Dr Chris Fay, CBE, FRSE, FREng; ✉ Merrifield, Links Road, Bramley, Guildford, Surrey GU5 0AL (☎ 01483 893112, fax 01483 894421)

FAY, Margaret; CBE (2010, OBE 2004); da of Oswald Allen (d 1993), and Joan, *née* Davis; *b* 21 May 1949; *Educ* South Shields GS for Girls; *m* 1, 1968 (m dis 1978), Matthew Stoker; 1 s (Graeme b 1972); m 2, 1982 (m dis 1993), Peter Fay; partner, David; *Career* Tyne Tees Television: joined as accounts clerk 1981, house services mangr properties and facilities 1984, TV prodn servs mangr 1986, controller of ops 1988, dir of ops 1995–97, md and gen mangr 1997–2003; chm One NorthEast 2003–12; dir Newcastle Gateshead Initiative 1999–; non-exec dir Darlington Building Soc 2000–; govr Teesside Univ 1998–; *Recreations* entertaining advertisers at local premier league football grounds; *Style—* Mrs Margaret Fay, CBE

FAY, Stephen Francis John; s of Gerard Fay (d 1968), and Alice, *née* Bentley (d 1969); *b* 14 August 1938; *Educ* Highgate Sch, Univ of New Brunswick Canada (BA, MA), LSE; *m* 1964, Prudence, da of Alan Butcher; 1 s (Matthew b 1967), 1 da (Susanna b 1969); *Career* journalist with: Glasgow Herald 1961–64, Sunday Times 1964–84, Independent on Sunday 1989–91; ed Business Magazine 1986–89, dep ed Independent on Sunday 1996–98, arts and cricket correspondent 1998–2012, ed Wisden Cricket Monthly 2001–05; winner of Special Award Br Press Awards 1987 and 1989; *Publications* The Great Silver Bubble (1982), The Ring (1984), Portrait of an Old Lady (1986), Powerplay, The Life and Times of Peter Hall (1995), The Collapse of Barings (1996); *Recreations* attending plays, watching cricket, drinking wine; *Clubs* Garrick, MCC; *Style—* Stephen Fay, Esq; ✉ 5A Furlong Road, London N7 8LS (☎ 020 7607 8950, e-mail stephen@sandpfay.co.uk)

FAYLE, Michael John; s of late D W Fayle, of the Isle of Man; *b* 22 November 1953; *Educ* Wade Deacon GS Widnes, Douglas HS for Boys; *m* 1975, Vivien; 1 s (Thomas Edward b 1993); *Career* articled clerk to J G Fargher of B Sugden & Co Chartered Accts IOM 1972–77; ptnr: J G Fargher & Co 1982–86, KPMG 1986–; chm IOM Soc of Chartered Accountants 1991; chm Friends of Manx Nat Heritage 2004–, chm Br Assoc of Friend of Museums 2011–; FCA 1983 (ACA 1977); *Recreations* collecting, gardening, fishing, running, skiing; *Style—* Michael J Fayle, Esq; ✉ Ballaqueeney Lodge, Ballaquayle Road, Douglas, Isle of Man IM2 5DD (☎ 01624 675725); KPMG LLC, Heritage Court, 41 Athol Street, Douglas, Isle of Man IM1 1LA (☎ 01624 681043, fax 01624 681098, e-mail mfayle@kpmg.co.im)

FAZAN, Claire; *Educ* LSE (LLB); *Career* slr specialising in clinical negligence litigation; ptnr: Bindman & Partners 1989–2003 (latterly head of clinical and personal injury), Irwin Mitchell 2003–07, Leigh Day & Co 2007–; memb Law Soc 1985 (memb Clinical Negligence Panel); *Publications* Medical Negligence Litigation, A Practitioner's Guide (co-author); *Style—* Ms Claire Fazan; ✉ Leigh Day & Co Solicitors, 25 St John's Lane, London EC1M 4LB (☎ 020 7650 1200)

FEAN, Sir (Thomas) Vincent; KCVO; *b* 20 November 1952, Burnley, Lancs; *Educ* St Theodore's RC Secdy Sch Burnley, Univ of Sheffield; *m* 1978, Anne Marie, *née* Stewart; 2 da (Catherine b 1979, Louise b 1981), 1 s (Dominic b 1983); *Career* diplomat; entered HM Dip Serv 1975, Arabic language trg 1977–78, 3 sec Baghdad 1978, posted Gaborone 1979, 2 then 1 sec Damascus 1979, 1 sec UKREP Brussels 1985–89, 1 sec FCO 1990–92, cnsllr Paris 1992–96, FCO 1996–99, dir Asia Pacific Trade Partners UK 1999–2002, high cmmr to Malta 2002–06, ambass to Libya 2006–10, consul gen to Jerusalem 2010–; *Style—* Sir Vincent Fean, KCVO; ✉ c/o FCO, King Charles Street, London SW1A 2AH (☎ 00218 21 740 7644, e-mail vincent.fean@fco.gov.uk)

FEAR, Kevin; s of Derek Fear (d 2006), and Gwen, *née* Roddy; *b* 12 June 1963, Watford; *Educ* Douai Sch Berks, Univ of Southhampton (BA), Univ of Nottingham (PGCE); *m* 1986, Denise, *née* Wilson; 1 da (Emma b 3 Feb 1999), 1 s (Adam b 6 Feb 2001); *Career* teacher and head of history King's Sch Chester 1986–2000; Nottingham HS: dep headmaster 2000–07, headmaster 2007–; *Recreations* following fortunes of Arsenal FC;

Clubs East India, Lansdowne; *Style*— Kevin Fear, Esq; ✉ Nottingham High School, Waverley Mount, Nottingham NG7 4ED (☎ 0115 978 6056, e-mail fear.kd@ nottinghamhigh.co.uk, Twitter @kevinfear)

FEARN, Baron (Life Peer UK 2001), of Southport in the County of Merseyside; Ronald Cyril (Ronnie) Fearn; OBE (1985); s of James Fearn (d 1972), of Southport, and Martha Ellen, *née* Hodge (d 1995); *b* 6 February 1931; *Educ* King George V GS Southport; *m* 11 June 1955, Joyce Edna, da of John Dugan (d 1945), of Southport; 1 s (Hon Susan Lynn b 1959), 1 s (Hon Martin John b 1962); *Career* Nat Serv RN; bank official Royal Bank of Scotland plc 1947–87; MP (Lib Dem) Southport 1987–92 and 1997–2001; Lib Dem spokesman: on health and tourism 1988–89, on local govt, tport and tourism 1989–92, on tourism 1997–2001; cncllr Sefton MBC 1974–2016; FCIB; *Recreations* badminton, sport, athletics, drama, politics; *Style*— The Lord Fearn of Southport, OBE, FCIB

FEARNLEY, Prof Stella Marie; *Educ* Astley GS, Univ of Leeds (BA); *Career* Price Waterhouse 1970–73, Grant Thornton 1973–86, then sr lectr Bournemouth Univ, then Grant Thornton lectr in accounting Univ of Southampton, then prof of accounting Univ of Portsmouth, currently prof of accounting Bournemouth Univ; memb Nat Cncl ICAEW 1991–2004; memb Professional Oversight Bd 2004–10; past pres Southern Soc of CAs; FCA 1978; *Recreations* music, theatre, walking, sailing; *Style*— Prof Stella Fearnley; ✉ Department of Accounting and Finance, The Business School, Bournemouth University, 89 Holdenhurst Road, Bournemouth BH8 8EB

FEARNLEY-WHITTINGSTALL, Hugh Christopher Edmund; s of Robert Fearnley-Whittingstall, of Glos, and Jane, *née* Lascelles; *b* 14 January 1965; *Educ* Eton, St Peter's Coll Oxford (BA); *Partner* Marie Derôme; 2 s (Oscar b 3 March 1999, Alfred b 21 March 2003), 1 da (Louisa b 15 Feb 2010); *Career* writer, broadcaster, chef; sous chef River Café Hammersmith 1989, ed The Magazine 1991, assoc ed Redwood Publishing 1992–93, prodr BBC Science 1993–94 (The Maggot Mogul 1993, Sleeping It Off 1994), fndr KEO Films (with Andrew Palmer) 1996; produced/presented: A Cook on the Wild Side (Channel 4) 1996–97, Escape to River Cottage (Channel 4) 1998–99; presenter: TV Dinners (Channel 4) 1997–99, Return to River Cottage (Channel 4) 2000, River Cottage Forever (Channel 4) 2002, Treats from the Edwardian Country House (Channel 4) 2002, Beyond River Cottage, The River Cottage Road Trip, The River Cottage Treatment, Hugh's Chicken Run, River Cottage Autumn 2008, River Cottage Summer 2009, River Cottage Winter 2009, Hugh's Fish Fight (Channel 4) 2010 and 2011, River Cottage Every Day 2010; contrib/columnist: Independent on Sunday, Sunday Telegraph, Sunday Times, Observer, Sunday Express; weekly food column Guardian Weekend magazine; patron: Farmers Markets 2002, FAMRA; supporter and campaigner various food prodn and environmental issues especially: Friends of the Earth, Soil Assoc, Fairtrade Fndn, Dorset Wildlife Tst; Glenfiddich Award for Best Food TV Prog (for A Cook on the Wild Side) 1998, Glenfiddich Trophy 2002, Best Feature BAFTA (for Hugh's Fish Fight) 2011, Best Popular Factual And Features Prog RTS Award (for Hugh's Fish Fight) 2012; *Books* Cuisine Bon Marché (1995), A Cook on the Wild Side (1997), Chindogu: 101 Unuseless Japanese Inventions (ed, 1997), The Very Best of TV Dinners (1999), The River Cottage Cookbook (2001), The River Cottage Year (2003), The River Cottage Meat Book (2004, Andre Simon Award), The River Cottage Family Cookbook (2005), Hugh Fearlessley Eats It All: Dispatches from the Gastronomic Frontline (2006), The River Cottage Fish Book (2007, Andre Simon Award), River Cottage Everyday (2009), River Cottage Everyday Veg (2011); *Recreations* cooking, fishing, scuba diving, vegetable gardening, charcuterie; *Style*— Hugh Fearnley-Whittingstall, Esq; ✉ c/o Anthony Topping, Greene and Heaton, 37 Goldhawk Road, London W12 8QQ (☎ 020 8749 0315)

FEARON, Christopher (Chris); s of John Fearon, and Grainne, *née* McAlinden; *b* 24 October 1980, Newry, NI; *m* 24 July 2011, Catherine, *née* Barter; *Career* head chef Deans at Queens Belfast 2008–; television appearances incl Great British Menu (BBC 2) 2011 (winner, cooked starter for the People's Banquet) and 2012; *Style*— Chris Fearon, Esq; ✉ Deanes at Queens, 1 College Gardens, Belfast BT9 6BQ

FEARON, Daniel; s of Henry Bridges Fearon (d 1995), of Maidenhead, Berks, and Alethea, *née* McKenna (d 1994); *b* 14 October 1944; *Educ* Canford; *m* 20 Feb 1971, Karen Dawn, da of Clifford M Wark (d 2005), of Toronto, Canada; 1 s (James Adrian b 1978), 1 da (Letitia Jane b 1981); *Career* Sotheby & Co 1963–69, Parke Bernet NY 1969–70, Spink & Son 1970–86; md Glendining & Co 1986–93, W & F C Bonham & Sons 1993–2000, professional numismatic conslt 2000–; memb Br Numismatic Soc 1960 (memb Cncl 1986); memb Worshipful Co of Drapers 1970; FRNS 1968–2005; *Books* Catalogue of British Commemorative Medals (1984), Victorian Souvenir Medals (1986); *Style*— Daniel Fearon, Esq; ✉ e-mail info@danielfearon.com, website www.danielfearon.com

FEARON, Prof Douglas Thomas; s of Henry Dana Fearon (d 1987), and Frances Hudson, *née* Eubanks (d 1995); *b* 16 October 1942; *Educ* Williams Coll Williamstown Massachusetts (BA), Johns Hopkins Univ Sch of Med Baltimore Maryland (MD); *m* 26 May 1977, Clare MacIntyre, da of Burrows J Wheless; 1 da (Elizabeth MacIntyre b 5 Feb 1982), 1 s (Thomas Henry b 22 Oct 1984); *Career* residency (internal med) Johns Hopkins Hosp Baltimore 1968–70, Maj US Army Med Corps 1970–72 (Bronze Star); Harvard Med Sch Boston: research fell in med 1972–75, instr in med 1975–76, asst prof of med 1976–79, assoc prof of med 1979–84, prof of med 1984–87; prof of med Johns Hopkins Univ and dir Grad Immunology Prog 1987–93, Wellcome Tst research prof of med Univ of Cambridge Sch of Clinical Med and princ research fell Wellcome Tst 1993–, fell Trinity Coll Cambridge, emeritus Sheila Joan Smith prof of immunology Univ of Cambridge, Walter B Writson prof of pancreatic cancer research Weill Cornell Med Coll NY; hon conslt in med Addenbrooke's Hosp Cambridge 1993–; Helen Hay Whitney Fndn research fellowship 1974–77, Merit Award Nat Insts of Health 1991, Lee C Howley Sr Prize for Arthritis Research Arthritis Fndn 1991; former memb Research Ctees Arthritis Fndn and American Heart Fndn; former memb Research Sub-ctee Arthritis and Rheumatism Cncl; author of scientific pubns in the field of immunology; memb Editorial Bd: Clinical and Experimental Immunology, Immunity, Jl of Experimental Med; fell Trinity Coll Cambridge 2001; memb: American Soc for Clinical Investigation 1979, Assoc of American Physicians 1984, Assoc of Physicians of GB and I 1994, European Molecular Biology Orgn 2000, Nat Acad of Sciences USA 2001; fell American Assoc for the Advancement of Science 1990, fell Acad of Medical Sciences 1998, fell Royal Soc 1999, memb American Acad of Arts and Sciences 2000 (fell 1999), FRCP 1994; *Recreations* tennis, golf; *Clubs* Country (Brookline, Massachusetts); *Style*— Prof Douglas Fearon; ✉ Senior Group Leader, CRUK Cambridge Institute, Li Ka Shing Centre, Robinson Way, Cambridge CB2 0RE (☎ 01223 769565, fax 01223 769881, e-mail dtf1000@cam.ac.uk)

FEATHER, Prof John Pliny; s of Harold Renton Feather (d 1968), and Ethel May, *née* Barrett (d 1966); *b* 20 December 1947; *Educ* Heath Sch Halifax, The Queen's Coll Oxford (Hastings scholar, MA, BLitt), Univ of Cambridge (MA), Loughborough Univ (PhD); *m* 10 July 1971, Sarah, da of Rev Arthur Winnington Rees (d 1991), and Sarah Muriel Rees (d 1988); *Career* ed Scolar Press 1970–71, asst librarian Bodleian Library Oxford 1972–79, fell Darwin Coll Cambridge 1977–78, Munby fell in bibliography Univ of Cambridge 1977–78; Loughborough Univ: lectr 1979–84, sr lectr 1984–87, prof of library and info studies 1987–, head of Dept of Info and Library Studies 1989–94 and 2003–06, dean of educn and humanities 1994–96, pro-vice-chllr 1996–2000, dean Grad Sch 2010–14, emeritus prof 2014–; memb numerous nat and int professional ctees; fell Library Assoc 1986, FRSA 1996; *Books* English Book Prospectuses – An Illustrated History (1984), The Provincial Book Trade in Eighteenth-Century England (1985), A Dictionary of Book History (1986), A History of British Publishing (1988, revised edn 2006), Preservation

and the Management of Library Collections (1991, revised 1997), The Information Society (1994, revised 1998, 2000, 2004, 2008, 2011 and 2013), Publishing, Piracy and Politics (1994), The Wired World (with James Dearnley, 2001), Publishing: Communicating Knowledge in the 21st Century (2003); *Recreations* cookery, photography; *Clubs* Athenaeum; *Style*— Prof John Feather; ✉ Loughborough University, Leicestershire LE11 3TU (e-mail j.p.feather@lboro.ac.uk)

FEATHERBY, William Alan; QC (2008); s of Joseph Alan Featherby, of Cranleigh, Surrey, and Patricia Annie, *née* Davies; *b* 16 May 1956; *Educ* Haileybury, Trinity Coll Oxford (MA); *m* 12 April 1980, Clare Francis, da of Ian Richard Posgate, of Henley-on-Thames, Oxon; 5 s (Francis Alan b 1982, George Ian b 1986, John William b 1991, St John James Milton b 1993, William David b 1995), 5 da (Victoria Clare b 1985, Elizabeth Anne b 1988, Margaret Lucy b 1989, Eleanor Mary b 1990, Sarah Jane Webster b 1992); *Career* called to the Bar Middle Temple 1978; currently in private practice South Eastern Circuit, recorder South Eastern Circuit 2002–; *Publication* A Yorkshire Furrow (1993); *Recreations* reading, writing, opera and music, children; *Clubs* Carlton; *Style*— William Featherby, Esq, QC; ✉ 12 King's Bench Walk, Temple, London EC4Y 7EL (☎ 020 7583 0811, fax 020 7583 7228)

FEATHERSTONE, Jane; da of John Robert Featherstone, of Hemel Hempstead, and Elizabeth Ann, *née* Atherton; *b* 24 March 1969, Stirling; *Educ* Old Palace Sch Croydon, Univ of Leeds (BA); *Career* jt md Kudos Film and TV Ltd (with Stephen Garrett, qv); prodr: Touching Evil 1 and 2 (ITV), Sex 'n' Death (BBC2), Glasgow Kiss (BBC1); exec prodr: Pure, Spooks (MI5) 1, 2, and 3 (BBC1), Pleasureland (Channel 4), Comfortably Numb (Channel 4), Hustle 1 (BBC1), Hustle 2 (BBC1), Spooks 4 (BBC1); memb BAFTA 1996–; *Awards* incl: BAFTA nomination Best Drama Series and RTS Soc Award nomination Best Behind the Scenes Newcomer for Touching Evil 1 and 2, BAFTA nomination Best Single Film for Sex 'n' Death, various awards at festivals incl Berlin, Emden and BIFA for Pure; for Spooks (MI5) 1, 2, and 3 incl: BAFTA Award Best Drama Series, Broadcast Award Best Drama Series 2003 (nomination 2004), RTS Award Best Drama Series 2004 (nomination 2003), nomination Banff Rockie Award Best Continuing Series 2003 and 2004, nomination Indie Award Best Prodn of the Year and Best Drama, nomination BAFTA Craft Award Editing Fiction/Entertainment; *Recreations* cinema, sailing, skiing, riding; *Clubs* Soho House; *Style*— Ms Jane Featherstone; ✉ Kudos Film and TV Ltd, 12–14 Amwell Street, London EC1R 1UQ (☎ 020 7812 3270)

FEATHERSTONE, Baroness (Life Peer UK 2015), of Highgate in the London Borough of Haringey; Rt Hon Lynne Choona Featherstone; PC (2014); da of Joseph Woolf Ryness (d 1967), of London, and Gladys, *née* Schneider (d 1991); *b* 20 December 1951; *Educ* South Hampstead HS, Oxford Poly; *m* 30 April 1982 (m dis 2002), Stephen Featherstone; 2 c; *Career* ldr Oppn Haringey Cncl 1998–2002; memb London Assembly GLA (Lib Dem) London (list) 2000–05; MP (Lib Dem) Hornsey and Wood Green 2005–15; Parly under-sec of state Home Office 2010–12, Parly under-sec Dept for Int Devpt 2012–14, min of state Home Office 2014–15; *Publications* Marketing and Communication Techniques for Architects (1992), Equal Ever After: the fight for same-sex marriage and how I made it happen (2016); *Recreations* tennis, architecture, food, film; *Clubs* Liberal; *Style*— The Rt Hon the Baroness Featherstone, PC; ✉ House of Commons, London SW1A 0PW (☎ 020 8340 5459, e-mail featherstonel@parliament.uk)

FEAVER, William Andrew; s of Douglas Russell Feaver (d 1997), and Katherine Muriel Rose, *née* Stubbs (d 1987); *b* 1 December 1942; *Educ* St Albans Sch, Nottingham HS, Keble Coll Oxford; *m* 1, 1964, Anne Victoria Turton; *m* 2, 1985, Andrea Gillian Lester Rose; 6 c (Jane b 14 Oct 1964, Emily b 27 April 1966, Jessica b 20 Aug 1969, Silas b 1 Oct 1970, Dorothy b 11 May 1985, Alice b 21 Oct 1986); *Career* South Stanley Boys' Modern Sch Co Durham 1964–65, Royal GS Newcastle upon Tyne 1965–71, Univ of Newcastle upon Tyne (James Knott fell) 1971–73; art critic: Newcastle Jl 1968–73, London Magazine 1970–74, Art International 1970–74, Listener 1971–75, Sunday Times Magazine 1972–75, Vogue 1972–95, Financial Times 1974–75, Art News 1974–, The Observer 1975–98, various other pubns, radio and TV; exhibition organiser; work incl: George Cruikshank (V&A) 1974, Thirties (Hayward Gallery) 1979, Peter Moores Liverpool exhibitions 1984 and 1986, Lucian Freud (Kendal) 1996, Michael Andrews (Tate Gallery) 2001, Lucian Freud (Tate Britain) 2002, John Constable (with Lucian Freud, Grand Palais Paris) 2002, Lucian Freud (Wallace Collection) 2004, Lucian Freud (Museo Correr Venice) 2005; painter; exhibitions incl: Piers Feetham 2005, Northumbria Univ Gallery 2008; visiting prof Nottingham Trent Univ 1994–; memb: Art Panel Arts Cncl 1974–78, Art Ctee Nat Gallery of Wales 1991–, Academic Bd Prince of Wales Drawing Sch 2006–; tstee Ashington Gp 1989–; Critic of the Year Nat Press Awards 1983 (commended 1986); *Books* The Art of John Martin (1975), Masters of Caricature (1980), Pitman Painters (1988, adapted for the stage by Lee Hall 2007), James Boswell: Unofficial War Artist (2006), Lucian Freud (2007), Frank Auerbach (2009); *Recreations* painting; *Style*— William Feaver, Esq; ✉ 1 Rhodesia Road, London SW9 9EJ (020 7737 3386); Rogers Coleridge and White (Agent)

FEDER, Ami; s of Joseph Feder (d 1985), and Nicha, *née* Dornstein (d 2000); *b* 17 February 1937; *Educ* Hebrew Univ of Jerusalem, LSE; *m* 26 March 1970, Frances Annabel, da of late Michael August; 1 da (Shelley b 1972), 1 s (Ilan b 1974); *Career* Israeli Army 1956–58; called to the Bar Inner Temple 1965, memb Israel Bar, head of chambers Chambers of Ami Feder Lamb Building 1995–2013; currently in practice SE Circuit; memb: Hon Soc of Inner Temple (elected Master of the Bench 2015), London Common Law and Commercial Bar Assoc (LCLCBA), Criminal Bar Assoc, European Criminal Bar; *Recreations* sport, music, theatre; *Style*— Ami Feder, Esq; ✉ Chambers: Lamb Building, Temple, London EC4Y 7AS (☎ 020 7797 7788, fax 020 7353 0535, e-mail afeder@ lambbuilding.co.uk, website www.lambbuilding.co.uk); Office (Israel): Adam Law Offices, The Tower – 15th Floor, 3 Daniel Frisch Street, Tel-Aviv 64731 (☎ 00 972 3 607 8888, fax 00 972 3 607 8889, e-mail feder@adam-law.com)

FEE, Mary; MSP; s of Andrew Rutherford (d 1987), and Marion Beryl, *née* Berry (d 1978); *b* 23 March 1954, Edinburgh; *m* 22 Oct 1977, Brian; 2 s (Michael and Stephen); *Career* Bank of Scotland 1972–74, British Telecom 1974–84, Tesco Retail 1990–2011, Local Authy cncllr 2007–12, MSP (Lab) W of Scotland 2011–, convener Equal Opportunities Ctee 2012–; shop steward USDAW 1990–2011; *Recreations* reading, walking; *Style*— Ms Mary Fee, MSP; ✉ The Scottish Parliament, Edinburgh EH99 1SP (☎ 0131 348 6391, e-mail mary.fee.msp@scottish.parliament.uk, website www.maryfee.msp.com, Twitter @maryfeemsp)

FEGGETTER, Jeremy George Weightman; TD (1986), QHS (1992), DL (1999); s of George Y Feggetter (d 2000), of Newcastle upon Tyne, and Doris, *née* Weightman (d 1997); *b* 5 May 1943; *Educ* Harrow, Univ of Durham (MB BS); *Career* sr res assoc Dept of Surgery Univ of Newcastle upon Tyne 1972–74, sr urological registrar Newcastle Gen Hosp 1975–76, sr surgical registrar Royal Victoria Infirmary Newcastle upon Tyne 1976–78 (house offr 1966–67, demonstrator in anatomy 1967–68, SHO 1968–69, registrar 1969–72), RSO St Paul's Hosp London 1978–79, conslt urologist Freeman Hosp and Wansbeck Hosp 1979–2010, conslt urologist Newcastle Nuffield Hosp 1979–; FRCS; OStJ 1990; *Recreations* aviation, travel; *Clubs* RSM, Army and Navy; *Style*— Jeremy Feggetter, Esq, TD, DL; ✉ Newcastle Nuffield Hospital, Clayton Road, Newcastle upon Tyne NE2 1JP (☎ 0191 281 6131)

FEINSTEIN, Elaine Barbara; da of Isidore Cooklin (d 1974), and Fay, *née* Compton (d 1973); *b* 24 October 1930; *Educ* Wyggeston GS Leicester, Newnham Coll Cambridge; *m* 1956, Dr Arnold Feinstein (d 2002); 3 s (Adam b Feb 1957, Martin b March 1959, Joel b June

1964); *Career* poet and novelist; judge Gregory Poetry Awards Soc of Authors 1986–91, judge Heinemann Awards Royal Soc of Literature 1990, chm of judges T S Eliot Award 1994; winner Cholmondeley Award for Poetry 1990; memb Exec Ctee English Centre Int PEN 1989–, memb Cncl RSL 2008–; Hon DLitt Univ of Leicester 1990, Rockefeller Fndn fell at Bellagio 1998; FRSL 1980; *Novels* The Circle (1970), The Amberstone Exit (1972), The Glass Alembic (1973, US title The Crystal Garden), Children of the Rose (1975), The Ecstasy of Dr Miriam Garner (1976), The Shadow Master (1978), The Survivors (1982), The Border (1984), Mother's Girl (1988, shortlisted for LA Times Fiction Prize 1990), All You Need (1989), Loving Brecht (1992), Dreamers (1994), Lady Chatterley's Confession (1995), Dark Inheritance (2000), The Russian Jerusalem (2008); *Poetry* In a Green Eye (1966), The Magic Apple Tree (1971), At the Edge (1972), The Celebrants and Other Poems (1973), Some Unease and Angels – Selected Poems (1977), The Feast of Eurydice (1980), Badlands (1987), City Music (1990), Selected Poems (1994), Daylight (1997), Gold (2001), Collected Poems (2002), Collected Poems (2002), Talking to the Dead (2007); trans: The Selected Poems of Marina Tsvetayeva (1971), Three Russian Poets – Margarite Aliger, Yunna Morits and Bella Akhmadulina (1976), Bride of Ice: New Selected Poems by Marina Tsvetaeva (2009); ed: Selected Poems of John Clare (1968), New Poetry (1988); *Biographies* Bessie Smith (1986), A Captive Lion – The Life of Marina Tsvetayeva (1987), Lawrence's Women – The Intimate Life of D H Lawrence (1993), Pushkin (1998), Ted Hughes: The Life of a Poet (2001), Anna of all the Russias: The life of Anna Akhmatova (2005); *Stories* Matters of Chance (1972), The Silent Areas (1980), New Stories (jt ed with Fay Weldon, 1979); *Television* Breath (BBC Play for Today, 1975), Lunch (dir Jon Amiel, 1981), 12-part series on The Edwardian Country Gentlewoman's Diary (1984), A Brave Face (BBC, 1985), A Passionate Woman (series on life of Marie Stopes, 1990), The Brecht Project (series on life of Bertolt Brecht); *Radio* plays: Echoes (1980), A Late Spring (1981), A Day Off (1983), Marina Tsvetayeva – A Life (1985), If I Ever Get On My Feet Again (1987), The Man in her Life (1990), Foreign Girls (1993), Winter Journey (1995), Women in Love (4 part adaptation, 1996), Book at Bedtime (10 part adaptation of Lady Chatterley's Confession,1996), Cloudberries (1999); *Recreations* theatre, music, travel, the conversation of friends; *Style*— Ms Elaine Feinstein; ✉ c/o Gill Coleridge, Rogers Coleridge & White, 20 Powis Mews, London W11 (✆ 020 7221 3717, fax 020 7229 9084, e-mail gillc@rcwlitagency.demon.co.uk)

FELD, Robert Philip; s of Alfred Feld (d 1990), and Lily, *née* Green (d 1997); *b* 3 January 1953; *Educ* Brighton & Hove Sussex GS, Imperial Coll of Sci and Technol; *m* 6 March 1987, Tara Louise, da of Edward Scannell (d 1996); 2 s (Daniel Mark Joseph b 1988, Joshua Alfred b 1991); *Career* md Resort Hotels plc 1983–94, chm Aubrey Business Group 1994–96, project co-ordinator Eplon Engrg 2000–03, chief exec Aerospace and Technical Engineering 2003–07, chief exec Surrey Business Consulting 2007–10; Freeman City of London; FIH, FRSA; *Recreations* aviation, cricket, yachting; *Clubs* City Livery; *Style*— Robert Feld, Esq; ✉ Aubrey House, The Green, Rottingdean, Brighton BN2 7HA (✆ 01273 303884, fax 01273 303884, e-mail rfeld6776@aol.com)

FELDMAN, Baron (Life Peer UK 1995), of Frognal in the London Borough of Camden; Sir Basil Feldman; kt (1982); s of Philip Feldman, and Tilly Feldman; *b* 23 September 1926; *Educ* Grocers' Sch; *m* 1952, Gita, da of Albert Julius (d 1964); 2 s, 1 da; *Career* chm: Martlet Services Gp Ltd 1973–81, Solport Ltd 1980–85, Watchpost Ltd 1983–; Gtr London area Nat Union of Cons and Unionist Assocs: dep chm 1975–78, chm 1978–81, pres 1981–85, vice-pres 1985–; Nat Union of Cons and Unionist Assocs: dep chm 1982–85, chm 1985–86, vice-pres 1986–, chm Exec Ctee 1991–96 (memb 1975–98); chair Cons Conf Blackpool 1985; author of several party booklets and pamphlets; jt chm Cons Pty's Impact 80s Campaign 1982–90; memb: Policy Gp for London 1975–81 and 1984–, Nat Campaign Ctee 1976 and 1978, Advsy Ctee on Policy 1981–84, Ctee for London 1984–90, Cons Pty Bd of Treasurers 1996–, treas Cons Pty 1996–; vice-pres Gtr London Young Cons 1975–77; pres: Richmond and Barnes Cons Assoc 1976–84, Hornsey Cons Assoc 1978–82; patron Hampstead Cons Assoc 1981–86, contested GLC elections Richmond 1973; memb: GLC Housing Mgmnt Ctee 1973–77, GLC Arts Ctee 1976–81; dir Young Entrepreneurs Fund 1985–94, memb Free Enterprise Loan Soc 1977–84; chm: Better Made in Britain Campaign 1983–98 (also fndr), The Quality Mark 1987–92, Shopping Hours Reform Cncl 1988–94, Better Business Opportunities 1990–98, London Arts Season 1993–96, Festival of Arts and Culture 1994–95, Renaissance Forum 1996–2010 (pres 2010–); membre consultatif Institutional Internat de Promotion et de Prestige Geneva (affiliated to UNESCO) 1978–93; memb: Post Office Users' Nat Cncl 1978–81, English Tourist Bd 1986–96; chm: Clothing EDC (NEDO) 1978–85, maker/user working party (NEDO) 1988–89; chm Salzburg Festival Tst 1998–2003 (vice-chm 1997–98); Silver Medal of Honour Salzburg 2003; FRSA 1987; *Books* Some Thoughts on Job Creation (for NEDO, 1984), Constituency Campaigning – a guide for Conservative Party workers; *Recreations* travel, golf, tennis, theatre, opera; *Clubs* Carlton; *Style*— The Rt Hon Lord Feldman; ✉ House of Lords, London SW1A 0PW

FELDMAN, Prof David John; s of Alec Feldman (d 1976), and Valerie Annette, *née* Michaelson; *b* 12 July 1953, Hove, E Sussex; *Educ* Brighton Hove and Sussex GS, Exeter Coll Oxford (MA, DCL); *m* 4 Sept 1983, (Naomi) Jill, *née* Newman; 1 da (Rebecca Jane b 14 March 1985), 1 s (Jonathan Alec b 26 March 1987); *Career* Univ of Bristol: lectr in law 1976–89, reader in law 1989–92; Univ of Birmingham: Barber prof of jurisprudence 1992–2000, prof of law 2000–04; Univ of Cambridge: fell Downing Coll 2003–, Rouse Ball prof of English law 2004–, chm Faculty Bd of Law 2006–09, chm Faculty Bd Human, Social and Political Sciences 2013–16; visiting fell ANU 1989; legal advsr Jt Select Ctee on Human Rights Houses of Parl 2000–04; judge Constitutional Ct of Bosnia and Herzegovina 2002–10 (vice-pres 2006–09); memb European Gp of Public Law, memb Soc of Legal Scholars (pres 2010–11); memb Justice; hon bencher Lincoln's Inn 2003, academic associate 39 Essex Chambers; Hon LLD Univ of Bristol 2013; Hon QC 2008; FBA 2006, FRSA; The Law Relating to Entry, Search and Seizure (1986), Criminal Confiscation Orders: The New Law (1988), Civil Liberties and Human Rights in England and Wales (1993, 2 edn 2002), Corporate and Commercial Law: Modern Developments (jt ed, 1996), English Public Law (ed, 2004, 2 edn 2009), Law in Politics, Politics in Law (ed, 2013), Cambridge Companion to Public Law (jt ed, 2015); *Recreations* music, cooking, dog walking; *Style*— Prof David Feldman; ✉ Faculty of Law, University of Cambridge, 10 West Road, Cambridge CB3 9DZ (✆ 01223 762122, fax 01223 330055, e-mail djf41@cam.ac.uk)

FELDMAN, Dr Keith Stuart; s of Reuben Feldman (d 1999), and Karola, *née* Landau (d 1977); *b* 29 July 1943; *Educ* Christ's Coll Finchley, Imperial Coll of Science and Technol London (BSc, PhD); *m* 8 July 1971, Teresa Ann, da of Simon Wallace (d 2000), and, Miriam, *née* Cohen (d 1985); 1 da (Cordelia b 15 May 1979), 1 s (Alexander b 15 Dec 1981); *Career* fndr Inter-Bond Services Ltd 1969–81, sr exec Datastream International Ltd 1979–81, dir Carr Kitcat & Aitken Ltd (formerly Galloway & Pearson) 1981–93, res actuary Robert Fleming & Co Ltd 1993–98, ind consulting actuary 1999–; FIA 1976, memb Int Stock Exchange 1984; *Publications* The Zilch in General Relativity (1965), Dispersion Theory Calculations for Nucleon-Nucleon Scattering (1965), A Model to Explain Investment Trust Prices and Discounts (1977), The Gilt Edged Market Reformulated (1977), AIBD Yield Book (1979), Report on the Wilkie Stochastic Investment Model (1992), Report of the Fixed Interest Working Group (1997); *Recreations* chess, skiing; *Clubs* Argonauts; *Style*— Dr Keith Feldman; ✉ Skybreak, The Warren, Radlett, Hertfordshire WD7 7DU (✆ 01923 853777, e-mail keith.feldman@btinternet.com)

FELDMAN, Dr Michael Morris; s of Louis Feldman (d 1975), and Shura Miller (d 1981); *b* 3 December 1938; *Educ* King Edward VII Sch Johannesburg, UCL (BA), UCH Univ of London (MPhil); *m* 7 Jan 1960, Wendy Bankes, da of Arthur Gerald Bankes Morgan (d 1975); 2 da (Melanie Jane Bankes b 1960, Susan Rose b 1964), 1 s (Matthew Richard Bankes b 1969); *Career* house officer UCH 1966, conslt psychotherapist Bethlem Royal and Maudsley Hosp 1975–98 (registrar 1969–72), sr lectr Inst of Psychiatry 1982– (lectr 1974–75), training analyst Inst of Psycho-Analysis 1983 (assoc member 1975, full member 1981); MRCP, FRCPsych; *Books* Psychic Equilibrium and Psychic Change: Selected Papers of Betty Joseph (co-ed, 1989), The Oedipus Complex Today: Clinical Implications (jtly, 1989), Doubt, Conviction and the Analytic Process (2009); *Recreations* gardening, music, photography, inland waterways; *Style*— Dr Michael Feldman; ✉ 32 Southwood Avenue, London N6 5RZ

FELDMAN, Dr Paul; *Educ* Univ of St Andrews (BSc), Warwick Business Sch Univ of Warwick (PhD); *m* 6 August 1982, Lesley, *née* Gray; 2 da (Amy, Hannah); *Career* conslt James Martin Assocs 1985–88, conslt Arthur D Little 1988–89, banking, savings and mortgage dir Nationwide Building Soc 1989–2005, sr vice pres Operations EMEA First Data Int 2006–07, chief information offr Barclaycard Barclays Bank 2007–10, IS dir Cancer Research UK 2010–12, chief technol offr Practical Law Co 2012–13, chief technol offr Legal UKI Thomson Reuters 2013–14, chief technol offr/ chief info offr Intellectual Property Office 2015, exec ptnr Gartner 2015, chief exec Jisc 2015–; *Recreations* cinema, music, gardening, golf, reading, travel, walking; *Style*— Dr Paul Feldman; ✉ Jisc, One Castlepark, Tower Hill, Bristol BS2 0JA

FELDMAN OF ELSTREE, Baron (Life Peer UK 2010), of Elstree in the County of Hertfordshire; Rt Hon Andrew Simon Feldman; PC (2015); s of Malcolm Roger Feldman, and Marcia, *née* Summers; *b* 25 February 1966, London; *Educ* Haberdashers' Aske's, BNC Oxford (BA), Inns of Court Law Sch; *m* 1999, Gabrielle Josephine Gourgey; 2 s, 1 da; *Career* called to the Bar 1991; mgmnt conslt Bain & Co 1988–90, commercial barr 1 Essex Ct 1991–95, dir Jayroma (London) Ltd 1995–; Cons Pty: dep treas 2005–08, chief exec 2008–10, co-chm 2010–15, chm Bd 2010–, chm 2015–; memb Bd Cons Pty Fndn 2010–; *Recreations* tennis, golf, skiing, reading; *Clubs* Carlton, George; *Style*— The Rt Hon the Lord Feldman of Elstree; ✉ House of Lords, London SW1A 0PW

FELL, Alison; da of Andrew Fell (d 1970), and Doris Johnstone (d 2007); *b* 4 June 1944; *Educ* Kinloch Rannoch Sch, Lochmaben Sch, Lockerbie Acad, Dumfries Acad, Edinburgh Coll of Art (Dip Sculpture, post-dip scholarship and travelling scholarship); *m* 1964 (m dis), Roger Coleman, *qv*, s of Ronald Coleman; 1 s (Ivan b 1967); *Career* poet and novelist; co-fndr: The Welfare State Theatre Leeds 1969, The Women's Street Theatre Gp; journalist: Ink, Oz, Time Out; memb Spare Rib Editorial Collective 1975–79 (latterly fiction ed); writer in residence: C Day Lewis fell London Borough of Brent 1978, London Borough of Walthamstow 1981–82; tutor at writing workshops in arts centres across UK, writer in action SE Arts Kent 1985, tutor Arvon Fndn 1985–; writer in residence NSW Inst of Technol 1986, writing fell UEA 1998, Royal Literary Fund fell UCL 2002–03, res fell Middlesex Univ 2003–06, Royal Literary Fund fell Courtauld Inst 2006–; Univ of Southampton: lectr in creative writing 2008–, prof of creative writing 2014–16; has recited at various arts venues throughout UK; subject of Whispers in the Dark (BBC TV Scotland) 1995; awarded Alice Hunt Bartlett Prize (Nat Poetry Soc) for first collections 1985; memb Greater London Arts Lit Panel 1984–86; memb: Soc of Authors, RSL; *Books* Hard Feelings (ed, 1979), The Grey Dancer (1981), Every Move You Make (1984), Truth, Dare or Promise (contrib, 1985), The Bad Box (1987), The Shining Mountain (1987, 2 edn 1988), Close Company – Stories of Mothers and Daughters (contrib, 1988), Sex and the City (contrib, 1989), Whose Cities? (contrib, 1991), Winters Tales (contrib, 1991), Mer de Glace (1991, Boardman Tasker award for mountain lit), The Pillow Boy of the Lady Onogoro (1994), The Mistress of Lilliput (1999), Tricks of the Light (2003), The Element -Inth in Greek (2012); *Poetry* Kisses for Mayakovsky (1984), The Crystal Owl (1988), Dreams, like heretics (1997), Lightyear (2005); *Plays* Mapping the Edge (jtly, performed Crucible Theatre Sheffield 2001, adapted for BBC Radio 2001); *Anthologies* The Seven Deadly Sins (ed and contrib, 1988), The Seven Cardinal Virtues (ed and contrib, 1990), Serious Hysterics (ed and contrib, 1992); poetry in anthologies: Licking The Bed Clean (1978), Bread and Roses (1979), One Foot on the Mountain (1979), Smile Smile Smile Smile (1980), Angels of Fire, Apples and Snakes, The New British Poetry, Is That The New Moon?, Anthology of Scottish Women's Poetry (1991), The Faber Book of 20th Century Scottish Verse (1992), The Faber Book of Movie Verse (1993), 20th Century Scottish Literature (2001), Red Sky at Night – Scottish Poetry (2003); stories in anthologies: Sex and the City (1992), Infidelity (1993), Bad Sex (1993), Shouting it Out (1996); *Style*— Ms Alison Fell; ✉ c/o Tony Peake, Peake Associates, PO Box 66726, London NW5 9FE (✆ 020 7681 4307, e-mail tony@tonypeake.com)

FELL, Sir David; KCB (1995, CB 1990); s of Ernest Fell (d 1964), of Belfast, NI, and Jessie, *née* McCreedy (d 1981); *b* 20 January 1943; *Educ* Royal Belfast Academical Instn, Queen's Univ Belfast (BSc); *m* 22 July 1967, Sandra Jesse, da of Hubert Moore (d 1982), of Co Fermanagh, NI; 1 da (Victoria b 1972), 1 s (Nicholas b 1976); *Career* sales mangr Rank Hovis McDougall 1965–66, teacher Belfast Model Sch 1966–67, res assoc Queen's Univ Belfast 1967–69; NI civil serv: asst princ Miny of Agric 1969–72, princ Miny of Commerce 1972–77, under sec Dept of Commerce 1981–82 (asst sec 1977–81), dep chief exec Industrial Devpt Bd for NI 1982–84, perm sec Dept of Econ Devpt 1984–91; head NI Civil Serv and second perm under sec of state NI Office 1991–97; chm: Boxmore Int 1998–2000, Northern Bank Ltd 1998–2005, National Irish Bank 1999–2005, Prince's Tst NI 1999–2005, Harland & Wolff Gp plc 2001–02, Titanic Quarter Ltd 2001–04, Titanic Properties Ltd 2001–04, Goldblatt McGuigan 2005–12, Chesapeake Corporation USA 2005–09 (dir 2000–09), Canal Corporation USA 2009–11, Novenso Ltd (formerly Litelighting Ltd) 2010–12; dir: Dunloe Ewart plc 1998–2002, Nat Aust Gp (Europe) Ltd 1998–2012, Fred Olsen Energy ASA 1999–2003, Clydesdale Bank plc 2005–12; pro-chllr Queen's Univ Belfast 2005–14 (dir Fndn Bd 2003–09); novelist 2015–; Hon DUniv Ulster, Hon LLD Queen's Univ Belfast 2014; CIMgt, FIB; *Books* The Gemelli Retribution (2015); *Recreations* rugby, music, travel, grandchildren; *Clubs* Belfast Old Instonians; *Style*— Sir David Fell, KCB; ✉ The Queen's University Belfast, University Road, Belfast BT7 1NN

FELL, Heather; da of Nicholas Fell, of Merrivale Farm, Yelverton, Devon, and Doreen, *née* Hutchings; *b* 3 March 1983, Plymouth; *Educ* Brunel Univ (BSc); *Career* modern pentathlete; Gold medals individual and team and Silver medal team relay World Junior Championships Athens 2003, Gold medal team relay and Silver medal individual European Championships Riga 2007, Gold medal World Cup Millfield 2008 (Bronze medal individual Moscow 2007 and Kladno 2008), Silver medal Budapest Indoor Championships 2008, Silver medal team World Championships Budapest 2008, Silver medal individual Olympic Games Beijing 2008, Silver medal individual World Cup Final Portugal 2008, Gold medal team and Silver medal individual European Championships 2009; memb Health Professions Cncl 2004; *Recreations* watersports, horse racing (as a spectator!), skiing, travelling, theatre, tennis (playing and watching), rugby (watching); *Clubs* Kelly Coll, Plymouth Fencing, Tavistock Athletics; *Style*— Miss Heather Fell; ✉ Merrivale Farm, Princetown, Yelverton, Devon PL20 6ST (✆ 01822 890251, e-mail heatherfell@hotmail.co.uk, website www.heatherfell.co.uk, Twitter @heatherfellnews); Mission Sports Management, 1st Floor, Park House, 14 Northfields, London SW18 1DD (✆ 020 8704 4165, fax 020 8704 4169, e-mail andy@missionsports.com)

FELLNER, Eric; CBE (2005); *Educ* Cranleigh Sch, Guildhall Sch of Music and Drama; *m* (m dis), Gaby Dellal; 3 c; partner, Laura Bailey, *qv*; 2 c; *Career* prodr; co-chm (with Tim

F

Bevan, *qv*) Working Title Films 1992–, launched Working Title 2 (with Tim Bevan) 2002; co-prodr Billy Elliot – The Musical 2005; govr BFI 2003–; 26 BAFTA Awards, 6 Academy Awards; *Film* Sid and Nancy 1986, Straight to Hell 1987, Pascali's Island 1988, The Rachel Papers 1989, Hidden Agenda 1990, Year of the Gun 1991, Liebestraum 1991, A Kiss Before Dying 1991, Wild West 1992, Frankie's House 1992, Romeo is Bleeding 1993, Posse 1993, No Worries 1993, The Hawk 1993, Four Weddings and a Funeral 1994, The Hudsucker Proxy 1994, Loch Ness 1995, Panther 1995, French Kiss 1995, Moonlight and Valentino 1995, Dead Man Walking 1995, Fargo 1996, Bean 1997, The Matchmaker 1997, The Borrowers 1997, The Hi-Lo Country 1998, Elizabeth 1998, The Big Lebowski 1998, What Rats Won't Do 1998, Notting Hill 1999, Plunkett & Macleane 1999, Oh Brother, Where Art Thou? 2000, The Man Who Cried 2000, Captain Corelli's Mandolin 2001, Bridget Jones's Diary 2001, The Man WhoWasn't There 2001, Long Time Dead 2001, 40 Days and 40 Nights 2002, Ali G Indahouse 2002, About A Boy 2002, The Guru 2002, My Little Eye 2002, The Shape of Things 2003, Thirteen 2003, Johnny English 2003, Ned Kelly 2003, The Italian Job 2003, Love Actually 2003, Shaun of the Dead 2004, Gettin' Square 2004, The Calcium Kid 2004, Thunderbirds 2004, Wimbledon 2004, Bridget Jones: The Edge of Reason 2004, Rory O'Shea Was Here 2004, The Interpreter 2005, Nanny McPhee 2005, Pride and Prejudice 2005, Mickybo & Me 2005, No 2 2006, Sixty Six 2006, United 93 2006, Catch a Fire 2006, The Golden Age 2007, Atonement 2007, Mr Bean's Holiday 2007, Hot Fuzz 2007, Gone 2007, Smokin' Aces 2007, Definitely Maybe 2008, Wild Child 2008, Burn After Reading 2008, Frost/Nixon 2008, The Boat That Rocked 2009, State of Play 2009, The Soloist 2009, Greenzone 2010, Nanny McPhee and the Big Bang 2010, Senna 2010, Paul 2010, Tinker Tailor Soldier Spy 2011, Johnny English Reborn 2011, Contraband 2012, Big Miracle 2012, Anna Karenina 2012, Les Miserables 2012, I Give It A Year 2013; *Style*— Eric Fellner, Esq, CBE; ✉ Working Title Films Ltd, 26 Aybrook Street, London W1U 4AN (✆ 020 7307 3000)

FELLOWES, Baron (Life Peer UK 1999), of Shotesham in the County of Norfolk; Sir Robert Fellowes; GCB (1998, KCB 1991, CB 1987), GCVO (1996, KCVO 1989, LVO 1982), QSO (1999), PC (1990); s of Sir William Albemarle Fellowes, KCVO (d 1986), agent to HM at Sandringham 1936–64, and Jane Charlotte (d 1986), da of Brig-Gen Algernon Francis Holford Ferguson; bro of Thomas Fellowes, *qv*; *b* 11 December 1941; *Educ* Eton; *m* 20 April 1978, Lady (Cynthia) Jane Spencer, da of 8 Earl Spencer; 2 da (Laura Jane b 1980, Eleanor Ruth b 1985), 1 s (Alexander Robert b 1983); *Career* Lt Scots Guards 1960–63; dir Allen Harvey & Ross (discount brokers and bankers) 1968–77, private sec to HM The Queen 1990–99 (asst private sec 1977–86, dep private sec 1986–90); chm Barclays Private Bank, non-exec dir SAB Miller plc 1999–2010; chm Prison Reform Tst 2001–08; tstee: Rhodes Tst 1999–2010, Winston Churchill Meml Tst 2001–16 (chm 2009–16), Mandela Rhodes Fndn 2003–10, Global Warming Policy Fndn 2009–; vice-chm Cwlth Educn Tst 2006–16, chm Voices Fndn 2004–12, memb Bd Br Library 2007–16, memb Cncl King Edward VII Hosp Sister Agnes 2010–13; pres Advsy Cncl Goodenough Coll 2008–14; Liveryman Worshipful Co of Goldsmiths; *Recreations* watching cricket, golf, reading; *Clubs* White's, Pratt's, MCC; *Style*— The Rt Hon the Lord Fellowes, GCB, GCVO, QSO, PC; ✉ House of Lords, London SW1A 0PW

FELLOWES, Thomas William; s of Sir William Albemarle Fellowes, KCVO, DL (d 1986), and Jane Charlotte (d 1986), da of Brig-Gen Algernon Francis Holford Ferguson; bro of Baron Fellowes, GCB, GCVO, QSO, PC (Life Peer), *qv*; *b* 3 November 1945; *Educ* Eton; *m* 1, 1968 (m dis 1972), Caroline Moira, da of Capt D J R Ker, MC, of Portavo, Co Down; m 2, 1975, Rosamund Isobelle, da of Bernard van Cutsem, and Lady Margaret Fortescue; 2 da (Catherine b 1977, Mary b 1978); *Career* dir Gerrard and National Discount Co Ltd 1973, dep chm Gerrard & National Holdings plc 1989–96, ret; non-exec dir: James Purdey & Sons Ltd 1991–2005, Hyperion Insurance Gp 1998–2001; chm London Discount Market Assoc 1995–97; conslt and non-exec dir Christie's International UK Ltd 1997–2009, conslt Julius Baer International 2002–; cmmr for Public Works Loans 1997–2001; chm of govrs Royal Hosp Sch Holbrook 1999–2003; Liveryman Worshipful Co of Ironmongers; *Clubs* Pratt's, White's, Royal Worlington Golf; *Style*— Thomas Fellowes; ✉ The Old Rectory, Barking, Ipswich, Suffolk IP6 8HH (✆ and fax 01449 723060, e-mail tommy@twfellowes.co.uk)

FELLOWES OF WEST STAFFORD, Baron (Life Peer UK 2011), of West Stafford in the County of Dorset; Julian Alexander Fellowes (aka Kitchener-Fellowes, registered by College of Arms 1998); DL (2009); s of Peregrine Edward Launcelot Fellowes (d 1999), of Chipping Campden, and Olwen Mary, *née* Stuart-Jones (d 1980); *b* 17 August 1949, Cairo, Egypt; *Educ* Ampleforth, Magdalene Coll Cambridge (MA), Webber Douglas Academy of Drama; *m* 28 April 1990, Emma, LVO (2000), da of Hon Charles Kitchener, gniece of 1 Earl Kitchener of Khartoum, Lady-in-Waiting to HRH Princess Michael of Kent; 1 s (hon Peregrine Charles Morant Kitchener b 1991); *Career* actor, writer, lecturer and producer; chm RNIB Talking Books Appeal 2005–, vice-pres Weldman Hospicecare Tst; Paul Harris fell Rotary Club of GB; Hon DLitt Bournemouth Univ; *Theatre* West End appearances incl: Joking Apart (Globe), Present Laughter (Vaudeville), Futurists (NT); Mary Poppins (writer of book for stage musical, New Amsterdam Theatre NY, Variety Club Musical Theatre Award 2005); *Television* incl: The Greater Good (BBC), Sharpe's Regiment (Sharpe Films), Killing me Softly (BBC), Aristocrats (BBC/RTE), Monarch of the Glen (BBC); co-prodns as dir of Lionhead incl: Married Man (with LWT), Little Sir Nicholas (with BBC); writer/adaptor Little Lord Fauntleroy (BBC, winner of 1995 Int Emmy Award); writer/prodr The Prince and the Pauper (BBC, BAFTA nomination 1996), Julian Fellowes presents Most Mysterious Murders (BBC), Never Mind the Full Stops (BBC 4); writer, creator and prodr Downton Abbey (ITV), writer Titanic (ITV); *Film* actor: Fellow Traveller, Damage, Shadowlands, Regeneration, Tomorrow Never Dies, Place Vendôme; writer: Piccadilly Jim, Vanity Fair, Young Victoria; writer/prodr Gosford Park (an original screenplay for Robert Altman); writer and dir: Separate Lies, From Time to Time; *Awards* New York Film Critics' Circle for Best Screenplay of 2001, Best Screenplay of 2001 National Film Circle (US), Writers' Guild Award for Best Original Screenplay of 2001, Best Screenwriter of 2001 ShoWest Distributors Award, Walpole Medal for Outstanding Achievement, Academy Award for Best Original Screenplay of 2001, Best Directorial Debut of 2005 (for Separate Lies) Nat Bd of Review; for Downton Abbey: Outstanding Writing in a Mini-Series, Movie or Dramatic Special Emmy Award 2011, Best Mini-Series, Movie or Dramatic Special Emmy Award 2011, Best Miniseries – Television or Film Golden Globe, Best Drama Nat Television Award 2012, 2013 and 2015; *Books* Snobs (2004), The Curious Adventures of the Abandoned Toys (2007), Past Imperfect (2008), Downton Abbey The Complete Scripts Season One (2012), Downton Abbey The Complete Scripts Season Two (2013), Downton Abbey The Complete Scripts Season Three (2014); *Recreations* history, building; *Clubs* Boodle's, Annabel's, Pratt's; *Style*— The Lord Fellowes of West Stafford, DL; ✉ c/o Independent Talent, 40 Whitfield Street, London W1T 2RH

FELLS, Prof Ian; CBE (2000); s of Dr Henry Alexander Fells, MBE (d 1975), of Sheffield, and Clarice, *née* Rowell (d 1996); *b* 5 September 1932; *Educ* King Edward VII Sch Sheffield, Trinity Coll Cambridge (MA, PhD); *m* 17 Aug 1957, Hazel Denton, da of Donald Murgatroyd Scott, of Sheffield; 4 s (Nicholas Scott b 1959, Jonathan Wynne b 1961, Alastair Rowell b 1963, Crispin Denton b 1966); *Career* cmmnd RCS 1951, Chief Wireless Offr Br Troops in Austria 1952; lectr and dir of studies Dept of Fuel Technol and Chem Engrg Univ of Sheffield 1958–62, reader in fuel sci Univ of Durham 1962–75, prof of energy conversion Univ of Newcastle upon Tyne 1975– (public orator 1971–74), exec David Davies Inst of Int Affairs 1975–2002, pres Inst of Energy 1978–79; memb: Sci Consultative Gp BBC 1976–81, Electricity Supply Res Cncl 1979–89, Cncl for Nat Academic Awards 1988–92; life vice-pres Int Centre for Life Newcastle upon Tyne 1996–, chm New and Renewable Energy Centre Blyth 2002–05, special advsr Energy, Cwlth and Business Cncl 2011–; dir Penultimate Power UK Ltd 2013–; involved with various TV series incl: Young Scientist of the Year, The Great Egg Race, Earth Year 2050, Take Nobody's Word for It, Tomorrow Tonight, QED, What If? The Lights Go Out, Horizon; Hatfield Meml Medal and Prize 1974, Beilby Meml Medal and Prize 1976, Sir Charles Parsons Meml Medal and Prize 1988, Royal Soc Faraday Medal 1993, Melchett Medal Inst of Energy 1999, Collier Medal Royal Soc 1999, Kelvin Medal Royal Philosophical Soc of Glasgow 2002; Higginson Lecture Univ of Durham 1999, Hunter Meml Lecture IEE 2000, Hawksley Meml Lecture IMechE 2001; FREng 1979, FInstE, FIChemE, FRSE 1996; *Books* UK Energy Policy Post-Privatisation (1991), Moving Ahead (1992), Energy for the Future (1995), Global Warming (1996), World Energy 1923–1998 and Beyond (1998), A Pragmatic Energy Policy for the UK (2008); *Recreations* sailing, cross-country skiing, energy conversation, painting; *Clubs* Naval and Military; *Style*— Prof Ian Fells, CBE, FRSE, FREng; ✉ 29 Rectory Terrace, Newcastle upon Tyne NE3 1YB (✆ and fax 0191 285 5343, e-mail ian@fellsassociates.com)

FELSTEAD, Peter John Raymond; s of Peter John William Felstead (d 1991), of E Grinstead, W Sussex, and Brenda Florence, *née* Scott (d 2007); *b* 27 October 1964, Cuckfield, Sussex; *Educ* Sackville Comp Sch E Grinstead, Univ of Manchester (BA); *m* 1, May 1993 (m dis 2004); 2 s (Joshua William Taylor b 11 June 1995, Charles William Taylor Bradley b 15 Aug 1997); m 2, 20 Sept 2014, Jessica Louise Wilson, 1 da (Josephine Florence Elizabeth b 4 June 2012); *Career* Jane's Information Gp: sub-ed and reporter Jane's Defence Weekly 1989–95, ed Jane's Intelligence Review 1997–99 (dep ed 1995–97), managing ed Security Business Unit 1999–2000, managing ed web content 2000–03, ed Jane's Defence Weekly 2003–; *Recreations* photography, films, military and aviation history, mountain biking, motoring, wargaming; *Style*— Peter Felstead, Esq; ✉ IHS Jane's, Sentinel House, 163 Brighton Road, Coulsdon, Surrey CR5 2YH (✆ 020 3253 2215, e-mail peter.felstead@ihs.com)

FELTON, Thomas Andrew (Tom); *b* 22 September 1987, London; *Career* actor; *Film* incl: Anna and the King 1999, Harry Potter and the Philosopher's Stone 2001, Harry Potter and the Chamber of Secrets 2002, Harry Potter and the Prisoner of Azkaban 2004, Harry Potter and the Goblet of Fire 2005, Harry Potter and the Order of the Phoenix 2007, The Disappeared 2008, Harry Potter and the Half-Blood Prince 2009, Harry Potter and the Deathly Hallows: Part 1 2010, Harry Potter and the Deathly Hallows: Part 2 2011, Rise of the Planet of the Apes 2011, From the Rough 2012, Night Wolf 2012, The Apparition 2012, Therese Raquin 2012, Attachment 2012; *Style*— Mr Tom Felton; ✉ c/o Michael Duff, Troika, 3rd Floor, 74 Clerkenwell Road, London EC1M 5QA

FELTWELL, Dr John Stewart Edmonds; s of Ray Parker Feltwell (d 1994), of Eastbourne, and Edna Mary, *née* Edmonds (d 1992); *b* 9 April 1948; *Educ* Sutton Valence, Royal Holloway Coll London (BSc, PhD), Univ of Kent at Canterbury (Dip Adult and Further Educn), King's Coll London (Dip EC Law); *m* 21 July 1979, Carol Lynn, da of Kenneth Thomas Mellor; 1 da (Zoë Ellen Victoria b 16 March 1985), 1 s (Thomas Edgar Ray b 17 May 1989); *Career* scientist and conslt ecologist; asst biology teacher Sutton Valence Sch 1973–78; prop: Wildlife Matters (consultancy and publisher) 1978–, Garden Matters 1993–, Garden Matters and Wildlife Matters Photographic Libraries; author of 43 books on entomology and natural history for children and adults, trans into 30 languages, also numerous scientific and popular articles and reviews; currently chartered biologist, chartered environmentalist and chartered ecologist; tstee Brazilian Atlantic Rainforest Tst (BART); memb Environmental Law Fndn 1997, life memb Int Dendrological Assoc; Freeman: Worshipful Co of Poulters 1993, City of London 1994; fell Assoc of Lawyers and Legal Advsrs 1997; corp memb Inst of Environmental Mgmnt and Assessment; FRES 1970, FLS 1970, CBiol 1970, FIBiol 1993; *Books* incl: Biology and Biochemistry of the Large White (1982), Butterflies and Other Insects of Britain (1984), Discovering Doorstep Wildlife (1985), Natural History of Butterflies (1986), Naturalist's Garden (1987), Animals and Where They Live (1988, published in 27 countries), A Guide to Countryside Conservation (1989), The Story of Silk (1990), Butterflies: A Practical Guide (1990), Beekeeping: A Practical Guide (1991), Slugs, Snails and Earthworms (1991), Recycling in the School Environment (1991), Meadows: A History and Natural History (1992), Pocket Guide to European Butterflies (1992), Butterflies and Moths (Dorling-Kindersley Eyewitness series, 1993), Encyclopaedia of Butterflies of the World (1993), Butterflies and Moths, Nature Facts (1993), Bugs, Beetles and Other Insects (1993), Live Oak Splendor, Gardens Along the Mississippi (1994), Pocket Guide to North American Butterflies (1994), Butterflies of North America Folio Edition (1994), Butterflies of Europe Folio Edition (1994), The Conservation of Butterflies in Britain, past and present (1995), A Creative Step by Step Guide to Climbers and Trellis Plants (1996), Wide World of Animals (1996), Spectacular Hanging Baskets (1996), Pocket Guide of Butterflies of Britain and Europe (1998), Clematis for all Seasons (1999), Geraniums and Pelargoniums (2001), Clematis and Climbers (2003), Bumblebees (2006), Rainforests (2008), Honeybees (2012), The Queen's Mulberries (jtly); *Recreations* observing nature, especially in rainforests; *Clubs* Farmers; *Style*— Dr John Feltwell; ✉ Marlham, Henley's Down, Battle, East Sussex TN33 9BN (✆ 01424 830566, e-mail john@wildlifematters.com, website www.wildlifematters.com, www.rainforestmatters.com and www.drjohnfeltwell.com)

FELTWELL, Robert Leslie (Bob); s of Ray Parker Feltwell (d 1994), of Eastbourne, E Sussex, and Edna Mary, *née* Edmonds (d 1992); *b* 15 February 1944; *Educ* King Edward VI Sch Norwich, Univ of London (BSc(Econ)); *m* 22 July 1967, Christine Renée, da of Richard Henry John Rees (d 2001), of Horsham, W Sussex; 2 da (Alison Mary b 1970, Elizabeth Jane b 1972); *Career* family farm Hartfield Sussex 1962–67, grad apprentice then prodn mangr Rolls-Royce Ltd Aero Engines 1967–70, telephone prodn mangr ITT UK and Belgium 1970–76, gen mangr Western Incubators Ltd 1976–78, overseas devpt mangr Pauls International Ltd 1978–79, prodn dir Eastern Counties Farmers Ltd 1979–90, chief exec and dir Suffolk C of C, Industry and Shipping 1990–2006, elected dir Br Chambers of Commerce Ltd 1999–2004; dir: Suffolk TEC 1993–2001, Business Link for Suffolk Ltd 1995–2006, Project for a University for Suffolk Company Ltd 1997–2005, Suffolk LSC 2001–04, BLS Enterprises Ltd 2001–15, Genix Holdings Ltd 2006–15, Otley Coll Enterprises Ltd 2009–14, Easton Leisure Ltd 2012–14, EOC SPV Ltd 2014–, Bentley Community Shop CIC 2015– (chm 2015), EOS Enterprises 2015–; memb Bentley Playing Fields Soc 2007–; treas Br C of C Execs 1993–2005, regnl sec E of England Cs of C 1993–2006, dir E of England Chambers of Commerce Ltd 1997–2006, hon memb Suffolk Chamber of Commerce Industry and Shipping 2006–; fndr memb University for Suffolk Task Gp 1994–2005; memb Standards Ctee Babergh DC 2008–12; ldr 35 UK Trade Missions to Brazil, Malaysia, Singapore, Hong Kong, Shanghai, South Korea, Vietnam and Thailand 1993–2005; young enterprise business advsr 2007–09; regular broadcaster and writer on business and int trade; govr: Otley Coll of Agriculture and Horticulture 2008–12 (chm 2009–12), Suffolk One Ipswich (formerly SWISS Sixth Form Sch Ipswich) 2008–12, Easton and Otley Coll 2012–; memb Bentley Parish Cncl 2007–, memb Cncl Suffolk Agricultural Assoc 2010–; Freeman City of London 1993, Liveryman Worshipful Co of Poulters 1994; MIEx 1995, CCMI (MIMgt 1979); *Recreations* travel, tennis; *Clubs* Farmers, Ipswich Rotary; *Style*— Bob Feltwell, Esq; ✉ Woodfield, Bentley, Ipswich, Suffolk IP9 2DH (e-mail bobfeltwell@talk21.com)

FENBY, Jonathan Theodore Starmer; CBE; s of Charles Fenby (d 1974), and June, *née* Head; *b* 11 November 1942; *Educ* King Edward's Sch Birmingham, Westminster, New Coll

Oxford (BA); *m* 1 July 1967, Renée; 1 da (Sara b 1970), 1 s (Alexander b 1972); *Career* corr bureau chief Reuters and ed Reuters World Serv 1963–77, corr The Economist France and West Germany 1982–86, home ed and asst ed The Independent 1986–88, dep ed The Guardian 1988–93 (dir 1990–95); ed: The Observer 1993–95, South China Morning Post 1995–99, Business Europe 2000–01; assoc ed Sunday Business 2000–01, co-fndr and editorial dir earlywarning.com 2004, managing ptnr Trusted Sources, fndr and md China Research 2006; memb Bd China Dialogue; research assoc SOAS London, assoc LSE and RIIA; contrib to Br, American, French and Japanese newspapers and magazines, broadcaster in GB, France, Switzerland, USA, Canada and the Far East; conf speaker GB, France, USA and Far East; Chevalier de la Légion d'Honneur and l'Ordre Nationale du Mérite (France); *Books* The Fall of the House of Beaverbrook (1979), Piracy and the Public (1983), The International News Services (1986), On The Brink, The Trouble With France (1998, revised edns 2002 and 2004, new edn US 2014), Comment peut-on être français? (1999), Dealing with the Dragon (2000), Generalissimo: Chiang Kai-shek and the China He Lost (2003), The Sinking of the Lancastric (2005), Alliance (2006), The Seventy Wonders of China (2007), Struggling Giant (foreword, 2007), China's Journey (2008), The Dragon Throne (2008 and 2015), The Penguin History of Modern China (2008), The General: Charles de Gaulle and the France He Saved (2010), Tiger Head Snake Tails – China Today (2012), The Siege of Tsingtao (2014), Will China Dominate the 21st Century? (2014), The History of Modern France (2015, updated paperback edn 2016); *Recreations* belote, walking, jazz; *Style—* Jonathan Fenby, CBE; ✉ 101 Ridgmount Gardens, London WC1E 7AZ (☎ 020 7323 0547, fax 020 7323 0579, e-mail jtfenby@hotmail.com); Trusted Sources, 48 Charlotte Street, London W1T 2NS

FENELEY, Mark Roger; s of Roger Charles Leslie Feneley, of Bristol, and Patricia; *b* 8 September 1961, Bristol; *Educ* Clifton (headmaster's scholarship, music scholarship, Douglas Fox Challen Gold Medal), CCC Cambridge (Smythe exhibition, Smythe scholarship, MA, MB BChir, MD), Guy's Hosp Med Sch London; *m* 1 (m dis); m 2, 14 July 2000, Sandra Sue Haskell, *née* Ingraham; 2 s (Ricky James b 10 Dec 1967, Anthony Scott b 28 Oct 1979), 1 da (Kim Marie b 19 May 1970); *Career* house surgn and house physician Guy's Hosp London 1987–88, demonstrator in anatomy Univ of Cambridge 1988–89, basic surgical trg posts Bart's Hosp London 1989–91, registrar (gen surgery) Ipswich Hosp 1991–92, research registrar Dept of Urology Bart's London 1992–94, sr registrar (urology) Bart's and Royal London Hosps London 1994–98, post doctoral fell James Buchanan Brady Urological Inst Johns Hopkins Hosp Baltimore MD 1998–2000, conslt urological surgn Nottingham City Hosp 2000–02, dir of postgrad med educn and clinical tutor Nottingham City Hosp 2002, conslt urological oncological surgn UCL Hosps 2003– (clinical lead in urology 2008–09, hon sr lectr in urological oncological surgery Inst of Urology 2004–), hon conslt urologist Whittington Hosp NHS Tst London 2009–, hon conslt urologist Royal Free Hosp NHS Fndn Tst London 2011–15; Hunterian prof RCS 1997; Section of Urology RSM Travelling Fellowship to USA 1997, Br Jl of Urology and Br Assoc of Urology Travelling Fellowship 1998, AstraZeneca Travelling Fellowship 2002, British Urological Fndn preceptorship to Monsoura Egypt 2006; full memb Br Assoc of Urological Surgns, corresponding memb American Assoc of Urological Surgns; memb: Oncology Section Br Assoc of Urological Surgns, Section of Urology RSM (jr rep and elected memb Cncl 1996–98), Soc for Study of Androgen Deficiency (memb Ctee 2002–, vice-chm 2003–05, chm 2005–07 and 2010–), BMA, Cambridge Med Soc, European Assoc of Urology; FRCS 1991, FRSM 1994, FRCS (Urology) 1997; *Publications* Textbook of Prostate Cancer: Principles and Practice (jt ed, 2005), Therapeutic Opportunities in Prostate Cancer (jt ed, 2007), Treatment Methods for Early and Advanced Prostate Cancer (jt ed, 2008), Handbook of Urological Surgery (jt ed, 2008); numerous book chapters and articles in professional jls relating to urological oncology, prostate diseases and prostate cancer screening; *Recreations* music; *Style—* Mr M R Feneley; ✉ Department of Urology, UCLH NHS Foundation Trust, 250 Euston Road, Ground Floor Central Wing, London NW1 2PG (website www.markfeneley.com)

FENHALLS, Richard Dorian; s of Roydon Myers and Maureen Fenhalls; *b* 14 July 1943; *Educ* Hilton Coll Univ of Natal (BA), Christ's Coll Cambridge (MA, LLM); *m* 1967, Angela Sarah, *née* Allen; 1 s, 1 da; *Career* Goodricke & Son, Attorney SA 1969–70, Citibank 1970–72; sr vice-pres: Marine Midland Bank 1972–77, American Express Bank 1977–81; dep chm and chief exec Guinness Mahon & Co Ltd 1981–85, chm Henry Ansbacher & Co Ltd and chief exec Henry Ansbacher Holdings plc 1985–93, chief exec Strand Partners Ltd 1993–; *Recreations* historic car rallying; *Clubs* Royal Ocean Racing, Royal Southern Yacht (Hamble), Royal Thames Yacht, Veteran Car Club of Great Britain; *Style—* R D Fenhalls, Esq; ✉ 6 Pembridge Place, London W2 4XB; Strand Partners Limited, 26 Mount Row, London W1K 3SQ (☎ 020 7409 3494, fax 020 7491 0899)

FENN, Robert Dominic Russell; *m* Julia, *née* Lloyd Williams; 2 s; *Career* diplomat; Belize/Guatemala Desk FCO 1983–85, 3 sec The Hague 1985–88, 2 sec Lagos 1988–89, South Africa Desk FCO 1989–92, 1 sec UK Mission NY 1992–97, 1 sec Rome 1997–2001, dep head Southern European Dept FCO 2001–04, dep high cmmr Nicosia 2004–08, high cmmr Brunei 2009–13, head Human Rights and Democracy Dept 2013–; *Style—* Mr Robert Fenn; ✉ c/o FCO, King Charles Street, London SW1A 2AH

FENNELL, Alister Theodore (Theo); s of Alister Fennell, and Verity Fennell; *Educ* Eton (cricket XI), Byam Shaw Sch of Art; *m* 1977, Louise *née* MacGregor; 2 da (Emerald, Coco); *Career* silversmith with Edward Barnard, started own business 1975, Theo Fennell plc (jewellers with outlets worldwide); memb Ctee: Nordorff Robins Music Therapy (NRMT), Elton John Aids Fndn; *Recreations* reading, drawing, talking, golf, cricket, playing guitar, musical theatre; *Clubs* MCC, I Zingari, Chelsea Arts, Sunningdale, Saints & Sinners, Tramp; *Style—* Theo Fennell, Esq

FENNER, John Ronald; OBE (1997); s of Louis Finkel (d 2000), and Claire, *née* Lubkin (d 1975); *b* 7 December 1935; *Educ* Brunswick Sch Haywards Heath, Tonbridge, UCL (LLB); *m* 24 March 1963, Gillian Adelaide, da of Stanley Joshua Simmons (d 1982), and Hettie, *née* Helman (d 1966); 2 s (Robert Matthew b 19 June 1965, Adam Edward b 28 Feb 1972), 1 da (Harriet Jane b 25 May 1967 d 1971); *Career* served articles Zeffertt Heard & Morley Lawson 1956–59, ptnr Lionel Leighton & Co 1962–70; Berwin Leighton: fndr ptnr 1970, managing ptnr 1980–84, chm 1984–90, sr ptnr 1990–94; fndr ptnr and sr ptnr Fenners 1994–2003, ptnr Maclay Murray & Spens 2003–05, sr conslt Pinsent Masons 2005–09, special advsr Mayor's Fund for London 2009–13; lectr Univ of the Third Age London 2012–; chm: Nat Cncl for Jews in the former Soviet Union 1989–93, BURA (British Urban Regeneration Assoc) 1991–99 (tstee BURA Charitable Tst 1993–2009), British Friends of Israel Philarmonic Orch Fndn 1993–96, Legacy Ctee Norwood Ravenswood; tstee and dir RICS Research Fndn 2001–05; chm of appeal Nightingale House 1986–93; memb Cncl Local Investment Fund 1995–99, vol memb Kids' Co 2013–; Freeman City of London, Master Worshipful Co of Fletchers 2002 (memb Ct of Assts, tstee Charitable Tst 1998–), memb Worshipful Co of Chartered Surveyors (memb Charity Ctee 2008–15, memb Educn Ctee 2008–, memb Ct of Assts 2013–); memb: Law Soc 1959, Southwestern Legal Fndn (USA) 1985, Int Bar Assoc 1985, City of London Slrs' Co; Grotius Prize 1960; *Recreations* history, theatre, opera; *Clubs* RAC; *Style—* John Fenner, Esq, OBE; ✉ 19 Avenue Close, Avenue Road, London NW8 6BX (☎ 020 7586 2282, e-mail johnronaldfenner@msn.com)

FENTIMAN, Prof Ian Stuart; s of Harold Latter Fentiman (d 1989), and Vida Frances, *née* Jones; *b* 23 June 1945; *Educ* Trinity Sch of John Whitgift, King's Coll Hosp London (MB BS, MD, DSc); *Career* conslt surgn Guy's Hosp 1982–, prof of surgical oncology Univ of London; Arris and Gale lectr RCS 1978; LRCP, FRCS (MRCS), fell Assoc of Surgns; *Books* Detection and Treatment of Early Breast Cancer (1991, 2 edn 1998), Prevention of Breast Cancer (1993), Breast Cancer (1994), Cancer in the Elderly: Research and Treatment (1994), Atlas of Breast Examination (1997), Challenges in Breast Cancer (1999); *Style—* Prof Ian Fentiman; ✉ Research Oncology, 3rd Floor Bermondsey Wing, Guy's Hospital, St Thomas Street, London SE1 9RT (☎ 020 7188 4245, fax 020 7403 8381, e-mail ian.fentiman@gstt.nhs.uk); 148 Harley Street, London W1G 7LG (☎ 020 7284 0068, fax 03333 441114)

FENTON, Maria Elizabeth Josephine; *b* 9 May 1956; *Educ* St Mary's Providence Convent, Kingston Univ, Coll of Law Guildford (BA); *Career* admitted slr of the Supreme Ct 1980; gp private banking legal advsr HSBC (Holdings) plc 1992–2007, legal counsel Kleinwort Benson Bank Ltd 2008–16; memb Law Soc; *Style—* Mrs Maria Fenton

FENTON, Dr Mark Alexander; s of Prof George Wallace Fenton (d 2000), and Dr Sylvia Fenton, *née* Hepton; *b* 20 October 1965; *Educ* Brentwood Sch, Peterhouse Cambridge (BA), Anglia Ruskin Univ (MSc, PhD); *Career* teacher Boswells Sch Chelmsford 1988–91, head of history and politics King Edward VI Sch Chelmsford 1991–97 (sr teacher 1994–97), dep head Sir Joseph Williamson's Mathematical Sch Rochester 1997–2001, headmaster Dr Challoner's GS Amersham 2001–16 (seconded pt/t to Br Cncl SLANT Project Trinidad and Tobago 2007–11), chief master King Edward's Sch Birmingham 2016–; nat ldr of educn 2009–, memb Headmasters' and Headmistresses' Conf 2010–, chm GS Heads Assoc 2012–13; dir Ramsey Singers 1987–; chm Bucks Schs Cricket Assoc 2004–, tstee Cricket Fndn 2005–08, youth cricket dir Bucks Cricket Bd 2012–; chair Bucks Acad of Sch Leadership 2005–08, govr Berkhamsted Sch 2013–; tstee Int Boys Sch Coalition 2014–; exec headteacher Ealing Fields Academy Tst 2014–16; *Recreations* choral singing and conducting; watching, playing and coaching cricket; *Clubs* MCC, Lansdowne, RSM, East India; *Style—* Dr Mark Fenton; ✉ King Edward's School, Edgbaston Park Road, Birmingham B15 2UA (☎ 0121 472 1672, e-mail office@kes.org.uk)

FENTON, Shaun Alan; *Educ* Haberdashers Askes Sch, Keble Coll Oxford (MA, PGCE); *Career* headteacher Sir John Lawes Sch Harpenden, headmaster Pate's GS (named Sunday Times School of the Year), headmaster Reigate GS 2012–; memb HMC 2012– (additional memb 2005–12); appearance on The One Show, regular contrib The Telegraph; tstee AQA; *Style—* Shaun Fenton, Esq; ✉ Reigate Grammar School, Reigate Road, Reigate, Surrey RH2 0QS (e-mail headmaster@reigategrammar.org, website www.reigategrammar.org)

FENWICK, (John) Andrew; s of John James Fenwick, of London, and Muriel Gillian, *née* Hodnett; *b* 8 October 1959; *Educ* Eton, Univ of Exeter (BA), Harvard Business Sch (PMD Program); *m* 10 Sept 1994, (Fiona) Jane Morgan, da of Hubert John Watkins, of Presteigne, Powys; 4 s (Mungo b 3 Nov 1997, Theodore, Samuel, Inigo (triplets) b 18 Sept 2003); *Career* accountant Deloitte Haskins & Sells 1982–86, fin PR Broad St Assocs London 1986–87, gp fin dir Brunswick Group LLP 1987– (vice-chm 2011–), dir Fenwick Ltd 1999–; govr New Kings Primary Sch Fulham 1993–2015 (chair 1996–2015); non-exec dir Royal Parks Agency 2003–; tstee: PSP Assoc 1998–2012, Royal Parks Fndn 2003– (vice-chm 2012–); govr and chair Thomas's Acad Fulham (formerly New Kings Primary Sch) 2015–; Freeman City of London 1990, Liveryman Worshipful Co of Mercers 1992 (Freeman 1990); FCA 1995 (ACA 1985); *Recreations* travel, horticulture; *Style—* Andrew Fenwick, Esq; ✉ Brunswick Group LLP, 15 Lincoln's Inn Fields, London WC2A 3ED (☎ 020 7404 5959, fax 020 7831 2823, e-mail afenwick@brunswickgroup.com)

FENWICK, Maj Charles Xtafer Sebastian; LVO (1977); s of David Fenwick (d 1982); *b* 7 April 1946; *Educ* Ampleforth; *m* 1997, Sara Elizabeth, da of late Col E Jewson, MC, DL, TD, and Mrs Jewson, and wid of late David Nickerson; *Career* Maj, Regt Offr Grenadier Guards 1965–78, tutor to HH Sheik Maktoum Bin Rashid Al Maktoum Ruler of Dubai 1968–69, asst private sec to HRH The Duke of Edinburgh 1975–77; chm BPN Ltd, chm Int Garden Centre Assoc H H (Br Gp) Ltd 1984–, chm The Chelsea Gardener 1984–, chm Myriad Enterprises 2007–; *Clubs* Turf, Pratt's; *Style—* Maj Charles Fenwick, LVO; ✉ Higham Place, Higham, Suffolk CO7 6JY; 4 Ladbroke Terrace, London W11 3PG

FENWICK, Maj Justin Francis Quintus; QC (1993); s of David Fenwick (d 1982), and Maita Gwladys Joan, *née* Powys-Keck (d 2007); *b* 11 September 1949; *Educ* Ampleforth, Clare Coll Cambridge (MA); *m* 21 June 1975, Marcia Mary, da of Archibald Dunn (d 1977), of Layham, Suffolk; 3 da (Corisande Mary b 1983, Rosamund Xanthe b 1985, Madeleine Isobel b 1988), 1 s (Hubert George Francis b 3 Aug 1990); *Career* Grenadier Gds 1968–81: Maj and Adj 2 Bn 1977–79, Extra Equerry to HRH The Duke of Edinburgh 1979–81; called to the Bar Inner Temple 1980 (bencher 1997); recorder 1999–, head of chambers 2000–05, dep judge of the High Court 2003–; dir: By Pass Nurseries Ltd 1982–, Bar Mutual Indemnity Fund 1998–2013 (chm 1999–2013); cmmr Royal Hosp Chelsea 2011–; *Recreations* shooting, reading, wine; *Clubs* Garrick; *Style—* Justin Fenwick, Esq, QC; ✉ 4 New Square, Lincolns Inn, London WC2A 3RJ (☎ 020 7822 2000)

FENWICK, Sir Leonard Raymond; kt (2008), CBE (2000); s of Leo Stanislaws Fenwick (d 1983), of Newcastle upon Tyne, and Hilda May, *née* Downey (d 1989); *b* 10 August 1947; *Educ* West Jesmond and John Harlay Schs Newcastle upon Tyne; *m* 1969, Jacqueline; 1 da (Kate b 1982); *Career* NHS: joined 1965, various posts in health serv mgmnt in NE England and Humberside 1966–74, admin then gen mangr Freeman Hosp since 1975, chief exec Freeman Gp of Hosps NHS Tst 1990–; cncllr Tyne & Wear CC 1981–86; Freeman City of Newcastle upon Tyne, memb Worshipful Co of Shipwrights 1968, chm Stewards Ctee of Incorporated Cos and Ct of Guild of City of Newcastle upon Tyne; memb Inst of Health Servs Mgmnt 1972; *Style—* Sir Leonard Fenwick, CBE; ✉ The Freeman Group of Hospitals, High Heaton, Newcastle upon Tyne NE7 7DN (☎ 0191 284 3111, fax 0191 213 1968)

FENWICK, Mark Anthony; s of John Fenwick, of Newcastle upon Tyne, and Sheila E M, *née* Edwards; *b* 11 May 1948; *Educ* Millfield; *m* 9 Nov 1972, Margaret Kathleen, da of Col Frederick Roger Hue Williams (d 1987), of Newbury, Berks; 1 da (Mia b 14 April 1978), 1 s (Leo b 26 Sept 1980); *Career* chm Fenwick Ltd 1997–, mangr Roger Waters 1992–; *Recreations* music, outdoor activities; *Style—* Mark Fenwick, Esq; ✉ Fenwick Ltd, New Bond Street, London W1A 3BS (☎ 020 7499 7275, fax 020 7629 1186, e-mail markfenwick@mfm.demon.co.uk)

FENWICK, Rt Rev Dr Richard David; *see:* St Helena, Lord Bishop of

FENWICK, Trevor James; s of Leslie Fenwick, of London, and Mabel Alice, *née* Lee; *b* 28 February 1954; *Educ* Highgate Sch, Univ of Essex (BA); *m* Jane Seton Hindley; 3 s (James b 1987, Edward b 1989, Charles b 1991); *Career* exec chm Euromonitor Int Ltd 1988– (dir 1980–), pres Euromonitor International Inc 1993–; dir: Data Publishers Assoc 1997– (chm 1993–97 and 2008–), Professional Publishers Assoc 2011–; pres Euro Assoc of Directory and Database Publishers 2002–04; memb: Bd Confdn of Info Communication Industries, Cncl Advtg Assoc 1997–2010, Advsy Panel on Public Sector Information 2003–08, Legal Deposit Advsy Panel 2005–10; DPA George Henderson Award 2011; govr Stationers' Crown Woods Acad 2014–, govr St Bride Fndn 2015–, tstee Stationers' Fndn 2016–; hon fell Ravensbourne 2014; Ct Asst Worshipful Co of Stationers and Newspaper Makers 2010–; FCIM; *Publications* Copyright in the Digital Age: Industry Issues and Impacts (ed); *Clubs* West Mersea Yacht, Reform; *Style—* Trevor Fenwick, Esq; ✉ Euromonitor International Ltd, 60–61 Britton Street, London EC1M 5UX

FERADAY, Caroline Emma; da of Allen and Gillian Feraday; *b* 25 May 1977, Chatham, Kent; *Educ* Rochester GS, Mid Kent Coll of Higher and Further Educn; *Career* TV and radio broadcaster; presenter: Capital Radio 1995–2001, Sky One 1999–2000, Travel Channel 2000–03, BBC Radio 5 Live 2001–03, LBC 97.3 2003–07, South East Today

(BBC) 2007–, Sky News 2009–10, This Morning (ITV) 2011–12, BBC London 94.9 2012–, GMTV, Sky Travel, Living TV, Comedy Store LA, Flappers Comedy Club LA; Outstanding Contribution to Radio and Journalism Prince Philip Medal 2007; *Recreations* running, movies, travel; *Style—* Ms Caroline Feraday; ✉ website www.carolineferaday.com; Twitter @carolineferaday; c/o Jane Compton, Compton Management, London

FERDINAND, Rio Gavin; s of Julian Ferdinand and Janice Ferdinand; bro of Anton Ferdinand (professional footballer, Sunderland FC), cous of Les Ferdinand (former England int footballer); *b* 7 November 1978, Peckham, London; *Career* professional footballer; clubs: West Ham United 1993–2000 (first team debut 1996), Leeds United 2000–02 (transferred for then Br record fee), Manchester United 2002– (transferred for then Br record fee, winners FA Premiership 2003, 2007, 2008, 2009, 2011 and 2013, winners UEFA Champions League 2008, finalists FA Cup 2005 and 2007); captained Manchester United FC to winners of FA Premiership and UEFA Champions League 2008; England: 81 caps, 3 goals, memb World Cup squad 1998, 2002 and 2006, capt 2010–11; co-fndr White Chalk Music 2005–, co-fndr Next Generation TV & Film, presenter Rio's World Cup Wind-Ups 2006, exec prodr Dead Man Running (film) 2009; *Style—* Mr Rio Ferdinand; ✉ c/o Jeff Weston at SEM Group, 98 Cockfosters Road, Barnet, Hertfordshire EN4 0DP (☎ 020 8447 4250)

FERGUS, Jeffrey John (Jeff); s of George M Fergus (d 1979), of Glasgow, and Catherine, *née* Fellowes; *b* 23 March 1949; *Educ* Crookson Castle Sch Glasgow, Univ of Strathclyde (BA); *m* 18 March 1989, Emily, da of Leslie Kark; 2 s (Frederick George Arthur b 1 April 1991, Charles William Merry b 26 May 1993); *Career* Leo Burnett advtg agency: joined Account Mgmnt Dept 1969, appointed to bd 1975, head of dept 1979–83, dep md 1980–83; md Grandfield Rork Collins 1983–86; Leo Burnett: md and chief exec 1986–94, regnl md Asia and the Pacific 1994–97, gp pres Europe, Africa, ME and Asia Pacific 1997–2001; dir Chartmille Roche 2005–, non-exec dir McDonald's Restaurants UK 2004–10; tstee Ronald McDonald House Charities 2008–, chm of tstees Ronald McDonald House Charities 2011–, dir Scottish Baroque Ensemble 2013–; chm Alumni Fund Bd Univ of Strathclyde 1990–94, memb Ct Univ of Strathclyde 2003–12; Hon DUniv Strathclyde 2009; MCIM 1980, MIPA 1982; *Clubs* Annabel's, Caledonian; *Style—* Jeff Fergus, Esq; ✉ 3 Fawcett Street, London SW10 9HN (☎ 020 7352 1322, fax 020 7351 7780)

FERGUS-THOMPSON, Gordon; s of George Leonard Thompson (d 1986), of Leeds, and Constance, *née* Webb (d 2005); *b* 9 March 1952; *Educ* Temple Moor GS Leeds, Royal Manchester Coll of Music; *Career* concert pianist; debut Wigmore Hall 1976; performed as soloist with orchs incl: The Philharmonia, English Chamber Orch, City of Birmingham Symphony Orch, Royal Liverpool Philharmonic, Hallé Orch, Bournemouth Symphony Orch, BBC Symphony Orchs; regular broadcaster BBC Radio 3, toured extensively throughout Europe as recitalist and soloist with the Göteborg Symphony Orch and the Residente Orch of the Hague, also Australia, Japan, China, Singapore, South Africa and USA; awarded Calouste Gulbenkian fellowship 1978; prof of piano Royal Coll of Music 1996–; FRCM 2010; *Recordings* incl: Complete Works of Ravel (2 Vols) 1992, Complete Works of Debussy (5 vols, winner solo instrumental section Music Retailers Assoc awards 1991) 1989, Complete Works of Scriabin (Vol 1 – Sonatas 4, 5, 9 and 10 and Studies Opus 42, winner Solo Instrumental Section MRA awards 1992) 1990, Rachmaninoff Études-Tableaux 1990, Bach transcriptions 1990, Two Rachmaninoff Sonatas 1987, Balakirev and Scriabin Sonatas 1987, Scriabin Vol 2 (Sonatas 2 and 3 and Studies Op 8) 1994, Scriabin Vol 3 (Preludes Op 2–17) 1994, Headington Piano Concerto 1997, Scriabin Vol 4 (The Complete Mazurkas) 2000, Scriabin Vol 5 (Preludes Op 22–74 and Impromptus Op 2, 7 & 10) 2001; *Recreations* art, chess, cooking, tennis, humour; *Style—* Gordon Fergus-Thompson, Esq; ✉ Royal College of Music, London SW7 2BS (☎ 07590 515645, e-mail gfergusthompson@rcm.ac.uk, website www.gordonfergusthompson.com)

FERGUSON; *see also:* Johnson-Ferguson

FERGUSON, Sir Alexander Chapman (Alex); kt (1999), CBE (1995, OBE 1984); s of Alexander Beaton Ferguson (d 1979), and Elizabeth, *née* Hardy (d 1986); *b* 31 December 1941, Govan, Glasgow; *Educ* Govan High Sr Secdy Sch; *m* 12 March 1966, Catherine Russell, da of Hugh Holding (d 1952); 3 s (Mark b 18 Sept 1968, Jason, Darren (twins) b 9 Feb 1972); *Career* football manager; player: Queen's Park 1958–60, St Johnstone 1960–64, Dunfermline Athletic 1964–67, Glasgow Rangers 1967–69, Falkirk 1969–73, Ayr United 1973–74, two Scot League caps; mangr: E Stirling 1974, St Mirren 1974–78 (First Div champions 1976–77), Aberdeen 1978–86, Scot nat team 1985–86 (asst mangr under Jock Stein 1985–86), Manchester United 1986–2013, ret; honours with Aberdeen: winners Euro Cup Winners' Cup 1983, winners Super Cup 1983, Premier Div champions 1980, 1982 and 1984, winners Scot FA Cup 1982, 1983, 1984 and 1986, winners Scot League Cup 1985; honours with Manchester United: winners FA Cup 1990, 1994, 1996, 1999 and 2004, winners Charity Shield/Community Shield 1990, 1993, 1994, 1996, 1997, 2003, 2007 and 2008, winners Euro Cup Winners' Cup 1991, winners Super Cup 1991, winners Rumbelows Cup 1992, winners FA Premier League Championship 1993, 1994, 1996, 1997, 1999, 2000, 2001, 2003, 2007, 2008, 2009, 2011 and 2013, winners European Champions League 1999 and 2008, Carling Cup 2006 and 2009; Manager of the Year Scotland 1983–85, Manager of the Year England 1993–94 and 1998–99; Lifetime Achievement Award BBC Sports Personality of the Year Awards 2001; Freeman: Aberdeen 1999, Glasgow 1999, Manchester 1999; Hon MA: Univ of Salford 1996, Univ of Manchester 1997; Hon Dr jur: Robert Gordon Univ Aberdeen 1997, Univ of St Andrews 2002; Hon MSc Manchester Met and UMIST (jtly) 1998, Hon DLitt Glasgow Caledonian Univ 2001, Hon Doc Univ of Stirling, Hon Doc Univ of Strathclyde, Hon Dr of Science Univ of Science; *Books* A Light in the North (1985), Alex Ferguson – Six Years at United (1992), Just Champion (1993), A Year in the Life (1995), A Will to Win (1997), Managing My Life (1999), The Unique Treble (2000); *Recreations* golf, snooker; *Style—* Sir Alex Ferguson, CBE; ✉ ACF Promotions, 24 Alderley Road, Wilmslow SK8 1PC (☎ 01625 535294)

FERGUSON, Prof Allister Ian; *b* 10 December 1951; *Educ* Univ of St Andrews (BSc, PhD), Univ of Oxford (MA); *Career* visiting scholar Stanford Univ 1977–79; postdoctoral fell: Univ of St Andrews 1979–80, Univ of Oxford 1980–83; sr lectr Univ of Southampton 1987–88 (lectr 1983–87); Univ of Strathclyde: prof of photonics 1989–, tech dir Inst of Photonics 1995–, dep princ 2004–11; Lindemann fell 1977–79, SERC postdoctoral fell 1981–86; author of numerous pubns and chapters in books; Neil Arnott prize 1974, NPL Metrology award 1983; fndr Microlase Optical Systems Ltd; ed-in-chief JPhysD: Applied Physics 1998–2003; fell Optical Soc of America 1997; FInstP 1990, FRSE 1993, FIEEE 2000, FFCS; *Style—* Prof Allister I Ferguson, FRSE; ✉ Department of Physics, University of Strathclyde, John Anderson Building, Glasgow G4 0NG (☎ 0141 548 3359, fax 0141 552 2891, e-mail a.i.ferguson@strath.ac.uk)

FERGUSON, Andrew James; s of K W E Ferguson, of Camberley, Surrey, and Sally, *née* Wragg (now Mrs Moore), of Market Harborough, Leics; *b* 22 September 1958; *Educ* St Chad's Cathedral Sch Lichfield, King's Sch Worcester, Br Sch of Osteopathy London (Dip, MSc); *m* May 1991, Louise, da of Nigel Mizen, of Dunsfold, Surrey; 2 c; *Career* in private osteopathic practice London 1980–, lectr Br Sch of Osteopathy 1982–86, osteopath to English Nat Ballet Sch 1992; memb Gen Osteopathic Cncl; *Books* Back and Neck Pain (1988); *Recreations* watching dance, gardening, writing; *Style—* Andrew Ferguson, Esq; ✉ 15 Pembridge Road, London W11 3HG (☎ 020 7937 2298)

FERGUSON, Duncan George Robin; s of Dr Robert Lewis Ferguson (d 1998), and Kathleen Iris Ferguson, *née* Mackness; *b* 12 May 1942, Edinburgh; *Educ* Fettes, Trinity Coll Cambridge (MA); *m* 1966, Alison Margaret, da of James Simpson; 1 da (Sarah b 1967), 2 s (Alexander b 1969, Jason b 1971); *Career* actuarial student Bacon & Woodrow 1965–69, actuary Metropolitan Life Cape Town 1969–73, dir Int Eagle Star 1974–88, ptnr Bacon & Woodrow (latterly B&W Deloitte) 1988–2003 (sr ptnr 1994–2003); chm: Alba Life, Royal & Sun Alliance Life Holdings; non-exec dir: Halifax plc 1994–2001, Henderson Gp plc 2004–; pres Inst of Actuaries 1996–98 (memb Cncl 1989–2000), memb Cncl Int Actuarial Assoc 1996–2002; FIA 1970; *Recreations* hunting, theatre; *Style—* Duncan Ferguson, Esq

FERGUSON, George Robin Paget; CBE (2010); s of Robert Spencer Ferguson, MVO, of Pewsey, Wilts, and Eve Mary, *née* Paget; *b* 22 March 1947; *Educ* Wellington, Univ of Bristol (BA, BArch); *m* 24 May 1969, (Aymée) Lavinia, da of Sir John Clerk, 10 Bt, of Penicuik House, Midlothian; 2 da (Alice b 1971, Corinna b 1979), 1 s (John b 1974); *Career* architect; fndr practice 1972; Ferguson Mann: ptnr 1979–87, md 1988–; fndr Acanthus Associated Architectural Practices Ltd 1986–, dir Concept Planning Group (masterplanners At Bristol harbourside project) 1991–96; dir Tobacco Factory Enterprises Ltd, dir Boats at Bristol (ferry) Ltd, fndr dir Acad of Urbanism 2005–, dir Canteen West Ltd 2009–, dir The Harbourside (Bristol) Ltd 2010–; tstee Demos think tank 2007–10; Living Landmarks Big Lottery Ctee 2006–07; creator of Bristol Brunel Mile, fndr and dir Bristol Beer Factory 2005; pres RIBA 2003–05; instigator of notion of x-listing (ugly buildings) 2004–; columnist By George! column Bristol Evening Post 2008–; pres Avon Youth Assoc; tstee Br Cathedral Tst, tstee Gtr Bristol Fndn 1995–2001, patron Care & Repair, tstee Arnonlfini Art Gall 2008–; Bristol City cncllr (Lib) 1973–79, Parly candidate (Alliance) Bristol W1983–87; television and radio incl The Architecture Show 1998, Demolition (Channel 4) 2005, Building Britain (BBC 1) 2007; pres Bristol Soc of Architects 1993–94; High Sheriff Bristol 1996–97; winner RIBA, RICS and Civic Tst awards; memb Soc of Merchant Venturers 1995; Hon MA Univ of Bristol 1999, Hon PhD UWE 2003; RIBA 1972 (pres 2003–05), RWA 1997; *Books* Races Against Time (1983); *Recreations* travel, people, ideas, making things happen; *Clubs* Chelsea Arts; *Style—* George Ferguson, CBE; ✉ Ferguson Mann Architects, Royal Colonnade, 18 Great George Street, Bristol BS1 5RH (☎ 0117 929 9293, fax 0117 929 9295, e-mail gferguson@fm-architects.co.uk, website www.fm-architects.co.uk)

FERGUSON, Gerrard Murray (Gerry); s of John Murray Ferguson (d 1976), of Tanworth in Arden, Warks, and Dorothy Maude Nathalie, *née* Havill; *b* 23 July 1953, Manchester; *Educ* Abbey Sch Ashurst Wood, Epsom Coll, Univ of Birmingham (LLB); *m* 1, 1981 (m dis 2012), Nancy Elizabeth, *née* Woodyatt; 2 s (Henry, Sam); m 2, 10 Oct 2015, Jane Elisabeth Millington; *Career* admitted slr; articled clerk J W Ward & Son 1976–78, slr then ptnr Mowbray Woodwards 1979–89, ptnr Withy King LLP (formerly Withy King & Lee) 1989–12, ret; former claimant clinical negligence specialist; memb Action Against Medical Accidents (AvMA) Specialist Clinical Negligence Panel and Law Soc Clinical Negligence Accreditation Scheme, Legal Aid Bd, Legal Services Cmmn ctees, NHS Ind Complaints Advocacy pilots; memb Law Soc 1981–2012; former int memb American Assoc for Justice; *Recreations* travel, motor sport and rugby photography; *Clubs* Bath Rugby; *Style—* Gerry Ferguson, Esq; ☎ 0121 476 5597, mobile 07831 718728, e-mail fergusongerry409@yahoo.com

FERGUSON, James Gordon Dickson; s of Col James Dickson Ferguson, OBE, ERD, DL (d 1979), and Jean, *née* Gordon (d 1996); *b* 12 November 1947; *Educ* Cargilfield Sch Edinburgh, Winchester, Trinity Coll Dublin (BA); *m* 20 June 1970, Nicola Hilland (d 2007), da of Walter G H Stewart; 2 s (Jim, William), 1 da (Jessica); *Career* Stewart Ivory & Co Ltd (formerly Stewart Fund Managers Ltd): joined 1970, dir 1974–, chm 1989–2000; chm: Value and Income Tst plc, The Scottish Oriental Smaller Cos Tst plc, The Monks Investment Tst plc, North American Income Tst plc, Northern 3 VCT plc, Amati Global Inv Ltd; dir The Independent Investment Tst plc, former dep chm Assoc of Investment Tst Cos; govr Gordonstoun Sch; *Recreations* country pursuits; *Clubs* New (Edinburgh); *Style—* James Ferguson, Esq; ✉ 25 Heriot Row, Edinburgh EH3 6EN

FERGUSON, Jeremy John; s of Archibald John Lindo Ferguson (d 1975), of Great Missenden, Bucks, and Ann Meryl, *née* Thomas (d 1991); *b* 12 November 1935; *Educ* Stowe; *m* 1, 19 July 1958, Josephine Mary, *née* Hitchcock (d 1995), 1 s (Paul b 1962), 1 da (Elizabeth b 1966); m 2, 21 June 1997, Gillian Marjorie Heal, *née* Stronach; *Career* ptnr: Seldon Ward & Nuttall 1960–74, Jeremy Ferguson & Co 1974–91, Chanters Barnstaple 1986–91, Chanter Ferguson Bideford & Barnstaple 1991–; dep coroner N Devon 1964–74, hon slr (memb and past pres) Bideford C of C, fndr and sec Bideford Devpt Project, pres Law Soc Motor Club, pres Devon and Exeter Law Soc 2002–03, memb Legal Aid Area Ctee, vice-pres Legal Aid Cmmn of the Fedn of European Bars 2003–04, memb Devon and Exeter Law Soc Mediation Ctee; civil mediation trainer to: Law Socs of Zimbabwe, Kenya, Hong Kong, Uganda and Tanzania, Polish Mediation Assoc, Multi Door Court Abuja Nigeria, Mombasa Law Soc; presenter Mediation TV 2008–09; legal advsr Divorce Aid; presenter of papers on civil mediation to Cwlth Law Assoc; shortlisted Slr of the Year 2007; hon life memb Devon and Somerset Law Soc; *Publications* A Practical Guide to Time Limited and Small Claims Civil Mediation; *Recreations* flying (PPL), civil mediation, video photography; *Style—* Jeremy Ferguson, Esq; ✉ Overskern, Churchill Way, Appledore, N Devon EX39 1PA (☎ 01237 474855, e-mail jeremy.ferguson273@btinternet.com); 17 The Quay, Bideford, North Devon EX39 2EN (☎ 01237 478751, fax 01237 470893); Bridge Chambers, Barnstaple, North Devon EX31 1HF (☎ 01237 427911, e-mail jeremy.ferguson@wollenmichelmore.co.uk)

FERGUSON, Kenneth Gordon; OBE (1990); s of late James Ferguson, of Aberdour, Fife, and late Blanche Stockdale, *née* MacDonald; *b* 17 February 1944, Edinburgh; *Educ* Leith Acad, Heriot-Watt Univ, Napier Coll; *m* 21 Aug 1970, Jennifer Day, da of late Hugh MacTaggart Love, and late Margaret, *née* Anderson; 2 da (Amanda b 11 Aug 1971, Rebecca b 19 June 1975); *Career* chartered quantity surveyor; trainee Robert T B Gilray 1962–67; asst: Boyden and Cockrane 1967–69, City of Edinburgh Architect's Dept 1969–71, Todd and Ledson 1972–79; sr ptnr Kenneth Ferguson and Partners 1979–; vice-pres SCUA 1985–87, memb Edinburgh City Cncl 1977–92, chm Advsy Bd Commercial Unit Cardonald Coll Glasgow 1992–97; tstee dir Castles of Scotland Building Preservation Tst 1994–; incorporate CIOB 2000 (assoc CIOB 1991); FRICS 1979 (ARICS 1969); *Recreations* visiting and advising on historic buildings; *Clubs* Scottish Arts; *Style—* Kenneth G Ferguson, Esq, OBE; ✉ Stoneheap Farm House, Stoneyburn, West Lothian EH47 8EH (☎ 01501 763497, mobile 07946 471826, e-mail kenneth.g.ferguson@btinternet.com)

FERGUSON, Prof Mark William James; CBE (1999); s of late James Ferguson, of Marple Bridge, Cheshire, and Elanor Gwendoline, *née* McCoubrey; *b* 11 October 1955, Belfast; *Educ* Coleraine Academical Inst, Queen's Univ Belfast (BSc, BDS, PhD, DMedSc); *m* (m dis); 3 da (Fleur Marcia b 9 Sept 1987, Astrid Olivia b 8 May 1991, Eanna Sorcha b 30 April 2002); *Career* Winston Churchill fell 1978, lectr in anatomy Queen's Univ Belfast 1979–84, prof of basic dental sci and head Dept of Cell and Structural Biol Univ of Manchester 1984–, dean Sch of Biological Sciences Univ of Manchester 1994–99; fndr, dir, ceo and chm Renovo 1998–2012, DG Science Fndn Ireland 2012–; chief scientific advsr Govt of Ireland 2012–; faculty day lectr and visiting prof Univ of the Witwatersrand Johannesburg 1994; chm Health and Life Scis Panel UK Govt Technol Foresight Prog, pres Med Section BAAS, pres Craniofacial Soc, sec and pres European Tissue Repair Soc; fndr chm Manchester Biosciences Incubator 1995–99; memb: HE Cncl for Eng Basic Med and Dental Scis Panel 1996–2007, Scientific Ctee Br Cncl 1998–2001, Genome Valley Steering Gp 2000–01, Ctee on Safety of Medicines Biologicals Sub-Gp 1999–2005, UKTI UK Life Sci Mktg Strategy Bd 2008–12, Int Cncl for Science (ICU) Ctee 2015; chair EU Country Review of Hungarian Research and Innovation System; pres Manchester Medical Soc 2009–10; Colyer Prize RSM 1980, Alan J Davis Achievement Award American Dental Assoc 1981, Conway Medal Royal Acad of Med in Ireland 1985, Darwin lectr BAAS 1987, Distinguished Scientist Award Int Assoc for Dental Research Washington 1988, Pres's Medal BAOMS 1990, John Tomes Prize RCS 1990, Steager lectr NYU 1992, Teale lectr RCP 1994, 86th Kelvin lectr IEE 1995, JJ Pindborg Int Prize for research in oral biology 1996, Sheldon Friel Medal and lectr Euro Orthodontic Soc 1996, Broadhurst lectr Harvard Med Sch 1996, Carter Medal Soc for Human Genetics 1997, Charles Tomes lectr and Medal RCS 1998, Int Assoc for Dental Research Craniofacial Biology Award 2000, Northcroft lectr British Orthodontic Soc 2001, Lawdon-Brown lectr RCP 2002, European Sci Prize (jtly) 2002, NW Dir of the Year IOD 2006, Technol Pioneer World Economic Forum Davos 2007, Fergal Nally lectr RCSI 2013, Sir Bernard Crossland lecture Queen's Univ Belfast 2015; Hon FFDRCSI 1990, Hon FDS (RCSEd) 1997, FMedSci 1998, FIAcadE 2014; *Publications* The Structure, Development and Evolution of Reptiles (1984), Crocodiles and Alligators: an Illustrated Encyclopaedic Survey by International Experts (1989), Cleft Lip and Palate: Long Term Results and Future Prospects (1990), Egg Incubation, Its Effects on Embryonic Development in Birds and Reptiles (1991), Gray's Anatomy (38 edn), The Structure, Development and Evolution of Teeth (2000); also author of over 300 papers and books on: palate devpt, wound healing, sex determination, alligators and crocodiles; *Recreations* scientific research, biology, travel, wildlife, reading, antiques; *Style—* Prof Mark Ferguson, CBE; ✉ Science Foundation Ireland, Wilton Park House, Wilton Place, Dublin 2, Ireland (☎ 00353 1 607 3175, fax 00353 1 607 3163, e-mail mark.ferguson@sfi.ie, website www.sfi.ie)

FERGUSON, Prof Niall Campbell; s of Dr James Campbell Ferguson, and Molly Archibald, *née* Hamilton; *b* 18 April 1964; *Educ* Glasgow Acad, Magdalen Coll Oxford (BA, DPhil); *m* 1, 1994 (m dis 2011), Susan Margaret Douglas Ferguson, *qv*, *née* Douglas; 2 s, 1 da; m 2, Ayaan Hirsi Ali; 1 s; *Career* Hanseatic scholar Hamburg 1986–88, res fell Christ's Coll Cambridge 1989–90, official fell and lectr Peterhouse Cambridge 1990–92; Univ of Oxford: lectr in modern history 1992–2000, prof of political and financial history 2000–02, visiting prof in modern European history 2003–09; John E Herzog prof of financial history Leonard N Stern Sch of Business NYU 2002–04, Lawrence A Tisch prof of history Harvard Univ 2004–, William Ziegler prof of business admin Harvard Business Sch 2006–11; Philippe Roman visiting prof LSE 2010–11; Houblon-Norman fell Bank of England 1998–99, sr fell Hoover Inst Stanford Univ 2003–, sr res fell Jesus Coll Oxford 2003; ed Jl of Contemporary History 2004–08, contrib to English Historical Review, Past & Present, Economic History Review and Jl of Economic History; TV presenter: Empire 2003, American Colossus 2004, War of the World 2006, Ascent of Money 2008, Civilization 2011; Paper and Iron: Hamburg business and German Politics in the Era of Inflation 1897–1927 (1995), Virtual History: Alternatives and counterfactuals (ed, 1997), The World's Banker: The history of the house of Rothschild (1998), The Pity of War (1998), The Cash Nexus (2001), Empire: How Britain made the modern world (2003), Colossus: The rise and fall of the American Empire (2004), The War of the World: History's age of hatred (2006), The Ascent of Money: A Financial History of the World (2008), High Financier: The Lives and Time of Siegmund Warburg (2010), Civilization: The West and the Rest (2011); *Recreations* double bass, journalism, skiing, surfing; *Clubs* Beefsteak, Savile, RAC, Gridiron, Brook; *Style—* Prof Niall Ferguson; ✉ Minda de Gunzberg Center for European Studies, Harvard University, 27 Kirkland Street, Cambridge, MA 02138, USA (☎ 00 1 617 495 4303, fax 00 1 617 495 8509, website www.niallferguson.com)

FERGUSON, Nicholas Eustace Haddon; CBE (2013); s of Capt Derrick Ferguson, RN (d 1992), of Craigard, Tighnabruaich, Argyll, and Betsy, *née* Eustace; *b* 14 October 1948; *Educ* Winchester, Univ of Edinburgh (BSc Econ), Harvard Business Sch (MBA, Baker scholar); *m* 18 Dec 1976, (Margaret) Jane Dura, da of Robert Collin, of Hook Norton, Oxon; 2 s (Alexander b 1978, Thomas b 1985), 1 da (Cornelia b 1979); *Career* venture capitalist; Schroders: joined 1980, chm Schroder Ventures Ltd 1984–2001, non-exec dir Schroders plc 2001–04, dir J Henry Schroder Wagg and Co Ltd, chief exec Schroder Ventures International Investment Trust plc, dir of several Schroder Gp cos; chm SVG Capital plc 2005–12 (dir 1996–), chm Br Sky Broadcasting Gp plc 2012– (non-exec dir 2004–); chm Courtauld Institute of Art, Int Students Club (C of E) Ltd; *Recreations* sailing, skiing; *Clubs* Brooks's; *Style—* Nicholas Ferguson, Esq, CBE

FERGUSON, Patricia; MSP; *b* 24 September 1958, Glasgow; *Educ* Garnethill Convent Secdy Sch Glasgow, Glasgow Coll of Technol; *m* Bill Butler; *Career* health serv admin 1978–90, admin Scottish Trades Union Congress 1990–94, organiser Scottish Lab Party 1994–96, Scottish offr Scottish Lab Party 1996–99, MP (Lab) Glasgow Maryhill 1999–; MSP (Lab): Glasgow Maryhill 1999–2011, Glasgow Maryhill & Springburn 2011–; Scottish Parl: min for parly business 2001–04, min for tourism, culture and sport 2004–07; *Style—* Ms Patricia Ferguson, MSP; ✉ The Scottish Parliament, Edinburgh EH99 1SP

FERGUSON, Dr Roger; s of Dr Alan Hudspeth Ferguson (d 1967), and Betty Fielding, *née* Willatt; *b* 23 August 1946, Nottingham; *Educ* City Sch Lincoln, Univ of Birmingham (MB ChB, MD); *m* 12 Jan 1974, Ruth Elizabeth, da of Prof Harold Spencer, of Willaston, Cheshire; 3 da (Sarah Helen b 1975, Jean Alison b 1976, Fiona Jane b 1978); *Career* med registrar Worcester Royal Infirmary 1970–73, res registrar Birmingham Gen Hosp 1973–75, sr med registrar Nottingham Gen Hosp and Derby Royal Infirmary 1975–79; conslt physician and gastroenterologist: Arrowe Park Hosp Wirral 1979–2007, BUPA Murrayfield Hosp (now Spire Murrayfield) Wirral 1980–14; external professional advsr to the Health Cmmr for England (Ombudsman) 1998–14; formerly chm Mersey Region Conslts and Specialists Ctee; GMC: former chm Fitness to Practice Ctee, former chm Registration Appeals Panel; medical memb First Tier Tbnl Social Entitlement Chamber; examiner in med Univ of Liverpool until 2014; memb: Midland Gastroenterological Soc, Northern Gastroenterological Soc, Br Soc of Gastroenterology; formerly memb Central Conslts and Specialists Ctee; former chm Wirral Wine Soc; FRCP 1987 (MRCP 1972), FRSM; *Books* Text Book of Gastroenterology (contrib, 1990 and 1993); *Recreations* swimming, golf, music, reading; *Clubs* Robin Hood Golf, Royal Over-Seas League; *Style—* Dr Roger Ferguson; ✉ 89 Bidston Road, Oxton, Prenton, Wirral, Merseyside CH43 6TS (☎ 0151 652 3722, fax 0151 670 9536, e-mail rferg10186@aol.com)

FERGUSON-SMITH, Prof Malcolm Andrew; s of Dr John Ferguson-Smith (d 1978), of Strathtay, Perthshire, and Ethel May, *née* Thorne (d 1993); *b* 5 September 1931; *Educ* Stowe, Univ of Glasgow (MB ChB); *m* 11 July 1960, Marie Eve, da of Stanislaw Franciszek Gzowski (d 1981); 3 da (Anne b 1961, Nicola b 1965, Julia b 1976), 1 s (John b 1970); *Career* prof of med genetics Univ of Glasgow 1973–87, dir West of Scot Regnl Genetics Serv 1973–87, ed-in-chief Prenatal Diagnosis 1980–2006, prof of pathology Univ of Cambridge 1987–98, hon conslt in med genetics Addenbrooke's Hosp 1987–98, dir E Anglian Regnl Genetics Serv 1987–95, emeritus fell Peterhouse Cambridge 1998– (fell 1987–98), research prof Dept of Veterinary Med Univ of Cambridge 1998–; Makdougall-Brisbane Prize Royal Soc of Edinburgh 1988; memb Neurology Bd MRC 1974–76, vice-pres Genetical Soc 1978–81; pres: Clinical Genetics Soc 1979–81, Perm Ctee Int Congress of Human Genetics 1986–91, European Soc of Human Genetics 1997–98, Int Soc for Prenatal Diagnosis 1998–2002, Assoc of Clinical Cytogenetics 2002–05; memb Cncl RCPath 1983–86, fndr memb Exec Ctee Human Genome Orgn 1988–92, WHO advsr in human genetics 1988–98, memb Cell Bd MRC 1989–93; Hon DSc: Strathclyde 1992, Glasgow 2002; FRCP (Glasgow) 1974, FRCPath 1978, FRSE 1978, FRS 1983, foreign memb Polish Acad of Sci 1988, FRCOG 1993, FMedSci 1998, HM Associate RCVS 2002, foreign memb Nat Acad of Med of Buenos Aires 2002; *Books* Early Prenatal Diagnosis (1983), Prenatal Diagnosis & Screening (1992), Essential Medical Genetics (6 edn, 2011); *Recreations* sailing, swimming, fishing; *Style—* Prof Malcolm Ferguson-Smith, FRS, FRSE; ✉ Department of Veterinary Medicine, University of Cambridge, Madingley Road, Cambridge CB3 0ES (☎ and fax 01223 766496, e-mail maf12@cam.ac.uk, website www.vet.cam.ac.uk/genomics)

FERGUSSON, Rt Hon Sir Alexander Charles Onslow; kt (2016), PC (2010); s of Lt Col the Rev Simon C D Fergusson (d 1981), of Alton Albany, Ayr, and Auriole Kathleen, *née* Hughes-Onslow; *b* 8 April 1949, Leswalt; *Educ* Eton, WSAC Auchincruive; *m* 20 June 1974, Jane Merryn, da of Bertram Barthold; 3 s (Iain Alexander Onslow b 24 June 1975, Dougal George Onslow b 31 Jan 1977, Christopher David Onslow b 22 April 1986); *Career* farmer 1970–99; MSP (Cons): Scotland S 1999–2003, Galloway and Upper Nithsdale 2003–11, Galloway & West Dumfries 2011–16; presiding offr Scottish Parl 2007–11; memb: Scottish Landowners Fedn, Blackface Sheepbreeders Assoc; *Recreations* curling, rugby, folk music; *Style—* The Rt Hon Sir Alexander Fergusson; ✉ Grennan, Dalry, Kirkudbrightshire DG7 3PL (☎ 01644 430250, e-mail acofergusson@gmail.com)

FERGUSSON, Rev Prof David; OBE (2016); s of Thomas E Fergusson, and Charis Fergusson; *b* 3 August 1956, Glasgow; *Educ* Kelvinside Acad Glasgow, Univ of Glasgow (MA), Tübingen Univ, Univ of Edinburgh (BD), Univ of Oxford (DPhil), Yale Univ; *m* Margot; 2 s (Mark, Calum); *Career* pt/t tutor Dept of Moral Philosophy Univ of Glasgow 1977, asst min St Nicholas' Church of Scotland Lanark 1983–84, assoc min St Mungo's Church of Scotland Cumbernauld 1984–86, pt/t lectr in systematic theology Univ of Glasgow 1984–86, lectr in systematic theology Univ of Edinburgh 1986–90, prof of systematic theology Univ of Aberdeen 1990–2000, prof of divinity Univ of Edinburgh 2000–; visiting lectr United Church of Japan 2002, Gifford lectr Univ of Glasgow 2008, Warfield lectr Princeton Theological Seminary 2009; pres Soc for the Study of Theology 2000–02 (memb Ctee 1994–97), sec Edinburgh Theological Club 1987–90; conslt ed and dir Scottish Jl of Theology 1993–, chair Editorial Bd Theology in Scotland 1993–, co-ed Eerdmans Guides to Theology series 1998–; memb Editorial Bd: Int Jl of Systematic Theology 1999–, Jl for the Study of the Christian Church 2001–; Cunningham lectr Univ of Edinburgh 1996, Bampton lectr Univ of Oxford 2001; tstee John Hope Tst 1995–; Chaplain-in-Ordinary to HM The Queen in Scotland 2015; Hon DD Univ of Aberdeen 2014; FRSE 2004, FBA 2013; *Books* Bultmann (1992), John Macmurray: The Idea of the Personal (1992), Christ, Church and Society: Essays on John Baillie and Donald Baillie (ed, 1993), The Future of the Kirk: Theology in Scotland Occasional Paper No 2 (ed with D W D Shaw, 1997), John and Donald Baillie: Selected Devotional Writings (ed, 1997), The Cosmos and the Creator: Introduction to the Theology of Creation (1998), Community, Liberalism and Christian Ethics (1998), The Future as God's Gift: Explorations in Christian Eschatology (ed with Marcel Sarot, 2000), Northern Accents: Aberdeen Essays on Preaching (ed with Alan Main, 2001), John Macmurray: Critical Perspectives (ed with Nigel Dower, 2002), Church, State and Civil Society (2004), Scottish Philosophical Theology (2007), Faith and its Critics (2009), Blackwell Companion to 19th Century Theology (2010), Cambridge Dictionary of Christian Theology (2011), Creation (2014), Cambridge Companion to Reformed Theology (2016); also author of contribs to several books; *Recreations* golf, football; *Clubs* New (Edinburgh), Mortonhall Golf; *Style—* The Rev Prof David Fergusson, OBE; ✉ New College, Mound Place, Edinburgh EH1 2LX (☎ 0131 650 8912, fax 0131 650 7952. e-mail david.fergusson@ed.ac.uk)

FERGUSSON, HE George Duncan Raukawa; s of Brig Sir Bernard Fergusson (Baron Ballantrae, Life Peer) (d 1980), by his w Laura Margaret Grenfell (d 1979) (*see* Peerage Baron Grenfell 1976); *b* 30 September 1955, Coupar Angus, Scotland; *Educ* Hereworth Sch NZ, Eton, Magdalen Coll Oxford (BA); *m* 10 Jan 1981, Margaret Sheila, da of Michael John Wookey, of Camberley, Surrey; 3 da (Laura (Mrs Kenworthy) b 1982, Alice (Mrs Drew) b 1986, Elizabeth b 1991), 1 s (Alexander b 1984 d 2005); *Career* Murray & Tait Slrs 1977–78; joined NI Office 1978, seconded to NI Dept of Commerce 1979–80, first sec Dublin 1988–91 (transferred to Dip Serv 1990), FCO London 1991–93, first sec Seoul 1994–96, head of Republic of Ireland Dept FCO 1997–99, consul-gen Boston 1999–03, on loan to Cabinet Office 2003–06, high cmmr to New Zealand and Samoa and govr of Pitcairn 2006–10, FCO London 2010–12, govr of Bermuda 2012–; *Style—* HE Mr George Fergusson; ✉ Government House, 11 Langton Hill, Pembroke HM13, Bermuda (☎ 001 441 292 3600)

FERLEGER BRADES, Susan Deborah; da of Alvin Ferleger, and Beatrice, *née* Supnick; *b* 7 July 1954; *Educ* Courtauld Inst of Art (MA), Univ of Mass, Amherst/Barnard Coll Columbia Univ NY (BA, magna cum laude, Phi Beta Kappa); *m* 1, 1979, Peter Eric Brades (m dis 2001); 1 s (b 1989); m 2, 2006, Rhett Davies; *Career* curatorial co-ordinator Solomon R Guggenheim Museum NY 1975–79; res Whitechapel Art Gallery London 1979–80; Hayward Gallery: Arts Cncl of GB/South Bank Centre exhbn organiser 1980–88, sr exhbn organiser 1988–93, dep dir 1993–96, dir 1996–2004, purchaser Arts Cncl Collection 1983–2004; visual arts advsr John Lyons Charity 2004–; art conslt London Library 2005–10; former memb Visual Arts Advsy Ctee Br Cncl; memb: South Bank Employers' Gp Public Art Gp, Visual Arts and Galleries Assoc (VAGA); former patron The Nat Children's Art Awards; tstee IVAM Centro Julio Gonzalez Valencia Spain 2000–04; awarded: Nat Endowment for Arts fell 1975–76, Smithsonian Inst travel grant for museum professionals 1977; ICOM; *Publications* Dictionary of National Biography (contrib, 2007); *Style—* Ms Susan Ferleger Brades

FERMONT, Dr David Calvin; s of David Andre Fermont, of Esher, Surrey, and Edith Mary, *née* Kew; *b* 31 October 1946; *Educ* Cheltenham Coll, Middx Hosp Med Sch (MB, BS); *m* 28 Sept 1974, Linda Jane, da of Maj Geoffrey Noel Marks, of Hove, E Sussex; 1 da (Sara Louise b 7 June 1980), 1 s (James Alexander b 29 July 1983); *Career* conslt oncologist and dir Cancer Centre Mount Vernon Hosp, Northwick Park and St Marks Hosps 1983–; chm Hillingdon HA Dist Med Ctee, memb Hillingdon DHA Mgmnt Bd; med exec dir: Mount Vernon Hosp Tst, Mount Vernon and Watford Hosp NHS Tst; memb Br Inst of Radiology, FRCS, FRSM, FRCR; *Books* numerous med pubns; *Recreations* cricket; *Style—* Dr David Fermont; ✉ Cancer Centre, Mount Vernon Hospital, Northwood, Middlesex HA6 2RN (☎ 01923 844231, fax 01923 844138)

FERMOY, 6 Baron (I 1856); Maurice Burke Roche; s of 5 Baron Fermoy (d 1984), and Lavinia, *née* Pitman (who m 2, 1995, Nigel E Corbally Stourton); *b* 11 October 1967, London; *Educ* Eton; *m* 26 March 1998, Tessa Fiona, da of late Maj David Kayll of Briantspuddle, Dorset; 2 da (Hon Arabella Elizabeth b 18 March 1999, Hon Eliza Lavinia b 9 Nov 2000); *Heir* bro, Hon Hugh Roche; *Career* Page of Honour to HM Queen Elizabeth The Queen Mother 1982–85, former Capt The Blues and Royals; with Bass Taverns 1995–99, fndr and dir Horse Fair Properties Ltd 1999–; dir Oxford Street Connections 2008–; memb Cherwell DC 2000–04, tstee Countyside Learning 2012–15, jt hon sec Warwickshire Hunt 2014–; *Recreations* hunting, shooting, gardening; *Clubs* Rag; *Style—* The Rt Hon Lord Fermoy; ✉ Handywater Farm, Sibford Gower, Banbury, Oxfordshire OX15 5AE (e-mail maurice@fermoy.co.uk)

FERN, Prof Dan; s of George Fern (d 1967), of Gainsborough, and Gwen Fern (d 1981); *b* 1 July 1945; *Educ* Queen Elizabeth GS Gainsborough, Manchester Coll of Art and Design, RCA; *m* 1969, Kate Fern; 2 da (Zoë b 1976, Ella b 1979), 1 s (Hugo b 1985); *Career* graphic artist; Royal Coll of Art: head of illustration 1986–, prof of illustration 1989–,

F

head Sch of Communication Design 1993–, prof of graphic art and design 1994–; *Solo Exhibitions* Print and Collage Constructions (Curwen Gallery London) 1982, Collage, Print and Type Constructions (Curwen Gallery) 1985, Recent Work (Entrepotdok Amsterdam) 1986, Mapworks (Pentagram Gallery) 1994, Box Set (Pentagram Gallery) 1994; *Group Exhibitions* incl: Art/Work (Nat Theatre) 1979, Homage to Herge (Joan Miro Fndn Barcelona) 1984, Art Meets Science (Smiths Gallery London) 1988, Image and Object (Nat MOMA Kyoto Japan) 1990, Gate 14 (RCA) 1993, Collage (England & Co) 1993, Collage (Tate Gallery North) 2000, exhbn of original posters cmmned to mark the centenary of Henri de Toulouse-Lautrec (Centre Pompedou Paris and Stedelijk Museum Amsterdam) 2001–02, Permanent Collection V&A; clients incl: Sunday Times Magazine, Radio Times, New Scientist, Decca Records, Penguin Books, Pan Books, J Walter Thompson, Young and Rubicam, Conran Design, Michael Peters Group, Pentagram, Thames Television, Assoc of Illustrators, The Royal Court Theatre, Royal Acad London; cmmnd work incl: video on drawing (for Faber-Castell) 1993, film on Deutsche Romantik theme (for South Bank Centre and Goethe Inst) 1994, film for Harrison Birtwistle Festival (premiered South Bank) 1996; lectr and speaker various conferences and workshops; head Educn Ctee Assoc of Illustrators 1977–79, memb various jury panels; twice winner of both Gold & Silver D & AD awards; FRCA, FCSD, FRSA; *Books* Works with Paper (1990); *Recreations* opera and other performing arts, mountaineering, astronomy, cycling, collecting (books, stamps, printed ephemera); *Style*— Prof Dan Fern; ✉ 58 Muswell Road, London N10 2BE (✆ 020 8883 5604); Communication, Art and Design, Royal College of Art, Kensington Gore, London SW7 (✆ 020 7584 5020, fax 020 7225 1487)

FERNANDES, Suella; MP; da of Chris Fernandes, and Uma, *née* Pillay; *b* 3 April 1980, London; *Educ* Queen's Coll Cambridge (MA), Université Paris 1 Panthéon-Sorbonne (LLM); *Career* called to the Bar Middle Temple 2005, barr No 5 Chambers London 2005–, admitted NY Bar 2006, Treasy counsel 2010–15; Pegasus scholarship 2010; MP (Cons) Fareham 2015–; *Recreations* cinema, reading, travel; *Style*— Ms Suella Fernandes, MP; ✉ House of Commons, London SW1A 0AA (✆ 020 7219 3000, e-mail suella@suellafernandes.co.uk, website www.suellafernandes.co.uk, Twitter @SuellaFernandes)

FERNEYHOUGH, Prof Brian John Peter; s of Frederick George Ferneyhough (d 1982), and Emily May, *née* Hopwood (d 1992); *b* 16 January 1943; *Educ* Birmingham Sch of Music, Royal Acad of Music, Royal Conservatory Amsterdam, Musikakademie Basel; *m* 19 May 1990, Stephanie Jan, *née* Hurtik; *Career* prof of composition Musikhochschule Freiburg 1973–86, composition lectr Darmstadt Summer Sch 1976–96, leader composition master class Civica Scuola di Musica di Milano 1984–87, composition teacher Royal Conservatory of The Hague 1986–87, ldr composition master class Fndn Royaumont 1990–, prof of music Univ of Calif San Diego 1987–99, William H Bonsall prof of music Stanford Univ 2000–, chair of poetics Mozarteum Salzburg 1995; memb: Jury Gaudeamus Int Composition Competition 1984 (Netherlands), Int Jury for World Music Days of Int Soc for Contemporary Music (Finland 1978, Hong Kong 1989), Akademie der Künste Berlin 1996–, Bayrische Akademie der schönen Künste 2005; Koussevitzky prize 1978, Royal Philharmonic Soc Award 1995, Ernst von Siemens Music Prize 2007; ARAM 1990, hon fell Birmingham Conservatoire 1996, FRAM 1998, memb Royal Swedish Acad of Music 2009; Chevalier de l'Ordre des Arts et des Lettres (France) 1984; *Compositions* incl: Sonatas for String Quartet 1967, Transit 1975, Time and Motion Studies I-III 1974–77, La Terre est un Homme 1979, Carceri d'Invenzione 1981–86, La Chute d'Icare 1988, Fourth String Quartet 1990, Bone Alphabet, Allgebrah 1991, Terrain 1992, On Stellar Magnitudes 1994, String Trio 1995, Incipits 1996, Flurries 1997, Unsichtbare Farben 1998, Doctrine of Similarity 1999, Shadowtime 1999–2004, Plotzlichkeith 2006, Chronos-Aion 2008, Fifth String Quartet 2007, Dum Transisset 2007, Sisyphus Redux 2009, Sixth String Quartet 2010, Finis Terrae 2012, Inconjunctions 2014, Contraccolpi 2015; *Recreations* reading, wine, cats; *Style*— Prof Brian Ferneyhough; ✉ Stanford University, Department of Music, Braun Music Center, 541 Lausen Mall, Stanford, CA 94305–3076 USA (e-mail brian.ferneyhough@stanford.edu)

FERNIE, Prof Eric Campbell; CBE (1995); s of Sidney Robert Fernie (d 1988), of Johannesburg, South Africa, and Catherine Reid, *née* Forrest (d 1959); *b* 9 June 1939, Edinburgh; *Educ* Marist Brothers Coll Johannesburg, Univ of the Witwatersrand (BA); *m* 28 Nov 1964, (Margaret) Lorraine, da of John Henry French, of Norfolk; 2 da (Lyndall *b* 1965, Jessica *b* 1969), 1 s (Ivan *b* 1969); *Career* sr lectr UEA 1974–84; Univ of Edinburgh: Watson Gordon prof of fine art 1984–95, dean Faculty of Arts 1989–92; dir Courtauld Inst of Art 1995–2003; cmmr: English Heritage 1995–2001, Royal Cmmn on the Historical Monuments of England 1997–99; chm Ancient Monuments Bd Scotland 1989–95; pres Soc of Antiquaries of London 2004–07 (vice-pres 1992–95), vice-pres: Public Monuments and Sculpture Assoc 2000–12; tstee: National Galleries of Scotland 1991–97, Heather Tst for the Arts 1997–2002, Scotland Inheritance Fund 1994–2004; memb Br Acad Corpus of Romanesque Sculpture Ctee; Hon DLitt UEA; FSA 1973, FSA Scot 1986, FRSE 1993, FBA 2002; *Books* The Communar and Pitancer Rolls of Norwich Cathedral Priory (1972), The Architecture of the Anglo Saxons (1983), Medieval Architecture and its Intellectual Context (1990), An Architectural History of Norwich Cathedral (1993), Art History and its Methods (1995), The Architecture of Norman England (2000), Romanesque Architecture (2014); *Style*— Prof Eric Fernie, CBE, FBA, FSA, FSA Scot, FRSE

FERNIE, Dr (Crawford) George MacDougall; s of George Fernie (d 2000), and Joan Fisher, *née* MacDougall (d 2003); *b* 5 October 1954, Glasgow; *Educ* Hyndland Sr Secdy Sch Glasgow, Univ of Glasgow (MB, ChB, DFM, MPhil), Univ of Strathclyde (LLB); *m* 12 Oct 1984, Isobel, *née* Kerr; 1 da (Anne Fiona Eadie *b* 10 Aug 1970), 2 s (Keith Ian Johnson *b* 7 Jan 1973, Campbell Crawford *b* 2 Jan 1985); *Career* house offr surgical paediatrics Royal Hosp for Sick Children Glasgow 1977–78, house offr Dept of Med Raigmore Hosp Inverness 1978, SHO Dept of Neurosurgery Inst of Neurological Sci Glasgow 1978–79, SHO Dept of Obstetrics & Gynaecology Stobhill Hosp Glasgow 1979, princ in gen practice Portland Park Lanarkshire 1979–1991, pt/t GP deputising Emergency Med Serv Bellshill 1979–80, pt/t casualty offr Royal Hosp for Sick Children Glasgow 1980–81, undergrad teaching in gen practice 1980–87, GP trainer 1987–91, princ in gen practice Canonbie 1991–96; Univ of Glasgow: hon research fell in clinical forensic med 1994–97, lectr 1996–, hon sr lectr in clinical forensic med 2001–; examiner for Dip of Forensic Med for Soc of Apothecaries in London 1996–2013; med advsr Hamilton DC 1990–91, sr medico-legal advsr Medical Protection Soc 2009–13, sr medical reviewer for Scotland 2013–; dep police surgn (Q Div) Strathclyde Police 1988–91, princ police surgn Annandale and Eskdale 1991–96, princ police surgn (K Div) Strathclyde Police 1996–2004, forensic med examiner Lothian & Borders Police 2004–05; memb: GP Clinical Advsy Panel Medical and Dental Defence Union of Scotland 1991–96 (med advsr 1996–2009, head Medical Div 2009), West of Scot Faculty Bd RCGP 1991–98, Cncl Scottish Medico-Legal Soc 1992–2002 and 2003–06, Tech Sub Gp to advise Strathclyde Police 1997–2004, Educn & Research Ctee Assoc of Police Surgns 1998–; Assoc of Forensic Physicians: memb Cncl 1996–2006, pres-elect 2002–04, pres 2004–06; memb Int Editorial Bd Jl of Clinical Forensic Med 2001–; BMA: memb UK Cncl 2004–06, memb Scot Cncl 2005–; memb Forensic Med Ctee 2001–14 (chm 2002–10); author of various pubns incl articles and commentaries in learned jls, and chapters in Encyclopaedia of Forensic and Legal Medicine (2005 and 2015); FRCGP 2004 (MRCGP 1984), FFLM RCP (registrar 2006–11, pres 2011–13), FRCPE 2011, FRCP London 2014; *Recreations* bearded collies, reading, hill walking; *Style*— Dr George Fernie; ✉ e-mail cgmf@btinternet.com; Healthcare

Improvement Scotland, Gyle Square, 1 South Gyle Crescent, Edinburgh EH12 9EB (✆ 0131 623 4756, fax 0131 240 1878, e-mail georgefernie@nhs.net)

FERRAN, Prof Eilis Veronica; da of Edward Gerald Ferran, and Kathleen Mary, *née* Best; *b* 14 March 1962, Belfast; *Educ* Univ of Cambridge (BA, PhD); *m* 27 June 1992, Roderick Cantrill; 1 da (Aoife *b* 6 Nov 1994), 1 s (Oliver *b* 11 Nov 1997); *Career* admitted slr 1986; articled clerk Coward Chance 1984–86; St Catharine's Coll Cambridge: coll lectr 1986–88, fell 1987–, dir of studies 1988–, tutor 1999–2000; Univ of Cambridge: asst lectr 1988–91, lectr 1991–2000, reader in corporate and commercial law 2000–05, prof of company and securities law 2005–, co-dir Centre for Corporate and Commercial Law 2006– (asst dir 1997–99, dir 1999–2003); legal conslt: Slaughter and May 1989–2000, Herbert Smith 2003–12; jt ed: Jl of Corporate Law Studies, CUP Int Corporate Law and Capital Market Regulation Series; visiting prof Univ of Hong Kong 2002, Chapman Tripp fell Univ of Victoria NZ 2004, res assoc European Corporate Governance Inst, visiting prof Law Faculty Univ of Auckland 2009, visiting prof Harvard Law Sch 2010, JM Keynes Univ of Cambridge fell 2011; special advsr: Parly Jt Ctee on the Draft Financial Services and Markets Bill 1999, House of Commons Select Ctee on Educn and Employment 2000–01, specialist advsr House of Lords EU Ctee Inquiry on Reform of EU Banking Sector 2012; chair Faculty Bd of Law 2012–; FBA 2013; *Books* Guide to the Financial Services Act 1986 (jtly, 2 edn 1989), Mortgage Securitisation: Legal Aspects (1992), Company Law and Corporate Finance (1999), Boyle and Birds Company Law (jtly, 2000), Building an EU Securities Market (2004), Current Law Annotated Guide to the Companies Act 2006 (jtly, 2007), Principles of Corporate Finance Law (2008), The Regulatory Aftermath of the Global Financial Crisis (jtly, 2012); author of various chapters and articles in learned jls; *Style*— Prof Eilis Ferran; ✉ St Catharine's College, Cambridge CB2 1RL (✆ 01223 338335, fax 01223 338340); Law Faculty, University of Cambridge, 10 West Road, Cambridge CB3 9DZ (✆ 01223 330033, e-mail evf1000@cam.ac.uk)

FERRELL, Prof William Russell (Bill); *b* 5 March 1949, St Louis, Missouri; *Educ* St Aloysius Coll Glasgow, Univ of Glasgow (MB ChB, PhD); *Career* jr house offr posts in surgery (Southern Gen Hosp Glasgow) and med (Stirling Royal Infirmary) 1973–74, sessional clinical work 1974–, visiting res fell Dept of Orthopaedic Surgery Univ of Western Aust 1984; Univ of Glasgow: lectr in physiology 1977–89, sr lectr 1989–91, reader 1991–93, head of physiology 1993–94, head of biomedical scis 1994, reader in clinical physiology 1997–2002, prof of clinical physiology 2002–; visiting prof: Dept of Surgery Univ of Calgary 1996, Univ of Paisley 1999–; expert referee: Jl of Physiology, Experimental Physiology, Jl of Rheumatology, Br Jl of Pharmacology, Clinical Sciences, Brain, Brain Research, Annals of the Rheumatic Diseases; memb MRC Advsy Panel 1997–2005; memb: Physiological Soc 1981, BMA, Br Soc of Med and Dental Hypnosis, Euro Neuropeptide Club, Br Soc for Rheumatology; FRCPGlas 1996; *Recreations* classical music, reading, electronics, skiing, tennis, DIY; *Style*— Prof Bill Ferrell; ✉ Room 2.71, New Lister Building, Glasgow Royal Infirmary, 10–16 Alexandra Parade, Glasgow G31 2ER(✆ 0141 201 8627, e-mail william.ferrell@glasgow.ac.uk)

FERRERS, 14 Earl (GB 1711); Sir Robert William Saswalo Shirley; 20 Bt (E 1611); s of 13 Earl Ferrers, PC, DL (d 2012); *b* 29 December 1952; *Educ* Ampleforth; *m* 21 June 1980, Susannah Mary, da of late Charles Edward William Sheepshanks (d 1991), of Arthington Hall, Otley, W Yorks; 1 da (Hon Hermione Mary Annabel *b* 11 Dec 1982), 2 s (William Robert Charles, Viscount Tamworth *b* 10 Dec 1984, Hon Frederick James Walter *b* 2 June 1990); *Heir* s, Viscount Tamworth; *Career* teaching in Kenya under CMS Youth Service Abroad Scheme 1971–72; articled to Whinney Murray & Co (chartered accountants) 1972–76, asst mangr Ernst & Whinney (now Ernst & Young) 1976–82, gp auditor and sr treasy analyst with BICC plc 1982–86, gp fin controller Viking Property Gp Ltd 1986, dir Viking Property Gp Ltd 1987–88, dir Norseman Holdings Ltd (formerly Ashby Securities Ltd) 1987–92 (and assoc cos 1988–92); md: Ruffer Management Ltd 1999–2011 (dir 1994–), Ruffer LLP 2004–11 (non-exec dir 2011–); dir Derbyshire Student Residences Ltd 1996–2003; dir Assoc of Private Client Investment Mangrs and Stockbrokers (APCIMS) 2007–13; tstee: Auckland Castle Tst 2012–15, Orders of St John Care Tst 2013–; FCA; Kt SMOM 2005; *Recreations* the British countryside and related activities, the garden; *Clubs* Boodle's, Pratt's; *Style*— The Earl Ferrers; ✉ Ditchingham Hall, Ditchingham, Norfolk NR35 2JX

FERRIS, Dr Elizabeth Anne Esther; da of Roy Ferris (d 1975), and Dorothy Philomena, *née* Roth (d 1990); *b* 19 November 1940; *Educ* Francis Holland Sch Clarence Gate, Middlesex Hosp Med Sch Univ of London (MB BS); *m* Julian Melzack; 1 da (Sophie *b* 1978); *Career* doctor and former int springboard diver; achievements as diver: represented GB 1957–64, Bronze medal Cwlth Games Cardiff 1958, Bronze medal Olympic Games Rome 1960, Gold medals springboard and highboard World Student Games Sofia 1961, Silver medal Cwlth Games Perth 1962; freelance journalist, writer and broadcaster on sport, women and sport, sports med, alternative med, health fitness 1968–; doctor specialising in: acupuncture 1972–86, autogenic trg 1980–96, sports psychology 1980–96; therapist cnsllr 1989–; research fell Dept of Nutrition KCL 1999–; fndr and life vice-pres The Olympians, co-fndr World Olympians Assoc (vice-pres 1995–2007); memb: Int Olympic Ctee Cmmn on Women and Sport 1995–, Admin Cncl of the Int Ctee for Fair Play, World Cncl for Nutrition, Fitness and Health, IAAF Workshop on Gender Verification in Sport 1990–; awarded Bronze medal of the Olympic Order by Int Olympic Ctee for work with women in sport 1980; *Books* Forty Plus (1992); *Videos* Bodyplan (1992); *Style*— Dr Elizabeth Ferris; ✉ Green Dragon House, Filkins, Lechlade, Gloucestershire GL7 3JG

FERRY, Bryan; CBE (2011); s of Frederick Charles Ferry (d 1984), and Mary Ann, *née* Armstrong (d 1991); *b* 26 September 1945; *Educ* Washington GS, Univ of Newcastle; *m* 1, 26 June 1982 (m dis 2003), Lucy Margaret Mary, da of Patrick Helmore; 4 c (Otis *b* 1 Nov 1982, Isaac *b* 16 May 1985, Tara *b* 6 Jan 1990, Merlin *b* 5 Dec 1990); *m* 2, 4 Jan 2012, Amanda Sheppard; *Career* vocalist and fndr memb Roxy Music 1971, solo recording artist; recordings with Roxy Music: Roxy Music 1972, For Your Pleasure 1973, Stranded 1973, Country Life 1974, Siren 1975, Viva 1976, Manifesto 1979, Flesh & Blood 1980, Avalon 1982, The High Road 1983, Streetlife 1986; solo recordings: These Foolish Things 1973, Another Time Another Place 1974, Let's Stick Together 1976, In Your Mind 1977, The Bride Stripped Bare 1978, Boys and Girls 1985, Bête Noire 1987, Taxi 1993, Mamouna 1994, As Time Goes By 1999, Frantic 2002, Dylanesque 2007; Bryan Ferry and Roxy Music Video Collection 1996; *Style*— Bryan Ferry, Esq, CBE

FERSHT, Prof Sir Alan Roy; kt (2003); s of Philip Joseph Fersht (d 1970), and Betty, *née* Mattleson (d 2003); *b* 21 April 1943; *Educ* Sir George Monoux GS, Gonville & Caius Coll Cambridge (MA, PhD); *m* 18 Aug 1966, Marilyn, da of Montague Persell (d 1973); 1 da (Naomi *b* 1970), 1 s (Philip *b* 1972); *Career* memb scientific staff MRC Laboratory of Molecular Biology Cambridge 1969–77 and 2010–, Wolfson res prof Royal Soc and prof of chemistry Imperial Coll London 1978–88, Herchel Smith prof of organic chemistry Univ of Cambridge 1988–2010, dir MRC Centre for Protein Engrg 1989–2010, master Gonville and Caius Coll Cambridge 2012–; Gabor Medal Royal Soc 1991, Davy Medal Royal Soc 1998, Anfinsen Award Protein Soc 1999, Stein and Moore Award Protein Soc 2001, Bader Award American Chemical Soc 2005, Linderstrøm Lang Medal 2005, Royal Medal Royal Soc 2008, Wilhelm Exner Medal (Austria) 2009; Hon PhD: Univ of Uppsala 1999, Univ of Brussels 1999, Weizmann Inst 2005, Hebrew Univ 2006, Aarhus Univ 2008; fell Imperial Coll London 2004; memb EMBO 1980, FRS 1983, memb Academia Europaea 1989, FMedSci 2007, hon foreign memb American Acad of Arts and Scis 1988, memb American Philosophical Soc 2008, foreign assoc Nat Acad of Sci USA, foreign memb Accademia Nazionale dei Lincei 2013; *Books* Enzyme Structure and Mechanism (1978,

1985), Structure and Mechanism in Protein Science (1998), Jaques Staunton Chess Sets 1849–1939 (2007), Jaques Staunton and British Chess Company Sets (2010); *Recreations* chess, horology, bird photography; *Clubs* Oxford and Cambridge; *Style*— Prof Sir Alan Fersht, FRS; ✉ Master's Lodge, Gonville and Caius College, Trinity Street, University of Cambridge CB2 1TA (☎ 01223 332431); MRC Laboratory of Molecular Biology, Francis Crick Avenue, Cambridge CB2 0QH (☎ 01223 267083)

FESTING, Andrew Thomas; MBE (2008); s of Field-Marshal Sir Francis Festing, GCB, DSO, DL (d 1971), of Birks, Northumberland, and Mary Cecilia, *née* Riddell (d 1992); *b* 30 November 1941; *Educ* Ampleforth, RMA Sandhurst; *m* 1968, Virginia Mary, da of Lt-Gen Sir Richard Fyffe, CBE, DSO, MC; 1 da (Charlotte (Hon Mrs Hepburne-Scott) b 1975); *Career* cmmnd Rifle Bde until 1968; head English Picture Dept Sotheby & Co 1977–81, full time portrait painter 1981–; commissions incl: HM The Queen, HM Queen Elizabeth The Queen Mother, The Princess Royal, Cardinal Hume, House of Lords, House of Commons, Speaker Boothroyd; Hon DLitt Northumbria Univ 2010; RP 1992 (pres 2002–08); *Recreations* hunting, shooting, fishing, gardening; *Style*— Andrew Festing, Esq, MBE, PPRP; ✉ 3 Hillsleigh Road, London W8 7LE

FETHERSTONHAUGH, Guy; QC (2003); s of Theobald Fetherstonhaugh (d 1990), and Genevieve, *née* Moreau (d 2009); *b* 29 January 1955, Malaya; *Educ* Stonyhurst, Univ of Bristol; *m* 23 March 1991, Alexia, *née* Lees; 1 da (Rosie b 15 June 1992), 2 s (Tom b 13 May 1994, Ned b 1 May 1996); *Career* Royal Green Jackets 1978–82; called to the Bar 1983, practising barr 1985–; bencher Inner Temple; Hon RICS 2011, FCIArb (memb 2014); *Books* Handbook of Rent Review (co-author, 2000), Commonhold (co-author, 2004); *Recreations* gardening, cycling, woodwork; *Clubs* Rifles' Officers', RAC; *Style*— Guy Fetherstonhaugh, Esq, QC; ✉ c/o Falcon Chambers, Falcon Court, London EC4Y 1AA (☎ 020 7353 2484)

FEUCHTWANGER, Antonia Mary; *see:* Cox, Antonia Mary

FEWSTER, Dr Kevin; AM (2001); Geoffrey Fewster and Audrey; *b* Perth, Australia; *Educ* Australian Nat Univ (BA), Univ of NSW (PhD); *m* Carol Scott, 1 da; *Career* dir South Australian Maritime Museum Port Adelaide 1984–89, dir Australian Nat Maritime Museum Sydney 1989–99, dir Powerhouse Museum Sydney 2000–07, dir Royal Museums Greenwich (formerly Nat Maritime Museum) 2007–; pres Int Congress of Maritime Museums 1996–99 and 2013–15, chm Cncl Australasian Museum Directors 2004–07; FRSA; *Books* Bean's Gallipoli: The Diaries of Australia's Official War Correspondent (ed, 1983, 1990, 2007), Gallipoli – The Turkish Story (with V Basarin, H Hurmuz Basarin, 1985, 2003); *Style*— Dr Kevin Fewster, AM, FRSA; ✉ Royal Museums Greenwich, London SE10 9NF

FEWTRELL, Nicholas Austin; s of Austin Alexander Fewtrell (d 1994), of Birmingham, and Marjorie Edna, *née* Kimberlin (d 1996); *b* 1 July 1955; *Educ* Bramcote Hills GS, QMC London (LLB); *m* 26 Nov 1983, Mahshid, da of Kazem Pouladdej (d 1998), of Tehran, Iran; 1 da (Stephanie Roxanne b 6 June 1989), 1 s (Alexander Darius b 7 June 1991); *Career* called to the Bar Inner Temple 1977; in practice Northern Circuit 1978–, recorder of the Crown Court 2003–; memb: Personal Injuries Bar Assoc, Professional Negligence Bar Assoc, Northern Circuit Cammercial Bar Assoc; *Recreations* golf, football, travel; *Clubs* Ringway Golf; *Style*— Nicholas Fewtrell, Esq; ✉ 18 St John Street, Manchester M3 4EA (☎ 0161 278 1800, fax 0161 835 2051, e-mail nickfewtrell@18sjs.com)

FFORDE, Catherine Rose (Katie); da of Michael Gordon-Cumming (d 1979), and Barbara, *née* Laub (d 1996); *b* 27 September 1952; *Educ* Assoc Arts Sch Wimbledon; *m* 1972; 2 s, 1 da; *Career* writer 1984–; former sec; prop (with husband) Narrow Boat Hotel; govr Rodborough Co Primary Sch; memb: Soc of Authors, Romantic Novelists' Assoc; *Books* Living Dangerously (1995), The Rose Revived (1996), Wild Designs (1996), Stately Pursuits (1997), Life Skills (1999), Thyme Out (2000), Artistic Licence (2001), Highland Fling (2002), Paradise Fields (2003), Restoring Grace (2004); *Recreations* gardening, singing, dogs; *Style*— Katie Fforde; ✉ c/o Press Department, Arrow, Random House, Vauxhall Bridge Road, London SW1 2SA (e-mail katiefforde@katiefforde.com)

FIDDES, Michael John Alexander; s of Alexander John Scott Fiddes, of Cockfield, Suffolk, and Ann Chalcraft, *née* Forde; *b* 20 November 1959, Southsea, Hants; *Educ* Westbourne House Chichester, Marlborough, Trinity Coll Oxford (BA); *m* 18 June 1983, Julia, *née* Curry; 5 s (George b 6 Aug 1984, Edward b 31 Oct 1988, Archie b 17 Nov 1992, Hamish b 26 Nov 1994, Miles b 27 March 1998); *Career* Strutt and Parker: joined 1982, equity ptnr 1994, head Rural Div 2005; MRICS 1986; *Recreations* golf, cricket, tennis, Red Poll cows; *Clubs* Oxford and Cambridge, Felsham Farmers and Landowners, Aldeburgh Golf; *Style*— Michael Fiddes, Esq; ✉ Hammond Hall, Drinkstone Green, Bury St Edmunds, Suffolk IP30 9TL (☎ 01449 737779); Strutt and Parker, 13 Hill Street, Berkeley Square, London W1X 8DL (☎ 020 7318 5192, e-mail michael.fiddes@struttandparker.com)

FIDGEN, Roger Stewart; s of Eric Frank Fidgen, and Vera, *née* Clark; *b* 14 May 1946; *Educ* Sherborne; *m* 1, 10 Nov 1971 (m dis 1988), Sarah Dorothy, da of William Nevill Dashwood Lang (d 1988); 2 s (Patrick b 1973, Robert b 1976), 1 da (Joanna b 1979); m 2, 20 May 1988, Jennifer Godesen, da of Stanley Angold; *Career* Sub Lt RNR 1969–72; chartered quantity surveyor; sr ptnr Gardiner and Theobald 2000–04; non-exec chm Waterman Gp 2005–14; pres Br Cncl for Offices 2002; govr Sherborne Sch; Liveryman Worshipful Co of Barbers; FRICS; *Recreations* fishing, shooting, sailing, skiing; *Clubs* Boodle's, Royal Thames Yacht, Flyfishers'; *Style*— Roger Fidgen, Esq; ✉ Wield House Farm, Upper Wield, Alresford, Hampshire SO24 9RS (☎ 01420 564292)

FIDLER, Prof Peter; CBE (2012, MBE), DL (Tyne and Wear); *Career* vice-chllr and chief exec Univ of Sunderland 1999–2014 (pres 2014–); *Style*— Prof Peter Fidler, CBE, DL; ✉ University of Sunderland, Edinburgh Building, City Campus, Chester Road, Sunderland SR1 3SD

FIDLER, Peter John Michael; s of Dr Harry Fidler, of Bramhall, Cheshire, and Lilian, *née* Kahn; *b* 16 March 1942; *Educ* Bradford GS, St John's Coll Oxford (MA); *m* 19 July 1984, Barbara Julia Gottlieb, da of Harold Pinto, of Wembley, Middx; 1 s (David Robert b 1985), 2 step da (Clare Rachel b 1973 d 2014, Katherine Anna b 1977), 1 step s (Richard Charles b 1979); *Career* admitted slr 1967; articled clerk Peacock Fisher & Finch (now Field Fisher Waterhouse) 1964–67, Coward Chance 1967–72, DJ Freeman 1972–84, ptnr Stephenson Harwood 1984–2002, conslt Pinsents 2002–04, conslt CMS Cameron McKenna LLP 2004–08, special counsel Edwards Wildman Palmer UK LLP 2008–12; memb: City of London Solicitors Co, Law Soc, City of London Law Soc; rep GB at croquet 1974; *Books* Sheldon's Practice and Law of Banking (now Sheldon and Fidler's, asst ed 1972, ed 1982), contributed chapters to Corporate Administrations and Rescue Procedures (I Fletcher, J Higham and W Trower, 2004) and to The Law of Insurance Broking; *Recreations* music, theatre; *Style*— Peter Fidler, Esq; ✉ 237 West Heath Road, London NW3 7UB (☎ 020 8455 2247)

FIELD, Rt Hon Frank; PC (1997), MP; s of late Walter Field, and Annie Field; *b* 16 July 1942; *Educ* St Clement Danes GS, Univ of Hull; *Career* former lobbyist, memb TGWU, cncllr Hounslow 1964–68, Parly candidate (Lab) S Bucks 1966; dir Child Poverty Action Gp 1969–79, fndr and dir Low Pay Unit 1974–80; MP (Lab) Birkenhead 1979–, oppn spokesman on educn 1979–81, Parly conslt to Civil and Public Servs Assoc, front bench oppn spokesman on health and social security 1983–84, chm Select Ctee on Social Servs 1987–97; min of state for welfare reform DSS 1997–98; Hon LLD Univ of Warwick, Hon DSc Univ of Southampton, hon doctorate Univ of Liverpool 2006, Hon DSc Univ of Buckingham 2009; hon fell: South Bank Univ, Univ of Kent at Canterbury; *Books* Unequal Britain (1974), To Him Who Hath: A Study of Poverty And Taxation (co author, 1976), Inequality In Britain: Freedom, Welfare and The State (1981), Poverty and Politics (1982), The Minimum Wage: Its Potential And Dangers (1984), Freedom And Wealth In A Socialist Future (1987), The Politics of Paradise (1987), Losing Out: The Emergence of Britain's Underclass (1989), An Agenda for Britain (1993), Europe isn't Working (jtly, 1994), Beyond Punishment: Pathways from Workfare (jtly, 1994), Making Welfare Work (1995), How to Pay for the Future: Building a Stakeholders Welfare (1996), Stakeholder Welfare (1997), Reforming Welfare (1997), Reflections on Welfare Reform (1998), The State of Dependency, Welfare Under Labour (2000), Making Welfare Work: Reconstructing Welfare for the Millennium (2001), Universal Protected Pension: Modernising Pensions For The Millenium (report by Pensions Reform Gp, 2001), Welfare Titans: How Lloyd George and Gordon Brown Compare and Other Essays on Welfare Reform (2002), Universal Protected Pension: The Follow-Up Report (2002), Neighbours from Hell: The Politics of Behaviour (2003), Attlee's Great Contemporaries (2009), Saints and Heroes (2010); as ed: 20th Century State Education (co-ed, 1971), Black Britons (co-ed, 1971), Low Pay (1973), Are Low Wages Inevitable? (1976), Education And The Urban Crisis (1976), The Conscript Army: A Study of Britain's Unemployed (1976), The Wealth Report (1979, 2 edn 1983), Policies Against Low Pay: An International Perspective (1984); *Style*— The Rt Hon Frank Field, MP; ✉ House of Commons, London SW1A 0AA (☎ 020 7219 3000)

FIELD, Sir Malcolm David; kt (1991); s of Maj Stanley Herbert Raynor Field (d 1970), of Selsey, W Sussex, and Constance Frances, *née* Watson; *b* 25 August 1937; *Educ* Highgate Sch, London Business Sch; *m* 1, 1963 (m dis 1970), Jane, da of James Barrie; m 2, 1974 (m dis 1982), Anne Carolyn, *née* Churchill; 1 da (Joanna Clare b 1974); m 3, 2001, Anne Charlton; *Career* 2 Lt WG 1956–58; dir WH Smith & Son Ltd; W H Smith Group plc: dir 1974, md wholesale 1978, md retail 1978, gp md 1982–94, gp chief exec 1994–96, chm W H Smith Group (USA) Inc 1988; chm: NAAFI 1986–93 (non-exec dir 1973–93, dep chm 1985), CAA 1996–2001; chm: Sofa Workshop Ltd 1998–2002, Tube Lines Ltd 2003–06, Aricom 2003–09 (merged with Peter Hambro Mining); non-exec dir: MEPC plc 1989–99, Scottish & Newcastle plc 1993–99, The Stationery Office 1996–2001, Walker Greenbank 1997–2002, Evolution (formerly Beeson-Gregory) 1999–2005, Odgers 2002–, Linden Homes 2001–07, Hochschild Mining plc 2006–16 (sr ind dir), Petropavlovsk (formerly Peter Hambro Mining) 2009–, Odgers Berndston 2010–16; dir Ferrexpo 2016–; non-exec memb Advsy Bd Phoenix Fund Mangrs 1992–96; policy advsr DFT (formerly DTLR) 2001–06; govr Highgate Sch (dep chm 1999–2005), pres Devon Gardens Tst 2006–15, memb Cathedral Cncl Exeter 2009–15; CIMgt 1988; *Recreations* tennis, watching cricket, golf, collecting watercolours and modern art; *Clubs* Garrick, MCC; *Style*— Sir Malcolm Field; ✉ 21 Embankment Gardens, London SW3 4LH

FIELD, Mark Christopher; MP; s of Major Peter Field (d 1991), of Reading, Berks, and Ulrike, *née* Peipe; *b* 6 October 1964; *Educ* Reading Sch, St Edmund Hall Oxford (MA), Coll of Law Chester; *m* 1, 1994 (m dis 2006), Michèle Louise Acton; m 2, April 2007, Victoria Margaret Philadelphia, da of late Dr Geoffrey Elphicke; 1 s (Frederick William Crispian b 19 Dec 2007), 1 da (Arabella Matilda Catherine b 18 June 2011); *Career* trainee slr Richards Butler 1988–90, slr Freshfields 1990–92, dir Kellyfield Consulting (specialist recruitment/headhunting) 1994–2001; slr of Supreme Court (non-practising); MP (Cons) Cities of London and Westminster 2001–; memb Select Ctee on Lord Chllr's Dept 2003, oppn whip 2003–04, shadow min for London 2003–05, shadow fin sec to the Treasy May-Dec 2005, shadow culture min 2005–06, memb Procedure Ctee 2008–10, memb Intelligence and Security Ctee 2010–; memb Standing Ctee on: Proceeds of Crime Act 2002, Enterprise Act 2002, Finance Act 2002, Licensing Act 2003, Housing Act 2004, Railways Act 2005, Finance Act (No 2) 2005, Registration of Financial Servs (Land Transactions) Act 2005, Nat Insur Contributions Act 2006, Nat Lottery Act 2006, Crossrail Act 2008, Nat Insur Contribution Act 2008, Finance Act 2008, Business Rates Supplements Act 2009, Finance Act 2009; chm All-Pty Gp on Private Equity and Venture Capital, vice-chm All Pty Gp on Football, vice-chm All Pty Gp on Bangladesh; cncllr Kensington and Chelsea BC 1994–2002; memb Advsy Bd London Sch of Commerce 2005–, advsr Cains 2011–, advsr Elwood and Atfield 2011–; regular broadcaster on BBC Radio 4, BBC 5 Live, BBC 1, BBC 2 and Sky News; Freeman City of London; *Publications* incl: chapter in A Blue Tomorrow – New Visions for Modern Conservatives (2001), chapter in Reforming the City (2009), Between the Crashes (2013), A View From Two Cities (2014); regular articles on economics and financial affairs for nat newspapers; *Recreations* sports including cricket and football, researching local history, wandering around London, avid listener to popular and rock music; *Clubs* Carlton (hon memb), RAC (hon memb); *Style*— Mark Field, Esq, MP; ✉ House of Commons, London SW1A 0AA (☎ 020 7219 8155)

FIELD, Sir Richard; kt (2002); s of Robert Henry Field, and Ivy May, *née* Dicketts; *b* 17 April 1947; *Educ* Ottershaw Sch, Univ of Bristol (LLB), LSE (LLM); *m* 1, 31 Aug 1968, Lynne (d 2007), da of Ismay Hauskind; 2 da (Rachel Eva b 3 June 1974, Beatrice Jasmine b 17 June 1981), 2 s (Matthew Ismay b 15 Feb 1978, Thomas Richard b 26 Nov 1988); m 2, 23 May 2009, Marion Nitch-Smith; *Career* asst prof Faculty of Law Univ of Br Columbia 1969–71, lectr Hong Kong Univ 1971–73, assoc prof Faculty of Law McGill Univ Montreal 1973–77; called to the Bar Inner Temple 1977 (bencher); QC 1987, dep judge of the High Court 1998, recorder 1999, judge of the High Court of Justice (Queen's Bench Div) 2002–14 (ret), presiding judge Western Circuit 2009, judge in charge of the Commercial List 2014; appointed to Cayman Islands Ct of Appeal and Dubai DIFC Ct; Cheng Yu Tung visiting prof Faculty of Law Hong Kong Univ 2014–15; *Recreations* opera, theatre, cinema; *Clubs* Garrick; *Style*— Sir Richard Field

FIELD, Cncllr Richard Clive; s of Lt Col N J L Field, OBE (d 2010), and Hon Mrs G Field *née* Gridley (d 2001), of Wye, Kent; *b* 31 July 1947, London; *Educ* Oakham Sch; *m* 1976, Susan Rosemary Hunter, *née* Pearson; 2 s (James Peter b 1978, Christopher Guy b 1981); *Career* advtg and publicity exec and property negotiator (country) Knight Frank & Rutley 1965–75, advtg and publicity mangr Jones Lang Wootton 1975–79, dir of mktg Savills 1979–84, dir of mktg Chestertons 1984–85, mktg dir and dir Main Bd Martlet Property Services plc/GA Property Services 1985–89, mktg and Bd dir Debenham Tewson and Chinnocks 1988–90, mktg and Bd dir Wasps Promotions Ltd 1990–91, dir of mktg RFU England 1992–98, ceo Richard Field Sponsorship and Sport Mktg Consultancy 1998–2000, conslt/mangr and head Gp Corp Affrs N M Rothschild & Sons Ltd 2000–02, ceo Richard Field Property Search 2004–; cncllr Wandsworth Borough 2014, dep mayor of Wandsworth 2014/15, mayor of Wandsworth 2016–17; dep chm Educn and Children's Servs OSC, chm Educn Standards Gp (ESG), chm Junior Citzens Scheme; memb: Licensing Ctee, Audit Ctee, Standards Ctee; memb Cons Pty (treas Wandsworth and Tooting); special operations regulator Exercise Watchtower 2015; RICS visiting lectr Coll of Estate Mgmnt Univ of Reading; former mentor Prince's Tst, involved with Acads and Free Schs Cmmn; MIPR 1971, MCIM 1973; *Recreations* cricket, gardening, music, fly fishing, studying military history and the heritage of Wandsworth; *Clubs* Vines Soc; *Style*— The Worshipful the Mayor of Wandsworth, Councillor Richard Field; ✉ e-mail rf@rfps.co.uk, website www.rfps.co.uk, Twitter @_RichardField_

FIELD, Prof Stephen John (Steve); CBE (2010); s of Derek Field, of Marple, Cheshire, and Yvonne, *née* Corke; *b* 22 June 1959, Stourbridge, W Midlands; *Educ* Marple Hall GS, Univ of Birmingham (MB ChB), Univ of Dundee (MMEd); *m* 21 Oct 1992, Lynn, *née* Kennedy; 2 da (Alice Elizabeth, Helen Marie (twins) b 30 Oct 1994); *Career* GP Corbett Medical Practice Droitwich Spa 1987–97, GP princ Bellevue Med Centre (now called Modality Partnership) Edgbaston 1997–, medical dir (primary care) NHS West Midlands 2010–11; regnl advsr and dir of postgrad GP educn W Midlands 1995–2001, rgnl

F

postgrad dean NHS W Midlands Workforce Deanery 2001–07, dep nat medical dir and dir of health inequalities NHS England 2012–13, chief inspector of general practice Care Quality Cmmn 2013–; non-exec dir UCL Partners 2012–; hon prof of med educn Univ of Warwick 2002–, hon prof of med Univ of Birmingham 2003–; chm Cncl RCGP 2007–10, chm NHS Future Forum 2011–12; memb Postgrad Med Educn and Trg Bd 2003–10, chm Nat Inclusion Health Bd 2010–16; faculty Harvard Univ (Harvard Macy prog for leaders in healthcare and educn); tstee Nishkam Healthcare Tst 2013–; DUniv Univ of Staffordshire 2006, Hon MSc Univ of Worcester 2010, Hon DSc Keele Univ 2011, DUniv Birmingham City Univ 2012, Hon DSc Univ of Exeter 2015; DRCOG 1987, DipMEd 1994, FRCGP 1997 (MRCGP 1987), ILTM 2001, FHEA 2007, MAcadMEd 2008, FRCP 2009, FFPH 2011, fell Faculty of Medical Leadership and Mgmnt 2012; *Publications* numerous pubns in med and educn jls 1994–; numerous books and teaching materials on communication skills, med educn, med career, primary care and health service policy; *Recreations* tennis, theatre, family, hill walking, a wonderful flat coat retreiver called Hattie; *Style*— Prof Steve Field, CBE; ✉ e-mail steve.field@cqc.org.uk

FIELD-JOHNSON, Nicholas Anthony; s of Henry Anthony Field-Johnson (d 1988), and Magdalena, née von Evert (d 1971); b 28 March 1951; *Educ* Harrow, Univ of Oxford (MA, treas Oxford Union), Harvard Business Sch (MBA); m Sarah Katherine, née Landale; 3 s (Anthony Russell b Oct 1984, Ben Sebastian b May 1986, Oliver Nicholas b Dec 1988); *Career* corporate financier Citibank NA London 1974–78, investment advsr Atlantic Richfield Co Los Angeles 1979–82, gen mangr World Trade Bank Los Angeles 1983–85, head of M&A Dresdner Bank AG London 1986–90, dir NM Rothschild & Sons Ltd 1990–91, ceo Case International Holdings Ltd 1992–98, md (UK) Alexander Dunham & Case Capital 1998–2003, md Fraser Finance 2004–; MInstD; *Recreations* fishing, sailing, shooting, tennis, food and travel; *Clubs* Carlton; *Style*— Nicholas Field-Johnson, Esq; ✉ Rose Cottage, Asthall Leigh, Witney OX29 9PX (☎ 01993 878309, mobile 07712 577089, e-mail nfjuk@yahoo.com); Fraser Finance Limited, 33 St James's Square, London SW1Y 4JS (☎ 020 7661 9331, e-mail nicholas@fraserfinance.com, website www.fraserfinance.com)

FIELDEN, Dr Christa Maria; da of Ludwig Robert Peix (d 1974), and Margaret Freer-Hewish, née von Neumann (d 2013); b 28 June 1943; *Educ* Hampshire Co HS for Girls, Univ of London (BSc, MSc, PhD); m 29 Jan 1964 (m dis 1983), Christopher James Fielden; 2 s (James b 15 July 1966, William b 4 Oct 1968 d 1989); *Career* with Civil Serv 1970–74, head Computer Dept CNAA 1974–75, called to the Bar Lincoln's Inn 1982, in practice SE Circuit; FSS 1982; *Style*— Miss Christa Fielden; ✉ 9 Woburn Court, Bernard Street, London WC1 (☎ 020 7837 8752); Chambers of Lord Gifford, QC, 1 Mitre Court Buildings, Temple, London EC4Y 7BS (☎ 020 7452 8900)

FIELDEN, Dr Jonathan Mark; s of Barry Fielden (d 1984), and Margaret, née Shaw; b 9 September 1963; *Educ* Bedford Sch, Univ of Bristol (BSc, MB ChB); m 29 Sept 1990, Catherine Ruth, née Emerson; 1 s (Alexander David); *Career* house offr Bristol Royal Infirmary 1988–89, SHO (med) Southmead Hosp and Bristol Royal Infirmary 1989–91; SHO (anaesthetics): Southmead 1991, Bath 1992–93; registrar (Bristol Anaesthetic Trg Scheme) 1993–96, provisional fell in anaesthesia St Vincent's Hosp Sydney Aust 1994–95, specialist registrar Wessex rotation 1996–98, conslt in anaesthesia and intensive care med Royal Berkshire Hosp 1998–; memb Central Consultants & Specialists Ctee 1999–; memb Cncl: BMA 1992–94 and 1996–98 (memb Jr Doctors Ctee 1986–87, 1992–94 and 1995–98), Royal Coll of Anaesthetists 1997–2001; MRCP, FRCA; *Recreations* sport, opera, hill walking, travel, healthy cynicism; *Style*— Dr Jonathan Fielden; ✉ Intensive Care Unit, Royal Berkshire Hospital, London Road, Reading RG1 5AN

FIELDING, Daryl; da of Benjamin Payne, and Muriel, née Matthews (d 1992); b 25 October 1957; *Educ* Univ of London (BSc); m 19 Sept 1983, Bruce John Fielding; *Career* account dir Abbott Mead Vickers 1986–89, bd dir Lowe Howard Spink 1989–96, BMP 1996–98, managing ptnr Ogilvy 1998–; memb D&AD, MIPA; *Recreations* opera, travel, scuba diving, Scotland; *Style*— Mrs Daryl Fielding; ✉ Ogilvy, 10 Cabot Square, London E14 4QB (☎ 020 7345 3231)

FIELDING, David Ian; s of William Fielding, and Nora, née Kershaw; b 8 September 1948; *Educ* Central Sch of Art and Design; *Career* theatre director and designer; designer for Pet Shop Boys World Tour 1991 and the album Very; *Theatre* as dir prodns incl: Britannicus (Crucible Sheffield), The Intelligence Park (Almeida Festival), The Hypochondriacs (Citizens Glasgow), Elisabeth II (Gate), The Eve of Retirement (Gate), The New Menoza (Gate), Betrayal (Citizens Glasgow), The Park (RSC, The Pit) 1995, Back to Methuselah (RSC); design cmmns RSC incl: The Tempest, The Plain Dealer, Restoration, King Lear; other design credits incl: Scenes from an Execution (Almeida), Mother Courage (RNT) 1995; *Opera* as dir prodns for Garsington Opera incl: Capriccio, Daphne, Idomeneo, Die Ägyptische Helena, Die liebe der Danae, Intermezzo, Die schweigsame Frau, Arabella; other credits incl: Elisa E Claudio (Wexford Festival Opera), Soundbites (ENO), The Turk in Itlay (ENO), Tannhäuser (Opera North), Rinaldo (Grange Park), The Turn of the Screw (Grange Park), Charodeika (Grange Park), Eliogabalo, The Love of Three Oranges, Tristan und Isolde; Wexford Festival Opera design cmmns incl: Medea in Corinto, Giovanna D'Arco, Hans Heiling, La Legenda Di Sakuntala, The Turn of the Screw; design cmmns for Scottish Opera incl: Seraglio, Die Fledermaus, Rigoletto, Wozzeck, The Rise and Fall of the City of Mahagonny; designs for Welsh Nat Opera incl: The Turn of the Screw, Il Trovatore, Elektra; designs for Kent Opera incl: Ruddigore, The Marriage of Figaro, King Priam (also filmed); designs for ENO incl: Rienzi, Mazeppa, Xerxes, Simon Boccanegra, Clarissa, A Masked Ball, Don Carlos, Street Scene (co-prod Scottish Opera); other prodns incl: Der Fliegende Holländer (Royal Opera House), La Clemenza Di Tito (Glyndebourne); cmmns abroad incl: The Rake's Progress (Netherlands Opera), Werther (Nancy Opera), Iolanthe (Komische Oper Berlin), Don Carlos (San José Symphony), Idomeneo (Vienna State Opera), Jules César (Paris Opera), The Ring Cycle (New Nat Theatre Tokyo); *Recreations* bridge, crosswords, Central American archaeology, gardening; *Style*— David Fielding, Esq

FIELDING, Emma Georgina Annalies; da of John Fielding, and Sheila, née Brown; b Catterick, Yorks; *Educ* RSAMD; m 17 May 2004, Michael Ashcroft; 1 s (Ernest George b 1 Aug 2008); *Career* actor; assoc artist RSC; *Theatre* credits incl: Jane Eyre in Jane Eyre (Crucible Sheffield), Thomasina in Arcadia (RNT), Agnes in School for Wives (Almeida), Penthea in Broken Heart (RSC), Hermia in A Midsummer Night's Dream (RSC), Viola in Twelfth Night (RSC), Ira in 1953 (Almeida), Ellie Dunn in Heartbreak House (Almeida), Lady Teazle in The School for Scandal (RSC), Alison in Look Back in Anger (RNT), Sarah in Spinning Into Butter (Royal Court), Private Lives (Albery Theatre (Olivier Award nomination Best Supporting Actress 2002)), Isabella in Measure for Measure (RSC), Imogen in Cymbeline (RSC), Playing with Fire (RNT), Eleanor/Esme in Rock n Roll (Duke of York's Theatre), Decade at St Katharine Dock, The King's Speech (Wyndham's Theatre), Heartbreak House (Chichester Festival Theatre), In the Republic of Happiness (Royal Court), Rapture, Blister, Burn (Hampstead Theatre), The Massive Tragedy of Madame Bovary! (Liverpool Everyman); *Television* credits incl: Mary Shelley in Dread Poets Society (BBC), Becky in Tell Tale Hearts (BBC), Joan in The Maitlands (BBC), Elizabeth in Drover's Gold (BBC), Isobel in Dance to the Music of Time (Dancetime), Frances in A Respectable Trade (BBC), Elizabeth Lack in Wings of Angels (BBC), Beatrice in Big Bad World (Carlton), Josie in Other People's Children (BBC), The Ghost Squad, Cranford, Cranford II, Midsomer Murders, Kidnap and Ransom, The Suspicions of Mr Whicher, George Gently, Father Brown, Death in Paradise, The Game, Silk, DCI Banks, New Tricks, Foyle's War, This Is England 90, Capital, Arthur and

George, Close to the Enemy, Dark Angel; *Film* Mary in Pandemonium (Mariner Films), DCI Pryce in Shooters (Coolbeans Films), Helga in Discovery of Heaven (Mulholland Films), The Other Man, Mabel in The Great Ghost Rescue, The Briny (short), I Do (short); *Awards* Carleton Hobbs Radio Award 1991, Ian Charleson Award (for School for Wives) 1993, London Critics' Circle Most Promising Newcomer (for Arcadia and School for Wives) 1993, Dame Peggy Ashcroft Award for Best Actress (for Twelfth Night and The Broken Heart) 1995, Theater World Award Outstanding Broadway Debut (for Private Lives); *Publications* Twelfth Night: Actors on Shakespeare (2002); *Recreations* hill walking, gardening; *Style*— Ms Emma Fielding; ✉ c/o Rebecca Blond Associates, 69a Kings Road, London SW3 4NX (☎ 020 7351 4100)

FIELDING, Helen; *Educ* Wakefield Girls' HS, St Anne's Coll Oxford; *Career* novelist; Publishing News Br Book Awards Book of the Year 1997; *Books* Cause Celeb (1995), Bridget Jones's Diary (1996), Bridget Jones: The Edge Of Reason (1999), Olivia Joules and the Overactive Imagination (2003), Bridget Jones: Mad About the Boy (2013); *Recreations* hiking, swimming, reading, movies, salsa; *Style*— Ms Helen Fielding; ✉ c/o Viking Publicity, 375 Hudson Street, New York 10014, USA

FIELDING, Sir Leslie; KCMG (1987); o s of Percy Archer Fielding (d 1963), and Margaret, née Calder Horry (d 1999); b 29 July 1932; *Educ* Queen Elizabeth's Sch Barnet, Emmanuel Coll Cambridge (MA), SOAS Univ of London, St Antony's Coll Oxford (MA); m 1978, Dr Sally Patricia Joyce Fielding, FSA, da of late Robert Stanley Thomas Stibbs Harvey; 1 s, 1 da; *Career* joined Foreign Serv 1956, Tehran 1957–60, FO 1960–64, Singapore 1964, chargé d'affaires Phnom Penh 1964–66, Paris 1966–70, FCO 1970–73; transferred to European Cmmn in Brussels 1973, head of delgn Cmmn of European Communities in Japan 1978–82, DG for external rels European Cmmn in Brussels 1982–87; vice-chllr Univ of Sussex 1987–92 (memb Univ Ct 2000–), memb High Cncl European Univ Inst Florence 1988–92, chm UK Nat Curriculum Working Gp for Geography 1989–90; currently lectr in history; hon pres Univ Assoc for Contemporary European Studies 1990–2000; memb: Japan-European Community Assoc 1988–98, UK-Japan 2000 Gp 1993–2001; advsr: IBM Europe 1989–95, Panasonic Europe 1990–96; memb House of Laity Gen Synod C of E 1990–92, reader C of E 1981–2007 (emeritus 2007–, served Dioceses of Exeter, Tokyo, Gibraltar, Chichester and Hereford); hon fell: Emmanuel Coll Cambridge 1990, Sussex European Inst 1993–; sometime fell St Hilda's Coll Oxford; Hon LLD Univ of Sussex 1992; FRSA 1989, FRGS 1991; Grand Offr of the Order of St Agatha (San Marino) 1987, Knight Cdr of the Order of the White Rose (Finland) 1988, Silver Order of Merit with Star (Austria) 1989; *Publications* Traveller's Tales (contrib, 1999), More Travellers' Tales (contrib, 2005), Before the Killing Fields: Witness to Cambodia and the Vietnam War (2007), Kindly Call Me God: The Misadventures of Fielding of the FO, Eurocrat Extraordinaire and Vice-Chancellor Semipotentiary (2009), Twilight Over The Temples: The Close of Cambodia's Belle Epoque (2011), The Mistress of the Bees (2011), Mentioned In Despatches: Phnom Penh, Paris, Tokyo, Brussels: Is Diplomacy Dead? (2012), Memories of Britain's European Pioneers 1973 (contrib, 2013), Is Diplomacy Dead? (2014), Germansweek and Its Parish Church (2014), Domesday, Book of Judgement (2014); *Recreations* living in the country; *Clubs* Travellers; *Style*— Sir Leslie Fielding, KCMG; ✉ Wild Cherry Farm, Elton, Ludlow, Shropshire, SY8 2HQ (website www.lesliefielding.com)

FIELDING, Noel; b 21 May 1973, London; *Educ* Croydon Art Coll, Bucks Chilterns UC; *Career* comedian and actor; *Stand Up* Voodoo Hedgehog (Edinburgh Fringe Festival and Her Majesty's Theatre London) 2002 (Outstanding Achievement in Comedy Time Out Award 2002) and (Melbourne Int Comedy Festival) 2003; *Television* incl: Garth Marenghi's Dark Place (Channel 4) 2004, The Mighty Boosh (BBC3 and BBC2) 2004–07 (also writer), Nathan Barley (Channel 4) 2005, IT Crowd (Channel 4) 2006–07, Noel Fielding's Luxury Comedy (E4) 2012–; team capt Never Mind the Buzzcocks (BBC2) 2007–, panelist The Big Fat Quiz of the Year (Channel 4) 2007 and 2011; *Style*— Noel Fielding; ✉ c/o PBJ and JBJ Management, 22 Rathbone Street, London W1T 1LA

FIENNES, Joseph Alberic; b 26 May 1970, Salisbury, Wilts; *Educ* Guildhall Sch of Music and Drama; m 2009, Maria Dolores Dieguez; 2 da (b 2010 and 2011); *Career* actor; *Theatre* Real Classy Affair (Royal Court), Edward II (Sheffield Crucible), Love's Labour's Lost (Nat Theatre), Epitaph for George Dillon (Comedy); West End incl: The Woman in Black, A View from the Bridge, A Month in the Country; RSC incl: Son of Man, Les Enfants du Paradis, Troilus and Cressida, The Herbal Bed, As You Like It; *Television* The Vacillations of Poppy Carew 1995, FlashForward 2009–10; *Films* Stealing Beauty 1996, Martha, Meet Frank, Daniel and Laurence 1998, Elizabeth 1998, Shakespeare in Love 1998, Forever Mine 1999, Rancid Aluminium 2000, Enemy at the Gates 2001, Dust 2001, Killing Me Softly 2001, The Great Raid 2003, Luther 2003, Leo 2003, The Merchant of Venice 2003, Sinbad: Legend of the Seven Seas 2003, Man to Man 2004, Darwin Awards 2004, Running with Scissors 2005, Goodbye Bafana 2006, The Escapist 2008, You Me and Captain Longbridge 2008, Spring 1941 2008, Against the Current 2009, Vivaldi 2010; *Style*— Joseph Fiennes, Esq; ✉ c/o Ken McReddie, 11 Connaught Place, London W2 2ET (☎ 020 7499 7448)

FIENNES, Ralph Nathanial; s of Mark Fiennes (d 2004), of London, and Jennifer, née Lash (d 1993); b 22 December 1962; *Educ* St Kieran's Coll Kilkenny Ireland, Bishop Wordsworth Sch Salisbury, Chelsea Sch of Art, RADA (Kendal Award, Forbes-Robertson Award, Emile Littler Award); *Career* actor; memb Br Actors' Equity Assoc; Outstanding Contrib to Br Cinema Br Ind Film Award 2011; *Theatre* Twelfth Night, A Midsummer Night's Dream and Ring Round the Moon (all The Open Air Theatre) 1985, Night and Day and See How They Run (both Theatr Clwyd), Me Mam Sez, Don Quixote and Cloud Nine (all Oldham Coliseum) 1986, Romeo & Juliet and A Midsummer Night's Dream (both Open Air Theatre) 1986, Six Characters in Search of an Author, Fathers and Sons and Ting Tang Mine (all NT) 1987–88, The Plantagenets, Much Ado about Nothing, King John, The Man Who Came to Dinner, Playing with Trains, Troilus and Cressida, King Lear and Love's Labour's Lost (all RSC) 1988–91, Hamlet (Hackney Empire and Broadway) 1995 (Tony Award for Best Actor), Ivanov (Almeida) 1997, Brand (RSC) 2003, Julius Caesar (Barbican) 2005, Faith Healer (Gate Theatre Dublin and Broadway) 2006, First Love (Sydney Festival); *Films* A Dangerous Man: Lawrence After Arabia, Wuthering Heights, The Baby of Macon, The Cormorant, Schindler's List (BAFTA Award for Best Supporting Actor, London Film Critics' British Actor of the Year Award), Quiz Show, Strange Days, The English Patient, Oscar and Lucinda, The Avengers, Onegin, A Taste of Sunshine, The End of the Affair, Spider, Wallace and Gromit: The Curse of the Were-Rabbit, Harry Potter and the Goblet of Fire, The Constant Gardener (Best Actor Evening Standard British Film Awards, Best British Actor London Film Critics' Circle Awards), The White Countess, Bernard and Doris, Harry Potter and the Order of the Phoenix, In Bruges, The Duchess, The Hurt Locker, The Reader, Nanny McPhee and the Big Bang, Clash of the Titans, Cemetery Junction, Harry Potter and the Deathly Hallows: Part 1, Coriolanus (also dir), Page Eight, Harry Potter and the Deathly Hallows: Part 2, Clash of the Titans 2, Great Expectations, Skyfall, The Grand Budapest Hotel; *Recreations* reading; *Style*— Ralph Fiennes, Esq

FIENNES, Sir Ranulph (TWISLETON-WYKEHAM-); 3 Bt (UK 1916), of Banbury, Co Oxford; OBE (1993); s of Lt-Col Sir Ranulph Twisleton-Wykeham-Fiennes, 2 Bt, DSO (d 1943, gs of 17 Baron Saye and Sele), and Audrey Joan, née Newson (d 2004); b 7 March 1944, (posthumously); *Educ* Eton, Mons Offr Cadet Sch; m 1, 11 Sept 1970, Virginia Frances (d 2004), da of Thomas Pepper (d 1985); m 2, 12 March 2005, Louise Millington; 1 da (Elizabeth Grace b 2006); *Career* Capt Royal Scots Greys, Capt 22 SAS Regt 1966, Capt

Sultan of Oman's Armed Forces 1968–70; exec conslt for Western Europe to Chm Occidental Petroleum Corp 1984–90; author and explorer; leader of first polar circumnavigation of earth (The Transglobe Expedition) that arrived back in UK in Sept 1982 after 3 years non-stop travel, first man (with colleague) to reach both Poles by surface travel, achieved world record for unsupported northerly travel reaching 88 degrees and 28 minutes Siberian Arctic 1990, leader of Ubar Expedition which discovered the lost city of Ubar 1992, record unsupported Polar trek of 1,272 miles in 96 days 1992–93 (also with colleague first unsupported crossing of Antarctic Continent), completed seven marathons on seven continents in seven days 2003, second in North Pole Marathon 2004, climbed North face of the Eiger 2007, climed to the summit of Mount Everest 2009 (oldest Briton); hon dir of science Univ of Chester 2014–; Hon DSc Loughborough Univ; Hon Dr: UCE 1995, Univ of Portsmouth 2000, Univ of Glasgow 2002, Univ of Sheffield 2005, Abertay 2007, Univ of Glamorgan 2012; *Awards* French Parachute Wings 1968, Dhofar Campaign Medal 1968, Sultan of Oman's Bravery Medal 1970, Man of the Year Award 1982, Livingstone Gold Medal Royal Scottish Geographical Soc 1983, Gold Medal NY Explorers Club 1984, Fndr's Medal RGS 1984, The Polar Medal 1984 with Bar 1995 by HM the Queen (first wife was first female recipient), ITV Award for the event of the decade 1990, Explorers Club (Br Chapter) Millennium Award for Navigation 2000, Oldie of the Year Award 2004, ITV Greatest Briton (Sport) 2007, Top UK Charity Fundraiser Just Giving Award 2010; *Books* Talent for Trouble (1968), Icefall in Norway (1971), The Headless Valley (1972), Where Soldiers Fear to Tread (1975), Hell on Ice (1978), To the Ends of the Earth: Transglobe Expedition 1979–82 (1983), Bothie The Polar Dog (jtly with first wife, 1984), Living Dangerously (1987), The Feather Men (1991), Atlantis of the Sands – The Search for the Lost City of Ubar (1992), Mind Over Matter (1993), The Sett (1996), Fit For Life (1998), Beyond the Limits (2000), The Secret Hunters (2002), Captain Scott (biography, 2003), Mad, Bad – Dangerous to Know (2007), Mad Dogs and Englishmen (2009), My Heroes (2011), Heat (2015); *Recreations* skiing, photography; *Clubs* Guild of Vintners, Travellers (hon memb), Highland Soc of London; *Style—* Sir Ranulph Fiennes, Bt, OBE

FIETH, Robin Paul; s of Eric Fieth (d 2007), and Eileen, *née* Miller (d 2000); *b* 8 December 1963, Sheffield; *Educ* Downside, Durham Univ (BA); *m* 7 Sept 1991, Fiona Mary Gair, *née* MacGregor; 2 da (Jessica b 3 May 1994, Alice b 28 March 1996), 1 s (Jonathan b 22 June 2000); *Career* sr mangr Price Waterhouse Bristol 1986–96, fin dir GiroVend Cashless Systems plc 1996–2000, gp fin dir Transacsys plc 2000–01, dir of fin ICAEW 2002–07, exec dir Members and Ops ICAEW 2007–13, chief exec BSA 2013–; dir Lending Standards Bd 2014–15, memb Exec Ctee European Assoc of Co-operative Banks 2014–; tstee: The Downside Settlement 2002–06, Chartered Accountants' Benevolent Assoc 2010–; FCA (memb ICAEW 1990); *Style—* Robin Fieth, Esq; ✉ Building Societies Association, 6th Floor, York House, 23 Kingsway, London WC2B 6UJ

FIFE, Jonathan Keith (Jon); s of Donald Ralph Fife, and Marjorie Eileen Fife; *b* 18 September 1948, Aberdeen; *Educ* Leeds Modern Sch, Lincoln Coll Oxford (BA); *m* 31 Dec 1974, Jean Margaret, *née* Northedge; 1 s (Edward James b 17 June 1978), 2 da (Katherine Alice, Rebecca Ann (twins) b 30 Jan 1981); *Career* admitted slr 1973; Waterhouse & Co: joined as trainee, slr 1973, ptnr 1978; currently sr ptnr Field Fisher Waterhouse (also head Commercial and Finance Gp); memb City of London Slrs Co; *Recreations* opera, football, golf; *Style—* Jon Fife, Esq; ✉ Field Fisher Waterhouse, 35 Vine Street, London EC3N 2AA (☎ 020 7861 4170, fax 020 7488 0084, e-mail jon.fife@ffw.com)

FIGES, Prof Orlando Guy; s of John Figes (d 2003), and Eva, *née* Unger; *b* 20 November 1959, London; *Educ* Univ of Cambridge (BA, PhD); *m* 1990, Stephanie, *née* Palmer; 2 da (Lydia, Alice (twins) b 1993); *Career* Univ of Cambridge: research fell Trinity Coll 1984–87, asst lectr History Faculty 1987, coll lectr and dir of studies Trinity Coll 1988, lectr History Faculty 1987; prof of history Birkbeck Coll London 1999–; Leverhulme Tst Sr Research Fellowship 1995–96, Leverhulme Tst Institutional Grant 1999–2001, British Acad Sr Research Fellowship 2000–01; for A People's Tragedy: Wolfson Prize for History 1997, NCR Book Award 1997, WH Smith Literary Award 1997, Longman/History Today Book of the Year Award 1997, LA Times Book Prize 1997; FRSL; *Publications* Peasant Russia, Civil War: The Volga Countryside in Revolution 1917–1921 (1989, 2 edn 1999), A People's Tragedy: The Russian Revolution 1891–1924 (1996), Interpreting the Russian Revolution: The Language and Symbols of 1917 (with Boris Kolonitskii, 1999), Natasha's Dance: A Cultural History of Russia (2002), The Whisperers: Private Life in Stalin's Russia (2007), Cinema: The Last Crusade (2010); also author of numerous chapters in books, articles and published lectures; *Recreations* soccer, gardening, wine; *Style—* Prof Orlando Figes; ✉ Birkbeck College, Malet Street, London WC1E 7HX (☎ 020 7631 6299, e-mail o.figes@bbk.ac.uk)

FIGGURES, Lt-Gen Andrew Collingwood; CB (2009), CBE (1998); s of Colin Norman Figgures, and Ethel Barbara, *née* Wilks; *b* 13 November 1950; *Educ* Loughborough GS, Welbeck Coll, RMA Sandhurst, St Catharine's Coll Cambridge (MA), Open Univ (MBA); *m* 1978, Poppy Felicity Ann, *née* Ogley; 1 da; *Career* cmmnd 1970, served UK, Cyprus, BAOR, former Yugoslavia, Iraq; student: Army Staff Coll Camberley, Higher Cmd and Staff Coll, RCDS; Cdr Equipment Support Land Cmd 1995, DOR (Land)/DEC(DBE) MOD 1999–2000, capability mangr (manoeuvre) MOD 2000–03, Dep Cmdg Gen Combined Jt Task Force 7 2003–04, Master Gen of the Ordnance and tech dir Defence Procurement Agency (DPA) and Defence Logistics Orgn (DLO) 2004; Col Cmdt REME 2002–; CEng 1991, FIMechE 1992, FIET 2006, FRAeS 2006; *Clubs* Leander; *Style—* Lt-Gen Andrew Figgures, CB, CBE; ✉ e-mail andrew.figgures944@mod.uk

FILBY, Ian; s of Peter Filby, of Bristol, and Paquita, *née* Garrido (d 1998); *b* 27 January 1959, Finchley, London; *Educ* Queen Elizabeth's Hosp Bristol, St Catharine's Coll Cambridge (BA, Soccer blue); *m* 1 June 1991, Susan, *née* Woo; 2 da (Luisa Lara b 27 Jan 1992, Francesca Linda b 17 March 2001), 1 s (Laurence Leon b 25 Aug 1993); *Career* Boots Co plc: retail buying 1981, sales and mktg dir Fads/Homestyle 1997; Boots the Chemists: dep dir trading 2001–03, commercial dir lifestyle 2003–05, exec dir beauty and lifestyle 2005–07, exec trading dir 2007–09; ceo DFS Furnishings 2010–, chm Shoezone plc 2014; chm Policy Bd Br Retail Consortium (BRC) 2014; *Recreations* golf, cricket, off-piste skiing, saxophone, good eating and drinking, triathlons; *Clubs* Belton Woods Golf, Belvoir CC; *Style—* Ian Filby, Esq; ✉ DFS Furniture Company Limited, Redhouse Interchange, Adwick-le-Street, Doncaster DN6 7NA

FILKIN, Elizabeth Jill; CBE (2014); da of John Tompkins, and Frances Trollope; *b* 24 November 1940; *Educ* Univ of Birmingham (BSocSci), Brunel Univ; *m* 2, 1974 (m dis 1994), Geoffrey Filkin, CBE (now Lord Filkin (Life Peer)), *qv*; 3 da; m 3, 1996, Michael John Honey; *Career* organiser Sparkbrook Assoc Birmingham 1961–64, res fell Anglo-Israel Assoc London and Israel 1964, lectr and researcher Univ of Birmingham 1964–68, lectr National Inst for Social Work London 1968–71 (also community worker N Southwark), community work services offr London Borough of Brent Social Services Dept 1971–75, lectr in social studies Univ of Liverpool 1975–83, chief exec National Assoc CAB 1983–88, asst chief exec London Docklands Devpt Corp 1991–92 (dir Community Servs 1988–91), The Adjudicator in The Adjudicator's Office 1993–99, Parly Cmmr for Standards 1999–2002; cmmr Audit Cmmn 1999–2004, chm ATVOD (Assoc for TV on Demand) 2004–, dep chm Regulatory Decisions Ctee FSA 2005– (memb 2002–), chm Appts Gp RPSGB 2005–, chm Advtg Advsy Ctee 2005–, chm HB and Senator Capital 2005–; non-exec dir: Britannia Building Soc 1992–98, Hay Management Consultants 1992–98, Logica plc 1995–99, Stanelco plc 2003–, Jarvis plc 2003–; non-exec advsr Weatherall Green & Smith 1997–99; former chm Rainer Fndn; chm Advsy Cncl Centre for Socio-Legal Studies Wolfson Coll Oxford 1995–2000; memb Cncl: Royal Holloway Coll London 1995–97 (dep chm Bd Govrs), Univ of E London 1997–2003; Special Award Zurich/Spectator Parly Awards 2001; Hon PhD: Brunel Univ 2002, South Bank Univ 2003; City fell Hughes Hall Cambridge 2003–06; *Books* The New Villagers (1969), What Community Worker Needs to Know (1974), Community Work & Caring for Children (1979), Caring for Children (1979), Women and Children First (1984); *Recreations* swimming, walking; *Style—* Elizabeth Filkin, CBE

FILKIN, Baron (Life Peer UK 1999), of Pimlico in the City of Westminster; (David) Geoffrey Nigel Filkin; CBE (1997); s of Donald Geoffrey Filkin (d 1994), and Winifred, *née* Underwood; *b* 1 July 1944; *Educ* King Edward VI GS Birmingham, Clare Coll Cambridge (MA), Univ of Manchester (DipTP); *m* 1, (m dis), Elizabeth Filkin, *qv*; 3 da (Fiona, Victoria, Beatrice); m 2, 28 May 2005, Brigitte Paupy; *Career* GVSO in Ghana, town planner Redditch Development Corporation 1969–72, mangr Housing Aid Centre Brent 1972–75, dir of housing and dep chief exec Merseyside Improved Housing 1975–79, dir of housing Ellesmere Port 1979–82, dir of housing Greenwich 1982–88, chief exec Reading BC 1988–91, sec Assoc of District Councils 1991–97, policy analyst and writer 1997–; Lord in Waiting (Govt whip) 2001–, Parly under sec of state Home Office 2002–03, Parly under sec of state Dept of Constitutional Affrs 2003–04, Parly under sec of state DfES 2004–05, chm Parly All-Pty Business Services Gp 2000–01, advsr Environment Ctee House of Commons until 2001, chm Merits Ctee House of Lords 2005–09, chm House of Lords Public Services and Demographic Change Ctee 2012–13; non-exec dir New Local Govt Network until 2001, local govt advsr to Joseph Rowntree Fndn until 2001, fndr chm Public Serv Reform Gp 2005–07, fndr chm 2020 Public Servs Tst 2008–10; advsr: Govt of South Africa until 2001, Serco until 2013; non-exec dir Accord plc until 2008; advsr: Capgemini until 2012, NSL until 2013; fndr and chm The Parliament Choir 2001–02; chm Beacon Cncl Advsy Panel 1999–2001; chm St Albans Cathedral Music Tst until 2012, chair Centre for Ageing Better 2014–; memb Soc of Local Authy Chief Execs; former MRTPI; *Publications* Ready for Ageing (report); *Recreations* walking, opera, music, bird watching; *Style—* The Rt Hon the Lord Filkin, CBE; ✉ House of Lords, London SW1A 0PW (☎ 020 7219 0640)

FILOCHOWSKI, Prof (Edward) Jan; *Educ* Univ of Cambridge (MA), Univ of Newcastle upon Tyne (MA); *m* Dr Naomi Judith Fulop; 1 s (Tom), 1 da (Kate); *Career* chief-exec NHS Hosp Tsts at: Poole 1992–97, Southmead 1998–99, Medway 1999–2002, Bath 2002–03, W Herts 2007–12, Gt Ormond St Hosp 2012–13; visiting fell Harvard Univ 1997–98, NHS Univ fell and sr assoc Judge Business Sch Univ of Cambridge 2004–05, visiting prof Brunel Univ 2004–; MHSM; *Publications* Too Good to Fail? (2013); *Style—* Jan Filochowski

FINALDI, Dr Gabriele; s of Remo Finaldi, and Iwonka Finaldi; *b* 28 November 1965; *Educ* Courtauld Inst of Art (PhD); *m* 1987, Maria Inés Guerrero Parra; 5 da (Marta b 1988, Carmen b 1989, Cristina b 1991, Ana Maria b 1998, Paola b 2005), 1 s (Francesco b 1995); *Career* art historian and curator; curator Later Italian and Spanish Painting Nat Gallery 1992–2002, dep dir Collections and Research Museo del Prado, dir Nat Gallery London 2015–; *Style—* Dr Gabriele Finaldi; ✉ National Gallery, Trafalgar Square, London WC2N 5DN

FINBOW, Roger John; s of Frederick Walter Finbow, of Sudbourne, Suffolk, and Olivia Francis, *née* Smith; *b* 13 May 1952; *Educ* Woodbridge Sch, Mansfield Coll Oxford (MA); *m* 23 May 1984, Janina Fiona (Nina), da of late John Doull; 3 da (Romy b 1985, Georgina b 1987, Isobel b 1989); *Career* Ashurst LLP (formerly Ashurst Morris Crisp) London: articled clerk 1975–77, asst 1977–83 (Paris 1978–79), assoc 1983–85, ptnr 1985–2009, conslt 2009–; chm Ctee City Slrs Educnl Tst; memb Mansfield Coll Devpt Bd; memb Competition and Markets Authy; chm Disciplinary Panel Br Univs and Colls Sport, chm Seckford Fndn, chm Ipswich Town plc, tstee Legal Educn Fndn; *Books* UK Merger Control: Law and Practice (jtly, 1995, 2 edn 2005); *Recreations* cars, collecting model cars, keeping fit, football spectating, ballet, motorbiking; *Style—* Roger Finbow, Esq; ✉ Yew Tree House, Lower Street, Higham, Colchester, Essex CO7 6JZ (☎ 01206 337378, e-mail rogerfinbow@angliamail.com); Ashurst LLP, Broadwalk House, 5 Appold Street, London EC2A 2HA (☎ 020 7638 1111, fax 020 7638 1112, e-mail roger.finbow@ashurst.com)

FINCH, Alison Mary; da of Joseph Finch (d 2012), and Sheila, *née* Richardson (d 2008); *b* 26 April 1948, London; *Educ* Blackheath HS GDST, Girton Coll Cambridge (entrance scholar, BA, PhD, maj state studentship); *m* 17 March 1979, Malcolm Bowie (d 2007); 1 s (Sam b 18 Jan 1980), 1 da (Jess b 10 April 1984); *Career* asst lectr and lectr Dept of French Univ of Cambridge 1978–93; fell in French: Churchill Coll Cambridge 1972–93, Jesus Coll Oxford 1993–95, Merton Coll Oxford 1995–2003, Churchill Coll Cambridge 2003– (vice-master 2005–06 and 2008–12, acting master 2012); chair Sub-Faculty of French Univ of Oxford 2000–03; memb Soc of French Studies 1972; co-ed French Studies 2002–05, gen ed Modern Humanities Research Assoc Translation Series 2009–; memb Amnesty Int, memb Labour Pty; memb MHRA 1974; Officier dans l'Ordre des Palmes Académiques (France) 2000; *Publications* Proust's Additions: The Making of A la Recherche du Temps Perdu (1977), Stendhal: La Chartreuse de Parme (1984), Concordance de Stendhal (1991), Women's Writing in Nineteenth-Century France (2000), French Literature: A Cultural History (2010); numerous articles and reviews 1974–; *Recreations* singing, swimming, travel, theatre; *Clubs* Oxford & Cambridge; *Style—* Prof Alison Finch; ✉ Churchill College, Cambridge CB3 0DS (e-mail amf1000@cam.ac.uk)

FINCH, Charles (ne Charles Ingle-Finch); s of Peter Finch, and Yolanda Turnbull; grand s of George Ingle-Finch, the mountaineer; *b* 15 August 1962, London; *m* Sydney Ingle-Finch, *qv*; *Career* film prodr; ceo Finch & Ptnrs; films incl: Mike Bassett: England Manager 2001, Spider 2002, Fat Slags 2004, Ghosts 2006, Camille 2007, Ruby Blue 2007, Battle for Haditha 2007, The Mutant Chronicles 2008; publisher Finch's Quarterly Review; *Style—* Charles Finch, Esq; ✉ Finch & Partners, 29–37 Heddon Street, London W1B 4BR

FINCH, Prof Dame Janet Valerie; DBE (2008), DL; da of Robert Bleakley Finch (d 1975), of Liverpool, and Evelyn Muriel, *née* Smith; *b* 13 February 1946; *Educ* Merchant Taylors' Sch for Girls, Bedford Coll London (BA), Univ of Bradford (PhD); *m* 1, 1967 (m dis 1981), Geoffrey O Spedding; m 2, 1994, David H J Morgan; *Career* research asst Dept of Anthropology Univ of Cambridge 1969–70, postgraduate research student Univ of Bradford 1970–73, lectr in sociology Endsleigh Coll of Educn Hull 1974–76; Lancaster Univ: lectr in social admin 1976–84, sr lectr 1984–88, prof of social relations 1988–, head Dept of Applied Social Science 1988–91, memb Senate 1984–87 and 1989–91, memb Academic Planning Ctee 1989–, chair Equal Opportunities Ctee 1990–93, memb Staffing Ctee 1991–93, pro-vice-chllr 1992–95; vice-chllr Keele Univ 1995–2010; hon prof of sociology Univ of Manchester 2010–; Universities UK: memb Sutherland Ctee (Academic Standards Gp) 1988–92, pt/t secondment to the Academic Audit Unit 1990–91, memb Jt Working Party with the Br Acad on postgraduate studentships in the humanities 1991–92, chair Health Professions Ctee 1996–2000, chair Jt Equality Steering Gp 2001–07, memb Exec 2002–05, chair Health Ctee 2003–07; memb Bd Quality Assurance Agency for HE 1997–2004, memb Strategic Research Ctee HEFCE 2003–06; Br Sociological Assoc: memb Nat Exec 1980–84, chair Exec 1983–84; ESRC: memb Research Centres Bd 1992–93, memb Cncl 1993–97, chair Research Grants Bd; memb Advsy Gps 1990–92: Nursing Research Unit KCL, Home Office project on Imprisonment and Family Ties Univ of Cambridge, Rowntree project on Young People and Housing Univ of Kent; memb: various Ctees CNAA 1982–92, Professoriate Standing Ctee Sheffield Poly (now Sheffield Hallam Univ) 1989–92, External Panel of Experts in Social Admin Univ of London 1990–

93, Bd Staffs Environmental Fund Ltd 2000–04, Cncl for Science and Technology 2004–11 (ind co-chair 2007–11), MRC 2014– (also chair Audit Ctee); chair: Preston Cncl for Racial Equality 1982–86 (exec memb 1977–86), Bd Staffs Connexions Ltd 2002–04, Working Gp, Expanding Access to Published Research Findings 2011–13, Governing Bd The Life Study 2011–15, Main Panel C Research Excellence Framework 2014, Nursing and Midwifery Cncl 2015–; tstee Nat Centre for Social Research 2002–12 (chair of tstees 2007–12); memb N Western RHA 1992–96; non-exec dir: Office for Nat Statistics 1999–2008, Identity and Passport Serv 2008–13; chair Bd Ombudsman Services Ltd 2010–16; govr: Edge Hill Coll 1990–92, Sheffield Hallam Univ 1992–95, Stoke-on-Trent Sixth Form Coll 1999–2002, Manchester Met Univ 2002–11; Hon DLitt UWE 1997, Hon DSc Univ of Edinburgh 2000, Hon DSc Univ of Southampton 2001, Hon DEd Univ of Lincoln 2002, Hon DEd Queen Margaret UC Edinburgh 2003; hon fell Royal Holloway Coll London 1999, hon fell Liverpool John Moores Univ 2001; AcSS 1999; *Books* Married to the Job: Wives' Incorporation in Men's Work (1983), Education as Social Policy (1984), Research and Policy: the Uses of Qualitative Methods in Social and Educational Research (1986), Family Obligations and Social Change (1989), Negotiating Family Responsibilities (with J Mason, 1993), Wills Inheritance and Families (jtly, 1996), Passing On (with J Mason, 2000); also author of numerous book chapters and of articles in refereed jls; *Clubs* Athenaeum; *Style—* Prof Dame Janet Finch, DBE, DL, AcSS

FINCH, John; *b* 8 September 1965; *Educ* Univ of Hull (BSc); *m* 6 Dec 1995, Hilary June *née* Lodge; 1 da (Bethany Jane b 22 Feb 1997); *Career* Mercury Communications 1987–94, Heinz 1994–96, Unipart Gp of Cos 1996–98, Nat Bank of Kuwait 1998–2002, SHL plc 2002–05, global chief info offr Experian 2005–13, exec dir for info services and chief info offr Bank of England 2013–; strategic tech advsr RSM; memb Cncl and Audit Ctee Univ of Nottingham, non-exec dir OPP Ltd; *Recreations* cricket, motorsport, music; *Style—* John Finch, Esq; ✉ Bank of England, Threadneedle Street, London EC2R 8AH (john.finch@bankofengland.co.uk)

FINCH, Michael James (Mick); s of Reginald James Finch, of Chadwell Heath, Essex, and Florence Anne, *née* Selby; *b* 6 July 1957; *Educ* Ravensbourne Coll of Art (BA), RCA (MA), Terra Summer Residency (sr scholar); *Partner* Bridget Strevens; 1 da (Ella); *Career* painter; chair Fndn Parsons Sch of Design Paris 1996–98 (prof 1992–98), head of painting Kent Inst of Art and Design 1998–99, prof of fine art Ecole des Beaux-Arts de Valencienne 1999–2007, 2D pathway ldr BAFA Central St Martins London 2008–; one man shows: Pomeroy Purdy Gallery 1990 and 1992 (curator 1988–91), Purdy Hicks Gallery 1994, Art et Patrimoine (Paris), Le Carré (Lille), Galerie é of (Paris), Galerie Agart (France) 2004, Galerie Pitch (Paris) 2005, Gallery 33 (Berlin) 2006 and 2007, Galerie Christian Aubert Paris 2008; included in various gp shows; paintings in collections: Peterborough City, Unilever, Burston, County NatWest, BDO Binder Hamlyn, Colas, Deutsch Bank; assoc ed Jl of the Visual Arts, ed Jl of Visual Art Practice no 8.1/2 2008; regular contrib Contemporary magazine and The Burlington magazine; Unilever award 1985, Burston award 1985, Ile de France FRAC; *Clubs* Groucho; *Style—* Mick Finch, Esq; ✉ 59 Rue de Meaux, Senlis 60300, France (✆ 00 33 44 60 94 20, fax 00 33 44 60 00 00, e-mail mick@mickfinch.com, website www.mickfinch.com)

FINCH, Paul Anthony; s of Ellis Finch (d 2005), and Eleanor, *née* Jones; *b* 5 October 1953, Ormskirk, Lancs; *Educ* Ormskirk GS, Univ of Newcastle upon Tyne, Coll of Law Chester; *m* 19 July 1980, Kay McDonald; *Career* admitted slr 1978; asst slr: Runnymede BC 1979–82, North Tyneside MBC 1982–86; slr Clifford Chance 1986–90, ptnr Dickinson Dees 1991– (slr 1990); memb: Law Soc 1978– (memb Planning and Environmental Ctee 1996–2006, Cncl memb for Northumbria 2008–), Newcastle upon Tyne Law Soc 1990–; *Publications* Notes to Leasehold Reform Housing and Urban Development Act 1993; contrib: Rights of Way Law Review, Compass Property Law Review; *Recreations* hockey, golf, cross country skiing, squash, gardening; *Clubs* Northumbria St George's Hockey, Longhirst Hall Golf; *Style—* Paul Finch, Esq; ✉ Dickinson Dees, One Trinity Gardens, Broad Chare, Newcastle NE1 2HF (✆ 0191 279 9311, fax 0191 230 8501, e-mail paul.finch@dickinson-dees.com)

FINCH, Sir Robert Gerald; kt (2005), JP (1992); s of Brig J R G Finch, OBE, and Patricia Hope, *née* Ferrar (d 1999); *b* 20 August 1944; *Educ* Felsted; *m* Patricia Ann; 2 da (Alexandra b 8 May 1975, Isabel b 8 June 1978); *Career* articled clerk Monro Pennefather & Co 1963–68; Linklaters: joined 1969 (Linklaters and Paines), ptnr 1974–, head Property Dept 1996–99; non-exec chm Liberty International 2005–; dir Int Fin Services London (IFSL) 2001; cmdt HAC 1992; Blundell Memorial lectr; memb Cncl St Paul's Cathedral 2000; tstee Morden Coll 2002; govr: Christ's Hosp 1992–, Witley Sch 1992–, Coll of Law 2000–; church cmmr 1999–; Alderman City of London, Sheriff City of London 1999–2000, HM Lt City of London 2003, Lord Mayor of the City of London 2003–04; Master Worshipful Co of Slrs 2000–01, Liveryman Worshipful Co of Innholders, Hon Liveryman Worshipful Co of Chartered Surveyors 2001, Ct Asst 2001, Hon Freeman Worshipful Co of Environmental Cleaners; memb Law Soc 1969; Hon FRICS; *Recreations* sailing, hill walking, skiing, ski mountaineering; *Clubs* Itchenor Sailing, Alpine Ski, Ski Club of Great Britain, Little Ship; *Style—* Sir Robert G Finch; ✉ Linklaters, One Silk Street, London EC2Y 8HQ

FINCH, Stephen John; s of Harry John Finch, of New Malden, Surrey, and Evelyn Louise, *née* Baggs; *b* 28 November 1950, Carshalton, Surrey; *Educ* Raynes Park GS, Univ of London (LLB); *Children* 4 s (Stuart John b 9 March 1977, Matthew Edward b 19 Jan 1979, Peter Thomas b 23 Feb 1985), 1 da (Eva Grace b 17 July 2013); *Career* admitted slr 1975; articles Messrs Withers 1973–75, commercial slr Sydney 1975–76, mangr slrs office London 1976–78, asst gp slr Lloyds Bowmaker Gp 1978–82, co slr Citibank International 1982–85, ptnr Hill Bailey 1985–89, ptnr Salans 1989–2012 (chm 2005–), ptnr Locke Lord (head Banking Dept); former memb Legislation, E-banking and Non-Prime Finance Ctees Finance and Leasing Assoc; *Publications* Practical Commercial Precedents (contrib to Consumer Credit Section); author of articles on UK retail banking law and European law devpts for the UK finance and banking industry; *Style—* Stephen Finch, Esq; ✉ Locke Lord, 201 Bishopsgate, London EC2M 3AF (✆ 020 7861 9011, fax 020 7785 9016, e-mail sfinch@locklord.com)

FINCH-SAUNDERS, Janet; AM; *Educ* Llandrillo Coll; *m* Gareth; 2 c; *Career* memb Nat Assembly for Wales (Cons) Aberconwy 2011–; shadow min for social services 2011–12, shadow min for local govt 2012–; *Style—* Ms Janet Finch-Saunders, AM; ✉ Highbank, Bodafon Road, Llandudno, Conwy LL30 3BA (e-mail janet@finch-saunders.co.uk); National Assembly for Wales, Cardiff Bay, Cardiff CF99 1NA (✆ 0300 200 7454, mobile 07540 964676, e-mail janet.finch-saunders@assembly.wales)

FINCHAM, Peter Arthur; *b* 26 July 1956; *Educ* Tonbridge, Churchill Coll Cambridge (MA); *Career* television producer; Talkback Productions: joined 1985, md 1986–2001, chief exec and jt dir of progs 2001–03; chief exec talkbackTHAMES 2003–05, controller BBC1 2005–07, dir of television ITV 2008–; exec prodr: Smith & Jones 1989–98, The Day Today 1994, Knowing Me Knowing You with Alan Partridge 1994, They Think It's All Over 1995, Never Mind the Buzzcocks 1996, Brass Eye 1997, The 11 O'Clock Show 1998, Big Train 1998, Shooting the Past 1999, Smack the Pony 1999, Jam 2000, Da Ali G Show 2000 and 2003, Meet Ricky Gervais 2000, Sword of Honour 2001, In a Land of Plenty 2001, Perfect Strangers 2001, Ali G Indahouse (feature film) 2002, Liar 2002, Bo' Selecta 2002, The Lost Prince 2003, Green Wing 2004; Indie-Vidual Award 2001; *Style—* Peter Fincham, Esq

FINDLATER, Will; *b* 18 November 1980; *Educ* Univ of Bristol (BA); *Partner* Hannah Millard; 1 s (Fred b 9 Aug 2011), 1 da (Ivy b 2015); *Career* editorial asst What Hi-Fi? Sound and Vision Magazine 2003–04; Stuff magazine: news ed 2004–07, commissioning ed 2007–09, dep ed 2009–10, ed 2010–, global online ed 2013–14, ed-in-chief 2014–15; ed-in-chief BikeRadar 2015–16; ed-in-chief Haymarket Creative Solutions 2016–; *Style—* Will Findlater, Esq; ✉ Haymarket Media Group, Bridge House, 69 London Road, Twickenham, Middlesex TW1 3SP (website www.haymarket.com, Twitter @willfindlater)

FINDLAY, Donald Russell; QC (Scot 1988); s of James Findlay (d 1980), of Edinburgh, and Mabel, *née* Muirhead (d 1985); *b* 17 March 1951, Cowdenbeath, Fife; *Educ* Harris Acad Dundee, Univ of Dundee (LLB), Univ of Glasgow (MPhil); *m* 28 Aug 1982, Jennifer Edith, *née* Borrowman; *Career* lectr in law Heriot-Watt Univ Edinburgh 1975–76, advocate 1975–; past chm: Advocates Criminal Law Gp, Faculty of Advocates Criminal Practices Ctee, Think Twice Campaign; chm Faculty of Advocates Criminal Bar Assoc; Lord Rector Univ of St Andrews (ret 1999); vice-pres Assoc for Int Cancer Research; chm Faculty Services Ltd 2003–05, vice-chm Glasgow Rangers FC (resigned 1999), chm Cowdenbeath FC 2011–; memb: Lothian Health Bd 1987–91, Faculty of Advocates 1975; FRSA; *Publications* Three Verdicts (1998); *Recreations* Glasgow Rangers FC, Cowdenbeath FC, Egyptology, The Middle East, travel, ethics, challenging authority; *Clubs* RAC, Glasgow Rangers Bond, RAC (Glasgow); *Style—* Donald R Findlay, Esq, QC

FINDLAY, Gordon Francis George; s of Francis Gordon Findlay (d 1975), of Edinburgh, and Muriel Arras Maitland; *b* 9 February 1950; *Educ* George Watson's Coll Edinburgh, Univ of Edinburgh (BSc, MB ChB); *m* 5 April 1975, Andrea May, da of Lt Ewart Leslie Cooper, of Buxted, Surrey; 1 s (Iain b 5 Jan 1978), 2 da (Claire b 10 Oct 1980, Emma b 27 Dec 1985); *Career* conslt neurosurgeon with special interest in spinal disease Walton Hosp Liverpool 1983–; extensive pubns in jls and textbooks on spinal disease; memb Br Soc of Neurosurgeons; fndr memb: Br Cevical Spine Soc, Euro Spine Soc; FRCS 1978; *Recreations* family, golf, music; *Style—* Gordon Findlay, Esq; ✉ Walton Hospital, Department of Neurosciences, Rice Lane, Liverpool L9 1AR (✆ 0151 525 3611)

FINDLAY, Neil; MSP; s of Ian Findlay, and Margaret, *née* McAuley; *b* Broxburn, W Lothian; *Educ* BA, PGCE; *m* Fiona, *née* Miller; 1 da (Chloe); *Career* bricklayer 1987–97, teacher 2003–11; local govt cncllr 2003–12, MSP (Lab) Lothians 2011–; founding memb, dir Fauldhouse Community Devpt Tst (former co sec); memb: Educnl Inst of Scotland (EIS) Trade Union, Gen Teaching Cncl for Scotland, Unite the Union; *Recreations* golf, going for a pint, gardening, cooking; *Clubs* Greenburn Golf; *Style—* Neil Findlay, Esq, MSP; ✉ The Scottish Parliament, Edinburgh EH99 1SP

FINDLAY, Ralph; s of James Findlay, and Margaret Findlay; *b* 9 January 1961, Manchester; *Educ* James Gillespie's HS Edinburgh, Univ of Edinburgh; *m* Louise; 1 s (Andrew b 1994), 1 da (Annabel b 1996); *Career* formerly: financial controller Geest plc, treasy mangr Bass plc; Marston's plc: memb Bd 1996–, fin dir 1996–2001, chief exec 2001–; chm Br Beer and Pub Assoc 2010–11; non-exec dir and chm Audit Ctee Bovis Homes plc 2015–; chair Cncl and pro-chllr Keele Univ 2014–; FCA; *Style—* Ralph Findlay, Esq; ✉ Marston's plc, Marston's House, Brewery Road, Wolverhampton WV1 4JT

FINDLAY, Richard; CBE (2013); *b* 5 November 1943, Berlin; *Educ* Royal Scottish Acad of Music and Dramatic Art Glasgow; *m*; 3 c; *Career* work in TV, radio, newspapers, Govt of Saudi Arabia and COI London; chief exec Scottish Radio Holdings; chm: STV Gp plc, Iatros Ltd; dir Youth Media Ltd; former govr RSAMD, chair RSAMD Fndn, founding chm Nat Theatre of Scotland; *Recreations* sailing, music, golf; *Clubs* Scottish Arts; *Style—* Richard Findlay, Esq, CBE; ✉ STV Group plc, Pacific Quay, Glasgow G51 1PQ (✆ 0141 300 3940, fax 0141 300 3260)

FINDLAY, Richard; s of Ian Macdonald Semple Findlay (d 2009), and Kathleen, *née* Lightfoot (d 2012); *b* 18 December 1951, Torphins, Aberdeenshire; *Educ* Gordon Schs Huntly, Univ of Aberdeen (LLB); *Partner* Gerald McGolgan (civil partnership 3 Nov 2007); *Career* trainee slr Wilsone & Duffus, asst slr Maclay Murray & Spens 1975–79, ptnr Ranken & Reid SSC 1979–90, ptnr Tods Murray LLP 1990–2012 (conslt 2012–13), entertainment lawyer and business affrs conslt 2013–15; pt/t lectr on law of film Napier Univ Edinburgh 1997–2015; dir: Krazy Kat Theatre Co 1984–86, Gallus Theatre Co Ltd 1996–98, Dance Base Ltd 1997–98, Lothian Gay & Lesbian Switchboard Ltd 1998–2002, Royal Lyceum Theatre Co Ltd 1999–2013 (vice-chm 2000–13), Edinburgh Music Theatre Co Ltd 1985–88, Audio Description Film Fund Ltd 2000–09, The Hill Adamson 2002–12, Scottish Screen 2003–07, Scottish Screen Enterprises Ltd 2003–07, Luxury Edinburgh Ltd 2006–12, Scottish Documentary Inst 2014–; Stills – Scotland's Centre for Photography 2015–; chm: Red FM Ltd 2004–05, David Hughes Dance Productions Ltd 2012–15; co sec: Assoc of Integrated Media Highlands and Islands, Gay Men's Health Ltd, Edinburgh Int Jazz and Blues Festival, Castle Hotel Mgmnt Co Ltd 2009–12; managing ed i2i 1995, Scotland ed Methuen Amateur Theatre Handbook, memb Advsy Editorial Bd The Firm Magazine 2009–12; memb: Advsy Bd Screen Acad Scotland, Int Assoc of Entertainment Lawyers 1990–2012, BAFTA 1990– (memb Mgmnt Ctee 1998–2004), New Producers Alliance 1993–98, IBA 1993–99, Writers' Guild 1993–2002, Arts & Business Placement Scheme 1994–2012, Int Entertainment and Multimedia Law and Business Network 1995–2010, Scottish Media Lawyers Soc 1995–10, Inst of Art and Law 1996–98, Theatrical Mgmnt Assoc 2000–12, RTS 2003–05; tstee: Peter Darrel Tst 1996–2004, Frank Mullen Tst 2004–08; hon patron Pitlochry Festival Theatre 2013–; *Recreations* music, theatre, opera, cinema, photography, Scottish politics, history and culture, cycling; *Style—* Richard Findlay, Esq; ✉ 1 Darnaway Street, Edinburgh EH3 6DW (✆ 0131 226 3253, mobile 07850 327725, e-mail richard@darnaway.co.uk, website http://about.me/richardfindlay, Twitter @RichardFindlay)

FINE, Anne; OBE (2003); da of Brian Laker (d 1989), and Mary Baker; *b* 7 December 1947; *Educ* Northampton HS for Girls, Univ of Warwick (BA); *m* 3 Aug 1968 (m dis 1990), Kit Fine, s of Maurice Fine; 2 da (Ione b 3 Aug 1971, Cordelia b 26 Feb 1975); *Career* writer; memb Soc of Authors; FRSL 2003; *Awards* Scot Arts Cncl Book Award 1986, Smarties Award 1990, Guardian Children's Fiction Award 1990, Carnegie Medal 1990 and 1993, Children's Author of the Year Award Br Book Awards 1990 and 1993, Whitbread Award for a children's book 1993, Whitbread Children's Book of the Year (for The Tulip Touch) 1997, Children's Laureate 2001–03; *Books* for children incl: The Summer House Loon (1978), The Other Darker Ned (1979), The Stone Menagerie (1980), Round Behind the Icehouse (1981), The Granny Project (1983), Madame Doubtfire (1987, filmed 1993), Crummy Mummy and Me (1988), The Country Pancake (1989), Goggle-Eyes (1989, adapted for BBC), Bill's New Frock (1989), The Book of the Banshee (1991), Flour Babies (1993), The Diary of a Killer Cat (1994), Step by Wicked Step (1995), The Tulip Touch (1996), Bad Dreams (2000), Up on Cloud Nine (2002), The More, The Merrier (2003), Frozen Billy (2004), The Road of Bones (2006), Eating Things on Sticks (2009), The Devil Walks (2011), Trouble in Toadpool (2012), Blood Family (2013) Blue Moon Day (2014); books for adults: The Killjoy (1986), Taking the Devil's Advice (1990), In Cold Domain (1994), Telling Liddy (1998), All Bones and Lies (2001), Raking the Ashes (2005), Fly in the Ointment (2008), Our Precious Lulu (2009); *Recreations* walking, reading; *Style—* Mrs Anne Fine, OBE, FRSL; ✉ c/o David Higham Associates, 7th Floor Waverley House, 7–12 Noel Street, London, W1F 8GQ (✆ 020 7437 7888, fax 020 7437 1072)

FINE, Dr Jeffrey Howard; s of Nathan Fine (d 2008), and Rebecca, *née* Levi (d 2011); *b* 5 October 1955; *Educ* The Howardian HS Cardiff, Bart's Med Coll London (MB BS); *m* 1 May 1993, Kirsty Elizabeth, da of Adolf Knul, of Hilversum, Holland; 1 s (Alexander David b 27 June 1990), 1 da (Charlotte Anne b 19 May 1992); *Career* professorial registrar Acad Unit of Psychiatry Royal Free Hosp London 1981, registrar in psychological med

Nat Hosp for Nervous Diseases London 1982–83, MO Home Office 1981–89, gen med practice London 1985, Euro neuroendocrine advsr Eli Lilly Pharmaceuticals Co 1986–87, private med psychiatric practice 1987–; completed London marathon 1983; freedom and key Kansas City Missouri USA 1976; MRCPsych 1984, FRSM 1987; memb: BMA 1980, Euro Assoc and Int Coll of Neuropsychopharmacology, Br Assoc of Neuropsychiatry 1988, Assoc of Independent Drs 1989; *Publications* author of papers on depression, light and obesity (Jl of Affective Disorder, 1987); *Recreations* jazz, tennis, sailing; *Clubs* Ronnie Scott's, West Heath Lawn Tennis; *Style*— Dr Jeffrey H Fine; ✉ 22 Harley Street, London W1G 9PL (☎ 020 7636 7661, e-mail jhfine@doctors.org.uk)

FINER, Prof Nicholas; s of Sir Morris Finer (d 1974), and Edith, *née* Rubner; *b* 24 December 1949, London; *Educ* The Hall Sch Hampstead, Mill Hill Sch, UCL (BSc, MB BS); *m* 1 March 1975, Susan, da of Prof Charles Dent, CBE (d 1975); 3 da (Emily b 30 Nov 1976, Sarah, Louise (twins) b 2 Aug 1978); *Career* hon conslt physician Guy's Hosp, hon sr lectr United Med and Dental Schs of Guy's and St Thomas' Hosp 1988–99 (lectr 1981–88), conslt physician and dir Research Dept Luton and Dunstable Hosp 1988–2002, hon conslt physician Addenbrooke's Hosp Cambridge 2002–09 (visiting specialist 1996–2002), visiting prof Univ of Luton 1996–2006, hon conslt physician UCH 2007–09, sr res assoc Univ of Cambridge, clinical dir Wellcome Tst Clinical Res Facility 2002–09, hon prof of medicine UCL Inst of Cardiovascular Science 2009–; chm Assoc for The Study of Obesity 1993–96, chm World Obesity Fedn – Clinical Care (formerly Int Assoc for Study of Obesity) 2010–16, sr princ clinical scientist Global Med Affrs Mgmnt Novo Nordisk A/S 2016–; Bissest Hawkins Medal RCP 2013; FRCP 1994 (MRCP 1977); *Books* contrib: Health Consequences of Obesity (1988), Progress in Sweeteners (1989), Handbook of Sweeteners (1991), Obesity (1997), Encylopedia of Nutrition (1998), Obesity and Metabolic Disorders (2005), ABC of Obesity (2007), A Modern Epidemic (2012), Oxford Handbook of Endocrinology and Diabetes 3rd Edition (2013), Endocrine and Metabolic Medical Emergencies (2014), Oxford Desk Reference: Endocrinology (2014), Clinical Dilemmas in Non-Alcoholic Fatty Liver Disease (2016); *Style*— Prof Nicholas Finer; ✉ websites www.uclh.nhs.uk/ourservices/consultants/pages/profnickfiner.aspx, www.ucl.ac.uk/obesity/staff, https://iris.ucl.ac.uk/iris/browse/profile?upi=NFINE27

FINGLETON, Dr John; s of Brendan Fingleton, of Cullenagh, Portlaoise, Ireland, and May, *née* McHugh; *b* 21 September 1965; *Educ* TCD (scholar, BA), Nuffield Coll Oxford (MPhil, DPhil); *Career* research offr Fin Markets Gp LSE 1991, lectr in economics TCD 1991–2000, chair Irish Competition Authy 2000–05, chief exec OFT 2005–12; European Centre for Advanced Research in Economics Université Libre de Bruxelles 1995, visiting scholar Grad Sch of Business Univ of Chicago 1998–2000; chm Assoc of Competition Economics 2002–07, chair Steering Ctee Int Competition Network 2009–, bd memb several jls specialising in competition policy; *Publications* Competition Policy and the Transformation of Central Europe (jtly, 1996), The Dublin Taxi Market: Re-regulate or Stay Queuing? (1998), The Economy of Ireland: Policy and Performance of a Small European Economy (contrib, 7 edn 2000); author of pubns in learned jls; *Style*— Dr John Fingleton

FINIGAN, John Patrick; s of John Joseph Finigan (d 1991), of Sale, Cheshire, and Mary Matilda Finigan (d 1983); *b* 12 November 1949; *Educ* Ushaw Coll Durham, St Bede's Coll Manchester, Cncl of Legal Educn London, Univ of Manchester, Harvard Law Sch, Fletcher Sch of Law and Diplomacy Tufts Univ; *m* 6 Dec 1976, Elizabeth, da of Joseph Liew, of Bandar Seri Begawan, Brunei; 1 s (Damien b 1980), 1 da (Emily Jane b 1982); *Career* slr; Standard Chartered Bank (UK, Germany, Brunei, Hong Kong, Indonesia and UAE) 1967–78, investment banking National Bank of Abu Dhabi 1978–82, fndr Investment Banking then branch gen mangr London Nat Bank of Kuwait 1983–95 (also founding gen mangr NKB (International) plc), gen mangr and chief exec Qatar National Bank 1995–2001, advsr to min of finance State of Qatar 2001–02, ceo National Bank of Oman (SAOG) 2002–; barr-at-law Lincoln's Inn; AIB 1970, ACIS 1973, FCIB 1980, FRSA 1988, MSI 1994; *Recreations* tennis, squash, music, literature, travel; *Clubs* Oriental, Overseas Bankers'; *Style*— John Finigan, Esq; ✉ e-mail finiganjohn@hotmail.com

FINK, Prof George; s of John H Fink (d 1965), and Therese, *née* Weiss; *b* 13 November 1936, Vienna; *Educ* Melbourne HS, Univ of Melbourne (MB BS, MD), Hertford Coll Oxford (DPhil); *m* 1959, Ann Elizabeth, da of Mark Langsam; 1 da (Naomi b 1961), 1 s (Jerome b 1965); *Career* jr and sr house offr Royal Melbourne and Alfred Hospitals Victoria Aust 1961–62, demonstrator in anatomy Monash Univ Victoria 1963–64, Nuffield Dominions demonstrator Univ of Oxford 1965–67, sr lectr in anatomy Monash Univ Victoria 1968–71, lectr Univ of Oxford 1971–80, offical fell in physiology and med Brasenose Coll Oxford 1974–80, dir MRC Brain Metabolism Unit 1980–99, hon prof Univ of Edinburgh 1984–99, vice-pres Research Pharmos Corp 1999–2003 (conslt 2003), dir Psychiatric Neuroscience Mental Health Research Inst Aust 2003–04, dir Mental Health Research Inst Aust 2004–06 (hon prof res fell 2007–); prosector in anatomy Univ of Melbourne 1956 (hon prof Centre for Neuroscience and Dept of Psychiatry 2007–13, prof fell Florey Inst of Neuroscience and Mental Health 2013–); Royal Soc and Israel Acad exchange fell Weizmann Inst 1979, Wolfson lectr Univ of Oxford 1982, Walter Cottman fell and visiting prof Monash Univ 1985 and 1989, first G W Harris Prize lectr Physiological Soc Cambridge 1987, Arthur M Fishberg visiting prof The Mt Sinai Med Sch NYC 1988, visiting prof of neurobiology Mayo Clinic Rochester Minnesota 1993, visiting prof Dept of Neurobiology Rockefeller Univ 1996–; memb: Cncl of the Euro Neuroscience Assoc 1980–82 and 1994–96, Mental Health Panel Wellcome Tst 1984–89, Steering Ctee Br Neuroendocrine Gp 1984–88 (tstee 1990–2000), Co-ordinating Ctee ESF Network on Neuroimmunomodulation 1990–92; chm External Monitoring Panel and 5 Year Review Ctee EU Biomedicine Prog; memb Physiological Soc, memb Pharmacological Soc, sr memb Soc for Endocrinology (UK), emeritus memb Endocrine Soc (USA), emeritus memb Soc for Neuroscience (USA), memb Int Brain Research Orgn, memb Int Soc for Neuroendocrinology, memb European Neuroendocrine Assoc (pres 1991–95), memb BMA, emeritus memb Genetics Soc of America, memb Int Coll of Neuro-Psychopharmacology 2012; hon memb Br Soc for Neuroendocrinology 2005; Lifetime Achievement Award Int Soc Psychoneuroendocrinology (ISPNE) 2000; FRSE 1989, FRSA 1996, FRCPEd 1998, FRSB 2015; *Books* Neuropepides – Basic and Critical Aspects (jt ed, 1982), Neuroendocrine Molecular Biology (jt ed, 1986), Transmitter Molecules in the Brain (1987), Neuropeptides: A Methodology (jt ed, 1989), Encyclopedia of Stress (ed-in-chief, 2000, BMA Commendation for Mental Health, 2 edn 2007), Stress Science: Neuroendocrinology (2009), Stress Consequences: Mental, Neuropsychological and Socioeconomic (2009), Stress of War, Conflict and Disaster (2010), Handbook of Neuroendocrinology (2012), Stress: Concepts, Cognition, Emotion and Behavior: Handbook of Stress Series Volume 1 (2016); author of over 360 scientific pubns, mainly on neuroendocrinology, neuropharmacology, neuroendocrine molecular biology and psychoneuroendocrinology; *Recreations* scuba diving, skiing, reading biographies and science jls; *Style*— Prof George Fink, FRSE, FRSB; ✉ Mental Health Research Institute, Florey Institute of Neuroscience and Mental Health, Level 5, Kenneth Myer Building, At Genetics Lane on Royal Parade, University of Melbourne Vic 3010, Australia (☎ 00 61 3 9035 6634, e-mail georgefink1@hotmail.com or gfink@mhri.edu.au or george.fink@florey.edu.au website www.georgefink.com)

FINK, Graham Michael; s of Horace Bertram Fink, of Oxford, and Margaret May, *née* Betts; *b* 7 September 1960, Portsmouth, Hants; *Educ* Wood Green Comp Sch Oxford, Banbury Sch of Art, Univ of Reading; *Career* French Gold Abbott advtg agency 1980–81, Collett Dickenson Pearce 1981–87, head of art WCRS 1987, gp head Saatchi & Saatchi 1987–90, creative dir Gold Greenless Trott 1990–94, commercials and music videos dir Paul Weiland Film Co 1995, fndr thefinktank 2001, exec creative dir M&C Saatchi 2005–2011, chief creative offr Ogilvy China 2011–; advtg awards incl: Cannes Lions Grand Prix, D&AD, LIAA, One Show, Clios, 4 BAFTAs; memb: Creative Circle, D&AD (pres 1996); hon doctorate Bucks New Univ 2005; RBAC, FRSA; *Style*— Graham Fink, Esq, FRSA, RBAC

FINK, Baron (Life Peer UK 2011), of Northwood in the County of Middlesex; Stanley Fink; s of late Louis Fink, and Janet Fink; *b* 15 September 1957; *Educ* Manchester Grammar, Trinity Hall Cambridge (MA); *m* 1981, Barbara, *née* Paskin; 2 s (Alexander b 12 March 1987, Jordan b 18 May 1994), 1 da (Gabriella b 5 Sept 1989); *Career* CA Arthur Andersen 1979–82, fin planning Mars Confectionary 1982–83, vice-pres Citibank NA 1983–86; Man Group plc: joined as dir 1987, gp fin dir 1992, md asset mgmnt 1996, ceo 2000–07, non-exec dep chm 2007–08, chm Strategic Investment Ctee; ceo Int Standard Asset Mgmnt (ISAM) 2008–; memb Inquiry Team Twenty-First Century Investments; treas Cons Pty; chm Ctee Evelina Children's Hosp Appeal, tstee ARK; ACA; *Recreations* golf, skiing, tennis; *Style*— The Lord Fink

FINKELSTEIN, Baron (Life Peer UK 2013), of Pinner in the County of Middlesex; Daniel Finkelstein; OBE (1997); *b* 30 August 1962; *Educ* LSE; *Career* ed Connexion 1990–92, dir Cons Research Dept 1995–97, political advsr to William Hague (as ldr of the oppn) 1997–2001; The Times: joined 2001, comment ed 2004–08, chief leader writer 2008–10, exec ed 2010–; regular columnist The Jewish Chronicle; *Style*— The Lord Finkelstein, OBE; ✉ The Times, 3 Thomas More Square, London E98 1XY

FINLAY, Rev Canon Dr Hueston Edward; s of Sydney Perry Finlay, of Portlaoise, and Vera, *née* Burns; *b* 23 May 1964, Portlaoise, Ireland; *Educ* Wesley Coll Dublin, TCD (BAI, BTh, MA), Univ of Cambridge (MA), KCL (PhD); *m* 19 August 1989, Annegret; 1 da (Svea Deirdre b 6 Jan 1992), 2 s (Lars Christopher b 30 July 1996, Karsten Alexander b 24 Nov 1999); *Career* Brown & Root Ltd London 1985–86, curate St Canice's Cathedral Kilkenny 1989–92, curate Univ Church of Gt St Mary Cambridge and chaplain Girton Coll Cambridge 1992–95, dean Magdalene Coll Cambridge 1995–2004 (also tutor and affliated lectr Divinity Faculty 1996–2004), canon Coll of St George Windsor 2004–, warden St George's House Windsor 2009, hon treas St Patrick's Cathedral Dublin 2011; author of various articles on philosophy and theology; *Recreations* chess, badminton, mathematics; *Style*— The Rev Canon Dr Hueston Finlay; ✉ The Chapter Office, Windsor Castle, Windsor, Berkshire SL4 1NJ (☎ 01753 848887, e-mail diagacht@hotmail.com)

FINLAY, Ian Gardner; s of John Gardner Finlay, of Ladybank, Fife, and Margaret Finlay, of Lothian; *Educ* Univ of St Andrews (BSc), Victoria Univ of Manchester (MB ChB); *m* 21 March 1981, Patricia Mary, *née* Whiston; 1 da (Nicola b 24 March 1984), 1 s (Euan b 20 Feb 1986); *Career* jr surgical trainee Royal Infirmary Manchester 1976–78, registrar in surgery W of Scotland Registrar Rotational Trg Scheme 1978–83, sr surgical registrar Glasgow Royal Infirmary 1983–87, clinical asst Univ of Minnesota 1985, sr registrar in colorectal surgery St Mark's Hosp London 1986, conslt colorectal surgn Dept of Coloproctology Royal Infirmary Glasgow (organised and developed dept as first unit of its type in UK) and hon sr lectr Univ of Glasgow 1987–; Patey Prize Surgical Research Soc 1982, Research Award American Soc of Colon and Rectal Surgns 1987, Audiovisual Prize Assoc of Surgns 1990, Moynihan Prize (jtly) Assoc of Surgns of GB and I 1995; memb Cncl Br Assoc of Coloproctology RSM 1991–; author of over 100 pubns incl book chapters, editorials and original articles relating to topics in coloproctology; FRCSGlas (hon treas and memb Cncl), FRCSEd 1993; *Recreations* golf, sailing, skiing, ornithology and antique furniture; *Clubs* Glasgow Golf, Glasgow Cricket, Scottish Royal Automobile; *Style*— Ian Finlay, Esq; ✉ Department of Coloproctology, Ward 61, Royal Infirmary, Glasgow G31 2ER (☎ 0141 211 4084, fax 0141 211 4991)

FINLAY, Ronald Adrian; s of late Harry Finlay, of London, and late Tess, *née* Matz; *b* 4 December 1956; *Educ* UCS London, St John's Coll Cambridge (MA); *m* 1992, Jennifer, *née* Strauss; 2 da; *Career* Br Market Research Bureau 1979–81, Merrill Lynch 1982–83, dir Valin Pollen Ltd 1986–90 (joined 1983); Fishburn Hedges: dir 1991–2012, dep chm 1999–2000, md 2000–03, ceo 2003–06; Ron Finlay Communications 2010–, ceo Senet Gp 2014–16; memb Ind Complaints Panel Portman Gp 2011–; tstee Women & Children First (UK) 2007–12, tstee SJP Charitable Tst 2013–; memb Market Research Soc 1996 (assoc 1980); FRSA 2007, MCIPR 2013, MCIM 2014; *Recreations* cycling, hill walking, bridge; *Style*— Ron Finlay, Esq; ✉ 12 Grey Close, London NW11 6QG (☎ 020 8455 1367, e-mail ron@ronfinlaycomms.co.uk)

FINLAY OF LLANDAFF, Baroness (Life Peer UK 2001), of Llandaff in the County of South Glamorgan; Ilora Gillian Finlay; da of late Prof Charles Beaumont Benoy Downman, of New Malden, Surrey; *b* 23 February 1949; *Educ* Wimbledon HS GPDST (head girl), St Mary's Hosp Med Sch London (entrance scholarship, MB BS); *m* 1972, Andrew Yule Finlay, s of late Henry Variot Langwill Finlay; 1 s (Hon Malcolm Charles b 1976), 1 da (Hon Sarah Elise b 1978); *Career* conslt in palliative med and med dir Holme Tower Marie Curie Centre Penarth 1987–2001, conslt in palliative med 1993– and team ldr for chronic pain services Velindre NHS Tst Oncology Centre Cardiff 1993–2008, hon prof of palliative med Univ of Wales Coll of Med (UWCM, now Cardiff Univ) 1996–, vice-dean (exec) Sch of Med UWCM 1999–2004, vice-dean (postgrad) Sch of Med Cardiff Univ 2004–05; professorial assoc Dept of Med Univ of Melbourne 1996–2001, hon prof of palliative med Ulyanovsk Univ 1999–2001, visiting prof Johanna Bijtel Lehrstuhle Groningen Univ 2000–02, hon prof Groningen Univ 2004–09; dir Inst of Med Ethics 2002–04, dir Living and Dying Well 2010–; chair: Wales Palliative Care Strategy Implementation Gp 2008–, Welsh Medical and Dental Academic Advsy Bd 2012–14, Nat Cncl for Palliative Care 2015–; memb: Science Ctee Cancer Research UK 2002–04, Advsy Cncl on Misuse of Drugs Act Home Office 2002–09, Ctee on Safety of Meds 2002–09, Expert Advsy Panel Exec Meds Control Agency 2002–09, UK Drugs Policy Cmmn 2008–12; non-exec dir Gwent HA 1996–2000; ed Palliative Care Today 1991–2003, memb Editorial Bd Med Humanities 2001–08, sr med ed Jl of Evaluation in Clinical Practice 2002–08, memb Int Editorial Bd Lancet Oncology 2002–08; pres: Chartered Soc for Physiotherapy, MS Cymru 2004–07; pres RSM 2006–08, vice-pres NSPCC Cymru 2004–07, pres BMA 2014–15; memb: Assoc for Palliative Med of GB and I (chair 1995–98), BMA (memb Ethics Ctee 2009–), Med Women's Fedn (pres 2000–02); Sarah Davis Meml Tst Lecture Univ of Dublin 1998, Dame Hilda Rose Meml Lecture Med Women's Fedn 1999, Dorothy Rees Meml Lecture 2003, Annual Public Lecture Cardiff Law Sch 2003, The Cardiff Lecture 2003, Stevens Lecture RSM 2009, Roscoe Lecture 2011, Rosemary Rue Lecture 2012, Riddell Lectures 2014; Upjohn Essay Prize RCGP 1983, Silver Medal Computers in Med BMA 1992, Healthcare IT Effectiveness Award NHS Exec and NHS Staff Coll Wales 1999; sits as crossbench peer in House of Lords; memb Select Ctee: Science and Technol 2002–2008 (chair Allergy Inquiry), Assisted Dying for the Terminally Ill Bill 2004–06, Mental Health Bill 2005–06, Public Service and Demographic Change 2012–13; memb Stakeholder Bd First Great Western 2003–09; vice-pres Fund for the Meml to the Women of World War II 2005–06; patron: Shalom Hospice Tst, Student for Kids Int Projects (SKIP), Action on Smoking and Health (ASH) (Wales), Cardiff and the Vale Youth Orch, MS Cymru, MNDA Cymru, Student Volunteering Cardiff; memb: Inst of Welsh Affrs, Wales Medico-Legal Soc, Royal Soc of Arts; govr Howell's Sch Llandaff GDST 2002–06, assoc GDST 2007–; Woman into Science and Technol 1996, Welsh Woman of the Year 1996–97, Outstanding Achievement Charity Champion Award 2007, Peer of the Year Dods & Scottish Widows Women in Public Life Awards 2008; Hon DSc: Univ of Glamorgan 2002, Univ of Wales 2005; hon fell:

F

Cardiff Univ 2002, Univ of Wales Inst Cardiff; DRCOG 1974, DCH 1975, FRCGP 1992 (MRCGP 1981), FRCP 1999 (LRCP 1972, MRCP 1997), FHEA 2007 (ILTM 2001), FRSM, Hon FRCS 2009 (MRCS 1972) founding FLSW 2010, FMedSci 2014; *Publications* Care of the Dying – A Clinical Handbook (jtly, 1984), Cancer Patients and their Families at Home, Resource Book (jtly, 1989, 2 edn 1994), The Effective Management of Cancer Pain (jtly, 2000, 2 edn 2003), Medical Humanities (jtly, 2002), Oral Care in Advanced Disease (jtly, 2005), Communication in Cancer Care (jtly, 2009); also author of numerous book chapters and papers in learned jls; *Style—* The Rt Hon the Lady Finlay of Llandaff; ✉ House of Lords, London SW1A 0PW (☎ 020 7219 6693, e-mail finlayi@parliament.uk)

FINLAYSON, Dr Niall Diarmid Campbell; OBE (1998); s of Dr Duncan Iain Campbell Finlayson, of Edinburgh, and Helen Rita, *née* Blackney; *b* 21 April 1939, Georgetown, Guyana; *Educ* Loretto, Univ of Edinburgh (BSc, MB ChB, PhD); *m* 12 Aug 1972, Dale Kristin, da of Dr Richmond Karl Anderson, of Chapel Hill, North Carolina, USA; 1 da (Catriona b 1973), 1 s (Iain b 1977); *Career* asst prof of med Cornell Univ Med Coll NY 1970–72, conslt physician Royal Infirmary Edinburgh 1973–2003, hon sr lectr in med Univ of Edinburgh Med Sch 1973–2003; pres Royal Coll of Physicians of Edinburgh 2001–04 (registrar 1997–99, vice-pres 1999–2000), teaching fell Univ of Edinburgh 2004–; chief medical offr Royal London Insurance (formerly Bright Grey Insurance) 2003–; chm LifeCare (Edinburgh) Ltd 2005–15; memb: BMA, Br Soc of Gastroenterology, Br Assoc for the Study of the Liver; FRCP, FRCPEd; *Books* Diseases of the Gastro Intestinal Tract and Liver (jtly, 3 edn 1997); *Recreations* music, history; *Style—* Dr Niall Finlayson, OBE; ✉ 10 Queen's Crescent, Edinburgh EH9 2AZ (☎ 0131 667 9369, e-mail ndc.finlayson@which.net)

FINN, Johanna Elizabeth; da of Bartholomew Anthony Finn, of London, and Anna Maria, *née* Kreuth; *b* 30 August 1951, London; *Educ* Convent of the Sacred Heart London, UCL (BSc); *m* (m dis); 2 s (Benedict Daniel Siddle b 20 Jan 1982, Leo Dominic Siddle b 1 Oct 1984), 1 da (Chloe Anneliese Siddle b 22 June 1990); *Career* KCH London 1972–73, nat admin trainee NHS Nat Training Scheme SE Thames RHA 1973–75, Northwick Park Hosp Harrow Middx 1975–77, Withington Hosp S Manchester 1977–79, sector admin W Middx Univ Hosp Isleworth 1979–82, unit admin St Mary's Hosp Paddington 1982–85, acting dep dist admin Paddington & N Kensington Health Authy 1985–86; unit gen mangr: Mile End Hosp and Bethnal Green Hosp Tower Hamlets 1986–89, Community & Priority Services Tower Hamlets 1989–90; chief exec The Royal London and Assoc Community Services NHS Trust 1990–91, regnl dir of corp affairs NW Thames RHA 1991–93, chief exec The West Suffolk Hosps Tst 1993–2001, dir of med undergraduate clinical placements NHS Workforce Devpt Confedn (Norfolk, Suffolk, Cambs) 2001–03, mgmnt conslt 2003–; dir Suffolk TEC 1994–2001, memb Suffolk LSC 2001–08 (chm 2007–08), memb LSC East of Eng Regnl Cncl 2008–10, lay memb W Suffolk Clinical Commissioning Gp 2012–; govr W Suffolk Coll 2004–15; assoc memb Inst of Health Service Mangrs 1975–; *Publications* Booklet for Patients – Localised Prostate Cancer (2009), Booklet for Patients – Enlarged Prostate (2009), Trends in Urology & Mens Health (contrib, 2011); *Recreations* music, theatre, reading, wine and food, bridge; *Clubs* NHS Oldfogies; *Style—* Miss Johanna Finn; ☎ 01284 764973

FINNEGAN, Prof Ruth Hilary; OBE (2000); da of Prof Tom Finnegan (d 1964), and (Lucy) Agnes, *née* Campbell (d 1995); *b* 31 December 1933; *Educ* Londonderry HS, The Mount Sch York, Somerville Coll Oxford (BA, Dip Anthropology, BLitt), Nuffield Coll Oxford (DPhil); *m* 1963, David John Murray, s of Jowett Murray; 3 da (Rachel Clare b 1965, Kathleen Anne b 1967, Brigid Aileen b 1969); *Career* teacher Malvern Girls Coll 1956–58, lectr in social anthropology Univ Coll of Rhodesia and Nyasaland 1963–64, sr lectr in sociology Univ of Ibadan Nigeria 1967–69 (lectr 1965–67), sr lectr in comparative social instns Open Univ 1972–75 (lectr in sociology 1969–72); Univ of the South Pacific Suva Fiji: reader in sociology 1975–78, head sociology discipline 1976–78; Open Univ: sr lectr 1978–82, reader 1982–88, prof of comparative social instns 1988–99, visiting res prof social sciences 1999–, emeritus prof 2002–; visiting prof of anthropology Univ of Texas at Austin 1989; memb SSRC/ESRC Social Anthropology and Social Affrs Standing Ctees 1978–86 (vice-chm Social Affrs Ctee 1985–86), memb Cncl Br Acad 2001–04; vice-chair Governing Body SOAS Univ of London 2003–06; pres Mount Old Scholars Assoc 2003–05; jt founding ed Family and Community History (jl) 1998–2002, hon ed Man (jl of Royal Anthropological Inst) 1987–89; assoc memb Finnish Literature Soc 1989, folklore fell Finnish Acad of Sci and Letters 1991, hon memb Assoc of Social Anthropologists of the UK and the Cwlth 2002; hon fell Somerville Coll Oxford 1997; FBA 1996; *Books* Survey of the Limba people of northern Sierra Leone (1965), Limba stories and story-telling (1967), Oral literature in Africa (1970, 1976, 3 edn 2011), Modes of thought. Essays on thinking in Western and non-Western societies (co-ed, 1973), Oral poetry: its nature, significance and social context (1 edn 1977, 2 edn 1992), The Penguin book of oral poetry (ed, 1978, published as A World treasury of oral poetry, 1982), Essays on Pacific literature (co-ed, 1978), Concepts of Inquiry (ed jtly, 1981), New approaches to economic life (ed jtly, 1985), Information Technology: social issues (ed jtly, 1987), Literacy and orality: studies in the technology of communication (1988), The hidden musicians: music-making in an English town (1989, 2 edn 2007), Oral traditions and the verbal arts: a guide to research practices (1992), From family tree to family history (co-ed, 1994), Sources and methods for family and community historians: a handbook (co-ed, 1994), South Pacific oral traditions (co-ed, 1995), Project reports in family and community history (CD-ROM, co-ed, 1996, 1997, 1998, 1999, 2000, 2001), Tales of the City (1998), Communicating: The Multiple Modes of Human Interconnection (2002, 2 edn 2014), Participating in the Knowledge Society: Researchers beyond the university walls (ed, 2005), The Oral and Beyond: Doing things with words in Africa (2007), Why Do We Quote? The Culture and History of Quotation (2011), Peace Writing (ed, 2013), Cato's Distichs (ed, 2013), Where is Language? (2015), Black Inked Pearl: A Girl's Quest (novel, 2015); also author of articles in learned jls; *Recreations* singing in local choirs, walking; *Style—* Prof Ruth Finnegan, FBA; ✉ Faculty of Social Sciences, The Open University, Walton Hall, Milton Keynes MK7 6AA (☎ 01908 654515, e-mail r.h.finnegan@open.ac.uk)

FINNERTY, Her Hon Judge Angela; da of late Michael Finnerty, and Mary, *née* Woolfrey; *b* 22 March 1954; *Educ* Bury Convent GS, Univ of Leeds (LLB), Coll of Law London; *m* 11 Feb 2012, His Hon Judge Heaton, QC, *qv*; 1 s (Thomas William England b 14 Oct 1982), 1 da (Elisabeth Louise England b 11 Oct 1984) from a previous relationship; *Career* called to the Bar Middle Temple 1976 (Harmsworth scholar); practising barr Park Lane Chambers Leeds (formerly 37 Park Square) 1977–2000; asst recorder 1994, recorder 1998, circuit judge (NE Circuit) 2000–, designated family judge for N Yorks 2010; *Style—* Her Hon Judge Finnerty; ✉ York County Court, Piccadilly House, 55 Piccadilly, York YO1 9WL

FINNEY, Patricia Deirdre Emöke; da of His Hon Judge Finney (d 1999), and Daisy Gizella Emöke, *née* Veszy; *b* 1958; *Educ* Henrietta Barnett Sch London, Wadham Coll Oxford (BA); *m* 1981, Christopher Alan Perry (d 2002), s of William J Perry; 1 da (Alexandra b 1987), 2 s (William b 1989, Luke b 1996); *Career* incl: TV reviewing The Evening Standard, sub-editing, running a medical jl, sec, freelance journalism, pt/t work in social servs, corp entertaining, selling advtg; dir Climbing Tree Books Ltd; four times runner-up Catherine Pakenham Award; memb NUJ; also writes under pseudonym P F Chisholm; *Radio plays* The Flood (R3, 1977), A Room Full of Mirrors (R4, 1988, first prize Radio Times Drama Awards); *TV plays* Biology Lessons (1986, second prize Radio Times Drama Awards); *Novels* A Shadow of Gulls (1977, David Higham Award for Best First Novel), The Crow Goddess (1978), Firedrake's Eye (1992), Unicorn's Blood (1998), Gloriana's Torch (2003), Do We Not Bleed (2013); As P F Chisholm: A Famine of Horses (1994), A Season of Knives (1995), A Surfeit of Guns (1996), A Plague of Angels (1998), A Murder of Crows (2010); *Non-fiction* Writeritis (2012), How to Beat Your Son at Computer Games (2012), 3 Steps to a Great Eating Habit (2013); *Children's Books* I, Jack (2000), Jack and Police Dog Rebel (2002), Jack and the Ghosts (2013), An Air of Treason (2014), four books in the Lady Grace series (Assassin, Betrayal, Conspiracy, Feud); *Recreations* history, music, making things, science, martial arts (3rd dan black belt in Taekwondo); *Style—* Ms Patricia Finney; ✉ agent Jane Conway-Gordon (☎ 020 7371 6939); website www.patriciafinney.com

FINNIGAN, Judith (Judy); da of John Finnigan (d 1984), and Anne Finnigan; *b* 16 May 1948; *Educ* Manchester High Sch for Girls, Univ of Bristol (BA); *m* 1; 2 s (Thomas, Daniel (twins) b 2 March 1977); m 2, 21 Nov 1986; Richard Madeley, *qv*; 1 s (Jack b 19 May 1986), 1 da (Chloe b 13 July 1987); *Career* television presenter; researcher Granada TV 1971–73, reporter Anglia TV 1974–77; presenter Granada TV 1980–2001, presenter Cactus TV 2001–09 (Richard and Judy (Channel 4 then UKTV) until 2009, Br Book Awards (Channel 4) 2004–09); *Awards* RTS Team Award for This Morning 1994, Most Popular Daytime Programme National Television Awards 1998, 1999, 2000 and 2001; *Style—* Ms Judy Finnigan; ✉ c/o James Grant Management, 94 Strand on the Green, Chiswick, London W4 3NN (☎ 020 8742 4950, fax 020 8742 4951)

FINNIGAN, Stephen James (Steve); CBE (2010), QPM (2006); s of James Francis Finnigan, and Veronica, *née* Ramsey d 1999); *b* 29 June 1957, Liverpool; *Educ* St John's Coll Cambridge (MA, Dip), Open Univ; *m* Jackie; 1 s (Adam), 1 da (Grace); *Career* joined Merseyside Police 1976; Lancs Constabulary: Asst Chief Constable 2001–02, Dep Chief Constable 2002–05, temp Chief Constable 2005–07, Chief Constable 2007–; chair Police Sport UK, chair Performance Mgmnt Coordination Ctee, memb Lancs Partnership Against Crime; memb Lancs Area Ctee Prince's Tst, pres Lancs Boys' and Girls' Clubs, vice-pres Lancs Outward Bound Assoc, vice pres NW Police Benevolent Fund; hon fell Univ of Central Lancs, visiting fell Edge Hill Univ Business Sch; *Style—* Steve Finnigan, Esq, CBE, QPM; ✉ Lancashire Constabulary Headquarters, Saunders Lane, Hutton nr Preston PR4 5SB (☎ 01772 412221, fax 01772 614916)

FINNIS, Prof John Mitchell; s of Maurice Meredith Steriker Finnis (d 1995), of Adelaide, and Margaret McKellar, *née* Stewart; *b* 28 July 1940; *Educ* St Peter's Coll, St Mark's Coll Adelaide (LLB), Univ of Oxford (DPhil); *m* 20 June 1964, Marie Carmel, *née* McNally; 3 da (Rachel b 1965, Catherine b 1971, Maria b 1974), 3 s (John-Paul b 1967, Jerome b 1977, Edmund b 1984); *Career* assoc in law Univ of Calif Berkeley 1965–66; Univ of Oxford: fell and praelector in jurisprudence Univ Coll 1966–2010, Rhodes reader in laws of Br Cwlth and US 1972–89, prof of law and legal philosophy 1989–2010; vice-master University Coll Oxford 2001–10; prof and head Law Dept Univ of Malawi 1976–78, Huber distinguished visiting prof Boston Coll 1993–94, visiting prof of law Univ of Oxford 2010–; Biolchini Family prof of law Univ of Notre Dame Indiana USA 1995–; called to the Bar Gray's Inn 1970; special advsr to Foreign Affrs Ctee of House of Commons on the role of UK Parliament in Canadian Constitution 1980–82; memb Int Theological Cmmn Vatican 1986–92; memb Pontifical Acad for Life 2001–; hon fell UC Oxford 2011–; Hon LLD Univ of Notre Dame Australia 2011; FBA 1990; *Books* Natural Law and Natural Rights (1980, 2 edn 2011), Fundamentals of Ethics (1983), Nuclear Deterrence, Morality and Realism (1987), Commonwealth and Dependencies Halsbury's Laws of England (vol 6 1971, 2003, vol 13 2009), Moral Absolutes (1991), Aquinas: Moral, Political and Legal Theory (1998), Collected Essays (5 Vols, 2011); *Style—* Prof John Finnis, FBA; ✉ e-mail john.finnis@law.ox.ac.uk

FINSBERG, Baroness (Yvonne) Elizabeth (Yvonne Sarch); da of Albert Wright (d 1971), and Edith Abigail, *née* Bingham, of Strabane, NI (d 1997); *b* 13 November 1940, Londonderry, NI; *Educ* Clarendon Sch N Wales, Trinity Coll Dublin (MA), Univ of Manchester (DMS), Univ of London (MA, DipFE); *m* 1, 1967 (m dis 1988), Michael Sarch; 2 s (Patrick b 1968, Adam b 1970); m 2, 1990, Baron Finsberg MBE, JP (Life Peer, d 1996); *Career* Home Office 1963–65, headmistress Fir Close Sch Lincs 1965–67, lectr Brunel Univ 1967–70, tutor Open Univ 1970–72, conslt James Morrell & Assocs 1972–75, independent economist and managing conslt UK and USA 1975–88, Korn/Ferry International 1988–91, fndr dir Sarch Search International (SSI) 1990–, exec search ptnr Howgate Sable & Partners London 1995–99; memb Lord Chancellor's Consultative Panel on Legal Services 2000–04; pres Bevin Boys Assoc 1996–2012; memb Cncl: RSA 1992–99, Int Centre for Briefing Farnham Castle 1992–99 (chm 2000–03); memb International Women's Forum; vice-pres John Grooms 1999–2001; govr Royal Sch Hampstead 1997–2000; chm Fairfax Residents' Assoc 2003; pres Atlantic Project Bluebell Railway 2005–, patron Cheltenham Festivals 2007; *Books* How to be Headhunted (1990), How to be Headhunted Across Europe (1992), How to be Headhunted Again and Again (1999); *Recreations* thinking, travelling, tapestry; *Style—* Elizabeth Finsberg; ✉ Myrtle House, 3 The High Street, Fairford GL7 4AD (☎ 01285 711102, e-mail elizabethfinsberg@yahoo.com)

FIONDA, Andrew; s of Frederick Fionda, and Sarah Fionda; *b* Middlesbrough; *Educ* Trent Poly Nottingham (BA Fashion), Royal Coll of Art (MDes); *Career* fashion designer; former experience with established Br design houses incl Marks & Spencer and Alexon Internation, fndr ptnr own label Pearce Fionda (with Ren Pearce, *qv*) 1984–94, co-designer (with Ren Pearce) Pearce II Fionda collection for Designers at Debenhams 1997–; New Generation Designers of the Year (Br Fashion Awards) 1995, Newcomers Award for Export (Br Knitting and Clothing Export Cncl/Fashion Weekly) 1995, World Young Designers Award (Int Apparel Fedn Istanbul) 1996, Glamour Category Award (Br Fashion Awards) 1997; worldwide stockists incl: Liberty, Harrods, Harvey Nichols and Selfridges (UK), Saks 5th Avenue and Bergdorf Goodman (USA), Lidia Shopping (Italy), CRC (Thailand), Brown Thomas (Ireland); gp exhbns incl: Design of the Times (RCA) 1996, The Cutting Edge of British Fashion 1947–1997 (V&A) 1997; regular guest fashion critic This Morning (ITV) 2004–; *Style—* Andrew Fionda

FIREMAN, Bruce Anthony; s of Michael Fireman (d 1982), of Vinnitsa, Ukraine; *b* 14 February 1944; *Educ* Kilburn GS, Jesus Coll Cambridge (open scholar); *m* 1968, Barbara, *née* Mollett; *Career* slr 1970; dir Corp Fin Charterhouse Japhet 1974–86, chm Fireman Rose Ltd 1986–2013, conslt Gordon Dadds LLP 2013– ; conslt on media and communications Guinness Mahon & Co Ltd 1991–93, seconded as md London News Radio Ltd 1993–94 (non-exec dir 1994–), returned to Guinness Mahon & Co as md media and communications 1994–98; md corporate fin Investec Henderson Crosthwaite 1998–2001, chm Metrodome Group plc 2001–05, sr ptnr Sylvester Media 2006–; dir: Newspaper Publishing plc (The Independent) 1986–93, D G Durham Group plc 1988–93, Culver Holdings plc 1991–2003, The Wyndham Motor Group plc 1998–2000, World Travel Holdings plc 2000–06; arbitrator Securities and Futures Authy 1992–2003; memb Law Soc; *Clubs* Garrick; *Style—* Bruce Fireman, Esq; ✉ 1 Wood Lane, London N6 5UE (☎ 020 8444 7125, e-mail bruce.fireman@sylvestermedia.com)

FIRN, Stephen Christopher; OBE (2014); *Career* chief exec Oxleas NHS Fndn Tst 2002–; *Style—* Stephen Firn, Esq, OBE; ✉ Oxleas NHS Foundation Trust, Pinewood House, Pinewood Place, Dartford, Kent DA2 7WG

FIRTH, Colin; CBE (2011); s of David Firth, and Shirley Firth; *b* 10 September 1960, Hants; *Educ* Montgomery of Alamein Sch, Winchester, Drama Centre London; *Career* actor; *Theatre* credits incl: Bennett in Another Country (Queens) 1983, Dubedat in Doctor's Dilemma (Bromley and Guildford) 1984, Felix in The Lonely Road (Old Vic) 1985, Eben in Desire Under The Elms (Greenwich) 1987, Aston in The Caretaker 1991, Chatsky

(Almeida) 1993, Walker in Three Days of Rain (Donmar Warehouse) 1999; *Television* Dutch Girls (LWT) 1984, Lost Empires (Granada) 1985–86, Tumbledown (BBC) 1987 (RTS Best Actor Award, BAFTA nomination), Out Of The Blue (BBC) 1990, Hostages (Granada) 1992, Master of the Moor (Meridian) 1993, The Deep Blue Sea (BBC) 1994, Pride and Prejudice (BBC) 1994 (Broadcasting Press Guild Award for Best Actor), The Turn of the Screw 1999, Donovan Quick 1999; *Radio* Two Planks and a Passion (BBC) 1986, The One Before The Last (BBC) 1987; *Film* Another Country 1983, Camille 1984, A Month in the Country 1986, Apartment Zero 1988, Valmont 1988, Wings of Fame 1989, Femme Fatale 1990, The Hour of the Pig 1992, Good Girls 1994, Circle of Friends 1995, The English Patient 1996, Fever Pitch 1996, My Life So Far 1997, The Secret Laughter of Women 1997, Shakespeare in Love 1998, The Secret Laughter of Women 1998, My Life So Far 1999, Blackadder Back and Forth 1999, Relative Values 2000, Londinium 2000, Bridget Jones' Diary 2001, The Importance of Being Earnest 2002, Hope Springs 2003, What a Girl Wants 2003, Girl with a Pearl Earring 2003, Love Actually 2003, Trauma 2004, Bridget Jones: The Edge of Reason 2004, Where the Truth Lies 2005, Mamma Mia! 2008, Easy Virtue 2008, Dorian Gray 2009, A Single Man 2009 (Best Actor London Film Critics' Circle Award 2010, Best Actor BAFTA 2010), St Trinian's 2: The Legend of Fritton's Gold 2009, A Christmas Carol 2009, The King's Speech 2010 (Best Actor Br Independent Film Award 2010, Best Actor (Drama) Golden Globe 2011, Outstanding Lead Actor Screen Actors Guild Award 2011, Actor of the Year London Critics' Circle Film Award 2011, Best Leading Actor BAFTA 2011, Best Actor Acad Award 2011), Tinker Tailor Soldier Spy 2011; *Style*— Colin Firth, Esq, CBE; ✉ c/o Independent Talent, 40 Whitfield Street, London W1T 2RH (☎ 020 7636 6565, fax 020 7323 0101)

FIRTH, Prof David; s of Allan Firth, and Betty, *née* Bailey; *Educ* Queen Elizabeth GS Wakefield, Trinity Hall Cambridge (MA), Imperial Coll London (MSc, DIC, PhD); *Career* lectr Imperial Coll London 1986–87, asst prof Univ of Texas at Austin 1987–89, lectr and sr lectr Univ of Southampton 1989–93, sr fell in statistics for the social sciences Univ of Oxford and Nuffield Coll Oxford 1993–2003, prof Univ of Warwick 2003–; professorial fell Economic and Social Research Cncl 2003–06; ed Jl of the Royal Statistical Soc B 1998–2001, author of numerous publications in scientific jls; chm Research Section RSS 2001–03 (hon sec 1994–96), memb Nat Statistics Methodolgy Advsy Ctee 2001–; memb RSS 1982 (Guy Medal in Bronze 1998, Guy Medal in Silver 2012), memb Int Statistical Inst 1998; fell Br Acad 2008; *Recreations* water polo, wheel building; *Style*— Prof David Firth; ✉ Department of Statistics, University of Warwick, Coventry CV4 7AL (☎ 024 7657 2581, fax 024 7652 4532, e-mail d.firth@warwick.ac.uk)

FIRTH, David; né David Coleman; s of Ivor Firth Coleman (d 1991), of Bedford, and Beatrice, *née* Jenkins (d 1990); *b* 15 March 1945, Bedford; *Educ* Bedford Modern Sch, Univ of Sussex (BA), Guildhall Sch of Music and Drama; *m* 2 Jan 1969, Julia Elizabeth, da of Albert Gould; 2 s (Matthew b 24 Sept 1973, Ben b 3 March 1980); *Career* actor, writer and singer; *Theatre* incl: Notes from Underground (Garrick) 1967, RSC 1967–70, The Courier 1776 (Albery, nominated Most Promising Actor in Plays and Players Awards) 1970, Gawain and the Green Knight (Phoenix Leicester) 1972; NT 1973 incl: Macbeth, The Cherry Orchard, Measure for Measure; other credits incl: Hedda (Roundhouse) 1980, Hamlet (Piccadilly) 1982, Marilyn (Adelphi) 1983, Poppy (Adelphi) 1983, The Importance of Being Earnest (Ambassadors) 1984, The Ratepayers Iolanthe (Phoenix) 1984, Canary Blunt (Latchmere) 1985, The Metropolitan Mikado (Queen Elizabeth Hall) 1985, The Phantom of the Opera (Her Majesty's) 1986 and (Royal Albert Hall) 2011, King Lear (Old Vic) 1988, The Hunting of the Snark 1991, A Tree Grows in Brooklyn (Barbican) 1992, Jubilee (Barbican) 1992, Assassins (Donmar) 1992, Knickerbocker Holiday (Barbican) 1993, Follies (Brighton) 1993, Forty Years On (West Yorkshire Playhouse) 1994, Love Life (Barbican) 1995, Passion (Queens) 1996, The Fix (Donmar) 1997, Die Fledermaus (Arts) 1998, On A Clear Day (Barbican) 1998, Good Grief (Yvonne Arnaud, Guildford) 1998, HMS Pinafore (Royal Festival Hall) 1999, Susanna's Secret (Drill Hall) 1999, Jubilee (Her Majesty's and BBC Radio 3) 1999, Der Kuhandel (Barbican and BBC Radio 3) 2000, Journey's End (Drill Hall) 2000, Cenerentola (Music Theatre London) 2001, Cat on a Hot Tin Roof (Lyric) 2001, Relatively Speaking (Secombe Theatre Sutton) 2002, Our Song (tour) 2003, Coward and Others 2004, The Man Who... (Orange Tree Richmond) 2005, The Shell Seekers (tour) 2006, Yellow Lines (Oval House) 2007, Park Avenue (Lilian Bayliss Theatre) 2008, Dirty Dancing (Aldwych Theatre) 2008, Phantom of the Opera (Royal Albert Hall) 2011, Around the World (Sadlers Wells) 2013; *Television* incl: Search for the Nile, Eyeless in Gaza, Love Story, Armchair Theatre, Village Hall, Terra Firma, Love for Lydia, Wings, Raffles, Saint Joan, The Gondoliers, Nanny's Boy, Troilus and Cressida, Sorry I'm A Stranger Here Myself, Lucky Jim, Yes Minister, Drummonds, Cardtrick, Singles, One Way Out, Stay Lucky, Murder East Murder West, Poirot, Between the Lines, The Late Show, Wycliffe, Holby City, Swallow, Doctors, The Bill, Waking the Dead, Casualty, Midsomer Murders; *Film* Out on a Limb 1985, The Upside of Anger 2004; *Writing* for TV and theatre incl: Sorry I'm A Stranger Here Myself 1980, The Live Rail 1982, Canary Blunt 1985, Cause for Complaint 1986, Oblique Encounter and Sod's Law 1987, Home James 1989, Shelley 1990, Otherwise You'd Cry 1992, A Real Farce 1998, Damaged Goods 1999, The Hidden Hand 2002; *Style*— David Firth, Esq; ✉ e-mail firthdavid@gmail.com; c/o Conway van Gelder Grant, 8–12 Broadwick Street, London W1F 8HW

FIRTH, Simon Nicholas; s of Graham Alfred Firth, of Lincs, and Janice, *née* Todd; *b* 21 October 1963, Sheffield; *Educ* Nottingham HS, ChCh Oxford (MA, pres Univ Law Soc 1986), Guildford Coll of Law; *Career* admitted slr 1989; asst slr Linklaters & Paines 1989–96 (articled clerk 1987–89), ptnr Linklaters 1996– (trainee devpt ptnr 2002–13); memb Financial Markets Ctee 2014–; visiting prof Univ of Law 2015–; *Books* Derivatives: Law and Practice (2003); *Style*— Simon Firth, Esq; ✉ Linklaters, One Silk Street, London EC2Y 8HQ (☎ 020 7456 3764, fax 020 7456 2222, e-mail simon.firth@linklaters.com)

FIRTH, Prof William James; s of William John Flett Firth (d 1993), and Christina May Coltart, *née* Craig (d 1994); *b* 23 February 1945, Holm, Orkney; *Educ* Perth Acad, Univ of Edinburgh (BSc, capt Univ hockey team), Heriot-Watt Univ (PhD); *m* 15 July 1967, Mary MacDonald, da of Charles Ramsay Anderson (d 1972), and Margaret, *née* Robertson (d 2008); 2 s (Michael John Charles b 11 Feb 1973, Jonathan William b 25 Aug 1975); *Career* reader Dept of Physics Heriot-Watt Univ 1984–85 (asst lectr 1967–69, lectr 1969–82, sr lectr 1982–84), Freeland prof of natural philosophy Dept of Physics and Applied Physics Univ of Strathclyde 1985–2010 (head of dept 1990–93 and 2001–04, emeritus prof 2015–); visiting prof Arizona Center for Mathematical Sciences Tucson USA 1989–95; Royal Soc euro fell Univ of Heidelberg 1978–79; chm Ctee of Scottish Professors of Physics 1992–96; ed: Progress in Quantum Electronics 1984–89, Cambridge Studies in Modern Optics 1986–92; FInstP 1997 (MInstP 1972), FRSE 1989, fell Optical Soc of America 1996 (memb 1986); *Publications* author of over 250 scientific articles; *Recreations* golf, the universe and everything; *Style*— Prof William Firth, FRSE; ✉ Department of Physics, University of Strathclyde, John Anderson Building, 107 Rottenrow, Glasgow G4 0NG

FIRTH-BERNARD, Christopher (Chris); s of Charles George Dickenson Firth-Bernard (d 1988), and Monica Margaret, *née* Henshaw (d 1977); *b* 27 December 1954, Chichester; *Educ* Bishop Luffa Sch Chichester; *m* 4 March 1995, Ann Marie Thérèse, *née* Pochon, 3 s (Joseph Charles b 4 Jan 2002, Jack Christopher b 14 Oct 2003, Alistair Donald b 5 Oct 2005); *Career* The Mount Hotel Tettenhall Wood 1971, The Royal Hotel Bognor Regis 1972–74, The Noke Hotel St Albans 1974–76, The Grand Hotel Krasapolski Amsterdam 1976–77; chef de partie The Royal Norfolk Hotel Bognor Regis 1977–78, chef de partie The Dolphin and Anchor Hotel Chichester 1978, sous chef Avisford Park Hotel Arundel 1978–79; head chef: The Feathers Inn Wadesmill 1979–81, Green End Park Hotel Herts 1981–86, Summer Isles Hotel Achiltibuie 1986– (1 Michelin Star 1998); runner-up in the food category Scotland on Sunday Glenfiddich Spirit of Scotland Awards 1998, Scottish Chef of the Year 1998; *Recreations* photography, art, ornithology; *Style*— Chris Firth-Bernard, Esq

FISCHEL, David Andrew; *b* 1 April 1958; *Career* Intu Properties plc (formerly Liberty International plc then Capital Shopping Centres Gp plc): joined 1985, fin dir 1988–92, md 1992–, chief exec 2001–; ACA 1983; *Style*— David Fischel; ✉ Intu Properties plc, 40 Broadway, London SW1H 0BT (☎ 020 7960 1207, mobile 07710 582843, e-mail david.fischel@intu.co.uk, website www.intugroup.co.uk)

FISCHEL, Robert Gustav; QC (1998); s of Bruno Rolf Fischel (d 1977), and Sophie Kruml (d 1993); *b* 12 January 1953; *Educ* City of London Sch, Univ of London (LLB), Coll of Law; *m* 1, 1989 (m dis 1997); 1 da (Lujzka Beatrice b 3 Oct 1992); m 2, 1999, Anna Louise Landucci; 1 da (Isabella Sophie b 5 June 1999); *Career* called to the Bar Middle Temple 1975, dir Int Catering Associates Ltd 1995; Freedom of the City of London; *Recreations* skiing, tennis, fine food and wine, cooking; *Clubs* Royal Over-Seas League; *Style*— Robert Fischel, Esq, QC

FISCHER, Dr Albert; *b* 27 May 1957, Amsterdam; *Educ* Leyden Univ (PhD); *Career* formerly: head of devpt Reed Elsevier Science, ptnr Green Ptnrs, managing ptnr and co-fndr Planet Capital; md Yellow & Blue Investment Mgmnt BV; non-exec chm: Planet Health Care plc 2001–10, Locamation BV, Cuculus GmbH, Triogen Gp BV; non-exec dir Vayon Gp Ltd; *Recreations* travelling to remote areas, sport, scuba diving, marathon running; *Clubs* Amsterdam Private Equity, Amstel; *Style*— Dr Albert Fischer; ✉ Yellow & Blue Investment Management, Kernkade 10, 3542 CH Utrecht, The Netherlands

FISCHER, Max Alfred; s of Alfred Fischer (d 1984), of Germany, and Lisa Fischer; *b* 31 August 1951; *Educ* Germany; *m* 1 Aug 1979, Susan Fischer; 2 s (Neil William b 7 Nov 1980, Daniel Alfred b 15 Sept 1982), 1 da (Selina Olive b 3 May 1988); *Career* chef; apprentice chef Lüneburg, subsequently commis chef Hotel Erbrinz 1969–72, demi chef Restaurant Nicholas Paris 1972–74, chef de partie Bell Inn Aston Clinton 1974–76, head chef Schloss Hotel Kronberg 1977–80, proprietor Fischer's Restaurant 1981–88, chef and proprietor Fischer's Baslow Hall 1989–; Michelin Star 1994–, Egon Ronay Restaurant of the Year 1995, 8 out of 10 Good Food Guide 2002, Johannsens Most Excellent UK Restaurant 2002; hon dr Sheffield Hallam Univ 2013; *Recreations* gardening; *Style*— Max Fischer, Esq; ✉ Baslow Hall Ltd, Calver Road, Baslow, Derbyshire DE45 1RR (☎ 01246 583259, fax 01246 583818, website www.fischers-baslowhall.co.uk)

FISCHER, Stefanie Margaret; da of Leonhard Fischer, of Wellington NZ, and Margaret June, *née* McLeod; step da of Prof Tom Keightley Ewer, OBE (d 1997); *b* 28 February 1955; *Educ* Redland HS Bristol, Girton Coll Cambridge (MA Arch, DipArch); *Career* architect specialising in the design of bldgs for cinema and media incl works to listed buildings; former princ Burrell Foley Fischer LLP Architects and Urban Designers; clients incl Royal Soc, Royal Acad for Engrg and Acad of Med Sciences, consultancy servs to BFI and UK Film Cncl; external examiner Univs of Westminster and Bath, examiner in professional practice Bartlett Sch of Architecture; work widely published in nat and architectural press; past memb Church Buildings Cncl, past memb Architecture Advsy Ctee Arts Cncl of England, past enabler Cmmn for Architecture and Built Environment (CABE); regnl chair RIBA Awards: Wales 1998, Southern Region 1999, London 2000; RIBA: memb Educn and Professional Standards Ctee, memb Appts Gp, memb Industry Practice Ctee, memb Pres's Theme Gp (client and consumer); memb ARCUK 1981, RIBA 1981, FRSA; *Recreations* opera, film, exhibitions, drama, dance, classical music, travel, literature, swimming, trekking; *Style*— Ms Stefanie Fischer; ✉ Burrell Foley Fischer LLP Architects, Studio 9, 14 Southgate Road, London N1 3LY (☎ 02076 206114, e-mail s.fischer@bff-architects.co.uk)

FISH, Prof Sir David; kt (2014); *Career* academic clinical neurologist Nat Hosp for Neurology and Neurosurgery UCL, med dir Specialist Hosps Clinical Bd UCL Hosps NHS Fndn Tst, md UCLPartners 2009–; *Style*— Prof Sir David Fish

FISH, David Thomas; QC (1997); s of Tom Fish (d 1987), and Gladys, *née* Durkin (d 1995); *b* 23 July 1949; *Educ* Ashton-under-Lyne GS, LSE (LLB); *m* 1989, Angelina Brunhilde, da of Arthur Dennett (decd); 1 s (Thomas b 8 Aug 1992), 1 da (Clementine b 20 March 1994); *Career* called to the Bar Inner Temple 1973; recorder of the Crown Court 1994–2006; non-exec chm 32 Red plc 2005–; *Recreations* horse racing, golf; *Style*— David Fish, Esq, QC; ✉ Deans Court Chambers, 24 St John Street, Manchester M3 4DF (☎ 0161 214 6000)

FISH, Dr Michael John; MBE (2004); s of Aubrey John Richard Fish (d 1970), of Eastbourne, and Dora, *née* Amos (d 1970); *b* 27 April 1944, Eastbourne, E Sussex; *Educ* Eastbourne Coll, City Univ; *m* 21 Sept 1968, Susan Mary, *née* Page; 2 da (Alison Elizabeth b 9 May 1971, Nicola Katherine b 25 Nov 1975); *Career* meteorologist and sr broadcast meteorologist; Meteorological Office Gatwick Airport 1962–65, posted to Bracknell as scientific offr 1965–67; BBC Weather Centre (London Weather Centre until 1991): joined 1967, higher scientific offr 1971–89, sr scientific offr 1989–2004; first radio broadcasts 1971 (BBC), first TV broadcasts 1974; ret from Meteorological Office 2004, occasionally presents weather on BBC South East; numerous appearances on TV and radio in various light entertainment and factual progs; latterly appearances in: Play What I Wrote (tour), French Paste (Shaw Theatre); famous for the 'hurricane gaffe' Oct 1987; features in opening ceremony London Olympics 2012; also co-ordinator trg courses for TV weather crews in Africa, meteorological conslt for numerous pubns and cos, specialist and lectr on climate change, travel writer and storm-chaser; after dinner speaker, narrator of voice-overs and award ceremony host; patron of several charities incl Age UK and Woodland Tst; TV Weather Presenter of the Year TRIC Awards 2004, The Greatest Br Weather Veteran 2011; Tie Man of the Year four times in the 1990s, believed to be the longest serving broadcast meterologist in the world; Hon DSc: City Univ 1996, Univ of Exeter 2005; Freeman City of London 1997; FRMetS 1965; *Publications* Storm Force: Britain's Wildest Weather (with Ian McCaskill and Paul Hudson); author of numerous articles on the weather for the nat press and other publications; *Recreations* travel, wine and good food, playing with my granddaughter; *Style*— Dr Michael Fish, MBE; ✉ c/o Knight Ayton Management, 29 Gloucester Place, London W1U 8HX (☎ 020 3795 1806); e-mail michael@michael-fish.com, websites www.michael-fish.com, www.fish4weather.com and www.michaelfish.org, Twitter @Fish4Weather

FISHBURN, (John) Dudley; s of late Eskdale Fishburn and Bunting Fishburn; *b* 8 June 1946; *Educ* Eton, Harvard; *m* 1981, Victoria, da of Sir Jack Boles and step da of Lady Anne Boles (da of 12 Earl Waldegrave); 2 da (Alice b 1982, Honor b 1984), 2 s (Jack b 1985, Marcus b 1987); *Career* journalist; The Economist 1979–2003; MP (Cons) Kensington 1988–97, PPS at the Foreign and Commonwealth Office 1989–90 and the DTI 1990–93; non-exec dir: HSBC Bank plc, Household International (Chicago), Henderson Smaller Cos Tst plc, Altria Inc, Beazley Gp plc; int advsr TT International 1997–; govr Peabody Tst; *Clubs* Brooks's; *Style*— Dudley Fishburn, Esq; ✉ 7 Gayfere Street, London SW1P 3HN (☎ 020 7976 0733)

FISHER, Adrian; s of Dr James Frederick Fisher, of Bournemouth, Dorset, and Rosemary, *née* Sterling-Hill; *b* 5 August 1951, Bournemouth, Dorset; *Educ* Oundle, Portsmouth Poly; *m* 1, 10 June 1975, Dorothy Jane, *née* Pollard; 2 da (Felicity Grace (Mrs Nichols) b 4 June 1976, Katherine Clare (Mrs Pickles) b 19 Dec 1978); m 2, 27 Aug 1997, Marie Ann, *née*

F

Butterworth; 1 s (Wilfred Edward b 28 June 1998), 2 step s (Julian Charles Mittra, Aidan James Mittra), 1 step da (Monica Kathleen Mittra); *Career* maze designer; over 600 mazes created in 30 countries since 1979, fndr Adrian Fisher Design Ltd; designed: world's first cornfield maize maze Pennsylvania 1993 (and 300 maize mazes since), 42 hedge mazes (incl at Leeds Castle, Blenheim Palace and Scone Palace), puzzles for World Puzzle Championships 2001–; pioneer of: brick-path-in-grass mazes, 45 modern Mirror Mazes (incl at Wookey Hole Caves, Hamburg Dungeon, Warwick Castle, Tokyo Dome, Palace of Sweets Wildwood NJ, Navy Pier Chicago IL, Hollywood Wax Museum Pigeon Forge TN and PortAventura theme park Spain), design of 55-storey The Maze Tower Dubai, foaming fountain water mazes, walk-through parting waterfalls, foaming fountain gates, wrought-iron maze gates in mazes; inventor 7-sided Fisher Paver system for decorative brick paving, co-inventor Mitre Tile system for paving, tiling and decorative patterns (incl Mitre Mosaic at SciTec Building Oundle Sch); Destination Imagination Resorgimento Award 2003, Absolut Vodka Int Artist 2002 (created Absolut Amaze Oxo Gallery London), gold medallist Liverpool Int Garden Festival 1984, six Guinness world records for progressively larger cornfield maize mazes 1993–2003; dir 1991 – The Year of the Maze tourism campaign, memb European Bd of Themed Entertainment Assoc 2006; The Art of the Maze (1990), Secrets of the Maze (1997), Mazes and Follies (2004), Mazes and Labyrinths (2004), The Amazing Book of Mazes (2006); *Recreations* gardening, photography, water-colour painting, recreational mathematics, keeping sheep; *Clubs* Worshipful Co of Gardeners of London, Worshipful Soc of Apothecaries of London; *Style*— Adrian Fisher, Esq; ✉ Adrian Fisher Design Ltd, Portman Lodge, Durweston, Dorset DT11 0QA (✆ 01258 458845, e-mail adrian@adrianfisherdesign.com, website www.adrianfisherdesign.com)

FISHER, Andrew Charles; s of Harold Fisher, of Barbados, and Jessie, *née* Tombleson (now Mrs Stanley); *b* 22 June 1961, Aldershot; *Educ* Univ of Birmingham (BSc); *m* 1, 15 Aug 1987 (m dis 2009), Bernadette Ann, *née* Johnson; 2 s (Christopher Andrew b 6 May 1988, Harry Lawrence b 8 May 1993); *m* 2, 23 May 2009, Caroline Gina, *née* Moss; 1 da (Gabriella Rose Mercury b 7 Jan 2008); *Career* mktg mangr Unilever plc 1982–87, ptnr Coopers & Lybrand Mgmnt Consultancy 1987–91, sales and mktg dir Equitor Div Standard Chartered Bank 1991–94, md Rangeley Co Ltd 1994–97, strategic advsr NatWest Wealth Mgmnt 1997–98, gp commercial dir Coutts NatWest Gp 1998–2000, chief exec Coutts Gp 2000–02, ptnr Carlyle Gp 2002–03, chief exec CPP Gp 2003–04, chief exec Cox Insurance Holdings plc 2004–05, chm and chief exec JS & P Ltd 2004–, chief exec Towry Law Gp 2006– (chm 2006–07); non-exec dir Benfield Gp Ltd 2003–08; govr Sandhurst Sch; MInstD; *Recreations* skiing, golf, scuba diving, flying; *Clubs* Wentworth, Mosimann's; *Style*— Andrew Fisher, Esq

FISHER, Charles Murray; s of Kenneth John Fisher (d 1996), of Cheltenham, Glos, and Beryl Dorothy, *née* Pearman; *b* 24 December 1949; *Educ* Cheltenham Coll, St Edmund Hall Oxford, Harvard Business Sch; *m* 29 Sept 1984, Denise Ellen, *née* Williams (d 2008); 2 da (Louisa Dora b 13 Dec 1985, Jasmine Diana b 24 June 1987); *Career* chm Sharpe & Fisher plc 1989–99; non-exec dir: South West Electricity plc 1990–95, Baggeridge Brick plc 1996–2005, Travis Perkins plc 2000–04, Delta plc 2000–06, Grafton Gp 2009–; chm: The Summerfield Charitable Tst 1999–2010, Mowlem plc 2002–05 (non-exec dir 1993); *Recreations* tennis, travel, reading; *Clubs* MCC, Turf; *Style*— Charles Fisher, Esq; ✉ Loumin Estates Ltd, 2 Cromwell Place, London SW7 2JE (✆ 020 7036 0222)

FISHER, David Paul; QC (1996); s of Percy Laurence Fisher (d 1964), and Doris Mary, *née* Western (d 2000); *b* 30 April 1949; *Educ* Felsted, Coll of Law, Inns of Court Sch of Law; *m* 1, 18 Sept 1971, Cary Maria Cicely (d 1977), da of Charles Egan Lamberton; 1 da (Clair Helen Maria b 14 Dec 1976); *m* 2, 7 July 1979, Diana Elizabeth, da of John Harold Dolby (d 1962); *Career* called to the Bar Gray's Inn 1973 (bencher 2003), recorder of the Crown Court 1991– (asst recorder 1987); head of chambers 2010–15, ret; memb: Gen Cncl of the Bar 1997–2000, Advocacy Studies Bd 1997–2001, Criminal Procedure Rule Ctee 2004–08; *Recreations* travel, sport, gardening, cinema; *Style*— David Fisher, Esq, QC; ✉ 21 College Hill, London EC4R 2RP (✆ 020 3301 0910, fax 3301 0911)

FISHER, Duncan Mark; OBE (2009); s of Humphrey Fisher, and Helga, *née* Kricke; *b* 3 November 1961, Amman, Jordan; *Educ* Univ of Cambridge (BA, MPhil), SSEES Univ of London (MA); *m* 30 Dec 1987, Clare, *née* Warren; 2 da (Miriam b 19 Sept 1996, Abigail b 11 Nov 2000); *Career* fndr and ceo East West Environment 1989–95, fndr, ceo then tstee Travel Fndn 1994–2008, co-fndr and ceo Fatherhood Inst 1999–2009, memb Bd Equal Opportunities Cmmn 2004–07, fndr Kids in the Middle 2012–, starting online publishing of child and family research 2013–; *Publications* Baby's Here! Who Does What? (2010); *Recreations* making lists, eating very good chocolate, singing, taking my children to things; *Clubs* Chocolate; *Style*— Duncan Fisher, OBE; ✉ 37 Upper House Farm, Crickhowell NP8 1BZ (✆ 07950 028704, e-mail mail@duncanfisher.com, website www.duncanfisher.com)

FISHER, Gillian Elizabeth; da of Norman James Fisher, of Oadby, Leics, and Patricia Jean, *née* Warrington; *b* 12 March 1955; *Educ* Beauchamp Coll Oadby, Univ of Warwick (LLB), Royal Coll of Music (ARCM); *m* 11 Feb 1983, Brian Christopher Kay, *qv*, s of Noel Bancroft Kay; *Career* soprano; concert singer, mainly Baroque and Classical repertoire; professional debut Queen Elizabeth Hall 1979; has sung at numerous major venues and festivals worldwide incl: Royal Opera House Covent Garden (debut 1981), Royal Festival Hall, Barbican Hall, Edinburgh Festival (debut 1984), BBC Proms (regular soloist since debut 1985), Three Choirs Festival, Bath and York Festivals, Paris, Monte Carlo, Madrid, Vienna, Milan, Venice, Cologne, Frankfurt, Concertgebouw Amsterdam, Brussels, Oslo, New York (debut Lincoln Centre 1983, further tours 1988 and 1989), Japan and Far East (debut 1987, further tours 1989 and 1992), Australia (debut Sydney Opera House 1992); has worked with numerous major conductors incl: John Eliot Gardiner, Trevor Pinnock, Christopher Hogwood, Robert King, Roger Norrington, Ton Koopman; *Recordings* numerous incl: Purcell Complete Odes and Welcome Songs (with King's Consort under Robert King, Hyperion, 8 CDs), Pergolesi Stabat Mater (with King's Consort and Michael Chance under Robert King, Hyperion, Gramophone Critics' Choice 1988), Great Baroque Arias (with King's Consort, Pickwick, in US classical top ten for several months 1988), Handel Duets (with James Bowman and King's Consort), Purcell's The Fairy Queen (with The Sixteen under Harry Christophers, Collins Classics), Purcell's King Arthur (with Monteverdi Choir under John Eliot Gardiner, Erato), Purcell's Dioclesian and Timon of Athens (with Monteverdi Choir under Gardiner, Erato), various Handel works with London Handel Orch under Denys Darlow, Bach Cantatas (with The Sixteen under Harry Christophers), Monteverdi Vespers (with Kammerchor Stuttgart, Deutsche Harmonia Mundi); *Recreations* reading, gardening, watching cricket; *Style*— Ms Gillian Fisher

FISHER, Prof John Robert; s of John Robert Fisher, of Barrow-in-Furness, Cumbria, and Eleanor, *née* Parker; *b* 6 January 1943; *Educ* Barrow GS, UCL (BA, MPhil), Univ of Liverpool (PhD); *m* 1 Aug 1966, (Elizabeth) Ann, da of Stephen Gerard Postlethwaite, of Barrow-in-Furness, Cumbria; 3 s (David John b 27 Sept 1967, Nicholas Stephen b 10 Dec 1970, Martin Joseph b 27 Aug 1973); *Career* Univ of Liverpool: lectr 1966–75, sr lectr 1975–81, dir Inst of Latin American Studies 1983–2001, dean Faculty of Arts 1986–92, prof 1987–2010, pro-vice-chllr 1995–98, emeritus prof 2010–; chm: Soc of Latin American Studies 1986–88 (treas 2004–), Anglo-Chilean Soc 1998–2000; pres Euro Assoc of Historians of Latin America 1996–99 (gen sec 1987–93, treas 2002–14), pres Int Congress of Americanists 2000–06 (vice-pres 1997–2000, and 2009–12); FRHistS 1975; Gt Offr Sun of Peru 2008; *Books* Government and Society in Colonial Peru (1970), Silver Mines and Silver Miners in Colonial Peru (1976), Commercial Relations between Spain and Spanish America 1778–1797 (1985), Peru (1989), Reform and Insurrection in Bourbon, New Granada and Peru (1990), Trade, War and Revolution (1992), The Economic Aspects of Spanish Imperialism in America (1997), El Perú Borbónico 1750–1824 (2000), Bourbon Peru 1750–1824 (2003), Una Historia de la Independencia del Perú (2009); *Recreations* theatre, music, walking, gardening, travel; *Style*— Prof John Fisher; ✉ University of Liverpool, PO Box 147, Liverpool L69 7WW (✆ 0151 677 9091, e-mail fisher@liverpool.ac.uk)

FISHER, Jonathan Simon; QC (2003); s of Aubrey Fisher; *b* 24 February 1958; *Educ* St Dunstan's Coll, N London Poly (BA), St Catharine's Coll Cambridge (LLM); *m* 21 Dec 1980, Paula Yvonne, da of Rev Louis Goldberg (d 1988); 2 s (Benjamin b 1984, David b 1990), 2 da (Hannah b 1987, Leah b 1995); *Career* called to the Bar Gray's Inn 1980, ad eundem Inner Temple 1985; registered practitioner Dubai Int Fin Ct 2015; standing counsel to Inland Revenue (Central Criminal Court and London Crown Courts) 1991–2003; visiting prof: Cass Business Sch City Univ London 2004–07, LSE 2006– (visiting fell 2004–06), City Univ London 2011–12, Hebrew Univ Jerusalem 2013–14 and 2015–16; cmmr Bill of Rights Cmmn Miny of Justice 2011–12; chm Fraud Advsy Panel Special Project Gp on Fraud Investigation and Prosecution 2006, dir and tstee Fraud Advsy Panel 2006–10; chm of research Soc of Cons Lawyers 2006–10 (memb Exec Ctee 2005–06 and 2011–, hon sec 2015); memb: Steering Gp Assets Recovery Agency 2003–06, Legal Panel Accountancy Investigation and Disciplinary Bd 2005–09; hon memb Steering Ctee London Fraud Forum 2007–, specialist advsr to the House of Commons Treasy Ctee 2014–; gen ed Lloyds Law Reports: Financial Crime 2008–; authorised tsts and estates practitioner Soc of Tst and Estate Practitioners (STEP) 2010; Hon LLD UWE 2015; chartered tax advsr and fell Chartered Inst of Taxation 2009; *Books* Pharmacy Law and Practice (co-author, 1995, 5 edn 2013), Law of Investor Protection (co-author, 1997, 2 edn 2003), A British Bill of Rights and Obligations (2006), Fighting Fraud and Financial Crime (2010), The Anti-Money Laundering Disclosure Regime and the Collection of Revenue in the United Kingdom (2010), Rescuing Human Rights (2012), Policing the Financial Markets: Risk and Recklessness (chapter 2 in Fighting Financial Crime in the Global Economic Crisis, 2014), The British Bill of Rights, Protecting Freedom Under the Law (article in Politeia, 2015), Strengthening the Restraint and Confiscation Regime (article in Criminal Law Review, 2015), Criminal forms of high frequency trading on the financial markets (article in Law and Financial Markets Review, co-author, 2015); *Recreations* theatre, football, arts, history, travelling; *Clubs* Carlton, Walbrook, Virgin Active; *Style*— Jonathan Fisher, Esq, QC; ✉ Devereux Chambers, Queen Elizabeth Building, Temple, London EC4Y 9BS (e-mail fisher@devchambers.co.uk)

FISHER, Richard; QC (2015); *Educ* Univ of Bristol (LLB); *Career* called to the Bar 1994; *Style*— Richard Fisher, Esq, QC; ✉ Doughty Street Chambers, 54 Doughty Street, London WC1N 2LS

FISHER, Rick; s of Samuel M Fisher (d 2011), and Helene, *née* Korn (d 1973); *b* 19 October 1954; *Educ* Haverford HS Philadelphia, Dickinson Coll Carlisle Pennsylvania; *Career* lighting designer; Bronze medal for lighting design World Stage Design Exhbn Toronto, Helpmann Award (Australia) 2008, LSI Lighting Designer of the Year 2008, Tony Award 2009, Drama Desk Award 2009, Outer Critics Circe NYC Award 2009; fell Assoc of Lighting Designers (former chm); *Theatre* RNT: Landscape with Weapon, Honour, Blue/Orange, Albert Speer, Widowers Houses, Black Snow, Peer Gynt, The Coup, An Inspector Calls (Tony Award 1994, Drama Desk Award 1994, Olivier Award nomination 1993, Ovation and Drama Circle Awards LA 1996), Pericles (Olivier Award nomination 1995), Machinal (Olivier Award 1994), What the Butler Saw, Under Milk Wood, Blinded by the Sun, The Designated Mourner, Fair Ladies at a Game of Poem Cards, Death of a Salesman, Lady in the Dark, Chips With Everything (Olivier Award 1998), Flight, Betrayal, Mother Clap's Molly House, The Winter's Tale, Jerry Springer – The Opera, Waste 2016; Royal Court: Three Birds Alighting in a Field, King Lear, Hysteria (Olivier Award 1994), Six Degrees of Separation, Bloody Poetry, The Old Neighbourhood (Duke of York's), Via Dolorosa (West End and Broadway), Serious Money, Far Away, My Zinc Bed, A Number, Tribes; RSC: Temptation, Restoration, Some Americans Abroad (also Lincoln Center NYC and Broadway), Two Shakespearean Actors, The Virtuoso, 'Tis Pity She's a Whore, Artists and Admirers, All's Well That Ends Well, The Gift of the Gorgon, Elgar's Rondo, The Broken Heart, A Russian in the Woods, Merchant of Venice, Richard III, Galileo; other prodns incl: The Audience (West End and Broadway), Moonlight (Almeida), A Walk in the Woods (Comedy Theatre), Lobby Hero, The Life of Stuff, Threepenny Opera, The Maids, Boston Marriage, Philanthropist, Old Times, Betrayal (all Donmar Warehouse), Rat in the Skull (Duke of York's), Disney's Hunchback of Notre Dame (Berlin), Billy Elliot: The Musical (Victoria Palace Theatre, Broadway and Australia), Tin Tin (Barbican), The King and I, Sweeney Todd (Paris), Sound of Music (Buenos Aires), Tiger Country, No Naughty Bits, Farewell to the Theatre, Chariots of Fire (all Hampstead Theatre), Sunny Afternoon (Hampstead Theatre and West End); *Opera* incl: Betrothal in a Monastery (Glyndebourne), Fiery Angel and Turandot (both Bolshoi Moscow), A Midsummer Night's Dream (Fenice Venice), Gloriana, La Bohème, L'Étoile, Peter Grimes (Opera North), The Magic Flute (Teatro Regio, Parma), Flying Dutchman (Opera Bordeaux), La Traviata (Paris Opera), The Fairy Queen, Dr Ox's Experiment, Verdi's Requiem, Turandot (ENO), Musica Nel Chiostro (3 seasons, Batignano Italy), Tsarina's Slippers (ROH), Wozzeck (ROH), 22 operas for Santa Fe Opera over 15 years; *Ballet* numerous dance pieces for The Kosh and Adventures in Motion Pictures incl Swan Lake (West End and Broadway); *Recreations* cycling, travel, camping; *Style*— Rick Fisher; ✉ c/o Denis Lyne Agency, 503 Holloway Road, London N19 4DD (✆ 020 7272 5020)

FISK, Prof David John; CB (1999); s of late John Howard Fisk, and Rebecca Elizabeth, *née* Haynes; *b* 9 January 1947; *Educ* Stationers' Company's Sch Hornsey, St John's Coll Cambridge (MA, ScD), Univ of Manchester (PhD); *m* 1972, Anne Thoday; 1 s, 1 da; *Career* DOE (now DETR): Building Res Estab 1972, higher sci offr 1972–73, sr sci offr 1973–75, princ sci offr 1975–78, sr princ sci offr and head Mechanical and Electrical Engrg Div 1978–84, asst sec Central Directorate of Environmental Protection 1984–87, dep chief scientist 1987–88, chief scientist 1988–, dir Environment and Int Directorate 1995–98, dir Central Strategy Directorate 1999–; visiting prof Univ of Liverpool 1988–, Royal Acad of Engrg prof of engrg for sustainable devpt Imperial Coll London; memb Steering Gp Building Futures; author of numerous papers on building sci, systems theory and economics; FCIBSE 1983, CEng 1983, FREng 1998; *Books* Thermal Control of Buildings (1981); *Style*— Prof David Fisk, CB

FITT, Prof Alistair; *Career* head Sch of Mathematics then pro-vice-chllr (Int) Univ of Southampton, pro-vice-chllr for research and knowledge exchange Oxford Brookes Univ, vice-chllr Oxford Brookes Univ 2015–; *Style*— Prof Alistair Fitt; ✉ Oxford Brookes University, Headington Campus, Gipsy Lane, Oxford OX3 0BP (website www.brookes.ac.uk)

FITTON-BROWN, HE Edmund; *Career* diplomat; China Desk FCO 1984–86, Finnish language trg, third then second sec Helsinki 1986–89, Information Dept FCO 1989–90, Arabic language trg 1990–92, ME Dept FCO 1992–93, first sec Cairo 1993–96, ME Dept FCO 1996–98, first sec Kuwait 1998–2001, dep head Dept ME and N Africa Directorate FCO 2001–03, cnsllr Cairo 2003–05, cnsllr Riyadh 2005–06, head Dept ME and N Africa Directorate FCO 2006–09, Italian language trg then cnsllr Rome 2009–11, cnsllr Dubai 2011–14, ambass to Yemen 2015–; *Style*— HE Edmund Fitton-Brown, Esq

FITZALAN HOWARD, Richard; *Educ* Ampleforth, Corpus Christi Coll Oxford; *Career* Fleming Family & Partners: ceo FF&P Asset Mgmnt Ltd 2000–10, chm Stonehage Fleming Investment Mgmnt 2010–; dir: JPMorgan Smaller Companies Investment Tst, Gabelli Value Plus + Trust plc; Pres Br Order of Malta; tstee: Dulverton Tst, Coll of Arms Tst, Order of St John Care Tst; *Style—* Richard Fitzalan Howard, Esq; ✉ Stonehage Fleming, 15 Suffolk Street, London SW1Y 4HG

FitzGERALD, Sir Adrian James Andrew Denis; 6 Bt (UK 1880), of Valencia, Co Kerry; The 24th Knight of Kerry (first recorded use of title 1468; The Green Knight); s of Sir George FitzGerald, 5 Bt, MC, 23 Knight of Kerry (d 2001); *b* 24 June 1940; *Educ* Harrow; *Heir* cous, Anthony D FitzGerald; *Career* hotelier 1983–90; ed Monday World 1967–74; Royal Borough of Kensington and Chelsea: cnclr 1974–2002, mayor 1984–85, chm Educn and Libraries Ctee 1995–98, chm Highways & Traffic Ctee 1999–2001; dep ldr London Fire and Civil Def Authy 1989–90, pres Anglo Polish Soc 2002– (chm 1989–92), vice-chm London Chapter Irish Georgian Soc 1990–2009, pres Benevolent Soc of St Patrick 1997–2014, govr Cardinal Vaughan Meml Sch 1999–2009 and 2010–13 (vice-chm 2002–03, chm 2003–09), pres Irish Assoc SMOM 2009–15, patron London Irish Centre 2009–, vice-pres Friends of the Ordinariate of our Lady of Walsingham 2011–, patron Latin Man Soc 2012–; Knight Grand Cross of Honour and Devotion in Obedience SMOM; *Publications* O'Connell: Education, Church and State (contrib, 1992), The Knights of Glin (contrib, 2009); *Clubs* Pratt's, Kildare Street and Univ, Beefsteak; *Style—* Sir Adrian FitzGerald, Bt, The Knight of Kerry; ✉ 16 Clareville Street, London SW7 5AW; Glenshelane House, Cappoquin, Co Waterford, Ireland

FITZGERALD, Christopher Francis; s of late Lt Cdr Michael Francis FitzGerald, RN, of Hove, E Sussex, and late Anne Lise, *née* Winther; *b* 17 November 1945; *Educ* Downside, Lincoln Coll Oxford (MA); *m* 1, 1968 (m dis 1984), Jennifer, *née* Willis; 1 s (Matthew b 1973), 2 da (Francesca b 1975, Julia b 1978); m 2, 1986, Jill, *née* Freshwater; 2 step da (Joanna b 1978, Victoria b 1979); *Career* admitted slr 1971; Slaughter and May: ptnr 1976–95, exec ptnr fin 1986–90, partnership Bd 1986–95; gen counsel and memb Exec Dirs' Ctee NatWest Group 1995–2000, dir The Intercare Gp plc 2001–03; chm The Macfarlane Tst 2007–12; dir: City Merchants High Yield Tst plc 2007–12, Mimecast Ltd 2007–; chm Regulatory Decisions Ctee FSA 2001–04, memb Financial Reporting Review Panel 2006–12; memb Fin Ctee Lincoln Coll Oxford 2003–; *Recreations* travelling, going to the opera, theatre and classical concerts, appreciating fine wines; *Style—* Christopher FitzGerald, Esq; ✉ 26 Lower Addison Gardens, London W14 8BQ

FITZGERALD, Edward Hamilton; CBE (2008), QC (1995); *b* 1953; *Educ* Univ of Oxford (BA), Univ of Cambridge (MPhil); *Career* called to the Bar 1978; practising barr specialising in criminal law, public law, judicial review and int human rights law, jt head Doughty Street Chambers; hon fell CCC Oxford; *Style—* Edward Fitzgerald, Esq, CBE, QC; ✉ Doughty Street Chambers, 54 Doughty Street, London WC1N 2LS

FITZGERALD, Michael John; s of Albert William Fitzgerald (d 1980), of West Chiltington, W Sussex, and Florence Margaret Fitzgerald, *née* Stannard (d 1981); *b* 14 May 1935; *Educ* Caterham Sch; *m* 9 June 1962, Judith-Ann, da of Dr A C Boyle, of Iping, W Sussex; 2 s (Alistair b 1964, Malcolm b 1966), 1 da (Aimee-Louise b 1970); *Career* CA; vice-pres and gen mangr Occidental International (Libya) Inc 1985–96, exec vice-pres Occidental International Oil Inc 1987–96; dir: Langham Publishing Ltd 1985–2000, Canadian Occidental North Sea Petroleum Ltd 1987–96, Hardy Exploration and Production (India) Inc 1999–2000, Mercury Oil and Gas Ltd 2001–07, Kew Electrical Distributors Ltd 2002–11; md OVP Associates Ltd 1996–; MInstPet, MInstD; *Recreations* golf, gardening, cricket, opera; *Clubs* West Sussex Golf, Travellers; *Style—* Michael J Fitzgerald, Esq; ✉ OVP Associates Ltd, The Stone House, Church Street, West Chiltington, West Sussex RH20 2JW (☎ 01798 812258, fax 01798 815597)

FITZGERALD, Niall William Arthur; KBE (2002); s of William FitzGerald (d 1972), and Doreen, *née* Chambers; *b* 13 September 1945, Sligo; *Educ* St Munchins Coll Limerick, UCD (MCom); *m* 1, 2 March 1970 (m dis 2003), Monica Mary, da of John Cusack (d 1985); 1 da (Tara b 5 Dec 1973), 2 s (Colin b 30 Jan 1976, Aaron b 24 March 1982); m 2, 27 Sept 2003, Ingrid van Velzen; 1 da (Gabriella b 21 April 2001); *Career* Unilever: joined Unilever Ireland as accountant 1967, various positions with subsids Paul & Vincent, Lever Bros Ireland and W & C McDonnell, Unilever Head Office London 1972–76 (PA to fin dir 1974–76), overseas commercial offr 1976–78, commercial offr N American ops 1978–80, finance dir Unilever South Africa (Pty) Ltd 1980–82, md Van den Bergh & Jurgens (Pty) Ltd South Africa 1982–85, gp treas London 1985–86, finance dir 1986–89, main bd dir Unilever plc and Unilever NV 1987–2004, edible fats and dairy co-ordinator 1989–90, detergents co-ordinator 1991–95, vice-chm Unilever plc 1994–95, exec chm Unilever plc 1996–2004, vice-chm Unilever NV 1996–2004; non-exec chm Reuters plc 2004–08 (non-exec dir 2003–08), dep chm Thomson Reuters 2008–11; chm Nijaco Ltd 2006–, chm Hakluyt & Co Ltd 2008–13 (chm Int Advsy Bd 2013–); non-exec dir: Bank of Ireland 1990–99, Prudential Corporation 1992–99, Merck 2000–03, Ericsson 2000–02; sr advsr Allen & Co; former memb Advsy Bd Spencer Stuart; former chm Europe Ctee CBI, co-chm Conference Bd (US) 2003–05, co-chm Transatlantic Business Dialogue 2004–05; former memb: Kok Cmmn on the Lisbon Agenda, Accounting Standards Review Ctee, US Business Cncl, Int Policy Cncl for Agriculture and Trade, Int Business Cncl (chm 2006–08), Fndn Bd World Economic Forum; former memb advsy bodies incl: Pres of S Africa's Int Investment Advsy Cncl, Advsy Bd Tsinghua Univ; memb Mitsubishi Int Advsy Ctee 2014–; chm of tstees Br Museum 2006–14, chm Nelson Mandela Legacy Tst (UK) 2005–08, co-chair Investment Climate Facility for Africa 2005–10, tstee Leverhulme Tst (chm 2013–), chm Munster Rugby Bd 2013–, chm Brand Learning 2013–; patron Br Irish Chamber of Commerce 2015–; chm Michael Smurfit Graduate Business Sch UCD 2014–; pres Advertising Assoc 2000–05; Distinguished Service Award Irish PM 2015; FCT 1986 (former memb Cncl), FRSA; *Recreations* opera and jazz, Irish rugby, supporting Manchester United, running (slowly), playing golf (poorly), creating an exotic garden in Sussex, observing humanity; *Clubs* RAC; *Style—* Niall FitzGerald, KBE, DSA; ✉ 103 Mount Street, 2nd Floor, London W1K 2TJ

FITZGERALD, Peter Gilbert; OBE (1993), DL (Cornwall 1999); s of P H FitzGerald (d 1995), and Hilda Elizabeth, *née* Clark (d 2010); *b* 13 February 1946; *Educ* Harvey GS Folkestone; *m* 5 Dec 1970, Elizabeth Thora, da of F L Harris (d 1970), of Cornwall; 1 s (Timothy b 24 Oct 1973); *Career* chartered accountant; dir: Valor Vanguard Ltd 1965–66, FitzGerald Lighting Ltd 1973–2008, Bodmin & Wenford Railway plc 1985–, FitzGerald Lighting Cornwall Ltd 2009–; chm Cornwall Economic and Tourism Forum 1992–99; burgess Bodmin 2001–; FCA 1972; *Recreations* cycling, walking, transport; *Style—* Peter G FitzGerald, Esq, OBE, DL; ✉ FitzGerald Lighting Cornwall Ltd, Normandy Way, Bodmin, Cornwall PL31 1EX (☎ 01208 79402)

FITZGERALD, Rodney A; *Career* qualified CA Hays Allan & Co 1979; fin dir Meespierson ICS Ltd until 1999, ceo Walker Crips Gp plc 2007– (joined as fin dir 1999); *Style—* Rodney FitzGerald, Esq; ✉ Walker Crips Group plc, Finsbury Tower, 103–105 Bunhill Row, London EC1Y 8LZ

FITZGERALD, Tara Anne Cassandra; da of Michael Callaby (d 1979), and Sarah Geraldine Fitzgerald; *b* 18 September 1967; *Educ* Walsingham Girls' Sch, The Drama Centre London; *m* Dec 2000, John Shahnazarian (d 2005); *Career* actress; prodr A Family Man (short film); *Theatre* incl: Angela Caxton in Our Song (Apollo and Bath Theatre Royal) 1992/93, Ophelia in Hamlet (Hackney Empire and Belasco Theatre NY) 1995, Antigone 1999, Blanche Du Bois in A Streetcar Named Desire (Bristol Old Vic) 2000, Nora in A Doll's House (Birmingham Rep) 2004, Mara in Clouds (Cambridge Arts) 2004, Vera Claythorne in And Then There Were None (Gielgud Theatre) 2005–06, The Misanthrope (Comedy Theatre) 2009–10, A Doll's House (Donmar Warehouse) 2009, Sylvia in Broken Glass (The Tricycle and West End) 2011, Beatrice in Farewell to the Theatre (Hampstead Theatre) 2012, Hermione in A Winter's Tale (RSC) 2013; *Television* incl: Polly Cuthbertson in The Camomile Lawn (Channel 4) 1992, Dolly Stokesay in Anglo-Saxon Attitudes (Thames), The Step-daughter in Six Characters in Search of An Author (BBC 2), Catherine Pradier in Fall from Grace (SkyTV) 1994, Poppy Carew in The Vacillations of Poppy Carew (Carlton) 1994, The Tenant of Wildfell Hall 1996, Marian in The Women in White (Carlton) 1997, Beth March in Little White Lies (BBC TV) 1998, Lady Dona St Colomb in Frenchman's Creek (Carlton) 1998, Zoe in In the Name of Love (Meridian) 1999, Monica Jones in Love Again (BBC 2) 2003, Kit Ashley in The Virgin Queen (BBC) 2005, Aunt Reed in Jane Eyre (BBC) 2006, Eve Lockhart in Waking the Dead (BBC) 2006–11, The Body Farm 2011, Selyse Baratheon in Game of Thrones 2012–, Marie de Medici in The Muskateers 2013; *Films* incl: Nancy Doyle in Hear My Song 1992, Estella Campion in Sirens 1993, Adele Rice in A Man of No Importance 1994, Betty from Cardiff in The Englishman Who Went Up a Hill But Came Down a Mountain 1994, Gloria in Brassed Off 1995, Daisy in Conquest 1998, Snow Angel in Childhood 1997, Kris in New World Disorder 1998, Susan Whitmore in Dark Blue World 2000, Clara Salvador in Secret Passage 2001, Topaz in I Capture the Castle 2001, Mum in Five Children and It 2003, Inessa Nesterov in Child 44 2013; *Awards* Drama Desk Award for outstanding featured actress in a play (for Hamlet), Reims Television Festival Best Actress 1999 (for Frenchman's Creek); *Recreations* music, cinema, painting, friends, theatre; *Clubs* Quo Vadis; *Style—* Ms Tara FitzGerald; ✉ c/o Lindy King, United Agents Limited, 12–26 Lexington Street, London W1F 0LE (☎ 020 3214 0800, fax 020 3214 0801, website www.unitedagents.co.uk)

FITZHERBERT, Sir Richard Ranulph; 9 Bt (GB 1784), of Tissington, Derbys; o s of Rev David Henry FitzHerbert, MC (d 1976), and Charmian Hyacinthe (d 2006), da of late Samuel Ranulph Allsopp, CBE, DL; suc unc, Sir John Richard Frederick FitzHerbert, 8 Bt 1989; *b* 2 November 1963; *Educ* Eton; *m* 1, 17 April 1993 (m dis 2007), Caroline Louise, da of Maj Patrick Shuter, of Ashbourne, Derbys; 1 s (Frederick David b 23 March 1995), 1 da (Francesca Norah b 21 April 1998); m 2, 28 Oct 2011, Fiona Alison, da of late Dr and Mrs John Fitzgerald; *Heir* s, Frederick FitzHerbert; *Career* pres: Derbys Community Fndn 1995–, Derbys Rural Community Cncl 1995–, Derbys Scouting Assoc 2004–; cnclr Derbys Dales District Cncl 2011–; patron Soc of Derbys Golf Captains 2006–, memb Bd HHA 2010–; *Recreations* cricket, field sports, restoring family estate and campaigning against excessive rules and regulations; *Clubs* MCC, White's, Stansted Hall CC, Parwich RBLCC, I Zingari; *Style—* Sir Richard FitzHerbert, Bt; ✉ Tissington Hall, Ashbourne, Derbyshire DE6 1RA (e-mail tisshall@dircon.co.uk, website www.tissingtonhall.co.uk)

FITZHERBERT-BROCKHOLES, Francis Joseph; eldest s of Michael John Fitzherbert-Brockholes (d 1998); *b* 18 September 1951; *Educ* Oratory Sch, CCC Oxford (MA); *m* 7 May 1983, Jennifer, da of Geoffrey George Watts, of Grassdale, Wandering, W Aust; 1 da (Susannah Louise b 23 Feb 1984), 2 s (Thomas Antony b 8 Nov 1985, George Frederick b 1 March 1988); *Career* called to the Bar 1975, admitted New York Bar 1978; in chambers Manchester 1976–77, assoc Cadwalader Wickersham & Taft 1977–78, ptnr White & Case 1985– (assoc 1978–85); *Style—* Francis Fitzherbert-Brockholes, Esq; ✉ White & Case LLP, 5 Old Broad Street, London EC2N 1DW (☎ 020 7532 1000, fax 020 7532 1001)

FITZMAURICE, Kevin; s of Charles Michael Fitzmaurice, and June, *née* Ward; *b* 12 June 1963; *Educ* LAMDA (Dip Stage Mgmnt); *m* 28 July 2001 (m dis), Rebecca Johnson; 1 da (Alice Clare b 3 March 2007), 1 s (Robert Charles b 23 Oct 2008); *Career* line prodr Almeida Theatre 1997–2001 (prodns incl: The Iceman Cometh, Richard II, Coriolanus), exec dir Young Vic Theatre 2001–09 (incl redevpt 2004–06; prodns incl: A Raisin in the Sun, Simply Heavenly, Tintin), prodr RSC 2009– (prodns incl: A Midsummer Night's Dream, The Homecoming, Comedy of Errors, Written on the Heart, A Life of Galileo, A Mad World My Masters, Love's Labour's Lost and Won, Christmas Truce, Death of a Salesman, Don Quixote); tstee LAMDA 2008–; *Style—* Kevin Fitzmaurice, Esq; ✉ Royal Shakespeare Company, Royal Shakespeare Theatre, Stratford Upon Avon, Warwickshire CV37 6BB

FITZPATRICK, Francis Paul Oliver; QC (2015); s of Thomas Fitzpatrick (d 1986), and Concepta, *née* Coote; *b* 16 April 1967, Birmingham; *Educ* Handsworth GS, Worcester Coll Oxford (MA, BCL); *m* 26 July 1997, Jessica, *née* Blakemore; 1 s (Thomas Francis Dante b 18 Feb 2003), 1 da (Miranda Grace b 21 Oct 2004); *Career* tutor in law Merton Coll Oxford 1989–91; called to the Bar Inner Temple 1990; *Recreations* cricket, fashion, opera, reading, sailing, skiing, tennis, travel, walking; *Style—* Francis Fitzpatrick, Esq, QC; ✉ 11 New Square, Lincoln's Inn, London WC2A 3QB

FITZPATRICK, Frank; s of Sean Fitzpatrick, and Constance Fitzpatrick (d 1999); *b* 1 March 1958; *Educ* St Chad's Coll Wolverhampton, Lancaster Univ (BA), Inst of Educn Univ of London (PGCE), Univ of Surrey (MA), Univ of Leicester (MBA); *m* 10 June 1997, Eugenia Lisboa; 2 da (Sara b 4 May 1993, Emma b 27 June 1997); *Career* teacher of English and teacher trainer Spain, Italy and UK 1983–94; Br Cncl: dir of studies Barcelona 1994–97, dir Oporto 1997–2000, asst dir Greece 2000–02, dir Peru 2002–06, dir and cultural attaché Macedonia 2006–; *Publications* A Teacher's Guide to Practical Pronunciation (1995); various teaching and teacher training articles in educn jls incl: Modern English Teacher, Practical English Teacher, The Teacher Trainer; *Style—* Frank Fitzpatrick, Esq; ✉ British Council, Bulevar Goce Del?ev 6, PO Box 562, 1000 Skopje, Republic of Macedonia (☎ 00 389 2 3135 035, fax 00 389 2 3135 036, e-mail frank.fitzpatrick@britishcouncil.org.mk, website www.britishcouncil.org/macedonia)

FITZPATRICK, James (Jim); MP; s of James Fitzpatrick, of Glasgow, and Jean, *née* Stones; *b* 4 April 1952; *Educ* Holyrood Sr Secdy Glasgow; *Children* 1 s (James b 1981), 1 da (Helen b 1982); *Career* with London Fire Brigade 1974–97, memb Nat Exec Cncl Fire Brigades Union 1988–97; MP (Lab): Poplar and Canning Town 1997–2010, Poplar and Limehouse 2010–; asst Govt whip 2001–02, a Lord Cmmr (Govt whip) 2002–03, vice-chamberlain HM's Household 2003–05, min for London 2005, Parly sec ODPM 2005–06, Parly under sec of state DTI 2006–09, min of state for farming and the environment 2009–10; vol agent Barking Constituency Lab Pty 1986–92, memb Exec London Lab Pty 1988–, chm Gtr London Lab Pty 1991–; govr Eastbury Comp Sch 1993–2000; awarded Fire Brigade Long Service and Good Conduct Medal; *Recreations* reading, football (West Ham United), TV and film; *Style—* Jim Fitzpatrick, MP; ✉ House of Commons, London SW1A 0AA (☎ 020 7219 5085 or 020 7219 6215, e-mail jim.fitzpatrick.mp@parliament.uk)

FITZPATRICK, Joe; MSP; s of Joseph Kelly Fitzpatrick, and Margaret M, *née* Crabb (d 2006); *b* 1 April 1967, Dundee; *Educ* Whitfield HS, Inverness Coll of Further and Higher Educn, Univ of Abertay Dundee (BSc); *Career* asst to Shona Robison, MSP 1999–2007, cnclr Dundee City Cncl 1999–2007, asst to Stewart Hosie, MSP 2005–07; MSP (SNP): Dundee West 2007–11, Dundee City West 2011–; memb NUJ; *Style—* Joe Fitzpatrick, Esq, MSP; ✉ The Scottish Parliament, Edinburgh EH99 1SP (☎ 01382 623200, fax 01382 903205, e-mail parliament@joefitzpatrick.net)

FITZPATRICK, Martin David; s of Francis Arthur Fitzpatrick, and Rosaria Anna Trofimena, *née* di Palma; *b* 10 July 1967, London; *Educ* Bancroft's Sch Essex, Balliol Coll Oxford (MA), GSM (Dip), Nat Opera Studio London; *m* 17 April 2001, Emer, *née* McGilloway; 1 da (Elizabeth Mary b 12 May 2002), 1 s (David James b 17 Jan 2005); *Career* music staff

F

Scottish Opera 1991–94, chorus master Opera North 1994–98, head of music Royal Danish Opera 1998–2001, head of music ENO 2003–; *Style—* Martin Fitzpatrick, Esq

FITZPATRICK, (Francis) Michael John; s of Francis Latimer FitzPatrick (d 1982), of East Bergholt, Suffolk, and Kathleen Margaret, *née* Gray (d 1997); *b* 14 July 1938; *Educ* Brentwood Sch; *m* 4 April 1964, Patricia Hilbery, OBE, da of Sir George Frederick Chaplin, CBE, DL, JP (d 1975), of Great Warley, Essex; 1 s (Richard b 1965), 1 da (Kathryn b 1967); *Career* chartered surveyor; Freeman City of London; FRICS; *Recreations* music, travel, wine, voluntary work; *Clubs* Royal Over-Seas League; *Style—* Michael J FitzPatrick, Esq; ✉ Bramling House, Hop Meadow, East Bergholt, Suffolk CO7 6QR

FITZPATRICK, Nicholas David; s of Prof Reginald Jack Fitzpatrick, of Heswall, Merseyside, and Ruth, *née* Holmes; *b* 23 January 1947; *Educ* Bristol GS, Univ of Nottingham (BA); *m* 23 Aug 1969, (Patricia) Jill, da of Peter Conway Brotherton; 1 da (Paula b 14 Dec 1973), 1 s (Daniel b 12 Jan 1976); *Career* trainee analyst Friends Provident 1969–72, equity mangr Abbey Life 1972–76, equity mangr then investment mangr BR Pension Fund 1976–86, ptnr and investment specialist Bacon & Woodrow 1986–2002, global investment ldr Hewitt Assocs 2002–05, assoc BESTrustees 2006–; FIA 1974, FSIP 2007; *Recreations* rugby, canal boats, woodturning; *Style—* Nicholas Fitzpatrick, Esq; ✉ Sommarlek, Woodhurst Park, Oxted, Surrey (☎ 01883 717927, e-mail ndfitz@gmail.com)

FITZSIMONS, Prof James Thomas; s of Robert Allen Fitzsimons, FRCS, and Dr Mary Patricia Fitzsimons, *née* McKelvey; *b* 8 July 1928; *Educ* St Edmund's Coll Ware, Gonville & Caius Coll Cambridge (MB BChir, MA, PhD, MD, ScD); *m* 1961, Aude Irène Jeanne, da of Gén Jean Etienne Valluy, DSO; 2 s, 1 da; *Career* house appts Leicester Gen and Charing Cross Hosps 1954–55; Flying Offr then Flight Lt RAF Inst of Aviation Med 1955–57; Univ of Cambridge: MRC scholar Physiological Lab 1957–59, demonstrator in physiology 1959–64, lectr 1964–76, reader 1976–90, prof of med physiology 1990–95, emeritus prof 1995–; Gonville & Caius Coll Cambridge: fell 1961–, tutor 1964–72, lectr in physiology 1964–93, dir of studies in med 1978–93, pres 1997–2005; memb: Physiological Soc Ctee 1972–76 (chm 1975–76), International Union of Physiological Sciences (IUPS) Cmmn on Physiology of Food and Fluid Intake 1973–80 (chm 1979–80); Royal Soc rep British Nat Ctee for Physiological Scis 1976–80; ed Biological Reviews 1984–95; Distinguished Career Award Soc for the Study of Ingestive Behavior 1998; Hon MD Lausanne 1978; FRS 1988; *Books* The Physiology of Thirst and Sodium Appetite (1979); author of scientific papers in professional jls; *Style—* Prof James Fitzsimons, FRS; ✉ Gonville & Caius College, Cambridge CB2 1TA (☎ 01223 332429, e-mail jtf10@cam.ac.uk)

FITZWALTER, Raymond Alan; s of Robert Fitzwalter (d 1997), of Bury, Lancs, and Lucy, *née* Fox (d 2000); *b* 21 February 1944; *Educ* Derby Sch, LSE (BScEcon); *m* 1, 6 Aug 1966 (m dis 1993), Mary, da of Richard Towman (d 1989), of Bury, Lancs; 2 s (Stephen Anthony b 24 Nov 1968, Matthew Paul b 11 Aug 1970), 1 da (Kathryn Anne b 16 Dec 1974); m 2, 7 May 1994, Ann Luise Nandy, da of Baron Byers (Life Peer, d 1984); *Career* Bradford Telegraph and Argus: trainee journalist 1965–67, feature writer 1967–68, dep news ed 1968–70; Granada TV: exec prodr World in Action 1986–93 (researcher 1970–75, prodr 1975–76, ed 1976–86), commissioning exec news and current affrs 1987–89, head of current affrs 1989–93, exec prodr What The Papers Say and drama documentaries 1989–93; independent prodr Ray Fitzwalter Associates Ltd 1993–; visiting fell Univ of Salford 1993–2002 (visiting prof 2002–10); northern rep and memb Cncl PACT 1994–2002, chm Campaign for Quality Television 1995–2006, chm Editorial Bd Bureau of Investigative Journalism 2009–; CPU scholar to Pakistan 1969, Young Journalist of the Year IPC Awards 1970 (commended 1968), BAFTA award best factual series for World in Action 1987, RTS awards for World in Action 1981, 1983 and 1985, BAFTA Desmond Davis award for outstanding creative contrib to TV 1991; FRTS 1993; *Books* Web of Corruption: The Story of John Poulson and T Dan Smith (with David Taylor, 1981), The Dream that Died: the rise and fall of ITV (2008); *Recreations* chess, naval history, a garden; *Style—* Raymond Fitzwalter, Esq; ✉ Ray Fitzwalter Associates, Stone Cottage, 115 Holcombe Old Road, Holcombe, Bury, Lancashire BL8 4NF (☎ 01706 828054, e-mail ray@fitzwalter.co.uk)

FITZWILLIAMS, Duncan John Lloyd; s of Charles Collinsplat Lloyd Fitzwilliams, (d 1984), of Newcastle Emlyn, Carmarthenshire, and Rosamond Muriel, *née* Hill (d 2003); *b* 24 May 1943; *Educ* Harrow, St Edmund Hall Oxford (MA); *m* 1, 1968, Hon Sarah Samuel, da of 4 Viscount Bearsted; m 2, 1978, Anna, da of Gp Capt Rex Williams, of Newton Ferrers, Devon; 2 da (Angharad, Victoria), 1 s (Logie); *Career* chm and jt fndr CASE plc 1969–88; dir: Foreign and Colonial Investment Trust plc 1973–91, Foreign and Colonial Pacific Investment Trust plc 1975–89, Anvil Petroleum plc 1975–85, Flextech Holdings plc 1976–86, Walker Greenbank plc 1977–88, Venture Link Ltd (chm) 1978–87, Henry Venture Fund II Inc (USA) 1985–, Lazard Leisure Fund 1986–94, Bespak plc 1986–2000 (Audit and Remuneration Ctee), Oakes Fitzwilliams & Co Ltd 1987–, Axa Fund Managers SA 2000– (chm Audit Ctee); co chm Quadrant Healthcare plc 1992–2000; memb Bd City Friends of Templeton Coll Oxford, former memb Info Technol Panel LSE; govr Harrow Sch; coracle champion of River Teifi 1956; MIIMR 1974; *Recreations* fishing, golf, history; *Clubs* White's, MCC, Berkshire Golf, The Brook (NY); *Style—* Duncan Fitzwilliams, Esq; ✉ Fisher's Copse House, Bradfield, Reading, Berkshire RG7 6LN (☎ 0118 974 4527); Nash Fitzwilliams & Co Ltd, 49 Albemarle Street, London W1S 4JR (☎ 020 7355 0450, fax 020 7355 0451, e-mail dfitzwilliams@nashfitzwilliams.com)

FITZWILLIAMS, Richard Brathwaite Lloyd; s of Maj Robert Campbell Lloyd Fitzwilliams, TD (d 2001), and Natalie Jura Stratford, *née* Mardall (d 1965); the family has four registered Royal Descents from Ethelred II (Ethelred the Unready), Edward I (through the Howards), Edward III and Malcolm II, King of Scots, all through Richard Fitzwilliams' ggg grandmother Jane Maria, da and co-heir of Adm Richard Brathwaite; *b* 14 October 1949; *Educ* Univ of Cape Town (BA, three Lestrade scholarships); *m* 16 Nov 1981 (m dis 1995), Gillian, da of Frederick William Savill, of Blaby, Leics; *Career* worked on project for Shadow Min of Educn United Party SA 1972, Europa Publications London 1972–2001, ed Int Who's Who 1975–2001, head Fitzwilliams Assocs 2001–; PR conslt: Belgravia Gallery, Maria Andipa Gallery 2001, RSPP 2002–, Fedn of Br Artists 2002–, The Threadneedle Prize 2008–12, The Lynn Painter-Stainers Prize 2009–13; acts for the artist Daphne Todd and the sculptress Shenda Amery; promoter of numerous art exhibitions; over 600 TV interviews and many on radio as royal commentator, film critic, arts reviewer and contrib: CNN, Sky News, Arise Tv, BBC Breakfast TV, BBC News Channel, ITV News, Al Jazeera, Channel 4, Channel 5, BBC World, CBC, CTV, BBC Radio 4, BBC Radio 2, BBC Wales, BBC Ulster, BBC Scotland, BBC GNS, TalkSport, Radio 5 Live, LBC, BBC London, BBC World Serv, Talk Radio, RTE, Radio New Zealand, Newstalk (Ireland), Newstalk ZB (NZ); film critic: Talk Radio Europe (Spain) 2007–, Siren FM (Lincoln) 2011–; film awards commentator Oscars, Golden Globes, BAFTAs; contrib London and UK Datebook 1997–, also articles in Daily Express, Cwlth Jl of Int Affrs and CNN.com; gives talks to clubs and societies and also guest lectr to several univs (topics incl Mutiny on the Bounty (has a family connection with Capt Bligh), royal matters, portraiture, the honours system and Who's Who); memb: Hampstead and Highgate Cons Assoc (former memb Town and Frognal Ward Ctee, former memb Exec Cncl), YMCA; *Recreations* cinema, theatre, entertaining, travel, swimming, exploring large cities; *Clubs* Naval and Military; *Style—* Richard B L Fitzwilliams, Esq; ✉ Fitzwilliams Associates, 84 North End Road, London NW11 7SY (☎ 020 8455 7393, mobile 07939 602749, e-mail richardfitzwilliams@hotmail.com, website www.richardfitzwilliams.com, Twitter @rfitzwilliams)

FIVET, Edmond Charles Paul; CBE (2008); *b* 12 February 1947, London; *Educ* St Marks Sch London, RCM (ARCM), Coll of St Mark & St John London (CertEd), Open Univ (pt/t BA), City Univ (pt/t MA); *m*; 1 step s; 2 c from previous m; *Career* professional freelance teacher and performer 1965–71, head of brass Surrey CC 1971–73, dir Jr Dept RCM 1983–89 (registrar 1973–82), princ Royal Welsh Coll of Music and Drama 1989–2007, fndr and dir of music Prometheus Orch 2008–; external examiner for BMus Birmingham Conservatoire 1995–98; Assoc Bd of the Royal Schs of Music: examiner 1977–92, memb Consultative Ctee 1984–86, memb Examinations Bd 1986–89, memb Diploma Bd 2009–11; music dir Audi Jr Musician (nat competition for 12–16 year olds) 1986–97, chair Concert Promoters Gp Making Music 2011–15, chair of adjudicators Bromsgrove Int Young Musicians Comp 2011–; memb: Nat Assoc of Youth Orchs 1983–84, Working Party Nat Fndn for Educnl Research LEA Instrumental Provision 1986–88, Ctee Welsh Colls of HE 1989–2007, Assoc of Euro Conservatoires 1989–2007, Conservatoires UK 1990–2007, Ctee Nat Centre for Dance and Choreography 1994–96, HE Wales 1996–2007; vice-pres Arts Cncl Richmond-upon-Thames (memb Exec Ctee 1982–86, vice-chm 1984–86), chm Richmond Music Festival 1985–94, chair Bury St Edmunds Concert Club 2007–, music dir Aldeburgh Music Club Choir 2007–, music dir Phoenix Singers 2008–12; chm Nat Youth Arts Focus Gp 1998–2005; memb: Music Ctee Welsh Arts Cncl 1991–94, Music Ctee Cardiff Int Festival 1992–95, Arts Cncl of Wales 2000–06; tstee Millennium Stadium Charitable Tst 2002–05; Hon Doctorate Univ of Glamorgan 2008; FRCM 1988, Hon FBC 2005, FRWCMD 2007; *Recreations* golf, reading, theatre, music, current affairs; *Clubs* Savile, Aldeburgh Golf; *Style—* Edmond Fivet, Esq, CBE; ✉ Fair Winds, 11 North Warren, Aldeburgh, Suffolk IP15 5QF(☎ 01728 454992, e-mail edmond@fivet.co.uk)

FLACK, Mervyn Charles; s of Maj Henry George Flack (d 1978), and Marjorie, *née* Lofthouse (d 1991); *b* 30 June 1942; *Educ* Raynes Park Co GS, Northampton Coll of Advanced Technol; *m* 5 Oct 1963, Margaret Elizabeth, da of George Robert Cumnock (d 1983); 1 s (James b 3 Nov 1969), 1 da (Emma b 2 Oct 1975); *Career* asst statistician, res analyst Gillette Industries Ltd 1962–67, co statistician Marplan Ltd 1967–69, chief statistician Attwood Statistics Ltd 1969–70, dir Opinion Research Centre 1971–79, dep md Louis Harris International 1978–79 (res dir 1973–78); chm City Research Associates Ltd 1980–2000, dir Applied Research & Communications Ltd 1995–2000, chm and chief exec City Research Group plc 1990–2000, dir Yankee Delta Corp Ltd 2001–03 and 2005–, sr ptnr Mervyn Flack & Associates, dir Charterhouse Research Ltd 2004–; memb: Market Research Soc, Cncl Assoc of Br Market Research Cos 1981–84, Cncl Br Market Research Assoc 1998–99; author various articles on market research; memb Aircraft Owners and Pilots Assoc, memb Goodwood Road Racing Club; MInstD; FSS 1963, FIS 1978 (MIS 1964), FMRS 2010 (MMRS 1968); *Recreations* private pilot, food, wine; *Style—* Mervyn Flack, Esq; ✉ Mervyn Flack & Associates, Maldons, Pendell Road, Bletchingley, Surrey RH1 4QH (☎ 01883 740370, e-mail mervyn@maldons.co.uk)

FLAHIVE, His Hon Judge Daniel Michael; *Career* called to the Bar 1982; recorder 2003, circuit judge (South Eastern Circuit) 2009–; judicial memb Parole Bd 2010–13; *Style—* His Hon Judge Flahive; ✉ c/o The South Eastern Circuit, 289–293 High Holborn, London WC1V 7HZ

FLANAGAN, Andrew Henry; s of Francis Andrew Desmond Flanagan, of Glasgow, and late Martha Gilmour White, *née* Donaldson; *b* 15 March 1956; *Educ* Hillhead HS Glasgow, Univ of Glasgow (BAcc); *m* 21 March 1992, Virginia Annette, da of James Richard Alastair Walker; *Career* articled clerk Touche Ross 1976–79, audit sr Price Waterhouse 1979–81, fin mangr ITT Europe Inc 1981–86, dir of fin Europe PA Consulting Group 1986–91, gp fin dir The BIS Group Ltd 1991–93; SMG plc (formerly Scottish Television plc then Scottish Media Group plc): gp fin dir 1994–96, md 1996, chief exec 1996–2006; chief exec NSPCC 2008–13, Civil Service cmmr for Scotland 2013–; chm Fleming Media until 2009; non-exec dir Scottish Rugby, non-exec dir NHS N & E London Cmmng Support 2013–, non-exec dir NHS Business Services Authy 2014–, non-exec dir CIPFA Business Services Ltd 2014–, non-exec dir Criminal Injuries Compensation Authy 2014–, chm Scottish Police Authy 2015–; Union 2000–05; MICAS; *Recreations* golf, jogging, skiing, cinema, reading, television; *Style—* Andrew Flanagan, Esq

FLANAGAN, Mary; da of Martin James Flanagan (d 1981), and Mary, *née* Nesbitt (d 1977); *b* 20 May 1943, Rochester, NH, USA; *Educ* Brandeis Univ (BA); *Career* writer; began writing 1979; works to date: Bad Girls (collection of short stories, 1984), Trust (1987), Rose Reason (1991), The Blue Woman (collection of short stories, 1994), Adèle (1997); critic for: Sunday Times, Evening Standard, New Statesman, The Independent, The Observer, The New York Times Book Review, Art Quarterly; teacher of creative writing: UEA 1995 and 1997, Birkbeck Coll London 2004–12, City Lit 2006–16; memb: Soc of Authors 1986, PEN (English and American) 1990; Royal Literary Fund Fellowship Univ of Leicester 2001–03; *Recreations* gardening, music, environmental campaigner; *Style—* Ms Mary Flanagan; ✉ c/o Clare Alexander, Aitken/Alexander Associates, 18–21 Cavaye Place, London SW10

FLANDERS, Stephanie Hope; da of Michael Flanders (d 1975), and Claudia Davis (d 1998); *b* 5 August 1968; *Educ* Balliol Coll Oxford, Harvard Univ; *Partner* John Arlidge; 1 s (Stanley b 2006), 1 da (Claudia b 2008); *Career* ldr writer and columnist FT 1994–97, speechwriter and advsr to US Treas Sec 1997–2001, NY Times 2001, economics ed Newsnight (BBC 2) 2002–08, economics ed BBC 2008–; visiting fell Nuffield Coll Oxford 2008–; memb Gen Cncl Royal Economic Soc; *Style—* Ms Stephanie Flanders; ✉ Room 4220, Television Centre, Wood Lane, London W12 7RJ

FLANNAGAN, Mark; *b* 16 March 1963, Newcastle-upon-Tyne; *Educ* Univ of St Andrews (MA); *Career* asst dir Action on Smoking and Health 1986–93, sr press offr BBC 1993–96, asst dir external affrs Royal Coll of Nursing 1996–97, campaigns dir Diabetes UK 1997–2000, ind conslt 2000–04, dir of communications and campaigning Crisis 2004–05, md New Tricks Communications Ltd 2005–08, dir of policy and communications Royal Coll of GPs 2008–10, chief exec Beating Bowel Cancer 2010–; chair Groundwork West London 2005–08, non-exec dir Groundwork London 2008–11; *Style—* Mark Flannagan, Esq; ✉ 94 Broadway, Knaphill, Woking, Surrey GU21 2RH (☎ 01483 838169, mobile 07827 276507, Twitter @markflannceo); Beating Bowel Cancer, Harlequin House, 7 High Street, Teddington TW11 8EE (☎ 08450 719300, direct tel 020 8973 0007, e-mail mark.flannagan@beatingbowelcancer.org, website www.beatingbowelcancer.org)

FLATHER, Gary Denis; OBE (1999), QC (1984); s of Joan Ada, *née* Walker; *b* 4 October 1937; *Educ* Oundle, Pembroke Coll Oxford; *m* Shreela (The Baroness Flather), *qv*, da of Aftab Rai; *Career* 2 Lt 1 Bn York and Lancaster Regt 1956–58, Hallamshire Bn TA 1958–61; called to the Bar Inner Temple 1962 (bencher and memb Scholarships Ctee 1995), recorder of the Crown Court 1986–2010 (asst recorder 1983–86), dep judge of the High Court 1997–2010; memb Panel of Chairmen ILEA Disciplinary Tbnl 1974–90, asst Parly boundary cmmr 1982–90, inspr DTI for enquiries under Fin Servs Act 1987–88; chm (jtly): Police Disciplinary Appeal Tbnl 1987–, MOD Police Disciplinary Appeal Tbnl 1991–; legal memb Mental Health Review Tbnl 1987–2010; legal assessor: GMC 1987–95, Gen Dental Cncl 1987–95, RCVS 2000–08; chm: Statutory Ctee Royal Pharmaceutical Soc of GB 1990–2000, Disciplinary Ctee CIM 1995, Special Educational Needs and Disability Tbnl (SENDIST) 2004–08, Private Patients' Forum 2011–12; dir Fearnehough (Bakewell) Ltd 1990–2002; escort to Mayor Royal Borough of Windsor and Maidenhead 1986–87, vice-pres Community Cncl for Berkshire 1987–2001, ind person Royal Borough of Windsor and Maidenhead 2012–; pres Maidenhead Rotary 1990–91; chm Bar Cncl

Disability Ctee 1990–2002, memb Bar Cncl Equal Opportunities Ctee 1998–2002, hon memb of the Bar 2002; tstee: ADAPT 1995–2006, The Disabled Living Fndn 1997–2003; cmmr Royal Hosp Chelsea 2005–11; Hon MRPharmS 2001; *Recreations* travel, music, dogs, coping with Multiple Sclerosis; *Style*— Gary Flather, Esq, OBE, QC; ✉ 4/5 Gray's Inn Square, London WC1R 5AY (☎ 020 7404 5252, e-mail garyflather@hotmail.co.uk)

FLATHER, Baroness (Life Peer UK 1990), of Windsor and Maidenhead in the Royal County of Berkshire; Shreela Flather; JP (1971), DL (Berks 1994); da of Rai Bahadur Aftab Rai (d 1972), and Krishna Rai (d 1989); *Educ* UCL (LLB, fell); *m* Gary Denis Flather, QC, *qv*; 2 s (Hon Paul, Hon Marcus); *Career* called to the Bar Inner Temple; infant teacher ILEA 1965–67; teacher of English as second language: Altwood Comp Sch Maidenhead 1968–74, Broadmoor Hosp 1974–78; cncllr Royal Borough of Windsor and Maidenhead 1976–91; pres Cambs Chilterns and Thames Rent Assessment Panel, vice-pres Building Socs Assoc 1976–91; vice-chm and fndr memb Maidenhead Community Rels Cncl, vice-chm Maidenhead Volunteer Centre, vice-chm and memb Mgmnt Ctee CAB, vice-chm Estates and Amenities and Leisure Ctees Royal Borough of Windsor and Maidenhead; fndr New Star Boys' Club for Asian boys, fndr summer sch project for Asian children in Maidenhead; sec Windsor and Maidenhead Cons Gp, sec and organiser Maidenhead Ladies' Asian Club 1968–78; community rels advsr Berks Girl Guides, race rels tutor for sr police offrs' courses; memb: Lord Chllr's Legal Aid Advsy Ctee 1958–88, W Met Conciliation Ctee of Race Rels Bd 1973–78, Cons Women's Nat Ctee 1975–89, Swann Ctee (enquiry into educn of children from ethnic minority gps) 1979–85, Cmmn for Racial Equality 1980–86, Bd of Visitors Holloway Prison 1981–83, Police Complaints Bd 1982–85, HRH Duke of Edinburgh's Ctee of Enquiry into Br Housing 1984–85, Broadmoor Hosp Bd 1987–88, Berks FPC 1987–88, BBC South and East Regnl Advsy Ctee, Dist Youth and Community Ctee, UK delgn to Econ and Social Ctee EC 1987–90, Exec Ctee Anglo-Asian Cons Soc, Social Security Advsy Ctee 1987–90, Servite Houses Ctee of Mgmnt, Nat Union Exec Ctee Cons Pty 1989–90, exec ctees of Br sections Int Unions of Local Authys, LWT Prog Advsy Bd 1990–93, Select Ctee Medical Ethics 1993–94, Bar Cncl Equal Opportunities Ctee 2002–03; non-exec dir: Thames Valley Training and Enterprise 1990–93, United News and Media (Meridian Broadcasting Ltd) 1991–2001; dir: Daytime TV Ltd 1978–79, Marie Stopes Int 1996–, Cable Corp 1997–2000, Kiss and Magic FM Ltd 2000–02, Bookpower 2001–07; chm: STARFM 101.6, Local Independent Radio Slough, Windsor and Maidenhead 1992–97, Ethics Ctee Broadmoor Hosp 1993–97, Alcohol Education and Research Cncl 1995–2002, Memorial Gates Tst 1998–2009 (meml now on Constitution Hill), Club Asia 2002–06; vice-chm Indo-Br Parly Gp, tstee Sir William Borlase Sch Marlow 1991–97; pres: Broadmoor League of Friends 1991–98, Berkshire Community Cncl 1991–98, Soc of Friends of the Lotus Children 1996–99, Global Money Transfer Ltd 1997–2001, Alumni Assoc of UCL 1998–2000; vice-pres: Assoc of District Cncls 1990–97, Townswomens Guilds, Servite Houses Housing Assoc, Careers Nat Assoc, Br Assoc of Counselling and Psychotherapy 1999–; vice-chm The Refugee Cncl 1991–96; patron Corona Worldwide; memb: Thames and Chilterns Tourist Bd 1987–88, Spoore Merry and Rixman Fndn, Poole's Charity, Ring's Charity, Hillingdon Hosp Tst 1990–98; UK rep on EU Advsy Cmmn on Racism and Xenophobia 1995–97; govr: Slough Coll of HE 1984–89, Cwlth Inst 1993–98; tstee: Rajiv Gandhi (UK) Fndn 1993–2001, Pan African Health Fndn 2004–12; memb: Cncl of Winston Churchill Meml Tst 1993–2008, Cncl of St George's House Windsor Castle 1996–2002, UK Advsy Cncl Asia House, Advsy Cncl American Intercontinental Univ 2004–06; lay memb UCL Cncl 2000–06; patron L'Orchestre du Monde 2014–, patron Women's Cncl; Mayor Royal Borough of Windsor and Maidenhead 1986–87 (Dep Mayor 1985–86); Hon Dr Open Univ 1994, Hon LLD Univ of Leeds 2008, hon doctorate Univ of Northampton 2010; Asian of the Year Asian Who's Who 1996, Asian Jewel Award 2003; FRSA 1999; Pravasi Diwas Samman (India) 2009; *Books* Woman – Acceptable Exploitation for Profit (2010); *Recreations* travel, cinema; *Style*— The Baroness Flather, JP, DL, FRSA; ✉ House of Lords, London SW1A 0PW (fax 01628 675355)

FLAUX, Hon Mr Justice; Sir Julian Martin Flaux; kt (2007); s of Louis Michael Flaux (d 2003), of Malvern, Worcs, and Maureen Elizabeth Brenda, *née* Coleman; *b* 11 May 1955; *Educ* King's Sch Worcester, Worcester Coll Oxford (MA, BCL); *m* 24 Sept 1983, Matilda Christian, da of Michael Hansard Gabb, of Canterbury, Kent; 3 s; *Career* called to the Bar Inner Temple 1978; in practice 1979–2007, QC 1994, recorder, judge of the High Court 2007–, presiding judge of the Midland Circuit 2010–13; *Recreations* walking, reading, opera; *Clubs* Garrick; *Style*— The Hon Mr Justice Flaux; ✉ Royal Courts of Justice, Strand, London WC2A 2LL

FLECK, Andrew; *Career* head Ashville Coll until 2010, head Sedbergh Sch 2010–; *Style*— Andrew Fleck, Esq

FLECK, Prof Norman A; *b* 11 May 1958; *Educ* Friends' GS Lisburn, Jesus Coll Cambridge (Coll Scholar, Rex Moir Prize, Percival Prize, Baker Prize, Keller Prize, MA), Pembroke Coll Cambridge (PhD); *Career* research fell Pembroke Coll Cambridge 1983–84, visiting scholar Harvard Univ 1984–85, research fell NASA Langley 1985; Univ of Cambridge: lectr in engrg 1985–94, fell Pembroke Coll 1985–, reader in mechanics of materials 1994–97, prof of mechanics of materials 1997–, also currently dir Cambridge Centre for Micromechanics; visiting scholar Harvard Univ 1989, 1993 and 1995; memb Editorial Bd: Jl of Composites: Technology and Research, Mechanics of Composite Materials and Structures; conslt: Thomas Broadbent & Sons, Cegelec, London International Group, Weston Medical Ltd; author of numerous book chapters and articles in learned jls; hon doctorate Einhoven Univ 2014; foreign assoc US Nat Acad of Engrg 2014; FIMMM 1997, CEng 1997, FRS 2004, FREng 2008; *Style*— Prof Norman Fleck; ✉ Engineering Department, University of Cambridge, Trumpington Street, Cambridge CB2 1PZ (☎ 01223 748240, fax 01223 332662, e-mail nafl@eng.cam.ac.uk)

FLECK, Richard John Hugo; CBE (2009); s of Peter Hugo Fleck (d 1975), and Fiona Charis Elizabeth Miller; *b* 30 March 1949; *Educ* Marlborough, Univ of Southampton (LLB); *m* 1983, Mary, da of Wing Cdr Frederick Thomas Gardiner, DFC; 1 da (Sara Katherine Victoria b 10 May 1987), 1 s (Peter Frederick Hugo b 3 March 1990); *Career* ptnr Herbert Smith 1980–2009 (joined 1971); chair Int Ethics Standards Bd for Accountants Advsy Gp 2006–13, chm Financial Reporting Review Panel 2012–15; dir Nat Audit Office 2009–12; memb: Auditing Practices Ctee 1986–91, Auditing Practices Bd 1991–2012 (chm 2003–12), Financial Reporting Cncl Ltd 2004–13; chm Incorporated Cncl of Law Reporting for England and Wales 2012–, memb Int Ethics Standards Bd for Accountants 2015–; chm Holburne Museum 2012–; Freeman City of London, Master Worshipful Co of Tallow Chandlers 2016–17; memb Law Soc; *Recreations* sailing, real tennis, golf, shooting, rackets; *Clubs* MCC, Royal Ocean Racing, Athenaeum, City Law, Jesters, Itchenor Sailing, Petworth House Tennis, Royal Yacht Squadron; *Style*— Richard Fleck, Esq, CBE; ✉ Herbert Smith Freehills LLP, Exchange House, Primrose Street, London EC2A 2EG (☎ 020 7374 8000)

FLEETWOOD, Sheriff Gordon; WS (1995); s of John Edward Fleetwood, of Lossiemouth, Morayshire, and Isabel Ann, *née* Roy; *b* 3 October 1951, Elgin, Morayshire; *Educ* Elgin Academy, Univ of Edinburgh (LLB); *m* 15 Nov 1975, Jean Swanson, *née* Arthur; 2 da (Jennifer b 1981, Gillian b 1983); *Career* slr; More & Co 1977–82, Sutherland & Co 1982–86, Fleetwood & Robb 1986–2004; pt/t sheriff 2003–14, Sheriff of Grampian, Highlands & Islands 2014–; memb Parole Bd for Scotland 2010–14; *Recreations* curling, salmon fishing; *Style*— Sheriff Gordon Fleetwood; ✉ Inverness Sheriff Court, The Castle, Inverness

FLELLO, Robert; MP; *b* 14 January 1966, Birmingham; *Educ* King's Norton Boys' Sch, UCNW Bangor; *Career* Inland Revenue 1987–89, Price Waterhouse 1989–95, Arthur Andersen 1995–99, Platts Flello Ltd 1999–2004, Malachi Community Tst 2004–05, MP (Lab) Stoke-on-Trent S 2005–; cncllr (Lab) Birmingham City Cncl 2002–04, regnl organiser Lab Pty 2004–05; memb: Co-op Pty, TGWU, Amicus, Unity; *Style*— Robert Flello, Esq, MP; ✉ House of Commons, London SW1A 0AA

FLEMING, David; OBE (1997); s of Jack Fleming, of Leeds, and Doreen, *née* Wordsworth; *b* 25 December 1952; *Educ* Temple Moor GS Leeds, LSE, Univ of Leeds (BA), Univ of Leicester (MA, PhD); *Partner* Alison Jane Hastings; 4 c (Breton b 31 August 1973, Mitya b 16 July 1983, Callum b 17 June 1987, Ruby b 8 June 2001); *Career* curator: Yorkshire Museum of Farming 1981–83, Collection Servs Leeds Museums 1983–85; princ keeper of museums Hull Museums 1985–90, dir Tyne & Wear Museums 1991–2001 (asst dir 1990–91), dir Nat Museums & Galleries on Merseyside 2001–; pres Museums Assoc; tstee: Nat Football Museum, St George's Hall Liverpool; AMA 1986, FRSA 1997; *Style*— Dr David Fleming, OBE; ✉ National Museums & Galleries on Merseyside, PO Box 33, 127 Dale Street, Liverpool L69 3LA (fax 0151 478 4321)

FLEMING, Prof George; *b* 16 August 1944, Glasgow; *Educ* Univ of Strathclyde (BSc), Univ of Strathclyde/Stanford Univ (PhD); *Career* vice-pres/dir Hydrocomp International California and Glasgow 1969–77, conslt Watson Hawksley High Wycombe 1980–92; Univ of Strathclyde: lectr 1971–76, sr lectr 1976–82, reader 1982–85, vice-dean Faculty of Engrg 1984–87, personal prof 1985–86, chair prof Dept of Civil Engrg 1986–2002 (emeritus prof 2002–), dir Water and Environmental Mgmnt Unit 1986–2002 (Better Environment Award for Industry RSA 1987), head Div of Water Engrg and Environmental Mgmnt 1989–2002, head Dept of Civil Engrg 1991–93, chm Mgmnt Gp David Livingstone Inst 1992–2002, md Centre for Environmental Mgmnt Studies Ltd 1993–, md Envirocentre 1996–2007 (chm 2007–), memb Senate 1996–2002, dir Centre for Environmental Mgmnt Res 1998–2002; visiting prof Padova Univ Italy 1980–88; conslt Clydeport Ltd (formerly Clyde Port Authy) 1987–2000, dir Scottish Consultants International 1987–91; memb: Scottish Exports Forum 1985, Overseas Projects Bd DTI 1991–95, Br Cncl Environment Sci & Engrg Advsy Cncl 1998–2000, Smeatonian Soc for Civil Engrs 1998–; chm: Glasgow and W of Scotland Assoc of Civil Engrs 1984–85, Cncl ICE 1985–89, Environment Ctee SERC 1985–89, Engrg Ctee Royal Acad of Engrg 1988–91, Scottish Contaminated Land Forum 1995–96, Advsy Panel Land Tst 1997, Steering Gp Telford Challenge 1998–2001, Engrgs Against Poverty 2001–, Clyde River Fndn 2000–03, ICE Cmmn on River Flood Risk Mgmnt 2001–02; pres ICE 1999–2000 (vice-pres 1996–99); non-exec dir: WRAP 2001–07, Br Waterways 2001–07, Port of Tyne 2005–10; conslt to numerous nat and int orgns incl: UN Food and Agriculture Orgn, ILO, World Meteorological Orgn; conslt to govt agencies incl: Scottish Devpt Agency, S of Scotland Electricity Bd, Central Electricity Generating Bd; conslt to private companies incl: Babtie Shaw and Morton, Binnie and Partners, Mott MacDonald, Bovis, Wimpey Waste; significant projects incl: dams in Kenya Labuan and Brunei, Strathclyde Park Reservoir, Dinorwig Power Station Project, reservoir mgmnt in the Alps, flood control in California, Chicago and Brazil; hon memb Br Hydrological Soc 2000, fell Transport Res Fndn 2001; FICE, FREng 1987, FRSE 1992 (memb Cncl 1995), FCIWM 2002; *Books and Publications* research pubns incl contribs to 11 books and over 200 pubns in jls; has produced 4 video documentaries and a perm exhbn; *Style*— Prof George Fleming, FRSE, FREng, FICE, FCIWM, CEnv; ✉ EnviroCentre Ltd, Craighall Business Park, 8 Eagle Street, Glasgow G4 9XA (☎ 0141 341 5040, e-mail gfleming@envirocentre.co.uk)

FLEMING, Grahame Ritchie; QC (Scot, 1990); s of late Ian Erskine Fleming, of Forfar, and Helen, *née* Wallace; *b* 13 February 1949; *Educ* Forfar Acad, Univ of Edinburgh (MA, LLB); *m* 1, 23 June 1984, Mopsa Dorcas (d 2008), eld da of Gerald Neil Robbins; 1 da (Leahna Damaris Robbins b 23 Aug 1985); *m* 2, 13 July 2013, Evelyn Mary, da of David Sheriff Whitson Donaldson; *Career* called to the Scottish Bar 1976, standing jr counsel to the Home Office in Scotland 1986–89, sheriff of the Lothians and Borders at Linlithgow 1993–2009, sheriff of the Lothian and Borders at Livingston 2009–14; *Recreations* travel, food, rugby; *Style*— Sheriff Grahame Fleming, QC; ✉ Advocates' Library, Parliament House, Edinburgh EH1 1RF

FLEMING, Prof Ian; s of David Alexander Fleming (d 1988), and Olwen Lloyd, *née* Jones (d 1996); *b* 4 August 1935; *Educ* King Edward VI Sch Stourbridge, Pembroke Coll Cambridge (MA, PhD, ScD); *m* 1, 3 Aug 1959 (m dis 1962), Joan, *née* Irving; *m* 2, 12 Nov 1965, Mary Lord Bernard; *Career* postdoctoral res Harvard Univ 1963–64; Univ of Cambridge: fell Pembroke Coll 1962–2002 (res fell 1962–64), demonstrator 1964–65, asst dir of res 1965–80, lectr 1980–86, reader in organic chemistry 1986–98, prof of organic chemistry 1998–2002, emeritus prof 2002–; RSC: memb 1962, Tilden lectr 1981, prize for organic synthesis 1983; FRS 1993; *Books* Spectroscopic Methods in Organic Chemistry (1966, 6 edn 2007), Selected Organic Syntheses (1973), Frontier Orbitals and Organic Chemical Reactions (1976), Comprehensive Organic Synthesis (jt ed, 1991), Pericyclic Reactions (1998, 2 edn 2015), Science of Synthesis Vol 4 (ed, 2001), Molecular Orbitals and Organic Chemical Reactions – Student Edition (2009), Molecular Orbitals and Organic Chemical Reactions – Reference Edition (2010); *Recreations* watching films, reading, music; *Style*— Prof Ian Fleming, FRS; ✉ Department of Chemistry, University of Cambridge, Lensfield Road, Cambridge CB2 1EW (☎ 01223 336372, e-mail if10000@cam.ac.uk)

FLEMING, Robert (Robin); CBE (2013), DL (Oxon 1989); s of Maj Philip Fleming (d 1971), of Barton Abbey, Oxon, and Joan Cecil, *née* Hunloke (d 1991); *b* 18 September 1932; *Educ* Eton, RMA Sandhurst; *m* 28 April 1962, Victoria Margaret, da of Frederic Howard Aykroyd (d 1978); 1 da (Joanna Kate (Mrs James King) b 19 Nov 1963), 2 s (Philip b 15 April 1965, Rory David b 5 June 1968); *Career* serv Royal Scots Greys 1951–58; joined Robert Fleming 1958, dir Robert Fleming Trustee Co Ltd 1961– (chm 1985–91), dir Robert Fleming Investment Trust Ltd 1968–2000, chm Robert Fleming Holdings Ltd 1990–97 (dir 1974–97, dep chm 1986–90); tstee BFSS 1975–96; High Sheriff Oxon 1980; *Recreations* most country pursuits; *Style*— Robin Fleming, Esq, CBE, DL; ✉ 15 Suffolk Street, London SW1Y 4HG (☎ 020 3696 6700, fax 020 3696 6701)

FLEMYNG, Jason; s of Gordon Flemyng; *b* 25 September 1966, Putney, London; *Educ* London Acad of Music and Dramatic Art; *m* 2008, Elly Fairman; *Career* actor; jt prop The Duchess Battersea; *Television* incl: Doctor Finlay 1993–94, Tess of the D'Urbervilles 1998, Tube Tales 1999, Primeval 2009–11; *Film* incl: The Jungle Book 1994, Rob Roy 1995, Stealing Beauty 1996, Hollow Reed 1996, Indian Summer 1996, Beck 1997, The James Gang 1997, The Life of Stuff 1997, Spice World 1997, Clueless 1998, Shuttle 1998, Deep Rising 1998, Lock, Stock and Two Smoking Barrels 1998, Bruiser 2000, Snatch 2000, Anazapta 2001, The Body 2001, Rock Star 2001, From Hell 2001, The Bunker 2001, Flipped 2001, Mean Machine 2001, Below 2002, The League of Extraordinary Gentlemen 2003, Drum 2004, Layer Cake 2004, Seed of Chucky 2004, A Woman in Winter 2005, Transporter 2 2005, Telling Lies 2006, Rollin' with the Nines 2006, The Half Life of Timofey Berezin 2006, Stardust 2007, Mirrors 2008, Shifty 2008, The Curious Case of Benjamin Button 2008, Solomon Kane 2009, City of Life 2009, Clash of the Titans 2010, Kick-Ass 2010, X-Men: First Class 2011, Hanna 2011, Jack Falls 2011, Ironclad 2011; *Style*— Jason Flemyng, Esq

FLESCH, Michael Charles; QC (1983); s of Carl Franz Flesch (d 2008), and Ruth, *née* Seligsohn (d 1987); *b* 11 March 1940; *Educ* Gordonstoun, UCL (LLB, 1st XV rugby, 1st VI tennis); *m* 2 Aug 1972, Gail, *née* Schrire; 1 da (Dina b 1973), 1 s (Daniel b 1976); *Career* called to the Bar Gray's Inn 1963 (Lord Justice Holker sr scholarship, bencher

F

1992); Bigelow teaching fell Univ of Chicago 1963–64, pt/t lectr in revenue law UCL 1965–82, practice at Revenue Bar 1966– (chm Revenue Bar Assoc 1993–95), chm Taxation and Retirement Benefits Ctee of Bar Cncl 1985–93; govr Gordonstoun Sch 1976–96; *Recreations* all forms of sport; *Clubs* Arsenal FC, MCC, Brondesbury Lawn Tennis and Cricket; *Style—* Michael Flesch, Esq, QC; ✉ Gray's Inn Chambers, Gray's Inn, London WC1R 5JA (☎ 020 7242 2642, fax 020 7831 9017)

FLETCHER, Andrew Fitzroy Stephen; QC (2006); s of late (Maj) Fitzroy Fletcher, of Castle Cary, Somerset, and Brygid, *née* Mahon; *b* 20 December 1957; *Educ* Eton, Magdalene Coll Cambridge (MA); *m* 1 Sept 1984 (m dis 1999), Felicia, da of Maj John Philip Pagan Taylor (d 1986); 2 s (Thomas b 1987, James b 1989); m 2, 28 July 2010, Eri, da of Tadeshi Aso; 3 s (Thomas, James, Alexander), 1 da (Milli); *Career* 2 Lt Welsh Gds 1976; called to the Bar Inner Temple 1980; Freeman City of London 1986, Liveryman Worshipful Co of Grocers 1994 (Freeman 1986); *Recreations* travel, real tennis, reading; *Clubs* Boodle's, Pratt's, MCC; *Style—* Andrew Fletcher, Esq, QC; ✉ 3 Verulam Buildings, Gray's Inn, London WC1R 5NT (☎ 020 7831 8441, e-mail afletcher@3vb.com)

FLETCHER, Prof Anthony John; s of John Molyneux Fletcher (d 1986), and Isabel Clare (Delle), *née* Chenevix-Trench; *b* 24 April 1941; *Educ* Wellington, Merton Coll Oxford (MA); *m* 1, 29 July 1967 (m dis 1999), Tresna Dawn, da of Charles Henry Railton Russell; 2 s (Crispin b 1970, Dickon b 1972); m 2, 6 Sept 2006, Brenda Joan, da of Richard Burdon Knibbs; *Career* history teacher King's Coll Sch Wimbledon 1964–67, successively lectr, sr lectr then reader Dept of History Univ of Sheffield 1967–81, prof Dept of History Univ of Durham 1987–95, prof Dept of History Univ of Essex 1995–2000, dir and gen ed Victoria County History Univ of London 2001–03; Leverhulme res fell 1999–2000; pres Ecclesiastical History Soc 1996–97; vice-pres Royal Hist Soc 1997–2001; auditor HEQC 1994–97; Quality Assurance Gp (QAA) 1997–2001, (chair Hist Benchmarking Gp 1998); FRHistS; *Books* Tudor Rebellions (1967), A County Community in Peace and War: Sussex 1600–1660 (1975), The Outbreak of the English Civil War (1981), Order and Disorder in Early Modern England (ed with J Stevenson, 1985), Reform in the Provinces (1986), Religion, Culture and Society in Early Modern Britain (ed jtly, 1994), Gender, Sex and Subordination in England 1500–1800 (1995), Childhood in Question (ed with S Hussey, 1999), Growing Up in England: The experience of Childhood 1600–1914 (2008), Life, Death and Growing Up on the Western Front (2013); *Recreations* theatre, music, opera, walking; *Style—* Prof Anthony Fletcher; ✉ 40 Coachman's Court, Station Road, Moreton-on-Marsh, Glos GL56 0DE (☎ 01608 651125, e-mail afletcher1@btinternet.com)

FLETCHER, Rt Rev Colin William; *see:* Dorchester, Bishop of

FLETCHER, Ian Macmillan; s of John Malcolm Fletcher, JP (d 2004), of Gourock, Scotland, and Jane Ann Cochran Fletcher (d 1980); *b* 16 February 1948; *Educ* Greenock Acad, Univ of Glasgow (LLB); *m* 15 Jan 1977, Jennifer Margaret (d 2007), da of Capt John Brown William Daly, MN (d 1972), of Glasgow; 2 da (Elizabeth Jane b 4 Aug 1978, Eleanor Kathleen b 21 Aug 1985), 1 s (Richard John Malcolm b 13 Jan 1980); *Career* admitted slr: Scotland 1971, England 1978; asst slr Richards Butler 1977–79; ptnr: MacRoberts 1980–87, Richards Butler 1987–99, Stephenson Harwood 1999–2008; dir, gen counsel and co sec NIRAH Hldgs Ltd 2007–14, non-exec chm London office Brinkmann & Ptnr (Germany) 2007–12, currently conslt for sales of corporate assets and real estate, conslt Peerpoint (Allen & Overy LLP) 2015–; former co sec Chilton Brothers Ltd; memb Cncl: Insolvency Lawyers Assoc Ltd 1989–2001 (past pres), Law Soc of Scotland 1992–2001 (convener Insolvency Slrs' Ctee 1993–2009), Assoc of Business Recovery Professionals (R3) 1994–2002; memb: Law Soc, Law Soc of Scotland, Soc WS, Int Bar Assoc (memb Creditors Rights and Insolvency section of Section on Business Law 1984–2008), Soc of Scottish Lawyers London (past pres), DTI Insolvency Regulation Working Party 1996–98; former memb City of London Slrs Co (formerly vice-chm Insolvency Law Sub-Ctee); authorised insolvency practitioner until 2013; memb London Symphony Chorus 2011–; WS, LTCL, LRAM, ARCO, MInstD, FABRP; *Books* The Law and Practice of Receivership in Scotland (jtly, 1987, 3 edn 2005), Insolvency and Finance in the Transportation Industry (jtly, 1993), The Law and Practice of Corporate Administrations (jtly, 1994, 2 edn 2004), Guide to Transnational Insolvency (jt ed, 1999); *Recreations* music, golf, swimming; *Clubs* Caledonian (tstee Common Good Fund); *Style—* Ian Fletcher, Esq, WS; ✉ e-mail ianmfletcher@btinternet.com

FLETCHER, Janis Richardson (Jan); OBE; *Career* entrepreneur, int property investor and developer, healthfood manufacturer and retailer and restaurateur; chm and financial interests in: Montpellier Estates Gp 1983–, Unique Restaurants Ltd 1984–, Bee Health Gp 1984–, Rougemont Estates 2009–; Govt advsr and memb Sec of State's Entrepreneurs Forum 2010–; founding chm Marketing Leeds 2004–08; memb: Int Businesswomen's Forum, Health Food Managers Assoc (HFMA); non-exec dir Skipton Building Soc 1995–2005; Veuve Clicquot Business Woman of the Year 1994, Yorkshire Woman of the Year 1995, BusinessAge Top 40 under 40 Award 1995, named one of Britain's Top 20 Entrepreneurs 2009; Hon DLitt 2009; FSA; *Recreations* business, current affairs, sport and fitness, theology; *Style—* Ms Jan Fletcher, OBE

FLETCHER, John W S; CBE; *Educ* Uppingham, Teesside Poly (H Dip Civil and Structural Engrg); *m* 1964, Jacqueline; 2 s, 1 da; *Career* Cleveland Bridge and Engineering Company (acquired by Cementation 1968, pt of Trafalgar House 1970): joined as trainee civil engr 1959, dir 1968–75, md 1975–82, divnl md and main Bd dir Trafalgar House plc 1982; mktg and business devpt dir Kvaerner ASA and chm and md Kvaerner Corp Devpt Ltd until 1999; chm Pacific Energy Ltd 1996–2007; currently: chm Gulf Minerals Ltd, chm Asian Cleveland Ltd, dir Somerley Gp Ltd, dir Somerley Int Ltd, dir Trafalgar House Construction (Jersey) Ltd; *Recreations* sailing; *Clubs* RAC, Royal Hong Kong Yacht, Hong Kong Jockey; *Style—* John W S Fletcher, CBE; ✉ Somerley International Limited, 20th Floor, China Building, 29 Queen's Road Central, Hong Kong (☎ 00 852 3769 0038, e-mail john.fletcher@somerleygroup.com, website www.somerley.com.hk)

FLETCHER, Prof John Walter James; s of Roy Arthur Walter Fletcher, MBE (d 1994), of Sherborne, Dorset, and Eileen Alice, *née* Beane (d 2002); *b* 23 June 1937; *Educ* Yeovil Sch, Trinity Hall Cambridge (BA, MA), Univ of Toulouse (MPhil, PhD); *m* 14 Sept 1961, Beryl Sibley, da of William Stanley Connop (d 1963), of Beckenham, Kent; 1 da (Harriet b 1972), 2 s (Hilary b 1976, Edmund b 1978); *Career* lectr in English Univ of Toulouse 1961–64, lectr in French Univ of Durham 1964–66; UEA: lectr in French 1966–68, reader in French 1968–69, prof of comparative literature 1969–89, pro-vice-chllr 1974–79, prof of European literature 1989–98, emeritus prof 1998–; hon sr res fell in French Univ of Kent 1997–; memb: Soc of Authors, Translators' Assoc; *Books* The Novels of Samuel Beckett (1964), Samuel Beckett's Art (1967), New Directions in Literature (1968), Claude Simon and Fiction Now (1975), Novel and Reader (1980), Alain Robbe-Grillet (1983), The Georgics (by Claude Simon, trans 1989, Scott Moncrieff prize for translation from French 1990), The Red Cross and the Holocaust (trans 1999), About Beckett (2003), A Pocket Philosophical Dictionary (by Voltaire, trans 2011), Three Strong Women (by Marie NDiaye, trans 2012); *Recreations* food and wine, listening to Monteverdi and Schubert; *Style—* Prof John Fletcher; ✉ School of European Culture and Languages, University of Kent, Canterbury CT2 7NF (e-mail jwjf@kent.ac.uk, website http://www.societyofauthors.org/profiles/writers/john-wj-fletcher)

FLETCHER, Jo(anna) Louise (GOULD-); da of Colin Adrian Gould-Fletcher, of London, and Edwina Charlotte, *née* Dean; *Educ* Queen Elizabeth's Sch Faversham; *m* 20 May 2005, Ian Charles Drury; *Career* The Whitstable Times & Kentish Observer 1978–81 (jr reporter, sr reporter, film critic); sr reporter: The Hillingdon Mirror 1981–82, The Middlesex Advertiser & Gazette 1982–83, The Ealing Gazette 1983; freelance journalist 1983–88, film critic and columnist News of the World 1991–93 (joined 1988); conslt ed: Headline Book Publishing plc 1986–88, Mandarin Books 1988–91, Pan Books 1991–94; assoc publisher Victor Gollancz Ltd 1994–2010, publisher and dir Jo Fletcher Books Ltd 2011–; contributing ed Science Fiction Chronicle NY 1982–2008; sometime guest lectr UCLA and Loyola USA, specialist tutor DipHE Univ of E London; memb: Bd World Fantasy Convention 1979–, Bd World Fantasy Awards Administration, World Horror Convention 1989–91; tstee: Horror Writers' Assoc 1989–99, Richard Evans Fund; memb: NUJ 1979, Science Fiction and Fantasy Writers of America 1987; Karl Edward Wagner British Fantasy Award 1997, The World Fantasy Award 2002, GOH World Horror Convention 2002, GOH World Fantasy Convention 2011, GOH Br Fantasy Convention 2015; *Books* Gaslight & Ghosts (ed, 1988), Horror At Halloween (ed, 1995), Secret City: Strange Tales of London (1997), Shadows of Light and Dark (1998), Off the Coastal Path (ed, 2010); *Recreations* history, travel, book collecting, singing; *Style—* Ms Jo Fletcher; ✉ 24 Pearl Road, Walthamstow, London E17 4QZ (☎ 020 8521 3034, e-mail jo.fletcher@jofletcherbooks.co.uk)

FLETCHER, Kim Thomas; s of Jack Fletcher, and Agnes, *née* Coulthwaite; *b* 17 September 1956; *Educ* Heversham GS, Hertford Coll Oxford (BA); *m* May 1991, Sarah Sands; 1 s (Rafe b 1992), 1 da (Matilda b 1994), 1 step s (Henry Sands b 1985); *Career* journalist; The Star Sheffield 1978–81, The Sunday Times 1981–86 (Home Affairs corr, Labour corr), The Daily Telegraph 1986–87, The Sunday Telegraph 1988–98, ed Independent on Sunday 1998–99, editorial dir Hollinger Telegraph New Media 2000–03, conslt ed The Daily Telegraph 2001–03, editorial dir Telegraph Gp Ltd 2003–05, ptnr Brunswick Gp 2007–; jt Reporter of the Year 1982; *Recreations* football, theatre; *Clubs* Groucho; *Style—* Kim Fletcher, Esq

FLETCHER, Martin Anthony; s of Anthony Travers Nethersole Fletcher, of Brandeston, Suffolk, and Nancy Evelyn, *née* Scott (d 1994); *b* 7 July 1956, Knighton, Wales; *Educ* Uppingham, Univ of Edinburgh, Univ of Pennsylvania (MA); *m* 10 Oct 1981, Catherine Jane, *née* Beney; 1 s (Barnaby Martin b 12 April 1986), 2 da (Hannah Catherine b 2 June 1984, Imogen Nancy b 26 April 1989); *Career* writer and journalist; North Herts Gazette 1980–82, Daily Telegraph 1982–83; The Times: lobby corr 1986–89, Washington corr 1989–92, US ed 1992–96, NI corr 1997–99, Brussels corr 1999–2002, foreign ed 2002–06, assoc ed 2006–13; *Books* The Good Caff Guide (1980), Almost Heaven (2000), Silver Linings (2013); *Recreations* tennis, squash, skiing, children; *Style—* Martin Fletcher, Esq; ✉ c/o The Times, 1 London Bridge Street, London SE1 9GF

FLETCHER, Michael; s of Richard Fletcher (d 1990), of Cardiff, and Catherine, *née* Thomas (d 1981); *b* 11 March 1945; *Educ* Whitchurch GS Cardiff, AA Sch of Arch (AADipl); *m* 1, 1969 (m dis 1982), Lesley Saunders; 1 s (Luke Fletcher b 1973), 1 da (Daisy Fletcher b 1977); m 2, 1990, Malory Massey; 1 da (Vita Massey Fletcher b 1992); *Career* architect; Farrell Grimshaw Architects 1970–72, assoc Wolff Olins design consultancy 1972–78, fndr ptnr Fletcher Priest Architects 1978–, fndr Fletcher Priest Bösl (German office) 1993–; RIBA: memb Cncl 1993–99, chm Clients Advsy Serv 1994–99, vice-chm London Region 1996, vice-pres client and consumer affrs 1997; RIBA 1972, FIMgt 1973; *Awards* Civic Tst commendation (for Babmaes St offices) 1989, Br Cncl of Offices Bldg of the Year Award and Br Inst of Facilities Mgmnt Bldg of the Year Award for Powergen offices 1996, and for Leo Burnett's offices 1997; *Recreations* water sports; *Style—* Michael Fletcher, Esq; ✉ Fletcher Priest Architects, Middlesex House, 34/42 Cleveland Street, London W1T 4JE

FLETCHER, Sheriff Michael John; s of Walter Fletcher (d 1992), and Elizabeth, *née* Pringle (d 1986); *b* 5 December 1945; *Educ* Dundee HS, Univ of St Andrews (LLB); *m* 19 Oct 1968, Kathryn Mary, da of John Bain, and Helen *née* Gorrie; 2 s (Christopher Michael b 13 Sept 1971, Mark Richard b 11 March 1977); *Career* apprentice slr Kirk Mackie and Elliot Edinburgh 1966–68; slr (ptnr): Ross Strachan & Co Dundee 1968–88, Hendry & Fenton Dundee 1988–92, Miller Hendry Dundee 1992–94; ed Scot Civil Law Reports 1999–; sheriff: S Strathclyde Dumfries and Galloway (at Dumfries) 1994–99, Lothian and Borders (at Edinburgh) 1999–2000, Tayside Central and Fife (at Perth) 2000–14; Retired Sheriff's Cmmn 2014–; memb Sheriff Court Rules Cncl 2002–10, memb Judicial Studies Ctee 2006–12, pres Sheriffs' Assoc 2009–11 (vice-pres 2008–09), regnl vice-pres for Atlantic and Mediterranean Cwlth Magistrates and Judges Assoc 2012–; *Publications* Delictual Damages (co-author); *Recreations* golf, gardening, learning Japanese; *Style—* Sheriff Michael Fletcher; ✉ Sheriff Chambers, Tay Street, Perth PH2 8NL

FLETCHER, (Peter) Neil; s of Alan Fletcher, of Thurnby, Leics (d 2007), and Ruth Fletcher (d 1961); *b* 5 May 1944, Blackpool, Lancs; *Educ* Wyggeston Boys' GS Leicester, City of Leeds Coll of Educn, Univ of London (BA), London Business Sch (MBA 1994); *m* 9 Sept 1967, Margaret Mary, da of Anthony Gerald Monaghan (d 1967); 2 s (Ben b 25 May 1971, Sam b 18 July 1974); *Career* teacher Leeds 1966–68; lectr in further educn: Leeds 1969–70, Harrow 1970–73, Merton 1973–76; educn offr (and head Educn Dept) NALGO 1991–93 (princ admin offr 1976–91), dir strategic projects UNISON 1994–95 (educn offr 1993–94), mgmnt conslt 1995–98 and 2003–; fndr and dir Strategy in Educn plc 2007–; head of educn, culture and tourism Local Govt Assoc 1998–2003; cncllr London Borough of Camden 1978–86 (dep ldr 1982–84); ILEA: memb 1979–90, chm Further and Higher Educn Sub-Ctee 1981–87, ldr 1987–90; chm: Assoc of Metropolitan Authorities Educn Ctee 1987–90 (memb 1981–90), Cncl of Local Educn Authorities 1987–90; govr: Penn Sch Bucks 1985–2006, LSE 1990–2001; chair Governing Body London Inst (now Univ of Arts) 1985–99, chair of govrs City Lit Inst 2003–06 (govr 1996–2006); advsr London Skills and Employment Bd 2006–08; FRSA 1989; hon fell Coll of Preceptors 1990; hon res assoc, IoE UCL 2015–;; *Recreations* cooking, walking, theatre, cricket, football; *Clubs* Royal Over-Seas League; *Style—* Neil Fletcher, Esq; ✉ 42 Narcissus Road, London NW6 1TH (☎ 020 7435 5306, mobile 07775 841427, e-mail neil@neilfletcher.org.uk)

FLETCHER, Dr (Archibald) Peter; s of Walter Archibald Fletcher (d 1970), and Dorothy Mabel Fletcher; *b* 24 December 1930; *Educ* Kingswood Sch Bath, London Hosp Med Coll, UCL, St Mary's Hosp Med Sch, MB BS (London), PhD (London); *m* 1972, Patricia Elizabeth Samson, *née* Marr; 3 s, 2 da; *Career* sr lectr in chemical pathology St Mary's Hosp London 1967–70, head of biochemistry American Nat Red Cross 1970–73, princ med offr and med assessor to Ctee on Safety of Medicines 1977, chief scientific offr and sr princ med offr DHSS 1978, res physician Upjohn Int 1978–80, sr med offr DHSS 1978–79; currently ptnr Pharma Services International and conslt to pharmaceutical industry; ptnr Documenta Biomedica, med dir IMS International, dir PMS International Ltd; *Publications* numerous papers in scientific and med jls on: glycoproteins, physical chemistry, metabolism of blood cells, safety evaluation of new drugs; *Recreations* gardening, cooking; *Clubs* Royal Society of Medicine; *Style—* Dr Peter Fletcher

FLETCHER, Philip A; *Career* M P Evans Gp plc: joined 1982, dir 1987–, md 1991–, exec chm 1999–2005; former exec dir: Bertam Hldgs plc, Lendu Hldgs plc; FCA; *Style—* Philip Fletcher, Esq; ✉ M P Evans Group plc, 3 Clanricarde Gardens, Tunbridge Wells, Kent TN1 1HQ

FLETCHER, Philip John; CBE (2006); s of late Alan Philip Fletcher, QC, and Annette Grace, *née* Wright; *b* 2 May 1946; *Educ* Marlborough, Trinity Coll Oxford (MA); *m* 1977, Margaret Anne, *née* Boys; 2 da (Helen b 1978 d 1989, Sarah b 1982); *Career* DOE: joined 1968, dir Central Fin 1986–89, dir (grade 3) Planning & Devpt Control 1990–93, chief exec PSA Services and Property Holdings 1993–94, dep sec (grade 2) Cities and Countryside 1994–95; receiver for Metropolitan Police District 1996–2000; DG Water Services 2000–06, chm Ofwat 2006–12; memb Archbishops' Cncl C of E 2007–16, memb

Ofqual Bd 2010–16, chair Mission and Public Affrs Cncl 2012–16; hon life memb ACPO 2000; *Style—* Philip Fletcher, CBE; ✉ 20 Calais Street, London SE5 9LP

FLETCHER, Phillip Douglas; s of Herbert Fletcher, and Mona Fletcher; *b* 16 September 1957, Barbados; *Educ* Georgetown Univ (Bachelor of Science in Foreign Service (BSFS)), Fletcher Sch of Law and Diplomacy Tufts Univ (MA), Univ of California Berkeley (JD); *m* 1984, Elena; 1 s (Phillip b 1991), 2 da (Emily b 1995, Sarah b 1996); *Career* slr specialising in project finance; Milbank, Tweed, Hadley & McCloy LLP: assoc 1983–92, ptnr 1993–, managing ptnr Europe 1995–; *Clubs* Roehampton; *Style—* Phillip Fletcher, Esq; ✉ Milbank, Tweed, Hadley & McCloy LLP, 10 Gresham Street, London EC2V 7JD (☎ 020 7615 3002, e-mail pfletcher@milbank.com)

FLETCHER, Robin Charles; s of Brian (who d 2013) and Elaine Fletcher *née* Bottomley; *b* 11 February 1966; *Educ* Rugby, South Glamorgan Inst (NCTJ), Univ of South Wales (MBA), Cardiff Univ (MPhil); *m* 2012, Tish*née* Bourke; 2 da (Olivia b 07/07/07, Yasmine 05/04/10); *Career* reporter Birmingham Post and Mail 1984–89, sr ed Midland Weekly Newspapers and ed Solihull News 1990–92; ed: Northampton Chronicle and Echo 1992–94, West Lancashire Evening Gazette 1994–95, Wales on Sunday 1996, South Wales Echo 1996–2001; communications dir Trinity Mirror Regionals 2002–03; founding dir Reflex Business Servs Ltd 2003–11, communications and performance dir Aster Gp 2011–14; nat dir Boarding Schools Assoc 2014–16, chief exec Boarding Schools Assoc 2016–; dir: Northampton Mercury Co Ltd 1994, Blackpool Gazette & Herald Ltd 1994–95; dir/tstee Cobalt Medical Imaging 2008–14; Guild of Editors: memb 1993–2001, vice-chm Gen Purposes Ctee 1996, hon sec S Wales region 1996 and 1999 (pres 1997–98 and 1999–2001); media advsr Wales Advsy Bd Business In the Community 2001–03; non-exec dir Williams Ross Ltd 2006–08; highly commended Regional Ed of the Year Newspaper Focus Awards 1994; highly commended IOIC Internal Communicator of the Year 2012 and 2013; hon fell Cardiff Met Univ (formerly Univ of Wales Inst Cardiff); FRSA 1999; *Recreations* squash, reading, writing, country walking, piano composition; *Style—* Robin Fletcher, Esq; ☎ 07770 738220, e-mail robin@boarding.org.uk

FLETCHER, Prof Roger; s of Harry Fletcher (d 1942), and Alice, *née* Emms (d 1996); *b* 29 January 1939; *Educ* Huddersfield Coll, Univ of Cambridge (MA), Univ of Leeds (PhD); *m* 23 Sept 1963, Mary Marjorie, da of Charlie Taylor (d 1970), of Harrogate; 2 da (Jane Elizabeth b 17 Nov 1968, Sarah Anne b 13 Sept 1970); *Career* lectr Univ of Leeds 1963–69, princ scientific offr AERE Harwell 1969–73; Univ of Dundee: sr lectr and reader 1973–84, prof 1984–2005, emeritus prof 2005–; Royal Medal RSE 2008; hon prof Univ of Edinburgh; FIMA, FRSE 1988, FRS 2003; *Books* Practical Methods of Optimization Vol I (1980), Vol 2 (1981); *Recreations* hill walking, bridge; *Style—* Prof Roger Fletcher, FRS, FRSE; ✉ Department of Mathematics, University of Dundee, Dundee DD1 4HN (☎ 01382 384490, e-mail fletcher@maths.dundee.ac.uk)

FLETCHER, HE Thomas Stuart Francis; CMG (2011); *b* 27 March 1975, Kent; *Educ* Harvey GS Folkestone, Hertford Coll Oxford (BA); *m* Louise Fitzgerald; 2 s (Charles b 2007, Theodore b 2011); *Career* diplomat; desk offr ME Peace Process FCO 1997–98, second sec political Nairobi 1998–2002, private sec to Baroness Amos, *qv*, and Chris Mullin FCO 2002–04, first sec Paris 2004–07, private sec for foreign affrs to the PM and PM's principal advsr on NI 2007–11, ambass to Lebanon 2011–; *Recreations* cricket, travel, walking; *Clubs* Cwlth, Strollers CC; *Style—* HE Mr Thomas Fletcher, CMG; ✉ c/o FCO (Beirut), King Charles Street, London SW1A 2AH (website www.lebanon.fco.gov.uk, Twitter @hmatomfletcher)

FLETCHER ROGERS, Helen Susan; *née* Stewart; da of Peter Alexander Stewart (d 1995), and Jessie Mary, *née* Sykes (d 1978); *b* 24 September 1941; *Educ* Greenhead HS Huddersfield, UCL; *m* 28 Sept 1972, David Geoffrey Fletcher Rogers, s of Murray Rowland Fletcher Rogers (d 1991); 2 s (Anthony, Jonathan); *Career* called to the Bar Gray's Inn 1965; PA Thomas & Co 1964–67; Kodak Ltd 1967–99 (Euro gen counsel 1995–99), Lawyers in Business 2001–06; memb: Valuation Tbnl for England 2004–13, Qualifications Ctee Bar Standards Bd 2007–13; non-exec dir: Tropix Healthcare Ltd 2001–09, Keswick Timeshare Ltd 2001–09; tstee Northwick Park Inst for Medical Research 1994–2006; vice-chm Northwick Park and St Mark's Hosp NHS Trust 1992–96; memb Advsy Cncl Br Inst of Int and Comparative Law 2001–, hon sec Bar Assoc for Commerce, Finance and Industry (BACFI) 2010–12 (hon treas 2007–10); dir Keswick Bridge Owners' Club Ltd 2005–09 (sec 2013–); hon sec Friends of HMS Conway 2004–, hon sec Totternhoe Sch Tst 2011–; *Books* Butterworths Encyclopaedia of Forms and Precedents Vol 16a (contrib on patents and designs); Microfilm and the Law; *Recreations* walking, working, theatre, music; *Clubs* Army and Navy; *Style—* Mrs Helen Susan Fletcher Rogers; ✉ Conway House, 5 Furlong Lane, Totternhoe, Dunstable, Bedfordshire LU6 1QR (☎ and fax 01582 472300)

FLIGHT, Baron (Life Peer UK 2011), of Worcester in the County of Worcestershire; Howard Emerson Flight; s of Bernard Thomas Flight (d 1990), of Devon, and Doris Mildred Emerson, *née* Parker (d 1999); *b* 16 June 1948; *Educ* Brentwood Sch, Magdalene Coll Cambridge (MA), Univ of Michigan Business Sch (MBA); *m* 1973, Christabel Diana Beatrice, da of Christopher Paget Norbury (d 1975), of Worcs; 3 da (Catherine b 1975, Josephine b 1986, Mary Anne b 1988), 1 s (Thomas b 1978); *Career* jt md Guiness Flight Global Asset Mgmnt 1986–98; chm: CIM Investment Mgmnt Ltd 2006–, Flight and Ptnrs 2007–, Downing Opportunities VCT 1 plc 2009–, Aurora Investment Tst plc 2011–; dir: Investec Asset Mgmnt 1998–, Marechale plc 2006–, Metro Bank plc 2010–, Edge Performance VCT plc 2011–, RSFX Ltd 2015–; conslt: TISA 2000–, Duff & Phelps 2005–, Arden plc 2014–; MP (Cons) Arundel and S Downs 1997–2005 (Parly candidate (Cons) Bermondsey and Southwark both elections 1974); shadow economic sec to Treasy 1999–2001, shadow Paymaster Gen 2001–02, shadow chief sec to the Treasy 2002–04, dep chm Cons Pty and special envoy to the City of London 2004–05, memb House of Lords EU Economic and Finance Ctee 2011–15, memb House of Lords Delegated Powers and Regulatory Reform Ctee 2015–; chm EIS Assoc 2005–; cmmr Guernsey Financial Services Cmmn 2005–; govr Brentwood Sch; tstee: The Elgar Fndn, Africa Research Inst; chm 1900 Club; Liveryman Carpenter's Co; FRSA; *Books* All You Need to Know About Exchange Rates (jtly, 1988); *Recreations* skiing, classical music, fruit farming, gardening; *Clubs* Carlton, Pratt's, Boodle's; *Style—* The Lord Flight; ✉ Flight & Partners, 6 Barton Street, London SW1P 3NG (☎ 020 7222 7559, fax 020 7976 7059, e-mail hflight@btinternet.com)

FLINN, Anthony James; s of Anthony Flinn, and Maureen, *née* Rouke; *b* 19 February 1980, Liverpool; *Career* restaurateur; prop and exec head chef: Anthony's Restaurant Leeds 2004–13, Anthony's at Flannels Leeds 2005–; prop Anthony's Patisserie Leeds 2007–, Piazza by Anthony Leeds 2008–; 3 AA Rosettes; *Recreations* shooting, photography; *Style—* Anthony Flinn, Esq; ✉ Anthony's Restaurant, 19 Boar Lane, Leeds LS1 6EA (☎ 0113 245 5922, website www.anthonysrestaurant.co.uk)

FLINT, Prof Anthony Patrick Fielding; *b* 31 August 1943; *m* 1967 (m dis 1996), Chan Mun Kwun; 2 s; *Career* research fell Depts of Physiology and Obstetrics and Gynaecology Univ of Western Ontario 1969–72, sr research biochemist Dept of Obstetrics and Gynaecology Welsh Nat Sch of Med 1972–73, lectr Nuffield Dept of Obstetrics and Gynaecology Univ of Oxford 1973–77; AFRC: sr scientific offr 1977–79, princ scientific offr 1979–85, sr princ scientific offr 1985–87, visiting scientist 1987–95; dir Inst of Zoology Univ of London 1987–93, dir of science Zoological Soc 1987–93; prof of animal physiology Univ of Nottingham 1993–; memb numerous ctees and editorial bds; author of over 240 pubns in scientific journals; Medal Soc for Endocrinology 1985, Medal of Polish Physiological Soc 1990; memb: Biochemical Soc 1967, Soc for Endocrinology 1973, Soc for the Study of Fertility 1973, Blair-Bell Research Soc 1974, Physiological Soc 1979; FIBiol 1982; *Clubs* Zoological; *Style—* Prof Anthony Flint; ✉ School of BioSciences, University of Nottingham, Sutton Bonington, Loughborough, Leicestershire LE12 5RD (e-mail anthony.flint@nottingham.ac.uk)

FLINT, Rt Hon Caroline Louise; PC (2008), MP; da of late Wendy Flint, *née* Beasley; *b* 20 September 1961; *Educ* Twickenham Girls' Sch, Richmond Tertiary Coll, UEA (BA); *m* 1, (m dis); 1 s, 1 da; m 2, Phil Cole; 1 step s; *Career* mgmnt trainee GLC/ILEA 1984–85, policy offr ILEA 1985–87, head Women's Unit NUS 1988–89, equal opportunities offr Lambeth Cncl 1989–91, welfare and staff devpt offr Lambeth Cncl 1991–93, sr researcher/political offr GMB 1994–97, MP (Lab) Don Valley 1997–; PPS: to Peter Hain, MP, *qv* (at FCO then DTI) 1999–2001, to Rt Hon Dr John Reid, MP, *qv*, 2002–03; Parly under-sec of state Home Office 2003–05, Parly under-sec of state for public health 2005–06, min of state for public health Dept of Health 2006–07, min of state for employment and welfare reform and min for Yorks and the Humber 2007–08, min of state for housing and planning 2008, min of state for Europe 2008–09, shadow sec for communities and local govt 2010–11, shadow sec of state for energy and climate change 2011–15; chair All-Pty Parly Gp on Childcare 1997–2003; parly advsr to Police Fedn for England and Wales 1999; memb: Educn and Employment Select Ctee 1997–99; chm Working for Childcare 1991–95 (memb 1989–); govr Strand-on-the-Green Sch Chiswick 1993–97; assoc ed Renewal 1995–2000 (memb Policy Advsy Bd 2000–01); memb: Fabian Soc, Community, GMB, Progress; *Recreations* cinema, leisure time with family and friends; *Style—* The Rt Hon Caroline Flint, MP; ✉ House of Commons, London SW1A 0AA (☎ 020 7219 4407); Constituency Office, Meteor House, First Avenue, Auckley, Doncaster DN9 3GA (☎ 01302 623330, e-mail caroline.flint.mp@parliament.uk, website www.carolineflint.org)

FLINT, Charles John Raffles; QC (1995); *Career* called to the Bar 1975, jr counsel to the Crown (common law) 1991–95; *Style—* Charles Flint, Esq, QC; ✉ Blackstone Chambers, Temple, London EC4Y 9BW

FLINT, Prof Colin David; s of Oswald George Flint (d 1981), of London, and Maud Elisabeth, *née* Hayes (d 2004); *b* 3 May 1943; *Educ* Leyton HS, Imperial Coll London (BSc, DIC, PhD, DSc); *m* 3 Aug 1968, Florence Edna, da of Charles Cowin (d 1970), of Isle of Man; 2 s (Richard Charles b 6 March 1972, Peter David Clucas b 25 July 1974); *Career* NATO postdoctoral fell Univ of Copenhagen Denmark 1967–69, prof of chemistry Birkbeck Coll London 1981– (lectr 1969–76, reader chemical spectroscopy 1976–81, head of dept 1979–86), emeritus prof of chemistry Univ of London 2003–; visiting prof: Univ of Virginia USA 1982, Univ of Chile 1985, 1987, 1991 and 1994, Tech Univ of Graz Austria 1986 and 1989, Univ of Copenhagen 1988, Univ of Padova 1991, Univ of Graz 1995 and 1996; UK co-ordinator DFID-Chiang Mai Univ Thailand Water Resource Centre Project 1988–; author of about 200 pubns in learned jls; ARCS, FRSC, CChem; *Books* Vibronic Processes in Inorganic Chemistry (ed, 1989); *Recreations* travel; *Style—* Prof Colin Flint; ✉ 34 Woolhampton Way, Chigwell Row, Essex (☎ 020 8500 6373, e-mail chigwell999@hotmail.com)

FLINT, David; s of David Flint, of Glasgow, and Dorothy, *née* Jardine; *b* 7 July 1955, Glasgow; *Educ* HS of Glasgow, Univ of Glasgow (LLB, LLM), Europa Inst Univ van Amsterdam (DiplCEI); *m* 27 Oct 1979, Marie, *née* Hepburn; 2 da (Jennifer b 22 June 1983, Aimée b 19 Sept 1990); *Career* MacRoberts LLP slrs: asst Corp and Commercial Dept 1979–84, ptnr Corp and Commercial Dept 1984–, currently sr ptnr and head IP Technology & Communications Gp; former memb Nominet UK Ind Experts Panel, former memb Jt Working Party of Scot, Eng and Northern Irish Law Socs and Bars on Competition Law 1981, former Corrs Panel Computer Law and Security Report; coordinator Infobank Current Comment Business Law Review 1997; chm: European Gp Scottish Lawyers 1985–95, Intellectual Property Sub-Ctee Int Business Law American Bar Assoc; NP 1980; licensed insolvency practitioner; memb: Law Soc of Scotland 1979, Insolvency Practitioners' Assoc 1990; assoc memb American Bar Assoc; FRSA 1998, FABRP 1998; *Publications* Liquidation in Scotland (1987, 2 edn 1990), Greens Scottish E-commerce Handbook (2000, and supplements), MacRoberts Scottish Liquidation Handbook (4 edn 2010); contrib on competition law to Stair Memorial Encyclopaedia and Halsbury's Laws of England; book chapters on data protection, insolvency, employee use of internet and e-mail; articles in legal, business and trade magazines; *Recreations* reading, music; *Style—* David Flint, Esq; ✉ MacRoberts, 60 York Street, Glasgow G2 8JX (☎ 0141 303 1100, fax 0141 332 8886, e-mail df@macroberts.com)

FLINT, Douglas Jardine; CBE (2006); s of Prof David Flint, and Dorothy, *née* Jardine; *b* 8 July 1955; *Educ* Univ of Glasgow (BAcc), Harvard Business Sch (PMD); *m* 25 May 1984, Fiona Isobel Livingstone, *née* McMillan; 2 s (Jamie Livingstone b 3 May 1989, Stuart David b 19 Jan 1991), 1 da (Catriona Lindsay b 13 Aug 1992); *Career* KPMG (formerly Peat Marwick Mitchell & Co): articled clerk 1977–80, accountant 1980–88, ptnr 1988–95; HSBC Holdings plc: gp fin dir 1995–2010, chm 2010; non-exec dir BP plc 2005–11; memb: ACT 1996, UK Accounting Standards Bd; CA 1980; *Recreations* golf; *Clubs* Caledonian, Rye Golf, Denham Golf; *Style—* Douglas Flint, Esq, CBE; ✉ HSBC Holdings plc, 8 Canada Square, London E14 5HQ (☎ 020 7991 2888, fax 020 7991 4675)

FLINTER, Prof Frances Anne; *née* Morgan; *b* 31 January 1959, London; *Educ* City of London Sch for Girls, Guy's Hosp Med Sch (MD, MB BS); *m* 1979, David Flinter; 2 da; *Career* conslt clinical geneticist Guy's and St Thomas' NHS Tst 1994–, prof of clinical genetics KCL, clinical dir Children's Services and Genetics Evelina Children's Hosp Guy's and St Thomas' NHS Fndn Tst 2000–07; memb Human Genetics Cmmn, pres Clinical Genetics Soc 2009–11; author of pubns on clinical genetics (inherited renal diseases, prenatal diagnosis and preimplantation genetic diagnosis); Elizabeth Wherry Award for research into renal disease BMA 1992; FRCP, FRCPCH; *Recreations* classical music (pianist and viola player); *Style—* Prof Frances Flinter; ✉ Genetics Department, 7th Floor, Borough Wing, Guy's Hospital, London SE1 9RT (☎ 020 7188 4627, e-mail frances.flinter@gstt.nhs.uk)

FLINTOFF, Andrew; MBE (2006); s of Colin Flintoff, and Susan Flintoff; *b* 6 December 1977, Preston; *m* Rachael; 1 da (Holly b 6 Sept 2004), 2 s (Corey b 8 March 2006, Rocky b 7 April 2008); *Career* professional cricketer with Lancashire CCC 1995–2010; England: 79 test matches, 141 one-day ints, 7 Twenty20 appearances, first team debut v South Africa 1998, one-day int debut v Pakistan 1999, memb team World Cup 1999, 2003 and 2007, memb squad Twenty20 World Cup 2007, memb team touring Pakistan and Sri Lanka 2000–01, Zimbabwe, India and NZ 2001–02, Bangladesh and Sri Lanka 2003, West Indies 2004 and 2009, South Africa 2004–05, Pakistan 2005, Australia 2006–07, India 2008; memb winning Ashes team 2005 (Man of the Series, Compton Miller Medal); panel memb A League of Their Own (Sky 1) 2010–, presenter Freddie's World of Sport (BBC Radio 5 Live) 2011; One-Day Int Player of the Year Int Cricket Cncl (ICC) Awards 2004, Player of the Year Professional Cricketers' Assoc 2004 and 2005, Player of the Year (jt winner) ICC Awards 2005, BBC Sports Personality of the Year 2005; Freeman City of Preston 2005; *Books* Being Freddie: The Story So Far (2006, Tesco Sports Book of the Year), Freddie My World, Andrew Flintoff: Ashes to Ashes; *Style—* Andrew Flintoff, Esq, MBE; ✉ c/o Katie Lydon, M&C Saatchi Merlin, 36 Golden Square, London W1F 9EE

FLÖCKINGER, Gerda; CBE (1991); da of Karl Flöckinger (d 1950), of Austria, and Anna, *née* Frankl (d 1985); *b* 8 December 1927; *Educ* Maidstone Girls' GS, Dorchester Co HS, S Hampstead HS, St Martin's Sch of Art (NDD), Central Sch of Art; *m* 1954 (m dis 1962); *Career* artist, jewellery designer/maker, lectr and photographer; emigrated from

Innsbruck to London 1938, naturalised British subject 1946; fndr course in modern experimental jewellery Hornsey Coll of Art 1962–68; work featured in more than 49 books, numerous pubns, articles, leaflets and catalogues, public lectures and book Pioneers of Modern Craft Crafts Cncl 1995; Goldsmiths' Hall Travel Award 1956; Freeman Worshipful Co of Goldsmiths 1998; hon fell Univ of the Arts 2006; *Solo Exhibitions* Crafts Centre London 1968, V&A 1971, City of Bristol Museum and Art Gallery 1971, Dartington Cider Press Gallery 1977, V&A 1986, Solo Showcase Exhbn Crafts Cncl Shop at V&A 1991, Electrum Gallery London 2007; *Group Exhibitions* incl: Philadelphia Museum of Art, Norway, Tokyo, Expo Osaka, Ashmolean Museum, Künstlerhaus Vienna, Schmuckmuseum Pforzheim, Nat Museum of Wales, The Netherlands, ICA 1954–64, Arnolfini Gallery Bristol 1962–73, The Observer Jewellery Exhbn (Welsh Arts Cncl touring) 1973–74, Treasures of London (Goldsmiths' Hall London) 1976–77, Diamond Story (Electrum Gallery) 1977, Objects The V&A Collects (V&A) 1978, British Women's Art (House of Commons) 1981, Sotheby's Craft Exhbn (Sotheby's London) 1988, Ornamenta (Pforzheim Germany) 1989, British Jewellery (Crafts Cncl London) 1989, Christie's Amsterdam 1990, 20th Anniversary Exhbn (Mobilia Gallery, formerly Electrum Gallery) 1991, What Is Jewellery? (Crafts Cncl) 1994, British Jewellery Exhbn (Mainz) 1995, British Master Goldsmiths (Goldsmiths' Hall London) 1997, Introducing Contemporary British Jewellery (Soc of Arts & Crafts Boston) 1998, Made to Wear: Creativity in Contemporary Jewellery (Central St Martins) 1998, 50th Anniversary Exhibition (Contemporary Applied Arts) 1998, British Gold – Italian Gold (Scottish Gallery and Graziella Grasetto Gallery Studio Milan) 1998, Jewellery Moves (Royal Scottish Museum Edinburgh) 1998, Sofa (USA) 1998–2009, The Pleasures of Peace: Craft Art and Design in Britain 1939–68 (Sainsbury Centre for Visual Arts) 1999, 25 Years of Contemporary British Craft (Crafts Cncl) 1999, Treasures of the 20th Century (Goldsmiths' Hall London) 2000, Het Versierde Ego – Het Kunstjuweel in de 20ste EEUW (Antwerp) 2000, Paper Plastics Palladium and Pearls (Lesley Craze Gallery) 2000, The Ring (Mobilia Gallery Cambridge MA, Wustum Museum Racine WI and tour) 2001–, Int Art and Design Fair NY 2003, Love Story (Goldsmiths' Hall London) 2003, Collect (V&A) 2003–11, trio exbhn with Wendy Ramshaw and David Watkins (V&A) 2006, Jewelry by Artists: The Daphne Farago Collection (Boston Museum of Fine Art), Past, Present and Future (Electrum Gallery London 40th anniversary exhbn) 2011, British Design 1948–2012 Innovation in the Modern Age (V&A) 2012, Art for the Ear, the Art of the Ring (Mobilia Gallery Cambridge MA) 2012, Contemporary Visions of the Necklace (Mobilia Gallery) 2012, Objects of Status, Power and Adornment (Mobilia Gallery) 2013, The Art of the Ring (Mobilia Gallery) 2014, 30 Years in the Making (Lesley Craze closing exhbn) 2014, A Sense of Jewellery (The Goldsmiths' Centre London) 2015; *Work in Public Collections* City of Bristol Museum and Art Gallery, Royal Museum of Scotland Edinburgh, Goldsmiths' Hall London, Crafts Cncl London, V&A, Castle Museum Nottingham, Schmuckmuseum Pforzheim Germany, Centre Pompidou Paris (slides), Boston Museum of Fine Art; work also in many private collections internationally; *Representing Galleries* Mobilia Gallery Cambridge MA USA; *Books* incl: Jewellery Concepts and Technology (1982), The Fontana Dictionary of Modern Thought (1984), Pioneers of Modern Craft (1997), Dictionary of Women Artists (1997), Contemporary Applied Arts – 50 Years of Craft (1998), Dictionnaire International Du Bijou (1998), Crafts in Britain in the 20th Century (1999), The Ring – Design Past and Present (1999), Design Sourcebook: Jewellery (1999), 25 Years of Crafts Council Shop at the V&A (1999), Jewels and Jewellery (by Clare Philips, 2004), New Directions in Jewellery (2005), Masters: Gold (2008), Vintage Jewellery (foreword, 2010); *Recordings* The National Life Story Collection British Library Sound Archive (2000); *Recreations* gardening (hybridising Iris Germanica), growing camellias, Siamese cats, pistol shooting; *Style—* Gerda Flöckinger, CBE; ✉ c/o Crafts Council Islington, 44A Pentonville Road, London N1 9BY; c/o Mobilia Gallery (e-mail mobiliaart@verizon.net); c/o Tatjana Marsden, Marsden Woo Gallery, 17–18 Great Sutton Street, London EC1V 0DN

FLOOD, Dr David Andrew; s of Frederick Joseph Alfred Flood, of Selsey, W Sussex, and June Kathleen, *née* Alexander; *b* 10 November 1955, Guildford, Surrey; *Educ* Royal GS Guildford, St John's Coll Oxford (MA), Clare Coll Cambridge (PGCE); *m* 26 June 1976, Alayne Priscilla, da of late Maurice Ewart Nicholas, of Farnborough, Hants; 2 da (Olivia Kathryn b 1979, Annalisa Harriet b 1989), 2 s (Christopher Nicholas b 1982, Joshua Samuel b 1986); *Career* asst organist Canterbury Cathedral 1978–86, music master King's Sch Canterbury 1978–86; organist and master of choristers: Lincoln Cathedral 1986–88, Canterbury Cathedral 1988–; pres Cathedral Organists' Assoc 2016–19; organist for: enthronement of Archbishop Runcie 1980, visit of Pope John Paul II 1982; musical dir for: enthronement of Archbishop Carey 1991, Lambeth Conf 1998 and 2008, enthronement of Archbishop Williams 2003, enthronement of Archbishop Welby 2013; asst dir Canterbury Choral Soc 1978–85, fndr and dir Canterbury Cantata Choir 1985–86; musical dir: Lincoln Choral Soc 1986–88, Canterbury Music Club 1984–86 and 1988–, Whitstable Choral Soc 1995–, Canterbury Singers 1996–99; pres Cathedral Organists Assoc 2016; visiting prof Canterbury Christ Church Univ 2011; visiting fell St John's Coll Durham 2007, hon fell Canterbury Christ Church Univ 2008; hon sr memb Darwin Coll Univ of Kent, Kent ambass 2015; Hon DMus Univ of Kent 2002; FRCO 1976, memb Royal Soc of Musicians 1997; Hon FGCM 2000; *Recreations* travel, motoring, DIY; *Style—* Dr David Flood; ✉ 6 The Precincts, Canterbury, Kent CT1 2EE (☎ 01227 865242, fax 01227 865222, e-mail davidf@canterbury-cathedral.org)

FLOOD, Debbie; da of Edward John Flood, and Barbara Margaret, *née* Houston; *b* 27 February 1980, Harrogate, N Yorks; *Educ* Univ of Reading (BSc); *Career* amateur rower; memb Leander Club (first ever female capt); achievements incl: Bronze medal double sculls World Junior Championships 1998, Gold medal double sculls Under 23 World Championships 1999, Gold medal single sculls Under 23 World Championships 2000, winner double sculls World Cup 2002, winner quadruple sculls World Cup 2004, Silver medal quadruple sculls Olympic Games Athens 2004, Gold medal quadruple sculls World Championships 2006 and 2007, Silver medal quadruple sculls Olympic Games Beijing 2008, Gold medal quadruple sculls World Championships 2010, sixth place quadruple sculls Olympic Games London 2012; indoor rowing: jr champion British Indoor Rowing Championships 1997, jr champion World Indoor Rowing Championships 1998, under 23 champion British Indoor Rowing Championships 1999; former prison offr, currently working for Christians in Sport; *Style—* Miss Debbie Flood

FLOOD, Michael Donovan (Mik); s of late Gp Capt Donovan John Flood, DFC, AFC, of Wyton, and Vivien Ruth, *née* Alison; *b* 7 May 1949; *Educ* St George's Coll Weybridge, Llangefni County Sch Anglesey; *m* 1, 1975 (m dis 1989), Julie, da of Paul Ward; 1 da (Amy Louise b 8 April 1976); m 2, 2001 (m dis 2012), Ionela, da of Constantin Niculae; *Career* fndr and artistic dir Chapter Arts Centre Cardiff 1970–81, devpt dir Baltimore Theater Project 1981–82, administrator Pip Simmons Theatre Gp 1982–83, freelance prodr 1983–85; dir: Watermans Arts Centre Brentford 1985–90, Inst of Contemporary Arts 1990–97; int arts and cultural policy conslt 1997–; chm: Bd London Electronic Arts 1997–2001, The Lux Centre for Film, Video and Digital Arts 1998–2001; pres Informal European Theatre Meeting (IETM) 1998–2002; prodr: Woyzeck (open air prodn with Pip Simmons Theatre Gp) 1976, Deadwood (open air prodn with Son et Lumière Theatre Gp, Time Out award winner) 1986, Offshore Rig (open air prodn with Bow Gamelan Ensemble) 1987; dir Pip Simmons Theatre Gp 1977–81, co-fndr Nat Assoc of Arts Centres 1976; memb: Assessment Ctee West Midlands Arts Assoc 1976, Film Ctee Welsh Arts Cncl 1976–80, Exec Ctee SE Wales Arts Assoc 1980–81, Ct Royal Coll of Art 1990–97, Panel of Assessors Arts Cncl of England Arts for Everyone Lottery Fund 1997–2001, Bd European Forum for Arts and Heritage 2004–08, Bd Thames Festival 2004–08; awarded HRH Queen Elizabeth II Silver Jubilee Medal for outstanding services to the arts and community 1977; *Recreations* sailing, ichthyology; *Clubs* Groucho; *Style—* Mik Flood, Esq; ✉ 1 Marshall House, Dorncliffe Road, London SW6 5LF (☎ 020 7736 8668, e-mail mik@mikflood.com, website www.mikflood.com)

FLOOD, Thomas Oliver (Tom); CBE (2004); s of Thomas Flood (d 1988), of Newbridge, Co Kildare, and Elizabeth, *née* O'Byrne; *b* 21 May 1947, Dublin; *Educ* Dominican Coll Newbridge, UCD (BA); *Partner* Paul Cornes (civil partnership 2006); *Career* A E Herbert Ltd (machine tools) 1969–70, W S Atkins (consulting engrs) 1970–72; 3M United Kingdom plc: Market Research Dept 1972–73, mktg Industrial Products 1973–75, mktg Packaging Systems Gp 1975–77, sales mangr Strapping Systems 1977–79, sales and mktg mangr Decorative Packing 1979–82, gp mktg mangr Packaging Systems 1982–86; BTCV (formerly British Tst for Conservation Volunteers): mktg dir 1986–90, dep chief exec 1990–92, chief exec 1992–2012; chair: DEFRA Water Leadership Innovation Gp 2013–, DEFRA The Lost Effra Project 2013–, DEFRA Civil Soc Partnership Network 2015–; co-chair DEFRA Civil Soc Advsy Bd (formerly DEFRA Third Sector Advsy Bd) 2009–; memb: UK Biodiversity Steering Gp, Environment Advsy Task Force Gp, New Deal Taskforce, Home Office Working Gp on Barriers to Volunteering, British Citizenship 1999, Home Office Ctee on Public Liability, Home Office Ctee Governance Strategy Gp 2003, Groundwork Light Touch Review ODPM 2004, Cleaner, Safer, Greener Communities CRG 2004, Third Sector Taskforce on Climate Change, The Environment and Sustainable Devpt 2009–; memb Bd ACEVO 2011–12, chair ACEVO Solutions Ltd 2011–, ind non-exec dir EST Ltd 2014–; vice-pres Conservation Volunteers 2012–16, tstee and memb Audit Ctee Energy Saving Tst 2012–, ambass FoodCycle 2012–13, memb Ctee Queens Award for Voluntary Service 2012–, vice-pres CPRE 2013–, memb Cncl Nat Tst 2013–15, chair Energy Saving Tst Fndn 2014–, dir UK Water Partnership 2015–, chair DEFRA Civil Soc Partnership Network 2015–; patron Knowledge Peers 2011; Liveryman Worshipful Co of Water Conservators 2016; FRSA 1996, CCMI 2010 (FCIM 1996); *Recreations* cinema, cooking, opera, theatre, walking; *Clubs* Royal Cwlth; *Style—* Tom Flood, Esq, CBE; ✉ Flat 18, 6 Pear Tree Court, London EC1R 0DW (☎ 020 7336 8239, mobile 07711262198, e-mail tomnflood@hotmail.co.uk)

FLORENCE, Prof Alexander Taylor; CBE (1994); s of Alexander Charles Gerrard Florence (d 1985), and Margaret, *née* Taylor (d 2003); *b* 9 September 1940, London; *Educ* Queen's Park Sch Glasgow, Univ of Glasgow (BSc, PhD), Royal Coll of Science and Technol, Univ of Strathclyde (DSc); *m* 1, 1964 (m dis 1995), Elizabeth Catherine, *née* McRae; 2 s (Graham b 1966, Alastair b 1969), 1 da (Gillian b 1972); m 2, 2000, Dr Florence Madsen, da of Bernard Madsen, of Paris; *Career* prof of pharmacy Univ of Strathclyde 1976–88 (lectr in pharmaceutical chemistry 1966–72, sr lectr 1972–76), dean Sch of Pharmacy Univ of London 1989–2006 (prof emeritus 2006–); pres European Assoc Faculties of Pharmacy 1997–2001, pres Controlled Release Soc 2002–03, vice-pres Federation Internationale Pharmaceutique 1998–2000; memb Ctee on Safety of Meds 1982–98 (chm Sub-Ctee on Chemistry Pharmacy and Standards 1989–98); ed-in-chief Int Jl of Pharmaceutics 2009–15 (ed-in-chief Europe 1997–2008); Founders Award Controlled Release Soc 2009; Hon Dr: Hoshi Univ Tokyo 2003, Univ of Strathclyde 2004, Danish Univ of Pharmaceutical Sciences Copenhagen 2006, UEA 2007, Univ of London 2009; FRSC 1977, FRSE 1987, FRPharmS 1987, FRSA 1989; *Books* Solubilization by Surface Active Agents (with P H Elworthy and C B Macfarlane, 1968), Surfactant Systems (with D Attwood, 1983), Physicochemical Principles of Pharmacy (with D Attwood, 1983, 6 edn 2015), Physical Pharmacy (with David Attwood, 2008, 2 edn 2012), Introduction to Clinical Pharmaceutics (2010); *Recreations* music, painting, writing; *Style—* Prof Alexander Florence, CBE, FRSE; ✉ 18 Marine Parade, Dundee DD1 3BN (e-mail ataylorflorence@aol.com); La Providence G, 7 rue Sincaire, Nice 06300, France

FLORENCE, David; s of George Florence, of Edinburgh, and Jill, *née* Ramage; *b* 8 August 1982, Aberdeen; *Educ* Stewarts Melville Coll Edinburgh, Univ of Nottingham (BSc); *Career* canoeist; debut competition 1997, memb Br sr team (C1 class) 2001–; achievements incl: Bronze medal World Cup series La Seu d'Urgell leg 2005, Gold medal World Cup series Augsburg leg 2006, Bronze medals World Cup series Prague and Augsburg legs 2007, Silver medal slalom C1 Olympic Games Beijing 2008, Silver medal C2 team World Championships 2009, Silver medal C2 team European Championships 2009, Bronze medal C2 World Championships 2010, 2 Bronze medals C2 and C2 team European Championships 2010, Bronze medal C2 team World Championships 2011, Silver medal C2 Olympic Games London 2012; *Recreations* skiing, golf, tennis, languages, bagpipes; *Clubs* Forth Canoe (Edinburgh); *Style—* David Florence, Esq; ✉ website www.davidflorence.com

FLORENCE, Dr Peter; MBE (2005); s of Norman Florence (d 1996), and Rhoda Lewis; *b* 4 October 1964, Kingston; *Educ* Ipswich Sch, Jesus Coll Cambridge (MA), Université de Paris-Sorbonne; *m* 12 Oct 1996, Becky Shaw; 4 s (Isaac b 25 Aug 1997, Ru b 13 Nov 2000, Morgan, Jacob (twins) b 10 March 2005); *Career* dir Hay Festival 1988–; advsr: FLIP (Festa Literária Internacional de Parati) Brazil, Festival Literatura Mantova; Hon DLitt Univ of Glamorgan, Hon DLitt Open Univ; fell Hereford Art Coll, creative fell Univ of Wales Bangor, fell Univ of Cardiff, fell Royal Welsh Coll of Music and Drama; *Publications* Ox-Tales Anthologies: Earth, Air, Fire, Water (co-ed, 2009), Ox-Travels Anthology (co-ed, 2011), Ox-Crimes Anthology (co-ed, 2014); *Recreations* family, food, walking; *Clubs* Hawks' (Cambridge), Groucho; *Style—* Dr Peter Florence, MBE; ✉ The Hay Festival, Drill Hall, Lion Street, Hay HR3 5AD

FLOUD, Prof Sir Roderick Castle; kt (2005); s of Bernard Francis Castle Floud (d 1967), and Ailsa, *née* Craig (d 1967); *b* 1 April 1942; *Educ* Brentwood Sch, Wadham Coll Oxford (MA), Nuffield Coll Oxford (DPhil); *m* 6 Aug 1964, Cynthia Anne, da of Lt Col Leslie Harold Smith, OBE, of Leicester; 2 da (Lydia b 1969, Sarah b 1971); *Career* lectr in econ history: UCL 1966–69, Univ of Cambridge 1969–75; fell and tutor Emmanuel Coll Cambridge 1969–75, prof of modern history Birkbeck Coll London 1975–88, visiting prof Stanford Univ 1980–81, provost and prof London Guildhall Univ (formerly City of London Poly) 1988–2002, vice-chancellor London Metropolitan Univ (merger of London Guildhall Univ and Univ of North London) 2002–04, pres London Met Univ 2004–06 (prof emeritus 2006–), acting dean Sch of Advanced Study Univ of London 2007–09; vice-pres European Univ Assoc 2005–07, chair Standing Ctee for Social Sciences European Science Fndn 2007–15; memb: ESRC 1993–97, Cncl Universities UK (formerly CVCP) 1997–2005 (vice-pres 1998–2001, pres 2001–03), Tower Hamlets Coll Corp 1997–2001, London Devpt Partnership Bd 1998–2001, Cncl Gresham Coll 1998–2014; fell Birkbeck Coll 1995, assoc memb Nuffield Coll Oxford 2007–16, provost Gresham Coll London 2008–14 (hon fell 2014–); Liveryman Co of Information Technologists 2003–15 (Freeman 1996), Liveryman Worshipful Co of Educators (Master 2005–06); Hon DLitt City Univ 1999, hon fell Wadham Coll Oxford 1999, hon fell Emmanuel Coll Cambridge 2003; academician Academy for the Learned Societies in the Social Sciences (AcSS) 2000; hon DLitt Univ of Westminster 2006; FRHistS 1980, FRSA 1989, FBA 2002, memb Academia Europaea 2012; *Books* An Introduction to Quantitative Methods for Historians (1973, 1979), Essays in Quantitative Economic History (ed, 1974), The British Machine Tool Industry 1850–1914 (1976), The Economic History of Britain since 1700 (co-ed, 1981, 4 edn 2014), The Power of the Past: Essays in Honour of Eric Hobsbawm (co-ed, 1984), Height, Health and History: Nutritional Status in the United Kingdom 1750–1980 (with K Wachter and A Gregory, 1990), The People and the British Economy 1830–1914 (1997),

Health and Welfare during Industrialization (co-ed 1997), London Higher (co-ed, 1998), The Changing Body: Health, Nutrition and Human Development in the Western World since 1700 (with R W Fogel, B Harris and S C Hong, 2011), The Cambridge Economic History of Modern Britain (co-ed, 2014), Health, Mortality and the Standard of Living in N America Since 1700 (ed, with R W Fogel, B Harris and S C Hong, 2014); also author of numerous articles and reviews; *Recreations* walking, skiing, theatre; *Clubs* Athenaeum; *Style—* Prof Sir Roderick Floud; ✉ Duck Bottom, 15 Flint Street, Haddenham, Buckinghamshire HP17 8AL (☎ 01844 291086, e-mail roderick.floud@btinternet.com)

FLOWER, Andrew (Andy); OBE (2011); s of William Frank Flower, and Jean Frances Flower; *b* 28 April 1968, Cape Town; *Educ* Vainona HS; *Career* former cricketer (wicketkeeper/batsman); club sides: Mashonaland 1993–94, Essex CCC 2002–06; Zimbabwe 1992–2003: 63 Tests (25 as capt incl first Test victory v Pakistan 1995), 213 one-day ints; England team: asst coach 2007–09, dir 2009–; world record holder: highest Test innings by a wicketkeeper (232 not out v India 2000), highest Test partnership between brothers (with Grant Flower, 265 runs); Zimbabwe Cricketer of the Year 1997, 1998, 2000 and 2001, Zimbabwe Sportsperson of the Year 2000–01, Int Cricketer of the Year 2000–01, Wisden Cricketer of the Year 2002; *Recreations* squash, tennis, reading, martial arts, adventure sports; *Style—* Andy Flower, Esq, OBE

FLOWER, Dr Antony John Frank (Tony); s of Frank Robert Edward Flower (d 1977), of Clyst Hydon, Devon, and Dorothy Elizabeth (d 1999), *née* Williams; *b* 2 February 1951; *Educ* Chipping Sodbury GS, Univ of Exeter (BA, MA), Univ of Leicester (PhD); *Career* graphic designer 1973–76, first gen sec Tawney Soc 1982–88, co-ordinator Argo Venture 1984–; fndr memb SDP 1981, memb Cncl for Soc Democracy 1982–83; dir: Res Inst for Econ and Social Affrs 1982–92, Argo Tst 1986–, Healthline Health Info Serv 1986–88, Health Info Tst 1987–88 (tstee 1988–90), Centre for Educnl Choice 1988–90, Environmental Concern Centre in Europe 1990–92; dir of devpt Green Alliance 1991–92; sec Ecological Studies Inst 1991–92, conslt mangr Construction Industry Environmental Forum 1992–96; chm: Inst of Community Studies 2001–05 (dep dir 1994–2005, tstee 1993–2005, sr fell), Mutual Aid Centre 2001–05 (tstee 1990–2005, dep dir 1994–2005), Young Fndn (merged Inst of Community Studies and Mutual Aid Centre) 2005–07; chm: Education Extra 2001, ContinYou 2003–04; conslt: Joseph Rowntree Reform Tst Ltd 1993–2003, Family Covenant Assoc 1994–, Cambridge Female Educn Tst 1999–2003; GAIA: memb Cncl 1988–2000, ed Tawney Journal 1982–88; co-fndr and managing ed Samizdat magazine 1988–91; assoc: Open Coll of the Arts 1988–, Redesign Ltd 1989–94, Nicholas Lacey and Partners (architects) 1989–, IPPR 1989–95, Rocklabs (Geological Analysts) 1993–; memb Advsy Bd The Earth Centre 1990–2000; patron: Tower Hamlets Summer Univ 1995–2007, National Space Science Centre 1996–; *Books* Starting to Write (with Graham Mort, 1990), The Alternative (with Ben Pimlott and Anthony Wright, 1990), Young at Eighty (ed with Geoff Dench and Kate Gavron, 1995), Guide to Pressure Groups (consultant ed, PMS, 1995), Trusting In Change (2004); *Recreations* collecting junk, making and restoring musical instruments; *Style—* Dr Tony Flower; ✉ 18 Victoria Park Square, London E2 9PF (☎ 020 8980 6263, fax 020 8980 0701)

FLOWER, Prof Roderick John; s of Gp Capt Leslie Ralph Flower MBE, MM (d 1994), of Stubbington, Hants, and Audrey Ellen, *née* Eckett (d 1991); *b* 29 November 1945; *Educ* Kingwell Court Sch, Woodbridge Sch, Univ of Sheffield (BSc, Thomas Woodcock Physiology Prize), Univ of London (PhD, DSc); *m* 1994, Lindsay Joyce, da of Henry Arthur Joseph Riddell; *Career* sr scientist Dept of Prostaglandin Res Wellcome Research Labs Kent 1975–84 (memb of staff 1973–75), head Sch of Pharmacy and Pharmacology Univ of Bath 1987–89 (prof of pharmacology 1984–89), prof of biochemical pharmacology Bart's and the Royal London Sch of Med and Dentistry 1989– (head Div of Pharmacology 1998–2003); Br Pharmacological Soc: memb 1974, chm Ctee 1989–92, meeting sec 1998–2000, pres 2001–03, Sandoz Prize 1978, Gaddum Meml Lecture and Medal 1986; William Withering Lecture RCP 2003, Bayliss-Starling Prize Physiological Soc 2006; Hon LLD Univ of Bath 2011, Hon DSc Univ of Sheffield 2016; memb Biochemical Soc 1985, FMedSci 2001, fell Academia Europaea 2003, FRS 2003, fell Br Pharmacological Soc 2004, FSB 2011; *Publications* Glucocorticoids (jtly, 2001), Rang & Dale's Pharmacology (jtly, 8 edn 2014); *Recreations* photography, the history of pharmacology; *Clubs* Athenaeum; *Style—* Prof Roderick Flower; ✉ Department of Biochemical Pharmacology, The William Harvey Research Institute, St Bartholomew's and the Royal London School of Medicine and Dentistry, Charterhouse Square, London EC1M 6BQ (☎ 020 7882 8781, fax 020 7882 5655, e-mail r.j.flower@qmul.ac.uk)

FLOWERS, Angela Mary; da of Charles Geoffrey Holland (d 1974), of Ashford, Kent, and Olive Alexandra, *née* Stiby (d 1987); *b* 19 December 1932; *Educ* Westonbirt Sch, Wychwood Sch Oxford, Webber Douglas Sch of Singing & Dramatic Art (Dip); *m* 1, 1952 (m dis 1973), Adrian Flowers; 3 s (Adam b 1953, Matthew, *qv*, b 1956, Daniel b 1959), 1 da (Francesca b 1965); m 2, 2003, Robert Heller, *qv*; 1 da (Rachel Pearl b 1973); *Career* worked in stage, film and advtg until 1967, fndr Angela Flowers Gallery Lisle St 1970 (Portland Mews W1 1971–78, Tottenham Mews W1 1978–88, Richmond Rd E8 1988–2002), chm Angela Flowers Gallery plc 1989–, promotes encourages and shows the work of young emerging and established artists; Hon DUniv East London 1999; sr fell RCA 1994; *Recreations* singing, piano, trombone; *Clubs* Groucho; *Style—* Miss Angela Flowers; ✉ Flowers East, 82 Kingsland Road, London E2 8DP (e-mail angelaflowers1932@gmail.com, website www.flowerseast.com)

FLOWERS, Matthew Dominic; s of Adrian John Flowers, of London, and Angela Mary Flowers, *qv*; *b* 8 October 1956; *Educ* William Ellis GS; *m* 2006, Emily Jane; 2 da (Grace b 2009, Melody b 2011), 2 s from previous marriages (Patrick b 1987, Jackson b 1995); *Career* asst Angela Flowers Gallery 1975–78, mangr and keyboard player for pop group Sore Throat 1975–81, played in various other bands including Blue Zoo (Cry Boy Cry Top Twenty hit 1982, led to two appearances on Top of the Pops) 1981–83; Angela Flowers Gallery: pt/t asst 1981–83, mangr 1983–88, md 1988–; fndr: Flowers West Santa Monica 1998, Flowers Central Cork St W1 2001, Flowers New York 529 West 20th St NYC 2003; publisher (with ed, Mike von Joel) State of Art newspaper 2005–09; govr Byam Shaw Sch of Art 1990–2000; memb: Cncl Mgmnt of Art Servs Grants 1987–92, Bradford Print Biennale Ctee 1989, Organising Ctee of London Art Fair 1989–95, Exec Soc of London Art Dealers 1993–96, Organising Ctee Miami Art Fair 1995, Patrons of New Art (Tate Gallery) 1995–99, Organising Ctee Toronto Art Fair 2003–07; non-exec dir of DACS 2008–; *Books* Publisher of many books including monographs on Nicola Hicks, Patrick Hughes, Josef Herman, Jack Smith and Bernard Cohen; and surveys such as British Figurative Art (Part One: Painting; Part Two: Sculpture) and British Abstract Painting; *Recreations* music, chess, soccer; *Style—* Matthew Flowers, Esq; ✉ Flowers Gallery, 82 Kingsland Road, London E2 8DP (☎ 020 7920 7777, fax 020 7920 7770, e-mail info@flowersgalleries.com)

FLOYD, Rt Hon the Lord Justice; Sir Christopher David Floyd; kt (2007), PC (2013); s of David Floyd, journalist, and Hana, *née* Goldman; *b* 20 December 1951; *Educ* Westminster, Trinity Coll Cambridge (MA); *m* 1974, Rosalind Jane, *née* Arscott; 1 s, 2 da; *Career* called to the Bar Inner Temple 1975 (bencher 2001), memb Irish Bar 1989, QC 1992, head intellectual property chambers at 11 South Square Gray's Inn 1994–2007, asst recorder Patents Co Court 1994–2000, dep High Court judge Patents Court 1999, recorder 2000–07, judge of the High Court of Justice (Chancery Div) 2007–13, a nominated judge of the Patents Court 2007–13 (judge in charge 2011–13), a Lord Justice of Appeal 2013–; a dep chm Copyright Tbnl 1996–2007, memb Bar Cncl Professional Conduct and Complaints Ctee 1999–2002, memb Bar Cncl 2000–04, memb Bar Cncl European Ctee 2003–04; chm: Intellectual Property Bar Assoc 2000–04, Competition Appeal Tbnl 2008–13, QC Appointments Complaints Ctee 2013–; writer of various articles in jls; *Recreations* cycling, walking, tennis, watching cricket; *Clubs* Garrick; *Style—* The Rt Hon the Lord Justice Floyd; ✉ Royal Courts of Justice, Strand, London WC2A 2LL

FLOYD, Sir Giles Henry Charles; 7 Bt (UK 1816); s of Lt-Col Sir John Duckett Floyd, 6 Bt, TD (d 1975); *b* 27 February 1932; *Educ* Eton; *m* 1, 23 Nov 1954 (m dis 1978), Lady Gillian Moyra Katherine Cecil, da of 6 Marquess of Exeter, KCMG; 2 s (David Henry Cecil b 1956, Henry Edward Cecil b 1958 d 2013); m 2, 1985, Judy Sophia, er da of late William Leonard Tregoning, CBE, of Landue, Launceston, Cornwall, and formerly w of Thomas Ernest Lane, of Tickencote Hall, Stamford; *Heir* s David Floyd; *Career* farmer; dir Burghley Estate Farms 1958–; High Sheriff of Rutland 1968; Liveryman Worshipful Co of Skinners; *Recreations* fishing; *Clubs* Turf; *Style—* Sir Giles Floyd, Bt; ✉ Tinwell Manor, Stamford, Lincolnshire PE9 3UF (☎ 01780 762676)

FLOYD, Richard Eaglesfield; s of Harold Bailey Floyd (d 1999), and (Edith) Margeret, *née* Griffith (d 1954); *b* 9 June 1938, Purley, Surrey; *Educ* Dean Close Sch Cheltenham; *m* 1995, Linda Ann Robinson, *née* Newnham; *Career* articled clerk Fincham Vallance & Co 1956–61 (sr clerk 1961–62 and 1964–65), insolvency administrator Cork Gully 1965–70, ptnr Floyd Nash & Co (latterly Richard Floyd & Co) 1971–2009 (held appts as administrative receiver, administrator, liquidator and tstee), conslt Baker Tilly 1997–2000, with Jeremy Knight & Co LLP 2009–; author of numerous articles on insolvency matters in specialised jls; memb Editorial Advsy Bd Tolley's Insolvency Law and Practice 1985–2007; Freeman City of London 1985, Liveryman Worshipful Co of Basketmakers 1998; FCA; *Books* with I S Grier: Voluntary Liquidation and Receivership (1985, 4 edn, 1999), Personal Insolvency – A Practical Guide (with F Brumby and S P E Knight, 1987, 4 edn 2012), Corporate Recovery: Administration Orders and Voluntary Arrangements (1995); *Recreations* poetry, mountain walking; *Style—* Richard Floyd, Esq; ✉ 29 Roseacre Garden, Chilworth, Guildford, Surrey GU4 8RQ (☎ 01483 302782)

FLOYER, Cecile Anne (Ceal); da of David Cornish Floyer (d 1996), of Devon, and Gerlinde Moger, *née* Mayer; *b* 18 April 1968, Karachi, Pakistan; *Educ* Goldsmiths Coll London (BA); *Career* artist; work in public collections at MOMA San Francisco and Denver Art Museum; Philip Morris Scholarship Künstlerhaus Bethanien Berlin 1997, Paul Hamlyn Award 2002; *Selected Solo Exhibitions* Tramway Project Room Glasgow 1996, Anthony Wilkinson Fine Art London 1996, Gavin Brown's Enterprise NYC 1996, Galleria Primo Piano Rome 1996 and 1997, City Racing London 1997, Herzliya Museum of Art Tel Aviv 1997, Lisson Gallery London 1997 and 2002, Künstlerhaus Bethanien Berlin 1998, Casey Kaplan NYC 1999, Kunsthalle Bern 1999, Pinksummer Genova 2000 and 2002, Ikon Gallery Birmingham 2001, Inst of Visual Arts Milwaukee 2001, Massive Reduction (Peer Shoreditch Town Hall London) 2001, Ceal Floyer/MATRIX 192 37' 4' (Univ of Calif Berkeley Art Museum) 2001, X'rummet (Statens Museum for Kunst Copenhagen) 2002, Index (Swedish Contemporary Art Fndn Stockholm) 2002, Casey Kaplan NYC 2003, Portikus Frankfurt 2003, Kabinett füm Aktulle Bremerhaven; *Selected Group Exhibitions* Fast Surface (Chisenhale Gallery London) 1993, Fast Forward (ICA London) 1994, Making Mischief (St James's Street London) 1994, Freddy Contreras/Ceal Floyer (The Showroom London) 1995, General Release: Young British Artists at Scuola di San Pasquale (Venice Biennale) 1995, Just Do It (Cubitt Gallery London) 1995, 4th Istanbul Biennale 1995, British Art Show 4 (Manchester, Edinburgh and Cardiff) 1995, Five Artists (Frith Street Gallery London) 1995, Oporto Festival of Contemporary Art 1996, Life/Live (Musée d'Art Moderne de la Ville de Paris and Centro Cultural de Belem Lisbon) 1996–97, Snowflakes Falling on the International Dateline (Casco Utrecht) 1997, Belladonna (ICA London) 1997, Treasure Island (Centro de Art Moderna/Calouste Gulbenkian Fndn Lisbon) 1997, Sentimental Education (Cabinet Gallery London) 1997, Urban Legends – London (Staatliche Kunsthalle Baden-Baden) 1997, Belladonna, A Selection (The Minories Colchester) 1997, You Are Here (RCA London) 1997, I Luoghi Ritrovati (Centro Civico Per L'Arte Contemporanea La Grancia Serre di Rapolano Siena) 1997, Material Culture: the object in British art in the 80's and 90's (Hayward Gallery London) 1997, Projects (Irish MOMA) 1997, Pictura Britannica (Museum of Contemporary Art Sydney and tour) 1997, Genius Loci (Kunsthalle Bern) 1998, Martin Creed, Ceal Floyer, John Frankland (Delfina Studios London) 1998, Dimensions variable (Br Cncl touring exhbn) 1998, Sunday (Cabinet Gallery London) 1998, Seamless (De Appel Fndn Amsterdam) 1998, In the Meantime (Galeria Estrany-de la Moto Barcelona) 1998, Real/Life – New British Art 1998–1999 (Tochigi Prefectural Museum of Fine Arts and tour) 1998, Drawing Itself (London Inst Gallery) 1998, Recent British Art at Kunstraum (Kunstraum Innsbruck) 1998, Then and Now (Lisson Gallery London) 1998, Every Day (11th Biennale in Sydney) 1998, Malos Habitos (Soledad Lorenzo Madrid) 1998, Triennale der Kleinplastik (Stuttgart) 1998, Thinking Aloud (South Bank Centre touring exhbn) 1998, minimalisms (Akademie der Künste Berlin) 1998, Richard Wentworth & Ceal Floyer (Galerie Carlos Poy Barcelona) 1998 (Galeria Rafael Ortiz Seville 1999), Looking at Ourselves: Works by Women Artists from the Logan Collection (MOMA San Francisco) 1999, Inside Out (Overgaden – Kulturministeriets Udstillningshus for Nutidig Kunst Copenhagen) 1999, On Your Own Time (PS1 Contemporary Art Center NYC) 1999, This Other World of Ours (TV Gallery Moscow) 1999, Luminous Mischief (Yokohama Portside Gallery Kanagawa) 1999, Mirror's Edge (Bild Museet Umeå and tour) 1999, Tramway Glasgow 1999, Peace (Museum für Gegenwarts Kunst Zurich) 1999, Trace (Tate Gallery Liverpool Liverpool Biennale) 1999, From There To Here – Art From London (Konsthallen Gothenburg) 1999, Edit (Badischer Kunstverein Karlsruhe) 2000, Crossroads: Artists in Berlin (Communidad de Madrid) 2000, Quotidiana (Castello di Rivoli Turin) 2000, Drive (Govett-Brewster Art Gallery New Plymouth) 2000, Making Time: Considering Time as a Material in Contemporary Video & Film (Palm Beach ICA) 2000, Extra Ordinary (James Cohan Gallery NYC) 2000, Film/Video Works – Lisson Gallery at 9 Keane Street (Lisson Gallery London) 2000, A Shot in the Head (Lisson Gallery London) 2000, Action, we're filming (Villa Arson Nice) 2000–01, City Racing 1988–1998: a partial account (ICA London) 2001, Nothing (NGCA Sunderland and tour) 2001, Squatters #1 (Witte de With Center for Contemporary Art Rotterdam and Museu de Serralves Porto) 2001, Media Connection (Palazzo delle Esposizioni Rome) 2001, Passion (Galerie Ascan Crone Hamburg and Berlin) 2001, Loop – Alles auf Anfang (Kunsthalle der Hypo-Kulturstiftung Munich) 2001, Sunday Afternoon (303 Gallery NYC) 2002, Colour White (De La Warr Pavilion Bexhill on Sea) 2002, Liminal Space (Center for Curatorial Studies Bard Coll Annadale-on-Hudson) 2002, Tempo (MOMA NYC) 2002, Four women and one pregnant man (Galleri MGM Oslo) 2002, Invitation (Museum für Moderne Kunst Frankfurt am Main) 2002, poT (Liverpool Biennial of Contemporary Art and tour) 2002, Loop. Back to the Beginning (Contemporary Arts Center Fifth Street Space Cincinnati) 2002, 40 Jahre: Fluxus und dir Folgen (Kunstsommer Wiesbaden 2002) 2002, Spiritus (Magasin 3 Stockholm) 2003, Perfect Timeless Repetition (c/o Atle Gerhardsen Berlin) 2003, Band Wagon Jumping (Norwich Gallery) 2003, Lapdissolve (Casey Kaplan NYC) 2003, Days Like These (Tate Britain) 2003, 50th Venice Biennale (Italian Pavillion) 2003; *Public Collections* Tate Collection, Museum für Moderne Kunst Frankfurt, Contemporary Art Soc Collection; *Screenings* The Meaning of Life (Part II) (CCA Glasgow and Art Nolde Stockholm) 1996, Such is Life (Serpentine Gallery Bookshop London) 1996, Fourth Wall – Waiting (Public Art Devpt Tst in assoc with RNT London) 1999; *Style—* Ms Ceal Floyer; ✉ Lisson Gallery (London) Ltd, 67 Lisson Street, London NW1 5DA (☎ 020 7724 2739, fax 020 7724 7124)

F

FLYNN, David Owen; s of Vincent Flynn, and Margaret, *née* Healy; *b* 16 August 1976, London; *m* 6 July 2013, Kam Kandola Flynn; *Career* Endemol UK: dep creative dir until 2007, md Brighter Pictures 2007–09, jt md Remarkable Television 2009–13 (creator and exec prodr: The Million Pound Drop Live, The Bank Job, The Common Denominator, Pointless), chief creative offr Endemol UK 2013–; co-chair Digital Bd; *Style—* David Flynn, Esq; ✉ Endemol UK, Shepherd's Building Central, Charecroft Way, Shepherd's Bush, London W14 0EE

FLYNN, Sister Ellen; da of Daniel Flynn, and Doris, *née* Ilott; *b* 15 February 1953, Nairobi, Kenya; *Educ* St Mary's Hereford, Christ's Coll Liverpool (BEd, Dip, DSLitt); *Career* teacher 1981–88, liturgy/music conslt 1989–99; The Passage: ceo 2000–09, chair 2009–; provincial cncllr Leadership Team of Sisters Nationally; tstee Depaul Tst 2000–13, chair DCSVP Services 2014–; Daughter of Charity of St Vincent de Paul; *Recreations* music; *Style—* Sister Ellen Flynn

FLYNN, Paul Phillip; MP; s of James Flynn (d 1939), and Kathleen Rosien, *née* Williams (d 1988); *b* 9 February 1935; *Educ* St Illtyd's Coll Cardiff, UC Cardiff; *m* 1, 6 Feb 1962, Ann Patricia; 1 da (Rachel Sarah b 1963 d 1979), 1 s (James Patrick b 1965); m 2, 31 Jan 1985, Lynne Samantha; *Career* chemist in steel indust 1955–81; since worked in local radio and as research asst to Euro MP Llewellyn Smith; MP (Lab) Newport W 1987–, oppn front bench spokesman on Welsh affrs May 1988–97, oppn front bench spokesman on social security Nov 1988–90, sec of state for Wales and shadow ldr House of Commons 2016–; *Books* Commons Knowledge: How to be a Backbencher (1997), Baglu 'Mlaen (1998), Dragons Led by Poodles (1999); *Clubs* Ringland Labour, Pill Labour; *Style—* Paul Flynn, Esq, MP; ✉ House of Commons, London SW1A 0AA (☎ 020 7219 3478, e-mail paulflynnmp@talk21.com, website paulflynnmp.co.uk)

FLYNN, Rachel Elizabeth; da of John Flynn, of Norwich, and Jennifer, *née* Bacon; *b* 28 June 1968, Norwich, Norfolk; *Educ* Norwich HS GPDST, Norwich Sch of Art, Univ of Durham (BA), Coll of Law York; *m* 11 Jan 1997, Rae Guest; *Career* trainee slr Townsends 1992–94; Taylor Vinters: slr 1994–2005, ptnr 2005–14; conslt slr Keystone Law 2015–; racing and stud book dir Weatherbys 2014–15; memb: Law Soc, Employment Lawyers' Assoc, Thoroughbred Breeders' Assoc, Amateur Jockeys' Assoc; Veterinary Notes for Horse Owners (contrib, 2002); *Recreations* horse racing, riding out, breeding racehorses; *Clubs* The Jockey Club Rooms; *Style—* Ms Rachel Flynn; ✉ Keystone Law, 53 Davies Street, London W1K 5JH (☎ 020 7152 6550, mobile 07739 642812, e-mail rachel.flynn@keystonelaw.co.uk)

FLYNN, Roger Patrick; s of Peter Daniel Flynn, of Sidmouth, Devon, and Shirley Josephine, *née* Kent (d 1996); *b* 4 November 1962, Sidmouth, Devon; *Educ* The King's Sch Devon, Imperial Coll London (BSc); *m* 9 August 1986, Lisa Martine, *née* Eyre; 2 da (Katie Rebecca b 29 May 1990, Lucy Abigail b 19 June 1994); *Career* with Arthur Andersen & Co 1984–88, commercial dir and gp fin dir Virgin Communications (int media gp of Virgin plc) 1991–95 (corp fin exec 1988–91), gen mangr World Sales and Distribution British Airways plc 1995–98, md Prudential Retail (subsid of Prudential plc) 1998–2000, chief exec BBC Ventures Gp Ltd 2000–04, chief exec Springboard Gp Ltd 2004–, pres int SDI Media Gp Inc 2006–09; chair Want2Bthere Ltd 2011–, chair Olive Communitcations Ltd 2013–; memb Magic Circle; memb Royal Inst of GB 1985, ACA 1988, RTS 2001; *Recreations* fitness, physics, reading, magic; *Style—* Roger Flynn, Esq; ✉ 29 Farm Street, Mayfair, London W1J 5RL (☎ 020 7355 9851, e-mail roger@springboard.uk.com)

FLYNN, Sarah Anne Judith; *see:* Markham, Sarah Anne Judith

FOAD, James; *b* 20 March 1987, Southampton, Hants; *Educ* Sophie, *née* Hutchinson; 1 da (Erin Foad); *Career* rower; achievements incl: winner Henley Royal Regatta (Britannia Cup) 2008 and (Silver Goblets and Nickels Challenge Cup), Silver medal (eights) World Championships 2010 and 2011, Bronze medal (eights) Olympic Games 2012, Silver medal (coxless pair) World Championships 2014, Gold medal (coxless pair) European Championships 2015; *Clubs* Molesey Boat, Itchen Imperial Rowing; *Style—* James Foad, Esq; ✉ 8 Ennerdale Gardens, West End, Southampton, Hampshire SO18 3NR

FOALE, Marion Ann; da of Stuart Donald Foale (d 1972), and Gertrude Lillian Maud, *née* Rayner; *b* 13 March 1939; *Educ* SW Essex Tech and Sch of Art, Sch of Fashion Design RCA (DesRCA, designed Queen's Mantle for OBE); *Children* 1 da (Polly Jones b 14 Dec 1972), 1 s (Charley Jones b 25 Jan 1977); *Career* fashion designer; fndr ptnr (with Sally Tuffin) Foale and Tuffin Ltd Carnaby Street 1961–72, signed with Puritan Fashions NY for 'Youth Quake' 1965; clothes designer for films: Kaleidoscope (with Susannah York) 1966, Two for the Road (with Audrey Hepburn) 1966; fndr own label Marion Foale (predominately producing hand knitwear) 1982–; exhibition Foale & Tuffin (Fashion and Textile Museum London) 2009–10; *Books* Marion Foale's Classic Knitwear (1987); *Recreations* painting; *Style—* Ms Marion Foale; ✉ Just Knitting Ltd, The Cottage, 133A Long Street, Atherstone, Warwickshire CV9 1AD (☎ 01827 720333, fax 01827 720444, e-mail foale@talk21.com)

FOALE, Dr Rodney Alan; s of Maurice Spencer Foale, of Melbourne, Australia, and Lyle Gwendolin, *née* Wallace; *b* 11 September 1946; *Educ* Scotch Coll Melbourne, Univ of Melbourne Med Sch; *m* 1980 (m dis 2008), Lady Emma Cecile Gordon, er da of the Marquis of Aberdeen and Temair; 2 s (Archie Alexander b 17 Sept 1984, Jamie Alexander b 1 April 1986); m 2, 2010 (m dis 2014), Dr Samina Showghi; 1 da (Amelia Jasmine b 15 Sept 2007); *Career* St Vincent's Hosp Univ of Melbourne 1972–73, med offr Australian Himalayan Expdn through India and Kashmir 1974–75, registrar Nat Heart Hosp 1975–79, clinical res fell Harvard Univ and MIT, Massachusetts Gen Hosp 1980–82, sr registrar in cardiology Hammersmith Hosp 1982–85, conslt cardiologist and clinical dir of cardiovascular science St Mary's Hosp 1985–98, dir of surgery and cardiovascular science St Mary's Hosp Tst 1998–; hon sr lectr Hammersmith Hosp 1985–98, hon sr lectr Imperial Coll 1998–; recognised teacher Univ of London 1985–; FACC 1986, FESC 1988, FRCP 1994 (MRCP 1976); *Recreations* various indoor and outdoor pursuits; *Clubs* Flyfishers', Oriental, Chelsea Arts, Shell Collectors; *Style—* Dr Rodney Foale; ✉ 66 Harley Street, London W1G 7HD (☎ 020 7323 4687, fax 020 7631 5341, e-mail raf@smht-foale.co.uk)

FOGEL, Steven Anthony; s of Joseph Gerald Fogel, JP, and Benita Rose Fogel; *b* 16 October 1951; *Educ* Carmel Coll, KCL (LLB, LLM); *m* 2 Jan 1977, Joan Selma, da of Curtis Holder (d 1972); 1 da (Frances Leah), 2 s (George Curtis, Jonathan Raphael); *Career* admitted slr 1976; sr ptnr Titmuss Sainer Dechert 1998–2000; managing ptnr (London) Dechert 2000–12, chm Uropharma 2012–; chm Sparrows Capital Ltd 2013–, non-exec dir memb Bd King & Wood Mallesons SJ Berwin LLP 2013–14; non-exec dir memb EMEA Bd King & Wood Mallesons LLP 2014–; memb Bd of Mgmnt Investment Property Forum 2002–07 (chm 2002–03); memb Anglo American Real Property Inst; tstee: Motivation 1992–2015, Advsy Bd CWM 2008–10, Bd Univ of London 2009–, Advsy Bd Landon Tsts 2009–; Freeman: City of London, Worshipful Co of Slrs; ACIArb; *Books* The Landlord and Tenant Factbook (jtly, 1992), Privity of Contract, A Practitioner's Guide (jtly, 1995, 3 edn 2000), Handbook of Rent Review (co-ed, 3 edn 2000); *Recreations* swimming, jazz, skiing; *Style—* Steven Fogel, Esq

FOGELMAN, Prof Ignac; s of Richard Fogelman (d 1975), and Ruth, *née* Tyras (d 1995); *b* 4 September 1948; *Educ* HS of Glasgow, Univ of Glasgow (BSc, MB ChB, MD); *m* 18 March 1974, Coral Niman, da of Harvey Norton (d 1980); 1 da (Gayle b 1974), 1 s (Richard b 1982); *Career* Guy's Hosp: conslt physician 1983–, dir Nuclear Med Dept 1988–97, dir Osteoporosis Screening and Res Unit 1988–, chm Bd of Examiners MSc in Nuclear Med 2001–; chm Specialist Advsy Ctee in Nuclear Med 1990–93, chm Densitometry Forum of the Nat Osteoporosis Soc 1999–2005; memb Bd and tstee Nat Osteoporosis Soc 1977–88 and 2002–08; memb Int Skeletal Soc 1988; FRCP 1987; *Books* Bone Scanning in Clinical Practice (1987), An Atlas of Clinical Nuclear Medicine (with M Maisey, 1988), An Atlas of Planar and Spect Bone Scans (with D Collier, 1988, 2 edn with L Holder, 2000), Bone Metastases (with R Rubens, 1991), The Evaluation of Osteoporosis (with H Wahner, 1994, 2 edn with G Blake, 1999), Skeletal Nuclear Medicine (with D Collier and L Rosenthall, 1996); *Recreations* bridge, theatre, opera, food, wine, music, books, travel; *Style—* Prof Ignac Fogelman; ✉ Department of Nuclear Medicine, Guy's Hospital, St Thomas Street, London SE1 9RT (☎ 020 7188 4114, fax 020 7188 4119)

FOGLE, Benjamin Myer (Ben); s of Dr Bruce Fogle, MBE, DVM, MRCVS, and Julia Foster; *b* 3 November 1973, London; *Educ* Bryanston, Univ of Portsmouth; *m* 2 Sept 2006, Marina, da of Hon Dr Jonathan Hunt; 1 s (Ludo), 1 da (Iona); *Career* TV presenter: BBC Countryfile, Animal Park, Wild in Africa, One Man and His Dog, Wild in California, Cash in the Attic, Crufts, Extreme Dreams with Ben Fogle, Through Hell and High Water, Holiday, New Lives in the Wild, Secrets of Scotts Hut, Swimming with Crocodiles, Harbour Lives, Extreme Dreams, On Thin Ice, Ben Fogle's Year of Adventures; journalist: The Telegraph, Sunday Times, Countrylife, The Guardian, NY Times, The Independent; ocean yachtmaster, RNR midshipman 1994–98, world record holder Atlantic rowing La Gomera to Antigua route (with James Cracknall, *qv*) 2005, walked to the South Pole with (with James Cracknall); pres Cncl for Nat Parks; tstee Royal Parks Fndn; ambass: WWF, Tusk; supporter: Duke of Edinburgh Awards, Hearing Dogs, RNLI, Centrepoint, Shelterbox; Freedom City of London; hon doctorate Univ of Portsmouth; FRGS; *Publications* The Tea Time Islands (2003), Offshore (2006), The Crossing (2006), Race to the Pole (2009), The Accidental Adventurer (2011), The Accidental Naturalist (2012); *Recreations* ocean rowing, desert marathons, exploration; *Style—* Ben Fogle, Esq; ✉ c/o Arlington Enterprises Limited, 1–3 Charlotte Street, London W1T 1RD (☎ 020 7580 0702, fax 020 7580 4994, e-mail hilary@arlington-enterprises.co.uk); website www.benfogle.com

FOLEY, His Hon Judge John Dominic; s of Cyril Patrick Foley (d 1972), of Bristol, and Winifred Hannah, *née* McAweeny (d 1980); *b* 17 January 1944; *Educ* St Brendan's Coll Bristol, Univ of Exeter (LLB, pres Bracton Law Soc, 1st XV rugby); *m* 1978 (m dis 1986), Helena Frances, da of Dr Kemp McGowan; 2 da (Jessica Rosalind b 23 Sept 1978, Helena Rachel b 25 Nov 1980); *Career* called to the Bar Inner Temple 1968, in practice Western Circuit 1969–, attorney-gen special prosecutor NI 1971–73, recorder of the Crown Court 1990–94 (asst recorder 1986–90), circuit judge (Western Circuit) 1994–2009; vice-pres Immigration Appeal Tbnl 1998–2005, memb Special Immigration Appeals Cmmn 2002–05 (investigating judge 2006–09); ind arbitrator (rugby discipline) Int Rugby Bd and RFU 2006–09; *Recreations* cricket, rugby, travel (especially the Caribbean), theatre, rock and blues; *Clubs* Somerset CCC, Bristol RFC, Clifton RFC, Carlton CC Barbados, Barbados Cricket Assoc; *Style—* His Hon Judge Foley

FOLEY, Lt-Gen Sir John Paul; KCB (1994, CB 1991), OBE (1979), MC (1976), DL (Herefordshire 2005); s of Maj Henry Thomas Hamilton Foley, MBE (d 1959), of Stoke Edith, Herefords, and Helen Constance Margaret, *née* Pearson (d 1985); *b* 22 April 1939; *Educ* Bradfield Coll (Mons OCS), Army Staff Coll; *m* 3 June 1972, Ann Rosamund, da of Maj John William Humphries; 2 da (Annabel b 11 July 1973, Joanna b 8 May 1976); *Career* Lt Royal Green Jackets 1959–60, Capt Royal Green Jackets 1961–69, Maj RMCS 1970, Army Staff Course Camberley 1971, Sqdn Cdr 22 SAS 1972–74, Brigade Maj 51 Inf Bde Hong Kong 1974–76, Lt Col dir staff Camberley 1976–78, Cmdg Offr 3 Bn 1978–80, Cmdt jr div Staff Coll Warminster 1981–82, Brig and arms dir MOD (dir SAS) 1983–85, student RCDS 1986, chief Br mission to Soviet forces E Germany 1987–89, Maj Gen central staffs MOD 1989–92, Cdr Br Forces Hong Kong 1992–94, Col Cmdt The Light Div 1994–97, chief Defence Intelligence 1994–97, ret 1998; Lt-Govr Guernsey CI 2000–05, High Sheriff Herefords and Worcs 2006–07, Vice Lord-Lt Herefords 2010–14, ret; Freeman City of London 1970, memb Ct of Assts Worshipful Co of Skinners 1996–2000 (Freeman 1965, Liveryman 1972); KStJ 2001; Offr Legion of Merit (USA) 1997; *Recreations* tennis, golf, walking, shooting, reading; *Clubs* Boodle's; *Style—* Lt-Gen Sir John Foley, KCB, OBE, MC, DL

FOLLAND, Nick James; s of James Charles Folland, of Ilfracombe, Devon, and Susan Rosemary Carpenter; *b* 6 October 1965, Emsworth, W Sussex; *Educ* Reading Sch, Univ of Bristol (LLB), Guildford Law Sch; *m* 15 May 1993, Emma, *née* Dunstone; 1 da (Dominique Beatrice b 11 April 1996), 1 s (Jack Charles b 5 July 1997); *Career* admitted slr: England and Wales 1993, Hong Kong 1995; slr Linklaters 1991–96, legal advsr then sr legal advsr Cable & Wireless plc 1996–2000, co sec and head of legal 365 Corporation plc 2000–01, co sec and gp legal dir Emap plc 2001–07, dir Emap Business International 2003–07, legal and corp responsibility dir Kingfisher plc 2007–12, legal and corp responsibility dir B&Q plc 2008–11 (memb Bd 2009–11), gp corp affrs dir Net Positive 2012–, ceo Crown Prosecution Service 2016–; treas Br American Project 1999–2002; *Recreations* running, cycling, sailing, skiing, expedition travel; *Style—* Nick Folland, Esq

FOLLETT, Prof Sir Brian Keith; kt (1992); *b* 22 February 1939; *Educ* Bournemouth Sch, Univ of Bristol (BSc, PhD), Univ of Wales (DSc); *m* Lady (Deb) Follett; 1 da (Karen Tracy Williams b 4 June 1965), 1 s (Richard James b 1 May 1968); *Career* NIH res fell Washington State Univ 1964–65, lectr in zoology Univ of Leeds 1965–69, lectr, reader then prof of zoology Univ of Wales Bangor 1969–78, prof of zoology Univ of Bristol 1978–93, vice-chllr Univ of Warwick 1993–2001, visiting prof of biology Univ of Oxford 2001–; chm: AHRC 2000–07, Br Library Advsy Cncl 2001–07, Teacher Trg Agency (now Teaching Agency) 2003–09, STEM Advsy Forum 2006–11; chair Royal Soc investigation into scientific aspects of livestock disease epidemics 2001–03; memb: Univs Funding Cncl 1988–91, Higher Educn Funding Cncl 1991–96, AFRC 1982–88, BBSRC (formerly AFRC) 1994–2001; tstee British Museum (Natural History) 1988–99, Royal Cmmn on Environmental Pollution 2000–05; author of over 250 scientific papers published in fields of reproductive physiology and biological clocks and of various reports for Government; Hon LLD Univ of Wales 1992, Hon FLA 1997, Hon DSc Univ Tek Malaysia 1999, Hon DSc Univ of Leicester 2001, Hon LLD Univ of Calgary 2001, Hon DLitt Univ of Oxford 2002, Hon DSc Univ of Warwick, Hon LLD Univ of St Andrews 2002, Hon DSc UEA 2004, Hon DSc Univ of London 2004, Hon DSc Univ of Bedfordshire 2008, Hon DSc Univ of Bournemouth 2008 ,Hon DSc Univ of Lancaster 2012; FRS 1984 (biological sec and vice-pres 1987–93); *Recreations* history; *Style—* Prof Sir Brian Follett, FRS; ✉ 120 Tiddington Road, Stratford-upon-Avon, Warwickshire CV37 7BB

FOLLETT, Kenneth Martin (Ken); s of late Martin Dunsford Follett, and late Lavinia Cynthia, *née* Evans; *b* 5 June 1949, Cardiff; *Educ* Harrow Weald GS, Poole Tech Coll, UCL (BA); *m* 1, 5 Jan 1968 (m dis 1985), Mary Emma Ruth, da of Horace Henry Elson (d 1988), of Kinson, Bournemouth; 1 s (Emanuele b 13 July 1968), 1 da (Marie-Claire b 11 May 1973); m 2, 8 Nov 1985 (Daphne) Barbara Follett, *qv*; *Career* journalist: S Wales Echo 1970–73, London Evening News 1973–74; dep md Everest Books 1976–77 (editorial dir 1974–76); author 1977–; pres Dyslexia Inst 1998–2008, chm Nat Year of Reading 1998–99, chair Reading is Fundamental (UK) 2005–10; Bd dir Nat Acad of Writing 2003–10; memb: Stevenage Lab Party, Liberty, Amnesty, Authors' Guild USA 1979; currently pres Stevenage Community Tst (chair 2005–13), tstee Nat Literary Tst 2005–10, patron Stevenage Home-Start, govr Roebuck Primary Sch and Nursery 1998–2008 (chm of govrs 2001–05); fell UCL 1995; Hon DLitt: Univ of Glamorgan, Saginaw Valley State Univ, Univ of Exeter; FRSA 2000; *Books* Eye of the Needle (1978, Best Novel Edgar Award, film 1982), Triple (1979), The Key to Rebecca (1980, film 1985), The Man from St Petersburg (1982), On Wings of Eagles (1983), Lie Down With Lions (1986, film 1994), The Pillars of the Earth (1989, film 2010), Night over Water (1991), A Dangerous Fortune

(1993), A Place Called Freedom (1995), The Third Twin (1996, film 1997), The Hammer of Eden (1998), Code to Zero (2000), Jackdaws (2001), Hornet Flight (2002), Whiteout (2004), World Without End (2007, film 2012), Fall of Giants (2010), Winter of the World (2012), Edge of Eternity (2014); *Recreations* bass guitarist of Damn Right I Got the Blues; *Clubs* Groucho, Athenaeum; *Style—* Ken Follett, Esq; ✉ website www.ken-follett.com

FOLLEY, Malcolm John; s of John Trevail Folley (d 1998), of Peacehaven, E Sussex, and Rosina, *née* O'Hara (d 1975); *b* 24 April 1952; *Educ* Lewes Co GS for Boys; *m* 5 June 1976, Rachel, da of Peter Ivan Kingman; 2 da (Siân Trevail b 27 July 1987, Megan Trevail b 19 Dec 1988); *Career* sports writer; indentured Sussex Express and County Herald 1968–72; news ed: Wimpey News 1972–73, Hayter's Sports Agency 1973; sports reporter: United Newspapers (London-based) 1973–75, Daily Express 1975–82, Mail on Sunday 1982–83; tennis corr Daily Mail 1984–86, dep ed Sportsweek 1986–87, sr sports writer Daily Express 1987–92, chief sports reporter Mail on Sunday 1992–2014 (dep sports ed 1992); highly commended Magazine Sports Writer of the Year 1986, Sports Reporter of the Year 1991, highly commended Sports News Reporter of the Year 2004; *Books* Hana: the Autobiography of Hana Mandlikova (co-author, 1989), A Time to Jump: the Authorised Biography of Jonathan Edwards (2000), Finding My Feet – The Autobiography of Jason Robinson (co-author, 2003), Borg versus McEnroe (2005), My Colourful Life, From Red to Amber (co-author with Ginger McCain, 2005), Senna versus Prost (2009), Monaco (2017); *Recreations* golf, skiing, tennis; *Style—* Malcolm Folley, Esq; ✆ 07831 135087, e-mail 24folleym@gmail.com, Twitter @malcolmfolley

FOLWELL, Nicholas David; s of Alfred Thomas Folwell (d 1975), and Irmgard Seefeld, of Market Drayton; *b* 11 July 1953; *Educ* Spring Grove GS, Middx Royal Acad of Music, London Opera Centre; *m* 1, (m dis 1995), 31 Jan 1981, Anne-Marie, da of George Ives; 1 s (Alexander Thomas b 22 July 1981), 1 step s (Adrian Marshal Matheson-Bruce b 15 Aug 1974); m 2, 13 July 1996, Susanna, da of David Tudor Thomas; *Career* baritone; also teaches vocal technique; joined Welsh Nat Opera 1978, first professional role The Bosun in Billy Budd 1978; later WNO roles incl: Marchese in La Traviata 1979, Melot in Triston Und Isolde 1979, Ottone in The Coronation of Poppea 1980, Figaro in The Marriage of Figaro 1981 and 1987, Melitone in La Forza del Destino 1981, Leporello in Don Giovanni 1982, Klingsor in Parsifal 1983, Pizarro in Fidelio 1983, Alberich in Das Rheingold 1983, Schaunard in La Bohème 1984, Alberich in Siegfried and Götterdämmerung 1985; other roles incl: Beckmesser in The Mastersingers of Nuremberg (Opera North) 1985, Leporello in Don Giovanni (Opera North) 1986, The Four Villians in The Tales of Hoffmann (Scottish Opera) 1986, Tonio in Pagliacci (ENO) 1986, Alberich in Der Ring (WNO at Covent Garden) 1986, The Poacher in The Cunning Little Vixen (WNO) 1987, Father in The Seven Deadly Sins (Royal Festival Hall) 1988, Figaro in The Marriage of Figaro (Scottish Opera) 1987, Papageno in The Magic Flute (ENO) 1988, Marullo in Rigoletto (Frankfurt Opera) 1988, Alberich in Das Rheingold (Scottish Opera) 1989, Koroviev in Der Meister und Margarita (world premiere, Paris Opera) 1989, Creon and The Messenger in Oedipus Rex (Scottish Opera) 1990, Melitone in La Forza del Destino (Scottish Opera) 1990, The Poacher in The Cunning Little Vixen (Royal Opera) 1990, Pizarro in Fidelio (Glyndebourne) 1990, Figaro in Le Nozze di Figaro (Opera Zuid Holland) 1991, Mutius in Timon of Athens (ENO) 1991, Chief of Police in Lady Macbeth of Mtsensk (ENO), Falke in Die Fledermaus (ENO), Figaro in Le Nozze di Figaro (Glyndebourne) 1992, Alberich in Das Rheingold (Opera de Nantes) 1992, Ottokar in Der Freischutz (Zwingenberg) 1993, Count Laski in Le Roi Malgré Lui (Opera North) 1994, Masetto in Don Giovanni (New Israeli Opera) 1994, title role in Der Kaiser von Atlantis (Liege) 1994, title role in Blond Eckbert (ENO) 1995, Lysiart in Euryanthe (QEH) 1995, title role in Rigoletto (Opera South) 1995, The Forester in The Cunning Little Vixen (ENO) 1995, Sancho in Don Quichotte (ENO) 1996, title role in Der Fliegende Hollander (Chelsea Opera QEH) 1996, Major Mary in Die Soldaten (ENO) 1996, title role in Bluebeards Castle (QEH) 1997, The Music Master in Ariadne on Naxos (ENO) 1997, Mr van Tricasse in Dr Ox's Experiment (ENO) 1998, Alberich in Das Rheingold (Longborough Festival) 1998, The Old Man in Purgatory (Dublin) 1999, L'Elisir d'Amore (Kinsale) 1999, Hunding in Die Valküre (Longborough Festival) 1999, Scarpia in Tosca (Isle of Man) 1999, The Stranger in the Dreaming of the Bones (world premier, Dublin) 2000, Germont in La Traviata (Opera Cork) 2000, Don José in Maritana (Waterford) 2000, Sharpless in Madama Butterfly (Holland Park) 2000, Escamillo in Carmen (Cork) 2000, title role in Rigoletto (Glasgow) 2001, Forester in The Cunning Little Vixen (ENO) 2001, Méphistopélès in Faust et Hélèn (QEH) 2002, Simone Trovai in Violante (QEH) 2002, Sharpless in Madama Butterfly (ENO) 2002, Alberich and Hunding in The Ring (LFO) 2002, Don Inigo Gomez in L'Heure Espagnol (Opera Zuid) 2003, L'Horloge and Le Chat in L'Enfant et les Sortileges (Opera Zuid) 2003, Pizarro in Fideolio (Opera Holland Park) 2003, Benoit & Alcindoro in La Boheme (Opera Holland Park) 2004, Pope Clement VI in Light Passing (York and BBC Radio 3) 2004, Idraote in Armida (Channel 4) 2005, Maestro di casa, Dumas and Schmidt in Andrea Chénier (Opera Holland Park) 2005, Alberich in Siegfried (Royal Danish OPera Copenhagen) 2006, The Host in Sir John in Love (ENO) 2006, The Bosun in Billy Budd (ENO) 2006, Monterone in Rigoletto (Opera Holland Park) 2006, Antonio in The Marriage of Figaro (ENO) 2007, Alberich in Das Rheingold (Loughborough Festival Opera) 2007, Don Alfonso in Cosi fan Tutte (Loughborough Festival Opera) 2007, Bartolo in Il Barbiere di Siviglia (Scottish Opera) 2007, The Doctor in Punch and Judy (Music Theatre Wales Covent Garden) 2008, Mumlal in The Two Widows (Scottish Opera) 2008, Dreieinigkeitsmoses in Aufstieg und fall der Stadt Mahogonny (Anger/Nantes Opera and Opera de Lille) 2009, Charles in For You (Music Theatre Wales) 2009, Alberich in Das Rheingold (Nationale Reisopera Holland) 2009, (Opera North) 2011 and (Longborough Festival Opera, Nationale Reisopera Holland and Den Nye Opera Norway) 2011, Kuligin in Katya Kabanova (ENO) 2010, Antonio in Le Nozze di Figaro (ROH) 2010, Brander in The Damnation of Faust (ENO) 2011, Nachtigal in Die Meistersinger von Nurnberg (ROH) 2011, Scarpia in Tosca (Kensington Symphony Orch) 2012, Antonio in Le Nozzedi Figaro (Glyndebourne Festival Opera) 2012 and 2013, Alberich in Götterdämmerung (Nationale Reisopera Holland) 2012, Theatre Manager and Banker in Lulu (Welsh Nat Opera) 2013, Tiger Brown in Dreigroschenoper (London Philharmonic Orch) 2013, Alberich in Das Rheingold and Gunther in Götterdämmerung (Opéra de Dijon) 2013, Filip in The Jakobin (Buxton Festival) 2014, various roles in The Trial by Philip Glass (World Premier, Music Theatre Wales) 2014, Ortel in The Mastersingers of Nuremberg (ENO) 2015, Benoit and Alcindoro in La Bohème (Grange Park Opera) 2015, Abimelech in Samson et Dalila (Grange Park Opera) 2015, Alcade in The Force of Destiny (ENO) 2015, Alberich in Das Rheingold (Saffron Opera Gp) 2016; recital tour with Lesley Garrett, CBE *qv*, 2010; also numerous classical concerts in UK and abroad; ARAM; *Recordings* incl: Tristan und Isolde (as Melot), Jailer in Tosca, Klingsor in Parsifal, Rimsky-Korsakov Christmas Eve, Tchaikovsky Vakula The Smith, The Cunning Little Vixen (as the Poacher), Der Zwerg (as the Haushofmeister), Pish Tush in The Mikado, Samuel in Pirates of Penzance, also A Dream of Paradise (solo album); *Recreations* golf; *Style—* Nicholas Folwell, ARAM; ✉ e-mail n-s@nfolwell.co.uk; Helen Sykes, Artists' Management (✆ 020 8780 0060, fax 020 8780 8772, e-mail info@helensykesartists.co.uk)

FONSECA, Jose Maria; da of Amador Francis Gabriel Fonseca (d 1984), of Abergavenny, Gwent, and Kathleen, *née* Jones; *b* 9 January 1944; *Educ* Sacred Heart Convent Highgate, Ursuline Convent San Sebastian Spain, Ursuline Convent St Pol de Leon Brittany, St Godric's Secretarial Coll Hampstead; *m* 1, 1975 (m dis 1982); m 2, 1985, Dick Kries; *Career* secretary, waitress, mangr of boutique, worked in model agency English Boy 1966–68, fndr Models One 1968–; *Style—* Mrs Jose Fonseca

FONTAINE, Senior Master Barbara Janet; da of John Fontaine, and Brenda, *née* Taylor; *b* 29 December 1953, Stockport; *Educ* Stockport HS for Girls, KCL (LLB); *m* 1 Sept 1990, Trevor Watkins; 2 s (Edward, James b 4 March 1993 (twins)); *Career* articles Bird & Bird 1976–78, admitted slr 1978, sr slr Hill Dickinson & Co 1978–83, sr slr Clifford Chance (formerly Coward Chance) 1983–87, ptnr Baker & McKenzie Hong Kong 1987–93; Sr Master (Queen's Bench Div) 2014– (Dep Master 1997, Master 2003), Queen's Remembrancer 2014–; hon bencher Gray's Inn 2015–; gen ed The White Book; memb Law Soc 1978–; *Recreations* reading, skiing, travel, theatre; *Clubs* Royal Hong Kong Yacht, Ladies' Recreation Hong Kong; *Style—* Senior Master Fontaine; ✉ Royal Courts of Justice, Room E101, Strand, London WC2A 2LL

FOOKES, Baroness (Life Peer UK 1997), of Plymouth in the County of Devon; Janet Evelyn Fookes; DBE (1989), DL (E Sussex 2001); da of Lewis Aylmer Fookes (d 1978), and Evelyn Margery, *née* Holmes (d 1996); *b* 21 February 1936; *Educ* Hastings and St Leonards Ladies' Coll, Hastings HS for Girls, Royal Holloway Coll London (BA); *Career* teacher 1958–70, chm Educn Ctee Hastings County Borough Cncl 1967–70 (memb 1960–61 and 1963–70); MP (Cons): Merton and Morden 1970–74, Plymouth Drake 1974–97; chm: Educn, Arts and Home Office Sub-Ctee of Expenditure Ctee 1975–79, Parly Animal Welfare Gp 1985–92, House of Lord's Refreshment Ctee 2003–07; vice-chm All-Pty Mental Health Gp 1985–92 (sec 1979–85); memb: Select Ctee on Home Affrs 1983–92, Cwlth War Graves Cmmn 1987–97, Armed Services Parly Scheme 2001–, Select Ctee considering the Hybrid CrossRail Bill 2008, Select Ctee on Communications 2010–15, Delegated Powers and Regulatory Reform Select Ctee 2013– (chm 2015–); dep speaker and second dep chm of Ways and Means 1992–97 (memb Speaker's Panel of Chairmen 1976–97), dep speaker House of Lords 2003; fell Industry and Parl Tst; memb: Cncl RSPCA 1973–92 (chm 1979–81), Cncl Stonham Housing Assoc 1980–92, Cncl SSAFA – Forces Help 1980–97, Cncl of Mgmnt Coll of St Mark and St John 1989–2004; pres Sussex branch SSAFA/Forces Help 2007, pres War Widows' Assoc 2006–; govr Kelly Coll 2002–14; Hon Freeman City of Plymouth 2000; *Recreations* swimming, theatre, gardening, yoga; *Style—* The Baroness Fookes, DBE, DL; ✉ House of Lords, London SW1A 0PW (✆ 020 7219 5353, fax 020 7219 5979)

FOOKES, Prof Peter George; s of George Ernest James Fookes (d 1980), of Reigate, Surrey, and Ida Corina, *née* Wellby (d 1988); *b* 31 May 1933; *Educ* Reigate GS, QMC and Imperial Coll London (BSc, PhD, DSc(Eng)); *m* 1, 4 Dec 1962, Gwyneth Margaret, da of Harry William Jones, of Stratford-upon-Avon, Warks; 3 da (Jennifer Marjorie b 7 Sept 1963, Anita Janet, Rosemary Eleanor (twins) b 19 Dec 1971), 2 s (Gregory Peter Gwyn b 20 Oct 1964, Timothy David b 17 July 1968); m 2, 25 July 1987, Edna May, da of John Arthur Nix, of Surbiton, Surrey; *Career* formerly chemical/soils lab technician, co engrg geologist Binnie & Ptnrs 1960–65, lectr in engrg geology Imperial Coll London 1966–71, conslt engrg geologist in private practice 1971–; visiting prof: of geomaterials QMC London 1979–96, of geology City Univ London 1991–2010, of engrg geology Univ of Newcastle 1993–96; distinguished research fell Univ of Oxford 2001; Br Geotechnical Soc Prize 1981 and 2000, William Smith Medal Geological Soc 1985, First Glossop Lectr and Medal Geological Soc 1997; ICE: Telford Premium 1981, Overseas Premium 1982 and 1992, George Stephenson Gold Medal 1990, Webb Prize 1990, Coopers Hill War Meml Medal and Prize 1992; author of over 200 published professional papers and books; memb: Geologists Assoc 1956, Br Geotechnical Soc 1963, Br Acad of Experts 1989; hon prof Univ of Birmingham 1999; Hon Dr of Science Univ of Plymouth 2005; FGS 1960, Companion ICE 1966, FIMMM 1977, CEng 1977, FIGeol 1986, CGeol 1990, FREng 1991, Hon FICT 1992, FRSA 1994, Hon FRGS 2003; *Recreations* industrial archaeology, narrow boating (life memb Kennet & Avon Canal Tst), steam railways (life memb: Mid-Hants Railway Preservation Soc, The Southern Steam Tst, Swanage Railway); *Style—* Prof Peter Fookes, FREng; ✆ 01329 835650

FOOT, Michael David Kenneth Willoughby; CBE (2003); s of Kenneth Willoughby Foot (d 1980), and Ruth Joan, *née* Cornah (d 1998); *b* 16 December 1946; *Educ* Latymer Upper Sch, Pembroke Coll Cambridge (MA), Yale Univ (MA); *m* 16 Dec 1972, Michele Annette Cynthia, da of Michael Stanley Macdonald, of Kingsgate, Kent; 1 s (Anthony b 5 June 1978), 2 da (Helen b 28 Oct 1980, Joanna b 22 July 1985); *Career* Bank of England: joined 1969, mangr Gilt-Edged Div 1981, mangr Money Market Div 1983, head Foreign Exchange Div 1988–90, head Euro Div 1990–93, head of banking supervision 1993–94, dep dir supervision and surveillance 1994–96, dir of banking supervision 1996–98; md Deposit Takers and Markets Directorate FSA 1998–2004, advsr to the chm and chief exec FSA 2004–, inspr Banks and Tst Cos Bahamas 2004–07, chm Promontory Financial (UK) Ltd 2007–12 (global vice-chm 2012–); UK alternate dir to IMF 1985–87; author of ind review for HM Govt on Br offshore finance centres 2009; hon pres ACI (UK) 2002–04; FCIB 2002 (AIB 1973); *Recreations* church singing, chess; *Clubs* RAF; *Style—* Michael Foot, Esq, CBE; ✉ 30 Old Broad Street, London EC2N 1HT

FOOT, Prof Rosemary June; da of Leslie William Foot, MBE (d 1993), and Margaret Lily Frances, *née* Fidler (d 1986); *b* 4 June 1948; *m* 27 Aug 1996, Timothy Kennedy; *Career* lectr in int relations Univ of Sussex 1978–90, prof of int relations St Antony's Coll Oxford 1996–2014, John Swire sr research fell in the int relations of E Asia 1990–2014, sr research fell dept of politics and in relations Univ of Oxford 2015–, emeritus fell St Anthony's Coll 2015–; Fulbright/American Cncl of Learned Societies Scholar Columbia Univ NY 1981–82, visiting exchange scholar People's Univ Beijing 1986, visiting fell Center for Int Studies Princeton Univ 1997, visiting Kiriyama prof for Pacific Rim studies Univ of San Francisco 2002, visiting fell Belfer Center for Sci and Int Affrs Kennedy Sch of Govt Harvard Univ 2006, visiting S Rajaratnam prof of strategic studies Inst of Def and Strategic Studies Nanyang Technol Univ Singapore 2006; Sir Howard Kippenberger visiting chair in strategic studies Univ of Victoria Wellington NZ 2014, visiting fell Nobel Inst Oslo 2014–; FBA 1996; *Books* The Wrong War: American Policy and the Dimensions of the Korean Conflict 1950–53 (1985), A Substitute for Victory: The Politics of Peace Making at the Korean Armistice Talks (1990), Migration: The Asian Experience (ed with Prof Judith M Brown, *qv*, 1994), The Practice of Power: US Relations with China since 1949 (1995), Hong Kong's Transitions, 1842–1997 (ed with Prof Judith M Brown, 1997), Rights Beyond Borders: The Global Community and the Struggle over Human Rights in China (2000), Order and Justice in International Relations (ed with Dr Andrew Hurrell and Prof John L Gaddis, 2003), US Hegemony and International Organizations (ed with Prof S Neil Macfarlane and Prof Michael Mastanduno, 2003), Human Rights and Counterterrorism in America's Asia Policy (2004), Does China Matter? A Reassessment (ed with Prof Barry Buzan, 2004), Framing Security: US Counter-terrorist Policies and Southeast Asian Responses (2008), China, the United States and Global Order (with Andrew Walter, 2011), China Across the Divide: the domestic and global in politics and society (2013), The Oxford Handbook of the International Relations of Asia (ed w Prof Saadia M Pekkanen and Prof John Ravenhill, 2014); *Recreations* walking, music, sailing; *Style—* Prof Rosemary Foot, FBA; ✉ St Antony's College, Oxford OX2 6JF (e-mail rosemary.foot@sant.ox.ac.uk) www.sant.ox.ac.uk/people/rosemary-foot

FOOTMAN, Timothy James (Tim); s of Michael Footman, and Caroline, *née* Edgeworth; *b* 7 May 1968; *Educ* Churcher's Coll Petersfield, Appleby Coll Oakville Ontario, Univ of Exeter (BA); *m* 22 Sept 2000, Boonratana Ngam-Akson; *Career* freelance journalist and editor; *Publications* The Push Guides (ed, 1994–97), Guinness World Records (ed, 1999–

F

2001), Welcome To The Machine: OK Computer and the Death of the Classic Album (2007), The Noughties 2000–2009: A Decade That Changed the World (2009), Leonard Cohen: Hallelujah – A New Biography (2009); contrib: The Guardian, MOJO, Time Out, Perigosto Stick; *Recreations* music of all flavours, cinema, modern art, walking the dog; *Style*— Tim Footman, Esq

FOOTTIT, Camilla; *née* Stephens; da of Mark Stephens, of Muchhadham, Herts, and Suzanne Elizabeth, *née* Malfroy; *b* 5 August 1970, Birmingham; *m* 1 May 2004, James Hugh Percival; 1 da (Kate Lilla Mary *b* 16 Aug 2007), 1 s (Jack Anthony *b* 29 Dec 2008); *Career* fndr Higgidy 2004–; *Books* The Higgidy Cookbook (2013); *Style*— Mrs Camilla Foottit; ✉ Higgidy, 60 Dolphin Road, Shoreham-by-Sea, West Sussex BN43 6PB

FOPP, Dr Michael Anton; s of late Sqdn-Ldr Desmond Fopp, AFC, AE, and Edna Meryl; *b* 28 October 1947; *Educ* Reading Blue Coat Sch, City Univ (MA, PhD); *m* 5 Oct 1968, Rosemary Ann, da of late V G Hodgetts, of Ashford, Kent; 1 s (Christopher Michael *b* 5 April 1973); *Career* Commercial and Instrument Rated pilot 1980–2010; keeper Battle of Britain Museum 1982–85 (dep keeper 1979–81), co sec Hendon Museums Trading Co Ltd 1981–85, visiting lectr City Univ 1984–93; dir London Tport Museum 1985–87, DG RAF Museums 1988–2010, public speaker 2010–; chm: Museum Documentation Assoc 1992–98, chm Air Pilots Tst 2010–, Air Safety Tst 2010–; pres Int Assoc of Tport Museums 1992–98, vice-pres London Underground Railway Soc; Freeman City of London 1980, Liveryman Hon Co of Air Pilots 1987 (Master 2010–11); DSc (hc) City Univ; FMA 1990, FRAeS 2001; *Publications* The Battle of Britain Museum (1981), The Bomber Command Museum (1982), Washington File (1983), The Royal Air Force Museum (1984), RAF Museum Children's Activity Book (ed, 1985), The RAF Museum (1992), High Flyers (ed, 1993), Museum and Gallery Management (1997), The Tradition is Safe (2003); author of articles published in various aviation and museum related publications; *Recreations* Oriental cookery, writing, RC yacht racing, flying, gliding; *Clubs* RAF, Air Sqdn; *Style*— Dr Michael A Fopp; ✉ Honourable Company of Air Pilots, Cobham House, 9 Warwick Court, Gray's Inn, London WC1R 5DJ

FORBES; *see also:* Stuart-Forbes

FORBES, Prof Charles Douglas; s of John Forbes (d 1985), and Annie Robertson, *née* Stuart (d 1982); *b* 9 October 1938; *Educ* HS of Glasgow, Univ of Glasgow (MB ChB, MD, DSc); *m* 6 March 1965, Janette MacDonald, da of Ewan Robertson (d 1980); 2 s (John Stuart *b* 20 Dec 1967, Donald Alexander Ewan *b* 20 Sept 1971); *Career* lectr med Univ of E Africa Nairobi 1965–66, Fulbright fell American Heart Assoc 1968–70, sr lectr then reader in med Univ of Glasgow 1972–86 (lectr in therapeutics 1962–65), prof of med Univ of Dundee 1987–; author of specialist books on blood coagulation and thrombosis; FRCPG 1974, FRCPE 1976, FRCP 1978, FRSA 1990, FRSE 1992; *Recreations* gardening, walking; *Style*— Prof Charles Forbes, FRSE; ✉ East Chattan, 108 Hepburn Gardens, St Andrews, Fife KY16 9LT (☎ 01334 472428)

FORBES, Very Rev Dr Graham John Thomson; CBE (2004); s of John Thomson Forbes (d 1986), of Edinburgh, and Doris, *née* Smith; *b* 10 June 1951; *Educ* George Heriot's Sch Edinburgh, Univ of Aberdeen (MA), Univ of Edinburgh (BD), Edinburgh Theol Coll; *m* 25 Aug 1973, Jane, da of John Tennant Miller, of Edinburgh; 3 s (Duncan, Andrew, Hamish); *Career* curate Old St Paul's Edinburgh 1976–82; provost: St Ninian's Cathedral Perth 1982–90, St Mary's Cathedral Edinburgh 1990–; non-exec dir Radio Tay 1986–90; fndr Canongate Youth Project Edinburgh, pres Lothian Assoc of Youth Clubs 1986–, HM (lay) Inspr of Constabulary for Scotland 1995–98; chm: Scottish Exec MMR Expert Gp 2001–02, Scottish Criminal Cases Review Cmmn 2002–10, UK Ctee on Ethical Aspects of Pandemic Influenza 2006–, Mental Welfare Cmmn for Scotland 2011–, Office of the Scottish Charity Regulator (OSCR) 2011–, Ctee of Scottish Univ Chairs 2015–; dir Theological Inst of the Scottish Episcopal Church 2002–04; memb: Scottish Community Educn Cncl 1981–87, Children's Panel Advsy Ctee Tayside 1986–90, Parole Bd for Scotland 1990–95, Scottish Consumer Cncl 1995–98, GMC 1996–2008, Clinical Standards Board for Scotland 1999–2005, Historic Buildings Cncl for Scotland 2000–02, Scottish Cncl Royal Coll of Anaesthetists 2001–04, Security Vetting Appeals Panel 2009–15, Armed Forces Pay Review Body 2009–14; chair Ct Edinburgh Napier Univ 2012–; Hon DUniv Edinburgh Napier, Hon LLD Univ of Aberdeen 2015; *Recreations* fly fishing, running; *Style*— The Very Rev the Provost of St Mary's Cathedral Edinburgh; ✉ 8 Lansdowne Crescent, Edinburgh EH12 5EQ (☎ 07711 199297); St Mary's Cathedral, Palmerston Place, Edinburgh EH12 5AW (☎ 0131 225 6293, e-mail provost@cathedral.net)

FORBES, Admiral Sir Ian Andrew; KCB (2003), CBE (1994); *b* 24 October 1946; *Educ* Eastbourne Coll; *m* 12 April 1975, Sally; 2 da; *Career* joined RN 1965; commands: HMS Kingfisher, HMS Diomede, HMS Chatham, HMS Invincible, UK Task Gp, UK Surface Fleet; Mil Advsr to High Rep in Sarajevo 1996–98, Supreme Allied Cdr Atlantic 2002–03, Dep Supreme Allied Cdr Transformation 2003–04; RAF Staff Coll Bracknell 1983, RCDS 1994; Queen's Commendation for Valuable Service 1996, first recipient Inaugural NATO Meritorious Service Medal 2003, US Legion of Merit 2004; sr exec advsr Booz & Co, sr exec advsr Strategy& and PwC; assoc fell RUSI, chm Naval Review, pres Forces Pension Soc; memb Windsor Leadership Tst; chm Cncl Eastbourne Coll and St Andrews Sch Eastbourne 2005–13, memb Advsy Bd Occidental Univ Calif; hon citizen Norfolk Virginia; *Recreations* history, gardening, golf, tennis; *Clubs* Army and Navy, Pilgrims; *Style*— Admiral Sir Ian Forbes, KCB, CBE; ✉ c/o Victory Services Club, Seymour Street, London W2 2HF

FORBES, 23 Lord (Premier S Lordship before July 1445); Malcolm Nigel Forbes; DL (Aberdeenshire 1996); s of 22 Lord Forbes, KBE (d 2013); *b* 6 May 1946; *Educ* Eton, Univ of Aberdeen; *m* 1, 30 Jan 1969 (m dis 1982), Carole Jennifer Andrée, da of Norman Stanley Whitehead (d 1981), of Aberdeen; 1 s (Neil Malcolm Ross *b* 10 March 1970), 1 da (Joanne Carole *b* 23 April 1972); *m* 2, 15 Feb 1988, Mrs Jennifer Mary Gribbon, da of Ian Peter Whittington (d 1991), of Tunbridge Wells, Kent; *Heir* s, Neil Forbes; *Career* dir: Instock Disposables Ltd, Castle Forbes Collection Ltd; farmer and landowner; *Recreations* skiing, shooting, golf; *Clubs* Pilgrims, Eton Ramblers, XL, Aboyne Golf, W Aberdeenshire Golf Soc; *Style*— The Lord Forbes, DL; ✉ Castle Forbes, Alford, Aberdeenshire AB33 8BL (☎ 01975 562524, e-mail office@castle-forbes.com)

FORBES, Neil; s of Keith Alexander Forbes, of Limoges, France, and Margaret Hannah-Crawford Forbes, *née* Mayne; *b* 7 October 1970; *Educ* Wavell Comp Sch, Farnborough Tech (City and Guilds), Perth Tech (City and Guilds); *m* 13 April 1998, Sarah, da of Douglas Stuart Grant Fowler; 2 s (Oscar Douglas *b* 25 July 2001, Louis Alexander *b* 9 April 2005); *Career* chef; experience The Waterside Inn and Le Manoir Quat'Saisons; commis chef Ballathie House, chef de partie The Peat Inn, sous chef Kinnaird, head chef Royal Scotsman train, head chef Braeval Restaurant, head chef Nairns, currently exec chef Atrium and Blue restaurants Edinburgh; guest chef Saturday Kitchen (BBC 2); *Awards* finalist Young Scottish Chef of the Year 1991, finalist Young Chef of the Year 1992, Michelin Star, 3 AA Rosettes, 5 out of 10 Good Food Guide 1999, Acorn winner 1997, Best Restaurant Edinburgh The List magazine 2004–05; *Publications* Consumables (recipe book for the Royal Scotsman train, 1996), Scotland on a Plate (contrib), Edinburgh on a Plate (contrib); *Recreations* sports cars, eating out, reading cookery books, interior design; *Clubs* Acorn; *Style*— Neil Forbes, Esq

FORBES, Prof Ronald Douglas; s of William Forbes (d 1960), and Agnes Jane Campbell, *née* McIldowie (d 2004); *b* 22 March 1947, Braco, Perthshire, Scotland; *Educ* Morrison's Acad Crieff, Edinburgh Coll of Art (DA, SED postgrad scholarship), Jordanhill Coll of Educn Glasgow; *m* 2, 1985, Sheena Henderson Bell, da of Arthur Bell; 2 da (Abigail,

Susan Bell), 1 s (Ian William Lorne); *Career* artist; lectr Bell Coll Hamilton 1972–73, Leverhulme sr art fell Univ of Strathclyde 1973–74, head of painting Crawford Sch of Art Cork 1974–78, artist in residence Livingston W Lothian 1978–80, lectr Glasgow Sch of Art 1979–83, head of painting Duncan of Jordanstone Coll of Art and Design Univ of Dundee 1995–2001 (MFA prog dir 1983–95), visiting prof in fine art Univ of Abertay Dundee 2003–, Leverhulme artist-in-residence Scottish Crop Research Inst 2005–09; res Hobart Centre for the Arts Univ of Tasmania 1995; subject of numerous art catalogues; fndr Glasgow League of Artists 1971, tstee Perthshire Public Art Tst 1994–2000; prof memb SSA 1972, RSA 2005 (ARSA 1996), RGI 2014; *Awards* first prize first Scottish Young Contemporary Exhbn 1967, RSA Guthrie Award 1979, Scottish Arts Cncl Award (for film making) 1979, Scottish Arts Cncl Studio Award Amsterdam 1980, RSA Highland Soc of London Award 1996, RSA Gillies Award (to visit India) 1999; *Solo Exhibitions* Compass Gallery Glasgow 1973, Goethe Inst Glasgow 1974, Collins Gallery Glasgow 1974, Drian Galleries London 1975, Cork Art Soc Gallery 1976 and 1978, Project Arts Centre Dublin 1976, The Lanthorn Livingston 1980, Forebank Gallery Dundee 1980, Third Eye Centre Glasgow 1980, Compass Gallery Glasgow 1983, Drian Galleries London 1984, Babbity Bowster Glasgow 1986, Seagate Gallery Dundee 1990 and 1995, Perth Museum and Art Gallery 1991, Maclaurin Art Gallery Ayr 1991, An Lanntair Gallery Stornoway 1995, Plimsoll Gallery Hobart Tasmania 1995, NS Gallery Glasgow 1996, De Keerder Kunstkamer Netherlands 1997, Zaks Gallery Chicago USA 1999, SIU Museum (Carbondale) USA 1999, VRC, DCA Dundee 2000, ROSL Galleries London and Edinburgh 2000–01, Vardy Gallery Sunderland 2001, Crawford Arts Centre St Andrews 2003, Smith Gallery and Museum Stirling 2005, Hannah Maclure Centre Univ of Abertay Dundee 2005 and 2009, Hamnavoe Gallery Aberdeen 2007, Hope Gateway Centre Botanics Edinburgh 2010, Collins Gallery Glasgow 2010, Perth Museum and Art Galleries 2011; *Work in Collections* incl: Arts Cncl NI, Cork Municipal Art Gallery, Dundee Museums and Art Galleries, Hunterian Gallery Glasgow, Museum Narodowego Gdansk, Smith Art Gallery Stirling (Scottish Arts Cncl Bequest), Perth Museum and Art Galleries, Ross Harper and Murphy Collection Glasgow, Univ of Strathclyde, Univ of Abertay Dundee, Rare Books Collection State Library of Qland; *Curated Exhbns* incl: Scottish Arts Cncl Touring Exhbn (Arts Cncl Belfast, Fruit Market Gallery Edinburgh, Collins Gallery Glasgow, Aberdeen Art Gallery) 1978–79, Netherlands Touring Exhbn (Hoensbruck, Roermond, Maastricht and Liege) 1983, Nature: Only and Idea (Galerie Trace Maastricht) 2002, Parallel Paths (RSA) 2006, Lifecycles (Tatha Gallery) 2014, The Newport Circle (Tatha Gallery) 2015; *Films* Between Dreams (1974), She (1974), TV 74 (1974), Sonnet (1975), Portfolio (1975), Behaviour Patterns (1977), Happy Day (1979), Incident (1981), The Illusionist (2005), By Any Other Name (2009), Joking Apart (2011), Only Make Believe (2014); documentary films: Two Painters (1978), Three Artists (1982), (mind)games (2005); *Recreations* theatre, cinema, gardening, laughing; *Style*— Prof Ronald Forbes, RSA; ✉ 13 Fort Street, Dundee DD2 1BS (☎ 01382 641498, e-mail ronnieforbes@blueyonder.co.uk, website www.ronald-forbes.com)

FORBES, Sandra Elizabeth Margaret (Mrs Nigel Websper); da of Albert Forbes, of Sion Mills, Co Tyrone, and Mary, *née* Hempton; *b* 8 April 1965, Strabane, NI; *Educ* Strabane GS, Univ of Manchester (LLB), Chester Law Coll; *m* 19 Sept 2001, Nigel Websper; 2 da (Olivia, Sienna (twins) *b* 27 April 2005); *Career* slr; Frere Cholomeley 1989–91, Burges Salmon 1991–2014, gp gen counsel and company sec National Express Gp plc 2014–16; govr UWE 2011–; *Recreations* cooking, reading, theatre; *Style*— Ms Sandra Forbes; ☎ 07970 515262, e-mail sandyforbes24@gmail.com

FORBES, Prof Sebastian; s of Dr Watson Forbes (d 1997), and Mary Henderson, *née* Hunt (d 1997); *b* 22 May 1941; *Educ* UCS Hampstead, Royal Acad of Music, Univ of Cambridge (MA, MusD); *m* 1, 1968 (m dis 1977); 2 da (Joanna *b* 1971, Emily *b* 1974); *m* 2, 24 Sept 1983, Tessa; 1 s (Alistair *b* 1984), 1 da (Nicola *b* 1986); *Career* prodr BBC (sound) 1964–67; lectr Univ Coll of N Wales Bangor 1968–72; Univ of Surrey: lectr 1972–, prof of music 1981–, emeritus prof 2006–; conductor incl: Horniman Singers 1981–90, Claud Powell Chamber Orchestra 2006–, Surrey Cantata 2008–; organist East and West Clandon 2006–; princ compositions incl: five string quartets 1969 (two), 1981, 1996 and 2000, Essay for Clarinet and Orchestra (1970), Death's Dominion (1971), Symphony in Two Movements (1972), Sinfonias 1 (1967, rev 1989), 2 (1978) and 3 (1990), Sonata for 21 (1975), Voices of Autumn, 8 Japanese Tanka for choir and piano (1975), Sonata for 8 (1978), Violin Fantasy No 2 (1979), Evening Canticles (Aedis Christi 1 (1980), Aedis Christi 2 (1984), St Pancras (2008)), Sonata for 17 (1987), Bristol Mass (1990), Hymn to St Etheldreda (1995), Sonata-Rondo for piano (1996), Rawsthorne Reflections for organ (1998), Sonata for 15 (2001), Interplay 2 for four pianists (2002), Duo for clarinet and piano (2003), Hurrah! for Brunel, cantata for young voices (2007), St Andrews Solo for viola (2009), Southwold Sonatina for treble recorder and piano (2013), Choral prelude on Gott der Vater wohn' uns bei for organ (2015); memb Performing Rights Soc; LRAM, ARCM, ARCO, ARAM, FHEA; *Style*— Prof Sebastian Forbes; ✉ Octave House, Boughton Hall Avenue, Send, Woking, Surrey GU23 7DF (e-mail s.forbes@surrey.ac.uk, websites www.sebastianforbes.com and www.surreycantata.com)

FORBES WATSON, Anthony; *Educ* Univ of York (BA); *m* Jenny; 2 c; *Career* ceo Penguin UK 1996–2005, publishing conslt 2005–08, md Pan Macmillan 2008–; pres UK Publishers Assoc 2002–03; *Style*— Anthony Forbes Watson, Esq; ✉ Pan Macmillan Publishers, 20 New Wharf Road, London N1 9RR

FORD; *see also:* St Clair-Ford

FORD, Lt-Col Sir Andrew Charles; KCVO (2012); *b* 5 February 1957; *Educ* King's Coll Taunton, RMA Sandhurst; *m* 25 May 1985, Rosalind, *née* Birkett; 2 s (Edward *b* 19 Dec 1986, Thomas *b* 9 Sept 1988); *Career* Grenadier Guards: 2 Lt 1977, Lt 1979, Capt 1983, Maj 1989, Lt-Col 1998; Welsh Guards 1999–2005, ret; comptroller Lord Chamberlain's Office 2006–; *Style*— Lt-Col Sir Andrew Ford, KCVO; ✉ Lord Chamberlain's Office, Buckingham Palace, London SW1A 1AA

FORD, Prof David Frank; Hon OBE (2013); s of George Ford (d 1960), of Dublin, and Phyllis Mary Elizabeth, *née* Woodman; *b* 23 January 1948; *Educ* The High Sch Dublin, Trinity Coll Dublin (fndn scholar, BA, Berkeley gold medal), St John's Coll Cambridge (scholar, MA, Naden research student, PhD), Yale Univ (Henry fell, STM); *m* 1982, Deborah Perrin, da of Rev Prof Daniel Wayne Hardy; 3 da (Rebecca Perrin *b* 1985, Grace *b* and d 1988, Rachel Mary *b* 1989), 1 s (Daniel George *b* 1991); *Career* research Tübingen Univ 1975; Univ of Birmingham: lectr in theol 1976–90, sr lectr 1990–91; Univ of Cambridge: regius prof of divinity 1991–2015, fell Selwyn Coll 1991–, fndn memb Trinity Coll 1991–2015, chm Faculty Bd of Divinity 1993–95, memb Syndicate Cambridge Univ Press 1993–2005, chm Centre for Advanced Religious and Theol Studies 1995–2012, memb Mgmnt Ctee E Asia Inst 2001–09, Gomes lectr Emmanuel Coll 2003, dir Cambridge Interfaith Prog 2003–15; McDonald distinguished scholar 2010–, princ investigator Religion and the Idea of a Research Univ Project 2011–13; vice-pres Bible Soc 1993–, memb Soc for Biblical Literature 1996–, pres Soc for the Study of Theol 1997–99; memb Cncl of 100 Ldrs World Economic Forum West-Islamic Dialogue 2004–08; visiting fell Yale Univ 1982, Donnellan lectr TCD 1984, Hollis lectr Church of S India 2002, Ebor lecture Univ of York 2006, Stephenson lectures Univ of Sheffield 2007, Pope John Paul II annual lecture on interreligious understanding Angelicum Univ Rome 2011; memb: AHRB Peer Review Coll 2005–11, Ctee of Mgmnt Centre for Medical Genetics and Policy 2005–10; memb Editorial Bd: Modern Theology, Scottish Jl of Theology, Teaching Theology and Religion; theol conslt L'Arche Int Fndn 1992–, theol conslt Primates' Meeting Anglican Communion 2000, 2001, 2002 and 2003; church warden St Luke's Church Bristol St

Birmingham 1979–84, lay canon Birmingham Cathedral 2007–, lay canon Ely Cathedral 2011–; memb: Faith and Order Advsy Gp C of E 1988–90, Bishop's Cncl Birmingham Dio 1989–91, Theol Working Gp on C of E Urban Policy 1989, Archbishop of Canterbury's Urban Theol Gp 1991–95, Cncl Ridley Hall Theol Coll 1991–2006, Mgmnt Ctee Soc for Scriptural Reasoning 1997–, C of E Doctrine Cmmn 1998–2003, Building Bridges Seminars (Christian-Muslim) (Lambeth 2002, Qatar 2003 and 2011), Bd Center for Comparative Scripture Study Minzu Univ Beijing 2012–, Advsy Bd Responsability, Soc for the Study of Theology, Int Bd of Advsrs John Templeton Fndn 2008–11, Bd of Reference Westminster Abbey Inst 2014–; chm Westcott House Theol Coll 1991–2006, co-chair Global Covenant Ptnrs 2015–, chair Theological Reference Gp Church of England Fndn for Educational Leadership 2015–; memb Mgmnt Ctee Newhaven Housing Assoc 1978–84, govr Lea Mason Sch 1984–91; tstee: Henry Martyn Tst 1991–, Golden Web Fndn 2006–12, Center of Theological Inquiry Princeton 2007– (memb 2003–); Sternberg Interfaith Gold Medallion 2008, Conventry Int Prize for Peace and Reconciliation 2012; memb American Acad of Religion; Hon DD Univ of Birmingham 2000, Hon DD Univ of Aberdeen 2016, Hon DD Univ of Bolton 2016, Hon DLitt DSVV Univ Hardiwar India 2016; *Books* Barth and God's Story: Biblical Narrative and the Theological Method of Karl Barth in the Church Dogmatics (1981), Jubilate: Theology in Praise (with Daniel W Hardy, 1984, 2 edn 2005), Meaning and Truth in 2 Corinthians (with F M Young, 1988), The Modern Theologians (1989, 3 edn 2005), A Long Rumour of Wisdom: Redescribing Theology (1992), The Shape of Living (1997, 2 edn 2002), Self and Salvation. Being Transformed (1999), Theology: A Very Short Introduction (1999), The Promise of Scriptural Reasoning (ed with C C Pecknold, 2006), Musics of Belonging: The Poetry of Michael O'Siadhail (ed with Marc Caball, 2006), Christian Wisdom: Desiring God and Learning in Love (2007), Shaping Theology (2007), The Future of Christian Theology (2011), The Drama of Living (2014), Say But the Word, Poetry as Vision and Voice by Micheal O'Siadhail (ed, with Margie M Tolstoy, 2015); *Recreations* family life, ball games, poetry, drama, kayaking, walking; *Style—* Prof David Ford, OBE; ✉ Selwyn College, Grange Road, Cambridge CB3 9DQ (e-mail dff1000@cam.ac.uk)

FORD, David R J; MLA; s of Eric Ford (d 1992), of Penarth and Orpington, and Jean, *née* McPhillimy (d 2007); *b* 24 February 1951, Bromley, Kent; *Educ* Dulwich Coll, Queen's Univ Belfast (BSc), NI Poly (CQSW); *m* 1975, Anne, *née* Murdock; 3 da, 1 s; *Career* staff vol Corrymeela Community 1972–73, social worker then sr social worker Northern Health and Social Servs Bd 1973–90, gen sec Alliance Pty 1990–98, MLA (Alliance) S Antrim 1998–, ldr Alliance Pty 2001– (chief whip 1998–2001); *Style—* David Ford, Esq, MLA; ✉ Feamore, Barnish, Kells, Co Antrim BT42 3PR; Parliament Buildings, Stormont, Belfast BT4 3XX (☎ 028 9052 1314, fax 028 9052 1313, e-mail david.ford@allianceparty.org)

FORD, (James) Glyn; s of Ernest Benjamin Ford (d 1990), of Glos, and Matilda Alberta James (d 1986); *b* 28 January 1950, Gloucester; *Educ* Marling Sch Stroud, Univ of Reading (BSc), UCL (MSc); *m* 1, 1973 (m dis), Hazel Nancy, da of Hedley John Mahy (d 1969), of Guernsey; 1 da (Elise Jane b 1981); m 2, 1992 (m dis), Daniela Zannelli; 1 s (Alessandro Aled b 1996); *Career* undergraduate apprentice BAC 1967–68, course tutor in oceanography Open Univ 1976–78, teaching asst UMIST 1977–78; res fell Univ of Sussex 1978–79; Univ of Manchester: res fell 1976–79, lectr 1979–80, sr res fell Prog of Policy Res in Engrg Sci and Technol 1980–84, hon visiting res fell 1984–; visiting prof Univ of Tokyo 1983; Parly candidate (Lab) Hazel Grove Gen Election 1987; MEP (Lab): Gtr Manchester East 1984–99, SW England 1999–2009; chm Ctee of Inquiry into Growth of Racism and Fascism in Europe for Euro Parl 1984–86, vice-chm Security and Disarmament Sub Ctee of Euro Parl 1987–89, rapporteur Ford Report Ctee of Inquiry into Racism and Xenophobia 1989–90, ldr European Parly Labour Party 1989–93 (dep ldr 1993–94), first vice-chm Socialist Gp Euro Parl 1989–93; chief observer EU (Indonesia) 2004 and (Aceh Indonesia) 2006–07; pres: Euro Parl Chapter, Interparliamentary Cncl Against Anti-Semitism; memb: Nat Exec Ctee Lab Party 1989–93, TU Liaison Review Gp into Trade Union links 1992–93, Consultative Ctee on Racism and Xenophobia 1994–98, nat treas Anti-Nazi League 1995–; dir Pol Int Ltd 2009–; Ldr Lab Pty Nat Policy Forum 2010– (representing SW England); *Publications* The Future of Ocean Technology (1987), Fascist Europe (1992), Evolution of a European (1993), Changing States (1996), Making European Progress (2001), North Korea on the Brink: Struggle for Survival (2008, trans into Japanese 2008 and Korean 2009), Left in Europe (2008), Our Europe, Not Theirs (ed, 2013, 2 edn 2016); author of various articles in jls of politics, sci and technol; *Clubs* Groucho, Soho House; *Style—* Glyn Ford, Esq; ✉ The Belle Vue Centre, 6 Belle Vue Road, Cinderford, Gloucestershire GL14 2AB

FORD, Graham; s of James Ford, GM, of Tunbridge Wells, and Muriel Betty, *née* Whitfield; *b* 8 May 1950; *Educ* St Dunstan's Coll Catford, Medway Coll of Design; *m* 4 June 1977, Rachel Anne, da of Prof H W F Saggs; 2 s (Joseph b 1 March 1978, Oscar b 8 Feb 1989), 2 da (Charlotte b 14 May 1980, Florence b 30 Nov 1986); *Career* photographer; asst to David Davies, Bob Croxford and David Thorpe 1968–76, freelance 1977–; clients incl: Volvo, Parker Pens, Benson & Hedges, Silk Cut, Sainsbury's, Levis, BMW, Whitbread, Absolut Vodka, Land Rover, Oxfam, NSPCC, RSPCA, COI; work held in the V&A London, Lurzers archive and private collections; Grand Prix Cannes; 25 gold and silver awards from: D&AD, Campaign, Assoc of Photographers, NY One Show, Cannes, Art Dirs' Club of Italy, Art Dirs' Club of Europe, Eurobest, Kodak; *Books* Bill Brandt The Assemblages; *Recreations* family, sailing, photography, wine, silversmithing; *Clubs* Deben Yacht; *Style—* Graham Ford, Esq; ✉ Topfields, Fen Walk, Woodbridge, Suffolk IP12 4BH (☎ 01394 383751, e-mail graham@grahamford.co.uk)

FORD, Baroness (Life Peer UK 2006), of Cunninghame in North Ayrshire; Margaret Anne Ford; da of Edward Garland (d 1993), and Susan, *née* Townsley; *b* 16 December 1957; *Educ* St Michael's Acad Kilwinning, Univ of Glasgow (MA, MPhil); *m* 1990, David Arthur Bolger; 2 c from previous m (Michael b 14 Aug 1984, Katharine b 4 April 1986); *Career* Scottish sec BIFU 1982–87, managing conslt Price Waterhouse 1987–90, dir of personnel Scottish Homes 1990–93, md Eglinton Management Centre 1993–2002, chm Lothian Health Bd 1997–2001, fndr, dep chm and non-exec dir Goodpractice.net 2000–05 (formerly chief exec), chm English Partnerships 2002–07, chm Irvine Bay Urban Regeneration Co 2006–; non-exec dir: Scottish Prison Serv 1994–98, Ofgem 2000–03, Thus Group plc 2002–05, Serco plc 2003–; memb: Industrial Tbnl Panel 1984–90, Scottish Business Forum 1997–; lay advsr HM Inspectorate of Constabulary 1993–; FRSA; *Recreations* family, golf, sports, bridge, painting, cooking, current affairs; *Style—* The Rt Hon the Lady Ford

FORD, Richard James Cameron; s of Bernard Thomas Ford (d 1967), of Burbage, Wilts, and Eveline Saumarez Ford (d 1952); *b* 1 February 1938; *Educ* Marlborough; *m* 27 Sept 1975, Mary Elizabeth, da of James Arthur Keevil; 3 s (James Richard Keevil b 26 July 1976, Charles John Cameron b 26 July 1978, William Bernard Saumarez b 29 May 1980); *Career* admitted slr 1961, ptnr Ford and Ford 1965, sr ptnr Ford Gunningham and Co 1970–2001, sr ptnr Wood Awdry & Ford 2002 (ptnr 2001–05, conslt 2005–08), conslt Thring Townsend Lee & Pemberton (now Thrings) 2008–; dir: Ramsbury Building Society 1984–86, West of England Building Society 1986–89, Regency and West of England Building Society 1989–90, Portman Building Society 1990; tstee Glos and Wilts Law Soc 1983–2005 (pres 1982–83); memb Salisbury Diocesan Synod 1985–93, lay chm Pewsey Synod 1987–93; memb: Wyvern Hosp Mgmnt Ctee 1967–70, Swindon Hosp Mgmnt Ctee 1970–74, Wilts AHA 1974–82; vice-chm Swindon HA 1982–87; memb Cncl Law Soc 1992–2002, chm Wills and Equity Ctee 2000–2004; clerk to Cncl Marlborough Coll 1994–2004; memb Ctee Marlborough and Dist Housing Assoc 1978–2007 (chm 1990–2007); *Recreations* riding, sailing; *Clubs* Royal Solent Yacht; *Style—* Richard Ford, Esq; ✉ The White Cottage, 8 Eastcourt, Burbage, Wiltshire SN8 3AE; Thrings, Drakes Way, Swindon, Wiltshire (☎ 01672 512265, fax 01672 514891)

FORD, Richard John; s of Arthur William Ford (d 1992), of Christchurch, Dorset, and Violet, *née* Banbury; *b* 10 April 1949; *Educ* Hove Co GS for Boys, Portsmouth Poly Sch of Architecture (BA), Poly of Central London (DipArch); *m* Janet Kathleen; 1 s (Edward Richard b 5 Feb 1984); *Career* student Portsmouth Poly and Poly of Central London 1976–80; exec creative dir responsible for all creative product Landor Associates: Europe 1984–98, New York 1998–; cmmns incl identity and environmental design for: British Airways 1984, Chase Manhattan Bank Europe 1985, Royal Jordanian Airline and Alfred Dunhill 1986, BAe and Abbey National 1987, Cepsa Petroleum Spain and Ballantyne Cashmere 1988, Emlak Bank Turkey 1989, Deutsche Shell 1990, Egnatia Bank Greece 1991, Seville Expo and Neste Petroleum Finland 1992, Lincoln Mercury USA, Telia (Swedish Telecom) and Cathay Pacific Airline 1993, Royal Mail and Delta Air Lines USA 1994, Montell (Worldwide) and KF (Swedish Co-op) 1995, Reuters (Worldwide) and Air 2000 (UK) 1996, Credit Lyonnais 1997, Shell International Petroleum and Compaq Computers (USA) 1998, Hyperion Software and Textron (USA) 1999; RIBA 1983; *Style—* Richard Ford, Esq

FORD, Vicky; MEP; *née* Pollock; *b* NI; *Educ* Trinity Coll Cambridge; *m* Hugo; 1 da (Elizabeth), 2 s (Edward, Anthony); *Career* vice-pres JP Morgan 1988–2000, md Bear Stearns Int 2000–03; Cons candidate Birmingham Northfield 2005; South Cambs DC: cncllr 2006–09, portfolio holder for community devpt 2006–07, portfolio holder for finance and resources 2007–09; MEP (Cons) East of England 2009–; Cons spokesman for economic and monetary affrs 2009–11, Cons spokesman for industry, research and energy 2011–13; substitute memb Environment, Public Health and Food Safety Ctee 2012–14, chm European Parliament Internal Market and Consumer Protection Ctee 2014–, memb Conference of Ctee Chairs 2014–; formerly: dep chm SE Cambs Cons Assoc, dep chm Cambs and Beds Area Cons; *Style—* Mrs Vicky Ford, MEP; ✉ Shirley House, 23 London Street, Swaffham, Norfolk PE37 7DD

F

FORD DAVIES, Dr Oliver Robert; s of Robert Cyril Davies (d 1974), of Ealing, London, and Cicely Mary, *née* Ford (d 1990); *b* 12 August 1939; *Educ* King's Sch Canterbury, Merton Coll Oxford (DPhil, pres OUDS); *m* Jenifer Armitage, da of Edward Armitage; 1 da (Miranda Katherine Emmerson b 1975); *Career* actor; lectr in history Univ of Edinburgh 1964–66; seasons at: Birmingham, Cambridge, Leicester, Oxford, Nottingham; hon assoc artist RSC; *Theatre* 34 prodns with RSC incl: Henry IV, Henry V, Henry VI, Henry VIII, As You Like It, Coriolanus, Love's Labour's Lost, The Greeks, Troilus and Cressida, The Love Girl and The Innocent, The Forest, Measure for Measure, Waste (also Lyric 1985), The Danton Affair, Principia Scriptoriae, Merry Wives of Windsor, Jekyll and Hyde, Hamlet 2008, Love's Labour's Lost 2008–09, Written on the Heart 2011–12, Richard II, Henry IV and Henry V (China and New York) 2016; RNT 1988–91: The Shaughraun, Hamlet, Lionel Espy in Racing Demon (Olivier Award for Actor of the Year), The Shape of the Table, The Absence of War 1993, Playing with Fire 2005, Galileo 2006, St Joan 2007, Much Ado About Nothing 2007, All's Well That Ends Well 2009; other credits incl: Bishop Talacryn in Hadrian VII (Mermaid, Haymarket) 1968–69, Tonight at Eight (Hampstead, Fortune) 1971–72, Mary Rose 1972, Heartbreak House (Yvonne Arnaud Guildford and Haymarket) 1992, Ivanov (Almeida) 1997, Naked (Almeida) 1998, Richard II and Coriolanus (Almeida/Gainsborough) 2000, King Lear (Almeida) 2002, Absolutely! (perhaps) (Wyndham's) 2003, King Cromwell, The Linden Tree, Larkin with Women (Orange Tree Richmond), The Crucible (Regents Park) 2010, Goodnight Mr Tom (Chichester and Phoenix) 2011–13; *Television* incl: Cause Celebre, A Taste for Death, Death of a Son, A Very British Coup, Inspector Morse, The Police, The Cloning of Joanna May, Anglo-Saxon Attitudes, The Absence of War, Truth or Dare, A Royal Scandal, A Dance to the Music of Time, Kavanagh QC, David Copperfield, The Way We Live Now, Bertie and Elizabeth, Sparkling Cyanide, The Badness of King George IV, Spooks, Foyle's War, Midsomer Murders, Marple, 37 Days, Apocalypse Slough; *Film* incl: Defence of the Realm, Scandal, The Danish Girl, Sense and Sensibility, Mrs Brown, Mrs Dalloway, Star Wars I and II, Johnny English, The Mother, The Deep Blue Sea; *Books* God Keep Lead out of Me – Shakespeare on War and Peace (jtly, 1985), Playing Lear (2003), King Cromwell (2005), Performing Shakespeare (2007); also written plays produced by Orange Tree Theatre, ATV and BBC Radio; *Recreations* music, history, carpentry; *Style—* Dr Oliver Ford Davies; ✉ c/o Caroline Dawson Associates, 167–9 Kensington High Street, London W8 6SH (☎ 020 7937 2749)

FORD-HUTCHINSON, Sally Mary Ann (Mrs Anthony Yeshin); da of Peter William Scott Ford-Hutchinson (d 1961), and Giuseppina Adele, *née* Leva; *b* 20 August 1950; *Educ* Holy Trinity Convent, Bristol Poly (HND, DipM), Lampeter Univ (MA); *m* 2 June 1977, Anthony David Yeshin; 2 s (Mark b 26 Dec 1979, Paul b 31 May 1983); *Career* res exec Leo Burnett Advertising Agency 1972–74, Benton & Bowles 1974–77; res mangr H J Heinz Ltd 1977–79, head Res Dept Wasey Campbell Ewald 1979–83, memb Planning Dept Grandfield Rork Collins 1983–86; DMB&B 1986–2000: dir, head Planning Dept and memb Mgmnt Ctee until 1996, a global planning dir 1996–2000; md The Thinking Shop 2000–; winner commendation IPA Advtg Effectiveness award; tstee The Vincent Wildlife Tst; fell MRS, FIPA, FRAI; *Recreations* opera, walking in the country, reading; *Style—* Ms Sally Ford-Hutchinson; ☎ 07785 290119, e-mail sally@ford-h.fsnet.co.uk

FORDE, Prof Michael Christopher; s of Michael Forde (d 1953), of Sale, Cheshire, and Mary (d 1980), *née* Murphy; *b* 15 February 1944; *Educ* De La Salle Coll Pendleton, Univ of Liverpool (BEng), Univ of Birmingham (MSc, PhD, SERC res student); *m* 1968, Edna, da of Griffith Williams; 1 s (Nicholas Simon b 1971), 1 da (Helen Louise b 1975); *Career* site civil engr Lehane Mackenzie & Shand Ltd/Christiani-Shand 1966–68; Co Surveyors Dept Cheshire CC Highway Design and Geotechnics 1968–69; Univ of Edinburgh: lectr in civil engrg 1973–84, sr lectr in civil engrg 1984–89, Carillion prof of civil engrg construction 1990–, head Inst Research in Engrg 1998–2001; ed-in-chief Construction and Building Materials Elsevier Ltd; chair: Railway Engrg Conf London 2009, Structural Faults and Repair Conf Edinburgh 2010; memb Assessment Panel Large Structural and Building Systems Prog Nat Science Fndn Washington DC 1993–2001; memb Int Standards Ctee Réunion Internationale des Laboratoires d'Essais et de Recherches sur les Matériaux et les Constructions (RILEM) MS 127 1992–; chm Ctee: American Concrete Inst ACI 228 1999– (also chair), Nat Res Cncl (USA) Transportation Research Bd AFF40, AFF40(1), AFP10-3 1998–, Euro Working Gp on Acoustic Emission 1978–, Inst Civil Engrs R&D Panel 1988–90, Inst Civil Engrs Ground Bd 1988–92, BSI No BDB/1 1989–92, BSI No B/153/1 1992–2000, Br Inst Non-Destructive Testing Res Exec Ctee 1988–96, exec chm MESIN Inst of Engrg and Technol; author of 280 papers published in scientific and learned jls; CEng 1973, FInstNDT 1989, FIET 1995, FIHT 1998 (MIHT 1969), FICE 1998, FREng 1999, FRSE 2006; *Publications* author of 280 papers published in scientific and learned jls; *Recreations* armchair cricketer, classic cars; *Clubs* Royal Scots; *Style—* Prof Michael Forde; ✉ University of Edinburgh, School of Engineering and Electronics, The Kings Buildings, Edinburgh EH9 3JL (☎ 0131 650 5721, fax 0131 452 8596, mobile 07831 496 249, e-mail m.forde@ed.ac.uk, website www.railwayengineering.com)

FORDHAM, John Michael; s of John William Fordham, and Kathleen Mary Fordham; *b* 15 December 1948; *Educ* Dulwich Coll, Gonville & Caius Coll Cambridge (BA, MA); *m* 28 Oct 1972 (m dis 2009), Sarah Anne, da of Denis Victor Burt; 1 da (Rebecca Kate b 1977), 1 s (Benjamin John b 1979); *Career* admitted slr 1974, ptnr Stephenson Harwood 1979–, head of commercial litigation 1995–; mediator (CEDR accredited); vice-pres Sutton CC; *Recreations* cricket, abstract art and jazz, rugby and tennis (observer); *Style*— John Fordham, Esq; ✉ Flat 6, 7 St George's Square, London SW1V 2HX (☎ 020 7821 9928, e-mail john.fordham@shlegal.com)

FORDHAM, Prof (Sigurd) Max; OBE (1994); s of Dr Michael Scott Montague Fordham (d 1995), of Jordans, Bucks, and Molly, *née* Swabey (d 1941); *b* 17 June 1933; *Educ* De Carteret Sch Jamaica, Dartington Hall Sch Totnes, Trinity Coll Cambridge (MA), Nat Coll of Heating Ventilation Refrigeration and Fan Engrg (William Nelson Haden scholar); *m* 24 Sept 1960, Thalia Aubrey, da of late Dr Reginald John Dyson; 3 s (Jason Christopher Lyle b 26 Sept 1962, Cato Michael Sigurd b 17 Nov 1964, Finn William Montague b 12 Nov 1967); *Career* Nat Serv Pilot Fleet Air Arm RN 1952–54; devpt engr Weatherfoil Heating Systems Ltd 1958–61, Ove Arup & Ptnrs Building Gp (later Arup Assocs) 1961–66, fndr Max Fordham & Ptnrs 1966– (constituted as co-op practice 1974), fndr ptnr Max Fordham Assocs 1984–, memb Max Fordham LLP 2001–; dir: Nestar Ltd 1987–2000, Panopus Printing Ltd 1987–2000, National Engineering Specification 1987–98, Max Fordham Consulting Ltd 2004–; visiting prof in building and design Univ of Bath 1990–; external examiner: Architectural Assoc 1991–97 and 2007–11, Univ of Edinburgh 1992–94, Univ of Cambridge Sch of Architecture 1996–99; chm Working Gp for Communications for Building IT 2000, chm Res Sub Ctee for Intelligent Façades for the Centre for Window & Cladding Technol 1993–; CIBSE: accreditation panelist 1989–, memb Cncl 1993–96 and 2000–, pres 2001–02 (vice-pres 1999, pres elect 2000–01), awarded Gold Medal 1997; Prince Philip Designers Prize 2008; FCIBSE 1971 (MCIBSE 1964), FRSA 1982, CEng 1987, Hon FRIBA 1992, FREng 1992, RDI 2008; *Publications* A Global Strategy for Housing in the Third Milleneum – The Envelope of the House in Temperate Climates (Royal Soc, 1992), Building Happiness (contrib, 2008), also numerous tech papers and articles; *Style*— Professor Max Fordham, OBE, FREng; ✉ Max Fordham LLP, 42/43 Gloucester Crescent, London NW1 7PE (☎ 020 7267 5161, fax 020 7482 0329, e-mail max@maxfordham.com and max@maxf.co.uk)

FORDHAM, Michael John; QC (2006); s of John Skidmore Fordham, of Wantage, Oxon, and Margaret, *née* Armstrong; *b* 21 December 1964; *Educ* Spalding GS, Hertford Coll Oxford (BA, BCL, Hockey blue), Univ of Virginia Sch of Law (LLM); *m* 17 April 1993, Alison Jane, *née* Oxley; 2 da (Anna Caitlin b 19 Oct 1994, Lois Rebekah b 11 Dec 1998), 1 s (Bradley John b 7 April 1997); *Career* called to the Bar Gray's Inn 1990 (Karmel, Prince of Wales and Mould scholarships 1989, bencher); barr: 3 Gray's Inn Place 1990–94, Blackstone Chambers 1994–; recorder 2010–, visiting judge Upper Tbnl 2012–, dep High Court judge 2013; counsel Burns Inquiry on hunting with dogs; coll lectr in admin law Hertford Coll Oxford, visiting fell Bingham Centre for the Rule of Law, visiting prof Middlesex Univ; co-ed Judicial Review jl; memb: Attorney Gen's Panel of Counsel, Advsy Bd Br Inst of Int and Comparative Law; memb Admin Law Bar Assoc; Human Rights Lawyer of the Year 2005, Jr Barr of the Year Public Law 2005, Bar Pro Bono Award 2006, Public Law and Human Rights QC of the Year 2008; *Publications* Judicial Review Handbook (6 edn 2012), Immigration Detention and the Rule of Law (2013), Streamlining Judicial Review (2014); *Recreations* hockey; *Clubs* St Albans Hockey (pres); *Style*— Michael Fordham, QC; ✉ mikefordham@hotmail.co.uk; Blackstone Chambers, Temple, London EC4Y 9BW (☎ 020 7583 1770, fax 020 7822 7350, e-mail michaelfordham@blackstonechambers.com)

FOREMAN, Michael; s of Walter Foreman (d 1938), of Lowestoft, Suffolk, and Gladys, *née* Goddard (d 1982); *b* 21 March 1938; *Educ* Notley Road Secdy Modern, Lowestoft Sch of Art, RCA (USA scholar, MA, Silver medal); *m* 22 Dec 1980, Louise Amanda, da of Basil Gordon Phillips; 3 s (Mark b 1961, Ben b 1982, Jack b 1986); *Career* illustrator; former: art dir Playboy, King and Ambit magazines, prodr animated films in Scandinavia and for BBC; regular contrib American and European magazines, held exhibitions Europe, America and Japan; awards: Aigle d'Argent at Festival International du Livre France 1972, Francis Williams Prize V&A Museum and Nat Book League 1972 and 1977, Kate Greenaway Medal 1982 and 1989, Smarties Grand Prix 1994, Graphic Prize Bologna, Kurt Maschler Award; Hon Dr Univ of Plymouth 1998; memb: AGI 1972, RDI 1986; Hon FRCA 1989; *Books* as author and illustrator: The Perfect Present (1967), The Two Giants (1967), The Great Sleigh Robbery (1968), Horatio (1970), Moose (1971), Dinosaurs & All That Rubbish (1972), War & Peas (1974), All The King's Horses (1976), Panda's Puzzle & His Voyage of Discovery (1977), Panda & The Odd Lion (1980), Trick A Tracker (1982), Land of Dreams (1982), Cat & Canary (1984), Panda & The Bunyips (1984), Panda & The Bushfire (1985), Ben's Box (1986), Ben's Baby (1987), The Angel & The Wild Animal (1988), War Boy (1989), One World (1990), Michael Foreman's World of Fairy Tales (ed, 1990), Michael Foreman's Mother Goose (1991), The Boy Who Sailed with Columbus (1991), Jack's Fantastic Voyage (1992), Grandfather's Pencil & The Room of Stories (1993), War Game (1993), Dad! I Can't Sleep (1994), Surprise! Surprise! (1995), After The War Was Over (1995), Seal Surfer (1996), The Little Reindeer (1996), Panda (1996), Look! Look! (1997), Angel and the Box of Time (1997), Jack's Big Race (1998), Chicken Licken (1998), The Little Red Hen (1999), Michael Foreman's Christmas Treasury (ed, 1999), Rock-A-Doodle Do! (2000), Memories of Childhood (2000), Cat in a Manger (2000), Saving Sinbad! (2001), Wonder Goal (2002), Dinosaur Time (2002), Michael Foreman's Playtime Rhymes (2002), Evie and the Man Who Helped God (2003), Hello World (2003), Cat on the Hill (2003), Can't Catch Me (2005), Classic Fairy Tales (2005), Norman's Ark (2006), Mia's Story (2006), Fox Tale (2006), The Littlest Dinosaur (2008), The Littlest Dinosaur's Big Adventure (2009), A Child's Garden (2009), Why The Animals Came To Town (2010), Fortunately, Unfortunately (2010), Superfrog! (2011), Oh! If Only... (2011), Friends (2012), Newspaper Boy and Origami Girl! (2012), Superfrog and the Big Stink! (2013), The Amazing Tale of Ali Pasha (2013), I Love You Too! (2013), Cat and Dog (2014), The Seeds of Friendship (2015), The Little Bookshop and the Origami Army (2015), A Life in Pictures (2015); and 177 books illustrated for other authors from Shakespeare and Dickens to Michael Morpurgo; *Clubs* Chelsea Arts; *Style*— Michael Foreman, Esq

FOREMAN-PECK, Prof James Stanley; s of John Foreman-Peck (d 1984), and Muriel Joan Foreman-Peck (d 1999); *b* 19 June 1948; *Educ* Alleyn's Sch Dulwich, Univ of Essex (BA), LSE (MSc, PhD); *m* 22 June 1968, Lorraine, da of Walter Alexander McGimpsey; 1 s (Alexander b 1978), 1 da (Eleanor b 1985); *Career* economist Electricity Cncl 1971–72, lectr in econs Thames Poly 1972–79, lectr in econs Univ of Newcastle upon Tyne 1979–88, visiting assoc prof Univ of Calif 1981–82, prof of econ history Univ of Hull 1988–90, fell St Antony's Coll Oxford and univ lectr in econ history 1990–98, prof of economics Cardiff Business Sch 2002–, dir Welsh Inst for Res in Economics and Devpt 2002–, head of economics Cardiff Univ 2015–; economic advsr HM Treasy 1999–2002; cnclr London Borough of Greenwich 1978–79, pres European Historical Economic Soc 1999–2001; memb: Amnesty Int, Nat Tst, Royal Econ Soc, Econ History Soc; *Books* A History of the World Economy: International Economic Relations since 1850 (1983, 2 edn 1994), European Telecommunications Organisations (ed, 1988), New Perspectives on the Late Victorian Economy (ed, 1991), Public and Private Ownership of Industry in Britain 1820–1990 (1994), The British Motor Industry (1995), Smith and Nephew in the Healthcare Industry (1995), Globalisation in History (1998), European Industrial Policy (1999); *Recreations* music, literature; *Style*— Prof James Foreman-Peck; ✉ Cardiff Business School, Cardiff University, Cardiff CF10 3EU (☎ 029 2087 6395, e-mail foreman-peckj@cardiff.ac.uk)

FORFAR, Dr (John) Colin; s of Prof J O Forfar, MC, of Edinburgh, and Isobel Mary Langlands; *b* 22 November 1951; *Educ* Edinburgh Acad, Univ of Edinburgh (BSc, MD, PhD), Univ of Oxford (MA); *m* (m dis); 1 da (Katriana Louise b 1981); *Career* reader in cardiovascular med Univ of Oxford 1985–86, physician and conslt cardiologist Oxford RHA 1986–; chm Oxford Heart Centre; author of numerous med pubns; chair (cardiovascular, renal, diabetes, respiratory and allergy) Expert Advsy Gp Cmmn on Human Medicines; memb: Br Cardiac Soc (former local sec), MRS, Oxford Med Soc; FRCPE 1987, FRCP 1991; *Recreations* walking, squash; *Style*— Dr Colin Forfar; ✉ Beckley Manor, Beckley, Oxford OX3 9TG (☎ 01865 358231); Department of Cardiology, John Radcliffe Hospital, Oxford OX3 9DU (☎ 01865 220326, fax 01865 220252)

FORGE, Anna; da of Kenneth Baynton Forge (d 1976), and Rosaline, *née* Shaw (d 1984); *b* 12 May 1951, Bromley, Kent; *Educ* Bromley GS for Girls, Univ of Kent at Canterbury (BA), Coll of Law; *Family* 1 da (Beth b 22 May 1970), 1 s (Omar Ben b 27 Nov 1993); *Career* admitted slr 1982; articled clerk rising to asst head of legal servs London Borough of Southwark 1979–88, asst slr rising to ptnr Berwin Leighton 1989–99, ptnr Mayer Brown Rowe and Maw LLP 1999–2007, ptnr McGrigors LLP 2007–11, conslt Pinsent Masons LLP 2012–; CEDR accredited mediator; *Publications* Butterworth's Local Government Finance (co-author, 2000); *Recreations* ballet, travel, reading, theatre; *Style*— Miss Anna Forge; ✉ Pinsent Masons LLP, 30 Crown Place, Earl Street, London EC2A 4ES (☎ 020 7054 2642, fax 020 7054 2501, e-mail anna.forge@pinsentmasons.com)

FORGE, Gilly Rosamund; da of John Bliss Forge, of Cirencester, Glos, and Margaret, *née* Whitwell (d 1966); *b* 27 February 1956; *Educ* The Abbey Malvern, New Hall Boreham, Trinity Coll Dublin (LLB); *Career* milliner; former journalist, estab millinery business 1989; designers worked with incl: Jean Muir, Anouska Hempel, Caroline Charles, Amanda Wakeley; model hat range sold exclusively, diffusion range sold in major retailers throughout UK, Europe, USA and Japan, and by mail order in UK; designer to Chester Jeffries glove mfrs 1992–96; *Style*— Miss Gilly Forge

FORRES, 4 Baron (UK 1922); Sir Alastair Stephen Grant Williamson; 4 Bt (UK 1909); s of 3 Baron Forres (d 1978), by his 1 w, Gillian Ann Maclean, *née* Grant; *b* 16 May 1946; *Educ* Eton; *m* 2 May 1969, Margaret Ann, da of late George John Mallam, of Mullumbimby, NSW; 2 s (Hon George b 1972, Hon Guthrie b 1975); *Heir* s, Hon George Williamson; *Career* chm Agriscot Pty Ltd; dir Jaga Trading Pty Ltd; Australian rep Tattersalls; *Clubs* Australian Jockey, Tattersalls (Sydney), Sydney Turf; *Style*— The Rt Hon the Lord Forres

FORREST, Alexander (Sandy); s of William Forrest, and Mary, *née* Kirk; *b* 19 July 1953; *Educ* St John's GS, Hamilton Acad, Univ of Strathclyde (BA); *m* 4 Sept 1980 (m dis 2014), Elspeth McInnes Paton; 2 s (Alasdair, Jonathan); *Career* Strathclyde Police: joined 1974, Supt and Dep Divnl Cdr 1992–94, Chief Supt and head Traffic Dept 1994–97, Chief Supt and Divnl Cdr 1997–99; Asst Chief Constable (Scot) Br Transport Police 1999–2001, Dep Chief Constable and HM's Asst Inspr of Constabulary for Scot 2001–03, dir Cncl for Healthcare Regulatory Excellence (CHRE) 2003–07, chief exec NHS24 2007; Atos: assoc ptnr 2008, gen mangr, client exec UK&I Cyber Security 2016–; lay memb Bar Standards Bd for Eng and Wales 2006–07; hon sec Assoc of Scot Police Supts 1994–98 (memb Police Negotiating Bd, memb Police Advsy Bd for Scot); Police Long Service and Good Conduct Medal, Queen's Jubilee Medal; CMILT, FRSA 2007; *Recreations* skiing, motorcycling and cycling; *Style*— Sandy Forrest, Esq; ✉ 4 Triton Square, Regent's Place, London NW1 3HG (e-mail sandy.forrest@atos.net)

FORREST, Dr John Richard; CBE (2002); s of Prof John Samuel Forrest, and Ivy May Ellen, *née* Olding; *b* 21 April 1943; *Educ* KCS Wimbledon, Sidney Sussex Coll Cambridge (BA, MA), Keble Coll Oxford (DPhil); *m* 1, 8 Sept 1973 (m dis), Jane Patricia Robey, da of John Robey Leech, of Little Hockham Hall, Norfolk; 2 s (Nicholas John b 1975, Alexander Iain b 1980), 1 da (Katharine Elizabeth b 1977); m 2, Diane Martine James; *Career* UCL: lectr 1970–79, reader 1979–82, prof 1982–84; tech dir Marconi Defence Systems Ltd 1984–86, dir of engrg IBA 1986–90, chief exec National Transcommunications Ltd 1991–94, dep chm NTL Group Ltd 1994–96, chm Brewton Gp Ltd 1994–99; dir: Egan International Ltd 1994–, Loughborough Sound Images plc 1996–98, Screen plc 1996–99, Drake Automation Ltd 1996–99, Tricorder Technology plc 1997–2001, 3i Gp plc 1997–2004, Blue Wave Systems Inc 1998–2001 (chm 2000–01), Morgan Howard Int Gp Ltd 1999–2000; chm Human IT Ltd 2000–03, exec chm Cellular Design Services Ltd 2003–05; dep chm: Surrey Satellite Technology Ltd 2006–, Omniglobe Networks Ltd 2006–, System C Healthcare plc 2007– (dir 2005–); chm Advsy Bd Interregnum plc 2003–06; chm UK Govt Spectrum Mgmnt Advsy Gp 1998–2003; sr vice-pres Royal Acad of Engrg 1999–2002 (hon sec (electrical engrg) 1995–97, vice-pres 1997–99); memb Cncl Brunel Univ 1996–99, pro-chllr Univ of Surrey 2005–; Hon DSc City Univ 1992, Hon DTech Brunel Univ 1995; Hon FBKSTS 1990; FIEE 1980, FREng 1985, FRSA 1987, FRTS 1990, FInstD 1991; Chevalier de l'Ordre des Arts et des Lettres (France) 1990; *Recreations* theatre, music, reading, sailing, mountain walking; *Style*— Dr John Forrest, CBE, FREng; ✉ mobile 07785 251734, e-mail johnrforrest@aol.com

FORREST, Nigel; s of Wing Cdr Gerald Vere Forrest (d 2000), of Sydney, Aust, and Elizabeth, *née* Burnett (d 1991); *b* 12 September 1946; *Educ* Harrow, Oriel Coll Oxford (MA), INSEAD (MBA); *m* 22 Nov 1980, Julia Mary, da of Philip Nash (d 1970), of Dorking, Surrey; 1 s (Dominic b 18 April 1982), 1 da (Harriet b 9 Feb 1984); *Career* commercial technol sales mangr Rolls Royce Ltd 1972 (grad trainee 1969), mangr Lazard Bros & Co Ltd 1978 (exec 1973), dep md Nomura International plc 1989–96 (assoc md 1986, exec dir 1983, mangr 1981), sr conslt NatWest Markets 1996–98, dir Nashbrook Partners Ltd 1998–, dir Amicus Expert Witness Ltd 1999–2001; chm Fundraising Ctee Highbury Roundhouse 1978–81; MCSI, FRSA; *Publications* The Channel Tunnel – Before The Decision (1973), The Court Jester (trans, 2009), Kraftwerk Publikation (co-author, 2012); author of five financial training books 1996; *Style*— Nigel Forrest, Esq, FRSA; ✉ Nashbrook Partners Ltd, Moor House, Arbrook Lane, Esher, Surrey KT10 9EE (☎ 07768 728619)

FORREST, Prof (Alexander) Robert Walker; s of Alexander Muir Forrest (d 2002), of Boston, Lincs, and Rose Ellen, *née* Ringham (d 1976); *b* 5 July 1947, Glasgow; *Educ* Stamford Sch, Univ of Edinburgh (BSc, MB ChB), Cardiff Law Sch (LLM); *m* Wendy S Phillips, da of Ian Phillips, of Millom, Cumbria; 2 s (Michael b 1981, David b 1984); *Career* conslt chem pathologist Royal Hallamshire Hosp 1981–98; Univ of Sheffield: clinical lectr in human metabolism and clinical biochemistry 1981–98, hon lectr in forensic toxicology 1985–98, prof of forensic toxicology 1998–2005, prof of forensic chemistry 2005–16; conslt clinical chemist and forensic toxicologist Sheffield Teaching Hosps NHS Fndn Tst 2005–07; HM sr coroner for S Lincs 2012–16; visiting prof of forensic toxicology Univ of Bradford 1996–2000, hon prof Faculty of Health and Wellbeing Sheffield Hallam Univ 2008–, hon prof Sch of Law Univ of Sheffield; asst coroner S Yorks (W) 1988–91 and 1993– (dep coroner 1991–93), asst coroner Hull 2008–; pres Forensic Science Soc 2005–07; memb: Coroners' Soc of England and Wales, Soc of Forensic Toxicologists, Selden Soc, Ecclesiastical Law Soc, Canon Law Soc; memb Editorial Bd Science and Justice 2007–; FRSC 1985, FRCPE 1989, FRCPath 1992 (MRCPath 1980), FRCP 1992, fell Faculty of Forensic and Legal Medicine (FFFLM) 2005 (vice-pres Medical Coroners), fell American Acad of Forensic Sciences (FAAFS) 2010; *Recreations* photography, computers, books, cats; *Clubs* Athenaeum; *Style*— Prof Robert Forrest

FORREST, Prof (Archibald) Robin; s of Samuel Forrest (d 1982), of Edinburgh, and Agnes Dollar, *née* Robin (d 2009); *b* 13 May 1943, Glasgow; *Educ* Daniel Stewart's Coll

Edinburgh, Univ of Edinburgh (BSc), Trinity Coll Cambridge (PhD); *m* 7 April 1973, Rosemary Ann, da of Ralph Kenneth Foster (d 1983), of Grantham, Lincs; 1 s (Matthew b 1975), 1 da (Susanna b 1977); *Career* asst dir of research Computer Laboratory Cambridge Univ 1971–74 (tech offr Engrg Dept 1968–71); visiting prof: Syracuse Univ NY 1971–72, Univ of Utah 1979, Univ of São Paulo 1996; visiting expert Beijing Inst of Aeronautics and Astronautics 1979, prof of computing science UEA 1980–2008 (reader in computing studies 1974–80, emeritus prof 2008–), visiting scientist Xerox Palo Alto Research Centre 1982–83; hon prof Shandong Univ 2003; CEng, CMath, CITP, FBCS, FIMA 1978; *Recreations* collecting wine, reading maps, rowing St Ayles skiffs; *Style*— Prof Robin Forrest, ✉ 3 Highlands, Folgate Lane, Old Costessey, Norwich NR8 5EA (📞 01603 742315)

FORRESTER, Prof Alexander Robert (Alex); OBE (1998); s of Robert James Forrester (d 1977), and Mary, *née* Gavin; *b* 14 November 1935, Kelty, Fife; *Educ* Univ of Heriot-Watt (BSc), Univ of Aberdeen (DSc, PhD); *m* 1961, Myrna Ross, da of James Doull; 3 da (Deborah Mary b 1964, Melanie Claire b 1966, Stephanie Emma b 1969), 1 s (James Gregor b 1970); *Career* professional football player Third Lanark FC 1958–59; Univ of Aberdeen: asst lectr 1963–64, lectr 1964–76, sr lectr 1976–81, reader 1981–85, prof 1985–, head Dept of chemistry 1987–89, dean 1989–, vice-princ 1990–, dean and vice-princ 1995–; chm Techfest-Stetpoint 2009–13; dir: Univ of Aberdeen research and industrial service (AURIS) 1990– (chm 2003–08), Offshore Medical Support 1992–96, Nat Collection of Industrial and Med Bacteria 1997–; memb: Cncl RSC 1987–90, Ctee of Scottish National Library 1988–93, Cncl Perkin Division 1991–94, Scottish Higher Education Funding Cncl Ctees, Ctees of Scottish Higher Education Principals (COSHEP), Cncl RSE 1998–; FRSC 1982, FRSE 1985; *Publications* Stable Organic Radicals (1968); and also author of many learned papers in academic jls; *Recreations* golf, reading, organising other people, cricket, rugby; *Clubs* Deeside Golf, Aberdeen Grammar Rugby (pres 2006–07); *Style*— Prof Alex Forrester, OBE, FRSE; ✉ 210 Springfield Road, Aberdeen (📞 01224 313367, fax 01224 272082)

FORRESTER, Ian Stewart; QC (Scot 1988); s of Alexander Roxburgh Forrester (d 1976), of Glasgow, and Elizabeth Richardson, *née* Stewart (d 1947); *b* 13 January 1945; *Educ* Kelvinside Acad Glasgow, Univ of Glasgow (MA, LLB), Tulane Univ of Louisiana New Orleans (MCL); *m* 7 March 1981, Sandra Anne Thérèse, da of M C Keegan, of Jefferson, Louisiana; 2 s (Alexander Stewart Daigle b 24 Sept 1982, James Roxburgh b 29 May 1985); *Career* European lawyer after training in Glasgow, New Orleans, NY and Edinburgh; estab ind chambers Brussels (with Christopher Norall) 1981 (now known as White & Case), practising before Euro Cmmn and Courts; admitted Faculty of Advocates 1972, admitted Bar State of NY 1977, called to the Bar Middle Temple 1996 (bencher 2012), admitted Bar Brussels 2000; chm: Br Cons Assoc in Belgium 1982–86; hon prof Univ of Glasgow 1991–; memb: Dean's Advsy Bd Tulane Univ Law Sch, American Bar Assoc, The Stair Soc; tstee EU Baroque Orch; elder St Andrew's Church of Scotland Brussels; Hon LLD Univ of Glasgow 2009; *Publications* The German Civil Code (1975), The German Commercial Code (1979), author of numerous articles and chapters on EC law and policy in The Oxford Yearbook of European Law, International Antitrust Law, The European Law Review, The Common Market Law Review, Legal Issues of European Integration, European Intellectual Property Review; *Recreations* politics, wine, cooking, restoring old houses; *Clubs* Athenaeum, International Château Sainte-Anne (Brussels), Royal Yacht of Belgium; *Style*— Ian Forrester, Esq, QC; ✉ 73 Square Marie-Louise, 1000 Brussels, Belgium; 62 Rue de la Loi, 1040 Brussels, Belgium (📞 00 32 2 2191620, fax 00 32 2 2191626, e-mail iforrester@whitecase.com)

FORSTER, Prof Anthony; *Educ* Univ of Hull (BA), Univ of Oxford (MPhil, DPhil), Univ of Nottingham (PGCert); *Career* army offr RCT 1985–91; stipendiary lectr St Hilda's Coll Oxford 1995–96, lectr Sch of Politics Univ of Nottingham 1996–2000; KCL: dir of research and sr lectr 2000–02, reader in European foreign and security policy Defence Studies Dept 2002; Univ of Bristol: prof of politics 2002–04, dir Governance Research Centre 2002–06, head Dept of Politics 2004–06; Durham Univ: exec dean (Social Sciences and Health) and prof of politics 2006–08, pro-vice-chllr (Educn) 2008–11, dep vice-chllr 2011–12; vice-chllr Univ of Essex 2012–; fell Leadership Fndn for HE 2014; FHEA 2007, FAcSS 2009, FRSA 2010; *Books* Britain and the Maastricht Negotiations (1999), The Making of Britain's European Foreign Policy (with Alasdair Blair, 2001), Euroscepticism in Contemporary British Politics: opposition to Europe in the British Conservative and Labour Parties since 1945 (2002), Reshaping Defence Diplomacy: New Roles for Military Cooperation and Assistance, Adelphi Paper 365 (with Andrew Cottey, 2004), Armed Forces and Society in Europe (2006), Out of Step: The Case for Change in British Armed Forces (with Tim Edmunds, 2007); edited collections: The Challenge of Military Reform in Postcommunist Europe: Building Professional Armed Forces (with Tim Edmunds and Andrew Cottey, 2002), Democratic Control of the Military in Postcommunist Europe (with Andrew Cottey and Tim Edmunds, 2002), Soldiers and Societies in Postcommunist Europe, Legitimacy and Change (with Tim Edmunds and Andrew Cottey, 2003), Civil-Military Relations in Postcommunist Europe (with Tim Edmunds and Andrew Cottey, 2006); *Recreations* 20th Century architecture; *Style*— Prof Anthony Forster; ✉ University of Essex, Wivenhoe Park, Colchester CO4 3SQ (Twitter @Forster_Anthony)

FORSTER, Jonathan; s of Dr Robert Forster (d 2009), of Yorks, and Marie, *née* Bateman (d 2012); *b* 18 December 1954, Leeds; *Educ* Shrewsbury, Univ of Leeds (BA); *m* 28 July 1979, Paula, *née* Crowther; 2 da (Sarah b 1 March 1982, Clare b 5 April 1984); *Career* English teacher Hymers Coll Hull 1978–83, head of English and housemaster Strathallan Sch 1983–1992, princ Moreton Hall Sch 1992–; govr various schs, advsr to academies and free schs; memb Soc of Heads, memb GSA 1992; FRSA 1993; *Recreations* cricket, golf, reading, travel, walking; *Clubs* Hull Literary, Army & Navy; *Style*— Jonathan Forster, Esq; ✉ Moreton Hall, Weston Rhyn, Oswestry, Shropshire SY11 3EW (📞 01691 776020, e-mail brownr@moretonhall.com, forsterj@moretonhall.com, website www.moretonhall.org)

FORSTER, Karen Elizabeth (KT); da of Timothy George Naylor, and late Victoria Josephine, *née* Barnes-Forster; *b* Epsom, Surrey; *Educ* Brighton, Hove and Sussex Sixth Form Coll, Oxford Brookes Univ (BA); *Career* rights dir Studio Editions Ltd 1993–95, rights dir Random House Ltd 1995–96, int sales dir Virgin Publishing Ltd 1996–2000, dep md Virgin Publishing Ltd 2000, md Virgin Books Ltd 2000–07, literary agent, talent mangr, non-exec dir, media conslt and publishing conslt 2008–; magistrate Central London Bench 2010–, magistrate London Family Panel 2012–; official Surrey County Athletics 2012–, official Regnl S of Eng Athletics 2013–; ind memb Panel Own Life Ltd 2013–; MInstD 2002; *Recreations* parenting, reading, music; *Style*— Ms KT Forster; ✉ e-mail ktforster@googlemail.com

FORSTER, Margaret; da of Arthur Gordon Forster, and Lilian, *née* Hind; *b* 25 May 1938; *Educ* Somerville Coll Oxford; *m* 1960, (Edward) Hunter Davies, *qv*; 1 s, 2 da; *Career* author; FRSL 1974; *Books* incl: Dames's Delight (1964), Georgy Girl (1965), Elizabeth Barrett Browning (1988), Have the Men Had Enough? (1989), Daphne du Maurier (1993), Hidden Lives (1995), Shadow Baby (1996), Rich Desserts & Captain's Thin: A Family & Their Times – social history of Carr's of Carlisle 1831–1931 (1997), Precious Lives (memoir, 1998), Good Wives? Mary, Fanny, Jennie and Me, 1845–2001 (2001), Diary of an Ordinary Woman (2003), Is There Anything You Want? (2005), Keeping the World Away (2006); *Style*— Miss Margaret Forster, FRSL; ✉ 11 Boscastle Road, London NW5 1EE

FORSTER, Prof (A) Paul; MBE (2016); s of Alfred Forster (d 1965), of Reading, and Dorothy Forster (d 1984); *b* 19 February 1942; *Educ* Stoneham Sch Reading, Univ of Nottingham (BA); *m* 1965, Patricia, *née* Hammond, 2 da (Simone b 19 Sept 1968, Eleanor b 1 Oct 1971); *Career* mktg exec; Cadbury Schweppes plc 1962–72: gen mangr Retail CTN Stores, mktg mangr confectionary Count Line Market; ptnr Lippa Newton Ltd (advtg agency) 1972–74, KMPH Group plc 1974–77 (md PLN Partners Ltd), Saatchi & Saatchi Group plc 1977–79 (md Roe Downton Ltd); Euro RSCG (formerly Colman RSCG Group) 1979–94: md until 1988, chief exec and chm communications group of companies 1988–94; non-exec dir N Brown Group plc 1993–99, chief exec Lifetime Business Group 1994–2000, ceo Euro Customer Mgmnt Centre Dimension Data plc; chm CVC Associates 2003–; visiting prof and memb Advsy Bd Nottingham Business Sch 1993–2011, dep chm Bd of Govrs Nottingham Trent Univ 1993–2007, visiting prof and memb Advsy Bd Birmingham City Univ Business Sch 2011– (chair Advsy Bd 2011–); chm Bd of Tstees Prostate Cancer UK 2004–13, assoc memb Hospice of St Francis 2011–; MCIM, FRSM; *Publications* Serving Them Right (1998); *Recreations* tennis, theatre; *Clubs* Royal Society of Medicine, The Marketing Society; *Style*— Prof Paul Forster, MBE, 📞 07973 891211, e-mail paul.forster@cvcuk.com

FORSTER, Rt Rev Peter Robert; *see:* Chester, Bishop of

FORSYTH, Sir Bruce Joseph (né Forsyth-Johnson); kt (2011), CBE (2006, OBE 1998); s of John Frederick Forsyth-Johnson (d 1961), and Florence Ada Forsyth-Johnson (d 1957); *b* 22 February 1928; *Educ* Latimer Sch Edmonton; *m* 1, 1951 (m dis), Olivia, da of Calvert, of NI; 3 da (Debbie b 1955, Julie b 1958, Laura b 1964); *m* 2, 24 Dec 1973 (m dis), Anthea, da of Bernard Redfern, of Torquay; 2 da (Charlotte b 1976, Louisa b 1977); *m* 3, 15 Jan 1983, Wilnelia, da of Enrique Merced, of Puerto Rico; 1 s (Jonathan Joseph b 1986); *Career* entertainer and television host; FBA 2008; *Theatre* Little Me (original Br prodn) 1964, Travelling Music Show 1978, One Man Show (Winter Garden NY 1979, Huntington Hartford Los Angeles 1979, London Palladium); numerous extensive tours UK, NZ and Aust; *Television* incl: Sunday Night at the London Palladium 1958–63, Piccadilly Spectaculars, Bruce Forsyth Show (ATV), The Generation Game (BBC, 1971–77 and 1990–94), Bruce's Big Night (LWT) 1978, Play Your Cards Right 1980–87 (ten series) and 1994–, Slingers Day (Thames) 1985–86, Hollywood or Bust 1984, You Bet! (LWT) 1987–89, Takeover Bid (BBC) 1990–91, Bruce's Guest Night (BBC) 1992–93, Bruce's Price is Right 1996, Strictly Come Dancing 2002–13; numerous specials incl: Bring on the Girls (Thames) 1976, Bruce and More Girls (Thames) 1977, Bruce Meets the Girls, The Forsyth Follies, Sammy and Bruce (with Sammy Davis Jr), The Entertainers (with Rita Moreno), The Muppet Show, The Mating Season, The Canterville Ghost; *Films* Star 1968, Can Heironymous Merkin Ever Forgive Mercy Humppe and Find True Happiness 1969, Bedknobs and Broomsticks 1971, The Seven Deadly Sins 1971, Pavlova 1984; *Awards* Daily Mirror National TV Award 1961, Variety Club Showbusiness Personality of the Year 1975, The Sun TV Personality of the Year 1976 and 1977, TV Times Favourite Male TV Personality 1975, 1976 and 1977, TV Times Favourite Game Show Host 1984, BBC TV Personality of the Year 1991, Lifetime Achievement Award for Variety 1995, Special Recognition Award Nat Television Awards 2011; *Recreations* golf, tennis; *Clubs* Tramp, Crockfords; *Style*— Sir Bruce Forsyth, CBE; ✉ Bruce Forsyth Enterprises Ltd, Straidarran, Wentworth Drive, Virginia Water, Surrey GU25 4NY (📞 and fax 01344 844056)

FORSYTH, Frederick; CBE (1997); s of Frederick William Forsyth (d 1991), and Phyllis, *née* Green (d 1989); *b* 25 August 1938, Ashford, Kent; *Educ* Tonbridge (scholar); *m* 1, 1974, Carole Ann, *née* Cunningham; 2 s (Frederick Stuart b Sept 1977, Shane Richard b June 1979); *m* 2, 1994, Sandy Molloy; *Career* RAF 1956–58; reporter Eastern Daily Press 1958–61, foreign corr Reuters News Agency 1961–65, reporter/corr BBC 1965–68, freelance war corr 1968–70; novelist and columnist 1971–; *Publications* The Biafra Story (non-fiction, 1969), Day of the Jackal (novel, 1971), eleven further novels, two novellas, two anthologies of short stories; *Recreations* scuba diving, game fishing; *Clubs* Saints and Sinners; *Style*— Frederick Forsyth, Esq, CBE; ✉ c/o Ed Victor Limited, 6 Bayley Street, London WC1B 3HE (📞 020 7304 4100, fax 020 7304 4111)

FORSYTH, (Robert) Justin Alexander; s of Robert Forsyth, and Maureen, *née* Irvine; *b* 17 June 1965, Paisley, Renfrewshire; *Educ* Oxford Poly (BA); *m* 21 April 2012, Lisa, *née* Stevens; 1 s (Arthur Stanley b 11 Jan 2013); *Career* Oxfam: advsr on Africa 1989–95, int advocacy dir Washington DC 1995–99, policy dir 1999–2002, dir campaigns and policy 2003–05; special advsr to PM 2005–08, PM's dir strategic communications 2008–10, chief exec Save the Children UK 2010–; *Recreations* reading, tennis, African history, politics; *Style*— Justin Forsyth, Esq; ✉ Save the Children, 1 St John's Lane, London EC1M 4AR (📞 020 7012 6400, email j.forsyth@savethechildren.org.uk, website www.savethechildren.org.uk, Twitter @justinforsyth)

FORSYTH, Dr Michael Graham; s of Eric Forsyth, of Wallasey, Merseyside, and Lucy Rebecca, *née* de Jong; *b* 26 November 1951, Tynemouth, Tyne and Wear; *Educ* Univ of Liverpool Sch of Architecture (BA, BArch), British Sch at Rome, Univ of Bristol (PhD); *m* 1 Sept 1975 (m dis), Vera, da of Nicos Papaxanthou, of Nicosia, Cyprus; 1 s (James b 28 Sept 1983), 2 da (Antonia b 18 Dec 1985, Henrietta b 18 March 1988); *Career* architectural practice Toronto 1976–79, res fell Univ of Bristol 1984–90 (lectr 1979–84), dir Plato Consortium Ltd Bath 1985–2002, ptnr Forsyth Chartered Architects Bath 1987–; Univ of Bath: sr visiting lectr 1996–99, MSc dir of studies in Conservation of Historic Buildings 1999–, sr lectr 1999–; awarded: Rome Scholarship in Architecture 1975, nineteenth annual ASCAP Deems Taylor award for books on music; many articles reviews and radio broadcasts; memb: Selection Board Br Sch at Rome 1987–93, Exec Ctee Friends of Bristol Art Gallery 1985–90, Exec Ctee Friends of Victoria Art Gallery Bath 1994–97 (chm 1995–97), Arts and Humanities Research Cncl Peer Review Coll 2009–; assessor Register for AABC 1998–2009; tstee Bath Preservation Tst 2008– (memb Renovations Ctee 1989–98); hon sec Soc of Rome Scholars 1984–89; RIBA 1979, ARCUK 1979; *Books* Buildings for Music: The Architect, the Musician, and the Listener from the Seventeenth Century to the Present Day (1985), Auditoria: Designing for the Performing Arts (1987), Bath: Pevsner Architectural Guide (2003), Understanding Historic Building Conservation (ed, 2007), Structures and Construction in Historic Building Conservation (ed, 2007), Materials and Skills for Historic Building Conservation (ed, 2007), An Outline of European Architecture (contrib, 2009), Palaces of Music: opera houses of Europe (jtly, 2010), Domes: a journey through European architectural history (jtly, 2011), Interior Finishes and Fittings for Historic Building Conservation (jt ed, 2012), Gardens and Landscapes in Historic Building Conservation (contrib, Marion Harney ed, 2014), Hermitage – A Palace and a Museum (jtly, 2014); *Recreations* the violin; *Clubs* Chelsea Arts; *Style*— Dr Michael Forsyth; ✉ 19 Lansdown Crescent, Bath BA1 5EX; University of Bath, Department of Architecture and Civil Engineering, Bath BA2 7AY (📞 01225 383016, fax 01225 386691, e-mail m.forsyth@bath.ac.uk)

FORSYTH OF DRUMLEAN, Baron (Life Peer UK 1999), of Drumlean in Stirling; Michael Bruce Forsyth; kt (1997), PC (1995); s of John Tawse Forsyth, and Mary Watson; *b* 16 October 1954; *Educ* Arbroath HS, Univ of St Andrews (MA); *m* 1977, Susan Jane, da of John Bryan Clough; 1 s, 2 da; *Career* nat chm Fedn of Cons Students 1976, memb Westminster City Cncl 1978–83, MP (Cons) Stirling 1983–97; PPS to Foreign Sec 1986–87, Parly under sec of state Scottish Office 1987–90; min of state: Scottish Office 1990–92, Dept of Employment 1992–94, Home Office 1994–95; sec of state for Scotland 1995–97; memb House of Lords Ctee on Monetary Policy 1999–2001, memb Jt Ctee on Reform of the House of Lords; dir Flemings 1997–2000, vice-chm Investment Banking Europe

JP Morgan 2000–01, dep chm JP Morgan UK 2001–05, sr md Evercore Ptnrs 2007–12 (sr advsr 2006–07), chm Safor Ltd 2012–; non-exec dir: J&J Denholm Ltd 2005–, NBNK Investments plc 2010–12; dir Hyperion Insurance Gp 2012–; chm Tax Reform Cmmn 2005–06, memb Lords Economic Affrs Select Ctee, memb Lords Select Ctee on Barnett Formula, memb review of Mull of Kyntire helicopter crash; chm Scottish Cons Pty 1989–90; dir Centre for Policy Studies 2006–; patron: Craighalbert Centre, CINI (UK) 2008–13; memb Devpt Bd Nat Portrait Gallery 2000–03; *Recreations* mountaineering, gardening, photography, astronomy, skiing; *Clubs* Sloane; *Style—* The Rt Hon the Lord Forsyth of Drumlean, PC; ✉ House of Lords, London SW1A 0PW

FORSYTHE, Dr (John) Malcolm; s of Dr John Walter Joseph Forsythe (d 1988), and Dr Charlotte Constance Forsythe, *née* Beatty (d 1981); *b* 11 July 1936; *Educ* Repton, Guy's Med Sch London (BSc, MB BS, MRCS, DObstRCOG), Univ of N Carolina, LSHTM (MSc); *m* 1, 28 Oct 1961 (m dis 1984), Delia Kathleen, da of late Dr J K Moore; 3 da (Suzanne Delia, Nicola Kathleen (twins) b 9 July 1962, Sarah Louise b 16 May 1969), 1 s (Marcus John Malcolm b 30 Sept 1965); m 2, 27 Jan 1984, Patricia Mary Murden, *née* Barnes; *Career* house surgn Guy's 1961–62, house offr Farnborough 1962, house physician Lewisham 1962–63, GP Beckenham 1963–65, MO Birmingham Regnl Hosp Bd 1965–68, princ asst sr admin MO Wessex RHB 1968–72, dep sr admin medical offr SE Met RHB 1972–73 (acting sr admin medical offr 1973–74), area MO Kent AHA 1974–78; regnl MO SE Thames RHA 1978–89 (dir of planning 1983–89), regnl MO and dir of Public Health and Serv Devpt SE Thames RHA 1989–92, dir Inst of Public Health 1990–91, prof of public health Univ of Kent Canterbury 1992–2001, sr lectr KCH Med Sch London 1992–2006, chm SW Kent PCT 2001–04; visiting prof Univ of N Carolina 1973, 1976 and 1993, adjunct prof St George's Univ Sch of Medicine Grenada WI 1995–; memb: Bd Public Health Laboratory Serv 1985–95, Bd of Mgmnt Horder Centre for Arthritis 1992–, BUPA Ltd 1993–2007, Hyde Housing Assoc 1999–2007 (memb In Touch Bd 2006–10), Bd Horder Centre 2001–04; chm: GMC Working Party on assessment in public health med 1995–97, Bd Tunbridge Wells Primary Care Gp 1998–2001, West Kent Primary Care Tst 2001–04; pres Epidemiology and Public Health Section RSM 1998–2000 (vice-pres 2001–02), sec Retired Fells Soc RSM 2006–10 (vice-chm 2010–11); hon conslt in public health med: Camberwell HA 1992–94, King's Coll Hosp Tst 1994–2001; memb Editorial Bd RCP 1999–2003; tstee: Sick Doctors' Tst 1996–2009, Sussex Tst for the Elderly 2004–11; chm Ind Remuneration Panel Tunbridge Wells BC, Sevenoaks DC and Tonbridge and Malling BC 2001–07, memb Bd Chichester Diocesan Housing Assoc 2000–07, treas John Fry Soc Guy's Hosp 2012–; Allen Daley Memorial Prize 1969, Jack Maser Fellowship American Hospital Assoc 1974, Cncl of Europe Fellowship 1977, Silver Core Award Int Medical Informatics Assoc 1977; FFPHM, FRCP; *Recreations* ornithology, bridge; *Clubs* RSM; *Style—* Dr Malcolm Forsythe; ✉ Buckingham House, 1 Royal Chase, Tunbridge Wells TN4 8AX

FORSYTHE, Max; *b* 2 May 1944, Staffs; *Educ* Newry GS, Belfast Coll of Art, London Coll of Printing; *m* Jane; 2 c; *Career* photographer; early career experience as art dir working at various advtg agencies incl Collett Dickenson Pearce; dir of various TV commercials and photographer (specialising in location and reportage photography for advtg indust) since 1972; campaign work for int accounts incl: Nike, Parker Pens, Bacardi, Teachers Whisky, P&O Cruises, Club Mediterranee, Bergasol, Hawaiian Tropic, Heineken, Ilford, and car mfrs Audi, Mercedes, Citroën, Range Rover, Vauxhall, BMW, Rolls Royce; numerous awards for photography in UK, USA and Europe incl: 5 Silvers (D&AD), Bronze Lion for direction (Cannes); first one-man exhbn Hamiltons Gallery London 1984; work in the collections of RPS and Nat Museum of Photography; chm Assoc of Photographers 1994; *Style—* Max Forsythe; ✉ website www.maxforsythe.com

FORTE, Hon Sir Rocco; kt (1995); o s of Baron Forte (Life Peer) (d 2007); *b* 18 January 1945; *Educ* Downside, Pembroke Coll Oxford (MA); *m* 15 Feb 1986, Aliai, da of Prof Giovanni Ricci, of Rome; 2 da (Lydia Irene b 1987, Irene Alisea b 1988), 1 s (Charles Giovanni b 6 Dec 1991); *Career* chm and chief exec Forte plc (formerly Trusthouse Forte plc) 1983–96 (chm 1993–96), currently chm and chief exec Rocco Forte Hotels; former memb: Br Tourist Authy, Grand Cncl Hotel and Catering Benevolent Assoc; Liveryman Worshipful Co of Bakers; FHCIMA, FCA, FInstD; Cavaliere di Gran Croce Order of Merit of the Italian Republic; *Recreations* golf, fishing, shooting, triathlon; *Clubs* Garrick, Whites; *Style—* The Hon Sir Rocco Forte; ✉ Rocco Forte Hotels, 70 Jermyn Street, London SW1Y 6NY (☎ 020 7321 2626, fax 020 7312 2424)

FORTESCUE, Hon Seymour Henry; s of 6 Earl Fortescue, MC, TD (d 1977), and his 2 w Hon Sybil Mary (d 1985), da of 3rd Viscount Hardinge; *b* 28 May 1942; *Educ* Eton, Trinity Coll Cambridge (MA), London Business Sch (MSc); *m* 1, 25 July 1966 (m dis 1990), Julia, o da of Sir John Arthur Pilcher GCMG (d 1990); 1 da (Marissa Clare b 20 Oct 1973), 1 s (James Adrian b 15 April 1978); m 2, 23 Aug 1990, Jennifer Ann Simon; 1 da (Alexandra Kate b 10 July 1991); *Career* dir Visa International 1981–91, chief exec Barclaycard 1982–85, dir UK Retail Servs Barclays Bank plc 1987–91 (gen mangr 1985–87), dir of finance and fundraising ICRF 1991–96, chief exec Health Educn Authy 1996–99; chief exec Banking Code Standards Bd 1999–; govr Oundle Sch 1999–2003; hon treas Lepra 1986–96, chm BookPower; memb Ct of Assts Worshipful Co of Grocers (Master 1997–98); *Recreations* gardening, travel, walking, country pursuits, opera; *Style—* The Hon Seymour Fortescue; ✉ Flat 2, 28 Hyde Park Gardens, London W2 2NB (☎ 020 7706 7457, fax 020 7661 9784, e-mail seymourfortescue@bcsb.org.uk); The Old School House, Denchworth, Wantage, Oxfordshire OX12 0DX (☎ 01235 868592)

FORTEY, Prof Richard Alan; s of Frank Allen Fortey (d 1965), and Margaret Zander Winifred, *née* Wilshin; *b* 15 February 1946; *Educ* Ealing GS for Boys, Univ of Cambridge (BA, PhD, Harkness Prize, ScD); *m* 1, 1968, Bridget Elizabeth Thomas; 1 s (Dominic b 21 Jan 1970); m 2, 1977, Jacqueline Francis; 2 da (Rebecca b 5 Oct 1978, Julia 30 Oct 1981), 1 s (Leo b 23 July 1986); *Career* sr scientific offr British Museum (Natural History) 1973–77 (jr research fell 1970–73), Howley visiting prof Memorial Univ of Newfoundland 1977–78, individual merit promotion for research distinction Natural History Museum 1986–2006 (princ scientific offr 1978–86), Collier prof in the public understanding of science and technol Univ of Bristol 2002–03, visiting prof Univ of Oxford 2000–11; Lyell Medal Geological Soc 1996, Frink Medal Zoological Soc 2001, Lewis Thomas Prize Rockefeller Univ 2003, Zoological Medal Linnean Soc 2006, Michael Faraday Award Royal Soc 2006, R C Moore Medal Society of Economic Paleontologists and Mineralogists 2008, Lapworth Medal Palaeontological Assoc 2014, Medal of the Paleontological Soc USA 2016; Hon DSc: St Andrew's Univ 2007, Open Univ 2007, Univ of Birmingham 2010, Univ of Leicester 2014; memb: Br Mycological Soc, Geological Soc of London (pres 2007); FGS 1981, FRS 1997, hon fell BAAS 2008, FRSL 2010; *Books* Fossils, the Key to the Past (1982), The Hidden Landscape (The Natural World Book of the Year Award, 1993), Life: an unauthorised biography (1997), Trilobite! (2000), The Earth: an intimate history (2004), Dry Store Room No 1 (2008), Survivors (2011), The Wood for the Trees (2016); also author (under pseudonym) Roderick Masters' Book of Money-Making Schemes (1981); *Recreations* fungi of all sorts, humorous writing, East Anglia (especially Suffolk), beer and wine; *Clubs* Lucretians; *Style—* Prof Richard Fortey, FRS; ✉ The Natural History Museum, Cromwell Road, South Kensington, London SW7 5BD (☎ 020 7942 5493, fax 020 7942 5546, e-mail raf@nhm.ac.uk)

FORTH, Dr Michael William; s of William Henry Forth (d 1990), and Gwendoline Forth (d 1994); *b* 17 August 1938; *Educ* KCL and KCH Med Sch (MB BS, LRCP, AKC, DPM); *m* 21 Feb 1970, Dr Margaret Foster, da of Lt Col R T Robertson, of Cape Town; 1 s (Robert William b 17 Feb 1974); *Career* conslt psychiatrist and sr lectr Royal Liverpool Hosp 1977–97; Mental Health Act cmmr 1984–86, regnl advsr in psychiatry Mersey Region 1987–91, med dir N Mersey Community Tst 1991–95, med dir W Cheshire Tst 1995–96; RCPsych: chm NW Div 1990–94, memb Cncl 1994–97, memb Ct of Electors 1994–2001 memb Mental Health Review Tbnl 1983–; memb Bd Cheadle Royal Charitable Tst 2000–03; FRCPsych 1986 (MRCPsych), MRCS; *Recreations* golf, music, crosswords; *Clubs* Royal Over-Seas League; *Style—* Dr Michael Forth; ✉ 139 Hough Green, Chester CH4 8JR (☎ 01244 671845, e-mail michaelforth@hotmail.com)

FORTNUM, Prof Rebecca; da of John Fortnum, and Eve, *née* Lomas, of London; *b* 19 September 1963; *Educ* Camden Sch for Girls London, Camberwell Sch of Arts and Crafts London, Corpus Christi Coll Oxford (BA), Univ of Newcastle upon Tyne (MA); *m* Richard Elliott; 1 s (Marlow b 19 Sept 1999), 1 da (Stella b 2 Jan 2002); *Career* artist; fell Skowhegan Sch of Painting and Sculpture ME 1991, visiting fell in painting Winchester Sch of Art 1992–93, sr lectr Painting Dept Norwich Sch of Art 1993–99, sr lectr in art Wimbledon Sch of Art 1999–2004, research fell in art Lancaster Univ 2004–, visiting artist Sch of the Art Inst Chicago 2006, reader in fine art Univ of the Arts London 2008– (sr lectr 2006–08), prof of fine art Middx Univ 2013; visiting lectr at numerous art colls and univs; author of numerous articles in art jls and nat press; *Solo Exhibitions* incl: Contra Diction (Winchester Gall) 1993, Smith-Jariwala Gall London 1994, Third Person (Kapil Jariwala Gall London) 1996, Solipsist (Angel Row Gall Nottingham) 2000, The Drawing Gallery London 2005, Absurd Impositions (V&A Museum of Childhood) 2011, Self Contained (Museum of London) 2013; *Awards incl* Pollock-Krasner Fndn NYC 1991, British Cncl travel award to Botswana 1993, Abbey scholarship Br Sch in Rome 1997, AHRB 2004, Arts Cncl of England 2005 and 2012, AHRC 2005; *Publications* Contemporary British Women Artists: In their own words (2007), Writing – In and Outside – Drawing (2012), Self Contained (2013), On Not Knowing: How Artists Think (2013); *Style—* Prof Rebecca Fortnum; ✉ e-mail rebecca@elliottfortnum.co.uk

FORWOOD, Sir Nicholas James; kt (2016), QC (1987); s of late Lt-Col Harry Forwood, RA, and Wendy, *née* French-Smith; *b* 22 June 1948; *Educ* Stowe, St John's Coll Cambridge (MA); *m* 4 Dec 1971, Sally Diane, da of His Hon Judge Basil Gerrard (decd), of Knutsford, Cheshire; 3 da (Victoria b 1974, Genevra b 1976, Suzanna b 1979), 1 s (Thomas b 1990); *Career* called to the Bar Middle Temple 1970, called to the Irish Bar 1981; judge Gen Court of the EU 1999–2015; pres 7th Chamber 2007–10, pres 2nd Chamber 2010–13; *Recreations* golf, opera, skiing, sailing, shooting, walking across Europe; *Clubs* Oxford and Cambridge; *Style—* Sir Nicholas Forwood, QC; ✉ Brick Court Chambers, 7–8 Essex Street, London WC2R 3LD

FOSKETT, Hon Mr Justice; Sir David Robert; kt (2007); s of late Robert Frederick Foskett, of Worcs, and late Ruth, *née* Waddington; *b* 19 March 1949; *Educ* Warwick Sch, KCL (LLB, pres Union); *m* 11 Jan 1975, Angela Bridget, da of late Maj Gordon Jacobs, MBE; 2 da; *Career* called to the Bar Gray's Inn 1972 (bencher 1999), QC 1991, recorder 1995–2007, dep judge of the High Court 1998–2007, judge of the High Court of Justice (Queen's Bench Div) 2007–; memb Civil Procedure Rule Ctee 1997–2001, chm Law Reform Ctee Bar Cncl 2005–07, memb Civil Justice Cncl 2012–15; pres: KCL Assoc 1997–2000, Old Warwickian Assoc 2000 and 2014; memb Cncl KCL 2010–; FCIArb, FKC; *Books* Foskett on Compromise (1980, 8 edn 2015); *Recreations* music, theatre, poetry, cricket, golf; *Clubs* Athenaeum, MCC, Woking Golf, G10; *Style—* The Hon Mr Justice Foskett; ✉ Royal Courts of Justice, Strand, London WC2A 2LL

FOSSEY, Ann; da of Reginald Fossey, and Mary Fossey; *b* 20 August 1948; *m* 3 April 1971, Hellmuth Berendt, s of Earnst Berendt; 2 s (Max b 2 July 1978, Thomas b 14 Dec 1981); *Career* dir Paul Winner Mktg Communications 1971–83, head PR Div Brompton (subsid of Lowe Howard Spink) 1983–85; Good Relations: joined as head of Consumer Div 1988, md 1999–2007, chm 2007–; memb Mktg Soc, FIPR; *Style—* Ms Ann Fossey; ✉ Good Relations, Holborn Gate, 26 Southampton Buildings, London WC2A 3PQ (☎ 020 7861 3142, fax 020 7861 3131)

FOSTER, Alison Lee Caroline (Lady Havelock-Allan); QC (2002); da of Leslie Francis Foster (d 1985), of Sussex, and Marie Ann, *née* McIntosh-Hudson; *b* 22 January 1957, Sussex; *Educ* Bexhill GS for Girls, Jesus Coll Oxford (exhibitioner, BA), Courtauld Inst of Art (MPhil), City Univ London (Dip), Inns of Ct Sch of Law; *m* 22 May 1986, Sir Mark Havelock-Allan, Bt (His Hon Judge Havelock-Allan); 2 da (Miranda Anthonia Louise b 29 July 1993, Hannah Marie Josephine b 18 Oct 1997), 1 s (Henry Caspar Francis b 6 Oct 1994); *Career* called to the Bar Inner Temple 1984 (bencher 2002); pupil then tenant 39 Essex Street Chambers 1985–, dep High Court judge (Chancery Div) 2008; legal advsr Ethical Ctee Br Psychoanalytical Soc; *Recreations* painting, gardening; *Clubs* Groucho, RAC; *Style—* Miss Alison Foster, QC; ✉ 39 Essex Street, London WC2R 3AT (☎ 020 7832 1111)

FOSTER, Andrew Kevin; CBE (2005); s of Kevin William Foster, of Cheshire, and Doreen Foster (d 1981); *b* 3 March 1955; *Educ* Millfield, Keble Coll Oxford (BA); *m* 1981, Sara Gillian, da of Donald Daniels; 2 da (Anna Kate b 1982, Grace Elizabeth b 1989), 1 s (Thomas Don b 1984); *Career* mktg mangr Rowntree Mackintosh 1976–81, dir Worldcrest Ltd 1981–; non-exec dir Wrighton NHS Tst 1991–92, chm West Lancs NHS Tst 1992–96, chm Wigan & Leigh NHS Tst 1996–2001, policy dir HR NHS Confederation 1998–2001, dir of HR Dept of Health 2001–06, dir of HR Blackpool, Fylde and Wyre Hosps NHS Tst 2006–07, chief exec Wrightington and Wigan and Leigh NHS Fndn Tst 2007–, interim chief exec Heart of England NHS Fndn Tst 2015; *Recreations* golf; *Clubs* Ormskirk Golf; *Style—* Andrew Foster, Esq, CBE; ✉ Wrightington, Wigan & Leigh NHS Foundation Trust, Royal Albert Edward Infirmary, Wigan Lane, Wigan, WN1 2NN (☎ 01214 240278, e-mail andrew.foster@wwl.nhs.uk)

FOSTER, Sir Andrew William; kt (2001); s of George William Foster, and Gladys Maria Foster; *b* 29 December 1944; *Educ* Abingdon Sch, Newcastle Poly (BSc), LSE (Post Grad Dip Social Studies); *m* 1, 1967 (m dis 2000), Christine Marquiss; 1 s, 1 d; m 2, 2001, Jadranka Porter; *Career* social worker 1966–71, area social servs offr 1971–75, asst dir of social servs Haringey 1975–79; dir of social servs: Greenwich 1979–82, N Yorks 1982–87; regnl gen mangr Yorks RHA 1987–91, dep chief exec NHS Mgmnt Exec 1991–92, controller Audit Commission 1992–2003, dep chm RBC 2003–, chair Further Educn Review Gp for Sec of State for Educn 2005, chm 2020 Public Servs Cmmn 2008–; non-exec dir: National Express Gp plc 2004–, Nestor Healthcare Gp 2004–, Liberata 2004–06, Prudential Health Ltd 2004–; non-exec dir Sport England 2003–09; chm: Athletics Review Gp 2004, Cwlth Games England 2007–, Capital Prog in FE Review 2009, Intercity Express Prog Review 2010; *Recreations* golf, walking, travel, theatre, food, wine; *Style—* Sir Andrew Foster; ✉ 269 Lauderdale Mansions, Lauderdale Road, London W9 1LZ

FOSTER, Rt Hon Arlene Isobel; PC (2016), MLA; da of John William Kelly, and Julia Georgina, *née* Sills; *b* 17 July 1970, Enniskillen, Co Fermanagh; *Educ* Collegiate GS for Girls Enniskillen, Queen's Univ Belfast (LLB), Inst of Professional Legal Studies Queen's Univ Belfast (Cert); *m* 24 Aug 1995, William Brian Johnston Foster; 1 da (Sarah Georgia b 25 April 2000), 2 s (George Nathaniel b 15 May 2002, William Benjamin Thomas b 18 Sept 2006); *Career* admitted slr NI 1996; slr in private practice 1996–2003 (pt/t slr 2003–07); MLA (DUP) Fermanagh & South Tyrone 2003–, min of environment 2007–08, min of enterprise, trade and investment 2008–15, min of finance 2015–16; acting first min of NI 2010, first min of NI 2016–; cnclr Fermanagh Dist Cncl 2005–07 and 2008–; Devolved Parliamentarian of the Year Women in Public Life Award 2008; *Recreations* reading, walking; *Style—* The Rt Hon Arlene Foster, MLA; ✉ 27 East Bridge Street, Enniskillen, Belfast BT74 7BW (☎ 028 66 320722, e-mail arlene.foster@niassembly.gov.uk and first.minister@executiveoffice-ni.gov.uk)

FOSTER, Brendan; CBE (2008, MBE 1976); s of Francis Foster, and Margaret Foster; *b* 12 January 1948; *Educ* St Joseph's GS Co Durham, Univ of Sussex (BSc), Carnegie Coll Leeds (DipEd); *m* 1972, Susan Margaret, da of Kenneth Frank Alston, of Clacton, Essex; 1 s (Paul b 1977), 1 da (Catherine b 1979); *Career* sch teacher St Joseph's GS Hebburn 1970–74, recreation mangr Gateshead Metropolitan Borough Cncl 1974–81, chm Nike (UK) Ltd 1981–87 (md Nike Europe), md Nova International Ltd 1987–; former athlete; Cwlth Games medals incl: Bronze 1500m 1970, Silver 5000m 1974, Bronze 5000m 1978, Gold 10,000m 1978; Euro Championships medals incl: Bronze 1500m 1971, Gold 5000m 1974; Olympic Games Bronze medal 10,000m 1976; world record holder: 2 miles 1973, 3000m 1974; UK record holder: 10,000m 1978, 1500m, 3000m, 2 miles, 5000m; BBC commentator on athletics 1980–; chm Great North Run 1981–; Hon MEd Univ of Newcastle, Hon DLitt Univ of Sussex, fell Sunderland Poly; *Style*— Brendan Foster, Esq, CBE; ✉ Nova International, Newcastle House, Albany Court, Monarch Road, Newcastle upon Tyne NE4 7YB

FOSTER, Prof Brian; OBE (2003); *b* 4 January 1954, Crook, Co Durham; *Educ* Wolsingham Secdy Sch, Queen Elizabeth Coll London (Dillon Prize, Andrewes Prize, BSc), Univ of Oxford (MA, DPhil); *m* 1983, Sabine Margot; 2 s (Paul Kai b 1989, Mark Kristian John b 1992); *Career* research assoc: Rutherford Appleton Lab 1978–82, Imperial Coll of Science and Technol 1982–84; Univ of Bristol: lectr Dept of Physics 1984–92, PPARC advanced fell 1991–97, reader Dept of Physics 1992–96, head Particle Physics Gp 1992–2003, prof of experimental physics 1996–2003, emeritus prof 2003; prof of experimental physics Univ of Oxford 2003– (head Subdepartment of Particle Physics 2004–11), professorial fell Balliol Coll Oxford 2003–, Alexander von Humboldt prof Univ of Hamburg and DESY 2011–; numerous positions with ZEUS experiment DESY Hamburg 1985– (incl spokesman 1999–2003), actg dir Adams Inst for Accelerator Science Univ of Oxford/Royal Holloway Univ of London 2004–05; involved with numerous cncls, ctees and panels incl: memb Particle Physics Ctee SERC 1986–90, chm Nuclear and Particle Physics Division Inst of Physics 1989–93, memb Scientific Cncl Deutsches Elektronen Synchrotron Hamburg 1999–2010, memb PPARC 2001–07 (chm Particle Physics Ctee 1996–99, co-chm Science Ctee 1996–99 (memb 2001–07)), chm European Ctee for Future Accelerators 2002–05 (and ex-officio memb Cncl CERN), European dir of global design effort for Int Linear Collider 2005–13, European dir Linear Collider Collaboration 2013–, memb Main Panel B and chm Physics Subpanel Research Excellence Framework 2011–15; advsr to govt oppn spokesmen on science and technol 1993–97; Special European Physical Soc Prize in Particle Physics (awarded jtly for discovery of the gluon) 1995, Research Prize Alexander von Humboldt Fndn 1999, Max Born Medal and Prize Deutsche Physikalische Gesellschaft/Inst of Physics 2003, Alexander von Humboldt Fndn Research Professorship 2010; MRI 1979, FInstP 1992 (memb Cncl 2009–13), memb BAAS 1993 (recorder Physics Section 1994–97), FRS 2008 (memb Cncl 2015–18); *Publications* Topics in High Energy Particle Physics (ed, 1988), 40 Years of Particle Physics (jt ed, 1988), Electron-Positron annihilation Physics (ed, 1990); author of numerous articles in learned jls; *Recreations* football (supporter of Sunderland FC), golf, cricket, skiing, walking, history, politics, biography, music, playing the violin, collecting first editions of books (particularly modern novels); *Style*— Prof Brian Foster, OBE, FRS; ✉ Denys Wilkinson Building, University of Oxford, Keble Road Oxford OX1 3RH (☎ 01865 273323, fax 01865 273417, e-mail b.foster@physics.ox.ac.uk); FLA, DESY, Notkestrasse 85, 22607 Hamburg, Germany

FOSTER, Christopher Kenneth; s of Kenneth John Foster (d 1982), of Sunningdale, Berks, and Christina Dorothy, *née* Clark; *b* 5 November 1949; *Educ* Harrow HS; *Career* chm and dir Springwood Books Ltd 1975–; dir: Chase Corporation plc 1985–87, Trafalgar House plc 1988–90, Wiggins Gp plc 1993–2005, Active Energy plc 2007–12, Alpha Prospects plc 2008–, Clean Tech Assets plc (formerly TXO plc) 2012–; Lord of the Manor of Little Hale; *Recreations* golf, music, art; *Clubs* Sunningdale Golf, Lansdowne, Annabel's; *Style*— Christopher Foster, Esq; ✉ Springwood House, The Avenue, Ascot, Berkshire SL5 7LR (☎ 01344 628753); 31 Queens Gate, Kensington, London SW7 5JA (☎ 07525 688741, e-mail christopher.foster9@btinternet.com)

FOSTER, Christopher Norman; s of Maj-Gen Norman Leslie Foster, CB, DSO (d 1995), and Joan, *née* Drury (d 1991); *b* 30 December 1946, Dublin; *Educ* Westminster; *m* 1981, Anthea Jane, *née* Sammons; 2 s (Nicholas b 9 July 1983, Piers b 18 April 1986); *Career* Cooper Bros & Co 1965–73, mangr Racing Dept then dir Weatherbys 1973–90; Jockey Club: sec 1983–90, Keeper of the Match Book 1983–, exec dir 1993–2006, conslt 2006–; vice-chm Int Fedn of Horseracing Authorities 2000–2007, tstee Retraining of Racehorses 2006–, dir Wincanton Racecourse 2006–, dir Nat Stud 2008–; govr Westminster Sch 1990–; FCA 1979 (ACA 1969); *Recreations* racing, shooting, golf, fishing, gardening; *Clubs* MCC, St Enodoc; *Style*— Christopher Foster, Esq; ✉ The Old Vicarage, Great Durnford, Salisbury, Wiltshire SP4 6AZ (☎ 01722 782773); The Jockey Club, 75 High Holborn, London WC1V 6LS (☎ 020 7611 1800, fax 020 7611 1899, e-mail christopher.foster@thejockeyclub.co.uk)

FOSTER, Rt Rev Christopher Richard James; *see:* Portsmouth, Bishop of

FOSTER, Giles Henry; s of Stanley William Foster (d 1986), and Gladys Maude, *née* Moon (d 2005); *b* 30 June 1948; *Educ* Monkton Combe Sch, Univ of York (BA), RCA (MA); *m* 28 Sept 1974, Nicole Anne, da of Alan Coates, of London; 2 s (George b 1982, William b 1987); *Career* film and TV dir; *Television* incl: Unknown Heart, The Other Wife, Shades of Love, The Four Seasons, Starting Over, Summer Solstice, Foyle's War (BAFTA nomination), Bertie and Elizabeth, The Prince and the Pauper, Relative Strangers, Coming Home, Oliver's Travels, The Rector's Wife, Adam Bede, The Lilac Bus, Monster Maker, Northanger Abbey, Hotel du Lac (BAFTA Award and ACE Award), Silas Marner (co-adaptor, BAFTA nomination), Dutch Girls, The Aerodrome, Last Summer's Child, The Obelisk, five scripts by Alan Bennett (incl Talking Heads: A Lady of Letters, BAFTA nomination); *Films* incl: Devices and Desires (Grierson Award), Consuming Passions, Tree of Hands; *Clubs* Groucho; *Style*— Giles Foster, Esq; ✉ e-mail ghf@clara.co.uk; c/o Laura Rourke, Independent Talent Group (☎ 020 7636 6565, e-mail laurarourke@independenttalent.com)

FOSTER, Jacqueline; MEP; da of Samuel Renshaw (d 1985), and Isabella, *née* Brennan (d 2001); *b* 30 December 1947, Liverpool; *Educ* Prescot Girls' GS; *m* (m dis 1981) Peter Laurance Foster; *Career* Cabin Services BEA/BA 1969–81 and 1985–99, area mangr Austria Horizon 1981–85; fndr memb and offr Cabin Crew '89 (Trade Union for UK Airline Crew) 1989–99; MEP (Cons) NW England 1999–2004 and 2009–, Cons tport spokesman 2001–04 and 2009–; chm Backbench Ctee of MEPs 1999–2004, dep ldr Cons MEPs 2013–; aerospace conslt 2004; head European Affrs Aerospace, Space & Defence Assoc of Europe 2005–09; *Recreations* winter sports, golf; *Clubs* Carlton, European Aviation, Royal Aeronautical Soc (Brussels Branch); *Style*— Mrs Jacqueline Foster, MEP

FOSTER, Dr James Michael Gerard; s of Dr Robert Marius Foster (d 2013), and Margaret Rhona, *née* Holland; *b* 19 December 1949, Cambridge; *Educ* King's Sch Canterbury, St Bart's Hosp Med Coll, Univ of London (Crawford exhibition, MB BS, MRCS LRCP), Univ of Wales Coll of Med (MSc); *m* 22 Nov 1986, Felicity Patricia, da of late Dr Charles Mathurin Vaillant; 2 s (Charles James Vaillant b 2 March 1989, Simon James Holland b 16 Nov 1991); *Career* extern in pediatrics Tucson Medical Centre Arizona 1973, house physician Luton and Dunstable Hosp Luton 1975, house surgn Royal Berks Hosp Reading 1975; SHO St Bart's Hosp London: in neurosurgery and cardiothoracic surgery 1976–77, in anaesthesia 1977–79; registrar in anaesthesia St George's Hosp London 1979–81; sr registrar: in anaesthesia Guy's Hosp London 1981–84, in pain med Sir Charles Gairdner Hosp Perth Western Australia 1984 (King's Fund travelling fellowship bursary); conslt: in anaesthesia and pain med St Bart's Hosp London 1985–2000, in pain med Frimley Park Hosp Surrey 2001–12, in pain med King Edward VII's Hosp London 2001–12; hon sr lectr St Bart's Hosp Med Coll; memb: London Pain Forum (sr fell); FRCA, DA, FFPMRCA; *Sporting Achievements* incl: Kenya Coast Open jr tennis champion 1968, ascent of Mt Kilimanjaro Tanzania 1969, represented Dubai UAE at rugby union 1974, West Australian Marathon 1984, capt Halford Hewitt Golf Team 2000–01; *Books* Terminal Care Support Teams (contrib, 1990), Coloproctology and the Pelvic Floor (contrib, 1992), Hospital-Based Palliative Care Teams (contrib, 1998); *Recreations* family, golf, photography, travel; *Clubs* RSM, Fountain, The Berkshire Golf (capt 2013), Royal Cinque Ports Golf, RPS; *Style*— Dr James Foster; ✉ Heathend Lodge, Windsor Road, Ascot, Berkshire SL5 7LQ (☎ 01344 621549); Private Consulting Rooms, The Princess Grace Hospital, 47 Nottingham Place, London W1U 5LZ (☎ 020 7486 1234, fax 020 7034 5042); The Princess Margaret Hospital, Osborne Road, Windsor, Berkshire SL4 3SJ (☎ 01753 743434, fax 01753 471474)

FOSTER, His Hon Judge Jonathan Rowe; QC (1989); s of Donald Foster (d 1980), and Hilda Eaton, *née* Rowe (d 2001); *b* 20 July 1947; *Educ* Oundle, Keble Coll Oxford (exhibitioner); *m* 1978, Sarah; 4 s; *Career* called to the Bar Gray's Inn 1970 (bencher 1998); recorder of the Crown Court 1988–2004, treas Northern Circuit 1992–97, dep judge of the High Court (Family Div 1994–2012, Queen's Bench Div 1998–2015), head 18 St John Street Chambers 1998–2004, circuit judge (Northern Circuit) 2004–15; memb: Criminal Injuries Compensation Bd 1995–2000, CICAP 1996–2004; govr Ryley's Sch 1990–2006, tstee Acorn Recovery Projects 2012–; *Recreations* outdoor activities, golf, bridge; *Clubs* St James Manchester, Hale Golf, Bowdon Lawn Tennis; *Style*— His Hon Judge Foster, QC; ✉ Manchester Crown Court, Minshull Street, Manchester M1 3FS (☎ 0161 954 7500)

FOSTER, Michael Robert; s of Robert O Foster (d 1996), and Nannette, *née* Howat; *b* 6 July 1941; *Educ* Felsted, Woodberry Forest Sch Virginia USA (ESU exchange scholar), AA Sch of Arch (AADipl), Univ of Essex (MA); *m* 17 Sept 1971, Susan Rose, *née* Bolson; 3 s (Jamie b 15 Sept 1973, Tom b 15 April 1976, Marcus b 11 July 1978); *Career* architect; asst Stillman & Eastwick-Field London and Skidmore Owings & Merrill Chicago 1965–66, asst and job architect YRM Architects and Planners 1966–69, full-time teacher Dept of Arch Poly of Central London 1970–71 (pt/t 1968–70), ptnr The Tooley & Foster Partnership (architects, engrs and designers) 1971–; pt/t teacher: Environmental Design Dept Wimbledon Sch of Art and in history and contextual studies Dept of Arch Poly of Central London 1971–73, Sch of Environmental Design RCA 1973–76, Schs of Arch and 3 Dimensional Design Kingston Poly 1975–79; pt/t lectr in history of design Middx Poly fndn course 1977–79; external examiner: interior design course Sch of 3 Dimensional Design Kingston Poly 1982–84, degree course in architecture South Bank Univ 1989–93, degree and dip course in architecture Univ of Portsmouth 1999–2002, Manchester Met Sch of Architecture 2003–06; Architectural Assoc: unit master Sch of Arch 1979–83, memb Cncl 1986–93, pres 1989–91; ARCUK: memb Educn Grants Panel Bd of Educn 1975–82, memb Cncl 1992–93; sec Standing Conf of Heads of Schs of Arch 1995–2003; project ldr NVQ/SVQ in Architectural Studies level 5 1998–; RIBA architect accredited in building conservation 2004–; tstee Geffrye Museum 1990–97 (chm Friends of Geffrye Museum 1981–90); RIBA 1968, MCSD 1981, memb L'Ordre des Architectes (France) 1991; *Books* The Principles of Architecture: Style, Structure and Design (1983); occasional contrib: AA Quarterly, Architect's Jl, Town and Country Planning, The Architect, Building Design; *Recreations* sailing, painting and drawing; *Style*— Michael Foster; ✉ The Tooley & Foster Partnership, Warwick House, Palmerston Road, Buckhurst Hill, Essex IG9 5LQ (☎ 020 8504 9711, fax 020 8506 1779, e-mail mfoster@tooleyfoster.com)

FOSTER, Neil William Derick; s of William Robert Brudenell Foster (d 1992), and Jean Leslie, *née* Urquhart (d 1986); bro of Richard Francis Foster, *qv*; *b* 13 March 1943; *Educ* Harrow, Aix en Provence Univ; *m* 2 Sept 1989, Anthea Caroline, da of Ian Gibson Macpherson, MC (d 2011); 1 da (b 21 Nov 1992); *Career* underwriting memb Lloyd's 1971–, dir John Foster & Sons plc 1975–93, dir and past chm Norfolk Churches Tst 1976–2007, dir Norfolk Marketing Ltd 1985–95; gen cmmr of income tax 1992–2002 (vice-chm Dereham Div 1996); past chm: East Anglia Div Royal Forestry Soc, The Game Conservancy Norfolk, East Anglia region Timber Growers Assoc, CLA Norfolk; chm: Upper Nar Internal Drainage Bd 1993–2004, HHA East Anglia, Lexham Parish Meeting 1992–; church warden St Andrew's E Lexham, govr Beeston Primary Sch 2001–04, memb Norfolk Rivers Bd 2005–; High Sheriff Norfolk 1999–; Liveryman Worshipful Co of Clothworkers 1965 (4th Warden 1995, 2nd Warden 1996, Master 2009); *Recreations* shooting, forestry, gardening; *Clubs* Boodle's, Norfolk; *Style*— Neil Foster, Esq; ✉ Lexham Hall, King's Lynn, Norfolk PE32 2QJ (☎ 01328 701 341); The Estate Office, Lexham Hall, King's Lynn, Norfolk PE32 2QJ (☎ 01328 701 288, fax 01328 700 053)

FOSTER, Nigel Pearson; s of Gordon Pearson Foster (d 1985), of Wilmslow, Cheshire, and Margaret Elizabeth, *née* Bettison (d 1989); *b* 18 February 1952; *Educ* Oswestry Sch; *m* 20 May 1988, Mary Elizabeth, da of Edward Bangs; 1 da (Elizabeth Margaret b 9 June 1990), 1 s (Charlie Edward b 13 Oct 1994); *Career* Rowlinson-Broughton 1969–72, Clough Howard Richards Manchester 1972–74, prodn asst Royds Manchester 1974–76, account exec The Advertising and Marketing Organisation 1976–79, TV prodr Wasey Campbell Ewald 1980–82 (account exec 1979–80), TV prodr Foote Cone Belding 1982–84; head of TV KMP 1984–86; J Walter Thompson: TV prodr 1986–89, head of TV UK 1989–96, exec dir of TV prodn Europe (and subsequently EMEA) 1996–2007; ptnr Shaw Independent Producers 2008–; FIPA; *Style*— Nigel Foster, Esq

FOSTER, Richard Anthony (Tony); s of Donald Foster (d 2000), of Bishop's Stortford, Herts, and Jean Foster; *b* 2 April 1946; *Educ* King Edward VI GS Chelmsford, St Peter's Coll Birmingham, Cardiff Coll of Art; *m* 1968, Ann Margaret, da of Donald Partington (d 1987), and Joan Partington (d 1985); *Career* artist; art teacher Leicester, Cayman Is and Cornwall 1968–75, visual arts co-ord S Hill Park Arts Centre Bracknell 1976–78, visual arts offr South West Arts 1978–84, professional artist 1984–; co-fndr with Jonathan Harvey and James Lingwood of TSWA; winner Yosemite Renaissance Prize 1988, RGS Cherry Kearton Meml Medal 2002; FRGS 1993; *Solo Exhibitions* incl: Royal Watercolour Soc London 1985, Yale Center for British Art New Haven Conn 1985, Francesca Anderson Gallery Boston Mass 1985 and 1988, City of Edinburgh Art Centre 1987, Ecology Centre London 1987, Calif Acad of Sciences San Francisco 1987, Smithsonian Inst Washington DC 1989, Newlyn Orion Penzance 1990, Montgomery Gallery San Francisco 1990, 1993 and 1995, Royal Albert Museum Exeter 1993 and 1998, Harewood House Yorks 1993 and 1998, Royal Botanic Gardens Kew 1995, Sun Valley Center for the Arts & Humanities, Meyerson & Nowinski Seattle 1997 and 1999, RGS London 1998, Montgomery Gallery San Francisco 1999, 2001 and 2003, Eyre Moore Gallery Seatle 1999, World Views (retrospective), Frye Art Museum Seattle 2000 and 2003, Graham Gallery New York 2000 and 2003, Nat Museum of Natural History Wyoming 2004, John Mitchell & Sons 2005, Royal Cornwall Museum 2008, Royal Watercolour Soc 2008, Gerald Peters Gallery 2008, Phoenix Art Museum 2009; *Collections* Denver Art Museum, Phoenix Art Museum, Sierra Nevada Museam of Art, Autry Center for Western Art LA, Stanford Univ Calif, Mesa Verde Nat Park; *Art Projects* incl: Travels Without a Donkey in the Cevennes (with James Ravilious) 1982, Thoreau's Country (walks and canoe journeys in New England) 1985, John Muir's High Sierra 1986–87, Exploring the Grand Canyon 1988–89, Rainforest Diaries (Costa Rica) 1991–93, Arid Lands (walks across deserts) 1993–95, Ice and Fire (series of paintings about volcanoes) 1996–98, WaterMarks (paintings of river journeys) 1998–2003, After Lewis and Clark – Explorer Artists and the American West (Sun Valley Center for the Arts, 2000) and Boise Art Museum (2001); Paint the Fire (BBC Radio 4 documentary) 1999, Escuela y Clinica Tony Foster (constructed and opened in El Chorro Honduras, 2001); Searching for a Bigger Subject 2005–07 (first artist to have painted all three faces of Everest and highest large-scale watercolour painted on site (3ft x 6ft at 17,400 ft), Sacred Places (Gerald Peter Gallery Santa Fe and NY) 2011–12, Museum of Northern Arizona 2013 (entire exhibition purchased for donation to Foster Art and Wilderness Fndn inc 2014 with a dedicated exhbn space in Palo Alto CA, opening 2015), major painting included in 'Leonardo da Vinci's Codex Leicester and the Power of Observation' Phoenix Art Museum Arizona 2015; TV documentaries: The Man Who Painted Everest (Sky Artsworld) 2006 and (PBS) 2009, Artistes d'en Haut (Painting Mont Blanc, 60 min documentary for French TV); *Publications* Painting at the Edge of the World: The Watercolours of Tony Foster (2008); *Recreations* snooker, walking, travel, scuba diving; *Style*— Tony Foster; ✉ 1 Well Street, Tywardreath Par, Cornwall PL24 2QH (☎ 01726 815300, website www.tony-foster.co.uk)

FOSTER, Richard Francis; s of William Robert Brudenell Foster (d 1992), of Lexham Hall, King's Lynn, and Jean Leslie, *née* Urquhart (d 1986); bro of Neil Foster, *qv*; *b* 6 June 1945; *Educ* Harrow, Trinity Coll Oxford, Studio Simi Florence, City & Guilds of London Art Sch; *m* 1970 (m dis 1984), Hon Sarah Rachel Jane Kay-Shuttleworth (now Hon Mrs Figgins), da of 4 Baron Shuttleworth (d 1975); 2 da (Henrietta Victoria (Mrs Benjamin Stanton) b 10 Aug 1973, Georgiana Pamela b 2 May 1975), 1 s (Edward William Thomas b 7 March 1978); *Career* landscape and portrait painter; numerous public and private portrait cmmns; artist accompanying HRH Prince of Wales's official visit to S America 2009; Lord Mayor's Award for London Landscapes 1972, Burke's Peerage Fndn Award for Portraiture 2016; Brother Art Workers' Guild; RP (vice-pres 1991–94, hon treas 2003–06); *Exhibitions* solo exhbns incl: Jocelyn Feilding Fine Art 1974, Spink & Son Venice 1978, Spink & Son India 1982, 1991 and 1997, Spink & Son Egypt 1984, Rafael Valls Ltd 1999, Partridge Fine Art 2003, Indar Pasricha Fine Art 2005, The Gallery Cork St 2008 and 2013; gp exhbns incl: Royal Soc of Portrait Painters (annually) 1969–, Royal Acad (most years) 1972–; *Recreations* travel, country sports, family life; *Clubs* Chelsea Arts, Pratt's; *Style*— Richard Foster, Esq; ✉ 5A Clareville Grove, London SW7 5AU (☎ 020 7244 7164, e-mail info@richardfoster.co.uk, website www.richardfoster.co.uk)

FOSTER, His Hon Judge Richard John Samuel; s of Samuel Geoffrey Foster (d 1968), and Beryl Constance, *née* Seabourne (d 2015); *b* 28 May 1954, Worcester; *Educ* Bromsgrove Sch Worcs, Coll of Law Guildford; *m* 1, 10 Oct 1980, Ann, *née* Scott (d 2002); 1 da (Charlotte Emma Scott b 15 Nov 1984); m 2, 5 April 2004, Susan Claire, *née* Brodie; 1 step-da (Claire Georgina Emily Sansome b 13 Nov 1983), 1 step-s (James David Thomas Sansome b 11 May 1985); *Career* slr Dawson and Co 1979–81, slr Barlow Lyde and Gilbert 1981–86; Vizards: ptnr 1986–98, jt sr ptnr 1998–99; sr ptnr Vizard Oldham 1999–2002, ptnr Weightman Vizards 2002–04; recorder 1998–2004, dep High Court judge 2003–, circuit judge 2004–, resident judge Luton Crown Court 2012–; memb Consistory Court Dio of St Albans 2000–04, memb Appeal Court United Grand Lodge 2011–; memb Bd Bedfordshire Probation Serv 2006–10; Hon recorder of Luton 2013–; chm of tstees Royal Br Legion Pension Fund 2003–04, tstee Bromsgrove Sch Fndn 2011–; *Publications* Local Authority Liability (jt ed, 6 edn 2016); *Recreations* running smallholding, bridge, golf; *Clubs* Reform, Andratx Golf (Mallorca); *Style*— His Hon Judge Richard Foster; ✉ Luton Crown Court, 7 George Street, Luton, Bedfordshire LU1 2AA (☎ 01582 522000, fax 01582 522001, e-mail hhjudge.foster@judiciary.gsi.gov.uk)

FOSTER, Robert; s of David Foster, of Ascot, and Amelia, *née* Morris; *b* 12 May 1943; *Educ* Oundle, CCC Cambridge (MA); *m* 1967, Judy, *née* Welsh; 1 s (Alan b 30 March 1976), 1 da (Joanna b 2 April 1978); *Career* electrical engr: Parkinson Cowan Ltd 1964–66, Automation Ltd 1966–71, Post Office Telecommunications 1972–77; DTI: princ 1977–84, asst sec 1984–91, dir Aerospace and Def Industries Directorate 1992–97, dir Innovation Policy and Standards 1998–2000; chief exec Competition Cmmn 2000–04; cmmr Nat Lottery Cmmn 2005–12, cmmr Gambling Cmmn 2013–; non-exec dir Jersey Competition Regulatory Authy 2004–12, chair Equinox Care, vice-chair King's Coll Hosp NHS Tst 2004–12; memb Advsy Cncl Oxford Capital Ptnrs; CEng, FIET, FRAeS; *Recreations* music, golf, reading, theatre; *Clubs* RSA; *Style*— Robert Foster, Esq; ✉ 9 Holmdene Avenue, Herne Hill, London SE24 9LB (e-mail fosterrobert@gmail.com); National Lottery Commission, 101 Wigmore Street, London W1U 1QU

FOSTER, Rosalind Mary (Mrs R M Englehart); da of Ludovic Anthony Foster (d 1990), of Greatham Manor, Pulborough, W Sussex, and Pamela Margaret, *née* Wilberforce (d 1997); *b* 7 August 1947; *Educ* Cranborne Chase Sch, Lady Margaret Hall Oxford (BA); *m* 2 Jan 1971, Robert Michael Englehart, QC, *qv*, s of Gustav Axel Englehart (d 1969), of London; 2 da (Alice b 1976, Lucinda (Mrs David Dalhuisen) b 1978), 1 s (Oliver b 1982); *Career* called to the Bar Middle Temple 1969 (bencher 1996), recorder of the Crown Court 1987–98; tribunal judge Mental Health Review Tbnl 2003–; memb Advsy Cncl Winston Churchill Memorial Tst 2012–; FRSA 2002; *Publications* Learning Medicine: How to become and remain a good doctor (co-author, 2007); *Recreations* theatre, travel; *Style*— Miss Rosalind Foster; ✉ 2 Temple Gardens, The Temple, London EC4Y 9AY (☎ 020 7822 1200, e-mail rfoster@2templegardens.co.uk)

FOSTER, Roy William John; s of Francis Edwin Foster (d 1997), and Marjorie Florence Mary, *née* Chapman (d 1944); *b* 25 May 1930, London; *Educ* Rutlish Sch; *m* 6 Sept 1957, Christine Margaret, da of Albert Victor Toler (d 1972); 2 s (Nicholas Charles Roy b 23 April 1960 d 1969, Richard James b 25 March 1964); *Career* Nat Serv RAF 1953–54, cmmnd PO 1953; qualified CA 1955, ptnr Coopers & Lybrand (and predecessor firms) 1960–90; memb Cncl: CBI 1986–96, ICRF (latterly Cancer Research UK) 1998–2003; Freeman City of London; Liveryman: Worshipful Co of Painter Stainers (memb Ct of Assts), Worshipful Co of CAs; CTA (formerly ATII) 1964, FCA 1965; *Recreations* rugby and cricket watching, theatre, travel; *Clubs* RAF, HAC, MCC, City Livery; *Style*— Roy Foster, Esq; ✉ Paddock House, 16 Paul's Place, Farm Lane, Ashtead, Surrey KT21 1HN (☎ and fax 01372 270079)

FOSTER OF BATH, Baron (Life Peer UK 2015), of Bath in the County of Somerset; Rt Hon Donald (Don) Foster; PC (2010); s of late Rev J A Foster, and late I E Foster; *b* 31 March 1947; *Educ* Lancaster Royal GS, Keele Univ (BA, CertEd), Univ of Bath (MEd); *m* 31 Dec 1968, Victoria Jane Dorcas, *née* Pettegree; 1 s, 1 da; *Career* science teacher Sevenoaks Sch 1969–75, science project dir Resources for Learning Devpt Unit Avon Educn Authy 1975–80, lectr in educn Univ of Bristol 1980–89, mgmnt conslt Pannell Kerr Forster 1989–92; cncllr Cabot Ward Avon CC 1981–89 (chm Educn Ctee 1987–89), Parly candidate (Alliance) Bristol E 1987, MP (Lib Dem) Bath 1992–2015; Lib Dem spokesman on: educn and trg 1992–94, educn and employment 1994–99, environment, tport, regions and social justice 1999–2001, tport, local govt and regions 2001–02, tport 2002–03, culture, media and sport 2003–; Parly under sec of state for communities and local govt 2012–, chief whip (Lib Dem) 2013–15, dep chief whip (govt) 2013–15, Controller of the Household 2013–15; memb Parly Office of Sci and Technol 1992–94, memb Educn and Employment Select Ctee 1996–99; vice-chm: Nat Campaign for Nursery Educn 1993–98 (pres 1998–2001), Br Assoc for Central and Eastern Europe 1994–97; hon pres Br Youth Cncl 1993–99; hon fell Bath Coll of HE; CPhys, MInstP; *Publications* Resource Based Learning in Science (1979), Science with Gas (1981), Aspects of Science (1984), Reading About Science (1984), Nuffield Science (1986), Teaching Science 11–13 (jt ed, 1987), Education: Investing in Education (1994), Making the Right Start: Nursery Education and Care (1994), From the Three Rs to the Three Cs: A Personal View of Education (2003); *Recreations* classical music, travel, sport; *Style*— The Rt Hon the Lord Foster of Bath; ✉ e-mail fosterdon@parliament.uk

FOSTER OF BISHOP AUCKLAND, Baron (Life Peer UK 2005); Derek Foster; PC (1993), DL (Co Durham 2001); s of Joseph Foster (d 1959), and Ethel, *née* Ragg (d 1982); *b* 25 June 1937; *Educ* Bede GS Sunderland, St Catherine's Coll Oxford; *m* 1972, (Florence) Anne, da of Thomas Bulmer, of Sunderland; *Career* youth and community worker 1970–73, further educn organiser 1973–74, asst dir of educn Sunderland Cncl 1974–79, chm N of England Devpt Cncl 1974–76, memb Tyne & Wear CC and Sunderland BC; MP (Lab) Bishop Auckland 1979–2005, memb House of Commons Trade & Industry Select Ctee 1980–82, additional oppn spokesman Social Security 1982, oppn whip 1982, PPS to Neil Kinnock 1983–85, oppn chief whip 1985–95, memb Shadow Cabinet 1985–97, shadow chllr of the Duchy of Lancaster 1995–97, chm House of Commons Employment Select Ctee 1997–2001, co-chm House of Commons Educn & Employment Select Ctee 1997–2001; memb: House of Commons Ecclesiatastical Ctee 1997–, House of Commons Liaison Ctee 1997–2001; exec memb Br-American Parly Gp 1997–2005; chm PLP: Employment Ctee 1980–81, Econ and Fin Ctee 1981–82; offr PLP 1985–95, ex-officio memb Lab Pty Nat Exec 1985–95, memb Advsy Ctee for Registration of Political Parties 1998–2005; hon pres Br Youth Cncl 1984–86, past vice-pres Christian Socialist Movement; chm: North Regional Information Soc Initiative 1996–2002, Pioneering Care Partnership 1997–2003, Nat Prayer Breakfast 1997–99, Manufacturing Industry Gp 1998–2005, Bishop Auckland Devpt Co Ltd, NE Pharmaceutical Gp, Bishop Auckland Town Forum 2002, NE e-Learning Fndn 2003, Heritage Lottery Fund NE; vice-chm: Youthaid 1979–85, Youth Affairs Lobby 1984–86; pres SW Durham Training 2003–07; memb Standards and Privileges Ctee 2003–05; non-exec dir Northern Informatics 1998; memb Nat Advsy Bd Salvation Army 1995–98, chm of tstees Bowes Museum; tstee: Auckland Castle, e-Learning Fndn 2001, Beamish Museum; memb Fabian Soc; patron Stockton and Darlington Railways Assoc; companion Inst of Lighting Engrs 2001–; fell Industry & Parly Tst; DCL Univ of Durham 2006; *Recreations* brass bands, male voice choirs, soccer, cricket; *Style*— The Rt Hon Lord Foster of Bishop Auckland, PC, DL; ✉ 3 Linburn, Rickleton, Washington, Tyne & Wear NE38 9EB (☎ 0191 417 1580)

FOSTER OF THAMES BANK, Baron (Life Peer UK 1999), of Reddish in the County of Greater Manchester; Sir Norman Robert Foster; OM (1997), kt (1990); s of Lilian and Robert Foster, of Manchester; *b* 1 June 1935; *Educ* Univ of Manchester Sch of Architecture (DipArch, CertTP), Yale Univ Sch of Architecture (MArch); *Career* Nat Serv RAF 1953–55; architect; fndr Foster Assocs 1967 then Foster + Partners 1996 (chm); winner of over 100 national and international competitions since 1979 for projects incl: Sainsbury Centre Norwich, Renault Centre Swindon, Willis Faber and Dumas Ipswich, The Sackler Galleries at the Royal Acad, Hongkong and Shanghai Bank HQ Hong Kong, Carré d'Art Nîmes, Bilbao Metro System, HQ Commerzbank Frankfurt, Hearst HQ NY, Millennium Bridge London, British Museum Great Court London, New German Parliament Reichstag Berlin, Hong Kong Int Airport Chek Lap Kok, Duisburg Inner Harbour, King's Cross Masterplan, 30 St Mary Axe London, McLaren Technol Centre, Millau Viaduct, West Kowloon Cultural District Hong Kong, Marseille Vieux Port France, Kuwait Airport, Haramain High Speed Rail Saudi Arabia, Sheikh Zayed Nat Museum Abu Dhabi, GLA HQ London, Great Glass House, National Botanical Garden of Wales, Masterplans London, Rotterdam, Stockholm, Gomera, Barcelona, Mallorca, Berlin, Nîmes, Cannes and Greenwich, Stansted Airport London, int airport Beijing, Centers for Science Research Stanford Univ, Supreme Court Singapore, univ campus Petronas Malaysia, Museum of Fine Arts Boston, Winspear (opera house) Dallas, Wembley Stadium, Murezzan St Moritz, Masdar City and Masdar Inst Abu Dhabi, Sperone Westwater NY, Circle Bath Hosp Bath, BMCE Banks Morocco, The Index Dubai, The Troika Kuala Lumpur, Bodegas Port Faustino Winery Spain, YachtPlus 40 Signature Series, Net Jets interior, 425 Park Avenue NY, Chateau Margaux Winery Bordeaux; conslt architect UEA 1978–87; teacher 1967–77: London Poly, Bath Acad of Arts, Univ of Pennsylvania, AA; visiting prof Urban Research Bartlett Sch of Architecture 1998–99; over 680 awards for design excellence incl: 62 RIBA, 24 Civil Tst, 14 BCI, 15 BCO, FT Industrial Architecture Award 1967, 1970, 1971, 1974, 1981, 1984 and 1993, Structural Steel Award 1972, 1978, 1980, 1984, 1986, 1992 and 2000, RS Reynolds Award 1976, 1979 and 1986, International Prize for Architecture 1976 and 1980, Ambrose Congreve Award 1980, Royal Gold Medal for Architecture 1983, Premio Compasso d'Oro Award 1987, PA Innovations Award 1988, Interiors USA Award 1988, 1992, 1993 and 1994, Kunstpreis Berlin Award 1989, RIBA Tstees Medal 1990, Mies van der Rohe Pavilion Award 1991, Gold Medal French Académie de Paris, Arnold W Brunner Meml Prize NY 1992, RFAC & Sunday Times Best Building of the Year Award 1992, ICE Merit Award 1992, ISE Special Award 1992, Concrete Soc Award 1992 and 1993, Benedictus Award 1993, Gold Medal American Inst of Architects 1994, Bund Deutsche Architekten Award 1994, Queen's Award for Export Achievement 1995, CSD Medal for lifetime achievement in design 1997, Prince Philip Designer Prize 1997, Pritzker Architecture Prize 1999, Walpole Medal of Excellence 1999, Le Prix Europeene de l'Architectúre de la Fndn Europeene de la Culture Europa 1999, Special Prize at 4th Int Biennial of Architecture São Paulo Brazil 1999, Visual Arts Award 2000, 5th South Bank Show Award 2001, Auguste Perret Prize 2002, Praemium Imperiale (Japan) 2002, Prince Philip Designers Prize 2004, World Solar Prize 2005, Br Cncl for Offices Pres's Award 2005, AJ 100 Most Admired Architect 2006–08, Medal of Honour for Services to Anglo-German Relations Br-German Assoc 2006, Madrid Creative Award 2006, Lynn S Beedle Achievement Award Cncl on Tall Buildings and Urban Habitat 2007, ULI Germany Leadership Award 2007, Grand DAI Award for Building Culture 2008, China Friendship Award 2008, Prince of Asturias Award for the Arts 2009, Save the Children Award Spain 2011, UN Assoc of NY Humanitarian Awards 2009, Save the Children Award Spain 2011, German Sustainability Award 2012, Soane Fndn Honours 2013, Blueprint Magazine Award for Architecture 2013, Gold Medal Award European Merit Fndn and Order of Architects and Consulting Engrs Luxembourg 2014, Noguchi Award 2014, Menschen in Europa Art Award 2014, The State Prize of Peace and Progress of the First President of the Republic of Khazakstan 2014, Louis Kahn Memorial Award 2015, Twenty Years of Excellence Award Architects' Journal 2015, AJ120 Most Admired Architect 2015, Gullion d'Or Award 2015, Sidney L Strauss Award New York Society of Architects 2015, Peace and Progress Prize of the President of Khazakstan 2015; TV documentaries incl: BBC Omnibus 1981, 1995 and 1999, Anglia Enterprise 1983, BBC Late Show 1990 and 1991, Building Sites 1991, The Limit 1998, Pinnacle Europe CNN 1999, South Bank Show 2001; film How Much Does Your Building Weigh Mr Foster 2010; featured in numerous international pubns and jls; exhbns of work held in: London, NY, Paris, Cologne, Copenhagen, Bordeaux, Lyon, Nîmes, Tokyo, Berlin, Madrid, Barcelona, Milan, Venice, Florence, Hong Kong, Antwerp; work in permanent collections of MOMA NY and Centre Pompidou Paris; vice-pres AA 1974 (memb Cncl 1973), memb RIBA Visiting Bd of Educn 1971 (external examiner 1971–73); memb Cncl RCA 1981; assoc Académie Royale de Belgique, memb Ordre Français des Architectes, hon memb Bund Deutsche Architekten 1983, hon fell American Inst of Architects 1980, foreign memb Royal Acad of Fine Arts Sweden 1995, offr Order of Arts and Letters Miny of Culture France 1994, memb European Acad of Sciences and Arts 1996, foreign memb American Acad of Arts and Sciences 1996, corresponding memb Dept of Fine Arts Croatian Acad 2015; IBM fell 1980, hon fell Kent Inst of Art and Design 1994; hon prof Univ of Buenos Aires 1997; Hon LittD UEA 1980, Hon DSc Univ of Bath 1986; Hon Dr: RCA 1991, Univ of Valencia 1992, Univ of Humberside 1992,

London Inst 2001, Ben Gurion Univ of The Negev (Lifetime Achievement Award) 2001, Robert Gordon Univ 2002, Univ of Durham 2002, Universidad Politécnica de Madrid 2012; Hon LLD: Univ of Manchester 1993, Technical Univ of Eindhoven 1996, Univ of Oxford 1996; Hon DLit Univ of London 1996, Hon DSc (Eng) UCL 2009; RIBA 1965, FCSD 1975, ARA 1983, RDI 1988, Hon FREng 1995, Hon FRIAS 2000, Hon ICE 2001; Commander's Cross of the Order of Merit (Germany) 1999, Orden Pour le mérite für Wissenschaft und Künste (Germany) 2002, Knight Cdr's Cross of Order of Merit (Germany) 2009; *Books* The Work of Foster Associates (1978), Norman Foster, Buildings and Projects, Vols 1, 2, 3, 4 (1989–90), Foster Associates (1991), Norman Foster Sketches (1991), Recent Works Foster Associates (1992), Sir Norman Foster (1997), Norman Foster, selected and current works of Foster and Partners (1997), Norman Foster – 30 Colours (1998), The Norman Foster Studio (2000), The Reichstag: The Parliament Building by Norman Foster (2000), Rebuilding the Reichstag (2000), On Foster ... Foster On (2000), Norman Foster Works: Vol 1 (2003), Vol 2 (2005), Vol 3 (2006), Vol 4 (2004), Vol 5 (2009), Vol 6 (2013), Foster 40 (2007), Norman Foster: A Life in Architecture (biography by Deyan Sudjic, 2010), Norman Foster: Drawings 1958–2008 (2010), Series of Monographs (2011), Norman Foster in the 21st Century (in AV Monograph 163–164, 2013), Moving. Norman Foster on Art (2013), Museum of Fine Arts Boston (2013), Norman Foster Works 6 (2014), Building with History (2015), Norman Foster: Progettazione integrate dal design alla pianificazione (2016), Foster + Partners (in UED 098, 2016); *Recreations* flying, skiing, running; *Style*— The Rt Hon the Lord Foster of Thames Bank, OM; ✉ Foster + Partners, Riverside Three, 22 Hester Road, London SW11 4AN (☎ 020 7738 0455, fax 020 7738 1107/1108, e-mail enquiries@fosterandpartners.com)

FOULKES, Gary Spencer; *b* 12 August 1979, Liverpool; *m* 20 Nov 2010, Sarah Bridge; 1 s (Caspian Seiji b 30 May 2014); *Career* chef de partie: Rhodes & Co Manchester 1998–2000, Richard Neat Oxo Tower 2001, Aubergine 2001–03; sous chef The Vineyard at Stockcross 2003–05; The Square: sous chef 2005–13, head chef 2013–, exec chef Angler at South Place Hotel 2016–; *Recreations* skiing, tennis, travel, scuba diving, dining out; *Style*— Gary Foulkes, Esq; ✉ South Place Hotel, 3 South Place, London EC2M 2AF (Twitter @garyfoulkes)

FOULKES, Nicholas; s of James Foulkes, and Regine, *née* Richter; *b* 2 December 1964, Aberystwyth; *Educ* Christ's Hosp, Hertford Coll Oxford; *m* 23 Sept 1989, Alexandra, *née* Holloway; 2 s (Maximilian Anton b 28 May 1996, Frederick Alexander b 9 May 1999); *Career* ed London Life Evening Standard 1990–92, assoc ed ES Magazine Evening Standard 1992–94; author, curator and journalist 1994–, luxury ed GQ, contributing ed Vanity Fair, editorial dir Finch's Quarterly Review, contrib ed The Rake, contrib ed Spear's, columnist Country Life, dir freelance contrib to Independent on Sunday, Daily Telegraph, Mail on Sunday, Evening Standard, Spectator, Newsweek and other newspapers and periodicals; Havana Man of the Year 2007, Int Best Dressed List 2011; *Publications* incl: Dressed to Kill: James Bond the Suited Hero (contrib, 1996), Turnbull and Asser (1997), Evening Standard Restaurant Guide (2000), Last of the Dandies: The Scandalous Life and Escapades of Count d'Orsay (2003), Marbella Club: The First Fifty Years (2005), The Bentley Miscellany (2005), The Bentley Era: The Fast and Furious Story of the Fabulous Bentley Boys (2006), Dunhill by Design (2006), Dancing into Battle: A Social History of the Battle of Waterloo (2006), The Trench Book (2007), The Carlyle (2007), Zadora Timepieces (2007), Mikimoto (2007), Cigor Style (2008), High Society, The History of America's Upper Class (2008), Gentlemen & Blackguards: Gambling Mania and the plot to steal the Derby of 1844 (2010), The Official History of Meissen Porcelain (2010), The History of Neapolitan Tailoring (2010), Bals (2011), Gioielleria Nardi (2012), Swans, Legends and the Jet Society (2013), The Impossible Collection of Watches (2014), The Marbella Club (2015), Savile Row and America (2015), Bernard Buffet, The Invention of the Modern Mega-Artist (2016); *Recreations* playing backgammon, eating at Riva, visiting tailors, watchmakers and cigar factories; *Clubs* White's; *Style*— Nicholas Foulkes, Esq; ✉ c/o Luigi Bonomi Associates, 91 Great Russell Street, London WC1B 3PS (☎ 020 7637 1234)

FOULKES, Prof (Albert) Peter; s of Henry Foulkes (d 1990), of Yorks, and Edith Cavell, *née* O'Mara (d 1989); *b* 17 October 1936; *Educ* Univ of Sheffield (BA), Univ of Cologne, Univ of Tulane (PhD); *m* 1959, (Barbara) Joy, da of William Joseph French (d 1981); 2 da (Imogen b 21 May 1960, Juliet b 26 Nov 1961); *Career* prof Stanford Univ 1965–75, prof of German Univ of Wales 1977–; Alexander Von Humboldt fell 1972; Inst of Linguists: memb Cncl 1982–89, chm Examinations Bd 1985–90, tstee 1986–90, vice-pres 1990–98; FIL 1982; *Books* The Reluctant Pessimist, Franz Kafka (1967), The Search for Literary Meaning (1975), Literature and Propaganda (1983), Tales from French Catalonia (2000); *Recreations* gardening, rambling, theatre, conjuring, photography; *Style*— Prof Peter Foulkes; ✉ 20L Kilbryde Cresent, Dunblane, Scotland FK15 9BA (e-mail peter_foulkes@orange.fr)

FOULKES, Thomas Howard Exton (Tom); OBE (2012); s of Maj Gen Thomas H F Foulkes (d 1986), and Delphine, *née* Smith; *b* 31 August 1950; *Educ* Clifton, Sandhurst, RMCS Shrivenham (BSc), Open Univ (MBA), RCDS; *m* 14 August 1976, Sally, *née* Winter; 2 da (Emma-Jane b 23 March 1982, Kate b 13 June 1987); *Career* cmmnd RE 1971, regtl duties RE 1971–82, Defence Equipment Procurement (bridges) 1982–89, CO 28 Amphibious Engr Regt 1989–92; Defence Equipment Procurement: project mangr Gen Engr Equipment 1992–95, equipment support mangr 1995–97; RCDS 1997–98, promoted to rank of Brig 1998, project mangr CAPITAL 1998–99, dir Army Estates Orgn 1999–2002; DG ICE 2002–11, chm Victoria BID Ltd 2011–15; pres Cwlth Engrs Cncl 2010–11, dir Engineering-UK 2007–11, memb Centre for Smart Infrastructure and Construction (CSIC) Steering Gp Univ of Cambridge 2011–; pres Royal Engrs Assoc FC 1992–2002; chm Cyntra Ltd Ltd 2009–11; memb Smeatonian Soc of Civil Engrs; visiting prof Univ of Surrey 2010; Freeman Worshipful Co of Engrs; CEng, FIMechE 1995, FICE 1996, MInstRE 2007, FIET 2008, FAPM 2008; *Publications* Monuments in Whitehall: A Walk With Heroes (series, 1985–95); author of various titles on military bridging and procurement of weapon systems 1982–98; *Recreations* skiing, cycling, gardening, studying philosophy; *Clubs* Athenaeum; *Style*— Tom Foulkes, Esq, OBE

FOULKES OF CUMNOCK, Baron (Life Peer UK 2005), of Cumnock in East Ayrshire; George Foulkes; PC (2002), JP (Edinburgh 1975); s of late George Foulkes, and Jessie M A W Foulkes (decd); *b* 21 January 1942; *Educ* Keith GS, Haberdashers' Aske's, Univ of Edinburgh; *m* 1970, Elizabeth Anna, da of William Hope; 2 s, 1 da; *Career* pres: Univ of Edinburgh Students Rep Cncl 1963–64, Scottish Union of Students 1965–67; rector's assessor at Univ of Edinburgh; dir: Enterprise Youth 1968–73, Age Concern Scotland 1973–79; cncllr and bailie Edinburgh City Cncl 1970–75, chm Lothian Region Educn Ctee 1974–79, cncllr Lothian Regnl Cncl 1974–79; chm: Educn Ctee Convention of Scot Local Authorities 1976–79, Scottish Adult Literacy Agency 1977–79; MP (Lab): S Ayrshire 1979–83, Carrick, Cumnock and Doon Valley 1983–2005; MSP (Lab) Lothians 2007–11; memb Commons Select Ctee on Foreign Affrs 1981–83, jt chm Commons All-Pty Pensioners' Ctee 1983–97; front bench oppn spokesman: Euro and Community Affrs 1983–85, Foreign Affrs 1985–92, Defence 1992–93, Overseas Devpt 1994–97; Parly under-sec of state for international devpt 1997–2001, min of state for Scot 2001–02, memb Intelligence and Security Ctee 2007–10; memb: House of Lords EU Select Ctee 2011–15, House of Lords EU Sub Ctee on Social Affrs and Consumer Protection 2011–, Jt Ctee on Nat Security Strategy 2011–14; UK delegate to: Parly Assembly of Cncl of Europe 2002–05 and 2016–, Assembly WEU 2002–05; memb: Exec Cwlth Parly Assoc (UK), Inter Parly Union (GB) 2002–05, Exec Ctee of Socialist Int (SI) 2002–05, Bd Westminster Fndn for Democracy 2007–13; dir Cooperative Press Ltd 1990–97, chm John Wheatley Centre 1991–97; treas Parliamentarians for Global Action (International) 1993–97, treas Climate Parliament 2014–16; chm Heart of Midlothian FC 2004–05; pres Caribbean-Britain Business Cncl 2002–10, pres Caribbean Cncl 2010–16; vice-chair Age Scotland 2014–16, chair Age Scotland 2016–; William Wilberforce Medal 1998; *Recreations* boating, supporting Heart of Midlothian FC; *Style*— The Rt Hon the Lord Foulkes of Cumnock, PC; ✉ House of Lords, London SW1A 0PW

FOULSTON, Robert; *Educ* Silcoates Sch Wakefield, Univ of Newcastle (LLB), Coll of Law; *Career* articled clerk Freshfields Bruckhaus Deringer 1987, articled clerk/slr DJ Freeman & Co 1987–89, lawyer SG Archibald 1989–90, lawyer Euro Equity Origination Credit Lyonnais Securities 1990–91; Bankers Tst: lawyer and vice-pres 1991–94, lawyer and dir Distressed Products 1994–96, md 1996–99; md Deutsche Bank 1999–2001, md and head European Distressed Products Deutsche Bank 2001–05, chief exec Retail Motor Industry Fedn (RMI) 2009–11, chm and shareholder Remit Gp 2008–, ptnr Acuity Legal Ltd 2015–; ptnr Adam Street Advsrs 2015–; chm and owner ITEC 1998–; *Style*— Robert Foulston, Esq; ✉ Remit Group, 201 Great Portland Street, London W1W 5AB

FOUNTAIN, Desmond Hale; s of Desmond Oswald Trevor Fountain (d 1976), of Calpe Alicante, Spain, and Ruth Emily, *née* Masters (d 1993); *b* 29 December 1946, Bermuda; *Educ* Whitney Inst Bermuda, Normanton Coll, Stoke-on-Trent Coll of Art, Exeter Coll of Art (DipAD), Univ of Bristol (CertEd, ATD); *m* 1, 1969 (m dis 1998), Miranda Mary Campbell, *née* Hay; 1 da (Annabel Emily Clare b 1975), 1 s (Luke Desmond Hugh b 1981); m 2, Eleonora Valerie (Luli) *née* Maunder, formerly Whitelockel; 3 step c (Katherine, Nicholas, James); *Career* sculptor; prize for art (aged 6 years) in adult exhibition Br Cncl Sierra Leone 1953; pres Exeter Coll of Art Student's Cncl 1968, SW rep for NUS 1968; fndr Bermuda Fine Art Tst private bill passed 1982; fndr The Bridge House Gallery 1976, fndr tstee The Bermuda National Gallery 1992, fndr Desmond Fountain Gallery 2000, grand opening The (New) Desmond Fountain Gallery Mandarin Oriental's Elbow Beach Hotel Paget Bermuda 2011; award from Miny of Cultural Affairs; Lifetime Achievment Award Govt of Bermuda 2003; FRBS 1985; *Exhibitions and Galleries* Bermuda Soc of Arts 1958, Exe Gallery Devon 1968, Exeter City Museum and Art Gallery 1969 and 1970, Spectrum Designs Ltd Devon 1969, Univ of Bristol 1970, City Hall Bermuda (two man show) 1972, City Hall Bermuda (four man show) 1973, Country Art Gallery USA 1974, Bermuda Soc of Arts Gp Show 1974, City Hall Bermuda (three man show) 1975, Bridge House Art Gallery Bermuda (fndr Desmond Fountain) 1976, Newport USA 1976, The Int Gallery Bermuda (three man show) 1977, St George's Gallery Middx 1977, Windjammer Gallery Bermuda 1980, 1981, 1985, 1986, 1989, 1993 and 1998, Bermuda Soc of Arts Members Show 1980, Glen Gallery Canada 1981, South African Gallery London 1981, Poole Fine Art USA 1981, Boston Fine Art Inc 1981, Coach House Gallery Guernsey 1983, Sally Le Gallis Jersey 1983, Renaissance Gallery USA 1983 and 1986, Alwin Gallery Summer Exhibition London 1985, Alwin Gallery UK 1986 and 1987, RSBS USA 1986, Br Sculptors Art Centre Bermuda 1987, Art Expo LA 1987, World Congress USA 1987, The Sculpture Gallery Bermuda 1989, Pinehurst Gallery NC 1990, Hartley Hill Gallery Calif 1992–93, E S Lawrence Gallery Aspen 1993, Cavalier Galleries Stamford 1993, RSBS Chelsea Harbour 1993, L'Ortolan Sculpture Garden Berks 1993, Perry House Galleries Alexandria USA 1994, Bruton Street London 1994, Cavalier Galleries Greenwich CT, NY and Nantucket 2003, 2004 and 2005, Royall Fine Art Tunbridge Wells 2005, jt show Cork St Gallery 2008, In Family Unity – Unity of the World (travelling exhibition in Russia) 2012–13, Windjammer 2 Gallery Bermuda 2013–, Mark Twain (Masterworks Bermuda) 2014; *Solo Exhibitions* incl: H A & E Smith Ltd Bermuda 1975, A S Cooper & Sons Gallery 1976, Hamma Galleries Bermuda 1978, Alwin Gallery London 1980, Bacardi Int 1982, Falle Fine Art Jersey 1995 and 1997, Cavalier Gallery USA 1995, Coutts Bermuda 1996; *Major Commissions* sculpture of Sir George Somers for St George's unveiled by HRH Princess Margaret 1981–84, medallions in silver, gold and platinum featuring a portrait of HRH Princess Margaret 1985, public memorial Greece 1993–94, sculpture of Mark Twain unveiled at Directors' Circle preview of Bermuda Nat Gall retrospective 1994–95, sculpture of The Spirit of Bermuda: Johnny Barnes 1997–98, Heroes of the Oz Trial UK 1997–2000, lifesize Jorgen Svendsen for Belzona in Harrogate 2002, Sarah (three times lifesize nude, World Sculpture Park Changchun) 2006, Matriarch (private location Austria) 2010, Life Size Bacchus (in bronze, one casting per major wine region, also to be cast in a French edition of 8 plus 4 artist copies) 2014, posthumous bust of Robert Clements; *Collections* Nemacolin Woodlands, The Hardy Family Art Collection/Mark Twain; *Publications* Desmond Fountain: Sculptor (2003), The Hardy Family Art Collection, The Garden of Heroes and Villains: Felix Dennis, Who's Who in Art; *Recreations* sailing, boating in general, antiques, collecting art, property restoration, oenology, guitar, singing, composing, driving, creating in one way or another and smelling the roses!; *Clubs* Royal Bermuda Yacht, Bermuda Boat and Canoe; *Style*— Desmond Fountain, Esq; ✉ Tangible Investments Ltd, PO Box FL 317, Flatts FL BX, Bermuda (e-mail (preferred) desfountain@mac.com, website www.desmondfountain.com, Facebook The Desmond Fountain Gallery and Desmond Fountain)

FOURMAN, Prof Michael Paul; s of Prof Lucien Paul Rollings Fourman (d 1968), of Leeds, and Dr Julia Mary, *née* Hunton (d 1981); *b* 12 September 1950, Oxford; *Educ* Allerton Grange Sch Leeds, Univ of Bristol (BSc), Univ of Oxford (MSc, DPhil); *m* 12 Nov 1982 (m dis 2001), Jennifer Robin, da of Hector Grainger Head (d 1970), of Sydney, Aust; 1 da (Paula b 1984), 2 s (Maximillian b 1987, Robin b 1992); *Career* jr res fell Wolfson Coll Oxford 1974–78, JF Ritt asst prof of mathematics Columbia Univ NY 1976–82; Dept of Electrical and Electronic Engrg Brunel Univ: res fell 1983–86, Hirst reader in integrated circuit design 1986, prof of formal systems 1986–88; Univ of Edinburgh: prof of computer systems 1988–, head of informatics 1994–97 and 2001–09, head of computer sci 1995–98; FBCS 2005, FRSE 2010; *Recreations* cooking, sailing; *Clubs* Royal Forth Yacht; *Style*— Prof Michael Fourman; ✉ School of Informatics, University of Edinburgh, Informatics Forum, Crichton Street, Edinburgh EH8 9AB (☎ 0131 651 5615, e-mail michael.fourman@ed.ac.uk)

FOVARGUE, Yvonne Helen; MP; *née* Gibbon; da of late Kenneth Gibbon, and Renee, *née* Reed; *b* 29 November 1956, Sale, Gtr Manchester; *Educ* Sale GS, Univ of Leeds (BA); *m* 3 March 2009, Paul Kenny; 1 da (Victoria b 24 Sept 1984); *Career* housing offr 1979–86, chief exec St Helens CAB 1986–2010; cncllr Warrington Cncl 2004–10, MP (Lab) Makerfield 2010–, oppn whip 2011–12, shadow transport min 2012–13, shadow defence min 2013–14, shadow young people's min 2014–15, shadow veterans' min 2015–; chair All Pty Parly Gp on: Debt and Personal Finance 2011–, Legal Aid 2011–14; memb St Helens Cncl for Voluntary Serv 2003–10; *Recreations* reading crime fiction; *Clubs* MENSA; *Style*— Ms Yvonne Fovargue, MP; ✉ website www.yvonnefovargue.com, Twitter @Y_FovargueMP, Facebook Yvonne4Makerfield

FOWKE, Philip Francis; s of Francis Henry Villiers (d 1974), and Florence, *née* Clutton (d 2000), of Gerrards Cross; *b* 28 June 1950; *Educ* Gayhurst Sch, Downside, began piano studies with Marjorie Withers, ARAM (awarded scholarship to study piano at RAM with Gordon Green, OBE); *m* 5 May 1999, Elizabeth Margaret Turnbull; *Career* concert pianist; Wigmore Hall debut 1974, Royal Festival Hall debut 1977, Proms debut 1979, US debut 1982; performs regularly with all leading Br orchs and for BBC Radio, toured extensively in Europe; performances incl: Lambert Piano Concerto BBC Proms 2001, Warsaw Concerto BBC Proms 2003, world première of Richard Bissell Rhapsody for Piano and Orchestra Royal Festival Hall 2003; contrib Times Literary Supplement, music magazines and obituaries for nat press; prof of piano Royal Acad of Music 1981–91, prof of piano Welsh Coll of Music and Drama 1994–95, head Keyboard Dept Trinity Coll of Music London 1995–99 (sr fell 1998), currently sr fell of keyboard TrinityLaban Conservatoire of Music & Dance London (formerly Trinity Coll of Music); recitalist and piano tutor Dartington International Summer Sch 1996, 1997 and 2000, vice-chm European Piano Teachers' Assoc (UK), warden Performers and Composers Section ISM 2004–05, regular tutor and recitalist Chetham's Int Summer Sch and Festival for Pianists; first prize Nat Fedn of Music Socs Award 1973, BBC Piano Competition 1974; Winston Churchill Fellowship 1976; FRAM; *Recordings* incl: Virtuoso Piano Transcriptions, Complete Chopin Waltzes, Chopin Sonatas Nos 2 and 3, Bliss Piano Recital, Bliss Piano Concerto (with Liverpool Philharmonic and David Atherton), Britten Scottish Ballad (with City of Birmingham Orch and Simon Rattle), Finzi Grand Fantasia and Toccata (with Liverpool Philharmonic and Richard Hickox), Rachmaninoff Piano Concerto No 2 and Rhapsody on a Theme from Paganini (with Royal Philharmonic and Yuri Temirkanov), Ravel Piano Concertos (with London Philharmonic and Serge Baudo), Saint-Saëns Carnival of Animals (with Scot Nat Orch and Sir Alexander Gibson), Tchaikovsky Piano Concertos Nos 1 and 2 (with London Philharmonic and Wilfried Boettcher), Delius Piano Concerto (with Royal Philharmonic and Norman del Mar), Hoddinott Piano Concerto No 1 (with Royal Philharmonic and Barry Wordsworth), film scores incl Warsaw Concerto (with RTE Concert Orch and Proinnsias O Duinn), Cyril Scott Piano Quartet and Quintet (with The London Piano Quartet), Alan Bush Piano Quartet (with The London Piano Quartet), Other Love Songs (with The Prince Consort); *Recreations* architecture, monasticism; *Clubs* Cavendish, Royal Over-Seas League, Savage; *Style*— Philip Fowke, FRAM; ✉ e-mail philipfowke@aol.com, website www.philipfowke.co.uk; c/o Patrick Garvey Management (☎ 0845 130 6112, e-mail patrick@patrickgarvey.com)

FOWLE, (William) Michael Thomas; CBE (2000); s of William Thomas Fowle (d 1968), of Salisbury, Wilts, and Nancy, *née* Williams (d 1971); *b* 8 January 1940, Madras, India; *Educ* Rugby, Clare Coll Cambridge (MA); *m* 1 (m dis), Judith Anderson; m 2, Margaret Dawes; 1 da (Emma Curtis), 1 s (John), 1 step s (James Smith); *Career* KPMG: ptnr 1976–99, sr UK banking and fin ptnr 1986–90, chm KPMG Banking & Finance Group 1989–93, sr UK audit ptnr 1990–93, sr ptnr London office and SE Region 1993–98, chm KPMG India 1996–2000; dir: Norwich and Peterborough Building Soc 1999–2006, ICICI Bank UK Ltd 2003–11, Vedanta Resources plc 2003–05; chief treas St John Ambulance 1999–2002, chair Place2Be 1999–, govr Sadler's Wells 1996–2003, dir Ind Schs Cncl 2009–10; govr Rugby Sch 1988–2009 (chm 2002), treas The Prince's Drawing Sch 2004–10, tstee Prince's Sch of Traditional Art 2010–, chair Chartered Accountants' Livery CHarity 2014–; Liveryman Chartered Accountants Livery Co (Master 2013–14); FCA (ACA 1965); *Recreations* collecting, boating; *Clubs* Athenaeum; *Style*— Michael Fowle, Esq, CBE; ✉ 31 Myddelton Square, London EC1Y 1RB (☎ 020 7278 8064, mobile 07802 806534, e-mail michael@fowle.uk.com)

FOWLER, Alan Roy; s of Ronald James Fowler (d 2009), and Mary Ellen, *née* Baines (d 2004); *b* 20 September 1958, London; *Educ* London Oratory; *m* 1981, Marie-Yvonne, *née* Binsted; *Career* slr specialising in pensions law; Lovells 1987–98, Charles Russell 1998–2000, Ashursts 2000–03, head of pensions law Stevens & Bolton 2003–11, conslt in UK and offshore pensions 2011–; memb Assoc of Pension Lawyers 1989; *Recreations* private light aviation, hill walking; *Style*— Alan Fowler, Esq

FOWLER, Prof Alastair David Shaw; CBE (2014); s of David Fowler (d 1939), and Maggie, *née* Shaw (d 1976); *b* 17 August 1930; *Educ* Queens Park Sch Glasgow, Univ of Glasgow, Univ of Edinburgh (MA), Pembroke Coll Oxford, The Queen's Coll Oxford (MA, DPhil, DLitt); *m* 23 Dec 1950, Jenny Catherine, da of Ian James Simpson (d 1981), of Giffnock House, Helensburgh; 1 da (Alison b 1954), 1 s (David Simpson b 1960); *Career* jr res fell The Queen's Coll Oxford 1955–59, visiting instr Univ of Indiana 1957–58, lectr UC Swansea 1959–61, fell and tutor of English literature BNC Oxford 1962–71, regius prof of rhetoric and English literature Univ of Edinburgh 1972–84 (univ fell 1984–87 and 2007–); Univ of Virginia: visiting prof 1969, 1979 and 1985–90, prof of English 1990–98; visiting prof Columbia Univ 1964, memb Inst for Advanced Study Princeton 1966 and 1980, visiting fell Cncl of Humanities Princeton Univ 1974, fell Humanities Res Centre Canberra 1980, visiting fell All Souls Coll Oxford 1984, visiting prof Univ of Wales Lampeter 1996; external assessor Open Univ 1972–77; advsy ed: Word and Image 1984–91 and 1992–97, Connotations 1990–98, New Literary History 1972–2003, English Literary Renaissance 1978–2003, Swansea Review, The Seventeenth Century 1986–2003, Translation and Literature 1990–2015; memb: Harrap Academic Advsy Ctee 1983–89, Scottish Arts Cncl 1976–77, Nat Printed Books Panel 1977–79, Carlyle Soc (hon vice-pres 1972), English Union Edinburgh (pres 1972), Renaissance Soc, Renaissance English Text Soc, Soc Emblem Studies, Spenser Soc, Bibliographical Soc Edinburgh, Assoc of Literary Scholars and Critics, RSL, Soc of Authors, AUT 1971–84, Agder Akademi 2003; honoured scholar Milton Soc of America 2013; FBA 1974; *Books* Spenser and the Numbers of Time (1964), The Poems of John Milton (with John Carey, 1968), Triumphal Forms (1970), Conceitful Thought (1975), Catacomb Suburb (1976), From the Domain of Arnheim (1982), Kinds of Literature (1982), A History of English Literature (1987), The New Oxford Book of Seventeenth Century Verse (1991), The Country House Poem (1994), Time's Purpled Masquers (1996), Paradise Lost (1998, 2 edn 2015), Renaissance Realism (2003), How to Write (2006), Literary Names (2012); *Clubs* Oxford and Cambridge; *Style*— Prof Alastair Fowler, CBE, FBA; ✉ 11 East Claremont Street, Edinburgh EH7 4HT (☎ 0131 556 0366)

FOWLER, Prof Christopher Gordon; s of Gordon Fowler, of Cardiff, and Elizabeth Aled, *née* Biggs; *b* 19 March 1950; *Educ* King Alfred's GS Wantage, Middx Hosp Med Sch, Univ of London (BSc, MB BS); *m* 1, 15 Dec 1973 (m dis 1996), Dr Clare Juliet Fowler, *qv*, da of Peter Amyas Wright, of Horton-on-Studley, Oxon; 1 s (William b 9 Aug 1980), 1 da (Alice b 28 June 1977); m 2, 20 Dec 1996, Mary Jane, da of Jeffrey John Absalom, of East Horsley, Surrey; 1 da (Molly b 12 July 2001); *Career* sr lectr in urology London Hosp Med Sch 1988 (lectr 1982), conslt urologist The London Hosp and Newham Health Dist 1988, currently dean for educn Queen Mary Univ of London; author of articles and chapters on fibreoscopy, laser surgery and uro-neurology; FRCS (Urol), FRCP, FHEA; *Recreations* family; *Clubs* Y; *Style*— Prof Christopher Fowler

FOWLER, Prof Clare Juliet; CBE (2012); da of Peter Wright, of Oxford, and Dr Jean Crum; *b* 1 July 1950; *Educ* Wycombe Abbey, Middx Hosp Med Sch (MB BS, MSc); *m* 1, 1973 (m dis 1996); 1 da (Alice Clare b 28 June 1977), 1 s (William Gordon Peter b 9 Aug 1980); m 2, 2000, Peter Bevan; *Career* sr registrar in clinical neurophysiology Middx Hosp and Nat Hosp 1984–86; conslt in clinical neurophysiology: Bart's 1987–89, Middx and UCH 1987–; conslt in uro-neurology Nat Hosp for Neurology and Neurosurgery 1987–, prof Inst of Neurology UCL 1998– (reader 1998–2001), dep med dir UCLH 1998–2001, caldicott guardian UCLH 2000–09; memb: Cncl EEG Soc 1987–91, Cncl Neurology Section Standing Ctee RSM; chm: Clinical Autonomic Research Soc 1990–92 (hon sec 1986–89), SUBDIMS; hon sec Br Soc of Clinical Neurophysiology 1992–95, memb Ethics Ctee Int Continence Soc 2008– (memb Scientific Ctee 1995–97); FRCP; *Books* Neurology of Bladder, Bowel and Sexual Dysfunction (1999), Pelvic Organ Dysfunction in Neurological Disease (2010); *Recreations* gardening, grandchildren; *Clubs* Athenaeum; *Style*— Prof Clare Fowler, CBE; ✉ Flat 12, 31 Marsham Street, London SW1P 3DW

FOWLER, James Christopher; s of Donald Fowler (d 2003), and Sheila, *née* Brown; *b* 22 October 1962, Zürich, Switzerland; *Educ* New Coll Sch Oxford (chorister), Merchant Taylors' Sch Northwood (music scholar), New Coll Oxford (choral scholar, MA); *m* 21 July 1984, Dr Charlotte, *née* Bonner-Morgan; 2 s (Alexander b 9 Dec 1989, Luke b 15 Feb 1992); *Career* advtg exec Publicis, MWP and Saatchi Gp 1985–91; teacher St John's Coll Cardiff 1991–99, head of sixth form Brentwood Sch 1999–2002, dep head Highgate Sch 2002–06; headmaster Aldenham Sch Elstree 2006–; princ examiner WJEC 1993–2006; inspr Ind Schs Inspectorate; memb HMC 2006; *Recreations* skiing, sailing, choral music, opera, cricket; *Clubs* East India, Lansdowne; *Style*— James Fowler, Esq; ✉ Headmaster's House, Aldenham School, Aldenham Road, Elstree, Hertfordshire WD6 3AJ (☎ 01923 854419, e-mail head@aldenham.com)

FOWLER, Jennifer Joan; da of Russell Aubrey Fowler (d 1971), and Lucy, *née* Tobitt (d 1995); *b* 14 April 1939; *Educ* Bunbury HS, Univ of W Aust (BA, BMus, DipEd); *m* 18 Dec 1971, John Bruce, s of Maj Frederick Paterson (d 1983); 2 s (Martin b 1973, Adrian b 1976); *Career* composer; major works: Hours of the Day (for 4 singers, 2 oboes and 2 clarinets) 1968, Ravelation (for string quintet) 1971, Veni Sancte Spiritus (for 12 solo singers) 1971, Chant with Garlands (for orchestra) 1974, Voice of the Shades (for soprano, oboe, violin) 1977, When David Heard (for choir and piano) 1982 (revised 2007), Echoes from an Antique Land (for ensemble) 1983, Lament (for baroque oboe, viol) 1988, And Ever Shall Be (for mezzo and ensemble) 1989, Reeds, Reflections (for oboe and string trio) 1990, Plainsong for Strings (for string orchestra) 1992, Lament for Dunblane (SSATB) 1996, Singing the Lost Places (for soprano and large ensemble) 1996, Eat and be Eaten (collection of songs for 6 singers) 1998–2000, Magnificat 2 (for soprano and ensemble) 2000, Spiral (for flexible ensemble) 2001, Magnificat and Nunc Dimittis (for choir and (optional) organ) 2002, Hymn for St Brigid (SATB) 2002, Apsaras Flying (for 3 recorders, cello and harpsichord) 2003, Streaming Up (for small ensemble) 2004, Towards Release (various instrumentations) 2004, Letter from Haworth (for soprano and ensemble) 2005, Line Spun with Stars (trio) 2006, Threaded Stars 2 (for solo harp) 2006, Bone Dance (trombone quartet) 2006, Lament (for 3 viols) 2007, Concerto (for alto saxophone and orch) 2010, Uncoiling (for solo oboe and piano) 2011, Three Cellos 2012, Magnificat 3 (for sporano, flute, cello and piano) 2012, Viola Solo (for unacoompanied viola) 2013; int prizes: Acad of the Arts Berlin, Radcliffe Award of GB, Gedok Prize Mannheim, Miriam Gideon Prize USA, Christopher Bodman Meml Prize, Sylvia Glickman Meml Prize, Marin Goleminov Int Composition Contest; memb: Br Acad of Composers and Songwriters, Women in Music (UK), Sound and Music, Int Alliance for Women in Music; *Recreations* literature, gardening; *Style*— Ms Jennifer Fowler; ✉ 21 Deodar Road, Putney, London SW15 2NP (e-mail 100611.2060@compuserve.com, website www.impulse-music.co.uk/fowler.htm)

FOWLER, Keith Harrison; s of Lancelot Harrison Fowler (d 1970), and Enid Florence, *née* Stow (d 1990); *b* 20 May 1934, London; *Educ* Aldenham; *m* 22 July 1961, Vicki Belinda, *née* Pertwee; 2 da (Annabel b 1964, Penelope b 1969), 1 s (Justin b 1966); *Career* Lt Army Suez Canal; exec chm Edman Communications Group plc 1977–88, chief exec Cresta Corporate Services Ltd 1988–89, dir Cresta Holdings Ltd 1988–89, chief exec Euro RSCG Marketing Group Ltd 1990–95; dir Pertwee Holdings Ltd 1982–92; chm: Cousins Communications Ltd 1996–99, Willox Ambler Rodford Law Ltd 1996–, Ninah Consulting Ltd 1998–99, Empire Design Ltd 2000–14; dir: Invision Microsystems Ltd 1998–99, Harrison Portfolio Ltd 1998–; dir Nat Advertising Benevolent Soc 1978–; chm Winchester House School Trust Ltd 1968–2011; chm Abbeyfield Soc (Great Missenden) 1991–2011, dir/tstee Abbeyfield Soc UK 2010–15, dir/tstee Abbeyfield Fndn 2015–; ACIS; *Recreations* painting, classic cars, pictures; *Clubs* Arts, Solus, Lord Taverners; *Style*— Keith Fowler, Esq; ✉ The Old Manse, Martinsend Lane, Great Missenden, Buckinghamshire HP16 9BH (☎ 01494 866431, e-mail keith.fowler@arrewig.com)

FOWLER, Neil Douglas; s of Arthur Vincent Fowler (d 1996), of Essex, and Helen Pauline, *née* Douglas (d 1990); *b* 18 April 1956; *Educ* Southend HS for Boys, Univ of Leicester (BA); *m* 9 June 1989, Carol Susan, da of Kenneth Sydney Eric Cherry; 1 da (Helen Christine b 28 Jan 1993), 1 step s (Maurice Christopher John Volans b 13 March 1976); *Career* trainee (later sr reporter) Leicester Mercury 1978–81, dep news ed (later asst chief sub ed) Derby Evening Telegraph 1981–84, asst to the ed (later asst ed) Lincolnshire Echo 1984–85; ed: Lincolnshire Echo 1985–87, Derby Evening Telegraph 1987–91, The Journal Newcastle upon Tyne 1991–94, The Western Mail Cardiff 1994–2002; prop Neil Fowler Communications 2002–03, ceo and publisher Toronto Sun 2003–; pres Soc of Editors 1999–2000; FRSA 1999; *Awards* newspaper industry awards: North East Newspaper of the Year 1992, Best Use of Photography 1993, highly commended Best Use of Colour 1993 and 1994, Regnl Newspaper of the Year 1994, Regnl Newspaper Ed of the Year 1994 (highly commended 1993); Daily Newspaper of the Year Welsh Press Awards 1999, 2000 and 2002, Welsh Journalist of the Year 1999; *Recreations* cricket, cinema, music of Frank Zappa; *Clubs* Essex CCC; *Style*— Neil Fowler, Esq; ✉ The Toronto Sun, 333 King Street East, Toronto, Ontario M5A 3X5, Canada (☎ 1 416 947 2222, fax 1 416 947 3119)

FOWLER, Baron (Life Peer UK 2001), of Sutton Coldfield in the County of West Midlands; Rt Hon Sir (Peter) Norman Fowler; PC (1979); s of N F Fowler (d 1964), of Chelmsford, Essex, and Katherine Fowler; *b* 2 February 1938; *Educ* King Edward VI Sch Chelmsford, Trinity Hall Cambridge; *m* 1, 1968 (m dis 1976), Linda Christmas; m 2, 1979, Fiona Poole, da of John Donald; 2 da (Hon Kate Genevieve b Nov 1981, Hon Isobel Geraldine b July 1984); *Career* with The Times 1961–70 (special corr 1962–66, home affrs 1966–70), memb Editorial Bd Crossbow 1962–69; MP (Cons): Nottingham S 1970–74, Sutton Coldfield Feb 1974–2001; PPS NI Office 1972–74, oppn spokesman Home Affrs 1974–75; chief oppn spokesman: Social Servs 1975–76, Tport 1976–79; min Tport 1979–81; sec of state: Tport 1981, Social Servs 1981–87, Employment 1987–90; special advsr to PM 1992 gen election; chm Cons Pty 1992–94, shadow sec of state for the Environment, Tport and the Regions 1997–98, shadow home sec 1998–99; dep chm Assoc of Cons Peers 2006–10 (memb Exec 2001–05), chm House of Lords Select Ctee on BBC Charter 2005–06, chm House of Lords Select Ctee on Communication 2006–10, chm House of Lords Select Ctee on HIV/AIDS 2011; chm: Midland Ind Newspapers 1991–98, National Housebuilding Cncl 1992–98, Regnl Ind Media (publishers of the Yorkshire Post gp of newspapers) 1998–2002, Numark 1998–2006, Aggregate Industries plc 2000–06 (non-exec dir 2010–13); non-exec dir: NFC plc 1990–97, Holcim 2006–10, ABTA 2010–, Int AIDS Vaccine Initiative; *Books* After the Riots (1979), Ministers Decide (1991), A Political Suicide (2008, shortlisted Channel 4 Political Books Award), AIDS: Don't Die of Prejudice (2014); *Style*— The Rt Hon the Lord Fowler, PC

FOWLER, Richard Thomas; s of Arthur Fowler (d 1984), and Joan Eileen Fowler (d 2010); *b* 8 September 1950; *Educ* Holme Valley GS, Loughborough Coll of Art & Design, Ravensbourne Coll of Art & Design (BA); *m* 11 Aug 1984, Jane Lesley, da of Col W P Fletcher; 1 s (Daniel John Fletcher b 6 Sept 1987), 1 da (Bryony Anne b 29 July 1990); *Career* memb design staff British Museum then display offr International Harvester Company of GB Ltd 1974–80, exhibit designer Science Museum 1980–83, head of design Nat Museum of Photography, Film and Television Bradford 1983–89, visiting designer Computer Museum Boston 1989–90, head of design Eureka! (educnl museum for children) 1990–93, fndr/designer Richard Fowler Assocs 1994–; current work incl: Galleries of Justice Museum, Kirkcudbright Galleries, Warrior Treasures: Saxon Gold from the Staffordshire Hoard at the Royal Armouries, Accessible Steam Heritage (ASH) project at the Bluebell Railway; chm Museum Design Gp 1992–95; memb Museums Assoc; FCSD; *Recreations* drawing, morris dancing, fly fishing, vintage motorcycling; *Clubs* White Rose Morris Men, Gold Star Owners', Halifax Vandals RUFC; *Style*— Richard

Fowler, Esq; ✉ RFA Design, D214, Dean Clough, Halifax, West Yorkshire HX3 5AX (☎ 01422 300012, e-mail richard.fowler@rfadesign.com)

FOWLER, Sheila Patricia; da of George William Spurs (d 1975), of Sunderland, and Lillian Bean, *née* Callum (d 1986); *b* 22 April 1946; *Educ* St Anthony's GS Sunderland, Monkwearmouth Coll Sunderland, Univ of Sunderland (HNC Business Studies); *m* 1 March 1976, Richard Fowler (d 2005), s of Richard Fowler; *Career* local govt offr Sunderland BC 1962–65, industrial market research offr rising to PRO Corning Glass Co Sunderland 1965–71; PRO: Washington Devpt Corp 1971–72, N of England Devpt Cncl (Promotions) 1972–74; industrial devpt offr Cleveland CC 1974–79, PR dir Sweetman Marketing Ltd Middlesbrough 1979–82, princ Sheila P Fowler Associates 1982–; ICP Promotional Achievement Award USA 1984, 1986 and 1987; FIPR 1987 (MIPR 1971); *Recreations* golf, reading, travelling, Spanish culture; *Clubs* Hartlepool Golf, Real Club de Campo (Malaga); *Style—* Mrs Sheila Fowler; ✉ Sheila P Fowler Associates, 10 Holyrood Crescent, Hart Village, Hartlepool TS27 3BB (☎ and fax 01429 272553, e-mail sheilafowlerpr@aol.com)

FOX, Dr Adam Tobias; s of Danny Fox (d 2004), and Shirley, *née* Cohen; *b* 10 April 1972; *Educ* Haberdashers' Aske's, Univ of Cambridge, UCL; *m* 14 March 1999, Tanya Lisa, *née* Meltzer; 1 s (Ethan b 24 August 2002), 1 da (Charlotte b 17 July 2005); *Career* clinical lead for allergy Guys & St Thomas' Hosp; allergy rep British Paediatric Allergy, Immunology and Infectious Diseases Gp Royal Coll of Paediatrics and Child Health, paediatric rep Joint Clinical Immunology and Allergy Ctee Royal Coll of Physicians, rep Specialised Paediatric Allergy Services NHS England Nat Clinic Reference Gp; KCL: reader, dir Allergy Acad; tstee and chm Health Advsy Bd Allergy UK; advsy panels for numerous charities incl NICE and ASA; sec BSACI; govr N London Collegiate Sch; Univ of Cambridge Raymond Horton-Smith Prize, Paediatric Allergist of the Year Allergy UK 2007, Britain's Best Children's Doctors The Times Magazine 2012; FRCPCH 2010; ✉ Dept of Paediatric Allergy, St Thomas' Hospital, London SE1 7EH (website www.adamfox.co.uk, Twitter @dradamfox)

FOX, Sir Chris; kt (2006), QPM (1997); s of Douglas Charles Fox (d 2010), and Olive Eileen Fox (d 2007); *b* 21 July 1949; *Educ* Robert Gordon's Coll Aberdeen, West Bridgford GS Nottingham, Loughborough Univ (BSc, Dip); *m* 1972, Carol Anne, da of Dennis Wortley, of Loughborough, Leics; 2 da (Sarah b 13 July 1975, Kathryn b 7 December 1976), 1 s (Robert b 31 July 1984); *Career* uniform and CID roles in Nottingham and Mansfield 1972–88, div cdr Nottingham N 1988–90, dep chief constable Warks 1994–96, chief constable Northants 1996–2003, pres ACPO 2003–06 (first full-time pres); lead nat police response to Jan 2005 tsunami and July 2005 terror attacks; chm Civil Nuclear Police Authy 2009–11, tstee Police Fndn; top mgmnt prog 1995; fell Univ of Northampton 2006; Companion Chartered Mgmnt Inst 2005; *Recreations* golf, inshore sailing; *Style—* Sir Chris Fox, QPM

FOX, Baron (Life Peer 2014), of Leominster in the County of Herefordshire; Christopher Francis Fox; *Career* dir of communications GKN 2012–; Lib Dems: dir of policy and communications 2008, ceo 2010; *Style—* The Lord Fox; ✉ House of Lords, London SW1A 0PW

FOX, Edward Charles Morice; OBE (2003); eld s of Maj Robin Fox, MC, Virtuti Militari (Poland), RA (d 1971), of Cuckfield, W Sussex, and Angela Muriel Darita, *née* Worthington (d 1999); bro of James Fox, *qv*, and Robert Fox, *qv*; *b* 13 April 1937; *Educ* Harrow; *m* 1, 1958 (m dis), Tracy Reed, da of late Anthony Pelissier, of Sussex; 1 da (Lucy Arabella (now Viscountess Gormanston) b 1960); m 2, Joanna David, *qv*; 1 da (Emilia Rose Elizabeth Fox, *qv*, b 31 July 1974), 1 s (Frederick Samson Robert Morice b 1989); *Career* late Coldstream Gds, 2 Lt Loyal N Lancs Regt; stage, screen and television actor 1958–; trained RADA; *Theatre* incl: Knuckle (Comedy) 1973, The Family Reunion (Vaudeville) 1979, Anyone for Denis (Whitehall) 1981, Quartermaine's Terms (Queen's) 1981, Hamlet (Young Vic) 1982, Interpreters (Queen's) 1985, Let Us Go Then You and I (Lyric) 1987, The Dance of Death (Manchester) 1987, The Admirable Crichton (Haymarket) 1988, Another Love Story (also dir, Leicester Haymarket) 1990, The Philanthropist (West End), My Fair Lady (tour) 1992, Quartermaine's Terms 1993, The Father 1995, A Letter of Resignation (Comedy and Savoy Theatres) 1997–98, The Browning Version 2000, The Twelve Pound Look 2000, The Winslow Boy (nat tour) 2002, The Old Masters (Comedy Theatre) 2004, You Never Can Tell (Garrick Theatre) 2005–06, Legal Fictions (Nat Town and Savoy Theatre) 2007–08, Lloyd George Knew My Father (nat tour) 2009, An Evening with Anthony Trollope (one man show, nat tour) 2010, Trollope in Barsetshire (Riverside Studios) 2011, Four Quartets (Riverside Studios) 2011, The Audience (Gielgud Theatre) 2013; *Television* incl: Hard Times 1977, Edward and Mrs Simpson 1978 (BAFTA Award for Best Actor 1978, TV Times Top Ten Award for Best Actor 1978–79, Br Broadcasting Press Guild TV Award for Best Actor 1978, Royal TV Soc Performance Award 1978–79), Gulliver's Travels 1995, Daniel Deronda 2002; *Film* incl: The Go-Between 1971 (Soc of Film and TV Arts Award for Best Supporting Actor, 1971), The Day of the Jackal 1973, A Doll's House 1973, Galileo 1976, The Squeeze 1977, A Bridge Too Far 1977 (BAFTA Award for Best Supporting Actor), The Duellists 1977, The Cat and the Canary 1977, Force Ten from Navarone 1978, The Mirror Crack'd 1980, Gandhi 1982, Never Say Never Again 1983, The Dresser 1983, The Bounty 1984, The Shooting Party 1985, A Month by the Lake 1996, Prince Valiant 1997, Nicholas Nickleby 2003; *Recreations* music, gardening; *Clubs* Savile; *Style—* Edward Fox, Esq, OBE

FOX, Emilia; da of Edward Fox, and Joanna David, *qqv*; *b* 1974; *Educ* Bryanston, Univ of Oxford (BA); *m* 2005 (m dis 2010), Jared Harris, s of Richard Harris (d 2002), the actor; partner, Jeremy Gilley; 1 da (Rose b Nov 2010); *Career* actress; *Theatre* The Cherry Orchard 1997, Katherine Howard 1998, Good (Donmar Warehouse) 1999, Richard II 2000, Coriolanus 2000, Les Liasons Dangereuses 2003; *Television* incl: Pride and Prejudice 1995, Bright Hair 1997, Rebecca 1997, The Round Tower 1998, The Scarlet Pimpernel 1998, Bad Blood 1998, Shooting the Past 1999, David Copperfield 1999, Bad Blood 1999, Other People's Children 2000, Randall & Hopkirk (Deceased) 2000, Helen of Troy 2002, Henry VIII 2003, Silent Witness VIII 2004, Silent Witness IX 2005, The Virgin Queen 2005, Miss Marple: The Moving Finger 2005, Silent Witness X 2006, Fallen Angel 2006, Born Equal 2006, Silent Witness XI 2007, Ballet Shoes 2007, The Game's Up 2008, Consuming Passions 2008, Silent Witness XII 2008, Silent Witness XIII 2009, Merlin 2009–11, Who Do You Think You Are 2010; *Films* The Pianist 2001, The Soul Keeper 2001, Three Blind Mice 2002, The Republic of Love 2002, The Life & Death of Peter Sellars 2003, Things to do Before You're 30 2003, The Tiger in the Snow 2004, Keeping Mum 2005, Cashback 2005, Honeymoon 2006, Flashbacks of a Fool 2007, Dorian Gray 2009, Way to Live Forever 2009, A Thousand Kisses Deep 2010, All For The Best 2011; Tric Award for Best Newcomer, Cult TV Best Actress Award, Best Actress in Italy; *Style—* Miss Emilia Fox

FOX, Gerald Marcus; s of Edwin Fox (d 2005), and Joscelyn, *née* Steele, of London; *b* 14 July 1963, Johannesburg; *Educ* Harrow, Harvard Coll (John Harvard scholarship, BA), Worcester Coll Oxford (OUDS, winner Oxford and Cambridge Photography Competitions); *Partner* Josephine Lindop; 2 da (Francesca b 1 Sept 2006, Chloe b 15 April 2010); *Career* broadcaster, prodr and dir; dir South Bank Show 1992–, drama dir Channel 4 and LWT 1992–98; series ed Cool Brittannia, Opening Shot, Fresh and Sampled; writer, prodr and dir: Johnny and the Dead (ITV) 1994 (Chicago Film Festival Golden Bear), Sitting Ducks 2003 (also actor), Mother's Milk 2011; dir: Children of the Guatemalan Dump (Best Film Adult and Children's Jury Chicago Children's Film Festival), The Fundamental Gilbert and George 1997 (Huw Wheldon Award BAFTA, RTS Best Arts Film Award 1998, Grand Prize Int Festival of Films on Art), This Is Not An Exit: The Fictional World of Bret Easton Ellis 2000; prodr and dir Leaving Home, Coming Home: A Portrait of Robert Frank 2005 (RTS Best Arts Film Award, Best Documentary in the Arts Grierson Award 2005, Int Festival of Films on Art Grand Prize 2005), Together We Can (RAI/FAO Special Award Prix Italia 2002); portrait of Cildo Mereilles for South Bank Show and Tate Gallery 2008, Venice in Venice exhibition Venice 2009; special film screenings of work Nat Gallery of Art, Washington DC and Met Museum of Art NY 2009; retrospective festival of films Nat Portrait Gallery London 2011, major career retrospective and Hommage Award Festival of Films on Art Montreal 2013; Angel Peace Award Monte Carlo Film Festival 2012, Inyathelo Award for Int Philanthropy to S Africa 2012; chm of charitable fndns in UK and SA; memb BAFTA 1996; *Solo Art Exhibitions* Living London (176 London) 2008 (Pick of the Week The Guardian and Time Out, Critics' Choice The Times), Concrete and Glass (London) 2008 (Time Out and Guardian Critics' Choice), Venice in Venice (Venice Biennale) 2009, Venetian Impressions (Eleven Fine Art London) 2010 (Critics' Choice FT and The Times), Nudes Moving (Eleven Fine Art London) 2012; *Recreations* tennis, photography, travel, cinema, dance, horse racing, music, skiing; *Clubs* Soho House, Groucho; *Style—* Gerald Fox, Esq; ✉ 60 Elgin Crescent, London W11 2JJ (☎ 020 7221 0117, e-mail geraldmfox@aol.com)

FOX, James; s of Maj Robin Fox, MC, Virtuti Militari (Poland), RA (d 1971), of Cuckfield, W Sussex, and Angela Muriel Darita, *née* Worthington (d 1999); bro of Edward Charles Morice Fox, OBE, *qv*, and Robert Michael John Fox, *qv*; *b* 19 May 1939; *Educ* Harrow; *m* 15 Sept 1973, Mary Elizabeth, da of Maj Allan Piper, of Wadhurst, E Sussex; 4 s (Thomas b 1975, Robin b 1976, Laurence b 1978, Jack b 1985), 1 da (Lydia b 1979); *Career* actor; *Television* incl: A Question of Attribution 1991, Headhunters 1993, The Choir (BBC) 1994, The Old Curiosity Shop (Disney Channel, Cable TV) 1994, Gullivers Travels (Channel 4) 1995, Elgar's 10th Muse (Channel 4) 1995, Metropolis 2000, The Lost World (BBC/AE TV) 2001, Suez 2007, Harley Street 2008, Merlin 2012; *Film* The Servant 1963, Those Magnificent Men in Their Flying Machines 1963, King Rat 1964, Thoroughly Modern Millie 1966, Isadora 1967, Performance 1969, Runners 1982, A Passage to India 1984, The Russia House 1990, Patriot Games 1992, The Remains of the Day 1993, Anna Karenina 1997, Jinnah 1998, Micky Blue Eyes 1998, Up At The Villa 1999, Sexy Beast 2000, The Golden Bowl 2000, The Mystic Masseur 2001, The Prince and Me 2004, Charlie and the Chocolate Factory 2005, Mr Lonely 2006, Sherlock Holmes 2009, WE 2010, Effie 2011, A Long Way From Home 2012; *Books* Comeback An Actor's Direction (1983); *Recreations* Russian language experience and culture; *Style—* James Fox, Esq; ✉ c/o Dalzell & Beresford Ltd, 26 Astwood Mews, London SW7 4DE

FOX, James George; s of George Romney Fox (d 1968), of Falmouth, Cornwall, and Barbara Muriel, *née* Twite (d 1994); *b* 14 May 1943; *Educ* Eton, Univ of Newcastle upon Tyne (BA), Univ of Pennsylvania (MBA); *m* 4 May 1974, Rebecca Jane, da of Charles Wright, of Canyon, Texas; 2 da (Rachel b 1975, Sarah b 1979), 2 s (Francis b 1977, Romney b 1981); *Career* dir: Hill Samuel Investment Management 1968–78, Falmouth Hotel plc 1981–92, Warburg Investment Management 1982–85; md: Deutsche Trust Managers 1985–2003, Deutsche Equity Income Trust plc 1991–2003, Anglo & Overseas Tst plc 1992–2003, Deutsche Latin American Companies Tst plc 1994–2004, JPMorgan American Investment Tst plc 2003–13, Miton Worldwide Growth Tst 2004–; *Recreations* sailing; *Clubs* Athenaeum; *Style—* James Fox; ✉ Trewardreva, Constantine, Falmouth, Cornwall (☎ 01326 340207); 57 Andrewes House, Barbican, London EC2 (☎ 020 7638 9103)

FOX, Jonathan Andrew; MBE (2013); *b* 30 May 1991, Plymouth, Devon; *Career* Paralympic swimmer; achievements incl: Silver medal men's 100m backstroke Paralympics Beijing 2008, two Silver (50m freestyle and 100m freestyle) and three Gold medals (400m freestyle, 100m backstroke and 4x100m freestyle relay) IPC European Championships 2009, Bronze medal 400m freestyle and Gold medal 100m backstroke IPC World Championships 2010, Gold medal 100m backstroke Paralympic World Cup 2010, two Bronze (4x100m freestyle relay and 4x100m medley relay), one Silver (50m freestyle) and three Gold medals (100m freestyle, 400m freestyle and 100m backstroke) IPC European Championships 2011, Gold medal 100m backstroke Paralympic Games 2012; *Style—* Jonathan Fox, Esq, MBE

FOX, Prof Keith A A; *b* 27 August 1949; *Educ* Univ of Edinburgh (BSc, MB ChB); *m* Aileen E M, *née* Paterson; 1 da (Natalie), 1 s (Alastair); *Career* asst prof in internal med (cardiology) Washington Univ Sch of Med St Louis 1983–85, sr lectr in cardiology and hon conslt cardiologist Univ of Wales Coll of Med Cardiff 1985–89, currently Duke of Edinburgh prof of cardiology Univ of Edinburgh (head Div of Med and Radiological Sciences 2000–10); int ed European Heart Jl; memb Editorial Bd: Heart, Coronary Artery Disease USA, Br Jl of Cardiology, Acute Coronary Syndromes; author of 585 peer reviewed scientific and medical pubns, mainly on the mechanisms and management of acute coronary artery disease; chair Clinical Prog Ctee European Soc of Cardiology 2012–; memb: Cncl on Basic Sci American Heart Assoc 1984, Cncl Br Heart Fndn 1997–2000, Bd European Soc of Cardiology 2008–10; memb Assoc of Physicians of GB and I 1991–; pres Br Cardiovascular Soc 2009–12, pres Action on Smoking and Health Scotland; Stelios Nicolaides Prize RCPEd, Silver Medal European Soc of Cardiology 2011, Mackenzie Medal Br Cardiovascular Soc 2013; FRCP 1987 (MRCP 1977), FESC 1988, FMedSci 2001, FRCPEd, FACC; *Recreations* hill walking, cycling; *Style—* Prof Keith A A Fox; ✉ Centre for Cardiovascular Science, Chancellor's Building, University of Edinburgh, 49 Little France Crescent, Edinburgh EH16 4SB

FOX, Kerry Lauren; da of Thomas Albert Fox, and Margaret Doris, *née* Poole; *Educ* Hutt Valley HS NZ, NZ Drama Sch Toi Whakaari; *Career* actress; *Theatre* Gothic But Staunch (The Depot), Jism (Bats Theatre), Bloody Poetry (Circa Theatre Wellington), Cosi (Belvoir St Theatre Sydney), The Maids (Donmar Warehouse), I Am Yours (Royal Court Theatre), In Flame (New Ambassadors Theatre), Cruel and Tender (Vienna Festival, The Young Vic); *Television* Mr Wroe's Virgins, A Village Affair, Saigon Baby, The Affair (nomination Best Actress Cable Ace Awards), Deja Vu, 40, The Murder Room, Nostradamus; *Film* incl: An Angel at My Table 1990 (Elvira Notari Award Venice Film Festival, Best Actress NZ Film Awards, Best Actress San Sebastian Film Festival), The Last Days of Chez Nous 1991, Friends 1993, The Last Tattoo 1994, Shallow Grave 1994 (Best Film Award for Acting Dinard Film Festival), Country Life 1994, The Hanging Garden 1997, Welcome to Sarajevo 1997, The Sound of One Hand Clapping 1998, Wisdom of Crocodiles 1998, To Walk With Lions 1999, The Darkest Light 1999, Fanny & Elvis 1999, Intimacy 2000 (Silver Bear for Best Actress Berlin Film Festival), The Point Men 2001, The Gathering 2002, Black and White 2002, So Close to Home 2003, Niceland 2004, Rag Tale 2005, Bright Star 2009; *Style—* Ms Kerry Fox; ✉ c/o ARG Management, 4 Great Portland Street, London W1W 8PA (☎ 020 7436 6400)

FOX, Prof Kim Michael; s of Lt-Col Michael Allen Fox (d 1980), of Edinburgh, and Veronica Venetia, *née* Sweeney (d 2015); *b* 17 June 1948; *Educ* Fort Augustus Abbey Sch, Univ of St Andrews (MB ChB, MD); *m* 11 March 1995, Karen, *née* Summers; 1 s (Michael James b 6 March 1978), 1 da (India Charis b 14 Nov 1998); *Career* conslt cardiologist at The Royal Brompton Hosp; prof of clinical cardiology and head Nat Heart and Lung Inst Imperial Coll; ed and author of textbooks in cardiology, ed Euro Heart Jl; FRCP 1988, fell Euro Soc of Cardiology (pres); *Books* Diseases of the Heart (ed, 1988, 2 edn 1996), Wolfe Atlases of Cardiology; *Style—* Prof Kim Fox; ✉ The Royal Brompton Hospital, Sydney Street, London SW3 6NP (☎ 020 7351 8626)

FOX, Rt Hon Dr Liam; PC (2010), MP; s of William Fox, and Catherine Fox; *b* 22 September 1961; *Educ* St Brides HS East Kilbride, Univ of Glasgow (MB ChB, MRCGP); *m* Dec 2005, Dr Jesme Baird; *Career* gen practitioner, also Army MO (civilian) RAEC and divnl surgn St John Ambulance; nat vice-chm Scottish YCs 1983–84, sabbatical as guest of US State Dept studying drug abuse and Republican campaigning techniques 1985; individual speaking prize World Debating Competition Toronto 1982, best speaker's trophy Univ of Glasgow 1983; Parly candidate (Cons) Roxburgh and Berwickshire 1987, MP (Cons) Woodspring 1992–; PPS to Rt Hon Michael Howard as Home Sec 1993–94, asst Govt whip 1994–95, Lord Cmmr HM Treasy (sr Govt whip) 1995–96, Parly under-sec of state FCO 1996–97; oppn front bench spokesman on constitutional affrs (Scotland) 1997–98, oppn frontbench spokesman on constitutional affrs 1998–99, shadow sec of state for Health 1999–2003, co-chm Cons Pty 2003, shadow foreign sec 2005, shadow defence sec 2005–10, sec of state for defence 2010–11, sec of state for int trade and pres Bd of Trade 2016–; memb Scottish Select Ctee 1992–93; sec Cons Backbench Health Ctee 1992–93, sec Cons West Country Members Ctee 1992–93, candidate Cons Pty leadership election 2005; *Style*— The Rt Hon Dr Liam Fox, MP; ✉ House of Commons, London SW1A 0AA (☎ 020 7219 4198)

FOX, Richard John; s of Dennis William Fox (d 1956), of Bristol, and Winifred Joan Fox (d 1998); *b* 23 December 1943; *Educ* Cotham GS, Bristol, Univ of Wales Cardiff (BSc(Econ)); *m* Sandra Wynne; 2 c (Mark Douglas b 1970, Helen Victoria b 1971); *Career* CA; Grace Darbyshire & Todd Bristol (now KPMG) 1965–71 (articled clerk 1965–68), Coopers & Lybrand London (now PricewaterhouseCoopers) 1971–78; ptnr: Mazars Neville Russell London 1978–87, KPMG 1987–93, The Learning Corporation 1993–; qualified facilitator and leadership coach; memb Int Coach Fedn; fndr and patron Guildford Business Forum; fndr memb Guildford Chamber Choir, memb St Saviour's Church Guildford; ACA 1968; *Publications* Creating a Purposeful Life; *Recreations* trekking, music especially choral, the countryside, reading; *Clubs* Glyndebourne, Royal Acad of Arts; *Style*— Richard J Fox, Esq; ✉ 35 Mountside, Guildford, Surrey GU2 4JD (e-mail richard@purposefullives.com, website www.purposefullives.com)

FOX, Prof Robert; s of Donald Fox (d 1972), and Audrey Hilda, *née* Ramsell (d 1993); *b* 7 October 1938; *Educ* Doncaster GS, Oriel Coll Oxford (MA, DPhil); *m* 20 May 1964, Catherine Mary Lilian, da of Dr Edmund Roper Power (d 1990); 3 da (Tessa b 1967, Emily b 1969, Hannah b 1972); *Career* asst master Tonbridge Sch 1961–63, Clifford Norton jr research fell The Queen's Coll Oxford 1965–66, prof of history of science Lancaster Univ 1987–88 (lectr 1966–72, sr lectr 1972–75, reader 1975–87), dir Centre de Recherche en Histoire des Sciences et des Techniques Cité des Sciences et de l'Industrie CNRS Paris 1986–88, asst dir Science Museum 1988, prof of history of science Univ of Oxford and fell Linacre Coll Oxford 1988–2006, hon fell Oriel Coll Oxford 2007; George Sarton Medal 2015, Alexandre Koyré Medal 2015; pres: Br Soc of the History of Science 1980–82, Int Union for the History and Philosophy of Science 1995–97 (first vice-pres Div of History of Science 1989–93, pres Div of History of Science 1993–97), European Soc for the History of Science 2003–06; FSA 1989; Chevalier dans l'Ordre des Palmes Académiques 1998, Chevalier dans l'Ordre des Arts et des Lettres 2006; *Books* The Caloric Theory of Gases from Lavoisier to Regnault (1971), Sadi Carnot. Réflexions sur la Puissance Motrice du Feu (1978, 1986, 1988 and 1992), The Organization of Science and Technology in France 1808–1914 (ed with G Weisz, 1980), The Culture of Science in France 1700–1900 (1992), Education, Technology and Industrial Performance in Europe 1850–1939 (ed with A Guagnini, 1993), Science, Industry and the Social Order in Post-Revolutionary France (1995), Technological Change (ed, 1996), Luxury Trades and Consumerism in Ancien Régime Paris (ed with A J Turner, 1998), Natural Dyestuffs and Industrial Culture in Europe, 1750–1880 (ed with A Nieto-Galan, 1999), Laboratories, Workshops and Sites (with A Guagnini, 2000), Thomas Harriot. An Elizabethan Man of Science (ed, 2000), Franco-British Interactions in Science since the Seventeenth Century (ed with B Joly, 2010), Thomas Harriot: Mathematics, Exploration and Natural Philosophy in Early Modern England (ed, 2012), The Savant and the State: Science and Cultural Politics in Nineteenth-Century France (2012), The Oxford Handbook of the History of Physics (ed, with J Z Buchwald, 2013); *Clubs* Athenaeum; *Style*— Prof Robert Fox, FSA; ✉ Museum of the History of Science, Broad Street, Oxford OX1 3AZ (☎ and fax 01865 512787, e-mail robert.fox@history.ox.ac.uk)

FOX, Robert Michael John; s of Maj Robin Fox, MC, Virtuti Militari (Poland), RA (d 1971), of Cuckfield, W Sussex, and Angela Muriel Darita (d 1999), *née* Worthington; bro of Edward Charles Morice Fox, OBE, *qv*, and James Fox, *qv*; *b* 25 March 1952; *Educ* Harrow; *m* 1, 26 Feb 1974 (m dis), Celestia, da of Henry Nathan Sporborg, CMG (d 1985); 2 da (Chloe Victoria b 24 May 1976, Louisa Mary b 18 July 1983), 1 s (Sam Henry b 24 June 1978); m 2, 16 Dec 1990 (m dis), Natasha Jane (actress Natasha Richardson, d 2009), da of Tony Richardson (d 1991) and Vanessa Redgrave, CBE, *qv*; m 3, 31 Jan 1996, Fiona, o da of late John Golfar; 1 s (Joseph Marlon Barnaby b 6 July 1995), 1 da (Molly Elizabeth b 24 January 1998); *Career* producer; actor When Did You Last See My Mother? (Royal Court) 1970, asst dir Royal Court Theatre 1971–73, PA to Michael White (Michael White Ltd) 1973–80, fndr Robert Fox Ltd 1980; *Theatre* prodns incl: Goose Pimples (Evening Standard Drama Desk Award for Best Comedy), Anyone for Denis?, exec prodr Another Country (Olivier Award for Best Play), Crystal Clear, The Seagull, Torch Song Trilogy, Interpreters, Orphans, J J Farr, Chess, Lettice & Lovage (Evening Standard Drama Desk Award for Best Comedy), Anything Goes, A Madhouse in Goa, Burn This, The Big Love, When She Danced, The Ride Down Mt Morgan, Vita and Virginia, Three Tall Women (Evening Standard Best Play Award), Skylight, Who's Afraid of Virgina Woolf , Master Class, Edward Albee's A Delicate Balance, Amy's View, Closer, The Judas Kiss, The Blue Room, The Boy From Oz (Australia), Little Malcolm and his Struggle Against the Eunuchs, The Lady in the Van, The Caretaker, The Breath of Life, Gypsy, The Boy From Oz, Salome: The Reading, The Pillowman, Hedda Gabler, The Vertical Hour, Frost/Nixon, The Lady from Dubuque, The Harder they Come, South Downs, The Audience, Stephen Ward, Fatal Attraction; *Television* Oscar's Orchestra (BBC TV childrens animation series), Working with Pinter; *Film* A Month by the Lake, Iris, The Hours, Closer, Notes on a Scandal; *Style*— Robert Fox, Esq; ✉ Robert Fox Ltd, 6 Beauchamp Place, London SW3 1NG (☎ 020 7584 6855, fax 020 7225 1638, e-mail robert@robertfoxltd.com)

FOX, Robert Trench (Robin); CBE (1993); s of Waldo Trench Fox (d 1954), of Penjerrick, Falmouth, Cornwall; *b* 1 January 1937; *Educ* Winchester, UC Oxford (MA); *m* 1962, Lindsay Garrett, da of Sir Donald Forsyth Anderson (d 1973); 2 da (Fenella Garrett (Mrs John Dernie) b 23 Oct 1964, Tamara Forsyth (Mrs Robert Onslow) b 24 June 1967), 2 s (Barclay Trench b 27 April 1971, Caspar Lloyd b 6 Oct 1972); *Career* dir Kleinwort Benson Ltd 1972–85, vice-chm Kleinwort Benson Group 1986–96, pres Kleinwort Benson Asia 1997–99; chm: Lombard Risk Conslts Ltd 2000–15, InvestUK 2014–; chm Export Guarantees Advsy Cncl 1992–98; *Recreations* shooting, walking, sailing; *Clubs* Brooks's; *Style*— Robin Fox, Esq, CBE; ✉ The Garden House, Cheriton, Alresford, Hampshire SO24 0QQ (☎ 01962 771230)

FOX, Ronald David (Ronnie); s of Walter Fox (d 1985), and Eva Fox (d 2010); *b* London; *Educ* Mercers Sch, City of London Sch, Lincoln Coll Oxford (MA); *m* 11 Feb 1973, Sonya; 1 da (Susan), 1 s (Michael); *Career* admitted slr 1972; ptnr Oppenheimers 1974–88, ptnr Denton Hall 1988–89, sr ptnr Fox Williams 1989–2005, princ Fox 2006–; slr of the Higher Cts; memb Int Bar Assoc 1984– (chm Practice Mgmnt Sub-Ctee 1995–98, chm Sr Lawyers Ctee 2008–10); fndr and hon memb Assoc of Partnership Practitioners; Law Soc: co-opted memb Completion Cheque Scheme Working Pty 1981–82, memb Standing Ctee on Co Law 1985–89, memb Cncl Membership Ctee 1990–97, memb Steering Ctee Law Mgmnt Section 1998–99, memb Employment Law Ctee 2001–04, memb Remuneration Ctee 2005–10, memb Communications Ctee 2014; City of London Law Soc City of London Slrs Co: memb Problems of Practice Sub-Ctee 1985–93, Working Pty (preparing evidence of City Slrs to Lady Marre's Ctee on the future of the legal profession) 1986, co-ordinator Survey on City Slrs' Attitudes to Multi-Disciplinary Practices 1987, memb Ctee 1988–2001; chm Working Pty (preparing the response of City Slrs to the Govt Green Paper on the Work and Organisation of the Legal Profession) 1989, memb Euro Employment Lawyers Assoc 1999–; numerous presentations to IBA ctees on the legal profession and management, rapporteur at NY, Hong Kong, Cannes and Barcelona IBA conferences; motoring corr City Solicitor (newsletter of the City of London Law Soc) 2006–16; nominated Star of the Year 2000 by Legal Business Magazine, Distinguished Serv award City of London Slrs' Co 1989, ranked leading partnership and employment lawyer in The Legal 500 and Chambers' Directory and by Super Lawyers; memb Appeal Bd Tank Museum 2008–10; Liveryman Worshipful Co of Slrs 1984 (memb Ct of Assts 1991, Jr Warden 1996, Sr Warden 1997, Master 1998); hon memb Assoc of Fells and Legal Scholars of the Centre for Int Legal Studies; *Books* Due Diligence, Disclosures and Warranties in Corporate Acquisition Practice – the United Kingdom (1988, 2 edn 1992), International Business Transactions-Service Agreements for Multinational Corporate Executives in the United Kingdom (1988), Payments on Termination of Employment (1981, 3 edn 1990), Legal Aspects of Doing Business in England & Wales (1984, 2 edn 1990), International Professional Practice – England and Wales (1992), Product Tampering in the United Kingdom (1993), Professional Secrecy in Europe – England and Wales (2013); also author of numerous articles on legal and management topics; *Recreations* opera, theatre, cinema, swimming, skin diving and scuba diving, motoring and other forms of transport, management studies, health benefits of chocolate, impact of The Archers on life; *Clubs* RAC (memb Pall Mall Ctee 2006–12, memb Bd 2012–), City of London; *Style*— R D Fox, Esq; ✉ Fox, 78 Cornhill, London EC3V 3QQ (☎ 020 7618 2400, fax 020 7618 2409, mobile 07836 238436, e-mail rdfox@foxlawyers.com, website www.foxlawyers.com, Skype foxlawyers)

FOX-ANDREWS, (Jonathen) Mark Piers; s of His Hon Judge James Roland Blake Fox-Andrews, QC (d 2002), and (Angela) Bridget, *née* Swift (d 1991); *b* 7 May 1952; *Educ* Eton, Trinity Hall Cambridge (MA); *m* 22 Sept 1984, Rosemary Anne, da of Dennis Jenks; 2 s (Maximillian George b 28 March 1987, Alfred James b 3 Dec 1993), 2 da (Florence Rose b 14 July 1989, Constance Augusta b 26 Jan 1992); *Career* Drexel Burnham Lambert: trader 1977–80, mangr Singapore Office 1980–83, mangr Sydney Office 1984, md (Futures Ltd) London Office 1984–90; Sabre Fund Mgmnt Ltd 1990–93; md: Mees Pierson Derivatives Ltd 1993–97, ADM Investor Services Int Ltd 1998–2013; *Books* Futures Fund Management (1991), Derivatives Markets and Investment Management (1995); *Clubs* Garrick, Hurlingham; *Style*— Mark Fox-Andrews, Esq; ✉ 20 Cheyne Gardens, London SW3 5QT (☎ 07768 155105, e-mail mfamanagement@outlook.com)

FOXALL, Colin; CBE (1995); s of Alfred George Foxall, of Chatham, Kent, and Ethel Margaret, *née* Hall; *b* 6 February 1947; *Educ* Gillingham GS; *m* 28 Sept 2013, Helen Patricia Kaye; 2 s from a previous relationship (Ian b 1981, Neil b 1984); *Career* Dept of Trade 1974–75; NCM Credit Insurance Ltd (formerly ECGD until privatisation 1991): joined 1966, asst sec 1982–86, gp dir/under sec of insurance servs 1986–91, chief exec and md 1991–97; chief exec and md NCM Holdings (UK) Ltd, vice-chm Managing Bd NCM NV 1996–97, reinsurance and mgmnt conslt 1998–, dir Radian Asset Assurance Ltd 2003–08; chm Rail Passenger Ctee Wales 2004–05, memb Br Tport Authy 2005–13, chm Passenger Focus 2005–15; advsr Benfield Gp 2007–10, advsr First Gp 2015–; MIEx, FICM; *Recreations* farming, cycling, walking; *Style*— Colin Foxall, CBE; ✉ 3 Fayre Gardens, Fairford GL7 4NU

FOXALL, Prof Gordon Robert; s of Gordon William Foxall (d 1978), of Birmingham, and Marion, *née* Radford; *b* 16 July 1949, West Bromwich; *Educ* Holly Lodge Sch, Univ of Salford (BSc, MSc), Univ of Birmingham (PhD, DSocSc), Univ of Strathclyde (PhD), Open Univ (MSc); *m* 26 June 1971, Jean, da of William Morris, of Birmingham; 1 da (Helen b 1977); *Career* Univ of Newcastle upon Tyne 1972–79, Univ of Birmingham 1980–83, reader Cranfield Inst of Technol 1983–86; prof Univ of Strathclyde 1987–90, prof Univ of Birmingham 1990–97, distinguished research prof Univ of Wales Cardiff 1997–98, prof of consumer behaviour and hon prof of psychology Keele Univ 1998–2001, distinguished research prof Univ of Cardiff 2002–; Maynard Phelps distinguished lectr Univ of Michigan 1988–91, sabbatical visitor Balliol Coll Oxford 1993–94, Winegard visiting prof Univ of Guelph Ontario 1994, visiting prof Univ of S Aust 1994, visiting prof of economic psychology Univ of Durham 2008–, visiting prof The Marketing Sch Univ of S Australia Adelaide 2015–16; FBPsS 1996, CPsychol 1988, fell Br Acad of Mgmnt, FAcSS; *Books* Consumer Behaviour (1980), Marketing Behaviour (1981), Strategic Marketing Management (1981), Consumer Choice (1983), Corporate Innovation (1984), Marketing in the Service Industries (1986), Consumer Behaviour in Theory and in Practice (1986), Consumer Psychology (1990), Consumer Psychology for Marketing (1994), Consumers in Context (1996), Marketing Psychology (1997), Consumer Behaviour Analysis (2002), Context and Cognition (2004), Understanding Consumer Choice (2005), Explaining Consumer Choice (2007), Behavioral Economics of Brand Choice (2007), Interpreting Consumer Choice (2010), The Marketing Firm: Economic Psychology of Corporate Behaviour (with Kevin Vella, 2011), Handbook of Developments in Consumer Behaviour (with Victoria Wells, 2012), The Routledge Companion to Consumer Behavior Analysis (2015), Addiction as Consumer Choice: Exploring the Cognitive Dimension (2016); *Recreations* reading, walking, writing, seeking more extravert recreations; *Clubs* Reform; *Style*— Prof Gordon Foxall; ✉ Consumer Behaviour Analysis Research Gp, Cardiff University, Aberconway Building, Colum Drive, Cardiff CF10 3EU (e-mail foxall@cf.ac.uk, website www.business.cardiff.ac.uk/contact/staff/foxall and www.dur.ac.uk/dbs/about/contact_us/staff-alpha/?id=6232)

FOY, John Leonard; QC (1998); s of late Leonard James Foy, and late Edith Mary, *née* Hanks, of Bucks; *b* 1 June 1946; *Educ* Dartford GS, Univ of Birmingham (LLB); *m* 1972, Colleen Patricia, *née* Austin (d 2006); 1 s (Daniel James b 25 May 1988); *Career* called to the Bar Gray's Inn 1969 (bencher 2004); recorder 2000, judge Mental Health Restricted Cases Panel; memb: Personal Injuries Bar Assoc, Professional Negligence Bar Assoc; *Recreations* sports, especially football, rugby and horse racing; *Style*— John Foy, Esq, QC; ✉ 9 Gough Square, London EC4A 3DG (☎ 020 7832 0500, fax 020 7353 1344)

FOYLE, (William Richard) Christopher; DL (Essex 2007); s of (William) Richard Foyle (d 1957), and Alice (later Mrs Harrap, d 1998), da of Eugen Kun, of Vienna; the Foyles are an ancient W Country family (*see* Burke's Landed Gentry, 18 Edn, vol 3); *b* 20 January 1943, London; *Educ* Radley; *m* 27 July 1983, Catherine Mary, da of Rev David William Forrester Jelleyman, of Melbourn, Cambs; 1 s (Alexander b 1968), 3 da (Charlotte b 1984, Annabel b 1985, Christine b 1987); *Career* trained in publishing and bookselling in London, Tuebingen, Berlin, Helsinki and Paris; mangr W & G Foyle Ltd 1965–72, ptnr Emson & Dudley and dir Emson & Dudley Securities Ltd 1972–78, prop Christopher Foyle Aviation (Leasing) Co 1977–2003; chm: Air Foyle Ltd 1978–2000, Air Foyle Executive Ltd 1988–2005, Charters Ltd 1994–2002, Air Foyle Passenger Airlines Ltd 1994–, Air Foyle Holding Co Ltd 1996–, Br Cargo Airline Alliance 1998–2007, CityJet 1999–2000, W&G Foyle Ltd Booksellers 1999–, Noved Investment Co 2000–, Air Foyle

Heavylift Ltd 2001–08; non-exec dir Air Charter Service plc 2007–12; tstee and memb Bd International Air Cargo Assoc 1992– (pres, ceo and chm of Bd 1997–99), vice-pres Guild of Aviation Artists, chm The Air League 2006–08 (dep pres 2008–), pres Air League of Monaco 2013–; tstee Foyle Fndn 2006–08, patron Book Trade Benevolent Soc; pres Maldon Golf Club 2000–08; IFW special achievement award 1997, inducted in TIACA Air Cargo Hall of Fame 2007, RICS East of England Historical Building Conservation Award 2008 (for Beeleigh Abbey), RICS Nat Award for Best Conserved and Restored Historical Building in UK 2008 (for Beeleigh Abbey); Freeman City of London, Liveryman Guild of Air Pilots and Air Navigators; Lord of the Manors of Beeleigh, Great Bromley, Martells Hall, Great Holland and Fordham Hall; FRAeS 1997, FCILT 1998, FRGS 2000, fell Aspen Inst, FRHS; Chevalier de la Confrérie des Chevaliers du Tastevin 2008; *Books* Foyles: A Celebration (jtly, 2003), Foyle's Philavery (2007), Foyle's Further Philavery (2008), Pioneers to Partners: A Photographic History of British Aircraft from 1945 (jtly, 2009), Beeleigh Abbey – A History and Guide (2012); *Recreations* travel, flying, reading non-fiction; *Clubs* White's, Royal Air Squadron, Annabel's, Garrick, Soc of Bookmen, Soc of Authors, Essex, Monte Carlo, Yacht Club of Monaco, Automobile Club of Monaco, Caribou (Aspen), CREM (Monaco), BAM (Monaco), Churchill (Monaco); *Style—* Christopher Foyle, Esq, DL; ✉ Tolhurst Fisher, Marlborough House, Victoria Road South, Chelmsford, Essex CM1 1LN

FOYLE, John Lewis; s of Roland Bernard Foyle (d 1996), of Portsmouth, Hants, and Rose Vera, *née* Taylor; *b* 7 June 1948; *Educ* Portsmouth Northern GS, St John's Coll Cambridge (MA); *m* 19 Feb 1972, Patricia Mary, da of John Victor Ketteringham (d 1986), of Ruthin, Clwyd; 3 s (James b 1972, Thomas d 1978, William b 1980); *Career* sec: Inflation Accounting Steering Gp 1976–78, Jt Exchanges Ctee 1982–96, ECOFEX 1988–96; dep chief exec London Int Fin Futures Exchange 1981–, dir Assoc of Futures Brokers and Dealers 1985–91; FCA 1973; *Recreations* sport, music; *Style—* John Foyle, Esq; ✉ Brookmead, Moat Farm Chase, Chipping Hill, Witham, Essex CM8 2DE; LIFFE, Cannon Bridge House, 1 Cousin Lane, London EC4R 3XX (☎ 020 7623 0444, fax 020 7588 3624)

FRACKOWIAK, Prof Richard Stanislaus Joseph; s of Capt Joseph Frackowiak, of London, and Wanda, *née* Majewska; *b* 26 March 1950, Kensington, London; *Educ* Latymer Upper Sch, Peterhouse Cambridge (MB BChir, MA, MD), UCL (DSc); *m* 1, 19 Feb 1972 (m dis 2002), Christine Jeanne Françoise, da of Louis Thepot, of St Cloud, France; 1 s (Matthew), 2 da (Stephanie, Annabelle); m 2, 11 Dec 2004, Laura Frances, da of Neville Spinney, of Orford, Suffolk; *Career* sr lectr and hon conslt Hammersmith Hosp and Nat Hosp for Neurology and Neurosurgery 1984–94, asst dir MRC Cyclotron Unit 1988–94, prof of clinical neurology Univ of London 1991–94; dean Inst of Neurology 1998–2003, prof and head Wellcome Dept of Cognitive Neurology, dir Leopold Muller Functional Imaging Lab 1994–2003, Wellcome Tst princ clinical research fell 1994–2004, dir Dept d'Etudes Cognitives Ecole Normale Supereure Paris 2004–09 (currently permanent visitor), chef de déparement des neurosciences cliniques et médecin chef de service de neurologie 2009–15, professeur ordinaire ad hominem Université de Lausanne et Centre Hospitalier Universitaire Vaudois Switzerland, adjunct prof École Politechnique Fédérale de Lausanne Switzerland; formerly scientific advsr to DG Institut National de la Santé et de la Recherche Médicale (INSERM) France 2004–14; adjunct prof of neurology Cornell Univ Med Sch 1992–; Sackler visiting prof Cornell Med Sch 1994, visiting prof Université Catholique de Louvain 1996–97, Geschwind visiting prof Harvard Med Sch 1999, Rogowski visiting prof Yale Med Sch 2001, hon prof Inst of Neurology UCL; chair Medical Science Ctee Science Europe 2012–15; co-dir (medical) Human Brain Project 2013–16; memb: Health and Medical Div American Acads of Science, Academia Europaea, Belgian Neurological Soc, Académie Royale de Medecine Belge, Canadian Neurological Soc; foreign associate Academie Nationale de Medecine, hon foreign memb Société Française de Neurologie, hon memb American Neurological Assoc, foreign assoc Polish Acad of Science; numerous named lectureships on the subject of functional neuro imaging; Hon Dr Univ of Liège 1999; Ipsen Prize 1997, Wilhelm Feldberg Prize 1996, Klaus Joachim Prize 2004; FRCP 1987, FMedSci 1998 (former memb Cncl); *Publications* Human Brain Function (2 edn, 2003); over 400 peer-reviewed articles in scientific jls; *Recreations* motorcycling, travel; *Clubs* Athenaeum; *Style—* Prof Richard Frackowiak

FRADD, Dr Simon Oakley; s of Frederick Ronald Fradd, of Otford, Kent, and Beryl Grace, *née* Milledge; *b* 20 April 1950; *Educ* Sevenoaks Sch, W Kent Coll Tunbridge Wells, KCL (BSc), Westminster Med Sch London; *m* 1 May 1976 (m dis), Elizabeth Harriett, da of Norman Allen Birtwhistle; *Career* house surgn Westminster Med Sch 1977; SHO: in paediatrics Queen Mary's Roehampton 1978, in neonatology Whittington Hosp London 1979, in A/E then orthopaedics St George's Tooting 1980–81; registrar: in surgery Burton Gen Hosp Burton-on-Trent 1981–84, in urology Univ Hosp of Wales Cardiff 1984–85; GP trainee: Burton-on-Trent 1985–86, under Dr Saunders Nottingham 1986–87, Castle Donington Leics 1987; GP princ Saunders & Fradd Nottingham 1988–; chm: Hosp Doctors' Assoc 1979–82, Negotiators' Hosp Jr Staff Ctee 1986–87 (dep chm 1984–86), Jr Membs' Forum BMA 1990, Doctor Patient Partnership 1997–; dep chm Gen Practitioners Ctee of BMA 1997–; memb Med Practices Ctee 1989–93, Gen Med Servs Ctee negotiator 1993–; memb GMC 1989–; Freeman City of London 1976, Liveryman Worshipful Co of Needlemakers 1976, Liveryman Worshipful Soc of Apothecaries 1993; Hon FAMGP 1998, Hon MRCGP 2000, FRCS; *Books* Hospital Doctors' Association Guide to Your Rights (jtly, 1981), Making Sense of Partnerships (jtly, 1994), Nottingham Non-Fundholder Project, Members Reference Book RCGP (1995); *Recreations* DIY, gardening, skiing, gliding; *Style—* Dr Simon Fradd; ✉ 67 New Concordia Wharf, Mill Street, London SE7 2BB; Greenwood and Sneinton Family Medical Centre, 249 Sneinton Dale, Sneinton, Nottingham NG3 7DQ (☎ 0115 948 4999, mobile 078 6069 3315)

FRAME, Frank Riddell; *b* 15 February 1930; *Educ* Univ of Glasgow (MA, LLB); *m* 1958, Maureen Milligan; 1 s, 1 da; *Career* admitted slr 1954; North of Scotland Hydro-Electric Board 1955–60, UK Atomic Energy Authy 1960–68, The Weir Group plc 1968–76 (dir 1971–76); The Hongkong and Shanghai Banking Corporation: joined as gp legal advsr 1977, exec dir 1985, dep chm 1986–90; advsr to Bd HSBC Holdings plc 1990–98; dir Northumbrian Water Gp Ltd 2012–; former chm: South China Morning Post Ltd, Far Eastern Economic Review Ltd, Wallem Gp Ltd; former dir: Marine Midland Banks Inc, Swire Pacific Ltd, The British Bank of the Middle East, Consolidated Press International Ltd, Securities and Futures Commission Hong Kong, Baxter International Inc, Edinburgh Dragon Tst plc, Northern Gas Networks Ltd; Hon DUniv Glasgow 2001; *Publication* The Law relating to Nuclear Energy (with Prof Harry Street); *Clubs* Brooks's; *Style—* Frank Frame, Esq; ✉ The Old Rectory, Bepton, Midhurst, West Sussex GU29 0HX

FRAME, Roger Campbell Crosbie; s of late Andrew Crosbie Frame, of Giffnock, Glasgow, and late Jessie Caldwell, *née* Campbell; *b* 7 June 1949; *Educ* Glasgow Acad; *m* 10 Sept 1973, Angela Maria, da of late Louis Evaristi, of Giffnock, Glasgow; 2 s (Nicholas Roger b 1976, Mark Christopher b 1980), 1 da (Lorenza Charlotte b 1988); *Career* chartered accountant; dir: Camos Ltd, Frame & Co Management Services Ltd; treas Glasgow Gp of Artists 1983–89; sec: Royal Scottish Soc of Painters in Watercolour (RSW) 1986–99 (currently hon memb, hon fell 1999), Glasgow Eastern Merchants and Tradesman Soc (ret 1999); chm: Int Sch of Florence 2004–08 (dir and govr 2003–08), American Schools Abroad Inc 2004–08; chm James Cusator Wards Fund (Univ of Glasgow) 1984–99, deacon Incorporation of Coopers of Glasgow 1985–86, offr Incorporation of Weavers of Glasgow (ret 1999); Freeman: City of Glasgow, City of London; fell Univ of Glasgow 1999; *Recreations* clay pigeon shooting, art; *Style—* Roger C C Frame, Esq; ✉ Dunglass, 56 Manse Road, Bearsden, Glasgow G61 3PN

FRAME, Ronald William Sutherland; s of late Alexander Frame, and late Isobel, *née* Sutherland; *b* 23 May 1953, Glasgow; *Educ* The HS of Glasgow, Univ of Glasgow (Foulis scholarship, MA, Bradley Medal), Jesus Coll Oxford (BLitt); *Career* writer 1981–; prose fiction, radio and television plays; *Awards* jt winner Betty Trask Prize 1984, Samuel Beckett Prize 1986, TV Industries Panel Most Promising Writer New to TV 1986, Saltire Prize Scottish Book of the Year 2000, Barbara Gittings Honor Award American Library Assoc 2003; *Television Scripts* Paris (1985), Out of Time (1987), Ghost City (1994), A Modern Man (1996), 4 Ghost Stories for Christmas (2000), Darien: Disaster in Paradise (2003), Cromwell (2003), The Two Loves of Anthony Trollope (contrib, 2004); *Radio Scripts* incl: The Lantern Bearers (1997), The Hydro (1997, second series 1998, third series 1999), Havisham (1998), Maestro (1999), Pharos (2000), Sunday at Sant' Agata (2001), Don't Look Now (adapted, 2001), Greyfriars Bobby (2002), The Servant (adapted, 2005), The Razor's Edge (adapted, 2005), A Tiger for Malgudi (adapted, 2006), The Blue Room (adapted, 2007), The Shell House (2008), Blue Wonder (2008), Monsieur Monde Vanishes (adapted, 2009), Pinkerton (2010), Sunday (adapted, 2010), Striptease (adapted, 2010), The Other Simenon 1, In Case of Emergency, The Cat, The Little Man from Archangel (all adaptations, 2011), The Other Simenon 2: Teddy Bear, The Neighbours, The Venice Train (all adaptations, 2012), The Dreamer (2012), Before the Fact (adapted, 2013), The Other Simenon 3, Three Beds in Manhattan, The Confessional, A New Lease of Life (all adaptations, 2014); *Novels and Short Story Collections* Winter Journey (1984, 3 Sony Radio Award nominations 1985), Watching Mrs Gordon (1985), A Long Weekend with Marcel Proust (1986), Sandmouth People (1987), A Woman of Judah (1987), Paris: A Television Play (1987), Penelope's Hat (1989), Bluette (1990), Underwood and After (1991), Walking My Mistress in Deauville (1992), The Sun on the Wall (1994), The Lantern Bearers (1999), Permanent Violet (2002), Time in Carnbeg (2004), Unwritten Secrets (2010), Havisham (2012); weekly Carnbeg short story in The Herald 2008 and The Scotsman 2008–09, regular contrib Scottish Review of Books Sunday Herald; *Recreations* walking in the wind, eavesdropping; *Style—* Ronald Frame, Esq; ✉ website www.carnbeg.com; c/o Faber & Faber Ltd, Bloomsbury House, 74–77 Great Russell Street, London WC1B 3DA (☎ 020 7927 3800, fax 020 7927 3801, e-mail qapublicity@faber.co.uk); c/o Laura Macdougall, Tibor Jones and Associates, 2–6 Atlantic Road, London SW9 8HY (☎ 020 7733 0555, e-mail laura@tiborjones.com)

FRAMLINGHAM, Baron (Life Peer UK 2011), of Eye in the County of Suffolk; Sir Michael Nicholson Lord; kt (2001); s of John Lord, and Jessie, *née* Nicholson; *b* 17 October 1938; *Educ* Christ's Coll Cambridge (MA); *m* 1965, Jennifer Margaret, *née* Childs; 1 s, 1 da; *Career* formerly farmer, aboricultural conslt; Parly candidate Manchester Gorton 1979; MP (Cons): Suffolk Central 1983–97, Suffolk Central and Ipswich N 1997–2010; PPS to Rt Hon John MacGregor as Min of Agric, Fisheries and Food 1984–85 and as Chief Sec to the Treasy 1985–87; dep speaker 2001–10; Parly delg to Cncl of Europe and WEU 1987–91; memb Select Ctee on Agric 1983–84, memb Select Ctee for the Parly Cmmr for Admin (Ombudsman), 2 dep chm Ways & Means and dep speaker 1997–2010; cncllr: N Beds BC 1974–77, Beds CC 1981–83; pres Arboricultural Assoc 1989–95; *Recreations* golf, sailing, trees; *Style—* The Lord Framlingham; ✉ House of Lords, London SW1A 0PW

FRAMPTON, Ronald Arthur (Ron); s of Arthur John Frampton (d 1991), of Axminster, Devon, and Dorothy May, *née* Churchill (d 1995); *b* 19 October 1940; *Educ* Axe Valley Sch, Exeter Coll; *m* 30 Dec 1970, Marianne Stiegler; 1 da (Stefanie Daniela b 13 April 1972), 1 s (Magnus John b 7 Sept 1975); *Career* photographer, photographic conslt and lectr specialising in portraiture, architecture, landscape and documentary photography, acknowledged expert in fine monochrome printing; lectr in applied photography: St Clare's Coll (AEC) Devon 1992–2003, Somerset Coll of Arts and Technol 1985–; visiting lectr and tutor 1986– incl: Dillington House Coll 1995–, Urchfont Manor Coll 1992–94, Symondsbury Coll Dorset 1988–95, RPS 1993–, Univ of Bath 1995–99; reg conslt: CGLI, BIPP, RPS; dep chm Applied and Professional Adjudicating Panel (Associateship and Fellowship) RPS 1999–; elected memb Section 7 Admissions and Qualifications Bd BIPP 1993–, elected memb Applied Distinctions Adjudicating Panel (Associateship and Fellowship) RPS 1994; BIPP Peter Grugeon Meml Award for Best Fellowship Portfolio 1991, Fenton Medal RPS (hon memb); ARPS, FBIPP, FRPS 1991, FMPA 1996; *Publications* exhbn catalogues incl: Fifty Photographers (1996), Beyond the Hills (1999), A Sense of Place (2000); books: Shadows In Time – Images from the West Country (2002), Beyond the Vale – Images from the West Country (2004); RPS pubns: Gaining the RPS Associateship and Fellowship in Applied Photography, Gaining the RPS Licentiateship, The Wide Field of Applied Photography, Assessment Criteria: RPS – Associateship and Fellowship in Applied Photography; contrib: The Photographer, RPS Jl; *Recreations* landscape, ecology, ecclesiastical architecture, social history, environment and natural history; *Style—* Ron Frampton, Esq; ✉ Rose Cottage, Valley Lane, Churchill, Axminster, Devon EX13 7LZ (☎ and fax 01297 33428)

FRANCE, Elizabeth Irene; CBE (2002); da of Ralph Salem, of Leicester, and Elizabeth Joan, *née* Bryan; *b* 1 February 1950; *Educ* Kibworth Beauchamp GS, UCW Aberystwyth (BSc Econ); *m* 24 July 1971, Dr Michael William France, s of Bert France (d 1976); 2 s, 1 da; *Career* Home Office: admin trainee 1971–77, princ (grade 7) 1977–86, grade 5 1986–94; Data Protection Registrar/Info Cmmr 1994–2002, chief ombudsman tOSl 2002–09, chair Office for Legal Complaints 2009–14, chair Security Industry Authy 2014–; memb Cmmn for the Control of Interpol Files 1998–2005, memb Br Transport Police Authy 2010–, memb Ofgem Enforcement Decision Panel 2014–, chair Police Advsy Bd for England and Wales 2014–, dep chair Regulatory Decisions Ctees FCA and PSR 2015–; memb Aarhus Convention Compliance Ctee 2002–05; non-exec dir Serious Organised Crime Agency 2005–10; memb Ct Univ of Manchester 2002–16, memb Cncl Univ of Wales Aberystwyth 2005–08, vice-pres Aberystwyth Univ 2008– (currently pro chllr); DSc (hc) De Montfort Univ 1996, Hon DLitt Loughborough Univ 2000, Hon DLaws Univ of Bradford 2002; fell Univ of Wales Aberystwyth 2003; FRSA, FICM; *Style—* Mrs Elizabeth France, CBE; ✉ Security Industry Authority (☎ 020 7025 4114, website www.sia.homeoffice.gov.uk)

FRANCE, Roger; s of late Harry Edmund France, and Ellen May, *née* Dark; *b* 7 January 1938; *Educ* Bedford Sch, Linacre Coll Oxford (MSc), Univ of York (scholar, MA), Imperial Coll London (scholar, DIC), Architectural Assoc (exhibitioner, AADipl), Poly of Central London (DipTP), CertTheol; *m* 1968, Dr Venetia Margaret King (d 2007); *Career* architect and town planner; architectural asst: Schs Div Middx CC 1961–62, Maguire and Murray 1962–63; asst architect Research Gp Town Devpt Div GLC 1963–65 (Housing Design Award Miny of Housing and Local Govt 1964, Civic Trust Design Award 1965), princ planning offr London Borough of Southwark (ldr Special Areas Gp) 1966–70, princ Roger France & Associates 1968–82; sr lectr in town planning N London Poly 1970–75, sr lectr in Urban Conservation and Renewal Oxford Poly 1975–92 (Oxford Brookes Univ 1992–94), visiting lectr Dept of Land Economy Univ of Cambridge 1991–92, visiting scholar Univ of Cambridge Inst of Educn 1993–94, visiting lectr Dept of Town and Regnl Planning Univ of Sheffield 1996–98, visiting scholar Dept of Geography Univ of Cambridge 1999–2000, Dept of Architecture and Civil Engineering Univ of Bath 2000–03; official lectr Civic Tst 1986–90; Register of Expert Witnesses 1995, specialist assessor and memb Visiting Panel Welsh Funding Cncl 1995–96, specialist advsr Design and Historic Environmental Panel RTPI 1996–98; advsr Bldgs Ctee Victorian Soc 1972–86,

F

chm annual conservation offrs' confs Univ of Oxford 1975–85, sec Inst of Religion and Medicine Oxford 1982–86, appointments advsr Oxford Diocesan Advsy Ctee 1982–87, tstee Oxford Preservation Tst 1982–90, memb Assoc for Study of Conservation of Historic Bldgs 1982–93; caseworker Cncl for Br Archaeology 1982–86, ind memb BSI Ctee B/209–7 for BS 7913:1998 1986–97, memb Educn Ctee Int Cncl of Monuments and Sites 1990–2006, examiner and dir of educn and trg IHBC(E) 2014–; fndr memb Assoc for Small Historic Towns and Villages 1989– (tstee 1991–98, hon memb 1998); fndr memb, convenor and chm Conservation Course Dirs' Forum 1991–2008; memb Soc for the Protection of Ancient Buildings and Georgian Gp; chm King St Neighbourhood Assoc Cambridge 1996–; hon memb: Assoc of Conservation Offrs 1984, Nat Tst for Historic Preservation of America 1985; memb Green Coll Oxford 1986; Freeman City of London 1994, Liveryman Worshipful Co of Chartered Architects 1994 (Master of Students 1995–2006, Master 2009–10), memb Coll of Readers 2000, licensed Reader Church of England (Gt St Mary's Cambridge 2003, Sidney Sussex Coll Cambridge 2003–08 and Queens' Coll Cambridge 2012–, chaplain Worshipful Co of Educators 2007–14), Liveryman Worshipful Co of Educators 2013 (fndr Ct memb Guild of Educators 2001); ARIBA 1964 (memb RIBA Visiting Panel 2004–05), MRTPI 1974, FRGS 1989, IHBC 1998, ILTM 2002, FHEA 2007, FRSA 2008; Commander Order of St Lazarus 2013; *Publications* Chester: a Study in Conservation (contrib, 1969), Look Before You Change (1985), Marston, a Case for Conservation (1988), Methods of Environmental Impact Assessment (contrib, 1995), Darwin College: A Portrait (contrib, 2013); numerous reviews and articles for pubns incl: RTPI Jl, The Planner, ASCHB Transactions, Heritage Outlook, Context; *Recreations* music, antiques – furniture and friends; *Clubs* Hawks', Cambridge; *Style*— Roger France, Esq; ✉ 32 Manor Place, Cambridge CB1 1LE (☎ 01223 358236)

FRANCE-HAYHURST, Jeannie; da of William Smith (d 1950), of Banffshire, and Mair, *née* Davies (d 1979); *b* 20 January 1950; *Educ* Towyn GS, Univ of Wales, Inns of Court Sch of Law; *m* 1, 1978 Anthony Jamieson; 1 s (Charles b 1979); *m* 2, James France-Hayhurst, s of late Robert France Hayhurst; 2 da (Lucinda b 1984, Serena b 1986); *Career* called to the Bar Gray's Inn 1972, pupillage and practice 1974–78, lectr in law 1972–78, slr 1980–86, recalled to the Bar 1987, recommenced practice (Northern Circuit) 1992; memb Ctee Family Law Bar Assoc; vice-chm Eddisbury Conc Constituency Assoc, Parly candidate (Cons) Montgomery 1992, cncllr (Cons) Cheshire CC 2000–01; chair Women's Enterprise Network 1989–90, vice-chair Chester Cathedral Devpt Tst; *Recreations* family, friends, the countryside, music, antiques; *Style*— Ms Jeannie France-Hayhurst; ✉ 1 Stanley Place Chambers, 1 Stanley Place, Chester CH1 2LU

FRANCIS, Andrew James; s of Frank Sidney Francis, DFC (d 1971), of Ashtead, Surrey, and Ann, *née* Velody (d 1994); *b* 1 November 1953; *Educ* City of London Freeman's Sch, Keble Coll Oxford (MA); *m* 18 Dec 1982, Victoria Louise, da of Francis Henry Gillum-Webb (d 1972), of Weybridge, Surrey; 1 s (Hugo), 3 da (Amelia, Alexandra, Charlotte (twin with Hugo)); *Career* called to the Bar Lincoln's Inn 1977 (bencher 2009); in practice at Chancery Bar 1979–; *Books* Restrictive Covenants and Freehold Land – A Practitioner's Guide, Rights of Light – The Modern Law (co-author), Private Rights of Way (co-author), Inheritance Act Claims – Law Practice and Procedure, Contentious Probate Claims (co-author); *Style*— Andrew Francis, Esq; ✉ Serle Court, 6 New Square, Lincoln's Inn, London WC2A 3QS (☎ 020 7242 6105, fax 020 7405 4004, e-mail afrancis@serlecourt.co.uk)

FRANCIS, Barney; s of Tony Francis, and Jane Francis; *b* 23 June 1971, Leicester; *Educ* Univ of Liverpool (BA); *m* 16 Dec 2000, Amy; 2 s (Freddie, George); *Career* Granada TV 1993–96, Sky TV 1996–98, BBC 1998–99, Sky Sports 1999– (md 2009–); *Style*— Barney Francis, Esq; ✉ British Sky Broadcasting Ltd, 6 Centaurs Business Park, Grant Way, Isleworth, Middlesex TW7 5QD

FRANCIS, Clare Mary; MBE (1978); da of Owen Francis, CB, and Joan St Leger, *née* Norman; *b* 17 April 1946; *Educ* Royal Ballet Sch, UCL (BSc Econ); *m* 1977 (m dis 1985), Jacques Robert Redon; 1 s (Thomas Robert Jean b 1978); *Career* writer; transatlantic singlehanded crossing 1973, first woman home Observer Singlehanded Transatlantic Race and holder women's record 1976, first woman skipper Whitbread Round The World Race 1977–78; chm Soc of Authors 1997–99, chm PLR advsy ctee 2000–03; fell UCL 1979, hon fell UMIST 1981; *Books* non-fiction: Come Hell or High Water (1977), Come Wind or Weather (1978), The Commanding Sea (1981); fiction: Night Sky (1983), Red Crystal (1985), Wolf Winter (1987), Requiem (1991), Deceit (1993), Betrayal (1995), A Dark Devotion (1997), Keep me Close (1999), A Death Divided (2001), Homeland (2004), Unforgotten (2008); *Recreations* opera, theatre; *Style*— Ms Clare Francis, MBE

FRANCIS, Clive; s of Raymond Francis (d 1987), of Brighton, E Sussex, and Margaret, *née* Towner; *b* 26 June 1946; *Educ* Ratton Secdy Modern Sch, RADA; *m* May 1989, Natalie, da of Martin Ogle, OBE; 1 da (Lucinda b Dec 1989), 1 s (Harry b Feb 1992); *Career* actor; caricaturist 1983–; five solo exhibitions; designer various theatre posters and book covers; *Theatre* West End incl: The Servant of Two Masters, Three, The Mating Game, Bloomsbury, The Return of A J Raffles, The Rear Column, The School for Scandal, Benefactors, The Importance of Being Earnest, Single Spies, A Small Family Business and 'Tis Pity She's a Whore (RNT), What The Butler Saw, An Absolute Turkey, Gross Indecency, Entertaining Mr Sloane, The Shakespeare Revue, The Lavender Hill Mob, Travels With My Aunt, Never So Good (NT), Enron (Coward Theatre and UK tour), The Reluctant Debutante (UK tour), The Madness of George III (Apollo Theatre), A Christmas Carol (one-man show, nationwide); for RSC incl: A Christmas Carol, Three Hours After Marriage, Troilus and Cressida; Chichester Festival Theatre incl: Monsieur Perichon's Travels, The Circle, Look After Lulu; Orange Tree Theatre Richmond: The Woman Hater, The Skin Game; other theatre incl: The Dresser, The Hypochondriac; *Television* incl: Poldark, Entertaining Mr Sloane, As You Like It, Masada, The Critic, A Married Man, The Far Pavilions, Yes Prime Minister, Oedipus, Adventures of Sherlock Holmes, After The War, The Rear Column, Quartermain's Terms, Old Flames, Lipstick on your Collar, The 10%ers, The Queen, New Tricks; *Film* Mr Turner, Laughlines (1989), Sir John, The Many Faces of Gielgud (1994), There is Nothing Like a Dane! (1998), There is Nothing Like a Thane! (2001), A Star is Drawn; adapted The Hound of the Baskervilles, Our Man in Havana, Three Men in a Boat, The Loved One, Susan Hill's The Small Hand, A Christmas Carol, Thark and Alice the Musical! for the theatre; *Recreations* walking, exploring England, twentieth century first editions, the Temple to Shakespeare (built by David Garrick); *Clubs* Garrick; *Style*— Clive Francis, Esq; ✉ e-mail cflampoons@btinternet.com, website www.actorclivefrancis.com and www.clivefrancisachristmascarol.com; c/o Simon Beresford, Paddock Suite, The Courtyard, 55 Charterhouse St, London EC1M 6HA (☎ 020 7336 0351, email mail@dbltd.co.uk)

FRANCIS, Prof Hywel; *b* 6 June 1946; *Educ* Whitchurch GS, Univ of Wales Swansea (BA, PhD); *Career* prof of continuing educn Univ of Swansea 1992–99, policy advsr on lifelong learning DfEE 1997–2000, special advsr to Sec of State for Wales 1999–2000; MP (Lab) Aberavon 2001–15, chair Welsh Affrs Ctee 2001–10, chair Jt Ctee on Human Rights 2010–; emeritus prof Univ of Swansea; fndr S Wales Miners' Library 1973, chair Welsh Congress in Support of Mining Communities 1984–86; vice-pres: Carers UK, Nat Inst of Adult Continuing Educn (NIACE); Hon DLitt Univ of Swansea; *Clubs* Aberavon RFC, Seven Sisters RFC, Ospreys RFC; *Style*— Prof Hywel Francis

FRANCIS, Dr John Michael; s of William Winston Francis (d 1939), of Haverfordwest, Pembs, and Beryl Margaret, *née* Savage (d 2003); *b* 1 May 1939; *Educ* Gowerton GS, Royal Coll of Science, Imperial Coll London (BSc, ARCS, PhD, DIC); *m* 14 Sept 1963,

Eileen, da of Hugh Foster Sykes (d 1977), of Whitley Bay, Northumberland; 2 da (Sarah Katherine b 1966, Rachel Victoria b 1968); *Career* R&D Dept CEGB 1963–70, first dir Soc Religion and Technol Project Church of Scot 1970–74, sr res fell in energy studies Heriot-Watt Univ 1974–76, asst sec Scottish Office 1981–84 (princ 1976–80), dir (Scotland) Nature Conservancy Cncl GB 1984–91 (memb Advsy Ctee 1974–76), chief exec Nature Conservancy Cncl for Scotland 1991–92, sr policy advsr The Scottish Office 1992–99; visiting fell Inst for Advanced Studies in the Humanities Univ of Edinburgh 1988, visiting fell Centre for Values and Social Policy Univ of Colorado at Boulder 1991; contribs to numerous professional and scientific jls; conslt (science, technol and social ethics) World Cncl of Churches Geneva 1971–83, rep UN Environment Conf Stockholm 1972; chm: Ctee on Society Religion and Technol Church of Scot 1980–94, Edinburgh Forum 1986–92; chair UK Nat Cmmn for UNESCO 2000–03, chair Sector Ctee Sustainable Devpt, Peace and Human Rights UK UNESCO 1999–2003, conslt and advsr UNESCO 2003–, dep chair UNESCO Scotland 2007–10, memb Governing Bd UNESCO Centre for Water Law, Policy and Sci Univ of Dundee 2008–; chair/convenor UN Assoc Edinburgh 2006–07; memb Cross Pty Gp on Int Devpt Scottish Parliament 1999–; memb: Oil Devpt Cncl for Scot 1973–76, Ind Cmmn on Tport 1974, Cncl Nat Tst for Scot 1984–92, Crown Estate Cmmn Advsy Ctee on Marine Fish Farming 1989–92, Scottish Universities Policy Research and Advice (SUPRA) network 1999–2009, Church and Nat Ctee Church of Scotland 2000–05, Exec Ctee Centre for Theology and Public Issues Univ of Edinburgh 2004–10, Steering Gp Scottish Sustainable Devpt Forum 2004–10, Church and Soc Cncl Church of Scotland 2005–12; memb St Giles' Cathedral Edinburgh; chm Francis Gp conslts (Europersona (trade mark)) 1991–99, professional memb World Futures Soc Washington DC 1991–2001, memb Reference Gp Millennium Project Washington DC 1992–, chair Scotland Node, Millennium Project 2014–, memb John Muir Tst, tstee RSE Scotland Fndn 2004–07; hon fell Univ of Edinburgh 2000–10; FRIC 1969, FRSGS 1990, FRSE 1991, FRZS Scot 1992; *Books* Scotland in Turmoil (1973), Changing Directions (jtly, 1974), Scotland's Pipedream (1974), The Future as an Academic Discipline (jtly, 1975), Scottish Oil Shakedown (1975), Facing up to Nuclear Power (1976), The Future of Scotland (jtly, 1977), North Sea Oil and the Environment (jtly, 1992), Democratic Contracts for Sustainable and Caring Societies (jtly, 2000); also author of review papers: Nature Conservation and the Voluntary Principle (1994), Nature Conservation and the Precautionary Principle (1996), The Reconstruction of Civil Society (1996), The Uncertainties of Nature Conservation and Environmental Protection (1997), Conserving Nature: Scotland and the Wider World (jtly, 2005); *Recreations* travels in France, tennis, theatre, writing on values and ethics; *Style*— Dr John M Francis, FRSE; ✉ e-mail john.m.francis@btinternet.com

FRANCIS, Mark Robert; s of Cecil Francis, and Lilian Louisa, *née* Richards; *b* 6 September 1962, Newtownards, Co Down; *Educ* Scabo HS Newtownards, Regent House GS Newtownards, St Martin's Sch of Art (BA), Chelsea Sch of Art (MA); *Career* artist; Grand Prize Tokyo Int Print Exhbn 1993, Irish MOMA/Glen Dimplex Artists Award 1996, Public Art Devpt Tst Mark Francis/Nicky Hurst 2004; *Solo Exhibitions* incl: Thumb Gallery London 1990, Jill George Gallery London 1992, Manchester City Art Gallery 1994, Galerie Thieme & Pohl Darmstadt 1995, Kerlin Gallery Dublin 1995, 1997, 2000 and 2003, Maureen Paley Interim Art London 1994, 1995, 1998, 2000, 2003 and 2004, Bloom Gallery Amsterdam 1996, Terra Nova – New Territories (Harewood House Leeds) 1996, Galerie Anne de Villepoix Paris 1996, 1998 and 2002, Mary Boone Gallery NY 1997 and 1999, Galerie Martina Detterer Frankfurt 1997, Kohn Turner Gallery LA 1998, Galerie Wilma Lock St Gallen 1999 and 2002, Kohji Ogura Gallery Nagoya 1999, Milton Keynes Gallery 2000, New Paintings (Galerie Reinhard Hauff Stuttgart) 2001, Michael Kohn Gallery LA 2003, Drawings (Thomas Schulte Galerie Berlin) 2003, New Paintings (Thomas Schulte Galerie Berlin) 2004, Interim Art (Maureen Paley London) 2004, New Prints (Marlborough Graphics London) 2004, Galerie Forsblom Helsinki 2005, Galerie Wilma Lock St Gallen 2005; *Group Exhibitions* incl: Summer Show (Tom Caldwell Gallery Dublin) 1983, New Contemporaries (Mall Galleries London) 1983, Stowells Trophy (Royal Acad of Arts London) 1984, Summer Show (Tom Caldwell Gallery Belfast) 1984, Athena Int Awards (Mall Galleries London) 1985, ILEA Class of 86 (Royal Festival Hall London) 1986, On The Wall Gallery Belfast 1986, Christie's New Contemporaries (RCA London) 1989, 5 Abstract Painters (Thumb Gallery London) 1989, Four Painters (New Acad Gallery London) 1990, Arco '92 (Madrid) 1992, Whitechapel Open (Whitechapel Art Gallery London) 1992, New Displays (Tate Gallery London) 1992, European Parl touring exhbn (Belfast, Edinburgh, Zürich, Brussels and London) 1992–93, Another Country (Rebecca Hossack Gallery London) 1993, Snap Shots (Eagle Gallery London) 1993, Contemporary Art at the Courtauld Inst (Courtauld Inst of Art London) 1993, Paintmarks (Kettles Yard Gallery Cambridge) 1994, Recent British Art (Richard Salmon Gallery London) 1994, The Curators Egg (Anthony Reynolds Gallery London) 1994, Mark Francis/Brad Lahore (Hervé Mikaeloff Gallery Paris) 1994, Testing the Water (Tate Gallery Liverpool) 1995, From Here (Karsten Schubert/Waddington Galleries London) 1995, Painters' Opinion (Bloom Gallery Amsterdam) 1995, Absolut Vision – New British Paintings in the 1990s (MOMA Oxford) 1996, Black Grey & White (Galerie Bugdahn und Kaimer Düsseldorf) 1996, British Abstract Art III (Flowers East Gallery London) 1996, Residue (Douglas Hyde Gallery Dublin) 1997, Beau Geste (Angles Gallery LA) 1997, Surface (Gow Langsford Gallery Auckland) 1997, Interior (Maureen Paley Interim Art London) 1997, Sensation-Young British Artists from the Saatchi Collection (Royal Acad of Arts London and Museum für Gegenwart Berlin) 1997–98, Post Naturamnach der Natur (Stadt Münster) 1998, POSTMARK: An Abstract Effect (Site Santa Fe New Mexico) 1999, Contemporary Painters Negociate Small Truths (Blamton Museum of Art Univ of Texas) 1999, Premio Michetti (Palazzo San Domenico Museo Michetti) 2000, Shifting Ground: Fifty Years of Irish Art 1950–2000 (Irish MOMA Dublin) 2000, Wreck of Hope (The Nunnery London) 2000, Irish Art Now: From the Poetic to the Political (Chicago Cultural Center) 2000, Fluid (Wolverhampton City Art Gallery and Galerie Wilma Lock St Gallen) 2001, The Rowan Collection Contemporary British and Irish Art (Irish MOMA Dublin) 2002, Eight New Paintings (Kerlin Gallery Dublin) 2002, The Saatchi Gift (Talbot Rice Gallery Edinburgh) 2002, Prospects and Drawing Prize (Essor Project Space London) 2002, John Moores (Walker Art Gallery Liverpool) 2002 and 2003, Before and After Science (Marella Arie Contemporanea Milan) 2003, Size Matters (Arts Cncl England touring exhbn) 2005, After the Thaw (AIB Art Collection Crawford Municipal Art Gallery Cork) 2005; *Work in Collections* incl: Unilever plc, Metropolitan Museum NY, Tate Gallery London, European Parl, Manchester City Art Gallery, Contemporary Art Soc, V&A, Machida City Museum of Graphic Art Tokyo, St Peter's Coll Oxford, de Young Memorial Museum San Francisco, Irish MOMA Dublin, St Louis Museum, Ulster Museum, Saatchi Collection London, Caldic Collection Amsterdam, NatWest Gp Art Collection London, Lambert Collection Zürich, Deutsche Bank, Br Cncl, Southampton City Art Gallery, Merrill Lynch Int Bank London, Merrill Lynch & Co Inc NY, Govt Art Collection, Goldman Sachs Int; *Style*— Mark Francis, Esq; ✉ 12 Grove Park, London SE5 8LR

FRANCIS, Mary Elizabeth; CBE (2005); da of Frederick Henry George (d 1978), and Barbara Henrietta, *née* Jeffs (d 1985); *b* 24 July 1948; *Educ* James Allen's Girls' Sch, Newnham Coll Cambridge (exhibitioner, MA); *m* 24 Nov 2001, Ian Ferguson Campbell Rodger, s of Dr David Rodger; *Career* res asst All Souls Coll Oxford 1970–73; Civil Service Dept and HM Treasy 1973–90, Corp Fin Dept Hill Samuel & Co Ltd 1984–86 (on secondment), asst then fin cnsllr Br Embassy Washington DC 1990–92, econ and domestic affrs private sec to PM 1992–95, dep private sec to HM The Queen 1995–99, DG Assoc of Br Insurers 1999–2005; non-exec dir: Bank of England until 2007, Centrica plc 2004–, Aviva plc 2005–, St Modwen Properties plc 2005–, Alliance & Leicester plc 2007–; dir International Financial Services London; govr Pensions Policy Inst; memb PCC; memb Bd Almeida Theatre; *Recreations* reading, swimming, walking, theatre; *Style—* Mrs Mary Francis, CBE

FRANCIS, Nicholas; QC (2002); s of Peter Francis (d 1973), and Jean Griffiths, *née* Beatt; *b* 22 April 1958, Penarth; *Educ* Radley, Downing Coll Cambridge (MA), Inns of Court Sch of Law; *m* 9 Sept 2000, Penny Seguss; 1 da (Joanna b 2 April 1979), 2 s (Oscar b 24 Sept 2001, Fox b 27 March 2005); *Career* called to the Bar 1981; recorder 1999– (asst recorder 1998–99), dep high ct judge 2011–; memb: Family Law Bar Assoc 1990, Int Acad of Matrimonial Lawyers 2003; *Books* International Pre-Nuptial and Post-Nuptial Agreements (general ed and contributing author); *Recreations* sailing; *Clubs* Royal Solent Yacht; *Style—* Nicholas Francis, Esq, QC; ✉ 29 Bedford Row, London WC1R 4HE (☎ 020 7404 1044, e-mail nfrancis@29br.co.uk)

FRANCIS, Penelope Julia Louise (Penny); da of Vincent Robert Paul Palmer, of Pont Royal, France, and Cynthia Ann Palmer; *b* 9 November 1959; *Educ* St Anne's Coll Sanderstead, Univ of Bristol (LLB); *m* 8 June 1985, Barry Hugh Francis, s of Stanley Francis; *Career* asst slr Beachcroft Stanleys 1984–89 (articled clerk 1982–84); Lawrence Graham: asst slr 1989–91, ptnr 1991–94, equity ptnr 1994–, formerly head Property Litigation Dept, head Property Dept 1998–2002, managing ptnr 2002–08, sr ptnr 2008–; memb Bd Centrepoint 2001–; memb Law Soc 1984; *Recreations* Middle and Far East travel, ballet, eating; *Style—* Mrs Penny Francis; ☎ 020 7379 0000, e-mail penny.francis@lg-legal.com

FRANCIS, Richard Maurice; s of Hugh Elvet Francis, QC (d 1986), and Emma Frances Wienholt, *née* Bowen (d 2006); *b* 28 June 1946; *Educ* Mill Hill Sch London, Univ of Durham (BA); *m* 2 Oct 1993, Victoria Adzoa, da of Godslove C Acolatse (d 2004), of Accra, Ghana; 1 da; *Career* called to the Bar Gray's Inn 1974; in practice Wales & Chester Circuit 1976–, in practice as a mediator 1996–; memb: Family Bar Assoc, Family Mediators Assoc; Golden Cross of the Polish Republic 1985; *Books* The British Withdrawal from the Baghdad Railway Project (1973), A History of Oakley Park Church (1976); *Recreations* family, reading books and quality newspapers, listening to BBC Radios 3 and 4; *Style—* Richard Francis, Esq; ✉ 9 Park Place, Cardiff CF10 3DP (☎ 029 2038 2731, fax 029 2022 2542); The Mediation Practice Ltd, 9 Park Place, Cardiff CF10 3DP (☎ 029 2070 0131, fax 029 2070 6828)

FRANCIS, Sir Robert Anthony; kt (2014), QC (1992); s of John Grimwade Francis, and Jean Isobel, *née* Wilson; *b* 4 April 1950; *Educ* Uppingham, Univ of Exeter (LLB, pres Guild of Students 1971–72); *m* 1, 1976 (m dis 2005), Catherine, da of John Georgievsky; 2 da (Anna Elizabeth b 1979, Helen Alexandra b 1981), 1 s (Nicholas John b 1985); m 2, 2007, Alison Meek, *qv*; *Career* called to the Bar Inner Temple 1973 (bencher 2002); tenant Serjeants Inn Chambers 1973– (jt head of chambers 2000–10), asst recorder of the Crown Court 1996–2000, recorder of the Crown Court 2000–, dep judge of the High Court 2014; chm Professional Negligence Bar Assoc 2004–05, vice-chm Trg for the Bar Cmmn Bar Cncl 2008–09, chm Mid Staffordshire NHS Fndn Tst Public Inquiry 2010–13, chm Educn and Trg Ctee Inner Temple 2009–13, cmmr and non-exec dir Care Quality Cmmn 2013–, chm Freedom to Speak Up Review 2014; pres Patients Assoc 2013, tstee Point of Care Fndn 2014, tstee Prostate Cancer Research Centre 2014, patron Florence Nightingale Fndn 2014; Hon FRCA; *Publications* Medical Treatment Decision and the Law (co-author, 2001, 2 edn 2010); *Recreations* cricket; *Style—* Sir Robert Francis, QC; ✉ Serjeants Inn Chambers, 85 Fleet Street, London EC4Y 1AE (e-mail rfrancis@serjeantsinn.com)

FRANCIS, Simon James; s of Mark William Francis, and Elisabeth Ann Francis; *Educ* Univ of Exeter (BSc, England students hockey and basketball); *m* 23 May 1998, Laura Jane; 2 da (Tabitha Ann b 22 Oct 1999, Poppy Isobel b 29 July 2002); *Career* media buying/planning Zenith Media 1990–94, gp media dir Leo Burnett 1994–98, managing ptnr and planning dir then futures dir MindShare 1998–2002, dir of strategic planning OMD Europe 2002–; accounts incl: BA, Kraft, Reckitt & Colman, Kellogg's, Procter & Gamble, IBM, Nike; IPA Advtg Effectiveness Award 1995; *Recreations* fly fishing, outdoor pursuits; *Style—* Simon Francis, Esq

FRANCKE, Ann; *Educ* Stanford Univ (BA), Columbia Univ (MBA, MS); *Career* gen mangr/category dir cosmetics Procter & Gamble 1986–99, European vice-pres Mars 1999–2002, dir of strategic mktg Boots Gp 2003, chief mktg offr Yell Gp 2004–06, pres and co-fndr Beautorium LLC 2007–09, global managing dir BSI Gp 2009–12, ceo CMI 2012–; memb Marketing Gp of GB; Hon DBA: UWE, Nottingham Trent Univ; Hon DUniv Oxford Brookes Univ; CCMI 2012, CMgr 2012; *Publications* FT Guide to Management (2013); *Clubs* WACL; *Style—* Ms Ann Francke; ✉ Chartered Management Institute, 77 Kingsway, London WC2B 6SR

FRANCOIS, Rt Hon Mark Gino; PC (2010), MP; s of Reginald Francois (d 1979), of Basildon, Essex, and Anna, *née* Carloni; *b* 14 August 1965; *Educ* Nicholas Comp Basildon, Univ of Bristol (BA), KCL (MA); *m* 30 June 2000 (m dis 2006), Karen, da of Tony Thomas, Sr; *Career* cncllr Basildon DC 1991–95 (vice-chm Housing 1992–95); MP (Cons): Rayleigh 2001–10, Rayleigh and Wickford 2010– (Parly candidate (Cons) Brent E 1997); oppn jr whip 2002–04, shadow economic sec to the Treasy 2004–05, shadow paymaster gen 2005–07, shadow Europe min 2007–10, memb Shadow Cabinet 2009–10, vice-chamberlain of HM Household (Govt whip) 2010–12, min of state for defence personnel, warfare and veterans 2012–13, min of state for the Armed Forces 2013–15, min of state for communities and resilience Dept for Communities and Local Govt 2015–; memb Environmental Audit Ctee House of Commons 2001–05; pres Palace of Westminster Lions Club 2006–12; fell Huguenot Soc of GB and I 2001–; Freeman City of London 2004; *Recreations* travel, walking, reading, history (particularly military history); *Clubs* Carlton, Rayleigh Conservative, Smuggler's Den Hullbridge; *Style—* The Rt Hon Mark Francois, MP; ✉ House of Commons, London SW1A 0AA (☎ 020 7219 3000)

FRANK, Sir (Robert) Andrew; 4 Bt (UK 1920), of Withyham, Co Sussex; s of Sir Robert John Frank, 3 Bt (d 1987), and his 2 w Margaret Joyce, *née* Truesdale (d 1995); *b* 16 May 1964; *Educ* Eton; *m* 1, 23 June 1990 (m dis 2010), Zoë Alia, er da of S A Hasan, of Windsor, Berks, and Pauline, *née* Davidson; m 2, 26 April 2014, Dr Rehanwant Singh Gomez, er s of Angelus Gomez, and Rabinder Kaur, of Kuala Lumpur, Malaysia; *Heir* none; *Career* retailer/prodr 1986–98, event mgmnt trg conslt 1998–; *Recreations* theatre, croquet, travel; *Style—* Sir Andrew Frank, Bt; ✉ Carrick, Gorse Ride North, Finchampstead, Berkshire RG40 4ES (e-mail sirafrank@thamesinternet.com)

FRANK, Prof Andrew Oliver; s of Ernest Oliver Frank (d 1993), of Haywards Heath, W Sussex, and Doris Helen Frank (d 1985); *Educ* Kingswood Sch Bath, Middx Hosp Med Sch (MB BS); *Career* lectr in med Univ of Malaya 1974–76, sr registrar in med rheumatology and rehabilitation Salisbury Health Dist 1977–80; Northwick Park Hosp and Inst of Med Res: conslt physician in rehabilitation med and rheumatology 1980–2009, clinical dir of orthopaedics, rheumatology and rehabilitation 1990–95; conslt in rehabilitation med Disablement Servs Centre Royal Nat Orthopaedic Hosp 1997–2009; prof (assoc) Centre for Research in Rehabilitation College of Health and Life Sciences Mary Seacole Building Brunel Univ London 1997–; Med Disability Soc (now Br Soc of Rehab Med): fndr and hon sec 1984–87, regional co-ordinator 1995–97, chm Educn Ctee 1996–99, pres 2000–02, chm Vocational Rehabilitation Working Pty 1999–2000, chair Special Interest Gp in Vocational Rehabilitation 2004–07; chm NW Thames Physical Disability Advsy Gp 1992–94, regnl advsr rehabilitation med 1996–2006, clinical chair NHS Modernisation Agency Wheelchair Collaborative 2002–04, medical dir Kynixa Ltd 2007–09; memb: Disability Ctee RCP 1979–87, Soc of Research into Rehabilitation 1982 (memb Cncl 1995–97 and 2000–02), N Thames Regnl Trg Ctee 1996–2006, SAC Rehabilitation Med 1998–99, Int Assoc for the Study of Pain 1994–2009, Rehabilitation Med Ctee 2000–02, Posture and Mobility Gp 2002–09, RSM; professional memb Vocational Rehabilitation Assoc; tstee Vocational Rehabilitation Assoc 2006– (chair Professional Devpt Ctee 2007–09, vice chair of tstees 2008–09, chair of tstees 2009–13, hon life memb 2013–), fndr memb and tstee UK Rehabilitation Cncl 2008–13, fndr memb Cncl for Work and Health 2009–13; finalist Hospital Doctor Innovations Award 2006, Rehabilitation First Outstanding Individual Achievement Award 2013; Hon DSc Brunel Univ 2003; professional memb Vocational Rehabilitation Assoc 2010; FRCP 1990 (MRCP), FHEA 2007; *Books* Disabling Diseases: Physical, Environmental and Psychosocial Management (with G P Maguire, 1989), Vocational Rehabilitation: The Way Forward (2000, 2 edn 2003), Low Back Pain: Diagnosis and Management (2001), Improving Services for Wheelchair Users and their Carers: Good Practice Guide; numerous pubns on back and neck pain, rehabilitation, vocational rehabilitation and powered wheelchairs; *Recreations* bridge, family, music, walking; *Style—* Prof Andrew Frank; ✉ PO Box 727, Rickmansworth WD3 0HS (☎ 01923 284972)

FRANK, David Thomas; s of Thomas Frank (d 1984), of Robertsford, Shrewsbury, and Margaret McCrea, *née* Cowan (d 2006); *b* 29 April 1954; *Educ* Shrewsbury, Univ of Bristol (LLB); *m* 10 July 1982, Diane Lillian, da of Stephen Nash Abbott, of Farnham Common, Bucks; 1 da (Lucinda b 1986), 1 s (Charles b 1988); *Career* admitted slr 1979; Slaughter and May: asst slr 1979–86, ptnr 1986–, head of Capital Markets 1993–2001, practice ptnr 2001–; *Recreations* lawn tennis, cars, shooting; *Style—* David Frank, Esq; ✉ Slaughter and May, One Bunhill Row, London EC1Y 8YY (☎ 020 7600 1200, fax 020 7090 5000, e-mail david.frank@slaughterandmay.com)

F

FRANK, Joanna Helen Louise; da of Sir Douglas Frank, QC, and late Sheila, *née* Beauchamp; *Educ* Oxford HS GDST, Univ of Warwick (BA); *Career* with Pan Books 1987–90, commissioning ed Random House 1990–92, editorial dir of fiction Simon & Schuster UK Ltd 1992–97, dir and agent A P Watt Literary Agency 1997–; *Recreations* walking, reading, cinema, cooking; *Clubs* Soho House; *Style—* Ms Joanna Frank; ✉ A P Watt Ltd, 20 John Street, London WC1N 2DR (☎ 020 7282 3109, fax 020 7282 3412)

FRANKLIN, Daniel John (Dan); s of Michael Howard Franklin, of Manningtree, Essex, and Suzanne Mary, *née* Cooper (d 1992); *b* 2 May 1949; *Educ* Bradfield, UEA (BA); *m* 29 June 1985, Lucy, da of Michael Hughes-Hallett, of Barton-on-the-Heath, Glos; 2 da (Lettice, Mary (twins) b 1 March 1990); *Career* editorial dir William Heinemann 1987, publisher Secker & Warburg 1988, publishing dir Jonathan Cape 1993–; *Style—* Dan Franklin, Esq; ✉ Jonathan Cape, 20 Vauxhall Bridge Road, London SW1V 2SA (☎ 020 7840 8400, fax 020 7233 6117)

FRANKLIN, Prof Ian Maxwell; s of Edwin William Franklin, of London, and Elizabeth Joyce, *née* Kessler; *b* 6 September 1949; *Educ* Owen's Boys Sch Islington, Univ of Leeds (BSc, MB ChB), UCL (PhD); *m* 1, 19 July 1975 (m dis 2010), Anne Christine, da of Harry Norman Bush, of Leeds; 1 s (Matthew Charles Maxwell b 1988), 1 da (Sophie Rose b 1991); m 2, 24 Sept 2011, Joyce Poole; *Career* MRC res fell UCL Hosp London 1977–80, sr registrar haematology UCL Hosp and Hosp for Sick Children Gt Ormond St London 1980–82, conslt haematologist Queen Elizabeth Hosp Birmingham 1982–92, dir of haematology Central Birmingham HA 1989–91, dir Bone Marrow Transplant Unit and conslt haematologist Royal Infirmary Glasgow 1992–96 (hon conslt 1996–); prof of transfusion med Univ of Glasgow 1996–2010; dir Glasgow and W of Scotland Blood Transfusion Centre 1996–97, nat med and sci dir Scottish Nat Blood Transfusion Serv 1997–2010, medical and scientific dir Irish Blood Transfusion Serv 2011–13; Br Soc for Haematology: scientific sec 1995–98, memb Ctee 2002–05; memb Advsy Ctee on the Safety of Blood, Tissues and Organs (SaBTO) 2008–10; tstee Thrombosis UK 2010– (chair of tstees 2016–); memb: American Soc of Hematology, Assoc of Physicians of GB & Ireland; FRCP 1990 (MRCP 1977), FRCPGlas 1994, FRCPEd 1996, FRCPath (memb Cncl 2002–05); *Recreations* aerobics, triathlon, cycling, music, unpublished writing, fashion, opera; *Style—* Prof Ian Franklin; ✉ 22 Ambra Vale, Cliftonwood, Bristol BS8 4RW (☎ 07717 532308)

FRANKLIN, John Richard; s of Richard Franklin (d 2007), and Jean, *née* Pearson; *Educ* Lockyer HS, Ipswich GS, Univ of Southern Qld (BA, Dip Teaching), Univ of New England (MEd Admin); *Career* teacher Qld Educn Dept 1976–79, housemaster, OC cadet unit and head of sr sch Toowoomba GS 1980–88, teacher Sedbergh Sch 1989, teacher Marlborough Coll 1989–92, dep headmaster St Peter's Coll Adelaide 1993–98, headmaster Ardingly Coll 1998–2007, head master Christ's Hosp 2007–; Liveryman Worshipful Co of Salters 2014–; memb: HMC 1998, SHA 1998; *Recreations* golf, music, theatre, cooking, travel; *Clubs* East India, Lansdowne; *Style—* John Franklin, Esq; ✉ Christ's Hospital, Horsham, West Sussex RH13 0LJ (☎ 01403 247432, fax 01403 255283, e-mail hmsec@christs-hospital.org.uk)

FRANKLIN, Paul J; *b* Cheshire; *Educ* Cheshire Sch of Art and Design, Ruskin Sch of Art, St John's Coll Oxford; *Career* computer artist Psygnosis 1992–94, computer animator Moving Picture Co 1994–98, co-fndr Double Negative Visual Effects 1998– (currently sr in-house visual effects supervisor and creative dir); film projects incl: Enemy at the Gates 2001, Captain Corelli's Mandolin 2001, Revelation 2001, Pitch Black 2002, Below 2002, Die Another Day 2002, Johnny English 2003, To Kill a King 2003, The League of Extraordinary Gentlemen 2003, Resident Evil: Apocalypse 2004, Sahara 2005, Batman Begins 2005, The Da Vinci Code 2006, Harry Potter and the Order of the Phoenix 2007, The Dark Knight 2008, Harry Potter and the Half-Blood Prince 2009, Inception 2010 (Best Visual Effects Acad Award 2011, Best Special Visual Effects BAFTA 2011), The Dark Knight Rises 2012, Interstellar 2014 (Best Visual Effects Acad Award 2015, Best Special Visual Effects BAFTA 2015), Mission: Impossible – Rogue Nation 2015, Captain America 2016, Life 2017; memb: BAFTA 2002–, AMPAS 2011–; *Publications* Gravitational Lensing by Spinning Black Holes in Astrophysics, and in the Movie Interstellar (Inst of Physics Jl of Classical and Quantum Gravity 2015, with Oliver James, Eugenie von Tunzelmann and Kip S Thorne), Visualizing Interstellars Wormhole (American Jl of Physics, with Oliver James, Eugénie von Tunzelmann and Kip S Thorne); *Style—* Paul Franklin, Esq; ✉ Double Negative Visual Effects, 160 Great Portland Street, London W1W 5QA

FRANKLIN, Prof Robin James Milroy; s of Sir Michael Franklin, KCB, CMG, of Barnet, Herts, former perm sec Dept of Trade and MAFF, and Dorothy, *née* Fraser; *b* 25 August 1962, Barnet, Herts; *Educ* Haberdashers' Aske's, RVC Univ of London (BVetMed), UCL (BSc), Univ of Cambridge (PhD); *m* 31 July 1999, Dr Barbara Skelly; 2 s (George b 2003, Toby b 2007); *Career* Dept of Vet Med Univ of Cambridge: Wellcome Tst res fell 1991–94, Wellcome Tst res career devpt fell 1994–99, Wellcome Tst proleptic lectr 1999–2000, sr lectr in experimental neurology 2000–02, reader in experimental neurology 2002–05, prof of neuroscience 2005–; fell Pembroke Coll Cambridge 1996–; Cavanagh Prize Br Neuropathological Soc 2004; author of over 160 articles in scientific jls; MRCVS 1988, FRCPath 2007 (MRCPath 2001); *Recreations* walking, reading, birdwatching, fly fishing; *Style—* Prof Robin Franklin; ✉ Department of Veterinary Medicine, University of Cambridge, Madingley Road, Cambridge CB3 0ES

FRANKLIN, Prof Simon Colin; s of Colin Franklin, of Culham, Oxon, and Charlotte, *née* Hajnal-Konyi; *b* 11 August 1953, London; *Educ* UC Sch, King's Coll Cambridge (BA), St Antony's Coll Oxford (DPhil); *m* 24 Dec 1975, Natasha, *née* Gokova; 1 s (Andrei b 21 Feb 1979), 1 da (Marina b 29 June 1981); *Career* research fell Clare Coll Cambridge 1980–

83; Dept of Slavonic Studies Univ of Cambridge: lectr in Russian 1983–99, reader in Slavonic studies 1999–2003, prof of Russian studies 2003–04, prof of Slavonic studies 2004–, head Sch of Arts and Humanities 2009–14; memb Bd of Tstees European Univ of St Petersburg 2010–; chm Pushkin House Tst 2005–09; Alexander Nove Prize 2003, ESSA Distinguished Scholarship Award 2006, Lomonosov Gold Medal Russian Acad of Sciences 2008; FBA 2012; *Books* The Emergence of Rus, c750–1200 (jtly, 1996), Writing, Society and Culture in Early Rus c950–1300 (2002), National Identity in Russian Culture (jtly, 2004); *Recreations* football, theatre, gardening; *Style*— Prof Simon Franklin; ✉ Clare College, Cambridge CB2 1TL (☎ 01223 333263, e-mail scf1000@cam.ac.uk)

FRANKS, Michael; s of Jacob Franks, MD (d 1976), and Janet Lilian Green (d 1978); *b* 6 May 1928, Kingsclere, Hants; *Educ* Epsom Coll, Merton Coll Oxford (MA), Gray's Inn; *m* 1, 1962 (m dis 1978), Anne, yr da of Sir David George Home, 13 Bt; 2 da (Lucinda b 1964, Miranda b 1966); m 2, 1980, Nicola Stewart, da of Col George Harcourt Stewart Balmain (d 1962); *Career* Sub-Lt RNVR 1951–53 (Nat Service); called to the Bar Gray's Inn 1953; in practice Chancery Bar 1953–59; Royal Dutch/Shell 1959–69; dir Beaverbrook Newspapers 1969–73; chm: Clyde Paper Co 1971–76, Schwarzkopf UK 1981–86; dep chm Goodhead Gp plc 1985–91; chm: Innsite Hotel Services 1987–90, Silicon Bridge 1989–96; dir: Select Appointments plc 1987–99 (chm 1991–92); strategic conslt South & West Investments; *Publications* Limitations of Actions (1959), The Clerk of Basingstoke – A Life of Walter de Merton (2003), The Basingstoke Admiral: A Life of Sir James Lancaster (2006), The Count, the Atlantic and the City – Sir Walter Ralegh v William Sanderson (2009); *Recreations* sailing, skiing, travel, writing history; *Clubs* Royal Thames Yacht; *Style*— Michael Franks, Esq; ✉ Field House, Mapledurwell, Basingstoke, Hampshire RG25 2LU (☎ 01256 464861)

FRANKS, Prof Stephen; *b* 14 September 1947; *Educ* Woodhouse GS Finchley, UCL (MB BS 1970, MD 1978); *m* 31 Aug 1972, Victoria Elizabeth, *née* Nunn; 2 s (Benjamin Paul b 8 May 1975, Joshua Jeremy b 17 Nov 1980), 1 da (Sarah Anne b 21 Jan 1977); *Career* postdoctoral res fell in endocrinology McGill Univ Montreal Canada (MRC travelling res fell, JB Collip fell) 1977–79, lectr in med Univ of Birmingham 1979–82, prof of reproductive endocrinology Imperial Coll Sch of Med at St Mary's Hosp (St Mary's Hosp Med Sch until merger) 1988– (sr lectr 1982–88); visiting prof and Griff Ross Meml lectr Nat Inst of Health Bethesda MD USA Oct 1996, Carl Gemzell lectr Univ of Uppsala Sweden 1990, Van Campenhout lectr Canadian Fertility and Andrology Soc 2002, Feldberg Prize lectr Univ of Aachen 2002, Patrick Steptoe Meml medal lectr Br Fertility Soc Glasgow 2006; ed Clinical Endocrinology 1994–96, author of over 200 peer-reviewed pubns; memb: Soc for Endocrinology (memb Ctee 1989–92, ed Newsletter 1992–, gen sec 1996–, chm 1999–), BMA; Medal lectr: Clinical Endocrinology Tst 1998, Soc for Endocrinology 1999; Hon MD Univ of Uppsala Sweden 1995; FRCP 1988 (MRCP 1972), FRCOG (ad eundem) 2000, FMedSci 2000; *Recreations* music, theatre, tennis; *Style*— Prof Stephen Franks; ✉ Institute of Reproductive and Developmental Biology, Imperial College London, Hammersmith Hospital, London W12 0NN (☎ 020 7594 2109/2176, e-mail s.franks@imperial.ac.uk)

FRANKS, Stephen George; s of Geoffrey Raymond Franks (d 1988), and Jean Margaret, *née* Macaree; *b* 18 September 1955; *Educ* De-Burgh Sch Epsom; *m* Sarah, da of Tony Bagnall Smith; 3 s (Archie George b 4 Oct 1986, Henry James b 14 Sept 1989, Fergus William b 25 Feb 1992); *Career* designer Lock and Petersen 1979–82; sr designer: Tayburn London 1982–83, Landsdown Euro 1983–84; ptnr and design dir Coley Porter Bell 1984–95, in own co Franks and Franks 1995–; memb D&AD 1980; FRSA 1994; *Style*— Stephen Franks, Esq

FRANSMAN, Laurens Francois (Laurie); QC (2000); s of Henri Albert Fransman, of Johannesburg, South Africa, and Stanmore, London, and Hannah Lena, *née* Bernstein; *b* 4 July 1956; *Educ* King David HS, Linksfield Johannesburg, Univ of Leeds (LLB); *m* 1, 7 Aug 1977 (m dis 1985), Claire Frances, da of Prof Colin Howard Ludlow Goodman (d 1990), of Mill Hill, London; 1 s (Piers b 1980); m 2, 9 July 1994, Helena Mary, da of Leonard George Cook (d 2001), of Caterham, Surrey; 1 s (Lindsey b 1997), 1 s (Elliot b 2000); *Career* barr, author; called to the Bar Middle Temple 1979, barr-at-law 2 Garden Ct Temple 1987–; UK contrib ed Immigration Law and Practice Reporter NY 1985, memb Editorial Bd Immigration and Nationality Law and Practice 1987–, memb Editorial Bd Immigration and International Employment Law 1999–2001; Halsbury's Laws of England (4 edn): conslt in nationality law 1991 issue, co-ordinating ed and princ contributor Br Nationality, Immigration and Asylum 2002 issue (conslt ed 5 edn 2011); fndr Immigration Law Practitioners' Assoc 1983 (chm, memb Exec Ctee); memb: Cncl of Europe/Commission Internationale de l'Etat Civil ad hoc Ctee of Experts on Citizenship 1992, Bar Euro Gp, Administrative Law Bar Assoc, Liberty, Lawyers for Liberty; *Books* British Nationality Law and the 1981 Act (1982), Tribunals Practice and Procedure (jtly, 1985), Immigration Emergency Procedures (jtly, 1986, 2 edn 1994), Fransman's British Nationality Law (1989, 3 edn 2011), The Constitution of the United Kingdom (contrib, 1991), Strangers and Citizens (contrib, 1994), Citizenship and Nationality Status in the New Europe (contrib, 1997), Immigration, Nationality and Asylum Under the Human Rights Act 1998 (jt ed and contrib, 1999), Immigration Law and Practice (contrib, 2001), Macdonald's Immigration Law & Practice (contrib, 5 edn 2001, 6 edn 2005, 7 edn 2008), Max Planck Encyclopaedia of Public International Law (contrib, 2009), Blackstone's Guide to The Borders, Citizenship and Immigration Act 2009 (jtly, 2010); *Recreations* guitar playing, history, geology, food, music, theatre; *Style*— Laurie Fransman, Esq, QC; ✉ Garden Court Chambers, 57–60 Lincoln's Inn Fields, London WC2A 3LS (☎ 020 7993 7600, fax 020 7993 7700)

FRASE, (Antony) Richard Grenville; s of Flt Lt Stanislaw Frase (d 1957), and Joy, *née* Thompson; *b* 8 July 1954; *Educ* Royal GS Newcastle upon Tyne, Repton, Trinity Coll Cambridge (MA); *m* 26 May 1990, Sarah-Louise, da of John and Margaret Walker, of Château de Thury, Burgundy; 1 s (James Grenville b 8 April 1992), 1 da (Amelia b 28 Feb 1995); *Career* 2 Lt TAVR 1976–78; admitted slr 1981, asst slr Allen & Overy 1981–83 (articled 1978–80), ptnr Denton Hall 1988–93 (asst slr 1983–87), counsel MeesPierson ICS Ltd 1993–95, head of litigation Personal Investment Authy 1995–98, ptnr Dechert 2005– (of counsel 1999–2004); sometime course co-ordinator and lectr dips in fin servs and capital markets law London Met Univ and Univ of Reading 2007–08; seconded to SFA 1989–91; memb: SFA Arbitration Panel 1992–2002, Arbitration Panel London Metal Exchange 1993–2005; govr St Edmund's Sch Godalming 2013–; memb HAC Co of Pikemen and Musketeers; ACIArb 1993; *Publications* The Euromoney Guide to World Equity Markets (contrib, 1991–2000), Futures Trading, Law and Regulation (contrib, 1993), Hedge Funds Law and Regulation (contrib, 2000), Exchanges Law and Regulation (ed and contrib, 2001), Practitioner's Guide to the FSA Regulation of Designated Investment Business (contrib, 2002, 3 edn 2007), Law and Regulation of Investment Management (2004, 2 edn 2012), Commercial Mortgage-backed Securitisation (contrib, 2006), Practitioner's Guide to MiFID (contrib, 2007), Hedge Funds and the Law (ed and contrib, 2010); *Recreations* neoplatonism, art, history; *Clubs* Reform, HAC; *Style*— Richard Frase, Esq; ✉ Dechert LLP, 160 Queen Victoria Street, London EC4V 4QQ (☎ 020 7184 7000)

FRASER, Dr Andrew Kerr; s of Sir William Kerr Fraser, GCB, FRSE, *qv*, and Lady Marion Fraser, LT, *née* Forbes; *Educ* George Watson's Coll Edinburgh, Univ of Aberdeen, Univ of Glasgow; *m* 1, 20 April 1985 (m dis), Geraldine, da of Brendan Martin, of Dublin; 3 s (Alasdair b 29 Sept 1988, Colum b 17 Feb 1990, Moray b 20 Jan 1995), 1 da (Roseanne b 25 Feb 1992); m 2, 21 Sept 2012, Barbara Allison; *Career* med dir Nat Servs Div Common Servs Agency NHS in Scotland Edinburgh 1993–94, dir of public health/chief admin med offr Highland Health Bd Inverness 1994–97, dep chief med offr Scottish Exec 1997–2003; Scottish Prison Service: head of health 2003–06, dir of health and care 2006–12; dir of public health science NHS Health Scotland 2012–; FRCPEd 1997, FFPHM 1999, FRCPGlas 2001; *Recreations* music, mountain walking; *Style*— Dr Andrew Fraser; ✉ Gyle Square, NHS Health Scotland, 1 South Gyle Crescent, Edinburgh EH12 9EB

FRASER, Angus Robert Charles; MBE (1999); s of Donald Fraser, and Irene, *née* Tonge; *b* 8 August 1965; *Educ* Gayton HS Harrow, Orange Hill Senior HS; *Career* professional cricketer; Middlesex CCC 1984–2002 (awarded county cap 1988); England: memb tour Australia and NZ 1990–91, memb team touring West Indies 1993/94, Australia 1994/95, South Africa 1995/96, West Indies 1998 (best bowling figures 8–53 in Port of Spain), memb winning team v South Africa 1998, memb squad Emirates Trophy 1998, memb team touring Australia 1998/99, 46 test matches, 42 one-day ints, best bowling 8–53; honours with Middlesex: County Championship 1985, 1990 and 1993, Nat West Trophy 1988, Benson & Hedges Cup 1986, Nixdorf Computers Middlesex Player of the Year 1988 and 1989, one of Wisdens 5 Cricketers of the Year 1996; currently cricket writer The Independent, summariser BBC Test Match Special; qualified cricket coach; *Recreations* wine, golf, watching Liverpool FC and rugby internationals, anything in sport but racing; *Style*— Angus Fraser, Esq, MBE

FRASER, Lady Antonia; DBE (2011, CBE 1999); *née* Pakenham; da of 7 Earl of Longford, KG, PC (d 2001), and Elizabeth, Countess of Longford, CBE (d 2002); *b* 27 August 1932; *Educ* St Mary's Convent Ascot, LMH Oxford; *m* 1, 25 Sept 1956 (m dis 1977), Rt Hon Sir Hugh Fraser, MBE, PC, MP (d 1984), s of 16 Lord Lovat; 3 da (Rebecca (Mrs Edward Fitzgerald) b 1957, Flora Fraser, *qv*, b 1958, Natasha (Mme Fraser-Cavassoni) b 1963), 3 s (Benjamin b 1961, Damian b 1964, Orlando b 1967); m 2, 27 Nov 1980, Harold Pinter, CH, CBE (Nobel Laureate, d 2008); *Career* writer; chm: Soc of Authors 1974–75, Crimewriters' Assoc 1985–86; co-tstee Authors' Fndn 1984–; pres English PEN 1988–89; Norton Medlicott Medal Historical Assoc 2000; FRSL 2003; *Books* incl: Mary Queen of Scots (James Tait Black Memorial Prize 1969), Cromwell our chief of Men (1973), James I & VI of England and Scotland (1974), Kings and Queens of England (ed, 1975), King Charles II (1979), The Weaker Vessel (Wolfson History Award 1984), Boadicea's Chariot: The Warrior Queens (1988), Quiet as a Nun (1977), Cool Repentance (1980), The Wild Island (1978), Oxford Blood (1985), Your Royal Hostage (1987), A Splash of Red (1981, basis TV series Jemima Shore 1983), Jemima Shore's First Case (1986), The Cavalier Case (1990), Jemima Shore at the Sunny Grave (1991), The Six Wives of Henry VIII (1992), The Pleasure of Reading (ed, 1992, reissued 2015), The Gunpowder Plot (1996, CWA Non-Fiction Dagger 1996, published in US as Faith and Treason: the story of the Gunpowder Plot, St Louis Literary Award 1996), Marie Antoinette: the journey (2001, Franco-British Soc Literary Award 2002), Love and Louis XIV (2006), Must You Go? My Life with Harold Pinter (2010), Perilous Question: The Drama of the Great Reform Bill 1832 (2013, published in US as Perilous Question: Britain on the Brink of Revolution), My History: A Memoir of Growing Up (2015); *Recreations* swimming, grandchildren; *Style*— Lady Antonia Fraser, DBE; ✉ c/o Curtis Brown Group Ltd, 28–29 Haymarket, London SW1Y 4SP (☎ 020 7396 6600, fax 020 7396 0110)

FRASER, Prof Derek; s of Jacob Fraser, of Birmingham, and Dorothy, *née* Hayes; *b* 24 July 1940; *Educ* King Edward's Camp Hill Sch Birmingham, Univ of Leeds (BA, MA, PhD); *m* 1962, Ruth, *née* Spector; 2 s (Philip Neal b 1963, Adam Jason b 1970), 1 da (Clio Lynn b 1965); *Career* sch teacher Birmingham 1962–65; sr lectr, reader then prof of modern history Univ of Bradford 1965–83, prof of English history UCLA 1982–84, HM's Inspector of Schs history and higher educn 1984–88, staff inspector for higher educn DES 1988–90; Sheffield City Poly: asst princ (on secondment), dep princ 1991–92; vice-chllr Univ of Teesside 1992–2003; Andrew W Mellon distinguished visiting prof Franklin and Marshall Coll Penn 1979; chm Ind Football Cmmn 2001–08, ind football ombudsman 2008–; chm Standards Verification UK 2005–11, dir Lifelong Learing UK 2011–13; memb Bd NE RDA 1998–2001; visiting prof: Univ of Vermont 1980, Stanford Univ 1981; Levinson Scholar in Residence St Andrew's Sch Delaware 2014; dir English Bridge Union County Tournament 2008–; FRHistS 1980; *Books* Urban Politics in Victorian England – The Structure of Politics in Victorian Cities (1976), Power and Authority in the Victorian City (1979), The Evolution of the British Welfare State (1984, 5 edn 2017), The Welfare State (2000); *Recreations* music, bridge, film, watching football; *Style*— Prof Derek Fraser; ✉ Independent Football Ombudsman, Suite 49, 33 Great George Street, Leeds LS1 3AJ (e-mail contact@theifo.co.uk)

FRASER, Prof Donald Gordon; s of Dr Gordon Fraser (d 2001), and Kathleen, *née* Benson; *b* 30 October 1949, Edinburgh; *Educ* Univ of Edinburgh (BSc), Univ of Oxford (MA, DPhil); *m* 27 June 1970, Anna, *née* Fojtíková; 1 s (Andrew Gordon b 7 Dec 1971), 1 da (Elizabeth Anna b 4 Oct 1974); *Career* geologist; jr research fell Merton Coll Oxford 1974–76, asst prof in mineralogy Columbia Univ NY 1976; Univ of Oxford: lectr in geochemistry 1976–96, prof of earth sciences 1996–, chm Fraser Ctee on the future structure of sci in Oxford 1988–90, chm Bd Faculty of Physical Sciences 1994–96 (vice-chm 1992–94), memb Univ Cncl 2006–, sr proctor 2008–09; governing body fell Wolfson Coll Oxford 1977–78, currently tutorial fell in geology Worcester Coll Oxford; sr visiting scientist Max-Planck Inst für Chemie Mainz 1980–81, sr research assoc CNRS Nice 1984–85, JSPS fell Inst for the Study of the Earth's Interior Misasa 1997–98, visiting assoc Div of Geological and Planetary Scis Calif Inst of Technol 1998, visiting assoc Beckman Inst Calif Inst of Technol 1998–99, Centre of Excellence research fell Inst for the Study of the Earth's Interior Misasa 2001–02; advsy ed Physics of the Earth and Planetary Interiors 1992–99; chm and md Statistical Sciences (UK) Ltd, dir Prolysis Ltd 2001–03; conslt: Shell, Chevron, Deminex Ltd, Greig Fester Ltd, Clyde Petroleum Ltd, Phillips Petroleum (Norway) Ltd; dir NATO Advanced Study Inst Thermodynamics in Geology 1976; sec European Assoc for Geochemistry 1987–89; memb: Int Advsy Panel Centre of Excellence Prog Inst for the Study of the Earth's Interior Misasa 2003–, CODATA Task Gp on Geothermodynamic Data Int Cncl of Scientific Unions; *Books* Elementary Thermodynamics for Geologists (with B J Wood, 1976), Thermodynamics in Geology (1977); *Recreations* skiing, poetry, golf, music; *Style*— Prof Donald Fraser; ✉ Department of Earth Sciences, University of Oxford, South Parks Road, Oxford OX1 3AN

FRASER, Flora; da of Rt Hon Sir Hugh Fraser, MBE, PC, MP (d 1984), and Lady Antonia Fraser, DBE, *qv*; *b* 30 October 1958; *Educ* St Paul's Girls' Sch, Wadham Coll Oxford; *m* 1, 1980 (m dis 1992), Robert Powell-Jones (d 1998); 1 da (Stella Powell-Jones b 15 May 1987); m 2, 1997 (m dis 2010), Peter Soros; 2 s (Simon Tivadar Soros b 10 March 1998, Thomas Hugh Soros b 3 May 1999); *Career* writer 1981–; tstee Nat Portrait Gallery 1999–2008; co-fndr: Elizabeth Longford Prize for Historical Biography 2003, Elizabeth Longford Awards for Historical Biographers 2003–15; judge Guggenheim-Lehrman Prize for Military Biography 2014–; memb Exec Ctee Friends of the Nat Libraries, memb Wadham Devpt Cncl Oxford 2011–; patron FreeOpenAirTheatre.org 2013–; *Books* Double Portrait (1983), Maud: The Diaries of Maud Berkeley (1985), Beloved Emma: The Life of Emma, Lady Hamilton (1986), The English Gentlewoman (1987), Tamgar (1990), The Unruly Queen: The Life of Queen Caroline (1996), Princesses: The Six Daughters of George III (2004), Venus of Empire: The Life of Pauline Bonaparte (2009), George & Martha Washington: A Revolutionary Marriage (2015, George Washington Book Prize 2016); *Recreations* swimming in Greece; *Clubs* Literary Soc; *Style*— Miss Flora Fraser;

✉ c/o Georgina Capel, Capel & Land, 29 Wardour Street, London W1D 6PS (☎ 020 7734 2414)

FRASER, Helen Jean Sutherland; CBE (2010); da of George Sutherland Fraser (d 1980), and Eileen Lucy, *née* Andrew; *b* 8 June 1949; *Educ* Collegiate Girls' Sch Leicester, St Anne's Coll Oxford (MA); *m* 16 April 1982, Grant James McIntyre, s of Athol McIntyre, of Cornwall; 2 da (Blanche b 1980, Marina b 1983); *Career* editorial dir William Collins 1977–87, publisher William Heinemann 1987–91, publisher Heinemann/Mandarin 1991–92, md Reed Trade Books 1996–97 (publishing dir 1992–96), md Gen Div Penguin Books (i/c Viking, Hamish Hamilton, and Michael Joseph imprints) 1997–2001, md Penguin UK 2001–09, chief exec Girls' Day Sch Tst 2010–; *Style—* Ms Helen Fraser, CBE; ✉ The Girls' Day School Trust, 100 Rochester Row, London SW1P 1JP (☎ 020 7393 6690)

FRASER, Sir Iain Michael; 3 Bt (UK 1943), of Tain, Co Ross; s of Maj Sir James David Fraser, 2 Bt (d 1997), and (Edith) Maureen, *née* Reay; *b* 27 June 1951; *Educ* Trinity Coll Glenalmond, Univ of Edinburgh (BSc); *m* 1, 1982 (m dis 1991), Sherylle Ann, da of Keith Gillespie, of Wellington, NZ; 1 da (Joanna Karen b 1983), 1 s (Benjamin James b 1986); m 2, 2004, Anne, da of Dr David Sim; *Heir* s, Benjamin Fraser; *Career* restaurant owner; *Style—* Sir Iain Fraser, Bt

FRASER, Ian; *Educ* Univ of Oxford (MA), Harvard Univ (MBA); *Career* mktg mangr Exxon Corporation 1977–83, divnl md Raychem Corporation 1983–91, gp md Reliance Security Gp plc 1991–98, ceo and memb Bd Brammer plc 1998–; CCMI 2007, FRSA 2008; *Style—* Ian Fraser, Esq; ✉ Brammer plc, St Ann's House, 1 Old Market Place, Knutsford, Cheshire WA16 6PD

FRASER, (Alexander) James (Jamie); s of Gen Sir David Fraser, GCB, OBE, DL, of Hants, and Julia, *née* De la Hey; *b* 30 June 1960, Cirencester, Glos; *Educ* Eton, RMA Sandhurst; *m* 12 April 1997, Stephanie, *née* Struthers; 3 da (Iona b 12 March 1999, Mary b 26 Sept 2000, Alice b 6 Feb 2004); *Career* cmmned Grenadier Gds 1980–89, David S Smith (Holdings) plc 1989–2001 (investor rels mangr 1992–97), dir Hamilton & Inches Ltd 2001– (md 2003–); memb Royal Co of Archers; MInstD; *Recreations* piping, golf, shooting; *Clubs* Pratts; *Style—* Jamie Fraser, Esq; ✉ Craigmaddie, Milngavie, Glasgow G62 8LB (☎ 0141 956 7866)

FRASER, John Arthur; *b* 8 August 1951, Melbourne, Aust; *Educ* Monash Univ Aust (BEcon); *Career* min (economic) Aust Embassy Washington DC USA 1985–88, dep sec (economic) Aust Treasy 1990–93, dir Aust Stock Exchange 1997–2003, chm and ceo UBS Global Asset Mgmnt 2001–, memb Gp Exec Bd UBS 2002–; govr Marymount Int Sch Kingston-upon-Thames 2007–; *Recreations* sailing, rugby; *Clubs* Oriental, Walbrook, Australian (Sydney); *Style—* John A Fraser, Esq; ✉ UBS Global Asset Management, 21 Lombard Street, London EC3V 9AH (☎ 020 7901 6200)

FRASER, Murdo; MSP; *b* 1965, Inverness; *Educ* Inverness Royal Acad, Univ of Aberdeen (LLB, Dip); *m* 1994, Emma Jarvis; 1 s (b 2008), 1 da (b 2009); *Career* slr and assoc Ketchen and Stevens WS until 2001, MSP (Cons) Mid-Scotland and Fife Aug 2001–; Scottish Parl: spokesman for enterprise and lifelong learning 2003–07, dep ldr Scottish Cons 2005–11, spokesman on educn and lifelong learning 2007–10, spokesman on health and wellbeing 2010–1, convenor Economy, Energy and Tourism Ctee 2011–; chm Scottish Young Conservatives 1989–91, chm Nat Young Conservatives 1991–92; Parly candidate (Cons): E Lothian 1997 (UK Parl), N Tayside 1999, 2003 and 2007 (Scot Parl) and 2001 (UK Parl), Perthshire N 2011 (Scot Parl); *Publications* Defending our British Heritage (1993), Full Fiscal Freedom (1998), Scotland and the Euro (1999), The Blue Book (2006), The Rivals: Montrose and Argyll and the struggle for Scotland (2015); *Recreations* hill walking, football, classic cars, Scottish history; *Style—* Murdo Fraser, Esq, MSP; ✉ The Scottish Parliament, Edinburgh EH99 1SP (☎ 0131 348 5293, fax 0131 348 5934, e-mail murdo.fraser.msp@scottish.parliament.uk)

FRASER, Prof Robert W; *b* 23 December 1955, Adelaide, Aust; *Educ* Univ of Adelaide (BEc), Univ of Oxford (MPhil, DPhil); *m* 16 Sept 2006, Janet Elaine Haddock-Fraser; 2 s (Matthew b 23 May 1989, Adam b 18 March 1995) and 1 da (Clair b 1 May 1991) by previous m; *Career* prof and dep head Sch of Economics Univ of Kent 2008–; pres Agricultural Economics Soc 2013–14; memb Editorial Bd: Jl of Agricultural Economics, Australian Jl of Agricultural and Resource Economics; distinguished fell Australian Agricultural and Resource Economics Soc 2008; *Style—* Prof Robert Fraser; ✉ School of Economics, Keynes College, University of Kent, Canterbury (e-mail r.w.fraser@kent.ac.uk)

FRASER, His Hon Judge; Cdre Robert William Fraser; MVO (1994); s of Gordon Smith Fraser (d 1988), and Kathleen Mary, *née* Blood; *b* 23 September 1955, Birkenhead, Merseyside; *Educ* Birkenhead Sch, Univ of Liverpool, RCDS, All Souls Coll Oxford; *m* 31 March 1990, Isobel Patricia Mary, *née* Clapham; 2 da (Alexandra b 30 Sept 1994, Annabel b 13 Aug 1996); *Career* joined Royal Navy 1974; called to the Bar 1984; equerry to HRH the Prince of Wales 1991–94, recorder 2001, sec to COS Ctee 2004–05, dir Naval Legal Servs 2005–07, circuit judge (South Eastern Circuit) 2007–; *Publications* Seaford House Papers (2002); *Recreations* sailing, skiing; *Style—* His Hon Judge Fraser, MVO; ✉ c/o The South Eastern Circuit, 289–293 High Holborn, London WC1V 7HZ

FRASER, Prof Ronald Strathearn Smith (Ron); s of Allan Fraser (d 1965), and Elizabeth, *née* Smith; *b* 10 July 1944; *Educ* Univ of Edinburgh (BSc, PhD, DSc); *m* 11 April 1987, Dr Hilary Margaret, *née* Haigh; 2 da (Rosalind Jane Strathearn b 4 Feb 1989, Eleanor Mary Haigh b 28 Aug 1990); *Career* res scientist Max-Planck Inst für Biologie Tübingen 1968–70, res fell Medical Res Cncl Dept of Zoology Univ of Edinburgh 1970–77, princ scientific offr and head Biochemistry Section Nat Vegetable Res Station Wellesbourne 1977–87; Inst of Horticultural Research: head Plant Science Div 1987–90, head of Station Inst of Horticultural Research Littlehampton 1987–96, dir of res in crop protection 1990–96; chief exec Soc for General Microbiology 1996–; hon lectr: Sch of Pure and Applied Biology Univ of Wales 1980–94, Dept of Microbiology Univ of Birmingham 1981–95; hon prof Sch of Biological Scis Univ of Birmingham 1995–98; hon visiting prof Sch of Biological Sciences Univ of Manchester 2000–03; memb Soc for Gen Microbiology; FIHort 1989; *Books* Mechanisms Of Resistance To Plant Diseases (1985, 2 edn 2000), The Biochemistry Of Virus-Infected Plants (1987), Recognition and Response In Plant Virus Interactions (1990); *Recreations* hill walking, music; *Style—* Prof Ron Fraser

FRASER, Sean; s of Ricky Fraser, and Susan, *née* Cochrane; *b* 30 April 1990, Edinburgh; *Educ* Lasswade HS; *Career* Paralympic swimmer; achievements incl: Bronze medal 100m backstroke Paralympics Beijing 2008, European record holder 50m and 100m backstroke (shortcourse), British record holder 100m backstroke and 50m freestyle (longcourse); *Clubs* Midlothian/Warrender Swim; *Style—* Sean Fraser, Esq; ✉ c/o British Paralympic Association, 40 Bernard Street, London WC1N 1ST

FRASER, Sir Simon; KCMG (2013, CMG 2009); *Career* civil servant; head of cabinet to Trade Cmmr European Cmmn 2004–08, DG for Europe and globalisation FCO 2008–09, perm sec Dept for Business, Innovation and Skills 2009–; *Style—* Sir Simon Fraser, KCMG; ✉ Department for Business, Enterprise and Regulatory Reform, 1 Victoria Street, London SW1H OET

FRASER, Sheriff Simon William Hetherington; s of late George MacDonald Fraser, of Baldrine, IOM, and late Kathleen Margarette, *née* Hetherington; *b* 2 April 1951; *Educ* Glasgow Acad, Univ of Glasgow (LLB); *m* 1, 7 Sept 1979 (m dis 2009), Sheena Janet, *née* Fraser; 1 da (Julie Katyana b 10 Dec 1981); m 2, 20 Feb 2010, Fiona; *Career* apprentice slr Kerr Barrie & Duncan Slrs Glasgow 1971–73, asst slr McGrigor Donald Slrs Glasgow 1973–75, ptnr Flowers & Co Slrs Glasgow 1976–89 (asst slr 1975–76), temp sheriff 1987–89, sheriff of N Strathclyde at Dumbarton 1989–2014; pres Glasgow Bar Assoc 1981–82, memb Cncl Sheriffs' Assoc 2007–10; *Recreations* watching Partick Thistle, cricket; *Clubs* Avizandum; *Style—* Sheriff Simon Fraser

FRASER, William; OBE (2006); s of William Fraser, OBE (d 1981), and Annie Betah, *née* Gardiner (d 1996); *b* 14 March 1938, Nottingham; *Educ* Forest Sch London; *m* Jan 1965, Penelope, *née* Hinds Howell; 2 da (Camilla Anne Davison b 9 Jan 1967, Emma Mary b 7 June 1968); *Career* Nat Serv 2nd Lt Queen's Own Cameron Highlanders 1957–59 (seconded for service to Ghana Army 1958–59); stockbroker City of London 1959–2008, associated with J M Finn & Co 1977–2008; memb Common Cncl City of London 1981– (past chm Music, Educn and City Bridge Tst Ctees, past chm City Lands and Bridge House Estates Ctee); chm: Partnership For Young London 1997–, City of London Acad Southwark 2003–, Met Public Gardens Assoc 2009–, Horlock Educnl Tst 2011–; tstee Central Fndn Schs of London; Master Worshipful Co of Gardeners 2006–07, Liveryman Worshipful Co of Musicians; MSI; *Recreations* sport, gardening, theatre, music; *Clubs* City Livery (pres 1991); *Style—* William Fraser, Esq, OBE; ✉ 1 Alleyn Road, Dulwich, London SE21 8AB (☎ 020 8670 4770, e-mail william.fraser@cityoflondon.gov.uk)

FRASER, Prof William Duncan (Bill); s of Brian Wadsworth Fraser, of Formby, Lancs, and Susan Cochrane Fraser (d 2003); *b* 16 May 1955, Glasgow; *Educ* Allan Glen's Sch Glasgow, Univ of Glasgow (BSc, MB ChB, MD); *m* 3 Aug 1989, Aileen Agnes; 2 da (Helen Jean b 19 July 1983, Karen Susan b 5 March 1987), 1 s (Brian James b 5 July 1990); *Career* house offr Southern Gen Hosp Glasgow 1982–83, sr registrar Royal Infirmary Glasgow 1986–91 (registrar 1983–86), conslt (locum) Regina Gen Hosp Saskatchewan 1990; Royal Liverpool Univ Hosp: sr lectr 1991–98, reader and hon conslt 1998–2000, prof and hon conslt 2000–, head Metabolic Bone Disease Unit; chm: Scientific Prog Ctee Assoc of Clinical Biochemists Focus 1999, Scientific Ctee Assoc of Clinical Biochemists 1999–2003; med advsr Nat Osteoporosis Soc; ed: Jl of Endocrinology, Calcified Tissues International; author of more than 150 peer-reviewed scientific papers on bone and calcium metabolism 1986–; ACB Fndn Award 2006; FRCPath 1997 (MRCPath 1989), MRCP 1999; *Recreations* golf, guitar, violin; *Style—* Prof Bill Fraser; ✉ University Department of Clinical Chemistry, Duncan Building, Royal Liverpool University Hospital, Prescot Street, Liverpool L69 3GA (☎ 0151 706 4247, fax 0151 706 5813, e-mail w.d.fraser@liv.ac.uk)

FRASER, Prof William Irvine; CBE (1998); s of Duncan Fraser (d 1979), and Muriel, *née* Macrae (d 1977); *b* 3 February 1940; *Educ* Greenock Acad, Univ of Glasgow (MB ChB, MD, DPM); *m* 1 Oct 1964, Joyce Carroll, da of Douglas Gilchrist (d 1978); 2 s (Ewen Duncan b 31 May 1966, Alan Douglas b 1 Sept 1968); *Career* physician supt and dir Fife Mental Handicap Servs 1974–78, hon sr lectr in psychology Univ of St Andrews 1973–89, pt/t sr lectr Univ of Edinburgh 1974–89, conslt psychiatrist Royal Edinburgh Hosp 1978–79, ed Jl of Intellectual Disability Research 1982–2003, currently prof emeritus of learning disability Univ of Wales Coll of Med; Burden Neurological Inst Prize medallist for research into mental handicap 1989, Int Assoc for Sci Study of Intellectual Disabilities Distinguished Achievement Award for Scientific Literature 1996; memb Gen Projects Ctee Mental Health Fndn 1981–87, co-dir Welsh Centre for Learning Disability 1994–2002; pres Welsh Psychiatric Soc 2006–12, chair Autism Cymru; FRCPsych 1978 (former chm Welsh Div), FRCPEd 2000, FMedSci 2001; *Books* Communicating with Normal and Retarded Children (with R Grieve, 1981), Caring for People with Learning Disabilities (1997), Seminars in Learning Disability (with M Kerr, 2003); *Style—* Prof William Fraser, CBE; ✉ e-mail fraser_bill@yahoo.com

FRASER, Sir William Kerr; GCB (1984, KCB 1979, CB 1978); s of late Alexander Macmillan Fraser, and Rachel, *née* Kerr; *b* 18 March 1929; *Educ* Eastwood Sch, Univ of Glasgow (MA, LLB); *m* 1956, Marion Anne, *née* Forbes, (Lady Marion Fraser, LT); 3 s (1 of whom Dr Andrew Fraser, *qv*), 1 da; *Career* joined Scot Home Dept 1955, perm under sec of state Scot Office 1978–88 (dep sec 1975–78); princ and vice-chllr Univ of Glasgow 1988–95, chm Royal Cmmn on the Ancient and Historical Monuments of Scotland 1995–2000; chllr Univ of Glasgow 1996–2006; Hon LLD Univs of Aberdeen, Glasgow and Strathclyde; Hon Dr Univ of Edinburgh; Hon FRCP (Glasgow), FRSE 1985, Hon FRSAMD 1995; *Clubs* New (Edinburgh); *Style—* Sir William Fraser, GCB, FRSE; ✉ Broadwood, Edinburgh Road, Gifford, East Lothian EH41 4JE (☎ and fax 01620 810319)

FRATER, Alexander Russell; s of Dr Alexander Smail Frater (d 1972), and Lorna Rosie, *née* Fray (d 1986); *b* 3 January 1937; *Educ* Scotch Coll Melbourne, Univ of Melbourne, Univ of Durham, Univ of Perugia; *m* 1963, Marlis, da of Erwin Pfund; 1 da (Tania Elisabeth b 1964), 1 s (Alexander John b 1969); *Career* asst ed Punch 1963–66, retained writer The New Yorker 1964–68, staff writer Daily Telegraph Magazine 1966–77, asst ed Radio Times 1977–79; The Observer: asst ed magazine 1979–84, dep ed magazine 1984–86, chief travel corr 1986–98; TV presenter: The Last African Flying Boat (BBC) 1990 (BAFTA Award for Best Single Documentary), Monsoon (BBC) 1991, In the Footsteps of Buddha (BBC) 1993; Br Press Award commendations 1982 and 1989, Br Press Award Travel Writer of the Year 1990, 1991 and 1992, Best Radio Feature Travelex Travel Writers' Awards 2000, overall winner Travelex Travel Writers' Awards 2000; patron Darjeeling Children's Tst 2009–10; *Books* Stopping-Train Britain (1983), Great Rivers Of The World (ed, 1984), Beyond The Blue Horizon (1986, Top Ten Books on Aviation The Guardian 2003), Chasing The Monsoon (1990, shortlisted Thomas Cook Travel Book of the Year Award, Br Book Award, McVitie's Prize, Top Ten Travel Books Daily Telegraph 2011), Tales From The Torrid Zone (2004), The Balloon Factory (2008); *Recreations* books, walking; *Style—* Alexander Frater, Esq; ✉ c/o Aitken Alexander Associates, 18–21 Cavaye Place, London SW10 9PT

FRAWLEY, Dr Tom J; CBE; *Career* sr health service mangr 1978–2000, assembly ombudsman for NI and NI cmmr for complaints 2000–; memb Exec Ctee Ombudsman Assoc 2012–; *Style—* Dr Tom Frawley, CBE; ✉ Office of the Assembly Ombudsman and Northern Ireland Commissioner for Complaints, Progressive House, 33 Wellington Place, Belfast BT1 6HN

FRAY, Prof Derek John; s of Arthur Joseph Fray (d 2000), of London, and Doris Lilian Wilson (d 1981); *b* 26 December 1939; *Educ* Emanuel Sch, Imperial Coll London (BSc Eng, ARSM, PhD, DIC, state scholar, royal scholar), Univ of Cambridge (MA); *m* 14 Aug 1965 (m dis 2002), Mirella Christine Kathleen, da of Leslie Honey, of Thames Ditton, Surrey; 1 s (Shelton Lanning b 1972), 1 da (Justine Chloe b 1974); *Career* asst prof of metallurgy MIT 1965–68, gp ldr Res Dept Imperial Smelting Corp Ltd Avonmouth Bristol 1968–71, univ lectr Dept of Materials Sci and Metallurgy Univ of Cambridge 1971–90; Fitzwilliam Coll Cambridge: fell 1972–90, librarian 1973–74, tutorial and estates bursar 1974–86, bursar 1986–88, professorial fell 1996–; prof of mineral engrg and head Dept of Mining and Mineral Engrg Univ of Leeds 1991–96, prof of materials chemistry Dept of Materials Sci and Metallurgy Univ of Cambridge 1996– (head of dept 2001–06, dir of research and emeritus prof of extraction materials chemistry 2007–); visiting prof Univ of Leeds 1996–, hon prof of science and technol Beijing 1995–, hon prof Hebei Poly Univ 2006–, hon prof Liaonong Univ of Sci and Technol 2010–; dir: EMC Ltd, Camfridge Ltd, Inotec AMD Ltd, Chinuka Ltd, Welding Alloys Gp Ltd; memb: Inst of Materials, Soc of Chemical Industry, AIME; Sidney Gilchrist Thomas lectr 2003; MIM 1966, FIMM 1988 (memb Organizing Ctee for extraction metallurgy 1981–85 and 1987, and for pyrometallurgy 1987, memb Editorial Bd, memb Cncl), FREng 1989, FRSC 2005, FRS 2008; *Awards* Matthey prize 1967, AIME Extractive Metallurgy Technol award 1980, Sir George Beilby medal 1981, Nuffield SERC visiting fellowship 1981, Bd of Review AIME 1985, Kroll medal and prize Inst of Metals 1987, John Phillips medal 1991, TMS

F

Distinguished Extractive Metallurgy Lectr 2000, Billiton Medal 2001, IMM 2001, Reactive Metals Award 2002, TMS 2002, Gold Medal IMMM 2003, Armourers and Braziers' Medal and Prize Royal Soc 2003, Reactive Metals Technol Award TMS 2004, Fedn of European Materials Socs Materials Innovation Prize 2009, Fray Int Symposium Cancun 2011, Max Bredig Award US Electrochemical Soc 2012, Futers Gold Medal IMMM 2015, Sydney Gilchrist Lecture 2016; *Books* Worked Examples in Mass and Heat Transfer in Materials Technology (1983); author of over 420 papers and over 300 published patents; *Recreations* cinema, walking, reading; *Style*— Prof Derek Fray, FRS, FREng; ✉ 7 Woodlands Road, Great Shelford, Cambridge CB22 5LW (☎ 01223 842296); Department of Materials Science and Metallurgy, University of Cambridge, 27 Charles Babbage Road, Cambridge CB3 0FS (☎ 01223 334306, fax 01223 334567, e-mail djf25@cam.ac.uk)

FRAYLING, Prof Sir Christopher John; kt (2001); s of Maj Arthur Frederick Frayling, OBE (d 1993), and Barbara Kathleen, *née* Imhof (d 2001); *b* 25 December 1946; *Educ* Repton, Churchill Coll Cambridge (scholar, MA, PhD); *m* 1981, Helen Ann Snowdon; *Career* lectr in history Univ of Exeter 1971–72, film archivist Imperial War Museum 1972–73, lectr in history of ideas Univ of Bath 1973–79; Royal Coll of Art: prof of cultural history 1979–2009 (prof emeritus 2009), pro-rector 1992–96, rector 1996–2009; visiting prof Shanghai Univ of Technol E China 1991; Arts Council of GB: memb Photography Panel 1983–85, chm Art Projects Ctee 1985–88, memb Cncl 1987–2000, chm Visual Arts Panel 1987–94 (dep chm 1984–87), chm Film, Video and Broadcasting Panel 1994–2000, chm Educn and Trg Panel 1996–98; chair Arts Cncl England 2004–09 (memb 1987–2000); V&A Museum: tstee 1983–2009, memb Advsy Bd 1981–83, ex officio memb Bd 1997–2009, memb Educn Ctee, chm Bethnal Green Museum Ctee, chm Contemporary Programme; govr BFI 1982–86 and 2009– (chm Educn Ctee 1983–86); chm: Crafts Study Centre Bath 1981–2004, Free Form Arts Trust 1984–89, Design Industries Gp DTI 1999–2001, Design Gp of Liturgical Ctee 1998–2000, Design Cncl 2000–04, Royal Mint Design Advsy Ctee 2001–11; memb: Crafts Cncl 1982–85 (chm Educn and Pubns Ctees), Nat Advsy Body Working Party on Higher Educn in the Arts 1985–88, Advsy Bd Inst of Contemporary Art, ARTEC (educn and technol gp), New Millennium Experience Co Litmus Group 1998–2000, Bd Design Museum, Arts and Humanities Research Bd 1999–2004; tstee Holburne of Menstrie Museum Bath 1983–2000, tstee Royal Mint Museum 2010–; writer and presenter of numerous TV series incl: The Art of Persuasion (Channel 4) 1984, Busting the Block (Channel 4) 1986, Cinema Profiles (BBC 2) 1984–90, The Face of Tutankhamun (BBC 2) 1993, Strange Landscape – the illumination of the Middle Ages (BBC 2) 1994–95, Nightmare – the birth of horror (BBC 1) 1996–97, Hotseat (Artsworld) 2000–01; RSA Bicentennial Medal 2001, Misha Black Meml Medal 2003, Maitland Medal 2006, da Vinci Medal 2009; fell Churchill Coll Cambridge 2009; hon fell: Humberside Poly 1991, Kent Inst of Art and Design 1997, Hereford Coll of Art 2010; Hon DLitt Univ of NSW; Hon Dr: Staffordshire Univ, UWE, Univ of Bath, Univ of Lancaster, Univ of the Arts, Univ of Brighton, Royal Coll of Art, Sheffield Hallam Univ; hon RIBA 2005, life fell RSA 2006 (FRSA 1984), FCSD 1994; *Books* Napoleon Wrote Fiction (1972), The Vampyre – Lord Ruthven to Count Dracula (ed, 1977), The Schoolmaster and the Wheelwrights (1980), Spaghetti Westerns – Cowboys and Europeans from Karl May to Sergio Leone (1981), The Royal College of Art: one hundred and fifty years of art and design (1987), The BFI Companion to the Western (co-ed, 1988), Vampyres – Lord Byron to Count Dracula (1991), Beyond the Dovetail – crafts, skill and imagination (ed, 1991), Clint Eastwood – a critical biography (1992), The Face of Tutankhamun (1992), The Art Pack (with Helen Frayling, 1992), Strange Landscape (1994), Things to Come – a film classic (1995), Design of the times (with Claire Catterall, 1996), Nightmare – the birth of horror (1996), Spaghetti Westerns (rev ed, 1998 and 2005), The Royal College of Art – One Hundred Years of Art and Design (1999), Sergio Leone – something to do with death (2000), The Hound of the Baskervilles (ed, 2001), Dracula (ed, 2003), Once Upon a Time in Italy (2005), Ken Adam – the Art of Production Design (2006), Mad, Bad and Dangerous – the Image of the Scientist in Film (2006), Ken Adam Designs the Movies (2009), Horace Walpole's Cat (2009), Craftsmanship: Towards a new Bauhaus (2011); numerous articles in learned and rather less learned journals and exhbn catalogues on aspects of Euro and American cultural history; *Recreations* finding time; *Style*— Prof Sir Christopher Frayling

FRAYN, Michael; s of late Thomas Allen Frayn, and late Violet Alice, *née* Lawson; *b* 8 September 1933; *Educ* Kingston GS, Emmanuel Coll Cambridge; *m* 1, 1960 (m dis 1989), Gillian, *née* Palmer; 3 da; m 2, 5 June 1993, Claire Tomalin, *qv*; *Career* author and playwright; columnist: The Guardian 1959–62 (reporter 1957–59), Observer 1962–68; recipient of numerous drama awards, Special Olivier Award 2013; hon fell Emmanuel Coll Cambridge 1985; Hon DPhil Univ of Cambridge 2001; FRSL 1969, CLit 2007; *Stage Plays* The Two of Us 1970, The Sandboy 1971, Alphabetical Order 1975, Donkeys' Years 1976, Clouds 1976, Balmoral 1978 (new version Liberty Hall 1980), Make and Break 1980, Noises Off 1982 (film 1991), Benefactors 1984, Look Look 1990, Here 1993, Now You Know 1995, La Belle Vivette (opera) 1995, Copenhagen 1998, Alarms & Excursions 1998, Democracy 2003, Afterlife 2008, Matchbox Theatre 2015; *Television* plays and films incl: Jamie, On a Flying Visit 1968, Birthday 1969, Clockwise 1986, First and Last 1989, A Landing on the Sun 1994, Remember Me? 1997; documentaries incl: Second City Reports 1964, One Pair of Eyes 1968, Laurence Sterne Lived Here 1973, Imagine a City Called Berlin 1975, Vienna: The Mask of Gold 1977, Three Streets in the Country 1979, The Long Straight (Great Railway Journeys of the World) 1980, Jerusalem 1984, Prague: the Magic Lantern 1994, Budapest: Written in Water 1996; comedy series: Beyond a Joke 1972, Making Faces 1975; *Translations of Plays* incl: The Cherry Orchard, Three Sisters, The Seagull, Uncle Vanya, Wild Honey (all Chekhov), The Fruits of Enlightenment (Tolstoy), Exchange (Trifonov), Number One (Anouilh), The Sneeze (Chekhov Short Plays); *Novels* incl: The Tin Men (1965, Somerset Maugham Award), The Russian Interpreter (1966, Hawthornden Prize), Towards the End of the Morning (1967), A Very Private Life (1968), Sweet Dreams (1973), The Trick of It (1989), A Landing On The Sun (1991, Sunday Express Book of the Year Award), Now You Know (1992), Headlong (1999, shortlisted for Booker Prize 1999), Spies (2003, Whitbread Novel of the Year 2003), Skios (2012); *Non-fiction* incl: Constructions (philosophy, 1974), Celia's Secret (with David Burke, 2000), The Human Touch: Our Part in the Creation of a Universe (2006), Collected Columns (2007), Travels with a Typewriter (2009), My Father's Fortune (2010, PEN Ackerley Prize); several volumes of collected writings and translations incl Stage Directions: Writing on Theatre 1970–2008; *Style*— Michael Frayn; ✉ c/o Greene & Heaton Ltd, 37 Goldhawk Road, London W12 9PU (☎ 020 8749 0315, fax 020 8749 0318)

FRAZER, Christopher Mark; s of Michael Leslie Frazer, of Twickenham, Middx, and Pamela Mary, *née* Stoakes; *b* 17 June 1960; *Educ* KCS Wimbledon, St John's Coll Cambridge (exhibitioner, Macaulay scholar, McMahon law student, MA, LLM, coll prizeman); *m* 20 May 1989, Victoria Margaret, da of John Peter Hess, of Chorlton-by-Backford, Cheshire; 1 s (Thomas Michael John b 19 June 1994), 1 da (Laura Charlotte Mary b 31 Aug 1996); *Career* called to the Bar Middle Temple 1983, ad eundem Inner Temple; in practice Midland, Western and SE circuits; dep district judge of the High Court and Co Court (Western Circuit) 1997–2001, recorder of the Crown Court 2000–; memb Gen Cncl of the Bar 1989–94 and 2000–, chm Bar Conf 1994, chm BARMARK panel 1999–2001; chm Editorial Bd Counsel magazine 1995–99; chm Young Barristers' Ctee of England and Wales 1991; Parly candidate (Cons) Peckham 1992, sec Soc of Cons Lawyers 1988–89 and 1998–2000; chm London West Cons Euro Constituency Cncl 1994–97; common councilman Corp of London 1986–95; Freeman City of London 1986; *Books* Thoughts for a Third Term (1987), Privatise the Prosecutors (1993); *Recreations* dinghy sailing, Classic FM, amusing my children; *Clubs* Guildhall, West Wittering Sailing; *Style*— Christopher Frazer, Esq; ✉ 2 Harcourt Buildings, Temple, London EC4Y 9DB (☎ 020 7353 6961, fax 020 7353 6968)

FRAZER, Lucy; QC (2013), MP; *m* David; 2 c; *Career* MP (Cons) SE Cambridgeshire 2015–; *Style*— Ms Lucy Frazer, QC, MP; ✉ House of Commons, London SW1A 0AA

FREAN, Jenny (Jennifer Margaret); da of Theodore John Farbridge (d 1984), of Lymington, Hants, and Isobel, *née* Reid Douglas (d 1988); *b* 17 April 1947; *Educ* City of London Sch for Girls, Hornsey Coll of Art (BA), Royal Coll of Art (MA); *m* 1970, Patrick Frean, s of Denis Frean, CBE; 1 da (Holly Thea b 1978); *Career* design conslt Centro Design Montefibre Milan 1974, fndr Jenny Frean Associates (textile design studio) 1975, portraitist 1984–86, fndr First Eleven Studio (textile designers) 1986; RDI 1998; *Recreations* music especially opera, all art forms, gardening; *Style*— Mrs Jenny Frean, RDI; ✉ e-mail jennyfrean@firstelevenstudio.com

FREARS, Stephen Arthur; s of Dr Russell E Frears (d 1977), of Nottingham, and Ruth M Frears (d 1971); *b* 20 June 1941; *Educ* Gresham's, Trinity Coll Cambridge (BA); *m* 1, 1967 (m dis 1973), Mary K, *née* Wilmers; 2 s (Sam b 1972, William b 1973); m 2, Anne Rothenstein; 1 s (Francis Frears b 1983), 1 da (Lola Frears b 1985); *Career* film director; pres of jury Cannes Film Festival 2007; *Films* Gumshoe 1971, Bloody Kids 1980, Going Gently 1981, Saigon 1983, Walter 1982, The Hit 1984, My Beautiful Launderette 1985, Prick up Your Ears 1986, Sammy and Rosie Get Laid 1987, Dangerous Liaisons 1989, The Grifters 1990, Accidental Hero 1992, The Snapper 1994, Mary Reilly 1995, The Van 1996, The Hi-Lo Country 1997, High Fidelity 1999, Liam 2001, Dirty Pretty Things 2002, The Deal 2003, Mrs Henderson Presents 2004, The Queen 2005, Chéri 2008, Tamara Drewe 2009, Lay the Favorite 2011, Mohammed Ali's Greatest Fight 2012, Philomena 2013, The Program 2015, Florence Foster Jenkins 2015, Victoria and Abdul 2016; *Style*— Stephen Frears, Esq; ✉ c/o Casarotto Ramsay Associates, Waverley House, 7–12 Noel Street, London W1F 8GQ (☎ 020 7287 4450, fax 020 7287 9128)

FREDERIKSEN-WALMSLEY, Heather; MBE (2013); *née* Frederiksen; da of John Frederiksen, of Leigh, Lancashire, and Lynne Mary, *née* Coop; *b* 30 December 1985, Billinge, Merseyside; *m* 27 Sept 2013, Paul Walmsley; 1 da (Molly b 13 Feb 2014); *Career* Paralympic swimmer; achievements incl: 2 Gold medals and 2 Silver medals Br Championships 2008, Gold medal (100m backstroke), 2 Silver medals (100m freestyle and 400m freestyle) and Bronze medal (200m individual medley) Paralympic Games 2008, Gold medal (100m backstroke) and 3 Silver medals (400m freestyle, 100m freestyle and 4x100m medley relay) Paralympic Games 2012; current holder of 5 world records (50m freestyle, 100m freestyle, 200m freestyle, 400m freestyle and 100m backstroke); *Clubs* City of Salford, City of Manchester Aquatics Swim Team; *Style*— Mrs Heather Frederiksen-Walmsley, MBE; ✉ c/o Matt Kendrew, ISM Ltd, Cherry Tree Farm, Cherry Tree Lane, Rostherne, Cheshire WA14 3RZ (☎ 01565 832100, e-mail matt@sportism.net); c/o Graham S Leigh (agent), Maple House, Haymarket Street, Bury, Greater Manchester BL9 0AR (☎ 0161 764 1818, mobile 07836 336028, fax 0161 761 6699, e-mail gsl@glplaw.com)

FREEDEN, Prof Michael Stephen; s of Herbert Freeden, and Marianne Freeden; *b* 30 April 1944; *Educ* Hebrew Univ of Jerusalem (BA), Univ of Oxford (MA, DPhil); *m* 1968, Irene Gerszzon; 1 s (Jonathan Gabriel b 1969), 1 da (Daniella Leora b 1972); *Career* lectr and sr lectr Univ of Haifa 1972–77, visiting fell St Antony's Coll Oxford 1977–78; Mansfield Coll Oxford: fell and tutor 1978–2011, sr tutor 1982–89, professorial fell 1996–2011; Univ of Oxford: chm Sub-Faculty of Politics 1991–93, prof of politics 1997–2011, dir Centre for Political Ideologies 2002–11, emeritus prof of politics 2011–; prof of political theory Univ of Nottingham 2013–15, professorial research assoc SOAS Univ of London 2016–; founding ed Jl of Political Ideologies 1996, assoc ed Oxford DNB 1993–2004; Br Acad research readership 1989–91, ESRC professorial fellowship 2004–07, Leverhulme emeritus fell 2016–; Medal for Science Bologna Univ 2012, Sir Isaiah Berlin Prize for Lifetime Contrib to Political Studies Award UK Political Studies Assoc 2012; FRHistS 1980, FAcSS 2016; *Books* The New Liberalism: An Ideology of Social Reform (1978), Liberalism Divided: A Study in British Political Thought 1914–1939 (1986), Reappraising J A Hobson: Humanism and Welfare (ed, 1990), Rights (1991), Ideologies and Political Theory: A Conceptual Approach (1996), A Very Short Introduction to Ideology (2003), Liberal Languages (2005), The Meaning of Ideology: Cross-Disciplinary Perspectives (2007), The Political Theory of Political Thinking (2013), The Oxford Handbook of Political Ideologies (ed, 2013), Liberalism: A Very Short Introduction (2015); *Recreations* second-hand book collecting, urban photography; *Style*— Prof Michael Freeden; ✉ Mansfield College, Oxford OX1 3TF (☎ 01865 270999, e-mail michael.freeden@mansfield.ox.ac.uk)

FREEDLAND, Michael Rodney; s of David Freedland, and Lily, *née* Mindel; *b* 18 December 1934; *Educ* Luton GS; *m* 3 July 1960, Sara, da of Abram Hockerman; 2 da (Fiona Anne b 1963, Daniela Ruth b 1964), 1 s (Jonathan Saul b 1967); *Career* journalist for local newspapers 1951–60, Daily Sketch 1960–61; freelance journalist 1961–; contrib: The Times, Sunday Telegraph, The Guardian, Economist, Spectator, The Observer, Daily Express, Sunday Express; broadcaster 1962– (progs incl You don't have to be Jewish (BBC and LBC) 1971–94 and various progs on BBC Radio 2); wrote Jolson (musical show, opened London 1995); *Books* 40 books incl: Al Jolson (1971), Irving Berlin (1973), Fred Astaire (1976), Gregory Peck (1979), The Warner Brothers (1982), Danny Kaye (1987), Leonard Bernstein (1987), Jane Fonda (1988), Dustin Hoffman (1989), Kenneth Williams (1990), André Previn (1991), Music Man (1994), Sean Connery, A Biography (1994), All The Way, A Biography of Frank Sinatra (1997), Bob Hope (1998), Bing Crosby (1998), Michael Caine (1999), Doris Day (2000), Some Like It Cool (2002), Liza with a 'Z' (2004), Dean Martin, King of the Road (2004), Confessions of a Serial Biographer (autobiography, 2005), Witch Hunt In Hollywood: McCarthyism's War on Tinseltown (2009), The Men Who Made Hollywood (2009), Judy Garland: The Other Side of the Rainbow (2011), Elvis Memories (2013), Man on the Rock (2013); *Recreations* reading, being with my family; *Style*— Michael Freedland, Esq; ✉ 152 Albany, Manor Road, Bournemouth Dorset BH1 3EW (☎ 01202 801787, mobile 07767 622586)

FREEDMAN, Cyril Winston; s of Sydney Freedman (d 1951), and Irene Rosalind, *née* Anekstein; *b* 31 August 1945; *Educ* Brighton Coll, Brighton Coll of Art and Design (Dip Graphic Art and Design); *m* 25 March 1970, Christine Mary, da of Cecil Shipman, of Swanwick, Derbys; 1 s (Mark b 1973), 1 da (Anna b 1977); *Career* chm: CWF Advertising Ltd 1971–74, Halls Homes and Gardens 1978–80 (md 1977–78, dir 1974–81); dir Pentos plc and subsidiaries 1979–81, chm Serco Ryan Ltd 1982–87, chief exec WBH Group Ltd (subsidiary of Lopex plc) 1985–88, dir Armour Automotive Products Group (subsidiary of Armour Trust plc) 1985–91; chm: Deeko plc 1988–90 (dir 1986–90), Hennell plc 1988–94, Worth Fine Fragrances plc 1992–97, Lighterlife UK Ltd 2005–08; dir Apax Partners & Co Ventures Ltd (formerly known as Alan Patricof Associates Ltd) 1988–95; exec chm S Daniels plc 1997–2002 (dep chm and chief exec 1995–97), non-exec chm Lloyd Maunder Property Hldgs Ltd 2004–09; dir: New Covent Garden Soup Co 1989–2002, Stead & Simpson Group 1992–2007; non-exec dir David Morris Int Ltd 2004–; FInstD, MCIM; *Recreations* painting, travel, collecting fine art; *Style*— Cyril Freedman, Esq; ✉ Minety House, The Green, Minety, Malmesbury, Wiltshire SN16 9PL (☎ 01666 860433, e-mail cyrilfreedman@aol.com)

FREEDMAN, Dr Danielle Beverley; *b* 28 August 1953; *Educ* Woodhouse GS London, Royal Free Hosp Sch of Med London (Winifred Ladd scholar, MB BS, Edith Peachy Phipson prize); *m* (m dis); 1 s; *Career* Royal Free Hosp London: house physician and house surgn posts 1977–78, SHO in clinical pathology 1978–79, registrar Dept of Chemical Pathology 1979–81; clinical lectr (sr registrar) Dept of Chemical Pathology Courtauld Inst of Biochemistry Middx Hosp Med Sch London 1981–84; Luton and Dunstable Hosp NHS Tst: conslt chemical pathologist and assoc physician in clinical endocrinology and metabolism 1985–, clinical dir of pathology 1990–, clinical dir of pathology and pharmacy 1993–, medical dir Luton and Dunstable Hosp 2005–; regnl postgraduate dean rep Univ of London and Univ of Cambridge; nat surveyor King's Fund Organisational Audit (Accreditation UK), nat inspr Clinical Pathology Accreditation (CPA) UK Ltd, memb Nat Working Pty for implementation of clinical guidelines; past chm Clinical Biochemistry Sub-Ctee NW Thames RHA; RCPath: chair SAC Clinical Biochemistry 2005–, former memb Cncl, memb Standing Ctee for Chemical Pathology, memb Nat Clinical Audit Ctee, RCPath rep Assoc of Clinical Biochemists Cncl, memb Standing Ctee on RCPath Academic Activities, memb Pubns Ctee, RCPath rep NHS Mgmnt Exec working with professions to develop service specifications, E Anglia rep for chemical pathology; Assoc of Clinical Biochemists: memb Scientific Ctee, sr ed Venture Pubns Gp, chm Jt Working Gp looking at near patient testing, chm Educn Ctee, Nat Ames Award and Medal for Research 1981, Prize for Clinical Audit 1992; FRCPath 1995; *Books* A Short Textbook of Chemical Pathology (ed), Clinical Chemistry (ed); numerous pubns in academic jls; *Style*— Dr Danielle Freedman; ✉ The Luton and Dunstable Hospital NHS Trust, Lewsey Road, Luton LU4 0DZ (☎ 01582 497212, fax 01582 497387)

FREEDMAN, His Hon Judge Jeremy Stuart; *b* 20 April 1959, Newcastle upon Tyne; *Educ* Oundle, Univ of Manchester (BA), City Univ (Dip); *m* 12 Aug 1989, Julia, *née* Chapman; 1 da (Lucy b 3 Dec 1990), 1 s (Nicholas b 7 July 1993); *Career* called to the Bar 1982; asst recorder 1998, recorder 2000, head of chambers 2003–10, circuit judge (North Eastern Circuit) 2013–; *Recreations* cinema, golf, opera, skiing, tennis, travel, walking; *Clubs* Northern Counties, Northumberland Golf; *Style*— His Hon Judge Jeremy Freedman; ✉ Newcastle-upon-Tyne Combined Court, The Law Courts, The Quayside, Newcastle-upon-Tyne NE1 3LA

FREEDMAN, Rt Hon Prof Sir Lawrence David; KCMG (2003), CBE (1996), PC (2009); s of Lt Cdr Julius Freedman, RN (d 1987), and Myra, *née* Robinson (d 1995); *b* 7 December 1948; *Educ* Whitley Bay GS, Univ of Manchester (BA), Univ of York (BPhil), Univ of Oxford (PhD); *m* 1974, Judith Anne, da of Harry Hill, and Stella Hill; 1 s (Samuel b 1981), 1 da (Ruth b 1984); *Career* teaching asst Dept of Politics Univ of York 1971–72, res (prize) fell Nuffield Coll Oxford 1974–75, lectr in politics (pt/t) Balliol Coll Oxford 1975, research assoc IISS 1975–76, research fell on British foreign policy RIIA 1976–78, head of policy studies RIIA 1978–82, prof of war studies KCL 1982–2014, vice-princ KCL 2003–13; columnist: The Independent 1987–93, The Times 1993–2000, FT 2000–; specialist advsr House of Commons Defence Ctee 1980–97; memb: Current Affrs Advsy Gp Channel 4 1986–87, Govt and Law Ctee Economic and Social Res Cncl 1982–87, Cncl IISS 1984–92 and 1993–2002, Cncl David Davies Meml Inst 1990–95, Cncl SSEES Univ of London 1996–99, Expert Panel on Strategic Defence Review MoD 1997–98, Iraq Inquiry 2009–16; memb Editorial Bd: Foreign Policy, Int Security, Political Quarterly, Intelligence and National Security; tstee Imperial War Museum 2001–09; FKC 1992, FBA 1995; *Books* US Intelligence and the Soviet Strategic Threat (1977, reprinted with new foreword 1986), Britain and Nuclear Weapons (1980), The Evolution of Nuclear Strategy (1981, 3 edn 2003), The Troubled Alliance: Atlantic Relations in the 1980s (ed, 1983), Nuclear War and Nuclear Peace (jtly, 1983, 2 edn 1988), The Atlas of Global Strategy (1985), The Price of Peace: Living with the Nuclear Dilemma (1986), Britain and the Falklands War (1988), US Nuclear Strategy: A Reader (co-ed, 1989), Military Power in Europe: Essays in Memory of Jonathan Alford (ed, 1990), Signals of War: The Falklands Conflict of 1982 (jtly, 1990), Britain in the World (jtly, 1991), The Gulf Conflict 1990–91 (jtly, 1993), Military Intervention in European Conflicts (ed, 1994), War: A Reader (ed, 1994), Strategic Coercion (ed, 1998), The Politics of British Defence 1979–1998 (1999), Kennedy's Wars (2000), The Cold War (2001), Superterrorism (ed, 2002), Deterrence (2004), The Official History of the Falklands Campaign (2 vols, 2005), A Choice of Enemies (2009), Strategy: A History (2013); *Recreations* political cartoons; *Style*— The Rt Hon Prof Sir Lawrence Freedman, KCMG, CBE, FBA; ✉ e-mail lawrence.freedman@kcl.ac.uk

FREEDMAN, Michael John; s of late Joseph Leopold Freedman, of London, and late Rosa Annie, *née* Bosman (d 1987); *b* 4 July 1946; *Educ* Clifton, Christ's Coll Cambridge; *m* 1973, Pamela Dawn, da of late Cyril Kay, and late Hilda Kay; 1 da (Natalie Kay b 31 Jan 1976), 1 s (Jonathan Leonard b 13 April 1979); *Career* mktg mangr Royal Angus Hotels 1965–69; mktg dir: Securadet Ltd 1969–72, Paul Kaye Studio Ltd 1972–; chm Cover Shots International 1990–2000, chm Artica Galleries Ltd 2005–10; memb Cncl BIPP 1989–2001; FBIPP, FMPA; *Recreations* badminton, swimming, reading, walking, backgammon; *Style*— Michael Freedman, Esq; ✉ Paul Kaye Studio Ltd, 63 Gordon Avenue, Stanmore, Middlesex HA7 3QR (e-mail mf@pkstudio.demon.co.uk)

FREELAND, Rowan Charles Bayfield; s of Col Paul Rowan Bayfield Freeland (d 2005), and Susanna Brigitta Elizabeth, *née* Burch (d 2011); *b* 13 December 1956; *Educ* Wellington, St Catherine's Coll Oxford (BA); *m* 12 Dec 1987, Davina Alexandra Claire, da of Maj Dennis Edward Salisbury (d 1964); 3 da (Marigold Claire Salisbury b 31 Oct 1990, Constance Margaret Alexandra b 12 Nov 1992, Beatrix Emily Faith b 1 June 1995); *Career* admitted slr 1982; ptnr Simmons & Simmons LLP 1988– (head Munich Office 2013–15); chm Intellectual Property Lawyers' Assoc 2014– (sec 2006–14); chm London Mozart Players 2011–16 (sec 1984–2012); *Recreations* family, opera, gardening, reading; *Style*— Rowan Freeland, Esq; ✉ Simmons & Simmons LLP, CityPoint, One Ropemaker Street, London EC2Y 9SS (☎ 020 7825 4447, e-mail rowan.freeland@simmons-simmons.com)

FREELAND, His Hon Judge Simon Dennis Marsden; QC (2002); s of Dennis M Freeland, and Rosemary Turnbull Tarn, *née* Menzies; *b* 11 February 1956; *Educ* Malvern Coll, Univ of Manchester (LLB); *m* 12 Feb 2002, Anne Elizabeth; 1 da (Ruby Anastasia b 3 July 2004), 1 s (George Arthur Menzies b 23 March 2006); *Career* called to the Bar Gray's Inn 1978; barr specialising in police law, recorder 1999–2007, head of chambers 5 Essex Court 2002–07, circuit judge (SE Circuit) 2007–; memb: Personal Injury Bar Assoc, SE Circuit Exec Ctee; *Recreations* walking, horse racing, good food and fine wine, family; *Style*— His Hon Judge Freeland, Esq, QC; ✉ Snaresbrook Crown Court, 75 Hollybush Hill, Snaresbrook, London E11 1QW

FREEMAN, Andrew Lawrence D; s of Richard D Freeman, and Diana L, *née* Cranwell; *b* 4 March 1963; *Educ* Balliol Coll Oxford (BA), Merton Coll Oxford (sr scholar); *m* Hazel Mary Mills; 2 s (Luke Edward Freeman-Mills b 1991, Maximilian James Downing Freeman-Mills b 1993); 1 da (Georgia Beatrice Rose Freeman-Mills b 1997); *Career* Financial Times: stockmarket reporter 1988, Euromarket reporter 1989, Lex Column 1990–92; The Economist: banking corr 1992–94, American finance ed 1995–97, Euro business corr 1999–2004, dep business affrs ed 2004–; ed fin servs Economist Intelligence Unit 1997–99; *Publications* The Armoire de Fer and the French Revolution (1990), Seeing Tomorrow: Rewriting the Rules of Risk (jtly, 1998), The Risk Revolution (2000); *Style*— Andrew Freeman, Esq; ✉ The Economist, 25 St James's Street, London SW1A 1HG

FREEMAN, David Charles; s of Howard Wilfred Freeman, of Sydney, Australia, and Ruth Adair, *née* Nott; *b* 1 May 1952; *Educ* Sydney GS, Univ of Sydney (BA); *m* 1 May 1985 (m dis 2012), Marie Louise, da of (Francis) John Angel (d 1968); 1 da (Catherine Elinor b 13 May 1989), 1 s (Lachlan John b 28 Feb 1993); *Career* opera prodr; fndr and dir: Opera Factory Sydney 1973–76, Opera Factory Zurich 1976–99, Opera Factory London 1981–98, Opera Factory Films Ltd 1991–; assoc artist ENO 1981–95; prodns incl: Monteverdi's Orfeo (ENO) 1981, Birtwistle's Punch and Judy (OFL) 1981, The Mask of Orpheus (ENO) 1986, Cosi Fan Tutte (OFL) 1986, Glass's Akhnaten (Houston, NY and London), Prokofiev's The Fiery Angel (St Petersburg, Covent Garden, Metropolitan NYC) 1992, Zimmermann's Die Soldaten (ENO) 1996, Madame Butterfly (Albert Hall) 1998, Wozzeck (Brussels) 2008; theatre: Goethe's Faust I and II (Lyric Hammersmith) 1988, adapted and directed Malory's Le Morte d'Arthur I and II (Lyric Hammersmith) 1990, The Bacchae (Xenakis' music for play) 1993, The Winter's Tale (opening season Shakespeare's Globe Theatre) 1997, Tosca (Royal Albert Hall) 1999, Carmen (Royal Albert Hall) 2002, Handel's Messiah (Royal Danish Opera) 2012; 8 TV prodns incl: Punch and Judy (Channel 4) 1985, all three Mozart/da Ponte operas (viz Cosi fan Tutte, Don Giovanni and The Marriage of Figaro) for Channel Four 1989–91; Chevalier de l'Ordre des Arts et des Lettres (France) 1985; *Style*— David Freeman, Esq; ✉ 37 Hazelmere Road, London NW6 7HA (e-mail dmfreeangel@hotmail.com)

FREEMAN, George William; MP; s of Arthur Robert Freeman, and Joanna, *née* Philipson; *b* 12 July 1967, Cambridge; *Educ* Radley Coll, Univ of Cambridge (BA); *m* 12 Oct 1996 (m dis 2016), Eleanor; 1 da (Ruby b 15 March 2001), 1 s (Frank b 25 March 2003); *Career* parly offr NFU 1990–92, fndr Local Identity Agency 1992–96, dir Early Stage Ventures Merlin Biosciences 1996–2001, ceo Amedis Pharmaceuticals Ltd 2001–03, md and chm 4D Biomedical Ltd 2003–10; MP (Cons) Mid Norfolk 2010– (parly candidate Stevenage 2005), PPS to Min for Climate Change 2010, govt advsr on life sciences 2011, min for life sciences 2014–; fndr The Norfolk Way 2007–; tstee Cambridge Union Soc 2005–08, memb Bd Greater Cambridge Partnership 2005–09; *Recreations* sailing, wild fowling; *Style*— George Freeman, Esq, MP; ✉ House of Commons, London SW1A 0AA (☎ 020 7219 1940, e-mail george.freeman.mp@parliament.uk, website www.georgefreeman.co.uk)

FREEMAN, HE Dr John; CMG; *m*; 2 c; *Career* diplomat; head S Africa Section FCO 1986–89, Senate liaison Br Military Govt Berlin and subsequently head Political Section Berlin 1989–91, dep head Eastern (later Central) European Dept and then head Security Co-ordination Dept FCO 1991–94, dep high cmmr and commercial and economic counsellor Singapore 1994–97, ambass and perm rep to UN agencies Vienna 1997–2001, dep perm rep NATO and alternate rep N Atlantic Cncl Brussels 2001–04, ambass and perm rep to UN Conf on Disarmament Geneva 2004–06 (ambass for multilateral arms control 2005–06), dep DG Orgn for the Prohibition of Chemical Weapons The Hague 2006–11, ambass to Argentina 2012–16 (non-resident ambass to Paraguay 2012–13); *Publications* Britain's Nuclear Arms Control Policy 1957–68, Security and the CSCE Process; *Recreations* walking, attending opera and music festivals, writing; *Clubs* Reform, Tigre Boat; *Style*— HE Dr John Freeman, CMG; ✉ c/o FCO (Buenos Aires), King Charles Street, London SW1A 2AH

FREEMAN, Jonathan; s of Garth Freeman, and Gillian, *née* Robinson; *b* 14 July 1969, Cricklade, Wiltshire; *Educ* St Anne's Coll Oxford (MA), Univ of Southern Calif (MA, Dean's scholar); *m* 20 Aug 1994, Tamzin, *née* Easton; 4 da (Chloë Rebecca, Lauren Molly, Lily Rachel, Grace Elizabeth); *Career* graduate teaching asst Univ of Southern Calif 1990–92; sr civil servant: Lord Chllr's Dept, Cabinet Office, Dept of Constitutional Affairs and Dept of Communities and Local Govt 1992–2008; Mosaic: sr operations dir 2008–11, md 2012–; sr mentoring advsr The Careers and Enterprise Co; memb Nat Advsy Bd: Naz Legacy Fndn, Patchwork Fndn; advsr: British Inspiration Trust, The Great British Community; memb Assoc of Chief Executives of Voluntary Orgns; Annemarie Schimmel Award for Championing a Muslim Cause Muslim News Awards for Excellence 2016, Certificate of Recognition of Contribution to Education in the UK Naz Legacy Fndn; *Publications* incl articles in TES and Huffington Post; *Recreations* cycling; *Clubs* Royal Over-Seas League; *Style*— Jonathan Freeman, Esq; ✉ Mosaic, The Prince's Trust, The Prince's Trust Morgan Stanley Centre, William Cotton Place, 124 St Paul's Way, London E3 4QA (e-mail jonathan.freeman@princes-trust.org.uk, website www.mosaicnetwork.co.uk, Twitter @jonathanfreeman)

FREEMAN, Prof Michael David Alan; s of Raphael Freeman, of London, and Florence, *née* Wax; *b* 25 November 1943; *Educ* Hasmonean GS Hendon, UCL (LLB, LLM); *m* 23 July 1967, Vivien Ruth, da of Sidney Brook, of Leeds; 1 da (Hilary Rachel b 1971), 1 s (Jeremy Simon Richard b 1973); *Career* called to the Bar Gray's Inn 1969; lectr in law: E London Coll of Commerce 1965–66, Univ of Leeds 1967–69 (asst lectr 1966–67); reader in law UCL 1979–84 (lectr 1969–79), prof of English law Univ of London (tenable at UCL) 1984–2013 (emeritus prof 2013–), fell UCL 2000–; fell Gray's Inn 2008; ed: Annual Survey of Family Law 1983–95, Current Legal Problems 1992–2004, Int Jl of Children's Rights 1992–, Int Jl of Law in Context 1995–2003; dir of trg Nicholson Graham and Jones 1989–91; formerly govr S Hampstead HS; Hamlyn lectr 2015; FBA 2009; *Books* incl: Introduction to Jurisprudence (1 edn 1972, 9 edn 2014), The Children Act 1975 (1976), Violence in the Home (1979), Cohabitation Outside Marriage (1983), The Rights and Wrongs of Children (1983), Essays in Family Law (1986), Dealing With Domestic Violence (1987), Medicine Ethics and the Law (1988), Children, their Families and the Law (1992), The Ideologies of Children's Rights (1992), The Moral Status of Children (1997), Science in Court (1998), Law and Literature (1999), Law and Medicine (2000), Children's Rights (2004), Children, Medicine and the Law (2005), Children's Health and Children's Rights (2006), Law and Sociology (2006), Law and Psychology (2007), The Best Interests of the Child (2007), Law and Philosophy (2008), Understanding Family Law (2008), Law, Mind and Brain (2009), Family Values and Family Justice (2010), Ethics of Public Health (2010), Law and Neuroscience (2010), Law and Childhood Studies (2011), John Austin and his Legacy (2012), Law and Language (2012), Law and Global Health (2014), The Definition of a Child (2015), The Human Rights of Children (2015), A Magna Carta for Children (2016); *Recreations* opera, theatre, cricket, literature; *Clubs* Middlesex CCC; *Style*— Prof Michael Freeman; ☎ 020 7679 1443, fax 020 7387 9597

FREEMAN, Peter Geoffrey; *b* 12 December 1955; *Educ* St Paul's, Balliol Coll Oxford (BA); *m* 1983, Tania, *née* Bromley-Martin; 1 s, 4 da; *Career* admitted slr 1981; DJ Freeman 1979–81, co-fndr and chief exec Argent Gp 1981–1998 (non-exec dir 1998–), fndr and chm Freeman Business Information plc (formerly Freeman Publishing) 1999–; chm: MGT plc, Puma Brandenburg 2006–09, Investment Property Forum 2008; non-exec dir: Land Securities plc 2002–04, MEPC; publisher Freeman's Guide to the Property Industry; jt winner (with bro, Michael) Property Personality of the Year 1996; memb Law Soc; *Recreations* family, reading, tennis, cycling, jogging, olive oil prodn; *Style*— Peter Freeman, Esq; ✉ Argent Group plc, 5 Albany Courtyard, Piccadilly, London W1J 0HF (☎ 020 7734 3721, fax 020 7734 4474)

FREEMAN, Peter John; CBE (2010), Hon QC (2010); s of Cdr John Kenneth Herbert Freeman, LVO, RN (ret), of Bath, and Jean Forbes, *née* Irving (d 2008); *b* 2 October 1948; *Educ* Kingswood Sch Bath (scholar), Goethe Inst Berlin, Trinity Coll Cambridge (exhibitioner, MA), Inns of Court Sch of Law, Université Libre de Bruxelles (Licence Spéciale en Droit Européen); *m* 1972, Elizabeth Mary, da of Frank and Barbara Rogers (d 2009); 2 da (Catharine b 1 Nov 1977, Sarah b 20 July 1988), 2 s (Christopher b 29 May 1979, Henry b 22 March 1983); *Career* called to the Bar Middle Temple 1972 (readmitted 2015), requalified as slr 1977; Simmons & Simmons: joined 1973, ptnr 1978–2003, head EC and Competition Law Gp 1987–2003, managing ptnr Commercial and Trade Law Dept 1994–99; chm Competition Cmmn 2006–11 (dep chm 2003–06), sr conslt Cleary Gottlieb Steen & Hamilton LLP 2011–13, chm Competition Appeal Tbnl 2013– (memb 2011); memb

F

Lloyds Enforcement Tbnl Panel 2012–; memb Advsy Bd Int Competition Law Forum, memb Scientific Bd Revista di Concorrencia e Regulação; distinguished fell Regulatory Policy Inst Oxford; *Publications* Butterworths Competition Law (jt gen ed 1991–2005, consulting ed 2005–); *Recreations* naval history, music; *Clubs* Oxford and Cambridge, Reform; *Style*— Peter Freeman, Esq, CBE, QC; ✉ Competition Appeal Tribunal, Victoria House, Bloomsbury Place, London WC1A 2EB (e-mail peter.freeman@catribunal.org.uk)

FREEMAN, Richard Downing; OBE; s of John Lawrence Freeman (d 1989), of Victoria, Aust, and Phyllis Jean, *née* Walker (d 1984); *b* 28 September 1936; *Educ* Trinity GS Melbourne, Univ of Melbourne (BComm, MComm, Lacrosse blue); *m* 21 May 1960, Diana Lynne, da of Harold Thomas Cranwell; 3 s (Christopher Thomas b 7 Aug 1961, Andrew Lawrence Downing b 4 March 1963, Timothy David b 4 Dec 1965); *Career* economist; British Petroleum: joined group as jr exec BP Australia 1955, Cooper trainee BP London then BP Germany, asst aviation mangr BP Australia until 1963; lectr then sr lectr and actg prof Univ of Melbourne (concurrently economic advsr Ctee for Economic Devpt Australia) 1963–70, economic advsr then sr economic advsr HM Treay 1971–73, head of div OECD Paris 1973–84, corporate chief economist ICI plc 1984–97 (conslt 1997–98), advsr KPMG 1996–2002; review and assoc ed Economic Record 1965–70, ed OECD Economic Outlook 1976–78; CBI: memb Economic Situation Ctee 1984–92, memb Working Gps on Inflation and on Economic and Monetary Union 1990, chm Working Gp on Environmental Economic Instruments 1990–97, memb Economic Affrs Ctee 1992–96, memb Sub-Ctee on Monetary Policy 1992–93; ESRC: memb Economic Ctee 1985–88, memb Industry Economy and Environment Ctee 1988–92, memb Cncl 1993–97, chm Research Centres Bd 1994–96, chm Research Priorities Bd 1996–97; NEDO: memb Chemical Trade Ctee 1985–86, memb City and Industry Finance Ctee 1988–90; chm: Economic Appraisal Ctee Chemical Industries Assoc 1984–97, Economic Ctee CEFIC 1989–92; memb: Croham Ctee on Exchange Rates 1985–86, Cncl Soc of Business Economists 1985–97, Res Ctee RIIA 1988–91, Cncl Royal Economic Soc 1989–94, Business and Trade Bd Chemical Industries Assoc 1989–97, Innovation Advsy Bd Action Gp on Industry-City Communications 1990–91, Environmental Policy Gp ICAEW 1991–92, Innovation Advsy Bd DTI 1991–93, Cncl Inst of Fiscal Studies, Ctee Centre for Economic Policy Performance LSE, Cncl Intellectual Property Inst; fell Soc of Business Economists; *Publications* author of various articles in jls and chapters in books, incl Environmental Costs and International Competitiveness (in Green Futures for Economic Growth, ed Terry Barker and David Cope 1991), The Future of UK Manufacturing (in jl The Business Economist, Spring 1991), How the UK Economy Should Be Run in the 1990s (editorial of The Business Economist, Winter 1992); *Clubs* Woking Lawn Tennis and Croquet; *Style*— Richard Freeman, Esq, OBE; ✉ Cranford, Coley Avenue, Woking, Surrey GU22 7BS (☎ 01483 772247, fax 01483 831001, e-mail rdfreeman@tiscali.co.uk)

FREEMAN, Baron (Life Peer UK 1997), of Dingley in the County of Northamptonshire; Rt Hon Roger Norman Freeman; PC (1993); s of Norman and Marjorie Freeman; *b* 27 May 1942; *Educ* Whitgift Sch, Balliol Coll Oxford (MA); *m* 1969, Jennifer Margaret, OBE, *née* Watson; 1 s, 1 da; *Career* pres OUCA 1964; md Bow Publications 1968 (former memb Cncl and treas Bow Group), md Lehman Brothers 1972–83 (joined Lehman Bros US 1969); Parly candidate (Cons) Don Valley 1979, MP (Cons) Kettering 1983–97; Parly under sec of state: armed forces MOD 1986–88, Dept of Health 1988–90; min of state: for public transport Dept of Tport 1990–94, for defence procurement MOD 1994–95; Chllr of the Duchy of Lancaster and cabinet min for public serv 1995–97; currently chm Advsy Bd PricewaterhouseCoopers; non-exec dir: Parity Gp plc 2011–, ITM PLC 2011–; fndr memb Hundred Gp of UK CA Fin Dirs; FCA 1978; *Publications* incl: Pensions Policy, Professional Practice, A Fair Deal for Water, Democracy in the Digital Age, All Change: British Railway Privatisation; *Recreations* sailing; *Clubs* Carlton; *Style*— The Rt Hon the Lord Freeman, PC; ✉ House of Lords, London SW1A 0PW

FREEMAN-ATTWOOD, Prof Jonathan; s of H W Freeman-Attwood, of Haddenham, Bucks, and M D S, *née* Philips; *b* 4 November 1961, Woking, Surrey; *Educ* Univ of Toronto (BMus) ChCh Oxford (MPhil); *m* 1 Dec 1990, Henrietta Paula Christian, *née* Parham; 1 da (Jessica b 12 Feb 1993), 1 s (Thomas b 13 April 1995); *Career* trumpet player, recording producer and writer; Royal Acad of Music: vice-princ and dir of studies until 2008, princ 2008–; prof Univ of London 2001–, visiting prof KCL 2007–; chm: Mendelssohn Scholarship Fndn, Lucille Graham Tst, Harriet Cohen Tst, Winifred Christie Tst, Artistic Advsy Ctee Garsington Opera; vice-pres National Wind Orchestra of GB; patron: London Youth Choirs, Cavatina Chamber Music Trst, Lionel Tertis Festival and Competition; tstee: Countess of Munster Tst, Young Classical Artists Tst, SAGA at Br Library, Assoc Bd Royal Schs of Music, Univ of London 2010–15, Garsington Opera 2012–, Christ Church Cathedral Music Tst 2012–; several BBC and Gramophone Awards as prodr (incl Gramophone Record of the Year 2010) and many other awards (incl Diapason d'Or); Hon RAM 1997, FKC 2009, FRNCM 2013; *Solo Recordings* Albinoni and Contemporaries 1993, Bach Connections 1998, The Trumpets that Time Forgot 2004, La Trompette Retrouvée 2007, Trumpet Masque 2008 (Recording of the Year High Fidelity 2008), Romantic Trumpet Sonatas by Mendelssohn, Schumann and Grieg 2011, A Bach Notebook for Trumpet 2013, Vocalises by Fauré 2014 (world premiere), The Neoclassical Trumpet (2015); prodr of over 200 commercial recordings; *Publications* New Grove (contrib, 2 edn 2000), The Re-Imagined Trumpet (series ed, 2014–); regular contrib to CUP, BBC Radio 3 broadcasts and reviewer, essay writer for recording labels incl Warner, EMI, Deutsche Gramophone and Universal; *Recreations* cricket, reading, walking, French wine chateaux; *Clubs* RAM Club (pres 2006–07), Five Elms; *Style*— Prof Jonathan Freeman-Attwood; ✉ Royal Academy of Music, Marylebone Road, London NW1 5HT (☎ 020 7873 7377, fax 020 7873 7314, e-mail j.freeman-attwood@ram.ac.uk, website www.ram.ac.uk)

FREEMANTLE, Glenn; s of Brian Leslie Freemantle, and Doreen, *née* Bell; *b* 20 May 1959, Uxbridge; *m* 16 Oct 1982, Alison, *née* Duffy; 3 s (Danny b 14 Oct 1985, Nick b 27 June 1988, Olly b 11 July 1992); *Career* sound designer; *Film* incl: Yentl 1983, Legend 1985, Little Buddha 1993, Backbeat 1994, Hackers 1995, Wing Commander 1999, The Beach 1999, Bridget Jones's Diary 2001, Bridget Jones: The Edge of Reason 2004, Love Actually 2003, V for Vendetta 2005, 28 Weeks Later 2007, Sunshine 2007, Golden Compass 2007, Slumdog Millionaire 2008 (Best Sound BAFTA 2009), Gravity 2013 (Best Sound BAFTA 2014, Best Sound Editing Golden Reel Award Motion Picture Sound Editors USA 2014, Best Sound Editing Acad Award 2014), The Book Thief 2013; *Recreations* cinema, gardening, golf, motorsport, music, travel, walking; *Style*— Glenn Freemantle, Esq; ✉ Sound 24, Pinewood Road, Iver, Buckinghamshire SL0 0NH

FREER, Mike; MP; *b* 29 May 1960; *Career* cncllr Barnet Cncl 1990–94 and 2002–10 (ldr 2006–10), MP (Cons) Finchley and Golders Green 2010–; *Style*— Mike Freer, Esq, MP; ✉ House of Commons, London SW1A 0AA

FREESTONE, Susan Mathilda (Sue); da of Charles Anthony Freestone, of Canada, and June Freestone (d 1991); *b* 27 March 1948; *Educ* Westdale Collegiate Sch Canada, North London Poly (BA(Eng)); *m* 1, 1966 (m dis 1978), Anthony Ashley Frank Meyer; 1 da (Sophie Mathilda Barbadee b 1972); partner, 1978–85, Donald John Macintyre, *qv*; 1 s (James Kenneth Freestone Macintyre b 1979); m 2, 1989, Vivian Louis White; *Career* bookseller 1966–69, business forecaster IBM 1969–72, ed William Heinemann 1984–1990, ed dir: Mandarin Books 1990–91, Jonathan Cape 1991; publishing dir Hutchinson 1992–; *Recreations* walking the dog; *Style*— Ms Sue Freestone; ✉ Hutchinson, Random House, 20 Vauxhall Bridge Road, London SW1V 2SA (☎ 020 7840 8400, fax 020 7233 7870)

FREETH, Peter Stewart; s of Alfred William Freeth, of Fovant, Wilts; *b* 15 April 1938; *Educ* King Edward's GS Aston, Slade Sch of Fine Art London, Br Sch of Rome; *m* 5 August 1967, Mariolina, da of Prof Leonardo Meliadò, of Rome; 2 s (Dylan b 5 July 1969, Paul b 1 July 1972); *Career* artist; tutor in printmaking Royal Acad Schs 1967–; pt/t posts: Colchester Sch of Art, Camden Inst, Kingsway Coll; RE 1987, RA 1992 (ARA 1990); *Solo Exhibitions* Christopher Mendez Gallery London 1987 and 1989, Royal Acad 1991, S Maria Gradillo Ravello Italy 1997, Mary Kleinman Gallery London 1998, Bankside Gallery London 2001, ChCh Coll Gallery Oxford 2005, North House Gall Manningtree 2006, Tennant Room Royal Acad 2008–09; *Public Collections* Br Museum, V&A, Arts Cncl, Fitzwilliam Museum, Ashmolean Museum, Govt Art Collection, Metropolitan Museum NYC, Nat Gallery Washington DC, Harvard Univ, Hunterian Museum and Art Gall Glasgow, Pallant House Gallery Chichester; *Awards* Prix de Rome 1960, Royal Acad Best Print Prize 1986, Wakayama Biennale Print Prize 1989, Hunting Print Prize 2002 and 2004; *Recreations* music, reading; *Style*— Peter Freeth, Esq, RA, RE; ✉ c/o The Royal Academy, London W1V 0DS

FREI, Matt; s of Peter Frei, of Baden-Baden, and Anita Frei; *b* 26 November 1963; *Educ* Westminster, St Peter's Coll Oxford (MA); *Partner* Penelope Quested; *Career* BBC Radio: disc jockey German Service 1986–87, prodr Current Affairs World Service 1987–88, reporter Jerusalem 1988–89, corr Bonn 1989–91, corr Foreign Affairs 1991–92, corr S Europe Rome 1992–97, corr Asia 1997–2003, corr Washington DC 2003–07; presenter BBC World News America 2007, Washington corr Channel 4 News 2011–; regular contrib: The Spectator, London Review of Books, Wall Street Journal; *Clubs* Gridiron (Oxford), Travellers (assoc memb); *Style*— Matt Frei, Esq

FRENCH, Prof Charles Andrew Ivey; s of Prof G S French, of Dundas, Canada, and Iris, *née* Ivey; *b* 27 April 1954, Hamilton, Canada; *Educ* Parkside HS Dundas, Univ of Wales Cardiff (BA), Inst of Archaeology Univ of London (MA, PhD); *Partner* Katarzyna Gdaniec; 2 s (Theodore b 21 Nov 1995, Hugh b 8 Dec 1998); *Career* palaeoenvironmentalist and asst dir Fenland Archaeological Tst 1983–92; Univ of Cambridge: lectr 1992–2000, sr lectr in archaeological science and head Dept of Archaeology 2000–05, reader in geoarchaeology 2006–12, prof of geoarchaeology 2012–; tstee Fenland Archaeological Tst; CMIFA 1983; *Books* The South-West Fen Dyke Survey (1993), Excavation of the Deeping St Nicholas Barrow Complex (1994), Geoarchaeology in Action: Studies in soil micromorphology and landscape evolution (2003), Archaeology and Environment of the Etton Landscape (2005), Prehistoric landscape development and human impact in the upper Allen valley, Cranborne Chase, Dorset (2007), A handbook of geoarchaeological approaches for investigating landscapes and settlement sites (2015); *Style*— Prof Charles French; ✉ Department of Archaeology, University of Cambridge, Downing Street, Cambridge CB2 3DZ (☎ 01223 333533, fax 01223 333503, e-mail caif2@cam.ac.uk)

FRENCH, Christopher; *b* 28 July 1950; *Educ* Roan GS for Boys; *Family* 1 da (Sally b 1977), 1 s (James b 1983); m, 25 June 2001, Marian Ann; *Career* Nationwide Building Society: trainee mangr 1971, branch mangr 1978, sec 1985; Nationwide Anglia Building Society: asst gen mangr 1988, gen mangr 1990, divnl dir 1991–92; chief operating offr National Home Loans plc 1993–95, chief exec Norland Capital Ltd (Kensington Mortgage Company) 1995–98; md: The Oxford Mortgage Company 1998–2004, Rosedale Mortgage Services Ltd 2003–, The Mortgage Marketing Centre 2003–; dir Lambeth Building Society 1999–2006; chm: Nationwide Building Society Staff Assoc 1980–82, Fedn of Building Society Staff Assocs 1980–81; FCIB 1978, DMS 1985, FRSA 1993; *Recreations* music, history; *Style*— Christopher French, Esq; ✉ e-mail chris-french@hotmail.co.uk

FRENCH, David; s of Capt Godfrey Alexander French, CBE, RN (d 1988), of Stoke Abbott, Dorset, and Margaret Annis, *née* Best (d 1999); *b* 20 June 1947; *Educ* Sherborne, St John's Coll Durham (BA); *m* 3 Aug 1974, Sarah Anne, da of Rt Rev Henry David Halsey (d 2009), former Bishop of Carlisle; 4 s (Thomas b 1978, Alexander b 1980, William b 1983, Hal b 1993); *Career* with Nat Cncl of Social Serv 1971–74, head Social Servs Dept RNID 1974–78, dir of serv C of E Children's Soc 1978–87, ceo RELATE Nat Marriage Guidance 1987–95, conslt on Family Policy 1995–97, ceo Commonwealth Inst 1997–2002, ceo Westminster Fndn for Democracy 2003–09; partner Hilliard French Exec Coaching 2014–; advsr European Partnership for Democracy 2010–12; assoc dir Transform 2011–, exec dir Alexandria Tst 2011–14; chm: London Corrymeela Venture 1974–76, St Albans Int Organ Festival 1985–87, The Twenty-First Century Fndn 1996–2001; memb: Governing Cncl Family Policy Studies Centre 1988–2001, Cncl UK Assoc for Int Year of the Family 1993–95, Bd ACENVO 1995–96, Cncl St Albans Cathedral 1996–99; tstee: Charity Appointments 1984–91, British Empire and Commonwealth Museum 1999–2003, Round Table Cwlth Jl of Int Affrs 2001–08; Liveryman Worshipful Co of Glaziers 1990; MCIPD 1970, FRSM 1989, FRSA 1993; *Recreations* challenging projects; *Style*— David French, Esq; ✉ Molly Bawn, Stoke Abbott, Beaminster, Dorest DT8 3JT (e-mail david@conveners.eu)

FRENCH, Douglas Charles; s of Frederick Emil French, of Surrey, and late Charlotte Vera, *née* Russell; *b* 20 March 1944; *Educ* Glyn GS Epsom, St Catharine's Coll Cambridge (MA), Inns of Court Sch of Law; *m* 1978, Sue, da of late Philip Arthur Phillips; 2 s (Paul b 1982, David b 1985), 1 da (Louise b 1983); *Career* dir PW Merkle Ltd 1972–87 (exec 1966–71); called to the Bar Inner Temple 1975; Parly candidate Sheffield Attercliffe 1979, MP (Cons) Gloucester 1987–97, special advsr to Chllr of Exchequer 1982–83 (asst to Rt Hon Sir Geoffrey Howe QC, MP 1976–79), chm Westminster and City Programmes 1997– (md 1979–87); PPS to the Min of State: FCO 1988–89, ODA 1989–90, MAFF 1992–93, Local Govt and Planning 1993–94; PPS to Sec of State for Environment 1994–97; barr; chm Bow Group 1978–79; former: chm All-Pty Building Socs Gp, vice-chm All-Pty Occupational Pensions Gp, vice-chm All-Pty Central Asia Gp, sec All-Pty Insurance and Financial Servs Gp; pres: Gloucester Cons Club 1989–97, Glyn Old Boys' Assoc 2005–11, Old Glynians' 2011; govr Glyn Sch Epsom 2000–15 (vice-chm 2003–, chm 2006–09); *Recreations* skiing, gardening, squash; *Clubs* RAC; *Style*— Douglas French, Esq; ✉ 231 Kennington Lane, London SE11 5QU (☎ 020 7582 6516, fax 020 7582 7245)

FRENCH, Jim; CBE (2009); *Career* Caledonian Airways Ltd 1970–80, Air UK Ltd 1980–90; Flybe: joined 1990, commercial dir, dep chief exec then chief operating offr, ceo 2001–, exec chm 2005–; Airline Exec of the Year Regnl Airline World 2002 and 2004; *Style*— Jim French, Esq, CBE

FRENCH, John Patrick; MBE (1981), JP (Carmarthenshire 1995); s of Francis George French (d 1985), of Sharow, Nr Ripon, and Doris Maud French; *b* 4 February 1945; *Educ* RMA Sandhurst, Army Staff Coll, Open Univ (BA); *m* 8 Feb 1986, Monica Mary Aitken; 4 s (Nicholas b 19 Nov 1970, Thomas b 9 Nov 1981, James b 1 July 1986, Edward b 16 Sept 1987), 2 da (Penny b 31 Jan 1972, Joanna b 21 Nov 1978); *Career* RCT: joined 1964, SOI Logistics MOD London 1985–88, CO 7 Tank Transporter Regt Germany 1988–90; chief exec: Dyfed Family Health Servs Authy 1990–96, Wales Tourist Bd 1996–; *Style*— John French, Esq, MBE; ✉ Wales Tourist Board, Brunel House, 2 Fitzalan Road, Cardiff CF2 1UY (☎ 029 2047 5201, fax 029 2047 5320, mobile 077 7836 2565)

FRENK, Prof Carlos Silvestre; s of Silvestre Frenk, of Mexico City, and Alicia, *née* Mora; *b* 27 October 1951, Mexico City; *Educ* Univ of Mexico (BSc, Gabino Berreda medal), Univ of Cambridge (PhD); *m* 9 Dec 1978, Susan Frances, *née* Clarke; 2 s (David b 22 Oct 1985, Stephen b 31 Aug 1989); *Career* postdoctoral research fell Univ of Calif Berkeley 1981–83, asst research physicist Univ of Calif Santa Barbara 1983–85, postdoctoral research fell Univ of Sussex 1983–85; Univ of Durham: lectr in astronomy 1985–91, reader in physics 1991–93, prof of astrophysics 1993–2001, Ogden prof of fundamental physics 2001–, dir Institute for Computational Cosmology 2001–; memb SERC (later PPARC): Educn, Trg and Fellowships Panel 1990–91, Theory Grants Panel 1991–94, Astronomy and Astrophysics Ctee 1991–94, UK Dark Matter Experiment Review Panels 1991–, Bd Isaac Newton Gp of Telescopes 1994–99 (chm 1997–99), Intercouncil High Performance Computation Mgmnt Ctee 1996–97, Astronomy Ctee 1996–99, Jt Astrophysics and Particle Physics Supercomputing Panel 1996–, First and Planck Instrument Review Panel 1997 (chm); Royal Soc: memb Sectional Ctee 2006–08, memb Educn Ctee 2007–13, chm Int Newton Fellowships 2008–, memb Cncl 2013–, memb Public Engagement Ctee 2013–, memb Grants and Awards Ctee 2014–; memb Wakeham Review of Physics in the UK 2008; organiser and memb organising ctees of scientific confs, delivered numerous lectures at major int confs and popular science events; author of over 400 articles in scientific jls, ed of 2 books; Br Cncl fell 1976–79, Nuffield Fndn science research fell 1991–92, Sir Derman Christopherson fell Univ of Durham 1992–93, PPARC sr fell 1996–99, Leverhulme research fell 2000–01; Royal Soc Wolfson Research Merit Award 2006, European Research Cncl Advanced Investigator Award 2010, Gruber Cosmology Prize 2011, Alexander von Humboldt Research Award 2012, Ludwig Bierman Lectures 2013, RAS Gold Medal 2014; FRS 2004; *Recreations* literature, ski training; *Style—* Prof Carlos Frenk; ✉ Institute for Computational Cosmology, Department of Physics, Ogden Centre for Fundamental Physics, Science Laboratories, South Road, Durham DH1 3LE (☎ 0191 334 3641, fax 0191 334 3645, e-mail c.s.frenk@durham.ac.uk)

FRERIS, Marika; da of Leonard Freris, of Herts, and Delphine, *née* Squire; *b* 24 July 1962; *Educ* Loreto Coll Sch for Girls, Imperial Coll London (BSc); *Career* sr research asst Dept of Molecular Biology The Wellcome Research Labs Beckenham 1983–85, clinical research scientist Dept of Clinical Immunology and Chemotherapy The Wellcome Fndn Beckenham 1985–89; Hill & Knowlton (UK) Ltd: account dir Eurosciences 1989–91, assoc dir Eurosciences 1991–94, dir Healthcare 1994–96; md: Churchill Communications Europe 1996–98, OCC Europe 1998–2000; owner and md Nyxeon 2000–; memb: Amnesty Int, ActionAid, Oxfam, Nat Trust, Friends of the Earth, IPR, BAJ, RCSA; tstee and memb Bd Age UK Camden; MInstD; *Style—* Ms Marika Freris; ✉ Nyxeon, 37–41 Bedford Row, South Entrance, London WC1R 4JH (☎ 020 7663 2252, fax 020 7663 2251, e-mail mfreris@nyxeon.com)

FRESHWATER, Timothy George (Tim); s of George John Freshwater (d 1986), and Rosalie, *née* MacLauchlan (d 1987); *b* 21 October 1944; *Educ* Eastbourne Coll, Emmanuel Coll Cambridge (MA, LLB); *m* 1984, Judy, *née* Lam (d 2011); *Career* Slaughter and May: joined 1967, ptnr 1975, seconded to Hong Kong office 1979–85, ptnr London (corp fin) 1985–96; Jardine Fleming Gp: joined 1996, chm 1999–2000; vice-chm Goldman Sachs (Asia) LLC 2001–11, chm Grosvenor Asia Ltd 2008–13; dir: Swire Pacific Ltd, Corney & Barrow Ltd, Hong Kong Exchanges and Clearing Ltd, Savills plc; pres Law Soc Hong Kong 1984–85, co-chm Jt Working Party on China of Law Soc and the Bar 1990–96; memb: Int Ctee Law Soc 1994–96, Hong Kong Panel on Takeovers and Mergers 1997–99, Hong Kong Trade Devpt Cncl 2006–12, Ct Hong Kong Univ of Science and Technol, Hong Kong Financial Services Devpt Cncl; *Books* The Practitioner's Guide to the City Code on Take-Overs and Mergers (contrib); *Clubs* Hong Kong, Shek-O Country, Boodle's Portland, Sunningdale; *Style—* Tim Freshwater; ✉ e-mail tim@timfreshwater.com

FRETER, Michael Charles Franklin; s of Leslie Charles Freter, of Sidmouth, Devon, and Myra, *née* Wilkinson; *b* 29 October 1947; *Educ* Whitgift Sch, St Edmund Hall Oxford (BA); *m* 2 June 1979, Jan, da of Brian Wilson, of Ealing, London; *Career* sr brand mangr Elida Gibbs Ltd 1970–76, account dir BBDO Advertising Ltd 1976–78, exec dir McCann-Erickson Advertising Ltd 1988–94 (joined 1978), managing ptnr The Imagination Brokers 1994–96, ptnr SWK London Ltd (formerly Summerfield Wilmot Keene Ltd) 1996–2006, princ The Imagination Brokers 2006–; *Style—* Michael Freter, Esq; ✉ 7 Sherbrooke Way, Worcester Park, Surrey KT4 8BG

FRETWELL, Clive; s of Derek Ernest Fretwell, of Yorkshire, and Doris Jean, *née* Mitchell; *b* 16 September 1961; *m* 18 Sept 1982, Julie, da of late Richard Sharrock; 2 da (Selina-Jane b 10 Oct 1984, Claire Louise b 14 Jan 1986); *Career* head chef Le Manoir aux Quat'Saisons 1986–97 (commis chef 1982–86), dir Le Petit Blanc École de Cuisine 1991–96, chef conslt Nico Central Midland Hotel Manchester 1997–98, head chef Restaurant Itsu London 1998–2001 (awarded Best Oriental Restaurant 1999–2000), exec chef and dir Brasserie Blanc 2002–; winner Boccuse d'Or Individual Gold Medal 1991 and 1993; *Recreations* cycling, skiing; *Style—* Mr C Fretwell; ✉ e-mail clive.fretwell@virgin.net

FREUD, Anthony Peter; OBE (2006); s of Joseph Freud (d 1998), of London, and Katalin, *née* Löwi (d 1990); *b* 30 October 1957; *Educ* KCS Wimbledon, King's Coll London (LLB), Inns of Court Sch of Law; *m* Colin Ure; *Career* pupillage as barr 1979–80; theatre mangr Sadler's Wells Theatre 1980–84, co sec and dir of opera planning WNO 1984–92, exec prodr (opera) Philips Classics Productions (The Netherlands) 1992–94, gen dir WNO 1994–2006, gen dir and ceo Houston Grand Opera 2006–11, gen dir Lyric Opera of Chicago 2011–; dir National Opera Studio 1994–2005, chm Opera Europa 2002–05, chm Opera America 2008–12, dir Opera America 2012–16; lectr in law Univ of Chicago 2016–; chm of jury Cardiff Singer of the World Competition 1995–2005; tstee NESTA 2004–05; memb Hon Soc of Gray's Inn 1979; hon fell Cardiff Univ 2002; *Recreations* the Arts, cooking, travel; *Style—* Anthony Freud, Esq, OBE; ✉ Lyric Opera of Chicago, 20 N Wacker Drive, Chicago, IL 60606, USA (e-mail afreud@lyricopera.org)

FREUD, Baron (Life Peer UK 2009), of Eastry in the County of Kent; David Anthony Freud; PC (2015); s of Anton Walter Freud (d 2003), and Annette Vibeke, *née* Krarup (d 2000); *b* 24 June 1950, London; *Educ* Whitgift Sch, Merton Coll Oxford (MA); *m* 1978, Priscilla Jane, *née* Dickinson; 1 s (Hon Andrew Alexander 1981), 2 da (Hon Emily Annette b 1983, Hon Juliet Sophie b 1986); *Career* journalist Western Mail 1972–75, Financial Times 1976–83 (writer Lex column 1979–83), S G Warburg (later known as UBS Investment Bank) 1984–2003 (global head of transport, leisure, business services, ret as vice-chm); ceo Portland Tst 2005–08 (tstee 2006–); advsr on welfare reform to Sec of State for Work and Pensions 2008–09, min for welfare reform and parly under-sec of state Dept for Work and Pensions 2010–15, min of state for welfare reform Dept for Work and Pensions 2015–; *Publications* Freud in the City (2006), Reducing Dependency Increasing Opportunity (ind report to DWP, 2007); *Recreations* skiing, cycling, swimming; *Style—* The Rt Hon Lord Freud, PC; ✉ House of Lords, London SW1A 0PW

FREUD, Emma Vallency; OBE (2011); da of Sir Clement (Raphael) Freud (d 2009), and June Beatrice (Jill), *née* Flewett; *b* 25 January 1962; *Educ* St Mary's Convent, Queen's Coll London, Univ of Bristol, Royal Holloway Coll London (BA); *Partner* Richard Curtis, CBE, *qv*; 1 da, 3 s; *Career* assoc film prodr, script ed and broadcaster; backing singer to Mike Oldfield on Tubular Bells tour 1978, memb The Girls (cabaret band) 1984–2004, co-dir and musical dir Open Air Theatre Regent's Park 1985–86; columnist Tatler 2011–, columnist Telegraph 2015– (Columnist of the Year Glamour Awards 2016); contrib to: Times Magazine, The Guardian, The Telegraph, Sunday Times, The Mirror, Radio Times; chm Christmaz Quiz NT 2000–; dir Red Nose Day 2000–, key memb Make Poverty History campaign and co-prodr Live 8 concerts 2005, patron White Ribbon Alliance 2008–13, dir Red Nose Day USA 2015–; *Television* incl: Six O'Clock Show 1986–88, Pillowtalk 1987–89, The Media Show 1989–91, Turner Prize 1991, Everyman 1992–94, BAFTA Awards 1994, Edinburgh Nights 1994–96, Theatreland 1996–98; script ed to Richard Curtis on: The Vicar of Dibley 1995–2007, Doctor Who 2010; *Radio* incl: Loose Ends (BBC Radio 4) 1987–, morning show BBC GLR 1988–90, lunchtime show BBC Radio 1 1995–96; *Theatre* NT Live 2009–; *Film* script ed to Richard Curtis on: Four Weddings and a Funeral 1994, Bean 1997, Notting Hill 1999, Bridget Jones's Diary 2001, Love Actually 2004; assoc prodr: The Boat That Rocked 2009, About Time 2013, Esio Trot 2014; *Recreations* Lego, colouring in; *Style—* Ms Emma Freud, OBE; ✉ Portobello Studios, 1st Floor, 138 Portobello Road, W11 2DZ

FREUD, Esther Lea; da of Lucian Freud, OM, CH (d 2011), and Bernardine Coverley; *b* 2 May 1963; *Educ* Michael Hall Sch, Drama Centre London; *Career* writer; actress 1983–91; *Books* Hideous Kinky (1992), Peerless Flats (1993), Gaglow (1997), The Wild (2000), The Sea House (2003), Love Falls (2007), Lucky Break (2011); *Style—* Miss Esther Freud; ✉ c/o Clare Conville, Conville & Walsh, 2 Granton Street, London W1F 7QL

FREUD, Matthew; s of Sir Clement Freud (d 2009), and June, *née* Flewitt; *b* 2 November 1963; *Educ* Westminster, Pimlico; *m* 1 (m dis), Caroline Hutton; 2 s (George Rupert b 3 Oct 1995, Jonah Henry b 1 April 1997); m 2 (m dis), Elisabeth Murdoch, *qv*, da of Rupert Murdoch; 1 da (Charlotte Emma b 17 Nov 2000), 1 s (Samson Murdoch b 13 Jan 2007); *Career* chm Freuds 1990–; tstee Comic Relief; *Style—* Matthew Freud, Esq; ✉ freuds, No 1 Stephen Street, London W1T 1AL (☎ 020 3003 6300, fax 020 3003 6303)

FREUDENHEIM, Adam; *Educ* Harvard Univ (AB), Univ of Cambridge (MPhil); *Career* actg publicity mangr Granta Books 1998, commissioning ed Yale Univ Press 1998–2004, publisher Penguin Classics and Reference 2004–12, publisher and md Pushkin Press Ltd 2012–; *Style—* Adam Freudenheim, Esq; ✉ Pushkin Press, 71–75 Shelton Street, London WC2H 9JQ

FREUDMANN, Dr Steven; s of Max Freudmann (d 1967), and Eleanor, *née* Hughes; *b* 15 June 1949, Wrexham, Clwyd; *Educ* Grove Park GS, Kingston Univ; *m* 1971 (m dis); 1 s (Matthew b 15 Aug 1971), 1 da (Rosie b 30 Aug 1975); partner, Cristina Fernandez; 2 s (Hugo b 22 May 2002, Max b 12 Dec 2005); *Career* md Majestic Travel 1967–2009, chm Advantage Travel Centres 2004–08, chm Triton Travel Gp 2006–, chm Alpha Prospects plc 2008–; dir ABTA 1991–2009 (chm 1991–97, pres 1997–2000), chm Inst of Travel and Tourism (ITT) 2001–; ITT Odyssey Award 1999; Hon Dr Leeds Met Univ 2009; fell ITT 1968, FTS 1998; *Recreations* all sport, gardening, mountain climbing; *Style—* Dr Steven Freudmann; ✉ Brook House, Worthenbury, Wrexham, Clwyd LL13 0FD (e-mail steven@itt.co.uk)

FREWER, Prof Richard John Barrett; s of Dr Edward George Frewer (d 1972), and Bridget Audrey Christina Pennefather, *née* Ford (d 1994); *b* 24 January 1942; *Educ* Shrewsbury, Gonville & Caius Coll Cambridge (choral scholar, MA), AA (AADip); *m* 19 July 1969, Carolyn Mary, da of Thomas Arthur Butler (d 1969); 1 da (Emelye b 1971); *Career* project architect Univ Centre Cambridge (listed grade 2) HKPA 1964–65, architect Arup Assocs 1966–91 (ptnr 1977–91, conslt 1991–98); major works incl: Zunz House Wimbledon (listed Grade 2), Sir Thomas White Bldg, St John's Coll Oxford (with Sir Philip Dowson), Theatre Royal Glasgow, Glasgow Scottish Opera, Liverpool Garden Festival Hall, Baburgh DC Offices Suffolk, Stockley Park Arena Heathrow; chair prof of architecture Univ of Bath 1991–2000; chair prof of architecture Univ of Hong Kong 2000–05, teaching fell Univ of Bath 2005–; architectural conslt 2005–; chair Construction Industry Cncl Educn Forum 1997–2000; tstee Holbourne Museum 1993–2000; professional tenor soloist, Bach specialist, Lieder and Oratorio repertoire; Grabowski Connell postgrad scholarship and Philharmonia's Martin scholarship; RIBA (ret), Hon HKIA, ARB; *Publications* Hin Tan: A Journey in Steel (2010); *Recreations* painting, gardening; *Style—* Prof Richard Frewer; ✉ Alma Cottage, Charlcombe, Bath BA1 8DR (☎ 01225 316485, e-mail richardfrewer@hotmail.com)

FREWIN, Jonathan Mayo; *b* 15 May 1955; *Educ* LCP; *Career* art ed Haymarket Publishers London 1976–77 and 1979–81, art dir Morgan Grampian London 1977–79, art dir PCI mgmnt consultancy New York 1981–84, prof Parsons Sch of Design New York 1984–88, pres/creative dir Frewin Shapiro Inc New York 1984–89, ptnr/creative dir ACFS Berkshire 1989–93, jt chief exec/creative dir Red Cell Glasgow 1993–2006, exec creative dir/md LHA 2006–09, creative dir Frewin Design Consultancy 2009–; *Style—* Jonathan Frewin, Esq

FREYBERG, 3 Baron (UK 1951); Valerian Bernard Freyberg; o s of 2 Baron Freyberg, OBE, MC (d 1993), and Ivry Perronelle Katharine, *née* Guild; *b* 15 December 1970; *Educ* Eton, Camberwell Coll of Arts, Slade Sch of Fine Art (MA); *m* 27 April 2002, Dr Harriet Rachel, da of late John Atkinson; 1 s (Hon Joseph John b 21 March 2007), 2 da (Martha Rachel Ivry b 21 Jan 2009, Stella b 2012); *Heir* s, Hon Joseph Freyberg; *Career* artist; memb Design Cncl 2001–04; elected hereditary crossbench peer 1999; *Recreations* beekeeping, music, cycling; *Style—* The Rt Hon the Lord Freyberg

FREYD, Michael; s of Cecil Freyd (d 1971), and Joan, *née* Woodhead (d 1960); *b* 5 June 1948; *Educ* Burnage GS Manchester, Univ of Hull (BSc); *m* 21 March 1971, Marilyn Sharon (Lyn), da of Ivor Paul Levinson (d 1960); 1 s (Mark b 29 Aug 1979), 2 da (Danielle b 14 June 1972, Elana b 7 May 1976); *Career* dep md UBS (formerly Phillips & Drew) (joined 1969, ptnr 1980–94, memb Option Ctee 1986–92), dir (with responsibility for mktg and business devpt) Prolific Objective Asset Management Ltd 1994–; memb Soc of Investment Analysts; MSI; *Recreations* golf, skiing, bridge, chess; *Style—* Michael Freyd, Esq; ✉ Prolific Objective Asset Management Ltd, Austin Friars House, 2–6 Austin Friars, London EC2N 2HE (☎ 020 7628 3717)

FRIDD, Nicholas Timothy; s of Norman Sidney Fridd, and Beryl Rosamond, *née* Phillips; *b* 21 September 1953; *Educ* Wells Blue Sch, ChCh Oxford (MA); *m* 14 Sept 1985, Fiona Bridgnell, da of Dr Keir Mackessack-Leitch; 1 da (Charlotte Mary b 11 Jan 1988), 1 s (John Bridgnell b 2 Nov 1989); *Career* called to the Bar Inner Temple 1975; *Books* Basic Practice in Courts, Tribunals and Inquiries (1989, 3 edn 2000); *Recreations* carpentry, walking disused railways; *Style—* Nicholas Fridd, Esq; ✉ Manor Farm, East Horrington, Wells, Somerset BA5 3DP (☎ 01749 679832, fax 01749 679849); Albion Chambers, Broad Street, Bristol BS1 1DR (☎ 0117 927 2144, fax 0117 926 2569)

FRIEDLEIN, Ashley; *b* 22 June 1972, London; *Educ* Univ of Cambridge; *Career* prodr Cambridge Film and Television 1995–96, prodr/project mangr FT.com 1996–97, Wheel 1997–2001, co-fndr and ceo Econsultancy 2002–; *Books* Web Project Management: Delivering Successful Commercial Web Sites (2000), Maintaining and Evolving Successful Commercial Websites: Managing Change, Content, Customer Relationships and Site Measurement (2002); *Style—* Ashley Friedlein, Esq; ✉ Econsultancy, 4th Floor, Wells Point, 79 Wells Street, London W1T 3QN

FRIEDMAN, Brian Sydney; s of Roy Friedman, of London, and Denise Adele, *née* Salter; *b* 25 February 1957; *Educ* Highgate Sch, St John's Coll Cambridge (MA); *m* 1983, Frances Patricia, *née* Davey; 1 da (Emma b 24 April 1987), 1 s (Jonathan b 1 March 1989); *Career* chartered accountant; Coopers & Lybrand 1978–84, Stoy Benefit Consulting 1985–94, ptnr and global head of Human Capital Services Andersen 1994–; pres Soc of Share Scheme Practitioners 1995–; ACA 1981, FTII 1988, MIPD 1990; *Books* Effective Staff Incentives (1991), Company Car Taxation (1993), Pay and Benefits Handbook (1994), Delivering on the Promise (1998); *Recreations* children, travel, football, reading; *Style—* Brian Friedman, Esq; ✉ Andersen, 1 Surrey Street, London WC2R 2PS (☎ 020 7438 2238, e-mail brian.friedman@uk.andersen.com)

FRIEDMAN, David Peter; QC (1990); s of Wilfred Emanuel Friedman (d 1973), and Rosa, *née* Lees (d 1972); *b* 1 June 1944; *Educ* Tiffin Boys' Sch, Lincoln Coll Oxford (MA, BCL); *m* 29 Oct 1972, Sara Geraldine, da of Dr Sidney Linton; *Career* called to the Bar 1968, recorder 1998–2005, bencher Inner Temple 1999; *Recreations* good food (cooked by others), reading; *Clubs* Lansdowne; *Style—* David P Friedman, Esq, QC; ✉ 4 Pump Court, Temple, London EC4Y 7AN (☎ 020 7842 5555, fax 020 7583 2036)

FRIEDMAN, Maria; da of Leonard Matthew Friedman (d 1994), of Edinburgh, and Clair Llewellyn Friedman; *b* 19 March 1960; *Educ* E Barnet Comp Sch, Arts Educnl Sch Golden Lane London; *Children* 2 s (Toby Oliver Sams-Friedman b 26 Nov 1994, Alfie Olegovich Poupko Friedman b 21 July 2002); *Career* actress and singer; *Theatre* RNT incl: Ghetto (Evening Standard Award for Best Play 1990), Sunday in the Park with George (Olivier Award for Best Musical 1991), Square Rounds, Lady in The Dark 1997; other prodns incl: Blues in the Night (Donmar Warehouse, Piccadilly), April in Paris (Ambassadors) 1994, The Break of Day (Royal Court) 1995, Passion (Queen's, Olivier Award for Best Actress in a Musical 1997) 1996, Chicago (Adelphi) 1998–99, Witches of Eastwick (Theatre Royal) 2000, Maria Friedman Live One Woman Show (Ambassadors) 2002, Ragtime (Piccadilly Theatre, Olivier Award for Best Actress in a Musical 2004) 2003, The Woman in White (Palace and Marquis Broadway, What's On Stage Award and Olivier Award nomination for Best Actress in a Musical, Theatre World Award for Outstanding Broadway Debut) 2004–05, Sweeney Todd (Royal Festival Hall) 2007, Maria Friedman Re-arranged (Trafalgar Studios and Menier Chocolate Factory) 2008, The King and I (Royal Albert Hall) 2009; dir Merrily We Roll Along (Harold Pinter Theatre) 2013 (Best Musical Revival Olivier Award 2014); *Concerts* venues incl: Barbican, Royal Festival Hall, Palladium, Drury Lane, Albert Hall, St David's Hall; By Special Arrangement (Donmar Warehouse, Olivier Awards Best Entertainment 1995), By Extra Special Arrangement (Whitehall) 1995, Henley Festival 1999, Last Night of the Proms 2002, From London to New York (Cafe Carlyle) 2003, By Special Arrangement (Cafe Carlyle) 2004, Palais De La Musica (Barcelona and Madrid) 2007, BBC Proms in the Park (Hyde Park and Glasgow) 2008, BBC's Friday Night is Music Night: Disney Celebration (Lyceum) 2008, Christmas in New York (Lyric) 2008, Love Songs for the Movies (Waterfront Hall Belfast) 2008, Maria Friedman sings Stephen Sondheim (Cadogan Hall) 2008, Maria Friedman Sings The Great British Songbook (Shaw) 2009, New York Moments (Lincoln Centre NY) 2009, BBC Radio 3 In Tune: Countdown to the Proms (RCM) 2010, BBC Proms (Royal Albert Hall) 2010, Maria Sings Stephen Sondheim (Cadogan Hall) 2010; *Television* incl: Me and the Girls, Blues in the Night, Red Dwarf, Casualty, Frank Stubbs Promotes, War Oratorio, In Deep, Orlando, Black Daisies for the Bride; *Film* Joseph and the Amazing Technicolour Dreamcoat; *Albums* solo recordings: Maria Friedman, Maria Friedman Live, Broadway Baby, Now and Then, Maria Friedman Celebrates The Great British Songbook; contrib to numerous cast recordings; *Style*— Ms Maria Friedman; ✉ c/o agent Liz Roberts (☎ 07905 490080, e-mail whitch_one@hotmail.com)

FRIEDMAN, Sonia; OBE (2016); da of Leonard Friedman, and Clair Friedman; *Educ* St Christophers Letchworth, Central Sch of Speech and Drama; *Career* theatre prodr; head Mobile Prodns and Theatre for Young People RNT 1989–93, co-fndr Out of Joint Prodns (with Max Stafford-Clark, *qv*) 1993, fndr Sonia Friedman Prodns (SFP, subsid of Ambassador Theatre Gp) 2002; prodns with Out of Joint incl: The Queen and I, The Libertine, The Steward of Christendom, The Break of Day, The Positive Hour, Shopping and Fucking, Our Lady of Sligo, Blue Heart; programmed at New Ambassadors Theatre: Stones in His Pockets, Drummers, Some Explicit Polaroids, Krapp's Last Tape, Our Late Night, Al Murray the Pub Landlord, Jane Eyre, Mother Courage and Her Children, A Doll's House, The Mill on the Floss, The Vagina Monologues, One for the Road, Boston Marriage, Abigail's Party; theatre prodns and co-prodns with SFP in the West End and/or on Broadway incl: The Book of Mormon, Shakespeare in Love, 1984, King Charles III, Electra, Sunny Afternoon, The River, Hamlet, Ghosts, Mojo, The Sunshine Boys, Twelfth Night/Richard III, Chimerica, Old Times, Merrily We Roll Along, Nice Work If You Can Get It, La Cage Aux Folles, A Chorus of Disapproval, Legally Blonde The Musical, Hay Fever, Absent Friends, Master Class, Private Lives, Jerusalem, The Mountaintop, Top Girls, Bertrayal, Much Ado About Nothing, Arcadia, The Children's Hour, Clybourne Park, A Flea in her Ear, Shirley Valentine/Educating Rita, La Bete, All My Sons, The Prisoner of Second Avenue, Othello, A View from the Bridge, A Little Night Music, The Norman Conquests, After Miss Julie, Dancing at Lughnasa, Boeing-Boeing, Maria Friedman Re-Arranged, The Play's The Thing, No Man's Land, The Seagull, Under the Blue Sky, That Face, Rock'N'Roll, Dealer's Choice, In Celebration, The Dumb Waiter, Love Song, Bent, Donkey's Years, Eh Joe, Faith Healer, Shoot the Crow, Otherwise Engaged, As You Like It, The Home Place, Noises Off, Whose Life is it Anyway?, By the Bog of Cats, The Woman in White, Guantanamo: Honour Bound to Defend Freedom, Endgame, Jumpers, Calico, See You Next Tuesday, Hitchcock Blonde, Absolutely! (Perhaps), Sexual Perversity in Chicago, Ragtime, What the Night Is For, On An Average Day, Afterplay, Up for Grabs, Benefactors, Lobby Hero, Maria Friedman Live, Mind Games, A Day in the Death of Joe Egg, A Servant to Two Masters, Gagarin's Way, Port Authority, Spoonface Steinberg, Speed-the-Plow, In Flame, The Mystery of Charles Dickens, The Late Middle Classes, Last Dance at Dum Dum, King of Hearts, Is He Dead?; *Style*— Ms Sonia Friedman, OBE; ✉ Sonia Friedman Productions, Duke of York Theatre, 104 St Martin's Lane, London WC2N 4BG (☎ 020 7845 8750, fax 020 7845 8759, website www.soniafriedman.com)

FRIEDMANN, Julian; *b* 1944, South Africa; *Educ* Univ of York (BA), SOAS Univ of London (MA), LSE; *Career* jt md Blake Friedmann Literary Agency; ed ScriptWriter magazine (new www.twelvepoint.com) 2001–10; EU Media 1 project: creator and former head of studies Prog for the Int Launch of TV Series (PILOTS), UK co-ordinator European Audiovisual Entrepreneurs (EAVE) prodr trg prog; dir: www.scriptwritermagazine.com, www.twelvepoint.com; visiting lectr: Univ of Brussels, Munich Film Sch, Masterschool Drehbuch Berlin, Liverpool John Moore Univ, London Coll of Printing, RCA, Nat Film & TV Sch, Northern Sch of Film and TV Leeds, De Montfort Univ (also estab masters degree in TV scriptwriting); former advsr Euro Film Coll Ebeltoft Denmark; former memb: Euro Jury Emmy nominations, Jury Grierson Documentary Award; memb July BAFTA TV Awards; exec prodr: Innocent (feature film), Benedict's Brother (feature film); *Books* How to Make Money Scriptwriting, Writing Long-Running Television Series (ed, 2 vols), The Insider's Guide to Writing for Television; *Recreations* gardening, astronomy; *Style*— Julian Friedmann, Esq; ✉ Blake Friedmann Literary Agency, 1st Floor, Selous House, 5–12 Mandela Street, London NW1 0DU (e-mail julian@blakefriedmann.co.uk, website www.blakefriedmann.co.uk and www.julianfriedmann.com)

FRIEDRICH, William Michael (Bill); s of William E Friedrich, and Elizabeth C, *née* Kline; *Educ* Babylon HS, Union Coll (cum laude), Columbia Law Sch (Dr Jur); *Career* assoc Thacher, Proffitt & Wood 1974–75, ptnr Shearman & Sterling 1983–95 (assoc 1975–83), gen counsel British Gas 1995–97, gen counsel BG plc 1997–2005, dep chief exec BG Gp plc 2000–; non-exec dir Royal Bank of Scotland 2006–; memb American Bar Assoc; *Recreations* field sports, riding, tennis; *Clubs* Union (NY), Mountain Lake, Tamarack (NY), Norfolk (CT); *Style*— W Friedrich, Esq; ✉ BG Group plc, 100 Thames Valley Park Drive, Reading, Berkshire RG6 1PT (☎ 0118 929 3367, fax 0118 929 3327, mobile 07785 950 648, e-mail william.friedrich@bg-group.com)

FRIEL, Anna; *b* 12 July 1976, Rochdale; *Children* 1 da (Gracie Ellen Mary b 9 July 2005), with David Thewlis, *qv*; *Career* actress; *Theatre* Look Europe 1999, Closer 2000, Lulu 2001, Breakfast At Tiffany's 2009–10; *Television* incl: GBH 1991, Emmerdale 1992, Medics 1993, Brookside 1993–95, Cadfael 1996, Tales from the Crypt 1996, Our Mutual Friend 1998, The Tribe 1998, Fields of Gold 2002, Watermelon 2003, Perfect Strangers 2004, The Jury 2004, Pushing Daisies 2007–09, Without You 2011; *Films* incl: The Stringer 1997, The Land Girls 1998, St Ives 1998, A Midsummer Night's Dream 1999, Rogue Trader 1999, Mad Cows 1999, Sunset Strip 2000, An Everlasting Piece 2000, The War Bride (nominee Best Actress Canadian Acad Award) 2000, Me Without You 2001, Timeline 2002, Land of the Lost 2009, London Boulevard 2010, You Will Meet a Tall Dark Stranger 2010, Limitless 2011; *Awards* Best Newcomer TV Quick Awards 1994, Best Actress Nat TV Awards 1995, Best Actress Smash Hits Poll Award Winner 1995, Best Supporting Actress (for Closer) Drama Desk Awards NY 1999; *Style*— Ms Anna Friel; ✉ c/o Conway van Gelder Ltd, 18–21 Jermyn Street, London SW1Y 6HP (e-mail annafriel@annafriel.com)

FRIEND, Lionel; s of Norman Alfred Child Friend (d 1991), and Moya Lilian, *née* Dicks (d 2003); *b* 13 March 1945, London; *Educ* Royal GS High Wycombe, RCM, London Opera Centre; *m* 1969, Jane, da of Norman Edward Hyland; 1 s (Toby Thomas b 1984), 2 da (Clea Deborah b 1972, Corinne Jane b 1977); *Career* conductor WNO 1969–72, Glyndebourne Festival and Touring Opera 1969–72; 2 Kapellmeister Staatstheater Kassel Germany 1972–75; staff conductor ENO 1976–89; music dir: Nexus Opera 1981–, New Sussex Opera 1989–96; conductor-in-residence Birmingham Conservatoire 2003–10, music dir Br Youth Opera 2015–; guest conductor: Philharmonia, City of Birmingham Symphony Orch, BBC Symphony Orch, Royal Ballet, Orchestre National de France, Nouvel Orchestre Philharmonique, Austrian Radio Symphony Orch, Swedish Radio Symphony Orch, Hungarian State Symphony Orch, Budapest Symphony Orch, Scot Chamber Orch, London Sinfonietta, Nash Ensemble, Opéra Nat de la Monnaie, Oper Frankfurt, LA Opera, Opera Australia, Royal Danish Opera, Polish Nat Opera, Portland Opera, Opera Zuid, NZ Opera; recordings incl works by Bliss, Brian, Britten, Debussy, Durkó, Colin Matthews, David Matthews, Anthony Milner, Payne, Poulenc, Schönberg, Souster, Stravinsky, Tavener and Turnage; *Recreations* reading, theatre; *Style*— Lionel Friend, Esq; ✉ 136 Rosendale Road, London SE21 8LG (☎ 020 8761 7845, website www.lionelfriend.com)

FRIEND, Mark; s of Prof John Friend, and Carol, *née* Loofe; *b* 23 November 1957; *Educ* Gonville & Caius Coll Cambridge (BA), Institut D'Etudes Européennes Brussels (Licence Spéciale en Droit Européen); *m* 19 May 1990, Margaret DeJong; 2 s; *Career* admitted slr 1982, ptnr (specialising in competition law and regulation) Allen & Overy 1990–; author of numerous contribs to legal periodicals on competition law; *Recreations* music, golf, art, classic cars, wine; *Clubs* RAC, Dulwich and Sydenham Hill Golf, Aldeburgh Golf; *Style*— Mark Friend, Esq; ✉ Allen & Overy LLP, One Bishops Square, London E1 6AD (☎ 020 3088 0000, fax 020 3088 0088)

FRIEND, Prof Sir Richard Henry; kt (2003); s of John Henry Friend, and Dorothy Jean, *née* Brown; *b* 18 January 1953; *Educ* Rugby, Trinity Coll Cambridge (MA, PhD); *m* 1979, Carol Anne Maxwell, *née* Beales; 2 da (Rachel Frances b 31 July 1981, Lucy Alexandra 14 Feb 1984); *Career* res fell St John's Coll Cambridge 1977–80; Univ of Cambridge: demonstrator in physics 1980–85, lectr 1985–93, reader 1993–95, Cavendish prof of physics 1995–; visiting prof Univ of Calif Santa Barbara 1986–87, visiting fell Royal Instn London 1992–98, Mary Shepard B Upson visiting prof Cornell Univ USA 2003, Kelvin lectr IEE 2004; Nuffield Sci res fell 1992–93; chief scientist Cambridge Display Technol Ltd 1997–2000; chief scientist and dir Plastic Logic Ltd 2000–04; J V Boys prize Inst of Physics 1988, interdisciplinary award RSC 1991, Hewlett-Packard Prize European Physical Soc 1996, Rumford Medal Royal Soc 1998, Italgas Prize for Research and Technological Innovation 2001, MacRoberts Prize Royal Acad of Engrg 2002, Silver Medal Royal Acad of Engrg 2002, Faraday Medal Inst of Electrical Engrgs 2003, Gold Medal European Materials Research Soc 2003, Descartes Prize European Cmmn 2003, Rhodia de Gennes Prize 2008; hon fell Trinity Coll Cambridge 2004; Hon DUniv: Linköping Sweden 2000, Mons Belgium 2002, Nijmegen 2008; FRS 1993, FREng 2002, FIEE 2002, Hon FRSC 2004, Hon FInstP 2008 (MInstP 1988, FInstP 1997); *Publications* author of numerous papers on solid state and chemical physics in scientific journals; *Style*— Prof Sir Richard Friend, FRS; ✉ University of Cambridge, Cavendish Laboratory, Madingley Road, Cambridge CB3 0HE (☎ 01223 337218, fax 01223 353397, e-mail rhf10@cam.ac.uk)

FRIEND, Rupert; *Career* actor; *Television* Sex Lies and Cyberspace 2000, Homeland 2012–; *Film* Babe B Movie 2000, The Libertine 2004, Pride and Prejudice 2005, Mrs Palfrey at the Claremont 2005, The Decameron 2006, The Moon and Stars 2006, The Last Legion 2006, Outlaw 2007, Jolene 2007, The Boy in Striped Pyjamas 2008, The Young Victoria 2009, Chéri 2009, The Kid 2010, Lullaby for Pi 2010, 5 Days of War 2011, Renee 2012; *Theatre* numerous performances at venues incl Royal Nat Theatre, The Globe Theatre, Cliveden Open Air Theatre; Outstanding New Talent Award Golden Satellite Awards 2005, nominated Best Newcomer Br Ind Film Awards 2005; *Style*— Rupert Friend, Esq; ✉ c/o Independent Talent Group, 40 Whitfield Street, London W1T 2RH (☎ 020 7636 6565, fax 020 7323 0101)

FRIEND, Tony Peter; s of H John Friend (d 1992), and Daphne Denise, *née* Cavanagh (d 2013); *b* 30 October 1954, London; *Educ* Highgate Sch, City of London (accountancy fndn course); *m* 25 Sept 1982, Antoinette (Toni) Julie, da of Thomas Brennan; 3 s (William Alexander Goodwin b 9 July 1988, Thomas Christopher Goodwin b 1 June 1991, John Sebastian Goodwin b 7 April 1994); *Career* Pannell Kerr Forster CAs 1974–79 (qualified 1978), Grindlay Brandts/Grindlays Bank/ANZ 1979–86; County NatWest: dir NatWest Wood Mackenzie 1986–94, dir of investment banking NatWest Markets 1995; md Ludgate Communications 1996–97; dir: Ludgate Group 1996–97, Ludgate Communications Inc 1996–97; managing ptnr and dir Instinctif Ptnrs (formerly College Hill) 1998–2015, ind Bd advsr with portfolio of roles 2015–; memb Nat Exec Assoc of Student Accountants 1974–79; Duke of Edinburgh Gold and Silver Awards 1971; Liveryman Worshipful Co of CAs in England and Wales; memb: Faculty of Fin and Mgmnt ICA, Investor Rels Soc; FCA, ACInstT, MSI; *Recreations* sports, travel, theatre; *Clubs* MCC (cricket and real tennis), Dedanist Soc, Old Cholmeleian Soc, Sports and Football, Totteridge Cricket, South Herts; *Style*— Tony Friend, Esq; ✉ Cambridge House, 19 Prince of Wales Drive, London SW11 4SB (☎ 07798 864995, e-mail tony@tfommunications.com)

FRIER, Prof Brian Murray; s of William Murray Frier (d 2014), of Edinburgh; *Educ* George Heriot's Sch Edinburgh, Univ of Edinburgh (BSc, MB ChB, MD); *m* Isobel Margaret, da of Dr Henry Donald Wilson (d 1991), of Edinburgh; 1 da (Emily Margaret); *Career* jr med appts Edinburgh and Dundee 1972–76, research fell in diabetes and metabolism Cornell Univ NY 1976–77, sr med registrar Edinburgh 1978–82; conslt physician: Western Infirmary and Gartnavel Gen Hosp Glasgow 1982–87, Royal Infirmary Edinburgh 1987–2012; Univ of Edinburgh: former pt/t reader in medicine, currently hon prof of diabetes; author of numerous publications on diabetes and hypoglycaemia; chm Hon Advsy Panel on Diabetes and Driving (UK) 2001–12, former chm Diabetes Research in Scotland (Chief Scientist Office); former govr George Heriot's Tst Edinburgh; memb: Diabetes UK (R D Lawrence lectr 1986, Banting meml lectr 2009), Assoc of Physicians GB and I, Euro Assoc for the Study of Diabetes, American Diabetes Assoc, Assoc of Br Clinical Diabetologists; Somogyi Award Hungarian Diabetes Assoc 2004; FRCPE 1984 (vice-pres 2008–12), FRCPG 1986; *Books* Hypoglycaemia and Diabetes: Clinical and Physiological Aspects (jt ed with B M Fisher, 1993), Hypoglycaemia in Clinical Diabetes (jt ed with B M Fisher, 1999, 3 edn, jt ed with S R Heller and R J McCrimmon, 2014), Insulin Therapy: a Pocket Guide (with M W J Strachan, 2013); *Recreations* cinema, music, opera, reading, travel, walking, rugby (spectating); *Clubs* Heriot's FP, Heriot's Rugby; *Style*— Prof Brian M Frier; ✉ 100 Morningside Drive, Edinburgh EH10 5NT (☎ 0131 447 1653); University of Edinburgh, BHF Centre for Cardiovascular Science, The Queen's

Medical Research Institute, Little France, Edinburgh EH16 4TJ (e-mail brian.frier@ed.ac.uk)

FRIER, (Gavin Austin) Garry; s of Gavin Walter Rae Frier (d 1985), and Isabel Fraser, *née* Austin (d 1981); *b* 18 May 1953; *Educ* Hutchesons' Boys Glasgow, Univ of Strathclyde (BA); *m* 1978, Jane Carolyn, da of John Keith Burton, of Glasgow; 1 s (Stuart Austin b 1981); *Career* CA; dir County Bank Ltd (renamed County Natwest Ltd) 1985–87; chief exec: Ferrum Holdings plc 1987–94, Williams de Broë plc Edinburgh 1995–97; dir A R Brown McFarlane Ltd 1993–, dir of corp fin Charterhouse Securities Edinburgh 1997–2002, dir of corp fin ING Barings Edinburgh 2003, chief exec Corp Governance Advsrs Ltd; MICAS 1978; *Recreations* tennis, shooting, skiing; *Clubs* New (Edinburgh); *Style—* Garry Frier, Esq; ✉ garryfrier@aol.com

FRISCHMANN, Dr Wilem William; CBE; s of Lajos Frischmann (d 1944), of Hungary, and Nelly Frischmann (d 1945); *Educ* Hammersmith Coll of Art and Building, Imperial Coll of Sci and Technol (DIC), City Univ of London (PhD); *m* 1 Sept 1957, Sylvia, da of Maurice Elvey (d 1980), of Glasgow; 1 s (Richard Sandor), 1 da (Justine Elinor); *Career* CJ Pell & Partners 1956–68 (ptnr 1961–68), sr ptnr Pell Frischmann & Ptnrs 1968–, chm Pell Frischmann Group 1984–; chm Conseco International Ltd; Hon DSc City Univ 1997; FREng 1985, FCGI, FIStructE, MConsE, MASCE; MSISdeFr; *Recreations* tennis, swimming, skiing; *Clubs* Arts; *Style—* Dr Wilem Frischmann, CBE, FREng; ✉ Pell Frischmann, 5 Manchester Square, London W1A 1AU

FRITCHIE, Baroness (Life Peer UK 2005), of Gloucester in the County of Gloucestershire; Dame Irene Tordoff (Rennie) Fritchie; DBE (1996); da of Charles Fredrick Fennell (d 1975), and Eva, *née* Tordoff; *b* 29 April 1942; *Educ* Ribston Hall GS for Girls; *m* 21 Oct 1960, Don Jamie Fritchie (d 1992), s of Frederick Fritchie; 2 s (Charles Eric b 14 March 1962 d 1991, Hon Andrew Peel b 30 Sept 1965); *Career* early career experience in family hotel Royal George Birdlip, admin offr Endsleigh Insurance Brokers 1970–73, sales trg offr Trident Insurance Ltd 1973–76, head of trg confs and specialist trg advsr on women's devpt Food and Drink Industrial Trg Bd 1976–80, conslt Social Ecology Associates 1980–81, dir Transform Ltd conslts on organisational change 1981–85, The Rennie Fritchie Consultancy 1985–89, md Working Choices Ltd 1989–91, Mainstream Devpt Consultancy 1991–; chair Nominet 2010; vice-chair Stroud and Swindon Building Soc 1995–2008; cmmr for public appts 1999–2005; chair: Gloucester HA 1988–92, S Western RHA 1992–94, S and W RHA 1997–98, 2gether Gloucester NHS Fndn Tst 2008–12; memb NHS Policy Bd 1994–96, chair Nat Advsy Gp on Nursing 1996, memb GMC 1996–99, pres Br Assoc of Medical Mangrs 1997–99, pres Chronic Pain Coalition 2005–08, pres Hospital Caterers Assoc 2009–10; Home Sec's rep on Selection Panel for Independent Membs of Police Authorities 1995–99; visiting faculty memb HSM Univ of Manchester 1994–99; non-exec bd memb Br Quality Fndn 1996–99; patron: Winston's Wish 1996–99, Women in Banking & Finance 2008–12; memb Working Parties: on women in NHS, examining non-exec bd membership for the public sector 1996; memb: Assoc Media Literacy Gp, All-Pty Parly China Gp, All Pty Gp for Educn, All Pty Gp on Libraries and Info Mgmnt, Br-American Parly Gp, All Pty Australian and NZ Gp, All Pty London 2012 Olympic and Paralympics Gp, All Pty Parly Gp on Taxation, All Parly Gp on Mental Health, All Pty Parly Gp on Ageing and Older People, Bd UK Shared Business Services 2013–15, House of Lords Audit Ctee 2015; memb and dep chair Audit Advsy Ctee Scottish Public Services Ombudsman 2007–10, chair Ind Appointments Selection Bd RICS 2006–12, memb Sounding Bd Health, Work and Wellbeing 2007, memb Bd BAMM Leadership Standards Scrutiny and Strategy Bd 2009–, memb Penna Public Service Advsy Bd 2015; formerly: bd memb Nat Centre for Mental Health, non-exec dir Inst of Health Servs Mgmnt Consultancy; hon visiting prof (with chair in creative leadership) Univ of York 1996–2008, pro-chllr Univ of Southampton 1998–2007 (chair Cncl 1998–99); memb Editorial Bd: Revans Inst for Action Learning, Research and Practice Jl, Whitehall and Westminster World 2006–08; patron: Lord Mayor's Appeal 2000–01, Pied Piper Appeal 2002–; ambass Winstons Wish 2002–06; memb Br and I Ombudsman Assoc 2002, vice-chair Br Lung Fndn 2006–10, chair Web Science Res Initiative Univ of Southampton/MIT 2006–09, chair Lloyds Bank Fndn in Eng and Wales 2015; Royal Aeronautical Soc and Parly memb Air League; chllr Univ of Gloucestershire 2012; fell C&G, fell Sunningdale Inst Nat Sch of Govt 2005–12; Hon DPhil Univ of Southampton 1996; Hon DUniv: York 1998, Oxford Brookes 2001, Queen's Univ Belfast 2005; Hon Dr of Laws Univ of St Andrews 2002, Hon Dr Open Univ 2003, DLitt (hc) Univ of Hull 2006; CIMgt 2001; *Books* Working Choices (1988), The Business of Assertiveness (1991), Resolving Conflicts in Organisations; *Recreations* family, reading, gardening, swimming, theatre, cooking, The Archers and Coronation Street; *Style—* The Rt Hon the Baroness Fritchie, DBE; ✉ Mainstream Development, 51 St Paul's Road, Gloucester GL1 5AP (☎ and fax 01452 414542); House of Lords, London SW1A 0PW

FRITH, Prof Christopher Donald (Chris); s of late Donald Alfred Frith, OBE, and late Mary Webster, *née* Tyler; bro of Prof Simon Frith, *qv*; *b* 16 March 1942, Cross in Hand, E Sussex; *Educ* Christ's Coll Cambridge (MA), Univ of London (Dip Abnormal Psychology, PhD); *m* 1966, Prof Uta Frith, *qv*; 2 s; *Career* research worker Dept of Psychology Inst of Psychiatry 1965–75, scientist Div of Psychiatry Clinical Research Centre MRC 1975–92, special appt MRC Cyclotron Unit Hammersmith Hosp 1992–94, Wellcome princ research fell Funtional Imaging Lab UCL 1994–2007, currently emeritus prof in neuropsychology Wellcome Tst Centre for Neuroimaging; Niels Bohr visiting prof MindLab Aarhus Univ; memb Editorial Bd Science 1999–2009; fell All Souls Coll Oxford; memb: Academia Europaea 1999, Assoc for the Scientific Study of Consciousness (pres 2001); guarantor Brain 1999–2010; Kenneth Craik Award St John's Coll Cambridge 1999, European Latsis Prize 2009 (jtly with Uta Frith), Fndn Fyssen Prize 2009; Hon DUniv: Paris-Lodron Salzburg 2003, York 2004; FMedSci 1999, FRS 2000, fell AAAS 2001, FBA 2008; *Publications* The Cognitive Neuropsychology of Schizophrenia (1992, Br Psychological Soc Book Award 1996), Human Brain Function (co-author, 1997), A Very Short Introduction to Schizophrenia (co-author, 2003), The Neuroscience of Social Interaction (co-author, 2004), Making Up the Mind (2007, Br Psychological Soc Book Award 2008); author of more than 400 pubns in peer-reviewed jls; *Recreations* music, computer programming; *Style—* Prof Chris Frith; ✉ Wellcome Trust Centre for Neuroimaging, University College London, 12 Queen Square, London WC1N 3BG (☎ 020 7833 7457, fax 020 7813 1445, e-mail cfrith@fil.ion.ucl.ac.uk)

FRITH, Mark; *b* 22 May 1970; *Educ* Gleadless Valley Sch Sheffield, Univ of East London; *Career* ed coll magazine 'Overdraft' 1989–90 (writer 1988–89); Smash Hits: writer 1990–93, features ed 1993–94, ed 1994–96; ed Sky Magazine 1996–97, ed Special Projects 1997–98, ed Heat Magazine 1999–2008, ed Time Out 2009–11, editorial dir Bauer Media 2011–; PPA Consumer Magazine Editor of the Year 2001 and 2002; *Publications* The Best of Smash Hits (ed, 2006); *Style—* Mark Frith, Esq; ✉ Bauer Media, Endeavour House, 189 Shaftesbury Avenue, London WC2H 8JG

FRITH, Rt Rev Richard Michael Cokayne; *see:* Hull, Bishop of

FRITH, Prof Simon; s of late Donald Alfred Frith, OBE, and late Mary Webster, *née* Tyler; bro of Prof Chris Frith, *qv*; *Educ* Univ of Oxford, Univ of Calif; *Career* Tovey chair of music Univ of Edinburgh 2006–; fndr memb Int Assoc for the Study of Popular Music, founding ed Popular Music, chair of judges Mercury Music Prize 1992–; *Style—* Prof Simon Frith; ✉ School of Arts, Culture & Environment, University of Edinburgh, Alison House, 12 Nicolson Square, Edinburgh EH8 9DF

FRITH, Prof Uta; Hon DBE; *née* Aurnhammer; *b* 25 May 1941, Rockenhausen, Germany; *Educ* Universität des Saarlandes Saarbrücken, Univ of London (Dip Abnormal Psychology, PhD); *m* Prof Chris Frith, *qv*; 2 s; *Career* MRC scientist 1968–2006; prof of cognitive devpt UCL 1996–2006 (emeritus prof 2006–); chartered clinical psychologist; memb: Experimental Psychology Soc, Br Neuropsychological Soc, American Psychological Soc, Soc for Neuroscience; memb Editorial Bd: Cognition, Jl of Child Psychology and Psychiatry; President's Award Br Psychological Soc 1990; Hon Dr: Univ of Göteborg Sweden 1998, Univ of St Andrews 2000, Univ of Palermo 2004, Univ of York 2004, Univ of Nottingham 2007; hon fell Newnham Coll Cambridge 2008; memb Academia Europaea 1992; FBA 2001, FMedSci 2001, FRS 2005, Hon FBPsS 2006 (FBPsS 1990); Autism – Explaining the Enigma (2 edn 2003), Autism in History: The Case of Hugh Blair of Borgue (with Rab Houston, 2001); *Style—* Prof Uta Frith, DBE; ✉ Institute of Cognitive Neuroscience, University College London, Alexandra House, 17 Queen Square, London WC1N 3AR (☎ 020 7679 1177, e-mail u.frith@ucl.ac.uk)

FROGGATT, Joanne; *b* 23 August 1980; *m* 2012, James Christian Cannon; *Career* actress; *Television* incl: Nature Boy 2000, Other People's Children 2000, Lorna Doone 2000, Paradise Heights 2002, The Stretford Wives 2002, Danielle Cable: Eyewitness 2003, Island at War 2004, Life on Mars 2006, See No Evil: The Moors Murders 2006, The Street 2006, Murder in the Outback 2007, Robin Hood 2009, Downton Abbey 2010– (Best Supporting Actress Golden Globes 2015), The Royle Family Christmas Special 2010, Moving On – The Butterfly Effect 2010, True Love 2012, Secrets – The Lie 2014, Dark Angel 2016; *Theatre* incl: Be My Baby (Soho Theatre) 2000, Playhouse Creatures (W Yorks Playhouse) 2003, Who's Afraid of Virginia Woolf? (Royal Exchange Manchester) 2007, All About My Mother (Old Vic) 2007, The Knowledge/Little Platoons (Bush Theatre) 2011; *Film* incl: In Our Name 2010 (Most Promising Newcomer Br Ind Film Award), Filth 2012, You Want Me to Kill Him? 2012, Still Life 2012, Starfish 2016, A Street Cat Named Bob 2016, A Storm in the Stars 2016, One Last Thing 2016; *Style—* Ms Joanne Froggatt; ✉ c/o John Grant, Conway Van Gelder Grant, 3rd Floor, 8–12 Broadwick Street, London W1F 8HW; PA Vanessa Green (e-mail vgreen@dsl.pipex.com)

FROOME, Christopher Clive (Chris); OBE (2016); s of Clive Froome, and Jane, *née* Flatt; *b* 20 May 1985, Nairobi, Kenya; *Partner* Michelle Cound; *Career* cyclist; memb: Team Konica Minolta 2007, Team Barloworld 2008–09, Team Sky 2010–; achievements incl: winner stage 2 Tour of Mauritius 2005, winner Tour of Mauritius 2006 (winner stages 2 and 3), second place stage 3 and winner stage 5 Giro delle Rigione 2007, winner stage 6 Tour of Japan 2007, Bronze medal (road cycling race) All-Africa Games 2007 (representing Kenya), second place Giro del Capo 2008, third place Giro Dell'Appennino 2008, winner Giro del Capo II 2009, second place Br Nat Time Trial Championships 2010, third place Tour of Beijing 2011, second place Vuelta a España 2011 (winner stage 17 and second place stage 10), fourth place Criterium du Dauphine 2012, second place Tour de France 2012 (winner stage 7), Bronze medal (time trial) Olympic Games 2012, winner Tour of Oman 2013 (first stage 5), winner Criterium Int 2013 (winner stage 3), second place Tirreno-Adriatico 2013 (winner stage 4), winner Tour de Romandie 2013 (winner prologue), winner Criterium de Dauphine 2013 (winner stage 5), winner Tour de France 2013 (winner stages 8, 15 and 17), Bronze medal (time trial) Olympic Games 2016; *Style—* Mr Chris Froome, OBE; ✉ e-mail info@chris-froome.com

FROST, Alan John; DL (Dorset, 2010); s of Edward George Frost (d 1981), and Ellen Lucy, *née* Jamieson (d 1979); *b* 6 October 1944; *Educ* Stratford Co GS, Univ of Manchester (BSc); *m* 15 Dec 1973, Valerie Jean, da of Francis David Bennett; 2 s (Christopher, Patrick); *Career* investment dir Abbey Life Gp 1986–89, md Abbey Life Assurance Co Ltd 1989–98, dir Lloyds Abbey Life plc 1989–96, gp chief exec United Assurance Gp plc 1998–2000; chm: Queen Mab Consultancy Ltd 2001–04, Car Crash Line Gp plc 2002–04 (non-exec dir 2002–06), Teachers' Building Soc 2004–10 (non-exec dir 2001–10); non-exec dir: INVESCO Pensions Ltd 2001–, NFU Mutual Insurance Co Ltd 2002–09, Hamworthy plc 2004–12; regular columnist in The Actuary Magazine 2002–08; chm: Dorset Opera 2004–, Bournemouth Chamber Music Soc 2012–; chm Bd of Govrs Bournemouth Univ 2004–10 (memb 2001–10, dep chm 2003–04); vice-chm St Peter's (Bournemouth) Devpt Project 2015–; former dir: Dorset TEC, Bournemouth Orchestras; former chm S Wessex Industrial Project Duke of Edinburgh's Award; former visiting fell European Centre for Corporate Governance Bournemouth Univ; High Sheriff Dorset 2011–12; Freeman City of London 1986, Master Worshipful Co of Actuaries 2004–05 (Liveryman 1986–); Hon DBA Bournemouth Univ 2011; FIA 1970, FIMgt 1990–2009; A General Introduction to Institutional Investment (with D P Hager, 1986), Debt Securities (with D P Hager, 1990), A Light Frost (2005); *Recreations* opera, genealogy; *Clubs* Reform; *Style—* Alan Frost, Esq, DL; ✉ 20 Little Forest Road, Bournemouth, Dorset BH4 9NW (☎ 01202 764734, e-mail mail@alanfrost.co.uk, website www.alanfrost.co.uk)

FROST, David George Hamilton; CMG (2006); s of George Frost, and Margaret, *née* Murfin; *b* 21 February 1965, Derby; *Educ* St John's Coll Oxford (BA); *m* 1993, Jacqueline Elizabeth, *née* Dias; 1 da (Jennifer b 1998), 1 s (Joshua b 2000); *Career* joined FCO 1987, second sec Br High Cmmn Nicosia 1989–90, seconded to KPMG 1990–92, first sec UK perm rep to EU 1993–96, first sec UK mission to UN 1996–98, private sec to Perm Under Sec 1998–99, dep head EU Dept FCO 1999–2001, economic cnsllr Br Embassy Paris 2001–03, dir EU (internal) FCO 2003–06, ambass to Denmark 2006–08, dir for strategy and policy planning FCO 2008–10, int trade dir Dept for Business, Innovation and Skills 2010–; *Style—* David Frost, Esq, CMG

FROST, David Stuart; CBE (2011), DL (W Midlands 2012); s of George William Stuart Frost, and Winifred Leslie, *née* Stuart; *b* 22 February 1953, Corbridge, Northumberland; *Educ* Thames Poly (BA), Poly of the South Bank (Dip); *m* June 1981, Mari, *née* Doyle; 2 da (Hannah b 11 June 1988, Sophie b 26 May 1990); *Career* economist London C of C 1976–79; Walsall C of C: dir of servs 1975–86, chief exec 1986–96; chief exec: East Mercia C of C 1996–2000, Coventry and Warks C of C 2000–02; DG Br Chambers of Commerce 2003–11; chm: Nat Cncl of Grad Entrepreneurship 2005–13, Vinspired 2012–, Nat Numeracy 2013–15, Stoke on Trent and Staffs Local Enterprise Partnership 2014–, Coventry Univ Coll 2015–; Master Worshipful Co of Loriners 2013; Hon DUniv Birmingham City Univ 2008; FRSA, FIOD, CCMI; *Publications* Health at Work – an independent review of sickness absence (2011); *Recreations* cycling, motorcycling; *Clubs* Naval and Military, Walsall, Bishopsgate Ward; *Style—* David Frost, Esq, CBE, DL; ✉ 5 Norfolk Gardens, Sutton Coldfield, West Midlands B75 6SS (e-mail david@david-frost.co.uk)

FROST, Nicholas John (Nick); *b* 28 March 1972, Dagenham, Essex; *Career* actor and writer; *Television* incl: Spaced 1999–2001, Man Stroke Woman 2005–07, Hyperdrive 2006–07; *Film* incl: Shaun of the Dead 2004, Kinky Boots 2005, Penelope 2006, Hot Fuzz 2007, Wild Child 2008, The Boat That Rocked 2009, Paul 2011 (also writer (with Simon Pegg, *qv*)), Attack the Block 2011, The Adventures of Tintin: The Secret of the Unicorn 2011, Snow White and the Huntsman 2012; *Style—* Mr Nick Frost; ✉ c/o Hamilton Hodell, Fifth Floor, 66–68 Margaret Street, London W1W 8SR

FROW, Ben Brummell; s of Gerald Frow (d 2005), and Sally, *née* Miles; *b* 14 July 1961, London; *Educ* Woodberry Down Comp Sch; *Partner* Nigel Bond (civil partnership 5 Jan 2007); *Career* head of features and factual entertainment Channel 4 1999–2004, controller of features and entertainment Channel 5 2004–07, dir of programming TV3 2007–13, dir of programmes Channel 5 2013–; *Recreations* shopping, eating out, interior design, reading, dog welfare; *Style—* Ben Frow, Esq; ✉ Channel 5, 10 Lower Thames Street, London EC3R 6EN (☎ 020 8612 7691, e-mail ben.frow@five.tv)

F

FRY, Anthony Michael; s of Denis Seymour Fry (d 2004), of Worthing, W Sussex, and Trixie, *née* Barter (d 1998); *b* 20 June 1955; *Educ* Stonyhurst, Magdalen Coll Oxford (MA, Atkinson Prize, treas Oxford Union), Harvard Business Sch (AMP); *m* 27 July 1985, Anne Elizabeth, da of Harry Birrell; 1 da (Sophie Alexandra b 18 April 1991), 2 s (Edward Harry Seymour b 21 Jan 1993, Hugo Benedict Cameron b 28 Nov 1996); *Career* N M Rothschild & Sons Ltd 1977–96: joined 1977, mangr International Pacific Corp Melbourne (renamed Rothschild Australia 1983) 1980–85, exec dir corp fin 1985–96; md: Barclays de Zoete Wedd 1996–97, Credit Suisse First Boston 1997–2004; head of UK investment banking Lehman Brothers 2004–08 (latterly sr advsr), sr md of corp advsy Evercore Ptnrs Inc 2008–10 (latterly sr advsr); chm: CALA Gp 2010–, Espirito Santo Investment Bank 2011–; non-exec dir: Southern Water plc 1994–96, John Mowlem & Co 1998–2005, BSI 2000–04, Panel on Takeovers and Mergers 2006–, Dairy Crest Gp plc 2007– (chm 2010–), Control Risks 2008–; chm Opera at the Garden 1994–98, vice-chm British Lung Fndn 1990–2002, chm LCC 2010–12, chm FA Premier League 2013–, chm FA 2013–; memb: Exec Bd LAMDA 1998–2004, Exec Bd Edinburgh Int Television Festival 1999–2011, Devpt Bd The Sixteen 2003–12, BBC Tst 2009–13, Bd LL Online 2009–, Bd ENO 2009–13, Paintings in Hospitals 2009–12, Advsy Bd Project Assocs 2012–, Advsy Bd Bord Intelligence 2012–; tstee: Nat Film and TV Sch (NFTS) 1992–96, National History Museum Development Tst 1993–98; memb Int Advsy Bd SOAS 2004– (chm Devpt Bd 2009–); govr Godolphin & Latymer Sch 2003–12; memb Guild of Bonnetmakers Glasgow; FRSA; *Recreations* opera, theatre, cricket; *Clubs* Soho House, Paramount, Australian, Armadillos CC, Incogniti CC, The Blake, Saracens RFC, Sussex CCC, Surrey CCC, Capital, Century, Searcys, Pasley-Tyler; *Style*— Anthony Fry, Esq; ✉ Espirito Santo Investment Bank, 10 Paternoster Row, London EC4M 7AL (☎ 020 3364 6723)

FRY, Dominic Lawrence Charlesworth; s of Richard Noël Fry, of Lyme Regis, Dorset, and Jean Marianne, *née* Brunskill-Davies; *b* 28 August 1959; *Educ* Christ's Hosp, Faculté des Lettres Université Paul Valéry III Montpellier, Univ of North Carolina (Morehead scholar, BA); *m* 5 March 1993, Ann-Marie, *née* Finn; *Career* with various consultancies 1982–90; UK communications dir AT&T UK 1990–95, gp communications dir Eurotunnel plc 1995–96, corp rels dir J Sainsbury plc 1996–2000, corp affairs dir Scottish Power plc 2000–05, conslt Tulchan Communications 2006–09, dir of communications Marks and Spencer plc 2009–; PRO Award for Excellence in Public Relations (AT&T) 1993; co-ordinator of arts sponsorship for the Almeida Theatre London 1990–95 (memb Cncl 1998–), small business mentor Prince's Youth Business Tst, head teacher and mentor; memb: ABSA, Business in the Arts Initiative, Soil Assoc; MIPR 1983; *Recreations* sailing, tennis, reading, rugby football; *Clubs* Reform; *Style*— Dominic Fry, Esq

FRY, Fiona; da of Terence Roche (d 1998), and Margaret Roche (d 2008); *b* 17 July 1959, Cuckfield, Sussex; *Educ* Convent of the Holy Child Jesus Mayfield, Univ of Aston in Birmingham (BSc); *m* 22 Sept 1990, Christopher Fry; 3 s (Max b 8 May 1994, Henry b 8 May 1996, Arthur b 25 Jan 2001); *Career* Peat Marwick Mitchell & Co 1981–85, Arthur Young McLelland Moores & Co 1985–87, London Stock Exchange 1987–89, head of investigations FSA 1990–98, ptnr and memb UK Bd KPMG 1998–; chair of corporate sponsor recruitment Juvenile Diabetes Research Fndn 2006–08; ACA 1985; *Clubs* Chichester Yacht; *Style*— Mrs Fiona Fry; ✉ KPMG, 8 Salisbury Square, London EC4Y 8BB

FRY, Gregory J (Greg); s of Wilfred John Fry; *b* 29 April 1957, Surrey; *Educ* Lord Wandsworth Coll Hants; *m* 4 April 2015, Cassandra, *née* Beilby; *Career* dir Berkeley Gp Hldgs plc, chm St George plc 1996–; FCA; *Clubs* Richmond Rugby; *Style*— Greg Fry, Esq; ✉ St George plc, St George House, 76 Crown Road, Twickenham TW1 3EU (☎ 020 8917 4000)

FRY, John; *Educ* Jesus Coll Cambridge (MA), INSEAD (MBA); *Career* former chief exec Archant, ceo Johnston Press plc 2009–; *Style*— John Fry, Esq; ✉ Johnston Press plc, 108 Holyrood Road, Edinburgh EH8 8AS

FRY, Michael Edward (Mike); JP (Manchester 1996); s of Stanley Edmund Fry, of Preston, Lancs, and Margaret, *née* Hunt; *b* 16 January 1958; *Educ* Univ of Newcastle upon Tyne (BA), Univ of Leeds (MA); *Career* graduate NHS admin job placements in Bath, Winchester, Newport IOW and Alton Hants 1980–82, admin St Martin's and Claverton Downs Hosps Bath 1982–84, dep admin and subsequent head of admin Freeman Gp of Hosps Newcastle upon Tyne 1984–88, unit gen mangr Christie Hosp S Manchester HA 1988–91, first chief exec Christie Hosp NHS Tst 1991–2000, first chief exec 28 St John Street Barr Chambers 2000–02, first chief exec St Johns Buildings Barr Chambers 2002–04; devpt dir Catalyst Healthcare 2007–08 (gen mangr 2004–07), founding ptnr MFIM 2008–; tstee Sir Edward Holt Tst 2008; hon fell Univ of Manchester 1992; RSM 2013; *Recreations* motor sport, football, opera; *Style*— Mike Fry, Esq; ✉ Caution Cottage, Burford Lane, Lymm, Cheshire WA13 9JN (e-mail fry1234@btinternet.com)

FRY, Lt-Gen Sir Robert Alan; KCB (2005), CBE (2002, MBE 1980); s of Raymond Mills Fry (d 2002), and Elizabeth, *née* Bryon; *b* 6 April 1951; *Educ* Penarth GS, Univ of Bath (BSc, LLD), KCL (MA, US Naval Inst Int Essay Prize); *m* 16 July 1977, Elizabeth, *née* Woolmore; 2 da (Katherine b 21 Dec 1979, Claire b 8 July 1984); *Career* in commerce NYC 1972–73; cmmnd Royal Marines 1973 (mentioned in despatches 1979); COS 3 Commando Bde 1989–91, CO 45 Commando Gp 1995–97, Cdr 3 Commando Bde 1999–2001, Cmdt-Gen Royal Marines 2001–02, Dep Chief Jt Ops 2002–03, DCDS (Commitments) 2003–, Dep Cmdg Gen Coalition Forces Iraq; ceo Hewlett Packard Defence and Security 2007–12; Jt Cdr's Commendation 1992; contrib articles to jls incl RUSI Magazine and US Naval Inst Magazine, columnist Prospect Magazine 2010–; exec chm McKinney Rogers 2010–, chm Albany Assocs 2012–; visiting prof KCL 2014–; Freeman City of London, Liveryman Worshipful Co of Plaisterers; US Legion of Merit 2006; *Publications* Wars in Peace (2015); *Recreations* Welsh rugby, film, photography, walking; *Clubs* Special Forces; *Style*— Lt-Gen Sir Robert Fry, KCB, CBE

FRY, Roger Gordon; kt (2012), CBE (2012); s of Gordon Edmund Fry (d 1993), and Doris Amelia Chopping (d 2008), of Portsmouth; *b* 10 January 1943, Portsmouth; *Educ* GS Portsmouth, Univ of London; *m* 31 Oct 1993, Begoña Jauregui; 2 s, 3 da; *Career* former teacher in secdy schs and univ; chm King's Educn Gp, fndr 9 Br int schs in UK, Spain, Lativa and Panama, fndr and chm King's Gp Acads UK (4 acads in S England); chm Cncl of British Int Schs 1996–2011 (pres 2011–), dir Ind Sch Cncl 2008–11; memb: Worshipful Co of Carmen 2002, Worshipful Co of Educators 2012; Hon DLitt Univ of Portsmouth, hon fell Trinity Coll Oxford; *Recreations* travel, world religions, gastronomy, classic cars; *Clubs* East India, Public Schools, Royal Naval (Portsmouth), Club Financiero Genova (Madrid), Real Gran Peña (Madrid); *Style*— Sir Roger Fry, CBE; ✉ Kings Group, Oldwood Road, Tenbury Wells, Worcestershire WR15 8PH (☎ 01905 814020, e-mail roger.fry@kingsgroup.org, website www.kingsgroup.org)

FRY, Stephen John; s of Alan John Fry, ARCS (Lt REME), of Booton, Norfolk, and Marianne Eve, *née* Newman; *b* 24 August 1957; *Educ* Uppingham, Queens' Coll Cambridge (MA); *m* 17 Jan 2015, Elliott Spencer; *Career* actor and writer; weekly Fry on Friday column in The Daily Telegraph 1989–91, technol columnist The Guardian 2007–; memb Bd and ambass Norwich City FC 2010–; patron: Friends for Life THT, Freeze (nuclear disarmament charity), Norwich Play House, Prisoners Abroad; memb: Amnesty Int, Comic Relief, Hysteria Tst; former rector Univ of Dundee; *Theatre* appeared with Cambridge Footlights in revue The Cellar Tapes at Edinburgh Festival 1981 (Perrier award, televised BBC 1982); Latin (Scotsman Fringe First award 1980 and Lyric Hammersmith 1983), Forty Years On (Chichester Festival and Queen's Theatre London) 1984, The Common Pursuit (Phoenix Theatre London) 1988, Look Look (Aldwych) 1990; re-wrote script for musical Me and My Girl 1984 (London, Broadway, Sydney), Homesick (West End) 1995, Twelfth Night (Globe) 2012 (Best Supporting Actor in a Play Whatsonstage Award 2013); *Television* incl: Alfresco (Granada) 1982–84, The Young Ones (BBC) 1983, Happy Families (BBC) 1984, Saturday Night Live (Channel 4) 1986–87, Blackadder's Christmas Carol (BBC) 1988, Blackadder Goes Forth (BBC) 1989, A Bit of Fry and Laurie (4 series, BBC) 1989–94, Jeeves and Wooster (Granada) 1991–93, Stalagluft (Yorkshire) 1993, Cold Comfort Farm (BBC) 1994, Gormenghast (BBC) 1999, Surrealismo (BBC) 2001, QI (BBC) 2003– (Comedy Panel Show Nat Television Award 2013), Absolute Power (BBC) 2003–05, Fortysomething (ITV) 2003, Tom Brown's Schooldays (ITV) 2004, Bones 2007 and 2009, Kingdom (ITV) 2007–09, Stephen Fry in America (BBC) 2008, The Borrowers 2011, The Bleak Old Shop of Stuff 2011; *Radio* incl: Loose Ends 1986–87, Whose Line Is It Anyway? 1987, Saturday Night Fry 1987, 2004, narrator in Vanity Fair (BBC Radio 4) 2004; *Film* The Good Father, A Fish Called Wanda 1988, A Handful of Dust, Peter's Friends 1992, IQ 1995, Wilde 1997, Gosford Park 2001, Thunderpants 2002, Harry Potter and the Chamber of Secrets 2002, dir and screenwriter Bright Young Things 2003, Tooth 2004, The Life and Death of Peter Sellers 2004, MirrorMask 2005, The Hitchhiker's Guide to the Galaxy 2005, A Cock and Bull Story 2005, V for Vendetta 2005, Stormbreaker 2006, House of Boys 2009, Alice in Wonderland 2010, Animals United 2010, Sherlock Holmes: A Game of Shadows 2011, The Hobbit: An Unexpected Journey 2012, The Hobbit: There and Back Again 2013; *Books* The Liar (1991), Paperweight (1992), The Hippopotamus (1994), Making History (1996), Moab Is My Washpot (1997), The Stars' Tennis Balls (2000), The Ode Less Travelled (2005), The Fry Chronicles (2010, Biography of the Year Galaxy Nat Book Award 2010); *Recreations* chess, computing, dining out, light alcoholic refreshments; *Clubs* Oxford and Cambridge, Chelsea Arts, Groucho, Savile, Dorchester, Browns; *Style*— Stephen Fry, Esq; ✉ website www.stephenfry.com, Twitter @stephenfry; c/o Hamilton Hodell, 5th Floor, 66–68 Margaret Street, London W1W 8SR

FRYDENSON, Henry; MBE (2012); s of Samuel Frydenson, and Barbara Frydenson; *b* 9 November 1954; *Educ* Hasmonean GS for Boys, UCL (LLB); *m* Aug 1980, Sarah, da of Samuel Reifer; 6 s (Alan, Jonathan, Martin, Sheldon, Andrew, Simon), 1 da (Deborah); *Career* admitted slr 1981; ptnr Berwin Leighton Paisner (formerly Paisner and Co) 1984–2006 (joined 1979), conslt Baker & McKenzie 2006–07, conslt Mishcon de Reya 2007–10, sr ptnr Frydenson & Co 2010–; chm Assoc of Contentious Tst and Probate Specialists (ACTAPS); memb: Soc of Tst and Estate Practitioners (STEP), Medico-Legal Soc, Trust Law Ctee, Charity Law Assoc, Public Guardianship Consultative Forum, Solicitors' Assoc of Higher Court Advocates, Law Soc; official slr and public tstee User Gp, CEDR accredited mediator; Queen's Diamond Jubilee Medal 2012; Freeman City of London 1984; *Recreations* first aid, walking; *Style*— Henry Frydenson, Esq, MBE; ✉ e-mail henry@frydenson.co.uk

FRYER, John Beresford; s of Reginald Arthur Fryer (d 1966), and Joyce Edith Fryer (d 1986); *b* 18 February 1945; *Educ* Chigwell Sch; *m* 1, 3 April 1971, Jennifer Margaret Glew (d 1995); 2 da (Polly Jane b 12 Dec 1976, Sally Ann b 31 March 1980); m 2, 3 Aug 1996 (m dis 2009), Gillian Holmes; 2 da (Roseanna Iris Joyce b 30 Aug 1997, Elizabeth Lily Jamie b 7 Aug 2000), 1 s (Jonathan Arthur Clive b 1 Nov 2002); *Career* sub ed and reporter: local newspapers in East London and Essex 1963–67, Daily Sketch 1967–68, London Evening Standard 1968–69; labour corr then labour ed Sunday Times 1969–82, industrial corr (formerly labour corr) BBC News 1982–97, assignments ed BBC Economic Affrs Unit 1997–99, ed Radio and New Media, Economics and Business Centre BBC News 1999–2002, head of press office and events FSA 2002–04, journalist and broadcaster 2004–, fndr West Park Communications 2004–; Parly candidate (Lab): Harwich 1974 (Feb and Oct), Buckingham 1979; memb Radio Acad; *Recreations* tennis, watching West Ham United FC; *Style*— John Fryer, Esq; ✉ e-mail johnberesfordfryer@yahoo.co.uk

FRYER, Martin John; s of David Ivor Fryer (d 1971), and June Laurie, *née* Bradley; *b* 3 September 1956; *Educ* Christ Church Cathedral Sch Oxford, Radley, CCC Cambridge (MA); *Career* VSO teacher Lawas Sarawak 1978–80, sponsorship asst Jacob de Vries Ltd 1981–82, VSO field co-ordinator Bangkok 1982–85; British Council: regnl offr E Europe and N Asia Dept 1986–87, asst regnl dir São Paulo 1987–90, corp planning offr London 1990–93, dir Istanbul 1993–99, head country services 1999–2001, dir Barcelona 2001–04, dir Argentina 2004–08; strategic campaigns and partnerships conslt FCO 2008–10, dir progs Br Cncl Pakistan 2010–13, dir Br Cncl S Korea 2013–; *Recreations* music, reading, travel; *Style*— Martin Fryer, Esq

FUKUDA, Haruko; OBE (2000); da of Masaru Fukuda (d 1984), and Yoko, *née* Tanaka; *b* 21 July 1946, Tokyo; *Educ* Western Jr HS Washington DC, Channing Sch London, New Hall Cambridge (MA); *Career* Atlantic Trade Study/Trade Policy Research Centre 1968–70, ODI 1970, World Bank (IBRD) Washington DC 1971, Vickers da Costa & Co Ltd 1972–74, ptnr James Capel & Co 1974–88, vice-chm Nikko Europe plc 1988–98, chief exec World Gold Cncl 1999–2002, sr advsr Lazard 1999–2004, chm Caliber Global Investment Ltd 2005–08; non-exec dir: Foreign & Colonial Investment Tst 1988–2005, Investec plc 2003–, Aberdeen Asian Smaller Companies Investment Tst plc 2003–, AB Volvo 2003–06, Global Resources Investment Tst plc 2014–; DSc (hc) City Univ 2000; FCSI, memb Stock Exchange 1980, FRSA; *Publications* Britain in Europe: Impact on the Third World (1973), Japan and World Trade: Years Ahead (1974); *Recreations* gardening, reading, art, cooking; *Clubs* Athenaeum; *Style*— Miss Haruko Fukuda, OBE; ✉ Flat 1, 33 Ennismore Gardens, London SW7 1AE (☎ 020 7589 0406, fax 020 7584 6898); 43 St James's Place, London SW1A 1NS (☎ 020 7495 8800, fax 020 7629 4010, e-mail harukofukuda@harukofukuda.com)

FULANI, Dan; *see:* Hare, John Neville

FULFORD, Rt Hon Lord Justice; Sir Adrian Bruce Fulford; kt (2002), PC (2013); s of late Gerald John Fulford, and late Marie Bettine, *née* Stevens; *b* 8 January 1953; *Educ* Elizabeth Coll Guernsey, Univ of Southampton (BA); *Partner* Jose Luis Tejado Zambrano (civil partnership 5 Dec 2009); *Career* housing advsr Housing Aid Centre Shelter 1974–76, called to the Bar Middle Temple 1978, in practice 1978–2002, QC 1994, recorder of the Crown Court, judge of the High Court of Justice (Queen's Bench Div) 2002–13, judge at the Int Criminal Court 2003–12, presiding judge of the first trial at the ICC Thomas Lubanga Dyilo, presiding judge SE Circuit 2010–12, a Lord Justice of Appeal 2013–, dep sr presiding judge 2015–16, sr presiding judge 2016–; pres Trial Div 2009–12, memb Advsy Ctee on Nominations of Judges ICC 2015–; *Publications* A Criminal Practitioner's Guide to Judicial Review and Case Stated, UK Human Rights Reports (ed), Archbold International (gen ed); *Recreations* tennis, golf, riding; *Clubs* Garrick; *Style*— The Rt Hon Lord Justice Fulford; ✉ Royal Courts of Justice, London WC2A 2LL (☎ 020 7947 6000)

FULFORD, Prof Kenneth William Musgrave (Bill); s of Kenneth Fulford (d 1979), and Violet Emily, *née* Robinson (d 1978); *b* 10 December 1942, Lincoln; *Educ* Aldenham Sch Herts, Univ of Cambridge, Middx Hosp Medical Sch (Burney Award), Univ of London (PhD), Univ of Oxford (DPhil); *m* 1964, Jane, *née* Bradshaw; 2 s (Charles b 8 Feb 1969, William b 28 April 1975), 1 da (Hannah b 30 Oct 1970); *Career* house offr Middx Hosp and Mt Vernon Hosp 1967–69, research registrar then sr registrar in immunology Middx Hosp 1970–74, trg rotation Inst of Psychiatry and Maudsley Hosp London 1974–77, clinical lectr Dept of Psychiatry Univ of Oxford 1977–83, research psychiatrist and hon conslt psychiatrist Univ of Oxford 1983–, prof of philosophy and mental health Univ of Warwick 1995– (estab centre of excellence for interdisciplinary field of philosophy and psychiatry), special advsr for values-based practice Dept of Health 2005–, co-dir Inst for

Philosophy, Diversity and Mental Health Univ of Central Lancs 2006–, memb Faculty of Philosophy Univ of Oxford 2007–, fell St Cross Coll Oxford 2008–; fndr and ed Philosophy, Psychiatry & Psychology jl, lead series ed Int Perspectives in Philosophy and Psychiatry; chair Philosophy and Humanities Section and co-chair Conceptual Issues Workgroup World Psychiatric Assoc, co-chair Philosophy and Humanities Section Assoc of European Psychiatrists; fndr Int Network for Philosophy and Psychiatry; FRCPsych 1994 (MRCPsych 1976), FRCP 1999 (MRCP 1970); *Publications* incl: Moral Theory and Medical Practice (1989), In Two Minds: A Casebook of Psychiatric Ethics (co-author, 2000), Healthcare Ethics and Human Values (co-ed, 2002), Nature and Narrative: An Introduction to the New Philosophy of Psychiatry (co-ed, 2003), Whose Values? A Workbook for Values-Based Practice in Mental Health Care (2004), Oxford Textbook of Philosophy and Psychiatry (co-author, 2006); *Recreations* walking; *Style—* Prof Bill Fulford; ✉ Room A-133, The Medical School, University of Warwick, Coventry CV4 7AL (☎ 024 7652 4961, fax 024 7657 3079, e-mail k.w.m.fulford@warwick.ac.uk)

FULFORD, Robert Ian; s of (Howard) Bruce Fulford, of Colchester, Essex, and Mary Elizabeth, *née* Frost; *b* August 1969, Essex; *Educ* Colchester Royal GS, St Aidan's Coll Durham, Univ of Essex (BSc); *m* Susan Margaret, *née* Chapman; *Career* croquet player; World champion: 1990, 1992, 1994, 1997, 2002; Br Open Champion 1991, 1992, 1996, 1998, 2003, 2004, 2006, 2007, 2008 and 2014; President's Cup winner: 1989, 1998, 1999, 2001, 2002, 2006, 2008, 2009, 2010, 2011 and 2012; NZ Open champion 1993, 2000, 2005 and 2006; memb GB team winning MacRobertson Shield: 1990, 1993, 1996, 2000, 2003 (capt), 2006 (capt), 2010; currently accountant MSX Int; ACA; *Recreations* bridge, chess, hockey, film, piano; *Style—* Mr Robert Fulford; ✉ e-mail rifulford@msn.com

FULLER, John Leopold; s of Roy Broadbent Fuller (d 1991), and Kathleen, *née* Smith (d 1993); *b* 1 January 1937; *Educ* St Paul's, New Coll Oxford (MA, BLitt, Newdigate prize); *m* 1960, Cicely Prudence, da of Christopher Martin; 3 da (Sophie b 1961, Louisa b 1964, Emily b 1968); *Career* poet and writer; visiting lectr SUNY Buffalo NY 1962–63, asst lectr in English Univ of Manchester 1963–66, fell and tutor in English Magdalen Coll Oxford 1966–2002 (emeritus fell 2002–); Geoffrey Faber Award 1974, Cholmondeley Award, Whitbread Prize 1983, Forward Prize 1996; FRSL 1980, fell English Assoc (FAE) 2001; *Poetry* Fairground Music (1961), The Tree That Walked (1967), Cannibals and Missionaries (1972), Epistles to Several Persons (1973), Squeaking Crust (1974), The Mountain in the Sea (1975), Lies and Secrets (1979), The Illusionists (1980), Waiting for the Music (1982), The Beautiful Inventions (1983), Come Aboard and Sail Away (1983), Partingtime Hall (with James Fenton, 1987), The Grey Among the Green (1988), The Mechanical Body (1991), Stones and Fires (1996), Collected Poems (1996), Now and for a Time (2002), Ghosts (2004), The Space of Joy (2006), Song & Dance (2008), Pebble & I (2010), Writing the Picture (with David Hurn, 2010), Dream Hunter (libretto of opera with Nicola LeFanu, 2011), New Selected Poems 1983–2008 (2012), Sketches from the Sierra de Tejeda (2013) The Dice Cup (2014), You're Having Me On (2014), Gravel in my Shoe (2015), AWOL (with Andrew Wynn Owen, 2015); *Fiction* The Last Bid (1975), The Extraordinary Wool Mill (1980), Flying to Nowhere (1983), The Adventures of Speedfall (1985), Tell It Me Again (1988), The Burning Boys (1989), Look Twice (1991), The Worm and the Star (1993), A Skin Diary (1997), The Memoirs of Laetitia Horsepole (2001), Flawed Angel (2005); *Criticism* Dramatic Works of John Gay (ed, 1983), A Reader's Guide to W H Auden (1970), The Sonnet (1972), The Chatto Book of Love Poetry (ed, 1990), W H Auden: a Commentary (1998), W H Auden: poems selected by John Fuller (2000), The Oxford Book of Sonnets (2000), Alexander Pope: poems selected by John Fuller (2008), Who is Ozymandias? and other puzzles in poetry (2011); *Recreations* music, chess; *Style—* John Fuller, Esq, FRSL; ✉ 4 Benson Place, Oxford OX2 6QH (☎ and fax 01865 556154, e-mail john.fuller@magd.ox.ac.uk); c/o United Agents, 12–26 Lexington Street, London W1F 0LE (☎ 020 3214 0800, fax 020 3214 0801, website www.unitedagents.co.uk)

FULLER, His Hon Judge Jonathan Paul; QC (2002); *Career* called to the Bar 1977; asst recorder then recorder 2000, circuit judge (Western Circuit) 2014–; *Style—* His Hon Judge Fuller, QC; ✉ c/o Courts of Justice, Deansleigh Road, Bournemouth, Dorset BH7 7DS

FULLER, Martin Elliott; *b* 9 February 1943, Leamington Spa, Warks; *Educ* Mid-Warks Coll of Art, Hornsey Coll of Art; *m* Margaret, *née* Rand (wine writer); *Career* artist; awarded Guggenheim-McKinley scholarship (American Art Workshop Italy) 1964, worked in Italy and America, now in London; work in collections incl Leamington Art Gallery and Museum and V&A Museum; appeared on Private Passions with Michael Berkeley (BBC Radio 3) 2001; Discerning Eye Award Modern Painters Magazine 1996, Hunting Art Prize 1997; *Solo Exhibitions* incl: Midland Art Centre Birmingham 1968, Arnolfini Gallery Bristol 1968 and 1971, Centaur Gallery Bath 1969, Bristol Art Gallery 1970, Camden Art Centre London 1971, Bear Lane Gallery Oxford 1971 and 1973, Festival Gallery Bath 1973, Grabowski Gallery London 1973, Thumb Gallery London 1976 and 1979, Oxford Gallery 1983, RZA Galerie Düsseldorf 1983, Austin Desmond Fine Art 1985 and 1990, On The Wall Gallery Belfast 1987, Hendriks Gallery Dublin 1987, Retrospective curated by William Packer (Leamington Spa Art Gallery and Museum) 2001, Cassian Devere Cole Fine Art London 2001, Adam Gallery 2005, Stour Gallery 2006, John Bloxham Gall London 2007 and 2008; *Group Exhibitions* incl: Hunterian Museum Univ of Glasgow 1997, KDK Gallery London 1997, Jonathan Clark Fine Art London (two-man show with Edward Burra) 2003, Adam Gallery London 2005, Drawing Gallery London 2006; *Commissions* incl: New Mexico 1990, Mural NY 1992/93, Times Mirror International Publishers Ltd London 1995, Dubai 1996, Chelsea and Westminster Hosp Arts Project London 1997, Railtrack Collection London 1998, Leamington Art Gallery and Museum Collection 2001, Waldorf Hotel London 2004, Radisson Hotel Cork 2005, six paintings (Dorchester Collection, whole of Floor 7 45 Park Lane); *Recreations* jazz, modern opera, Wagner, church crawling; *Clubs* Chelsea Arts, Groucho, Garrick, Academy, Blacks, Savile; *Style—* Martin Fuller, Esq; ✉ Studio II, 3 Stewart's Place, Blenheim Gardens, London SW2 5AZ (☎ 020 8678 6008, e-mail martin@martinfuller.net, website www.martinfuller.net)

FULLER, Paul Maurice; CBE (2016), QFSM (2008); s of Brian Fuller, of Alvechurch, Worcs, and Linda, *née* Peters; *b* 16 February 1960, St Albans, Herts; *Educ* Elmbridge Sch Cranleigh, Radyr Comp Sch, Southbank Univ (BSc, MSc), Fire Serv Coll Moreton-in-Marsh; *m* 5 July 1979 (m dis 1994), Claire Ellen, *née* Williams; 1 da (Amy Sarah b 18 Dec 1979), 1 s (Ben Maurice b 30 March 1981); m 2, 15 March 1997, Helen Elizabeth, *née* Davey; 1 da (Jessica Alice b 11 March 2008); *Career* recruit rising to station offr and advanced trg instr W Midlands Fire Service 1978–87, station cdr rising to asst divnl offr W Sussex Fire Brigade 1987–89, asst divnl offr Staffs Fire & Rescue Serv 1990–94, dep divnl cdr rising to asst chief fire offr Wilts Fire Brigade 1994–2002, chief fire offr Beds and Luton Combined Fire Authy 2002–; pres Chief Fire Offrs Assoc 2014/2015, dep chair Fire Sector Fedn, memb FIRESA Cncl; memb: Beds and Luton Chief Execs' Forum, Beds and Luton Local Resilience Forum Exec Gp; advsr Beds and Luton LGA; chair of tstees Children's Burns Tst, tstee Firefighters Charity, tstee Beds Police Partnership Tst; memb Instn for Supervision and Mgmnt 1995, FIFireE 2008 (memb 1984); *Recreations* scuba diving, motorcycling, swimming, walking, reading; *Style—* Paul M Fuller, Esq, CBE, QFSM; ✉ 12 Tulip Tree Close, Bromham, Bedfordshire MK43 8GH (☎ 01234 824175); Chief Fire Officer, Bedfordshire and Luton Fire & Rescue Service, Southfields Road, Kempston, Bedfordshire MK42 7NR (☎ 01234 845017, e-mail paul.fuller@bedsfire.com)

FULLER, Richard; MP; *b* Bedford; *Educ* Univ of Oxford (BA), Harvard Business Sch (MBA); *Career* MP (Cons) Bedford 2010–; *Style—* Richard Fuller, Esq, MP; ✉ House of Commons, London SW1A 0AA

FULLER, Simon; *m* 2008, Natalie; 1 da (b Dec 2010); *Career* with Chrysalis Music until 1985; estab 19 Entertainment 1985 (sold 2005; more than 75 UK no1 and 250 Top 40 singles and albums), estab XIX Mgmnt 2009, brands incl 19TV, 19 Recordings, 19 Mgmnt and Popworld; mangr of artists and celebrities incl: Paul Hardcastle, Annie Lennox, Eurythmics, Spice Girls, S Club 7, S Club Juniors, Will Young, Gareth Gates, David and Victoria Beckham; prodr and creator Pop Idol (ITV) 2001 (BAFTA Award, Golden Rose of Montreux 2002), prodr American Idol (Fox Network) 2002; charity projects incl: Greenpeace, Amnesty Int, Prince's Tst; *Style—* Simon Fuller, Esq

FULTON, (Robert) Andrew; s of late Rev Robert Morton Fulton, and late Janet White, *née* Mackenzie; *b* 6 February 1944; *Educ* Rothesay Acad, Univ of Glasgow (MA, LLB); *m* 29 Aug 1970, Patricia Mary Crowley; 2 s (Daniel Robert b 8 Oct 1972, Edward Patrick b 8 Sept 1974), 1 da (Joanna Mary b 9 May 1979); *Career* HM Dip Serv; third sec FCO 1968, third then second sec Saigon 1969–72; first sec: Rome 1973–77, E Berlin 1978–81, FCO 1981–84; cnsllr: Oslo 1984–87, FCO 1987–89, UK Mission to UN NY 1989–92, FCO 1993–94, Washington 1995–99; chm: Advsy Bd Proudfoot Consltg 2002–09, EdoMidas 2003–09, nation1 2005–08, GPW 2006–, Advsy Bd Huntswood 2006–09, Vioearth Ltd 2012–, Advsy Bd INSP 2012–; int business advsr: Memex Technol 2003–11, Dynamic Knowledge Corp 2005–08, Armor Gp Int 2006–10; sr advsr: Source 8 2009–11, Indigo Vision 2010–11 (non-exec dir 2011–); chm: Scottish Cons and Unionist Party 2008–11, Scot N American Business Cncl 2000–09 (pres 2009–); dir Scot Control Risks Gp 2002–06; visiting prof Sch of Law Univ of Glasgow 1999–2003; *Recreations* golf, national hunt racing, reading, cinema; *Clubs* New (Edinburgh); *Style—* Andrew Fulton, Esq; ✉ 7 Crown Road South, Glasgow G12 9DJ (☎ 0141 337 3710, e-mail afulton@gpwltd.com)

FULTON, Rev John Oswald; s of Robert Fulton (d 1994), of Clydebank, and Margaret, *née* Wright (d 2008); *b* 9 July 1953; *Educ* Clydebank HS, Univ of Glasgow (BSc, BD); *m* 1989, Margaret, da of Robert Wilson (d 1981), of Glasgow; 1 da (Ruth Janet b 6 Sept 1991); *Career* United Free Church of Scotland: ordained 1977, min Croftfoot Glasgow 1977–94, gen sec 1994–; convener Ctee on Trg for the Miny 1984–89, moderator Presbytery of Glasgow and The West 1987–88 and 2012–13, convener Ctee on Miny and Home Affrs 1989–93, moderator Gen Assembly 2000–01, moderator Presbytery of West 2012–13; govr Hamilton Coll 2007–13; *Recreations* gardening, photography, music, reading; *Style—* The Rev John Fulton; ✉ 12 Peveril Avenue, Burnside, Rutherglen, Glasgow G73 4RD (☎ 0141 630 0068); United Free Church of Scotland, 11 Newton Place, Glasgow G3 7PR (☎ 0141 332 3435, fax 0141 333 1973, e-mail johnofulton@talktalk.net)

FULTON, (Paul) Robert Anthony; s of George Alan Fulton (d 1981), and Margaret, *née* Foxton (d 2001); *b* 20 March 1951; *Educ* Nunthorpe GS York, Churchill Coll Cambridge (BA); *m* 1981, Lee Hong Tay; *Career* civil servant Home Office 1973–2003; positions incl: private sec to perm sec, dir Prison Industries and Farms 1991–96, princ fin offr 1996–2000, dir of strategy and performance 2000–02, implementation dir ARA 2002–03; tstee/vice-chair/chair SOVA 2004–12; chair DuCane Housing Assoc 2004–11, chair CHAS (Central London) Ind Housing and Debt Advice Serv 2006–10, memb Finance and Audit Ctee Skills for Justice 2008–10, tstee Salvaire 2012–; treas: Clinks 2009–, Concern and Help for East Elmbridge Retired 2009–; *Recreations* learning new things, re-learning old things; *Style—* Robert Fulton, Esq; ✉ 1 Meadow Close, Hinchley Wood, Esher, Surrey KT10 0AY (robert@fulton-web.com)

FULTON, Lt-Gen Sir Robert Henry Gervase; KBE (2005); s of James Fulton (d 1993), and Cynthia, *née* Shaw (d 2005); *b* 21 December 1948, London; *Educ* Eton, UEA (BA); *m* 16 Aug 1975, Midge, *née* Free; 2 s (James b 1977, Mark b 1980); *Career* cmmnd RM 1972, 42 Commando 1973–75, 40 Commando 1976–78, instr Sch of Signals Blandford 1978–80, Army Staff Coll Camberley 1980–81, instr Jr Div Staff Coll 1981–83, 42 Commando 1983–85, SO2 Ops HQ Trg Reserves and Special Forces RM 1985–87, SO2 Commitments Dept of Cmdt Gen RM 1987–90, SO1 Directing Staff Army Staff Coll Camberley 1990–92, CO 42 Commando 1992–94, asst dir CIS Op Regts CGRM 1994–95, RCDS 1996, cmd 3 Commando Bde 1997–2001, capability mangr Information Superiority MOD 2001–03, DCDS (Equipment Capability) 2003–06; Govr and C-in-C Gibraltar 2006–09, ceo Global Leadership Fndn 2010–; memb Cncl RUSI 2003; chm Aske Bd of Govrs Haberdashers' Aske's Schs Elstree; Liveryman Worshipful Co of Haberdashers; KStJ 2009, King of Arms Order of the British Empire 2011–; *Recreations* playing and watching sport, military history; *Clubs* Army and Navy, MCC; *Style—* Sir Robert Fulton, KBE; ✉ Global Leadership Foundation, 1 Knightsbridge Green, London SW1X 7NE

FURBER, (William) James; s of Frank Robert Furber, of Blackheath, London, and Anne Wilson, *née* McArthur; *b* 1 September 1954, London; *Educ* Westminster, Gonville & Caius Coll Cambridge (MA); *m* 22 Oct 1982 (m dis 2010), Rosemary Elizabeth, *née* Johnston; 1 da (Elizabeth Sarah Anne b 29 Nov 1984), 2 s (Robert William Johnston b 10 Aug 1986, Charles James Haslett b 1 Jan 1989); *Career* admitted slr 1979; Farrer & Co: joined 1976, assoc ptnr 1981–85, ptnr 1985–, sr ptnr 2008–11; slr to the Duchy of Cornwall 1994–; treas Lowtonian Soc 2003–, sec St Bartholomew's Medical Coll Tst 1996–2012; tstee: Leonard Cheshire Fndn 2000–06, Arvon Fndn 2000–07, Trinity Coll of Music Charitable Tst 2005–; sec Art Workers Guild 2007–10; reader C of E 1991–2009; memb: Law Soc 1979–, City of Westminster and Holborn Law Soc 1981– (pres 1996–97); tstee Univ of Cambridge Musical Soc 2014–; *Publications* Encyclopedia of Forms and Precedents (Vol 36 (Sale of Land), 1990); *Recreations* golf, literature, wine, laughter, avoiding boring people; *Clubs* Garrick, Bucks, Hawks, R&A, Royal St George's Golf, Royal West Norfolk Golf, Royal Blackheath Golf, Hon Co of Edinburgh Golfers; *Style—* James Furber, Esq; ✉ Farrer & Co, 66 Lincoln's Inn Fields, London WC2A 3LH (☎ 020 3375 7000, e-mail james.furber@farrer.co.uk)

FURBER, (Robert) John; QC (1995); s of Frank Robert Furber, of Blackheath, London, and Anne Wilson, *née* McArthur; *b* 13 October 1949; *Educ* Westminster, Gonville & Caius Coll Cambridge (MA); *m* 1, 16 April 1977, (Amanda) Cherry, da of Frederick Colbran Burgoyne Varney, OBE; 1 s (Thomas b 1980), 2 da (Sophia b 1983, Olivia b 1989); m 2, 22 Jan 2011, Dr Virginia Taylor, da of Thomas Philip Taylor, MBE; *Career* called to the Bar Inner Temple 1973; chm Property Bar Ass 2011–14; chm Field Lane Fndn 2004–06 and 2009–12; *Books* jt ed: Halsbury's Laws of England (Landlord and Tenant) (1981), Hill and Redman's Law of Landlord and Tenant (1981–2016), Halsbury's Laws of England (Compulsory Acquisition) (1996), Guide to Commonhold and Leasehold Reform Act (2002); *Recreations* literature, music, cricket; *Clubs* Buck's, Beefsteak, Pratt's; *Style—* John Furber, Esq, QC; ✉ 1 Hallgate, Blackheath Park, London SE3 9SG (☎ 020 8852 7633); Wilberforce Chambers, 8 New Square, Lincoln's Inn, London WC2A 3QP (☎ 020 7306 0102)

FURBER, Prof Stephen Byram; CBE (2008); s of Benjamin Neil Furber, of Marple, Cheshire, and Margaret, *née* Schofield; *b* 21 March 1953, Manchester; *Educ* Manchester Grammar, St John's Coll Cambridge (Baylis scholar, BA), Univ of Cambridge (PhD); *m* 6 Aug 1977, Valerie Margaret, da of Reginald Walter Elliott; 2 da (Alison Mary b 4 Jan 1982, Catherine Margaret b 10 April 1984); *Career* Rolls-Royce research fell Emmanuel Coll Cambridge 1978–81; princ designer BBC microcomputer hardware 1981–82; hardware design engr and design mangr Acorn Computers Ltd Cambridge 1981–90; princ hardware architect of the ARM 32-bit RISC microprocessor 1983; Univ of Manchester: ICL prof of computer engrg Dept of Computer Science 1990, head Dept of Computer Science 2001–04; dir: Manchester Informatics Ltd 1994–2010, Cogency Technol Inc

F

Toronto 1997–99, Cogniscience Ltd 2000–, Transitive Technologies Ltd 2001–04, Silistix Ltd 2004–06; led research gp which developed AMULET1 won BCS Award 1995, BBC Micro and ARM both won Acorn Queen's Award for Technol, Royal Acad of Engrg Silver Medal 2003, Royal Soc Wolfson Research Merit Award 2004–09, IET Faraday Medal 2007, Millennium Technol Prize Laureate Technol Acad of Finland 2010, IEEE Computer Soc Computer Pioneer Award 2013; memb PCC St Chad's Handforth (Anglican); fell Computer History Museum CA 2012; Hon DSc Univ of Edinburgh 2010, Hon DSc Anglia Ruskin Univ 2012; FBCS 1997 (MBCS 1992), CEng, FREng 1999, FRS 2002, FIET 2004, FIEEE 2005; *Publications* VLSI RISC Architecture and Organisation (1989), ARM System Architecture (1996), ARM System-on-Chip Architecture (revised edn, 2000); author of over 150 papers; *Recreations* 6 string and bass guitar (church music group); *Style*— Prof Stephen Furber, CBE, FRS, FREng; ✉ School of Computer Science, University of Manchester, Oxford Road, Manchester M13 9PL (✆ 0161 275 6129, fax 0161 275 6236, e-mail steve.furber@manchester.ac.uk)

FURMANOVSKY, Jill; da of Jack Furmanovsky, and Eva Furmanovsky; *b* 1953, Bulawayo, Rhodesia; *Educ* Claremont Sch Kenton, Harrow Sch of Art, Central Sch of Art; *m*; 1 da; *Career* photographer; in-house photographer Rainbow Theatre 1972–79, freelance photo journalist 1970s and 1980s (contrib Sounds, Melody Maker, NME, Smash Hits and The Face); fndr JFA Studio 1982 (extending photography coverage to incl advtg and fashion), fndr Rockarchive.com 1998; work featured in Sunday Times, The Observer, The Guardian, Q Magazine and others; stills photographer on films: Sister My Sister 1992, Institute Benjamenta 1993, Carrington 1994, Secret Agent 1995; official photographer to pop group Oasis; *Exhibitions* Was There Then – Oasis (touring London, Manchester, Glasgow and Europe) 1997; author of articles published in Photography Magazine 1987 and Br Journal of Photography 1990–91; *Awards* incl: Nikon Honourable Award 1984, Diamond Euro Music Photographer of the Year 1987, Ilford Award 1990, The Observer Portrait Award 1992, Kodak Gold Award 1994, Woman of the Year for the Music Industry and Related Media 1998, Lifetime Achievement Award Record of the Day Magazine 2012; *Books* The Moment – 25 Years of Rock Photography (1995), Was There Then – Oasis A Photographic Journey (1997); *Style*— Ms Jill Furmanovsky; ✉ e-mail jill@rockarchive.com, website www.rockarchive.com

FURMSTON, Prof Michael Philip; TD; s of Joseph Philip Furmston (d 1987), of Chipstead, Surrey, and Phyllis, *née* Clowes (d 2004); *b* 1 May 1933; *Educ* Wellington, Exeter Coll Oxford (MA, BCL), Univ of Birmingham (LLM); *m* 26 Sept 1964, Ashley Sandra Maria, da of Edward Cope, of Cumnor, Oxon; 7 da (Rebecca b 1967, Rachel b 1969, Charlotte b 1971, Clare b 1973, Alexandra b 1975, Antonia b 1978, Olivia b 1979), 3 s (Simon b 1977, Thomas b 1981, Timothy b 1983); *Career* Nat Serv RA 1951–53, cmmnd 2 Lt 1952, TA serv 1953–78 (Maj 1966); lectr in law: Univ of Birmingham 1957–62, Queen's Univ Belfast 1962–63; fell Lincoln Coll Oxford and lectr in law 1964–78; Univ of Bristol: prof of law 1978–98, dean Faculty of Law 1980–84 and 1995–98, pro-vice-chllr 1986–89 (emeritus prof 1998–); Singapore Mgmnt Univ: prof of law 2007–15, dean of law 2007–2012, emeritus prof 2015–; prof of law Sunway Univ Malaysia 2015–; bencher Gray's Inn 1989; chm Comec 1996–2000; Freeman Worshipful Co of Arbitrators; Hon DUniv Open Univ 2010; *Books* Cheshire Fifoot and Furmston's Law of Contract (ed, 8 to 16 edns, 1972–2012), A Building Contract Casebook (with V Powell-Smith, 1984, 5 edn 2012), The Law of Tort: Policies and Trends in Liability for Damage to Property and Economic Loss (ed, 1986), You and the Law (ed with V Powell-Smith, 1987), Sale and Supply of Goods (1996, 3 edn 1999), Contract Formation and Letters of Intent (1997), The Law of Contract (ed, 1999, 4 edn 2010, 5 edn 2015), Contract Formation (with G J Tolhurst, 2010), Commercial and Consumer Law (with Jason Chuah, 2010, 2 edn 2013), Privity of Contract (with G J Tolhurst, 2015); *Recreations* chess (rep British team in 2 correspondence olympiads), dogs, watching cricket; *Clubs* Reform, Naval and Military, MCC; *Style*— Prof Michael Furmston, TD; ✉ 51 Grenville Court, Bridgwater, Somerset TA6 3TY (e-mail michaelfurmston@hotmail.com); Faculty of Law, University of Bristol, Wills Memorial Building, Queens Road, Bristol BS8 1RJ (✆ 0117 954 5301, fax 0117 922 5136); Room AE 726, Level 7, Sunway University, 5A Jalan Universiti, Bandar Sunway, 47500 Selangor Darul Ehsan, Malaysia

FURNEAUX, Paul; s of James Furneaux, of Aberdeen, and Nora Mavis, *née* Davidson; *b* 2 March 1962; *Educ* Aberdeen GS, Edinburgh Coll of Art (BA, postgrad Dip), Tama Art Univ Tokyo (MA); *Partner* Ruth Hollyman; 1 da (Silvie Rose Holly Furneaux); *Career* artist; Edinburgh Coll of Art: pt/t lectr in drawing and painting 1992–96 and 2000–03, teacher Summer Sch 1992–96; first artist in residence Center for Contemporary Printmaking Norwalk CT 2003; currently artist running workshops in contemporary Japanese woodblock printing at Edinburgh Print Workshop and other nat and int venues; professional memb Soc of Scottish Artists, professional memb Aberdeen Artists Soc 1994, RSA 2007; *Solo Exhibitions* incl: Foyer Gall Aberdeen 2000, Genkan Gall Tokyo American Club 2001, Stone Cut Wood Cut (Royal Museum Edinburgh) 2001, Edinburgh Festival Exhbn (Firth Gall Edinburgh) 2001, Hönran Gall Falun Sweden 2002, Northern Light Gall Stockholm 2003, New Works (Center for Contemporary Printmaking CT) 2003, Blue Flowers Red Shadows (Patriot Hall Gall Edinburgh) 2005, Woodcuts (The Friends Room RSA) 2007, Woodblock Prints (Patriot Hall Gall Edinburgh) 2007, Echo (Station K Studios Sandnes Norway) 2007, Notes on a Landscape (i2 Open Eye Galley Edinburgh) 2009, Paul Furneaux: Mokuhanga (Edinburgh Printmakers Gallery) 2011, Indigo (two person with Alan Kilpatrick, Patriothall Gallery Edinburgh) 2011, New Works (two person with Niamh Flangan, Graphic Studio Gallery Dublin) 2012, Paul Furneaux, (Claremont Gallery Aberdeen) 2013, Inside: Outside (Open Eye Gallery Edinburgh) 2014, Japanese Woodcut Prints (Printmaking Studio Academy of Fine Arts Gent Belgium) 2014 *Group Exhibitions* incl: Connections 2000 (invited artist, RSA), Opening Exhbn (Gallery Vallmer Ljubjana Slovenia) 2001, Ink from Wood – Two Traditions (Center for Contemporary Printmaking Norwalk CT) 2003, The Directors Choice (Open Eye Gall Edinburgh) 2004, Cross Flows Five Int Artists (Shin Pu Kan Gall Kyoto) 2004, Tokyo Int Mini-print Triennial (Tama Art Univ) 2005, Urban Landscapes (Open Eye Gall Edinburgh) 2006, Crossflows (Numthong Gall Bangkok) 2006, Royal Acad Summer Exhbn 2007, Preview (Open Eye Gall) 2007, 40 Years of Original Prints (Edinburgh Printmakers) 2007, Footprint (First International Biennale Centre for Contemporary Printmaking Connecticut USA) 2008, Yard Art The Repeat Performance of Thought (Roof Gallery Tokyo) 2008, Japanese Wave New Shores, Contemporary Japanese woodcut prints from Scotland, Finland and Japan (Northern Print Gallery Newcastle) 2010, Summer Exhbn (RA London) 2010 and 2012–14, Annual Exhbn (Royal Scottish Academy Edinburgh) 2011, 2012 (invited artist, Artists' Studios) and 2013–14, Reflection: selected exhbn from recipients of Visual Arts Awards Scheme 2000–2010 (City Art Centre Edinburgh) 2011, The Scottish Summer Exhbn (Fleming Collection London) 2011, In Japan: highlights of academicians projects in contemporary Japan (Royal Scottish Academy) 2011, Annual Exhbn (Royal Glasgow Institute) 2012, Weaving the Century: Tapestry from Dovecot Studios 1912–2012 2012, Natural Curiosity (Patriothall Gall Edinburgh) 2012, Prints 21 (Tokyo Metropolitan Museum Tokyo in celebration of 80th anniversary of the Japanese Print Association (invited artist)) 2012, Exhbn of the Six Autumn 2012 Mokuhanga Residents (CfSHE Annex Gallery Tokyo) 2013, Soc of Scottish Artists Annual 2013, Royal Scottish Soc of Painters in Watercolour Annual Exhbn 2013, Visual Arts Scotland Annual Exhbn 2013, Mokuhanga Prints: Riding the Great Wave (Richard F Brush Art Gall St. Lawrence Univ Canton USA) 2013, Scottish Art Today (Bohun Gallery Oxfordshire) 2014, National Open Art Competition Exhbn (Somerset

House London) 2014; *Work in Collections* City Art Centre Edinburgh, Jean F Watson Bequest Purchase, Aberdeen Art Gall, Heriot-Watt Univ, Edinburgh Coll of Art, Royal Scottish Acad, BBC Scotland, Cornhill Hosp Aberdeen, Eastern Gen Hosp Edinburgh, Aberdeen City Library, Forester Hill Hosp Aberdeen, Art in Hosps Tst, Harry and Margery Boswell Art Collection Univ of St Andrews, Royal Scottish Museum, Univ of Edinburgh Royal Infirmary, St Andrew's House Scottish Exec, Falun city Sweden, Dalrus Region Sweden; *Awards* Royal Scottish Acad Keith Prize 1986, Edinburgh DC Spring Fling first prize for painting 1986, Young Scottish Artist of the Year 1987, Clason-Harie Bursary for Postgrad Exhbn 1987, Print Prize 1987, Largo Award Edinburgh Coll of Art, Sunday Times Scotland Mayfest Award for Visual Art 1989, Royal Over-Seas League Prize 1989, Alistair E Salvesen Art scholar 1990, Royal Scottish Acad Meyer Openheim Prize 1991, Soc of Scottish Artists J F M Purchase Prize 1991, Royal Scottish Acad Ireland Alloys Award 1994, Br Cncl travel grant to travel and exhibit in Mexico 1994, Japanese Govt (Monbusho) scholarship 1996–2000, research student and masters course in Japanese woodblock printing techniques Tama Art Univ of Tokyo 1997–2000, National Year of the Artist residency at Nat Museum of Scotland Edinburgh 2001, Dundee Contemporary Arts Technical Training Award, Aberdeen Artists Shell Expro Award, Hope Scott Assistance Grant 2003, Professional Devpt Award Scottish Arts Cncl 2003 and 2004, Shell Expro Award (Bronze) Aberdeen Artists 71 2005, Grampian Health Center Purchase Award 2005, Scottish Arts Club Award 2005, Soc of Scottish Artists Website Award 2007, RSA John Murray Thomson Award 2007, SSA North Sea Project Award (for residency at K. Studios Sandnes Norway) 2007, Visual Arts Awards 2009 and 2011, City of Edinburgh Cncl supporting residency at Graphic Print Studio Dublin 2009, PF Charitable Award Visual Arts Scotland Annual Exhbn 2010, Royal Scottish Acad William Gilles Bequest 2011, Hope Scott Tst Award 2011, GB Sasakawa Fndn Grant 2011, House for an Art Lover Award Royal Glasgow Inst Annual Exhbn 2012, John Gray Award Royal Scottish Soc of Painters in Watercolour Annual Exhbn 2013, Richard Coley Award for Sculptors Visual Arts Scotland Annual Exhbn 2013, Turtleton Tst Award for a Scottish Artist Nat Open Art Competition 2014, Roy Wood Print Prize Royal Scottish Acad Open Exhbn 2014, prize winner Nat Open Art Competition London 2015, Orrin Trust Award Scotland 2015, Deloitte Prize Soc of Scottish Artists Annual Exhbn; exhbn curator (contemporary Japanese woodblock print makers) Japan 2001 Edinburgh Printmakers Gallery 2001, invited artist Luboradón 2001 (international printmaking symposium and workshop) Poland 2001, artist in residence Center for Contemporary Printmaking CT 2003, artist residency for 2 months in Bjerkriem Norway, micro residency Edinburgh Sculpture Workshop 2009, Mokuhanga Innovation Laboratory (MI-LAB) Lake Kawaguchi Int artist-in-residence prog for mid-career print artists; regular exhibitor RSA; *Publications* Paul Furneaux, Mokuhanga: selected works 1987–2011 (with essays by Rebecca Salter, RA and Arthur Watson, PRSA), Paul Furneaux Outside: Inside, A Contemporary Use of Japanese Woodcut Printing (with introduction 'Paul Furneaux In Conversation with Michael Phillips' and essays by Arthur Watson, PRSA and Prof Paul Gladston); *Recreations* hill walking; *Style*— Paul Furneaux, RSA; ✉ WASPS Patriot Hall Studios, Studio 108, Edinburgh; 36 Rodney Street, Edinburgh EH7 4DX (✆ 0131 556 0710, e-mail mail@paulfurneaux.com, website www.paulfurneaux.com)

FURNELL, Prof James Rupert Gawayne; s of Percy Gawayne Furnell (d 1986), of London, and Margaret Katherine Aslett, *née* Wray (d 1979); *b* 20 February 1946; *Educ* Leighton Park Sch Reading, Univ of Aberdeen (MA), Univ of Glasgow (DCP), Univ of Stirling (PhD), Univ of Dundee (LLB, Dip LP); *m* 14 Sept 1974, Lesley Anne, da of John Ross, of Glasgow; 1 s (Alistair b 1976), 1 da (Rachael b 1978); *Career* clinical psychologist Royal Hosp for Sick Children Glasgow 1970–72, conslt clinical psychologist (child health 1980–98), memb Forth Valley Health Bd 1984–87; admitted Faculty of Advocates and called to Scottish Bar Parliament House Edinburgh 1993; visiting prof Caledonian Univ of Glasgow 1996–; memb Nat Consultative Ctee in Professions Allied to Med 1984–87, chm Div of Clinical Psychology Br Psychological Soc 1988–89; assoc ed Criminological and Legal Psychology 1997–2000; hon fell Univ of Edinburgh 1987–2000; FBPsS; *Recreations* flying, cross country skiing; *Clubs* Royal Northern and Univ (Aberdeen); *Style*— Prof James Furnell; ✉ Glensherup House, Glendevon, Perthshire

FURNELL, Stephen George; s of George Edward Furnell (d 1971), of Kettering, Northants, and Norah Delia, *née* Barritt (d 1995); *b* 30 June 1945; *Educ* Kettering GS, Cambridgeshire HS, Leicester Poly (Dip); *m* 12 Feb 1972, Maxine, da of Harry Smith (d 1989), of Edmonton, London; 2 s (Thomas b 1972, Henry b 1982); *Career* Architects Dept Leicester CC 1967, ptnr TP Bennett 1987–93 (joined 1969), fndr Furnell Associates 1993–; ARIBA 1970, MCSD 1987; *Recreations* cricket, golf, photography, painting; *Style*— Stephen Furnell, Esq; ✉ Furnell Associates, 444 Coulsdon Road, Old Coulsdon, Surrey CR5 1EE

FURNESS, His Hon Mark Richard; s of Sqdn Ldr Thomas Hogg Baitey Furness, (Ret), of Cardiff, and Pip, *née* Harris; *b* 28 November 1948; *Educ* Hereford Cathedral Sch, St John's Coll Cambridge (MA); *m* 20 April 1974, Margaretta, da of William Trevor Evans; 1 s (David b 21 Oct 1978), 1 da (Emma b 24 Oct 1979); *Career* called to the Bar Lincoln's Inn 1970; recorder of the Crown Court 1996–98 (asst recorder 1992–96), circuit judge 1998–2016, ret; chm: Social Security Appeal Tbnl 1988–94, Disability Appeal Tbnl 1990–98; *Recreations* bridge, DIY, travel, literature, theatre, opera, motoring; *Clubs* Cardiff & County, Saba Rock Yacht, Bay Gp Investments; *Style*— His Hon Mark Furness; ✉ Pontypridd County Court, Courthouse Street, Pontypridd, CF37 1JR (✆ 01443 490800)

FURNISS, Eugenie; da of John Valentine Furniss, and Susan, *née* Manley Casimir; *b* 3 December 1972, London; *Educ* Queen Anne's Caversham, Univ of Exeter; *m* Dec 2008, Guy Nixon; 2 s (Stanley b 28 Jan 2008, Rex b 5 Feb 2011); *Career* William Morris Endeavor Entertainment Ltd 1997–2012 (head London Literary Div 2007–12), md Furniss Lawton 2012–; memb Assoc of Authors' Agents; *Recreations* running, medieval churches, politics, environmental issues; *Style*— Mrs Eugenie Furniss; ✉ Furniss Lawton, 94 Strand on the Green, Chiswick, London W4 3NN (✆ 020 8987 6804)

FURNISS, (Mary) Jane; CBE (2012); da of Eric Richard Sanders (d 1965), and Catherine Bennett, *née* Coghlan (d 2008); *b* 28 March 1954, Burton on Trent, Staffs; *Educ* Burton on Trent Girls' HS, Univ of Bradford (BSc), Univ of York (MSc, CQSW); *m* 13 Aug 1977, David Kenneth Furniss; *Career* various roles as probation offr rising to asst chief probation offr W Yorks Probation Serv 1978–95; HM Inspectorate of Probation: HM inspector of probation 1995–97, HM asst chief inspector of probation 1997–99, hm dep chief inspector of probation 1999–2001; sr civil servant responsible for various aspects of govt policy and progs of reform in the field of criminal justice 2001–06, chief exec Ind Police Complaints Cmmn 2006–13; former memb Audit and Risk Ctee Children's Cmmr, non-exec memb Slrs Regulation Authy 2012– (sr ind dir 2014–), non-exec memb Nat Crime Agency 2013; tstee Crisis until 2016 (dep chair of tstees 2013–16), former tstee Nicro UK, bd mentor Critical Eye 2013–, memb Judging Panel Contrarian Prize 2013–, chair Judging Panel Criminal Justice Alliance Awards 2015–, tstee Cumberland Lodge Windsor Great Park 2016–; *Recreations* listening to music, art, travelling the world, running; *Style*— Ms Jane Furniss, CBE; ✉ e-mail jane.furniss@btinternet.com

FURSDON, (Edward) David; o s of Maj-Gen (Francis William) Edward Fursdon, CB, MBE (d 2007), and Joan Rosemary, *née* Worssam; succeeded uncle as owner of 750 year old Fursdon family estate in Devon 1981; *b* 20 December 1952; *Educ* Sherborne, St John's Coll Oxford (scholar, MA, Cricket blue), RAC Cirencester; *m* 7 Oct 1978, Catriona Margaret, da of Geoffrey Crichton McCreath, of Berwick-upon-Tweed; 3 s (Oliver b 1980, Thomas b 1982, Charles b 1986); *Career* 6 QEO Gurkha Rifles 1972; MOD (Whitehall and UN Geneva) 1975–79, secdy teacher 1979–84, ptnr Stags auctioneers 1994–2007; rural conslt 2008–; cmmr Crown Estate 2008–15 (Bd cnsllr 2015–16), cmmr English Heritage 2010–14; CLA: chm Devon branch 1997–99, chm Legal and Parly Ctee 1999–2003, exec 1996– (chm 2003), dep pres 2003–05, pres 2005–07; chm Beeswax (Dyson) Farming Ltd (formerly Beeswax Farming Ltd) 2014–; memb Bd of Tstees Nat Tst 2016–; chm: SW Chamber of Rural Enterprise 2010–14, SW Bd 2012 Games 2010–12, SW Rural and Farming Network 2013–, DEFRA/Industry Future of Farming Review 2013; memb: Bd HHA 2004–15, Rural Ctee Duchy of Cornwall 2008–, Bd SW Regnl Devpt Agency 2010–12; chm Cadbury Parish Meeting 1982–; govr Blundell's Sch 1984–2011 (chm 2000–11); High Sheriff Devon 2009–, Lord Lt Devon 2015– (DL 2004–15); FRICS, FAAV, FRAgS; *Recreations* sport, travel, trees; *Clubs* MCC, Vincent's (Oxford), Farmers; *Style*— David Fursdon, Esq; ⌗ Fursdon, Cadbury, Exeter EX5 5JS (☏ 01823 445030, e-mail david@fursdon.co.uk)

FURSE, Dame Clara Hedwig Frances; DBE (2008); *Educ* St James's Sch Malvern, LSE (BSc(Econ)); *m*; 3 c; *Career* with Heinold Commodities Ltd 1979–83; Phillips & Drew/UBS: joined 1983, dir 1988–90, exec dir 1992–95, md 1995–96, global head of futures 1996–98; gp chief exec Credit Lyonnais Rouse 1998–2000, chief exec London Stock Exchange plc 2001–09; LIFFE: bd dir 1990–99, dep chm 1997–99, chm Strategy Working Gp 1994–95, chm Membership and Rules Ctee 1995–97, chm Fin Ctee 1998–99; bd dir: Euroclear plc 2002–, LCH Clearnet 2004, Legal and General Gp plc 2009–13, Nomura Holdings Inc 2010–, Amadeus IT Holding 2010–; non-exec memb Dept of Work and Pensions 2011–, memb Fin Policy Ctee Bank of England 2013–; tstee RICS 2002; *Style*— Dame Clara Furse, DBE

FURST, Stephen Andrew; QC (1991); *Career* called to the Bar Middle Temple 1975, recorder 1999–, dep High Court judge 2010–; *Style*— Stephen Furst, Esq, QC; ⌗ Keating Chambers, 15 Essex Street, London WC2R 3AU (☏ 020 7544 2600)

FURTADO, Peter Randall; s of Robert Audley Furtado (d 1992), and Marcelle Elizabeth, *née* Whitteridge (d 1992); *b* 20 May 1952; *Educ* Whitgift Sch, Oriel Coll Oxford (BA, Dip Art History); *m* 1983, Ann, *née* Swoffer; 3 da (Tamzin Eiko Swoffer b 1985, Robyn Freya b 1991, Joanna Eveline b 1991); *Career* sr ed Hamlyn Books 1977–83, freelance ed 1983–87, sr ed Equinox Books 1987–91, exec ed Andromeda Books 1991–97, ed History Today 1998–2008; chm Shintaido Fndn 1994–97 and 2002–09, lead conslt SiftGroups Ltd 2010–; dir Int Shintaido Fedn 2004–; Hon DLitt Oxford Brookes Univ 2009; FRHistS 2002; *Books* managing ed: Ordnance Survey Atlas of Great Britain (1981), Illustrated History of the 20th Century (10 vols, 1989–92), Cassell Atlas of World History (1996), 1001 Days that Changed the World (2008), Living Histories: Restoration England (2010), History's Daybook (2011); *Recreations* cycling, saxophone, moving meditation; *Style*— Peter Furtado, Esq; ⌗ 1 Marlborough Court, Duke Street, Oxford OX2 0QT (☏ 01865 251234, e-mail peter@historyfm.co.uk)

FURZE, Jane; s of Arthur Furze, and Mary, *née* Baldwin, of Clevedon; *b* 20 March 1965, Clevedon, Somerset; *Educ* Clevedon Comp Sch, Christ's Coll Cambridge (BA); *m* 29 Nov 2013, Alan M J Bush; *Career* head of mktg Kraft Foods until 2011, dir Cheltenham Literature Festival 2011–; *Recreations* gardening, reading, travel, walking; *Style*— Ms Jane Furze; ⌗ Cheltenham Festivals, 109–111 Bath Road, Cheltenham, Gloucestershire GL53 7LS

FYFE, Brig Alastair Ian Hayward; DL (Somerset 1995); s of Archibald Graham Fyfe (d 1979), of Misterton, Somerset, and Alison Amy, *née* Hayward (d 1982); *b* 21 October 1937; *Educ* Lancing, RMA Sandhurst, Staff Coll Camberley; *m* 15 Aug 1964, Deirdre Bettina, da of Air Cdre James Maitland Nicholson Pike, CB, DSO, DFC (d 1999), of Watlington, Oxon; 1 da (Nicola b 22 June 1966), 1 s (Andrew b 31 Aug 1967); *Career* cmmnd Duke of Cornwall's LI 1958, cmd 1 Bn LI 1980–82 (Adj 1968–69), mil attaché Moscow 1988–91, hon ADC to HM The Queen 1989–91, regimental sec LI (Somerset) 1991–99, Hon Col Somerset ACF 1995–2002, Dep Hon Col Rifle Volunteers 1999–2007; fell Woodard Schs Corp 1995–, vice-provost Western Div Woodard Schs 2000–04; chm: Somerset ACF Tst 1999–2010, Somerset Mil Museum Tst 1999–2011; govr: King's Hall Sch 1992–2007, King's Coll Taunton 1992–2007; High Sheriff Somerset 2006–07; *Recreations* music, watching cricket and football; *Clubs* Army and Navy; *Style*— Brig Alastair Fyfe, DL

FYFE, Cameron Stuart; s of James Fyfe, of Dumfries, and Kathleen, *née* Hardman (d 1976); *b* 27 July 1954; *Educ* Dumfries Acad, Univ of Edinburgh (LLB); *m* 12 June 1995, Nuala McGrory; 2 da (Caitlin b 14 June 1996, Cara b 2 Dec 2002), 2 s (Michael b 2 May 1998, Sean b 21 June 2004), 1 step s (Mark b 17 Jan 1988); *Career* apprentice then asst slr Cornillon Craig & Co Edinburgh 1976–80; Ross Harper & Murphy: asst slr Edinburgh 1980–81, ptnr Court Dept East Kilbride 1981–89, i/c Head Office 1989–94, managing ptnr 1994–99, head Litigation Dept until 2011; currently conslt Drummond Miller Slrs; winner first Scottish case for annulment of arranged marriage; *Books* Layman's Guide to Scotland's Law (1995); *Recreations* golf, tennis, fishing, hill climbing, painting, writing, guitar; *Clubs* Hilton Park Golf, Univ of Glasgow Tennis; *Style*— Cameron Fyfe, Esq; ⌗ Drummond Miller LLP, 65 Bath Street, Glasgow G2 2DD (☏ 0141 332 0086)

G

GABRIEL, Peter; *b* 13 February 1950; *Educ* Charterhouse; *Career* rock singer and songwriter; co-fndr Genesis 1966 (with Mike Rutherford, *qv*, and Tony Banks); albums with Genesis: From Genesis to Revelation 1969, Trespass 1970, Nursery Cryme 1971, Foxtrot 1972, Genesis Live 1973, Selling England by the Pound 1973, The Lamb Lies Down on Broadway 1974; left gp to pursue solo career 1975; solo albums: Peter Gabriel I 1977, II 1978, III 1980 and IV 1982, Peter Gabriel Plays Live 1983, So 1986, Shaking the Tree 1990 (compilation), Us 1992, Secret World 1995, Ovo 2000, Up 2002, Big Blue Ball 2008, Scratch My Back 2010; singles include: Solsbury Hill, Sledgehammer, Family Snapshot, Mercy Street, Shaking the Tree, Don't Give Up, San Jacinto, Here Comes the Flood, Red Rain, Games Without Frontiers, Shock the Monkey, I Have the Touch, Big Time, Zaar, Biko, In Your Eyes; soundtrack albums: Birdy, Passion (for Last Temptation of Christ), Long Walk Home (for Rabbit Proof Fence) 2002; Ivor Novello Lifetime Achievement Award 2007, Time 100 Most Influential People Award 2008, Polar Music Prize 2009; fndr: World of Music Arts and Dance (WOMAD) 1982, Real World Group (developing projects in arts and technol) 1985, Real World Studios 1986, Real World Records 1989, Real World Multimedia 1994; launched Witness (human rights prog) 1992; CD-Rom releases: XPLORA, EVE; Hon DMus Univ of Bath 1996; *Books* Genesis: Chapter and Verse (with other band members, 2007); *Style*— Peter Gabriel, Esq; ✉ c/o Real World Studios, Box Mill, Box, Wiltshire SN13 8PL

GADHIA, Jayne-Anne; CBE (2014); *b* 19 October 1961, Stourbridge, W Midlands; *Educ* Royal Holloway Coll London; *Career* RBS 2001–06, ceo Virgin Money plc 2007–; *Publications* Empowering Productivity: Harnessing the Talents of Women in Financial Services (response to request from HM Treasury to lead a review into the representation of women in senior managerial roles in the financial services industry); *Style*— Ms Jayne-Anne Gadhia, CBE; ✉ Virgin Money plc, Jubilee House, Gosforth, Newcastle upon Tyne NE3 4PL

GADSBY, Dr Roger; MBE (2009); s of Frank William Gadsby, and Nellie Irene Gadsby; *b* 2 March 1950; *Educ* King Henry VIII Sch Coventry, Univ of Birmingham Med Sch (BSc, MB ChB); *m* 19 Oct 1974, Pamela Joy, da of Clifford Raine; 1 da (Emma Elizabeth b 1 Nov 1978), 1 s (Andrew David b 6 Sept 1981); *Career* postgrad med trg Birmingham and Stoke on Trent 1974–77, trainee in gen practice 1977–79, ptnr in gen practice Nuneaton 1979–2010, GP clinical lead Nat Diabetes Audit 2012–; assoc clinical prof Warwick Med Sch Univ of Warwick 1992–, visiting prof Inst of Diabetes in Older People (IDOP) Univ of Beds 2009–; memb various ctees Diabetes UK (formerly Br Diabetic Assoc); memb Cncl RCGP 1994–99 (chm Midland Faculty 1996–1999); chm of tstees Pregnancy Sickness Support; FRCGP 1992 (MRCGP); *Publications* Delivering Quality Diabetes Care in General Practice (2005), Vital Diabetes Management (with w, Pam Gadsby), Diabetes and Ednocrine Disorders in Primary Care (2009); author of several chapters in textbooks and of more than 300 articles and papers about diabetes care and pregnancy sickness symptoms; *Recreations* jogging, gardening; *Style*— Dr Roger Gadsby, MBE; ✉ Warwick Medical School, University of Warwick, Coventry CV4 7AL (☎ 02476 573101, e-mail r.gadsby@warwick.ac.uk or rgadsby@doctors.org.uk)

GAGE, Deborah Pamela; da of late Quentin Henry Moreton Gage, and late Hazel Olive, *née* Swinton-Home; *b* 26 March 1950, Lusaka, Zambia; *Educ* Moira House Eastbourne, Study Centre of the Fine & Decorative Arts London (dip); *Career* Antique Porcelain Co/Antique Co of New York Inc NYC 1971–78, ind dealer 17th/18th c Euro decorative arts and paintings and late 19th/early 20th c French & British pictures 1981–; non-exec dir AXA Art Insurance Ltd; treas Nat Antique & Art Dealers Assoc of America NYC 1974–78; fndr and tstee The Charleston Trust 1979–88 (opened Charleston Farmhouse Sussex, home of the artists Vanessa Bell and Duncan Grant, to public 1985), ttstee Michael L Rosenberg Fndn; memb US and Kenya Bds Lewa Wildlife Conservancy Kenya; *Books* Tobacco Containers and Accessories – Their Place in Eighteenth Century European Social History (with Madeleine Marsh, 1988); *Recreations* travel, photography, riding; *Clubs* Muthaiga (Kenya); *Style*— Miss Deborah Gage; ✉ Deborah Gage (Works of Art) Ltd, 38 Old Bond Street, London W1S 4QW (☎ 020 7493 3249, fax 020 7495 1352, e-mail debo@deborahgage.com)

GAGE, 8 Viscount (I 1720); Sir (Henry) Nicolas Gage; 15 Bt (E 1622); also Baron Gage of Castlebar (I 1720), and Baron Gage (GB 1790), of High Meadow, Co Gloucester; yr s of 6 Viscount Gage, KCVO (d 1982), and his 1 w, Hon Alexandra Imogen Clair Grenfell (d 1969), da of 1 Baron Desborough; suc his bro, 7 Viscount Gage (d 1993); *b* 9 April 1934, Firle, E Sussex; *Educ* Eton, ChCh Oxford; *m* 1, 1974 (m dis 2002), Lady Diana Adrienne Beatty, da of 2 Earl Beatty (d 1972); 2 s (Hon Henry William b 1975, Hon David Benedict b 1977); m 2, 2009, Alexandra Murray Templeton; 1 s (Hon John Valentine b 31 July 2009); *Heir* s, Hon Henry Gage; *Career* 2 Lt Coldstream Gds 1953; dir Firle Estate Co; *Style*— The Rt Hon the Viscount Gage; ✉ Firle Place, Lewes, East Sussex BN8 6LP (☎ 01273 858535, fax 01273 858188); The Cottage, Charwelton, Daventry, Northamptonshire (☎ 01327 60205)

GAIMAN, Neil Richard; s of David Bernard Gaiman, and Sheila Gaiman; *b* 10 November 1960; *Educ* Whitgift Sch, Ardingly; *m* 1 (m dis 2008), Mary Therese, *née* McGrath; 1 s (Michael Richard b 21 July 1983), 2 da (Holly Miranda b 26 June 1985, Madeleine Rose Elvira b 28 Aug 1994); m 2, Jan 2011, Amanda McKinnon Palmer; *Career* writer of modern comics, award-winning books for children and adults, TV and film scripts, songs and poetry; prof in the arts Bard College USA; creator of Sandman series DC Comics, co-originator and ed The Utterly Comic Comic Relief Comic (Comic Relief 1991), creator Neverwhere (6 part TV series BBC TV) 1996 (film script currently being prepared), scriptwriter Princess Mononoke 1998 (film released 1999), writer/dir of short films A Short Film about John Bolton 2002 and Statuesque 2009, scriptwriter Mirrormask 2005, scriptwriter (with Roger Avary) Beowulf 2007, prodr Stardust 2007, scriptwriter Doctor Who episodes The Doctor's Wife 2011 and Nightmare in Silver 2013, articles in Time Out, The Sunday Times, The Guardian, Punch, The Observer Colour Supplement, songwriter The Flash Girls; chm Soc of Strip Illustration 1988–90; memb: Science Fiction Fndn 1988–92, Comic Art Museum Florida; dir Comic Book Legal Defense Fund; patron: Open Rights Gp, Science Fiction Fndn, Bookend Tst (Tasmania); hon fell Liverpool Sch of Arts; Hon DFA Univ of the Arts Philadelphia 2012; *Awards* incl: Best Graphic Novel The Eagle for Violent Cases 1988, Best Writer The Eagle of American Comics 1990, World Fantasy Award for Sandman #19 1991, Best Writer Will Eisner Comic Indust for Sandman 1991, 1992, 1993 and 1994, Best Continuing Series Will Eisner for Sandman 1991, 1992 and 1993, Best Writer Austrian Prix Vienne 1993, Best Collection Int Horror Critics' Guild for Angels and Visitations 1994, Best Int Writer Kemi (Finland) 1994, Lucca Best Writer (Italy) 1997, Best Foreign Writer Max Und Moritz (Germany) 1998, Sproing (Norway) 1998, Bob Clampett Humanitarian Award 2007, Newbery Medal for The Graveyard Book 2009, Carnegie Medal for The Graveyard Book 2010, Kurt Vonnegut Jr Award for Literature 2010, Boston Public Library Literary Lights for Children 2010, Galaxy Award for Most Popular Foreign Author (China) 2010, Book of the Year Br Nat Book Award for The Ocean at the End of the Lane 2013, Best Fantasy Novel Locus Award for The Ocean at the End of the Lane 2014, Best Fantasy Goodreads Choice Award for Trigger Warning 2015; also 1 BAFTA, 4 Hugos, 2 Nebulas, 1 World Fantasy Award, 4 Bram Stoker Awards, 17 Locus Awards, 2 Br Science Fiction Awards, 1 Br Fantasy Award, 3 Geffens, 1 Int Horror Guild Award and 2 Mythopoeic Awards; *Books* Ghastly Beyond Belief (1985), Don't Panic (1987), Good Omens (co-author with Terry Pratchett, 1990), Now We Are Sick (Poetry, 1991), The Golden Age (1992), Angels and Visitations (1993), The Day I Swapped My Dad For Two Goldfish (book for children, 1997), Stardust (1997), SMOKE & MIRRORS: Short Fictions and Illusions (collection of short fiction, 1998), American Gods (2001), Coraline (2002), The Wolves in the Walls (2003), Marvel 1602 (2003), Sandman: Endless Nights (2003), Anansi Boys (2005), Fragile Things: Short Fictions and Wonders (2006), The Graveyard Book (2008), Who Killed Amanda Palmer (2008), Odd and the Frost Giants (2008, World Book Day book), A Little Gold Book of Ghastly Stuff (2011), Chu's Day (2013), Make Good Art (2013), The Ocean at the End of the Lane (2013), Fortunately the Milk (2013), The Truth is a Cave in the Black Mountains (2014), Chu's First Day at School (2014), The Graveyard Book Graphic Novel, Volumes 1 & 2 (2014), The Sleeper and the Spindle (2014), Hansel and Gretel (2014), Trigger Warning (2015), The View from the Cheap Seats (2016); *Publications* collections of Sandman graphic novels incl: Preludes and Nocturnes, The Doll's House, Dream Country, Season of Mists, A Game of You, Fables and Reflections, Brief Lives, World's End, The Kindly Ones, The Wake (1996); other graphic novels incl: Violent Cases (1987), Black Orchid (1988), Signal to Noise (1992, subsequently broadcast as a radio play by BBC Radio 3 1996), Death: The High Cost of Living (1993), Mr Punch (1994), Death: The Time of Your Life (1997), The Last Temptation (acknowledged inspiration for the Alice Cooper album of the same title); *Recreations* making things up, keeping bees; *Style*— Neil Gaiman; ✉ website www.neilgaiman.com, Twitter @neilhimself; c/o Merrilee Heifetz, Writers House, 21 West 26th Street, New York, NY 10010, USA (☎ 001 212 685 2605, fax 001 212 685 1781, e-mail mheifetz@writershouse.com)

GAINSFORD, Ronald Francis; OBE (2010); *m* Roseanne; 4 c; *Career* chief exec Trading Standards Inst 2002–; *Style*— Ronald Gainsford, Esq, OBE; ✉ The Trading Standards Institute, 1 Sylvan Court, Sylvan Way, Southfields Business Park, Basildon SS15 6TH

GAISMAN, Jonathan Nicholas Crispin; QC (1995); o s of Peter Gaisman, of Kirdford, W Sussex; *b* 10 August 1956; *Educ* Eton, Worcester Coll Oxford (BCL, MA); *m* 24 April 1982, Teresa Mignon (Tessa), MBE (1991), eldest da of Sir John Jardine Paterson, of Norton Bavant, Wilts; 2 da (Clementine b 1986, Imogen b 1987), 1 s (Nicholas b 1989); *Career* called to the Bar Inner Temple 1979 (bencher 2004); recorder 2000–09 (asst recorder 1998–2000); a dir: English Chamber Orchestra and Music Soc 1992–96, Int Musicians' Seminar Prussia Cove 1994–, Streetwise Opera 2002–, Music at Plush 2011–; FRSA 1997; *Recreations* the arts, travel, country pursuits; *Clubs* I Zingari, Beefsteak; *Style*— Jonathan Gaisman, Esq, QC; ✉ 7 King's Bench Walk, Temple, London EC4Y 7DS (☎ 020 7910 8300)

GAITSKELL, Robert; QC (1994); s of Stanley Gaitskell (d 1967), and Thelma Phyllis, *née* Holmes (d 1987); *b* 19 April 1948; *Educ* Hamilton HS Zimbabwe, Univ of Cape Town (BSc(Eng)), KCL (PhD, AKC); *m* 1974, Dr Deborah Lyndall Bates; 1 da (Kezia Lyndall b 2 Nov 1983); *Career* graduate trainee Reyrolle Parsons 1971–73, engr Electricity Dept Bulawayo Zimbabwe 1973–75, electrical engr GEC (SA) 1975–76; called to the Bar Gray's Inn 1978 (bencher Gray's Inn 2003), in practice 1979–, recorder 2000–10 (asst recorder 1997–2000); lectr Centre of Construction Law & Mgmnt KCL 1993–2003; senator Engrg Cncl 1997–2002; vice-pres IEE 1998–2001, chm IET/IMechE Jt Ctee on Model Forms 2001–; past chm: Mgmnt Div IEE, Professional Gp on Engrg and the Law; legal columnist Engrg Mgmnt Jl 1993–2003; memb Ctee London Common Law and Commercial Bar Assoc 1985–2000, memb Barristers Ctee Gray's Inn 2002–03; Liveryman Worshipful Co of Engrs 1997, Liveryman Worshipful Co of Arbitrators 2002 (memb Ct of Assts 2010–); accredited and registered mediator CEDR 1999; FIET, CEng, FCIArb, FIMechE; *Recreations* Methodist local preacher, theatre, walking; *Clubs* Athenaeum; *Style*— Dr Robert Gaitskell, QC; ✉ Keating Chambers, 15 Essex Street, London WC2R 3AA (☎ 020 7544 2600, fax 020 7544 2700, e-mail rgaitskell@keatingchambers.com)

GALASKO, Prof Charles Samuel Bernard; s of David Isaac Galasko (d 1951), and Rose (d 1996); *b* 29 June 1939; *Educ* King Edward VII Sch Johannesburg, Univ of Johannesburg (MB BCh, ChM); *m* 29 Oct 1967, Carol, da of Michael Lapinsky; 1 da (Deborah b 1970), 1 s (Gavin b 1972); *Career* med trg Johannesburg Gen Hosp 1963–66, lectr Univ of the Witwatersrand 1964–66; registrar: Hammersmith Hosp 1967–69, Royal Postgrad Med Sch 1967–69; sr registrar Radcliffe Infirmary and Nuffield Orthopaedic Centre Oxford 1970–73; conslt orthopaedic surgn Hammersmith Hosp 1973–76 (dir of orthopaedic surgery), asst dir Div of Surgery Royal Postgrad Med Sch 1973–76 (dir of orthopaedic surgery), prof of orthopaedic surgery Univ of Manchester 1976–2004; hon conslt orthopaedic surgn: Manchester Children's Hosp Tst 1976–2002 (Sir Arthur Sims Cwlth prof 1998), Salford Royal Hosps NHS Tst 1976–2005 (dir Educn and Trg 2003–05); contrib over 300 published articles; temp advsr World Health Authy 1981; chm Award Ctee SICOT 1984–87 and 1990–93, treas Int Assoc Olympic Med Offrs 1988–2000, memb Med Ctee British Olympic Assoc 1988–2003, vice-chm English Olympic Wrestling Assoc, chm Br Amateur Wrestling Assoc 1992–96 (vice-pres 1996–2001); pres: SIROT 1990–93 (memb Prog Ctee 1981–84, memb Exec Ctee 1981–96, prog chm 1984–87, chm Membership Ctee 1987–90), Br Orthopaedic Assoc 2000–01 (memb Cncl 1988–91, chm Acad Bd 1998–2002, vice-pres 1999–2000), Faculty of Sports and Exercise Med 2006–09; vice-pres: Section of Oncology RSM 1987 (memb Cncl 1980–87), RCS 1999–2001 (memb Cncl 1991–2003, chm Hospital Recognition Ctee 1992–95, chm Trg Bd 1995–99); chm: Assoc of Profs of Orthopaedic Surgery 1983–86, Jt Ctee of Higher Surgical Trg (GB and

I) 1997–2000, Intercollegiate Academic Bd of Sport and Exercise Med 2002–05; Hon MSc Univ of Manchester 1980; Hunterian prof RCS 1971, SICOT fell 1972, ABC fell 1978, Aust Cwlth fell 1982; fndr memb: Int Orthopaedic Res Soc, Metastatis Res Soc, South African Surgical Res Soc; memb Br Orthopaedic Res Soc, hon fell South African Orthopaedic Assoc, emeritus fell American Orthopaedic Assoc, hon memb American Fracture Assoc, corresponding memb Columbian Soc of Orthopaedic Surgery and Traumatology, hon fell Br Orthopaedic Assoc 2013, hon fell Faculty of Sport and Exercise Medicine 2014; FRCS (England), FRCSEd, FMedSci, fell Faculty of Sports and Exercise Med (FFSEM) Ireland, FFSEM UK, Hon FCMSA; *Books* Radionuclide Scintigraphy in Orthopaedics (jt ed, 1984), Principles of Fracture Management (ed, 1984), Skeletal Metastases (1986), Neuromuscular Problems in Orthopaedics (ed, 1987), Recent Developments in Orthopaedic Surgery (jt ed, 1987), Current Trends in Orthopaedic Surgery (jt ed, 1988), Imaging Techniques in Orthopaedics (jt ed, 1989); over 450 other publications; *Recreations* sport, music, theatre, travel; *Style*— Prof Charles Galasko; ✉ 72 Gatley Road, Gatley, Cheshire SK8 4AA (fax 0161 428 4558)

GALATOPOULOS, Stelios Emille; s of John Galatopoulos (d 1978), of Nicosia, Cyprus and Athens, and Maria, *née* Stylianaki (d 1948); *b* 2 August 1932; *Educ* Hellenion Sch Nicosia, The English Sch Nicosia, Univ of Southampton (BSc(Eng)); *Career* civil and structural engr; designer: T C Jones 1954–55, Kellogg Int Corp 1956–60; designer and head of Civil and Structural Dept Tripe and Wakeham (chartered architects) London and Cyprus for Akrotiri Strategic Base 1960–66, freelance engr 1967–72, designer Pell Frischmann 1972–75, freelance engr 1975–, lectr, concert presenter and compere; opera and music critic-journalist: Music and Musicians, Records and Recordings, Lirica nel Mondo (Italy), Opera, Musical America; broadcaster: BBC, CBC (Cyprus), RTE (Dublin) America, Germany, Austria; vice-pres Opera Italiana 1985; memb Soc of Authors 1971; *Books* Callas La Divina (1966), Italian Opera (1971), Callas Prima Donna Assoluta (1976), Maria Callas: Sacred Monster (1998), Bellini: Life, Times, Music (2002); *Recreations* opera, theatre, ballet, concerts, tennis, swimming, skiing, travel; *Style*— Stelios Galatopoulos, Esq; ✉ Flat 4, 47 Sheen Road, Richmond, Surrey TW9 1AJ (☎ 020 8332 0336)

GALBRAITH, Anne; CBE (2010); *b* 1940; *Educ* Univ of Durham (LLB); *m* 1965, John Galbraith; 1 s (b 1970), 1 da (b 1971); *Career* chm Newcastle CAB 1982–87, memb Northern RHA 1988–91, chm Royal Victoria Infirmary and Associated Hosps NHS Tst 1991–98, special tstee Newcastle Univ Hosps 1992–98, tstee Rothley Tst 1994– (currently chair), PM's advsr Citizens' Charter Advsy Panel 1994–97, memb Cncl on Tbnls 1997–2003, chair Prescription Pricing Authy 2000–06, non-exec dir NHS Business Servs Authy 2006–14; currently chair Valuation Tbnl Service; chm Cncl Univ of Durham 2006–12; *Recreations* gardening; *Style*— Mrs Anne Galbraith, CBE; ✉ Valuation Tribunal Service, 120 Leman Street, London E1 8EU

GALBRAITH, Jeremy; *b* 14 August 1966; *Educ* King's Sch Worcester, Univ of Leeds Faculty of Law (LLB); *Career* researcher to Dr Keith Hampson, MP 1988–89, conslt Market Access International 1989–95 (dep md 1994–95); md: Burson-Marsteller Public Affairs London 1995–99, Burson-Marsteller Europe Government Relations 1996–99, Burson-Marsteller Brussels 2000–07; ceo Burson-Marsteller EMEA 2007–, global chm public affrs Burson-Marsteller 2010–14, global chief strategy offr Burson-Marsteller 2014–; Parly candidate (Cons) Newham NE 1992; *Recreations* tennis, running, opera, film and restaurants; *Style*— Jeremy Galbraith, Esq; ✉ Burson-Marsteller, 37 Square de Meeus, B-1000 Brussels, Belgium (☎ 00 322 743 6611, fax 00 322 733 6611, e-mail jeremy.galbraith@bm.com)

GALE, Baroness (Life Peer UK 1999), of Blaenrhondda in the County of Mid Glamorgan; Anita Gale; da of Arthur Victor Gale (decd), and Lillian Maud Gale (decd); *b* 28 November 1940, Blaenrhondda, Mid Glamorgan; *Educ* Treherbert Secdy Modern Sch, Pontypridd Tech Coll, UC Cardiff (BSc); *m* 1959 (m dis 1983); 2 da; *Career* sewing machinist 1955–56 and 1965–69, shop asst 1956–59; joined Lab Pty 1966, former shop steward Tailors and Garment Workers Union 1967–70, women's offr and asst organiser Wales Lab Pty 1976–84, gen sec Wales Lab Pty 1984–99; sits as Lab peer in House of Lords; oppn whip 2010–13; memb: Information Ctee 2000–03, Select Ctee on Info, Jt Ctee on Statutory Investments 2004–07, EU Select Ctee Sub-Ctee G on Social Policy and Consumer Affrs 2006–09, Work of Arts Ctee 2010–12 and 2013–; jt sec Assoc Parly Gp for Animal Welfare 2001–10 (memb 2000–, vice-chair 2000–01), chair All Pty Parly Gp for Parkinson's 2008 (co-chair 2015–), chair Lab Pty Parly Women's Ctee 2013–; memb: Inter Parly Union 1999–, All-Pty Parly Gp for Children in Wales (jt sec 2006–09), All-Pty Gp on Smoking and Health, All-Pty Arts and Heritage Gp, British/Taiwan Parly Friendship Gp; memb Parly Assemby Cncl of Europe 2008–10; GMB Union (Lab Organisers Branch): memb 1976–, chair Wales and SW section 1986–99, equal opportunities offr 1991–99; memb Welsh Lab Women's Ctee 1999, cmmr for Wales The Women's Nat Cmmn 2004–09; vice-chair Lab Animal Welfare Soc 1999–; pres Treherbert and Dist Branch Br Legion 2002–, patron Kidney Wales Fndn 2008–, pres Nat Assoc of Old Age Pensioners of Wales 2010–, patron Bees for Devpt 2013–, pres Cardiff and Dist Rhondda Soc 2014–; memb: Bevan Fndn, Parkinson's UK; memb: IPU 1999–, CPA 2007–; Val Feld Welsh Woman of the Year Award 2005; *Recreations* walking, swimming, travel; *Style*— The Rt Hon the Lady Gale; ✉ House of Lords, London SW1A 0PW (☎ 020 7219 8511, e-mail galea@parliament.uk)

GALE, Sir Roger James; kt (2012), MP; s of Richard Byrne Gale, and Phyllis Mary, *née* Rowell (d 1948); *b* 20 August 1943; *Educ* Hardye's Sch Dorchester, GSM; *m* 1, 1964 (m dis 1967), Wendy Dawn Bowman; m 2, 1971 (m dis), Susan Sampson; 1 da (Misty); m 3, 1980, Suzy Gabrielle, da of Thomas Leopold Marks (d 1972); 2 s (Jasper, Thomas); *Career* formerly: reporter BBC Radio, prodr BBC Radio 4 Today Show, dir BBC Children's TV, prodr and dir Thames Children's TV, editor Teenage Unit Thames; Parly candidate (Cons) Birmingham Northfield (by-election) 1982, MP (Cons) Thanet N 1983–; PPS to min of state for the Armed Forces 1992–94, a vice-chm Cons Pty 2001–03; Parly ldr UK Delgn Parly Assembly of the Cncl of Europe 2015–; chm All-Pty Animal Welfare Gp 1992–98, pres Cons Animal Welfare Gp; fell: Indust and Parl Tst, Parl and Armed Forces Fellowship, Parl and Police Fellowship; memb Speaker's Chm Panel 1997–; special constable 2002–06; chm Try Angle Awards Fndn 2000–, tstee Soc for the Protection of Animals Abroad (SPANA) 2010– (chm of tstees until 2015); hon memb Br Veterinary Assoc 2010–; *Recreations* swimming, sailing; *Clubs* Farmers', Lord's Taverners, Soc of Knights Batchelor; *Style*— Sir Roger Gale, MP; ✉ House of Commons, London SW1A 0AA (e-mail galerj@parliament.uk, website www.rogergale.co.uk)

GALEAZZI, Mara; da of Faustino Galeazzi, of Italy, and Anna Maria, *née* Folchi; *b* 25 November 1973, Chiari, Italy; *Educ* La Scala Milan; *m* 23 Aug 2008, Jügen Volckaerts; 1 c (Maia Anya b 20 April 2012); *Career* ballet dancer; danced with: Ashely Page Co (Scottish Ballet), Irek Mukamedov Co; princ Royal Ballet 2003–13 (joined 1992), ret; also danced with: Stuttgaert Co, Rome Co; involved with: Dancing for the Children, Gt Ormond St Hosp, Soroptimist; Cavaliere al Merito della Republica Italiana; *Performances* incl: Anastasia, Juliet, Lise, Firebird, Gamzatti, Giselle, Manon, Les Corsaire, Tatiana, Mathilde Kschessinska, Mary Vetsera, Marie Larisch, Myrtha, Calliope, Lescaut's Mistress, Aurora (Awakening pas de deux), Queen of the Dryads, The Leaves are Fading, Scènes de ballet, Agon, Thaïs pas de deux, Voices of Spring, Swan Lake, Sleeping Beauty, Cinderella, My Brother, My Sisters, Song of the Earth, Fearful Symmetries, Symphony in C, Agon, Apollo, Symphonic Variations, Concerto, Raymonda Act III, The Judas Tree, Danses concertantes, Las Hermanas, Street Dancer in Don Quixote, Young Wife in La Ronde, Pierrot Lunaire, Volontaries, Chroma, Infra, Limen, Talisman pas de deux, Two-Part Invention, Cheating, Lying, Stealing, Tidelines, Masquerade, Hidden Variables, This House Will Burn, Les Saisons; *Recreations* cinema, music, opera, travel, ballet; *Style*— Miss Mara Galeazzi; ✉ c/o The Royal Ballet, Royal Opera House, Covent Garden, London WC2E 9DD; websites www.maragaleazzi.com, www.dancingforthechildren.com, Twitter @maragaleazzi

GALGANI, Franco; s of Piero Galgani, of Leghorn and Vilia Galgani; *b* 28 March 1949; *Educ* Saffi Secdy Sch Florence Italy, Florence Hotel Sch Florence (Nat Dip), Open Univ UK (BA); *m* 1, 1967 (m dis 1977), Mary Ellen, *née* McElhone; 3 s (Lorenzo b 1968, Riccardo b 1969, Giancarlo b 1971); m 2, 1981, Lynne, *née* MacDonald; 1 da (Daniela b 1983); *Career* restaurateur; industrial trg 1963–68: Alberg Ristorante L'Elba nr Grosseto Italy, Grand Hotel Florence, Hotel Iselba Island of Elba, Hotel de la Plage St Raphael France, Hotel Baglioni Florence, Grand Hotel Florence, George Hotel Keswick Eng, Hotel Parco Rimini Italy; food and beverage supervisory and mgmnt appts 1968–76: Granville Restaurant Glasgow, MacDonald Hotel (Thistle) Giffnock Glasgow, Stuart Hotel (Thistle) and Bruce Hotel (Swallow) E Kilbride Strathclyde; mangr and ptnr Balcary Bay Hotel Scot 1976–82; gen mangr: Buchanan Arms Hotel Loch Lomond Scot 1982–85, Stakis Dunkeld House Perthshire Scot 1985–86, Marine Highland Hotel Troon Ayrshire Scot 1986–91, Carlton Highland Hotel Edinburgh 1991–98; mktg dir Scottish Highland Hotels plc 1996–99; conslt and advsr to hospitality industry 1999–2001, dir of sales N Br Tst Gp 2001–03, divnl md Crerar Hotels 2003–04, mangmnt conslt 2004–; former memb: Bd of Dirs Ayrshire Tourist Bd, Cncl Ayr Coll of Further Educn, Glasgow Coll of Food Technol; former chm Edinburgh Principal Hotels Assoc; bd dir Edinburgh and Lothians Tourist Bd; Master Innholders Award 1989, Scottish Highland Hotels Group Mangr of the Year 1990; Freeman City of London; FHCIMA 1989; *Recreations* travel, theatre and classical music, outdoor pursuits with family; *Style*— Franco Galgani, Esq; ✉ 8 Newington Road, Edinburgh EH9 1QS (e-mail franco@galgani.co.uk)

GALIONE, Prof Antony; s of Angelo Galione, of Faulkbourne, Essex, and Margaret, *née* Cole; *b* 13 September 1963; *Educ* Felsted (Lord Butler of Saffron Walden scholar), Trinity Coll Cambridge (sr scholar, MA, PhD); *m* 22 Aug 1992, Angela Jane, da of John Clayton, and Jane Clayton, of Thorp Arch, W Yorks; *Career* Johns Hopkins Univ: Harkness fell 1989–91, Dmitri d'Arbeloff fell in biology 1990–91; Univ of Oxford: Beit meml fell for med research Dept of Pharmacology 1991–94, Hayward jr research fell Oriel Coll 1992–95, lectr in med sciences St Hilda's Coll 1993–95, Wellcome Tst career devpt fell Dept of Pharmacology 1994–97, Staines med research fell Exeter Coll 1995–98, lectr in molecular and cellular biochemistry St Catherine's Coll 1997–98, Wellcome Tst sr fell in basic biomedical science Dept of Pharmacology 1997–2005, fell and tutor in biochemical pharmacology New Coll 1998–2005, titular prof of pharmacology 2002–05, prof of pharmacology and head of dept 2006–, professorial fell Lady Margaret Hall 2006–, extraordinary lectr in pharmacology New Coll 2006–; Herbert Rand visiting fell Marine Biological Lab Woods Hole MA 1993; memb Physiology and Pharmacology Panel Wellcome Tst 2002–05, memb Basic Science Interest Gp Wellcome Tst 2006–; ed Biochemical Jl 1997–2006, memb Editorial Bd Zygote 1998–, author of scientific papers on cell signalling in jls incl Nature, Science and Cell; memb: American Biophysical Soc 1995–, Br Marine Biological Assoc 1995–, Br Pharmacological Soc 1997–, Br Neuroscience Assoc 1997–; Novartis Prize Br Pharmacological Soc 2001; MA (by incorporation) Univ of Oxford 1992; FMedSci 2010, FRS 2016; *Recreations* Egyptology, riding, Jack Russell terriers, gardening; *Style*— Prof Antony Galione; ✉ University Department of Pharmacology, Mansfield Road, Oxford OX1 3QT (☎ 01865 271633, fax 01865 271853, e-mail antony.galione@pharm.ox.ac.uk)

GALL, Henderson Alexander (Sandy); CMG (2011), CBE (1988); s of Henderson Gall (d 1963), of Banchory, Scotland, and Jean, *née* Begg (d 1970); *b* 1 October 1927, Penang; *Educ* Glenalmond, Univ of Aberdeen (MA); *m* 11 Aug 1958, Eleanor Mary Patricia Anne, da of Michael Joseph Smyth (d 1964), of London; 3 da (Fiona Deirdre b 7 May 1959, Carlotta Maire Jean b 2 Nov 1961, Michaela Monica b 27 March 1965), 1 s (Alexander Patrick Henderson b 17 June 1960); *Career* Nat Serv RAF 1945–48; foreign corr Reuters 1953–63 (Berlin, Nairobi, Suez, Geneva, Bonn, Budapest, Johannesburg, Congo); ITN: foreign corr 1963–92 (ME, Africa, Vietnam, Far East, China, Afghanistan, Pakistan, Gulf War), newscaster 1968–90 (News at Ten 1970–90); prodr/presenter/writer of documentaries, subjects incl Cresta Run 1970 and 1985, King Hussein 1972, Afghanistan 1982, 1984 and 1986, George Adamson 1989, Richard Leakey 1995, Empty Quarter 1996, Veil of Fear (World in Action) 1996, Imran's Final Test 1997, Sandy's War (Tonight with Trevor McDonald) 2001, Afghanistan: War Without End (History Channel) 2004; freelance writer; independent TV prodr 1993–; chm Sandy Gall's Afghanistan Appeal (SGAA) 1986–; rector Univ of Aberdeen 1978–81; Sitara-i-Pakistan 1985, Lawrence of Arabia Medal RSAA 1987; Hon LLD Univ of Aberdeen 1981; *Books* Gold Scoop (1977), Chasing the Dragon (1981), Don't Worry About the Money Now (1983), Behind Russian Lines, an Afghan Journal (1983), Afghanistan: Agony of a Nation (1988), Salang (1989), George Adamson: Lord of the Lions (1991), A Year in Kuwait (1992), News from the Front (1994), The Bushmen of Southern Africa: Slaughter of the Innocent (2001), War Against the Taliban: Why It All Went Wrong in Afghanistan (2012); *Recreations* gardening, swimming; *Clubs* Turf, St Moritz Tobogganing (hon memb); *Style*— Sandy Gall, Esq, CMG, CBE; ✉ Doubleton Oast House, Penshurst, Tonbridge, Kent TN11 8JA (fax 01892 870977, e-mail henderson.alexander.gall@gmail.com); Sandy Gall's Afghanistan Appeal (SGAA), Doubleton Oast House, Penshurst, Kent TN11 8JA (e-mail sgaa@btinternet.com); TV agent: Knight Ayton Management, 35 Great James Street, London WC1N 3HB (☎ 020 7931 4400)

GALLACCIO, Anya; *b* 1963, Scotland; *Educ* Kingston Poly, Goldsmiths Coll London; *Career* artist; residencies: int artist in residence Art Pace (San Antonio TX) 1997, Sargeant Fellowship (Br Sch at Rome) 1998, Kanazawa Coll of Art 1999, 1871 Fellowship (Rothemere American Inst, Univ of Oxford and San Francisco Art Inst) 2002; Paul Hamlyn Award for Visual Artists 1999, nominated Turner Prize 2003; *Solo Exhibitions* incl: red on green (ICA London) 1992, Stephen Friedman London 1995, Keep off the grass (Serpentine Gallery Lawn London) 1997, Chasing Rainbows (Bloom Gallery Amsterdam, Delfina London) 1998, Glaschu (Tramway at Lanarkshire House Glasgow) 1999, All the rest is silence Anya Gallaccio at Sadler's Wells (Sadler's Wells London) 1999, blessed (Lehmann Maupin Gallery NY) 2001, beat (Duveen Sculpture Cmmn Tate Britain London) 2002, Turner Prize Exhibition (Tate Britain London) 2003, Ikon Birmingham 2003, Lehmann Maupin Gallery NY 2004, Silver Seed (Mt Stuart Tst Isle of Bute) 2005, The Look of Things (Palazzo delle Papesse Siena Italy) 2005, One Art (Sculpture Centre NY) 2006, Galeria Leme Sao Paulo 2006, Three Sheets to the Wind (Thomas Dane Gallery London) 2007; *Group Exhibitions* incl: Freeze (Surrey Docks London) 1988, A Group Show (Barbara Gladstone Gallery NY, Stein Gladstone Gallery NY) 1992, Pictura Britannica ART FROM BRITAIN (Museum of Contemporary Art Sydney, Art Gallery of S Aust, Te Papa Wellington) 1997, The Greenhouse Effect (Serpentine Gallery London) 2000, In Print (Br Cncl touring exhibition) 2002–03, Rose c'est la vie – On Flowers in Contemporary Art (Tel Aviv Museum of Art) 2004, Domestic (Futility) (New Art Centre Wilts) 2004, Art of the Garden (Tate Britain) 2004, Von Pop bis Heute (Kunstalle Bielefeld) 2004, Turning Points: 20th Century British Sculpture (Tehran Museum of Contemporary Art) 2004, Forest (Wolverhampton Art Gallery and tour) 2004, Flowers observed, flowers transformed (Andy Warhol Museum) 2004, Lustewarande 04: Disorientation of Beauty (Tilburg Netherlands) 2004, Sad Songs (Univ Galleries Illinois State Univ) 2005, Monuments for the USA (White Columns NY) 2005, Forest (Oriel

G

Davies Gallery Newtown Wales) 2005, If it didn't exist you'd have to invent it (The Showroom London) 2006, Too Much Love (Angeles Gallery LA) 2006, Toutes Compositions (Counter Gallery London) 2006, Core, (Illumitate Productions London) 2006, Wood for the Trees and Falling Leaves (Gimpel Fils London) 2007, Chanel Pushkin (State Museum of Fine Arts Moscow) 2007, Turner Prize: A Retrospective (Tate Britain, Moscow Museum of Modern Art and Mori Art Museum Tokyo) 2007; *Work in Public Collections* incl: Br Cncl Collection London, Museum of Contemporary Art Sydney, Tate London, V&A London; *Publications* subject of: Anya Gallaccio: beat (by Mary Horlock, Heidi Reitmaier and Simon Schama) 2002, Anya Gallaccio: Chasing Rainbows (essay by Ralph Rugoff, 1999), Silver Seed: Anya Gallaccio (2005), The Look of Things (essays by Lorenzo Fusi, Jordan Kaplan and Mark Gisbourne) 2005; featured in Ikon Catalogue (2003); *Style*— Ms Anya Gallaccio; ✉ c/o Lehmann Maupin, 540 West 26 Street, NY, USA (✆ 00 1 212 255 2923, fax 00 1 212 255 2924)

GALLACHER, Dr Stephen John; *b* 29 May 1961; *Educ* St Aloysius' Coll Glasgow, Univ of Glasgow (MB ChB, MD); *Career* jr house offr: (med) Univ Dept of Med Glasgow Royal Infirmary 1983–84, (surgery) Dept of Surgery Duke Street Hosp Glasgow 1984; SHO/ registrar (med rotation) Southern Gen Hosp Glasgow 1984–87, lectr in med Univ Dept of Med Glasgow Royal Infirmary 1990–95 (registrar in med 1987–90), conslt physician with an interest in diabetes and endocrinology Southern Gen Hosp NHS Tst 1995–2015 then Queen Elizabeth Univ Hosp 2015–; memb Cncl RCPSGlas 1993–95; FRCP (Edinburgh and Glasgow); *Publications* author of over 50 pubns in the field of metabolic bone diseases; *Style*— Dr Stephen Gallacher; ✉ Queen Elizabeth University Hospital, 1345 Govan Road, Glasgow G51 4TF (✆ 0141 201 1100)

GALLAGHER, Edward Patrick; CBE (2001); s of Charles Henry Gallagher (d 1977), and Lucy Georgina, *née* Gardiner (d 1996); *b* 4 August 1944; *Educ* Univ of Sheffield (BEng, Dip Business Studies, Mappin medal, John Brown award); *m* 3 April 1969, Helen, da of Ronald George Wilkinson; 2 s (James Edward b 16 Feb 1975, Robert Daniel b 28 July 1977); *Career* systems analyst Vauxhall Motors 1963–68, corp planning mangr Sandoz Products Ltd 1968–70, computer servs mangr Robinson Willey Ltd 1970–71; Black and Decker: fin mangr 1971–73, prodn mangr 1973–78, dir Mktg Servs 1978–79, dir Serv and Distribution 1979–81, dir Business Analysis based USA 1981–83, dir Market and Product Devpt 1983–86; Amersham International: dir Corp Devpt 1986–88, divnl chief exec 1988–90, mfrg dir 1990–92; chief exec and memb Bd: Nat Rivers Authy 1992–95, Environment Agency 1995–2001; dir ECUS 2001–11; chair: Health and Safety Ctee Engrg Employers Fedn 2001–04, Environmental Vision 2003–11 (memb 2001–11), Energy and Environment Policy Ctee IEE 2003–04 (memb 1999–2004), Pesticides Forum 2003–06, Advsy Bd Centre for Social Economic Res on Global Environment (CSERGE) 2004–07 (memb 2001–07), Energywatch 2004–08, Enviro-fresh Ltd 2004–07, Renewable Fuels Agency 2007–11, Centre for Low Carbon Futures 2009–14; vice-pres Cncl for Environmental Educn 1997–2006; memb: English Tourism Sustainability Task Force 1999–2000, Royal Acad of Engrs Sustainable Devpt Educn Working Gp 1999–2003, Cncl English Nature 2000–06, Awards Ctee Royal Acad of Engrg 2001–04, Bd Consumer Focus 2007–11; special advsr Maidenhead Waterways Restoration Gp 2007–; patron Environmental Industries Cmmn 2001–13; civil servs cmmr 2001–06; memb Cncl Univ of Bristol 1994–97 (memb Fin Advsy Gp 1994–2000); Middlesex Univ: memb Faculty of Technology Advsy Gp 1994–97, visiting prof Business Sch and Faculty of Technol 1994–97, visiting prof Sch of Health, Biological and Environmental Sci 1997–, chair Bd of Govrs 2001–04 (govr 1994–2000), dep chm 2000–01), chm Audit Ctee 1996–2000, chm Governance Ctee 2000–01, chm Planning and Resources Ctee 2000–01; tstee: Living Again Tst, Royal Hosp for Neurodisability 1993–2003; Freeman City of London, Liveryman Worshipful Co of Water Conservators (memb Ct of Assts 1999–2001); Hon DEng Univ of Sheffield 1996; Hon DSc: Univ of Tomsk Russia 1998, Univ of Plymouth 1998, Brunel Univ; Hon DUniv Middx 2005; CEng, FIEE 1990, MRI 1992, FCIWEM 1994, FRSA 1995–2007, CIMgt 1996, FREng 1997; *Recreations* the countryside, tennis, playing the guitar, clocks; *Style*— Edward Gallagher, CBE, FREng; ✉ 154 Whyteladyes Lane, Cookham, Berks SL6 9LA

GALLAGHER, Eileen; *Educ* Queen Margaret's Acad Ayr, Univ of Glasgow (MA), Univ of Wales Coll of Cardiff (NCTJ Cert); *Career* freelance journalist 1980–84 (for newspapers incl Glasgow Herald and Daily Record); Scottish Television: joined as press offr 1984, head of prog planning 1987–91, head Broadcasting Div 1991–92, concurrently i/c scheduling Children's ITV for ITV Network 1991–92, dir of broadcasting and main bd dir Scottish Television plc (now Scottish Media Group plc) 1992–94; md Broadcasting Granada/LWT 1994–96, md LWT and dep md Granada UK Broadcasting 1996–98, co-fndr and md Shed Productions 1998–, md Ginger Television 1999; non-exec dir Britt Allcroft 1998–; *Style*— Ms Eileen Gallagher

GALLAGHER, Jock James Young; s of Joseph Gallagher (d 1938), and Margaret, *née* Young (d 1984); *b* 31 March 1938, Greenock, Scotland; *Educ* Greenock HS; *m* 31 Dec 1970, Sheenagh Glenn, da of Richard Jones (d 1958); *Career* journalist with various newspapers 1958–66; BBC: news prodr 1966–70, head network radio 1980–89 (ed 1970–80), head special projects 1989–90; md BroadVision 1990–2003; chm The Health Independent Ltd 1999–2004, chm Press Freedom Network; dir Centre for Freedom of the Media 2008–; hon lectr Univ of Sheffield; exec dir Assoc of Br Eds 1990–99, ed British Editor 1990–99; memb: Communications Sector Ctee UK UNESCO 2000–03, WM Ctee Further Educ Funding Cncl 1997–2001, FCO Panel on Free Expression; vice-chm Kidderminster Coll 1996–2001; past pres Radio and TV Industries Club (Midlands), vice-pres Birmingham Press Club, dir Bewdley Festival Ltd 1988–, pres The Young Prog 2006–; memb Fed Exec Lib Dems 2002–06 and 2013–14, chair Membership Working Gp 2013; past pres Wyre Forest Lib Dems, vice-pres Lib Dems Parly Candidates Assoc 2005– (chm 2002–05), pres W Midland Lib Dems 2010–, chair Lib Dems Parly Candidates Assoc General Task Force 2010; Euro Parly candidate (Lib Dem) for Hereford and Shropshire 1994, Parly candidate (Lib Dem) Birmingham Edgbaston 1997; Magnus Magnusson Medal ICS 2010, Inveramsay Medal (Young Prog) 2012; hon memb Soc of Editors; memb: Chartered Inst of Journalists, Radio Acad, Assoc of Euro Journalists; founding fell Inst of Contemporary Scotland (dep chair 2006); *Books* History of the Archers (1975), Portrait of A Lady – biography of Lady Isobel Barnett (1980), The Life And Death of Doris Archer – biography of Gwen Berryman (1981), To The Victor The Spoils (1986), Return to Ambridge (1987), Borchester Echoes (1988), The Archers Omnibus (1990), Europress (1992), Laurie Lee: A Many-coated Man (1998), Scotland's Global Empire@ a chornicle of great Scots (2013); also ed Who's Who in the Liberal Democrats (1998, 2000, 2002 and 2004); *Recreations* golf, reading, politics; *Clubs* Kidderminster Golf, Victory Services; *Style*— Jock Gallagher, Esq; ✉ e-mail jyg@cix.co.uk

GALLAGHER, Kelly Marie; MBE (2014); *b* 18 May 1985, Bangor, Co Down; *Educ* Univ of Bath (BSc); *Career* Paralympic skier (most decorated Br alpine skier at World Championship level); Gold medal (giant slalom, with Claire Robb) NZ Winter Games 2009; with Charlotte Evans: Silver medal (slalom) and Bronze medal (giant slalom) IPC World Championships 2011, Gold medal (slalom) Europa Cup Finals 2011, Gold medal (slalom) World Cup Finals Sochi 2013, Gold medal (Super-G competition) 2014; currently statistician NI Statistic and Research Agency; Hon Dr Queen's Univ Belfast 2015; *Style*— Ms Kelly Gallagher, MBE; ✉ c/o British Paralympic Association, 60 Charlotte Street, London W1T 2NU

GALLAGHER, Noel David Thomas; s of Peggy Gallagher; er bro of Liam Gallagher, *qv*; *b* 29 May 1967, Manchester; *m* 1, 6 June 1997 (m dis 2001), Meg Mathews; 1 da (Anaïs);

m 2, 18 June 2011, Sara MacDonald; 2 s (Donovan, Sonny Patrick); *Career* former roadie The Inspiral Carpets, fndr memb (lead guitarist/backup vocals/songwriter) Oasis 1991–2009, solo (as Noel Gallagher's High Flying Birds) 2011–; *Albums* with Oasis: Definitely Maybe 1994 (entered UK charts no 1, fastest selling debut album in British history), (What's the Story) Morning Glory? 1995 (UK no 1), Be Here Now 1997 (UK no 1), The Masterplan 1998 (compilation, UK no 2), Familiar to Millions 2000 (live album, UK no 5), Heathen Chemistry 2002 (UK no 1), Don't Believe the Truth 2005 (UK no 1); solo Noel Gallagher's High Flying Birds 2011 (UK no 1); contrib Help (Warchild album) 1995; *Singles* top 10 UK singles with Oasis incl: Live Forever (no 10), Cigarettes & Alcohol (no 7), Whatever (no 3), Some Might Say (no 1), Roll With It (no 2), Wonderwall (no 2), Don't Look Back in Anger (no 1), D'You Know What I Mean (no 1), Stand By Me (no 2), All Around the World (no 1), Go Let It Out (no 1), Who Feels Love (no 4), Sunday Morning Call (no 4), The Hindu Times (no 1), Stop Crying Your Heart Out (no 2), Little By Little/She is Love (no 2), Songbird (no 3), Lyla (no 1), The Importance of Being Idle (no 1), Let There Be Love (no 2); solo: The Death of You and Me 2011, AKA...What A Life! 2011; other contribs for artists incl The Chemical Brothers; *Awards* incl: Best New Group Brit Awards 1995, Best Group and Best Album ((What's the Story) Morning Glory?) Brit Awards 1996, Best Group and Best Song (Wonderwall) MTV Music Awards 1996, nominated Best Song (Wonderwall) Grammy Awards 1997, Best British Band NME Awards 2009, Brits Album of 30 Years ((What's the Story) Morning Glory?) Brit Award 2010, NME Godlike Genius Award 2012, Outstanding Collection Ivor Novello Award 2013; *Style*— Noel Gallagher; ✉ c/o Big Brother Recordings Ltd, PO Box 29479, London NW1 6GG

GALLAGHER, (Arthur) Robin; s of Hon James Albert Gallagher (d 1965), of York, and Winifred Mary, *née* Dill (d 1994); *b* 7 April 1941, Rhyl; *Educ* St Bede's Coll Manchester; *m* 1, 1969 (m dis 1992), 2 da (Kirsten b 8 March 1974, Kate b 1 Dec 1977); *m* 2, 1998, Christine Lloyd; 1 step da (Sarah Jane Lloyd, b 14 March 1979), 1 step s (Michael Midgley b 17 Feb 1970); *Career* Lt RNR 1960–66; articled clerk Royce, Peeling, Green & Co 1957–63, Whinney Smith and Whinney 1963–66, Touche Ross and Co Manchester and Leeds 1966–74, Ladyship Int Gp 1974–80, Whitecroft plc 1980–81, dir Antler Property Corp plc 1981–94, md Wellholme Ltd 1988–95; dir and dep chm: Towngate plc 1990–2014 (conslt 2014–), Brigdale Ltd 1990–2014; chm Oakland Securities Ltd 1991–96; jt fndr Save Baguley Hall Campaign 1966; vice-pres Leeds Jr C of C 1973–75; fell ICAEW 1963; *Publications* The Battle for Bligny Hill 6 June 1918 (2002), The Woods of Longley Old Hall (2003), 100 Years of Toulston Polo Club (with Sarah Lloyd, 2013); *Recreations* old buildings, 17th century oak furniture, polo; *Clubs* Army and Navy, RNR Offrs, Toulston Polo, Liverpool Master Mariners; *Style*— Robin Gallagher, Esq; ✉ Longley Old Hall, Longley, Huddersfield HD5 8LB (✆ 01484 430852, mobile 07703 314282, e-mail gallagher@longleyoldhall.co.uk, website www.longleyoldhall.co.uk)

GALLAGHER, Stephen Kent; *b* 13 October 1954; *Educ* Eccles GS, Univ of Hull (BA); *Career* writer and director; with: Documentaries Dept Yorkshire TV, Presentation Dept Granada TV 1975; freelance writer 1980–, exec prodr ABC Signature 2014–15; radio plays incl: The Last Rose of Summer 1977, Hunter's Moon 1978, The Babylon Run 1979, A Resistance to Pressure 1980, The Kingston File 1987, By The River, Fontainebleau 1988, The Horn 1989, Life Line 1992; TV work: Warriors' Gate (BBC) 1981, Terminus (BBC) 1984, Moving Targets (BBC) 1988, Chimera (Zenith/Anglia) 1991, Here Comes The Mirror Man (YTV) 1995, Oktober (adapted and directed for Carnival Films/LWT) 1998, The Kingdom of Bones (BBC Films) 2001, The Memory of Water (Carnival) 2004, Eleventh Hour (series creator and episodes, ITV) 2005, The Cup of Silence (Carnival) 2006, Life Line (Carnival/BBC) 2007, Eleventh Hour (format creator and episodes, CBS/Warner) 2008, Crusoe (series developer and lead writer, Power/NBC Universal) 2008, The Forgotten (co-exec prodr, ABC/Warner/Jerry Bruckheimer Television) 2009, Silent Witness: The Legacy (BBC) 2013 (Best TV Drama European Science TV and New Media Awards), Stan Lee's Lucky Man (Carnival/Sky) 2016; memb: Writers Guild of GB (Northern chair 1994–96), Writers Guild of America (East), Henry Irving Soc, Br Fantasy Soc; *Publications* novels incl: Chimera (1982), Follower (1984), Valley of Lights (1987), Oktober (1988), Down River (1989), Rain (1990), The Boat House (1991), Nightmare, With Angel (1992), Red, Red Robin (1995), White Bizango (2002), The Spirit Box (2005), The Painted Bride (2006), The Kingdom of Bones (2007), The Bedlam Detective (2012), The Authentic William James (2016); non fiction incl Journeyman (2000); writings also incl short fiction and criticism collected in Out of his Mind (Br Fantasy Award 2004) and Plots and Misadventures (2007); *Style*— Stephen Gallagher, Esq; ✉ c/o The Agency, 24 Pottery Lane, Holland Park, London W11 4LZ (website www.stephengallagher.com, weblog www.stephengallagher.co.uk)

GALLAGHER, Tony; *b* 1964; *Educ* Finchley Catholic HS, Univ of Bristol, City Univ London; *Career* former asst ed Daily Mail; Daily Telegraph: dep ed 2007–09, ed 2009–14; *Style*— Tony Gallagher, Esq

GALLAGHER, William John Paul (Liam); s of Peggy Gallagher; yr bro of Noel Gallagher, *qv*; *b* 21 September 1972, Manchester; *m* 1, 7 April 1997 (m dis 2000), Patsy Kensit; 1 s (Lennon); *m* 2, 14 Feb 2008 (m dis 2014), Nicole Appleton; 1 s (Gene); *Career* formerly with band The Rain, fndr memb (lead vocals) Oasis 1991–2009, memb Beady Eye 2009–; fndr Pretty Green (clothing label); *Albums* with Oasis: Definitely Maybe 1994 (entered UK charts no 1, fastest selling debut album in British history), (What's the Story) Morning Glory? 1995 (UK no 1), Be Here Now 1997 (UK no 1), The Masterplan 1998 (compilation, UK no 2), Familiar to Millions 2000 (live album, UK no 5), Heathen Chemistry 2002 (UK no 1), Don't Believe the Truth 2005 (UK no 1); with Beady Eye: Different Gear, Still Speeding 2011, BE 2013; contrib Help (Warchild album) 1995; *Singles* top 10 UK singles with Oasis incl: Live Forever (no 10), Cigarettes & Alcohol (no 7), Whatever (no 3), Some Might Say (no 1), Roll With It (no 2), Wonderwall (no 2), Don't Look Back in Anger (no 1), D'You Know What I Mean (no 1), Stand By Me (no 2), All Around the World (no 1), Go Let It Out (no 1), Who Feels Love (no 4), Sunday Morning Call (no 4), The Hindu Times (no 1), Stop Crying Your Heart Out (no 2), Little By Little/She is Love (no 2), Songbird (no 3), Lyla (no 1), The Importance of Being Idle (no 1), Let There Be Love (no 2); with Beady Eye incl The Roller 2011; *Awards* incl: Best New Group Brit Awards 1995, Best Group and Best Album ((What's the Story) Morning Glory?) Brit Awards 1996, Best Group and Best Song (Wonderwall) MTV Music Awards 1996, nominated Best Song (Wonderwall) Grammy Awards 1997, Best British Band NME Award 2009, Brits Album of 30 Years ((What's the Story) Morning Glory?) Brit Award 2010; *Recreations* supporting Man City; *Style*— Liam Gallagher; ✉ c/o Big Brother Recordings Ltd, PO Box 29479, London NW1 6GG

GALLARD, HE Jill; *née* Parkinson; *Educ* Univ of Edinburgh; *m* Dominic; 2 s; *Career* diplomat; desk offr for Spain and Portugal Consular Dept FCO 1991–93, consular attaché for Olympic Games Barcelona 1992, desk offr for Bulgaria and Romania Central European Dept FCO 1993–94, intern European Cmmn 1994, third sec political Madrid 1994–97, second sec EU/economic Madrid 1997–99, head Turkey Section Southern European Dept FCO 1999–2001, dep head Common Foreign and Security Policy Team FCO 2003, head Political and EU/Economic Sections Prague 2004–07, private sec to Perm Under Sec FCO 2007–08, asst dir of operations HR Directorate FCO 2008–10, ambass to Portugal 2011–14, human resources dir FCO 2014–; *Style*— HE Mrs Jill Gallard; ✉ c/o FCO, King Charles Street, London SW1A 2AH

GALLEMORE, Michael; s of Ronald Gallemore (d 1988), of Chapel-en-le-Frith, Derbys, and Mary, *née* Slater, of Rhos-on-Sea, Colwyn Bay; *b* 3 November 1944; *Educ* Manchester

Central GS; *m* 7 July 1967, Janetta Florence, da of Frank and Ada Reeves (d 1985); 1 s (Alexander Michael b 3 Nov 1974); *Career* interviewer Nat Rheumatism Survey 1961, joined Stewart & Hartleys news agency Manchester as reporter 1962, contrib various series to nat newspapers on subjects incl drugs, crime and the judicial system; Mirror Group Newspapers 1964–93: joined staff of Daily and Sunday Mirror 1964, worked as reporter, art ed, sub-ed, led attempted mgmnt buyout of MGN, managing ed (North) MGN 1985–88; The Sporting Life: managing ed 1988, ed 1989–93, md 1989–92; responsible for editorial launch of The European and Racing Times (NY), left MGN 1993; Barkers Trident Communications Corp publishers 1993–2000, commercial dir/ed Action Line magazine, Racing International, European Senior Tour and European Tour Golf Magazines and various other racing and sporting magazines; dep chm and ed-in-chief London & Edinburgh Publishing plc 1996–; ed-in-chief and md Worldwide Sporting Pubns Ltd Wimslow & Dubai 2000–; Jockey Club point-to-point course inspr 1994 (point-to-point clerk of the course); memb Br Field Sports Soc; *Books* ed: All Such Fun (by Michael Pope, 1992), A Year in Red Shirts (by Jack Berry); *Recreations* hunting, point-to-point riding, race riding, golf, rugby, soccer, cricket, tennis, squash, former semi-professional soccer and rugby league player; *Clubs* Shrigley Hall Country, Racehorse Owners' Assoc, Point-to-Point Owners' Assoc; *Style*— Michael Gallemore, Esq; ✉ Browside Farm, Stoneheads, Whaley Bridge, High Peak, Derbyshire SK23 7BB (☎ 01663 732841, e-mail mikeg@sportingpublications.com); Worldwide Sporting Publications Ltd, 54 Alderley Road, Wilmslow, Cheshire SK9 1NY

GALLIANO, John Charles; CBE (2001); s of John Joseph Galliano, of Gibraltar, and Anita, *née* Guillen; *b* 28 November 1960; *Educ* Wilson's GS Camberwell, City and East London Coll of Textiles and Art and Design, St Martin's Sch of Art; *Career* fashion designer; head of: Givenchy (Paris) 1995–96, Dior (Paris) 1996–2011; work on permanent display The Museum of Costume Bath 1987; creative dir Maison Martin Margiela 2014–; British Designer of the Year (British Fashion Awards) 1987, 1994, 1995 and (jtly with Alexander McQueen) 1997; hon fell London Inst 1997; *Style*— John Galliano, Esq, CBE

GALLIE, Prof Duncan Ian Dunbar; CBE (2009); s of Ian Gallie, and Elsie, *née* Peers; *Educ* St Paul's (scholar), Magdalen Coll Oxford (demyship, BA), St Antony's Coll Oxford (DPhil); *m* Martine, *née* Jurdant; 2 da (Natasha, Justine); *Career* res fell Nuffield Coll Oxford 1971–73, lectr in sociology Univ of Essex 1973–79, reader in sociology Univ of Warwick 1979–85, official fell Nuffield Coll Oxford 1985–2014, Emeritus Fell Nuffield Coll 2014–; prof of sociology Univ of Oxford 1996–; dir ESRC Social Change and Econ Life Initiative 1985–90, advsr Comitè National d'Evaluation de la Recherche 1991, co-ordinator EU Employment, Unemployment and Social Exclusion Prog 1995–98; memb Scientific Ctee: Institut de Recherche sur les Sociétés Contemporaines (IRESCO) 1989–93, Institut Fédératif de Recherche sur les Économies et les Sociétés Industrielles (IFRESI) 1993–98; memb: EU Advsy Gp on Social Scis and Humanities in the European Research Area 2002–06, Strategic Advsy Bd Danish Nat Inst of Social Research, Expert Gp on Psychological Risks at Work French Miny of Work 2008–10, Scientific Cncl Paris Sch of Economics 2009–, Sci Cncl CREST-GENES 2010–; Distinguished Contribution to Scholarship Award American Sociological Assoc 1985; memb Br Sociological Assoc; FBA 1995 (vice-pres 2004–06, foreign sec 2006–11); *Books* In Search of the New Working Class (1978), Social Inequality and Class Radicalism in France and Britain (1985), Restructuring the Employment Relationship (jtly, 1998), Welfare Regimes and the Experience of Unemployment (jtly, 2000), Why we need a New Welfare State (jtly, 2002), Resisting Marginalization (jtly, 2004), Employment Regimes and the Quality of Work (jtly, 2007), Economic Crisis, Quality of Work and Social Integration (jtly, 2013), Unequal Britain at Work (jtly, 2015); *Recreations* travelling, music, museum gazing; *Style*— Prof Duncan Gallie, CBE, FBA; ✉ 149 Leam Terrace, Leamington Spa, Warwickshire CV31 1DF; Nuffield College, Oxford OX1 1NF (☎ 01865 278586, e-mail duncan.gallie@nuffield.ox.ac.uk)

GALLIGAN, Prof Denis James; s of John Felix Galligan (d 1973), and Muriel Maud, *née* Johnson; *b* 4 June 1947, Dalby, Australia; *Educ* Downlands Coll Toowoomba, Univ of Queensland (LLB), Univ of Oxford (MA, BCL, DCL); *m* 20 June 1972, Martha Louise, da of Alfred Lewis Martinuzzi, of Innisfail, Queensland; 1 da (Francesca Louise b 22 Feb 1975), 1 s (Finbar John b 10 Sept 1977); *Career* lectr Faculty of Law UCL 1974–76, pt/t lectr Magdalen Coll Oxford 1975, fell Jesus Coll Oxford and CUF lectr Univ of Oxford 1976–81, sr lectr Faculty of Law Univ of Melbourne 1982–84, dean Faculty of Law Univ of Southampton 1987–90 (prof 1985–93), prof of socio-legal studies and dir Centre for Socio-Legal Studies Univ of Oxford 1993–; fell Wolfson Coll Oxford; Jean Monnet prof Università degli Studi di Siena 2003–, visiting prof Central European Univ Budapest 1993–2004; pres UK Assoc for Legal and Social Philosophy 1989–91, conslt OECD Paris 1995–97; assoc ed Oxford DNB; memb Socio-Legal Studies Assoc; called to the Bar Gray's Inn, barr Supreme Court Queensland; fndn academician Acad of Social Sciences;; *Books* Essays in Legal Theory (1984), Law, Rights and the Welfare State (1986), Discretionary Powers: A Legal Study of Official Discretion (1986), Procedure (1992), Administrative Law (1992), Australian Administrative Law (1993), Socio-Legal Readings in Administrative Law (1995), Socio-Legal Studies in Context (1995), Due Process and Procedural Fairness (1996), Administrative Justice in the New European Democracies (1998), Administrative Law in Central and Eastern Europe (1998), Law and Informal Practices (2003), Law in Modern Society (2006), The Social and Political Foundations of Constitutions (jt ed, 2013), Constitutions and the Classics: A Selection of British, French and American Authors from Fortescue to Bentham (ed, 2013); *Recreations* reading, gardening; *Style*— Prof Denis Galligan; ✉ The Rosery, Beckley, Oxford OX3 9UU (☎ and fax 01865 351281); Centre for Socio-Legal Studies, Manor Building, Oxford OX1 3UQ (☎ 01865 284220, fax 01865 284221, e-mail denis.galligan@csls.ox.ac.uk); Wolfson College, Oxford OX2 6UD

GALLIMORE, Michael; s of John Gallimore (d 1998), of Surbiton, Surrey, and Rita Ida Doreen, *née* Clarke (d 2014); *b* 8 March 1958; *Educ* Kingston GS, St Catharine's Coll Cambridge (MA, capt Univ Hockey Club, Hockey blue); *m* 29 July 1983, Jane Frances, da of Alfred Aspinall, of Southport, Merseyside; 1 s (William Mark b 1990), 1 da (Claire Edith b 1994); *Career* admitted slr 1983, ptnr Hogan Lovells Int LLP 1988–; memb: Law Soc 1983, City of London Slrs' Co 1983; England hockey int; *Recreations* golf, hockey, theatre; *Clubs* Porters Park Golf, Ladykillers Hockey, Hawks' (Cambridge); *Style*— Michael Gallimore, Esq; ✉ Hogan Lovells International LLP, Atlantic House, Holborn Viaduct, London EC1A 2FG

GALLIMORE, Patricia Mary; da of Capt Charles Philip Gallimore, RN (d 1988), and Elizabeth St John, *née* Benn (d 1977); *b* 7 August 1944; *Educ* Hermitage House Sch Bath, Westbourne Sch Glasgow, St Margaret's Sch Sutton Coldfield, Birmingham Sch of Speech & Drama; *m* 7 April 1973, Charles Gardner, s of John Gardner; 1 s (Thomas Charles b 27 May 1977), 1 da (Harriet Mary Elizabeth b 26 July 1982); *Career* radio actress 1965–; twice memb BBC Radio Drama Co; leading roles in plays and serials incl: War and Peace, The Forsyte Saga, Wuthering Heights, Cold Comfort Farm, Waggoners Walk (BBC Radio 2) 1969–71, Pat Archer in The Archers (BBC Radio 4) 1974–; TV appearances incl: Spy-Ship (BBC), Aliens in the Family (BBC), Kinsey (BBC), Jupiter Moon (BSB); author Organic Year: A Guide to Organic Living (2000); has recorded over 200 titles for audiobooks; winner BBC Student Radio Drama Prize (now Carleton Hobbs Award) 1965, winner Audiofile's Earphone Awards 2008 (for Queen Camilla by Sue Townsend), winner Audiofile's Earphone Awards 2015 (for Tall Poppies by Janet Woods); *Recreations* swimming, reading, walking, enjoying time with friends and family; *Style*— Patricia Gallimore; ✉ c/o The Archers, BBC, The Mailbox, Birmingham B1 1RP

GALLOWAY, George; s of George Galloway, of Dundee, and Sheila Reilly; *b* 16 August 1954; *Educ* Harris Acad; *m* 1, 1979 (m dis), Elaine, da of James Fyffe, of Dundee; 1 da (Lucy b 1982); m 2, 2000, Dr Amineh Abu-Zayyad; *Career* labourer jute & flax industry 1973, prodn worker Michelin Tyres 1973, organiser Dundee Lab Pty 1977, dir War on Want 1983; MP: (Lab) Glasgow Hillhead 1987–97, (Lab until 2003 then Respect 2004–05) Glasgow Kelvin 1997–2005, (Respect) Bethnal Green & Bow 2005–2010, (Respect) Bradford W 2012–15; Hilal-i-Quaid-i-Azzam decoration for servs to the movement for the restoration of democracy in Pakistan 1990, Hilal-i-Pakistan decoration for work on self-determination for Jammu and Kashmir 1996; Debater of the Year Zurich/Spectator Parly Awards 2001; appeared in Celebrity Big Brother (Channel 4) 2006; *Books* Downfall – The Ceausescus and the Romanian Revolution (jtly, 1991), I'm Not the Only One (2004), Mr Galloway Goes to Washington (2005), The Fidel Castro Handbook (2006); *Recreations* sport, films, music; *Style*— George Galloway, Esq; ✉ House of Commons, London SW1 0AA

GALLOWAY, Janice; da of late James Galloway, and Janet Clark McBride (d 1982); *b* 2 December 1955; *Educ* Ardrossan Acad, Univ of Glasgow; *Children* 1 s (James b 21 Feb 1992); m Aug 2006, Jonathan May; *Career* writer, sometime English teacher; TLS res fell British Library 1999, visiting prof Dept of Creative Writing Univ of Stirling 2013–14, inaugural Scottish Writing Fell Univ of Otago at Dunedin NZ 2014; E M Forster Award 1994; *Books* The Trick is to Keep Breathing (1990, SAC Award, MIND/Allan Lane Award), Blood (1991, SAC Award), Foreign Parts (1994, McVitie's Prize for Scottish Writer of the Year 1994, SAC Award), Where You Find It (1996), Pipelines (with Anne Bevan, 2000), Clara (2002, Saltire Soc Scottish Book of the Year Award 2002), Boy Book See (2002), Monster (libretto, with Sally Beamish, 2002), Rosengarten (with the sculptor Anne Bevan, 2004), This is Not About Me (2008, SMIT Non-Fiction Book of the Year), Collected Stories (2009), All Made Up (2011, Creative Scotland Book of the Year), Things Unseen (contrib, 2013), The Magic Box (contrib, 2014), Jellyfish (short stories, 2016); *Style*— Ms Janice Galloway; ✉ c/o Jonathan Cape, 20 Vauxhall Bridge Road, London SW1V 2SA; c/o Blake Friedmann Agency, First Floor, Selous House, 5–12 Mandela Street, London NW1 0DU (☎ 020 7387 0842); c/o Pru Rowlandson, Granta Books, 12 Addison Avenue, Holland Park, London W11 4QR; website www.janicegalloway.net

G

GALLOWAY, Rev Prof Peter John; OBE (1996), JP (City of London 1989); s of Henry John Galloway (d 1986), and Mary Selina, *née* Beshaw (d 2009); *b* 19 July 1954; *Educ* Westminster City Sch, Univ of London (BA, PhD), Brunel Univ (DLitt); *Partner* Michael Russell Stewart Turner (civil partnership 2008); *Career* ordained: deacon 1983, priest 1984; curate: St John's Wood London 1983–86, St Giles-in-the-Fields London 1986–90; vicar Emmanuel West End Hampstead London 1990–2008 (priest-in-charge 1990–95), chaplain Queen's Chapel of the Savoy 2008–, chaplain Royal Victorian Order 2008–; area dean: North Camden 2002–07, Surrogate 2006–; chm of govrs Emmanuel Sch 1990–2008, visiting prof in politics and history Brunel Univ 2008–; St John Ambulance: asst DG 1985–91, dep DG 1991–99, chm Nat Publications Ctee 1988–95; memb Lord Chancellor's Advsy Ctee (City of London) 1994–2000 and 2005–11 (vice-chm 2008–11) and (Central and S London) 2012–13, chm of the Bench 2001–04 (dep chm 2000), chm Gtr London Bench Chairmen's Forum 2004 (dep chm 2003); chm The Goldsmiths' Soc 1997–2007 (vice-chm 1991–97); vice-chm Convocation Univ of London 1999–2003 (actg chm 2001–03), chm Univ of London Convocation Tst 2005–12; memb Cncl: Goldsmiths Coll London 1993–99, Univ of London 1999–2008, Heythrop Coll 2006–14; tstee St Gabriel's Tst 2001–04, govr St Olave's and St Saviour's GS 2010– (vice-chm 2012–13, chm 2013–), govr St Olave's and St Saviour's Schs Fndn 2013–; Order of St John of Jerusalem: memb Chapter-Gen 1996–99, memb Priory of England Chapter 1999–2013, sub dean Priory of England 1999–2007 (registrar 2007–); Award of Merit Orders and Medals Research Soc 2013; Freeman City of London 1995, chaplain to HRH The Princess Royal as Master Worshipful Co of Butchers 2010–11; hon fell Goldsmiths Coll London 1999; FSA 2000; KStJ 1997 (ChStJ 1992), Offr Order of the Crown of Romania 2013; *Books* The Order of St Patrick 1783–1983 (1983), Henry F B Mackay (1983), Good and Faithful Servants (jtly, 1988), The Cathedrals of Ireland (1992), The Order of the British Empire (1996), Royal Service (jtly, vol 1, 1996), The Most Illustrious Order (1999), A Passionate Humility, Frederick Oakeley and the Oxford Movement (1999), The Cathedrals of Scotland (2000), The Order of St Michael and St George (2000), Companions of Honour (2002), The Order of the Bath (2006), The Order of the Thistle (2009), The Queen's Chapel of the Savoy (2009), Exalted, Eminent and Imperial: Honours of the Raj (2014), The Royal Victorian Order (2016); *Recreations* reading, writing, book collecting, solitude; *Clubs* Athenaeum (memb Gen Ctee 2011–14), Beefsteak; *Style*— The Rev Prof P J Galloway, OBE, JP, FSA; ✉ The Queen's Chapel of the Savoy, Savoy Hill, London WC2R 0DA

GALLOWAY, Bishop of (RC) 2015; Rt Rev William Nolan; *Career* ordained priest 1977; asst priest Our Lady of Lourdes East Kilbride 1978–80, asst priest St David's Plains 1980–83, vice-rector Scots Coll Rome 1983–90, asst priest St Bridget's Baillieston 1990–94, parish priest Our Lady of Lourdes East Kilbride 1994–2015; *Style*— The Rt Rev the Bishop of Galloway

GALLWEY; *see:* Frankland-Payne-Gallwey

GALMICHE, Daniel Michel; s of Daniel Galmiche (d 1994), and Anne-Marie, *née* Calame; *b* 18 January 1958, Lure, France; *Educ* Lycee Hotelier de Strasbourg, Lycee Mixte de Lure; *m* (m dis); partner, Claire Marchionne; 1 s (Antoine-Daniel b 4 Feb 2000); *Career* trained with the Roux bros at Le Gavoche 1977–78; head chef: Knockinaam Lodge Hotel Portpatrick 1986–93 (1 Michelin Star 1990), The Duxton Hotel Singapore 1993–95; exec chef Penina Meridian Golf and Resort Hotel Alvor 1995–96, chef mangr Harveys Restaurant Bristol 1996–2003 (1 Michelin Star); exec chef: L'Ortolan Shinfield 2003–04 (1 Michelin Star), Cliveden House Hotel Taplow 2004–08 (1 Michelin Star), Forbury Hotel 2008–; resident writer for Reading Evening Post Food Monthly (jt winner UK Supplement of the Year Regional Press Awards 2007); memb: Acad Culinaire of GB, World Master Chef Soc, Soil Assoc Judging Panel for Organic Food; conslt Steelite Int; TV appearances incl: The Greatest Dishes in the World (Sky), Too Many Cooks (HTV), Saturday Kitchen (BBC); Master Chef of the Year Scotland 1989; *Style*— Daniel Galmiche, Esq

GALSWORTHY, Sir Anthony Charles; KCMG (1999, CMG 1985); s of Sir Arthur Norman Galsworthy, KCMG (d 1986), and Margaret Agnes, *née* Hiscocks (d 1973); *b* 20 December 1944; *Educ* St Paul's, CCC Cambridge (MA); *m* 30 May 1970, Jan, da of Dr A W Dawson-Grove; 1 s (Andrew b 1974), 1 da (Carolyn b 1975); *Career* Far East Dept FCO 1966–67, language student Hong Kong 1967–69, third sec (later second sec) Peking 1970–72, Rhodesia Dept FCO 1972–74, private sec to min of state 1974–77, first sec Rome 1977–81, first sec (later cnsllr and head of Chancery) Peking 1982–84, head Hong Kong Dept FCO 1984–86, princ private sec to sec of state for Foreign and Cwlth Affrs 1986–88, visiting res fell RIIA 1988–89, sr Br rep Sino-Br Jt Liaison Gp on Hong Kong 1989–93, chief of assessments staff Cabinet Office 1993–95; dep under sec of state FCO 1995–97, ambass China 1997–2002; advsr Bd Standard Chartered Bank 2002–14; dir Bekaert SA 2004–14, dir WWT Consulting Ltd 2009–; scientific assoc Nat History Museum 2001–; memb Foreign Affrs Advsy Ctee Royal Soc 2003–; tstee Wildfowl and Wetland Tst 2002–09, tstee Br Tst for Ornithology 2002–06, dir Earthwatch (Europe) 2002–06; hon fell Royal Botanic Gardens Edinburgh 2001–, hon prof Kunming Inst of Botany Chinese Acad of Sciences 2002–; Order of the Lion of Finland 1975, Order of Adolph of Nassau

(Luxembourg) 1976; *Publications* The Eupithecia of China: a Revision (with Dr V Mironov, 2014); *Recreations* ornithology, wildlife; *Style—* Sir Anthony Galsworthy, KCMG

GALSWORTHY, Stamford (Sam); s of Arthur Michael Galsworthy, and late Charlotte Helena Galsworthy; *b* 20 May 1976, Truro, Cornwall; *Educ* Radley, Univ of the W of England; *m* Kitty Harvie; 1 da (Isadora Prudence Grace b 11 Nov 2014); *Career* export manager Fuller Smith & Turner 2001–06, co-fndr Sipsmith Independent Spirits 2007–; *Style—* Sam Galsworthy, Esq

GALTON, Prof David Jeremy; s of Maj Ernest Manuel Galton, and Cecilia, *née* Leyburn; *b* 2 May 1937; *Educ* Highgate Sch, Univ of London (MD, DSc); *m* 11 April 1967, (Gwynne) Merle; 1 da (Clare Judith b 1968), 1 s ((James) Seth b 1970); *Career* conslt physician St Bartholomew's Hosp 1971–, conslt physician i/c Moorfields Eye Hosp 1974–, prof Univ of London 1987–; chm Clinical Science 1979–81, sec Euro Atherosclerosis Soc; memb: Med Res Soc 1971, Assoc Physicians UK 1975, RSM; *Books* The Human Adipose Cell (1971), Molecular Genetics of Common Metabolic Disease (1985), Hyperlipidaemia in Practice (1991); *Recreations* skiing, sailing, music; *Style—* Prof David Galton; ✉ St Bartholomew's Hospital, West Smithfield, London EC1 (☎ 020 7882 6018, fax 020 7882 6064, e-mail d.j.galton@qmul.ac.uk)

GALTON, Raymond Percy (Ray); OBE; s of Herbert Galton, and Christina Galton; *b* 17 July 1930; *Educ* Garth Sch Morden; *m* 1956, Tonia Phillips (d 1995); 1 s, 2 da; *Career* scriptwriter and author (in collaboration with Alan Simpson, OBE, *qv*); *Theatre* incl: Way Out In Piccadilly 1966–67, The Wind in the Sassafras Trees 1968, Albert och Herbert (Sweden) 1981; with John Antrobus: When Did You Last See Your Trousers 1987–88 (nat tour 1994), Steptoe and Son – Murder at Oil Drum Lane (Comedy Theatre and nat tour) 2006; *Radio* incl: Hancock's Half Hour 1954–59, The Frankie Howerd Show, Back with Braden, Steptoe and Son 1966–73, The Galton & Simpson Radio Playhouse 1998–99, Galton and Simpson's Half Hour (Radio 2) 2009, The Missing Hancocks 2014; *Television* incl: Hancock's Half Hour 1956–61, Citizen James 1961, BBC Comedy Playhouse, Steptoe and Son 1962–74, Galton and Simpson Comedy 1969, Milligan's Wake, Frankie Howerd, Clochemerle 1971, Casanova 1973, Dawson's Weekly 1975, The Galton and Simpson Playhouse 1976–77, Camilo e Filho (Portugal Steptoe) 1995, Paul Merton In Galton & Simpson's... (series) 1996 and 1997; with Johnny Speight: Spooner's Patch 1977–81, Pfeifer (Germany) 2000; with John Antrobus: Room at the Bottom 1986–87, Get Well Soon 1997; *Film* incl: The Rebel 1960, The Bargee 1963, The Wrong Arm of the Law 1964, The Spy with the Cold Nose 1966, Loot 1970, Steptoe and Son 1971, Steptoe and Son Ride Again 1973, Den Siste Fleksnes (Norway) 1974, Le Petomane 1977; with Andrew Galton: Camping (Denmark) 1990; *Awards* John Logie Baird award for outstanding contribution to TV, Writers' Guild award (twice), Guild of TV Producers and Directors 1959 Merit Awards for Scriptwriters of the Year, Screenwriters' Guild Best TV Comedy Series (for Steptoe and Son) annually 1962–65, Dutch TV Best Comedy Series (for Steptoe and Son) 1966, Screenwriters' Guild Best Comedy Screenplay (for Steptoe and Son) 1972, Banff Festival Best TV Comedy (for Room at the Bottom) 1987, Writer's Guild of GB Lifetime Achievement Award 1997, BPI Gold Disc for BBC radio collection Hancock's Half Hour 1998, fell BAFTA 2016 (with Alan Simpson, OBE); *Books* Hancock (1961), Steptoe and Son (1963), The Reunion and Other Plays (1966), Hancock Scripts (1974), The Best of Hancock (1986), Hancock – The Classic Years (1987), The Best of Steptoe and Son (1988), Steptoe and Son (2002), Fifty Years of Hancock's Half Hour (2004), The Masters of Sitcom from Hancock to Steptoe (2011); *Style—* Ray Galton, Esq, OBE; ✉ c/o Tessa Le Bars, 54 Birchwood Road, Petts Wood, Kent BR5 IN2 (e-mail tessa.lebars@ntlworld.com, website www.galtonandsimpson.com)

GALVIN, Chris; s of Kathleen, *née* Grover; *b* 12 October 1958, Romford, Essex; *Educ* Westminster Kingsway Coll, W London Univ (BSc); *Career* The Ritz, The Lanesborough Hotel, Manage a Trois NY, Conran Restaurants, The Wolseley; proprietor (with bro Jeff Galvin, *qv*) Galvin Restaurants: Galvin Bistrot de Luxe 2005–, Galvin at Windows 2006–, Galvin La Chapelle 2009–, Pompadour by Galvin and Galvin Brasserie de Luxe 2012–, Galvin Demoiselle 2012, Galvin HOP 2016, Galvin at The Athenaeum 2016, The Centurion 2016, The Green Man 2016; *Books* Galvin: a Cookbook deluxe (2011); *Recreations* sailing, gastronomy; *Style—* Chris Galvin, Esq; ✉ Galvin Restaurants, 19 Newman Street, London W1T 1PF (☎ 020 7299 0444, fax 020 7299 0445)

GALVIN, Jeff; s of Frank Galvin, of Southend on Sea, Essex, and Kathleen, *née* Grover; *b* 1 December 1969, Chelmsford, Essex; *Educ* Thurrock Tech Coll (City & Guilds), Westminster Coll (Dip), MCA; *Career* chef; sous chef Chez Nico Park Lane London 1994–97, head chef Marco Pierre White at the Oak Room 1999, head chef L'Escargot 2000– (1 Michelin Star); proprietor (with bro Chris Galvin, *qv*) Galvin Restaurants: Galvin Bistrot de Luxe 2005–, Galvin at Windows 2006–, Galvin La Chapelle 2009–, Pompadour by Galvin and Galvin Brasserie de Luxe 2012–, Galvin Demoiselle 2012, Galvin HOP 2016, Galvin at The Athenaeum 2016, The Centurion 2016, The Green Man 2016; finalist Academy Annual Awards of Excellence 1991; Hon MSc Univ of West London; Master of Culinary Arts 2014; *Books* Galvin: a Cookbook de Luxe (2011); *Recreations* running, golf, cooking; *Style—* Jeff Galvin, Esq; ✉ Galvin Restaurants, 19 Newman Street, London W1T 1PF (☎ 020 7299 0447, fax 020 7299 0445)

GALWAY, Sir James; kt (2001), OBE (1977); s of James Galway; *b* 8 December 1939, Belfast; *Educ* Royal Coll of Music, Guildhall Sch of Music, Conservatoire National Supérieur de Musique Paris; *m* 1; 1 s; m 2; 1 s, 2 da (twins); m 3, 1984, Jeanne Cinnante; *Career* flute-player; princ flute: London Symphony Orch 1966, Royal Philharmonic Orch 1967–69, Berlin Philharmonic Orch 1969–75; solo career 1975–, soloist/conductor 1984–, princ guest conductor London Mozart Players 1999–; artist laureate Ulster Orch; records for Sony BMG; Grand Prix du Disque 1976 and 1989, President's Merit Award Nat Acad of Recording, Arts and Science 2004; James Galway rose by David Austin, *qv*, displayed Chelsea Flower Show 2000; hon fell Guildhall Sch of Music 2003; Hon MA Open Univ 1979, Hon Dr Univ of St Andrews; Hon DMus: Queen's Univ Belfast 1979, New England Conservatory of Music 1980; Officier de l'Ordre des Arts et des Lettres (France) 1987; *Publications* Flute (Yehudi Menuhin Music Guide Series, 1982), James Galway – An Autobiography (1978), The Man with the Golden Flute – Sir James, A Celtic Minstrel (2009); *Recreations* music, swimming, walking, theatre, films, TV, chess, backgammon, talking to people; *Style—* Sir James Galway, OBE; ✉ c/o International Classical Artists (☎ 00 44 20 3405 6314, website www.icartists.co.uk)

GAMBACCINI, Paul Matthew; s of Mario Matthew Gambaccini, of Westport, CT, and Dorothy, *née* Kiebrick; *b* 2 April 1949; *Educ* Staples HS, Dartmouth Coll (BA), UC Oxford (MA); *m* in NY 2012, Christopher Sherwood (UK civil partnership 2012); *Career* broadcaster and music journalist; with Rolling Stone Magazine 1970–77; host: Ivor Novello Awards 1987–, Music Industry Trust's Man of the Year Award 1997–2012, Sony Radio Awards 1999–2008, BBC Jazz Awards 2005–08, Parliamentary Jazz Awards 2005–12; News Int visiting prof of broadcast media Univ of Oxford 2009; ambass Prince's Tst 2009–; Philanthropist of the Year 1995; Sony Radio Awards: Best Music Broadcaster 2002 (nominated 1999, 2001, 2006, 2008 and 2011), Best Music Documentary 2003, The Gold Award 2007; *Radio* BBC Radio One 1973–86 and 1991–93, BBC Radio Four 1974–, Capital Radio 1986–91, Classic FM 1992–95, 1998–2002 and 2007–08, BBC Radio Three 1995–96, BBC Radio Two 1998–, Jazz FM 2003–05; *Television* incl: Omnibus (BBC 1), Pebble Mill at One (BBC 1), Summer Festivals (BBC 2), The Other Side of the Tracks (Channel 4) 1983–85, TV-am 1983–92, Television's Greatest Hits (BBC 1), GMTV 1993–96, Call My Bluff (BBC) 1998–2003, Sing It Back (ITV) 2007, Celebrity Mastermind (BBC) 2010 (winner); *Books* Guinness Book of British Hit Singles (co-ed, 10 edns), Guinness Book of British Hit Albums (co-ed, 7 edns), Radio Boy (1986), Television's Greatest Hits (1993), Love Letters (1996), Close Encounters (1998), Theatre: The Ultimate Man (co-author, 2000), Love, Paul Gambaccini (2015); *Recreations* films, theatre, British Softball Federation Hall of Fame 2007, comic books; *Style—* Paul Gambaccini; ☎ 020 7401 6753, e-mail paulgambaccini@hotmail.com

GAMBLE, Prof Andrew Michael; s of Marcus Elkington Gamble, of Sevenoaks, Kent, and Joan, *née* Westall; *b* 15 August 1947; *Educ* Brighton Coll, Queens' Coll Cambridge (BA), Univ of Durham (MA), Gonville & Caius Coll Cambridge (PhD); *m* 15 June 1974, Christine Jennifer, da of Allan Edwin Rodway; 1 s (Thomas Simon b 7 March 1977), 2 da (Corinna Lucy b 25 Feb 1980, Sarah Eleanor b 3 August 1983); *Career* Univ of Sheffield: lectr in politics 1973–82, reader 1982–86, prof 1986–, pro-vice-chllr 1994–98; visiting prof: Univ of Kobe 1990, Univ of Hitotsubashi 1992, Univ of Chuo 1994; dir Political Econ Res Centre 1998–; Isaac Deutscher Meml Prize 1972, Mitchell Prize 1977; memb: Political Studies Assoc, Br Int Studies Assoc; jt ed: Political Quarterly, New Political Economy; FRSA 1999, FBA 2000, AcSS 2002; *Books* The Conservative Nation (1974), Britain in Decline (1981), The Free Economy and the Strong State (1988), Hayek: The Iron Cage of Liberty (1996), Politics and Fate (2000), Between Europe and America: The Future of British Politics (2003); *Recreations* music, books, walking; *Style—* Prof Andrew Gamble; ✉ Department of Politics, University of Sheffield, Sheffield S10 2TU (☎ 0114 222 1651, fax 0114 273 9769)

GAMBLE, David Martin; s of Rev Alfred Edward Gamble, of Scotland, and Yvonne, *née* Cornforth (d 1973); *b* 10 March 1953; *Educ* Soham Village Coll, Ealing Sch of Photography; *m* Lora Fox Gamble; 1 s (Zachariah Fox Gamble); *Career* photographer Observer Life Magazine 1984–; other magazines incl: Independent, Sunday Times, Telegraph, Traveller Magazine, Time-Life, Fortune (NY), Paris Match, The New Yorker Magazine, Newsweek (NY); photographic subjects incl: Martin Amis, The Dalai Lama, José Carreras, Lord (Jacob) Rothschild, Robet Altman, Alan Rickman, Karsh of Ottowa; exhibitions incl: Arles 1987 (jtly), Assoc of Photographers Gallery 1987, Kodak Euro Exhibition 1988, World Press Awards 1989, Les Portes d'Europe (Provence) 1992; winner Kodak Grande Prix Euro Award France 1987; film documentary: Faces 1989, Groucho, Portraits Exhibition London 1996; exhibition Andy Warhol House 1998; memb AFAEP; painter; pt/t artist in residence École National de la Photographie; *Recreations* watching cricket, jazz, photography; *Clubs* Groucho; *Style—* David Gamble, Esq; ☎ 020 7284 0757

GAMBLE, Richard Arthur; s of Arthur Gamble (d 1985), of New Malden, Surrey, and Grace Emily, *née* Little (d 1997); *b* 19 September 1939; *Educ* Raynes Park County GS; *m* 26 April 1966, Elizabeth Ann, da of Edward Godwin Atkyns; 2 s (Simon b 1967, James b 1970); *Career* articled clerk W J Gilbert & Co CAs London 1957–62, asst mangr Turquand Youngs & Co CAs 1962–66, dir and co sec Lee Davy Gp Ltd 1966–68, dir and sec Hamilton Smith Lloyd's Brokers 1968–70, fin dir Lowndes Lambert Intl Lloyd's Brokers 1970–76, European fin dir Data 100/Northern Telecom Systems 1976–80, fin dir McDonnell Douglas Information Systems and dir McDonnell Douglas UK 1980–84, dep chief fin offr Br Airways 1984–89; Royal Insurance Hldgs plc: gp fin dir 1989–91, gp chief operating offr 1991, gp chief exec 1992–96; gp chief exec Royal & Sun Alliance Insurance Gp plc 1996–98; non-exec chm Denne Gp Ltd 2001–03 (non-exec advsr 1999–2001); non-exec dir: Excel Airways Gp plc 2003–06, Highway Insurance Hldgs plc 2003–08 (chm 2006–08), Equity Syndicate Mgmnt Ltd Lloyds Syndicate 2011–13; chm The Policyholders' Protection Bd 1994–98, memb Advsy Ctee on Business and the Environment (ACBE) (chm Fin Sector Working Gp 1993–96), dir Assoc of Br Insurers 1992–96; tstee Crimestoppers 1995–, pres GB Wheelchair Basketball Assoc 1997–; govr RSC 1997–2002; FCA, CIMgt; *Recreations* watching all sports, playing golf, walking, theatre, family, cricket, motorsport, music, opera, tennis, travel; *Clubs* Beaconsfield Golf, Falmouth Rugby (vice-pres), Falmouth Cricket (vice-pres); *Style—* Richard Gamble, Esq; ✉ 77 St John's Road, Penn, Buckinghamshire HP10 8HU

GAMBLE, Thomas (Tom); s of Thomas Gamble (d 1987), of Stockton-on-Tees, and Dorothy, *née* Naylor (d 1986); *b* 6 February 1924; *Career* artist; served RN 1942–46; formerly sr lectr Loughborough Coll of Art and Design; Turner Award and Medal 2012; Freeman City of London, Liveryman and Gold Medalist Worshipful Co of Painter/Stainers; memb Artworkers' Guild, fell Royal Watercolour Soc; *Exhibitions* incl: Royal Acad, Royal Watercolour Soc, Bankside Gallery (Sunday Times and Singer & Friedlander), Hunting Gp Prizes, Royal Festival Hall, The Arts Club, Painters Hall, Paterson's Gallery Albermarle St London, Brian Sinfield, Milne and Moller, Burlington Fine Art, Woodgates Gallery East Bergholt, American Watercolour Soc, Canadian Watercolour Soc, Exposicion Internacional de Acuarela Barcelona; *Work in Collections* incl Lloyd's of London, Middlesbrough Art Gallery, Loughborough Univ of Technol, Leics CC, Notts CC, Arts Club, Intelligence Corps and several private galleries; *Clubs* Arts; *Style—* Tom Gamble, Esq, RWS; ✉ 10 Blythe Green, East Perry, Huntingdon, Cambridgeshire PE28 0BJ (☎ 01480 810468)

GAMBLES, Dr Ian; *Educ* Balliol Coll Oxford (BA), Georgetown Univ (MSc), Princeton Univ (PhD); *Career* former dir of nat infrastructure Planning Inspectorate Dept for Communities and Local Govt, dir Forestry Cmmn England 2013–; *Books* Making the Business Case (2009); *Style—* Dr Ian Gambles; ✉ Forestry Commission, Foss House, King's Pool, 1–2 Peasholme Green, York YO1 7PX

GAMBON, Sir Michael John; kt (1998), CBE (1990); s of Edward Gambon, and Mary Gambon; *b* 19 October 1940; *Educ* St Aloysius Sch for Boys London; *m* 1962, Anne Miller; *Career* actor; formerly engrg apprentice; Liveryman Worshipful Co of Gunmakers; Hon DLitt 2002; *Theatre* incl: first stage appearance Edwards/Mac Liammoir Dublin 1962, Nat Theatre, Old Vic 1963–67, RSC Aldwych 1970–72, Norman Conquests (Globe) 1974, Otherwise Engaged (Queen's) 1976, Just Between Ourselves (Queen's) 1977, Alice's Boys (Savoy) 1978; National Theatre: Galileo 1980 (London Theatre Critics' Best Actor Award), Betrayal 1980, Tales From Hollywood 1980, A Chorus of Disapproval 1985 (Olivier Best Comedy Performance Award), Tons of Money 1986, A View from the Bridge 1987 (Evening Standard Best Actor Award, Olivier Award, Plays and Players London Theatre Critics' Award, Variety Club Best Stage Actor Award), A Small Family Business 1987, Mountain Language 1988, Skylight (Olivier Award nomination for Best Actor 1996) 1995, Volpone (Evening Standard Best Actor Award) 1995; King Lear and Cleopatra (RSC Stratford and Barbican) 1982–83, Old Times (Haymarket) 1985, Uncle Vanya (Vaudeville) 1988, Veterans' Day (Haymarket) 1989, title role in Othello 1990, Taking Steps 1990, Man of the Moment (Globe) 1990, Tom Driberg MP in Tom and Clem (Aldwych) 1997, The Unexpected Man (Duchess) 1998, Juno and the Paycock (Dublin) 1999, Cressida (Albery) 2000, The Caretaker (Comedy Theatre, Variety Club Best Stage Actor Award) 2000, Henry IV Parts One and Two (RNT) 2005; *Television* incl: The Singing Detective 1986 (BAFTA Best Actor Award 1987), Maigret (Granada) 1991, The Entertainer (BBC) 1993, Faith (Central) 1994, Wives and Daughters (BBC) 1999 (BAFTA Best Actor Award, Royal Television Soc Best Actor Award), Longitude (Granada) 1999 (BAFTA Best Actor Award), Family Tree 2000, Endgame (Beckett on Film series) 2001, Perfect Strangers 2001, Path To War 2002, The Lost Prince 2003, Angels in America 2003, Joe's Palace 2007, Cranford 2007, Emma 2009, Doctor Who 2010; *Films* incl: The Cook, The Thief, His Wife and Her Lover 1989, The Heat of the Day 1989, Paris by Night 1989, A Dry White Season 1990, Mobsters 1990, Toys 1991, Clean Slate 1992, Indian Warrior 1993, Browning Version 1993, Two Deaths 1994, Man Of No Importance 1994, Bullet To Beijing 1994, Midnight In Moscow 1994, The Innocent Sleep 1995, Mary

Reilly 1996, Nothing Personal 1996, The Gambler 1997, Sleepy Hollow 1997, Last September 1998, Dancing at Laugnasa 1998, Plunkett and Macleane 1998, The Insider 1998, End Game 1999, High Heels – Low Life 2000, Charlotte Gray 2000, Gosford Park 2001, Ali G The Movie 2000, The Actors 2002, Open Range 2003, Sylvia 2003, Harry Potter and the Prisoner of Azkaban 2004, Being Julia 2004, Sky Captain and the World of Tomorrow 2004, Layer Cake 2004, The Life Aquatic with Steve Zissou 2004, Harry Potter and the Goblet of Fire 2005, The Omen 2006, Amazing Grace 2006, The Good Night 2007, Harry Potter and the Order of the Phoenix 2007, Brideshead Revisited 2008, Harry Potter and the Half-Blood Prince 2009, Fantastic Mr Fox 2009, The Book of Eli 2010, The King's Speech 2010, 2010 Harry Potter and the Deathly Hallows: Part 1 2010; *Recreations* flying, gun collecting, clock making; *Style—* Sir Michael Gambon, CBE; ✉ c/o Independent Talent, Oxford House, 76 Oxford Street, London W1N 0AX (✆ 020 7636 6565, fax 020 7323 0101)

GAMMELL, Sir William (Bill); kt (2006); *b* 29 December 1952; *Educ* Fettes, Univ of Stirling (BA); *m* Janice; 3 s, 1 step s; *Career* fndr and chief exec Cairn Energy plc 1980–, non-exec chm Cairn India; dir: Scottish Inst of Sport 1999–2008, Artemis VCT Tst 2003–09, sportscotland 2008–; fndr and chm Winning Scotland Fndn 2006–; memb: Br Olympic Advsy Bd 2006–, Govt Asia Task Force 2007–, UK Indian Business Cncl 2007–; Ernst & Young UK Entrepreneur of the Year 2004, Business Insider Elite Leader of the Year 2004, IOD Scotland Dir of the Year 2006, Entrepreneurial Exchange Hall of Fame 2006; Hon DBA Napier Univ 2005, Hon DUniv Stirling 2006, Hon DEng Heriot Watt Univ 2007, Hon DEd Univ of Abertay 2009; formerly rugby player, memb Scotland nat team 1977–80; *Style—* Sir Bill Gammell; ✉ Cairn Energy plc, 50 Lothian Road, Edinburgh EH3 9BY (✆ 0131 475 3000, fax 0131 475 3030)

GAMMIE, Malcolm James; CBE (2005), QC (2002); s of Maj James Ian Gammie, MC (d 1987), of Bickley, Kent, and Florence Mary, *née* Wiggs (d 2016); *b* 18 February 1951; *Educ* Edge Grove Sch Aldenham, Merchant Taylors', Sidney Sussex Coll Cambridge (MA); *m* 21 Dec 1974, Rosalind Anne, da of William James Rowe (d 1997), of Bromley, Kent; 3 da (Helen Victoria b 10 Feb 1979, Isabel Margaret Ruth b 19 Feb 1985, Catharine Alice Louise b 17 Feb 1988), 1 s (Christopher James b 18 May 1981); *Career* called to the Bar Middle Temple 1997; judge First-tier Tbnl (Tax Chamber) and p/t judge Upper Tbnl (Tax and Chancery) 2009–; Linklaters & Paines: articled clerk 1973–75, slr Tax Dept 1975–78 and 1985–87, ptnr 1987–97; dep head of Tax Dept CBI 1978–79; dir: Nat Tax Office Thomson McLintock & Co 1979–84, Nat Tax Servs KMG Thomson McLintock 1984–85; ed Law and Tax Review 1982–88, contrib to Financial Times on tax matters 1983–87; memb 1987–97: Special Ctee of Tax Law Consultative Bodies, Taxation Ctee IOD, City of London Slrs Co; chm Law Soc's Revenue Law Ctee 1996–97; Inst for Fiscal Studies: memb Cncl 1985–2001, chm Capital Taxes Working Pty 1986–92, chm Exec Ctee 1991–97; Chartered Inst of Taxation: memb Cncl 1983–96, chm Tech Ctee 1990–92 and 1994–95, pres 1993–94; memb Perm Scientific Ctee Int Fiscal Assoc 1998–2008 (former vice-chm Br Branch Ctee); memb Cabinet Office: Taxation Deregulation Gp 1993–97, Fiscal Studies Working Pty Advsy Cncl on Sci & Technol 1993; Inst for Fiscal Studies (IFS) Tax Law Review Ctee: memb 1994–97, research dir 1997–2014, chm 2014–; London C of C and Industry: former memb, memb Cncl 1989–92, chm Taxation Ctee 1989–92; dep special cmmr and pt/t chm VAT & Duties Tbnl 2002–09; sec and memb Cncl Assoc of Taxation Technicians 1989–91, memb Tax Professionals' Forum 2010–; visiting professorial fell Centre for Commercial Law Studies QMC London, research fell Inst for Fiscal Studies 1997–, Unilever prof of int business law Leiden Univ The Netherlands 1998, visiting prof of int tax law Univ of Sydney 2000 and 2002, visiting prof of tax law LSE 2000–, adjunct prof of tax law Sydney Univ 2008–; memb Soc for Advanced Legal Studies 1997–; FRSA 1993; *Books* Taxation Publishing, Tax on Company Reorganisations (with Susan Ball, 1980, 2 edn 1982), Tax Strategy for Companies (1981, 3 edn 1986), Stock Relief (with D Williams, 1981), Tax Focus on Interest and Discounts (with D Williams, 1983), Tax Strategy for Directors, Executives and Employees (1983, 2 edn 1985), Land Taxation (ed, 1985–), Whiteman on Capital Gains Tax (with P Whiteman, QC, and Mark Herbert, 1988), The Process of Tax Reform in the United Kingdom (1990); Butterworths Tax Handbooks (conslt ed, 1994–2004); *Recreations* music, church architecture; *Style—* Malcolm Gammie, Esq, CBE, QC; ✉ Chambers of Lord Grabiner, QC, 1 Essex Court, Temple, London EC4Y 9AR (✆ 020 7583 2000, fax 020 7583 0118, e-mail mgammie@compuserve.com, websites www.malcolmgammie.com and www.oeclaw.co.uk)

GAMMON, Philip Greenway; s of Stanley Arthur John Gammon (d 1979), of Chippenham, Wilts, and Phyllis Joyce, *née* Paul (d 1998); *b* 17 May 1940, Chippenham, Wilts; *Educ* Chippenham GS, Royal Acad of Music (scholar), Badische Musikhochschule Karlsruhe; *m* 1963, Floretta, da of Konstantin Volovinis; 2 s (Paul Christopher b 1968, Anthony John b 1970); *Career* pianist; dep piano teacher Royal Acad of Music and Royal Scottish Acad of Music 1964, pianist Royal Ballet Covent Garden 1964–68, princ pianist Ballet For All 1968–71, pianist Royal Ballet 1971–2005 (princ pianist 1999–2005); solo pianist and conductor London Contemporary Dance 1979; tours of many countries incl Brazil, USSR, Aust, China, Japan, S Korea, Argentina and Israel; first orchestral arrangement of La Chatte Metamorphosée en Femme by Offenbach (Staatsoper Vienna, Royal Opera House Covent Garden) 1985, arrangement of MacMillan's Winter Dreams by Tchaikovsky 1991; ARCM 1968, FRAM 2002 (ARAM 1991); *Performances* major solo performances with Royal Ballet incl: The Four Temperaments 1973, Elite Syncopations 1974, A Month in the Country 1976, La Fin du Jour 1979, Rhapsody 1980, Return to the Strange Land 1984, Rubies 1989, Winter Dreams 1991, Ballet Imperial 1994, Duo Concertant 1995, Mr Worldly Wise 1996, Marguerite and Armand 2000, Symphonic Variations 2000, The Concert 2000, Ballet Imperial, Rhapsody, Symphonic Variations, Dances at a Gathering; other performances as solo pianist incl: concert for 50th Anniversary of Royal Ballet (with Royal Liverpool Philharmonic Orchestra, Philharmonic Hall Liverpool) 1981, gala performance celebrating 100 years of Performing Arts (Metropolitan Opera House NY) 1984, meml serv for Sir Frederick Ashton Westminster Abbey 1988, meml serv for Dame Margot Fonteyn 1991 and for Sir Kenneth MacMillan 1993 Westminster Abbey, Symphony Hall Birmingham, Queen Elizabeth Hall (part of Sir Roger Norrington's Tchaikovsky Week-End) 1998; as conductor incl: Coppélia (Ballet for All, debut, Theatre on the Green Richmond) 1970, Royal Ballet Touring Company 1976, Sleeping Beauty (Royal Ballet, Royal Opera House debut) 1978, Royal Ballet Sch performances (Royal Opera House) 1987, 1989, 1990 and 1992, Chance to Dance ROH Educn 2002 and 2005; conducting assignments with Royal Ballet incl: Ondine 1989, The Planets 1990, The Prince of the Pagodas 1990; recent guest conducting assignments incl: Hong Kong Ballet (Grand Cultural Centre Hong Kong) 1996, Nat Ballet of Portugal (San Carlos Theatre and Centro Cultural de Belém Lisbon) 1997, Rivoli Theatre Porto 1998; *Awards* Assoc Bd Gold medal Grade 8 1954, Recital Diploma 1960, Walter MacFarren Gold medal 1961, Karlsruhe Culture prize 1962, Performer's Dip Badische Musikhochschule Karlsruhe 1963, Royal Ballet Gold Medal 2011; *Recordings* incl: Elite Syncopations (Continental Record Distributors), A Month in the Country (EMI Int Classical Div), Winter Dreams (NVC Arts, Teldec Video), Marguerite et Armand (Liszt sonata DVD) 2004; presenter Music and Reminiscence (memoirs with Royal Ballet and music); *Recreations* walking, reading, holidaying in Greece; *Style—* Philip Gammon, Esq; ✉ 19 Downs Avenue, Pinner, Middlesex HA5 5AQ (✆ 020 8866 3260, e-mail pggammon@gmail.com)

GANDY, David James; s of Christopher Gandy, and Brenda, *née* Rabey; *b* 19 February 1980, London; *Educ* Billericay Sch, Cheltenham Univ; *Career* model; various worldwide campaigns incl: Light Blue and Light Blue 2 Dolce & Gabbana 2007 and 2009, Martini 2011, M&S Collezione 2012; guest ed ES Magazine, writer Vogue.com, GQ magazine and GQ.com 2010, other appearances in V Man, Details, Shortlist Mode, L'Officiel Hommes, Velour, Tetu, Twist and Style Man; spoken at Oxford Union, memb Ctee London's Collections, ambass Battersea Dogs Home; GQ Int Man of the Year, Glamour Int Man of the Year, Shortlist Award; *Recreations* sport, food and drink, cars, watches, motor racing; *Style—* Mr David Gandy; ✉ c/o Heidi Beattie, Select Model Management, 27–35 Mortimer Street, London W1T 3JG (e-mail heidi@selectmodel.com); c/o Charl Hickson (e-mail charl@monsta.biz)

GANELLIN, Prof (Charon) Robin; s of Leon Ganellin (d 1969), and Beila, *née* Cluer (d 1972); *b* 25 January 1934, London; *Educ* Harrow Co GS, QMC London (BSc, PhD), Univ of London (DSc); *m* 1, 27 Dec 1956, Tamara (d 1997), da of Jacob Greene (d 1988); 1 da (Nicole b 1960), 1 s (Mark b 1963); *m* 2, 23 July 2003, Monique, da of Gérard Lehmann (d 2005); *Career* res chemist Smith Kline & French Labs Ltd 1958–59, res assoc MIT 1960, vice-pres Smith Kline & French Research Ltd 1984–86 (vice-pres res 1980–84, dir 1978–86, head of chemistry 1962–78, medicinal chemist 1961–62); Smith Kline & French prof of medicinal chemistry UCL 1986–2003 (emeritus prof of medicinal chemistry 2003–), dir Upjohn Euro Discovery Unit UCL 1987–93; hon prof Univ of Kent 1979–89; chm Soc for Drug Res 1985–87; pres IUPAC Medicinal Chemistry 2000–01, chm IUPAC Sub Ctee of Medicinal Chemistry and Drug Devpt 2002–12; Prix Charles Mentzer 1978; Royal Soc of Chemistry: Medicinal Chemistry Medal 1977, Tilden Medal 1982, Adrien Albert Medal 1999; Div of Medicinal Chemistry Award American Chemical Soc 1980, Soc Chemistry Indust Messel Medal 1988, Soc for Drug Res Award for Drug Discovery 1989, USA Nat Inventors Hall of Fame 1990, Nauta Award for Pharmacochemistry from the European Fedn for Medicinal Chemistry 2004, Pratesi Medal Medicinal Chemistry Div Societa Chimica Italiano 2006, American Chemical Soc Div of Medicinal Chemistry Hall of Fame 2007; fell Queen Mary & Westfield Coll London 1992, emeritus fell IUPAC Div VII 2014; Hon DSc Aston Univ 1995; hon memb European Histamine Research Soc 2007; FRSC 1968, FRS 1986, CSci 2004, foreign corresponding academician Spanish Royal Acad of Pharmacy 2006; *Books* Pharmacology of Histamine Receptors (1982), Frontiers in Histamine Research (1985), Dictionary of Drugs (1990), Medicinal Chemistry (1993), Dictionary of Pharmacological Agents (1997), Analogue-based Drug Discovery (2006, Vol II 2010, Vol III 2013), Practical Studies in Medicinal Chemistry (web edn, 2007, print edn 2011), Introduction to Biological and Small Molecule Drug Research and Development: theory and case studies (jt ed, 2013), Analogue-based Drug Discovery, Vol III (2013); *Recreations* music, sailing, walking, theatre; *Clubs* Royal Soc; *Style—* Prof Robin Ganellin, FRS; ✉ Department of Chemistry, University College London, 20 Gordon Street, London WC1H 0AJ (✆ 020 7679 4624, e-mail c.r.ganellin@ucl.ac.uk)

GANESH, Janan; *b* 18 February 1982, Nigeria; *Career* researcher Policy Exchange 2005–07, political corr The Economist 2007–12, currently political columnist FT; *Style—* Janan Ganesh, Esq; ✉ Financial Times, Number One Southwark Bridge, London SE1 9HL

GANGULI, Pablo; *b* 23 November 1983, Kolkata, India; *Career* entrepreneur and festival dir; fndr: Liberatum, Connect UK 2002; creator and dir of several festivals and special UK cultural diplomacy celebrations (arts, opera, literature, film, fashion, design) in Papua New Guinea, New Delhi, Mumbai, Moscow, St Petersburg and Marrakech 2001–09, ventures in Brazil, USA, Spain, China, Turkey and Italy 2010–11; *Style—* Pablo Ganguli, Esq

GANS-LARTEY, Joseph Kojo; s of Charles Botway Lartey (d 1977), of Ghana, and Felicia Adoley, *née* Gans-Boye (d 1995); *b* 28 August 1951; *Educ* Presbyterian Secdy Sch X'Borg Accra Ghana, Croydon Coll Surrey (HNC), Ealing Coll of Higher Educn (LLB), LSE (LLM); *m* 28 Oct 1978, Rosmarie, da of Harold Ramrattan (d 1987), of Trinidad and Tobago; 1 da (Josephine Annmarie Laatele b 11 Sept 1985), 1 s (Charles Andrew b 10 April 1990); *Career* sr enrolled psychiatric nurse 1978–82 (trainee 1974–76, enrolled 1976–78), sr legal asst RAC 1985–86, crown prosecutor 1986–, sr crown prosecutor 1989–, princ crown prosecutor 1990–, prosecution team ldr 1995, borough crown prosecutor 2005; memb: Hon Soc of Lincoln's Inn 1983, Bar of Trinidad and Tobago 1984; nominated a Times Lawyer of the Week 2000; *Recreations* sports, international relations, reading, writing, parenting; *Style—* Joseph Gans-Lartey, Esq; ✉ The Crown Prosecution Service, 12th Floor, Southern House, Wellesley Grove, Croydon CR9 1DY (✆ 020 8662 2880, fax 020 8662 2843, e-mail ganslartey@aol.com)

GAPES, Michael John (Mike); MP; s of Frank late Gapes, and Emily Gapes; *b* 4 September 1952; *Educ* Buckhurst Hill County HS, Fitzwilliam Coll Cambridge (MA), Middx Poly; *Career* VSO teacher Swaziland 1971–72, sec Cambridge Students' Union 1973–74, chm Nat Orgn of Lab Students 1976 (vice-chm 1975); Lab Pty: nat student organiser 1977–80, research offr Int Dept 1980–88, sr int offr 1988–92; Parly candidate (Lab) Ilford N 1983, MP (Lab/Co-op Pty) Ilford S 1992–; PPS to Paul Murphy, MP, *qv*, 1997–99, PPS to Rt Hon Lord Rooker, *qv*, 2001–02; chm Foreign Affairs Select Ctee 2005–10 (memb 1992–97 and 2010–), memb Defence Select Ctee 1999–2001 and 2003–05; chm UN Parly Gp 1997–2001; vice-chair PLP Defence Ctee 1992–94 and 1996–97, chair PLP Children and Families Ctee 1993–94; chm Westminster Fndn for Democracy 2002–05; memb: Co-op Pty, UNITE; vice-pres Ilford Football Club; memb: RIIA 1996–, Cncl RIIA 1996–99, Cncl VSO 1997–2011; *Recreations* watching football and cricket, blues and jazz music; *Clubs* West Ham Supporters', Ilford and Woodford Royal Airforce Assoc; *Style—* Mike Gapes, Esq, MP; ✉ House of Commons, London SW1A 0AA (✆ 020 7219 6485, fax 020 7219 0978, e-mail mike.gapes.mp@parliament.uk)

GARBUTT, Graham Bernard; *b* 16 June 1947; *Educ* Univ of Bath (BSc, BArch), Univ of Sheffield (MA); *Career* urban renewal co-ordinator Haringey BC 1974–80, policy and prog planning offr Hackney BC 1980–87, dir S Canning Town and Custom House Project Newham BC 1987–90, chief exec Gloucester City Cncl 1990–2001, regnl dir Govt Office for W Midlands ODPM 2001–05, ceo Countryside Agency/Cmmr for Rural Communities 2005–09, UK rep EUROPA Univs Network 2010–; England rep European Assoc of State Territorial Representatives 2002–05 (pres 2005); advsr OECD Territorial Review of Chile 2009–10, chair Cheltenham Devpt Task Force 2010–; visiting lectr AA Grad Sch 1976–82, visiting prof of governance and devpt Univ of W of England 2010–; patron Friends of Cheltenham CAB 2010–11; *Recreations* family, visual arts, architecture, cycling, garden; *Style—* Graham Garbutt, Esq; ✉ Faculty of Environment and Technology, Frenchay Campus, Coldharbour Lane, Bristol BS16 1QY (e-mail graham.garbutt@uwe.ac.uk)

GARBUTT, John; *b* 14 June 1954; *Educ* LSE; *m* 14 June 2014, Solangela, *née* Tangarife; 1 s (Simon b 1989); *Career* investment analyst Rowe & Pitman Hurst-Brown 1975–77, pension fund mangr ICI 1977–79, investment and unit tst mangr Touche Remnant 1979–84, institutional fund mangr Schroders 1984–87, dir Institutional Funds Kleinwort Benson Investment Mgmnt 1987–91, dir Asset Mgmnt HSBC 1991–2013; non-exec dir and chm Remuneration Ctee Stobart Gp 2014–; memb: UK Soc of Investment Professionals, CFA Inst of the UK; visiting prof and memb Advsy Bd Faculty of Business and Law London Met Univ, hon visiting prof Univ of West London; memb Cncl Royal Soc of St George (City Branch), vice-chm Parochial Church Cncl and churchwarden St Stephen Walbrook Church, alderman Walbrook Ward in the City of London; chm Int Students Tst, life vice-pres Br Red Cross, tstee Asthma UK; Liveryman: Worshipful Co of Weavers (Renter Bailiff), Worshipful Co of Joiners and Ceilers (ct asst), Worshipful

Co of Int Bankers; ct asst Guild of Freemen of the City of London; FCISI, FRSA, FRGS; *Recreations* travel, ethnic art, chess; *Clubs* City Livery (sr pres), Walbrook Ward (pres), Coleman Street Ward, Ward of Cheap; *Style—* John Garbutt, Esq; ✉ Stobart Group Ltd, 22 Soho Square, London W1D 4NS

GARBUTT, Nicholas Martin Antony; s of Anthony Joseph Garbutt, of Manchester, and Norah, *née* Payne; *b* 21 June 1959; *Educ* Xaverian Coll Manchester, Oriel Coll Oxford (BA, Judo half blue); *m* 3 Sept 1988, Frances, da of Francis Burscough, of Preston; *Career* journalist; reporter: Ashton-under-Lyme Reporter 1980–83, Chester Evening Leader 1983–84, Telegraph and Argus Bradford 1984; mgmnt trainee Liverpool Echo 1987–88 (reporter 1984–87), news ed Daily Post Liverpool 1988–89, asst ed Sunday Tribune Dublin 1989–90, ed The Irish News Belfast 1990–94, dep ed Belfast Telegraph 1994–96, dir of business devpt Belfast Telegraph Newspapers 1996–99, head of corp relations for Ireland Nat Australia Bank 1999, head of corp relations for Europe Nat Australia Bank 2000–02, md Asitis Consulting 2004–; *Recreations* study of Irish History and Culture, martial arts; *Style—* Nicholas Garbutt, Esq

GARDAM, Jane Mary; OBE (2009); da of William Pearson (d 1988), of Coatham, N Yorkshire, and Kathleen Mary, *née* Helm (d 1988); *b* 11 July 1928; *Educ* Saltburn HS for Girls, Bedford Coll London; *m* 20 April 1954, David Hill Gardam, QC, *qv*, s of Harry Hill Gardam; 2 s (Tim, *qv*, b 1956, Thomas b 1965), 1 da (Catharine b 1958); *Career* novelist; travelling librarian Red Cross Hospital Libraries 1951, sub ed Weldon's Ladies Jl 1952, asst literary ed Time and Tide 1952–54; memb Ctee: NSPCC, PEN; HonDLitt Univ of Teesside 2002; FRSL 1976–81; *Novels* A Long Way from Verona (1971), The Summer After the Funeral (1973), Bilgewater (1977), God on the Rocks (1978), The Hollow Land (1981, Whitbread Award), Bridget and William (1981), Horse (1982), Kit (1983), Crusoe's Daughter (1985), Kit in Boots (1986), Swan (1987), Through The Doll's House Door (1987), The Queen of the Tambourine (1991, Whitbread Award), Faith Fox (1996), The Green Man (1998), The Flight of the Maidens (2001); trilogy: Old Filth (2009), The Man in the Wooden Hat (2011), Last Friends (2013); *Short Stories* A Few Fair Days (1971), Black Faces, White Faces (1975, David Highams Award, Winifred Holtby Award), The Sidmouth Letters (1980), The Pangs of Love (1983, Katherine Mansfield Award 1984), Showing The Flag (1989), Going in to a Dark House (1994, PEN Silver Pen Award), Missing the Midnight (1997); *Non-Fiction* The Iron Coast (1994); *Recreations* botanical; *Clubs* Arts, PEN, University Women's; *Style—* Jane Gardam, OBE; ✉ Haven House, Sandwich, Kent CT13 9ES (☎ office 01304 612680)

GARDAM, Timothy David; s of David Hill Gardam, QC, of Sandwich, and Jane Gardam, FRSL, *qqv*, *née* Pearson; *b* 14 January 1956; *Educ* Westminster, Gonville & Caius Coll Cambridge (MA); *m* Kim Scott (d 2002), da of Capt Gordon Walwyn, RN, CVO, of Warblington; 2 da; *Career* BBC: trainee 1977, prodr Newsnight 1979–82, exec prodr Timewatch 1982–85, exec prodr Bookmark 1984–85, output ed Newsnight 1985–86, dep ed Gen Election 1987, ed Panorama 1987–90, ed Newsnight 1990–93, head of weekly progs News & Current Affrs 1994–96; controller of news, current affairs and documentaries Channel 5 Broadcasting 1996–98, dir of progs Channel Four TV 1998–2002, dir of TV Channel Four 2002–03; princ St Anne's Coll Oxford 2004–, chair Reuters Inst for the Study of Journalism Univ of Oxford; non-exec dir SMG plc until 2007, non-exec memb Bd Ofcom 2008–; *Recreations* gardening, ruins; *Style—* Timothy Gardam, Esq; ✉ St Anne's College, Oxford OX2 6HS

GARDEN, Dr (David) Graeme; OBE (2011); s of Robert Symon Garden (d 1982), of Preston, Lancs, and Janet Anne, *née* McHardy; *b* 18 February 1943; *Educ* Repton, Emmanuel Coll Cambridge (BA), King's Coll Hosp (MB BChir); *m* 1, 16 March 1968 (m dis 1981), (Mary) Elizabeth, da of Clive Wheatley Grice (d 1979); 1 s (John b 9 June 1975), 1 da (Sally b 2 April 1971); m 2, 12 Feb 1983, Emma, da of John David Valentine Williams; 1 s (Thomas b 2 Dec 1984); *Career* actor and writer; writer and performer: I'm Sorry I'll Read That Again (radio), I'm Sorry I Haven't A Clue (radio), The Goodies (TV), Do Go On (radio), The Motion Show (radio), If I Ruled the World (TV); writer for TV with Bill Oddie: Doctor In The House, Doctor At Large, The Astronauts; presenter Bodymatters BBC TV; theatre: NT, Royal Court, Royal Exchange Manchester, Cambridge Theatre Co; author: The Magic Olympical Games (NT), Horse and Carriage (play); writer and dir trg films Video Arts; *Books* The Seventh Man (1981), The Skylighters (1987), Stovold's Mornington Crescent Almanac (2002); *Recreations* TV, fishing; *Style—* Dr Graeme Garden, OBE; ✉ c/o Emma Darrell Management, North Vale, Shire Lane, Chorleywood, Hertfordshire WD3 5NH (☎ 01923 284061, fax 01923 284064)

GARDEN, Prof (Olivier) James; CBE (2014); s of James Garden, OBE, (d 1992) and Marguerite Marie Jeanne, *née* Vourc'h (d 2010); *b* 13 November 1953; *Educ* Lanark GS, Univ of Edinburgh (BSc, MB ChB, MD); *m* 15 July 1977, Amanda Gillian, da of late Austin Merrills, OBE, of Dunbar; 1 s (Stephen James b 21 July 1988), 1 da (Katherine Laura b 13 Aug 1991); *Career* lectr in surgery Univ Dept of Surgery Glasgow Royal Infirmary 1985–88, chef de clinique Unit de Chrurgie Hepatobiliare Hôpital Paul Brousse Villejuif France 1986–87; Univ Dept of Surgery Royal Infirmary Edinburgh: sr lectr in surgery 1988–97, prof of hepatobiliary surgery 1997–2000, regius prof of clinical surgery 2000–; clinical dir Scottish Liver Transplant Unit Royal Infirmary Edinburgh 1994–2005, head Sch of Clinical Sciences and Community Health Univ of Edinburgh 2002–06, dir Masters in Surgical Sciences Univ of Edinburgh 2007–12, dir Surgical Distance Learning Univ of Edinburgh 2010–; surgn to HM The Queen in Scotland 2004–; Br Jl of Surgery Soc Ltd: dir 2002–, co sec 2003–12, chm 2012–; ed-in-chief HPB 2009–19, pres Int Hepato-Panncreato-Biliary Assoc 2012–14; vice-chm Edinburgh World Heritage Tst 2015–; FRCSGlas 1981, FRCSEd 1994, FRCPEd 2003, Hon FRACS 2007, Hon FRCPS (Canada) 2007, FRSE 2013, Hon FACS 2014, Hon FRCSEng 2015, Hon Fell Coll of Surgns of Hong Kong 2015, Hon FRCSI 2015; *Books* Principles and Practice of Surgical Laparoscopy (1994), Intraoperative and Laparoscopic Ultrasonography (1995), Color Atlas of Surgical Diagnosis (1995), A Companion to Specialist Surgical Practice (8 vols, 1997, 5 edn 2013), Liver Metastasis: Biology, Diagnosis and Treatment (1998), General Surgery: Principles and International Practice (2009), Principles and Practice of Surgery (6 edn, 2012); *Recreations* heritage, golf, skiing, food, wine; *Clubs* Craigielaw Golf, New; *Style—* Prof James Garden, CBE; ✉ University Department of Surgery, The Royal Infirmary, Edinburgh EH16 4SA (☎ 0131 242 3614, fax 0131 242 3617, e-mail ojgarden@ed.ac.uk)

GARDEN, Ralph; s of George Garden (d 1996), and Phillippa Mary, *née* Hills; *b* 21 April 1950; *Educ* Robert Gordon's Coll Aberdeen, Univ of Aberdeen (MA); *m* 1978, Katharine Margaret, da of Patrick Linton; 2 s (Philip b 1982, David b 1986), 1 da (Kay b 1983); *Career* various positions rising to client services dir Scottish Widows 1972–96, with Govt Actuary's Dept 1997–98, chief exec Scottish Public Pensions Agency 1998–2005, head of facilities and estates Scottish Exec 2005–09; FFA; *Recreations* golf, curling, hill walking; *Style—* Ralph Garden, Esq

GARDEN OF FROGNAL, Baroness (Life Peer UK 2007), of Hampstead in the London Borough of Camden Susan Elizabeth Garden; PC (2015); *née* Button; da of Henry George Button (d 2008), and Peggy, *née* Heslop (d 1972); *b* 22 February 1944; *Educ* Westonbirt Sch, St Hilda's Coll Oxford (MA); *m* 13 Nov 1965, Timothy Garden (Air Marshal the Lord Garden, KCB, Life Baron, d 2007); 2 da (Hon Alexandra Sarah b 1970, Hon Antonia b 1971); *Career* secdy sch teacher in UK and Germany 1965–85; City and Guilds of London Inst: joined 1988, mangr 1990–2000, conslt 2000–08; chm Assoc of Sr Membs St Hilda's Coll Oxford 1996–2000, tstee Oxford Univ Soc 2001–05 (vice-chm 2005–07); memb Lib Dem Federal Conference Ctee 2004–08; advsr Citizens Advice Bureaux 1982–87, pres Relate Central Middx 1997–2002, caseworker SSAFA 2001–05, Lib Dem whip House of Lords 2008–10, Baroness-in-waiting 2010, Govt whip and spokesperson for DCMS, Dept of Business, Innovation and Skills and DFE 2010–12, Govt whip and spokesperson for Dept of Business, Innovation and Skills, DFE and MOD 2012–13, dir UK-Japan 21st Century Gp 2013–, Govt whip and spokesperson for Women and Equalities, DFE and DEFRA 2014–15, dep chm of Ctees 2015–; memb Cncl Air League 2012–; patron: Hampstead Counselling Service 2009–, UK Defence Forum 2010–; Master World Traders' Co 2008–09 (Liveryman 2000–); FRSA 1993, FCGI 2010, Hon Fell Chartered Inst of Linguists (CIL) 2012; *Clubs* Nat Lib, RAF; *Style—* The Rt Hon the Baroness Garden of Frognal; ✉ House of Lords, London SW1A 0PW (e-mail gardens@parliament.uk or sue.garden@blueyonder.co.uk)

GARDINER, Barry; MP; *b* 10 March 1957; *Educ* Glasgow HS, Haileybury, Univ of St Andrews, Harvard Univ (J F Kennedy scholar), Univ of Cambridge (MA); *m* 29 July 1979, Caroline, *née* Smith; 3 s, 1 da; *Career* former int arbitration company dir, MP (Lab) Brent N 1997–; PPS to Beverley Hughes, MP, *qv*, 2002–06, Parly under sec NI Office 2004–05, Parly under sec DTI 2005–06, Parly under sec of state DEFRA 2006–07, PM's special envoy for forestry 2007–08, PPS to Peter Mandelson, *qv*, BERR 2008–10, Ldr of the Oppn's special envoy for climate change and the environment 2011–13; shadow min of state for natural environment 2013–15, shadow min of state for energy and climate change 2015–, shadow sec of state for int trade 2016–; chair GLOBE Int 2012–13, vice-pres Europe Globe Int 2015–; chair: Lab Friends of Israel, Lab Friends of India, All-Pty Gp on UK India Trade and Investment, All-Pty Parly Gp on Leasehold Reform, All-Pty Gp on Sports and Leisure, All-Pty Gp on Olympics, Public Accounts Select Ctee; Cambridge City Cncl: cncllr 1988–94, mayor 1992–94; fell Linnean Soc; *Recreations* singing in choir, playing music, spending time with family, bird watching, hiking; *Style—* Barry Gardiner, Esq, MP; ✉ House of Commons, London SW1A 0AA (☎ 020 7219 4046, e-mail gardinerb@parliament.uk, website www.barrygardiner.com)

GARDINER, David Alfred William; DL (Berks 1992); s of Neil William Gardiner (d 1973), of Great Auclum, Burghfield Common, Berks, and Norah, *née* Clegg (d 1963); *b* 11 April 1935; *Educ* Winchester, Imperial Coll London, Harvard Business Sch; *m* 1963, Carolyn Georgina, da of Thomas Humphrey Naylor (d 1966), of Ashton, Chester; 2 s (James b 1965, Andrew b 1971), 1 da (Georgina (Mrs Charles Mullins) b 1968); *Career* Lt Grenadier Gds 1953–55; dir Huntley & Palmers Ltd and associated cos 1961–83; farmer and landowner; High Sheriff Berks 1988–89; chm Berks CLA 1989–92, pres Newbury and Royal Co of Berks Show 1993, chm Mid and W Berks Local Access Forum 2003–05; fndr-chm Green Lanes Environmental Action Movement (GLEAM) 1995–, fndr chm Green Lanes Protection Gp 2005–; *Recreations* field sports; *Style—* David Gardiner, Esq, DL; ✉ The Old Rectory, Lilley, Newbury, Berkshire RG20 7HH (☎ and fax 01488 638227, e-mail davidgardiner@waitrose.com)

GARDINER, Sir John Eliot; kt (1998), CBE (1990); s of Rolf Gardiner, and Marabel, *née* Hodgkin; *b* 20 April 1943; *Educ* Bryanston, King's Coll Cambridge (MA), King's Coll London (Cert); *m* 1, 1972 (m dis 1980), Cherryl ffoulkes; m 2, 1981 (m dis 1997), Elizabeth Suzanne, *née* Wilcock; 3 da; m 3, 2001, Isabella de Sabata; *Career* conductor; studied with Thurston Dart 1965–66 and Nadia Boulanger in Paris 1967–68; fndr and artistic dir: Monteverdi Choir 1964, Monteverdi Orchestra 1968, English Baroque Soloists 1978, Orchestre Révolutionnaire et Romantique 1989; youngest conductor Henry Wood Promenade concert Royal Albert Hall 1968; concert debut Wigmore Hall 1966; operatic debut: Sadler's Wells Opera London Coliseum 1969, Royal Festival Hall 1972, Royal Opera House 1973, Vienna Philharmonic 1995, Glyndebourne, London Philharmonic, London Symphony, Berlin Philharmonic 1997, Zurich Opera 1998, La Scala Milan 2001; guest conductor with maj orchestras in: Amsterdam, Paris, Brussels, Geneva, Frankfurt, Dresden, Leipzig, London, Munich, Vienna, Berlin; US/Canadian debuts: Dallas Symphony 1981, San Francisco Symphony 1982, Carnegie Hall NY 1988, Toronto Symphony 1988, Boston Symphony 1991, Cleveland Orchestra 1992, NY Philharmonic 2002, Chicago 2004, Pittsburgh Symphony 2004; Euro music festivals incl: Aix-en-Provence, Aldeburgh, Bath, Berlin, Edinburgh, Flanders, Holland, City of London, Lucerne, Salzburg, BBC Proms; revived works of: Purcell, Handel, Rameau (world stage première of opera Les Boréades in Aix-en-Provence 1982), Berlioz (world première of Messe Solenelle at Westminster Cathedral 1993); princ conductor: CBC Vancouver Orchestra 1980–83, NDR Symphony Orchestra Hamburg 1991–94; Opéra de Lyon: musical dir 1982–88, chef fondateur 1988; artistic dir: Göttingen Handel Festival 1981–90, Veneto Music Festival 1986; performed, recorded and broadcast Bach Cantata Pilgrimage with Monteverdi Choir and English Baroque Soloists 1999–2000; has made over 250 recordings; pres Bach Archive Leipzig 2014; visiting fell Peterhouse Cambridge 2008–09, hon fell King's Coll Cambridge 2014; Hon DUniv Lumière de Lyon 1987, Dr (hc) New England Conservatory of Music Boston 2005, Hon Dr of Musicology Univ of Pavia 2006, Hon DMus Univ of St Andrews 2014, Hon DMus Univ of Cambridge 2015; Commandeur de l'Ordre des Arts et des Lettres (France) 1997 (Officier 1988), Das Verdienst Kreuz 1st Class (Germany) 2005, Chevalier Legion d'Honneur (France) 2010; hon FKC 1992, Hon FRAM 1992, Hon FBA 2015; *Awards* Grand Prix du Disque 1978, 1979, 1980 and 1992, Prix Caecilia 1982, 1983 and 1985, Edison award 1982, 1986, 1987, 1988, 1989, 1996 and 1997, Arturo Toscanini Music Critics award 1985 and 1986, Nat Acad of Recording Arts and Sciences nominations 1986, 1987, 1989, 1997, 2000 and 2001, Deutscher Schallplattenpreis 1986, 1994 and 1997, IRCA prize Helsinki 1987, 15 Gramophone awards incl Record of the Year 1991 and Artist of the Year 1994, Conductor of the Year Cannes Classical Music Awards 1995, Handel Halle Prize 2001, Robert Schumann Prize 2001, La Medalla Internacional Complutense Madrid Univ 2001, Leonie Sonning Prize (Denmark) 2005, Bach-Medaille City of Leipzig 2005, RAM and Kohn Fndn Bach Prize 2008, Special Achievement Award 2010; *Publications* Music in the Castle of Heaven: A Portrait of Johann Sebastian Bach 2013; *Recreations* forestry, organic farming; *Style—* Sir John Eliot Gardiner, CBE

GARDINER, Prof John Graham; s of William Clement Gardiner (d 2003), of Ilkley, W Yorks, and Ellen, *née* Adey (d 1976); *b* 24 May 1939; *Educ* King Edward VI GS Birmingham, Univ of Birmingham (BSc, PhD); *m* 29 Dec 1962, Sheila Joyce, da of Cecil Walter Andrews (d 1958); 2 da (Tabitha Jane b 19 July 1966, Emily Josephine 12 Dec 1972), 1 s (Benjamin John b 21 Oct 1967); *Career* pre-univ apprenticeship GEC Coventry 1957–58, Racal postdoctoral research fell Univ of Birmingham 1964–66, software engr Racal Research Ltd Tewkesbury 1966–68, sr engr Racal (Slough) Ltd 1968; Univ of Bradford: lectr 1968–72, sr lectr 1972–78, reader in electronic engrg 1978–86, chm Postgrad Sch of Info Systems Engrg 1984–88, prof of electronic engrg 1986–, head Dept of Electronic and Electrical Engrg 1993–96, dean of engrg and physical scis 1996–2002, dir Centre for Industrial Collaboration 2006–; hon pres Br Royal Univ Kurdistan 2009–; dir: Aerial Facilities Ltd 1974–90, Nortel (Communications) Ltd 1976–96, Aerial Group Ltd 1990–97, Compec Ltd 1996–, Ventures & Consultancy Bradford Ltd 1996–2005; conslt: Telecommunications Div DTI 1987–96, EC DG XIII 1988–91 and 1994; nat co-ordinator Link Personal Communications Programme 1987–93, chm Professional Gp E8 IEE 1990–93; CEng 1971, MIERE 1971, FIEE 1984 (MIEE 1971), FREng 1994, SMIEEE 1996, FRSA 1996; *Books* Mobile Communication Systems (with J D Parsons, 1989), Personal Communication Systems (with B West, 1995); *Recreations* music – occasionally performing, but mostly, these days, listening; *Style—* Prof John Gardiner, FREng; ✉ 1 Queen's Drive Lane, Ilkley, West Yorkshire LS29 9QS (☎ 01943 609581, e-mail compecjg@aol.com); School of Engineering, Design and Technology, University of Bradford, Richmond Road, Bradford BD7 1DP (☎ 07968 756477)

GARDINER, John Ralph; QC (1982); *b* 28 February 1946; *Educ* Bancroft's Sch Woodford, Fitzwilliam Coll Cambridge (MA, LLM); *Career* called to the Bar Middle Temple 1968 (Harmsworth scholar, bencher); practising barr specialising in revenue law, currently head of chambers 11 New Square; supervisor in law Univ of Cambridge 1968–72; memb Bar Cncl 1982–86, treas Senate of Inns of Court and Bar Cncl 1985–86; memb Revenue Bar Assoc; *Style*— John Gardiner, Esq, QC; ✉ 11 New Square, Lincoln's Inn, London WC2A 3QB

GARDINER, Dr Julie Patricia; da of Norman Arthur Gardiner, of Warminster, Wiltshire, and Jean Margaret, *née* Driver; *b* 9 March 1958; *Educ* High Wycombe HS for Girls, Univ of Reading (BA, PhD); *m* 1, 1981 (m dis 1994), John Arthur Davies; m 2, 1998, Michael John Allen; *Career* freelance archaeologist (projects incl E Hants field survey, Cranborne Chase project, Hengistbury Head) 1983–84, asst then managing ed E Anglian Archaeology Norfolk Archaeological Unit 1984–89, managing ed Cncl for British Archaeology 1989–91, reports mangr Wessex Archaeology 1991–2009, managing ed Oxbow Books 2009–; dir Prehistoric Society Ltd 1991–; Prehistoric Soc: memb Cncl, ed PAST newsletter 1991–94, ed Proceedings 1994– (asst ed 1993); memb Inst of Field Archaeologists 1986 (ed Occasional Papers series 1991–93); FSA, MIFA; *Publications* Archaeology of the Mary Rose (Vols 1–5, 2003); author and ed of numerous articles and monographs incl definitive account of excavations of Stonehenge (1995); *Recreations* gardening, art, cinema, walking; *Style*— Dr Julie Gardiner, FSA; ✉ Oxbow Books Ltd, 10 Hythe Bridge Street, Oxford OX1 2EW (☎ 01865 241249, e-mail jpg@oxbowbooks.com)

GARDINER OF KIMBLE, Baron (Life Peer UK 2010), of Kimble in the County of Buckinghamshire; John Eric Gardiner; s of Anthony Ernest Fiddes Gardiner (d 2005), and Heather Joan, *née* Robarts (d 2015); *b* 17 March 1956, London; *Educ* Uppingham, Royal Holloway Coll London (BA); *m* 22 May 2004, Olivia Mirabel, *née* Musgrave; *Career* private sec to: Rt Hon Kenneth Baker, MP 1989–90, Rt Hon Chris Patten, MP 1990–92, Rt Hon Sir Norman Fowler, MP 1992–94, Rt Hon Jeremy Hanley, MP 1994–95, Rt Hon Brian Mawhinney, MP 1995; party whip 2010–12, Govt whip 2012–, currently Capt Queen's Body Guard of the Yeomen of the Guard (dep chief whip in House of Lords); Govt spokesman: Business, Innovation and Skills 2012–13, Cabinet Office 2012–15, Energy and Climate Change 2012–15, Dept for Culture, Media and Sport 2013–15, DEFRA; memb Select Ctee HIV and AIDS in the UK 2010–11; farmer, ptnr C M Robarts & Son 1992–; Countryside Alliance: dir of political affrs 1995–2004, dep chief exec 2004–10, exec dir and memb Bd 2010–12; chm Vale of Aylesbury Hunt 1992–2006, pres Bucks Agricultural Assoc 2007; *Recreations* hunting, gardening; *Clubs* Pratt's; *Style*— The Lord Gardiner of Kimble; ✉ House of Lords, London SW1A 0PW (e-mail gardinerj@parliament.uk)

GARDNER; *see also:* Bruce-Gardner

GARDNER, Brenda Ann Ellen; da of Michael Sweedish (d 1999), of Canada, and Flora, *née* Gibb; *b* 1 June 1947, Vancouver, Canada; *Educ* Univ of Saskatchewan (BA, BEd), Washington Univ; *m* 1968, (James) Douglas Gardner (d 1986), s of James Gardner; *Career* teacher USA and UK 1968–72, asst ed Penguin Books 1972–77; ed: W H Allen 1977–79, E J Arnold 1979–81, Evans 1981–83; md and chair Piccadilly Press 1983–2013, publisher Piccadilly Press (part of Bonnier Gp 2013–; chair Children's Book Circle 1981–82; chair Mgmnt Ctee Castlehaven Community Assoc; winner Women in Publishing Pandora Award 1999; *Recreations* reading, swimming, tennis, yoga, theatre, films; *Style*— Ms Brenda Gardner; ✉ Hot Key/Piccadilly Press, Northburgh House, 10 Northburgh Street, London EC1V 0AT (☎ 020 7490 3875, e-mail b.gardner@piccadillypress.co.uk)

GARDNER, Brian Patrick; s of late T C Gardner, CBE, of Whittlesford, Cambs, and B T Gardner; *b* 17 July 1948; *Educ* St George's Coll Harare, Beaumont Coll, Univ of Oxford (MA, BM BCh); *m* 18 Oct 1980, Stephanie Catherine Mary, da of Dr Faller (d 1980); 5 da (Catherine b 1982, Laura b 1984, Annabelle b 1989, Edel b 1991, Felicity b 1998), 4 s (Paul b 1983, Martin b 1988, Benedict b 1994, Liam b 1996); *Career* various jr med posts 1974–79, registrar in neurosurgery Royal Victoria Hosp Belfast 1980–82, sr registrar in spinal injuries Mersey Regnl Spinal Cord Injuries Centre Southport 1982–85, conslt surgn in spinal injuries Nat Spinal Injuries Centre 1985–; memb BMA; FRCS 1980, FRCP 1995 (MRCP 1978), FRCPEd 1996; *Recreations* family, walking, rugby; *Style*— Brian Gardner, Esq; ✉ 2 Northumberland Avenue, Aylesbury, Buckinghamshire HP21 7HG (☎ 01296 423420, fax 01296 424627, e-mail office@bgardner.co.uk); National Spinal Injuries Centre, Stoke Mandeville Hospital, Aylesbury, Buckinghamshire HP21 8AL

GARDNER, Christopher James Ellis; QC (1994); s of James Charles Gardner (d 1984), of Dartmouth, and Phillis May, *née* Wilkinson; *b* 6 April 1945; *Educ* Rossall Sch, Fitzwilliam Coll Cambridge (MA); *m* 1972, Arlene Sellers; 1 s (Simon James b 19 Feb 1973), 1 da (Sophie Ruth b 16 Aug 1978); *Career* called to the Bar Gray's Inn (Lord Justice Holker sr exhibitioner) 1968, recorder of the Crown Court 1993–, chief justice Turks & Caicos Islands 2004–07; chief justice of Falklands, S Sandwich and S Georgia, Br Antarctic Territory and Br Indian Ocean Territory 2007–15; chartered arbitrator, accredited mediator; fell Soc for Advanced Legal Studies, FIArb, FRSM, fell Cwlth Judicial Educn Inst; *Recreations* open air theatre, bell ringing, cooking curries, boating, ballet; *Clubs* Royal Dart Yacht, Dartmouth Yacht, Garrick; *Style*— Christopher Gardner, QC; ✉ Old Rose Cottage, Cheriton, Hampshire SO24 0QA (☎ 01962 771580, mobile 07788 748191, e-mail cgqc@hotmail.com, website www.cgqc.com)

GARDNER, Dr David Alan; s of John Lawrence Gardner (d 1997), and Alice Winifred, *née* Cattermole; *b* 29 April 1938; *Educ* Minchenden Sch Southgate, Univ of Leeds; *m* 17 Sept 1966, Gillian Ann, da of Capt Edmund Patrick Flowers, of Bangor, N Wales; 4 da (Philippa b 1967, Amanda b 1969, Samantha b 1971, Jemima b 1974), 3 s (Leon b 1977, Oliver b 1980, Joshua b 1985); *Career* registrar Guy's Hosp London 1968–70, conslt pathologist Kensington Chelsea and Westminster Hosp 1973–74, conslt pathologist UCH 1974– (sr registrar 1971–73, sr lectr 1974–); chm: S Camden Pathology Ctee, NE Thames Regnl Biochemistry Ctee; memb NE Thames Regnl Scientific Ctee; FRCPath 1984 (MRCPath 1971), MRCS, LRCP; *Recreations* British campaign medals, golf; *Style*— Dr David Gardner; ✉ 200 Sandridge Road, St Albans, Hertfordshire AL1 4AL (☎ 01727 862019, e-mail dagardner@ntlworld.com)

GARDNER, Douglas Frank; s of Lt Ernest Frank Gardner (decd), and Mary, *née* Chattington (decd); *b* 20 December 1943, London; *Educ* Woolverstone Hall, Coll of Estate Mgmnt, Univ of London (BSc); *m* 5 Sept 1978, Adèle, da of Maj Charles Macmillan Alexander, 1 s (Mark b 1972), 2 da (Teresa b 1971, Amy b 1979); *Career* chief exec Properties Div Tarmac plc 1976–83; Brixton Estate plc: md 1983–93, chm 1993–2000, chm Brixton Investments Ltd and Brixton France SA; chm: Industrial Devpt Partnership II 2000–07, Industrial Realisation plc 2000–, Nuffield Hospitals 2001–09 (govr 1995–2009), City & Provincial Securities LLP 2007–08 (dir 2008–11); Halverton REIM LLP: chm 2004–07, dir GPT Halverton Ltd 2007–09; dir: INVESCO UK Property Income Tst Ltd 2004–12, Hirco plc 2006–11, Invista Real Estate Mgmnt Hldgs plc 2010–12; ptnr Adams Row Capital LLP; memb Investment Ctee European Industrial Partnership; FRICS; *Recreations* tennis, opera; *Clubs* Queen's; *Style*— Douglas Gardner, Esq; ✉ 10 Stavordale Lodge, 10–12 Melbury Road, London W14 8LW

GARDNER, Prof Julian; *b* 6 May 1940; *Educ* Balliol Coll Oxford (BA), Courtauld Inst of Art (Dip History of Art, PhD), British Sch at Rome (Rivoira Scholar); *Career* lectr Courtauld Inst of Art 1966–74; Univ of Warwick: fndn prof in the history of art 1974–2006, pro-vice-chllr 1987–91 and 1995–98, sometime memb numerous ctees and policy gps; dir AHRB Centre for the Study of Renaissance Élites and Court Cultures 2002–05; visiting research prof: Max-Planck-Gesellschaft Bibliotheca Hertziana Rome 1983–85 and 1992, Kuratorium Kunsthistorisches Institut Florence 1993–2003, Institut Nationale d' Histoire de l'Art Paris 1999–; distinguished visiting prof of mediaeval studies Univ of Calif Berkeley 2000, visiting prof Harvard Univ 2003, visiting prof Harvard Univ Center for Italian Renaissance Studies Villa e Tatti Florence 2005–06, Kress prof Nat Gallery of Art Washington 2011–12; membre titulaire Comité Internationale d'Histoire de l'Art 1990–2000; memb Editorial Bd: Burlington Magazine, Arte Cristiana, Revue de l'Art, Perspective; FSA 1977; *Books* The Tomb and the Tiara. Curial tomb sculpture in Italy & Avignon 1200–1400 (1992), Patrons, Painters and Saints (1993), Giotto and his Publics (2011), The Roman Crucible (2013); *Style*— Prof Julian Gardner, FSA; ✉ History of Art Department, University of Warwick, Coventry, Warwickshire CV4 7AL (☎ 024 7652 8339, fax 024 7652 3006, e-mail julian.gardner@warwick.ac.uk)

GARDNER, Prof Sir Richard Lavenham; kt (2005); s of Allan Constant Gardner (d 1943), of Beare Green, Surrey, and Eileen May Alexander, *née* Clarke (d 1961); *b* 10 June 1943; *Educ* St John's Leatherhead, St Catharine's Coll Cambridge (PhD); *m* 14 Dec 1968, Wendy Joy, da of Charles Hampton Trevelyan Cresswell (d 1989), of Cobham, Surrey; 1 s (Matthew Thomas b 18 April 1985); *Career* research asst Physiological Laboratory Univ of Cambridge 1969–73, lectr Dept of Zoology Univ of Oxford 1973–77, student ChCh Oxford 1974– (now emeritus), Henry Dale research prof Royal Soc 1978–2003, Edward Penley Abraham research prof Royal Soc 2003–08, hon dir Developmental Biology Unit ICRF 1985–96; pres Inst of Biology 2006–08; hon prof Univ of York 2007–; ind memb Advsy Bd for the Research Cncls 1990–93; Scientific Medal Zoological Soc of London 1977, March of Dimes Prize in Developmental Biology 1999, Royal Medal Royal Soc 2001, Albert Brachet Prize Belgian Royal Acad of Sciences, Letters and Fine Arts 2004; Hon ScD Univ of Cambridge 2012; memb Academia Europaea 1989; FRS 1979; *Publications* original articles and reviews in various jls incl Nature, Proceedings of the National Academy of Sciences (USA), Transactions of the Royal Society & Development; *Recreations* sailing, painting, ornithology, music; *Style*— Prof Sir Richard Gardner, FRS; ✉ Department of Biology, University of York, Heslington, York YO10 5DD (e-mail rg534@york.ac.uk)

GARDNER, Dr Rita Ann Moden; CBE (2003); da of John William Gardner, of Holsworthy, N Devon, and Evelyn, *née* Moden; *b* 10 November 1955; *Educ* Huntingdon GS, UCL (BSc), Wolfson Coll Oxford (DPhil); *partner* 1982–, Dr Martin Eugene Frost; *Career* lectr in geography KCL 1979–94, dir Environmental Sci Unit and reader in environmental sci Queen Mary & Westfield Coll London 1994–96, dir and sec RGS (with Inst of Br Geographers) 1996–; sec-gen EUGEO (European Geographical Socs Cncl) 2002–12; non-exec dir Br Antarctic Survey 2011–14; author numerous papers in academic jls; memb: Benchmarking Steering Gp QAA (Quality and Assurance Agency of the HE Funding Cncl for Eng) 2003–07, Sci, Engrg and Environment Advsy Ctee Br Cncl 2002–07, Archives Task Force Dept for Culture Media & Sport 2002–04, Educn and Governance Advsy Gp Br Cncl 2007–10, BIS Working Gp on Open Access to Scholarly Publishing 2011–13, Geography Expert Advsrs Gp Dept for Educn 2011–14, Cncl AcSS 2013–, Cncl Assoc of Learned and Professional Society Publishers (ALPSP) 2013–16; non-political advsr on geography to Dept for Children, Schs and Families 2006–09; tstee WWF-UK 2001–04, tstee World Conservation Monitoring Centre 2008–11; co-chair Exhibition Road Cultural Gp 2004–09; awarded Busk Medal (for contribs to geomorphology) 1995, AAG Ronald F Abler Distinguished Service Honors American Assoc of Geographers (AAG) 2015, Scottish Geographical Medal Royal Scottish Geographical Soc 2016; Hon Dr: Univ of Gloucester 2003, Univ of Southampton 2004; hon fell QMC 2002; FRGS 1979, FAcSS 2015; *Books* Mega-Geomorphology (1981), Landshapes (1986), Landscape in England and Wales (1994); *Recreations* contemporary architecture, gardening, dance, travel, good food and wine; *Style*— Dr Rita Gardner, CBE; ✉ Royal Geographical Society (with IBG), 1 Kensington Gore, London SW7 2AR (☎ 020 7591 3010, e-mail director@rgs.org)

GARDNER, Sir Roy Alan; kt (2002); s of Roy Thomas Gardner (d 2000), and Iris Joan (d 1999); *b* 20 August 1945; *Educ* Strode's Sch Egham; *m* 1969, Carol Ann, *née* Barker; 1s, 2 da; *Career* accountant Concorde Project BAC Ltd 1963–75, fin dir Marconi Space & Defence Systems Ltd 1975–1984, fin dir Marconi Co Ltd 1984–85, exec dir STC plc 1986–91, md STC Communications plc 1989–91, chief operating offr Northern Telecom Europe Ltd 1991–92, md GEC Marconi Ltd 1992–94, exec dir British Gas plc 1994–97, chief exec Centrica plc 1997–2006; chm: Manchester United plc 2001–05 (non-exec dir 2000–05), Compass Gp 2006–14 (non-exec dir 2005–), Plymouth Argyle FC 2009–10, Connaught plc 2010, Enserve Gp Ltd (formerly Spice Ltd) 2010–14, Mainstream Renewable Power Ltd 2011– (dir 2008–); non-exec dir Laporte plc 1996–2001,ind non-exec dir William Hill plc 2014–, non-exec chm Serco Gp plc 2015–; sr advsr Credit Suisse 2006–, dir Willis Gp Hldgs Ltd 2006–16; chm Advsy Bd Energy Futures Lab Imperial Coll London 2007–; pres Carers UK, chm Nat Modern Apprenticeship Task Force 2003–05, chm Apprenticeship Ambassadors Network 2014, pres Energy Inst 2007; tstee Devpt Tst 1997–; CIMgt, FRSA, FCCA 1980, FRAeS 1992, FCGI; *Recreations* golf, running; *Clubs* Annabel's, Brooks's, Mark's; *Style*— Sir Roy Gardner

GARDNER, Dr William Norman; s of Norman Charles Gardner (d 1979), of Sydney, Aust, and Ngaire Jean, *née* Dawson (d 1995); *b* 24 January 1943; *Educ* Penrith HS, Univ of Sydney (MB BS), Univ of Oxford (DPhil); *m* 1, 1971 (m dis 1974), Lydia, *née* Sinclair (d 1999); m 2, 1981, Jane Elizabeth, da of Alan Maurice Stainer (d 1990), of Kidlington, Oxon; 3 s (Timothy b 1981, Nicholas b 1985, Joseph b 1988); *Career* med house appts Sydney and Royal Adelaide Hosps 1966–68, sr house appt Brompton, London Chest and Westminster Hosps 1969–71, Wellcome grad student then MRC res offr Dept of Physiology and then Nuffield Inst Oxford 1971–80, memb Wolfson Coll Oxford until 1983, sr lectr and hon conslt physician King's Coll Sch of Med 1987–99 (lectr in med Dept of Thoracic Med 1981–87), conslt physician Eastbourne District Gen Hosp 2006–11; locum conslt chest physician in various hosps incl Ealing Hosp 2014–15 and N Middlesex Univ Hosp 2015–16; reader and hon conslt physician GKT Sch of Medicine 1999–2004; Euro Respiratory Soc: chm Control of Breathing Gp 1993–95, head Clinical Physiology Assembly 1995–97; memb Br Thoracic Soc 1981; author of various articles on respiratory and foetal physiology, respiratory med and hyperventilation syndromes; FRCP 1991 (MRCP 1971); *Recreations* piano, sailing; *Clubs* Cruising Assoc; *Style*— Dr William Gardner; ✉ 92 Holmdene Avenue, London SE24 9LE (☎ 07710 641261, e-mail wngardner2000@yahoo.co.uk)

GARDNER OF PARKES, Baroness (Life Peer UK 1981), of Southgate in Greater London, and of Parkes in the State of New South Wales and Commonwealth of Australia; (Rachel) Trixie Anne Gardner; AM, JP (N Westminster Inner London 1971); da of Hon (John Joseph) Gregory McGirr (d 1949; MLA, NSW State Govt), and late Rachel, *née* Miller; *b* 17 July 1927; *Educ* Monte Sant Angelo Coll N Sydney, Univ of Sydney (BDS); *m* 1956, Kevin Anthony Gardner (d 2007, Lord Mayor of Westminster 1987–88), s of late George Gardner, of Sydney, Australia; 3 da (Hon Sarah Louise (Hon Mrs Joiner) b 1960, Hon Rachel Trixie (Hon Mrs Pope) b 1961, Hon Joanna Mary b 1964 (Hon Mrs Everett)); *Career* dental surgeon; memb: Westminster City Cncl 1968–78, GLC Havering 1970–73, Enfield-Southgate 1977–86; Parly candidate (Cons): Blackburn 1970, N Cornwall 1974; govr National Heart Hosp 1974–90, memb Industrial Tbnl Panel for London 1974–97, Br chm European Union of Women 1978–82, nat women's vice-chm Cons Party 1978–82, UK rep on UN Status of Women Cmmn 1982–88, memb LEB 1984–90; dir: Gateway Building Society 1987–88, Woolwich Building Society 1988–93; vice-pres: Bldg Socs

G

Assoc 1985–90, Nat House Building Cncl 1990–2002; vice-chm NE Thames RHA 1990–94, UK chm Plan International 1989–2003, chm Suzy Lamplugh Tst 1993–96, chm Royal Free Hampstead NHS Tst 1994–97; tstee Parly Advsy Cncl on Tport Safety 1992–98; House of Lords: dep speaker 1999–2002, dep chm of Ctees, memb Info Select Ctee 2003–05, memb Delegated Powers Ctee 2005–; hon vice-pres Br Legion Women's Section 2003–07; Dip Cordon Bleu Paris 1956, memb The Cook Soc UK 1993– (chm 1996); Univ of Sydney Alumni Award for Int Achievement 2010, Award for Peer Contribution to Central Lobby 2012 Dods Politics 2012; hon fell Univ of Sydney 2005, hon fell Sancta Sophia Coll Univ of Sydney 2013; Hon Dr Middlesex Univ 1997; *Recreations* gardening, cooking, travel, historic buildings, family life; *Style*— The Rt Hon Baroness Gardner of Parkes, AM; ✉ House of Lords, London SW1A 0PW

GARDNER-THORPE, Dr Christopher; s of Col Sir Ronald Gardner-Thorpe, GBE, TD, JP (d 1991), and Hazel Mary St George, *née* Dees; *b* 22 August 1941; *Educ* St Philip's Sch London, Beaumont Coll, St Thomas' Hosp Med Sch London (MB BS), Univ of London (MD); *m* 1 April 1967 (m dis 1988), Sheelah, da of Dr Edward Irvine (d 1993), of Exeter; 2 s (Damian, James), 3 da (Catherine, Anne, Helen); *Career* conslt neurologist SW Regnl Health Authy (duties principally Exeter, Plymouth and N Devon) 1974–2006, hon tutor in neurology Post Grad Med Sch Univ of Exeter 1983–90; regnl advsr in neurology RCP Assoc of Br Neurologists 1997–2002; fndr chm Devon and Exeter Medico-Legal Soc 1996–2004 (pres 2004–); memb Int League Against Epilepsy 1969–, fndr memb and hon tres SW Eng Neurosciences Assoc 1981–2001, fndr memb S Eng Neurosciences Assoc, memb Res Ctee of the World Fed of Neurology 1998–2011, sec and treas World Fedn of Neurology Research Gp on the History of the Neurosciences 1998–2011; memb: Harveian Soc 1966–, SW Physicians Club 1974–, Devon and Exeter Med Soc 1974– (hon asst sec 1978–81, hon sec 1981–85, hon reporting sec 1989–98, pres-elect 1998–99, pres 1999–2000, curator 2001–09), chm of tstees Northcott Devon Med Fndn 2002– (memb Advsy Ctee 1983–2002), memb Med Soc of London 2001–; ed various books and papers on epilepsy and other neurological topics; fndr hon med advsr Devon Sports Assoc for the Disabled 1976–, memb Northumbrian Pipers Soc 1976–, pres Meryon Soc 2001–06, fell Linnean Soc 2005–, dep pres Faculty of the History and Philosophy of Medicine 2014–; HM Lieut City of London 1981–; Freeman City of London 1978, Liveryman Worshipful Co of Barbers 1980, lectr, examiner and course dir DHMSA Worshipful Soc of Apothecaries; FRSM 1968, FRCP 1985, FRSA 1997, FACP 2001, FRCPEd 2015; OStJ 1980; *Publications* Antiepileptic Monitoring (chief ed, 1977), James Parkinson 1755–1824 (1987), Stones Unturned (2000), The Book of Princetown (2003), The Royal Devon and Exeter Hosp 1941–2006 (jtly, 2008), Drake's Leat: Safe Water for a City (jtly, 2010); former ed Jl of Medical Biography, author of various papers on epilepsy and other neurological topics; *Recreations* music, travel, reading, photography, sailing, walking, medical history; *Clubs* Savile, Victory Services; *Style*— Dr Christopher Gardner-Thorpe; ✉ The Coach House, 1A College Road, Exeter EX1 1TE (✆ 01392 433941)

GAREL-JONES, Baron (Life Peer UK 1997), of Watford in the County of Hertfordshire; Rt Hon (William Armand Thomas) Tristan Garel-Jones; PC (1992); s of Bernard Garel-Jones, of Madrid, and Meriel, *née* Williams; *b* 28 February 1941; *Educ* King's Sch Canterbury; *m* 1966, Catalina, da of Mariano Garrigues, of Madrid; 4 s, 1 da; *Career* MP (Cons) Watford 1979–97; PPS to Barney Hayhoe 1981–82, asst Govt whip 1982–83, a Lord Cmmr of the Treasy 1983–86; HM Household: vice-chamberlain 1986–87, comptroller 1987–89, treas (dep chief whip) 1989–90; min of state for Europe FCO 1990–93; md UBS Investment Bank; *Recreations* collecting books; *Style*— The Rt Hon the Lord Garel-Jones, PC; ✉ House of Lords, London SW1A 0PW

GAREY, Prof Laurence John; *b* 18 July 1941, Peterborough; *Educ* Deacon's Sch Peterborough, Univ of Nottingham (state scholarship to read modern languages), Worcester Coll Oxford (Theodore Williams scholar in anatomy, MA), Dept of Human Anatomy Univ of Oxford (MRC trg scholar, DPhil, Rolleston meml prize), St Thomas' Hosp London (clinical scholar, BM BCh (Oxon)); *m*; 2 c; *Career* Reserve Offr (Pilot) Nottingham and Oxford Univ Air Sqdns RAF 1959–63; house offr in gen med Memorial Hosp Watford 1968; Univ of Oxford: departmental demonstrator Dept of Human Anatomy 1968–71, lectr Balliol and Merton Colls 1968–72, Schorstein research fell in med sci 1970–72; Sir Henry Wellcome travelling fell and visiting prof Dept of Physiology Univ of Calif Berkeley 1972–73; Univ of Lausanne: professeur asst Inst of Anatomy 1973–76, professeur associé Inst of Anatomy 1976–87, lectr Sch of Ergotherapy 1976–87; assoc prof Dept of Anatomy Nat Univ of Singapore 1987–90; Univ of London: prof and head Dept of Anatomy (Division of Neuroscience after merger) Imperial Coll Sch of Med at Charing Cross Hosp (Charing Cross and Westminster Med Sch until merger 1997) 1990–97, vice-pres Bd of Studies in Human Anatomy and Morphology 1993–95; prof and chm of Dept of Anatomy Faculty of Medicine and Health Sciences UAE Univ Al Ain 2000–04; chair Neuroscience Programmes Network Int Brain Research Orgn 2006–08; visiting fell Aust Nat Univ Canberra 1982, visiting prof Faculty of Medicine Kuwait Univ 1999; memb Editorial Bd: Biological Signals 1990–97, Jl für Hirnforschung 1992–93, Jl of Brain Research 1994–2000, Int Jl of Diabetes and Metabolism 2001–; assessor: HE Funding Cncl for Wales 1997, Quality Assurance Agency for HE 1998–2000; memb Ctee of Admin Neurobiology Research Gp Nat Cncl for Scientific Research Marseille 1979; Inst of Neurophysiology and Psychophysiology Marseille: memb Ctee of Admin 1977–81, scientific dir Dept of Cellular Neurobiology 1982–84; memb: London Ctee of Licensed Teachers of Anatomy 1990–2000 (chm 1993–2000), Panel of Examiners RCPS(Ed) 1993–98, Ct of Examiners RCS 1992–99; memb: Acad of Med of Singapore, Afro-Asia Oceania Assoc of Anatomists (memb Int Ctee 1988–), Anatomical Soc of GB and I (vice-pres 1994–), Assoc of Profs of the Univ of Lausanne (memb Ctee 1983–87), Aust Neuroscience Soc, Br Neuropathological Soc, Child Vision Research Soc, European Biomedical Research Assoc (fndr memb), European Brain and Behaviour Soc, European Neuroscience Assoc, Hong Kong Soc of Neurosciences, Int Brain Research Orgn (treas 1983–85), Nat Postgraduate Med Coll of Nigeria, NY Acad of Scis, Physiological Soc, RSM, Singapore Neuroscience Assoc (pres 1988–90), Soc for Neuroscience, Swiss Soc of Anatomists, Histologists and Embryologists, Swiss Soc of Cellular and Molecular Biology (vice-pres 1980–82), Union of Swiss Socs of Experimental Biology; hon memb Centre for Neuroscience UCL; *Books* Plastic and Reconstructive Surgery of the Orbitopalpebral Region (jtly, 1990); translations: Neuronal Man: The Biology of Mind (1985, 2 edn 1986), The Population Alternative (1986), Localisation in the Cerebral Cortex (1994), The Paradox of Sleep: The Story of Dreaming (1999, new edn 2001), New Research Findings on the Anatomy of the Cerebral Cortex of Special Relevance to Anthropological Questions (trans, 2004), The Castle of Dreams (trans, 2008), Your Brain and Your Self: What You Need to Know (trans, 2009); author of various scientific articles on neuroanatomy; *Style*— Prof Laurence J Garey

GARFIELD, John Samuel; s of Montagu Garfield (d 1976), of Hove, E Sussex, and Marguerite, *née* Elman (d 1983); *b* 13 February 1930; *Educ* Bradfield Coll, Emmanuel Coll Cambridge (MA, MB MChir); *m* 6 Oct 1962, Agnes Clara Teleki, da of Count Joseph Teleki de Szek (d 1985), of Pomaz, Hungary; 3 da (Stephanie b 1963, Johanna Francoise b 1965, Marie-Claire b 1969); *Career* jr specialist med RAMC 1956–58, conslt neurosurgeon 1968, hon emeritus Univ of Southampton Trust Hosps 1992–; numerous pubns on neurosurgical and medico-legal topics; former pres Soc of Br Neurological Surgns, memb Cncl Med Def Union; former chm Wessex Regnl Med Advsy Ctee; photographer; exhibitions in London, Winchester, Brussels, Ypres and Birmingham 1980–98; FRCS 1961, FRCP 1971; *Photographic Publications* The Fallen (1990 and 2014), The Eye, the Brain and the Camera (1993), History of EANS (1995), Rehearsal (2001), Teleki Houses in Transylvania and Hungary (2004), The Garden Gallery (2006), Images of Music (2011); *Clubs* Athenaeum; *Style*— John Garfield, Esq; ✉ Keyhaven, Hadrian Way, Chilworth, Southampton SO16 7HY (✆ 023 8076 7674)

GARFIELD, Simon Frank; s of Herbert Sidney Garfield (d 1973), and Hella Helene, *née* Meyer (d 1979); *b* 19 March 1960; *Educ* UCS Hampstead, LSE (BSc Econ); *m* 1, 1987 (m dis 2008), Diane, da of Rubin Samuels; 2 c; m 2, 2012, Justine, da of Ralph Kanter; *Career* sub ed Radio Times 1981, scriptwriter radio documentaries BBC 1981–82, ed Time Out magazine 1989–91 (writer 1982–88); news feature writer: Independent and Independent on Sunday newspapers 1990–96, Observer 2001–; documentary writer and presenter BBC Radio 4; Guardian/NUS Student Journalist of the Year 1981, BSME Ed of the Year (Time Out) 1989, Mind Journalist of the Year 2005; *Books* Expensive Habits: The Dark Side of the Music Industry (1986), The End of Innocence: Britain in the time of AIDS (1994, Somerset Maugham Prize 1995), The Wrestling (1996), The Nation's Favourite: The True Adventures of Radio 1 (1998), Mauve (2000), The Last Journey of William Huskisson (2002), Our Hidden Lives (2004), We Are At War (2005), Private Battles (2006), The Error World (2008), Mini (2009), Exposure: The Unusual Life and Violent Death of Bob Carlos Clarke (2009), Just My Type: A Book About Fonts (2011), On The Map (2012), To the Letter: A Journey Through a Vanishing World (2013), My Dear Bessie: A Love Story in Letters (ed, 2014), A Notable Woman: The Romantic Journals of Jean Lucey Pratt (ed, 2015), Timekeepers: 21 Stories About A Modern Obsession (2016); *Recreations* cycling, music, poker, cricket, cooking, Chelsea FC; *Clubs* Two Brydges Place; *Style*— Simon Garfield, Esq; ✉ c/o United Agents Ltd, 12–26 Lexington Street, London W1F 0LE (✆ 020 3214 0800, e-mail info@unitedagents.co.uk, website www.simongarfield.com)

GARFIT, (Charles) William Aikman; s of Brian Corringham Garfit (d 1997), of Harlton, Cambridge, and Myrtle Joan, *née* Robertson Aikman (d 1945); *b* 9 October 1944; *Educ* Bradfield Coll, Cambridge Sch of Art, Byam Shaw Sch of Art (scholar, Dip ILEA Cert), Royal Acad Sch of Art (Dip); *m* 23 July 1966, Georgina Margaret, da of Sir Norman Joseph, KCVO; 2 da (Jacquelyn Jean b 1969, Penelope Mina b 1971), 1 s (Henry Charles Joseph b 1975); *Career* artist specialising in river and water landscapes; work mostly by private commission since 1994 (incl commissions in UK, Iceland, Russia, USA, Brazil, France and Austria); monthly contrib Shooting Gazette 1995–; memb: Game Shooting Ctee BASC 1991–2002, Conservation Ctee Countryside Alliance 1998–2000, Judge Ctee Purdey Award 2002–; ptnr S Cambs Conservation Conslts 2015; RBA 1976; *Solo Exhibitions* incl: Waterhouse Gall London 1970, 1972 and 1974, Mall Galls London 1976, Stacey Marks Gall Eastbourne 1978, Tryon Gall London 1981, 1983, 1985, 1988, 1991 and 2009, Holland & Holland London 1994; *Awards* Laurent Perrier Award for Wild Game and Conservation Mgmnt 1988; selected for inclusion in: Shooting Times First XI Game Shots 1990, Sporting Gun Top 10 Pigeon Shots 1998, Shooting Gazette – Britain's Top Shots 1999, The Field – The 50 Best Shots 2002, 2008, 2009, 2010, 2011, 2012, 2013 and 2014, The Super XV Woodpigeon Shots Fieldsports magazine 2014; European 12 Bore Hammer Gun Champion 2001; Freedom of the City of London 2014, Liveryman Worshipful Co of Gunmakers 2015; *Publications* Conservation, Development and Management of Gravel Pits for Sports and Conservation (paper, 1983), Will's Shoot (book, 1993), Will's Shoot Revisited (2005), Will's Shooting Ways (2009), Will's Pigeon Shooting (2012); illustrator of over 30 country sporting, shooting and conservation books and magazines; *Recreations* wood pigeon and game shooting, game and conservation management, botany, ornithology; *Style*— William Garfit, Esq; ✉ The Old Rectory, Harlton, Cambridge CB23 1ES (✆ 01223 262563, fax 01223 264523, e-mail william.garfit@btinternet.com, website www.williamgarfit.co.uk)

GARLAND, Gary John Richard; s of William Garland (d 1993), and Evelyn Jobson; *b* 26 August 1958, South Shields; *Educ* Westoe Comp, South Shields Marine Coll, Newcastle Poly, Inns of Court Sch of Law; *Career* called to the Bar Inner Temple 1989; asylum support adjudicator 2000–, UN int prosecutor KFOR-Kosovo 2000–01, sr war crimes prosecutor Int Criminal Tbnl for the former Yugoslavia (ICTY) The Hague 2001–03, cmmr Ind Police Complaints Cmmn (IPCC) 2003–, dep district judge 2004–, cmmr for complaints HM Revenue and Customs 2006–, cmmr for complaints Serious Organised Crime Agency (SOCA) 2007–10; dep chief Legal Ombudsman for England & Wales; memb Bar Cncl 1991–2000; *Recreations* swimming, travel, theatre, life; *Style*— Gary Garland, Esq

GARLAND, Nicholas Withycombe; OBE (1998); s of Thomas Ownsworth Garland, and Margaret, *née* Withycombe (d 1998); *b* 1 September 1935; *Educ* Rongotai Coll NZ, Slade Sch of Fine Art; *m* 1, 1964 (m dis 1968), Harriet Crittall; m 2, 1969 (m dis 1994), Caroline Beatrice, da of Sir Peter Medawar; 3 s (Timothy William b 1957, Alexander Medawar (Alex) b 1970, Theodore Nicholas b 1972), 1 da (Emily b 1964); m 3, 1995, Priscilla Roth, *née* Brandchaft; *Career* political cartoonist: Daily Telegraph 1966–86 and 1991–, The Independent 1986–91; *Style*— Nicholas Garland, Esq, OBE; ✉ The Daily Telegraph, 111 Buckham Palace Road, London SW1W 0DT

GARLAND, Hon Sir Victor; KBE (1981); s of Idris Victor Garland; *b* 5 May 1934; *Educ* Hale Sch, W Aust Univ (BA); *m* 1960, Lynette Jamieson; 2 s, 1 da; *Career* RAAF 1951–52; practised as chartered accountant 1958–69; memb for Curtin (Lib) Aust Fed House of Reps 1969–81; Parly and ministerial positions: min assisting the Treas 1972 and 1975–76, min for Supply 1971–72, opposition chief whip 1974–75, chm Expenditure Ctee 1976–77, min for Special Trade Representations 1977–79 (incl GATT negotiations), min for Business and Consumer Affrs 1979–80; high cmmr for Aust in the UK 1981–83; non-exec dir Prudential Corporation plc 1984–93; dir: Henderson Far East Income Trust plc 1984– (chm 1990–), Mitchell Cotts plc 1984–87, Throgmorton Trust plc 1985–2006, Govett Funds Inc 1991–2000 (pres 1997–2000), Nelson Hurst 1993–97, Fidelity Asian Values 1996– (chm 2000–), other public companies; vice-chm: South Bank Bd 1986–2000, Royal Cwlth Soc for the Blind; Freeman City of London 1982, Liveryman Worshipful Co of Tallow Chandlers, Hon Freeman Worshipful Co of Butchers; FCA; *Clubs* White's, Weld (Australia); *Style*— Hon Sir Victor Garland, KBE

GARLAND-THOMAS, Her Hon Judge Jane Elizabeth; *Career* admitted slr 1980, dep district judge 1999–2001, district judge 2001–14, circuit judge (Wales Circuit) 2014–; *Style*— Her Hon Judge Garland-Thomas; ✉ c/o Swansea Civil and Family Justice Centre Hearing Centre, Caravella House, Quay West, Quay Parade, Swansea, South Wales SA1 1SP

GARLICK, Paul Richard; QC (1996); s of Arthur Garlick (d 1978), and Dorothy Sylvia, *née* Allan; *b* 14 August 1952; *Educ* Scarisbrick Hall Sch, Univ of Liverpool (LLB); *Career* called to the Bar Middle Temple 1974 (master of the bench 2005), standing counsel to HM Customs & Excise 1990–96, recorder (Western Circuit) 1997–; memb Hon Soc of Middle Temple 1972; *Recreations* music, travel, walking; *Style*— Paul Garlick, Esq, QC

GARMOYLE, Viscount; Hugh Sebastian Frederick Cairns; s and h of 6 Earl Cairns, CBE, *qv*; *b* 26 March 1965; *Educ* Eton, Univ of Edinburgh, London Coll of Law; *m* 19 Dec 1991, Juliet, o da of Andrew Eustace Palmer, CMG, CVO, of Little Missenden, Bucks; 1 s (Hon Oliver David Andrew b 7 March 1993), 2 da (Hon Tara Davina Amanda b 3 April 1995, Hon Harriet b 3 March 1998); *Career* Freshfields Slrs 1990–94; Cazenove & Co: joined 1994, ptnr 1999–2001, md 2001–03, md JPMorgan Cazenove 2004–; Liveryman Worshipful Co of Fishmongers; *Style*— Viscount Garmoyle

GARNER, Prof Alan; OBE (2001); s of Colin Garner (d 1983), of Cheshire, and Marjorie, *née* Greenwood Stuart (d 1997); *b* 17 October 1934, Congleton, Cheshire; *Educ* Manchester Grammar, Magdalen Coll Oxford; *m* 1, 1956, Ann, da of Harry Cook (d 1976), of Oxford; 1 s (Adam), 2 da (Ellen, Katharine); m 2, 1972, Griselda, da of Paul Greaves (d 1986), of

St Petersburg, Russia; 1 s (Joseph b 1973), 1 da (Elizabeth b 1975); *Career* author; Mil Serv Lt RA; memb Editorial Bd Detskaya Literatura Publishers Moscow; visiting prof Sch of Applied Sciences Univ of Huddersfield 2012; co-fndr Blackden Tst; World Fantasy Lifetime Achievement Award 2012; Hon DLitt Univ of Warwick 2010, Hon DLitt Univ of Salford 2011, Hon DUniv Huddersfield 2012, Hon DLitt Machester Met Univ 2013; FSA 2007, FRSL 2012; *Plays* Holly from the Bongs (1965), Lamaload (1978), Lurga Lom (1980), To Kill a King (1980), Sally Water (1982), The Keeper (1983), Pentecost (1997), Out of the Dark (2015); *Dance Drama* The Green Mist (1970); *Libretti* The Bellybag (1971), Potter Thompson (1972), Lord Flame (1996); *Films* The Owl Service (1969), Red Shift (1978), Places and Things (1978), Images (1981, First Prize Chicago Int Film Festival), Strandloper (1992); *Lectures* Powsels & Thrums: The Loom of Creation (inaugural Garner lecture Jodrell Bank Observatory) 2015; *Books* The Weirdstone of Brisingamen (1960), The Moon of Gomrath (1963), Elidor (1965), Holly from the Bongs (1966), The Old Man of Mow (1967), The Owl Service (1967, Library Assoc Carnegie Medal 1967, Guardian Award 1968), The Hamish Hamilton Book of Goblins (1969), Red Shift (1973), The Breadhorse (1975), The Guizer (1975), The Stone Book (1976, Phoenix Award Children's Book Assoc of US 1996), Tom Fobble's Day (1977), Granny Reardun (1977), The Aimer Gate (1978), Fairy Tales of Gold (1979), The Lad of the Gad (1980), A Book of British Fairy Tales (1984), A Bag of Moonshine (1986), Jack and the Beanstalk (1992), Once Upon a Time (1993), Strandloper (1996), The Little Red Hen (1997), The Voice that Thunders (1997), The Well of the Wind (1998), Approach to the Edge (1998), Thursbitch (2003), By Seven Firs and Goldenstone (2009), Boneland (2012), The Beauty Things (with Mark Edmonds, 2016); *Recreations* work; *Clubs* The Portico Library; *Style*— Prof Alan Garner, OBE, FRSL, FSA; ✉ Blackden, Holmes Chapel, Cheshire CW4 8BY; c/o Karolina Sutton, Curtis Brown, Haymarket House, 28–29 Haymarket, London SW1Y 4SP

GARNER, Dr John Angus McVicar; s of Edmund Garner (d 1998), and Catherine, *née* McVicar; *b* 4 September 1950, London; *Educ* Eltham Coll, Univ of Edinburgh (MB, ChB, DCH, DRCOG); *Children* 1 da (Victoria b 21 Sept 1976), 1 s (Douglas b 5 Sept 1981); *Career* various hosp appts 1974–79, princ GP St Triduana's Medical Practice 1980–2013 (sr ptnr 2005–13); chm: Scottish GPs 1992–95, BMA Cncl Scotland 1999–2004; vice-chm Medical and Dental Defence Union of Scotland 1995–; team ldr for performance GMC, tstee BMA Pension Fund, lay observer Cncl Law Soc of Scotland; FRCGP 1995; *Recreations* travel, philately, photography, ponds; *Clubs* New (Edinburgh); *Style*— Dr John Garner; ✉ 1 Drylaw Avenue, Edinburgh EH4 2DD (☎ 0131 467 4148, e-mail johngarne@aol.com); St Triduana's Medical Practice, 54 Moira Park, Edinburgh EH7 6RU (☎ 0131 657 3341, e-mail john.garner@lothian.scot.nhs.uk)

GARNER, Prof Paul; s of David Garner, of Liverpool, and Sylvia, *née* Card (d 1978); *b* 25 August 1955; *Educ* Spalding GS, UCL (MB BS, MD); *Career* surgical house offr UCH London 1979, med house offr Ninewells Hosp Dundee 1980; SHO: Withington Hosp Manchester 1980, N Staffs Hosp 1981, Booth Hall Hosp Manchester 1981–82; dist MO in charge Aitape PNG (VSO) 1982–84; PNG Inst of Med Research: epidemiologist Madang 1984–86, research dir Kunjingini 1986–87, offr i/c Madang 1987–88; research fell then lectr LSHTM 1988–94; Liverpool Sch of Tropical Med (LSTM): sr lectr 1994–, head Int Health Research Gp 1995–, personal chair 2001–; hon conslt in primary health care Liverpool Dist 1994–, hon research fell St George's Med Sch Grenada 1997–, hon prof Chongqing Med Univ 2004–, hon prof Christian Med Coll Vellore 2012–, hon prof Stellenbosch Univ; co-ordinator Int Artemisinin Study Gp Secretariat 1999–; memb: MRC Physiological Med and Infections Bd 1999–2003, MRC Audit Ctee 2002–08, WHO Malaria Treatment Guidelines Gp 2004–, WHO HIV Operational Guidelines Gp 2015–, WHO Expert Ctee on Essential Medicines 2015–; co-ordinating ed Cochrane Infectious Diseases Gp 1994–, section ed (infectious diseases) Clinical Evidence 1998–2011, specialist assoc ed Int Jl of Epidemiology 2000–, exec memb Co-ordinating Editors Bd Cochrane 2006–15; referee for jls incl BMJ and Lancet; FFPHM 2001 (MFPHM 2000); *Publications* 35 Cochrane reviews, 140 research papers and numerous other contribs to academic jls; *Recreations* running, military fitness, contemporary music, cooking and entertaining; *Style*— Prof Paul Garner; ✉ Liverpool School of Tropical Medicine, Pembroke Place, Liverpool L3 5QA (☎ 0151 705 3201, e-mail paul.garner@lstmed.ac.uk)

GARNER, Richard Clayton; s of Eric Walter Ernest Garner (d 1981), of London, and Dorothy Bertha, *née* Taylor (d 1995); *b* 12 February 1950; *Educ* Highgate Sch, Harlow Tech Coll (NCTJ Cert); *m* 29 Oct 1985, Anne (d 2008), da of George Wilkinson (d 2000); *Career* journalist; BBC News Information 1967–69, Islington and Camden Jls 1970–73, municipal corr Kent Evening Post 1973–77, educn corr then dep London ed Birmingham Evening Mail 1977–80, TES 1980–90, educn corr Daily Mirror 1990–2001, educn ed The Independent 2001–2016, columnist TES 2016–; memb NUJ 1970–; *Books* Midsummer Variations: an Anthology of Contemporary Poetry (1970); *Recreations* cricket (watching now!), going to the theatre; *Clubs* Middlesex CCC; *Style*— Richard Garner, Esq; ✉ 137 The Avenue, Hertford SG14 3DX (☎ and fax 01992 583366, mobile 07795 262670, e-mail richardcgarner8@outlook.com)

GARNER, Talitha (Tally); da of Anthony Garner, of London, and Krithia Wildfire; *b* 9 September 1977, London; *Educ* Ursuline Convent HS Wimbledon, Univ of Newcastle upon Tyne (BA), McGill Univ Montreal; *Partner* Thomas Hyde; *Career* prodr Lowe Lintas and Ptnrs 2001–02, agent representing screenwriters, dirs and film and TV rights Curtis Brown 2003– (joined as book-to-film agent 2002), jt fndr Cuba Pictures Prodn Co 2004–; *Style*— Miss Tally Garner; ✉ Curtis Brown Literary Agency, Haymarket House, 28–29 Haymarket, London SW1Y 4SP (☎ 020 7393 4458, fax 020 7393 4401, e-mail tally@curtisbrown.co.uk)

GARNETT, Adm Sir Ian David Graham; KCB (1998); s of Capt Ian Graham Hartt Garnett, DSC, RN (d 1996), and Barbara (d 1984); *b* 27 September 1944; *Educ* Canford Sch, BRNC Dartmouth; *m* 1973, Charlotte Mary, *née* Anderson; 1 s (b 1975), 2 da (b 1978 and 1982); *Career* joined RN 1962, appointed Lt 1967, flying trg 1968–69, HMS Hermes 814 Sqdn 1969–70, loan serv RAN 1971–72, HMS Tiger 826 Sqdn 1973–74, Warfare Offr 1974–76, Sr Pilot 820 Sqdn 1977–78, Dep Dir JMOTS 1978–80, CO HMS Amazon 1981–82, RN Staff Course 1983, Asst Dir Operational Requirements 1983–86, Capt Fourth Frigate Sqdn HMS Active 1986–88, RN Presentation Team 1988–89, Dir Operational Requirements 1989–92, Flag Offr Naval Aviation 1993–95, Dep SACLANT 1995–98, Chief of Jt Ops 1999–2001, COS SHAPE 2001–04, Commandant RCDS 2005–08; chm Chatham Historic Dockyard Tst 2005–16; cmmr Cwlth War Graves Cmmn 2006–11 (vice-chm 2008–11); memb Fleet Air Arm Officers' Assoc; *Recreations* my family and other matters; *Clubs* Royal Navy 1765 and 1785; *Style*— Sir Ian Garnett, KCB

GARNHAM, Caroline Xania; da of Edward Hatch (d 1981), of Guildford, and Elisabeth Houtman; *b* 10 October 1955; *Educ* George Abbott Sch for Girls Guildford, Univ of Exeter (BSc); *m* 1, 30 Dec 1977 (m dis 1984), Hugh Laurence Garnham, s of Jack Garnham; m 2, 9 Aug 1991 (m dis 2004), Michael Robert Little, *qv*; 1 s (Edward Charles Frank b 21 Nov 1992), 1 da (Georgia Elizabeth Medina b 10 Nov 1995); *Career* ptnr Private Capital Gp Simmons & Simmons, currently ceo Garnham Family Office Servs; fndr and dir www.familybhive.com; proposed and drafted The Executive Entity Act 2011 for The Bahamas; The Lawyer Top 5 Client Lawyer 2011; memb Law Soc; FTII; *Books* How to Win Business from Private Clients, Who Do You Trust When You Are Super Rich?; *Recreations* tennis, skiing, writing; *Style*— Ms Caroline Garnham; ✉ Flat 4, 6 Hyde Park Gardens, London W2 2LT (☎ 07979 188288)

GARNHAM, Hon Mr Justice; Sir Neil Garnham; QC (2001); *Career* called to the Bar 1982; asst recorder 1999, recorder 2000, dep judge of the High Court of Justice, judge of the High Court of Justice (Queen's Bench Div) 2015–; *Style*— The Hon Mr Justice Garnham, QC

GARNIER, Rt Hon Sir Edward Henry; kt (2012), PC (2015), QC (1995), MP; s of William d'Arcy Garnier (Col, late RA, d 1989), and Hon Mrs Garnier (*née* Hon Lavender Hyacinth de Grey, d 2010); *b* 26 October 1952; *Educ* Wellington, Jesus Coll Oxford (MA); *m* 17 April 1982, Anna Caroline, da of Michael James Mellows (d 1974), of Belton House, Rutland; 1 da (Eleanor Katharine Rose b 21 Sept 1983), 2 s (George Edward b 20 July 1986, James William b 21 Jan 1991); *Career* called to the Bar Middle Temple 1976 (bencher 2001), called to the NI Bar 2010; recorder of the Crown Court 2000–15 (asst recorder 1998–2000); vice-pres Hemsworth Cons Assoc; contested: Wandsworth BC by-election 1984, Tooting ILEA election 1986; Parly candidate (Cons) Hemsworth W Yorks 1987, MP (Cons) Harborough 1992–; PPS to mins of state for Foreign and Cwlth Affrs: Rt Hon Alastair Goodlad 1994–95, David Davis 1994–95; PPS to Rt Hon Sir Nicholas Lyell as Attorney Gen and to Sir Derek Spencer as Slr Gen 1995–97, PPS to Rt Hon Roger Freeman as chcllr Duchy of Lancaster 1996–97, oppn front bench spokesman Lord Chancellor's Dept 1997–99, shadow Attorney General 1999–2001, memb Exec Ctee to the 1922 Ctee 2001–2005, shadow Home Office min 2005–07, shadow min for justice 2007–09, shadow attorney gen 2009–10, HM slr gen 2010–12; memb Home Affrs Select Ctee 1992–95, sec Cons Backbench Foreign Affrs Ctee 1992–94, jt chm All-Pty Parly Knitwear and Textile Industry Gp 1992–94, treas All-Pty Br-Netherlands Parly Gp 2001–, jt chm All-Pty Br-Italian Parly Gp 2004–06, chm All-Pty Br-Liechtenstein Parly Gp 2004–10, memb Howard League Cmmn on Sex in Prisons 2012–14; UK election observer: Kenya 1992, Bosnia 1996; memb Advsy Bd Samaritans 2013–, tstee Prison Reform Tst 2015–; Parly fell St Antony's Coll Oxford 1996–97; Freeman City of London 2015; *Books* Halsbury's Laws of England (contrib, 4 edn), Bearing the Standard (jtly, 1991), Facing the Future (jtly, 1993), Lissack & Horlick on Bribery (contrib, 2 edn); *Recreations* cricket, shooting, opera; *Clubs* Pratt's, Vincent's (Oxford), Beefsteak, White's; *Style*— The Rt Hon Sir Edward Garnier, QC, MP; ✉ 1 Brick Court, Temple, London EC4Y 9BY (☎ 020 7353 8845, fax 020 7583 9144); House of Commons, London SW1A 0AA (☎ 020 7219 3000); website www.edwardgarnier.co.uk

G

GARNIER, Dr Jean-Pierre; *b* 31 October 1947; *Educ* Stanford Univ (Fulbright fell, French Govt scholar, MBA, pres Small Business Club), Univ Louis Pasteur France (PhD Pharmacology); *m*; 3 c; *Career* Mil Serv Med Corp France 1974–75; Pharmaceuticals Div Schering-Plough Corporation 1975–90: various sales and mktg posts France, Switzerland and Belgium 1975–78, dir of mktg Belgium subsid 1978–80, gen mangr Danish subsid 1980–82, gen mangr Portuguese subsid 1982–83, sr dir Mktg US Domestic Div 1983–84, vice-pres Mktg US Domestic Div 1984–85, sr vice-pres and gen mangr US Domestic Div 1985–88, pres US Pharmaceuticals Products Div 1989–90; SmithKline Beecham: pres America (US and Canada) 1990–93, memb Bd SmithKline Beecham Corporation 1992–, exec vice-pres Pharmaceuticals 1993–94, chm Pharmaceuticals 1994–96, pres Pharmaceuticals and Consumer Healthcare and chief operating offr 1996–2000; ceo GlaxoSmithKline 2000–; dir United Technologies Corporation; memb French/American C of C, tstee Eisenhower Exchange Fellowships Inc, emeritus tstee Acad of Natural Scis Philadelphia; former memb Bd of Tstees Massachusetts Eye and Ear Hosp; Communicator of the Year award Int Assoc of Business Communicators 1993, Chevalier de la Légion d'Honneur 1997; *Recreations* competitive tennis and paddle player, golf, wind surfing, skiing, bridge; *Style*— Dr Jean-Pierre Garnier; ✉ GlaxoSmithKline, One Franklin Plaza, PO Box 7929, Philadelphia, PA 19101–7929, USA (☎ 00 215 751 5810, fax 00 215 751 6546, e-mail jean-pierre.garnier@gsk.com)

GARNIER, Rear Adm Sir John; KCVO (1990, LVO 1965), CBE (1982); s of Rev Thomas Vernon Garnier (d 1939), and Helen Davis, *née* Stenhouse (d 1993); *b* 10 March 1934, Hemel Hempstead; *Educ* Berkhamsted Sch, BRNC Dartmouth; *m* 31 Dec 1966, Joanna Jane (Dodie), da of Alan Cadbury (d 1994), and Jane Cadbury, *née* Walker (d 2001); 2 s (Thomas b 1968, William b 1970), 1 da (Louisa b 1972); *Career* joined RN 1950, served HM Yacht Britannia 1956–57, HMS Tyne 1956, qualified navigation specialist 1959, Naval Equerry to HM The Queen 1962–65, cmd HMS Dundas 1968–69, Directorate of Naval Ops and Trade 1969–71, cmd HMS Minerva 1972–73, Def Policy Staff 1973–75, exec offr HMS Intrepid 1976, Asst Dir Naval Manpower Planning 1976–78, RCDS 1979, cmd HMS London 1980–81, Dir Naval Ops and Trade 1982–84, Cdre Amphibious Warfare 1985, Flag Offr Royal Yachts 1985–90, Extra Equerry to HM The Queen 1988–, Private Sec and Comptroller to HRH Princess Alexandra 1991–95; pres RNA Sherborne Branch 1997–; memb Cncl Shipwrecked Fishermen and Mariners' Royal Benevolent Soc 1996–2004; govr Sherborne Sch for Girls 1985–2004; Younger Bro of Trinity House 1974, Freeman City of London 1982; *Recreations* sailing, gardening, opera, golf, computers; *Style*— Rear Admiral Sir John Garnier, KCVO, CBE; ✉ Bembury Farm, Thornford, Sherborne, Dorset DT9 6QF

GARNIER, Mark Robert Timothy; MP; s of Peter Garnier, and Patricia, *née* Dowden; *b* 26 February 1963, London; *Educ* Charterhouse; *m* Caroline Louise, *née* Joyce; 2 s (Edward b 18 Jan 2002, George b 28 Dec 2007), 1 da (Jemima b 23 Aug 2003); *Career* md South China Securities 1989–95, dir Daiwa Europe 1995–96, assoc dir Edmond de Rothschild Securities 1996–97, assoc dir Bear Stearns 1997–98, ind hedge fund mangr 1999–2005, ptnr CGR Capital 2005–08, ptnr Severn Capital LLP 2008–11; cncllr Forest of Dean DC 2003–07, MP (Cons) Wyre Forest 2010–; memb Ct Worshipful Co of Coachmakers; FCISI, FRSA; *Clubs* RAC, Carlton, N London Rifle; *Style*— Mark Garnier, Esq, MP; ✉ House of Commons, London SW1A 0AA (☎ 020 7219 7198, e-mail mark.garnier.mp@parliament.uk, website www.markgarnier.co.uk)

GARNIER, Thomas Julian Cadbury; s of Rear Adm Sir John Garnier, KCVO, CBE, of Thornford, Dorset, and Joanna Jane (Dodie), *née* Cadbury; *b* 18 May 1968, Gibraltar; *Educ* Radley, Univ of Bristol (BSc), Univ of Oxford (PGCE); *m* 25 June 1994, Alexandra Mary, *née* Penny; 2 s (Philip b 5 Aug 2000, Peter b 28 Oct 2003); *Career* Seaman Offr RN 1987–94 (Navigating Offr HMS Brinton 1991–93); Abingdon Sch 1995–2005 (day housemaster 1998–2002, boarding housemaster 2002–05), headmaster Pangbourne Coll 2005–; memb Inst of Physics; Queen's Telescope 1988, Carl Zeiss Award 1991; *Recreations* sailing, rowing, singing; *Clubs* Leander; *Style*— Thomas Garnier, Esq; ✉ Pangbourne College, Pangbourne, Reading RG8 8LA (☎ 0118 984 2101, fax 0118 984 1239)

GARRAD, Charles William Wynne; s of Douglas Garrad, and Mary Ann Garrad; *Educ* Marlborough, Stourbridge Coll of Art, Cardiff Coll of Art (DipAD), Chelsea Sch of Art (HDA); *m* 1994, Mary Norden; *Career* artist, film prodn designer and dir; formerly teacher at various Br art schools; exhbns incl: Serpentine, Ikon, MCA Sydney; chm: Artsadmin, Shelagh Cluett Tst; *Television and Film* credits as designer incl: Amongst Women, The Englishman Who Went Up a Hill But Came Down a Mountain, The Serpent's Kiss, Paranoid, Waiting for Godot; credits as dir incl: Time Passing (BBC), That Time (Beckett on Film), Waiting for You (theatrical feature); *Recreations* cycling, cooking, eating; *Style*— Charles Garrad, Esq; ✉ website www.charlesgarrad.com

GARRATT, Prof Clifford John; s of John Taylor Garratt, and Ann, *née* Critchley; *Educ* Magdalen Coll Oxford, Bart's Med Sch London; *Children* 1 da (Lucy Rebecca b 8 Sept 1994); *Career* lectr Nat Heart and Lung Inst and hon sr registrar Royal Brompton Hosp 1992–93, Br Heart Fndn int fell 1996–97, prof of cardiology Univ of Manchester 2001–, hon conslt cardiologist Manchester Royal Infirmary 2001–; treas Br Pacing and Electrophysiology Gp 1999–; Guild Burgess of Preston; fell Euro Soc of Cardiology 1999;

FRCP 1997; *Publications* Mechanisms and Management of Cardiac Arrhythmias (2001); author of many other original articles relating to cardiac arrhythmias; *Recreations* fly fishing, skiing, wildlife photography; *Style*— Prof Clifford Garratt; ✉ Manchester Heart Centre, Manchester Royal Infirmary, Oxford Road, Manchester M13 9WL (☎ 0161 276 8858, fax 0161 276 4443)

GARRATT, Colin Dennis; s of Sqdn Ldr Dennis Herbert Garratt, of Uppingham, Leics, and Margaret Alice, *née* Clarke; *b* 16 April 1940; *Educ* Mill Hill Leicester; *m* Liu Yanchun; 1 da (Tamerlane b 29 April 2008); from previous marriages: 3 s (James Daniel b 2 Aug 1987, Dominion and Antaeus (twins) b 18 June 1999), 1 da (Marie-Louise b 3 June 1993); *Career* photographer, author and publisher; engaged in professionally documenting the last steam locomotives of the world 1969–; writer and illustrator of some 60 books incl Around the World in Search of Steam (autobiography, 1987); also noted audio-visual theatre shows based on global expeditions; currently dir Milepost 92 1/2 (picture library and photographers to the railway industry); latest expdns incl: Bihar and Assam 2007, Inner Mongolia 2008, Northern Manchuria 2009, Gobi Desert 2011; continuing to scour the earth to record imperilled survivors of the legendary age of steam; *Recreations* ornithology, politics, music, art, the appreciation of fine cigars; *Style*— Colin Garratt, Esq; ✉ Milepost 92 1/2, Newton Harcourt, Leicester LE8 9FH (☎ 0116 259 2068, e-mail studio@railphotolibrary.com, website www.railphotolibrary.com)

GARRATT, Sheryl; da of Frank Stephen Garratt, of Birmingham, and June Valerie, *née* Fray; *b* 29 March 1961; *Educ* Barr Beacon Comp Birmingham, UCL (BA); *m* 22 March 1994, Mark McGuire; 1 s (Liam James McGuire b 12 Feb 1996); *Career* freelance writer New Musical Express 1980–83, music ed City Limits 1983–86; freelance writer 1986–88: The Observer, The Sunday Telegraph, Honey, New York Rocker, The Face, News on Sunday, Looks; ed The Face 1989–95 (music/prodn ed 1988–89, winner Int Magazine of the Year PPA Awards 1994); freelance writer 1995–98: The Sunday Times, The Independent, The Guardian, Red, Elle and New Statesman; ed The Observer Life magazine 1998–2000, sr writer The Observer 2000–02; currently freelance for The Telegraph, The Times, Elle, Red, Grazia, Vanity Fair and GQ; *Books* Signed Sealed and Delivered (1984), Adventures in Wonderland (1998), Bliss to be Alive – The Collected Journalism of Gavin Hills (ed, 2000); *Recreations* drinking, dancing, cooking, reading, talking; *Style*— Ms Sheryl Garratt; ✉ 38 London Road, Deal, Kent CT14 9TE (e-mail sherylg1@mac.com)

GARRATT, Timothy George; s of George Herbert Garratt (d 1976), of Chichester, W Sussex, and Hylda Joyce, *née* Spalton (d 1958); *b* 7 September 1942; *Educ* Stowe; *m* 24 April 1965, Vanessa Ann, da of Charles Albert Wright (d 1980), of Chichester, W Sussex; 2 s (Alastair b 1969, James b 1973); *Career* chartered surveyor; ptnr Rendells Auctioneers Valuers & Estate Agents S Devon 1976–2011 (ret); memb Gen Cncl RICS 1969–73, memb Governing Cncl RICS 2011–15; chm: Devon and Cornwall Branch RICS 1989–90, Western Counties Agric Valuers' Assoc 1993–94; memb Cncl Livestock Auctioneers' Assoc 1992–95; pres Chagford and Dist Lions Club 1984–85 and 1992–93, zone chm Lions Club Int 1985–86; *Recreations* farming, gardening, country wine making, home butchery; *Style*— Timothy Garratt, Esq; ✉ Baileys Hey, Chagford, Devon TQ13 8AW (☎ 01647 433396)

GARRAWAY, Kathryn Mary (Kate); *b* 4 May 1967; *Educ* Fitzharrys Sch Abingdon, Bath Spa Univ (BA); *m* 1, 1998 (m dis 2002), Ian Rumsey; m 2, Sept 2005, Derek Draper; 1 da (Darcey Mary b 2006), 1 s (William b 2009); *Career* television broadcaster; prodn journalist, reporter and news presenter Central News 1995; presenter: Meridian Tonight (ITV) until 1997, BBC News 24 1997–98, Sunrise (Sky) 1998–2000, GMTV 2000–10, Daybreak 2010–; *Style*— Ms Kate Garraway; ✉ c/o Melanie Rockcliffe, TROIKA, 3rd Floor, 74 Clerkenwell Road, London EC1M 5QA

GARRETT, André Neil; s of Neil Garrett, of Marylebone, London, and Patricia, *née* Cainey; *b* 14 March 1972; *Educ* Beechen Cliff Sch Bath, Bath Coll of HE; *Career* chef: Hunstrete House Hotel Bath 1989–91, Chez Nico Park Lane London 1991–95, Bistro Bruno 1995–96, Nico Central 1996–99, Fine Dining Room Landmark Hotel 1999–2000; Orrery Restaurant: chef 2000–02, head chef 2002–06 (Michelin Star 2003–06); head chef Galvin @ Windows London Hilton on Park Lane 2006–13, exec head chef Cliveden House 2013–; Roux scholarship 2002, scholarship with Guy Savoy Paris 2003; 10th place Bucuse d'Or 2007; Master of Culinary Arts (MCA) 2005; *Recreations* cycling, reading, snowboarding, eating, motorcycle racing; *Style*— André Garrett, MCA

GARRETT, Graham Robert; s of Alan Garrett, of London, and Joan Garrett; *b* 10 July 1961, London; *Educ* Sir George Monoux Sr High London; *Partner* Jacqueline Hewitt; 1 s (Jake b 24 Dec 1991), 1 da (Jessica b 26 Oct 1993); *Career* restaurateur; professional musician 1979–91; chef dir Christoph's 1996–98, exec chef Nico Ladenis The Restaurant Partnership 1998–2000, chef patron The House Searcy Corrigan 2000–02, chef and owner The West House Kent 2002– (runner up Best Restaurant Outside London Harpers and Moët 2003, Michelin Star 2004–, 3 AA Rosettes 2008), exec chef/conslt Curlew Restaurant Bodiam Sussex (Michelin Star 2011), Kent Chef of the Year 2013; television appearances incl: A Taste of the South (ITV), Food Poker (BBC 2), Ramsay's Best Restaurant (Channel 4), Great British Menu BBC 2); memb World Master Chefs Soc 2007–; *Books* Sex, Drugs and Sausage Rolls – Recipes and Autobiography (2015); *Recreations* golf, food, travel; *Clubs* Chart Hills Golf, The Groucho; *Style*— Graham Garrett, Esq; ✉ website www.thewesthouserestaurant.co.uk

GARRETT, Lesley; CBE (2002); *b* 10 April 1955; *Educ* Royal Acad of Music (Countess of Munster Award, Decca-Kathleen Ferrier Memorial Prize), Nat Opera Studio; *m* 1991; 1 s, 1 da; *Career* soprano; studies with Joy Mammen; princ ENO 1984–98, memb bd dir ENO 1998–; previous engagements incl: Wexford Festival, WNO, Opera North, Buxton Festival, Glyndebourne; Gramophone Award for best selling classical artist of the year 1996; FRAM; *Roles* incl: title role in Mozart's Zaide, Susanna in The Marriage of Figaro, Despina in Cosi fan Tutte, Carolina in Cimarosa's The Secret Marriage, Atalanta in Xerxes, Eurydice in Orpheus in the Underworld, Bella in Tippet's Midsummer Marriage, Musetta in La Bohème, Adele in Die Fledermaus, Rose in Kurt Weill's Street Scene, Zelrina in Don Giovanni, Dalinda in Ariodante, title role in The Cunning Little Vixen, Jenny in Kurt Weill's The Rise and Fall of the City of Mahagonny, title role in La Belle Vivette, Rosina in The Barber of Seville; *Television* Jobs for the Girls (BBC 1), Viva La Diva (BBC 2), Lesley Garrett Tonight (BBC 2); *Recordings* DIVA! A Soprano at the Movies, PriMadonna, Simple Gifts, Soprano in Red 1995, Soprano in Hollywood 1996, A Soprano Inspired 1997, Lesley Garrett 1998, I Will Wait for You 2000, Travelling Light 2001, The Singer 2002, So Deep is the Night 2003; *Recreations* watching cricket; *Style*— Ms Lesley Garrett, CBE

GARRETT, Prof Malcolm Leslie; s of Edmund Garrett (d 1992), of Northwich, Cheshire, and Edna, *née* Mullin; *b* 2 June 1956; *Educ* St Ambrose Coll Altrincham, Univ of Reading, Manchester Poly (BA); *Career* fndr and design dir Assorted Images graphic design consultancy 1977–94, fndr and creative dir AMX interactive communications co 1994–2001, interactive design conslt 2001–03, Immersion Studios Toronto 2003–04, creative dir Applied Information Gp 2005–11; creative dir: 53k communications co 2011–12, IMAGES&Co 2013–, dynamo london, i-Design; co-curator Design Manchester 2013–; visiting prof: in interactive RCA, Central St Martin's Sch of Art, Univ of the Arts London; visiting lectr/teacher numerous univs in Europe and USA, external moderator Manchester Met Univ 2008–12; work exhibited in solo and group shows around the world 1981–; work in permanent collection Dept of Prints and Drawings V&A; chm Design Week Awards 1999–2000; memb: BAFTA Interactive Design Awards Ctee 1999–2003, Exec Ctee RDI 2008–, Sir Misha Black Awards Ctee 2011–; nominated Prince Philip Designers Prize 1998; Hon MA Univ of Salford 2000, Hon DDes Robert Gordon Univ 2005, Hon DDes Univ of the Arts 2013; RDI 2000 (Master of the Faculty 2013–15); memb: D&AD 1997–, BAFTA 1999–; FRSA 2006, FISTD 2009; *Books* Duran Duran – Their Story (with Kasper de Graaf, 1982), When Cameras Go Crazy – Culture Club (with Kasper de Graaf, 1983), Interference (with Nick Rhodes, 1984), Duran Duran – The Book of Words (ed with Kasper de Graaf, 1985), More Dark Than Shark (with Brian Eno, Russell Mills and Rick Poynor, 1986), New British Graphic Designers (with Neville Brody and Peter Saville, 1991), Malcolm Garrett – Ulterior Motifs (graphic devices 1977–91) (1991), The Graphic Beat Vol 1 (1992), Sublime (1992), 100 Best Album Covers (2000), Communicate: Independent British Graphic Design since the Sixties (ed with Rick Poynor, 2004), Duran Duran Unseen – Photographs by Paul Edmond (ed with Kasper de Graaf, 2005), Magazine – The Biography by Helen Chase (2009), Fuse 1–20 (2012); *Recreations* 1969 Plymouth Sport Fury; *Clubs* Phoenix Arts, Shoreditch House; *Style*— Prof Malcolm Garrett, RDI; ✉ IMAGES&Co Ltd, The Clarence Centre, 6 St George's Circus, London SE1 6FE (e-mail malcolm.garrett@images.co.uk, website www.images.co.uk and www.malcolmgarrett.com)

GARRETT, Stephen James; s of James Leslie Michael Peter Garrett, of Sussex, and Margot, *née* Fleischner; *b* 16 April 1957; *Educ* Westminster, Merton Coll Oxford (BA); *Career* exec chm Kudos Film and TV Ltd; *Style*— Stephen Garrett, Esq; ✉ Kudos Film & TV Ltd, 12–14 Amwell Street, London EC1R 1UQ (☎ 020 7812 3270)

GARRICK, Sir Ronald; kt (1994), CBE (1986), DL (Renfrewshire 1996); s of Thomas Garrick, and Anne, *née* MacKay; *b* 21 August 1940; *Educ* RCST Glasgow, Univ of Glasgow (BSc); *m* 1965, Janet Elizabeth Taylor Lind; 2 s, 1 da; *Career* Weir Group plc: joined G & J Weir Ltd 1962, md Weir Pumps 1981, md and chief exec 1982–99, chm 1999–2002; non-exec dir: Scottish Power plc 1992–99, Shell UK Ltd 1993–98, Bank of Scotland 2000–01, HBOS plc 2001– (dep chm 2003–); dir Devonport Management Ltd; dep chm Scottish Enterprise Bd 1991–96; memb: Scottish Cncl CBI 1982–90, Scottish Economic Cncl 1989–98, Scottish Business Forum 1998–99; memb Restrictive Practices Court 1986–96; memb Dearing Ctee of Inquiry into HE 1996–97; Univ of Strathclyde: visiting prof Mech Engrg Dept 1991–96, memb Gen Convocation 1985–96, memb Ct 1990–96; hon sec for mech engrg Royal Acad of Engrg 1991–94; Hon DUniv: Paisley 1993, Strathcylde 1994; Hon DEng Univ of Glasgow 1998; FREng (FEng 1984), FRSE 1992, FIMechE; *Style*— Sir Ronald Garrick, CBE, DL, FRSE, FREng; ✉ HBOS plc, The Mound, Edinburgh EH1 1YZ

GARRIDO, Damian Robin Leon; QC (2015); s of Robin John Garrido, and Karen Margaret, *née* Broome; *b* 7 June 1969, Manchester; *Educ* Manchester GS, Univ of Kent at Canterbury, City Univ London, Inns of Court Law Sch Gray's Inn; *m* 2015, Lucy Joanna, *née* Watts; *Career* called to the Bar 1993, Chambers of P F Singer QC 1993–2006, Chambers of F Judd QC 2006–; recorder (Family Court) 2012–, dep judge of the High Court of Justice (Family Div) 2016–; memb: Family Law Bar Assoc, Hon Soc of the Middle Temple 1993; *Books* Relocation – A Practical Guide (2013, 2 edn); *Recreations* motorsport, skiing; *Style*— Damian Garrido, Esq, QC; ✉ Harcourt Chambers, 2 Harcourt Buildings, London EC4Y 9DB (☎ 08445 617135, e-mail clerks@harcourtchambers.co.uk, website www.harcourtchambers.co.uk)

GARSIDE, HE Bernhard Herbert; s of Capt Roy Bernard Garside, and Gertrud Hedwig, *née* Blome; *b* 1962, Germany; *Educ* St Joseph's Coll Dumfries, Univ of Glasgow (MA); *m* Jennifer Susan, *née* Yard; *Career* diplomat; FCO: joined 1983, clerk Trade Relations & Exports Dept 1983–85, clerk West Indian & Atlantic Dept 1985–86, asst admin offr Masirah 1986–87, asst admin offr Dubai 1987–90, entry clearance offr Lagos 1990–94, desk offr Non Proliferation Dept 1994–95, head Diplomatic Bag Services 1995–97, head The Queen's Messengers 1997–99, HM consul Havana 1999–2002, consul gen Amsterdam 2003–07, head Illegal Immigration and Asylum Team Migration Directorate 2007, migration delivery offr to Sudan Khartoum 2007–08, business change mangr Finance Directorate 2008–10, dep head of mission Algiers 2011–15, ambass to Repub of El Savador 2015–; *Recreations* cinema, gardening, golf, music, skiing, scuba diving; *Style*— HE Mr Bernhard Garside; ✉ c/o FCO (San Salvador), King Charles Street, London SW1A 2AH

GARSIDE, Prof John; CBE (2005); s of James Eric Garside, and Ada Garside; *b* 9 October 1941; *Educ* Christ's Coll Finchley, UCL (state scholar, Salters' scholar, BSc(Eng), PhD, DSc(Eng)); *m* 1965, Patricia Louise Holtom; 1 s (Thomas b 1967), 1 da (Ruth b 1969); *Career* pt/t lectr Dept of Chemical Engrg Borough Poly London 1964–66, tech offr R&D Dept Imperial Chemical Industries Ltd Agric Div Billingham 1966–69, Fulbright sr scholar and visiting prof Dept of Chemical Engrg Iowa State Univ 1976–77, reader in chemical engrg UCL 1981 (lectr 1969–81); UMIST (now Univ of Manchester): prof of chemical engrg 1982–, head of dept 1983–88 and 1990–92, vice-princ for academic devpt and external affrs 1985–87, dep princ 1986–87, pro-vice-chllr 1997–2000, vice-chllr 2000–04; dep pro-vice-chllr Univ of Lancaster 2014– (memb Cncl 2012–); Monbusho/BC visiting prof Dept of Chemical Engrg Tokyo Univ of Agric and Technol 1992; memb: Engrg and Materials Science Panel Res Corp Tst 1985–88, Engrg Bd SERC 1990–93, Cncl IChemE 1992–1997 (pres 1994–95), NW Science Cncl 2000–04; European Fedn of Chemical Engrg: UK delg 2000–, memb Working Pty on Crystallization 1990–2000 (chm 1994–2000), vice-pres 2006–09; assoc ed Chemical Engrg Communications 1985–99, hon ed Trans IChemE 2000–06; fell UCL 1994; Hon LLD Univ of Manchester 2004, Hon DEng UMIST 2004; CEng 1969, FRSA 1985, FIChemE 1986, FREng 1988; *Recreations* music, gardening, sailing; *Clubs* Athenaeum; *Style*— Prof John Garside, CBE, FREng; ✉ Bryham House, Askham, Penrith CA10 2PU

GARSTON, Clive Richard; s of Henry Leslie Garston (d 1978), of Manchester, and Sheila Esther, *née* Cohen; *b* 25 April 1945, Blackpool; *Educ* Manchester Grammar, Univ of Leeds (LLB), Coll of Law; *m* 25 Feb 1973, Racheline Raymonde, da of Jacques Sultan; 1 s (Nicholas Nathan b 15 July 1974), 1 da (Louise Anne b 22 May 1978); *Career* slr; Hall Brydon Manchester: articled clerk 1966–68, asst slr 1968–71, ptnr 1971–78; sr ptnr Halliwell Landau Manchester 1989–95 (ptnr 1978–89 and 1995–2001), sr ptnr Halliwell Landau London 2001–07, conslt Davies Arnold Cooper LLP 2009–12, conslt DAC Beachcroft LLP 2011–; chm Ultimate Finance Gp plc 2007–12; non-exec dep chm The Inter Care Gp plc 1990–2002; memb: Law Soc 1968, International Bar Assoc, American Bar Assoc; FCSI; *Recreations* cricket, music, opera, swimming, skiing, travel, watching Manchester United; *Clubs* RAC, Lancashire CCC; *Style*— Clive R Garston, Esq; ✉ 100 Howard Building, 368 Queenstown Road, London SW8 4NR (☎ 020 7498 6053, mobile 07802 356614); Sandy Ridge, Bollinway, Hale, Cheshire WA15 0NZ (☎ 0161 904 9822); DAC Beachcroft LLP, 100 Fetter Lane, London EC4A 1BN (e-mail cgarston@dacbeachcroft.com)

GARTHWAITE, Nicholas; s of Anthony Garthwaite (d 1972), and Waveney Samuel (d 1986); *b* 26 March 1952; *Educ* Churchill Coll Cambridge (BA); *m* 2 April 1982, Caroline Catchpole Willbourne, da of Thomas Willbourne; 3 s; *Career* various posts in oil, electricity, European policy and energy efficiency divisions Dept of Energy 1973–86, managing conslt Telecommunications Gp Touche Ross Mgmnt Conslts 1986–94, dir of telecommunications Price Waterhouse Corporate Finance 1994–96, mgmnt conslt Cicero Strategy 1996–; non-exec chm Cicero Translations 1980–; Competition Cmmn (formerly Monopolies & Mergers Cmmn): memb Telecommunications Panel 1998–2007, memb Reporting Panel 2000–07, memb Code of Business Practice Complaints Adjudication Panel Assoc of Br Healthcare Industries 2008–; author of articles on telecommunications; memb Communications Mgmnt Assoc 1994; tstee and memb Honorary Devpt Advsy Bd Bampton Classical Opera; FRSA; *Recreations* crosswords, ballet, opera; *Style*— Nicholas

Garthwaite, Esq; ✉ Cicero Strategy, 6 St Petersburgh Place, London W2 4LB (✆ 020 7229 3256, e-mail nicholas.garthwaite@cicerostrategy.com)

GARTON ASH, Prof Timothy John; CMG (2000); s of John Garton Ash, and Lorna Garton Ash; *b* 12 July 1955; *Educ* Sherborne, Exeter Coll Oxford (BA), St Antony's Coll Oxford (MA), Free Univ W Berlin, Humboldt Univ E Berlin; *m* 1982, Danuta; 2 s (Thomas b 1984, Alexander b 1986); *Career* editorial writer on Central Euro affrs The Times 1984–86, foreign ed The Spectator 1984–90, columnist The Independent 1988–90, columnist The Guardian 2002–, regular contrib to New York Review of Books; fell: Woodrow Wilson Int Center for Scholars Washington 1986–87, St Antony's Coll Oxford 1990–, Hoover Inst Stanford Univ 2000–; prof of European studies Univ of Oxford 2004–; memb Bd of Govrs Westminster Fndn for Democracy 1992–2001; David Watt meml prize 1989, Commentator of the Year in Granada TV What the Papers Say Awards 1990, George Orwell Prize 2006; Hon DLitt Univ of St Andrews 2004, Hon DLitt Sheffield Hallam 2005, Hon DLitt Leuven 2011; FRSA, FRHistS, FRSL; Order of Merit (Poland) 1992, memb Berlin-Brandenburg Acad of Sci 1994, Order of Merit (Germany) 1995, Imre Nagy Meml Plaque (Hungary) 1995, Premio Napoli 1995, OSCE Prize for Journalism and Democracy 1998, Order of Merit (Czech Repub) 2003; *Books* Und Willst Du Nicht Mein Bruder Sein... Die DDR heute (1981), The Polish Revolution: Solidarity (1983, 3 edn 1999, Somerset Maugham award 1984), The Uses of Adversity (1989, Prix Européen de l'Essai 1989, 3 edn 1999), We The People (1990, 2 edn 1999), In Europe's Name (1993), The File: A Personal History (1997), History of the Present: Essays, Sketches and Despatches from Europe in the 1990s (1999), Free World (2004), Facts are Subversive (2009); *Recreations* travel; *Clubs* Frontline, Institut für die Wissenschaften vom Menschen (Vienna); *Style*— Prof Timothy Garton Ash, CMG; ✉ St Antony's College, Oxford OX2 6JF

GARTSIDE, Edmund Travis; TD (1968), DL (Gtr Manchester 1990); s of Col J B Gartside, DSO, MC, TD, JP, DL (d 1964), and Cora Maude, *née* Baker; *b* 11 November 1933; *Educ* Winchester, Trinity Coll Cambridge (MA); *m* 1, 29 Aug 1959 (m dis 1982), Margaret Claire, *née* Nicholls; 1 s (Michael Travis b 1961), 1 da (Vanessa Perry Anne (Mrs Anderson) b 1962); m 2, 5 May 1983, Valerie Cox, da of Cyril Vowels, of Instow, Devon; *Career* Nat Serv 2 Lt RE and Lancs Fusiliers 1952–54; TA: Lancs Fusiliers (Maj) 1954–67, E Lancs Regt 1967–68; chm and md Shiloh plc (formerly Shiloh Spinners Ltd) 1966– (mgmnt trainee 1957, dir 1960, gen mangr Roy Mill 1961–65, dep chm 1963–66, md 1965); dir Oldham and Rochdale Textile Employers' Assoc 1965–2000 (pres 1971–75), memb Central Ctee Br Textile Employers' Assoc 1969–89 (pres 1976–78); pres: Eurocoton 1985–87, Cncl of Br Cotton Textiles 1989–; memb Cncl: IOD 1974–2001, Shrievalty Assoc 1996–99; High Sheriff Gtr Manchester 1995–96; memb Ct Univ of Manchester 1979–94, govr Manchester GS 1984–98; CCMI, FInstD; *Clubs* Army and Navy; *Style*— Edmund Gartside, Esq, TD, DL

GARVEY, Prof Conall John; s of Col Sean Garvey, and Vona Garvey; *b* 9 August 1955; *Educ* NUI (MB, BCh, BAO), UC Galway (Gold medal in otorhinolaryngology, special prize in paediatrics), Newcastle Coll (Dip); *Children*; 4 c (Grainne b 15 July 1982, Darren b 3 March 1984, Fergal b 6 Nov 1985, Killian b 5 June 1988); *Career* radiologist; SHO UC Hosp Galway 1979–80, registrar then sr registrar Northwick Park Hosp & Clinical Research Centre Harrow 1980–86, conslt radiologist Liverpool HA 1986–2014, conslt in admin charge Sefton Gen Hosp 1986–93, clinical dir of radiology Royal Liverpool Univ Hosp 1995–2001 (chm Hosp Medical Bd 1997–99), nat clinical lead for radiology NHS Modernisation Agency 2001–05; hon prof Univ of Liverpool 2012–; chm: Dist Med Advsy Ctee Liverpool HA 1999–2001, Radiology Network Gp Merseyside & Cheshire Cancer Network 2002–05; RCR: memb Cncl 2001–04, FRCR examiner 2001–05, treas 2005–10; memb: Nat Bowel Cancer Expert Gp, Radiology Working Party (Nat Cancer Standards); Levy Prize RCR 1996; FRCR 1984; Disorders of the Small Intestine (contrib, 1985), Complications in Diagnostic Imaging (contrib, 1987), Exercises in Diagnostic Imaging: For MRCP and other higher qualifications (co-author, 1989); numerous articles and reviews for learned jls; papers for nat and int meetings and congresses; *Recreations* flying, golf; *Clubs* Prenton Golf, Southport & Merseyside Flying; *Style*— Prof Conall Garvey; ✉ e-mail conall.garvey@gmail.com

GARVIE, (Fiona) Jane; *b* 19 May 1956; *Educ* Westbourne Sch for Girls Glasgow, Univ of Glasgow (MA, LLB); *m* 1998, Andrew Hardie Primrose; *Career* Maclay Murray & Spens: legal apprentice 1979–81, asst slr 1981–84, seconded to Bristows, Cooke & Carpmael London 1984–85, litigation ptnr 1985–97, head Employment Law Unit 1995–97; fndr Garvie & Co (employment lawyers) 1997, ptnr and head of Employment Golds Slrs 2000–01, conslt 2001–02, employment judge Employment Tbnls (Scotland) 2002–; Int Bar Assoc: chm Discrimination and Gender Equality Ctee 1998–2002 (vice-chm 1996–98), memb SLP Cncl 2002–04; memb: Educn and Trg Ctee Law Soc of Scotland 1996–2000, Law Soc of Scotland 1981, Law Soc 1992; *Publications* Indirect Discrimination in Managing a Legal Practice (Int Legal Practitioner, Sept 1995); *Recreations* music, reading, gardening, walking, exploring cities; *Style*— Ms Jane Garvie; ✉ Central Office of Employment Tribunals, Eagle Buildings, 215 Bothwell Street, Glasgow G2 7TS (✆ 0141 204 0730)

GARVIE, Dr Wayne; s of George Garvie, of Suffolk, and Frances, *née* Passmore; *b* 9 September 1963; *Educ* Univ of Kent Canterbury (BA), Univ of Sheffield (PhD); *m* 1993, Tracey, *née* Stephenson; 2 da (Susie Lola b July 1999, Lara Honey b April 2002); *Career* Granada TV: sports researcher 1988–91, prodr 1991–96, dep dir of broadcasting 1996, dir of broadcasting 1996–98; head of entertainment and features BBC Prodn 1998–2000, head of music, entertainment and features BBC Prodn 2000–01, head Entertainment Gp BBC 2001–06, md of content and prodn BBC Worldwide 2006–10, md of int prodn All3Media 2011–; visiting prof of media Univ of Chester; tstee Nat Museum of Lab History, chair RTS (memb 1993); memb BAFTA; *Recreations* football, relentless child care, pottering around the garden and idleness; *Style*— Dr Wayne Garvie

GARWOOD, Prof Stephen John; s of Ronald David Garwood (d 1998), and Irene Gaynor, *née* Dawson; *b* 25 September 1951; *Educ* Barry Boys GS, Imperial Coll London (BSc(Eng), ACGI, PhD, DIC); *m* 20 Nov 1976, Rosemary Joy, *née* Mott; 1 da (Sophie Kate b 1 Nov 1980), 1 s (Thomas Stephen Frederick b 1 Sept 1982); *Career* Welding Inst: research engr rising to sr research engr 1976–80, section head 1980–89, head of engrg 1989–94, head of structural integrity 1994–96; tech dir RR&A 1996–98, dir of engrg and technol Rolls-Royce Marine Power 1998–2000; Rolls-Royce plc: dir of technol 2000–01, dir of materials 2001–05, dir engrg and technol – submarines Rolls-Royce Marine 2005–13; prof of structural integrity, mechanical engrg Imperial Coll London 2014–; non-exec dir Transport Systems Catapult; author of over 80 pubns in the field of structural intergrity of welded structures; visiting prof Imperial Coll London; 56th Hatfield Meml lecture 2008; Leslie Lidstone-Esab Gold Medal 1986; CEng 1981, FWeldI 1980, FIMechE 1987, FIMMM 2002, FREng 2002; *Clubs* hockey, squash, running; *Style*— Prof Stephen Garwood; ✉ Department of Mechanical Engineering, Imperial College London, Exhibition Road, London SW7 2AZ (e-mail s.garwood@imperial.ac.uk)

GASCOIGNE, Ian; *b* 7 July 1956, Plymouth, Devon; *Educ* Westfield Sch, Univ of Lancaster (BSc), Univ of Leicester (MA); *Career* St James's Place plc: joined 1991, memb Bd 1997–, gp sales dir 2003–; tstee St James's Place Fndn; *Recreations* watching Sheffield Wednesday FC, poker; *Style*— Ian Gascoigne, Esq; ✉ St James's Place plc, St James's Place House, Dollar Street, Cirencester, Gloucestershire GL7 2AQ

GASKELL, (Richard) Carl; s of (Henry) Brian Gaskell (d 1982), and Doris Winnifred, *née* Taylor; *b* 23 March 1948; *Educ* Gateway Sch Leicester, Univ of Newcastle upon Tyne (LLB); *m* 29 Dec 1973, Margaret Annette, da of Stanley Walter Humber; 1 s (Philip b 1975), 3 da (Victoria b 1976, Elizabeth b 1979, Gillian b 1983); *Career* called to the Bar Lincoln's Inn 1971, Midland & Oxford circuit, asst recorder of the Crown Court 1989–; chm Desford Branch Bosworth Cons Assoc; *Style*— Carl Gaskell, Esq

GASKIN, Prof John Charles Addison; s of Harry James Gaskin (d 1995), of Mixbury, Oxon, and Evelyn Mary Addison Gaskin, *née* Taylor (d 1989), of Aberdeen; *b* 4 April 1936; *Educ* City of Oxford HS, Univ of Oxford (MA, BLitt), Univ of Dublin (DLitt); *m* 20 May 1972, Diana Katherine, da of Maurice Dobbin (d 1969); 1 s (Rupert John Addison b 1974), 1 da (Suzette Jane Addison b 1975); *Career* Royal Bank of Scotland 1959–61; TCD: jr dean, lectr and prof of naturalistic philosophy 1963–97, fell 1978–; hon tutor Univ of Durham 1997–2010; cncllr Hesleyhurst 1997–; dir Music at Paxton Summer Festivals 2006–13; lectr with Westminster Classic Tours 2007–; *Books* incl: Hume's Philosophy of Religion (1978, 1988), The Quest for Eternity (1984), Varieties of Unbelief (1989), The Epicurean Philosophers (1994), The Dark Companion – Ghost Stories (2001), Tale sof Twilight and Borderlands (2005), A Doubt of Death (2011), The Traveller's Guide to Classical Philosophy (2011), Hobbes' Leviathan (ed, Folio Soc edn 2012), The Master of the House (2014); *Recreations* eating and dreaming, writing stories, old wine, gardening, walking, classical civilisation; *Clubs* Northern Counties (Newcastle); *Style*— Prof John C A Gaskin; ✉ Crook Crossing, Netherwitton, Morpeth, Northumberland NE61 4PY; Hatfield College, Durham DH1 3RQ

GASKIN, Malcolm Graeme Charles; s of Charles Augustus Gaskin (d 1981), of Blyth, Northumberland, and Jean, *née* Denton; *b* 27 February 1951; *Educ* Blyth GS, Manchester Poly, Sch of Art and Design; *m* Deborah Ann, da of Michael Loftus, of Osterley, Middx; 2 s (Jack Alexander, Lewis Ross (twins) b 1983), 1 da (Francesca Vita b 1985); *Career* art dir Leo Burnett 1973–77 (created 'Eau' campaign for Perrier); creative dir: TBWA 1977–81, Woollams Moira Gaskin O'Malley 1987–95, Osprey Park Agency 1995–96; creative dir Ford of Britain and head of art Ogilvy & Mather 1998–; advertising awards for Lego, Land Rover, CIGA, Nursing Recruitment and AIDS; pres Advertising Creative Circle; memb: Creative Circle, D&AD 1975; *Books* Design and Art Direction (1975); *Recreations* gardening, angling, hiking, art; *Clubs* Soho House; *Style*— Malcolm Gaskin, Esq; ✉ Ogilvy & Mather, 10 Cabot Square, Canary Wharf, London E14 4QB (✆ 020 7345 3000)

G

GASS, Lady; Dame Elizabeth Periam Acland Hood; DCVO (2014), JP (Somerset 1996); da of Hon (Arthur) John Palmer Acland-Hood, barrister (d 1964; s of 1 Baron St Audries, Barony extinct 1971), and Dr Phyllis Acland-Hood, *née* Hallett (d 2004); *b* 2 March 1940; *Educ* Cheltenham Ladies' Coll, Girton Coll Cambridge (MA); *m* 1975, Sir Michael David Irving Gass, KCMG (d 1983, sometime HM Overseas Civil Serv in W Africa, colonial sec Hong Kong, high cmmr for W Pacific, British high cmmr for New Hebrides); *Career* memb Somerset CC 1985–97, chm Exmoor National Park Ctee 1989–93, dir Avalon NHS Tst 1993–96; memb: Rail Users' Consultative Ctee for Western England 1992–99, Cncl Cheltenham Ladies' Coll 1992–2001, Wessex Regnl Ctee Nat Tst 1994–2002, Nat Exec Ctee CLA 1998–2003, Historic Houses Assoc Wessex Ctee 1998–, Cncl Univ of Bath 1999–2002, Wells Cathedral Cncl 2004–; tstee West of England Sch for Children with Little or No Sight 1996–2008; cmmr English Heritage 1995–2001; pres Royal Bath and West of England Soc 2002–03, patron, pres and memb of many Somerset charitable orgns; High Sheriff Somerset 1994, HM Lord-Lt Somerset 1998–2015 (DL 1995–98, Vice Lord-Lt 1996–98); *Recreations* gardening, music, archaeology; *Style*— Lady Gass, DCVO; ✉ Fairfield, Stogursey, Bridgwater, Somerset TA5 1PU (✆ 01278 732251, fax 01278 732277)

GASSON, Allan; s of Maj Dr John Gasson, RAF, DSO, DFC*, FRCS, and Valerie Gasson; *b* 18 November 1955; *Educ* Diocesan Coll Cape Town, Univ of Cape Town (BSc), INSEAD (MBA); *m* Rosemary; 1 s (Benjamin), 2 da (Amy, Julia); *Career* business devpt dir BET 1985–86, chief exec United Transport Line, conslt Bain & Co 1987–90, gen mangr Beverage Div then business devpt dir EMEA Dole Food Co 1990–92, fndr and md Burlington Conslts 1993–2005, head of M&A strategy Deloitte 2005–; *Publications* Intervention Strategies of Private Equity Firms in their Portfolios (2005); *Recreations* golf, tennis, sailing, skiing, opera, theatre; *Clubs* Worplesdon Golf, Hurlingham, Royal Cape Golf, Kelvin Grove Country; *Style*— Allan Gasson, Esq; ✉ Deloitte & Touche LLP, Athene Place, 66 Shoe Lane, London EC4A 3BQ

GASSON, Andrew Peter; s of Sidney Samuel Gasson, and Elsie Gasson; *b* July 1943; *Educ* Dulwich Coll, Henry Thornton GS, City Univ; *Career* in private practice (specialising in contact lenses) 1972–; pres Contact Lens Soc 1974–75; examiner: Spectacle Makers' Co, Coll of Optometrists 1975–84; memb: Contact Lens Ctee BSI 1980–82, Cncl Br Contact Lens Assoc 1986; vice-chm Ophthalmic Ethics Ctee London 2003–04; lectr at numerous sci meetings; chm Br Orthokeratology Soc 1997–2013; chm Wilkie Collins Soc 1981–; Freeman City of London, Liveryman Worshipful Co of Spectacle Makers; fell Br Contact Lens Assoc 2001; FRSM, FBOA, FCOptom, DCLP, FAAO, ARPS; *Books* The Contact Lens Manual (jtly, 1991, 4 edn 2010), The Good Cat Food Guide (jtly, 1992 and 2006), The Good Dog Food Guide (jtly, 1993), Wilkie Collins – an Illustrated Guide (1998), The Public Face of Wilkie Collins (jtly, 2005), Lives of Victorian Literary Figures: Wilkie Collins (jtly, 2007), The Lighthouse by Wilkie Collins (jt ed, 2013); *Recreations* antiquarian books, travel, photography, cricket, motoring, bridge; *Clubs* MCC, Surrey CCC; *Style*— Andrew Gasson, Esq; ✉ 6 De Walden Street, London W1G 8RL (✆ 020 7224 5959, e-mail lenses@andrewgasson.co.uk)

GAST, Alice; *Career* prof of chemical engrg Stanford Univ 1985–2001; MIT 2001–2006: vice-pres for research, assoc provost, Robert T Haslam chair in chemical engrg; pres Lehigh Univ Pennsylvania 2006–14, pres Imperial Coll 2014–; *Style*— Prof Alice Gast; ✉ Imperial College London, South Kensington Campus, London SW7 2AZ

GASTON, Prof (John Stanley) Hill; *b* 24 June 1952; *Educ* Royal Belfast Academical Instn, Lincoln Coll Oxford (MA), Univ of Oxford Med Sch (scholar, BM BCh), Univ of Bristol (PhD); *m*; 2 c (b 1981, b 1983); *Career* house surgn Basingstoke Dist Hosp then house physician Radcliffe Infirmary Oxford 1976, SHO in clinical haematology Royal Postgrad Med Sch London 1977, SHO in nephrology Southmead Hosp Bristol 1977–78, SHO/registrar rotation in gen med Southmead Hosp, Bristol Gen Hosp, Bristol Royal Infirmary and Torbay Dist Hosp 1978–80, Sir Michael Sobell cancer research fell Cancer Research Campaign Dept of Pathology Univ of Bristol 1980–83, hon registrar in med and rheumatology Dept of Med Bristol Royal Infirmary 1980–83, MRC travelling fell Div of Immunology Stanford Univ Med Center Calif 1984, clinical fell Div of Immunology Stanford Univ Med Sch 1985; hon conslt in rheumatology: Central Birmingham HA 1987–92, S Birmingham HA 1992–95; Univ of Birmingham: MRC research trg fell Dept of Rheumatology and hon sr registrar Dept of Med 1985–87, Wellcome sr research fell in clinical sci 1987–92, sr lectr in rheumatology 1992–94, reader in experimental rheumatology 1994–95, prof of experimental rheumatology 1995; prof of rheumatology Univ of Cambridge 1995–2015; clinical dir W Anglia Comp Local Research Network 2008–13; fell St Edmund's Coll Cambridge, visiting fell Univ of Turku Finland 1988 (Wellcome Tst grant 1989–92); Arthritis Research UK: memb Research Sub-Ctee 1992–95 and 2002–, chm Fellowship Ctee 1995–2000; numerous presentations at meetings and int confs, author of published papers, reviews, editorials and book chapters; asst ed: Rheumatology; memb: Assoc of Physicians, Br Soc for Rheumatology (Michael Mason Prize 1990, Heberden Round Medal 2011), Br Soc for Immunology, American Coll of Rheumatologists; FRCP, FMedSci 2001; *Recreations* travel, music, science and faith interactions; *Style*— Prof J S Hill Gaston; ✆ 01223 837554, mobile 07884 186139; University of Cambridge School of Clinical Medicine, Department of Medicine, Box 157,

Level 5, Addenbrooke's Hospital, Hills Road, Cambridge CB2 0QQ (✆ 01223 330161, fax 01223 330160, e-mail jshg2@medschl.cam.ac.uk)

GATENBY, Ian Cheyne; s of Lt-Col William Gatenby (d 1971), of Esher, Surrey, and Frances Alice, *née* Davies (d 1982); *b* 30 June 1942; *Educ* Royal GS Newcastle upon Tyne, Exeter Coll Oxford (MA); *m* 1, Jan 1973 (m dis 1989); 1 s (Piers b 5 Aug 1975), 1 da (Catherine b 9 April 1977); m 2, 30 April 1994, Anne Margaret, *née* Storrs; *Career* admitted slr 1968, assoc ptnr Lovell White & King 1973–77 (articled clerk then asst slr 1966–73); Cameron McKenna (formerly McKenna & Co): joined 1975, ptnr 1977–, currently sr planning ptnr; author of numerous articles on planning and rating; memb Law Soc 1988 (memb Planning Panel 1993); legal assoc RTPI 1993; *Recreations* skiing, sailing, English National Opera, gardening; *Clubs* Ski of GB, Ranelagh Sailing; *Style*— Ian Gatenby, Esq

GATES, Paul Winnett; OBE (2003); s of Harry Winnett Gates (d 1971), and Sylvia Edna Mellor (d 1969); *b* 26 April 1948; *Educ* Meols Cop HS Southport; *m* 2 Sept 1989, Elaine; 1 s (Allan b 11 Jan 1967), 1 da (Donna b 20 Feb 1971); *Career* Stirling Knitting 1965–77 (shop steward 1969–77); Nat Union of Hosiery and Knitwear Workers (NUHKW): dist offr NW 1977–82, NE dist sec 1984–90; Nat Union of Knitwear, Footwear and Apparel Traders (KFAT): nat offr 1990–94, gen sec 1994–2007; TUC: dir Partnership Inst 2000, dir Stakeholder Tstees Ltd 2001, memb Gen Cncl 2001–02; dir Skillfast-UK (Sector Skills Cncl for the Textile and Clothing Industry) 2002–09; ind memb Bd DTI 2005–07; tstee Gen Fedn of Trade Unions (GFTU) 1999–2007; memb: Nat Jt Industrial Cncl for the Knitting Industries 1975–2007, Footwear Industry Jt Consultative Ctee 1991–2007, Textile Industry Health and Safety Advsy Ctee (TEXIAC) 1995–2007, Textile & Clothing Strategy Gp (TCSG) 1999–2007, Exec Int Textile, Garment and Leather Workers' Fedn (ITGLWF) 1999–2007, Exec European Trade Union Fedn for the Textile, Clothing and Leather Industries (ETUC:TCL) 1999–2007, Lab Pty, Low Pay Cmmn, Central Arbitration Ctee, Employment Trbnls Panel; dir Bolton Bury TEC (BBTEC) 1989–94, memb Duke of Edinburgh Cwlth Study Conf 1984; memb Textiles Inst 1998; *Recreations* football, cricket, gardening; *Style*— Paul Gates, Esq, OBE; ✉ 1 Poolside Walk, Southport PR9 8NB

GATFIELD, Stephen John; s of Dennis Edward Gatfield, of Barnard Castle, Co Durham, and Hilary Marie Gatfield; *b* 2 September 1958; *Educ* Churcher's Coll Petersfield, City of London Freemans' Sch Ashtead, Univ of Bristol (BSc), IMD PED (Business Sch Mgmnt Dip); *m* 31 May 1992, Eliza, da of Dr Ronald Tepper; *Career* account planner Leo Burnett advtg 1981–84, account dir Grandfield Rork Collins 1984–85, gp account planner Saatchi & Saatchi 1985–86; StarCom (formerly Leo Burnett): bd dir 1987, head of account mgmnt 1988–90, dep md 1990–91, md 1991–96, chief exec 1992–97, md Asia/Pacific 1997–2000, chief operating offr LB Worldwide 2001–03; exec vice-pres of global ops and innovation Interpublic Gp 2004–06, exec vice-pres of network operations and strategy Interpublic Gp, ceo Lowe & Ptnrs Worldwide; co-chm Naked Communications 2011–; memb Asia Soc; memb: IPA, IDM, MRS 1981, Strategic Planning Soc 1990; *Recreations* tennis, golf, theatre, jazz, modern art; *Clubs* RAC, IMD Alumni, Seawanhaka Yacht; *Style*— Stephen Gatfield, Esq

GATISS, Mark; *b* 17 October 1966; *Educ* Bretton Hall Coll, Univ of Leeds (BA); *Career* actor, writer and comedian, memb The League of Gentlemen comedy gp; Hon DLitt Univ of Huddersfield; *Theatre* A Local Show for Local People (nat tour) 2000–01, Art (Whitehall Theatre) 2002, All About My Other (Old Vic) 2007, Season's Greetings (NT) 2010, The Recruiting Officer (Donmar Warehouse) 2012, Coriolanus (NT) 2013; *Television* The League of Gentlemen (BBC) 1999, 2000 and 2002, The League of Gentlemen Christmas Special (BBC) 2000, Surrealissimo (BBC) 2001, Dr Terrible's House of Horrible (BBC) 2001, Spaced (Channel 4) 2001, Nighty Night (BBC) 2004, Catterick (BBC) 2004, From Bard to Verse (BBC) 2004, Footballers' Wives (ITV) 2004, Miss Marple: Murder at the Vicarage (ITV 1) 2004, The Quartermass Experiment (BBC 4) 2005, Doctor Who: The Unquiet Dead (BBC) (writer) 2005, The Wind in the Willows 2006, Sense and Sensibility 2008, Clone 2008, Crooked House 2008, Worried About the Boy 2010, The First Men in the Moon 2010, Sherlock (BBC) 2010– (also writer), Being Human (BBC) 2012, Game of Thrones (HBO) 2014; *Radio* The Further Adventures of Sherlock Holmes (Radio 4) 2003, Nebulous (Radio 4) 2005; *Film* Now You See Her 2001, The Cicerones 2002, Bright Young Things 2003, Sex Lives of the Potatomen 2003, Matchpoint 2005, The Hitchhiker's Guide to the Galaxy 2005, Shaun of the Dead 2004, The League of Gentlemen's Apocalypse 2005, Starter for Ten 2006; *Awards* Perrier Award 1997, Sony Silver Award for Radio Comedy 1998, Golden Rose of Montreux 1999, BAFTA Award for Best Comedy 2000, RTS Award for Best Entertainment 2000, NME Award for Best TV Prog 2001, South Bank Show Award for Best Comedy 2003, Best Drama Series BAFTA 2011 (for Sherlock), Best Drama Series RTS Award 2011 (for Sherlock); *Books* Nightshade (1992), St Anthony's Fire (1994), The Roundheads (1997), Last of the Gaderene (1999), The Essex Files (with Jeremy Dyson, 1997), A Local Book for Local People (2000), The Vesuvius Club (2004), The Devil in Amber (2006), Black Butterfly (2008); *Recreations* painting; *Clubs* Soho House, Vesuvius; *Style*— Mark Gatiss, Esq; ✉ c/o PBJ Management, 7 Soho Street, London W1D 3DQ (✆ 020 7287 1112); c/o Curtis Brown Group Ltd, Haymarket House, 28–29 Haymarket, London SW1Y 4SP (✆ 020 7393 4400)

GATTI, Daniele; *b* 6 November 1961; *Educ* Artisit Liceo; *m* Silvia Chiesa; *Career* conductor; fndr and musical dir Stradivari (orchestra da camera) 1986–92, res conductor Pomeriffi Musicali Orchestra Milan 1986, AsLi Co 1988–89, conductor Teatro Comunale Bologna 1990–92, res conductor Accademia Nazionale di Santa Cecilia Orchestra 1993–97, princ guest conductor Royal Opera House 1994–97, music dir Royal Philharmonic Orch 1996–, music dir Teatro Comunale Bologna 1997–; conductor: Teatro alla Scala 1988, Rossini Opera Festival 1988 and 1998, Carnegie Hall NY 1990, Toronto Symphony Orch 1991, Los Angeles Philharmonic 1991, Orchestre Symphonique de Montréal 1993, Bayerische Rundfunk 1993, LSO 1993, Philadelphia Orch 1993, Cincinnati Symphony Orch 1994, Nat Symphony Orch Washington 1994, Chicago Symphony Orch 1994, 2001, San Francisco Symphony 1994, LPO 1994, White Nights Festival St Petersburg 1994, BBC Proms 1995 and 1997, New York Philharmonic 1996, 1998, 1999 and 2001, Berlin Philharmoniker 1997, Accademia di Santa Cecilia 1998, Orchestra Verdi di Milano 1998, Boston Symphony 1998 and 2001, Munich Philharmonic 1998, 2001 and 2002, Dresden Staatskapelle 1999 and 2002, Vienna State Opera 2002 and 2003, Israel Philharmonic 2002, Semperoper Dresden 2003; numerous performances with Royal Philharmonic Orch and Teatro Comunale di Bologna; tours with Royal Philharmonic Orch incl: Europe 1999, USA 1999, Germany, Italy, Spain and Belgium 2001–2002, Italy 2002, North America, Germany, Spain and Switzerland 2003–04; tours with Teatro Comunale di Bologna incl Japan 1998 and 2001; recordings on Decca and Sony Classical labels, exclusive recording with BMG Conifer; winner Int Prize Le Muse Florence 1996; *Recreations* reading, walking, football, chess; *Style*— Daniele Gatti, Esq; ✉ The Royal Philharmonic Orchestra, 16 Clerkenwell Green, London EC1R 0QT

GAUKE, Rt Hon David; PC (2016), MP; *Educ* Northgate HS, St Edmund Hall Oxford, Chester Coll of Law; *m* Rachel; 3 s (William b 2002, Robert b 2004, Henry b 2008); *Career* Parly research asst to Barry Legg MP 1993–94; slr: Richards Butler 1995–99, Macfarlanes 1999–2005; Parly candidate (Cons) Brent E 2001, MP (Cons) SW Hertfordshire 2005–; Exchequer sec to the Treasy 2010–14, fin sec to the Treasy 2014–16, chief sec to the Treasy 2016–; dep chair Brent E Cons Assoc 1998–2000; *Style*— The Rt Hon David Gauke, MP; ✉ House of Commons, London SW1A 0AA (✆ 020 7219 4459, fax 020 7219 4759, e-mail david@davidgauke.com, website www.davidgauke.com)

GAULT, David Thomas; s of William Gault (d 1989), and Irene Mable Bebe, *née* Tilbe (d 1993); *b* 21 March 1954, St Andrews, Fife; *Educ* Huntingdon GS, Bourne Sch Singapore, Coleraine Academical Instn, Univ of Edinburgh (MB, ChB, Rowing blue); *m* 6 May 1989, Debbi, *née* Hastings-Nield; 2 s (William George b 23 Jan 1990, Thomas Charles b 26 Jan 1993), 2 da (Sophie Margaux b 4 June 1991, Lauren Elizabeth b 24 Aug 1994); *Career* conslt plastic surgn: Mount Vernon Hosp 1991–2006, Gt Ormond St Hosp For Children 1999–2006, London Centre for Ear Reconstruction (private practice) 2006–; developed Ear Buddies, flushout technique for extravasation, and Gault technique for pinnaplasty, all now in use worldwide; C C Wu visiting prof Hong Kong 2004; memb Editorial Bd Jl of Cosmetic and Laser Therapy; Arnold Huddart Medal 1990, Daily Star Gold Award 1992, Hosp Dr Surgery Team of the Year (Merit) 2005; memb: Br Assoc of Plastic Surgns 1991, Br Assoc of Aesthetic Plastic Surgns 1993, European Assoc of Plastic, Reconstructive and Aesthetic Surgns 2000; 50 Ways To Hurt Yourself At Home – A Book of Cartoons (1997), Otolaryngology (contrib, 2008); author of numerous articles in learned jls; *Recreations* rowing, planting, painting; *Style*— David Gault, Esq; ✉ London Centre for Ear Reconstruction, The Portland Hospital, 205–209 Great Portland Street, London W1W 5AH (✆ 020 7935 7665 and 020 3393 1103, fax 01628 891334, e-mail dg@davidgault.co.uk, website www.davidgault.co.uk and www.earreconstruction.co.uk)

GAUNT, Jonathan Robert; QC (1991); s of Dr Brian Gaunt, and Dr Mary Joyce Gaunt, *née* Hudson; *b* 3 November 1947; *Educ* St Peter's Coll, Radley (exhibitioner), UC Oxford (scholar, BA), Lincoln's Inn (Mansfield scholar); *m* 18 Jan 1975, Lynn Adele, da of Terence Arthur John Dennis; 1 da (Arabella b 10 April 1985); *Career* called to the Bar Lincoln's Inn 1972 (bencher), jt head of chambers, dep judge of the High Court; *Books* Halsbury's Law of England vol 27 Landlord and Tenant (ed 1981 and 1994 edns), Gale on Easements (16 edn, 1996, 17 edn 2002, 18 edn 2008, 19 edn 2012); *Recreations* golf, sailing; *Style*— Jonathan Gaunt, Esq, QC; ✉ Falcon Chambers, Falcon Court, London EC4Y 1AA (✆ 020 7353 2484, fax 020 7353 1261, e-mail gaunt@falcon-chambers.com)

GAUTHIER, Alexis Pascal; s of Jean Pierre Gauthier (d 1989), and Colette Gauthier (d 1991); *b* 24 June 1973; *Educ* Avignon Hotellerie Sch; *Partner* Clive Chong (civil partnership 14 Feb 2006); 2 c (Arthur b 8 July 2005, Anaïs b 21 Aug 2008); *Career* Hotel Negresco Nice 1991–93, Le Louis XV Monte Carlo 1993–96, Roussillon Restaurant 1998–2010 (1 Michelin Star 2000–10, 3 AA Rosettes, Time Out Best Vegetarian Award 2000 and 2001), Gauthier Soho Restaurant 2010– (Michelin Star 2011–); *Style*— Alexis Gauthier, Esq; ✉ Roussillon, 16 St Barnabas Street, London SW1W 8PE (✆ 020 7730 5550, fax 020 7824 8617, e-mail alexis@roussillon.co.uk); Gauthier Soho, 21 Romilly Street, London W1D 5AF (✆ 020 7494 3111, e-mail a.gauthier@gauthiersoho.co.uk, Twitter @gauthiersoho)

GAVAGHAN, David; *Career* chief exec Strategic Investment Bd NI 2004–10, chief exec Titanic Quarter 2012–; *Style*— David Gavaghan, Esq

GAVAN, Peter Joseph; *b* 23 April 1951; *Educ* Knox Acad Haddington, Balliol Coll Oxford (MA); *m* Nicki Jane McHarg; 2 s (Alistair, Angus), 2 da (Ailsa, Isla); *Career* political journalist 1973–87, with Corp Affrs Div in the petrochemical industry 1987–89, dir issues mgmnt Burson-Marsteller 1989–92; dir corp affrs: Total (UK) 1992–95, National Grid Gp plc 1995–98, Invensys plc 1998–99, Viridian Gp plc 1999–2001, Severn Trent plc 2001–10; md Strategic Judgement Ltd 2010–; founding tstee, dir and co sec kidsinthemiddle.org.uk 2013–; MCIJ, FRSA; *Clubs* Royal Northern and University (Aberdeen); *Style*— Peter Gavan, Esq; ✉ Doonbrae, Blackcliffe, Welford, Warwickshire CV37 9UB (✆ 07771 355597)

GAVIN, Jamila Elizabeth; *née* Khushal-Singh; da of Terence Khushal Singh (d 1997), of Glos, and Jessica, *née* Dean (d 1997); *b* Mussoorie, India; *Educ* Notting Hill and Ealing HS, Trinity Coll of Music London (piano scholar), Paris (French Govt scholarship to study piano), Hochschule für Musik Berlin; *Career* author; studio mangr BBC Radio 1964–67, prodn asst/dir Music and Arts progs BBC 1967–71; author of plays: The Green Factor (musical), The God at the Gate (Play for Today BBC Radio 4) 2001, A Singer from the Desert Came 2008, Razia (Nat Youth Theatre); adapted Measure for Measure (Shakespeare Schs Festival), adapted Coram Boy (BBC Radio 4 Classic Serial) 2009; memb: PEN, Soc of Authors, West of England Writers, Bd Stroud Festival; patron Shakespeare Schs Festival, memb Bd Polka Theatre; supporter: The Coram Family, North South Travel, PEN, Amnesty Int; memb Lab Pty; FRSL 2015; *Books* The Magic Orange Tree and Other Stories (1979), Double Dare and Other Stories (1982), Kamla and Kate (1983), Digital Dan (1984), Ali and the Robots (1986), Stories from the Hindu World (1986), The Hideaway (1987), Three Indian Princesses: The Stories of Savitri, Damayanti, and Sita (1987), The Singing Bowls (1989), I Want to Be an Angel (1990), Kamla and Kate Again (1991), Forbidden Clothes (1992), Deadly Friend (1994), The Demon Drummer (1994, adapted as a play, performed at Cheltenham Literary Festival 1994), Pitchou (1994, republished as Fine Feathered Friend 1996), The Temple by the Sea (1995, republished in Three Indian Goddesses, 2001), A Singer from the Desert (1996), A Fine Feathered Friend (1996), The Mango Tree (1996), Presents (1996), Who Did It? (1996), The Wormholers (1996), Grandma's Surprise (1996), Our Favourite Stories: Children Just Like Me Storybook (1997), Just Friends (1997), Out of India: An Anglo-Indian Childhood (1997), Forbidden Memories (1998), Forbidden Dreams (1998), Someone's Watching, Someone's Waiting (1998), Monkey in the Stars (1998, dramatised and performed at Polka Theatre 2000), Star Child on Clark Street (1998), Coram Boy (2001, Whitbread Children's Book of the Year 2000, adapted by Helen Edmundson and performed by Nat Theatre 2006–07 and adapted for BBC Radio 4 Classic Serial 2008), The Girl who Rode on a Lion (republished in Three Indian Goddesses, 2001), Danger by Moonlight (2002), The Blood Stone (2003), Grandpa Chatterji's Third Eye (2006), Walking on my Hands, The Teenage Years (2007), Walking on my Hands (2007), The Robber Baron's Daughter (2008), The Whistling Monster (2009), Wherever I Lay Down My Head (2009), Alexander the Great: Man, Myth or Monster (2011), Tales from India (2011), School for Princes: Stories from the Panchatantra (2011), Blackberry Blue and other fairy tales (2013), The Man in Red Trousers (contrib to Stories of WW1 anthology, ed Tony Bradman, 2014), Only Remembered (contrib, WW1 anthology, ed Michael Morpurgo, 2014), The Blood Line (contrib to Haunted, collection of ghost stories, 2011); contrib to various educational schemes incl: All Aboard (1995), The Lake of Stars, Grandma's Surprise and The Mango Tree (1996, Storyworlds reading scheme); Surya Trilogy: The Wheel of Surya (1992, special runner-up Guardian Children's Fiction Award 1992), The Eye of the Horse (1994, short listed Guardian Children's Fiction Award), The Track of the Wind (1997, shortlisted Guardian Children's Fiction Award); Grandpa Chatterji series: Grandpa Chatterji (1993, shortlisted Smarties Award, adapted for TV 1996), Grandpa's Indian Summer (1995); *Recreations* music, theatre, art, walking, playing the piano; *Style*— Mrs Jamila Gavin; ✉ David Higham Associates Ltd, 7th Floor, Waverley House, 7–12 Noel Street, London W1F 8GQ (✆ 020 7437 7888, fax 020 7437 1072)

GAVIN, Kenneth George (Kent); s of George Henry Gavin (d 1970), of London, and Norah Sylvia, *née* Vine (d 1993); *b* 11 August 1939; *Educ* Tollington Park London; *m* (m dis), Thelma, *née* Diggins; 2 da (Stephanie Kim b 22 Dec 1961, Tracy June b 8 March 1963); *Career* Nat Serv RAF 1959–61; apprentice then freelance and staff photographer Keystone Press Agency, with Daily Mirror 1965–2004 (latterly chief photographer), prop Kent Gavin Associates; FRPS; *Awards* winner of over 143 incl: Br Press Photographer of the Year (four times), Royal Photographer of the Year (seven times), Royal Photographer of the Decade (twice), World Press News Feature Photographer of the Year, Ilford News Picture of the Age 25th Anniversary Photographic Awards 1992, Chairman's

Award (Lifetime Achievement Award) UK Picture Editors' Guild 2012; *Books* Flash Bang Wallop – Inside Stories of Fleet Street's Top Press Photographer, Princely Marriage (with Anthony Holden), Portraits of a Princess: Travels with Diana (2004), Kent Gavin: My Royal Appointments (2012); *Recreations* football, Arsenal FC; *Clubs* Tramp; *Style*— Kent Gavin, Esq; ✉ Kent Gavin Associates (e-mail kent.gavin@virgin.net, website www.kentgavinassociates.com)

GAVIN, Rupert; *Career* copywriter, account dir, equity ptnr, dir of Sharps (later Saatchi & Saatchi) 1976–87, exec vice-pres Dixons US 1987–89, commercial dir Dixons Gp plc 1989–92, dep md Dixons Stores Gp 1992–94; BT plc 1994–98: dir of Information, Communications and Entertainment, dir of Multimedia Services, md Consumer Div; chief exec BBC Worldwide 1998–2004, fndr Kingdom Media 2004, chm Contender Entertainment Gp 2004–06, chief exec Odeon/UCI Cinemas Gp 2005–14; dir and exec chm Incidental Colman 1981–, non-exec dir Virgin Mobile 2004–06; dir: Ambassador Theatre Gp 1999–2013, The Garden Centre Gp 2014–, Countrywide plc 2014–; chm Historic Royal Palaces 2015–, chm Honours Ctee (Arts and Media) 2016–; 9 Olivier Awards 1998–2014; Warden Worshipful Co of Grocers 2014; FRTS; *Recreations* theatre producer, writer, gardener; *Style*— Rupert Gavin, Esq

GAVRON, (Felicia) Nicolette (Nicky); AM; da of Clayton English Coates, and Elisabet Charlotta Horstmeyer; *Educ* Worcester GS, Courtauld Inst of Art; *m* 1967 (m dis 1987), Robert Gavron (Baron Gavron, CBE (Life Peer), *qv*); 2 da; *Career* lectr Camberwell and St Martins Schs of Art; elected Archway Ward Haringey Cncl (Lab) 1986 (chair various ctees incl Planning, Environment and Housing Ctees and Housing and Urban Aid Sub-Ctees) 1986–2002; London Planning Advsy Ctee (LPAC): memb and ldr Lab Gp 1989–97 and 1998–2000, dep chair 1989–94, chair 1994–97 and 1998–2000; ldr Lab Gp SE Regnl Planning Conf (SERPLAN) 1993–97, co-vice-chair London Pride Housing Initiative, rep LPAC on London Pride Partnership 1994–97, initiated and co-chair (with Lord Sheppard) London Pride Waste Action Prog 1995–97; GLA: memb London Assembly (Lab) Enfield & Haringey 2000–04, memb Sustainable Devpt Cmmn 2000–02, dep mayor 2000–03 and 2004–08, memb Met Police Authy 2000–08, Lab mayoral candidate 2002 (stepped aside 2003), vice-chair Climate Change Agency 2005–08, initiated C20 (later C40) Climate Leadership Gp 2005, chair Planning and Housing Cmmn 2008–12 (planning chair and vice-chair 2012–); memb Cmmn for Integrated Tport 1999–2002; chair Local Govt Assoc (LGA) Planning Ctee 1997–99 (vice-chair 1999–2000), chair LGA Futureswork on Reforming Local Planning 1997–2002; fndr Arts Line 1981; vice-chair Assoc of Met Authorities Devpt Cmmn 1996–98; memb Exec Gtr London Arts Assoc; vice-chair London Arts Bd 1992–2000; convenor London Arts and Regeneration Gp; chair London Assoc of Arts Centres (LAAC) 1983–89, Thames Advsy Gp 1994–97; memb Bd London First 1999–2004; chair Nat Planning Forum 1999–2002; advsr Urban Task Force 1998–2000; founding tstee Jackson's Lane Community Centre 1975–, chair Broadwater Farm Community Centre 2003–04, dir Broadwater Farm Enterprise Centre; memb Rotterdam Int Advsy Bd 2007–; vice-chair Global Urban Devpt 2009–; chief project advsr Economics of Green Cities Prog global collaborative project 2009–; hon advsr Jt US China Collaboration on Clean Energy 2009–; Hon Dr London Guildhall Univ 2001; FRSA, Hon FRIBA 2011; *Publications* London: World City Study (1992), Values Added (1997); various papers on new strategic authority for London; *Style*— Ms Nicky Gavron, AM; ✉ London Assembly, City Hall, Queens Walk, Southwark, London SE1 2AA

GAWKRODGER, Prof David John; *Educ* King Edward's Sch Bath, Univ of Birmingham (MB ChB, MD), Univ of Sheffield (DSc); *Career* house physician and surgn Queen Elizabeth Hosp Birmingham 1976–77, med sr house offr and registrar N Staffordshire Hosp Centre Stoke-on-Trent 1977–81, registrar and sr registrar in dermatology Royal Infirmary Edinburgh 1981–85, lectr in dermatology Univ of Edinburgh 1985–88, conslt dermatologist Royal Hallamshire Hosp Sheffield 1988–2012, hon prof of dermatology Univ of Sheffield 2003–; pres Section of Dermatology RSM 2007–08; ed Br Jl of Dermatology 1996–99 (co-ed 1994–96); hon sec Dowling Club 1987–88; memb Br Assoc of Dermatologists (hon treas 2004–07); MRCP, FRCPEd, FRCP; *Books* Skin Disorders in the Elderly (contrib, 1988), Immunology (contrib, 1985, 5 edn 1997), Dermatology – An Illustrated Colour Text (1992, 6 edn 2016), Textbook of Dermatology (contrib, 6 edn 2004); *Recreations* painting, drawing; *Style*— Prof David Gawkrodger; ✉ Department of Dermatology, Royal Hallamshire Hospital, Glossop Road, Sheffield S10 2JF (✆ 0114 271 1900)

GAWTHORPE, David J; *Educ* BSc; *Career* chief exec Castings plc; *Style*— David Gawthorpe, Esq; ✉ Castings plc, Lichfield Road, Brownhills, West Midlands WS8 6JZ

GAYLE, Mike; *b* 1970, Birmingham; *Career* writer and journalist; former features ed Just Seventeen and agony uncle Bliss, sometime model Benetton; contrib: FHM, More, Sky, Cosmopolitan, B Magazine, Sunday Times Style; columnist The Express; *Books* My Legendary Girlfriend (1998), Mr Commitment (1999), Turning Thirty (2000), Dinner for Two (2002), His 'n' Hers (2004), Brand New Friend (2005), Wish You Were Here (2007), The Life & Soul of the Party (2008), The To Do List (2009), The Importance of Being a Bachelor (2010), The Stag and Hen Weekend (2012); *Style*— Mike Gayle, Esq; ✉ c/o Emma Longhurst, Hodder and Stoughton, 338 Euston Road, London NW1 3BH (✆ 020 7873 6102, fax 020 7873 6123)

GAYLER, Paul Michael; MBE (2012); s of Stanley Joseph Gayler (d 1998), of Clacton-on-Sea, Essex, and Lilian May, *née* Hall (d 1993); *b* 7 July 1955; *Educ* Priory Comp Sch Dagenham, Grays Thurrock Tech Coll; *m* 30 June 1979, Anita Pauline, da of Alan Blackburn; 2 s (Lee Daniel b 24 July 1983, Ryan James b 25 April 1985), 2 da (Lauren Marie b 21 April 1987, Rosie Adele b 11 Feb 1992); *Career* chef; apprenticeship Palace Hotel Torquay 1974–75, trg Royal Garden Hotel London 1975–80, sous chef Dorchester Hotel London 1980–82; head chef: Inigo Jones Restaurant London 1982–89 (dir 1985–89), Halkin Hotel Belgravia 1990–91; exec chef Lanesborough Hotel London 1991–, conslt chef Tesco Food Stores; chm Pierre Taittinger 2000–; winner Mouton Cadet competition 1979–82, finalist Pierre Tattinger competition Paris (later Br judge), Catey Award for Outstanding Services to Hospitality for Hotel Industry 2012, various Gold & Silver medals Germany, Switzerland, Austria and Britain; judge Roux Scholarship 1989, 1990 and 1991; holder Matrise Escoffier Assoc Culinaire Française; Master Craftsman Cookery and Food Assoc, Palmes Culinaire Assoc Culinaire Française; memb: Académie Culinaire de France, Chefs and Cooks Circle, Guild de Fromagers de France, Craft Guild of Chefs, Master Chefs of GB; hon memb of Inst of Consumer Sciences; *Books* Virtually Vegetarian (1995), Great Value Gourmet (1996), Passion for Cheese (1997), Ultimate Vegetarian (1998), Passion for Vegetables (1999), Raising the Heat (2000), Passion for Potatoes (2001), Flavours of the World (2002), Healthy Eating for your Heart (2003), Mediterranean Cook (2004), Burgers (2004), Pure Vegetarian (2006), Steak (2006), World Breads (2006), World in Bite Size (2007), Paul Gayler's Sauce Book (2008), Sausages (2011), A Cook's Collection of Homemade Soups (2013); *Style*— Paul Gayler, Esq, MBE; ✉ The Lanesborough Hotel, Hyde Park Corner, London SW1X 7TA (chef's office ✆ 020 7333 7009, fax 020 7259 5606, e-mail pgayler@lanesborough.com, website www.paulgayler.co.uk)

GAYMER, Dame Janet Marion; DBE (2010, CBE 2004), Hon QC (2008); *née* Stringer; da of Ronald Frank Craddock (d 1994), of Nuneaton, Warks, and Marion Clara, *née* Stringer (d 1988); *b* 11 July 1947, Nuneaton, Warks; *Educ* Nuneaton HS for Girls, St Hilda's Coll Oxford (MA), LSE (LLM); *m* 4 Sept 1971, John Michael Gaymer, s of Kenneth John Gaymer (d 2001), of Great Bookham, Surrey; 2 da (Helen b 1977, Natalie b 1979); *Career* admitted slr 1973 (hon bencher Gray's Inn 2012); Simmons & Simmons: ptnr and head Employment Law Dept 1977–, sr ptnr 2001–06; cmmr for public appts 2006–10; chm Employment Law Ctee Law Soc 1993–96 (memb 1987), former chm Employment Law Sub-Ctee City of London Law Soc 1987; fndr chm and vice-pres Employment Lawyers Assoc 1993, fndr chm and hon chm European Employment Lawyers Assoc 1998; memb Editorial Advsy Bd: Sweet & Maxwell's Encyclopaedia of Employment Law 1987, Tolley's Health and Safety at Work 1995–2006; memb Advsy Bd Excello Law Ltd 2013–; memb: Justice Ctee Industrial Tbnls 1987, Cncl ACAS 1995–2001, Cncl Justice 1995– (also memb Exec Bd 1995–2003); memb Steering Bd Employment Tbnls Service 2001–06; chair: Employment Tbnl System Taskforce 2001–02, reconstituted Employment Tbnl System Taskforce 2003–06; co-chair Consultation Steering Panel Legal Educn and Trg Review 2011–13; ind memb Speaker's Ctee Ind Parly Standards Authy 2011–16, memb Bd Financial Ombudsman Service 2011–13, memb Mgmnt Bd House of Commons 2013–15 (actg chair 2014–15), chair House of Commons Administration Estimate and Members Estimate Audit Ctees 2013–, non-exec memb House of Commons Cmmn 2016–; hon fell St Hilda's Coll Oxford 2002– (visiting law fell 1998), hon visiting prof in the practice of strategy and human resources Faculty of Mgmnt Cass Business Sch 2008–14; memb Bd of Govrs Royal Shakespeare Co 1999–2009, memb Bd Int Women of Excellence 2004–15, memb Advsy Bd City Women's Network 2013– (patron 2007–13); tstee Employers Network for Equality and Inclusion (formerly Employers Forum on Age) 2008–13; patron: Assoc of Women Slrs 2000–13, Target (founding tstee 2008–12), Ovarian Cancer 2012–; The Times Woman of Achievement in the Law Award 1997, Ptnr of the Year The Lawyer/HIFAL Award 1998, Lifetime Achievement Award City of London Law Soc 2006; Hon Dr Univ of Surrey 2006; Hon LLD: Univ of Nottingham 2004, Coll of Law 2009, Univ of Westminster 2013, BPP Univ 2013; Freeman Worshipful Co of Slrs 1977, Liveryman City of London Slrs Co 2007; affiliate IPD, memb Law Soc; memb CIArb; FRSA; *Publications* The Employment Relationship (2001); *Recreations* watercolour and oil painting, swimming, theatre, music, opera; *Clubs* Athenaeum; *Style*— Dame Janet Gaymer, DBE, QC (Hon); ✉ The Nutcracker House, Effingham Common Road, Effingham, Surrey KT24 5JG (✆ 01372 452639, e-mail janet@janetgaymer.com, website www.janetgaymer.com)

G

GAYNER, Justin John Heydon; s of Dr John Gayner, and Jan, *née* Fairrie; *b* 30 August 1966, London; *Educ* Eton, Durham Univ (BA); *m* 4 Sept 2010, Anna, *née* Brewer; *Career* writer, broadcaster and prodr; journalist Daily Telegraph and Daily Mail 2002–05, commercial dir QI Ltd 2005–07, co-fndr and creative dir ChannelFlip 2007–; *Books* The Book of General Ignorance (jtly, 2008); *Clubs* Sunningdale Golf, Karmarama Table Tennis; *Style*— Justin Gayner, Esq; ✉ ChannelFlip Media, 41 Great Pulteney Street, London W1F 9NZ (e-mail justin@channelflip.com)

GAZDAR, Prof Gerald James Michael; s of John Gazdar (d 1966), of Hatfield, and Kathleen, *née* Cooper (d 1993); *b* 24 February 1950; *Educ* Heath Mount Sch, Bradfield Coll, UEA (BA), Univ of Reading (MA, PhD); *Career* Univ of Sussex: lectr in linguistics 1975–80, reader in linguistics 1980–84, reader in artificial intelligence and linguistics 1984–85, prof of computational linguistics 1985–2002 (emeritus prof 2002–), dean Sch of Cognitive and Computing Scis 1988–93, visiting prof Univ of Brighton 2007–; fell Center for Advanced Study in the Behavioral Scis Stanford Univ 1984–85; FBA 1988–2002; *Books* Pragmatics (1979), Order, Concord and Constituency (with Klein and Pullum, 1983), Generalized Phrase Structure Grammar (with Klein, Pullum and Sag, 1985), New Horizons in Linguistics II (with Lyons, Coates and Deuchar, 1987), Natural Language Processing in the 1980s (with Franz, Osborne, Evans, 1987), Natural Language Processing in Prolog/Lisp/Pop-11 (with Mellish, 1989); *Style*— Prof Gerald Gazdar; ✉ School of Science and Technology, University of Sussex, Brighton BN1 9QH (✆ 01273 678030, fax 01273 671320)

GAZE, Dr Mark Nicholas; s of John Owen Gaze (d 1987), and May Susan, *née* Skelton (d 2000); *b* 6 February 1958, Exeter; *Educ* Med Coll of St Bartholomew's Hosp Univ of London (MB BS MD); *m* 22 June 1987 (m dis 1997), Dr Janet Ann Wilson, da of Dr Henry Donald Wilson (d 1991); 1 s (Donald John b 1991); *Career* house surgn Southend Hosp Essex 1981–82, house physician St Bartholomew's Hosp London 1982; sr house offr in med: Severalls Hosp Colchester 1983, St Mary's Hosp Portsmouth 1983–85; registrar in radiation oncology Royal Infirmary and Western Gen Hosp Edinburgh 1985–87; lectr in radiation oncology: Univ of Edinburgh 1987–89, Univ of Glasgow 1989–92, sr registrar in clinical oncology Beatson Oncology Centre Glasgow 1992–93, conslt oncologist UCL Hosps and Great Ormond Street Hosp for Children 1993–, hon sr lectr UCL and Inst of Child Health Univ of London 1993–, chm London Trg Scheme for Clinical Oncolology London Deanery 2003–08, chm Radiotherapy Gp UK Children's Cancer Study Gp 2004–09, govr UCL Hosps NHS Fndn Tst 2007–10, chm Children's Cancer and Leukaemia Gp 2009–14; chm Collegiate Membs Ctee RCPE 1989–90 (memb Cncl 1988–90); RCR: memb Bd Faculty of Clinical Oncology RCR 1997–2000, memb Educn Bd Faculty of Clinical Oncology 2006–10, memb Cncl 2013–; memb Jt Cncl for Clinical Oncology 1998–2004; pres Section of Oncology RSM 2002–03 (memb Cncl 2000–11); chm Medical Ctee UCL Hosps 2006–07; MRCP 1984, FRCR 1988, FRCPEd 1995, FRCP 1999; *Books* Stell and Maran's Head and Neck Surgery (4 edn, 2000), Handbook of Community Cancer Care (2003); *Clubs* Reform; *Style*— Dr Mark Gaze; ✉ The Leys, Wofferwood Common, Stanford Bishop, Worcester WR6 5UA (✆ 01886 884140, e-mail markgaze@mac.com); Department of Oncology, University College Hospital, 250 Euston Road, London NW1 2PG(✆ 020 73447 9088, fax 020 3447 9055, e-mail mark.gaze@uclh.nhs.uk)

GAZE, Nigel Raymond; s of Raymond Ernest Gaze, of Knutsford Cheshire, and Beatrice Maud, *née* Caswell; *b* 11 February 1943; *Educ* Prescot GS, Univ of Liverpool (MB ChB), Univ of London (BMus); *m* 6 Aug 1966, Heather Winifred, da of Ronald Douglas Richardson, of Leeswood, Mold, Clwyd; 3 da (Julia b 4 Aug 1967, Celia b 23 March 1970, Mary b 7 Jan 1979), 3 s (Richard b 8 April 1972, Thomas b 27 Aug 1974, Harry b 29 March 1985); *Career* conslt plastic surgn Royal Preston and Blackpool Victoria Hosps 1980–; contrib various articles on med subjects in jls; organist, accompanist and composer; musical dir Elizabethan Singers, accompanied Hutton GS Chamber Choir on the record And My Heart Shall Be There, organist Clitheroe Assoc of Church Choirs and Fishergate Baptist Church, several published compositions for organ and choir; memb: Victorian Soc, RSCM, Preston Select Vestry, CPRE, Nat Tst, Br Inst of Organ Studies, Cncl Br Assoc of Aesthetic Plastic Surgns; memb: BMA, Br Assoc Plastic Surgns, Hospital Consultants and Specialists Assoc; FRCS, FRCSEd, FRCO, FTCL, FVCM, LRAM, MBAE; *Books* Year Book of Plastic Surgery (contrib, 1981); *Recreations* collecting books and interesting junk, architecture, DIY; *Style*— Nigel Gaze, Esq; ✉ Priory House, 35 Priory Lane, Penwortham, Preston, Lancashire PR1 0AR (✆ 01772 743821); Fulwood Hall Hospital, Midgery Lane, Fulwood, Preston, Lancashire PR2 5SX

GAZZARD, Prof Brian George; CBE (2011); s of Edward George Gazzard, and Elizabeth, *née* Hill; *b* 4 April 1946; *Educ* Univ of Cambridge (MA, MD); *m* 18 July 1970, Joanna Alice, da of Thomas Robinson Koeller; 3 s (Simon, Nicholas, Luke); *Career* sr registrar: Liver Unit KCH 1974–76, St Bartholomew's Hosp 1976–78; conslt physician and AIDS dir Westminster and St Stephen's Hosps 1978–; memb various ctees organising res and fin for AIDS patients; FRCP; *Books* Peptic Ulcer (1988), Gastroenterological Manifestations of AIDS, Clinics in Gastroenterology (1988); *Recreations* gardening; *Style*— Prof Brian Gazzard, CBE; ✉ Old Blew House, Dulwich Common, London SE21 (✆ 020 7693 1151); Chelsea and Westminster Hospital, London SW5 (✆ 020 8746 8239, fax 020 8834 4240, telex 919263 VHAG)

GAZZARD, Michael John (Mike); s of Kenneth Howard Gazzard, of East Molesey, Surrey, and Nancy Campbell, *née* Lawrence; *b* 20 June 1949; *Educ* Oakham Sch, Enfield Coll of Technol (BA), City Univ London (MSc); *m* Brenda, *née* Porth; 1 da (Hannah Sascha Louise b 9 July 1991), 1 s (George Alexander Howard b 5 March 1993); *Career* Student Trg Prog Simca Cars Paris 1969–70, market analyst Chrysler Int SA London 1972–73; VAG United Kingdom (formerly VW GB Ltd): Volkswagen product mangr (cars) 1973–76, area sales mangr 1976–79, Audi product mangr 1979–83; Toyota (GB) Ltd: advtg and sales promotion mangr 1983–91, mktg ops mangr 1991–93, dir of mktg ops 1993–94, dir of corp affrs and external communications 1994–96; mktg mangr Rolls-Royce and Bentley Motor Cars Ltd 1996–97, sr exec sales & mktg Rolls-Royce Motor Cars International SA 1997, md Custom Publishing Ltd 1998–, md Tee to Green Mktg Ltd 1999; dir Br Homes Awards 2007–; memb Inst of Mktg 1976, FIMI 1987, Hon FRIBA 2011; *Publications* Design: The Key to a Better Place (managing ed); *Recreations* golf, swimming, tennis, squash; *Clubs* Horsley Sports, Clandon Regis Golf; *Style—* Mike Gazzard, Esq; ✉ Fairway House, Clandon Regis, Epsom Road, West Clandon, Surrey GU4 7TT (☎ 01483 225221, fax 01483 225223, e-mail mike@teetogreen.com)

GEARY, Kevin; s of Frank Geary (d 1992), and Hilda, *née* Stott (d 2005); *b* 3 November 1951; *Educ* Manchester Grammar, Univ of Kent at Canterbury (BA, MA); *Children* 2 da (Kerry b 11 March 1977, Rachel b 9 June 1982); *Career* successively: ODI fell Miny of Finance Swaziland 1974–76, ptnr Coopers & Lybrand 1978–94, dir of business devpt Clifford Chance 1995–2001, currently md Cigamon Consulting Ltd; author of numerous pubns; *Recreations* travel, tennis, cooking, cycling, hiking, yoga; *Style—* Kevin Geary, Esq; ✉ Cigamon Consulting Ltd, 189 Andrewes House, Barbican, London EC2Y 8BA (☎ 020 7638 1323)

GEATER, Sara; da of Jack Robert Geater (d 1999), and Patricia, *née* Tapp; *b* 18 March 1955, Coventry, W Midlands; *Educ* LLB; *Partner* Felicity Milton (civil partnership June 2007); 1 s (Jack Geater-Milton b 2 Sept 2004 (twin)), 1 da (Molly Geater-Milton b 2 Sept 2004 (twin)); *Career* barr; formerly: line prodr and prodn accountant Channel 4, head of prodn HAL/Miramax Films, head of film and TV Avalon, dir of rights and business affrs BBC; head of commercial affrs Channel 4 2004–07; Talkback Thames: chief operating offr 2007–10, interim chief exec 2010, chief exec 2010–14, chair Pact 2014–; FRSA; *Style—* Ms Sara Geater; ✉ pact, 3rd Floor Fitzrovia House, 153–157 Cleveland St, London W1T 6QW

GEBBETT, Stephen Henry; s of Albert Gebbett, of Hundon, Suffolk, and Elsie Mary, *née* Kettle; *b* 24 January 1949; *Educ* Raynes Park Co GS, Univ of Wales (BSc Econ); *m* 22 Dec 1973, Linda Margaret; 1 s (Timothy Giles b 5 Oct 1976), 1 da (Kimberley Sarah b 13 May 1981); *Career* graduate trainee and assoc dir F J Lyons PR Consultancy 1970–76; Marketing Div Charles Barker (formerly Charles Baker Lyons): assoc dir 1976–79, dir 1979–86, md 1986–88, chief exec 1988–91, chm and chief exec 1991–92; dir Charles Barker BSMG (formerly Charles Barker plc) 1992–, md Charles Barker Marketing 1996–, creative dir Charles Barker BSMG Worldwide 1999–2000, sr conslt Hill and Knowlton 2000–03, dir PR Four Communications plc 2003–09 (conslt 2009–16), md Creative PR Counsel Ltd 2003–; FCIPR (MIPR 1976, FIPR 1998); *Recreations* squash, gardening, humour; *Style—* Stephen Gebbett, Esq; ✉ Creative PR Counsel Ltd, The Old Barn, 53, Longdown Lane North, Epsom, Surrery KT17 3JB (☎ 07413 033039, e-mail steve@thegebbetts.com, Twitter @sgebbett)

GÉBLER, Dr Carlo Ernest; s of Ernest Gébler (d 1998), and Edna, *née* O'Brien; *b* 21 August 1954, Dublin; *Educ* Bedales, Univ of York (BA), Nat Film and TV Sch, Queen's Univ (PhD); *m* Tyga; 2 da (India Rose b 1981, Georgia Madeleine b 1994), 3 s (Jack Redmond b 1987, Finn b 1990, Euan b 1998); *Career* author, script writer, film director; memb Aosdána (Eire) 1990; tutor of creative writing HM Prison Maze 1992–95, writer in residence HM Prison Maghaberry 1997–, Br Cncl int writing fell TCD 2004, Arts Cncl writing fell TCD 2006, visiting fell TCD 2009, 2010 and 2013, visiting Arts Cncl fell UCO 2014; Queens Univ Belfast: lectr in creative writing 2007–, Royal Literary Fund fell 2008 and 2009; *Films* writer and dir: Croagh Patrick 1977, The Beneficiary 1979, Over Here 1980, Rating Notman 1981, Country & Irish 1982, Two Lives: A Portrait of Francis Stuart 1985, George Barker 1987, August in July (writer) 1990, Plain Tales from Northern Ireland 1993, Life After Death 1994, The Widow's Daughter (writer) 1995, A Little Local Difficulty 1995, Baseball in Irish History 1996, Put to the Test 1998 (winner RTS Award for Best Regnl Documentary 1999), The Suspecting Glance: Conor Cruise O'Brien 2001, Student Life 2001, The Siege (writer and presenter) 2012; *Publications* The Eleventh Summer (1985), August In July (1986), Work and Play (1987), Driving through Cuba: An East-West Journey (1988), The TV Genie (1989), Malachy and his Family (1989), Life of a Drum (1990), The Witch That Wasn't (1991), The Glass Curtain: Inside an Ulster Community (1991), The Cure (1994), W9 & Other Lives (1996), How to Murder a Man (1998), Frozen Out (1998), The Base (1999), Father & I (2000), Caught on a Train (2001), August '44 (2003), The Siege of Derry: A History (2005), The Bull Raid (2005), A Good Day for a Dog (2008), My Father's Watch (with Patrick Maguire, 2008), The Dead Eight (2011), Confessions of a Catastrophist (2014), The Projectionist (2015), The Wing Orderly's Tales (2016); *Plays* How to Murder a Man (1995), The Dance of Death Parts I & II (adaptor, 1998), Ten Rounds (2002), Silhouette (2006), Henry & Harriet (2007), Adolf Gebler, Clarinettist (2008), The Room in the Tower (adaptor, 2009), Charles & Mary (2011), Belfast By Moonlight (2013), Walking to the Ark (2015); author of reviews, articles, short stories, travel pieces; contrib to short story collections: Travellers Tales, London Tales, 20 under 35, Winter's Tales 6, New Writing Two, Fatherhood, My Generation, New Writing 9; *Recreations* walking, travelling, reading; *Style—* Carlo Gébler, Esq; ✉ c/o Antony Harwood, 103 Walton Street, Oxford OX2 6EB (☎ 01865 559615, fax 01865 554173, e-mail ant@antonyharwood.com)

GEDDES, Prof Duncan Mackay; CBE (2012); s of Sir Reay Geddes, KBE (d 1998), and Imogen, *née* Matthey; *b* 6 January 1942; *Educ* Eton, Magdalene Coll Cambridge (MA), Westminster Med Sch (MB BS), Univ of London (MD); *m* 16 April 1968, Donatella Flaccomio Nardi Dei, da of Marchesa A Roselli del Turco Medici Tornaquinci; 2 s (Gavin b 27 Feb 1971, Acland b 3 March 1981), 1 da (Gaia b 5 April 1973); *Career* jr hosp appts Westminster, Hammersmith, Middx and Brompton Hosps 1971–78; conslt physician: London Chest Hosp 1978–87, Brompton Hosp 1978–2007; civilian conslt in diseases of the chest to: the Army 1988–2007, the Navy 1991–2007; dir: Finsbury Worldwide Pharmaceutical Tst 1995–2012, India Pharma Fund 2005–09; chm Bd National Asthma Campaign 1996–2003; memb Med Advsy Bd Transgene Spa 1997–2001; tstee Royal Brompton and Harefield Hosps Charitable Tst; Br Thoracic Soc: hon sec 1981–84, vice-pres 1999–2000, pres 2000–2001; FRCP 1982; *Books* Practical Medicine (1976), Airways Obstruction (1981), Respiratory Medicine (1990), Cystic Fibrosis (1994); author of over 250 scientific articles and invited chapters; *Recreations* tennis, golf, painting; *Clubs* Boodle's; *Style—* Prof Duncan Geddes, CBE; ✉ Royal Brompton Hospital, Fulham Road, London SW3 6NP (☎ 020 7352 8121, fax 020 7351 8999, e-mail dgeddes0@gmail.com)

GEDDES, 3 Baron (UK 1942), of Rolvenden; Euan Michael Ross Geddes; s of 2 Baron, KBE (d 1975), and Enid, *née* Butler (d 1999); *b* 3 September 1937; *Educ* Rugby, Gonville & Caius Coll Cambridge (MA), Harvard Business Sch; *m* 1, 1966, Gillian (d 1995), yr da of late William Arthur Butler, of Henley-on-Thames, Oxon; 1 da (Hon (Margaret) Clair b 1967), 1 s (Hon James George Neil b 1969); *m* 2, 1996, Susan Margaret, da of late George Harold Carter, of Kingswood, Surrey; *Heir* s, Hon James Geddes; *Career* Lt Cdr RNR (ret); House of Lords: elected hereditary peer 1999–, dep speaker 2000–, chm Sub-Ctee B (Energy, Tport and Industry) 1995–99, memb Procedure Ctee 2002–05, memb Sub-Ctee B (Internal Market) 2003–07, memb Liaison Ctee 2005–07, memb Refreshment Ctee 2007–; treas Assoc of Conservative Peers 2000–; life pres Trinity Coll London 2009–; *Recreations* golf, music, shooting, bridge, gardening; *Clubs* Brooks's, Hong Kong, Hong Kong Golf, Noble and Gentlemen's Catch; *Style—* The Lord Geddes; ✉ House of Lords, London SW1A 0PW (☎ 020 7219 6400, fax 020 7219 5979)

GEDDES, Prof John; *Educ* Manchester Grammar, Univ of Leeds; *Career* med trg in psychiatry Sheffield, Edinburgh and Oxford, currently head of dept and prof of epidemiological psychiatry Univ of Oxford, dir of R&D and hon conslt psychiatrist Oxford Health NHS Fndn Tst; *Publications* New Oxford Textbook of Psychiatry (jtly, 2 edn), Lecture Notes in Psychiatry (jtly), Pyschiatry Core Text (jtly); articles on mood disorders and schizophrenia; *Style—* Prof John Geddes; ✉ Department of Psychiatry, University of Oxford, Warneford Hospital, Oxford OX3 7JX (e-mail john.geddes@psych.ox.ac.uk)

GEDDES, Paul Robert; s of (William) Keith Elliott Geddes, OBE (d 1998), of Ambleside, Cumbria, and Anne, *née* Bolland; *b* 4 June 1969, Surrey; *Educ* Wilson's Sch Wallington, St Peter's Coll Oxford (MA, Domus music scholar); *m* 27 Aug 1994, Fiona, *née* Slater; 2 da (Sophia b 1 June 1998, Saskia b 4 Jan 2000); *Career* brand and mktg mangr Procter & Gamble 1990–97; Kingfisher plc: head of mktg Superdrug Stores plc 1997–99, mktg and business devpt dir Comet plc 1999–2001; mktg dir Argos Ltd 2001–04; RBS Retail Banking 2004–09: md products and mktg, chief exec retail banking; ceo Direct Line Gp (formerly RBS Insurance) 2009–; FCIBS; *Recreations* music (violin), travel; *Style—* Paul Geddes, Esq

GEDDES, Philip Clinton; s of David Geddes, and Audrey Clinton, *née* Phillips; *b* 26 August 1947; *Educ* Sherborne, Queens' Coll Cambridge; *m* 27 Oct 1984, Selina Valerie, da of Capt Derek Head, RNR; 3 s (David b 1985, James b 1989, Thomas Christian b 1991), 1 da (Emily Anne b 1993); *Career* gen trainee BBC 1970, prodr BBC features 1973–80, exec prodr TVS and head of sci and industry progs 1981–88; former ed Special Reports Financial Times TV; currently UK memb Mgmnt Bd of EU Fundamental Rights Agency (Vienna), prog coach UK Govt Growth Accelerator 2012–15; writer and conslt to businesses; tstee Gilbert White and Oates Museum; *Books* In the Mouth of the Dragon (1981), Inside the Bank of England (1988); *Plays* author and prodr An Evening with Rudyard Kipling (first staged Nov 2015); *Recreations* cricket; *Clubs* Ooty; *Style—* Philip Geddes, Esq; ✉ Manor Farm, Upper Wield, Alresford, Hampshire SO24 9RU (☎ 01420 562361, e-mail geddesp@msn.com)

GEE, Ali Jane; *Educ* Kingswood Sch Bath, UCL (BA); *Career* dir of planning Edelman until 2013; Fishburn: gp strategy and planning dir 2013, ceo 2013–; *Recreations* music, skiing; *Style—* Ms Ali Gee; ✉ Fishburn, 77 Kingsway, London WC2B 6SR (website www.thisisfishburn.com)

GEE, Kathryn Olive Perry (Kathy); MBE (2013); da of Dr Eric Arthur Gee, FSA (d 1989), of York, and Olive Mary, *née* Deer (d 1992); *b* 2 July 1951; *Educ* Mill Mount GS York, Univ of Exeter (BA), Univ of Leicester (postgrad cert in mus studies); *m* 1975 (m dis 1997), Julian Elsworth Tanner; *Career* heritage conslt and leadership coach; curator Cookworthy mus Devon and Wheal Martyn Mus Cornwall English China Clays 1973–84, freelance conslt 1983–90; dir W Midlands Regnl Museums Cncl 1990–2002, chief exec MLA W Midlands 2002–06, Volition Assocs 2006–; dep chair of govrs Univ of Wolverhampton 2003–, tstee Heritage Lottery Fund 2006–13, tstee Avoncroft Museum of Buildings 2009–; author of numerous articles; Dip in corp and exec coaching 2007, NLP practitioner 2007; FMA 1986 (AMA 1976); *Publications* five for Cookworthy Museum, two for Wheal Martyn Museum, four for Nat Trust, three books on local history, Museum Projects – a handbook for volunteers (1989), The Heritage Web – structures and relationships (1993), First Principles – a framework for museum development in the West Midlands (1996), Fast Forward (2000); *Recreations* poet, travel, gardening, theatre; *Style—* Ms Kathy Gee, MBE; ✉ Volition Associates, 43 High Street, Feckenham, Redditch, Worcestershire B96 6HW (e-mail kathy.gee@volitionassociates.co.uk)

GEE, Dr Maggie Mary; OBE (2012); da of Victor Gee, of Holt, Norfolk, and Aileen, *née* Church; *b* 2 November 1948; *Educ* Horsham HS for Girls, Somerville Coll Oxford (major open scholar, MA, BLitt), Wolverhampton Poly (PhD); *m* 1983, Nicholas Rankin; 1 da (Rosa b 1986); *Career* writer 1982–; writing fell UEA 1982, teaching fell Univ of Sussex 1996– (hon visiting fell 1986–), visiting lectr Univ of Northumbria 2000–02, visiting prof Sheffield Hallam Univ 2005–; chair RSL 2004–08 (memb Cncl 1999–); memb: Mgmnt Ctee Soc of Authors 1991–94, Govt Public Lending Right Ctee 2001–07; judge Booker Prize 1989; Hawthornden fell 1989, Northern Arts fell 1996; FRSL 1994; *Books* Dying In Other Words (1981), The Burning Book (1983), Light Years (1985), Grace (1988), Where are the Snows (1991), Lost Children (1994), The Ice People (1998), The White Family (2002, shortlisted Orange Prize for Fiction 2002, Impac Prize for Fiction 2004), The Flood (2004), My Cleaner (2005), The Blue (2006); *Recreations* film, visual arts, walking, swimming; *Style—* Dr Maggie Gee, OBE, FRSL; ✉ c/o Karolina Sutton, Curtis Brown, 5th Floor, Haymarket House, 28–29 Haymarket, London SW1Y 4SP

GEE, Stephen; s of Norman and Barbara Gee; *b* 18 February 1944; *Educ* Ardingly; *Career* Price Waterhouse CAs 1962–68, Forte plc 1968–70, Samuel Montagu & Co Ltd 1970–75, md Waterbrook Ltd 1975–82, fin dir and dep chm My Kinda Town plc 1982–97, md Wallace Clifton Ltd 1997–; dir: Ashtenne Holdings plc, English Country Inns plc; chm: Carluccio's Ltd, Henry J Beans plc; FCA; *Recreations* tennis, sailing, shooting; *Style—* Stephen Gee, Esq; ✉ Wallace Clifton Ltd, 1 Airlie Gardens, London W8 7AJ

GEE, Steven Mark; QC (1993); s of Dr Sidney Gee, of Regent's Park, London, and Dr Hilda Gee, *née* Elman; *b* 24 August 1953; *Educ* Tonbridge, BNC Oxford (open scholar, MA, Gibbs prize for law); *m* 13 June 1999, Meryll Emilie, *née* Bacri; 2 s (Alexander b 15 April 2000, Harry b 9 August 2001); *Career* called to the Bar Middle Temple (Harmsworth scholar, Senate of Inns of Court prizeman in Bar Finals) 1975, recorder and memb NY Bar, admitted Federal Courts of NY; in commercial practice, recorder, formerly standing jr counsel in export credit guarantee matters DTI, head of chambers Stone Chambers; FCIArb; *Books* Commercial Injunctions (5 edn 2004); *Recreations* marathon running; *Clubs* Serpentine Running, MCC; *Style—* Steven Gee, Esq, QC; ✉ 38 Eaton Terrace, London SW1W 8TS (☎ 020 7823 4660); Stone Chambers, 4 Field Court, Gray's Inn, London WC1 (☎ 020 7440 6900, fax 020 7242 0197, e-mail steven.gee@stonechambers.com)

GEE, Timothy Edward Daniel (Tim); s of Archibald Geoffrey Gee, of Northampton, and Rosemary Noel, *née* Foster; *b* 26 May 1962; *Educ* Bedford Sch, Worcester Coll Oxford (Simmons & Simmons open scholar, BA); *m* 3 July 1993, Anita Kau Heung; *Career* Baker & McKenzie: articled clerk 1984–86, based London 1986–88, Hong Kong 1989–90, Budapest 1991, ptnr (based London) 1992–, currently head Global M&A; memb Law Soc 1986, admitted slr Hong Kong 1989; *Recreations* rugby, fly fishing, wine; *Clubs* East India, Old Bedfordians, Hong Kong Football, The Flyfishers'; *Style—* Tim Gee, Esq; ✉ Baker & McKenzie, 100 New Bridge Street, London EC4V 6JA (☎ 020 7919 1000, fax 020 7919 1999, e-mail timothy.gee@bakernet.com)

GEEKIE, Rhondda; *née* Jennings; da of Joseph Jennings (d 2003), and Isabella, *née* Tasker; *b* 18 July 1949, Dundee; *m* 22 Jan 1972, Allan Geekie; 2 s (Neil b 30 Oct 1972, Iain b 20 July 1977), 1 da (Moira b 24 Oct 1974); *Career* cncllr E Dunbartonshire Cncl 1995– (ldr 2007–); chm Silver Birch (Scotland) Ltd, dir Citizens' Advice Bureau; JP 2003–07; *Recreations* volunteering, reading; *Style—* Councillor Rhondda Geekie; ✉ 59 Iona Way,

Kirkintilloch, Glasgow G66 3QB (☎ 0141 776 7812, e-mail rhonddageekie@hotmail.com); East Dunbartonshire Council, Kirkintillock G66 4TJ (☎ 0141 578 8000)

GEFFEN, Charles Slade Henry (Charlie); s of late Ernest (Bill) Geffen, and Bridget, *née* Slade Baker, of Milford, Surrey; *b* 19 September 1959, London; *Educ* Harrow, Univ of Leicester (LLB); *m* 17 May 1986, Rosey, da of Peter Valder, and late Rachel Valder; 1 da (Rebecca b 22 April 1990), 3 s (Jack b 19 Feb 1992, Benjamin b 23 March 1994, Oliver b 10 Oct 1998); *Career* slr; ptnr Ashurst 1991–2014 (memb Bd 1998–2013, sr ptnr 2009–13), ptnr and chair London Corp Practice Gibson Dunn & Crutcher 2014–; memb Bd of Tstees: Inst of Cancer Res 2014–, City Year UK 2014–; participates in Speakers for Schools; *Clubs* MCC; *Style—* C S H Geffen, Esq; ✉ Gibson Dunn & Crutcher, Telephone House, 2–4 Temple Avenue, London EC4Y 0HB (☎ 020 70714225, e-mail charlie.geffen@me.com)

GEIM, Prof Sir Andre Konstantin; kt (2012); *b* 21 October 1958, Sochi, Russia; *Educ* Moscow Inst of Physics and Technol (MSc), Inst of Solid State Physics Russian Acad of Sciences (PhD); *Career* Univ of Manchester: prof of physics 2001–07, dir Manchester Centre for Mesoscience and Nanotechnology 2002–, Langworthy prof 2007–, Regius prof 2013; Inst of Physics Mott Medal and Prize 2007, Körber European Science Award 2009, US Nat Acad of Science John J Carty Award for the Advancement of Science 2010, Royal Soc Hughes Medal 2010, Nobel Prize in Physics (jtly) 2010, Royal Soc Copley Medal 2013; hon doctorate: Delft Univ of Technol, ETH Zürich, Univ of Antwerp, Univ of Manchester; FRS 2007; Knight Cdr Order of the Netherlands Lion 2010; *Style—* Prof Sir Andre Geim; ✉ School of Physics & Astronomy, University of Manchester, Oxford Road, Manchester M13 9PL

GELARDI, Geoffrey Alan David; s of Albert Charles Gelardi, and Noreen, *née* Eagles; *b* 28 July 1953; *Educ* St George's Coll Weybridge Surrey; *m* 4 May 1984, Eileen Mary, da of William Sheridan; 3 da (Piera Maria b 27 Oct 1985, Georgina Maria b 28 Jan 1987, Olivia Maria b 29 April 1995); *Career* hotelier; various positions: Carlton Tower London 1970–71, Grand Hotel et Tivollier Toulouse 1971–72, London Hilton Hotel 1972–74; grad trainee prog Waldorf Astoria NYC 1974, co-ordinator of hotel opening and mangr Terrace Coffee Shop Hilton Hotel of Philadelphia 1975, asst to Food & Beverage Dir Waldorf Astoria 1976; dir of food & beverage ops: New York Statler Hilton NYC 1977, Arlington Park Hilton Chicago 1978, Resorts International Casino Hotel Atlantic City New Jersey 1979–81; resident mangr Plaza of the Americas Dallas 1981, mangr Remington Hotel Houston 1982; md Bel Air Hotel Los Angeles 1983–85, md/ptnr Sorrento Hotel Seattle 1985–90, md The Lanesborough London 1990–; *Recreations* squash, tennis, horse riding; *Clubs* RAC, Annabel's; *Style—* Geoffrey Gelardi, Esq; ✉ The Lanesborough, 1 Lanesborough Place, London SW1X 7TA

GELBER, David; s of Edward Gelber (d 1970), of Toronto, and Anna, *née* David (d 1974); *b* 10 November 1947; *Educ* Whittinghame Coll Brighton, Hebrew Univ Jerusalem (BSc), Univ of London (MSc); *m* 1, 1969 (m dis 1979), Laura Beare; 1 s (Jeremy Edward b 1973), 1 da (Amy b 1975); m 2, 1982, Vivienne, da of Harry Cohen, of Weybridge; *Career* Morgan Guaranty Tst 1975–76, vice-pres Citibank/Citicorp 1976–85, md (head of global swaps and foreign exchange options) Chemical Bank 1985–89, global mangr (head of swaps and options) Hong Kong Bank 1989–92, jt md James Capel Gilts Ltd 1992–94, chief operating offr Midland Global Markets, gp md Intercapital Ltd 1994–98, chief operating offr Intercapital plc 1998–2005; non-exec chm Walker Crips Weddle Beck plc 2007–; *Recreations* tennis, squash; *Clubs* RAC Cumberland Lt; *Style—* David Gelber, Esq

GELDARD, Robin John; CBE (1996); s of Cyril John Geldard (d 1984), of Thornton Dene, S Glamorgan, and Gertrude Nellie Lawrence (d 1971); *b* 9 August 1935; *Educ* Aldenham, Coll of Law; *m* 4 Sept 1965, Susan Elizabeth, da of Sir Martin Llewellyn Edwards (d 1987), of Lisvane, Cardiff; 2 s (Bruce b 1967, Michael b 1970), 1 da (Anna b 1972); *Career* recruit RM 1958, Mons Offr Cadet Sch, sr under off, cmmnd RM 1959, 2 Lt Commando Trg Unit, RM rugby team 1958–60; admitted slr; ptnr then sr ptnr Edwards Geldard 1962–95, asst registrar 1980–85; dir various cos 1980–95, memb Lloyd's 1986, dir Minories Underwriting Agencies Ltd until 1998, business conslt 1998–2013; pres: Cardiff Incorporated C of C and Industry 1987–89, Cardiff Incorporated Law Soc 1988–89 (vice-pres 1987–88), Federated Welsh C of C 1988–94 (vice-pres 1987–88), Assoc British Chambers of Commerce 1994–96 (dep pres 1992–94); hon consul for Japan at Cardiff 1993 and 1996; *Recreations* sailing, fly fishing, music, photography; *Clubs* Naval, Exeter Flotilla, River Yealm Yacht; *Style—* Robin Geldard, Esq, CBE; ✉ work ☎ 01752 873084, e-mail robin@rgeldard.plus.com

GELDOF, Bob; Hon KBE (1986); *b* 5 October 1951; *Educ* Blackrock Coll Dublin; *m* 1, 1986 (m dis 1996), Paula Yates (d 2000); 3 da (Fifi Trixibelle, Peaches Honeyblossom (d 2014), Pixie); 1 adopted da (Heavenly Hiraani Tigerlilly (da of Paula Yates and Michael Hutchence)); m 2, 2015, Jeanne Marine; *Career* former journalist with Georgia Straight Canada, NME and Melody Maker; fndr and memb Boomtown Rats 1975–86; organiser: Live Aid 1985, Live 8 2005; chm Band Aid Tst 1985–; former co-owner Planet 24, co-fndr Ten Alps Communications 1999; fndr: Deckchair.com, WapWorld; cmmr Cmmn for Africa, campaigner against Third World debt and supporter of numerous charities incl Make Poverty History and Drop the Debt; Hon Dr of Law: Univ of Dundee 2002, UC Dublin 2004; Hon DCL: UEA 2004, Univ of Newcastle upon Tyne 2007; Hon DUniv Roehampton Univ 2007, hon degree Univ for the Creative Arts 2010; Chavalier des Arts et des Lettres 2006; *Singles* co-writer (with Midge Ure, *qv*) Do They Know It's Christmas? (Band Aid) 1984, Do They Know It's Christmas? (Band Aid II) 1989, Do They Know It's Christmas? (Band Aid 20) 2004; *Albums* The Boomtown Rats: The Boomtown Rats 1977, Tonic for the Troops 1978, The Fine Art of Surfacing 1979, Mondo Bongo 1980, V Deep 1982, In the Long Grass 1984, The Best of The Boomtown Rats 2003; solo: Deep In the Heart of Nowhere 1986, The Vegetarians of Love 1990, The Happy Club 1992, Sex, Age & Death 2001; *Television* Grumpy Old Men (BBC) 2003, Geldof in Africa (BBC) 2005; *Film* Pink in Pink Floyd's The Wall, Harry 'Flash' Gordon in Number One (1985); *Awards* UN World Hunger Award, Irish Peace Prize, Rose d'Or Charity Award 2005, Lifetime Achievement Award Brit Awards 2005, Free Your Mind Award MTV 2005, Nobel Man of Peace Award 2005, The North-South Cncl Award 2005, Marketer of the Year Award EPM 2006, nominated 6 times for Nobel Peace Award (latest nomination 2007); *Publications* Is That It? (autobiography, 1986), Geldof in Africa (2005); *Style—* Bob Geldof, KBE; ✉ c/o Gina Nelthorpe-Cowne, Kruger Cowne Ltd, Unit 7C Chelsea Wharf, 15 Lots Road, London SW10 0QJ (☎ 020 7352 2277, e-mail gina@krugercowne.com)

GELLER, Jonny; s of Seymour Geller, and Joyce Calmus; *b* 6 August 1967, London; *Educ* City of London Sch, Univ of Warwick (BA), Drama Studio (postgrad degree); *m* 10 Sept 1995, Karen Mattison, MBE; 3 s (Ben b 9 July 1998, Joe b 22 Jan 2001, Noah b 6 Aug 2006); *Career* actor 1989–93; Curtis Brown: joined as asst 1993, agent 1995–, currently jt ceo and md Books Div; clients incl: Monica Ali, Ed Balls, William Boyd, Tracy Chevalier, Giles Coren, Howard Jacobson, John le Carré, David Lodge, David Mitchell, David Nicholls, *qqv*, Tony Parsons, Ruth Jones, Jay Rayner, Elif Shafak, Lisa Jewell, Jane Fallon, Adele Parks, Ian Fleming, Jonathan Freedland, Linda Grant, Matthew Syed, Nelson Mandela; memb: Agents Assoc, London Book Fair Advsy Bd; involved with: Cheltenham Literary Festival, World Book Night, The Reading Agency; Evening Standard London's 1000 Most Influential 2009–16, Literary Agent of the Year 2012, Debrett's 500 2015 and 2016, 100 Most Connected Men in Britain GQ 2015; *Books* New Beginnings (ed, 2005), Yes, But Is It Good For The Jews? (2006); *Recreations* cinema, reading, walking; *Style—* Jonny Geller, Esq; ✉ Curtis Brown Group Ltd, Haymarket House, 28–29 Haymarket, London SW1Y 4SP

GELLING, HE William John; OBE; *m* Lucy Elizabeth; *Career* diplomat; G8 sous-sherpa asst Economic Policy Dept FCO 2001–02, Urdu language trg 2002–03, second sec (counter-terrorism/internal) Islamabad 2003–06, first sec (political-military) Baghdad 2006–07, head Multilateral Team Iran Coordination Gp FCO 2007–09, private sec to the Foreign Sec FCO 2010–13, French language trg 2013, high cmmr to Rwanda and ambass to Burundi 2014–; *Style—* HE Mr William Gelling, OBE; ✉ c/o FCO (Kigali), King Charles Street, London SW1A 2AH

GEMMELL, Gavin John Norman; CBE (1998); s of late Gilbert Anderson Sloan Gemmell, of Gullane, E Lothian, and late Dorothy Maud Gemmell; *b* 7 September 1941; *Educ* George Watson's Coll; *m* 18 March 1967, Kathleen Fiona (Kate), *née* Drysdale; 2 da (Alison Fiona b 22 Aug 1969 d 2014, Lynsey Jane b 4 April 1975), 1 s (John Gilbert b 9 Sept 1971); *Career* CA 1964; Baillie Gifford & Co: investment trainee 1964, ptnr 1967, ptnr i/c pension fund clients 1973, sr ptnr 1989–2001; chm: Toyo Trust Baillie Gifford Ltd 1990–2001, Scottish Widows 2002–07, Gyneideas 2006–10, Archangels 2008–14; dir: Guardian Baillie Gifford 1991–2001, Archangels 2001–16, Lloyds TSB Group 2002–07; tstee: Nat Gallery of Scotland 1999–2007, Mpathy Medical Devices 2007–10, Flexitricity 2009–14, NetThings 2014–, Ateeda 2014–; chm Ct Heriot-Watt Univ 2002–08; Hon DUniv Heriot Watt Univ 2009; *Recreations* golf, travel; *Clubs* Gullane Golf, Hon Co of Edinburgh Golfers; *Style—* Gavin Gemmell, Esq, CBE; ✉ 14 Midmar Gardens, Edinburgh EH10 6DZ (☎ 0131 466 6367, e-mail gavingemmell@blueyonder.co.uk)

GEMMELL, Prof J Campbell; *b* Stirling, Scotland; *Educ* Univ of Aberdeen (BSc), Univ of Oxford (PhD); *m* 1992, Avril Gold; *Career* post-doc research lectr Christ Church Oxford 1985–89, ceo Scottish Environment Protection Agency 2003–12, chief exec South Australian Environment Protection Authority 2012–14, currently prof Univ of Glasgow 2014–; adjunct prof Univ of S Australia; ptnr Canopus Consulting; FRSA; *Books* chapters in Faure, M et al (2015), chapter in Pink, G and White, R (2015); *Clubs* SMWS Edinburgh; *Style—* Prof J Campbell Gemmell

GEMMELL, James Henry Fife; s of James Walter Shanks Gemmell (d 1962), and Vera McKenzie, *née* Scott (d 1990); *b* 17 May 1943; *Educ* Dunfermline HS, Univ of Edinburgh; *m* 27 Dec 1972, (Catherine) Morna Davidson, da of late John Wilson Gammie, of Elgin, Morayshire; 2 da (Caroline b 1974, Catriona b 1976); *Career* CA 1965; ptnr Fryer Whitehill and Co 1975–82; ptnr Horwath Clark Whitehill 1982–2003 (chm 1997–2002), chm Horwath Clark Whitehill Associates Ltd 1985–2003, memb Cncl Horwath International 1994–2002, chm Horwath International Europe 1996–2007; chm Bridford Career Mgmnt plc 1990–2000, conslt Siddall & Co Ltd 2004–08, dir Pharmovation 2005–10; ICAS: memb Cncl 1988–94, chm Fin and Gen Purposes Ctee 1990–94, Eng and Wales Area Ctee 1989–92, memb Discipline Ctee 1994–98; memb Accountancy and Actuarial Discipline Bd 2009–12; chm Flexlands Sch Educnl Tst Ltd 1988–2001; chm Woking Family Contact Centre 2006–, chm Friends of Woking Community Hosp 2008–13; Royal Hosp for Neuro Disability: treas 2011–, dep chm 2015–; hon fell Sch of Pharmacy Univ of London (treas 2000–10); FRSA; *Books* RICS Accounts Rules (1978), Insurance Brokers Accounts and Business Requirement Rules (1979), How to Value Stock (1983); *Recreations* gardening; *Clubs* Caledonian; *Style—* James Gemmell, Esq; ☎ 01483 764372, e-mail james.gemmell2@btinternet.com

GENN, Prof Dame Hazel Gillian; DBE (2006), Hon QC (2006); da of Lionel Genn (d 2004), and Dorothy, *née* Rosen (d 2014); *b* 17 March 1949, London; *Educ* Univ of Hull (BA), CNAA (LLB), Univ of London (LLD); *m* 1973, Daniel Appleby; 1 da (Beatrice Hope b 1977), 1 s (Matthew Felix b 1980); *Career* researcher: Inst of Criminology Cambridge 1972–74, Oxford Centre for Socio-Legal Studies 1974–85; successively lectr, reader, prof and head of dept Law Dept QMC London 1985–94, prof Faculty of Laws UCL 1994–; memb: Ctee on Standards in Public Life 2003–, Judicial Appts Cmmn 2006–, Sr Salaries Review Bd; chair Judicial Sub-Ctee 2013–; Hon LLD: Kingston Univ 2004, Univ of Edinburgh 2004, Univ of Leicester 2007; memb: Soc for Legal Scholars, Socio-Legal Studies Assoc; FBA 2000; *Publications* Hard Bargaining (1987), Paths to Justice (1999), Paths to Justice Scotland (2001), Tribunals for Diverse Users (2006), Judging Civil Justice (2009); *Recreations* walking, music; *Clubs* Athenaeum; *Style—* Prof Dame Hazel Genn, DBE; ✉ Faculty of Laws, University College London, Bentham House, Endsleigh Gardens, London WC1H 0EG (☎ 020 7679 1436, e-mail h.genn@ucl.ac.uk)

GENTLE, Mary; da of George William Gentle, of Dorset, and late Amy Mary, *née* Champion; *Educ* Bournemouth Univ (BA), Goldsmiths Coll London (MA), KCL (MA); *Career* author; computer game script and voice direction ZombieVille (1996); *Books* A Hawk in Silver (1977), Golden Witchbreed (1983), Ancient Light (1987), Scholars and Soldiers (1989), Rats and Gargoyles (1990), The Architecture of Desire (1991), Grunts! (1992), Left to His Own Devices (1994), A Secret History: The Book of Ash 1 (1999), Carthage Ascendant: The Book of Ash 2 (2000), The Wild Machines: The Book of Ash 3 (2000), Lost Burgundy: The Book of Ash 4 (2000), ASH: A Secret History (2000); as Roxanne Morgan: Dares (1995), Bets (1997), Game of Masks (1999); *Recreations* sword fighting, live role-play games; *Style—* Ms Mary Gentle

GENTLEMAN, David William; s of Tom Gentleman (d 1966), and Winifred Murgatroyd (d 1966); *b* 11 March 1930; *Educ* Hertford GS, St Albans Sch of Art, Royal Coll of Art (ARCA); *m* 1, 1953 (m dis 1966), Rosalind Dease; 1 da (Fenella); m 2, 1968, Susan, da of George Ewart Evans (d 1988), of Brooke, Norfolk; 1 s (Tom), 2 da (Sarah, Amelia); *Career* painter and designer; work incl: painting in watercolour, lithography, wood engraving, illustration, graphic design, posters, postage stamps, coins, Eleanor Cross mural designs for Charing Cross Underground Station 1979; memb: Cncl AGBI (Artists' Gen Benevolent Inst) 1970–, Alliance Graphique Internationale 1972–, Properties Ctee Nat Tst 1986–2005; Prince Philip Designers Prize 2007; RDI 1970; Hon FRIBA, Hon FRCA; *Solo Exhibitions* Watercolours (Mercury Gallery) 1970–2000, Watercolours and Designs (Royal Coll of Art) 2002, Watercolours (Fine Art Soc) 2004, 2007, 2010, 2012 and 2014; *Work in Collections* Tate Gallery, V&A, British Museum, Fitzwilliam Museum, various private collections; *Books* Design in Miniature (1972), David Gentleman's Britain (1982), David Gentleman's London (1985), A Special Relationship (1987), David Gentleman's Coastline (1988), David Gentleman's Paris (1991), David Gentleman's India (1994), David Gentleman's Italy (1997), The Wood Engravings of David Gentleman (2000), Artwork (2002), David Gentleman Design (2009), Ask the Fellows who Cut the Hay: illustrations (2010), London, You're Beautiful (2012), In the Country (2014); illustrations for many other books; edns of lithographs (1967–2008); *Style—* David Gentleman; ✉ 25 Gloucester Crescent, London NW1 7DL (☎ 020 7485 8824, e-mail d@gentleman.demon.co.uk)

GEORGE; *b* 1942, Devon; *Educ* Dartington Hall Adult Educn Centre, Dartington Hall Coll of Art, Oxford Sch of Art, St Martin's Sch of Art; *Career* artist, in partnership with Gilbert, *qv*, since 1967; shortlisted Turner Prize 1984, Turner Prize 1986; Living Sculpture incl: The Red Sculpture, 3 Living Pieces, Underneath the Arches, Our New Sculpture, Reading from a Stick; *Selected Two Person Exhibitions* Snow Show (St Martins Sch of Art London) 1968, Shit and Cunt (Robert Fraser Gallery London) 1969, The Paintings (Whitechapel Art Gallery London, Kunstverein Dusseldorf, Koninklijk Museum voor Schone Kunsten Antwerp) 1971–72, Dusty Corners (Art Agency Tokyo) 1975, Photo-Pieces 1971–1980 (Stedelijk van Abbemuseum Eindhoven, Georges Pompidou Centre Paris, Kunsthalle Bern, Whitechapel Art Gallery London) 1980–81, Gilbert & George (touring, galleries incl: Contemporary Arts Museum Houston, The Solomon R Guggenheim Museum NY, Milwaukee Art Museum Milwaukee) 1984–85, Pictures 1982 to 85 (Hayward Gallery London, Lenbachaus Munich, Palacio de Velazquez Madrid) 1987, For AIDS Exhibition (Anthony d'Offay Gallery London) 1989, The Cosmological Pictures

G

(touring, galleries incl: Palazzo delle Esposizioni Rome, Fundació Joan Miró Barcelona, Irish MOMA Dublin, Kunsthalle Zürich, Wiener Secession Vienna, Tate Gallery Liverpool) 1991–93, Gilbert & George China Exhibition (The Art Museum Shanghai, Nat Art Gallery Beijing) 1993, Shitty Naked Human World (Wolfsburg Kunstmuseum Germany) 1994, The Naked Shit Pictures (South London Art Gallery) 1995, New Testamental Pictures (Museo do Capodimonte Naples) 1998, Black White and Red 1971 to 1980 (James Cohan Gallery New York) 1998, The Rudimentary Pictures (inaugural exhibition, Milton Keynes Gallery) 1999, Nineteen Ninety Nine (Kunstmuseum Bohn, Museum of Contemporary Art Chicago, Museum Moderner Kunst Vienna) 1999–2001, Enclosed and Enchanted (MOMA Oxford) 2000, New Horny Pictures (White Cube London) 2001, Gilbert & George: A Retrospective (Sch of Fine Art Athens, Kunsthaus Bregenz) 2002, The Dirty Words Pictures (Serpentine Gallery London) 2002, Thirteen Hooligan Pictures (Bernier/ Eliades Athens) 2004, 20 London E1 Pictures (Modern Art Museum St Etienne, Kestner Gesellschaft Hannover) 2004–05, Gilbert & George (British Pavilion Venice Biennale) 2005, Brooklyn Museum of Art NY 2008, Philadelphia Museum of Art 2008, Jack Freak Pictures (CAC Malaga, Museum of Contemporary Art Zagreb, Palais des Beaux Arts Brussels) 2010, Deichtorhallen Hamburg 2011, Kunstmuseum Linz 2011, Laznia Centre for Contemporary Art Gdansk 2011–12; *Work in Collections* incl: Arario Gallery Chungnam, Astrup Fearnley Museet fur Moderne Kunst Oslo, Denver Art Museum, Nat Portrait Gallery London, San Francisco MOMA, Tate Modern London; *Style*— George; ✉ White Cube, 48 Hoxton Square, London N1 6PB (☎ 020 7930 5373, fax 020 7749 7480)

GEORGE, Andrew Henry; s of Reginald Hugh George, and Diana May, *née* Petherick; *b* 2 December 1958; *Educ* Helston Sch, Univ of Sussex (BA), UC Oxford (MSc); *m* 1987, Jill Elizabeth, da of late William Marshall, and Margery Marshall; 1 da (Morvah May b 15 Oct 1987), 1 s (Davy Tregarthen b 11 Sept 1990); *Career* rural offr Nottinghamshire Rural Community Cncl 1981–85, dep dir Cornwall Rural Community Cncl 1986–97; MP (Lib Dem) St Ives 1997–2015; shadow fisheries min 1997–2005, shadow disabilities min 1999–2001, PPS to Rt Hon Charles Kennedy, MP, *qv*, 2001–02, shadow sec of state for rural affrs and food 2002–05, shadow sec of state for int devpt 2005–06; vice-chair: All-Pty Parly Fisheries Gp, All-Pty Parly Planning and Housing Gp, All-Pty Parly Debt, Aid and Trade Gp, All-Pty Parly Tribal Peoples Gp; chair All-Pty Parly Global TB Gp, co-chair All-Pty Parly Gp for Water, chair All-Pty Parly Gp for Gypsy Roma Travellers, chair Grocery Market Action Gp, chair Mables Reunited; memb: Agriculture Select Ctee 1997–2000, Community and Local Govt Select Ctee 2008–10, Health Select Ctee; works alongside Mins in Dept for Food and Rural Affrs as Lib Dem lead in Commons, chairs Lib Dem DEFRA and DECC teams; pres Cncl for Racial Equality (Cornwall); memb: World Devpt Movement, Cornish Social and Economic Research Gp; *Books* Cornwall at the Crossroads (1989), A Vision of Cornwall (1994), A View from the bottom left-hand corner: Impressions of a raw recruit through parliamentary sketches and essays 1997–2002 (2002); The Natives are Revolting Down in the Cornwall Theme Park (in Cornish Scene, 1986); also author of numerous articles and booklets on rural and Cornish themes; *Recreations* swimming, cycling, football, rugby, cricket, walking, poetry, painting/drawing, singing, art, poultry keeping; *Clubs* Commons and Lords Rugby, Leedstown CC, Commons Football Team, Commons Cricket; *Style*— Andrew George, Esq; ✉ House of Commons, London SW1A 0AA (☎ 020 7219 4588, fax 020 7219 5572, e-mail bethany.fenton@parliament.uk); Trewella, 18 Mennaye Road, Penzance, Cornwall TR18 4NG (☎ 01736 360020, fax 01736 332866, e-mail cooperu@parliament.uk)

GEORGE, Andrew Neil; s of Walter George, of Edinburgh, and Madeleine, *née* Lacey (d 1961); *b* 8 October 1952; *Educ* Royal HS Edinburgh, Univ of Edinburgh (MA); *m* 1977, Watanalak, da of Kovit Chaovieng; 1 da (Arada Caroline b 1979), 1 s (Michael Alastair b 1982); *Career* HM Dip Serv 1974–: W Africa Dept FCO 1974–75, SOAS London 1975–76, third later second sec Bangkok 1976–80, S America Dept FCO 1980–81, W Africa Dept FCO 1981–82, Perm Under-Sec's Dept FCO 1982–84, first sec Canberra 1984–88, first sec (head of Chancery) Bangkok 1988–92, Repub of Ireland Dept FCO 1993–94, Eastern Dept FCO 1994–95, Non-Proliferation Dept FCO 1995–98, ambass to Paraguay 1998–2001, cnsllr Commercial Devpt Jakarta 2002, asst dir health and welfare FCO 2003–06, govr Anguilla 2006–; *Recreations* reading, golf, watching football; *Style*— Mr Andrew George

GEORGE, Prof Sir Charles Frederick; kt (1998); s of William Hubert George (d 1957), and Evelyn Margaret, *née* Pryce (d 2003); *b* 3 April 1941; *Educ* Oundle, Univ of Birmingham (BSc, MB ChB, MD); *m* 17 May 1969 (m dis 1973), Rosemary, da of late Edward Moore, JP; *Career* med registrar: Birmingham Gen Hosp 1968–69, Hammersmith Hosp London 1969–71; tutor in med and clinical pharmacology Royal Postgrad Med Sch London 1971–73; Univ of Southampton: sr lectr in med 1974–75, prof of clinical pharmacology 1975–99, dean of med 1986–90 and 1993–98; med dir Br Heart Fndn 1999–2004; pres BMA 2004–05 (chair Bds of Science and of Medical Educn 2005–09); chm Jt Formulary Ctee Br Nat Formulary 1986–2000; memb GMC (chm Educn Ctee 1994–99); chair Stroke Assoc 2009–13; hon fell Faculty of Pharmaceutical Med RCP 1989; BMA Gold Medal 2010; Hon DSc Univ of Birmingham 2003, Hon DM Univ of Southampton 2004, Hon DSc Univ of Leicester 2007; fndr FMedSci, FRCP 1978, FRSA 1993, FESC 2000, Hon FFPH 2004; *Books* Presystemic Drug Metabolism (with Renwick & Shand, 1982), Drug Therapy in Old Age (1998) with Woodhouse Denham and MacLennan; *Recreations* windsurfing, walking; *Clubs* Reform; *Style*— Prof Sir Charles George; ✉ 15 Westgate Street, Southampton SO14 2AY (☎ 023 8022 9100)

GEORGE, Charles Richard; QC (1992); s of Hugh Shaw George, CIE, IFS (d 1967), and Joan, *née* Stokes; *b* 8 June 1945; *Educ* Bradfield Coll, Magdalen Coll Oxford (MA), CCC Cambridge; *m* Joyce Tehmina, da of Rev Robert James Barnard; 2 da (Tara Sophie b 1978, Eva Jane b 1981); *Career* asst master Eton Coll 1967–72; called to the Bar: Inner Temple 1974 (bencher 2001); in planning, admin and Parly law practice 1975–2015, recorder of the Crown Court 1997–, dep High Court judge 2010–; chllr Diocese of Southwark 1996–2009, dean of the arches and auditor 2009–; memb House Cncl St Stephen's House Oxford 1999–2012, tstee and vice-pres Bradfield Club in Peckham, memb Ctee Sevenoaks Soc 2013–, chm Sevenoaks Conservation Cncl 2014–; *Books* The Stuarts An Age of Experiment (1973); *Recreations* jogging, history and travel; *Clubs* Garrick; *Style*— The Rt Worshipful Charles George, QC; ✉ Church Field, 2 Oak Lane, Sevenoaks, Kent TN13 1NF

GEORGE, Her Hon Judge Jane Elizabeth; *Educ* Girton Coll Cambridge (MA); *Career* admitted slr 1984, ptnr Rothera Dowson Slrs 1990–2006, dep dist judge 1998, dist judge 2007, circuit judge (Midland Circuit) 2014–; fee-paid legal memb Mental Health Review Tbnl 1995–2006; fndr memb Assoc of Road Transport Lawyers; dep diocesan registrar Southwell Dio 1996–2006; *Recreations* cinema, cricket, gardening, music, walking; *Style*— Her Hon Judge George; ✉ c/o Leicester County Court and Family Court, 90 Wellington Street, Leicester, Leicestershire LE1 6HG

GEORGE, Jill Findlay; da of Ronald Francis George (d 1987), and Joan Findlay, *née* Brooks (d 1987); *b* 12 September 1954; *Educ* St Margaret's Sch Bushey, Univ of Florence, Sheffield Coll of Art (BA); *Career* PR Dept V&A Museum 1972–74, antique shop N Devon 1976–77; Jill George Gallery (Thumb Gallery until 1991): joined 1978, dir 1981, co dir 1983, sole owner and dir 1986–; represented Herts in jr tennis; memb Ctee Art Business Design Centre 1989–92; memb Soc of London Art Dealers; *Recreations* theatre-going, films, music, tennis, classic car shows, croquet; *Clubs* Groucho, Chelsea Arts; *Style*— Ms Jill George; ✉ 16 Gillingham Road, London NW2 (☎ 020 8450 1867); Jill George Gallery, 38 Lexington Street, Soho, London W1F 0LL (☎ 020 7439 7343/7319, fax 020 7287 0478, e-mail info@jillgeorgegallery.co.uk)

GEORGE, Michael; s of John James George (d 1964), of Thorpe St, Andrew, Norwich, Norfolk, and Elizabeth, *née* Holmes; *b* 10 August 1950; *Educ* King's Coll Cambridge Choir Sch, Oakham Sch, RCM; *m* 15 July 1972, Julie Elizabeth Kennard (soprano), da of Stanley Kennard; 2 da (Lucy Elizabeth Sullivan b 27 May 1975, Emilie Jane b 1 Aug 1978), 1 s (Nicholas James Stanley b 19 Aug 1980); *Career* bass baritone; ranges from twelfth century to present day; has appeared at all maj festivals throughout Britain incl The Proms 1990 (4 separate concerts performing Bach, Janácek, Arvo Part and Renaissance music), The Three Choirs Festival and elsewhere with City of Birmingham Symphony, Scot Chamber and BBC Symphony Orchs; performed abroad 1990: Messiah (Italy, Spain, Poland and France), Mozart's Requiem (with Trevor Pinnock, Ottawa), Handel (California and Boston), Haydn's Creation (under Hogwood, Holland, Germany and Italy) *Recordings* incl: Carmina Burana (4 vols), Acis and Galatea, Haydn's Creation, Beethoven's Ninth Symphony, Missa Solemnis (with Hanover Band), Handel's Messiah, St John Passion (with The Sixteen), Handel's Joshua, Stravinsky's Le Rossignol (with BBC Symphony Orch), Holst's At the Boar's Head (under David Atherton), Elgar – Dream of Gerontius (EMI), Purcell – Complete Odes, Anthems & Songs (with The King's Consort, Hyperion); *Recreations* tennis, golf, food; *Clubs* Concert Golfing, Royal Mid-Surrey Golf; *Style*— Michael George, Esq

GEORGE, Nicholas; s of Wallace Yewdall Evelyn George, and Joy Isabel Gilbert, *née* Hickey; *b* 1 February 1954, London; *Educ* Radley; *m* Lady Marsha Fitzalan Howard; *Career* articled clerk Edward Moore & Sons 1973–77, Joseph Sebag & Co 1977–79, Rowe & Pitman 1979–81; dir: WI Carr Sons & Co 1981–86, BZW Securities 1986–93, Drayton Asia Trust plc 1989–93, BZW Asia 1991–93; dir and head of SE Asian equities and emerging market securities Robert Fleming Ltd 1993–97, dir Jardine Fleming Ltd 1997, md JP Morgan 1997–2001, md HSBC Securities (head of Asian corp broking) until 2002, co-fndr and dir KGR Capital Ltd 2002–; non-exec chm euNetworks Gp Ltd, chm Nutmeg Savings and Investments Ltd; non-exec dir: Millennium and Copthorne Hotels plc, euNetworks plc, GK Goh Hldgs; dir Henderson Far East Income Ltd; FCA 1978, AIIMR 1980; *Recreations* fishing, travelling, gardening, country pursuits; *Clubs* Hong Kong, City of London; *Style*— Nicholas George, Esq; ✉ LGT Capital Partners (UK) Ltd, 35 Dover Street, London W1S 4NQ

GEORGE, Russell Ian; AM; s of Richard George, and Janet, *née* Haynes; *b* 27 April 1974, Welshpool, Powys; *Educ* BA; *Career* memb Nat Assembly for Wales (Cons) Montgomeryshire 2011–, shadow sec for energy and sustainable devpt 2011–14, shadow min for agriculture and rural affrs 2014–16, shadow min for economy, tport and sport 2016–; *Style*— Russell George, Esq, AM; ✉ National Assembly for Wales, Cardiff Bay, Cardiff CF99 1NA (☎ 0300 200 7206, e-mail russell.george@assembly.wales, website www.russellgeorge.com, Twitter @Russ_George)

GEORGE, Terry; *b* Belfast, NI; *Career* filmmaker; *Films* incl: In the Name of the Father (writer and prodr) 1993 (nominated Oscar 1993), Some Mother's Son (writer and dir) 1996 (Young European Dir of the Year 1996), The Boxer (writer) 1997, A Bright Shining Lie (writer and dir) 1998, Hart's War (writer) 2002, Hotel Rwanda (writer, prodr and dir) 2004 (nominated Oscar 2004); *Television* The District (creator, writer and dir) 2000; *Style*— Terry George, Esq; ✉ c/o International Creative Management, 8942 Wilshire Boulevard, Beverly Hills, Los Angeles, USA, 90211 (☎ 00 1 310 550 4000, fax 00 1 310 550 4100)

GEORGIADIS, Philip Andrew; s of Jack Constantine Georgiadis, and Jean Alison, *née* Tytler; *b* 6 May 1962; *Educ* KCS Wimbledon, Univ of York (BA); *m* 23 Dec 1991, Penelope, da of John Granville Brenchley; 2 da (Olivia Florence b 13 June 1992, Bella Grace b 11 Oct 2002), 1 s (Toby Alexander (twin) b 11 Oct 2002); *Career* media exec Benton & Bowles advtg agency 1984–85 (joined as trainee media buyer 1983), media exec Ray Morgan & Partners Sept-Nov 1985; WCRS: media planner/buyer 1985–87, media mangr/assoc dir 1987–89, bd dir 1989–91, media dir Esprit Media 1990–91, exec media dir 1991–94, vice-chm 1994–95; chief exec Initiative Media 1995–98, fndr ptnr Walker Media 1998–; FIPA; *Recreations* travelling, golf; *Clubs* Park, Soho House; *Style*— Philip Georgiadis, Esq; ✉ Walkermedia, Middlesex House, 34 Cleveland Street, London W1P 5FB

GERADA, Prof Clare; MBE (2000); *b* 8 November 1959, Ibadan, Nigeria; *Educ* UCL; *m* Prof Sir Simon Wessely, *qv*; *Career* GP 1992–; immediate past chair Cncl RCGP; FRCPych, FRCGP, FRCP; Nat Order of Merit Award Malta 2012; *Style*— Prof Clare Gerada, MBE; ✉ Hurley Clinic, Ebenezer House, Kennington Lane, London SE11 4HJ

GERAGHTY, Barry; s of Thomas Geraghty, and Bea, *née* Monaghan; *b* 16 September 1979, Dublin; *Educ* St Michaels Sch Trim Co Meath; *m* 4 Jan 2010, Paula Heaphy; 2 da (Siofra b 14 Aug 2005, Orla b 2 May 2011), 1 s (Rian b 3 June 2015); *Career* jockey 1996–; races won incl: Aintree Grand Nat 2003, Champion Chase Cheltenham 2003, 2005, 2010, 2012 and 2013, Tingle Creek Chase 2003 and 2004, King George VI Chase 2004 and 2005, Cheltenham Gold Cup 2005 and 2013, Tingle Creek Chase 2012; 33 winners at Cheltenham Festival incl Champion Hurdle 2009 (rode 1000th winner 2009) and 2014; Irish Champion Jump Jockey 2002 and 2004; RTE Irish Sports Personality of the Year 2003; supporter: Fighting Blindness, Plan Sponsor a Child; *Recreations* golf, hunting, skiing, water skiing, Gaelic Athletic Assoc (hurling and football); *Clubs* Royal Tara Golf, Ward Union Stag Hunt; *Style*— Barry Geraghty; ✉ 5 Norman Grove, Ratoath, County Meath, Ireland

GERLIS, Dr Laurence; s of Toby Gerlis, of Herts, and Sylvia, *née* Sussman; *b* 17 May 1950; *Educ* City of London Sch (scholar), Clare Coll Cambridge (scholar, MA, MB BCh, William Butler prize in med), London Hosp (scholar, DipPharmMed, paediatrics & pathology prize); *m* 1971, Pauline Benveniste; 2 da (Melanie b 1974, Sarah b 1977), 1 s (Adam b 1982); *Career* Med Unit London Hosp 1974–76, med dir Novo Laboratories 1976–82, dir of clinical res Biogen Geneva 1982–85; radio doctor Talk Radio; currently: interest in diabetes care, private GP; visiting conslt King Edward VII Hosp Port Stanley; appearances on radio and TV med progs incl: LBC, BBC, Thames, C4, Br Med TV, Talk Radio; memb Faculty Pharmaceutical Physicians 1990; MRCP; *Books* Good Clinical Practice (1987, 2 edn 1989), Biotechnology Made Simple (1989), Consumer's Guide to Prescription Medicines (1990), Thomas Cook Health Passport (1990), Consumer's Guide to Non-Prescription Medicines (1991); *Style*— Dr Laurence Gerlis; ✉ e-mail dr@gerlis.com

GERMAIN, (Dennis) Richard; s of Capt Dennis George Alfred Germain (d 1956), and Catherine Emily Violet, *née* Tickner (d 2009); *b* 26 December 1945; *Educ* Mayfield Coll; *m* 7 Sept 1968, (Jadwiga) Anne Teresa, da of Zygfryd Nowinski (d 1988); 1 s (Richard b 1973), 1 da (Suzanne b 1976); *Career* called to the Bar Inner Temple 1968; memb Criminal Bar Assoc; *Recreations* cinema, photography, stamp collecting, antiques, gardening; *Style*— Richard Germain, Esq; ✉ Mander Lara, Oxford Road, Gerrards Cross, Buckinghamshire SL9 8TB (☎ 01753 885775, e-mail richardgermain@talktalk.net); 9 Bedford Row, London WC1R 4AZ (☎ 020 7489 2727, fax 020 7489 2728, e-mail richard.germain@9bedfordrow.co.uk)

GERMAN, Baron (Life Peer 2010), of Llanfrechfa in the County Borough of Torfaen; Michael James German; OBE (1997); s of Arthur Ronald German, of Cardiff, and Margaret Molly, *née* McCarthy, of Cardiff; *b* 8 May 1945, Cardiff; *Educ* St Illyd's Coll Cardiff, St Mary's Coll London (Cert Ed), Open Univ (BA), UWE (DipEd Mgmnt); *m* 5 Aug 2006, Veronica, *née* Hopkins; 2 da (Sophie Gemma Ann (Mrs Notley) b 27 Nov 1972, Laura Emily Jane (Mrs Toscano) b 28 Nov 1973); *Career* teacher 1963–90, dir

European Div Welsh Jt Educn Ctee 1990–99, memb Nat Assembly for Wales (Lib Dem) South Wales East 1999–2010; Nat Assembly for Wales: Lib Dem ldr 1999–2008, Dep First Min 2000–01 and 2002–03, min for Econ Devpt 2000–01, min for Rural Devpt and Wales Abroad 2002–03; memb Cardiff City Cncl 1983–96 (Lib Dem ldr 1983–96, jt ldr of cncl 1987–91); memb Lib Dem Fed Exec 1992–98, memb Lib Dem Fed Policy Ctee 2011–12, memb Advsy Ctee on Business Appts 2014–, treas Lib Dems 2015–; pres Dolen Cymru (The Wales Lesotho Link), pres Monmouth Brecon Abergavenny Canal Tst; vice-chair The Parliament Choir 2013–; chair Anglo-Azerbaijani Soc 2013–; *Recreations* travel, music; *Clubs* Nat Lib; *Style*— The Lord German, OBE; ✉ Twitter @mjgerman

GERRARD, David Lester; *b* 13 December 1942; *Educ* King Edward VI Sch Birmingham, Birmingham Coll of Art; *m* 6 April 1974, Catherine Robin; 2 da (Sophia Elizabeth b 22 March 1978, Charlotte Mary b 16 Oct 1980); *Career* industrial designer Robert Matthew Johnson-Marshall & Partners Edinburgh 1967–72, prod designer Pakistan Design Inst Karachi 1974–76, princ Gerrard & Medd (product, interior and furniture design consultancy) 1977–; external assessor Nat Coll of Art Lahore Pakistan 1976, visiting design lectr Dept of Architecture Nova Scotia Tech Coll Halifax 1977; memb Design for Transformation (projects in Romania and Slovakia); memb Bd Heritage Unit Robert Gordon's Univ Aberdeen 1993–; vice-pres CSD 1990–93 (chm Scottish Regn); awards: Scottish Designer of the Year 1980, Civic Trust award 1985; ASTD 1969, FCSD 1978; *Recreations* gardening, skiing, travelling, worrying; *Style*— David Gerrard, Esq

GERRIE, Malcolm; s of Athelstan Ross Gerrie, and Evelyn Gerrie; *Educ* various schs, Univ of Durham, Sunderland Poly (BEd); *Career* TV prodr; researcher Tyne Tees TV; creator The Tube and The White Room (both Channel 4); prodr for TV: The Brit Awards, Miss World, The Three Tenors, Glastonbury, BAFTA Film Awards; currently chief exec Initial; memb The Music Mangr' Forum Br Music Roll of Honour 2000; *Recreations* running, reading, cinema, eating, keeping fit, travel, music, music, music; *Style*— Malcolm Gerrie, Esq

GERSHON, Sir Peter Oliver; kt (2004), CBE (2000); s of Alfred Joseph Gershon (d 1970), and Gerta Gershon (d 1999); *b* 10 January 1947, Balham; *Educ* Reigate GS, Churchill Coll Cambridge (MA); *m* 17 April 1971, Eileen Elizabeth *née* Walker; 2 da (Katherine Helen b 25 Jan 1973, Jennifer Frances b 27 April 1980), 1 s (Timothy John b 29 Nov 1974); *Career* with ICL 1969–87 (memb Mgmnt Bd and dir Network Systems 1985–87); md: STC Telecommunications 1987–90, GPT Ltd 1990–94, Marconi Electronic Systems Ltd 1994–99; chief operating offr BAE Systems 1999–2000, chief exec Office of Government Commerce 2000–04; non-exec chm: Symbian 2004–08, Premier Farnell plc 2005–11 (non-exec dir 2004–11), General Healthcare Gp Ltd 2006–11, Vertex Ltd 2007–11; chm: Tate & Lyle plc 2009–, Nat Grid plc 2012– (dep chm 2011), Aircraft Carrier Alliance 2014–; memb UK Govt Efficiency Bd 2010–15; memb Advsy Bd Sutton Tst 2013–; Liveryman Worshipful Co of Info Technologists; Hon DTech Kingston Univ 2005, hon fell Cardiff Univ 2007, fell Imperial Coll London 2011; CCMI (CIMgt 1997), Hon FCIPS 2000, FREng 2001, FBCS 2005 (MBCS 1985), Hon FIEE 2005 (FIEE 1998); *Publications* Review of Civil Procurement in Central Government (1999), Independent Review of Public Sector Efficiency (2004), Independent Review of Ministerial and Royal Air Travel (2006), Independent Review of the Australian Government's Use of ICT (2008); *Recreations* swimming, reading, theatre, travel, cycling; *Style*— Sir Peter Gershon, CBE, FREng

GETHING, Vaughan; AM; *m* Michelle; *Career* slr and ptnr specialising in employment law Thompsons Solicitors; cncllr Cardiff City Cncl 2004–08, memb Nat Assembly for Wales (Lab) Cardiff S and Penarth 2011–; *Style*— Vaughan Gething, AM; ✉ National Assembly for Wales, Cardiff Bay, Cardiff CF99 1NA

GETHING, Prof William (Bill); s of Philip Gething (d 2006), and Dorothy, *née* Mortimer (d 2008); *b* 13 May 1952, Kuala Lumpur, Malaya; *Educ* Malvern Coll, CCC Cambridge (MA, DipArch); *m* 1999, Wendy Allan, *née* Seals; 2 c (Frederique b 4 Mar 1992, Charlie b 23 Feb 1995); *Career* architect and sustainability conslt; ptnr Feilden Clegg Bradley Studios 1993–2009, princ Bill Gething: Sustainability + Architecture 2009–, prof of architecture UWE 2013–; memb Cncl RIBA 2002–08 (President's sustainability advsr 2002–09), visiting prof of sustainability Univ of Bath; memb Carbon Tst Accreditation Bd 2006–09; vice-chair: BRE Global Governing Body, Architect's Cncl of Europe Task Force: Environment and Sustainable, CABE Ecotowns Review Panel; govr Bathford Primary Sch; *Publications* Photovoltaics in Buildings (with Randall Thomas, 1999), Rapid Assessments Checklist for Sustainable Buildings (with Dr William Bordass, 2006), The Environmental Handbook (with Peter Clegg, 2007), Design for Future Climate: opportunities for adaptation in the built environment (2010), Design for Climate Change (2013), Niche or Mainstream? The business case for adapting buildings to climate change (2015); *Recreations* saxophone, sketching; *Style*— Prof Bill Gething; ✉ Bill Gething: Sustainability + Architecture, Herons, High Street, Bathford, Bath BA1 7TH (☎ 07876 574821, e-mail bill@billgething.co.uk)

GETTY, Mark Harris; s of Sir Paul Getty, KBE, the philanthropist (d 2003), and Gail, *née* Harris; *b* 9 July 1960, Rome; *Educ* Taunton Sch, St Catherine's Coll Oxford (BA); *m* 16 Dec 1982, Domitilla, *née* Harding; 3 s (Alexander b 21 July 1984, Joseph b 23 Nov 1988, Julius b 25 May 1990); *Career* early career with Kidder Peabody and Hambros Bank Ltd; co-fndr and chm: Getty Investments LLC 1993–, Getty Images 1994–; chair Wisden 2003–, chair Nat Gallery; *Recreations* reading Burke's Peerage; *Style*— Mark Getty, Esq; ✉ Getty Images, 101 Bayham Street , London NW1 0AG

GHAFFARI, Dr Kamran; s of Mir Jalil Ghaffari, of Milan, Italy, and Aschraf Ghaffari; *b* 17 July 1948; *Educ* King's Sch Ely, Univ of Milan (MD); *m* 8 Nov 1986, Farnaz, da of Mir Jafar Ghaffari-Tabrizi; *Career* sr registrar and lectr in psychiatry St Thomas' Hosp 1984–86, md and conslt psychiatrist Psychiatric and Psychological Consultant Services Ltd 1987–91, conslt i/c Eating Disorders Unit Huntercombe Manor Hosp 1991–93, conslt psychiatrist in psychotherapy Ashford Hosp 1992–2002; W Middx Univ Hosp: conslt psychiatrist in psychotherapy 1992–2006, jt dir Psychological Therapy Serv 1996–2003, head Eating Disorders Serv 1996–2003; head of psychological therapy servs Cardinal Clinic 1992–2007; also conslt psychiatrist and psychoanalyst in private practice; chm BMA Local Negotiating Ctee for Hounslow and Spelthorne Community and Mental Health NHS Tst 1993–2000; memb Assoc of Psycho-analytic Psychotherapy in the NHS; memb RMS, FRCPsych, fell Br Psycho-analytic Soc; *Publications* The Function of Assessment within Psychological Therapies; author of professional papers on addiction, eating disorders, etc; *Recreations* theatre, bridge, chess, computer sciences; *Style*— Dr Kamran Ghaffari

GHANI, Nusrat; MP; da of Abdul Ghani, and Farzand Begum; *Educ* Burdesley Green Girls' Sch, Cadbury Sixth Form Coll, Univ of Central England (now Birmingham City Univ), Univ of Leeds (MA); *m* 2002, David Alexander Wheeldon; 1 da (Farah Mai, b 2006); *Career* campaigner (health) Age UK, health campaigner Breakthrough Breast Cancer, with BBC World Service and BBC World Service Tst; MP (Cons) Wealden 2015–; memb Home Affrs Select Ctee, co-chair All-Pty Parly Gp on Ageing and Older People, chair All-Pty Parly Gp on Eye Health and Visual Impairment (RNIB), offr All-Pty Parly Gp on Women in Parl, liason offr Cons Rural Affrs Gp; *Recreations* cinema, music, reading, skiing, travel, walking Ashdown Forest; *Style*— Ms Nusrat Ghani, MP; ✉ House of Commons, London SW1A 0AA (☎ 020 7219 4619, e-mail nusrat.ghani.mp@ parliament.uk, website www.nusghani.org.uk, Twitter @Nus_Ghani)

GHAZAL, Prof Peter; s of George Sabah Ghazal (d 2008), and Jean, *née* Chappell; *b* 21 August 1961; *Educ* Univ of Wales (BSc), Univ of Edinburgh (PhD); *m* 22 Dec 1985, Jacqueline Ann, *née* Bernklow; 1 da (Anna Lisa b 21 Oct 1992), 1 s (Andrew Peter b 14

Nov 1994); *Career* fell Nat Inst of Diabetes and Digestive and Kidney Diseases Lab of Biochemistry and Metabolism NIH Bethesda MD 1986–88; Scripps Research Inst La Jolla CA: sr research assoc Dept of Immunology 1988–90, asst prof Dept of Immunology and Dept of Neuropharmacology Div of Virology 1990–95, chair Pathogenesis Affinity Gp 1994–96, assoc prof Grad Prog in Macromolecular and Cellular Structure and Chemistry 1994–2000, assoc prof Dept of Immunology and Dept of Molecular Biology 1995–2000, adjunct prof Dept of Immunology 2000–08; Univ of Edinburgh: reader Section of Med Microbiology Lab of Clinical and Molecular Virology 2000–01, fndr and dir Scottish Centre for Genomic Technology and Informatics 2000–07, prof of molecular genetics and biomedicine (personal chair) 2001–, dir of studies Faculty of Med 2001–, fndr and head Div of Pathway Medicine 2007–13; lectr Grad Prog in Molecular Biology Univ of Calif San Diego 1995–97; memb Special Review Ctee: Nat Cancer Inst NIH 1992–93, Nat Inst for Neurological Disorders and Stroke NIH 1993; memb: Scientific Advsy Bd American Fndn for AIDS Research (AmFAR) 1992–, NASA review ctee for ground-based and small payload research in space life sciences 1995, US Army Med Research and Material Command (USAMRMC) review ctee for the breast cancer research prog 1996–2000, Organizing Ctee 22nd, 25th and 26th Int Herpesvirus Workshop 1997, 2000 and 2001 (also session chair), Nat Sciences and Engrg Research Cncl of Canada ad hoc review ctee 1998, Israel Science Fndn ad hoc review ctee 1999, Nat Cancer Inst NIH review panel on models for anti-cancer drug discovery 1999, Synergy Between Research in Medical Informatics, Bioinformatics and Neuorinformatics Belgian Presidency of the EU and EC 2001, Bd Faculty of 1000 2001–03, Scientific Advsy Ctee CHI- Integrated Bioinformatics: High throughtput information of pathways and biology Int Soc for Computational Biology Zurich 2002 (also session chair), Bd Connect Ltd 2002–04, Advsy Bd Bioarrays Europe 2002–07, Scientific Advsy Cncl Dublin Molecular Med Centre 2002–08, UK Research Cncls (UKRC) 2003, Strategy Panel BBSRC 2003–07, Wellcome Tst Technology Transfer Challenge Ctee 2003–08, MRC Infections and Immunity Bd 2004–09, Genome Canada 2004–09, NIH/NIAID Review Panels 2008–10 (memb Advsy Bd 2011–), Expert Panel for Networks of Centres of Excellence Canada, Bd Human Immunology Project NIH/NIAID 2011–; founding memb Scottish Bioinformatics Forum Scottish Enterprise 2002–, founding memb RNAi Global Initiative 2005–; chair Data Sharing Working Gp BBSRC 2006, chair Virus Advsy Bd Sanger Inst 2010–; co-fndr and chief scientific advsr ArrayJet Ltd 2001–07, co-fndr, non-exec dir and chief scientific advsr Lab901 Ltd 2002–08, co-fndr and dir Fios Genomics Ltd 2008–; sr scientific advsr Johnson & Johnson Inc 1997–2000; scientific advsr: Pharmacia Genetic Engrg Inc 1992–93, Isis Pharmaceuticals Inc 1994, Signal Pharmaceuticals Inc 1994–97, Allergan Inc 1996; assoc ed Virology 1996–2001; author of numerous articles and papers in learned jls; invited panellist Science and the Parliament RSC 2001, organiser and co-chair Biochip and Functional Genomics Workshop RSE and Wellcome Tst 2002, chair and invited keynote speaker 1st European Congress on Proteomics and Protein Arrays Copenhagen 2003; scholar Leukemia Soc of America 1993–98, Beacon Award, Chllr's Award; FMedSci 2015; *Recreations* sailing; *Clubs* Royal Gourock Yacht, Generation Science; *Style*— Prof Peter Ghazal; ✉ Divison of Pathway Medicine, The University of Edinburgh Medical School, Little France Crescent, Edinburgh EH16 4SB (☎ 0131 242 6242, fax 0131 242 6244, e-mail p.ghazal@ ed.ac.uk)

GHEE, Tony; *Educ* Univ of Adelaide (LLB); *Career* lawyer Ten Network Aust 1985–88, slr Denton Wilde Sapte 1990–94, ptnr Ashursts 1994–2003, ptnr Taylor Wessing 2003–15 (conslt 2015–); dir: SBS Discovery Media UK Ltd, CEE Broadcasting Ltd, P7S1 Broadcasting UK Ltd; memb: Br Literary Artistic Copyright Assoc, Australian Business in Europe; *Publications* Butterworths' Encyclopaedia of Forms and Precedents (contrib and ed of telecommunications section); *Style*— Tony Ghee, Esq; ✉ Taylor Wessing, 5 New Street Square, London EC4A 3TW (☎ 020 7300 7000, fax 020 7300 7100, e-mail a.ghee@taylorwessing.com)

GHOSH, Shiulie; da of Dr Salil K Ghosh, and Rose M Ghosh; *Educ* Teesside HS for Girls, St Mary's Sixth Form Coll Middlesbrough, Univ of Kent at Canterbury (BA); *m* 2001, Simon Torkington; 1 da (Maya Scarlett b 2003); *Career* BBC: prog asst Radio Cleveland 1989–90, trainee BBC News 1990–91, reporter and presenter BBC East Midlands 1991–93, reporter Countryfile 1993–95, reporter and presenter BBC Newsroom South East 1995–98; ITN: gen reporter 1998–99, home affrs corr and newscaster 1999–2002, home affrs ed and newscaster 2002–; Best TV Journalist BT Ethnic Multicultural Media Awards 2001; patron Int Care and Relief (ICR) Charity 2002–; *Recreations* scuba diving, travelling, reading; *Style*— Ms Shiulie Ghosh; ✉ ITN, 200 Gray's Inn Road, London WC1X 8XZ (☎ 020 7833 3000, fax 020 7430 4302, e-mail shiulie.ghosh@itn.co.uk)

GIBB, Frances Rebecca; da of Matthew Gibb, of Islington, London, and Bettina Mary, *née* Dawson; *b* 24 February 1951; *Educ* St Margaret's Sch Bushey, UEA (BA); *m* 5 Aug 1978, Joseph Cahill (d 2009); 3 s (Thomas b 3 Aug 1983, James b 19 April 1985, Patrick b 8 April 1989); *Career* news res asst Visnews 1973, trainee reporter Times Higher Education Supplement 1974–78, art sales corr Daily Telegraph 1978–80; The Times: reporter 1980–82, legal affairs corr 1982–, legal ed 1999–; visiting prof Queen Mary's Coll London, govr KCS Wimbledon; *Clubs* Reform; *Style*— Ms Frances Gibb; ✉ The Times, 1 Pennington Street, London E1 9XN (☎ 020 7782 5931)

GIBB, Nicolas John (Nick); MP; s of John McLean Gibb (d 1996), and Eileen Mavern Hanson Gibb; *b* 3 September 1960; *Educ* Maidstone GS, Roundhay Sch Leeds, Thornes House Sch Wakefield, Univ of Durham; *Career* tax accountant KPMG until 1997; MP (Cons) Bognor Regis and Littlehampton 1997–; shadow Treasy spokesman 1998–99, oppn Trade and Indust spokesman 1999–2001, memb Public Accounts Ctee 2001, memb Educn and Skills Select Ctee 2003–05, shadow min for schs 2005–10, min of state for schs 2010–12 and 2014–, memb PM's Policy Bd 2013; FCA; *Publications* Bucking the Market (1990), Maintaining Momentum (1994); *Style*— Nick Gibb, Esq, MP; ✉ House of Commons, London SW1A 0AA (☎ 020 7219 6374, fax 020 7219 1395)

GIBB, Stephen John; WS (1994); s of Andrew Gibb, of Glasgow, and Ann M Symington, *née* Bannon; *b* 17 July 1964, Paisley; *Educ* King's Park Secdy Sch Glasgow, Univ of Glasgow (LLB, DipLP); *m* 22 Sept 1989, Christine, *née* McLintock; 1 da (Alexandra Jane), 1 s (David John); *Career* admitted slr: Scot 1988, Eng and Wales 1993; Fyfe Ireland WS (formerly Bird Semple Fyfe Ireland WS): trainee 1986–88, slr 1988–91, assoc 1991–94, ptnr 1994–99; Shepherd+Wedderburn: ptnr 1999–, chief exec 2012–; memb: Law Soc of Scot 1988, Law Soc of Eng and Wales 1993; MInstD; *Recreations* golf, football, reading, guitar, family taxi service; *Clubs* Murrayfield Golf; *Style*— Stephen Gibb, Esq, WS; ✉ Kaimes Lodge, 4 Kaimes Road, Edinburgh EH12 6JS (e-mail gibbsinedinburgh@ hotmail.com); Shepherd+Wedderburn, 1 Exchange Crescent, Conference Square, Edinburgh EH3 8UL (☎ 0131 473 5211, fax 0131 228 1222, e-mail stephen.gibb@ shepwedd.co.uk)

GIBBARD, Prof Philip Leonard (Phil); s of Leonard Gibbard (d 1988), and Lorna Yvonne, *née* Lodge (d 1999); *b* 22 October 1949, Chiswick, London; *Educ* Isleworth GS, Univ of Sheffield (BSc), Darwin Coll Cambridge (PhD); *m* 19 Nov 2001, Ann Jennison (d 2013); *Career* Royal Soc European exchange fell Univ of Oulu Finland 1975–76, NRC research fell Univ of Western Ontario 1976–77; Univ of Cambridge: NERC post-doctoral research assoc 1977–80, Leverhulme Tst fell 1980–82, NERC sr post-doctoral research assoc 1983–84, asst dir of research Sub-Dept of Quaternary Research Dept of Botany 1984–94, Dept of Geography univ lectr in Quaternary geology 1995–2001 (fndr memb Godwin Inst of Quaternary Research), reader in Quaternary palaeoenvironments 2001–05, prof of quaternary palaeoenvironments 2005–; Int Union for Quaternary Research (INQUA):

corresponding memb Cmmn on Genesis of Quaternary Deposits 1978–86, jt chm Cmmn on Glaciation 1996–2003, memb Sub-Cmmn on European Quaternary Stratigraphy 1996–, sec Cmmn on Stratigraphy 1999–2003, ex-officio memb Stratigraphy and Chronology Cmmn 2003–; chm NE Atlantic Palaeoceanography and Climate Change Review Ctee NERC 1999, chair Sub-Cmmn on Quaternary Stratigraphy Int Cmmn on Stratigraphy 2002–, jt chm Anglo-French Gp Manche 1997–; memb: Int Geological Correlation Project (IGCP) 24 Ctee on Pre-Anglian Glaciation in GB 1979, CELIA/LIGA Workshop 1990, IGCP 253 End of the Pleistocene Fennoscandian Gp and Extra-Glacial Regions Gp, EC SHELF Gp 1993–97, PALTRANS Gp 1995–97, Earth Sciences Peer Review Ctee NERC 1996–99; co-ordinator BALTEEM Gp 1997–2002; Jl of Quaternary Science: book review ed 1985–89, dep ed 1988–89, ed 1990–94, asst ed 1995–96, currently memb Editorial Bd; memb Editorial Bd: Geological Magazine 1996–2006, Netherlands Jl of Geosciences 1998–, Geological Quarterly 1999–2009, Boreas 2000–, Jl of the Geological Society (advsy ed 2001–08), Quaternaire 2002–, Bulletin de la Société Géologique de France 2004–08; author of numerous chapters and articles in learned jls, book reviews, translations and websites; dosent (lectr for life) Dept of Geology Univ of Helsinki 1987, prof associé Univ de Caen-Basse Normandie 2001 and 2007–08, chercheur associé CNRS Caen 2002, visiting prof Universität für Bodenkultur Wien 2007; memb: Geologists' Assoc, Geological Soc (Stratigraphy Cmmn 1995–), Quaternary Research Assoc (memb Exec Ctee 1979–81, chm Lithostratigraphy Subctee 1980, hon sec 1981–85, vice-pres 1997–2001, chair Jt Assoc Quaternary Research 2001–04), American Quaternary Assoc, Geological Soc of Finland, Deutsche Quartärvereinigung, Assoc Française pour l'Etude du Quaternaire, Lapin Tutkimus Seura, Univ and Coll Union; sec-gen Int Cmmn on Stratigraphy 2016–20; Lyell Fund Prize Geological Soc 1999, André Dumont Medal Geologica Belgica 2014, James Croll Medal Quaternary Research Assoc 2014; Hon PhD Univ of Helsinki 2010, hon ScD Univ of Cambridge 2010; *Books* incl: Quaternary Geology of the Vale of St Albans: Field Guide (co-ed, 1978), Pleistocene History of the Middle Thames Valley (1985), Pliocene – Middle Pleistocene of East Anglia: Field Guide (co-ed, 1988), Glacial Deposits in Great Britain and Ireland (co-ed, 1991), The Pleistocene History of the Lower Thames Valley (1994), Glacial Deposits in North-East Europe (co-ed, 1995), Stratigraphical Procedure (jtly, 2002), Extent and Chronology of Glaciation (3 Vols, co-ed, 2004), Early-Middle Pleistocene Transitions: The Land-Ocean Evidence (co-ed, 2005), Quaternary Glaciations – Extent and Chronology: a closer look (co-ed, 2011), The Ice Age (with J Ehlers and P Hughes, 2016); *Recreations* jazz and blues music, modern architecture, art and design; *Style*— Prof Phil Gibbard; ✉ Cambridge Quaternary, Department of Geography, University of Cambridge, Downing Place, Cambridge CB2 3EN (☎ 01223 333924, fax 01223 333392, e-mail plg1@cam.ac.uk)

GIBBENS, Prof Nigel Paul; CBE (2016); s of Francis Bernard Gibbens, of Worth, Kent, and Pauline Carol, *née* Holmes (d 2014); *b* 1 March 1958, Dover; *Educ* RCVS London (BVetMed), Univ of Edinburgh (MSc); *m* 21 Nov 1981, Jane Crombie, *née* Stirling; *Career* vet practice Derbys 1981–83; vet service: Belize 1985–88, Yemen 1988–90, UK 1990–96; involved in veterinary and agriculture policy 1996–2008; chief veterinary offr 2008–; memb: Br Vet Assoc, Vet Public Health Assoc, Assoc of Govt Vets; MRCVS; *Recreations* cinema, gardening, music, travel, walking; *Style*— Professor Nigel Gibbens, CBE; ✉ c/o Defra, Nobel House, 17 Smith Square, London SW1P 3JR (☎ 020 7238 6495, e-mail nigel.gibbens@defra.gsi.gov.uk, website www.defra.gov.uk, Twitter @ChiefVetUK)

GIBBON, Lindsay Harwin Ward (Lin); da of James Ferguson Gibbon; *b* 29 November 1949; *Educ* Glasgow Sch of Art; *Children* 1 da (Katherine Jane Harwin Gibbon McGregor b 1985); *Career* dir Randak Design Consultants Ltd 1978– (graphic designer specialising in corp literature and packaging design); memb Bd of Dirs Scottish Design 1994–98, fndr chm Scottish Design Res Forum 1994–, memb: Bd of Dirs Glasgow 1999 Festival Co Ltd 1997–, judging panel Prince Philip Prize for Design 1999, 2000 and 2001; vice-pres CSD 2001– (pres 1998–2000); FCSD 1994, FRSA 2000; *Style*— Lin Gibbon; ✉ Sorisdale, by Lanark; Randak Design Consultants Ltd, Gordon Chambers, 90 Mitchell Street, Glasgow G1 3NQ (☎ 0141 221 2142, fax 0141 226 5096)

GIBBON-WILLIAMS, Andrew; s of Ivor James Williams (d 1990), of Barry, S Glamorgan, and Grace Mary, *née* Thomas; *b* 6 March 1954; *Educ* Barry Boys' GS, Edinburgh Coll of Art Univ of Edinburgh (Huntly-MacDonald Sinclair travelling scholarship, MA); *Career* artist and art critic; art critic The Sunday Times Scotland 1988–96, regnl art critic The Times 1988–97, regular contrib to BBC Arts progs; winner: Young Artist bursary Scottish Arts Cncl 1982, Warwick Arts Tst Artist award 1989; *Solo Exhibitions* 369 Gallery Edinburgh 1979, 1980, 1982 and 1986; *Group Exhibitions* incl: Scottish Painters (Chenil Gallery London) 1978, The Royal Scottish Academy 1980, Scottish Painting (Watts Gallery Phoenix) 1981, Best of 369 (St Andrews Festival) 1983, The Scottish Expression: 1983 (Freidus Ordover Gallery NYC) 1983, Peintres Contemporains Ecossais (Galerie Peinture Fraîche Paris) 1983, New Directions – British Art (Puck Building NYC) 1983, Chicago Int Art Exposition 1983–89, Int Contemporary Art Fair London 1984, Contemporary Scottish Art (Clare Hall Cambridge) 1984, Scottish Painting (Linda Durham Gallery Sante Fe) 1985, Scottish Art Since 1900 (Scottish Nat Gallery of Modern Art, Edinburgh and The Barbican Gallery, London 1989–90; *Work in Public Collections* incl: The Scottish Arts Cncl, Dundee Art Gallery, Glasgow Museums and Art Galleries, IBM UK Ltd, Philips Petroleum, Scottish Nat Gallery of Modern Art, City of Edinburgh Public Collection, The Warwick Arts Tst Collection, L&M Moneybrokers Ltd, NatWest Bank, The McDonald Corporation (USA); *Books* The Bigger Picture (1993), An American Passion (1995), Craigie: The Art of Craigie Aitchison (1996), William Roberts: An English Cubist (2005); *Recreations* travel, music, gardening; *Style*— Andrew Gibbon-Williams, Esq; ✉ e-mail andy1232@alice.it

GIBBONS, Prof Gary William; s of Archibald William Stallard Gibbons, and Bertha, *née* Bunn; *b* 1 July 1946; *Educ* Purley Co GS, St Catharine's Coll Cambridge (MA, PhD); *m* 1972, Christine, da of Peter Howden; 2 s (William Peter b 1979, Charles Arthur b 9 Aug 1981); *Career* DAMTP Univ of Cambridge: lectr 1980–90, reader 1990–98, prof of theoretical physics 1998–; fell Trinity Coll Cambridge 2002–; FRS 1999; *Publications* Euclidean Quantum Gravity (with S Hawking in World Scientific, 1993); also author of numerous research papers; *Recreations* listening to music and looking at paintings; *Style*— Prof Gary Gibbons; ✉ DAMTP, University of Cambridge, CMS, Wilberforce Road, Cambridge CB3 0WA (☎ 01223 337899, fax 01223 766865, e-mail gwg1@amtp.cam.ac.uk)

GIBBONS, Jeremy Stewart; QC (1995); s of Geoffrey Seed Gibbons (d 1998), of Bighton, Hants, and Rosemary Marion, *née* Stewart (d 1978); *b* 15 July 1949; *Educ* St Edward's Sch Oxford, Coll of Law Guildford; *m* 1, 1974, Mary Mercia, da of Rev Kenneth Sutton Bradley; 2 s (Edward b 16 April 1977, Tim b 13 Dec 1983), 2 da (Harriet b 21 Oct 1979 (decd), Polly b 27 March 1981); m 2, 1998, Sarah Valerie, da of Michael John Jenkins, FRICS; *Career* articled clerk 1967–71, called to the Bar Gray's Inn 1973, head of Chambers 1991–, recorder of the Crown Court 1993– (asst recorder 1989–93); *Recreations* skiing, cooking, gardening, carpentry; *Style*— Jeremy Gibbons, Esq, QC

GIBBONS, Dr John Ernest; CBE (2000); s of John Howard Gibbons (d 1979), and Lilian Alice, *née* Shale (d 1982); *b* 20 April 1940; *Educ* Oldbury GS, Birmingham Sch of Architecture (DipArch, DipTP), Univ of Edinburgh (PhD); *m* 3 Nov 1962, Patricia, da of Eric John Mitchell, of Albany, WA; 1 s (Mark b 16 March 1963), 2 da (Carey b 20 May 1964, Ruth b 29 July 1967); *Career* lectr: Aston Univ 1964–66, Univ of Edinburgh 1969–72; Scot Devpt Dept: princ architect 1972–74 and 1976–78, superintending architect 1978–82; res scientist CSIRO Melbourne 1975; SO: dep dir bldg directorate 1982–84, dir of bldg 1984–, chief architect 1984–2005; architectural advsr to the Scottish Parly 2001–; visiting prof Mackintosh Sch of Architecture Glasgow 2000–; memb: Cncl Edinburgh Architectural Assoc 1977–80, Cncl RIAS 1977–80, Cncl ARCUK 1984–, Design Cncl 1984–88; DUniv UCE; RIBA 1964, ARIAS 1967, FSA Scot 1984, FRSA 1987; *Clubs* New (Edinburgh); *Style*— Dr John Gibbons, CBE; ✉ Crichton House, Pathhead, Midlothian EH37 5UX (☎ 01875 320 085, mobile 07922 043089, e-mail jegibbons@btconnect.com); The Scottish Parliament, Parliament Headquarters, Edinburgh EH99 1SP

GIBBONS, Michael Robert; s of Rev Robert Gibbons (d 1980), and Audrey, *née* Bird; *b* 18 July 1957, Co Durham; *Educ* City of Leicester Boys' GS, KCL (BA, AKC, PGCE); *m* 28 July 1984, Penny, *née* Hewett; 1 s (Daniel Robert Peter b 17 May 1990), 1 da (Sarah Verity b 12 March 1993); *Career* asst master Ardingly Coll 1981–85, asst master Rugby Sch 1985–97 (housemaster 1992–97), second master Whitgift Sch 1997–2001, headmaster Queen Elizabeth GS Wakefield 2001–10, princ and ceo GS at Leeds 2010–; memb: HMC 2001; *Recreations* sport, travel, family; *Clubs* East India, Lansdowne; *Style*— Michael Gibbons, Esq; ✉ The Grammar School at Leeds, Alwoodley Gates, Harrogate Road, Leeds LS17 8GS (☎ 0113 229 1552, e-mail enquiries@gsal.org.uk, website www.gsal.org.uk)

GIBBONS, Paul; s of Norman Gibbons (d 1979), of Reading, Berks, and Irene, *née* Pantlin; *b* May 1947, Reading, Berks; *m* Sept 1967, Jennifer, *née* Harwood; 1 s (Peter Joseph b 21 Oct 1987); *Career* fndr and dir: Hurst Publishing Ltd (publishers of Auto Trader magazines) 1977–99, Leaderboard Golf Ltd (owners Sandford Springs, Chart Hills and The Oxfordshire golf clubs and Dale Hill Hotel and Golf Club) 2000–; supporter: Duke of Edinburgh Award Scheme, Sparks; MInstD; *Recreations* golf, swimming, walking; *Clubs* Publishers Golf Soc; *Style*— Paul Gibbons, Esq; ✉ Leaderboard Golf Limited, Leaderboard House, Sandford Springs, Wolverton, Tadley, Hampshire RG26 5RT (☎ 01635 291506, fax 01635 291501, e-mail lorrainew@leaderboardgolf.co.uk)

GIBBONS, Stephen John; s of John Gibbons, of Luton, Beds, and Wendy Patricia, *née* Luery; *b* 8 October 1956; *Educ* Bedford Modern Sch, Luton Sixth Form Coll, Dunstable Coll of FE, RCA (MA); *m* Valerie Anne, da of Michael Mercer; 1 da (Francesca Louisa b 29 Dec 1990), 1 s (Frederick Jim b 27 July 1993); *Career* graphic designer Minale Tattersfield 1982–84, ptnr The Partners 1985–96 (joined 1984), fndr ptnr Dew Gibbons 1997, exec dir Design Business Assoc 2012–; recipient 2 Silver D&AD Awards for environmental graphics and signing schemes, 2 Gold, 1 International Export, 2 Silver and 2 Bronze DBA Design Effectiveness Awards, Design Agency of the Year The Drum Network Awards 2014, 2 Gold Vertex Awards 2015, 1 Gold Transform Award 2015, 2 Silver Transform Awards 2015 and 2016, various others from CSD/Minerva Awards, XYZ Magazine Awards, Communication Awards in the Building Industry, Donside Graphic Design and Print Awards and Design Week Awards; work selected for various int awards/pubns incl: Art Dirs' Club of NY, PDC Gold Awards USA, Creativity USA, Communication Arts USA, Graphis Switzerland, Int Poster Biennale Poland; occasional design juror D&AD (memb Exec Ctee until 1998), lectr at various UK univs and seminars/confs on graphic design; external moderator BA Graphic Design Kingston Univ; *Publications* articles on design and marketing topics for SPC Magazine, articles on client relationships and educn for Design Week, articles on healthcare packaging for Retail Packaging Magazine and Packaging Gazette; *Style*— Stephen Gibbons, Esq; ✉ 6th Floor Studio, 45 Gee Street, London EC1V 3RS (☎ 020 7689 8999)

GIBBONS, Sir William Edward Doran; 9 Bt (GB 1752), of Stanwell Place, Middlesex; JP (S Westminster Inner London 1994); s of Sir John Edward Gibbons, 8 Bt (d 1982), and Mersa Wentworth, *née* Foster; *b* 13 January 1948; *Educ* Pangbourne Sch, RNC Dartmouth, Univ of Bristol (BSc), Univ of Southampton (MBA); *m* 1, 1972 (m dis 2004), Patricia Geraldine Archer, da of Roland Archer Howse; 1 da (Joan Eleanor Maud b 1980), 1 s (Charles William Edwin b 1983); m 2, 2004, Maggie Moone; *Heir* s, Charles Gibbons; *Career* Sealink UK: asst shipping and port mangr Parkeston Quay 1979–82, serv mangr Anglo-Dutch 1982–85, mangr Harwich-Hook 1985–87, gen mangr Isle of Wight Servs 1987–90; tport and mgmnt conslt 1990–94, dir Passenger Shipping Assoc 1994–, mktg dir European Cruise Cncl 2004–; chm Manningtree Parish Cncl 1985–87, chm Cncl of Travel and Tourism 1996–; non-exec memb IOW Dist Health Authy 1990–94; JP Portsmouth 1990–94, JP South Westminster Div Inner London Magistrates 1994–; Freeman Shipwright's Livery Co 2008–; hon MBA Univ of Southampton 1996, MCIT; *Style*— Sir William E D Gibbons, Bt; ✉ 1 West Walks, Dorchester, Dorset DT1 1RE

GIBBONS BURTON, Gemma Jeanette; *née* Gibbons; da of Jeanette Gibbons (d 2004); *b* 6 January 1987, Greenwich, London; *Educ* Univ of East London (BSc), Univ of Bath (FdSc), Univ of East London (PGCert); *m* 26 May 2013, Euan Burton, MBE; *Career* judoka; achievements incl: Bronze medal Birmingham World Cup 2008, Bronze medal World Univ Games 2009, Bronze medal Under 23 European Championships 2009, Silver medal Birmingham World Cup 2010, Bronze medal Suwon World Cup 2010, Bronze medal Apia World Cup 2011, Bronze medal Jeju World Cup 2011, Silver medal Bucharest World Cup 2012, Silver medal Tallinn World Cup 2012, Silver medal London Olympic Games 2012, Gold medal Br Open 2012, Gold medal Br Championships 2013, Gold medal German Grand Prix 2013, Bronze medal Russia Grand Slam 2013, Bronze medal Croatia Grand Prix 2013, Silver medal Commonwealth Games 2014, Gold medal European Open Czech Republic 2015, Gold medal Ulaanbaatar Grand Prix 2015, Bronze medal Tashkent Grand Prix 2015, Bronze medal Qingdao Grand Prix 2015, Bronze medal Jeju Grand Prix 2015, Bronze medal Tokyo Grand Slam 2015; UK sports ambass Cancer Research; *Clubs* Metro Judo; *Style*— Mrs Gemma Gibbons Burton; ✉ c/o British Judo Association, Suite B, Loughborough Technology Centre, Epinal Way, Loughborough LE11 3GE

GIBBS, Christopher Henry; 5 and yst s of Hon Sir Geoffrey Cokayne Gibbs, KCMG (d 1975; 2 s of 1 Baron Hunsdon of Hunsdon, 4 s of 1 Baron Aldenham, JP), and Helen Margaret Gibbs, CBE, JP, *née* Leslie (d 1979); *b* 29 July 1938; *Educ* Eton, Stanbridge, Université de Poitiers; *Career* art dealer (now ret); dir Christopher Gibbs Ltd; chm J Paul Getty Jr Charitable Tst; *Recreations* antiquarian pursuits, gardening; *Clubs* Beefsteak, Pratt's; *Style*— Christopher Gibbs, Esq; ✉ L6 Albany, Piccadilly, London W1J 0AZ (e-mail secretary@christophergibbs.com); El Foolk, 284 Rue de la Vieille Montagne, Tangiers, Morocco 90 000

GIBBS, Justin Geoffrey; s of David C L Gibbs (d 2009), and C Fleur *née* Mein; *b* 18 February 1969, Melbourne, Australia; *Educ* Melbourne Grammar, Eton, Monash Univ Australia (BEc); *m* 26 Jul 2006, Lucy, *née* Moore; 2 s (Christopher b 2 Nov 2007, Otto b 26 May 2009); *Career* banker 1994–2000, dir Liv-ex 2000–; *Recreations* horse racing, sailing, skiing, barbequing; *Clubs* White's, Turf, Melbourne, Victorian Racing, Melbourne Cricket, RGS; *Style*— Justin Gibbs, Esq; ✉ Liv-ex Ltd, Battersea Studios 2, 82 Silverthorne Road, London SW8 3HE

GIBBS, Marion Olive; CBE (2012); da of Harry Norman Smith, and Olive Mabel, *née* Lewis; *Educ* Pate's GS for Girls Cheltenham, Univ of Bristol (BA, PGCE, MLitt); *Career* asst mistress City of Worcester Girls' GS 1974–76, teacher Chailey Comp Sch 1977, head of sixth form, dir of studies and head of classics Burgess Hill Sch for Girls 1977–89, head of sixth form and head of classics Haberdashers' Aske's Girls' Sch 1989–91, HM's Inspector of Schs 1992–94, headmistress James Allen's Girls' Sch 1994–2015; tutor Open Univ 1979–91; chm Cncl JACT 2001–04; memb: Classical Assoc (memb Cncl 1984–87 and 1995–98, jt hon sec 1989–92), Hellenic Soc (memb Cncl 1997–2000 and 2008–11, chm Sch's Ctee 2002–09), Educn Ctee Woodward Corp 2015–; tstee: Dulwich Picture Gallery 1999–2001 and 2008–11, Arvon Fndn 2008–16, Charter MAT 2015–; FRSA 1997; *Publications* Greek Tragedy: An Introduction (1989), Two Sectors, One Purpose:

Independent Schools in the System (contrib, 2002), The Teaching of Classics (contrib, 2003), Heads: Leading Schools in the 21st Century (contrib, 2007); *Recreations* gardening, music, drama, keeping informed about the developing world; *Style—* Mrs Marion Gibbs, CBE; ✉ e-mail mog.gibbs1@btinternet.com

GIBBS, Stephen Cokayne; OBE (2001); 2 s of Hon Sir Geoffrey Gibbs, KCMG (d 1975), 2 s of 1 Baron Hunsdon of Hunsdon, JP, himself 4 s of 1 Baron Aldenham, JP, and Hon Lady Gibbs, CBE, JP (d 1979); *b* 18 July 1929; *Educ* Eton; *m* 1972, Lavinia Winifred, 2 da of Sir Edmund Bacon, 13 Bt, KG, KBE, TD (d 1982); 2 s, 1 da; *Career* 2 Lt KRRC, Maj QVR (TA) 1960–63 and Royal Green Jackets; dir: Charles Barker plc 1962–87, Vaux Group plc 1971–99; Nat Tst for Scotland: memb Exec Ctee 1987–97, memb Cncl 1991–96, chm Regnl Ctee Argyll, Lochaber & Western Isles 1995–2000; memb: RUCC for Scotland 1992–97, Deer Cmmn for Scot 1993–2000; chm: Isle of Arran District Salmon Fisheries Bd 1991–, Assoc of Deer Mgmnt Gps 1994–2005; *Recreations* shooting, stalking, gardening; *Clubs* Pratt's; *Style—* Stephen Gibbs, Esq, OBE; ✉ Dougarie, Isle of Arran KA27 8EB (☎ 01770 840229/840259, e-mail office@dougarie.com)

GIBBS-KENNET, Peter Adrian; s of Reginald Ernest Gibbs Gibbs-Kennet, DLI (ka WWII), and Ruth, *née* Wyatt (d 1991); *Educ* Plymouth and Mannamead Coll Devon, Oriel Coll Oxford (MA, post-grad Dip Ed, Coll VIII); *m* 12 July 1968, Anna Eleanor, da of Gp Capt Hugh Llewellyn Jenkins, MD, OStJ (d 2001), and Vivienne, *née* Pawson (d 2008); 1 s (Swithun Aurelian Wyatt b 6 July 1972); *Career* asst sec UCCA (now UCAS) until 1971, academic registrar Lanchester Poly (now Coventry Univ) 1971–80, dir of educn and practice standards RIBA 1980–95; devpt conslt: AA Sch of Architecture London 2000–02, Bartlett Sch of Architecture UCL 2000–05; founding jt ed and sec Editorial Bd The Jl of Architecture (Taylor and Francis/RIBA) 1995–; memb Registration Advsy Gp and R&D Ctee RIBA 2004–11; Freeman City of London 1994; FCMI 1981, FRSA 1982, Hon FRIBA 2002; *Recreations* inertia; *Clubs* Oxford and Cambridge; *Style—* Peter Gibbs-Kennet, Esq; ✉ Norwich Cottage, Bisley, Gloucestershire GL6 7AD (☎ 01452 770462, e-mail dli1944@aol.com)

GIBBY, Prof Mary; OBE (2010); *b* Doncaster; *Educ* Univ of Leeds (BSc), Univ of Liverpool (PhD); *Career* Br Museum (Natural History) 1974–2000, dir of science Royal Botanic Garden Edinburgh 2000–12; memb Scientific Advsy Ctee Scottish Natural Heritage 2001–07; *Style—* Prof Mary Gibby, OBE

GIBSON, Charles; QC (2001); *b* 1960; *Educ* Wellington, Univ of Durham (BA), Univ of London (Dip Law); *m*; 4 c; *Career* called to the Bar 1984; currently memb Henderson Chambers; recorder 2001–; accredited mediator; memb: Professional Negligence Bar Assoc, Common Law and Commercial Bar Assoc; *Publications* Group Actions: Product Liability Law and Insurance; *Style—* Charles Gibson, Esq, QC; ✉ Henderson Chambers, 2 Harcourt Buildings, Temple, London EC4Y 9DB

GIBSON, Christopher Allen Wood; QC (1995); s of Sir Ralph Brian Gibson, of London, and Ann Chapman, *née* Reuther; *b* 5 July 1953; *Educ* St Paul's, BNC Oxford (BA); *m* 4 Aug 1984, Alarys Mary Calvert, da of David Eaton, of Emsworth, Hants; 2 da (Harriet b 10 Dec 1984, Julia b 24 May 1987); *Career* called to the Bar Middle Temple 1976 (bencher 2003), recorder of the Crown Ct 2002–; memb Professional Conduct and Complaints Ctee of the Bar Cncl 1999–2002, chair Fitness to Practise Ctees Gen Pharmaceutical Cncl 2011–; memb Hon Soc of Middle Temple, FCIArb 1992; *Recreations* sailing, motorcycles, photography; *Clubs* Vincent's (Oxford); *Style—* Christopher Gibson; ✉ Outer Temple Chambers, The Outer Temple, 222 Strand, London WC2R 1BA (☎ 020 7353 6381)

GIBSON, Colin Raymond; s of Raymond Gibson (d 2011), and Muriel, *née* Power (d 1992); *b* 9 February 1957; *Educ* William Hulmes GS Manchester, Nat Cncl for Trg of Journalists Coll Preston (Dip); *m* 6 June 1987, Patricia Mary, da of David Coxon (d 2008); 1 da (Emma Catherine b 19 Aug 1989), 1 s (Michael Peter b 3 Aug 1993); *Career* sports writer; St Regis Newspapers Bolton (Stretford & Urmiston Jl) 1976–79, sports ed Messenger Newspapers Stockport 1979–80; sports corr: Daily Telegraph 1984 (joined 1980), Daily Mail 1984–86; chief sports writer Daily Telegraph 1986–93, sports ed Sunday Telegraph 1993–99, asst ed (sport) The Australian 1999–2001, sports ed Daily Mail 2001–2004, dir of communications FA 2004, head of communications ECB 2005–09, head of media and communications Int Cricket Cncl 2010–; memb: Sports Writers' Assoc of GB 1984, Football Writers' Assoc 1982; *Books* Glory, Glory Nights (1986), Football Association Publications (1990–93); *Recreations* golf, travel; *Style—* Colin Gibson, Esq

GIBSON, David Frank; s of Reginald James Gibson, of Warrington, Cheshire, and Emily, *née* Tanner; *b* 4 December 1946, Warrington, Lancs; *Educ* Boteler GS Warrington, UCL (BSc, DipArch); *m* 2 Sept 1969, Mary, da of John Greaves, of Warrington, Cheshire; 1 s (Timothy Edward Phillip b 1984), 1 da (Helen Emily Mary b 1988); *Career* architectural asst James Stirling and Ptnr 1968–70, assoc Colin St John Wilson and Ptnrs 1978–79 (architect 1971–79), studio tutor Bartlett Sch of Architecture 1979–88, Julian Harrap Architects 1981–84, assoc Alex Gordon and Partners 1985–87 (architect 1979–80), princ David Gibson Architects 1987–, prop Gibson Dennis Assocs 1998–; chm Islington Building Preservation Tst, chm Islington Soc; RIBA 1979, AABC 2012; *Recreations* architecture, bicycle maintenance, flying; *Style—* David Gibson, Esq; ✉ 22 St George's Avenue, London N7 0HD; David Gibson Architects, 3P Leroy, London N1 3QP (☎ 020 7226 2207, e-mail david@dgibarch.co.uk)

GIBSON, David William; s of John Love Gibson (d 1984), and Patricia Ann, *née* Cowcill (d 1984); *b* 19 May 1962; *Educ* Truro Boys' Sch, Univ of Kent at Canterbury (BA), Coll of Law; *m* (m dis), Marishelle, da of Donald Booth; 2 s (Angus Edmund b 16 Dec 1993, Alasdair Theodore b 9 May 1996); *Career* Alsop Wilkinson 1985–89, co sec and gp gen counsel Rexam plc (formerly Bowater plc) 1989–; memb Law Soc 1987; *Style—* David Gibson, Esq; ✉ Rexam plc, 4 Millbank, London SW1P 3XR (☎ 020 7227 4100, fax 020 7227 4139)

GIBSON, Elspeth; *Educ* Mansfield and Notts Coll of Art and Design (BTEC); *Career* fashion designer; work experience with Zandra Rhodes 1983, womenswear designer and pattern cutter Triangle Clothing Ltd London 1984–86, designer and pattern cutter Source Clothing London 1986, designer William Hunt London 1986–87, designer Coppernob Ltd London 1987–89, head of design Monix London 1989–94; freelance designer 1994–, commissions incl Debenhams childrenswear, founded Elspeth Gibson label, opened boutique 1998, launched bath products range 1999; Br Fashion Cncl New Generation Designer of the Year 1998, Best British Designer Elle Style Awards 1999, Glamour award nominee 1999, subject of V&A exhbn 2000; *Style—* Mrs Elspeth Gibson

GIBSON, Hon Hugh Marcus Thornely; DL; eldest s of Baron Gibson (d 2004); *b* 23 June 1946; *Educ* Eton, Magdalen Coll Oxford (BA); *m* 31 March 1967, Hon Frances Towneley, da of Hon Anthony Strachey (d 1955); 2 da (Effie Dione b 1970, Amelia Mary b 1973), 1 s (Jasper Tallentyre b 1975); *Career* dir Royal Doulton plc 1983–98, md Minton Ltd 1987–99, chief exec Royal Crown Derby Porcelain Co Ltd 1985–12 (chm 2007–12); Hon MUniv Derby 2004; *Books* A Case of Fine China: The Story of the Founding of Royal Crown Derby 1875–1890; *Recreations* National Trust, book collecting, wine, fishing; *Clubs* Reform, Brooks's; *Style—* Hon Hugh Gibson, DL; ✉ Penns in the Rocks, Groombridge, Tunbridge Wells TN3 9PA

GIBSON, Sir Ian; kt (1999), CBE (1990); s of Charles Gibson (d 1991), and Kate, *née* Hare (d 1971); *b* 1 February 1947; *Educ* Burnage GS, Univ of Manchester (BSc, vice-pres Union), London Business Sch; *m* 1, 1969 (m dis 1985), Joy Dorothy, da of Geoffrey Musker; 2 da (Janine Victoria , *qv*, b 17 June 1972, Sarah Rachel b 15 Feb 1975); m 2, 1988 (m dis 2010), Susan Margaret, da of John Lawrence Wilson; 1 s (Daniel Lancelot b 2 Nov 1989); m 3, 2010, Jane, da of William Blackburn; *Career* research asst ICI 1968, various industrial relations and mfrg mgmnt positions Ford Motor Co Ltd and Ford Werke AG Germany 1969–84; Nissan Motor Manufacturing (UK) Ltd: dir purchasing and prodn control 1984–87, dep md 1987–89, chief exec 1989–99; chm Nissan Yamato Engineering 1989–98, dir Nissan European Technology Centre 1990–2000, dir Nissan Motor GB 1992–2000, dir Nissan Motor Iberica SA 1996–2001, md Nissan Motor Iberica 1997–99, pres Nissan Europe NV 1999–2000 (vice-pres 1994–99), sr vice-pres Nissan Motor Co Ltd Japan 1999–2001, memb Supervisory Bd Nissan Europe NV 2000–2001; chm: Trinity Mirror plc 2006–12, W M Morrison Supermarkets plc 2008–15 (non-exec dir 2007–15); non-exec dir: Asda Group plc 1993–99 (dep chm 1996–99), Prodrive 2002, GKN plc 2002–08, Northern Rock plc 2002–08, BPB plc 2002–05 (dep chm 2003–04, chm 2004–05); memb Public Interest Body PWC 2010–; dir: Industry Forum 1997–2007, Centre for Life Tst 2001–11; chm: Ctee NEDO, Automotive Innovation and Growth Team 2001–03; pres SMMT 1999–2000 (vice-pres 1995–99); memb Bd Tyne & Wear Development Corp until 1998; memb Ct Bank of England 1999–2004; Mensforth Gold Medal IEE 1998, Castrol IMI Gold Medal 2002; Hon DBA Univ of Sunderland 1990, Hon DBA Univ of York St John 2015; FRSA 1990, CIMgt 1990, FInstP 1999; *Recreations* sailing, skiing; *Clubs* RAC; *Style—* Sir Ian Gibson, CBE

GIBSON, James Ernest; s of Joseph David Gibson, CBE (d 1992), and Emily Susan Gibson (d 1998); *b* 4 July 1960, Suva, Fiji; *Educ* Suva GS, Univ Coll Sch, Wadham Coll Oxford (MA); *m* 1, 1987 (m dis 1999), Rosemary, *née* Cameron; 1 da (Leonora b 1993); m 2, 2001, Michelle, *née* McAndrew; 2 da (Joeley b 2001, Milly b 2005); *Career* CA Arthur Andersen & Co until 1989, fin dir Heron Property 1989–94, fin dir Edge Properties plc 1994–98, ceo and co-fndr Big Yellow Gp plc 1998–; non-exec chm Anyjunk Ltd, shareholder dir Moby Self Storage Brazil; tstee London Children's Ballet; FCA; *Recreations* golf, tennis, non-fiction, rugby; *Clubs* Royal Overseas League; *Style—* James Gibson, Esq; ✉ Big Yellow Group plc, 2 The Deans, Bridge Road, Bagshot, Surrey GU19 5AT (e-mail jgibson@bigyellow.co.uk, website www.bigyellow.co.uk)

GIBSON, Jane; *Educ* Central Sch of Speech & Drama, Ècole Jacques Lecoq Paris; *Career* choreographer and dir; head of movement RNT; dir of movement RSC Acad 2002–; memb Advsy Panel to Dance Res Ctee Imperial Soc of Teachers of Dancing; assoc dir Cheek By Jowl; fndr memb Common Stock Theatre Co; *Theatre* movement/choreography since 1986; for RNT incl: A Matter of Life and Death, The Pied Piper, School for Wives, Yerma, Fuente Ovejuna, Hamlet, Ghetto, Peer Gynt, The Crucible, Richard III, Piano, Wind in the Willows, Arturo Ui, Angels in America, Black Snow, Pygmalion, Uncle Vanya, Rise and Fall of Little Voice, The Recruiting Officer, Sweeney Todd, Arcadia, Perestroika, Millennium Approaches, Broken Glass, Le Cid, The Merry Wives of Windsor, Volpone, Mother Courage and Her Children, La Grande Magia, Stanley, The Prince's Play, Blue Remembered Hills, Peter Pan, The Day I Stood Still, London Cuckolds, Not About Nightingales, An Enemy of the People, Mutabilitė, Flight, The Villains' Opera, Romeo and Juliet, The Cherry Orchard, Mother Clap's Molly House, Tartuffe, Mappa Mundi, The Mandate; for RSC incl: The Revenger's Tragedy, Much Ado About Nothing, The Plain Dealer, Macbeth, Don Juan, Elgar's Rondo, The School for Scandal, The Rivals, Twelfth Night; for Cheek By Jowl incl: Lady Betty, Sarah Sampson, Hamlet, Duchess of Malfi, Much Ado About Nothing, Homebody/Kabul, Twelfth Night (Moscow Theatre Assoc); other credits incl: Lear (Melbourne Theatre Co),The Merry Widow (Scottish Opera), Charlie Gorilla (Lyric Belfast), The Shaugraun (Abbey Theatre Dublin), Gawain (ROH), La Clemenza di Tito (Glyndebourne, also BBC), Emma (Cambridge Theatre Co), La Traviata (ROH), Force of Destiny and Mahagonny (ENO), Peter Pan (West Yorkshire Playhouse), The Rake's Progress (WNO), Julio Cesare (ROH), Flastaff (Salzburg), Le Noce di Figaro (Aix en Provence, Garsington), Don Giovanni (Garsington), Le Cid (Festival d'Avignon), Five Gold Rings (Almeida Theatre), Othello (Cheek by Jowl), The Importance of Being Earnest (Oxford Stage Co), Candida (Oxford Stage Co), Les Liaisons Dangereuses (Ambassadors Theatre), The Lady in the Van (Bath Theatre Royal), Blithe Spirit (Bath Theatre Royal and Savoy Theatre); as director for LAMDA credits incl: The Country Wife, Loot, The Fireraisers, The Bald Prima Donna, The Lover, Immodesty Blaize and the Adventures of Walter, Burlesque!; as co-dir with Sue Lefton credits incl: Lark Rise (Haymarket Leics and Almeida), Nana (for Shared Experience, Almeida and Mermaid), A Tale of Two Cities (Cambridge Theatre Co, Newcastle Theatre and tour), Hiawatha (Sheffield Crucible), A Working Woman (W Yorks Playhouse), Private Lives (Theatre Royal Bath), Great Expectations (RSC), The Changeling (Cheek by Jowl), Voyage Round My Father (Donmar Warehouse), Tom & Viv (Almeida) Cymbeline (Cheek by Jowl), 'Tis Pity She's a Whore (Southwark Playhouse), Our Country's Good (Liverpool Playhouse), A Midsummer Night's Dream (Sydney Theatre Co), Silverland (Lacuna Prodns), Kiss of the Spiderwoman (Donmar Warehouse), The Changeling (Cheek by Jowl), Troilus and Cressida (Cheek by Jowl), Andromache (Theatre de Bouffe du Nord Paris), Twelfth Night (Regent's Park Open Air Theatre), In a Forest Dark and Deep, When We Are Married, Waste (Almeida Theatre), Twelfth Night (Regent's park), Tombstone Tales (Arcola), Macbeth (Cheek By Jowl), Tiger Country (Hampstead Theatre Co), In a Forest Dark and Deep (Vaudeville Theatre), The Madness of George III (Theatre Royal Bath), Tis Pity She's a Whore (Barbican), The Pitchfork Disney (Arcola Theatre), Huis Clos (Donmar Warehouse), Troilus and Cressida (RSC and Wooster Gp), A Tender Thing (RSC), Ubu Roi (Barbican), Longing (Hampstead Theatre), Ubu Roi (Barbican), 'Tis Pity She's A Whore (Cheek by Jowl), Shakespeare in Love (Noël Coward Theatre), When the Terror is Over the Victims Will Dance (Drama Centre London); *Opera* The Rape of Lucretia (Aldeburgh Opera), La Traviata (ROH), Gawain (ROH), Mahagonny (ENO), The Force of Destiny (ENO), La Clemenza Di Tito (Glyndebourne), The Marriage of Figaro (Aix Enprovence), Julio Cesari (ROH), The Heart of Darkness (ROH), The Rape of Lucretia (Aldeburgh), Maometto Secondo (Garsington); *Televison* credits incl: Far From the Madding Crowd (Granada), Tom Jones (BBC), David (TNT), Emma (ITV/A&E), Scarlett (CBS TV), Pride and Preducice (BBC, Best Choreographer nomination Emmy Awards 1996), Great Expectations (BBC), Wives and Daughters (BBC), Madame Bovary (BBC), The Russian Bride (BBC), The Scarlet Pimpernel (BBC), Lorna Doone (BBC), Love in a Cold Climate (BBC), Night and Day (BBC), Daniel Deronda (BBC), Cambridge Spies (BBC), Charles II (BBC), Reversals (ITV), The Deal (Channel 4), Mansfield Park (ITV), Persuasion (ITV), Cranford Chronicles (BBC), Tess (BBC), Elizabeth I, Legenos (TNT), Mr Selfridge (ITV), Virtuoso (HBO); *Film* incl: Cousin Bette, Dracula, Sense and Sensibility, Firelight, Nancherro, Mansfield Park, Kate and Leopold, I Capture the Castle, Iris, The Girl with the Pearl Earring, Nanny McPhee, Pride and Prejudice, V for Vendetta, Perfume, The Golden Age, Atonement, Becoming Jane, Holiday, Death Defying Acts, And When Did You Last See Your Father?, Adam Resurrected, Brideshead Revisited, Nanny McPhee 2, Bel Ami, My Week With Marylyn, Oz: The Great and Powerful, A Little Chaos; *Style—* Ms Jane Gibson; ✉ c/o Independent Talent Group, 40 Whitfield Street, London W1T 2RH (☎ 020 7636 6565, fax 020 7323 9867)

GIBSON, Janine Victoria; da of Sir Ian Gibson, CBE , *qv*, of Gosforth, Newcastle upon Tyne, and Joy Gibson; *b* 17 June 1972; *Educ* Walthamstow Hall Sevenoaks, St John's Coll Oxford (BA); *m* 1999, Steve Busfield; 2 da (Martha Gibson Busfield b 6 Aug 2002, Kitty Gibson Busfield b 30 March 2006); *Career* journalist; dep ed Televisual 1995–97, int ed Broadcast 1997–98, media corr The Independent 1998; The Guardian: media corr 1998–2000, media ed 2000–03, ed G3 and ed-in-chief Media Guardian 2003–06, asst ed 2006, exec ed Guardian Unlimited 2007–09, ed guardian.co.uk 2009–11, ed-in-chief Guardian US 2011–14, dep ed 2014–15; ed-in-chief Buzzfeed UK 2015–; memb

Broadcasting Press Guild; *Publications* Guardian Media Directory (2007), Media 08 (2008); *Style—* Ms Janine Gibson; ✉ e-mail janine.gibson@buzzfeed.com

GIBSON, Dr John Robin; s of Norman John Gibson (d 1983), and Marie Louise Elizabeth, *née* Edwards (d 2009); *b* 16 December 1949, Kingston, Jamaica; *Educ* Eastwood HS Glasgow, Univ of Glasgow (MB ChB); *m* 25 April 1990, Sabina Silvia, da of Joachim Rosenthaler, of Basel, Switzerland; *Career* hosp MO Bulawayo 1974–77, med registrar Glasgow 1977, hon conslt dermatologist London Hosp 1983–89 (hon dermatology registrar and sr registrar 1978–82), head Dermatology Section Wellcome Res Labs Beckenham 1978–89, vice-pres of clinical res Bristol-Myers Squibb Co 1992–93 (dir 1989–90, exec dir 1990–92), sr vice-pres global devpt Allergan Inc 1993–2007; dir Somanta Ltd; volunteer clinical prof of dermatology: SUNY Buffalo 1992–2007, Univ of Calif Irvine 2001–07; pres and ceo Healthwise Int Inc, dir Geneve Bio Inc; chm British American Business Cncl Orange County; pres and ceo Jangus Music Inc; dir Green Kidz Inc; author multiple book chapters and papers on: dermatology, therapeutics, pharmacology, allergy; Freeman City of London 1987, Liveryman Worshipful Soc of Apothecaries 1988 (Yeoman 1982); memb: BMA, BAD, AAD; MRCP, FRCPG 1987, FRSM; *Recreations* guitar playing, song writing, bridge, squash; *Style—* Dr John R Gibson; ✉ 2368 Glenneyre Street, Laguna Beach, CA 92651, USA (☎ 949 376 9060, e-mail johnrobingibson@cox.net); 9 Cabo Del Sol, Denia, Alicante, Spain

GIBSON, Kenneth James; MSP; s of Kenneth George Gibson (d 1994), and Iris, *née* Arbuckle; *b* 8 September 1961; *Educ* Bellahouston Acad (biology and history prizes), Univ of Stirling (BA); *m* 1 June 1989, Lynda Dorothy, da of Peter Payne; 2 s (Ross Ewan Fraser b 16 Sept 1992, Lewis Duncan Callum b 13 August 1998), 1 da (Heather Kirsty Fiona b 8 July 1996); *Career* systems devpt offr Br Steel 1982–87, sponsorship advsr and visitor info mangr Glasgow Garden Festival 1987–88, pharmaceutical sales 1988–99; memb Glasgow DC 1992–96, memb Glasgow City Cncl 1995–99 (ldr of oppn 1998–99); MSP (SNP) Glasgow 1999–2003, MSP (SNP) Cunninghame North 2007–; Scot Parl: dep convenor Social Justice Ctee, memb Local Govt Ctee, convenor Cross Pty Gp on Tobacco Control, convenor Cross Pty Gp on Consumer Affrs; SNP: memb 1979–, memb NEC 1997–99 (vice-convenor Local Govt), shadow min for Local Govt 1997–2000, shadow min for Local Govt, Consumer Affrs and Urban Regeneration 2000–02, shadow min for Housing and Urban Regeneration 2002; hon patron Grandparents Apart Self-Help Gp; *Recreations* reading, theatre, cinema, opera, ballet, football and swimming; *Style—* Kenneth Gibson, Esq, MSP

GIBSON, Patricia; MP; da of James Duffy, and Eileen, *née* Doherty; *b* 12 May 1968, Glasgow; *Educ* Univ of Glasgow (MA); *m* 12 Oct 2007, Kenneth Gibson; *Career* secdy sch English teacher 1992–2015; memb Gen Teaching Cncl; MP (SNP) Ayrshire N and Arran 2015–; cncllr Glasgow City Cncl 2007–12; *Recreations* cinema, music, reading; *Style—* Ms Patricia Gibson, MP; ✉ House of Commons, London SW1A 0AA (Twitter @PGibsonSNP)

GIBSON, Paul Alexander; s of Wing Cdr L P Gibson (d 1954), and Betty, *née* Peveler; *b* 11 October 1941; *Educ* Kingswood Sch Bath, King's Coll London, Canterbury Sch of Architecture, Regent Street Poly Sch of Architecture; *m* 29 Aug 1969, Julia Rosemary, da of Leslie Atkinson; *Career* architect; Farrell Grimshaw Partnership 1968–69, lectr N Dakota State Univ USA 1969–70, Foster Associates 1970–72, private practice Sidell Gibson Partnership 1973–2002 (conslt 2002–); major projects incl: MEPC office buildings Frankfurt 1974, master plans Univ of Arack Iran and housing at Kermanshah Iran 1976, 25 varied housing schemes English Courtyard Assoc 1976–2001, office buildings and housing Frankfurt 1991, New Jewel House Tower of London 1993, appointed architect for Windsor Castle restoration 1994, 3 buildings at Brindley Place Birmingham 1995–2001, office building for Cazenove 2001; winner major architectural competition for Grand Buildings Trafalgar Square 1987; RIBA 1969; *Recreations* painting, music; *Style—* Paul Gibson, Esq

GIBSON, Rob McKay; s of John Gibson, and Elsie Gibson; *b* 16 October 1945, Glasgow; *Educ* Glasgow HS, Univ of Dundee (MA), Dundee Coll of Educn (DipEd, Teaching Dip); *Partner* Dr Eleanor Roberta Scott; *Career* Invergordon Acad: teacher of geography and modern studies 1973–74, asst princ teacher of guidance 1974–77; princ teacher of guidance Alness Acad 1977–95, writer and researcher 1995–2003; MSP (SNP): Highlands and Islands 2003–11, Caithness, Sutherland & Ross 2011–16; memb Tranpsort, Infrastructure and Climate Change Ctee and vice-convenor Educn, Lifelong Learning and Culture Ctee Scottish Parl, convenor Rural Affrs, Climate Change and Environment Ctee and memb Devolution (Further Powers) Ctee 2011–16; vice-pres Brittany Scotland Assoc, hon pres Kilt Society of France; *Books* The Promised Land (1974), Highland Clearances Trail (1983, new edn 2006), Toppling the Duke (1996), Plaids and Bandanas (2003); *Recreations* traditional music singer, organic gardener, hill walker, traveller; *Style—* Rob Gibson, Esq; ✉ Tir Nan Oran, 8 Culcairn Road, Evanton, Rossshire IV16 9YT (☎ 01349 830388, e-mail robgibson273@btinternet.com)

GIBSON, HE Robert Winnington; CMG (2011); *Career* diplomat; desk offr European Integration Dept FCO 1978–79, ME Center for Arabic Studies FCO 1979–80, HM vice consul Jeddah 1981–84, second sec UKREP Brussels 1984–85, second sec chancery Port of Spain 1986–89, head Peacekeeping and Finance Section UN Dept FCO 1989–93, head Saudi Arabian and Gulf Section ME Dept FCO 1993–95, first sec UK Delgn to OECD Paris 1995–99, dep head Whitehall Liaison Dept FCO 1999–2001, dep high cmmr and commercial counsellor Dhaka 2002–05, dep head of mission Baghdad 2006–07, dep high cmmr Karachi and dir UK Trade and Investment Pakistan 2008–11, high cmmr to Bangladesh 2011–16; *Style—* HE Mr Robert Winnington Gibson, CMG; ✉ c/o FCO (Dhaka), King Charles Street, London SW1A 2AH

GIBSON, Ven Terence Allen (Terry); s of Fred William Allen Gibson, of Boston, Lincs, and Joan Hazel, *née* Bishop; *b* 23 October 1937; *Educ* Boston GS, Jesus Coll Cambridge (MA), Cuddesdon Theol Coll; *Career* curate St Chad Kirkby Liverpool 1963–66, warden Centre 63 C of E Youth Centre and vicar for Youth Work 1966–75, rector of Kirkby Liverpool 1975–84, rural dean Walton Liverpool 1979–84; archdeacon of: Suffolk 1984–87, Ipswich 1987–; *Style—* The Ven the Archdeacon of Ipswich; ✉ 99 Valley Road, Ipswich, Suffolk IP1 4NF (☎ 01473 250333, fax 01473 286877)

GIBSON, Thomas Herbert; s of Clement Herbert Gibson (d 1976), of England and Argentina, and Marjorie Julia, *née* Anderson (d 1982); *b* 12 April 1943; *Educ* Eton; *m* 1966, Anthea Fiona Catherine (d 2010), da of late Lt-Col G A Palmer, RE; 3 s (Miles Cosmo Archdale b 1968, Sebastian Thomas Maximilian b 1972, Benjamin Hugh George b 1973); *Career* fndr chm Thomas Gibson Fine Art Ltd 1969–96, ret, fndr Thomas Gibson Fine Art Advsy Services 1996–; *Recreations* tennis; *Style—* Thomas Gibson, Esq; ✉ Thomas Gibson Fine Art Advisory Services, 39 St James's Street, London SW1A 1JD

GIBSON, Prof Vernon Charles; *Educ* Univ of Oxford (DPhil); *Career* NATO postdoctoral fell Caltech 1984–86, lectr in inorganic chemistry Univ of Durham 1986–93, prof of chemistry Univ of Durham 1993–95; Imperial Coll London: first holder Sir Geoffrey Wilkinson chair of chemistry 1995, currently Edward Frankland BP prof of inorganic chemistry, head Catalysis and Materials Research Section; R D Haworth Medal Univ of Sheffield 1980, BP Chemicals Young Univ Lectr 1990–93, Sir Edward Frankland fell RSC 1992–93, Corday-Morgan Medal and Prize RSC 1993–94, Joseph Chatt lectr RSC 2001, Tilden lectr RSC 2004–05; FRS 2004; *Clubs* Athenaeum; *Style—* Prof Vernon Gibson; ✉ Department of Chemistry, Imperial College London, South Kensington Campus, London SW7 2AZ

GIBSON, Hon William Knatchbull; 3 s of Baron Gibson (Life Peer, d 2004), and Elizabeth Dione (d 2012), da of Hon Clive Pearson; *b* 26 August 1951; *Educ* Eton, Magdalen Coll Oxford (BA); *m* 1988, Lori Frances, o da of Herbert Mintz, of Miami, FL; 1 s (Matthew Charles b 6 Dec 1990), 1 da (Sarah Claire b 29 Aug 1992); *Career* newspaper mangr with Westminster Press (industrial rels specialist 1976–82), Sloan fell London Grad Sch of Business Studies 1983, dir of admin Financial Times 1984–86, publisher of Financial Times magazines 1986–89, md Financial Times Business Information 1989–95; chm: Westminster Press Ltd 1996–97 (also chief exec), Dowell and Associates 2000–04, Kidsactive 2000–03, AYM 2002–04; dir: MQ Publications 1998–2003, Business in Focus Productions 1999–, Millbank Financial Services 2002–, Camellia plc 2014–; memb Newspaper Panel Competition Cmmn 1999–2006; *Recreations* music, opera, shooting, skiing; *Clubs* Garrick, Sussex; *Style—* The Hon William Gibson; ✉ 46 Victoria Road, London W8 5RQ; Newhouse Farm, Balcombe, West Sussex RH17 6RB

GIBSON HARRIS, Jeremy Miles (Jez); s of Leonard Miles Gibson Harris, and Jean Mary Royce, *née* Skinner; *b* 14 January 1960; *Educ* Shene GS, Richmond Coll, Sir John Cass Coll of Art; *m* 1994, Jayne Senft; 1 da (Eleanor Siân b 2 Aug 2000), 1 s (Sam George b 23 Sept 2007); *Career* worked in film industry 1980–; contrib special effects and animatronics on over 30 feature films; with Nick Maley's Make-Up EFX Ltd 1980, estab Crawley Creatures 1986; voting memb BAFTA; early animatronics work incl: The Dark Crystal 1981, Jabba the Hutt for Return of the Jedi 1982, Greystoke, Legend of Tarzan 1984; film projects incl: An American Werewolf in Paris, Blackadder Back & Forth, The Little Vampire, Tomorrow Never Dies; TV projects incl: Walking with Dinosaurs, Walking with Beasts, Sea Monsters, Primeval; jeweller and silversmith; gp exhbns incl: Jewellery Redefined, 30 Contemporary Jewellers, Period Homes and Gardens (sculpture exhbn), Oxford Artists; former rugby union player: London Welsh, Harlequins, Surrey Co; dir Time Bites Ltd (chocolate co); *Awards* for Walking with Dinosaurs: Team Production Award RTS Prog Awards 1999, Millennium Products award 1999, Best Documentary TRIC Awards 1999, Lead Special Effects Supervisor Primetime Emmy Awards 1999–2000; Design and Craft Innovation Award RTS Craft and Design Awards 1999–2000, Visual Effects BAFTA TV Crafts Awards 2002 and 2003; *Recreations* horse riding, kayaking, walking, travelling to exotic locations; *Clubs* Oxford Sculptors' Gp; *Style—* Jez Gibson Harris, Esq; ✉ Crawley Creatures Limited/i-bodi Ltd, Unit 8, Swan Business Centre, Osier Way, Buckingham MK18 1TB (☎ 01280 815300, website www.crawley-creatures.com and www.i-bodi.com)

GIBSON OF MARKET RASEN, Baroness (Life Peer UK 2000), of Market Rasen in the County of Lincolnshire; Anne Gibson; OBE (1998); da of Harry Tasker (d 1967), of Lincs, and Jessie, *née* Roberts (d 2002); *b* 10 December 1940; *Educ* Caistor GS, Chelmsford Coll of Further Educn, Univ of Essex (BA); *m* 1, 1962 (m dis 1985), John Donald Gibson; 1 da (Rebecca Bridgid b 1964); *m* 2, 1988, John Bartell, s of Henry Bartell (d 1983), of Liverpool; 1 step da (Sharon Jayne b 1965); *Career* full-time organiser Lab Pty (Saffron Walden) 1965–70, researcher House Magazine (jl of Houses of Parliament) 1975–77, Party candidate (Lab) Bury St Edmunds 1979, asst/asst sec and dep head Orgn and Industrial Rels Dept TUC (with special responsibility for equal rights area of work) 1977–87; nat offr Amicus with special responsibility for: voluntary sector and equal rights section 1987–96, policy and political work 1996–2000; memb: Gen Cncl TUC 1989–2000, Dept of Employment Advsy Gp on Older Workers 1993–96, Bd Bilbao Agency 1996–2000, Trade Union Sustainable Devpt Ctee 1999–2000, Parly and Scientific Ctee; memb Lab Pty: NEC Women's Ctee 1990–98, Nat Constitutional Ctee 1997–2000, Lab Pty Policy Reform 1998–2000, Foreign and Commonwealth Affrs Gp, Home Affrs Gp, Lab Pty Defence Gp; Equal Opportunities cmmr 1991–98, Health and Safety cmmr 1996–2000, dep Lord speaker 2008–; memb All-Pty Parly Gps: Adoption, Bolivia (chair), Brazil, Arts and Heritage, Asthma, BBC, Breast Cancer, Children, Corporate Social Responsibility (dep chair), Insurance and Fin Servs, Latin America (dep chair), Rail Freight, Safety and Health, Sex Equality, TU Gp of MPs and Peers, Rural Affrs, Food & Health Forum (treas); memb: Select Ctee on the EU 2001–05, Constitutional Bill Select Ctee, Lords Reform Ctee, BBC Charter Review Select Ctee 2005–06, Link Standing Ctee on Consumer Issues 2006–13, Jt Lords and Commons Constitutional Renewal Ctee 2008–10; chair: UMIST Research Gp on Bullying at Work 2003–05, DTI Research Gp on Bullying at Work 2004–08; dep chm House of Lords; memb English Beef and Lamb Exec (EBLEX); pres:Yeadon Air Training Cadets 2002–, RoSPA 2004–08 (dep chair 2001–04); memb: Air League Cncl 2005–, Air Cadet Cncl 2006–, Fawcett Soc, Fabian Soc, Unite (formerly Amicus); patron Happy Child 2010; *Publications* author numerous TUC and MSF Equal Opportunities Booklets incl Charter of Equal Opportunities For 1990s (1990); Disability and Employer – A Trade Union Guide (1989), Lesbian and Gay Rights in Employment (1990), Recruitment of Women Workers (1990), Part time Workers Rights (1991), Women in MSF (1991), Sexual Harassment at Work (1993), Caring – A Union Issue (1993); *Recreations* reading, theatre, knitting, embroidery; *Style—* The Rt Hon the Baroness Gibson of Market Rasen, OBE; ✉ House of Lords, London SW1A 0PW

GIBSON-BOLTON, Elaine; da of Robert William Holmes Gibson-Bolton, of Norwich, and Rosaleen Christabel, *née* Smyth; *b* 15 January 1962; *Educ* Wymondham Coll, Univ of Reading (LLB), Univ of Amsterdam (Dip), Coll of Law; *Career* admitted slr 1987; trainee slr Clifford Harris & Co 1985–87; slr: Holman Fenwick & Willan 1987–89, Freshfields 1989–93, SJ Berwin LLP 1993– (ptnr 1997–); memb: Assoc of Electricity Producers, Slrs European Gp, City of London Slrs, Competition Law Forum, Law Soc European Gp (LSEG), Bd Tomorrow's People; Competition Lawyer/Team of the Year Legal Business; memb Worshipful Co of Fuellers; memb: Law Soc 1987, Inst of Advanced Legal Studies; *Recreations* travel, theatre, film, gardening, koi; *Clubs* Century, European Aviation, Women in Media; *Style—* Ms Elaine Gibson-Bolton; ✉ SJ Berwin LLP, 10 Queen Street Place, London EC4R 1BE (☎ 020 7111 2463, fax 020 7111 2000, e-mail elaine.gibson-bolton@sjberwin.com)

GIBSON-SMITH, Dr Christopher (Chris); CBE (2011); *Educ* Univ of Durham, Univ of Newcastle upon Tyne (PhD), Stanford Univ (MSc); *m* Marjorie; 2 da (Emma, Sarah); *Career* BP plc: joined as exploration and production geologist 1970, chief geologist 1983, European chief exec BP Exploration 1992, chief operating offr BP Chemicals 1995, gp md 1997–2001; chm: National Air Traffic Services Ltd (NATS) 2001–05, London Stock Exchange plc 2003–, British Land Co plc 2007–12 (non-exec dir 2003–), Reform 2012–, Partnership 2013–; non-exec dir: Lloyds TSB plc 1999–2005, Powergen 2001–02, Qatar Financial Centre Authy; formerly: memb UK Sustainability Commission, memb Sloan Advsy Bd Stanford Business Sch, memb Cncl CBI Scotland, chm Business in the Arts Scotland, chm California Marine Mammal Centre; tstee: IPPR, Arts & Business; govr London Business School; hon fell Univ Col Durham; *Recreations* literature, music, art, skiing, sailing, golf; *Style—* Dr Chris Gibson-Smith, CBE; ✉ London Stock Exchange, 10 Paternoster Square, London EC4M 7LS

GIDDINGS, John; s of John Giddings, and Margaret McDougall; *b* 1 May 1953, St Albans, Herts; *Educ* St Albans Sch, Univ of Eeter; *m* 20 Jan 2007, Caroline, *née* Terry; 4 da (Alice Lloyds, Sara Birch, Lisa Birch, Kitty Giddings); *Career* music agent and promoter; MAM 1976–81, TBA Int 1981–86, fndr and md Solo Music Agency and Promotions 1986–; artists incl: David Bowie, The Rolling Stones, The Police, Lady Gaga, Pharrell Williams; memb: Agents Assoc, Assoc of Ind Festivals; Agent of the Decade; involved with Scouts and Dimbola Lodge Isle of Wight; *Recreations* cinema, motorsport, music, reading, walking; *Clubs* Hurlingham; *Style—* John Giddings, Esq; ✉ Solo, 4th Floor Chester

House, 81 Fulham High Street, London SW6 3JW (☎ 020 7384 6644, e-mail john@solo.uk.com, website www.solo.uk.com, Twitter @JohnGiddings01)

GIDDY, Pam; da of B S Giddy, of Coventry, and N K Giddy, *née* Pabla; *b* 5 April 1967, Coventry; *Educ* Lyng Hall Girls Sch Coventry, Sidney Stringer Sch Coventry, LSE (LLB); *Career* ed Violations of Rights pamphlets for Charter 88 1990–93, ed News & Careers Cosmopolitan magazine 1993–94, prodr BBC2 Newsnight 1994–99, dir Charter 88 democratic reform gp 1999–2001, fndr and dir POWER Inquiry 2004–; memb: Bd Joseph Rowntree Reform Trust Ltd, Content Bd Ofcom; *Recreations* swimming, reading; *Clubs* County Hall Westminster; *Style—* Ms Pam Giddy

GIDOOMAL, Balram (Ram); CBE (1998); *b* 23 December 1950, Mombasa, Kenya; *Educ* Christopher Wren Sch London, Imperial Coll London (BSc); *m* Sunita Shivdasani; 2 s (Ravi b 1979, Ricki b 1983), 1 da (Nina b 1981); *Career* research analyst in mgmnt science (with Civil Service grant) Imperial Coll London 1972–75, ops research analyst Lloyds Bank International London 1976–78; Inlaks Group: dep gp chief exec Head Office France then Geneva 1978–85, UK gp chief exec London then Scotland 1985–89, non-exec vice-chm London 1988–92; chm: Winning Communications Partnership Ltd, Traidcraft plc 2011–, Bd Dulas Ltd 2014–, Cotton Connect Ltd 2016–, Stewardship Services 2016–; strategic advsr: Vertex Law LLP 2011–13, Klaafs Ltd 2011–, United Business Machines Ltd 2011–; non-exec dir: Amsphere Ltd 2006–, Nirmaan Bharti SAAVS Lucknow 2007–09; fndr chm: Christmas Cracker Trust 1989–2000, South Asian Concern 1991–, South Asian Development Partnership 1993–, Business Link London (South) 1995–98; dir: Christian Research Assoc 1994–96, Nat Accreditation Bd Business Links DTI 1995–2000, Business Link London 1996–98, Far Pavilions Ltd 1998–2007; fndr dir and vice-chair South London Trg and Enterprise Cncl (SOLOTEC) 1991–97, ldr Christian Peoples Alliance 2000–04 (candidate for London Mayor and Greater London Assembly 2000 and 2004), fndr dir and former vice-chair African Caribbean Westminster Initiative 1998–2002, patron Small Business Bureau 1996–, pres National Information Forum 2003–09, vice-pres The Leprosy Mission 1999–, vice-pres Livability (formerly The Shaftesbury Soc), vice-pres Employee Ownership Assoc 2009–; dir: Epsom and St Helier NHS Tst 1999–2006 (chair Audit Ctee 2000–05), English Partnerships 2000–03 (memb Audit Ctee); chm: Business Link Nat Conference 1997, London Community Fndn 2001–03, London Sustainablility Exchange 2001–07, The Employability Forum 2003–09 (memb 2000–09), Nat Refugee Integration Forum (Employers Subgroup) 2003–06, Allia (formerly CityLife Industrial and Provident Soc) 2005–; memb Henderson's Global SRI Advsy Ctee 2004–10; chair Office of the Independent Adjudicator for HE 2009–; memb: Apples & Pears Res Cncl MAFF 1995–98, Bd Covent Garden Market Authy 1998–2004, Exec Ctee Assoc of Charitable Foundations 1995–98, Cabinet Office Better Regulation Task Force 1997–2002 (chair Anti Discrimination Sub-Gp 1998, chair Technol Means Business Cncl DTI 1998–2004), Cncl Britain in Europe, Advsy Ctee on Clinical Excellence Awards 2004–08, Cncl RSA 2004–09 (tstee 1998–2002), Complaints Audits Ctee UK Border Agency (formerly Home Office Immigration Nationality Database) 2005–08, External Relations Gp Water UK 2009–, Advsy Cncl Inst of Business Ethics 2009–, Bd Int Justice Mission Washington DC 2008–14, Bd Food Standards Agency 2014–; external memb Audit and Risk Assurance Ctee Equalities and Human Rights Cmmn 2010–14; business advsr for ethnic minorities The Prince's Tst 1991–2000, sec India Devpt Tst 1994–; tstee: Inst for Citizenship 2000, Timebank Charitable Tst 2001–04, Forum for the Future 2001–11, Trg for Life 2001–04, Care for Children 2010–13; memb Bd of Govrs James Allen Girls Sch 1997–2002; memb Bd Kings Coll Sch 1998–2011, govr The Health Fndn 2000–05; visiting prof of entrepreneurship and inner city regeneration Middx Univ; memb Cncl Bd Inst for Employment Studies 2001–10; St George's Hosp Med Sch Univ of London: memb Cncl 2002–09 (vice-chair 2006–09), memb Audit Ctee (chair 2006–09), chair Estates Project Bd 2005–09; crown appointee on Ct and Cncl Imperial Coll London 2002–09, chair Res Ethics Ctee Imperial Coll London 2006–09 (also chair Student Tstee Bd); hon memb Faculty of Divinity Univ of Cambridge 1997–, Dehejia fell Sidwell Friends Sch Washington DC 2008, Fellowship Imperial Coll (FIC) 2010; delivered Hansen Wessner Lecture 2000 at Saïd Business Sch Univ of Oxford; appeared on various TV and radio documentaries and progs on ethnic and business issues 1987–, subject of numerous newspaper articles; Freeman City of London, Liveryman Worshipful Co of Information Technolgists; LLD (hc) Univ of Bristol 2002, DLitt (hc) Nottingham Trent Univ 2003, Hon DUniv Middx; ARCS, FRSA, FCGI, CCMI (memb Bd); *Publications* Sari 'n' Chips (1993), Chapatis for Tea (1994), Karma 'n' Chips (1994), The Creative Manager (contrib), South Asian Development Partnership Population Report for Great Britain – The £5 billion Asian Corridor for Opportunities for TECS (with SOLOTEC), Lions Princesses, Gurus (1996), A Way of Life: Hinduism (1997), The UK Maharajahs (1997), Building on Success, The South Asian Contribution to UK Competitiveness (1997), How would Jesus vote? (2001), The British and how to deal with them: Doing Business with Britain's Ethnic Minorities (2001), Who Is My Neighbour? (2002), The Right Use of Money (contrib, 2004); Coming to Britain an Immigrant's Story (video), Songs of the Kingdom (music), Asia Worships (music); *Recreations* swimming, current affairs; *Style—* Ram Gidoomal, Esq, CBE; ✉ 14 The Causeway, Sutton, Surrey SM2 5RS (e-mail ramgidoomal@blueyonder.co.uk)

GIELGUD, Maina Julia Gordon; Hon AO (1991); da of Lewis Evelyn Gielgud (d 1953), and Elisabeth Sutton (author and actress under name of Zita Gordon; d 2006); niece of Sir John Gielgud; *b* 14 January 1945, London; *Educ* BEPC France; *Career* ballerina with: Cuevas Co and Roland Petit Co to 1963, Grand Ballet Classique de France 1963–67; princ ballerina: Béjart Co 1967–71, Berlin 1971, London Festival Ballet 1972–76, Sadler's Wells Ballet 1976–78; freelance ballerina and guest artist 1978–82, rehearsal dir London City Ballet 1982; artistic dir: Australian Ballet 1983–96, Royal Danish Ballet March 1997–99; artistic assoc Houston Ballet 2003–05, guest princ repetiteur English Nat Ballet 2007–12, artistic advsr Hungarian Nat Ballet 2014–, currently freelance staging, directing and coaching, taking master classes and jury member for int competitons; creations and choreographies: Steps Notes and Squeaks (London) 1978, Petit Pas et Crac (Paris) 1979, Ghosties and Ghoulies (London City Ballet) 1982, The Sleeping Beauty (Australian Ballet) 1984, Giselle (Australian Ballet) 1986, (Boston Ballet) 2002, 2006 and 2009, (Ballet du Rhin) 2003 and (Australian Ballet) 2007; *Style—* Ms Maina Gielgud, AO; ✉ Stirling Court, 3 Marshall Street, London W1F 9BD (e-mail mainagielgud@gmail.com)

GIEVE, Katherine Elizabeth; da of Charles Vereker (d 1996), and Patricia, *née* Kastelian (d 2001); *b* 26 June 1949, Oxford; *Educ* Merchant Taylors' Sch for Girls Liverpool, St Anne's Coll Oxford (BA); *m* 25 March 1972, John Gieve; 2 s (Daniel b 6 June 1980, Matthew b 31 Aug 1982); *Career* admitted slr 1978; slr: West Hampstead Law Centre 1978–83, Wilford McBain 1983–85, Family Rights Gp 1986–88; Bindmans LLP (formerly Bindman & Ptnrs): slr 1988–91, ptnr 1991–2014, head Family Dept 2003–14, conslt 2014–; memb Law Soc, fell Int Acad of Matrimonial Lawyers; *Publications* Cohabitation Handbook (1981), Balancing Acts: On Being a Mother (1989); *Recreations* yoga; *Style—* Ms Katherine Gieve; ✉ Bindmans LLP, 236 Gray's Inn Road, London WC1X 8HB (☎ 020 7833 4433, fax 020 7833 9792, e-mail k.gieve@bindmans.com)

GIFFORD, 6 Baron (UK 1824); Anthony Maurice Gifford; QC (1982); s of 5 Baron Gifford (d 1961), and (Ellice) Margaret, *née* Allen (d 1990); *b* 1 May 1940; *Educ* Winchester, King's Coll Cambridge; *m* 1, 22 March 1965 (m dis 1988), Katherine Ann, da of Max Mundy, of Kensington, London; 1 s (Hon Thomas Adam b 1967), 1 da (Hon Polly Anna b 1969); m 2, 24 Sept 1988 (m dis 1998), Elean Roslyn, da of Bishop David Thomas, of Kingston, Jamaica; 1 da (Sheba Chanel b 1992); m 3, 11 April 1998, Tina Natalia, da of Clement Goulbourne, of Kingston, Jamaica; *Heir* s, Hon Thomas Gifford; *Career* sat as Lab Peer in House of Lords until 1999; called to the Bar Middle Temple 1962; head of chambers 2000–; chm: Broadwater Farm Inquiry 1986, Liverpool 8 Inquiry 1989; attorney at law Jamaica 1990; sr ptnr Gifford, Thompson & Bright 1991–; chm: Ctee for Freedom Mozambique, Angola and Guiné 1968–75, N Kensington Law Centre 1974–77, Legal Action Gp 1978–81, Mozambique Angola Ctee 1984; vice-chm British Defence and Aid Fund 1985; *Books* Where's the Justice (1986), The Passionate Advocate (2007); *Style—* The Lord Gifford, QC; ✉ London Chambers, 1 Mitre Court Buildings, Temple, London EC4Y 7BS (☎ 020 7452 8900, fax 020 7452 8999, e-mail anthony.gifford@btinternet.com, website www.lmcb.com and www.gtbjamaica.com

GIFFORD, Prof Paul Peerless-Dennis; s of David Arthur Gifford, of Norwich, Norfolk, and Vera Rosina, *née* Palmer; *b* 23 April 1944, Chelsfield, Kent; *Educ* King Edward VI Sch Norwich, Univ of Cambridge (MA), Univ of Toulouse (Lès L, Dr 3e Cycle, Dès L); *m* 20 Sept 1969, (Irma) Cynthia Mary, da of Lt-Col AFS Warwick (d 1961); 2 da (Fiona b 20 Sept 1972, Joanne b 8 May 1975), 1 s (Gregory b 27 May 1979); *Career* Buchanan chair of French Univ of St Andrews 1987–2008; visiting res fell Girard Fndn (Imitatio) Univ of Stanford Calif 2009–12; Maître des Jeux L'Académie des Jeux Floraux 2014; *Books* Valéry – Le Dialogue des Choses Divines (1989), Reading Paul Valéry. Universe in Mind (1998), Voix, traces, avènement: l'écriture et son sujet (1999), Subject Matters (2000), 2000 Years (2002), Love, Desire and transcendence in French Literature: Deciphering Eros (2006), La Création en Acte (2006), Can We Survive our Origins? (2015), How We Became Human (2015); *Recreations* sailing, skiing, golf, tennis; *Style—* Prof Paul Gifford; ✉ 14 Sycamore Close, Wellesbourne, Warwickshire CV35 9SH; Department of French, University of St Andrews, Buchanan Building, St Andrews, Fife KY16 9PH (e-mail ppg@st-and.ac.uk)

GIFFORD, Sir (Michael) Roger; kt (2014); s of Prof Douglas Gifford (d 1991), and Hazel, *née* Collingwood (d 2010); *b* 3 August 1955; *Educ* Sedbergh, Trinity Coll Oxford (MA); *m* 1, 1983, Jane Lunzer; 2 da (Olivia b 1985, Augusta b 1989 d 1992), 3 s (Fergus b 1986, Fred b 1988, Hector b 1994); m 2, 2008, Clare, *née* Taylor; 1 da (Thea b 1993), 1 s (Frederick b 1996); *Career* SG Warburg & Co Ltd 1978; Skandinaviska Enskilda Bank: Corp Fin, Primary Debt and Equity Capital Markets Enskilda Securities 1982–90, head of capital markets 1990–93, head of London branch 1992–94, head of Tokyo branch 1994–99, UK country mangr 2000–; chm: Swedish C of C UK 2003–07, Assoc of Foreign Banks UK 2007–11; tstee: St Paul's Cathedral Fndn, St Paul's Cathedral Choir Sch 2006–11; govr: King Edward's Sch Witley, Bridewell Hosp 2005–15, Summer Fields Sch Oxford 2001–07; chm: English Chamber Orchestra & Music Soc 2001–, The Tenebrae Choir 2012–, From Sweden Festival 2004–06, Sibelius & Beyond Festival 2007; Alderman City of London (Cordwainer ward) 2004–, Sheriff City of London 2008–09, Lord Mayor of London 2012–13; chllr City Univ 2012–13; hon fell Guildhall Sch of Music and Drama 2013; memb: Worshipful Co of Musicians, Co of Security Professionals, Co of Cordwainers; Master Co of Int Bankers 2010–11, memb Guild of PR Practitioners; Hon LLD Univ of St Andrews 2013, Hon DSc City Univ 2013; Cdr of the Order of the Polar Star (Sweden) 2007 (Offr 2001), Cdr Order of the Lion (Finland) 2012, KStJ 2012, Order 5th Class (Kuwait) 2013; *Recreations* chamber music, singing, opera, gardening; *Clubs* Cordwainer Ward, Bread Street Ward, Royal Perth, Garrick; *Style—* Sir Roger Gifford; ✉ 40 Inverness Street, London NW1 7HB; SEB, 1 Carter Lane, London EC4V 5AN

GIFFORD, Zerbanoo; da of Bailey Irani, and Kitty Mazda; *b* 11 May 1950; *Educ* Roedean, Watford Coll of Technol, London Sch of Journalism, Open Univ (BA); *m* 14 Sept 1973, Richard David Gifford, s of David Arthur Gifford, of Norwich; 2 s (Mark Mazda b 28 Aug 1975, Alexander Justice (Wags) b 27 Feb 1979); *Career* Lib cncllr Harrow 1982–86; Parly candidate (Lib Alliance): Hertsmere 1983, Harrow East 1987; Parly candidate (Lib Dems) Hertsmere 1992; chm: Lib Pty Community Rels Panel 1985, Cmmn into Ethnic Involvement 1986; elected memb Lib Dem Federal Exec 1991–92, pres Hertsmere Lib Dems; memb Status of Women Cmmn 1987, former community affairs advsr to leader of Lib Democrats; advsr Home Sec's Race Relations Forum; former ed Libas magazine, runner-up Special Interest Magazine Ed of the Year 1988, columnist Lib Democrat News; memb Advsy Cncl The Prince's Youth Business Tst, dir Anti-Slavery Int, dir Charities Aid Fndn India, fndr dir The ASHA Fndn, fndr ASHA Centre; Freeman City of Lincoln Nebraska; Nehru Centenary Award from Non-Resident Indians' Assoc 1989, Asian City Club Annual Award 1990, nominee Women of Europe Award 1991, Int Woman of the Year for humanitarian work 2006, Splendor Award 2007; fell Nat Endowment of Sci, Technol and Arts (NESTA) 2004, FRSA; *Books* The Golden Thread (1990), Dadabhai Naoroji (1992), Asian Presence in Europe (1995), Thomas Clarkson and the Campaign against Slavery (1996), Celebrating India (1998), Confessions to a Serial Womaniser: Secrets of the World's Inspirational Women (2007), An Uncensored Life (biography, 2015); *Recreations* collecting antique embroidery, meeting extraordinary people; *Style—* Mrs Zerbanoo Gifford; ✉ ASHA Centre, Gunn Mill House, Lower Spout Lane, near Flaxley, Gloucestershire GL17 0EA (☎ 01594 822330, website www.ashacentre.org)

GILBART, Hon Mr Justice; Sir Andrew James Gilbart; kt (2014), QC (1991); s of Albert Thomas Gilbart (d 1975), and Carol, *née* Christie (d 2006); *b* 13 February 1950; *Educ* Westminster (Queen's Scholar), Trinity Hall Cambridge (MA); *m* 1, 20 Jan 1979 (m dis 2001), Morag, da of Robert Thomas Williamson (d 1990), and Agnes Buchanan Williamson, of Ayrshire; 1 s (Thomas Christie b 1980), 1 da (Ruth Alexandra b 1982); m 2, 6 Nov 2003, Paula Doone Whittell, da of Bill Fox (d 1975), and Doone Fox, of Ettington, Warks; 2 step s, 1 step da; *Career* called to the Bar Middle Temple 1972 (bencher 2000); in practice Northern Circuit and Planning and Environment Bar 1973–2004, recorder 1996–2004 (asst recorder 1992–96), head Kings Chambers Manchester and Leeds 2001–04, circuit judge (Northern Circuit) 2004–08, dep High Court judge 2005–14, sr circuit judge and Hon Recorder of Manchester 2008–13, judge of the High Court of Justice (Queen's Bench Div) 2014–; memb Restricted Patients Presidents Panel Mental Health Review Tbnl 2001–06, judicial memb Lands Tbnl 2006–08; *Recreations* history, theatre, walking, The Ariege, singing, computing, cooking; *Style—* The Hon Mr Justice Gilbart; ✉ Royal Courts of Justice, London WC2A 2LL

GILBERT; *b* 1943, Dolomites; *Educ* Wolkenstein Sch of Art, Hallein Sch of Art, Munich Acad of Art, St Martin's Sch of Art; *Career* artist, in partnership with George, *qv* since 1967; shortlisted Turner Prize 1984, Turner Prize 1986; Living Sculpture incl: The Red Sculpture, 3 Living Pieces, Underneath the Arches, Our New Sculpture, Reading from a Stick; *Selected Two Person Exhibitions* Snow Show (St Martins Sch of Art London) 1968, Shit and Cunt (Robert Fraser Gallery London) 1969, The Paintings (Whitechapel Art Gallery London, Kunstverein Dusseldorf, Koninklijk Museum voor Schone Kunsten Antwerp) 1971–72, Dusty Corners (Art Agency Tokyo) 1975, Photo-Pieces 1971–1980 (Stedelijk van Abbemuseum Eindhoven, Georges Pompidou Centre Paris, Kunsthalle Bern, Whitechapel Art Gallery London) 1980–81, Gilbert & George (touring, galleries incl: Contemporary Arts Museum Houston, The Solomon R Guggenheim Museum NY, Milwaukee Art Museum Milwaukee) 1984–85, Pictures 1982 to 85 (Hayward Gallery London, Lenbachaus Munich, Palacio de Velazquez Madrid) 1987, For AIDS Exhibition (Anthony d'Offay Gallery London) 1989, The Cosmological Pictures (touring, galleries incl: Palazzo delle Esposizioni Rome, Fundació Joan Miró Barcelona, Irish MOMA Dublin, Kunsthalle Zürich, Wiener Secession Vienna, Tate Gallery Liverpool) 1991–93, Gilbert & George China Exhibition (The Art Museum Shanghai, Nat Art Gallery Beijing) 1993, Shitty Naked Human World (Wolfsburg Kunstmuseum Germany) 1994, The Naked Shit Pictures (South London Art Gallery) 1995, New Testamental Pictures (Museo do

Capodimonte Naples) 1998, Black White and Red 1971 to 1980 (James Cohan Gallery New York) 1998, The Rudimentary Pictures (inaugural exhibition, Milton Keynes Gallery) 1999, Nineteen Ninety Nine (Kunstmuseum Bohn, Museum of Contemporary Art Chicago, Museum Moderner Kunst Vienna) 1999–2001, Enclosed and Enchanted (MOMA Oxford) 2000, New Horny Pictures (White Cube London) 2001, Gilbert & George: A Retrospective (Sch of Fine Art Athens, Kunsthaus Bregenz) 2002, The Dirty Words Pictures (Serpentine Gallery London) 2002, Thirteen Hooligan Pictures (Bernier/ Eliades Athens) 2004, 20 London E1 Pictures (Modern Art Museum St Etienne, Kestner Gesellschaft Hannover) 2004–05, Gilbert & George (British Pavilion Venice Biennale) 2005, Brooklyn Museum of Art NY 2008, Philadelphia Museum of Art 2008, Jack Freak Pictures (CAC Malaga, Museum of Contemporary Art Zagreb, Palais des Beaux Arts Brussels) 2010, Deichtorhallen Hamburg 2011, Kunstmuseum Linz 2011, Laznia Centre for Contemporary Art Gdansk 2011–12; *Work in Collections* incl: Arario Gallery Chungnam, Astrup Fearnley Museet fur Moderne Kunst Oslo, Denver Art Museum, Nat Portrait Gallery London, San Francisco MOMA, Tate Modern London; *Style*— Gilbert; ✉ White Cube,144–152 Bermondsey St, London SE1 3TQ ✆ 020 7930 5373, fax 020 7749 7480)

GILBERT, Christine; CBE; *Career* HM chief inspector of educn, children's servs and skills OFSTED 2006–11, currently chief exec Brent Cncl; *Style*— Ms Christine Gilbert, CBE

GILBERT, Prof Fiona Jane; da of Dr John Knight Davidson, OBE, of Glasgow, and Edith Elizabeth, *née* McKelvie; *b* 1 May 1956; *Educ* Hutchesons' Girls' GS, Univ of Glasgow (MB ChB), Univ of Aberdeen (DMRD); *m* 4 June 1982, Martin James Gilbert, *qv*, s of James Robert Gilbert, of Aberdeen; 1 s (Jamie b 1986), 2 da (Mhairi b 1989, Kirstin b 1992); *Career* conslt radiologist 1989–96, prof of radiology Univ of Aberdeen 1996–; dir NE Scotland Breast Screening Service 1989–2000; memb BMA 1978, FRCR 1986, FRCP 1991 (MRCP 1981), FRCPE 1994; *Recreations* sailing, skiing, tennis, theatre, classical music; *Style*— Prof Fiona Gilbert; ✉ 17 Rubislaw Den North, Aberdeen AB15 4AL; Department of Radiology, Lilian Sutton Building, University of Aberdeen, Foresterhill, Aberdeen AB25 2ZD (✆ 01224 559718, e-mail f.j.gilbert@abdn.ac.uk)

GILBERT, His Hon Francis Humphrey Shubrick; QC (1992); s of Cdr Walter Raleigh Gilbert, RN (d 1977), of Compton Castle, S Devon, and Joan Mary Boileau, *née* Willock (d 2001); *b* 25 January 1946; *Educ* Stowe, Trinity Coll Dublin (MA); *m* 19 April 1975, Sarah Marian, da of Col Douglas Kaye, DSO, DL (d 1996), of Brinkley Hall, Suffolk; 2 da (Emma b 11 Nov 1976, Rosella b 15 Feb 1979), 1 s (Raleigh b 28 Oct 1982); *Career* called to the Bar Lincoln's Inn 1970 (bencher 2000); recorder on Western Circuit, head of chambers Walnut House Exeter 1995–2001, circuit judge (Western Circuit) 2001–16, resident judge Plymouth 2006–12, recorder of Exeter 2012–16; pres Pegasus Club 2001; memb Devon CC 1977–85; *Recreations* sailing, shooting; *Clubs* Royal Yacht Sqdn; *Style*— His Hon Francis Gilbert, QC; ✉ e-mail francisgilbert@tiscali.co.uk

GILBERT, Martin James; s of James Robert Gilbert, of Aberdeen, and Winifred, *née* Walker; *b* 13 July 1955; *Educ* Robert Gordon's Coll, Univ of Aberdeen (MA, LLB); *m* 4 June 1982, Prof Fiona Jane Gilbert, *qv*, da of Dr John K Davidson; 1 s (Jamie), 2 da (Mhairi, Kirstin); *Career* CA 1981; Deloitte Haskins and Sells 1978–81, Brander and Cruickshank 1982–83; chief exec Aberdeen Asset Management plc (formerly Aberdeen Trust plc) 1991–, dir Aberdeen Development Capital plc 1986–2012, dir Aberdeen Asian Smaller Co Investment Trust 1995, chm Aberdeen Global Income Fund Inc 1998–2005, chm Aberdeen Asia-Pacific Income Fund 2000–05; non-exec chm: Firstgroup plc 1995–2013, Chaucer Holdings plc 1998–2011; non-exec dir Select International Funds plc 2007–2014, sr ind dir Sky plc 2011–, dep chm Sky plc 2016–; chm Practitioner Panel Prudential Regulation Authy 2013–; memb: Fin Servs Trade and Investment Bd UK Treasy, Fin Servs Advsy Bd Scottish Govt, Int Advsy Panel Monetary Authy of Singapore, Int Advsy Bd Br American Business; MICAS (vice-pres 2002–03); *Recreations* golf, hockey, skiing, sailing; *Clubs* Royal and Ancient (St Andrews), Royal Aberdeen Golf, Royal Selangor Golf, Gordonians HC, Royal Northern and Univ, Deeside Golf, Wimbledon Golf, Royal Thames Yacht, Leander; *Style*— Martin Gilbert; ✉ 17 Rubislaw Den North, Aberdeen AB15 4AL; Aberdeen Asset Management plc, 10 Queen's Terrace, Aberdeen AB10 1YG (✆ 01224 631999)

GILBERT, Prof (Geoffrey) Nigel; CBE (2016); s of Geoffrey Alan Gilbert, FRS, of Birmingham, and Lilo, *née* Czigler; *b* 21 March 1950; *Educ* King Edwards Sch Birmingham, Emmanuel Coll Cambridge (exhibitioner, BA, PhD, ScD); *m* 1974, Jennifer Mary, da of Henry Roe; *Career* lectr Univ of York 1974–76; Univ of Surrey: lectr 1976–84, reader 1984–91, prof of sociology 1991–, pro-vice-chllr 1997–2005, dir Centre for Research in Social Simulation; govr Nat Inst for Econ and Social Research; memb: Cncl Complex Systems Soc 2012–, Social Science Expert Panel DEFRA/Dept for Energy and Climate Change 2012–, Engrg Policy Ctee Royal Academy of Engrg 2012, Advisory Gp Future and Emerging Technologies (FET) EC 2014–; Nuffield sr res fellowship 1996; CEng 1990, FBCS 1997, FREng 1999, FAcSS 2000, FRSA 2005; *Publications* Modelling Society: an introduction to loglinear analysis for social researchers (1981), Accounts and Action (with P Abell, 1983), Opening Pandora's Box: a sociological analysis of scientists discourse (with M Mulkay, 1984), Social Action and Artificial Intelligence (with C Heath, 1985), Computers and Conversation (with P Luff and D Frohlich, 1990), Fordism and Flexibility: divisions and change (with R Burrows and A Pollert, 1991), Women and Working Lives: divisions and change (with S Arber, 1991), Researching Social Life (ed, 1992, 3 edn 2008), Analyzing Tabular Data: loglinear and logistic models for social researchers (1993), Simulating Societies: the computer simulation of social phenomena (with J Doran, 1994), Artificial Societies: the computer simulation of social life (with R Conte, 1995), Perspectives on HCI: Diverse Approaches (with A F Monk, 1995), Social Science Microsimulation (with K G Troitzsch, U Mueller and J E Doran, 1996), Humans, Computers and Wizards: Studying human (simulated) computer interaction (with R C Wooffitt, N Fraser and S McGlashan, 1997), Computer Simulations in Science and Technology Studies (with P Ahrweiler, 1998), Multi-agent Systems and Agent-based Simulation (ed with J S Sichman and R Conte, 1998), Simulation for the Social Scientist (with K G Troitzsch, 1999, 2 edn 2005), Agent-based Models (2007), Computational Social Science (ed, 2010), Viability and Resilience of Complex Systems (with G Deffuant, 2011), Modelling Norms (with C Elsenbroich, 2013), Simulating Innovation: Computer-based Tools for Rethinking Innovation (with C Watts, 2014); also author of six other books and over 200 articles in learned jls; *Recreations* cooking; *Style*— Prof Nigel Gilbert, CBE, FREng; ✉ Department of Sociology, University of Surrey, Guildford GU2 7XH (✆ 01483 689173, fax 01483 689551, e-mail n.gilbert@surrey.ac.uk)

GILBERT, Pippa Beryl; da of Philip Henry Crockett, MBE, and Beryl, *née* Wright (d 1969); *b* 23 July 1955; *Educ* Abbotsholme Sch; *m* 27 Aug 2003, Robert J Gilbert; *Career* dir: County Leatherwear 1976, Hustwick Ltd 1979, Toromed Ltd 1999; md: County Leatherwear (Tinter Ltd) 1987–, County Chamois Co Ltd 1987– (dir 1980); ptnr Heart of England Antiques 1987–; dir The Coventrian Partnership Ltd 2007–; assoc memb Int Export Assoc 1978, FInstD 1991; *Recreations* sailing, antique collecting, travel; *Style*— Mrs Pippa Gilbert; ✉ Chamant Manor, Old End, Appleby Magna, Derbyshire (e-mail blondepippa@aol.com)

GILBERT, Richard Simon; s of Nigel John Gilbert, of Emsworth, Hants, and Mair, *née* James; *b* 1 November 1957; *Educ* Sevenoaks Sch, Falmouth Sch of Art (BA), Wimbledon Sch of Art (BA), Chelsea Sch of Art (MA), Br Sch in Rome (Abbey Major scholar in painting), Sch of the Art Inst of Chicago (Harkness fell); *Career* self-employed fine artist; teacher: Sch of Art and Design Wellington Coll Berks 1994, Cheltenham Coll 2000, King's Sch Worcester 2007–11, Royal GS Worcester 2011–; Barclays Postgrad Painting award 1984; *Solo Exhibitions* Recent Work (Main Gallery Warwick Arts Trust London) 1986, Recent Work (Raab Gallery London) 1988, New Work (Raab Gallery London) 1992, Touching Silence (Hereford Museum and Art Gallery) 2002, Fourteen (Leominster Priory Church) 2001, Fourteen (Worcester Cathedral) 2006 and (St Martin's Arts Centre Birmingham) 2007, Getting Ahead (Dean Close Sch Cheltenham), Envisage (Wallspace Broadgate London), Opening the Wound (The Gallery Dean Close Sch Cheltenham); *Group Exhibitions* incl: Wet Paint (Festival Gallery Bath) 1984, CAS Market (Smiths Gallery London) 1984–87 and 1990, John Moores Fourteenth Nat Exhibition (Walker Art Gallery Liverpool) 1985, Forty European Artists (Raab Gallery) 1986, Athena Arts awards (Barbican) 1987, Art for the City (Lloyd's Building London) 1987, Fellowship Exhibition (Sch of Art, Inst of Chicago) 1989, The Landscape and the Cityscape (Raab Gallery London) 1990, Rome scholars 1980–90 (Gulbenkian Gallery RCA London) 1990, The Discerning Eye (Mall Gallery London) 1990, Six Young British Artists (Oviedo, Madrid, Barcelona) 1991–92, Royal Over-Seas League Exhibition (Rosl Houe London) 1992, CAS Market (Smiths Galleries London) 1992 and 1993, The Blue Gallery 1994 and 1995, The Beardsmore Gallery 2000 and 2002, Fine Edge 2001, Leominster 2001, Hereford Open Exhibition, Hereford Museum and Art Gallery, Sculpture in the Garden, Paydirt (Kentchurch Court Hereford); *Work in Collections* Contemporary Art Soc, Victoria Art Gallery Melbourne, Arthur Andersen plc, Barclays Bank plc, Business Design Centre, Leicester Educn Authy, Lloyds Bank of Spain and South America (Madrid), Pearl Life Assurance Co London, Rosehaugh Stanhope London, Clifford Chance London and NY, National Westminster Bank London, Caja de Ahorros de Segovia, Plymouth Art Gallery, Unilever plc and in private collections; *Style*— Richard Gilbert, Esq; ✉ The Creswells, Sutton St Nicholas, Hereford HR1 3AX (✆ 01432 880748, e-mail richard@creswells.co.uk)

GILBERT, Stephen David John Gilbert; *Educ* St Austell Coll, Univ of Wales Aberystwyth, LSE; *Career* cncllr: Restormel Borough Cncl 1998–2002, London Borough of Haringey 2002–05; MP (Lib Dem) St Austell and Newquay 2010–15; *Style*— Stephen Gilbert, Esq; ✉ 10 South Street, St Austell PL25 5BH; House of Commons, London SW1A 0AA

GILBERTSON, (Cecil) Edward Mark; s of Francis Mark Gilbertson (d 2004), and Elizabeth Margaret, *née* Dawson (d 2009); *b* 2 June 1949; *Educ* Eton; *m* 1, May 1975 (m dis 1980), Astrid Jane, da of late Lt-Col Vaughan; m 2, 3 Sept 1986, Nicola Leslie Bellairs, yr da of Maj J A B Lloyd Philipps (d 1974); 1 da (Georgina Charlotte Bellairs b 29 Oct 1987), 1 s (Harry Edward Bellairs b 20 Feb 1990); *Career* dir Brewin Dolphin Securities Ltd 1992–2009; tstee CPRW; *Recreations* shooting, real tennis, golf; *Clubs* MCC, Bristol and Bath Tennis, Cradoc Golf; *Style*— Edward Gilbertson, Esq; ✉ Cathedine Hill, Cathedine, Brecon, Powys LD3 7SX; Llangwarren Estate, Letterston, Pembrokeshire SA62 5UL

GILBEY, Sir (Walter) Gavin; 4 Bt (UK 1893), of Elsenham Hall, Essex; s of Sir (Walter) Derek Gilbey, 3 Bt (d 1991), and Elizabeth Mary, *née* Campbell; *b* 14 April 1949; *Educ* Eton; *m* 1, 1980 (m dis 1984), Mary, da of late William E E Pacetti, of Florida, USA; m 2, 1984 (m dis 1992), Anna, da of Edmund Prosser, of Cheshire; *Career* pres Great British Foods Inc; also works with abused children; *Recreations* golf, travel, anthropology; *Clubs* Army and Navy, Royal Dornoch Golf; *Style*— Sir Gavin Gilbey, Bt

GILCHRIST, Clive Mace; s of John Llewellyn Gilchrist (d 1986), and Ida, *née* Mace (d 1999); *b* 27 September 1950; *Educ* LSE (BSc Econ); *m* 1979, Angela Rosemary, da of Roger Watson Hagger; 2 da (Philippa Jane (Pippa) b 1985, Julia Joy b 1987); *Career* stockbroker; J & A Scrimgeour & Co 1972–75, Joseph Sebag & Co 1975–78; dep dir of investment Postel Investments Ltd 1978–87; dir: Argosy Asset Management plc 1987–91 (md Jan-May 1991), Aberdeen Asset Management plc 1991–2003; dep chm BESTrustees plc 2010–; Nat Assoc of Pension Funds: vice-pres 1992–94, chm Investment Ctee 1990–92, vice-chm Cncl 1990–92 (memb 1988–94); Assoc of Corporate Tstees: memb Cncl 1997–2003, chm Pensions Ctee 1997–2003; ASIP 1980, FCSI 1992 (MSI 1979), FRSA 1993; *Recreations* gardening, music, travel; *Style*— Clive Gilchrist, Esq; ✉ Ashleigh Grange, Westhumble, Dorking, Surrey RH5 6AY; BESTrustees plc, Five Kings House, 1 Queen Street Place, London EC4R 1QS (✆ 020 7332 4100, fax 020 7332 4108, e-mail clive.gilchrist@bestrustees.co.uk)

GILCHRIST, James; *Career* recitalist, oratorio and soloist; early career as doctor; tenor 1996–; appearances with orchestras incl: English Chamber Orch, City of London Sinfonia, Northern Sinfonia, Acad of Ancient Music, Scottish Chamber Orch, BBC Symphony Orch, Zürich Tonhalle Orch, St Louis Symphony Orch, Royal Concertgebouw Orch; opera appearances incl: Cosi Fan Tutte, Ariadne auf Naxos, Zaide, Alceste, King Arthur; *Recordings* incl: Bach Cantatas Vol 36 (2006), Die Schöne Müllerin (2009), Songs of Lennox Berkeley (2009), Earth, Sweet Earth & Britten Winter Words (2010), Schwanengesang (2010); *Style*— Mr James Gilchrist; ✉ c/o Sue Nicholls, Hazard Chase Ltd, 25 City Road, Cambridge CB1 1DP

GILCHRIST, Mary Ann; da of David Porter (d 1990), and Ruth, *née* Morris (d 1995); *b* 28 June 1951, London; *Educ* Edgbaston C of E Coll for Girls Birmingham; *m* 14 Jan 1978, Alan John Gilchrist; 1 da (Emma Elizabeth Ruth b 13 Aug 1987); *Career* restaurateur; nurse Radliffe Infirmary 1969–72, cook Jeanies Restaurant Oxford 1972–78, chef and prop 3 Conies Thorpe Mandeville 1982–87, chef Court House Hotel Newton Ferrers Devon 1987–90, chef and prop Carlton House Llanwrtyd Wells 1991–2005, chef and prop Carlton Riverside Llanwrtyd Wells 2005–; advsr: Mid Wales Food and Land Tst Initiative, Mid Wales Food and Tourism Partnership; memb: Masterchefs of GB, Slow Food Movement; *Awards* Good Food Guide Restaurant of the Year, Good Hotel Guide Cesar Award, True Taste Awards 2001, 2002, 2004 and 2005, AA Wales Restaurant of the Year 2007/08, semifinalist Great British Menu (BBC); *Recreations* travel, reading, cooking; *Style*— Mrs Mary Ann Gilchrist; ✉ 2 Cloth Hall, Dolecoed Road, Llanwrtyd Wells, Powys LD5 4RA (✆ 01591 610248, e-mail info@carltonriverside.com)

GILCHRIST, Maj Gen Peter; CB (2004); s of Col David Alexander Gilchrist (d 2003), and Rosemary, *née* Drewe; *b* 28 February 1952, Sidmouth, Devon; *Educ* Marlborough, RMA Sandhurst; *m* 5 Sept 1981, Sarah-Jane, da of late Lt-Col H S S Poyntz; 1 da (Joanne Elizabeth b 19 June 1983), 1 s (Alexander b 24 April 1985); *Career* troop ldr, nuclear, chemical and biological defence offr, and gunnery and intelligence offr Germany and NI 1972–76, long armour inf course 1977, gunnery instr 1978–80, ops offr and Adj 3 RTR 1980–82, Staff Coll Div 11 1983–84, Bde Maj 20 Armd Bde 1985–86, Sqdn Ldr 3 RTR Cyprus and Germany 1987–88, Mil Sec (MS) 1989, memb Directing Staff RMCS Shrivenham 1990–93, CO 1 RTR 1993–95, higher command and staff course 1996, Col Operational Requirements (OR) 1996–98, Brig PE 1998–2000, Master Gen of the Ordnance and exec dir Defence Procurement Agency 2000–04, Col Cmdt Royal Armd Corps 2000–04, Dep Col Cmdt RTR 2000–08, Dep Cmdg Gen Combined Forces Cmd Afghanistan 2004–05, head British Defence Staff and defence attaché Washington 2005–08, ret 2009; non-exec chm: Push Technol Ltd, Enterprise Control Systems Ltd; dir Synergie Global Ltd, sr ind dir Ricardo plc (chm Ricardo Remuneration Ctee); chm Bd of Tstees Tank Museum; MInstD; Bronze Star Medal (USA) 2006; *Recreations* field sports, sailing, skiing, gardening; *Clubs* Army and Navy; *Style*— Maj Gen Peter Gilchrist, CB

GILCHRIST, Susan Georgina; da of (Robert) David Gilchrist, of West Compton, Somerset, and Constance May, *née* Hodgson; *b* 26 May 1966; *Educ* Millfield, KCL (BA, L M Faithfull prize); *m* Dr Andrew Roberts; *Career* conslt Bain & Co 1987–90; City reporter: Mail on Sunday 1991–92, The Times 1993–95; currently gp chief exec Brunswick Group Ltd (ptnr 1995–); chm Southbank Centre 2016–; Specialist Writer of the Year Br Press

Awards 1992; *Recreations* literature, music, art, theatre, cinema, friends; *Clubs* 5 Hertford Street, Ivy; *Style—* Ms Susan Gilchrist; ✉ Brunswick Group Ltd, 16 Lincoln's Inn Fields, London WC2A 3ED (☎ 020 7404 5959, fax 020 7831 2823, mobile 07974 982301, e-mail sgilchrist@brunswickgroup.com)

GILDEA, Prof Robert Nigel; s of Denis Gildea, of London, and Hazel, *née* Walsh; *b* 12 September 1952; *Educ* Merton Coll Oxford (MA), St Antony's Coll Oxford, St John's Coll Oxford (DPhil); *m* 21 March 1987, Lucy-Jean Lloyd; 2 da (Rachel b 30 Sept 1989, Georgia b 28 Dec 1991), 2 s (William b 16 Nov 1994, Adam b 28 March 1997); *Career* jr research fell St John's Coll Oxford 1976–78, lectr in history KCL 1978–79, tutor in modern history Merton Coll Oxford 1979–2006; Univ of Oxford: reader in modern history 1996–2002, prof of modern French history 2002–06, prof of modern history 2006–, fell Worcester Coll 2006–, emeritus fell 2016–; Elie Halévy visiting prof Inst d'Etudes Politiques Paris 2000; FRHistS 1986, FBA 2010; Chevalier dans l'Ordre des Palmes Académiques (France) 1997; *Books* Education in Provincial France: A Study of Three Departments (1983), Barricades and Borders: Europe 1800–1914 (1987, 3 edn 2003), The Past in French History (1994), France since 1945 (1996, 2 edn 2002), Marianne in Chains: In Search of the German Occupation 1940–1945 (2002, Wolfson History Prize), Surviving Hitler and Mussolini: Daily Life in Occupied Europe (2006), Writing Contemporary History (2008), Children of the Revolution: The French 1799–1914 (2008), Europe's 1968: Voices of Revolt (2013), Fighters in the Shadows: A New History of the French Resistance (2015); *Recreations* music, walking, swimming, cooking, Oxford United; *Style—* Prof Robert Gildea; ✉ Worcester College, Oxford OX1 2HB (e-mail robert.gildea@history.ox.ac.uk)

GILDERNEW, Michelle; *Educ* St Catherine's Coll Armagh, Univ of Ulster; *Career* Sinn Féin rep to London 1997–98, memb NI Assembly 1998–2012 (dep chair Social Devpt Ctee 1999–2002, memb Centre Ctee 2000–02), MP (Sinn Féin) Fermanagh and S Tyrone 2001–15, Sinn Féin spokesperson on enterprise, trade and investment; *Style—* Ms Michelle Gildernew; ✉ House of Commons, London SW1A 0AA

GILES, Alan James; s of Ronald Giles, of Dorset, and Christine, *née* Bastable; *b* 4 June 1954; *Educ* Blandford Sch, Merton Coll Oxford (MA), Stanford Univ (MS); *m* 22 April 1978, Gillian, da of Norman Rosser; 2 da (Claire b 12 April 1984, Nicola b 20 April 1987); *Career* The Boots Co plc: buyer 1975–78, promotions mangr 1978–80, asst merchandise controller 1980–82; WH Smith Gp plc: devpt mangr 1982–85, merchandise controller 1985–88, exec dir 1995–98; ops and devpt dir Do It All 1988–92, md Waterstone's 1993–99, chief exec HMV Gp plc 1998–2006; non-exec dir: Somerfield plc 1993–2004, Wilson Bowden 2004–07, Rentokil Initial 2006–, Office of Fair Trading 2007–14, Competition and Markets Authy 2014–, Perpetual Income & Growth Investment Tst 2015–; chm Fat Face Gp 2006–13; MCIM; *Style—* Alan Giles, Esq

GILES, Prof Anthony Kent (Tony); OBE (1992); s of Harry Giles (d 1967), of Rochester, Kent, and Eva Gertrude, *née* Kent (d 1972); *b* 30 June 1928; *Educ* Sir Joseph Williamson's Mathematical Sch Rochester, Queen's Univ Belfast (BScEcon); *m* 1, 2 Jan 1954 (m dis 1985), Helen Elizabeth Margaret, da of J Charles Eaton (d 1968), of Londonderry; 3 da (Ann b 1954, Amanda b 1957, Alison b 1963), 1 s (John b 1960); m 2, 6 Aug 1987, Heather Constance, da of Frank H J Pearce (d 1987), of Durban, South Africa; 1 step s (Sean Hewson b 1971), 1 step da (Linda Hewson b 1975); *Career* PO (Personnel Selection) RAF 1947–49; asst agric economist and lectr Univ of Bristol 1953–59; Univ of Reading: lectr 1960–68, sr lectr 1968–83, dir Farm Mgmnt Unit 1979–91, prof of farm mgmnt and provincial agric economist 1983–93 (prof emeritus 1993–), chm Sch of Applied Mgmnt Studies 1986–91, hon res fell Rural History Centre 1994–; UK country rep Int Soc of Agric Economists 1973–87, chm UK Farm Business Survey Ctee 1975–92, nat chm Centre Mgmnt in Agric 1987–89, pres Agric Econ Soc 1988; active in Samaritans 1972–82 (dir Reading Branch 1978–80); FIMgt 1989, FIAgrM 1992; *Books* professional: Agricultural Economics 1923–73 (1973), The Farmer as Manager (1980, 2 edn 1990), Innovation and Conservation: Ernest Edward Cook and his Country Estates (jt ed, 1989), The Managers Environment (ed, 1990), Agricultural Economics at the University of Reading 1923–1993 (1993), Windows on Agricultural Economics and Farm Management (1993), See You at Oxford! A Celebration of Fifty Oxford Farming Conferences Over Sixty Years (1995), The Manager as Farmer – Wisdom from some I have known (1996), Case Studies in Agricultural and Rural Land Management (ed, 2 edn 1997), Owner, Occupier and Tennant: Reading University at Churn Farm 1969–96 (1998), A Thirty Year Gestation: The Origins, Development and Future of the Institute of Agricultural Management (1999), From 'Cow College' to Life Sciences: A Celebration of 75 Years of Reading University's Agricultural Faculty (2000), Twenty-five Years of the Edith Mary Gayton Memorial Lectures 1984–2008 (jt ed, 2008); non-professional: One Hundred Years With the Clifton Rugby Football Club (princ author, 1972), About Twenty Five Years of Cricket (1983), The Publications of A K Giles, 1955–93 (1994), Never Mind the Frills – An Autobiographical Sketch (1995), The Guv'nors (1997), Not Evacuated (2002), Part of All That I Have Met: A Personal Travelogue (2005), 21 for 4 (2005), Not to Be Squandered (2007), Chocks Away (2009), Without a Satnav (2010), How On Earth (2011), Unforgettable Moments (2014); *Recreations* watching sport (rugby and cricket), aviation, collecting books (especially early Penguins); *Clubs* Clifton Rugby Football, Penguin Collectors' Soc; *Style—* Prof Tony Giles, OBE; ✉ The Cottage, 63 Northumberland Avenue, Reading, Berkshire RG2 7PS (☎ 0118 975 2763)

GILES, Brian John; s of Alfred Giles (d 1984) of Kent, and Constance, *née* Barndon (d 1996); *b* 22 September 1941; *Educ* Westlands Sittingbourne; *m* 23 Feb 1963, Shirley Jennifer; 2 da (Sarah Louise b 24 June 1965, Philippa Clare b 30 April 1969); *Career* apprentice jockey Fairlawne Racing Stables 1958–62, ed Chaseform Raceform 1963–66; Daily Mail: equestrian corr 1967, Robin Goodfellow (main tipster) 1987–2006, Gimcrack 2007–; memb: Sports Writers' Assoc, Equestrian Writers Assoc; Horse Trials Gp Award of the Year for Servs to Sport 1990, Champion Tipster of Britain (Flat Season) 1999; *Books* How to Win on the Flat, Twenty-Five Years in Showjumping – a Biography of David Broome, So You Think You Know About Horses, Behind The Stable Door, SR Direct Mail Book of Eventing (with Alan Smith); *Recreations* reading, classical music; *Style—* Brian Giles, Esq; ✉ Daily Mail, Northcliffe House, Derry Street, Kensington, London W8 (☎ 020 7938 6203)

GILES, Capt John Edmunds Julian Norrie (Magoo); s of Lt Col Norrie Giles, and Patricia, *née* Railton; *b* 7 October 1964, Aldershot, Hants; *Educ* Eton, RMA Sandhurst; *m* Priscilla Williams; 1 s (Otis), 1 da (Lola); *Career* Coldstream Guards 1984–95 (ADC to Lt Gen Sir William Rous, temp equerry to HM The Queen); Garden House Sch 1995–2006 (head of boys 2000–06), head and fndr Knightsbridge Sch 2006–, jt fndr Knightsbridge Schs Int (KSI) 2009–; Bosnia UN Medal; *Books* The Magic T-shirt Shop (2015); *Recreations* sport (football, cricket, tennis), children, writing, drawing; *Clubs* Guards Cricket, Eton Ramblers, Queens, Worplesdon, Guards Golfing Soc, Royal Hosp; *Style—* Capt Magoo Giles; ✉ Knightsbridge School, 67 Pont Street, London SW1X 0BD (e-mail m.giles@knightsbridgeschool.com)

GILES, John Smart; s of Alexander Giles, of York, and Doreen, *née* Smart; *b* 30 March 1949; *Educ* Rutherford Coll Newcastle, Nunthorpe GS York; *m* 11 May 1971, Jacqueline, da of Gordon Leonard Clapham; 1 da (Claire Elizabeth b 1974); *Career* trainee/darkroom asst Westminster Press 1966–72, photographer Western Press/Yorkshire Evening Press 1972–88, staff photographer Press Association (NE) 1988–2006, chief photographer Press Association Photos 2006– (semi-ret 2012), photos ed major sports events Press Assoc; *Awards* Kodak, Fuji, Nikon, Canon Images of Life, UK Press Gazette, British Sports Cncl, Heineken Humour Awards, Whitbread Media Awards for sport, news and feature pictures, Press Gazette British Press Awards Sports Photographer 1997, BPA Photographer of the Year 2003, Barclays Premiership Shot of the Season 2007; *Recreations* tennis, sport; *Clubs* Appleton Roebuck Tennis; *Style—* John Giles, Esq; ✉ The Press Association, PA News Centre, 292 Vauxhall Bridge Road, Victoria, London (☎ 020 7963 7156, mobile 07860 167458)

GILES, Lt-Col Lucy Margaret; da of Marcus Giles, and Margaret, *née* Brown, of Somerset; *b* 3 June 1969, Yeovil, Somerset; *Educ* King Arthur's Sch Wincanton, Sexey's Sch Bruton, Univ of Exeter (BSc), Cranfield Univ (MA), Univ of Southampton (PGCE); *m* 28 March 1998, Nick Pond; 1 da (Jessica b 2004), 1 s (Alexander b 2008); *Career* cmmnd Royal Logistic Corps (RLC) 1992, 68 Sqdn RCT (later 68 Sqdn RLC) 1993, troop cdr 3 Close Support Regt RLC Abingdon (incl tour on Op GRAPPLE 5 Bosnia) 1994–95, Sqdn 2IC 3 Close Support Regt RLC Abingdon (incl tour of Bosnia) 1995–97, Sqdn 2IC then adjutant 29 Movement Control Regt RLC S Cerney 1998, Br Military Advsy and Trg Team SA 1999, SO3 Media Operations 5 Airborne Bde HQ Aldershot (detached for Op LANGER Int Force E Timor) 1999–2000, SO3 Media Operations 12 Mechanised Bde HQ Aldershot (tour of Bosnia as military spokesperson for Multinational Div (SW), detached for Op SILKMAN Sierra Leone and Foot and Mouth Crisis Cumbria) 2000–01, student on ACSC Jt Servs Command and Staff Coll (JSCSC) Shrivenham 2001–03, SO2 Gen Staff HQ NI 2003–05, OC 47 Air Dispatch Sqdn RLC Lyneham 2005–07 (overseeing AD operations in Iraq and Afghanistan and other locations), SO2 Orgn and Devpt HQ Directorate RLC Deepcut 2007–09, OC 86 Sqdn RLC 26 rg Regt Deepcut (including tour on Op Herrick 14/15 Afghanistan) 2009–11, SO1 Directing Staff Army Div JSCSC 2011–14, Cdr New Coll Royal Military Acad Sandhurst 2015–; chm UK Armed Forces Orienteering; memb Sandhurst Tst, guide leader Girl Guiding UK, ambass First Women UK; shortlisted Women in Defence Awards (Most Inspirational Award) 2016; Freeman of the City of London 1997, Liveryman Worshipful Co of Farriers 1997; *Recreations* walking, orienteering; *Clubs* Exeter Univ Alumni, British Orienteering (level 2 coach); *Style—* Lt-Col Lucy Giles; ✉ New College, RMAS, Camberley, Surrey GU15 4PQ (☎ 01276 412445, e-mail rmas-nc-comd@mod.uk)

GILES, Martin Peter; s of Peter James Wickham Giles (d 1977), and Jean Winifred, *née* Smith; *b* 13 September 1964; *Educ* Wymondham Coll, Lady Margaret Hall Oxford (MA); *m* 1993, Isabelle Sylvie, da of Jacques Lescent; 1 s (Thomas b 31 Dec 1994), 1 da (Margaux b 18 April 1997); *Career* Midland Bank International 1983–85, J P Morgan 1985–86; The Economist Newspaper 1988–: banking corr 1988–89, Euro business corr 1989–93, fin ed 1994–98; publisher CFO Europe 1998–2000, dir Economist Enterprises 2000–; *Recreations* wine tasting, sport; *Style—* Martin Giles, Esq; ✉ The Economist, 25 St James's Street, London SW1A 1HG

GILES, Prof Paul David; s of Peter Brian Giles (d 2006), of Southend-on-Sea, Essex, and Mary Alice, *née* Cope; *b* 13 September 1957, London; *Educ* ChCh Oxford (MA), Univ of Oxford (DPhil); *m* 1989 (m dis 2002), Nadine, *née* Cornwall; *Career* asst/assoc prof Portland State Univ Oregon 1987–94, lectr in American studies Univ of Nottingham 1994–99, lectr in American lit Univ of Cambridge 1999–2002, reader in American lit Univ of Oxford 2002–06, prof of American lit Univ of Oxford 2006–10, Challis prof of English Univ of Sydney 2011–; dir Rothermere American Inst Univ of Oxford 2003–08; pres Int American Studies Assoc 2005–07; memb: Br Assoc for American Studies 1985 (Arthur Miller Essay Prize 1999), Modern Language Assoc of America 1987 (William Riley Parker Essay Prize 2003); *Publications* Hart Crane: The Contexts of 'The Bridge' (1986), American Catholic Arts and Fictions: Culture, Ideology, Aesthetics (1992), Transatlantic Insurrections: British Culture and the Formation of American Literature 1730–1860 (2001), Virtual Americas: Transnational Fictions and the Transatlantic Imaginary (2002), Atlantic Republic: The American Tradition in English Literature (2006), Transnationalism in Practice: Essays on American Studies, Literature and Religion (2010), The Global Remapping of American Literature (2011); *Recreations* soccer, cricket, classical music, opera; *Style—* Prof Paul Giles; ✉ Department of English (A20), University of Sydney, Sydney, NSW 2006, Australia (e-mail paul.giles@sydney.edu.au)

GILFILLAN, Andrew Crawford; s of Robert Crawford Gilfillan (d 1995), and Joan, *née* Leslie; *b* 21 April 1952, Halifax, Yorks; *Educ* Bradford GS, Univ of Sussex (BA), Univ of Cambridge (MA); *m* 29 March 1980, Janet Elizabeth, *née* Allen; 1 s (Robert Crawford b 6 Jan 1982), 1 da (Jessica Elizabeth b 21 Nov 1986); *Career* CUP: dir educn 1995–2002, memb Press Bd 1995–, dir ELT 2002–04, md Cambridge Learning 2004–06, md Europe, ME and Africa 2007–; memb Bd Educnl Publishers Cncl 1994–2002; memb Wine Soc; Liveryman Worshipful Co of Stationers and Newspaper Makers; FRSA 2007; *Recreations* golf, walking, wine, guitars; *Clubs* Cambridge Univ Grads Centre, Brampton Park Golf; *Style—* Andrew Gilfillan, Esq; ✉ Cambridge University Press, Shaftesbury Road, Cambridge CB2 8RU (☎ 01223 315052, e-mail agilfillan@cambridge.org)

GILHOOLY, John; OBE (2013); s of Owen Gilhooly, and Helena, *née* Conway; *b* 15 August 1973, Limerick; *Educ* UC Dublin (BA); *Career* admin UC Dublin 1994–97, mangr Harrogate Int Centre 1997–99; Wigmore Hall: exec dir 1999–, artistic dir 2005–; artistic advsr London Music Masters 2012; chm: Royal Philharmonic Soc 2010–, Mahogany Opera Gp 2013–; patron: Irish Heritage 2010–, Corpus Christi RC Church Restoration Appeal 2012–, Cavatina Chamber Music Tst 2015; tstee Int Musicians Seminar Prussia Cove 2015–; Hon FRAM 2006, Hon RCM 2012, Hon FGS 2015, hon fell Royal Irish Acad of Music 2016; Knight Order of the White Rose of Finland 2015, Order of Merit of the Federal Repub of Germany 2016; *Style—* John Gilhooly, Esq, OBE; ✉ Wigmore Hall, 36 Wigmore Street, London W1U 2BP (☎ 020 7258 8266, website www.wigmore-hall.org.uk)

GILI, Katherine Montserrat; da of John Lluis Gili (d 1998), and Elizabeth Helen, *née* McPherson (d 2011); *b* 6 April 1948; *Educ* Wychwood Sch Oxford, Bath Acad of Art (BA), St Martin's Sch of Art; *m* 1986, Robert Persey; 1 s (Harry b 1987); *Career* sculptor; art lectr: Norwich Sch of Art 1972–84, St Martin's Sch of Art 1975–84, Wimbledon Sch of Art 1979–81, The City Lit 1985–95; visiting lectr: Kingston Univ 1989–2002, Kent Inst of Art and Design 1995–2001; ptnr Rokatha creative metalwork 1997–2013; exhibition selector for New Contemporaries 1978, Serpentine Summer Show 1979, Have you Seen Sculpture from the Body? (Tate Gallery) 1984; memb Anglo-Catalan Soc; Elephant Tst Award 1994, Jack Goldhill Award for Sculpture Royal Acad Summer Exhibition 2013; FRBS 1999; *Solo Exhibitions* Serpentine Gallery London 1977, Salander/O'Reilly Gallery New York 1981, Poussin Gallery London 2011; *Group Exhibitions* incl: MOMA Oxford 1973, Chelsea Gallery 1974, Stockwell Depot Annual exhibitions 1974–79, The Condition of Sculpture (Hayward Gallery) 1975, Silver Jubilee exhbn of contemporary British sculpture (Battersea Park) 1977, Hayward Annual (Hayward Gallery) 1979, UEA 1982, Yorkshire Sculpture Park 1983, Tate Gallery 1984, Cornerhouse Gallery Manchester 1986, Int Contemporary Arts Fair London 1986, Whitefriars Museum Coventry 1987, Centro Cultural del Conde Duque Madrid 1988, Greenwich Open Studios 1988–90 and 1992, Int Festival of Iron Cardiff 1989, Normanby County Park Scunthorpe 1990, New Art Centre Sculpture Garden at Roche Court 1991–97, South Bank Centre London 1993, Lewisham Sculpture Park Riverdale Gardens 1993–94, Charterhouse Gallery London 1994, The Living Room Gallery London 1994, Flowers East Gallery London 1995, 1998, 1999, 2001, 2002 and 2004, Mercury Gallery London 1996, Royal Acad Summer Exhbn London 1996–97, 2009 and 2013–15, Mount Ephraim Gardens 1997, RBS Summer Show 2000, 2001, 2002 and 2005, St Augustine's Abbey Canterbury 2003, Pride of the Valley Sculpture Park 2003–, Fe2 05 (Myles Meehan Gallery Darlington Arts Centre) 2005, Steel (Canary Wharf) 2006, Poussin Gallery London 2007, 18@108: Steel (RBS) 2008, Artist of the Day

G

(Flowers Gallery London) 2014; *Work in Collections* incl: City of Lugano Collection, Arts Cncl, Cartwright Hall Museum Bradford, Railtrack, General Electric USA, Henry Moore Inst; *Recreations* playing tennis, walking, listening to music; *Style—* Ms Katherine Gili; ☎ 01795 533235, e-mail katherine@persey.plus.com, website www.katheringili.com

GILL, A A; s of Michael Gill, of London, and Yvonne, *née* Gilan; *b* 28 June 1954; *Educ* St Christopher Sch Letchworth, St Martin's Sch of Art London, Slade Sch of Fine Art London; *Children* 1 da (Flora b 23 Dec 1991), 1 s (Hector b 30 April 1993); *Career* journalist, artist and cook; currently: TV and restaurant critic The Sunday Times; Columnist of the Year 1994, Food Writer of the Year (for work in Tatler) and Restaurant Writer of the Year (for work in The Sunday Times) Glenfiddich Awards 1996, Critic of the Year (for work in Sunday Times) British Press Awards 1997, Cover Award 1998; *Books* Sap Rising (1996), The Ivy: a restaurant and its recipes (1997), Starcrossed (1999), Le Caprice (1999); *Clubs* Chelsea Arts; *Style—* A A Gill, Esq; ✉ The Sunday Times, 1 London Bridge Street, London SE1 9GF (☎ 020 7782 5000)

GILL, Rt Hon Lord; Brian Gill; PC (2002); s of Thomas Gill (d 1986), of Glasgow, and Mary, *née* Robertson (d 1986); *b* 25 February 1942; *Educ* St Aloysius' Coll Glasgow, Univ of Glasgow (MA, LLB), Univ of Edinburgh (PhD); *m* 6 Sept 1969, Catherine, *née* Fox; 5 s (Brian John b 1970, Francis Damian b 1971, James Patrick b 1973, Michael Simon b 1974, Anthony Thomas b 1983), 1 da (Anne Lucy b 1978); *Career* called to the Scottish Bar 1967, Lincoln's Inn 1991 (hon bencher 2002); QC 1981, keeper Advocates Library 1987–94, senator Coll of Justice Scotland (Lord of Session) 1994, Lord Justice Clerk of Scotland and pres Second Div of the Court of Session in Scotland 2001–12, Lord Justice General of Scotland and Lord Pres of the Court of Session 2012–15; chm Scottish Law Cmmn 1996–2001, dep chm Copyright Tbnl 1989–94; chm RSAMD 1999–2006, chm Cncl RSCM 2010–; Hon LLD: Univ of Glasgow 1998, Univ of Strathclyde 2003, Univ of St Andrews 2006, Univ of Edinburgh 2007, Univ of Abertay 2008; DAcad RSAMD 2006; FRSAMD 2002, FRSE 2004; KSG 2011; *Books* Agricultural Tenancies (1982, 4 edn 2016), Scottish Planning Encyclopedia (gen ed, 1996); *Recreations* church music; *Clubs* Athenaeum, MCC; *Style—* The Rt Hon Lord Gill; ✉ e-mail lord.bgill@gmail.com

GILL, Christopher J F; RD (1971); s of late F A Gill, and late D H Gill, *née* Southan; *b* 28 October 1936; *Educ* Shrewsbury; *m* 2 July 1960, Patricia, da of late E V Greenway; 1 s (Charles b 1961), 2 da (Helen b 1963, Sarah b 1967); *Career* Lt Cdr RNR 1952–79; butcher and farmer, chm F A Gill Ltd 1968–2006; Wolverhampton BC: memb (Cons) 1965–72, chm Public Works Ctee 1967–69, chm Local Educn Authy 1969–70; MP (Cons) Ludlow 1987–2001 (Parly candidate (UKIP) 2010); former vice-chm Cons European Affairs Ctee, former vice-chm Cons Agric Ctee; memb UKIP Nat Exec Ctee 2007–10; hon pres The Freedom Assoc 2007– (hon chm 2001–07); Liveryman Worshipful Co of Butchers, Freeman City of London; *Publications* Whips Nightmare (2003), Cracking the Whip (2012); *Recreations* walking, sailing, golf, DIY; *Style—* Christopher Gill, Esq, RD; ✉ Talbot Court, Salop Street, Bridgnorth, Shropshire WV16 5BR (☎ 01746 219251)

GILL, Rev Dr David Christopher; s of Alan Gill (d 1940), and Muriel, *née* Hodgson (d 1985); *b* 30 July 1938; *Educ* Bellevue GS Bradford, Univ of St Andrews (MB ChB), Salisbury Theol Coll, Univ of Nottingham (Dip Theol and Pastoral Studies); *Career* TA OTC 1956–61, RAMC 1961–66, 153 Highland Field Ambulance, Capt, RARO 1966–; house offr, sr house offr then registrar 1963–66 (appts at Perth Royal Infirmary, Bridge of Earn Hosp and King's Cross Hosp Dundee), medical supt and dist MO Mkomaindo Hosp Masasi Mtwara Region Tanzania 1966–72 (regnl leprosy offr 1967–72), clinical asst Herrison Hosp and Yeovil Dist Hosp 1972–74, registrar then sr registrar psychiatry Knowle Hosp Fareham 1974–78, conslt psychiatrist Mapperley Hosp Nottingham 1978–95 (emeritus conslt 1995–), clinical teacher Univ of Nottingham Med Sch 1978–95, The Priory Clinic Nottingham 1993–2006 (med dir 1995–2006), ret; chm Collegiate Trainees Sub-Ctee Royal Coll of Psychiatrists 1976–78, chm Senior Med Staff Ctee Mental Illness Unit 1980–85, medical memb Mental Health Act Review Tbnl 2003–06; memb Nottingham Medico-Chirugical Soc; memb Cncl Univ of St Andrews; ordained: deacon 1981, priest C of E 1985, priest Russian Orthodox Church in GB 1995; rector Orthodox Parish of St Aidan and St Chad Nottingham 2003– (priest in charge 1995–2003), Ecumenical Patriarch Orthodox Church in GB and I; DObstRCOG 1965, DTM&H (Liverpool) 1968, DPM 1975, FRCPsych 1986 (MRCPsych 1976); author of papers on electro-convulsive therapy, and psychiatric aspects of paranormal and possession states; *Recreations* sailing, theatre, opera, gardening; *Clubs* Royal Yachting Assoc, Army Sailing Assoc, Naval; *Style—* The Rev Dr David Gill; ✉ 1 Malvern Court, 29 Mapperley Road, Nottingham NG3 5SS (☎ 0115 962 2351, e-mail frdgill@btinternet.com)

GILL, Prof (Evelyn) Margaret; OBE (2011); da of late William Alexander Morrison Gill, and late Eveline Elizabeth, *née* Duthie; *b* 10 January 1951, Edinburgh; *Educ* Mary Erskine Sch for Girls Edinburgh, Univ of Edinburgh (BSc), Massey Univ NZ (PhD), Open Univ (BA); *Career* researcher Grassland Research Inst 1976–89, prog mangr then dir of research Natural Resources Inst (research arm of ODA) 1989–96, chief exec Natural Resources International Ltd 1996–2000, chief exec and dir of research Macaulay Inst 2000–06, chief scientific advsr rural affrs and environment Scottish Govt 2006–11, prof of integrated land use Univ of Aberdeen 2006–, sr research fell Dept for Int Devpt 2009–16; chair Ind Science & Partnership Cncl Consultative Gp on Int Agricultural Research (CGIAR) 2014–; Hammond Prize Br Soc of Animal Science 1992; FRSE 2003; *Recreations* hill walking, classical music; *Style—* Prof Margaret Gill, OBE

GILL, Neena; *b* 24 December 1956, Ludhiania; *Educ* Liverpool Poly (BA), London Business Sch; *Career* worked for London Borough of Ealing 1981–83, princ housing offr UK Housing Tst 1983–86, chief exec Asra Gtr London Housing Assoc 1986–90, chief exec New London Housing Gp 1990–99; dir Dalston City Challenge, chair Hackney Housing Partnership, memb Bd Hackney 2000; MEP (Lab) W Midlands 1999–2009; European Parl: vice-pres S Asia Delgn, Lab spokesperson Budgets Ctee, memb Industry, External Trade, Research and Energy Ctee; trade union steward 1981–83, memb Gen Ctee Constituency Lab Pty 1995–97, memb Lab NEC Ethnic Minority Taskforce; *Publications* incl: Race and Housing, Women and Housing, Standards in Housing; *Style—* Ms Neena Gill; ✉ West Midlands European Office, Terry Duffy House, Thomas Street, West Bromwich B70 6NT

GILL, Nick; s of William Gill, of Carlisle, Cumbria, and Mary, *née* Russell; *b* 24 September 1961, Carlisle, Cumbria; *Educ* Manchester Poly (BA); *m* 1999, Laura, *née* Bailey; 1 da (Sara), 2 s (Jack, Tom); *Career* BMP DDB 1984–1998 (memb Bd 1992, creative dir 1995), creative dir Nike account Wieden and Kennedy 1998, Bartle Bogle Hegarty 1998– (memb Bd 1999, creative dir on numerous accounts incl Vodafone, Levi's, KFC, Boddingtons, Microsoft X-Box, Axe and Barnardo's); student awards winner D&AD 1982, 4 Gold Cannes Golden Lions (2 Silvers), 12 D&AD Silver Pencils, 8 Gold Br TV Advtg Awards (8 Silvers); *Recreations* music, art, looking after children; *Style—* Nick Gill, Esq; ✉ Bartle Bogle Hegarty, 60 Kingly Street, Soho, London W1B 5DS (☎ 020 7734 1677, fax 020 7437 3666, e-mail nick.gill@bbh.co.uk)

GILL, Peter; OBE (1980); s of George John Gill (d 1986, union rep Spillers Flower Mill Gen Strike 1926), and Margaret Mary, *née* Browne (d 1966); *b* 7 September 1939; *Educ* St Illtyd's Coll Cardiff; *Career* dramatic author and director; actor 1957–65; directed first prodn A Collier's Friday Night at the Royal Court 1965; plays directed incl: The Local Stigmatic 1966, Crimes of Passion 1967, The Daughter-in-Law 1967 (first prize Belgrade Int Theatre Festival 1968), The Widowing of Mrs Holroyd 1968, The Duchess of Malfi 1971, Twelfth Night 1974, As You Like It 1975, The Fool 1975, The Way of the World 1992, New England 1994, Uncle Vanya 1995, A Patriot for Me 1995; assoc artistic dir Royal Court Theatre 1970–72; dir Riverside Studios 1976–80; prodns: The Cherry Orchard (own version), The Changeling 1978, Measure for Measure 1979, Julius Caesar 1980; appointed assoc dir Nat Theatre 1980–97; prodns: A Month in the Country 1981, Don Juan 1981, Major Barbara 1982, Tales from Hollywood 1983, Venice Preserv'd 1984, Fool for Love 1984, The Garden of England 1985, The Murderers 1985, Mrs Klein 1988, Juno and The Paycock 1989; dir Nat Theatre Studio 1984–90; wrote and produced: The Sleepers Den 1966 and 1969, Over Garden's Out 1969, A Provincial Life (after Chekov) 1969, Small Change 1976 and 1983, As I Lay Dying (after Faulkner) 1985, In The Blue 1985, Mean Tears 1987, Cardiff East 1996; other plays incl: Three Sisters (new version) 1997, Friendly Fire 1999, The Seagull (RSC) 1999, The York Realist 2000 (also at Royal Court 2002), Original Sin (After Wedekind) 2002; other prodns incl: Tongue of the Bird, Ellen McLauglain (Almeida) 1997, Certain Young Men (Almeida) 1999, Speed the Plow (Ambassador's) 1999, Luther (RNT) 2001, Scenes From the Big Picture (RNT) 2003, Days of Wine and Roses (Donmar), George Dillon (Comedy Theatre) 2005, The Voysey Inheritance (RNT) 2006, Look Back in Anger (Bath) 2006; *Style—* Peter Gill, Esq, OBE; ✉ c/o Casarotto Ramsay and Associates Ltd, Waverley House, 7–12 Noel Street, London W1F 8GQ (☎ 020 7287 4450, fax 020 7287 9128)

GILL, Stephanie; *Educ* St John's Coll Cambridge; *Career* dep headteacher Kirby GS until 2014, princ Altrincham GS for Girls 2014–; *Style—* Ms Stephanie Gill

GILL, HE Stuart William; OBE (2015); *m* Maggie; 2 da (Elizabeth, Claire); *Career* diplomat; various positions Dept of Trade and Industry 1980–94, first sec and head of inward investment Chicago 1994–98, first sec and head of section UK Rep to EU Brussels 1998–2002; FCO: head of section EU-Asia and EU-US Europe Directorate 2002–06, dep head Far Eastern Gp Asia Pacific Directorate 2006–08; British consul-gen Melbourne 2008–12, ambass to Iceland 2012–16, high cmmr to Malta 2016–; *Style—* HE Mr Stuart Gill; ✉ c/o Foreign & Commonwealth Office (Reykjavik), King Charles Street, London SW1A 2AH

GILLAN, Rt Hon Cheryl; PC (2010), MP; da of late Adam Mitchell Gillan, and Mona Gillan; *b* 21 April 1952, Llandaff, Cardiff; *Educ* Cheltenham Ladies' Coll, Coll of Law, Chartered Inst of Marketing; *m* 7 Dec 1985, John Coates Leeming, s of James Arthur Leeming; *Career* with Int Mgnt Gp 1977–84, dir Br Film Year 1984–86, sr mktg conslt Ernst and Young 1986–91, mktg dir Kidsons Impey 1991–93; chm Bow Gp 1987–88, European Parly candidate (Cons) Gtr Manchester Central 1989; MP (Cons) Chesham and Amersham 1992–; Parly under sec of state DfEE 1995–97; oppn frontbench spokesman on trade and industry 1997–98, oppn frontbench spokesman on foreign and Cwlth affrs 1998–2001, oppn whip 2001–03, oppn frontbench spokesman Home Office 2003–05, shadow sec of state for Wales 2005–10, sec of state for Wales 2010–12; memb Select Ctee on: Science and Technol 1992–95, Procedures 1994–95, Public Administration 2014–; int treas CPA 2003–06; vice-chm 1922 Ctee 2015–; Liveryman Worshipful Co of Marketors; FCIM; *Recreations* golf, music, gardening; *Clubs* RAC; *Style—* The Rt Hon Cheryl Gillan, MP; ✉ House of Commons, London SW1A 0AA

GILLAN, Matthew Stewart (Matt); s of Kevin John Gillan, and Patricia Rose, *née* Simon; *b* 7 January 1981, Portsmouth, Hants; *Educ* Eggars Sch Alton; *Career* commis chef Hen and Chicken Alton 1997–98, chef de partie Hunters Restaurant Alresford 1998–99, jr sous chef Midsummer House Cambridge 1999–2003, demi chef Restaurant Gordon Ramsay 2003, sr chef de partie The Vineyard Stockcross 2003–04, Vue du Monde Melbourne 2005; head chef: Camellia South Lodge Hotel Horsham 2006–08, The Pass South Lodge Hotel Horsham 2008– (7/10 Good Food Guide 2012–, 4 AA Rosettes 2012–, Michelin star 2012–); *Recreations* mixed martial arts; *Style—* Matt Gillan, Esq; ✉ The Pass, South Lodge Hotel, Brighton Road, Lower Beeding, West Sussex RH13 6PS (☎ 01403 891711, website www.exclusivehotels.co.uk, Twitter @mattgillan)

GILLARD, David Owen; MBE (2008); s of Robert Gillard (d 1983), of Croydon, Surrey, and Winifred, *née* Owens (d 1981); *b* 8 February 1947; *Educ* Tavistock Sch Croydon; *m* 1994, Valerie Ann Miles; *Career* arts writer and critic; scriptwriter and asst dir Assoc Br Pathé 1967–70, film and theatre critic Daily Sketch 1970–71, opera critic Daily Mail 1971– (ballet critic 1971–88), instituted Drama Preview Pages in The Listener 1982, fndr ed Friends (ENO magazine) 1983–92; Radio Times: radio corr 1984–91, writer My Kind of Day 1992–2002, writer Face Behind the Voice feature 1996–, classical music ed 2001–02; compere: Silhouette Opera Charity Concerts 2002–, Candlelight Opera perfs 2007–; patron Regent Centre Christchurch Dorset 2011–; memb: NUJ 1963 (life memb 2007), Critics' Circle 1974 (hon memb 2014), Broadcasting Press Guild 1995; *Books* Oh Brothers! (play, 1971), Beryl Grey: A Biography (1977); *Recreations* hill walking, collecting children's books and signed first editions, amateur dramatics including pantomime (finalists (with Regent Rep) Sky Arts 1's Nation's Best Am-Dram competition 2012); *Style—* David Gillard, Esq, MBE; ✉ 1 Hambledon Court, 18 Arundel Way, Highcliffe, Dorset BH23 5DX (☎ and fax 01425 275796)

GILLEN, Dr David; *Educ* BSc, MD; *Career* vice-pres medical affrs Pfizer; MFOM; *Style—* Dr David Gillen

GILLEN, Rt Hon Lord Justice; Rt Hon Sir John Gillen; kt (1999); *b* 18 November 1947; *Educ* Methodist Coll Belfast, The Queen's Coll Oxford; *Career* called to the Bar Gray's Inn 1970; QC (NI) 1983, judge of the High Court of Justice in NI 1999–, Lord Justice of Appeal in NI 2014–; *Style—* The Rt Hon Lord Justice Gillen; ✉ c/o Royal Courts of Justice, Chichester Street, Belfast BT1 3JF

GILLER, Norman; *b* 18 April 1940; *Educ* Raine's Fndn GS Stepney; *m* 8 April 1961, Eileen (d 2006); 1 s (Michael), 1 da (Lisa); partner, Jackie Wright; *Career* copy boy London Evening News 1955–56, reporter, sub ed and layout designer Boxing News 1959–61, sports ed and layout designer Stratford Express 1961–62, sports sub ed Evening Standard 1962, sports sub ed and layout designer Daily Herald 1962–64, football reporter Daily Express 1964–66 (chief football reporter 1966–74), TV sports columnist Evening News 1977–80, The Times annual Jumbo Sports Crossword 1985–, TV sports columnist Sunday Express 1991–97, The Judge sports column The Sun 1995–, The Silver Surfer football column FC.com 2000–, nine years of newspaper columns with Eric Morecambe (Daily Express and Titbits magazine); chief scripwriter Laureus World Sports Acad Awards 2002–03; numerous freelance appts 1974–; deviser many newspaper games since 1974 incl: The Name Game The Sun 1974–, Sportsword crossword The Express 1992–, Times Test Crossword in The Times 2001–06 (all games and puzzles compiled in partnership with s Michael) and two board games (Namedropper! and Tiddlythinks!); creator Petrolheads (BBC TV), script writer for This Is Your Life (scripts written for George Shearing, Richard Branson, Nigel Mansell, Peter Alliss and many others); other TV credits incl: Stunt Challenge (ITV) 1984 and 1985, Stand and Deliver (Sky) 1995–97; writer and deviser: The Games of '48 (with Brian Moore, ITV), Eurovision Song Contest Preview 1992–93, Who's the Greatest (seven-part series, ITV); writer and deviser Ricky Tomlinson's TV Joke Shop; chief assoc to Brian Klein (On the Box Productions Ltd); co-prodr and writer of videos featuring Lawrence Dallaglio, Dickie Bird, Frankie Dettori, Gordon Ramsay, John Motson, Harry Carpenter, David Seaman, Ray Winstone and Vinnie Jones 1998–2008; also prodr and writer: Over the Moon (ITV), Frankly Bruno (Chrysalis), Football Trivial Pursuit (Telstar); PR for Joe Bugner and Frank Bruno; resident blogger Sports Journalists' Assoc; *Books* 99 to date (2015); ghostwriter of numerous works with sporting personalities incl: Banks of England (with Gordon Banks), Watt's My Name (with Jim Watt), The Seventies Revisited (with Kevin Keegan), Olympic Heroes (with Brendan Foster), How to Box (with Henry Cooper), The Glory and the Grief (with George Graham), Top Ten Cricket Book (with Tom Graveney), Know What I Mean?

and From Zero to Hero (with Frank Bruno), Denis Compton – the Untold Stories, While I've Still Got Lead in My Pencil (with Roy Ullyett), The Final Score (with Brian Moore), Banks vs Pele: The Save that Shook the World (with Terry Baker); Billy Wright: A Hero For All Seasons (2002), McFootball (2003), Football and All That (2004), Football My Arse, Reading My Arse, Cheers My Arse and Celebrities My Arse (all with Ricky Tomlinson, 2005–07), The Great Football Quiz Book (2005), Bobby Moore The Master, Henry Cooper A Hero for All Time; 20 books with Jimmy Greaves incl: This One's On Me, The Final (novel), The Boss (novel), The Sixties Revisited, It's A Funny Old Life, Saint and Greavsie's World Cup Special, Don't Shoot The Manager, Heroes and Entertainers (2007); other books incl: The Golden Milers, The Marathon Kings, The Olympics Handbook, This Sporting Laugh, Crown of Thorns, Mike Tyson, The Release of Power (with Reg Gutteridge), Golden Heroes (with Dennis Signy), six Carry On novels (1996), Mike Baldwin (biography, 2000), Footballing Fifties (2007), The Concorde Club: the first 50 years, The Lane of Dreams: the complete history of White Hart Lane (with Jimmy Greaves and Steve Perryman, 2009), Bill Nicholson Revisited, Danny Blanchflower: This WAS His Life, The Ali Files (2015); *Recreations* creating computer graphics and websites (including www.normangillerbooks.com), listening to light classics, playing banana-fingered jazz piano with SootsJazz promoter Jackie Wright, reading, travelling (38 countries to date), surfing the internet, following all major sports, teaching grandchildren the history of sport; *Clubs* The Concorde; *Style—* Norman Giller, Esq; ✉ e-mail author@normangillerbooks.com, website www.normangillerbooks.com, Facebook Norman Giller, Twitter @UncleNormanGiller)

GILLESPIE, Dr Alan Raymond; CBE (2003); s of Charles Gillespie (d 1984), and Doreen, *née* Murtagh; *b* 31 July 1950, NI; *Educ* Grosvenor HS Belfast, Univ of Cambridge (MA, PhD); *m* 27 June 1973, Ruth, *née* Milne; 1 s (Patrick b 1989), 1 da (Christianne b 1991); *Career* Citibank NA 1976–86, ptnr Goldman Sachs and Co 1986–99, chief exec Cwlth Devpt Corporation 1999–2002, chm NI Industrial Devpt Bd 1999–2001, chm Ulster Bank Gp 2001–08, chm Alliance & Leicester 2008; non-exec dir United Business Media plc 2008–; chm Int Finance Facility for Immunization 2005–; chair ESRC 2009–; patron Queen's Univ of Belfast Fndn; Hon DUniv Ulster, Hon LLD Queen's Univ Belfast; High Sheriff Co Down 2008; *Recreations* golf, tennis, sailing; *Clubs* Wisley Golf, St George's Hill Lawn Tennis; *Style—* Dr Alan Gillespie, CBE

GILLESPIE, Jonathan William James; s of J J M Gillespie, and P D, *née* Evans; *b* 6 December 1966, Luton, Beds; *Educ* Bedford Modern Sch, Selwyn Coll Cambridge (MA, PGCE); *m* 8 Aug 1992, Caroline, *née* Hotchkiss; 2 s; *Career* asst master Highgate Sch 1990–97; Fettes Coll: head of modern languages 1997–2001, housemaster Moredun House 2001–06; head master: Lancing Coll 2006–14, St Albans Sch 2014–; FRSA; *Recreations* Highland bagpipe, hockey, cricket, golf, hill walking; *Style—* Jonathan Gillespie, Esq; ✉ St Albans School, Abbey Gateway, St Albans AL3 4HB (☎ 021727 515085, fax 01727 843447, e-mail hm@st-albans-school.org.uk)

GILLESPIE, (Joseph Andrew) Robert; s of John Robert Gillespie, and Honora Margaret, *née* Littlefair; *b* 14 April 1955, Nottingham; *m* 19 Sept 1987, Sally, *née* Powell; 3 da (Imogen b 17 Feb 1988, Isabel b 7 Feb 1996, Elizabeth b 19 April 1998); *Career* Price Waterhouse 1977–81, S G Warburg & Co Ltd 1981, head of UK investment banking SBC Warburg 1995, head of European investment banking UBS Warburg 1997; UBS Investment Bank: global head of investment banking 1999–2005, vice-chm 2005–08; chm Somerset House Tstees Ltd, chm Boat Race Co Ltd, vice-pres Save the Children, memb Bd NSPCC, memb Cncl Univ of Durham; CA 1980; *Recreations* sailing, golf, shooting; *Clubs* Leander, Oriental; *Style—* Robert Gillespie, Esq

GILLETT, Christopher John; yr s of Sir Robin Danvers Penrose Gillett, 2 Bt, GBE, RD; *b* 16 May 1958, London; *Educ* Durlston Court Sch, Pangbourne Coll, King's Coll Cambridge (choral scholar, MA), Royal Coll of Music (studied under Robert Tear and Edgar Evans), Nat Opera Studio; *m* 1984 (m dis), Julia, yr da of late W H Holmes, of Tunbridge Wells; 1 da (Tessa Holmes b 1987), 1 s (Adam Holmes b 1989); m 2, 1996, Lucy, da of H Schaufer, of Arizona USA; *Career* operatic and concert tenor; has worked with various major opera companies incl: New Sadler's Wells (over 150 performances), Royal Opera, ENO, Glyndebourne Touring Opera, Kent Opera, Music Theatre Wales, Opera Northern Ireland, LA Opera, La Scala Milan, Teatro Real Madrid, Teatre Liceu Barcelona; Liveryman Worshipful Co of Musicians; *Performances* operatic roles incl: Ferrando in Cosi fan Tutte (Glyndebourne Touring Opera), title role in Albert Herring (Glyndebourne Touring), Roderigo in Otello (Royal Opera House Covent Garden), Dov in The Knot Garden (Covent Garden), Pang in Turandot (Covent Garden), Hermes in King Priam (with Royal Opera Co in Athens), Nooni in The Making of the Representative for Planet Eight (with ENO at the London Coliseum and in Amsterdam), St Magnus in Peter Maxwell Davies' Martyrdom of St Magnus (Music Theatre Wales), Arbace in Idomeneo (English Bach Festival), Flute in A Midsummer Night's Dream (Aix-en-Provence Festival, Teatro Regio Turin, Ravenna Festival, ENO, Rome Opera) and Lysander in the same for Netherlands Opera and New Israeli Opera, Vasek in The Bartered Bride (Opera Northern Ireland), Pysander in Ulisse (Vlaamse Opera, Netherlands Opera), Tikhon Kabanova in Katya Kabanova (Glyndebourne Touring Opera), Gigolo in Rosa (Netherlands Opera), Aschenbach in Death in Venice (Genoa); concert performances incl: Stravinsky Cantata (with La Chapelle Royale under Philippe Herreweghe in Paris and Brussels), Haydn Creation (in Madrid), Handel Messiah (with The Sixteen Choir and Orch under Harry Christophers in the Netherlands), Nyman Songs, Sounds and Sweet Airs (with Michael Nyman Band in Japan), Bach St John Passion (Symphony Hall Birmingham and King's Coll Chapel Cambridge), Britten War Requiem (Teatro Colon Buenos Aires, Stuttgart, Rotterdam, Amsterdam, Taipei), Bach's St Matthew Passion (RFH with Bach Choir), Britten Nocturne (Philadelphia Orch), Peter Grimes (LSO); *Recordings* incl: Elgar The Kingdom (with London Philharmonic under Leonard Slatkin, RCA), The Beggar's Opera (Decca), Albert Herring (Naxos), Oliver Knussen Double Bill (Deutsche Grammophon); *Publications* Who's My Bottom? (2010), Scraping the Bottom (2014); various articles in The Observer, Opernwelt and at www.sinfinimusic.com; *Style—* Christopher Gillett, Esq; ✉ 3 Woolley Street, Bradford on Avon, Wiltshire BA15 1AD (☎ and fax 01225 865701, e-mail mail@christophergillett.co.uk, website www.christophergillett.co.uk); agent Musichall (website www.musichall.uk.com)

GILLFORD, Lord; Patrick James Meade; o s and h of 7 Earl of Clanwilliam, *qv*; *b* 28 December 1960; *Educ* Eton, RMA Sandhurst; *m* 1989 (m dis 1992), Serena Emily, da of Lt-Col Brian Lockhart; 1 da (Hon Tamara Louise (Meade) b 1990); m 2, 1995, Cara, da of Paul de la Peña, of Elmley Castle, Pershore, Worcs; 1 s (Hon John Maximillian b 1998), 1 da (Hon Natalya Katherine Sophia b 1999); *Career* Coldstream Gds 1979–83, Hanson plc 1983–90, seconded to The Rt Hon Douglas Hurd, *qv*, 1985–86, Ian Greer Associates 1990–93, md Westminster Policy Partnership public affrs consltts 1993–96, chm The Policy Partnership 1996–; cncllr Royal Borough of Kensington and Chelsea 1990–98 (chm Traffic and Highways); dir Br Sch of Osteopathy 1997–99, chm Cleveland Bridge 2001–04, dir Polyus Gold 2006–, dir Cedar Ptnrs 2006–, dir Eurasia Drilling Corp Ltd 2008–; *Recreations* arabic, golf, skydiving, sub-aqua, helicopter flying; *Clubs* Turf, Pratt's, Mill Reef (Antigua), New Zealand Golf; *Style—* Lord Gillford; ✉ Gardant Communications, 51 Causton Street, London SW1P 4AT (☎ 020 7976 5555, fax 020 7976 5353, e-mail pgillford@gardantcommunications.com)

GILLHAM, Paul Maurice; s of Gerald Albert Gillham, and Doris, *née* Kinsey; *b* 26 November 1931; *Educ* RCM, GSM (LGSM), Christ's Coll Cambridge (MA); *m* 3 Sept 1960, Jane Marion, da of Sir George Pickering (d 1982); 1 da (Carola b 7 July 1963), 2 s (Adam b 27 Dec 1965, Dan b 13 April 1968); *Career* chm: Keith Prowse Group 1970–80, St Giles Properties Ltd 1980–, Patent Developments International Ltd 1980–, Actonbarn Ltd 1983–92, Gillham Hayward Ltd 1995–; pres Accusphyg LLC (USA) 1998–; dir: Wren Underwriting Agencies Ltd 1993–97, Daisy Chain (Hair and Beauty) Ltd 1997–, Cathedral Capital plc 1997–; chm LPO Cncl 1983–87; *Recreations* playing cello and piano, walking; *Style—* Paul Gillham, Esq; ✉ 3 Broadhatch Cottages, Bentley, Farnham, Surrey GU10 5JL (☎ 01420 22371)

GILLIAM, Terry Vance; s of James Hall Gilliam, and Beatrice, *née* Vance; *b* 22 November 1940; *Educ* Occidental Coll (BA); *m* 1973, Maggie Weston; 1 s (Harry Thunder), 2 da (Amy Rainbow, Holly Dubois); *Career* actor, director, writer, animator; assoc ed Help! magazine 1962–64, freelance illustrator 1964–65, advertising copywriter and art dir 1966–67; exec prodr Complete Waste of Time (Monty Python CD-Rom) 1995; contrib to Spellbound Hayward Gallery 1996; visiting prof RCA 1997; govr BFI 1997–; Hon DFA: Occidental Coll 1987, RCA 1989; Hon Dr Wimbledon Sch of Art 2004; fell BAFTA 2009; Chevalier Ordre Des Artes et Lettres 2014; *Television* resident cartoonist We Have Ways of Making You Laugh 1968, animator Do Not Adjust Your Set 1968–69, animator, actor and co-writer Monty Python's Flying Circus 1969–76 and 1979; animator: The Marty Feldman Comedy Machine 1971–72, The Do-It-Yourself Film Animation 1974; presenter The Last Machine (BBC series) 1995; *Film* co-writer, actor and animator: And Now For Something Completely Different 1971, Monty Python and The Holy Grail 1974 (also co-dir), Monty Python's Life of Brian 1978, Monty Python Live at The Hollywood Bowl 1982, Monty Python's The Meaning of Life 1983; animator and writer The Miracle of Flight 1974; co-writer/dir: Jabberwocky 1976, Time Bandits (also prodr) 1980, Brazil 1985, The Adventures of Baron Münchhausen 1988, The Fisher King 1991, Twelve Monkeys 1995, Fear & Loathing in Las Vegas 1998, The Brothers Grimm 2005, Tideland 2005, The Imaginarium of Dr Parnassus 2009, The Wholly Family 2011; dir The Zero Theorem 2013; subject of Lost in La Mancha 2002; actor: Neuf Mois Ferme 2014, Jupiter Ascending 2014, Absolutely Anything 2014; *Stage* Monty Python Live (Mostly) 2014; *Albums* Monty Python's Flying Circus (jtly, 1970), Another Monty Python Record (jtly, 1971), Monty Python's Previous Record (jtly, 1972), The Monty Python Matching Tie and Handkerchief (jtly, 1973), Monty Python Live at Drury Lane (jtly, 1974), Monty Python and the Holy Grail (jtly, 1975), Monty Python Live at City Centre (jtly, 1976), The Monty Python Instant Record Collection (jtly, 1977), Monty Python's Life of Brian (jtly, 1979), Monty Python's Contractual Obligation Album (jtly, 1980), Monty Python Live at the Hollywood Bowl (jtly, 1981), Monty Python's The Meaning of Life (jtly, 1983), Monty Python The Final Rip Off (jtly, 1987), Monty Python Sings (jtly, 1989), Fear & Loathing in Las Vegas (soundtrack, produced jtly, 1998); *Opera* The Damnation of Faust (ENO) 2011, Benvenuto Cellini (ENO) 2014; *Books* The Cocktail People (1966), Monty Python's Big Red Book (jtly, 1977), Monty Python's Papperbok (jtly, 1977), Monty Python and The Holy Grail (jtly, 1977), Monty Python's Life of Brian (jtly, 1979), Animations of Mortality (1979), Time Bandits (jtly, 1981), Monty Python's The Meaning of Life (jtly, 1983), The Adventures of Baron Münchhausen (jtly, 1989), Monty Python's Just the Words (jtly, 1989), Not the Screenplay of Fear & Loathing in Las Vegas (jtly, 1998), Dark Knights and Holy Fools (1998), Gilliam on Gilliam (1999), The Pythons: An Autobiography (2003), Dreams & Nightmares: Terry Gilliam & The Brothers Grimm, Gilliamesque (2014); *Recreations* sitting extremely still for indeterminate amounts of time; *Style—* Terry Gilliam, Esq; ✉ c/o Jenne Casarotto, Waverley House, 7–12 Noel Street, London W1F 8GQ (☎ 020 7287 4450, fax 020 7287 9128, e-mail jenne@casarotto.uk.com)

GILLICK, Liam; *b* 13 April 1964; *Educ* Univ of London, Goldsmiths Coll; *Career* artist; prof Columbia Univ NY 1997–2012, grad Ctee memb Bard Coll NY 2008–; selected to represent Germany for 53rd Venice Biennale 2009; nominated: Turner Prize 2002, Vincent Award Stedelijk Museum Amsterdam 2008; *Solo Exhibitions* incl: The Wood Way (Whitechapel Gall London) 2002, A Short Text on the Possibility of Creating an Economy of Equivalence (Palais de Tokyo) 2005, Three Perspectives and a short scenario (Witte de With, Rotterdam, Kunsthalle Zurich and MCA Chicago) 2008–10, Kunst und Ausstellungshalle de Bundesrepublik Deutschland 2010; *Public Commissions and Projects* incl: Home Office London 2005, Dynamica Building Guadalajara Mexico 2009; *Public Collections* incl: Govt Art Collection, Arts Cncl, Tate Britain, Museum of Modern Art NY, Guggenheim Museum NY, Hirshhorn Museum Washington DC, Museum of Contemporary Art Chicago; *Publications* incl Proxemics: Selected Writing 1988–2006 (2006), All Books (2009), Meaning Liam Gillick (2009); contrib to many art magazines and jls incl Parkett, Frieze, Art Montly, October and Art Forum; *Style—* Liam Gillick, Esq; ✉ c/o galleries: Casey Kaplan NY (website www.caseykaplangallery.com), Esther Schipper Berlin (www.estherschipper.com), Maureen Paley London (www.maureenpaley.com), Eva Presenhuber Zurich

GILLIE, Dr Oliver John; s of John Calder Gillie, of Tynemouth, Northumberland, and Ann, *née* Philipson; *b* 31 October 1937, North Shields, Tyneside; *Educ* Bootham Sch York, Univ of Edinburgh (BSc, PhD), Stanford Univ; *m* 3 Dec 1969 (m dis 1988), Louise, da of Col Phillip Panton; 2 da (Lucinda Kathrine b 1970, Juliet Ann b 1972); m 2, 2 Oct 1999, Jan, da of Leo Thompson; 2 s (Calder Thompson b 1994, Sholto Douglas b 1997); *Career* lectr in genetics Univ of Edinburgh 1961–65, Nat Inst for Medical Research Mill Hill 1965–68, IPC Magazines 1968–70, Haymarket Publishing 1970–72, med corr The Sunday Times 1972–86; The Independent: med ed 1986–89, special corr 1989–94; freelance journalist 1994–, fndr Health Research Forum 2004; asst ed Public Health Nutrition; collaborator VIDAL trial vitamin D; Royal Jubilee Medal; FRSA; *Books* incl: The Sunday Times Book of Body Maintenance (jtly, 1978), The Sunday Times Guide to the World's Best Food (jtly, 1981), The Sunday Times Self-Help Directory (jtly, 1982), The ABC Diet and Bodyplan (jtly, 1984), Regaining Potency (1995), Escape from Pain (1997), Food for Life (1999), Sunlight Robbery (2004), Vitamin D, Sunlight and Health (2006), Scotland's health deficit: An explanation and a plan (2008), 'Controlled trials of vitamin D, causality and type 2 statistical error' (in Public Health Nutrition, 2014); *Recreations* sailing, climbing Munros; *Clubs* RSM, RSA; *Style—* Dr Oliver Gillie; ✉ 68 Whitehall Park, London N19 3TN (☎ 020 7561 9677, e-mail olivergillie@blueyonder.co.uk, website www.healthresearchforum.org.uk)

GILLIES, Crawford; s of Robert Gillies (d 2002), and Euphemia, *née* Rennie; *b* 1 May 1956, Edinburgh; *Educ* Univ of Edinburgh (LLB), Harvard Business Sch (MBA, Baker scholar); *m* 1978, Alison, *née* Farquhar; 3 s (Callum b 1990, Fraser b 1992, Alasdair b 1997); *Career* ptnr Bain & Co 1988–2005 (md Europe 2001–05); chm: Control Risks Gp plc 2006–, Hammonds 2006–09, Scottish Enterprise 2009–15; dir: Standard Life plc 2007–16, MITIE Gp plc 2012–15, Barclays plc 2014–, SSE plc 2015–; ACA 1980; *Recreations* trees, rugby, golf; *Clubs* Caledonian; *Style—* Crawford Gillies, Esq; ✉ e-mail cg@crawfordgillies.co.uk

GILLIES, Prof Malcolm George William; AM (2013); s of Frank Douglas Gillies, of Canberra, Aust (d 1988), and Beatrice Mary Belle, *née* Copeman (d 1997); *b* 23 December 1954, Brisbane, Aust; *Educ* ANU (BA), Univ of Queensland (DipEd), Univ of Cambridge (MA), KCL (MMus), Univ of London (PhD), Univ of Melbourne (DMus); *Partner* David Adrian Pear; *Career* tutor, lectr then sr lectr Univ of Melbourne 1982–92, prof and dean of music Univ of Queensland 1992–99, exec dean and pro-vice-chllr Univ of Adelaide 1999–2001, dep vice-chllr (educn) ANU 2002–06, vice-pres (devpt) ANU 2006–07, vice-chllr and pres City Univ London 2007–09, vice-chllr London Met Univ 2010–14; chair London Higher 2010–14; pres: Aust Acad of the Humanities 1998–2001, Nat Acads Forum 1998–2002, Aust Cncl for the Humanities, Arts and Social Sciences 2004–06; emeritus prof London

G

Met Univ 2014–, emeritus prof Australian Nat Univ 2015–, visiting prof King's Coll London 2015–; Deems Taylor Award American Soc of Composers, Authors and Publishers 2007; fell Aust Acad of the Humanities 1992, fell Aust Coll of Educators 2005, FRSA 2008, FIOD 2015; Bartók in Britain (1989), Bartók Remembered (1990), The Bartók Companion (ed, 1993), The All-Round Man (jt ed, 1994), Grainger on Music (jt ed, 1999), Portrait of Percy Grainger (jt ed, 2002), Self-Portrait of Percy Grainger (jt ed, 2006), Bartók Connections (2007); *Recreations* swimming, the arts, travel, the 1890s; *Clubs* IoD (London); *Style*— Prof Malcolm Gillies, AM

GILLIES, Prof Pamela; CBE (2013); *b* 13 February 1953, Dundee; *Educ* Univ of Aberdeen (BSc, PGCE, MEd), Univ of Nottingham (MMedSci, PhD); *Career* conslt Global Prog on AIDS (latterly UNAIDS) WHO 1989–, exec dir of research Health Authy for England 1996–99, prof of public health Royal Coll of Physicians of London 2002, visiting prof of health and human rights Harvard Univ, princ and vice-chllr Glasgow Caledonian Univ 2006–; memb: Bd Scottish Inst for Excellence in Social Work Educn 2006–08, Univs UK Research Policy Ctee; tstee Carnegie Tst for the Univs of Scotland, tstee British Cncl 2008–14; tstee Saltire Fndn; author of over 100 academic jls and Govt reports; FAcSS 2005, hon fell Royal Coll of Physicians of Glasgow 2007, Harness fell Cwlth Fund of NY, FRSA, FFPH, FRSE; *Recreations* tennis, horticulture, Women Dirs on UK Bds Gp; *Style*— Prof Pamela Gillies, CBE; ✉ c/o Julie Burns, executive assistant (☎ 0141 331 3112, e-mail julie.burns@gcu.ac.uk)

GILLIES, Stuart; *Career* formerly with: Riche Stockholm, Lord Byron Hotel Rome, Le Caprice London; Daniel's NY 1995–97; Gordon Ramsay Hldgs: head chef The Connaught 2002–03, chef patron Boxwood Café 2003–, chef patron Gordon Ramsay Plane Food Heathrow Airport Terminal 5 2008–, chef dir Savoy Grill 2010–, md 2011–; television appearances incl: GMTV, Masterchef Goes Large, Saturday Kitchen, Great British Menu; regular columnist Men's Health; *Style*— Mr Stuart Gillies; ✉ Gordon Ramsay Holdings, 1 Catherine Place, London SW1E 6DX

GILLIES, Prof William; s of Iain Gillies (d 1989), and Mary Kyle, *née* Cathie (d 1999); *b* 15 September 1942, Stirling, Scotland; *Educ* Oban HS, Univ of Edinburgh (MA), Univ of Oxford (MA); *m* 24 June 1972, Valerie Roselyn Anna, da of Peter John Simmons, of Edinburgh; 1 s ((John) Lachlan b 1973), 2 da (Maeve b 1974, Mairi b 1982); *Career* Dublin Inst for Advanced Studies 1969–70, prof of Celtic Univ of Edinburgh 1979–2009 (lectr 1970–79); visiting prof of Celtic languages and literatures Harvard Univ 2009–10 and 2013–15; dir Pittencrieff Int plc 2008–; hon professorial fell Univ of Edinburgh 2009–; Hon DLitt Univ of Ulster 2006; FSA Scot 1975, FRSE 1990, FRHistS 2002; *Books* Criticism and Prose Writings of Sorley Maclean (ed, 1985), Gaelic and Scotland (ed, 1989), Survey of the Gaelic Dialects of Scotland (gen ed, 1994–97), Celtic Connections 1 (ed, 1999), Celtic Connections 2 (ed, 2005); *Style*— Prof William Gillies, FRSE; ✉ 67 Braid Avenue, Edinburgh EH10 6ED (☎ 0131 447 2876, e-mail williamgillies@hotmail.com); University of Edinburgh, 50 George Square, Edinburgh EH8 9JU (e-mail w.gillies@ed.ac.uk); Harvard University, Warren House, Barker Center, Quincy Street, Cambridge, MA 02138, USA (☎ 001 617 495 1208, e-mail wgillies@fas.harvard.edu)

GILLIGAN, Andrew Paul; s of Kevin Anthony Gilligan, and Ann Elizabeth *née* Roberts; *Educ* Grey Court Sch, Richmond & Kingston Coll of FE, St John's Coll Cambridge; *Career* Cambridge Evening News 1994–95, foreign desk Sunday Telegraph 1995, def corr Sunday Telegraph 1995–99, def and dip corr Today Prog BBC Radio 4 1999–2004, former columnist Evening Standard; cycling cmmr for London 2013–; MRUSI, MRAeS; *Recreations* hill walking, architecture, riding on buses; *Style*— Andrew Gilligan, Esq

GILLIGAN, Prof Christopher Aidan; CBE (2015); s of William Christopher Gilligan (d 1995), and Kathleen Mary, *née* Doyle (d 2003); *b* 9 January 1953, New Ross, Ireland; *Educ* Keble Coll Oxford (MA), Wolfson Coll Oxford (DPhil), Univ of Cambridge (MA, ScD); *m* 21 Dec 1974, Joan Margaret, *née* Flood; 3 da (Clare Siobhan b 20 April 1978, Helen Mairead b 19 March 1984, Elizabeth Anne b 30 April 1987), 1 s (Richard Aidan John b 16 April 1980); *Career* Univ of Cambridge: demonstrator Dept of Applied Biology 1977–82, lectr Dept of Applied Biology 1982–89, lectr Dept of Plant Sciences 1989–95, fell King's Coll 1988– (professorial fell 1999), reader in mathematical biology Dept of Plant Sciences 1995–99, prof of mathematical biology Dept of Plant Sciences 1999–, head Sch of Biological Scis 2009–13 (dep head and head-elect 2008–09); dep visiting prof Dept of Botany and Plant Pathology Colorado State Univ 1982, research fell Rothamsted Research 1998–2013, sr research fell Royal Soc Leverhulme Tst 1998–99, professorial res fell BBSRC 2005–10; chair: Scientific Advsy Cncl DEFRA 2011–14, Bd Cambridge Prog for Sustainability Leadership 2011–16, Jt Nature Conservation Ctee 2014–; memb: Cncl Nat Inst Agric Botany 1985–91, Governing Body Silsoe Res Inst 1998–2006, Cncl BBSRC 2003–10 (memb Strategy Bd 2005–09, chm Crop Science Review 2003–04), Advsy Ctee on Forest Res Forestry Cmmn 2006–09; advsr: Scottish Exec Environment and Rural Affrs Dept (SEERAD) 1998–2003, Inst Nat de la Recherche Agronomique (INRA) France 2003–05 (chair Cmmn d'Evaluation on Plant Health and Environment 2003); tstee Natural History Museum 2011–; pres Br Soc for Plant Pathology 2001, hon fell American Phytopathological Soc 2005; FRSS 1995; *Publications* Mathematical Modelling of Crop Disease (ed, 1985); numerous articles on botanical epidemiology, modelling in biology in mathematical and biology jls; *Recreations* family, running, reading, travel; *Style*— Prof Christopher Gilligan, CBE; ✉ Department of Plant Sciences, University of Cambridge, Downing Site, Cambridge CB2 3EA (☎ 01223 333900, fax 01223 333953, e-mail cag1@cam.ac.uk)

GILLILAND, Alan Howard; s of Wilfrid Howard Gilliland (d 1986), and Mary, *née* Miller (d 2004); *b* 7 January 1949; *Educ* Bedford Sch, PCL, AA Sch of Architecture; *m* 31 Oct 1975, Pauline, *née* Howkins; 5 s (Benjamin b 30 Jan 1976, Robert b 12 Dec 1980, Alexander b 4 Feb 1983, Oliver b 29 Jan 1985, Jack b 4 June 1988), 1 da (Emily b 24 Sept 1977); *Career* press photographer Evening Despatch Darlington 1979–86; editorial graphic artist: The Northern Echo 1986, London Daily News 1986–87; Daily and Sunday Telegraph: joined 1987, head Graphics Dept 1989–2005, graphics ed 1992–2005; currently prop: Raven's Quill Ltd, Alan Gililand Graphics, Straight-Taking Photgraphy; illustrator for architects incl John McAslan & Ptnrs and Kit Martin; Graphic Artist of the Year Br Press Awards 1988 and 1989 (commended 1990), Linotype Award for text and graphics (for Daily Telegraph) Newspaper Industry Awards 1990, Silver award for breaking news informational graphic Soc of News Design US 1989 (2 awards of excellence 1990, 1991, 1994, 1997, 1998 and 1999), jt winner Graphic Artist of the Year Br Press Awards 1991, highly commended Image of the Year Br Press Awards 1994, Team of the Year (for the war in Iraq) Br Press Awards 2004; *Books* incl: The Amazing Adventures of Curd the Lion and Us!) in the Land at the Back of Beyond (author and illustrator, 2008), The Flight of Birds (author, 2010), Ana Thema (author and illustrator, 2010), The Flight of Birds, White Edition (author, 2011); also illustrator of: three-book series for Osprey (Weapon, Raid, Duel), 72 non-fiction books for Penguin, 200-part Great Battles series, model village templates for Hachette Partworks; *Recreations* real tennis, walking, cycling, kayaking; *Clubs* Petworth House Real Tennis, Byte the Book, Assoc of Illustrators, Publishers Assoc; *Style*— Alan Gilliland, Esq; ✉ Raven's Quill Limited, The Gatehouse, Lincoln Road, Bloxholm, Lincolnshire LN4 3AT (website www.ravensquill.com, blog https://alangilliland.blogspot.com); Alan Gilliland Graphics (e-mail alan@ravensquill.com, website www.alangilliland.com)

GILLINGWATER, Richard; CBE (2008); *Educ* Univ of Oxford, IMD Lausanne (MBA); *Career* formerly: corporate finance dir Kleinwort Benson, jt head global corporate finance BZW, chm European investment banking Credit Suisse First Boston; fndr chief exec

Shareholder Exec Cabinet Office 2003–07, dean Cass Business Sch City Univ London 2007–; chm: Faber Music Ltd, CDL 2009–; dir Faber Music Holdings Ltd; non-exec dir: Kidde plc 2004–05, Qinetiq 2004–06, Tomkins plc 2005–, Debenhams plc 2006–, Scottish & Southern Energy plc 2007–; sr ind dir Hiscox 2011–; *Style*— Richard Gillingwater, Esq, CBE

GILLIONS, Paul; s of William Stanley Gillions (d 1972), and Marie Lilian, *née* Crawley; *b* 15 May 1950; *Educ* St Albans GS for Boys; *m* 5 June 1976, Grace Kathleen, da of David Adam Smith, and Kathleen Iris, *née* Towers; 2 da (Jennie b 1980, Laura b 1983); *Career* int PR conslt; Burson-Marsteller Ltd: main bd dir 1987–93, dir of issues mgmnt Burson-Marsteller Europe, memb Int Bd 1992–93; sr vice-pres and dir public policy and issues mgmnt Fleishman-Hillard 1993–96, sr vice-pres int public policy Fleishman-Hillard (Europe and USA) 1996–98, int md Burson-Marsteller 1998–2000; int conslt on public policy and issues mgmnt 2001–; govr memb and vol RNLI; *Publications* Exploring Public Relations (contrib, 2006 and 2009); *Recreations* rugby, sailing, boating; *Style*— Paul Gillions, Esq; ✉ 3 Whitehurst Avenue, Hitchin, Hertfordshire SG5 1SR (☎ 01462 621453, e-mail paulgillions@aol.com)

GILLMAN, Tricia; da of Dr Theodore Gillman (d 1971), of Cambridge, and Selma, *née* Cohen (d 1993); *b* 9 November 1951; *Educ* Univ of Leeds (BA), Univ of Newcastle upon Tyne (MFA); *m* 1989, Alexander Ramsay, s of Frank Raymond Faber Ramsay (d 1977); 1 s (Thomas Jesmond b 3 Jan 1990); *Career* artist; teacher: various posts 1977–83 (Newcastle Poly, Univ of Leeds, Ravensbourne Sch of Art, Lanchester Poly, Birmingham Poly, Edinburgh Sch of Art, Univ of Reading, Chelsea Sch of Art), St Martin's Sch of Art 1983–99, RCA 1988–95; *Solo Exhibitions* Parkinson Gallery Leeds 1978, Sunderland Arts Centre 1982, Arnolfini Gallery Bristol 1985, Benjamin Rhodes Gallery London 1985, 1987 and 1993, Laing Gallery Newcastle (touring) 1989–90, Gardner Centre Brighton 1994, Art Space Gallery London 1996, Jill George Gallery London 1997, 1999 and 2002; *Group Exhibitions* incl: Northern Art Assoc Exhibition (Shipley Art Gallery and tour) 1978, St Martin's Painters (Seven Dial Gallery) 1982, Summer Show II (Serpentine Gallery) 1982, John Moores Liverpool Exhibition XIV (Walker Art Gallery) 1985, Thirty London Artists (Royal Acad of Art) 1985, Malaysian and British Exhibition Paintings and Prints (National Art Gallery, Kuala Lumpur, Singapore and Hong Kong) 1986, Britain in Vienna (Kunsthaus Vienna) 1986, London Group (RCA and tour) 1987, Summer Show (Royal Acad of Art) 1987 and 2003, John Moores Exhibition (Liverpool) 1989, Tricia Gillman and Richard Gorman: Small Paintings (Benjamin Rhodes Gallery) 1989, Homage to the Square (Flaxman Gallery) 1990, Works on Paper (Benjamin Rhodes Gallery) 1990, Forces of Nature (Manchester City Art Gallery and tour) 1990, Br Cncl and Royal Coll of Art touring exhibition of Eastern Europe 1990, Art '91 (London Contemporary Art Fair Olympia) 1991, Peter Stuyvesant Touring Exhibition (Zaragoza and Seville, Spain) 1991, The Discerning Eye (Mall Galleries) 1991, John Moores Exhibition (Liverpool) 1991, The New Patrons (Christie's London) 1992, 20th Century Women's Art (New Hall Cambridge) 1992, 3 Ways (RCA touring exhbn to Central Europe) 1992, London Group (Morley Coll London) 1992, Chicago Art Fair 1993, 3 Artists (Benjamin Rhodes Gallery) 1994, Harlech Biennale (Wales) 1994, Summer Show (RA) 1994, Harlech Biennale (Wales) 1995, Solo Show (Art Space Gallery) 1996, 20th Century Art Fair (London) 1996, 1997, 1998 and 1999, Solo Show (Gil George Gallery) 1997, Art '97 (Business Design Centre London) 1997, Hunting Group Art Prize (travelling show) 1997, Critic's Choice (New Academy Gallery) 1997, Summer Show (Royal Acad of Arts) 1997, 3x3 (Art Space Gallery) 1997, Art '98 (Business Design Centre London) 1998, Art '99 (Business Design Centre London) 1999, Santa Fe Art Fair 1999, 2K, 2K (Jill George Gallery London) 2000, Art 2000 (Business Design Centre London) 2000, 20/21 British Art Fair (RCA) 2000, Cheltenham International Drawing Exhibition 2000, Hunting Group Art Prize (RCA) 2000, Toronto International Art Fair 2000 and 2001, Palm Springs International Art Fair 2001, Art Palm Beach 2002, Art 2002 (Business Design Centre London) 2002, Roya Acad Summer Exhibition (Royal Acad of Arts London) 2003 (nominated for Delenney Prize) and 2004, Walk Gallery London 2004, Bankside Gallery London 2004; *Work in Collections* public collections: Contemporary Arts Soc, Univ of Leeds, Television South West, The Stuyvesant Fndn, Stanhope Properties plc, Herbert Art Gallery Coventry, Unilever plc; private collections in: Britain, Belgium, Holland, Japan, Thailand, USA, Italy; *Style*— Ms Tricia Gillman; ✉ c/o Jill George Gallery, 38 Lexington Street, Soho, London W1R 3HR (☎ 020 7439 7319, fax 020 7287 0478)

GILLOTT, Roland Charles Graeme; s of John Arthur Gillott (d 1982), of Northwood, Middx, and Ursula Mary, *née* Bailey (d 1983); *b* 22 August 1947; *Educ* Haileybury; *m* 25 Oct 1975, (Bridget) Rae, da of Lesley Bentley Jones (d 1959), of Northwood, Middx; 2 da (Shanta b 21 April 1978, Lissa b 1 Jan 1981), 1 s (Adrian b 20 Oct 1979); *Career* admitted slr 1972 (now non-practising), ptnr Radcliffes (now RadcliffesLeBrasseur) 1979–2013 (managing ptnr 2004–13); churchwarden St Michaels and All Angels Amersham 1991–95 and 2001–03; pres Churches on the Hill Amersham (COTHA) 2001–05, govr Merchant Taylors' Sch 2005–, tstee Haileybury Soc 2013– (pres-elect 2015–16); Liveryman: Worshipful Co of Merchant Taylors 1979, Worshipful Co of Info Technologists 1995; memb Law Soc; *Recreations* walking, photography; *Clubs* MCC, RAC, Travellers, City Livery; *Style*— Roland Gillott, Esq; ✉ Glenwayth, Hervines Road, Amersham, Buckinghamshire HP6 5HS (☎ 01494 722674, e-mail roland.gillott@btinternet.com)

GILMORE, David; s of David Gilmore, and Dora, *née* Baker; *b* 7 December 1945, London; *Educ* Alleyn's Sch Dulwich; *m* 23 Sept 1978, Fiona, da of J P R Mollison; 3 s (Charles b 1982, George b 1985, Edward b 1989); *Career* artistic director; appts incl: Watermill Theatre, Nuffield Theatre Southampton, currently artistic dir St James Theatre London; prodns incl: Nuts (Whitehall), Daisy Pulls it Off, Lend Me a Tenor (both Globe), The Resistible Rise of Arturo Ui, Beyond Reasonable Doubt (both Queen's), The Hired Man (Astoria), Cavalcade (Chichester), Song and Dance (Sydney, Melbourne and Adelaide), Glen Garry Glenross (Brussels), Fatal Attraction (Haymarket), Mandragola (RNT), Casablanca (Whitehall), A Swell Party (Vaudeville), Radio Times (Queen's), Grease (Dominion and Australian Arena Tour), As you Like it (Chicago), Chapter Two (Queen's), Alone Together (Hong Kong and Beijing), Là Haut (Lyon and Paris), Happy Days (Olympic Superdome Sydney), Gasping (Hong Kong), The Jamie Oliver Stage Show (London and Aust), Footloose (Capitol Sydney), Hair (Berlin and Paris), Noises Off (nat tour), Steel Magnolias (nat tour); *Recreations* golf, gardening; *Clubs* Garrick; *Style*— David Gilmore, Esq; ✉ agent: Lesley Duff, Diamond Management (☎ 020 7631 0400, e-mail ld@diman.co.uk)

GILMORE, Fiona Catherine; da of Robin (Dick) Triefus (d 1983), and Jean Margaret, *née* Herring (da of Alfred Herring, VC); *b* 7 November 1956; *Educ* Queenswood Sch Hatfield (scholar), Univ of Cambridge (MA); *m* 5 May 1979 (m dis 2004), Richard John Maurice Gilmore (d 2010), s of Richard Thomas Gilmore; 3 s (Daniel b 1986, Alexander b 1989, Edward b 1993); *Career* Ted Bates Advertising Agency London 1977–78, Benton & Bowles Advertising Agency London 1978–84, md Michael Peters & Ptnrs 1987–90 (devpt dir 1984, mktg dir 1985), md Lewis Moberly 1990–91, fndr ptnr and ceo Springpoint (brand and corp identity positioning and design consultancy) 1991–2003, fndr ptnr and chm Acanchi 2003–; speaker CBI conf 1986; memb: CBI Vision 2010 Gp 1986–87, NEDO Maker User Working Pty 1988, Milk Mktg Bd 1988, GCSE Modern Language Working Pty 1989; govr Centre for Info on Language Teaching and Res 1987, chm Design Effectiveness Awards Scheme 1988–89; non-exec dir RSPB 1994, non-exec memb Bd United Learning Tst 2003–10, non-exec dir CAMFED 2011–; advsr Lambeth Palace 1992–98, memb Cncl Water Aid 1997–2003; memb RSA; *Books* Brand Warriors (ed,

1997), CBI Growing Business Handbook (contrib, 1997), Warriors on the High Wire (2001), Brand Warriors China (2003); *Recreations* family, skiing, tennis, walking, opera; *Clubs* Reform; *Style*— Mrs Fiona Gilmore

GILMORE, Margaret; da of Rev Canon Norman Gilmore (d 1996), and Barbara, *née* Elcoat; *b* 9 February 1956, Nqutu, South Africa; *Educ* N London Collegiate Sch, Westfield Coll London (BA); *m* 10 July 1993, Eamonn Matthews; 1 s (Christopher b 21 Jan 1998); *Career* reporter Kensington Post 1977–79, corr IRN 1979–84, reporter BBC NI 1984–85; corr: Newsnight 1986–89, This Week 1989–92, Panorama 1993–95, BBC News 1995–97, Environment BBC News 1997–2000, Home and Legal Affrs BBC News 2000–07; memb Bd Food Standards Agency 2008–14, non-exec dir and memb Human Fertilisation and Embryology Authy 2015–; sr research fell RUSI 2007–14 (sr assoc fell 2014–); TV News Environment Corr of the Year Br Environment and Media Awards 1997; *Publications* The Terrorist Hunters (jtly, 2009); *Recreations* playing the piano, family and friends, supporting Reading FC; *Style*— Mrs Margaret Gilmore; ✉ c/o Knight Ayton Management, 35 Great James Street, London WC1N 3HB (e-mail margaretgilmore@btinternet.com, website www.margaretgilmore.com)

GILMORE, Rosalind Edith Jean; CB (1995); da of Sir Robert Brown Fraser, OBE (d 1984), and Betty, *née* Harris (d 1984); *b* 23 March 1937; *Educ* King Alfred Sch London, UCL (BA), Newnham Coll Cambridge (MA); *m* 17 Feb 1962, Brian Terence Gilmore, CB, s of John Henry Gilmore; *Career* HM Treasy: appointed 1960, asst princ 1960–62, asst private sec to Chllr of Exchequer 1962–65, princ 1965, resigned to accompany husb to Washington; exec asst to Econ Dir International Bank for Reconstruction and Development 1966–67; HM Treasy: reinstated 1968, princ private sec to Paymaster Gen 1973, princ private sec to Chllr of Duchy of Lancaster 1974, asst sec 1975, head of Fin Inst Div 1977–80 (Banking Act 1979, Credits Unions Act 1979), press sec to Chllr of Exchequer 1980–82, head of Information 1980–82; gen mangr corp planning Dunlop Ltd 1982–83, dir of mktg National Girobank 1983–86, marketing conslt FI Group plc (Software) 1986–89; memb Fin Servs Act Tbnl 1986–89, full-time chm and first cmmr Building Societies Cmmn 1991–94 (dep chm 1989–91), dir SIB 1993–96, memb Regulatory Bd Lloyds of London 1995–98 (dir of regulation 1995), memb Lloyds Prudential Supervisory Gp 1998–2001; chm: Arrow Broadcasting (CLT subsid) 1994–97, Homeowners Friendly Society Ltd 1996–98; dir: Mercantile Group plc, Mercantile Credit Co Ltd, London and Manchester Group plc 1986–89, BAT Industries plc 1996–98, Zurich Financial Services AG 1998–2007, TU Fund Managers Ltd 2000–; IWF London: fndr memb 1983, pres 1986–89 and 2001–; vice-pres: Building Socs Assoc 1995–, Int Women's Forum 1997–2001; chm Leadership Fndn Washington DC 2005–07 (dir 1997–2007, also ex officio dir Int Women's Forum Washington DC 2005–); cmmr National Lottery 2000–02; memb: Ct Cranfield Univ (formerly Cranfield Inst of Technol) 1992–, Cncl Royal Coll of Music 1997–2007; dir: Opera North 1993–98, Moorfields Eye Hosp Tst 1994–2000; directing fell St George's House Windsor Castle 1986–89; fell UCL 1988, hon fell Newnham Coll Cambridge 1995 (assoc fell 1986–95); FRSA 1985, CIMgt 1992, Hon RMC 2009; *Publications* Mutuality for the Twenty First Century Centre for the Study of Financial Innovation (1998); *Recreations* music, reading, languages, Greece; *Clubs* Athenaeum; *Style*— Mrs Rosalind Gilmore, CB; ✉ 3 Clarendon Mews, London W2 2NR (✆ and fax 020 7402 8554)

GILMORE, Sheila; *b* 1 October 1949, Aberdeen; *Educ* Univ of Kent at Canterbury, Univ of Edinburgh; *m* Brian; 4 c; *Career* cncllr Edinburgh DC 1991–2007, MP (Lab) Edinburgh E 2010–15; *Style*— Mrs Sheila Gilmore; ✉ House of Commons, London SW1A 0AA

GILMOUR, David Jon; CBE (2003); s of Douglas Graham Gilmour, and (Edith) Sylvia, *née* Wilson; *b* 6 March 1946; *Educ* Perse Sch for Boys, Cambridge Coll of Arts & Technol; *m*; 7 c; *Career* musician and singer; with Pink Floyd 1968–; albums with Pink Floyd incl: Atom Heart Mother (1970), Dark Side of the Moon (1973), The Wall (1979), The Final Cut (1983), A Momentary Lapse of Reason (1987), The Division Bell (1994), Pulse (1995); solo albums: David Gilmour (1978), About Face (1984), In Concert (live, 2002); Lifetime Achievement Ivor Novello Award 2008; *Recreations* literature, films, aviation, sailing; *Style*— David Gilmour, Esq, CBE

GILMOUR, (Hon) Sir David Robert; 4 Bt (UK 1926), of Liberton and Craigmillar, Co Midlothian; s of Baron Gilmour of Craigmillar, PC (3 Bt, Life Peer, d 2007), and Lady Caroline Margaret Montagu Douglas Scott (d 2004), da of 8 Duke of Buccleuch and Queensberry; *b* 14 November 1952; *Educ* Eton, Balliol Coll Oxford; *m* 1975, Sarah Anne, da of late Michael Bradstock, of Clunas, Nairn; 3 da (Rachel b 1977, Katharine b 1984, Laura b 1985), 1 s (Alexander b 1980); *Heir* s, Alexander Gilmour; *Career* writer; contrib: Spectator, Literary Review, New York Review of Books; Alistair Horne fell St Antony's Coll Oxford 1996–97; FRSL; *Books* Dispossessed: The Ordeal of The Palestinians 1917–80 (1980), Lebanon: The Fractured Country (1983), The Transformation of Spain: From Franco to the Constitutional Monarchy (1985), The Last Leopard: A Life of Giuseppe di Lampedusa (1988), The Hungry Generations (1991), Cities of Spain (1992), Curzon (1994, Duff Cooper Prize), The French and their Revolution (ed, 1998), Paris and Elsewhere (ed, 1998), The Long Recessional: The Imperial Life of Rudyard Kipling (2002, Elizabeth Longford Prize), The Ruling Caste: Imperial Lives in the Victorian Raj (2005), The Pursuit of Italy: A History of a Land, its Regions and their Peoples (2011); *Recreations* cricket, gardening, opera; *Clubs* Brooks's; *Style*— Sir David Gilmour, Bt, FRSL; ✉ The Barn House, Alkerton, Oxfordshire OX15 6NL (✆ 01295 678673, e-mail gilmourdr@aol.com)

GILMOUR, Ewen Hamilton; s of Lt Cdr Patrick Dalrymple Gilmour (d 1988), and Lorna Mary, *née* Dore (d 2011); *b* 16 August 1953; *Educ* Rugby Sch, Downing Coll Cambridge; *m* 3 June 1978, Nicola, da of Maarten Van Mesdag; 3 s (James b 1980, Rowallan b 1982, Fergus b 1985), 1 da (Iona b 1990); *Career* CA; KPMG 1974–80, Charterhouse Bank Ltd 1980–93 (dir 1987), Lloyd's of London 1993–95, Amlin plc 1995–98, chief exec Chaucer Holdings plc 2000–09 (dir 1998–2009), dep chm Lloyd's of London 2006–10; chm: Hampden Agencies Ltd 2010–, Antares Managing Agency Ltd 2014–, Starstone Underwriting Ltd 2015–; memb Lloyd's Enforcement Bd 2012–; FCA 1979 (ACA); *Recreations* cricket, golf, tennis; *Clubs* Boodles, City of London, Invalids, I Zingari, MCC, Butterflies, Armadillos, Stragglers of Asia, Band of Brothers, Royal Wimbledon Golf; *Style*— Ewen Gilmour, Esq; ✉ 20 Arthur Road, London SW19 7DZ

GILMOUR, His Hon Nigel Benjamin Douglas; QC (1990); s of Benjamin Waterfall Gilmour (d 1967), and Barbara Mary, *née* Till (d 2001); *b* 21 November 1947; *Educ* Tettenhall Coll, Univ of Liverpool (LLB); *m* 1972, Isobel Ann Harborow; 2 da (Katy b 28 Feb 1977, Alison b 1 Oct 1988); *Career* called to the Bar Inner Temple 1970, recorder 1990–, circuit judge (Northern Circuit) 2000–13; memb Hon Soc of Inner Temple; *Recreations* wine, gardening; *Style*— His Hon Nigel Gilmour, QC

GIMBLETT, Richard; s of Frederick Gareth Robert Gimblett, of Yorks, and Margaret, *née* Cornford; *b* 7 April 1959, London; *Educ* Desborough Comp Sch Maidenhead, Jesus Coll Oxford (BA), Inns of Court Sch of Law; *m* 21 March 1987, Ruth, *née* Dyson; 1 s (Alexander James Leathley b 12 Aug 1988), 1 da (Hannah Catherine Elizabeth b 4 July 1990); *Career* called to the Bar 1982, admitted slr 1990; private practice barrister 1983–84, legal advsr CAA 1985–88, barr and slr Norton Rose 1988–94, Barlow, Lyde & Gilbert: slr 1994–1996, ptnr 1996–; memb Law Soc 1990; dir FTO Tst Fund Ltd 1994–; *Recreations* golf, hill running, reading; *Style*— Richard Gimblett, Esq

GINSBERG, Prof Lionel; s of Henry Ginsberg (d 1989), of London, and Rosalind, *née* Veltman; *b* 18 April 1955; *Educ* Haberdashers' Aske's, Middx Hosp Med Sch Univ of London (BSc, PhD, MB BS, Betuel prize); *m* m 1, 8 June 1980, Dr Andrea Marguerite Cobon (d 1995), da of Herbert Frederick Cobon (d 2006); 2 da (Amelia b 16 Feb 1984, Constance May b 1 June 1989), 2 s (Louis b 12 July 1985 d 26 Nov 1985, Tobias b 11 Jan 1988); m 2, 4 April 1998, Sue, *née* Byford; *Career* MRC res student Dept of Biology as Applied to Med Middx Hosp Med Sch 1976–79, visiting specialist Nat Insts of Health Bethesda Maryland USA 1981, house physician The Middx Hosp 1982–83, house surgn N Middx Hosp 1983; SHO: in gen med (endocrinology and metabolism) Hammersmith Hosp 1983–84, in neurology The Nat Hosp Queen Square 1984; resident med offr in cardiology Nat Heart Hosp 1984–85, locum med registrar St Mary's Hosp Paddington 1985; registrar: in med (endocrinology) Hammersmith Hosp 1985, in neurology Royal Free Hosp 1985–87, in neurology The Nat Hosps 1987–88; visiting scientist Nat Insts of Health Bethesda Maryland 1988–89, clinical lectr in neurology Univ of Cambridge and hon sr registrar in neurology Addenbrooke's Hosp 1990–92, sr lectr in neurology Royal Free Hosp Sch of Med and Inst of Neurology Univ of London 1992–98, hon sr lectr in neurology Univ of London 1998–2005, campus sub-dean and student support tutor UCL Medical Sch 2005–, prof of clinical neurology UCL 2010–; conslt neurologist: Royal Free Hosp 1992–, Princess Grace Hosp 1998–2000, King's Oak Hosp Enfield 1999–2005, Nat Hosp for Neurology and Neurosurgery Queen Square 1992–98 (hon conslt 1998–), Queen Elizabeth II Hosp Welwyn Garden City 1992–98, Chase Farm Hosp Enfield 1998–2005, UCL Hosps 2010–; memb Assoc of Br Neurologists 1992 (memb Cncl 2008–12, hon treas 2011–15); FRCP, FHEA; *Books* Lecture Notes on Neurology (1999, 2005 and 2010); also author of numerous research articles in academic jls; *Recreations* pianoforte, walking, reading; *Style*— Prof Lionel Ginsberg; ✉ Department of Clinical Neurosciences, Royal Free Hospital, Pond Street, London NW3 2QG (✆ 020 7317 7543, e-mail lionel.ginsberg@nhs.net)

GIRVAN, Rt Hon Sir (Frederick) Paul Girvan; kt (1995), PC (2007); s of Robert Frederick Girvan (d 2000), of Holywood, Belfast, and Martha Patricia, *née* Barron (d 1989); *b* 20 October 1948; *Educ* Larne GS, Belfast Royal Acad, Clare Coll Cambridge (BA), Queen's Univ Belfast; *m* 20 July 1974, Karen Elizabeth, *née* Joyce; 1 da (Rebecca Jane b 19 March 1977), 2 s (Brian Richard b 12 Dec 1978, Peter Michael b 19 Jan 1980); *Career* called to the Bar NI 1971, called to the Inner Bar (QC) 1984, jr crown counsel (Chancery) 1981–84, judge of the High Court of Justice NI 1995–2007, chancery judge 1997–2004, a Lord Justice of Appeal NI 2007–15; hon bencher Gray's Inn; chm NI Law Reform Advsy Ctee 1997–2004 (memb 1994–2004); memb Standing Advsy Ctee on Human Rights 1985–87; chllr Archdiocese of Armagh; *Recreations* reading, travel, badminton, cycling, walking, modern languages, cooking, golf; *Style*— The Rt Hon Sir Paul Girvan

G

GISSING, Jason; s of Graham Gissing, and Mikiko Gissing; *b* 25 October 1970; *Educ* Oundle, Worcester Coll Oxford; *m* 2002, Katinka, *née* Naess; 2 s, 2 da; *Career* Goldman Sachs 1992–2000, co-fndr and commercial dir Ocado 2000–14, ret (full-year maiden profit on sales of £1 billion 2014, Which? Online Retailer of the Year 2009, 2010, 2011, 2012 and 2014, The Grocer Green Retailer of the Year 2009, Oracle World Retailer of the Year 2010); supporter: Greenpeace, Rootcamp; *Recreations* tennis, skiing, football, yoga, history; *Clubs* Queens, Campden Hill Lawn Tennis, 5 Hertford St; *Style*— Jason Gissing, Esq; ✉ e-mail jason@jasongissing.com

GITSHAM, Julian Mark; s of Michael Leonard Gitsham, and Sylvia, *née* Wood; *b* 11 May 1965; *Educ* Knutsford Co HS, Oxford Poly (BA, DipArch, Dip Urban Design, Les Townshend Award, Barton Willmore Prize); *m* 31 Aug 1987, Nicola Sarah, *née* Hyde; 2 da (Honor Olivia b 22 April 1998, Phoebe Hope b 18 Sept 2000); *Career* architect; architectural asst Aldington Craig and Collinge Architects 1989–92, project architect Hants Co Architects Dept 1992–95; projects incl: Hants Record Office (RIBA Award, Civic Tst Award), Tadley Library, Hackney Community Coll (RIBA Award, Civic Tst Award), South Downs Coll, Glen House Children's Secure Unit; sr architect Portcullis House London Michael Hopkins and Partners 1996–99, ptnr Feilden Clegg Bradley Architects LLP 1999–2014, principal Hassell 2014–; projects incl: housing Peabody Tst Fulham, new museum millennium project RAF Hendon, new museum devpt RAF Museum Cosford, mixed use project Mildmay Mission Hosp, Shoreditch Tabernacle Baptist Church and Peabody Tst, housing Venture Devpts Putney; Housing Design Award 1999; ARB 1990, RIBA 1990; *Recreations* waterskiing, cinema, music, mountain biking; *Clubs* Oxford Wakeboard and Ski; *Style*— Julian Gitsham, Esq; ✉ Hassell, Level 2, Morelands, 17 – 21 Old Street, Clerkenwell, London EC1V 9HL

GITTUS, Prof John Henry; *b* 25 July 1930; *Educ* Univ of London (BSc, DSc), KTH Stockholm (DTech); *m* 23 May 1953, Rosemary Ann, da of John Geeves; 1 s (Michael John b 7 April 1954), 2 da (Sara Ann b 19 Aug 1956, Mary Ann b 8 Aug 1958); *Career* res worker Br Cast Iron Res Assoc 1951–56 (apprentice 1947–51), gp ldr Mond Nickel R&D Laboratories Birmingham 1956–60; UKAEA: res mangr Springfields 1960–80, head of water reactor fuel devpt 1980–81, head Atomic Energy Tech Branch Harwell 1981–83, dir of water reactor res Harwell 1981–83, dir of safety 1983–87, dir of communications 1987–89; dir gen Br Nuclear Industry Forum 1989–93 (currently conslt); fndr sr ptnr John Gittus & Associates (sci and public affrs consultancy) 1993–, sr ptnr NUSYS (nuclear conslts) Paris 1995–; working memb Lloyd's Nuclear Syndicate 1996–; conslt: Argonne Nat Laboratory Chicago 1968, Oak Ridge Nat Laboratory Tennessee 1969, ESKOM South Africa 1997–, GE Healthcare (Amersham, radio-pharmaceuticals) 1999–, Cox Insurance Holdings plc 1999–2002, Chaucer Holdings plc 2002–, NECSA South Africa 2006–; Regents prof UCLA 1990–, prof Univ of Plymouth 1997–, Royal Acad of Engrg prof 2006–; visiting prof: École Polytechnique Fédérale Lausanne Switzerland 1976, Univ of Nancy 1985; interpreter's certificate in French; FREng 1989, FIMechE, FIM, FIS, memb Mensa; *Books* Uranium (1963), Creep, Viscoelasticity and Creep-Fracture in Solids (1976), Irradiation Effects in Crystalline Solids (1980); *Recreations* old motor cars, golf, swimming; *Clubs* IOD, RSM; *Style*— Prof John Gittus, FREng; ✉ Chaucer Holdings plc, 9 Devonshire Square, Cutlers Gardens, London EC2M 4WL (✆ 020 7397 9700, mobile 07775 898449, e-mail john@gittus.com)

GIVAN, Paul Jonathan; MLA; *b* 12 October 1981, Lisburn, Co Antrim; *Educ* Laurelhill Community Coll Lisburn, Univ of Ulster; *Career* MLA (DUP) Lagan Valley 2010–; *Style*— Paul Givan, Esq, MLA; ✉ Northern Ireland Assembly, Parliament Buildings, Belfast BT4 3XX

GIVEN, Andrew Ferguson; s of Edward F Given, CMG, CVO, of Lymington, and Philida Naomi, *née* Bullwinkle; *b* 14 November 1947; *Educ* Charterhouse, Lincoln Coll Oxford; *m* 18 Sept 1971 (sep), Morwenna, da of Frederic Neil Ritchie, of Italy; 2 da (Davina, Catriona); *Career* asst to md Union Corp UK Ltd 1969–73, exec dir James Finlay Corporation 1974–75; Northern Telecom Ltd (Canada): various positions 1977–82, asst treas 1982–83, treas and controller Bell-Northern Research 1984–87, vice-pres finance Northern Telecom Europe 1987–88; gp finance controller Plessey Group plc 1988–89, gp finance dir then dep chief exec Logica plc 1990–2002; non-exec dir: Spectris plc 2001–, VT Gp plc 2002–, Spirent Communications plc until 2006, Morgan Crucible Co plc 2007–; FRSA; *Recreations* sailing, photography, travel, running; *Clubs* Army and Navy; *Style*— A F Given

GIZZI, Julian Anthony; s of Antonio Gizzi, and Vilma Gizzi; *b* Hove, E Sussex; *Educ* Downside, Magdalene Coll Cambridge (MA); *Career* admitted slr 1981; ptnr Beachcroft LLP (formerly Beachcroft Wansbroughs) 1986– (slr 1981–86); memb Structure and Governance Working Gp Dearing Ctee 1993; FRSA 1997; *Publications* Duties and Powers (1996), Butterworths' Law of Education (gen ed, 2000), VAT for Solicitors (3 edn, 2002); *Style*— Julian Gizzi, Esq; ✉ Beachcroft LLP, 100 Fetter Lane, London EC4A 1BN (✆ 020 7242 1011, fax 020 7894 6640, e-mail jgizzi@beachcroft.co.uk)

GLADSTONE, Emma; da of Tim Gladstone, and Caroline, *née* Crawley; *b* 12 November 1960, London; *Educ* Camden Sch for Girls, Manchester Univ (BA), Trinity Laban (PGCert); *m* 17 April 2004, Barnaby Stone; 1 da (Matilda Gladstone b 11 March 1994); 1 step s (Matthew), 1 step da (Mair); *Career* ind dancer 1977–1997, assoc dir The Place Theatre 1997–2003, artistic prodr and programmer Salder's Wells Theatre 2005–13, artistic dir Rolex Mentor Protégé Arts Weekend Venice 2013, artistic dir and chief exec Dance Umbrella 2013–; mentor Dance UK Leverhulme Tst, advsr Family Arts Campaign PAL Labs, memb What Next?, memb Nat Dance Network; hon fell Trinity Laban 2014; RSA 2014; *Books* Body Language #1–7 (ed, 2012); *Clubs* 2 Brydges Place; *Style*— Ms Emma Gladstone; ✉ Dance Umbrella, 1 Brewery Square, London SE1 2LF (☎ 020 707 1200, e-mail emmag@danceumbrella.co.uk, Twitter @gladstone_bag)

GLADSTONE OF CAPENOCH, Robert Hamilton; er s of John Gladstone of Capenoch, TD (d 1977), and his 2 w, Diana Rosamond Maud Fleming, *née* Hamilton; gggs of Thomas Steuart Gladstone, JP, who acquired Capenoch 1850; *b* 17 July 1953; *Educ* Eton, Magdalene Coll Cambridge (MA); *m* 16 Jan 1982, Margaret Jane, da of Brig Berenger Colborne Bradford, DSO, MBE, MC, of Kincardine, Kincardine O'Neil, Aberdeenshire; 2 s (John, Harry (twins) b 3 March 1983), 1 da (Catharine b 13 April 1986); *Career* chartered surveyor; John Sale & Partners 1974–78, Smiths-Gore 1978–2013; FRICS 1989 (ARICS 1977); *Clubs* Whistle, '71; *Style*— Robert Gladstone of Capenoch; ✉ Capenoch, Thornhill, Dumfriesshire (☎ 01848 330261)

GLADWELL, David John; s of Leonard Butterworth Gladwell (d 1971), of Clayhidon Devon, and Violet Rita, *née* Lloyd-Jones (d 1977); *b* 13 March 1947, Llandrillo yn Rhôs, Sir Ddinbych; *Educ* Blundell's, Univ of Exeter (LLM), Queen Mary Coll London (Dip), Univ of Greenwich (MSc); *m* 24 June 1988, Ragnhild, *née* Kuhbier; 1 step s (Olok Dominic Banerjee b 1972); *Career* J Henry Schroder Wagg Merchant bankers 1966–69, called to the Bar Gray's Inn 1972 (bencher 2004), practising barr 1972–74, Office of the Registrar of Criminal Appeals 1974–81; Lord Chllr's Dept: Private Law Div 1982–87, Int Div 1988–93, head Law Reform Div 1993–96, head Civil Justice Div 1996–99, head of sr judicial appts 1999–2001, chm Review of Criminal Immunity of the State 2001–03, head Constitutional Policy 2003, head Civil Appeals Office and Master in the Court of Appeal Civil Div 2003–07, cnsllr 2007–; hon cnsllr Oxleas NHS Tst 2007–, hon amputee rehabilitation cnsllr Guy's and St Thomas' NHS Tst 2010–15; adjunct prof Sturm Coll of Law Univ of Denver 2007–08; chm: Working Gp on the Establishment of the Patents County Court 1986–87, Cncl of Europe Euro Ctee on Legal Co-operation 1992–93 (vice-chm 1991–92), Cncl of Europe Working Gp on Efficiency of Justice 1999–2000; sec Judicial Working Gp on Ethics 2002; memb: Editorial Advsy Panel Intellectual Property in Business 1988–92, Cncl of Europe Missions to Russian Fedn 1997–2006 and Ukraine 2010–11, Civil Justice Cncl 1998–2000, CEDR Advsy Cncl 1998–2000, Working Gp on a single European Patent Court 1999–2000, Exec Ctee Anglo-Russian Law Assoc 2002– (tstee 2009–), European Bd Int Assoc for Ct Administration 2005–07; memb: EU Assessment Missions to Albania and Croatia 2002 and Ukraine 2006, UK Govt Assessment Mission to Turkey 2003, Cwlth Assessment Missions to Zambia 2007 and Guyana 2008; workshops for the Palestinian judiciary 2014; accredited mediator CEDR; fell Soc for Advanced Legal Studies 1999 (memb Advsy Cncl 2003–07), memb Br Assoc for Counselling and Psychotherapy (MBACP Registered and Accredited) 2008; *Publications* The Exhaustion of Intellectual Property Rights (1986), Patent Litigation (1989), The Patents County Court (1989), Are You Ready for Woolf? (1999), The Civil Justice Reforms in England and Wales (1999), Modern Litigation Culture (2000), Judicial Appointments (2001), Legal Aid in the Republic of Georgia (jtly, 2002), Legal Aid in Montenegro (jtly, 2002), Mediation and the Courts (2004), Manual of Civil Appeals (contrib ed, 2004), Legal Aid in Ukraine (2008), School is only one Influence on Children (2014), The Experience of Sudden Disability (2015), Ethics and Research into Vulnerable Groups (2015); *Recreations* pretending not to be frightened on Crib Goch, seeking new experiences, concert and opera-going; *Clubs* Garrick; *Style*— David Gladwell, Esq; ✉ Rosemary Lane, Clayhidon, Cullompton, Devon EX15 3PG (e-mail counsellor@unseen.is, website http://davidgladwell-counsellor.london/)

GLAISTER, Lesley Gillian; da of Leonard Oliver Richard Glaister (d 1981), and Maureen Jillian, *née* Crowley; *b* 4 October 1956; *Educ* Deben HS Felixstowe, Open Univ (BA), Univ of Sheffield (MA); *m* 1, 1976 (m dis 1984), Christopher French; 2 s (Joseph William French b 1978, Joshua James French 1981); 1 s by subsequent partner (Leo Stewart-Glaister b 1988); m 2, 1993 (m dis 1998), Dr Robert Murphy; m 3, 2001, Andrew Greig; *Career* adult educn tutor 1982–90, full time writer and teacher of creative writing 1990–; winner: Somerset Maugham Award 1991, Betty Trask Award 1991; memb Soc of Authors 1991; FRSL 1994; *Plays* Birdcalls (Crucible Theatre Sheffield) 2003; *Books* Honour Thy Father (1990), Trick-or-Treat (1991), Digging to Australia (1992), Limestone and Clay (1993), Partial Eclipse (1994), Private Parts of Women (1996), Easy Peasy (1997), Sheer Blue Bliss (1999), Now You See Me (2001), As Far As You Can Go (2004), Nina Todd Has Gone (2007); *Style*— Ms Lesley Glaister, FRSL; ✉ c/o Bill Hamilton, A M Heath & Co, 6 Warwick Court, London WC1R 5JD (☎ 020 7242 2811)

GLAISTER, Prof Stephen; CBE (1998); *Educ* Univ of London (PhD); *Career* LSE: teaching asst 1968–69, lectr in econs 1969–74 and 1977–78, Rees Jeffreys res fell in social and environmental aspects of the devpt of roads and road transport 1974–77, Cassel reader in econs 1978–94, chm Academic Studies Ctee 1991–93, Cassel reader in econ geography 1994–98, assoc 1999–; prof of transport and infrastructure Dept of Civil and Environmental Engrg Imperial Coll London 1998–, dir Railway Technol Strategy Centre Imperial Coll London 1998–; partnership dir Tube Lines 2009–10; dir RAC Fndn 2008–; econ advsr: Br Rail Policy Unit and InterCity Strategy 1980–93, Office of Gas Supply 1996–2002; econ advsr and non-exec memb Advsy Bd Rail Regulator 1993–2001, special advsr Parly Select Ctee on Transport 1981–83 and 1988–90, advsr to buses sub-gp Cmmn for Integrated Transport 1999–2003; memb: Ind Advsy Ctee on Trunk Road Assessment 1977–81, Jt Sci Res Cncl/Social Sci Res Cncl Transport Ctee 1978–80, Non-Exec Bd London Regnl Transport 1984–93, London First Transport Initiative 1995–2002, Central London Ptnrship Advsy Gp 1997–2002, Review of Road Charging Options for London Working Gp 1998–2000, Advsy Ctee Centre for the Study of Regulated Industries 1999–, Steering Gp for Road Pricing Feasibility Study Dept for Transport 2003–; Transport for London: memb Bd 2000–08, memb Surface Panel 2000–08, memb Fin Panel 2000–08, memb Fin Ctee 2000–08, memb Rail Panel 2000–03, vice-chair Underground Advsy Panel 2003–08; ed Economica 1979–82, managing ed Jl of Transport Economics and Policy 1987–99; tstee Rees Jeffreys Road Fund 1979; fell Tport Research Fndn; FICE, FCGI; *Style*— Prof Stephen Glaister, CBE; ✉ RAC Foundation, 89 Pall Mall, London SW1Y 5HS (☎ 020 7747 3485, mobile 07973 206389, e-mail stephen.glaister@racfoundation.org, website www.racfoundation.org)

GLANFIELD, Jonathan James (Joe); s of Robert Glanfield, of Exmouth, Devon, and Beverley Glanfield; *b* 6 August 1979, Sutton, Surrey; *Educ* Exmouth Community Coll; *Career* yachtsman; achievements (with Nick Rogers, *qv*) in 470 class incl: fourth place Olympic Games Sydney 2000, Silver medal World Championships 2001, Bronze medal European Championships 2002, Silver medal Pre-Olympics Athens 2003, Gold medal Princes Sofia Regatta Palma 2004, Bronze medal World Championship 2004, Silver medal Olympic Games Athens 2004, Gold medal European Championships 2004 and 2005, Gold medal Qingdao Int Regatta 2006, Gold medal Skandia Sail for Gold Regatta 2006, Gold medal Rolex Miami OCR 2007, Silver medal Olympic Test Event Qingdao 2007, Silver medal Olympic Games Beijng 2008; ranked No 1 (470 class) Int Sailing Fedn (ISAF) world rankings 2004; *Style*— Joe Glanfield, Esq; ✉ website www.rogersglanfield.com

GLANVILLE, Brian Lester; s of James Arthur Glanville (d 1960), and Florence, *née* Manches (d 1984); *b* 24 September 1931; *Educ* Charterhouse; *m* 1959, Elizabeth Pamela de Boer, da of Fritz Manasse (d 1961); 2 s (Mark, Toby), 2 da (Elizabeth, Josephine); *Career* novelist, journalist, playwright; football corr and sports columnist: The Sunday Times 1958–92, The People 1992–96, The Times 1996–98, The Sunday Times 1998–; lit advsr Bodley Head 1958–62; *Books* novels incl: Along The Arno, The Bankrupts, Diamond, The Rise of Gerry Logan, The Olympian, A Roman Marriage, The Artist Type, A Second Home, The Financiers, A Cry of Crickets, The Comic, Kissing America, The Catacomb, Dictators; short story collections: A Bad Streak, The Director's Wife, The Thing He Loves, The King of Hackney Marshes, Love is Not Love; Football Memories (autobiography), Story of the World Cup, The Arsenal Stadium History, England's Managers, stage musical Underneath The Arches (co-author, 1981–83), A Visit to the Villa (play for stage and radio), The Real Arsenal; *Style*— Brian Glanville, Esq; ✉ 160 Holland Park Avenue, London W11 4UH (☎ 020 7603 6908)

GLASER, Prof Mark Gordon; s of Asher Alfred Glaser (d 1987), and Minnie, *née* Nasilewitz (d 1983); *b* 1 December 1944; *Educ* St Clement Dane's GS, Charing Cross Hosp Med Sch (MB BS, MRCS LRCP, DMRT); *Career* conslt in radiotherapy and oncology Charing Cross Hosp 1980–, hon conslt radiotherapist Hammersmith Hosp and Postgrad Med Sch 1980–, clinical teacher Univ of London 1981–, clinical dir Riverside HA Cancer Servs 1990–, dir Depts of Radiotherapy Hammersmith and Charing Cross Hosp 1994–, chief of cancer services Imperial Coll Healthcare NHS Tst 2008–13, dep clinical prog dir (cancer and surgery) Imperial Coll Healthcare NHS Tst 2011–13; visiting prof Yale Univ USA 1984, visiting prof and research scholar Massachusetts Gen Hosp Boston (Harvard Univ) 2006–, visiting prof Dept of High Energy Physics Imperial Coll London 2012–; author of papers on cancer and radiation therapy; memb Univ of London: Senate 1981–, Military Educn Ctee 1982–84, Central Research Fund Ctee 1982–84, Collegiate Cncl 1987–89, Academic Cncl 1989–; chm Gunnar Nilsson Cancer Treatment Fund 2000–, medical advsr Maggie's Centres 2013–; FFR RCSI 1977, FRCR 1978; *Recreations* walking, philosophy, comparative religion; *Clubs* Reform; *Style*— Professor Mark Glaser; ✉ Department of High Energy Physics, Imperial College London, Blackett Laboratory, Prince Consort Road, London SW7 2BW (☎ 020 7594 7823)

GLASGOW, Edwin John; CBE (1998), QC (1987); s of Richard Edwin Glasgow, and Mary, *née* Markby; *b* 3 August 1945; *Educ* St Joseph's Coll Ipswich, UCL; *m* 1967, Janet, *née* Coleman; 1 s (Oliver Edwin James b 17 Jan 1971), 1 da (Louise Victoria Mary b 20 March 1972); *Career* Met Police 1961–64; called to the Bar Gray's Inn 1969 (bencher 1994); barr specialising in commercial litigation, administrative and public law and public inquiries, currently memb of chambers 39 Essex St; inquiries incl: Bradford Fire, Hillsborough, Piper Alpha, Herald of Free Enterprise, Guiness DTI, Guildford Four, Alison Halford, Bloody Sunday; chm Fin Reporting Review Panel 1991–98; vice-chm Thames Ditton CC 2001–; tstee: London Opera Players, Harlequin FC (chm), Mary Glasgow Language Tst (chm); Lawyer of the Year Legal Business Awards 2005; *Recreations* music, family, France; *Clubs* RAC (steward); *Style*— Edwin Glasgow, Esq, CBE, QC; ✉ Copper Hall, Thames Ditton, Surrey KT7 0BX; Entrechaux, Vaulcluse, France; 39 Essex Street, London WC2R 3AT (☎ 020 7832 1111)

GLASGOW, 10 Earl of (S 1703); Patrick Robin Archibald Boyle; DL (Ayrshire 2000); also Lord Boyle (S 1699), Lord Boyle of Kelburn (S 1703), Baron Fairlie (UK 1897); s of Rear Adm 9 Earl of Glasgow, CB, DSC (d 1984), and his 1 wife Dorothea (d 2006), only da of Sir Archibald Lyle, 2 Bt; *b* 30 July 1939; *Educ* Eton, Sorbonne; *m* 29 Nov 1975, Isabel Mary, da of George Douglas James; 1 s (Hon David Boyle b 1978), 1 da (Lady Alice Dorothy b 1981); *Heir* s, Hon David Boyle (Viscount of Kelburn); *Career* Sub-Lt RNR 1960; known professionally as Patrick Boyle; asst dir Woodfall Films 1961–64, freelance asst dir 1965–68, TV documentary producer/dir Yorkshire Television 1968–70, freelance TV documentary producer/dir working for BBC, Yorkshire Television, ATV, Central and Scottish Television 1971–81; formed Kelburn Country Centre (a leisure park created from part of the family estate) 1977, currently managing Kelburn Country Centre; sits as Lib Dem in House of Lords 2004–; chm Largs Viking Festival 1981–85, dir Ayrshire and Arran Tourist Bd 1999–2000 and 2003–04; *Recreations* theatre, cinema, opera; *Style*— The Rt Hon the Earl of Glasgow, DL; ✉ Kelburn, Fairlie, Ayrshire KA29 0BE (☎ 01475 568204); Kelburn Country Centre, Fairlie, Ayrshire KA29 0BE (☎ 01475 568685); House of Lords, London SW1A 0PW (020 7219 5419)

GLASGOW AND GALLOWAY, Dean of; *see:* Duncan, Very Rev Dr Gregor

GLASGOW AND GALLOWAY, Bishop of 2010–; Rt Rev Dr Gregor Duthie Duncan; s of Edwin John Duncan (d 2001), of Largs, and Janet Brown, *née* Simpson (d 2009); *b* 11 October 1950; *Educ* Allan Glen's Sch Glasgow, Univ of Glasgow (MA), Clare Coll Cambridge (PhD), Oriel Coll Oxford (BA), Ripon Coll Cuddesdon; *Career* research asst Univ of Oxford 1976–80; ordained: deacon 1983, priest 1984; curate Oakham with Hambleton and Egleton and Braunston with Brooke 1983–86, chaplain Edinburgh Theol Coll 1987–89, rector St Columba's Largs 1989–99, rector St Ninian's Glasgow 1999–2010, dean Dio of Glasgow and Galloway 1996–2010; memb Gen Synod Scottish Episcopal Church 1990–98, 2000–03 and 2006– (former tutor Theol Inst); *Style*— The Rt Rev the Bishop of Glasgow and Galloway; ✉ Bishop's Office, Diocese of Glasgow and Galloway, 5 St Vincent Place, Glasgow G1 2DH

GLASS, David Peter; s of Max Glass, of Lisbon, Portugal, and Sigrid, *née* Dressler; *b* 9 December 1957, Zurich, Switzerland; *Educ* Boundstone Comp Sch, London Sch of Contemporary Dance, Ecole Etienne Decroux Paris, Alvin Ailey Sch New York, Jean Louis Barrault Carré Sch Paris; *m* 2000, Valerie Sophie Berdaa; *Career* writer and dir 1982–; dancer and mime artist with Community Arts Theatre 1976–77, street theatre France, England and Italy 1977, began int solo career 1977; written and directed shows incl: Phoenix Dance Co, English Dance Theatre, Nottingham Playhouse, Crucible Theatre, Mime Theatre Project, Scottish Opera, Opera Circus, Scottish Chamber Orchestra, Hong Kong Symphony Orchestra, Playbox Theatre Co, Yellow Earth Theatre Co, Polka Theatre's Tate Gallery Centenary prodn; artistic dir David Glass Ensemble 1989–; David Glass Ensemble prodns incl: first adaptation of Popeye 1989, Bozo's Dead 1990, Gormenghast 1991–94, Les Enfants du Paradis 1993, The Mosquito Coast (Young Vic) 1995, Lucky (Young Vic) 1995 (also at Purcell Room 1996), first musical adaptation of La Dolce Vita 1996, Glassworks (performed internationally) 1996–98, The Lost Child Trilogy 1998–2000: The Hansel Gretel Machine, The Lost Child, The Red Thread (performed internationally), Off the Wall (UK tour) 2000, Unheimlich Spine (Riverside Studios London) 2001 2001; assoc dir feature film Beg!, movement conslt Mad and her Dad (Lyric) 1995; artistic dir Br Summer Sch of Mime, fndr and artistic dir of Southern Int Mime Festival; teacher Central Establishment of Physical Theatre, guest tutor/mentor Central Sch of Speech and Drama; memb Panel Arts Cncl; *Style*— David Glass, Esq

GLASS, Deborah Anne; OBE (2012); da of Reuben Glass, of Melbourne, Aust, and Pauline, *née* Ritcher; *b* 15 September 1959; *Educ* Monash Univ Melbourne (BA, LLB); *m* 14 Nov 1997, Jonathan Mirsky; *Career* sr dir Hong Kong Securities and Futures Cmmn 1989–98, chief exec Investment Mgmnt Regulatory Orgn 1998–2000, memb Police Complaints Authy 2001–04, chair Kensington and Chelsea Ind Custody Visitors Panel 2002–04, Ind Police Complaints Cmmn 2004–14 (dep chair 2008–14), ombudsman State of Victoria Australia 2014–; *Publications* contrib to Oxford Jl of Policing; *Recreations* keeping fit and enjoying life with family and friends; *Style*— Ms Deborah Glass, OBE; ✉ Victorian Ombudsman, Level 1, 459 Collins Street, Melbourne 3000, Australia

GLASSON, Prof John; s of John Glasson, and Olive, *née* Palmer; *b* 2 April 1946; *Educ* LSE (BSc), Lancaster Univ (MA); *m* 29 June 1968, Carol; 2 da (Rebecca b 16 March 1971, Claire b 2 May 1974); *Career* economist and planner Craigavon Devpt Corp 1968–69; Oxford Poly (latterly Oxford Brookes Univ): lectr, sr lectr then princ lectr Sch of Planning 1969–80, head Sch of Planning 1980–2003, dir Impacts Assessment Unit 1980–, pro-vice-chllr (research and consultancy) 1998–2002, research dean Sch of Built Environment 2002–07, founding dir Oxford Inst for Sustainable Devpt 2004– (prof emeritus 2007–); registered commr UK Infrastructure Planning Cmmn 2010–; visiting prof: Curtin Univ W Aust 2002–13, UCLan 2007–12; memb: UK DOE Planning Research Advsy Gp 1991–96, HEFCE Research Assessment Panel 1992, 1996 and 2001, ESRC Trg Bd 1998–2004, Strategic Planning Advsy Gp SE of Eng Regnl Assembly; dir Oxfordshire Econ Observatory 2001–; MRTPI 1971, MIMgt 1984, FRSA 1992, Academician AcSS 2009; *Publications* Introduction to Regional Planning (1992), Towards Visitor Impact Management (1995), Introduction to Environmental Impact Assessment (1995, 4 edn 2012), Contemporary Issues in Regional Planning (2002), Regional Planning (2007); ed Natural and Built Environment Series 1993–, Contemporary Issues in Australian Urban and Regional Planning (2015); *Recreations* long distance walking, jogging, running, leisure travel, cinema, reading; *Style*— Professor John Glasson; ✉ Oxford Brookes University, Headington, Oxford OX3 0BP (☎ 01865 483401, fax 01865 483559, e-mail jglasson@brookes.ac.uk)

GLASSPOOL, Frank Harry; s of Lesley William George Glasspool (d 1936), and Isobel, *née* Highfield (d 1992); *b* 14 May 1934; *Educ* Duke of York Royal Mil Sch; *m* 1, 1 April 1961 (m dis 1981), Olive, da of Charles Geddes (d 1982); 1 da (Wendy b 25 Jan 1963), 1 s (Stephen b 2 Nov 1964); m 2, 25 Feb 1984, Rosemary Esther, da of George Edward Saunders; 2 step s (Simon b 21 Dec 1963, Timothy b 7 Oct 1965), 1 step da (Juliette b 25 July 1971); *Career* sr engr Kellogg Int 1961–68, sr ptnr Glasspool & Thaiss 1968–2005 (conslt 2005–); past pres Rotary Club Berkhamsted Bulbourne; CEng, FIStructE 1974, MConsE 1979; *Recreations* tennis, photography, golf; *Clubs* Berkhamsted Bulbourne Rotary; *Style*— Frank Glasspool, Esq; ✉ Barncroft, Peggs Lane, Buckland, Aylesbury, Buckinghamshire HP22 5HX (e-mail frankandrosemary@talktalk.net)

GLASSPOOL, Jonathan; s of Michael Glasspool, and Anna Glasspool; *b* 18 March 1965; *Educ* Tonbridge (music scholar), Trinity Coll Oxford (exhibitioner, BA), Univ of Bristol (MA), Warwick Business Sch (MBA); *m* 1999, Alysoun Owen; 2 da (Alice Rose b 2000, Elizabeth b 2006), 1 s (Theo b 2002); *Career* head of publishing Inst of Mgmnt 1990–93, publisher Butterworth-Heinemann Reed Elsevier plc 1993–98, appointed product dir electronic media div Bloomsbury Publishing plc 1999, dep md A&C Black Ltd 2003, currently md Bloomsbury Academic & Professional and pres Bloomsbury USA; chair Industry Advsy Bd Oxford Brookes Univ, memb Commercial Bd ICAEW; tstee Publishing Trg Centre; memb Elysian Singers London; FRSA; *Publications* Business – the Ultimate Resource (ed, 2002, 3 edn 2011); *Recreations* chamber music; *Style*— Jonathan Glasspool, Esq; ✉ Bloomsbury Academic & Professional, 50 Bedford Square, London WC1B 3DP

GLASTONBURY, Virginia; *née* Cooper; da of Rt Hon Sir Frank Cooper, GCB, CMG (d 2002), and Peggy, *née* Claxton (d 2004); *b* Bromley, Kent; *Educ* Bromley HS GPDST, Lady Margaret Hall Oxford (MA), Coll of Law; *m* 25 Oct 1980, Richard Glastonbury; 1 step s (Simon Richard b 6 Nov 1970); *Career* admitted slr 1982; specialises in PFI/PPP, projects and general real estate; joined as articled clerk Denton Hall & Burgin 1980; Denton Hall: ptnr 1988–2000, memb Bd 1995–2000, managing ptnr UK 1999–2000; Dentons UKMEA LLP (formerly Denton Wilde Sapte then SNR Denton UK LLP): memb Bd 2000–05, managing ptnr UK 2000–02, chief exec 2002–05, ptnr 2005–; memb Law Soc; FRSA; *Recreations* grandchildren, motor sports, travel; *Clubs* IoD (City branch), RSA; *Style*— Mrs Virginia Glastonbury; ✉ Dentons UKMEA LLP, One Fleet Place, London EC4M 7WS (☎ 020 7320 6226, fax 020 7246 7777, e-mail virginia.glastonbury@dentons.com)

GLAZER, Prof Anthony Michael (Mike); *Educ* Univ of St Andrews (BSc), Univ of London (PhD); *Career* postdoctoral asst rising to dir Wolfson Unit for the Sudy of Dielectric Materials Cavendish Lab Univ of Cambridge 1969–76, official fell and tutor in physics Jesus Coll Oxford 1976–, appointed lectr in physics Univ of Oxford 1976, currently emeritus prof of physics Univ of Oxford; visiting prof Univ of Warwick; emeritus fell Jesus Coll Oxford; fndr Oxford Cryosystems; pres British Crystallographic Assoc 1996; *Books* Space Groups for Solid State Scientists (with Gerald Burns, 1978, 3 edn 2012), The Structures of Crystals (1987), Statistical Mechanics: A Survival Guide (with J S Wark, 2001); *Recreations* aviation; *Style*— Prof Mike Glazer; ✉ Condensed Matter Physics, Clarendon Laboratory, Parks Road, Oxford OX1 3PU

GLEADELL, Colin Francis; s of Maj Gen Paul Gleadell, CB, CBE, DSO (d 1988), and Mary, *née* Montgomerie Lind (d 1994); *b* 17 December 1946; *Educ* Downside, Churchill Coll Cambridge (MA); *m* 1988, Sophie Barbara Estella, da of Ernle David Drummond Money; 1 da (Rose Montgomerie b 7 Sept 1993), 1 s (Benjamin Ernle Alexander b 23 July 1998); *Career* res Paul Mellon Fndn for Br Art 1968–71, mangr Crane Arts London 1971–73, freelance art conslt and pt/t musical dir NEMS Records 1974–78, head Modern Art Dept Bonham's Auctioneers 1979–81, freelance art conslt 1982–85, features ed Galleries Magazine 1985–97, salesroom corr Art Monthly 1986–, London corr Art Newsletter 1996–, art sales corr The Daily Telegraph 1997–, art market corr Artnet News 2014–; memb Advsy Ctee 20th Century Br Art Fair 1987–; conslt BBC TV: The Great Picture Chase 1990, Relative Values 1991, Eric Hebborn, Portrait of a Master Forger 1991, Sister Wendy's Grand Tour 1993; art conslt Channel 4 News 1999–; memb Int Assoc of Art Critics 1987; *Publications* numerous exhibition catalogues and articles in specialist art magazines; *Style*— Colin Gleadell, Esq; ✉ e-mail colin@glead.freeserve.co.uk

GLEDHILL, Rt Rev Jonathan Michael; *see:* Lichfield, Bishop of

GLEDHILL, Keith Ainsworth; MBE (1994), DL (Lancs 1986); s of Norman Gledhill (d 1970), of Blackpool, and Louise, *née* Ainsworth (d 1988); *b* 28 August 1932; *Educ* Arnold Sch Blackpool; *m* 7 July 1956, Margaret Irene, da of Joseph Bramwell Burton (d 1970); 1 s (Ian C b 1958); *Career* jr offr MN 1950–54; Nat Serv RAF 1954–56; Norman Gledhill & Co Ltd 1956–65, Delta Metal Co Ltd 1965 (sr exec contract); fndr: Gledhill Water Storage Ltd 1972, Nu-Rad Ltd 1974, Thermal Sense (Energy Conservation Systems) Ltd 1979; past chm Foxton Dispensary Tst, past vice-chm Blackpool and Fylde Soc for the Blind, past govr Skelton Bounty Tst, past chm St John Ambulance Cncl for Lancs, chm Governing Cncl Arnold Sch 1983–97, current pres St John Ambulance Cadets of Lancs, vice-pres Lancs Cncl Vol Youth Servs; past chm Lancs Youth Clubs Assoc, past offr Rotary Int; High Sheriff Lancs 1992, Vice Lord-Lt Lancs 2002–05; Freeman City of London, Liveryman Worshipful Co of Plumbers; FInstD 1968, MInstP 1970; KStJ; *Recreations* golf; *Clubs* Royal Lytham and St Anne's Golf, Fylde RUFC; *Style*— Keith Gledhill, Esq, MBE, DL, KStJ; ✉ Broken Hill, 35 South Park Drive, Blackpool, Lancashire FY3 9PZ (☎ 01253 764462)

GLEDHILL, His Hon Judge Michael Geoffrey James; QC (2001); *Educ* ChCh Oxford; *m* Elizabeth Ann Miller, *née* Gordon; *Career* called to the Bar Middle Temple 1976 (bencher 2007); recorder 1998, circuit judge (South Eastern Circuit) 2008–; dep chllr Diocese of Salisbury 2008–15; *Style*— His Hon Judge Gledhill, QC; ✉ c/o The South Eastern Circuit, 289–293 High Holborn, London WC1V 7HZ

GLEDHILL, Ruth; da of late Rev Peter Gledhill, and Bridget Mary, *née* Rathbone; *b* 15 December 1959, Loughton, Essex; *Educ* Thomas Alleyne's GS Uttoxeter, LCP (HND), Birkbeck Coll London (Cert Religious Studies); *m* 1, 1989 (m dis 1993), John Edward Stammers; m 2, 1996 (m dis 2003), Andrew Daniels; m 3, 2006, Alan Franks; 1 s (Arthur Peter Gledhill b 27 Oct 2001); *Career* indentured Birmingham Post & Mail 1982–84, gen news reporter Daily Mail 1984–87; The Times: home news reporter 1987–90, religion corr 1990–, columnist At Your Service (Times Weekend) 1996–, blog Articles of Faith; regular radio and TV appearances on religious affrs; highly commended Templeton Prize for Religious Reporting 1998, nominated Specialist of the Year UK Press Awards 2004, Andrew Cross Religion Writer of the Year 2004, nominated Digital Journalist of the Year UK Press Awards 2009; *Books* Birmingham is Not a Boring City (co-author, 1984), The Times Book of Best Sermons (ed and introduction, 1995, 1996, 1997 and 1998), At A Service Near You (1996), The Times Book of Prayers (ed, 1997); *Recreations* playing with my son, playing the guitar, reading and writing fiction; *Clubs* Reform, London Rotary; *Style*— Ms Ruth Gledhill; ✉ home ☎ 020 8948 5871; The Times, 1 Pennington Street, London E98 1TT (☎ 020 7782 5001, fax 020 7782 5988, e-mail ruth.gledhill@thetimes.co.uk, blog www.timesonline.co.uk/gledhill)

GLEESON, Dermot James; s of Patrick Joseph Gleeson (d 2006), of Cheam, Surrey, and Margaret Mary, *née* Higgins (d 1998); *b* 5 September 1949; *Educ* Downside, Fitzwilliam Coll Cambridge (open scholarship, MA); *m* 6 Sept 1980, Rosalind Mary Catherine, da of Dr Charles Edward Moorhead (d 1953), of Chipping Campden, Glos; 1 da (Catherine b 1981), 1 s (Patrick b 1984); *Career* Cons Res Dept 1974–77 (acting dir 1979), European Cmmn (cabinet of Christopher Tugendhat) 1977–79, EEC rep of Midland Bank Brussels 1980–82; MJ Gleeson Group plc: joined 1982, chief exec 1988–1994, chm 1994–; dir: The Housing Corporation 1990–95, Construction Industry Training Bd 1995–2002; chm Major Contractors Gp 2003–05; govr BBC 2000–06, memb BBC Tst 2006–08; chm of govrs Rydes Hill Prep Sch 2014–; *Clubs* Beefsteak (chm 2004–07), RAC, Brooks's; *Style*— Dermot Gleeson, Esq; ✉ Hook Farm, White Hart Lane, Wood Street Village, Surrey GU3 3EA (☎ 01483 236210); M J Gleeson plc, Integration House, Rye Close, Ancells Business Park, Fleet, Hants GU51 2QG (☎ 012 5236 0300)

GLEN, Iain Alan Sutherland; s of James Robert Glen, and Alison Helen, *née* Brown; *b* 24 June 1961, Edinburgh; *Educ* RADA (Bancroft Gold Medal); *Career* actor; Hon LLD Univ of Aberdeen 2004; *Theatre* incl: The Blue Room (Donmar Warehouse and Broadway, Best Actor Broadway Drama League Award, nomination Best Actor Olivier Awards), Martin Guerre (West End, nomination Best Actor in a Musical Olivier Awards), The Broken Heart (RSC), Henry V (RSC, nomination Evening Standard Awards), Here (Donmar Warehouse), Macbeth (Tron Theatre, Mayfest Award for Best Actor), King Lear (Royal Court), Coriolanus (Chichester Festival Theatre), Hamlet (Bristol Old Vic, Ian Charleson Award), Hapgood (West End), Road (Royal Court), Edward II (Royal Exchange Manchester), A Streetcar Named Desire (RNT), The Seagull (Edinburgh Fesitval), Hedda Gabler (Almeida Theatre and West End, Olivier Award for Best Revival), The Crucible (RSC, Olivier nomination for Best Actor, Olivier Award for Best Revival), Scenes from a Marriage (Coventry Belgrade and West End), Wallenstein (Minerva Theatre), Separate Tables (Chichester Festival Theatre), Ghosts (West End, also dir), Uncle Vanya (Print Room), Fortune's Fool (The Old Vic); *Television* incl: Will You Love Me Tomorrow, The Fear, Adam Bede, Frankie's House, Trial & Retribution, Wives & Daughters, Death of a Salesman (nomination BAFTA Awards), The Picnic, Glasgow Kiss, Anchor Me, The Relief of Belsen (BAFTA nomination), The Diary of Anne Frank, Kidnapped (BBC), Into The Storm (HBO), Game of Thrones (HBO), Spooks (BBC), Strike Back (Sky), The Jack Taylor Series, Downton Abbey (ITV), Prisoners' Wives, Henry IV Part II (BBC), Breathless (ITV), Ripper Street (BBC), Borgia 2 (Canal Plus); *Film* incl: Paris By Night, Mountains of the Moon (Best Actor Evening Standard Awards), Rosencrantz and Guildenstern Are Dead, Fools of Fortune, Silent Scream (Silver Bear for Best Actor Berlin Film Festival, Michael Powell Award, Scottish BAFTA Awards), Young Americans, Tombraider, Keeper Of My Soul, Spy Sorge, Song for a Raggy Boy, Man to Man, Tara Road, Small Engine Repairs, Resident Evil, Kingdom of Heaven, Vagabond Shoes (short film, Grand Jury Prize Lille Short Film Festival, BAFTA Audience Award), Mrs Radcliffe's Revolution, Churchill and War, Pope Joan, Harry Brown, The Iron Lady, Kick Ass 2; *Recreations* most sports, playing guitar and piano, singing; *Style*— Iain Glen

GLEN, John Philip; MP; s of Philip Glen, of Lacock, Wilts, and Thalia, *née* Mitchenere; *b* 1 April 1974, Bath; *Educ* King Edward's Sr Sch Bath (head boy), Mansfield Coll Oxford (MA, pres JCR), Univ of Cambridge (MBA); *m* Emma Caroline, *née* Stephens; 1 step-s (William b 29 April 1999), 1 step-da (Emily b 1 Nov 2001); *Career* parly researcher to Gary Streeter, MP, *qv*, and Michael Bates (now The Lord Bates, *qv*) 1996–97, strategy conslt Accenture (formerly Andersen Consulting) 1997–2004, dir Cons Research Dept 2005–06, sr advsr and global head of strategy Acenture 2006–10; MP (Cons) Salisbury 2010–, memb Defence Select Ctee 2010–12, PPS to Rt Hon Eric Pickle, MP, *qv*, 2012–; memb Bd Centre for Policy Studies 2009–11; *Publications* There is Such Thing as Society (contrib, 2002), Completing the Reform, Freeing the Universities (2013); *Recreations* church, family, squash, eating out; *Clubs* National; *Style*— John Glen, Esq, MP; ✉ Morrison Hall, 12 Brown Street, Salisbury SP1 1HE (☎ 01722 323050); House of Commons, London SW1A 0AA (e-mail john.glen.mp@parliament.uk)

GLENDAY, Craig Douglas; *b* 31 May 1973, Dundee; *Career* founding ed The X Factor magazine 1993–96, prodr/ed Trinity Mirror 2000–01, ed-in-chief Guinness World Records 2002–; chm Stephen Sondheim Soc; *Style*— Craig Glenday, Esq; ✉ Guinness World Records, 12th Floor, South Quay Plaza 3, South Quay Building, 183 Marsh Wall, London E14 9SH

GLENDINNING, (Hon) Victoria (Hon Mrs O'Sullivan); CBE (1998); er da of Baron Seebohm, TD (Life Peer, d 1990), and Evangeline (d 1990), da of His Hon Sir Gerald Berkeley Hurst, QC; *b* 23 April 1937; *Educ* St Mary's Wantage, Millfield, Somerville Coll Oxford (MA), Univ of Southampton (Dip Social Admin); *m* 1, 1958 (m dis 1981), Prof (Oliver) Nigel Valentine Glendinning; 4 s; m 2, 1982, Terence de Vere White (d 1994), s of Frederick S de Vere White; m 3, 1996, Kevin O'Sullivan; *Career* author and journalist; head Booker Prize panel 1992; pres English Centre PEN 2001 (vice-pres 2003), vice-pres RSL 2000; hon fell Somerville Coll Oxford 2004; Hon DLitt: Univ of Southampton 1994, Univ of Ulster 1995, Univ of Dublin 1995, Univ of York 2000; FRSL; *Books* A Suppressed Cry (1975), Elizabeth Bowen – Portrait of a Writer (1977), Edith Sitwell – A Unicorn among Lions (1981, Duff Cooper Award and James Tait Black Award), Vita (1983, Whitbread Biography Award), Rebecca West (1987), Hertfordshire (1989), The Grown Ups (1989), Trollope (1992, Whitbread Biography Award), Electricity (1995), Sons and Mothers (ed with Matthew Glendinning, 1996), Jonathan Swift (1998), Flight (2002), Leonard Woolf (2006), Love's Civil War: Elizabeth Bowen & Charles Ritchie 1941–73 Letters and Diaries (ed, 2009), Raffles and the Golden Opportunity (2012); *Clubs* Athenaeum; *Style*— Victoria Glendinning; ✉ c/o David Higham Associates Ltd, 7th Floor, Waverley House, 712 Noel Street, London W1F 8GQ (☎ 020 7437 7888)

GLENDONBROOK, Baron (Life Peer UK 2011), of Bowdon in the County of Cheshire; Sir Michael David Bishop; kt (1991), CBE (1986); s of Clive Leonard Bishop (d 1980); *b* 10 February 1942; *Educ* Mill Hill Sch; *Career* chm: British Midland plc 1978–2009 (joined 1964), British Regional Airlines Group plc 1982–2001, Manx Airlines 1982–2001, Loganair 1983–97, Channel 4 Television 1993–1997 (dep chm 1991–93); dep chm Airtours plc 1996–2001 (dir 1987–2001); dir: Williams plc 1993–2001, Kidde plc 2000–02; memb: E Midlands Electricity Bd 1980–83, E Midlands Bd Central Independent Television plc

G

1981–90; life pres D'Oyly Carte Opera Tst; *Clubs* Brooks's, St James's (Manchester); *Style—* The Lord Glendonbrook, CBE; ☎ 01530 564388

GLENN, Christine; *Career* called to the Bar Gray's Inn 1980; chief exec Inner London Magistrates' Courts' Serv 1995–2001, ceo Parole Bd for England and Wales 2001–09, chief parole cmmr for NI 2011–; immigration judge Asylum and Immigration Tbnl 2001–13; FRSA 2008; *Recreations* music, opera, travel; *Style—* Ms Christine Glenn; ✉ Mezzanine Floor, Laganside Courts, Oxford Street, Belfast BT1 3LL (☎ 028 9054 5900, e-mail christine.glenn@parolecomni.org.uk)

GLENN, Jonathan; *Career* formerly: global head of fin Celltech Gp plc, chief fin offr Akubio Ltd; Consort Medical plc: gp fin dir 2006–07, chief exec 2007–; *Style—* Jonathan Glenn, Esq; ✉ Consort Medical plc, Ground floor, Suite D, Breakspear Park, Breakspear Way, Hemel Hempstead HP2 4TZ

GLENN, His Hon Judge Paul Anthony; s of Sidney Glenn (d 2009), and Nora, *née* Lavin (d 2006); *b* 14 September 1957, Newcastle-under-Lyme; *Educ* St Joseph's Coll Stoke-on-Trent, Univ of Liverpool (LLB); *m* 31 Aug 1985, Diane, *née* Burgess; 2 s (George Francis b 5 April 1987, Robert William b 3 Sept 1988); *Career* called to the Bar Gray's Inn 1983; clerk Cheshire Magistrates' Courts 1981–85, prosecuting slr Co Prosecuting Slrs' Office Cheshire 1985–87, sr crown prosecutor CPS Cheshire and Staffordshire 1987–90, practicing barr 1990–2004 (memb of chambers 4 Fountain Court and Citadel Chambers), recorder of the Crown Court 2001–04, circuit judge (Midland Circuit) 2004–, hon recorder Stoke-on-Trent; *Recreations* football, rugby, cricket; *Style—* His Hon Judge Glenn; ✉ c/o Stoke-on-Trent Combined Court Centre, Bethesda Street, Hanley, Stoke-on-Trent ST1 3BP

GLENNIE, Hon Lord; Angus James Scott Glennie; s of Robert Nigel Forbes Glennie, of London and Sussex, and Barbara Scott, *née* Nicoll (d 1987); *b* 3 December 1950; *Educ* Sherborne, Trinity Hall Cambridge (exhibitioner, MA); *m* 3 Oct 1981, Patricia Jean, da of His Hon Andrew James Phelan; 3 s (Alasdair Lewis Scott b 3 April 1983, Patrick James Nicoll b 27 July 1987, Pierce Nicholas Forbes b 11 Jan 1990); 1 da (Aisling Frances Robertson b 19 April 1985); *Career* called to the Bar Lincoln's Inn 1974, QC 1991; called to the Scottish Bar 1992, QC (Scot) 1998, senator Coll of Justice 2005–; memb Gibraltar Bar; farmer 1991–; assoc memb London Maritime Arbitrators' Assoc; *Recreations* sailing, real tennis, skiing; *Style—* The Hon Lord Glennie; ✉ Court of Session, Parliament House, Edinburgh EH1 1RQ

GLENNIE, Dame Evelyn Elizabeth Ann; DBE (2007, OBE 1993); da of Herbert Arthur Glennie, of Ellon, Aberdeenshire, and Isobel Mary, *née* Howie; *b* 19 July 1965, Aberdeen; *Educ* Ellon Acad Royal Acad of Music; further studies in Japan on Munster Tst Scholarship; *Career* solo musician (timpani and percussion); debut recital Wigmore Hall 1986, BBC Prom debut 1989; first ever solo percussion recital 1989, Last Night of the Proms 1994, other Proms appearances in 1992, 1996, 1997, 1998, 1999, 2000, 2004 and 2007; concerts with numerous orchs worldwide as percussion soloist incl: LSO, Philharmonia, London Sinfonietta, Northern Sinfonia, Eng Chamber, RTE (Dublin), Ulster Orch, BBC Scottish Symphony, Finnish Radio Symphony, Trondheim Symphony (Norway), Los Angeles Philharmonic, NY Philharmonic, Detroit Symphony, Nat Symphony (Washington), St Louis Symphony, Orchester der Deutschen Oper Berlin; concert tours of: Europe, Australia, USA, S America, Japan, Middle East, NZ, Far East, UK; composer original music for TV, radio and films; numerous concerts and recitals as a percussion soloist and Great Highland bagpiper; guest appearances and presenter on TV and radio; appeared in Touch the Sound; recordings: Bartók Sonata for Two Pianos and Percussion (with Sir Georg Solti and Murray Perahia 1987, Grammy awards 1989 and 2001), Rhythm Song (1989), Light in Darkness (1990), Last Night of the Proms 100th Season (1995), Dancin', Rebounds, Veni Veni Emmanuel, Wind in the Bamboo Grove, Drumming, Her Greatest Hits, The Music of Joseph Schwantner, Street Songs, Reflected in Brass, Shadow Behind the Iron Sun, UFO; several pieces composed for her by: John McLeod, Richard Rodney Bennett, Dominic Muldowney, James MacMillan, Geoffrey Burgon, Dave Heath, Thea Musgrave, Jonathan Harvey, Askell Masson, John Psathas, Mark Anthony Turnage; awarded: Gold Medal Shell LSO music scholarship 1984, Munster Tst scholarship 1986, Leonardo de Vinci Prize 1987, Charles Heidsieck Instrumentalist of the Year Award 1991; voted by Jr Chamber as one of ten outstanding young people in the world 1989, Scotswoman of the Decade for the 1980s; motivational speaker; Hon DMus: Univ of Aberdeen 1991, Univ of Portsmouth 1995, Univ of Bristol 1995, Loughborough Univ 1995, Univ of Southampton, Univ of Exeter; Hon DLitt Univ of Warwick 1993, Hon LLD Univ of Dundee 1996; FRCM 1991, FRAM 1992, FRSE 2005; *Books* Good Vibrations (autobiography, 1990), Cinematic Film – Touch the Sound (2004); *Recreations* reading, walking, music, antiques, psychology; *Style—* Dame Evelyn Glennie, DBE; ✉ The Office of Evelyn Glennie, Unit 6 Ramsay Court, Kingfisher Way, Hitchingbrooke Business Park, Huntingdon, Cambridgeshire PE29 6FY (☎ 01480 459279, fax 01480 451610, e-mail brenda@evelyn.co.uk, website www.evelyn.co.uk)

GLENTON, Anthony Arthur Edward; CBE (2000, MBE Mil 1983), TD (1974), DL (Northumberland 1990); s of Lt-Col Eric Cecil Glenton (d 1978), of Gosforth, Newcastle upon Tyne, and Joan Lydia, *née* Taylor; *b* 21 March 1943; *Educ* Merchiston Castle Sch Edinburgh; *m* 8 April 1972, Caroline Ann, da of Maurice George Meade-King, of Clifton, Bristol; 1 da (Sophie b 1974), 1 s (Peter b 1977); *Career* joined TA 1961, Lt-Col 1984, cmd 101 (Northumbrian) Field Regt RA (V) 1984–86, Col 1986, dep cdr 15 Inf Bde 1986–89; ADC to HM the Queen 1987–89; TA Col advsr to GOC Eastern Dist 1990–94, chm North of England RFCA 2000–03; Hon Regtl Col 101 (Northumbrian) Regt RA (V) 2005–10; sr ptnr Ryecroft Glenton Chartered Accountants Newcastle upon Tyne; chm: SSAFA – Forces Help Northumberland Branch 1989–, Newcastle Building Society 1993–98 (dir 1987–2008), Port of Tyne Authy 1994–2005, Charles W Taylor Ltd 1996–2003; Vice Lord Lt Northumberland 2013–; Freeman City of London, Liveryman Worshipful Co of Chartered Accountants; FCA 1971; *Recreations* shooting, sailing, contemporary art; *Clubs* Army and Navy; *Style—* Anthony Glenton, Esq, CBE, TD, DL, FCA; ✉ Whinbank, Rothbury, Northumberland NE65 7YJ (☎ 01669 620361); 32 Portland Terrace, Jesmond, Newcastle upon Tyne NE2 1QP (☎ 0191 281 1292)

GLENTORAN, 3 Baron (UK 1939); Sir (Thomas) Robin Valerian Dixon; 5 Bt (UK 1903), CBE (1992, MBE 1969), DL (1979); er s of 2 Baron Glentoran, KBE, PC (d 1995), and Lady Diana Mary Wellesley (d 1984), er da of 3 Earl Cowley; *b* 21 April 1935; *Educ* Eton; *m* 1, 1959 (m dis 1975), Rona Alice Gabrielle, da of Capt George Cecil Colville, CBE, RN, of Bishop's Waltham, Hants; 3 s (Hon Daniel George b 1959, Hon Andrew Wynne Valerian b 1961, Hon Patrick Anthony b 1963); m 2, 1979 (m dis 1988), Alwyn Gillian, da of Hubert A Mason, of Donaghadee, Co Down; m 3, 1990, Mrs Margaret Anne Murphy, *née* Rainey; *Heir* s, Hon Daniel Dixon; *Career* 2 Lt Grenadier Gds 1954, Capt 1958, Maj 1966; non-exec chm Redland of NI 1996–98 (md 1972–96); oppn House of Lords spokesman: agric, fisheries and food until 2001, environment, food and rural affrs 2001–02, NI 2001–, DTI 2004–05; memb Millennium Cmmn until 2006; *Recreations* sailing, skiing; *Clubs* Royal Yacht Squadron, Royal Cruising, Irish Cruising; *Style—* The Lord Glentoran, CBE, DL; ✉ 16 Westgate Terrace, London SW10 9BJ (☎ 020 7730 7190, e-mail rg@glentoran.demon.co.uk); House of Lords, London SW1A 0PW (e-mail glentoranr@parliament.uk)

GLICK, Ian Bernard; QC (1987); s of Dr Louis Glick (d 1989), and Phyllis Esty, *née* Barnett (d 2008); *b* 18 July 1948; *Educ* Bradford GS, Balliol Coll Oxford (MA, BCL); *m* 14 Dec 1986, Roxane Olivia Sarah, da of Dr R Eban, and Mrs Sylvia Levin; 3 s (Louis Daniel b 22 March 1991, Joseph Adam b 30 May 1992, Saul David b 27 Dec 1994); *Career* called to the Bar Inner Temple 1970 (bencher 1997); jr counsel in common law to the Crown 1985–87, standing counsel in export credit cases to DTI 1985–87; chm Commercial Bar Assoc (COMBAR) 1997–99; *Style—* Ian Glick, Esq, QC; ✉ 1 Essex Court, Temple, London EC4Y 9AR (☎ 020 7583 2000, fax 020 7583 0118)

GLOAG, Ann Heron; OBE (2004); *Career* co-fndr Stagecoach Gp 1980 (exec dir 1980–2000, non-exec dir 2000–); bd memb Mercy Ships; fndr and tstee: Balcraig Fndn, Gloag Fndn, Freedom from Fistula Fndn; Businesswoman of the Year Award, European Women in Achievement Award, Susan B Anthony Humanitarian of the Year Award 2009, Eleanor Roosevelt Award for Outstanding Achievement 2011; Order of the Star of Africa 2009; *Style—* Ms Ann Gloag, OBE

GLOBE, Hon Mr Justice; Sir Henry Brian Globe; kt (2011), QC (1994); s of Theodore Montague Globe (d 2007), of Liverpool, and Irene Rita, *née* Green; *b* 18 June 1949; *Educ* Liverpool Coll, Univ of Birmingham (LLB, Hockey blue); *m* 11 June 1972, Estelle, da of Irene Levin (d 1995), and Israel Levin (d 1998); 2 da (Danielle Rebecca (Mrs Ohana) b 5 Feb 1976, Amanda Jane (Dr Dee) b 3 Sept 1978); *Career* called to the Bar Middle Temple 1972 (bencher 2005); jr Northern Circuit 1974; standing counsel to: Dept of Social Security 1985–94, HM Customs & Excise 1992–94; recorder 1991–2003 (asst recorder 1988–90), circuit judge (Northern Circuit) 2003, sr circuit judge (crime) 2003–11, resident judge Liverpool 2003–11, hon recorder Liverpool 2003–11, judge of the High Court of Justice (Queen's Bench Div) 2011–, presiding judge North Eastern Circuit 2013–16; treas Northern Circuit 2001–03; memb: Bar Cncl 2001–03, Criminal Ctee Judicial Studies Bd 2001–05, Criminal Justice Cncl 2004–10, Sentencing Cncl 2010–15; govr King David Schs Liverpool 1979–2001, chm of govrs King David HS 1990–2000, tstee King David Fndn 2001–13; hon fell Liverpool John Moores Univ 2013; Hon LLD Univ of Liverpool 2015; *Recreations* tennis, bridge, cycling; *Style—* The Hon Mr Justice Globe; ✉ Royal Courts of Justice, Strand, London WC2A 2LL (e-mail mrjustice.globe@ejudiciary.net)

GLOCER, Thomas Henry (Tom); s of Walter Glocer (d 1973), of NY, and Ursuala, *née* Goodman; *b* 8 October 1959, NY; *Educ* Columbia Univ (BA), Yale Univ (JD); *m* 5 Aug 1988, Maarit Hannele, *née* Leso; 1 da (Mariana b 1 June 1998), 1 s (Walter b 6 Jan 2000); *Career* attorney Davis Polk and Wardwell 1984–93, Reuters Gp plc 1993–2008 (chief exec 2001–08), chief exec Thomson Reuters Corp 2008–; dir Merck & Co Inc; memb: Cncl on Foreign Rels, Bd of Dirs Partnership for NYC, Int Business Cncl World Economic Forum, Columbia Coll Bd of Visitiors, President's Cncl on Int Activities Yale Univ, European Business Ldrs Cncl, Int Advsy Bd Br American Business Inc, Int Business Advsy Cncl Lodnon, Madison Cncl Library of Congress; memb Advsy Bd: Tate Museum, Whitney Museum, Univ of Cambridge Business Sch, NYC Investment Fund, Judge Inst of Mgmnt Univ of Cambridge; *Publications* Coney Island: A Voyage of Discovery (computer game, 1984); *Recreations* tennis, windsurfing, skiing; *Clubs* Queens Tennis; *Style—* Tom Glocer, Esq; ✉ Thomson Reuters Building, 3 Times Square, New York, NY 10036, USA (☎ 001 646 223 7788, fax 001 646 223 7780, e-mail thomas.glocer@thomsonreuters.com)

GLOSTER, Rt Hon the Lady Justice; Dame Elizabeth Gloster; DBE (2004), PC (2013); da of Peter Gloster (d 1991), and Betty Mabel, *née* Read (d 2005); *b* 5 June 1949; *Educ* Roedean, Girton Coll Cambridge (BA); *m* 1, 29 Oct 1973 (m dis 2005), Stanley Eric Brodie, QC, *qv*, s of Dr Abraham Brodie (d 1978); 1 da (Sophie Rebecca b 12 Sept 1978), 1 s (Samuel Rufus b 14 Jan 1981); m 2, 15 March 2008, Sir Oliver Bury Popplewell, s of Frank Popplewell, OBE (d 1965); *Career* called to the Bar 1971: Inner Temple (bencher 1992), Bermuda, Gibraltar, IOM; memb Lincoln's Inn (ad eundem) 1974, memb Panel of Jr Counsel representing DTI in co matters 1982–89, QC 1989, recorder 1995–2004 (asst recorder 1991–95), judge of the High Court of Justice (Queen's Bench Div Commercial Ct) 2004–13, judge in charge Commercial Court 2010–12, a Lady Justice of Appeal 2013–; assoc memb (as barr) Insolvency Lawyers' Assoc 1991–2004, pt/t memb Civil Aviation Authy 1992–93, judge of the Courts of Appeal of Jersey and Guernsey (pt/t) 1994–2004; patron London Branch CIArb; *Style—* The Rt Hon the Lady Justice Gloster, DBE

GLOUCESTER, Dean of; *see:* Bury, Very Rev Nicholas

GLOVER, Prof Dame Anne; DBE (2015, CBE 2009); *Educ* Univ of Edinburgh, Univ of Cambridge (PhD); *m* 1996, Ian George; *Career* prof Sch of Med Sciences Univ of Aberdeen, tech dir Remedios 1999–2002; chief scientific advsr for Scotland 2006–11, chief scientific advsr to the Pres European Cmmn 2012–15, vice-princ External Affrs Univ of Aberdeen 2015–; memb Cncl NERC 2001–11, chair UK Collaborative on Devpt Sciences 2009–11, pres Assoc of Science Educn Scotland 2009–10, chair Carnegie Tst for the Univs of Scotland 2015–, memb Bd Scottish Enterprise 2015–, memb Bd Offshore Renewable Energy Catapult 2016–; tstee: CL:AIRE 2004, African Agriculture Technology Fndn (AATF) 2015–, Centre for Agriculture and Biosciences Int (CABI) 2016–; Woman of Outstanding Achievement in Science, Engrg and Technol 2008; fell American Acad of Microbiology 1995, FRSE 2005, FRSB 2006, FRSA 2008, hon fell Soc for Gen Microbiology 2012, hon fell Academia Europea 2014, FRSC 2014, fell European Acad of Scis and Arts 2015, FRS 2016; *Recreations* sailing; *Style—* Prof Dame Anne Glover, DBE, FRS; ✉ University of Aberdeen, University Office Room 180, Old Aberdeen, AB25 (e-mail l.a.glover@abdn.ac.uk)

GLOVER, Anne Margaret; CBE (2006); Prof John Glover, and Dr Mary Glover; *b* 6 February 1954, Liverpool; *Educ* Clare Coll Cambridge (MA), Yale Sch of Mgmnt (MPPM); *Career* venture capitalist; early career with Cummins Engine, subsequently conslt and mangr Bain & Co then memb investment team Apax Partners & Co Ventures, chief operating offr Virtuality Gp plc 1993–95, fndr Calderstone Capital Ltd (advsr to IT start-up cos) 1996, co-fndr and chief exec Amadeus Capital Partners Ltd 1997–; non-exec dir: Optos plc 1996–, Future Cities Catapult 2015–; chm BVCA 2004–05 (memb Cncl 1998–, vice-chm 2003–04); memb DTI Technology Strategy Bd 2005–12, memb European Research and Innovation Advsy Bd, chm EVCA (now known as Invest Europe) 2014–15; memb Bd: Glysure, Covestor Inc, Nomad plc, Royal Soc Enterprise Fund; memb Private Equity Advsy Bd London Business Sch; Hon FREng 2008; *Style—* Ms Anne Glover, CBE; ✉ Amadeus Capital Partners Limited, 16 St James's Street, London SW1A 1ER

GLOVER, Prof David Moore; *b* 28 March 1948; *Educ* Broadway Tech GS Barnsley, Fitzwilliam Coll Cambridge (BA), UCL (PhD); *Career* Damon Runyon postdoctoral res fell Stanford Univ 1972–75; Imperial Coll of Science and Technol London: lectr in biochemistry 1975–81, sr lectr 1981–83, reader in molecular genetics 1983–86, prof of molecular genetics and dir Eukaryotic Molecular Genetics Gp Cancer Research Campaign 1986–89 (jt dir 1979–86), head Dept of Biochemistry 1988–89; Univ of Dundee: prof of biochemistry 1989–92, prof of molecular genetics Dept of Anatomy and Physiology 1992–99; Arthur Balfour prof of genetics Univ of Cambridge 1999–2015, dir of research Dept of Genetics Univ of Cambridge 2015–; fell Fitzwilliam Coll 2004–; chief scientist Polgen Div Cyclacel Ltd 1999–2009; ed Jl of Cell Science, ed in chief Royal Soc's Open Biology; Cancer Research Campaign Career Devpt Award 1979–89; memb: EMBO 1978, Human Genome Orgn 1990; FRSE 1992, FRS 2009; *Books* Frontiers in Molecular Biology (series ed); author of over 250 scientific pubns; *Style—* Prof David M Glover, FRS, FRSE; ✉ Cancer Research UK Cell Cycle Genetics Research Group, University of Cambridge, Department of Genetics, Cambridge CB2 3EH (e-mail d.glover@gen.cam.ac.uk)

GLOVER, Edward Charles; CMG (2003), MVO (1976); s of Edward Leonard Glover (d 1989), and Mary Glover (d 2015); *b* 4 March 1943; *Educ* Univ of London (BA, MPhil); *m* Dame Audrey Frances Glover, DBE, CMG; 2 da (Caroline b 21 April 1973, Charlotte b 25 Feb 1976), 2 s (Rupert b 18 Oct 1980, Crispin b 28 Jan 1983), and 1 s decd (d 1977); *Career* HM Dip Serv: SE Asian Dept FCO 1969–71, private sec to High Cmmr to Aust 1971–73, second sec Washington DC 1973–77, delgn sec and third ctee rep UK Delgn to UN

Law of the Sea Conf 1978–80, on secondment to Guinness Peat Group 1980–83, Arms Control and Disarmament Dept FCO 1983–85, Br Mil Govt Berlin 1985–89, dep head Near East and N African Dept FCO 1989–91, head Mgmnt Review Staff FCO 1991–94, dep head of mission Brussels 1994–98, high cmmr to Guyana and ambass to Surinam 1998–2002, Quality and Efficiency Unit FCO 2002–03, ret; short term conslt DFID support to the Min of Foreign Affairs Macedonia 2003–05, FCO advsr on foreign affrs to: Iraqi Min of Foreign Affrs 2004–05; short term conslt DFID support to office of Prime Minister Kosovo 2006–07, assoc conslt to Miny of Foreign Affrs Sierra Leone 2008, assoc conslt Public Administration Int 2009–13; dir Foreign and Cwlth Assoc 2011– (dir Communication 2015–); assoc fell Centre for Caribbean Studies Univ of Warwick (chair Warwick Caribbean Scholarship Fund 2016); chm Bd of Tstees Iwokrama Int Rainforest Centre Guyana 2005–12; chm NW Norfolk Decorative and Fine Arts Soc 2003–06, tstee King's Lynn Preservation Tst 2003–, tstee Size of Wales 2013–; author 2014–; contrib articles to The New Economy and G8 Climate Change Addressing the Challenge; memb: RIIA 1969, Hakluyt Soc, Alliance of Independent Authors 2014–; *Books* The Music Book (2014), Fortune's Sonata (2015), A Motif of Seasons (2016); *Recreations* tennis, watercolour painting, reading (biographies), ran 2014 London Marathon and 2015 Hampton Court Half Marathon; *Clubs* Brooks's, The Norfolk Club (Norwich); *Style—* Edward Glover, Esq, CMG, MVO; ✉ The Oak House, Thornham, Norfolk PE36 6LY (e-mail edward.glover@btopenworld.com)

GLOVER, Helen; MBE (2013); *b* 17 June 1986, Truro, Cornwall; *Educ* Univ of Wales Inst Cardiff; *Career* rower; achievements incl: Silver medal (coxless pair) World Championships 2010, Silver medal (coxless pair) World Championships 2011, Gold medal (coxless pair) Olympic Games 2012, Gold medal (coxless pair) World Championships 2013, 2014 and 2015, Gold medal (coxless pair) Olympic Games 2016; *Clubs* Minerva Bath; *Style—* Ms Helen Glover, MBE; ✉ c/o MTC (UK) Ltd, 71 Gloucester Place, London W1U 8JW

GLOVER, Prof Jane Alison; CBE (2003); da of late Robert Finlay Glover, TD, and late Jean, *née* Muir, MBE; *b* 13 May 1949; *Educ* Monmouth Sch for Girls, St Hugh's Coll Oxford (MA, DPhil); *Career* conductor; musical dir Glyndebourne Touring Opera 1982–85, musical dir London Choral Soc 1983–99; artistic dir London Mozart Players 1984–91, princ conductor Huddersfield Choral Soc 1989–96, music dir Music of the Baroque (Chicago) 2002–, dir of opera Royal Acad of Music 2009–16; appeared with many orchs and opera cos incl: Glyndebourne Festival Opera 1982–, BBC Proms 1985–, ROH 1988–, ENO 1989–, Opera Australia 1996–, Glimmerglass Opera 1994–, Staatsoper Berlin, Met Opera, New York Philharmonic Orchestra, Cleveland Orchestra, Philadelphia Orchestra; prof Univ of London 2010–; regular broadcaster on TV and radio, regular recordings; sr research fell St Hugh's Coll Oxford 1982 (hon fell 1991); govr BBC 1990–95; NY City Opera Gen Dir's Cncl Award for Outstanding Achievement 2001; Hon DMus: Univ of Exeter 1986, Cncl for Nat Acad Awards 1991, Univ of London 1992, City Univ 1994, Univ of Glasgow 1997; Hon DUniv Open Univ 1988; Hon DLitt: Loughborough Univ of Technol 1988, Univ of Bradford 1992; memb Worshipful Co of Haberdashers; RSA 1988, FRCM 1993, Hon RAM 2014; *Books* Cavalli (1978), Mozart's Women (2005); *Recreations* theatre, walking, skiing, watching tennis; *Style—* Prof Jane Glover, CBE

GLOVER, Julian Wyatt; CBE (2013); s of (Claude) Gordon Glover (d 1975), of Arkesden, Essex, and Honor Ellen Morgan, *née* Wyatt (d 1998); *b* 27 March 1935; *Educ* St Paul's, Alleyn's Sch Dulwich, RADA; *m* 1, 1957 (m dis 1966), Dame Eileen Atkins, DBE *qv*; m 2, 28 Sept 1968, Isla Blair, *qv*; 1 s (Jamie Blair b 10 July 1969); *Career* actor; Nat Serv 2 Lt RASC 1954–56; started out as spear-carrier Shakespeare Meml Theatre Stratford-upon-Avon 1957; Liveryman Worshipful Co of Dyers 1956; *Theatre* incl: Aufidius in Coriolanus and Warwick in Henry VI (RSC) 1977, Habeas Corpus, Educating Rita, The Aspern Papers, Never The Sinner, title role in Henry IV Parts I and II RSC 1991–92 (winner Best Supporting Actor Olivier Award 1993), All My Sons 1992, Cyrano de Bergerac (Haymarket) 1992–93, An Inspector Calls (RNT, Aldwych) 1993–94, Chips With Everything (RNT) 1996–97, Prayers of Sherkin (Old Vic) 1997, Waiting for Godot (Peter Hall Co) 1998, Phedre and Britannicus (Albery) 1998, A Penny For a Song (Whitehall), Prospero in The Tempest (Nuffield Theatre), In Praise of Love (nat tour), title role in King Lear (Shakespeare's Globe), Macbeth (Albery), Taking Sides (nat tour) 2003–04, Galileo's Daughter (Peter Hall season Bath) 2004, The Dresser (nat tour and Duke of York's) 2004–05, John of Gaunt in Richard II (Old Vic) 2005, Mikhail Gorbachev in The President's Holiday (Hampstead Theatre) 2008, Oliver (Theatre Royal Drury Lane) 2009; theatre seasons with: RSC (8 seasons, Cassius and Friar Lawrence 1995–96), Prospect, The Old Vic and Nat Theatre Companies; dir Hamlet (Norwich Playhouse) 1996, Voysey Inheritance (NT) 2006, Shadowlands (Salisbury) 2007, Maurice's Jubilee (Edinburgh Festival) 2012 and (tour) 2013, The Scottsboro Boys (Young Vic) 2013 and (Garrick Theatre) 2014, John of Gaunt in Richard II (RSC Barbican and Brooklyn Acad of Music) 2015/16; *Television* incl: An Age of Kings, Z-Cars, Dombey and Son, By The Sword Divided, Wish Me Luck, Spy Trap, Cover Her Face, Warburg, Man of Influence, Darling Buds of May, Money for Nothing, Degrees of Error, Taggart, The Chief 1995, The Infiltrator, Cadfael, The Midsomer Murders, Born and Bred, Trial & Retribution, Silent Witness, Game of Thrones, Merlin, Atlantis, Spies of Warsaw 2012; *Films* incl: Tom Jones, For Your Eyes Only, The Fourth Protocol, I Was Happy Here, Star Wars, The Empire Strikes Back, Cry Freedom, Biko, Treasure Island, Indiana Jones and the Last Crusade, King Ralph, Vatel, Harry Potter and the Chamber of Secrets, Two Men Went to War, Troy, The Young Victoria, The Timber 2012; *Books* Beowulf (1987 and 1995, republished 2005); *Style—* Julian Glover, Esq, CBE; ✉ c/o Conway van Gelder Ltd, 8–12 Broadwick Street, London W1F 8HW (☎ 020 7287 0077, fax 020 7287 1940)

GLOVER, Richard Gordon Finlay; s of Robert Finlay Glover, of Malvern, Worcs, and Jean, *née* Muir; *b* 3 August 1952; *Educ* Tonbridge, Univ of Strasbourg, CCC Oxford (BA); *m* 4 Oct 1980, Teresa Anne, da of Richard Ingram Lindsell; 1 s (Thomas Finlay b 19 Jan 1984), 1 da (Alice Catherine b 31 July 1987); *Career* ICI 1974–80, Grand Metropolitan 1980–86, United Biscuits 1986–88, sr search conslt Whitehead Mann 1988–90, chief exec BSM Group plc 1997–99 (md 1990–97), md RAC Business Services 1999, chief exec ATC Group 2000–03, chief exec ATC Int Holdings 2003–; chm Haberdashers' Aske's Fndn of Academies 2004–; Liveryman Worshipful Co of Haberdashers 1977; FRSA 1993; *Recreations* Welsh rugby, cinema, squash; *Style—* Richard Glover, Esq; ✉ ATC (International Holdings) Limited, Suite 6 & 7, The Old Office Block, 16 Elmtree Road, Teddington, Middlesex TW11 8ST (☎ 020 8977 8429)

GLOVER, Stephen Charles Morton; s of Prebendary John Morton Glover (d 1979), and Helen Ruth, *née* Jones (d 1984); *b* 13 January 1952; *Educ* Shrewsbury, Mansfield Coll Oxford (MA); *m* 1982, Celia Elizabeth, da of Peter Montague; 2 s (Edmund b 1983, Alexander b 1987); *Career* leader and feature writer Daily Telegraph 1978–85 (parliamentary sketch writer 1979–81), foreign ed The Independent 1986–89 (co-fndr 1986), ed The Independent on Sunday 1990–91, assoc ed (politics) The Evening Standard 1992–95; columnist: Daily Telegraph 1996–98, The Spectator 1996–2005, Daily Mail 1998–, The Independent 2005–12; dir Newspaper Publishing plc 1986–92; *Books* Paper Dreams (1993), Secrets of the Press (ed, 1999); *Clubs* Garrick; *Style—* Stephen Glover, Esq

GLUCK, Malcolm; s of Harry Gluck (d 1986), of Hove, E Sussex , and Ivy, *née* Messer (d 1982); *b* 23 January 1942; *Educ* Drury Fall Sch Hornchurch, Watford Coll of Art, Fairkytes and Harrow Lodge public libraries; *m* 1, 1969 (m dis 1976), Marilyn Janet Day; 1 s (Ben b 1982, with Patricia Wellington); m 2, 1984 (m dis 2003), Susan Ashley; 1 da (Alexandra Ashley Harriet b 1986), 1 s (Joseph Augustus Ashley b 1989); *Career* author; oily rag Rotary Hoes Ltd 1957, apprentice Ford Motor Co 1957–60, trainee salesman Kingsland Shoes Ltd 1960, poet 1960–61, office boy Stratford East Waste Paper Mill Ltd 1961, cost clerk Hackney Springs & Screws Ltd 1961, clerk Spillers Pet Food 1961, asst to domestic supt Mile End Hosp 1961, jr sec Motor Agents Assoc 1961–62, student Watford Coll of Art 1962–63; copywriter: SH Benson (trainee) 1963, Press & Gen Publicity 1963–64, Arks Publicity 1964–65, Streets Advtg 1965, Mclaren Dunkley Friedlander 1965–66, Doyle Dane Bernbach NY (sr) 1969; copy chief Doyle Dane Bernbach London 1971–73 (copywriter 1966–69, gp head/assoc dir 1970–71), co-prop, sales dir and games developer Intellect Games Ltd 1973–75, creative dir Drakes Jarvis & Gluck Ltd 1973–75, script writer and contrib Punch 1976, conslt creative dir Pincus Vidler Arthur Fitzgerald 1976–77, dir/sr copywriter Abbott Mead Davies Vickers 1977–80, sr copywriter Collet Dickenson Pearce 1980–84, dir Olgivy & Mather 1984–85, exec creative dir Lintas 1986–88, creative dir Priestley Marin-Guzman & Gluck 1989–92; writer Superplonk wine column The Guardian 1989, publisher Adze Magazine 1992, conslt wine ed Sainsbury's Magazine 1993–2001, wine ed Cosmopolitan magazine 1995–96, wine corr The Guardian 1996–, co-prop Superplonk Online Ltd 2000–, writer Party Paupers column The Guardian 2002; compiler/presenter Vintage Classics Deutsche Grammophon 1996; presenter: Nosh & Plonk (jtly, video) 1993, Gluck Gluck Gluck (BBC 2) 1996, The World of Wine (video and DVD) 2003; involved with: CND 1957–73, Anti-Apartheid Movement 1970–92, Lab Pty Advtg Advsy Gp 1978–80; memb Circle of Wine Writers; *Awards* over 200 awards 1966–92 from D&AD, Br Advtg Film Awards, Br Creative Circle and overseas incl: Best Trade Advtg Copy 1966, Best Colour Advertisement 1967, Best Black & White Newspaper Advertisement Copy 1968, Best Newspaper Colour Advertisement 1972, Best Animated Commercial 1971, Best Travel Advtg Campaign 1979, Best Cinema Commercial 1980, Best Use of Celebrity in a TV Commercial 1982, Best Outdoor Poster 1987, Most Original Animated Commercial 1988; *Books* Superplonk (annually, 1991–), Supernosh (with Anthony Worral Thompson, *qv*, 1993), Gluck's Guide to High Street Wine (1995), Gluck on High (1996), Gluck Gluck Gluck (1996), Summerplonk (1997 and 1998), Streetplonk (1997, 1998, 1999 and 2000), The Sensational Liquid – Gluck's Guide to Wine Tasting (1999), Wine Matters – Why Water Just Won't Do (2003), New Media Language (contrib, 2003), Superplonk – The Top One Thousand (2005), Supergrub (2005), The Simple Art of Marrying Food and Wine (with Mark Hix, 2005), Malcolm Gluck's Brave New World (2006), Chateau Lafite 1953 and Other Stories (2010), Five Tons of Jam – The Poetry of John Orland (2010), Random Oxidation (2017); *Recreations* novels (European and American), poetry, music (classical and jazz piano), chess, cooking (European, Oriental), cycling, language study, London cemeteries, photography, crosswords, film, travel; *Clubs* Groucho, Frontline; *Style—* Malcolm Gluck, Esq; ✉ c/o Ed Victor Limited, 6 Bayley Street, Bedford Square, London W1B 3HB

GLURJIDZE, Elena; da of Levan Glurjidze, of St Petersburg, Russia, and Valentina, *née* Mikhailova; *b* 11 May 1974, Tbilisi, Georgia; *Educ* Tbilisi Choreographic Sch, Vaganova St Petersburg Acad of Russian Ballet; *m* 3 April 2004, Prince Kakhaber Abashidze; 1 s (Alexander Nicholas b 1 Oct 2004); *Career* ballerina; formerly with: Russian Ballet Co St Petersburg, St Petersburg State Academic Ballet Theatre, St Petersburg Ballet Theatre of Konstantin Tatchkin; English Nat Ballet: princ dancer 2002–07, lead princ 2007–; roles incl: Giselle in Giselle, Kitri in Don Quixote, Aurora in Sleeping Beauty, Clara in The Nutcracker, Odette and Odile in Swan Lake, Cinderella in Cinderella, Swanild in Coppelia, Virginia in The Canterville Ghost; guest dancer World Ballet Stars Festivals Ukraine; memb Equity; Bronze medal 8th Moscow Int Competition of Ballet Artists 1997, winner 8th Paris Int Competition of Soloists 1998, Best Ptnr 7th Perm Open Competition 2002; *Recreations* growing exotic flowers, collecting pictures, visiting parks throughout Europe with my son and husband; *Style—* Mrs Elena Glurjidze; ✉ 17 Aylmer Road, London W12 9LG (☎ 07967 008776, e-mail elenaglurjidze@gmail.com); c/o English National Ballet, Markova House, 39 Jay Mews, London SW7 2ES

GLYNN, (Brian) David; s of William Arthur Glynn, CBE (d 1976), and Norah Haden, *née* Mottram; *b* 30 May 1940; *Educ* Epsom Coll, Guy's Hosp Dental Sch (BDS Univ of London, LDS RCS Eng, DGDP RCS Eng, represented hockey and shooting teams), Univ of Oregon Dental Sch (Newland Pedley scholar); *m* 16 May 1964, Judith Mary, da of George Charles English, CBE; 2 da (Amanda Jayne b 18 March 1968, Nicola Louise b 17 June 1970); *Career* dental surgeon; Dept of Conservation Dentistry Guy's Hosp: pt/t registrar 1967–74, pt/t jr lectr 1974–76, pt/t sr demonstrator 1976–79; in private practice 35 Devonshire Place W1 1979– (pt/t 1967–74); chm Compudent Ltd 1984–95; Fédération Dentaire Internationale: conslt Scientific Programme Ctee 1989, conslt Cmmn of Dental Practice on Computer Aided Diagnostics 1990; lectr on use of computers in gen dental practice, author of numerous papers and courses on restorative dentistry, responsible for use of closed circuit TV in teaching at Guy's Hosp (prodr various films); memb: BDA, American Dental Soc of London (sec 1972–75, pres 1992–93); fell Int Coll of Dentists 1981 (gen sec Euro section 1984–92, vice-pres 1992–93, pres 1994–95, int pres 1999 (pres-elect 1998)); *Publications* Use of Closed Circuit TV (Medical and Biological Illustration, 1973); various papers to American Dental Soc of London; *Recreations* fly fishing, skiing, sailing, tennis, flying, twin and single engine aircraft; *Clubs* Fly Fishers; *Style—* David Glynn, Esq; ✉ Glynn Setchell and Allan, 35 Devonshire Place, London W1N 1PE (☎ 020 7935 3342/3, fax 020 7224 0558)

GOAD, Dame Sarah Jane Frances; DCVO (2012), JP (1974); da of Uvedale Lambert, and Diana, *née* Grey (d 1944); step da of Melanie Grant Lambert, of Denver, Colorado; *b* 23 August 1940; *Educ* St Mary's Wantage; *m* 1961, Timothy Francis Goad, DL; 1 da, 2 s; *Career* dir Tilburstow Farms Co Ltd 1963–70, ptnr Lambert Farmers 1970–94; memb Surrey Magistrates' Soc 1987–93, dep chm Family Panel 1992–97; HM Lord-Lt Surrey 1997–2015; chm Southwark Cathedral Cncl 2000–08, lay canon Southwark Cathedral 2004–15; pres Yvonne Arnaud Theatre 2004–15; tstee and chm: Love Walk (home for disabled) 1984–98, Surrey Care Tst 1987–97; tstee: St Mark's Fndn 1971–, Surrey History Tst 1999–, Chevening Estate 2001–12; govr: St Stephen's C of E Sch 1970–90, Hazelwood Sch 1979–84; hon fell Royal Holloway Coll 2013; DStJ 1997; *Recreations* books, buildings, arts; *Style—* Dame Sarah Goad, DCVO; ✉ Prickloves Farmhouse, South Park, Bletchingley, Surrey RH1 4NE

GOBITS, Rolph; s of Ben Gobits (d 1957), and Ruth, *née* Reinheimer; *b* 19 September 1947, The Hague, Netherlands; *Educ* Bournemouth & Poole Coll of Art (BA), RCA (scholar, MA, Daily Telegraph Magazine Award); *m* 1, 15 Dec 1978 (m dis 2002), Amanda, *née* Currey; 2 da (Tamara b 8 Sept 1974, Anoushka b 13 June 1981); m 2, Dec 2005, Mrs Yulia Globina; *Career* photographer; clients incl: Mercedes Benz, BMW, Audi, Volkswagen, General Motors, IBM, Apple, British Airways, TWA, Hyatt Hotels, American Express, Forte Hotel Group, AT&T, Texaco, Spalding, Bosch, Morgan Grenfell Merchant Bank, Natwest, Orient Express, Gucci, IPC Publications, French Tourist Office, Jersey Tourist Office, Scottish Tourist Office, Marconi, Granada, Red Cross, Hewlett Packard, Compaq, Mobil Oil, US Postal Services, Br Tourist Office, BT, Chrysler Corp, United Technologies in USA, Credit Suisse Gp, Royal Mail, Sotheby's, Chrystal Cruises, Guardian Newspapers, Air Canada; dir lensmodern.com (gallery and picture library); exhbn: The Travelling Entertainers 2007, Naarden Festival Holland 2007; 3 private exhbns Moscow 2009–10, 2 one-man shows in Moscow galleries 2009, 2 one-man shows in Vladivostok galleries 2010, show in Life The Gallery Farnham, private exhbn at the Arka Gallery Vladivostok Russia 2013; masterclasses in Moscow and Vladivostok; 1 of 7 dirs of an internet-based photographic gallery and library called Lensmodern which

G

represented over 200 award-winning photographers from all over the world; commissioned to set up Dept of Photography in Faculty of Art, Culture in Sport Far Eastern Federal Univ Russia 2013; visiting prof Graphic Design Dept Far Eastern Federal Univ 2013–14; vice-chm Assoc of Photographers; *Awards* Arts Council Bursary 1974; D&AD: Silver Award for most oustanding advertising colour photograph 1979, special mention for consumer campaign 1981, Silver Award (Netherlands club) for most outstanding advertising colour photograph 1984, Silver Award for most outstanding consumer campaign 1984, Silver Award (France club) for VW campaign 1992; Campaign Press Advertising: Silver Award for best use of colour 1983, Silver Award for best media advertisement 1983, Silver Award for best travel advertisement 1985, Silver and Bronze Awards for best business advertisement 1986; Advertising Festival Gold Award for best advertisement in Europe Cannes 1992; Assoc of Photographers: Silver Award 1995, Judges Choice 2000 and 2002, Merit Award 2001; The Morton Kirschner Photography Award (Holland): Gold Award 1999, Bronze Award 2000; *Recreations* photography, reading, chess; *Style*— Rolph Gobits, Esq; ✉ Rolph Gobits Studio Ltd, The Coach House, 1 Winfrith Road, London SW18 3BE (☎ 07785 292599, website www.gobitsphoto.com)

GOBLE, Prof Carole Anne; CBE (2014); George John Goble, and Barbara Mary, *née* Davey; *b* 10 April 1961, Maidstone, Kent; *Educ* Univ of Manchester (BSc); *m* 23 July 2003, Ian David Cottam; *Career* Computer Science Dept Univ of Manchester: lectr 1985–95, sr lectr 1995–2000, prof 2000–; co-fndr Open Middleware Infrastructure Inst 2006–10, EIC Jl Web Semanic; co-fndr Software Sustainability Inst 2010; dep dir Elixir UK 2013; fndr e-Science Gp; memb BBSRC Cncl 2013–; chair BBSRC appts bd 2014–, chair 13th Intl Semantic Web Conf 2014; res and technol innovations in e-sci, in partnership with int researchers in life sci, biodiversity, astronomy, chemistry, social sci; Microsoft Research Jim Gray e-Science Award 2008; FBCS 2005, FREng 2010; *Publications*author of over 300 pubns in e-sci, information systems, knowledge management, semantic web, distributed computing and scholarly communication; *Recreations* music festivals, shopping; *Style*— Prof Carole Goble, CBE; ✉ Kilburn Building, School of Computer Science, University of Manchester, Oxford Road, Manchester M13 9PL (☎ 0161 275 6195, e-mail carole.goble@manchester.ac.uk, website https://sites.google.com/site/carolegoble, Twitter @CaroleAnneGoble)

GODBER, John; s of Harry Godber, and Dorothy, *née* Deakin; *b* 18 May 1956; *Educ* Minsthorpe HS, Bretton Hall Coll (BEd), Univ of Leeds (MA, MPhil, PhD (unfinished research thesis)); *m* 12 Sept 1993, Jane, da of Clifford Thornton; 2 da (Elizabeth b 29 Oct 1994, Martha b 10 Aug 1997); *Career* playwright and dir; former head of drama Minsthorpe HS, artistic dir Hull Truck Theatre Co 1984–; visiting prof Liverpool Hope Univ 2004, hon lectr Bretton Hall Coll 2006, prof of drama Univ of Hull; Hon DLitt: Univ of Hull 1988, Humberside and Lincolnshire Univ 1997; DUniv OU 2005; FRSA 2004; *Theatre* Cramp (NSDF) 1981, September in the Rain (Hull Truck Theatre Co) 1984, Blood Sweat and Tears (Hull Truck Theatre Co), Bouncers (London, Eur and USA, Edinburgh Fringe First Award 1984, seven Drama Critics Circle Awards, five Joseph Jefferson Awards), Up 'N' Under II, Shakers (with Jane Thornton, London, Aust and USA), Teechers (Arts Theatre London, Aust and USA), Salt of the Earth (Edinburgh Fringe First Award, Joseph Jefferson Award), On the Piste 1991, Happy Families, April in Paris 1992, The Office Party (Nottingham Playhouse nat tour) 1992, Happy Jack (Hull Truck Theatre Co and tour, Edinburgh Fringe Festival Award) 1982, Up 'N' Under (Fortune Theatre London and tour, Edinburgh Fringe First Award, Olivier Comedy of the Year Award) 1984, Passion Killers (Derby Playhouse) 1994, Lucky Sods (Hull Truck Theatre Co) 1995, Gym and Tonic (Hull Truck Theatre Co) 1996, Weekend Breaks (Hull Truck Theatre Co) 1997, It Started With a Kiss 1998, Unleashed 1999, Thick as a Brick 1999, Reunion 2002, Men of the World 2001, Screaming Blue Murder 2003, Fly Me to the Moon 2004, Going Dutch (Hull Truck Theatre Co) 2004, Wrestling Mad (Hull Truck Theatre Co) 2005, Christmas Crackers 2006, Crown Prince 2007; *Television* incl: Blood Sweat and Tears (BBC 2), The Ritz (BBC 2), The Continental (BBC Christmas Special), My Kingdom for a Horse (film for BBC) 1991, Chalkface (BBC) 1991, Bloomin Marvellous (BBC 1) 1997, Thunder Road (writer and dir, film for BBC) 2003, Thick as a Brick (film for BBC) 2005, Oddsquad (BBC) 2005 (BAFTA Best Schools Drama 2005, BAFTA Best Screenplay 2005); numerous episodes of Brookside, Crown Court and Grange Hill; *Film* Up 'N' Under (writer and dir) 1998; *Style*— John Godber, Esq

GODBOLD, Brian Leslie; OBE (2007); s of Leslie Robert Godbold (d 1970), and Eileen Rosalie, *née* Hodgkins (d 2011); *b* 14 July 1943; *Educ* Elmbridge Sch Cranleigh, Walthamstow Sch of Art (NDD), RCA Fashion Sch; *Career* designer Jovi NY 1965–67, head of tailoring Wallis Shops 1967–69; head of design: Cojana 1970–74, Baccarat/Wetherall (headed team that designed BA uniform 1976) 1974–76; Marks & Spencer: exec head of design 1976–93, design dir 1993–98; dep chm Br Fashion Cncl 1997–2000 (sponsored by Marks & Spencer), non-exec dir George at Asda 2000–06, strategic fashion retail and design conslt 2000–; dir Ramon Gurillo Ltd 2004–; RCA: vice-chm Cncl 2000–03 (memb 1993–2006), sr fell 2006; memb: Design Cncl 1998–2001, Advsy Bd of Fashion Merchandise Mgmnt Course Westminster Univ 1999–, Advsy Bd India Int Fashion Week 2009–; photographer, exhibited Summer Open (Assoc Gallery London) 2000, one-man exhbn (Egg London) 2001, Morocco (one-man exhbn, Seu-Xerea Valencia) 2008; memb Br Friends of Shenkar Israel; Hon DDes: Univ of Southampton 1994, Univ of Westminster 1999; hon fell Shenkar Coll of Engrg and Design Israel 1999; FRSA, FCSD; *Recreations* antique collecting, decorating, gardening; *Style*— Brian Godbold, Esq, OBE; ✉ e-mail briangodbold43@aol.com

GODDARD, (Charles) Anthony Ashton; s of David Rodney Goddard, of Lympstone, Devon, and Susan, *née* Ashton; *b* 30 September 1954, Kuala Lumpur; *Educ* Radley, Emmanuel Coll Cambridge (MA); *m* 15 Sept 1979, Caroline Felicity, *née* Wells; 2 da (Chloe Elizabeth Ashton b 3 Nov 1981, Henrietta Louise b 6 Sept 1983), 1 s (Samuel Harry b 11 May 1985); *Career* ICI plc: joined 1976, regnl exec N Europe 1985–89, sales and mktg dir chemical products 1989–93, sales and mktg dir ICI C&P Ltd 1993–98; assoc ptnr strategy practice and ldr UK chemicals practice Accenture (formerly Andersen Consulting) 1998–2002, headmaster Aysgarth Sch 2002–15 (govr 1991–2002); govr Tudor Hall Sch 1988–2002, govr Abberley Hall Sch 2011–; ldr of house parties Stewards' Tst; *Recreations* sailing, tennis, golf, family; *Style*— Anthony Goddard, Esq; ✉ Rookwood Lodge, Rookwood Rd, West Wittering, Chichester, W. Sussex PO20 8QL

GODDARD, Prof John Burgess; OBE (1986); s of Burgess Goddard, of Rickmansworth, Herts, and Maud Mary, *née* Bridge (d 1970); *b* 5 August 1943; *Educ* Latymer Upper Sch, UCL (BA), LSE (PhD); *m* 24 Sept 1966, Janet Patricia, da of Stanley James Peddle (d 1956), of Rickmansworth, Herts; 2 da (Jane Elizabeth b 1 Dec 1970, Jennifer Anne b 7 Nov 1974), 1 s (David Jonathan b 4 August 1976); *Career* lectr LSE 1968–75, Leverhulme fell Univ of Lund Sweden 1974 (Leverhulme emeritus fell 2008–10); Univ of Newcastle upon Tyne: Henry Daysh prof Regnl Devpt Studies 1975–2008 (emeritus prof 2008–), dir Centre of Urban and Regnl Devpt Studies 1977–98, head Geography Dept 1980–87, dean Faculty of Law, Environment and Social Sciences 1994–98, pro-vice-chllr 1998–2001, dep vice-chllr 2001–08, dir Newcastle Initiative Ltd 1988–94; NESTA visiting fell 2008–09; memb: N Econ Planning Cncl 1976–79, Exec Ctee Newcastle Common Purpose 1989–93; govr and memb Employment and Fin Ctee Univ of Northumbria at Newcastle (formerly Newcastle Poly) 1989–98; memb: Port of Tyne Authy 1990–93, Human Geography Ctee SSRC 1976–79, Editorial Bd Environment and Planning 1988–91; ed Regional Studies 1979–84; advsr: CBI Task Force on Urban Regeneration 1987–88, House of Commons Trade and Indust Select Ctee 1994–95; memb: Exec Ctee Regnl Studies Assoc 1979–84, Editorial Bd BBC Domesday Project 1985–86, Jt Ctee ESRC and Nat Sci Fndn of America on Large Scale Data Bases 1986–87; dir ESRC Prog on Info and Communication Technologies 1992–93; chm: The Assoc of Dirs of Res Centres in the Social Scis (DORCISS) 1990–97, Assoc of Research Centres in the Social Sciences (ARCISS) 1997–99, NE Regnl Ctee Community Fund 2002–06, Advsy Gp on Widening Participation in Horizon 2020 EC 2014–; memb: Tyne & Wear C of C 1982–95, Advsy Bd of the Natural Environment and Land Use Programme 1991–95, R&D Ctee Northern RHA 1993–94, Econ Advsy Ctees, Exec Ctee Univ for the North East 2000–08, Constitutional Forum Newcastle City Cncl 2001, Newcastle Partnership, Tyne & Wear Sub-Regional Partnership, Bd Newcastle City Centre Partnership (NE1 Ltd) 2008–, Lead Expert Gp Foresight Land Use Futures Prog, Cncl St Nicholas Cathedral Newcastle 2011–, Bd Campaign for the Social Sciences 2014–, Advsy Gp on Science With and For Society in Horizon 2020 EC 2014–; tstee: Together Newcastle 2013–, Newcastle Cathedral 2016–, Tyne Rowing Club 2016–; Lord Dearing Lifetime Achievement Award for HE 2012; fell UCL 2011; MIBG 1966, memb Regnl Studies Assoc 1966, FRGS 1988 (Victoria medal 1992), FRSA 1993, fell Acad of Learned Socs in the Social Scis 2003 (memb Cncl 2013), fell Academia Europaea 2016–; *Books* numerous books and pubns incl: Office Linkages and Location (1973), Office Location in Urban and Regional Development (1975), British Cities: An Analysis of Urban Change (with N A Spence, 1981), Economic Development Policies: an evaluation study of the Newcastle Metropolitan Region (with F Robinson and C Wren, 1987), Higher Education and Regions: Globally Competitive and Locally Engaged (2007), The University and the City (with Paul Vallance); *Recreations* rowing, walking; *Clubs* Northern Counties, Athenaeum, Tyne Rowing (chm 2008–11); *Style*— Prof John Goddard, OBE; ✉ Centre for Urban and Regional Development Studies, Newcastle University, Newcastle upon Tyne NE1 7RU (☎ 0191 222 7732, fax 0191 232 9259, e-mail john.goddard@ncl.ac.uk, website www.ncl.ac.uk/curds/people/profile/john.goddard)

GODDARD, Rt Rev John William; s of Rev William Goddard, and Anna-Elizabeth, *née* Notley; *Educ* Wells Cathedral Sch, St Chad's Coll Durham (BA, DipTh); *m* Vivienne, *née* Selby, 2 s (Michael 1976, Gareth 1979); *Career* ordained: deacon 1970, priest 1971; curate Southbank 1970–74, curate Cayton with Eastfield 1974–75, vicar Ascension Middlesbrough 1975–82, rural dean of Middlesbrough 1981–87, vicar All Saints Middlesbrough 1982–88, canon and prebend of York 1987–88, vice-princ Edinburgh Theol Coll 1988–92, team rector of Ribbleton 1992–2000, bishop of Burnley 2000–14; race and justice cmmr Churches Together 2002, Archbishop's advsr on inter-faith issues in Northern Province, chair NW Forum of Faiths; memb Task Force Burnley '01, govr Burnley FE Coll; *Recreations* canal narrow boat, gardening, socialising, golf; *Style*— The Rt Rev John Goddard; ✉ Church House, Cathedral Close, Blackburn BB1 5AA (☎ 01253 503087, e-mail bishop.burnley@blackburn.anglican.org)

GODDARD, Rt Rev John William; *see:* Burnley, Bishop of

GODDARD, Martyn Stanley; s of Thomas Raymond Goddard (d 1982), and Winifred Florence, *née* Eastman (d 1998); *b* 9 October 1951; *Educ* Mandville Co Secdy Sch, Aylesbury Coll of Further Educn, Harrow Coll of Technol and Art (Dip Applied Photography); *m* Beverley Margret Ballard; 2 da (Lauren b 7 June 1985, Grace Natalie b 8 May 1990); *Career* photographer; asst to Gered Mankowitz and Denis Waugh 1975–76, freelance photographer IPC Young Magazine Group 1976–77; assignments 1977–91: Sunday Telegraph Magazine, Sunday Express Magazine, You Magazine, advtg projects (incl devpt of markets for car photography in Br and American magazines); editorial and advtg work 1991–; exhibitions incl: Blondie in Camera (Mirandy Gallery) 1978, Montserrat Studio (Lincoln Centre NY) 1979, 10 x 6 Group (Battersea Arts Centre, Neal St Gallery) 1981, Polaroid Time Zero (tour of UK) 1981, Human Views 1977–81 (J S Gallery London) 1981, National Portraits (Nat Theatre) 1983, Faces of Our Time (Nat Theatre tour) 1985, The Car (V&A) 1986, Rock'n'Roll and Speed (Exposure Gallery) 2007; Jet Media Excellence Award for Photography 1996, Hyundi Photographic Award for Motoring Photography 2002, 2004, 2005 and 2006; FBIPP; *Books* An Omlette and three glasses of wine (2012); *Publications* The Original Aston Martin; *Recreations* historic rally car driving, black and white photographic diary, mountain biking; *Clubs* Historic Rally Car; *Style*— Martyn Goddard, Esq; ✉ Martyn Goddard Photography, 5 Jeffrey's Place, London NW1 9PP (e-mail photo.mg@virgin.net, website www.martyngoddard.com)

GODDARD, Prof Peter; CBE (2002); s of Herbert Charles Goddard (d 1971), and Rosina Sarah, *née* Waite (d 1991); *b* 3 September 1945; *Educ* Emanuel Sch London, Trinity Coll Cambridge (MA, PhD, ScD); *m* 24 Aug 1968, Helen Barbara, da of Francis Fraser Ross (d 1991), of Alne, N Yorks; 1 da (Linda b 1973), 1 s (Michael b 1975); *Career* res fell Trinity Coll Cambridge 1969–73, visiting scientist CERN Geneva Switzerland 1970–72 and 1978, lectr in applied mathematics Univ of Durham 1972–74; St John's Coll Cambridge: lectr in mathematics 1975–91, fell 1975–94 and 2004–, tutor 1980–87, sr tutor 1983–87, master 1994–2004; Univ of Cambridge: univ asst lectr 1975–76, univ lectr 1976–89, reader in mathematical physics 1989–92, prof of theoretical physics 1992–2004, dep dir Isaac Newton Inst for Mathematical Sciences 1991–94 (hon fell 2011–), chm Local Examination Syndicate 1998–2003, memb Cncl 2000–03; Inst for Advanced Study Princeton dir 2004–12, prof 2012–16, emeritus prof 2016–; visiting prof Univ of Virginia Charlottesville 1983; govr: Berkhamsted Sch and Berkhamsted Sch for Girls 1985–96, Emanuel Sch 1992–2003, Shrewsbury Sch 1994–2003, Hills Road Sixth Form Coll Cambridge 1999–2003 (chm 2001–03); memb: Inst for Theoretical Physics Univ of Calif Santa Barbara 1986 and 1990, Inst for Advanced Study Princeton 1974 and 1988, London Mathematical Soc 1989 (pres 2002–03), Cncl Royal Soc 2000–02; Dirac medal and prize International Centre for Theoretical Physics 1997; hon fell Trinity Coll Dublin 1995, hon fell Trinity Coll Cambridge 2009; FRS 1989, FInstP 1990, FRSA 1998; *Recreations* mathematical physics, informal flower arranging, idle thought; *Style*— Prof Peter Goddard, CBE, FRS; ✉ Institute for Advanced Study, Einstein Drive, Princeton, NJ 08540, USA (☎ 001 609 734 8335)

GODDARD, Philip Norman; s of Norman Goddard (d 1984), of Templecombe, Somerset, and Rose May, *née* Pitman (d 2002); *b* 28 October 1948; *Educ* Brunel Univ (BTech), Univ of Bath (MSc); *m* 1973, Elizabeth Louise; 1 da (Joanna Louise b 1979), 1 s (Edward Philip b 1982); *Career* Westland Helicopters Ltd: head of Advanced Engrg 1989–90, chief systems engr 1990–92, dir of engrg 1992–, tech dir, now consIt; CEng, MIMechE, FREng 1997; *Recreations* vintage cars and motorcycles, golf; *Style*— Philip Goddard, Esq, FREng; ✉ Brympton Barn, Middle Chinnock, Crewkerne, Somerset TA18 7PN (☎ 01935 881948, e-mail philipgoddard323@btinternet.com)

GODDEN, (Anthony) Nicholas; s of late Tony and Molly Godden; *b* 21 February 1945; *Educ* Wellington, INSEAD; *m* 1967, Joanna Stephanie, *née* Wheeler; 2 s (James Musgrave b 1970, Peter William b 1984), 2 da (Katharine Jane b 1972, Alexandra Mary 1982); *Career* trainee accountant Ernst & Young 1963–67, fin dir Cleghorn & Harris Ltd South Africa 1967–73, chief accountant Mars Ltd 1973–75; Raychem Ltd: fin dir 1975–93, chm and md 1993–96; chm Lloyd's Superannuation Fund 1999–2011, chm Coors Brewers Pensions Ltd 2005–15, tstee Remploy Pension Scheme 2007–, chm Smith's Industries Pension Scheme 2014–, chm Lloyd's Register Superannuation Fund Assoc 2014–; memb Cncl CBI 1994–96; dir East Wilts Healthcare NHS Tst 1993–97, chm Swindon & Marlborough NHS Tst 1997–2003, chm North Bristol NHS Tst 2003–05; dir Wiltshire TEC 1994–97; FCA 1967; *Recreations* sailing, gardening; *Style*— Nicholas Godden, Esq

GODDIN, Richard William; s of William Frederick Goddin (d 1967), and Audrey Joan, *née* Stearn (d 2003); *b* 17 May 1943; *Educ* Perse Sch Cambridge, Univ of Westminster Sch of Mgmnt Studies (DMS, Urwick medal), Henley Mgmnt Coll; *m* 15 June 1985, Margaret

Ann, da of Reginald Barlow (d 1957), and Doris, *née* Russell (d 1999); 2 s (James William b 1987, Thomas Richard Druce b 1991); *Career* sr mangr Nat West Bank plc 1977–83, treas Lombard North Central plc 1983–86, dep treas Nat West plc 1986–87; County NatWest Ltd: exec dir 1987–88, head Global Funding Gp Treasury 1989–92, md Global Money Markets 1992–97, dir BOE NatWest South Africa 1996–97, md Gp Treasury 1997–2000, md Treasury Risk Associates Ltd 2001–10; dir: Ashwell Property Gp plc 2001–09 (chm 2008–09), Greenways Ravenswood Ltd 2004–09, Br Microlight Aircraft Assoc Ltd 2012–15; ACIB, FRSA, CMAe; *Recreations* flying, croquet, country life; *Clubs* Royal Aero, Croquet Assoc, Red Baron Flying, Whitehill Farm Aero; *Style*— Richard Goddin, Esq; ✉ Belmington Close, Meldreth, Cambridgeshire SG8 6NT

GODFREY, Andrew Paul; s of Bernard Russel Godfrey, of Dunblane, and Carol Emma Elise, *née* Leonhardt; *b* 12 August 1953; *Educ* Morrison's Acad Crieff Perthshire, Univ of Edinburgh (BSc Econ); *m* Irene, da of Robert Simpson, MBE; 2 s (Paul Douglas b 24 Oct 1982, Stuart Mark b 22 Feb 1985); *Career* Grant Thornton: regnl managing ptnr for Scot and NI; fin advsr and auditor various cos Scotland; ACA 1977; *Recreations* golf; *Clubs* Gleneagles Golf, Dunblane Golf; *Style*— Andrew Godfrey, Esq; ✉ Faery Knowe, St Mary's Drive, Dunblane FK15; Grant Thornton, 95 Bothwell Street, Glasgow G2 7JZ (☎ 0141 223 0000, fax 0141 223 0001, mobile 079 7615 5860)

GODFREY, Daniel; s of Gerald Michael and Anne Sheila Godfrey; *b* 30 June 1961; *Educ* Westminster, Univ of Manchester (BA); *m* July 1994, Frederiki, da of Iwan Perewiznyk, and Maroulla Perewiznyk; 3 s (Jonathan Joseph b 21 July 1981, Antony James b 14 June 1984, Benjamin David Sydney b 2 June 1997), 1 da (Mia Christina b 7 July 1987); *Career* proprietor The Sharper Image (mktg and media relations conslts) 1991–94, mktg dir Flemings 1994–98, DG Assoc of Investment Cos 1998–2009, communications dir Phoenix Gp 2009–12, chief exec Investment Assoc 2012–15; chm Personal Finance Educn Gp 2000–03, ind dir The Investment Forum 2014–; *Recreations* raising children, watching football; *Clubs* Inst of Contemporary Arts, IOD; *Style*— Daniel Godfrey, Esq

GODFREY, (William) Edwin Martindale; s of Ernest Martindale Godfrey (d 1974), of Chesterfield, Derbys, and Anna Lol Tedde, *née* Maas; *b* 20 October 1947; *Educ* Repton, Queens' Coll Cambridge (MA); *m* 10 Sept 1977, Helen Ann, da of Dr John Arthur Clement James (d 1996), of Northfield, Birmingham; 2 s (William b 1978, Thomas b 1980), 1 da (Alice b 1983); *Career* admitted slr 1971; asst slr Norton Rose Botterell and Roche 1971–72; Simmons & Simmons: asst slr 1972–76, ptnr 1977–, head of commercial gp 1993–2002, int managing ptnr 1995–96, seconded as dep chief exec Private Fin Panel 1997, head of major projects 1998–2002; Int Bar Assoc: vice-chm Ctee on Anti Tst Law 1981–86, chm Sub-Ctee on Structure and Ethics of Business Law 1990–94 (vice-chm 1988–90), memb Standing Ctee on Professional Ethics 1990–, memb Cncl Section on Business Law 1994–98, memb Standing Ctee on Int Legal Practice 1995–2000 (chm 1997–2000), memb Standing Ctee on Multi-Disciplinary Practice 1995–; memb Advsy Bd Int and Comparative Law Center S Western Legal Fndn Dallas 1991; dir Shape London 1998–; hon legal advsr Hertford CAB until 1995; Freeman: City of London Solicitors' Co 1990, City of London 1991; memb: Law Soc 1971, City of London Law Soc 1990 (chm Commercial Law Sub-Ctee 1998–), Int Bar Assoc, Hertford Deanery Synod 1990–94; govr Abel Smith Jr Mixed Infants Sch Hertford 1992–2000; FRSA 1994; *Books* Joint Ventures in Butterworths Encyclopaedia of Forms & Precedents (ed 5 edn, 1990), Law Without Frontiers (ed, 1995), Butterworths PFI Manual (jt ed, 1998); *Style*— Edwin Godfrey, Esq; ✉ Simmons & Simmons, CityPoint, One Ropemaker Street, London EC2Y 9SS (☎ 020 7628 2020, fax 020 7628 2070, telex 888562)

GODFREY, Howard Anthony; QC (1991); s of Emanuel Godfrey (d 1991), and Amy, *née* Grossman (d 2011); *b* 17 August 1946; *Educ* William Ellis Sch, LSE (LLB); *m* 3 Sept 1972, Barbara, da of John Ellinger, of London; 2 s (Timothy b 1975, James b 1980); *Career* asst lectr in law Univ of Canterbury NZ 1969, pt/t tutor Dept of Law LSE 1970–72; called to the Bar Middle Temple 1970 (bencher 2004), ad eundem Inner Temple 1984; practising SE Circuit 1972–, recorder Crown Court 1992–; called to the Bar Turks and Caicos Islands 1996; fell Soc for Advanced Legal Studies 1998; *Recreations* wine and food, humour; *Style*— Howard Godfrey, Esq, QC; ✉ 2 Bedford Row, London WC1R 4BU (☎ 020 7440 8888, fax 020 7242 1738)

GODFREY, Paul; s of Peter Godfrey, of Exeter, and Valerie, *née* Drake; *b* 16 September 1960; *Career* playwright, director and screenwriter; dir Perth Repertory Theatre Scotland 1983–84, Eden Court Theatre Inverness 1985–87 (estab touring co); *Plays* Inventing A New Colour (NT Studio 1987, Royal Court 1988), A Bucket of Eels 1988, Once in a While the Odd Thing Happens (RNT) 1990, The Panic (Royal Opera) 1991, The Blue Ball (RNT) 1995, Catalogue of Misunderstanding 1998, Tiananmen Square (BBC Radio) 1999, The Oldest Play 2000, Linda 2000; Trilogy of Plays from Difference Sources: The Modern Husband (ATC) 1995, The Invisible Woman (The Gate) 1996, The Candidate (Manchester Royal Exchange) 1997; Collected Plays: Volume One (1998); *Screenplays* The Best Sex of My Life (2001), A Map of the City (2004), Goodbye Hobberdy Jack! (2006), Dickens in New York (2006), Park & Ride (2006); *Awards* incl: Arts Cncl Trainee Directors bursary 1983, Arts Cncl Playwrights Award 1989, David Harlech Meml Bursary 1990, Stephen Arlen Award 1991, Arts Cncl Playwrights' Award 1992 and 1998, Wingate Scholarship 1996; *Style*— Paul Godfrey

GODFREY, Dr Richard Charles; s of Thomas Charles Godfrey (d 1965), of Watford, Herts, and Joan Eva, *née* Clayton; *b* 8 September 1940; *Educ* Watford GS, Peterhouse Cambridge (MA), UCL (MD); *m* 8 June 1968, Jane Catherine, da of Stanley Goodman, of Reigate, Surrey; 3 s (Thomas b 1970, Robin b 1974, Matthew b 1975), 1 da (Sarah b 1971); *Career* Univ of Southampton: lectr in med 1972–76, conslt physician 1976–2002, clinical sub-dean 1984–89; Overseas Devpt Admin prof of med Moi Univ Kenya 1991–94, health advsr Merlin 2002–07; warden Farley Hosp Almshouses 1981–2011, organ conslt to Salisbury Diocesan Advsy Ctee; church and concert organist, music teacher; tstee Humanitarian Aid Relief Tst 2007–09; MD, FRCP, ARCO; *Recreations* association croquet; *Style*— Dr Richard Godfrey; ✉ Dashwood, Lyme Road, Up Lyme, Lyme Regis DT7 3UY (☎ 01297 445709, mobile 07884 387663)

GODFREY-ISAACS, Laura; *b* 22 July 1964; *Educ* Kingston Poly, Brighton Poly (BA), Slade Sch of Art London, RCA (PhD); *Career* artist; sr lectr: Winchester Sch of Art, Univ of Southampton, Kent Inst of Art and Design; visiting lectr at numerous art colls incl Tate Gallery, Whitechapel Gallery, Barbican and Camden Art Centre; artist in residence: Pratt Inst Brooklyn NYC 1988–89, Tate Gallery Liverpool 1990; dir Home prodn co 1998–; public art projects with numerous galleries and museums; *Solo Exhibitions* Monima Gallery London 1987, Morgan's Gallery London 1987, Tate Gallery Liverpool 1990, Sue Williams Gallery London 1991 and 1993, John Milton Gallery London 1991, Physical Encounters (Gardner Arts Centre Univ of Sussex touring to Royal Festival Hall Galleries London) 1992, Robert Hossack Gallery London 1994, Condeso Lawler Gallery NYC 1994, John Jones Gallery London 1995; *Group Exhibitions* incl: Al Fresco Exhibition (RA) 1988, Whitechapel Open Studio Exhibition 1989, View of the New (Royal Over-Seas League London) 1991, John Moores Exhibition (Walker Art Gallery Liverpool) 1991, Roses are Red (Br Cncl touring exhbn of UK and Bulgarian artists to Polvdiv Bulgaria and London) 1991, invited artist Whitechapel Open 92, Festival International de la Peinture Cannes (Br Cncl rep artist with Saleem Arif, *qv*) 1992, Women's Art at New Hall Cambridge 1992, Somatic States (Middlesex Univ and Norwich Art Gallery) 1992, Riverside Open (Riverside Studios London) 1993, Skin (Antonio Barnola Gallery Barcelona) 1993, Wit and Excess (Sydney, Brisbane, Melbourne and Adelaide) 1994, It's a Pleasure (South Bank London) 1995, Stereo-Tip (Soros Centre for Contemporary Art Ljubljana Slovenia) 1995; *Collections* incl: Momart, New Hall, Arts Cncl of GB, Contemporary Arts Soc; *Awards* Jacob Mendelsohn scholarship 1986, McDonald fellowship from Pratt Inst NYC 1988, Boise fellowship from Slade Sch of Art London 1988, Fulbright fellowship for residency in NYC 1988, Momart fellowship for residency at Tate Gallery Liverpool 1990; *Style*— Ms Laura Godfrey-Isaacs

GODLEY, Adam; s of Samuel Jack Godley, and Gladys, *née* Gainsboro; *b* 1964, Amersham, Bucks; *Educ* Rickmansworth Sch; *Career* actor; *Theatre* West End: An Inspector Calls (Westminster Theatre), June Moon (Vaudeville Theatre), The Revengers Comedies (Strand Theatre), The Wood Demon (Playhouse Theatre), The Importance of Being Earnest (Haymarket Theatre), Private Lives (Albery Theatre and Richard Rogers Theater NY, Outstanding Broadway Debut Theatre World Award), The Rivals (Albery Theatre); Royal Court Theatre: Mr Kolpert, Mouth to Mouth (nomination Best Supporting Actor Olivier Awards), Rain Man (Apollo Theatre, nomination Best Actor Olivier Award, nomination Best Actor WOS Award); Donmar Warehouse: Cabaret, The Front Page; NT: Cleo, Camping, Emanuelle and Dick (nomination Best Supporting Actor Olivier Awards), Mr A's Amazing Maze Plays, Watch on the Rhine, Close of Play, The Pillowman, Paul, Two Thousand Years, From Morning To Midnight; RSC: Three Hours After the Marriage, The White Devil, The General From America, A Midsummer Night's Dream, From Morning To Midnight; plays at Scarborough: Eden End, The Ballroom, The Beaux Strategem, Man of the Moment, Taking Steps, Othello; other credits incl: The Critic (Royal Exchange Theatre Manchester), A Going Concern (Hampstead Theatre), Dear Charles (Guildford Theatre), Hippolytus (Gate Theatre), Zero Hour (Edinburgh Festival), Anything Goes (Stephen Sondheim Theatre NY, Outer Critics Circle Award, nomination Drama Desk Award, nomination Tony Award); *Television* Cor Blimey!, Sword of Honour, Margery and Gladys, Hawking, The Young Visiters, Nuremburg, Terminator: The Sarah Connor Chronicles, Breaking Bad, The Old Curiosity Shop, Numb3rs, Mad Men, Merlin, Dollhouse, Marple: The Secret of Chimneys, Case Histories, Lie To Me, Harry's Law, The Spies of Warsaw, A Young Doctor's Notebook, Homeland, Suits, Manhattan, Perception, Powers; *Radio* incl: The Frederica Quartet, The School for Scandal, The Ghost Train, Birdsong, Forty Years On, Les Liaisons Dangereuses, Tess of the D'Urbevilles; *Film* Thunderpants, And Now... Ladies and Gentlemen, Bride of Ice, Around the World in 80 Days, Love Actually, Charlie and the Chocolate Factory, Nanny McPhee, Elizabeth – The Golden Age, Son of Rambow, X-Files: I Want to Believe, The Special Relationship, Wilde Salome, The Forger, Battleship, The Theory of Everything, The BFG, De Premier; *Style*— Adam Godley, Esq; ✉ c/o Sue Latimer, ARG, 4 Great Exmoor Street, London W10 6BD (☎ 020 7436 6400, fax 020 7436 6700, e-mail latimer@argtalent.com)

GODLEY, Georgina Jane (Mrs Sebastian Conran); da of Michael Godley, and Heather, *née* Couper; *b* 11 April 1955; *Educ* Putney HS, Thames Valley GS, Wimbledon Art Sch, Brighton Poly (BA), Chelsea Sch of Art (MA); *m* 16 April 1988, Sebastian Conran, s of Sir Terence Conran; 2 s (Samuel Orby Conran b 12 May 1989, Maximillian Anthony Rupert Conran b 4 April 1995); *Career* picture restorer 1978–79, menswear designer Browns London and Paris 1979, ptnr designer Crolla London 1980–85, fndr and designer own label Georgina Godley (retail outlets from London to USA and Japan, and illustrations and articles in all maj fashion pubns); currently style dir Habitat; sr lectr St Martin's Sch of Art and Sch of Fashion and Textiles RCA; *Style*— Ms Georgina Godley

GODMAN, Jo; da of Frank Alfred Leonard, of Dernford Hall, Swefling, Suffolk, and Amelia Emma, *née* Day; *b* 29 May 1944; *Educ* Camden Sch for Girls, Holborn Coll of Law, Languages and Commerce; *m* 11 March 1967, Keith William Godman, s of William Christopher Godman; *Career* girl friday Chapman Raper TV commercials prodn co 1965–67, prodn asst Geoffrey Forster Associates 1967–71, prodr for Tom Bussmann of Bussmann Llewelyn 1972–80 (prodn asst 1971–72), co-fndr Patterson Godman Ltd 1980–83, md RSA Films Ltd (Ridley Scott Associates) 1983–96; fndr Godman Ltd 1997–; has produced numerous commercials winning awards at D&AD, British TV Awards, Cannes and Clio NY; *Recreations* cinema, gardening, ballet, cooking, swimming; *Clubs* Groucho, Women in Advertising, Soho House; *Style*— Jo Godman

GODSAL, Philip Caulfeild; s of Maj Philip Hugh Godsal (d 1982), of Iscoyd Park, Whitchurch, Shropshire, and Pamela Ann Delisle, *née* Caulfeild (d 2004); *b* 10 October 1945; *Educ* Eton; *m* 1, 29 Nov 1969 (m dis 1985), Lucinda Mary, da of Lt Cdr Percival Royston Dancy; 3 s (Philip Langley b 28 June 1971, Benjamin Rupert Wilmot b 17 June 1976, Thomas Henry b 3 Aug 1977), 1 da (Laura Sophie b 24 May 1973); m 2, 2 July 1986, Selina Baber, da of Thomas William Brooke-Smith (d 1991), of Canford Cliffs; 3 step da (Zoe Christina b 1974, Lucinda Selina b 1976, Christina Juliet b 1980); *Career* farmer, land agent and chartered surveyor; formerly ptnr Savills Norwich, ptnr John German Shrewsbury 1984–97, sr ptnr Carter Jonas Shrewsbury 1997– (now conslt); chm Historic Houses Assoc for Wales 1989–91, chm N Wales Region Timber Growers UK 1989–91, sec Shropshire Rural Housing Assoc 1988–95; pres Iscoyd and Fenns Bank CC; Regnl Ctee National Trust: chm Mercia 2000–02, vice-chm West Midlands 2002–06; High Sheriff Clwyd 1993–94; FRICS; *Recreations* shooting, forestry, reading; *Clubs* MCC, Farmers', Frontline, Lancashire CCC; *Style*— Philip Godsal, Esq; ✉ Wolvesacre Mill, Agden, Whitchurch, Shropshire SY13 3RE; Carter Jonas, Chartered Surveyors and Property Consultants, South Pavilion, Sansaw Business Park, Hadnall, Shrewsbury SY4 4AS (☎ 01939 210113, e-mail philip.godsal@carterjonas.uk)

GODSIFF, Roger; MP; s of late George Godsiff, and Gladys Godsiff; *b* 28 June 1937; *Educ* Catford Comp Sch; *m* Julia Brenda; 1 s, 1 da; *Career* formerly political offr APEX then sr research offr GMB; Parly candidate Birmingham Yardley 1983; MP (Lab): Birmingham Small Heath 1992–97, Birmingham Sparkbrook and Small Heath 1997–2010, Birmingham Hall Green 2010–; House of Commons: chm All-Pty Kashmir Parly Gp 1992–2004, chm Br-Japanese Parly Gp 1997–; cnclIr London Borough of Lewisham 1971–90 (Lab chief whip 1974–77, mayor 1977); chm Charlton Athletic Charitable Tst; Japanese Order of the Rising Sun Gold and Silver Star 2014; *Recreations* sport, particularly football; *Clubs* Charlton Athletic Supporters', Rowley Labour; *Style*— Roger Godsiff, Esq, MP; ✉ House of Commons, London SW1A 0AA

GODSMARK, His Hon Judge Nigel Graham; QC; s of Derek Godsmark (d 2013), and Betty Howard, *née* Young (d 2011); *b* 8 December 1954, London; *Educ* Queen Mary's GS Basingstoke, Univ of Nottingham; *m* 17 July 1982, Priscilla, *née* Howitt; 2 da (Katherine b 25 Oct 1988, Anna b 24 Dec 1991), 1 s (Christopher b 11 July 1995); *Career* called to the Bar 1979; asst recorder 1999, recorder 2000, circuit judge (Midland Circuit) 2012–, dep judge of the High Court 2013, designated civil judge for Notts, Derbys and Lincs 2013–; hon prof of law Univ of Nottingham 2009; *Style*— His Hon Judge Godsmark, QC; ✉ Nottingham Combined Court Centre, Canal Street, Nottingham NG1 7EL

GODWIN, Prof Richard John (Dick); s of John Leige Godwin (d 1992), of Nettlebed, Oxon, and Kathleen Alice, *née* Hands (d 1971); *b* 20 April 1947; *Educ* Nat Coll of Agric Engrg (BSc), Univ of Illinois (MS), Univ of Reading and Nat Coll of Agric Engrg (PhD); *m* 15 July 1975, Jill Banfield, da of J Fisher; *Career* res and teaching asst Dept of Agric Engrg Univ of Illinois 1968–70; Cranfield Univ at Silsoe (formerly Nat Coll of Agric Engrg and Silsoe Coll): res scholar 1970–73, res offr 1974–76, lectr in applied soil mechanics 1977–81, sr lectr in soil dynamics 1981–85, asst dir of R&D 1979–84, dir of res 1984–99, prof and head of agric and environmental engrg 1985–96, dean Faculty of Agric Engrg, Food Prodn and Rural Land Use 1990–93, prof and head of agric and biosystems engrg 1996–99, prof and head Inst of AgriTechnology 1999–2001, prof and ldr Engrg Gp Nat Soil Resources Inst 2001–, dir of postgrad res 2001–07; pro-vice-chllr Cranfield Univ 1993–

G

96; external examiner: Univ of the W Indies 1987–91, Harper Adams Agric Coll 1994–97, UC Dublin 1996–2000, Univ of Aberdeen, Univ of Newcastle upon Tyne, Univ of SA, Asian Inst of Technol; referee and memb Editorial Bd Jl of Agric Engrg Res 1984–; assoc ed: Jl of Terramechanics, Soil Use and Management; visiting prof Harpur Adams Univ Coll; pres IAgrE 1994–96; chm Douglas Bomford Tst 2008–12 (tstee 1994–2008), memb Bd of Tstees Claas Fndn 1999–2008; hon prof Czech Univ of Life Sciences; Award of Merit IAgrE; Dr (hc) Slovak Univ of Agriculture 2008, DSc (hc) Harper Adams UC 2012; fell American Soc of Agric Engrs 1994 (int dir 1992–94, John Deere Medal 2005); CEng (IAgrE), CEnv, Hon FIAgrE 2000, FREng 2001, FRAgS 2009, Hon FRASE; *Publications* numerous articles and papers in learned jls; *Recreations* gardening, walking, DIY, photography; *Style—* Prof Dick Godwin; ✉ Dick Godwin Associates Limited, 9 Holly Walk, Silsoe, Bedford MK45 4EB (☎ 01525 86153, e-mail r.godwin@iagre.biz)

GODWIN, Tim; OBE (2003), QPM (2009); *Educ* Haywards Heath GS, Warsash Coll of Nautical Studies, Univ of Portsmouth (BA), Univ of Cambridge (Dip); *Career* joined Sussex Police 1981, Met Police 1999–2012 (Dep Cmmr 2008–12, acting Cmmr 2011); *Style—* Tim Godwin, Esq, OBE, QPM

GODWIN-AUSTEN, Dr Richard Bertram; s of R Annesley Godwin-Austen, CBE (d 1977), and Kathleen Beryl Godwin-Austen (d 1995); *b* 4 October 1935; *Educ* Charterhouse, St Thomas' London Hosp (MB BS, MD); *m* 1, 12 Aug 1961, Jennifer Jane (d 1996), da of Louis Sigismund Himely; 1 s (Jonathan Reade b 1962), 1 da (Alice Amelia b 1964); m 2, 15 Nov 1997, (Deirdre) Sally, da of Gerald Stark Toller; *Career* sr registrar Inst of Neurology Queen Sq London 1967–70, conslt neurologist Univ Hosp Nottingham 1970–98; clinical teacher (former chm) of neurological sciences Nottingham until 1998; memb Med Advsy Panel Parkinson's Disease Soc; pres Assoc of British Neurologists, vice-pres Euro Fedn of Neurological Socs, delegate to Euro Bd of Neurology, sec and treas gen World Fedn of Neurology; High Sheriff Notts 1994–95; FRCP 1976; *Books* The Parkinson's Disease Handbook (1984), The Neurology of the Elderly (1989), Seizing Opportunities – The Reminiscences of a Physician (2008); *Recreations* gardening, dessert wines; *Clubs* Garrick, RSM; *Style—* Dr Richard Godwin-Austen; ✉ 15 Westgate, Southwell, Nottinghamshire NG25 0JN

GOETZ, Michael Steven (Mike); s of Richard T Goetz (d 2004), and Nancy Feltner, *née* Worthington, of Melbourne, FL; *b* 7 August 1956, Columbus, OH; *Educ* Ohio State Univ (BA), Boston Univ Sch of Law (JD); *m* 15 Oct 1988, Dr Senah E Green; 3 s (Jonathan Richard b 12 July 1991, Christopher Robert b 26 Oct 1992, William Hunter b 1 March 1994); *Career* admitted NY State Bar 1988; slr specialising in banking; practised NY 1986–2000, ptnr White & Case LLP London 2000–08 (co-head Banking and Capital Markets Gp), ptnr Freshfields Bruckhaus Deringer London 2008–09, ptnr (managing ptnr London) Ropes and Gray LLP 2009–; *Style—* Mike Goetz, Esq

GOGGINS, Rt Hon Paul Gerard; MP, PC (2009); s of John Goggins, and Rita Goggins (d 1991); *b* 16 June 1953; *Educ* St Bede's Sch Manchester, Ushaw Coll Durham, Birmingham Poly, Manchester Poly; *m* 1977, Wyn, da of Tom Bartley (d 1991); 2 s (Matthew b 1980, Dominic b 1985), 1 da (Theresa b 1982); *Career* residential child care offr Liverpool Catholic Social Servs 1974–76, offr i/c residential children's home Wigan MBC 1976–84, project dir NCH Action for Children in Salford 1984–89, nat dir Church Action on Poverty 1989–97; MP (Lab) Wythenshawe and Sale E 1997–; PPS to Rt Hon John Denham MP, *qv*, 1998–2000, PPS to Rt Hon David Blunkett MP, *qv*, 2000–03, Parly under sec of state Home Office 2003–06, Parly under-sec of state NI Office 2006–07, min of state NI Office 2007–10; memb Social Security Select Ctee 1997–98; fndr chm UK Coalition Against Poverty; cncllr Salford City Cncl 1990–98; *Recreations* football (Manchester City FC), walking and music; *Style—* The Rt Hon Paul Goggins, Esq, MP; ✉ House of Commons, London SW1A 0AA (☎ 020 7219 3000); ☎ 0161 499 7900

GOH, Dr Beng Tin; *b* 14 May 1953; *Educ* Univ of Singapore (MB BS), Univ of London (Dip Dermatology), Soc of Apothecaries (Dip Venereology); *m* 17 Dec 1978, Dr Tiak Nyar Sim; 2 da (Po-Siann b 18 May 1983, Po-Laine b 20 Jan 1985); *Career* registrar in genitourinary med King's Coll Hosp London 1980–81, sr registrar in genitourinary med Royal London Hosp and Moorfields Eye Hosp London 1982–85, conslt in genitourinary med Barts NHS Tst and Moorfields Eye Hosp London 1985–2012 (emeritus conslt physician Barts Health NHS Tst 2013–), int conslt advsr Guangdong Provincial Dermatology Hosp Guangzhou China 2013–; author of papers on syphilis incl guidelines, oculo-genital infections, chlamydia and sexual health in ethnic groups; past examiner Soc of Apothecaries' Dip in Genitourinary Med; hon treas Chinese Nat Healthy Living Centre London; FRCP; *Recreations* travelling, photography; *Style—* Dr Beng Tin Goh; ✉ Ambrose King Centre, The Royal London Hospital, Whitechapel, London E1 1BB (☎ 020 7377 7309, e-mail beng.goh@bartshealth.nhs.uk)

GOLD, Antony; s of Ellis Neville Gold, of Liverpool, and Sonya, *née* Greene; *b* 26 August 1958; *Educ* Birkenhead Sch, Univ of Manchester (LLB), Chester Law Coll; *m* 3 Oct 1983, Sally Jane, da of late Eddie Perkin; 2 da (Clara Wendy b 21 June 1989, Martha Amanda b 27 May 1998), 1 s (Alastair b 5 March 1992); *Career* asst slr Hammelburger Marks Manchester 1983–84 (articled clerk 1980–83); Eversheds: asst slr/assoc Alexander Tatham Manchester (now part of Eversheds) 1984–88, ptnr 1988–, UK head of litigation 1993–98, head of litigation Eversheds Manchester 1995–2001, head of intellectual property Eversheds Leeds/Manchester 2001–03, head Retail Sector Gp 2005–, head of intellectual property Eversheds 2007–08; acted for investors in Barlow Clowes case 1988–89, for local authorities in BCCI case 1991–92 and numerous other cases involving financial collapse, professional negligence and intellectual property; memb: Law Soc 1983, Int Arbitration Club, Int Trademark Assoc 2000; *Recreations* reading, mountaineering; *Style—* Antony Gold, Esq; ✉ Eversheds House, 70 Great Bridgewater Street, Manchester M1 5ES (☎ 0845 497 8204, fax 0161 832 5337, e-mail antonygold@eversheds.com)

GOLD, David; *b* 9 September 1936, London; *m* (m dis), Beryl Hunt; 2 da (Jacqueline Gold *qv*, Vanessa); *Career* businessman; owner: Gold Gp Int, Sport Newspapers 1986–2007, Birmingham City FC 1993–2009, West Ham United FC 2010–; winner Int Malta Air Rally 1981 and 1982; *Recreations* flying (PPL holder 40 years, helicopter licence 10 years), golf; *Style—* David Gold, Esq; ✉ Twitter @davidgoldwhu

GOLD, Baron (Life Peer UK 2011), of Westcliff-on-Sea in the County of Essex; David Laurence Gold; s of Michael Gold (d 1980), and Betty, *née* Levitt; *b* 1 March 1951; *Educ* Westcliff HS, LSE (LLB); *m* 27 Aug 1978, Sharon; 1 da (Amanda b 30 March 1981), 2 s (Alexander b 23 Jan 1983, Edward b 5 Oct 1985); *Career* admitted slr 1975; Herbert Smith: ptnr 1983–, head of litigation 2003–05, sr ptnr 2005–10; pres Southend & Westcliff Hebrew Congregation 1997–2006; memb Ctee Br Israel Law Assoc 1997–98, memb Ctee Br Overseas Trade Gp for Israel 1998–2000; govr LSE 2009–; Freeman City of London Slrs' Co; memb Law Soc; *Recreations* theatre, cinema, bridge, travel, family; *Style—* The Lord Gold; ✉ Herbert Smith, Exchange House, Primrose Street, London EC2A 2HS (☎ 020 7374 8000, fax 020 7374 0888, e-mail david.gold@herbertsmith.com)

GOLD, Jacqueline; CBE (2016); da of David Gold, and Beryl Hunt; *b* 16 July 1960; *Educ* Baston Old Sch; *m* 1, 20 Aug 1980 (m dis 1990), Tony D'Silva; m 2, 15 May 2010, Daniel Cunningham; 1 da (Scarlett Rose b 5 May 2009); *Career* Ann Summers: joined as wages clerk 1979, launched party plan 1981, dir 1987, md and chief exec 1993–; vice-pres Children's Tst 2012–, patron Breast Cancer Campaign; Working Women Mean Business Award 1993, Gucci Business Age 40 Under 40 Award 1995, shortlisted London Entrepreneur of the Year 2001, shortlisted Nat Business Awards Entrepreneur of the Year 2003, Business Communicator of the Year 2004, Inspirational Woman of the Year 2012, TiE Female Entrepreneur of the Year 2013; *Books* Good Vibrations (autobiography, 1995), A Woman's Courage (autobiography, 2007); *Recreations* football, yoga; *Style—* Ms Jacqueline Gold, CBE; ✉ Ann Summers, Gold Group House, Godstone Road, Whyteleafe, Surrey CR3 0GG; publicist Shelley Frosdick, PHA Media (☎ 020 7025 1373, e-mail shelley@pha-media.com)

GOLD, His Hon Judge Jeremy Spencer; QC (2003); s of late Alfred Gold, and Ruby Caroline, *née* Reid (d 2003); *b* 15 July 1955, London; *Educ* Brighton, Hove and Sussex GS, Univ of Kent at Canterbury (BA); *m* 19 Sept 1976, Joanne Lesley, *née* Driver; 3 da (Laura b 3 Dec 1979, Jessica b 28 July 1982, Tasha b 20 May 1986); *Career* called to the Bar 1977; criminal barr 1977–2009, asst recorder 1999, recorder 2000, circuit judge (South Eastern Circuit) 2009–; *Recreations* theatre, travel, good company, Brighton & Hove Albion FC, Lancing Wanderers FC; *Style—* His Hon Judge Gold, QC; ✉ Leeds Crown Court, High Street, Lewes, East Sussex BN7 1YB (☎ 01273 480400)

GOLD, Kevin; *Career* slr; articled Lovell White Durrant, ptnr Bayer Rosin until 1995, Mishcon de Reya 1995– (managing ptnr 1997–); *Style—* Kevin Gold, Esq; ✉ Mishcon de Reya, Summit House, 12 Red Lion Square, London WC1R 4QD

GOLD, Murray Jonathan; s of Leonard Gold, and Suzanne Gold; *b* 1969; *Educ* Portsmouth GS, CCC Cambridge; *Career* writer and composer; memb: Writer's Guild, PRS, Mechanical Copywright Protection Soc; *Theatre* as composer incl: Hove (RNT) 1993, Transit Hotel (Battersea Arts Centre) 1995, Dr Faustus (Young Vic) 2002; as writer incl: Glue Wedding (Battersea Arts Centre), Resolution (Battersea Arts Centre), Exodus (Battersea Arts Centre), Candide (adaptation, Gate Theatre and RNT Studio) 1997, 50 Revolutions (Whitehall Theatre) 1999; *Television* composer: Vanity Fair (BBC) 1998 (Best Original Score RTS 1999, nomination Best Theme TRIC Awards 1999), Queer as Folk (Channel 4) 1999 and 2000 (nomination Best Original Score RTS 1999, nomination Best Original Music for TV BAFTA Awards 1999 and 2000), Love in the 21st Century (Channel 4) 1999, Clocking Off (Channel 4) 2000, Randall & Hopkirk (Deceased) (BBC) 2000, Shameless (series 1–5 (co-writer, series 3–5), Channel 4) 2004–08, Casanova (Channel 4) 2005, Dr Who (series 1–4, BBC) 2005–08, Torchwood (co-writer, series 1 and 2, BBC) 2007–08; sometime writer Family Affairs (Channel 5); *Radio* writer Electricity (BBC Radio 3) 2000 (Best New Radio Play Soc of Authors 2001, adapted for stage Bush Theatre 2002); *Films* composer: Mojo 1997, Beautiful Creatures 2000, Wild About Harry 2000, Miranda 2002, Alien Autopsy 2006, Mischief Night 2006, I Want Candy 2006, Death at a Funeral 2007; *Recreations* music, theatre, film, pubs, cricket, football, history; *Clubs* Century; *Style—* Murray Gold, Esq; ✉ c/o Manners McDade Artist Management, 46 Copperfield Street, London SE1 0DY (☎ 020 7928 9939, e-mail info@mannersmcdade.co.uk)

GOLD, Nina; *Educ* Christ's Coll Cambridge (MA); *Career* casting director; memb: BAFTA, Acad of Motion Picture Arts and Sciences 2011; *Film* incl: Twin Town 1997, The Borrowers 1997, Topsy Turvy 1999, Love's Labour's Lost 2000, Mike Bassett: England Manager 2001, The 51st State 2001, Max 2002, The Life and Death of Peter Sellers 2004, Vera Drake 2004, Brothers of the Head 2005, The Illusionist 2006, Starter for 10 2006, Amazing Grace 2006, Hot Fuzz 2007, Beowulf 2007, The Edge of Love 2008, Eastern Promises 2008, Happy-Go-Lucky 2009, Bright Star 2009, Nowhere Boy 2009, A Christmas Carol 2009, Red Riding 2009, The King's Speech 2010, Another Year 2010, My Week with Marilyn 2011 (Artios Award 2012), Jane Eyre 2011, Attack the Block 2011, Wild Bill 2011, The Iron Lady 2011, Prometheus 2012, Les Misérables 2012, Shadow Dancer 2012, Sightseers 2012, In Fear 2012, The World's End 2013, A Long Way Down 2013, Rush 2013, How I Live Now 2013, Dom Hemingway 2013, The Counselor 2013; *Television* incl: Tipping the Velvet 2002, The Virgin Queen 2005, Rome 2005–07, Longford 2006, John Adams 2008 (Outstanding Casting Emmy Award 2009), Einstein and Eddington 2008, The Devil's Whore 2008, Small Island 2009, The Special Relationship 2010, Any Human Heart 2010, The Crimson Petal and the White 2011, Game of Thrones 2011–, Secret State 2012, Restless 2012; *Theatre* Ecstasy 2011, The Audience 2013; *Style—* Ms Nina Gold

GOLDACRE, Prof Michael John; s of Reginald Goldacre (d 1983), and Patricia Goldacre (d 1986); *b* 3 January 1944, Melbourne, Aust; *Educ* Bec Sch London, Magdalen Coll Oxford (BA), UCH London (BM BCh); *m* 1973, Susan Maria; 4 s (Ben b 1974, Joshua b 1981, Raphael b 1983, Alexander b 1985); *Career* Univ of Oxford: clinical lectr in social and community med 1974–, dir Unit of Health-Care Epidemiology 1986–, UK Med Careers Research Gp 1993–, prof of public health 2002–; fell Magdalen Coll Oxford 1985– (tutor for grads 1993–95, dean of degrees 1993–2011); scientific dir SE England Public Health Observatory 2000–05; author of approximately 350 papers on epidemiology, public health and health servs research in med jls; FFPH, FRCP; *Style—* Prof Michael Goldacre; ✉ Nuffield Department of Population Health, University of Oxford, Old Road Campus, Old Road, Oxford OX3 7LF

GOLDBERG, Andrew (Andy); OBE (2011); s of Arnold Goldberg, of Cardiff, and Lillian, *née* Diamond; *b* 28 July 1970; *Educ* Imperial Coll London (MB BS), Univ of London (MD); *m* 16 Dec 2004, Adi Balogh; 3 c (Jack b 2007, Taylor b 2009, Robert b 2011); *Career* conslt orthopaedic and trauma surgeon Northampton Gen Hosp 2009–10, conslt orthopaedic surgeon Royal Nat Orthopaedic Hosp and clinical sr lectr in trauma and orthopaedics UCL 2010–; chief investigator TARVA Trial (www.anklearthritis.co.uk); memb: Br Orthopaedic Assoc, Br Orthopaedic Foot and Ankle Soc, American Orthopaedic Foot and Ankle Soc (AOFAS), RSM; FRCSI 1997, FRCS 1998 (TR&Orth 2006); *Publications* Surgical Talk (1999, 3 edn 2012), Clinical Talk (series ed, 2005–), over 70 peer reviewed pubns and book chapters; *Recreations* travel, photography, music, tennis, reading, wine tasting; *Style—* Mr Andy Goldberg, OBE; ✉ The Wellington Hospital, St John's Wood, London NW8 9LE (☎ 020 7042 1828, e-mail goldbergpp@gmail.com, website www.myankle.co.uk)

GOLDBERG, David Gerard; QC; s of Arthur Goldberg (d 1982), of Plymouth, and Sylvia, *née* Stone; *b* 12 August 1947; *Educ* Plymouth Coll, LSE (LLB, LLM); *m* 22 Dec 1981 (m dis 2003), Alison Ninette, da of Jack V Lunzer, of London; 1 s (Arthur b 1986), 1 da (Selina b 1984); *Career* called to the Bar Lincoln's Inn 1971 (bencher 1997), in practice at Revenue Bar; case note ed British Tax Review 1975–87, author of numerous articles on taxation and company law, chm of the tstees Surgical Workshop for Anatomical Prosection 1994–; Philip Hardman Meml Lecture 1995; *Books* An Introduction to Company Law (jtly, 1987), The Law of Partnership Taxation (jtly, 1987); *Recreations* reading, letter writing, thinking; *Style—* David Goldberg, Esq, QC; ✉ Gray's Inn Tax Chambers, 36 Queen Street, London EC4R 1BN (☎ 020 7242 2642, fax 020 7831 9017, e-mail dg@taxbar.com)

GOLDBERG, Rabbi Dr David J; OBE (2004); s of Percy Selvin Goldberg (d 1981), and Frimette, *née* Yudt (d 1980); *b* 25 February 1939; *Educ* Manchester Grammar, Lincoln Coll Oxford (MA), Trinity Coll Dublin, Leo Baeck Coll London; *m* 1969, Carole-Ann, da of Sydney Marks; 1 s (Rupert Alexander Ian b 1 Feb 1974), 1 da (Emily Catherine Toby b 18 Jan 1977); *Career* rabbi Wembley and Dist Liberal Synagogue 1971–74; The Liberal Jewish Synagogue: assoc rabbi 1975–86, sr rabbi 1986–2004, emeritus rabbi 2004–; Robert Waley-Cohen travelling scholarship 1978; chm ULPS Rabbinic Conf 1983–85 and 1995–97, vice-chm Cncl of Reform and Liberal Rabbis 1984 and 1993–95, co-chm London Soc of Jews and Christians 1989–2004 (co-pres 2004–); Interfaith Gold Medallion (for outstanding contribution to interfaith understanding) 1999, Premio Iglesias (for Italian edn of To the Promised Land) 1999; DD (hc) Univ of Manchester 2000; *Books* The Jewish People (1987, new edn 1989), To the Promised Land (1996), Progressive Judaism Today (ed, 1997), Liberal Judaism: The First 100 Years (ed, 2004), The Divided Self (2006), This Is Not the Way (2012), The Story of the Jews (2014); *Recreations* fell walking, travel, watching cricket, listening to music, reading; *Style—* Rabbi Dr David J Goldberg, OBE; ✉ The Liberal Jewish Synagogue, 28 St John's Wood Road, London NW8 7HA (☎ 020 7286 5181, fax 020 7266 3591, e-mail djg@bartvillas.org.uk)

GOLDBERG, Jonathan Jacob; QC (1989); s of Rabbi Dr Percy Selvin Goldberg (decd), and Frimette, *née* Yudt (decd); *b* 13 November 1947; *Educ* Manchester Grammar, Trinity Hall Cambridge (MA, LLB); *m* 7 Nov 1980 (m dis 1991), Alexis Jane, da of Sir George Martin, CBE, *qv*; 1 da (Natasha Jane Frimette b 22 Dec 1982), 1 s (Saul Percy Laurence b 22 Sept 1985); *Career* called to the Bar Middle Temple 1971, practising SE Circuit, recorder of the Crown Court 1993–; memb NY State Bar 1985, Int Presidency of the Int Assoc of Jewish Lawyers and Jurists 1999–; memb SE and Northern Circuits; *Recreations* reading, films, music, wine; *Style—* Jonathan Goldberg, QC; ✉ 30 Ely Place, London EC1N 6TD (☎ 020 7400 9600, fax 020 7400 9630)

GOLDBERG, Melvin Douglas (Mel); s of Louis Goldberg, and Rebecca, *née* Caplin; *b* 5 June 1937, London; *Educ* Westminster City Sch, St John's Coll Cambridge (MA); *Children* 2 s (Alexander Douglas, Richard Douglas), 1 da (Nora Eden); *Career* admitted slr 1963; sr ptnr Mel Goldberg Law LLP; pres and fndr memb Br Assoc for Sport and Law, memb Sport Dispute Resolution Panel of Mediators; past chm Amateur Swimming Assoc, former ceo Int Squash Players' Assoc; memb: Sports Ctee Variety Club of GB, Ctee Anti-Slavery Int, Ctee Sport Against Addiction; Sports Business 12th Most Influential Sports Lawyer in the World; memb Law Soc; *Books* The Final Score (co-author); *Recreations* cinema, cricket, motorsport, music, opera, reading, skiing, tennis; *Style—* Mel Goldberg, Esq; ✉ Mel Goldberg Law, Media House, 4 Stratford Place, London W1C 1AT (☎ 020 7355 0310, fax 020 7355 0322, e-mail mg@melgoldberg.co.uk)

GOLDENBERG, Philip; s of Nathan Goldenberg, OBE (d 1995), and Edith, *née* Drusinsky (changed to Dee, d 2010); *b* 26 April 1946; *Educ* St Paul's, Pembroke Coll Oxford (MA); *m* 1, 16 Aug 1969 (m dis 1975), Dinah Mary Pye; m 2, 12 Oct 1985, Lynda Anne, *née* Benjamin; 3 s (Jonathan b 1986 d 2009, Benjamin b 1990, Joshua b 1994), 1 da (Philippa b 1988); *Career* admitted slr 1972, asst slr Linklaters & Paines 1972–82, ptnr SJ Berwin 1983–2004 (asst slr 1982–83); conslt Michael Conn Goldsobel 2004–16, chm Mission Capital plc 2008–11; sec Oxford Univ Lib Club 1966, pres Watford Lib Assoc 1980–81, vice-chm Home Counties Regnl Lib Pty 1976–78 and 1980–81; Lib Pty: Cncl 1975–88, Nat Exec Ctee 1977–87, Candidates Ctee 1976–85, Assembly Ctee 1985–87; Lib Dems: memb Federal Conf Ctee 1988–92, Federal Policy Ctee 1990–92, pres Woking Lib Dems 1992–94, treas SE Region 1999–2001, chair SE Region 2001–04, Panel of potential nominees for interim peerages 1999–, memb Federal Appeals Panel 2000–10 (chair 2006–10), memb English Lib Dems Exec 2001–06 (vice-chair 2004–06); Parly candidate: (Lib) Eton and Slough 1974 (twice) and 1979, (Lib/SDP Alliance) Woking 1983 and 1987, (Lib Dem) Dorset and E Devon (Euro) 1994, Woking (Lib Dem) 1997; memb Woking BC 1984–92 and 2003–08 (chm Highways Ctee 1988–90, dep ldr Exec 2006–07, chm Overview and Scrutiny Ctee 2007–08); former memb Exec Ctee Wider Share Ownership Cncl, memb Cncl Electoral Reform Soc 1978–82; CBI: memb London Regnl Cncl 1989–95, memb Nat Cncl 1992–2004, memb Fin and Gen Purposes Ctee 1994–2004; RSA: legal advsr Tomorrow's Company Inquiry 1995, tstee 2004–09, treas 2005–09; memb: Working Party DTI Company Law Reform Project 1998–99, Federal Tst Working Party on Corporate Social Responsibility 2001–02; jt author original Constitution of the Lib Democrats 1988; advsr on formation of Lab/Lib Dem Jt Cabinet Ctee 1997, advsr on procedural provisions of Scottish Coalition Agreement 1999, advsr on procedural provisions of UK Coalition Agreement 2010; memb Cncl City in Europe 2001–04; jt ed New Outlook 1974–77, memb Editorial Advsy Bd Business Law Review 1994–2004; tstee Tuberous Sclerosis Assoc 2000– (chm 2010–14), memb Mgmnt Ctee Woking People of Faith 2010–15 (tstee 2013–); govr: Slough Coll of Higher Educn 1980–86, Annie Lawson Sch Ravenswood Village 1997–2005; burials offr Guildford Synagogue 2009–; memb Law Soc; FRSA 1992, FSALS 1997; *Books* Fair Welfare (1968), Sharing Profits (with Sir David Steel, 1986), CCH's Company Law Guide (3 edn 1990, 4 edn 1996), SJ Berwin's Business Guide to Directors' Responsibilities (2001); *Recreations* family, friends; *Clubs* National Liberal; *Style—* Philip Goldenberg, Esq; ✉ Toad Hall, White Rose Lane, Woking, Surrey GU22 7LB (☎ 01483 765377, fax 01483 764970, e-mail philipglibdem@gmail.com)

GOLDIE, Baroness (Life Peer UK 2013), of Bishopton in the County of Renfrewshire; Annabel MacNicoll Goldie; DL (Renfrewshire); da of Alexander Macintosh Goldie, and Margaret MacNicoll Goldie; *Educ* Greenock Acad, Univ of Strathclyde (LLB); *Career* ptnr Donaldson Alexander Russell & Haddow Glasgow 1978–2006; MSP (Cons) West of Scotland 1999–2016, ldr Scottish Conservatives 2005–11; memb Advsy Bd West of Scotland Salvation Army; elder Church of Scotland; *Recreations* gardening, cycling, bird watching, music; *Style—* The Baroness Goldie, DL; ✉ House of Lords, London SW1A 0PW (e-mail goldiea@parliament.uk)

GOLDIE, Ian William; *Educ* Trinity Coll Glenalmond, Jesus Coll Cambridge (MA); *Children* 2 s (Stuart, Daniel) 1 da (Emily); *Career* ptnr Slaughter and May 1983–2005, legal dir Frontier Power 2009–; *Recreations* golf, rugby, skiing; *Clubs* Royal St George's Golf, Woking Golf; *Style—* Ian Goldie

GOLDING, Baroness (Life Peer UK 2001), of Newcastle-under-Lyme in the County of Staffordshire; Llinos (Llin) Golding; da of Rt Hon Ness Edwards (d 1968; MP for Caerphilly 1939–68), and Elina Victoria (d 1988); *b* 21 March 1933; *Educ* Caerphilly Girls' GS, Cardiff Royal Infirmary Sch of Radiography; *m* 1, June 1957 (m dis 1971), John Roland Lewis; 1 s (Hon Stephen), 2 da (Hon Caroline (Hon Mrs Eardley), Hon Janet d 2009); m 2, 8 Aug 1980, John Golding (d 1999); *Career* sec Newcastle Dist Trades Cncl 1976–86, memb N Staffs DHA 1983–86; MP (Lab) Newcastle-under-Lyme 1986–2001 (by-election), W Midlands whip 1987–92; oppn frontbench spokesperson on: Social Security 1992–93, Children and the Family 1993–95, Food Agriculture and Rural Affrs 1995–97; memb Select Ctee on Culture, Media and Sport 1997–2001; chm All-Pty Parly Gp on Children, treas All-Pty Parly Gp on Racing and Bloodstock Industries, sec All-Pty Angling Gp 2007–; cmmr Cwlth War Graves 1993–2002; memb BBC Advsy Cncl 1989–92; chm Fishing Ctee Countryside Alliance 2005; admin steward Br Boxing Bd of Control; chm Citizen Card; former tstee NSPCC, chm Second Chance charity for children; memb: NUPE, Soc of Radiographers; *Recreations* fishing, horse racing; *Style—* The Baroness Golding

GOLDING, Dr Richard James Arthur; s of late Arthur Bertram Golding, and late Bridget Elizabeth, *née* Mahoney; *b* 13 April 1952; *Educ* Queen Elizabeth's Sch for Boys Barnet, Wadham Coll Oxford (MA, DPhil); *Career* stockbroker and investment banker 1976–; Simon and Coates 1976–81, ptnr Grieveson Grant and Co 1984–86 (joined 1981), dir Kleinwort Benson Ltd 1986–92, commercial dir Principal Fin Nomura International plc 1992–99, dir Annington Homes plc 1996–99, dir Thorn plc 1998–99, md Anthem Corporate Finance Ltd 2002–14; visiting researcher Economics Dept City Univ 2007–; memb London Mathematical Soc; FInstP, FCISI, MIMA; *Clubs* Oxford and Cambridge; *Style—* Dr Richard Golding

GOLDINGAY, Rev Prof John Edgar; s of Edgar Charles Goldingay (d 1974), and Ada Irene, *née* Horton (d 2001); *b* 20 June 1942, Birmingham; *Educ* King Edward's Sch Birmingham, Keble Coll Oxford (BA), Univ of Nottingham (PhD), Lambeth (DD); *m* 1, 28 Aug 1967, Ann Elizabeth (d 2009), da of Arthur Wilson (d 1971); 2 s (Steven b 1968, Mark b 1971); m 2, 8 Dec 2010, Kathleen Scott; *Career* ordained: deacon 1966, priest 1967; asst curate Christ Church Finchley 1966–69; St John's Coll Nottingham: lectr 1970–88, princ 1988–97; currently prof Fuller Theol Seminary Pasadena, California; priest-in-charge St Barnabas Pasadena; *Books* How to Read the Bible (1977), Songs from a Strange Land (1978), Approaches to Old Testament Interpretation (1981), Theological Diversity and the Authority of the Old Testament (1987), Word Biblical Themes: Daniel (1989), Models for Scripture (1994), Models for the Interpretation of Scripture (1995), After Eating the Apricot (1996), To the Usual Suspects (1998), The Vital Connection (1998), Men Behaving Badly (2000), Isaiah (2001), Walk On (2002), Old Testament Theology Vol 1 (2003), Vol 2 (2006) and Vol 3 (2009), The Message of Isaiah 40–55 (2005), Psalms 1–41 (2006), Isaiah 40–55 (2006), Psalms 42–89 (2007), Psalms 90–150 (2008), Nahum, Habakkuk, Zephaniah, Haggai (2009), Genesis for Everyone (2010), Exodus and Leviticus for Everyone (2010), Numbers and Deuteronomy for Everyone (2010), Key Questions about Christian Faith (2010), Joshua, Judges and Ruth for Everyone (2011), 1 and 2 Samuel for Everyone (2011), Key Questions about Biblical Interpretation (2011), 1 and 2 Kings for Everyone (2011), Remembering Ann (2011), 1 and 2 Chronicles for Everyone (2012), Ezra, Nehemiah and Esther for Everyone (2012), Job for Everyone (2013), Isaiah 56–66 (2013), Psalms for Everyone Part One (2013), Psalms for Everyone Part Two (2014), Proverbs Ecclesiastes Song of Songs for Everyone (2014), The Theology of the Book of Isaiah (2014), Isaiah for Everyone (2015), Do We Need the New Testament (2015), Jeremiah for Everyone (2015), An Introduction to the Old Testament (2015), Lamentations and Ezekiel for Everyone (2016), Daniel and the Twelve Prophets for Everyone (2016), Biblical Theology (2016); *Recreations* The Old Testament, jazz, blues, rock music; *Style—* The Rev Prof John Goldingay; ✉ 111 South Orange Grove Boulevard, Apt 108, Pasadena, CA 91105, USA (☎ 626 405 0626, fax 626 584 5251, e-mail johngold@fuller.edu, website www.johngoldingay.com)

GOLDMAN, Ian John; s of Morris Lewis Goldman, of Liverpool, and Tina, *née* Kleinman (d 1992); *b* 28 January 1948; *Educ* Liverpool Coll, LSE (LLB); *m* 9 Sept 1970, Diane Elizabeth, JP, da of William Shipton (d 1984), of London; 3 da (Vikki b 1972, Katie b 1975, Charlotte b 1979); *Career* admitted slr 1971, princ Louis Godlove & Co 1971; dir: Commercial & Financial Investments Ltd 1972–2009, Goldman Investments Ltd 1972–90; sr ptnr: Godlove Pearlman 1991–96, Godloves 1996–2008 (conslt 2008–10); non-exec dir (vice-chm) Leeds Teaching Hosps NHS Tst 1998–2005; memb: Leeds Family Practitioner Ctee 1985–90, Leeds East HA 1988–90, Leeds Law Soc Ctee 1988–2002 (pres 1998–99), Nat Exec Ctee Jewish Nat Fund of GB 1981–87 (chm Leeds Dist 1981–84); vice-chm Leeds Family Health Services Authy 1990–96, chm Leeds Med Service Ctee 1985–96, chm Leeds Restaurant Assoc 2009–10; hon slr Leeds Jewish Welfare Bd 1995–2005, hon life vice-pres Leeds Jewish Rep Cncl 2004– (pres 2001–04); dir Casa Mia Hldgs Ltd 2008–10; tstee Overseas Partnering and Trg Initiative 2003–; memb Law Soc 1971; FInstD 1990; *Style—* Ian Goldman, Esq; ✉ Godloves, 8–16 Dock Street, Bridge End, Leeds LS10 1LX (e-mail ian@iangoldman.co.uk)

GOLDMAN, Lisa; *Career* co-fndr and artistic dir Red Room 1995–2006, artistic dir Soho Theatre 2006–; *Style—* Ms Lisa Goldman; ✉ Soho Theatre, 21 Dean Street, London W1D 3NE

GOLDREIN, Iain Saville; QC (1997); s of Neville Clive Goldrein, CBE, of Crosby, Liverpool, and Sonia Hannah Jane, *née* Sumner; *b* 10 August 1952; *Educ* Merchant Taylors', Hebrew Univ Jerusalem, Pembroke Coll Cambridge (Squire scholar, exhibitioner, Ziegler Prize); *m* 18 May 1980, Her Hon Judge Margaret Ruth de Haas, QC, *qv*, da of late Josef de Haas, and Lilo de Haas, of Altrincham, Manchester; 1 s (Alastair Phillip b 1 Oct 1982), 1 da (Alexandra Ann b 22 Feb 1985); *Career* called to the Bar Inner Temple 1975 (Duke of Edinburgh scholar); in practice London and Northern Circuit, dep High Court judge, recorder of the Crown Court, acting deemster Isle of Man; memb Mental Health Review Tbnl 1999–2003; visiting prof (Sir Jack Jacob chair in litigation) Nottingham Trent Univ, visiting prof (chair in law and genetics) Univ of Bolton; memb Int Advsy Bd Centre for Islamic Finance Univ of Bolton; memb Middle Temple; ed-in-chief Genetics Law Monitor 2000–02, ed Coram Genetics Law Jl; memb: Int Cncl of Experts Hong Kong, Advsy Cncl Centre for Oppn Studies Westminster, Advsy Bd Faith in the Future, Liverpool Mayoral Cmmn on Environmental Sustainability, Steering Bd Cornerstone Fndn Liverpool; Companion Acad of Experts (BAE Register of Mediators); Hon LLD Univ of Bolton; FSALS, FRSA; *Books* Personal Injury Litigation, Practice and Precedents (with Her Hon Judge Margaret de Haas, QC, 1985), Ship Sale and Purchase, Law and Technique (1985, ed-in-chief 2 edn, 1993, 4 edn 2003 with Clifford Chance, 5 edn 2008 with Clyde & Co, 6 edn 2012), Commercial Litigation, Pre-Emptive Remedies (with His Hon K H P Wilkinson, 1987 and 1991, with His Hon Judge Kershaw, QC, 1996, and The Rt Hon Lord Justice Jacob, 2003, 2 int edition 2012), Butterworths' Personal Injury Litigation Service (with Her Hon Judge Margaret de Haas, QC), Pleadings: Principles and Practice (with Sir Jack Jacob, 1990), Bullen and Leake and Jacob's Precedents of Pleadings (gen ed 13 edn with Sir Jack Jacob, 1990), Structured Settlements (ed in chief with Her Hon Judge Margaret de Haas, QC, 1993 and 1997), Medical Negligence: Cost Effective Case Management (with Her Hon Judge Margaret de Haas, QC, 1997), Insurance Disputes (co-ed, 1999, 3 edn 2012), Civil Court Practice (co-ed, annually 1999–2013), Personal Injury Major Claims Handling: Cost Effective Case Management (co-ed with Her Hon Judge Margaret de Haas, QC and John Frenkel, 2002), Judicial Review of Human Rights (with Lord Clyde and Mr Justice Elias, 2002), Child Case Management Practice (with Mr Justice Ryder, 2 edn 2012), Media Access to the Family Courts (2009), Privacy Injunctions and the Media: A Practice Manual (2012), Hong Kong Civil Procedure (advsy ed, 2013–14), Hong Kong Bullen and Leake's Precedents of Pleadings (advsy ed, 2013), Malaysia Civil Procedure (int advsy ed, 2013–14); *Recreations* Classical Hebrew, classical music, history, anything aeronautical, classical motor vehicles; *Style—* Iain Goldrein, Esq, QC; ✉ Coram Chambers, 9–11 Fullwood Place, London WC1V 6HG; Number 7, Harrington Street, Liverpool L2 7QS (☎ 0151 242 0707, fax 0151 236 1120, mobile 0831 703156, e-mail ian.goldrein@7hs.co.uk); KCH Chambers, 1 Oxford Street, Nottingham NG1 5BH

GOLDRING, Rt Hon Sir John Bernard; kt (1999); s of Joseph Goldring (d 1980), and Marianne Goldring; *b* 9 November 1944; *Educ* Wyggeston GS Leicester, Univ of Exeter; *m* 2 Jan 1970, Wendy Margaret Lancaster, da of Ralph Lancaster Bennett (d 1980); 2 s (Jeremy b 1971, Rupert b 1974); *Career* called to the Bar Lincoln's Inn 1969 (bencher 1996); QC 1987, standing prosecuting counsel to Inland Revenue (Midland & Oxford Circuit) 1985–87, recorder Midland & Oxford Circuit 1987, dep sr judge Sovereign Base Areas Cyprus 1991, dep judge of the High Court 1995, judge Courts of Appeal Jersey and Guernsey 1998, judge of the High Court of Justice 1999–2008, presiding judge Midland Circuit 2002–05, cmmr Judicial Appts Cmmn 2006–08, Lord Justice of Appeal 2008–14, dep sr presiding judge for England and Wales 2008–10, sr presiding judge for England and Wales 2010–; *Recreations* gardening, skiing; *Clubs* Athenaeum; *Style—* The Rt Hon Sir John Goldring; ✉ Royal Courts of Justice, Strand, London WC2A 2LL

GOLDRING, Mark; CBE (2008); *Educ* Univ of Oxford, LSE; *Career* previously with Dept for Int Devpt, Oxfam and UN Devpt Prog; chief exec: VSO 1999–2008, Mencap 2008–13, Oxfam GB 2013–; *Style—* Mark Goldring, Esq, CBE; ✉ Oxfam, Oxfam House, John Smith Drive, Cowley, Oxford OX4 2JY

GOLDSACK, His Hon Judge Alan Raymond; QC (1990), DL (South Yorkshire 2009); s of Raymond Frederick Goldsack, MBE (d 1985), of Hastings, and Mildred Agnes, *née* Jones (d 2000); *b* 13 June 1947; *Educ* Hastings GS, Univ of Leicester (LLB); *m* 21 Aug 1971, Christine Marion, da of Frank Leslie Clarke, MBE; 3 s (Ian b 1974, Richard b 1977, Stephen b 1980), 1 da (Tessa b 1975); *Career* called to the Bar Gray's Inn 1970 (bencher 2003), recorder 1988–94, circuit judge (NE Circuit) 1994–2002, sr circuit judge 2002–2013,

G

hon recorder of Sheffield 2002–2013; memb parole bd of eng and wales; DL (South Yorkshire 2009); *Recreations* gardening, walking; *Style*— His Hon Judge Goldsack, QC, DL; ✉ The Old Rectory, Braithwell, Rotherham S66 7AF (☎ 01709 812167)

GOLDSCHMIED, Marco; s of Guido Rodolfo Goldschmied, and Elinor Violet, *née* Sinnott; *b* 28 March 1944; *Educ* Rudolf Steiner Sch Milan, Liceo Manzoni Milan, William Ellis GS London, AA Sch of Architecture (Dipl), Univ of Reading (MSc); *m* 1969, Andrea, *née* Halvorsen; 4 s, 1 da; *Career* architect; assoc ptnr Piano + Rogers 1971–77; Richard Rogers Partnership: fndr ptnr 1977–84, md 1984–89; md Richard Rogers Architects Ltd London 1989–2004, chm River CADS Ltd, vice-pres and dir Richard Rogers Japan KK, chm Thames Wharf Studios; projects incl: masterplanning Heathrow Terminal 5 1990, Learning Resource Centre Thames Valley Univ 1996 (RIBA Award 1998), Europier passenger terminal Heathrow 1996 (RIBA Award 1997, Br Steel Award 1997), Greenwich peninsula masterplan 1997, offices and residential Mercedes Benz Berlin 1998, Lloyd's Register of Shipping HQ London 1999, Daiwa Europe office devpt London 1999, Bordeaux Law Courts 1998, Montevetro riverside residential 1999, Millennium Dome 1999, offices and laboratories Gifu Japan 1999; teacher: AA 1971, Glasgow Sch of Art 1999; external examiner Mackintosh Sch; lectr RIBA 1981–99, also lectr at Univs incl: Darmstadt, Vienna, Manchester, Westminster, Glasgow; RIBA: chm Awards Gp, memb Cncl, memb Int Affairs Bd, memb Educn Review Gp, pres 1999–2001; memb: Br Cncl of Offices, ARB Cncl, ARB Euro Advsy Gp, Univ of Reading Construction Forum, Building Awards Jury 1998–99; *Books* Architecture 98 (1998), Visions of the 21st Century (ed, 2000); *Recreations* 20th century history, architecture, skiing, meditation, cooking, The Simpsons; *Style*— Marco Golschmied, Esq

GOLDSMITH, Harvey Anthony; CBE (1996); s of Sydney Goldsmith, and Minnie Goldsmith; *b* 4 March 1946; *Educ* Christ's Coll, Brighton Coll of Technol; *m* 4 July 1971, Diana; 1 s (Jonathon b 28 July 1976); *Career* concert promoter and prodr; ptnr Big O Posters 1966–67, merged with John Smith Entertainments Ltd 1970, fndr Harvey Goldsmith Entertainments Ltd 1976, acquired Allied Entertainments Group 1984, formed Classical Productions (with Mark McCormack) 1986; staged first free open air concert Parliament Hill Fields 1968, fndr concerts Roundhouse Camden 1968, cr Crystal Palace Garden Party series 1969–72; promoter: Aida 1988, Carmen 1989, Pavarotti in the Park 1991, Tosca 1991, The 3 Tenors 1996; vice-pres: Music Users' Cncl, REACT; chm Concert Promoters Assoc, vice-chm Prince's Tst Action Mgmnt Bd; memb Bd: London Tourist Bd, Prague Heritage Fund; tstee: Band Aid, Live Aid Foundation, Royal Opera House, CST; memb Communication Gp Red Cross; Int Promoter of the Year 1994–97, Ambassador for London Judges Award 1997; *Recreations* golf; *Clubs* RAC, Hartsbourne Golf, Vale de Lobo Golf; *Style*— Harvey Goldsmith, Esq, CBE; ✉ Harvey Goldsmith Entertainments Ltd, Greenland Place, 115–123 Bayham Street, London NW1 0AG (☎ 020 7482 5522, fax 020 7428 9252)

GOLDSMITH, Baron (Life Peer UK 1999), of Allerton in the County of Merseyside; Peter Henry Goldsmith; PC (2002), QC (1987); s of Sydney Elland Goldsmith, and Myra, *née* Nurick; *b* 5 January 1950; *Educ* Quarry Bank HS Liverpool, Gonville & Caius Coll Cambridge (MA), UCL (LLM); *m* Joy, *née* Elterman; 3 s (James b 1978, Jonathan b 1983, Benjamin b 1985), 1 da (Charlotte b 1981); *Career* called to the Bar Gray's Inn 1972 (bencher 1994); in practice SE Circuit, jr counsel to the Crown in Common Law 1985–87, recorder of the Crown Court 1991–, dep judge of the High Court 1994–; attorney gen 2001–07; Euro chm of litigation Debevoise & Plimpton LLP 2007–; chm Bar of England and Wales 1995; memb Gen Cncl of the Bar 1992–96 and 2001– (chm Legal Servs Ctee 1991–93, vice-chm 1994, chm Int Relations Ctee 1996); pres Bar Pro Bono Unit (chm 1995–2000) 2001–, chm Fin Reporting Review Panel 1997–2000 (memb 1995–2000), memb Advsy Bd Cambridge Centre for Commercial and Corporate law 1998–; memb Cncl Public Concern at Work 1995–97; Int Bar Assoc: chm Standing Ctee on Globalisation of Law 1995–98, chm Ctee 1 IBA Human Rights Inst 1995–98, memb Cncl 1996–, co-chm IBA Human Rights Inst 1998–2001; co-chm Twinning Ctee 1996–98; memb Exec Ctee GB-China Centre 1996–2001; PM's personal rep Convention For a European Union Charter of Fundamental Rights 1999–2000; memb Jt Select Ctee on Human Rights 2001; elected to American Law Inst 1997; Avocat Paris Bar 1997; *Style*— The Rt Hon the Lord Goldsmith, PC, QC

GOLDSMITH, Walter Kenneth; s of Lionel Goldsmith (d 1981), and Phoebe Goldsmith (d 2004); *b* 19 January 1938; *Educ* Merchant Taylors'; *m* 1961, Rosemary Adele, da of Joseph Salter (d 1970); 2 s, 2 da; *Career* chartered accountant Mann Judd & Co 1964–66, mgmnt conslt McLintock Mann & Whinney Murray 1964–66, with Black & Decker Ltd 1966–79 (md 1974, chief exec and European dir 1975, corp vice-pres and pres Pacific Int Ops 1976–79), dir gen IOD 1979–84, chm Korn Ferry International Ltd 1984–86 (chief exec 1984–85), gp planning and mktg dir Trusthouse Forte plc 1985–87, chm Food From Britain 1987–90; chm: Ansoll Estates Ltd 1990–98, Flying Flowers Ltd 1990–99, Betterware plc 1990–95, Beagle Holdings Ltd 1992–2008, Fitness First plc 1997–2003, Estates & Mgmnt Ltd 2006–, Mercury Gp plc 2006–09; dir: Bank Leumi (UK) plc 1984–2013, Isys plc 1987–97, British Food and Farming Ltd 1990–2014, Guiton Gp 1998–2006, Asite plc 1998–, Visonic Ltd 2005–10, Energy Technique plc 2007–16; advsr Rotch Gp 1996–; memb: Eng Tourist Bd 1982–84, Br Tourist Authy 1984–86; co-creator Festival of Food and Farming 1989 and 1992, memb Cncl Royal Agric Soc of Eng 1990–95; co-fndr Israel Diaspora Tst 1982, memb Br Overseas Trade Gp for Israel 1984–91 (chm 1987–91), treas Leo Baeck Coll 1987–89, chm of tstees Jewish Music Inst 2003–08 (vice-pres 2008–), memb Advsy Bd SOAS 2009–11; Liveryman Worshipful Co of CAs in Eng and Wales 1985, Freeman City of London; FCA, FRSA; *Publications* The Winning Streak (with D Clutterbuck, 1984), The Winning Streak Workout Book (1985), The New Elite (with Berry Ritchie, 1987), The Winning Streak Mark 2 (1997); *Recreations* music, property; *Style*— Walter Goldsmith, Esq

GOLDSMITH, (Frank) Zac; MP; s of Sir James Goldsmith (d 1997), and Lady Annabel Goldsmith, *née* Vane-Tempest Stewart; *b* 20 January 1975; *Educ* Eton; *m* 1 (m dis 2010), Sheherazade, *née* Ventura-Bentley; 2 da (Uma Romaine, Thyra Amber), 1 s (James Edward); m 2, 2013, Alice Miranda, da of late Hon Amschel Mayor James Rothschild; *Career* Redefining Progress (RP) San Francisco 1995–96, Int Soc for Ecology and Culture (ISEC) California, Bristol and Ladakh 1996–98, dir and ed The Ecologist 1997–2010; memb Advsy Bd JMG Fndn; memb Bd: Fundación Ecológicà de Cuixmala, Royal Park Fndn, Countryside Restoration Tst, Rainforest Fndn, Green Aliance Tst, Aspinall Fndn; Beacon Prize for Philanthropy 2003, Global Green Award for Environmental Leadership 2004; MP (Cons) Richmond Park 2010–; *Clubs* 5 Hertford St, Travellers; *Style*— Zac Goldsmith, MP; ✉ 372 Upper Richmond Road West, London SW14 7JU (☎ 020 8878 7866)

GOLDSPINK, Prof Geoffrey; s of James Albert Goldspink (d 1992), and Muriel, *née* Gee; *b* 2 April 1939; *Educ* Univ of Hull (BSc), Trinity Coll, Univ of Dublin (PhD, ScD), FRSC; *m* 31 Dec 1960, Barbara, da of Frederick Staniforth (d 1966); 3 s (Mark Richard b 6 Jan 1962, Paul Harvey b 28 April 1964, Andrew Jeffrey b 27 Jan 1966); *Career* prof and head of zoology Univ of Hull, visiting prof Univ of Nairobi, Agassiz visiting prof Harvard Univ, prof of anatomy and cell biology Tufts New England Med Centre Boston USA; Univ of London: fndr chair of veterinary molecular and cellular biol, dir of molecular and cellular biol RVC London, currently emeritus prof Royal Free and UCL Med Schs; discovered Mechano Growth Factor (MGF, responsible for increasing muscle strength and repair, being developed by the pharmaceutical industry for treatment of muscle loss in the elderly and several diseases), scientific advsr and using MRG for tissue repair in human and veterinary medicine; *Books* Growth and Differentiation of Cell in Vertebrate Tissues, Mechanics and Energetics of Animal Locomotion; *Recreations* restoration of houses of historical interest, music; *Style*— Prof Geoffrey Goldspink; ✉ Brambledene, East Common, Harpenden, Hertfordshire AL5 1DQ

GOLDSPINK, Robert Andrew; s of late Canon R W Goldspink, of Fenstanton, Cambs, and Kathleen Edith, *née* Betts; *b* 8 August 1949; *Educ* Eltham Coll, Fitzwilliam Coll Cambridge (Squire scholar, Rebecca Flower scholar, MA, LLM); *m* 1 Sept 1973, Dr Margo Diane Dunlop, da of Roy Graham Dunlop, MBE (d 1989); 1 s (James Elliot b 1985), 1 da (Jesse Lorraine b 1991); *Career* articled clerk Wild Hewitson & Shaw Cambridge 1973–75, supervisor in constitutional legal studies Fitzwilliam and Christ's Colls Cambridge 1973–75, slr Freshfields 1975–80; Denton Hall: joined 1980, ptnr 1981–97; Morgan Lewis & Bockius LLP: ptnr 1997–2009, managing ptnr London 2004–09; accredited mediator, lectr on legal subjects 1975–; non-exec dir Serious Fraud Office 2010–; dir: Opportunity Int UK 2009–, Opportunity Tanzania Ltd 2010–; memb: Marriot Ctee proposing revisions to English arbitration law, Jt Working Pty Gen Cncl of the Bar and the Law Soc reviewing English civil courts and court procedures 1993, Court of Appeal Mediation Steering Ctee 1997–2003, Commercial Court Users' Ctee 2003–09; memb Law Soc; *Publications* International Commercial Fraud (co-ed); *Recreations* gardening, music, travel; *Clubs* Cwlth; *Style*— Robert A Goldspink, Esq; ✉ The White House, 19 Buckden Road, Brampton, Cambridgeshire PE28 4PR (e-mail robert.a.goldspink@gmail.com)

GOLDSTAUB, Thomas Charles; s of Werner Fritz Goldstaub, and Beate Charlotte, *née* Muller; *b* 2 September 1953; *Educ* Forest Sch; *m* 4 June 1985, Jane Hilary Elizabeth, da of Gordon Heslop Procter; 1 da (Tabitha Sophie b 11 Dec 1985), 1 s (Rollo Alexander b 16 April 1989); *Career* md Fred & Warner Ltd 1983–86 (sales and mktg dir 1979–82), special projects dir Garrard & Co 1987–88, mktg dir Mappin & Webb 1989–90, md Fintex of London 1993–2006 (dep md 1991–93), sales and mktg dir Charles Clayton 2006, ceo TG Consulting 2007–; Freeman City of London 1986, Liveryman Worshipful Co of Upholders 1986; *Books* What Do You Call A Kid (1985); *Recreations* sailing, skiing, classic cars; *Style*— Thomas Goldstaub, Esq

GOLDSTEIN, Prof Harvey; s of Jack Goldstein (d 1991), and Millicent Goldstein (d 1945); *b* 30 October 1939; *Educ* Hendon GS, Univ of Manchester (BSc), UCL (Dip Statistics); *m* 1970, Barbara, *née* Collinge; 1 s (Thomas Gregory b 1977); *Career* research asst Dept of Statistics UCL 1962–64, lectr in statistics Inst of Child Health Univ of London 1964–71, head of Statistics Section Nat Children's Bureau 1971–76, prof of statistical methods Inst of Educn Univ of London 1977–2005, prof of social statistics Univ of Bristol 2005–; jt ed Jl of the Royal Statistical Soc 2015–18; jt dir WHO collaborating centre on child growth and devpt 1989–, jt dir Int Centre for Research on Assessment 1992–2005, assoc dir Int Sch Effectiveness and Improvement Centre 1993–2005; visiting lectr in biostatistics Univ of Wisconsin 1968; visiting prof: Ontario Inst for Studies in Educn Toronto Canada July-Aug 1983 and 1986 (adjunct prof 1987–90), UEA 1992–; adjunct prof Australian Catholic Univ 2014–; memb Ed Bd Annals of Human Biology 1974–90, assoc ed Jl of Educnl and Behavioural Statistics 1988–, exec ed Assessment in Educn 1993–; govr: St James' CE Primary Sch Haringey 1982–90, Tetherdown Primary Sch Haringey 1987–89; fndn govr William Ellis Sch London 1993–96; tstee Longview 2005–; memb: Biometric Soc, Soc for the Study of Human Biology, American Statistical Assoc, Psychometric Soc, Br Educnl Research Assoc, Nat Cncl on Measurement in Educn, Int Statistical Inst 1987–; Hon DUniv Open Univ 2001; CStat, FSS (memb Cncl 1973–77 and 2000–04, Guy Medal in Silver 1998), FRSA 1991–99, FBA 1996; *Publications* Multilevel Statistical Models (4 edn, 2011); over 350 academic pubns; *Recreations* tennis, walking, cycling, playing the flute; *Style*— Prof Harvey Goldstein, FBA; ✉ Graduate School of Education, University of Bristol, Bristol BS8 1JA (e-mail h.goldstein@bristol.ac.uk)

GOLDSTEIN, Dr Michael; CBE (1997); s of Jacob Goldstein (d 1945), of London, and Sarah, *née* Goldberg (d 2001); *b* 1 May 1939; *Educ* Hackney Downs GS London, Northern Poly (BSc, PhD, DSc); *m* 5 May 1962 (m dis 2009), Janet Sandra, da of Henry Arthur Skevington (d 1979), of London; 1 s (Richard b 1968); *Career* successively lectr, sr lectr then princ lectr Poly of North London (formerly Northern Poly) 1963–73; Sheffield Poly: head Dept of Chemistry 1974–83, dean of the Faculty of Science 1979–83; vice-chllr Coventry Univ (formerly Coventry Poly) 1987–2004 (dep dir 1983–87); author of many scientific articles and several review chapters in books 1962–84 and of articles on educn and educn mktg 2004–10; chm Chemistry Bd CNAA 1978–84, involved with local, regnl and nat sections of Royal Soc of Chemistry (pres Educn Div 1993–95, chm Educn and Qualifications Bd 1995–99) and various local/regnl orgns and gps, chm Cncl for the Registration of Forensic Practitioners 2005–08; chm UCAS 1997–2001, memb Bd Universities and Colleges Employers Assoc (UCEA) 1994–2001, chm States of Jersey HE Devpt Gp 2005–08, memb Bd Fndn Degree Forward 2006–10, memb States of Jersey Skills Bd 2008–15; chm Heist 2004–06, dep chm CVOne Ltd 2002–08, dir ContinYou Ltd 2003–10; chm cre8us (formerly Creative Partnerships Coventry) 2004–10; memb Bd: Coventry, Solihull and Warwickshire Partnerships Ltd 1994–2004, The City Centre Co (Coventry) Ltd 1997–2002, Coventry and Warwickshire LSC 2001–07; memb W Midlands Sub-Ctee Advsy Ctee for Clinical Excellence 2008–10, memb Ind Monitoring Bd HM Prison/Young Offenders' Inst Swinfen Hall 2012–; chair Coventry and Warks NHS Partnership Tst 2010–11 (non-exec dir 2006–09, vice-chair 2009–10), chair Search and Governance Ctee Solihull Coll 2006–12 (memb 2003–06); tstee Community Educn Devpt Centre 1996–2003, panellist Judicial Appointments Cmmn 2012–; Hon DSc Univ of Warwick 2003; hon fell Univ of Worcester 1998; CChem, FRSC 1973 (MRSC 1967), Hon FCGI 1994; *Books* Three Lives in Education: Reflections of an Anglo-Jewish Family (jtly, 2009, 2 edn 2012), John Hibbs: His Journey by Bus, Coach and Train (jtly, 2015); *Recreations* DIY, Coventry City FC, classic Rupert Bear; *Style*— Dr Michael Goldstein, CBE; ✉ 78 Whitehouse Drive, Lichfield, Staffordshire WS13 8FE (☎ 01543 418063, e-mail michael.goldstein@btinternet.com, LinkedIn www.linkedin.com/profile/view?id=123242576&trk=nav_responsive_tab_profile)

GOLDSTEIN-JACKSON, Kevin Grierson; JP (Poole 1990); s of Harold Grierson Jackson (d 1992), and Winifred Jackson (d 2013); *b* 1946; *Educ* Univ of Reading (BA), Univ of Southampton (MPhil); *m* 6 Sept 1975, Jenny Mei Leng, da of Ufong Ng, of Malaysia; 2 da (Sing Yu b 1981, Kimberley b 1984); *Career* Staff Rels Dept London Tport 1966, Scottish Widows Pension and Life Assurance Soc 1967, prog organiser Southern TV 1970–73, asst prodr HK/TVB Hong Kong 1973, freelance writer and TV prodr 1973–75, fndr and dir Thames Valley Radio 1974–77, head of film Dhofar Region TV Serv Sultanate of Oman 1975–76, asst to head of drama Anglia TV 1977–81; TSW – Television South West: fndr controller and dir of progs 1981–85, jt md 1981–82, chief exec 1982–85; dir ITV Pubns 1981–85; dir of private cos; artist; contrib FT 1986–; govr Lilliput First Sch Poole 1988–93; Freeman City of London 1996; FRSA 1978, FCMI 1982, FInstD 1982, FFA 1988, FRGS 1989; *Books* incl: The Right Joke for the Right Occasion (1973), Experiments with Everyday Objects (1976), Dictionary of Essential Quotations (1983), Share Millions (1989), The Public Speaker's Joke Book (1991), The Astute Private Investor (1994), Quick Quips (2002); *Recreations* writing, painting, TV, films, music, haiku; *Style*— Kevin Goldstein-Jackson, Esq; ✉ c/o Alcazar, 18 Martello Road, Branksome Park, Poole, Dorset BH13 7DH

GOLDSTONE, Prof Anthony Howard; CBE (2008); *b* 13 September 1944; *Educ* Univ of Oxford (MA, BM BCh); *Career* house physician in med Chase Farm Hosp Enfield 1969, house surgn Edgware Gen Hosp 1969–70, resident clinical pathologist Guy's Hosp 1970, registrar in haematology Western Infirmary Edinburgh 1971–72 (SHO in med 1970–71), res fell in clinical immunology Cancer Research Campaign Edinburgh Royal Infirmary 1972–73, sr registrar in haematology Addenbrooke's Hosp and Dept of Haematological Med Univ of Cambridge 1973–76, postgraduate dean Sch of Med UCL 1984–87, med dir UCL Hosp NHS Tst 1992–2000, dir N London Cancer Network 2000–09; currently: conslt clinical haematologist, prof Sch of Med UCL, chm Royal Nat Orthopaedic Hosp NHS Tst 2011–; dir Clinical Directorate in Haematology Bloomsbury District 1991–93; chm: Registry of Transplant in Lymphoma Euro Bone Marrow Transplant Gp 1984–92, Med Ctee UCH 1986–88, NE Thames Regnl Haematologists 1988–92, Working Gp Bloomsbury Haematologists 1988–92; FRCP(Edin) 1979, FRCP 1983 (MRCP 1971), FRCPath 1987 (MRCPath 1975); *Books* Leukaemia, Lymphoma and Allied Disorders (jtly, 1976), Examination Haematology (1977), Synopsis of Haematology (1983), Clinics in Haematology: Autologous Bone Marrow Transplantation (ed, 1986); author of numerous book chapters and papers in scientific jls; *Recreations* following Manchester City to ever greater glory, Porsches, grandchildren and being walked by the dog; *Style—* Prof Anthony Goldstone, CBE; ✉ University College Hospital, 235 Euston Road, London NW1 2BU (☎ 020 3447 1528, fax 020 7387 3025, e-mail anthony.goldstone@uclh.nhs.uk)

GOLDSTONE, Anthony Keith; s of Myer Charles Maurice Goldstone (d 1987), and Rose, *née* Kessly (d 1987); *b* 25 July 1944; *Educ* Manchester Grammar, Royal Manchester Coll of Music; *m* 26 July 1989, Caroline Anne Clemmow, pianist, da of David Menzies Clemmow; *Career* pianist; appears as soloist, in duo with wife Caroline Clemmow and as memb various chamber ensembles; fndr Musicians of the Royal Exchange 1978; has worked with all major Br symphony orchs, performed at numerous Br and international festivals and BBC Prom concerts (incl Last Night); FRMCM 1973; *Recordings* incl: Chopin Piano Solos (vols 1, 2 and 3), Schubert Piano Solos and Schumann Piano Solos, Lyapunov Solos, Schubert Solo Masterworks Series, Beethoven Solos, Unheard Mozart, Tchaikovsky – Rare Transcriptions and Paraphrases Vols 1 and 2, A Night at the Opera, The Piano at the Carnival, The Piano at the Ballet, Britten Resonances (piano solos by Britten and others), Parry Piano Solos on Parry's Piano, Elgar Piano Solos on Elgar's Piano, Holst and Lambert Piano Solos, Piano Music from Castle Howard, Beethoven Fourth Concerto (with RPO under Norman Del Mar), Pitfield First Concerto, Saint-Saëns Carnival of Animals (with RPO under Owain Arwel Hughes), Berkeley and Debussy Duos (with James Galway on flute), Beethoven Piano Quartets (with Cummings String Trio), Sibelius Piano Quintet (with Gabrieli String Quartet), Alkan Concerto da Camera No 2 and Bombardo-Carillon (with Morhange Ensemble and Caroline Clemmow respectively), Mendelssohn Complete Sonatas for Violin and Piano (with Yossi Zivoni), Holst Quintet for Piano and Wind and Jacob Sextet for Piano and Wind (with Elysian Wind Quintet); with w, Caroline Clemmow: A Moyzes (solos and two pianos), Holst Planets (two pianos), The Virtuoso Piano Duo (two pianos), Schubert Piano Duet Cycle, The Unauthorised Schubert Piano Duos (vols 1, 2 and 3), Britten and McPhee (two pianos), Gál Piano Duos, Soler Double Concertos (two pianos), Russian Tableaux (solos and piano duets), Paradise Gardens (solos and piano duets), Herzogenberg (solos and piano duos), Explorations (solos and piano duos), George Lloyd Music for Two Pianos, Virtuoso Variations (various piano duets), Tchaikovsky Piano Duets, Dvořák and Mendelssohn Symphonies, Orientale, Graham Whettam (solos and piano duos), Grieg for Piano Duo, Mozart on Reflection (two pianos), Chopin for Piano Duo, The Jazz Age for Piano Duo, Alkan Piano Duos, Delicias (Spanish piano duos), Magical Places (symphonic poems for piano duet), Brian Chapple (solos and piano duos), Gershwin and Ravel for Piano Duo, Rimsky-Korsakov Scheherazade (piano duets), Romantic Duet Sonatas, Duet Lollipops, Romantic Duet Waltzes, Romantic Duet Suites; *Recreations* antique maps and clocks, the Yorkshire Dales, birdwatching; *Style—* Anthony Goldstone, Esq; ✉ Walcot Old Hall, Alkborough, North Lincolnshire DN15 9JT (☎ 01724 720475, fax 01724 721599, e-mail akgoldstone@aol.com, website www.divine-art.com/AS/goldstone.htm)

GOLDSTONE, His Hon Judge (Leonard) Clement; QC (1993); s of Maurice Goldstone (d 1980), and Maree, *née* Lewis; *b* 20 April 1949; *Educ* Manchester Grammar, Churchill Coll Cambridge (BA); *m* 20 August 1972, Vanessa, da of Donald Forster, and Muriel Forster; 3 s (Simon Lewis b 27 Dec 1973, Jonathan Andrew b 11 Oct 1976, Maurice James b 24 May 1980); *Career* called to the Bar Middle Temple 1971; recorder 1992–2002, treas Northern Circuit 1998–2001, circuit judge (Northern Circuit) 2002– (sr circuit judge 2011–); pres Mental Health Review Tbnl (restricted cases) 1999–; *Recreations* golf, bridge, theatre, music; *Clubs* Dunham Forest Golf & Country (Altrincham); *Style—* His Hon Judge Goldstone, QC

GOLDSTONE, Jonny; *b* 11 October 1976; *Educ* Manchester Grammar, Univ of Cambridge; *m* Sarah; *Career* admitted slr 2002; co-fndr (with Tom Pakenham, *qv*) Green Tomato Cars 2006–13 (vice-pres 2013–15), fndr Piccnicc Consulting 2015–; memb Advsy Bd Hubbub Online 2008–; *Style—* Jonny Goldstone, Esq

GOLDSWORTHY, Andy; OBE (2000); s of Prof Fredrick Alan Goldsworthy, and Muriel, *née* Stanger; *b* 25 July 1956; *Educ* Wheatlands Secdy Modern Sch, Harrogate HS, Bradford Art Coll, Preston Poly; *m* Judith Elizabeth, da of Barry Gregson, and Audrey, *née* Jackson; 2 s (James b 8 Oct 1987, Thomas b 15 Dec 1994), 2 da (Holly b 4 April 1990, Anna b 5 Feb 1993); *Career* artist/sculptor; *Solo Exhibitions* incl: Evidence (Coracle Press Gallery London) 1985, Rain, Sun, Snow, Mist, Calm (The Henry Moore Centre for the Study of Sculpture, Leeds City Art Gallery and Northern Centre for Contemporary Art Sunderland touring) 1985, Winter Harvest (Book exhbn with John Fowles, Scottish Arts Cncl) 1987, Fabian Carlsson Gallery London 1987, Gallery Takagi Nagoya 1988, Yurakucho Asahi Gallery Tokyo and Osaka 1988, Mountain and Coast Autumn into Winter 1987 (also at Fabian Carlsson Gallery London 1988), Touching North (Anne Berthoud Gallery London and Graeme Murray Gallery Edinburgh) 1989, Black in Black (Fabian Carlsson Gallery London) 1989, Snowballs in Summer (Old Museum of Tport Glasgow) 1989, Leaves (The Natural History Museum London) 1989, Garden Mountain (Centre D'Art Contemporain Castres) 1990, Hand to Earth – Sculpture 1976–90 (retrospective exhbn touring Leeds City Art Gallery, Royal Botanic Garden Edinburgh, Stedelijke Musea Gouda and Centre D'Art Contemporain Toulouse) 1990–91, Drawings (Aline Vidal Gallery Paris) 1990–91, With Nature (Galerie Lelong NY and Chicago Arts Club) 1991, Sand Leaves (Chicago Arts Club) 1991, With Nature (Galerie Lelong NYC) 1991, Mid Winter Muster (Adelaide Festival) 1992, Verden Und Vergehen (Museum Bellerine Zurich) 1992, California Project (Haines Gallery San Francisco) 1992, Stone Sky (Galerie St Anne Brussels) 1992, Ile de Lassiuiere 1992, Flow of Earth (exhbn and film, Castlefield Gallery Manchester) 1992, Hard Earth (Turske Hue-Williams Gallery London) 1992, Australia, NZ and Japan 1993, Mid-Winter Muster (Harwood House) 1993, Wood Land (Galerie Lelong NY) 1993, Tochigi Museum of Fine Art 1993, Setagaya Museum of Fine Arts Tokyo 1994, Aline Vidal Gallery Paris 1994, Hue-Williams Fine Art London 1994, Laumeier Sculpture Park St Louis 1994, Oriel Gallery Cardiff 1994, Haines Gallery San Francisco 1994, San José Museum of Art 1995, Galerij S65 Belgium 1995, Galerie Lelong NY 1995, Musée de Digne 1995, Green on Red Gallery Dublin 1995, Tuillehouse Carlisle 1996, Margaret Harvey Gallery St Albans 1996, Michael Hue-Williams London 1996, Galerie Lelong NY 1996, Haines Gallery San Francisco 1996, Penrith Museum 1997, Musee d' Art Contemporain Montreal 1998, Galerie Lelong Paris 1998, Springer & Winckler Galerie Berlin 1998, Ingelby Gallery Edinburgh 1998, Andy Goldsworthy (Michael Hue-Williams Fine Art London) 1999, Andy Goldsworthy (Storm King Art Centre NY), Time (Barbican Centre London, Michael Hue-Williams Fine Art London) 2000, Gigne Works Hotel Scribe Paris 2000, Herbert Johnson Museum of Art Cornell Univ NY 2000, Site Santa Fe 2000, Galerie Lelong NY 2000, Time (Abbot Hall Art Gallery and Museum) 2001, Silent Spring (Gallerie Lelong Paris) 2001, Time (Springer & Winckler Galerie Berlin) 2001, Journey (Galerie S65 Aalst) 2002; *Group Exhibitions* incl: Place (Gimpel Fils Summer Show London) 1983, Sculpture in the Open Air (Yorkshire Sculpture Park) 1983, Salon D'Automne (Serpentine Gallery London) 1984, The Possibilities of Space – Fifty Years of British Sculptors' Drawings (Musee de Beaux Arts De Besançon, Kirlees Museums tour) 1987–88, Apperto 88 (Venice Biennale) 1988, Through the Looking Glass – Photographic Art in Britain 1945–1989 (Barbican Art Gallery London) 1989, Leaves (Atelier des Enfants, Centre Georges Pompidou Paris touring) 1990, Attitudes to Nature (Ile De Vassiviere) 1991, Shared Earth (Br-Russian art, UK tour) 1991, Goldsworthy and Girke (Fruitmarket Gallery Edinburgh) 1992, Galerie Lelong NY 1993, Impermanence (Alderich MOMA) 1993, Parc de la Courneuve (Paris installation) 1993, Morecambe Bay Works (Lancaster, Scott Gallery and Storey Inst) 1993, Tikon (project, Denmark) 1993, Trees (Kunstierwerkstatt Lotheringstrasse Munich) 1993, Time Machine (British Museum London) 1994; *Selected Works* Breath of Earth (San José Museum of Art) 1995, Four Stones (Galerij S65 Aalst) 1995, Black Stones, Red Pools (Galerie Lelong NY) 1995, Earth Memory (Musée de Digne les Baines) 1995, A Clearing of Arches. For The Night (Hathill Sculpture Fndn) Goodwood Sussex 1995, For the Night (Green on Red Gallery Dublin) 1995, Time Machine (Museo Egizio Turin) 1995, Vegetal (dance collaboration with Ballet Atlantique La Rochelle) 1995, clay floor installation (Glasgow MOMA) 1996, Printemps de Cahors 1996, Northern Rock Art (DLI Museum and Durham Art Gallery) 1996, Sheepfolds (Tulliehouse Carlisle) 1996, Sheepfolds (Margaret Harvey Gallery St Albans) 1996, Wood (Michael Hue-Williams Fine Art London, Galerie Lelong NY, Haines Gallery San Francisco) 1996, Andy Goldsworthy (Anchorage Museum of Art) 1996, Northern Exposure (Harris Gallery Preston) 1997, Andy Goldsworthy – Sheepfolds (Penrith Museum) 1997, Northern Lights (Mercer Art Gallery Harrogate) 1997, Obsession + Devotion (Haines Gallery) 1997, Andy Goldsworthy – Sheepfold Drawings (Egremont West Cumbria) 1998, Arch (Musée d'Art Contemporain de Montreal) 1998, Goldsworthy (Galerie Lelong Paris) 1998, Etre Nature (Foundation Cartier Paris) 1998, Installation und Photographie (Springer & Winckler Galerie Berlin) 1998, Project 8 (Total Museum Korea) 1998, Andy Goldsworthy (Staatsbosbeheer Netherlands) 1999, Arches (Plymouth Art Centre) 1999, Maison European Paris 2001; *Film* Two Autumns (ACGB/Channel 4), Flow of Earth (Granada), Rivers and Tides (Mediopolis Berlin/Skyline Edinburgh) 2000; *Publications* Rain sun snowhail mist calm (1985), Mountain and Coast Autumn into Winter (1987), Parkland (1988), Leaves (1989), Garden Mountain (1989), Touching North (1989), Andy Goldsworthy (1989), Sand Leaves (1991), Hand to Earth (1991), Ice and Snow Drawings (1992), Two Autumns (1993), Stone (1994), Black Stones, Red Pools (1995), Sheepfolds (1996), Wood (1996), Cairns (1997), Andy Goldsworthy (1998), Arch (with David Craid, 1999), Wall (2000), Time (2000); *Style—* Andy Goldsworthy, Esq, OBE; ✉ c/o Michael Hue-Williams Fine Art Ltd, 21 Cork Street, London W1X 1HB (☎ 020 7434 1318, fax 020 7434 1321)

GOLDTHORPE, Dr John Harry; CBE (2002); s of Harry Goldthorpe (d 1989), of Great Houghton, Barnsley, and Lilian Eliza Goldthorpe (d 2002); *b* 27 May 1935; *Educ* Wath-upon-Dearne GS, UCL (BA), LSE, Univ of Cambridge (MA), Univ of Oxford (MA); *m* 1963, Rhiannon Esyllt, da of late Isaac Daniel Harry; 1 s (David Daniel Harry), 1 da (Siân Elinor); *Career* lectr Faculty of Econ and Politics Univ of Cambridge 1961–69 (fell King's Coll 1960–69), official fell Nuffield Coll Oxford 1969–2002 (emeritus fell 2002–), visiting prof Cornell Univ 2003–06, visiting prof Centre for Longitudinal Studies Inst of Educn Univ of London 2008–11, distinguished sr research fell Dept of Social Policy and Intervention Univ of Oxford 2012–15; pres Int Sociological Assoc Ctee on Social Stratification 1982–85; Br Acad assessor ESRC 1988–92, chm Social Studies Section Br Acad 1992–94; Hon Fil Dr Univ of Stockholm 1990; memb Academia Europaea 1988. foreign memb Royal Swedish Acad of Sciences 2001; FBA 1984, FRSS 2016; *Books* The Affluent Worker – Industrial Attitudes and Behaviour (jtly, 1968), The Affluent Worker – Political Attitudes and Behaviour (jtly, 1968), The Affluent Worker in the Class Structure (jtly, 1969), The Social Grading of Occupations – A New Approach and Scale (jtly, 1974), Social Mobility and Class Structure in Modern Britain (2 edn, 1987), The Constant Flux – A Study of Class Mobility in Industrial Societies (jtly, 1992), On Sociology (2000, 2 edn 2007), From Indifference to Enthusiasm: Patterns of Arts Attendance in England (jtly, 2008), Sociology as a Population Science (2016); *Recreations* bird watching, cryptic crosswords; *Style—* Dr John Goldthorpe, CBE, FBA; ✉ 32 Leckford Road, Oxford OX2 6HX (☎ 01865 556602); Nuffield College, Oxford OX1 1NF (☎ 01865 278559, fax 01865 278621, e-mail john.goldthorpe@nuffield.ox.ac.uk)

GOLDWAG, Wanda Celina; *b* Rugby, Warks; *Educ* LSE (BSc); *m* 29 June 2013, Catherine Worboyes (civil partnership converted); *Career* exec dir AIR MILES 1996–2000; advsr Smedvig Venture Capital 2000–; non-exec dir True North Human Capital 2008–, cmmr Civil Service Cmmn 2012–; memb QC Appointments Panel 2016–; *Style—* Ms Wanda Goldwag; ✉ Civil Service Commission, Room G/8 Ground Floor, 1 Horse Guards Road, London SW1A 2HQ

GOLOMBOK, Prof Susan Esther; da of Benzion Golombok, of Glasgow, and Clara, *née* Panice; *b* 11 August 1954, Glasgow; *Educ* Univ of Glasgow (BSc), Inst of Educn Univ of London (MSc), Inst of Psychiatry Univ of London (PhD); *m* 21 Feb 1979, Prof John Rust; 1 s (Jamie Carlos b 25 March 1985); *Career* research psychologist Inst of Psychiatry Univ of London 1977–86, lectr, sr lectr, reader then prof of psychology City Univ London 1987–2005, dir Centre for Family Research and prof of family research Univ of Cambridge 2006–; *Publications* Bottling it Up (jtly, 1985), Modern Psychometrics (jtly, 1989), Gender Development (jtly, 1994), Growing up in a Lesbian Family (jtly, 1997), Parenting: What Really Counts? (2000), Modern Families: Parents and Children in New Family Forms (2015); pubns in academic jls; *Recreations* cinema, cooking, design; *Style—* Prof Susan Golombok; ✉ Centre for Family Research, University of Cambridge, Free School Lane, Cambridge CB2 3RQ (☎ 01223 334510, fax 01223 330574, e-mail seg42@cam.ac.uk, website www.cfr.cam.ac.uk)

GOMBRICH, Prof Richard Francis; *b* 17 July 1937; *Educ* St Paul's (scholar), Magdalen Coll Oxford (Demy scholar, MA, DPhil), Harvard Univ (AM); *Career* Univ of Oxford: lectr in Sanskrit and Pali 1965–76, governing body fell Wolfson Coll 1966–76, Boden prof of Sanskrit and professorial fell Balliol Coll 1976–2004, fndr and academic dir Oxford Centre for Buddhist Studies 2002– (pres 2009–); Benjamin Meaker visiting prof Univ of Bristol 1981–82, visiting prof École des Hautes Études en Sciences Sociales 1982, Stewart visiting fell Princeton Univ 1986–87, Numata visiting prof SOAS 2006; gen ed Clay Sanskrit Library 2000–08; memb: Advsy Cncl V&A 1978–83, Theological and Religious Studies Bd Cncl for Nat Academic Awards 1983–90, Cncl Soc for S Asian Studies 1986–92, Cncl Royal Asiatic Soc 1989–90, Academia Europaea 1990–, Pubns Ctee Royal Asiatic Soc 1991–92; pres Pali Text Soc 1994–2002 (hon sec and treas 1981–94); gen ed Jl of Oxford Centre for Buddhist Studies 2011–; hon fell Int Assoc for Buddhist Studies 2008; Hon DLitt Kalyani Univ 1991, Hon DEd De Montfort Univ 1996; S C Chakraborty medal Asiatic Soc 1993; Sri Lanka Ranjana 1994, Vacaspati Tirupati 1997; *Books* Precept and Practice: Traditional Buddhism in the Rural Highlands of Ceylon (1971), The World of Buddhism: Buddhist Monks and Nuns in Society and Culture (jt ed, 1984), Theravâda Buddhism: A Social History from Ancient Benares to Modern Colombo (1988, 2 edn 2006), Buddhism Transformed: Religious Change in Sri Lanka (jtly, 1988), How Buddhism Began (1996, 2 edn 2006), Kindness and Compassion as Means to Nirvana

(1998), What the Buddha Thought (2009); author of over 100 articles in learned jls; *Style—* Prof Richard Gombrich; ✉ Oxford Centre for Buddhist Studies, Wolfson College, Oxford OX2 6UD

GOMERSALL, Sir Stephen John; KCMG (2000, CMG); s of Harry Raymond Gomersall (d 1976), and Helen Gomersall (d 1995); *b* 17 January 1948; *Educ* Forest Sch, Queens' Coll Cambridge (MA), Stanford Univ (MA); *m* 26 Oct 1975 (m dis 2006), Lydia, da of E W Parry; 2 s (Timothy b 1978, Simon b 1980), 1 da (Emily b 1982); *Career* FCO: entered 1970, Political Section Tokyo 1972–77, Rhodesia Dept and private sec to Dep Foreign Min 1977–82, Political Section Washington 1982–86, econ cnsllr Tokyo 1986–90, head of security policy 1990–94, ambass and dep perm rep UK Mission to the UN 1994–98, dir of int security 1998–99, ambass to Japan 1999–2004; chief exec and gp chm Hitachi Europe 2004–13; currently: Bd dir Hitachi Ltd, dep chm Hitachi Europe, dir Hitachi Rail Europe, dir Horizon Nuclear Power Ltd, dir JPMorgan Japanese Investment Tst; memb Advsy Cncl LSO; *Recreations* music, golf, tennis, skiing; *Style—* Sir Stephen Gomersall, KCMG; ✉ 24 Windsor Court, Moscow Road, London W2 4SN

GOMEZ, Jill (Countess of Northesk); da of Albert Clyde Gomez, and Denise Price Denham; *b* New Amsterdam, Br Guiana; *Educ* RAM, Guildhall Sch of Music; *m* 28 Nov 2010, 15 Earl of Northesk, *qv*; *Career* opera and concert singer; FRAM; after twice winning John Christie Award at Glyndebourne made operatic debut as Adina in L'Elisir d'Amore (Glyndebourne Touring Opera) 1968; masterclass teacher: RAM, Guildford Sch of Music and Drama, Trinity Colls of Music, Britten-Pears Sch Aldeburgh; adjudicator: Edward Boyle Memorial Prize, Wingate Scholarship, Dartington Hall Music Festival, Cardiff Singer of the Year (with Edward Seckerson for BBC 2); *Opera* roles with Glyndebourne Festival Opera incl: Mélisande in Pelléas et Mélisande 1969, title role in La Calisto 1970, Anne Trulove in The Rake's Progress 1975, Helena in A Midsummer Night's Dream 1984; debut ROH 1970, cr role of Flora in Tippett's The Knot Garden, subsequent roles incl: Tytania in A Midsummer Night's Dream, Lauretta in Gianni Schicchi; roles with English Opera Gp incl: Ilia in Idomeneo, Governess in The Turn of the Screw (with Peter Pear's final appearance as Quint); roles with Scottish Opera incl: Leïla in Les Pêcheurs de Perles (Scottish Opera) 1982–83, Pamina in The Magic Flute, Elizabeth in Elegy for Young Lovers, the Countess in The Marriage of Figaro, Fiordiligi in Cosi fan Tutte, Anne Trulove in The Rake's Progress; other roles incl: cr role of Countess in Thea Musgrave Voice of Ariadne (Aldeburgh) 1974, title role in Thaïs (Wexford) 1974, Jenifer in The Midsummer Marriage (WNO) 1976, cr title role in William Alwyn's Miss Julie for radio 1977, Tatiana in Eugene Onegin (Kent Opera) 1977, Donna Elvira in Don Giovanni (Ludwigsburg Festival) 1978, cr title role in BBC world première of Prokofiev's Maddalena 1979, Fiordiligi in Cosi Fan Tutte (Bordeaux) 1979, 8th Book of Madrigals (Zurich Opera, première, Zurich Monteverdi Festival) 1979, Violetta in La Traviata (Kent Opera at Edinburgh Festival) 1979, Cinna in Lucio Silla (Zurich) 1981, Governess in The Turn of the Screw (Geneva) 1981, Cleopatra in Giulio Cesare (Frankfurt) 1981, Teresa in Benvenuto Cellini (Berlioz Festival, Lyon) 1982, Governess in The Turn of the Screw (ENO) 1984, Donna Anna in Don Giovanni (Frankfurt Opera 1985, Kent Opera 1988), Amyntas in Il Re Pastore (Kent Opera) 1987, cr role of the Duchess in Powder her Face (Cheltenham Festival and Almeida Theatre) 1995; *Concerts and Recitals* in Austria, Belgium, France, Germany, Hong Kong, Italy, Netherlands, Scandinavia, Spain, Switzerland, Thailand, West Indies, UK and USA; with conductors incl: Boulez, Britten, Curtis, Davis, Del Mar, Haitink, Kubelik, Mackerras, Marriner, Norrington, Previn, Rattle, Solti; masterclasses, festival appearances incl: Aix-en-Provence, Aldeburgh, Bath, Bergen, Cheltenham, Edinburgh, Flanders, Florence, Glyndebourne, Prague, Spoleto, Versailles and BBC Proms; progs incl: A Spanish Songbook, Night and Day (cabaret), Fortunes of Love and War: a musical portrait of the Napoleonic era (devised by her for the 1998 Géricault exhbn Fitzwilliam Museum and later Wigmore Hall), A Bouquet from the Pleasure Gardens: Theatre songs and English Opera airs of the late 18th century (Cambridge Spring Concerts) 2007; *Recordings* incl: Monteverdi Vespro della Beata Vergine 1610, Rameau La Danse, Handel Admeto, Acis and Galatea, Ode to St Cecilia, three recital discs of French, Spanish and Mozart songs (with John Constable), Britten Quatre Chansons Françaises (premiere recording), Ravel Trois Poèmes de Mallarmé, Canteloube Chants d'Auvergne, Britten Les Illuminations, Villa Lobos Bachianas Brasileiras No 5, Samuel Barber Knoxville, Summer of 1915, Cabaret Classics with John Constable, South of the Border (...Down Mexico Way), Britten's Blues (incl songs by Cole Porter, premiere recording), cmmnd David Matthews work Cantiga – The Song of Inês de Castro, Mahler/Matthews Seven Early Songs (premiere recordings), A Spanish Songbook (with John Constable), cr role of Duchess in Thomas Adès Powder Her Face (premiere recording, nominated for a Grammy award 2000); *Recreations* swimming, pilates, Alexander technique, cycling, theatre, walking in the Cairngorms; *Style—* Miss Jill Gomez; ✉ e-mail jillgomez@btopenworld.com

GOMMON, Peter Nicholas; s of David Edward Gommon (d 1987), and Jean, *née* Vipond; *b* 19 December 1945; *Educ* Northampton GS, Univ of Liverpool (BArch), City of Birmingham Poly (DipLA), Univ of Central England (MA); *m* 21 July 1973, Moira Joan, da of Leonard Thomas Maguire (d 1990), of Millhouses, Sheffield; 3 s (David b 28 Dec 1974, Joseph b 7 Aug 1976 d 1986, Edward b 19 Oct 1978); *Career* architect and landscape architect; dir Ainsley Gommon Architects Ltd 1981–2010, ret (winners of 30 Nat and Int Awards for community projects, landscape and architecture); currently conslt to Ainsley Gommon Architects; external examiner Sch of Landscape Manchester Metropolitan Univ 1998–2001; memb: St Saviour Devpt Ctee; RIBA 1975, CMLI 1982, FRSA 1992; *Recreations* art, theatre, music, agriculture, motor cycling, bass player with 'Orange Zebra'; *Clubs* TOMCC; *Style—* Peter Gommon, Esq; ✉ 46 Shrewsbury Road, Oxton, Birkenhead CH43 2HZ (☎ 0151 653 7204, e-mail pierregommon@btinternet.com); Ty Joseff, 6 Pen y Fron, Penmon, Ynys Môn, Gwynedd; Ainsley Gommon Architects, 1 Price Street, Birkenhead Merseyside L41 6JN (website www.ainsleygommonarchitects.co.uk)

GONTARSKI, Steven; *b* 1972, Philadelphia, USA; *Educ* Brown Univ USA (BA), Goldsmiths Coll London (MA); *Career* artist; *Solo Exhibitions* Steven Gontarski: The Unbalance of Boredom (Taché-Lévy Gallery Brussels) 2000, White Cube 2000, Le Consortium Dijon 2003, Prophet (Karyn Lovegrove Gallery LA) 2003, Gandy Gallery Prague 2004, Zero (The Economist Plaza London) 2004, December Morning Prophecy (Inside the White Cube London) 2004, The Visitors (Groninger Museum Groningen) 2005, pkm gallery Seoul 2006; *Group Exhibitions* American Beauty (Brown Univ RI USA) 1994, Looking Out, Putting Out (450 Broadway Gallery NY) 1995, Imaginary Beings (Exit Art/The First World NY) 1995, Sweat (Exit Art/The First World NY) 1996, Humdrum (The Trade Apartment London) 1997, Cloth Bound (Laure Genillard Gallery London) 1998, Die Young Stay Pretty (ICA London) 1998, Neurotic Realism Part I (Saatchi Gallery London) 1999, Nurse (Johnen & Schöttle Gallery Cologne) 1999, Heart + Soul (60 Long Lane London) 1999, Din (4x4 Gallery Amsterdam) 1999, Drawing Exhbn (Taché-Lévy Gallery Brussels) 2000, Drawings (Sommer Contemporary Art Tel Aviv) 2000, Heart + Soul (Sandroni Rey Venice Calif) 2000, Hard Candy (42 Westbourne Gardens London) 2000, Hardy Candy Berlin (Galerie Wieland Berlin) 2000, Conversation (Milton Keynes Gallery) 2000, A very nice film club (Vilma Gold Gallery London) 2000, Chantal Joffe and Steven Gontarski (One in the Other London) 2001, Mind the Gap (Wetterling Gallery Stockholm) 2001, Freestyle: Werke Aus der Sammlung Boros (Museum Morsbroich Leverkusen) 2001, Jam: Tokyo-London (Barbican Gallery London) 2001, We Set Off in High Spirits (Matthew Marks Gallery NY) 2001, Friends of Mine (Gallery Muu Helsinki) 2001, Jam: Tokyo-London (Tokyo City Opera Gallery) 2002, Electric Dreams (Curve Gallery London) 2002, Guided by Heroes (Z33 Hasselt) 2003, Coollustre (Collection Lambert en Avignon) 2003, Dornbracht/Statements 7 Venice 2003, Dirty Pretty Things (The Ship London) 2003, Game Over (Grimm/Rosenfield Munich) 2003, Roll Out (Karyn Lovegrove Gallery LA) 2003, The Future Lasts a Long Time (TalEsther Gallery Tel Aviv) 2004, Suejin Chung, Meena Park, Steven Gontarski (Kukje Gallery Seoul) 2004, Nachtelijke Uitspattingen/Nocturnal Emissions (Groninger Museum Groningen) 2004, Kingdom (Market Gallery Glasgow) 2004, The Future Lasts a Long Time (Le Consortium Dijon) 2005, Pour de Vrai Musée des Beaux Arts Nancy 2005; *Style—* Steven Gontarski, Esq; ✉ Studio ☎ 020 7377 5665, fax 020 7377 5665, mobile 07958 372093, e-mail info@stevengontarski.com, website www.stevengontarski.com

GONZALEZ-BUNSTER, Carolina; *b* 22 March 1983, Greenwich, CT, USA; *Educ* Georgetown Univ (BA), LSE (MSc), Said Business Sch Oxford (MBA); *Career* analyst Clinton Climate Initiative 2006–07, financial analyst Goldman Sachs 2007–08, fndr Walkabout Fndn 2008–; Woman of the Future Award 2010; listed in: Sunday Times 30 Women Under 30 2011, Evening Standard London's 1000 Most Influential People 2011; *Style—* Ms Carolina Gonzalez-Bunster; ✉ Ignite, Walkabout, 15A Ives Street, London SW3 2ND (website www.walkaboutfoundation.org, Twitter @walkabout2011)

GOOCH, Charles Albert; s of Ernest Edward Gooch; *b* 15 September 1938; *Educ* Coleman St Ward Sch London; *m* 1974, June Margaret, *née* Reardon; 2 da (Charlotte b 1976, Jessica b 1978); *Career* former chm Shaw & Marvin plc; chm: Buckland Securities Ltd, MacNiven-Cameron plc; dir MacNiven & Cameron Developments Ltd; Liveryman Worshipful Co of Stationers and Newspaper Makers; *Style—* Charles Gooch, Esq; ✉ Buckland Securities Ltd, Buckland House, 1 Thomas More Way, London N2 0UL (☎ 020 8432 8726, fax 020 8346 9608)

GOOD, Anthony Bruton Meyrick; OBE; s of Meyrick George Bruton Good, and Amy Trussell; *b* 18 April 1933, Sutton, Surrey; *Educ* Felsted; *m* 29 Sept 2010, Dr Iris Good; 2 da (1 decd); *Career* mgmnt trainee Distillers Group 1950–52, editorial asst Temple Press Ltd 1952–55, PR offr Silver City Airways (PR/marketing Br Aviation Servs Ltd) 1955–60, fndr and chm Good Relations Gp plc 1961–89; chm: Cox & Kings Ltd 1975– (dir 1971–), Good Relations (India) Ltd 1988–, Cox & Kings (India) Ltd 1988– (dir 1980–), Good Consultancy Ltd 1989–, Flagship Gp Ltd 1999–2011, Miller Insurance Gp Ltd 2000–04, The Tranquil Moment Ltd 2000–07, Sage Organics Ltd 2000–09, Tulip Star Hotels Ltd 2000–, Outright Mktg and Distribution Ltd (formerly Q-Link Int Ltd) 2000–14, Relish Events Ltd 2001–06, Nutrahealth plc 2004–15, Marlin Gp Hldgs plc 2012–14; dir: IM Gp Ltd 1977–98, Arcadian International plc 1995–98, Care First Gp plc 1996–98, Gowrings plc 2004–05, Obento Ltd 2004–13, Benney Watches plc 2007–13, I-Connections UK Ltd 2008–, DQ Entertainment plc 2008–13, Outright Communication Ltd 2009–15, All About Brands plc 2010–12; dir UK India Business Cncl (India) Ltd 2005–14; Hon FIoD, FCIPR; *Recreations* travel, reading, theatre; *Clubs* RAC; *Style—* Anthony Good, Esq, OBE; ✉ Clench House, Wootton Rivers, Marlborough, Wiltshire SN8 4NT (☎ 01672 810670); Clench Lodge, Wootton Rivers, Marlborough, Wiltshire SN8 4NT (☎ 01672 810126, e-mail tony@tonygood.co.uk)

GOOD, Rev Dr (George) Harold; OBE (1985, MBE 1970); s of Rev Robert James Good (d 1976), and Doris, *née* Allen (d 1979); *b* 27 April 1937, Londonderry, NI; *Educ* Methodist Coll Belfast, Edgehill Theol Coll Belfast, Christian Theol Seminary Indianapolis; *m* 11 Aug 1964, Clodagh Anne, da of Charles Coad, of Waterford; 3 da (Carolyn b 3 July 1965, Sharon b 18 Nov 1967, Denise b 9 May 1972), 2 s (Jonathan b 11 March 1970, Richard b 23 Aug 1972); *Career* ordained minister Methodist Church in Ireland 1962; served circuits: Co Armagh, Dublin, Waterford, Belfast, Co Down; min to youth 1st Methodist Church Warren Ohio, pt/t chaplain HMP Crumlin Rd Belfast, pt/t chaplain Belfast City Hospital; pres Methodist Church in Ireland 2001–02; dir Corrymeela Community Centre for Reconciliation 1973–78; NI supplementary benefits cmmr 1974–80, NI memb Social Security Advsy Ctee 1980–98, chair and review of NI Cncl of Social Service 1982–83, chm Personal Social Services Advsy Ctee DHSS 1984–92, memb NI Human Rights Cmmn 1999–2004; chm NI Assoc for Care and Resettlement of Offenders 1992–2001, memb Methodist Cncl on Social Responsibility, fndr memb Healing Through Remembering project; chair Advice Services Alliance 2005–11; patron: Habitat for Humanity, The Leprosy Mission; govr Greenwood House Assessment Centre, govr Methodist Coll Belfast; ind witness to decommissioning of weapons of the IRA 2005; jt recipient René Cassin Peace Award Basque Govt 2005, World Methodist Cncl Peace Prize 2007, jt recipient Gandhi Fndn Int Peace Award 2008; DUniv (hc): Queen's Univ Belfast 2008, Univ of Ulster 2008, Open Univ 2010; DD (hc) Ohio Wesleyan Univ 2010, DD (hc) Christian Theological Seminary Indianapolis 2015; *Recreations* travel, painting, photography, sea angling, DIY; *Style—* The Rev Dr Harold Good, OBE; ✉ 4 Brown's Park, Marino, Holywood, Co Down BT18 0AB (☎ 028 9042 1464, e-mail harold.good@irishmethodist.org)

GOODALL, Caroline Mary Helen; da of Capt Peter Goodall, CBE, TD (d 1995), of Wetherby, W Yorks, and Sonja Jeanne, *née* Burt; sis of Charles Peter Goodall, *qv*; *b* 22 May 1955; *Educ* Queen Ethelburga's Sch, Newnham Coll Cambridge (MA); *m* 1 Oct 1983, (Vesey) John Hill, s of Maj Vesey Michael Hill (d 1972); *Career* asst slr Slaughter and May 1980–84 (articled clerk 1978–80); Herbert Smith: asst slr 1984–87, ptnr 1987–2009, head Corp Div 2000–05, conslt 2009–; memb: Company Law Ctee Law Soc 2006–09, Companies Ctee CBI; non-exec dir: SVG Capital plc 2010–14, Grant Thornton LLP 2010–, Next plc 2013–; tstee and non-exec dir Woodland Tst 2009–12, memb Cncl Nat Tst 2010– (tstee 2012–); memb: American Bar Assoc 2000–09, Worshipful Co of Slrs, Law Soc, Int Bar Assoc; assoc fell Newnham Coll Cambridge 2005–08; MInstD, FRSA; *Recreations* tennis, theatre, sailing, fell walking; *Clubs* Roehampton, Brancaster Staithe Sailing, Athenaeum; *Style—* Miss Caroline Goodall; ✉ Herbert Smith Freehills, Exchange House, Primrose Street, London EC2A 2HS (☎ 020 7374 8000, fax 020 7374 0888, e-mail caroline.goodall@hsf.com)

GOODALL, Howard; CBE (2011); s of Geoffrey Goodall, and Marion, *née* Smith; *b* 26 May 1958, Bromley, Kent; *Educ* Stowe, Lord Williams's Sch Thame, ChCh Oxford (MA); *m* 2000, Val Fancourt; *Career* composer; television presenter: Choir of the Year (BBC), Chorister of the Year (BBC), Young Musician of the Year (BBC), Howard Goodall's Organworks (Channel 4) 1996, Howard Goodall's Choirworks (Channel 4) 1998, Howard Goodall's Big Bangs (Channel 4) 2000 (Huw Wheldon Award BAFTA 2000), Howard Goodall's Great Dates (Channel 4) 2002, Howard Goodall's 20th Century Greats (Channel 4) 2004, Howard Goodall's How Music Works (Channel 4) 2006, The Story of Music (BBC 2) 2013; presenter and composer in residence Classic FM 2008–15; nat ambass for singing 2007–11; Br Acad of Composers and Songwriters Gold Badge Award, Making Music Sir Charles Grove Prize for Outstanding Contribution to British Music 2007; hon doctorate Bishop Grosseteste Univ Coll Lincoln, hon doctorate Univ of Bolton; ARCO; *Works* musical theatre: The Hired Man 1984, Girlfriends 1986, Days of Hope 1991, Silas Marner 1993, The Kissing-Dance 1999, The Dreaming 2001, A Winter's Tale 2005, Two Cities 2006, Love Story 2010, Bend It Like Beckham 2015; television themes: Red Dwarf, Blackadder, Mr Bean, The Thin Blue Line, The Vicar of Dibley, The Catherine Tate Show, QI; choral works: Missa Aedis Christi 1993, Love Divine 2000, In Memoriam Anne Frank 2001, Winter Lullabies 2005, Veni Sancte Spiritus 2008, Eternal Light: A Requiem 2008, Enchanted Voices: The Beatitudes 2009, Pelican in the Wilderness 2010, Rigaudon Queen Elizabeth II Diamond Jubilee Regatta 2012, Sure of the Sky: Des Himmels Sicher 2014; *Style—* Howard Goodall, Esq, CBE; ✉ website www.howardgoodall.co.uk, Twitter

@Howard_Goodall; c/o PBJ and JBJ Management, 22 Rathbone Street, London W1T 1LA; c/o Faber Music (publisher)

GOODBAND, Philip Haydon; s of Philip Aubrey Goodband, of Camberley, Surrey, and Edith Emma Haydon Goodband; *b* 26 May 1944; *Educ* Strode's Sch UK, Dijon France; *m* 1; 1 da (Emily Victoria b 19 Sept 1973), 2 s (Charles Lindsey Haydon b 15 June 1975 d 1975, Henry Lindsey Charles b 24 Oct 1978); m 2, 2 Oct 2004, Ann Marie, da of Frederick Deluca, of Stockton CA; *Career* MW; Vintners scholar 1970; dir: Gilbey SA France 1972–73, Stowells of Chelsea 1981–86 (buyer 1973–80); Grants of St James's: wine buying, quality and logistics 1986–88, md Wine Div on Trade 1988–92, business devpt dir 1992–94; princ Philip Goodband Int Wine Consultancy 1994–; chm Inst of Masters of Wine 1984–85, dir Wine Devpt Bd 1980–92, dir Wine Standards Bd UK 1999–2007; chair of judges Int Wine and Spirit Competition 2002–; tstee Wine and Spirit Trade Benevolent Soc 1986–89; frequent public speaker and lectr; life memb Academie du Champagne; Freeman: City of London 1972, Worshipful Co of Haberdashers 1972 (Clothed 1975); FBBI 1968; Compagnon du Beaujolais 1978, membre de L'Ordre St Etienne France 1981, Cavaleiro da Confraria do Vinho do Porto Portugal 1987, Chevalier des Coteaux de Champagne 1989, Commndeur and Conseiller d'Honneur to the Grand Conseil de Bordeaux 1996–; *Recreations* travel, tennis, theatre, food and wine; *Clubs* City of London, Dorking Lawn Tennis and Squash; *Style—* Philip Goodband, MW; ✉ Philip Goodband MW, 21 Grenehurst Park, Capel, Dorking, Surrey RH5 5GB (☎ 01306 712173, mobile 07973 119891, e-mail phg@philipgoodband.com, website www.philipgoodband.com)

GOODBODY, Michael Ivan Andrew; s of Llewellyn Marcus Goodbody (d 1989), of Ardclough Lodge, Straffan, Co Kildare, and Eileen Elizabeth, *née* Bourke; *b* 23 January 1942; *Educ* Kingstown Sch Dublin; *m* 9 March 1968, Susannah Elizabeth, da of Donald Guy Pearce (Capt Ayrshire Yeomanry RA, ka 1944); 2 da (Sarah b 1970, Perry b 1976), 1 s (Guy b 1972); *Career* Lt TA, 289 Parachute Battery RHA; stockbroker Smith Rice & Hill 1962–74, private client stockbroker Capel-Cure Myers 1974–88, dir: Capel-Cure Myers Capital Management Ltd 1988–98, Capel-Cure Sharp 1998–2000, Carr Sheppards Crosthwaite 2001–06; hon treas Colne Stour Countryside Assoc; MSI; *Books* The Goodbody Family of Ireland (1979), The Goodbodys – Millers, Merchants and Manufacturers (2011); *Recreations* family history, genealogy, countryside conservation; *Style—* Michael Goodbody, Esq; ✉ The Old Rectory, Wickham St Paul's, Halstead, Essex CO9 2PJ

GOODBURN, Andrew Robert; s of Robert Goodburn, and Peggy, *née* Barrett; *b* 5 January 1947; *Educ* Harrow HS, Monkton House Sch; *m* 28 June 1969, Elizabeth Ann, da of Joseph Henry Dunn; 3 s (Giles Andrew b 11 Nov 1972, Henry Robert b 18 April 1974, Benjamin Joseph b 24 June 1978), 1 da (Anne-Marie b 19 May 1980); *Career* Peat Marwick Mitchell & Co 1964–70 (articled clerk, audit sr); Bowthorpe Holdings plc 1970–81: gen mangr Hellermann Cassettes (fin controller), fin dir Hellermann Deutsch, commercial dir Bowthorpe EMP, mktg dir Hellermann Electric; ptnr Grant Thornton 1987–91 (joined as sr mgmnt consIt 1982), head of fin consultancy Price Waterhouse (Redhill Office) 1991–93, commercial dir Ricardo Hitec 1993–94, fin dir Ricardo Aerospace 1994, fin dir Ricardo Consulting 1995–97, gp fin dir Ricardo Gp plc 1997–2007; non-exec dir Caffyns plc 2004–14; FCA (ACA 1969); *Recreations* tennis, golf, travel, gardening; *Clubs* Thurlestone Golf, Royal Ashdown Forest Golf; *Style—* Andrew Goodburn, Esq; ✉ Deacons Hay, Beaconsfield Road, Chelwood Gate, East Sussex RH17 7LG (☎ 01825 740225, e-mail andrew.goodburn@me.com)

GOODCHILD, Peter Robert Edward; s of Douglas Richard Geoffrey Goodchild, MBE (d 1989), of Angmering Village, W Sussex, and Lottie May, *née* Ager (d 2000); *b* 18 August 1939; *Educ* Aldenham, St John's Coll Oxford (MA); *m* 1968, Penelope-Jane, da of Dr William Pointon-Dick (d 1956), and Gwendoline Honora, *née* Pearse (d 2007); 2 da (Abigail b 1971, Hannah b 1974); *Career* prodr Horizon BBC TV 1965–69 (winner Soc of Film and TV Arts Mullard Award for Science Broadcasting 1967, 1968 and 1969), ed Horizon BBC TV 1969–76 (winner BAFTA Award for Best Factual Series 1972 and 1974, winner Italia Prize for Factual Programmes 1973 and 1975), exec prodr drama prodns 1977–80 (including Marie Curie 1977 and Oppenheimer 1980 which both won BAFTA Awards for Best Series), prodr Bread or Blood 1980, head of science and features BBC TV 1980–84 (initiating programme QED), head of plays BBC TV 1984–89 (initiating Screen Two, Screen One and Screenplay), exec prodr and prodr Film Dept BBC 1989–94; prodr: The March 1990 (winner One World TV Premier Network award), Adam Bede 1991, Trust Me 1992, Return to Blood River 1994, Black Easter 1994 (winner Gold Award Chicago Film Festival 1996), King of Chaos 1998 (BAFTA nominee 1998); dir: Stone City Films 1995–98, Green Umbrella Features 1998–2004; pres Dunchideock Treacle Miners 2000–, vice-pres Exeter Rowing Club 2002–; CChem, FRSC; *Books* Shatterer of Worlds (the life of J Robert Oppenheimer, 1980), The Real Dr Strangelove (the life of Edward Teller, 2004); *Radio Plays* incl: The Great Tennessee Monkey Trial 1991, The Chicago Conspiracy Trial 1993 (NY Radio Festival Gold Award 1995), Nuremberg 1996, In the Name of Security 1998, Lockerbie on Trial 2001, Great Monkey Trial 2009; *Stage Plays* The Real Dr Strangelove 2006, The Great Monkey Trial (US tour) 2006, Edward and Oppie 2009 (US tour 2010–11); *Recreations* rowing, music, gardening; *Clubs* Oxford and Cambridge; *Style—* Peter Goodchild, Esq; ✉ Dunchideock House, Dunchideock, Exeter EX2 9TS

GOODCHILD, Tim; *Educ* Guildford Coll of Art, Wimbledon Coll of Art (Arts Cncl scholar); *Career* designer; designed costumes for opening ceremony The 2002 Commonwealth Games Manchester, forthcoming prodns incl The Talking Cure (Josefstadt Theatre Vienna), Elf musical (UK premiere), Putting It Together (London premiere), The Nutcracker (Houston Ballet Company); *Theatre* over 70 West End prodns incl: Hadrian VII 1969, Richard II 1969, Cowardy Custard 1972, Gone with the Wind (Theatre Royal) 1972, Show Boat (Adelphi Theatre), Hans Andersen (Palladium Theatre), Pump Boys and Dinettes 1983, Bus Stop 1990, Pirandello's Henry IV 1990, Our Song 1992, Chapter Two 1996, Quartet 1999, Strangers on a Train 2013; over 20 prodns for The New Shakespeare Co incl: My Fair Lady 1979, Oklahoma (also Aust) 1980, Little Shop of Horrors 1983, Blondel 1983, Café Puccini 1986, Five Guys Named Moe (also Broadway and Aust) 1990, Hey Mr Producer 1998; for RSC prodns incl: The Taming of the Shrew 1993/94, The Relapse 1995, Zenobia 1995, Three Hours After Marriage 1996, The Merry Wives of Windsor 1996; for Chichester Festival Theatre: School for Scandal, Love for Love, Blithe Spirit, R Love J, The Royal Baccarat Scandal; other prodns incl: Antony and Cleopatra (Egyptian Nat Theatre) 1978, Cyrano de Bergerac (Stratford Ontario Festival Theatre), The Corsican Brothers (Abbey Theatre Dublin), Peter Pan (McLab Theatre Canada), Gigi (Volksoper Vienna) 1999, Lettice and Lovage (UK tour), Falstaff (Chartelet Theatre Paris), Noel Coward's Star Quality (world premiere, UK tour and West End), Taboo (Boy George musical London and Broadway), We Will Rock You (Queen tribute musical Dominion Theatre, Las Vegas, Germany, Russia, Australia, Tokyo, South Africa, Spain), Suspension (Bristol Old Vic); *Opera* Sadler Wells Opera Co: The Mikado 1983, HMS Pinafore (also City Center NY) 1983, Gondoliers 1984; other prodns incl: La Traviata (WNO), The Mikado (Australian Opera Co), The Tales of Hoffman (Victoria State Opera Co), Mephistopheles (ENO) 1999, La Bohème (Kirov Opera), The Tales of Hoffman (Huston Grand Opera), Salome (NYC Opera), Le nozze di Figaro (LA Opera Co), La Vie Parisienne (ENO), La Traviata (Royal Danish Opera, WNO), Falstaff (Chatelet Theatre Paris), Roméo et Juliette (LA Opera), Sir John in Love (ENO), 2006, Don Carlo (LA Opera) 2006, Die Meistersinger von Nürnberg (LA Opera) 2006–07, The Marriage of Figaro (LA Opera); *Ballet* numerous prodns incl: Swan Lake (Moscow National Ballet, Moscow, UK, world tour) 1988, The Look of Love (BBC2), A Simple Man (BBC2, BAFTA Award), The Fool on The Hill (Aust State Ballet and TV film), Don Quixote (Northern Ballet Theatre); *Awards* Green Room Award Best Operatic Design (for The Tales of Hoffman, Aust), Olivier Award for Best Costume Design (for The Relapse) 1997, Olivier Awards for Best Costume Design and Best Set Design (for Three Hours After Marriage) 1998; nominations incl: The Theatre LA Ovations Award for Best Set (for Five Guys Named Moe), Sammy Award (for The Fool on the Hill), Whatsonstage Award for Best Design (for Strangers on a Train), Olivier Award for Best Design (for Strangers on a Train); *Style—* Tim Goodchild, Esq; ✉ c/o Simpson Fox Associates Ltd, 6 Beauchamp Place, London SW3 1NG (☎ 020 7434 9167, fax 020 7494 2887)

GOODE, Prof Anthony William; s of late William Henry Goode, of Tynemouth, and Eileen Veronica, *née* Brannan; *b* 3 August 1944; *Educ* Corby Sch, Univ of Newcastle upon Tyne Med Sch (MB BS, MD); *m* Dr Patricia Josephine, da of late Michael and Mary Flynn; *Career* surgical appts Newcastle upon Tyne teaching hosps and demonstrator anatomy Univ of Newcastle upon Tyne 1968–74, various appts Univ of London teaching hosps 1975–; clinical dir Helicopter Emergency Medical Service Royal London Hosp 1997–99; currently: prof of endocrine and metabolic surgery Univ of London, hon conslt surgn Royal London Hosp and Bart's, hon prof Dept for Biological and Med Systems Imperial Coll London, ed-in-chief Med Science and the Law; res programmes related to: nutrition, metabolism, endocrinology in surgery, role of microgravity res in future med and surgical devpt; pres Br Acad of Forensic Sciences; hon sec and treas Br Assoc Endocrine Surgns 1982–97 (fndr memb 1980); tstee Smith & Nephew Fndn 1990–; hon memb The Hunterian Soc (orator 1999); Freeman City of London 1994, Liveryman Worshipful Soc of Apothecaries 1997; memb: RSM 1972, Int Soc Surgery 1985, New York Acad Sciences 1987; fell American Coll of Surgeons 2000, FRCS 1972; *Books* contrib numerous surgical textbooks; ed-in-chief Medicine Science and the Law; *Recreations* music (especially opera), cricket, literature; *Clubs* Athenaeum, MCC, Cross Arrows CC; *Style—* Prof Anthony Goode; ✉ The Surgical Unit, The Royal London Hospital, Whitechapel, London E1 1BB (☎ 020 7377 7000)

GOODE, Matthew; s of late Anthony John James Goode, and Jennifer Ann, *née* Cowling; *b* 3 April 1978, Exeter, Devon; *Educ* Univ of Birmingham, Webber Douglas Acad; *Career* actor; *Theatre* Blood Wedding (Mercury Theatre Colchester), The Tempest (Mercury Theatre Colchester); *Television* Inspector Lynley 2003, He Knew He Was Right 2004, A Murder is Announced 2005, My Family and Other Animals 2005; *Film* Confessions of an Ugly Stepsister 2002, South From Granada 2003, Chasing Liberty 2004, Match Point 2005, Imagine Me and You 2005, My Family and Other Animals 2005, Copying Beethoven 2006, The Lookout 2007, Brideshead Revisited 2008, Watchmen 2009, A Single Man 2009, Leap Year 2010, Cemetery Junction 2010, Burning Man 2011; *Style—* Matthew Goode, Esq; ✉ c/o Dalzell & Beresford Ltd, 26 Astwood Mews, London SW7 4DE (☎ 020 7341 9411, fax 020 7341 9412, e-mail mail@dbltd.co.uk)

GOODE, Prof Sir Royston Miles (Roy); kt (2000), CBE (1994, OBE 1972), QC (1990); s of Samuel Goode (d 1968), of Portsmouth, Hants, and Blooma, *née* Zeid (d 1984); *b* 6 April 1933; *Educ* Highgate Sch, Univ of London (LLB, LLD); *m* 18 Oct 1964, Catherine Anne, da of Jean Marcel Rueff, and Marianne Rueff; 1 da (Naomi b 1965); *Career* Nat Serv RASC 1955–57; admitted slr 1955, ptnr Victor Mishcon & Co 1963–71 (conslt 1971–88); QMC London: prof of law 1971–73, Crowther prof of credit and commercial law 1973–89, dean Faculty of Law and head dept 1976–80; hon pres Centre Commercial Law Studies 1989– (fndr and dir 1979–89), Norton Rose prof of English law Univ of Oxford 1990–1998 (emeritus prof 1998–), fell St John's Coll Oxford 1990–98 (emeritus fell 1998–); pres Cncl Int Postgrad Law Sch Belgrade 2002–04; transferred to the Bar Inner Temple 1988 (hon bencher); chm Pension Law Review Ctee 1992–93; UK rep and memb Governing Cncl UNIDROIT Rome 1989–2003; memb Cncl Br Acad 2007–; Freeman City of London; hon fell Queen Mary & Westfield Coll London 1991; Hon DSc (Econ) Univ of London 1996, Hon LLD UEA 2003, Hon LLD Coll of Law 2011; FBA 1988, FRSA 1990; *Books* Hire-Purchase Law and Practice (2 edn 1970), Legal Problems of Credit and Security (5 edn 2013 (ed Louise Gulliver)), Commercial Law (4 edn 2009 (ed Ewan McKendrick)), Payment Obligations in Commercial and Financial Transactions (2 edn 2009 (ed Charles Proctor)), Proprietary Rights and Insolvency in Sales Transactions (3 edn 2010 (ed Simon Mills)), Principles of Corporate Insolvency Law (4 edn 2011), Official Commentary on the Convention on International Interests in Mobile Equipment and Aircraft Protocol (3 edn 2013), Official Commentary on the Convention and International Interests in Mobile Equipment and Space Protocol (2013), Official Commentary on the Convention on International Interests in Mobile Equipment and Luxembourg Protocol (2 edn 2014); *Recreations* chess, walking, browsing in bookshops; *Clubs* Reform; *Style—* Prof Sir Roy Goode, CBE, QC, FBA; ✉ 42 St John Street, Oxford OX1 2LH

GOODENOUGH, Alan; *b* 7 December 1943; *Career* unit gen mangr Excel Bowling 1964–66, gen mangr and regnl dir Bingo and Social Clubs Rank Organisation plc 1966–71, main bd dir Pleasurama plc 1972–88, md Casinos, Hotels and Holiday Businesses and main bd dir Mecca Leisure Group plc 1988–90, fndr and chm Lyric Hotels 1990–, non-exec chm Time Line (bus and coach operator) 1990–, chief exec London Clubs International plc 1993– (brought co to UK stock market 1994); MInstD 1990; *Style—* Alan Goodenough, Esq; ✉ London Clubs International plc, 10 Brick Street, London W1Y 8HQ (☎ 020 7518 0000, fax 020 7518 0174)

GOODERHAM, Peter Olaf; CMG (2007); s of Leonard Eric Gooderham (d 2000), and Gerd, *née* Huseby (d 2005); *b* 29 July 1954; *Educ* Univ of Newcastle (BA), Univ of Bristol (PhD); *m* 1985, Carol-Anne, *née* Ward; *Career* diplomat; mgmnt trainee Industrial Facts and Forecasting 1975–76; res fell: Univ of Essex 1979–81, Univ of Birmingham 1981–83; asst desk offr Falkland Islands Dept FCO 1983–85, 1 sec Arms Control UK Delgn NATO 1985–87, head Nigeria Section West Africa Dept FCO 1987–90, first sec (economic) Riyadh 1990–93, dep head Security Policy Dept FCO 1993–96, cnsllr Economic and Social Cncl UK Mission NY 1996–99, political cnsllr Br Embassy Washington DC 1999–2003, UK rep EU Political and Security Ctee UK Representation in Brussels 2003–04, dir ME and North Africa Dept DFSD 2004–07, perm rep UK Mission to the UN Geneva 2008–; *Style—* Peter Gooderham, Esq, CMG; ✉ UK Mission, 58 Avenue Louis Casai, Case Postale 6, 1216 Cointrin, Geneva, Switzerland (☎ 0041 022 918 2358, fax 0041 022 918 2377)

GOODEVE, (John) Anthony; s of Cdr Sir Charles Frederick Goodeve, OBE (d 1980), of London, and Janet Irene, *née* Wallace (d 1993); *b* 4 August 1944; *Educ* Canford Sch; *m* 30 March 2007, Elaine Day, *née* Langston;1 da (Claire Michelle b 29 May 1982); *Career* RNR 1963–66; Shell Mex and BP Ltd 1964–78 (latterly with Shell UK Oil), md Dupré Vermiculite Ltd 1978–79, gp mktg exec Wood Hall Building Group Ltd 1979–80, chief exec and md Grosvenor Property & Finance Ltd 1980–2009, md Grosvenor Investment Planning Ltd 1997–; Freeman City of London 1969, Liveryman Worshipful Co of Salters 1969 (Renter 1996, memb Ct of Assts 1998, Master 2004–05); FIoD; *Recreations* politics, boating, skiing, photography, swimming; *Clubs* IOD; *Style—* Anthony Goodeve, Esq; ✉ Highfields House, 4 Prospect Lane, Harpenden, Hertfordshire AL5 2PL

GOODEY, Felicity Margaret Sue; CBE (2001), DL (Gtr Manchester 1998); da of Henry E A Goodey (d 2001), and Susan, *née* Fong (d 2002); *b* 25 July 1949, Plymouth, Devon; *Educ* St Austell GS, St Hugh's Coll Oxford (BA); *m* 31 Aug 1973, John R Marsh; 2 s (Alexander James b 28 Oct 1980, Christopher Henry b 8 March 1985); *Career* trainee journalist rising

G

to sr corr BBC 1971–85, self-employed with BBC contracts (presenter Radio 4 and BBC NW) and presenter and ind prodr TV documentaries 1985–99, owner and mangr Felicity Goodey & Associates 1990–98, dir Precise Communications 1998–2001; chair: Lowry Operational Co 1994–2003, Lowry Devpt Co 1994–2003, Lowry Tst 1994–2004; hon life pres The Lowry 2004–; interim chief exec mediacity:uk 2005–07; non-exec dir Nord Anglia plc 1999–2007, dir Unique Communications Gp 2001–05 (non-exec dir 2005–07); chair: Cultural Consortium NW 1999–2004, NW Tourism 2003–11, Central Salford Urban Regeneration Co 2004–11, Univ Hosp of S Manchester 2008–15; non-exec dir: Excellence Northwest 1993–2004, Sustainability NW 1994–98, NW Devpt Agency 1998–2002, Manchester Cwlth Games Ltd 1997–2002, Manchester C of C and Industry 1999–2014; memb Cncl AHRC 2003–07, memb Advsy Cncl Manchester Business Sch 2009–; hon vice-pres NW Riding for the Disabled 1978–, tstee Friends of Rosie 1992–, memb Bd Going for Green 1994–98, govr Manchester GS 1994–2008, memb Bd Paterson Cncl (Christie Hosp) 1996–98, chair Macmillan Day Care Hospice 1997–99, chair Smart project for First Step Tst 2005–13, chair Creative Industries in Salford 2006–08, memb Panel Regnl Growth Fund 2011–15, pres Cheshire Wildlife Tst 2011–; memb Bd: Royal Northern Coll of Music 2014–, Buxton Opera Festival 2014–, Royal Northern Coll of Music 2014–; chm Buxton Festival 2015–; Goldstone Award, Blue Circle Award; Hon Col 207 Manchester Field Hosp 2009–14; Hon LLD Univ of Manchester, Hon DLitt Manchester Met Univ, Hon DLitt Univ of Salford; hon fell: Bolton Inst, Univ of Central Lancs; Paul Harris fell 2013; Hon FRIBA 2004, FRSA 2006; *Recreations* family, theatre, opera; *Clubs* Oxford & Cambridge, RSA; *Style—* Ms Felicity Goodey, CBE, DL; ✉ The Buxton Festival, 3 The Square, Buxton, Derbyshire SK17 6AZ (website www.buxtonfestival.co.uk)

GOODFELLOW, John Graham; *b* 10 January 1947; *Educ* Allan Glen's Sch Glasgow; *Career* cashier rising to asst mangr programming Burnley Building Soc Glasgow 1964–82, asst gen mangr i/c IT National & Provincial Building Soc 1983–84; Skipton Building Society: asst gen mangr then gen mangr i/c IT and admin 1984–91, chief exec and dir 1991–; chm Business Link North Yorkshire, dir N Yorks TEC; MIDPM, FRSA; *Style—* John Goodfellow, Esq; ✉ Skipton Building Society, The Bailey, Skipton, North Yorkshire BD23 1DN (☎ 01756 705000, fax 01756 705703)

GOODFELLOW, Prof Dame Julia; DBE (2010, CBE 2001); *Educ* Univ of Bristol, Open Univ (PhD), Stanford Univ Calif; *Career* vice-master Birkbeck Coll London 1998–2002, chief exec Biotechnology and Biological Sciences Research Cncl 2002–07, vice-chllr Univ of Kent 2007–; chair Br Science Assoc 2009–; memb: Cncl for Science and Technol 2011–, Science and Technol Facilities Cncl 2011–; Hon DSc: Univ of Strathclyde, Univ of Bristol, Durham Univ; Hon DUniv Essex, Hon DSc Univ of Edinburgh; hon fell Birkbeck Coll London; FMedSci, FInstP, FSB; *Style—* Prof Dame Julia Goodfellow, DBE; ✉ University of Kent, Canterbury, Kent CT2 7NZ

GOODHART, Prof Charles Albert Eric; CBE (1997); s of Prof Arthur Lehman Goodhart, KBE (d 1978), sometime master UC Oxford, of NY, and Cecily Agnes Mackay, *née* Carter (d 1985); *b* 23 October 1936; *Educ* Eton, Trinity Coll Cambridge (BA, Adam Smith prize), Harvard Univ (PhD); *m* 2 July 1960, Margaret Ann (Miffy), da of Prof Sir Eric Smith, KBE (d 1990), of Plymouth; 3 da (Lucy b 1963, Alice b 1968, Sophie b 1970), 1 s (William b 1965); *Career* prize fell Trinity Coll Cambridge and asst lectr Univ of Cambridge 1963–65, economic advsr Dept of Econ Affrs 1965–66, lectr LSE 1966–68, advsr on domestic monetary policy then chief econ advsr Bank of England 1968–85, advsr on financial stability to the govr Bank of England 2002–04; Norman Sosnow prof of banking and fin LSE 1985–2002; non-exec dir Gerrard Group plc 1987–96; memb: Exchange Fund Advsy Ctee Hong Kong 1988–97, Monetary Policy Ctee Bank of England 1997–2000; FBA 1990; *Books* The New York Money Market and the Finance of Trade 1900–1913 (1969), The Business of Banking 1891–1914 (1972), Money Information and Uncertainty (1973, 2 edn 1989), Monetary Theory and Practice (1984), The Evolution of Central Banks (1988), The Central Bank and the Financial System (1995), The Regulatory Response to the Financial Crisis (2009), The Basel Committee on Banking Supervision (2011); *Recreations* sheep, walking; *Style—* Prof Charles Goodhart, CBE, FBA; ✉ 27 Abbotsbury Road, London W14 8EL (☎ 020 7603 5817); Halford Manor, South Tawton, Okehampton, Devon EX20 2LZ (☎ 01837 840354, e-mail caegoodhart@aol.com); London School of Economics and Political Science, Houghton Street, London WC2A 2AE (☎ 020 7955 7555, e-mail c.a.goodhart@lse.ac.uk)

GOODHART, Baron (Life Peer UK 1997), of Youlbury in the County of Oxfordshire; Sir William Howard Goodhart; kt (1989), QC (1979); 2 s of Prof Arthur Lehman Goodhart, KBE (hon), QC (d 1978), and Cecily, *née* Carter; *b* 18 January 1933; *Educ* Eton, Trinity Coll Cambridge, Harvard Law Sch; *m* 21 May 1966, Hon Celia Herbert, da of 2 Baron Hemingford (d 1982); 1 s, 2 da; *Career* Nat Serv 1951–53; called to the Bar Lincoln's Inn 1957 (bencher 1986); chm Exec Ctee Justice (Br Section Int Cmmn of Jurists) 1988–94 (vice-chm 1978–88); memb: Cncl of Legal Educn 1986–92, Conveyancing Standing Ctee Law Cmmn 1987–89, Int Cmmn of Jurists 1993–2008 (memb Exec Ctee 1995–2002, vice-pres 2002–06), Ctee on Standards in Public Life 1997–2003, Select Ctee on Delegated Powers 1998–2002 (chm 2006–10), Select Ctee on the EU 1998–2001 and 2005–06, Jt Ctee on Reform of the House of Lords 2002–03; resigned House of Lords 2015; contested Kensington: SDP 1983, SDP/Alliance 1987, Lib Dem 1988; Parly candidate (Lib Dem) Oxford W and Abingdon 1992; chm: SDP Cncl Arrangements Ctee 1982–88, Lib Dem Conf Ctee 1988–91, Lib Dem Lawyers' Assoc 1988–91; memb Lib Dem Policy Ctee 1988–97; tstee Campden Charities 1975–90, chm Univ of Cambridge Ct of Discipline 1992–2001; *Style—* The Lord Goodhart, QC

GOODHEW, David; *b* 11 June 1971, London; *Educ* Cardinal Vaughan Meml Sch, CCC Oxford; *m* 21 July 2012, Dr Céline Haines; 1 s (Thibault b 26 Dec 2014); *Career* asst teacher Bancroft's Sch Essex 1994–98, asst master Eton 1998–2000, head of classics Bristol GS 2000–05, dir of studies Arnold Sch Lancs 2005–08, dep head Durham Sch 2008–12, head Latymer Upper Sch Hammersmith 2012–; govr: Glendower Prep Sch 2013–, Dauntsey's Sch 2014–; FRSA; *Recreations* classical music (violin), cycling; *Clubs* East India, Lansdowne; *Style—* David Goodhew, Esq; ✉ Latymer Upper School, King Street, Hammersmith, London W6 9LR (Twitter @latymerhead)

GOODHEW, Prof Peter John; s of Philip Arthur Goodhew (d 1979), and Sheila Mary Goodhew; *b* 3 July 1943; *Educ* Kings Coll Sch, Univ of Birmingham (BSc, PhD, DSc); *m* 27 July 1968, Gwendoline Diane, da of Frederick Fletcher; 1 s (Robert b 1972), 1 da (Laura b 1974); *Career* prof: Univ of Surrey 1986–89 (lectr 1968, reader 1982), Dept of Engrg Univ of Liverpool 1990– (dean of engrg 1995–98, pro-vice-chllr 1998–2001, head of dept 2002–04); CEng 1978, FIM 1983, CPhys 1985, FInstP 1990, FREng 2002; *Books* Specimen Preparation in Materials Science (1972), The Operation of The Transmission Electron Microscope (1984), Specimen Preparation for TEM of Materials (1984), Thin Foil Preparation for Electron Microscopy (1985), Electron Microscopy and Analysis (1975, 3 edn 2001), Light Element Analysis in the TEM (1988), Introduction to Scanning Transmission Electron Microscopy (1998); *Recreations* wood turning, reading; *Style—* Prof Peter Goodhew; ✉ Department of Engineering, University of Liverpool, Liverpool L69 3GH (☎ 0151 794 4665, e-mail goodhew@liv.ac.uk)

GOODIN, His Hon Judge David Nigel; s of Nigel Robin Fyson Goodin (d 1998), and Diana, *née* Luard; *b* 31 March 1953, Cheltenham, Glos; *Educ* King's Sch Ely, Coll of Law; *m* 1, 1993 (m dis 2003); 2 s (Mark David b 8 Dec 1994, George Luard Fyson b 6 Feb 1998); m 2, 2010, Catherine Mary, da of James Maurice Robson; 1 step-da, 1 step-s; *Career* slr in private practice Suffolk 1980–2003, recorder 2000–03 (asst recorder 1996–2000), circuit judge 2003–, resident judge Ipswich Crown Court 2009–; *Recreations* family and friends; *Clubs* Peelers, Suffolk; *Style—* His Hon Judge Goodin; ✉ The Crown Court, 1 Russell Road, Ipswich, Suffolk IP1 2AG (☎ 01473 228500)

GOODING, Christopher Anderson; s of late Frank L Gooding, and Maureen Gooding; *b* 27 May 1957; *Educ* St Lawrence Coll Ramsgate, Brünel Univ (LLB); *m* Natasha Miriam, da of Jafr Khajeh, of Woking; *Career* admitted slr 1981; ptnr: Clyde & Co 1985–96 (joined 1981), LeBoeuf Lamb Greene & MacRae 1996–99, Howard Kennedy 1999–2009, Fasken Martineau 2009–; *Recreations* sailing; *Style—* Christopher Gooding, Esq

GOODING, HE Mark; OBE (2011); s of Air-Vice Marshal Keith H Gooding (d 2001), and Jean Gooding; *b* 17 December 1974; *Educ* Lady Margaret Hall Oxford (MA); *Partner* Dr Christopher McCormick (civil partnership 2005); *Career* diplomat; desk offr EU Dept FCO 1999–2000, consul (politics, economics, PPA) Shanghai 2002–04, team ldr EU Budget Team FCO 2004–06, private sec to the Foreign Sec FCO 2006–08, dep high cmmr Sri Lanka and the Maldives 2008–11, ambass to Cambodia 2011–14, min cnsllr (political) Br Embassy Beijing 2014–; *Style—* Mr Mark Gooding, OBE; ✉ c/o FCO, King Charles Street, London SW1A 2AH

GOODING, Mel; s of Frederick Gooding (d 1990), and Kathleen, *née* Cox; *b* 3 June 1941; *Educ* Northgate GS for Boys Ipswich, Univ of Sussex (BA, MA); *m* 1967, Esther Rhiannon Coslette, da of Ceri Richards; 2 s (Francis b 1974, Thomas b 1979); *Career* lectr in English, pedagogics and communication various London colls 1966– (notably Sidney Webb Coll of Educn 1972–80 and City of London Poly 1980–94), sr res fell Edinburgh Sch of Art 1998–2005, visiting prof Wimbledon Sch of Art 2006–08; contrib numerous articles to art press since 1980 incl: Arts Review, Artscribe, Flash Art, Art Monthly; contrib numerous introductions and essays to exhibition catalogues 1979–; curator of exhibitions incl: Ceri Richards (with Bryan Robertson, Tate Gallery) 1981, Ceri Richards Graphics (Nat Gallery of Wales and tour) 1979–80, Poetry into Art (UEA and Nat Library of Wales) 1982, F E McWilliam (Tate Gallery) 1989, Michael Rothenstein Retrospective (Stoke-on-Trent City Art Gallery and tour), Wilhelmena Barns-Graham (Trinity Hall) 2008, Drawings of Wilhelmena Barns-Graham (Pier Gallery Stromness) 2009; author and publisher (with Bruce McLean) of seven artists' books 1985–90; *Publications* incl: Ceri Richards Graphics (1979), F E McWilliam (1989), Michael Rothenstein The Retrospective (1989), The Phenomenon of Presence Frank Auerbach (1989), The Experience of Painting (1989), Malevich A Box (with Julian Rothenstein, 1990), Bruce McLean (1990), John Hoyland (1990), William Alsop Architect (1992), Michael Rothenstein's Boxes (1992), Patrick Heron (1994), Mary Fedden (1995), Plecnik's National and University Library of Slovenia (1997). Terry Frost: Art and Images (2000), Promenade (2001), Movements in Modern Art – Abstract Art (2001), Gillian Ayres (2001), Ceri Richards (2003), Song of the Earth (2003), John Hoyland (2006), Herman de Vries (2006), A2Z (2006), Merlyn Evans (2009), Frank Bowling (2011); *Recreations* walking, bird watching; *Style—* Mel Gooding; ✉ 62 Castelnau, Barnes, London SW13 9EX (☎ 020 8748 4434)

GOODISON, Sir Nicholas Proctor; kt (1982); yr s of Edmund Harold Goodison, of Radlett, Herts, and Eileen Mary Carrington, *née* Proctor; *b* 16 May 1934; *Educ* Marlborough, King's Coll Cambridge (MA, PhD); *m* 18 June 1960, Judith Nicola, o da of Capt Robert Eustace Abel Smith (ka 1940), Grenadier Gds; 1 s, 2 da; *Career* H E Goodison & Co (later Quilter Goodison & Co, now Quilter & Co Ltd): joined 1958, ptnr 1962, chm 1975–88; chm Stock Exchange 1976–88 (memb Cncl 1968–88), chm TSB Group plc 1989–95, dep chm Lloyds TSB Group plc (following merger) 1995–2000; dir: General Accident plc 1987–95, Corus plc (formerly British Steel plc) 1989–2002 (dep chm 1993–99); pres: Int Fedn of Stock Exchanges 1985–86, Br Bankers' Assoc 1991–96, Heads, Teachers & Industry 1999–2002; vice-chm ENO 1980–98 (dir 1977–98); chm: Courtauld Inst of Art 1982–2002 (memb Bd 2002–09), Nat Art Collections Fund 1986–2002 (memb Ctee 1976–2002), Crafts Cncl 1997–2005, Retirement Income Reform Campaign 2001–09, Burlington Magazine Ltd 2002–07, Burlington Magazine Fndn 2002–07 (tstee 1975–), National Life Story Collection 2003–15 (tstee 2003–15, advsr 2015–); tstee: Nat Heritage Meml Fund 1988–97, Harewood House Tst 1989–, Kathleen Ferrier Meml Fund; pres Furniture History Soc 1990–, pres Walpole Soc 2007–, hon keeper of furniture Fitzwilliam Museum Cambridge; memb: Cncl Industrial Soc 1976–2000, Royal Cmmn on Long-Term Care for the Elderly 1997–99, Further Educn Funding Cncl 1999–2001, Advsy Bd Judge Inst of Mgmnt Univ of Cambridge 1999–2002; ldr and author Goodison Review HM Treasy 2003 (report Securing the Best for our Museums: Private Giving and Government Support published 2004); govr Marlborough Coll 1981–97; CINOA Prize for Lifetime Achievement in Arts 2004, Robinson Medal V&A Museum 2007; Liveryman: Worshipful Co of Goldsmiths, Worshipful Co of Clockmakers; Hon DLitt: City Univ 1985, Univ of London 2003; Hon LLD Univ of Exeter 1989, Hon DSc Aston Univ 1994, Hon DArt De Montfort Univ 1998, Hon DCL Univ of Northumbria 1999; hon fell King's Coll Cambridge, hon fell Courtauld Inst of Art; hon fell Royal Acad, sr fell RCA 1991, Hon FRIBA 1992, hon fell City and Guilds; CIMgt, FCIB 1989 (vice-pres 1989), FBA, FSA, FRSA; Chevalier de la Legion d'Honneur 1990; *Publications* English Barometers 1680–1860 (1968, 2 edn 1977), Ormolu – The Work of Matthew Boulton (1974, revised as Matthew Boulton: Ormolu 2002), These Fragments (2005); author of many papers and articles on the history of furniture, clocks and barometers; *Recreations* history of furniture and decorative arts, music and opera, walking; *Clubs* Athenaeum, Beefsteak, Brooks's; *Style—* Sir Nicholas Goodison; ✉ PO Box 2512, London W1A 5ZP

GOODLAD, Baron (Life Peer UK 2005), of Lincoln in the County of Lincolnshire; Sir Alastair Robertson Goodlad; KCMG (1997), PC (1992); yst s of late Dr John Fordyce Robertson Goodlad, of Lincoln, and Isabel, *née* Sinclair; *b* 4 July 1943; *Educ* Marlborough, King's Coll Cambridge (MA, LLB); *m* 1968, Cecilia Barbara, 2 da of Col Richard Hurst (s of Sir Cecil Hurst, GCMG, KCB), by his w Lady Barbara, *née* Lindsay (6 da of 27 Earl of Crawford (and Earl Balcarres), KT, PC); 2 s; *Career* Parly candidate (Cons) Crewe 1970; MP (Cons): Northwich Feb 1974–83, Eddisbury 1983–99; asst Govt whip 1981–82, a Lord Cmmr of the Treasy 1982–84, jt vice-chm Cons Pty Trade Ctee 1979–81 (jt hon sec 1978–), hon sec All-Pty Heritage Gp 1979–81; memb Select Ctee Agriculture 1979–81, Parly under sec of state at Dept of Energy 1984–87; chm NW Area Cons Membs of Parly 1987–89, chm All-Pty Gp for Refugees 1987–89; memb Select Ctee on Televising Proceedings of the House, comptroller Her Majesty's Household and sr govt whip 1989, treas of HM Household and dep chief whip 1990–92; min of state FCO 1992–95; Parly sec to the Treasy (Govt chief whip) 1995–97, shadow int devpt sec 1997–98; high cmmr to Australia 2000–05; chm House of Lords Select Ctee on the Constitution 2007–10 (memb 2006–), chm House of Lords Select Ctee on Merits of Statutory Investments 2010–; memb House of Commons bridge team in matches against Lords 1982–85, pres Water Companies Assoc 1989; *Clubs* Brooks's, Beefsteak, Pratt's; *Style—* The Lord Goodlad, KCMG, PC; ✉ House of Lords, London SW1A 0PW

GOODMAN, Prof Andrew David; s of Bernard Goodman (d 2009), and Helène, *née* Greenspan (d 1984); *b* 4 June 1956; *Educ* Queen Elizabeth's Sch Barnet, Univ of Southampton (LLB), Rushmore Univ (MBA), Birkbeck Coll London and Nixon Univ LA (UAE Campus) (PhD); *m* (m dis 2010); 4 s (Adam Howard b 1986, Simon Nicholas b 1989, Sam Alexander b 1991, James Aidan Lewis b 1996); *Career* called to the Bar Inner Temple 1978 (master of the bench 2009); registered CEDR mediator 1992–, advocacy trainer NITA (UK) 2000, advocacy trainer Nottingham Law Sch 2001, expert UK Panel Nominet 2001–03, prof of conflict mgmnt and dispute resolution studies Rushmore Univ USA 2003–, advocacy trainer Inner Temple 2012–; memb Attorney-Gen's Pro-Bono Panel

Judicial Assistance Network 2013; visiting lectr in dispute resolution Univs of Southampton, Cardiff, Reading and Northumbria, London Met Univ, Manchester Met Univ, BPP UC and Coll of Law, visiting lectr Dubai Real Estate Inst; course dir RICS Accredited Mediator Training 2007–; dir XPL Professional Skills Training 2006, convenor Standing Conference of Mediation Advocates 2007, memb Civil Mediation Cncl 2007, memb Ind Standards Cmmn Int Mediation Inst, dir Higher Educn Disputes Advsy Service, dir Assoc for Mediation Assessors Trainers and Instructors (AMATI) 2014; memb Editorial Bd Jackson ADR Handbook 2013, guest ed ADR Commercial Law Jl of Nepal, memb Editorial Bd Mediation Theory and Practice; FCIArb 2001, FInstCPD 2005, FRSA 2007; *Books* The Court Guide (1980, 20 edn 2012), The Bar Diary (1982, 1983, 1984), Gilbert and Sullivan At Law (1983), The Royal Courts of Justice Guide (1985), Gilbert and Sullivan's London (1988, 2 edn 2000), The Prison Guide (1999), The Walking Guide to Lawyer's London (2000, 2 edn 2010), What's it Worth? Awards of General Damages in Non-Personal Injury Claims (2004), How Judges Decide Cases – Reading, Writing and Analysing Judgments (2005), Influencing the Judicial Mind – Effective Writing Advocacy in Practice (2006), Mediation Advocacy (2007, 2 edn 2011, Hong Kong edn 2012, Nigeria edn 2012), Inner Temple Yearbook (ed, 2007–09), Small Claims Procedure: A Practical Guide (2008), Small Claims in the County Court – A Guide to Mediation and Litigation (5 edn 2011), Effective Written Advocacy (2012); *Recreations* travel, music, Victorian theatre; *Style*— Prof Andrew Goodman; ✉ 1 Chancery Lane, London WC2A 1LF (☎ 0845 634 6666, fax 0845 634 6667, e-mail agoodman@1chancerylane.com, websites www.xpl-pst.com, www.mediationadvocates.org.uk, www.amati.org.uk, www.1chancerylane.com)

GOODMAN, Dr Dougal Jocelyn; OBE (2012); *Educ* Univ of Cambridge, Stanford Univ; *m* 1978, Penny; 1 s (Alexander), 1 da (Lucy); *Career* Cavendish Lab Univ of Cambridge 1973–79, Hokkaido Univ Japan 1979–80, BP 1980–95, dep dir Br Antarctic Survey 1995–2000, currently chief exec Fndn for Science and Technol and conslt (strategy and risk); Polar Medal 1998; FREng 2005; *Recreations* travel in the Arctic and Antarctic regions, sailing; *Clubs* Athenaeum, Royal Harwich Yacht; *Style*— Dr Dougal Goodman, OBE, FREng; ✉ The Foundation for Science and Technology, 10 Carlton House Terrace, London SW1Y 5AH

GOODMAN, Helen; MP; *b* 2 January 1958, Nottingham; *Educ* Lady Manners Sch Bakewell, Somerville Coll Oxford; *Career* former civil servant HM Treasy, former head of strategy The Children's Soc; MP (Lab) Bishop Auckland 2005–; parly under-sec of state for pension reform 2009–10, shadow justice min 2010–11, shadow culture, media and sport min 2011–14, shadow welfare reform min 2014–; memb: Amnesty Int, Christian Socialist Movement, Public Accounts Ctee 2005–07; *Style*— Ms Helen Goodman, MP; ✉ House of Commons, London SW1A 0AA

GOODMAN, Henry; twin s of late Hyman Goodman, and late Fay, *née* Tobias; *b* 23 April 1950; *Educ* CFS GS, RADA (J Barton Prize, Poel Prize, Shereck Award); *m* Sue, *née* Parker; 1 s (Ilan b 31 Oct 1981), 1 da (Carla b 25 May 1986); *Career* teacher, director and actor; teacher and ldr various workshops incl: Guildhall Drama Sch, BADA, RNT, RNT Studio; artistic dir: Roundabout Theatre Co 1975, Peoples Space Theatre 1981; lectr in Drama and Movement Rhode Univ South Africa 1974–75; judge BBC Radio int playwriting competition 2014; patron Eastside Educn Tst; *Theatre* RNT: Roy Cohn in Angels in America, Mickey in After the Fall, Dr Baugh in Cat on a Hot Tin Roof, Steve/Les in Decadence, Beatrice and Benedick, Nathan Detroit in Guys and Dolls, Gellburg in Broken Glass (also West End); RSC: Rocky Gravo in They Shoot Horses Don't They, Kitely in Every Man in his Humour, Lefer in Henry V, Prince de Condé in The Devils, Stalin/Azhog in Redstar, Dromio of Ephesus in Comedy of Errors (Best Newcomer Olivier Awards 1983), Voltore in Volpone, Harry in The Time of Life, Stravinsky in Astonish Me, Jacques in Jacques and His Masters, Arch of Canterbury and Norfolk in Henry VIII, Klyestakov in Government Inspector, Shylock in The Merchant of Venice (Best Actor Critics Circle Awards 1999, Best Actor Olivier Awards 2000), Tartuffe in Tartuffe, Lopakhin in Cherry Orchard, Groucho Marx in Groucho, Capt Hook in Peter Pan, Richard III, Volpone 2015; West End: Buddy Fidler in City of Angels, Hal in Kvetch; Tricycle Theatre: Agent in Lady Sings the Blues, Simon in A Free Country, Goldberg in Birthday Party; other credits incl: Charles Guiteau in Assassins (Olivier Award for Best Actor in a Musical, Donmar Warehouse), Freud in Hysteria (Royal Court and Duke of Yorks, Olivier Best Actor Award nomination 1995), Billy Flynn in Chicago (Adelphi), Mark in Art (Wyndhams Theatre), Serge in Art (Royale Theatre NY), Eddie in Feelgood, Max Bialystock in The Producers (St James Theatre NY), Tevye in Fiddler on the Roof (Crucible Sheffield); dir of various plays incl: The Promise (Arbizov), Metamorphosis, Agamemnon (Best Dir Award), Decadence, Bye Bye Blues, Neighbours, Epsom Wells, Berlin Kabarett, Metropolis Kabarett, Tartuffe (Broadway), Fiddler on the Roof, The Line, Duet for One, Yes Prime Minister, The Resistible Rise of Arturo Ui (Chichester Festival Theatre) 2012 and (Duchess Theatre West End) 2014 (nominated Best Actor Olivier Awards 2014, TMA Best Actor Award, Theatregoer Awards), Volpone (RSC) 2015; *Television* incl: Lovejoy, Rides, Spinoza, Maigret, The Gravy Train II, Zorro, El CID, Gentlemen and Players, London's Burning, This is David Lander, Bust, After the War, 99 to 1, Sherlock Holmes, The Chain, Pompei in Measure for Measure (BBC), David Siltz in Dennis Potter's Cold Lazarus (BBC/Channel 4), Xmas (TV film, Channel 4), Unfinished Business (BBC) 1997–98, Foyle's War, Murder Investigation Team, Murder in Suburbia, Lehman Brothers Something for Nothing (BBC), New Tricks (BBC) 2013, Nixon's The One (Sky Arts) 2013, Midsomer Murders (ITV) 2014, Penny Dreadful (Sky Atlantic) 2014, Alan Turing (Channel 4) 2014, London Spy (BBC 2) 2015; *Radio* Gentlemen Prefer Blondes, The Prisoner in Prisoner of Papa Stour, André Gregory in Dinner with André, David Selznik in Diaries of David Selznik, Jackson in The Nuremberg Trials, title role in Beaumarchais, defence lawyer in No2 Goering, Woody Allen in Retribution, Lavoisier in Breath of Fresh Air, Teddy in Talking Towers, Adam in East of Eden, Berlioz in Fantastic Symphony, Alan Jay Lerner Diaries, Monsieur Ibrahim (writer and performer, winner Sony Award), Les Miserables, Thinking of Leaving your Husband, Goldfinger; narrator The Autograph Man (audiobook), reader Mitterand (Book of the Week BBC Radio 4), reader Deep South (Book of the Week BBC Radio 4); *Film* Secret Weapon, Queen of Hearts, Son of the Pink Panther, Mary Reilly, The Saint, Private Parts, Broken Glass, Notting Hill, The Life and Death of Peter Sellers, Out on a Limb, Colour Me Kubrick, Taking Woodstock, The Damned United, The Surprise 2014, Woman In Gold 2014, Captain America: The Winter Soldier 2014, Adam Jones 2014, Avengers: Age of Ultron 2015, Altamira 2015, Trotsky: The Chosen 2015; *Recordings* Enoch Arden by Richard Strauss 2014, Liszt Odyssey of Love (with Lucy Parham) 2014; live concerts in role of Liszt, Chopin, Schumann and Debussy with Lucy Parham; *Style*— Henry Goodman, Esq; ✉ c/o Markham Froggatt & Irwin, 4 Windmill Street, London W1T 2HZ (☎ 020 7636 4412)

GOODMAN, Prof John Francis Bradshaw; CBE (1995); s of Edwin Goodman (d 1979), and Amy Bradshaw, *née* Warrener (d 1989); *b* 2 August 1940; *Educ* Chesterfield Sch, LSE (BSc), Victoria Univ of Manchester (MSc), Univ of Nottingham (PhD); *m* 12 Aug 1967, Elizabeth Mary, da of Frederick William Towns (d 1993), of Romiley, Gtr Manchester; 1 da (Clare b 1970), 1 s (Richard b 1972); *Career* personnel offr Ford Motor Co 1962–64, lectr in industrial economics Univ of Nottingham 1964–69, industrial rels advsr NBPI 1969–70, sr lectr in industrial rels Univ of Manchester 1970–74; UMIST (now Univ of Manchester): Frank Thomas prof of industrial rels 1975–2002, vice-princ 1979–81, head Manchester Sch of Mgmnt 1977–79, 1986–88 and 1989–94, emeritus prof 2002–; visiting prof of industrial rels: Univ of WA 1981 and 1984, McMaster Univ 1985, Auckland Univ 1996; tstee Withington Girls Sch 1986–97 (govr 1980–92); pres: Br Univs Industrial Rels Assoc 1983–86, Manchester Industrial Rels Soc 1984–2002; chm: Professional Football Negotiating and Consultative Ctee 2000–, Police Arbitration Tribunal 2003–14; dep chm: Wood St Mission Manchester 1986–2004, Central Arbitration Ctee 1998–2011; memb: Cncl ESRC 1993–97, Cncl ACAS 1987–98, Panel of Arbitrators ACAS 1980–; CCIPD 1986; *Books* Shop Stewards (1973), Rule-making and Industrial Peace (1977), Ideology and Shop-floor Industrial Relations (1980), Employment Relations in Industrial Society (1984), Unfair Dismissal Law and Employment Practice (1985), New Developments in Employee Involvement (1992), Industrial Tribunals and Workplace Disciplinary Procedures (1998); *Recreations* mountain walking (Munro-ist, 1997), football, golf; *Style*— Prof John Goodman, CBE; ✉ 2 Pott Hall, Shrigley Road, Pott Shrigley, Macclesfield, Cheshire SK10 5RT (☎ 01625 572480)

GOODMAN, Jonathan Richard; s of Stanley Goodman, and Terry, *née* Asher; *Educ* St Paul's (fndn scholar), Pembroke Coll Oxford (open and closed scholarships, MA); *Career* md Bounty Books 1983–86, publisher Hamlyn Octopus 1986–90, fndr and chm Carlton Books 1992–; patron: Artangel, Tate Galleries; *Recreations* sport, table tennis; *Clubs* Groucho, Century; *Style*— Jonathan Goodman, Esq; ✉ Carlton Publishing Group, 20 Mortimer Street, London W1T 3JW (☎ 020 7612 0406, fax 020 7612 0408, e-mail jgoodman@carltonbooks.co.uk)

GOODMAN, Margaret Beatrice (Maggie); da of John Bertram Goodman (d 1985), and Cissie Phyllis, *née* Kay (d 1952); *b* 26 November 1941; *Educ* Plymouth HS for Girls, Coll of Commerce Univ of Birmingham; *m* 1988, Dr Anthony Harold Mercer Gaze (d 2000), s of William Mercer Gaze; *Career* asst ed New Era Magazine 1960–62, Honey Magazine 1962–67 (sub ed, showbusiness ed, features ed, asst ed), asst ed rising to ed Petticoat magazine 1967–69, freelance feature writer 1969–71, dep ed Cosmopolitan 1971–79, fndr ed Company 1979–88, launch ed Hello! (with Maggie Koumi, *qv*) 1988–93, head Magazine Devpt Gp The National Magazine Company 1994–96, freelance conslt and writer 1996–, ed Home & Life 1997–2000; awards for Hello!: Consumer Magazine of the Year PPA and Media Week 1990, Magazine of the Year Br Press Circulation Awards 1991, Editors of the Year for gen interest magazine BSME 1991; memb BSME 1978–91 (chm 1982); *Books* Every Man Should Have One (jt author, 1971); *Style*— Ms Maggie Goodman; ✉ 15a Upper Park Road, London NW3 2UN (☎ 020 7722 3889)

GOODMAN, Prof Martin David; s of Cyril Joshua Goodman, and Ruth, *née* Sabel; *b* 1 August 1953; *Educ* Rugby, Trinity Coll Oxford (MA, DPhil, DLitt); *m* 1976, Sarah Jane, da of John Lock; 2 s (Joshua b 1982, Alexander b 1984), 2 da (Daisy b 1987, Charlotte b 1992); *Career* Kaye jr research fell Oxford Centre for Postgrad Hebrew Studies 1976–77, lectr in ancient history Univ of Birmingham 1977–86; Univ of Oxford: fell Oxford Centre for Hebrew and Jewish Studies 1986–, sr research fell St Cross Coll 1986–91, lectr in Roman history Christ Church 1988–, Hebrew Centre lectr in ancient history 1990–91, univ reader in Jewish studies and professorial fell Wolfson Coll 1991–96, prof of Jewish studies 1996–, hon fell Trinity Coll 2010–; fell Inst for Advanced Studies Hebrew Univ of Jerusalem 1993; pres Br Assoc for Jewish Studies 1995, pres Oxford Centre for Hebrew and Jewish Studies (acting pres 1995–96), 1999–2000 and 2013–14; sec Euro Assoc for Jewish Studies 1994–98; review ed Jl of Roman Studies 1993–98 (ed 1999–2003), jt ed Jl of Jewish Studies 1995–99; hon DLitt Univ of Southampton 2015; FBA 1996; *Books* State and Society in Roman Galilee, AD 132–212 (1983, 2 edn 2000), On the Art of the Kabbalah (jt trans, 1983, 2 edn 1993), The History of the Jewish People in the Age of Jesus Christ (jt ed, 1986–87), The Ruling Class of Judaea: the origins of the Jewish revolt against Rome, AD 66–70 (1987, reprinted 1988, 1989, 1991, paperback 1993), The Essenes according to the Classical Sources (with Geza Vermes, 1989), Mission and Conversion: proselytizing in the religious history of the Roman Empire (1994), The Roman World 44 BC- AD 180 (1997, 2 edn 2012), Jews in a Graeco-Roman World (ed, 1998, paperback 2004), Apologetic in the Roman World: Pagans, Jews and Christians (jt ed, 1999), Representations of Empire: Rome and the Mediterranean World (jt ed, 2002), The Oxford Handbook of Jewish Studies (ed, 2002), Judaism in the Roman World: Collected Essays (2007), Rome and Jerusalem (2007), Abraham, the Nations and the Hagarites (jt ed, 2010), Rabbinic Texts and the History of Late-Roman Palestine (jt ed, 2010), Toleration within Judaism (jtly, 2013); also author of over 35 articles and 100 reviews; *Style*— Prof Martin Goodman, FBA; ✉ The Oriental Institute, University of Oxford, Pusey Lane, Oxford OX1 2LE (☎ 01865 278208, fax 01865 278190)

GOODMAN, Richard Antony; s of Antony Marlow Goodman (d 1999), of Leicester, and Florence, *née* Sowry (d 1994); *b* 17 June 1952, Northampton; *Educ* Dunstable GS, Selwyn Coll Cambridge (MA); *m* 14 April 1979, Julie, da of John Edwin Williams, of Chilham, Kent; 2 s (Thomas b 1982, William b 1986), 1 da (Charlotte b 1989); *Career* admitted slr 1976; ptnr: Cameron Markby Hewitt (now Cameron McKenna) 1981–2002, KLegal 2002–03, Watson Farley & Williams LLP 2003–14 (conslt 2014–); memb Law Soc; *Recreations* music, garden, photography; *Style*— Richard Goodman, Esq; ✉ Watson Farley & Williams LLP, 15 Appold Street, London EC2A 2HB (☎ 020 7814 8164, fax 020 7814 8141, e-mail rgoodman@wfw.com)

GOODMAN, Prof Roger James; s of late Cyril Joshua Goodman, and late Ruth, *née* Sabel; *b* 26 May 1960, Burnham-on-Crouch, Essex; *Educ* Rugby, King Edward VI GS Chelmsford, Univ of Durham (BA), Univ of Oxford (DPhil); *Partner* Carolyn Joy Dodd; 2 s (Samuel John b 17 Sept 1991, Joseph James b 26 Aug 1994), 1 da (Abigail Anne b 24 Nov 1999); *Career* Nissan jr research fell in the social anthropology of Japan St Antony's Coll Oxford 1985–88, lectr Japan-Europe Industry Research Centre Imperial Coll London 1988–89, reader in Japanese studies Dept of Sociology Univ of Essex 1989–93; Univ of Oxford: lectr in the social anthropology of Japan 1993–2003, Nissan prof of modern Japanese studies 2003–, head Social Scis Div 2008–; fell St Antony's Coll Oxford 1993– (actg warden 2006–07); chair Endowment Ctee Japan Fndn 1999–2006; chair AcSS 2015–; *Books* Japan's 'International Youth': The Emergence of a New Class of Schoolchildren (1990), Ideology and Practice in Modern Japan (co-ed, 1992), Case Studies in Human Rights in Japan (co-ed, 1996), The East Asian Welfare Model: Welfare Orientalism and the State (co-ed, 1998), Children of the Japanese State: The Changing Role of Child Protection Institutions in Contemporary Japan (2000), Family and Social Policy in Japan: Anthropological Approaches (ed, 2002), Can the Japanese Reform Their Education System? (co-ed, 2003), Global Japan: The Experience of Japan's New Minorities and Overseas Communities (co-ed, 2003), The 'Big Bang' in Japanese Higher Education: The 2004 Reforms and the Dynamics of Change (co-ed, 2005), Aging in Asia (co-ed, 2007), A Sociology of Japanese Youth: From Returnees to NEETs (co-ed, 2012), Higher Eudcation and the State: Changing Relationships in Europe and East Asia (co-ed, 2012); *Recreations* hockey coach; *Style*— Prof Roger Goodman; ✉ Nissan Institute of Japanese Studies, 27 Winchester Road, Oxford OX2 7NA (☎ 01865 274576, fax 01865 274574, e-mail roger.goodman@nissan.ox.ac.uk)

GOODMAN, Steven; *b* 10 July 1961, London; *Educ* UMIST (BSc), Inst of Mktg (Dip), DipCAM; *m* Sharon; 2 da (Ella b 2005, Ruby b 2008); *Career* The Media Business 1983, press dir Mediacom 1999, md print trading GroupM 2005–; memb Bd Audit Bureau of Circulation (ABC), memb Ctee of Advertising Practice Gen Media Panel, chair IPA Press Directors Bd; FIPA 2009 (MIPA 1989); *Recreations* clay pigeon shooting, classic cars; *Clubs* AMOC; *Style*— Steven Goodman, Esq; ✉ GroupM, 26 Red Lion Square, London WC1R 4HQ (e-mail steve.goodman@groupm.com)

GOODMAN, Prof Timothy Nicholas Trewin; s of J Vincent Goodman (d 1971), and Eileen M Sherwell; *b* 29 April 1947; *Educ* Judd Sch Tonbridge, St John's Coll Cambridge (open scholar, BA), Univ of Warwick (MSc), Univ of Sussex (DPhil); *m* 1 Dec 1973, Choo-Tin, da of Nam-Sang Soon; 3 c (Joy b 12 Feb 1976, Kim b 6 May 1978, Ruth b 28 Oct 1981); *Career* VSO teacher King Edward VII Sch Taiping Malaysia 1973, teacher St Andrew's Secdy Sch Singapore 1974–75, lectr Universiti Sains Malaysia 1975–79, lectr Univ of Dundee 1979–90, full prof Texas A&M Univ 1990–91, prof of applied analysis Univ of Dundee 1994–2008 (reader 1992–94, emeritus prof 2008–); memb Edinburgh Mathematical Soc 1979; FRSE 1997; *Publications* author of over 150 academic papers in learned jls; *Recreations* Scottish country dancing, hill walking, music; *Style*— Prof Timothy Goodman, FRSE; ✉ e-mail tntg2@cam.ac.uk

GOODSON-WICKES, Dr Charles; DL (Gtr London 1999, rep DL London Borough of Islington 2011–); s of Ian Goodson Wickes, FRCP (d 1972), of Stock Harvard, Essex, and Monica Frances Goodson-Wickes; *b* 7 November 1945; *Educ* Charterhouse, St Bartholomew's Hosp, Inner Temple; *m* 17 April 1974, Judith Amanda, da of late Cdr John Hopkinson, RN (d 1978), of Stamford, Lincs; 2 s (Edward b 1976, Henry b 1978); *Career* consulting physician, co dir, business conslt and charity chief exec; called to the Bar 1972; house physician Addenbrooke's Hosp Cambridge 1972; Surgn Capt The Life Gds (served BAOR, NI, Cyprus) 1973–77, Silver Stick MO, Household Cavalry 1977, RARO 1977–2000, re-enlisted as Lt-Col for Gulf Campaign 1991 (served Saudi Arabia, Iraq, Kuwait); specialist physician St Bartholomew's Hosp 1977–80, conslt physician BUPA 1977–86, occupational physician 1980–94; former med advsr: Barclays Bank, RTZ, Hogg Robinson, Standard Chartered, Norwegian Directorate of Health, British Alcan, McKinsey, Christies, etc; dir: Nestor Healthcare Group plc 1993–99, Gyrus Gp 1997–2007, Devpt Bd Royal Inst of Chartered Surveyors 2010–14, Medarc Ltd; currently dir Thomas Greg and Sons Ltd (chm 2011) and other cos; Parly candidate (Cons) Islington Central 1979, MP (Cons) Wimbledon 1987–97; PPS to Rt Hon Sir George Young, Bt, MP: as Min of State for Housing and Planning 1992–94, as Fin Sec to Treasy 1994–95, as Sec of State for Tport 1995–96; formerly: vice-chm Def Ctee and Constitutional Affrs Ctee, memb Jt Ctee Consolidation of Bills, memb Select Ctee Armed Forces Bill 1990, sec Arts and Heritage Ctee; BOC fell Industry and Parly Tst 1991; vice-chm Cons Foreign and Cwlth Cncl 1997–2012, patron Hansard Soc 2003–; chief exec London Playing Fields Fndn 1998–2007 (chm 1997–98), memb London Sports Bd 2000–03; publisher Beaumont Fox as literary executor of his great grandfather Sir Frank Fox, OBE 2014–; former memb: Med Advsy Ctee Industry Soc, Fitness Advsy Panel IOD; treas Dr Ian Goodson Wickes Fund for Handicapped Children 1979–88; chm Asbestos Licensing Regulations Appeals Tbnl 1982–87, chm BFSS 1994–97 (memb Public Affrs Ctee 1980–87), patron Countryside Alliance 2003– (fndr chm 1997–99), vice-pres Gt Bustard Gp 2008–, memb Advsy Cncl Inst for the Study of the Americas Univ of London 2010–12; govr Highbury Grove Sch 1977–85, vice-pres Ex-Servs Mental Welfare Soc (Combat Stress) 1990–, chm The Rural Tst 1999–2014, DG Canning House 2010–12; memb HAC 2013, Freedom City of London 2014; *Books* The New Corruption (1984), Another Country (contrib, 1999); *Recreations* hunting, shooting, real tennis, gardening, travel, history; *Clubs* Boodle's, Pratt's, MCC; *Style*— Dr Charles Goodson-Wickes, DL; ✉ Watergate House, Bulford, Wiltshire (☎ 01980 632344); 37 St James's Place, London SW1 (☎ 020 7629 0981); Medarc Limited (e-mail cgw@medarc-limited.co.uk)

GOODWILL, Robert; MP; s of late Robert William Goodwill, and late Joan, *née* Breckon; *b* 31 December 1956; *Educ* Bootham Sch York, Univ of Newcastle upon Tyne (BSc); *Family* 3 c; *Career* farmer 250 acre family farm, md Mowthorpe (UK) Ltd, MEP (Cons) Yorkshire and the Humber 1999–2004 (Parly candidate: Cleveland and Richmond 1994, Yorkshire S (by election) 1998), MP (Cons) Scarborough and Whitby 2005– (Parly candidate (Cons): Redcar 1992, NW Leicestershire 1997); European Parl: memb Environment, Public Health and Consumer Policy Ctee 1999–2004, vice-chm '79 Back Bench Ctee 1999–2002, memb Delgn to Belarus, Ukraine and Moldova 1999–2004, dep ldr Cons in the the European Parl 2003–04; House of Commons: memb Select Ctee on Tport 2005–06, oppn whip 2006–07, shadow tport min 2007–10, asst whip 2010–; past chm: NFU Local Branch, Count Commodity Ctee; cncllr Terrington Parish Cncl 1987–99; *Recreations* cooking, eating out, languages, steam ploughing, engineering; *Clubs* Farmers; *Style*— Robert Goodwill, Esq, MP; ✉ House of Commons, London SW1A 0AA

GOODWIN, Prof Guy Manning; s of Kenneth Manning Goodwin (d 1974), and Constance, *née* Hudson; *b* 8 November 1947; *Educ* Manchester Grammar, Exeter Coll Oxford (MA, DPhil, BM BCh, Martin Wronker Prize in Med); *m* 1971, Philippa Catherine, *née* Georgeson; 2 da (Frances Eleanor b 28 Dec 1977, Rosalind Mary b 6 Oct 1981); *Career* scholar MRC 1968–71, fell by examination Magdalen Coll Oxford 1971–76, research assoc Univ of Washington Seattle USA 1972–74, house physician Nuffield Dept of Clinical Med Oxford 1978–79, house surgn Horton Gen Hosp Banbury 1979, SHO Professorial Unit Brompton Hosp London 1980, registrar Rotational Trg Scheme in Psychiatry Oxford 1980–83, MRC clinical trg fell and hon sr registrar MRC Clinical Pharmacology Unit Radcliffe Infirmary Oxford 1983–85, clinical lectr and hon sr registrar Univ Dept of Psychiatry Oxford 1985–86, MRC clinical scientist, hon conslt psychiatrist and hon sr lectr 1986–95, prof of psychiatry Univ of Edinburgh 1995–96, W A Handley prof of psychiatry Univ of Oxford 1996–; author of original papers in physiology, neuropharmacology and psychiatry; pres Br Assoc for Psychopharmacology 2002–04; FRCPsych, FMedSci; *Recreations* football, opera and hill walking; *Style*— Prof Guy Goodwin; ✉ Department of Psychiatry, Warneford Hospital, Headington, Oxford OX3 7JX (☎ 01865 226451, fax 01865 204198, e-mail guy.goodwin@psych.oxford.ac.uk)

GOODWIN, Jonathan; s of Philip Goodwin, and Ann Goodwin; *b* 12 November 1972, London; *Educ* Charterhouse, Univ of Nottingham (BA); *m* 25 June 2011, Flora, *née* Hesketh; 4 s (Archie b 17 Aug 1999, Patrick b 14 Sept 2003, Thaddeus b 28 Jan 2005, Joseph b 17 March 2014), 1 da (Olivia b 22 Nov 2000); *Career* assoc Apax Partners until 1997, md Talk Radio 1997–2000, fndr LongAcre Partners 2000 (sold 2007), fndr Founders Forum 2005, co-fndr PROfounders Capital 2010, fndr Lepe Partners 2011–; *Recreations* sailing, shooting, skiing, tennis; *Clubs* Queens Tennis, Royal Yacht Squadron; *Style*— Jonathan Goodwin, Esq; ✉ Lepe Partners, 17 Old Court Place, London W8 4PL (website www.lepepartners.com)

GOODWIN, Dr Neil; CBE (2007); s of James Goodwin (d 1996), of Salford, and Dorothy Goodwin (d 1986); *b* 1 March 1951; *Educ* N Salford Co Secdy Sch, London Business Sch (MBA), Manchester Business Sch (PhD); *m* 1, 1980 (m dis 1992), Sian Elizabeth Mary, *née* Holliday; 2 s (Matthew Thomas James b 17 Dec 1981, Owen David Neil b 29 March 1987); m 2, 2006, Christine Hannah; 1 step-s (Benjamin Philip Hannah), 1 step-da (Charlotte Faye Hannah); *Career* various NHS managerial positions Manchester, Liverpool and W Midlands 1969–81, St Albans 1981–84, gen mangr Central Middlesex Hosp 1985–88, gen mangr St Mary's Hosp Paddington 1988–92; chief exec: St Mary's Hosp NHS Trust 1992–94, Manchester HA 1994–2002, Gtr Manchester SHA 2002–06; chair London Cancer Alliance 2012–16, chair Healthcare Support (Newcastle) Ltd 2014–16; non-exec dir UK Transplant Authority 2000–05, dir Goodwin Hannah Ltd 2006–14, chair Aintree Univ Hosp NHS Fndn Tst 2014–, ind chair NHS Eastern Cheshire Caring Together Bd 2016–; visiting prof of leadership studies: Univ of Manchester 2004–15, UCL 2009–12, Univ of Durham 2010–13; friend Lloyd George Museum Wales; CHSM 2006 (MHSM 1980, FHSM 1991); *Publications* Leadership in Healthcare: A European Perspective (2005); also book contribs and numerous articles on health services and public health leadership, hosp mgmnt incl customer care, personal devpt for chief execs and public consultations; *Recreations* photography; *Style*— Dr Neil Goodwin, CBE

GOODWIN-BRIGGS, Vivien Catherine; *née* Kirby; da of John Crompton Kirby (d 1975), of Birmingham, UK, and Gwendoline Carole, *née* Sproston; *b* 19 June 1964, Syosset, NY; *Educ* Chaminade Coll Prep HS, Univ of Calif Santa Barbara (BFA); *m* 1 16 Aug 1989 (m dis 2011), Alan Goodwin, s of Alfred Stanley Goodwin; 1 da (Abigail Chelsea b 1 Feb 1996); 2 16 July 2015, Andrew John Briggs, s of Peter Briggs; *Career* Samuel French Ltd: asst to performing rights dir 1988–90, asst to md 1991–98, admin dir 1998–99, md 2000–12; md R&H Theatricals Europe Ltd 2012–; memb: Noel Coward Advsy Ctee 2005–12, Masterclass Devpt Bd 2007–10, Terence Rattigan Centenary Ctee 2009, Musical Theatre Network 2013–; tstee Terence Rattigan Charitable Tst 2014–; *Recreations* amateur dramatics, running, swimming, reading; *Clubs* Dartford Roadrunners, Geoffrey Whitworth Theatre, Club at The Ivy; *Style*— Mrs Vivien Goodwin; ✉ R&H Theatricals Europe Ltd, 71–91 Aldwych House, Aldwych, London WC2B 4HN (☎ 020 7054 7200, mobile 07711 393129, fax 020 7054 7290, e-mail vivien.goodwin@rnh.com)

GOODWORTH, Simon Nicholas; s of Michael Thomas Goodworth, of Broadstone, Dorset, and Lorna Ruth, *née* Skerret; *b* 9 August 1955; *Educ* Solihull Sch W Midlands, Univ of Manchester (LLB); *m* 1991, Doris, da of Jun Yip Sew Hoy, of Outram, NZ; 2 da; *Career* admitted slr 1980; ptnr: Theodore Goddard 1986–2002 (res ptnr NY 1991), Covington & Burling 2002– (specialist in mergers and acquisitions, and in private equity funds and private equity); memb Law Soc; *Recreations* tennis, squash, theatre, music (violin, piano, guitar); *Style*— Simon N Goodworth, Esq; ✉ Covington & Burling, 265 Strand, London WC2R 1BH (☎ 020 7067 2013, fax 020 7067 2222, e-mail sgoodworth@cov.com)

GOODYER, Prof Ian Michael; s of Mark Leonard Goodyer, and Belle, *née* Warwick; *b* 2 November 1949; *Educ* Kingsbury HS, Univ of London; *m* Jane Elizabeth, da of late Frank Goodliffe Akister; 1 s (Adam b 19 Nov 1981), 1 da (Sarah b 17 April 1983); *Career* clinical posts in med, surgery and paediatrics 1974–76, postgraduate trg in psychiatry Univ of Oxford 1976–79, res fell Brown Univ RI 1979–80, sr registrar Newcastle HA 1980–83, conslt and sr lectr Univ of Manchester 1983–87, prof Univ of Cambridge 1992–2000 (lectr 1987–92); fell Wolfson Coll Cambridge; sec-gen Int Assoc of Child Psychiatry 1992–2000; FRCPsych, FRCPCH, FMedSci; *Books* Life Experiences, Development and Child Psychiatry (1991), The Depressed Child Adolescent (1995, 2 edn 2001), Unipolar Depression: A Lifespan Perspective (2003), The Origins of Common Mental Illness (jtly, 2005), Social Cognition and Developmental Psychopathology (jtly, 2008); *Recreations* keeping fit, golf, music; *Clubs* Royal Soc of Medicine; *Style*— Prof Ian Goodyer; ✉ Developmental Psychiatry, Department of Psychiatry, Douglas House, 18B Trumpington Road, Cambridge CB2 8AH (☎ 01223 746162, fax 01223 746003, e-mail ig104@cam.ac.uk)

GOOLEY, Michael David William (Mike); CBE (2007); s of Denis David Gooley, and Lennie Frances May, *née* Woodward; *b* 13 October 1936, Sheffield; *Educ* St George's Coll Weybridge, RMA Sandhurst; *Family* 3 da (Katherine Mary Veronica b 1962, Jennifer Samantha b 1967, Siobhan Hilary Eila b 1975), 1 s (Tristan Patrick b 1973); m, 8 Sept 2000, Fiona Kathleen, *née* Leslie; *Career* Br Army: enlisted 1955, cmmnd 2 Lt S Staffs Regt 1956, joined 22 SAS 1958 (served Malaya and Arabian Peninsula), Adj 21 SAS 1961–63, 1 Bn Staffords 1963 (served Kenya), 22 SAS 1964 (served Malay Peninsula, Borneo and Saudi Arabia), ret 1965; mil advsr to Royalist Yemeni Army 1965–69, fndr and chm Trailfinders Ltd 1970–; fndr tstee Mike Gooley Trailfinders Charity; FInstD 1978, FRGS 1996, hon life fell RSA 2005; *Recreations* travel, aviation, wining and dining, sport; *Clubs* Special Forces (tstee 1993–2007); *Style*— Mike Gooley, Esq, CBE; ✉ Trailfinders, 9 Abingdon Road, London W8 6AH

GOOSE, His Hon Judge Julian Nicholas; QC (2002); *Career* called to the Bar 1984; asst recorder 1999, recorder 2000, circuit judge (North Eastern Circuit) 2013–; *Style*— His Hon Judge Goose, QC; ✉ Sheffield Combined Court Centre, The Law Courts, 50 West Bar, Sheffield S3 8PH

GOPAL-CHOWDHURY, Paul; *b* 1949; *Educ* Camberwell Sch of Art, Slade; *Career* artist; Boise Travelling Scholarship and French Govt Scholarship 1973–74; lectr: Chelsea Sch of Art 1973–74 (pt/t 1975–77), Fine Art Dept Univ of Leeds (pt/t) 1975–77, Byam Shaw Sch of Art (pt/t) 1975–77; Gregory fell Univ of Leeds 1975–77; artist-in-residence Gonville & Caius Coll Cambridge and Kettle's Yard Gallery Cambridge 1983–84; *Solo Exhibitions*: Art Gallery Newcastle Poly 1980, Arts Centre Folkestone 1980, Ian Birksted Gallery 1981 and 1984, Kettle's Yard Gallery Cambridge (and tour to Axiom Gallery Cheltenham and Oldham Art Gallery) 1984–85, Benjamin Rhodes Gallery 1986, 1988 and 1991, Quay Arts Centre IOW 1988; *Group Exhibitions* incl: London Gp 1971, Royal Acad Summer Exhbn (1972, 1974, 1978, invited artist 1988), Royal Soc of Oil Painters 1973, John Moores Exhbn (Liverpool) 1974, Hayward Annual 1979 and 1981, Serpentine Summer Show 3 1979, Whitechapel Open (Whitechapel Gallery) 1980 and 1983, Imperial Tobacco Portrait Awards (Nat Portrait Gallery) 1980, 1981 and 1985, A Taste of Br Art Today (Brussels) 1981, Ian Birksted Gallery (NY) 1981, Heads (Lamont Gallery London) 1992, Royal Acad Summer Exhbn (invited artist) 1992 and 1993, Beautiful Blooms (Lamont Gallery London) 1993; *Public Collections*: Bolton Art Gallery, Chase Manhattan Bank NY, Chelmsford and Essex Museum, Contemporary Art Soc, de Beers Ltd, Doncaster Museum and Art Gallery, Newcastle Poly; 2nd prize Imperial Tobacco Portrait Award (Nat Portrait Gallery) 1982; *Publications* articles incl: My Painting (Artscribe), Painting From Life (Hayward Annual 1979 Catalogue), Portrait of the Artist (Artist's and Illustrator's Magazine 1986), Reviving the Figurative Tradition (Landscape 1987); *Style*— Paul Gopal-Chowdhury, Esq

GORDON; *see also:* Duff Gordon, Smith-Gordon"

GORDON, Andrew Mark Ainslie; s of Robert W A Gordon, of Graveley, Cambridgeshire, and Pamela Pheby, *née* Roberts; *b* 23 January 1969, Nocton, Lincolnshire; *Educ* St Columba's Coll St Albans, Univ of Kent at Canterbury (BA); *partner* Joanna Anderson; 2 s (Hal Riley b 30 Jan 2005, Logan Griff b 27 June 2008); *Career* jr press offr Hodder & Stoughton 1992–93; Little, Brown & Co UK: copywriter 1994–95, desk ed 1995–98, commissioning ed 1998–2000; sr ed Time Warner UK 2000–01, editorial dir Simon & Schuster UK 2001–07, literary agent David Higham Associates 2007– (dir 2011–); *Recreations* reading, collecting film posters; *Clubs* MCC, Century, RAF; *Style*— Andrew Gordon; ✉ c/o David Higham Associates, 7th Floor, Waverley House, 7–12 Noel Street, London W1F 8GQ (e-mail andrewgordon@davidhigham.co.uk)

GORDON, Bryony; *Career* journalist and author; columnist The Daily Telegraph and Sunday Telegraph; *Books* The Wrong Knickers: A Decade of Chaos (2014), Mad Girl (2016); *Style*— Ms Bryony Gordon

GORDON, Christopher James; s of (Alexander) Esmé Gordon, RSA, FRIBA (d 1993), and Betsy Ballment, *née* McCurry (d 1990); *b* 3 December 1944, Edinburgh; *Educ* Edinburgh Acad, Univ of St Andrews (MA), Br Sch of Archaeology Athens, Poly of Central London (Dip Arts Admin); *m* 27 June 1970, Susan Merriel, da of Bonham Bazeley, DSC; 1 da (Antonia b 4 Dec 1973), 3 s (Alexander b 4 Oct 1975, Rupert b 2 Sept 1978, Adam b 24 July 1981); *Career* trainee mangr Williamson Magor & Co (tea estates) Calcutta 1967–69, asst music offr Arts Cncl of GB 1969–72, theatre and mktg mangr Hampstead Theatre 1973, sr arts offr/festival admin London Borough of Camden 1973–77, co arts offr Hampshire CC 1977–85, exec dir Cncl of Regnl Arts Assocs 1985–91, chief exec English Regnl Arts Bds 1991–2000, freelance conslt in cultural policy and mgmnt; external examiner: MA Arts Admin Leicester Poly 1986–91, MA Euro Cultural Mgmnt Univ of Warwick 1993–96, occasional lectr 1993–, assoc fell 1998–; memb Cncl Univ of

Southampton 1998–2004; visiting prof: Univ of Bologna 2002–, Univ of Turin 2004–08, London City Univ 2007–13; lectr on cultural policy: Dijon, Barcelona, Turin, Salzburg; chair Festivals Panels Gr London Arts Assoc 1976–77; memb: Nat Film & Video Forum BFI 1991–2000, Planning and Devpt Bd Arts Cncl of GB 1986–91; Southern Arts Assoc: chair General Arts, chair Festivals Panels, memb Exec Ctee, memb Gen Cncl; chair Cncl of Europe Evaluation of Cultural Policy in: Latvia 1997–98, Italy 1995, Cyprus 2004, Turkey 2009–13; chair Advsy Bd Fondazione Fitzcarraldo Turin 1999–2012; hon treas Euro Forum for the Arts & Heritage (EFAH) 1996–99; chair Fondation Marcel Hicter (European Dip); memb: Bd Bournmouth Orch 1982–90, Bd Nuffield Theatre Southampton 2003–11; Winchester Cathedral Fabric Ctee 1996–; tstee Portsmouth Theatre Royal 1985–99, tstee and chair Hants Sculpture Tst 1987–2013; memb Editorial Bd Int Jl of Cultural Policy; FRSA; *Books* Cultural Policy in Italy (1995), Cultural Policy in Latvia (1997), European Perspectives on Cultural Policy (UNESCO 2001), Cultural Policy in Cyprus (2003), Gambling on Culture (2004), Cultural Policy and Social Inclusion (2004), Cultural Policy in Turkey (2013), Rebalancing Our Cultural Capital (jtly, 2013), Policy for the Lottery, the Arts and Community in England (2014); articles in academic jls, research on London bias in arts funding in England (www.GPSCulture.co.uk); *Recreations* travel, music, art, history, archaeology; *Style*— Christopher Gordon, Esq; ✉ 28 Cornes Close, Winchester, Hampshire SO22 5DS (☎ 01962 864204, e-mail christophergordon@compuserve.com, website www.gpsculture.co.uk)

GORDON, Prof David; s of Lawrence Gordon (d 1992), and Pattie, *née* Wood (d 2008); *b* 23 February 1947, Croydon; *Educ* Magdalene Coll Cambridge (open scholar, MA, MB, BChir), Westminster Med Sch London; *m* Dr C Louise, *née* Jones; 1 da (Henrietta Katherine b 1984), 3 s (Frederick Samuel b 1986, Nathaniel Charles b 1988, Theodore William b 1990); *Career* sr lectr then hon sr lectr in medicine St Mary's Hosp Medical Sch London 1980–94 (research and academic appts 1972–80, also asst dir Medical Unit 1980–83), hon conslt physician St Mary's Hosp London 1980–94; Wellcome Tst: asst dir 1983–89, prog dir 1989–98, dir of special initiatives 1998–99; Univ of Manchester (formerly Victoria Univ of Manchester): prof of medicine 1999–2008, dean Faculty of Medicine, Dentistry, Nursing and Pharmacy 1999–2004, vice-pres and dean Faculty of Medical and Human Science 2004–06, vice-pres 2006–08, emeritus prof of medicine 2008–; conslt Health Sector Reform Project Miny of Health Azerbaijan 2010–11; visiting prof Univ of Copenhagen 2007– and several other visiting professorships; chair Cncl of Heads of Medical Schs 2003–06, pres Assoc of Med Schs in Europe 2004–11, pres World Fedn for Medical Educn 2015–; dep chm ORPHEUS 2005–10; former memb: Scottish Office Dept of Health Chief Scientist Ctee, Exec Cncl Assoc of Medical Research Charities, Research Ctee HEFCE, CVCP Task Force on Clinical Academic Careers; memb Editorial Bd Trends in Molecular Medicine; author of pubns in scientific jls incl: Lancet, BMJ, Jl of Physiology, American Jl of Physiology, Clinical Science, Molecular Medicine Today; memb: Acad of Medical Sciences (memb various ctees), Assoc of Physicians, Med Pilgrims, 1942 Club; medical referee Civil Serv 1989–94; FRCP 1989 (MRCP 1972), FMedSci 1999; *Publications* pubns on medicine, physiology and medical education in journals and elsewhere; *Style*— Prof David Gordon; ✉ World Federation for Medical Education, 13A Chemin du Levant, 01210 Ferney-Voltaire, France (e-mail gordoncph@gmail.com)

GORDON, David Michael (Dave); OBE (2013); *b* 24 May 1951, London; *Educ* Harrow Co GS, Univ of Warwick (BA); *m* 6 Sept 1980, Barbara; 2 da (Caroline b 1 Aug 1983, Judith b 4 Oct 1985); *Career* radio studio mangr 1972–79, sr prodr Radio Sport 1983–85 (prodr 1979–83); BBC: joined as asst prodr TV Sport 1985, worked on Grandstand and Sportsnight, exec ed Grandstand 1997–2001 (asst ed 1991–97), head Major Events BBC Sport 2001–13, actg dir BBC Sport 2005, currently sports broadcasting conslt; covered numerous sporting events incl: 10 Olympic Games, 7 Winter Olympics, 8 Cwlth Games, London Marathon, Great North Run, Wimbledon; winner of numerous awards incl BAFTAs, RTS Lifetime Achievement Award 2013; *Recreations* supporting Fulham FC, learning to play the saxophone; *Style*— Dave Gordon, Esq, OBE; ✉ e-mail davegordon.sport@gmail.com

GORDON, David Sorrell; s of Sholom Gordon (d 1965), and Tamara (Tania) Gordon (d 1994); *b* 11 September 1941; *Educ* Clifton, Balliol Coll Oxford (BA), LSE, Harvard Business Sch (AMP); *m* 1, 1963 (m dis 1969), Enid Albagli; m 2, 1974, Maggi McCormick; 2 s; *Career* chartered accountant Thomson McLintock (now KPMG) 1965–68; The Economist: journalist 1968–78, prodn and devpt dir The Economist Newspaper Ltd 1978–81, gp chief exec The Economist Newspaper Ltd 1981–93; chief exec Independent Television News Ltd (ITN) 1993–95; business advsr 1995–96, sec Royal Acad of Arts 1996–2002, ceo and dir Milwaukee Art Museum 2002–; dir: The Financial Times Group Ltd 1983–93, Mediakey plc 1996–2001, Profile Books 1996–, Financial News 1999–2006 (chm 2001–2006), Dice Inc 2006–; chm Contemporary Art Soc 1992–98, memb Bd South Bank Centre 1986–96, govr BFI 1983–91, memb Ct of Govrs LSE 1990–2000, tstee: Tate Gallery 1993–98, Architecture Fndn 1992–2002; FCA; *Books* Newspaper Money (jtly with Fred Hirsch, 1975); *Recreations* movies, magic lanterns; *Clubs* Garrick; *Style*— David Gordon, Esq; ✉ Milwaukee Art Museum, 700 North Art Museum Drive, Milwaukee, Wisconsin 53202, USA (☎ 00 1 414 224 3200)

GORDON, His Hon Judge (Cosmo) Gerald Maitland; s of John Kenneth Maitland Gordon, CBE (d 1967), of Farnham, Surrey, and Erica Martia, *née* Clayton-East (d 1983), of London; *b* 26 March 1945; *Educ* Eton; *m* 4 July 1973, Vanessa Maria Juliet Maxine, *née* Reilly-Morrison; 2 s (James Cosmo Alexander b 11 Oct 1975, George William Robert b 6 June 1978); *Career* called to the Bar Middle Temple 1966 (bencher 2003), recorder of the Crown Court 1986–90 (asst recorder 1982–86), circuit judge (SE Circuit) 1990–, permanent judge Central Criminal Ct 1994–; Cncl of Royal Borough of Kensington and Chelsea: memb 1971–90, chm Works and Town Planning Ctees, dep leader 1982–88, mayor 1989–90; Liveryman Merchant Taylors Co 1995; *Style*— His Hon Judge Gordon; ✉ Central Criminal Court, Old Bailey, London EC4M 7EH (☎ 020 7248 3277)

GORDON, Ian; s of James Donald Gordon, of Montrose, Angus, and Winifred, *née* Thomson (d 1985); *b* 15 August 1957; *Educ* Biggar HS, Univ of Edinburgh (LLB); *m* 22 July 1988, (Mary) Angela Joan, da of Donald Macdonald, of Isle of Lewis; 1 s (James Alexander Donald b 22 April 1992), 1 da (Juliet Emily Katherine b 1 August 1994); *Career* McGrigors (formerly McGrigor Donald): apprentice 1979–81, slr 1981, ptnr 1983–; ptnr Pinsent Masons following merger with McGrigors 2012–; memb: Law Soc of Scotland 1981, Assoc of Pension Lawyers 1986 (memb Ctee and former chm Scottish Gp); NP 1981; *Publications* Battling with Courage (PLC Pensions, 2014); *Recreations* hillwalking, tourism, getting out and about; *Style*— Ian Gordon; ✉ Pinsent Masons LLP, 141 Bothwell Street, Glasgow G2 7EQ (☎ 0141 567 8557, e-mail ian.gordon@pinsentmasons.com)

GORDON, John Keith; s of Prof James Edward Gordon, and Theodora Mary Camilla, *née* Sinker; *b* 6 July 1940; *Educ* Marlborough, Trinity Coll Cambridge (MA), Yale Univ (Henry fell), LSE; *m* 14 Aug 1965, Elizabeth, da of Maj A J Shanks (d 1962); 2 s (Timothy Alan b 1971, Alexander Keith b 1973); *Career* Dip serv; entered FCO 1966, Budapest 1968–70, seconded to Civil Serv Coll 1970–72, FCO 1972–73, UK Mission Geneva 1973–74, head of Chancery and consul Yaoundé 1975–77 (concurrently chargé d'affaires Gabon and Central African Repub), FCO 1977–80, cultural attaché Moscow 1980–81, Office of UK Rep to EC Brussels 1982–83, UK perm delg to UNESCO Paris 1983–85, head Nuclear Energy Dept FCO 1986–88, left FCO 1990; dep and policy dir Global Environment Res Centre 1990–94; ind conslt and analyst 1994–; Parly candidate (Lib Dem) Daventry 1997; special advsr UNED-Forum 1998–2004; memb UK Nat Cmmn for UNESCO 2003–07; pres Cncl for Educn in World Citizenship 2006–09, chair S Oxon Sustainability (SOS) Gp 2011–, vice-chair Oxon LEADER Prog 2015–; *Publications* Institutions and Sustainable Development: Meeting the Challenge (with Caroline Fraser, 1991), 20/20 Vision: Britain, Germany and a New Environmental Agenda (with Tom Bigg, 1993), Canadian Round Tables (1994), Edward Wakefield – Aviator, Soldier, Philanthropist (2015); author of other contributions to books, symposia and periodicals; *Recreations* walking, books, history; *Clubs* RSA, Nat Liberal; *Style*— John Gordon, Esq; ✉ Well House, Reading Road, Wallingford, Oxfordshire OX10 9HG

GORDON, Lyndall Felicity; da of Harry Louis Getz (d 1969), of Cape Town, South Africa, and Rhoda Stella Press (d 1999); *b* 1941, Cape Town, South Africa; *Educ* Good Hope Seminary Cape Town, Univ of Cape Town (BA Hons), Columbia Univ NY (PhD); *m* 1963, Prof Siamon Gordon, *qv*; 2 da (Anna b 9 Aug 1965, Olivia Jane b 26 Nov 1978); *Career* Univ of Oxford: Rhodes fell 1973–75, lectr Jesus Coll 1977–84, CUF lectr in English 1984–95, Dame Helen Gardner fell St Hilda's Coll 1984–95, sr research fell St Hilda's Coll 1995–; asst prof Columbia Univ 1975–76; Eliot meml lectr RSL 2003; memb: PEN, Virginia Woolf Soc; FRSL 2002; *Publications* Eliot's Early Years (1977, reprinted 1988, Rose Mary Shaw Prize Br Acad), Eliot's New Life (1988, Southern Arts Prize), Virginia Woolf: A Writer's Life (1984, winner James Tait Prize for Biography), Shared Lives (1992, revised edn 2005), Charlotte Brontë: A Passionate Life (1994, Cheltenham Prize for Lit, revised edn 2008), A Private Life of Henry James: Two Women and His Art (1998, revised edn 2012), Vindication: A Life of Mary Wollstonecraft (2005), Lives Like Loaded Guns: Emily Dickinson and her Family's Feuds (2010), The Imperfect Life of T S Eliot (2012), Divided Lives: Dreams of a Mother and Daughter (2014); author of numerous essays in various pubns; *Recreations* reading, ballet; *Style*— Lyndall Gordon; ✉ St Hilda's College, Oxford OX4 1DY; c/o Isobel Dixon, Blakefriedmann Agency, 122 Arlington Road, London NW1 7HP (☎ 020 7284 0408, e-mail isobel@blakefriedmann.co.uk, website www.lyndallgordon.net)

G

GORDON, (George) Michael Winston; s of Winston Gordon, of Clonallon Rd, Warrenpoint, NI, and Marjorie Georgina Gordon; *b* 8 May 1937; *Educ* Queen's Univ Belfast (BSc, MSc), Univ of NSW (MEngSc); *m* 11 Aug 1966, Narelle Helen, da of Flt Lt Kenneth Charles Nicholl (decd), of Sydney, NSW, Aust; 3 s (Matthew b 9 Sept 1967, Nicholas b 24 May 1969, Benjamin b 8 Feb 1976); *Career* grad trainee Metropolitan Vickers 1958–60; design engr: Bristol Aircraft Co 1961–62, Amalgamated Wireless Australasia 1962–67; conslt: PA Management Consultants Aust, Singapore, Malaysia and NI 1967–76, Booz Allen and Hamilton Algeria 1976–77; dir: NI Devpt Agency 1977–80, American Monitor 1980–82, BIS London 1982–93 (chief operating offr); md LINK Training 1993–97; dir and chief operating offr The Spring Group plc (formerly CRT plc) 1994–2001, dir Microgen plc 1995–98, chm Talent Technol Pty Ltd 2002–07, dir Previsor 2007–10, chm and dir A4e Pty Ltd 2009–13 (dir 2014–), prop, chm and dir Pareto Pty Ltd 2013–; MIEE (NY), FInstD; *Recreations* swimming (Australian record holder in 1500m butterfly); *Clubs* Returned Servicemen League (Harbord NSW); *Style*— Michael Gordon, Esq; ✉ Shell Cottage, 3 Collingwood Street, Manly, NSW, Australia (mobile 0403 642079, e-mail george.cordon@bigpond.com)

GORDON, Prof Peter; s of Louis Gordon (d 1969), and Anne, *née* Schultz (d 1941); *b* 4 November 1927; *Educ* Univ of Birmingham (DipEd), LSE (BSc, MSc), Inst of Educn Univ of London (PhD); *m* 30 March 1958, Tessa Joan, da of Bernard Leton, of Stanmore, Middlesex; 1 da (Pauline Amanda b 24 June 1961), 1 s (David Nicholas b 12 April 1965); *Career* RAF in England and India 1945–48; teacher primary and secdy schs 1951–65, HM inspr of schs 1965–73; Inst of Educn Univ of London: lectr 1973–76, reader 1976–82, prof of history of educn 1982–93; FRHistS 1982, FSA 1991; *Books* The Victorian School Manager (1974), The Cabinet Journal of Dudley Ryder, Viscount Sandon (with Christopher Howard, 1974), Curriculum Change in the 19th and 20th Centuries (with Denis Lawton, 1978), Games and Simulations in Action (with Alec Davidson, 1978), Theory and Practice of Curriculum Studies (1978), Philosophers as Educational Reformers (with John White, 1979), Selection for Secondary Education (1980), The Study of Education: Inaugural Lectures (1980, 1988, 1995), The Red Earl: The Papers of the Fifth Earl Spencer of Althorp 1835–1910 (1981, 1986), The Study of the Curriculum (ed 1981), A Guide to English Educational Terms (with Denis Lawton, 1984), HMI (with Denis Lawton, 1987), Dictionary of British Educationists (with R Aldrich, 1989), History of Education: The Making of a Discipline (with R Szreter, 1989), Education and Policy in England in the Twentieth Century (ed 1991), Teaching the Humanities (ed 1991), The Wakes of Northamptonshire (1992), Dictionary of Education (with Denis Lawton, 1993, 2 edn 1996), International Yearbook of History Education (jt ed, 1995), A Guide to Educational Research (ed, 1996), Biographical Dictionary of North American and European Educationists (with Richard Aldrich, 1997), Royal Education: Past, Present and Future (with Denis Lawton, 1999), Politics and Society: The Journals of Lady Knightley of Fawsley 1885–1913 (1999), Dictionary of British Women's Organisations 1825–1960 (with David Doughan, 2001), International Review of History Education (jt ed, 2001), A History of Western Educational Ideas (with Denis Lawton, 2002), Dictionary of British Education (with Denis Lawton, 2003), Understanding History: Recent Research in History Education (jt ed 2005), Musical Visitors to Britain (with David Gordon, 2005), Women, Clubs and Associations in Britain (with David Doughan, 2006), The Political Diaries of the Fourth Earl of Carnarvon, 1857–1890: Colonial Secretary and Lord-Lieutenant of Ireland (2009); *Recreations* music, architecture; *Style*— Prof Peter Gordon, FSA; ✉ Birtsmorton, 58 Waxwell Lane, Pinner, Middlesex HA5 3EN (☎ 020 8868 7110)

GORDON, Richard John Francis; QC (1994); s of John Bernard Basil Gordon, of London, and Winifred Josephine, *née* Keenan; *b* 26 November 1948; *Educ* St Benedicts Sch, ChCh Oxford (MA), UCL (LLM); *m* 13 Sept 1975, Jane Belinda, da of Anthony George Lucey, of Welburn, N Yorks; 2 s (Edmund John Anthony b 17 June 1982, Adam Richard Cosby b 25 Oct 1985); *Career* called to the Bar Middle Temple 1972; ed Crown Office Digest 1988–, broadcasts and articles on admin law in legal periodicals and other pubns; Freeman City of London; FRGS, ACIArb; *Books* The Law Relating to Mobile Homes and Caravans (2 edn, 1985), Judicial Review Law and Procedure (1985); *Recreations* modern fiction, theatre, cricket; *Style*— Richard Gordon, Esq, QC; ✉ 39 Essex Street, London WC2R 3AT (☎ 020 7583 1111, fax 020 7353 3978)

GORDON, Maj-Gen Robert Duncan Seaton; CMG (2005), CBE (1994); s of Col Jack Gordon (d 2005), and Joan, *née* Seaton (d 1981); *b* 23 November 1950; *Educ* Wellington Coll, St Catharine's Coll Cambridge (MA); *m* 1979, Virginia (Gina), da of Dr and Mrs William Brown of Toronto, Canada; 2 s (Seaton b 1981, Charlie b 1985); *Career* cmmnd 17/21 Lancers 1970; Army Staff Coll Shrivenham and Camberley 1982, COS 4 Armoured Bde 1983–84, Lt Col 1987, Military Asst to C in C BAOR/NORTHAG 1987–90, CO 17/21 Lancers 1990–92, Full Col 1993, Sec Chief of Staff's Ctee MOD 1993–94; Higher Cmd and Staff Course 1994; Brig 1994, Cdr 19 Mechanised Bde 1994–96, RCDS 1996, Dir Army PR 1997–99, Maj-Gen 1999, GOC 2 Div York 1999, GOC 2 Div Edinburgh 2000–02, Col Cmdt RAVC 2001–07, Force Cdr UN Mission to Ethiopia and Eritrea 2002–04, ret Army 2005; currently: conslt on peacekeeping, md Robert Gordon Consulting Ltd, sr advsr to UNDP on security strategy in Iraq; govr Edinburgh Castle 2000–02; Queen's Commendation for Valuable Service (Bosnia) 1995; MRUSI 1974; *Recreations* history, offshore sailing, countryside sports, tennis, bad golf; *Clubs* Cavalry and Guards'; *Style*— Maj-Gen Robert Gordon, CMG, CBE

GORDON, (Prof) Robert Patterson; s of Robert Gordon (d 1976), and Eveline, *née* Shilliday; *b* 9 November 1945; *Educ* Methodist Coll Belfast, St Catharine's Coll Cambridge (Jarrett exhibitioner and scholar, John Stewart of Rannoch Hebrew scholar, sr scholar, Bender prize, Tyrwhitt's Hebrew scholar, Mason prize, MA, PhD, LittD); *m* 1970, Helen Ruth, *née* Lyttle; 2 s ((Christopher) Graham b 17 Nov 1975, Alasdair Robert b 3 Oct 1985), 1 da ((Nicola) Claire b 19 Sept 1977); *Career* lectr in Hebrew and Semitic languages Univ of Glasgow 1970–79 (asst lectr Hebrew and Old Testament 1969–70), regius prof of Hebrew Univ of Cambridge 1995–2012 (lectr in Old Testament 1979–95); fell: St Edmund's Coll Cambridge 1985–89, St Catharine's Coll Cambridge 1995–2012 (emeritus fell 2012–); memb Fndn Trinity Coll Cambridge 1995–2012; McManis lectures Wheaton ILL 1990, Macbride sermon Oxford 2000, Didsbury lectures Manchester 2001, Biblical Studies Lectrs Samford Univ Birmingham AL 2004, etc; sec Int Orgn for the Study of the Old Testament 2001–04; memb: Soc for Old Testament Study (pres 2003), Br Assoc of Jewish Studies; consltg ed New Int Dictionary of Old Testament Theology and Exegesis 1997, review ed Vetus Testamentum 1998–2009, ed Hebrew Bible and Its Versions 2001–15; memb Editorial Bd Vetus Testamentum 1995–2015; tstee Spalding Tsts; FBA 2011; *Books* 1 and 2 Samuel (1984, Chinese edn 2002), 1 and 2 Samuel. A Commentary (1986, reprinted 2004), The Targum of the Minor Prophets (with K J Cathcart, 1989), Studies in the Targum to the Twelve Prophets (1994), Wisdom in Ancient Israel (jt ed, 1995), The Place is too Small for us (ed, 1995), The Old Testament in Syriac According to the Peshitta Version: Chronicles (1998), Hebrews: A New Commentary (2000, 2 edn 2008), Holy Land, Holy City (2004), The Old Testament in its World (jt ed, 2005), Hebrew Bible and Ancient Versions (2006), The God of Israel (ed, 2007), Thus Speaks Ishtar of Arbela (jt ed, 2013), Leshon Limmudim (jt ed, 2013), Genesis 1–11 in its Ancient Context (2015), Syriac Peshitta Bible with English Translation: Chronicles (2016); *Recreations* jogging, local history (N Ireland), otopianistics; *Clubs* National, Carrickfergus Gasworks Preservation Soc; *Style*— Robert Gordon; ✉ St Catharine's College, Cambridge CB2 1RL (e-mail rpg1000@cam.ac.uk)

GORDON, Robert Smith Benzie; CB (2000); s of William Gladstone Gordon (d 1980), and Helen Watt, *née* Benzie (d 2003); *b* 7 November 1950; *Educ* The Gordon Schs Huntly, Univ of Aberdeen (MA); *m* 2 July 1976, Joyce Ruth, da of Stephen Cordiner; 2 da (Rachel Joyce b 19 Oct 1978, Jennifer Claire b 18 March 1984), 2 s ((Robert Stephen) Niall b 20 March 1980, David William James b 20 May 1989); *Career* Scottish Office: admin trainee 1973, various trg appointments, princ Scot Devpt Dept 1979–85, asst sec and private sec to sec of state for Scotland 1985–87, asst sec Dept of Agric and Fisheries 1987–90, asst sec mgmnt and orgn and industrial relations 1990–91, dir of admin servs 1991–, under sec 1993–97, head of Constitution Gp 1997–98, head of Scottish Exec Secretariat 1999–2001, head Fin and Central Servs Dept 2001–2002, chief exec Crown Office and procurator fiscal serv and head of legal and parly servs Scottish Exec 2002–04, head Justice Dept and head of legal and parly servs Scottish Exec 2004–07, DG justice and communities Scottish Govt 2007–10, assoc Kynesis Consultants; chair Audit and Accountability Ctee Police Investigations and Review Cmmr; chair Bd Bethany Christian Tst, chair Provincial Standing Ctee Scottish Episcopal Church, chair Bd Safe Families for Children Scotland; Warden Incorporation of Goldsmiths City of Edinburgh; *Style*— Robert Gordon, Esq, CB; ✉ e-mail robertgordon@blueyonder.co.uk

GORDON, Roderick Caryl Patrick Ramsay (Roddy); s of John Ramsay Gordon (d 1997), and Jean Carlyle, *née* Irvine; *b* 17 March 1959, Hanover, Germany; *Educ* Charterhouse, Univ of Bristol (LLB); *m* 5 Sept 1992, Katharine Elizabeth, *née* Morton; 2 s (Thomas Patrick b 25 March 1995, James Harry b 12 Sept 1997); *Career* offr 4/7 Royal Dragoon Gds 1981–84; admitted slr 1988; trainee Braby & Waller 1986–88, slr Masons 1988–1993, ptnr Robert Muckle 1993–2001, ptnr Watson Burton LLP 2001–13, ptnr DAC Beachcroft LLP 2013–; memb: Law Soc 1988–, Technol and Construction Slrs Assoc; MCIArb, CEDR accredited mediator; *Recreations* skiing, sailing, riding, golf; *Clubs* Cavalry and Guards', Northern Counties; *Style*— Roddy Gordon, Esq; ✉ DAC Beachcroft LLP, Wellbar Central, 36 Gallowgate, Newcastle upon Tyne NE1 4TD (☏ 0191 404 4018, e-mail rgordon@dacbeachcroft.com)

GORDON, Prof Siamon; s of Jonah Gordon (d 1955), of South Africa, and Liebe, *née* Solsky (d 1988); *b* 29 April 1938; *Educ* SACS Cape Town, Univ of Cape Town (MB ChB), Rockefeller Univ (PhD); *m* April 1963, Dr Lyndall Gordon, *qv*, da of Harry Getz; 2 da (Anna b 9 Aug 1965, Olivia Jane b 26 Nov 1978); *Career* registrar Dept of Pathology Univ of Cape Town Med Sch 1963–64 (intern Dept of Med and Surgery 1962–63), res asst Wright-Fleming Inst of Microbiology St Mary's Hosp Med Sch 1964–65, asst prof and assoc physician Lab of Cellular Physiology and Immunology Rockefeller Univ 1971–76 (res assoc and asst physician Lab of Human Genetics 1965–66); Univ of Oxford: visiting scientist Dept of Biochemistry 1974–75, fell Exeter Coll 1976–, Newton-Abraham lectr in pathology 1976–91, reader in experimental pathology Sir William Dunn Sch of Pathology 1976–89, prof of cellular pathology 1989–91, Glaxo prof of cellular pathology 1991–2008 (emeritus 2008–), acting head of dept 2000–01; scholar Leukemia Soc of America Inc 1973–76 (special fell 1971), adjunct assoc prof Rockefeller Univ 1976–, Br Cncl visiting prof and lectr Hebrew Univ 1994, visiting fell NCI/ NIAID NIH 2009–10; Friederich Sasse Award in immunology 1990, Medal of the Polish Soc of Haematology and Transfusion Med 1997; memb Editorial Bd: Jl of Cell Science 1982–90, Progress in Leukocyte Biology 1987, American Jl of Respiratory Cell and Molecular Biology 1989–91, Jl of Experimental Medicine 1993–, Jl of Leukocyte Biology 1998–2006, Immunology 2000–, Marie T Bonazinga Award Soc of Leukocyte Biology 2003; memb: Lister Scientific Advsy Ctee 1987–92, Br Soc for Immunology, Br Soc for Cell Biology, American Soc for Cell Biology, Soc for Leukocyte Biology, Henry Kunkel Soc; hon memb Assoc of Assoc of American Immunologists 2004; DSc (hc) Univ of Cape Town 2002; FMedSci 2003, FRS 2007; *Books* Macrophage Biology and Activation, Current Topics in Microbiology and Immunology (ed, 1992), Legacy of Cell Fusion (ed, 1994), Phagocytosis – The Host (V5) and Microbial Invasion (V6) Advances in Cell and Molecular Biology of Membranes and Organelles (ed, 1999), The Macrophage as Therapeutic Target (ed, 2003); author of articles in various scientific jls; *Recreations* reading, music, history; *Style*— Prof Siamon Gordon; ✉ Sir William Dunn School of Pathology, University of Oxford, South Parks Road, Oxford OX1 3RE (☏ 01865 275500, fax 01865 275515, e-mail siamon.gordon@path.ox.ac.uk)

GORDON, Tanya Joan (Mrs Tanya Sarne); OBE (2011); da of Jean-Claude Gordon, of Bayswater, London, and Daphne Thomas, *née* Tucar (d 1976); *b* 15 January 1945; *Educ* Godolphin & Latymer Sch, Univ of Sussex (BA); *m* 1969 (m dis), Michael Sarne, s of Alfred Schener; 1 s (William Gordon b 30 May 1972), 1 da (Claudia Aviva b 17 Jan 1970); *Career* model 1963–64, asst to Cultural Attaché Persian Embassy 1966–67, asst to Lit Agent Kramers 1967–68, freelance reader for Universal Film Studios 1967–68, supply teacher of history for GLC (mainly at St Martin's-in-the-Field) 1968–69, spent two years in Brazil helping husband make a film (Intimidade), working as a tour guide for Brazil Safaris and modelling 1973–75, sales dir Entrepas Ltd 1976–78, fndr Miz (fashion business) 1978–83, fndr Ghost 1984–2006, ind fashion designer 2006–; fndr memb Fashion Indust Action Gp, memb Br Fashion Cncl; *Recreations* cooking, tennis, acquiring property and the obvious; *Clubs* Groucho, Campden Hill Tennis; *Style*— Ms Tanya Gordon, OBE

GORDON CLARK, Robert Michael; *b* 8 May 1961, Derby; *Educ* St John's Sch Leatherhead, Univ of Southampton; *m* Elizabeth, *née* Day; 2 da (Anya, Imogen); *Career* formerly dir of communications and mktg then dep chief exec London First; London Communications Agency: co-fndr, chm and md 1999–2010, exec chm 2010–, clients incl Benson Elliot, Brockton Capital, King's Cross Central Ltd Partnership, LCR, Lee Valley Regnl Park Authy, Mace, Market Tech and St George plc; dir Shannon and Clark Prodns Ltd 2008–11, non-exec dir Hayes Davidson 1999–2010; tstee Thames Festival 2005–13 (chm 2013–), govr and chair Devpt Ctee St John's Sch Leatherhead 1996–2011; MCIPR; *Recreations* theatre, cricket; *Clubs* Questors Theatre, HAC Cricket (vice-pres); *Style*— Robert Gordon Clark, Esq; ✉ London Communications Agency, 8th Floor Berkshire House, 168–173 High Holborn, London WC1V 7AA (☏ 020 7612 8480, e-mail rgc@londoncommunications.co.uk, website www.londoncommunications.co.uk)

GORDON LENNOX, Maj-Gen Bernard Charles; CB (1986), MBE (1968); s of Lt-Gen Sir George Gordon Lennox (d 1988), and Nancy Brenda, *née* Darell (d 1993); *b* 19 September 1932; *Educ* Eton (page of honour to HM The King 1946–49), Sandhurst; *m* 1958, Sally-Rose, da of John Weston Warner (d 1981); 3 s (Edward Charles b 1961, Angus Charles b 1964, Charles Bernard b 1970); *Career* cmd 1 Bn Grenadier Gds 1974–75, GSO 1 RAF Staff Coll 1976–77, Brig 1977, Cdr Task Force H, Dep Cdr and COS SE Dist UKLF 1981–83, Maj-Gen 1982, Br Cmdt and GOC Br Sector Berlin 1983–85, sr Army memb RCDS 1986–87, Lt-Col Grenadier Gds 1989–95; dir Regions Motor Agents Assoc 1988–89; chm Guards Polo Club 1992–99; *Recreations* country sports, cricket, squash, music; *Clubs* Army and Navy, MCC; *Style*— Maj-Gen B C Gordon Lennox, CB, MBE; ✉ The Estate Office, Gordon Castle, Fochabers, Morayshire IV32 7PQ

GORDON OF STRATHBLANE, Baron (Life Peer UK 1997), of Deil's Craig in Stirling; James Stuart Gordon; CBE (1984); s of James Edward Gordon (d 1975), of Glasgow, and Elsie, *née* Riach (d 1984); *b* 17 May 1936; *Educ* St Aloysius' Coll, Univ of Glasgow (MA, winner Observer Mace and Best Individual Speaker, pres Union); *m* 1971, Margaret Anne, da of Andrew Kirkwood Stevenson (d 1968), of Glasgow; 1 da (Hon Sarah Jane b 1972), 2 s (Hon Michael Stevenson b 1974, Hon Christopher James b 1976); *Career* political ed STV 1965–73; md Radio Clyde 1973–96; chm: Scottish Radio Holdings plc (parent co) 1996–2005 (chief-exec 1991–96), Scottish Tourist Bd 1998–2001 (memb 1997–2001), RAJAR (Radio Audience Research) 2003–06; dir: Johnston Press plc 1996–2007, The Active Capital Trust plc until 2009; chm: Scottish Exhibition Centre 1983–89, Advsy Gp on Listed Sports Events on TV 1997–98; memb: Scottish Devpt Agency 1981–90, Ct Univ of Glasgow 1984–97, Ctee of Inquiry into Teachers' Pay and Conditions 1986, Ctee on Funding of the BBC 1999; tstee: National Galleries of Scotland 1998–2002, John Smith Meml Tst 1995–2007; Sony Award for Outstanding Services to Radio 1984, Lord Provost's Award for Public Service 1996; Hon DLitt Glasgow Caledonian Univ 1994, Hon DUniv Glasgow 1998; fell Radio Acad 1994; *Recreations* walking, skiing, genealogy; *Clubs* New (Edinburgh), Glasgow Art, Prestwick Golf; *Style*— The Lord Gordon of Strathblane, CBE; ✉ House of Lords, London SW1A 0PW (☏ 020 7219 1452, fax 020 7219 1993)

GORDON WALKER, Hon Alan Rudolf; er (twin) s of Baron Gordon-Walker, CH, PC (Life Peer, d 1980); *b* 1946; *Educ* Wellington, ChCh Oxford (MA); *m* 1976, Louise Frances Amy, da of Gen Sir Charles Henry Pepys Harington, GCB, CBE, DSO, MC; 1 s (Thomas b 1978), 1 da (Emily b 1981); *Career* former md: Hodder and Stoughton, Pan Macmillan Ltd, Cassells; chm Umbria Press 1997–; *Clubs* MCC, Hurlingham; *Style*— The Hon Alan Gordon Walker

GORDON-SAKER, Master; Andrew Stephen; s of Vincent Gordon-Saker, and Gwendoline Alice, *née* Remmers; *b* 4 October 1958; *Educ* Stonyhurst, UEA (LLB); *m* 28 Sept 1985, Liza Helen Gordon-Saker, *qv*, da of William James Marle; 1 da (Francesca b 1989), 1 s (Edward b 1991); *Career* called to the Bar Middle Temple 1981; in practice 1981–2003, dep taxing master of the Supreme Court 1994–2003, costs judge 2003–, costs offr Supreme Court 2010–, sr costs judge (chief taxing master) 2014–; memb Eastern Region Legal Aid Area Ctee 1995–2003; cncllr London Borough of Camden 1982–86; contributing ed Butterworths Costs Service 2006–, contributing ed Civil Procedure (The White Book) 2012–; *Recreations* gardening, construction; *Clubs* Trumpington Bridge; *Style*— Master Gordon-Saker; ✉ Royal Courts of Justice, Strand, London WC2A 2LL

GORDON-SAKER, Her Hon Judge Liza Helen; da of William James Marle, of Chislehurst, Kent, and Doreen Maud, *née* Adams; *b* 30 November 1959; *Educ* Farrington's Sch Chislehurst, UEA (LLB); *m* 28 Sept 1985, Andrew Stephen Gordon-Saker, *qv*, s of Vincent Gordon-Saker, of Norwich; 1 da (Francesca b 1989), 1 s (Edward b 1991); *Career* called to the Bar Gray's Inn 1982; in practice 1983–2009, dep district judge 2006–10, district judge of the principal registry of the family division 2010–14, circuit judge (South Eastern Circuit) 2014–; dir Bar Mutual Indemnity Fund Ltd 1988–2002; Freeman City of London 1984; *Recreations* golf; *Style*— Her Hon Judge Gordon-Saker

GORDON-SMITH, William Haydn; s of Cyril Smith, ISO (d 1993), and Joyce Muriel, *née* Davies (d 2001); *b* 14 March 1944; *Educ* Richmond Hill Sch Sprotbrough, West End Co Sch Bentley, Doncaster Tech Coll; *Career* writer and local architectural historian; civil servant Ministry of Pensions & Nat Insurance 1962–89, proprietor The Lodge Gallery Cusworth Park Doncaster 1972–77, Clerk Parish Cncls of Norton and High Melton 1972–78, agent to Cusworth Estate and tstee Cusworth Church Lands 1971–, fndr Cusworth Hall Gardens Tst 2013; memb Doncaster Civic Tst; assoc Bibliotheca Alexandrina – Alexandria and Mediterranean Research Centre; Lord of the Manor of Cusworth in the former W Riding of Yorkshire, Arms granted by College of Arms London 1991; *Books* Cusworth Hall (1964), Sprotbrough Hall (1966), Askern Spa (1968), Sprotbrough Colliery (1968), Cusworth Hall and the Battie-Wrightson Family (1990), Cantley Hall (1992), El'Onsuleya – The Former British Consulate-General, Alexandria (2010), Campsall Hall (2012); series of fifty illustrated articles on the Country Houses of Doncaster (1964) for Doncaster Gazette and South Yorkshire Times; *Style*— W H Gordon-Smith, Esq; ✉ 7 Christ Church Terrace, Thorne Road, Doncaster, South Yorkshire DN1 2HU (☏ 07732 323903, mobile 00 20 10 655 9893); 13 Rue Kamel El Kilani, Flat 2, Alexandria, Egypt (☏ 00 20 10 0655 9893)

GORE, His Hon Judge Allan Peter; QC (2003); *b* 25 August 1951, Sydney, Australia; *Educ* Purley GS for Boys, Trinity Hall Cambridge (BA, LLB), Coll of Law Chancery Lane; *m* 1, 1981 (m dis 1998); 3 da (Rachael, Lauren, Hannah); m 2, 2016, Alison Taylor; *Career* called to the Bar Middle Temple 1978; tenant: 2 Plowden Buildings 1979–82, 5 Essex Court 1982–91, 12 King's Bench Walk 1991–2010; recorder 2000–10 (asst recorder 1999–2000), circuit judge 2010, sr circuit judge 2011–, designated civil judge for Greater Manchester; lectr then sr lectr in law Poly of the South Bank London 1975–81, instr Inns of Court Sch of Law 1986–90; memb Exec Ctee: Personal Injury Bar Assoc 1994–2003, Assoc of Personal Injury Lawyers 1995–2006 (pres 2005); ADR accredited mediator 2005; *Recreations* sport, food, travel, reading, film and theatre, music, modern art; *Style*— His Hon Judge Gore, QC; ✉ Manchester Civil Justice Centre, 1 Bridge Street West, Manchester M60 9DJ (☏ 0161 240 5000)

GORE BROWNE, Alexandra Victoria (Alex); da of Anthony Giles Spencer Gore Browne (d 2014), and Penelope Anne Courtenay Jones, *née* Thomson; *b* 24 August 1975; *Educ* Francis Holland Sch (scholar), Chelsea Coll of Art, Central St Martins (BA, Queens scholarship); *Career* asst Edina Ronay 1997, freelance work for Donna Karan, Gap and Warner Bros 1998–99, knit conslt for Matthew Williamson, Ghost, Joseph and Alexander McQueen (designed and made showpieces for autumn/winter 2001) 2000, consultancy alex gore browne for dcc Dawson Int 2001, fndr own label knitwear 2001, knit conslt Nina Ricci 2013–14, knit conslt Alexander McQueen 2015–; exhibited: London Designers Exhbn spring/summer 2002 and autumn/winter 2002; New Generation sponsorship by Marks and Spencer and Topshop; visiting lectr Central St Martins 2004–; *Clubs* Chelsea

Arts, Soho House; *Style*— Miss Alex Gore Browne; ✉ Eaton Dovedale Farm, Doveridge, Ashbourne, Derbyshire DE6 5LP (☎ 01889 590420, e-mail alex@alexgorebrowne.com, website www.alexgorebrowne.com)

GORE-BOOTH, Sir Josslyn Henry Robert; 9 Bt (I 1760), of Artarman, Sligo; o s of Sir Angus Josslyn Gore-Booth, 8 Bt (d 1996), and Hon Rosemary Myra, *née* Vane (d 1999), da of 10 Baron Barnard, CMG, OBE, MC, TD; *b* 5 October 1950; *Educ* Eton, Balliol Coll Oxford (BA), INSEAD (MBA); *m* 1980, Jane Mary, da of Hon Sir (James) Roualeyn (Hovell-Thurlow-) Cumming-Bruce (d 2000); 2 da (Mary Georgina b 1985, Caroline Sarah b 1987); *Heir* kinsman, Julian Gore-Booth; *Career* dir Kiln Cotesworth Corporate Capital Fund plc 1993–97; chm Herriot Hospice Homecare 2007–13; patron Sacred Trinity Salford; *Recreations* shooting, cooking; *Style*— Sir Josslyn Gore-Booth, Bt; ✉ Home Farm, Hartforth, Richmond, North Yorkshire DL10 5JS (☎ 01748 826781)

GORELL, 5 Baron (UK 1909); John Picton Gorell Barnes; s of late Hon Ronald Alexander Henry Barnes; *b* 29 July 1959, London; *Educ* Univ of Staffs; *m* 1989, Rosanne, *née* Duncan; 1 s (Hon Oliver), 1 da (Hon Demelza Eleanor); *Career* assoc ptnr Wilson & Ptnrs (now LSH), Gorell Barnes Chartered Surveyors; tstee Northants Community Fndn; Liveryman Worshipful Co of Weavers; MRICS; *Recreations* sailing, gun dogs, Stoke City FC; *Style*— The Lord Gorell; ✉ Fieldways, Ringstead Road, Great Addington, Kettering, Northamptonshire NN14 4BW

GORELL BARNES, Chris; s of Henry Gorell Barnes, and Gillian Caruthers; *b* 31 May 1974, London; *Educ* Bedales, European Business Sch; *Partner* Martha Lane Fox (Baroness Lane Fox); 2 s (Milo, Felix b 2016 (twins)); *Career* entrepreneur and investor; acct mangr Rapier 1998–2000, exec prodr Tsunami Films 2000–02, fndr and exec prodr Method Films 2002–04, dir Eagle Eye Solutions 2007–, fndr and ceo Adjust Your Set 2008–; co-fndr and tstee Blue Marine Fndn 2008–; *Recreations* film and cinema, sailing, travel, walking, diving; *Clubs* Mark's, 5 Hertford Street, Soho House; *Style*— Chris Gorell Barnes, Esq; ✉ Adjust Your Set, 7–10 Charlotte Mews, London W1T 4EF (e-mail alice.shaw-beckett@adjustyourset.com)

GORHAM, Karen Marisa; *see:* Sherborne, Bishop of

GORHAM, Martin Edwin; OBE (2005); s of Clifford Edwin Gorham (d 1983), and Florence Ada, *née* Wright; *b* 18 June 1947, Laindon, Essex; *Educ* Buckhurst Hill Co HS, QMC London (BA); *m* 1, 1968 (m dis 1998), Jean McNaughton, *née* Kerr; m 2, 1998, Sally, *née* Fletcher; 1 step da; *Career* administrative trg NHS 1968–70; dep hosp sec: Scarborough Hosp 1970–72, Doncaster Royal Infirmary 1972–75; hosp administrator: Northern Gen Hosp Sheffield 1975–82, Lodge Moor Hosp Sheffield 1983; head of corp planning Newcastle HA 1983–86, unit gen mangr Norfolk and Norwich Hosps Acute Unit 1986–90, dep regnl gen mangr South West Thames RHA 1990–92, chief exec London Ambulance Serv 1992–96, dir of projects S Thames Regnl Office NHS Exec 1996–98, chief exec Nat Blood Service 1998–2005, chief exec NHS Blood and Transplant (NHSBT) 2005–07, dir Gorham Partnership Ltd 2007–12, dir Douglas-Gorham Partnership Ltd 2008–15; pres European Blood Alliance 2001–07 (hon past pres 2014–), tstee Princess Royal Tst For Carers 2001–06, memb ISBT Fndn Bd 2013–; memb Royal Soc of Medicine; MHSM, Dip HSM; *Recreations* walking, music, reading, gardening, travelling and the arts in general, sport (cricket and skiing); *Style*— Martin Gorham, Esq, OBE; ✉ 20 Grange Road, Bishops Stortford, Hertfordshire CM23 5NQ (☎ 01279 501876, mobile 07711 447265, e-mail martin.gorham@yahoo.co.uk)

GORING, George Ernest; OBE (1992); *b* 19 May 1938; *Educ* Cheltenham, Ecole Hoteliere Lausanne, Westminster Coll; *Career* md and prop The Goring Hotel and Manoir de Lezurec France; chm Master Innholders 1988, pres Reunion des Gastronomes 1988–90; chm London Div BHRCA 1989–92, chm Pride of Britain Hotel Consortium 1997–2000; jt master Mid Surrey Farmers' Draghounds 1993; Hotelier of the Year 1990, membre d'honneur Clefs d'Or; Liveryman Worshipful Co of Distillers; fell Tourism Soc, Master Innholder, FHCIMA; *Recreations* horseracing, hunting, the sea; *Style*— George Goring, Esq, OBE; ✉ The Goring Hotel, Beeston Place, Grosvenor Gardens, London SW1W 0JW

GORING, Lesley Susan; da of Walter Edwin Goring (d 1983), and Peggy Lambert; *b* 23 March 1950; *Educ* Northfields Sch for Girls; *Career* fashion PR conslt; PA to mangr Biba 1965–67, press offr Mr Freedom 1967–72, Lynne Franks PR 1972–75; fndr and proprietor: Goring Public Relations 1975–, Lesley Goring Fashion Show Production 1980–; *Recreations* music, social gatherings, pets; *Style*— Ms Lesley Goring; ✉ Lesley Goring Show Production, 81 Oyster Wharf, 18 Lombard Road, London SW1 3RR (e-mail lesley.goring@btconnect.com)

GORLOV, Alison Mary Haymon; *née* Haymon; da of Mark Haymon (d 1992), of London, and Sylvia Theresa, *née* Rosen (d 1995), of Norwich; *b* 7 September 1951, London; *Educ* Walthamstow Hall Sevenoaks, Coll of Law London; *m* 16 Nov 1975, Peter Gorlov; 4 da (Rebecca b 1 Aug 1982, Sarah b 30 May 1984, Jessica b 2 July 1987, Naomi b 4 May 1992); *Career* admitted slr 1975; appointed Roll A Parly agent 1978; ptnr: Sherwood & Co 1978–90 (asst slr 1975), Winckworth Sherwood (following merger) 1990–; memb Law Soc, memb and past pres Soc of Parly Agents; *Recreations* reading, listening to classical music, writing, walking, history; *Style*— Mrs Alison Gorlov; ✉ Minerva House, 5 Montague Close, London SE1 9BB (☎ 020 7593 5005, e-mail agorlov@wslaw.co.uk)

GORMAN, Prof Neil Thomson; DL (Notts 2007); s of Stewart Gorman (d 1996), and Madge Isabella, *née* Thomson (d 2006); *b* 10 September 1950, Wolverhampton; *Educ* Univ of Liverpool (BVSc, Edgar Golding Prize in Anatomy, Pathology Prize, Clinical Vet Prize), Univ of Cambridge (Horserace Betting Levy Bd PhD Research Fellowship, PhD); *m* 16 Aug 1975, Susan Mary, *née* Smith; 1 da (Felicity Jane b 4 Jan 1981), 1 s (James Muir b 28 Dec 1983); *Career* postdoctoral research assoc MRC Centre Cambridge 1977–81, jr research fell Wolfson Coll Cambridge 1978–81, asst prof Dept of Med Sciences Sch of Vet Med Univ of Florida 1981–84 (concurrently asst prof Dept of Comparative and Experimental Pathology and Dept of Med Microbiology and Immunology Coll of Med), lectr in vet med and oncology Dept of Clinical Vet Med Univ of Cambridge 1984–87, tutor in vet med Christ's Coll Cambridge 1985–87, fell Wolfson Coll Cambridge 1986–87, prof of vet surgery and head Dept of Vet Surgery Glasgow Univ Vet Sch 1987–93, head of research Waltham Centre for Pet Nutrition 1993–97, vice-pres R&D Mars Petcare Europe 1997–99 (European dir of R&D 1997), vice-pres R&D (petcare) Masterfoods Europe 2000–01, global dir (science and technology platforms) Masterfoods Europe 2001–03, vice-chllr Nottingham Trent Univ 2003–14; visiting prof Coll of Vet Med Michigan State Univ 1986, Evelyn Williams visiting prof Faculty of Vet Science Univ of Sydney 1988, adjunct prof Dept of Med Sciences Coll of Vet Med Univ of Florida 1987–93; hon prof Faculty of Vet Med Univ of Glasgow; memb Research Assessment Exercise for Vet Med, Agric and Food Science 2001; delivered numerous lectures and presentations worldwide; RCVS: memb Vet Nursing Ctee 1990–99 (chm 1995–99), memb Cncl 1990–, memb Educn Ctee 1991–93, memb Specialisation and FE Ctee 1995–98, chm Fin and Gen Purposes Ctee 1996–97, memb External Affrs Ctee 1996–, jr vice-pres 1996–97, pres 1997–98, sr vice-pres 1998–99, memb Advsy Ctee 2000–; Br Small Animal Vet Assoc (BSAVA): memb Scientific Ctee 1978–81, memb Educn Ctee 1986–90, memb Congress Ctee 1987–90, jr vice-pres 1990–91, pres 1992–93 (pres-elect 1991–92), sr vice-pres 1993–94; AFRC: memb Visiting Panels to BBSRC Insts 1989 and 1993, memb Agric Research Grant Ctee 1990–93, memb BBSRC Network Gp 1996–; memb Cncl Animal Welfare Cncl 1999–; memb: American Assoc of Immunologists, Br Assoc of Immunology, American Assoc of Vet Immunologists, Br Vet Cancer Soc, American Vet Cancer Soc, European Vet Cancer Soc, NY Acad of Sciences, BVA, BSAVA, Br Soc of Gen Microbiology, American Vet Med Assoc; Wellcome Tst Travel Award 1980, American Assoc of Immunologists Travel Award 1983, WHO Int Cancer Technol Transfer (ICRETT) Fellowship 1986, Diplomate American Coll of Vet Internal Med (Oncology) 1988; involved with: BioCity Nottingham Ltd, Experience Nottinghamshire; memb Ct Univ of Liverpool, hon fell Wolfson Coll Cambridge 2006, hon fell St Edmund's Coll Cambridge 2006; Hon DVMS Univ of Glasgow 2004, Hon DVSc Univ of Liverpool 2006, Hon DVetMed Royal Veterinary Coll Univ of London 2012; FRCVS 1981 (MRCVS 1974), FRSA 2008; *Publications* Advances in Veterinary Immunology and Immunopathology (ed with F J Bourne, 1983, 2 edn 1985), Contemporary Issues on Small Animal Medicine Volume 6 – Oncology (1986), Clinical Veterinary Immunology (with R E W Halliwell, 1988), Basic and Applied Chemotherapy in Veterinary Practice (with J M Dobson, 1992), Canine Medicine and Therapeutics (ed, 1998); also author of book chapters, refereed articles and conf proceedings; *Recreations* opera, golf, sport; *Clubs* Caledonian; *Style*— Prof Neil Gorman, DL; ✉ e-mail neil.gorman@ntu.ac.uk

GORMLEY, Sir Antony Mark David; kt (2014), OBE (1997); s of Arthur John Constantine Gormley (d 1977), of Hampstead, London, and Elspeth, *née* Braüninger; bro of Brendan Gormley, MBE, *qv*; *b* 30 August 1950; *Educ* Ampleforth, Trinity Coll Cambridge (MA), Goldsmiths Coll London (BA), Slade Sch of Fine Art UCL (Higher Dip Fine Art); *m* 14 June 1980, Emelyn Victoria (Vicken), da of Maj (Ian) David Parsons, of Broxbourne, Herts; 2 s (Ivo b 16 March 1982, Guy b 17 June 1985), 1 da (Paloma b 20 July 1987); *Career* artist and sculptor; memb Arts Cncl of England 1998–; tstee Br Museum 2007–; major cmmn incl Angel of the North 1997 (Civic Tst Award 2000); winner Turner Prize 1994, South Bank Art Award 1999, Br D&AD Silver Award for Illustration 2000, Bernard Heilinger Award for Sculpture 2007, Obayashi Prize Japan 2012, Praemium Imperiale Japan 2013; hon fell: Goldsmiths Coll London 1998, RIBA 2001, Jesus Coll Cambridge 2003, Trinity Coll Cambridge 2003; hon doctorate: Univ of Sunderland 1998, UCE 1998, Open Univ 2001, Univ of Cambridge 2003, Univ of Newcastle upon Tyne 2004, Univ of Liverpool 2006, UCL 2006; FRSA 2000, RA 2003; *Solo Exhibitions* most recent incl: Domain Field (The Great Hall Winchester) 2004, Mass and Empathy (Fundacao Gulbenkain Lisbon) 2004, Clearing (White Cube London and Galerie Nordenhake Berlin) 2004, Fai Spazio, Prendi Posto (Poggibonsi part of Arte 'all Arte 9 Italy) 2004, Asian Field (Johnan High School Tokyo) 2004, Unform (Yale Centre for Br Art) 2004, Antony Gormley Display (Tate Britain) 2004, Antony Gormley: New Works (Sean Kelly Gallery NYC) 2005, ANtony Gormley (Glyndebourne Opera House) 2005, Another Place (Crosby Beach Merseyside) 2005, Altered States (Galleria Mimmo Scognamiglio Naples) 2006, You and Nothing (Xavier Hufkens Brussels) 2006, Critical Mass (Museo D'Arte Contemporanea Donna Regina Napoli) 2006, Blind Light (Hayward Gallery) 2007, Spacetime (Mimmo Scognamiglio Arte Contemporanea Milan) 2007, Feeling Material (Deutscher Bundestag Gallery Berlin) 2007, Blind Light (Sean Kelly Gallery NY) 2007, Ataxia (Anna Schwartz Gallery Melbourne) 2007, Firmament (White Cube Mason's Yard London) 2008, Another Singularity (Galleri Andersson Sandstrom Sweden) 2008, Lot (Castle Cornet Guernsey) 2008, Drawings 1981–2001 (Galerie Thaddaeus Ropac Paris) 2008, Clay and the Collective Body (Helsinki) 2009, One and Other (fourth plinth commission Trafalgar Square) 2009, Domain Field (Garage Centre for Contemporary Culture Moscow) 2009, Breathing Room II (Sean Kelly Gallery NY) 2010, Firmament IV (Anna Schwartz Gallery Sydney) 2010, Critical Mass (De La Warr Pavillion Bexhill-on-Sea) 2010, Test Sites (White Cube Mason's Yard London) 2010, Event Horizon (Madison Sq Art NY) 2010, Memes (Melbourne) 2011, Flare II (Salisbury Cathedral) 2011, For the Time Being (Galerie Thaddaeus Ropac Paris) 2011, Two States (Harewood House Yorks) 2011, Still Standing (State Hermitage Museum St Petersburg) 2011, Vessel (Galleria Continua San Gimignano Italy) 2012, Still Being (CCBB Sao Paulo) 2012, according to a given mean (Xavier Hufkens Brussels) 2013, Meter (Galerie Thaddaeus Ropac Salzburg) 2013, States and Conditions (White Cube Hong Kong) 2014, Expansion Field (ZPK Berne Switzerland) 2014, Second Body (Galerie Thaddaeus Ropac Paris) 2015, Human (Forte di Belvedere Florence Italy) 2015, Land (various UK sites) 2015, Event Horizon (Hong Kong) 2015–16, Host (Galleria Continua Beijing) 2016, Construct (Sean Kelly Gallery) 2016, Cast (Alan Cristea Gallery London) 2016; *Group Exhibitions* Objects and Sculpture (ICA London) 1981, Br Sculpture of the 20th Century (Whitechapel Art Gallery London) 1981, Venice Biennale 1982 and 1986, Biennale de São Paulo 1983, Int Survey MOMA NY 1984, British Art Now: A Subjective View (touring exhbn Japan) 1990–91, Inheritance and Transformation (Irish MOMA Dublin) 1991, Natural Order (Tate Gallery Liverpool) 1992, Images of Man (Isetan Museum of Art, Tokyo/Daimura Museum, Umeda-Osaka/Hiroshima City Museum of Contemporary Art) 1992, The Human Factor: Figurative Sculpture Reconsidered (Albuquerque Museum) 1993, HA HA: Contemporary British Art in an 18th Century Garden (Killerton Park) 1993, The Fujisankei Biennale (Hakone Open-Air Museum) 1993, From Beyond the Pale: Part One (Irish MOMA Dublin) 1994, Sculptors' Drawings from the Weltkunst Collection (Tate Gallery London) 1994, Contemporary British Art in Print (Scot Nat Gallery of Modern Art Edinburgh and Yale Center for Br Art New Haven) 1995, Glaube, Hoffnung, Liebe und Tod (Kunsthalle Vienna) 1995, Un Siècle de Sculpture Anglaise (Jeu de Paume Paris) 1996, Betong (Konsthall Malmö) 1996, A Ilha Do Tesouro (Centro de Arte Moderna Jose de Azeredo Perdigao Lisbon) 1997, L'Empreinte (Centre Georges Pompidou Paris) 1997, Material Culture: The Object in British Art of the 1980's and 90's (Hayward Gallery) 1997, Arte Urbana (Expo '98 Lisbon) 1998, Presence: Figurative Art at the End of the Century (Tate Gallery Liverpool) 1999, Trialogo Rome 2000, Tate Liverpool 2004, Millennium Galls Sheffield 2005, Figure/Sculpture Vienna 2005, Henry Moore – Epoch und Echo (Künzelsau Germany) 2005, Zero Degrees (Sadler's Wells) 2005, Space: Now & Then (Funamend Fndn Tilburg) 2005, to the Human Future (Mito Contemporary Art Center Japan) 2006, Asian Field (Sydney Biennale) 2006, 60 Years of Sculpture (Arts Cnsl Collection Yorks Sculpture Park) 2006, Turner Prize: A Retrospective (Tate Britain) 2007, Reflection (Pinchuk Art Centre Kiev) 2007, Fourth Plinth Proposals (Nat Gallery) 2008, Gravity: Ernesto Esposito Collection (Spain) 2008, Genesis – The Art of Creation (Bern) 2008, Locked In (Luxembourg) 2008, History in the Making (Mori Art Museum Tokyo) 2008, En Perspective (Musée des Beaux-Arts de Caen) 2008, Kivik Art 08 (Kivik Art Centre Sweden) 2008, Statuephilia (Br Museum) 2008, Earth: Art of a Changing World (Royal Acad) 2009), Visceral Bodies (Vancouver Art Gallery) 2010, XIV International Sculpture Biennale of Carrara 2010, A Serpentine Gesture and Other Prophecies (49 Nord 6 Est Franc Lorraine Metz) 2011, TRA: Edge of Becoming (Palazzo Fortuny Venice) 2011, Summer Exhibition (Royal Acad) 2011, The Last Days of Pompeii (Getty Villa California) 2012, Unlimited Bodies (Paris 2012), Uncommon Ground (UK, touring 2013), Body & Void: Echoes of Henry Moore (Perry Green UK 2014), A Walk Through British Art (Tate Britain) 2015, Tuileries 2015 (Jardin des Tuileries Paris) 2015, Scape 8: New Intimacies (Christchurch New Zealand) 2015, Found (The Foundling Museum London) 2016; *Books, Publications and Catalogues* most recent incl: Antony Gormley Drawing (2002), Antony Gormley: Workbooks 1 1977–1992 (2002), Antony Gormley (2002), Asian Field (2003), Antony Gormley: Standing Matter (2003), Domain Field (2003), Making Space (2004), Domain Field at Winchester: Antony Gormley (2004), Broken Column (2004), Mass and Empathy (2004), Antony Gormley: Inside Australia (2005), Antony Gormley: Asian Field (2005), Asian Field: Makers and Made (2006), Fai Spazio Prendi Posto/Making Space Taking Place (2006), Antony Gormley: Breathing Room (2006), Intersezioni 2: Time Horizon (2006), Antony Gormley (2007), Antony Gormley: Blind Light (2007), Antony Gormley: Bodies in Space (2007), Acts, States, Times, Perspectives (2008), Between You and Me (2008), Antony Gormley (2009), Antony Gormley – Another

G

Singularity (2009), Gormley on Guernsey (2009), Ataxia II (2009), Antony Gormley (2009), AG – Antony Gormley (2010), Aperture (2010), Exposure (2010), One and Other (2010), Event Horizon (2010), Drawing Space (2010), Memes (2011), For the Time Being (2011), Horizon Field (2011), Still Standing (2011), Horizon Field Hamburg (2012), Corpos Presentes Still Being (2012), Vessel (2012), According to a Given Mean (2013), Firmament and Other Forms (2013), Model (2013), Meter (2013), States and Conditions Hong Kong (2014), Expansion Field (2014), Room (2014), Second Body (2015), Human (2015), Antony Gormley On Sculpture (2015), Event Horizon Hong Kong (2016), Land (2016); *Recreations* sailing, skiing, walking; *Style—* Sir Antony Gormley, OBE, RA; ✉ e-mail admin-work@antonygormley.com

GORMLEY, Sir (Paul) Brendan; KCMG (2014), MBE (2001); s of Arthur John Constantine Gormley (d 1977), and Elspeth, *née* Brauninger; bro of Antony Gormley, OBE, *qv*; *b* 2 September 1947, London; *Educ* Strasbourg Univ, Trinity Coll Cambridge (MA); *m* 14 Sept 1974, Sally Henderson; 2 s (Thomas J b 4 April 1977, Titus D b 12 July 1981), 1 da (Chloe A b 22 Feb 1979); *Career* former social worker and monk; Oxfam: country dir Niger 1976–78, regnl dir W Africa 1978–83, country dir Egypt 1983–85, positions at Oxfam HQ 1985–2000, Africa dir 1991–2000; ceo DEC 2000–12, lead conslt PBG Consulting 2012–; lead expert RHEG 2012–, chair CDAC Network 2013–, chair INGO Accountability Charter co 2014–; tstee: Noel Buxton Tst, One World Media, Age Int; *Recreations* sailing, golf; *Style—* Sir Brendan Gormley, KCMG, MBE; ✉ Foxburrow Barn, Hailey, Witney OX29 9UH (☎ 01993 773592, e-mail gormley.dec@btinternet.com)

GORNA, Christina; da of John Gorna, of Hale, Cheshire, and Muriel Theresa Gorna; *b* 19 February 1937; *Educ* The Hollies Convent, Loreto Convent Llandudno, Univ of Manchester (LLB), Univ of Neuchâtel (Dip Swiss and Int Law), Sorbonne (Dip French Civilisation), Br Cncl scholar; *m* 6 July 1963, Ian Davies (d 1996), s of Reginald Beresford Davies, of Timperly, Cheshire; 1 da (Samantha Jane b 14 Jan 1964), 1 s (Caspar Dominick John b 11 May 1966); *Career* barr, writer, broadcaster and columnist; called to the Bar Middle Temple 1960 (Harmsworth Scholar); sr lectr Coventry Univ 1973–79, in practice specialising in criminal, family, professional negligence, licensing and media law 1980–, former head Castle Chambers Exeter, ldr Cathedral Chambers Exeter; regulator: ABIA, security industry 2003–; numerous TV and radio appearances incl: Question Time, Any Questions?, Woman's Hour, Kilroy, The Time The Place, Great Expectations, Behind the Headlines, Central Weekend, Advice Shop, The Verdict, Esther – You Are What You Wear, Points of Law, Ready Steady Cook; presenter: Careering Ahead, Experts Exported, The Flying Brief (TV series), Check it Out (consumer series); regular contrib: GMTV, UK Living, Westcountry TV, Viva Radio, Talk Radio, London Talk Radio, Gemini Radio, Channel 1, TLC, The Right Thing, Radio 5 Live, BBC Radio Sussex, Liberty Radio (legal corr), BBC Radio London (also legal corr); occasional contrib five TV, Great Lives 'Vivien Leigh' (BBC Radio 4); judge Sex in Court (series, E4), The Flying Brief (series, Channel 4), Real Women 2012; profile writer, gossip columnist, book, theatre and art reviewer, public speaker, debater and fashion model; columnist The Universe; profiled in City Magazine 1998 and Express Echo 1999; memb: SW Rent Assessment Tbnl 1999, Bd Amazonia (radical women's theatre gp) 2002–, Advsy Body Women in Prison, Prison Reform Tst, Sub-Ctee ABIA, London Ladies Ctee Cancer Research Campaign, Western Circuit, 300 Gp, Charter 88, Assoc of Women Barristers, Thomas More Soc, Assoc of Catholic Lawyers, Media Soc, Church Cncl St Michael's English Church Beaulieu-sur-Mer Cote d'Azur; hon pres Network West, chair Network Far West; lady ambass Lady Magazine; FRSA 1994; *Books* Company Law, Leading Cases on Company Law, Questions and Answers on Company Law, Lies and Misdemeanours, Seize the Day (contrib); *Recreations* reading, swimming, performing and visual arts, art collecting, visiting galleries, writing, painting, clothes (especially hats); reading and writing poetry; *Clubs* Groucho, Network; *Style—* Miss Christina Gorna; ✉ Chelsea Chambers, 10A Kempsford Gardens, London SW5 9LH (☎ 020 7370 0434); 4 Paper Buildings, Temple, London EC4Y 7EX (☎ 020 7353 3366); clerk: Jan Wood (☎ 01392 204259); agent: Jacque Evans (☎ 020 8699 1202, mobile 07775 565101)

GORNALL, Alastair Charles; s of J I K Gornall, of Odiham, Hants, and E C Gornall, *née* Leighton; *b* 6 June 1956; *Educ* Stowe, RMA Sandhurst (RAF flying scholarship); *m* 1986, Sarah, *née* McCall; 3 c; *Career* Lt 17/21 Lancers; Business Week International NY 1979–81; md: Scope Communications 1981–90, Consolidated Communications Management Ltd 1990–2001, Madsen Gornall Ashe 2002–04; chief exec Reed Exhibitions 2004–; *Recreations* boating; *Clubs* Cavalry and Guards', Annabel's; *Style—* Alastair Gornall, Esq; ✉ Reed Exhibitions Ltd, Oriel House, 26 The Quadrant, Richmond, Surrey TW9 1DL

GORNICK, Naomi; da of Abraham Harris (d 1989), and Rachel Harris (d 1992); *Educ* Montreal Canada, Willesden Sch of Art, PCL; *m* Bruce Gornick; 1 s (Simon), 1 da (Lisa); *Career* design mgmnt conslt; assoc prof of design mgmnt; dir MA Design Strategy and Innovation Brunel Univ 1993–; advsr: Middlesex Univ, De Montfort Univ, industrial clients incl Raychem, London Underground; ed Debrett's Interior Design Collection 1988 and 1989; Chartered Soc of Designers: memb Cncl 1992–, vice-pres 1986–89, fndr chm Design Mgmnt Gp 1981–86; course ldr RCA 1989–91; memb Steering Ctee on Design Mgmnt Courses CNAA, memb Bd of Tstees Worldesign Fndn USA 1993–, chm Design Selection Ctees Design Cncl, panel judge for Design Centre Awards 1989; FCSD, FRSA; *Clubs* Chelsea Arts; *Style—* Naomi Gornick

GORRINGE, Christopher John; CBE (1999); s of Maurice Sydney William Gorringe (d 1981), and Hilda Joyce, *née* Walker (d 2012); *b* 13 December 1945, Walton-on-Thames, Surrey; *Educ* Bradfield, RAC Cirencester; *m* 17 April 1976, Jennifer Mary, da of Roger and Mary Chamberlain; 2 da (Kim b 13 April 1978, Anna b 24 Feb 1981); *Career* asst land agent Iveagh Tstees Ltd (Guinness Family) 1968–73, chief exec All Eng Lawn Tennis and Croquet Club Wimbledon 1983–2005 (asst sec 1973–79, sec 1979–83); pres Ind Schs Tennis Assoc 2008; hon fell Univ of Roehampton 1998; ARICS 1971; *Publications* Holding Court (2009); *Recreations* lawn tennis, golf; *Clubs* All England Lawn Tennis, Queen's, Jesters, Int LTC of GB, St George's Hill Lawn Tennis, Rye Lawn Tennis (pres); *Style—* Christopher Gorringe, Esq, CBE

GORROD, Prof John William; s of Ernest Lionel Gorrod (d 1981), and Caroline Rebecca, *née* Richardson (d 1990); *b* 11 October 1931; *Educ* Univ of London (DSc, PhD), Chelsea Coll London (Dip), Brunel Coll of Advanced Technol (HNC); *m* 3 April 1954, Doreen Mary (d 2012), da of George Douglas Collins (d 1992); 1 da (Julia b 8 June 1959), 2 s (Simon b 5 April 1962, Nicholas b 16 July 1966); *Career* res fell Dept of Biochemistry Univ of Bari Italy 1964, res fell Royal Cmmn for the Exhibition of 1851 1965–67, lectr in biopharmacy Chelsea Coll London 1968–80 (reader 1980–84), prof of biopharmacy and head Chelsea Dept of Pharmacy KCL 1984–89, res prof Faculty of Life Sciences KCL 1990–97 (head of Div of Health Sciences 1988–90), prof emeritus Univ of London 1997–, prof of toxicology Univ of Essex 1997–; memb Canada Research Chairs Program Coll of Reviewers 2001–; pres Int Soc for the Study of Xenobiotics (ISSX) 2000–01; govr Ipswich Hosp Tst 2010–14; Silver Galen medal Comenius Univ Bratislava 2012; memb: Assoc for Res in Indoor Air 1989, Air Tport Users' Ctee CAA 1990–92, Assocs for Res in Substances of Enjoyment 1990–97, Cncl Indoor Air Int 1990–98; cncllr Polstead Parish Cncl 1999–2003; corresponding memb German Pharmaceutical Soc 1985; hon fell: Pan/Hellenic Pharmaceutical Soc 1987, Turkish Pharmaceutical Assoc 1988, Bohemslovaca Pharmaceutical Soc 1991, Sch of Pharmacy Univ of London 2002; FRSC 1980, Hon MRPharmS 1982, FRCPath 1984, FKC 1996, CBiol, FRSB; *Books* Drug Metabolism in Man (1978), Drug Toxicity (1979), Testing for Toxicity (1981), Biological Oxidation of Nitrogen in Organic Molecules (1985), Biological Oxidation of Nitrogen (1978), Metabolism of Xenobiotics (1988), Development of Drugs and Modern Medicines (1986), Molecular Basis of Human Disease (1989), Molecular Basis of Neurological Disorders and Their Treatment (1991), Nicotine and Related Tobacco Alkaloids: absorption, distribution, metabolism and excretion (1993), Analytical Determination of Nicotine and Related Compounds and Their Metabolites (ed, with Peyton Jacob III, 1999); *Recreations* reading travel and biographies; *Clubs* Athenaeum; *Style—* Prof John Gorrod; ✉ The Rest Orchard, Polstead Heath, Suffolk CO6 5BG (☎ 01787 211752); Biological Sciences, University of Essex, Wivenhoe Park, Essex CO4 3SQ (e-mail jgorr@essex.ac.uk)

GORST, Brenda Anne; *see:* Brenda Coleman

GORTY, Peter; s of Nathan Gorty, and Bella, *née* Lancet; *b* 3 November 1944; *Educ* Owens Sch Islington, LSE (LLB); *m* 20 Sept 1970, Mariana; 1 s (Andrew), 1 da (Helen); *Career* articled clerk Gilbert Samuel & Co 1967–69, asst slr Withers 1969–70, ptnr specialising in banking and energy law Nabarro Nathanson 1972– (asst slr 1970–72); *Recreations* all sports, reading, theatre, architecture; *Style—* Peter Gorty, Esq; ✉ Nabarro Nathanson, 50 Stratton Street, London W1X 5NX (☎ 020 7493 9933, fax 020 7629 7900)

GOSCHEN, 4 Viscount (UK 1900); Giles John Harry Goschen; s of 3 Viscount Goschen, KBE (d 1977), and his 2 w Alvin, *née* England; *b* 16 November 1965; *m* 23 Feb 1991, Sarah, yr da of late A G Horsnail, of Clophill, Beds; 2 da (Hon Annabel Sophie Moyana b 7 July 1999, Hon Auriel Elizabeth Caroline b 9 Jan 2004), 1 s (Hon Alexander John Edward b 5 Oct 2001); *Heir* s, Hon Alexander Goschen; *Career* a Lord in Waiting to HM the Queen 1992–94; Parly under sec of state Dept of Tport 1994–97; with Investment Banking Div Deutsche Bank AG (formerly Deutsche Morgan Grenfell) 1997–2000, dir Barchester Advisory Ltd 2000–02, Korn/Ferry Int 2005–; *Style—* The Viscount Goschen; ✉ House of Lords, London SW1A 0PW

GOSDEN, John Harry Martin; s of John Montague Gosden (d 1967), and Peggie Gosden; *b* 30 March 1951; *Educ* Eastbourne Coll, Emmanuel Coll Cambridge (MA, Athletics blue); *m* 1982, Rachel Dene Serena Hood; 2 s (Sebastian b 1983, Thaddeus b 1995), 2 da (Serena b 1985, Theodora b 1990); *Career* racehorse trainer; asst trainer: Sir Noel Murless 1974–76, Dr Vincent O'Brien 1976–77; trainer: USA 1979–88, England 1989–; achievements as trainer USA: among top ten 1982–88, leading trainer Calif meets, 8 state champions, 3 Eclipse Award winners; achievements as trainer UK: trained over 2400 winners in UK, trained fastest 1000 winners in UK (incl over 200 Gp race winners), trained 4 St Leger winners (Shantou 1996, Lucarno 2007, Arctic Cosmos 2010, Masked Marvel 2011), Derby winner (Benny the Dip) 1997, Br 1000 Guineas winner (Lahan) 2000, French 1000 Guineas (Zenda and Valentine Waltz), Breeders Cup Classic winner (Raven's Pass) 2008, Arlington Million winner (Debussy) 2010, Dubai Sheema Classic winner (Dar Re Mi) 2010, Irish St Leger winner (Duncan) 2011, Br King George and Queen Elizabeth Diamond Stakes winner (Nathaniel) 2011, Eclipse Stakes winner (Nathaniel) 2012, Irish Oaks winner (Great Heavens) 2012, Coronation Stakes winner (Fallen For You) 2012, Irish 2000 Guineas (Kingman) 2014, St James's Palace Stakes (Kingman) 2014, Sussex Stakes (Kingman) 2014, Prix Jacques le Marois (Kingman) 2014, Prince of Wales Stakes (The Fugue) 2014, Epsom Oaks (Taghrooda) 2014, King George & Queen Elizabeth II Stakes (Taghrooda) 2014, Epsom Derby, Prix L'Arc de Triomph, Irish Champion Stakes and Eclipse (Golden Horn) 2015, Prix de Diane (Star of Seville) 2015; Champion Trainer Flat 2012 and 2015 (record prize money), Top Trainer Royal Ascot 2012, Champion Miler (Kingman) 2014, Champion 3-year-old Filly (Taghrooda) 2014, Champion 3-year-old colt (Golden Horn) 2015; Sussex Martlets schoolboy cricketer 1967–68, memb Blackheath Rugby Club 1969–70, memb Br under 23 rowing squad 1973; *Recreations* opera, skiing, polo, environmental issues; *Style—* John H M Gosden, Esq; ✉ Clarehaven Stables, Bury Road, Newmarket, Suffolk CB8 7BY (☎ 01638 565400, fax 01638 565401, e-mail jhmg@johngosden.com)

GOSLING, Christopher Spencer; DL (Essex 1995); *b* 22 August 1942; *Educ* Eton, RAC Cirencester; *m* 24 June 1967, Juliet Mary, *née* Stanton; 2 da (Venetia Rachel b 2 Oct 1969, Larissa Catherine b 9 Dec 1971), 1 s (Alexander Edward Spencer b 1 July 1975); *Career* farmer; family partnership 1964–, sole proprietor 1979–; conslt land agent and rural estate mgmnt Strutt & Parker Chelmsford 1964–98, ret; Country Landowners' Assoc: memb Cncl 1982–88, chm Essex Branch 1983–86, memb Agricultural & Land Use Sub-Ctee 1985–88; memb Cncl Essex Agricultural Soc (Essex Show) 1981–99 (chm 1991–95), steward Int Pavilion Royal Show 1987–92; chm Essex Branch Game Conservancy Cncl 1983–86; memb: British Field Sports Soc, Essex Agric Assoc; High Sheriff Essex 1993–94; *Recreations* shooting, stalking, tennis, windsurfing, skiing, travel, golf; *Clubs* Beefsteak, Essex, Hintlesham Golf; *Style—* Christopher Gosling, Esq, DL; ✉ Byham Hall, Great Maplestead, Halstead, Essex CO9 3AR (☎ 01787 460134, fax 01787 461463, e-mail chrisgos@byhamhall.co.uk)

GOSLING, His Hon Judge Jonathan Vincent Ronald; *Career* called to the Bar 1980; asst recorder then recorder 2000, circuit judge (Midland Circuit) 2009–; *Style—* His Hon Judge Gosling; ✉ Derby Combined Court, Morledge, Derby DE1 2XE

GOSLING, Paula Louise (Mrs John Hare); da of A Paul Osius (d 1986), and Sylvie, *née* Van Slembrouck (d 1986); *b* 12 October 1939; *Educ* Mackenzie HS, Wayne State Univ (BA); *m* 1, 1968 (m dis 1979), Christopher Gosling, s of Thomas Gosling; 2 da (Abigail Judith b 1970, Emily Elizabeth b 1972); m 2, 1981, John Anthony Hare, s of John Charles Hare; *Career* copywriter: Campbell-Ewald USA 1962–64, C Mitchell & Co London 1964–67, Pritchard-Wood London 1967–68, David Williams Ltd London 1968–70; copy conslt: C Mitchell & Co 1970–72, ATA Advertising Bristol 1977–79; crime writer 1979–; Arts Achievement Award Wayne State Univ 1994; Crime Writers' Assoc: memb Ctee 1984–90, chm 1988–89; memb: Soc of Authors, ALCS, Mensa; *Books* A Running Duck (1978, US title Fair Game, John Creasey Meml Award for Best First Crime Novel 1978, made into film for Japanese TV and into film Cobra and film Fair Game 1995), The Zero Trap (1979), Mind's Eye (as Ainslie Skinner 1980, US title The Harrowing), Loser's Blues (1980, US title Solo Blues), The Woman in Red (1983), Monkey Puzzle (1985, Gold Dagger Award for Best Crime Novel 1986), The Wychford Murders (1987), Hoodwink (1988), Backlash (1989), Death Penalties (1991), The Body in Blackwater Bay (1992), A Few Dying Words (1993), The Dead of Winter (1995), Death and Shadows (1999), Underneath Every Stone (2000), Ricochet (2002), Tears of the Dragon (2004); author of numerous serials and short stories incl Mr Felix (nominated Best Short Story MWA 1987); *Recreations* needlework, kite-flying; *Style—* Ms Paula Gosling; ✉ c/o Greene and Heaton Ltd, 37 Goldhawk Road, London W12 8QQ (☎ 020 8749 0315, fax 020 8749 0318)

GOSLING, Timothy Job; s of Prof Raymond George Gosling, and Mary Warren Job; *b* 23 August 1966, Kingston, Jamaica; *Educ* St Edmunds Sch Canterbury, Central Sch of Art and Design, Central St Martins (BA); *Career* asst designer for Miss Saigon and Starlight Express NY tours 1987–89, dir and ptnr David Linley's 1989–2005, fndr Gosling (designer of furniture and bespoke interiors) 2005–; memb British Interior Design Assoc 1999–; Freeman City of London, Liveryman Worshipful Co of Furniture Makers; *Publications* Gosling Classic Design for Contemporary Interiors (2009), London Secrets, A Draughtman's Guide (2012), Classic Contemporary: The DNA of Furniture Design (2015); *Clubs* Athenaeum (memb Arts Ctee), Beefsteak; *Style—* Timothy Gosling, Esq; ✉ Sycamore House, 4 Old Town, London SW4 0JY (☎ 020 7498 8335, e-mail tim@tgosling.com)

GOSPER, Brett; s of Richard Kevan Gosper, of Melbourne, Aust, and Jillian Mary, *née* Galwey (d 1981); *b* 21 June 1959; *Educ* Scotch Coll Melbourne, Monash Univ Melbourne (BA); *m* 1, 1989 (m dis), Laurence, *née* Albes; 1 s (Jonathan Kevan Thomas b 24 June 1990); m 2, 1998, Elizabeth, *née* Bernsen; 1 da (Ella Jillian b 22 June 1999), 1 s (Matt

William Svend b 15 March 2001); *Career* advtg exec; account exec Ogilvy & Mather Melbourne 1981–82, gp account dir Ogilvy & Mather Paris 1982–89, dir rising to dep md BDDP Paris 1989–93, fndr md BDDP Frankfurt 1993–94, chm and chief exec Euro RSCG Wnek Gosper London 1994–2003, memb Bd Euro RSCG Worldwide 1996–2003, memb Bd Media Planning Worldwide 1998–2003, chief exec McCann-Erickson NY 2003–04, pres NY Gp TWBA 2004–; *Recreations* rugby; *Clubs* Melbourne Rugby Union (Best Club Player Award 1978, 1979 and 1980, rep Victoria, Queensland and Australia), Racing Club de France (memb rugby team 1981–90, Best Club Player Award 1987, rep French Barbarians v All Blacks 1986), MCC (life memb), Castel (Paris), Melbourne Cricket; *Style*— Brett Gosper, Esq

GOSS, Hon Mr Justice; Sir James Richard William Goss; kt (2014), QC (1997); s of His Hon Judge W A B Goss (d 1963); *b* 12 May 1953; *Educ* Charterhouse, UC Durham (BA); *m* 1982, Dawna Elizabeth, *née* Davies; 2 s, 3 da; *Career* called to the Bar Inner Temple 1975 (bencher 2000); recorder 1994–2009, circuit judge (North Eastern Circuit) 2009–11, sr circuit judge and hon recorder Newcastle upon Tyne 2011–14, judge of the High Court of Justice (Queen's Bench Div) 2014–; *Style*— The Hon Mr Justice Goss; ✉ Royal Courts of Justice, Strand, London WC2A 2LL

GOSWAMI, Prof Usha Claire; *b* 21 February 1960; *Educ* St John's Coll Oxford (BA, sr scholarship, DPhil), Inst of Educn Univ of London (PGCE); *Career* pt/t lectr in psychology Univ of Warwick 1985, actg fell for psychology St John's Coll Oxford 1985, lectr in psychology St John's Coll and Merton Coll Oxford 1986 and 1988–89, jr research fell Merton Coll Oxford 1986–87 and 1988–89, Harkness fell Univ of Illinois 1987–88, univ lectr in experimental psychology Univ of Cambridge 1990–97, prof of cognitive developmental psychology Inst of Child Health and fell Inst of Cognitive Neuroscience UCL 1997–2002, prof of educn Univ of Cambridge 2002–10, prof of cognitive developmental neuroscience Univ of Cambridge 2010–; fell St John's Coll Cambridge 1990–; Faculty of Educn Univ of Cambridge: memb Faculty Bd, memb Strategy Ctee, memb Research Ctee; memb: Research Steering Ctee Dept of Human Communication Sciences UCL, Bd Faculty of Social and Political Sciences Univ of Cambridge, Appointments Ctees UCL, Birkbeck Coll London, Inst of Psychology KCL and Univ of Cambridge; external examiner: Univ of Oxford, Univ of Kent at Canterbury, Univ of Burgundy, Univ of Edinburgh, Univ of Hong Kong, Univ of Newcastle, Univ of Essex; advsr Nat Curriculum Cncl for the Teaching of English 1992, conslt Nat Literacy Project 1997; UK memb Managing Ctee European Concerted Action on Learning Disorders as a Barrier to Human Devpt COST A8 1995–2000; memb: Research Grants Bd ESRC 1998–2000, Neurosciences and Mental Health Bd MRC 1999–2003, Dir's Advsy Gp Social, Genetic and Developmental Psychiatry Research Centre KCL 2000–05, Cross-Bd Gp MRC 2001–03, Sr Advsy Bd Nat Center for Developmental Science in the Public Interest Cornell Univ; ed Applied Psycholinguistics, ed Developmental Science (Fast Track), reviewer for numerous pubns; memb Editorial Bd: Jl of Child Psychology and Psychiatry, Jl of Experimental Child Psychology, Cognitive Development, Dyslexia, Reading Research Quarterly, Reading & Writing, Psychological Bulletin, Applied Psycholiguistics; reviewer: Wellcome Tst, MRC, ESRC, Nuffield Fndn, Social Sciences and Humanities Research Cncl of Canada, Australian Research Cncl; chosen speaker Br Psychology Soc Millennium Event 2001, Broadbent Lecture Br Psychology Soc Annual Conf 2003, delivered numerous invited addresses at confs and symposia worldwide; Nat Acad of Educn Spencer Fellowship 1990–92, Alexander von Humboldt Research Fellowship 1995–96, Leverhulme Major Research Fellowship 2009–11; first runner-up American Psychology Assoc Outstanding Dissertation of the Year Award 1989, Br Psychology Soc Spearman Medal 1992, Norman Geschwind-Rodin Prize 1992; *Publications* Phonological Skills and Learning to Read (with P E Bryant, 1990), Analogical Reasoning in Children (1992), Cognition in Children (1998), Blackwells Handbook of Childhood Cognitive Development (ed, 2002, 2 edn 2010), Cognitive Development: The Learning Brain (2008); also author of numerous jl articles and book chapters; *Style*— Prof Usha Goswami; ✉ Department of Experimental Psychology, University of Cambridge, Downing Street, Cambridge CB2 3EB (☎ 01223 767635, fax 01223 333564)

GOTCH, Prof Frances Margaret; *née* Gore; da of Geoffrey Gore (d 1994), and Queenie, *née* Rawlings (d 1988); *b* 29 January 1943, London; *Educ* Univ of Oxford (MSc, DPhil); *m* 1 Feb 1964, Michael Gotch, s of Leonard Gotch; 3 da (Lisa Helen b 1966 d 2003, Emma Sophie b 1969, Sharon Mandy (adopted 1973) b 1960); *Career* formerly research scientist Nuffield Dept of Med then univ lectr Inst of Molecular Med Oxford, currently prof and head Dept of Immunology Imperial Coll Chelsea & Westminster Hosp London; author of over 200 pubns in peer reviewed jls since 1970; FRCPath; *Recreations* reading, painting, keep-fit; *Style*— Prof Frances Gotch; ✉ Department of Immunology, Imperial College of Science, Technology & Medicine, Chelsea & Westminster Hospital, 369 Fulham Road, London SW10 9NH (☎ 020 3315 8257, fax 020 3315 5997, e-mail f.gotch@imperial.ac.uk)

GOTO, Prof John; *b* 1949, Stockport; *Educ* Berks Coll of Art, St Martin's Sch of Art (BA); *Career* artist; pt/t lectr: Camberwell Sch of Art 1979–81, Poly of Central London 1979–87, Oxford Brookes Univ 1979–99, Ruskin Sch of Drawing & Fine Art Univ of Oxford 1987, Univ of Derby 2000–03; prof of fine art Univ of Derby 2003–13 emeritus prof of Fine Art 2014–; visiting lectr to numerous art colls since 1979; Br Cncl scholar: Paris 1977, Prague 1978; artist fell Girton Coll Cambridge 1988–89, vice-chm Visual Arts Panel Southern Arts Assoc 1989–90; *Solo Exhibitions* incl: Goto Photographs 1971–81 (The Photographer's Gallery) 1981, Goto Photographs 1975–83 (PPS Galerie Gundlac Hamburg) 1983, ULUV Gallery Prague (Br Cncl Exhibition) 1983, Moravian Gallery Bruno Czechoslovakia 1983 (touring Czechoslovakia and Spain 1983–85), Sites of Passage (Fischer Fine Art and Ashmolean Museum Oxford) 1986 and 1988, Terezin (Cambridge Darkroom, John Hansard Gallery Southampton, Cornerhouse Manchester and Raab Galerie Berlin) 1988–89, The Atomic Yard (Kettle's Yard Cambridge and Raab Gallery) 1993, The Scar (Benjamin Rhodes Gallery London, Manchester City Galleries and John Hansard Gallery Univ of Southampton) 1993, John Goto (touring Russia) 1994–95, The Framers' Collection (Portfolio Gallery Edinburgh) 1997, The Commissar of Space (MOMA Oxford) 1998, NPG2000 Exhibition of Cmmn Artist (Nat Portrait Gallery London) 1999, Capital Arcade (Korea, Sweden and UK tour) 1999 and 2000, High Summer (London, Edinburgh, Netherlands, Oporto and UK tour) 2001–02, Loss of Face (Tate Britain) 2002–03, Ukadia (Djanogly Art Gallery) 2003 (also at Galeria f5.6 Munich and Gallery On Seoul 2005), John Goto's New World Circus (nat tour) 2006–07 and (tour Finland to Poland) 2008–09, Floodscapes (Gallery On Seoul and UK tour) 2006–08, Dance to the Muzik of Time (Dominique Fiat Gallery Paris) 2008, Dance to the Muzik of Time (Gallery On Seoul) 2009, Mosaic (Edinburgh Printmakers Gallery) 2011, Jazz (Gallery On Seoul) 2011, Dreams of Jelly Roll (Freud Museum London) 2012, Sweet Augmentations (Galerie Dominique Fiat Paris) 2012–13, 1977: Lewisham and Belleville (Art Jericho Oxford) 2013, Three Series by John Goto (Gallery On, Seoul Korea) 2014, Two Days at Oxford (OFS Gallery Oxford) 2016; *Group Exhibitions* incl: Painting/Photography (Richard DeMarco Gallery) Edinburgh 1986, Next/Tomorrow (Kettle's Yard Cambridge) 1986, Fifteen Studios (MOMA Oxford) 1986, Romantic Visions (Camden Arts Centre) 1988, Blasphemies Ecstasies & Cries (Serpentine Gallery) 1989, Photographic Art in Britain 1945–89 (Barbican), Metamorphosis (Raab Gallery Millbank) 1989, After Auschwitz: Responses to the Holocaust in Contemporary Art (Royal Festival Hall and UK tour) 1995–96, Trade (Winterthur, Rotterdam) 2001–02, Sight Seeing (Graz) 2003, Collage (Bloomberg Space London) 2004, Identity_Factories (Mir Gallery Bucharest) 2005, John Goto's New World Circus (Lodz Art Centre Poland and Voipaala Arts Centre Finland) 2008, High Summer (Haus de Fotografie Dr Robert-Gerlich-Museum Burghausen) 2009, F5.6 Special Edition (Galerie F5.6 Munich) 2009, Royal Scottish Acad 184th Annual Exhibition (invited artist) 2010, Elders Project Elsewhere Idyll and Friction in the Landscape (Sint-Michielsgestel Holland) 2010, Art of Faith: 2000 Years of Religious Art in Norfolk (Norwich Castle Museum) 2010, Persistence of Vision (Gregory J Peterson Collection NY Acad of Arts) 2011, Imagine Earth (Hangaram Art Museum Seoul) 2011, An Uncommon Past (curator and exhibitor, The New Media Gallery Sichuan Fine Art Inst Chongqing China) 2012, Medusa Caravage Salon Saison Nouvelles Vagues (Palais de Tokyo Paris) 2013, Back in the Day (The Drum Birmingham) 2013, Telling Pictures (Gallery On Seoul) 2014, Territory and Community (Yoseu Int Art Festival Korea) 2014, Konstellationen Galerie F5.6 Munich 2014; *Catalogues* Shotover (1984), Terezin (1988), The Atomic Yard (1990), The Scar (1993), Commissar of Space (1998), The National Portrait Gallery: An Architectural History (2000), Ukadia (2003), Carro Electrico 104 (2005), New World Circus (2006), Floodscapes (2006), Dance to the Muzik of Time (2009), Lovers' Rock (2013); *Recreations* jazz, political and art history; *Style*— Prof John Goto; ✉ website www.johngoto.org.uk; f5.6 Galeria Munich (website www.f5komma6.de); Galerie Dominique Fiat Paris (website www.dominiquefiat.com)

GOTTELIER, Patrick George Campbell; s of Alfred John Dunhill Gottelier, of Penzance, Cornwall, and Freda Joan Gottelier; *b* 20 November 1951; *Educ* Birmingham Poly, Central Sch of Art (BA); *m* 3 Dec 1982, (Catherine) Jane, da of Prof Charles Lewis Foster; 2 s (Thomas Charles Morehead b 13 Feb 1988, William John de Chermont b 13 April 1991); *Career* fndr dir (with w) Artwork specialising in knitwear 1977–, estab diffusion label Artwork Blue 1990, expanded into fashion related products with ranges of toiletries and cosmetics successfully launched 1997; stockists incl Harvey Nichols and Whistles of London and numerous others worldwide, show regularly London, NY and Paris; *Recreations* photography, sailing, walking, travel, cooking; *Clubs* Chelsea Arts; *Style*— Patrick Gottelier, Esq

G

GOUDIE, Prof Andrew Shaw; s of William Cooper Goudie, and Mary Isobel, *née* Pulman (d 1992); bro of (Thomas) James Cooper Goudie, QC, *qv*; *b* 21 August 1945; *Educ* Dean Close Sch Cheltenham, Trinity Hall Cambridge (MA, PhD); *m* 21 March 1987, Heather Ann, da of John Viles, of Chelmsford, Essex; 2 da (Amy Louise b 7 June 1988, Alice May b 25 May 1991); *Career* Univ of Oxford: lectr in geography and fell Hertford Coll 1976–84, prof of geography 1984–, head of dept 1984–94 and 2002–03, pres Oxford Univ Devpt Prog and pro-vice-chllr 1995–97, master St Cross Coll 2003–11, dir China Centre 2011–13; FRGS 1970; *Books* The Human Impact, The Nature of the Environment, Environmental Change, Geomorphological Techniques, Duricrusts, The Warm Desert Environment, Land Shapes, Discovering Landscape in England and Wales, The Prehistory and Palaeogeography of the Great Indian Desert, Chemical Sediments in Geomorphology, Climate, The Earth Transformed, Salt Weathering Hazards, Encyclopedia of Global Change, Great Warm Deserts of the World, Desert Dust in the Global System, The Oxford Companion to Global Change, Wheels Across the Desert, Handbook of Geomorphology, Arid and Semi-arid Geomorphology, Landscapes and Landforms of Namibia (with Heather Viles), Geomorphology in the Anthropocene (with Heather Viles), Great Desert Explorers; *Recreations* old books, old records, gardening; *Clubs* Geographical; *Style*— Prof Andrew Goudie; ✉ School of Geography and the Environment, Oxford OX1 3QY (☎ 01865 285072, fax 01865 285073)

GOUDIE, Prof Andrew William; CB (2011); s of Britton Goudie, and Joan Goudie; *b* 3 March 1955; *Educ* Queens' Coll Cambridge (Wrenbury scholar, BA Econs, MA, PhD), Open Univ (BA Maths & Stats); *m* 1978, Christine Lynne Hurley; 2 s, 2 da; *Career* Univ of Cambridge: research offr Dept of Applied Econs 1978–85, res fell Queens' Coll 1981–83, fell and dir of studies Robinson Coll 1983–85; sr econ World Bank Washington 1985–90, sr econ advsr Scottish Office 1990–95, princ econ OECD Devpt Centre Paris 1995–96, chief econ DFID 1996–99; Scottish Exec and Scottish Govt: chief econ advsr 1999–2011, DG Economy Dept 2003–11; special advsr to Princ and visiting prof Univ of Strathclyde 2011–; Hon DLitt Univ of Strathclyde 2003; FRSE; *Publications* articles in learned jls incl: Econ Jl, Jl Royal Statistical Soc Economica, Scottish Jl Political Economy; *Style*— Prof Andrew Goudie, CB

GOUDIE, (Thomas) James Cooper; QC (1984); s of William Cooper Goudie (d 1981), and Mary Isobel, *née* Pulman (d 1992); bro of Prof Andrew Shaw Goudie, *qv*; *b* 2 June 1942; *Educ* Dean Close Sch Cheltenham, LSE (LLB); *m* 30 Aug 1969, Mary Teresa (Baroness Goudie), *qv*, da of Martin Brick; 2 s (Hon Martin b 5 July 1973, Hon Alexander b 14 July 1977); *Career* slr 1966–70, called to the Bar Inner Temple 1970 (bencher 1991); SE Circuit 1970–, recorder 1985–2008, dep judge of the High Court (Queen's Bench Div) 1995–; chm Bar European Gp 2001–03, dep chm Info Tbnl 2000–12, pres Nat Security Panel 2007–12; memb Brent Cncl 1967–78 (latterly ldr), Party candidate (Lab) Brent North 1974; past chm: Admin Law Bar Assoc, Law Reform Ctee, Bar Cncl, Soc of Labour Lawyers; govr LSE 2001–; FCIArb; *Style*— James Goudie, Esq, QC; ✉ 11 King's Bench Walk, Temple EC4Y 7EQ (☎ 020 7632 8500, fax 020 7583 9123/3690)

GOUDIE, Baroness (Life Peer UK 1998), of Roundwood in the London Borough of Brent; Mary Teresa Goudie; da of Martin Brick, and Hannah Brick (d 1992); *b* 2 September 1946; *Educ* Our Lady of the Visitation Sch, Our Lady of St Anselm Sch; *m* 30 Aug 1969, James Goudie, QC, *qv*; 2 s (Hon Martin b 5 July 1973, Hon Alexander b 14 July 1977); *Career* asst dir Brent People's Housing Assoc 1977–81, sec Lab Pty Solidarity Campaign 1981–87, dir Hansard Soc 1985–89, dir House magazine 1989–90, public affrs manger World Wide Fund for Nature (UK) 1990–95, ind public affrs conslt 1995–98, strategic and mgmnt conslt 1998–; House of Lords: EC Law and Institutions Sub-Ctee 1998–2001, Procedure Ctee 2001, Finance and Staff Sub-Ctee 2002, Info Ctee 2002; memb Lab Pty 1964–, memb Lab Parly Gen Election Campaign Team 1998–2001, liaison peer for home affrs 1998–2001, vice-chair Lab Peers 2001–03; memb Brent Cncl 1971–78 (chm various ctees and also dep whip); sec Scottish Industry Forum; memb: Soc of Lab Lawyers, Fabian Soc, Industry Forum, Centre for Scottish Policy, Devpt Ctee Community Service Volunteers 1996–, Inter-Parly Union; patron: NI Voluntary Tst, National Childbirth Tst, Generation Sci Club; memb Ct Napier Univ; Hon LLD Napier Univ 2000; *Recreations* Labour Pty, family, reading, travel, food, wine, art, gardening; *Style*— The Rt Hon the Baroness Goudie; ✉ House of Lords, London SW1A 0PW (☎ 020 7219 5880)

GOUGH, Denise; da of Gerard Gough, and Angela, *née* Hughes; *b* 28 February 1980, Ireland; *Educ* Acad of Live and Recorded Arts (Acting Dip); *Career* actress; involved with Era 50:50 for gender inequality in the arts; *Film* incl: Outlanders 2007, The Kid 2010, Robin Hood 2010, Complicit 2013, The Quiet Roar 2014, Jimmy's Hall 2014, The Duchess of Malfi 2015; *Television* incl: Waking the Dead (BBC 1) 2009, Silent Witness (BBC 1) 2010, Titanic: Blood and Steel (CBC) 2012, What Remains (BBC 1) 2013, Stella (Sky 1) 2014; *Theatre* incl: Desire Under the Elms (Lyric Hammersmith) 2012, Our New Girl (Bush Theatre) 2012, The Duchess of Malfi (Sam Wanamaker Playhouse) 2014, People, Places and Things (NT and West End) 2015–; *Awards* Best Newcomer Critics Circle Award 2010, Best Actress Critics Circle Award 2016, Best Actress Olivier Award 2016; *Recreations* cinema, walking, theatre, yoga; *Style*— Ms Denise Gough; ✉ c/o Independent Talent, 40 Whitfield Street, London W1T 2RH (☎ 020 7636 6565)

GOUGH, Prof Douglas Owen; s of Owen Albert John Gough, of Romford, Essex, and Doris May, *née* Camera; *b* 8 February 1941; *Educ* Hackney Downs GS, St John's Coll Cambridge (MA, PhD, Strathcona award); *m* 16 Jan 1965, Rosanne Penelope, da of Prof (Charles)

Thurstan Shaw; 2 da (Kim Ione May b 30 July 1966, Heidi Natasha Susan b 25 Feb 1968), 2 s (Julian John Thurstan b 29 Sept 1974, Russell Edward William b 18 Aug 1976); *Career* res assoc Jt Inst for Laboratory Astrophysics and Dept of Physics and Astrophysics Univ of Colorado 1966–67, sr postdoctoral res assoc Goddard Inst for Space Studies 1967–69; Univ of Cambridge: memb graduate staff Inst of Theoretical Astronomy 1969–73, fell Churchill Coll 1972–, lectr in astronomy and applied mathematics 1973–85, reader in astrophysics 1985–93, prof of theoretical astrophysics 1993–2008, dir Institute of Astronomy 1999–2004; consulting prof of physics Stanford Univ 1996–2015; memb Bd of Dirs Møller Centre for Continuing Educn Churchill Coll Cambridge 1992–97; visiting memb Courant Inst of Mathematical Scis 1967–69, astronome titulaire associé Observatoires de France 1977, dir de recherche associé CNRS Observatoire de Nice 1977–78, SRC sr fell 1978–83, professeur associé Univ of Toulouse 1984–85, hon prof of astronomy Queen Mary & Westfield Coll London 1986–2006, fell Jt Inst for Laboratory Astrophysics 1986–, visiting fell Japan Soc for the Promotion of Sci 2005, visiting prof Aarhus Univ 2006, Leverhulme emeritus fell 2008–11 and 2016–18, research assoc Univ of Calif Santa Cruz 2010, invitation fell Japan Soc for the Promotion of Science 2012, fell Nat Astronomical Observatory of Japan 2014, visiting scientist High Altitude Observatory Boulder 2014–, Cambridge-Hamied visiting fell Mumbai 2015, distinguished visiting prof Univ of Mumbai 2015, sr visiting research assoc Stanford Univ 2016; Sir Joseph Larmor lectr Cambridge Philosophical Soc 1988, Wernher von Braun lectr Nat Aeronautics and Space Admin 1991, Morris Loeb lectr in physics Harvard Univ 1993, Bishop lectr Columbia Univ 1996, Halley lectr Univ of Oxford 1996, R J Tayler meml lectr RAS 2000, Colloquium Ehrenfestii Inst Lorentz 2003, Vainu Bappu lectr 2008; second prize Gravity Res Fndn 1973, James Arthur prize lectr Harvard Univ 1982, William Hopkins prize Cambridge Philosophical Soc 1984, George Ellery Hale prize American Astronomical Soc 1995, Eddington medal RAS 2002, Gold Medal RAS 2010; foreign memb Royal Danish Acad of Sciences and Letters 1998, NASA Gp Achievemtn Award for SDO Sci Investigation 2012; FRAS 1966, FRS 1997, FInstP 1997; Mousquetaire d'Armagnac 2001; *Books* Problems of Solar and Stellar Oscillations (ed, 1983), Seismology of the Sun and the Distant Stars (ed, 1986), Challenges to Theories of the Structure of Moderate-Mass Stars (jt ed, 1991), Models of Ordinary Astrophysical Matter (jt ed and contrib, 2004), The Scientific Legacy of Fred Hoyle (ed, 2005); author of 350 research papers in scientific jls and books; *Recreations* cooking, listening to music; *Style*— Prof Douglas Gough, FRS; ✉ 3 Oxford Road, Cambridge CB4 3PH (☎ 01223 360309); Institute of Astronomy, Madingley Road, Cambridge CB3 0HA (☎ 01223 337548, fax 01223 337523, e-mail douglas@ast.cam.ac.uk)

GOUGH, Ian; s of Malcolm Gough, and Sandra, *née* Carol; *b* 10 November 1976, Panteg, Wales; *Educ* Llantarnam Comp; *Career* rugby union player; Toronto Nomads 1995, Newport RFC 1996–98 and 2000–03, Pontypridd RFC 1998–2000, Newport Gwent Dragons 2003–07, Ospreys 2007–13; Wales 1998: 64 caps, debut 1998, winners Six Nations Championship (Grand Slam) 2005 and 2008; currently conslt and schs ambass ESS Wales; *Books* From the Ground Up, A Life Less Ordinary (autobiography, 2015); *Recreations* golf, scuba diving, off roading, flying, windsurfing, cinema, travel, PPL flying, motorbikes, stand up paddle boarding, cycling; *Style*— Ian Gough, Esq; ✉ Ospreys Rugby Liberty Stadium, Landore, Swansea SA1 2FA

GOUGH, Prof Piers William; CBE (1998); s of late Peter Gough, and late Daphne Mary Unwin, *née* Banks; gs of Leslie Banks, the actor; *b* 24 April 1946; *Educ* Uppingham, AA Sch of Architecture (AADipl); *m* 8 June 1991 (m dis), Rosemary Elaine Fosbrooke, da of Robert Bates; 1 s (Clement Rahwangi b 3 Jan 2007); *Career* architect; ptnr CZWG Architects 1975–; princ works: Phillips West 2 London W2 1976, China Wharf London SE1 1988, CDT Building 1988, Street-Porter House London EC1 1988, The Circle London SE1 1990, Crown Street Regeneration Project Gorbals Scotland 1991–, Westbourne Grove Public Lavatories 1993, 1–10 Summers Street Clerkenwell 1994, two Boarding Houses 1994, Soho Lofts Wardour Street London 1995, Cochrane Sq Glasgow 1995 (1999), Leonardo Centre 1995, 19th and 20th Century Galleries Nat Portrait Gallery London 1996, Brindleyplace Cafe Birmingham 1997, Bankside Lofts London 1999, The Glass Building Camden London 1999, Green Bridge Mile End Park 2000, Office at Edinburgh Park 2000, Tunnel Wharf Rotherhithe London 2001, Allen Jones' Studio Ledwell 2001, Samworth's Girls' Boarding House Uppingham Sch 2001, Bankside Central 2001, Suffolk Wharf at Camden Lock London 2002, Fulham Island London 2002, Queen Elizabeth Square and Crown Street Corner Gorbials 2003–04, Regency Galleries at Nat Portrait Gallery 2003, Bling Bling Building Liverpool 2006, South Central Building 2006, Arsenal Masterplan 2000 incl Vision 7 N7 2007, Drayton Park N5 2008, Canada Water Library 2009, Fortune Green London NW6 2010, Almeida Centre London N1 2010, Queensland Road N7 2010, Maggie's Centre Nottingham 2011; exhbns: Lutyens (Hayward Gallery) 1982, Gilbert (Royal Acad) 1985, CZWG 68–88 (RIBA Heinz Gallery) 1988, Soane (Royal Acad) 1999, Saved! (Hayward Gallery) 2003–04; pres AA 1995–97 (memb Cncl 1970–72 and 1991–99); memb Design Review Ctee Cmmn for Architecture and the Built Environment (CABE) 1999; cmmr English Heritage 2000–07 (memb London Advsy Ctee 1995–2003, memb Urban Panel 1999–2003), cmmr Cmmn for Architecture and the Built Environment 2007–, memb London Legacy Devpt Corp (LLDC) Devpt Control Ctee 2013–; prof of architecture Royal Acad 2013; RIBA Gold Medal Panel 2000; tstee: Chisenhale Gallery 1993–2002, Artangel 1994–2003, Kent Design Champion 2004–08; Hon DUniv Middx 1999, hon fell Queen Mary Univ of London 2001; RIBA, FRIAS, RA 2002 (memb Cncl 2011–); *Publications* English Extremists (1988); The Shock of the Old (Channel 4); *Recreations* parties; *Style*— Prof Piers Gough; ✉ CZWG Architects LLP, 17 Bowling Green Lane, London EC1R 0QB (☎ 020 7253 2523, mobile 07973 666121, fax 020 7250 0594, e-mail mail@czwgarchitects.co.uk)

GOUGH, 5 Viscount (UK 1849); Sir Shane Hugh Maryon Gough; 5 Bt (UK 1842); also Baron Gough of Chinkangfoo and of Maharajpore and the Sutlej (UK 1846); s of 4 Viscount Gough, MC, JP, DL (d 1951, ggs of Field Marshal 1 Viscount, KP, GCB, GCSI, PC, whose full title was Viscount Gough of Goojerat in the Punjaub and of the City of Limerick. His brilliant exploits in the two Sikh Wars resulted in the annexation of the Punjab to British India), by his w Margaretta Elizabeth (d 1977), da of Sir Spencer Maryon-Wilson, 11 Bt; *b* 26 August 1941; *Educ* Winchester; *Career* late Lt Irish Gds; stockbroker Laurence Keen & Gardner (and successor firms) 1968–97; chm: Mastiff Electronic System Ltd, Barwell plc and associate cos, Charlwood Leigh Ltd; chm: Gardners Tst for the Blind, Cecilia Charity for the Blind, Schizophrenia Research Tst; memb Assembly RNIB, tstee Spirit of Scotland, memb Cncl Fairbridge; Sr Grand Warden United Grand Lodge of England 1984–86; FRGS; Priory of Scotland, Military and Hospitaller Order of St Lazarus; *Clubs* White's, Pratt's; *Style*— The Rt Hon the Viscount Gough; ✉ Keppoch Estate Office, Strathpeffer, Ross-shire IV14 9AD (☎ 01997 421224); 17 Stanhope Gardens, London SW7 5RQ; c/o John Mitchell Fine Paintings, 44 Old Bond Street, London W1S 4gb (☎ 020 7491 4344, fax 020 7493 5537)

GOULD, Deborah Jane (Debby); da of Frank Cotterill (d 1981), and Lily, *née* Matthews; *b* 11 March 1960, Bedhampton, Hants; *Educ* Portsmouth GS for Girls, Univ of Portsmouth (BSc, MSc), Univ of York (Cert); *m* 13 Aug 1983 (m dis 2001), Robert Gould; 2 s (Will b 12 Jan 1988, Josh b 20 Nov 1989); partner, Stephen Evans; *Career* registered gen nurse 1981, registered midwife 1984; midwife Portsmouth NHS Tst 1984, clinical practice devpt midwife Guy's and St Thomas' Hosp Tst 1997–98, high care mangr Southampton Univ Hosps Tst 1998–2001, head of midwifery Winchester and Eastleigh Healthcare Tst 2001, conslt midwife Queen Charlotte's and Chelsea Hosps London 2001–04, actg head of midwifery and gynaecology St George's Hosp London 2004–05, head of midwifery and sr nurse for gynaecology Mayday Univ Hosp Croydon 2005, currently head of midwifery UCH; memb Cncl Royal Coll of Midwives 2000– (dep chair 2005–; memb various ctees and working parties incl: Educn and Research Gp 2001–05, Finance and Governance Ctees 2005, Professional Policy Gp 2005–), memb NICE Topic Selection Panel for Children, Adolescence and Maternity; writer Birth Rite column Br Jl of Midwifery 2000–, author of articles in professional jls, presentations at numerous nat and int confs on midwifery and motherhood; *Style*— Miss Debby Gould; ✉ University College London Hospital, Elizabeth Garrett Anderson Hospital, Huntley Street, London WC1E 6DH (☎ 0845 155 5000, fax 020 7383 3415)

GOULD, Jonathan; s of Cedric Gould (d 1956), of London, and Joan Wilson, *née* Spiers (d 1983); *b* 1 April 1952; *Educ* Hurstpierpoint Coll, Univ of Bristol (LLB); *m* 4 May 1991, Elizabeth Ann Mackie; *Career* Allen & Overy: articled 1974–76, asst slr 1976–81, ptnr 1982–2003, res ptnr Hong Kong 1988–96; gp gen counsel and dir Jardine Matheson Ltd 2004–09, sr advsr Allen Overy Hong Kong 2009–; *Clubs* Hong Kong, Shek O; *Style*— Jonathan Gould, Esq; ✉ Allen & Overy, 9th Floor, Three Exchange Square, Central, Hong Kong (☎ 00 852 2974 7101, fax 00 852 2974 6999)

GOULD, Jonathan Leon (Jonny); s of Robert Gould (d 2002), and Yvonne Gould; *b* 5 June 1967; *Educ* Handsworth GS Birmingham; *Career* reporter Supercall Sport 1988, sports ed Beacon Radio 1988–90, reporter BBC World Service, LBC, IRN, ITN, BFBS and BSkyB 1990–92, head of sport ITN Radio/IRN 1992–95, md Sportsmedia Broadcasting Ltd 1992–2014, md Radio & Social Media Broadcasting Ltd 2014–; morning sports reporter Talk Radio 1995–99; presenter: Five News and Sport 1997–2000, ITV Sport 2000–02, Football Italia (Channel 4) 2001–02, Euro Fever 2000–, talkSPORT Radio 2009–13, Breakfast Show Sport Smooth Radio 2012–14, Breakfast Show Sport BBC Radio 2 2014–; touchline reporter Prem Plus, narrator Stars in Fast Cars (BBC 1) 2006, newspaper reviewer Sky News 2008–, sports pundit Sky News 2009–, int football expert Al Jazeera English 2010–, sports pundit ESPN 2011; sports columnist LJN Newspaper 2003–05; exec dir Inst of Sports Sponsorship 1994–2005; blogger soccermongery.com 2007–; *Recreations* cycling, Aston Villa, property, travel, English language and literature, improvisational comedy; *Clubs* Soho House; *Style*— Jonathan Gould, Esq; ✉ Radio & Social Media Broadcasting Ltd, Suite 16, Linen House, 253 Kilburn Lane, London W10 4BQ (☎ 020 8964 6555, e-mail jonny.gould@sportsmedia.co.uk, website www.sportmedia.co.uk and www.jonnygould.com, Twitter @jonnygould)

GOULD, HE Matthew Steven; MBE (1997); *b* 20 August 1971; *m* Celia Jane Leaberry; 2 da (Rachel Elizabeth Leaberry b April 2011, Emily Rebecca Leaberry b May 2013); *Career* diplomat; asst desk offr (NATO/Bosnia) Security Policy Dept FCO 1993–94, second sec Manila 1994–97, speech writer to Foreign Sec FCO 1997–99, dep head Consular Div FCO 1999–2001, political counsellor Islamabad 2002–03, dep head of mission Tehran 2003–05, foreign and security policy counsellor Washington 2005–07, private sec for foreign affrs to PM 2007, princ private sec to Foreign Sec 2007–10, ambass to Israel 2010–; *Style*— HE Mr Matthew Gould, MBE; ✉ c/o FCO (Tel Aviv), King Charles Street, London SW1A 2AH

GOULD, Richard; s of Bobby Gould; *b* 14 March 1970, London; *Educ* Bristol GS, Royal Military Academy Sandhurst, Harvard Business Sch; *m* 1993, Rebecca Gould; *Career* offr Royal Tank Regiment 1988–2000; Bristol City FC until 2005; chief exec: Somerset CCC 2005–11, Surrey CCC 2011–; *Recreations* cycling, shooting; *Style*— Richard Gould, Esq; ✉ Surrey County Cricket Club, Kia Oval, Kennington, London SE11 5SS

GOULD, Emeritus Prof Warwick; s of Leslie William Gould, and Fedora, *née* Green; *b* 7 April 1947; *Educ* Brisbane GS, Univ of Queensland (BA); *m* Deirdre Josephine Ellen Toomey; *Career* Royal Holloway Univ of London (formerly Royal Holloway and Bedford New Coll London): lectr in English language and literature 1973–86, sr lectr 1986–91, reader in English literature 1991–95; research reader Br Acad 1992–94; Univ of London: memb Academic Cncl 1990–94, memb Senate 1990–94 and 2000–, memb Academic Ctee 1994–2000, memb Cncl 1995–2000 and 2002–, prof of English literature 1995–; Sch of Advanced Study Univ of London: prog dir Centre for English Studies 1997–99 (dep prog dir 1994–97), dir Inst of English Studies 1999–2013, dep dean 2000–03, sr research fell Inst of English Studies 2013–; acting dir Inst of Cwlth Studies 2009; Cecil Oldman Meml Medal for Bibliography and Textual Criticism Univ of Leeds 1993, Br Acad President's Medal 2012; FRSL 1997, FRSA 1998, FEA 1999; *Publications* Yeats Annual (ed, 1983–), Joachim of Fiore and the Myth of the Eternal Evangel (jtly, 1987, 2 edn Joachim of Fiore and the Myth of the Eternal Evangel in the Nineteenth and Twentieth Centuries 2001), The Secret Rose: Stories by W B Yeats (jt ed, 1981, 2 edn 1992), The Collected Letters of W B Yeats, Vol 2 1896–1990 (jt ed, 1997), Gioacchino da Fiore e il Mito dell'Evangelo Eterno Nella Cultura Europea (jtly, 2000), W B Yeats Mythologies (jt ed, 2005); *Recreations* book collecting; *Style*— Emeritus Prof Warwick Gould; ✉ Institute of English Studies, Senate House, Malet Street, London WC1E 7HU (☎ 020 7862 8673, fax 020 7862 8720, e-mail warwick.gould@sas.ac.uk)

GOULD OF POTTERNEWTON, Baroness (Life Peer UK 1993), of Leeds in the County of West Yorkshire; Joyce Brenda Gould; da of Solomon Joseph Manson; *b* 29 October 1932; *Educ* Roundhay Sch for Girls, Bradford Tech Coll; *m* 1952 (sep), Kevin Gould; 1 da (Hon Jeannette b 1953); *Career* dispensing chemist 1952–65; Labour Party: asst regnl organiser and women's offr Yorks 1969–75, asst nat agent and chief women's offr 1975–85, dir of organisation Lab Pty 1985–93, front bench spokesperson on Citizen's Charter 1993–95, oppn front bench spokesperson on women's affrs 1996–97, a Baroness in Waiting (Govt whip) 1997–98 (oppn whip 1994–97), Dept Liaison Peer to Leader of House of Lords Baroness Jay of Paddington 1998–; memb Independent Commn on Voting Systems; formerly: exec memb Women's Nat Cmmn, Lab Pty sec Nat Jt Ctee Working Women's Organisations, sec Yorks Nat Cncl of Civil Liberties, memb Ctee Campaign Against Racial Discrimination, memb Home Office Ctee on Electoral Matters, dir Maries Stopes International; pres: Br Epilepsy Assoc, Family Planning Assoc; vice-pres: Socialist Int Women 1979–85, Population Concern; dir: Diaroma Art, Studio Upstairs; chair and tstee Mary Macarthur Holiday Homes Tst; author of numerous pamphlets on feminism, socialism and sexism; memb: Fabian Soc, Hansard Soc, Howard League, Bevan Soc, Lab Electoral Reform Soc; *Style*— The Rt Hon Baroness Gould of Potternewton; ✉ House of Lords, London SW1A 0PW

GOULDING, Sir (William) Lingard Walter; 4 Bt (UK 1904), of Millicent, Clane, Co Kildare, and Roebuck Hill, Dundrum, Co Dublin; er s of Sir (William) Basil Goulding, 3 Bt (d 1982), and Hon Valerie Hamilton Monckton (d 2003), o da of 1 Viscount Monckton of Brenchley; Sir Lingard is tenth in descent from William Goulding, who arrived in Ireland as a member of Oliver Cromwell's army; *b* 11 July 1940, Dublin; *Educ* Winchester, Trinity Coll Dublin (BA, HDipEd); *Heir* yr bro, Timothy Goulding; *Career* with Conzinc Rio Tinto of Aust 1963–66, Goulding Fertilisers and Rionore Kilkenny 1966–70; racing driver; teacher Brook House Sch 1970–74, headmaster Headfort Sch 1977–2001 (asst master 1974–77); memb Inc Assoc of Prep Schs 1975–; jr coach and curator Goodwood Cricket Club Adelaide 2005–, teacher and cricket coach St Peter's Adelaide 2007–12, coach Christian Brothers Coll Adelaide 2013–; *Books* 'Your Children Are Not Your Children' – The Story of Headfort School (2012); *Recreations* cricket, motorsport, music, reading, tennis, squash, running; *Style*— Sir Lingard Goulding, Bt; ✉ The Habitaunce, Headfort, Kells, Co Meath, Republic of Ireland

GOULDING, Paul Anthony; QC (2000); s of Byron Goulding, and Audrey, *née* Lansdown; *b* 24 May 1960; *Educ* Latymer Sch Edmonton, St Edmund Hall Oxford (MA, BCL); *m*

16 June 1984, Rt Rev June Osborne, Dean of Salisbury; 1 da (Megan b 11 Jan 1990), 1 s (Tom b 16 June 1992); *Career* tutor in law St Edmund Hall Oxford 1982–84; called to the Bar Middle Temple 1984 (bencher); vice-pres Employment Lawyers' Assoc 2000–04 (chm 1998–2000), memb Bd European Employment Lawyers Assoc 2001–05, specialist memb FA Judicial Panel; *Books* European Employment Law and the UK (2001), Employee Competition: Covenants, Confidentiality and Garden Leave (2007, 3 edn 2016), Playing Contracts in Sport: Law & Practice by Lewis & Taylor (3 edn 2014); *Recreations* football, rugby, opera, golf; *Clubs* Reform; *Style*— Paul Goulding, Esq, QC; ✉ Blackstone Chambers, Blackstone House, Temple, London EC4Y 9BW (☎ 020 7583 1770, fax 020 7822 7350, e-mail paulgoulding@blackstonechambers.com, website www.blackstonechambers.com)

GOULTY, Alan Fletcher; CMG (1998); s of Anthony Edmund Rivers Goulty (d 2002), and Maisie Oliphant, *née* Stein (d 2014); *b* 2 July 1947; *Educ* Bootham Sch York, CCC Oxford (MA); *m* 30 July 1983, Lillian Craig, da of Rev Dr Hendon Mason Harris Jr (d 1981), and Marjorie Elizabeth Weaver (d 2005); 1 s (Alastair Charles b 16 Dec 1970); *Career* third sec: FCO 1968–69, MECAS 1969–71, Beirut 1971–72; second sec: Khartoum 1972–75, FCO 1975–77; first sec: Cabinet Office 1977–80, Washington 1981–85, FCO 1985–87; cnsllr and head Near East and North Africa Dept FCO 1987–90, dep head of mission Cairo 1990–95, ambass to Sudan 1995–99, dir Middle East FCO 2000–02, UK special rep Sudan 2002–04, ambass to Tunisia 2004–08, UK special rep Darfur 2005–06; fell Weatherhead Center for Int Affrs Harvard Univ 1999–2000, sr scholar later global fell Woodrow Wilson Int Center for Scholars 2009–15, adjunct prof Georgetown Univ 2010–11; Grand Cordon du Wissam Alaouite (Morocco) 1987; *Recreations* sport, chess, bird-watching; *Clubs* MCC, Travellers, Royal Over-Seas League; *Style*— Alan Goulty, CMG; ✉ c/o Travellers Club, 106 Pall Mall, London SW1Y 5EP (e-mail alan.goulty@verizon.net)

GOVE, Rt Hon Michael; PC (2010), MP; *b* 26 August 1967, Edinburgh; *Educ* Robert Gordon's Coll Aberdeen, Univ of Oxford; *Career* journalist; reporter Aberdeen Press and Journal 1989, researcher and reporter Scottish Television 1990–91, reporter BBC News and Current Affrs 1991–95, journalist The Times 1995–; MP (Cons) Surrey Heath 2005–, shadow min for housing 2005–07, shadow sec of state for children, schs and families 2007–10, sec of state for educn 2010–14, chief whip 2014–15, sec of state for justice 2015–; chm Policy Exchange until 2005; *Books* Michael Portillo: The Future of the Right (1995), Celsius 7/7 (2006); *Style*— The Rt Hon Michael Gove, MP; ✉ House of Commons, London SW1A 0AA (website www.michaelgove.com)

GOVETT, (Clement) John; LVO (1990); s of Clement Charles Govett (d 1963), and Daphne Mary, *née* Norman (d 1964); *b* 26 December 1943; *Educ* St Paul's, Pembroke Coll Oxford (MA); *m* 14 June 1975, Rosalind Mary, da of Geoffrey Fawn (d 1988); 3 da (Helen b 1977, Sarah b 1978, Joanna b 1981); *Career* Price Waterhouse 1966–69, dir J Henry Schroder Wagg & Co Ltd 1980–90 (joined 1969); Schroder Investment Management Ltd: dep chief exec 1987–94, chm 1995–96; gp md asset mgmnt Schroders plc 1996–98; chm Schroder Split Fund plc 1993–2000; dir: INVESCO City & Commercial Trust plc (formerly New City & Commercial Investment Trust plc) 1993–2001, Derby Trust plc 1995–2003, Schroder Emerging Countries Fund plc 1996–2003, Schroder Ventures International Investment Tst plc 1996–2004, Peel Hotels plc 1998–2015; *Books* Cranley Letters (2009); *Recreations* bridge, golf, gardening; *Clubs* Brooks's; *Style*— John Govett, Esq, LVO; ✉ 29 Marchmont Road, Richmond, Surrey TW10 6HQ (☎ 020 8940 2876)

GOWAN, David John; CMG (2005); s of late Prof Ivor Lyn Gowan, and Gwendoline Alice, *née* Pearce, of Colwall, Herefordshire; *b* 11 February 1949, Oxford; *Educ* Nottingham HS, Ardwyn GS Aberystwyth, Balliol Coll Oxford (MA); *m* 10 Aug 1975, Marna Irene, da of Rhondda Williams; 2 s (Richard Vernon b 20 Sept 1978, Edward William b 29 April 1982); *Career* asst princ MOD 1970–73, Home Civil Serv 1973–75; HM Dip Serv: second sec FCO 1975–76, Russian language trg 1976–77, second then first sec Moscow 1977–80, first sec FCO 1981–85, head of Chancery and consul Brasilia 1985–88, on secondment to Cabinet Office 1988–89, asst head Soviet Dept FCO 1989–90, on secondment as cnsllr Cabinet Office 1990–91, cnsllr (commercial and Know How Fund) Moscow 1992–95, cnsllr and dep head of mission Helsinki 1995–99, cnsllr FCO 1999–2000, min Moscow 2000–03, ambass to Serbia and Montenegro 2003–06; St Antony's Coll Oxford: sr assoc memb 1999–2000, guest memb 2007–10; hon sr res fell Univ of Birmingham 2008–11; memb: Bishop's Cncl 2007–, Synod Dio in Europe 2008–, Cncl Keston Inst 2009–; chm Russian Booker Ctee 2012–15; *Publications* How the EU can help Russia (2000); *Recreations* reading, walking, travel, music, theatre; *Clubs* Athenaeum; *Style*— David Gowan, Esq, CMG; ✉ 8 Blackmore Road, Malvern, Worcestershire WR14 1QX (☎ 01684 565707, e-mail david.gowan@btinternet.com)

GOWAR, Martyn Christopher; s of T W Gowar (d 1987), of Ewell, Surrey, and M A Gowar, *née* Bower (d 1986); *b* 11 July 1946; *Educ* KCS Wimbledon, Magdalen Coll Oxford (MA); *m* 1971, Susan Mary, da of D B H Scotchmer; 3 s (Jonathan b 1973, Michael b 1975, Alexander b 1978); *Career* Lawrence Graham: articled clerk Lawrence Graham & Co 1967, ptnr 1973–2006, sr ptnr 1997–2002, conslt 2006–08; conslt Penningtons 2008–09, ptnr McDermott Will & Emery 2009–14 (sr counsel 2014–); memb: Int Ctee Soc of Tsts & Estate Practitioners (STEP), Cncl Inst of Advanced Legal Studies; vice-pres (Europe) Int Acad of Estate & Tst Law; taxation ed Law Soc Gazette 1979–94; frequent lectr on taxation and tst topics; govr St Paul's Cathedral Sch until 2014, tstee Ashley Family, chm Ashley Family Fndn; memb Addington Soc; Liveryman Worshipful Co of Glaziers; Liveryman Worshipful Co of Tax Advsrs; CTA (Fell) 1981 (CTA 1976); *Publications* Trusts in Prime Jurisdiction (contrib, 2010); regular contrib to STEP Jl and SPEAR'S Wealth Magazine; *Recreations* golf, cricket, gardening; *Clubs* MCC, Lord's Taverners, In and Out, Hankley Common Golf, Rye Golf, London Slrs' Golf Soc; *Style*— Martyn Gowar, Esq; ✉ McDermott Will & Emery UK LLP, Heron Tower, 110 Bishopsgate, London EC2N 4AY (☎ 020 7577 6900, fax 020 7577 6950, e-mail mgowar@mwe.com)

GOWER, David Ivon; OBE (1992); s of Richard Hallam Gower (d 1973), and Sylvia Mary, *née* Ford (d 1986); *b* 1 April 1957; *Educ* King's Sch Canterbury, UCL; *m* 18 Sept 1992, Thorunn Nash; 2 da (Alexandra Sylvia b 25 Sept 1993, Samantha Erna b 28 May 1996); *Career* former professional cricketer; Leicestershire CCC 1975–89 (capt 1984–86 and 1988–89), Hampshire CCC 1990–93 (winners NatWest Trophy 1991 and Benson & Hedges Cup 1992); England: debut 1978, 117 test caps, capt 1984–86 and 1989 (total 32 tests as capt), 114 one day int appearances, highest score 215 v Aust Edgbaston 1985, third highest scoring English player in test matches with 8,231 runs incl 18 centuries (broke Geoff Boycott's previous record v Pakistan Old Trafford 1992), ret from first class cricket 1993; cricket corr Sunday Express 1993–95; joined Test Match Special team BBC 1994, memb BBC TV Cricket Commentary Team 1994–99; team capt They Think it's All Over (BBC TV) 1995–2003, presenter Sky TV International Cricket 1999–; columnist: The Sun 2000–01, The Sunday Times 2002–14; Hon MA: Univ of Southampton, Loughborough Univ; hon doctorate: Winchester Univ, De Montfort Univ 2014; *Books* David Gower: the Autobiography (with Martin Johnson, *qv*, 1992), David Gower: An Endangered Species (autobiography with Simon Wilde, 2014), David Gower's 50 Greatest Cricketers of All Time (2015); *Recreations* tennis, skiing, Cresta run, safari; *Clubs* St Moritz Tobogganing, East India, MCC, Groucho, Garrick; *Style*— David Gower, Esq, OBE

GOWER, His Hon Judge Peter John; QC (2006); s of His Hon John Hugh Gower, QC, and Shirley, *née* Darbourne (d 2012); *b* 30 November 1960, Tonbridge, Kent; *Educ* Lancing, Christ Church Oxford (MA, Classics scholar); 7 Aug 1993, Emma Margaret, *née* Clout; 2 s (James b 11 Aug 1996, Tom b 2 Dec 1999); *Career* called to the Bar Lincoln's Inn 1985 (Hardwicke scholar), standing counsel DTI (now Dept for Business, Innovation and Skills) 1991–2006; recorder 2002–12, circuit judge (South Eastern Circuit) 2012–; chm Kent Bar Mess; *Recreations* cricket, gardening, fishing; *Style*— His Hon Judge Gower, QC; ✉ Croydon Crown Court, The Law Courts, Altyre Road, Croydon, Surrey CR9 5AB (☎ 020 8410 4700, e-mail HHJudge.GowerQC@judiciary.gsi.gov.uk)

GOWER-SMITH, (Nicholas) Mark; s of Charles Samuel Smith (d 1983), of Tunbridge Wells, and Margaret Brenda, *née* Isaac; *b* 20 March 1955; *Educ* The Skinners' Sch Tunbridge Wells, City of London Poly; *m* 25 July 1987 (m dis 2010), Christine Lorraine, *née* Allan; 2 s (Charles Edward b 1989, James Andrew b 1993); *Career* CA; sr ptnr Norman Cox & Ashby 1984–; prop Gower-Smith & Co 1984–; dir St John and Red Cross Defence Medical Welfare Serv 2008–13; organist St John's Church Tunbridge Wells 1992–; Freeman City of London 1991, Master Worshipful Co of Tobacco Pipe Makers and Tobacco Blenders 2014–15 (Liveryman 1991, memb Ct of Assts 2007, Warden 2011–14), Freeman Worshipful Co of Musicians 2016; FCA, FRSA 1994; memb Order of the Hospital of St John of Jerusalem 2013 (Esq 2006); *Recreations* music, opera, heraldry, photography, the work of A W N Pugin; *Style*— Mark Gower-Smith, Esq; ✉ Grosvenor Lodge, 72 Grosvenor Road, Tunbridge Wells, Kent TN1 2AZ (☎ 01892 522551)

GOWERS, Andrew Richard David; s of Michael David Warren Gowers, of Haywards Heath, W Sussex, and Florence Anne Dean, *née* Sykes; *b* 19 October 1957; *Educ* Trinity Sch Croydon, Gonville & Caius Coll Cambridge (MA); *m* 1982, Finola Mary, *née* Clarke; 1 s, 1 da; *Career* Reuters: grad trainee 1980, Brussels Bureau 1981–82, Zurich corr 1982–83; Financial Times: foreign staff 1983–84, agric corr 1984–85, commodities ed 1985–87, ME ed 1987–90, features ed 1990–92, foreign ed 1992–94, dep ed 1994–97, acting ed 1997–98, ed-in-chief Financial Times Deutschland Hamburg 1998–2001, ed 2001–05; Lehman Brothers: head of corp communications, advtg and brand and mktg strategy Europe 2006–07, global co-head corp communications, mktg and brand mgmnt 2007–08; columnist Sunday Times 2005–; ldr Gowers Review of Intellectual Property for HM Treasy 2005–06; jt winner Guardian/NUS Student Journalist of the Year award 1979; *Books* Behind the Myth: Yasser Arafat and the Palestinian Revolution (1990, reissued as Arafat: The Biography 1994); *Recreations* cinema, reading, opera, music of all kinds; *Style*— Andrew Gowers, Esq

G

GOWERS, Polly; OBE (2012); *Career* fndr and ceo Everyclick 2005–; *Style*— Ms Polly Gowers, OBE; ✉ Everyclick, Basepoint Business Centre, Crab Apple Way, Vale Business Park, Evesham WR11 1GP

GOWERS, Prof Sir (William) Timothy; kt (2012); s of the late Patrick Gowers, of London, and Caroline Molesworth, *née* Maurice; *b* 20 November 1963; *Educ* Eton, Trinity Coll Cambridge (BA, Cert of Advanced Study in Mathematics, PhD); *m* 1, 1988 (m dis 2007), Emily Joanna, da of Sir Keith Thomas; 2 s ((William) John b 1992, Richard Humphrey b 1994), 1 da (Madeline Margaret b 1997); m 2, Julie, da of Alain Barrau; 1 s (Octave b 2007), 1 da (Esther b 2010); *Career* research fell Trinity Coll Cambridge 1989–93; UCL: lectr 1991–94, reader 1994–95; Univ of Cambridge: lectr 1995–98, Rouse Ball prof of mathematics 1998–; Jr Whitehead Prize London Mathematical Soc 1995, European Mathematical Soc Prize 1996, Fields Medal 1998; int memb American Philosophical Soc 2010; Hon DSc Univ of St Andrews 2013; hon fell UCL 1999; FRS 1999; *Publications* Mathematics: A Very Short Introduction (2002), The Princeton Companion to Mathematics (ed, 2008); various research papers in mathematical jls; *Recreations* jazz piano; *Style*— Prof Sir Timothy Gowers; ✉ Centre for Mathematical Sciences, Wilberforce Road, Cambridge CB3 0WB (☎ 01223 337973, e-mail wtg10@dpmms.cam.ac.uk)

GOWING, Nik; s of Donald James Graham Gowing (d 1969), and Prof Margaret Mary Gowing, *née* Elliott (d 1998); *b* 13 January 1951; *Educ* Latymer Upper Sch, Simon Langton GS Canterbury, Univ of Bristol (BSc); *m* 10 July 1982, Judith Wastall, da of Dr Peter Venables, of Andover, Hants; 1 da (Sarah Margaret b 21 Dec 1983), 1 s (Simon Donald Peter b 9 Feb 1987); *Career* reporter Newcastle Chronicle 1973–74, presenter-reporter Granada TV 1974–78; ITN: joined 1978, Rome corr 1979, Eastern Europe corr 1980–83, foreign affrs corr 1983–87, dip corr 1987–89, dip ed and newscaster Channel 4 News 1989–96; co-presenter The World This Week 1990–92; main presenter: BBC World News TV 1996–2014, BBC News 1996–2014; conslt: in media and conflict mgmnt, Carnegie Cmmn on Prevention of Deadly Conflict 1996–97, Euro Community Humanitarian Office (ECHO) 1997–; memb: Governing Body Br Assoc for Central and Eastern Europe 1997–2008, Academic Cncl Wilton Park Conference Centre 1998–2012, Cncl RIIA 1998–2004, Strategy Ctee Project on Justice in Times of Transition 2000–, Editorial Bd Press and Politics Jl Harvard Univ, Ctee Rory Peck Tst 1995–, Steering Ctee Konigswinter Conf 1999–; vice-chm Bd of Govrs Westminster Fndn for Democracy 1996–2005, govr Ditchley Fndn 2000–; fell Kennedy Sch of Govt Harvard Univ 1994, visiting fell Int Affairs Keele Univ, visiting fell Reuters Inst Oxford Univ 2008–09; visiting prof depr social sci and public policy King's College London 2014–; memb: Exec Cncl RUSI 2005–10 (memb Advsy Cncl 2011–16, tstee 2016–), RIIA, RTS, Cncl ODI 2007–14; hon degree Univ of Exeter 2012 hon degree LLB Univ of Bristol 2015; *Books* The Wire (1988), The Loop (1993), Skyful of Lies and Black Swans (2009), Thinking the Unthinkable (2016); *Recreations* cycling, skiing, authorship, lecturing and chairing conferences; *Clubs* Savile; *Style*— Dr Gowing; ✉ e-mail gowing.nik@gmail.com

GOYMER, His Hon Judge Andrew Alfred; s of Richard Kirby Goymer (d 1986), and Betty Eileen, *née* Thompson (d 2012); *b* 28 July 1947, Bromley, Kent; *Educ* Dulwich Coll, Pembroke Coll Oxford (Hull scholar, MA); *m* 30 Sept 1972, Diana Mary, da of Robert Harry Shipway, MBE, (d 1999); 1 s (Patrick b 1977), 1 da (Eleanor b 1980); *Career* Gerald Moody entrance scholar 1968, Holker sr exhibitioner 1970, Arden Atkin and Mould prizeman 1971; called to the Bar Gray's Inn 1970, admitted to the Bar NSW Aust 1988; memb SE Circuit 1972–99, recorder of the Crown Court 1991–99 (asst recorder 1987–91), circuit judge 1999–; memb Forensic Sci Advsy Cncl 2007–14, asst sec Cncl of HM Circuit Judges 2012– (memb Ctee 2009–, chm Criminal Sub-Ctee 2014–); *Style*— His Hon Judge Andrew Goymer; ✉ 6 Pump Court, Temple, London EC4Y 7AR (☎ 020 7797 8400)

GOZNEY, Sir Richard Hugh Turton; KCMG (2006, CMG 1993), CVO (2009); s of Thomas Leonard Gozney (d 1991), of Oxford, and Elizabeth Margaret Lilian, *née* Gardiner (d 1998); *b* 21 July 1951; *Educ* Magdalen Coll Sch Oxford, St Edmund Hall Oxford (open scholar, BA); *m* 1982, Diana Edwina, da of David Brangwyn Harvey Baird; 2 s (James b 1987, Alexander b 1990); *Career* vol teacher Rusinga Secdy Sch Kenya 1970; HM Dip Serv: joined FO 1973, third sec Jakarta 1974–78, second sec Buenos Aires 1978–81, first sec and head of Chancery Madrid 1984–88, asst private sec later private sec to Foreign Sec (Geoffrey Howe, John Major then Douglas Hurd) 1989–93, attachment to RIIA 1993, high cmmr to Swaziland 1993–96, head Security Policy Dept FCO 1996–97, chief of assessments staff Jt Intelligence Orgn 1998–2000, ambass to Indonesia 2000–04, high cmmr to Nigeria 2004–07 (concurrently non-resident ambass to Benin and Equatorial Guinea), govr and C-in-C Bermuda 2007–12; Lt Govr Isle of Man 2016–; non-exec dir ARM plc 2013–15, strategic advsr Green Park Worldwide 2014–, conslt Guardian Global Resources 2014–; tstee Langham Dome (Norfolk) 2012–16, Orangutan Fndn 2014–; *Publications* Gibraltar and the EU (1993), Birds of the Abuja Golf Course (2007); *Recreations* birdwatching, walking, sailing; *Style*— Sir Richard Gozney, KCMG, CVO; ✉ Government House, Isle of Man IM3 1RR (e-mail gozneyrichard@gmail.com)

GRABARZ, Robert Karl; *b* 3 October 1987, Enfield, Gtr London; *Educ* Longsands Coll St Neots; *Career* athlete (high jump); achievements incl: Gold medal European

Championships 2012, Bronze medal Olympic Games 2012; *Style—* Mr Robert Grabarz; ✉ website www.jccm-uk.com

GRABINER, Baron (Life Peer UK 1999), of Aldwych in the City of Westminster; Anthony Stephen Grabiner; QC (1981); s of Ralph Grabiner (d 1985), and Freda, *née* Cohen (d 1989); *b* 21 March 1945, Hampton Court, Middlesex; *Educ* Central Fndn Boys' GS London, LSE, Univ of London (LLB, LLM); *m* 18 Dec 1983, Jane Aviva, da of late Dr Benjamin Portnoy, of Hale, Cheshire; 3 s (Joshua b 1986, Daniel b 1989, Samuel b 1994), 1 da (Laura Sarina b 1992); *Career* called to the Bar Lincoln's Inn 1968 (bencher 1989); standing jr counsel to the DTI Export Credits Guarantee Dept 1976–81, jr counsel to the Crown 1978–81, recorder S Eastern Circuit 1990–99, dep High Ct judge 1998–; head of chambers 1995–; treas Lincoln's Inn 2013; non-exec chm Arcadia Gp Ltd 2002–; chm Ct of Govrs LSE 1998–2007 (memb 1990–, vice-chm 1993–98); non-exec dir Wentworth Golf 2005–; memb Ctee Surrey CCC 2011–; hon fell LSE 2009, elected master of Clare Coll Cambridge 2014–; *Books* Sutton & Shannon on Contracts (7 edn, 1970), Banking Documents in Encyclopedia of Forms and Precedents (1986), The Informal Economy (report for HM Treasury, 2000); *Recreations* golf, theatre; *Clubs* Garrick, RAC, MCC; *Style—* The Rt Hon Lord Grabiner, QC; ✉ The Master's Lodge, Clare College, Trinity Lane, Cambridge CB2 1TL (✆ 01223 333207, e-mail asg43@cam.ac.uk)

GRABINER, Michael; CBE (2012); s of Henry Grabiner, of London, and Renee, *née* Geller; *b* 21 August 1950, St Albans, Herts; *Educ* St Albans Sch, King's Coll Cambridge (MA Econ, pres Students' Union 1972–73); *m* 30 May 1976, Jane Olivia, *née* Harris; 3 s, 1 da; *Career* joined Post Office 1973, personal asst to MD Telecommunications 1976–78, London Business Sch (Sloan Programme) 1980–81; rejoined BT: dep dir of mktg 1984–85, gen mangr Northern London Dist 1985–88, gen mangr City of London Dist 1988–90, dir quality and orgn 1990–92, dir global customer serv Business Communications Div 1992–94, dir BT Europe 1994–95; former memb Bd: BT Telecommunicaciones SA Spain, VIAG InterKom Germany, Telenordia Sweden, Albacom Italy; chief exec Energis plc 1996–2001; ptnr Apax Ptnrs 2002–09, chm Spectrum Strategy Consultants 2003–06, chm Synetrix Holdings Ltd 2004–06, ptnr Portland Place Advsrs LLP 2012–; non-exec dir: Littlewoods plc 1998–2002, Emblaze Systems 2000–05, Chelsfield plc 2002–04, Telewest Global Inc 2004–06, Tim Hellas 2005–06, Bezeq 2006–10, Pelephone 2008–10; cncllr London Borough of Brent 1978–82 (chm Devpt Ctee 1980–82), dir East London Partnership 1994–95, chm Partnerships for Schools 2005–12, non-exec dir Centre for Effective Dispute Resolution 2012–; treas Reform Synagogues of GB 2002–05, chm UK Jewish Film Festival 2004–06, chm UK Movement for Reform Judaism 2005–08, chm World Union for Progressive Judaism 2011–15, chm of govrs Jewish Community Secondary Sch 2009–13; chm ResponseAbility 2008–11; Freeman City of London 1995–, memb Worshipful Co of Info Technologists; *Style—* Michael Grabiner, Esq, CBE; ✉ e-mail mike@grabiner.net

GRACE, Prof John; *b* 19 September 1945; *Educ* Bletchley GS, Univ of Sheffield (BSc, PhD); *m* Elizabeth, *née* Ashworth; 2 s (Stewart, Thomas), 1 da (Josephine); *Career* Univ of Edinburgh: lectr 1970–85, reader 1985–92, prof of environmental biology 1992–, head Inst of Ecology and Resource Mgmnt 2000–02, head Inst of Atmospheric and Environmental Sci 2005–07, emeritus prof 2010–; Br Ecological Soc: memb Cncl 1983–89, co-ed Functional Ecology 1987–99, pres 2002–03; served on several ctees incl Terrestrial Life Scis Trg Ctee NERC 1986–89; section ed Encyclopaedia of Ecology and Environmental Management; pres: Botanical Soc of Scotland 2012–, Scottish Forestry Tst 2012–, Science Advsy Ctee Royal Botanic Garden Edinburgh 2014–; memb: Soc for Experimental Biology, Int Soc for Biometeorology; delivered Africanus Horton Meml lectr Freetown Sierra Leone 1988 (among others); jury memb Premi Ramon Margalef d'Ecologia Catalunya; awarded medal Univ of Helsinki 1994, BES medal 2007; FRSE 1994, FIBiol; *Books* Plant Response to Wind (1977), Plant Atmosphere Relationships (1983); also author of over 200 book chapters and papers in refereed jls; *Recreations* gardening, bridge, outdoor pursuits; *Style—* Prof John Grace, FRSE; ✉ School of GeoSciences, University of Edinburgh, Crew Building, West Mains Road, Edinburgh EH9 3JN (✆ 0131 650 5400, fax 0131 662 0478, e-mail jgrace@ed.ac.uk)

GRACE, John Oliver Bowman; QC (1994); s of Oliver Jelf Grace, MBE, TD, DL (d 1996), of Hollingbourne, Kent, and Marjorie Foster, *née* Bowman (d 2007); *b* 13 June 1948; *Educ* Marlborough, Univ of Southampton (LLB); *m* 1973, Carol, da of Canon Jack Roundhill; 2 s (Edward Oliver b 2 Jan 1977, George William Jack b 11 June 1980), 1 da (Eleanor Rose b 26 Nov 1983); *Career* called to the Bar Middle Temple 1973 (bencher 2001); memb: Professional Negligence Bar Assoc, London Common Law and Commercial Bar Assoc; conslt ed Lloyds Law Reports-Medical; chm Mental Health Research UK; *Recreations* gardening, music, reading, cricket, France, sailing, bricklaying, modern art; *Clubs* 4 W's, Band of Brothers Cricket, Old Stagers, Whitstable Yacht; *Style—* John Grace, Esq, QC; ✉ 3 Serjeants' Inn, London EC4Y 1BQ (✆ 020 7427 5000, e-mail jgrace@3sergeantsinn.com)

GRACHVOGEL, Maria; s of Joseph George Grachvogel, of London, and Margaret Mary, *née* McHugh; *b* 11 July 1969; *Educ* Holy Family Convent Sch Enfield, St Angelas RC Sch Palmers Green; *Career* fashion designer; self-employed (with ptnr Plaze Xarizienne) 1988–90, launched Maria Grachvogel Collection 1991, first exhibited London Fashion Week 1994, first catwalk show London Fashion Week 1995; launched: G Collection at Debenhams 1997, Maria Grachvogel Couture Collection 2000, Maria Grachvogel flagship store Sloane St London 2001, Maria Grachvogel Bridal 2002; Br Apparel Export Award for Small Business 1998; *Recreations* travel, art, dance, architecture and interiors, food, cooking, entertaining; *Style—* Ms Maria Grachvogel; ✉ Maria Grachvogel Ltd, 162 Sloane Street, London SW1X 9BS (✆ 020 7245 9331, fax 020 7245 9332, e-mail sales@mariagrachvogel.com)

GRADE OF YARMOUTH, Baron (Life Peer UK 2011), of Yarmouth in the County of Isle of Wight; Michael Ian Grade; CBE (1998); s of late Leslie Grade and n of late Lords Grade and Delfont; *b* 8 March 1943; *Educ* Stowe, St Dunstan's Coll; *m* 1, 1967 (m dis 1981), Penelope Jane, *née* Levinson; 1 s (Jonathan), 1 da (Alison); m 2, 1982 (m dis 1991), Hon Sarah Jane Lawson (d 2008), yst da of (Lt-Col) 5 Baron Burnham, JP, DL (d 1993); m 3, 1998, Francesca Mary, *née* Leahy; 1 s (Samuel); *Career* sports columnist Daily Mirror 1964–66 (trainee journalist 1960), theatrical agent Grade Organisation 1966, jt md London Management and Representation 1969–73, dir of progs and memb Bd LWT 1977–81 (dep controller of progs 1973), pres Embassy TV LA 1982–83, chm and chief operating offr The Grade Co (ind TV and motion picture prodn co) 1983–84, controller BBC1 1984–86, dir of progs BBC TV 1986–87, chief exec Channel 4 1988–97; First Leisure plc: non-exec dir 1991–97, non-exec chm 1994–97, exec chm 1997–98, chief exec 1998–99; non-exec chm Pinewood/Shepperton Film Studios 2000–, chm of govrs BBC 2004–06, exec chm ITV plc 2007–09; non-exec chm: VCI plc 1994–98, Octopus Publishing Gp 2000–01, Hemscott.net 2000–06, Camelot Gp 2002–04 (non-exec dir 2000), Ocado 2006–13, James Grant Gp 2010–12; non-exec dir: Charlton Athletic FC plc 1997–2009, New Millennium Experience Co 1998–2001, Digitaloctopus 2000–01, SMG plc 2003–04, WRG 2011–; memb Cncl LAMDA 1981–, pres RTS 1995–97, chm Devpt Cncl RNT 1997–2004, chm Index on Censorship 2000–04, vice-pres BAFTA 2004–; memb Bd of Tstees Writers and Scholars Educnl Tst 2000–04; Broadcasting Press Guild Harvey Lee Award for outstanding contribution to broadcasting 1997, RTS Gold Medal 1997; *Recreations* entertainment; *Style—* The Lord Grade of Yarmouth, CBE; ✉ c/o Pagefield, The Courtyard Studio, 18 Marshall Street, London W1F 7BE

GRADON, Michael; s of late Oswald Gradon, of Cambridge, and Judy, *née* Foster (d 2005); *b* 7 April 1959, Pembury, Kent; *Educ* Haileybury, Downing Coll Cambridge (Tennis and Real Tennis blue); *m* 26 March 1983, Jill, *née* Cottrell; 2 s (Andy b 28 Dec 1989, David b 11 May 1992); *Career* P&O (The Peninsular and Oriental Steam Navigation Co) 1986–2006: joined as commercial slr 1986, head Gp Legal Dept 1991, gp legal dir 1994, co sec 1996, memb Bd 1998–2006, dir commercial and legal affrs 2002–06, chm P&O Estates 2005–06, chief exec London Gateway 2005–06; sr ind dir Modern Water 2007–15; dir: Grosvenor 2007–15, Genesis Lease 2007–10, Exclusive Hotels 2009–, Aercap NV 2010–; memb Ctee of Mgmnt Wimbledon Championships 2004–; *Recreations* cricket, tennis, golf; *Clubs* All England Lawn Tennis, Tandridge Golf, Hawks, Rye Golf; *Style—* Michael Gradon, Esq

GRADY, Prof Monica Mary; CBE (2012); *b* 15 July 1958; *Educ* Univ of Durham (BSc), Darwin Coll Cambridge (PhD); *Career* formerly head Meteorite Team Dept of Mineralogy Nat History Museum (currently scientific assoc); Open Univ: prof of planetary and space sciences 2005–, dir Cosmochemistry Research Gp, head Dept of Physical Sciences 2011–15; hon prof of meteoritics UCL; collaborated with Jo Brady on Constructing Space sci-art project 2003–04; *Publications* incl: Catalogue of Meteorites (2000), Search for Life (2001), Astrobiology (2001), Atlas of Meteorites (2013); *Style—* Prof Monica Grady, CBE; ✉ Department of Physical Sciences, The Open University, Walton Hall, Milton Keynes MK7 6AA

GRAEF, Roger Arthur; OBE (2006); s of Dr Irving Philip Graef (d 1978), of New York City, and Gretchen Waterman Graef (d 1984); *b* 18 April 1936; *Educ* Horace Mann Sch NY, Putney Sch VT, Harvard Univ (BA); *m* 1, 26 Nov 1971 (m dis 1985), Karen Bergemann (d 1986); 1 da (Chloe Fay b 26 Nov 1972), 1 s (Maximilian James b 26 July 1979); m 2, 26 July 1986, Susan Mary, da of Sir Brooks Richards, KCMG, DSC (d 2002), of Dorset; *Career* writer, criminologist, producer, broadcaster and director; dir 26 plays and operas USA and two dramas for CBS TV; dir Period of Adjustment (Royal Court); co-designer London Transport Bus Map, pt/t lectr Assoc Sch of Architecture; memb Bd Govrs BFI 1975–79; memb Bd: London Transport Exec 1976–79, Channel 4 1980–85; memb Cncl: ICA 1971–83, BAFTA 1976–77, Howard League for Penal Reform; chm Study Gp for Public Involvement in Planning DOE 1975–77, fndr ICA Architectural Forum, expert memb Euro Analytical Coll of Crime Prevention 1993–97, fell Mannheim Centre of Criminology LSE, News International visiting prof of broadcast media Univ of Oxford 1999–2000, visiting prof Univ of London 2000–01; special advsr Paul Hamlyn Fndn 1999–; media columnist The Times 1992–94; numerous articles in: The Sunday Times, Times, Daily Mail, Evening Standard, The Independent, The Observer, Daily Telegraph, Mail on Sunday, The Guardian, Police Review; columnist Community Care; memb Br Soc of Criminology, pres Signals Int Tst 1991–98; tstee: Koestler Award Tst 1997–, Butler Tst 1997–2001, Grierson Award Tst 1997–, Mental Health Fndn 1998–2000; patron: RAPT, Waterville Youth Club, Grassmarket Theatre, Irene Taylor Tst, Exploring Parenthood, Voice of the Child in Care, Friends United, Crime Concern (memb Bd of Tstees 2002–03); chm: Theatre de Complicité 1991–, Book Aid 1992–93, Youth Advocate Prog 2003–; memb: Devpt Control Review (Dobry Ctee) DOE 1975–77, Ctee for Control of Demolition DOE 1976, Advsy Bd Oxford Probation Studies Unit, US/UK Fulbright Cmmn 1998–, Child and Adolescent Mental Health Cmmn 1998–2000, Ind Advsy Gp Met Police 1999–, Advsy Bd John Grieve Centre 2002–, Bd of Tstees The Photographers' Gallery 2002–06, Prince's Tst Surviving Damage in Childhood Panel; James Cameron meml lectr 2007; fell BAFTA 2004 (for lifetime achievment), fell Royal Television Soc; *Television* incl: The Space Between Words (BBC/KCET) 1972, A Law in the Making: Four Months Inside The Ministry (Granada) 1973, Inside The Brussels HQ (Granada) 1975, Is This the Way to Save a City? (BBC) 1976, Decision: Steel, Oil, Rates (ITV/Granada) 1976, Pleasure at Her Majesty's (Amnesty/BBC) 1977, Decision: British Communism (ITV/Granada) 1977 (RTS Award 1978), The Secret Policeman's Ball (Amnesty Int/ITV) 1978, Italy: Chain Reaction (Granada) 1979, Police (series, BBC) 1980–82 (BAFTA Award 1982, TV Critics' Circle Award, Cannes Festival European TV Award), Police: Operation Carter 1981–82, Nagging Doubt (Channel 4) 1984, Comic Relief (BBC) 1985, Maybe Baby (BBC) 1985, Closing Ranks (Zenith/Central ITV) 1987, The Secret Life of the Soviet Union (Channel 4) 1990, Turning the Screws (Channel 4) 1993, Look at the State We're In (BBC) 1995, In Search of Law and Order – UK (Channel 4) 1995, Breaking the Cycle (ITV) 1996, In Search of Law and Order – USA (PBS/Channel 4) 1997–98, Keeping it in the Family (Channel 4) 1998, Masters of the Universe (Channel 4) 1999, Race Against Crime (Channel 4) 1999, The Siege of Scotland Yard (Channel 4) 1999; exec prodr: Life After Murder (BBC) 2000, Not Black and White (Channel 4) 2001, Police (BBC) 2001, September Mourning (ITV) 2002, Rail Cops (BBC) 2003 and 2004–05, The Truth About Potters Bar? (BBC) 2003, Who Am I Now? (BBC/BBC Scotland) 2003, Care Specials (Channel Five) 2003, Malaria: Fever Road (BBC/PBS) 2004, The Protectors (BBC) 2004, Rail Cops 2 (BBC) 2004, Who Killed PC Blakelock? (BBC) 2004, Remember the Secret Policeman's Ball? (BBC) 2004, Chinatown (BBC 2) 2004, Who Killed my Child? (Channel 4) 2005; series ed: Who Is? (BBC) 1967–68, Inside Europe (ITV) 1978–79, Signals (Channel 4) 1991–92, Breaking the Rules (BBC) 1998, Who's Your Father? (Channel 4) 2000, Feltham Sings! (Channel 4/Century Films) 2004 (BAFTA Award); exec prodr: Welcome to Potters Bar (BBC 1) 2004, Murder Blues (BBC 1) 2005, Who Killed My Baby (Channel 4) 2005, Classroom Chaos (Five) 2005, What Killed My Dad? (BBC 1), Panorama: What Future for Kurt? 2005, This World: Property to Die For (BBC 2) 2006, Blood and Land (BBC 2) 2006, Panorama: Rape on Trial 2006, Potters Bar – Search for the Truth (BBC 1) 2006, Hold Me Tight, Let Me Go (BBC 4) 2007, Race for the Beach (BBC 1) 2007, The Burning Season (BBC) 2007, Searching for Madeline (Channel 4) 2007, The Millionaire and Murder Mansion (Channel 4) 2009, Panorama: May Contain Nuts (BBC 1) 2009, The Truth About Crime (BBC 1) 2009; *Internet Productions* Web Lives (itv.com) 2007; *Radio* incl: Living Dangerously (1995), The Illusion of Information (2001), Any Questions, PM, The World Tonight, Front Row, Today Programme; *Film* GM or Not? (corporate video) 2003; *Books* Talking Blues – The Police in Their Own Words (1989), Living Dangerously – Young Offenders in Their Own Words (1993), Why Restorative Justice? (2000); *Recreations* tennis, music, photography, Dorset; *Clubs* Beefsteak, Groucho, Pilgrims; *Style—* Prof Roger Graef, OBE; ✉ 72 Westbourne Park Villas, London W2 5EB (✆ 020 7286 0333 or 020 7727 7868, e-mail rogerg@filmsofrecord.com)

GRAF von EINSIEDEL, Andreas Jean-Paul; s of Wittigo Graf von Einsiedel (d 1980), of Frankfurt am Main, Germany, and Walburga, *née* Graefin von Oberndorff; *b* 28 January 1953, Heidelberg; *Educ* Marquartstein Bavaria, PCL (BA); *m* 1, 2 June 1979 (m dis 1992), Harriet Angela Victoria, da of Henry George Austen de L'Etang Herbert Duckworth (d 1992); 3 s (Orlando Ernle Benedict b 19 Aug 1980, Evelyn b 26 Aug 1982 d 2004, Robin b 12 April 1988), 1 da (Gwendolen b 24 Jan 1985); m 2, 11 Dec 2012, Johanna Thornycroft, *née* Corbin; *Career* internationally renowned interiors photographer; work published regularly in many leading national and international interior magazines; *Style—* Andreas Graf von Einsiedel; ✉ 72–80 Leather Lane, London EC1N 7TR (✆ 020 7242 7674, fax 020 7831 3712, e-mail andreas@einsiedel.com, website www.einsiedel.com)

GRAFF, Laurence; OBE (2013); s of Harry Graff, and Rebecca, *née* Segal; *b* 13 June 1938, London; *Educ* St George's East London; *m* 24 Dec 1962, Anne-Marie, *née* Bessiere; 2 s (Francois b 12 Oct 1963, Stephane b 26 April 1965), 1 da (Kristelle b 8 Feb 1980); *Career* jeweller; apprentice Hatton Garden, fndr Graff 1960 (opened first maj retail store Knightsbridge London 1974, currently 49 stores worldwide incl corporate offices in NY, Hong Kong, Japan, Geneva and London; memb: Exec Ctee Guggenheim Museum Int

Dir's Cncl, Int Cncl Tate Modern, Int Cncl Berggruen Museum Berlin, Christie's Advsy Bd; int tstee Museum of Contemporary Art LA, memb Bd of Govrs Tel Aviv Museum of Art; Queen's Award to Industry 1973, Queen's Award for Export Achievement 1977 and 1994, Queen's Award for Enterprise 2006, Queen's Award for Int Trade 2014; *Books* Graff: The Most Fabulous Jewels in the World (2007), GRAFF (2015); *Recreations* collector of contemporary and modern art, skiing, sailing; *Clubs* Annabel's, Harry's Bar, George, Mark's, The Arts Club, 5 Hertford Street; *Style*— Laurence Graff, Esq, OBE; ✉ Graff Diamonds International, 28–29 Albemarle Street, London W1S 4JA (☎ 020 7584 8571, e-mail penny@graffdiamonds.com)

GRAFFTEY-SMITH, John Jeremy (Jinx); s of Sir Laurence Barton Grafftey-Smith, KCMG, KBE (d 1989), and Mrs Vivien Isobel Tennant-Eyles, *née* Alderson (d 1995); *b* 13 October 1934; *Educ* Winchester, Magdalen Coll Oxford (MA); *m* 23 Jan 1964, Lucy, da of Mrs Ciceley Fletcher, of Dorset; 2 s (Alexander b 1967, Toby b 1970), 1 da (Camilla b 1968); *Career* 2 Lt Oxfordshire & Bucks LI 1953–55; banker; Samuel Montagu 1958–66, Wallace Bros 1966–76, res dir Allied Med Gp Saudi-Arabia 1977–81, London rep Nat Commercial Bank of Saudi-Arabia 1982–2002 (sr advsr 2002–05); sr advsr Merchant Bridge & Co Ltd, ret 2009; dir Angelic Record Prodns Ltd, co sec Angelic Union Ltd; patron Bucks branch Br Red Cross 2014–; memb Worshipful Co of Int Bankers; *Recreations* golf, poetry, music, wine; *Clubs* Lansdowne, City of London, Rifles, Buckingham Golf, Mentmore Golf and Country; *Style*— Jinx Grafftey-Smith, Esq; ✉ Burcott Hill, 39 Soulbury Road, Burcott LU7 0JU (☎ 01296 688252, e-mail jinxgs80@gmail.com)

GRAFTON, Fortune, Duchess of; (Ann) Fortune FitzRoy; GCVO (1980, DCVO 1970, CVO 1965); o da of late Capt (Evan Cadogan) Eric Smith, MC, LLD; *m* 12 Oct 1946, 11 Duke of Grafton (d 2011); 2 s, 3 da; *Career* SRCN Great Ormond St 1945, pres W Suffolk Mission to the Deaf, nat vice-pres Br Royal British Legion Women's Section 2003–; govr: Felixstowe Coll, Riddlesworth Hall; JP: Co of London 1949, Co of Suffolk 1972; memb Bd of Govrs Hosp for Sick Children Great Ormond St 1952–66; patron: Great Ormond St Nurses League, West Suffolk Relate; vice-pres Trinity Hospice (Clapham Common) 1951; Lady of the Bedchamber to HM The Queen 1953–66, Mistress of the Robes to HM The Queen 1967–; pres W Suffolk Decorative and Fine Art Soc; patron: Clarence River Historical Soc Grafton NSW Aust 1980, Guildhall String Ensemble 1988; pres Br Heart Fndn Bury St Edmunds Branch Suffolk 1992; *Style*— Fortune, Duchess of Grafton, GCVO; ✉ 14 Whitelands House, Cheltenham Terrace, London SW3 4QX (☎ 020 7730 1950)

GRAFTON-GREEN, Patrick; s of George Grafton-Green (d 1990), of London, and Brigid Anna, *née* Maxwell (d 1991); *b* 30 March 1943; *Educ* Ampleforth, Wadham Coll Oxford (MA); *m* 18 Sept 1982, Deborah Susan, da of Raymond Goodchild; 2 s (Nicholas Patrick James b 4 Nov 1983, Patrick William Peter b 18 April 1987), 2 da (Charlotte Brigid Kate b 3 Sept 1985, Lucy Anna Clare (twin) b 18 April 1987); *Career* Addleshaw Goddard (formerly Theodore Goddard): articled clerk 1966–68, staff slr 1969–73, ptnr 1973–2006, memb Mgmnt Ctee 1991–92 and 1997–2006, head Media & Sports Gp 1992–2006, sr ptnr 1997–2003, chm 2003–2006; sr ptnr Michael Simkins LLP 2006–; regular speaker at confs on taxation of entertainers and businesses operating in media sector; memb Law Soc 1969; *Recreations* music, theatre, cricket, horseracing; *Clubs* MCC, Middlesex CCC; *Style*— Patrick Grafton-Green, Esq; ✉ Michael Simkins LLP, Lynton House, 7–12 Tavistock Square, London WC1H 9LT (☎ 020 7874 5634, fax 020 7874 5601, e-mail paddy.graftongreen@simkins.com)

GRAHAM, Alan Philip; s of Aaron Goldstein (d 1981), of Edgware, Middx, and Helen, *née* Brown; *b* 4 December 1947; *Educ* Orange Hill Boys' GS; *m* Jennifer, da of Charles Phillips; 2 da (Caroline Louise b 14 Jan 1977, Lucie Vanessa b 11 April 1979); *Career* merchant banker; N M Rothschild & Sons Group: Credits Div 1967–68, money market dealer 1968–69, assigned to Manchester Branch 1969–71, Foreign Exchange and Bullion Dealing Room 1971–77, mangr 1974, md and chief exec NMR Metals Inc NY (memb Precious Metals Ctee NY Commodity Exchange) 1977–79, asst dir 1980, Int Banking Div London 1980–83, exec dir and head Banking Div N M Rothschild & Sons (CI) Limited Guernsey and dir Old Court Currency Fund Ltd 1984–88, exec dir N M Rothschild & Sons Limited 1988– (dir Treasy Div and head Treasy Admin), non-exec dir N M Rothschild & Sons (CI) Ltd, md N M Rothschild & Sons (Singapore) Ltd 1992–94; non-exec dir SFO 2004–; chm of tstees Motor Neurone Disease Assoc, tstee WIZO UK; Freeman City of London 1977; memb Chartered Inst of Bankers 1967; *Recreations* soccer, music, theatre, tennis; *Clubs* Overseas Bankers'; *Style*— Alan Graham, Esq; ✉ N M Rothschild & Sons Ltd, New Court, St Swithin's Lane, London EC4P 4DU

GRAHAM, Sir Alexander Michael; GBE (1990), JP (City of London 1979); s of late Dr Walter Graham, and late Suzanne, *née* Simon; *b* 27 September 1938; *Educ* St Paul's; *m* 6 June 1964, Carolyn, da of Lt Col Alan Wolryche Stansfeld, MBE; 3 da; *Career* Nat Serv 1957–59, cmmnd Gordon Highlanders, TA 1959–67; Frizzell Group Ltd: joined 1957, md 1973–90, dep chm 1990–93; chm Firstcity Insurance Brokers Ltd 1993–98; underwriting memb Lloyd's 1978–98; chm: Employment Conditions Abroad Ltd 1993–2005, Euclidian plc 1994–2001, Folgate Insurance Company Ltd 1995–2001 (dir 1975–2005); pres British Insurance Law Assoc 1994–96, vice-pres Insurance Inst of London; Mercers' Co: Liveryman 1971–, memb Ct of Assts 1980, Master 1983–84; memb Ct of Common Cncl City of London 1978–79, alderman Ward of Queenhithe 1979–2004, pres Queenhithe Ward Club 1979–2004, Sheriff City of London 1986–87, HM Lt City of London 1989–2004, Lord Mayor of London 1990–91; Hon Freeman: Merchant Adventurers of York 1983–, Worshipful Co of Insurers 1992–; Hon Liveryman Worshipful Co of Chartered Secs and Admins 1992–; govr: Hall Sch Hampstead 1975–93, Christ's Hosp Sch 1979–2004, King Edward's Sch Whitley 1979–2004, St Paul's Girls' Sch 1980–93 and 2004–09, St Paul's Sch 1980–2009 (chair 2004–09), City of London Sch 1983–85, City of London Girls' Sch 1992–95; memb Cncl Gresham Coll 1983–93, chllr City Univ 1990–91, memb Ct Univ of Herts; chm of tstees: United Response 1993–2002, Morden Coll 1996–2013 (tstee 1988–2013); tstee Temple Bar Tst 1992–2005, hon life memb Macmillan Cancer Relief 1993–; memb Exec Ctee Army Benevolent Fund 1991–98, chm Nat Employers Liaison Ctee for TA and Reserve Forces 1992–98; pres: Civil Serv Motoring Assoc 1993–2006, Old Pauline Club 2001–03 (formerly vice-pres); vice-pres N Herts Garden Hospice 1991–2015; Hon DCL City Univ 1990, Hon DLitt Univ of Hertfordshire 2016; Gentleman Usher of the Purple Rod Order of the Br Empire 2000–13; FCII 1964, FBIIBA 1967, FInstD 1975, FCIS 1990, FRSA 1980, CIMgt 1991; Commandeur l'Ordre du Tastevin 1985, Order of Wissam Alouite (Morocco) 1987, KStJ 1990 (chm Cncl Order of St John Herts 1993–2001), Grand Cross Order of Merit (Chile) 1991, Vigneron d'Honneur et Bourgeois de St Emilion 1999; *Recreations* wine, calligraphy, genealogy, music, reading, silver, bridge, sports (golf, swimming, shooting and avoiding gardening); *Clubs* Garrick, City Livery, Royal Worlington and Newmarket Golf, Mid Herts Golf; *Style*— Sir Alexander Graham, GBE; ✉ Walden Abbotts, Whitwell, Hitchin, Hertfordshire SG4 8AJ (☎ and fax 01438 871997)

GRAHAM, Sir (John) Alistair; kt (2000); s of Robert Graham (d 1968), and Dorothy, *née* Horner (d 1995); *b* 6 August 1942; *Educ* Royal GS Newcastle upon Tyne; *m* 1967, Dorothy Jean, da of James Clark Wallace, of Morpeth, Northumberland; 1 da (Polly b 1972), 1 s (Richard b 1974); *Career* asst sec, asst gen sec and gen sec Civil and Public Service Assoc 1966–86, dir The Industrial Soc 1986–91, chief exec Calderdale and Kirklees Trg and Enterprise Cncl Ltd 1991–96, chief exec Leeds Trg and Enterprise Cncl 1996–2000; chm: Parades Cmmn NI 1997–2000, Police Complaints Authy 2000–04, West Yorks SHA 2002–03, British Tport Police Authy 2004–08, Ctee on Standards in Public Life 2004–07 (memb 2003–), PhonepayPlus (formerly Ind Ctee for the Supervision of Standards of Telephone Info Servs (ICSTIS)) 2006–13; Northern and Yorks regnl cmmr NHS Appts Cmmn 2003, non-exec dir Information Cmmn 2003–09; memb: Fitness to Practice Ctee Gen Optical Cncl, Employment Appeals Tbnl until 2012, QC Appts Panel 2010–15; visiting prof Imperial Coll London 1982–91, visiting fell Nuffield Coll Oxford 1984–92; hon vice-pres Opera North; non-exec dir Durham CCC; Hon Dr: Open Univ, Univ of Bradford; FCIPD (FIPD 1989); *Publications* Palgrave Annual Political Review (contrib); *Recreations* music, theatre; *Clubs* Lansdowne; *Style*— Sir Alistair Graham; ✉ e-mail grahama8@hotmail.com

GRAHAM, Andrew John Noble; CBE (2002); s and h of Sir John Graham, Bt, GCMG, *qv*, and Marygold, *née* Austin; *b* 21 October 1956; *Educ* Eton, Trinity Coll Cambridge (BA); *m* 7 July 1984, Susan Mary Bridget, *née* O'Riordan; 3 da (Katharine Rose b 31 July 1986, Louisa Christian b 19 April 1988, Isabella Alice b 8 Jan 1993), 1 s (James Patrick Noble b 15 March 1990); *Career* Argyll and Sutherland Highlanders (Princess Louise's): cmmnd 1979, CO 1995–97, Col of Regt 2000–06; Col Royal Regt of Scotland 2007–; Army Staff Coll Camberley 1988, Higher Command and Staff Course 1998, Cdr 3 Inf Bde 1999–2001, Dir Army Resource and Plans MOD 2001–03, DCG MNC-Iraq 2004, DG Army Recruiting and Trg 2004–07, Col Cmdt RAVC 2007–, dir Defence Acad 2008–; Dep Col Cmdt AGC (ETS) 2006–; memb Counsel Queen's Body Guard for Scotland (Royal Co of Archers); *Recreations* piping, all sports, family, animals, destructive gardening, reading (history, travel); *Style*— A J N Graham, Esq, CBE; ✉ c/o Regimental Headquarters, The Royal Regiment of Scotland, The Castle, Edinburgh EH1 2YT

GRAHAM, Brett; s of Geoff Graham, and Jenny, *née* Curry; *b* 8 March 1979, Aust; *Educ* Newcastle HS NSW, Hunter Inst of Tech and HE Newcastle Aust; *Career* restaurateur; Scratchleys on The Wharf Aust 1995–97, Banc Restaurant Aust 1997–2000, jr sous chef Square Restuarant Mayfair London 2000–04, chef and proprietor The Ledbury Restaurant Notting Hill London 2005– (1 Michelin Star 2005 (rising to 2 Michelin Stars 2010), 3 AA Rosettes 2007), co-proprietor Harwood Arms Fulham (1 Michelin Star); Josephine Pignolet Award 1999, Young Chef of the Year 2002; *Recreations* shooting, horse riding; *Style*— Brett Graham, Esq; ✉ 80 Blenheim Crescent, Notting Hill, London W11 1NZ (☎ 020 7792 0854); The Ledbury, 127 Ledbury Road, Notting Hill, London W11 2AQ (☎ 020 7792 8570, fax 020 7792 9191, e-mail brett@theledbury.com)

GRAHAM, Cathryn Judith; da of Kenneth Graham, and Dorothy, *née* Jefferson; *b* 28 March 1955; *Educ* Univ of Birmingham (BMus), Royal Northern Coll of Music; *Career* repetiteur and vocal coach Stockholm 1978–92 (worked with Folkoperan, Vadstena Acad, State Opera Sch, Kulturama, Norrlands Opera, Nat Touring Theatre and Dramatiska Ensemble), admin asst ENO Contemporary Opera Studio 1993, exec dir SPNM 1994–97, md London Sinfonietta 1997–2006, dir of music Br Cncl 2006–; memb: Nat Music Cncl 1994–97, Advsy Cncl Br Music Info Centre 1994–97, Bd Assoc of Br Orchs 1998–2006, Bd NMC Recordings 2000–, Bd Kings Place Music Fndn 2006–07; *Recreations* theatre, visual arts, walking; *Clubs* Groucho; *Style*— Ms Cathryn Graham; ✉ British Council, 10 Spring Gardens, London SW1A 2BN (☎ 020 7389 3087, fax 020 7389 3088, e-mail cathy.graham@britishcouncil.org)

GRAHAM, Christopher Sidney Matthew; s of David Maurice Graham (d 1999), and Rosemary West, *née* Harris (d 1988); *b* 21 September 1950, London; *Educ* Canterbury Cathedral Choir Sch, St Edward's Sch Oxford (music scholar), Univ of Liverpool (BA, pres Guild of Undergraduates); *m* 2010, Mary Crockett; *Career* news trainee rising to TV and radio prodr BBC 1973–87 (progs incl A Word in Edgeways, File on 4, Nationwide and Timewatch); prodr A Week in Politics (Channel 4) Brook Productions Ltd 1987–1988, dep ed Money Programme BBC 1988–89, asst ed BBC TV news 1989–90, managing ed news progs BBC 1990–95, sec BBC 1996–99 (dep sec 1995–96), DG ASA 2000–09, Information Cmmr 2009–16; chm European Advertising Standards Alliance (EASA) 2003–05 (vice chair 2001–03), vice-chm Article 29 Working Party (EU Data Protection Authorities) 2012–14; non-exec dir Electoral Reform Servs Ltd 2001–09, lay rep Bar Standards Bd 2006–09; memb (Lib) Liverpool City Cncl 1971–74; govr Liverpool Inst HS 1972–74; memb Ct Univ of Bath 1998–99; vice-pres Cncl Univ of Liverpool 2016–; Parly candidate (Lib) N Wilts 1983 and 1987; tstee: BBC Children in Need 1997–99, Cedar Tree Community Project 2007–09; *Recreations* music, writing, history; *Style*— Christopher Graham, Esq; ✉ The University of Liverpool, Foundation Building, 765 Brownlow Hill, Liverpool L69 7ZX

GRAHAM, David Warwick; s of Peter Graham, of Edinburgh, and Maureen, *née* Ramsay; *b* 25 November 1960; *Educ* George Watson's Coll Edinburgh, Univ of Aberdeen (BA), Univ of Stirling (MBA); *m* 30 April 1993, Kirsty, *née* Gunn; 2 da (Amelia Elizabeth Lyon b 20 Jan 1999, Katherine Rae Sutherland b 5 Sept 2001); *Career* sales rep David Flatman 1983–87; Phaidon Press: sales rep 1987–91, sales mangr 1991–94, sales dir 1994–97; md: Canongate Books 2000–06, Granta 2006–; *Recreations* fishing; *Clubs* Scottish Arts; *Style*— David Graham, Esq; ✉ Granta, 2–3 Hanover Yard, Noel Road, London N1 8BE (☎ 020 7704 9776)

GRAHAM, Sir James Bellingham; 11 Bt (E 1662), of Norton Conyers, Yorkshire; er s of Wing Cdr Sir Richard Bellingham Graham, 10 Bt, OBE, JP, DL (d 1982), and Beatrice Mary, OBE, *née* Hamilton-Spencer-Smith (d 1992); *b* 8 October 1940; *Educ* Eton, ChCh Oxford; *m* 1986, Halina, yr da of late Major Wiktor Grubert, soldier and diplomat; *Career* researcher in fine and decorative arts Cecil Higgins Museum and Art Gallery 1980–96, curator (with wife) of Norton Conyers and its collections 1996–; *Books* Cecil Higgins, Collector Extraordinary (jtly with wife, 1983), A Guide to the Cecil Higgins Museum and Art Gallery (jtly with wife, 1987), Guide to Norton Conyers(1976, several subsequent edns); contrib of exhibition reviews (jtly with wife); *Recreations* visiting museums and historic houses, travel; *Style*— Sir James Graham, Bt; ✉ Norton Conyers, Wath, nr Ripon, North Yorkshire HG4 5EQ

GRAHAM, Jefferson; MBE; *b* 24 February 1960; *Educ* Ardrossan Acad; *m* 3 May 1991, Inge Renée Van Zijll De-Jong; 1 s (Stanley b 29 Sept 1992); *Career* residential care offr Strathclyde Regnl Cncl, presenter BBC Radio Scotland Glasgow, Radio Forth Edinburgh, presenter and head of music West Sound Radio Ayr, presenter Moray Firth Radio Inverness, prodr and presenter Capital Radio London, presenter, prog controller and dep gen mangr Radio Luxembourg (Luxembourg and London), presenter and programming conslt Atlantic 252 Dublin, prog dir Red Rose Gold and Red Rose Rock FM, main bd dir and tstee Red Rose Community Tst, presenter WZZR Miami, exec prodr daytime progs and music manager BBC Radio 1; gp prog dir Independent Radio Group, channel mangr WilliamHillRadio.com, presenter Gaydio, media and programming conslt and broadcaster 2003–; tutor in radio Univ of Westminster; New York Festival International Programming Award; memb: Radio Acad, Brit Award Voting Acad, Equity; Special Constable Lancs Constabulary (Inspr, divnl offr); Long Service and Good Conduct Medal, Queen's Royal Jubilee Medal; *Style*— Jefferson Graham, Esq, MBE; ✉ 36 Cunnery Meadow, Leyland, Lancashire PR25 5RL (☎ 07973 800259, e-mail jeff.graham@jesting.com, Twitter @iChuff)

GRAHAM, John Malcolm; s of Malcolm Pullen Graham (d 1989), of Oxford, and Edna Stanhope, *née* Davis (d 1991); *b* 9 February 1940; *Educ* Uppingham, Pembroke Coll Oxford (MA, BM BCh), Middx Hosp; *m* 15 Jan 1966, Sandy Judy, da of Wing Cdr Eduardo Walpole Whitaker, DFC (d 1985); 1 s (Alastair b 25 April 1966), 2 da (Harriet b 9 June 1976, Emily b 17 Jan 1978); *Career* conslt ENT surgn UCH, Middx and Royal Nat Throat, Nose and Ear Hosp 1979–2010 (currently emeritus surgn); ENT conslt Med Fndn for Victims of Torture 1991–, chm Med Ctee St Luke's Hosp for the Clergy London

G

1992–2002 (memb Cncl 2004–16); fndr pres Br Assoc for Paediatric Otorhinolaryngology 1991–93, pres Section of Otology RSM 2003–04, chm Br Cochlear Implant Gp 2001–05, elected UK Cncl memb European Fedn of Otolaryngological Socs (EUFOS) 1994–2004, gen sec European Soc of Paediatric Otorhinolaryngology 2010–16 (pres 2002–06); founding ed Cochlear Implants International 2000–; patron: Music and the Deaf, LINK Centre; Cutlers' Surgical Prize 1997, W J Harrison Prize 2003, Walter Jobson Horne Prize BMA 2005; Freeman City of London 1988, Liveryman Worshipful Soc of Apothecaries; DM (Lambeth) 1998; memb: BMA, RSM; miembro correspondiente Societad del ORL de Uruguay; FRCS, FRCSE; *Publications* Ballantyne's Deafness (ed, 7 edn), Pediatric ENT (2007); author of sci papers and contrib to chapters on subjects incl: airway management in premature infants, tinnitus in adults and children, cochlear implants, electric response audiometry; *Recreations* music, construction, verse; *Style*— John Graham, Esq; ✉ 150 Harley Street, London W1G 7LQ (e-mail john.graham10@virgin.net)

GRAHAM, Sir John Moodie; 2 Bt (UK 1964), of Dromore, Co Down; s of Sir Clarence Johnston Graham, 1 Bt (d 1966); *b* 3 April 1938; *Educ* Trinity Coll Glenalmond, Queen's Univ Belfast (BSc); *m* 1970 (m dis 1982), Valerie Rosemary, da of late Frank Gill, of Belfast; 3 da (Suzanne Margaret b 1971, Alyson Rosemary b 1974, Lucy Christina b 1978); partner, David J Galway (civil partnership Jan 2006); *Heir* none; *Career* pres N Ireland Leukaemia Res Fund, dir John Graham (Dromore) Ltd, Electrical Supplies Ltd, Concrete (NI) Ltd, Ulster Quarries Ltd, G H Fieldhouse Plant (NI) Ltd; memb Lloyds 1978; ret 1983; *Style*— Sir John Graham, Bt; ✉ 1 Station Road, Holywood BT18 0BP (✆ 028 9042 3390, e-mail sirjg@btinternet.com)

GRAHAM, Leona; *b* 18 January 1971; *Educ* Univ of Warwick (BA); *Career* radio presenter: Choice 102.2 Birmingham 1995, Power FM 1995–96, 96.4 The Eagle 1996–98, Surf 107.2 1998–99, Core Digital Radio 1999–2000, Virgin Radio (now Absolute Radio) 2000–; voice-over artiste: ITV, BBC, Sky, Channel 4, Radio 1; *Style*— Ms Leona Graham; ✉ c/o Rhubarb Agency ✆ 020 8742 8683, website www.rhubarbvoices.co.uk; e-mail leona@leonagraham.com, website www.leonagraham.com

GRAHAM, (John) Michael Denning; s of William Graham (d 1962), of Glasgow, and Inez Reid (d 1988); *b* 7 September 1944; *Educ* Royal Belfast Academical Inst, Queen's Univ Belfast (LLB); *m* 25 July 1970, Christina Jeanne, da of Ronald Ernest Sinclair, of Cladyhood, NI; 2 s (David William Denning b 1974, Richard Anthony Denning b 1976); *Career* formerly sr ptnr Paterson Robertson & Graham Slrs (Glasgow, Kirkintilloch, Clydebank and Lennoxtown), currently dir of business law MacRoberts, Solicitors (Glasgow and Edinburgh); chm NHS Tbnl for Scotland, chm National Appeal Panel Pharmaceutical Lists; judge Tbnls Judiciary; non-exec dir John Smith & Son (Glasgow) Ltd 1988–2000; pt/t lectr and tutor Glasgow Grad Law Sch, lectr in law Univ of Glasgow and Univ of Strathclyde; returning offr Community Cncl Elections 1982–96, pt/t chm Rent Assessment Ctee Glasgow and West of Scotland 1983–98, dir Glasgow Slrs' Property Centre 1993–99; non-exec dir W Glasgow Hosps Univ NHS Tst 1994–99; deacon Incorporation of Fleshers of Glasgow 1993–94; memb Law Soc of Scotland, chm (Scotland) Int Client Counselling Competition, former chm West of Scotland IoD; fell Caledonian Univ Glasgow (govr 1991–98); FRSA; *Recreations* tennis, skiing, golf, hang-gliding; *Clubs* Western (Glasgow); *Style*— Michael Graham, Esq; ✉ Clairmont, 11 Winton Drive, Glasgow G12 0PZ (✆ 0141 334 7988, e-mail jmd.graham@ntlworld.com); Ben Lochan, Lochgoilhead, Argyll; MacRoberts, Solicitors, 60 York Street, Glasgow (✆ 0141 303 1100, fax 0141 303 1100, e-mail mike.graham@macroberts.com)

GRAHAM, Prof Neil Bonnette; s of George Henry Graham (d 1979), of Liverpool, and Constance, *née* Bonnette (d 1986); *b* 23 May 1933; *Educ* Alsop HS Liverpool, Univ of Liverpool (BSc, PhD); *m* 16 July 1955, Marjorie, da of William Edwin Royden (d 1937), of Liverpool; 1 s (Paul b 19 Sept 1957), 3 da (Kim b 7 Oct 1959, Michele b 14 May 1965, Lesley b 6 Aug 1967); *Career* res scientist Canadian Industries Ltd McMasterville PQ Canada 1956–67, gp head ICI Petrochemical and Polymer Laboratory Runcorn Cheshire 1967–73 (former assoc gp head), fndr and tech dir Polysystems Ltd Clydebank 1980–90, co-fndr and ceo Smart Tech Ltd 2000–, co-fndr and ceo Ecoco Ltd 2000–05, co-fndr and scientific dir Ocutec Ltd 2001–; res prof of chemical technol Univ of Strathclyde 1983–97 (Young prof 1973–83, prof emeritus 1997–); expert advsr on active med implants to Sec of State 1993–2010; memb Dept of Health Medicines Div Regulatory Advsy Ctee on Dental and Surgical Materials 1978–86; tstee: McKinnon McNeil Tst, James Clerk Maxwell Tst; memb Scot Bd of Mission Aviation Fellowship (MAF) 2000–12; deacon Bearsden Baptist Church 1998–2004; holder of more than 100 patents; Leblanc Medal 1956, Potts Medal 1970, Lifetime Achievement Award Nexxus Scotland 2010; ALCM, CChem, CSci, FRSC, FCIC, FIM, FRSE; *Recreations* walking, sailing, music; *Style*— Prof Neil Graham, FRSE; ✉ 6 Kilmardinny Grove, Bearsden, Glasgow G61 3NY (✆ 0141 942 0484, e-mail neilbgraham@msn.com)

GRAHAM, Sir Peter; KCB (1993, CB 1982), QC (1990); o s of Alderman Douglas Graham, CBE (d 1981), of Huddersfield, W Yorks, and Ena May, *née* Jackson (d 1982); f was Mayor of Huddersfield 1966–67, and Freeman of Borough 1973; family motto Verborum vi Vincimus; *b* 7 January 1934; *Educ* St Bees Sch Cumberland (scholar), St John's Coll Cambridge (scholar, MA, LLM); *m* 1, Judith Mary, da of Charles Dunbar, CB; 2 s (Ian b 1960, Alistair b 1962); m 2, Anne Silvia, da of Benjamin Arthur Garcia; m 3, Janet, da of Capt William Eric Walker, TD; *Career* Lt RNR 1952–55, served as pilot Fleet Air Arm; called to the Bar: Gray's Inn 1958 (bencher 1992), Lincoln's Inn 1982; joined Parly Counsel Office 1959, Parly counsel 1972–86, second Parly counsel 1987–91, first Parly counsel 1991–94, conslt in legislative drafting 1994–; *Recreations* playing keyboards, good food and wines, gardens, classic and vintage cars; *Clubs* The Sette of Odd Volumes; *Style*— Sir Peter Graham, KCB, QC; ✉ Le Petit Château, La Vallette, 87190 Magnac Laval, France

GRAHAM, Richard; MP; *Educ* ChCh Oxford; *m* Anthea; 3 c; *Career* MP (Cons) Gloucester 2010–; PM's trade envoy: for Indonesia 2013–, for ASEAN 2015–, for Malysia and Philippines 2016–; tstee Gloucestershire Community Fndn; *Clubs* MCC, Gloucester City Winget Cricket, Lords and Commons Cricket; *Style*— Richard Graham, MP; ✉ House of Commons, London SW1A 0AA (e-mail richard.graham.mp@parliament.uk, website www.richardgraham.org, Twitter @RichardGrahamMP)

GRAHAM, Rigby; MBE (2010); s of Richard Alfred Graham (d 1971), of Leicester, and Helen Sutherland Downie (d 1967); *b* 2 February 1931; *Educ* Wyggeston Sch, Leicester Coll of Art & Design (Sir Jonathan North bronze and silver medals); *m* 1953, Patricia, da of Horace Dormer Green; 1 da (Eleonora b 1968); *Career* De Montfort Univ (formerly Leicester Poly): princ lectr, assoc fell 1983; Hon DLitt Univ of Leicester 2008; *Solo Exhibitions* Gadsby Gallery Leicester 1963, 1966, 1969, 1971, 1974, 1978, 1980 and 1981, Great Yarmouth Art Gallery 1964, Mowbray Gallery Sunderland 1965, Compendium Gallery Birmingham 1966, Crescent Theatre Gallery Birmingham 1967, Kings Lynn Festival 1967, Griffin Garnett Galleries Shrewsbury 1969, St Peter Port Guernsey 1970, Pacifica Library Sharp Park California 1976, Menlo Park Civic Centre California 1976, Victoria Galleries Harrogate 1977, Retrospective Hemel Hempstead Pavilion 1977, Rawlins Art Centre Quorn 1978, Bosworth Gallery Desford 1979 and 1981, Wymondham Art Gallery 1979 and 1984, Coach House Gallery Guernsey 1981, Drew Edwards Keene Gallery 1983, Woodquay Gallery Galway 1984, Phoenix Gallery Amsterdam 1985, Artifact Gallery Leicester 1986, Bottle Kiln Gallery W Hallam 1986, David Holmes Art Gallery Peterborough 1988–94, Warwick Museum and Art Gallery 1992, Goldmark Gallery Uppingham 1987, 1989, 1991, 1992, 1994, 1997, 1999 and 2000, Navenby 1992, Bleddfa Tst Gallery Powys 1990, Manchester Poly 1990, Univ of Wales Aberystwyth 1989, Carnegie Museum Melton Mowbray 1999, Snibston Discovery Park Coalville 1999, Retrospective Exhibition New Walk Museum Leicester 1999, Manchester Metropolitan Univ 2001, Yarrow Gallery Oundle 2005, Gascoigne Gallery Harrogate 2006; *Film* John Clare – A Painter in Search of a Poet (Channel 4) 1991, Rigby Graham's Irish Voyage 2003 (video/DVD), John Piper 2010 (jtly, DVD); *Books* The Pickworth Fragment (1966), Slieve Bingian (1968), The Casquets (1972), Ruins (with Michael Felmingham, 1972), John Piper 1973, Deserted Cornish Tin Mines (1975), String & Walnuts (1978), Seriatim (1978), Graham's Leicestershire (1980), A Broken String of Beads (1980), Sketchbook Drawings (1989), Kippers & Sawdust (1992), Cyril on the Grand Tour (1999), A Paper Snowstorm (jtly, 2005), Pennant and his Welsh Landscapes (2006), Epistola Caledoniensa (jtly, 2009), Outposts Theater (jtly, 2010), Enthiusiasm and Laughter (jtly, 2008), Christmas Cards of Rigby Graham (jtly, 2011), Rigby Graham in Print (2012); *Recreations* Italian opera, reading; *Style*— Rigby Graham; ✉ c/o Mike Goldmark, Goldmark Gallery, Uppingham, Rutland LE15 9SQ (✆ 01572 821424); website www.rigbygraham.com

GRAHAM, (George Malcolm) Roger; OBE (1987); s of William George Blampied Graham (d 1943), and Enid, *née* Townsley (d 1970); *b* 10 May 1939; *Educ* Mill Hill Sch, Fitzwilliam Coll Cambridge; *m* Irene Helen Leyden, *née* Martin; 1 s, 2 da; *Career* various appts in heavy electrical and aircraft industries 1961–62, major account mangr IBM 1965–67 (joined 1962), md ASAP Consultants Ltd 1967–69; BIS Gp Ltd: joined 1969, involved in mgmnt buy-in 1980 and sale to NYNEX Corp 1986, various positions rising to chm and chief exec until 1993; dir: Close Brothers Corporate Finance plc 1995–2001, Scottish Life Assurance Co Ltd 1999–2001; chm: Computer People plc then Delphi Gp plc 1994–96, Mantix Systems Ltd 1994–2006, Gresham Computing 1997–2001, Active Hotels plc 2001–04, Maxima Hldgs plc (formerly Azur Gp plc) 2001–04, Transversal Corp Ltd, Reviewworld Ltd; NATS Tech Bd advsr 2011–15; dir Better Cities Ltd; pres: UK Computing Servs Assoc 1981–82, European Computing Servs Assoc 1986–88; first chm World Computing Serv Indust Forum, fndr chm Computing Servs Indust Trg Cncl; patron Prince's Tst; vice-chm Mill Hill Sch 1996–2006 (govr 1986), memb Campaign Cncl Fitzwilliam Coll Cambridge; Freeman City of London 1988; Liveryman: Worshipful Co of Glovers 1988, Worshipful Co of Information Technologists 1992 (Master 2004–05); *Books* The Handbook of Computer Management (with R B Yearsley, 1973), Information 2000 – Insights into the Coming Decades in Information Technology (1989); *Recreations* landscape gardening, opera, private flying; *Clubs* Oxford and Cambridge; *Style*— G M R Graham, Esq, OBE; ✉ Gaston House, Gaston Green, Bishop's Stortford, Hertfordshire CM22 7QS

GRAHAM, Ross King; *b* 1947, London; *Educ* Loretto; *m* Jillie; 3 da (Kirsty, Charli, Jo); *Career* chartered accountant; ret; dir Misys plc 1987–2003; ptnr Arthur Young 1981–87, dir Misys plc 1987–2003 (finance dir 1987–97, corp devpt dir 1997–2003); non-exec dir various cos incl: Wolfson Microelectronics plc 2003–14, Psion plc 2005–12, Acambis plc 2004–09, Patientline plc 2006–08; chm: Keywords Studios plc 2013–, Airthmetica Ltd 2013–, SME Capital Finance Ltd (sr ind dir); FCA, FIPA (ret); *Recreations* golf, tennis, mental conundra; *Clubs* Blackwell Golf, Sunningdale Golf, Trevose Golf, Queens, Caledonian; *Style*— Ross K Graham, Esq; ✉ c/o Mail Boxes etc, Unit 180, 61 Praed Street, London W2 1NS (mobile 07771 834202, e-mail ross.graham@outlook.com)

GRAHAM, Sandra Denise; da of late James Graham, of Poole, Dorset, and late Joyce N Elizabeth, *née* Botham; *Educ* Fylde Lodge HS Stockport, Manchester Polytechnic (BA); *Career* admitted slr 1984; formerly ptnr Penningtons, currently conslt Horsey Lightly Fynn, specialist in liquor licensing and entertainment law and food law, other specialisms incl planning law and private client law; nominated as one of ldrs in their field by Chambers and ptnrs in directory 1995–96 and 1996–97; chm Bournemouth and Dist Young Slrs' Gp 1991–92, treas Nat Young Slrs' Gp 1990–92 (Bournemouth and Dist rep 1985–92); memb: Bournemouth and Dist Law Soc (memb Gen Ctee 1990–93), Law Soc, Inst of Licensing; affiliate memb Inst of Acoustics; dir Bournemouth Area Hospitality Assoc; tstee and non-exec dir BHLive; vice-chair and sec (SW region) Inst of Licensing; Notary Public; *Recreations* gardening (memb RHS), cake decorating (memb Br Sugarcraft Guild), sailing, music, travel; *Style*— Ms Sandra Graham

GRAHAM, Prof Stephen Douglas Nelson; s of David Douglas Nelson Graham, and Doreen Bramfit, *née* Lowerson; *b* 26 February 1965, Tynemouth; *Educ* Univ of Southampton (BSc), Univ of Newcastle upon Tyne (MPhil), Victoria Univ of Manchester (PhD); *m* 1996, Annette Marie Kearney; 2 s (Ben b 1998, Oliver b 2000); *Career* urban planner Sheffield City Cncl 1989–1992, lectr rising to prof of urban technol Univ of Newcastle upon Tyne 1992–2004, prof of human geography Univ of Durham 2004–10, prof of cities and society Sch of Architecture, Planning and Landscape Newcastle Univ 2010–; visiting prof: Dept of Urban Studies and Planning MIT 1999–2000, Centre for Sustainable Urban and Regnl Futures Univ of Salford 2003–04; conslt UN Centre for Human Settlements; Br Acad reader 2003–05; *Books* Telecommunications and the City (with S Marvin, 1996), Splintering Urbanism (with S Marvin, 2001), Cities, War and Terrorism (ed, 2004), Cybercities Reader (ed, 2004), Disrupted Cities (ed, 2009), Cities Under Siege (2010); *Recreations* cycling; *Style*— Prof Stephen Graham; ✉ School of Architecture, Planning and Landscape, Newcastle University, Newcastle upon Tyne NE1 7RU

GRAHAM, Teresa Colomba; CBE (2008, OBE 1998); da of Albert Rea (d 1986), and Anna, *née* Mastroianni; *b* 8 March 1956; *Educ* La Sagesse Convent GS Newcastle upon Tyne, Univ of Newcastle upon Tyne (BA); *m* (m dis); *Career* Price Waterhouse CAs: Newcastle upon Tyne Office 1977–88 (qualified 1980), seconded to Govt Enterprise and Deregulation Unit 1987, London Office 1988–90 (advsr to Govt on deregulation); Baker Tilly: joined 1989, former head Business Serviced Dept, currently sr advsr, chair Salix Finance; non-exec dir Br Business Bank 2014–; mentor and advsr to CW Communications, Yesrenewables and Spotlight; advsr SME issues ICAEW; former chm Regulatory Bd RICS, chair Administrative Burdens Advsy Bd HMRC; dep chair Govt's Better Regulation Cmmn 1997–2007, non-exec memb Office of Tax Simplification, non-exec memb Steering Bd Small Business Serv DTI 2000–06, memb Small Business Cncl DTI 2003–06; former chm Educnl Policy Ctee RSA; former memb: Ctee for Smaller Entities (CASE) Accounting Standards Bd, Parly Ministerial Gp on Access Business, Advsy Ctee ONS; chm London Soc of CAs 1994–95, former chm London Entrepreneurs' Club, patron Network; govr Bromley Coll 1993–94, former dir Business Link S London; fell Newcastle Univ 2013 (memb Ct); Young Accountant of the Year 1988, Outstanding Achievement Award ICEAW 2007; FCA 1992 (ACA 1982), FRSA 1993, Hon FRICS 2012; *Publications* Graham Review on Pre-packaged Administrations (2014); *Recreations* opera, driving, reading; *Style*— Mrs Teresa Graham, CBE; ✉ 9 Eccleston Square, London SW1V 1NP (e-mail teresa@teresagraham.co.uk)

GRAHAM, Tim; *Career* photographer currently specialising in travel, nature and environment images and for 40 years in photographing the Royal Family and world culture, people, places and scenes during travels to more than 100 countries; subjects incl: Royal Family, Heads of State, VIPs; sittings: the eight reigning European monarchs (photographed at Windsor Castle), the Royal Family (group of 28 at Clarence House), HM The Queen and HRH The Duke of Edinburgh, The Prince and Princess of Wales, Prince William and Prince Harry, Princess Alice, Prince Edward, The Duke and Duchess of Gloucester and family, Prince and Princess Michael of Kent and family, Prince Albert of Monaco, Margaret Thatcher; exhibition Royal Photographs RA 1984; *Books* On the Royal Road (1984), The Prince and Princess of Wales – In Person (1985), The Prince and Princess of Wales – In Private, In Public (1986), Diana – HRH The Princess of Wales (1988), Charles and Diana – A Family Album (1991), Diana, Princess of Wales – A

Tribute (1997), Dressing Diana (1998), The Royal Year, Jubilee: A Celebration of 50 Years of the Reign of Her Majesty Queen Elizabeth II (2002), William (2003); *Recreations* photography, wine, food, travel, cars, countryside, preservation of the environment and wildlife; *Style*— Mr Tim Graham; ✉ Tim Graham Picture Library (e-mail mail@timgraham.co.uk, website www.timgrahamstock.com and www.gettyimages.com)

GRAHAM, Tony; s of David and Freda Graham; *b* 23 November 1951, London; *Educ* Orange Hill GS, Univ of Kent (BA), Didsbury Coll of Educn Univ of Manchester (PGCE); *Career* drama teacher Central Fndn Girls' Sch London 1975–83, Fulbright exchange to Olney HS Philadelphia 1983–84, head of drama Haverstock Sch London 1984–86, memb ILEA Drama Advsy Team 1986–88; TAG Theatre Co: Scottish Arts Cncl assoc dir bursary 1989, artistic dir 1992–97; artistic dir Unicorn Theatre for Children 1997–2011, freelance theatre dir 2011, dir Nat Theatre Co Korea 2013, 2014 and 2016, creative assoc Belgrade Theatre Coventry 2014; visiting artist NYU 2012, visiting prof Rose Bruford Drama Sch 2012 (hon fell 2011); built new award-winning theatre 2005; memb Bd Oily Cart Theatre; Edinburgh Festival Critics Prize (for Lanark) 1995, Equity/TMA Barclays Award Best Production of a Children's Play (for Tom's Midnight Garden) 2001; memb: Equity, TYA (UK), Action for Children's Arts, SDUK; *Style*— Tony Graham; ✉ 26 Balfour Road, London N5 2HE (e-mail tg@tgraham.demon.co.uk)

GRAHAM, (Arthur) William; JP (1979); s of William Douglas Graham (d 1970), and Eleanor Mary Scott, *née* Searle (d 2013); *b* 18 November 1949; *Educ* Blackfriars Sch, Coll of Estate Mgmnt London; *m* 20 June 1981, Elizabeth Hannah, da of Joshua Griffiths, of Gwent; 1 s (William James b 1982), 2 da (Sarah Jane Mary b 1984, Hannah Victoria b 1987); *Career* cncllr: Gwent CC 1986–90, Newport BC 1988–2002 (ldr Cons Gp 1992–2002), Newport City Cncl 2002–04; memb Nat Assembly for Wales (Cons) S Wales E 1999–2016; shadow min for the economy, science and tport, chief whip, shadow ldr of the house 2000–09, Assembly cmmr for resources, chair Enterprise & Business Ctee 2014–16; chm Newport Harbour Cmmrs; govr Rougemont Sch Tst 1991–2006; FRICS 1974; *Recreations* breeder of pedigree Suffolk sheep, foreign travel; *Clubs* Carlton, Pall Mall; *Style*— William Graham, Esq; ✉ The Volland, Lower Machen, Newport, Gwent NP10 8GY (☎ 01633 440419, fax 01633 440751); National Assembly for Wales, Cardiff CF99 1NA (☎ 0300 200 7234, e-mail william.graham@assembly.wales)

GRAHAM OF EDMONTON, Baron (Life Peer UK 1983), of Edmonton in Greater London; (Thomas) Edward Graham; PC (1998); s of Thomas Edward Graham, of Newcastle upon Tyne; *b* 26 March 1925; *Educ* WEA Co-Op Coll, Open Univ (BA); *m* 1950, Margaret Golding, da of Frederick and Alice Golding, of Dagenham; 2 s (Hon Martin Nicholas b 1957, Hon Ian Stuart b 1959); *Career* various posts Co-operative Movement 1939–; memb and leader Enfield Cncl 1961–68, national sec Co-Op Party 1967–74, MP (Lab and Co-Op) Enfield Edmonton Feb 1974–83, PPS to Min of State Prices and Consumer Protection 1974–76, lord cmmr Treasury 1976–79; oppn front bench spokesman on Environment 1980–83; oppn House of Lords spokesman on Sport, Defence, N Ireland 1983; oppn whips office, oppn chief whip 1990–97, chm Lab Peers Gp; chm United Kingdom Co-operative Cncl 1997–; Hon MA 1989; pres Inst of Meat; Hon Freeman Worshipful Co of Butchers, Freeman London Borough of Enfield; FIMgt, FRSA; *Style*— The Rt Hon the Lord Graham of Edmonton, PC; ✉ 2 Clerks Piece, Loughton, Essex IG10 1NR (☎ 020 8508 9801); House of Lords, London SW1 (☎ 020 7219 6704)

GRAHAM-BROWN, James Martin Hilary; s of L H Graham-Brown, of Burton, Leics, and E C Graham-Brown, *née* Blaxland; *b* 11 July 1951; *Educ* Sevenoaks Sch, Univ of Kent (BA), Univ of Bristol (MPhil); *m* 30 Sept 1978, Susan Leslie, *née* Clarke; 2 da (Annie b 14 Dec 1985, Isobel b 15 July 1987); *Career* professional cricketer: Kent CCC 1970–76, Derbys CCC 1977–79; dep head Bournemouth Sch 1988–92, head Truro HS 1992–2000, head Royal HS Bath GDST 2000–09; chief examiner English A Level Cambridge Univ Bd 1986–94; *Plays* Leaving Samson (1994), Crisis (1998), Speaking Ill of the Dead (2000), Marital Moments (2001), Redeeming Lizzie Reeve (2002), She's Gone Then (2003), You'll Never Guess What? We went to school with Tina Goddard (2004); *Recreations* writing plays, directing productions; *Style*— James Graham-Brown, Esq

GRAHAM-BROWN, Prof Robin Alan Charles; s of Maj Lewis Hilary Graham-Brown (d 2003), of Burton on the Wolds, Leics, and Elizabeth Constance, *née* Blaxland (d 2008); *b* 14 August 1949, Broadstairs, Kent; *Educ* Sevenoaks Sch, Royal Free Hosp Sch of Med (BSc, MB BS); *m* 13 Sept 1975, Dr Margaret Marie Rose Anne Graham-Brown, da of late Dr Robert Graham; 3 s (James Robert Philip b 1980, Matthew Paul Mark b 1982, John Joseph Dominic b 1986); *Career* conslt dermatologist Leicester Royal Infrirmary 1983–2013; currently: emeritus (and hon) conslt dermatologist Univ Hosps of Leicester, conslt dermatologist Loughborough Hosp, visiting conslt dermatologist Gibraltar Health Authy; hon sr lectr Univ of Leicester Sch of Med 1993, hon prof Coll of Medicine Biological Sciences & Psychology Univ of Leicester 2016; pres British Assoc of Dermatologists 2005–06 (local sec 1987–88); ed British Jl of Dermatology 2001–04; FRCP 1990 (MRCP 1976), FRCPCH 2005, KCHS; *Books* Skin Disorders in the Elderly (1988), Lecture Notes: Dermatology (1990, 11 edn 2017), Colour Atlas and Text of Dermatology (1998, 2 edn 2007), Dermatology: Fundamentals of Practice (2008) and numerous chapters and peer-reviewed publications; *Recreations* horse riding, cricket, music (especially choral and opera); *Clubs* MCC, Dowling, American Dermatological Assoc (hon int memb), Catenian Assoc, Quorn Hunt Supporters Assoc; *Style*— Prof Robin Graham-Brown; ✉ Killiecrankie, 46 Barrow Road, Burton on the Wolds, Loughborough, Leicestershire LE12 5TB (☎ 01509 880558); Spire Leicester Hospital, Gartree Road, Oadby LE2 2FF (☎ 0116 265 3690)

GRAHAM-DIXON, Andrew Michael; s of Anthony Philip Graham-Dixon, QC, and Margaret Suzanne, *née* Villar; *b* 26 December 1960; *Educ* Westminster, ChCh Oxford (MA), Courtauld Inst; *m* 8 June 1985, Sabine Marie, *née* Pascale Tilly; 2 da (Eleanor b 1986, Florence b 1989), 1 s (Arthur b 1992); *Career* art critic The Independent 1986–98, princ art critic Sunday Telegraph 2004–06 (art columnist Sunday Telegraph magazine 2001–06); assoc prof of history of art London Inst 1997–; BP Arts Journalist of the Year 1987 and 1988, Hawthornden Prize for Art Criticism 1991; memb Advsy Ctee Hayward Gallery 1991–96; writer and presenter: A History of British Art (6-part series, BBC2) 1996, Renaissance (6-part series, BBC2) 1999, The Secret of Drawing (4-part series, BBC2) 2005, The Art of Eternity (3-part series, BBC4) 2007, The Art of Spain (3-part series, BBC4) 2008; presenter The Culture Show (BBC2) 2005–; *Books* Howard Hodgkin (1992), A History of British Art (1996), Paper Museum (1996), Renaissance (1999), In the Picture (2003), Michelangelo and the Sistine Chapel Ceiling (2008); *Recreations* snooker, golf; *Clubs* Camden Snooker Centre, Muswell Hill Golf; *Style*— Andrew Graham-Dixon, Esq; ✉ 21 Croftdown Road, London NW5 1EL

GRAHAM-DIXON, Dr Francis; s of Michael Stuart Graham-Dixon (d 2001), and Anita, *née* Falkenstein (d 2000); *b* 21 March 1955; *Educ* Stowe, Univ of London (BA), Univ of Sussex (MA, DPhil); *m* 25 July 2007, Alexandra Noble; 2 s (Freddie b 1981, Charlie b 1984), 1 da (Celia b 1989); *Career* Sotheby's London 1973–78, Record Merchandisers 1978–79, Warner Brothers 1979–80, Logorhythm Music 1980–81, BBC 1982–87, Francis Graham-Dixon Gallery London 1987–2003, Univ of Sussex 2006–09, St Antony's Coll Oxford 2013; Fellowship Humboldt Univ Berlin 2009; govr Winchester Sch of Art 1989–93; AHRC Doctoral Research Award 2005–08, German History Society Bursary 2006; *Books* Journal of War and Cultural Studies Vol 1 (contrib, 2008), New Readings (contrib, 2008), German History Vol 28 (contrib, 2010), The Lost Decade: the 1950s in European History, Politics, Society and Culture (contrib, 2011), Jazz Journal (contrib, 2011–), Social and Education History (contrib, 2013), The Allied Occupation of Germany – The Refugee Crisis, Denazification and the Path to Reconstruction (2013); *Recreations* endurance running, jazz, fine art, our Jack Russell terriers; *Clubs* MCC, Sheen Shufflers Running; *Style*— Dr Francis Graham-Dixon; ✉ e-mail fgrahamdixon@btinternet.com

GRAHAM-HALL, John; s of Leonard G Hall, of Northwood, and Betty, *née* Minns; *b* 23 November 1955; *Educ* Malvern Coll, King's Coll Cambridge (MA), RCM (Tagore Gold Medal); *m* 1990, Helen, da of John Williams; 2 da (Katharine b 31 Aug 1990, Emily b 6 Dec 1992); *Career* opera singer; tst ENO Benevolent Fund *Major roles* incl: Britten's Albert Herring (Glyndebourne 1985–90, ROH 1989), Aschenbach in Death in Venice (Glyndebourne) 1989, (Monnaie) 2009, (La Scala) 2011 and (ENO and Amsterdam) 2013, Herod in Salome (ENO) 1999 and 2005, Mime in Ring Cycle (ENO) 2002–04, Tanzmeister in Strauss's Ariadne (ROH) 2002–06, Perela in Dusapin's Perela (Unomo di Fumo Paris and Montpellier) 2003, Tikhon in Janacek's Katya Kabanova (Lyon) 2005 and (ENO and Monnaie) 2010, Michel in Martinu's Julietta (Paris) 2006, Poesta in Mozart's Finta Giardiniera (Salzberg) 2006, Govenor and Vanderdendur in Bernstein's Candide (Naples) 2007 and (Rome) 2012, Shuisky in Moussorgsky's Boris Godunov (ENO) 2008, Beadle in Sondheim's Sweeney Todd (Chatelet) 2011, Peter Grimes (La Scala) 2012, Basilio in Mozart's Figaro (Met and Aix-en-Provence) 2012; *Concerts* Evangelist in St Matthew Passion and St John Passion (various) 1985–2011, Carmina Burana (various) 1993–2013, War Requiem (various) 1998–2011, Dream of Gerontius 3 Choir Festival 2011; *Recordings* Britten: Albert Herring (DVD, Glyndebourne, 1985), Figaro (2002), Mozart's Magic Flute (2004), Finta Giardiniera (Salzburg, 2006), Salome (CD, 2008), Ariadne (CD, 2010), Peter Grimes (La Scala, 2012), Death in Venice (ENO, 2013); *Books* My Wife the Diva (novel, 2013); *Recreations* cookery, bridge; *Style*— John Graham-Hall, Esq; ✉ c/o Musichall, Oast House, Hollow Lane, East Hoathly, East Sussex BN8 6QX (☎ 01825 840437)

GRAHAME, Christine; MSP; da of Christie Herkes Grahame, and late Margaret, *née* Brealey; *b* 9 September 1944, Burton on Trent; *Educ* Boroughmuir Sr Secdy Sch, Univ of Edinburgh (MA, LLB, DipEd, DipLP, NP); *m* (m dis); 2 s (Angus b 14 Jan 1971, Niall b 1 Nov 1974); *Career* MSP (SNP): Scotland South 1999–2011, Midlothian S, Tweeddale & Lauderdale 2011–; convenor: Justice 1 Ctee 2001–03, Health and Community Care Ctee 2003–04, Health and Sport Ctee 2007–, Justice Ctee 2011–16; shadow spokesperson Social Justice 2004–07; sec Parly website, memb Cross-Pty Gp on Animal Welfare; dep presiding offr Scottish Parliament 2016–; patron Scottish Heart At Risk Testing, patron Jam; memb NUJ; *Recreations* malt, gardening; *Style*— Ms Christine Grahame, MSP; ✉ The Scottish Parliament, Edinburgh EH99 1SP (e-mail christinegrahame.msp@scottish.parliament.uk, website www.christinegrahame.com)

GRAINGE, Lucian Charles; CBE (2010); s of Cecil Grainge (d 1984), and Marion Grainge (d 1994); *b* 29 February 1960, London; *Educ* Queen Elizabeth GS Barnet; *m* 30 June 2002, Caroline, *née* Lewis; 1 s (Elliot b 6 Nov 1993), 1 da (Alice b 7 March 2000), 1 step da (Betsy b 22 Dec 1987); *Career* head creative dept April Music/CBS 1981 (plugger 1979), dir and gen mangr RCA Music (now BMG Music Publishing) 1982–85, A&R dir MCA UK 1985–86, md Polygram Music Publishing UK 1986–1993, md Polydor 1997–99 (gen mangr A&R and business affrs 1993–97), chm Universal Music UK 2001–08 (dep chm 1999–2001), chm and ceo Universal Music Gp Int 2005–10, co-ceo Universal Music Gp 2010–11, chm and ceo Universal Music Gp 2011–; memb Bd: Int Fedn of Phonographic Industy 2005–, Vivendi 2010–13, Activision Blizzard 2011–13, DreamWorks Animation 2013–, Northeastern Univ 2013; Music Industry Tsts' Award 2008, Billboard Magazine Power 100 2013, 2015 and 2016, President's Merit Award (Icon Award) The Recording Acad 2014, Spirit of Life Award City of Hope 2015; UK Business ambass 2012–; tstee American Friends of the Royal Fndn of the Duke and Duchess of Cambridge and Prince Harry 2011–; Officier des Arts et des Lettres 2011; *Recreations* soccer, automobiles; *Style*— Lucian Grainge, Esq, CBE; ✉ Universal Music Group, 2220 Colorado Avenue, Santa Monica, CA90404, USA (☎ 001 310 865 1823, fax 001 310 865 3230, e-mail lucian.grainge@umusic.com or laura.savage@umusic.com)

GRAINGER, His Hon Judge Ian David; s of David Grainger (d 1985), and Edna, *née* Rudrum (d 2011); *b* 1 August 1956, Kingston-upon-Hull; *Educ* Tynemouth HS, Tynemouth Coll, UC Oxford (MA), Univ of London (BA), UCL (MA); *Career* called to the Bar 1978, bencher Inner Temple 2008; practised in commercial law One Essex Court 1979–2009, recorder 2003, circuit judge (South Eastern Circuit) 2009–; memb Cncl and chair Audit Ctee Roehampton Univ 2003–09, memb Bd of Tstees Univ of London 2008–14; vice-chm Br Italian Soc 2007–09; *Publications* An Introduction to the Civil Procedure Rules (jtly, 1999, 2 edn as The Civil Procedure Rules in Action (2000)); *Recreations* Italy and all things Italian, reading, classical music, walking; *Style*— His Hon Judge Grainger; ✉ Reading Crown Court, Old Shire Hall, The Forbury, Reading RG1 3EH

GRAINGER, Dr Katherine; CBE (2013, MBE 2006); *b* 12 November 1975, Glasgow; *Educ* Univ of Edinburgh (LLB), Univ of Glasgow (MPhil), KCL (PhD); *Career* rower; achievements incl: Bronze medal (eights) World Championships 1997, Silver medal (quadruple sculls) Olympic Games 2000, Gold medal (coxless pairs) World Championships 2003, Silver medal (coxless pairs) Olympic Games 2004, Gold medal (women's quad) World Championships 2005, Gold medal (women's quad) World Championships 2006, Gold medal (women's quad) World Championships 2007, Silver medal (quadruple sculls) Olympic Games 2008, Silver medal (women's single scull) World Championships 2009, Gold medal (double sculls) World Championships 2010, Gold medal (double sculls) World Championships 2011, Gold medal (double sculls) Olympic Games 2012, Silver medal (double sculls) Olympic Games 2016; chllr Oxford Brookes Univ 2015–; *Style*— Dr Katherine Grainger, CBE

GRAINGER, Richard; *b* 6 July 1960; *Educ* Durham Sch, St Edmund Hall Oxford; *m* Sept 1989, Alice Miranda Cockburn; 4 da; *Career* qualified CA Pice Waterhouse; Hill Samuel Bank Ltd 1987–96, Close Brothers Corporate Finance Ltd 1996–2009, founding ptnr Dunelmia Ptnrs 2009–14; non-exec chm Safestore Hldgs Ltd 2008–13 (memb Bd 2007–13), chm IPES (Hldgs) Guernsey 2008–13, non-exec dir Palmer & Harvey plc 2012–, non-exec chm Harrington Brooks Ltd 2013–, non-exec dir McKay Securities plc 2014–; ACA; *Recreations* skiing, shooting, golf; *Style*— Richard Grainger; ☎ 07785 386172

GRAINGER, Steve; MBE (2007); s of Malcolm Grainger, and Patricia Grainger; *b* 5 March 1966, Saltburn by the Sea, N Yorks; *Educ* Saltscar Comp Sch Redcar, Sir William Turner's Sixth Form Coll Redcar, Leeds Poly (BA); *m* 8 April 1989, Julie; 2 da (Amie b 8 Oct 1991, Hayley b 11 Oct 1995); *Career* Mansfield DC 1987–89, Notts CC 1989–92, Nat Coaching Fndn 1992–95, various positions Youth Sport Tst 1995–2011 (chief exec 2004–11), rugby devpt dir RFU 2011–; *Recreations* athletics, skiing, foreign travel; *Style*— Steve Grainger, Esq, MBE; ✉ RFU, Rugby House, Twickenham Stadium, 200 Whitton Road, Twickenham TW2 7BA

GRAMMENOS, Prof Costas Theophilos; Hon CBE (2008); s of Cdr Theophilos C Grammenos (d 1998), and Argyro, *née* Spanakos (d 1996); *b* 23 February 1944; *Educ* Third State Sch of Athens, Pantion Univ (BA), Univ of Wales (MSc), City Univ (DSc); *m* 20 Nov 1972, Anna, da of Prof Constantinos A Papadimitriou (d 1994); 1 s (Theophilos b 6 April 1975); *Career* Nat Serv Greek Navy 1968–70; Nat Bank of Greece 1962–75 (shipping fin expert, head office 1973–74); independent researcher and advsr 1977–82; Sir John Cass Business Sch City of London (formerly City Univ Business Sch): visiting prof 1982–86, fndr and head Int Centre for Shipping, Trade and Finance 1984–, prof of shipping, trade and finance 1986–, acting dean 2000, dep dean 2001–10; pro-vice-chllr City Univ 1998–2012; fndr and chm City of London Biennial Meetings 1999–; visiting prof Univ of Antwerp 2000–; memb: Bd of Dirs Alexander S Onassis Public Benefit Fndn 1995–, BIMCO Bd of Govrs (Educn) 1995–, American Bureau of Shipping 1996–,

Baltic Exchange 1997–; non-exec memb Bd Marfin Investment Gp (MIG) 2007–10; pres Int Assoc of Maritime Economists 1998–2002, founding tstee Inst of Marine Engrs Meml Fund 2000–, founder pres Int Hellenic Univ Greece 2006–; hon fell Inst of Marine Engrs Science and Technol 2008–; Seatrade Personality of the Year 1998; Freeman of the City of London 2000, Liveryman Worshipful Co of Shipwrights 2002; FRSA 1996; Archon Ecumenical Patriarchate of Constantinople 1994; FCIB 2004; *Books* Bank Finance for Ship Purchase (1979), The Handbook of Maritime Economics and Business (ed, 2002, 2 edn 2010); author of various academic papers and studies on shipping finance; *Recreations* music, theatre, walking; *Clubs* Travellers; *Style—* Prof Costas Th Grammenos, CBE; ✉ Sir John Cass Business School, City of London, 106 Bunhill Row, London EC1Y 8TZ (☎ 020 7040 8671, fax 020 7040 8895)

GRAMS, Gerry; *b* 29 July 1959; *Educ* Mackintosh Sch of Arch Glasgow Sch of Art (DipArch, W Sommerville Shanks legacy, Bram Stoker medal, ARIAS (Rowan Anderson Award); *Career* architectural apprentice: Murray and Manson Architects Glasgow 1980–81, McGurn Logan and Duncan Architects Glasgow 1982; architect McGurn Logan Duncan and Opfer Glasgow 1983–96 (assoc dir 1988–96), fndr ptnr Bonar & Grams Architects 1996; projects incl: Tron Theatre, Glassford Court, private house for Robbie Coltrane, Bellgrove Cross/Graham Square housing for Molendinar Park HA, The Piping Centre Glasgow, Refurbishment of the Clydeway Centre Glasgow, Kelvin Square Housing Development Glasgow, Shelbourne Hotel Health Club Dublin; city design advsr Glasgow City Cncl; pt/t design tutor (fndn course) Dept of Architecture Univ of Strathclyde 1989–96; dir Workshop and Artists Studio Provision Scotland Ltd (WASPS); *Competitions* second prize Crown Street Masterplan 1990, first prize Darnley Masterplan 1991; *Exhibitions* Royal Scottish Acad Summer Exhibition 1984, For a Wee Country... (RIAS Jubilee Travelling Exhibition) 1990; *Style—* Gerry Grams, Esq

GRAN, Maurice Bernard; s of Mark Gran (d 1965), of London, and Deborah, *née* Cohen (d 1986); *b* 26 October 1949; *Educ* William Ellis GS London, UCL (BSc); *m* Carol James; 1 da (Jessica b 21 June 1985), 1 s (Thomas b 23 May 1988); *Career* mgmnt trainee Dept of Employment, various mgmnt appts Employment Services Agency 1974–80, television scriptwriter 1980–; creator and writer (with Laurence Marks, *qv*): Holding the Fort 1979–82, Roots, Shine on Harvey Moon 1982–85 and 1995, Roll Over Beethoven, Relative Strangers, The New Statesman 1987–91, Birds of a Feather 1989–99 and 2014–16, Snakes and Ladders, So You Think You've Got Troubles, Get Back, Love Hurts 1991–93, Wall of Silence (film) 1993, Goodnight Sweetheart 1994–99, Mosley (min-series) 1997, Dirty Work 2000, Believe Nothing 2002, Playing God (Stephen Joseph Theatre Scarborough) 2005, New Statesman (Trafalgar Studios London and tour) 2006–07, Dreamboats and Petticoats (Savoy Theatre London and nat tour) 2009 and (Playhouse Theatre London and nat tours) 2010–14 (Best Musical Olivier Award nominee 2010), Von Ribbentrop's Watch (Oxford Playhouse and tour) 2010, Birds of a Feather Live – nat tour 2011–13, Save the Last Dance for Me (nat tours 2012–13 and 2016), Dreamboats and Miniskirts (Windsor and nat tour) 2014–15, Love Me Do (Watford Palace Theatre) 2014; radio plays (with Laurence Marks): My Blue Heaven trilogy (Radio 4), Dr Freud Will See You Now Mrs Hitler (Radio 4), Von Ribbentrop's Watch (Radio 4), Love Me Do (Radio 4); fndr (with Laurence Marks and Allan McKeown, *qv*) Alomo Productions 1988 (now part of Thames Talkback plc); memb Cncl BAFTA 1994–95; *Awards* Silver Medal Int Film and TV Festival NY for Relative Strangers 1985, Int Emmy for The New Statesman 1988, BAFTA Best Comedy Award for The New Statesman 1990, Mitsubishi TV Sitcom of the Year for Birds of a Feather 1991, Mitsubishi TV Drama of the Year for Love Hurts 1991, BAFTA Writer's Award (jtly with Laurence Marks) 1992; *Books* with Laurence Marks: Holding the Fort (1981), The New Statesman Scripts (1992), Dorien's Diary (1993); *Recreations* watching football, buying clothes, fell walking, theatre, cinema; *Clubs* Groucho, Arsenal FC, BAFTA; *Style—* Maurice Gran, Esq; ✉ website www.marksandgran.com

GRANATT, Michael Stephen Dreese; CB (2001); s of Arthur Maurice Granatt, and Denise Sylvia, *née* Dreese; *b* 27 April 1950, London; *Educ* Westminster City Sch, Queen Mary Coll London; *m* Jane, *née* Bray; 1 s, 3 da; *Career* sub-ed Kent Sussex Courier 1974, press offr Dept of Employment 1979–81, press offr Home Office 1981–83, sr info offr then head of info Dept of Energy 1983–89, dir of public affrs Met Police 1989–92, dir of communication DOE 1992–95, dir of communication Home Office 1995–98, DG Govt Info Communication Service (GICS) 1998–2003 (head of Civil Contingencies Secretariat 2001–02), ptnr Luther Pendragon 2004–; chair Club of Venice 2000–, chair UK Press Card Authy 2004–; sr assoc fell Defence Acad of the UK 2004–09; govr and tstee Mary Hare 2004– (chair 2010–), tstee Deafness Research UK 2008–; CIPR Stephen Tallents Medal 2002; FIPR 2000; *Recreations* photography, reading science fiction, walking the dogs; *Clubs* Savage; *Style—* M S D Granatt, CB, FCIPR; ✉ e-mail mikegranatt@luther.co.uk

GRANDAGE, Michael; CBE (2011); *b* 2 May 1962; *Educ* Humphry Davy GS Penzance, Central Sch of Speech and Drama; *Partner* Christopher Oram (civil partnership); *Career* theatre dir and prodr; artistic dir Crucible Theatre Sheffield 1999–2005, artistic dir Donmar Warehouse 2002–12, artistic dir Michael Grandage Company 2012–; Hon DUniv: Sheffield Hallam 2002, Sheffield 2004, Univ of London 2015; hon fell: Central Sch of Speech and Drama 2008 (pres 2009–), Royal Welsh Coll of Music and Drama 2014; Award for Excellence in Int Theatre Int Theatre Inst 2006; *Productions* Crucible Theatre Sheffield: What the Butler Saw 1997, Twelfth Night 1998, The Country Wife 2000, As You Like It 2000 (also Lyric Theatre Hammersmith; Best Dir Evening Standard Awards, Best Dir Critics Circle Awards, South Bank Show Award for Theatre), Edward II 2001, Don Juan 2001, Richard III 2002, The Tempest 2002 (also The Old Vic London), A Midsummer Night's Dream 2003, Suddenly Last Summer (also Albery Theatre London) 2004, Don Carlos 2004 (also Gielgud Theatre London, Best Dir Evening Standard Award); Donmar Warehouse: Good 1999, Passion Play 2000 (also Comedy Theatre London; Best Dir Evening Standard Award, Best Dir Critics Circle Award, nomination Best Dir Olivier Award), Merrily We Roll Along 2000–01 (3 Olivier Awards incl Best Musical, Best Dir Critics Circle Award), Privates on Parade 2001–02 (3 nominations Olivier Awards), The Vortex 2002–03, Caligula 2003 (Best Dir Olivier Award), After Miss Julie 2003–04, Pirandello's Henry IV 2004, Grand Hotel, the Musical 2004 (Best Musical Olivier Award), The Wild Duck 2005 (Best Dir Critics Circle Award), Guys and Dolls (Donmar at the Piccadilly Theatre, Best Musical Olivier Award) 2005, The Cut 2006, Frost/Nixon 2006 (also Broadway, nomination Best Dir Tony Award), Don Juan in Soho 2006, John Gabriel Borkman 2007, Othello 2007 (Best Dir Evening Standard Theatre Award 2008), The Chalk Garden 2008 (Best Dir Evening Standard Theatre Award 2008), Ivanov 2008 (Best Dir Evening Standard Theatre Award 2008), Twelfth Night 2008, Madame de Sade 2009, Hamlet 2009 (also Broadway), Red 2009 (also Broadway, Best Dir Tony Award, Drama Desk Award), King Lear 2010 (Best Dir Critics Circle Award), Luise Miller 2011, Richard II 2012 (Evening Standard Award for Ten Years at the Donmar); Almeida Theatre: The Doctor's Dilemma 1998, The Jew of Malta 1999; Glyndebourne Opera: Billy Budd 2009, Nozze di Figaro 2012; Michael Grandage Company at the Noel Coward Theatre London: Privates on Parade 2012, Peter and Alice 2013, The Cripple of Inishmaan 2013, A Midsummer Night's Dream 2013, Henry V 2013, Photograph 51 2015; Evita (Adelphi Theatre London) 2006 and (Broadway) 2012, Danton's Death (NT) 2010, Madama Butterfly (Houston Grand Opera) 2010, Don Giovanni (Met Opera) 2011; *Film* Genius 2016; *Books* A Decade at the Donmar 2002–2012 (2012); *Style—* Michael Grandage, Esq, CBE; ✉ Michael Grandage Company, Fourth Floor, Gielgud Theatre, Shaftesbury Avenue, London W1D 6AR (☎ 020 3582 7210, e-mail mg@michaelgrandagecompany.com)

GRANGE, Sir Kenneth Henry; kt (2013), CBE (1984); s of Harry Alfred Grange, and Hilda Gladys, *née* Long; *b* 17 July 1929; *Educ* Willesden Coll of Art; *m* 21 Sept 1984, Apryl Jacqueline, da of Deric Swift; *Career* tech illustrator RE 1947–48; architectural asst Bronek Katz & Vaughan 1949–50; designer: Gordon Bowyer 1950–52, Jack Howe & Partners 1952–58; fndr Kenneth Grange Design London 1958–72, fndr ptnr Pentagram Design Ltd 1972–; memb Bd of Dirs Shakespeare Globe Centre 1997–; winner: 10 Design Cncl Awards, Duke of Edinburgh Prize for Elegant Design 1963, CSD Gold Medal (for lifetime's achievement in design) 1996, Prince Philip's Designers Prize 2001; work represented in collections of: V&A, Design Museum London, State Museum Munich; one man shows: Kenneth Grange at the Boilerhouse V&A 1983, The Product Designs of Kenneth Grange of Pentagram XSITE Tokyo Japan 1989; juror BBC Design Awards 1996; Master Faculty of Royal Design for Industry 1985–87 (memb 1969); memb Cncl and memb Advsy Bd on Product Design Design Cncl (industrial design advsr 1971), memb Ct RCA; Hon Doctorate: RCA 1985, De Montfort Univ 1998, Univ of Staffs 1998, Open Univ 2003; Hon DUniv Heriot-Watt 1986, Hon DUniv Plymouth 2013; FCSD 1965 (pres 1987–89), RDI 1969 (Master of Faculty 1982–84); *Books* Living by Design (jtly 1977), The Compendium (jtly, 1993), Kenneth Grange Making Britain Modern (2011); *Recreations* building; *Style—* Sir Kenneth Grange, CBE, RDI; ✉ Pentagram, 11 Needham Road, London W11 2RP

GRANT, Andrew William; DL (Worcs 2006); s of Francis Denis Grant, of Worcestershire; *b* 11 April 1945; *Educ* Belmont Abbey Hereford; *m* 1995, Beatrice Irene Helen Victoria, da of (John) Miles Huntington-Whiteley, *qv*; 2 s (Frederik Francis Thomas Augustus b 1999, Ludovic William Miles Hubertus b 2002); *Career* chartered surveyor and landowner; prop Andrew Grant estate agents and surveyors 1971–; CLA: memb Cncl 1996–2012, pres Worcs branch 2002–05 (vice-chm 1996–99, chm 1999–2002), chm W Midlands Regnl Ctee 2004–07; hon vice-pres Worcester branch Br Red Cross; tstee: Elizabeth FitzRoy Support 1993–2014, Worcester and Dudley Historic Churches Assocs; govr St Richard's Hospice 1979–89 (patron 2006–), chm St Mary's Convent Sch 1989–99, pres Worcester Cons Assoc 2006–, tstee Worcester Community Fndn; High Sheriff Herefords and Worcs 2005–06; FRICS; KM 2004; *Recreations* shooting; *Clubs* Brooks's, White's, Blackwell Golf; *Style—* Andrew Grant, Esq, DL; ✉ Bransford Manor, Worcester WR6 5JG (☎ 01886 832368, e-mail andrewgrantdl@gmail.com)

GRANT, Anthony Ernest; OBE (2005); s of Ernest Grant (d 1985), and Doris, *née* Hughes (d 1991); *b* 23 April 1940; *Educ* King Edward VII GS Sheffield, Keble Coll Oxford (MA); *m* 14 April 1962, Darel Avis, da of Frederick John Atkinson (d 1980); 3 da (Henrietta (Mrs Michael Flood) b 1965, Sarah (Mrs Angus Ward) b 1966, Philippa (Mrs Matthew Odell) b 1969); *Career* Coopers & Lybrand CAs 1961–96; chm Leeds Financial Services Initiative 1993–94; non-exec dir: Rocom Group Ltd 1996–2001, Leeds Building Soc 1996–2006, John Cotton Gp Ltd 1997–, TVision Technology Ltd 2002–07; pres W Yorks CAs 1993–94, pres Leeds C of C 1996–99, chm W Yorks Employer Coalition 2000–05, dep chm Leeds Met Univ 1990–91; tstee: Thackray Medical Museum 2004–09, W Yorks Police Community Tst 2006–12, Friends of Cudeca Hospice 2009–14; High Sheriff W Yorks 2011–12; *Clubs* Oxford and Cambridge; *Style—* Anthony Grant, Esq, OBE; ✉ 63 Old Park Road, Leeds LS8 1JB (☎ 0113 266 3721, e-mail anthony.grant@oprleeds.co.uk)

GRANT, Charles Peter; CMG (2013); s of Peter Forbes Grant (d 1974), and Elizabeth Ann, *née* Shirreff; *b* 9 October 1958, Oxford; *Educ* Marlborough, Univ of Cambridge, Univ of Grenoble; *Career* early career with Euromoney; The Economist: City writer 1986–89, in Brussels 1989–93, writer on British affrs London 1993–94, defence ed 1994–98; dir Centre for European Reform 1998– (fndr 1995); dir British Cncl 2002–08; memb: Bd Edam (Turkish Centre for Economic and Foreign Policy Studies), Bd Terra Nova (France), Bd Moscow Sch of Political Studies; Prix Stendhal Adelphi Fndn 1992; Chevalier de l'Ordre Nationale du Mérite (France) 2003, Bene Merito (Poland) 2015, Star of Italy 2015; *Publications* Delors: Inside the House that Jacques Built (1994); author of numerous pubns and essays for Centre for European Reform; *Recreations* hill walking, music; *Clubs* Reform; *Style—* Charles Grant, Esq, CMG; ✉ Centre for European Reform, 14 Great College Street, London, SW1P 3RX (☎ 020 7233 1199, fax 020 7233 1117, e-mail charles@cer.org.uk)

GRANT, Dr Sir David; kt (2016), CBE; *Educ* King's Sch Tynemouth, Univ of Durham (PhD); *Career* md Dowty Electronics Ltd 1984–88, technical dir Dowty Gp 1988–91, technical dir GEC plc 1991, vice-chllr Cardiff Univ 2001–; vice-pres Royal Acad of Engrg; IEE Mensforth Gold Medal 1996; FREng, FLSW, CEng, FIET; *Style—* Dr Sir David Grant, CBE; ✉ Vice-Chancellor's Office, Cardiff University, Cardiff CF10 3AT

GRANT, Helen; MP; *b* 28 September 1961, London; *Educ* Univ of Hull, Coll of Law Guildford; *m* 1991, Simon; 2 s; *Career* admitted slr 1988; estab Grants Slrs 1996; non-exec dir Croydon NHS Primary Care Tst 2005–07; MP (Cons) Maidstone and The Weald 2010–, under-sec of state for justice and under sec for women and equalities 2012–14, min for sport and tourism 2013–15; *Style—* Mrs Helen Grant, MP; ✉ House of Commons, London SW1A 0AA

GRANT, Hugh John Mungo; s of James Murray Grant, of Chiswick, and late Fynvola Susan, *née* MacLean; *b* 9 September 1960; *Educ* Latymer Upper Sch, New Coll Oxford (scholarship, BA); *Career* actor; began career in theatre performing Jockeys of Norfolk (written with Chris Lang & Andy Taylor); prodr Simian Films; *Films* incl: Privileged, Maurice (Best Actor Venice Film Festival 1987 (jtly with James Wilby)), White Mischief, Rowing with the Wind, The Dawning, The Bengali Night, The Lair of the White Worm, Impromptu, The Big Man, Bitter Moon, Night Train to Venice, The Remains of the Day, Sirens, Four Weddings and a Funeral (Best Actor BAFTA Awards 1995, Best Actor in a Comedy Golden Globe Awards 1995, Peter Sellers Award for Comedy Evening Standard British Film Awards 1995), An Awfully Big Adventure, Restoration, The Englishman Who Went Up a Hill But Came Down a Mountain, Nine Months, Sense & Sensibility, Extreme Measures, Notting Hill (Peter Sellers Award for Comedy Evening Standard British Film Awards 2000, Best British Actor Empire Film Awards 2000, nomination Best Actor in a Comedy Golden Globe Awards 2000), Mickey Blue Eyes, Small Time Crooks, Bridget Jones' Diary (Peter Sellers Award for Comedy Evening Standard British Film Awards 2002), About a Boy (Best British Actor Empire Film Awards 2003, Best British Actor London Critics Circle Film Awards 2003), Two Weeks Notice, Love Actually, Bridget Jones: The Edge of Reason, American Dreamz, Music and Lyrics, Did You Hear About The Morgans?, The Pirates! In an Adventure with Scientists!, Cloud Atlas; *Style—* Hugh Grant, Esq; ✉ c/o Laura Scully, Second Floor, 42 Westbourne Grove, London W2 5SH (☎ 020 7284 0263, fax 020 7482 6714)

GRANT, Sir Ian David; kt (2010), CBE (1988), DL (Perth and Kinross 2010); s of Alan Howison Brewster Grant (d 1974), and Florence Ogilvie, *née* Swan (d 2006); *b* 28 July 1943; *Educ* Strathallan Sch, E of Scotland Coll of Agric (Dip); *m* 19 July 1968, Eileen May Louisa, da of Alexander Yule; 3 da (Catherine Louise b 10 Jan 1970, Jane Belle b 14 July 1971, Rosanne Elaine b 1 March 1974); *Career* dir East of Scotland Farmers 1976–2002, chm Copa Cereals Gp Brussels 1982–86, pres NFU Scotland 1984–90 (vice-pres 1981–84), chm Grains Gp Int Fedn of Agric Producers 1984–89; dir: Clydesdale Bank plc 1989–97, NFU Mutual Insurance Soc 1990–2008 (dep chm 2003–2008), Scottish and Southern Energy plc (formerly Scottish Hydro Electric plc) 1992–2003 (dep chm 2000–03); chm Crown Estate 2002–09 (cmmr 1996–2009); chm: Scottish Tourist Bd 1990–98 (memb Bd 1988–98), Cairngorms Partnership 1998–2003, Scot Exhbn Centre Ltd 2002–

13 (dep chm 2001, dir 1998–); memb: Cncl CBI Scotland 1984–96, Bd Br Tourist Authy 1990–98; tstee: NFU Mutual Charitable Trust 2009–, Queen Elizabeth Castle of Mey Trust 2010–; FRAgS; *Recreations* gardening, travel, reading, music; *Clubs* Royal Smithfield (vice-pres); *Style*— Sir Ian Grant, CBE

GRANT, Prof Ian Philip; s of Harold H Grant (d 1981), and Isabella Henrietta, *née* Ornstien (d 1980); *b* 15 December 1930; *Educ* St Albans Sch, Wadham Coll Oxford (open scholar, MA, DPhil); *m* 1958, Beryl Cohen; 2 s (Paul Simon b 1960, David Michael b 1962); *Career* princ scientific offr UKAEA Aldermaston 1961–64 (sr scientific offr 1957–61); Pembroke Coll Oxford: Atlas research fell (jt appt with SRC Atlas Computer Lab) 1964–69, tutorial fell in mathematics 1969–98 (fell emeritus 1998–), actg master 1984–85; Univ of Oxford: univ lectr in mathematics 1969–90, reader in mathematical physics 1990–92, prof of mathematical physics 1992–98 (prof emeritus 1998–); visiting prof: McGill Univ Montreal 1976, Åbo Akademi Finland 1977, Inst de Fisica Univ Nacional Autónoma de México 1981; chm Oxford Synagogue and Jewish Centre 1985–2004; govr: Royal GS High Wycombe 1981–2000, St Paul's Sch London 1993–2001; memb London Mathematical Soc 1977; CMath 1992; FRAS 1964, FRS 1992, FInstP 2005; *Publications* Relativistic Quantum Theory of Atoms and Molecules (2006), author of papers in learned jls on relativistic quantum theory in atomic and molecular physics, and on radiative transfer theory in astrophysics and atmospheric science; *Recreations* walking, music, conversation; *Style*— Prof Ian Grant, FRS; ✉ Mathematical Institute, University of Oxford, Andrew Wiles Building, Radcliffe Observatory Quarter, Woodstock Road, Oxford OX2 6GG (e-mail ipg@maths.ox.ac.uk)

GRANT, Dr Jane Wentworth; *née* Gibbons; *b* 28 April 1942, Dorchester; *Educ* Univ of Bristol (BA), Inst of Educn Univ of London (PGCE), Univ of Essex (MA, MPhil), Univ of Lagos (Cert Yoruba), Univ of Kent (PhD); *m* Neville J H Grant; 2 s, 1 da; *Career* various English teaching posts Dar-es-Salaam and England 1964–69, lectr Univ of Lagos 1971–73, educn offr/admin African Arts in Educn Project 1980–84, devpt offr Policy and Promotions Dept Nat Cncl for Voluntary Orgns 1984–89, dir Nat Alliance of Women's Orgns 1989–94, former consit and researcher on governance of women's orgns; non-exec dir Oxleas Mental Health Tst 2003–; reader Queen's Anniversary Prizes for Higher and Further Educn; memb: Advsy Cncl Global Fund for Women, Advsy Gp, Nat Alliance of Women's Orgns, Women's Studies Network, Int Working Gp of Women's Nat Cmmn; govr Churchfield Sch; FRSA; *Books* In the Steps of Exceptional Women: The Story of the Fawcett Society (2016); author of numerous pubns on multi-cultural educn and women's issues, incl The Governance of Women's Organisations Towards Better Practice (2002); *Clubs* Commonwealth, Fawcett Soc, Women's Int League for Peace and Freedom, UNA-UK; *Style*— Dr Jane Grant; ✉ Apt 6 Bardon Lodge, 17 Stratheden Road, Blackheath, London SE3 7TE (☎ 020 8858 8489, e-mail jane.wentworthgrant@gmail.com)

GRANT, Prof John; s of John Grant, of Bedlington, and Ivy Grant; *b* 8 January 1948; *Educ* Bedlington GS, Univ of Leeds (BSc, Brodetsky prize), Univ of Newcastle upon Tyne (PhD); *m* Elizabeth, da of Robert Foster, and Ivy Foster; 2 da (Julie b 22 Nov 1972, Lara b 11 July 1974), 1 s (David b 8 May 1981); *Career* senior sci offr RAE Farnborough 1972–79; Parsons Power Generation Systems (Rolls-Royce Industrial Power Group): princ design engr 1979, chief devpt engr 1991, dir Turbine-Generator Devpt 1994, tech dir 1996–97; engrg dir Siemens Power Generation 1997–2003; visiting prof in principles of engrg design Univ of Newcastle upon Tyne 1997–2004, ret; author of numerous tech papers in jls and conf and seminar proceedings; Alan Marsh Meml Award RAeS 1976; FIMechE 1991, FREng 1996; *Recreations* gardening, church; *Style*— Prof John Grant, FREng; ☎ 01670 791836, e-mail shamels@tiscali.co.uk

GRANT, John Albert Martin; s of late Walter Grant, and Irene, *née* Smyth; *b* 13 October 1945, Belfast; *Educ* Campbell Coll Belfast, Queen's Univ Belfast (BSc), Cranfield Sch of Mgmnt (MBA), Univ of Bolton (DEng); *m* 1971, Corinne, da of late John Porter, and Sally Porter; 2 da (Joanna b 27 March 1974, Nicola b 9 June 1976), 1 s (James b 23 April 1979); *Career* Ford of Europe: treas 1985–87, vice-pres Business Strategy 1987–88; exec dir Corp Strategy Ford Motor Co (US) 1989, exec dep chm Jaguar Ltd 1990–92; fin dir: Lucas Industries plc 1992–96, Lucas Varity plc 1996; chief exec Ascot plc 1997–2000; chm: Hasgo Group Ltd 2000–09, Peter Stubs Ltd 2000–05, The Royal Automobile Club Motor Sports Assoc Ltd 2002–05, Torotrak plc 2005–11 (non-exec dir 1998–2005), Surion Energy Ltd 2009–10, Gas Turbine Efficiency plc 2010–11; non-exec dir: National Grid plc 1995–2006, Corac plc 2000–06, Royal Automobile Club Ltd 2004–10, MHP SA 2006–, Melrose plc 2006–, Pace plc 2008–15, Wolfson Microelectronics plc 2011–14, Augean plc 2015–, Touch Bionics Ltd 2015–; chm Br Racing Drivers' Club Ltd 2013–; memb FIA World Motorsports Cncl 2003–05; FCT 1976; *Recreations* motor sport, skiing, opera; *Clubs* RAC, BRDC; *Style*— Mr John Grant; ✉ The Malthouse, Manor Lane, Claverdon, Warwick CV35 8NH (☎ 01926 842459 (office), e-mail johngrant13@btconnect.com)

GRANT, Prof John Paxton; s of John Dickson Grant (d 1968), and Jean Ramsay, *née* Paxton (d 1993); *b* 22 February 1944; *Educ* George Heriot's Sch, Univ of Edinburgh (LLB, Lord President Cooper prize), Univ of Pennsylvania (LLM); *m* 1983, Elaine Elizabeth, da of Eric Roy McGillvray Sutherland; *Career* lectr in public law: Univ of Aberdeen 1967–71, Univ of Dundee 1971–74; Faculty of Law Univ of Glasgow: sr lectr 1974–88, prof 1988–99, dean 1985–89 and 1992–96; prof of law Lewis and Clark Sch of Law Portland Oregon 1999–, prof emeritus Univ of Glasgow 1999–; ed The Juridical Review 1988–99; *Books* Independence and Devolution: The Legal Implications for Scotland (1976), The Impact of Marine Pollution (with Cusine, 1980), The Encyclopaedic Dictionary of International Law (with Parry, 1986), Legal Education 2000 (1989), English-Estonian Law Glossary (1993), English for Lawyers (1994), The Lockerbie Trial Briefing Handbook (1999, 2 edn 2000), The Encyclopaedic Dictionary of International Law (with Barker, 2 edn 2003), The Lockerbie Trial: A Documentary History (2004), International Law Deskbook (2005); *Recreations* walking, travelling; *Style*— Prof John Grant

GRANT, Dr John William; s of late John MacDonald Grant, and Isabella Grigor Clark, *née* Morrison; *b* 27 May 1953; *Educ* Dingwall Acad Ross & Cromarty, Univ of Aberdeen (MB ChB, MD); *m* 14 Nov 1980, Daniela, da of Hans Felix, of Bex, Switzerland; 2 da (Joanna b 1983, Marsali b 1986); *Career* registrar pathology Ninewells Hosp Dundee 1979–81, sr registrar in neuropathology and histopathology Southampton Gen Hosp 1981–86, Oberarzt Inst of Pathology Univ of Zürich Switzerland 1986–88; conslt histopathologist Addenbrooke's Hosp Cambridge 1988–, assoc lectr Univ of Cambridge 1989–, fell Emmanuel Coll Cambridge; MA Univ of Cambridge 1995; memb: BMA, Pathological Soc, Br Neuropathology Soc, Swiss Neuropathology Soc, ACP; FRCPath 1996 (MRCPath 1984); *Recreations* skiing, photography, squash; *Style*— Dr John W Grant; ✉ 243 Hinton Way, Great Shelford, Cambridge CB2 5AN; Histopathology Department, Box 235, Addenbrooke's Hospital, Hills Road, Cambridge CB2 2QQ (☎ 01223 216744, fax 01223 216980, e-mail jwg21@cam.ac.uk)

GRANT, Prof Sir Malcolm John; kt (2013), CBE (2003); s of Francis William Grant (d 1987), and Vera Jessica, *née* Cooke; *b* 29 November 1947; *Educ* Waitaki HS Oamaru, Univ of Otago (LLB, LLM, LLD); *m* 13 July 1974, Christine Joan, da of Thomas John Endersbee, ISO (d 1986); 2 s (Nikolas b 1976, Thomas b 1980), 1 da (Joanna b 1978); *Career* sr lectr in law (former lectr) Univ of Southampton 1972–86, prof of law UCL 1988–91 (sr lectr 1986–88), prof of land economy Univ of Cambridge 1991–2003; fell Clare Coll Cambridge 1991–, pro-vice-chllr Univ of Cambridge 2002–03, provost and pres UCL 2003–13, univ advsr Arizona State Univ 2015–, memb Int Cncl of Russian Fedn Govt on 5–100 Univ Improvement Prog 2013–; cmmr for local govt for England 1992–2002; chm Local Govt Cmmn 1996–2002 (dep chm 1995–96), chm Agric and Environment Biotechnology Cmmn 2000–05, chm Steering Bd Nat GM Public Debate 2003–04, memb Standards Ctee GLA 2000–08 (chair 2004–08), memb ESRC 2008–11, memb HEFCE 2009–15, pres Cncl for At-Risk Academics 2013–; called to the Bar Middle Temple 1998 (bencher 2005); ed Encyclopaedia of Planning Law and Practice 1982–2005 (conslt ed 2005–), conslt ed Encyclopaedia of Environmental Law 1993–; tstee: Ditchley Fndn 2002–11, Somerset House 2014–; govr London Business Sch 2003–13, govr Royal Instn 2006–10, chm Russell Gp of UK Research Univs 2006–09, memb Hong Kong Univs Grants Ctee 2007–15, chm NHS Commissioning Bd (now NHS England) 2011–, chllr Univ of York 2015–; dir Genomics England Ltd 2014–; Br business ambass 2008–; Hon LLD Univ of Otago 2006, Hon LLD UCL 2013; life hon memb NZ Resource Mgmnt Law Assoc 2000; Hon MRTPI 1994, Hon ARICS 1995; FAcSS 2001; Officier dans l'Ordre Nationale de Mérite (France) 2004; *Books* Planning Law Handbook (1981), Urban Planning Law (1982, supplement 1989), Rate Capping and the Law (1984, 2 edn 1986), Permitted Development (1989, 2 edn 1996), Singapore Planning Law (1999), Environmental Court Report (2000); *Recreations* opera, gardening, forestry, health, grandchildren; *Style*— Prof Sir Malcolm Grant, CBE

GRANT, Nicholas; s of Hugo Moore Grant (d 1987), of Edinburgh, and Cara Phyllis, *née* McMullen-Pearson (d 2007); *b* 24 March 1948; *Educ* Durham Sch, Univ of London (LLB), Univ of Warwick (MA); *m* 5 Nov 1977, Rosalind Louise, da of Winston Maynard Pipe; 1 s (Robert b 1979), 1 da (Rosemary b 1981); *Career* head of res and PR Confedn of Health Serv Employees 1972–82, dir of communications Lab Pty 1983–85, public affrs advsr to Mirror Group Newspapers 1985–89; currently ceo Mediatrack Research Ltd; memb: (Lab) Lambeth BC 1978–84, West Lambeth DHA 1982–84; Parly candidate (Lab) Reigate 1979; assoc Market Res Soc; fell Int Assoc for the Measurement and Evaluation of Communication (FIAMEC, past pres), FCIPR, FRSA; *Books* Economics of Prosperity (contrib, 1980), Political Communication for British General Election (1983); *Recreations* hill walking, history, chess, music, running; *Style*— Nicholas Grant, Esq; ✉ Tigh na Clachan, Fearnan, Perthshire PH15 2PF; Mediatrack Research Ltd, 61 Queen Square, Bristol BS1 4JZ (☎ 020 7430 0699, e-mail ngrant@mediatrack.com)

GRANT, Patrick James; s of James Grant, and Susan *née* Fitzearle; *b* 1 May 1972, Edinburgh; *Educ* Univ of Leeds (BEng), Said Business Sch Oxford Univ (MBA); *Career* dir Norton & Sons; Menswear Designer of the Year British Fashion Cncl 2010–; hon professorship Sch for Business and Society Glasgow Caledonian Univ; *Style*— Mr Patrick Grant; ✉ 16 Savile Row, London W1S 3PL

GRANT, Sir Paul Joseph Patrick; kt (2009), DL (London, 2009); s of Thomas Grant (d 1988), and Teresa, *née* Walsh (d 1995); *b* 16 May 1957, Liverpool; *Educ* Salesian Coll Bootle, Univ of Hull (BA), Univ of Durham (PGCE), Univ of London (MA); *m* Aug 1996, Deniece, *née* Jones; 3 da (Niamh b 23 May 1994, Sorcha b 22 April 1999, Alannah b 6 May 2003); *Career* history teacher Whitby Sch 1979–87 (teacher exchange Port Macquarie HS NSW 1986), head of history St Bonaventure's Newham 1987–90 (head of Year 11 1989–90); Robert Clack Sch Dagenham: head of humanities 1990–, sch professional tutor 1994–, headteacher 1997–; hon fell Faculty of Educn Univ of Hull 2012, visiting prof of educn Faculty of Health, Social Care and Educn Anglia Ruskin Univ 2012; conslt headteacher: Nat Coll for Sch Leadership, Specialist Schs and Acads Tst; memb: Educn Bd Business in the Community, SHA 1997–, Orgn for Sch Ldrs, Premier League Educn Advsy Bd 2013–; Prince of Wales Teaching Inst 2003–, tstee Robert Clack School of Science Alumni 2011–; Nat Ldr of Educn 2014; Freedom of Borough of Barking and Dagenham 2010; DLitt (hc) Univ of Hull 2011; *Publications* Changing Times (1990); *Recreations* holidaying in France, sport particularly football (Liverpool FC and Everton FC), reading historical/political suspense novels during holiday time, film, cinema, Lancs CC, cycling; *Clubs* Imperial Knights; *Style*— Sir Paul Grant, DL; ✉ Robert Clack School, Gosfield Road, Dagenham RM8 1JU (☎ 020 8270 4227, e-mail pgrant@robert-clack.bardaglea.org.uk)

GRANT, Rhoda; MSP; da of Donald and Morag MacCuish, of Kenmore; *b* 26 June 1963; *Educ* Plockton HS, Inverness Coll of Further and Higher Educn, Open Univ (BSc); *m* 4 Aug 1989, Mark Grant; *Career* Unison 1993–99; Highland Regnl Cncl 1987–93; MSP (Lab) Highlands & Islands 1999–2003 and 2007–; *Style*— Mrs Rhoda Grant, MSP; ✉ The Scottish Parliament, Edinburgh EH99 1SP

GRANT, Richard E; *b* 5 May 1957; *Educ* Waterford-Kamthlaba Mbabane, Univ of Cape Town (BA); *m* 1 Nov 1986, Joan Washington, *qv*; 1 da (Olivia b 4 Jan 1989); *Career* actor; *Theatre* co-fndr Troupe Theatre Co Cape Town 1980–82; credits incl: Man of Mode (Orange Tree) 1983, A Midsummer Night's Dream and Merry Wives of Windsor (Regents Park) 1984, Tramway Road (Lyric Hammersmith) 1984, The Importance of Being Earnest (Aldwych) 1993, The Play What I Wrote (West End) 2002, Otherwise Engaged (Criterion Theatre) 2006, My Fair Lady (Sydney Opera Co) 2008; *Television* for BBC incl: Honest Decent and True 1985, Here is the News 1988, Suddenly Last Summer 1992, Bed 1994, Karaoke (with Channel Four) 1995; A Royal Scandal 1996, The Scarlet Pimpernel 1998, Agatha Christie's Nemesis 2006, Mumbai Calling 2008, The Fear 2012, Art of Paradise 2012, Hotel Secrets 2012, Dr Who Christmas Special 2012, Girls 2013, Hotel Secrets 2013, Downton Abbey 2014; *Film* incl: Withnail and I 1986, Warlock 1988, How to Get Ahead in Advertising 1988, Mountains of the Moon 1988, Killing Dad 1989, Henry and June 1989, LA Story 1990, Hudson Hawk 1990, The Player 1992, The Age of Innocence 1992, Dracula 1993, Prêt a Porter 1994, Cool Light of Day 1994, Jack & Sarah 1995, Portrait of a Lady 1995, Twelfth Night 1995, The Serpent's Kiss 1996, Food of Love 1996, Keep The Aspidistra Flying 1997, St Ives 1997, Spiceworld The Movie 1997, The Match 1998, A Christmas Carol 1999, Trial and Retribution 1999, The Little Vampire 1999, Hildegarde 2000, Gosford Park 2001, The Hound of the Baskervilles 2002, Monsieur N. 2003, Bright Young Things 2003, Tooth 2004, Colour Me Kubrick 2004, Wah-Wah 2004 (writer and dir), Garden of Eden 2008, The Iron Lady 2011, Dom Hemmingway 2012; *Books* With Nails (1996), By Design (1998), Wah Wah Diaries (2006); *Recreations* scuba diving, building dolls houses, photography; *Style*— Richard E Grant, Esq; ✉ c/o ARG Talent, 4A Exmoor Street, London W10 6BD (☎ 020 7436 6400, website www.richard-e-grant.com)

GRANT, Susan Lavinia; da of Donald Blane Grant, of Dundee, Scotland, and Lavinia Ruth, *née* Ritchie; *b* 29 January 1948; *Educ* St Leonard's Sch St Andrews Scotland, Goldsmiths Coll London; *m* 1, 1969 (m dis 1973), Charles Sharpe; m 2, 1975 (m dis 1983), Ian Woolgar; 1 da (Lavinia Unity b 1977), 1 s (Edward Rupert b 1980); *Career* res exec J Walter Thompson 1968–74, researcher BBC Publications then publicity exec BBC TV 1974–78, publicity mangr Hamlyns 1978–82, account mangr then account dir Good Relations 1982–86, fndr dir and memb Bd The Communication Group 1986–; currently fndr ptnr Grant Butler Coomber Group; MIPR; *Recreations* tennis, golf, waterskiing, Scotland, painting; *Clubs* Riverside Racquets, Panmure Golf; *Style*— Ms Susan Grant

GRANT OF DALVEY, Sir Patrick Alexander Benedict; 14 Bt (NS 1688), of Dalvey; Chieftain of Clan Donnachaidh Grants; s of Sir Duncan Alexander Grant of Dalvey, 13 Bt (d 1961), of Polmaily, Glen Urquhart, Inverness-shire, and Joan Penelope, *née* Cope (d 1991); *b* 5 February 1953; *Educ* Fort Augustus Abbey Sch, Univ of Glasgow (LLB); *m* 1981 (m dis 2005), Dr Carolyn Elizabeth, da of Dr John Highet, of Pollokshields, Glasgow; 2 s (Duncan Archibald Ludovic b 1982, Neil Patrick b 21 Oct 1983); *Heir* s, Duncan Grant of Dalvey; *Career* deerstalker/gamekeeper 1969–71, inshore fisherman/skipper Scottish Highlands W Coast 1971–76; chm and md Grants of Dalvey Ltd 1987–; chm The Clan Grant Museum Tst, former chm The Clan Grant Soc; winner Queen's Award for Export 1992, Highland Business Award 1995; *Recreations* deerstalking, Scottish piping; *Clubs* New

G

(Edinburgh); *Style*— Sir Patrick Grant of Dalvey, Bt; ✉ Tomintoul House, Flichity, Farr, Inverness-shire IV1 2XD; Grants of Dalvey Ltd, Alness, Ross-shire IV17 0XT

GRANT OF MONYMUSK, Sir Archibald; 13 Bt (NS 1705), of Cullen, Co Buchan; s of Capt Sir Francis Cullen Grant, 12 Bt (d 1966, himself tenth in descent from Archibald Grant, whose f d 1553 and whose er bro John was ancestor of the Barons Strathspey), by his w Jean, only da of Capt Humphrey Tollemache, RN (s of Hon Douglas Tollemache, 8 s of 1 Baron Tollemache); *b* 2 September 1954, London; *Educ* Trinity Coll Glenalmond, RAC Cirencester (Dip Farm Mgmnt); *m* 1, 31 Dec 1982 (m dis 2010), Barbara Elizabeth, eldest da of Andrew Garden Duff Forbes, of Druminnor Castle, Rhynie, Aberdeenshire, and Mrs Alison Forbes; 2 da; m 2, 28 July 2012, Fiona Mary Julia, eldest da of late Sir Duncan Grant, and late Lady Grant; *Career* farmer; *Recreations* hill walking, shooting, water divining; *Clubs* Royal Northern; *Style*— Sir Archibald Grant of Monymusk, Bt; ✉ House of Monymusk, Monymusk, Inverurie AB51 7HL (☎ 01467 651220); Estate Office, Monymusk, Inverurie AB51 7HL (☎ 01467 651333, fax 01467 651250, e-mail ag@monymusk.com, website www.monymusk.com)

GRANT PETERKIN, Joanna; da of Sir Brian Young, and Fiona Marjorie, *née* Stewart (d 1997); *b* 4 July 1949, Windsor; *Educ* Downe House, Wycombe HS, Univ of Durham (BA), Univ of Oxford (PGCE); *m* Maj-Gen Peter Grant Peterkin, CB, OBE, *qv*; 1 da (Alexandra (Mrs James Burton) b 1975), 1 s (James b 1977); *Career* St Paul's Girls' Sch: teacher 1989–96, advsr on univ entrance 1996–98; head St George's Sch Ascot 1999–2005, educn conslt 2005–; govr: St John's Sch Leatherhead until 2013, Downe House 2010–, Malvern Coll 2011–14, Gordonstoun 2013–; memb Ctee Westminster Under Sch 2008–, tstee North Foreland Lodge Tst until 2013; *Recreations* playing the piano and cello, dance, film, visiting churches, most music; *Style*— Mrs Joanna Grant Peterkin; ✉ Grange Hall, Forres Moray IV36 2TR (☎ 01309 672742); 20 Bridstow Place, London W2 5AE (☎ 07765 676879, e-mail grantpeterkinj@gmail.com)

GRANT PETERKIN, Maj-Gen (Anthony) Peter; CB (2003), OBE (1990); s of Brig James A Grant Peterkin (d 1981), and Dorothea, *née* Chapman; *b* 6 July 1947; *Educ* Ampleforth, RMA Sandhurst, Univ of Durham (BA, MSc); *m* 1974, Joanna Grant Peterkin , *qv*, da of Sir Brian Young; 1 s, 1 da; *Career* Cdr 24 Airmobile Bde 1993–94, RCDS 1995, dep mil sec 1996–98, md OSCE mission to Kosovo 1999, GOC 5 Div 2000, mil sec and chief exec Army Personnel Centre 2001–03, serjeant at arms House of Commons 2005–08; chm: Saigon Children's Charity, Bee House Educn, Highlanders' Museum; *Clubs* Army and Navy; *Style*— Maj-Gen Peter Grant Peterkin, CB, OBE; ✉ Grange Hall, Forres, Moray IV36 2TR (☎ 01309 672742, e-mail petergp@yahoo.com)

GRANTCHESTER, 3 Baron (UK 1953); Christopher John Suenson-Taylor; s of 2 Baron Grantchester, CBE, QC (d 1995), and Betty, *née* Moores; *b* 8 April 1951; *Educ* Winchester, LSE (BSc); *m* 1973 (m dis 2001), Jacqueline, da of Dr Leo Jaffé; 2 da (Hon Holly Rachel b 1975, Hon Hannah Robyn b 1984), 2 s (Hon Jesse David b 1977, Hon Adam Joel b 1987); *Heir* s, Hon Jesse Suenson-Taylor; *Career* dairy farmer and cattle breeder; pres Western Holstein Club 1999–2000, chm SW Cheshire Dairy Assoc; pres and dir Royal Assoc of Br Dairy Farmers 2001–04; former memb Cncl Holstein Soc Exec; former memb Cncl: RASE Cheshire Agric Soc; Supreme Dairy Female RASE 1990 and 1991; dir Five Six (Liverpool) Ltd, chm Dairy Farmers of Britain 2008–09; UK Parliament: memb Sub Ctee D EU Ctee 1997–99, memb Hybrids Ctee 2004–, opposition whip 2010–; tstee Fndn for Sport and the Arts; *Recreations* soccer; *Style*— The Rt Hon the Lord Grantchester; ✉ Lower House Farm, Back Coole Lane, Audlem, Crewe, Cheshire (☎ 01270 811363)

GRANTHAM, Bishop of 2015–; Rt Rev Dr Nicholas Alan Chamberlain; s of Alan Roger Chamberlain, and Pauline Biggs, of Old Basing, Hants; *b* 25 November 1963, Chiswick; *Educ* Christleton County HS Chester, St Chad's Coll Durham Univ (BA, PhD), Univ of Edinburgh (BD); *Career* ordained: deacon 1991, priest 1992; St Mary Cockerton Co Durham, curate then team vicar St Francis's Church Newton Aycliffe Co Durham 1994–98, priest-in-charge St Barnabas's Church Burnmoor Co Durham 1998–2006, vicar Parish of St George and St Hilda Jesmond Dio of Newcastle 2006–15; *Recreations* cinema, music, reading, running, travel, walking; *Clubs* Northern Counties; *Style*— The Rt Rev the Bishop of Grantham; ✉ Edward King House, Minster Yard, Lincoln LN2 1PU (☎ 01522 504090)

GRANTLEY, 8 Baron (GB 1782); Richard William Brinsley Norton; s of 7 Baron Grantley, MC (d 1995), and Lady Deirdre Elisabeth Freda Hare, da of 5 Earl of Listowel; *b* 30 January 1956; *Educ* Ampleforth, New Coll Oxford (MA, pres Oxford Union); *Heir* bro, Hon Francis Norton; *Career* merchant banker; Conservative Research Dept 1977–81, cllr RBK&C 1982–86, Parly candidate (Cons) 1983, former ldr UK Independence Pty in the House of Lords; former dir Morgan Grenfell Int Ltd, dir project and export fin HSBC Bank plc 1997–2005; dir Hosp of St John and St Elizabeth 2008–12; Knight SMOM; *Recreations* Bridge, smoking; *Clubs* Pratt's, Polish; *Style*— The Rt Hon the Lord Grantley; ✉ 8 Halsey Street, London SW3 2QH

GRATTAN, Prof Kenneth Thomas Victor; s of William Grattan (d 1983), and Sarah Jane Grattan (d 1978); *b* 9 December 1953; *Educ* Lurgan Coll Co Armagh, Queen's Univ Belfast (BSc, Dunville Scholar, PhD), City Univ London (DSc); *m* 28 Sept 1979, Lesley Sharon, da of Robert George Allen (d 2003); *Career* postdoctoral research asst Dept of Physics Imperial Coll of Sci and Tech London 1978–83; City Univ London: lectr in measurement and instrumentation 1983–87, sr lectr 1987–88, reader 1988–91, prof of measurement and instrumentation 1991–2013, head Dept of Electrical, Electronic & Information Engrg 1991–2001, assoc dean Sch of Engrg and Mathematical Sciences 2001–06, dep dean Sch of Engrg and Mathematical Sciences 2006–08, dean Sch of Informatics and Sch of Egrg and Mathematical Sciences 2008–12; dean City Grad Sch 2012–; George Daniels prof of scientific instrumentation Royal Acad of Engrg 2013–; ed Measurement 2001–; pres Int Measurement Confedn (IMEKO) 2015–; numerous invited lectures and talks to professional bodies and int meetings; Liveryman Worshipful Co of Scientific Instrument Makers 1995 (steward 1998–2011, asst 2011–); FInstP 1992 (memb 1984, Optics and Photonics Division Prize 2010), FIET (FIEE 1992, memb 1985), FInstMC 1995 (memb 1986, Callendar Medal 1992, vice-pres 1996–99, pres 2000, Hartley Medal 2012), FREng 2008; *Publications* Concise Encyclopedia of Measurement and Instrumentation (with L Finkelstein, 1994), Optical Fiber Sensor Technology Vols I-V (with B T Meggitt, 1995, 1997, 1999 and 2000), Fiber Optic Fluorescence Thermometry (with Z Y Zhang, 1995); also author of over 800 papers on measurement, instrumentation and optics in leading int professional jls incl Physical Review, Review of Scientific Instruments, Sensors and Actuators and IEEE Transactions; *Recreations* philately, travel, photography, church affairs; *Style*— Prof Kenneth Grattan; ✉ City Graduate School, City University London, Northampton Square, London EC1V 0HB (☎ 020 7040 8120, e-mail k.t.v.grattan@city.ac.uk)

GRATWICKE, His Hon Judge Charles James Phillip; s of Maj Phillip Gratwicke (d 1993), and Maeve, *née* Power (d 1978); *b* 25 July 1951, Taunton, Somerset; *Educ* St Bernadine's Franciscan Coll Buckingham, St John's Coll Southsea, Univ of Leeds (LLB); *m* 31 Aug 1981, Jane Vivien, *née* Meyer; 2 s (James Phillip b 19 Dec 1983, Robert Charles b 1 Nov 1987), 1 da (Amy Jane b 3 Feb 1986); *Career* called to the Bar Middle Temple 1974; barr 1974–2003, asst recorder 1998–2000, recorder 2000–03, circuit judge 2003–, resident judge Chelmsford Crown Court 2012–, hon recorder of Chelmsford 2013; pt/t chm Disciplinary Ctee: Potato Mktg Bd 1988–2003, Milk Mktg Bd 1990–2000; *Recreations* long distance walks, sailing, travel, London in all its forms, marine paintings and all things maritime; *Clubs* Nat Lib Club, Seven Seas, Chelmsford, Essex; *Style*— His Hon Judge Gratwicke; ✉ The Crown Court, New Street, Chelmsford CM1 1EL (☎ 01245 603091)

GRAVES, Christopher; *b* 6 April 1956; *Educ* Westminster Sch, Queens' Coll Cambridge (MA, DipArch); *m* 17 May 1986, Amanda, *née* Mayhew; 2 da (Stephanie, Arabella), 1 s (Benedict); *Career* architect Trehearne and Norman 1981–85, dir Tudor Tst 1986–; RIBA 1983; *Style*— Christopher Graves, Esq; ✉ The Tudor Trust, 7 Ladbroke Grove, London W11 3BD

GRAY, Adam; s of David Mackrow Gray (d 2001), and Jillan Spensley, *née* Marsh Jones; *b* 21 October 1969; *Educ* Northampton Coll of FE; *Career* chef; Four Seasons Restaurant Inn on the Park Hotel London 1989–92, Le Manoir aux Quat'Saisons Oxford 1993–94, conslt chef Coral Reef Club Barbados 1994–95, head chef The Millennium Chelsea Hotel 1997–98, head chef Coast Restaurant London 1998–99 (Time Out Best Large Restaurant Award 1998), head chef city rhodes London 2001–03 (1 Michelin Star, 2 AA Rosettes, no 1 City Restaurant Hardens Restaurant Guide), head chef Rhodes Twenty Four 2003–11, exec head chef Skylon 2013–; *Publications* Mushrooms – Recipes from Leading Chefs (1998); *Recreations* cycling, swimming; *Style*— Adam Gray, Esq

GRAY, Alasdair James; s of Alex Gray (d 1973), and Amy, *née* Fleming (d 1952); *b* 28 December 1934; *Educ* Whitehill Secdy Sch, Glasgow Sch of Art (BA); *m* 1, 1961, Inge Sørensen; 1 s (Andrew); m 2, 1991, Morag McAlpine; *Career* pt/t art teacher and muralist 1958–62, theatrical scene painter Pavilion Vaudeville and Glasgow Citizens' Theatre 1963–64, painter and playwright 1964–76, artist recorder Peoples' Palace Glasgow (local history museum) 1977, writer in residence Univ of Glasgow 1977–80, novelist and playwright 1981–; assoc prof of creative writing Glasgow Univ 2001–03; murals in: Scottish USSR Friendship Soc, Greenhead Church of Scotland Bridgeton, Belleisle Street Synagogue Glasgow, Riverside Restaurant Bar Kirkfield Bank (painted 1969, restored 2009), Greenfield Church of Scotland Clarkston, Palacerigg Nature Reserve, Abbots House History Museum Dunfermline 1995, Ubiquitous Chip Restaurant Glasgow 2000, Oran Mor Leisure Centre Glasgow 2004; memb Soc of Authors; *Awards* for writing incl: Scottish Arts Cncl, Saltire Soc, Times, Guardian 1993, Whitbread 1993; *Books* Lanark: A Life in Four Books (1981), Unlikely Stories Mostly (1983), 1982 Janine (1984), The Fall of Kelvin Walker (1985), Lean Tales (with James Kelman and Agnes Owen, 1985), Saltire Self Portrait (1988), Old Negatives: 4 Verse Sequences (1989), Something Leather (1990), McGrotty and Ludmilla (1990), Why Scots Should Rule Scotland 1992 (1992), Poor Things (1992), Ten Tales Tall and True (1993), A History Maker (1994), Mavis Belfrage and Four Shorter Stories (1996), Why Scots Should Rule Scotland 1997 (1997), Working Legs: A Play for People Without Them (1997), Introduction to the Book of Jonah (1999), The Book of Prefaces (2000), Sixteen Occasional Poems (2000), A Short Survey of Classic Scottish Writing (2001), The End of Their Tethers: Thirteen Sorry Stories (2003), How We Should Rule Ourselves (with Adam Tomkins, 2005), Old Men in Love (2007), Fleck: A verse comedy derived from Goethe's Tragedy of Faust (2008), A Gray Play Book (2009), A Life in Pictures (2010), Collected Verses (2010), Every Short Story (collection, 2012), Of Me and Others – personal essays (2014), Independence Political Essays (2014); *Recreations* liking the English; *Style*— Alasdair Gray, Esq; ✉ art dealer: Sorcha Dallas, 5–9 St Margaret's Place, Glasgow G1 5JY (☎ and fax 0141 553 2662, e-mail sorcha@sorchadallas.com, website www.sorchadallas.com); literary agent (fiction): Zoe Waldie, Rogers, Coleridge & White Ltd, 20 Powis Mews, London W11 1JN (☎ 020 7221 3717, fax 020 7229 9084, e-mail info@rcwlitagency.com or zoewaldie@rcwlitagency.com, website www.rcwlitagency.com); literary agent (non-fiction): Jenny Brown, Jenny Brown Associates, 33 Argyle Place, Edinburgh EH9 1JT (☎ 0131 229 5334, e-mail info@jennybrownassociates.com, website www.jennybrownassociates.com); agent for play permissions: Nick Quinn, The Agency (London) Ltd, 24 Pottery Lane, London W11 4LZ (☎ 020 7727 1346, e-mail nquinn@theagency.co.uk)

GRAY, Alistair William; s of John Lambert Gray (d 1980), of St Andrews, and Agnes Roberts, *née* Pow; *b* 6 September 1948; *Educ* Madras Coll St Andrews, Univ of Edinburgh (MA); *m* 7 April 1972, Sheila Elizabeth, da of Walter Harold Rose, of Preston, Lancs; 2 da (Kathryn Julia b 1976, Nicola Elizabeth b 1978); *Career* asst mill mangr Wiggins Teape Ltd 1970–72, divnl mangr Unilever Ltd 1972–78, exec dir John Wood Group plc 1978–81, dir strategic mgmnt consltg Arthur Young 1982–87, dir of strategy PA Consulting Group 1987–91 (assoc 1991–), fndr own co Genesis Consulting 1991–; non-exec dir: Highland Distilleries plc, AorTech International plc; chm Collections Group Ltd; visiting lectr Univ of Strathclyde; chm: Scottish Inst of Sport, Devpt Ctee Euro Hockey Fedn (memb Exec); hon pres Scottish Hockey Union; Burgess of Aberdeen 1980; FInstM, ACMA, MInstD, MIMgt, FIMC, MRSH; *Books* The Managers Handbook (1986); *Recreations* hockey, golf, squash; *Clubs* Western Hockey, New Golf (St Andrews), Royal Northern and Univ; *Style*— Alistair Gray, Esq

GRAY, Sir Bernard Peter; kt (2015); s of Peter Michael Gray, of Weston, Herts, and Mary Angela, *née* Murphy; *b* 6 September 1960, Redhill, Surrey; *Educ* Hitchin Boy's GS, Univ of Oxford (MA), London Business Sch; *Career* FT Gp 1989–97 (sometime columnist Lex), MOD 1997–99, United Business Media 1999–2005 (latterly ceo CMP Information), chief exec TSL Education 2005–; non-exec dir Cable & Wireless 2003–; Def Journalist of the Year RAeS 1996; *Publications* Beginners' Guide to Investment (1991 and 1993); *Recreations* motor sport, opera, cinema; *Style*— Sir Bernard Gray; ✉ TSL Education, Admiral House, 66–68-East Smithfield, London E1 1BX

GRAY, Bryan Mark; CBE (2009, MBE 2001), DL (Cumbria 2010); s of Clifford Benjamin Gray (d 2003), and June Mary, *née* Turner (d 2007); *b* 23 June 1953; *Educ* Wath-upon-Dearne GS, Univ of York (BA); *m* 31 July 1976, Lydia, *née* Wallbridge; 3 s (Robert b 12 April 1982, Philip b 29 May 1985, Michael b 24 May 1988); *Career* various positions ICI 1974–93, chief exec Baxi Group Ltd 1993–2000 (dep chm 2000–04), chm Baxi Technologies 2001–08; chm: Westmorland Ltd 2005–, Urban Splash Hotels 2006–09, Peel Media 2008–11; non-exec dir: Energetix Gp plc 2006–08, United Utilities Water plc 2008–09; pres Soc of Br Gas Industries 2000–01, dep pres Assoc of European Heating Industries, chm Central Heating Information Cncl until 2003; chm: CBI NW 2000–02, Northwest Devpt Agency 2002–09; memb Bd: NW Cultural Consortium 2003–09, Liverpool Culture Co 2003–09; memb LSC 2004–08; memb Lake District Nat Park Authy 2006–14, chm Lowther Castle and Gardens Tst 2007–, chm Churches Tst for Cumbria 2008–15, lay canon Carlisle Cathedral 2014–; pro-chllr Lancaster Univ 2003–13; hon prof Univ of Nottingham 2003–; vice-pres Preston North End FC (chm 1994–2001); memb Advsy Bd Nat Railway Museum 2011–; tstee: Nat Museums Liverpool 2004–12, Nat Football Museum (fndr chm until 2001); High Sheriff Lancs 2003–04; FRSA; *Recreations* reader Dio of Cumbria, life memb Nat Tst, football; *Style*— Bryan Gray, Esq, CBE, DL; ✉ e-mail bryan.gray@bryangray.co.uk

GRAY, (John) Charles Rodger; CMG (2004); s of Very Rev Dr John R Gray (d 1984), of Dunblane, Perthshire, and Mrs John R Gray; *b* 12 March 1953; *Educ* HS of Glasgow, Univ of Glasgow (MA); *m* 1988, Anne-Marie Lucienne Suzanne, *née* de Dax d'Axat; 3 s (Louis b 1995, Alexander b 1997, Thomas b 2000); *Career* diplomat; entered HM Dip Serv 1974, served West African Dept FCO 1974–76, third later second sec Warsaw 1976–79, Eastern European and Soviet Dept FCO 1979–83, UK Delgn to OECD Paris 1983–87, on secondment to Cabinet Office 1987–89; FCO: dep head Central African Dept 1989, dep head Central European Dept 1989–92, head Eastern Adriatic Dept 1992–93; cnsllr and head of Chancery Jakarta 1993–96, fell Center for Int Affrs Harvard Univ 1996–97, cnsllr Washington 1997–2001; FCO: attached to Counter Terrorism Policy Dept 2001, head Middle East Dept 2002–04, Iran co-ordinator 2004–05; ambass to Morocco 2005–08, HM Marshal of the Diplomatic Corps 2008–14; *Recreations* history; *Clubs* New

(Edinburgh); *Style—* Charles Gray, Esq, CMG; ✉ 23 Drayton Court, Drayton Gardens, London SW10 9RH

GRAY, David; s of John Allan Gray (d 1993), of Leeds, and Vena Isabel, *née* Woods (d 2008); *b* 9 January 1955; *Educ* Leeds GS, Univ of Cambridge; *m* 26 May 1984, Julie Marie, da of Anthony Sergeant; *Career* Eversheds: joined as trainee 1977, equity ptnr 1982, head of corp Leeds and Manchester 1995, head of corp and dep managing ptnr Leeds and Manchester 1998, regnl managing ptnr Leeds and Manchester 2000, managing ptnr 2003–09, chm Eversheds Int 2009–13; non-exec dir DWF LLP 2013–; pro-chllr and chair Cncl Univ of Leeds 2013–; *Recreations* golf, racing, Liverpool FC; *Clubs* Alwoodley Golf, Ganton Golf; *Style—* David Gray, Esq; ☏ 07721 612580, e-mail david.gray13@hotmail.co.uk

GRAY, David John; s of James Vincent Gray (d 1989), of Liverpool, and Jeanne Winifred Veronica, *née* Lamb; *b* 2 March 1959; *Educ* Liverpool Bluecoat Sch, Univ of Bristol (BA); *m* 18 Aug 1990, Hilary Jane Rosemary, *née* Fletcher; 2 da (Olivia Scarlet b 22 Aug 1994, Katja Elizabeth b 14 July 1997); *Career* display sales exec Centaur Communications 1984–85, account mangr Pilgrim Communications 1985–87, planning dir Design in Action until 1996 (joined 1987), ceo Creative Leap 1996–; *Recreations* mountaineering, cookery; *Style—* David Gray, Esq

GRAY, Prof Douglas; s of Emmerson Walton Gray, and Daisy Gray; *b* 17 February 1930; *Educ* Wellington Coll NZ, Victoria Univ of Wellington (MA), Univ of Oxford (MA); *m* 3 Sept 1959, Judith Claire, da of Percy Campbell; 1 s (Nicholas b 1961); *Career* asst lectr Victoria Univ of Wellington 1953–54; Univ of Oxford: lectr in English Pembroke and Lincoln Colls 1956–61, fell in English Pembroke Coll 1961–80 (emeritus fell 1980–), univ lectr in English language 1976–80, JRR Tolkien prof of English literature and language 1980–97, professorial fell Lady Margaret Hall 1980–97 (hon fell 1997–); Hon LittD Victoria Univ of Wellington 1995; FBA 1989; *Books* Themes & Images in the Medieval English Religious Lyric (1972), A Selection of Religious Lyrics (1975), Robert Henryson (1979), The Oxford Book of Late Medieval Verse and Prose (1985), Selected Poems of Robert Henryson and William Dunbar (1998), The Oxford Companion to Chaucer (2003), Later Medieval English Literature (2008), From the Norman Conquest to the Black Death (2011), The Phoenix and the Parrot: Skelton and the Language of Satire (2012), Simple Forms, Essays on Medieval English Popular Literature (2015); *Style—* Prof Douglas Gray, FBA; ✉ 31 Nethercote Road, Tackley, Oxford OX5 3AW (☏ 01865 274300)

GRAY, Duncan Alexander James; *b* 3 January 1968; *Educ* Robert Gordon's Coll Aberdeen, UC Oxford (BA, pres Oxford Union); *Partner* Eve Tomlinson; 2 c (Louie b 18 November 1997, Teddy b 27 July 2000); *Career* researcher GLR 1989–90 (Round at Chris's), writer Londoner's Diary Evening Standard 1991; Planet 24: devpt writer and researcher 1991–92 (Big Breakfast), researcher 1992 (The Best of The Word 2), asst prodr 1992 (The Big Breakfast End of Year Show), asst prodr 1992–93 (The Word), devpt prodr 1993, prodr 1993–94 (The Word), series prodr 1994 (Surf Potatoes), series ed 1994–95 (The Word); prodr Talk Back Productions 1995–96 (Brass Eye), creative dir Planet 24 USA 1996–97; exec prodr: Planet 24 1997–98 (The Big Breakfast), Channel Four TV Corp 1997–98 (Jo Whiley Show); controller of entertainment: Granada TV 1998–2003, Granada Content 2002–03, head of entertainment and reality programming ABC Television 2003–06, controller of entertainment ITV 2006–08; BSkyB: commissioner of entertainment 2009–10, head of entertainment Sky 1, Sky 2 and Sky 3 2010–; *Style—* Duncan Gray, Esq

GRAY, Dr Henry Withers; s of Henry Withers Gray (d 1958), and Jean Allen, *née* Cross (d 1994); *b* 25 March 1943, Glasgow; *Educ* Rutherglen Acad, Univ of Glasgow (MD); *m* 5 July 1967, Mary Elizabeth, MBE, da of Angus Henry Shaw, BEM (d 1996); 1 s (Stuart Henry b 1968), 2 da ((Elizabeth) Anne b 1970 d 2007, Karen Louise b 1981); *Career* conslt physician in med and nuclear med 1977–2007, ret; medical advsr Univ of Strathclyde 2000–12, ret; FRCP 1978, FRCPG 1984, FRCR 2003; *Recreations* piping, photography; *Clubs* Lowland and Borders Pipers Soc (LBPS); *Style—* Dr Harry Gray; ✉ 4 Winton Park, E Kilbride, Glasgow G75 8QW (☏ 01355 229525, e-mail harry.gray@blueyonder.co.uk)

GRAY, Iain Cumming; MSP; s of Robert Gray, and Catherina Gray; *b* 7 June 1957; *Educ* Inverness Royal Acad, Univ of Edinburgh (BSc); *m* 1997, Gillianne Gray, da of William McCormack; 1 da (Shelley b 1980); 2 step da (Caitlin Dalgleish b 1979, Lindsay Dalgleish b 1981); *Career* physics teacher 1978–86, campaigns mangr Oxfam Scot 1986–99; MSP (Lab): Edinburgh Pentlands 1999–2003, E Lothian 2007–; dep min of Justice 1999–2001, min for Social Justice 2001–02, min for Enterprise, Tport and Lifelong Learning 2002–03, special advsr under sec of state Alistair Darling, MP 2003–07; ldr Scottish Lab Pty 2008–11 and (actg) 2015; memb Advsy Ctee Centre for Scottish Public Policy; memb Amnesty Int, chair Hibernian Community Fndn; *Recreations* football (Hibernian FC season ticket holder), reading, hillwalking, martial arts; *Style—* Iain Gray, Esq, MSP

GRAY, Prof Iain Gilmour; CBE (2014); *Career* md and gen mangr Airbus UK until 2007, chief exec InnovateUK 2007–14; dir of aerospace Cranfield Univ; chm Bristol Aero Collection; CEng, FREng, FRAeS (Gold Medal 2007); *Style—* Prof Iain Gray, CBE; ✉ Director of Aerospace, School of Aerospace, Transport and Manufacturing (SATM), Building 83, Cranfield University, Bedfordshire MK43 0AL (e-mail i.gray@cranfield.ac.uk)

GRAY, James; MP; s of late Very Rev John R Gray, and Dr Sheila Gray; *b* 7 November 1954; *Educ* Glasgow HS, Univ of Glasgow, Christ Church Oxford; *m* 1 (m dis 2008), Sarah; 2 s (John, William), 1 da (Olivia); m 2, 2009, Philippa Gay Mayo, *née* Keeble; 3 step-c; *Career* mgmnt trainee P&O 1977–78, shipbroker and dept mangr Anderson Hughes Ltd 1978–84, md GNI Freight Futures Ltd 1985–92, sr mangr GNI Ltd (futures brokers) 1990–92, special advsr to Michael Howard, MP and then John Gummer, MP as secs of state for the environment 1992–95, dir Westminster Strategy Ltd (public affrs conslts) 1995–97, MP (Cons) Wiltshire N 1997– (Parly candidate Ross, Cromarty and Skye 1992); House of Commons: oppn whip 2000–01, shadow min for defence 2001–02, shadow min for environment, food and rural affairs 2002–05, shadow sec of state for Scotland 2005, memb DETR Select Ctee 1997–2000, memb DEFRA Select Ctee 2007–10, chm Parly Gp on MS 2003–11, chm Parly Gp for Army 2004–10, memb Cons Defence and Security Policy Gp 2006–07, memb Speaker's Panel of Chairmen 2010–, memb Procedure Ctee 2010–15, memb Finance and Services Ctee 2010–14, chm All Party Parly Gp for Armed Forces 2010–, chm Armed Forces Parly Tst 2013–, memb Defence Select Ctee House of Commons 2013–, chair All Pty Parly Gp for Polar Regions 2015–, memb Admin Ctee House of Commons 2015–; dep chm Wandsworth Tooting Cons Assoc 1994–96, chm Cons Rural Action Gp 2003–04; memb Baltic Exchange 1978–91 and 1997–, dir Baltic Futures Exchange 1989–91; convenor Poles Apart Conference RUSI 2013, led UK Delgn to Arctic Circle Conference Reykjavik 2014; grad RCDS 2003; vice-chm Charities Property Assoc 2001–09; pres Chippenham Branch Multiple Sclerosis Soc; chm Horse and Pony Taxation Ctee 1999–2002, conslt Br Horse Ind Confedn 1999–2002, pres Assoc of Br Riding Schs 2002–; Freeman City of London; memb Ct of Assts HAC 2002–07; *Books* Financial Risk Management (1985), Futures and Options for Shipping (1987, winner Lloyd's of London Book Prize), Shipping Futures (1990), Crown Versus Parliament: Who Decides on Going to War (2004), Poles Apart (2013), Who Takes Britain to War? (2014); *Recreations* the countryside and riding horses, British heritage and local history; *Clubs* Pratt's, Chippenham Constitutional (pres), Royal Wootton Bassett Cons, HAC (vice-pres Saddle); *Style—* James Gray, Esq, MP; ✉ House of Commons, London SW1A 0AA (☏ 020 7219 6237)

GRAY, Prof John Clinton; s of William John Gray (d 1998), and Edith Grace, *née* Tooke (d 1993); *b* 9 April 1946; *Educ* Sir Joseph Williamson's Mathematical Sch Rochester, Simon Langton GS Canterbury, Univ of Birmingham (BSc, PhD), Univ of Cambridge (MA); *m* 1971 Julia, *née* Hodgetts; 1 s (Christopher Clinton b 12 June 1977), 1 da (Stephanie Louise b 25 July 1980); *Career* univ research fell Univ of Birmingham 1970–73, research biochemist UCLA 1973–75; Univ of Cambridge: SRC fell 1975–76, demonstrator 1976–80, lectr 1980–90, reader in plant molecular biology 1990–96, prof of plant molecular biology Dept of Plant Sciences 1996–2011 (emeritus prof of plant molecular biology 2011–), head Dept of Plant Sciences 2003–09; science research fell Nuffield Fndn 1983–84, sr research fell Royal Soc Leverhulme Tst 1991–92; non-exec dir Horticulture Research International 1997–2003; memb SERC Biological Sciences Ctee 1990–93, memb Cncl Sainsbury Lab 1999–2008; tstee Science and Plants for Schools (SAPS) 1991–2008, plant science advsr Gatsby Charitable Fndn 1996–2008; memb EMBO 1994–; *Publications* Ribulose Bisphosphate Carboxylase-Oxygenase (ed with R J Ellis, 1986), Plant Trichomes (ed with D L Hallahan, 2000); also author of papers in scientific jls and stamp magazines; *Recreations* growing plants, mountains, collecting stamps; *Clubs* Midlands Assoc of Mountaineers; *Style—* Prof John Gray; ✉ 47 Barrons Way, Comberton, Cambridge CB23 7EQ (e-mail jcg2@cam.ac.uk); Robinson College, Grange Road, Cambridge CB3 9AN

GRAY, John F; s of Frederick Gray (d 2006), and Miriam Gray (d 1980); *b* 27 January 1944; *Educ* Thomas Richard's Tech Inst Tredegar, Coll of Distributive Trades London (DipCAM); *m* Sandra, da of D Reginald Jones; 1 da (Louise b 13 Aug 1976); *Career* successively admin offr, admin mangr and promotions mangr Methodist Assoc of Youth Clubs 1969–77 (elected hon pres 1976), launched Fundraising Dept Methodist Homes for the Aged 1977–81, dir advocacy National Children's Home 1980–90, with Princess Royal Tst for Carers 1990–91; dir corporate communications Br Red Cross 1991–2000, chm European Red Cross and Red Crescent Public Support Gp 1992–2001, vice-chm International Red Cross and Red Crescent Communications Forum 1996–2001, public affrs advsr Br Red Cross 2000–09, advsr on global fundraising practices International Red Cross and Red Crescent Movement; md Stayahead Consultancy 2000–10, chief exec UCLH Charitable Fndn 2007–14, ret; chm London Inst of Fundraisers 1991–95, co-fndr and fell Inst of Fundraising (formerly Inst of Charity Fundraising Mangrs, exec memb 1982–88, chm Int Ctee 1997–), chm European Fundraising Network 1999–2002, pres European Fundraising Assoc (EFA) 2002–05; memb: American Nat Soc of Fundraising Execs, IPR Fellows Forum 1996–; memb Editorial Bd Charity Magazine 1995–98; frequent guest lectr at various fundraising and communications confs; external examiner DipPR CAM 1993–2000; memb Appeal Ctee Central Hall Westminster 1992–99, tstee IPR Benevolent Fund 1999–2004; pres St David's Day in London Celebration 2004–05 (vice-pres 2002–04); lay preacher Methodist Church, appointed circuit steward E Sussex Methodist Church 2014–; Freeman City of London 1988, Liveryman Worshipful Co of Feltmakers 1998–2005, memb Ct Guild of PR Practitioners 2000 (Master 2004); FIPR, MIPR 1976, FRSA, FCAM 2000; *Awards* National Children's Home Order of St Christopher 1989, Br Red Cross Badge of Honour for Distinguished Service 1997, named as one of PRWeek's 100 most influential PR figures in the UK 2005, named in the PR Week Power Book as one of the most influential people in PR 2007, 2008 and 2009; *Books* Organizing Special Events (co-author, 2000); *Recreations* music, theatre, travel; *Clubs* Royal Over-Seas League; *Style—* John F Gray, Esq; ✉ 47 Downside Close, Eastbourne, East Sussex BN20 8EL (☏ 01323 646699, e-mail johnfgray@btconnect.com)

GRAY, Prof John Nicholas; s of Nicholas Chatt Wardle Gray (d 1985), and Joan, *née* Bushby (d 1990); *b* 17 April 1948, South Shields, Tyne and Wear; *Educ* South Shields Grammar-Tech Sch for Boys, Exeter Coll Oxford (MA, DPhil); *m* 1988, Mieko, *née* Kawai; *Career* lectr in political theory Univ of Essex 1973–76, fell and tutor in politics Jesus Coll Oxford 1976–98, prof of politics Univ of Oxford 1996–98, prof of European thought LSE 1998–2007, emeritus prof Univ of London 2008–; visiting prof in govt Harvard Univ 1986, Olmstead visiting prof in social philosophy Yale Univ 1994; Hon DUniv Open Univ 2006; *Publications* Mill on Liberty: A Defence (1983, 2 edn 1996), Hayek on Liberty (1984, 3 edn 1998), Liberalism (1986, 2 edn 1995), Liberalisms: Essays in Political Philosophy (1989), Post-Liberalism: Studies in Political Thought (1993), Beyond the New Right: Markets, Government and the Common Culture (1993), Enlightenment's Wake: Politics and Culture at the Close of the Modern Age (1995), Isaiah Berlin (1995), Endgames: Questions in Late-Modern Political Thought (1997), Voltaire and Enlightenment (1998), False Dawn: The Delusions of Global Capitalism (1998, 3 edn 2002), Two Faces of Liberalism (2000), Straw Dogs: Thoughts on Humans and Other Animals (2002), Al Qaeda and What It Means To Be Modern (2003, 2 edn 2007), Heresies: Against Progress and Other Illusions (2004), The Political Theory of John Gray (contrib, 2007), Black Mass: Apocalyptic Religion and the Death of Utopia (2007, Lannnan Fndn Notable Book Award 2008), Gray's Anatomy: Selected Writings (2009, new edn 2016), The Immortalization Commission: Science and the Strange Quest to Cheat Death (2011), The Silence of Animals: On Progress and Other Modern Myths (2013), The Soul of the Marionette: A Short Inquiry Into Human Freedom (2015), The Soul of the Marionette: A Short Inquiry Into Human Freedom (2015); *Style—* Prof John Gray; ✉ c/o Tracy Bohan, The Wylie Agency UK, 17 Bedford Square, London WC1B 3JA (☏ 020 7908 5900, fax 020 7908 5901, e-mail tbohan@wylieagency.co.uk)

GRAY, Keith Sydney; *b* 19 February 1972; *Educ* The Lindsey Sch Cleethorpes; *Partner* Jasmine Fassl; 1 da (Clara Anna Helen b 7 Feb 2012); *Career* children's and young adult author and reviewer; *Books* Creepers (1996, shorlisted Guardian Children's Fiction Award 1997), From Blood: Two Brothers (1997, nominated for Library Assoc Carnegie Medal 1998), Hunting the Cat (1997), Dead Trouble (1997), Happy (1998), The Runner (1998, winner Silver Medal Smarties' Children's Book Award 1998), £10,000 (2001), Warehouse (2002, shortlisted Guardian Children's Fiction Award 2002, shortlisted Scot Arts Cncl Book Awards 2003, winner Angus Book Award 2003), Malarkey (2003, shortlisted Book Trust Teenage Prize 2003), The Fearful (2005), Ostrich Boys (2008, shortlisted for Costa Book Award, CILIP Carnegie Medal, winner Scottish Children's Book Award; adapted for stage (Birmingham Rep) 2011); anthologies: Losing It (ed, 2010), Next (ed, 2012); *Style—* Keith Gray, Esq; ✉ c/o Lucy Juckes, Jenny Brown Associates, 33 Argyle Place, Edinburgh EH9 1JT (e-mail lucy@jennybrownassociates.com); website www.keith-gray.com

GRAY, Prof Kevin John; s of the late Bryce Holmes Gray, and late Priscilla Margaret, *née* McCullough; *b* 1951; *Educ* Trinity Hall Cambridge (MA, PhD, LLD, Yorke prize), Univ of Oxford (DCL); *m* 1996, Susan Francis (d 2014); *Career* fell Queens' Coll Cambridge 1975–81, lectr in law Univ of Cambridge 1978–90, fell Trinity Coll Cambridge 1981–90, advocate 1986–88, research fell ANU 1990 (visiting fell 1979, 1989, 1998 and 2005–06), Drapers' prof of law Univ of London 1991–93, sr research fell St John's Coll Oxford 1993–94, prof of law Univ of Cambridge 1993–2011 (emeritus prof of law 2011–), professorial fell Trinity Coll Cambridge 1993– (dean 2006–15 (actg dean 2004–05)), prof of law Nat Univ of Singapore 2008–; visiting prof: Univ of Osaka 2001, Univ of NSW 2003, Univ of Stellenbosch 2005 and 2008, Univ of Tasmania 2006, Nat Univ of Singapore 2006 and 2007; overseas research fell Nat Research Fndn of South Africa 2005, Leverhulme Tst major Research Fellowship 2008–11, fell Stellenbosch Inst for Advanced Study 2009–, distinguished visiting mentor Australian Nat Univ Coll of Law 2015; called to the Bar Middle Temple 1993 (elected bencher 2014); memb Soc of Legal Scholars 1975, assoc memb Académie Internationale de Droit Comparé 1995, memb peer review coll

G

Arts and Humanities Research Cncl (AHRC) 2004–07; hon memb Property Bar Assoc 2016; Distinguished Gifford Lecture Univ of Hawaii 2010; jr and sr int athlete 1968–69, memb Access and Conservation Ctee Br Mountaineering Cncl 2002–06; FBA 1999; *Books* Reallocation of Property on Divorce (1977), Elements of Land Law (1987, 5 edn with S F Gray 2009), Land Law (with S F Gray, 1999, 7 edn 2011); other books and articles on law, legal theory, human rights and the environment; *Recreations* mountaineering and rock climbing; *Style*— Prof Kevin Gray, FBA; ✉ Trinity College, Cambridge CB2 1TQ (☎ 01223 338497)

GRAY, Lauren Alexandra; *b* 3 November 1991, Stirling, Scotland; *Educ* Univ of Glasgow; *Career* curler; achievements incl: Gold medal World Championships 2013, Bronze medal Winter Olympic Games 2014; currently exec search researcher Odger Berndtson; *Recreations* cinema, golf, motorsport, music, reading, sailing, skiing, tennis, travel; *Style*— Ms Lauren Gray; ✉ c/o British Curling, The Royal Caledonian Curling Club, Cairnie House, Ingleston, Newbridge, Midlothian EH28 8NB

GRAY, Matthew Walter; s of Matthew Dunlop Ferguson Gray (d 1982), and Eileen Mary, *née* Joyce (d 1989); *b* 18 April 1969, Elderslie, Renfrewshire; *Educ* Gryffe HS Houston, Napier Poly Edinburgh (BA); *Career* exec chef Inverlochy Castle Hotel Fort William 2001–09 (3 AA Rosettes 2001–09, 1 Michelin Star 2001–09), chef patron Chez Roux at La Torretta Lake Resort and Spa TX USA 2009–12 (exec chef 2012–13); dir food and beverage concept devpt Valor Hospitality Atlanta GA USA 2013–; *Style*— Matthew Gray, Esq; ✉ Valor Hospitality Partners, 2100 Powers Ferry Road SE, Suite 150, Atlanta GA 30339 (e-mail mgray@valorhospitality.com)

GRAY, Neil; MP; *Career* MP (SNP) Airdrie and Shotts 2015–; *Style*— Neil Gray, MP; ✉ House of Commons, London SW1A 0AA

GRAY, Peter Francis; s of Rev George Francis Selby Gray; *b* 7 January 1937, London; *Educ* Marlborough, Trinity Coll Cambridge; *m* 1978, Fiona Bristol; 2 s (Augustus b 1979, Julius b 1981); *Career* Nat Serv Lt Royal Fus attached to 4 King's African Rifles Uganda 1956–58; with HM Foreign Serv 1963–64, SG Warburg & Co 1964–66, Cooper Brothers & Co 1966–69, Samuel Montagu & Co 1970–77, head Investment Div Crown Agents for Oversea Govts and Admins 1977–83, md Touche Remnant & Co 1983–87; chm: Exmoor Dual Investment Tst plc 1988–98, Aberdeen Lloyd's Insurance Tst plc 1993–98, Finsbury Income & Growth Investment Tst plc 1993–2004, Supervisory Bd Postbank and Savings Bank Corp (Hungary) 1998, Close Finsbury Euro-Tech Tst plc 2000–06, Hampden Capital plc 2001–07, Anglo Japanese Investment Corporation plc 2006–12, New Europe Property Investments plc 2007–09, Berkeley Capital Ltd 2009–, KB Re Ltd 2010–15; dir: TR Industrial & General Tst plc 1984–88, New Zealand Investment Tst plc 1988–2003, Gartmore Value Investments plc 1989–94, Gartmore Distribution Tst plc 1993–2002, F&C Private Equity Tst plc 1994–2002, Graphite Enterprise Tst plc 2002–09, UTI India Pharma Fund Ltd 2005–10, Farida (Europe) Ltd 2008–; dir Advsy Bd: Mellenthin Corporate Finance 2004–, Al Farida Investments 2007–15, Official Monetary and Financial Instns Forum (OMFIF) 2013–; dep chm Assoc of Investment Tst Cos 1985–87; memb Int & Diplomatic Exchange 2016–; FCA; *Recreations* literature and music; *Clubs* Brooks's, City of London; *Style*— Peter Gray, Esq; ✉ 26 Ursula Street, London SW11 3DW

GRAY, Richard Innes John; s of James Gray, of Falkirk, and Jean, *née* Paterson; *b* 30 November 1953, Falkirk; *Educ* Graeme HS Falkirk, Univ of Strathclyde (BSc); *m* 5 July 1975, Ann, da of George Crozier; 1 da (Lynsey Elizabeth b 26 Dec 1980), 1 s (Steven James George b 22 Nov 1986); *Career* engr; ICI: plant engr 1975–82, standards engr 1982–85, engrg mangr 1985–88; Courtaulds Chemicals: ops mangr 1988–92, site mangr 1992–95, site dir 1995–2000; site dir and dir of health, safety and environment Acetate Products Ltd 2000–07; CSWDC Ltd: tech dir 2007–08, jt md 2008–10, md 2010–15, non-exec chm 2015–; fin dir PREWIN Fndn 2016–; non-exec dir: Derwent Cogeneration Ltd 2002–07, Engrg and Technol Bd 2002–05, Environmental Servs Assoc 2009– (hon treas 2010–); IMechE: chm 2001–03, hon treas (E Midlands Regn) 2003–, chm Educn Awards Ctee 2013–; Freeman City of London 2003, Liveryman Worshipful Co of Engrs 2004–14; CEng 1982, FIMechE 1992 (MIMechE 1982), MCIWEM 2010; *Publications* Sea-level ~ 400 000 years ago (MIS 11): analogue for present and future sea-level? (in Climate of the Past, 5, 1853–1882, 2009); *Recreations* fitness training, travel; *Style*— Richard Gray, Esq; ✉ CSWDC Ltd, Bar Road, Coventry CV3 4AN (e-mail richard.gray@cswdc.co.uk, website www.cswdc.co.uk)

GRAY, Prof Richard John; s of George Ernest Gray (d 1991), and Helen, *née* Cox (d 2007); *b* 5 January 1944; *Educ* Tiffin Sch, St Catharine's Coll Cambridge (open scholar, BA), Univ of Cambridge (PhD); *m* 1, 1965 (m dis), Joyce Mary, *née* Gray; 1 da (Catharine Emma b 6 April 1966), 1 s (Ben Thomas b 21 May 1972); m 2, 1990, Sheona Catherine, da of Ian Binnie; 1 da (Jessica Vivien b 7 April 1991), 1 s (Jack Ewan George b 12 March 1993); *Career* sr research scholar St Catharine's Coll Cambridge 1966–67, Harkness fell Univ of N Carolina and Univ of Calif 1967–69; Dept of Literature Univ of Essex: lectr 1969–76, sr lectr 1976–80, reader 1981–90, prof 1990–; Robert E McNair visiting prof Univ of S Carolina 1993, Barbara Lester Methvin visiting distinguished prof of Southern literature Univ of Georgia 2009; memb Int Cncl Centre for the Study of Southern Culture Univ of Mississippi 1979, memb Exec Ctee Br Assoc for American Studies 1990–2002; assoc ed Jl of American Studies 1990–97, ed Jl of American Studies 1997–2002; Inaugural Eccles Centre lectr Br Library 2004, Sarah Tryphene Phillips lectr Br Acad 2005, Lamar Lectr US 2006; FBA 1993; *Books* American Verse of the Nineteenth Century (ed, 1973), American Poetry of the Twentieth Century (ed, 1976), The Literature of Memory: Modern Writers of the American South (1977), Robert Penn Warren: A Collection of Critical Essays (ed, 1980), American Fiction: New Readings (ed, 1983), Writing the South: Ideas of an American Region (1986, C Hugh Holman Award, revised edn 1992), American Poetry of the Twentieth Century (1990), The Complete Poems and Selected Essays of Edgar Allan Poe (ed, 1993), The Life of William Faulkner: A Critical Biography (1994), The Selected Poems of Edgar Allan Poe (ed, 1996), Southern Aberrations: Writers of the American South and the Problems of Regionalism (2000), Companion to the Literature and Culture of the American South (2004), A History of American Literature (2004, 2 edn 2011), A Web of Words: The Great Dialogue of Southern Literature (2007), Translatlantic Exchanges: The South in Europe – Europe in the American South (ed, 2007), A Brief History of American Literature (2011), After the Fall: American Literature since 9/11 (2011), A History of American Poetry (2015); *Recreations* cinema, wine tasting, running, tennis, gardening, travel; *Style*— Prof Richard Gray, FBA; ✉ Berri-Dene, Anglesea Road, Wivenhoe, Colchester, Essex CO7 9JS (☎ 01206 823118); Department of Literature, University of Essex, Wivenhoe Park, Colchester, Essex CO4 3SQ (e-mail grayr@essex.ac.uk)

GRAY, Sir William Hume; 3 Bt (UK 1917), of Tunstall Manor, Hart, Co Durham; s of late William Talbot Gray (d 1971), s of 2 Bt, and Rosemarie Hume, *née* Elliott-Smith; suc gf, Sir William Gray, 2 Bt, 1978; Sir William Cresswell Gray, 1 Bt, was chm William Gray & Co Ltd, a memb of Lloyd's Register Ctee and fndr of the S Durham Steel and Iron Co Ltd in 1889; *b* 26 July 1955; *Educ* Eton, Poly of Central London (DipArch); *m* 1, 1984 (m dis 1998), Catherine, yst da of late John Naylor, of The Mill House, Bramley, Hants; 1 s (William John Cresswell b 1986), 2 da (Octavia b 1987, Clementine b 1990); m 2, 2001, Juliet, da of D J Jackson, of Headlam, Co Durham; 1 s (Theodore James b 2007), 1 da (Tilly Alexandra Eveleigh b 29 Oct 2009); *Heir* s, William Gray; *Career* architect William Gray Associates; dir: Eggleston Hall Ltd 1998, Meals in Fields Ltd 2006; High Sheriff Co Durham 1998–99; *Style*— Sir William Gray, Bt; ✉ Egglestone Hall, Eggleston, Barnard Castle, Co Durham

GRAY-CHEAPE, Hamish Leslie; JP (Warwickshire 1985), DL (Warwickshire 1990); s of Lt-Col Leslie George Gray-Cheape, MBE, JP, DL (d 1991), of Carse Gray, Forfar, Angus, and Dorothy Evelyn, *née* Thomas (d 1986); *b* 18 March 1942; *Educ* Eton; *m* 6 Oct 1965, Fiona Mariella, da of Brig Sir Harry Ripley Mackeson (d 1964, 1 Bn late Royal Scots Greys); 2 s (James b 1968, George b 1971); *Career* Capt Grenadier Gds 1961–71; farmer 1972–; High Sheriff of Warwickshire 1984, Vice Lord-Lt Warks 2008–; memb Queen's Body Guard for Scotland (Royal Co of Archers) 1972; *Style*— Hamish Gray-Cheape, JP, DL; ✉ Great Alne, Warwickshire (☎ 01789 488420); Hill House, Walcote, Alcester, Warwickshire B49 6LZ

GRAYLING, Prof Anthony Clifford; s of Henry Clifford Grayling (d 1988), and Ursula Adelaide, *née* Burns (d 1969); *b* 3 April 1949; *Educ* Univ of London (BA), Univ of Sussex (BA, MA), Univ of Oxford (DPhil); *m* 1, 1970, Gabrielle Yvonne, da of Dr Joseph Smyth, of Rottingdean, E Sussex; 1 s (Anthony Jolyon Clifford b 1971), 1 da (Georgina Evelyn Ursula b 1975); m 2, 2012, Katie Hickman; 1 da (Madeleine Catherine Jennifer b 1999); *Career* lectr in philosophy St Anne's Coll Oxford 1984–91; Birkbeck Coll Univ of London: lectr 1991–98, reader in philosophy 1998–2005, prof of philosophy 2005–11, master New Coll of the Humanities 2011–; visiting prof Univ of Tokyo 1998; Leverhulme Tst fell 1999, Jan Huss fell 1994 and 1996; ed Online Review, gen ed Russell series; memb Editorial Bd: Prospect magazine, Reason and Practice magazine, Russell Newsletter; columnist: The Guardian 1999–2002, The Times 2003–04; cmmr Drug Testing in the Workplace Enquiry, memb Joseph Rowntree Fndn Social Evils Enquiry 2008; judge Booker Prize 2003, chm of judges Booker Prize 2014; memb Aristotelian Soc 1986– (hon sec 1992–98), vice-pres Br Humanists Assoc 2000–; FRSL, FRSA; *Books* An Introduction to Philosophical Logic (1982, 3 edn1997), The Refutation of Scepticism (1985), Berkeley: The Central Arguments (1986), Wittgenstein (1988), The Long March to the Fourth of June (with Xu You Yu, under the pseudonym Li Xiao Jun, 1991), China: A Literary Companion (with Susan Whitfield, 1993), Russell (preface, 1995), Philosophy 1: A Guide Through the Subject (introduction and ed, 1995), Philosophy 2: Further Through the Subject (introduction and ed, 1998), Moral Values (1998), The Quarrel of the Age: The Life and Times of William Hazlitt (introduction, 2000), The Meaning of Things (introduction, 2001), The Reason of Things (2002), What is Good? (2003), The Mystery of Things (2004), The Heart of Things (2005), Descartes (2005), Among the Dead Cities (2006), The Form of Things (2006), Towards the Light (2007), Against All Gods (2007), The Choice of Hercules (2007), Truth, Meaning and Realism (2007), Scepticism and the Possibility of Knowledge (2008), Ideas that Matter (2009), Liberty in the Age of Terror (2009), To Set Prometheus Free (2009), Thinking of Answers (2010), The Good Book (2011), The God Argument (2013), The Challenge of Things (2015); *Recreations* opera, theatre, travel, reading, walking,ballet; *Clubs* Athenaeum, Beefsteak, Groucho; *Style*— Prof A C Grayling; ✉ c/o Catherine Clarke, Felicity Bryan Agency, North Parade, Oxford

GRAYLING, Rt Hon Chris; PC (2010), MP; s of John Grayling, of Knutsford, Cheshire, and Elizabeth , *née* Arculus; *b* 1 April 1962; *Educ* Royal GS High Wycombe, Sidney Sussex Coll Cambridge (MA); *m* 1987, Susan, da of Peter Dillistone (d 1996); 1 s, 1 da; *Career* prodr BBC News 1985–88, prodr then prog ed Business Daily Channel 4 1988–91, BBC Enterprises 1991–93; dir: Workhouse Ltd 1993–95, Charterhouse Productions 1993, SSVC Gp 1995–97; md Burson-Marsteller 1997–2001; MP (Cons) Epsom and Ewell 2001–, oppn whip 2002, shadow health min 2002–03, shadow educn min 2003–05, shadow health min 2005, shadow ldr of the House of Commons 2005, shadow sec of state for tport 2005–07, shadow sec of state for work and pensions 2007–09, shadow home sec 2009–10, min of state for employment 2010–12, Lord Chllr and sec of state for justice 2012–15, Lord Pres of the Cncl and ldr of the House of Commons 2015–16, sec of state for transport 2016–; *Publications* The Bridgewater Heritage (1984), A Land Fit for Heroes (1985), Just Another Star? Anglo-American Relations Since 1945 (co-author, 1988); *Recreations* golf, cricket, family; *Style*— The Rt Hon Chris Grayling, MP; ✉ House of Commons, London SW1A 0AA (☎ 020 7219 8226, e-mail graylingc@parliament.uk); 212 Barrett Wood Lane, Ashtead, Surrey KT21 2DB (☎ 01372 271036, fax 01372 270154)

GRAZEBROOK, Adrian Michael; TD (1974); s of Brig (Tom) Neville Grazebrook, CBE, DSO (d 1967), of Sheepscombe House, Glos, and (Marion) Betty, *née* Asplin; *b* 25 March 1943; *Educ* Sherborne; *m* 22 Sept 1984, Susan Mary, da of (Frank) Geoffrey Outwin (d 2005), of Barnwood, Gloucester; *Career* cmmnd TA 1962, Lt-Col 1984–90; admitted slr 1966; ptnr Wilmot & Co 1968–; vice-pres Racehorse Owners' Assoc 1995–96, dir Br Horseracing Bd 2003–07; memb Law Soc 1966; *Recreations* racing, choral singing; *Clubs* Army and Navy, Turf; *Style*— Adrian Grazebrook, Esq, TD; ✉ The Shepherd's Cottage, Hilcot End, Ampney Crucis, Cirencester, Gloucestershire GL7 5HG (☎ 01285 851507); Wilmot & Co Solicitors LLP, 38 Castle Street, Cirencester, Gloucestershire GL7 1QH (☎ 01285 650551, fax 01285 654007, mobile 07831 496608, e-mail agrazebrook@wilmots.co.uk)

GREATOREX, Barbara; da of Benjamin John Jackson, of Bicester, Oxon, and Millicent Clare Jackson (d 1989); *b* 11 March 1951, Bicester, Oxon; *Educ* Bicester Sch, Univ of Warwick (BSc), Univ of York (PGCE), Open Univ (MA), Master NLP Practitioner; *Children* 2 s (Thomas Edward b 26 March 1978, Samuel John b 12 June 1979), 1 da (Sarah Ellen b 30 March 1981); *Career* sr teacher Joseph Rowntree Sch York 1984–97, dep headteacher Wolverhampton Girls' HS 1997–2002, headteacher Wallington HS for Girls 2002–12; involved with RSPB; *Recreations* birding, hill walking, yoga; *Style*— Mrs Barbara Greatorex

GREATOREX, Raymond Edward (Ray); s of Percy Edward Greatorex (d 1985), and Lilian Alice Greatorex (d 1986); *b* 28 May 1940; *Educ* Westcliff HS, Lewes Co GS; *m* Barbara Anne; 1 da (Joanna b 16 Sept 1974); *Career* CA 1964; ptnr: Sydenham & Co 1970, Hodgson Harris 1980, Hodgson Impey 1985, Kidsons Impey 1990; chm HLB Int 1994–99, nat managing ptnr HLB Kidsons 2000–02, exec chm Baker Tilly 2002–06; Freeman City of London, Liveryman Worshipful Co of Farriers (Master 2002–03); FCA; *Recreations* racehorse owner, football, cricket, travelling, gardening, reading; *Clubs* East India, MCC; *Style*— R E Greatorex; ✉ Beeches Brook, Wisborough Green, West Sussex RH14 0HP (☎ 01403 700796, e-mail ray.greatorex@outlook.com)

GREATREX, Thomas James (Tom); s of Simon Greatrex (d 2001), and Brenda, *née* King, of Budleigh Salterton, Devon; *b* 30 September 1974, Ashford, Kent; *Educ* Judd Sch Tonbridge, LSE (BSc); *m* 28 June 2003, Laura, *née* Orrock; 2 da (Katherine, Jessica (twins) b 18 Nov 2009); *Career* parly asst Oppn Whip's Office 1996–97, special advsr to Govt Chief Whip 1997–98, special advsr to Min of Agriculture 1998–99, rgnl organiser GMB Trade Union 1999–2003, head of policy and public affrs E Dunbartonshire Cncl 2004–06, dir of corp affrs NHS 24 2006–07, special advsr to Sec of State for Scotland 2007–10, MP (Lab) Rutherglen and Hamilton W 2010–15; chief exec Nuclear Industry Assoc 2015–; founding chair Fulham Supporters Tst; *Recreations* football, family; *Clubs* Blantyre Miners' Welfare; *Style*— Tom Greatrex, Esq; ✉ e-mail tomgreatrex1974@gmail.com, Twitter @TomJGreatrex

GREAVES, Baron (Life Peer UK 2000), of Pendle in the County of Lancashire; Anthony Robert (Tony) Greaves; s of late Geoffrey Lawrence Greaves, of Bradford, W Yorks; *b* 27 July 1942; *Educ* Queen Elizabeth GS Wakefield, Hertford Coll Oxford (BA), Univ of Manchester; *m* 1968, Heather, da of late Graeme Baxter, of Sevenoaks, Kent; 2 da (Hon Victoria Louise b 1978, Hon Helen Zoë Elizabeth Marie b 1982); *Career* teacher Colne GS and Nelson and Colne Coll 1968–73, organising sec Assoc of Lib Cnsllrs 1977–85, mangr Hebden Royd Publications Ltd 1985–90; *Style*— The Lord Greaves; ✉ House of Lords, London SW1A 0PW

GREAVES, Gerard Marshall; s of William Greaves, of London, and Suzanne, *née* Smith; *b* 28 August 1966, New Mills, Derbys; *Educ* Merchant Taylors' Sch Northwood, Holland Park Comp London, Univ of Liverpool (BA); *m* 25 June 1994, Lisa, *née* Sewards; 2 s (Callum b 2 Sept 1996, Timon b 18 Dec 1998), 1 da (Tegan b 7 Aug 2004); *Career* reporter Bromley Post 1988, reporter Fleet Street News Agency 1989; Daily Express: reporter 1990, educn corr 1992, dep news ed 1993, NY corr 1995, foreign corr 1996; dep ed Daily Mail Weekend magazine 2000, ed Mail on Sunday Live magazine 2005 (Magazine of the Year Br Press Awards 2008), dep ed Mail on Sunday 2012–16, dep ed Daily Mail 2016–; *Style*— Gerard Greaves, Esq; ✉ Mail on Sunday, 2 Derry Street, London W8 5TT (☎ 020 7938 6000)

GREAVES, (Ronald) John; s of Ronald Greaves, and Rose Mary, *née* Nugent; *b* 7 August 1948; *Educ* Douay Martyrs Ickenham, Central London Poly (LLB); *m* 1, 3 July 1970 (m dis 1980), Angela, da of Stanley Menze; m 2, Margaret Dorothy, da of Denis John O'Sullivan, of Lincolnshire; 1 da (Caroline Frances b 28 July 1984), 1 s (Patrick John b 30 Sept 1987); *Career* called to the Bar Middle Temple 1973; dep dist judge Magistrates Ct 1999–; Parly candidate (Lab) St Albans 1979; memb Justice Ctee of Compensation for Wrongful Imprisonment; tstee Chilterns Multiple Sclerosis Centre 2005–; *Style*— John Greaves, Esq; ✉ Adams House, London Road, Rickmansworth, Hertfordshire WD3 1JT (☎ and fax 01923 776878); 9–12 Bell Yard, London WC2A 2LF (☎ 020 7400 1800, fax 020 7404 1405, DX LDE 390)

GREEN, Alan; s of William Green, of Belfast, and Margaret, *née* Leckey; *b* 25 June 1952, Belfast; *Educ* Methodist Coll Belfast, Queen's Univ Belfast (BA); *m* 29 March 1980, Brenda Collette; 1 da (Sarah b 14 June 1983), 1 s (Simon b 19 May 1986); *Career* football commentator, broadcaster and writer; BBC Radio: joined as news trainee London 1975, current affrs presenter and reporter on radio and TV NI, joined BBC Radio Sport 1982, currently sr football commentator BBC Radio 5 Live and World Football (BBC World Service); currently freelance broadcaster and writer; Sony Awards: Sports Broadcaster of the Year 1997, Speech Broadcaster of the Year 2002; memb Radio Acad Hall of Fame 2007; *Publications* The Green Line (autobiography, 2000); *Recreations* golf, travel; *Style*— Alan Green, Esq; ✉ BBC Sport (Radio), MediaCityUK, Salford M50 2EQ (☎ 0161 335 6647, e-mail alan.green23@btopenworld.com)

GREEN, Alison Anne; da of Sam Green, CBE, of Bromley, Kent, and Lilly, *née* Pollak; *b* 18 March 1951; *Educ* Bromley HS, UCL (LLB, LLM), Univ of Louvain; *m* 20 April 1991, Thomas Francis Conlon; 1 da (Samantha Alice Green Conlon); *Career* called to the Bar Middle Temple 1974; lectr in law Univ of Surrey 1976–78; tutor in law: QMC London 1978–79, UCL 1979–81; chair Br Insurance Law Assoc 1994–96 (vice-chair 1992–94, vice-pres 1999–); vice-chair Bar Law Reform Ctee, memb Panel of Arbitrators of AIDA Reinsurance & Insurance Arbitration Soc, memb Disciplinary Panel Bar Cncl 2000–05; chm of tstees Br Insurance Law Assoc Charitable Tst; accredited mediator; pt/t judge of the Upper Tbnl 2009–; *Books* Insurance Contract Law (ed advsr 1988), Insurance Law: An Introduction (contrib, 2007), Consumer Insurance Law: Disclosure, Representations and Basis of the Contract Clauses (contrib, 2013); *Recreations* music, tennis, ballet; *Clubs* Hurlingham; *Style*— Miss Alison Green; ✉ 2 Temple Gardens, Temple, London EC4Y 9AY (☎ 020 7822 1200, fax 020 7822 1300, e-mail agreen@2tg.co.uk or ali88green@aol.com, website www.2tg.co.uk)

GREEN, Wing Cdr Andrew Duncan; OBE (1997); *b* 30 July 1962, Atherstone, Warks; *Educ* St Olave's GS Orpington, Worcester Coll Oxford (MA); *m* 2008, Emma; *Career* fighter pilot RAF; first person to break the sound barrier on land, broke the World Land Speed Record 1997 (also first supersonic record), broke Diesel Land Speed Record 2006; *Recreations* motorsport, sailing, flying; *Style*— Wing Commander Andrew Green, OBE

GREEN, Andrew James (Andy); s of Phil Green (d 2001), and Judy Green (d 1996); *b* 7 September 1955; *Educ* King Edward's Sch for Boys Edgbaston, Univ of Leeds (BSc); *m* 6 July 2014, Susan Elizabeth Jukes; *Children* 2 s (James Edward b 5 June 1986, Alastair Philip b 25 Nov 1993), 1 da (Alix Evelyn b 14 June 1988); *Career* Shell 1976–84, Deloitte Haskins & Sells 1984–86; BT Gp: joined 1986, ceo BTOpenworld 1999–2001, bd dir BT Gp plc 2001–07, ceo BT Global Services (previously BT Ignite) 2001–07; ceo Logica 2008–12; chair: DockOn AG 2012–, npGroup 2013–; non-exec dir ARM Hldgs plc 2011–; chair Connected Digital Economy Catapult 2013–; co-chair UK Space Leadership Cncl and pres UK Space 2010–, chair e-skills UK 2010–; FRSA; *Recreations* cricket, scuba diving, travel; *Clubs* Chartered Mgmnt Inst; *Style*— Andy Green, Esq; ✉ e-mail pat@andyjgreen.co.uk, website www.andyjgreen.co.uk

GREEN, Ann Margaret; CBE (2010); *b* Chester; *Career* chm Bd and chllr York St John Univ; chm: Hadrian's Wall Tst, Bd York Theatre Royal, York Guildhall Orchestra; FRSA 1977, FCMI 1995; *Style*— Ms Ann Green, CBE; ✉ York St John University, Lord Mayor's Walk, York YO31 7EX

GREEN, Anthony Eric Sandall; s of Frederick Sandall Green (d 1961), of London, and Marie-Madeleine (Mrs Joscelyne), *née* Dupont; *b* 30 September 1939; *Educ* Highgate Sch, Slade Sch of Fine Art (Dip Fine Art); *m* 29 July 1961, Mary Louise, da of Gordon Roberts Cozens-Walker (d 1981); 2 da (Katharine Charlotte b 1965, Lucy Rebecca b 1970); *Career* artist; Harkness fellowship USA 1967–69, fell UCL 1991–; tstee Royal Acad of Arts 2000–08; over 100 one-man shows worldwide; exhbns incl Fine Art Soc 2004; featured artist at Royal Acad Summer Exhbn 2003; UK public collections: Tate, V&A, Arts Cncl of GB, Br Cncl, and others; foreign public collections: Metropolitan Museum of Art NYC, various museums in Japan and Brazil, and others; hon fell Wolfson Coll Cambridge 2015; hon doctorate Univ of Buckingham 2011; RA 1977; *Books* A Green Part of the World (with Martin Bailey, 1984); *Recreations* family, travel; *Style*— Anthony Green, Esq, RA; ✉ Mole End, 40 High Street, Little Eversden, Cambridge CB23 1HE (☎ 01223 262292)

GREEN, (Michael James) Bay; s of Patrick Green, OBE, DFC, and Eileen Brenda, *née* Green; *b* 4 June 1943; *Educ* Harrow; *m* 26 Aug 1971, Ann Eila, da of James Kennedy Elliott, OBE, and Elfie Claire Temple, *née* Reed; 1 s (Edward James Patrick b 27 Nov 1973), 1 da (Caroline Eila b 6 Oct 1975); *Career* articled clerk Peat Marwick Mitchell & Co 1960–65, mangr G W Green & Sons 1965–71; Kleinwort Benson Ltd: joined 1971, dir 1978, chm and md Kleinwort Benson Australia Ltd 1981–84; head of corporate finance and md Hill Samuel Bank Ltd 1988–91; Kleinwort Benson Group plc: dir 1991–1998, head Financing and Advsy Div 1994–96, gp vice-chm 1996–98; vice-chm Dresdner Kleinwort Benson 1998–2000, vice-chm Dresdner Kleinwort 2000–09; dir: RPC Gp plc 1998–2009, Invensys plc 2005–14, Axis-Shield plc 2005–11, Help the Hospices 2005–15; specialist advsr to Markets Div Financial Conduct Authy until 2015; FCA; *Recreations* opera, shooting, yachting; *Clubs* Boodle's; *Style*— Bay Green, Esq; ✉ 75 Burton Court, Franklins Row, London SW3 4SX

GREEN, Brian Russell; QC (1997); s of Bertram Green (d 1992), and Dora, *née* Rinsler (d 2001); *b* 25 July 1956; *Educ* Ilford Co HS for Boys, St Edmund Hall Oxford (scholar, BA, BCL); *m* 2 Oct 1994, Yvonne, da of Charles Mammon; 1 s (Bertram b 1998), 1 da (Rachael b 1999); *Career* lectr in law LSE 1978–85, tutor in jurisprudence St Edmund Hall Oxford 1978–80, called to the Bar Middle Temple 1980 (Lloyd Jacob Memorial Exhibition 1980, Astbury Law Scholar 1980), in practice 1981–; memb: Revenue Law Ctee Law Soc 1994–, Assoc of Pension Lawyers, Revenue Bar Assoc, Chancery Bar Assoc, Soc of Trust & Estate Practitioners, Assoc of Contentions Tst and Probate Specialists; *Publications* author of various articles in legal periodicals; *Recreations* arts, cooking, dining, gardening, skiing, travel, walking/trekking; *Style*— Brian Green, QC; ✉ Wilberforce Chambers, 8 New Square, Lincoln's Inn, London WC2A 3QP (☎ 020 7306 0102, fax 020 7306 0095, e-mail bgreen@wilberforce.co.uk)

GREEN, Prof Brynmor Hugh (Bryn); OBE (1995); s of Albert Walter Green (d 1971), and Margaret Afona, *née* Griffiths (d 1971); *b* 14 January 1941; *Educ* Dartford GS, Univ of Nottingham (BSc, PhD); *m* 14 Aug 1965, Jean, da of (Thomas) Norman Armstrong (d 1981); 2 s (David Ellis, Simon Gareth); *Career* lectr Dept of Botany Univ of Manchester 1965–67; Nature Conservancy Cncl: dep and SE regnl offr 1967–74, chief sci team 1974; Wye Coll London: lectr and sr lectr 1974–87, Sir Cyril Kleinwort prof of countryside mgmnt 1987–96, emeritus prof 1996–; chm Working Party on Flora, Fauna and Landscapes Cncl of Europe 1971–73, memb Eng Ctee Nature Conservancy Cncl 1983–90, countryside cmmr 1984–93, chm Landscape Conservation Working Gp Int Union for the Conservation of Nature 1992–98, vice-pres Kent and Sussex Farming and Wildlife Advsy Gp 2002–12, chm White Cliffs Countryside Mgmnt Project 1990–96 and 2008–11, vice-pres Kent Wildlife Tst 2002–, memb Nat Tst SE Regnl Ctee 2007–10; Churchill fell 1999; *Books* Countryside Conservation (1981, 3 edn, 1996), The Diversion of Land (with C Potter et al, 1991), The Changing Role of the Common Agricultural Policy (with J Marsh et al, 1991), Threatened Landscapes (with W Vos et al, 2001), Natural Kent (2008); contrib sci papers to numerous jnls and books; *Recreations* golf, watercolour sketching, ornithology; *Style*— Prof Bryn Green, OBE; ✉ Heatherbank, 49 Brockhill Road, Saltwood, Hythe, Kent CT21 4AF (☎ 01303 261093, e-mail mabr08@dial.pipex.com)

GREEN, Charles; s of Jacob Green, of Leicester, and Anna, *née* Ostersetzer; *b* 26 March 1950; *Educ* London Sch of Film Technique; *m* 28 May 1972, Toni, da of Leibish and Mania Engelberg, of Antwerp, Belgium; 1 s (Kenny b 23 Jan 1975), 2 da (Michelle b 4 June 1977, Davina b 6 Jan 1986); *Career* photographer; opened portrait studio Edgware 1978; Master Photographer of the Year Award 1985, Court of Honour Award of Excellence Professional Photographers Soc of NY USA 1986, 12 Kodak Gold Awards for tech excellence and creativity 1988–95, Gold Certificate for Achievement World Cncl of Professional Photographers 1989; exhibitions: The Forgotten People 1990, Epcot Centre Florida (portraits chosen by Professional Photographers of America) 1990–91, Leaders of GB Into the 21st Century 1995; awarded Masters and Craftsman Degree in Photography Professional Photographers of America 1991, official photographer for investitures at Buckingham Palace 1992–; Master of Electronic Imaging (MEI), Master Photographer, FASP, FBIPP 1985 (ABIPP 1983), FMPA, FRPS, FRSA; *Books* Shooting For Gold (1987), Create The Image (2004); *Style*— Charles Green; ✉ Charles Green Photography, Grosvenor House, 1 High Street, Edgware, Middlesex HA8 7TA (☎ 020 7993 8093, fax 020 8952 3388, e-mail portraits@charlesgreen.com, website www.charlesgreen.com)

GREEN, Chris; MP; *Career* MP (Cons) Bolton W 2015–; *Style*— Chris Green, Esq, MP; ✉ House of Commons, London SW1A 0AA

GREEN, Christopher Edward Wastie (Chris); s of James Wastie Green, and Margarita, *née* Mensing; *b* 7 September 1943; *Educ* St Paul's, Oriel Coll Oxford (MA); *m* 1966, Mitzie, da of Dr Petzold; 1 da (Carol b 1969), 1 s (James b 1971); *Career* British Rail: mgmnt trainee 1965, area mangr Hull 1973, passenger ops mangr BRB 1978, regnl ops mangr Scotland 1980, dep gen mangr ScotRail 1983, gen mangr ScotRail 1984, md Network South East 1990–91 (dir 1986), md InterCity 1992–94, md ScotRail 1994–95; chief exec English Heritage March 1995–96 (cmmr July 1995–96), md (Gibb Rail) Gibb Ltd (formerly Sir Alexander Gibb & Partners) 1996–99, chief exec Virgin Trains 1999–2005; dir: Eurotunnel plc, Network Rail 2005–; pres Railway Study Assoc 1997–98, pres Railway Convalescent Homes 2002–, memb Advsy Panel Railway Heritage Tst 2003–; memb Advsy Bd Cranfield Univ 1996–99; Hon DUniv Univ of Central England 2002; Hon DBA IMC 2002; FCIT; *Recreations* canal boating, architecture, music, hill walking; *Style*— Chris Green, Esq

GREEN, Emeritus Prof Christopher John Charles; OBE (1995); s of late Eric Frederick Green, and late Muriel Mary, *née* Rice; *b* 3 November 1942, Ipswich, Suffolk; *Educ* Northgate GS for Boys Ipswich, Univ of Leeds (BA, PhD); *m* 3 Aug 1968, Sylvia Alice, da of Robert Buckenham, and Doris Buckenham; 2 s (Jonathan James b 13 Dec 1971, Richard Charles b 27 April 1975); *Career* lectr Enfield Coll of Technol 1971–73 (Hockerill Coll 1968–71), sr lectr Middx Poly 1973–76, head of dept Essex Coll of HE 1981–89 (Chelmer Coll of HE 1976–81), project dir Essex Centre Anglia Coll of HE 1989–91, prof of continuing and adult educn Anglia Poly Univ (formerly Anglia Poly) 1991–2004 (dir Regnl Office 1992–2004); chm Four Counties Gp of HE Instns, business ldr Aimhigher: Partnerships for Progression in the East of England 1995–2004; sr music critic East Anglian Daily Times, regular columnist for Archant Newspapers, Essex Chronicle and Today Magazines; artistic dir: Trianon Music Gp 1959–, Ipswich Festival 1980–83, Anglia Singers 1988–; chm: Nat Assoc of Youth Orchestras 1975–78, Chelmsford and Dist Mental Health Centre 1983–2003, Ipswich Arts Assoc 1989–; chair Friends of Braintree Community Hosp; Hon DUniv: East Anglia, Essex; assoc fell Br Psychological Soc 1989, memb Critics Circle; *Recreations* reading, music, theatre; *Style*— Emeritus Prof Christopher Green, OBE; ✉ website www.tmg.org.uk

GREEN, Colin Raymond; s of Dr Gerald Herman Green, of London, and Maisie, *née* Benkwich; *b* 16 April 1949; *Educ* Hampton GS, LSE (LLB), Coll of Law, Wujs Inst Arad Israel; *m* 1975, Hazel Ruth, *née* Lateman; 1 s (Samuel Nathan b 1983), 1 da (Hanna Judith b 1985); *Career* admitted slr 1973, asst slr Paisner & Co 1973–74 (articled clerk 1971–73), ptnr Clintons 1975–77 (asst slr 1974–75); British Telecommunications plc: legal asst The Post Office (before demerger of British Telecom) 1977–81, head of privatisation Legal Div British Telecom 1981–84, head of M&A Legal Div 1984–85, dir Commercial Dept 1985–89, slr and chief legal advsr 1989–94, gp commercial dir and sec 1994–2002, memb Exec Ctee 1996–2002, dir BT Property Ltd 1991–99, tstee BT Pension Scheme 1994–2002, chm BT Telecommunications SA 2001–02; chm Hermes Group Pension Fund 2002–12; dir: VIO Worldwide Ltd 1998–2001, Airtel Movil SA 1999–2001, ECI Telecom Ltd 2002–09, Radware Ltd 2009–11; dir CEDR 1995–99; dir Nightingale Hammerson 2003–, chm Green Aid 2004–; voluntary advsr Citizen's Advice Kingston 2002–, tstee Refugee Action 2013–; memb Law Soc 1973; *Recreations* football, reading, theatre, walking, music (playing and composing); *Style*— Colin Green, Esq

GREEN, Rt Hon Damian Howard; PC, MP; s of Howard Green, of Shiplake, Oxon, and late Audrey Edith, *née* Lyons; *b* 17 January 1956; *Educ* Reading Sch, Balliol Coll Oxford (MA, pres Oxford Union); *m* 1988, Alicia Hester Collinson, *qv*, da of late Judge Jeffreys Collinson; 2 da (Felicity b 1990, Verity b 1993); *Career* prodr/presenter Financial World Tonight BBC Radio 4 1978–82, economics scriptwriter ITN Channel 4 News 1982–84, news ed (Business News) The Times 1984–85, business ed Channel 4 News 1985–87, dep ed Business Daily Channel 4 1987–92, special advsr PM's Policy Unit 1992–94; subsequently public affrs conslt; Parly candidate (Cons) Brent E 1992; MP (Cons) Ashford 1997–; oppn front bench spokesman on educn and employment 1998–99, environment spokesman 1999–2001, shadow sec of state for Educn and Skills 2001–03, shadow sec of state for Transport 2003–04, shadow immigration min 2005–10, min of state for immigration 2010–12, min of state for policing and criminal justice 2012–14, sec of state for work and pensions 2016–; chm Parly Mainstream 2003–10, all-pty BBC Gp 2014–; memb European Scrutiny Ctee 2015–; memb Select Ctee on: Culture, Media and Sport 1997–98, Procedure; vice-pres Tory Reform Gp; *Publications* ITN Budget Factbook (1984, 1985 and 1986), A Better BBC (pamphlet for Centre for Policy Studies, 1991), The Cross Media Revolution (co-author, 1995), Communities in the Countryside (Social Market Fndn,

G

1996), Regulating the Media in the Digital Age (1997), The Four Failures of the New Deal (Centre for Policy Studies, 1998), Restoring the Balance (Tory Reform Group, 2000), Better Learning (2002), Controlling Economic Migration (with David Davis, 2006); *Recreations* cricket, football, opera, theatre; *Clubs* MCC; *Style—* The Rt Hon Damian Green, MP; ✉ website www.damiangreen.org.uk; House of Commons, London SW1A 0AA (☎ 020 7219 3000)

GREEN, Sir (Gregory) David; KCMG (2004, CMG 1999); s of Thomas Dixon Green, of Fulford, York, and Mabella Mary, *née* Walley; *b* 2 December 1948; *Educ* The Leys Sch Cambridge, Keswick Hall Coll of Educn Norwich, Trinity Hall Cambridge (BEd); *m* 10 Sept 1977, Corinne, da of Anthony Bernard Butler; 3 da (Hannah Mabella b 1978, Emily Corinne b 1980, Frances Ethel Rosalind b 1982); *Career* teacher of English West Pakistan (VSO) 1967–68, teacher of art/head of first year Northcliffe Comp Sch 1972–75, teacher of art/head of year Aston Comp Sch Rotherham 1975–76, dir Children's Relief Int/The Cambridge Project Save the Children 1976–79; Save the Children: staff devpt and trg offr 1979–82, dep dir of personnel 1983, dir of personnel 1983–88, dir of personnel and admin 1988–90; dir VSO 1990–99, DG British Cncl 1999–2007; memb Advsy Panel Mgmnt Devpt Unit NVCO 1985–86, memb VSO Cncl 2000–08; chair: Dartington Hall Tst 2007–15 (tstee 2006–09), Royal Cwlth Soc 2008–09, Prince's Sch of Traditional Arts 2008–, Dash Arts 2010–16, Soumik Datta Arts 2013–; memb Laurence Olivier Award Panel 1985, tstee and memb Cncl English Stage Co 2005–, govr Univ of the Arts London 2008–, tstee Finnish Inst in London 2015–, tstee Africa's Voices Fndn 2015–; dir Cinderella (by Peter Maxwell Davies, Queen Elizabeth Hall) 1990; exhibition of paintings held 1978; Freeman: City of Freetown 2004, City of London 2006; MIPM 1987, FRGS, hon fell Coll of Teachers; *Publications* Chorus (1977), Drawing on Experience (2011); *Recreations* theatre, music, painting, travel; *Style—* Sir David Green, KCMG

GREEN, David John Mark; CB (2011), QC (2000); s of John Geoffrey Green, of Woodford Green, Essex, and Margaret Green; bro of Geoffrey Green, *qv*; *b* 8 March 1954; *Educ* Christ's Hosp, St Catharine's Coll Cambridge (MA); *m* 7 June 1980, Katherine, da of James Sharkey, of Woodford Green; 1 s (Dominic James Millican), 2 da (Clemency Alice, Leonora Isabel); *Career* Def Intelligence Staff MOD 1975–78; called to the Bar Inner Temple 1979 (bencher 2008); recorder of the Crown Court 2000–, dir Revenue and Customs Prosecutions Office (RCPO) 2004–10, dir Serious Fraud Office 2012–; Liveryman Worshipful Co of Gardeners (memb Ct of Assts 2007–); *Clubs* Garrick; *Style—* David Green, Esq, CB, QC

GREEN, Dr David William; s of late William Edward Green, and late Joy Doris, *née* Powell; *b* 5 March 1950; *Educ* Penarth GS, Fakenham GS, King's Coll Hosp Med Sch (MB BS), Open Univ (MBA); *Career* conslt anaesthetist KCH; visiting prof of regional anaesthesia Univ of Western Ontario 1987, asst prof Univ of Texas SMS at Dallas, hon sr lectr King's Health Partners; past pres Section of Anaesthesia RSM; memb: BMA, American Soc of Anaesthesiologists; FRCA 1977; *Books* A New Short Textbook of Anaesthetics (jtly, 1986), Anaesthesia and Perioperative Care (jtly, 1994), Fundamentals of Perioperative Management (jtly, 2003); *Recreations* classical music; *Clubs* Royal Overseas League, Osler Club of London; *Style—* Dr David Green; ✉ 10 Gladstone Road, Fakenham, Norfolk NR21 9BZ

GREEN, Frank; CBE (2013); *Career* formerly teacher, chief exec Leigh Academies Tst (LAT) 2009–14, nat schs cmmr 2014–; *Style—* Frank Green, Esq, CBE; ✉ Department for Education, Sanctuary Buildings, Great Smith Street, London SW1P 3BT

GREEN, Geoffrey David; s of Ronald Green (d 1977), of Enfield, and Ivy May, *née* Steggles (d 1988); *b* 17 March 1946; *Educ* George Spicer Central Sch Enfield; *m* 3 April 1969, Rosmarie, da of Dominik Raber, of Affoltern Am Albis, Switzerland; 2 da (Natasha b 1970, Vanessa b 1972); *Career* dir: Bisgood 1985–, County Securities 1986–, County NatWest 1986–90, County NatWest Wood MacKenzie 1988–90; MSI 1992 (memb Stock Exchange 1970); *Recreations* cycling, gardening, travel, local history, reading; *Style—* Geoffrey Green, Esq; ✉ Hadleigh, 35 Carnaby Road, Broxbourne, Hertfordshire EN10 7EG

GREEN, Geoffrey Edward; s of Edward Bowyer Green (d 1990), of Beaconsfield, Bucks, and Clara Jane, *née* Allen (d 1972); *b* 27 March 1929; *Educ* Royal GS High Wycombe, Univ of London (LLB), Law Soc's Coll of Law; *m* 2 Jan 1954, Joy Anne, da of William Robert Willcocks (d 1963), of Beaconsfield, Bucks; 1 da (Nichola Joy (Mrs Blunt) b 1955 d 2001); *Career* admitted slr 1951, NP 1969; asst to Sir Cullum Welch, Bt, PA to Sir Frank Medlicott, CBE, MP 1952–54, sole practice and ptnr in central London 1954–61, practice in Beaconsfield 1962–97; pt/t specialist law lectr 1983–94; underwriting memb Lloyd's 1972–2003; memb Law Soc delgn to European Commision 1972, memb first delgn of Parly candidates (Cons) to European Parl 1973; Parly candidate (Cons) Manchester Openshaw 1974; fndr memb Central and S Middx Law Soc (former memb Cncl); memb: Soc of Cons Lawyers (memb Exec Ctee 1974–77), Law Soc, Soc of Notaries, City of London Law Soc, Berks, Bucks and Oxon Law Soc; life vice-pres Old Wycombiensian Assoc 2004; Freeman City of London 1951, Liveryman Worshipful Co of Slrs of the City of London 1974; granted armorial bearings by Coll of Arms 1986; *Recreations* reading, travel, gardening, spending time with my grandchildren, Alexander Philip Blunt (Alex, b 1978) and Anna Louise Luty, née Blunt (Anna, b 1987); *Style—* Geoffrey Green, Esq

GREEN, Geoffrey Stephen; s of John Geoffrey Green, of Essex, and Margaret Rowena, *née* Millican; bro of David Green, CB, QC, *qv*; *b* 3 September 1949; *Educ* Forest Sch, St Catharine's Coll Cambridge (MA); *m* 1 (m dis 1980), Fiona Mary Inglis; m 2, 30 Dec 1982, Sarah Charlton Chesshire, da of Wing Cdr Arthur Chesshire; 3 s (Alexander Thomas Charlton b 29 Dec 1983, Frederick Robert b 3 June 1986, Henry George Rollo b 30 July 1990); *Career* admitted slr 1975; Ashurst LLP (formerly Ashurst Morris Crisp): ptnr 1979–2013, head Corporate Dept 1994–98, sr ptnr 1998–2008, head of Asia practice Hong Kong 2009–13, sr conslt Asia 2013–; currently non-exec dir various cos; chm Financial Reporting Review Panel; *Recreations* tennis, cricket, golf; *Clubs* Hurlingham, Oriental Club; *Style—* Geoffrey Green, Esq

GREEN, Prof Jennifer Clare; *née* Bilham; da of Philip Leo Bilham, and Brenda Hastings, *née* Colyer; *b* 30 December 1941; *Educ* Sutton HS, St Hugh's Coll Oxford (scholar, MA, DPhil); *m* 2 Jan 65, Malcolm Leslie Hodder Green; 2 s (Russell Philip Malcolm b 30 Jan 1969, Matthew Charles Hereward b 20 Dec 1973), 1 da (Sophie Ann Jennifer b 1 Sept 1970); *Career* Turner and Newall res fell 1966–69, fell St Hugh's Coll Oxford 1969–2009 (emeritus fell 2009–), prof of chemistry Univ of Oxford 1999–2009 (emeritus prof 2009–); chm Atalanta's Fund; FRSC; *Publications* author of 350 research papers in scientific journals; *Style—* Prof Jennifer Green; ✉ Inorganic Chemistry Laboratory, South Parks Road, Oxford OX1 3QR (☎ 01865 272600)

GREEN, Jill; *b* 10 July 1959; *Educ* MSc, BA; *m* Anthony Horowitz, *qv*; 2 s (b 1989, b 1991); *Career* grad trainee rising to mktg mangr (Spain) Thomson Holidays 1980–83, account mangr Allen Brady Marsh Advtg 1983–84, account dir McCann Erickson Advtg 1984–87, sr account dir Abbott Mead Vickers Advtg Agency 1987–90; Red Rooster Films & TV Entertainment: head of children's programming rising to prodr/exec prodr 1991–95, dep md 1994–96, md 1996–98; fndr Greenlit Productions (specialising in major drama and feature films) 1998–; jury memb/chm of various TV awards incl BAFTA, RTS and int EMMYs; *Recreations* design, films, remote traveller, roller blading; *Clubs* RTS, National Film Theatre, National Geographic Society; *Style—* Mrs Jill Green; ✉ Greenlit Productions Ltd, 14/15 D'Arblay Street, London W1V 3FP (☎ 020 7287 3545, fax 020 7439 6767)

GREEN, Dr John Edward; s of John Green (d 1957), and Ellen, *née* O'Dowd (d 1974); *b* 26 August 1937; *Educ* Birkenhead Inst GS, St John's Coll Cambridge (MA, PhD); *m* 12 June 1959, Gillian Mary, da of Harold Barker Jackson (d 1988); 1 da (Imogen b 1964), 1 s (John b 1966); *Career* student apprentice Bristol Aircraft Ltd 1956, tech asst De Havilland Engine Co 1959–61, dir project time and cost analysis MOD (PE) HQ 1981–84, dep head of defence staff and min-cnsllr defence equipment Br Embassy Washington 1984–85, dep dir aircraft Royal Aircraft Estab 1985–87 (aerodynamics 1964–81, head various res divs 1971–78, head Aerodynamics Dept 1978–81); Aircraft Research Association Ltd: chief exec 1988–95, chief scientist 1995–2014; visiting prof Coll of Aeronautics 1996–2004; Royal Aeronautical Soc: memb Cncl 1986–2000, hon treas 1992–96, vice-pres 1992–95, pres-elect 1995–96, pres 1996–97; UK rep Int Cncl of Aeronautical Sciences 1986–2000 (pres 1996–98, life memb 2002, Maurice Roy Medal 2006, hon fell 2008), Cranfield Univ: memb Court 1988–2008, memb Cncl 1995–2005, visiting prof 1996–2004; CEng 1972, FRAeS 1978, FREng 1994, fell American Inst of Aeronautics and Astronautics (FAIAA) 1999, correspondent l'Académie de l'Air et de l'Espace 2010; *Recreations* mountain walking (Munroist 1994), music; *Style—* Dr John Green, FREng; ✉ 1 Leighton Street, Woburn, Milton Keynes MK17 9PJ (☎ and fax 01525 290631, e-mail greens@wobumhc.freeserve.co.uk)

GREEN, Dr John Timothy; s of Thomas Albert Green (d 1978), of Birmingham, and Joan, *née* Chamberlain; *b* 1 January 1944; *Educ* King Edward's Five Ways Sch Birmingham, Queens' Coll Cambridge (fndn scholar, MA, PhD); *m* 1985, Susan Mary, da of David Harold Shattock; 1 s (Thomas William b 16 Nov 1988); *Career* Queens' Coll Cambridge: bye fell 1970–72, dean 1972–77, tutor 1977–80, sr tutor 1977–80, fell and lectr in mathematics 1972–93, life fell 1993–; chief exec RSM 1993–96; dir Historic Properties (London) English Heritage 1997–98; sec Faculty of Med Imperial Coll of Sci, Technol & Med London 1998–2004, chief co-ordinating offr Imperial Coll London 2004–10; recruitment advsr FCO 1992–99; dir: South Leicestershire Garages 1985–95, Pennant Hotels 1987–95, RSM Press Ltd 1993–96, RSM Support Services Ltd 1993–96, RSM Foundation Inc NY 1993–96; vice-chm Project Hope 1995–2001; dir Kennedy Inst of Rheumatology 1999–2010, dir Assoc of Research Mangrs and Administrators 2008–10, dir MyChoice Data Systems Ltd 2009–16; tstee: Harpur Tst 1984–87, London First Medicine 1995–96; chm Alexander Street Press LLP 2010–, assoc Harvey Nash plc 2010–, chm Astins Ltd 2011–; conslt: Arup 2004–11, Elsevier 2010–; ind dir 3i plc 1996–2007; non-exec dir: Chadwyck-Healey Ltd 1997–99, NW London Hosps Tst 2001–10, Imperial Coll Bioincubator Ltd 2004–07, Burlington Danes Ltd 2004–07, MyAction Ltd 2009–10; govr: Hills Road Sixth Form Coll Cambridge 1993–98, Perse Sch Cambridge 2001–08; contrib to Jl of Fluid Mechanics and other scientific pubns, advsr to Lord Darzi's review of NHS 2008; *Recreations* opera, music, fell-walking; *Style—* Dr John T Green

GREEN, Jonathon Simon; s of Arthur Green (d 1989), of London, and Salome, *née* Morris (d 2011); *b* 20 April 1948; *Educ* Bedford Sch, Brasenose Coll Oxford; *Partner* Susan Ford; 2 s (Lucien b 29 Sept 1977, Gabriel b 10 May 1982); *Career* freelance writer, broadcaster, editor and lexicographer 1969–; *Books* Contemporary Dictionary of Quotations (1982, revsd edn 1989 and 1996), Newspeak – A Dictionary of Jargon (1983), The Dictionary of Contemporary Slang (1984, revsd edn 1993 and 1996), The Slang Thesaurus (1986), The Dictionary of Jargon (1987), Days in the Life – Voices from the English Underground 1961–71 (1988), The Encyclopedia of Censorship (1990), Them – Voices from the Immigrant Community in Contemporary Britain (1990), Neologisms – A Dictionary of Contemporary Coinages (1991), It – Sex Since the Sixties (1993), Slang Down the Ages (1994), Chasing the Sun: Dictionary Makers and the Dictionaries they Made (1996), All Dressed Up: The Sixties and the Counter-Culture (1998), The Cassell Dictionary of Slang (1998), Cassell's Rhyming Slang (2000), Chambers Slang Dictionary (2008), Green's Dictionary of Slang (2010), Odd Job Man: Some Confessions of a Slang Lexicographer (2014), Language! 500 Years of the Vulgar Tongue (2014), Slang: a Very Short Introduction (2016); *Style—* Jonathon Green, Esq; ✉ c/o Coombs Moylett & Maclean Literary Agency 120 New Kings Road London SW6 4LZ (*Tel* 02087 400454

GREEN, Lucinda Jane; MBE (1977); da of Maj-Gen George Erroll Prior-Palmer, CB, DSO (d 1977), by his 2 w, Lady Doreen, *née* Hope (d 1998); sis of Simon Prior-Palmer, *qv*; *b* 7 November 1953; *Educ* St Mary's Sch Wantage, Idbury Manor; *m* 1981 (m dis 1992), David Michael Green, yr s of late Barry Green, of Brisbane, Aust; 1 s (Frederick b 1985), 1 da (Lissa b 1989); *Career* three day eventer; winner Badminton Horse Trials Championships 1973, 1976, 1977, 1979, 1983 and 1984, Individual Euro Championships 1975 and 1977, memb Br team Olympic Games Montreal 1976, memb Euro Championship winning team Burghley 1977, memb World Championship team Kentucky 1978, memb World Championship winning Br 3-Day Event Team Luhmühlen 1982 (also winner of individual championship), Silver medal Euro Championship Frauenfeld 1983, Team Silver medal Olympic Games LA 1984, memb winning Euro Championship team Burghley 1985; coach cross-country clinics worldwide 1989–; dir British Eventing 1997–2002; selector Br 3-Day Event Team 1999–2008 (chm of selectors 2003); co-presenter of 6-part documentary Horses (Channel 4) 1986–87, presenter Rural Rides (Meridian TV) 1997–98, commentator for BBC and satellite TV; commentated on all equestrian events at Olympic Games: Barcelona (for BBC) 1992, Atlanta (for Channel 7 Aust) 1996, Sydney (for Channel 7 Aust) 2000, Athens (for Channel 7 Aust) 2004, London 2012 (for Channel 9 Aust); editorial conslt Eventing magazine 1989–92, columnist Riding magazine 1993–2010, regular contrib Daily Telegraph; memb Cncl Sport England 1999–2003; FRSA 2000; *Books* Up, Up and Away (1978), Four Square (1980), Regal Realm (1983), Cross Country Riding (1986), The Young Rider (1993); *Clubs* Mount Kenya Safari; *Style—* Mrs Lucinda Green, MBE; ✉ The Tree House, Appleshaw, Andover, Hampshire SP11 9BS (☎ 01264 771133)

GREEN, Dr Malcolm Robert; s of Frank Green (d 1970), and Margery Isabel Green (d 1997); *b* 4 January 1943; *Educ* Wyggeston GS Leicester, Magdalen Coll Oxford (MA, DPhil); *m* 18 Dec 1971, Mary Margaret, da of Leonard Charles Pratley (d 1987); 2 da (Eleanor b 1975, Sally b 1978), 1 s (Alasdair Calum b 1981); *Career* lectr in Roman history Univ of Glasgow 1967–98; memb: Corpn of Glasgow 1973–75, Strathclyde Regnl Cncl 1975–96, City of Glasgow Cncl 1996–2007; chm: Scottish Teachers and Lectrs Negotiating Ctee 1977–90, Nat Ctee for In-Serv Trg of Teachers 1977–86, Educn Ctee of Convention of Scottish Local Authorities 1978–90, Scottish Ctee for Staff Devpt in Educn 1987–91, Educn Ctee City of Glasgow Cncl 1995–99; business mangr 1999–2005; vice-chair West of Scotland Rgnl Equality Cncl, chair Scottish Alliance of Regnl Equality Cncls 2012–; Scottish cmmr MSC 1983–85, fin chm Scottish Examination Bd 1984–90; active in community based housing assoc movement 1975–; FSQA; *Style—* Dr Malcolm Green; ✉ 4A Hughenden Gardens, Glasgow G12 9XW (☎ 0141 339 2007)

GREEN, Rev Dr (Edward) Michael Bankes; s of Rev Edward Bankes Green (d 1985), and Beatrice Emily, *née* Smith (d 1980); *b* 20 August 1930; *Educ* Clifton, Exeter Coll Oxford (scholar, BA), Queens' Coll and Ridley Hall Cambridge (BA, BD, Fencing blue, Carus New Testament and Selwyn New Testament prizes), Univ of Toronto (Lambeth DD); *m* 12 Sept 1957, Rosemary Wake, da of Lt-Col Charles Felix Stoehr, OBE (d 1932); 2 s (Timothy b 1960, Jonathan b 1966), 2 da (Sarah b 1962, Jenny b 1964); *Career* Nat Serv Lt RA 1953–55; ordained: deacon 1957, priest 1958; curate Holy Trinity Eastbourne 1957–60; tutor in New Testament: London Coll of Divinity 1960–69, Univ of London 1960–69, Univ of Nottingham 1969–75; canon of Coventry 1970, princ St John's Coll Nottingham 1969–75, rector St Aldate's Church Oxford 1975–86, prof of evangelism Regent Coll Vancouver 1987–92, advsr in evangelism to Archbishops of Canterbury and York 1992–

2002, sr research fell Wycliffe Hall Oxford 1997–2005, co-rector Holy Trinity Church Raleigh NC 2005–07, chaplain Oxford Centre for Christian Apologetics 2008–; pres Christian Union Oxford 1955–57, memb Studiorum Novi Testamenti Societas 1960, conslt Lambeth Conf 1968, memb Anglican Doctrinal Cmmn 1969–75; DD (Lambeth) 1996; *Books* Called to Serve (1964), Evangelism in the Early Church (1970), I Believe in the Holy Spirit (1975), You Must Be Joking (1976), The Truth of God Incarnate (ed 1977), I Believe in Satan's Downfall (1981), To Corinth With Love (1982), Evangelism through the Local Church (1990), Who Is This Jesus? (1990), On Your Knees, My God, Good News is for Sharing, Acts for Today, New Testament Spirituality, How Can I Lead a Friend to Christ? (1995), Critical Choices (1995), Strange Intelligence (1996), Evangelism for Amateurs (1998), After Alpha (1998), Bible Reading for Amateurs (1999), Churchgoing for Amateurs (2000), The Message of Matthew (2000), Asian Tigers for Christ (2001), Adventure of Faith (2001), 30 Years that Changed the World (2002), A Prayer Journey with the Apostle Paul (2004), The Books the Church Suppressed (2005), You cannot be serious (2005), I'd like to believe, but... (2005), In Search of Spirituality (2007), Bible-reading: a Beginners' Guide (2009), Lies, Lies, Lies! (2009), Compelled by Joy (2011), Jesus for Sceptics (2013), When God Breaks In (2014); *Recreations* fishing, walking, gardening; *Style*— Rev Canon Dr Michael Green; ✉ Hilltop, Lodge Hill, Abingdon, Oxfordshire OX14 2JD (e-mail embgreen@gmail.com)

GREEN, Prof Michael Boris; s of Absalom Green, of London, and Genia, *née* Osherovitz; *b* 22 May 1946; *Educ* William Ellis Sch, Churchill Coll Cambridge (BA, PhD); *Career* res fell: Inst for Advanced Study Princeton NJ 1970–72, Cavendish Laboratory Cambridge 1972–77, Dept of Theoretical Physics Oxford 1977–79; Nuffield science fell 1984–86, prof Physics Dept QMC London 1985–93 (lectr 1979–85), John Humphrey Plummer prof of theoretical physics Univ of Cambridge 1993–; sr fell SERC 1986–91 (advanced fell 1977–79), distinguished Fairchild fell Caltech 1990; Maxwell medal and prize Inst of Physics 1987, Hopkins prize Cambridge Philosophical Soc 1987, Dirac medal Int Centre of Theoretical Physics 1989, Heinemann prize American Physical Soc 2002, Dirac medal and prize Inst of Physics 2004; FInstP, FRS 1989; *Books* Superstring Theory Vols 1 and 2 (with J H Schwarz and E Witten, Cambridge University Press, 1987); *Style*— Prof Michael Green, FRS; ✉ Department of Applied Mathematics and Theoretical Physics, Silver Street, Cambridge CB3 9EW (☎ 01223 330884)

GREEN, Michael Philip; s of Cyril Green, and Irene, *née* Goodman; *b* 2 December 1947; *Educ* Haberdashers' Aske's; *m* 1, 12 Oct 1972 (m dis 1989), Hon Janet Frances, da of Baron Wolfson, FBA (Life Peer), *qv*; 2 da (Rebecca b 1974, Catherine b 1976); m 2, 15 June 1990, Theresa (Tessa), *née* Buckmaster; 3 s (Oliver Charles b 1992, Theodore Samuel b 1994, Jack Benjamin Maurice b 1997), 1 da (Marina Jacqueline b 2001); *Career* chm Carlton Communications plc 1983–2003; dir Tangent Industries Ltd; non-exec dir: Reuters Holdings plc 1992–99, Independent Television News Ltd, Thomson, GMTV Ltd; chm: The Media Tst, Tangent Charitable Tst; tstee Sainsbury Centre for Mental Health; *Recreations* bridge, television; *Clubs* Portland; *Style*— Michael Green, Esq

GREEN, Hon Mr Justice; Sir Nicholas Nigel Green; kt (2013), QC (1998); s of John Reginald Green, of Warwickshire, and Pauline Barbara; *b* 15 October 1958; *Educ* King Edward's Camp Hill Sch Birmingham, Univ of Leicester (LLB), Univ of Toronto (LLM), Univ of Southampton (PhD); *m* 22 Sept 1990, Fiona Clare, da of Alan Lindsay Cramb (d 1997); 1 da (Natasha Victoria Green b 17 May 1992), 1 s (Alexander John Green b 18 Aug 1994); *Career* called to the Bar Inner Temple 1986 (bencher 2002), with Brick Court Chambers; recorder of the Crown Court 2004–, judge of the High Court of Justice (Queen's Bench Div) 2013–; memb Supplementary Panel Treasury Counsel 1997–98; lectr Univ of Southampton 1981–85, pt/t lectr UCL 1985–87; chm Bar European Gp 1999–2001, memb Bar Cncl 2001–10 (vice-chm 2009–, vice-chm Int Rels Ctee 2000–02, chm European Ctee 2003–06, chm Legal Servs Ctee 2006–08), memb Gen Mgmnt Ctee of the Bar 2001–10, memb Exec Ctee Inner Temple 2003–06, chm Bar Cncl of England and Wales 2010, chm Advocacy Trg Cncl 2011–; hon prof of law Univ of Leicester; *Publications* Commercial Agreements and Competition Law: Practice and Procedures in the UK and EEC (1986, 2nd ed 1997); *Recreations* swimming (swam for England 1976 and English Univs 1978–79), family, collecting Victorian watercolours; *Style*— The Hon Mr Justice Green; ✉ Royal Courts of Justice, Strand, London WC2A 2LL

GREEN, Dame Pauline; DBE (2003); *née* Wiltshire; da of Bertram William Wiltshire (d 1975), of Bracknell, Berks, and Lucy, *née* Vella; *b* 8 December 1948; *Educ* John Kelly Secdy Modern Girls' Sch, Kilburn Poly, Open Univ (BA), LSE (MSc); *m* 6 March 1971 (m dis 2003), Paul Adam Green, s of Charles Henry Green, of Southampton; 1 s (Simon Timothy b 23 April 1974), 1 da (Ruth Charlotte b 20 Oct 1976); *Career* met police offr 1969–74, subsequently asst teacher Special Educn Unit London Borough of Barnet, pt/t lectr Barnet Coll of FE 1980–85, asst Parly offr Co-operative Union (responsible for Euro affairs) 1985–89; MEP (Lab) London North 1989–99, MEP (Lab) London 1999 (lead candidate regnl list); ldr: Euro Parly Lab Pty 1993–94, Parly Gp Pty of Euro Socialists 1994–99; vice-pres Socialist International 1994–99; Lab Pty spokesperson on public health and consumer protection 1989–93, pres All-Pty Gp on Consumer Affairs 1989–94, memb Bureau of Socialist Gp 1991–99; chief exec Co-operatives UK Ltd 2000–09, memb Co-operative Cmmn (sponsored by PM, Tony Blair, *qv*) 2000–07, pres Int Co-operative Alliance 2009–15; memb: Lab Pty NEC 1993–99, Co-operative Pty, USDAW; Grand Gold Cross with Star (Austria), Cdr of the Order of Honour (Greece), Grand Cdr of the Order of Merit (Cyprus); *Books* Embracing Cyprus – the path to unity in the new Europe (2003); *Recreations* music, reading; *Style*— Dame Pauline Green

GREEN, Prof Peter James; s of Frank Arthur Green (d 1981), and Joyce Maureen, *née* Walder (d 1975); *b* 28 April 1950, Solihull; *Educ* Solihull Sch, Univ of Oxford (BA), Univ of Sheffield (MSc, PhD); *m* 25 June 1984, Elizabeth Jane Bennett, *née* Styles; 2 da (Sarah Jane (Ms Lyall) b 1970, Katherine (Mrs Walker) b 1972); *Career* lectr in statistics Univ of Bath 1974–78, sr lectr in statistics Univ of Durham 1986–89 (lectr 1978–86); Univ of Bristol: prof of statistics 1989–2011, Henry Overton Wills prof of mathematics 2003–11, emeritus prof of statistics and professorial research fell 2011–; distinguished prof of statistics Univ of Technology Sydney 2011–; ed Statistical Science 2014–16; visiting assoc prof Univ of Wisconsin 1984–85; Royal Statistical Soc: Guy Medal in Bronze 1987, Guy Medal in Silver 1999, pres 2001–03; pres Int Soc for Bayesian Analysis 2007; Royal Soc Wolfson Research Merit Award 2006; FIMS 1991, CStat 2000, FRS 2003, fell Int Soc for Bayesian Analysis 2017; *Publications* Nonparametric Regression and Generalised Linear Models (1994), Highly Structured Stochastic Systems (ed, 2003); author of numerous papers in academic jls; *Recreations* biking, running, mountains; *Clubs* Mendip Hills Hash, Weston Athletic; *Style*— Prof Peter Green; ✉ School of Mathematics, University of Bristol, Bristol BS8 1TW (☎ 0117 928 7967, fax 0117 928 7999, e-mail p.j.green@bristol.ac.uk)

GREEN, Philip Ernest; s of Ernest Frederick Green, of Ashington, Dorset, and Doreen, *née* Baker; *b* 26 October 1956, Erith, Kent; *Educ* Chislehurst and Sidcup GS, Collingwood Coll Univ of Durham (BA); *m* 21 July 1979, Jane Elizabeth, *née* Ardouin; 2 s (James Edward b 7 Sept 1982, Thomas Paul b 9 April 1984); *Career* various appts Br Aerospace 1979–94; Meggitt plc: gp co sec 1994–99, gp corporate affrs dir 1999–2016, memb Bd 2001–, exec dir of commercial and corporate affrs 2016–; govr Queen Elizabeth's Sch Wimborne 1999–2007; non-exec dir Poole Hospital NHS Fndn 2015–; FCIS 1988 (ACIS 1982); *Recreations* Southampton FC supporter, Bournemouth Symphony Orchestra concerts; *Style*— Philip Green, Esq; ✉ Meggitt plc, Atlantic House, Aviation Park West, Bournemouth International Airport, Christchurch, Dorset BH23 6EW (☎ 01202 597597, e-mail philip.green@meggitt.com)

GREEN, Philip Nevill; CBE (2014); s of Harry Nevill Green (d 1974), and Sheila Jose, *née* Emery; *b* 12 May 1953; *Educ* Queen Mary's GS Walsall, Univ of Wales (BA), London Business Sch (MBA); *m* 27 Aug 1977, Judith Anne, *née* Rippon; 2 da (Kathryn Jane (Katie) b 12 Nov 1979, Jemma Clare b 8 Oct 1982); *Career* vice-pres Crayonne USA Inc 1977–80, md Coloroll Gp plc 1980–90, chief operating offr DHL Worldwide Express NV (Europe/Africa) 1990–99, chief operating offr Reuters Gp plc 1999–2003, ceo P&O Nedlloyd Ltd 2003–05, ceo United Utilities plc 2006–11, advsr to PM on corporate responsibility 2011–; non-exec dir: SKF Gothenberg 2000–06, Tibco Software 2002–03, Lloyds TSB Group plc 2007–09, Business in the Community 2008–14; chm: BakerCorp 2011–, Clarkson plc 2013–14, Carillion 2014– (memb Bd 2011–); chm designate Williams & Glyn, sr ind dir Saga 2014–; non-exec chm Trading for Good 2013–15; tstee: Int Sch of Brussels 1993–99, Philharmonia 2000–14, Missionary Aviation Fellowship (MAF) 2004–06; chm: Sentebale 2011–, Bible Soc 2012–15; memb Advsy Bd London Business Sch 2000–06; *Recreations* cricket, travel, walking, theatre, opera; *Clubs* RAC, MCC; *Style*— Philip Green, Esq, CBE; ✉ Carillion plc, 25 Maddox Street, London W1S 2QN

GREEN, Richard David; s of Bernard Green, and late Flora Amelia, *née* Wartski; *b* 25 May 1944; *Educ* Highgate Sch, The Queen's Coll Oxford (BA); *m* Jan 1994, Hazel Ann *née* Spittle; *Career* PA to Chairman/Managing Director John Wyeth & Co Ltd 1966–67; Keyser Ullman Investment Management Ltd: investment analyst 1967–68, gp economist and fund mangr 1970–72; Hill Samuel Investment Management Ltd: economist Research and Unit Trust Management 1973, instn fund mangr 1974–76, sr investment mangr 1976–77 (dir 1979); former dir Hill Samuel Investment Management (global investment) 1981, sr exec advsr/exec dir and chief investment offr Daiwa International Capital Management (UK) Ltd 1988–; memb: Soc of Business Economists, London Oil Analysts Gp, Inst of Investment Mgmnt and Res; *Recreations* travel, dog walking, charities, reading, water sports, art, theatre; *Style*— Richard Green, Esq; ✉ 45B Netherhall Gardens, Hampstead, London NW3 5RL (☎ 020 7435 3497)

GREEN, Samuel; QC (2015); s of Rev Norman Green, and Mildred, *née* Bond (d 2003); *b* 30 December 1975, Ballymena, NI; *Educ* Trinity Coll Cambridge (Whittaker Scholar, MA); *m* 2003, Lynn; 1 da (Ruby); *Career* called to the Bar (Lincoln's Inn) 1998; called to the Bar (NI) 2007; *Recreations* cycling, boxing, keeping fit; *Style*— Samuel Green, Esq, QC

GREEN, Simon Charles; s of Thomas Eric Green, of Great Longstone, Derbys, and Barbara Ann, *née* Morritt (d 1975); *b* 8 September 1961; *Educ* Worksop Coll, Aberystwyth Univ, Manchester Poly; *m* 28 April 1990, Helen Claire, da of Rodney Jameson; 1 da (Sophie Roseanna b 28 April 1991), 1 s (Sam Thomas b 13 Oct 1993); *Career* jr art dir Saatchi & Saatchi advtg 1982–86; art dir rising to gp head/bd dir: WCRS 1986–90, Still Price Lintas 1990–93; fndr ptnr Addition Marketing until 1993, jt creative/bd dir BDDH 1993–97, ptnr and jt creative dir Partners BDDH 1997–; awards: numerous from annual awards incl British TV, Campaign Press & Poster, Cannes Film Festival, NY Festival, Creative Circle, One Show, Clio, etc, 1983–; memb D&AD; *Recreations* photography, painting; *Clubs* Hogarth Health; *Style*— Simon Green, Esq

GREEN, Vivien; da of William Richard Green, and Violet, *née* Summers; *Career* literary agent; with: Curtis Brown Ltd 1968–71, Richard Scott Simon Ltd 1971–89, Anthony Sheil Assocs 1989–90, Sheil Land Assocs 1990–; pres Assoc of Authors' Agents; *Recreations* the company of friends; *Style*— Miss Vivien Green

GREEN OF DEDDINGTON, Baron (Life Peer 2014) of Deddington in the County of Oxfordshire; Sir Andrew Fleming Green; KCMG (1998, CMG 1991); s of Gp Capt Joseph Henry Green, CBE (d 1970), and Beatrice Mary, *née* Bowditch (d 1997); *b* 6 August 1941; *Educ* Haileybury, Magdalene Coll Cambridge (MA); *m* 21 Sept 1968, Catherine Jane, da of Lt Cdr Peter Norton Churchill, RN (d 1940); 1 da (Diana b 1970), 1 s (Stephen b 1973); *Career* short serv cmmn Royal Greenjackets 1962–65; joined Dip Serv 1965, MECAS Lebanon 1966–68, second sec Aden 1968–70, asst political agent Abu Dhabi 1970–72; first sec: FCO 1972–77, UK Delgn OECD Paris 1977–79, FCO 1979–82; political cnsllr Washington 1982–85, consul-gen and head of Chancery Riyadh 1985–88, cnsllr FCO 1988–91, HM ambass Syria 1991–94, asst under-sec (Middle East) FCO 1994–96, HM ambass Saudi Arabia 1996–2000; chm: Migrationwatch UK 2001–, Medical Aid for Palestinians 2002–05; *Recreations* tennis, bridge; *Style*— The Lord Green of Deddington, KCMG; ✉ 89 St Georges Square, London SW1V 3QW

GREEN OF HURSTPIERPOINT, Baron (Life Peer UK 2010), of Hurstpierpoint in the County of West Sussex; Stephen Keith Green; s of Dudley Keith Green, and Dorothy Rosamund Mary, *née* Wickham; *b* 7 November 1948; *Educ* Lancing, Univ of Oxford (BA), MIT (MSc); *m* 31 July 1971, Janian Joy; 2 da (Suzannah Joy b 29 June 1974, Ruth Madalene b 16 Feb 1977); *Career* Miny of Overseas Devpt 1971–77, mgmnt conslt McKinsey & Co Inc 1977–82, Hong Kong & Shanghai Banking Corporation Ltd 1982–92; HSBC Holdings plc: gp treas 1992–98, exec dir investment banking and markets 1998–2003, gp chief exec 2003–06, gp chm 2006–10; Govt trade and investment min 2011–13; chm Int Advsy Cncl Br C of C 2014–16; tstee Br Museum 2005–10, chm Nat History Museum 2014–; non-stipendiary min Anglican Church; *Books* Serving God? Serving Mammon? (1996), Good Value: Reflections on Money, Morality and an Uncertain World (2009), Reluctant Meister: How Germany's Past is Shaping Its European Future (2014), The European Identity – Historical and Cultural Realities We Cannot Deny (2015); *Recreations* opera, European literature, walking; *Clubs* Athenaeum; *Style*— The Lord Green of Hurstpierpoint

GREEN-ARMYTAGE, John McDonald (Jock); *b* 6 June 1945; *Educ* McGill Univ Montreal (BA), Columbia Univ NY (MBA); *m* 1977, Susan Rosemary, da of Lt-Col Hugh Shelley Le Messurier and Rosemary Alice Champney (maternal gda of 21 Baron Forbes and paternal ggda of Sir James Walker, 1 Bt, of Sand Hutton); 1 s (Matthew b 1978), 3 da (Anna b 1981, Camilla b 1983, Elizabeth b 1985); *Career* N M Rothschild & Sons Ltd: exec 1970–77, exec dir 1977–82, non-exec dir 1988–97; ceo The Guthrie Corporation 1982–88, jt chm and chief exec Kelt Energy plc 1990–91, non-exec chm, chief exec then dep chm William Baird plc 1992–96, non-exec dir then chm Amec plc 1996–2011; currently chm: JZ International, Star Capital Partners; non-exec dir M P Evans Gp plc; *Clubs* Turf, Brooks's, Guards Polo (chm); *Style*— Jock Green-Armytage, Esq

GREEN-PRICE, Sir Robert John; 5 Bt (UK 1874), of Norton Manor, Radnorshire; s of Capt Sir John Green-Price, 4 Bt (d 1964); *b* 22 October 1940; *Educ* Shrewsbury; *Heir* cous, Simon-Green Price; *Career* landowner; Capt (ret) RCT; ADC to Govr of Bermuda 1969–72; lectr in English: Teikyo Univ 1975–82, Chiba Univ of Commerce 1982–; pt/t lectr: Keio Univ 1977–97, Waseda Univ 1986–97; guest lectr NHK Radio 1978–83, asst prof of English Chiba Univ of Commerce Japan until 1997; *Recreations* travel; *Style*— Sir Robert Green-Price, Bt

GREENALL, Hon Gilbert; CBE (1993); 2 s of 3 Baron Daresbury (d 1996); *b* 16 August 1954; *Educ* Eton, RMA Sandhurst, Univ of Bristol (MB ChB), INSEAD (MBA); *m* 1983 (m dis 2008), Sarah Elizabeth, er da of Ian C Mouat, of Stetchworth, Suffolk, and former w of Robert Greville Kaye Williamson; 3 s (Gilbert Edward b 1984, Frederick John b 1986, Alexander b 1988), 1 da (Amelia Frances b 1990); *Career* humanitarian relief co-ordinator: Thai/Cambodian border 1979, Karamoja Uganda 1980–81, Iran 1991, Iraq 1991; UK relief co-ordinator Northern Iraq for ODA 1991, Br Govt rep on EC/UN Mission to Baghdad and Iran/Iraq border 1991, Br Govt humanitarian relief prog for Bosnia 1992, Somalia 1993 and Angola 1993, head EC Task Force for the former Yugoslavia 1992–93, Br Govt assessment of humanitarian progs in Azerbaijan, Armenia and Georgia 1994–, Br Govt

G

advsr on volcanic emergency Montserrat 1995, ODA advsr to GOC Multinational Div SW IFOR Bosnia 1996, Dept for Int Devpt advsr to Perm Jt Force HQ Northwood 1997; memb UN Asessment and Coordination Team (OCHA) 1997–, missions to Irian Jaya 1997, Afghanistan 1998, China 1998, Albania 1999, Kosovo 1999, East Timor 1999, Mozambique 2000, Palestinian occupied territories (West Bank and Gaza Strip) 2000, Sri Lanka 2003; DfID: advsr to Joint Task Force Sierra Leone 2000, advsr to 16 Air Assault Bde Macedonia 2001, head of mission Kabul Afghanistan 2001, humanitarian advsr Br Embassy Iraq 2004; MOD strategic review of the Balkans 2002, advsr Br Govt Post Conflict Reconstruction Unit 2005, Indian Ocean tsunami 2005, Pakistan earthquake 2005, advsr GOC UN Interim Force in Lebanon (UNIFIL) 2006, UN mission Bukavu earthquake Democratic Repub of Congo 2008, Libyan migrant emergency 2011, flash floods Comoros Islands 2012; High Sheriff Herefords and Worcs 2009; Hon MD Univ of Bristol 2006; *Recreations* flying, skiing; *Clubs* White's; *Style—* The Hon Gilbert Greenall, CBE, MD; ✉ Bromesberrow Place, Ledbury, Herefordshire HR8 1RZ

GREENAWAY, Prof Sir David; kt (2014), DL (Nottinghamshire 2009); s of David Greenaway (d 1986), and Agnes MacKechnie, *née* Parker (d 1999); *b* 20 March 1952, Glasgow; *Educ* Eastbank Acad Glasgow, Henry Mellish GS Nottingham, Liverpool Poly (BSc), Univ of Liverpool (MCom), Univ of Nottingham (DLitt); *m* (Susan) Elizabeth, da of William Hallam, of Strelley, Nottingham; 2 s (Stuart David b 1978, Daniel Christopher b 1980); *Career* lectr in econs Leicester Poly 1975–78, prof of economics Univ of Buckingham 1986–87 (lectr sr lectr and reader 1979–86); Univ of Nottingham: prof of economics 1987–, pro-vice-chllr 1994–2001 and 2004–08, vice-chllr 2008–; visiting prof: Lehigh Univ Pennsylvania 1982 and 1987, Claremont Graduate Sch California 1989, 1990, 1991 and 1993; conslt: UNIDO 1983 and 1985, World Bank 1986, 1988 and 2005, Euro Cmmn 1991, GATT 1992, HM Treasy 1993, UNCTAD 1993, Asian Devpt Bank 1997, Caribbean Regional Negotiating Machinery 2000–, Dept for Tport 2003–04; jt managing ed The World Economy, assoc ed The Economic Jl; chm: HEFC Research Assessment Panel for Economics 1999–2001 and 2005–08, Ind Review of Postgrad Med Educn and Trg 2011–13, Bd of Tstees CASE Europe 2014–, Russell Gp Univs 2015–; memb: ESRC Cncl 1997–2001, Armed Forces Pay Review Body 1998–2010 (chm 2004–10), Sr Salaries Review Body 2004–10; govr NIESR 1995–; non-exec dir: Nottingham HA, QMC Hosp Tst 2001–04; Hon Col E Midlands Offr Trg Corps 2013–, hon citizen Ningbo China 2012; hon fell Liverpool John Moores Univ 2012, Hon LLD Univ of Liverpool 2016; memb: Royal Econ Soc 1978 (memb Cncl and Exec 1991–97), Euro Econ Assoc, American Economic Assoc; *Books* An Introduction to International Economics (1979), International Trade Policy (1983), Current Issues in International Trade (1985), The Economics of Intra Industry Trade (1986), Pioneers of Modern Economics in Britain (1989), Current Issues in Macroeconomics (1989), Economic Analysis of Regional Trading Agreements (1989), Trade and Industrial Policy in Developing Countries (1993), Macroeconomics – Theory and Policy in the UK (3 edn with G K Shaw, 1993), Globalisation and Productivity Growth (2005), Globalisation and Labour Market Adjustment (2008), Handbook of International Trade (2011); *Recreations* football, wine, travel, cycling; *Clubs* Army and Navy; *Style—* Prof Sir David Greenaway, DL; ✉ Vice-Chancellor's Office, University of Nottingham, University Park, Nottingham NG7 2RD

GREENBERG, Daniel Isaac; Dr Morris Greenberg, of London, and Dr Gillian Greenberg, *née* Freeman; *b* 5 September 1965; *Educ* City of London Sch, Trinity Coll Cambridge, Inns of Court Sch of Law; *m* 1988, Julia Sharon Becker; 4 c (Yisroel Meir b 1989, Avrohom Boruch b 1992, Shira Chana b 1996, Elisheva Rivka b 1999); *Career* called to the Bar 1988; legal advsr Lord Chllr's Dept 1988–91, counsel Parly Counsel Office 1991–2010, conslt Berwin Leighton Paisner LLP 2010–; gen ed Westlaw UK Annotated Statutes 2008–; advsr Jewish Assoc for Business Ethics 2005–; govr: Ind Jewish Day Sch 1994–2009, Hasmonean HS 2007–; participant in numerous Jewish communal and educational projects; *Publications* Stroud's Judicial Dictionary (7 edn 2006), Craies on Legislation (9 edn 2008), Jowitt's Dictionary of English Law (3 edn 2010), Laying Down the Law (2011); occasional articles on Jewish law in The Jewish Chronicle 1996–; *Recreations* Talmudic study, family life; *Clubs* North Hendon Adas Yisroel; *Style—* Daniel Greenberg, Esq; ✉ Berwin Leighton Paisner LLP, Adelaide House, London Bridge, London EC4R 9HA

GREENBERG, Her Hon Judge Joanna Elishever Gabrielle; QC (1994); da of Ivan Marion Greenberg (d 1966), and Doris, *née* Sandground (d 1990); *b* 28 November 1950, London; *Educ* Brondesbury and Kilburn HS for Girls, King's Coll London (LLB); *Career* called to the Bar Gray's Inn 1972 (bencher 2002); recorder 1995– (asst recorder 1992–95), circuit judge (SE Circuit) 2014–; chm Police Appeals Tbnls 1997–2014; *Style—* Her Hon Judge Greenberg, QC; ✉ Wood Green Crown Court, Woodall House, Lordship Lane, London N22 5LF

GREENBERG, Simon Marc; Benson Greenberg, and Judith, *née* Ashley; *b* 26 July 1969; *Educ* Christ's Coll Finchley, Univ of Exeter (BA), City Univ (Dip Newspaper Journalism), Harvard Business Sch; *m* 2013, Fran Jefferson; 3 c; *Career* journalist; jr reporter Hornsey Jl 1991–92; Mail on Sunday: sports reporter, asst sports ed, dep sports ed 1992–97; sports ed Evening Standard 1997–2000, assoc ed and head of sport News of the World 2000–02, asst ed (sport) Evening Standard 2002–04, communications and public affrs dir Chelsea FC 2004–09, COS England 2018 World Cup Bid 2009–10, dir of corporate affrs News Int 2011–, sr vice-pres and global head of rights News Corp 2013–; exec memb Mgmnt and Standards Ctee News Corp 2011–13; *Awards* Br Sports Journalism Sports Reporter of the Year 1994, UK Press Gazette/Br Press Awards Sports News Reporter of the Year 1994; *Recreations* all sport, films, music; *Clubs* Soho House; *Style—* Simon Greenberg; ☎ 07786 688627, e-mail sgreenberg@newscorp.com

GREENBURY, Toby Jonathan; s of Coleman Leonard Greenbury (d 1989), of Henley-on-Thames, Oxon, and Hannah Judith Pamela Greenbury; *b* 18 September 1951; *Educ* Clifton, UCL; *Career* asst slr Stephenson Harwood 1976–79 (articled clerk 1974–76, seconded assoc Lord Day & Lord NY 1976–77); D J Freeman: asst slr 1979–80, ptnr 1980–2001, sr ptnr 2001–03; ptnr Olswang 2003–; Freeman: City of London 1987, Worshipful Co of London Slrs 1985; memb: Law Soc, NY Bar; *Recreations* gardening, polo, riding, music; *Clubs* Hurlingham, City; *Style—* Toby Greenbury, Esq; ✉ Olswang, 90 High Holborn, London WC1V 6XX (☎ 020 7067 3000, fax 020 7067 3999, e-mail toby.greenbury@olswang.com)

GREENE, Dr Alice Mary; da of Col Charles Westland Greene, Indian Med Servs, ret (d 1984), and Dr Elizabeth M Greene, *née* Rees, Capt RAMC, ret (d 2003); *b* 19 September 1952; *Educ* Wesley Coll Dublin, Trinity Coll Dublin (MB BCh, BAO, BA), City & Guilds of London Art Sch (postgrad dip); *Career* Sir Patrick Dun's Hosp Dublin 1977–78, St James' Hosp 1978–79, Crumlin Children's Hosp Dublin 1980, registrar in med Royal London Homoeopathic Hosp 1982–83, GP NHS practice 1983–87, opened private practice Hampstead 1983–89, Letchworth Centre for Homoeopathic and Complementary Med 1985–91, private practice Harley St 1989–; lectr: Br Autogenic Soc, Homeopathic Physicians Teaching Gp Oxford 1991–; postgrad qualifications: DCH, DObst 1980, Family Planning Cert 1980, Dip Autogenic Psychotherapy 1988, Dip Psychosynthesis 1995, UKCP Registered Psychotherapist, H. Dip Architectural Carving 2010; MRCGP 1981, fell Br Autogenic Soc 2000 (chairwoman 1997–2000), fell Faculty of Homeopathy (FFHom) 2001 (memb 1982); *Publications* Passionate Medicine – Making the transition from conventional medicine to homeopathy (jtly, 2005); *Style—* Dr Alice Greene; ✉ The Fourth Floor Flat, 86 Harley Street, London W1G 7HP (☎ 020 7580 4188, e-mail algreene@globalnet.co.uk, website www.dralicegreene.com)

GREENE, Graham Carleton; CBE (1986); er s of late Sir Hugh Carleton Greene; *b* 10 June 1936, Berlin; *Educ* Eton, UC Oxford (MA); *m* 1, 1957 (m dis), Hon Judith Margaret, da of late Baron Gordon-Walker, CH, PC (Life Peer); m 2, 1976 (m dis 1984), Sally Georgina Horton, da of Sidney Wilfred Eaton; 1 s; *Career* merchant banking Dublin, New York and London 1957–58; publishing: Secker & Warburg Ltd 1958–62, Jonathan Cape 1962–90 (dir 1962–90, md 1966–88); dir: Chatto, Virago, Bodley Head and Jonathan Cape 1969–88 (chm 1970–88), Random House UK Ltd 1988–90, Jackdaw Publications (chm 1964–88), Cape Goliard Press 1967–88, Guinness Mahon Holdings 1968–79, Australasian Publishing Co Pty 1969–88 (chm 1978–88), Sprint Productions 1971–80, Book Reps (NZ) 1971–88 (chm 1984–88), CVBC Services Ltd (chm 1972–88), Guinness Peat Group plc 1973–87, Grantham Book Storage Ltd (chm 1974–88), Triad Paperbacks Ltd 1975–88, Chatto, Virago, Bodley Head and Jonathan Cape Australia Pty Ltd (chm 1977–88), Greene King plc 1979–2004, Statesman & Nation Publishing Co Ltd 1980–85 (chm 1981–85), Statesman Publishing Co Ltd 1980–85 (chm 1981–85), New Society (chm 1984–86), Random House Inc 1987–88, Jupiter Int Green Investment Trust plc 1989–2001, Henry Sotheran Ltd 1990–, Ed Victor Ltd 1991–, Rosemary Sandberg Ltd 1991–2002, Libra KFT (Budapest) 1991–, London Merchant Securities plc 1996–2007 (chm 2000–07), Garsington Opera Limited 1996– (chm 2006–09); pres Publishers Assoc 1977–79 (memb Cncl 1969–88); memb: Book Devpt Cncl 1970–79 (dep chm 1972–73), Int Ctee Int Publishers Assoc 1977–88 (Exec Ctee 1981–88), Groupe des Editeurs de Livres de la CEE (EEC) 1977–86 (pres 1984–86), Arts Cncl Working Party Sub Ctee on Public Lending Right 1970, Paymaster Gen's Working Party on Public Lending Right 1970–72, Bd British Cncl 1977–88; chm Nat Book League 1974–76 (dep chm 1971–74), memb Gen Ctee Royal Literary Fund 1975; chm Museums and Galleries Cmmn 1991–96; British Museum: tstee 1978–2002, chm of tstees 1996–2002; vice-chm British Museum Devpt Tst 1993–2004 (chm 1986–93), pres British Museum Fndn Inc 1989–90, chm British Museum Co Ltd 1988–96, dir American Friends of British Museum 1990–2002; vice-pres GB-China Centre 1997– (chm 1986–97); memb Bd: Sainsbury Inst of Study of Japanese Arts and Culture 1999–, Stiftung Hans Arp und Sophie Taeuber-Arp 1999–; tstee Trollope Soc 1989–2004, memb Cncl Stiftung Temple Gift 2001–, chm Compton Verney House Tst 2005–13 (govr 1995–2013); Freeman City of London 1960, Liveryman Fishmongers' Co 1960; Hon DLitt Keele Univ 2002, Hon DCL UEA 2002, Hon DLitt Buckingham Univ 2004; Chevalier de l'Ordre des Arts et des Lettres (France) 1985; *Style—* Graham Greene, Esq, CBE; ✉ e-mail grahamc.greene@virgin.net

GREENE, His Hon Judge Maurice Alan; s of late Jack Greene, and late Freda, *née* Redler; *b* 1960, Salford; *Educ* Stand GS Whitefield, Liverpool John Moores Univ, Inns of Ct Sch of Law, Univ of Leicester; *m* 1986, Amanda, *née* Ashe; 2 da (Sarah b 1989, Rebecca b 1992); *Career* called to the Bar 1982; dep district judge 1999, recorder 2002, circuit judge (Northern Circuit) 2012–; liaison judge Tameside Magistrates Court 2013–; memb Hon Soc of the Inner Temple; *Recreations* watching sport, dog walking, crime fiction, history; *Style—* His Hon Judge Maurice Greene; ✉ Manchester Crown Court, The Court House, Minshull Street, Manchester M1 3FS

GREENE, Moya Marguerite; *b* 10 June 1954, Newfoundland, Canada; *Educ* Memorial Univ of Newfoundland (BA), Osgoode Hall Law Sch, York Univ Toronto (LLB); *Career* sr policy advsr Labour Code Reform Labour Canada 1982–84, transportation and privatisation specialist Privy Cncl Office (Econ) 1984–86, dir of intergovernmental affrs Consumer and Corp Affrs 1986–87, dir of social policy Federal-Provincial Relations Office 1987–89, dir of general policy Human Resources Devpt Canada 1989–91, asst dep min Transport Canada 1991–96, md Investment Banking and Infrastructure Finance TD Securities 1996–2000, sr vice-pres and chief admin offr Canadian Imperial Bank of Commerce 2000–03, sr vice-pres operational effectiveness Bombardier 2003–05, pres and chief exec Canada Post 2005–10, chief exec Royal Mail 2010–; vice-chm Bd Purolator Courier Ltd 2005–10; memb Bd: Canada Post Corp 2005–10, Royal Mail 2010–; memb Bd Tim Hortons 2008–; memb IOD; *Recreations* opera, reading, walking; *Clubs* Athenaeum, 5 Hertford; *Style—* Ms Moya Greene; ✉ Royal Mail Group Ltd, 100 Victoria Embankment, London EC4Y 0HQ (☎ 020 7449 8101, e-mail lisa.agnew@royalmail.com)

GREENE, His Hon Judge Peter Livesey; *Career* admitted slr 1972; dep district judge (princ registry Family Div) 1999, district judge (prince registry Family Div) 2004, circuit judge (SE Circuit) 2011–; *Style—* His Hon Judge Greene; ✉ Peterborough Combined Court Centre, Crown Buildings, Rivergate, Peterborough PE1 1EJ

GREENFIELD, Dr Christopher John; s of Leonard George Greenfield (d 1991), of Oldland Common, nr Bristol, and Betty Joan, *née* Griffiths (d 2008); *b* 28 December 1948; *Educ* Kingswood GS, Univ of Leeds (BA), Michigan State Univ (MA), Univ of Bristol (MEd, EdD); *m* 23 June 1984, Gillian, da of George Orme (d 1984), of Newcastle upon Tyne; 1 s (George b 1987), 1 da (Laura b 1989); *Career* researcher Rowntree Tst 1971–73, asst to Richard Wainwright MP 1974–77, teacher in Huddersfield and Bahrain 1978–82, Quaker ME sec 1982–86, headmaster Sidcot Sch 1986–97, princ Sherborne Sch Int Coll 1997–2013, headmaster British/Georgian Sch Tbilisi 2013–16 (emeritus headmaster 2016–); Parly candidate: (Lib) Leeds NE 1974, (Lib) Leeds W 1979, (Lib Dem) Kingswood 2001; chm: Quaker Headteachers' Conf 1991–94, Assoc of Int Study Centres 2001–04, Rowntree Reform Tst 2010–13 (tstee 1983–, vice-chm 2006–10); vice-chm: Assoc of Educnl Guardians of Int Students 2000–04, Boarding Sch Assoc 2008– (chm 2009–10); memb: Leeds CC 1973–76, W Yorks CC 1976–80, Winscombe PC 1988–97, Long Sutton PC 1997–99 and 2008–13, Boarding Schools Assoc Exec 2006–11, Taiwan Panel Br Cncl 2007–10; tstee AEGIS 2008–11; fell CCC Cambridge 1995–96; *Publications* White Robed Queen (1994), By Our Deeds (1997), The Bridge (ed, 2000), World Class (with P Hardaker, 2005), Schooling in England (2007), Bridge to Success (ed, 2008), Living and Learning at School in England (2010), BGS Grammar in Columns (w T Japaridze 2014), Truly World Class (w P Hardaker 2015); *Recreations* Caucasian affairs, education in Georgia; *Clubs* National Liberal; *Style—* Dr Christopher Greenfield; ✉ 319 Russell Court, London WC1H 0NH (e-mail cjgreenfield@outlook.com)

GREENFIELD, Jonathan (Jon); s of John Frederick Greenfield, of Hatfield, and Mary Decimer, *née* Metivier; *b* 17 April 1959; *Educ* Hatfield GS, Univ of Manchester Sch of Architecture (BA, BArch); *m* 10 Aug 1991, Margaret Mary; 1 s (Patrick Peter b 22 Sept 1992), 1 da (Rosemary Anne b 31 May 1994); *Career* architect; office jr Sir Basil Spence Partnership 1978, trg with Trevor Dannatt & Partners 1980–81; project architect Chapman Taylor Partners (shopping devpts in Stockport and Coventry), assoc dir Pentagram Design Ltd (reconstruction of Shakespeare's Globe in Southwark, campaign designs for the Rose Theatre Tst); estab Parameta Architects 1997; UNESCO travelling scholar Verona 1980, winner Mid Herts Rotary debating competition 1976; RIBA; *Books* Shakespeare's Globe Rebuilt (contrib, 1997); *Recreations* drawing and painting; *Clubs* Friends of Shakespeare's Globe; *Style—* Jon Greenfield, Esq; ✉ The Mill House, Burnthouse Lane, Silfield, Wymondham, Norfolk NR18 9NP (☎ 01953 602084)

GREENFIELD, Baroness (Life Peer UK 2001), of Ot Moor in the County of Oxfordshire; Susan Adele Greenfield; CBE (2000); da of Reginald Myer Greenfield, and Doris Margaret Winifred Greenfield; *b* 1 October 1950, London; *Educ* Godolphin & Latymer Sch, St Hilda's Coll Oxford (MA, DPhil); *m* 1991 (m dis 2003), Prof Peter William Atkins, *qv*; *Career* travelling scholarship to Israel 1970, MRC res scholarship Dept of Pharmacology Oxford 1973–76, Dame Catherine Fulford sr scholarship St Hugh's Coll 1974, J H Burn Tst scholarship Dept of Pharmacology Oxford 1977, MRC trg fell Lab of Physiology Oxford 1977–81, Royal Soc Study Visit Award Coll de France Paris 1978, MRC-INSERM French Exchange fell Coll de France Paris 1979–80; Univ of Oxford: jr res fell Green Coll 1981–84, tutorial fell in med Lincoln Coll 1985–, univ lectr in synaptic pharmacology 1985–, prof of pharmacology 1996–; dep dir Squibb Projects 1988–95; Gresham chair of physic Gresham Coll London 1995–98; dir Royal Instn of GB 1998–2010 (Fullerian prof of physiology 1998–); visiting fell in neurosciences Inst La Jolla CA 1995, distinguished visiting scholar Queen's Univ Belfast 1996; Royal Instn Christmas lectr 1994 (first woman to present series); columnist Independent on Sunday 1996–98, Brain Story (series, BBC2) 2000; tstee Science Museum 1998–; chllr Heriot-Watt Univ; fell World Economic Forum 2001–10; CEO and fndr Neuro-Bio 2013–; Michael Faraday Award Royal Soc 1998, Woman of Distinction of the Year Jewish Care 1998, Woman of the Year The Observer 2000; hon fell Univ of Cardiff 2000; awarded 31 honorary degrees; Hon FRCP 2000; Ordre National de la Legion d'Honneur 2003, Australian Medal for Medical Res 2010; *Books* Mindwaves (co-ed with C B Blackmore, 1987), Journey to the Centers of the Brain (with G Ferry, 1994), Journey to the Centers of the Mind (1995), The Human Mind Explained (ed, 1996), The Human Brain: A Guided Tour (1997), Brain Power (ed, 2000), Brain Story (2000), The Private Life of the Brain (2000), Tomorrow's People (2003), ID: The Quest for Identity in the 21st Century (2008), You & Me: The Neuroscience of Identity (2011), 2121: A Tale from the Next Century (2013), Mind Change (2014), A Day in The Life of The Brain (2016); author of 200 published res papers; *Recreations* squash, dancing; *Clubs* The Hospital (London); *Style*— The Baroness Greenfield, CBE; ✉ Lincoln College, Oxford OX1 3DR (☎ 01235 42083, email sagpa@susangreenfield.com)

GREENGRASS, Paul; *b* 13 August 1955, Cheam, Surrey; *Educ* Queen's Coll Cambridge; *Career* film dir; pres Directors UK; *Film* Bloody Sunday (also writer) 2002, The Bourne Supremacy 2004, United 93 (also writer and prodr) 2006 (Best Dir BAFTA 2007), The Bourne Ultimatum 2007, Green Zone 2010 (also prodr), Captain Phillips 2013; *Style*— Mr Paul Greengrass; ✉ c/o Creative Artists Agency, 2000 Avenue of the Stars, Los Angeles, CA 90067, USA

GREENGROSS, Baroness (Life Peer UK 2000), of Notting Hill in the Royal Borough of Kensington and Chelsea; Lady Sally R; OBE (1993); *née* Michaels; *b* 29 June 1935; *Educ* Brighton & Hove HS, LSE (BA); *m* 26 May 1959, Sir Alan Greengross, *qv*; 3 da (Stephanie Gail b 24 April 1960, Joanna Louise b 31 Oct 1961, Claire Juliet b 10 Feb 1964), 1 s (Mark Peter b 6 Nov 1962); *Career* former linguist, exec in industry, lectr and researcher; vice-pres Age Concern England 2002– (asst dir 1977–82, dep dir 1982–87, DG 1987–2000), chief exec Int Longevity Centre UK 2004– (chair 2000–04); chair Experience Corps 2001–06, co-chair Alliance for Health and the Future 2003–, chair Advsy Ctee English Longitudinal Study on Ageing Int Centre for Health and Soc UCL (also chair Crucible Project), sec-gen Eurolinkage 1981–2001, hon memb Bd of Dirs Int Fedn on Ageing, memb Bd HelpAge Int; jt chm Bd Age Concern Inst of Gerontology KCL 1987–2000, exec chair Millennium Debate of the Age 1998–2000, chair Advsy Ctee New Dynamics of Ageing; cmmr Equality and Human Rights Cmmn 2007–12; fndr: Age Resource, Employers' Forum on Age, Ageing Well Prog, Exchange on Ageing Law and Ethics; memb: Bd Campaign for Learning 1999–, Advsy Ctee Federal Tst, Ofcom Advsy Ctee on Older and Disabled People 2004–06; pres: Pensions Policy Inst 2004– (memb 2001–), Coll of Occupational Therapists 2008–; patron: Action on Elder Abuse 1994–, Sheffield Inst for Studies on Ageing 1999–, Groundwork Fndn 1999–, Pennell Initiative 1999–2004, Age Concern Espana 2000–, Care and Repair England 2000–, Ransackers, Int Consortium for Intergenerational Progs; UK Woman of Europe 1990, Int Women's Forum Women That Make a Difference Award 1998; vice-chm Britain in Europe Campaign 2000–06; chair All Party Gps on: Corp Social Devpt 2001–, Old and Young Together – Intergenerational Futures 2008–, Incontinence 2008–; hon vice-pres Royal Soc for Promotion of Health; Hon DLitt: Univ of Ulster 1994, Brunel Univ 2002, Keele Univ 2004; Hon DUniv: Kingston and St George's, Exeter 2000, Leeds Met 2003, Open Univ 2002; FRSH 1989, FRSA 1989, Hon FIA 2000; *Books* Ageing, an Adventure in Living (ed, 1985), The Law and Vulnerable Elderly People (ed, 1986), Living, Loving and Ageing (1989), and others; *Recreations* countryside, music; *Clubs* Hurlingham, Reform; *Style*— The Rt Hon the Baroness Greengross, OBE; ✉ House of Lords, London SW1A 0PW (☎ 020 7219 3000)

GREENHALGH, David Anthony; s of Rowland William Greenhalgh (d 1972), and Barbara Emily, *née* Edwards (d 1989); *b* 4 December 1943; *Educ* Sedbergh; *m* 24 May 1980, Jill Marian, da of John Donaldson (d 2001); 1 s (Thomas William Michael Iain b 26 Nov 1991); *Career* articled clerk March Pearson & Skelton Manchester 1963–68; admitted slr 1968; Linklaters: joined 1969, tax ptnr 1974–93, head of Tax Dept 1989–93, corp ptnr 1994–99; conslt: Carey Olsen 2000–03, Charles Russell Speechlys LLP 2005–15; dir St George's Hill Golf Club (Holdings) Ltd 2001–09; memb Revenue Law Sub-Ctee City of London Law Soc 1974–91; Freeman City of London 1991; memb Law Soc 1968; *Recreations* golf, gardening; *Clubs* City of London, St George's Hill Golf, West Sussex Golf, Wisley; *Style*— David Greenhalgh, Esq; ✉ Pine Close, Camp End Road, St George's Hill, Weybridge, Surrey KT13 0NU

GREENHALGH, Matt; s of Philip Greenhalgh, and Rita, *née* Roberts; *b* Salford; *Educ* Loreto Coll Manchester, Univ of Chester; Nicola Shindler, *qv*; *Career* screenwriter; *Television* incl Clocking Off (BBC 1), Burn It (BBC) 2003, Cold Feet (ITV), Legless (Channel 4) 2005; *Film* Control 2007 (Carl Foreman BAFTA 2008), Nowhere Boy 2009 (nominated BAFTA 2010), The Look of Love 2014; *Recreations* nature; *Style*— Matt Greenhalgh, Esq; ✉ c/o Sue Rodgers, Independent Talent Group Ltd, 40 Whitfield Street, London, W1T 2RH

GREENHALGH, Richard; *Career* chm: Unilever UK 1998–2004, First Milk 2004–; non-exec chm CARE International UK 2004–, non-exec dir Rank Gp plc 2004–; advsr: Calor SA, All Nippon Airways; chm: Cncl for Industry and HE, Nat Coll for Sch Leadership 2000–04, Templeton Coll Oxford 2004–; memb Bd Int C of C 2000–04, memb Cncl Royal Society of Arts; CCMI 2004; *Style*— Richard Greenhalgh, Esq

GREENHALGH, Robert (Bob); s of Robert Greenhalgh (d 1994), of Lancs, and Bertha Platt (d 1980); *b* 15 March 1942; *Educ* Lancaster Royal GS, Open Univ (BA); *m* 17 July 1965, Elizabeth, da of John Richard Higdon (d 1995), of Kent; *Career* princ RNIB Nat Rehabilitation Centre 1975–83, princ of trg S Regnl Assoc for the Blind 1983–92, sr ptnr Bob Greenhalgh and Partners (t/a Iridian) 1992–94, specialist in visual disability 1994–; hon chm: Mobility of the Blind Assoc 1973–76, Partially Sighted Soc 1980–88 and 1998–; hon treas Leonardo European Vision Rehabilitation Educn and Trg Assoc (LEVRETA); Freeman City of Lancaster; *Recreations* music, good food, writing; *Style*— Bob Greenhalgh, Esq; ✉ 43 Marine Drive, Hest Bank, Lancaster LA2 6ED (☎ 01524 824878, e-mail bobgreenhalgh@btinternet.com)

GREENHALGH, Prof Roger Malcolm; s of Maj John Greenhalgh (d 1977), and Phyllis, *née* Poynton (d 2002); *b* 6 February 1941; *Educ* Ilkeston Sch, Clare Coll Cambridge (MA, MD MChir), St Thomas' Hosp; *m* 30 July 1964, Karin Maria, da of Dr Karl Gross, and Lucia, *née* Hammer; 1 s (Stephen John, *qv*, b 4 Sept 1967), 1 da (Christina Elizabeth b 26 June 1970); *Career* house surgn St Thomas' Hosp London 1967, lectr in surgery Bart's 1972–76; Charing Cross and Westminster Hosp Med Sch (now Imperial Coll Sch of Med since merger 1997): hon conslt surgn 1976–, sr lectr in surgery 1976–81, prof of surgery (Univ of London) 1982–, chm Dept of Surgery Charing Cross and Westminster Med Sch 1989–97, clinical dean 1991–93, dean 1993–97, head Dept of Acute and Reconstructive Surgery Imperial Coll Sch of Med 1997–, head Dept of Vascular Surgery Imperial Coll 1997–2006; emeritus prof of surgery and head Imperial Coll Vascular Surgery Research Gp 2006–; BIBA Medical: dir 1999–, md 2012–16, chm 2016–; chm Charing Cross Symposium Prog 1978–; pres of surgery Euro Union of Med Specialties 1998–2002, pres Euro Bd of Surgery 2002–06, pres European Fedn of Surgical Specialties Union Européenne des Médecins Spécialistes (UEMS) 2004–08; chm Med Cncl Charing Cross and Westminster Hosps 1992–93, chm Directorate of Surgery Hammersmith Hosps Tst 1993–98, chief of Vascular Service Hammersmith Hosps Tst 1998–2002; hon conslt surgn: Hammersmith Hosp Tst, Chelsea and Westminster Hosp Tst, Chelsea Royal Hosp, Queen Mary's Hosp Roehampton; Hunterian prof RCS of Eng 1980, Protem prof Brigham Hosp Harvard 1984, Boone-Powell prof Baylor Univ Dallas 1984, Hunter Sweaney prof Duke Univ North Carolina 1991, Sir Peter Freyer lectr Univ of Galway 1995, Mannick prof Brigham Hosp Harvard 1996, Scott-Heron lectr Univ of Belfast 1999, Wattie Fletcher lectr 2004, Kinmonth lectr RCS 2004; sometime examiner Univ of Cambridge, Univ of London, Univ of Edinburgh, Univ of Bristol, Univ of Leicester, Nat Univ Ireland, Univ of Southampton, Univ of Birmingham and Univ of Hong Kong; memb Scientific Ctee on Tobacco and Health (formerly Ind Scientific Enquiry into Smoking and Health) 1979–, sec gen and chm Exec Ctee Assoc of Int Vascular Surgns 1982–2005, chm Liaison Ctee Bioengrg Centre Roehampton 1985–88, vice-pres Section of Surgery RSM 1986, chm Riverside Med Cncl 1992–93, pres Vascular Soc GB & I 1999–2000 (vice-pres 1998–2000) 1998–99, memb Abdominal Aortic Aneurysm Nat Screening Prog Advice Gp (formerly Working Pty) 2004–, Dept of Health memb NICE Approval Ctee for Endovascular Aneurysm Repair 2008–, memb Bd MRC 1998–2002 (advsr 2002–, memb Coll of Experts 2002); chm of tstees European Soc for Vascular Surgery 1987–2006 (offr and memb Cncl 1987–93), memb Cncl Assoc of Surgns of GB and Ireland 1987–90 and 1993–2008, hon life pres European Bd of Vascular Surgery 2005–; chm Editorial Bd European Jl of Vascular Surgery 1986–93, memb Editorial Bd Annals of Surgery 1991, memb Jl of Vascular and Endovascular Therapy 2001; hon memb: Southern Africa Vascular Surgery Soc 1989, Polish Surgical Soc 1991, Hellenic Surgical Soc 1991, Mediterranean League of Angiology and Vascular Surgery 1991, Canadian Vascular Soc 1991, German Vascular Soc 1992, European Soc for Vascular Surgery 1993, Brazilian Soc of Angiology and Vascular Surgery 1993, Hellenic Vascular Surgical Soc 1995, Mediterranean League of Vascular Surgeons 1996, Aust Vascular Society 2002, Soc for Vascular Surgery 2003, Swiss Vascular Soc 2003, European Venous Forum 2007, Int Union of Angiology 2008, Soc for Vascular Surgeons 2011; Distinguished Person's Award European Soc for Vascular Surgery 2002, Michael van Vloten Lecture Eindhoven 2003, Lifetime Achievement of Vascular and Endovascular Surgery Arizona Heart Inst 2011; vice-pres London branch Br Red Cross Soc 1992–; hon citizen Kranidi Greece 2006; Liveryman: Worshipful Co of Barbers, Worshipful Soc of Apothecaries; Hon Dr (summus cum laude): Warsaw Med Acad 2003, Athens Univ 2005; Moynihan fell Assoc of Surgeons 1974, ad hominem FRCS(Ed) 1999; FRCS 1971, hon fell Br Soc for Interventional Radiology 2004, Hon FRCS(I) 2007; *Books* Progress in Stroke Research (1978), Smoking and Arterial Disease (1979), Hormones and Vascular Disease (1980), Femoro Distal Bypass (1981), Extra Anatomical Bypass and Secondary Arterial Reconstruction (1982), Progress in Stroke Research 2 (1983), Vascular Surgical Techniques (1984), Diagnostic Techniques and Investigative Procedures (1985), Vascular Surgery – Issues in Current Practice (1986), Indications in Vascular Surgery (1987), Limb Salvage and Amputation in Vascular Surgery (1988), Vascular Surgical Techniques – An Atlas (2 edn 1989, 3 edn 1994, 4 edn 2001), The Cause and Management of Aneurysms (1990), The Maintenance of Arterial Reconstruction (1991), Emergency Vascular Surgery (1992), Surgery for Stroke (1993), Vascular Imaging for Surgeons (1995), The Trials and Tribulations of Vascular Surgery (1996), Clinical Surgery (ed, 1996), Inflammatory and Thrombotic Problems in Vascular Surgery (1997), Indications in Vascular and Endovascular Surgery (1998), The Durability of Vascular and Endovascular Surgery (1999), Vascular and Endovascular Opportunities (2000), The Evidence for Vascular and Endovascular Reconstruction (2002), Vascular and Endovascular Controversies (2003, updated edns 2009 and 2012), Vascular and Endovascular Challenges (2004, updated edns 2007 and 2010), Towards Vascular and Endovascular Consensus (2005, updated edns 2008 and 2011), More Vascular and Endovascular Controversies (2006), More Vascular and Endovascular Challenges (2007), Born to be a Surgeon (2011), Vascular and Endovascular Controversies Update (2012), Vascular and Endovascular Challenges Update (2013), Vascular and Endovascular Consensus Update (2014), Vascular and Endovascular Controversies Update (2015), Vascular and Endovascular Challenges Update (2016); *Recreations* tennis, snorkelling; *Clubs* Athenaeum, Garrick; *Style*— Prof Roger Greenhalgh; ✉ 271 Sheen Lane, London SW14 8RN (☎ 020 8878 1110); Department of Surgery, Charing Cross Hospital, London W6 8RF (☎ 020 8846 7316, fax 020 8846 7330, e-mail r.greenhalgh@imperial.ac.uk)

GREENHALGH, Stephen John; s of Prof Roger Greenhalgh, *qv*, and Mrs Karla Greenhalgh; *b* 14 September 1967; *Educ* St Paul's, Trinity Coll Cambridge; *Children* 3 c; *Career* ldr Hammersmith and Fulham Cncl 2006–12, dep mayor for policing and crime London 2012–; memb Cons Pty; *Style*— Stephen Greenhalgh, Esq; ✉ MOPAC, City Hall, The Queen's Walk, More London, London SE1 2AA

GREENING, Rt Hon Justine; PC (2012), MP; *b* 30 April 1969, Rotherham, S Yorks; *Educ* Oakwood Comp, Univ of Southampton, London Business Sch (MBA); *Career* audit mangr Price Waterhouse 1991–96, finance mangr GlaxoSmithKline 1996–2002, finance mangr Centrica plc 2002–05, MP (Cons) Putney 2005– (Parly candidate (Cons) Ealing, Acton and Shepherds Bush 2001), shadow economic sec to the Treasy 2007–09, shadow communites and local govt min 2009–10, economic sec to the Treasy 2010–11, sec of state for transport 2011–12, sec of state for int devpt 2012–16, sec of state for educn and min for women and equalities 2016–; *Style*— The Rt Hon Ms Justine Greening, MP; ✉ House of Commons, London SW1A 0AA (☎ 020 7219 8300, e-mail greeningj@parliament.uk, website www.justinegreening.co.uk); Constituency Office ☎ 020 8946 4557

GREENISH, Damian John William; s of John William Anthony Graham Greenish (d 2000), and Sonia Petre, *née* Redfern (d 2006); *b* 20 December 1950, London; *Educ* Harrow, Univ of Warwick (BA); *m* 1, 13 Feb 1982, Bettina Mary, *née* Knudtzon; 2 s (Rupert Peter William b 7 Jan 1983, Adam Damian b 9 Feb 1985); m 2, 3 Nov 1989, Joanne Marie, *née* Paterson; 1 s (Frederick John Montrose b 28 Dec 1990), 1 da (Louisa Marie Redfern b 2 Jan 1994); *Career* admitted slr 1979; ptnr Lee & Pembertons 1980–2000; Pemberton Greenish LLP: co-fndr 2000, sr ptnr 2000–12, chm 2012–14, conslt 2016–; chm Chelsea Soc 2012–; hon pres ALEP 2010–; memb Law Soc; *Publications* Hague on Leasehold Enfranchisement (co-author, 1999, 6 edn 2014); *Recreations* fishing, shooting, cricket; *Clubs* Armadillo Cricket, Piltdown Golf, Chelsea Arts; *Style*— Damian Greenish, Esq; ✉ Frensham House, Piltdown, East Sussex TN22 3XN (☎ 01825 722291, e-mail damian@greenishconsulting.com); 45 Cadogan Gardens, London SW3 2AQ (☎ 020 7591 3350, fax 020 7591 3300, e-mail d.greenish@pglaw.co.uk)

GREENISH, Rear Adm Philip Duncan; CBE (2003); s of late Cdr Geoffrey Greenish, OBE, RN, and late Alice Greenish; *b* September 1951; *Educ* Cheltenham Coll, Univ of Durham (BSc); *m* 1972, Wendy, *née* Midmer; 2 s, 1 da; *Career* Capt Weapon Trials and Acceptance 1992–94, MA to Chief of Defence Procurement 1994–96, RCDS 1997; dir: Operational Requirements (Sea Systems) 1997–99, Equipment Capability (Above Water Battlespace) 1999–2000; COS to C-in-C Fleet: Corp Devpt 2000–02, Support 2002–03; chief exec Royal Acad of Engrg 2003–; memb: CCLRC 2005–07, STFC 2007–11, EngineeringUK 2007–, Cncl Univ of Southampton 2011–; ADC to HM The Queen 1997–2000; tstee: Daphne Jackson Tst 2004–15, Science Media Centre 2011–; CEng 1989, FIEE 2001; *Recreations* tennis, golf, skiing, music, gardening; *Style*— Rear Adm Philip Greenish, CBE; ✉ Royal Academy of Engineering, 3 Carlton House Terrace, London SW1Y 5DG

G

GREENLAW, Lavinia; da of Griffith John Keith Greenlaw, and Patricia Elizabeth Lindsay, *née* Mackintosh; *b* 30 July 1962, London; *Educ* Anglo-European Sch, Kingston Univ (BA), London Coll of Printing (Dip), Courtauld Inst (MA); *Children* 1 da (Georgia Elizabeth Ardizzone b 16 Nov 1987); *Career* poet and novelist; former ed and arts administrator; freelance writer, critic and broadcaster 1994–; residences incl Science Museum and Royal Festival Hall; prof of poetry UEA 2007–13; Wellcome Engagement fell 2013–; FRSL; *Awards* Eric Gregory Award 1990, Arts Cncl Writers' Award 1995, Forward Prize for Single Poem 1997, Wingate Scholarship 1998, NESTA Fellowship 2000, Spycherleuk Literaturpreis 2002, Cholmondeley Award 2003, Prix du Premier Roman 2003, Soc of Authors Travelling Scholarship 2005, Ted Hughes Award for New Work in Poetry 2011; *Poetry* Night Photograph (1993), A World Where News Travelled Slowly (1997), Thoughts of a Night Sea (jtly, 2002), Minsk (2003), The Casual Perfect (2011); *Fiction* Mary George of Allnorthover (2001), An Irresponsible Age (2006); *Opera* libretti: Hamelin (2003), Minsk (2005), Peter Pan (2013); *Non-fiction* The Importance of Music to Girls (memoir, 2007), Questions of Travel: William Morris in Iceland (2011); *Opera* Minsk (2005); *Style*— Ms Lavinia Greenlaw; ✉ c/o Kate Burton, Faber & Faber, Bloomsbury House, 74–77 Great Russell Street, London WC1B 3DA ☎ 020 7927 3800, fax 020 7927 3801, e-mail kate.burton@faber.co.uk)

GREENLY, Simon Stafford; s of Raymond Henry Greenly (d 2005), of Corsham, Wilts, and Brenda Margaret Agnes, *née* Stafford (d 1986); *Educ* Uppingham, Univ of London (BSc), Geneva Univ; *m* (m dis 2012) Aug 2004, Marilyn Jane Morris; *Career* Beecham Group 1967–71; dir: Stafford Robert and Partners 1972–96, Lloyd Instruments plc 1985–87, Harlequin Financial Services 1998–2005, Warren & Son 2006–08, Snows 2007–08, Notcutts Gp 2014–16, Lewis Live 2014–; ptnr Cranleigh LLP 2014–, ptnr Cranleigh Merchant Venturers LLP 2014–; chm: Les Routiers 1983–90, Greenly's Management Consultants 1983–2000, ATA Selection plc 1986–88, Greenly's Holdings 1988–, GSL Systems 1991–93, Celemi UK 1993–96, Campaign for Learning 1997–2002, Leadership Alliance 1998–2001, Harlequin Leasing 1999–2000, Peter Honey Publications 2000–02, Harlequin Thoroughbred Racing 2003–04, Lucas & Greenly 2003–06, MaST International plc 2004, Winchester Capital Ptnrs 2005–09; chm Hants C of C 2010–12; visiting entrepreneur Univ of Portsmouth 2010–13; tstee: Windsor Leadership Tst 1995–2000, Bon Pere Tst 2000–; *Publications* Climate Audit (Tomorrow's Company Inquiry, 1998); *Recreations* fly fishing, racing, riding, gardening, fine wine, dancing; *Clubs* RAC, RSYC, GRRC, GAC; *Style*— Simon Greenly, Esq; ✉ Church End Annex, Bucks Head Hill, Meonstoke, Hampshire SO32 3NA (☎ 01489 878102)

GREENO, Edward Patrick; *Educ* Cranleigh Sch, KCL; *m* (m dis); 3 c; *Career* admitted slr: UK 1983, Hong Kong 1989; Herbert Smith: articled clerk 1981–83, asst slr 1983–89, ptnr 1989–2013; Quinn Emanuel Urquhart & Sullivan LLP 2013–; int arbitrator 2001–; memb Law Soc; MCIArb 1989; *Recreations* music, sailing, tennis, Italy, golf, rugby; *Clubs* St George's Hill LTC, St George's Hill Golf, 606, Athenaeum, Kandahar; *Style*— Edward Greeno, Esq; ✉ Quinn Emanuel Urquhart & Sullivan LLP, One Fleet Place, London EC4M 7RA (☎ 020 7653 2000, e-mail tedgreeno@quinnemanuel.com)

GREENOUGH, Alan Edward; s of Edward Greenough (d 1986), and Nancy Dewar, *née* Houghton (d 2004); *b* 14 July 1949; *Educ* Cowley GS St Helens, Univ of Bristol (LLB); *m* 1, 1975 (m dis 1998), Sheila Mary, da of Francis Thomas Collins, of Rainhill, Merseyside; 2 da (Emma b 10 June 1978, Kate b 16 April 1980); m 2, 1999, Pamela Tracey, da of Derek Coldwell, of Ludlow, Salop; 1 da (Victoria b 3 April 2000); *Career* slr specialising in M&A and private equity; ptnr: Alsop Wilkinson 1979–94 (sr ptnr Manchester office 1989, sr corp fin ptnr NW 1989), Pinsent Curtis Biddle 1994–2004 (nat head of corp fin 1996–2004), White & Case 2004–06, Hogan Lovells Int LLP 2006– (head int private equity practice 2006–14, ptnr in charge Legal Services Centre 2015–); memb Law Soc; *Recreations* most sports; *Style*— Alan Greenough, Esq; ✉ 27 Woodchester Park, Beaconsfield, Buckinghamshire HP9 2TU; Hogan Lovells International LLP, Atlantic House, Holborn Viaduct, London EC1A 2FG

GREENSLADE, Brian Carol; s of Ivor Greenslade (d 2000), and Ethel, *née* Radford (d 2001); *b* 25 December 1948, N Molton, Devon; *Educ* S Molton Community Coll; *m* 16 Aug 1975, Margaret, *née* Carter; 1 s (Robert b 17 March 1979), 1 da (Kathryn b 17 Sept 1982); *Career* bank clerk National Westminster Bank 1966–70, accounting asst ICC Ltd 1970–72, fin controller Selkirk Manufacturing Ltd 1972–95; cncllr Devon CC 1985– (ldr 1993–), cncllr N Devon Dist Cncl 1991– (ldr 2011); memb: Devon and Cornwall Police Authy 1989– (chm 1999–2003), Assoc of Police Authorities 1997– (dep chair 2001), Assembly of Euro Regions 1993– (vice-pres 2000); memb Lib Dem Party; inc company and commercial accountant 1977; *Recreations* reading, travelling; *Style*— Councillor Brian Greenslade; ✉ 2 Longpiece, Marwood, Barnstaple, North Devon EX31 4DT (☎ 01271 372065, fax 01271 378524, e-mail brian.greenslade@devon.gov.uk)

GREENSLADE, Prof Roy; *b* 31 December 1946, Dulwich, London; *Educ* Dagenham County HS, Univ of Sussex (BA); *Career* journalist; with Barking Advertiser 1962–66; sub ed: Lancashire Evening Telegraph 1966–67, Daily Mail Manchester 1967–69; dep chief sub ed The Sun 1969–71 and 1971–73, sub ed Daily Mirror 1971, pt/t sub ed Sunday Mirror 1975–79, news reader BBC Radio Brighton 1975–76, Daily Express and Daily Star 1979–81 (leaving as features ed), asst features ed The Sun 1981–86, managing ed (News) Sunday Times 1986–90, ed Daily Mirror 1990–91, conslt ed News International 1991, freelance 1992–, columnist The Guardian and The Observer 1996–2005, columnist Daily Telegraph 2005–; presenter Talk TV (Granada/BSkyB) 1996–97; dir: Impact Books 1993–98, Choocleus Ltd 1996–; presenter Mediumwave (BBC Radio 4); prof of journalism City Univ London 2003–; Hon DLitt Brighton 1999; *Books* Goodbye to the Working Class (1975), Maxwell's Fall (1992), Press Gang (2003); *Style*— Roy Greenslade, Esq; ✉ c/o Peters, Fraser and Dunlop, Derby House 34–43 Russell Street London WC2B 5HA (☎ 020 7344 1000)

GREENSTOCK, Sir Jeremy Quentin; GCMG (2003, KCMG 1998, CMG 1991); s of John Wilfrid Greenstock (d 1992), of Sheepscombe, Glos, and his 1 w, Ruth Margaret, *née* Logan (d 1973); *b* 27 July 1943; *Educ* Harrow, Worcester Coll Oxford (exhibitioner, BA, Rackets blue, Tennis blue); *m* 12 April 1969, Anne Derryn Ashford Hodges, da of William Anthony Ashford Hodges, of Fritton, Norfolk; 2 da (Katherine b 1970, Alexandra b 1975), 1 s (Nicholas b 1973); *Career* asst master Eton 1966–69; HM Dip Serv: joined 1969, MECAS 1970–72, second then first sec Dubai 1970–74, private sec to HM Ambass Washington 1974–78, planning staff, personnel ops, Near E and N African Depts FCO 1978–83, commercial cnsllr Jeddah and Riyadh 1983–86, head of Chancery Paris 1987–90, asst under sec of state Western and Southern Europe FCO 1990–93, min Washington 1994–95, dep under sec Middle East and Eastern Europe FCO 1995, political dir FCO 1996–1998, UK perm rep to the UN NY and UK rep on the Security Cncl 1998–2003, UK special rep for Iraq 2003–04; dir Ditchley Fndn 2004–2010, chm Gatehouse Advsy Ptnrs 2010–, chm Lambert Energy Advsy 2012– (non-exec dir 2010–), co-chm European Eminent Persons Gp on the Middle East 2012–; non-exec dir De La Rue 2005–13; special advsr: BP 2004–10, Forward Thinking 2006–; tstee Int Rescue Ctee (UK) 2005–12, chm UN Assoc UK 2011–16; memb Cncl Chatham House 2011–; King of Arms Order of St Michael and St George 2007–; *Recreations* reading, music, travel, sport; *Style*— Sir Jeremy Greenstock, GCMG; ✉ 3 Cornwall Gardens, London SW7 4AJ

GREENWELL, Sir Edward Bernard; 4 Bt (UK 1906), of Marden Park, Godstone, Co Surrey and Greenwell, Wolsingham, Co Durham; DL (1988); s of Capt Sir Peter McClintock Greenwell, 3 Bt, TD, DL (d 1978), and (Jean) Henrietta Rose (who m 2, Hugh Kenneth Haig, TD), da of Peter Haig Thomas and Lady Alexandra, *née* Agar, 2 da of 4 Earl of Normanton, DL; *b* 10 June 1948; *Educ* Eton, Univ of Nottingham (BSc), Cranfield Inst of Technology (MBA); *m* 1974, Sarah Louise (d 2010), da of Lt-Col Philip Maitland Gore-Anley (d 1968), of Sculthorpe House, Fakenham; 3 da (Belinda Clayre b 1977, Lucy Rose b 1979, Daisy Julia b 1983), 1 s (Alexander Bernard Peter b 1987); *Heir* s, Alexander Greenwell; *Career* farmer; pres Country Land and Business Assoc 2001–03; *Clubs* Turf; *Style*— Sir Edward Greenwell, Bt, DL; ✉ Gedgrave Hall, Woodbridge, Suffolk IP12 2BX

GREENWOOD, His Hon Judge Alan Eliezer; s of Rabbi Isaac Hans Grunewald (d 1998), and Martha Grunewald (d 1987); *b* 5 June 1947; *Educ* Hasmonean GS, UCL (LLB); *m* 15 June 1975, Naomi, *née* Ohayon; 2 s (Ilan Anthony b 20 Sept 1977, Doron Joshua b 10 Jan 1982), 1 da (Dalia Karen b 1 May 1979); *Career* called to the Bar Middle Temple 1970; asst recorder 1992–96, recorder 1996–2000, circuit judge (SE Circuit) 2000–; memb: Criminal Bar Assoc (treas 1993–97), Gen Cncl of the Bar 1993–95, United Jewish Israel Appeal (UJIA) Bench and Bar Ctee; *Recreations* five-a-side football, tennis, skiing, cycling, theatre, film, travel; *Style*— His Hon Judge Greenwood; ✉ Harrow Crown Court, Hailsham Drive, Harrow, Middlesex HA1 4TU (☎ 07930 348228, e-mail hhjudge.greenwood@judiciary.gsi.gov.uk)

GREENWOOD, Brian John; s of Ronald Greenwood (d 1979), and Marianne Luise, *née* Weiss; *b* 15 April 1950; *Educ* Forest Sch, Univ of Southampton (LLB); *m* 1 July 1978, Julia Le Messurier, da of Alan Le Messurier Scott; 4 s (Jonathan Ronald b 9 April 1981, James Alan b 1 Oct 1985, Alexander Brian, Benjamin John (twins) b 5 Oct 1989), 1 da (Jacqueline Rachel b 10 April 1983); *Career* articled clerk City of Westminster 1973–76, admitted slr 1976, asst slr S Yorks CC 1976–78, asst co slr Kent CC 1980–82 (sr asst slr 1978–80), chief slr Beds CC 1982–85, ptnr and head Planning and Environmental Law Gp Norton Rose 1988– (joined 1985), head Evironment and Planning Gp Taylor Wessing 2007–09, head of planning and environmental law Osborne Clarke 2009–, ptnr and head of infrastructure, planning and environment Winckworth Sherwood LLP 2015–; visiting lectr on planning and environmental law Coll of Law 1988–93; Law Soc: exec memb Local Govt Gp 1979–85, memb Planning and Environmental Law Ctee 1989– (chm 1996–), chm Environmental Law Sub-Ctee 1995–; chm Planning and Environmental Law Sub-Ctee City of London Law Soc 1990–95; memb: CBI Environmental Protection Panel, Int Bar Assoc; Liveryman Worshipful Co of Slrs 1989 (memb of Ct 1992, Master 2003–04), Liveryman Worshipful Co of Gardeners 2005; FRSA; *Books* Basic Planning Law and Practice (1989), Butterworths Planning Law Encyclopaedia (1990), Butterworths Planning Law Handbook, Planning and Compensation Act 1991 (1991), Environmental Regulation and Economic Growth (contrib), Planning Law and Practice; *Recreations* family, violin, classical music, sport; *Style*— Brian Greenwood, Esq; ✉ Winckworth Sherwood, Minerva House, 5 Montague Close, London SE1 9BB (☎ 020 7593 5016)

GREENWOOD, HE Judge Sir Christopher John; kt (2009), CMG (2002), QC (1999); s of late Capt Murray Guy Greenwood, and late Diana Maureen, *née* Barron; *b* 12 May 1955; *Educ* Wellingborough Sch, Magdalene Coll Cambridge (MA, LLB); *m* 5 Aug 1978, Susan Anthea, da of late Geoffrey James Longbotham, and late Patricia Longbotham; 2 da; *Career* called to the Bar Middle Temple 1978 (bencher 2003); practising barr Essex Court Chambers 1995–2009, judge of the Int Ct of Justice 2009–; Univ of Cambridge: fell Magdalene Coll 1978–96, dir of studies in law 1982–96, tutor 1989–96, dean 1982–87, lectr Faculty of Law 1984–96 (asst lectr 1981–84); prof of int law LSE 1996–2009; dir of studies in public int law Hague Academy of Int Law 1989; visiting prof: West Virginia Univ 1986, Mississippi Univ 1989, Marburg Univ 1991; hon fell Magdalene Coll 2009, hon fell Lauterpacht Centre for Int Law 2009; memb Panel of Arbitrators: Law of the Sea Convention, Int Centre for the Settlement of Investment Disputes; *Publications* Essays on War in International Law (2006); jt ed Int Law Reports; articles in legal periodicals; *Recreations* politics, biography, reading novels; *Clubs* Athenaeum, Oxford and Cambridge, De Witte Society, Haagsche; *Style*— HE Judge Sir Christopher Greenwood, CMG, QC; ✉ International Court of Justice, Peace Palace, Carnegieplein 2, 2517 KJ The Hague, The Netherlands (☎ 0031 70 302 2323, fax 0031 70 364 9928, e-mail c.greenwood@icj-cij.org)

GREENWOOD, Jeremy John; s of Basil Procter Greenwood (d 1963), of Langham, Norfolk, and Stephanie Kathleen, *née* Davidson Houston, MBE (d 1988); *b* 30 March 1936; *Educ* Haileybury, Peterhouse Cambridge (MA); *m* 26 Oct 1963, Annabel Elizabeth Marie-Gabrielle, da of Noel Carlile (d 1945); 1 s (Simon Harry b 1966), 2 da (Elinor Rose b 1971, Gemma Charlotte b 1972); *Career* cmmnd 1st King's Dragoon Gds 1956–59; publisher; various positions with Cassell, Pergamon and Hutchinson Presses; dir Trade Div Cassell Ltd 1977–81; proprietor and md Quiller Press 1981–2002, proprietor JJG Publishing 2003–; govr Runton Hill Sch for Girls 1984–88, chm branch Arthritis Research Cncl; *Books* Sefton – Horse For Any Year (1983); *Recreations* horses, shooting, golf, tennis, theatre; *Clubs* Cavalry and Guards', Royal West Norfolk Golf, MCC; *Style*— Jeremy Greenwood, Esq; ✉ Sparrow Hall, Hindringham, Fakenham, Norfolk NR21 0DP (e-mail greenwood.quiller@btopenworld.com)

GREENWOOD, (Kathryn) Sarah; da of David Greenwood, and Carmel, *née* Coady; *b* 9 March 1960, Newcastle upon Tyne; *Educ* Wimbledon Sch of Art (BA, Arts Cncl bursary); *m* (m dis); 1 s (Mackintosh Muggleton b 31 May 1994); *Career* production designer; designed extensively for theatre 1982–85; BBC: joined as asst designer 1985, designer 1986, sr designer 1994; freelance 1997–; memb: AMPAS, Art Directors' Guild, BAFTA; *Commercials* American Express, Chanel; *Television* incl: Later with Jools Holland (BBC) 1993–95 (series 1, 2 and 5), The Late Show (BBC) 1994, Black Daisies for the Bride (BBC) 1994, Bore of the Year Awards (BOFTY) (BBC) 1995, The King of Hearts (Channel 4) 1995, After Miss Julie (BBC) 1996, The Tenant of Wildfell Hall (BBC) 1996 (Production Design RTS Award 1997), The Moonstone (BBC) 1996, Nature Boy (BBC) 2000, Bodily Harm (Channel 4) 2001–02, Ready When You Are Mr McGill (WTTV) 2002, Charles II (BBC) 2002–03; *Film* incl: Keep the Aspidistra Flying 1997, The Governess 1997, Esther Khan 1998, This Year's Love 1998, Born Romantic 1999–2000, Pride and Prejudice 2003–04, Starter for Ten 2005, Atonement 2006 (Best Prodn Design BAFTA 2008), Miss Pettigrew Lives for a Day 2007, The Soloist 2007–08, Sherlock Holmes 2008–09, Hanna 2009–10, Sherlock Holmes II 2010–11, Anna Karenina 2011–12, Tarzan 2012–13; *Recreations* cinema, gardening, sailing, skiing, travel, walking; *Style*— Ms Sarah Greenwood; ✉ c/o Independent Talent Group Ltd, Oxford House, 76 Oxford Street, London W1D 1BS (☎ 020 7636 6565)

GREER, Adrian; CMG (2004); s of David Smith Greer (d 1989), and Christine, *née* Dawson; *b* 26 April 1957; *Educ* Queen Mary's GS Walsall, Univ of St Andrews (MA); *m* 1985, Diana, *née* Cuddy; 3 da (Joanna b 27 Dec 1985, Christina b 21 Sept 1987, Hazel b 7 Aug 1996), 1 s (Christopher b 25 June 1992); *Career* auditor NAO 1979–84; Br Cncl: devpt offr London 1984–85, devpt mangr Japan 1985–88, project mangr London 1988–89, chief accountant 1989–91, dir Lesotho and Swaziland 1991–93, dir Zambia 1993–96, dir Europe, Asia and Americas Devpt Services 1996–2000, dir Russia 2000–04, dir Learning, Creativity and Society 2004–07, rgnl dir East Asia 2007–10, dir Global Network 2010–12, chief operating offr 2012–; memb Ct Univ of St Andrews 2016–; CIPFA 1984, FRSA; *Recreations* running, cycling, swimming; *Clubs* Dulwich Runners, Vets Athletic; *Style*— Adrian Greer, Esq, CMG; ✉ e-mail adrian.greer@sky.com

GREER, Prof Germaine; *b* 29 January 1939, Melbourne, Australia; *Educ* Star of the Sea Convent Gardenvale, Univ of Melbourne (Diocesan and Sr Govt scholar, BA), Univ of Sydney (MA), Univ of Cambridge (Cwlth scholar, PhD); *Career* broadcaster, journalist, columnist and reviewer 1972–; sr tutor in English Univ of Sydney 1963–64, asst lectr then lectr in English Univ of Warwick 1967–72, lectr throughout N America with

American Program Bureau 1973–78, lectr to raise funds for Tulsa Bursary and Fellowship Scheme 1980–83, prof of modern letters Univ of Tulsa 1980–83 (visiting prof Graduate Faculty of Modern Letters 1979), dir Stump Cross Books 1988–, special lectr and unofficial fell Newnham Coll Cambridge 1989–98, prof of English and comparative literary studies Univ of Warwick 1998–2003, special supervisor in English Newnham Coll Cambridge 2008–; fndr ed Tulsa Studies in Women's Literature 1981, fndr dir Tulsa Centre for the Study of Woman's Literature; Hon Dr: Univ of Grittith 1996, Univ of York Toronto 1999, UMIST 2000; hon degree Univ of Essex 2003, Hon DLitt Anglia Poly Univ 2003, LLD (hc) Univ of Melbourne 2003, Hon DLitt Sydney Univ 2005; Centenary Medal Australian Living Treasure Nat Tst Award 2003; *Publications* The Female Eunuch (1969), The Obstacle Race: The Fortunes of Women Painters and their Work (1979), Sex and Destiny: The Politics of Human Fertility (1984), Shakespeare (1986), The Madwoman's Underclothes (selected journalism, 1986), Kissing the Rod: An Anthology of Seventeenth Century Women's Verse (ed with Susan Hastings, Jeslyn Medoff, Melinda Sansone, 1988), Daddy, We Hardly Knew You (1989, winner J R Ackerley Prize and Premio Internazionale Mondello), The Uncollected Verse of Aphra Behn (ed, 1989), The Change: Women, Ageing and the Menopause (1991), Slip-Shod Sibyls: Recognition, Rejection and The Woman Poet (1995), The Whole Woman (1999), John Wilmot, Earl of Rochester (1999), 101 Poems by 101 Women (ed, 2001), The Boy (2003), Poems for Gardeners (ed, 2003), Whitefella Jump Up The Shortest Way to Nationhood (2004), Shakespeare's Wife (2007), On Rage (2008), White Beech (2014); Stump Cross Books incl: The Uncollected Works of Aphra Behn, The Collected Works of Katherine Philips, the Matchless Orinda (3 vols), The Surviving Works of Anne Wharton; *Style*— Prof Germaine Greer; ✉ c/o Aitken Alexander Associates, 291 Gray's Inn Road, London WC1X 8QJ

GREER, Prof Ian Andrew; *b* 16 April 1958; *Educ* Allan Glen's Sch Glasgow, Univ of Glasgow (MB ChB, MD); *Career* SHO, res fell and registrar posts in obstetrics and gynaecology, gen med, haemostasis and thrombosis Univ Dept of Med Royal Infirmary Glasgow and Glasgow Royal Maternity Hosp, lectr and hon sr registrar in obstetrics and gynaecology Univ of Edinburgh, Edinburgh Royal Infirmary and Simpson Meml Maternity Pavilion 1987–90, clinical res scientist and clinical conslt MRC Reproductive Biology Unit Edinburgh, hon sr lectr Dept of Obstetrics and Gynaecology Univ of Edinburgh and hon conslt obstetrician and gynaecologist Simpson Meml Maternity Pavilion 1990–91, Muirhead prof and head Dept of Obstetrics and Gynaecology Univ of Glasgow, hon conslt obstetrician Glasgow Royal Maternity Hosp and hon conslt gynaecologist Glasgow Royal Infirmary 1991–2006; Univ of Glasgow: regius prof 2000–06, head Div of Developmental Med 2002–06, dep dean Faculty of Med 2003–06; dean and prof of obstetric med Hull York Medical Sch and hon conslt obstetrician Hull and East Yorks Hosps NHS Tst 2007–10; currently: provost and exec pro-vice-chllr Faculty of Health and Life Sciences Univ of Liverpool, chief exec Liverpool Health Partners, chair Northern Health Science Alliance; Gold Medal RCOG 1987, William Blair Bell meml lectr RCOG 1989, Bernhard Baron travelling scholar RCOG 1989, Watson Prize lectr RCPS 1990; chm Subspeciality Ctee RCOG 1995–98, chair Nat Advsy Ctee Centre for Maternal and Child Enquiries 2006–, chair MRC Translational Stem Cell Research Ctee 2007–; non-exec dir Hull and E Yorks NHS Tst 2008–10; memb: Soc for Gynaecologic Investigation, Int Soc for Thrombosis and Haemostasis, Int Soc of Obstetric Medicine, MacDonald Obstetric Medicine Soc; fell Faculty of Sexual & Reproductive Healthcare (FFSRH), FRCOG, FRCPGlas, FRCPEd, FRCP, FRCPI, FAE, FMedSci; *Books* Haemostasis and Thrombosis in Obstetrics and Gynaecology (ed, 1992), Thrombosis in Obstetrics and Gynaecology (ed, 1997), Mosby's Color Atlas and text of Obstetrics and Gynaecology (jt ed, 2000), Antenatal Disorders for the MRCOG (jtly, 2000), The Menopause in Practice (jtly, 2002), Problem-based Obstetrics and Gynaecology (jtly, 2003), Venous Thrombosis in Women, Pregnancy, the Contraceptive Pill and HRT (2003), Pregnancy: The Inside Guide (2003), Practical Obstetric Haematology (jtly, 2006), Preterm Labour (jt ed, 2006), Women's Vascular Health (ed, 2007), Maternal Medicine (ed, 2007), Textbook of Periconceptional Medicine (ed, 2009), Fertility and Conception (2007); author of numerous medical pubns; *Style*— Prof Ian Greer; ✉ Foundation Building, University of Liverpool, Brownlow Hill, Liverpool L69 7ZX

GREER, Prof (Alan) Lindsay; s of Alan Greer (d 1994), and Helena, *née* Lindsay; *b* 19 June 1955, Ballymena, Co Antrim; *Educ* Trinity Hall Cambridge (MA, PhD); *Career* Div of Applied Sciences Harvard Univ: NATO research fell 1980–81, asst prof of applied physics 1981–84; Dept of Materials Sci and Metallurgy Univ of Cambridge: sr asst in research 1984–88, lectr 1988–96, reader in microstructural kinetics 1996–2001, prof of materials sci 2001–, dep head of dept 2001–05, head of dept 2006–; Sidney Sussex Coll Cambridge: fell 1984–, tutor for grad students 1987–96, vice-master 2004–; invited prof Inst Nat Poly de Grenoble 1994, Clark Harrison distinguished visiting prof of physics Center for Materials Innovation Washington Univ St Louis MO 2005, advsy prof Chongqing Univ People's Republic of China 2005–; ed Philosophical Magazine 2003–; author of over 300 papers in materials science (rapid solidification, metallic glasses, nanocrystalline alloys, nucleation, multilayers, electromigration), ed of proceedings, author of chapters in books; Zacharaisen Award Jl of Non-Crystalline Solids 1989, Light Metals Award Minerals, Metals & Materials Soc 1998, Cast Shop Technol Award Minerals, Metals & Materials Soc 1999, Cook-Ablett Award IMMM 2000, Pilkington Prize Univ of Cambridge 2000, Sr Scientist Medal Int Symposium on Metastable and Nano Materials 2000, Honda Medal Tohoku Univ 2004, Hume-Rothery Prize IMMM 2006; CEng 1981, MIMMM 1981, FRSA 1993; *Recreations* archery; *Style*— Prof Lindsay Greer; ✉ Sidney Sussex College, Cambridge CB2 3HU (☎ 01223 338836, fax 01223 338884, e-mail alg13@cam.ac.uk); University of Cambridge, Dept of Materials Science & Metallurgy, Pembroke Street, Cambridge CB2 3QZ (☎ 01223 334308, fax 01223 334567)

GREGOR, Zdenek Jiri; s of Prof Ota Gregor, and Miroslava Gregor; *b* 27 March 1948; *Educ* Prague 7 HS, Westminster Med Sch of London; *m*; 1 s (Benjamin b 1973), 1 da (Camilla b 1977); *Career* house appts Westminster Hosp 1971–72, res surgical offr Moorfields Eye Hosp 1976–79, asst prof Univ of Southern Calif LA 1980–82, sr lectr ophthalmology Univ of London 1982–83, conslt ophthalmic surgn Moorfields Eye Hosp 1983–, numerous pubns and chapters on disorders and surgical treatment of the retina and the vitreous 1975–; memb: Oxford Ophthalmological Congress 1979, Euro Flouroscein Angiography Club 1977, Macular Soc of the US, Retina Soc of the US, Scientific Advsy Cncl, Opportunities for the Disabled; LRCP 1971, FRCS 1977, FRSM 1986 (and memb), fell Coll Ophthalmologists 1988; *Recreations* music, skiing; *Style*— Zdenek Gregor, Esq; ✉ 94 Harley Street, London W1N 1AF (☎ 020 7935 0777, fax 020 7935 6860); Moorfields Eye Hospital, City Road, London EC1V 2PD (☎ 020 7253 3411, fax 020 7253 4696, telex 266129)

GREGORY, Prof Alan; s of William Raymond Gregory, and Margaret Mary, *née* Richards; *b* 19 March 1954, Mountain Ash, Wales; *Educ* St Bartholomew's GS Newbury, LSE (MSc); *m* 1 (m dis), Barbara Elaine, *née* Arnold; m 2, Julie Mary, *née* Whittaker; *Career* CA 1974; successively mgmnt trainee, accountant and mangr BR 1971–76, budgets controller Green Shield Stamps 1977, lectr SW London Coll 1977–78, sr lectr in accounting Luton Coll of HE 1978–83, sr lectr Brighton Poly 1983–86, princ lectr City of London Poly 1986–89, lectr in accounting and finance Univ of Exeter 1989–95, prof of accounting Univ of Glasgow 1995–96, prof of business studies Univ of Wales Aberystwyth 1996–97, prof of corporate finance Univ of Exeter 1997–; memb Competition Cmmn (now Competition and Markets Authy) 2001–09, academic advsr Cost of Capital Gp 2009–, md AGRF Ltd; fell CIMA 1986 (assoc 1978); *Publications* Valuing Companies (1992), Management Accounting in Hotel Companies (jtly, 1995), Cost of Capital in the UK (jtly, 1999), Recent Advances in Mergers and Acquisitions Vol 1 (ed jtly, 2000), Strategic Valuation of Companies (2 edn, 2001), Recent Advances in Mergers and Acquisitions Vol 2 (ed jtly, 2003); numerous pubns in leading jls incl: Jl of Empirical Finance, Jl of Business Finance and Accounting, European Financial Management, Jl of Accounting and Public Policy, Accounting and Business Research, Economic Jl; *Recreations* painting, sailing, skiing; *Style*— Prof Alan Gregory; ✉ School of Business and Economics, University of Exeter, Room 214, Streatham Court, Rennes Drive, Exeter EX4 4PU (e-mail a.gregory@ex.ac.uk)

GREGORY, Alex; MBE (2013); *b* 11 March 1984, Cheltenham, Glos; *Educ* Univ of Reading; *Career* rower; achievements incl: Gold medal (coxless fours) World Championships 2009, fourth (coxless fours) World Championships 2010, Gold medal (coxless fours) World Championships 2011, Gold medal (coxless fours) Olympic Games 2012; *Clubs* Leander; *Style*— Mr Alex Gregory, MBE

GREGORY, David Noel; s of Charles Cope Gregory, and Caroline Ada Gregory; *b* 25 December 1944; *Educ* Hillcroft Sch London; *m* 19 Aug 1972, Angela Mary, da of Ernest James Day; 1 da (Claire Louise b 9 Feb 1975), 1 s (Daniel Mark b 24 Feb 1977); *Career* CA; articled clerk Evans Peirson & Co, gp fin controller James Walker Goldsmith & Silversmith plc; fin dir: Instore Enterprises Ltd (subsid Debenhams), Eurobrands Ltd (subsid Remy Martin & Co) 1987–90; gp fin dir: Freetraders Group Ltd 1991–95, Oxbridge Group Ltd 1995–97, Alfano Bros Ltd; md DG Corporate Services Ltd 1997–; FCA (ACA 1969), ATII 1971, FCCA 1980, MBCS 1981, JDipMA 1981, DipM 1990, MCIM 1990; *Clubs* Twickenham on Thames Rotary; *Style*— David Gregory, Esq; ✉ DG Corporate Services Ltd, 15 Orchard Rise, Richmond, Surrey TW10 5BX

GREGORY, Derek Edward; s of Edward Gregory (d 1970), of Ilkeston, and Hilda, *née* Stokeley (d 1989); *Educ* Ilkeston GS; *m* 1, 16 June 1962, Marjorie (d 1984), da of Lloyd Priest Newcastle (d 1976); 1 s (Philip Edward b 1965), 1 da (Tina Louise b 1968); m 2, 13 Dec 1986, Kate (d 2007); *Career* fndr and sr ptnr Gregory Priestley & Stewart CA's Ilkeston and Long Eaton 1970–; treas Stanton by Dale CC 1958–; FCA 1961; *Recreations* golf, cricket, gardening; *Style*— Derek Gregory, Esq; ✉ Rosemary Cottage, Bowling Close, Stanton By Dale, Ilkeston, Derby (☎ 0115 932 2047); Gregory Priestley & Stewart, 16 Queen Street, Ilkeston, Derbyshire (☎ 0115 932 6726)

GREGORY, John Kennedy; s of William John Gregory, of North Tawton, Devon, and Irene Kennedy, *née* Heath; *b* 19 March 1958, Crediton, Devon; *Educ* Blundell's, Brooke Univ Oxford (BA); *partner* Marilyn Ann Walker; 1 da (Jordan b 20 Nov 1989); *Career* mktg mangr Aust and NZ Nippon Int Containers 1980–82, gen mangr Aust, NZ and S Pacific Transamerica ICS Ltd 1982–85; Gregory Distribution: md 1985–2003, chief exec 2003–; business advsr South West Acad of Fine and Applied Art, tstee Devon Air Ambulance; MCIT 1998; *Recreations* golf, tennis, skiing; *Clubs* Exeter Golf and Country; *Style*— John Gregory, Esq; ✉ Reeds, The Retreat Drive, Topsham, Devon EX3 0LS (☎ 01392 877564, e-mail johng@gdl.uk.com)

GREGORY, John Raymond; s of Raymond Gregory (d 1988), of Congleton, Cheshire, and Ivy Charlotte, *née* Bourne (d 1993); *b* 18 April 1949; *Educ* St Ambrose Coll Hale Barns, Univ of Hull; *m* 11 April 1981, Fiona Mary Kristin, da of Donald Walker (d 1997); 2 s (Gordon b 1981, Lawrence b 1984), 2 da (Victoria b 1983, Elizabeth b and d 1987); *Career* called to the Bar Middle Temple 1972, in practice 1973–; memb Chancery Bar Assoc; chm Stretford Constituency Cons Assoc 1980–82; Parly candidate (Cons) Stretford and Urmston 1997; *Recreations* swimming, archaeology, writing, painting; *Clubs* Lancashire CCC; *Style*— John Gregory, Esq; ✉ Deans Court Chambers, 24 St John Street, Manchester M3 4DF (☎ 0161 214 6000, e-mail johnraymondgregory@hotmail.com)

GREGORY, Prof Kenneth John; CBE (2007); s of Frederick Arthur Gregory (d 1969), of Belper, Derbys, and Marion, *née* Yates (d 1981); *b* 23 March 1938; *Educ* Herbert Strutt Sch Belper, UCL (BSc, PhD, DSc); *m* 25 Aug 1962, Margaret (Christine), da of Lawrence Wilmot (d 1974), of Belper, Derbys; 2 da (Caroline b 1964, Sarah b 1966), 1 s (Jonathon b 1971); *Career* reader in physical geography Univ of Exeter 1972–76 (lectr 1962–72), prof Univ of Southampton 1976–92 (dean of sci 1984–87, dep vice-chllr 1988–92), warden Goldsmiths Coll London 1992–98, Leverhulme emeritus fell 1998–2001; visiting lectr Univ of New England Armidale NSW Aust 1975, distinguished visiting prof Arizona State Univ 1987, visiting prof Univ Kebangsaan Malaysia 1987; vice-chair Governing Body Univ of Southampton Solent 1999–2007; memb Cncl Brunel Univ 2010– (dep chair 2015–); Linton Award Br Geomorphological Res Gp 1999, Geographical Medal Royal Scottish Geographical Soc 2000; Hon DSc: Univ of Southampton 1997, Univ of Greenwich 1997; DUniv (hc) Southampton Solent 2008; hon fell Goldsmiths Coll 1998; fell UCL 1999; Freeman: City of London 1997, Worshipful Co of Goldsmiths 1997 (Liveryman 1998); FRGS 1962 (Back Award 1980, Founder's Medal 1993), CGeog 2001, FBSG 2013 (pres 2009–14); *Books* Southwest England (with A H Shorter and W L D Ravenhill, 1969), Drainage Basin Form and Process (with D E Walling, 1973), River Channel Changes (ed, 1977), Geomorphological Processes (with E Derbyshire and J R Hails, 1979 and 1980), Horizons in Physical Geography (ed with M J Clark and A M Gurnell, 1988), The Nature of Physical Geography (1985), Temperate Palaeohydrology (ed with L Starkel and J B Thornes, 1989), Global Continental Palaeohydrology (ed with L Starkel and V Baker 1995), Global Continental Changes: the context of palaeohydrology (ed with J Branson and AG Brown 1996), Evaluating Teacher Quality in Higher Education (ed with R Aylett, 1996), Fluvial Geomorphology of Great Britain (ed, 1997), Palaeohydrology and Environmental Change (ed with G Benito and V R Baker, 1998), The Changing Nature of Physical Geography (2000), Palaeohydrology: Understanding Global Change (ed with G Benito, 2003), River Channel Management (with P W Downs, 2004), Physical Geography (ed 4 vols, 2005), Environmental Sciences: A companion primer (jtly, 2008), The Earth's Land Surface (2010), The SAGE Handbook of Geomorphology (ed with A S Goudie, 2011), The Basics of Geomorphology: Key Concepts (with J Lewin, 2014); *Recreations* gardening, travel; *Style*— Prof Kenneth Gregory, CBE; ✉ 9 Poltimore Road, Guildford, Surrey GU2 7PT (☎ 01483 821123, e-mail k.j.gregory@ntlworld.com)

GREGORY, Lesley; *Educ* Charlton Park Sch Cheltenham, Somerville Coll Oxford (BA, Hockey blue), Coll of Law; *m*; 3 c; *Career* articled Courts & Co 1983; Memery Crystal: slr 1983–88, ptnr (specialising in corporate and commercial law) 1988–, chief exec 2010–; non-exec dir Accuma plc 2006–10; memb Nominated Advisors (NOMAD) Ctee Quoted Companies Alliance; Lawyer Magazine Hot 100 Lawyer 2012, highly commended Legal Business Woman of the Year Law Soc Excellence Awards 2014; memb Law Soc; *Recreations* tennis, running, theatre, opera; *Style*— Ms Lesley Gregory; ✉ Memery Crystal, 44 Southampton Buildings, London WC2A 1AP (☎ 020 7242 5905, fax 020 7242 2058, e-mail lgregory@memerycrystal.com)

GREGORY, Rear Adm (Alexander) Michael; OBE (1987); s of Vice Adm Sir George David Archibald Gregory, KBE, CB, DSO (d 1975), of Greymount, Alyth, Perthshire, and Florence Eve Patricia, *née* Hill; *b* 15 December 1945; *Educ* Marlborough, BRNC Dartmouth; *m* 13 June 1970, Jean Charlotte, da of Lt Cdr Gerald Robin Muir, OBE (d 1991), of Braco Castle, By Dunblane, Perthshire; 4 da (Charlotte b 1971, Katherine b 1973, Helen b 1979, Sarah b 1982); *Career* HMS Albion and HMS Aisne 1965–66, HMS Narwhale 1966–67, HMS Otter 1967–68, HMS Warspite 1968–70, HMS Courageous 1970–73, HMS Odin (based in Australia) 1973–75, i/c HMS Finwhale 1976–78, HMS Repulse 1978–80, staff of US Third Fleet Hawaii 1980–82, i/c HMS Renown 1982–85, Cdr Tenth Submarine Sqdn and i/c HMS Resolution 1985–86, Jt Servs Def Coll 1987, MOD

G

Directorate of Naval Warfare 1987–88, i/c HMS Cumberland 1988–90, capt Tenth Submarine Sqdn 1990–92, MOD Naval Staff 1992–93, naval attaché Washington 1994–97, flag offr Scotland N England and NI 1997–2000; chief exec METCOM 2001–03, chief exec Energy Industries Cncl 2004–07; lieut Queen's Bodyguard for Scotland (Royal Co of Archers); Lord-Lt Dunbartonshire 2008–; *Recreations* fishing, skiing, gardening; *Style*— Rear Adm Michael Gregory, OBE

GREGORY, Nicholas; *Educ* St John's Coll Camb, Univ of Reading; *Career* army offr Worcs and Sherwood Foresters Regt 1987–92, trainee surveyor Chesterton 1993–96, fund mangr UBS Global Asset Mgmnt (UK) Ltd 1996–2002, dir Castlemore Securities Ltd 2002–05, jt chief exec The Local Shopping REIT plc until 2013(dir 2005–13), currently jt md Waypoint Asset Mgmnt Ltd; MRICS 1995; *Style*— Nicholas Gregory, Esq; ✉ Waypoint Asset Management Limited, 2nd Floor, 86 Brook Street, London W1K 5AY

GREGORY, Dr Paul Duncan; s of Thomas Gregory, of Troon, and Elsie, *née* Millward; *b* 1 December 1954; *Educ* Marr Coll Troon, Univ of Edinburgh (BCom, PhD); *m* 21 July 1978, Catherine Margaret, da of James Campbell, of Troon; 1 s (James Alexander b 1985), 1 da (Jennifer Alison b 1987); *Career* oil analyst Wood Mackenzie & Co Ltd 1981–85, asst dir Hill Samuel 1986–87, dir County Natwest Securities 1989–92 (assoc dir 1988–89); md: Wood Mackenzie Consultants Ltd 1994–2001 (dir 1992–94), NatWest Markets 1995–98, Bankers Tst International 1998–99, Deutsche Bank 1999–2001; Wood Mackenzie Ltd: chief exec 2001–07, dep chm 2007–09, chm 2009–15; chm Lingo24 Ltd 2015–; *Books* Factors Influencing the Export Performance of the Scottish Manufacturing Sector of the Offshore Supplies Industry (1982), World Offshore Markets: Can Britain Compete? (1986); *Recreations* golf, gardening; *Clubs* Renaissance Golf, Royal Troon Golf, Loch Lomond Golf; *Style*— Dr Paul Gregory; ✉ 25 Greenhill Gardens, Edinburgh EH10 4BL (☎ 0131 447 7935); Lingo24 Ltd, 18 Torpichen Street, Edinburgh EH3 8JB (mobile 07799 343305, e-mail paul.gregory@lingo24.com)

GREGORY, His Hon Judge Peter Joseph; s of Patrick Brian Gregory, and Sheila, *née* Kennedy, of Belfast; *b* 18 September 1958, Belfast; *Educ* St MacNissi's Coll Garron Tower, Univ of Manchester (LLB), Inns of Court Law Sch; *m* 4 Sept 1982, Jennifer, *née* Jones; 4 s (Joseph, Matthew, Adam, Liam), 1 da (Roisin); *Career* called to the Bar (Gray's Inn) 1982; recorder 2002, circuit judge (Northern Circuit) 2015–; *Recreations* music, reading, football, beer; *Style*— His Hon Judge Peter Gregory; ✉ Liverpool Civil and Family Court, 35 Vernon Street, Liverpool L2 2BX

GREGORY, His Hon Judge Philip John; s of John Godfrey Gregory, of Alvechurch, Worcs, and Winifred, *née* Groves (d 1982); *b* 13 January 1953, Birmingham; *Educ* Moseley GS Birmingham, Pembroke Coll Oxford (MA), Inns of Court Sch of Law; *m* 14 April 1979, Deborah, *née* Lane; 2 da (Hannah b 26 Dec 1982, Elizabeth b 6 Sept 1985), 1 s (Thomas b 18 Aug 1991); *Career* called to the Bar 1975; recorder 1999–2004 (asst recorder 1997–99), circuit judge 2004–; *Recreations* tennis, golf, reading; *Style*— His Hon Judge Gregory; ✉ Birmingham Crown Court, 1 Newton Street, Birmingham B4 7NA

GREGORY, Dr Philippa; da of Arthur Percy Gregory (d 1955), of Nairobi, and Elaine, *née* Wedd (d 1983); *b* 9 January 1954; *Educ* Duncan House Sch for Girls' Clifton, Colston's Girls' Sch Bristol, Univ of Sussex (BA), Univ of Edinburgh (PhD); *m* Anthony Mason; 1 da (Victoria Elaine Chislett b 31 Jan 1982), 1 s (Adam Gregory Carter b 20 Jan 1993); *Career* work on: newspaper in Portsmouth 1972–75, prodr BBC Radio 1978–82; guest reviewer Sunday Times 1989–; *Books* Wideacre (1987), The Favoured Child (1989), Princess Florizella (1989), Meridon (1990), Florizella and the Wolves (1991), The Wise Woman (1992), Mrs Hartley and the Growth Centre (1992), Florizella and the Giant (1992), Fallen Skies (1993), The Little Pet Dragon (1994), A Respectable Trade (1995), Diggory and the Boa Conductor (1996), Perfectly Correct (1996), The Little House (1997), Earthly Joys (1998), Virgin Earth (1999), Zelda's Cut (2000), The Other Boleyn Girl (2001, Parker Pen Novel of the Year 2001), The Queen's Fool (2003), The Virgin's Lover (2004), The Constant Princess (2005), The Boleyn Inheritance (2006), The Other Queen (2008), The White Queen (2009), The Red Queen (2010), The Lady of the Rivers (2011), The Women of the Cousins' War (2011), The Kingmaker's Daughters (2012), Changeling (2012), Stormbringers (2013), The White Princess (2013), Fools Gold (2014), The King's Curse (2014); screenplays: Mrs Hartley and the Growth Centre (BBC 2, 1995), A Respectable Trade (BBC 1, 1997), The Other Boleyn Girl (BBC 2, 2003 and Columbia Pictures, 2008), The Little House (ITV, 2010), The White Queen (BBC, 2013); documentaries: The Real White Queen and Her Rivals (BBC, 2013); *Style*— Dr Philippa Gregory

GREGORY, Richard John; OBE (2004); s of John Gregory, and Joan, *née* Slingsby; *b* 18 August 1954; *Educ* Danum GS Doncaster; *Career* industrial corr Morning Telegraph 1977–79, news ed Granada TV 1979–81; Yorkshire Television: news ed 1981–82, prodr 1982–84, ed Calendar 1984, head of news 1991–92, controller of regnl progs 1992–93, memb Bd 1993, dir of regnl progs 1993–95, dir of broadcasting 1995–96, md Yorkshire Television (Broadcasting) 1996–97, md Yorkshire Television 1997–2002; chair: Northern Media Sch 1996–2001, Yorkshire Initiative 1997–2000, Yorkshire Int Business Convention Ltd 1999–2003, Regional Leadership Team Yorkshire and Humber Business in the Community 2001–, Imagesound plc 2002–; dep chair Yorkshire Forward 1999–; memb: Bd Yorkshire Arts 2000–02, Cncl Inst of Employment Studies 2002–, Bd Yorkshire Cultural Consortium 2002–04; chair Yorkshire Bank 2004–; non-exec dir: Clydesdale Bank 2000–, Business in the Community Ltd 2001–, National Australia Group Europe Ltd 2004–, Sheffield Univ Enterprises Ltd 2005–; tstee dir Sheffield Galleries and Museums Tst 2002–, chair Sheffield Hallam Univ 1999–2003 (sometime govr and dep chm); *Recreations* Peak District; *Style*— Richard Gregory, Esq, OBE

GREGSON, Charles Henry; s of Geoffrey Gregson (d 2006), of Somerset, and Anne Gregson (d 2002); *b* 7 June 1947; *Educ* Harrow, Trinity Hall Cambridge (MA); *m* 26 Sept 1972, Caroline, *née* Blake; 2 s (Oliver b 14 Feb 1978, James b 22 June 1982); *Career* admitted slr 1972; with Clifford-Turner & Co Slrs 1970–74; United Business Media plc (formerly Mills & Allen International and MAI plc): joined 1974, md Shepperton Studios Ltd 1975–80, co sec 1976–77, chief exec MAI Money Brokers (later Garban plc) 1980–98, chm ICAP plc (formerly Garban plc) 1998–; non-exec dir Provident Financial plc 1995– (dep chm 2000–); dir Public Catalogue Fndn; *Recreations* gardening, deerstalking, racing; *Clubs* Turf; *Style*— Charles Gregson, Esq; ✉ PR Newswire Europe Ltd, 209–215 Blackfriars Road, London SE1 8NL (☎ 020 7454 5144, fax 020 7454 5331, e-mail charles.gregson@prnewswire.com)

GREGSON, Edward; s of Edward Gregson (d 1978), and May Elizabeth, *née* Eaves (d 1985); *b* 23 July 1945; *Educ* Manchester Central GS, Royal Acad of Music (GRSM, LRAM, Battison Haynes, Edward Hecht and Frederick Corder Memorial Prizes (all for composition), Univ of London (BMus); *m* 1967, Susan Carole; 2 s (Mark Edward b 1968, Justin Serge b 1970); *Career* lectr in music Rachel McMillan Coll 1970–76, sr lectr then reader rising to prof of music Goldsmiths Coll London 1976–96, princ RNCM 1996–2008 (emeritus prof 2008); also composer; dir: Performing Right Soc 1995–, Hallé Concerts Soc 1998–2006; govr and feoffee Chethams Sch of Music 1996–; govr Assoc Bd of RSM 1996–2008; tstee Nat Fndn for Youth Music 1999–2003; chm Conservatoires UK 2004–08; memb: Composers' Guild of GB (vice-chm 1976–78), Assoc of Professional Composers (chm 1989–91), Br Acad of Composers and Songwriters 1992–; memb Bd Cultural Consortium for englandnorthwest 2003–04; hon prof of music Univ of Manchester 1996–2008; Hon DMus Univ of Sunderland 1996, Hon DArts Manchester Met Univ 2003, Hon DMus Lancaster Univ 2006, Hon DUniv Univ of Central England 2007, Hon DMus Univ of Manchester 2008, Hon DMus Univ of Chester 2009; fell Dartington Coll of Arts 1997, fell Leeds Coll of Music 2008; FRAM 1990, Hon FLCM 1998, CRNCM 2008 (FRNCM

1999), FRCM 2000; *Compositions* incl: Oboe Sonata 1965, Brass Quintet 1967, Music for Chamber Orchestra 1968, Horn Concerto 1971, Essay (for brass band) 1971, Tuba Concerto 1976, music for York Cycle of Mystery Plays 1976 and 1980, Connotations (for brass band) 1977, Metamorphoses 1979, Trombone Concerto 1979, The Salamander and the Moonraker (children's cantata, text by Susan Gregson) 1980, Fairground Songs (text by Susan Gregson) 1982, Trumpet Concerto 1983, Piano Sonata 1983, Contrasts – a concerto for orchestra 1983 (revised 2002, re-titled Concerto for Orchestra), Dances and Arias (for brass band) 1984, Festivo 1985, Missa Brevis Pacem 1988, Celebration 1991, The Sword and the Crown (based on music from RSC history play prodns 1988 and 1990) 1991, Of Men and Mountains (for brass band) 1991, Blazon 1992, Clarinet Concerto 1994, Concerto for Piano and Wind 1995, The Kings Go Forth 1996, Stepping Out (for string orchestra) 1996, A Welcome Ode 1997, Three Matisse Impressions (for recorder, string orchestra, harp and percussion) 1997, And the Seven Trumpets 1998, The Dance, forever the Dance (for mezzo-soprano, choir and orchestra) 1999, Violin Concerto 2000, The Trumpets of the Angels (for brass band and organ) 2000, Occasional Fanfares (for orchestra) 2002, Romance for Treble Recorder and String Quartet 2004 (also in piano version), An Age of Kings (for brass band, male chorus, mezzo-soprano solo, harp and piano) 2004, Shadow of Paradise (oboe and percussion) 2005, Saxophone Concerto 2006, A Song for Chris (concerto for cello and chamber orchestra) 2007, Rococo Variations (brass band) 2008, Remember (soprano and ensemble) 2008, Goddess (string orchestra) 2009, Tributes (clarinet and piano) 2010, Aztec Dances (flute of recorder and piano) 2010, Dream Song (orchestra) 2010, An Album for my Friends (piano) 2011, Triptych (solo violin) 2011, Symphony in two movements (brass band) 2012, Of Distant Memories (Music in an Olden Style) (brass band) 2013, Aztec Dances (concerto for flute and ensemble) 2013, Trombone Concerto (brass band version) 2013, Three John Donne Settings (choir SATB) 2013, Peace Perfect Peace (choir SATB) 2013, Horn Concerto (orchestral version) 2013, Remember (solo, children's choir, orchestra) 2014, String Quartet 2014, Cornet Concerto 2016, The Trumpets of Angels (new performing edn 2016); *Recordings* incl: commercial recordings on the Chandos, Olympia, Doyen, Sony and Polyphonic labels, plus broadcasts on BBC TV, BBC Radio 2 and 3, Classic FM and many other int radio stations; *Publications* Composers on Composing (in band Vol 3, ed Mark Camphouse, 2007), My New Music – Dream Song for Orchestra (in Musical Opinion, 2010), Arnold the Symphonist (in Composers on the Nine, ed Paul Harris 2011), Gregson: The Manchester Years (1996–2013) (Hindmarsh, Paul in Manchester Sounds Vol 9, 2013); *Recreations* food, wine, watching sport, walking the dogs; *Style*— Prof Edward Gregson; ✉ e-mail edward.gregson@btinternet.com, websites www.edwardgregson.com, www.musicsalesclassical.com

GREGSON, Prof Sir Peter John; kt (2011), DL (2007–13); s of Howard Davenport Gregson, and Susan Katharine, *née* Lunn; *b* 3 November 1957, Scotland; *Educ* Imperial Coll London (BSc, Bessemer Medal, PhD, Matthey Prize); *m* 13 Aug 1983, Rachael Kathleen, *née* McClaughry; 3 da (Eleanor Margaret b 18 Aug 1991, Maria Katharine b 26 July 1994, Christina Rosalind b 26 Jan 1999); *Career* Univ of Southampton 1983–2004, pres and vice-chllr Queen's Univ Belfast 2004–13, chief exec and vice-chllr Cranfield Univ 2013–; non-exec dir Rolls-Royce Gp plc 2007–12; strategic advsr Lockheed Martin UK 2016–; memb: User Panel EPSRC 2004–07, Cncl CCLRC 2004–07, Cncl Assoc of Cwlth Univs 2011–14; chair MK 2050 Futures Cmmn 2015–16; author of numerous scientific papers in learned jls on the engineering performance of aerospace materials and computational and experimental modelling of load bearing medical devices; Donald Julius Groen Prize of IMechE 1993, Rosenhain Medal and Prize Inst of Materials 1996, Flax Tst Prize 2010; Hon DSc: Bengal Engrg and Sci Univ 2008, NUI 2008, Univ of Southampton 2009, Soka Univ Japan 2011, Queen's Univ Belfast 2014; CEng 1986, FIMMM 1998, FREng 2001, FIEI 2004, FCGI 2006, FIAI 2007, MRIA 2007; *Recreations* music (chair St Albans Int Organ Festival), gardening, tennis, sailing; *Clubs* Athenaeum; *Style*— Prof Sir Peter Gregson; ✉ Vice-Chancellor's Office, Cranfield University, Cranfield, Bedfordshire MK43 0AL (☎ 01234 754014, e-mail vc@cranfield.ac.uk)

GREGSON, Simon (né Simon Gregory); *b* 2 October 1974, Manchester; *Career* actor; Steve McDonald in Coronation Street (ITV) 1989–; Best Couple Inside Soap Award 2003 (jtly), Best Storyline Br Soap Award 2004 (jtly), Best Actor in a Br Soap Manchester Evening News TV and Theatre Award 2004, Most Popular Character in Br Soap UK.gov.com online poll 2009, Most Favourite Character in Soap virginmedia.com 2009, Best Soap Actor TV Choice & TV Quick Awards 2009; *Recreations* boating, shooting; *Style*— Mr Simon Gregson; ✉ c/o Langford Associates, 17 Westfields Avenue, Barnes, London SW13 0AT

GREIG, Geordie Carron; s of Sir Carron Greig, and Monica, *née* Stourton; *b* 16 December 1960; *Educ* Eton, St Peter's Coll Oxford (MA); *m* 1995, Kathryn Elizabeth, *née* Terry; 1 s (Jasper b 30 April 1998), 2 da (Monica, Octavia (twins) b 11 June 2000); *Career* reporter: South East London and Kentish Mercury 1981–83, Daily Mail 1984–85, Today 1985–87; The Sunday Times: reporter 1987–89, arts corr 1989–91, New York corr 1991–95, literary ed 1995–99; ed Tatler 1999–2009, ed London Evening Standard 2009–10, editorial dir The Independent and London Evening Standard 2010–12, ed The Mail on Sunday 2012–; dir London Evening Standard and Independent Print Ltd 2009–; tstee Raisa Gorbachev Fndn 2005–12, tstee Friends of the Nat Libraries 2013–; FRSA 2006; *Books* Louis and the Prince (1999, reprinted as The King Maker 2012), Breakfast with Lucian (2013); *Style*— Geordie Greig, Esq; ✉ The Mail on Sunday, Northcliffe House, 2 Derry Street, London W8 5TS

GREIG, Dr Kenneth Muir; s of Walter Davidson Greig, of Edinburgh, and Margaret, *née* Muir (d 1997); *b* 30 March 1960; *Educ* George Heriot's Sch Edinburgh, Worcester Coll Oxford (MA), Univ of Edinburgh (PhD); *m* June 1987, Josephine Claire Berenice, da of Prof Anthony Taylor; 1 da (Matilda Louise b 13 June 1992), 1 s (Lachlan Walter b 5 Dec 1996); *Career* exploration geologist BP 1984–87; mathematics teacher and housemaster Christ's Hosp 1987–93, head of mathematics and dir of studies Dollar Acad 1993–2000, headmaster Pangbourne Coll 2000–05, rector Hutchesons' GS Glasgow 2005–16, headmaster Brighton Coll Al Ain UAE 2016–; *Recreations* natural science, beachcombing, smallholding, watching sport; *Clubs* East India, Western, Caledonian; *Style*— Dr Kenneth Greig; ✉ Brighton College Al Ain, PO Box 101110, Abu Dhabi, United Arab Emirates (e-mail headmaster@brightoncollegealain.ae)

GREIG, Tamsin; *b* 23 February 1967; *Educ* Camden Sch for Girls, Univ of Birmingham (BA); *m* Richard Leaf; 2 s, 1 da; *Career* actress; *Radio* The Archers (BBC Radio 4) 1991–; *Television* Black Books 2000–04, When I'm Sixty-Four 2004, Green Wing (Channel 4) 2004–06 (Best Comedy Performance RTS Award 2005), Love Soup 2005–08, The Diary of Anne Frank (BBC) 2009, Emma (BBC) 2009, Going Postal 2010, Friday Night Dinner 2011, Episodes (BBC) 2011–, White Heat 2012; *Film* Shaun of the Dead 2004, Captain Eager and the Mark of Voth 2008, Tamara Drewe 2010, Arthur Christmas 2011; *Theatre* Beatrice in Much Ado About Nothing (RSC) 2006–07 (Laurence Olivier Award, Best Shakespearean Performance Critics' Circle Theatre Award), King John (RSC) 2006–07, The God of Carnage (Gielgud Theatre) 2008, Gethsemane (RNT) 2008, The Little Dog Laughed (Garrick) 2010 (Best Supporting Actress in a Play What's On Stage Award 2011), In The Beginning (Westminster Abbey); *Style*— Ms Tamsin Greig; ✉ c/o Sally Hope Associates, 108 Leonard Street, London EC2A 4XS

GRENIER, David Arthur; s of Rev George A Grenier (d 1973), and Dorothy Anita, *née* Burn (d 1990); *b* 12 August 1931; *Educ* St John's Sch Leatherhead, Jesus Coll Cambridge (MA), Sorbonne; *m* 25 Aug 1959, Janet Elizabeth, da of Ralph Thompson (d 1989); 3 s (Lewis b 1962, Julian b 1968, Michael b 1969); *Career* Capel-Cure Myers Ltd: dep chm 1975–77, chm 1977–79; ptnr Scott Goff Hancock & Co 1980–82, sr ptnr Scott Goff Layton & Co 1982–86, dir Smith New Court plc 1986–88, chief exec Independent Investment Mgmnt Ltd 1989–98 (chm 1998–2001), conslt 2001–02; chm of tstees Cancer Research UK pension scheme 2003–06; Freeman City of London, Liveryman Worshipful Co of Painter Stainers; ASIP 1968, FRSA 1992; *Recreations* opera, golf; *Clubs* Oxford and Cambridge, Coningsby, W Berks Golf; *Style—* David Grenier, Esq; ✉ The Mill House, Great Shefford, Hungerford, Berkshire RG17 7DR

GRESTY, Deborah Susan; da of Alexander William Gresty, and Barbara Joan Nash, *née* Perry; *b* 3 April 1953; *Educ* Birkenhead HS, Merchant Taylors' Sch, Univ of Nottingham (BA), Oxford Centre of Mgmnt Studies; *m* Peter Warland, s of Charles Warland; *Career* magazine publisher; Thomson Publications: grad trainee 1974, advertisement sales exec Pins & Needles 1975, dep advertisement mangr Living 1977 (advertisement sales exec 1976); Slimming Magazine: advertisement mangr 1979, advertisement dir 1980, dir 1981, publisher 1982–84; publisher/dir Working Woman 1984–85; publisher: Brides and Setting Up Home 1985–90, House & Garden 1990–96, Condé Nast Traveller 1997–; bd dir Condé Nast 1993–; *Recreations* tennis, cricket, classical music, opera, theatre; *Style—* Ms Deborah Gresty; ✉ Condé Nast, Vogue House, Hanover Square, London W1R 0AD (☎ 020 7499 9080)

GRESTY, Hilary Marion Bell; da of late Allan Bell Gresty, and Joy Margaret, *née* Coltham; *b* 24 February 1954; *Educ* Oxford Girls' HS, Univ of Exeter (BA), UCL (MA), Courtauld Inst London (MPhil); *Partner* Edward Macready Dickinson; 3 s (Edmund Gresty Dickinson b 12 June 1992, Arthur Gresty Dickinson b 16 Feb 1994, Roland Gresty Dickinson b 1 Feb 1997); *Career* research asst Royal Library Windsor 1977, library res asst Tate Gallery London 1978–81, curator Kettle's Yard Univ of Cambridge 1983–89, freelance writer, lectr, curator and visual arts conslt 1989–; dir VAGA (Visual Arts & Galleries Assoc) 1991–2012; princ lectr (p/t) Sch of Fine and Performing Arts Univ of Lincoln 2013–; *Exhibitions* incl: 1965–1972 – when attitudes became form (1984), Pounds Artists (1985), C R W Nevinson (1988); progs incl work with Susan Hiller, Nan Hoover, Ron Haselden, Mary Kelly, Richard Layzell and Charlie Hooker; *Catalogues* incl: Christopher Wood – his early years (Newlyn Art Gallery, 1989), Ron Haselden (Serpentine Gallery, 1990), Alison Wilding (Newlyn Art Gallery, 1993), Other Criteria: Sculpture in 20th Century Britain (contrib, Henry Moore Inst Leeds, 2003); *Books* British Sculpture 1960–90 (contrib), Postmodern Art: theory into practice (contrib 1996), Sculpture in 20th Century Britain (contrib, Henry Moore Inst Leeds, 2003), Keith Arnatt (Maureen Paley Gallery, 2012); *Clubs* RSA; *Style—* Ms Hilary Gresty, FRSA; ✉ The Old Village School, Witcham, Ely, Cambridgeshire CB6 2LQ (☎ 01353 776296, e-mail hilary.gresty@gmail.com)

GRETTON, Lady; Jennifer Ann Gretton; JP; *née* Moore; *b* 14 June 1943, St Ives, Cornwall; *m* 3 Baron Gretton (d 1989); 1 s, 1 da; *Career* mangr Stapleford Estate 1989–; HM Lord-Lt Leics 2003– (DL Leics 2001); pres: Melton Mowbray and Dist Model Engrg Soc 1989–, Rural Community Cncl Leics and Rutland 1994, Leics Orgn for the Relief of Suffering (LOROS) 1999, Cncl St John Ambulance 2003–, E Midlands Reserve Forces and Cadets Assoc (EMRFCA) 2003–, Army Benevolent Fund Leics and Rutland Ctee 2003–, Leics Historic Buildings Tst 2006–, Leics and Rutland branch SSAFA 2008–; vice-pres: Cncl Leics Scouts 2003–, EMRFCA Co Ctee 2003–, Leics and Rutland Branch Magistrates Assoc 2004–; memb: Ctee Leics and Rutland CLA 1989–2007, Student Affrs Ctee and Advsy Cncl Harlaxton Manor (Br campus of Univ of Evansville) 1989–2006, Environment and Water Ctee CLA 1994–98; patron: Royal Leics Regt Museum Appeal 2003–08, Change Ashby Now (CAN) 2003–, Leics and Rutland Wildlife Tsts 2004–, Leicester City Male Voice Choir 2005–, Leics Early Music Assoc 2006–; ambassador Nat Forest 2005–; church warden All Saints Somerby 1992–95, memb Ctee Somerby PCC 1991–, memb Cncl Leicester Cathedral 2003–09; patron of five parishes; restored Stapleford Miniature Railway 1995, instigated Stapleford Steam Rally 1996; memb Oakham Sch Choral Soc; LLD (Hon) Univ of Leicester, DUniv (Hon) Loughborough, Hon DLitt De Montfort Univ; *Recreations* sport, music, steam; *Style—* Jennifer, Lady Gretton, JP; ✉ Holygate Farm, Holygate Road, Stapleford, Melton Mowbray, Leicestershire LE14 2SG (☎ 01572 787540, fax 01572 787516)

GREVILLE, Michael; *b* 1962; *Educ* Eton, Univ of Bristol (LLB); *Career* called to the Bar 1985, admitted slr 1990; Watson, Farley & Williams: head Litigation Gp 1996–2001, managing ptnr 2001–14; *Clubs* Royal Ocean Racing (hon treas 1999–2010, Vice-Cdre 2010, Cdre 2011–14), Royal Yacht Squadron; *Style—* Michael Greville, Esq; ✉ Watson, Farley & Williams, 15 Appold Street, London EC2A 2HB

GREY, Sir Anthony Dysart; 7 Bt (UK 1814), of Fallodon, Northumberland; s of Capt Edward Elton Grey (d 1962), and Nancy, *née* Meagher; suc gf, Sir Robin Edward Dysart Grey, 6 Bt (d 1974); *b* 19 October 1949; *Educ* Guildford GS Perth (Aust); *m* 1, 1970 (m dis), Donna, da of Donald Daniels, of London; m 2, 1993, Alison Turner; 3 da (Matilda Jessie b 4 Jan 1994, Lucinda Jane b 25 Jan 1996, Sophie Diana b 7 Jan 2002), 1 s (Thomas Jasper b 30 April 1998); *Heir* s, Thomas Grey; *Recreations* fishing, painting; *Style—* Sir Anthony Grey, Bt; ✉ c/o 38 King's Park Road, Perth, Western Australia 6005, Australia

GREY, Prof Christopher John; s of Alan Grey (d 2005), and Madeleine, *née* Beck; *b* 5 December 1964, Sanderstead, Surrey; *Educ* Trinity Sch Croydon, Univ of Manchester (BA, PhD); *m* 11 April 1992, Nathalie, *née* Mitev; *Career* ESRC fell UMIST 1990–93, lectr then sr lectr Univ of Leeds 1993–98; Judge Business Sch Univ of Cambridge: lectr, sr lectr then reader 1999–2005, prof of organizational theory 2005–07, sr res assoc 2007–12; fell Wolfson Coll Cambridge 2002–11; Univ of Warwick: prof of organizational behaviour 2007–12, head of industrial relations and organizational behaviour 2008–10; prof of organizational studies Royal Holloway Univ of London 2012– (dir of research 2013–), affiliated prof Univ Paris-Dauphine 2013–; visiting fell Stockholm Univ 1995–2002, visiting prof Copenhagen Business Sch 2011; Leverhulme Major Research Fell 2010–12; ed-in-chief Management Learning 1999–2005, assoc ed Organization 2011–; chair Mgmnt Research Advsy Forum Nat Coll for Sch Leadership 2002–07, memb Nat Educnl Research Forum 1999–2003; FAcSS 2015–; *Books* Secrecy at Work (2016), Critical Management Studies (2016); *Publications* Rethinking Management Education (1996), Making Up Accountants (1998), Essential Readings in Management Learning (2004), Studying Organizations (2005, 2008 and 2012), The Oxford Reader in Critical Management Studies (2005), Decoding Organization (2012),; *Recreations* cricket, cookery, collecting vintage ashtrays; *Style—* Prof Christopher Grey; ✉ School of Management, Royal Holloway, University of London, Egham, Surrey TW20 0EX (☎ 01784 276213, fax 01784 276100, e-mail chris.grey@rhul.ac.uk)

GREY-THOMPSON, Baroness (Life Peer UK 2010), of Eaglescliffe in the County of Durham; Dame Carys Davina (Tanni) Grey-Thompson; DBE (2005, OBE 2000, MBE 1993); *b* 26 July 1969, Cardiff; *Educ* Loughborough Univ (BA); *m* Dr Ian Thompson; 1 da (Carys); *Career* wheelchair athlete; achievements incl: Bronze medal 400m Paralympics Seoul 1988, 2 Silver medals (100m and 200m) and Bronze medal 400m World Championships Assen 1990, 4 Gold medals (100m, 200m, 400m and 800m) and Silver medal 4 x 100m Paralympics Barcelona 1992, winner London Marathon 1992, 1994, 1996, 1998, 2000 and 2001, 4 Gold medals (100m, 200m, 400m and 800m), Silver medal 5000m and Bronze medal 10000m World Championships Berlin 1994, Gold medal 800m and 3 Silver medals (100m, 200m and 400m) Paralympics Atlanta 1996, 2 Gold medals (200m and 400m) and Silver medal 800m World Championships Birmingham 1998, 4 Gold medals (100m, 200m, 400m and 800m) Paralympics Sydney 2000, 2 Gold medals (100m and 400m) Paralympics Athens 2004, 2 Gold medals (100m and 400m) Paralympic World Cup 2005, Gold medal 200m, Silver medal 400m and Bronze medal 800m World Championships Assen 2006, Silver medal 200m Paralympic World Cup 2007; BBC Wales Sports Personality of the Year 1992, 2000 and 2004, BBC Sports Personality of the Year Helen Rollason Award 2000; ret 2007; non-exec dir UK Athletics 2007–12, memb Bd London Marathon 2007–, memb Bd TfL 2008–, memb Bd London Legacy Devpt Corp; sits in House of Lords as crossbench peer 2010–; patron Paralympics GB, vice-pres Royal Br Legion Women's Section; tstee: Laureus Sport for Good Fndn, Jane Tomlinson Tst, Tony Blair Fndn, Duke of Edinburgh Award, Wembley Nat Stadium Tst; pro-chllr Staffs Univ until 2013; hon doctorates: Univ of Glasgow, Loughborough Univ, Staffs Univ, Mancester Met Univ, Southampton Univ, Univ of Surrey, York and Ripon Coll, Teesside Univ, Leeds Met Univ, Univ of Wales, Open Univ, Herriot Watt Univ, Univ of Exeter, Univ of Hull, Sheffield Hallam Univ, Leicester Univ, Oxford Brookes Univ, Newcastle Univ, Univ of Glamorgan 2001, Univ of Wales Newport 2003, Univ of Bath 2013, Univ of E London 2013; Hon DLitt Univ of Oxford 2013; fell Univ of Swansea 2001; hon fell: Univ of Cardiff 1997, Liverpool John Moores 2005, Univ of Wales Inst Cardiff 2001; *Style—* The Baroness Grey-Thompson, DBE

GRIBBIN, Dr John Richard; *b* 19 March 1946, Maidstone, Kent; *Educ* Maidstone GS, Univ of Sussex (BSc, MSc), Univ of Cambridge (PhD); *m* 1966, Mary, *née* Murray; 2 s (Jonathan b 1972, Benjamin b 1976); *Career* Nature magazine 1970–75, visiting fell Social Policy Research Unit 1975–78, physics conslt New Scientist 1978–98, visiting fell in astronomy Univ of Sussex 1998–; FRAS, FRMetS, FRSL, FRSA; *Non-Fiction* incl: Genesis: The origins of man and the universe (1981), In Search of Schrodinger's Cat (1984), In Search of the Double Helix (1985), In search of the Big Bang (1986), The Omega Point: The search for the missing mass, and the ultimate fate of the universe (1987), The One Per Cent Advantage (with Mary Gribbin, 1988), The Hole in the Sky (1988), Cosmic Coincidences: Dark matter, mankind and anthropic cosmology (with Martin Rees, 1989), Hothouse Earth: The Greenhouse Effect and Gaia (1990), Children of the Ice (with Mary Gribbin, 1990), Blinded by the Light: The secret life of the sun (1991), The Matter Myth (with Paul Davies, 1991), Stephen Hawking: A life in science (with Michael White, 1992), In Search of the Edge of Time: Black holes, wormholes and time machines (1992), In the Beginning: The birth of the living universe (1993), Albert Einstein: A Life in Science (with Michael White, 1993), Being Human (with Mary Gribbin, 1993), Schrodinger's Kittens and the Search for Reality (1995), Darwin: A life in science (with Michael White, 1995), Richard Feynman: A Life in Science (1997), Origins (1997), Q is for Quantum: An Encyclopedia of Particle Physics (1998), Almost Everyone's Guide to Science: The Universe, Life and Everything (1998), The Birth of Time: How Astronomers Measured the Age of the Universe (1999), What's the Big Idea? Chaos and Uncertainty (with Mary Gribbin, 1999), Deep Space (1999), The Search for Superstrings, Symmetry, and the Theory of Everything (1999), Stardust (with Mary Gribbin, 2000), Ice Age (with Mary Gribbin, 2001), The First Chimpanzee (2001), Space: Our Final Frontier (2001), Science: A History (2002), The Science of Philip Pullman's His Dark Materials (with Mary Gribbin, 2003), The Men who Measured the Universe (with Mary Gribbin, 2004), Deep Simplicity (2004), Big Numbers (with Mary Gribbin, 2004), The Fellowship: the story of a revolution (2005), The Universe: A Biography (2007), Flower Hunters (with Mary Gribbin, 2008), He Knew He was Right (with Mary Gribbin, 2009), In Search of the Multiverse (2010), From Here to Infinity (with Mary Gribbin, 2011), Planet Earth (with Mary Gribbin, 2011), Not Fade Away (2012), Erwin Schrodinger (2012), Computing with Quantum Cats (2013); *Fiction* Double Planet (with Marcus Chown, 1988), Father to the Man (1989), Reunion (with Marcus Chown, 1991), Ragnarok (with David Compton, 1991), Innervisions (1993), Timeswitch (2009), The Alice Encounter (2011); *Recreations* watching cricket, cooking, chess; *Clubs* Kent CCC; *Style—* Dr John Gribbin

GRICE, Sir Paul Edward; kt (2016); s of Kenneth William Grice, and Maureen, *née* Power; *b* 13 October 1961; *Educ* Archbishop Holgate's Sch York, York Coll of Arts and Technol, Univ of Stirling (BSc); *m* 1987, Elaine Rosie; 2 da; *Career* civil servant; Dept of Transport 1985–87, DOE 1987–92; Scottish Office: head Housing and Regeneration Branch 1992–95, head Mgmnt and Change Unit 1995–97, head of div Constitution Gp Referendum Scotland Bill 1997–98, dir of implemenation 1998–99; clerk and chief exec Scottish Parliament 1999–; memb ESRC 2009–15; memb Ct Univ of Stirling 2005–13; tstee Bank of Scotland Fndn 2011–, memb Bd Edinburgh Int Festival 2013–; Hon FRIAS 2006; *Style—* Sir Paul Grice; ✉ The Scottish Parliament, Edinburgh EH99 1SP

GRIEF, Alison; QC (2015); da of Ken Grief, and Sheila Grief; *b* Margate; *Educ* King Ethelbert Sch Birchington Kent, Middlesex Poly (LLB); *m* 30 Aug 2002, Martin King; 2 s (Billy Grief-King, Toby Grief-King); *Career* called to the Bar Inner Temple 1990 (Yarborough-Anderson scholar), recorder 2012; asst coroner: Mid Kent and Medway 2008–, Herts 2012–; memb: Bar Pro Bono Unit, Family Law Bar Assoc, Assoc of Lawyers for Children, Lawyers for Liberty, Family Mediation Assoc; *Recreations* gardening, reading, walking; *Style—* Ms Alison Grief, QC; ✉ 1st Floor, 4 Paper Buildings, Temple, London EC4Y 7EX

GRIEVE, Alan Thomas; CBE (2003); s of Lewis Miller Grieve (d 1963), of Stanmore, Middx, and Doris Lilian, *née* Amner (d 1975); *b* 22 January 1928; *Educ* Aldenham, Trinity Hall Cambridge (MA, LLM); *m* 1, 1957 (m dis 1971), Anne, da of Dr Lawrence Dulake, of Reigate, Surrey; 1 da (Amanda (Baroness Harlech) b 1958), 2 s (Charles b 1960, Ivan b 1962); m 2, 1971, Karen Louise, da of Michael de Sivrac Dunn (d 2000), of Honiton, Devon; 1 s (Thomas de Sivrac b 1973), 1 da (Lara b 1974); *Career* Nat Serv 2 Lt 14/20 King's Hussars, Capt City of London Yeo TA; admitted slr 1953; sr ptnr Taylor Garrett; conslt Taylor Wessing; dir: Baggeridge Brick plc 1964–2003, Stenham plc 1971–94, Medical Insurance Agency Ltd 1976–92, Reliance Resources Ltd 1978–97, Wilson Bowden plc 1993–96, Vaudeville Theatre Ltd 1998–2001, Savoy Theatre Mgmnt Ltd 1998–2004, Hereford Mappa Mundi Tstee Co Ltd 1998–2011, Jerwood Space Ltd 1998–, Theatre Enterprises Ltd 2001–04, Jerwood Gallery Ltd 2008–, and other cos; chm Jerwood Fndn 1977–; patron Brendoncare for the Elderly; tstee: Oakham Sch 1973–93, Br Racing Sch 1986–94, RCP 2007–10 (memb Fin and Gen Purposes Bd 1986–92); memb Educnl Assets Bd 1988–90, hon memb Cncl Royal Court Theatre; hon Vice Cdre Sea Cadets Assoc; ambass The Samaritans 1999–; memb Law Soc; Hon FRCP 2002, Hon FTCL 2002; *Books* Purchase Tax (1958); *Recreations* performing and visual arts, country life, collecting; *Clubs* Boodle's, Hawks' (Cambridge); *Style—* Alan Grieve, Esq, CBE; ✉ Stoke Lodge, Clee Downton, Ludlow, Shropshire SY8 3EG (☎ 01584 823413, fax 01584 823419); Jerwood, 7 St Stephen's Mews, London W2 5QZ (☎ 020 7792 1410, fax 020 7792 1539, e-mail alan.grieve@jerwood.org, website www.jerwood.org)

GRIEVE, Rt Hon Dominic Charles Roberts; PC (2010), QC (2008), MP; s of Percy Grieve, QC (d 1998), and Evelyn, *née* Mijouain (d 1991); *b* 24 May 1956; *Educ* Westminster, Magdalen Coll Oxford (MA), Central London Poly (Dip Law); *m* 6 Oct 1990, Caroline, da of Geoffrey Hutton; 2 s (James b 17 April 1994, Hugo b 29 Aug 1995); *Career* called to the Bar Middle Temple 1980 (bencher 2004); Parly candidate (Cons) Norwood 1987; MP (Cons) Beaconsfield 1997–; oppn frontbench spokesman for Scot 1999–2001, shadow min Home Office 2001–03, shadow attorney gen 2003–09, shadow home sec 2008–09, shadow sec of state for justice and shadow Lord Chllr 2009–10, Attorney-Gen for England and Wales and Advocate Gen for NI 2010–14; memb Select Ctee: Statutory Instruments 1997–2001, Environmental Audit 1997–2001; memb Ctee of Standards and Privileges 2015–, chm Intelligence and Security Ctee of Parl 2015–; cncllr London Borough of Hammersmith and Fulham 1982–86, vice-chm Fulham Cons Assoc 1988–91; hon recorder Royal Borough of Kingston upon Thames 2012; memb John Muir Tst, pres Franco-British Soc, vice-chm Franco-British Cncl 2010–, Luxembourg Soc; lay visitor to police stations 1990–96; govr Ditchley Fndn 2010–16 (tstee 2016–); *Recreations* scuba diving, skiing, fell walking, travel, architecture; *Clubs* Garrick; *Style—* The Rt Hon Dominic Grieve, QC, MP; ✉ House of Commons, London SW1A 0AA (✆ 020 7219 6220)

GRIEVE, His Hon Judge Michael Robertson Crichton; QC (1998); *Career* called to the Bar 1975; asst recorder 1998, recorder 2000, circuit judge (South Eastern Circuit) 2011–; *Style—* His Hon Judge Grieve, QC; ✉ Southwark Crown Court, 1 English Grounds, London SE1 2HU

GRIFFIN, Prof Brian James; s of James Henry Griffin (d 1985), and Edith Moore (d 2008); *b* 13 April 1948; *Educ* Halesowen Tech Sch, Dudley Tech Coll, Manchester Poly Sch of Photography (ONC, Dip Photography, Dip Assoc of Manchester); *m* 1, July 1980 (m dis 2001), Frances Mary, da of Morris Newman; 1 da (Layla Sky b Jan 1982), 1 s (Danz James Sky b Aug 1983); m 2, March 2003, Brynja Sverrisdottrr, da of Sverirr Thorolfson; *Career* trainee draughtsman 1964–66, trainee estimator 1966–69, photography student 1969–72, photographer 1972–90, film dir 1990–; writer and dir of short film: Claustrofoamia 1994, The Curl 1996, Xmas Steps 1998; Premi Al Llibre Fotografic award for Work (Primavera Fotografica '90 Barcelona); hon doctorate Birmingham City Univ 2014; Hon FRPS 2006; Freeman City of Arles (France); *Books* Brian Griffin Copyright (1978), Power (1980), Open (1985), Portraits (1987), Work (1988), Brian Griffin Influences (2005), The Water People (2006), Baugur: The Movie (2006), team (2007), The Black Kingdom (2013), Business As Usual (2013), Heaven Street (2015); *Recreations* speedway racing; *Style—* Prof Brian Griffin; ✉ Flat 11, Canada Wharf, 255 Rotherhithe Street, London SE16 5ES (✆ 07836 687166, website www.briangriffin.co.uk)

GRIFFIN, Christopher John (Chris); s of Peter J C Griffin; *b* 22 July 1957; *Educ* Woodhouse Grove Sch, Bradford Coll of Art and Design, Sheffield City Poly (BA); *m* 1988, Emma Victoria; 2 da (Evangeline Olivia b 1994, Sophie Georgina b 1996); *Career* Metal Box plc 1979–85, MBO of design div Metal Box plc to form Packaging Innovation Ltd (now Pi3, PIglobal) 1984, md PI Design International 1995, ceo Museum of Brand Packaging and Advtg 2003; Innovator of the Year Award Inst of Packaging 1992; hon doctorate Univ of Beds; dir Mktg Soc (memb 1985); FIP (memb 1980); *Publications* author of various conf proceedings covering design, research and IT; *Style—* Chris Griffin, Esq; ✉ PI, 1 Colville Mews, Lonsdale Road, London W11 2AR (✆ 020 7908 0800, fax 020 7908 0950)

GRIFFIN, Prof George Edward; s of Herbert Griffin (d 1973), of Hull, and Enid Mary, *née* Borrill; *b* 27 February 1947; *Educ* Malet Lambert Sch Hull, KCL (BSc), St George's Hosp Med Sch (MB BS), Univ of Hull (PhD); *m* 15 April 1972, Daphne Joan (d 1998), da of Lionel Haylor, of Romford; 2 s (James Edward b 1978, Andrew John b 1980), 1 da (Joanna Mary b 1983); *Career* Harkness fell Harvard Univ Med Sch 1975–76; St George's Hosp Med Sch (now St George's Univ of London): house physician 1974 and reg medicine Royal Postgrad Medical Sch 1975–79, lectr 1979–83, dept head of communicable diseases 1990–2012, chm of med 1994–2003; Wellcome Tst: sr lectr 1983–89, reader in med 1989–92, conslt physician 1983–, prof of infectious diseases and med 1992–; sec MRS 1988–95; memb: Public Health Lab Serv Bd 1995–2001, MRC (UK) Physiological Med and Infection Bd 1995–2000, Wellcome Tst Int Interest Panel 2002–05, Fellowship Ctee Wellcome Tst-India Alliance, Bd Public Health England 2013–, Scientific Advsy Bd Sanofi 2013–; expert advsr House of Lords Ctee Fighting Infection 2002–03, Cncl Acad Medical Sciences 2004–06; chair Advsy Ctee on Dangerous Pathogens Dept of Health/HSE/DEFRA 2005–15, chair Scientific Advsy Bd Xellia Pharmaceuticals 2014–; various pubns on pathogenesis of infection, immunological and metabolic responses to infection and vaccines; FRCP, FRCPI, FMedSci (foreign sec 2013–); *Recreations* mountain walking, gardening, cricket, travel; *Clubs* RAC, MCC; *Style—* Prof George Griffin; ✉ Institute of Infection and Immunity, St George's, University of London, Tooting, London SW17 0RE (✆ 020 8725 0905, e-mail ggriffin@sgul.ac.uk)

GRIFFIN, Kevin Anthony; s of Patrick Anthony Griffin, of Harrow, Middx, and Patricia Barbera, *née* Squirrell; *b* 13 October 1964; *Educ* Watford Coll; *m* 2 Dec 1994, Sharon Theresa, da of Robert Gumley; 3 s (Oliver Robert b 29 March 1991, Patrick Dennis Richard b 14 Sept 1992, Thomas b 14 Sept 1994); *Career* photographer; asst to Jerry Oke, Paul Wakefield and Don McCullin 1986–89, freelance 1989–; memb Assoc of Photographers 1995; *Exhibitions* various American galleries, Hamiltons Gallery 1993; *Awards* D&AD (for best use of colour photography in advtg) 1989, Assoc of Photographers (for best colour cmmnd series) 1995; *Recreations* football, reading, cooking; *Style—* Kevin Griffin, Esq; ✉ website www.kevingriffinphoto.com

GRIFFIN, Paul; s of Reginald Stuart Griffin, and Sylvia Mary, *née* Toyn; *b* 29 December 1955; *Educ* Humberston Fndn GS, Magdalen Coll Oxford (MA, BCL); *m* 16 April 1983, Janet Mary, da of Cecil Sidney Turner; 1 da (Leonie Sabrina b 20 May 1991), 1 s (Alexander Jake b 25 Sept 1994); *Career* called to the Bar Gray's Inn 1979, practising barr; memb Bar Cncl of England and Wales 1995–98, lay memb Practice Regulation Review Ctee ICA 1995–; memb: Ctee London Common Law and Commercial Bar Assoc 1987–98, COMBAR; *Recreations* restoring our French property, collecting furniture art books and wine, gardening, travel, skiing, music; *Style—* Paul Griffin, Esq

GRIFFIN, Prof Roger Francis; s of Ernest James Griffin (d 1959), and Dorothy Maud, *née* Brenchley (d 1992); *b* 23 August 1935, Banstead, Surrey; *Educ* Caterham Sch, St John's Coll Cambridge (major open scholar, BA, PhD, ScD); *m* 30 July 1966 (m dis 2003), Rita Elizabeth Mary, *née* Gasson; 2 s (Rupert Ivor James b 11 Jan 1971, Richard Joseph b 6 July 1977); *Career* Carnegie fell Mt Wilson Observatory Calif 1960–61, jr asst observer Cambridge Observatories 1962–65, research fell St John's Coll Cambridge 1962–65, Mr & Mrs John Jaffé research fell Royal Soc 1965–70, conslt astrophysicist to St John's Coll Cambridge 1970–72, John Couch Adams astronomer 1972–92, fell St John's Coll Cambridge 1972– (memb Cncl 1976–81, sec Cncl 1977–81), asst dir of research Inst of Astronomy Univ of Cambridge 1973–92, prof of observational astronomy Univ of Cambridge 2001–02 (reader 1992–2001); guest investigator, visiting assoc and visiting observer at several observatories in Europe and the Americas; ed The Observatory Magazine 1963–85; memb: Br Astronomical Assoc 1949, Royal Astronomical Soc 1957 (memb Cncl 1968–70 and 1988–90), Int Astronomical Union 1961 (pres Radial Velocity Cmmn 1973–76), Astronomical Soc of the Pacific 1965, Astronomical Soc of India 1983; Sir Henry Strakosch Award to visit South African observatories 1958, Jackson-Gwilt Medal and Gift Royal Astronomical Soc 1980, int conf held in honour 1991; *Publications* A Photometric Atlas of the Spectrum of Arcturus (1968), A Photometric Atlas of the Spectrum of Procyon (with R E Griffin, 1979); numerous papers in professional jls incl more than 250 in one particular series; *Recreations* joinery, running (completed London Marathon eleven times, 2014 time 4 hrs 48 mins); *Clubs* Cambridge Univ Hare and Hounds; *Style—* Prof Roger Griffin; ✉ The Observatories, Madingley Road, Cambridge CB3 0HA (✆ 01223 337536, fax 01223 337523)

GRIFFITH, Nia; MP; *b* 4 December 1956; *Educ* Univ of Oxford, UCNW; *Career* joined Lab Pty 1981; teacher, sometime Educn advsr and Estyn Schools Inspector, head of languages Morriston Comp Swansea; MP (Lab) Llanelli 2005–, shadow sec of state for Wales 2015–; *Style—* Ms Nia Griffith, MP; ✉ House of Commons, London SW1A 0AA

GRIFFITH JONES, His Hon Judge Richard Haydn; s of Wyn Griffith Jones (d 2008), and Mary, *née* Alston (d 1986); *b* 29 June 1951; *Educ* Solihull Sch, Univ of Leeds; *m* 1974, Susan, *née* Hale; 1 da (Katherine b 6 Aug 1979), 3 s (David b 1 July 1982, Robert b 7 July 1986, Haydn b 16 Aug 1988); *Career* called to the Bar 1974, recorder 1994–99, circuit judge (Midland Circuit) 1999–; hon recorder of Coventry 2011, resident judge Warwick and Coventry Crown Courts; *Publications* Sins of the Fathers (1974); *Recreations* poultry keeping, watching association football; *Style—* His Hon Judge Griffith Jones; ✉ Warwickshire Justice Centre, Newbold Terrace, Leamington Spa (✆ 01926 682428)

GRIFFITH WILLIAMS, Sir John Griffith Williams; kt (2007); s of Griffith John Williams, and Alison Rundle, *née* Bennett; *b* 20 December 1944; *Educ* Kings Sch Bruton, The Queen's Coll Oxford (BA); *m* 3 April 1971, Mair, only da of Rt Hon Sir Tasker Watkins, VC, GBE, DL; 2 da (Joanna Kate b 5 June 1972, Sarah Jane b 18 May 1976); *Career* Lt Royal Welch Fus (TA) (cmmnd 1964), Welsh Volunteers (TAVR) 1967–71; called to the Bar Gray's Inn 1968 (bencher 1994); memb Wales & Chester Circuit (treas 1993–95, ldr 1996–98), recorder 1984–2000, QC 1985, dep judge of the High Court (Queen's Bench Div) 1995–2000, circuit judge 2000–01, sr circuit judge and hon recorder of Cardiff 2001–07, judge of the High Court of Justice (Queen's Bench Div) 2007–14 ret, presiding judge Wales Circuit 2010–; chllr Diocese of Llandaff 1999– (dep chllr 1996–99); asst cmmr to Parly Boundary Cmmn for Wales 1994–2000; memb Bar Cncl 1990–92; fell Woodard Corp (Western Div) 1994–2002, hon fell Univ of Cardiff 2008; Hon LLD Univ of S Wales 2013; *Recreations* golf; *Clubs* Cardiff and County, Royal Porthcawl Golf; *Style—* Sir John Griffith Williams; ✉ c/o Royal Courts of Justice, Strand, London WC2A 2LL

GRIFFITH-JONES, His Hon Judge David Eric; QC (2000); s of Sir Eric Griffith-Jones, KBE, CMG, QC (d 1979), and Lady (Mary) Patricia Griffith-Jones (d 2005); *b* 7 March 1953; *Educ* Marlborough, Univ of Bristol; *m* 1984, Virginia Ann Meredith, da of Sydney Brown and Annemie Brown; 2 s (Frederick Newton b 13 July 1985, Robert Peter b 18 Jan 1987), 1 da (Harriette Anna b 3 June 1991); *Career* called to the Bar Middle Temple 1975; recorder 1997–2007 (asst recorder 1992–97), asst boundary cmmr 2000–, circuit judge (South Eastern Circuit) 2007–; legal memb: Sport Resolutions Arbitration Panel 2000, Panel of Sports Arbitrators CIArb 2002–; p/t pres Mental Health Review Tbnl 2002–, chm ICC Drugs Appeal Tbnl 2004, 2005, 2006 and 2007, legal memb Parole Bd 2009–15; CIArb accredited mediator 2003, ACAS arbitrator 2007–; chm Appeal Ctee LTA 2004–06; FCIArb 1991; *Books* Law and the Business of Sport (1997), Sport: Law and Practice (contrib, 2008, 3rd ed 2014); *Recreations* sport, travel, woodturning, skydiving, the blues; *Clubs* Falconhurst Cricket, Sevenoaks Rugby Football, Royal Cinque Ports Golf, Royal Ashdown Forest Golf; *Style—* His Hon Judge David Griffith-Jones, QC; ✉ c/o Judicial Secretariat for London and the South East, 3rd Floor, 1 Queen Victoria Street, London EC4N 4XY

GRIFFITH-JONES, John; s of late Mervyn Griffith-Jones, and late Joan, *née* Baker; *b* 11 May 1954; *Educ* Trinity Hall Cambridge (MA); *m* 1990, Cathryn Mary Stone; 1 s, 1 da; *Career* Peat Marwick Mitchell (now KPMG): joined 1975, sr ptnr KPMG UK 2006–12; chm Financial Conduct Authy 2013–; memb Advsy Bd Judge Business Sch; dir Nat Numeracy Tst; served TA (Royal Green Jackets) 1975–90; Liveryman Worshipful Co of Skinners; *Recreations* tennis, sailing, bridge; *Style—* John Griffith-Jones, Esq; ✉ Financial Conduct Authority, 25 North Colonnade, Canary Wharf, London E14 5HS (✆ 020 7066 1000, e-mail john.griffith-jones@fsa.gov.uk)

GRIFFITHS; *see also:* Norton-Griffiths

GRIFFITHS, Alan Paul; s of Emrys Mathias Griffiths, and Jane, *née* Griffiths; *b* 21 September 1953; *Educ* St Davids Sch, Jesus Coll Oxford (MA, BCL); *Career* fell and tutor in law Exeter Coll Oxford 1977–88, called to the Bar Gray's Inn 1981, practising barr; chm: MOMA Oxford 1990–2000, Oxfordshire Community Rels Cncl 1978–80; memb: Commercial Bar Assoc (memb Ctee 1992–, memb Exec 1992–95), Admin Law Bar Assoc; vice-chm Nat Ctee Child Poverty Action Gp 1987–91; memb Oxford City Cncl 1980–88 (ldr and chm Fin Ctee); *Style—* Alan Griffiths, Esq; ✉ 1 Essex Court, Temple, London EC4Y 9AR (✆ 020 7583 2000, fax 020 7583 0118, e-mail agriffiths@oeclaw.co.uk)

GRIFFITHS, Andrew James; MP; *b* 19 October 1970, Dudley, W Midlands; *m* 28 Sept 2013, Kate Elizabeth, *née* Kniveton; *Career* former COS to: Rt Hon Theresa May, MP, Rt Hon Hugo Swire, MP, Rt Hon Eric Pickles, MP, *qqv*; MP (Cons) Burton 2010–; PPS to Brandon Lewis, MP and Rt Hon Mark Francois, MP, *qqv* Dept for Communities and Local Govt 2015–; *Style—* Andrew Griffiths, Esq, MP; ✉ House of Commons, London SW1A 0AA (✆ 020 7219 7029, e-mail andrew.griffiths.mp@parliament.uk, website www.andrewgriffithsmp.com, Twitter @agriffithsmp)

GRIFFITHS, Courtenay; QC (1980); *b* Kingston, Jamaica; *Educ* LSE (LLB); *m* Angela; 2 s (Marcus, Adam); *Career* called to the Bar Gray's Inn (bencher); practising barr specialising in criminal justice; recorder 1999–; legal asst Police Support Ctee GLC 1981–84, Revson fell City Coll City Univ NY 1984–85; previously chair: Public Affairs Ctee, Race Rels Ctee of the Bar Cncl; Hon LLD Leeds Met Univ, Hon LLD Coventry Univ; *Recreations* Liverpool FC, West Indies cricket supporter; *Clubs* MCC; *Style—* Courtenay Griffiths, Esq, QC; ✉ Garden Court Chambers, 57–60 Lincoln's Inn Fields, London WC2A 3LS (✆ 020 7993 7754, fax 020 7993 7700)

GRIFFITHS, Prof Hugh Duncan; s of Gordon Hugh Griffiths, of Weymouth, Dorset, and Morag Gordon, *née* Nicholson; *b* 22 March 1956; *Educ* Hardye's Sch Dorchester, Keble Coll Oxford (open scholar, MA), Univ of London (PhD, DSc(Eng)); *m* 25 March 1989, Morag Shearer, da of George Muirhead Kirkwood, of Isle of Arran, Scotland; 2 da (Siân Helen b 7 March 1992, Alexandra Rose b 8 June 1993); *Career* sr scientist Plessey Electronic Systems Research 1980–81 (scientist 1978–80); Dept of Electronic and Electrical Engrg UCL: assoc research asst 1982–85, lectr 1985–90, sr lectr 1990–93, prof 1993–06, head of dept 2001–06; princ Defence Coll of Mgmnt and Technol Cranfield Univ Shrivenham 2006–; chair Exec Ctee Campaign for Science and Engineering; hon ed IEE Proceedings on Radar, Sonar and Navigation 1994–; Liveryman Worshipful Co of Engrgs 2003; fell Inst of Acoustics 1994, FIEE 1995 (MIEE 1983), FREng 1997, FIEEE 1999; *Awards* Lord Brabazon Premium IERE (jtly) 1984, Young Scientist Award Int Union of Radio Sci 1990, AESS Radar Systems Panel Award IEEE 1996, Mountbatten Premium IEE (jtly) 1996, Maxwell Premium IEE (jtly) 1996; Modern Antennas (jtly, 1997, 2 edn 2005), Advances in Bistatic Radar (2007), also author of over 250 pubns in jls and conf proceedings; *Recreations* food and wine, most sports; *Style—* Prof Hugh Griffiths, FREng; ✉ 34 Rochester Square, London NW1 9RZ (✆ 020 7267 4009); Defence College of Management and Technology, Shrivenham, Cranfield University, Defence Academy of the United Kingdom, Wiltshire SN6 8LA (✆ 01793 785436, fax 01793 785546, e-mail h.griffiths@cranfield.ac.uk)

GRIFFITHS, Dr Hugh William; s of Peter Griffiths, of Downham, Essex, and Gwyneth Margaret, *née* Roberts; *b* 20 March 1957; *Educ* Brentwood Sch, Univ of Newcastle upon Tyne (MB BS); *m* 2, 30 May 1992, Caroline, da of James Evans, of Welwyn; *Career* house offr Darlington Meml Hosp 1980–81, Newcastle Rotational Trg Scheme in psychiatry 1982–85, res registrar MRC 1985–86, sr registrar Northern Regnl Rotation 1986–88, conslt psychiatrist: St George's Hosp 1988–92, Royal Victoria Infirmary Newcastle upon Tyne 1992–94; med dir Northumberland Mental Health Tst 1994–, dir of policy NHS Clinical Governance Support Team 2001–03, dep nat dir for mental health Dept of Health 2003–10, nat clinical dir for mental health Dept of Health 2010–13; hon clinical lectr Univ of Newcastle upon Tyne; FRCPsych 1999 (MRCPsych 1984); *Recreations* rugby union, skiing, motor sport, photography, flying, music; *Clubs* Newcastle Aero; *Style—* Dr Hugh Griffiths; ✉ e-mail hugh.griffiths@blueyonder.co.uk

GRIFFITHS, John; AM; s of Albert John Griffiths (d 1982), and Hannah, *née* O'Connor, of Newport; *b* 19 December 1956; *Educ* Duffryn Comp Sch, Newport FE Coll, UC Cardiff (LLB), Bristol Poly; *m* 1978, Alison Kim, da of Donald Henry Hopkins; 2 s (Lee John b 24 Nov 1976, Neil Darren b 17 Jan 1980); *Career* lectr in FE and HE 1988–89, prodn exec 1989–90, practising slr 1990–99; memb Nat Assembly for Wales (Lab Co-op) Newport East 1999–, dep min for econ devpt 2001–03, dep min for health & social servs

2003–07, dep min for educn (skills) 2007–09, counsel gen and ldr Legislative Prog 2009–, min for the environment and sustainable devpt 2011–13, min for culture and sport 2013–; *Recreations* cricket, tennis, badminton, running, reading; *Style—* John Griffiths, Esq, AM; ✉ National Assembly for Wales, Cardiff Bay, Cardiff CF99 1NA (☎ 02920 898303, fax 029 2089 8308, e-mail john.griffiths@wales.gov.uk)

GRIFFITHS, John Albert; s of late Richard Griffiths, and late Katie Joan, *née* Smithers; *b* 2 December 1943; *Educ* Tiffin Boys' Sch Kingston upon Thames; *m* Peggy-Ann Marie, *née* Waite, da of late Robert Mandel, of Alberta, Canada; 2 s (James Richard b 28 Feb 1980, Charles Robert b 25 July 1984); *Career* reporter then sub ed Surrey Herald Group 1961–64, ed Blackheath Reporter 1965–66, PR offr Mannix Heavy Construction Group Calgary 1966–67, news ed The Albertan (Calgary morning newspaper) 1967–68, night ed and motoring corr Calgary Herald 1968–70; Financial Times: foreign staff 1974–76, night foreign news ed 1977, dep foreign news ed 1978–80, specialist writer on world motor industry and motor sport 1980–2000, motoring ed 2000–; memb World Land Speed Record Team (Richard Noble, Black Rock Desert Nevada 1983, 468–633 mph) and writer subsequent film (For Britain and the Hell of it), holder World Land Speed Record for a fire engine (Black Rock Desert Nevada Nov 2 1982, 130 mph); *Recreations* motor racing (as driver); *Style—* John Griffiths, Esq; ✉ Financial Times, 1 Southwark Bridge, London SE1 9HL (☎ 020 7873 3000, e-mail john.griffiths@ft.com)

GRIFFITHS, John Egbert; s of Claude Griffiths (d 1975), and Edith May, *née* Bradley (d 2009); *b* 6 May 1939; *Educ* Tettenhall Coll Staffordshire (scholar), King's Coll Durham (BArch, scholar); *m* 12 Aug 1964 (m dis 1988); 2 da (Heidi Michelle b 1966, Sally Ann b 1969); *Career* architect and arbitrator; sr ptnr Mason Richards Partnership 1972–98; RIBA 1965, ACIArb 1976; Grand Offr: United Grand Lodge of Ancient Free and Accepted Masons of England, Supreme Grand Chapter of Royal Arch Masons of England; Dep Provincial Grand Master Masonic Province of Staffordshire 2005–09; *Books* The Evolution of a Small Town (1962); *Recreations* countryside pursuits, painting and sketching, watching rugby union football, running miniature steam trains on Welsh estate, conservation of ancient woodland and site of special scientific interest relating to bats on estate; *Clubs* Old Tettenhallians, Wolverhampton Masonic; *Style—* John Griffiths, Esq; ✉ Y Fron, Glascwm, Bwlch-y-Cibau, Llanfyllin, Montgomeryshire, Powys SY22 5LU (☎ 01938 500204)

GRIFFITHS, John Henry Morgan; MBE (2011); s of Sir Eldon Wylie Griffiths, and Sigrid, *née* Gante; *b* 3 December 1953; *Educ* Rugby, Emmanuel Coll Cambridge (MA); *m* 10 June 1994, Hilary R, elder da of John W Yeend, of Cheltenham, Glos; *Career* Lloyds Bank International 1975–79 (seconded to Bank of London & SA 1975–77, int mgmnt London 1977–79), Samuel Montagu & Co Ltd 1979–90 (syndications mangr 1981–83, dir and W Coast rep (USA) S M Inc 1983–87, exec dir 1986–90), dep gen mangr Nomura Bank International plc 1990–91, chief exec Lynton Bardwell Ltd 1993–, md CL BES Ltd 1993–; dir New Anglia Local Enterprise Partnership 2011–; chm West Suffolk Partnership 2004–; cncllr St Edmundsbury BC 1997– (ldr 2003–); *Recreations* fishing, tennis, shooting; *Clubs* Lord's Taverners; *Style—* John Griffiths, Esq, MBE; ✉ Lynton Cottage, Ixworth Thorpe, Suffolk IP31 1QR (☎ 07958 700434)

GRIFFITHS, (Susan) Lesley; AM; *b* 1960; *Career* memb Nat Assembly for Wales (Lab) Wrexham 2007–, dep min for science, innovation and skills 2009–11, min for health and social servs 2011–13, min for local govt and govt business 2013–15, min for communities and tackling poverty 2015–16, cabinet sec for rural affrs and environment 2016–; *Style—* Ms Lesley Griffiths, AM; ✉ National Assembly for Wales, Cardiff Bay, Cardiff CF99 1NA (website www.lesleygriffiths.org)

GRIFFITHS, Prof Matthew Thomas; *b* 11 May 1971, Blyth, Northumberland; *Educ* Sexeys Sch Somerset, Epsom and Kingston Coll of Nursing and Midwifery, Homerton Sch of Health Studies Homerton Coll Cambridge; *m* 22 May 1996, Donna, *née* Baker; 1 da (Hope Florence b 4 April 1996), 1 s (Oscar Thomas b 25 April 1998); *Career* registered nurse, advanced nurse practitioner and prescriber, pioneer in developing nurse prescribing worldwide; NHS 1989–98, 2000–02 and 2005–16, Cook UK 1998–2000, sr lectr Homerton Coll 2002–05, Vocare (contracted to NHS) 2016–; expert witness Apex Healthcare Assocs 2016–; professorial chair: Northampton Univ, UWE, Birmingham City Univ; nat advsr on prescribing and medicines mgmnt and conslt advsr RCN 2002–16; lectr/practitioner Festival Medical Servs 1993–, emergency practitioner British Assoc for Immediate Care (BASICS); memb Exec Cncl Resuscitation Cncl UK (first nurse ever elected) 2001–, memb Joint Formulary Ctee Br Nat Formulary 2014–16; memb Advsy Gps Shipman Inquiry and Dept of Health 2007–13; memb No 4626 Aeromedical Evacuation Sqdn Royal Auxiliary Air Force 1994–96; patron Community Heartbeat Tst; *Publications* Independent and Supplementary Prescribing An Essential Guide (with Molly Courtenay, 2005), Medications Safety – An Essential Guide (2012, highly commended Medical Book of the Year); *Clubs* Victory Services (London); *Style—* Prof Matthew Griffiths; ✉ e-mail matt@matt-griffiths.com, website www.matt-griffiths.com

GRIFFITHS, Sir Michael; kt (2014); s of David Wesley Griffiths (d 2005), and Muriel, *née* Belfield; *b* 23 September 1951, Wolverhampton; *Educ* Wolverhampton GS, Univ of York (BA), Univ of Sussex (PGCE), NPQH; *m* 27 July 1984, Kathryn Margaret, *née* Simister; 2 s (Matthew Adam b 29 April 1989, Daniel Jonathan b 26 May 1991); *Career* science teacher 1974–89, senior lecturer Sheffield City Polytechnic 1989–91, science adviser and inspector Sefton Local Authority; headmaster: Wallingford Sch Oxford 1999–2001, Northampton Sch for Boys 2001–14, ret; fndr and consIt SMG Education 2014–; pres Assoc of Sch and Coll Leaders 2012–13; FRSA 2007; *Recreations* golf, music, travel, Wolverhampton Wanderers; *Clubs* East India; *Style—* Sir Michael Griffiths; ✉ The Byre, Cattle End, Silverstone, Towcester, Northants NN12 8UX (e-mail mike.wwfc@btinternet.com); Northampton School for Boys, Billing Road, Northampton NN1 5RT

GRIFFITHS, Prof Paul David; *b* 30 January 1953; *Educ* St Bartholomew's Hosp Med Coll London (BSc, MB BS, MD, DSc (Med) 1995); *m* 1979, Brenda, *née* Attenborough; 3 s (Jonathon b 3 Aug 1984, Jamie b 24 May 1986, Ben b 25 Sept 1988); *Career* Fogarty int scholar Birmingham Alabama 1980–81, lectr Virology Dept St Bartholomew's Hosp 1980–82, prof Virology Dept Royal Free and Univ Coll Med Sch (formerly Royal Free Hosp Sch of Med) 1982– (currently head of dept); ed-in-chief Reviews in Med Virology, memb editorial bds of 8 other specialist jls, holder of numerous research grant awards, invited lectr at many int meetings, memb numerous ctees (local, nat and int); Ian Howat Prize in Med Microbiology 1975, Wheelwright's Prize for Paediatrics 1977, Lawrence Postgrad Research Scholarship 1979, Wellcome Award for Rapid Viral Diagnosis 1988, William Julius Mickle Fellowship 1991; memberships incl: Soc of Gen Microbiology 1982, Med Research Club 1988, Euro Gp for Rapid Viral Diagnosis, Br Soc for Antimicrobial Chemotherapy, Int AIDS Soc, Int Soc for Antiviral Research; FRCPath 1995, fell American Acad of Microbiology 2003; *Publications* author of over 200 original scientific papers and over 200 book chapters and invited reviews; *Recreations* family, music, bridge; *Style—* Prof Paul D Griffiths; ✉ Department of Virology, University College Medical School, Royal Free Campus, Rowland Hill Street, London NW3 2PF (☎ 020 7794 0500 ext 33210, fax 020 7830 2854)

GRIFFITHS, Peter Anthony; CBE (2013); s of Albert Griffiths (d 1981), of Swansea, and Grace, *née* Cousins (d 1962); *b* 19 May 1945; *Educ* Swansea Tech Coll; *m* 29 Oct 1966, Margaret, da of Alan Harris; 2 s (Neil b 9 Oct 1969, Kevin b 17 Aug 1971); *Career* dist administrator Medway HA 1976–81, actg area administrator Kent HA 1981–82, dist gen mangr Lewisham and N Southwark HA 1984–88 (dist administrator 1982–84), regnl gen mangr SE Thames RHA 1988–89, dep chief exec Dept of Health Richmond House London 1989–91, chief exec Guy's and Lewisham NHS Tst London 1991–93, on secondment to Dept of Health 1993, chief exec Health Quality Service (in assoc with King's Fund) 2000– (dep chief exec King's Fund 1994); chm Queen Victoria NHS Fndn Tst 2005–15 (chm Fndn Tst Network 2010–13); chm NHS Pensioners Tst; AHSM, AIMgt, memb RSA; *Recreations* golf, reading, gardening; *Style—* Peter Griffiths, CBE; ✉ Primrose Cottage, Primmers Green, Wadhurst, East Sussex TN5 6DU

GRIFFITHS, Peter Kevin; s of Denis Griffiths, of Cardiff, and Elsie Joyce, *née* Linck; *b* 15 October 1956; *Educ* Llanishen HS Cardiff, UC Cardiff (BA); *Career* studio mangr BBC 1978; prodr Radio 4: Womans Hour 1981–82, Features Dept 1982–83, presentation 1983–85, Network Features Dept Manchester 1985; sr prodr sport and ceremonial outside broadcasts Radio 2 and Radio 4 1985–90, sr prodr Features and Arts for Radio 4 and Radio 5 1990–97, prodn conslt to South African campaign using radio to offer opportunities for adult educn Johannesburg 1994–96, exec prodr BBC Features & Events Radio 1997–2010 (led BBC Radio's coverage of the funeral of Diana, Princess of Wales (winner Sony Gold Award) and coverage of the funeral of HM Queen Elizabeth The Queen Mother), ed live events BBC Radio and Music Prodn 2010– (events incl BBC at the Edinburgh Festivals), exec prodr responsible for Any Questions, In Touch, Loose Ends, Home Truths (winner 3 Sony Gold Awards 1999) and Radio 4 Food and Farming Awards, chief project mangr live events BBC Audio and Music Prodn 2008– (events incl Proms in the Park); memb Radio Acad; *Recreations* music, friends, tennis, books, history; *Style—* Peter Griffiths, Esq; ✉ British Broadcasting Corporation, Broadcasting House, Portland Place, London W1A 1AA (☎ 020 7765 0666, e-mail peter.griffiths@bbc.co.uk)

GRIFFITHS, (William) Robert; QC (1993); s of late William John Griffiths, of Haverfordwest, Dyfed, and Marjorie Megan, *née* Green; *b* 24 September 1948; *Educ* Haverfordwest GS, St Edmund Hall Oxford (open scholar, MA, BCL); *m* 10 March 1984, Angela May, da of Robert Victor Crawford, of Manchester; 2 da (Anna-Victoria Sophia b 7 Oct 1986, Helena Elizabeth Rose b 13 Sept 1989), 1 s (Charles William Alexander b 13 March 1991); *Career* called to the Bar Middle Temple 1974 (bencher 2004, special advocate 2004); jr counsel to the Crown (common law) 1989–93, legal practitioner New South Wales 1998–, Senior Counsel NSW 1999. jt head of chambers 4–5 Gray's Inn Square 2008–; chm Test Match Grounds Consortium 1998–2001, chm First Class Forum on Line Rights Working Pty 2000–01; MCC: memb Estates Ctee 1996–2004, memb Working Pty on Natwest Media Centre 1997–99, memb Staging Agreement Working Gp 1998, memb Internet and e-Commerce Ctee 2000–01, memb Cricket Ctee 2000–04 and 2008–14, memb Indoor and Coaching sub-Ctee 2000–10, memb Ctee 2000–01, 2001–03, 2006–09 and 2012–15, chm Laws Sub-Ctee 2008–14, chm Devpt Ctee 2009–12; memb Cncl and Bd Chamber of Commerce and Industry 2014–; chm Greyhound Racing Regulatory Bd and dir Greyhound Racing Bd 2015–; Freeman City of London 1997; *Recreations* philosophy, collecting modern first editions, cricket (represented Welsh secondary schools at cricket and rugby), collecting antiquaria and twentieth century British art; *Clubs* MCC, Lord's Taverners (tstee 2011–), Garrick; *Style—* Robert Griffiths, Esq, QC, SC; ✉ 4–5 Gray's Inn Square, Gray's Inn, London WC1R 5AY (☎ 020 7404 5252, fax 020 7242 7803); Selborne-Wentworth Chambers, 174 Phillip Street, Sydney, New South Wales, Australia 2000 (☎ 00 6 12 92 33 4081); Lascelles Great House, Holetown, Barbados, West Indies

GRIFFITHS, Sian; *Educ* Univ of Oxford (BA, MPhil); *Career* features ed Times Higher Educn Supplement 1987–2000; Sunday Times: dep ed supplements 2000–09, dep ed News Review 2009–13, educn ed 2013–; *Style—* Ms Sian Griffiths; ✉ Sunday Times, 3 Thomas More Street, London E98 1XY (Twitter @siangriffiths6)

GRIFFITHS, Prof Siân Meryl; OBE (2000); da of John Daniel Griffiths, of London, and Rosemary, *née* Quick; *b* 20 March 1952; *Educ* N London Collegiate Sch, Univ of Cambridge (MA), King's Coll Hosp Med Sch (MB BCh), Univ of London (MSc); *m* 1, 1978 (m dis 1986), Anthony Chu; 2 da (Jessica b 1979, Alexandra b 1980); m 2, 1987, Ian Wylie; 1 s (Sam b 1987); *Career* jr doctor 1977–80, trainee in public health med 1981–85, conslt in public health/dist med offr City of Hackney DHA 1985–87, conslt in public health Oxford RHA 1988–90, hon sr lectr St George's Hosp Med Sch London and regnl dir of public health SW Thames RHA 1990–94, dir of public health and health policy Oxfordshire HA 1994–2001, hon sr lectr Dept of Public Health and Primary Care Univ of Oxford 1995–, conslt in public health med Oxford Radcliffe Hosps NHS Tst, sr fell in public health Univ of Oxford, co-chair Hong Kong Govt's Expert Ctee into the SARS Epidemic 2003 (subsequently chair Monitoring Ctee); Chinese Univ of Hong Kong: prof of public health and dir Sch of Public Health Faculty of Med 2005–13, sr advsr int acad devpt 2012–, dir Centre for Global Health 2013–, emeritus prof 2014–; technical advsr of public health research Shenzhen Centre for Disease Control and Prevention 2006–09, specialist advsr Healthcare UK; visiting prof Oxford Brookes Univ 1997–2007, visiting prof Imperial Coll 2014–; pres Faculty of Public Health Med RCP 2001–04 (treas 1995–98, vice-pres 2000–01), memb Bd PMETB 2003–05, memb Nat Health Authy Bd of Qatar, memb 2008 Research Assessment Exercise for Epidemiology and Public Health; chair Pharmacy Healthlink 2003, co-chair Assoc of Public Health 1995–98; assoc memb Bd Public Health England 2014–; hon prof: Sch of Public Health Univ of Peking, Cardiff Univ; hon fell Cardiff Univ 2012, hon visiting fell Univ of Cambridge 2012–; hon doctorate Univ of the West of England 2007; memb: Bd New Opportunities Fund 1998–2004, BMA, Med Women's Fedn, Bd Health Protection Agency; FFPH, FRCP, FDSRCS, fell Hong Kong Acad of Medicine; *Books* Routledge Handbook of Global Public Health Asia (2014); *Recreations* family, film, opera; *Clubs* Athenaeum, Hong Kong Jockey; *Style—* Prof Siân M Griffiths, OBE; ✉ 2 Canal Yard, Thrupp, Kidlington, Oxfordshire OX5 1JZ (☎ 07429 082681, e-mail sian@sianmgriffiths.com)

GRIFFITHS, Stephen Gareth (Steve); s of Dr Thomas Edwin Teasdale Griffiths (d 1984), and Kathleen Isobel Maxwell (d 1989); *b* 2 February 1949; *Educ* Ysgol Syr Thomas Jones Amlwch Ynys Môn, Churchill Coll Cambridge (BA); *m* 25 March 1978 (m dis 2006), Lala Isla, da of Alfredo Isla García, of Madrid; 1 s (Pablo Siôn Isla Griffiths b 20 July 1979); *Career* poet, social and health policy specialist; work published in many magazines incl: Stand, Poetry Wales, Poetry Review, Literary Review, The Rialto, 2Plus2 (Geneva), New Welsh Review, La Traductière (Paris); poetry readings in Britain, France, Spain and USA, various BBC broadcasts; memb Exec Academi Gymreig (Eng Language Section Welsh Acad) 1989–95 (fell 1995); conslt: ODPM 2000–03, Dept of Health 2002–03; *Publications* The Green Horse (contrib, 1978), Anglesey Material (1980), Anglo-Welsh Poetry 1480–1980 (contrib, 1984), Civilised Airs (1984), Uncontrollable Fields (1990), Poetry Book Society Anthology (contrib, 1990), The Bright Field (contemporary poetry from Wales, contrib 1991), Selected Poems (1993), Poetry 1900–2000, One Hundred Poets from Wales (contrib, 2007), Landing (pamphlet, 2008), An Elusive State (2008); numerous pubns in social policy field on poverty, health inequality and supported housing for Joseph Rowntree Fndn Shelter and many local and health authorities; author of policy statements and guidance for Dept for Communities and Local Govt, Dept for Work and Pensions and Dept of Health; *Recreations* finding space and silence, eating and drinking, music, friendship; *Style—* Steve Griffiths; ✉ 6 Cleeve Hill, Forest Hill, London SE23 3DD (☎ 020 8291 3180)

GRIFFITHS, Trevor; s of Ernest Griffiths (d 1961), of Manchester, and Ann Veronica, *née* Connor (d 1976); *b* 4 April 1935; *Educ* St Bede's Coll Manchester, Univ of Manchester (BA); *m* 1, 13 March 1960, Janice Stansfield (d 1977); 2 da (Sian b 1965, Emma b 1967), 1 s (Joss b 1968); m 2, 6 June 1992, Gillian Cliff; *Career* playwright; work incl: The Wages of Thin (first prodn Stables Theatre Manchester 1969), The Big House (1972, BBC Radio 4 1969), Occupations (1980, Stables Theatre Manchester 1970), Lay By (jtly 1971,

G

Traverse Theatre Edinburgh 1971), Apricots (1978, Basement Theatre London 1971), Thermidor (1978, Edinburgh Festival 1971), Sam, Sam (1972, Open Space 1972), The Party (1974, NT 1973), All Good Men and Absolute Beginners (1977, BBC TV 1974), Comedians (1976, Nottingham 1975), Through The Night and Such Impossibilities (1977, BBC TV 1975), Bill Brand (Thames TV 1976), The Cherry Orchard (new English version 1978, Nottingham Playhouse 1977), Deeds (jtly, Nottingham Playhouse 1978), Sons and Lovers (1982, BBC TV 1981), Country (1981, BBC TV 1981), Reds (with Warren Beatty, 1981), Oi For England (1982, Central TV 1982), The Last Place on Earth (Central TV 1985), published as Judgement Over The Dead 1986, Real Dreams (1987, Williamstown Theatre Festival 1984), Fatherland (1987), Collected Plays for Television (1988), Piano (1990, NT 1990), The Gulf Between Us (West Yorkshire Playhouse Leeds, 1992), Thatcher's Children (Bristol Old Vic 1993), Hope in the Year Two (1994, BBC TV 1994), Who Shall Be Happy....? (stage version of Hope in the Year Two, Belfast Festival 1995), Food for Ravens (1998, BBC TV 1997), Camel Station (2001), These Are The Times: A Life of Thomas Paine (2005), A New World (stage version of These Are The Times, 2009), Habaccuc Dreams (2010); BAFTA Writers Award 1982, WGA Best Original Screenplay 1982 (for Reds), nominated Best Original Screenplay Acad Award 1982 (for Reds), RTS Best Regional Prog 1998 (for Food for Ravens), Gwyn A Williams Award BAFTA Cymru 1998 (for Food for Ravens); memb: Writers' Guild of America (West), AMPAS; *Publications* These Are The Times: A Life of Thomas Paine (2005), Trevor Griffiths Theatre Plays One (2007), Trevor Griffiths Theatre Plays Two (2007), Bill Brand – the screenplays (2010); *Recreations* chess, bridge, music, photography; *Style*— Trevor Griffiths; ✉ website www.trevorgriffiths.co.uk; c/o United Agents Limited, 12–26 Lexington Street, London W1F 0LE (☎ 020 3214 0800, fax 020 3214 0801, website www.unitedagents.co.uk)

GRIFFITHS, Wendy Jane; *b* 27 April 1957, Wales; *m* 23 Dec 1996, Jeremy Ross; 1 da (Katie); *Career* headmistress Tudor Hall Sch Banbury 2004–; *Style*— Miss Wendy Griffiths; ✉ Tudor Hall School, Wykham Park, Banbury, Oxfordshire OX16 9UR

GRIFFITHS OF BURRY PORT, Baron (Life Peer UK 2004); of Pembrey and Burry Port in the County of Dyfed; Rev Dr Leslie John Griffiths; s of Sydney John Griffiths (d 1987), and Olwen, *née* Thomas (d 1976); *b* 15 February 1942; *Educ* Univ of Wales (BA), Univ of Cambridge (MA), Univ of London (PhD); *m* 26 July 1969, Margaret, da of Alfred Rhodes (d 1989); 2 s (Hon Timothy b 24 Sept 1972, Hon Jonathan b 7 Jan 1974), 1 da (Hon Ruth b 29 Oct 1975); *Career* lectr Univ of Wales 1964–67; methodist min: Cambridge 1969–70, Haiti 1970–74 and 1977–80, Reading 1974–77, Loughton 1980–86, London 1986–91, Finchley and Hendon 1991–96, Wesley's Chapel 1996–; hon canon St Paul's Cathedral 2000, select preacher Westminster Abbey Lent 2001; pres Methodist Conf 1994; regular contribs to radio and TV broadcasting; chm: Methodist Church Caribbean and Latin American Ctee 1981–89, Churches Advsy Cncl for Local Broadcasting 1996–2000, Methodist Church Euro Reference Gp 1997–2000, Coll of Preachers 2004–10; chm All Party Parly Gp on Haiti 2010, memb Ecclesiastical Ctee in Parliament 2011; pres Boys' Brigade 2011; memb Bd: Addiction Recovery Fndn 1987–2003, Christian Aid 1990–98, Birnbeck Housing Assoc 1993–96; memb Sir Halley Stewart Tst and tstee Art and Christianity Enquiry; chair of tstees Central Fndn Schs 2012; chm of govrs Southlands Coll 1997–2003; fell: Sarum Coll 2001, Sion Coll 2002, Univ of Cardiff 2005, Univ of Wales Lampeter 2006, Harris Manchester Coll Oxon 2015; FLSW 2012; KStJ 1989; *Books* History of Methodism in Haiti (1991), Letters Home (1995), The Aristide Factor (1997), Worship and our Diverse World (1999), Voices From the Desert (2003), World Without End? (2007), View from the Edge (2010); *Recreations* rugby, snooker, reading, conversation; *Clubs* The Graduate Centre (Cambridge); *Style*— The Rt Hon the Lord Griffiths of Burry Port; ✉ 49 City Road, London EC1Y 1AU (☎ 020 7253 2262, fax 020 7608 3825, e-mail superintendent@wesleyschapel.org.uk)

GRIFFITHS OF FFORESTFACH, Baron (Life Peer UK 1991), of Fforestfach in the County of West Glamorgan; Brian Griffiths; s of Ivor Winston Griffiths and Phyllis Mary, *née* Morgan; *b* 27 December 1941; *Educ* Dynevor GS, LSE (BSc, MSc); *m* 18 Sept 1965, Rachel Jane, da of Howard Jones; 2 da (Hon Aeronwen Jane b 1968, Hon Owenna Mary Ruth b 1973), 1 s (Hon James Brian b 1970); *Career* lectr in economics LSE 1968–76 (asst lectr 1965–68), prof of banking and int fin City Univ 1977–85, dir Centre for Banking and Int Finance 1977–82, dean Business Sch City Univ 1982–85, visiting prof Rochester Univ USA 1972–73, prof of ethics Gresham Coll 1984–87, dir Bank of England 1984–86, head of Prime Minister's Policy Unit (Rt Hon Margaret Thatcher) 1985–90; int advsr and vice-chm Goldman Sachs (Int) 1991–; chm: Land Securities Trillium, Westminster Health Care 1998–2002, Centre for Policy Studies 1991–2000, Archbishop of Canterbury's Lambeth Tst; non-exec dir: Times Newspapers, Herman Miller, Service Master, English Welsh and Scottish Railway; chm Sch Examinations and Assessment Cncl 1991–93; *Books* The Creation of Wealth (1984), Morality and the Market Place (1989); *Clubs* Garrick; *Style*— The Rt Hon Lord Griffiths of Fforestfach; ✉ House of Lords, London SW1A 0PW

GRIGG, Christopher (Chris); s of Colin Grigg, and Ann Grigg; *b* 6 July 1959, Basingstoke, Hants; *Educ* King Edward VI Sch Southampton, Trinity Hall Cambridge (MA); *m* 1987, Fionna Stirling; *Career* Morgan Grenfell 1981–85; Goldman Sachs Int: joined 1985, md 1997–2000, ptnr 2000–04; Commercial Bank Barclays Bank plc: treas 2005–07, ceo 2007–08, chief exec Br Land Co plc 2009–; memb Exec Bd EPRA 2010; pres Br Property Fndn 2012– (vice pres until 2011), non exec dir BAE Systems 2013–; *Recreations* military history, skiing, golf, loyal support of England's cricket and rugby teams; *Style*— Chris Grigg, Esq; ✉ British Land plc, York House, 45 Seymour Street, London W1H 7LX

GRIGGS, Anita, *née* Falkner; *b* 25 January 1953, London; *Educ* Univ of York, Univ of London (PGCE); *m* ; 4 da; *Career* formerly head of economics: St Paul's Girls Sch, Godolphin and Latymer Sch; headmistress Falkner House 1999–; *Style*— Mrs Anita Griggs; ✉ Falkner House, 19 Brechin Place, London SW7 4QB

GRIGGS, His Hon Jeremy David; s of Celadon Augustine Griggs (d 2008), of East Brent, Somerset, and Ethel Mary (Maisie), *née* Anderson (d 1996); *b* 5 February 1945; *Educ* St Edward's Sch Oxford, Magdalene Coll Cambridge (MA); *m* 1, 1971 (m dis 1982), Wendy Anne Russell, *née* Culham; 2 s (Christopher b 1972, Tom b 1974), 1 da (Beth b 1976); *m* 2, 1985, Patricia Ann (the actress Patricia Maynard), da of Thomas Maynard (d 1991); 2 step da (Hannah Waterman b 1975, Julia Waterman b 1979); *Career* called to the Bar Inner Temple 1968; memb Western Circuit, recorder of the Crown Court 1990–95, circuit judge (Western Circuit) 1995–2010, designated civil judge for Devon and Cornwall 2006–10, dep circuit judge 2010–; Bar's rep CCBE 1990–94, vice-chm Br Romanian Legal Assoc 1991–95; chm London Choral Soc 1986–90; *Publications* A South African Childhood: Biographical notes on the life of Celadon Augustine Griggs; *Recreations* playing the piano, beekeeping, walking on Dartmoor, studying history; *Clubs* Victory Servs; *Style*— His Hon Jeremy Griggs; ✉ Exeter Combined Court Centre, Southernhay Gardens, Exeter EX1 1UH

GRIGGS, Patrick John Spear; s of John Garson Romeril Griggs (d 1987), of Jersey, CI, and Inez Frances, *née* Cole (d 1985); *b* 9 August 1939; *Educ* Stowe, Tours Univ France, Law Soc Sch of Law London; *m* 4 April 1964, Marian Patricia, da of John Pryor Birch, of Mere, Wilts; 3 s (Simon Richard b 1967, Edward John b 1969, William Robert b 1972); *Career* slr 1963; Ince and Co: joined 1958, ptnr 1966, sr ptnr 1989–95, conslt 1995–; sec and treas Br Maritime Law Assoc 1995–2005, pres Comité Maritime Int 1997–2004; chm Opera Rara 2004–12; Freeman City of London; *Books* Limitation of Liability for Maritime Claims (jtly, 1987, 4 edn 2005); *Recreations* tennis, skiing, walking, cycling, golf; *Clubs*

City of London; *Style*— Patrick Griggs, Esq, CBE; ✉ c/o Ince & Co, Aldgate Tower, 2 Leman Street, London E1 8QN (☎ 020 7481 0010, e-mail pm.griggs@yahoo.co.uk)

GRIGGS, Roy; s of Norman Edward Griggs, CBE, of London, and Livia Lavinia, *née* Levi; *b* 26 April 1950; *Educ* Westminster, Univ of Bristol (LLB); *m* 4 Jan 1975, Anita Gwendolyn, da of Humphrey Osmond Nunes (d 1972); 4 da (Flavia b 1979, Eleanor b 1982, Cordelia b 1986, Marina b 1989); *Career* slr Norton Rose Botterell and Roche 1975–84 (seconded to Hong Kong office 1981–83), ptnr and conslt CMS Cameron McKenna LLP (formerly Cameron Markby Hewitt) 1985– (joined as slr 1984); memb City of London Slrs' Co; memb Law Soc; *Recreations* bridge, sailing, opera, skiing; *Clubs* Itchenor Sailing; *Style*— Roy Griggs, Esq; ✉ CMS Cameron McKenna LLP, Mitre House, 160 Aldersgate Street, London EC1A 4DD (☎ 020 7367 2813, fax 020 7367 2000)

GRIGSON, Hester Sophia Frances (Sophie); da of Geoffrey Edward Harvey Grigson (d 1985), of Broad Town, Wilts, and Jane, *née* McIntire (d 1990); *b* 19 June 1959; *Educ* Oxford HS, UMIST (BSc); *m* 19 June 1992 (m dis 2005), William Black, s of Brian Black; 1 da, 1 s; *Career* freelance food writer and broadcaster, princ Sophie's Cookery School; cookery corr: Evening Standard 1986–93, Sunday Express Magazine 1988–91, Independent 1993–94, Sunday Times Magazine 1994–96, Independent on Sunday (restuarant reviewer) 1997–98; contrib various magazines, newspapers and radio progs incl Curious Cooks (Radio 4) 1994, columnist Waitrose Food Illustrated 2005; ptnr and contrib Food.com, chair Jane Grigson Tst, patron Oxford Children's Food Festival; memb Guild of Food Writers; *Television* for Channel 4 incl: Grow Your Greens/Eat Your Greens 1993, Travels à la Carte (with William Black) 1994, Sophie's Meat Course 1995, Taste of the Times 1997, Sophie Grigson's Herbs (BBC) 1998, Feasts for a Fiver (BBC) 1999, Sophie Grigson's Sunshine Food (BBC) 2000, Sophie's Weekends (UKTV) 2003, Grigson (UKTV) 2004, Sophie in the Souk (Travel Channel) 2009, Sophie in the Orient (Travel Channel) 2010; *Awards* Food Writer of the Year Restauranteur Assoc of GB 1992, Caroline Walker Award (Media) 1994, Magazine Cookery Writer of the Year Guild of Food Writers 1997, Cookery Journalist of the Year Guild of Food Writers 2001, Jacob's Creek Bronze Award for Best Hardcover Recipe Book (with William Black) 2003; *Books* Food for Friends, Sophie's Table, Sophie Grigson's Ingredients Book, The Students' Cook Book, Eat Your Greens, The Carved Angel Cook Book (with Joyce Molyneux), Travels à la Carte (with William Black), Sophie Grigson's Meat Course, Sophie Grigson's Taste of the Times (1997), Sophie Grigson's Herbs (1998), Sophie Grigson's Feasts for a Fiver (1999), Fish (with William Black, 1999), Sophie Grigson's Sunshine Food (2000), Organic (with William Black, 2001), The Complete Sophie Grigson Cookbook (2001), My Favourite Family Recipes (2003), Sophie Grigson's Country Kitchen (2003), The First-Time Cook (2004), Vegetables (2006), Spices (2011); *Style*— Ms Sophie Grigson; ✉ website www.sophiescookeryschool.com; c/o Deborah McKenna Ltd (☎ 020 8876 0051, fax 020 8392 2462)

GRIME, Geoffrey John; s of Sqdn Ldr John Frederic Grime, DFC (d 1997), of Blackpool, Lancs, and José Thompson, *née* Bennett (d 2006); *b* 7 February 1947; *Educ* Sedbergh; *m* 19 June 1971, Margaret Joyce, da of Stanley Hamilton Russell (d 2005), of St Helier, Jersey; 1 da (Caroline b 1973), 1 s (Charles b 1975); *Career* Coopers & Lybrand: joined 1969, ptnr 1972–95, sr ptnr 1990–95; chm: Abacus Financial Services Gp Ltd 1995–99, Jersey Finance Ltd 2000–03, EFG Offshore Ltd 2006–14, Jersey Electricity plc 2008–, Computer Patent Annuities Hldgs Ltd 2008–11; elected dep of St Mary (States of Jersey) 2002–05, Jurat Royal Ct of Jersey 2014–; hon treas: Jersey Arts Cncl until 1985, Br Heart Fndn Jersey until 1987, Jersey Church Schs Soc 1987–2004; Freeman: City of London 1975, Worshipful Co of Musicians 1977; FCA 1969; *Recreations* veteran and vintage cars; *Clubs* Brooks's, United (Jersey); *Style*— Geoffrey Grime, Esq; ✉ Pine Farm, Rue Des Landes, St Mary, Jersey JE3 3EE (☎ 01534 863840)

GRIME, Mark Stephen Eastburn; QC (1987); s of Roland Thompson, and late Mary Diana, *née* Eastburn, of Morfa Nefyn; *b* 16 March 1948; *Educ* Wrekin Coll, Trinity Coll Oxford (scholar, MA); *m* 29 July 1973, Christine, da of J H A Emck, of West Wittering, W Sussex; 2 da (Eleanor b 1977, Isabel b 1981); *Career* called to the Bar Middle Temple 1970 (bencher 1997); Northern Circuit 1970–, recorder 1990–2003, recorder technol and construction 1997–2003; chm: Disciplinary Appeal Tbnl UMIST 1980–, Northern Arbitration Assoc 1994–97 (memb Cncl 1990–98), Northern Circuit Med Law Assoc 2000–02; FCIArb 1996; *Recreations* antiquarian horology, sailing; *Style*— Stephen Grime, Esq, QC; ✉ Deans Court Chambers, 24 St John Street, Manchester M3 4DF (☎ 0161 214 6000, 07000 444943, fax 0161 214 6001, e-mail grime@deanscourt.co.uk)

GRIMMER, Gregory Charles (Greg); *b* 13 January 1966, Rusington, Sussex; *Educ* Thamesmead Sch, Torquay Boys' GS, Univ of W London (BA); *m* Lucy, *née* Boag; 1 s (Joseph), 1 da (Liberty); *Career* grad trainee rising to media gp manager Delaney Fletcher/Bozell 1987–91; CIA Medianetwork: sr media exec 1991, dir of press buying 1994, dir of client services 1997–98; strategic planner New PHD Gp 1998–99, managing ptnr Optimedia International Ltd 1999–; ZenithOptimedia: memb bd, commercial dir, md Zed 2005–08, fndr Hurrell, Moseley, Dawson and Grimmer 2008–13, global chief operating offr Fetch 2014–; Media Mind Winner 1994, Media Week Magazine Face to Watch 1995, Special Award for Integration IPA Effectiveness Awards 1996, Monte Carlo TV Effectiveness Winner 1997; MIPA; *Publications* contributing author Advertising Works 10 and Digital State, columnist mediatel.co.uk; *Recreations* skiing, cycling, tennis; *Clubs* Electric House, Soho House; *Style*— Greg Grimmer, Esq; ✉ e-mail greg@wearefetch.com

GRIMMETT, Prof Geoffrey Richard; s of Benjamin John Grimmett, of Birmingham, and Patricia Winifred, *née* Lewis; *b* 20 December 1950; *Educ* King Edward's Sch Birmingham, Univ of Oxford (MA, MSc, DPhil, DSc), Merton Coll Oxford (postmaster); *m* 2 Sept 1986, Rosine, da of Pierre Bonay; 1 s (Hugo b 16 May 1989); *Career* IBM res fell Univ of Oxford and New Coll Oxford 1974–76, prof of mathematics Univ of Bristol 1989–92 (lectr 1976, reader 1985), prof of mathematical statistics Univ of Cambridge 1992– (dir Statistical Lab 1994–2000, head Dept of Pure Mathematics and Mathematical Statistics 2002–07); visiting prof at Univs incl: Cornell, Arizona, Rome, Utah, UCLA, Br Columbia, Paris; professorial fell Churchill Coll Cambridge 1999–2013, hon fell Inst of Actuaries 1999, master Downing Coll Cambridge 2013; memb: GB fencing team 1973–77, Olympic foil team 1976; nat under 20 foil champion 1970; FRS 2014; *Books* Probability and Random Processes (1982, 3 edn 2001), Probability, An Introduction (1986, 2 edn 2014), Percolation (1989, 2 edn 1999), One Thousand Exercises in Probability (2001), The Random-Cluster Model (2006), Probability on Graphs (2010); *Recreations* mountaineering, music, canyoneering; *Clubs* Climbers', Alpine; *Style*— Prof Geoffrey Grimmett; ✉ Statistical Laboratory, University of Cambridge, Wilberforce Road, Cambridge CB3 0WB (☎ 01223 337958, fax 01223 337956, website www.statslab.cam.ac.uk/~grg/); Downing College, University of Cambridge, Cambridge CB2 1DQ

GRIMOND, Hon John Jasper; er s of Baron Grimond, TD, PC (Life Peer; d 1993), by his w, Laura, *née* Bonham Carter (d 1994); *b* 1946, Edinburgh; *Educ* Eton, Balliol Coll Oxford, Harvard Univ (Nieman fellow); *m* 1973, Kate, er da of Lt-Col Peter Fleming, OBE (d 1971), of Nettlebed, Henley-on-Thames; 3 da (Mary Jessie b 1976, Rose Clementine b 1979, Georgia Celia b 1983); *Career* The Economist: joined 1969, asst ed 1975–12, Br ed 1976–79, American ed 1979–88, foreign ed 1989–2002, writer-at-large 2002–12, contributing ed 2012–; columnist The Oldie 2014–; dir Fleming American Investment Trust 1991–2000; tstee: Prison Reform Tst 1995–2009, Kennedy Meml Tst 2006–, Rothschild Archive 2010–; Harkness fell 1974–75; *Books* The Economist Style Book (ed); *Style*— The Hon John Grimond; ✉ 49 Lansdowne Road, London W11 2LG

GRIMSHAW, Nicholas (Nick); s of Peter Grimshaw, and Eileen Grimshaw; *b* 14 August 1984, Manchester; *Educ* Univ of Liverpool; *Career* television and radio presenter; ambass Royal Acad of Arts, involved with BBC Children in Need and BBC Sport Relief; ambass London Collections Men; *Radio* BBC Radio 1: Switch (with Annie Mac) 2007, Weekend Breakfast Show 2008–09, 10pm-Midnight Show 2009–12, Breakfast Show 2012–; *Television* Freshly Squeezed (Channel 4), Sound (BBC 2), T4 (Channel 4), The Album Chart Show (Channel 4), New Look Style the Nation (Channel 4), Sweat the Small Stuff (BBC 3), X Factor (as judge, ITV) 2015–, Soundchain (as host, MTV) 2015–; *Recreations* music; *Style*— Mr Nick Grimshaw; ✉ c/o Money, 42A Berwick Street, London W1F 8RZ (☎ 020 7287 7490, e-mail caroline@moneymanagementuk.com, website www.moneymanagementuk.com, Twitter @grimmers)

GRIMSHAW, Sir Nicholas Thomas; kt (2002), CBE (1993); s of Thomas Cecil Grimshaw (d 1942), and Hannah Joan, *née* Dearsley; *b* 9 October 1939; *Educ* Wellington, Edinburgh Coll of Art, AA Sch of Architecture (AADipl); *m* 20 Oct 1972, Lavinia, da of John Russell, CBE, of New York; 2 da (Chloe b 1973, Isabel b 1977); *Career* chm: Nicholas Grimshaw & Ptnrs Ltd 1980–2007, Grimshaw Architects LLP 2007–; pres: AA 1999–2001, Royal Acad of Arts 2004–11; major projects incl: Zurich Airport redevelopment, Channel Tunnel terminal for BR Waterloo, Br Pavilion for Expo '92 Seville, Berlin Stock Exchange, BA Combined Operation Centre Heathrow, Camden Superstore for J Sainsbury, HQ for BMW Bracknell, HQ for Igus GmbH Cologne, factory for Herman Miller Bath, Oxford Ice Rink, Gillingham Business Park for Grosvenor Devpts, res centre for Rank Xerox, printing plant for Financial Times, regional HQ for Orange Telephones, restoration of Paddington Station for Railtrack, Caixa Galicia Art Fndn A Coruña, Western Region HQ for the RAC, Euro Inst of Health and Mgmnt Studies Univ of Surrey, The Donald Danforth Plant Science Centre St Louis, The Eden Project, Millennium Point Birmingham, The New Bath Spa, Nat Space Science Centre Leicester, the grandstand at Lords for the MCC, Ijburg Bridge and Biljmer Station for high speed trains Amsterdam, New Exhibition Hall at Site of Frankfurt Fair, headquarters and assembly plant for Rolls Royce Goodwood, New East Wing for RCA London, HQ for Lloyds TSB Gresham St London, Experimental Media and Arts Centre for Rensselaer Poly Inst NY, St Botolph's office bldg London, HQ for KPMG Berlin, Battersea Power Station, Spencer Street Station Melbourne Aust, ExCeL London Phase 2 Devpt, Cancer Research Centre UCL, Garibaldi Repubblica (fashion and events building) Milan, Adelaide Univ Project 2 Aust, Nat Steel Museum Monterrey Mexico, Fulton Street Station NY, Cutty Sark, Stanstead Airport masterplan for BAA, new academic bldg LSE, new academic bldg K2 London South Bank Univ, extension Queen's Museum of Art NY, Newport City Footbridge Wales, Arts and Innovation Centre Univ of Bangor, Pulkovo Airport St Petersburg, Newport Station, Miami Science Museum, Via Verde Housing Project NY, Nunawading Station Melbourne, Moenchengladbach masterplan 2012, Wimbledon masterplan 2012, Parramatta Tower Sydney 2012, HS2 Euston, Highpoint Shopping Centre Aust, Tirana masterplan, EDF Energy Sizewell, SITA Facility Suffolk, Heathrow Terminal 2B, NW Rail Link Aust, Jones Street Apartments, Stoke-on-Trent Bus Station, Reading Station 2013, Doherty Insatiate for Immunity and Infectious Disease Univ of Melbourne Queens Museum 2013, Pulkovo Airport St Petersburg, Fulton Centre NY 2014, SITA Energy from Waste Facility Univ of New South Wales New Materials Science Building Sydney 2015; major awards and commendations incl: RIBA Awards 1975, 1978, 1980, 1983, 1986, 1989–91, 1994, 1995, 1999, 2001, 2002, 2004, 2006, 2007, 2009, 2013 and 2014, FT Award for Industrial Architecture 1977, 1980, 1995 and 1997, Br Construction Industry Awards 1988, 1989, 1992, 1993, 1995, 1999, 2001 and 2010, Structural Steel Design Awards 1969, 1977, 1980, 1989, 1993, 1994, 1995, 1999, 2000–03, 2007, 2010, 2011, 2013 and 2014, Civic Tst Award 1978, 1982, 1989, 1990, 1991, 1995, 1996, 2003, 2007 and 2015, Architectural Design Award 1974, 1982 and 1983, Royal Fine Arts Cmmn Sunday Times 1989, 1993, 1994 and 2004, BBC Design Awards finalist 1990, Business and Indust Award Certificate of Merit 1977, Euro Award for Steel Structure 1981, Constructa Preis for Industrial Architecture in Europe 1990, Quaternario Fndn Int Award 1993, Mies van der Rohe Pavilion Award for Architecture 1994, Lubetkin Prize 2007, Royal Inst of Dutch Architects Building of the Year (for Bijlmer Sation) 2008, Brunel Award 2008, AIA Award 2009, Structural Egrg Award 2010, UK Commercial Property Award 2010, ICE Award 2011, AIA Housing Award 2013, AIA/HUD Secretary's Award 2013, Residential Architecture Award 2013, AIA Award of Merit 2014, AIA Medal of Honor 2015, AJ120 Building of the Year, Architectural Collaboration Award and New Practice of the Year 2015; visiting prof Univ of the Arts 2008–; Hon DLitt: London South Bank Univ, Univ of Edinburgh, Heriot Watt Univ, UCL; Hon Dr Poletechnico di Milano 2009; hon memb BDA, Hon FAIA, Hon FRIAS; RIBA 1967, FCSD 1969, RA 1994; *Books* Nicholas Grimshaw & Partners Ltd: Product and Process (jtly, 1988), Structure, Space and Skin: the work of Nicholas Grimshaw & Partners Ltd 1988–93 (1993), Architecture, Industry and Innovation: the work of Nicholas Grimshaw & Partners Ltd 1966–88 (jtly, 1995), Equilibrium: The Work of Nicholas Grimshaw & Partners Ltd 1993–2000 (2000), Capturing the Concept: The sketch books of Sir Nicholas Grimshaw, CBE, PRA 1981–2008, Grimshaw: Architecture The First 30 Years (2011); *Recreations* sailing, tennis; *Style*— Sir Nicholas Grimshaw, CBE, PPRA; ✉ Grimshaw Architects LLP, 57 Clerkenwell Road, London EC1M 5NG (☎ 020 7291 4141, fax 020 7291 4194)

GRIMSTON, Neil Alexander; TD (1982); s of Flt Lt Victor Gordon Manners Grimston (d 1966), and Adeline Jean Margaret, *née* Esson (d 1992); *b* 8 September 1947; *Educ* Inst of Leadership and Mgmnt (post-grad qualification in exec coaching and leadership mentoring); *m* 1, 19 July 1975, Berylanne (d 2003), da of David McNaught (d 1992), of Thames Ditton, Surrey; 1 s (Alexander b 1979), 1 da (Henrietta b 1984); *m* 2, 5 March 2011, Serena Standing, *née* Kittoe; *Career* Private HAC 1970 (vet memb 1971–), cmmnd 2 Lt TA RCT 1971, Lt 1972, Capt 1976, cmd ind unit with BAOR 1977–82, Capt RARO 1983–2002; with Hill Samuel 1967–70, discount broker Smith St Aubyn 1970–73, discount broker Page and Gwyther Group 1973–77; Chemical Bank 1977–92: vice-pres and mangr World Insurance Gp (Asia) 1982–84, head City Instns Gp 1985–87, dir Chemical Bank Tstee Co 1986–88, vice-pres and head of Fin Instns Gp 1987–92, memb Euro Mgmnt Ctee 1991–92; sr conslt dir Telos 1993–94, gp fin dir and memb Exec Mgmnt Ctee Telos Bioinformatik AG (Lucerne) 1994–95, dir Telos Consulting Inc (USA) 1994–95, chm Isisquest Ltd 1995–96, md Grimston & Co 1998–, dir and chief operating offr 5GM Ltd 2000–01, jt md eSecure Business Ltd 2001–04 (ceo 2003–04), md eAssure Gp 2004–07, chm Hanover Partnership Ltd 2005–16, memb Advsy Panel Devonshire Corporate Finance Ltd 2005–08, Hanover Fndn 2003–10 (dir 2008–10), chm Hanover Partnership for Schs and Acads 2010–11, non-exec dir Business Devpt Bd RICS 2010–15; business conslt 1992–, mentor and exec coach 1995–; vice-chm Twickenham Cons Assoc 1969–74, cncllr (Cons) London Borough of Richmond-upon-Thames 1971–74; memb approved list of Cons Pty potential candidates for Westminster and Euro Parls 1989–93, chm Oxshott and Stoke Cons Assoc 1989–91; memb: HAC 1970–2008, Millennium Masters Assoc, Alumnus London Business Sch, European Mentoring and Coaching Cncl, Royal Logistic Corps, Sandhurst Tst 2014, Dio of Ely Bd of Educn 2015–; chm Ermine St Church Acad 2015–; chm Westminster Adult Educn Service (Westminster City Cncl) 2011–15 (vice-chm 2006–11), approved sponsor of secondary schs Dept of Educn 2011; Freeman City of London 1971, Master Worshipful Co of Scriveners 1999–2000; fell Inst of Leadership and Mgmnt 2009; *Recreations* feature films, internet, networking, research, technology; *Clubs* Singapore Cricket, Army and Navy; *Style*— Neil A Grimston, Esq, TD; ☎ 07876 741907, e-mail neil.grimston@hanoverpartnership.com

GRIMSTON OF WESTBURY, 3 Baron (UK 1964); Sir Robert John Sylvester (Robin) Grimston; 3 Bt (UK 1952); er s of 2 Baron Grimston of Westbury (d 2003), and Hon June Mary, *née* Ponsonby, da of 5 Baron de Mauley; *b* 30 April 1951; *Educ* Eton, Univ of Reading (BSc); *m* 1984, Emily Margaret, da of Maj John Evelyn Shirley, of Ormly Hall, Ramsey, IOM; 2 da (Hon Charlotte Elgiva b 23 March 1991, Hon Philippa Margaret b 7 Oct 1995); *Career* Capt Royal Hussars (PWO) 1970–81; CA: Binder Hamlyn, Citicorp Scrimgeour Vickers Ltd, Matrix Securities Ltd, London Court Ltd; *Style*— The Lord Grimston of Westbury

GRIMSTONE, Sir Gerald Edgar (Gerry); kt (2014); s of Edgar Wilfred Grimstone (d 1986), and Dorothy Yvonne, *née* Martin (d 2016); *b* 27 August 1949, London; *Educ* Whitgift Sch, Merton Coll Oxford (MA, MSc); *m* 23 June 1973 (m dis 1995), Hon Janet Elizabeth Gudrun Suenson-Taylor, da of 2 Baron Grantchester, CBE, QC (d 1995); 1 s (Toby Stephen Gunnar b 1975), 2 da (Jenny Elizabeth May b 1979, Anna Rose Yvonne b 1982); *Career* Civil Serv 1972–86 (latterly asst sec HM Treasy); J Henry Schroder & Co Ltd: dir 1986–99, head Int Fin and Advsy Dept 1994–95, dep chm Schroder Asia Ltd, head of investment banking Asia-Pacific region 1994–97, head of investment banking North America (based in New York) 1997–98, vice-chm Schroders Investment Banking 1998–99; non-exec dir: Dairy Crest 1999–2007, Candover Investments plc 1999–2011 (chm 2006–11), Aggregate Industries 2000–04, RAF Air Cmd 2001–07, F&C Global Smaller Companies plc 2002–07 (chm 2004–07), Standard Life 2003– (chm 2007–), Deloitte LLP 2011–, TheCityUK (chm 2012–15); dep chm Barclays 2016–; advsr: FCO 1999–2000, HM Treasy 2008–10, MOD 2010– (lead non-exec dir 2011–); UK business ambass 2009–10, memb Bd Shareholder Exec 2009–16; memb Horserace Totalisator Bd 1999–2006; tstee RAF Museum 2008–; MSI; *Clubs* Athenaeum, RAF, China, Hong Kong, Caledonian; *Style*— Sir Gerry Grimstone; ✉ Standard Life plc, 30 Lothian Road, Edinburgh EH1 2DH

GRINDLAY, Bruce Colin Walter; s of Colin Grindlay, and Patricia, *née* Waight; *b* 7 September 1967, Surrey; *Educ* King's Coll Sch Wimbledon, St George's Sch Vancouver BC, Emmanuel Coll Cambridge (organ scholar, MA, MusB); *m* 5 Aug 1995, Elizabeth Jane, *née* Ruck; 1 da (Jessica b 13 July 1999), 1 s (Samuel b 10 July 2001); *Career* head of chapel music and housemaster Bedford Sch 1994–2001, dir of music Christ's Hosp 2001–09, headmaster Sutton Valence Sch 2009–; memb: MMA 1994, HMC 2009; Freeman Worshipful Co of Cooks; FRCO (also chm), memb Royal Candian Coll of Organists (ARCCO); *Recreations* music, opera, reading, golf, cooking, sailing; *Clubs* East India; *Style*— Bruce Grindlay, Esq; ✉ Sutton Valence School, North Street, Sutton Valence, Kent ME17 3HL (☎ 01622 845203, e-mail hm@svs.org.uk)

GRINYER, Clive Antony; s of Tony Grinyer, of Southampton, Hants, and Hazel Grinyer; *b* 29 July 1960; *Educ* Highcliffe Comp Sch, Brockenhurst Sixth Form Coll, Southampton Coll of Art, Central Sch of Art and Design; *m* 21 May 1988, Janis, da of late Philip Kirby; 2 s (Laurence Kirby b 16 June 1992, Miles Kirby b 3 Oct 1995); *Career* designer; Moggridge Associates UK and USA 1983–89, founding ptnr Tangerine design consultancy 1989, dir Samsung IDEO USA 1994–95, European design dir Samsung Electronics 1995–98, head of product design TAG Mclaren Audio 1998–2001, dir of design and innovation Design Cncl 2001–03, dir of customer experience Orange World 2003–06, dir of design Orange France Telecom Paris 2006–; dir of customer experience Barclays plc 2013–; monthly columnist Design Week magazine 2001–; tstee: RSA 2010–, Merton Music Fndn; visiting prof Glasgow Sch of Art; memb Design Advsy Bd Br Cncl; memb Jury: Millennium Product, RSA Student Award, D&AD Awards, Drum magazine Design 100; RSA Student Design Award 1982, Industrial Design Soc of America (IDSA) Awards for Ford car audio projects 1986, IDSA/Business Week Award for Samsung Europe products 1995; FRSA 1983, FCSD 1996; *Books* Smart Design (2003); *Recreations* sailing, classic Maseratis, guitarist; *Style*— Clive Grinyer, Esq; ✉ Barclays Plc 1 Churchill Place London E14 5HP

GROBEL, His Hon Peter Denis Alan Christian Joseph; s of Cyril Peter Grobel, and Kathleen, *née* Donaghy; *b* 11 August 1944; *Educ* Mount St Mary's Coll, UCL (LLB); *m* 1975, Susan, *née* Twemlow; 3 s, 1 da; *Career* called to the Bar Lincoln's Inn 1967; in practice Common Law Bar 1971–2001, recorder 1991–2001, circuit judge (SE Circuit) 2001–14; chm Special Educn Needs Tbnl 1994–2000; *Style*— His Hon Peter Grobel

GROCHOLSKI, Count Alexander Luan; head of the family; hereditary title of Count confirmed in Russia 1881; er s of Count Kazimierz Adam Grocholski (d 1994), and his 1 w, Elzbieta Zofia, *née* Countess Baworowska (d 1987); suc uncle Count Stanislas Bohdan Karol Grocholski (d 2002); *b* 30 August 1949; *Educ* French Lycée London, Study Centre for the History of the Fine and Decorative Arts London; *m* 1979, Bridget Caroline, da of Capt John Hamilton Fleming (d 1971); 1 da (Katherine Rose Mary b 1980); *Career* Phillips Son & Neale Ceramics Dept 1969–73, Sotheby's Valuation Dept 1973–78; Grocholski & Co Art and Antique Valuers and Consultants 1978–; *Recreations* reading, walking; *Style*— The Count Grocholski; ✉ 27 Baalbec Road, London N5 1QN (☎ 020 7226 8806)

GROCOCK, Dr Anne; da of Bon Grocock, and Grace Grocock; *b* 7 March 1947, Leicester; *Educ* Westonbirt Sch, St Anne's Coll Oxford (MA, DPhil); *Career* Univ of Oxford Dept of Human Anatomy: departmental demonstrator 1973–79, departmental research asst 1979–80 and 1982–85, ICRF research fell 1985–89; Univ of Oxford coll lectr in anatomy and endocrinology: Worcester Coll 1976–79, Magdalen Coll 1977–80, Merton Coll 1977–80 and 1985–89, Keble Coll 1984–89, Lincoln Coll 1986–89; bursar and official fell St Antony's Coll Oxford 1990–97, exec dir RSM 1997–2006, asst registrar Univ of Oxford 2006–10; dep chair Nat Museum of Science Industry 2002–06 (tstee 1996–2006, chm Audit Ctee 1997–2006); memb: Def Estates Audit Ctee 2005–10, DSDA Audit Ctee 2008–10, Standards Ctee Gen Optical Cncl 2010–; Univ of Oxford: advsr to women jr membs Merton Coll 1988–89, memb SCR Merton Coll 1990–, memb Equal Opportunities Ctee 1992–95, memb Estates Bursars' Standing Ctee 1994–97, tstee Staff Pension Scheme 1994–97, memb Audit Ctee 1995–97, pres Assoc of Sr Membs St Anne's Coll 1997–2000; memb Cncl of Mgmnt Jl of Reproduction and Fertility Ltd 1977–82, chm Reproduction Research Information Services Ltd 1988–93 (memb Cncl of Mgmnt 1976–81), memb Owners' Advsy Bd Veterinary Lab Agency (VLA) 2007–11; memb: Society for Reproduction and Fertility 1969–2009, Endocrine Soc 1975–2009, Assoc of Univ Administrators 1990–98; tstee: Oxford Soc 1995–2003, Royal Med Benevolent Fund 1998–2005, Nuffield Oxford Hosps Fund 2001– (chm 2005–); non-exec dir Oxford Health NHS Fndn Tst 2008–; pres Westonbirt Assoc 1989–97; memb Cncl Taunton Sch 1990–2001 (chair F&GP Ctee 1992–97), govr Westonbirt Sch 1991–97, memb Ct Imperial Coll London 2001–06; MInstD 1999, FRSA 2000–16; *Publications* author of numerous scientific papers; *Recreations* music, opera, travel, collecting sculpture and books; *Style*— Dr Anne Grocock

GROCOTT, Baron (Life Peer UK 2001), of Telford in the County of Shropshire; Bruce Joseph Grocott; PC (2002); s of Reginald Grocott, and Helen Grocott; *b* 1 November 1940; *Educ* Univ of Leicester, Univ of Manchester; *m* 1965, Sally Barbara Kay, *née* Ridgway; 2 s (Hon John b 1970, Hon Neil b 1974); *Career* lectr in politics 1965–74, television journalist and prodr Central Television 1979–87; MP (Lab): Lichfield and Tamworth 1974–79, The Wrekin 1987–97, Telford 1997–2001; PPS to: Min for Local Govt Planning 1975–76, Min of Agric 1976–78; formerly PPS to Rt Hon Tony Blair, *qv* 1994–2001; Lord in Waiting (Govt whip) 2001–02, Capt HM Body Guard of Hon Corps of Gentlemen-at-Arms (chief Govt whip, House of Lords) 2002–08; chllr Univ of Leicester; memb Bd Birmingham City Univ; *Clubs* Trench Labour; *Style*— The Rt Hon the Lord Grocott, PC

GROOM, Brian William Alfred; s of Fred Groom (d 1978), of Manchester, and Muriel Edith, *née* Linfoot; *b* 26 April 1955; *Educ* Manchester Grammar, Balliol Coll Oxford (BA); *m* 1980, Carola May, da of Peter Withington; 1 s (Jack Edward b 4 Oct 1984), 1 da (Elinor Rose b 6 Aug 1987); *Career* trainee reporter and sports ed Goole Times 1976–78; Financial Times: Syndication Dept 1978–79, sub ed int edn 1979–81, labour reporter and mgmnt feature writer 1981–85, UK news ed 1985–88; ed Scotland on Sunday 1994–97 (dep ed 1988–94); Financial Times: S of England corr and regions team ldr 1997–2000, political ed 2000–02, Europe Edn ed 2002–05, comment and analysis ed 2005–09, UK business and employment ed 2009–14; freelance ed conslt and writer 2014–; Pfizer award NCTJ 1978; *Recreations* cricket, football, walking, Britain's culture and history; *Style—* Brian Groom, Esq; ✉ Alphin House, 69 Chew Valley Road, Greenfield, Oldham, OL3 7JG (☎ 07785 956069, e-mail groombrian@hotmail.com)

GROOM, Jeremy Richard; s of Peter Farrant Groom, of Walton on Thames, and Anne, *née* Dainty; *b* 2 May 1948; *Educ* King's Sch Canterbury, Lincoln Coll Oxford; *m* 9 April 1983, Jennifer, da of Sir Norman Richard Rowley Brooke, CBE (d 1989), of Cardiff; 1 da (Camilla b 1984), 1 s (Pelham b 1989); *Career* ptnr Seymour Pierce and Co 1977–87 (joined 1972), dir Seymour Pierce Butterfield Ltd 1987–94, sr divnl dir Brewin Dolphin 1994–2014; memb Stock Exchange 1975, FSI 2000 (MSI (Dip) 1992); *Recreations* music, theatre, cricket; *Clubs* MCC; *Style—* Jeremy Groom, Esq; ✉ e-mail jeremy.groom@btinternet.com

GROOM, Michael John; s of Thomas Rowland Groom (d 1984), of Wolverhampton, and Eliza Groom (d 1971); *b* 18 July 1942; *Educ* St Chad's GS Wolverhampton, Cotton Coll; *m* 4 June 1966, Sheila Mary, da of Harold Cartwright, of Wolverhampton; 2 da (Nichola b 1971, Sally b 1975); *Career* chartered accountant; Michael Groom & Co 1971–76 and 1981–89, Tansley Witt 1976–80, Binder Hamlyn 1980–81, dir various cos, lectr in mgmnt and legislation; chm Consultative Ctee of Accountancy Bodies 2001–02, dep chm Financial Reporting Cncl 2001–02; memb: ICAEW (memb Cncl 1975–2004, former treas, chm 1998–99, pres 2001–02), City Takeover Panel; Hon DBA Univ of Wolverhampton 2003; Liveryman and Hon Memb Court Worshipful Co of Chartered Accountants; FCA 1964; *Books* ed/author 1975–81: Chartac Administration Manual, Chartac Accounting Manual, Chartac Auditing Manual, Chartac Taxation Manual, Chartac Accounting and Auditing Model File, Financial Management in the Professional Office, Cash Control in the Smaller Business, Budgeting and Cash Management; *Recreations* theatre, travel, food and wine, photography; *Clubs* Albert Lawn Tennis; *Style—* Michael Groom, Esq; ✉ 14 High Meadows, Compton, Wolverhampton WV6 8PH (☎ 01902 753816)

GROOME, Eur Ing Richard Leonard; s of Leonard William Edward Groome, OBE, of London, and Patricia Yvonne, *née* Holttum; *b* 9 June 1951; *Educ* Hertford GS, Univ of Nottingham; *m* 10 Sept 1977, Janet Mary, da of William Edward Seckington; 1 da (Emily Sara b 2 April 1984); *Career* prodn mangr Beecham Foods Ltd 1973–76, devpt mangr then tech servs mangr Express Foods Gp 1976–86, gp planning mangr then div mangr Elliott Presco Ltd 1986–90, gen mangr prodn Muller Dairy UK Ltd 1990–92, dir UK Elliott Gp Ltd 1992–2005, chief exec Manchester Salford Trafford NHS LIFT Co 2005–08, ops dir John Laing plc 2008–13, md WMS Ltd 2013–, dir and chair Solskin Ltd 2013–; UK delg for IChemE to Int Food Gp 1984–86; non-exec dir Shropshire HA 1996–2002, pres Conseil National Des Ingénieurs et des Scientifiques de France (CNISF) 2012, non-exec dir NW Ambulance NHS Tsst 2013–; treas Shropshire Rifle Assoc, clerk Alberbury with Cardeston PC; Freeman City of London, Warden Worshipful Co of Engineers; FIChemE 1984, FRSH 2005; *Recreations* photography, fine wines, golf; *Clubs* Farmers', St James' (Manchester), Wine Share, RAF; *Style—* Eur Ing Richard Groome; ✉ The Brooklands, Station Road, Westbury, Shrewsbury SY5 9DA (☎ 01743 884653, e-mail richard.groome@talk21.com)

GROSS, Howard Anthony; s of Harold Victor Gross (d 2005), and Pamela Alicia Tamara, *née* Rosen (d 1994); *b* 24 May 1948, Hoddesdon, Herts; *Educ* Minchenden Sch, City of London Coll; *m* 4 Nov 1973, Beverley, da of Bennett Teff, of Christchurch, Dorset; 2 da (Zoë b 1975, Amanda b 1978); *Career* chartered accountant; chief exec Gross Klein 1968– (Gross Klein Wood 2001–); fndr chm Hartley Computer User Gp 1979–82; chm: North London Chartered Accountants 1984–85, Heathfield Sch Parents' Assoc (GPDST) 1985–89, Solution 6 Accounts Computer User Group 1998–2000; London Soc of Chartered Accountants: elected memb 1984, hon treas 1990–93, pres 2001–02; memb Cncl ICAEW 2002– (non-exec dir 2012, chair Members Bd 2012–), vice-chair Soc of Professional Accountants 2010–; exec ed Accountants Digest 2001–06, memb Editorial Advsy Bd Economia 2012–; Freeman City of London 1990; FCA 1971, CTA 1972, FCCA 1980; *Recreations* jogging (completed London Marathon 1989), my granddaughters Charlotte and Tammy; *Style—* Howard Gross, Esq; ✉ Gross Klein, 5 St John's Lane, London EC1M 4BH (☎ 020 7549 1683, e-mail howard@grosskleinnet.com, website www.grosskleinnet.com)

GROSS, John Jacob; s of Abraham and Muriel Gross; *b* 12 March 1935; *Educ* City of London Sch, Wadham Coll Oxford; *m* 1965 (m dis), Miriam Gross, *qv*, da of Kurt May; 1 s (Thomas b 1966), 1 da (Susanna b 1967); *Career* former asst lectr Univ of London, fellow King's Coll Cambridge 1962–65, literary ed New Statesman 1973, ed Times Literary Supplement 1974–81, tstee Nat Portrait Gallery 1977–84, dep chm George Weidenfeld & Nicolson Ltd 1982–83, staff writer NY Times 1983–89, theatre critic Sunday Telegraph 1990–; FRSL; *Books* The Rise and Fall of the Man of Letters (1969, Duff Cooper Meml Prize), Joyce (1971), The Oxford Book of Aphorisms (ed, 1983), Shylock: A Legend and its Legacy (1992, Heinemann Prize), The Oxford Book of Comic Verse (ed, 1994), The New Oxford Book of English Prose (ed, 1998), A Double Thread (2001); *Style—* John Gross, Esq

GROSS, Dr Michael Lester Phillip; s of Harold Victor Gross, of Southgate, and Pamela Alicia Tamar, *née* Rosen; *b* 31 March 1952; *Educ* Minchenden Sch Southgate, Sidney Sussex Coll Cambridge (MA, MB BChir, MD), The London Hosp Med Coll; *m* 1, 30 July 1974, Jennifer Ruth, da of Lawrence Hoffman, of Edgware; 2 da (Louise b 1977, Jemma b 1981); m 2, Aug 2009, Karen Mary, da of Jos Staughton, and Jean Staughton; *Career* sr resident The Nat Hosp 1983–85, sr registrar St Mary's Hosp and The Nat Hosp 1985–89, conslt neurologist Clementine Churchill Hosp, dir of neurophysiology Clementine Churchill Harrow, dir of neurophysiology Spire Bushey Hosp; former chm Div of Neurological Sci and conslt neurologist Regnl Neurological Centre Royal Surrey Co Hosp Guildford and East Surrey Hosps (memb Regnl Neurosciences Advsy Ctee), former clinical dir The Royal and East Surrey Neurology Research Unit; scientific papers and int presentations on treatment of Guillain-Barré syndrome, inflammatory polyneuropathy, experimental allergic neuritis, plasma exchange, rejection encephalopathy, migraine and headache syndromes and gen neurology topics; memb: Assoc of Br Neurologists, Euro Neurological Soc, BMA, Int Headache Soc, World Fedn of Neurology; shortlisted UK Hosp Dr of the Year 1998 and 1999, elected to Tatler 250 (Best UK Specialists 2013); FRCP 1995; *Books* The Therapeutic Modification of Inflammatory Polyneuropathy (1987); *Recreations* bridge, tennis, photography, theatre; *Style—* Dr Michael Gross; ✉ 105 Nibthwaite Road, Harrow, Middlesex HA1 1TE (e-mail drgross@neurologyclinic.org.uk)

GROSS, Miriam Marianna; *née* May; da of Kurt May, of Frankfurt, Germany, and Vera Hermine, *née* Freiberg; *b* 12 May 1938; *Educ* Dartington Hall Sch, St Anne's Coll Oxford (MA, DipEd); *m* 1, 1965 (m dis), John Jacob Gross, *qv*, s of Abraham Gross; 1 s (Thomas b 1966), 1 da (Susanna b 1967); m 2, 1993, Sir Geoffrey Owen; *Career* The Observer: joined as asst literary ed, dep literary ed 1964–81, woman's ed 1981–84; ed Book Choice Channel 4 1986–90, arts ed Daily and Sunday Telegraph 1986–91, literary and assoc ed Sunday Telegraph 1991–2005, freelance journalist 2005–, sr ed Standpoint Magazine 2007–11; tstee Real Action 2014–; *Books* The World of George Orwell (1971), The World of Raymond Chandler (1976), So Why Can't The Read? (2010), An Almost English Life (2012); *Recreations* painting; *Style—* Ms Miriam Gross; ✉ 24a St Petersburgh Place, London W2 4LB (☎ 020 7727 2291)

GROSS, Rt Hon Lord Justice; Rt Hon Sir Peter Henry Gross; kt (2001), PC (2010); s of late Sam Lewis Gross, and Fanny Alice, *née* Cohen (d 2002); *b* 13 February 1952; *Educ* Herzlia Sch Cape Town, Univ of Cape Town (BBusSc, MBusSc, Rhodes scholar), Oriel Coll Oxford (MA, BCL, Eldon scholar); *m* 1985, Ruth Mary, *née* Cullen; 2 s (George William b 6 April 1989, Edmund Walter b 6 Aug 1992); *Career* called to the Bar Gray's Inn 1977 (bencher 2000), admitted to the Bar NSW 1986, QC 1992, recorder 1995–2001 (asst recorder 1991–95), judge of the High Court of Justice (Queen's Bench Div) 2001–10, presiding judge SE Circuit 2005–08, judge in charge of Commercial Court 2009–10, Lord Justice of Appeal 2010–, dep sr presiding judge for England and Wales 2011–12, sr presiding judge for England and Wales 2013–15; chm: London Common Law and Commercial Bar Assoc 1996–97, Educn and Trg Ctee Bar Cncl 1998–2000, Int Rels Ctee Bar Cncl 2001, Advsy Bd City Univ Inst of Law 2003–05; *Books* Legal Aid and Its Management (1976); *Recreations* jogging, cricket, sailing, cross-country skiing; *Clubs* Oxford and Cambridge; *Style—* The Rt Hon Lord Justice Gross; ✉ Royal Courts of Justice, Strand, London WC2A 2LL

GROSS, Prof Philip John; s of Juhan Karl Gross, and Mary Jessie Alison, *née* Holmes; *b* 27 February 1952, Delabole, Cornwall; *Educ* Devonport HS Plymouth, Univ of Sussex (BA), Poly of North London (Dip Librarianship); *m* 1; 1 da (Rosemary b 20 Aug 1978), 1 s (Jonathan b 20 March 1982); m 2, 8 April 2000, Zélie, *née* Marmery; *Career* poet; early career working in publishing and libraries; writer and creative writing educator; lectr in creative studies Bath Spa Univ Coll until 2004, professor of creative writing Univ of Glamorgan 2004–; first prize National Poetry Competition 1982, T S Eliot Prize 2009; *Poetry* Familiars (1983), The Ice Factory (1984), Cat's Whisker (1987), The Air Mines of Mistila (with Sylvia Kantaris, 1988), Manifold Manor (1989), The Son of the Duke of Nowhere (1991), The All-Nite Café (1993), I D (1994), Scratch City (1995), A Cast of Stones (1996), The Wasting Game (1998, shortlisted Whitbread Prize), Changes of Address (2001), I Spy Pinhole Eye (with Simon Denison, 2002), Mappa Mundi (2003), The Egg of Zero (2006, shortlisted Roland Mathias Prize), The Water Table (2009, T S Eliot Poetry Prize), Off Road To Everywhere (2010) Deep Field (2011), Later (2013), A Fold in the River (with Valerie Coffin Price, 2015), Love Songs of Carbon (2015); *Novels* The Song of Gail and Fludd (1991), Plex (1994), The Wind Gate (1995), Transformer (1996), Psylicon Beach (1998), Facetaker (1999), Going for Stone (2002), Marginaliens (2003), The Lastling (2003), The Storm Garden (2006); *Plays* Internal Affairs (shared 1 prize BBC W of Eng playwriting competition), Rising Star (1995); *Libretti* Snail Dreaming (1997), The King in the Car Park (2015); *Clubs* Religious Soc of Friends; *Style—* Prof Philip Gross; ✉ School of Humanities and Social Sciences, University of South Wales, Pontypridd CF37 1DL (website www.philipgross.co.uk)

GROSSART, Sir Angus McFarlane McLeod; kt (1997), CBE (1989), QC, DL; s of William John White Grossart, JP (d 1980), and Mary Hay, *née* Gardiner (d 2000); *b* 6 April 1937; *Educ* Glasgow Acad, Univ of Glasgow (MA, LLB); *m* 1978, (Marion) Gay Kerr, *née* Dodd; 1 da (Flure b 6 Dec 1982); *Career* CA 1962; advocate Scottish Bar 1963–69, chm and md Noble Grossart Ltd (merchant bank) 1969–; chm: Scottish Investment Trust plc 1974–2003, Lyon and Turnbull 1999–, Edinburgh Partners 2004–, Charlotte St Partners 2014–; dep chm Ronson Capital Partners 2011–; directorships incl: Edinburgh US Tracker Trust plc (formerly American Trust plc) 1973–07 (former chm), Royal Bank of Scotland plc 1982–2005, Royal Bank of Scotland Group plc 1985–2005 (vice-chm 1996–2005), BP Scot Advsy Bd 1990–2005, Trinity Mirror Gp plc 1998–2007, Scottish & Newcastle plc 1998–2008; non-exec chm: Scottish Daily Record, Sunday Mail 1998–2007, Scotland International 1999–, Scottish Futures Tst 2008–; chm of tstees Nat Galleries of Scot 1989–97, chm The Fine Art Soc 1998–2016, tstee and dep chm Nat Heritage Memorial Fund 1999–2005, chm Bd Nat Museums of Scotland 2006–12, tstee Glasgow Life 2007–, tstee High Steward of Scotland's Dumfries House Tst 2007–16, chm Burrell Renaissance 2013–, chm Edinburgh Int Cultural Summit 2014–; Livingston award Capt of Industry 1990, Lord Provost of Glasgow's Medal for Public Service 1997, Paolozzi Gold Medal 1997, Walpole Medal of Excellence 2003, NMS Gold Medal 2012; Hon LLD Univ of Glasgow 1985, Hon DBA Univ of Strathclyde 1998, Hon DLitt Univ of St Andrews 2004, Hon LLD Univ of Aberdeen 2006; FRSE 1998; *Recreations* golf, restoration of sixteenth century castle, Scottish painting, decorative and applied arts; *Clubs* New (Edinburgh), Royal and Ancient (St Andrews), Hon Co of Edinburgh Golfers; *Style—* Sir Angus Grossart, CBE, QC, DL; ✉ Noble Grossart Ltd, 48 Queen Street, Edinburgh EH2 3NR (☎ 0131 226 7011, fax 0131 226 3332)

GROSSART, Hamish McLeod; s of Kenneth William McFarlane Grossart, and Mairi, *née* Paterson; *b* 7 April 1957, Edinburgh; *Educ* Glasgow Acad, Univ of Stirling; *m* 1, 14 May 1981 (m dis), Fiona Jean McDonald; 2 da (Mhoraig Louise b 14 March 1987, Cathleen Maire b 28 May 1989); m 2, 7 Dec 1996 (m dis), Elaine Rosalind Mackenzie Simpson; 1 s (Ruairidh Sholto MacLeod b 8 Jan 1998), 1 da (Rosalind Sophie Mackenzie b 20 Nov 2000); m 3, 11 June 2010, Elizabeth Kythe Stirling, *née* Gray Muir; *Career* dir Noble Grossart Ltd 1982–83 (joined 1979, responsible for corp fin), fndr dir First Northern Corporate Finance Ltd 1983–86; EFT Group plc: dir (following merger with First Northern) 1986–97, md 1987–92, chm 1992–97; chm: Quality Care Homes plc 1992–94 (dir 1994–95), Scottish Highland Hotels plc 1992–99 (dir 1991–99), Eclipse Blinds plc 1994–98, Hicking Pentecost plc 1994–98 (dir 1991–98), Indigo Vision plc 1996–2002 and 2003–, Royal Doulton plc 1998–2005, Artemis Investment Mgmnt LLP 2011–16 (now non-exec dir); dep chm: Cairn Energy plc 1996–2010 (dir 1994–2010), Scottish Radio Holdings 1996–2006 (dir 1985–91 and 1993–2006), British Polythene Industries plc 2006–; dir: British Thornton Holdings plc 1991–94, Martin Currie Income & Growth Trust plc 1997–2005, Artemis Investment Mgmnt Ltd 1997–2011, Sigma Technology Group plc 2000–05, Lionheart plc 2001–04; govr Kilgraston Sch 1999–2004; *Recreations* my children, shooting, cooking, historic landscapes and buildings; *Style—* Hamish Grossart; ✉ Artemis Investment Management LLP, 14 Melville Street, Edinburgh

GROSSMAN, Prof Ashley Barry; s of Sidney Grossman (d 1966), of London, and Rose, *née* Green; *b* 20 February 1948; *Educ* Hasmonean GS, St Catharine's Coll Cambridge (open exhibitioner), UCH Med Sch London (Atkinson scholar, BA, BSc, MB BS, MD, Belasco medal, Univ Gold medal); *m* 1, 1971 (m dis 1982), Susan, da of Dr Dennis Friedman; 1 da (Emily Priscilla Sidonie b 7 July 1978); m 2, 1984, Deborah Foster, da of John Clark; 5 da (Sophie Eleanor b 28 April 1985, Annabel Clare b 9 Oct 1986, Camilla Rose b 14 Nov 1992, Cordelia Anne b 23 Nov 1996, Elizabeth Sîan Helen b 3 Aug 2000); *Career* hon conslt Dept of Endocrinology Bart's 1986–, prof Bart's Med Coll 1993– (lectr 1982–86, sr lectr 1986–90, reader 1990–93), prof of endocrinology Oxford Centre for Diabetes, Endocrinology and Metabolism Churchill Hosp Univ of Oxford 2011–; ed Frontiers of Hormone Research, former ed Clinical Endocrinology, memb Editorial Bd Pituitary, Functional Neurology and Jl of Clinical Endocrinology and Metabolism; former chm: UK and Ireland Neuroendocrine Tumour Soc, Advsy Bd European Neuroendocrine Tumour Soc; past pres European Neuroendocrine Assoc, past pres Soc for Endocrinology, pres The Pituitary Soc 2015–16; sr memb Assoc of Physicians; fell Green-Templeton Coll Oxford; FRCP, FMedSci; *Books* Neuroendocrinology: a Clinical Text (with Mary Forsling,

1986), Bailliere's International Clinics in Endocrinology: The Neuroendocrinology of Stress (1987), Psychoneuroendocrinology (1991), Clinical Endocrinology (ed, 1993 and 1997), Frontiers of Hormone Research (former ed-in-chief), Endocrinology (sr ed, 7 edn 2015), Oxford Desk Reference in Endocrinology (with Graham Eastell and Helen Turner, 2015); *Recreations* riding, skiing, walking, daughters; *Style—* Prof Ashley Grossman; ✉ 8 Ringwood Avenue, London N2 9NS (☎ 020 8444 8918); OCDEM, Churchill Hospital, Oxford OX3 7LE (☎ 01865 857308, fax 01865 857311, e-mail ashley.grossman@ocdem.ox.ac.uk)

GROSSMAN, Dr Loyd Daniel Gilman; CBE (2015, OBE 2003); s of David K Grossman (d 1982), of Boston, MA, and Helen Katherine, *née* Gilman (d 1985); *b* 16 September 1950; *Educ* Boston Univ (BA), LSE (MSc), Magdalene Coll Cambridge (MPhil, PhD); *m* 15 June 1985, Hon Deborah Jane, da of Baron Puttnam, CBE (Life Peer), *qv*, of London (dis 2005); 2 da (Florence Grace b 1989, Constance Catherine b 1992); *Career* Harpers & Queen: design ed 1981–84, restaurant critic 1981–89 and 1991–93; contrib ed Sunday Times 1984–86; deviser/writer/presenter: Through the Keyhole (formerly ITV, now BBC) 1983–2003, Behind the Headlines (BBC) 1989–92, Master Chef (BBC) 1990–2000, The Dog's Tale (BBC) 1993, Junior Masterchef (BBC) 1994–99, Off Your Trolley (BBC) 1995, Conspicuous Consumption 1996, The World on a Plate (BBC) 1997, Loyd on Location 1999–2001, History of British Sculpture (five) 2003; presenter: Composers at Home (BBC Radio 3), 2004–, Build Britain (BBC) 2007, Step Up to the Plate (BBC) 2008; songwriter and guitarist (with The New Forbidden, performances at various festivals incl Glastonbury, Vintage, Cornbury and Rebellion); memb: Bd mda (formerly Museum Document Assoc) 1998–2001, MLA (formerly Museums, Libraries and Archives Cncl then Resource: Cncl for Museums, Archives and Libraries) 1999–2007 (chm Designation Challenge Fund 2001–03), Bd Culture Northwest: Cultural Consortium for NW England 2002–09 (chm 2004–09), Bd Assoc of Leading Visitor Attractions 2013–; cmmr: Museums and Galleries Cmmn 1996–2000, Royal Cmmn on Historical Monuments of England 1999–2003; English Heritage: chm Museums and Collections Advsy Ctee 1997–2001, cmmr 1997–2003, memb Museum and Archives Panel 2001–03, chm Nat Blue Plaques Panel 2003–06; chm: Campaign for Museums 1995–2009, Museums and Galleries Month 2000 (co-chm 2001–08), The 24 Hour Museum 2000–05, Public Monuments and Sculpture Assoc 2001–07, Churches Conservation Tst 2007–16, Nat Museums Liverpool 2005–08, Heritage Alliance 2009–; vice-chm NW Regnl Cultural Consortium 2002–03, dep chair Liverpool Culture Co 2005–07; pres British Assoc of Friends of Museums 2005–14, vice-pres Merseyside Civic Soc 2007–08, pres NADFAS 2014–; tstee: Museum of Science and Industry in Manchester 1999–2002, St Deiniol's Library 2003–08 (fell 2008), Gladstone's Library 2014–; chm: Conservation Awards 1998–2003, Univ for the Creative Arts 2008–12; dep chair The Royal Drawing Sch 2014–, govr Building Crafts Coll 2014–; memb Cncl Br Sch at Rome 2013–; chm of judges Gulbenkian Prize for Museums 2004; patron: Historic Lincoln Tst, Haslemere Educational Museum, Cavell Nurses Tst, American Museum in Britain; vice-pres Sick Children's Tst, chm Better Hosp Food Panel NHS 2001–06, hon life memb The Dog's Tst; emeritus govr LSE 2009– (memb Ct of Govrs 1996–2009, memb Cncl 2003–08); Upper Warden Ct of Assts Worshipful Co of Art Scholars, Dealers and Collectors 2010–, Hon Liveryman Worshipful Co of Glaziers 2011–, Freeman City of London 2011, Liveryman Worshipful Co of Carpenters 2012–; Hon DLitt Univ of Chester 2007, Hon DArts Univ of Lincoln 2011, hon doctorate Univ of Essex 2014; FRSA, FSA, FSA Scot, FRSM; *Publications* The Social History of Rock Music (1975), Harpers & Queen Guide to London's 100 Best Restaurants (1987), The Dog's Tale (1993), Loyd Grossman's Italian Journey (1994), Courvoisier's Book of the Best (ed, 1994–96), The World on a Plate (1997), The 125 Best Recipes Ever (1998), Foodstuff (2002), Benjamin West and the Struggle to Be Modern (2015); articles on architecture, history, design and food in newspapers and magazines; *Albums* Ain't Doin' Nothin' (with The New Forbidden, 2010); *Recreations* fishing, scuba diving (PADI Divemaster), looking at buildings, tennis, chess, the Boston Red Sox, playing old Gibson and Gretsch guitars; *Clubs* Brooks's, Flyfishers', Hurlingham, Chelsea Arts, Oxford & Cambridge, Pilgrims, Piscatorial Soc, City Livery, London Sketch; *Style—* Dr Loyd Grossman, CBE, FSA

GROSSMAN, Russell; s of David Grossman, and Irene, *née* Ramm; *b* 7 April 1961, Blackpool, Lancs; *Educ* Arnold Sch Blackpool, UMIST (BSc), Univ of Salford (MSc); *m* 1 Sept 1985, Eunice Goodstone; 1 da (Gabriella b 15 March 1987), 3 s (Gavin b 26 March 1989, Jaimie b 19 July 1992, Harry b 28 June 1999); *Career* PR mangr Jubilee Line extension London Underground 1994–96, sr conslt Nichols Assocs 1994–97, dir of communications Royal Mail London 1997–99, head of int communications BBC 1999–2006, head of internal and change communications HMRC 2006–08, dir (later gp dir) of communications Dept for Business, Innovation and Skills (formerly Dept for Business, Enterprise and Regulatory Reform) 2008–15, dir of communications Office of Rail and Road 2015–; head of internal communications profession UK Govt Communications 2015–; int chair Int Assoc of Business Communicators 2014–15; accredited business communicator; FCIM, FCIPR, FRSA; *Style—* Russell Grossman, Esq; ✉ Office for Rail and Road, 1 Kemble Street, London WC2B 4AN

GROSZ, Stephen Ernest; Hon QC (2012); s of Joe Emil Grosz, and Teddy Grosz; *b* 14 April 1953, London; *Educ* William Ellis Sch, Clare Coll Cambridge (MA), Univ of Brussels (Licencié Spécial en Droit Européen); *m* 9 June 2012, Vicki Chapman; *Career* admitted slr 1978; Bindmans LLP: articles 1976–78, ptnr 1981–2013, sr consult 2013–; memb: Cncl Justice, Advsy Cncl Br Inst of Human Rights; chair Human Rights Ctee Law Soc 2014–15 (memb 2011–17); qualified civil and commercial mediator 2012; fell Bingham Centre for the Rule of Law 2013–; *Publications* Human Rights: The 1998 Act and the European Convention (jtly, 2000), Human Rights: Judicial Protection in the United Kingdom (jtly, 2008); *Recreations* swimming, singing, cycling, theatre; *Style—* Stephen Grosz, Esq, QC; ✉ Bindmans LLP, 236 Gray's Inn Road, London WC1X 8HB (☎ 020 7833 4433, fax 020 7837 9792, e-mail s.grosz@bindmans.com)

GROUND, (Reginald) Patrick; QC (1981); s of Reginald Ground (d 1975), of Pinner, Middx, and Ivy Elizabeth Grace, *née* Irving (later Mrs Alan Manser, d 1992); *b* 9 August 1932; *Educ* Beckenham and Penge County GS, Lycée Gay Lussac Limoges, Selwyn Coll Cambridge (exhibitioner, MA), Magdalen Coll Oxford (MLitt); *m* 1964, Caroline, da of Col J F C Dugdale (d 1991), of London; 3 s (Andrew b 1967, Richard b 1970, Thomas b 1974), 1 da (Elizabeth b 1969); *Career* Sub Lt RNVR Med Fleet 1955–56; called to the Bar Inner Temple 1960 (Inner Temple studentship and Foster Boulton prize 1958, bencher 1987); cncllr Hammersmith BC 1968–71, chm Ctees responsible for Health and Social Servs 1969–71; MP (Cons) Feltham and Heston 1983–92, PPS to the Slr Gen 1987–92; chm of tstees Daisy Tst 1981–, pres OUCA 1958, chm Fulham Soc 1975–95; *Recreations* lawn tennis, sailing, theatre, music, forestry, travel; *Clubs* Carlton, Brooks's, Queen's (tstee 2008–10); *Style—* Patrick Ground, Esq, QC; ✉ 13 Ranelagh Avenue, London SW6 3PJ (e-mail post@patrickground.com)

GROVE, Peter Ernest; s of Ernest Grove (d 1974), and Elsie May, *née* Silver; *b* 18 November 1949; *Educ* Heathcote Sch Chingford; *m* 27 Jan 1973, Catherine Anne, da of Joseph Frederick Jolly, of Wanstead, London; 1 s (Alexander b 28 April 1979), 2 da (Elizabeth b 10 Jan 1981, Caroline b 18 Jan 1982); *Career* dep underwriter: Willis Faber Underwriting Mgmnt Ltd 1977, Lloyd's Syndicates 197/726 561 & 566 1984, Bankside Syndicates Ltd 1987; active underwriter Lloyd's Syndicates 197 & 561 1988, dir QBE Hldgs (Europe) Ltd 1998, active underwriter Lloyd's Syndicate 2999 2003, chief underwriting offr QBE European Operations 2004–, dir QBE International Holdings (UK) plc 2004–; dir Minibus & Coach Club Ltd 2005–, dir British Marine Managers Ltd 2006–; *Recreations* chess, reading; *Style—* Peter Grove, Esq; ✉ QBE European Operations, Plantation Place, 30 Fenchurch Street, London EC3M 3BD (☎ 020 7105 4516, fax 020 7105 5020, e-mail peter.grove@uk.qbe.com)

GROVE, Valerie; da of Doug Smith (d 1973); *b* 11 May 1946; *Educ* Kingsbury Co GS, Girton Coll Cambridge (exhibitioner, MA); *m* 1, 1968, David Brynmor Jenkins; m 2, 1975, Trevor Charles Grove, s of Ronald Grove (d 1980); 3 da (Lucy b 1976, Emma b 1979, Victoria b 1981), 1 s (Oliver b 1983); *Career* reporter Shields Gazette 1965–66, feature writer Evening Standard 1968–87 (literary ed 1979–81 and 1984–87), columnist Sunday Times 1987–91, feature writer The Times 1992–2014; *Books* Where I Was Young – Memories of London Childhoods (1977), The Compleat Woman (1987), Dear Dodie (1996), Laurie Lee: The Well-loved Stranger (1999), A Voyage Round John Mortimer (2007), So Much to Tell: the life of Kaye Webb (2010), Grumbling at Large: Selected essays of J B Priestley (ed, 2016); *Recreations* tennis, archives; *Clubs* Coolhurst Tennis, Biographers'; *Style—* Mrs Valerie Grove; ✉ 14 Avenue Road, Highgate, London N6 5DW (☎ 020 8348 2621, e-mail vgrove@dircon.co.uk)

GROVE-WHITE, Prof Robin Bernard; s of Charles William Grove-White, of Amlwch, Gwynedd, and Mary, *née* Dobbs; *b* 17 February 1941; *Educ* Uppingham, Worcester Coll Oxford (BA), Bangor Univ (PhD); *m* 1, 1970 (m dis 1974), Virginia Harriet, da of Christopher Ironside, OBE; 1 s (William b 1973); m 2, 1979, Helen Elisabeth, da of Sir Francis Graham Smith, of Henbury, Cheshire; 1 da Ruth (b 1980), 2 s (Simon b 1982, Francis b 1986); *Career* freelance writer for TV, radio, press in US, Canada and UK 1963–71, asst sec Cncl for the Protection of Rural England 1972–80 (dir 1981–87), vice-chm Cncl for National Parks; research fell Centre for Environmental Technol Imperial Coll London 1987–89, dir Centre for Study of Environmental Change Lancaster Univ 1991–2000, prof of environment and soc Lancaster Univ 2000–05 (emeritus prof 2005–); forestry cmmr 1990–98, memb Agric and Environment Biotechnology Cmmn 2000–05; chm Greenpeace UK 1996–2004, pres N Wales Wildlife Tst 2010–; contrib to The Times, Guardian, New Scientist, Nature and numerous academic jls; High Sheriff Gwynedd 2011–12; Hon DSc Univ of Bath 2011; *Recreations* reading, walking, cricket; *Style—* Prof Robin Grove-White; ✉ Brynddu Llanfechell, Ynys Mon LL68 0RT (☎ 01407 710245)

G

GROVER, Rajiv; *Educ* Univ of London (BSc, MB BS, MD); *m* 1992, Nikita; 2 da (Serena, Sophia); *Career* conslt plastic surgeon NW London Regnl Centre Mount Vernon Hosp 2001–06, conslt plastic surgeon King Edward VII Hosp London 2002–, private practice Harley St; Hunterian prof RCS 1998–; memb Cncl Br Assoc of Aesthetic Plastic Surgeons 2004– (sec 2006–10, pres elect 2010–12, pres 2012–14); European Assoc of Plastic Surgeons Prize in Plastic Surgery 1996 and 1999, Br Assoc of Aesthetic Plastic Surgeons Hackett Prize in Aesthetic Plastic Surgery 1996 and 2000, American Assoc of Plastic Surgeons Gold Medal 2000, Br Jl of Plastic Surgery Mento Prize in Plastic Surgery 2001; FRCS 1993 (Hallet Prize and Gold Medal), FRCS(Plast) 2000; *Publications* Textbook of Facial Rejuvenation Surgery (jtly 2008); *Recreations* personal fitness, cycling, photography; *Clubs* Arts; *Style—* Rajiv Grover, Esq; ✉ 144 Harley Street, London W1G 7LE (☎ 020 7486 4301, website www.rajivgrover.co.uk)

GROVES, Brian Arthur; s of Alfred Edward Groves (d 1990), and Winifred May, *née* Sheen (d 1996); *b* 3 July 1933; *Educ* Bishop Wordsworth Sch Salisbury; *m* 1 Aug 1955, Daphne Frances, da of Frederick Gale (d 1957); 2 da (Heather b 1956, Beverley, b 1957); *Career* journalist 1950–71, motoring ed Daily Mail 1968–71, advtg and PR dir Nissan UK Ltd 1985–88 (mktg dir 1975–85), chm David Ruskin Ltd 1988–92, md AFG Ltd 1992–94, dir: Nissan UK Ltd 1994–2007, OMC Investments Ltd 2007–; *Recreations* golf, flying; *Style—* Brian A Groves, Esq; ✉ Sarum, Ivy Gates, St Peter Port, Guernsey (☎ 01481 727766, mobile 07781 127766)

GRUDER, Jeffrey Nigel; QC (1997); of Bernard Gruder (d 1996), and Lily Gruder (d 2003); *Educ* City of London Sch, Trinity Hall Cambridge (MA); *m* 1979, Gillian Vera, *née* Hyman; 2 da (Joanna b 7 July 1982, Katherine b 26 Nov 1989), 1 s (Jonathan b 25 June 1985); *Career* called to the Bar Middle Temple 1977 (bencher 2008); *Recreations* tennis, reading, art, theatre; *Style—* Jeffrey Gruder, Esq, QC; ✉ Essex Court Chambers, 24 Lincoln's Inn Fields, London WC2A 3ED (☎ 020 7583 2000, fax 020 7583 0118)

GRUENBERG, Erich; OBE (1994); *b* Vienna; *Educ* Jerusalem Conservatoire; *Career* violinist; concertmaster Stockholm Philharmonic Orch 1956–58; leader: LSO 1962–65, Royal Philharmonic Orch 1972–76, London Ensemble 1975–82; prof Royal Acad of Music, formerly prof Royal Coll of Music and Guildhall Sch of Music; chm of jury Yehudi Menuhin Int Competition for Young Violinists 1997–2002, involved in int masterclasses and juries worldwide; chm of tstees Hattori Fndn for Young Musicians; played with orchs incl: all major Br orchs, Sydney Symphony, Melbourne Symphony, Hungarian State Symphony; toured in: USA, Canada, S America, Aust, Holland, Germany, Spain, Italy, Scandinavia, Switzerland, USSR, Hungary, Far East; winner Carl Flesch Int Violin Competition; cmmnd numerous new works and given first performances incl: David Morgan Violin Concerto (with the Royal Philharmonic Orch and Sir Charles Groves, Royal Festival Hall) 1975, John McCabe Violin Concerto No 2 (cmmnd, performed with the City of Birmingham Symphony Orch and Chris Seaman) 1979, John Mayer's Sangit (cmmnd, performed with Bournemouth Symphony Orch) 1980 and Ragamalika for Violin and Tambura (cmmnd, performed Cheltenham Festival) 1989, Robin Holloway's Romanza (Promenade Concert, with Simon Rattle) 1982; Hon RAM, FGSM, FRCM; *Recordings* incl: Beethoven Violin Concerto (with the Philharmonia and Jascha Horenstein), Kreisler Pieces (also with the Philharmonia), Complete Beethoven Violin and Piano Sonatas (first recording by a Br artist), various works by Bach, Stravinsky, Messiaen, Durkó, Parry, Reizenstein and Vaughan-Williams; *Style—* Erich Gruenberg, Esq, OBE; ✉ 22 Spencer Drive, Hampstead Garden Suburb, London N2 0QX (☎ and fax 020 8455 4360)

GRUFFUDD, Ioan; *b* 6 October 1973, Cardiff; *Educ* RADA; *m* 14 Sept 2007, Alice Evans; 2 da (Ella Betsi Evans Griffith b 6 Sept 2009, Elsie Marigold Evans Griffith b 13 Sept 2013); *Career* actor; *Theatre* incl The Decameron (Gate Theatre), That Play Wot I Wrote (The Right Size, Wyndhams); *Television* incl: Austin, Pobol Y Cwm, William Jones, A Relative Stranger, Poldark, Hornblower (voted Best Actor in a Drama Series Biarritz Int TV Festival 1999), Great Expectations, Love in the 21st Century, Warriors, Hornblower II, Man and Boy, The Forsythe Saga, Hornblower III, Century City, Ringer 2011–12, Glee 2013, Forever (ABC) 2015; *Film* incl: Wilde 1997, Titanic 1997, Solomon and Gaenor 1999, Very Annie Mary 1999, Another Life 1999, Shooters 2000, 102 Dalmations 2000, Happy Now? 2001, Black Hawk Down 2001, The Gathering 2001, This Girl's Life 2003, King Arthur 2004, Fantastic Four 2005, Amazing Grace 2006, Fantastic Four: Rise of the Silver Surfer 2007, Tony Blair in W 2008, The Kid 2010, Sanctum 2011, Foster 2011, Horrible Bosses 2011, San Andreas 2015, Keep Watching 2016; *Style—* Ioan Gruffudd, Esq; ✉ c/o Framework Entertainment, 9057 Nemo Street, West Hollywood, CA 90069 (☎ 001 310 858 0333)

GRUFFYDD, Llyr Huws; AM; s of Peter Hughes Griffiths, and Meinir, *née* Lloyd; *b* 25 September 1970, Aberystwyth, Wales; *Educ* Ysgol Gyfun Bro Myrddin, UC of Wales Aberystwyth; *m* 20 Aug 2002, Delyth Ann, *née* Morris; 3 s (Bedwyr Clwyd, Osian Gwyn, Iwan Berwyn), 1 da (Anest Mair); *Career* youth devpt offr Menter Cwm Gwendraeth (Welsh language initiative) 1992–97, sr voluntary sector offr Wales Youth Agency and dir Cncl for Wales of Voluntary Youth Servs 1997–99, researcher and press offr for Jill Evans, MEP *qv* and Eurig Wyn 1999–2003, devpt mangr Menter a Busnes 2003–10, NE Wales consultancy mangr Nat Trust 2010–11, memb Nat Assembly for Wales (Plaid

Cymru) N Wales 2011–; *Style*— Llyr Gruffydd, Esq, AM; ✉ National Assembly for Wales, Cardiff Bay, Cardiff CF99 1NA

GRUNDY, Rev Canon Dr Malcolm Leslie; s of Arthur James Grundy (d 1993), and Gertrude Alice, *née* Carter (d 1995); *b* 22 March 1944, Biggleswade, Beds; *Educ* Sandye Place Sch, Mander Coll Bedford, King's Coll London (AKC), Open Univ (BA), Univ of Leeds (PhD); *m* 1972, Wendy Elizabeth, da of Stanley Gibson (d 1977); 1 s (Stephen James b 1973); *Career* architectural asst Bedford BC 1959–63, Community Serv Vols 1963–64, King's Coll London 1964–69, curate Doncaster Parish Church 1969–72, chaplain then sr chaplain Sheffield Industrial Mission 1972–80, dir of educn and community Dio of London 1980–86, team rector of Huntingdon 1986–91, hon canon of Ely 1987–94, dir Avec 1991–94, archdeacon of Craven (Dio of Bradford) 1994–2005, canon emeritus Bradford 2005–, dir Fndn for Church Leadership 2005–09; co-fndr: Edward King Inst for Miny Devpt, MODEM (chair 1999–2004); fndr ed Ministry jl 1986–; non-exec dir Yorkshire Culture 2004–08, tstee Women's Educn Partnership 2010–; visiting fell York St John Univ; *Books* Light in the City (1990), An Unholy Conspiracy (1992), Community Work (1995), The Parchmore Partnership (ed, 1995), Management and Ministry (1996), Understanding Congregations (1998), Faith On the Way (with Peter Ball, 2000), What They Don't Teach You at Theological College (2003), What's New in Church Leadership? (2007), Leadership and Oversight (2011), Multi-Congregation Ministry (2015); *Recreations* classic cars, gardening; *Style*— The Rev Canon Dr Malcolm Grundy; ✉ 11 Givendale Grove, York YO10 3QF (☎ 01904 422999, e-mail mlgweg@gmail.com)

GRUT, Lennart; *Educ* Loretto, Copenhagen Tech Univ (MSc); *Career* Folmer Anderson Associates Consltg Engineers Copenhagen 1966–68; sr engineer Ove Arup & Partners: London 1968–72, France 1972–75; md Arup France 1975–81, res and devpt dir UNITATA Bhd Malaysia 1981–83, Elga Services Pte Ltd Singapore (mgmnt conslts) 1983–86; Richard Rogers Partnership: dir, md Richard Rogers Gmbh Germany, dir Richard Rogers Japan, IT dir; *Projects* incl: Nantes and Epone shopping centres France, Marseille Airport Masterplan and extension France, Ct of Human Rights Strasbourg France, Bordeaux High Ct France, Potsdamer Platz devpt Berlin Germany, Skylight office and housing devpt Frankfurt Germany, Gifu Virtual Reality Res Centre Japan, new terminal Barajas Airport Madrid Spain, terminal 5 Heathrow Airport London; *Style*— Lennart Grut, Esq; ✉ Richard Rogers Partnership, Thames Wharf, Rainville Road, London W6 9HA

GRUZDYEV, Dmitri; s of Gennady Valyentinovich Gruzdyev, and Ludmilla Stepanovna Oulitina, of St Petersburg, Russia; *b* 27 April 1971; *Educ* Vaganova Acad of Ballet St Petersburg; *m* 1993, Sarah Victoria Arnott Gruzdeva, da of John Marshall; 2 s (Nicolas Alexander Gruzdev b 29 April 2003, Edward John Gruzdev b 4 Feb 2006); *Career* ballet dancer; Kirov 1989–93; English Nat Ballet: jr soloist 1993–95, soloist 1995, sr soloist 1995, princ dancer 1997–2006, sr princ dancer 2006–; *Recreations* cinema, motorcars, travelling, wine, gardening; *Style*— Dmitri Gruzdyev, Esq; ✉ English National Ballet, 39 Jay Mews, London SW7 2ES (☎ 020 8581 1245, fax 020 7225 0827)

GRYK, Wesley Casimir; s of Wesley Casimir Gryk, Sr (d 2001), and Bernice Bieluch Gryk (d 1993); *b* 12 May 1949, Manchester, CT; *Educ* East Catholic HS Manchester CT, Harvard Coll (BA), Warsaw Univ (Fulbright fell), Harvard Law Sch (JD); *Career* slr; memb NYC Bar; judicial clerk to Hon Constance Baker Motley (US district judge Manhattan NY) 1975–76, with Shearman and Sterling NY and Hong Kong 1976–80, dep rep and legal advsr to UNHCR 1980–81, dep legal advsr then dep head of the research dept Int Secretariat Amnesty Int 1981–86, slr B M Birnberg and Co 1988–94, fndr and sr ptnr Wesley Gryk Slrs LLP 1995–; former memb Cncl and Legal Affrs and Policy Bd Law Soc; former memb Bd: Refugee Legal Centre, Redress Tst, Legal Aid Practitioners Gp; travelled extensively on int human rights missions; fndr and vol UK Lesbian and Gay Immigration Gp; *Publications* AIDS: A Guide to the Law (1990), Advising Gay and Lesbian Clients (1999), Advising Clients with HIV and AIDS (2000); *Recreations* dancing, reading, travel; *Style*— Wesley Gryk, Esq; ✉ Wesley Gryk Solicitors LLP, 140 Lower Marsh, London SE1 7AE (☎ 020 7401 6887, fax 020 7261 9985, e-mail wesley@gryklaw.com)

GRYLLS, Bear; s of Sir Michael Grylls (d 2001), and Lady Grylls; *b* 7 June 1974; *Educ* Eton, Birkbeck Coll London; *m* 2000, Shara, *née* Cannings Knight; 3 s (Jesse b 10 June 2003, Marmaduke b 6 April 2006, Huckleberry b 15 Jan 2009); *Career* served as trooper E Sqdn 21 SAS Regt; youngest Br climber to reach summit of Mt Ama Dablam 1997, youngest Br climber to reach summit of Mt Everest 1998, motivational speaker, expdn ldr and TV personality 1998– (perfs incl: Oxford Union, RGS, Explorers Club, Scotland Yard, face of Sure for Men deodorant TV commercials), ldr Arnold & Son Trans Atlantic Arctic expdn 2003, ldr Mumm high altitude balloon dinner, ldr GKN Mission Everest paramotor flight; Chief Scout The Scout Assoc (youngest ever); nominated Boardman Tasker Mountain Literature Award 2000; ambass Prince's Tst; TV presenter: Escape to the Legion (series, Channel 4) 2005, Man vs Wild with Bear Grylls (6 seasons, Discovery Channel), Born Survivor: Bear Grylls (series, Channel 4), The Island With Bear Grylls (series, Channel 4, Best Reality and Constructed Factual Show BAFTA 2015), Mission Survive (ITV), Running Wild (NBC); Hon Lt Cdr RN, Hon Lt Col RM; *Books* Facing Up (2000), The Kid Who Climbed Everest (2001), Facing the Frozen Ocean (2004, shortlisted Sports Book of the Year), Born Survivor (Sunday Times Top 10 bestseller), Bear Grylls' great Outdoors Adventures (2008), Mud, Sweat and Tears (autobiography, 2011, no. 1 bestseller), A Survival Guide for Life (2012), True Grit (2013), Your Life: Train For It (2014), Extreme Food (2015), Ghost Fight (2015); *Children's Fiction* Mission: Survival: Gold of the Gods, Way of the Wolf, Sands of the Scorpion, Tracks of the Tiger, Claws of the Crocodile, Rage of the Rhino; *Recreations* climbing, sailing, martial arts, yoga, skydiving, piano and guitar, my wife Shara and our Welsh island hideaway; *Clubs* SAS Regt Assoc, Alpine, RGS; *Style*— Bear Grylls, Esq; ✉ website www.beargrylls.com

GRYLLS, Vaughan Frederick; s of late Herman Grylls, and late Muriel, *née* Butler; *b* 10 December 1943; *Educ* Newark Magnus GS, Slade Sch of Fine Art, UCL; *m* 1, 1973 (m dis 1988) Gillian Daniell; 1 da (Pinny); m 2, 1994, Polly Powell, *qv*; 1 da (Hattie), 1 s (George); *Career* lectr Univ of Reading 1970–71, lectr Homerton Coll Cambridge 1971–73, sr lectr Roehampton Inst 1974–84, prof Williams Coll Mass 1984–88, prof and dean of Sch of Art and Design Univ of Wolverhampton 1989–96, dir and chief exec Kent Inst of Art and Design 1996–2005, retired as founding chief exec Univ for the Creative Arts 2005 (prof emeritus 2006); fndr UK Arts and Design Insts Assoc (UKADIA) 2002, fndr The Lack of Principals 2007; dir Pavilion Books Gp Ltd 2015–; chair of govrs Dallington Sch London 2008–; currently parent rep Interview Panel for Conslt Appts Great Ormond St Hosp; FRSA 1995; *Exhibitions* numerous since 1970 incl: ICA, Whitechapel, Arnolfini, Photographers' Gallery London, Old Truman Brewery London, Sadler's Wells London, Piper Gallery London, GX Gallery London, London Gp; *Public Collections* Polaroid Inc, Unilever, Pfizer, Welsh Arts Cncl, Nat Museum of Media, Contemporary Arts Soc; *Publications* Oxford Then & Now (2009), Cambridge Then & Now (2011), I Brought This In Case – The 1960s, Four Art Schools and Me (2014), Hong Kong Then & Now (2016), Singapore Then & Now (2016); *Recreations* driving a Bristol 411, playing the piano in a pale imitation of Charlie Kunz; *Clubs* Chelsea Arts, Savile; *Style*— Vaughan Grylls; ✉ website www.vaughangrylls.com; c/o Anand Sagger (e-mail anand@gxgallery.com)

GUARD, Howard Anthony; DL (2010); s of Herbert William Guard (d 2001), of Knebworth, Herts, and Lilian Maud Guard (d 1995); *b* 27 February 1946, London; *Educ* Ardingly, Univ of Leeds (BA); *m* 1972, Sheila Kathleen, da of Reginald Hyder; 4 s (Thomas Benjamin b 1973, Charles William b 1975, Edward Oliver b 1979, George Henry Hubert b 1982); *Career* asst dir in feature films 1968–73, prodr working in advtg industry 1973–77, fndr Howard Guard Productions (making advtg films and documentaries) 1977–; dir Eton at Work 1995; tstee Nat Hosp Fndn of Neurosurgery London 1990–2010, chm St Albans Cathedral Fabric Tst 2007–13; High Sheriff Herts 2007–08; Freeman City of London 1995, Liveryman Worshipful Co of Barber-Surgns; Hon Dr Univ of Herts 2015; *Clubs* Groucho; *Style*— Howard Guard, Esq, DL; ✉ Netherwylde Farm, Radlett, Hertfordshire WD7 7HS

GUBBAY, Raymond; CBE (2001); s of David Gubbay, and Ida Gubbay; *b* 2 April 1946, London; *Educ* Univ Coll Sch Hampstead; *m* 1972 (m dis), Johanna Quirke; 2 da; *Career* concert, opera and ballet promoter; fndr Raymond Gubbay Ltd 1966; memb Bd Royal Philharmonic Orch, memb Bd of Govrs Central Sch of Ballet; Hon FRAM, Hon FTCL; *Recreations* living in France, my six grandchildren; *Style*— Raymond Gubbay, Esq, CBE; ✉ Raymond Gubbay Ltd, Dickens House, 15 Tooks Court, London EC4A 1QH

GUBBINS, Prof David; s of Albert Edmund Gubbins (d 1964), and Joyce Lucy Gubbins (d 1994); *b* 31 May 1947; *Educ* King Edward VI GS Southampton (fndn scholar), Trinity Coll Cambridge (exhibitioner, BA), Univ of Cambridge (PhD); *m* 20 May 1972, Margaret Stella, da of James Francis McCloy; 1 s (Matthew Jonathan b 5 Aug 1975), 2 da (Katherine Joyce b 6 April 1977, Clare Margaret b 1 Sept 1981); *Career* visiting research fell Univ of Colorado 1972–73, instr in applied mathematics MIT 1973–74, postdoctoral research asst and pt/t adjunct asst prof UCLA 1974–76; Univ of Cambridge: postdoctoral research asst Dept of Geodesy and Geophysics 1976–77, sr assoc in research Dept of Geodesy and Geophysics 1977–81, fell Churchill Coll and lectr in mathematics for natural sci 1978–90, asst dir of research Dept of Earth Sci 1981–89; Univ of Leeds: prof of geophysics Dept of Earth Sci 1989–2000, head of Geophysics 1989–2000 res prof of earth sci 2000–09, emeritus prof of Geophysics 2009–; research assoc: Inst of Geophysics and Planetary Physics, Scripps Inst of Oceanography Univ of California San Diego 2009–; hon prof Schs of Mathematics and Sch of Geosciences Univ of Sydney 2011–; pres Studies of the Earth's Deep Interior 1999–2003; Cecil and Ida Green Scholar: Inst of Geophysics and Planetary Physics, Scripps Inst of Oceanography 2000–01; memb: Royal Astronomical Soc 1972–, Soc of Exploration Geophysicists 1992–; Murchison Medal Geological Soc 1999, Gold Medal Royal Astronomical Soc 2003, John Adam Fleming Medal American Geophysical Union 2004, Chree Medal and Prize Inst of Physics 2005, Augustus Love Medal European Geosciences Union 2007, Arthur Holmes Medal and hon memb European Geosciences Union 2009; foreign memb Norwegian Acad of Sci and Letters 2005; fell American Geophysical Union (FAGU) 1985 (memb 1972), FInstP 1996; FRS 1996; *Books* Seismology & Plate Tectonics (1990), Time Series Analysis and Inverse Theory for Geophysicists (2004), Encyclopedia of Geomagnetism and Paleomagnetism (ed, 2007); *Recreations* swimming, sailing; *Clubs* Wigtown Bay Sailing; *Style*— Prof David Gubbins, FRS; ✉ School of Earth and Environment, University of Leeds, Leeds LS2 9JT (☎ 0113 343 2251, e-mail gubbins@earth.leeds.ac.uk)

GUBERT, Walter Alexander; *b* 15 June 1947; *Educ* Univ of Florence (LLD), INSEAD (MBA); *m* Caroline, *née* Espagno; 2 da (Amelie b 9 Feb 1979, Elsa b 6 June 1981); *Career* J P Morgan: asst vice-pres Chemicals Analyst Paris 1973–77, vice-pres Treasy Mgmnt Advsy London 1977–81, sr vice-pres Capital Markets NY 1981–87, chief exec J P Morgan Securities Ltd London 1987–90, chm London Mgmnt Ctee 1989–92, head M&A Europe 1989–92, md and co-head Investment Banking EMEA 1992–95, sr exec EMEA 1995–97, vice-chm 1998–2000, global head Investment Banking 1998–2000, vice-chm and memb Bd JPMorgan 1998–2000, chm JPMorgan Investment Bank 2001–04, chm JPMorgan Chase EMEA 2004–; memb Bd of Govrs South Bank Centre 2005–08; *Recreations* golf, tennis, sailing; *Clubs* Wisley, Queenwood; *Style*— Walter Gubert, Esq; ✉ J P Morgan, 25 Bank Street, Canary Wharf, London E14 5JP (☎ 020 7134 3978)

GUELLER, Simon Harris; s of Basil Gueller (d 1990), and Margaret Jane, *née* McDougal; *b* 15 August 1964; *m* 24 Aug 1990, Rena Tania, da of Yiftach Polushko; 2 da (Abigail Hannah b 31 Dec 1990, Zoe Nicole b 6 Aug 1998); *Career* chef; positions incl: Cardinal Wetherby, Prue Leith's outside catering, chef to commercial bank dir, Interlude de Tabaileau, Chelsea Wharfe, head chef Keats Hampstead, pastry chef Wood Hall; prop/chef: Millers Harrogate (joined as head chef) 1989–95, Rascasse Leeds 1995–2000, Guellers Rest Leeds 2000–02, head chef and proprietor The Box Tree Ilkley 2004–; *Awards* for Millers: Egon Ronay 1990–95, Egon Ronay Award for outstanding fish dishes 1991, Egon Ronay star 1995, Good Food Guide 3/5 1990–95, Good Food Guide Co Restaurant of the Year 1993, 3 AA rosettes 1993–95 (2 rosettes 1991–92), Michelin Red M 1995; Egon Ronay Regnl Chef of the Year 1996; for Rascasse: 3 AA rosettes, Egon Ronay star, Michelin star, Michelin Bib Gourmande, Good Food Guide 3*/5, Good Food Guide Regnl Restaurant of the Year, Egon Ronay Regnl Winner Customer Care Award 1997, Yorkshire Life Restaurant of the Year 1997; for Guellers Rest: Yorkshire Life Chef of the Year 2000, Good Food Guide Yorkshire Restaurant of the Year 6/10 2002, Michelin star 2002; for The Box Tree: Michelin star 2005–, 3 AA Rosettes 2005–; *Recreations* football, fishing, music, reading, road cycling; *Style*— Simon Gueller, Esq; ✉ The Box Tree, 35–37 Church Street, Ilkley, West Yorkshire LS29 9DR

GUEST, Richard John; s of Raymond Guest, and Irene, *née* Homes; *b* 9 February 1971, York; *Educ* Fulford Comp Sch Yorks; *m* 27 June 1998, Victoria, *née* Barber; 1 s (William John); *Career* restaurateur; apprenticeship Elliots Hotel York 1987–90, commis chef River Restaurant Savoy Hotel London 1990–93, chef de partie then sous chef Four Seasons Hotel 1993–97, head chef Maison Novelli London 1996–99 (Michelin Star, 3 AA Rosettes), head chef Castle Hotel Taunton 1999–2010 (Michelin Star until 2008, 3 AA Rosettes, Tatler Magazine Best Out of Town Restaurant, Hotel and Caterer Acorn Award), co-owner and chef Augustus 2010–; involvement with: Friends of the Earth, Taste of the West (demonstrating and judging); memb Slow Food Movement (represented Britain at Terre Madra Slow Food Movement in Turin); contributed promotional lit for EBLEX (English Beef and Lamb Execs); *Publications* Your Plaice or Mine (contrib, 1998), Jam with Lamb (2007, Best Local Cookery Book for the UK Gourmand World Cookbook Award 2007); contrib to various magazine incl Hotel & Caterer and Olive Magazine; *Recreations* reading books on food, cooking, keeping fit; *Style*— Richard Guest, Esq

GUEST ALBERT, Revel Sarah; *née* Guest; da of Hon Oscar Guest (d 1958), of Hereford, and Susan Kathleen, *née* Paterson (d 1982); *b* 14 September 1931, London; *Educ* Bedgebury Pk Sch, LSE; *m* 26 Aug 1963, Robert Alan Albert, s of James Albert, of Boston, USA; 1 s (Justin Thomas b 19 Feb 1965), 1 da (Corisande Charlotte b 10 March 1967); *Career* private sec to ldr Lib Pty (Jo Grimond) 1949–51, contested Gen Election and LCC 1951 and 1952, asst ed Time & Tide magazine 1953–55, press offr UK Cncl of the European Movement 1955–57, journalist Westminster Press 1957–59, researcher and prodr Panorama (BBC) 1959–67, bureau chief Public TV Laboratory of US 1967 and 1968, formed Transatlantic Films 1968; prodr and dir 1968–; work incl: Horse Tales, Science of Love, Extreme Body Parts, Trailblazers, The Three Gorges Dam, Treasures of the Yangtse River, Horse Tales, History's Turning Points I & II, Greek Fire, The Horse in Sport, The Monastery of Mount Sinai, A Year in the Life of Placido Domingo, Four American Composers, In Search of Paradise, Paris Lost, Feliks Topolski, Self Encounter – Man in a Fog, Bold as Brass, If It Moves Shoot It, Makin' It, Norman Mailer v Fun City USA; produced 15 operas and ballets from Covent Garden for BBC and NHK 1991–94; exec prodr War Horse 2011 (6 Oscar nominations); chm Hay on Wye Literary Festival 1997–2016 (pres emeritus 2016–); MRTS; *Books* Lady Charlotte – A Biography of the Nineteenth Century (1989), History's Turning Points (1995); *Recreations* horse training, gardening, MFH Golden Valley 1981–90; *Clubs* Turf; *Style*— Mrs Revel Guest Albert;

✉ Cabalva House, Whitney-on-Wye, Hereford HR3 6EX (☎ 01497 831232, mobile 07824 314411, e-mail revelguest@gmail.com)

GUEST GORNALL, Anthony Richard; s of Dr Richard Guest Gornall, and Emma Mildred, *née* Jackson; *Educ* Malvern Coll, Hertford Coll Oxford; *m* 1962, Judith, *née* Redmond, da of Dr Aidan Redmond, of London; 1 da (Lucy), 1 s (Richard); *Career* Cassell & Co Publishers 1960–62, Hutchinson & Co Publishers 1962–65, co-fndr Intercontinental Literary Agency 1965; hereditary memb Preston Guild; *Recreations* golf (winner Sunningdale Fndrs Singles 1994), reading, music, gardening; *Clubs* Oxford and Cambridge, Cheshire Pitt, Sunningdale Golf; *Style*— Anthony Guest Gornall, Esq; ✉ 2 Villiers House, Sunningdale, Berkshire SL5 9RZ (e-mail guestgornall@btinternet.com); c/o Intercontinental Literary Agency, Centric House, 391 Strand, London WC2R 0LT

GUGGENHEIM, John Michael; s of Michael Guggenheim, and Marjorie, *née* Horsfall; *b* 26 December 1967, Wakefield, W Yorks; *Educ* Bradford GS, Univ of Hull (LLB), Chester Law Sch; *m* 6 March 1999, Alison, *née* Balding; 3 da (Isobel Grace b 8 Feb 2003, Hannah Rose b 23 April 2005, Sophie Beatrice b 4 May 2007); *Career* admitted slr of Supreme Court 1994; ptnr Walker Morris 2000–08 (joined 1992), dir Petsco Ltd 2008–, ptnr Lentin Smith Property Mgmnt; *Recreations* music, football, golf; *Style*— John Guggenheim, Esq; ✉ White Cross, 8 Bradford Road, Guiseley Leeds West Yorkshire LS20 8NH

GUI, Gerald P H; s of Col George P C Gui, and Lily M F Gui; *b* 8 June 1962; *Educ* St Bees Sch Cumbria, UCL and Middx Hosp Med Sch London (MB BS, Suckling Prize in neurosciences, Univ of London Laurels), Univ of London (MS); *m* 8 Sept 1992, Corina R, da of Agustin Espinosa; 2 s (Adrian, Marcus (twins) b 26 May 2004); *Career* house surgn Whittington and Royal Northern Hosps 1986–97, house physician Queen Elizabeth II Hosp Welwyn Garden City 1987; SHO: in A&E Royal Free Hosp Med Sch London 1987–88 (also anatomy demonstrator), in cardiothoracic surgery Harefield Hosp 1988–89, in urology and gen and vascular surgery St George's Hosp London 1989–90; registrar in gen surgery: Basildon Hosp 1990–91 (with orthopaedics 1990), Bart's and Homerton Hosp 1991–92, N Middx Hosp London 1992–93; surgical res fell Professorial Surgical Unit Bart's 1993–94, lectr and sr registrar Univ Dept of Surgery St George's Hosp London 1994–96, sr registrar in gen surgery St Helier's NHS Tst Surrey 1996, conslt surgn and head Breast Diagnostic Unit Royal Marsden NHS Tst 1997–, hon sr lectr Inst of Cancer Res London 1997–, coll tutor RCS 1997–2005; Royal Marsden NHS Tst: memb Ctee for Clinical Res, memb Appts Ctee Basic Surgical Trg; memb Teaching Faculty FRCS Course RCS 1995–; examiner Univ of London 2001– (recognised teacher 1998–); involved with Br Cncl Link Project for devpt of breast cancer servs in Sri Lanka 2000–; conslt advsr Marks & Spencer Health Screen Project 1998–2001, symptomatic breast cancer rep London and Thames region Br Assoc of Surgical Oncology 2001–04; delivered numerous oral presentations and invited lectures to symposia and learned societies; chief ed (UK) Women's Oncology Review 2001–06; memb: BMA 1986–, GMC 1986–, Surgical Res Soc 1994–, Br Assoc of Surgical Oncology 1994–, Br Oncological Assoc 1994–, Br Breast Gp 1998– (memb Membership Ctee 2001–07); Surgical Res Soc Travel Award 1993, S Essex Med Educn and Res Tst Award 1993 and 1994, Surgn in Trg Medal RCS(Ed) 1994, Br Oncological Assoc Bursary 1994, RCS Fndn Inc NY Travelling Fellowship 1997 (held at Plastic and Reconstructive Surgery Unit Emory Univ Atlanta); represented Cumbria, UCL and Middx Hosp Med Sch in swimming, rep Univ of London in life saving; pres Univ of London Lifesaving Soc 1985–86 (treas 1981–85), tutor in resuscitation Essex Branch Royal Life Saving Soc 1984; friend ROH, memb Glyndbourne Festival Opera; fell Assoc of Surgns of GB and Ireland 1997 (memb 1996); FRCSEd 1990, FRCS 1991; *Publications* Breast Reconstruction: a woman's choice (contrib, 2002), Gray's Anatomy (contrib, 2008); numerous pubns of original work as scientific manuscripts on breast cancer diagnosis, clinical mgmnt, surgery, operative techniques and tumour biology in peer-reviewed jls; *Recreations* classical music, opera, piano, water sports; *Clubs* Royal Nautical (Santa Cruz); *Style*— Gerald Gui, Esq; ✉ Academic Surgery (Breast Unit), The Royal Marsden NHS Trust, Fulham Road, London SW3 6JJ (☎ 020 7808 2783, fax 020 7808 2673), 145 Harley Street, London W1G 6BJ (☎ 020 7487 5558, fax 020 7487 5559, e-mail gerald.gui@rmh.nhs.uk)

GUILBAUD, Patrick; s of Daniel Guilbaud, and Henriette Guilbaud; *b* 22 March 1952; *Educ* Aero Spatial Pont de Levallois; *m* 10 April 1976, Sally, *née* Lloyd Owen; 1 s (Charles b 24 June 1977), 1 da (Emilie b 22 Sept 1981); *Career* chef; Hotel Moderne Caen 1969, Br Embassy Paris 1970–71, Le Doyen Paris 1972, La Maree Paris 1973, Midland Hotel Manchester 1974; chef and owner: Le Rabelais 1976–80, Restaurant Patrick Guilbaud 1981–; winner numerous Irish and European restaurant awards, incl 2 Michelin Stars; memb Restaurant Assoc of Ireland; Chevalier de l'Ordre du Mérite, Chevalier de la Légion d'Honneur; *Books* Restaurant Patrick Guilbaud: The First Thirty Years; *Recreations* golf, skiing, boating; *Clubs* Royal Dublin Golf, Real Club de Golf Sotogrande, Real Club Valderrama; *Style*— Patrick Guilbaud, Esq; ✉ Restaurant Patrick Guilbaud, 21 Upper Merrion Street, Dublin 2, Ireland (☎ 00 353 1676 4192 , fax 00 353 1661 0052, e-mail rpguilbaud@eircom.net)

GUILD, Prof Elspeth; da of Carman Guild (d 2000), of Toronto, Canada, and Edith Ford Walker (d 1971); *b* 25 June 1954, Toronto, Canada; *Educ* Radboud Univ Nijmegen (PhD); *Career* slr Baileys Shaw & Gillett Slrs 1989–97, ptnr Kingsley Napley Slrs 1997–; prof Law Faculty Radboud Univ Nijmegen 2000–, prof of law Queen Mary Univ of London; memb Immigration Law Practitioners Assoc; *Publications* Immigration Law in the European Community (2001), Legal Elements of European Identity: EU Citizenship and Migration Law (2004), Security and Migration in the 21st Century (2009); *Style*— Prof Elspeth Guild; ✉ Kingsley Napley, Knights Quarter, 14 St John's Lane, London EC1M 4AJ (☎ 020 7814 1200, fax 020 7490 2288, e-mail eguild@kingsleynapley.co.uk)

GUILD, Rear Adm Nigel Charles Forbes; CB (2003); s of William John Forbes Guild (d 1982), and Joan, *née* Innes (d 1957); *b* 9 February 1949; *Educ* Bryanston, BRNC Dartmouth, Trinity Coll Cambridge (MA), Univ of Bristol (PhD), JSDC Greenwich; *m* 10 July 1971, Felicity Jean, da of Hugh Wilson; 2 s (Allan b 17 Feb 1979, Ian b 25 June 1982); *Career* joined RN 1966; served HMS Tenby, midshipman HMS Intrepid, served HMS Hermes, dep project manager Br Underwater Test and Evaluation Centre Range MOD Kyle of Lochalsh, Weapon Engr HMS Euryalus 1982, served STANAVFORLANT, Cdr DGFMP(N) 1984, Sqdn Weapon Engr IKARA Leanders tour, HMS Beaver Armilla patrol Gulf, Staff Weapons Engr Offr Flag Offr Sea Training, Capt 1990, Mil Asst to Chief of Defence Procurement MOD, Surface Flotilla Weapons Offr Fleet Command, Chief Staff Offr (Engrg) Flag Offr Surface Flotilla, Cdre 1996, dir Combat Systems and Equipments MOD Procurement Exec 1996–98, Dir Integrated Project Teams Smart Procurement Implementation 1998, Rear Adm 2000, Exec Dir 4(XD4) Defence Procurement Agency Exec Bd and Controller of the Navy 2000–03, Sr Responsible Owner Carrier Strike and Chief Naval Engr Offr 2004–09, ret; chm Bd Engrg Cncl 2011–; *Recreations* village pantomime, rowing (pres RN and RM ARA); *Style*— Rear Adm Nigel Guild, CB

GUILDFORD, Bishop of 2015–; Rt Rev Andrew John Watson; *Educ* Winchester, CCC Cambridge, Ridley Hall Cambridge; *Career* ordained 1987, curate St Peter's Ipsley Dio of Worcester 1987–91, curate St John and Peter's Notting Hill Dio of London 1991–96, vicar St Stephen's East Twickenham, area dean Hampton 2003–08, bishop of Aston 2008–14; *Style*— The Rt Rev the Bishop of Guildford

GUILLE, Very Rev John Arthur; s of Arthur Leonard Guille (d 1986), of Guernsey, and Winifred Maud, *née* Lane (d 2000); *b* 21 May 1949, Southwell; *Educ* Guernsey GS, Christ Church Coll Canterbury, Univ of London (CertEd), Salisbury and Wells Theological Coll, Univ of Southampton (CertTheol, BTh), Univ of Wales Lampeter (MA); *m* 10 July 1976, Susan; 2 da (Elizabeth Susan b 9 June 1981, Rose Ellen b 27 Feb 1983), 1 s (Peter John b 26 February 1987); *Career* head of religious educn: Stockbridge Co Secdy Sch 1970–72, St Sampsons Secdy Sch Guernsey 1972–73; ordained: deacon 1976, priest 1977; curate Chandlers Ford St Boniface and St Martins 1976–80; priest-in-charge: St John the Evangelist Surrey 1980–84, St Michael and All Angels Bournemouth 1983–84; vicar St John with St Michael 1984–89; chaplain: Talbot Heath Sch for Girls 1980–89, Le Monnaie Chapel 1989–99, Mitchell House/les Bourgs Hospice 1991–99; rector St Andre de la Pommeraye Guernsey 1989–99, vice-dean of Guernsey 1996–99, archdeacon of Basingstoke 1999–2000, residentiary canon of Winchester Cathedral 1999–2007, archdeacon of Winchester 2000–07, dean of Southwell 2007–14 (emeritus dean 2014–); *Publications* A Millennium of Archdeacons (2003); *Recreations* gardening, family history; *Style*— The Very Rev J Guille; ✉ Les Pelerins, Rue de la Planque, St Martin, Guernsey, Channel Islands GY4 6TH (☎ 01481 237168)

GUILOFF, Prof Roberto Jaime; s of Angel Guiloff-Luder (d 1980), of Chile, and Blanca Eva, *née* Davis (d 2014); *b* 4 March 1943, Santiago, Chile; *Educ* Instituto Nacional Santiago, Univ of Chile (honour scholar, BSc, LMed Surg, MD, LPhil), LMSSA; *m* 1, 3 Feb 1968 (m dis 1997); 1 s (Claudio b 10 Nov 1968), 1 da (Carolina b 1 May 1972); m 2, 6 April 1999, Dr Heather Angus-Leppan, da of Prof P Angus-Leppan (d 2001), of Australia; 2 da (Vivien b 17 April 1999, Angelica b 27 April 2001), 1 s (David b 13 July 2002); *Career* trg in neurology Univ of Chile Hosp 1967–72, asst prof of neurology Univ of Chile 1972–74, Queen Elizabeth II scholar (Br Cncl) Nat Hosp for Nervous Diseases 1972–73; registrar in neurology: St Thomas' Hosp 1973–74, Nat Hosps 1974–76; sr registrar in neurology Nat Hosp for Nervous Diseases, Royal Free Hosp and King's Coll Hosp 1976–81; conslt neurologist: Westminster and St Stephen's Hosp 1981–89, Westminster and Charing Cross Hosps 1989–93, Charing Cross and Chelsea and Westminster Hosps 1993–2008, Charing Cross Hosp 2008–; hon conslt neurologist Royal Brompton Hosp London 1993–2006, hon sr lectr in med (neurology) Imperial Coll Sch of Med at Charing Cross Hosp (Charing Cross and Westminster Med Sch until merger 1997) 1987–; dir: Neuromuscular Unit Charing Cross Hosp 1993–2008, Motor Neurone Disease Care and Research Centre Charing Cross Hosp 1994–2011; hon prof of neurology Univ of Chile 2008; sec for int affrs Section of Neurology RSM 1993–2001, sec and treas Motor Neurone Disease Ctee World Fedn of Neurology 1999–2005; hon sec Br Soc for Clinical Neurophysiology 1998–2000; memb: Br Soc for Clinical Neurophysiology 1979, Assoc of Br Neurologists 1981, RSM 1989, Br Peripheral Nerve Soc 2002– (memb cncl 2007–10), Medical Soc of London 2015–; pres: Section of Clinical Neurosciences RSM 2000–2001, W London Medico-Chirurgical Society 2003–2004; FRCP 1987 (MRCP); *Books* Sense Perception in Idealism and The Neurological Theory (1968), Neurological Aspects of Human Retroviruses (contrib chapter, 1992), Motor Neurone Disease (contrib chapter, 1994), Clinical Trials in Neurology (ed, 2001); papers on neurology and neurophysiology; *Recreations* opera, classical music, tennis, gym; *Style*— Prof Roberto Guiloff; ✉ Charing Cross Hospital, Fulham Palace Road, London W6 8RF (☎ 020 8846 1196, fax 020 8746 8420, e-mail r.guiloff@imperial.ac.uk)

GUILOR, Ralph John; s of John Kenneth Guilor, and Ingeborg Elizabeth, *née* Bambach; *b* 1 January 1955; *Educ* Dartford GS, Portsmouth Sch of Architecture (BArch, DipArch); *m* 1, 1979 (m dis 1990); 1 da (Rachel Elizabeth b 1983), 1 s (Edward Charles b 1985); m 2, 1991 (m dis 1992); m 3, 1995; *Career* architect Ralph Guilor Architects; Civic Tst Award 1986, Cheltenham Civic Tst Award 1986, 1996, 1998, 2000, 2001, 2002 and 2004; RIBA; *Recreations* music, art, sport; *Style*— Ralph Guilor, Esq; ✉ Ralph Guilor Architects, Priory Lawn, Priory Place, Cheltenham, Gloucestershire GL52 6HG (☎ 01242 251469, fax 01242 251609, e-mail ralph-guilor@supanet.com)

GUINNESS, (Cecil) Edward; CVO (1986); er s of John Cecil Guinness (d 1970, gs of Richard Samuel Guinness, whose great uncle Arthur was the founder of the family brewing firm), of Clarehaven, Parbold, Lancs, and Betty, *née* Knowles Davies (d 1976); *b* 1924; *Educ* Stowe, Univ of Belfast, Sch of Brewing Birmingham; *m* 1951, Elizabeth Mary Fossett, da of George Alan Thompson (d 1971), of Albrighton Hall, nr Wolverhampton; 3 da (1 of whom decd); *Career* served WWII Offr Cadet RA (invalided out); former vice-chm Guinness Brewing Worldwide; dir: Guinness plc 1971–89 (joined as jr brewer 1945), Wolverhampton and Dudley Breweries 1964–87; chm Harp Lager 1971–87; vice-pres Brewers' Soc (chm 1985–86); chm: UK Tstees Duke of Edinburgh's Cwlth Study Cons 1971–86, Fulmer PC 1973–91 (memb Gerrards Cross with Fulmer PCC 2002–06), Licensed Trade Charities Tst 1981–92, Governing Body Dame Alice Owen's Sch Potters Bar 1981–92, Wine and Spirit Trade's Benevolent Soc 1989–90, Exec Ctee Fulmer Sports and Community Assoc 2003–04; govr and memb Bd of Tstees Queen Elizabeth Fndn for Disabled People 1996–2012 (chm Devpt Tst 1993–96), patron Int Sch of Creative Art 2012–; pres: Performing Arts Centre Campaign Dame Alice Owen's Sch 1997–2002, Fulmer Recreation Ground Campaign 2000–03; former pres and memb Exec Ctee Licensed Victuallers Nat Homes (vice-pres 1991–92), memb Governing Body Lister Inst of Preventive Med 1968–2001, selected as original memb Amersham Area Advsy Team Thames Valley Police Authy 1994; Hon Asst Worshipful Co of Brewers (Master 1977–78); life memb Industrial Soc; Order of Mercy 2010; *Books* The Guinness Book of Guinness (1988), Fulmer's Fallen (co-author, 2009), A Brewer's Tale, Memoirs of Edward Guinness CVO (2014); *Recreations* gardening, writing; *Style*— C Edward Guinness, Esq, CVO; ✉ Huyton Fold, Fulmer Village, Buckinghamshire SL3 6HD (☎ 01753 663179)

GUINNESS, Lt Cdr Sir Howard Christian Sheldon; kt (1981), VRD (1953); s of Edward Douglas Guinness, CBE (d 1983), by his 1 w, Martha Letière, *née* Sheldon; er bro of Sir John Guinness, CB, *qv*; *b* 3 June 1932; *Educ* Eton; *m* 1958, Evadne, da of Capt Evan Gibbs, Coldstream Gds (n of 1 Baron Wraxall); 1 da (Annabel b 1959), 2 s (Christopher b 1963, Dominic b 1966); *Career* served RNR, Lt Cdr; joined S G Warburg & Co 1955, exec dir 1970–85; dir: Harris & Sheldon GP 1960–81, Quality Milk Producers 1988–, Riyad Bank Europe 1993–; dir and dep chm Youghal Carpets (Hldgs) 1972–80; chm N Hants Cons Assoc 1971–74; Wessex Cons Assoc: vice-chm 1974, chm 1975–78, treas 1978–81; dairy farmer, memb Cncl English Guernsey Cattle Assoc 1963–72; *Clubs* White's; *Style*— Lt Cdr Sir Howard Guinness, VRD; ✉ The Manor House, Glanvilles Wootton, Sherborne, Dorset DT9 5QF

GUINNESS, Jasmine; da of Patrick Guinness, and Liz, *née* Casey; *Educ* Headford Sch Kells Co Meath, St Columbas Coll Dublin, Winchester Sch of Art; *Children* 1 s; *Career* model; first job aged 9, full time aged 19; fndr and organiser Clothesline (exhbn, fashion show and auction) 2000–01, co-fndr Honeyjam 2006–; supporter of many charities; *Recreations* horse riding, tennis, reading, photography, teaching son how to play football; *Style*— Miss Jasmine Guinness

GUINNESS, Sir John Ralph Sidney; kt (1999), CB (1985); s of Edward Douglas Guinness, CBE (d 1983), by his 1 w, Martha Letière, *née* Sheldon; yr bro of Lt Cdr Sir Howard Guinness, VRD, *qv*; *b* 23 December 1935; *Educ* Rugby, Trinity Hall Cambridge; *m* 1967, Valerie (d 2014), da of Roger North, JP; 1 s, 1 da (and 1 s decd); *Career* Overseas Devpt Inst 1961–62; FO: joined 1962, Economic Relations Dept 1962–63, third sec UK Mission to UN NY 1963–64, seconded to UN Secretariat as special asst to dep under sec (later under sec Econ and Social Affrs) 1964–66, FCO 1967–69, first sec (econ) High Cmmn Ottawa 1969–72, seconded to Central Policy Review Staff (Cabinet Office) 1972–75 and 1977–79, alternate UK rep to Law of the Sea Conf 1975–77; transferred to Home Civil Serv 1980; Dept of Energy: under sec 1980–83, dep sec 1983–91, perm under sec 1991–92; chm British Nuclear Fuels plc 1992–99; chm Trinity Finance Gp Ltd 1999–2003; non-

G

exec dir: Guinness Mahon Holdings plc 1993–99, Ocean Group plc 1993–99, Mithras Investment Trust 1994–2006; tstee Prince's Youth Business Tst 1994–2000; govr Compton Verney House Tst 2000–03; tstee: Royal Collection Tst 2001–07, Nat Maritime Museum 2005–13; chm Reviewing Ctee on the Export of Works of Art 1995–2003, chair Expert Panel Heritage Lottery Fund 2005, memb Expert Panel Nat Heritage Memorial Fund 2006–13, tstee Heritage Conservation Tst 2007–; hon fell Univ of Central Lancashire 1999; *Recreations* iconography; *Clubs* Brooks's, Beefsteak; *Style*— Sir John Guinness, CB; ✉ 11 Swan Court, Chelsea Manor Street, London SW3 5RX (☎ 020 7352 6945)

GUINNESS, Lucinda Jane (Lulu); OBE (2006); da of Cdr Sir Miles James Rivett-Carnac, Bt, RN, DL, *qv*, of Martyr Worthy Manor, Hants, and April Sally, *née* Villar; *b* 29 May 1960; *Educ* Riddlesworth Hall Diss, Downe House, Queens Gate Sch London, Univ of Cape Town; *m* 11 Nov 1986, Valentine Guy Bryan Guinness, s of 3 Baron Moyne, *qv*; 1 da (Tara Victoria); *Career* handbag designer 1989–; launched career with Lulu Bag (signature briefcase design), subsequently moved into high fashion showing seasonally at The London Design Show and The Coterie NY; numerous stockists worldwide incl London, NY, Paris and Hong Kong; *Recreations* travel, reading, shopping; *Style*— Mrs Lulu Guinness, OBE

GUINNESS, Timothy Whitmore Newton (Tim); s of Capt Eustace Guinness, DSC, RN (d 1980), and Angela Beryl, *née* Hoare (d 1990); *b* 20 June 1947; *Educ* Eton, Magdalene Coll Cambridge (BSc Eng), MIT (MSc); *m* 6 June 1974, Beverley Anne, da of George Mills; 2 s (Edward, Harry), 2 da (Mary, Katherine); *Career* Baring Bros & Co Ltd 1970–77, Guinness Mahon & Co 1977–87 (investment dir 1982–87), chief exec Guinness Flight Global Asset Mgmnt Ltd 1987–97, chief exec Guinness Flight Hambro Asset Mgmnt Ltd 1997–98, chm Investec Guinness Flight 1998–2000, chm Investec Asset Mgmnt 2000–03, chm Guinness Atkinson Asset Mgmnt and Guinness Asset Mgmnt 2003–; dir: S R Europe Tst plc 2001–12, Investec High Income Tst plc 2001–09, Quayle Munro Hldgs plc 2007–12; chm: Brompton Bicycle Co Ltd 2000–, Atlantis Japan Growth Fund Ltd 2002–14; memb Ct of Assts Worshipful Co of Grocers; *Recreations* sailing, skiing, riding, walking; *Clubs* Whites, Travellers, MCC, Royal Yacht Sqdn, City Univ, Royal Inst, Pratts; *Style*— Tim Guinness, Esq

GULBENKIAN, (Basil) Paul (né Boghos Parsegh); s of Krikor Parsegh Gulbenkian (d 1968), of Beaulieu, Hants, and Vergine Gulbenkian (d 1965); *b* 23 March 1940; *Educ* KCS Wimbledon, LSE (LLB); *m* 1; 1 da (Vergine b 24 Nov 1968); m 2, 1 da (Sylvia b 27 July 1972); m 3, 15 Dec 1990, Jacqueline, da of late Bedros Chamlian; *Career* admitted slr 1965; ptnr Isadore Goldman 1970–89, sr ptnr Gulbenkian Harris Andonian and Isadore Goldman 1989–2005, sr ptnr Gulbenkian Andonian 2005–10, ret; asst recorder 1992–98, recorder 1998–2005; pt/t immigration adjudicator 1989–2005, immigration judge 2005–10; conslt: Claremont Richards Slrs 2010–, Gulbenkian Andonian Slrs 2010–, Meadows Ryan Slrs 2010–, OTS Slrs; asst cmmr to the Boundary Cmmn for England and Wales 2000–; chm Serv Mgmnt Ctee Camden CAB 1978–83, pres Holborn Law Soc 1984–85, memb Legal Aid Appeal Panel 1984–89; fndr memb: Slrs' Family Law Assoc (now Resolution), Immigration Law Practitioners' Assoc, Euro Immigration Lawyers' Gp (pres), Cncl of Immigration Judges; memb Int Assoc of Refugee Law Judges; hon pres: Benlian Tst, Essefian Tst; tstee: St Sarkis Charity Tst (hon chm 2005–), various tsts for benefit of Armenian Community, legal advsr/immigration conslt Anglo Cathay Enterprises (ACE); memb Law Soc 1961 (hon auditor 1988–89); hon consul (legal affairs) Embassy of the Republic of Armenia 1998–2012; Freeman City of London 2001; FRSA; *Publications* ed of two books on European immigration law; *Recreations* music, opera, theatre, good food and wine, walking; *Style*— Paul Gulbenkian, Esq

GULL, Prof Keith; CBE (2004); s of David Gull, and Doris, *née* Manging; *b* 29 May 1948, Middlesbrough; *Educ* Eston GS, Queen Elizabeth Coll London (BSc, PhD); *m* 1972, Dianne Hilary Leonora, *née* Elgar; 1 s (David Graeme), 1 da (Hannah Ruth); *Career* lectr, reader and prof Univ of Kent 1972–89, prof, research dean and head of dept Sch of Biological Sciences Univ of Manchester 1989–2002, prof of molecular microbiology Univ of Oxford 2002–, sr research fell Lincoln Coll Oxford 2002–09, princ St Edmund Hall Oxford 2009–; visiting fell Sandoz Forschungsinstitut Vienna 1978, visiting prof McArdle Lab for Cancer Research Univ of Wisconsin Madison 1982–83; chair Research Awards Advsy Ctee Leverhulme Tst, tstee Cancer Research UK 2003–08; author of over 300 scientific pubns; Hon DSc Univ of Kent 2008; FMedSci 1999, FRS 2003, memb EMBO 2011; *Recreations* fly fishing, painting; *Style*— Prof Keith Gull, CBE; ✉ Sir William Dunn School of Pathology, University of Oxford, South Parks Road, Oxford OX1 3RE (☎ 01865 285455, e-mail keith.gull@path.ox.ac.uk); St Edmund Hall, Oxford OX1 4AR (☎ 01865 279076, e-mail keith.gull@seh.ox.ac.uk)

GULLACHSEN, Lorentz; s of Willoughby (Gus) Gullachsen, of Stratford upon Avon, and Doris, *née* Price; *b* 18 March 1951; *Educ* Birmingham Poly Sch of Photography (Dip), Birmingham City Univ (MA); *m* 1982 (m dis 1991), remarried 1992 (m dis 1993), Maxine; 1 da (Laurie-Mo b 23 Nov 1983), 1 s (Jack Gustav b 19 April 1988); *Career* advertising and portrait photographer (specialising in location advtg shooting worldwide); fndr Pictures Studio Birmingham 1974–88, working from London 1988–, estab GULHOS (producing visual communication for the travel and hospitality industry) 2014–; numerous gp/association exhbns (incl Movers and Shakers (Birmingham Symphony Hall) 2005), has published extensively in all continents; visiting lectr Birmingham Inst of Art and Design, assoc lectr Univ of Derby; work archived at Birmingham Central Library and Nat Portrait Gall; Association of Photographers Awards incl Silver/Merits 1988–93 and Gold 1989, Gold Benson and Hedges Professional Awards 1990, Open W Midlands Biannual Arts Prize 2010; memb Assoc of Photographers 1977; *Recreations* photography, game shooting, surfing; *Clubs* Birmingham Press; *Style*— Lorentz Gullachsen, Esq; ✉ The Barn Studios, Preston Fields, Clifford Chambers, Stratford upon Avon CV37 8LA (☎ 07836 504777, e-mail lorentz@gullachsen.com, websites www.gullachsen.com and www.gulhos.com, Linkedin gullachsen)

GULLAN, Richard Wilson; s of Archibald Gordon Gullan, OBE, and Helena Gullan; *b* 1953; *Educ* Merchant Taylors', Med Coll of St Bartholomew's Hosp (BSc, MB BS); *m* 1979, Christine; 4 c; *Career* post-grad training in London, Manchester, Cambridge, Edinburgh and London 1977–88, conslt neurosurgeon 1988, sr neurosurgeon King's Coll Hosp and hon conslt neurosurgeon Maudsley and Bethlam Royal Hosp London, currently sr conslt neurosurgeon King's Coll Hosp London; ind practice: London Neurosurgery Partnership, Harley Street, Blackheath, Kent Inst of Medicine and Surgery; Liveryman Worshipful Soc of Apothecaries; memb: Soc of Br Neurological Surgns, Br Assoc of Spinal Surgeons, North American Spine Soc, Br Neuro-Oncology Soc, BMA; FRCP, FRCS 1982, FRSM; *Recreations* violinist (concertmaster European Doctor's Orch), golf; *Clubs* Royal St George's and Royal Cinque Ports Golf, Oxford and Cambridge, Bromley Music; *Style*— Richard Gullan, FRCP, FRCS; ✉ Clinical Neurosciences Centre (Neurosurgical Offices), King's College Hospital, Denmark Hill, London SE5 9RS (☎ 020 3299 3117, fax 020 3299 3280, e-mail richardgullan@nhs.net)

GULLICK, His Hon Stephen John; s of David Gullick (d 2007), and Evelyn, *née* Norton (d 2003); *b* 22 February 1948, Hitchin, Herts; *Educ* Taunton Sch, Univ of Birmingham; *m* 6 Jan 1973, Lesley; 2 s (Mathew b 9 April 1977, Daniel b 25 Nov 1982); *Career* called to the Bar Grays Inn 1971; practice as barrister North Eastern Circuit 1971–98, , standing counsel HM Customs and Excise North Eastern Circuit 1992–98, circuit judge 1998–2015, resident judge Bradford Crown Court 2001–09, hon recorder of Bradford 2002–09; *Style*— His Hon Stephen Gullick; ✉ St Albans Crown Court, Bricket Road, St Albans AL1 2JW

GULLIVER, Trevor; s of John Gulliver, and Eugenie Devose, *née* Barsley; *b* 29 July 1953; *Educ* Colfes Sch London, Bournemouth Univ; *m* 1984, Nicola; 2 s (Hugo, Bertie); *Career* restaurateur and mgmnt conslt; md Mobile Merchandising Co Ltd 1977–87, md Groupe Forest Hill UK 1987–91, founding ptnr The Fire Station Waterloo 1991–94 (Evening Standard Pub of the Year and other awards), ceo St John Restaurant Gp (https://www.stjohngroup.uk.com, incl HG Wines, St John Bakery and Boulevard Napoleon Winery La Liviniere, France) 1993– (numerous national and international awards), dir Vinum Restaurants Ltd (operating Cantina Vinopolis and Wine Wharf London) and Brew Wharf Ltd 1997–2011; creator of other restaurants incl: Putney Bridge, Wine Wharf at Borough Market, Bar Blue Bankside; wine columnist, food and wine judge, regular int speaker and retained conslt to projects in devpt; FCMI 1974; *Recreations* squash, the arts, wine; *Clubs* RAC; *Style*— Trevor Gulliver, Esq; ✉ St John Restaurant Group, 26 St John Street, London EC1M 4AY (☎ 020 7553 9842, e-mail PA: kitty@stjohnresaurant.com); Trevor Gulliver Consultancy (e-mail tg@trevorgulliver.com)

GUMBEL, Elizabeth-Anne; QC (1999); da of Walter Gumbel (d 1980), and Muriel Gumbel (d 1987), of London; *Educ* St Paul's Girls Sch, Wycombe Abbey, LMH Oxford (MA); *m* 1984, Michael Wainwright; 1 da (Ruth b 21 Oct 1988), 1 s (Mark b 6 Jan 1990); *Career* called to the Bar 1974; practising barrister specialising in clinical negligence and personal injury; memb Editorial Ctee Clinical Risk; memb: PNBA, PIBA, Family Law Bar Assoc; *Style*— Miss Elizabeth-Anne Gumbel, QC; ✉ Chambers of Philip Havers QC, 1 Crown Office Row, London EC4Y 7HH (☎ 020 7797 7500, fax 020 7797 7550, e-mail lizanne.gumbel@1cor.com)

GUMLEY, Frances; *see:* Gumley-Mason, Frances

GUMMER, Rt Hon Benedict Michael (Ben); PC (2016), MP; s of The Rt Hon the Lord Deben, *qv*, and Penelope Jane (Penny), *née* Gardner; *b* 19 February 1978, London; *Educ* St John's Coll Sch Cambridge, Tonbridge Sch, Peterhouse Cambridge; *Career* co dir 2001–10; MP (Cons) Ipswich 2010–; paymaster gen and min for the Cabinet Office 2016–; writer; *Books* The Scourging Angel: The Black Death in the British Isles (2009); *Style*— The Rt Hon Ben Gummer, MP; ✉ House of Commons, London SW1A 0AA (e-mail ben@bengummer.com)

GUNESEKERA, Romesh; *b* Colombo, Sri Lanka; *Career* author; FRSL 2004; Sri Lanka Ranjana 2005; *Books* Monkfish Moon (1992), Reef (1994), The Sandglass (1998), Heaven's Edge (2002), The Match (2006), The Spice Collector (2008), The Prisoner of Paradise (2012); *Style*— Romesh Gunesekera; ✉ website www.romeshgunesekera.com, Twitter @romeshg; A M Heath & Co Ltd, 6 Warwick Court, Holborn, London WC1R 5DJ

GUNEWARDENA, Desmond Anthony Lalith (Des); s of Neville Paul Kingsley Gunewardena, of Old Coulsdon, Surrey, and Muriel G, *née* Perera; *b* 11 August 1957, Kandy, Sri Lanka; *Educ* Wimbledon Coll, Univ of Bristol (BSc); *m* Aug 1991, Elizabeth, *née* Pask; 1 da (Saskia b April 1992), 1 s (Dominic b April 1994); *Career* CA 1981; Ernst & Young 1978–1984; Heron International: head of financial planning 1984–87, finance directorships 1987–89; finance dir Conran Roche 1989–91; Conran Holdings: finance dir 1991–95, ceo 1995–2006, dep chm 2006–; chm and chief exec D&D London 2006–; non-exec dir London First; FRSA 2002; *Recreations* tennis, skiing, chess; *Style*— Des Gunewardena, Esq; ✉ D&D London, 16 Kirby Street, London EC1N 8TS (☎ 020 7716 7800, e-mail des@danddlondon.com)

GUNN, Catherine Rachel (Cathy); da of late John Sinclair Gunn, of Auldearn, Nairn, and late Rosemary Elizabeth, *née* Williams; *b* 28 May 1954; *Educ* St Swithun's Sch Winchester, Univ of Durham (BA), Univ of Edinburgh (Dip Business Admin), Birkbeck Coll Univ of London (MA); *m* 1994, Charles Guybon Hutson; 1 s (Rollo Guybon Hutson, b 8 Nov 1994), 1 da (Tallulah Rosemary Hutson b 4 June 1996); *Career* investment analyst Touche Remnant & Co 1976–78; fin writer: Investors Chronicle 1978–80, The Times 1980–81, freelance 1981–83; fin writer and dep ed Financial Weekly 1983–86, City ed Today 1987–91 (dep City ed 1986–87), fin ed The People 1993–99, writer, broadcaster and freelance conslt 1991–; dir ArtHut Ltd 1999–, devpt mangr Chickenshed Theatre Co 2006–07, freelance arts and fundraiser 2007–, chair Islington Carers Centre 2009–13; FRSA; *Publications* Fraud: The Growth Industry of the Eighties (with Mihir Bose, 1989), Nightmare on Lime Street: Whatever happened to Lloyd's of London (1992 and 1993), High Street Robbery – How the Banks hold up their Customers (1993); *Recreations* arts, travel, writing; *Clubs* Academicians Room; *Style*— Cathy Gunn, FRSA; ✉ ArtHut Ltd, 116 Hazellville Road, London N19 3NA

GUNN, (Anthony) William; s of William Arthur Gunn, OBE (d 1988), of Alton, Hants, and Diana Elizabeth, *née* Taylor (d 1972); *b* 21 May 1946; *Educ* Radley, Corpus Christi Coll Oxford (MA), Walter Sichel scholarship, WSET dip (Rouyer Guillet cup); *m* 6 June 1970, Amanda Marson, 3 da of Anthony Stedman Till; 2 da (Fiona Elizabeth b 10 July 1973, Rachel Georgina b 20 July 1977); *Career* Grants of St James's Ltd 1968–81: wine buyer 1977–81, buying dir Hatch Mansfield & Co; controller Wines and Spirits ASDA Stores Ltd 1981–83; Dent & Reuss Ltd (H P Bulmer plc) 1983–90; md Pol Roger Ltd 1990–2007; Inst of Masters of Wine: chm 1997–98; chm MW Educn and Examination Bd 1999–2002; chm: French Wines Ctee Wine & Spirit Assoc 1980–81, Champagne Agents Assoc 1993;jury memb Gault-Millau 'Olympiades of Wines' 1977, judge various nat and int wine shows; pres Royal Warrant Holders' Assoc 2010–11; tstee Queen Elizabeth Scholarship Tst 2007–11; Freeman City of London 1988, Liveryman Worshipful Co of Fishmongers 1987; MW 1974; Chevalier de l'Ordre du Mérite Agricole 1983, Offr de l'Ordre des Coteaux de Champagne, Chevalier du Tastevin; *Books* contrib: Wines of the World (1981), The Wine Drinker's Handbook (1982), Which? Wine Guide (1983–86); *Recreations* fly fishing, travel, classical music and opera; *Clubs* Oxford and Cambridge; *Style*— William Gunn, Esq; ✉ The Stone Barn, Woolhope, Hereford HR1 4QR (☎ 01432 860624, e-mail derwentgunn@tiscali.co.uk)

GUNNING, Christopher; s of Alexis Lambertus Gunning (d 1962), of Cheltenham and London, and Janet Alice, *née* Bennett (d 1993); *b* 5 August 1944; *Educ* Hendon Co GS, Guildhall Sch of Music and Drama (BMus); *m* 17 June 1974, Annie Christine, da of Flt Lt Clifford William Cornwall Farrow (d 1985), of Bristol; 4 da (Olivia b 1975, Pollyanna b 1977, Verity b 1981, Chloe b 1985); *Career* composer; TV and film scores incl: Rogue Male 1975, Charlie Muffin 1979, Day of the Triffids 1981, Wilfred and Eileen 1981, Flame to the Phoenix 1982, East Lynne 1982, Children's Opera Rainbow Planet 1983, Rebel Angel 1987, Porterhouse Blue 1987 (BAFTA award for the Best Original TV Music), Agatha Christie's Poirot (BAFTA award for Best Original TV Music) 1989, When the Whales Came (Royal Premiere 1989, nominated British Film Institute Anthony Asquith award for Best Film Score 1990), Yorkshire Glory 1990, Under Suspicion 1991 (Ivor Novello award for Best Film Score), The Big Battalions 1992 (BAFTA nomination for Best TV Music), Midnight Movie 1993, The Glass Virgin 1995, The Affair 1995, All or Nothing at All, Middlemarch (BAFTA Award for Best TV Music), Karaoke and Cold Lazarus 1996 (nominated for Ivor Novello award), Rebecca 1997 (Ivor Novello Award for Best TV Score), Firelight 1997 (Ivor Novello Award for Best Film Score), The Last Train 1999, Anchor Me 2000, The Innocent 2000, Poirot 2001, Wild Africa 2001, Pollyanna 2002, The Boy David 2002, Flight of Fancy 2002, Rosemany and Thyme 2003, Five Little Pigs 2004, Death on the Nile 2004, The Hollow 2004, Sad Cypress 2004, La Mome 2006, La Vie en Rose 2007 (Best Original Film Score BAFTA), Grace of Monaco 2014; concert works incl: Concerto for Saxophone 1998, The Lobster 1998, String Quartet 1998, Aunt Vita 2001, Piano Concerto 2001, Symphony 2002, Symphony No 2 2003, Oboe Concerto 2004, Light and Dark Music for Strings 2005, Symphony No 3 2005, Symphony

No 4 2006, Concerto for Clarinet and Orchestra 2008, Symphony No 5 2010, Symphony No 6 2010, Concertino for Flute and Small Orchestra 2010, Concerto for Guitar and Orchestra 2011, Night Voyage 2012, Hector's Return 2012, Symphony No 7 2013, Trio for Violin, Cello and Piano 2014; Gold Badge Award BASCA 2011; ARCM, AGSM; *Books* First Book of Flute Solos, Second Book of Flute Solos, Really Easy Flute Book, Really Easy Trumpet Book, Really Easy Horn Book; *Recreations* walking, reading, horticulture; *Style*— Christopher Gunning, Esq; ✉ Woodleys, Croxley Haall Woods, Rickmansworth, Hertfordshire WD3 3BE (e-mail christopher@christopher-gunning.co.uk)

GUNSTON, Sir John Wellesley; 3 Bt (UK 1938), of Wickwar, Co Gloucester; o s of Sir Richard Wellesley Gunston, 2 Bt (d 1991), and his 2 w, Joan Elizabeth Marie, *née* Forde; *b* 25 July 1962; *Educ* Harrow, RMA Sandhurst; *m* 1 Sept 1990 (m dis 1998), Rosalind Gordon, yst da of Edward Gordon Eliott, of Bower's Mill House, nr Guildford, Surrey; 1 s (Richard St George b 3 July 1992); *Heir* s, Richard Gunston; *Career* cmmnd 1 Bn Irish Gds; chm The Rory Peck Tst and Award 1995–97, md Hard News Ltd 1998–, dir NWF Productions 1995–; memb Soc of Authors 1994; FRGS 1988, FRSAA 1995, FRAS 1998; *Clubs* Special Forces, Cavalry and Guards; *Style*— Sir John Gunston, Bt

GUPTARA, Prof Prabhu; *b* 5 February 1949, New Delhi, India; *Educ* St Stephen's Coll Delhi (BA, MA); *Career* univ lectr India 1970–79, mgmnt conslt and trainer 1979–95, fndr chm Prabhu Guptara Associates 1984–96, chm ADVANCE Management Training Ltd 1988–2003, gp dir Organisational Learning & Transformation Union Bank of Switzerland 1995–98, dir Orgn and Exec Devpt Wolfsberg (subsid of UBS AG) Switzerland 1999–2011, chm Relational Thinking Network 2013–15, exec dir Relational Analytics Ltd 2015–; fndr ed Organisations and People 1994–97; prof or visiting prof: Int Inst for the Mgmnt of Telecommunications Univ of Fribourg Switzerland, European Inst of Purchasing Mgmnt, INSEAD France, Carlson Sch of Business Univ of Minnesota, MIT USA, Univ of St Thomas USA, Univ of Keio Japan, Univ of Sogang Korea, Rotterdam Sch of Mgmnt Netherlands 1990–93; distinguished prof of global business, mgmnt and public policy William Carey Univ India 2009–; distinguished speaker IndUS Forum USA 2012; lectured at: UNCTAD, Cncl of Europe, Univ of London, Univ of Oxford, Univ of Sorbonne, Univ of Warwick, Assoc Bank Inst (Frankfurt), Henley Mgmnt Coll, Int Inst for Mgmnt Devpt (Lausanne), Sloane Sch of Mgmnt MIT, Int Mgmnt Assoc of Japan, Singapore Inst of Mgmnt, Keizai Koho Centre of the Keidanren Japan, Wharton Sch of Business Univ of Pennsylvania USA, Nat Univ of Singapore, Univ of Cambridge; contrib to Forward Press magazine (columnist), Gower Handbook of Management, Gower Handbook on Quality, International Encyclopaedia of Business and Management, International Indian magazine (columnist) and other reference books, as well as to numerous newspapers and magazines incl: FT, Daily Telegraph, The Times, The Guardian, The Spectator, New Statesman, New Society, International Management, Jl of Japanese Trade and Industry, Training & Development (columnist); memb Cncl: Inst of Mgmnt, Int Fedn of Trg and Devpt Orgns, Assoc for Mgmnt Educn and Devpt, Ridley Hall Fndn 1998–2003; memb Organising Ctee: stars08, stars09, stars10 and stars 11, Zermatt Summitt 2010 and 2011; memb Bd: Inst of Mgmnt Univ of St Gallen Switzerland 2007–, alpha-Medicus GmbH Munich 2015–; chair Career Innovation Res Gp 1998–, vice-chm Guildford Branch Inst of Trg and Devpt, judge MSC Nat Trg Awards 1988, judge Deo Gloria Award for Fiction 1990 (chm judges panel 1991 and 1992); govr Univ of Westminster (formerly Poly of Central London) 1989–92; Freeman: City of London, Worshipful Co of Info Technologists; currently or formerly MIMgt, MSPS, FRCS, FInstD, FIPD, FRSA; *Books* philosophy and spirituality related works: Indian Spirituality (1984), Yoga: a Christian Option? (jtly, 1985); business related works: The Basic Arts of Marketing (3rd edn, 1990), Top Executives in the Global 100 Companies and their IT-Competence (1998); ed: The Lotus: An Anthology of Indian Religious Poetry in English (1998), Leela Dharmaraj 1923–1972 Selected Poems (1979, 2 edn 1988); bibliographical work Black British Literature from the Eighteenth Century to the Present: The First Bibliography (1986); poems published in numerous jls and anthologies, articles published in numerous publications most recently Malayali Diaspora: From Kerala to the Ends of the World (2013); chapters in books: International Executive Development Programmes (ed Philip Sadler, 1996), The Gower Handbook of Management (ed John Lock, 1998), Leadership and Management in the 21st Century (ed Cary L Cooper, 2004), Der Geldcomplex -Kritische Reflexion unseres Geldsystems und mögliche Zukunftsszenarien (The Money Complex, critical reflections on our monetary systems and potential scenarios for the future, in the series St Galler Beiträge zur Wirtschaftsethik, ed M Weis and H Spitzeck, 2008), The Role of Law and Ethics in a Globalised Economy, Intellectual Property, Competition and Tax Law, Max Planck Institute Studies, Germany (ed Joseph Straus, 2009), Foundations of Contemporary Leadership: Contemporary Leadership Readings (ed Franco Gandolfini, 2011); foreword to Erfolgsfaktor Integrität: Wie Wirtschaft und Gesellschaft erneuert werden können (Johannes Grassl and Claude R Schmutz, 2010); *Recreations* poetry, hill walking, yoga, music, films, food; *Clubs* Arts Centre Group; *Style*— Prof Prabhu S Guptara; ✉ website www.prabhu.guptara.net and www.prabhuguptara.blogspot.com, Twitter @prabhuguptara

GURBANOV, HE Fakhraddin; *b* 3 September 1954, Baku, Azerbaijan; *Educ* Azerbaijan State Univ of Foreign Languages, Inst of Political Sciences Baku, JFK Sch of Govt Harvard Univ; *m* ; 1 da; *Career* Azerbaijani diplomat; dir Office of Information Miny of Foreign Affrs 1990–92, dir Office of Protocol Miny of Foreign Affrs 1992–93, 1 sec and consul Washington DC 1993–2001, ambass-at-large Western Hemisphere Miny of Foreign Affrs 2001–03, charge d'affaires Ottawa 2003–04, ambass to Canada 2004–07, ambass to the Ct of St James's 2007–14; pres Consular Corps of Washington DC 1996; *Style*— HE Mr Fakhraddin Gurbanov; ✉ Embassy of the Republic of Azerbaijan, 4 Kensington Court, London W8 5DL

GURDON, Prof Sir John Bertrand; kt (1995); s of late W N Gurdon, DCM, of Suffolk, and late Elsie Marjorie, *née* Byass; *b* 2 October 1933; *Educ* Eton, ChCh Oxford (BA, DPhil, Beit meml fell); *m* 1964, Jean Elizabeth Margaret Curtis; 1 s, 1 da; *Career* Gosney res fell Caltech 1962; Univ of Oxford: department demonstrator Dept of Zoology 1963–64, res fell ChCh 1962–72, lectr Dept of Zoology 1965–72; visiting res fell Carnegie Inst Baltimore 1965, head Cell Biology Div MRC Laboratory of Molecular Biology Cambridge 1979–83, Fullerian prof of physiology and comparative anatomy Royal Inst 1985–91, John Humphrey Plummer prof of cell biology and chm Wellcome/CRC Inst Cambridge 1991–2001, master Magdalene Coll Cambridge 1995–2002; fell: Churchill Coll Cambridge 1973–94, Eton Coll 1978–93; chm Co of Biologists Cambridge 2001–; govr Wellcome Tst 1995–2000; hon foreign memb: American Acad of Arts and Sciences, US Nat Acad of Sciences, Belgian Acad of Letters and Fine Arts 1984, Lombardy Acad of Sci Italy 1989, Academie des Sciences France 1990; foreign memb: American Philosophical Soc 1983, Inst of Med USA 2003; Liveryman Worshipful Co of Goldsmiths; hon fell: ChCh Oxford, Magdalene Coll Cambridge 2002, Churchill Coll Cambridge 2007; Hon DSc: Univ of Chicago 1978, Univ of Paris 1982, Univ of Oxford 1985, Univ of Hull 1998, Univ of Glasgow 2000, Univ of Cambridge 2007, Vrije Universiteit Brussel 2009, Andres Bello Univ Chile 2012, Rockefeller Univ NY 2014; Hon FRCP 2014; FRS 1971; *Awards* Albert Brachet Prize Belgian Royal Acad 1968, Scientific Medal Zoological Soc 1968, Feldberg Fndn Award 1975, Paul Ehrlich Award (Germany) 1977, Comfort Crookshank Award for Cancer Res 1983, William Bate Hardy Prize Cambridge Philosophical Soc 1984, Prix de Charles Leopold Mayer Acad des Scis France 1984, Ross Harrison Prize 1985, CIBA Medal Biochemical Soc 1985, Royal Medal Royal Soc 1985, Emperor Hirohito International Prize (Japan) 1987, Wolf Prize in Medicine (Israel) 1989, Jan Waldenstrom Medal 1991, Distinguished Serv Award (Miami) 1992, Jean Brachet Memorial Prize 2000, Conklin Medal 2001, Copley Medal Royal Soc 2003, Rosenstiel Basic Science Award (USA) 2009, Albert Lasker Award for Basic Medical Research 2009, Nobel Prize for medicine or physiology 2012; *Publications* Control of Gene Expression in Animal Development (1974); author of articles in numerous scientific journals (especially on nuclear transplantation); *Recreations* tennis, skiing, horticulture, lepidoptera; *Clubs* Eagle Ski; *Style*— Prof Sir John Gurdon, FRS; ✉ Whittlesford Grove, Whittlesford, Cambridge CB2 4NZ

GURR, Prof Sarah Jane; da of Denis Coates Smith, of Lyminge, Kent, and Marie Therese, *née* Robinson; *b* 7 May 1958, Cuckfield, Sussex; *Educ* King's Sch Canterbury, ICSTM (BSc, ARCS, PhD, DIC), Univ of Oxford (MA); *m* 9 July 1983, Dr Paul Andrew Gurr; 2 da (Charlotte Lucy b 29 June 1994, Alice Eugenie b 31 Dec 1996); *Career* post doctoral research fell Univ of St Andrews 1984–89, research fell and Royal Soc univ research fell Univ of Leeds 1989–92; Univ of Oxford: fell Somerville Coll 1992–, lectr 1992–2002, reader 2002–04, prof 2004–; Royal Soc Leverhulme Tst sr research fell 2002–03, NESTA fell 2004–07; dir Rothamsted Research 1999–2006; pres Br Soc for Plant Pathology 2009–10 (first woman); memb Ctee Biotechnology and Biological Sciences Research Cncl 2008–10; author of over 80 research papers and articles, ed of 2 books and various articles in popular press; govr: King's Sch Canterbury 1999–, Stowe Sch 2005–; Huxley medal 1998; *Recreations* wine, art, reading, plants; *Style*— Prof Sarah Gurr; ✉ Somerville College, Oxford OX2 6HD (☎ 01865 275813, e-mail sarah.gurr@plants.ox.ac.uk)

GURU-MURTHY, Krishnan; *b* 5 April 1970, Liverpool; *Educ* Queen Elizabeth's GS Blackburn, Hertford Coll Oxford (BA); *m* 6 Feb 2005, Lisa; *Career* broadcaster; BBC: Open to Question 1988–89, subsequently East 1989–91, Newsround 1991–94, Newsnight 1994–97, BBC News 24 1997–98; Channel 4: Channel 4 News 1998–, Dispatches, Going Cold Turkey, Britain's Deadliest Addictions, Powerhouse, Ask the Chancellors, Unreported World; *Clubs* Groucho, Ivy, Soho House; *Style*— Krishnan Guru-Murthy, Esq; ✉ c/o Noel Gay Artists, 19 Denmark Street, London WC2H 8NA (☎ 020 7836 3941); Channel 4 News, ITN, 200 Grays Inn Road, London WC1X 8XZ (e-mail krishnan@channel4.com, website www.channel4.com/news)

GUTCH, Richard Evelyn; s of Sir John Gutch (d 1988), and Diana Mary, *née* Worsley (d 2013); *b* 17 November 1946; *Educ* Winchester, Gonville & Caius Coll Cambridge (BA), UCL (MPhil); *m* 15 May 1971, Rosemary Anne Capel, da of John Alexander Pike; 2 s (James Alexander b 1974, Adam William b 1978); *Career* town planning posts in Camden and S Yorks 1970–76, sr lectr Planning Unit PCL 1976–80, policy co-ordinator (then asst to chief exec) London Borough of Brent 1980–85; asst dir Resource Devpt NCVO 1985–92, chief exec Arthritis Care 1992–2001, dir England and strategic progs Community Fund 2001–04, chief exec Futurebuilders England Ltd 2004–08, assoc Prospectus 2008–13; chm then treasurer Long Term Med Conditions Alliance 1993–96, chm then vice-chm ACEVO 1995–99; MRTPI 1972–80; FRSA 1992; *Publications* incl: Partners or Agents? (NCVO, 1990), Contracting Lessons from the US (NCVO, 1992), The Good Merger Guide for Charities (Eastside and Prospectus, 2012); *Recreations* the arts, walking, Venice, carpentry, gardening; *Style*— Richard Gutch, Esq; ✉ e-mail richardgutch@richardgutch.com

GUTHRIE, James Dalglish; QC (1993); s of Ronald Dalglish Guthrie (d 1982), and Nina, *née* Llewelyn (d 1987); *b* 21 February 1950; *Educ* Harrow, Worcester Coll Oxford (BA); *m* 1981, Lu, da of Mr and Mrs Nigel Page-Roberts; 1 da (Charlotte Elizabeth b 31 July 1985), 1 s (Robert James b 17 June 1989); *Career* called to the Bar Inner Temple 1975 (bencher 2000), memb chambers 3 Hare Court (formerly 1 Crown Office Row) 1975–, recorder 1999–, head chambers 2002–10; *Recreations* fishing, painting, travel; *Clubs* Turf; *Style*— James Guthrie, Esq, QC; ✉ 3 Hare Court, Temple, London EC4Y 7BJ (☎ 020 7415 7800, fax 020 7415 7811, e-mail james@guthrieqc.com)

GUTHRIE, Prof Peter Moir; OBE; s of William Moir Guthrie, Surrey (d 1989), and Mary Barbara, *née* McMaster (d 1991); *b* 21 February 1951, La Paz, Bolivia; *Educ* Merchiston Castle Sch Edinburgh, Imperial Coll London (BSc, ACGI, MSc, DIC); *m* 1979, Lorna Jane, *née* Cowcher; 1 s (Oliver Moir 20 Dec 1981), 1 da (Caroline Mary b 5 April 1985); *Career* asst engr VSO Kaduna Nigeria 1974; planning engr: Turriff Taylor Tarmac Ltd (Flotta Oil Terminal Orkney Islands) 1975, Turriff Taylor Ltd (Ahwaz Iran) 1976; engrg geologist Balfour Beatty Ltd (second Dartford Tunnel Project) 1976, engr Soil Mechanics Ltd 1977–78; Scott Wilson Kirkpatrick: engr 1978–79, chartered engr 1979–80, sr chartered engr 1980–85, asst princ engr 1985–86, princ engr 1986–87, assoc (head of mktg) 1987–90, ptnr 1990–95, dir 1995–2004, bd dir 1997–2004; non-exec dir Buro Happold 2010–; prof of engrg for sustainable devpt Univ of Cambridge 2000–; memb Science Advsy Cncl DEFRA 2007–12; author of several manuals and books; co fndr and vice-pres Red R Engineers for Disaster Relief; nat winner Beacon Prize for Giving 2004; Hon LLD Univ of Bristol 1994; FICE 1997 (MICE 1979), FREng 1998, FCGI 1999; *Recreations* skiing, golf, tennis; *Style*— Prof Peter Guthrie, OBE, FREng; ✉ Camrose House, 9 The Street, Old Basing, Hampshire RG24 7BW (☎ 01256 352175, fax 01256 476116); Engineering Department, Cambridge University, Trumpington Street, Cambridge CB2 1PZ (e-mail pmg31@cam.ac.uk)

GUTHRIE OF CRAIGIEBANK, Baron (Life Peer UK 2001), of Craigiebank in the City of Dundee; Field Marshal Charles Ronald Llewelyn Guthrie; GCB (1994, KCB 1990), LVO (1977), OBE (1980), DL (2009); s of Ronald Dalglish Guthrie (d 1982), of Chelsea, and Nina, *née* Llewelyn (d 1987); *b* 17 November 1938, London; *Educ* Harrow, RMA Sandhurst; *m* 11 Sept 1971, Catherine, da of Lt-Col Claude Worrall, MVO, OBE, Coldstream Gds (d 1973), of Avon Dassett, Warks; 2 s (Hon David Charles b 21 Oct 1972, Hon Andrew James b 3 Sept 1974); *Career* cmmnd Welsh Gds 1959, served BAOR and Aden, 22 SAS Regt 1965–69, psc 1972, mil asst to Chief of Gen Staff MOD 1973–74, Bde Maj Household Div 1976–77, CO 1 Bn Welsh Gds served Berlin and NI 1977–80, Col gen staff mil ops MOD 1980–82, cmd Br Forces New Hebrides 1980, 4 Armd Bde 1982–84, Chief of Staff 1 (Br) Corps 1984–86, GOC NE Dist cmd 2 Inf Div 1986–87, Asst Chief of the Gen Staff MOD 1987–89, Cmd 1 Br Corps 1990–91, C in C BAOR 1992–94, cmd Northern Army Gp 1992–93 (NORTHAG, now disbanded), Chief of the Gen Staff 1994–97, Chief of the Defence Staff April 1997–2001; Col Cmdt Intelligence Corps 1986–95; Col Life Guards (Gold Stick) 1999–; ADC Gen to HM The Queen 1993–2001; Col Cmdt SAS Regt 2000–09; pres: Army Saddle Club 1991–97, Army LTA 1991–99, Army Benevolent Fund 2002–12; tstee IISS; dir: N M Rothschild & Sons Ltd 2001–10, Petropavlovsk plc 2008–16; chm Hosp of St John and St Elizabeth 2008–, chm St John's Hospice 2013–; pres: Fedn of London Youth Clubs 2001–, Action Medical Research 2001–, Weston Spirit 2003–06; hon fell and visiting prof KCL 2001–, visiting prof St Mary's Univ Twickenham, memb Bd Moscow Sch of Political Studies 2002–, chllr Liverpool Hope Univ 2013–; Freeman City of London, Liveryman Worshipful Co of Painter-Stainers; Knight SMOM, KCSG, Cdr Legion of Merit (USA) 2001; *Publications* Just War (jtly, 2008); *Recreations* tennis, opera, travel; *Clubs* White's, All England Lawn Tennis, Cavalry and Guards, Beefsteak, Buck's; *Style*— Field Marshal the Rt Hon the Lord Guthrie of Craigiebank, GCB, LVO, OBE, DL; ✉ PO Box 25439, London SW1P 1AG

GUTTERIDGE, Prof Tom Michael Gillan; s of Herbert Thomas Gutteridge (d 1972), of Tynemouth, and Ethelie, *née* Boucher; *b* 2 February 1952, London; *Educ* Royal GS Newcastle upon Tyne, Univ of York (BA); *m* 1, 1981 (m dis 1993), Jillian, da of Capt C Carrington Barber; 2 s (Benjamin Leo Thomas, Sam Fredric), 2 da (Rebecca Holly, Anya Romanta); m 2, 2003 (m dis 2007), Rosetta, da of Angelo Santagati (d 2004); m 3, 2009,

G

Joanna, da of William Samuel Pine; 1 da (Isadora Clover); *Career* BBC: news trainee 1973–75, dir Nationwide, Tonight and Panorama 1975–79, prodr/dir Tonight in Town 1979, prodr Harty 1980, prodr/dir A Kick up the Eighties and The Hot Shoe Show 1981, exec prodr BBC TV Music & Arts 1982–85, dir BBC coverage of Gen Election 1983; Mentorn Gp: fndr chm and chief exec 1985–2000, exec chm 2000–03; chief exec Mentorn Barraclough Carey Productions 1997–2000; non-exec chm West One Television 1991–99; jt chm Space Productions 1994–2003; dir The Television Corp plc 2000–03; broadcasting conslt Camelot plc (Nat Lottery); chief exec Fremantle Media N America 2004–05; chm Vine Media 2006–16, chm Standing Stone Productions 2007–16; non-exec dir: Northern Film & Media 2009– (chm 2014–), Screenreach Interactive 2010–15; columnist Newcastle Journal 2007–; visiting prof Univ of Teesside 2008–; Mentorn prodns incl: Gerry Anderson's Space Precinct, 01 for London, Challenge Anneka, Today's the Day, The Bullion Boys, The Valley, The Fall of Saigon, Star for a Night, Cancer Wars, Question Time, The Clintons, Robot Wars, Queen and Country, Paradise Hotel; Fremantle prodns incl: American Idol, The Price is Right, Family Feud; Standing Stone Prodns incl: Loveland, Hot Seat, The Ideas Factory; prodns as freelance dir incl: Fire & Ice (LWT) 1985, The Sleeping Beauty (Anglia) 1986; exec prodr BattleBots Inc. 2016–; chm PACT 1993–94, memb Cncl Br Screen Advsy Cncl 1994–2004, chm Skillset North 2008–12; vice-chm RTS 2000–02; tstee: Nat Film and TV Sch Fndn, Tom Gutteridge Fndn; memb BAFTA, FRTS 1996; *Awards* BAFTA Award for The Hot Shoe Show 1984, Bronze Rose of Montreux for Fire & Ice 1985, Best Dir Int Monitor Awards LA for Fire & Ice 1985, Best Prog Int Monitor Awards for Sleeping Beauty 1986, Int Emmy nomination for I Drew Roger Rabbit 1987, Bronze Rose of Montreux, Best Prog Nat Viewers and Listeners' Assoc Awards for Challenge Anneka 1991, Silver Hugo Award Chicago and NY Film Festival Bronze Medal for Passport 1994, Silver medal for Best Children's Series NY Film and TV Festival for Early Bird 1994, Int Emmy for Best Drama for The Bullion Boys 1994; *Recreations* food, the countryside; *Clubs* Soho House, Chelsea Arts, Groucho, Century; *Style*— Prof Tom Gutteridge; ✉ e-mail tomgutteridge@aol.com, website www.tomgutteridge.com

GUY, Frances; da of David Guy (d 1996), and Elise, *née* Hendry; *b* 1 February 1959, Edinburgh; *Educ* Univ of Aberdeen (MA), Johns Hopkins Univ Bologna (Dip), Carleton Univ Ottawa (MA); *m* 1989, Hugo G Raybaudo; 2 da (Anaide b 14 Oct 1991, Nina b 2 May 1996), 1 s (James b 5 June 1993); *Career* diplomat; joined FCO 1985, dep head of mission Addis Ababa 1997, ambass to Yemen 2001–04, head Engaging with the Islamic World Gp FCO 2004–06, ambass to Lebanon 2006–11; *Recreations* running, swimming, tennis; *Clubs* Royal Cwlth Soc; *Style*— Frances Guy; ✉ c/o Foreign and Commonwealth Office, King Charles Street, London SW1A 2AH

GUY, Gillian; CBE (2015); *Educ* Univ of Bristol (LLB); *Career* formerly slr; ceo: London Borough 1994–2006, Victim Support 2006–10, Citizens Advice 2010–; memb: Cncl Sentencing 2010–13, Bd NAO 2012–15, Banking Standards Bd 2015–; *Style*— Ms Gillian Guy, CBE; ✉ Citizens Advice, 3rd Floor North, 200 Aldersgate Street, London EC1A 4HD

GUY, Dr John Alexander; *b* 16 January 1949; *Educ* Univ of Cambridge (Greene Cup Clare Coll, MA, PhD, York Prize for published work in legal history); *m* 1 (m dis 2004); 2 c; m 2, 14 May 2005, Julia Fox; *Career* research fell Selwyn Coll Cambridge 1970–73, asst keeper of public records Public Record Office London 1973–78, visiting lectr in British history Univ of Calif Berkeley 1977; Univ of Bristol: lectr in modern British history 1978–82, awarded tenure 1981, reader in British history 1982–90; John Hinkley visiting prof Johns Hopkins Univ 1990, Richard L Turner prof of humanities and prof of history Univ of Rochester 1990–92; Univ of St Andrews: prof of modern history 1992–2002, head Sch of History and Int Relations 1992–94, provost St Leonard's Coll 1994–97, vice-princ 1996–97, hon res prof 2002–09; fell Clare Coll Cambridge 2003– (visiting fell 2002–03); Marc Fitch research reader British Acad 1987–89; fell Leverhulme Trust Research 1997–98; currently historian, author and broadcaster; FRHistS 1977; *Publications* The Public Career of Sir Thomas More (1980), Tudor England (1988, paperback edn, 1990), The Reign of Elizabeth I: Court and Culture in the Last Decade (1995), The Tudor Monarchy (1997), Thomas More (2000), My Heart is My Own: The Life of Mary Queen of Scots (2004, Whitbread Biography of the Year 2004, Marsh Biography Prize 2005), A Daughter's Love: Thomas and Margaret More (2008), Thomas Becket: Warrior, Priest, Rebel, Victim (2012), The Children of Henry VIII (2013), The Tudors: A Very Short Introduction (2 revised edn, 2013), Henry VIII: The Quest For Fame (2014), Elizabeth – The Forgotten Years (2016); also author of nine other books, 54 articles and numerous book reviews; *Recreations* opera, theatre, art, animals; *Style*— Dr John Guy; ✉ Clare College, Cambridge CB2 1TL (e-mail jag64@cam.ac.uk); c/o Rogers, Coleridge and White, 20 Powis Mews, London W11 1JN (☎ 020 7243 6326, website www.johnguy.co.uk)

GUY, Prof Keith William Arthur; s of Kenneth Leonard Guy (d 1977), of Portsmouth Co, and Margaret Olive Jesse, *née* Rose; *b* 14 December 1943, Frilford Heath, Berks; *Educ* Southern GS, Imperial Coll London (BSc, MSc, PhD, ACGI, DIC); *m* 1, 5 April 1968 (m dis 1989), Penelope Ann, da of Peter Desmond Greenyer; 3 da (Tabitha Kate b 11 Sept 1971, Victoria Rose b 31 May 1973, Hannah Roberta b 9 Sept 1976 d 30 Sept 2003); m 2, 25 May 1991, Kathryn Elizabeth, da of Dr Norman Lawrence Franklin, CBE, FRS, FEng (d 1987); *Career* Air Products plc: joined 1970, mangr Staff Engrg 1974, mangr Engrg Design 1977, mangr Process and Proposals 1983, gp mangr Engrg 1985, tech dir 1987, mktg dir 1989, business devpt dir 1995–99, dir 1999–2001; dir and sr ptnr Spiritus Group Ltd 2001–09, managing ptnr Esprit Assocs (Europe) Ltd 2010–; dir Webaspx Ltd 2001; chm: Process Systems Enterprise Ltd 2001–15, Impact Faraday Ltd, Hyradix Inc 2005–07, Spiritus Consulting Europe Ltd 2008–10, Process Integration Ltd 2007–15, Process AIM Ltd 2015–; memb Advsy Bd Paros plc 2006–07; memb CEI 1979–83; Inst of Chem Engrs: chm London and SE Branch 1985–87, chm Engrg Practices Ctee 1989–99, chm Tech Bd 1996–2005, vice-pres 1999–2005; Royal Acad of Engrg: chm membership 1996–2000, chm President's Pro-active Gp 2001–07, memb Engrg Policy Bd 2005–; SERC (now EPSRC): appointments to Interdisciplinary Res Centre at Imperial Coll London 1989–2001, chm Process Engrg Ctee 1993–94, chm Chem Engrg Sub-Gp 1991–93, memb Clean Technol Mgmnt Ctee 1992–94; IMI (Process) STAG memb 1995–2001; memb Steering Panel Process Systems Gp Univ of Edinburgh 1992–96; external examiner: in chem engrg Univ of Bradford 1992–98, MSc int pollution mgmnt UMIST; visiting prof: Dept of Chem Engrg Univ of Bath 1994–2002, Imperial Coll of Science Technol and Med (ICSTM) London; visiting prof of chemical engrg Imperial Coll London 2009–; memb: Res Assessment Panel (Chemical Engrg) and teaching assessment specialist assessor (Chemical Engrg) 1995–97 and 1999–2002, Chemicals Foresight Panel 1996–99, Bd Crystal Faraday Partnership 2001–05; chm: Mgmnt Bd Inst of Applied Catalysis 1996–99 (ceo 1999–), Industrial Bd Univ of Sheffield 1998–2002, Industrial Advsy Bd ICSTM London 1999–, Industrial Advsy Bd UMIST, Impact Faraday Partnership 2001–09; tstee IChemE Benevolent Fund 2007– (chm 2014–); pres Mitcham and Morden Cons Assoc 1996–99 (chm 1983–88 and 1993–95); govr and chm Fin Ctee Hatfield Sch Merton 1998–2002; visiting prof of chemical engrg Univ of Manchester 2015–; Liveryman Worshipful Co of Scientific Instrument Makers 2003, Liveryman Worshipful Co of Engrs 2009; CEng 1975, CSci 2004, CEnv 2005; FIChemE 1981 (tstee Benevolent Fund 2008–), FREng 1988, FCGI 1998, FRSA 2009; *Publications* numerous papers and co authorships on engrg; *Recreations* bridge, politics, golf, book collecting, church, music, travel, food; *Clubs* Royal London Yacht, Island Sailing, City Livery Yacht; *Style*— Prof Keith Guy, FCGI, FREng, FRSA; ✉ Esprit Associates (Europe) Ltd, Clevedon, Windsor Road, Medstead, Hampshire GU34 5EF (☎ 01420 562802, fax 01420 561634, e-mail keith.guy@espritassociates.com)

GWENLAN, Gareth; OBE (2013); s of Charles Aneurin Gwenlan (d 1939), and Mary, *née* Francis (d 1980); *b* 1937, Brecon; *m* 1, 1962 (m dis); 1 s (Simon); m 2, 1986 (m dis 1993), Sarah Elizabeth Fanghanel; m 3, 2000, Gail Susan Evans; *Career* television executive producer and director; actor and theatre dir 1960–64, lectr in drama and opera Royal Northern Coll of Music 1964–65, joined BBC 1965, head Comedy Dept BBC TV 1983–90, head of comedy BBC Wales 2002–; over 200 prog credits incl: Woodhouse Playhouse 1977, The Fall and Rise of Reginald Perrin 1978–80, To The Manor Born 1978–81, Butterflies 1979–81, Solo 1980, Roger Roger 1988, Waiting for God 1990–96, The Legacy of Reginald Perrin 1996, Only Fools and Horses; 2 Br Acad Awards (12 nominations), Lifetime Achievement Award BAFTA 2014; md Watson Equestrian Partnership; hon fell Royal Welsh Coll of Music and Drama 1999; FRTS 1997; *Recreations* dressage; *Clubs* Garrick; *Style*— Gareth Gwenlan, Esq, OBE; ✉ Putley Mill, Putley, Herefordshire

GWYN, Philip Hammond Rhys; s of Brig Rhys Anthony Gwyn, OBE (d 1987), and Dorothy Eileen, *née* Macmillan; *b* 18 August 1944; *Educ* Eton, Trinity Coll Cambridge (MA); *m* 1, 1970, Susan Alice Margaret, da of Brig Derek Shuldham Schreiber, CVO (d 1972); 1 s (Hwfa b 1980), 3 da (Katherine b 1972, Anna b 1974, Christina b 1976); m 2, 2006, Martha Davidson Berry; *Career* called to the Bar Inner Temple 1968; chm Christie Gp plc, non-exec dir Alumasc Gp plc 1984–; *Recreations* sports, the arts; *Clubs* Brooks's, White's; *Style*— Philip Gwyn, Esq; ✉ Christie Group plc, Whitefriars House, 6 Carmelite Street, London EC4Y 0BS

GWYNNE, Andrew; MP; *b* 4 June 1974; *Educ* Egerton Park Community HS, Tameside Coll, NE Wales Inst, Univ of Salford; *Career* cncllr (Lab) Tameside MBC 1996–2008; European co-ordinator Arlene McCarthy MEP 2000–01, research asst to Andrew Bennett MP 2000–05, MP (Lab) Denton and Reddish 2005–, PPS to Rt Hon Baroness Scotland of Asthal (as Min of State Home Office) 2005–07, PPS to Rt Hon Jacqui Smith, MP (as Home Sec) 2007–09, PPS to Rt Hon Ed Balls, MP (as Sec of State for Children, Schs and Families) 2009–10, shadow min for tport 2010–11, shadow min for health 2011–; memb: Unite, GMB, Co-operative Party, Christian Socialist Movement; *Style*— Andrew Gwynne, Esq, MP; ✉ House of Commons, London SW1A 0AA

GWYNNE, Haydn; da of Guy Thomas Haydn Gwynne (d 1994), and Rosamond Noelle, *née* Dobson; *Career* actress; lecturer Facoltá di Economia E Commercio Rome Univ 1983–85; *Theatre* incl: debut Susan Dunedin in His Monkey Wife (Stephen Joseph Theatre Scarborough) 1986, West End debut Billie Burke in Ziegfeld (London Palladium) 1988; other roles incl: Millamant in The Way of the World (Theatre Royal Northampton) 1990, title role in Hedda Gabler (Bolton Octagon) 1990, Lady Macbeth in Macbeth (Ludlow Festival) 1991, Oolie/Donna in City of Angels (Prince of Wales) 1993 (nomination Best Actress in a Musical Olivier Awards 1993), The Memory of Water (Hampstead) 1996, Mrs Wilkinson in Billy Elliot the Musical (Victoria Palace) 2005–06 (nomination Best Actress in a Musical Olivier Awards 2006); Manchester Royal Exchange incl: The Bluebird of Unhappiness 1987, Mrs Gaylustre in The Cabinet Minister 1988, Sylvia in The Recruiting Officer 1992; RSC incl: Olivia in Twelfth Night (Stratford, Barbican) 1994–95, Helena in A Midsummer Night's Dream (Stratford) 1994–95, Solveig/Mother Aase in Peer Gynt (Swan Stratford, Young Vic) 1994–95; *Television* incl: What Mad Pursuit (BBC) 1986, Lovejoy (BBC) 1986, Call Me Mister (BBC) 1986, The Great Writers – Thomas Mann (LWT/Channel Four) 1987, After the War (Granada) 1987, Robyn Penrose in Nice Work (BBC) 1989, B B Miller in Time Riders (Thames) 1991, Alex in Drop the Dead Donkey (Channel Four) 1991–93 (nomination British Comedy Award and BAFTA Award), Portia in The Merchant of Venice (Channel Four) 1995, Hospital! (Channel Five) 1997, Verdict (Yorkshire) 1998, Dangerfield (BBC) 1998, Dr Joanna Graham in Peak Practice (Carlton) 1999–2000 (nominations RTS Award), Supt Susan Blake in Mersey Beat (BBC) 2001–02, Merseybeat (Best Actress RTS Awards 2002 and 2003), Emma in The Secret 2002, Midsomer Murders (ITV) 2004, Dalziel & Pascoe (BBC, Best Actress RTS Awards 2005), Absolute Power (BBC); *Film* incl: The Pleasure Principle 1990, Remember Me? 1996, The Heat of the Story 2004, These Foolish Things 2004; *Style*— Ms Haydn Gwynne; ✉ c/o Markham & Froggatt Ltd, Julian House, 4 Windmill Street, London W1P 1HF (☎ 020 7636 4412, fax 020 7637 5233)

GWYNNE, Richard; s of Dr Edward Ieuan Gwynne, of Ystrad-Rhondda, Mid Glamorgan, and Mary Teresa, *née* Downey; *b* 9 March 1955; *Educ* Porth County GS, Trinity Coll Cambridge (MA); *m* 6 May 1995, Susan Mary, *née* Paton; 1 s, 1 da; *Career* admitted slr 1979, ptnr Stephenson Harwood 1986–, chm Mgmnt Ctee Fulham Legal Advice Centre 1987–91; memb Worshipful Co of Slrs; memb IBA; *Publications* International Execution Against Judgement Debtors (contrib, 1993 and subseq edns), Structuring International Contracts (contrib, 1996); numerous articles on conflict of laws and banking law; *Recreations* opera, golf; *Style*— Richard Gwynne, Esq; ✉ 46 Lytton Grove, Putney, London SW15 2HE (☎ 020 8788 7567, e-mail richard.gwynne55@gmail.com); Stephenson Harwood, One Finsbury Circus, London EC4M 7SH (☎ 020 7329 4422, fax 020 7606 0822, e-mail richard.gwynne@shlegal.com)

GYIMAH, Samuel Phillip (Sam); MP; *b* 10 August 1976, Beaconsfield, Bucks; *Educ* Achimota Secdy Sch Ghana, Freman Coll Herts, Somerville Coll Oxford; *m* 29 Sept 2012, Dr Nicola Mary Black; 1 s (Ethan); *Career* with Goldman Sachs until 2003, entrepreneur 2003–10, chm Bow Gp 2006–07; MP (Cons) Surrey E 2010–, memb Int Devpt Select Ctee 2011–12, PPS to the PM 2012–13, Lord Cmmr of HM Treasy (Govt whip) 2013–14; Parly under-sec of state for childcare and educn 2014–, min for the constitution 2014–16; pres Oxford Union 1997; *Books* From the Ashes... The Future of the Conservative Party (ed, 2005), Beyond the Banks (with Nesta, 2011); *Style*— Sam Gyimah, Esq, MP; ✉ House of Commons, London SW1A 0AA (☎ 020 7219 3504, e-mail sam@samgyimah.com, website www.samgyimah.com)

GYNGELL, Skye; da of Bruce Gyngell (d 2000), and Lesley Ann Gyngell; *b* 6 September 1963, Sydney, Australia; *Educ* La Varenne Paris; *m* 1989 (m dis 1997), Tom Gore; 2 da (Holly, Evie); *Career* chef; formal trg La Varenne Paris; formerly with: Dodin-Bouffant Paris, The French House London, The Dorchester; currently head chef Petersham Nurseries Cafe (Michelin star 2011–); food writer Independent on Sunday New Review; *Books* A Year in my Kitchen (2006, Best Cookery Book Guild of Food Writers Award 2007), My Favourite Ingredients (2008), How I Cook (2010, Best UK Woman Chef Book Gourmand World Cookbook Award 2010); *Recreations* reading, cooking for family and friends, gardening; *Style*— Ms Skye Gyngell; ☎ 020 8605 3627, e-mail skyegyngell@hotmail.com; Petersham Nurseries, Church Lane, Off Petersham Road, Richmond, Surrey TW10 7AG

H

HAACKE, Norman Patrick von; s of Frederick and Margaret Haacke; *b* 15 March 1952; *Educ* St Joseph's Acad Blackheath, London Coll of Music (jr exhibitioner), St Catharine's Coll Cambridge (MA, MB BChir), Bart's Med Coll; *m* 17 Feb 1979, Jennifer Mary, da of Mathew Finbar Hunt (d 1986); 1 da (Georgina Alexandra Morgan b 4 Nov 1984), 1 s (Samuel James Finbar b 22 Aug 1982); *Career* house surgn Bart's 1976–77, house physician Royal Berkshire Hosp 1977, SHO Addenbrooke's 1977–78, sr registrar Royal Nat Throat, Nose and Ear Hosp 1983 (SHO 1980, registrar 1980–83), sr registrar Edinburgh Royal Infirmary 1983–87, conslt ENT surgn Southampton Univ Hosps 1987–2000, sr lectr in otolaryngology Univ of Southampton 1987–2000; currently conslt ENT surgn: Met Police Serv, Cromwell Hosp, Lister Hosp, Princess Grace Hosp, Portland Hosp for Women and Children, Wessex Nuffield Hosp, Chalybeate Hosp; med dir Wessex Regnl Hearing and Balance Centre 1987–97; examiner in fellowship Royal Coll of Surgns in Ireland; Lionel Colledge meml fell RCSE 1985–86; dir S of England Cochlear Implant Centre 1989–97; jt fndr and tstee All Hear Trust 1990–96; memb: Br Assoc of Otolaryngologists, Br Assoc for Paediatric Otorhinolaryngology, Otolaryngology Research Soc, S Western Laryngological Soc, Scottish Otolaryngological Soc, Euro Rhinologic Soc, American Rhinologic Soc, Euro Acad of Facial Plastic Surgery, BMA; FRCSI 1982, FRCS 1983, FRSM; *Publications* author of 3 chapters and over 40 papers on cochlear implantation, endoscopic sinus surgery and other aspects of ENT surgery; *Recreations* flying, sculpture and painting, music; *Style*— Norman Haacke, Esq; ✉ Chalybeate Hospital, Chalybeate Close, Tremona Road, Southampton S016 6UY (☎ 023 8076 4308, fax 023 8078 5621, e-mail haacke@entfacialplastic.com); 234 Great Portland Street, London W1W 5QT (☎ 020 7630 9599, fax 070 9203 9266, e-mail office@entfacialplastic.com)

HABERMAN, Prof Steven; s of Louis Haberman, of Essex, and Rita Lily, *née* Kaminsky; *b* 26 June 1951; *Educ* Ilford Co HS, Trinity Coll Cambridge (MA), City Univ (PhD, DSc); *m* 11 April 1976, Mandy Nicola Haberman, da of Arnold and Sylvia Brecker, of Herts; 1 s (Benjamin Adam b 18 Aug 1978), 2 da (Nadia Lia (twin) b 18 Aug 1978, Emily Michal b 15 Feb 1980); *Career* Prudential Assurance Co 1972–74, Govt Actuary's Dept 1977–97; City Univ: lectr Dept of Actuarial Sci 1974–79, sr lectr 1979–83, reader 1983–85, prof 1985–, dean Sch of Mathematics 1995–2002, dep dean Cass Business Sch 2002–12, dean Cass Business Sch 2012–15; memb: Cncl Inst of Actuaries 1986–91 and 1993–99, Morris Review Advsy Panel 2004–05, Bd for Actuarial Standards 2006–12; FIA 1975, ASA 1976, FSS 1979, FIMA 1996; *Books* Pensions: The Problems of Today and Tomorrow (1987), History of Actuarial Science (1995), Modern Actuarial Theory and Practice (1999, 2 edn 2005), Actuarial Models for Disability Insurance (1999), Modelling Longevity Dynamics for Pensions and Annuity Business (2009); *Recreations* reading, music, cinema, hiking; *Style*— Prof Steven Haberman; ✉ Cass Business School, City University London, 106 Bunhill Row, London EC1Y 8TZ (☎ 020 7040 8470, fax 020 7040 8899, e-mail s.haberman@city.ac.uk)

HABGOOD, Anthony John; s of John Michael Habgood, MC, and Margaret Diana Middleton, *née* Dalby; *b* 8 November 1946; *Educ* Gresham's, Gonville & Caius Coll Cambridge (MA), Carnegie Mellon Univ Pittsburgh (MS); *m* 29 June 1974, Nancy, da of Ray Nelson Atkinson, of San Mateo, CA; 1 da (Elizabeth Ann b 21 Sept 1975), 2 s (John Alan, George Michael (twins) b 14 Nov 1979); *Career* memb Mgmnt Exec Ctee Boston Consulting Gp Inc 1979–86 (dir 1976–86), dir then chief exec Tootal Group plc 1986–91, chief exec then chm Bunzl plc 1991–2009, chm Whitbread plc 2005–14; chm Ct Bank of England 2014–; chm: MHC UK Ltd 2006–07, RELX Gp (formerly Reed Elsevier plc and NV) 2009–, Preqin Ltd 2011–, Norwich Research Park 2013–16; non-exec dir: Geest plc 1988–93, Powergen plc 1993–2001, SVG Capital plc 1996–2009, National Westminster Bank plc 1998–2000, Marks & Spencer plc 2004–05, Norfolk and Norwich Univ Hosp Tst 2006–13; *Clubs* Brooks's, Royal Norfolk and Suffolk Yacht; *Style*— Anthony Habgood, Esq; ✉ RELX Group plc, 1–3 Strand, London WC2N 5JR (☎ 020 7166 5745, e-mail nuala.goldsboro@relx.com, website www.relx.com)

HACK, Jefferson; *b* 1971, Montevideo, Uruguay; *Educ* Pangbourne, London Coll of Printing; *Children* 1 da (Lila Grace b 29 Sept 2002, with Kate Moss, *qv*); *Career* magazine editor; Dazed & Confused: co-fndr 1991, editor 1991–2001, gp editorial dir 2001–; fndr: Another Magazine 2001, Another Man 2005; *Style*— Jefferson Hack, Esq; ✉ Dazed & Confused, 112–116 Old Street, London EC1V 9BG (☎ 020 7336 0766, fax 020 7336 0966)

HACKER, Richard Daniel; QC (1998); s of Samuel Hacker, of London, and Lilli Paula; *b* 1954; *Educ* Haberdashers' Aske's, Downing Coll Cambridge (MA), Wiener Anspach scholar 1976, Université Libre de Bruxelles (Licencié Speciale en Droit Européen); *m* 25 March 1988, Sarah Anne, da of Richard Millar, of Bath; 1 da (Rebecca Leonora b 23 Jan 1993); *Career* called to the Bar Lincoln's Inn 1977; Hardwicke scholar 1977, Lincoln's Inn Student of the Year Prize 1977, Gray's Inn 1989; asst parly boundary cmmr 1999; chm Inquiry Into Hertforshire Parly Constituency Boundaries 2000; called to the Bar Br Virgin Islands 2003; *Recreations* travel, gastronomy, opera; *Style*— Richard Hacker, QC; ✉ 3–4 South Square, Gray's Inn, London WC1R 5HP (☎ 020 7696 9900, fax 020 7696 9911)

HACKETT, Mark Christopher; *b* 13 February 1963; *Career* nat mgmnt trainee (W Midlands) Central Birmingham HA 1984–86, asst operational mangr St George's Hosp London 1986–88, business services mangr E Hosps Unit W Glamorgan 1988–90; Good Hope Hosp: dep unit gen mangr 1990–91, actg unit gen mangr 1991–93, exec dir 1993–95, dir of ops 1993–95, dir of devpt 1995; chief exec Birmingham Women's Hosp 1996–99, chief exec Royal Wolverhampton Hosps NHS Tst 1999– (formerly actg chief exec); chair: Regnl Risk Mgmnt Gp (part of Regnl Clinical Governance Framework) 1999, Wolverhampton Emergency Capacity Gp 1999–2001, Black Country Cancer Network 1999–, Wolverhampton Local Information Steering Gp 1999–; vice-chair Black Country Cardiac Network 2000–; memb: W Midlands Commnd Research Advsy Ctee 1996–2002, Expert Panel W Midlands Evidenced Based Med Union 1997–99, Dept of Health/MRC Advsy Ctee on Scientific Advances in Genetics 1998–2001, Regnl Organisational Developmental Gp 1998–2001, Chief Exec's Learning Set 1998–, Regnl Chief Execs Developmental Gp 1999–, Regnl Higher Awards Ctee 2002–, Regnl Postgrad Med Teaching Gp 2002–; reviewer and author of numerous articles in professional jls; *Recreations* sport, current affairs, my two children; *Style*— Mark Hackett, Esq; ✉ The Royal Wolverhampton Hospitals NHS Trust, New Cross Hospital, Wolverhampton, West Midlands WV10 0QP (☎ 01902 307999)

HACKING, 3 Baron (UK 1945); Sir Douglas David Hacking; 3 Bt (UK 1938); s of 2 Baron Hacking (d 1971); n of Hon Lady Waller (d 2010); *b* 17 April 1938; *Educ* Aldro Sch, Charterhouse, Clare Coll Cambridge (MA); *m* 1, 1965 (m dis), (Rosemary) Anne (who m subsequently, 1982, Antony Askew (decd), of Highgate, London), da of late Frank Penrose Forrest, FRCSE, of Lytchett Matravers, Dorset; 1 da (Hon Belinda Anne b 1966), 2 s (Hon Douglas Francis b 8 Aug 1968, Hon Daniel Robert b 27 May 1972); m 2, 1982, Dr Tessa Margaret Hunt, MB, MRCP, FRCA, er da of late Roland Hunt, CMG, of Whitchurch Hill, Berks; 3 s (Hon Alexander Roland Harry b 20 Jan 1984, Hon (Maxwell David) Leo b 8 July 1987, Hon Christian Eric George b 7 Dec 1989); *Heir* s, Hon Douglas Hacking; *Career* Nat Serv RN 1956–58; Lt RNR (ret); sat as a peer in House of Lords 1972–99 (memb Select Ctee on Euro Community 1989–93 and 1995–99); barr 1963–76, Harmsworth Major Entrance exhibitioner and Astbury scholar Middle Temple; attorney: New York State 1975, Simpson Thacher and Bartlett New York 1975–76; slr Supreme Court of Eng & Wales 1977–99; ptnr Richards Butler 1981–94, ptnr Sonnenschein 1994–99; int arbitrator 1997–, barr 1999–, chartered arbitrator 1999–, memb Littleton Chambers 2000–; observer of Human Rights Inst of Int Bar Assoc at the trial of the Chief Justice of Gibraltar 2001; Freeman: City of London, Worshipful Co of Merchant Taylors'; Liveryman Worshipful Co of Arbitrators; FCIArb 1979; *Publications* Well: Did You Get the Right Arbitrator? (2000); author of numerous articles on the law and arbitration; *Clubs* MCC, Reform; *Style*— The Rt Hon the Lord Hacking; ✉ 27 West Square, Kennington, London SE11 4SP (☎ 020 7735 4400, fax 020 7735 7337, website www.lordhacking.com); Littleton Chambers, 3 King's Bench Walk North, Temple, London EC4Y 7HR (☎ 020 7797 8600, fax 020 7797 8699, e-mail clerks@littletonchambers.co.uk)

HACKITT, Dame Judith Elizabeth; DBE (2016, CBE 2007); da of Kenneth George Hackitt (d 2010), and Rhoda, *née* Jeffcott (d 1986); *b* 1 December 1954, Nuneaton, Warks; *Educ* Queen Elizabeth Grammar Atherstone, Imperial Coll London (BSc); *m* 24 Sept 1977, David John Lea; 2 da (Alexandra b 4 Feb 1985, Kathryn b 16 Sept 1987); *Career* formerly: various process mgmnt roles Exxon Chemicals, gp risk mangr Elementis plc; DG Chemical Industries Assoc 2002–06, chair Health and Safety Exec (formerly Health and Safety Cmmn) 2007–16 (cmmr 2002–05), chair Engineering Employers Fedn 2016–; dir Chemistry for Europe project European Chemical Industry 2005–07; former non-exec dir Oxon Health Authy, non-exec dir Energy Saving Tst 2009–, non-exec dir High Value Manufacturing Catapult 2013–; hon vice-pres Instn of Occupational Safety and Health; tstee City & Guilds Gp 2015–; Top 50 Women in Engineering 2016; FIChemE 2001 (memb Cncl, pres 2013–14), FCGI 2007, FREng 2010; *Recreations* cinema, reading, travel; *Style*— Dame Judith Hackitt, DBE; ✉ EEF, Broadway House, Tothill Street, London SW1H 9NQ (e-mail chair@eef.org.uk)

HACKNEY, Jeffrey; s of Reginald Thomas Hackney, of Stoke-on-Trent, and Mildred Anne, *née* Stanway; *b* 5 January 1941; *Educ* Newcastle HS, Wadham Coll Oxford (BA, BCL, Vinerian scholar), UCL (Churchill Jenkinson prize); *m* 27 Oct 1962, Dr Ann Christine, da of Frank Swindells; 1 s (Daniel b 3 Nov 1965), 1 da (Lucy b 2 April 1967); *Career* called to the Bar Middle Temple 1966 (Blackstone scholar, Colombos prize), pupillages with Martin Nourse (now Lord Justice Nourse) and Nicolas Browne-Wilkinson (now Lord Browne-Wilkinson); St Edmund Hall: fell and tutor in law 1964–76, librarian 1966–72, sr tutor 1972–76, emeritus fell 1976–; Wadham Coll Oxford: fell and tutor in law 1976–2008, sec to Governing Body 1981–84, sr tutor 1986–88 and 2000, sub-warden 2002–03 and 2004–08, actg warden 2003–04, emeritus fell 2008–; University of Oxford: chm Law Faculty Bd 1977–79, Keeper of the Archives 1987–95, chm Libraries Bd 1988–91, Bodleian curator 1986–91, chm Gen Bd of the Faculties 1991–93, memb Hebdomadal Cncl 1991–95, chm Curators of the Sheldonian Theatre 1993–2011, chm Disciplinary Ct 1997–2002, Clerk of the Market 2010–; *Books* Understanding Equity and Trusts (1987); *Recreations* music, theatre; *Style*— Jeffrey Hackney, Esq; ✉ 25 Barton Lane, Headington, Oxford OX3 9JW (☎ 01865 61458); Wadham College, Oxford OX1 3PN (☎ 01865 277918)

HACKNEY, Dr Roderick Peter (Rod); s of William Hackney, and Rose, *née* Morris; *b* 3 March 1942; *Educ* John Bright's GS Llandudno, Sch of Architecture Univ of Manchester (MA, BA, ARCH, PhD); *m* Christine (Tina); 1 s (Roan b 27 April 1982); *Career* architect Expo 1967 monorail stations Montreal Canada 1965–66, housing architect Libyan Govt Tripoli 1967–68, asst to Arne Jacobson Copenhagen 1968–71, established practice of Rod Hackney Architect in Macclesfield 1972, established a number of offices throughout the UK 1975–87 and offices in Paris, Shenzhen and United Arab Emirates 1995–, set up Castward Ltd (building and devpt) 1983, designer (with Shenzhen Sch of Architecture) 2000 Housing Scheme Shenzhen China 2002, co-fndr and co-dir Kansara Hackney Ltd (lifestyle consltss) 2008–; RIBA: elected nat memb to the Cncl 1978, vice-pres 1981–83, memb 3 man delgn to USSR under Anglo-Soviet Cultural Agreement 1984, chm The Times-RIBA Community Enterprise Scheme 1985–89, pres 1987–89, memb Cncl 1991–99 and 2001–08, vice-pres int affrs 1992–99, hon librarian 1998–99, tstee Br Architectural Library Tst (RIBA Library) 1998–99, chm Br Architectural Library Tst 1999–2001, chm Discipline Hearings Panel 2001–02, Discipline Ctee 2002–08, memb Conservation Ctee 2010–, sr conservation architect 2011–; UIA: elected Cncl for Gp 1 1981, memb Editorial Bd Int Architect 1983, memb Editorial Bd Jl of Architect Theory and Criticism 1988, vice-pres 1985, pres 1987–90, memb Cncl 1991–2008, memb Gold Medal Jury 1993, co-ordinator corp plan 1993–2001, memb Int Jury World Student Architecture Prize 1998–99, memb World Habitat Awards Advsy Gp 2003; chm UN Best Practice Awards 2004, pres Int Cncl for Caring Communities (ICCC) NY 2010–; advsr on regeneration and inner city problems in Sweden, Italy and USA 1990–, advsr UNESCO Caribbean on Havana World Heritage Site 2009–, advsr Samba Bank Saudi Arabia on new Central Bank HQ Riyadh 2010–, advsr Lebanese Govt on Tripoli Int Fair; consult BBC TV documentary series Europe by Design 1991; other TV work incl: Build Yourself A House 1974, Community Architecture 1977, BBC Omnibus 1987, Europe By Design 1991, Question Time; radio incl: The Listener 1986, Any Questions 1987, Third Ear 1990, Call to Account 1992, Woman's Hour 1992, Common Ground 1996, The Today Programme, The World at One, The Tonight Programme; conslt World Architecture Review Agency Shenzen 1992–, int advsr Centre for Int Architecture Studies Univ of Manchester Sch of Architecture 1992–2008; vice-pres UN Int Students Competition 2012; visiting prof UP6 Paris 1984, pres Young Architect World Forum Sofia 1985, pres Building Communities Int Community Architecture Conf 1986, special prof in architecture Univ of Nottingham

1987–91, lectr tour of India (sponsored by Br Cncl) 1991, advsr to Mayor of Trento 1991, lectures in Sri Lanka (sponsored by Br Cncl) 1992, juror and advsr to DVA Int Competition Netherlands 1992, memb jury Int Students Competition Beijing 1998, advsr to Mayor of City of Meridian MS (Livable Southern Communities Conf) 1992, lecture Int Biennale for Architecture BA/93 Buenos Aires 1993, lecture Univ of Shenzhen World Architecture Review Agency 1993, lecture Inst of Architects Karachi 1993, conslt speaker Livable City Conf Meridian MS1994 and 1996, speaker Biennial conf on Architecture and Children 1999, speaker Caring Communites UN HQ 1999, speaker on sustainable housing Iran 2002, advsr Centre for Human Settlements International India 1994, conslt Chapman Clarke Films (Forever England, Central TV) 1995, visiting prof Royal Danish Acad of Fine Arts Copenhagen 1995, lectr Br-American-Canadian Assocs tour USA 1995, Int Conf Writers & Intellectuals Pakistan 1995, lecture Hogeschool Mideen Brabant & IHS Netherlands 1996, lecture Acad of Architecture Rotterdam 1996, visiting prof Sunshant Sch of Art & Architecture New Delhi 1997, lectr on community architecture and people planning TV Sch for Habitat Studies New Delhi 1997, visiting prof Coll of Architecture Xian Univ 1999–, keynote World Cncl of Genetics 2011; first prize: DOE Awards for Good Design in Housing 1975, St Ann's Hospice Architectural Competition 1976; Prix Int d'Architecture de l'Institut National du Logement 1979, commended RICS and The Times Conservation Awards 1980, highly commended DOE Awards 1980, commended The Civic Tst Awards 1980 and 1982, hon mention Sir Robert Matthews Award 1981, President's Award Manchester Soc for Architects 1982, commended Otis Award 1982; commendation Business Enterprise Award 1993, shortlisted Millennium Expo Competition Greenwich 1995, commended Natural Stone Award 1995, 96 citation World Habitat Awards 1995; Gold Medal: Bulgarian Inst of Architects 1983, Young Architect of the Biennale Sofia 1983; Award of Commendation Civic Tst Awards 1984, Grand Medal of the Federacion de Colegios de Arquitectos de la Republica Mexicana 1986, PA Award for Innovation in Building Design and Construction 1988, Past Pres' Medal UIA Lausanne 1998, attained ISO 9001 Certification BSI 1996; hon fell: American Inst of Architects 1988, Federacion de Colegios de Arquitectos de la Republica Mexicana 1988, United Architects of the Philippines 1988, Royal Architectural Inst of Canada 1990, Indian Inst of Architects 1990; hon memb: Consejo Superior de los Colegios de Arquitectos de España 1987, Architecture Soc of China 2003; chm of Tstees Inner City Tst 1986–96, presented the case for Int Year of Shelter for the Homeless to all Pty Confs 1986, pres Snowdonia Nat Park Soc 1987–2003; patron Llandudno Museum and Art Gallery 1988–2003, patron Dome Project Buxton 1999–2003; pres N Wales Centre of the Nat Tst 1990–; memb Advsy Ctee Int Cncl of Caring Communities NY 1998; hon memb Rural Buildings Preservation Tst 1994–2003, memb Assoc of Planning Supervisors 1996; FCIArb 1977, MCIOB 1987, FFB 1987, ARIBA 1969; *Books* The Good, The Bad and The Ugly (1990), music play (based on own work) Good Golly Miss Molly (West End, 1991), Icinquatenaire de l'Union Internationale des Architectes Paris (contrib, 1998), Healthy People (contrib, 2011); *Recreations* photography, travelling, walking, outdoor pursuits, looking at buildings, speaking at conferences; *Clubs* Cwlth; *Style*— Dr Rod Hackney; ✉ St Peter's House, Windmill Street, Macclesfield, Cheshire SK11 7HS (☎ 01625 431792, fax 01625 616929, e-mail roderick.hackney@gmail.com, website www.kansarahackney.com)

HACON, His Hon Judge Richard David; *Career* called to the Bar 1979; specialist circuit judge Intellectual Property Enterprise Court 2013–; *Style*— His Hon Judge Hacon; ✉ Intellectual Property Enterprise Court, The Rolls Building, 7 Rolls Building, Fetter Lane, London EC4A 1NL

HADDACKS, Vice Adm Sir Paul Kenneth; KCB (2000); s of Kenneth Alexander Haddacks (d 2002), and Edith Lillian, *née* Peardon (d 1979); *b* 27 October 1946; *Educ* Kingswood Sch Bath, BRNC Dartmouth, RN Staff Coll, Staff Coll Camberley, RCDS; *m* 1970, Penny Anne, da of late Prof D Robertson; 1 s (David Paul b 1973); *Career* joined RN 1964; commanded HM Ships: Scimitar 1971–72, Cleopatra 1981–82, Naiad 1982–83, Intrepid 1986–88; Cdr 1979, instr US Naval Acad 1979–80, Capt 1984, asst dir Naval Plans 1984–86, dep dir Naval Warfare 1988–89, Cdr RN Task Force Gulf 1990, Capt of the Fleet 1991–94, Rear Adm 1994, ACOS (Policy) to SACEUR 1994–97, Vice Adm 1997, UK Mil Rep at NATO HQ 1997–2000; dir Int Mil Staff NATO HQ 2001–04, Lt Govr Isle of Man 2005–11; chm Chichester Coll 2014–; chm Coastal Forces Heritage Tst 2016–; KStJ 2010; *Recreations* family and travel; *Style*— Vice Adm Sir Paul Haddacks, KCB; ✉ c/o Naval Secretary, Naval Command HQ, Portsmouth PO2 8BY

HADDEN, Abel Robert; s of Alan Edwin Robert Hadden (d 2003), and Carmen Clare, *née* Masters (d 1995); *b* 4 June 1953; *Educ* Westminster; *m* 1 (m dis 1984), Katherine, *née* Taylor; 1 s (Leo b 1983); m 2 (m dis 2002), Belinda, da of Dr Sir Reginald Frederick Brittain Bennett, VRD (d 2000); 1 da (Camilla b 1991); *Career* articled clerk Touche Ross 1972–75, Odhams & Gunn 1975–76, Charles Barker 1976–81, Abel Hadden Associates Ltd 1981–83, Good Relations Group/Lowe Bell Communications 1983–94, md Edelman London 1994–98, md Abel Hadden & Co 1998–2002, ptnr Bell Pottinger 2003–; IPR: memb 1976, memb Consltsʼ Gp 1979–84, memb Cncl 1981–84; CAM examiner 1984–92 (chief examiner 1988–92); DipCAM 1980, FCIPR 1993; *Recreations* allotment gardening, fishing, skiing, croquet; *Clubs* Hurlingham, White's, St Moritz Tobogganing, Chelsea FC; *Style*— Abel Hadden, Esq

HADDINGTON, 13 Earl of (S 1619) John George Baillie-Hamilton; also Lord Binning (S 1613) and Lord Binning and Byres (S 1619); only s of 12 Earl of Haddington, KT, MC, TD (d 1986), and Sarah, *née* Cook (d 1995); *b* 21 December 1941; *Educ* Ampleforth, Trinity Coll Dublin, RAC Cirencester; *m* 1, 19 April 1975 (m dis 1981), Prudence Elizabeth, da of Andrew Rutherford Hayles, of Bowerchalke, Wilts; m 2, 10 Dec 1984, Susan Jane Antonia, da of John Heyworth, of Bradwell Grove, Burford, Oxon; 1 s (George Edmund Baldred, Lord Binning b 27 Dec 1985), 2 da (Lady Susan Moyra b 15 July 1988, Lady Isobel Joan b 16 June 1990); *Heir* s, Lord Binning; *Career* farmer, fndr Save Our Songbirds (now Songbird Survival) 1998; *Recreations* beekeeping, keeping finches, field sports, photography, racing, cerealogy, fancy fowl; *Clubs* Turf, New, Puffins, Chelsea Arts; *Style*— The Rt Hon the Earl of Haddington; ✉ Mellerstain, Gordon, Berwicks TD3 6LG (e-mail hadders01@btinternet.com)

HADDON-CAVE, Hon Mr Justice; Sir Charles Anthony Haddon-Cave; kt (2011), QC (1999); s of Sir Philip Haddon-Cave, KBE, CMG (d 1999), and Elizabeth, *née* Simpson (d 2008); *b* 20 March 1956; *Educ* King's Sch Canterbury, Pembroke Coll Cambridge (MA); *m* 2 Aug 1980, Amanda Charlotte, da of Timothy James Law, of Godalming, Surrey; 2 da (Alexandra Charlotte b 11 Feb 1987, Florence Caroline b 8 Jan 1991); *Career* called to the Bar: Gray's Inn 1978 (bencher 2003), Hong Kong 1980; asst recorder 1998–2000, recorder 2000–11, judge of the High Court of Justice (Queen's Bench Div) 2011–; chm The Grange Festival 2015–; *Recreations* running, opera; *Clubs* Garrick, Royal Aeronautical Soc; *Style*— The Hon Mr Justice Haddon-Cave; ✉ Royal Courts of Justice, Strand, London WC2A 2LL

HADDOW, Christopher; QC (Scot 1985); s of Sir (Thomas) Douglas Haddow (d 1986), and Margaret, *née* Rowat (d 1969); *b* 15 May 1947, Edinburgh; *Educ* George Watson's Coll Edinburgh, Univ of Edinburgh (LLB); *m* 4 Aug 1970, Kathleen, *née* Bell; 3 s (Timothy Rowat b 28 July 1973, Robin Sinclair b 28 Aug 1975, Andrew Nicholas b 1 June 1978); *Career* admitted Faculty of Advocates 1971; *Publications* Armour on Valuation for Rating (jt ed, 1991–); *Recreations* classic cars, hockey; *Style*— Christopher Haddow, QC; ✉ c/o Alan Moffat, Advocates Clerk, Ampersand, Advocates' Library, Parliament House, Edinburgh EH1 1RF (☎ 0131 226 5710, e-mail alan.moffat@advocates.org.uk)

HADEN-GUEST, 5 Baron (UK 1950); Christopher Haden-Guest; s of 4 Baron Haden-Guest (d 1996), and his 2 w, Jean Pauline, *née* Hindes; *b* 5 February 1948; *m* 1984, Jamie Lee Curtis, the actress, da of Tony Curtis the actor, and Janet Leigh, the actress; 1 adopted da (Anne b 1986), 1 adopted s (Thomas b 1996); *Heir* bro, Hon Nicholas Haden-Guest; *Career* actor, director, writer and humour conslt; writer of comedy for: National Lampoon (in print and for National Lampoon Radio Hour), Lily Tomlin (Emmy Award), Saturday Night Live; co-writer and dir Family Tree (HBO and BBC) 2013; hon doctorate Berklee Sch of Music 2007; *Films* as as actor incl Nigel Tufnel in This is Spinal Tap 1984 (also scriptwriter); as dir incl: The Big Picture, Attack of the 50ft Woman, Waiting for Guffman, Almost Heroes, Best in Show 2000, A Mighty Wind 2003, For Your Consideration 2006; *Recreations* fly fishing; *Style*— The Rt Hon Lord Haden-Guest

HADEN-TAYLOR, Dr Anthony St John; s of Frank Pacey Haden-Taylor (d 1971), of Broughton House, Broughton Gifford, Wilts, and Enid Christine, *née* Bushnell (Mrs Bousfield, d 2012); *b* 26 March 1948, Newport, Monmouthshire; *Educ* King's Sch, Sherborne, Pacific Western Univ of Calif (BSc, MSc, PhD); *m* 15 April 1989 (m dis 2007), Hon Susan Rosemary, *née* Greenall, da of 3 Baron Daresbury (d 1996), and sis of Peter, 4 Baron Daresbury, and former w of David St C O Bruton; 2 da (Pandora Eleanor Christine b 7 Nov 1989 d 1990, Annabella Margaret Christine b 28 July 1995), 1 s (Albert Henry George b 26 Oct 1999); *Career* sr ptnr International Management Consultants SA 1970–82, chm Ashe Park Estate and Ashe Park Mineral Water Ltd 1976–83, chief exec Taylor Downs & Co 1987–91, sr ptnr The HT Partnership; chm: ReCycled Refuse International Ltd, ReCycled Refuse (Holdings) Ltd, Global Marine Shipping (No 10) Ltd; tstee Int Soc Security, memb Soc for the Environment; Liveryman and Freeman City of London 1982, Liveryman Worshipful Co of Basketmakers; chartered environmentalist (CEnv), memb Chartered Inst of Wastes Mgmnt (MICWM); *Publications* numerous publications on reusable energy, recycling and the environment; *Recreations* polo, shooting, golf, scuba diving, tennis, skiing, sailing; *Clubs* Annabel's, Royal Channel Islands Yacht; *Style*— Dr Anthony Haden-Taylor, CEnv, MICWM; ✉ Isis House, Route des Genet, St Brelade, Jersey JE3 8LE (e-mail chairman@rcinternational.com or ahadentaylor@gmail.com, website www.rcinternational.com and www.rcrusa.com)

HADGRAFT, Prof Jonathan; s of John William Hadgraft (d 1984), and Doris, *née* Ayres (d 1996); *b* 13 December 1950; *Educ* Queen Elizabeth's Sch Barnet, UC Oxford (MA, DPhil, DSc); *m* 1, 3 May 1975 (m dis 1996), Pauline Joyce, da of Thomas Henry Bilton, of Penarth, S Glamorgan; 1 da (Eleanor Tamsin); m 2, 16 June 1997, Isobel Joyce, da of James Ednie Dow, of Nottingham; *Career* lectr in pharmaceutical chemistry Univ of Strathclyde 1977–79, lectr in pharmacy Univ of Nottingham 1979–85, prof The Welsh Sch of Pharmacy 1985–2000; prof in medway sciences and dir skin and membrane research Univ of Greenwich 2000–04, prof Sch of Pharmacy Univ of London 2004–; CChem, FRSC 1983; *Style*— Prof Jonathan Hadgraft; ✉ The School of Pharmacy, University of London, 29–39 Brunswick Square, London WC1N 1AX (e-mail jonathan.hadgraft@btinternet.com)

HADOW, Rupert Nigel Pendrill (Pen); s of Nigel Philip Ian Hadow, of E Sussex, and Anne Pendrill, *née* Callingham; *b* 26 February 1962; *Educ* Harrow (first recorded runner of the 20-mile 'Long Ducker'), UCL (BA); *m* June 1995 (m dis), Mary Frances, da of late Archie Nicholson; 1 s (Wilf Pendrill b 19 Oct 1998), 1 da (Freya Alice b 12 April 2002); *Career* fndr The Polar Travel Co; promoter, organiser and professional guide numerous Arctic expdns; polar records held: organised first all-women expdn to N Geographic Pole 1997, first solo unsupported expdn to N Geographic Pole (first Briton unsupported to both N and S Geographic Poles); fndr Geo Mission Ltd/Catlin Arctic Survey 2008–12, fndr Arctic Mission Ltd (not-for-profit, central Arctic Ocean protection) 2016; hon vice-pres Royal Scottish Geographical Soc, hon vice-pres Scientific Exploration Soc, hon patron Br Exploring Soc; Hon LLD Univ of Exeter, Hon DSc Univ of Plymouth; *Books* SOLO: Alone and Unsupported to the North Pole (2004), Catlin Arctic Survey – Investigating the Changing Arctic Ocean Environment (2013); *Recreations* Dartmoor and the River Dart; *Clubs* RGS, MCC, Frontline; *Style*— Pen Hadow, Esq

HAGAN, David Lloyd; s of William Hamill Hagan (d 1984), of Liverpool, and Miriam Dilys, *née* Lloyd (d 1998); *b* 21 May 1946; *Educ* Merchant Taylors' Sch Crosby, Emmanuel Coll Cambridge; *m* 5 Dec 1981, Anita Janet Shepstone, da of Lennart Pettersson, of Karlstad, Sweden; 2 s (Charles b 1 Nov 1982, Felix b 14 March 1987), 1 da (Isabel b 4 Aug 1984); *Career* chm and chief exec Marlon House Holdings Ltd 1974–83, dir Medical and Professional Software Ltd 1984–2008, md Tullett & Tokyo Equities Ltd 1986–91; chm: David Hagan Ltd 1986–2008, Trio Holdings plc 1992–2005, Neptune Energy Ltd 2004–; dir Premier Renewable Enery Fund Ltd 2007–10; FCA 1970, ATII 1970, MSI; *Recreations* offshore powerboat racing (Class II World Champion 1979), boatbuilding; *Clubs* Royal Thames Yacht, Royal Lymington Yacht, The South West Shingles Yacht (Vice Cdr); *Style*— David Hagan, Esq; ✉ Eastwoods, Pitmore Lane, Sway, Lymington, Hampshire SO41 6BW

HAGERTY, William John Gell (Bill); s of William Hagerty, and Doris Julia, *née* Gell; *b* 23 April 1939; *Educ* Beal GS Ilford Essex; *m* 1, 1965 (m dis 1990), Lynda Ann, *née* Beresford; 1 s (William Daniel b 22 Jan 1970), 1 da (Faith Georgia b 5 March 1975); m 2, 1991, Elizabeth Ann Vercoe, *née* Latta; 1 s (Adam Benedict b 1 Dec 1993); *Career* local newspaper journalist 1955–58 and 1960–62; with: Sunday Citizen, Daily Sketch 1962–67; various editorial positions The Mirror Group 1967–85, managing ed (features) Today 1986–87, ed Sunday Today 1987–88, conslt to the publisher Hola! Magazine (conslt Hello! Magazine) 1987–88, dep ed Sunday Mirror 1988–90, dep ed Daily Mirror 1990–91, ed The People 1991–92, conslt Tribune 1993–, ed British Journalism Review 2002–12 (chm 2012–15, co-chm 2015–); theatre critic: Today 1993–95 (also film critic 1994–95), various publications 2003, The Sun 2004–09; tstee Journalists' Charity 2004– (chm 2011–12), dir London Press Club 2007–; *Books* Flash Bang Wallop! (with Kent Gavin, 1978), Read All About It (2003), Alastair Campbell Diaries (ed, 5 vols); *Recreations* watching cricket, jazz, lunch; *Clubs* Gerry's, Acts and Actors, Victory Services; *Style*— Bill Hagerty; ✉ 11 Strand on the Green, Chiswick, London W4 3PQ (☎ 020 8994 4966)

HAGGARD, Prof Mark Peregrine; CBE (2001); s of Capt Stephen H A Haggard (d 1943), and Morna Christian, *née* Gillespie (d 1977); *b* 26 December 1942; *Educ* Dollar Acad, Univ of Edinburgh (MA), Univ of Cambridge (PhD); *m* 22 Sept 1962, Elizabeth Gilmore, da of Thomas Jackson Houston (d 1943), of Hong Kong; 2 s (Stephen b 1963, Patrick b 1965); *Career* teaching offr and fell CCC Cambridge 1967–71, prof Queen's Univ Belfast 1971–76, dir MRC Inst Hearing Res 1977–2002, chief advsr Hearing Res Tst 1987–2002, MRC External Scientific Staff Cambridge 2002–; memb Neurosciences Bd MRC 1989–93, dep chm Health Serv and Public Health Res Bd MRC 1990–93, memb HTA Commissioning Bd 1999–; fell Acoustical Soc America 1982, FMedSci 1998; *Books* Hearing Science and Hearing Disorders (with M E Lutman, 1983), British Medical Bulletin: Hearing (with E F Evans, 1987), Screening Children's Hearing (with E A Hughes, 1991), Research in the Development of Services for Hearing-Impaired People (1993); *Recreations* extreme skiing, swimming, Byzantine art; *Style*— Prof Mark Haggard, CBE

HAGGER, Jonathan Osborne; s of Cyril Francis Osborne Hagger (d 1957), of Loughton, Essex, and Norah Harrison, *née* Broadley (d 1981); *b* 3 February 1949; *Educ* Chigwell Sch; *m* 27 April 1974, (Carol) Anne, da of Alan David Luton, of Loughton, Essex; 2 s (William b 1981, James b 1984); *Career* non-exec chm, dir and consIt; Edward Moore & Sons (Chartered Accountants) 1968–72, BUPA 1972–75, Willis Faber 1976–85; gp finance dir: Bain Clarkson 1985–89, FKB Group plc 1990; chief financial offr The Grosvenor

Estate 1991–2008; gp finance dir: Grosvenor Estate Holdings 1991–99, Grosvenor Gp Holdings 2000–03, Grosvenor Gp 2004–06; chm: Realty Insurances 1994–2013, G LHearn 2009–14; non-exec dir: Generation Life 2007–15, Brookfield Infrastructure Ptnrs 2008–12, Martins Properties 2008–, London Clinic 2008–09 (also tstee), Saunderson House 2012– (Investment Ctee 2008–); memb: Tax Deregulation Task Force 1996–97, American European Business Assoc 2002–09 (dir 2004–09), Policy Ctee Inst for Family Business 2006–08; Evaluation Ctee Coutts Nat Prize for Family Business 2007–10; chm: King Charles Music Soc 1988–2000, English Sinfonia 1995–2006; tstee Church of King Charles the Martyr 1996–; Liveryman Worshipful Co of Painter Stainers 2001; ARCM 1968, FCA 1972, FCT 1993; *Recreations* organist, opera, golf; *Style*— Jonathan Hagger, Esq; ✉ Saunderson House, 1 Long Lane, London EC1A 9HF (✆ 020 7315 650)

HAGGIE, Linford Richard David; s of David Haggie, and Fiona Knowles, *née* Worcester; *b* 15 August 1978, London; *Educ* Eton, Newcastle Univ; *m* 20 Sept 2010, Martina Alessandra, *née* Romieri; 1 da (Aurelia b 13 July 2013); *Career* md Graphic Alliance LLP; dir Austique Ltd; tstee Wheeleasy Fndn; *Clubs* Hurlingham, St Mortiz Tabogganing; *Style*— Linford Haggie, Esq; ✉ Graphic Alliance LLP, 1 Rosoman Place, London EC1R 0JY (✆ 020 7395 5770, e-mail linford@graphicalliance.co.uk, website www.graphicalliance.co.uk, Twitter @linfordhaggie)

HAGMAN, Eric; CBE (2003); s of Harald Hagman (d 1989), of Fairlie, Ayrshire, and Jessie Munro, *née* Henderson (d 2004); *b* 9 July 1946; *Educ* Kelvinside Acad, Univ of Glasgow; *m* 1; 2 s (Christian b 1972, Robin b 1974), 1 da (Victoria b 1978); *m* 2, Valerie Hagman; 2 step s (George b 1971, John b 1973); *Career* chartered accountant; trained Thomson McLintock, qualified 1969; Arthur Andersen: joined 1969, ptnr in Scot 1978, managing ptnr Glasgow 1979, regnl managing ptnr Scot 1983, chm Scotland 1998, UK sr ptnr for global markets, ret 2002; non-exec chm Matthew Algie, memb Advsy Bd AON UK, dir Saints plc, dir WA Baxter & Sons; past memb Advsy Bd UBS Wealth mgmnt; past chm: Audit Practice Ctee ICAS, Technical Liaison Ctee ICAS; past Cncl of CBI Scotland; former dir: British Polythene Industries plc, Celtic plc, Glen Gp plc, Scottish Enterprise, Scottish Financial Enterprise; former: pres Royal Glasgow Inst, chm RSAC, treas Police Dependents Tst, treas RCA London, tstee Scottish Nat Galleries, memb Bd Glasgow Sch of Art; *Recreations* sailing, skiing, tennis, art, travelling; *Clubs* Royal Scottish Motor Yacht, Clyde Corinthian Yacht; *Style*— Eric Hagman, Esq, CBE; ✉ Number Ten, 6 Mains Avenue, Giffnock, Glasgow G46 6QY (✆ 0141 620 0927, e-mail eric@erichagman.com)

HAGUE, Keith Douglas; *b* 17 February 1950, Sheffield, S Yorks; *Educ* BA, MSc; *m* Linda; 1 da (Rachel), 1 s (Scott); *Career* various positions NHS 1971–88, gen mangr BUPA Health Services Merseyside 1988–91, gen mangr BUPA Health Services Leicester 1991–95, int mktg dir Health Care Int Medical Centre Scotland 1995–97, regnl gen mangr Capio Health Services 1997–2003, ceo The Wellington Hosp London 2003–; dep chm Br Red Cross Medical and Science Ctee, hon sec Health Section Carlton Political Ctee; fundraiser Juvenile Diabetes Research Fndn; Companion Windsor Castle Coll of St George, World Fell Duke of Edinburgh World Fellowship 2009; MIOD; *Clubs* Carlton; *Style*— Keith Hague, Esq; ✉ The Wellington Hospital, Wellington Place, London NW8 9LE

HAGUE OF RICHMOND, Baron (Life Peer UK 2015), of Richmond in the County of North Yorkshire; Rt Hon William Jefferson Hague; PC (1995); s of Nigel Hague, of Wentworth, S Yorks, and Stella, *née* Jefferson; *b* 26 March 1961; *Educ* Wath upon Dearne Comp Sch, Magdalen Coll Oxford (MA, pres Oxford Union), INSEAD (MBA); *m* 19 Dec 1997, Ffion, da of Emyr Jenkins, *qv*; *Career* temp special advsr to Chancellor of Exchequer 1983, mgmnt conslt McKinsey and Co 1983–88; MP (Cons) Richmond (Yorks) 1989–2015; PPS to Rt Hon Norman Lamont as Chancellor of the Exchequer 1990–93, under-sec of state for social security 1993–94, min of state Dept of Social Security 1994–95, sec of state for Wales 1995–97; ldr Cons Pty and ldr of HM Opposition 1997–2001, shadow foreign sec 2005–10, foreign sec 2010–14, ldr of the House of Commons 2014–15; chm Int Democrat Union 1999–2002; political and econ advsr JCB 2001–09, political advsr Terra Firma Capital Partners 2002–09; non-exec dir: AES Engineering 2001–09, AMT-Sybex Ltd 2004–09; chair Int Advsy Gp Linklaters LLP 2015–, sr advsr Teneo 2015–; columnist Daily Telegraph 2015–; visiting prof in practice LSE Centre for Women, Peace and Security 2016–; dir: Intercontinental Exchange (ICE) 2015–, ICE Futures Europe 2015–; chm United for Wildlife Taskforce Royal Fndn of the Duke and Duchess of Cambridge and Prince Harry 2014–; chm RUSI 2015–; FRSL; *Books* William Pitt the Younger (2004, History Book of the Year Br Book Awards 2005), William Wilberforce (2007); *Style*— The Rt Hon the Lord Hague of Richmond; ✉ House of Commons, London SW1A 0AA (✆ 020 7219 3000)

HAIG, Matt; *Career* journalist and novelist; contrib: The Guardian, The Sunday Times, The Independent, The Sydney Morning Herald, The Telegraph; *Books* incl: The Last Family in England (2004), The Dead Fathers Club (2006), Shadow Forest (2007), The Possession of Mr Cave (2008), Runaway Troll (2008), The Radleys (2010), The Humans (2013), Echo Boy (2014), A Boy Called Christmas (2015), Reasons to Stay Alive (non-fiction, 2015); *Style*— Matt Haig, Esq

HAIGH, Simon Mark; s of Philip Haigh (d 2000), and Elaine, *née* Dickinson; *b* 22 July 1964, Huddersfield; *Educ* Newsome Secdy Modern Sch, Huddersfield Tech Coll (Dip); *m* 15 Jan 2000, Joanna Elizabeth, *née* Beech; 2 s (Joshua George Philip b 9 March 2001, Zack Andrew Arthur b 6 Nov 2007); *Career* chef: Hambleton Hall 1988–90, Manoir aux Quat Saisons 1990–92, Inverlochy Castle 1993–2001, Seaham Hall 2001–02, Mallory Court Hotel 2002–, exec chef Eden Hotel Collection (Mallory Court Hotel, Buckland Tout Saints Hotel, The Kings Hotel and The Arden Hotel); Michelin Star 15 years, 3 AA rosettes, 1 star Harden Guide, 1 star Egon Ronay (Best Desserts of Scotland 1998), Caterer & Hotelkeeper 30 Under 30 Acorn Award; *Publications* recipes in: Scotland on a Plate (2001), Chefs of Distinction (2002), Children in Need (2005), Soup Kitchen (2005), Dom Perignon 1998 Vintage The Collection (2005), Glorious-Eblex (2005), A Taste of Relais & Chateaux (2009); *Recreations* golf, dining out, spending time with family; *Clubs* Wilmslow Golf; *Style*— Simon Haigh, Esq; ✉ Mallory Court Hotel & Restaurant, Harbury Lane, Bishops Tachbrook, Leamington Spa, Warwickshire CV33 9QB (✆ 01926 330214, e-mail simon.haigh@mallory.co.uk)

HAILES, Julia Persephone; MBE (1999); da of Lt-Col John Martin Hunter Hailes, DSO (d 1995), of Stoke-sub-Hamdon, Somerset, and Marianne Carlyon, *née* Coates; *b* 23 September 1961; *Educ* St Mary's Sch Calne; *m* 1, (m dis 2010), Edward de Courcy Bryant; 3 s (Connor Carlyon b 1 Jan 1995, Rollo Jack b 22 Nov 1996, Monty Merlin b 12 Nov 1998); *m* 2, 2014, James Garner-Smith Macdonald; *Career* Leo Burnett Advertising 1981–83; dir: SustainAbility Ltd 1987–95 (memb Cncl 1995–2006), UK Eco-Labelling Bd 1992–98, Creative Consumer Co-operative Ltd (t/a Out of This World) 1994–2000, 5 St Lawrence Terrace Ltd 1995–, Six Fox Ltd 1996–98, Jupiter Global Green Investment Trust 2001–06; vice-chair Advsy Ctee on Consumer Products and the Environment (ACCPE) 1999–2005; writer regular monthly column for Planet Food BBC Online 2001–02; tstee: Haller Fndn 2003–15, Guild of Food Writers 2004–07, Ecos Tst 2005–08, Waste Watch 2010–11, Keep Britain Tidy 2011, E for Good Ltd 2011–13; memb Cncl Global 500 Forum 1992–96; elected to UN Global 500 Roll of Honour (for outstanding environmental achievements) 1989; dist cncllr S Somerset 1999–2003; *Books* Green Pages, The Business of Saving The World (1987), The Green Consumer Guide (1988), The Green Consumer's Supermarket Shopping Guide (1989), The Young Green Consumer Guide (1990), The Green Business Guide (1991), Holidays That Don't Cost the Earth (1992),

Manual 2000 Life Choices for the Future You Want (1998), The New Foods Guide (1999), The New Green Consumer Guide (2007); *Recreations* tennis, walking, bridge, photography; *Style*— Ms Julia Hailes, MBE; ✉ Hooke Farm, Hooke, Beaminster, Dorset DT8 3NZ (✆ 01308 861047, e-mail julia@juliahailes.com, website www.juliahailes.com, www.juliahailesblog.blogspot.com, Twitter @juliahailes)

HAILSHAM, 3 Viscount (UK 1929); Douglas Martin Hogg; PC (1992), QC (1990); also Baron Hailsham (UK 1928), of Hailsham, Co Sussex; and Baron Hailsham of Kettlethorpe (Life Peer UK 2015), of Kettlethorpe in the County of Lincolnshire; s of Baron Hailsham of St Marylebone, KG, PC (Life Peer 1970; suc as 2 Visc Hailsham 1950, disclaimed Viscountcy 1963; d 2001); *b* 5 February 1945; *Educ* Eton, ChCh Oxford (pres Oxford Union); *m* 6 June 1968, Hon Sarah Elizabeth Mary Hogg (Baroness Hogg, *qv*); 1 da (Hon Charlotte b 26 Aug 1970), 1 s (Hon Quintin b 12 Oct 1973); *Heir* s, Hon Quintin Hogg; *Career* called to the Bar Lincoln's Inn 1968; MP (Cons): Grantham 1979–97, Sleaford and N Hykeham 1997–2010; PPS to Leon Brittan as chief sec to Treasury 1982–83, asst Govt whip 1983–84, Parly under sec Home Office 1986–89, min of state for Industry and Enterprise 1989–90, min of state Foreign Office 1990–95, min of Agriculture, Fisheries and Food 1995–97; *Style*— The Rt Hon Douglas Hogg, QC, Viscount Hailsham

HAIN, Baron (Life Peer UK 2015), of Neath in the County of West Glamorgan; Rt Hon Peter Gerald Hain; PC (2001); s of Walter Hain, and Adelaine Hain; *b* 16 February 1950; *Educ* QMC London (BScEcon), Univ of Sussex (MPhil); *m* 1975 (m dis), Patricia Western; 2 s; *m* 2, 2003, Dr Elizabeth Haywood; *Career* head of res Union of Communication Workers 1987–91 (asst res offr 1976–87), MP (Lab) Neath 1991–2015 (Parly candidate (Lab) Putney 1983 and 1987); oppn whip 1995–96, oppn spokesman on employment 1996–97, Parly under-sec of state Welsh Office 1997–99, min of state FCO 1999–2000, min of state for Energy DTI 2001, min of state for Europe FCO 2001–02, sec of state for Wales 2002–08, Ldr of the House of Commons and Lord Privy Seal 2003–05, sec of state for NI 2005–07, sec of state for work and pensions 2007–08, sec of state for Wales 2009–10, shadow sec for Wales 2010–12; chm Stop the Seventy Tour campaign 1969–70, nat chm Young Libs 1971–73, press offr Anti-Nazi League 1977–80; *Books* Don't Play with Apartheid (1971), Community Politics (1976), Mistaken Identity (1976), Policing the Police (ed vol I, 1978, vol II 1980), Neighbourhood Participation (1980), Crisis and Future of the Left (1980), Political Trials in Britain (1984), Political Strikes (1986), A Putney Plot? (1987), The Peking Connection (1995), Ayes to the Left (1995), Sing the Beloved Country (1996), Mandela (2010), Outside In (2012), Ad & Wal (2014), Back to the Future of Socialism (2015); *Recreations* football, cricket, rugby, motor racing, supporting Chelsea FC and Neath RFC, rock and folk music; *Clubs* Resolven Rugby, Ynysygerwn CC; *Style*— The Rt Hon the Lord Hain; ✉ House of Lords, London SW1A 0PW (✆ 020 7219 3925, e-mail peter.hain@parliament.uk, Twitter @peterhain, website www.peterhain.org.uk)

HAIN, Robert Cameron; s of John MacFarlane Hain, and Beverley Jean, *née* Hendry; *b* 5 April 1953, Kingston, Ontario; *Educ* Univ of Toronto (BA), Univ of Oxford (MLitt); *m* 7 June 1991, Tracy; 2 c (Iska Simone, Kayla Cameron); *Career* vice-pres Atlantic Canada Royal Trust Corp of Canada 1988–90, vice-pres sales Royal Trust International and pres and ceo Royal Trust Bank (Switzerland) 1990–93; sr vice-pres then exec vice-pres Investors Gp Inc 1993–97, ptnr Ernst & Young 1997–98, sr vice-pres and head of global private banking CIBC Financial Gp 1998–99, global ptnr AMVESCAP plc 1999– (memb Exec Bd 2001–), pres and ceo AIM Funds Mgmnt Inc 1999–2002, ceo INVESCO UK and chm INVESCO Perpetual 2002–08, currently chm City Financial Investment Co Ltd; memb Nat Bd Canadian Mental Health Assoc 1987–89 (chair Toronto Bd 1980–88), memb Bd Canadian Psychiatric Research Fndn 1988–90, memb Fndn Bd St Michael's Hosp Toronto 2001; dir Nat Youth Orch of Canada 1988–92, chm Winnipeg Art Gallery 1996–97, tstee Nova Scotia Coll of Art and Design 2001–04; *Recreations* sailing; *Clubs* RAC, Phyllis Court, London Capital, Leander, Granite (Toronto), St Charles Golf and Country (Winnipeg), Royal Nova Scotia Yacht Sqdn; *Style*— Robert Hain, Esq; ✉ City Financial Investment Company Limited, 2 The Boulevard, City West One Office Park, Gelderd Road, Leeds LS12 6NT

HAINES, Prof Sir Andrew Paul; kt (2005); s of Charles George Thomas Haines, of Southall, Middx, and Lilian Emily, *née* Buck; *b* 26 February 1947; *Educ* Latymer Upper Sch, KCH Med Sch London (MB BS, MD); *m* 12 Feb 1982 (m dis 1989), June Marie Power; children, 2 s (Alexander b 7 Sept 1993, Adam b 19 Aug 1997); *m* 2, 14 March 1998, Dr Anita Berlin; *Career* house physician and surgn KCH 1969, SHO Nat Hosp for Nervous Diseases 1972, MO Br-Nepal Med Tst 1973, memb scientific staff MRC, Epidemiology and Med Care Unit Northwick Park Hosp 1974–86; pt/t sr lectr in gen practice: Middx Hosp Med Sch 1980–84, St Mary's Hosp Med Sch 1984–87; prof of primary health care UCL and subsequently Royal Free and Univ Coll Med Sch 1987–2000, dir London Sch of Hygiene and Tropical Med 2005–10 (dean 2001–05, prof of public health and primary care 2001–); dir of R&D: NE Thames RHA (pt/t secondment) 1993–95, NHS Exec N Thames 1995–96; author of papers on med subjects incl cardiovascular prevention, alcohol, care of the elderly and environmental issues; vice-pres MEDACT 1992–2010, hon conslt in public health Public Health England 2013–; memb: Cncl Int Physicians for the Prevention of Nuclear War 1982–85 (winners Nobel Peace Prize 1985), Public Health Laboratory Serv Bd 1983–86, Cncl Pugwash Orgn for Sci and World Affrs 1987–92 (winners Nobel Peace Prize 1996), Working Pty on Prevention RCP 1989–91, WHO/UNEP/WMO Task Gp on Health Impacts of Climate Change 1993–96, NHS Central R&D Ctee 1995–2001, Scientific Advisory Ctee Assoc of Medical Research Charities 1998–2004, London Health Cmmn 2000–09, Mgmnt Ctee King's Fund 2000–06, Res Strategy Ctee Public Health Lab Serv 2001–03, Dept of Health Patient Info Advsy Gp 2001–03, Dept of Health Advsy Gp on Refugee Health Professionals 2001–03, Health and Social Care Policy Ctee Universities UK 2001–10, WHO Advsy Ctee on Health Research 2004–08; lead author UN Intergovernmental Panel on Climate Change Working Gp 2 1993–2001 (winners Nobel Peace Prize 2007), chief of climate change (part-time) Health Protection Agency 2010–13, review ed Health Chapter UN Intergovernmental Panel on Climate Change 2011–14; chair: Health and Social Care Policy Ctee Universities UK 2007–09, WHO Task Force on Guidance for Health Systems Strengthening 2010–11; MRC: memb Health Servs Research Ctee 1989–92, memb Health Servs and Public Health Research Bd (chm 1996–98), memb Cncl 1996–98, memb Strategy Bd 2008–11, chair Global Health Gp 2008–11; chair: Tropical Health Educn Tst 2010–, Biomedical Grant Review Panel Multiple Sclerosis Soc 2010–12, Marie Curie Cancer Care Research Ctee 2011–, Research Strategy Ctee Multiple Sclerosis Soc 2012–; tstee Biobank UK 2011–, tstee Medical Research Fndn 2014–; hon fell UCL 2006, hon fell Faculty of Public Health 2009, hon fell KCL 2009, hon memb Nat Acad of Medicine of Mexico 2012; FFPHM 1991 (MFPHM 1987), FRCGP 1991 (MRCGP 1976), FRCP (London) 1992 (MRCP 1971), fndr FMedSci 1998, foreign assoc memb Inst of Medicine US Nat Acad of Sciences 2008, tstee RSM 2014; *Publications* co-ed of books and author of over 300 scientific papers, editorials, book chapters and reports on topics incl: epidemiology, evidence-based practice, implementing research findings, health policy and environmental health; *Recreations* cycling, environmental and security issues; *Style*— Prof Sir Andrew Haines; ✉ London School of Hygiene and Tropical Medicine, Keppel Street, London WC1E 7HT (✆ 020 7927 9238, e-mail andy.haines@lshtm.ac.uk)

HAIRD, Susan Margaret; CB (2007); da of Douglas Haird, and Myrah, *née* Owen; *b* 10 October 1952; *Educ* Dollar Acad, Univ of St Andrews (MA), Coll of Europe; *m* 1979, David Lee Simpson; 1 s (Mark Simpson b 24 May 1982), 1 da (Anna Simpson b 27 June

1984); *Career* DTI: joined 1976, private sec to Perm Sec 1978, private sec to Parly Under-Sec 1979, Commercial Relations and Exports Div 1980–84, Personnel Div 1985–89, Industrial Materials Div 1989, on loan Equal Opportunities Div Cabinet Office 1989–92, Atomic Energy Div 1992–96, Office of Manpower Econs 1996–99, dir Export Control 1999–2000, dir Export Control and Non-Proliferation 2000–02, dir HR and Change Mgmnt 2002–04, dep chief exec UK Trade and Investment 2004, currently European rep for British Columbia, vice-pres Canada UK Chamber of Commerce; non-exec dir Engrg Employers Fedn; memb Advsy Cncl Br Expertise; *Style—* Miss Susan Haird, CB

HAITINK, Bernard; Hon CH (2002), Hon KBE (1977); *b* 1929; *Career* conductor; chief conductor Concertgebouw Orchestra Amsterdam 1964–88, artistic dir and princ conductor London Philharmonic Orchestra 1967–79, musical dir Glyndebourne Opera 1978–88, musical dir ROH Covent Garden 1988–2002 (debut 1977), pres London Philharmonic Orchestra 1990–, music dir European Union Youth Orch 1994–99; princ guest conductor Boston Symphony 1995–, chief conductor Dresden Staatshapelle 2002–; guest conductor: Berlin Philharmonic, Bayerische Rundfunk, Vienna Philharmonic, Concertgebouw, Salzburg Festival, Berlin Festival, re-opening of Glyndebourne Opera 1994, Tanglewood Festival, LSO 1998; conductor laureate Concertgebouw Orchestra Amsterdam 1999; numerous recordings for EMI and Philips; awarded Bruckner Medal of Honour Bruckner Soc, hon gold medal Gustav Mahler Soc 1970, Erasmus prize Holland 1991, gold medal Royal Philharmonic Soc 1991, Olivier Award for Oustanding Achievement in Opera 1996; Hon DMus Univs of Oxford and Leeds; Order of Orange (Nassau), Chevalier de l'Ordre des Arts et des Lettres (France), offr Order of the Crown (Belgium); RAM, FRCM; *Style—* Bernard Haitink, Esq, CH, KBE; ✉ c/o Askonas Holt, Lincoln House, 300 High Holborn, London WC1V 7JH (☎ 020 7400 1700, fax 020 7400 1799, e-mail info@askonasholt.co.uk)

HAITSMA MULIER, Pieter Willem Gaspard; s of Jean Gaspard Haitsma Mulier (d 1980), of Malmesbury, Wilts, and Anna Maria Wilhelmina Jacoba Hope of Luffness, *née* Fabius; *b* 21 February 1969; *Educ* Rijks Univ Utrecht; *m* Nov 2006, HSH Princess Vanessa zu Sayn-Wittgenstein-Berleburg; *Career* Lt Col (reserve) Huzaren van Boreel Royal Netherlands Mil Acad 1993; head of sales Nomura Int 1995–98, princ Oakes Fitzwilliams & Co Ltd 1998–2001, head of private placement gp ARC Assocs 2001–02, fndr and ceo Mulier Capital Ltd 2003–; *Recreations* sailing, skiing, tennis; *Clubs* New (Edinburgh); *Style—* Pieter Haitsma Mulier, Esq; ✉ Luffness Castle, Aberlady EH3 0QB (☎ 01875 870218); Mulier Capital Limited, 19 Eccleston Square, London SW1V 1NS (☎ 020 7821 6111, fax 020 7821 5999, e-mail pieter@mulier.com)

HAJDUCKI, Andrew Michael; QC (Scot 1994); *b* 12 November 1952; *Educ* Dulwich Coll, Downing Coll Cambridge (MA); *m* 1, 1980 (m dis), Gayle Shepherd; 3 s (1 decd), 1 da; m 2, 2002, Katharine Lilli Dodd; *Career* called to the Bar Gray's Inn 1976, admitted Faculty of Advocates 1979, pt/t tutor Univ of Edinburgh 1979–81, reporter session cases 1980, temp sheriff 1987–99; safeguarder: Lothian Children's Panel 1987–96, East, West and Midlothian and City of Edinburgh 1996–97; arbiter (Scotland) Motor Insurers' Bureau Untraced Drivers' Scheme 2000–03; reporter Scottish Legal Aid Bd 1999–; candidate and agent (Lib) Scot 1978–85; FSA Scot 1990; *Publications* Scottish Civic Government Licensing Law (co-author, 1994, 3 edn 2009), Civil Jury Trials (1998, 2 edn 2006), Scottish Licensing Handbook (contrib, 1999), Renton and Brown's Statutory Offences (contrib, 2000); also author of books on railway history, author of various articles in legal jls; *Recreations* reading, travel; *Style—* Andrew Hajducki, Esq, QC; ✉ c/o Advocates' Library, Parliament House, Edinburgh EH1 1RF

HAJI-IOANNOU, Sir Stelios; kt (2006); s of Loucas Haji-Ioannou, of Athens, Greece, and Nedi Haji-Ioannou; *b* 14 February 1967; *Educ* Doucas HS Athens, LSE (BSc), City Univ (MSc); *Career* with Troodos Maritime 1989–91; fndr: Stelmar Tankers 1992, easyJet 1995, easyGroup 1998, easyInternetcafé 1999, easyCar 2000, easyValue 2000, easyMoney 2001, easyCinema 2003, easyBus 2004, easyHotel 2004, easyCruise 2004, easyPizza 2004, easyMusic 2004, easy4men 2004, easyJobs 2004, easyMobile 2005, easyOffice, easyWatch, easyVan, easyGym 2010, easyProperty 2014; European Communicator of the Year PR Week Awards 2000, GQ Man of the Year (entrepreneur) 2001, Ernst and Young Young Entrepreneur of the Year 2001; fndr chm Cyprus Marine Environment Protection Association (CYMEPA) 1992, fndr Stelios Philanthropic Fndn 2008, memb Cncl of Ambassadors WWF-UK; hon consul gen for the Republic of Cyprus to Monaco 2009; hon degree: Liverpool John Moores Univ, Cass Business Sch, Newcastle Business Sch, Cranfield Univ; *Recreations* serial entrepreneurship, yachting; *Style—* Sir Stelios Haji-Ioannou

HALAM, Ann; *see:* Jones, Gwyneth Ann

HALBERT, Bill; *Career* exec chm KCOM Gp plc 2009– (exec dep chm 2008–09); *Style—* Bill Halbert, Esq; ✉ KCOM Group plc, 37 Carr Lane, Hull HU1 3RE

HALBERT, His Hon Derek Rowland; s of late Ronald Halbert, and Freda Mabel, *née* Impett; *b* 25 March 1948; *Educ* King's Sch Chester, Selwyn Coll Cambridge (MA), Open Univ (BA), Univ of Chester (LLD); *m* 28 Sept 1972, Heather Rose, da of late Samuel Walter Ashe; 2 da (Sarah Lucy b 21 Jan 1979, Elizabeth Amy b 17 May 1983); *Career* called to the Bar Inner Temple 1971, in practice Wales & Chester Circuit 1972–95, recorder of the Crown Court 1991–95; circuit judge: Wales & Chester Circuit 1995–2007, Northern Circuit 2007–15, ret; designated civil judge: Cheshire and N Wales 2003–06, Cheshire 2007–; hon sr lectr in law Univ of Chester 2015–; *Clubs* Leander; *Style—* His Hon Derek Halbert; ✉ Chester Civil Justice Centre, Trident House, Little St John Street, Chester CH1 1SN

HALDANE OF GLENEAGLES, (James) Martin; 28th of Gleneagles; er s of James Haldane (d 1990), of Gleneagles, Auchterarder, and Joanna Margaret, *née* Thorburn; suc his kinsman, Alexander Chinnery Haldane, 27th of Gleneagles (d 1994); *b* 18 September 1941; *Educ* Winchester, Magdalen Coll Oxford; *m* 5 Oct 1968, Petronella Victoria, da of Sir Peter Scarlett, KCMG, KCVO; 1 s, 2 da; *Heir* s, James Alexander Haldane; *Career* chartered accountant; ptnr: Arthur Young 1970–89, Chiene & Tait 1989–2001 (chm 1998–2001); chm: Craighead Investments plc 1982–90, Queen's Hall (Edinburgh) Ltd 1992–2001, Shires Income plc 2003–08 (dir 1996–2008), Investors Capital Trust plc 2004–10 (dir 1995–2010); dir: Northern and Scottish Bd Legal and General Assurance Soc 1984–87, Scottish Life Assurance Co 1990–2001 (dep chm 1999–2001), Wellington Members Agency Ltd 1995–96, Stace Barr Wellington Ltd 1996–97, Stace Barr Angerstein plc 1997–2001; chm: Scottish Philharmonic Soc 1978–85, Scottish Chamber Orchestra 1981–85, Scottish Opera Endowment Tst 2011–15; memb: Cncl Edinburgh Festival Soc 1985–89, D'Oyly Carte Opera Tst 1985–92 and 2012–, Cncl Nat Tst for Scotland 1992–97, Ct Univ of Stirling 1997–2005; memb Queen's Body Guard for Scotland (Royal Co of Archers) (treas 1992–2001); chm of govrs Innerpeffray Library 1994–2005; Hon DUniv Stirling 2006; FRSA; *Recreations* music, golf, shooting; *Clubs* Brooks's, New (Edinburgh), Hon Co of Edinburgh Golfers; *Style—* Martin Haldane of Gleneagles; ✉ Gleneagles, Auchterarder, Perthshire PH3 1PJ (☎ 01764 682388 and 01764 682535, e-mail jmhaldane@gleneagles.org); 23 Northumberland Street, Edinburgh EH3 6LR (☎ 0131 556 2924)

HALDENBY, Andrew John; s of Gerald Haldenby (d 1978), and Elizabeth Haldenby; *b* 4 January 1972; *Educ* Univ of Cambridge (BA), Birkbeck Coll London (MSc); *m* 2003, Simone; 1 s (Charles b 2007), 1 da (Violet b 2009); *Career* researcher then head Political Section Cons Research Dept 1995–97, dir of studies Centre for Policy Studies 1998–99, dir of communications Business for Sterling 2000–01; Reform: co-fndr, dir of research 2001–05, dir 2005–; memb Mont Pelerin Soc 2011–; *Recreations* family, chess, reading, house music; *Style—* Andrew Haldenby, Esq; ✉ Reform, 45 Great Peter Street, London SW1P 3LT

HALE, Brenda Anne; MLA; *b* 29 January 1968, Belfast, NI; *Educ* Open Univ (BSc); *m* 25 July 1987, Capt Mark James Hale (ka 2009); 2 da (Victoria b 4 May 1993, Alexandra b 16 May 2001); *Career* MLA (DUP) Lagan Valley 2011–; memb: Br-Irish Parly Assembly 2012, North-South Parly Assoc 2012, Cwlth Parly Assoc 2013, NI Policing Bd 2014; NI ambass ABF The Soldiers' Charity; memb DUP 2011–; *Style—* Mrs Brenda Hale, MLA; ✉ Room 350, Parliament Buildings, Stormont, Ballymiscaw, Belfast BT4 3XX (website www.brendahale.co.uk)

HALE, Charles Martin; s of Charles Sidney Hale (d 1981), and Carmen, *née* de Mora (d 2001); *b* 19 January 1936, London; *Educ* St Bernard's Sch NY, Culver Mil Acad, Stanford Univ (BSc), Harvard Business Sch (MBA); *m* 11 Feb 1967, Kaaren Alexis; 2 da (Melissa b 18 May 1971, Amanda b 9 Nov 1976); *Career* USN: serv USS Union, Ensign i/c Boat Gp Div 1958, Lt 1960; gen ptnr Hirsch & Co London 1963–71, md and sr offr Europe AG Becker Inc 1971–83, gen ptnr Lehman Bros Kuhn Loeb Inc 1983–84, md and head Int Div Donaldson Lufkin & Jenrette Securities Corp 1984–95, chm Donaldson Lufkin & Jenrette Int 1996–2000; vice-chm Credit Suisse First Boston (Europe) Ltd 2000–01; exec chm, dir and mgmnt and exec ctee Polar Capital Partners 2002–; dir: Innospec (Nasdaq) 1998–2008, Eddington Capital Mgmnt 2006–10, Ridley Park Paragon Fund Ltd 2010–13; chm UK Assoc of NY Stock Exchange Membs 1989–91; memb: Advsy Cncl Inst of United States Studies 2000–03, Great Ormond St Hosp for Children Redevelopment Advsy Bd 2004–07, N American Advsy Cncl and William Pitt Gp Chatham House 2009–, Advsy Bd Perlus Fund 2013–, The Pilgrims, Le Cercle; *Recreations* tennis, travel, opera and philately; *Clubs* Boodle's, Hurlingham, Queenwood Golf, Harvard (NY), George, Mark's, City of London, Westmoor (Nantucket), Cliffside Beach (Nantucket), Anglers (Nantucket), Harry's Bar; *Style—* Charles Hale, Esq; ✉ 33 Lyall Mews, London SW1X 8DJ (☎ 020 7245 9916)

HALE, Julian Anthony Stuart; s of James Peter Rashleigh Hale (d 1981), and Gillian Mariette Stuart, *née* Mason; *b* 27 November 1940; *Educ* Winchester, ChCh Oxford (MA); *m* 1, 1963 (m dis 1970), Jennifer Monahan; m 2, 1971, Mary Kathleen Benét (d 1984); m 3, 1987, Helen Elizabeth Grace, da of Julian Likierman, of London; 2 da (Laura b 1972, Tamara b 1988), 1 s (Felix b 1990); *Career* books ed G G Harrap 1963–65, Italian prog organiser BBC External Servs 1972–73 (prodr and scriptwriter 1968–72), ed European Gazette 1973, writer 1973–; prodr BBC Radio 3 and 4 incl: In The Air, Wilko's Weekly, File On 4, Third Ear, Radio Lives 1979–94 (also presenter European Journeys); ind radio prodr 1994–; prodr Icon Books audiotapes 1996–; *Books* incl: Ceausescu's Romania (1971), Radio Power (1975), Snap Judgement (1974), Vicious Circles (1978), Midwinter Madness (1979), Black Summer (1982), Down Among the Stars (2009), Landscapes of the Imagination: The French Riviera (2009); *Style—* Julian Hale, Esq; ✉ 372 Cromwell Tower, Barbican, London EC2Y 8NB (☎ 020 7256 2566, e-mail jashale@btinternet.com)

HALE OF RICHMOND, Baroness (Life Peer UK 2004), of Easby in the County of Yorkshire; Dame Brenda Marjorie Hale; DBE (1994), PC (1999); da of Cecil Frederick Hale (d 1958), and Marjorie, *née* Godfrey (d 1981); *b* 31 January 1945; *Educ* Richmond HS for Girls Yorks, Girton Coll Cambridge (MA); *m* 1, 1968 (m dis 1992), Dr (Anthony) John Christopher Hoggett, QC, *qv*, s of Christopher Hoggett (d 1989), of Grimsby; 1 da (Julia b 1973); m 2, 1992, Prof Julian Thomas Farrand, QC, *qv*, s of John Farrand (d 1998); *Career* Univ of Manchester: asst lectr 1966, lectr 1968, sr lectr 1976, reader 1981, prof of law 1986–89; prof of English law KCL 1989–90 (visiting prof 1990–); visiting fell Nuffield Coll Oxford 1997–2005, visitor Girton Coll Cambridge 2004– (hon fell 1996–2004); law cmmr 1984–93; called to the Bar Gray's Inn 1969 (bencher 1994), QC 1989; asst recorder 1984–89, recorder of the Crown Court 1989–93, judge of the High Court of Justice (Family Div) 1994–99, liaison judge (Family Div) London 1997–99, Lord Justice of Appeal 1999–2004, Lord of Appeal in Ordinary 2004–09, a Justice of the Supreme Court 2009–13 (dep pres 2013–); chllr Univ of Bristol 2004–; pres UK Assoc of Women Judges 2004–, pres Int Assoc of Women Judges 2010–12; memb Cncl of Tribunals 1980–84; pres Nat Family Mediation 1994– (chm 1989–93), chair Mgmnt Ctee Royal Courts of Justice Advice Bureau 2002–03, memb Human Fertilisation and Embryology Authy 1990–93; jt gen ed Journal of Social Welfare Law 1978–84; managing tstee Nuffield Fndn 1987–2002; Hon LLD: Univ of Sheffield 1989, London Guildhall Univ 1996, Univ of Manchester 1997, Univ of Bristol 2002, Univ of Cambridge 2005, Univ of Hull 2006, KCL 2007, City Univ 2007, Univ of Oxford 2007, Univ of Reading 2007, Coll of Law 2008, Univ of West England 2008, Univ of Huddersfield 2009, Univ of Sussex 2009, Univ of Salford 2010, Georgetown Univ Washington DC 2010, Univ of Glasgow 2011, Univ of Kent 2011, Univ of Westminster 2011, Univ of Liverpool 2013, Univ of Swansea 2014, Univ of York 2015, Ulster Univ 2016; Hon DUniv: Essex 2005, Open Univ 2016; Hon FBA 2004, Hon FRCPsych 2007; *Books* Mental Health Law (1976, 5 edn 2010), Parents and Children (1977, 4 edn 1993), The Family Law and Society – Cases and Materials (with D S Pearl, 1983, 6 edn with D S Pearl, E Cooke and D Monk 2008), Women and the Law (with S Atkins, 1984), From the Test-tube to the Coffin – Choice and Regulation in Private Life (The Hamlyn Lectures, 1996); many contribs to legal texts and periodicals; *Recreations* domesticity, drama, duplicate bridge; *Clubs* Athenaeum; *Style—* The Rt Hon the Lady Hale of Richmond, DBE, PC; ✉ The Supreme Court of the United Kingdom, Parliament Square, London SW1P 3BD (☎ 020 7960 1980, e-mail justices@supremecourt.uk)

HALES, Antony John (Tony); CBE (2008); s of Sidney Alfred Hales (d 1985), and Margaret Joan, *née* Wood; *b* 25 May 1948, Blackpool; *Educ* Repton, Univ of Bristol (BSc); *m* Linda Christine, da of Hugh Churchlow; 4 c; *Career* Cadbury Schweppes: food salesman 1969–70, asst brand mangr milk products 1970–71, brand mangr biscuits 1971–74; foods mktg mangr Cadbury Typhoo 1974–79, mktg dir Joshua Tetley & Son Ltd 1979–83, md Halls Oxford and West Brewery Co 1983–85, md Ind Coope-Taylor Walker Ltd 1985–87, retail dir Allied Breweries Ltd 1987, md Ansells Ltd 1987–89; Allied Domecq plc (Allied-Lyons plc until 1994): dir 1989–99, chief exec J Lyons & Co Ltd 1989–91, gp chief exec 1991–99; chm: Navy, Army and Air Force Institutes Ltd 2001–08, Workspace Gp plc 2002–10, British Waterways 2005–12, NAAFI Pension Tstees 2009–, Canal and River Tst 2012–15, The Greenwich Fndn 2014–; non-exec dir: Hyder plc 1993–97, HSBC Bank 1994–2001, Aston Villa FC 1997–2006, Tempo Holdings Ltd 2000–01, David Halsall Int 2000–05, Reliance Security Gp 2001–05, SIS (Hldgs) Ltd 2002–10, International Personal Finance Gp plc 2006–, Services Sound and Vision Corp 2009–, WNO 2010–, Capital & Regional plc 2011–; chm Nat Manufacturing Cncl CBI 1993–95; Freeman City of London 1986, Liveryman Worshipful Co of Brewers 1986, The Greenwich Fndn 2014–; *Style—* Tony Hales, Esq, CBE; ✉ Belvoir House, Edstone Court, Wooton Wawen, Henley in Arden, Warwickshire B95 6DD

HALES, Lady Celestria Magdalen Mary; *née* Noel; da of 5 Earl of Gainsborough (d 2009); *b* 27 January 1954; *Educ* St Mary's Convent Ascot, St Hilda's Coll Oxford; *m* 1 March 1990, Timothy Manville Hales, o s of late S W M Hales, MC; 1 da (Catherine Rose Mary b 11 June 1990); *Career* social ed (as Lady Celestria Noel) Jennifer's Diary in Harpers & Queen 1992–98, ed PrivatAir the Magazine 2000–11, conslt to Debrett's 2013–; *Books* The Harpers & Queen Book of the Season (1994), Debrett's Guide to the Season (2000), Round the World in 60 Years – The Windsor Diamond Jubilee Pageant (2012), Debrett's Handbook (co-ed, 2014); *Style—* The Lady Celestria Hales; ✉ Castle Farmhouse, Mill Road, Maxey, Peterborough PE6 9EZ

HALES, Christopher James; s of James Camille Hales (d 1968), and Genefer Enid, *née* Ratcliff (d 2007); *b* 12 November 1952; *Educ* Westminster, Univ Hall (Univ of London external BA); *Career* called to the Bar Gray's Inn 1979; Treasy slr 1990–2003, lawyer Health and Safety Exec 2004–09, lawyer Govt Legal Dept (formerly Treasy slr) 2009–; *Recreations* composing songs, sport, art, karate, painting; *Style*— Christopher Hales, Esq; ✉ Government Legal Department, One Kemble Street, London WC2B 4TS (☎ 020 7210 2961, e-mail chris.hales@tsol.gsi.gov.uk)

HALEY, Geoffrey Norman (Geoff); s of Norman Haley (d 1966), of Pudsey, W Yorks, and Grace Ward, *née* Cooke (d 1983); *b* 12 October 1944; *Educ* Accrington GS, Univ of London (BL), Brunel Univ and Henley Mgmnt Coll (MBA), Inst of Mktg (DipM); *m* 22 Oct 1966, Doreen Haley, da of Leslie Veitch; 1 s (Paul b 5 Sept 1974), 1 da (Julie b 24 June 1977); *Career* admitted slr 1971, dep gp legal advsr Costain Gp 1974–78, dir Costain UK 1980–86 (legal advsr 1978–86), gen mangr Costain Ventures 1986–89; ptnr Theodore Goddard 1989–93, SJ Berwin & Co 1993–98, Arnold & Porter 1998–2000; legal advsr: Thames Barrier Consortium 1979–86, Channel Tunnel contractors Transmanche Link 1985; dir GKN Kwikform Ltd 1986–89, alternate dir Br Urban Devpt 1988–89; expert to European Cmmn; conslt advsr: UNCTAD Geneva, UNIDO Vienna; chm Int Project Finance Assoc 1998–; memb: Law Soc, Soc of Construction Law, Greenlands Assoc, Ascot Round Table, Panel Euro Centre for Infrastructure Studies Rotterdam; visiting prof London Met Univ; numerous articles in the field of construction law and private fin for transportation and infrastructure projects; Lord of the Manor of Kidderminster Burnell; MInstPet; *Books* A-Z of Boot Projects, Negotiating Infrastructure Agreements; *Recreations* swimming, cycling, walking; *Clubs* RAC; *Style*— Geoffrey Haley, Esq; ✉ Tanglewood, 39A Llanvair Drive, South Ascot, Berkshire SL5 9LW (☎ 01344 627311); International Project Finance Association, 2nd Floor, 150 Fleet Street, London EC4A 2DU(☎ 020 7427 0900, fax 020 7583 8020)

HALFON, Rt Hon Robert Henry; PC (2015), MP; *b* 22 March 1969; *Educ* Highgate Sch, Univ of Exeter (BA, MA); *Career* MP (Cons) Harlow 2010–; PPS to Rt Hon George Osborne, MP, Chllr of the Exchequer 2014–15, dep chm Cons Pty and min without portfolio Cabinet Office 2015–; exec memb 1922 Ctee 2010–14, memb Public Administration Select Ctee 2010–14, co-chm All-Pty Parly Skills and Apprenticeships Gp 2011–12, chm All-Pty Parly Fair Fuel Gp 2011–14, chm All-Pty Parly Literacy Gp 2012–13, vice-chm Kurdistan Region Parly Gp 2012–15, co-chm Brazil Parly Gp 2013–15; Nat Conservative Excellence Award for Social Action 2008, The House Magazine Transport Campaigner of the Year Dods Parly Awards 2014, Campaigner of the Year Spectator 2014; *Books* Stop the Union Bashing (2012); *Recreations* reading, Chelsea FC, horology; *Clubs* East India; *Style*— The Rt Hon Robert Halfon, MP; ✉ House of Commons, London SW1A 0AA (e-mail halfon4harlow@roberthalfon.com, website www.roberthalfon.com, Twitter @Halfon4HarlowMP)

HALFORD, Andy; s of Frank Halford, and Norma Halford; *b* 18 March 1959, Berks; *Educ* Bedford Sch, Univ of Nottingham (BA); *m* 1984, Alison; 3 s (Matthew, Christopher, Toby); *Career* chartered accountant; Price Waterhouse Nottingham and Durban 1980–92; East Midlands Electricity plc: business devpt dir 1992–95, IT dir 1995–97, gp finance dir 1997–98; Vodafone Gp plc: chief financial offr UK 1999–2001, chief financial offr North Europe, Middle East and Africa 2001–02, chief financial offr Verizon Wireless 2002–05, gp chief financial offr 2005–14; gp finance offr Standard Chartered Bank 2014–; FCA; *Recreations* property renovation, photography, cars, travel; *Style*— Andy Halford, Esq; ✉ Standard Chartered Bank, 1 Basinghall Avenue, London EC2V 5DD

HALFORD, John; s of Gordon Halford, of Bristol, and Mary, *née* Stevenson; *b* 28 May 1967, Newcastle; *Educ* Univ of Southampton (LLM, Sally Kiff Prize); *Career* admitted slr 1996; mangr and sr advsr immigration advice centre Bristol 1990–91, trainee and slr specialising in immigration cases with human rights dimension Humberside Law Centre 1992–98, slr Public Law Project 1998–2003 (currently memb Bd), ptnr Bindman & Ptnrs Solicitors 2003–; memb Mental Health and Disability Sub-Ctee and Domestic Human Rights Reference Gp Law Soc; memb: Admin Law Bar Assoc, Human Rights Lawyers' Assoc, Community Care Practitioners' Gp; *Publications* Butterworth's Health Services Law and Practice (co-author, 2001), Legal Action's Health Law Series (co-author), contrib to specialist legal pubns incl Judicial Review, Disabled Student Advisor and Legal Action; *Recreations* mountaineering, reading, music, theatre, film; *Style*— John Halford, Esq; ✉ Bindman & Partners Solicitors, 275 Gray's Inn Road, London WC1X 8QB (☎ 020 7833 4433, fax 020 7837 9792, e-mail j.halford@bindmans.com)

HALFORD, William Timothy (Tim); s of John Halford (d 2003), of Ripon, N Yorks, and Beatrice Margery Halford (d 1959); *b* 19 February 1947; *Educ* The Leys Sch Cambridge; *m* 1969 (m dis 2000), Andrea Rosemary, da of John Henry Lee (d 1968); 3 da (Amy Katherine b 15 Dec 1971, Joanna Alice b 8 Aug 1973, Harriet Louisa b 15 Nov 1975); *Career* PR consultancy 1966–75, vice-pres of Euro public affairs Occidental Petroleum Corp 1975–84, dir group public affairs Grand Metropolitan plc 1984–92, dir group PR Trafalgar House plc 1992–94, dir group corporate affrs Standard Chartered plc 1995–2002, dir Stonehenge Public Relations Ltd 2002–07; chm: Crechendo Ltd 1992–, Milford Collection Ltd 2009–; chm Ponthafren Assoc 2012–15; FCIPR; *Recreations* sailing, walking, theatre; *Style*— Tim Halford, Esq; ✉ Malt House, Llandyssil, Powys SY15 6LJ

HALIFAX, 3 Earl of (UK 1944); Sir Charles Edward Peter Neil Wood; 7 Bt (GB 1784); DL (1983); also Viscount Halifax (UK 1866), Baron Irwin (UK 1925); s of 2 Earl of Halifax (d 1980); *b* 14 March 1944; *Educ* Eton, ChCh Oxford; *m* 1976, Camilla, da of Charles Frank Johnston Younger, DSO, TD (d 1995), of Gledswood, Melrose, Roxburghshire; 1 s (James Charles, Lord Irwin b 1977), 1 da (Lady Joanna b 1980); *Heir* s, Lord Irwin; *Career* dep chm Christie's UK; JP 1985–2014; High Steward of York Minster 1988; KStJ; *Style*— The Rt Hon the Earl of Halifax, KStJ, DL; ✉ Garrowby, York YO41 1QD

HALL, Adrian; s of Cecil Herbert Wellington Hall, MBE (d 2003), and Jean Barbara, *née* Littlejohn; *b* 24 August 1963, Littlehampton, W Sussex; *Educ* Elgin Acad, Dorset Inst of HE; *m* 30 June 2007, Hilary Rhona Ellis; 3 s (Benjamin Daniel b 31 Jan 1990, Jacob Wellington b 2 Aug 1992, Fyfe Evan b 10 May 2009), 1 da (Ivy Agnes b 1 June 2012); *Career* archaeologist 1981–88; Civil Serv: exec offr Dept of Employment 1991–96, higher exec offr Dept of Employment 1997–99, head of housing and regeneration Govt Office for the South East, head of multimedia resources DfES 2002–05, prog dir personalised content DfES 2005–06; dir mobile learning Steljes Ltd 2006–08, dir Okapi Consultancy and EdTech Consultancy 2009–, int partnerships dir Renaissance Learning Ltd 2016–; memb Advsy Bd NESTA Futurelab 2002–06; md Int Gateway for Gifted Youth Univ of Warwick 2012–15, digital man Child to Child 2015–; *Recreations* mountain biking, cricket, travelling; *Style*— Adrian Hall, Esq; ✉ 13 Parkstead Road, London SW15 5HS; Okapi Consultancy Ltd, 13 Parkstead Road, London SW15 5HS (e-mail hally24@gmail.com)

HALL, Col Alan Edmund Matticot; MBE (2010), TD (1975), DL (London 1985); s of Maj Edmund Hall (d 1983), of Helston, Cornwall, and Norah, *née* Carrick (d 1985); *b* 7 October 1935, London; *Educ* Emanuel Sch, Churcher's Coll Petersfield, The GS Enfield; *m* 8 Feb 1958, Diane Mary, da of Robert William Keyte (d 1969), of Cliftonville, Kent; 2 da (Amanda b 1959, Nicola b 1962), 1 s (James b 1968); *Career* Nat Serv 1955–57, Territorial Serv RMP 1961–82; OC 44 Parachute Bde Provost Co 1965–67, OC 253 Provost Co 1969–76; appt Hon Col RMP TA 1977–82; memb Ctees Gtr London TAVRA: Exec and Fin, Gen Purpose and Fin, HQ, HQ Club (vice-chm (Army) 1992–2002)); Hon Col 36 Signal Regt 1990–2001; md: Ind Coope London 1973–77, Ind Coope Ltd 1978–80, Ind Coope East Anglia Ltd 1981–84, J & W Nicholson & Co 1984, Löwenbräu (UK) Ltd 1993–94 (dir of UK sales Löwenbräu Lager 1986–93); dir Infomatrix Ltd 1994–96; estab Alan Hall Associates 1994; dir Birchdeck Ltd 1998–2003 (chm 1998–2003); pres The Licensed

Victuallers National Homes 1990, pres Soc of Past Chairmen 1991 and 1995, former pres The Percheron Horse Soc, regnl chm The Wishing Well Appeal; pres: NE London SSAFA – Forces Help and FHS, Co of Gtr London NE Scout Assoc, Ilford Div St John Ambulance, Cystic Fibrosis Holiday Fund 2000–12; memb: NE London Nat Employers Liaison Ctee, Appeal Bd Redbridge Sports and Leisure 2009–12; patron: Haven House Fndn 1998–2014 (life pres 2014), Helen Rollason Cancer Care Appeal 2000, Abbess Adelicia Charity 2003–; vice-patron Peter May Meml Appeal; rep DL London Borough of Redbridge 1987–2010; chm Good Easter 2002– (parish cncllr 1999, vice-chm 2000–02); Freeman City of London 1984, Liveryman Worshipful Co of Broderers; FIMgt 1979; *Books* Seven Miles from Everywhere on the Way to Nowhere (2003); *Recreations* shooting, wood working, curry cooking, Jaguar cars; *Style*— Col Alan Hall, MBE, TD, DL; ✉ Pippins, Tye Green, Good Easter, Essex CM1 4SH (☎ 01245 231280, e-mail jaguarpippins@aol.com)

HALL, Ali; *Educ* Univ of Liverpool; *Career* former ed More magazine, currently ed Look magazine; *Style*— Ms Ali Hall; ✉ Look, IPC Media, Blue Fin Building, 110 Southwark Street, London SE1 0SU

HALL, Andrew; *Career* chief exec Qualifications and Curriculum Devpt Authy 2009–10 (acting chief exec 2008–09), ceo Assessment and Qualifications Alliance 2010–; *Style*— Andrew Hall, Esq; ✉ AQA, Devas Street, Manchester M15 6EX

HALL, Anthony Arthur; *b* 25 May 1939, London; *Educ* Sir George Monoux GS Walthamstow; *m* Valerie Christine; 1 s (Graham Anthony), 2 da (Alison Lindsay, Kathryn Lorna); *Career* with Barclays Bank Ltd 1955–65, Barclays Bank DCO (Dominion Colonial & Overseas, now Barclays International) 1965–71, N M Rothschild (CI) Ltd Guernsey 1971–72, Bank of London and Montreal Nassau Bahamas 1972–73, Italian International Bank (CI) Ltd Guernsey 1974–76, md Rea Brothers (Guernsey) Ltd 1976–95 (chm 1995–96), jt ceo Rea Brothers Group plc 1988–1995, currently non-exec dir and conslt to a number of quoted investment funds; ACIB, FIOD; *Recreations* flying (multi-engine instrument rated pilot), target pistol shooting, golf, chess, swimming; *Clubs* Royal Guernsey Golf; *Style*— Anthony Hall, Esq; ✉ Le Pavois, Marette de Haut, St Martin, Guernsey GY4 6JL (☎ 01481 235254, fax 01481 235395, e-mail tonyhallgy@aol.com)

HALL, Prof Christopher; s of Victor Hall (d 2000), and Doris, *née* Gregory (d 2012); *b* 31 December 1944, Henley-on-Thames, Oxon; *Educ* Royal Belfast Academical Inst, Trinity Coll Oxford (MA, DPhil, DSc); *m* 1966, Sheila (d 2006), da of Thomas H McKelvey; 1 da (Liza b 30 May 1971), 1 s (Benjamin b 8 July 1973); *Career* res assoc Electrochemistry Res Centre Case Western Reserve Univ, Cleveland Ohio USA 1970–71, sr res assoc Sch of Chemical Sci UEA 1971–72, lectr in building engrg UMIST 1972–83, head Rock and Fluid Physics Dept Schlumberger Cambridge Res 1983–88, head Chemical Technol Dept Dowell Schlumberger St Etienne France 1988–90, scientific advsr Schlumberger Cambridge Res 1990–99; Univ of Edinburgh: prof of materials and dir Centre for Materials Sci and Engrg 1999–2010, dir of res Sch of Engrg and Electronics 2002–08, sr hon professorial fell 2010–; visiting prof Univ of Manchester 1994–, visiting fell Princeton Univ 1998, visiting scientific advsr Schlumberger Cambridge Res 1999–2004, sr memb Robinson Coll Cambridge 1988–, sr memb Int Union of Testing and Res Laboratories for Materials and Structures; memb: EPSRC Structural Materials Coll 1994–2010, EPSRC Review Panel on Scanning Probe Microscopy 1998, Soc of Chemical Industry; Brian Mercer Award for Innovation Royal Soc 2001; FRSC 1980, FIMMM 1990, CEng 1990, FRSE 2010, FREng 2013; *Publications* Polymer Materials (1981, 2 edn 1989), Civil Engineering Materials (contrib), Water Transport in Brick, Stone and Concrete (with W D Hoff, 2002, 2 edn 2012), ICE Manual of Construction Materials (contrib), Materials: A Very Short Introduction (2014); numerous scientific papers on physical chemistry, materials sci and engrg in professional jls; *Style*— Prof Christopher Hall; ✉ 9A Church Street, Stapleford, Cambridge CB22 5DS (☎ 01223 844343); School of Engineering, University of Edinburgh, The King's Buildings, Edinburgh EH9 3JL (e-mail christopher.hall@ed.ac.uk)

HALL, Capt Christopher John Pepler; RD (1976, Bar 1986); s of Cdr Harry John Hall, DSO, DSC*, RD (d 1994), of Salisbury, Wilts, and Kathleen Gwladys, *née* Pepler (d 1994); *b* 30 December 1940, Zanzibar; *Educ* Marlborough, Univ of Edinburgh; *m* 1, 8 July 1967, Patricia Valerie (d 1992), da of Capt William Neil Kennedy Mellon Crawford, VRD, CA (d 1978); 5 s (Richard b 1969, Ian b 1970, David b 1972, Alistair, Stephen (twins) b 1976); *m* 2, 4 Nov 2000, Elizabeth Mary Stewart, da of Philip Ralph Scrafton, MPS, and wid of Finlay McLeay Morgan (d 1990); *Career* RNR 1960–92; Capt 1988, CO HMS Claverhouse Forth Division RNR 1983–89, Capt Mobilisation and Recruiting (Reserves) 1989–92, Hon ADC to HM The Queen 1991–92, Naval Vice-Chm Lowland RFCA 1992–2006; qualified CA 1966, Cooper Bros Mombasa 1967–68; ptnr: Davidson Smith Wighton and Crawford Edinburgh 1970–78, Turquands Barton Mayhew 1978–80, Ernst & Whinney 1980–82; md Hall Management Services Ltd 1982–93, sole prop CJP Hall CA 1989–2001; conslt to various charities 2001–; Scot Episcopal Church: convenor Finance Ctee 1991–96, diocesan sec and treas Diocese of Argyll and the Isles 1987–2001, convenor Provincial Investment Ctee 2000–06; chm Sea Cadet Assoc in Scotland 2006–12; *Recreations* sailing, travel, reading, theatre, Zanzibar Anglican cathedral restoration; *Clubs* Royal Scots (Edinburgh), RNSA, Mombasa (Kenya); *Style*— Christopher J P Hall, RD*; ✉ 15 Zetland Place, Edinburgh EH5 3LZ (☎ 0131 552 5991, e-mail cjph@challca.com)

HALL, Colin; s of Arthur Graham Henry Hall (d 1998), and Winifred Martha, *née* Gray (d 1979); *b* 23 April 1945; *Educ* Stationers' Company's Sch, Univ of Bristol (LLB); *m* 29 Sept 1973, Philippa Margaret, da of Hac Collinson, of Sway, Hants; 4 s (Nicholas Justin b 1976, Oliver Rupert b 1978, Giles Edward, Rupert Charles (twins) b 1981); *Career* HM Dip Serv 1966–68, admitted slr 1971, ptnr Slaughter and May slrs 1978–98 (joined 1969); dir The Woodland Tst 1998–; tstee The Tree Register of the British Isles 1992–; *Recreations* sailing, gardening, farming, forestry; *Style*— Colin Hall, Esq; ✉ The Oast House, West End, Frensham, Surrey GU10 3EP (☎ 01252 793422, fax 01252 795263)

HALL, Daniel Charles Joseph; s of Stuart Hall, of Wilmslow, Cheshire, and Hazel, *née* Bennett; *b* 29 August 1962; *Educ* Repton, Univ of Bristol (LLB), Coll of Law London; *m* 11 May 1996, Melanie Jane; 2 s (Benjamin b 24 Oct 1997, Giles b 25 Nov 2002), 1 da (Isabel b 25 April 2000); *Career* slr; trainee slr Eversheds 1985–87, slr Clifford Chance 1987–92, ptnr Eversheds 1992– (head of corporate 1999–); chm Hallé Orchestra Tstees, memb regnl ctee London Stock Exchange; memb Law Soc; memb BASC; *Recreations* golf, shooting, fishing; *Style*— Daniel Hall, Esq; ✉ Brookfield Farm, Ancoats Lane, Alderley Edge, Cheshire SK9 7TT (☎ 01565 872525); Eversheds, Eversheds House, 70 Great Bridgewater Street, Manchester M1 5ES (☎ 0845 497 9797, fax 0845 497 8888, e-mail danielhall@eversheds.com)

HALL, Prof Sir David Michael Baldock; kt (2003); s of Ronald Hall, and Gwen, *née* Baldock; *b* 4 August 1945; *Educ* Reigate GS, St George's Med Sch (MB BS); *m* 24 Aug 1966, Susan Marianne, da of Gordon Howard Luck; 2 da (Emma b 1969, Vanessa b 1971); *Career* paediatrician Baragwanath Hosp Johannesburg 1973–76, sr registrar Charing Cross Hosp 1976–78, conslt St George's Hosp 1978–93, prof of community paediatrics Children's Hosp Sheffield 1993–2005 (emeritus prof 2005–), currently hon prof of paediatrics Univ of Cape Town; hon conslt: The Spastics Soc (now Scope) 1982–86, Tadworth Ct 1986–92; med advsr Assoc for All Speech-Impaired Children 1981–86; pres RCPCH (formerly Br Paediatric Assoc) 2000–03 (academic vice-pres 1994–98); fndr memb Children's Head Injury Tst, patron Scope 2003–12; FRCP 1986 (MRCP 1972), FRCPCH; *Books* Health for all Children (1989, 4 edn 2003), The Child with a Disability (2 edn

1996), Child Surveillance Handbook (3 edn 2009); *Recreations* travel, reading, music; *Clubs* Rotary, Breede River Winelands; *Style*— Prof Sir David Hall; ✉ Storrs House Farm, Storrs Lane, Sheffield S6 6GY (☎ 0114 285 3177, fax 0027 86 661 8429, e-mail d.hall@sheffield.ac.uk)

HALL, Prof Denis R; *b* 1 August 1942, Cardiff; *Educ* Univ of Manchester (BSc), Bart's Med Coll London (MPhil), Case Western Reserve Univ Cleveland Ohio (PhD), Edinburgh Business Sch (MBA); *m*; 2 c; *Career* graduate asst/postdoctoral fell Dept of Electrical Engrg Case Western Reserve Univ Cleveland OH 1967–71, postdoctoral research fell (Nat Acad of Scis Award) NASA Goddard Space Flight Center Greenbelt MD 1971–72, sr research scientist Avco Everett Research Lab Boston MA 1972–74 (summer visiting research scientist 1986 and 1988), princ scientific offr Royal Signals and Radar Estab MOD 1974–79, sr lectr/reader in applied laser physics Dept of Applied Physics Univ of Hull 1979–87; Heriot-Watt Univ Edinburgh: prof of optoelectronics Dept of Physics 1987–, currently asst princ (research); pt/t GS teacher in physics and physical educn 1965–67; conslt Systems Electronics Inc Cleveland OH 1969–74; MOD research contract monitor (industrial and univ contracts) 1974–79, MOD delg on Int Tech Cooperation Panel (lasers and IR systems) 1975–79, chief project scientist UK Satellite Laser Ranging Facility Royal Greenwich Observatory 1979–83; dir Laser Applications Ltd Hull 1980–86; memb: Satellite Laser Ranging Steering Ctee Astronomy, Space and Radio Bd SERC 1979–84, Quantum Electronics Bd Euro Physical Soc 1988–94, E13 Gp Ctee IEE 1993–; chm Quantum Electronics Gp Ctee Inst of Physics 1991–94 (memb 1977–81 and 1986–89); memb: Sigma Xi (elected) 1971, IEEE-LEOS 1991, Optical Soc of America; CEng, FInstP 1985 (MInstP 1974), FIEE 1986 (MIEE 1985), FRSE 1991; *Publications* author/jt author of numerous pubns in learned jls and of invited and contributed papers; *Style*— Prof Denis R Hall, FRSE; ✉ Department of Physics, Heriot-Watt University, Riccarton, Edinburgh EH14 4AS (☎ 0131 451 3081)

HALL, Dinny (Mrs Brannigan); da of David Alexander Hall, of Shantock House, Bovingdon, Hertfordshire, and Susan Anne, *née* Martyr; *b* 28 April 1959; *Educ* Bourne Valley Comp, Herts Sch of Art and Design St Albans, Central Sch of Art and Design (BA); *m*; 1 s (Lorcan); *Career* jewellery designer; set up own business in Soho London 1983, launched first range of jewellery using gold and precious stones 1990, opened first shop Notting Hill 1992, second shop Chelsea 1995; clients incl Harvey Nichols, Browns, Harrods and many other prestigious stores worldwide; collections featured since 1985 in magazines incl: Vogue, Harpers & Queen, Elle, Sunday Times, Sunday Telegraph; Br Accessory Designer of the Year 1989; *Books* Creative Jewellery (1986); *Recreations* cooking, travelling, walking; *Clubs* Groucho; *Style*— Ms Dinny Hall

HALL, Douglas William Hugh (Dougie); *b* 24 September 1980, Dingwall, Highlands and Islands; *Educ* Glenalmond Coll, Univ of Strathclyde (BA); *Career* rugby union player (hooker); clubs: Edinburgh Rugby 2002–07, Glasgow Warriors 2007–; Scotland: 31 caps, debut v Wales 2003; *Style*— Mr Dougie Hall; ✉ c/o Glasgow Warriors, Firhil Stadium, Firhill Road, Glasgow G20 7AL

HALL, Edward Peter (Ed); s of Sir Peter Hall , *qv*, and Jacqueline Hall; *Educ* Bedales, Univ of Leeds, Mountview Theatre Sch; *m* Baroness Issy van Randwyck; 2 da (Georgia Molly Catherine, Savannah Perdita Maisy); *Career* artistic dir: Hampstead Theatre, Propeller Theatre Co; assoc dir: Old Vic Theatre, NT; Propeller Theatre Co prodns incl: Henry V, Comedy of Errors, Twelfth Night (Best Dir TMA Theatre Award 1999), Rose Rage (adaption of Henry VI part I-III, Drama Desk Broadway, Best Dir Olivier Award nomination, TMA Award), A Midsummer Night's Dream (TMA Award 2003, world tour 2009), The Winters Tale (The Watermill and tour, TMA Award nomination), Twelfth Night (Old Vic) 2007, Taming of the Shrew (Old Vic) 2008, The Merchant of Venice (world tour 2009); RSC prodns incl: Two Gentlemen of Verona, Henry V (South Bank Show Theatre Award 2010), Julius Caesar, Tantalus (also Denver); other prodns incl: Macbeth (Albery Theatre London), Hinge of the World (Guildford), The Constant Wife (Apollo Theatre), A Funny Thing Happened on the Way to the Forum (NT, Evening Standard and Olivier Award nomination), Edmund (NT), A Streetcar Named Desire (Roundabout Theatre NY), Once in a Lifetime (NT), Two Men of Florence (Huntington Theatre Boston), Enlightenment, Loyalty, Chariots of Fire, Raving, Sunny Afternoon (Best Musical Olivier Awards 2015), Wonderland (Evening Standard New Play Award), Rabbit Hole, Firebird; dir: Strike Back (Left Bank Films), Safari Strife (documentary, part of Cutting Edge series Channel 4), Kingdom (Parellel Fims, ITV), Spooks (Kudos, BBC 1, nominated Best Drama BAFTA), Trial and Retribution: Closure (La Plante Productions, ITV), Spooks (BBC 1), Restless (BBC 1), Downton Abbey (ITV), Partners in Crime (BBC 1); *Publications* Rose Rage; *Recreations* motorcycling, cricket, fishing; *Clubs* Two Brydges Place; *Style*— Edward Hall, Esq; ✉ c/o Casarotto Ramsay & Associates, 12 Noel Street, London W1F 8GQ; c/o Susan Weaving, Endeavour, 1325 Avenue of the Americas, New York NY 10019, USA (☎ 00 1 212 903 1100)

HALL, Fairfax Alexander Charles; s of Charles Francis Hall, and Diana Elizabeth Griselda Hall; *b* 16 November 1974, Truro, Cornwall; *Educ* Radley, Univ of Edinburgh (MA), Wharton Sch Univ of Pennsylvania (MBA); *m* Eloise Collet; 1 s (Alexander b 2007), 2 da (Emily b 2009, Orla b 2013); *Career* conslt LEK Consulting 1998–2002, strategy mangr Diageo 2004–07, co-fndr Sipsmith Independent Spirits 2007–; *Style*— Fairfax Hall, Esq

HALL, Fiona Jane; MBE; da of Edward Cutts (d 1985), and Dorothy Cutts (d 1995); *b* 15 July 1955, Swinton, Manchester; *Educ* Worsley Wardley GS, Eccles Coll, St Hugh's Coll Oxford (BA), Oxford Poly (PGCE); *m* 24 Sept 1975 (m dis), Michael Hall; 2 da (Catherine b 1979, Rosemary b 1982); *Career* pt/t teacher/tutor 1984–94, asst to Lib Dem cncllrs Newcastle upon Tyne 1994–97, press officer and researcher to Lib Dem MPs 1997–2004, MEP (Lib Dem) NE England 2004–14, currently sr policy advsr; *Style*— Ms Fiona Hall, MBE; ✉ The School House, Whittingham, Alnwick, Northumberland NE66 4UP(☎ 01665 574383)

HALL, Emeritus Prof George Martin; s of George Vincent Hall (d 1971), of Bridlington, E Yorks, and Dora Hortensia, *née* Beauchamp (d 2006); *b* 14 May 1944; *Educ* King Edward VI Sch Lichfield, UCL (MB BS, PhD), Univ of London (DSc); *m* 9 Jan 1964 (sep), Marion Edith, da of Frank Gordon Burgin, MBE, of Great Missenden, Bucks; 1 da (Katherine Elizabeth b 1965); *Career* prof of clinical anaesthesia Royal Postgrad Med Sch Univ of London 1989–92 (sr lectr 1976–85, reader 1985–89), fndn prof of anaesthesia St George's Hosp Med Sch Univ of London 1992–2013, emeritus prof Univ of London 2013–; chm to British Journal of Anaesthesia; contrib research papers on anaesthesia; sec Euro Soc of Anaesthesiology 2001–05; *Recreations* cycling, jazz, supporting Staffordshire; *Clubs* Farmers'; *Style*— Emeritus Prof George Hall; ✉ Department of Anaesthesia and Intensive Care Medicine, St George's Hospital Medical School, London SW17 0RE (☎ 07885 084086, e-mail georgemartinhall@gmail.com)

HALL, Gillian Mary; da of John Robert Hall (d 1990), and Mary, *née* Davison (d 2015); *b* 8 November 1960, North Shields, Tyne and Wear; *Educ* Central Newcastle HS, Newnham Coll Cambridge (Squire law scholar, MA), Chester Coll of Law; *m* 7 July 1995, (John) Richard Whitaker; 1 s (Daniel George b 9 Jan 1997), 2 step da (Hannah Dorothy b 1 Aug 1986, Rhoda Constance b 2 Aug 1990); *Career* slr; articled clerk Lovell White & King (now Hogan Lovells) 1983–85; Watson Burton LLP: slr 1985–88, ptnr 1988–2014, sr ptnr 2010–14, conslt 2014–; accredited mediator; memb Regnl Cncl CBI; memb Bd: NE Local Enterprise Partnership 2013–, Arch (Northumberland devpt co) 2014–; harbour cmmr Port of Blyth 2014–; memb Law Soc 1985; *Recreations* family, travel, cooking, literature; *Style*— Ms Gillian Hall; ✉ Watson Burton LLP, 1 St James' Gate, Newcastle upon Tyne NE99 1YQ (☎ 0191 244 4444, fax 0191 244 4500, e-mail gillian.hall@watsonburton.com)

HALL, Prof Ian Philip; s of Kenneth Hall, and June, *née* Dobson; *b* 6 March 1958; *Educ* Kirkham GS, Lincoln Coll Oxford (BA, BM BCh), Univ of Nottingham (DM); *m* 23 Oct 1982, Gillian Mary, da of Samuel Wright (d 1999); 3 da (Claire Elizabeth b 3 Aug 1988, Fiona Jane b 25 Nov 1990, Sarah Louise b 18 April 1997); *Career* registrar and res fell City and Univ Hosps of Nottingham 1986–92, MRC travelling fell Univ of Pennsylvania 1992–93, sr res fell Nat Asthma Campaign 1993–98, prof of molecular med Univ of Nottingham 1998–, non-exec dir Nottingham Univ Hosp Tst 2009–13, dean Univ of Nottingham Medical Sch 2009–15, dir Centre for Biomolecular Sciences Univ of Nottingham 2015–; memb Assoc of Physicians; FRCP; *Publications* author of over 150 papers and reviews on genetics of airway disease, pharmacogenetics and cell signalling; *Recreations* mountaineering, classical guitar, tennis, gardening; *Style*— Prof Ian Hall; ✉ Division of Respiratory Medicine, D Floor South Block, Queen's Medical Centre, Nottingham NG7 2UH (☎ 0115 823 1063, e-mail ian.hall@nottingham.ac.uk)

HALL, Janice Elizabeth (Jan); OBE (1996); da of John Brian Hall, and Jean, *née* Chadwick; *b* 1 June 1957; *Educ* Rutland Girls' HS, St Anne's Coll Oxford (MA); *Children* 1 s (Theo b 15 Feb 1996); *Career* mktg mangr Paints Div ICI 1979–83, chm and chief exec Coley Porter Bell 1983–94, Euro chief exec The GGT Group plc 1994–97, ptnr Spencer Stuart & Associates (exec search) 1997–2005, ptnr JCA Group (exec search) 2005–; sr non-exec dir First Choice Holidays plc 1994–2003; non-exec dir: Allied Maples Group Ltd 1988–91, BSM Group plc 1992–98, London First 1993–95, Veos Ltd 1998–2002; chm: Design Business Assoc 1988–90, Ashridge Coll Assoc 1990–92, DTI BOTB Small Firms Ctee 1992–96; memb: DTI Small Firms Advsy Group on the Single Market 1988–90, Southern Bd BR 1990–93, FO/DTI Br Overseas Trade Bd 1993–96, Dept of Employment TEC Assessors Ctee 1993–95, Advsy Bd Warwick Business Sch 1993–2008, Cmmn on Public Policy and Br Business 1995–97, President's Advsy Group on Competitiveness DTI 1997–99, Tate Corporate Advsy Gp 2009–, Advsy Bd SAID Business Sch 2010–, Evington Catalyst 2012–; memb Cncl: CSD 1988–91, IOD 1991–2005; chm Mktg Group of GB 1997–99, vice-pres Strategic Planning Soc 1995–2001; tstee Demos 1993–2000; hon prof Warwick Business Sch 1997–; FCSD 1989, FRSA 1990; *Books* Dementia Essentials: how to guide a loved one through Alzheimer's or dementia and provide the best care (2013); *Recreations* travel, food, music; *Style*— Ms Jan Hall, OBE; ✉ JCA Group, 55 Baker Street, London W1U 8EW

HALL, Jerry Faye; da of John P Hall (d 1977), and Marjorie, *née* Sheffield; *b* 2 July 1956; *m* 21 Nov 1990 (sep), Sir Michael Philip (Mick) Jagger; 2 da (Elizabeth b 2 March 1984, Georgia b 12 Jan 1991), 2 s (James b 28 Aug 1985, Gabriel b 9 Dec 1997); *Career* actress and model 1973–; has been in over 100 commercials and appeared on the cover of over 150 magazines; worked for all the major designers in Paris, London, New York, Milan and Tokyo; contracts/campaigns incl: Yves Saint Laurent (Opium perfume) 1975–82, Revlon Cosmetics 1976–89, L'Oriel Hair 1979–82, Thierry Mugler (Angel perfume) 1996–98; *Theatre* Bus Stop (New Jersey) 1988 (also West End 1990), The Graduate (West End) 2000, The Vagina Monologues (West End and Austin TX) 2001, The Play What I Wrote (West End and Belfast) 2001, Picasso's Women (UK tour) 2002, Benchmark (2003), The Graduate (US tour) 2003, Les Miserables (West End) 2004, Chitty Chitty Bang Bang (West End) 2004, The Phanton of the Opera (West End) 2004, Fame (West End) 2004, Anything Goes (West End) 2004, Blood Brothers (West End) 2004; *Television* numerous appearances incl: Andy Warhol Television (host) 1985, The David Letterman Show 1984, 1985, 1987, MTV Music News 1986, She's With Me (NBC pilot) 1986, Saturday Night Live (host) 1986, Hysteria II 1989, Clive James on the 80's (co-presenter) 1989, French and Saunders 1990, Bejewelled (TVS/Disney) 1990, The Detectives 1992, Cleudo (Granada) 1993, Jerry Hall's Gurus 2004, Popetown 2004; *Radio* The Betty Grable Story (Radio 3) 1995; *Video* Let's Stick Together (Bryan Ferry) 1976, The Price of Love (Bryan Ferry) 1977, Lady Godive (Simply Red) 1989; *Films* St Germain Des Pres Après Le Guerre 1974, Willie and Phil 1978, Urban Cowboy 1979, Jack and the Beanstalk 1982, The Emperor and the Nightingale 1982, Running out of Luck 1984, Galileus Mouse 1987, Batman 1988, Princess Carabou 1994, Savage Hearts 1994, Vampire in Brooklyn 1994, Diana and Me 1996, RPM 1996, Merci Docteur Rey 2001, Tooth 2004; *Books* Tall Tales (1985); *Style*— Ms Jerry Hall

HALL, John Peirs; s of late Dr Robert Noel Hall, and late Doreen Cecilia, *née* Russell; *b* 26 June 1940; *Educ* Stowe; *m* 1965, Sarah Gillian, da of Gerard Thorpe Page; 3 s (James b 6 April 1966, Charles b 6 May 1968, Freddie b 12 May 1977); *Career* trainee Read Hurst Brown Stockbrokers 1958–65; Wontner Dolphin & Francis (became Brewin Dolphin 1974 and then Brewin Holdings plc 1994): joined 1965, md 1987, ceo 1992–; Freeman City of London 1970, memb Ct of Assts Worshipful Co of Merchant Taylors; memb IMRO, MSI (memb Stock Exchange 1965); *Recreations* breeding British White cattle, sailing, golf; *Clubs* City of London, Royal Yacht Squadron, Island Sailing, Huntercombe Golf; *Style*— John Hall, Esq; ✉ Brewin Dolphin Holdings plc, 12 Smithfield Street, London EC1A 9BD (☎ 0845 213 1000, fax 0845 213 3587, e-mail john.hall@brewin.co.uk)

HALL, Jonathan James; s of Gordon Hall, and M Joyce, *née* Pratt; *b* 11 October 1960; *Educ* Marlborough, Univ of Bristol (BA), UCL (DipArch, MSc), KCL (MSc); *Career* architect; Building Design Partnership 1986–89, princ Allford Hall Monaghan Morris Architects LLP 1989–; clients incl: Joseph Rowntree Fndn, Peabody Tst, Derwent London, Great Portland Estates, Corporation of London, Barbican Arts Centre, Essex CC, British Cncl, Design Cncl, Centro; occasional lectr at various schs of architecture; external examiner: Sch of Architecture UCE 2001–03, De Montfort Univ 2004–; RIBA Awards for Architecture: for Poolhouse 1996, for Broadgate Club 1998, for Croydon Med Centre 1999, for Great Notley Sch and Work Learn Zone at Millennium Dome 2000, for Walsall Bus Station 2001, for Jubilee Sch and Clearwater Yard 2003, for Raines Court 2004, for Barbican Arts Centre and Unity Liverpool 2007; Royal Fine Art Cmmn Award (for Great Notley Sch), Royal Fine Art Cmmn Tst Award 2000; RIBA 1989, FCIArb 2005; *Recreations* walking, watching the occasional game of cricket; *Clubs* Surrey CC; *Style*— Jonathan Hall, Esq; ✉ Allford Hall Monaghan Morris Architects LLP, 5–23 Old Street, London EC1V 9HL (☎ 020 7251 5261, fax 020 7251 5123)

HALL, Maj Gen Jonathan Michael Francis Cooper; CB (1998), OBE (1987), DL (Dorset 2010); s of Charles Richard Hall; *b* 10 August 1944; *Educ* Taunton Sch, RMA Sandhurst; *m* 5 Oct 1968, Sarah Linda, *née* Hudson; 2 da (Candida Sarah b 1971, Rachel Katharine b 1973); *Career* cmmnd 3rd Carabiniers 1965, Staff Coll Camberley 1977, Cmd Offr Royal Scots Dragoon Guards 1984–86, Higher Cmd and Staff Course 1988, Cmd 12 Armoured Bde 1989–90, Royal Coll of Def Studies 1991, Dep Mil Sec (A) 1992–94, Dir RAC 1994–95, GOC Scotland and Govr Edinburgh Castle 1995–97; Lt Govr and cmmr Royal Hosp Chelsea 1997–2005, managing conslt Compton Fundraising Ltd 2006–; Hon Corps of Gentlemen at Arms 1999–2014 (standard bearer 2012–14); Col Cmdt: Scottish Div 1995–97, Royal Army Vet Corps 1995–2001; Col Royal Scots Dragoon Guards 1998–2003, vice-pres Royal Scots Dragoon Guards Cncl 2004–; HM's Cmmr Queen Victoria Sch Dunblane 1995–97; memb Ethical Review Process Ctee ICL 2003–09; vice-pres: Army Benevolent Fund Dorset 2008–16, Soc of Dorset Men 2010–14; tstee: Royal Armoured Corps War Memorial Benevolent Fund 1999–2011, VC and GC Benevolent Fund 2004–, Army Museums Ogilby Tst 2004–14; memb Sherborne Abbey Parochial Church Cncl 2006–16, vice-patron Nat Assoc of Almshouses Appeal 2012–13; govr Taunton Sch 2007–16, govr Blind Veterans UK (St Dunstans) 2011–, life memb Sandhurst Tst 2016–; hon assoc memb BVA (designated memb Ethics and Welfare Gp 2007–10); Freeman City of

London, Liveryman Worshipful Co of Farriers 2006–; FCMI (FIMgt) 1997; OStJ 1998 (chm and memb Cncl Dorset branch 2008–11), Knight Cdr of the Order of Francis I 2014; *Recreations* country pursuits, travel; *Clubs* Cavalry and Guards' (tstee 2007–14), MCC, Woodroffe's, Pratt's, Somerset County Cricket; *Style—* Maj Gen Jonathan Hall, CB, OBE, DL; ✉ Orchard House, Nether Compton, Sherborne, Dorset DT9 4QA (☎ 01935 812422, mobile 07884 421509, e-mail jmfc.hall@btinternet.com)

HALL, Lee; s of Peter Edward Hall, and Sylvia, *née* Rodgers; *Educ* Benfield Comp Sch Newcastle upon Tyne, Fitzwilliam Coll Cambridge (BA); *m* 2003, Beeban Kidron; 2 step c (Noah, Blaze); *Career* playwright; writer in residence: Live Theatre Newcastle upon Tyne 1997–98, RSC 1998–99; memb: BAFTA, Writers Guild of GB, Writers Guild of America, Acad of Motion Pictures; *Theatre* Mr Puntila and His Man Matti (trans, Almeida Theatre London) 1997, Cooking with Elvis (Live Theatre Newcastle upon Tyne and Whitehall Theatre London) 2000, A Servant to Two Masters (RSC at Young Vic) 2000, Billy Elliot the Musical (Victoria Palace Theatre) 2005; *Television* The Student Prince 1996; *Radio* I Luv You Jimmy Spud 1995 (Best Writing on Radio Sony Awards 1996), Spoonface Steinberg 1996 (Writers Guild Award 1997, Mental Health in the Media Award 1997); *Films* Billy Elliot 2000 (Best Screenplay Br Ind Film Awards 2000, nomination BAFTA Awards 2000, nomination Oscars 2000), Gabriel & Me 2001; *Publications* Spoonface Steinberg and Other Plays (1996), Cooking with Elvis (1999), A Servant to Two Masters (new adaptation, 2000), Pinocchio (new adaptation, 2000), Billy Elliot (screenplay, 2001), The Good Hope (new adaptation, 2001); *Recreations* buying books, sleeping and eating; *Style—* Lee Hall, Esq; ✉ c/o Judy Daish Associates, 2 St Charles Place, London W10 6EB

HALL, Mervyn Douglas; s of Matthew Douglas Hall (d 1965), of Windsor, and Maisie Eileen, *née* Allen; *b* 4 January 1949; *Educ* Windsor GS; *m* 14 April 1984, Valerie, *née* Nealson; 1 s (Nicholas James b 19 June 1974), 1 da (Suzannah Elizabeth b 27 July 1977); *Career* reporter: Windsor, Slough and Eton Express 1965–69, Shropshire Star 1969–70, Evening Post Luton 1970–73; sports ed LBC 1973–78; ITN: sports ed 1978–84, news ed 1984–89, ed Radio 1989–90, chief ed IRN 1990–93, sales dir 1993–95; int mktg mangr Reuters Media 1995–99, estab Salthouse Consultancy 1999; broadcast mangr All England Lawn Tennis Club; *Recreations* golf, reading, food and wine, rugby union; *Clubs* Phyllis Court (Henley-on-Thames); *Style—* Mervyn Hall, Esq

HALL, (Haddon) Michael (Mike); s of William Haddon Hall (d 1972), and Mildred, *née* Brown, of London; *b* 28 June 1945; *Educ* Aristotle Sch; *m* 1, 24 Jan 1970 (m dis 1976), Kathleen Mary, da of William Suggitt; m 2, 25 April 1981 (m dis 1986), Suzanne Marie, da of Ronald M Bell; m 3, 11 May 1989 (m dis 2002), Victoria Ann, da of Bryan John Vallas (d 1984); 1 s (Stephen b 6 Aug 1992); m 4, 19 April 2003, Maryna, da of Boris Vetrov; *Career* CA Barsham Nixon & Hamilton 1969–72 (joined as articled clerk 1961), qualified sr Stoy Hayward & Co 1972–74; Boty Cox Crawford & Ridley (merged Edward Moore & Sons 1975, which merged Rowland Nevill 1985 to become Moores Rowland, and with BDO Stoy Hayward 1999): audit mangr 1974–79, ptnr 1979–, equity ptnr 1983–2001; prop Haddon Hall 2001–; non-exec dir Croydon Business Venture Ltd 1990–96; FCA 1979 (ACA 1969); *Recreations* applied philosophy, shooting, reading science fiction, collecting collectables; *Clubs* Historical Breechloading Small-Arms Assoc (hon treas); *Style—* Mike Hall, Esq; ☎ and fax 01622 204325, car 07887 907485, e-mail hh006f6689@blueyonder.co.uk

HALL, Prof Michael Anthony; s of Frederick Lancelot Hall (d 1982), and Eva, *née* Bridgewood-Jeffes (d 1992); *b* 7 July 1940; *Educ* Rutherford GS, Imperial Coll London (BSc, PhD, DSc); *m* 25 Aug 1964, Gillian, da of Frederick Barrone (d 1975); 1 da (Sara Jayne Barrone b 1 June 1969); *Career* Univ of Calif Riverside 1964–67, Scottish Hort Res Inst 1967–68, dir and prof Inst of Biological Sciences UCW Aberystwyth 1968–; memb Malaysian Rubber Research Devpt Bd; 150 pubns in professional jls; FIBiol, FRSA, ARCS; *Books* Plant Structure, Function and Adaptation (1976); *Recreations* skiing, music; *Style—* Prof Michael Hall; ✉ Glascoed, Piercefield Lane, Penparcau, Aberystwyth SY23 1RX (☎ 01970 612465); Institute of Biological, Environmental and Rural Sciences, Aberystwyth University SY23 3DA (☎ 01970 622313, fax 01970 622350, e-mail mzh@aber.ac.uk, website www.aber.ac.uk/en/ibers/staff/staff-list/mzh/)

HALL, Michael Harold Webster; s of Dr L W Hall (d 2010), and Barbara, *née* Moss (d 1978); *b* 6 July 1957, Cambridge; *Educ* Cambridgeshire HS for Boys, Trinity Hall Cambridge (MA), Birkbeck Coll London (MA); *Career* ed Thames and Hudson Ltd 1982–89; Country Life: architectural writer 1989–95, architectural ed 1995–98, dep ed 1998–2004; ed Apollo 2004–10; chm Activities Ctee Victorian Soc; tstee: Emery Walker Tst, Marc Fitch Fund; Essay Medal Soc of Architectural Historians of GB 1991; FSA 2003; *Publications* The English Country House, from the archives of Country Life (1994), Gothic Architecture and its Meanings 1550–1830 (ed, 2002), Waddesdon Manor (2002, new edn 2012), The Victorian Country House (2009), George Frederick Bodley and the Later Gothic Revival in Britain and America (2014); *Style—* Michael Hall, Esq; ✉ e-mail michael@michaelhwhall.com

HALL, Michael Robert; DL (Derbys 2004); s of Robert Hall (d 1980), of Cheshire, and Hannah Hall (d 2001); *b* 9 May 1942; *Educ* William Hulme's Manchester; *m* 1, 1969 (m dis 1996), Irene Mavis, da of Percy Cuthbert Archer (d 1993), of Cheshire; 1 da (Kathryn Elizabeth b 1971), 1 s (Robert Anthony b 1974); m 2, 2002, Anne Hazel, da of Gordon Cross (d 1999); 1 step s (David Charles b 1977), 1 step da (Joanna Elizabeth b 1979); *Career* dir: Selective Fin Servs Ltd 1987–, Redmill Industries Ltd 1987–, Construction Cosmetics Ltd 1988–, Chesterfield Royal Hosp 2005–; former dep vice-chllr Univ of Derby; memb Derbyshire C of C; dir LSC; Hon DUniv Derby 2005; FCA 1975, FCMA 1977, FCT 1980, CGMA 2012; *Recreations* squash, walking, sailing; *Style—* Michael R Hall, Esq, DL; ✉ Derventio House, Ashford in the Water, Derbyshire DE45 1QP

HALL, Nigel John; s of Herbert John Hall, of Chipping Sodbury, Avon, and Gwendoline Mary, *née* Olsen; *b* 30 August 1943; *Educ* Bristol GS, West of England Coll of Art (NDD), RCA (MArtRCA), Harkness fellowship to USA; *m* 1986, Manijeh Yadegar; *Career* artist; tutor RCA 1971–74, princ lectr Chelsea Sch of Art 1974–81; memb: Panel CNAA 1975–76, Faculty of Prix de Rome 1979–83; RA 2003; *Solo Exhibitions* incl: Galerie Givaudan Paris 1967, Robert Elkon Gallery NY 1974, 1977, 1979 and 1983, Annely Juda Gallery London 1978, 1981, 1985, 1987, 1991, 1996, 2000, 2003, 2005, 2011 and 2016, Galerie Maeght Paris 1981 and 1983, Staatliche Kunsthaus Baden-Baden 1982, Nishimura Gallery Tokyo 1980, 1984 and 1988, Hans Mayer Gallery Düsseldorf 1989 and 1999, Garry Anderson Gallery Sydney 1987 and 1990, Galerie Ziegler Zurich 1986, 1988 and 1995, Fondation Veranneman Belgium 1987, 1995, 1997 and 2002, Park Ryu Sook Gallery Seoul 1997, 2000, 2005 and 2008, Konstruktiv Tendens Stockholm 2000, Sculpture at Schoenthal Monastery Switzerland 2001, Galleri C Hjärne Helsingborg 2004, Galerie Scheffel Bad Homburg 2004, 2007, 2011 and 2015, Kunsthalle Mannheim 2004, Galerie Lutz und Thalmann Zurich 2006, Centre Cultural Contemporani Pelaires Palma de Mallorca 2007, Yorks Sculpture Park 2008, Sala Pelaires Palma de Mallorca 2009, Galerie Andres Thalmann Zurich 2010 and 2012, Oklahoma City Art Center 2010, Royal Acad London 2011, Churchill Coll Cambridge 2013, Galerie Alvaro Alcazar Madrid 2015; *Group Exhibitions* incl: Documenta VI (Kassel) 1977, British Sculpture in the Twentieth Century (Whitechapel Gallery London) 1981, Aspects of British Art Today (Tokyo Metropolitan Museum) 1982, Carnegie International (Carnegie Inst Pittsburgh) 1982, Britannica: Thirty Years of Sculpture (Le Havre Museum of Fine Art) 1988, Blickachsen 4 (Bad Homburg) 2003, 2006 Beaufort (MOMA Ostend), Full House: Faces of a Collection (Kunsthalle Mannheim) 2006, British Art Plus (Museum Biedermann Donaueschingen Germany) 2015, Making It: Sculpture in Britain 1977–86 (Yorkshire Sculpture Park and tour) 2015, 10 Years (Galleria Alvaro Alcazar Madrid) 2016; *Commissions* Aust Nat Gallery Canberra, IBM London, Airbus Industrie Toulouse, Olympic Park Seoul, MOMA Hiroshima, British Petroleum London, Glaxo Research, Bank of America London, Bank for Int Settlements Basel; *Work in Public Collections* incl: Tate Gallery London, Musée Nat d'Art Moderne Paris, Nat Galerie Berlin, Tel Aviv Museum, Power Inst Sydney, MOMA NY; *Style—* Nigel Hall, Esq, RA; ✉ 11 Kensington Park Gardens, London W11 3HD (☎ 020 7727 3162); Annely Juda Fine Art, 23 Dering Street, London W1R 9AA (☎ 020 7629 7578)

HALL, Nigel Ruthven; s of Ruthven Oliphant Hall (d 1983), and Dr Zaida Mary Hall, *née* Megrah (d 2013); *b* 19 November 1960, London; *Educ* Winchester, Balliol Coll Oxford (Frazer entrance scholarship, Periam Prize, BA, BM BCh, DM); *m* 20 April 1991, Alison Elizabeth; da of Dr Philip Kenneth Wilson, of Ipswich, Suffolk; 1 da (Emma b 2 Dec 1995), 1 s (Benjamin b 21 Feb 1998); *Career* house offr: John Radcliffe Hosp Oxford 1985–86, Royal Berks Hosp Reading 1986; SHO: UCH London 1986–86, Middx Hosp Med Sch London 1987, Guy's Hosp Rotational Scheme in Surgery London 1987–89, Royal Marsden Hosp London 1989–90; registrar NW Thames Regnl HA (Hillingdon Hosp and St Mary's Hosp Paddington) 1990–91, ICRF clinical research fell in coloproctology and hon surgical registrar Dept of Surgery Gen Infirmary at Leeds and ICRF Genetic Epidemiology Lab St James's Univ Hosp Leeds 1992–94, registrar Royal Halifax Infirmary 1994–95, sr registrar Gen Infirmary at Leeds 1995–96 and 1997–98, sr registrar Huddersfield Royal Infirmary 1996–97, clinical fell in colon and rectal surgery Univ of Minnesota Minneapolis 1998–99, conslt colorectal and gen surgn Addenbrooke's Hosp Cambridge 1999–; assoc lectr Faculty of Clinical Medicine Addenbrooke's Hosp Cambridge 2005–; memb: BMA, Sections of Coloproctology and Surgery RSM, Assoc of Surgns of GB and I, Assoc of Coloproctology of GB and I, American Soc of Colon and Rectal Surgns; FRCS 1997; *Publications* numerous book chapters, reviews and articles in med jls; *Style—* Mr Nigel Hall; ✉ Department of Surgery, Box 201, Addenbrooke's Hospital, Hills Road, Cambridge CB2 0QQ (☎ 01223 348219, fax 01223 216015, e-mail nigel.r.hall@addenbrookes.nhs.uk, website www.cambridgebowelclinic.co.uk)

HALL, Sir Peter Reginald Frederick; kt (1977), CBE (1963); s of Reginald Edward Arthur Hall, and Grace, *née* Pamment; *b* 22 November 1930; *Educ* Perse Sch Cambridge, St Catharine's Coll Cambridge (MA); *m* 1, 1956 (m dis 1965), Leslie Caron, the actress; 1 s (Christopher), 1 da (Jennifer); m 2, 1965 (m dis 1981), Jacqueline Taylor; 1 s (Edward, *qv*), 1 da (Lucy); m 3, 1982 (m dis 1990), Maria Ewing, the mezzo-soprano; 1 da (Rebecca b 1982); m 4, 1990, Nicola (Nicki) Frei; 1 da (Emma b June 1992); *Career* director and producer of plays, films and operas; dir: Oxford Playhouse 1954–55, Arts Theatre London 1955–57; fndr Int Playwrights' Theatre 1957, md RSC 1960–68 (created the RSC as a permanent ensemble, and opened the RSC's London home at the Aldwych Theatre), co-dir RSC 1968–73, dir Nat Theatre of GB 1973–88, artistic dir Glyndebourne Festival Opera 1984–90, formed own prodn co Peter Hall Co Ltd 1988, artistic dir Old Vic 1996–; assoc prof of drama Univ of Warwick 1966–; memb Arts Cncl of GB 1969–72, fndr memb Theatre Directors' Guild of GB 1983; chllr Kingston Univ 2000–; Hon DLitt Univ of Reading 1973; Hon LittD: Univ of Liverpool 1974, Univ of Leicester 1977, Univ of Essex 1995, Univ of Cambridge 2003; Hon DUniv York 1966, Hon DUniv Cornell USA; Chevalier de l'Ordre des Arts et des Lettres (France); *Theatre* has directed over 150 major prodns in London, Stratford-upon-Avon and New York, including 19 Shakespeare plays, and the premieres of plays by Samuel Beckett, Harold Pinter, Tennessee Williams, Edward Albee, Jean Anouilh, Peter Shaffer, John Mortimer, John Whiting, Alan Ayckbourn; first prodns incl: Waiting for Godot (Arts Theatre London) 1955, Gigi 1956, Love's Labour's Lost 1956, Cat on a Hot Tin Roof 1958; RSC prodns incl: Twelfth Night 1958, 1960 and 1991, A Midsummer Night's Dream 1959 and 1963, Beckett 1961, The Collection 1962, The Wars of the Roses 1964 (televised for BBC 1965), The Homecoming 1965 and 1973, Macbeth 1967 and 1982, A Delicate Balance 1969, All's Well That Ends Well, The Gift of the Gorgon (also Wyndhams), Julius Caesar 1995; NT prodns incl: Bedroom Farce 1977, The Cherry Orchard 1978, Betrayal 1978 and 1980, The Importance of Being Earnest 1982, Yonadab 1985, Entertaining Strangers 1987, Antony and Cleopatra 1988, The Winter's Tale 1988, Cymbeline 1988, The Tempest 1988; Peter Hall Co prodns incl: Orpheus Descending (NY) 1988, The Merchant of Venice 1989, The Wild Duck (Phoenix) 1990, The Homecoming (Comedy Theatre) 1991, The Rose Tattoo (Playhouse) 1991, Tartuffe (Playhouse) 1991, Sienna Red 1992, An Ideal Husband (Globe) 1992, Four Baboons Adoring the Sun (NY) 1992, Lysistrata (Old Vic, Wyndhams) 1993, Separate Tables (Queens) 1993, Piaf (Piccadilly) 1993, An Absolute Turkey (Globe) 1993, On Approval (Playhouse) 1994, Hamlet (Gielgud Theatre) 1994, The Master Builder (Haymarket) 1995, Mind Millie for Me (Haymarket) 1996, The Oedipus Plays (Epidaurus and RNT) 1996, School for Wives 1996, A Streetcar Named Desire (Haymarket) 1997, Waste (Old Vic) 1997, The Seagull (Old Vic) 1997, Waiting For Godot (Old Vic) 1997, King Lear (Old Vic) 1997, The Misanthrope (Piccadilly) 1998, Major Barbara (Piccadilly) 1998, Filumena (Piccadilly) 1998, Kafka's Dick (Piccadilly) 1998, Amadeus (Old Vic) 1999, Measure for Measure 1999, A Midsummer Night's Dream (Ahmanson Theatre Los Angeles) 1999, Lennie (Queen's Theatre London) 1999, Amadeus (CTG/LA, Music Box NY) 1999, Cuckoos (CTG/LA) 2000, Tantalus (DCPA/Denver) 2000, Romeo and Juliet (MTA/LA) 2001, Japes (Haymarket) 2001, Tantalus (UK tour, Barbican RSC) 2001, Troilus & Cressida (TFNA/NY) 2001, Lady Windermere's Fan (Haymarket) 2002, Bacchi (NT, Epidaurus, Newcastle) 2002, Mrs Warren's Profession (Strand Theatre) 2002 (UK tour) 2003, Where There's A Will (UK tour) 2003, Betrayl (Theatre Royal Bath, UK tour) 2003, Design For Living (Theatre Royal Bath, UK tour) 2003, As You Like It (Theatre Royal Bath, UK and USA tour) 2003, Cuckoos (Barbican, Theatre Royal Bath, Happy Days (Arts Theatre London) 2003, Summer and Smoke (London) 2004, The Dresser (Duke of York's) 2005; *Operas* incl: The Magic Flute (Covent Garden) 1966, Eugene Onegin (Covent Garden) 1971, The Marriage of Figaro (Glyndebourne) 1973 and 1989, A Midsummer's Night Dream (Glyndebourne) 1981 and 1989, Macbeth (Metropolitan Opera NY) 1982, The Ring (Bayreuth) 1983, Figaro (Geneva) 1983, Carmen (Glyndebourne) 1985, Albert Herring (Glyndebourne) 1985 and 1986, (Covent Garden) 1989, Salome (LA 1986, Covent Garden 1988 and 1992, Chicago 1988), New Year (world premiere, Houston) 1989, The Magic Flute (LA) 1993, Simon Boccanegra (Glyndebourne) 1998, Midsummer Night's Dream (Glyndebourne), 2001, Othello (Glyndebourne) 2001, Othello (Chicago Lyric Opera) 2001, Albert Herring (Glyndebourne) 2002, The Marriage of Figaro (Lyric Opera of Chicago) 2003; *Films and Television* Work is a Four Letter Word 1968, A Midsummer Night's Dream 1969, Three into One Won't Go 1969, Perfect Friday 1971, The Homecoming 1973, Akenfield 1974, She's Been Away 1989, Orpheus Ascending 1991, The Camomile Lawn (Channel 4) 1991, Jacob (TNT/LUX) 1993, Never Talk to Strangers (TriStar Pictures) 1994–95, The Final Passage (Channel 4) 1995; *Awards* Tony Award: 1967 for Pinter's Homecoming, 1981 for Shaffer's Amadeus; Hamburg Univ Shakespeare Prize 1967, Standard Special Award 1979, Standard Award for Best Director 1981 and 1987, Standard Award for outstanding achievement in Opera 1981, Sidney Edwards Award for NT prodn of The Oresteia 1982, Olivier Theatre Award for lifetime achievement 1999; *Publications* The Wars of the Roses (with John Barton, 1970), translation of Ibsen's John Gabriel Borkman (with Inga-Stina Ewbank, 1975), Peter Hall's Diaries (1983), adaptation of George Orwell's Animal Farm (1986), adaptation of Ibsen's The Wild Duck (with Inga-Stina Ewbank, 1990), Making an Exhibition of Myself (autobiography, 1993), translation of Feydeau's An Absolute Turkey (with Nicki Frei,

H

1993), translation of Ibsen's The Master Builder (with Inga-Stina Ewbank, 1995), translation of Feydeau's L'Occupe toi d'Amelie – Mind Millie for Me (with Nicki Frei, 1996), The Necessary Theatre (1999), Exposed by the Mask (2000), Shakespeare's Advice to the Players (2003); *Clubs* Garrick, RAC; *Style*— Sir Peter Hall, CBE; ✉ Peter Hall Company, The Penthouse, 7 Leicester Place, London WC2H 7BP (☎ 020 7287 7122, fax 020 7287 7123)

HALL, Peter Ruthven; s of Ruthven Oliphant Hall (d 1983), and Lady Ramsbotham, *née* Zaida Mary Megrah (d 2013); *b* 16 February 1962; *Educ* Winchester, Univ of Bristol (BA), Oxford Poly (DipArch), Univ of Warwick (MA); *Career* set and costume designer; theatre conslt Theatreplan (ptnr 2004–13), theatre conslt Charcoalblue 2013–; theatre design conslt: Hudson Theatre NY, Center Stage Baltimore, Sadler's Wells East Olympic Park, W Yorks Playhouse Leeds, Alexandra Palace Theatre London, Hall for Cornwall Truro, Dorfman Theatre, NT, The Old Vic, York Theatre Royal, Citizens' Theatre Glasgow, new theatre for Luckley House Sch, Cobham, Southport Cultural Centre, Lime Tree Theatre Limerick, The Baths Hall Scunthorpe, Old Fire Station Oxford, Platform London, lecture theatre Sainsbury Laboratory Cambridge, Montaigne Theatre Notre Dame Sch Cobham, Crucible Theatre and Studio Sheffield, Theatre at the Mill Newtonabbey NI, refurbishment Eden Court Theatre Inverness, studios and cinemas; memb Br team Prague Quadrennial exhbn of stage design 1995 (Gold medal winners), memb Br team Prague Quadrennial exhbn of stage design 2003 (Golden Triga winners), exhibitor World Stage Design 2005 Toronto; SBTD: memb 1987–, ed newsletter 1994–2004, co sec; memb Theatre Designers' Ctee Equity; *Theatre* Love! Valour! Compassion! (Library Theatre Manchester), Long Day's Journey into Night (Theatre Royal Plymouth and Young Vic London), The Grapes of Wrath (Crucible Theatre Sheffield), Women of Troy (Gate Theatre London), Vassa Zheleznova (Gate Theatre London), The House of Bernard Alba (Oxford Playhouse); musical theatre incl: Sunset Boulevard (Sydmonton Festival), Tutankhamun (for Imagination), World Café (Edinburgh Festival), Joy to the World (for Imagination, Royal Albert Hall); *Opera* RNCM: Jenufa, Le nozze di Figaro, La Bohème, Albert Herring, Roberto Devereux; other operas incl: Der Stein der Weissen (Garsington Opera), The Turn of the Screw (Snape Maltings), Flavio (London Handel Festival), Ottone (London Handel Festival), L'Arlesiana (Holland Park Opera), Lakmé (Opera Ireland); costume designs incl: Tosca (Malmö Musiktheater), Madame Butterfly (Royal Danish Opera), The Turn of the Screw (Opera Northern Ireland), Zar und Zimmermann (Stadttheater Aachen), Don Giovanni (Vienna Kammeroper), Die Zauberflöte (Vienna Kammeroper); *Publications* Make SPACE! Design for Theatre and Alternative Spaces (with Kate Burnett, 1994), Time + Space: Design for Performance 1995–99 (with Kate Burnett, 1999), 2D>3D, Design For Theatre and Performance (with Kate Burnett, 2002), Theatre Buildings a Design Guide (contrib, 2010), Making the Scene (featured, 2010), World Scenography 1990–2005 (feaured, 2014); *Style*— Peter Ruthven Hall, Esq; ✉ Charcoalblue LLP, 17 Short Street, London SE1 8LJ

HALL, Philip David (Phil); s of Norman Philip Hall, of South Woodham Ferrers, Essex, and Olive Jean Hall; *b* 8 January 1955; *Educ* Beal GS, NCTJ Course Harlow Coll; *m* Marina; 2 da (Alice, Poppy), 1 s (William); *Career* reporter: Dagenham Post 1974–77, Ilford Recorder 1977–80; sub ed: Newham Recorder 1980–84, Weekend Magazine 1984–85; The People: reporter 1985–86, chief reporter 1986–89, news ed 1989–92, news ed Sunday Express 1992–93; News of the World: asst ed (features) 1993–94, dep ed 1994–95, ed 1995–2000; ed-in-chief Hello! 2001–02, editorial dir of devpt Trinity Mirror 2002–05, fndr and chm PHA Media 2005–; memb PCC 1998–99 and 2002–03; memb Editors' Ctee PPA 2002–03; *Recreations* golf, cinema, theatre; *Style*— Phil Hall, Esq

HALL, Richard John Jeaffreson; s of Rev Francis James Thomas Hall (d 1991), and Patricia Musgrave, *née* Parry; *b* 31 July 1945; *Educ* Westminster, ChCh Oxford (MA); *m* 1, 25 July 1970, Wendy Jane, *née* Thomas; 1 da (Rebecca b 28 Feb 1973), 1 s (Crispian b 15 Jan 1975); m 2, 17 June 1995, Sally Frances Mary, da of Geoffrey Cass; *Career* articled Smallfield Fitzhugh Tillett 1968–71; Binder Hamlyn: joined 1971, ptnr 1978–97 (seconded to Milan Div 1979–81), head Corp Services Div 1989–91, marketing ptnr 1992–94; dir of fin Royal Opera House 1997–98; dir of fin and mgmnt services SCOPE 1998–; memb Urgent Issues Task Force of Accounting Standards Board 1991–95; FCA (ACA 1971); *Recreations* tennis, squash, Italian opera; *Clubs* Hurlingham (memb Ctee 1997–2001, chm Fin Ctee 1998–2001), Cumberland Lawn Tennis; *Style*— Richard Hall, Esq; ✉ c/o SCOPE Ltd, 6 Market Road, London N7 9PW (☎ 020 7619 7100)

HALL, District Judge Richard V M; s of Geoffrey Herbert Hall, d 1977; and Mildred Hutchinson, *née* Brice (d 2006); *Educ* Bradford GS, Univ of Exeter (LLB), Coll of Law Guildford; m 1967 (m dis 1992); 3 s (Nicholas Adam John b 1 May 1968, Matthew Edward Jeremy b 20 October 1970, Richard William James b 15 March 1979); *Career* slr 1970–, lectr in law Teesside Poly 1970–71, prosecuting slr Teesside Police Authy 1971–72, ptnr Goodswens Solicitors Middlesbrough 1973–97; High Court NE Circuit: dep County Court registrar and dep district registrar 1984, district judge 1998– (dep 1990–98); hon slr Cleveland Community Relations Cncl 1973–97; chm Arbitration Cmmn Int Correspondence Chess Fedn 2004–; memb Law Soc 1970–; *Recreations* chess (Correspondence Chess Grand Master, runner up 25th World Correspondence Chess Championship), tennis, gardening, antiquarian chess books; *Clubs* Reform; *Style*— District Judge R V M Hall; ✉ Teesside Combined Court Centre, Russell Street, Middlesbrough TS21 2AE

HALL, Robert Stirling (Bob); s of William Smith (d 1995), and Margaret Ralston, *née* Inglesant (d 1997); *b* 2 January 1953; *Educ* Johnstone HS, Duncan of Jordanstone Art Coll (BArch); *m* Carole Ann, da of Thomas McKechnie; 1 da (Louise b 19 July 1983), 1 s (Robbie b 16 March 1985); *Career* architect; Irvine New Town Architects' Dept 1978–80; The Parr Partnership (formerly James Parr & Partners): joined 1980, assoc 1982–89 (responsible for opening Glasgow Office 1982), ptnr 1989–; projects incl: Scottish Exhbn and Conf Centre Glasgow 1985, Sun Microsystems Linlithgow 1990, Glasgow Airport stage 2 expansion 1994, NEC Semiconductors Livingston 1996, Siemens Microelectronics Newcastle 1997, Edinburgh Airport major devpt 1997; RIBA 1979, ARIAS 1979; *Recreations* badminton, golf, football; *Style*— Bob Hall, Esq

HALL, Simon Andrew Dalton; MBE (2006); s of late Peter Dalton Hall, CB, of Milton Keynes, Bucks, and late Stella Iris, *née* Breen; *b* 6 February 1955; *Educ* Ampleforth, St Catharine's Coll Cambridge (MA), Coll of Law; *m* 26 Aug 1978, late Teresa Ann, da of John Edmund Bartleet, of Great Tey, Essex; 2 da (Rachael b 16 June 1979, Sophie b 18 March 1988), 2 s (Eddie b 8 Dec 1980, Harry b 31 March 1983); *Career* slr; articled clerk Freshfields 1977–79, seconded to Cravath Swaine & Moore 1983–84, Freshfields NY office 1984–85 (ptnr 1985–); memb: Law Soc, City of London Slrs Co; *Books* Leasing Finance (jtly, 1997), Aircraft Financing (jtly, 1998); *Style*— Simon Hall, Esq, MBE; ✉ e-mail simonhall026@gmail.com

HALL, Steven Richard; s of Ernest Hall, and Eva, *née* Bartle; *b* 23 March 1956, Bradford; *Educ* Bradford GS, Blackpool GS, Blackpool VI Form Coll, Univ of Leeds (BA); *m* Lucie; 1 s (Christopher), 1 da (Sophie); *Career* product manager then sales exec Macmillan Press 1978–82, area sales manager UMI 1982–88, sales dir Chadwyck-Healey Ltd 1988–96, md Chadwyck-Healey Ltd 1996–99, sr vice-pres and gen manager Chadwyck-Healey Ltd/ProQuest Information and Learning 1999–2004, jl sales and mktg dir Blackwell Publishing Ltd 2004–07, commercial dir Wiley-Blackwell 2007–08, dir Steven Hall Consulting Ltd 2008–10, md Inst of Physics Publishing 2010–; *Recreations* tennis, skiing, travel, modern art and architecture; *Style*— Steven Hall, Esq; ✉ IOP Publishing, Temple Circus, Temple Way, Bristol BS1 6BE (☎ 0117 929 7481, e-mail steven.hall@iop.org)

HALL, Stuart; s of Charles Duell Hall (d 1994), and Amy, *née* Boucher (d 1985); *b* 16 August 1951; *Educ* Queens' Coll Cambridge 1969–72 (MA); *m* 22 April 1977, Rosemary Florence Monica, *née* Cockshutt; 2 da (Charlotte Jane b 3 Dec 1978, Lindsay May b 7 June 1982); *Career* slr specialising in professional liability and commercial litigation; ptnr: Dawson & Co 1976–85, Barlow Lyde & Gilbert 1985–; *Recreations* tennis, swimming, fishing, rugby; *Style*— Stuart Hall, Esq; ✉ Clyde & Co LLP, The St Botolph Building, 138 Houndsditch, London EC3A 7AR (☎ 020 7876 6508, e-mail stuart.hall@clydeco.com)

HALL, Timothy Francis (Tim); s of Ronald William Hall (d 1985), and Mary, *née* Briggs; *b* 29 November 1959; *Educ* Ashburton Sch, Canterbury Coll of Art (BA), Univ of London (DipArch); *m* 30 May 1999, Elizabeth Amy, da of Jonathon Foster; 1 da (Evalina Isabelle b 18 Nov 2001), 2 s (Benjamin Jonty Ronald b 25 Sept 2003, Arthur Kenneth b 10 July 2007); *Career* architect; sr designer Officescape 1985–86, sr designer Newman Levinson 1986–90; projects incl: competition-winning scheme for new theatres, shopping centre and offices in central Milton Keynes, competition-winning scheme for housing and golf club in Bushey; Lewis + Hickey Architects 1990–93, sr architect John Outram Associates 1993–94 (projects incl Judge Inst of Mgmnt Studies Cambridge), md Lewis + Hickey Architects 1993–; work featured in Architects Jl; supporter Elizabeth Finn Tst; FRIBA 1989; *Books* Habitation au Bord de l'Eau (1994); *Recreations* tennis, swimming, photography; *Clubs* Chelsea Football; *Style*— Tim Hall, Esq; ✉ Lewis + Hickey Architects, 17 Dorset Square, London NW1 6QB (☎ 020 7724 1611, fax 020 7724 2282, mobile 07702 096058, e-mail thall@lewishickey.com)

HALL, Prof Dame Wendy; DBE (2009, CBE 2000); *b* 25 October 1952, London; *Educ* Univ of Southampton; *m* Dr Peter Chandler; *Career* University of Southampton: head Sch of Electronics and Computer Science 2002–07, dean Faculty of Physical Sciences and Engrg 2010–14, currently prof of computer science and exec dir Web Science Inst; memb Cncl Royal Soc; FREng 2000, FBCS, FIET, FCGI 2002, FRS 2009; *Style*— Prof Dame Wendy Hall, DBE; ✉ Web Science Unit, University of Southampton, Southampton SO17 1BJ

HALL HALL, HE Alexandra Mary; da of Francis Alleyne Hall Hall (d 1986), and Mary, *née* Whittaker; *m* 2002, Daniel Charles Twining; 2 c; *Career* diplomat; joined FCO 1986, desk offr Thailand, Burma and Laos FCO 1987–88, Thai language trg 1988–89, second sec (political and press) Bangkok 1989–93, head of humanitarian affrs UN Dept FCO 1993–95, seconded to European Secretariat Cabinet Office 1995–97, Policy Planning Dept FCO 1997–98, head ME Peace Process Section FCO 1998–99, first sec (Latin America, Caribbean and Overseas Territories) Washington DC 1999–2001, head Press Office and embassy spokesperson Washington DC 2002–02, seconded to US State Dept 2002–04, head Human Rights, Democracy and Good Governance Dept FCO 2004–06, counsellor and head Political Section New Delhi 2006–07, dep head of mission Bogota 2009–11, ambass to Georgia 2013–; *Recreations* gardening, reading, skiing, tennis, travel, walking; *Style*— HE Ms Alexandra Hall Hall; ✉ c/o FCO (Tbilisi), King Charles Street, London SW1A 2AH

HALL OF BIRKENHEAD, Baron (Life Peer UK 2010), of Birkenhead in the County of Cheshire; Anthony William (Tony) Hall; CBE (2006); s of Donald William Hall, and Mary Joyce, *née* Wallwork; *b* 3 March 1951; *Educ* King Edward's Sch Birmingham, Birkenhead Sch, Keble Coll Oxford (MA); *m* 6 Aug 1977, Cynthia Lesley, da of Arthur Robin Davis; 1 da (Eleanor Alice Mary b 30 Jan 1986), 1 s (William Arthur Henry b 5 June 1989); *Career* BBC TV: joined as news trainee 1973, sr prodr World at One 1978, output ed Newsnight 1980, sr prodr Six O'Clock News 1984, ed Nine O'Clock News 1985, ed TV News and Current Affrs 1987–90, dir News and Current Affrs 1990–93, md News and Current Affrs 1993–96, chief exec BBC News 1996–2001; chief exec Royal Opera House 2001–13, DG BBC 2013–; chair: Theatre Royal Stratford East 2001–09, Sector Skills Cncl for the Creative and Cultural Industries 2004–09, Cultural Olympiad 2009–12, High House Production Park Ltd 2011–13; non-exec dir: HM Customs and Excise 2002–05, Channel 4 TV 2002–13 (dep chm 2012–13), British Cncl 2008–13, LOCOG 2009–12; patron Newsworld 1999–2000, memb Clore Leadership Bd 2005–10, memb Mayor of London's Cultural Forum 2006–13, tstee Paul Hamlyn Fndn 2011–, tstee Fndn Years Tst; contrib various pubns, memb Cncl Brunel Univ 1999–2002; memb House of Lords (cross-bench) 2010–; CMI Gold Medal 2010; Liveryman Worshipful Co of Painter Stainers 1985, Freeman City of London 1988; Hon DLitt Goldsmiths Coll London; hon visiting fell Dept of Journalism City Univ 1999, hon fell Keble Coll Oxford, hon fell Liverpool John Moores Univ; FRTS (vice-chm 1990–98, chm 1998–2000); *Books* King Coal – A History of The Miners (1981), Nuclear Politics (1984); *Recreations* opera, church architecture, walking; *Clubs* Reform, Garrick, Ivy; *Style*— The Lord Hall of Birkenhead, CBE; ✉ c/o Amanda Churchill or Rachel McQuinn, Director-General's Office, BBC Broadcasting House, Portland Place, London W1A 1AA

HALL-SMITH, Martin Clive William; s of (Sydney) Patrick Hall-Smith (d 2002), of Hove, E Sussex, and Angela Wilma, *née* Hall (d 1996); *b* 21 July 1948, Hove, Sussex; *Educ* Eton, Univ of Edinburgh (LLB), Selwyn Coll Cambridge (MA); *m* 17 Dec 1983, Victoria Mary, da of John Sherwood Stephenson (d 1992), of Wylam, Northumberland; 2 da (Rose b 1985, Katharine b 1987), 1 s (Edward b 1989); *Career* called to the Bar Inner Temple 1972; employment judge 2002–; pt/t chm of employment tbnls 1993–2002; Master Worshipful Co of Loriners 2004; *Recreations* music, skiing, gardening, Russian history; *Clubs* Brooks's; *Style*— M C W Hall-Smith, Esq; ✉ East Coombe, North Bank, Hassocks, West Sussex BN6 8J9 (☎ 01273 844379, e-mail martinhallsmith@gmail.com)

HALLETT; *see also:* Hughes Hallett

HALLETT, Prof Christine; *b* 1949; *Educ* Univ of Cambridge, Loughborough Univ (PhD); *Career* former civil servant DHSS; teaching and research posts Keele Univ and Univ of Leicester; Univ of Stirling: reader in social policy 1989–95, prof of social policy 1995–, princ and vice-chllr 2004–10 (formerly sr dep princ); Civil Service cmmr; chair Bd of Tstees UKCISA (UK Cncl for Int Student Affrs); FRSE 2002; *Publications* incl: The Personal Social Services in Local Government, Interagency Co-ordination in Child Protection, Child Abuse: Aspects of Interprofessional Co-operation (with O Stevenson), Co-ordination and Child Protection: a review of the literature (with E Birchall); also author of learned articles, monographs and edited works; *Recreations* golf, walking, tennis, music; *Style*— Prof Christine Hallett

HALLETT, Rt Hon Lady Justice; Rt Hon Dame Heather Carol; DBE (1999), PC (2005); da of Hugh Victor Dudley Hallett, QPM (d 1991), and Doris Viola, *née* Churchill; *b* 16 December 1949; *Educ* Brockenhurst GS, St Hugh's Coll Oxford, (MA); *m* 20 April 1974, Nigel Vivian Marshall Wilkinson, QC, *qv*, s of John Marshall Wilkinson (d 1993); 2 s; *Career* called to the Bar Inner Temple 1972 (bencher 1993); recorder of the Crown Court 1989, QC 1989, ldr SE Circuit 1995–97, dep judge of the High Court 1995, judge of the High Court of Justice (Queen's Bench Div) 1999–2005, presiding judge Western Circuit 2001–04, Lord Justice of Appeal 2005–; judicial appts cmmr 2006– (vice-chm Judicial Appointments Cmmn 2007); chm General Cncl of the Bar 1998, dir Public Affairs Bar Cncl 1993, chm Judicial Coll 2010, vice-pres Queen's Bench Div 2011, treas Inner Temple 2011, vice-pres Criminal Div Ct of Appeal 2011–; *Recreations* theatre, music; *Style*— The Rt Hon Lady Justice Hallett, DBE

HALLETT, Jeremy Norman; s of Maj Howard Samuel Hallett (d 1979), of Stourbridge, and Majorie Winnifred, *née* Harris (d 1981); *b* 3 May 1948; *Educ* Grange Secdy Modern Sch, Bluecoat Boys' Sch Stourbridge, Bromsgrove Coll of Educn, Inst of Health Servs Mgmnt (Dip Public Admin), Harvard Business Sch; *m* 1971, Pamela Anne Stephenson; 1 s (James Dominic), 1 da (Rebecca Louise); *Career* admin asst Warley BC 1970–71 (mgmnt grad trainee 1969–70), chief admin offr Walsall Co Borough 1971–74, unit admin Walsall HA

1974–77; Kidderminster HA: dep dist gen mangr 1978–82, dist admin 1982–83, dist gen mangr 1983–87; jt chief exec Gwent Health Cmmn 1993–96 (dist gen mangr 1988–92), chief exec Wilts HA 1996–2002, assoc conslt Nat PCT Devpt Prog 2002–07, chm Integrated Care Solutions 2008–; memb Nat Tst; MHSM; *Recreations* family, fishing, tennis, music; *Clubs* Harvard Business; *Style*— Jeremy N Hallett, Esq; ⊠ Old Toll House, Beckhampton, Marlborough, Wilts SN8 1QJ (☎ 07531 454298, e-mail jeremy.pam3@gmail.com)

HALLETT, Jess; da of Ray Hallett, and Patricia Harvey, *née* Lewis; *b* 14 December 1965, Devon; *Children* 1 s (Luca Birindelli b 16 Jul 2003), 1 da (Lara Kate Birindelli b 22 Nov 2007); *Career* former head booker Storm Models, currently ind casting dir; projects incl: Alexander McQueen 2002–, Ermenegildo Zegna, Marc by Marc Jacobs, Dunhill, Louis Vuitton, Fendi; *Style*— Ms Jess Hallett; ⊠ c/o Birgitta Toyoda, Streeters, 53– 55 Scrutton Street, London EC2A 4PJ (☎ 020 7253 3949, e-mail birgitta@streeterslondon.com, www.streeters.com)

HALLETT, Dr Michael John; s of Arthur Ronald Hallett (d 1979), of Weymouth, Dorset, and Dorothy Muriel, *née* Stone (d 2004); *b* 29 April 1940; *Educ* Weymouth GS, Bournemouth Municipal Coll of Art (Dorset County Athletics colours), Manchester Poly UMIST (MPhil), Birmingham Poly (Dip History of Art and Design), Univ of Bolton (PhD); *m* 1970, Carol Ann, da of Norman Maurice Flint; 1 da (Emily Jane b 22 May 1975), 1 s (William James b 11 July 1977); *Career* photographer Studio 5 1959–60; lectr in photography: Leicester Coll of Art and Design 1960–65, Bournemouth and Poole Coll of Art 1965–66; lectr then sr lectr in photographic studies Manchester Coll of Art and Design and Manchester Poly 1966–69 and 1970–75, visiting prof Sch of Photographic Arts and Scis Rochester Inst of Technol NY 1969–70; Univ of Central England in Birmingham (formerly Birmingham Poly): princ lectr Dept of Visual Communication 1975–82, head Sch of Photography 1975–78, princ lectr Sch of Theoretical and Historical Studies in Art and Design Birmingham Inst of Art and Design 1982–97; photographer, photohistorian, writer and biographer 1997–; conslt for documentary film Stefan Lorant: Man in Pictures (1997); memb: Nat Cncl Inst of Incorporated Photographers 1966–69, Associateship Panel and Fellowship Panel of History of Photography and Critical Writing Category RPS 1990–; chm Distinctions Panel Research, Educn and Application of Photography RPS 2004–07, chm Distinctions Advsy Bd RPS 2008–11 (chair Fellowship Bd 2008–11); chair Educn Working Gp 2011–13, dep chm Sector 7 Admissions and Qualifications Bd BIPP 1989–98; Kodak Colour scholar Eastman Kodak Co 1964, life memb Stockport Harriers & Athletic Club 1975; research fell Centre for Fine Art Research (CFAR) Birmingham City Univ 2014–, academic assoc Univ of Worcester 2016–; memb Euro Soc for the History of Photography 1981; FRSA 1964, FRPS 1967, FBIPP 1969, MIMgt 1976, FCSD 1977, ASICI 2014; *Books* Programmed Photography (with Jack Tait, 1967), Programmed Colour Photography (1970), Worcester Cathedral: A Grand View (1987), Arts Council Independent Photography Directory (with Barry Lane, 1989), Where to Study: Photography Film Video TV (1990, 1992, 1994, 1998 and 1999), Rewriting Photographic History (1990), The Real Story of Picture Post (1994), Bullring: the heart of Birmingham (2003), Stefan Lorant: Godfather of Photojournalism (2005), Picture Journalism (2009), Olympic Coast (2012), Never a Dull Moment (2013), A Hungarian in England (2013), Puerto del Carmen (2015), The Manchester/Liverpool Photography Circle 1840–1880 (2016); reg contrib British Journal of Photography, contrib British Journal of Photography Annual 1970–94; *Recreations* travel; *Style*— Dr Michael Hallett; ⊠ 134 Henwick Road, St John's, Worcester, WR2 5PB (☎ 01905 425547, e-mail hallettpic@aol.com, website www.michaelhallett.com)

HALLETT, Robert Leonard; s of Vernon Harold Leonard Hallett (d 1974), and Alma Victoria, *née* Braham (d 1999); *b* 9 March 1958, London; *Educ* Uckfield Sch, Lewes Tertiary Coll; *Partner* Isha Yvette Allen; 1 s (Scott Gabriel Leonard b 23 Jan 2004); *Career* dir DBA Ltd 1980–85, co-owner Trident Studios 1985–90; dir: Marshall Arts Ltd 1990–99, Meanfiddler Music plc 1999–2004; pres AEG Live Int 2004–; memb Exec Ctee CPA; *Style*— Robert Hallett, Esq; ⊠ AEG Live, 25 Canada Square, London E14 5LQ (☎ 020 7536 2645, fax 020 7536 2603, e-mail rob@aeglive.co.uk)

HALLEY, Ian Alexander; s of Alexander Halley, of St Michael, Suffolk, and Betty, *née* Sheward; *b* 7 January 1957; *Educ* Dr Challoner's GS, Univ of Nottingham (BA); *m* 29 Oct 1983, Diana Mary, da of Henry Colbert; 1 da (Emily Diana b 10 April 1989), 1 s (Daniel Alexander b 5 July 1992); *Career* advtg exec; Allen Brady & Marsh 1979–86, J Walter Thompson 1986–88, Ogilvy & Mather 1988–95, dir Collett Dickenson Pearce & Partners 1995–97, gp dir McCann-Erickson Advertising 1997–2004, Euro RSCG 2004–05, md Rees Bradley Hepburn 2005–; *Recreations* football, cars, Art Deco; *Style*— Ian Halley, Esq; ⊠ Rees Bradley Hepburn, Diddington Farm, Meriden, West Midlands CV7 7HQ (☎ 01675 443939)

HALLIDAY, Charlotte Mary Irvine; da of Edward Irvine Halliday (d 1984), of St John's Wood, London, and Dorothy Lucy, *née* Hatswell (d 1986); *b* 5 September 1935; *Educ* Froebel Sch, Wester Elchies Craigellachie, Francis Holland Sch London, Royal Acad (Silver Medal for drawing); *Career* artist; keeper New English Art Club 1989–; topographical cmmns incl: Royal Hospital Chelsea 1959, Shell Centre 1957–59, head office Barclays Bank 1961–68, headquarters BP, Barbican 1964, head office Willis Faber Dumas Tower Hill and Ipswich 1978, Mowlem Nat West Tower 1980, head office Singer & Friedlander 1982, Dixons 1982–86, Royal Opera House 1984, RAC Pall Mall 1985–86, Royal Soc of Medicine 1987, United Newspapers 1989, Union Discount Co Cornhill 1990, Salisbury Cathedral 1991, Selfridges 1991, Lord's Pavilion 1994, Trinity Coll of Music 1994, The Great Hall Lincoln's Inn 1994, The Monument for Mercury Asset Management 1995, UCL 1997, The Houses of Parliament from St Thomas' Hospital 2000, St Alban's Abbey 2006, The Supreme Court Parliament Square 2011; contrib to various gp exhbns and Summer Exhbns RA 1956–, 'one-man show' with Sally Hunter Fine Art 1998, Sheridan Russell Gallery 2002; memb NEAC 1961, RBA 1961–92, RWS 1976 (assoc 1971); *Awards* Lord Mayor's Art Awards 1962, 1963 and 1976, de Laszlo Medal RBA 1973, Spirit of London Awards 1978 and 1979; *Books* illustrations for Edwardian Architecture, A Biographical Dictionary (by A Stuart Gray, 1985), Fanlights – A Visual Architectural History (with A S Gray, 1990); *Recreations* amateur choral singing, walking in the Sussex Downs; *Style*— Miss Charlotte Halliday; ⊠ 36a Abercorn Place, St John's Wood, London NW8 9XP (☎ 020 7289 1924)

HALLIDAY, Prof Ian Gibson; CBE (2009); s of John Alexander Halliday, and Gladys, *née* Taylor; *b* 5 February 1940, Kelso, Roxburghshire; *Educ* Univ of Edinburgh (MA, MSc), Univ of Cambridge (PhD); *m* 27 July 1965, Ellenor Gardiner Hervey, *née* Wilson; 1 s (Robert Allan b 30 May 1970), 1 da (Katrina Ellenor b 31 July 1972); *Career* lectr, reader then prof Imperial Coll London 1968–93, prof and head of physics Univ of Wales Swansea 1993–98, chief exec PPARC 1998–2005, chief exec Scottish Univs Physics Alliance 2005–09, prof emeritus Univ of Edinburgh 2010–; pres European Science Fndn (ESF) 2006–, memb EU Research Advsy Bd (EURAB), UK delg CERN Cncl 1998–2005; author of many pubns on theoretical particle physics; FInstP, FRSE; *Recreations* golf, fishing; *Style*— Prof Ian Halliday, CBE; ⊠ Derwent House, Walkley Hill, Stroud, Gloucestershire GL5 3TX (☎ 01453 767073, e-mail ian.halliday@e-halliday.org); School of Physics, James Clerk Maxwell Building, The Kings Buildings, West Mains Road, Edinburgh EH9 3JY

HALLIGAN, Joseph; *b* 11 January 1988, Birmingham; *Educ* King Edward VI Five Ways Birmingham, Churchill Coll Cambridge; *Career* architect; founding memb Assemble (Turner Prize 2015); *Style*— Joe Halligan, Esq

HALLIGAN, Liam James; s of Martin Thomas Halligan, and Evelyn, *née* Thorp; *b* 29 April 1969, London; *Educ* John Lyon Sch Harrow (entrance scholarship, head boy), Univ of Warwick (BSc), St Antony's Coll Oxford (MPhil, memb Isis boat race crew); *Partner* Lucy Miranda Ward; 2 da (Ailis Rosa b 5 Aug 2000, Maeve Isabella b 19 Feb 2003), 1 s (Ned Tomas b 3 Jan 2006); *Career* economist, writer and broadcaster; econ intern IMF 1992, head of res Social Market Fndn 1993, economist Econ Miny Russian Govt 1994–95, Moscow reporter The Economist 1995–96, econ columnist Moscow Times 1995–96, political corr Financial Times 1996–98, econ corr Channel 4 News 1998–2006, economics ed Sunday Telegraph 2006–07 (economics commentator Telegraph Gp 2007–), chief economist Prosperity Capital Mgmnt (UK) 2007–10, chief economist Prosperity Capital Mgmnt (Russian Fedn) 2010–13, economist and strategist New Sparta Gp 2013–; editor-at-large Business New Europe 2014–; columnist: Sunday Business 2000–01, Sunday Telegraph 2001–06, GQ Magazine 2007–10; memb: Advsy Cncl Social Market Fndn, Risk Cmmn RSA, Soc of Business Economists, Advsy Cncl Centre for Competitive Advantage in the Global Economy Dept of Economics Univ of Warwick; Wincott Fndn Business Broadcaster of the Year 1999, Industrial Soc Prog of the Year 2001, Wincott Fndn Business Prog of the Year 2002 and 2006, Workworld Prog of the Year 2002, 2003, 2004 and 2007, Bradford & Bingley Personal Fin Award 2003, Best Broadcast Story Business Journalist of the Year 2004 and 2005, Br Press Awards Business and Finance Commentator of the Year 2007, Workworld Columnist of the Year 2007; *Publications* incl: Beyond Unemployment (with Robert Skidelsky, qv, 1993), Europe Isn't Working (with Frank Field, qv, MP, 1994), A Guide to Russia's Parliamentary Elections (1995), Lessons From Russia's Stabilisation Programmes (with Robert Skidelsky, 1996); author of numerous articles for Sunday Telegraph, The Economist Intelligence Unit and Wall St Jl; *Recreations* film, rowing, sailing, roller-skating, guitar, double bass, Irish traditional music, choral music; *Clubs* Groucho; *Style*— Liam Halligan, Esq; ⊠ New Sparta Group, 27a Floral Street, London WC2E 9EZ (e-mail l.halligan@newsparta.net)

HALLING, Prof Peter James; s of John Halling, of Heswall, Merseyside, and Enid Joyce, *née* Rutherford; *b* 30 March 1951; *Educ* Calday GS, Univ of Cambridge (BA), Univ of Bristol (PhD); *Career* research asst Biochemical Engrg Section UCL 1975–78, scientist Unilever Research Lab 1978–83; Univ of Strathclyde: lectr 1983–89, sr lectr 1989–90, prof 1990–; MRSC; FRSE 1996; *Recreations* orienteering; *Style*— Prof Peter Halling, FRSE; ⊠ 2/2, 34 Montague Street, Glasgow G4 9HX; Department of Pure & Applied Chemistry, University of Strathclyde, Glasgow G1 1XW (☎ 0141 552 4400, fax 0141 548 4822, e-mail p.j.halling@strath.ac.uk)

HALLISSEY, Michael; s of John Francis Hallissey, MBE (d 1986), and Mary, *née* Kendall (d 2011); *b* 6 March 1943; *Educ* Royal GS Lancaster, Magdalen Coll Oxford (MA); *Career* chartered accountant; PricewaterhouseCoopers (formerly Price Waterhouse before merger): staff accountant 1964–68, asst mangr Melbourne 1969–70, mangr Milan 1970–71, sr mangr London 1971–74, audit ptnr London 1974–79, practice devpt ptnr UK 1979–81, strategic planning ptnr UK 1981–82, corp fin ptnr London 1982–85, head of corp fin servs UK 1985–87, head of strategic planning Price Waterhouse World Firm 1987–88, dir of strategy Price Waterhouse Europe 1988–98; visiting fell The Business Sch Imperial Coll of Sci and Technol London 1998–2003; strategic conslt specialising in mgmnt of int business with particular reference to the availability and economics of energy resources and the economics of climate change 1998–; FCA 1968, FRSA; *Books* numerous articles on corp strategy, strategic planning, mergers and acquisitions; *Recreations* politics, sailing, music, opera, good food; *Style*— Michael Hallissey, Esq; ⊠ 66 Waterside Point, Albert Bridge, London SW11 4PD

HALLISSEY, Timothy Charles Daniel (Tim); s of Brendan Hallissey, and Josephine, *née* Peckham; *b* 3 December 1961, Hayes; *Educ* St Paul's RC Comp Haywards Heath; *m* 5 July 1986, Sharron McQuoid; 3 da (Leah Jo-Ann b 8 May 1987, Jennie Rebecca b 19 July 1988, Anna Harriett b 24 Apr 1990); *Career* reporter rising to chief sub-ed The News Portsmouth 1980–95; The Times: joined as sub-ed 1995, subsequently assoc sports ed, then dep sports ed, sports ed 2004–; The Times named Sports Newspaper of the Year 2005, 2009, 2010, 2011 and 2012, and Sports Team of the Year 2013; *Recreations* reading, travelling; *Style*— Tim Hallissey, Esq; ⊠ The Times, The News Building, 1 London Bridge Street, London SE1 9GF (☎ 020 7782 5759, e-mail tim.hallissey@thetimes.co.uk)

HALLIWELL, Prof Neil; *b* 20 July 1948; *Educ* Univ of Liverpool (BSc, PhD); *m* 1987, Tessa Jane; 2 da (Katherine b 18 June 1990, Elisabeth b 22 Jan 1993), 1 s (Andrew b 31 July 1995); *Career* scientific offr Atomic Energy Authy 1972–74; Univ of Southampton: research fell Dept of Aeronautics 1974–77, lectr Inst of Sound and Vibration Research 1977–87 (sr lectr 1987–90); Loughborough Univ: prof of optical engrg 1990–, head Dept of Mechanical Engrg 1992–97, dean of engrg 1997–2011, pro-vice-chllr (research) 2001–11, dep vice-chllr 2006–11; author of over 200 published research papers in field of laser technol for engrg application; sr memb Laser Inst of America; UK Prize for Metrology Nat Physical Laboratory 1992, Higher Doctorate (DSc) Univ of Southampton 1992; FInstP 1990, FIMechE 1991, FREng 1996, FSPIE 1997, fell Soc of Photo-Optical and Instrumentation Engrs (USA); *Recreations* match angling; *Style*— Prof Neil Halliwell, DSc, FREng

HALLS, Andrew David; s of Gerald Halls, and Barbara Halls; *b* 29 January 1959, Bristol; *Educ* Shenley Ct Sch Birmingham, Gonville & Caius Coll Cambridge (scholar, MA); *m* 1987, Veronique Le Droff; 2 da; *Career* English teacher Chigwell Sch 1981–84, English teacher Whitgift Sch 1984–88, head of English Bristol GS 1989–95, dep headmaster Trinity Sch 1995–98, master Magdalen Coll Sch Oxford 1998–2007, head master King's Coll Sch Wimbledon 2008–; *Publications* 14–18 – A New Vision for Secondary Education (contrib, 2013); *Recreations* family, reading, theatre, running; *Style*— Mr A D Halls; ⊠ King's College School, Wimbledon SW19 4TT (☎ 020 8255 5300)

HALSALL, Alan; *Educ* Newcastle Univ (LLB); *Career* owner: Halsall Toys 1979–2006, Silver Cross Ltd 2006–15 (also chm); fndr Skipton & Ripon Enterprise Gp 2005–; jt chm Business for Britain 2013–16, memb Bd Vote Leave 2015–16; govr Craven Community Coll 2012–14, chm Craven Educnl Tst 2014–; *Recreations* golf, horse racing; *Clubs* Carlton, Royal Lytham & St Anne's Golf; *Style*— Alan Halsall, Esq; ⊠ e-mail davidahalsall@gmail.com

HALSALL, Francesca Jean; *b* 12 April 1990; *Career* swimmer; achievements incl: Gold medal (4x100m medley) European Championships (Long Course) 2006, 2 Silver medals (4x100m medley and 4 x 100m freestyle) Cwlth Games 2006, Gold medal (4 x 100m medley) European Championships (Long Course) 2008, Silver medal (100m freestyle) and 3 Bronze medals (50m freestyle, 4x100m freestyle and 4x100m medley) World Championships (Short Course) 2008, Silver medal (100m freestyle) World Championships (Long Course) 2009, 2 Gold medals (100m freestyle and 4 x 100m medley), 2 Silver medals (100m butterfly and 4 x 100m freestyle) and Bronze medal (50m freestyle) European Championships (Long Course) 2010, Gold medal (50m butterfly), 3 Silver medals (50m freestyle, 4 x 100m freestyle and 4 x 100m medley) and Bronze medal (100m freestyle) Cwlth Games 2010, Bronze medal (50m freestyle) World Championships 2013; *Style*— Ms Francesca Halsall

HALSALL, Air Cdre Martin William; s of Bernard Holt Halsall, MC, of Market Harborough, Leics, and Emily Constance, *née* Sutton; *b* 10 February 1954, Melton Mowbray, Leics; *Educ* Becket Sch Nottingham, Univ of Salford, Univ of London (MBA); *m* 1, 18 August 1979 (m dis 2011), Elizabeth Ann, *née* Shaw; 2 s (Matthew b 5 Jan 1982, Alexander James b 18 Oct 1983), 1 da (Amy Victoria b 22 March 1992); *m* 2, 29 Dec 2015, Catherine Anne O'Neill; *Career* joined RAF 1974, pilot F4 Phantom Fighters 1976–1990 (exchange tour with JG71 'R' of the Luftwaffe 1983–86), Canadian Forces Cmd and Staff Coll Toronto 1990–91, First Offr cmdg Falkland Islands Air Wing 1995, Cdr Br Forces Italy 2000, Cdr Western Sovereign Base Area (Cyprus) and Station Cdr RAF Akrotiri 2001–03, Dep Cdr NATO Combined Air Ops Centre 3 Bodø Norway 2003–04, asst dir NATO Jt Air Power Competence Centre Kalkar Germany 2004–05; bursar Haileybury and Imperial Serv Coll 2006–08, ceo King's Gp (educn) Madrid 2008–09, chief ops offr INTO UEA London 2009–12, princ Greenwich Sch of Mgmnt Greenford 2012–14, interim chief operations offr Study Gp 2014–15, dir Glion Inst of HE London 2015, bursar Oratory Schs Assoc Woodcote 2016–; FCMI; *Recreations* golf, tennis, gardening; *Style—* Air Cdre Martin Halsall; ✉ 30 Blakes Avenue, New Malden, Surrey KT3 6RL (e-mail martinhalsall@gmail.com)

HALSEY, Simon Patrick; CBE (2015); s of Louis Arthur Owen Halsey, of Kingston upon Thames, Surrey, and Evelyn Elisabeth, *née* Calder; *b* 8 March 1958; *Educ* chorister New Coll Oxford, Winchester (music scholar), King's Coll Cambridge (choral scholar), Royal Coll of Music (conducting scholar); *m* 14 June 1986, Lucy Jane, da of Norman Linsley Lunt; 1 s (Jack b 31 July 1989), 1 da (Harriet b 10 June 1992); *Career* conductor Scottish Opera-Go-Round 1980–81, dir of music Univ of Warwick 1981–88; chorus dir: CBSO Chorus 1983–, Acad of Ancient Music 1988–91, Flemish Opera Antwerp 1990–94; assoc dir Philharmonia Chorus 1986–98, music dir City of Birmingham Touring Opera 1987–1997; principal conductor Rundfunkchor Berlin 2001–15, Conductor Laureate 2015–; artistic dir: Salisbury Festival 1988–93, BBC Nat Chorus of Wales 1995–2000; artistic advsr Schleswig-Holstein Musik Festival Choir 2014–, artistic dir Orfeó Català Choirs and artistic advsr Palau de la Música Barcelona 2016–; princ guest conductor: Netherlands Radio Choir 1997–2008, Sydney Philharmonia Choirs 1997–2000; chief conductor Netherlands Radio Choir 2002–08; principal conductor Choral Projects Northern Sinfonia of England 2005–12; has appeared as guest conductor with various major choirs and orchs incl: LSO, CBSO, English Chamber Orch, Scottish Chamber Orch, London Symphony Chorus, French, Swedish, Danish and Belgian Radio Choirs, Australian Chamber Orch, Hong Kong Philharmonic Orch; has made over 40 recordings on EMI, Chandos, Oiseau-Lyre, Harmonia Mundi, Coviello and Hyperion as chorus master and on Conifer as conductor; founding dir BBC Proms Youth Chorus 2012–, choral dir London Symphony Orch and Chorus 2012–; int chair of choral conducting Royal Welsh Coll of Music and Drama 2008–14, dir Youth Choral Prog Berliner Philharmoniker 2012–; prof and dir Choral Activities Univ of Birmingham 2012–; prof Univ of Birmingham 2012; conslt ed Faber Music Ltd; Grammy Award 2008, 2009 and 2011; Hon DUniv Central England 2000, Hon MA Univ of Warwick 2007, Hon DMus Univ of Birmingham 2008; Hon Fellship Royal Welsh Coll of Music and Drama 2015; Queen's Medal for Music 2015; Order of Merit 1st Class Federal Republic of Germany 2010; *Books* Schott Master Class Chorleitung (2011); *Recreations* architecture, food and wine, sport, English literature, travel; *Style—* Simon Halsey, Esq, CBE; ✉ 2 Brooke Close, Bridge End, Warwick CV34 6PE; c/o Susie McLeod, Intermusica Ltd, Chrystal Wharf, 36 Graham Street, London N1 8GJ (☎ 020 7608 9900, e-mail gevans@intermusica.co.uk)

HALUCH, (Stefan) James (Jim); s of late Stefan L Haluch, and late Elizabeth, *née* Wallace; *b* 9 March 1944, Bathgate, W Lothian; *Educ* St Mary's Acad Bathgate; *m* 25 May 1968, Joyce Vevers, da of late George S McClelland; 2 da (Helena b 1965, Shelagh b 1971), 2 s (James b 1969, Eoin b 1974); *Career* Inland Revenue 1962–65, The Scotsman Edinburgh 1965–70, business conslt and hotelier 1970–88, Sight & Sound Education Ltd 1988–91, head of mktg, head of corporate communications and assoc princ Telford Coll Edinburgh 1991–2006, business conslt Athol Consulting 2006–, dir Park Homes Scotland Ltd 2013–; dir/sec Willow Wood (West Lothian) Community Co Ltd 2007–; chm Isle of Arran Tourist Bd 1980–83, pres Isle of Arran Licensed Trade Assoc 1983–86; former councillor: Bathgate Town Cncl, W Lothian CC; FInstSMM, FCMI, FCIPD; *Recreations* music, travel, renewable energy, community development; *Style—* Jim Haluch, Esq; ✉ 11 Cuthill Brae, West Calder, West Lothian EH55 8QE (e-mail jim.haluch@btinternet.com)

HAM, Prof Christopher John (Chris); CBE (2004), DL (W Midlands 2013); s of Raymond Ham (d 1993), and Ann Ham (d 1993); *b* 15 May 1951, Cardiff; *Educ* Cardiff HS for Boys, Univ of Kent (BA, MPhil), Univ of Bristol (PhD); *m* 30 May 1980, Ioanna, *née* Burnell; 2 s (Alex b 6 Sept 1982, Matthew b 18 June 1989), 1 da (Jessica b 16 Dec 1985); *Career* research asst Nuffield Centre for Health Serv Studies Univ of Leeds 1975–77, lectr Sch for Advanced Urban Studies Univ of Bristol 1977–86, policy analyst King's Fund Inst and fell in health policy and mgmnt King's Fund Coll 1986–92, dir Health Servs Mgmnt Centre 1993–2000, dir (on secondment) Strategy Unit Dept of Health 2000–04, prof of health policy and mgmnt Univ of Birmingham 2004–14 (emeritus prof 2014–); chief exec King's Fund 2010–; advsr to numerous orgns incl: Health Ctee House of Commons, Audit Cmmn, Nat Audit Office, Dept of Health, BDA, BMA, NHS Confedn, RCP, Demos (memb Advsy Cncl), World Bank, WHO; former vice-pres Patients' Assoc, chair Int Soc on Priorities in Health Care 1998–2000, memb Social Policy Assoc 1977–, non-exec dir Heart of England NHS Fndn Tsts 2007–10, govr The Health Fndn 2006–10, memb Bd of Tstees Canadian Health Services Res Fndn 2006–10, sr assoc Nuffield Tst 2008–09; visiting prof Univ of Surrey 2009, visiting prof London Sch of Hygiene and Tropical Medicine 2011–; ed: State of Health series Open Univ Press 1991–2010, Health Servs Mgmnt series Open Univ Press 1994–; memb Editorial Bd: Policy and Politics 1984–89, Br Jl of Health Care Mgmnt 1996–2000, Health Expectations 1997–; reviewer and referee for numerous professional jls; Kellogg Fndn Fellowship to Nordic Sch of Public Health Gothenburg 1986; Donabedin Int Award 2013; Hon DLitt Univ of Kent 2012; FRSM 1993, fndr fell Acad of Med Sciences 1998, Hon FRCP 2004, Hon FRCGP 2008; *Publications* incl: Policy Making in the NHS: A Case Study of the Leeds Regional Hospital Board (1981), Health Policy in Britain (1982, 6 edn 2009), The Policy Process in the Modern Capitalist State (with M J Hill, 1984, 2 edn 1993), Managing Health Services: Health Authority Members in Search of a Role (1986), Health Check: Health Care Reforms in an International Context (with R Robinson and M Benzeval, 1990), The New NHS: Organisation and Management (1991), Management and Competition in the New NHS (1991, 2 edn 1997), Priority Setting Processes for Healthcare (with F Honigsbaum, J Calltorp and S Holmström, 1995), The NHS Guide (with S Haywood, 2 edn 1993), Priority Setting in Healthcare: Lessons for General Practice (1995), Public, Private or Community: What Next for the NHS? (1996), Health Care Reform: Learning From International Experience (ed, 1997), Tragic Choices in Health Care: The Case of Child B (with S Pickard, 1998), The Global Challenge of Health Care Rationing (ed with A Coulter, 2000), The Politics of NHS Reform 1988–97: Metaphor or Reality? (2000), Contested Decisions (with S McIver, 2000), Reasonable Rationing (ed with G Robert, 2003), NHS Mutual (with Jo Ellins, 2009), Medical Leadership (with Peter Spurgeon and John Clark, 2011); numerous book chapters, articles in newspapers and refereed jls, research reports, briefing papers and conf proceedings; *Recreations* sport, music, theatre, reading, travel; *Style—* Prof Chris Ham, CBE, DL; ✉ The King's Fund, 11–13 Cavendish Square, London W1G 0AN (☎ 020 7307 2400, e-mail c.ham@kingsfund.org.uk)

HAMBLEN, Nicholas Archibald; QC (1997); s of Derek Hamblen, and Pauline, *née* Morgan; *Educ* Westminster, St John's Coll Oxford (MA), Harvard Law Sch (LLM); *m* 1985, Kate Hamblen; 1 da (Eleanor b 1990), 1 s (Jamie b 1992); *Career* called to the Bar Lincoln's Inn 1981; specialist in commercial law especially shipping, int trade, insurance, arbitration; recorder 1999–; *Clubs* MCC, Hurlingham, Vincent's (Oxford); *Style—* Nicholas Hamblen, Esq, QC; ✉ 20 Essex Street, London WC2R 3AL (☎ 020 7583 9294, fax 020 7583 1341)

HAMBLIN, Brian James; s of Philip James Arthur Hamblin, of Orpington, and Freda Mary Hamblin; *b* 17 February 1954; *Educ* Cray Valley Tech HS, Lanchester Poly (BA); *m* 1, 1977 (m dis 2008), Jane Karen, da of W Alan Sutherland; 2 da (Elizabeth Jane b 7 April 1983, Victoria Claire b 6 Feb 1985), 1 s (Philip James b 4 July 1987); *m* 2, 2009, Nicola Jayne, da of A Whitehouse; *Career* articled clerk Warley & Warley 1975–76; PKF Leicester 1979–: asst mangr then sr audit mangr 1984–85, ptnr 1985–, managing ptnr and sr corp recovery ptnr 1986–, regnl managing ptnr for Midlands 1999–; memb Cncl R3 2010–; Hon BA Coventry Poly 1976; memb Inst of Taxation 1981, MIPA 1990, MSPI 1990 (chm Midlands Region); FCA; *Recreations* playing the trumpet, badminton, golf, church steward; *Clubs* Leicester Rotary; *Style—* Brian Hamblin, Esq; ✉ PKF, Pannell House, 159 Charles Street, Leicester, Leicestershire LE1 1LD (☎ 0116 250 4400, fax 0116 285 4651)

HAMBLING, Maggi; CBE (2010, OBE 1995); da of Harry Leonard Hambling (d 1998), of Hadleigh, Suffolk, and Marjorie Rose, *née* Harris (d 1988); *b* 23 October 1945; *Educ* Hadleigh Hall Sch, Amberfield Sch, Ipswich Sch of Art, Camberwell Sch of Art (DipAD Painting), Slade Sch of Fine Art (Higher Dip Fine Art), Boise travel award NY 1969; *Career* artist; first artist in residence Nat Gallery London 1980–81; Jerwood Painting Prize 1995; fell New Hall Cambridge 2003; Marsh Award for excellence in public sculpture 2005; Hon DLitt UEA 2000, hon fell Univ of the Arts London 2004; *Works in Public Collections* incl: Arts Cncl of GB, Birmingham City Art Gallery, Br Cncl, Br Museum, Christchurch Mansion Ipswich, Clare Coll Cambridge, Chelmsford and Essex Museum, Contemporary Art Soc, Eastern Arts Collection, Euro Parliament Collection, Fndn Du Musee De La Main Lausanne, GLC, Greene King Breweries, Gulbenkian Fndn, Haddo House Aberdeen, Harris Museum and Art Gallery Preston, HTV Bristol Imperial War Museum, Leics Educn Ctee, Minories Colchester, Morley Coll London, Nat Gallery, Nat Portrait Gallery, Petworth House, Rugby Museum, RAMC, Scottish Nat Gallery of Modern Art Edinburgh, Scottish Nat Portrait Gallery, Southampton Art Gallery, St Mary's Church Hadleigh Suffolk, St Mary's Coll Strawberry Hill London, St Mary's Hosp London, Tate Gallery, Unilever House London, Usher Gallery Lincoln, Whitworth Art Gallery Manchester, William Morris Sch London, Aust Nat Gallery Canberra, Hereford Cathedral, New Hall Cambridge, Yale Center for Br Art New Haven Conn, Templeton Coll Oxford, Univ of Warwick, Wakefield Art Gallery, Ashmolean Museum Oxford, Usher Gallery Lincoln, Government Art Collection, Castle Museum Norwich, Fitzwilliam Museum Cambridge, Barclay's Art Collection, Lady Margaret Hall Oxford; *Exhibitions* Hadleigh Gallery Suffolk 1967, Morley Gallery London 1973, Warehouse Gallery London 1977, Nat Gallery London 1981, Nat Portrait Gallery London and tour 1983, Serpentine Gallery London 1987, Richard Demarco Gallery Edinburgh 1988, Maclaurin Art Gallery Ayr 1988, Arnolfini Gallery Bristol and tour 1988, Bernard Jacobson Gallery London 1990, Yale Center for British Art New Haven Conn USA 1991, CCA Galleries London 1993, Northern Centre for Contemporary Art Sunderland 1993, Cornerhouse Manchester 1993, Angel Row Nottingham 1994, Christchurch Mansion Ipswich 1994, Harris Museum Preston 1994, Barbican Centre London 1994, Sculpture in Bronze Marlborough Fine Art 1996, National Portrait Gallery 1997, Yorkshire Sculpture Park 1997, Hugh Lane Gallery Dublin 1997, Monument to Oscar Wilde Adelaide Street London 1998, Good Friday Gainsborough's House Sudbury 2000, Marlborough Fine Art and Morley Gallery 2001, Very Special Brew Paintings Sotheby's 2003, North Sea Paintings Aldeburgh Festival Exhibition 2003, Scallop sculpture to celebrate Benjamin Britten Aldeburgh beach Suffolk 2003, Portraits of People and the Sea Marlborough Fine Art 2006, No Straight Lines (Fitzwilliam Museum and tour) 2007, Waves Breaking (Marlborough Graphics) 2007, Waves and Waterfalls (Abbot Hall Kendal) 2007 and (Marlborough Fine Art) 2008, Waterfalls and Slaughden Waves (Peter Pears Gallery Aldeburgh) 2008, George Always: Portraits of George Melly by Maggi Hambling (Walker Art Gallery Liverpool and Nat Portrait Gall London) 2009, The Sea (Lowry) 2009, The Brixton Heron Sculpture London SW9 2010, Maggi Hambling: the Wave (Fitzwilliam Museum Cambridge) 2010, Sea Sculpture, Paintings and Etchings (Malborough Fine Art London) 2010, Freud Museum London, SNAP (Aldeburgh Festival) 2012, Wall of Water (The Hermitage St Petersburg) 2013, The Winchester Tapestries unveiled (Winchester Cathedral) 2013, Walls of Water (National Gallery London) 2014, War Requiem and Aftermath (KCL Somerset House London) 2015; *Books* Maggi and Henrietta: Drawings of Henrietta Moraes by Maggi Hambling (2001), Maggi Hambling: The Works (2006), George Always (2009), You are the Sea (2009), The Sea (2009), The Aldeburgh Scallop (2010), War Requiem and Aftermath (2015); *Clubs* Chelsea Arts, The Ivy; *Style—* Miss Maggi Hambling, CBE; ✉ c/o Morley College, 61 Westminster Bridge Road, London SE1 7HT

HAMBRO, James Daryl; s of Jocelyn Olaf Hambro, MC (d 1994), and his 1 w, Ann Silvia, *née* Muir (d 1972); *b* 22 March 1949; *Educ* Eton, Harvard Business Sch; *m* Diana Cherry; 3 c; *Career* exec dir Hambros Bank 1972–85; md: J O Hambro Magan & Co 1988–94, J O Hambro & Co 1986–98; chm: J O Hambro Capital Mgmnt Ltd 1996–, Ashtenne Hldgs plc 1997–2005, ViCTory VCT, Hansteen Hldgs plc 2005–, James Hambro & Ptnrs LLP 2010–; dir: Primary Health Properties plc 1996–2016, Capital Opportunities Tst 1997–2003, Enterprise Capital Tst 1997–2003; dep chm Peabody Tst 1993–2006; chm: Int Students Tst 1988–2016, Henry Smith Charity 2007–15, Guide Dogs for the Blind Assoc 2016–; *Clubs* White's, Royal West Norfolk; *Style—* James Hambro; ✉ James Hambro & Partners LLP, 45 Pall Mall, London SW1Y 5JG (☎ 020 7078 0088)

HAMBRO, (George) Jay; s of Peter C P Hambro, and Karen G G, *née* Brodrick; *b* 24 September 1974, London; *Educ* Harrow, Univ of Newcastle (BA); *m* 14 June 2003, Alexandra Sophie, *née* Babington; 2 da (Zia Mary b 15 Sept 2005, Sasha Arabella b 9 Nov 2006); *Career* N M Rothschild & Sons Ltd 1997–2000, mangr HSBC Investment Bank 2000–03, dir Peter Hambro Mining plc 2003–06 (currently non-exec dir), chief exec Aricom plc 2006–09, chm IRC Gp 2010–; memb Worshipful Co of Goldsmiths; *Recreations* wine, field sports; *Clubs* White's; *Style—* Jay Hambro, Esq

HAMBRO, (Alexander) Richard; s of Jocelyn Olaf Hambro, MC (d 1994), by his 1 w, Ann Silvia, *née* Muir (d 1972); *b* 1 October 1946; *Educ* Eton; *m* 1, 1973 (m dis 1982), Hon Charlotte, da of Baron Soames, GCMG, GCVO, CH, CBE, PC; 1 da (Clementine b 1976, bridesmaid to Lady Diana Spencer at her marriage to HRH The Prince of Wales 1981); m 2, 12 July 1984 (m dis 1992), Juliet Mary Elizabeth Grana, da of Maj Thomas Harvey and Lady Mary Harvey; m 3, 1993, Mary Christine James, *née* Briggs; *Career* dir Hambros Bank 1979– (joined 1966), pres Hambro America Inc 1975–83, co-fndr J O Hambro & Co 1986; chm: J O Hambro Investment Management Ltd, I Hennig & Co diamond brokers 1987, Wiltons (St James's) Ltd 2003–, Inst of Cancer Research 2003, Smith's Holdings Ltd 2003–, The Money Portal plc 2003–; dir Mercantile Investment Tst plc 2006; pres Colon Cancer Concern 1997, dep pres Macmillan Cancer Relief 2001–; chm: Jt Br Cancer Charities, Newmarket Racecourses Tst 2004; tstee: The London Clinic 2000, Burdett Tst for Nursing; *Clubs* White's, RAC, The Brook (NY), Jockey; *Style—* Richard Hambro, Esq; ✉ Waverton House, Moreton-in-Marsh, Gloucestershire GL56 9TB

HAMBRO, Rupert Nicholas; CBE (2014); eldest s of Jocelyn Olaf Hambro, MC (d 1994), and his 1 w, Ann Silvia, *née* Muir (d 1973); *b* 27 June 1943, London; *Educ* Eton, Aix-en-Provence; *m* 1970, Mary Robinson, da of late Francis Boyer; 1 s, 1 da; *Career* accountant Peat Marwick Mitchell Co 1962–64; Hambros Bank Ltd: dir 1964–86, dep chm 1980–83, chm 1983–86; J O Hambro & Co Ltd: md 1986–94, chm 1994–99; non-exec founding ptnr Robinson Hamro Ltd 2010–, ptnr Hambro Perks 2012–; chm: J O Hambro Ltd 1986–,

Wilton's (St James') Ltd 1987–2003, J O Hambro Magan Ltd 1988–96, J O Hambro Magan Irby Holdings Ltd 1988–96, Hamleys of London 1989–94, Mayflower Corporation plc 1989–2004, Fenchurch plc 1993–97, Longshot plc 1996–2007, J O Hambro Mansford Ltd 1998–2008, Longshot Health and Fitness 1999–2007, Roland Berger & Partners Ltd 2000–03, Kapital Ventures plc 2001–06, Longshot Hotels Ltd 2001–04, Tanner Krolle Ltd 2002–06, Cazenove & Loyd Ltd 2004–, Lovedean Ltd 2008–10, Theo Fennell plc 2009–13, Sipsmith Ltd 2009–, Seenit Ltd 2015–; memb Bd of Dirs Anglo American Corp of SA Ltd 1981–97, memb Int Advsy Bd Montana AG 1988–2000; dir: The Telegraph plc 1986–2003 (dir Telegraph Advsy Bd 2002–03), Asset Trust plc 1987–90, Bank Gutmann AG 2000–, Bd Open Europe 2006–07; memb Bd: Chatsworth House Tst Ltd 1982–2004, Racecourse Holdings Tst 1985–94, Triton Europe 1987–90, Sedgwick Group plc 1987–92, Pioneer Concrete plc 1988–99, The Mayflower Corp plc 1988–2004, CTR Gp 1990–97, Abel Hadden and Co Ltd 1998–2001, KBC Peel Hunt plc 2000–03; non-exec dir Seenit Ltd 2015–; chm: Assoc of Int Bond Dealers 1979–82, Soc of Merchants Trading to the Continent 1995–2009; vice-patron RBS 1997–; chm of tstees: The Silver Tst 1987–; chm: Garfield Weston Boys' Club Tst 1991–2000, Woburn Golf and Country Club Ltd 1998–2003, Bd of Govrs Museum of London 1998–2005, The Walbrook Club Ltd 1999–2001, Third Space Gp Ltd 1999–2007, Jermyn Street Assoc 2000–03, Univ of Bath in Swindon 2000–07, The Walpole Ctee Ltd 2000–05, Old Etonian Tst 2001–, Woburn Enterprises Ltd 2003–11, Chiswick House and Gardens Tst 2005–11, Devpt and Strategy Bd ZSL 2013–; hon pres Br Assoc of Adoption and Fostering 2006–; treas Nat Art Collection Fund 1991–2003, chm of govrs Museum of London 1999–2005, dep chm Clubs for Young People (formerly NAYC) 2001–11, treas Business for Sterling 2002–07, co-chm Museum in Docklands 2003–05, memb Cncl and chm Devpt Bd RCA 2010–16, tstee Wallace Collection 2013–, chm Angel Club RCA 2015–16; Walpole Medal of Br Excellence 2005; Prime Warden Worshipful Co of Goldsmiths 2009–10; Univ of Bath: memb Cncl 2005–11, hon fell 1998–; Knight Falcon (Iceland) 1987, Baron of Denmark; *Recreations* country pursuits; *Clubs* White's, Walbrook, Jupiter Island (Florida), Groucho; *Style*— R N Hambro, Esq, CBE; ✉ Hambro Perks, 1 Queen Anne's Gate Building, 21 Dartmouth Street, London SW1H 9BP (☎ 020 3653 0329, e-mail ruperthambro@hambroperks.com)

HAMEED, Baron (Life Peer UK 2007), of Hampstead in the London Borough of Camden; Dr Khalid Hameed; CBE, DL (Gtr London 2007); s of Prof Dr M Abdul Hameed, and Rashida Abdul Hameed; *b* 1 July 1941; *Educ* Lucknow Univ India (BSc, DPA, MB BS, DSc), Univ of London (DTM&H), Univ of Middlesex (DLitt), Met Univ (DSc); *m* 1989, Dr Ghazala Afzal; 3 s, 3 da; *Career* ceo Cromwell Hosp London 1990–2005, chm Alpha Hosp Gp 2003–15, chm and chief exec London Int Hosp 2006–15; chm: Cwlth Youth Exchange Cncl 1999–2015, Cncl for Co-Existence 2006–; chm Woolfe Inst of Abrahamic Faiths 2007–16, tstee The Little Fndn, govr Int Students House, pres Friends of the Br Library, vice-patron Nat Almhouse Assoc; sits in House of Lords as crossbench peer 2007–; Sternberg Award for Interfaith Work 2006, Ambass of Peace Award 2007; High Sheriff Gtr London 2006–07; Freedom of the City of London 2010–; FRCP; *Clubs* Athenaeum, MCC, Mosimann; *Style*— The Lord Hameed, CBE, DL; ✉ House of Lords, London SW1A 0PW

HAMER, (Michael Howard) Kenneth; s of Mark Hamer (d 1970), and Feodora Leonora, *née* Abrahams (d 1958); *b* 27 July 1945; *Educ* Cheltenham Coll, Sidney Sussex Coll Cambridge (Evan Lewis-Thomas law student); *m* 20 Sept 1986, Victoria, da of Dr Thomas Walsh (d 1988); 1 da (Clara b 1989); *Career* practising barr; admitted slr 1968; called to the Bar: Inner Temple 1975, King's Inns Ireland 1998; recorder of the Crown Court 2000– (asst recorder 1991–2000); counsel for passenger gp at Southall and Ladbroke Grove rail accident inquiries 1997–2001; chair Home Office Review of Independent Membs of Police Authorities 2003–04; chair Appeal Ctee CIMA 2006–12; memb prosecuting panel for Conduct Ctee of the Bar Standards Bd; legal assessor to: GMC, Nursing and Midwifery Cncl, Gen Dental Cncl; jt ed Assoc of Regulatory and Disciplinary Lawyers Quarterly Bulletin, memb Cncl Incorporated Cncl of Law Reporting 2016–; memb Westminster City Cncl 1970–74; chair Iford Parish Meeting 2012–16 (vice-chair 2010–12); FCIArb 1999, accredited mediator 2002; *Publications* Professional Conduct Casebook (2013, 2 edn 2015); *Recreations* walking my dog, opera, arts; *Clubs* Carlton; *Style*— Kenneth Hamer, Esq; ✉ Iford Manor, Iford, Lewes, East Sussex BN7 3EU (☎ 01273 472832); Henderson Chambers, 2 Harcourt Buildings, Temple, London EC4Y 9DB (☎ 020 7583 9020, fax 020 7583 2686, e-mail khamer@hendersonchambers.co.uk)

HAMES, Christopher; QC (2015); s of Peter Hames, and Sheila, *née* Hickman; *b* 11 January 1964, Brentwood, Essex; *Educ* Univ of Sheffield (LLB); *m* 26 Aug 1989, Megan Butler; 1 s (Theo), 1 da (Tilly); *Career* called to the Bar 1987; memb Family Law Bar Assoc, affiliate memb Resolution Inner Temple, reviewer Bar Pro Bono Unit, Bar liaison offr Child Abduction Lawyers' Assoc (CALA); *Recreations* cricket, music, opera, tennis, travel, walking; *Style*— Christopher Hames, Esq, QC

HAMES, Duncan John; *b* Herts; *Educ* Watford GS for Boys, Univ of Oxford; *m* Jo Swinson; *Career* CGMA; conslt Deloitte 1998–2004, dir Chippenham Conslts Ltd 2005–10; cncllr W Wilts DC 2003–07, MP (Lib Dem) Chippenham 2010–15, PPS to the Dep PM 2012–15; memb Bd: SW RDA 2003–09 (chair Audit Ctee 2008–09), GB China Centre 2011–15, S London and Maudsley NHS Fndn Tst 2016– (chair Audit Ctee); dir Human Dances Ltd 2015–; assoc CIMA; *Style*— Duncan Hames, Esq; ✉ website https://uk.linkedin.com/in/duncanhames

HAMID, David; s of Osman Hamid, and Doreen Hamid; *b* 11 December 1951, Leicester; *Educ* Alleynes GS Stevenage, Univ of Bradford; *m* Gillian Joy; 1 da (Sarah), 3 s (Michael, Peter, Stephen); *Career* early career in mktg positions with: United Biscuits, Golden Wonder, Sony, Alfred Dunhill (latterly mktg dir Int Jewellery Division); Dixons Gp plc: joined 1986, roles incl mktg dir Supasnaps, md Dixons Financial Services, md Mastercare and gp md PC World, latterly gp chief operating offr, memb Bd 1997–2003; ceo Halfords 2003–05, ptnr OpCapita LLP (formerly Merchant Equity Ptnrs) 2006–; chm: Nationwide Autocentres 2005–10, Game Digital plc 2012–; dep chm MVideo Russia 2011–; chm Music for Youth; *Recreations* hockey, golf, guitar; *Clubs* RAC; *Style*— David Hamid, Esq

HAMILTON; *see also:* Stirling-Hamilton

HAMILTON, Duke of ; *see:* Hamilton and Brandon

HAMILTON, Abe; né Ayub; s of Yaqub Ali, and Roberta Austin (d 1993); *b* 4 January 1962, Manchester; *Educ* High Peak Coll of FE Buxton, Bournemouth & Poole Coll of Art & Design, Middx Poly; *Career* former chef; fashion designer 1986–; cmmnd by Browns to design a capsule collection for new store 1993, first show Harvey Nichols 1993, creative dir Aqua di Parma Milan 2001, loungewear collection for Debenhams High St Store London, collections sold to int boutiques and stores incl Barneys NY and Joyce Hong Kong; clients incl: Madonna, Kylie Minogue, Beyoncé, Iman, Helen Fielding, Tori Amos, Mary Telford; work featured in pubns incl: Vogue, Marie Claire, Elle; winner British Design – The New Generation category (British Fashion Awards) 1993; *Style*— Abe Hamilton, Esq; ✉ 9 Patmore House, Matthias Road, London N16 8LQ

HAMILTON, Andrew; MVO; s of Peter Hamilton, of Sussex, and Susie, *née* Blackwell; *b* 15 January 1950; *Educ* Univ Coll Sch, Coll of Estate Mgmnt Univ of Reading; *m* 23 July 1983, Fiona Ann, da of John Scott-Adie, of Perthshire; 2 s (Charles Scott-Adie b 1988, Malcolm Scott-Adie b 1991); *Career* dir: John D Wood SA 1975–77, Haslemere Estates plc 1977–86, Ranelagh Development Ltd 1986–91; Poundbury devpt dir Duchy of Cornwall 1991–, chm The Prince's Regeneration Tst 2004–08, devpt dir Knockroon 2009–14; FRICS 1986; *Recreations* opera, conservation, France; *Clubs* Boodle's, Annabel's; *Style*— Andrew Hamilton, Esq, MVO; ✉ c/o Round Hill House, Fawley, Henley-on-Thames, Oxfordshire RG9 6HU (☎ 01491 577846, mobile 07836 510101, e-mail andrewhamilton.roundhill@gmail.com)

HAMILTON, Sir Andrew Caradoc; 10 Bt (NS 1646), of Silvertonhill, Lanarkshire; s of Sir (Robert Charles) Richard Caradoc Hamilton, 9 Bt (d 2001); *b* 23 September 1953; *Educ* Charterhouse, St Peter's Coll Oxford (BA); *m* 26 Oct 1984, Anthea Jane, da of Frank Huntingford, of Hindhead, Surrey; 3 da (Alice b 4 Dec 1986, Harriet b 18 March 1989, Imogen Rosie b 6 Nov 1993); *Heir* kinsman, Paul Howden; *Career* schoolmaster 1976–89; tourist attraction prop 1989–; *Recreations* cricket, real tennis, art, music, family; *Clubs* MCC, Leamington Cricket, Leamington and Moreton Morrell Real Tennis; *Style*— Sir Andrew Hamilton, Bt

HAMILTON, Prof Andrew David; *Educ* Univ of Exeter (BSc), Univ of British Columbia (MSc), Univ of Cambridge (PhD); *Career* asst prof of chemistry Princeton Univ 1981–88, prof of chemistry Univ of Pittsburgh 1988–97, provost Yale Univ 2004–08 (joined 1997), vice-chllr Univ of Oxford 2009–15, pres NY Univ 2016–; Arthur C Cope Scholar Award American Chemical Soc 1999, Int Izatt Christiansen Award in Macrocyclic Chemistry American Acad of Arts and Sciences 2011; FRS 2004; *Style*— Prof Andrew Hamilton; ✉ New York University, New York, NY10012 USA

HAMILTON, His Hon Andrew N R; s of Robert Bousfield Hamilton (d 1949), and Margery Wensley Iorwerth Hamilton (d 1991); *b* 7 January 1947; *Educ* Cheltenham Coll, Univ of Birmingham (LLB); *m* 17 April 1982, Isobel Louise, *née* Goode; 1 s, 1 da; *Career* called to the Bar 1970; in practice from chambers in Nottingham 1971–2001, recorder of the Crown Court 1999–2001 (asst recorder 1993–99) circuit judge (Midland Circuit) 2001–16; external examiner Bar Vocational Course 1997–2000; chm Nottingham Civic Soc 1978–83, chm Nottingham Park Conservation Tst 1992–, chm Wollaton Historical and Conservation Soc 2011–; memb Nottingham City Cncl 1973–91; Hon Alderman City of Nottingham 1991; *Books* Nottingham's Royal Castle (1976, 5 edn 1999), Nottingham's Caves (1977, 4 edn 2004); *Recreations* tennis, golf, skiing; *Clubs* Nottingham and Notts United Services; *Style*— His Hon Andrew Hamilton; ✉ 39 Wollaton Vale, Wollaton, Nottingham NG8 2PD

HAMILTON, Anthony John; *Educ* Dulwich Coll, ChCh Oxford (MA, DPhil); *m* 1977 Angela Jane Lamboll, da of K C L Webb, Esq; *Career* Schroders 1969–72, Morgan Grenfell 1972–76; Wainwright Securities 1976–78, chm Fox-Pitt Kelton Gp 1994–2003 (joined 1978); chm: AXA Equity & Law plc 1995–2013, AXA UK plc 2000–13; non-exec dir: AXA Financial Inc (NY) 1995–2014, AXA (Paris) 1996–2013, Sun Life & Provincial Hldg plc 1997–2000, Swiss Re Capital Markets Ltd 2004–06, TAWA plc 2004–14; dir and tstee Game and Wildlife Conservation Tst 2009–; Chevalier de la Légion d'Honneur 2012; *Recreations* golf, country pursuits; *Clubs* Royal Ashdown Forest Golf, The Turf, Valderrama Golf (Spain), City of London, The Brook (NY); *Style*— Anthony Hamilton, Esq; ✉ The Red House, Crockham Hill, Kent TN8 6SX

HAMILTON, Rt Hon Lord Arthur Campbell; PC (2002); s of James Whitehead Hamilton (d 1954), of Glasgow, and Isobel Walker, *née* McConnell (d 1997); *b* 10 June 1942; *Educ* Glasgow HS, Univ of Glasgow, Worcester Coll Oxford (BA), Univ of Edinburgh (LLB); *m* 12 Sept 1970, Christine Ann, da of Thomas Carlyle Croll, of St Andrews, Fife; 1 da (Miranda b 1975); *Career* memb Faculty of Advocates 1968; standing jr counsel: Scot Devpt Dept 1975–78, Bd Inland Revenue (Scot) 1978–82; QC (Scot) 1982; Advocate Depute 1982–85, judge of the Courts of Appeal of Jersey and Guernsey 1988–95, senator of the Coll of Justice 1995–2005, Lord Justice Gen of Scotland and Lord Pres of the Court of Session 2005–12, judge of the Court of Appeal Botswana 2012–, arbitrator 2014–, judge Qatar Int Court 2015–; pres Pensions Appeal Tbnls for Scot 1992–95; hon fell Worcester Coll Oxford 2003; *Recreations* music, history; *Clubs* New (Edinburgh); *Style*— The Rt Hon Lord Hamilton; ✉ 8 Heriot Row, Edinburgh EH3 6HU (☎ 0131 556 4663)

HAMILTON, Caroline; da of Walter Hamilton (d 1988), and Jane, *née* Burrows; *Educ* Perse Sch for Girls Cambridge, Girton Coll Cambridge (BA, Hockey, Cricket and Athletics blues); *Career* entrepreneur and polar explorer; ldr first all-women expdn to North Pole McVitie's Penguin North Pole Relay 1997, ldr first Br all-women team to ski to South Pole 2000, memb M&G Investments North Pole Expdn 2002 (becoming first all-women team to ski to both poles); motivational speaker for businesses, lectr and after-dinner speaker, film and TV financier; investment banker: HSBC Samuel Montagu 1985–88, Dresdner Kleinwort Benson 1988–92; dir Screen Partners Gp 1993–2004, fdr Icebreaker Investment Gp, md Icebreaker Management Ltd 2004–; mangr under Mental Health Act 1995–2001, non-exec memb Wandsworth HA 1990–95, non-exec memb Bd Threshold Housing and Support 1996–2007; memb Cambridge Ospreys Alumni Ctee 2000–; fell British American Project 2003–; tstee CAMFED Int 2005–; *Books* South Pole 2000 (2000), To the Pole (2001); *Recreations* parties, travelling, sport; *Style*— Ms Caroline Hamilton; ✉ Icebreaker Management Limited, 46 Gresham Street, London EC2V 7AY (websites www.icebreakerfund.com and www.carolinehamilton.com)

HAMILTON, Sir David; kt (2016); s of David Hamilton (d 1993), and Agnes Gardner; *b* 24 October 1950; *m* 1 Aug 1969, Jean, da of James Macrae, and Mary Trench; 2 da (Shirley b 28 Sept 1971, Isla b 20 Sept 1975); *Career* coalminer Easthouses Colliery, Bilston Glen Colliery, Rufford Colliery, Notts and Monktonhall Colliery 1965–84 (NUM delegate Monktonhall Colliery 1965–85), supervisor Employment Trg Scheme Midlothian Cncl 1987–89, placement and trg offr Craigmillar Festival Soc 1989–92, chief exec Craigmillar Opportunities Tst 1992–2000, cncllr Midlothian Cncl 1995–2001; MP (Lab) Midlothian 2001–15, PPS to Rt Hon Ed Miliband, MP, *qv* 2008–10, oppn sr whip and Scottish whip 2010–; cabinet memb for strategic services incorporating economic devpt, transportation and strategic planning 1995–2001; memb: House of Commons: Procedures Select Ctee, Broadcasting Select Ctee, Scottish Affrs Select Ctee, Defence Select Ctee, European Scrutiny Ctee, European A Standing Ctee, Exec Ctee Scottish Gp of MPs, All-Pty Non Profit Making Members Club Gp, Br American Parly Gp (BAPG), Singapore Parly Gp, Cwlth Parly Assoc (CPA), Dept for Work and Pension Select Ctee; memb: NUM 1965–; *Style*— Sir David Hamilton; ✉ House of Commons, London SW1A 0AA (e-mail hamiltonda@parliament.uk, website www.davidhamiltonmp.co.uk); Midlothian Constituency Office, 95 High Street, Dalkeith, Midlothian EH22 1AX (☎ 0131 654 1585)

HAMILTON, Douglas (Doug); *Educ* RCA (MA); *Career* designer Rodolfo Bonetto Milan 1970, sr lectr in interior design Chelsea Sch of Art 1976–84, creative dir Wolff Olins 1995–2002 (memb MBO team 1997), currently global creative dir Hutchison Whampoa; former clients incl: Repsol, First Direct, Orange, Virgin, Goldfish, Channel 5, Go, ONDigital, Open, Sky, Odeon, Ikea, Indesit; speaker at London Business Sch and Domus Acad Italy; *Style*— Doug Hamilton, Esq

HAMILTON, Eben William; QC (1981); s of Rev John Edmund Hamilton, MC (d 1981), of Edinburgh, and Hon Lilias Hamilton, *née* Maclay (d 1966), eld da of 1 Baron Maclay, of Glasgow; *b* 12 June 1937; *Educ* Winchester, Trinity Coll Cambridge (MA); *m* 1985, Themy Rusi, da of Brig Rusi Bilimoria (d 1963), of Bellagio, Bombay, India; *Career* 4/7 Royal Dragoon Gds 1955–57, Fife and Forfar Yeo/Scottish Horse TA 1957–68; called to the Bar Inner Temple 1962 (bencher 1985), practising Chancery Bar 1962–, head of chambers 1990–2003, dep judge of the High Ct (Chancery Division) 1990–2005; admitted: Hong Kong Bar 1978, Singapore Bar 1982, Cayman Bar 2001; DTI inspr Atlantic Computers plc 1990–93; tstee Royal Scottish Corp 2008–; FRSA 1989; *Clubs* Garrick; *Style*— Eben Hamilton, Esq, QC; ✉ Barley Harbour, Newtowncashel, Co Longford, Ireland; 6 Stone Buildings, Lincoln's Inn, London WC2A 3XT (☎ 020 7242 7650)

HAMILTON, Fabian; MP; s of late Mario Reginald Uziell-Hamilton, and late Adrianne Uziell-Hamilton; *b* 12 April 1955, London; *Educ* Brentwood Sch, Univ of York; *m*

H

Rosemary Ratcliffe; 2 da (b 1984 and 1987), 1 s (b 1993); *Career* MP (Lab) Leeds NE 1997–, memb Foreign Affrs Select Ctee 2001–; tstee Nat Heart Research Fund; govr Northern Sch of Contemporary Dance; *Recreations* cycling, photography, MGs; *Style*— Fabian Hamilton, Esq, MP; ✉ constituency office: 335 Roundhay Road, Leeds LS8 4HT (☎ 0113 249 6600, e-mail gerry@leedsne.co.uk); House of Commons, London SW1A 0AA (☎ 020 7219 3493, fax 020 7219 4945, e-mail hamiltonf@parliament.uk)

HAMILTON, Francis Rowan Oldfield de Courcy; s of James Percival de Courcy Hamilton (d 1995), of Watlington, Oxon, and Elizabeth Millicent (d 1991), da of Maj-Gen Sir Louis Oldfield, KBE, CB, CMG, DSO; *b* 11 February 1940; *Educ* Winchester, ChCh Oxford; *m* 22 July 1972, Catherine Rae, da of Lt Cdr William Alastair Robertson, CBE, DSC and bar, RN (d 1998), of Gifford, E Lothian; 2 da (Antonia b 1977, Olivia b 1979), 1 s (Thomas b 1983); *Career* The Economist Intelligence Unit 1965–72 (dir Mexico Office from 1967), dir Samuel Montagu & Co Ltd 1978–86; chief of div and sr advsr Int Finance Corp Washington DC 1986–2003; chm: Melrose Arts Tst 2005–06, Borders Book Festival 2006–15 (dir 2015–), Lennoxlove Book Festival 2009–14; dir Penicuik House Preservation Tst 2010–, dir The Moffat Partnership Ltd (BritainsDNA/ScotlandsDNA) 2011–15; *Clubs* Travellers, New (Edinburgh), Queen's; *Style*— Francis de C Hamilton, Esq; ✉ Chesterhall, Eildon, Melrose, Roxburghshire TD6 9HE (☎ 01835 823372, e-mail frodech@gmail.com)

HAMILTON, (Alexander) Gordon Kelso; s of Arthur Hamilton Kelso Hamilton (d 1996), of Weybridge, Surrey, and Elizabeth Evelyn, *née* Williams; *b* 27 August 1945; *Educ* Charterhouse, Pembroke Coll Cambridge (MA); *m* 12 July 1980, France Elisabeth Mary Colette, da of Pierre Millet (d 1998), and Elizabeth Millet (d 1984); 1 s (Edward b 1984), 1 da (Georgina b 1986); *Career* ptnr: Mann Judd 1975–79, (following merger) Deloitte & Touche 1979–2006; memb Financial Reporting Review Panel 2002–11; tstee Pembroke Coll Cambridge (The Valence Mary (1997) Endowment Fund) 1985–90; RNID: memb Cncl of Mgmnt 1990–92, memb Fin Ctee 1990–96, tstee 1992–96, hon treas 1993–96; dir St George's Hill Golf Club Ltd 1980–96; tstee and dir Action on Addiction 1996–2007 (hon treas 2002–07); non-exec dir: Beazley plc 2006–13, Barloworld Ltd 2007–16, Nedbank Private Wealth Ltd 2008–, Aibel Gp Ltd 2008–10, Northamber plc 2010–15, Petra Diamonds Ltd 2011–, Atrium Underwriting Gp Ltd 2014–; *Recreations* golf; *Clubs* Royal & Ancient, The Berkshire, Brooks's, Buck's; *Style*— Gordon Hamilton, Esq; ✉ 51 Chelsea Square, London SW3 6LH

HAMILTON, (John Robert) Leslie; *b* 15 June 1952, Toronto, Canada; *Educ* Lurgan Coll NI, Queen's Univ Belfast (MB BCh, BAO), Univ of Northumbria (LLM); *m* 1980, Joy; 1 s (Stuart b 28 July 1981), 3 da (Suzanne b 5 Sept 1983, Carolyn b 3 July 1986, Fiona b 14 June 1988); *Career* successively: house offr Royal Victoria Hosp Belfast, tutor Dept of Physiology Queen's Univ Belfast, surgical registrar NI, sr surgical registrar Yorks RHA Leeds 1985–91 (and Gt Ormond St Hosp 1988–89), conslt cardiac surgn Freeman Hosp Newcastle upon Tyne 1991–2015; numerous invited lectures, presentations to learned socs and published articles; chm Intercollegiate Examination Bd FRCS Cardiothoracic 2004–06, memb Donation Ethics Ctee Acad of Medical Royal Colls 2010–12, dir for professional affairs RCS, pres North of England Medico-legal Soc (formerly vice-pres); asst coroner Durham and Darlington; memb: BMA, Soc for Cardiothoracic Surgery of GB and I (pres 2008–10), Br Congenital Cardiac Assoc, European Assoc for Cardiothoracic Surgery (memb Cncl 2010–12); FRCS 1981 (currently memb Cncl), FRCSEd(Cardiothoracic) 1988; *Recreations* family activities, local church; sport – ex athletics and rugby, golf, skiing, sailing (dinghy, Clipper 'Round the World' 2015/16 yacht race) and scuba diving; *Style*— Leslie Hamilton, Esq; ✉ The Old Barn, Low Gosforth Home Farm, Bridle Path, Newcastle upon Tyne NE3 5EU (e-mail lesliehamilton80@yahoo.co.uk)

HAMILTON, Lewis; MBE (2009); *b* 7 January 1985, Stevenage, Herts; *Career* motor racing driver; champion (with ASM F3 Dallara-Mercedes) F3 Euroseries 2005, champion (with ART Grand Prix) GP2 Series 2006, driver (with Vodafone McLaren Mercedes) Formula One 2007– (runner-up Drivers' Championship 2007, holds record for most consecutive podium finishes from debut, youngest driver to lead World Championship); grand prix victories: Canada 2007, USA 2007, Hungary 2007, Japan 2007, GB 2008, Germany 2008, Singapore 2009, Turkey 2010, Canada 2010, Belgium 2010, China 2011, Germany 2011, Abu Dhabi 2011, Montreal 2012, Hungary 2013, Italy 2014; Formula One World Champion 2008, 2014 and 2015; BBC Sports Personality of the Year 2014; *Style*— Lewis Hamilton, Esq, MBE

HAMILTON, Liam; *b* 12 August 1959, Glasgow; *Educ* Univ of Glasgow (MA); *m* Ilaria D'Elia; *Career* staff journalist STV 1981–84, with Border TV 1984–86 (ed: Answer the Question, Borderlive, Lookaround, Ten Thirty), prodr then news ed Central TV 1986–88 (credits incl: The Time The Place, Donahue in Britain, General Election coverage, Spitting Image), ed This Morning Granada TV 1988–92, ed and exec prodr GMTV 1992–95, dir of broadcasting LWT 1995–98, md LWT 1998–2000, chief operating offr Worldpop 2000–01, controller daytime ITV 2002–06, md Prospect Pictures 2006–; *Style*— Liam Hamilton, Esq

HAMILTON, Michael John; s of William E Hamilton (d 1985), of Guelph, Canada, and Jean, *née* Clark; *b* 24 October 1939; *Educ* Univ of Western Ontario (BA), Univ of Oxford (MA); *m* 20 Sept 1967, Irena, da of Albert Rudusans (d 1962); 1 s (Andrew), 3 da (Katharine, Anna, Nina); *Career* jt md Manufacturers Hanover Ltd 1969–73; exec dir: First Boston Corporation Europe Ltd 1973–78, Blyth Eastman Dillon Inc 1978–79; md Wallace Smith Trust Co Ltd 1980–91, fndr M J Hamilton & Co 1991–97, gp md Banco Finantia 1997–2009; dir: Midland Expressway Ltd 1992–96, Autostrade International SA 1993–94, Autostrade UK Ltd 1993–96, Hampton and Kempton Waterworks Railway Ltd, Finantia Securities Ltd; pres Autostrade International Equity Inc 1993–94; memb: Dulles Euro Advsy Bd Nippon Telephone and Telegraph Inc 1986–92, Bd of Mgmnt Dulles Greenway Virginia 1993–94; chm of tstees: Kempton Great Engine Tst, Guildhall Sch Tst 2000–09; chm Univ of Western Ontario UK Fndn 2007–09; tstee Startup, tstee Thames 21; hon fell Guildhall Sch 2004; *Recreations* tennis, opera, cottage; *Clubs* City of London; *Style*— Michael Hamilton, Esq; ✉ 10 St George's Road, St Margaret's, Twickenham TW1 1QR (e-mail mmjham16@aol.com)

HAMILTON, Dr Nigel; s of Sir Denis Hamilton (d 1988), and Olive, Lady Hamilton, *née* Wanless (d 2012); *b* 16 February 1944; *Educ* Westminster, Univ of Munich, Trinity Coll Cambridge (BA, MA), Groningen Univ (PhD); *m* 1, 1966, Hannelore Pfeifer (d 1973); 2 s (Alexander b 1967, Sebastian b 1970); m 2, 1976 (m dis 2005), Outi Palovesi; 2 s (Nicholas b 1977, Christian b 1980); m 3, 2006, Raynel Shepard; *Career* slave Andre Deutsch Publishing House 1965–66; fndr: The Greenwich Bookshop 1966, The Biography Bookshop 1987; author, lectr and broadcaster 1969–; dir British Inst of Biography 1996–2001; visiting prof Univ of Massachusetts Boston 1989–94, visiting prof of history Royal Holloway Coll London 1995–2000, prof of biography De Montfort Univ 1999–2000; jt chm BIORAMA Real Lives Centre Steering Ctee (project for a nat biographical arts centre) 1996–2000, visiting scholar George Washington Univ 2005, visiting scholar Georgetown Univ 2005; sr fell John W McCormack Grad Sch of Policy and Global Studies Univ of Massachusetts Boston 2000–; pres Biographers Int Orgn 2010–12, hon pres Société de Biographie Aix-Marseilles Univ 2015–; *Awards* Whitbread Prize for Best Biography 1981, Templer Award for Best Contrib to Mil History 1987, Blue Ribbon Award for Best Documentary (NY Film and Video Assoc) 1988, longlisted Nat Book Award (for FDR at War) 2014, shortlisted Plutarch Award (for FDR at War) 2015; *Books* Royal Greenwich (with Olive Hamilton, 1969), The Brothers Mann, The Lives of Heinrich and Thomas Mann (1978), Monty: The Making of a General (1981), Monty: Master of the Battlefield (1983), Monty: The Field-Marshal (1986), Monty, The Man Behind the Legend (1987), JFK: Reckless Youth (1992), Monty: The Battles of Field-Marshal Bernard Montgomery (1994), The Full Monty: Montgomery of Alamein 1887–1942 (2001), Bill Clinton: An American Journey (2003), Montgomery: D-Day Commander (2007), Biography: A Brief History (2007), Bill Clinton: Mastering the Presidency (2007), How to Do Biography: A Primer (2008), American Caesars: Franklin D Roosevelt to George W Bush (2010), The Mantle of Command: FDR at War 1941–42 (2014), Commander-in-Chief: FDR's Battle with Churchill 1943 (2016); *Television* writer and narrator of films incl: Monty, In Love and War (BBC TV, 1987), Frontiers, Finland and the Soviet Union (BBC TV, 1989); *Recreations* tennis; *Clubs* The Tavern; *Style*— Dr Nigel Hamilton; ✉ McCormack Graduate School of Policy and Global Studies, UMass Boston, 100 Morrissey Blvd, Boston 02125–3393, USA (☎ +1 617 287 5550, fax +1 617 287 5544, e-mail nigel.hamilton@umb.edu)

HAMILTON, Peter Brian; s of late Lt-Col Brian Hamilton, and Clara Maria, *née* Ertelthaler; *b* 7 February 1941; *Educ* Beaumont Coll, Plymouth Coll of Navigation (Dip); *m* 1 (m dis); 1 s (James Drummond Alexander b 11 Sept 1977); m 2, 1979, Rosalind Mary, da of Bernard James Sanger (d 1990); 1 s (Edward Peter Willoughby b 14 Nov 1980), 1 step da (Amanda Suzanne Jerrom b 25 Aug 1970), 1 step s (Charles Lindsay Jerrom b 11 May 1973); *Career* navigating offr Shell Tankers Ltd 1957–60, reporter and feature writer FT 1960–63, Young and Rubicam 1963–75 (exec, account dir, md), dir public affairs Gulf Oil Corporation (Europe Africa and ME) 1975–80, dir Good Relations Group plc 1980–84; gp md/dep chm The Communication Group plc 1985–; memb Falmouth Harbour Cmmn 2011–13; FCIPR 1998 (MCIPR 1966); *Recreations* sailing, gardening, music, wine; *Clubs* Royal Cornwall Yacht; *Style*— Peter Hamilton, Esq; ✉ Quay House, 2 Tinners Walk, Port Pendennis, Falmouth, Cornwall TR11 3XZ (☎ 01326 317471, e-mail peterhamilt@aol.com); The Communication Group plc, 19 Buckingham Gate, London SW1E 6LB (☎ 020 7630 1411, fax 020 7931 8010, e-mail phamilton@tcg.pr.co.uk)

HAMILTON, Peter Bryan; s of Brian Hamilton, of Hythe, Hants (d 2007), and Clara, *née* Marchi (d 2002); *b* 28 August 1956; *Educ* King Edward VI Sch Southampton, ChCh Oxford (MA); *m* 7 Aug 1993, Sylvie, *née* Vulliet; 2 da (Jessica b 29 Jan 1981, Anna b 14 May 1994); *Career* head of French Radley Coll 1981–89, head of modern languages Westminster Sch 1989–96 (also housemaster Wren's), headmaster King Edward VI Sch Southampton 1996–2002, headmaster Haberdashers' Aske's Boys' Sch 2002–; govr: Reddiford Sch, Lochinver House, Khrishna-Avanti Primary Sch; *Recreations* skiing, hill walking, karate, canoeing, opera; *Clubs* East India, Lansdowne; *Style*— Peter Hamilton, Esq; ✉ Haberdashers' Aske's Boys' School, Butterfly Lane, Elstree, Hertfordshire WD6 3AF (☎ 020 8266 1700, fax 020 8266 1800, e-mail hm@habsboys.org.uk)

HAMILTON, Simon; MLA; s of Frank Hamilton, and Muriel, *née* McClure; *b* 17 March 1977, Newtownards, Co Down; *Educ* Regent House Sch Newtownards, Queen's Univ Belfast (BA, BLegSc); *m* 14 Nov 2003, Nicola, *née* McAvoy; 2 s (Lewis b 25 Feb 2006, Kyle b 3 Dec 2008); *Career* auditor Pricewaterhouse Coopers 2001–03, press offr DUP 2003–07, MLA (DUP) Strangford 2007–; dep chair Finance and Personnel Ctee 2008–09, chair Social Devpt Ctee 2009–11, dep chair Environment Ctee 2011–13, assembly private sec to Min of Finance and Personnel 2011–13, min of finance and personnel 2013–15, min of health, social services and public safety 2015–16, min for the economy 2016–; hon memb CIPFA 2015; *Recreations* reading, travel, walking; *Style*— Simon Hamilton, Esq, MLA; ✉ Northern Ireland Assembly, Parliament Buildings, Belfast BT4 3XX (e-mail simon.hamilton@mla.niassembly.gov.uk, website www.simonhamilton.org, Twitter @simonhamilton)

HAMILTON, Sophie; da of Rev Dr P N Hamilton (d 1989), and G M Hamilton, *née* McAndrew; *b* 14 October 1955, London; *Educ* St Mary's Sch Calne, Marlborough, Clare Coll Cambridge (BA); *m* 27 Jan 1990, Prof Peter Goldie (d 2011); *Career* admitted slr 1979; articled clerk then asst slr Frere Cholmeley 1977–84, ptnr Frere Cholmeley Bischoff 1985–98 (recruitment ptnr 1985–88, trg ptnr 1988–90, head Property Dept 1989–92), ptnr Forsters 1998– (sr ptnr 2002–08); memb: Law Soc, Anglo-American Real Property Inst (treas 2006–08); chair Nottingham Law Sch Ltd 1991–98 (dir 1998–99), govr Nottingham Trent Univ 1991–98; chair Cheek by Jowl Theatre Co Ltd 1995– (dir 1981–); tstee Corporation of Church House 2009–; Freeman City of London, Liveryman Worshipful Co of Goldsmiths; Hon LLD Nottingham Trent Univ; *Recreations* theatre, reading, walking; *Style*— Mrs Sophie Hamilton; ✉ Forsters LLP, 31 Hill Street, London W1J 5LS (☎ 020 7863 8333, fax 020 7863 8444, e-mail sophie.hamilton@forsters.co.uk)

HAMILTON, Her Hon Susan; QC (1993); da of Leslie Edward Hamilton (d 1999), of Hove, E Sussex, and Olive Blossom, *née* King; *b* 30 December 1946; *Educ* Hove GS for Girls, Brighton Tech Coll; *m* 16 April 1977, Dr E P Kelly; 2 s (Thomas b 2 March 1982, Robert Eric b 16 Feb 1984); *Career* called to the Bar 1975; in practice 2 Mitre Court 1975–98, asst recorder 1993, recorder 1995, circuit judge (SE Circuit) 1998–2007; memb RHS; supporter: Barnardos, NSPCC, Nat Tst; *Books* Hamilton on Highways (1981), Halsbury's Laws: Highways vol 21 (1981 and 1995), Rating vol 39 (1982 and 1998); *Recreations* sailing, gardening, reading, music, holidays, travelling; *Clubs* Royal Southern Yacht; *Style*— Her Hon Susan Hamilton, QC; ✉ c/o Bromley County Court, College Road, Bromley, Kent BR1 3PX (e-mail shamilton@lix.compulink.co.uk)

HAMILTON, William McDonald (Bill); s of late Cdr James Hamilton, VRD, RNR, of St Andrews, Fife, Scotland, and Emily, *née* McDonald; *b* 22 September 1943; *Educ* Dundee HS, Monkwearmouth Coll Sunderland; *m* 5 Feb 1972, Gertrude Veronica, da of Michael Lee (d 1963), of Aughrim, Co Wicklow; 1 da (Claire b 1973), 1 s (David b 1980); *Career* reporter/newsreader Tyne Tees TV 1966–70, sports prodr BBC radio 1970–71, reporter/presenter Border TV 1971–73, reporter/presenter BBC TV Scotland 1973–80, home affrs corr BBC TV News 1981–88, news and sports corr BBC TV News 1988–97, freelance corr/presenter 1997–; vice-pres Anglo-Albanian Assoc; memb Football Referees' Assoc; Paul Harris fell Rotary Int; Order of Mother Teresa (Albania); *Books* I Belong to Glasgow (1975), Albania – Who Cares? (1992), Man on the Spot (2010); *Recreations* association football referee; *Style*— Bill Hamilton, Esq; ✉ 39 Waverley Road, St Albans, Hertfordshire AL3 5PH (☎ 01727 869604, e-mail info@billhamilton.co.uk)

HAMILTON OF EPSOM, Baron (Life Peer UK 2005), of West Anstey in the County of Devon; Sir Archibald Gavin (Archie) Hamilton; kt (1994), PC (1991); yr s of 3 Baron Hamilton of Dalzell, GCVO, MC, JP (d 1990), and Rosemary Olive, *née* Coke (d 1993); *b* 30 December 1941; *Educ* Eton; *m* 14 Dec 1968, Anne, da of late Cdr Trevelyan Napier, DSC, RN; 3 da; *Career* cncllr London Borough of Kensington & Chelsea 1968–71, MP (Cons) Epsom and Ewell 1978–2001; PPS to: sec of state Energy 1979–81, sec of state Tport 1981–82; asst govt whip 1982–84, lord cmmr to the Treasy 1984–86, Parly under sec of state (Def Procurement) 1986–87, PPS to PM 1987–88, min of state (Armed Forces) Min of Defence 1988–93; chm 1922 Ctee of Cons backbench MPs 1997–2001; dir: Leafield Engineering, Jupiter Dividend and Growth Tst, New Star Global Fund, Specialised Risk Mgmnt, Specialised Investigation Servs, MSB; *Style*— The Rt Hon the Lord Hamilton of Epsom, PC

HAMILTON-BURKE, Ian Douglas; s of John Douglas Burke (ka 1944), and Jean Hamilton, *née* Drane; *b* 14 October 1943, Bolton; *Educ* Liverpool Coll; *m* Joan, da of Harold Planche; 2 s (James Patrick Ian, Andrew Charles Raoul), 1 da (Victoria Roisin); *Career* Poulsoms CAs 1968–86; dir Minster Executive Ltd 1978–86; ptnr: Hodgson Impey CAs 1986–90, Pannell Kerr Forster CAs 1990–91, Hamilton-Burke Dufau Ltd CAs 1991–2009; dir:

Curtins Holdings plc 1990–2003, Curtins Gp plc 1997–2003, Westlink Gp Ltd 2005–07; fndn memb Liverpool Coll; TEP; FCA, FInstD; *Recreations* hockey, marathon running, fell walking; *Clubs* Liverpool Lyceum Soc; *Style—* Ian Hamilton-Burke, Esq; ✉ Bellisle, Quarry Street, Liverpool L25 6DY (☎ 0151 428 3199, e-mail ianhamiltonburke@yahoo.com); Hamilton-Burke Dufau Ltd, Hilltop Old Hall Road, Windermere LA23 1JA

HAMILTON-SHIELD, Prof Julian Paul; *b* 28 May 1961; *Educ* Clifton, Univ of Bristol (MB ChB, MD); *m* Olivia Plunkett; 1 s (Hugo), 3 da (Antonia, Leonora, Beatrice); *Career* house offr Bristol 1985–86, SHO Bristol and Gt Ormond St Hosp London 1986–90, registrar Queen Elizabeth Hosp for Children and Gt Ormond St Hosp London 1990–92; Univ of Bristol and Bristol Royal Hosp for Children: lectr 1995–97, sr lectr in child health 1997–2006, reader 2006–08, prof 2008–; Best Practice Award ASO 2005, Clinical Excellence Award BUPA Fndn 2006; MRCP 1987, FRCPCH 1997; *Publications* numerous peer-reviewed papers on diabetes and obesity in childhood and related metabolic conditions; *Recreations* my family, sport; *Style—* Prof Julian Hamilton-Shield; ✉ Institute of Child Health, UBHT Education Centre, Upper Maudlin Street, Bristol BS2 8AE

HAMLYN, Jane; da of late Paul Hamlyn; *Career* dir and fndr Frith Street Gallery 1989–, chair Paul Hamlyn Fndn 2004–; *Style—* Ms Jane Hamlyn; ✉ Frith Street Gallery, 17–18 Golden Square, London W1F 9JJ

HAMMERSLEY, Ben; *b* 3 April 1976, Leicester; *Educ* Loughborough GS; *Career* contrib ed WIRED magazine; PM's ambass to TechCity; FRGS, innovator-in-residence Goldsmiths Coll London; fell Robert Schuman Sch of Advanced Study Florence, fell Brookings Inst Washington DC; FRSA; *Publications* 64 Things You Need to Know Now for Then (2012); *Recreations* flying trapeze; *Clubs* Savage, Frontline; *Style—* Ben Hammersley, Esq; ✉ 78 York Street, London W1H 1DP (☎ 07515 353094, e-mail ben@benhammersley.com, website www.benhammersley.com, Twitter @benhammersley); c/o Kate Lossius, London Speaker Bureau, Kate@londonspeakerbureau.com

HAMMERSLEY, Philip Tom; CBE (2000, OBE 1989); s of Tom Andrew Hammersley (d 1959), of Buckhurst Hill, Essex, and Winifred Alice, *née* Moyns (d 1970); *b* 10 February 1931; *Educ* Bancroft's Sch, Imperial Coll London (BSc); *m* 24 July 1954, Lesley Ann, da of Norman Stuart Millage; 2 s (Mark Andrew b 10 April 1957, Paul David b 22 May 1962), 1 da (Alison Clare b 18 May 1960); *Career* plant then design engr ICI Plastic Div 1954–65; Clarks Ltd Street Somerset: chief engr 1965–68, prodn servs mangr 1968–70, dir Children's Div 1971–79; pres Stride Rite Footwear Inc (Stride Rite Corp) Boston MA 1979–81; British Shoe Corp Ltd: factories dir 1981–85, dir responsible for mfrg, personnel and info systems 1985–87, md Freeman Hardy Willis and Trueform 1987–89, commercial dir 1989–90; non-exec chm BSS Group plc Leicester 1995–99 (non-exec dir 1991–); chm: Cncl Shoe and Allied Trades Research Assoc 1983–86, E Midlands Regnl Cncl CBI 1988–90; pres Br Footwear Mfrs Fedn 1986–87; vice-chm Leics HA 1990–92; chm: Leicester Royal Infirmary NHS Tst 1992–97, Trent Regnl Office NHS Exec 1997–99, Univ Hosps of Leicester NHS Tst 2000–06; memb Cncl Univ of Leicester 1991–2004; tstee National Space Science Centre 1997–2001 and 2006–09, chm National Space Centre (Operations) Ltd 2001–09; Hon LLD Univ of Leicester 2008; Freeman City of London, Liveryman Worshipful Co of Pattenmakers 1983; Hon DBA De Montfort Univ 1999; CEng, MIMechE 1961, FRSA 1993; *Clubs* MCC, East India; *Style—* Philip Hammersley, Esq, CBE

HAMMON, Michael Antony; s of Arthur Stanley Hammon (d 1985), and Mary Augusta, *née* Salter (d 1993); *b* 5 March 1937; *Educ* Oundle; *m* Oct 1966 (m dis 1993), Letitia Sara, da of Henry Leslie Johnson (d 1991); 2 s (Charles b 1969, George b 1973), 2 da (Sara b 1970, Elizabeth b 1972); *Career* slr; in practice Hammon Slrs; cncllr: Warwick RDC 1965–70, Warks CC 1967–81 (chm Finance, Educn and Policy and Resources Ctees, ldr of Cncl 1976–81), Coventry City Cncl 1987–96 and 2010–; Dep Lord Mayor of Coventry 2014–15, Lord Mayor of Coventry 2015–16; pres Coventry Cons Assoc 2011–15; lawyer memb W Midlands Rent Assessment Panel 1982–86, press and PR offr Warks Law Soc 1984–89; chm Edenhurst Court (Torquay) Ltd 1998–2013, dir H H Goddard Ltd; *Recreations* gardening, photography; *Clubs* Naval and Military, Rotary Club of Coventry, Hereford Show Club (fndr memb and pres); *Style—* Michael Hammon, Esq; ✉ Hammons Solicitors, The Old Bank, 353 Walsgrave Road, Coventry CV2 4BG (☎ 024 7644 8585, fax 024 7644 5257, e-mail m.hammon@hammonssolicitors.co.uk)

HAMMOND, Sir Anthony Hilgrove; KCB (2000, CB 1992), QC (1997); s of Col Charles William Hilgrove Hammond (d 1985), and Jessie Eugenia, *née* Francis (d 1940); *b* 27 July 1940; *Educ* Malvern, Emmanuel Coll Cambridge (open scholar, MA, LLM); *m* 29 Sept 1988, Avril, *née* Collinson; *Career* admitted slr 1965, asst slr GLC (formerly London CC) 1965–68 (articled clerk 1962–65); Home Office: legal asst 1968–70, sr legal asst 1970–74, asst legal advsr 1974–80, princ asst legal advsr to Home Office and NI Office 1980–88, dep under sec of state and legal advsr 1988–92 (legal advsr NI Office 1988–92); slr DTI 1992–97; procurator gen and Treasy slr 1997–2000; standing counsel to Gen Synod C of E 2000–13; Freeman City of London 1991, Liveryman Worshipful Co of Glass Sellers 1992 (memb Ct of Assts 2000, Master 2007); *Recreations* bridge, music, birdwatching; *Clubs* Athenaeum; *Style—* Sir Anthony Hammond, KCB, QC; ✉ The White Cottage, Blackheath, Guildford, Surrey GV4 8RB (☎ 01483 892607)

HAMMOND, Dr Brian Robert; s of Dennis Francis Hammond, of Rustington, W Sussex, and Iris Margaret Rose Hammond; *b* 28 May 1953; *Educ* Battersea GS, Anglo-Euro Coll of Chiropractic (DC, Canadian Award for Academic Distinction), Univ of Surrey (PhD); *m* 5 Nov 1975, Elizabeth-Jane, da of David Frederick Vincent Craig; 1 da (Samantha Danielle b 26 July 1978), 1 s (Daniel Michael b 29 June 1980); *Career* practising chiropractor; clinic dir Sutton Chiropractic Clinic 1975–, ed Euro Jl of Chiropractic 1976–80, govr Anglo-Euro Coll of Chiropractic 1976–80, memb Gen Cncl Euro Chiropractors' Union 1976–80, external lectr Anglo-Euro Coll of Chiropractic 1980–, external examiner CNAA 1989–92, memb Euro Cncl on Chiropractic Educn 1989–96; memb Br Chiropractic Assoc 1975– (treas 1987–89), Soc for Back Pain Res 1977–, Nat Back Pain Assoc 1977–; *Books* The Detection of Spondylolysis using Lumbar Sonography (1984); *Recreations* bridge, badminton; *Clubs* New Malden Bridge; *Style—* Dr Brian Hammond; ✉ Sutton Chiropractic Clinic, 137 Brighton Road, Sutton, Surrey SM2 5SW (☎ 020 8661 1613, fax 020 8770 9517)

HAMMOND, Donald William; *b* 5 March 1948; *Educ* King's Sch Macclesfield, Lancaster Univ (BA), Manchester Business Sch (DBA); *m* 19 March 1982, Carole Isobel Hammond (d 2016); *Career* T & N plc 1969–73, Citibank NA 1974–76, Banco Hispano Americano Ltd 1976–86; dir: Edington plc 1986–90, Henry Cooke Group plc 1988–90, Waterwise Technology Ltd 1993–2012, TRUSTECH 2001–; cncllr Cheshire W and Chester 2011–; various co sec and non-exec dir roles; memb Inst Knowledge Transfer (IKT), FInstD, FRSA; *Recreations* riding, shooting, venture capital, Bordeaux wine; *Clubs* Manchester Tennis and Racquets; *Style—* Donald Hammond, Esq; ✉ The Butts, Smithy Lane, Great Budworth, Northwich, Cheshire CW9 6HL (e-mail don@don-hammond.com, website www.don-hammond.com)

HAMMOND, Prof Geoffrey Paul; s of Jack Hammond (d 1997), and Alice Kate, *née* Elliott (d 2008); *b* 3 May 1946; *Educ* South Bank Univ, Univ of Brighton, Cranfield Univ (MSc); *m* 1974, Judith Anne, da of Llewellyn Williams; 1 da (Katherine Lucy b 1976), 1 s (Benjamin David b 1978); *Career* refrigeration engineer 1963–68; design and devpt engr 1968–71; VSO lectr Uganda Tech Coll 1971–72; Dept of Applied Energy Cranfield Univ: research offr 1975, lectr 1976, sr lectr 1985, reader 1989; Univ of Bath: British Gas prof of environmental engrg 1990–94, head Sch of Architecture and Building Engrg 1992–94, prof of mechanical engrg 1995–, dir Int Centre for the Environment (ICE) 2003–08, fndr dir Inst for Sustainable Energy and the Environment (I-SEE) 2008–11; hon prof in sustainable bioenergy Univ of Nottingham 2010–; memb: Lab Pty 1974–, EPSRC/SERC panels covering the built environment, computational modelling, energy and post grad training 1985–, Bradford on Avon Oxfam Gp 1991–, B & NES Local Agenda 21 1996–97, Environment Agency's N Wessex Area Environment Gp 1998– 2006 (dep chm 2000–04, chm 2004–06); patron Bath Environment Centre 1994– (fndr tstee 1995–98); chair Combe Down Stone Mines Community Assoc 2000–02, tstee and memb Cncl Wilts Wildlife Tst 2004–11, chair Swindon Climate Change Action Plan Steering Gp 2005–11, memb (environment rep) Swindon Strategic Partnership 2005–10; Dufton Silver Medal CIBSE 1985, Willem van Gool Meml Lecture Economics and Mgmnt of Energy in Industry (ECEMEI) 3rd European Congress Estoril 2004, George Stephenson Prize IMechE 2009, James Watt Medal ICE 2015; CEng; FIMechE 1999 (MIMechE 1973); *Publications* Contributions to professional journals and conference proceedings in the areas of technology assessment of energy (including bioenergy and biofuel) systems, decarbonisation of industry, and transition pathways to a low carbon future, using a toolkit of methods derived from the engineering and environmental sciences; *Recreations* science/science fiction, hill walking, community activities; *Clubs* Bradford on Avon Film Soc; *Style—* Prof Geoffrey Hammond; ✉ Department of Mechanical Engineering, University of Bath, Claverton Down, Bath BA2 7AY (☎ 01225 386168, fax 01225 386928, e-mail ensgph@bath.ac.uk, website http://www.bath.ac.uk/mech-eng/people/hammond/index.html)

HAMMOND, Jane Dominica; da of Reginald Egbert Rolt Hammond (d 1967), and Nancy Mildred, *née* Hawtrey (d 1983); *b* 6 April 1934; *Educ* Queen Anne's Sch Caversham, Hampstead Secretarial Coll, CAM (Dip PR); *m* 1970, Rudolph Samuel Brown, JP (d 1986); 1 da (Louisa Catherine b 5 March 1974); *Career* secretarial work Publicity Dept BBC 1955–57, Press Office Swissair 1959–61, asst ed Dairy Industries 1961–64; NALGO (now UNISON): reporter Public Service (newspaper) 1964–65, Health Service PRO 1965–68; PRO St Teresa's Hosp 1968–70; sr info offr: London Borough of Hammersmith 1971–73, Community Rels Cmmn 1973–77 and its successor body Cmmn for Racial Equality 1977–78; ed Hollis PR Weekly 1978–80; chm and md Trident Public Relations Ltd 1980–2003, prop Trident Training Services 1988– (launched for client Afro Hair & Beauty annual exhbn in 1983 and ran it again in 1984 and 1985, ran its Press Office 1993); ed Rotary in London (quarterly magazine); memb Cncl IPR 1965–68, 1969–71 and 1995–97 (vice-chm Educn and Trg Ctee 1994–97, vice-chm Int Gp 2001), chm IPRA Cncl UK 2000–02, millennium fndr memb Guild of PR Practitioners; memb: PR Educators' Forum, Ethics Ctee and Press and PR Industrial Cncl NUJ 2004–07, NUJ Journalist Editorial Advsy Bd, PR and Communication Cncl, Professional Training Ctee 2014–; examiner CAM 1977–95, asst course dir annual Sr Int PR Courses 1991–96, lectr Westminster Coll 1991–, tutor PR Educn Tst (PRET) Distance Learning Prog 1991–2000, jt course dir annual int introductory and advanced PR courses RIPA International 1994–2003, external moderator 1995–99, course dir London Corp Trg Courses 1998–2010, examiner Holborn Coll 1999–2002, lectr Birkbeck Coll 1999–2000; NVQ assessor 1998–; memb Quaker Outreach London Ctee 1998–2000; fndr memb Women's National Cancer Control Campaign; memb NUJ, FCIPR 1981 (MIPR 1968), MIPRA 1996, FCAM 2000; *Publications* contrib chapter in The Practice of Public Relations (ed S Black, 1995), Government Relations with the Public in Romania (1998); presented paper on media measurement to Tehran Univ symposium 2005; *Recreations* reading, cooking, cycling, swimming; *Clubs* Rotary St Pancras (formerly Rotary Putney, pres 2000–01), Soc of Friends (Quakers); *Style—* Miss Jane Hammond; ✉ Trident Training Services, 46 La Providence, Rochester, Kent ME1 1NB (☎ 01634 847772, e-mail trident@btconnect.com, website www.tridenttraining.co.uk)

HAMMOND, (Jonathan) Mark; *Career* West Sussex County Cncl: dir of environment and devpt 2000–04, chief exec 2004–10; chief exec Equality and Human Rights Cmmn 2011–15; lay memb: Governing Body NE Hamps Clinical Commissioning Gp 2015–, Gen Pharmaceutical Cncl 2016–; visiting prof in public admin Canterbury Christchurch Univ 2011–; *Style—* Mark Hammond, Esq; ✉ e-mail mark.hammond4@nhs.net

HAMMOND, Prof Norman David Curle; s of William Hammond, and Kathleen Jessie, *née* Howes; *b* 10 July 1944; *Educ* Varndean GS, Peterhouse Cambridge (Trevelyan scholar, Leaf Student, Dip Classical Archaeology, MA, PhD, ScD); *m* 1972, Dr Jean Wilson, FSA, *qv*, da of Alan Wilson, and Beryl, *née* Wagstaff; 1 s (Gawain Jonathon Curle b 2 Dec 1975), 1 da (Deborah Julian Curle b 13 Sept 1982); *Career* Univ of Cambridge: research fell Centre of Latin American Studies 1967–71, Leverhulme research fell Centre of Latin American Studies 1972–75, research fell Fitzwilliam Coll 1973–75; sr lectr Univ of Bradford 1975–77, visiting prof of anthropology Univ of Calif Berkeley 1977; Rutgers Univ USA: visiting prof 1977–78, assoc prof 1978–84, prof of archaeology 1984–88; visiting prof Jilin Univ Changchun China 1981, Irvine chair of anthropology Calif Acad of Sciences 1984–85, Curl lectr RAI 1985, visiting prof Univ de Paris Sorbonne 1987, fell in pre-Columbian studies Dumbarton Oaks Washington 1988, assoc in Maya archaeology Peabody Museum Harvard Univ 1988–, prof of archaeology Boston Univ 1988–2010 (chm 2005–07, emeritus prof 2011–), visiting fell Worcester Coll Oxford 1989, academic tstee Archaeological Inst of America 1990–93, visiting fell Peterhouse Cambridge 1991 and 1996–97, visiting prof Rheinische-Wilhelms-Universität Bonn 1994, visiting fell McDonald Inst for Archaeological Research Univ of Cambridge 1997 and 2004 (sr fell 2008–), Rockefeller Fndn scholar 1997, visiting fell All Souls Coll Oxford 2004, visiting fell Clare Hall Cambridge 2004; Bushnell lectr Univ of Cambridge 1997, Stone lectr Archaeological Inst of America 1997–98, Brush lectr 2001, Brunswick distinguished lectr Metropolitan Museum 2001, Borowski lectr 2002, Reckitt lectr Br Acad 2006, Aronui lectr Royal Soc of NZ 2011, De Carle distinguished lectr Univ of Otago 2013; archaeology corr The Times 1967–, memb Editorial Bds various archaeological jls in UK and USA, contrib to various scientific jls, ed Afghan Studies 1976–79, consltg ed Library of Congress (HLAS) 1977–89, archaelogy consIt Scientific American 1979–95, archaelogy ed TLS 2009–11; memb various advsy bds Belize 1987–; excavations and surveys: Libya/Tunisia 1964, Afghanistan 1966, Belize 1970– (Lubaantun 1970, Nohmul 1973–86, Cuello 1976–2002, La Milpa 1992–2002), Ecuador 1972–84; Hon Phi Beta Kappa 1989, Hon DSc Univ of Bradford 1999; FSA 1974 (memb Cncl 1996–99, Soc Medal 2001), FBA 1998; *Publications* South Asian Archaeology (ed, 1973), Mesoamerican Archaeology New Approaches (ed, 1974), Lubaantun: a Classic Maya Realm (1975), Social Process in Maya Prehistory (ed, 1977), The Archaeology of Afghanistan (ed with F R Allchin, 1978), Maya Archaeology and Ethnohistory (ed with G R Willey, 1979), Ancient Maya Civilization (1982, 5 edn 1994), Archaeology Proceedings (gen ed, 8 vols), 44th International Congress of Americanists (1983–84), Nohmul: a prehistoric Maya community in Belize – Excavations 1973–1983 (1985), Cuello: an early Maya community in Belize (1991), The Maya (2000); papers in learned and unlearned jls; *Recreations* fine wine, intelligent women, opera; *Clubs* Athenaeum, Tavern (Boston); *Style—* Prof Norman Hammond, FSA, FBA; ✉ Wholeway, Harlton, Cambridge CB23 1ET (☎ 01223 262376)

HAMMOND, Rt Hon Philip; PC (2010), MP; s of Bernard Hammond, and Doris Hammond; *b* 4 December 1955; *Educ* Shenfield Sch Brentwood, UC Oxford (open scholar, MA); *m* 1991, Susan Carolyn, da of Mr and Mrs E Williams-Walker; 2 da (Amy Victoria Louise b 9 Sept 1994, Sophie Elizabeth Alice b 10 Oct 1996), 1 s (William Oliver James b 13 May 1999); *Career* asst to chm then marketing mangr Speywood Laboratories 1977–81, dir Speywood Medical Ltd 1981–83, established and ran medical equipment distribution business 1983–94 (concurrently dir various medical equipment manufacturing companies UK and Europe); dir: Castlemead Ltd 1984–2004, Castlemead Homes Ltd 1994–2004,

H

Consort Resources Ltd 2000–03; ptnr CMA Consultants 1993–95, conslt to Govt of Malawi 1995–97; MP (Cons) Runnymede and Weybridge 1997– (Parly candidate (Cons) Newham NE 1994); memb Environment Tport and Regions Select Ctee 1997–98; oppn frontbench spokesman on: health and social servs 1998–2001, trade and industry 2001–02, local and regnl govt 2002–05; shadow chief sec to Treasy 2005, shadow sec of state for work and pensions 2005–07, shadow chief sec to the Treasy 2007–10, sec of state for transport 2010–11, sec of state for defence 2011–14, foreign sec 2014–16, Chllr of the Exchequer 2016–; memb Trade and Industry Select Ctee 2002; *Clubs* Weybridge Conservative; *Style—* The Rt Hon Philip Hammond, MP; ✉ House of Commons, London SW1A 0AA (☎ 020 7219 4055, fax 020 7219 5851)

HAMMOND, His Hon Judge Simon Tristram; s of Philip Jones Hammond (d 1986), of Leicester, and Sylvia Dina, *née* Sillem (d 1988); *b* 5 January 1944; *Educ* Eastbourne Coll, Coll of Law; *m* 10 July 1976, Louise, da of Charles Duncan Weir, FRCS, MC; 2 da (Pollyann Lucy *b* 8 Feb 1980, Alicia Francesca *b* 18 Nov 1992), 1 s (Edward Charles *b* 2 Aug 1981); *Career* articled to Philip Jones Hammond 1962–67, admitted as slr 1967, ptnr Victor Lissack London 1970–76, ptnr Philip J Hammond & Sons Leicester 1977–93, recorder 1990–93 (asst recorder 1985–90), circuit judge (Midland & Oxford Circuit) 1993–, diversity and community rels judge for Leicester 2002–; memb: Law Soc's Standing Ctee on Criminal Law 1982–91, Crown Court Rules Ctee 1988–93, Enforcement Sub-Ctee Home Office Review of Magistrates' Court Procedure 1989–90, Coll of Law Advsy Bd 1992, Bd Leics and Rutland Probation Tst 2003–14, Judicial Studies Bd Equal Treatment Advsy Ctee 2006–10; asst cmmr to Parly Boundary Cmmn for England 1992; church warden; *Recreations* riding, skiing, vegetable gardening, food and wine, bread making; *Style—* His Hon Judge Simon Hammond; ✉ Department for Constitutional Affairs, Midland Circuit Office, Priory Court, 33 Bull Street, Birmingham B4 6DW (☎ 0121 681 3200)

HAMMOND, Stephen; MP; s of Bryan Norman Walter Hammond, and Janice Eve, *née* Yeoman; *b* 4 February 1962, Southampton; *Educ* King Edward VI Sch, QMC Univ of London; *m* 1991, Sally; 1 da (Alice); *Career* dir UK equities Dresdner Kleinwort Benson Securities 1991–98; Commerzbank Securities: joined 1998, dir pan European research 2000–03; MP (Cons) Wimbledon 2005– (Parly candidate (Cons): N Warks 1997, Wimbledon 2001), shadow tport min 2005–10, PPS to Sec of State Dept for Communities and Local Govt 2010–12, Parliamentary under sec of state for transport 2012–14; chm: APPG for Markets 2015, APPG for Infrastructure 2015; memb Treasy Select Ctee 2015–; cncllr Merton BC 2002–06; *Style—* Stephen Hammond, Esq, MP; ✉ House of Commons, London SW1A 0AA (e-mail hammonds@parliament.uk, website www.stephenhammondmp.co.uk)

HAMMOND, Suzanna Mary; *Educ* Convent of St Clotilde Lechlade, Portsmouth Coll of FE (Dip Business Studies), Univ of Sussex/Regent St Poly (Business Communications and Journalism Degree); *m*; 3 s; *Career* account exec Good Relations Ltd 1969–72, assoc dir heading Consumer Products Div Lexington International 1975–82 (account dir 1972–75), dep md Hill & Knowlton (UK) Ltd (following merger with Lexington International) 1985–87 (dir Consumer Mktg Gp 1982–84), md Ogilvy Adams & Rinehart 1987–93, chief exec Hammond PR 1993–; *Style—* Ms Suzanna Hammond

HAMMONDS, Peter James Scott; *b* 1 February 1954; *Educ* Douglas HS for Boys Isle of Man, Bedford Coll London (BA), LSE (MSc); *m* 27 Sept 1980, Hazel Frances; 2 da (Sophie Elizabeth *b* 27 June 1985, Henrietta Ellen *b* 21 Aug 1990); *Career* Sec and Slr's Office Central Electricity Generating Bd 1977–79; Lloyds Bank plc: joined Sec's Dept 1979, asst sec 1981–87, dep sec 1987–91, sec Lloyds Merchant Bank Ltd 1985–91; co sec National Westminster Bank plc 1991–; non-exec dir Proshare; ICSA: dep chm Co Secs' Forum, elected memb Cncl, vice-pres UK Cncl, treas and vice-pres Int Cncl, memb Int Disciplinary Tbnl, chm Admissions Ctee; assoc memb IOD (memb Professional Standards Ctee and Chartered Accreditation Bd); 3 times prizewinner for Gilbert Lectures on Banking; FRGS 1977, FCIS 1991 (ACIS 1980); *Recreations* heavy gardening; *Style—* Peter Hammonds, Esq

HAMNETT, Prof Andrew; s of Albert Edward Hamnett (d 1990), and Dorothy Grace, *née* Stewart (d 2000); *b* 12 November 1947; *Educ* William Hulme's GS Manchester, UC Oxford (open scholar, MA), St John's Coll Oxford (chemistry senior scholar, DPhil); *m* 2 April 1976, Suzanne Marie, da of Charles Parkin (d 1993); 3 da (Erica *b* 1979, Hilary, Gillian (twins) *b* 1981); *Career* jr research fell The Queen's Coll Oxford 1972–77, Killam research fell Univ of British Columbia 1974–76; Univ of Oxford: departmental research asst Inorganic Chemistry Lab 1977–80, lectr in inorganic chemistry 1980–89, successively fell by special election, fell then dean St Catherine's Coll 1980–89; Univ of Newcastle Upon Tyne: prof of physical chemistry 1989–2000, pro-vice-chllr 1993–97, dep vice-chllr 1997–2000; princ and vice-chllr Univ of Strathclyde 2001–09; pres Scottish Assoc of Marine Sciences 2010–13; memb then chm Physical Chemistry Sub-Ctee SERC 1988–94, dep chm Chemistry Ctee EPSRC 1993–94; currently chm Newcastle and District Soc of Organists, hon sec Northern Synod Tst United Reformed Church, pres Morpeth Rotary Club; FRSC 1991, FRSA 1997, FRSE 2002; *Books* Techniques and Mechanisms in Electrochemistry (with P A Christensen, 1994), Electrochemistry (with Carl Hamann and Wolf Vielstich, 1998); *Recreations* music (organist and pianist), languages, philately; *Style—* Prof Andrew Hamnett; ✉ University of Strathclyde, 16 Richmond Street, Glasgow G1 1XQ (☎ 0141 548 2099, fax 0141 553 1521)

HAMPSHIRE, Prof Michael John; CBE (1987); *b* 13 October 1939; *Educ* Heckmondwike GS, Univ of Birmingham (BSc, PhD); *m* 1962, Mavis, *née* Oakes; 1 da (Julie Louise *b* 1972); *Career* Univ of Salford: lectr 1964–71, sr lectr 1971–78, prof of solid state electronics 1978–83, prof of electronic info technol 1983–, chm Dept of Electronic and Electrical Engrg 1981–89, asst md Salford University Business Services (SUBS) Ltd tech conslts 1989–95; dir: SUBS Ltd 1989–98, Vertec Ltd 1991–98 (fndr chm 1981–91, co awarded N of England first prize in BTG Academic Enterprise Competition 1982), Cedeta Research Ltd 1991–92; conslt: Ferranti Semiconductors Ltd 1970–74, Volex Group plc 1977–99, Thorn EMI 1980–88; fndr chm: Mgmnt Ctee Calderdale Industrial Microelectronics Centre 1984–88, Mgmnt Ctee NW Microelectronics Awareness Prog 1986–89; chm: Mgmnt Ctee Microelectronics Awareness Scheme 1983–86, R&D Ctee Volex Group plc 1988–92; memb: SERC Nat Mgmnt Ctee for Teaching Company Scheme 1983–88, AMTEC Jt Bd of Studies 1986–88, Mgmnt Ctee Software Servs Div SUBS Ltd 1986–89; Techmart Technol Transfer Trophy 1984; author of numerous papers, theses and reports; Hon MIED 1981; FInstP 1971–2001, FIEE 1984–2001, CEng 1984, CPhys 1984, Hon FIED 2001; *Recreations* music, golf; *Style—* Prof Michael Hampshire, CBE; ✉ University of Salford Enterprises Ltd, Technology House, Lissadel Street, Salford, Manchester M6 6AP (☎ 0161 257 2700, fax 0161 257 2701)

HAMPSHIRE, Susan; OBE (1995); da of George Kenneth Hampshire (d 1964), and June Hampshire (d 1967); *Educ* Hampshire Sch Knightsbridge; *m* 1, 1967 (m dis 1974), Pierre Julian Granier-Deferre; 1 s 1 da (decd); *m* 2, 1981, Sir Eddie Kulukundis, OBE, *qv*; s of George Elias Kulukundis (d 1978); *Career* actress; Hon DLitt: Univ of London 1984, Univ of St Andrews 1986, Univ of Exeter 2001; Hon DEd Univ of Kingston 1994, Hon DArts Pine Manor Coll Boston USA 1994; *Theatre* incl: Express Bongo, Follow That Girl, Fairy Tales Of New York, The Ginger Man, Past Imperfect, The Sleeping Prince, She Stoops to Conquer, Peter Pan, A Doll's House, The Taming of The Shrew, Romeo and Jeanette, As You Like It, Miss Julie, The Circle, Arms and the Man, Man and Superman, Tribades, An Audience Called Edward, Crucifer of Blood, Night and Day, The Revolt, House Guest, Blithe Spirit, Married Love, A Little Night Music, The King and I, Noel and Gertie, Relative Values, Suzanna Andler, Black Chiffon, Relatively Speaking, Relative Values,

The Lady in the Van, Cinderella 2005–06 and 2006–07, The Bargain 2007, The Circle 2008, Pride and Prejudice 2009–10; *Television* incl: What Katy Did, The Andromeda Breakthrough, The Forsyte Saga 1970, Vanity Fair 1971, The First Churchills 1973, The Pallisers 1975, Dick Turpin 1980, Barchester Chronicles 1982, Leaving (2 series), Going to Pot I, II and III, Don't Tell Father, The Grand (series I & II), Coming Home, Nancherrow, Monarch of the Glen (7 series), Sparkling Cyanide, The Royal; *Film* incl: During One Night, The Three Lives of Thomasina, Night Must Fall, The Fighting Prince of Donegal, Paris in August, Monte Carlo or Bust, Violent Enemy, David Copperfield, A Time For Loving, Living Free, Baffled, Malpertius, Neither The Sea Nor The Sand, Roses and Green Peppers, Bang; *Awards* winner 3 Emmy Awards for Best Actress; *Books* Susan's Story, The Maternal Instinct, Lucy Jane at the Ballet, Lucy Jane on Television, Lucy Jane and the Dancing Competition, Lucy Jane and the Russian Ballet, Trouble Free Gardening, Every Letter Counts, Easy Gardening, Rosie's First Ballet Lesson; *Recreations* gardening; *Style—* Miss Susan Hampshire, OBE; ✉ c/o Chatto & Linnet (☎ 020 7349 7222, e-mail info@chattolinnet.com)

HAMPSON, Christopher; CBE (1994); s of Harold Ralph Hampson (d 1972), of Montreal, Canada, and Geraldine Mary, *née* Smith (d 1984); *b* 6 September 1931; *Educ* Ashbury Coll Ottawa, McGill Univ Montreal (BEng); *m* 18 Sept 1954, Joan Margaret Cassils, da of Lt-Col Arthur C Evans (d 1960), of Montreal, Canada; 3 da (Daphne Margaret (Mrs Kearns) *b* 1955, Sarah Anne (Mrs Clarridge) *b* 1958, Aimée Joan Geraldine (Mrs Pitman) *b* 1966), 2 s (Christopher Geoffrey *b* 1957, Harold Arthur *b* 1965); *Career* CIL Inc Canada: vice-pres and dir 1973–78, sr vice-pres and dir 1982–; md and ceo ICI Australia Ltd 1984–87, exec dir ICI plc 1987–94; non-exec chm: Yorkshire Electricity Group plc 1994–97, RMC Group plc 1996–2002 (non-exec dir 1994–2002), Br Biotech plc 1998–2002; dep chm Environment Agency 2000 (memb Bd 1995–2000); non-exec dir: SNC-Lavalin Group Inc 1993–2002, TransAlta Corporation 1994–2003, BG plc 1997–2000, Lattice Group plc 2000–02; formerly non-exec dir Costain Gp plc; CIMgt 1990; *Recreations* tennis, skiing; *Clubs* York (Toronto), Boodle's, Hurlingham; *Style—* Christopher Hampson, Esq, CBE; ✉ 77 Kensington Court, London W8 5DT (☎ 020 7376 1906)

HAMPSON, Christopher; s of Geoff Hampson, and Janice, *née* Morrison; *b* 31 March 1973, Manchester; *Educ* Royal Ballet Sch; *Career* choreographer; dancer English Nat Ballet 1992–99 (jr soloist 1995); roles incl: Drosselmeyer in The Nutcracker, Paris in Romeo and Juliet, The Headmistress in Graduation Ball, lead in Square Dance; ballet master City Ballet of London 1999– (ballet master for VIVA! Tour and Wayne Sleep's Dash and Aspects of Dance tours), artistic dir Scottish Ballet 2012–15, ceo and artistic dir Scottish Ballet 2015–; memb Sub-Ctee Benesh Inst, memb Bd Dance Base 2012–; winner Ursula Moreton Choreographic Competition Royal Ballet Sch 1992, Best Classical Choreography Critics' Circle Awards 2002, Barclay's Theatre Award for outstanding achievement in dance 2002; hon memb Dalcroze Soc; *Choreography* for English Nat Ballet: Perpetuum Mobile 1997, Country Garden 1998, Capriol Suite 1998, Concerto Grosso 1999, Double Concerto 2001; for City Ballet of London: Coda for Three Men 1998, Dinaresade 1999, Canciones 1999; other credits incl: Notturno (for Thomas Edur and Agnes Oaks) 1998, Carnival (NY Ballet) 1999, Malcolm Arnold Dances (Elmhurst) 2000, Anniversaire (English Nat Ballet Sch) 2000, Entrées (Royal Ballet Sch and English Nat Ballet Sch) 2000, Homage to a Princess (Rojo/Kobburg) 2000, A Christmas Carol (first full-length work, Royal Festival Hall) 2000, Songs Without Words (London Studio Centre/Images of Dance) 2001, Esquisses (English Nat Ballet Sch) 2001, Saltarello (Royal NZ Ballet) 2001, Double Concerto (English Nat Ballet) 2001, A Christmas Carol (St David's Hall Cardiff) 2002, Romeo and Juliet (Royal NZ Ballet) 2002, Nutcracker (English Nat Ballet) 2002, Trapeze (English Nat Ballet) 2003, Giselle (Nat Theatre Prague) 2004, Sinfonietta Giocosa (Atlanta Ballet) 2005, two solos for the Royal Acad of Dance Genée Int Ballet Competition 2006, Cinderella (Royal NZ Ballet) 2007, Three Dialogues (Royal Ballet Sch) 2007, Paganini Variations (Hong Kong Acad of Performing Arts) 2008, Capriol Suite (Ballet Central) 2008, Dear Norman (Royal Ballet) 2009, choreography for Royal Acad of Dance Solo Seal Award 2009, Silhouette (Royal NZ Ballet) 2010, Cinq Regards (Conservatoire de Paris) 2010, Rite of Spring (Atlanta Ballet) 2011, Storyville (Ballet Black) 2012, Hansel & Gretel (Scottish Ballet) 2013; *Recreations* wine, travel, theatre, reading, music, knitting, marathon running; *Style—* Christopher Hampson, Esq; ✉ e-mail chris@christopherhampson.com, website www.christopherhampson.com

HAMPSON, Sir Stuart; kt (1998), DL (Bucks 2015); *b* 7 January 1947; *Educ* St John's Coll Oxford (MA); *Career* with Civil Serv 1969–82 (successively Bd of Trade, FCO, Dept of Prices and Consumer Protection and Dept of Trade); John Lewis Partnership: joined 1982, md Tyrrell & Green until 1986, memb Bd 1986, dir of research and expansion 1986–93, dep chm 1989–93, chm 1993–2007; chm and first cmmr Crown Estate 2010–; memb Oxford Retail Gp 1987–93, a founding dep chm London First 1992–97; chm Royal Soc of Arts 1999–2001 (memb Cncl 1995–2009, treas 1997, dep chm 1998–99 and 2001–02), memb Royal Soc of Arts Inquiry into Tomorrow's Company, dir Centre for Tomorrow's Company 1996–99 (chm 1998–99); pres RASE 2005–06; High Sheriff of Bucks 2013–14; Hon DBA: Kingston Univ 1998, Southampton Solent Univ 2001, Middlesex Univ 2007; Hon DSc Univ of Bucks 2010, Hon LLD Univ of Warwick 2010; hon fell St John's Coll Oxford 2001; Hon FCGI 2002; *Style—* Sir Stuart Hampson, DL

HAMPTON, Christopher James; CBE (1999); s of Bernard Patrick Hampton, and Dorothy Patience, *née* Herrington; *b* 26 January 1946; *Educ* Lancing, New Coll Oxford (MA); *m* 1971, Laura Margaret de Holesch; 2 da; *Career* res dramatist Royal Court Theatre 1968–70, freelance writer 1970–; FRSL; Officier de l'Ordre des Arts et des Lettres (France) 1997; *Plays* When Did You Last See My Mother? 1966, Total Eclipse 1968, The Philanthropist 1970 (Evening Standard Best Comedy Award, Plays and Players London Theatre Critics Best Play), Savages 1973 (Plays and Players London Theatre Critics Best Play, Los Angeles Drama Critics' Circle Award for Distinguished Playwriting 1974), Treats 1976, The Portage to San Cristobal of A H (from George Steiner) 1982, Tales from Hollywood 1982 (Standard Best Comedy Award 1983), Les Liaisons Dangereuses (from Laclos) 1985 (Plays and Players London Theatre Critics Best Play, Standard Best Play Award 1986, NY Drama Critics' Circle Best Foreign Play Award 1987, Laurence Olivier Award 1986), White Chameleon 1991, Sunset Boulevard (book and lyrics) 1993 (Tony Awards for book and lyrics 1995), Alice's Adventures Under Ground 1994, The Talking Cure 2002, Dracula (book and lyrics) 2004, Waiting for the Barbarians (opera libretto) 2005, Embers 2006, Appomattox (opera libretto) 2007, Youth Without God 2009, Appomattox 2012, Stephen Ward (book and lyrics) 2013, The Trial (libretto) 2014; *Television* Able's Will BBC 1977, The History Man (from Malcolm Bradbury) BBC 1981, The Price of Tea 1984, Hotel du Lac (From Anita Brookner) BBC 1986 (BAFTA Best TV Film Award 1987), The Ginger Tree (from Oswald Wynd) BBC 1989, The Thirteenth Tale (BBC) 2013; *Film* A Dolls House 1973, Tales From the Vienna Woods 1979 (Screen International Award 1980), The Honorary Consul 1983, The Good Father 1986 (Prix Italia 1988), Wolf at the Door 1986, Dangerous Liaisons 1988 (Writers Guild of America Award, BAFTA Award, Academy Award), Carrington (also dir) 1995 (Special Jury Award Cannes Film Festival 1995), Total Eclipse 1995, Mary Reilly 1996, The Secret Agent (also dir) 1996, The Quiet American 2002, Imagining Argentina 2003 (also dir), Atonement 2007, Chéri 2009, A Dangerous Method 2011, Adore 2013, Ali and Nino 2015; *Translations* Marya (by Isaac Babel) 1967, Uncle Vanya (by Chekhov) 1970, Hedda Gabler (by Ibsen) 1970, A Doll's House (by Ibsen) 1971, Don Juan (by Molière) 1972, Tales from the Vienna Woods (by Horváth) 1977, Don Juan Comes Back from the War (by Horváth) 1978, Ghosts (by Ibsen) 1978, The Wild Duck (by Ibsen) 1979, The Prague

Trial (by Chéreau and Mnouchkine) 1980, Tartuffe (by Molière) 1983, Faith, Hope and Charity (by Horváth) 1989, Art (by Yasmina Reza) 1996 (Scott Moncrieff Prize 1997), An Enemy of the People (by Ibsen) 1997, The Unexpected Man (by Yasmina Reza) 1998, Conversations After a Burial (by Yasmina Reza) 2000, Life x 3 (by Yasmina Reza) 2000, Three Sisters (by Chekhov) 2003, The Seagull (by Chekhov) 2007, God of Carnage (by Yasmina Reza) 2008, Judgment Day (by Horváth) 2009, The Father (by Florian Zeller) 2014, The Mother (by Florian Zeller) 2015, Egmont (libretto from Goethe) 2015; *Publications* Hampton on Hampton (ed by Alistair Owen, 2005); *Recreations* travel, cinema; *Clubs* Dramatists'; *Style*— Christopher Hampton, Esq, CBE, FRSL; ✉ 2 Kensington Park Gardens, London W11 3HB; c/o Casarotto Ramsay & Assoc Ltd, Waverley House, 7–12 Noel Street, London W1F 8GQ (☎ 020 7287 4450, fax 020 7287 9128)

HAMPTON, Sir (Leslie) Geoffrey; kt (1998); s of Leslie Harold Hampton, and Irene, *née* Wain; *Educ* High Arcal GS Dudley, King Alfred's Coll Winchester (CertEd), Univ of Southampton (BEd), Univ of Birmingham (MEd); *m* Christine Joyce, da of Charles Edward Bickley; 2 s (Paul Geoffrey b 29 July 1979, Ian James b 15 May 1988); *Career* teacher rising to actg dep headteacher Pensnett Sch Dudley 1974–87, dep headteacher Buckpool 1987–93, headmaster Northicote Sch Wolverhampton 1993–99; Univ of Wolverhampton: dir Leadership Centre and dean Sch of Educn 1999–2006, pro-vice-chllr 2006–09, dep vice-chllr 2009–13, emeritus prof 2016–; chief exec Education Central 2013–16; memb: Police Consultative Ctee 1988–93, SHA 1989–, Nat Steering Gp Basic Skills Agency 1995–2007, Bd Nat Educn Business Partnerships 2007–09, Bd C of E Central Eudcn Tst (CECET); Govt appointee Special Measures Action Recovery Teams (SMART Initiative) 1997, co-dir Nat Information and Communication Technologies (ICT) Research Centre DFES 2001–03, chair (govt appointee) Walsall Educn Bd 2003, assoc dir Specialist Schs Tst 2005, chief advsr to Min for Schs for Black Country Challenge 2008–11, chair LEP Wolverhampton, chair Raising Achievement Board Lichfield Dio 2016, memb Music Educn Advsy Gp Associated Bds of the Royal Schs of Music (ABRSM) 2016; Hon DEd King Alfred's Coll Winchester 2003, KPMG prof of educn leadership 2005; *Publications* Transforming Northicote School – Pathfinders for Success (jtly, 2000), A Practical Guide to Teacher Professional Development (jtly, 2004); work features in Govt publications From Failure to Success (1996), Excellence in Schools (White Paper, 1997), and Trust Schools (DfES DVD, 2006); also contrib to Developing Quality Systems in Education (ed G Doherty, 1994); author of numerous articles on educn in jls; *Recreations* DIY, cycling, gardening; *Style*— Sir Geoffrey Hampton; ✉ University of Wolverhampton, Offices of the Vice-Chancellor, Wulfruna Street, Wolverhampton WV1 1SB (☎ 01902 322766, fax 01902 824345, e-mail g.hampton@wlv.ac.uk)

HAMPTON, 7 Baron (UK 1874); Sir John Humphrey Arnott Pakington; 7 Bt (UK 1846); s of 6 Baron (d 2003); *b* 24 December 1964; *Educ* Dyson Perrins C of E HS, Shrewsbury, Exeter Coll of Art and Design (BA); *m* 4 Oct 1996, Siena E E, yr da of Remo Caldato, of Rome; *Career* assoc dir Band and Brown Communications London; *Style*— The Rt Hon the Lord Hampton; ✉ e-mail johnnie@thirst-london.com

HAMPTON, Prof John Reynolds; s of Eric Albert Hampton (d 1979), of Gorleston, Norfolk, and Norah Kathleen, *née* Johnson (d 1981); *b* 8 November 1937; *Educ* Gresham's, Magdalen Coll Oxford (BA, DM, DPhil, MA, BM BCh), Radcliffe Infirmary Oxford; *m* 25 July 1964, Pamela Jean, da of Edmund Joseph Wilkins (d 1980), of Tunbridge Wells; 2 s (Christopher, Philip), 1 da (Joanna); *Career* house physician and surgn and SHO Radcliffe Infirmary 1963–64, jr lectr and lectr in med Univ of Oxford 1965–68, instr in med and jr assoc in med Harvard Univ and Peter Bent Brigham Hosp Boston 1968–69; Univ of Nottingham 1969–: lectr, sr lectr in med and hon conslt physician to Nottingham Hosps 1970–74, reader in med and conslt physician Queen's Med Centre 1974–79, prof of cardiology 1980–; sec Atherosclerosis Discussion GP 1978–81; memb: Br Cardiac Soc, Assoc of Physicians; FRCP 1975, FFPM, FESC; author of more than 400 scientific papers; *Books* incl: Integrated Clinical Science – cardiovascular disease (1983), The ECG in practice (1986, 3 edn 2003), The ECG Made Easy (4 edn, 1992, 8 edn 2008); *Recreations* sailing; *Style*— Prof John Hampton; ✉ Cardiovascular Medicine, D Floor, S Block, Queen's Medical Centre, Nottingham NG7 2UH (☎ 0115 970 9346, fax 0115 970 9384, e-mail jrhampton@doctors.net.uk)

HAMPTON, Sir Philip Roy; kt (2007); *Educ* Lincoln Coll Oxford (MA), INSEAD (MBA); *Career* CA 1978; with Coopers & Lybrand 1975–80, with Lazard Bros 1981–90, gp fin dir British Steel plc 1990–95, exec fin dir BG Group plc 1996–2000, gp fin dir BT plc 2000–02, gp fin dir Lloyds TSB Group plc 2002–04, chm J Sainsbury plc 2004–09, chm RBS Gp 2009–15, chm GlaxoSmithKline 2015–; non-exec dir: Belgacom 2004–10, Anglo American plc 2009–; ldr Hampton Review for HM Treasy 2004–05; *Style*— Sir Philip Hampton

HAMROUNI, Sandra Lesley; da of Vernon Carter (d 2001), and Patricia, *née* Barton; *b* 13 January 1958, Bradford, W Yorks; *Educ* Richmond Sch Yorks, Univ of Birmingham (BA), Inst of Educn Univ of London (PGCE, MA), Churchbridge Teachers' Centre (RSA Dip), CIM (Cert); *m* 29 April 1995, Lotfi Hamrouni; 2 s (Malik b 8 Feb 1997, Amir b 7 Jan 2001); *Career* English teacher: VSO Kenya 1979–81, Instituto Britannia Mexico 1981–82, Handsworth Wood Girls' Sch Birmingham 1982–83; British Cncl: English teacher Abu Dhabi 1984–86, dep dir of studies Cairo 1988–89, teaching centre mangr Tunis 1992–95, teaching centre mangr Damascus 1995–97, dir of trg and examination servs Muscat 1997–2002, teaching centre mangr Madrid 2002–04, country dir Bahrain 2004–; *Recreations* playing violin, music, opera, African and Arab literature, film, dance, running, weight training; *Clubs* Royal Over-Seas League; *Style*— Ms Sandra Hamrouni; ✉ British Council Bahrain, AMA Centre, PO Box 452, 146 Shaikh Salman Highway, Manama 356, Bahrain (☎ 00 973 17261555, fax 00 973 17241272)

HAMWEE, Baroness (Life Peer UK 1991), of Richmond upon Thames in the London Borough of Richmond upon Thames; Sally Rachel Hamwee; AM; da of late Alec Hamwee, and late Dorothy, *née* Saunders; *b* 12 January 1947; *Educ* Manchester HS for Girls, Univ of Cambridge (MA); *Career* slr; ptnr Clintons Slrs; cncllr London Borough of Richmond-upon-Thames 1978–98 (chm Planning Ctee 1983–87); chm London Planning Advsy Ctee 1986–94; pres ALDC (Lib Dem Cncllrs' Assoc) 1995–96; memb London Assembly GLA (Lib Dem) 2000–; GLA: dep chair 2000–01, 2002–03 and 2004–05, chair 2001–02, 2003–04 and 2005–08; chair London Assembly Budget Ctee 2000–08; Lib Dem frontbench spokesperson 1991–2009, Lib Dem spokesperson on home affrs House of Lords 2009–; former memb Select Ctees: Extradition Law, Inquiries Act 2005, Adoption Legislation, Secondary Legislation Scrutiny, Economic Affrs, Central/Local Govt Relations; chair All-Pty Parly Gp on Family Migration 2013, memb All-Pty Parly Gp on Immigration Detention 2015, memb Jt Ctee on Human Rights 2015–; vice-pres Town and Country Planning Assoc (former pres); former memb Cncl of Mgmnt Family Policy Studies Centre; memb: Cncl of Mgmnt Refuge, Advsy Bd Missing People, Advsy Gp Centre for Public Scrutiny; jt pres London Cncls, vice-pres Town and Country Planning Assoc; legal advsr The Simon Community; chm XFM Ltd 1996–98, former chair TCPA Inquiry 'Your Place or Mine?'; former memb: Cncl Parents for Children, Bd London First, Joseph Rowntree Fndn Inquiry, Planning For Housing; tstee: Rose Theatre Kingston 2009–, Safer London 2014–; patron PAC (post-adoption servs); vice-pres CIEH, FRSA; *Style*— Baroness Hamwee, AM; ✉ 101A Mortlake High Street, London SW14 8HQ

HANBURY, Heather; da of Douglas Adams, and Jane Campbell; *b* 20 September 1960, Belfast; *Educ* Univ of Edinburgh (MA), Wolfson Coll Cambridge (MSc), Inst of Educn London Univ (PGCE); *m* 24 April 1993, Roland Hanbury; *Career* mgmnt conslt Touche Ross 1986–93, VSO corp fundraiser 1994–96; Blackheath HS: head of upper sch, head of sixth form; head of sixth form Haberdashers' Aske's, dep head (Staff Welfare and Devpt) Latymer Upper Sch, headmistress Wimbledon HS 2008–14, headmistress Lady Eleanor Holles Sch 2014–; *Recreations* reading, travel, theatre, bridge; *Style*— Ms Heather Hanbury; ✉ The Lady Eleanor Holles School, Hanworth Road, Hampton, Middlesex TW12 3HF (☎ 020 8783 9703, e-mail heatherhanbury@lehs.org, website www.lehs.org.uk)

HANBURY, Margaret Elizabeth; da of Paul Barrett Hanbury (d 1999), and late Norah, *née* Stubbs; *b* 24 November 1946; *Educ* Leweston Manor Sherborne; *m* March 1978 (m dis 1999), Guillaume de Rougemont; 1 s (Henry Paul b 14 Sept 1981); *Career* literary agent; founded own agency 1983, clients incl J G Ballard, George Alagiah, Simon Callow, Jane Glover and Katie Price; memb Assoc of Authors' Agents; *Clubs* Bembridge Sailing; *Style*— Ms Margaret Hanbury; ✉ The Hanbury Agency, 28 Moreton Street, London SW1V 2PE (☎ 020 7630 6768)

HANBURY-TENISON, (Airling) Robin; OBE (1981), DL (Cornwall 2003); s of Maj Gerald Evan Farquhar Tenison (d 1954), of Co Monaghan, Ireland, and Ruth Julia Marguerite, *née* Hanbury (d 2000); *b* 7 May 1936; *Educ* Eton, Magdalen Coll Oxford (MA); *m* 1, 1959, Marika (d 1982), da of Lt-Col John Montgomerie Hopkinson (d 1989), of Sussex; 1 da (Lucy b 1960), 1 s (Rupert b 1970); m 2, 1983, Louella Gage, da of Lt-Col George Torquil Gage Williams, of Menkee, Cornwall; 1 s (Merlin b 1985); *Career* farmer, author, explorer, environmental and human rights campaigner; pres Survival Int 1984– (chm 1969–84), memb SW Regnl Panel MAFF 1993–96, chief exec Countryside Alliance (formerly BFSS) 1995–98; pres Rain Forest Club 2001–05, pres Cornwall Red Squirrel Project 2011–; RGS Patron's Medal 1979, Farmers Club Cup 1998, CLA Contribution to the Countryside Award 2000, Pio Manzù Medal Italy 2000, Mungo Park Medal Scot Royal Geographical Society 2001; Dr (hc) Univ of Mons-Hainant 1992, Hon DSc Plymouth Univ 2012; *Books* The Rough and The Smooth (1969), A Question of Survival (1973), A Pattern of Peoples (1975), Mulu – The Rain Forest (1980), The Yanomami (1982), Worlds Apart (1984), White Horses Over France (1985), A Ride along the Great Wall (1987), Fragile Eden (1989), Spanish Pilgrimage (1990), The Oxford Book of Exploration (1993), Jake's Escape (1996), Jake's Treasure (1998), Jake's Safari (1998), Worlds Within (2005), The Seventy Great Journeys in History (2006), Land of Eagles (2009), The Great Explorers (2010), Echoes of a Vanished World (2012), Beauty Freely Given (2012), The Modern Explorers (2013); *Recreations* travelling, conservation; *Clubs* Geographical, Pratt's, Travellers; *Style*— Robin Hanbury-Tenison, Esq, OBE, DL; ✉ Cabilla Manor, Cardinham, Bodmin, Cornwall PL30 4DW (☎ 01208 821224, fax 01208 821267, e-mail robin@cabilla.co.uk, website www.cabilla.co.uk and www.robinsbooks.co.uk)

H

HANCOCK, Prof Barry William; OBE (2009); s of George Llewellyn Hancock (d 2008), and Sarah Hancock (d 1973); *b* 25 January 1946; *Educ* E Barnet GS, Univ of Sheffield Med Sch (MB ChB, MD), Univ of London (DCH); *m* 5 July 1969, (Christine Diana) Helen, da of Alexander Moffatt Spray (d 1972); 1 da (Caroline b 1971), 1 s (David b 1974); *Career* medical registrar Professorial Therapeutics Unit Royal Infirmary Sheffield 1973–74, lectr in med and sr registrar Professorial Medical Unit Royal Hosp Sheffield 1974–78, hon conslt physician and oncologist Royal Hallamshire and Weston Park Hosps Sheffield 1978–88; Univ of Sheffield: sr lectr in med 1978–86, reader in med 1986–88, prof of clinical oncology 1988–2009, emeritus prof 2009–; formerly: dir Supraregional Gestational Trophoblastic Tumour Serv, YCR dir Cancer Research; pres Int Soc for the Study of Trophoblastic Disease; hon dir Trent Palliative Care Centre, divnl surgn N Derbys St John Ambulance Bde; Lord Mayor of Sheffield's Honours Award 1999, Sheffield Star Health Award 2002, Univ of Sheffield Centenary Medal 2005, Pfizer Excellence in Oncology Lifetime Achievement Award 2008, Gold Medal Int Soc for the Study of Trophoblastic Disease 2009, Sheffield City Cncl Sheffield Legends Award 2010; MRCP 1973, FRCP (London) 1985, FRCR 1994, FRCP (Edinburgh) 1995; *Books* Assessment of Tumour Response (ed, 1982), Immunological Aspects of Cancer (jt ed, 1985), Lymphoreticular Disease (jt ed, 1985), Lecture Notes in Clinical Oncology (jtly, 1986), Cancer Care in the Community (ed, 1996), Cancer Care in the Hospital (ed, 1996), Gestational Trophoblastic Diseases (jt ed, 1997, 3 edn 2009), Malignant Lymphoma (jt ed, 2000); *Recreations* railways, photography, philately, tennis; *Style*— Prof Barry Hancock, OBE; ✉ Treetops, 253 Dobcroft Road, Ecclesall, Sheffield S11 9LG (☎ 0114 235 1433); Academic Unit of Clinical Oncology, Weston Park Hospital, Whitham Road, Sheffield S10 2SJ (e-mail b.w.hancock@sheffield.ac.uk)

HANCOCK, Prof Gus; s of Reginald Hancock, and Mary Elizabeth Hancock; *b* 17 November 1944; *Educ* Harvey GS Folkestone, Dorking Co GS, Bangor GS, Trinity Coll Dublin (Louis Claude Purser entrance scholar, fndn scholar, BA, Gold medal) Peterhouse Cambridge (res studentship, Shell Petroleum postgrad res scholar, PhD); *m* 1971, Rosemary Margaret Nofolk Brown; 1 da, 1 s; *Career* postdoctoral res asst Dept of Chemistry Univ of Calif San Diego 1971–73, wissenschaftlicher angestellte (perm res offr) Fakultät f Physik Universität Bielefeld 1973–76; Univ of Oxford: fell Trinity Coll 1976–2012 (emeritus fell 2012–), lectr in physical chemistry 1976–96, prof of chemistry 1996–2012, head Dept of Physical and Theoretical Chemistry 2005–10; Stanford Univ: Fulbright fell 1982–83, visiting prof of chemistry 1989; ed: Research in Chemical Kinetics 1992–99, Comprehensive Chemical Kinetics 1992–99; chm Gas Kinetics Gp RSC 1988–90 (sec 1986–88); memb: Physical Chemistry Panel SERC 1990–93, Plasma and Ion Surface Engrg Panel 1990–, Structure, Bonding and Reaction Mechanisms Coll EPSRC 1995–2005, Marine and Atmospheric Sciences Panel NERC 1996–97, Atmospheric Sciences Panel NERC 1997–99, Upper Troposphere Lower Stratosphere Steering Gp NERC 1999–2004; Corday Morgan Medal and Prize RSC 1982, Reaction Kinetics Award RSC 1995, Japan Soc for the Promotion of Sci Fellowship 1997, 14th Italgas Prize for Sci and Technol for the Environment 2000, Polanyi Medal Gas Kinetics Gp RSC 2002, Reaction Dynamics Award RSC 2010; hon doctorate Univ of Cordoba Argentina 2013; *Publications* over 200 refereed pubns in scientific literature; *Style*— Prof Gus Hancock; ✉ Physical and Theoretical Chemistry Laboratory, Oxford University, South Parks Road, Oxford OX1 3QZ (☎ 01865 275439, fax 01865 275410, e-mail gus.hancock@chem.ox.ac.uk)

HANCOCK, Rt Hon Matthew; PC (2014), MP; *b* 2 October 1978; *Educ* King's Sch Chester, West Cheshire Coll, Univ of Oxford, Univ of Cambridge; *m* Martha, *née* Hoyer Millar; 1 da, 2 s; *Career* Border Business Systems, economist Bank of England 2000–05, COS to Rt Hon George Osborne, MP, *qv*, 2005–10; MP (Cons) W Suffolk 2010–, min for skills 2012–13, min of state for skills and enterprise 2013–14, min for energy, business, enterprise and Portsmouth 2014–15, paymaster general 2015–; *Books* Master of Nothing (with Nadhim Zahawi, MP, *qv*, 2011); *Style*— The Rt Hon Matthew Hancock, MP; ✉ House of Commons, London SW1A 0AA (☎ 020 7219 7186, e-mail matthew.hancock.mp@parliament.uk); ☎ 01638 576692, website www.matthewhancock.co.uk

HANCOCK, Michael Thomas (Mike); CBE (1992); *b* 9 April 1946; *m* 1967, Jacqueline, da of Sidney and Gwen Elliott; 1 s, 1 da; *Career* memb Bd of Dirs Drug Rehabilitation Unit Alpha Drug Clinic Droxford 1971–; memb Portsmouth City Cncl 1971– (Fratton Ward 1973–, ldr Lib Dem Gp 1989–97); Hampshire CC: memb 1973–, ldr of the oppn 1977–81 and 1989–93, ldr Lib Dem Gp 1989–97, ldr 1993–97; joined SDP 1981 (memb Nat Ctee 1984), Parly candidate (SDP) Portsmouth S 1983 (SDP/Alliance 1987), MP (SDP) Portsmouth S 1984–87, MP (Lib Dem) Portsmouth S 1997–2015; Lib Dem spokesman on defence 1997–; dir Daytime Club BBC 1987–90, chm Southern Branch NSPCC 1989–, dist offr for Hampshire, IOW and Channel Islands Royal Soc for Mentally Handicapped

Children and Adults 1989–97; memb: Br Delgn to UN 1983–84, Bureau of the Assembly of Euro Regions 1993–96, Congress of Local and Regnl Authorities of Europe (a body of the Cncl of Europe) 1994–97; vice-pres Atlantic Arc Cmmn of the Conf of Peripheral Maritime Regions 1994; tstee: Royal Marines Museum Portsmouth, Mary Rose; dir the Beneficial Fndn Portsmouth; contrib to various jls; hon award for contrib to Anglo-German rels Homborn W Germany 1981; *Recreations* people, living life to the full; *Style—* Mike Hancock, Esq, CBE; ✉ House of Commons, London SW1A 0AA (☎ 020 7219 5180); office: 1A Albert Road, Southsea, Hampshire PO5 2SE (☎ 023 9286 1055, fax 023 9283 0530); home: (☎ 01329 287340)

HANCOCK, Rt Rev Peter; *see:* Bath and Wells, Bishop of

HANCOCK, Roger Markham; s of late Howard Spencer Hancock, of Oxford, and late Marjorie Helen, *née* Skelcher; *b* 4 November 1942; *Educ* Southfield Sch Oxford; *m* 14 Aug 1968, Marian Sheila, da of late Arthur Herbert Holloway, of South Tawton; 1 da (Kirsty Sheila Bevis b 14 Aug 1975), 1 s (Mark Peter Skelcher b 25 Jan 1978); *Career* articled clerk Wenn Towsend Chartered Accountants Oxford 1959–65, mgmnt accountant British Motor Corp 1965, mangr Morris & Harper Chartered Accountants 1966; Whitley Stimpson & Partners: ptnr 1967–2003, managing ptnr 1987–95, sr ptnr 1995–2003; ptnr Moores Rowland Banbury 1979–99, memb Cncl Moores Rowland Int 1985–99; chm: Morris & Harper Ltd 1997–99 (dir), Nortec Training Agency Ltd 1997–2003 (dir 1986–2003); dir S H Jones (Wine and Spirit Merchants) Ltd 2004–; pres Banbury and Dist C of C 1989–90, FCA 1967 (ACA 1965); *Recreations* theatre, music, rugby football; *Style—* Roger Hancock, Esq

HANCOCK, Stephen Clarence; s of Norman Harry Hancock, of Brymore, West Parade, Llandudno, Wales, and Jean Elaine, *née* Barlow; *b* 1 November 1955; *Educ* King Edward VI Lichfield, City of Stoke-on-Trent Sixth Form Coll, Univ of Sheffield (LLB); *Career* admitted slr 1980; ptnr Herbert Smith Slrs 1986–2009 (articled clerk 1978–80, asst slr 1980–86), dir and gen counsel Wittington Investments Ltd 2009–; memb Worshipful Co of Slrs; *Style—* Stephen Hancock, Esq; ✉ Habendum Limited, Suite B, Skyway House, Parsonage Road, Takeley, Hertfordshire CM22 6PU

HAND, Prof David John; OBE (2013); s of Peter F Hand, of Lambert's Castle, Dorset, and Olive Margaret, *née* Abbott; *b* 30 June 1950, Peterborough; *Educ* Bournemouth Sch, Univ of Oxford (BA, capt Judo Team), Univ of Southampton (MSc, PhD); *m* 13 Aug 1993, Dr Shelley L Channon; 2 da (Rachel b 24 Jan 1983, Emily b 7 Feb 1986); *Career* statistician Inst of Psychiatry 1977–88, prof of statistics and head Statistics Dept Open Univ 1988–99, prof of statistics Imperial Coll London 1999–2011 (emeritus prof of mathematics 2011–); chief scientific advsr Winton Capital Mgmnt 2010–; non-exec dir UK Statistics Authy 2013–; memb Magic Circle 2015; Thomas L Saaty Prize for Applied Advances in the Math and Mgmnt Sciences 2001, Guy Medal in Silver RSS 2002; memb Int Statistical Inst 1988; FRSS 1973, CStat 1993, Hon FIA 1999, FBA 2003; *Books* Discrimination and Classification (1981), Finite Mixture Distributions (jtly, 1981), Kernel Discriminant Analysis (1982), Artificial Intelligence and Psychiatry (1985), Multivariate Analysis of Variance and Repeated Measures: a practical guide for behavioural scientists (jtly, 1987), The Statistical Consultant in Action (jt ed, 1987), Analysis of Repeated Measures (jtly, 1990), Artificial Intelligence Frontiers in Statistics (ed, 1993), AI and Computer Power (ed, 1994), A Handbook of Small Data Sets (jt ed, 1994), Elements of Statistics (jtly, 1995), Biplots (jtly, 1996), Practical Longitudinal Data Analysis (jtly, 1996), Construction and Assessment of Classification Rules (1997), Statistics in Finance (jt ed, 1998), Intelligent Data Analysis (jt ed, 1999, 2 edn 2003), Advances in Intelligent Data Analysis, IDA-99 (jt ed, 1999), Principles of Data Mining (jtly, 2001), Advances in Intelligent Data Analysis, IDA-01 (jt ed, 2001), Pattern Detection and Discovery (jt ed, 2002), Methods and Models in Statistics (jt ed, 2004), Measurement Theory and Practice (2004), Selected Statistical Papers of Sir David Cox (jt ed, 2005), Information Generation (2007), Statistics: a Very Short Introduction (2008), ROC Curves for Continuous Data (jtly, 2009), The Improbability Principle: Why Coincidences, Miracles and Rare Events Happen Every Day (2014), The Wellbeing of Nations: Meaning, Motive and Measurement (jtly, 2014); *Recreations* magic; *Style—* Prof David Hand, OBE; ✉ Department of Mathematics, Imperial College, 180 Queen's Gate, London SW7 2AZ (☎ 020 7594 2843, e-mail d.j.hand@imperial.ac.uk)

HAND, Graham Stewart; s of Ronald Charles Hand (d 2008), and Mary Fraser Hand (d 1992); *b* 3 November 1948; *Educ* Univ of Cambridge (MA); *m* 16 June 1973, Anne Mary Seton, *née* Campbell; 1 s (Nicholas b 27 Nov 1979), 1 da (Kate b 16 April 1984); *Career* with HM Forces 1969–80; joined HM Dip Serv 1980, UK Mission to UN (New York) 1981, Br Embassy Dakar 1982–85, FCO News Dept 1985–87, Br Embassy Helsinki 1987–90, Aid Policy Dept FCO/ODA 1990–92, head of human rights FCO 1992–94, dep high cmmr Lagos 1994–97, RCDS 1997, ambass to Bosnia-Herzegovina 1998–2001, chargé d'affaires Tajikistan 2002, ambass to Algeria 2002–04; chief exec British Expertise 2004–13 (dir 2013–), dir GSH Consulting Ltd 2013–, conslt FCO 2015–; co-ordinator UK Anti-Corruption Forum 2010–15; *Publications* Human Rights in British Foreign Policy (1997), Seaford Papers; *Recreations* golf, sailing, cooking, music, singing; *Clubs* Army Sailing Association; *Style—* Graham Hand, Esq; ☎ 07766 235805, e-mail graham@gshconsulting.co.uk, website www.gshconsulting.co.uk

HAND, His Hon Judge John Lester; QC (1988); s of John James Hand (d 1965), and Violet, *née* Middleton; *b* 16 June 1947; *Educ* Huddersfield New Coll, Univ of Nottingham; *m* 1, 17 Dec 1971 (m dis 1989), Helen Andrea, *née* McWatt; m 2, 6 April 1990, Lynda (Ray) Ferrigno Hand, da of Gisbert Mills (d 1985); 1 da (Theodora Isobel b 1991); *Career* called to the Bar Gray's Inn 1972 (bencher 1996), practising barrister 1972–2008, recorder of the Crown Court 1991–2008, former head of chambers, circuit judge (SE Circuit) 2008–; memb: Mental Health Review Tbnl, Employment Appeal Tbnl; *Recreations* motorcycling, windsurfing; *Style—* His Hon Judge Hand, QC; ✉ Central London County Court, 26–29 Park Crescent, London W1B 4HT

HANDCOCK, John Eric; CVO (2002, LVO 1991), DL (Royal Co of Berks 1986); s of Eric George Handcock (d 1979), and Gladys Ada Florence, *née* Prior (d 1997), of Windsor, Berks; *b* 7 October 1930, Reading, Berks; *Educ* Aldenham, KCL (LLB); *m* 1956, (Joan) Margaret (Peggy), da of Wilfred Joseph Bigg, CMG (d 1983), of Swanage, Dorset; 2 s (David, Jonathan), 2 da (Sandra, Nicola); *Career* admitted slr 1954; sr ptnr Lovegrove and Durant of Windsor, Slough and Ascot (subsequently Lovegrove & Eliot of Windsor and Egham) 1966–95, conslt 1995–99; pres Berks, Bucks and Oxon Incorporated Law Soc 1979–80, dir Solicitors' Benevolent Assoc 1981–88, pt/t chm Social Security Appeals Tbnls 1992–2000; Nat Assoc of Round Tables of GB and NI: chm Thames Valley Area 1964–65, memb Nat Cncl 1966–68, nat exec convenor Rules and Special Purposes 1968–70; pres Windsor District Chamber of Commerce 1960–61, 1961–62, 2012–13 and 2013–14; chm Berks Bucks and Oxon Prof Cncl 1981–82; govr: Upton House Sch Windsor 1965–99, St George's Choir Sch Windsor Castle 1975–96; capt lay stewards St George's Chapel Windsor Castle 1992–2010 (dep capt 1977–92, lay steward emeritus 2010–), tstee Prince Philip Tst for Windsor and Maidenhead 1977–2007 (hon sec 1977–2002); pres Windsor and Eton Operatic Soc 1961–, hon slr River Thames Soc 1962–2002 (life memb 1986, vice-pres 2003–06), pres Windsor Advsy Centre 1970–2011, patron Windsor and Eton Sea Cadets 1994–, life pres Windsor Local History Gp 2002, pres Friends of King Edward VII Hosp 2004–14, vice-pres Windsor Eton Choral Soc 2004–; Paul Harris fell Rotary International 1994; Freeman City of London 1984, Liveryman Worshipful Co of Spectacle Makers 2002–16 (Freeman 1984); Citoyen d'Honneur de la Ville Royale de Dreux 1976; *Publications* The Institute that Became an Institution: The History of the Royal Albert Institute and its Trust (2005), The Rotary Club of Windsor and Eton: The First 75 Years 1931–2006 (2006); *Recreations* history, European travel, wine, books; *Style—* John E Handcock, Esq, CVO, DL; ✉ Red Deer House, Kingswood Rise, Englefield Green, Surrey TW20 0NG (☎ 01784 434289)

HANDELSMAN, Harry; *b* Munich; *Children* 2 da (Maya Bodinger, Allegra Handelsman); *Career* fndr Manhattan Loft Corp 1992–, ptnr Ealing Studios; developer behind: Chiltern Firehouse, Bankside Lofts, Soho Lofts, Fitzrovia Apartments, Hackney Fashion Hub; responsible for restoration of St Pancras Renaissance Hotel (opened 2011), currently working on Manhattan Loft Gardens; Hon FRIBA; *Style—* Harry Handelsman, Esq; ✉ Manhattan Loft Corporation Ltd, Edison House, 223–231 Old Marylebone Road, London NW1 5QT

HANDLEY, Dr Anthony James; s of Wing Cdr Austyn James Handley, RAF (d 1985), of West Mersea, Essex, and Beryl Janet, *née* Ashling (d 1982); *b* 22 June 1942; *Educ* Kimbolton Sch, KCL, Westminster Hosp Med Sch (MB BS, MD), DipIMC RCS(Ed); *m* 3 Dec 1966, Jennifer Ann, da of Noël Lindsay Ross Kane (d 1986), of Colchester, Essex; 1 da (Juliette b 1971), 1 s (Simon b 1973); *Career* Maj RAMC (TA) 1970–94; conslt physician (cardiology) Colchester Hosp Univ NHS Fndn Tst (formerly NE Essex HA then Essex Rivers Healthcare NHS Tst) 1974–2002 (hon conslt physician 2003–), hon clinical tutor Charing Cross and Westminster Med Sch 1976–2002, clinical tutor Colchester Postgrad Med Centre 1980–85; chm: Basic Life Support Sub-Ctee Int Liaison Ctee on Resuscitation 1996–2005, Resuscitation Cncl (UK) 1997–2000 (hon sec 1986–97), Basic Life Support Sub-Ctee Resuscitation Cncl (UK) 2000–10, Basic Life Support Int Course Ctee European Resuscitation Cncl 2006–10; chief med advsr RLSS (UK) 1992–, hon med offr Irish Water Safety 2000–, conslt advsr British Airways; co sec and dir Resuscitation Cncl (UK) Trading Ltd; hon treas and dir European Resuscitation Cncl 2011–; memb: Br Cardiac Soc 1984, Editorial Bd Resuscitation; FRSM 1985, FRCP 1985; OStJ 1992; *Books* Thoracic Medicine (contrib, 1981), Life Support (ed, 1992, 5 edn 2006), Advanced Life Support (ed, 1994), ABC of Resuscitation (ed, 2003); *Recreations* swimming, music (euphonium player), beekeeping; *Style—* Dr Anthony J Handley; ✉ Hillcrest Cottage, Bartlow Road, Hadstock, Cambridge, CB21 4PF (☎ 01223 890999, e-mail tony.handley@outlook.com)

HANDLEY, Martin Hugh; s of Dr William Richard Cecil Handley (d 1997), and Irene Jessie, *née* Edwards (d 2010); *b* 8 July 1951, Oxford; *Educ* Bedales, CCC Cambridge (MA); *m* 1, 6 July 1974 (m dis 2000), Anne, *née* Clayton; 1 s (David Christopher b 17 Sept 1982), 1 da (Mika Elisabeth b 24 July 1984); m 2, 26 June 2009 (m dis 2016), Sarah Louise, *née* Walker; *Partner* Sally Scott; *Career* chorusmaster and conductor Australian Opera 1981–84, chorusmaster and conductor ENO 1984–90, head of music and conductor Royal Danish Opera 1997–99, princ conductor Carl Rosa Opera 2004–; music dir CoOpera Co 2012–15, music dir Tarantara 2015–; presenter: BBC World Service 1985–, BBC Radio 3 1998–; guest coach: Young Artists Prog ROH 2002–, Nat Opera Studio 2006–, Royal Acad of Music 2007–; *Recreations* Sussex countryside, food, wine, travel, Oxford United FC; *Style—* Mr Martin Handley; ✉ c/o BBC Radio 3, BBC Broadcasting House, London W1A 1AA (e-mail martin.handley@bbc.co.uk)

HANDOVER, Richard Gordon; CBE (2008); s of Gordon Frank James (d 1991), and Hilda, *née* Dyke (d 1981); *b* 13 April 1946, South Africa; *m* 1972, Veronica Joan, da of Arthur Woodhead; 2 da (Felicity Kate b 29 Jan 1979, Alexandra Veronica b 8 Feb 1981), 1 s (James Richard Nicholas b 9 Feb 1984); *Career* WHSmith: joined 1964, md Our Price 1989, md WHSmith News 1995, memb Bd 1995–2005, gp chief exec 1997–2003, chm 2003–05; chm Alexon plc 2008–; non-exec dir: Nationwide Building Soc 2000–07, Royal Mail Holdings plc 2003–; chm: Educn Leadership Team Business in the Community 1999–2008, Adult Learning Inspectorate 2001–07; *Recreations* tennis, golf, painting, running, travelling; *Style—* Richard Handover, Esq, CBE; ✉ e-mail r.handover@btinternet.com; Alexon Group plc, 40–48 Guildford Street, Luton LU1 2PB

HANDS, Rt Hon Greg; MP; *b* 1965, NY; *Educ* Dr Challoner's GS, Univ of Cambridge; *m* Irina; 1 da (b Feb 2006), 1 s (b July 2007); *Career* worked in banking until 1997, cnclr Hammersmith and Fulham BC 1998–2006 (ldr Cons Gp 1999–2003); MP (Cons): Hammersmith and Fulham 2005–10, Chelsea and Fulham 2010–; chief sec to the Treasy 2015–; memb: Cons Way Forward (CWF), Cons Friends of Israel, Fulham Soc, Chelsea Soc, Fulham and Hammersmith Historical Soc, Hammersmith and Fulham Historic Buildings Gp; *Clubs* Carlton, Chelsea Arts; *Style—* The Rt Hon Greg Hands, MP; ✉ House of Commons, London SW1A 0AA (website www.greghands.com)

HANDS, Guy; s of Christopher Hands, and Sally Hands; *b* 27 August 1959; *Educ* Judd Sch Tonbridge, Mansfield Coll Oxford (MA); *m* 1984, Julia Caroline, *née* Ablethorpe; 2 s, 2 da; *Career* head of Eurobond trading Goldman Sachs 1982–94 (trading 1986, head Global Asset Structuring Gp 1990), fndr and md Principal Finance Gp Nomura International plc 1994–2001, chm Terra Firma Capital Partners Ltd 2002–; *Recreations* films, wine, fine art, photography; *Style—* Guy Hands, Esq; ✉ Terra Firma, Capital Management Ltd, Royal Chambers, St Julian's Avenue, St Peter Port, Guernsey GY1 3RE (☎ 01481 754690)

HANDS, Philip; s of Christopher Dawson Hands, and Sally Frances, *née* Partridge; *b* 11 December 1962, Taplow, Bucks; *Educ* Judd Sch Tonbridge, Univ of Nottingham (LLB); *m* 21 Jan 1995, Samantha Dorothy, *née* Mayers; 1 s (Gage Stanley b 9 Aug 1999), 1 da (Octavia Jean b 9 Jan 2002); *Career* Beachcroft LLP (formerly Wansbroughs Willey Hargrave, then Beachcroft Wansbroughs): slr 1988–96, ptnr 1996–2007; princ Hands Law 2007–08, dir Hands Law Ltd 2008–11, chm Villa Saletta 2008–, ptnr Star Legal LLP 2011–14, dir Star Legal Ltd 2014–; memb: Law Soc 1988, Property Litigation Assoc 2000; *Recreations* cycling, sailing, skiing, golf; *Style—* Philip Hands, Esq; ✉ Star Legal Limited, 3 Richmond Hill, Clifton, Bristol BS8 1AT

HANDS, Terry; CBE (2007); *b* 9 January 1941; *Educ* Univ of Birmingham (BA), RADA; *m* 1, 1964 (m dis 1967), Josephine Barstow (now Dame Josephine Barstow, DBE, *qv*); m 2, 1974, (m dis 1980), Ludmila Mikael; 1 da (Marina); partner, 1988–96, Julia Lintott; 2 s (Sebastian, Rupert); m 3, 2002, Emma Lucia; *Career* theatre and opera director; fndr dir Liverpool Everyman Theatre 1964–66; RSC: artistic dir Theatreground (touring schs and community centres) 1966–68, assoc dir 1967, jt artistic dir 1978, chief exec 1986–91, dir emeritus 1991–; dir Clwyd Theatr Cymru 1997–2015; Hon DLitt Middlesex Univ, Hon DLitt Univ of Birmingham, Hon DLitt Univ of Liverpool, Hon PhD; hon fell: Shakespeare Inst, Welsh Coll of Music and Drama 2002, Glyndwr Univ, Bangor Univ; Chevalier de l'Ordre des Arts et des Lettres (France); *Theatre* dir many prodns for RSC incl: The Merry Wives of Windsor 1968 (revived 1975/76), Pericles 1969, Henry V, Henry IV Parts I and 2 (all transfered to Aldwych (centenary season Stratford)) 1975, Henry VI (all 3 parts, Stratford (1st time in entirety since Shakespeare's day, SWET Award for Dir of the Year)) 1977, Coriolanus 1977, As You Like It, Richard II and Richard III (the latter two completing the entire Shakespeare history cycle, begun 1975, with Alan Howard in leading roles, Stratford) 1982, Much Ado About Nothing (Stratford) 1982, Poppy (Musical of the Year), Cyrano de Bergerac (SWET Award for Best Dir, Barbican) 1983, Red Noses 1985, Singer 1989, The Seagull 1990, Tamburlaine (Evening Standard Award for Best Dir, transferred to Barbican) 1992–93, The Importance of Being Earnest (Birmingham Rep and Old Vic) 1995; for Clwyd Theatr Cymru: The Importance of Being Earnest 1997, Equus 1997, A Christmas Carol 1997, The Journey of Mary Kelly, The Norman Conquests 1998, Twelfth Night 1999, Macbeth 1999, Under Milk Wood 1999, Private Lives 2000, King Lear 2001, Bedroom Farce 2001, The Rabbit 2001, Rosencrantz and Guildenstern are Dead 2002, Betrayal 2002, Romeo and Juliet 2002, The Four Seasons 2002, Blithe Spirit 2003, The Crucible 2003, Pleasure and Repentance 2003, One Flew Over the

Cuckoo's Nest 2004, Brassed Off 2004, Troilus and Cressida 2005, Chorus of Disapproval 2006, Memory 2006, Arcadia 2007, Cherry Orchard 2007, Macbeth 2008, Noises Off 2009, Mary Stuart 2009, Pygmalion 2009, Arden of Faversham 2010, A Small Family Business 2010, Blackthorn 2011, The Taming of the Shrew 2011, As You Like It 2012, Boeing, Boeing 2012, The Winslow Boy 2013, Under Milk Wood 2014, Hamlet 2015; other credits incl: Richard III (Comedie Française) 1972 (Meilleur Spectacle de L'Année), Twelfth Night 1976 (Meilleur Spectacle de L'Année), Othello (Paris Opera, televised France 1978), Parsifal (Royal Opera House) 1979, Arden of Faversham (Schauspielhaus Zürich) 1992, Buffalo Bill Show (Recklinghausen) 1992, Simon Boccanegra (Bremen) 1992, Sag Mir Wo Die Blumen Sind (Berlin) 1993, Hamlet (Paris) 1994, Hadrian VII and The Visit (Chichester Festival Theatre) 1995, Merry Wives of Windsor (RNT 1995, NT Oslo 1995), The Pretenders (NT Oslo) 1996, The Seagull (NT Oslo) 1998, Macbeth (New York) 2000; conslt dir: Comedie Française 1975–80, Troilus and Cressida (Burgtheater Vienna) 1977, As You Like It (Burgtheater Vienna) 1979, Hamlet (Chicago Shakespeare Theatre) 2006; *Style*— Terry Hands, Esq, CBE; ✉ Clwyd Theatr Cymru, Mold, Flintshire CH7 1YA (☎ 01352 756 331)

HANDS, Dr Timothy Roderick; s of Roderick Kirton Hands (d 2015), and Catherine Ella, *née* Walker (d 2005); *b* 30 March 1956, London; *Educ* Emanuel Sch Battersea, Guildhall Sch of Music and Drama, KCL (BA, William Stebbing Prize, J S Brewer Prize, Early English Text Soc Prize, L M Faithful Prize, First Leathes Prize, Jelf Medallist), St Catherine's Coll Oxford (sr scholar), Oriel Coll Oxford (DPhil, R W B Burton sr scholar); *m* 9 April 1988, Jane Elizabeth Morrison, da of Ian Smart, of Wootton, Oxon, and Ann Smart (d 2010); 2 s (Nicholas b 31 July 1993, Edward b 15 July 1995); *Career* stipendiary lectr Oriel Coll Oxford 1985–86, asst master King's Sch Canterbury 1986–94 (housemaster Galpin's 1990–94), second master Whitgift Sch Croydon 1994–97, headmaster Portsmouth GS 1997–2007, master Magdalen Coll Sch 2007–16, headmaster Winchester 2016–; conductor Schola Cantorum of Oxford 1982–85, tstee Portmouth Cathedral 1999–2005, founding chm Portsmouth Festivities 2000–07 (chm of tstees and Bd of Dirs 2006–07, patron 2007–), bishop's rep Portsmouth Cathedral Cncl 2001–05, founding chm Oxford Festival of the Arts 2015–; memb: Admiralty Interview Bd 1998–2004, Editorial Bd Conference and Common Room 2000–12, ISC Working Gp on Access to Ind Educn 2000–03, DFES Independent State Sch Partnership Forum 2002–04, HMC and GSA Univs Ctee 2003–12 (co-chair 2005–12), Ctee HMC 2003– (chm S Central Div 2004–05, chm elect 2012–13, chm 2013–14, vice-chm 2014–15), External Advsy Bd Faculty of English Univ of Oxford 2006–, Ct Univ of Leicester 2008– ; tstee HMS Warrior 1860 2003–07; memb Cncl: Alleyn's Sch Dulwich 2005–08, Our Lady's Sch Abingdon 2007–12, Cheltenham Ladies Coll 2008–09, St Mary's Calne 2009–15, Bedales 2010–; AKC; *Books* A George Eliot Chronology (1989), Thomas Hardy: Distracted Preacher (1989), A Hardy Chronology (1992), Thomas Hardy: Writers in Their Time (1995), Ideas to Assemble (2006); author of chapters in books on Thomas Hardy, and of educational, literary and musical articles, editions and reviews; *Recreations* classical music, sport (especially rugby and cricket), writing; *Clubs* East India, Lansdowne; *Style*— Dr Timothy Hands; ✉ Witham Close, 62 Kingsgate Street, Winchester, SO23 9PF (☎ 01962 621100)

HANDY, Charles Brian; CBE (2000); s of Ven Brian Leslie Handy, Archdeacon of Kildare, and Joan Kathleen Herbert, *née* Scott; *b* 25 July 1932; *Educ* Bromsgrove Sch, Oriel Coll Oxford (MA), MIT (SM); *m* 5 Oct 1962, Elizabeth Ann, da of Lt-Col Rowland Fenwick Ellis Hill (d 1978); 1 da (Kate b 1966), 1 s (Scott b 1968); *Career* mktg exec Shell International Petroleum Co Ltd 1956–65, economist Charter Consolidated Co Ltd 1965–66, int faculty fell MIT 1966–67, London Business Sch 1967–95 (prof 1978–94), warden St George's House Windsor Castle 1977–81, writer and broadcaster 1981–; chm RSA 1986–88, memb CNAA 1988–91; Lifetime Achievement Award Thinkers 50 (2011), Irish Presidential Award for Overseas Service 2015; Hon DLitt: Bristol Poly 1988, UEA, Univ of Essex 2000, Univ of Hull 2000, Univ of Roehampton 2014; Hon DUniv Open Univ 1989, Hon DPhil Univ of Middlesex 1998; Hon DSc: Queen's Univ Belfast 1998, Univ of Exeter 1999; Hon DCL Univ of Durham 2000, Hon Dr Univ of Dublin 2006; hon fell: St Mary's Coll Twickenham 1999, Inst of Educn Univ of London 1999, City & Guilds 2000, Oriel Coll Oxford 2000; *Books* Understanding Organizations (1983), Future of Work (1984), Gods of Management (1985), Understanding Schools (1986), Understanding Voluntary Organizations (1988), The Age of Unreason (1989), Inside Organisations (1990), The Empty Raincoat (1994), Waiting for the Mountain to Move (1995), Beyond Certainty (1995), The Hungry Spirit (1997), The New Alchemists (1999), Thoughts for the Day (1999), The Elephant and the Flea (2001), Reinvented Lives (2002), Myself and Other Important Matters (2006), The New Philanthropists (2006), The Second Curve (2015); *Recreations* theatre, cooking, travel; *Style*— Charles Handy, Esq, CBE; ✉ Flat 2, 73 Putney Hill, London SW15 3NT (☎ 020 8788 1610, mobile 07932 062436); Old Hall Cottages, Bressingham, Diss, Norfolk IP22 2AG (☎ 01379 687546)

HANGARTNER, Dr (John) Robert Wilfred; s of John Hangartner, and Ita Patricia, *née* Brett; *b* 5 February 1955; *Educ* Merchant Taylors', Guy's Hosp Med Sch Univ of London (BSc, MB BS, MRCS, LRCP), Open Univ (MBA); *m* 1980, Jillian Mary, da of Martin Frederick Ansell; 1 da (Caroline Emma b 27 Feb 1987), 1 s (Christopher Robert b 12 May 1991); *Career* house offr gen med Lewisham Hosp 1979–80, SHO Guy's Hosp 1980–81 (house offr gen surgery 1980); St George's Hosp: SHO 1981–82, registrar (pathology) 1982–83, clinical lectr in histopathology Med Sch 1983–88; hon sr registrar SW Thames RHA 1983–88; Dept of Health: sr med offr 1988–91, sr princ med offr and divnl head 1993–97 (temp princ med offr 1991–93); CMO Guardian Health Ltd 1997–2000, sr med exec PPP Healthcare Ltd 1998–2000; princ dir Brett Cook Consulting Ltd 2001–15, clinical dir GSTS Pathology LLP 2009–14, clinical dir Viapath LLP 2014–; Guy's and St Thomas' NHS Fndn Tst: conslt pathologist (renal histopathology) 2002–, clinical dir Diagnostic and Therapeutic Services Directorate 2004, divnl dir Core Clinical Servs Div 2004–06; hon CMO Bass Healthcare Trustee Ltd 1998–2000; chm Hospital Jr Staff Ctee BMA 1984–85; former memb: Cncl BMA, Bd of Educn and Science BMA; FRSA 1994, FRCPath 1997 (MRCPath 1988); *Recreations* photography, sailing; *Style*— Dr Robert Hangartner; ✉ Brett Cook Consulting Ltd, 11 Annesley Road, Blackheath, London SE3 0JX (☎ 020 8319 3164, fax 020 8319 8775, e-mail jrwh5@mac.com)

HANHAM, Baroness (Life Peer UK 1999), of Kensington in the Royal Borough of Kensington and Chelsea; Joan Brownlow Hanham; CBE (1997); da of Alfred Spark, of Newcastle upon Tyne; *b* 23 September 1939; *Educ* Hillcourt Sch Dublin; *m* 1964, Dr Iain William Ferguson Hanham, s of Charles Hanham (d 2011); 1 s (Hon James Charles b 1971), 1 da (Hon Emma Margaret Juhasz b 1973); *Career* cncllr Royal Borough of Kensington and Chelsea (ldr 1989–2000); shadow min for local govt 2002–07, shadow min Home Office 2007–09, shadow min for transport 2009–10, Parly under-sec of state Dept for Communities and Local Govt 2010–; chm English Volunteering Devpt Cncl 2002–09, pres Volunteering England 2009–10, chm St Mary's Hosp Paddington 2000–07; *Style*— The Rt Hon the Baroness Hanham, CBE

HANKES, Sir Claude; KCVO (2006); *b* 8 March 1949; *Career* marco-strategic advsr; Manufacturers Hanover 1968–72, Robert Fleming & Co Ltd 1972–77 (dir 1974–77), dep chm Leutwiler and Partners Ltd 1992–96; chm: Mgmnt Ctee Price Waterhouse and Partners 1983–89, Shaw & Bradley Ltd 1993–, Advsy Ctee to Jordan on Strategic Policy Matters 1993–94; interim chm Roland Berger Strategy Consultants Ltd 2003–05; advsr: to Iraq 2003, to Governing Cncl Iraq 2003–04, to Iraq on macro strategic issues 2005–, Trade Bank of Iraq 2007–; masterminded resolution to South African debt crisis 1985–86, Nobel Report 1991, testified at US Congress on UN Oil for Food scandal 2004; tstee: Windsor Leadership Tst 1998–2007 (chm 2000–07), Hawthornden Int Retreat For Writers 2008–10; St George's House Annual Lecture: 'There is no answer without the wisdom of understanding' 2014; hon memb Coll of St George Windsor Castle, hon fell and life memb Cncl St George's House Windsor Castle 2006, hon fell CCC Oxford; *Recreations* photography (Jamie Hanks), gardening, reading; *Clubs* Turf; *Style*— Sir Claude Hankes, KCVO; ✉ e-mail officesirclaude@gmail.com

HANKEY, Dr the Hon Alexander Maurice Alers; s of 2 Baron Hankey, KCMG, KCVO (d 1996); hp of bro 3 Baron Hankey, *qv*; *b* 18 August 1947; *Educ* Rugby, Trinity Coll Cambridge, MIT (PhD), MERU (MSCI); *m* 1970 (m dis 1990), Deborah, da of Myron Benson, of Mass, USA; *Career* Greenlaw fell MIT 1969–71, Lindemann fellowship 1972–73 (held at Stanford Linear Accelerator Center), teacher of transcendental meditation 1973; Maharishi Int Univ USA: asst prof of physics 1973–74, associate prof 1974–75, prof 1975–78; prof of physics Maharishi Euro Res Univ of Switzerland and UK 1975–82, govr Age of Enlightenment 1977–, co dir Acad for the Sci of Creative Intelligence Mass 1978, dean Faculty Maharishi Int Academy UK 1985–86, registrar Maharishi Univ of Natural Law North of England Campus 1986–92, exec asst to Dr Geoffrey Clements 1998–2002, distinguished prof of yoga and physical sci Swami Vivekananda Yoga Anusandhana Samsthana (SVYASA) Bangalore 2007–, sr advsr Manipal Universal Learning Bangalore 2007; dean of foreign academic studies Indian Inst of Ayurveda Integrative Med 2009–11; memb Int Advsy Bd Inst of Applied Dermatology Kerala 2007–10; memb Editorial Bd: Jl of Alternative and Complementary Med 2003 (assoc ed 2009–), Evidence Based Complimentary and Alternative Medicine (eCAM) 2004–07, Int Jl of Yoga 2007–; exec ed Jl of Ayurveda Integrative Med 2009–11; Leverhulme Fndn res award 1986; chm East Grinstead TM Centre 1993–2007, memb Exec Cncl Natural Law Party of GB 1992–2001, sec Natural Law Pty of Sussex 1994–97; *Publications* The Sun's First Rays (poems); author of numerous scientific papers and articles particularly in critical phenomena, biophysics of complementary med and self-observing quantum systems; *Recreations* skiing, tennis, hiking; *Clubs* Royal Tennis; *Style*— Dr the Hon Alexander Hankey; ☎ 07710 534195 and 00 91 900 800 8789, e-mail alexhankey@gmail.com

HANKEY, 3 Baron (UK 1939); Donald Robin Alers Hankey; s of 2 Baron Hankey, KCMG, KCVO (d 1996), and his 1 w, Frances Bevyl, *née* Stuart-Menteth (d 1957); *b* 12 June 1938; *Educ* Rugby, UCL (Dip Arch); *m* 1, 1963 (m dis 1974), Margaretha, yr da of Cand Jur H Thorndahl, of Copenhagen, Denmark; m 2, 1974 (m dis 1994), Eileen Désirée, da of Maj-Gen Stuart Hedley Molesworth Battye, CB, of Fensacre House, Ascot, Berks; 2 da (Hon Fiona Bevyl b 1975, Hon Beatrice Eileen b 1978); m 3, 9 July 1994, June, da of late Dr Leonard Taboroff, and of Mrs Elsie Taboroff, of Palo Alto, CA; 1 s adopted (Hugh Michael Alers b 4 May 1997); *Heir* bro, Dr the Hon Alexander Hankey, *qv*; *Career* fndr chm: Intercol 1969, Intercol Int 1970, Gilmore Hankey Kirke (GHK) 1973–2000, Gilmore Hankey Kirke SA Paris 1974–80; conslt to: HRH King Khalid's Meml Mosque 1985–88, World Bank of Pakistan 1988–92, China 1992–2011 (Liaoning Urban Devpt, Shenyang, Ningbo, Cicheng, Shaoxing Cities conservation and regeneration, Lijiang post-earthquake reconstruction and conservation, Qongqing historic environment conservation, Leshan Grand Buddha World Heritage, WH Cities of Qufu and Zoucheng regeneration), St Petersburg 1996–97, ODA Calcutta Environmental Mgmnt and Action Plan 1996–98, cities of Shibam Zebid and San'a Yemen 1998–99, EU Sustainable Mgmnt of Built Heritage of Paramaribo 2000–01, Strategy and Action Plan for the Antiquities and Museums Sectors for the Supreme Cmmn for Tourism Surinam 2003–04, USAID Assessment of Dept of Antiquities and Proposals for a New Strategic Framework Jordan 2005, devpt of strategy for heritage mgmnt and strengthening Dept of Antiquities Jordan 2006–07, planning and architecture of Salt and Madaba Jordan, Moscow Convent of Sts Martha and Mary conservation architecture and reuse, Sharjah Conservation Masterplan of Central Region, Tate Gallery, Nat Maritime Museum, Nat History Museum, Banqueting House Whitehall, 6/7 Old Palace Yard, Admiralty Arch, Grange Northington, Lulworth Castle, Windsor Castle, Ashton Court Mansion, Bristol Harbourside, policy and planning of historical core of Yangon Myanmar 2015; fndr and chm All-Pty Gp on Architecture and Planning 1997–2000; pres ICOMOS (UK) 2007–13 (vice-chm 1997–2007), vice-chm MOD (Defence Estates Orgn) Historic Building Advsy Gp 1998–2003, chm Historic Building Advsy Gp Dept of the Environment, Community and Local Govt Repub of Ireland 2008–10; memb: ASCHB; RIBA, FRSA, FRAI, FSA; *Publications* Report on the Development of New Seville Jamaica (1991), Conservation in Pakistan (1992), The Walled City of Lahore (1993), Principles for the Recording of Monuments Groups of Buildings and Sites (1996), Cultural Heritage Protection Project for Yemen (1998), The City of Ningbo (1999), The City of Li Jiang (1999), Principles for the Management of the Historic Environment (2001), Strategy and Action Plan for the Antiquities and Museums of Kingdom of Saudi Arabia (2004), Overview of the Urban Heritage Sector in China (2005), Assessment of Department of Antiquities and Proposals for New Strategic Framework (2005); *Recreations* tennis, painting, music; *Clubs* RSA; *Style*— The Rt Hon the Lord Hankey; ✉ 8 Sunset Road, London SE5 8EA (☎ 020 7733 0453, mobile 07887 942431, e-mail hankeyd100@gmail.com)

HANLEY, Rt Hon Sir Jeremy James; KCMG (1997), PC (1994); s of Jimmy Hanley (d 1970), and Dinah Sheridan; *b* 17 November 1945; *Educ* Rugby; *m* 1, 1968 (m dis), Helene; 1 s (Jason b 1970); m 2, 1973, Verna, Viscountess Villiers, da of Kenneth Stott (d 1992), of Jersey; 1 s (Joel b 1974), 1 step da (Lady Sophia b 1971); *Career* CA; MP (Cons) Richmond and Barnes 1983–97 (Parly candidate (Cons) Lambeth Central (by-election) 1978 and 1979); vice-chm Cons Trade and Industry Ctee, memb House of Commons Select Ctee on Home Affrs; former memb: House of Commons Select Sub-Ctee on Race Relations and Immigration, Br-Irish Inter Parly Body; former sec All-Pty Gp for Europe; PPS to: Min of State at Privy Cncl Office, Min for Civil Serv and the Arts (Rt Hon Richard Luce, MP) 1987–90, Sec of State for the Environment (Rt Hon Christopher Patten, MP) 1990; Parly under-sec of state NI Office 1990–93 (min for Health, Social Servs and Agriculture 1990–92, min for Political Devpt, Educn and Community Relations 1992–93), min of state for Armed Forces MOD 1993–94, chm Cons Pty 1994–95, Cabinet min without portfolio 1994–95, min of state (for N Africa, ME, Indian Sub-Continent, SE Asia, Far East and Pacific, Overseas Trade) FCO 1995–97; Parly advsr Inst of CAs in England and Wales 1986–90; chm: International Trade & Investment Missions Ltd 1997–2002, AdVal Group plc 1998–2003, Brain Games Network plc 2000; non-exec dir: ITE Group plc 1998–2008, GTECH Hldgs Corp Inc 2001–06, Willis Towers Watson 2006–, Langbar Int Ltd 2006–, Blue Hackle Ltd 2006–10, Lottomatica SpA 2008–11, Nymex London Ltd 2008–09, Mountfield Gp plc 2008–09, Willis Ltd 2008–, London Asia Capital plc 2011–; sr conslt Kroll Assocs 2003–04; memb: Euro Advsy Bd Credit Lyonnais 2000–05, Advsy Bd Talal Abu-Ghazaleh International 2004–05; vice-pres Br-Iranian C of C 2002–06 (chm 2000–02); memb Bd Arab-Br C of C 1998–2011; Freeman City of London, Master Worshipful Co of CAs 2005–06, Liveryman Dyer's Co; FCA, FCIS; *Recreations* cookery, cricket, chess, languages, the arts; *Clubs* Lord's Taverners, Garrick, Pilgrims, Saints & Sinners; *Style*— The Rt Hon Sir Jeremy Hanley, KCMG; ✉ 6 Butts Mead, Northwood, Middlesex HA6 2TL (☎ 01923 826675)

HANLEY-BROWNE, Mark David; s of Alan Hanley-Browne, of Walton-on-Thames, Surrey, and Eileen, *née* Hankin; *b* 19 October 1961, Crawley, W Sussex; *Educ* St George's Coll Weybridge, Lady Margaret Hall Oxford (exhibitioner, MA), Homerton Coll Cambridge (PGCE); *m* 10 July 1993, Rachael, *née* Scott; *Career* asst master and biology teacher Sevenoaks Sch 1983–88, asst master and head of careers and HE Charterhouse 1988–97, dep head (pastoral) Highgate Sch 1997–2004, headmaster Emanuel Sch London 2004–;

fell commoner (sabbatical) St John's Coll Cambridge 1995; memb HMC 2004– (chair London HMC 2011–12, memb Univs Ctee 2015–); memb Guild of Freemen City of London; *Recreations* writing, travel, wine appreciation; *Clubs* East India, RAF, Lansdowne, Athenaeum; *Style*— Mark Hanley-Browne, Esq; ✉ Emanuel School, Battersea Rise, London SW11 1HS (☎ 020 8870 4171, fax 020 8877 1424, e-mail hm@emanuel.org.uk)

HANLEY-RYDER, Shirley Ann; *née* Farnworth; da of late Gerard Farnworth, and late Renee Winifred, *née* Royds; *b* 2 October 1956, Blackburn, Lancs; *Educ* Notre Dame GS Blackburn, Univ of Leicester (BSc); *m* 1, 25 June 1983 (m dis 1998), Dermot Joseph Hanley, s of Dr Donal Aloysius Hanley, and late Honora Eileen, *née* O'Mahony; 3 s (Christopher Jon b 17 May 1987, William Gerard b 5 March 1990, Simon James b 22 Jan 1992); m 2, 12 Jan 2002, Stephen Albert Ryder, s of late William Albert Ryder, and late Doris, *née* Hardy; *Career* grad trainee rising to PR account exec Octagon Marketing Consultants Ltd 1979–82, sr PR exec Byron Advertising Ltd 1982–84; QBO plc (latterly Bell Pottinger Ltd): campaign mangr 1984–86, campaign dir 1986–87, associate dir 1987–89, bd dir 1989, dep md 1991–2002; fndr: The Hanley Ryder Partnership 2002, EmPower Engagement Mktg Ltd 2004; ceo Grayling Int Moscow 2010–11, regnl dir Grayling Eurasia and SE Europe 2011–; independent PR advsr 2013–; MCIPR 1988; *Recreations* tennis, travel, entertaining, family life; *Style*— Mrs Shirley Hanley-Ryder; ✉ 21 Talbot Avenue, Bournemouth BH3 7HS (☎ 07836 514409, e-mail shirley@hr-p.co.uk)

HANNA, Hon Mr Justice Michael Anthony Patrick; s of Francis Hanna (d 1987), of Belfast and Dublin, and Mary Ida, *née* Conboy (d 1999); *b* 18 July 1953, Belfast; *Educ* St MacNissi's Coll Garron Tower, TCD (BA, LLB), King's Inns Dublin; *m* 2 Jan 1981, Philomena, *née* Connolly; 4 s (Francis b 22 Feb 1982, Michael b 24 May 1983, Patrick b 1 Aug 1984, Leo b 19 Oct 1994), 1 da (Aoife Maria b 14 Oct 1988); *Career* called to the Bar King's Inns Dublin 1977 (bencher), called to the Inner Bar 1996; judge of the High Court of Ireland 2004–; *Recreations* walking, travel, golf, reading, music, cinema; *Clubs* Kildare St and Univ, Skibereen Golf, Baltimore Sailing; *Style*— The Hon Mr Justice Michael Hanna; ✉ The High Court, Four Courts, Inns Quay, Dublin 7, Ireland (☎ 00 353 1 888 6000, fax 00 353 1 872 5669, e-mail michaelhanna@courts.ie)

HANNAFORD, Barry William; s of Albert Edward Hannaford (d 1984), and Ethel, *née* Cesana; *b* 25 June 1953; *m* Rowena; *Career* trainee lighting engr Thorn Lighting Ltd 1970–75, lighting engr Concord Lighting Ltd 1975–76 (dep mangr 1977–80), project sales mangr Erco Lighting Ltd 1980–85, dir Lighting Design Partnership 1987–96 (assoc 1985–86), ptnr DPA Lighting Conslts 1996– (dir DPA Dubai 2005–); noteable projects incl: James Bond film set Pinewood Studios, Newport and Sequoia Lodge Disney Hotels Paris, Opus Sacrum Warsaw, Hyatt Hotels, Palm Jumeirah Lighting Masterplan, Jansui Restaurant Burj al Arab, Arcapita HQ and Mosque Bahrain; *Publications* Lighting Design (jtly, Design Cncl); *Style*— Barry Hannaford, Esq

HANNAH, Christine Margaret (Chris); da of Robert Edwin Davies (decd), of Widnes, Cheshire, and Marion, *née* Rowley; *b* 9 October 1954; *Educ* Wade Deacon GS for Girls Widnes (head girl), Inst of Personnel Mgmnt, Lancaster Univ (MA); *m* 1, 27 March 1982, Philip Stephen Hannah (decd); 1 s (Benjamin Philip), 1 da (Charlotte Faye); m 2, 7 Sept 2006, Neil Goodwin; *Career* mgmnt trainee Marks & Spencer 1973–74, mgmnt trainee Mersey RHA 1974–75, dir of personnel Halton HA 1978–88, dir of personnel Chester HA 1988–90, head of HR Mersey RHA 1990–93, chief exec S Cheshire HA 1993–96, dir of strategic devpt NW Regnl Office NHS 1996–2001, chief exec Cheshire and Merseyside Strategic HA 2002–06, chair Skills for Health (sector skills cncl UK health sector) 2004–, dir Goodwin Hannah Ltd 2006–; *Recreations* theatre, literature, political history, travel; *Style*— Ms Chris Hannah; ✉ The Old School, Windmill Lane, Preston on the Hill, Warrington, Cheshire WA4 4AZ (☎ 01928 713932, fax 01928 716927, mobile 07867 538107, e-mail chris@goodwinhannah.co.uk)

HANNAH, David Stuart; s of Daniel Hannah, of Appleton, Warrington, and Phyllis, *née* Mottershead; *b* 1 January 1953; *Educ* Royal GS Lancaster, Univ of Liverpool (LLB); *Children* 1 da (Louise b 1979), 3 s (Daniel b 1981, Christopher b 1983, Michael b 1987); *Career* admitted slr 1977; tutor in law of equity and trusts Univ of Liverpool 1974–78; memb Legal Aid Area Ctee Chester 1981–, chm Educn Ctee Slrs Family Law Soc 1996–97; memb Nat Ctee SFLA 1996–97, fndr Ctee memb Br Assoc of Lawyer Mediators 1995, examiner and assessor to Law Soc Family Law Panel, memb Family Law Ctee Law Soc 1998–; Continuing Professional Devpt (CPD) assessor 1999–; *Recreations* swimming, photography, restoring classic cars; *Style*— David S Hannah, Esq; ✉ 1 Marlfield Road, Grappenhall, Warrington WA4 2JT (☎ 01925 264974); 1 Victoria Road, Stockton Heath, Warrington WA4 2AL (☎ 01925 261354)

HANNAH, Prof Leslie; s of Arthur Hannah (d 1969), and Marie, *née* Lancashire; *b* 15 June 1947; *Educ* Manchester Grammar, St John's Coll Oxford (MA), Nuffield Coll Oxford (DPhil); *m* 29 Dec 1984 (m dis 1998), Nuala Barbara Zahedieh, da of late Thomas Hockton, of Hove, E Sussex; 1 s (Thomas b 1988), 2 step da (Sophie b 1977, Miranda b 1981); *Career* res fell St John's Coll Oxford 1969–73, lectr in economics Univ of Essex 1973–75, lectr Univ of Cambridge 1975–78 (fell Emmanuel Coll, fin tutor 1977–78); LSE: dir Business Hist Unit 1978–88, prof 1982–97, pro-dir 1995–97, actg dir 1996–97, visiting prof 2008–; dean Business Sch City Univ 1997–2000; res fell Centre for Econ Policy Res London 1984–92, visiting prof Harvard Business Sch 1984–85, assoc fellow Centre for Business Strategy London Business School 1988–89, invited lectr at univs in USA Europe and Japan; dir various cos (dir NRG Victory Holdings 1987–93), dir London Economics 1992–2000 (fndr memb, subsequently specialist res consult), chief exec Ashridge 2000–03, prof Univ of Tokyo 2004–07 and 2012–13; referee/tstee for various res funding agencies, charities and jls; memb Social Sci Res Cncl (UK) 1982–84, chm Editorial Advsy Bd Dictionary of Business Biography 1979–85; *Books* The Rise of the Corporate Economy (1976, 2 edn 1983, Japanese edn 1987), Management Strategy and Business Development (ed, 1976), Concentration in Modern Industry: Theory, Measurement and the UK Experience (jtly, 1977), Electricity Before Nationalisation (1977), Engineers, Managers and Politicians (1982), Entrepreneurs and the Social Sciences (1984), Inventing Retirement: The Development of Occupational Pensions in Britain (1986), Electricity Privatisation and the Area Boards: the Case for 12 (jtly, 1987), Pension Asset Management: An International Perspective (ed, 1988), Barclays: The Business of Banking (jtly, 2001); *Recreations* reading, walking, talking; *Clubs* Reform; *Style*— Prof Leslie Hannah; ✉ 322 Lauderdale Tower Barbican London EC2Y 8NA

HANNAM, Steve; *b* 26 April 1949; *Career* non-exec dir and chm Devro plc 2009–; non-exec dir: Low & Bonar plc, AZ Electronic Materials Ltd, McBrides plc 2013–; *Style*— Steve Hannam, Esq; ✉ Devro plc, Moodiesburn, Chryston, Scotland G69 0JE

HANNAN, Daniel John; MEP; s of Hugh R Hannan (d 2000), of Brighton, and Lavinia, *née* Moffat; *b* 1 September 1971, Lima, Peru; *Educ* Marlborough, Oriel Coll Oxford (MA); *m* Sara, da of Jeffrey Maynard, and Margaret Maynard; 2 da (Annabel b 2002, Allegra b 2005); *Career* dir Euro Res Gp 1994–99, ldr writer Daily Telegraph 1996–2008, special advsr to Rt Hon Michael Howard, QC, MP, *qv*, 1997–99, MEP (Cons) SE England 1999–; *Publications* Time for a Fresh Start in Europe (1993), Britain in a Multi-Speed Europe (1994), The Challenge of the East (1996), A Guide to the Amsterdam Treaty (1997), Direct Democracy (2005), The Case for EFTA (2006), The Plan: Twelve Months to Renew Britain (2008); *Recreations* Shakespeare; *Clubs* Garrick, Pratt's; *Style*— Daniel Hannan, Esq, MEP

HANNAY, Anthony Hewitt Scott; s of Thomas Scott Hannay (d 1975), of Chorlton-by-Backford, Cheshire, and Doreen, *née* Paul (d 2006); *b* 2 May 1944; *Educ* Rugby, Univ of Liverpool (LLB); *m* 10 Oct 1970, Rosemary Susan, da of Maj Geoffrey Thomas St John Sanders, TD (d 1986), and Eleanor, *née* de Zoete (d 1988), of Cirencester, Glos; 1 da (Diana b 1973), 1 s (Andrew b 1975); *Career* admitted slr 1968; ptnr: Laces & Co 1970–88, Lace Mawer 1988–93 (conslt 1993–96), Anthony Hannay (slr) 1996–99; dir Liverpool Cncl of Social Service Inc 1994–2002; conslt Bullivant Jones 2000–04; memb Mgmnt Ctee RNLI 1986–2002 (memb Cncl 2002–14, vice-pres 2014–), chm Port and City of Liverpool Consultancy Gp RNLI (and predecessor branches) 1989–; memb: Mersey RHA 1988–90, Law Soc; CEDR accredited mediator 2011–; *Recreations* sailing, waterskiing (but no longer enough of either); *Style*— Anthony Hannay, Esq; ✉ The Stray, School Lane, Neston CH64 7TX (☎ 0151 336 8455, e-mail anthony@thehannays.co.uk)

HANNAY OF CHISWICK, Baron (Life Peer UK 2001), of Bedford Park in the London Borough of Ealing; David Hugh Alexander Hannay; GCMG (1995, KCMG 1986, CMG 1981), CH (2003); s of J G Hannay (d 1972), of Aston Tirrold, Oxon, and E M Hannay (d 1986), *née* Lazarus; *b* 28 September 1935; *Educ* Winchester, New Coll Oxford; *m* 1961, Gillian Rosemary (d 2015), da of H Rex (d 1962), of Exmouth, Devon; 4 s (Hon Richard, Hon Philip, Hon Jonathan, Hon Alexander); *Career* 2 Lt 8 King's Royal Irish Hussars 1954–56; HM Dip Serv: joined 1959, Tehran 1960–61, oriental sec Kabul 1961–63, Eastern Dept FO 1963–65, second then first sec UK Delgn to the EC 1965–70, first sec UK Negotiating Team with the Euro Community 1970–72, chef de cabinet to Sir Christopher Soames (vice-pres of Cmmn of Euro Community) Brussels 1973–77, head Energy Sci and Space Dept FCO 1977–79, head ME Dept FCO 1979, asst under sec of state (Euro Community) FCO 1979–84, min Washington 1984–85, ambass and UK perm rep to Euro Community 1985–90, ambass and UK permanent rep to UN and rep on Security Cncl 1990–95, ret; Br Govt special rep for Cyprus 1996–2003, PM's personal envoy to Turkey 1998, memb Cncl Britain in Europe 1999–2005, memb TANGGUH Ind Advsy Panel 2002–09, memb EU Select Ctee House of Lords 2002–06 and 2008–14, vice-chm All Party Parly Gp on the EU 2006–, memb Int Orgns Ctee 2007–08, jt convenor All Party Parly Gp on Global Security and Non-Proliferation 2008–, memb Exec Br American Parly Gp 2008–12, chair Sub-Ctee on Home Affrs 2010–14, chair All-Party Parly Gp on the UN 2011–, memb Top Level Gp on Multilateral Nuclear Disarmament and Non-Proliferation 2011–, chm All Party Parly Gp on the UN 2011–, memb Ctee on Arctic 2014–15, memb Ctee on Sexual Violence in Conflict 2015–16; chm Int Advsy Bd EDHEC Business Sch 2003–09, memb UN Sec-Gen's High Level Panel for Threats, Challenges and Change 2003–04, chair UN Assoc of the UK 2006–11, memb Advsy Bd GPW 2011–, memb Forum for Future of Europe 2013–, chair Sr European Experts Gp 2014–; dir Salzburg Seminar 2002–05, memb Advsy Bd Centre for European Reform 1997–, memb Advsy Bd Judge Business Sch Univ of Cambridge 2004–10; non-exec dir: Chime Communications plc 1996–2006, Aegis Gp plc 2000–03; govr Ditchley Fndn 2005–; pro-chllr Univ of Birmingham 2001–06 (memb Cncl and Ct 1999–), memb Cncl Univ of Kent 2009–15, pres Crown and Manor Club Hoxton 2010–; Hon DLitt Univ of Birmingham; hon fell New Coll Oxford; *Books* Cyprus: The Search for Solution (2004), New World Disorder: The UN after the Cold War – An insider's view (2008), Britain's Quest for a Role: Half a Century of Diplomacy Seen by One of Britain's Senior Ambassadors (2012); *Recreations* photography, travel, gardening; *Clubs* Travellers; *Style*— The Rt Hon the Lord Hannay of Chiswick, GCMG, CH; ✉ 3 The Orchard, London W4 1JZ (☎ 020 8987 9012)

HANRATTY, Judith Christine; CVO (2008), OBE (2002); da of John Edward Hanratty (d 1981), and Joyce, *née* Proudfoot (d 2000), of Waikanae, NZ; *b* 16 August 1943; *Educ* Chilton St James Sch, St Hilda's Collegiate Sch NZ, Victoria Univ of Wellington NZ (LLB, LLM, LLD); *Career* barrister: High Ct of NZ 1966, Supreme Ct of Victoria Aust 1980, Inner Temple 1987; co sec BP plc until 2003; dir: BP Pension Trustees Ltd 1992–2004, London Electricity plc 1995–97, Charles Taylor plc 2000–12, Partnerships UK plc 2001–05, BSI 2002–05, Partner Re 2005–16, England Golf 2012–16; memb: Insurance Brokers' Registration Cncl (Sec of State nominee) 1993–98, Listing Authy Ctee of FSA (formerly London Stock Exchange) 1996–2003, Competition Cmmn (formerly Monopolies and Mergers Cmmn) 1997–2003, Takeover Panel 1997–2003, Cncl Lloyd's 1998–2009 (chm Market Supervision and Review Ctee), Gas and Electricity Markets Authy 2004–10; chm Cwlth Inst 2002–15, chm Cwlth Educn Tst 2007–; chm Coll of Law 2004–05; fell Lucy Cavendish Coll Cambridge; FRSA 1994; *Recreations* golf, horticulture, croquet; *Clubs* Athenaeum, Royal Wellington Golf, Royal Wimbledon Golf, Wellington; *Style*— Miss Judith Hanratty, CVO, OBE; ✉ 36 Sloane Court West, London SW3 4TB; 341 Fergusson Drive, Heretaunga, Upper Hutt 5018, New Zealand

HANSCOMB, Christine; da of Ronald Hanscomb, and late Margaret Hanscomb; *b* 7 January 1946; *Educ* Ravensbourne Sch of Art Sunderland, Maidstone Sch of Art (BA); *m* David Versey, artist; 2 da (Crystal-Lily b 5 Nov 1976, Tara-Jade b 25 July 1984); *Career* Art Dept Vogue Magazine 1969–71, art dir Brides magazine 1971–76, art ed Vogue Magazine 1977, art dir Vogue Beauty Book 1978–81, freelance photographer 1979– (specialising in food, still life, children and underwater photography); cmmnd by most maj advtg agencies in London, Paris and Milan 1981–, and by pubns incl Vogue (London, Paris and NY), Country Living, Interiors, House and Garden, The Observer and Sunday Times; commercials dir with The Producers prodn co; *Books* English Country Style (1987); photographic illustrations for numerous cookery books incl: Madhur Jaffrey's A Taste of India, Antonio Carluccio's A Taste of Italy, Sir Terence and Lady Conran's The Cook Book, Sainsbury's The Book of Food, Nathalie Hambro's Visual Delights, Perfect Puddings, Water Babies and Aqua Yoga; *Recreations* films, music, art, deepsea scuba diving, the countryside, gardening; *Style*— Ms Christine Hanscomb; ✉ 11 Perseverance Works, 38 Kingsland Road, London E2 8DD (☎ 020 7739 0132, fax 020 7729 7066, e-mail mail@christinehanscomb.co.uk, website www.christinehanscomb.co.uk)

HANSELL, Matthew Simon; s of Barry Hansell, and Hilary, *née* Tombs; *b* 15 September 1961, Birmingham; *Educ* King Edward's GS Stourbridge, UWIST Cardiff, Coll of Law Chester; *m* 17 Dec 1988, Josephine Elizabeth, *née* Marshall; 1 s (Luke b 10 Oct 1994), 1 da (Amy b 14 Nov 1997); *Career* admitted slr 1985; articled clerk Manby & Steward 1983–85, MFG Slrs 1986–87, Martineau Johnson Slrs 1988–2004 (latterly ptnr and head of Private Client Gp), ptnr Mills & Reeve 2004– (ldr National Private Client Gp 2006–); memb: Law Soc (memb Capital Taxes Ctee), Soc of Tst and Estate Practitioners (STEP); Private Client Lawyer of the Year Birmingham Law Soc 2005, UK Regnl Legal Team of the Year STEP 2006/07; *Style*— Matthew Hansell, Esq; ✉ The Barn, 23 New Wood Lane, Blakedown, Kidderminster, Worcestershire DY10 3LD (☎ 01562 701238); Mills & Reeve, 78–84 Colmore Row, Birmingham B3 2AB (☎ 0121 456 8297, fax 0121 456 8483, e-mail matthew.hansell@mills-reeve.com)

HANSEN, Alan David; s of John McDonald Hansen, of Clackmananshire, Scotland, and Anne Peddie, *née* Gillon; *b* 13 June 1955; *Educ* Lornshill Acad; *m* 21 June 1980, Janette, da of James Harold Rhymes; 1 s (Adam John b 29 June 1981), 1 da (Lucy Grace b 23 Aug 1984); *Career* former professional footballer; Partick Thistle 1973–77, Liverpool FC 1977–91 (621 appearances, 8 League Championships, 3 European Cups, 2 FA Cups); currently commentator and analyst Sportsnight and Match of the Day BBC TV, presenter of football documentaries; *Recreations* golf, tennis; *Clubs* Hillside Golf, Southport and Birkdale Cricket; *Style*— Alan Hansen, Esq; ✉ c/o BBC TV Sports and Events Group, Kensington House, Richmond Way, London W14 0AX

HANSEN, Brent Vivian; s of Vivian Ernest Hansen (d 1988), of Christchurch, NZ, and Noeline, *née* Eathorne; *b* 14 September 1955; *Educ* St Andrew's Coll Christchurch, Univ of Otago (BA), Canterbury Univ Christchurch (MA), Christchurch Teachers' Coll (teaching cert); *m* 30 Aug 1986, Phillipa Jennie Dann, of NZ; 1 da (Marley Harriet b 22 April 1991), 1 s (Cassidy Jake b 8 Jan 1995); *Career* TV New Zealand: floor mangr, unit mangr and prodr 1978–82, prodr/dir Radio With Pictures 1982–86; MTV Networks Europe: news prodr 1987, dir of news 1987–88, head of prodn 1988–89, dir of programming and prodn 1989–94, pres and chief exec 1994–2005; pres of creative MTV International 2005–06; World Class New Zealander Award (creative div) 2006; memb Bd of Govrs South Bank Centre 2006–, non-exec dir FiveCool 2012–; memb BAFTA; *Recreations* collecting music, theatre and art enthusiast; *Clubs* BAFTA, Groucho; *Style*— Brent Hansen, Esq

HANSEN, Prof Jean-Pierre; s of Georges Hansen (d 1960), and Simone Hansen-Flohr (d 1986); *b* 10 May 1942; *Educ* Athénée Grand-Ducal de Luxembourg, Université de Liège (BA), Université de Paris (PhD); *m* 22 Dec 1971, Martine, da of late Henri Béchet; 1 da (Anne-Elise Nichols b 22 June 1976); *Career* research assoc CNRS 1967–73, prof of physics Université Pierre et Marie Curie Paris 1973–86, prof of physics and head Dept of Physics Ecole Normale Supérieure de Lyon 1986–97, prof of theoretical chemistry Univ of Cambridge and fell CCC Cambridge 1997–; visiting scientist Institut Laue-Langevin Grenoble 1980–81, visiting Miller prof Univ of Calif Berkeley 1991, visiting fell Balliol Coll and Physical Chemistry Laboratory Univ of Oxford 1994–95; memb: Société Française de Physique 1969, Institut Universitaire de France 1992–97; Grand Prix de l'Etat Academy of Science (France) 1991, Prix Spécial Société Française de Physique 1998, Liquid Matter Prize European Physical Soc 2005, Rumford Medal Royal Soc 2006, Berni Alder-CECAM Award of the European Physical Soc 2013; Dr (hc) Université de Liege 2008; FRSC 1998, FRS 2002; *Publications* Theory of Simple Liquids (monograph with I R McDonald, 1976, 4 edn 2013), Basic Concepts for Simple and Complex Liquids (monograph with J L Barrat, 2003); also author of over 300 papers in scientific jls; *Recreations* history of art, classical music, travelling around Italy; *Style*— Prof Jean-Pierre Hansen, FRS; ✉ Department of Chemistry, University of Cambridge, Lensfield Road, Cambridge CB2 1EW (☎ 01223 336376, fax 01223 336362, e-mail jph32@cam.ac.uk)

HANSFORD, Victoria; da of Stephen Hansford, of Farnborough, Hants, and Marion Mounsey, *née* Cullen; *b* 31 October 1979, Lewisham, London; *Educ* Leeds Met Univ (BA), Brunel Univ (MSc), Univ of Surrey (DUniv); *Partner* Tom Aggar, *qv*; *Career* Paralympic rower; GB Rowing 2006–; achivements incl Bronze medal mixed coxed four (with Alastair McKean, Naomi Riches, MBE, James Morgan, *qqv* and Alan Sherman) Paralympics Beijing 2008; SPLA devpt mangr Univ of Surrey 2002–; *Style*— Miss Victoria Hansford

HANSON, Andrew; s of John Hanson (d 1980), of London, and Nansi, *née* Hood Evans (d 2014); *b* 15 May 1961, Westminster, London; *Educ* Highgate Sch, Architectural Assoc Sch of Architecture, Univ of Edinburgh (DipArch); *m* 14 Oct 1995, Louise, *née* Davidson; 2 da (Lucy b 15 April 1998, Katy b 24 Nov 2000); *Career* fndr ptnr Circus Architects 1990–97; dir: Harper Mackay Architects 1997–2002, Hanson and Confederates 2002–12, Hanson Architects 2012–; memb: RIBA 1991 (memb Cncl 2002–08, chm RIBA London 2005–09), RIAS 2005, Wandsworth Cncl Design Review Panel 2013–; *Clubs* Scottish Arts, Electric House, Soho House; *Style*— Andrew Hanson, Esq; ✉ Hanson Architects, 7c Wellington Studios, Wellington Road, London NW10 5LJ (☎ 020 8962 6269, e-mail andrew@hansonarchitects.co.uk)

HANSON, Anthony David; s of William Gordon Hanson, OBE (d 1990) of Notts, and Dulce Durrant, *née* Snook (d 1996); *b* 13 April 1945, Notts; *Educ* Eton, Grenoble Univ; *m* April 1968, Rosemary Patricia (Rosi), *née* Ruddle; 1 s (Christopher Jeremy Piers b 1982); *Career* wine buyer André Simon Wines Ltd and Courtenay Wines (Int) London 1970, buying dir André Simon Wines Ltd 1975–77; Haynes Hanson & Clark (wine merchants): fndr 1978, md 1979–91, buying conslt 1991–; chm Inst of Masters of Wine 1998–99; conslt: LiquorLAND and Vintage Cellars Sydney 1997–, Saulnier Blache Conslts Paris 1991–; Christie's Int Wine Dept: sr dir 2000–02, sr conslt 2002–; judge: Aust Nat Wine Show Canberra 1987, Perth Wine Show 1992, NZ Nat Wine Awards Auckland 1993, Rutherglen Wine Show 1997, Royal Sydney Wine Show 2000; speaker: Pinot Noir Conference McMinnville OR 1991, The Bordeaux Debate l'Université de Bordeaux-Talence 1999; lectr Wine Australia Melbourne 1998, currently regular lectr; current writing incl christies.com and Decanter and Wine (China); co-scripted and co-presented Wines of Burgundy's Côte d'Or double video 1988, Burgundy corr Microsoft On-Line Wine Guide 1995–98; chm French Wine Ctee UK Wine and Spirit Assoc 1975, memb UK Govt Hospitality Wine Ctee 1989–2006; MW 1976, FRSA; *Publications* Burgundy (1982, 2 edn 1995, winner Best Wine Book André Simon Meml Award 1995, winner 1er Cru Award 1995, runner-up Prix du Champagne Lanson 1995); *Recreations* skiing, walking, reading, gardening; *Clubs* 1243 Bourgogne Soc (Beaune); *Style*— Anthony Hanson, Esq; ✉ Christie's International Wine Department, 8 King Street, St James's, London SW1Y 6QT (☎ 020 7226 4575, fax 020 7226 4575, mobile 07786 175570, e-mail ahanson@btconnect.com)

HANSON, Dr Brian John Taylor; CBE (1996); s of Benjamin John Hanson (d 1978), of Norwood Green, Middx, and Gwendoline Ada, *née* Taylor (d 1999); *b* 23 January 1939; *Educ* Hounslow Coll, Law Soc Coll of Law, Univ of Wales (LLM); *m* 10 June 1972, Deborah Mary Hazel, da of Lt-Col Richard Stewart Palliser Dawson, OBE (d 1994), of Stowting, Kent; 2 s (James b 1973, Crispin b 1982), 3 da (Sarah (Mme Guillaume Nicolas) b 1975, Rebecca (Mrs Hugh Stevens) b 1979, Alice b 1986); *Career* slr and ecclesiastical notary; slr in private practice 1963–65, slr Church Cmmrs for Eng 1965–70; Gen Synod of C of E: asst legal advsr 1970–74, legal advsr 1974–2001, registrar 1980–2001, memb Legal Advsy Cmmn 1980–2001 (sec 1970–86); legal advsr: House of Bishops 1974–2001, Archbishops' Cncl 1999–2001; registrar to the Convocation of Canterbury 1982–2001, guardian Shrine of Our Lady of Walsingham 1984–, Bishop's nominee on Chichester Diocesan Synod 1987– (chm Diocesan Bd of Patronage 1998–2014, chm Diocesan House of Laity and Synod, vice-pres 2001–15); memb Cncl: St Luke's Hosp for the Clergy 1985–2001, The Ecclesiastical Law Soc 1987–2003, Chichester Cathedral 2000–; reviewer Cmmn for Health Improvement 2001–05, jt sec Archbishop's Panel of Reference for the Anglican Communion 2005–07; assessor for notarial appeals 2001–; memb Appeals Tribunal Healthcare Cmmn 2005–; fell Woodard Corp 1987–; govr: St Michael's Sch Burton Park 1987–94, Pusey House Oxford 1993– (vice pres 2005–), Quainton Hall Sch 1994–2005; pres Soc for the Maintenance of the Faith 1999–; Archbishop's Nominee on St Luke's Res Fndn 1998–2007, assessor to the Archbishop of Canterbury for the Clergy Discipline Measure 2010–; memb: Law Soc 1963, Canon Law Soc of GB 1980, Ecclesiastical Law Assoc 1980; Warden of the Lower Liberty St Andrew Holborn 2002–13 (Warden emeritus 2013–), lay canon Gibraltar Cathedral 2003–13 (lay canon emeritus 2013–); Freeman City of London, Liveryman Worshipful Co of Glaziers and Painters of Glass; DCL (Lambeth) 2001; FRSA 1996; *Books* The Opinions of the Legal Advisory Commission (ed, 6 edn, 1985), The Canons of the Church of England (ed, 2 edn 1975, 4 edn 1986), Norwood Parish Church – A Short History (1970), Garth Moore's Introduction to English Canon Law (jtly, 3 edn, 1992), Atkin's Court Forms (ed Ecclesiastical vol, 1992, 1996, 2000); *Recreations* the family, gardening, genealogy; *Clubs* Royal Overseas League; *Style*— Dr Brian Hanson, CBE; ✉ Garden Cottage, Wappingthorn Farm Lane, Steyning, West Sussex BN44 3AG (☎ 01903 812214, e-mail brianhanson39@hotmail.com)

HANSON, Rt Hon David George; PC (2007), MP; s of late Brian Hanson, and Glenda Hanson; *b* 5 July 1957; *Educ* Verdin Comp Sch Winsford, Univ of Hull (BA, CertEd); *m* 6 Sept 1986, Margaret, *née* Mitchell; 2 s, 2 da; *Career* vice-pres Hull Univ Students' Union 1978–79, trainee Co-operative Union 1980–81, mangr Plymouth Co-operative 1981–82, various appts The Spastics Soc (now Scope) 1982–89, dir Re-Solv (Soc for Prevention of Solvent Abuse) 1989–92; MP (Lab) Delyn 1992– (also contested 1987); PPS to Chief Sec to The Treasy 1997–98, asst govt whip 1998–99, Parly under sec of state Wales 1999–2001, PPS to Rt Hon Tony Blair, MP, *qv*, 2001–05, min of state NI Office 2005–07, min of state Dept of Justice 2007–09, min of state for security, counter-terrorism, crime and policing 2009–10, shadow min Treasy 2010–11, shadow police min 2011–13, shadow immigration min 2013–15; sec PLP Heritage Ctee 1995–97; memb: Leadership Campaign Team 1995, Public Service Select Ctee, Justice Select Ctee 2015–, Speaker's Panel of Chairs 2015–; Parly candidate (Lab) Eddisbury 1983, Euro Parly candidate Cheshire W 1984; cncllr: Vale Royal BC 1983–91 (chm Econ Devpt Ctee and cncl ldr 1989–91), Northwich Town Cncl 1987–91; *Recreations* football, cinema, cooking; *Style*— The Rt Hon David Hanson, MP; ✉ 4 Trelawny Square, Flint, Flintshire CH6 JNN (☎ 01352 763159); House of Commons, London SW1A 0AA (020 7219 5064)

HANSON, Geoffrey; s of John Hanson (d 1967), of Witney, Oxon, and Grace Emily, *née* Elphick (d 1977); *b* 9 December 1939; *Educ* Eastbourne GS, Itchen GS Southampton, Trinity Coll of Music London (GTCL, LTCL, ATCL); *m* 5 Aug 1961 (m dis 1994), (Alice) Janet, MBE, da of Frank Wyatt (d 1948); *Career* conductor and composer; conductor London Ripieno Soc 1962–, prof Trinity Coll of Music London 1964–2004, conductor Square Singers of St James 1977–89; Telemann St Matthew Passion Camden Festival 1968; artistic dir East Finchley Arts Festival 1997; memb City of Westminster Arts Cncl; memb: Performing Rights Soc 1981, Incorporated Soc of Musicians 1983, Composers' Guild of GB 1983; hon fell Trinity Coll of Music London 1972; *Compositions* incl: 3 Pieces for Organ 1970, A Trilogy of Psalms for chorus and orchestra 1973, Brecon Ser 1974, concerto for piano and orchestra 1977, concerto for oboe and strings 1978, Sinfonia Amoris for soloists chorus and orchestra 1981, War! Cry War! for soloists chorus and orchestra 1986, concerto for violin and orchestra 1986, concerto for clarinet and strings 1987, concerto for viola and orchestra 1990, The Virgin Crown (opera) 1991, Te Deum (for Hanover Choir) 1993, Carols for Tring 1994, Piano Quintet 1995, Joan of Arc (opera) 1996, Concerto for Organ and Orchestra 1999, Cuthman's Journey (opera) 2000, Concerto for Flute and Strings (London Mozart Players) 2001, Requiem for chorus, soprano, soloist and organ 2002, Songs of War and Peace (Finchley Children's Music Gp) 2003, Concerto for Horn and Strings (London Mozart Players) 2004, Music for Strings (London Mozart Players) 2005, Rose (variations for organ) 2005, Conversation Piece (double concerto for violin, 'cello and orch, David Juritz, Sebastian Comberti and London Mozart Players) 2006, Piano Concerto no 2 (Rimantas Vingras and the London Mozart Players) 2007, Chamber Symphony (London Mozart Players) 2008, Five Nocturnes for Tenor and Chamber Orchestra (Ian Priestley – Tenor and London Mozart Players) 2009, St Cecilia (text Fleur Adcock, OBE, *qv*) 2009, Let the Pealing Organ Blow (for organ and orch, London Mozart Players) 2010, Sinfonia (for organ) 2011, Odyssey (for cello and orch, London Mozart Players) 2012, Ode to the Human Voice (text Fleur Adcock, OBE) 2012, Soliloquy (organ solo, Robert Munns) 2012; *Publications* Three Pieces for Organ, Lute Book Lullaby, People Look East, Down in yon Forest, Two Harvest Carols, Brecon Service; *Recreations* swimming, walking; *Style*— Geoffrey Hanson, Esq; ✉ 22 New Ash Close, London N2 8DQ (☎ 020 84449214, e-mail geoffreyhanson@btinternet.com)

HANSON, Sir John Gilbert; KCMG (1995), CBE (1979); s of Gilbert Fretwell Hanson (d 1981), and Gladys Margaret, *née* Kay (d 1991); *b* 16 November 1938; *Educ* Manchester Grammar, Wadham Coll Oxford (MA); *m* 1962, Margaret (d 2003), da of Edward Thomas Clark, MBE, of Oxfordshire; 3 s (Mark b 1966, Paul b 1967 (decd), James b 1971); *Career* WO 1961–63; Br Cncl: Madras India 1963–66, MECAS Lebanon 1966–68, Bahrain 1968–72, London 1972–75, Tehran Iran 1975–79, London 1979–82, RCDS 1983; min (cultural affrs) Br High Cmmn New Delhi 1984–88, dep dir gen Br Cncl 1988–92, dir gen Br Cncl 1992–98; warden Green Coll Oxford 1998–2006; memb Governing Cncl SOAS 1991–99; tstee Charles Wallace (India) Tst 1998–2000; pres: Br Skin Fndn 1997–2002, Bahrain-British Fndn 1997–2005, UK Cncl for Overseas Student Affairs 1999–2005; Hon Girdler The Girdlers' Co 2010; Hon DLitt Oxford Brookes Univ 1995, Hon Dr Univ of Lincolnshire & Humberside 1996, Hon Dr Univ of Greenwich 1996; hon fell: Wadham Coll Oxford, Green Coll Oxford 2006–08, Green Templeton Coll 2008–, St Edmund's Coll Cambridge; *Recreations* books, music, sailing, sport, travel; *Clubs* MCC, Gymkhana (Chennai); *Style*— Sir John Hanson, KCMG, CBE; ✉ Green Templeton College, Woodstock Road, Oxford OX2 6HG (☎ 01865 274 775, fax 01865 274 796)

HANSON, Hon Robert William; s of Baron Hanson (Life Peer, d 2004); *b* 3 October 1960; *Educ* Eton, St Peter's Coll Oxford; *m* 2010, Maria (Masha) Markova; *Career* NM Rothschild & Sons Ltd 1983–90 (asst dir 1990), dir Hanson plc 1992–97 (assoc dir 1990–92); chm: Hanson Pacific 1994–97, Hanson Transport Gp 1996– (dir 1990–), Hanson Capital Investments Ltd 1998–, Hanson Westhouse Ltd 2006–09, Strand Hanson 2009–; Liveryman Worshipful Co of Saddlers; *Recreations* hunting, shooting, tennis, golf; *Clubs* White's, Queen's, The Berkshire, The Brook (NY), Royal Thames Yacht; *Style*— The Hon Robert Hanson; ✉ Hanson Office, 26 Mount Row, London W1K 3SQ (☎ 020 7529 3725, e-mail rwhanson@hancap.com)

HANWORTH, 3 Viscount (UK 1936); Sir (David) Stephen Geoffrey Pollock; 3 Bt (UK 1922); also Baron Hanworth (UK 1926); s of 2 Viscount Hanworth (d 1996), and (Isolda) Rosamond, *née* Parker; *b* 16 February 1946; *Educ* Wellington, Guildford Tech Coll, Univ of Sussex; *m* 1968, Elizabeth, da of Lawrence Vambe, of Harare, Zimbabwe; 2 da (Hon Cecily Abigail Shona b 1971, Hon Charlotte Anne Catherine b 1973); *Career* lectr Queen Mary & Westfield Coll London, reader Queen Mary Univ of London, emeritus prof Univ of Leicester; *Publications* The Algebra of Economics (1979), A Handbook of Time-Series Analysis, Signal Processing and Dynamics (1999), Innovations in Multivariate Statistical Analysis (jt ed, 2000); *Style*— The Rt Hon the Viscount Hanworth; ✉ 12 Gladsmuir Road, London N19 3JX (☎ 020 7272 1023, e-mail pollockd@parliament.uk or stephen_pollock@sigmapi.u-net.com, website www.le.ac.uk/users/dsgp1)

HAQUE, Muhammed Luthful; QC (2015); s of Muhammed Serajul Hoque, and Dilwara Begum, of Loughborough; *b* 26 July 1973, Loughborough; *Educ* Loughborough GS, Hertford Coll Oxford; *m* 7 Oct 2006, Emma Louise, *née* Peacock; 2 da (Isabelle Amaya b 6 Sept 2009, Jessica Samira b 27 Aug 2011 (twin)), 1 s (Oliver Omar b 27 Aug 2011 (twin)); *Career* called to the Bar (Lincoln's Inn) 1997 (Sunley and Hardwicke Scholar); memb: Personal Injury Bar Assoc, London Common Law Bar Assoc, Professional Negligence Bar Assoc, TECBAR, Scholarships Ctee Lincoln's Inn; Lincoln's Inn advocacy tutor; *Recreations* cricket, golf, music, skiing; *Clubs* Leicestershire CCC, Sadlers Wells Dining; *Style*— Muhammed Haque, QC; ✉ Crown Office Chambers, 2 Crown Office Row, Temple, London EC4Y 7HJ

HARARI, Sammy; s of René David Harari, and Sandrine, *née* Olifson; *b* 4 April 1950; *Educ* Univ of Reading, Univ of Montpellier (BA); *Career* with Dunlop Ltd 1972–74, account dir Darcy Masius Benton & Bowles 1974–83, dir Yellowhammer 1983–86 (handled UK Govt first anti-heroin campaign), chief exec TBWA 1986–89 (responsible for UK Govt anti-AIDS campaign), fndr md Harari Page 1990–98, chm Travis Sully Harari Fndn 1998–99, worldwide creative dir Harari 1999– (devpt projects in Paris, London, NY and Koh Samui); MInstM, MIPA; *Style*— Sammy Harari, Esq; ✉ 1150 Park Avenue, Apartment PHD, New York, NY 10128, USA (☎ 00 1 212 876 8567, e-mail sammyharari@gmail.com)

HARBERTON, 11 Viscount (I 1791); Henry Robert Pomeroy; also Baron Harberton (I 1783); s of Hon Robert Pomeroy (d 1997), and (Winifred) Anne, *née* Colegate (d 2014); suc unc, 10 Viscount Harberton, 2004; *b* 23 April 1958, Hanover; *Educ* Eton, RAC Cirencester,

H

Univ of Reading; *m* 27 Oct 1990, Caroline, da of Jeremy Grindle; 2 s (Hon Patrick Christopher b 10 May 1995, Hon Hugh William b 18 April 1997); *Heir* s, Hon Patrick Pomeroy; *Career* Portman Estate 1982–88, P&O Properties 1988–92, TEAR Fund Ghana 1993–96, Action on Disability and Devpt 1997–2005, Send A Cow 2005–13, CHASE Africa 2013–; lay reader C of E; MRICS 1988; *Recreations* cycling, beekeeping; *Style*— The Rt Hon the Viscount Harberton; ✉ CHASE Africa (✆ 01373 836012, e-mail henrypomeroy@chaseafrica.org.uk)

HARBOR, John Liming; s of Jack Liming Harbor, of Swanage, and Isabel Katherine, *née* Lauder; *b* 11 March 1947; *Educ* Hurstpierpoint Coll; *m* 4 July 1970, Christine Elizabeth, da of John Walter De Foix Rawle; 1 da (Lucy Elizabeth b 12 May 1973), 1 s (Andrew Liming b 7 May 1979); *Career* audit supervisor London and Madrid Barton Mayhew (later merged with Ernst & Young) 1970–75, conslt to shipowners UK and Netherlands 1975–80, ptnr Bagshaws 1982–91 (joined 1980), sr insurance ptnr Moore Stephens (following merger with Bagshaws) 1991–; FCA (ACA 1970); *Recreations* golf, walking, cooking; *Style*— John Harbor, Esq; ✉ Moore Stephens, St Paul's House, 8–12 Warwick Lane, London EC4P 4BN

HARBORD, Richard Lewis; s of Lewis Walter Harbord, of Norwich, and Dorothy Florence, *née* Mobbs; *b* 30 April 1946, London; *Educ* Minchenden GS, Anglian Regnl Mgmnt Centre (MPhil), Henley Coll of Mgmnt (MPhil); *m* 2 May 1970, Jenny Ann, da of Herbert John Berry (d 1988); 3 s (Mark b 26 Aug 1971, Adam b 5 Oct 1975, Guy b 19 July 1984); *Career* chief exec London Borough of Richmond-upon-Thames 1988–99 (fin dir 1981–88), md London Borough of Hammersmith and Fulham 1999–2002, public sector conslt to central and local govt 2002–, chief exec Boston Borough Cncl 2009–14; dir: LDA plc, Public Sector Conslts Ltd 2002–; memb: Cncl Rating and Valuation Assoc 1987– (pres 1994–95 and 2013–14), Ct Univ of Surrey; chm Windlesham Community House Project; hon fell St Mary's Univ Twickenham 2001–; Freeman City of London 2008; memb IPFA 1967 (memb Cncl 2003–), memb BCS 1968, FCCA 1981, FRVA 1982, FRSA 1990; *Recreations* family; *Style*— Richard Harbord, Esq; ✉ Gooserye, Cooper Road, Windlesham, Surrey GU20 6EA (e-mail richard@harbord.net)

HARBORNE, Peter Gale; s of late Leslie Herbert Harborne, and late Marie Mildred Edith, *née* Suckling; *b* 29 June 1945; *Educ* King Edward's Sch Birmingham, Univ of Birmingham (BCom); *m* 24 July 1976, Tessa Elizabeth Harborne, da of late Dennis Frederick Joseph Henri, of Solihull, West Midlands; 2 s (James b 1980, Alexander b 1981); *Career* Home Civil Service 1966–72, HM Dip Serv 1972, first sec Ottawa 1974–75, first sec (commercial) Mexico City 1975–78, Lloyds Bank Int 1979–81, FCO 1981–83, first sec and head of Chancery Helsinki 1983–87, counsellor and dep head of mission Budapest 1988–91, FCO 1991–95, ambass to Slovak Republic 1995–98, high cmmr to Trinidad and Tobago 1999–2004; clerk advsr European Scrutiny Ctee House of Commons 2004–; *Recreations* cricket, tennis, the arts; *Clubs* MCC; *Style*— Peter Harborne, Esq

HARBOUR, Ivan; *Educ* Bartlett Sch of Architecture and Planning (UCL Environmental Design Prize); *Career* architect; YRM 1983, London Borough of Hackney 1983; Richard Rogers Partnership: joined 1985, dir 1993–; lectr: South Bank Univ, Strasbourg Univ, Univ of Melbourne, RIBA; *Projects* incl: Lloyd's of London, Reuters Data Centre, European Ct of Human Rights, Nice Masterplan, Lloyd's Register of Shipping Competition, Bordeaux Law Cts, Ile Seguin Paris Masterplan Competition, South Bank Centre Competition, VR Techno Centre Gifu Japan, Minami Yamashiro Sch Kyoto Japan, ParcBit Masterplan Mallorca, Fujita Restaurant Tokyo Japan, Electronic Arts HQ Competition, Museum of Islamic Art Quatar Competition, Madrid Airport, Nippon TV HQ Tokyo Japan, Antwerp Law Cts Competition, Nat Assembly for Wales Competition, Kyoto Retail Bldg Japan, Millennium Experience Rest Zone, Amano Laboratory Building; *Style*— Ivan Harbour, Esq; ✉ Richard Rogers Partnership, Thames Wharf, Rainville Road, London W6 9HA

HARBOUR, Malcolm John Charles; CBE (2013), MEP; s of John Harbour (d 1980), and Bobby Harbour (d 1995); *b* 19 February 1947, Woking, Surrey; *Educ* Gayhurst Sch Gerrards Cross, Bedford Sch, Trinity Coll Cambridge (MA), Aston Univ (Dip Mgmnt Studies); *m* 12 July 1969, Penny, *née* Johnson; 2 da (Louise b 1974, Katy b 1977); *Career* BMC Longbridge: engrg apprentice 1967, designer and devpt engr 1969–72, product planning mangr Rover-Triumph 1972–76, project mangr Medium Cars 1976–80, dir of business planning Austin Rover 1980–82, dir of mktg 1982–84, dir of sales UK and Ireland 1984–86, dir Overseas Sales 1986–89; fndr and ptnr Harbour Wade Brown Motor Industry Conslts 1989–99, jt fndr and dir Int Car Distribution Programme (ICDP) 1993–99, non-exec dir 1999–2006, co-fndr and project dir 3 Day Car Programme 1998–99; MEP (Cons) W Midlands 1999–, Cons spokesman Internal Market, co-ordinator EPP-ED Gp 2004–09, chm Internal Market and Consumer Protection Ctee 2009–; rapporteur: Motor Vehicle Fuel Tank Directive 1999, European Cmmn Personnel Reforms 2000–04, 2nd Generation Internet 2000–, Universal Service in Electronic Communications 2001 and 2008, Internal Market Strategy 2003, Motor Vehicle Type Approval 2007, Pre-Competitive Procurement 2008, Recreational Craft 2013; vice-chm STOA (Scientific and Technology Options Assessment) Panel, memb Cons Delegation Bureau 1999–2002, memb ECR Gp Bureau 2009–, vice-pres Cons Technol Forum 2011– (chm 2004–11); memb Delgn to Japanese Parl; co-chm: European Forum for the Automobile in Soc 2000–09, European Parl Ceramics Industry Forum 2000–; govr European Internet Fndn 2003–, dir EURIM 2004–, chm European Manufacturing Forum 2009; guardian Birmingham Assay Office 2007–; candidate (Cons) Euro elections 1989 and 1994, former chm Solihull Constituency, former rep Nat Union Trade and Industry Forum, former memb W Midlands Area Exec Cncl, memb Solihull Cons Assoc 1972–; Hon DSc Univ of Aston 2008; CEng, MIMechE, FIMI; *Publications* Winning Tomorrow's Customers (1997), Our Vision of Europe (contrib, EPP-ED Gp, 2001), many car industry reports published by ICDP; *Recreations* choral singing, motor sport, travel, cooking; political interests: European affairs, transport, competition policy, e-commerce, telecomms, automotive indust, ceramics indust; *Style*— Malcolm Harbour, Esq, CBE, MEP; ✉ ASP 13E130, European Parliament, 60 Rue Wiertz, B1047 Brussels (✆ 322 284 5132, fax 322 284 9132, e-mail malcolm.harbour@europarl.europa.eu); UK Office, 285 Kenilworth Road, Balsall Common, Coventry CV7 7EL (✆ 01676 530682, fax 01676 530658)

HARDEN, Peter William Mason; s of late John Henry Mason Harden, of Chester, and Susan Harden; *Educ* Trinity Coll Cambridge; *m* Francesca Elizabeth; 3 s, 1 da; *Career* co-fndr (with bro, Richard Harden, *qv*) Harden's Guides 1991–; FRSA; *Clubs* Hawks; *Style*— Peter Harden; ✉ Harden's Ltd, 8 Golden Cross House, 8 Duncannon Street, London WC2N 4JF (✆ 020 7839 4763, e-mail ph@hardens.com, website www.hardens.com)

HARDEN, Richard John Mason; s of late John Henry Mason Harden, and Susan Harden; *b* 26 July 1959, Chester; *Educ* King's Sch Chester, Christ's Coll Cambridge; *m* 29 Jan 2000, Jeanette, *née* Holland; 2 da; *Career* called to the Bar; credit analyst Baring Bros, mangr Samuel Montagu, co-fndr (with bro, Peter Harden, *qv*) Harden's 1991–; *Publications* London Restaurants (annually 1991–), and other listings info online and offline; *Style*— Richard Harden, Esq; ✉ (✆ 020 7839 4763, e-mail mail@hardens.com, website www.hardens.com)

HARDEN, Prof Ronald McGlashan; OBE (2003); s of Alexander Harden (d 1959), and Janet Roy, *née* McGlashan; *b* 24 December 1936; *Educ* Uddington GS, Univ of Glasgow (MB ChB, MD); *m* 4 Jan 1961, Sheila, da of James Harris (d 1956); 3 da (Susan b 28 Sept 1964, Valerie b 31 July 1966, Jennifer b 3 July 1968); *Career* res and clinical posts Western Infirmary Glasgow 1960–70, sr lectr in med Univ of Glasgow 1970–72, postgrad dean of med Univ of Dundee 1985–99 (dir centre for med educn and hon conslt physician 1972), dir Educ Devpt Unit Scottish Cncl for Postgraduate Med and Dental Educ 1999–, teaching dean Univ of Dundee Sch of Med 1994–; ed Medical Teacher and int authy on med educn with over 200 papers in scientific jls; sec/treas Assoc for Med Educn Europe, memb Exec Assoc for Study of Med Educn; FRCPGlas 1975, FRCPS Canada 1988, FRCSEd 1994; *Recreations* gardening; *Clubs* Royal Society of Medicine; *Style*— Prof Ronald Harden, OBE; ✉ Association for Medical Education in Europe, 12 Airlie Place, Dundee DD1 4HJ

HARDIE, Baron (Life Peer UK 1997), of Blackford in the City of Edinburgh; Andrew Rutherford Hardie; PC (1997), QC (Scot 1985); s of late Andrew Rutherford Hardie, and late Elizabeth Currie, *née* Lowe; *b* 8 January 1946; *Educ* St Modan's HS Stirling, Univ of Edinburgh (MA, LLB); *m* 16 July 1971, Catherine Storrar, da of late David Currie Elgin, of Edinburgh; 2 s (Hon Ewan b 1975, Hon Niall b 1981), 1 da (Hon Ruth b 1977); *Career* admitted slr 1971, admitted memb Faculty of Advocates 1973; advocate depute 1979–83, standing jr counsel City of Edinburgh DC 1983–85 (sr counsel 1987–97), dean Faculty of Advocates 1994–97 (treasurer 1989–94), Lord Advocate 1997–2000, Senator Coll of Justice (Lord of Session) 2000–12; convener Children in Scotland 1994–96, hon pres The Muir Soc 1994–2000, hon pres Capability Scotland 2012–; hon bencher Lincoln's Inn 1997; *Style*— The Rt Hon the Lord Hardie, PC, QC; ✉ House of Lords, London SW1A 0PW (✆ 020 7219 3000, e-mail hardiera@parliament.uk)

HARDIE, David; WS (1982); s of late John Hardie, and late Amy Alfreda, *née* Masey; *b* 17 September 1954; *Educ* Glasgow Acad, Greenock HS, Univ of Dundee (LLB); *m* 27 Feb 1981, Fiona Mairi, da of late Dr Alexander Donaldson Willox, MBE, of W Lothian; 3 s (Iain b 1981, Stewart b 1984, Alasdair b 1989); *Career* NP 1979, ptnr Dundas & Wilson CS LLP 1983– (formerly chm, managing ptnr, head of corporate and head of knowledge and learning); head of venture philanthropy Inspiring Scotland; NP: Law Soc of Scot, Int Bar Assoc; *Recreations* sailing, golf, swimming, cycling, motor cycling; *Style*— David Hardie, Esq, WS; ✉ Dundas & Wilson CS LLP, Saltire Court, 20 Castle Terrace, Edinburgh EH1 2EN (✆ 0131 200 7345, fax 0131 228 8888, e-mail david.hardie@dundas-wilson.com)

HARDIE, Brig Donald Graeme; CVO, TD, JP; s of Graeme Hardie, BEM, of Helensburgh, and Sheila Ramsay McLennan (d 1965); *b* 23 January 1936, Glasgow; *Educ* Larchfield, Blairmore, Merchiston Castle Sch Edinburgh; *m* 10 Feb 1961 (m dis 1995), Rosalind Allan Ker; 2 s (Fergus Allan Graeme b 15 Sept 1962, Adam Ker b 2 June 1964); m 2, 27 Dec 1999, Sheena Roome; *Career* mgmnt trainee UTR 1956–59, F W Allan & Ker Shipbrokers 1960–61; dir: J & G Hardie & Co Ltd 1961–2000, Gilbert Plastics 1973–76, Hardie Polymers Ltd 1981–2000; md: Hardie International Sales 2000–04, Preston Stretchform 2000–04; Nat Serv cmmnd 41 Field Regt RA 1954–56; TA service: 277 (A & S H) Field Regt RA 1956–66, CO G & SUOTC 1966–73, Col Lowlands 1973–76, Col DES 1976–80, Col Scot 1980–84, ACF Brig Scot 1985–87; Hon Col: 105 AD Regt RA (V) 1992–99, Glasgow & Lanarkshire ACF 1993–2000; Hon Col Commandant Royal Regiment of Artillery 2003–06; chm RA Cncl for Scot 1996–2001; vice-pres: ACFA Scot 1990–99, Nat Artillery Assoc 2002–; pres until 2007: SSAFA – Forces Help Dunbartonshire, Scouts Dumbarton area, Guides Dunbartonshire, Boys Brigade Lennox & Argyll; memb Highland Soc of London 2004–; patron: Cornerstone until 2008, Craigalbert Centre until 2008; chieftain Loch Lomond Games, pres Highland RFCA 2005–07, session clerk Luss Parish Church 2015–; HM Lord-Lt Dunbartonshire 1990–2007; keeper Dumbarton Castle 1996 (lifetime appt); memb Grand Antiquity Soc; FIMMM; KStJ; *Recreations* shooting, fishing, sailing, curling; *Clubs* Royal Northern & Clyde Yacht, Royal Scots; *Style*— Brig Donald Hardie, CVO, TD; ✉ East Lodge, Arden G83 8LX (✆ 01389 850790)

HARDIE, Gwen Waterston; da of James Waterston Hardie, and Anne, *née* Livingston; *b* 7 January 1962; *Educ* Inverurie Acad, Edinburgh Coll of Art (BA); *m* David Basson; *Career* artist; lectr and visiting artist to various art colls incl: Glasgow, Edinburgh, Sheffield Poly, St Martin's and Royal Coll of Art, Oxford Brookes Univ, Cleveland Univ, Ottawa Univ, NY Studio School, MICA Baltimore, Bridge St Studio Center Brooklyn; *Solo Exhibitions* Paton Gallery London 1986 and 1988, Fruitmarket Gallery Edinburgh (travelling Br show) 1987, Kettle's Yard Cambridge 1988, Scottish Nat Gallery of Modern Art Edinburgh 1990, Fischer Fine Art London 1990, Annely Juda Fine Art London 1994, Talbot Rice Gallery Univ of Edinburgh 1994, Jason and Rhodes Gallery London 1996 and 1998, Peterborough Museum & Art Gallery 1997, Ogilvie & Estill Conwy Wales 1997, Beaux Art London 1999, Lindsey Brown NY 2001, Alpan Gallery Huntington 2004, Dinter Fine Art NY 2005, Body Tondi (Bridge Street Studio Center NY) 2009, Boundaries (An Lanntair Stornoway Scotland) 2012 and (Taigh Chearsabhagh Lochmaddy Scotland) 2013, Skin Deep (Smoyer Gallery Roanoke College US) 2014; *Group Exhibitions* Contemporary Art for Museums – Contemporary Art Soc purchases 1982–84 (Sutton Place Guildford Surrey) 1985, Twelve British Artists (Künstlerhaus Vienna) 1986, The Human Touch (Fischer Fine Art London) 1986, Identity – Desire (Scottish Arts Cncl touring) 1986, The Self-Portrait – A Modern View (Artsite Bath) 1987, The Vigorous Imagination (Scottish Nat Gallery of Modern Art Edinburgh) 1987, The New British Painting (American touring) 1988–90, Scottish Art in the 20th Century (The Royal W of England Acad Bristol) 1991, Cabinet Paintings (Gillian Jason Gallery) 1991, Critics Choice (Bruton St Gallery) 1992, Artistic Associations (Gillian Jason Gallery) 1992, The Body Abstract – Somatic States (Quicksilver Gallery Univ of Middx) 1992, Festival Fourteen (Dunfermline Dist & City Museum) 1992, Foreground and Distances (Serpenti Galleria Rome and touring Europe) 1992–94, New Artists and Cabinet Art (both at Jason and Rhodes Gallery, London) 1995, Vigorous Imagination – 10 Years On (Scottish Gallery Edinburgh) 1997, John Moores Liverpool Exhibition (Jason and Rhodes Gallery London) 1998, 'Tech' Jason & Rhodes Gallery London 1998, Beaux Art London 1999, Quintet (Lennon Weinberg NY) 2000, Elizabeth Fndn for the Arts Studio Centre Open Studios (NY) 2000, Abstraction and Immanence (Times Square Gallery NY) 2001, Narcissus (Scottish National Gallery of Art Edinburgh) 2001, Landscape (Lindsey Brown Gallery NY) 2002, London Art Fair (Stephen Lacey Gallery) 2004, Brooklyn Artists (Alpan Gallery Huntington NY) 2005, Drawn (Dinter Fine Art NY) 2006, Closer (Alpan Gallery Huntington NY) 2006, Close (Dinter Fine Art NY) 2006, Radius (Metaphor Contemporary Brooklyn NY) 2007, The Dutch Barn Show (Rose Burlingham Fine Art Lindsey Brown Studio NY) 2008, McTears Auction and Galleries 2009 and 2010, The Edinburgh School (Lemon Street Gallery Truro) 2010, 400 Women (Shoreditch Town Hall) 2010, Tenwordsandoneshot (Kevin Krumniki online projects Germany) 2010, Portraiture: Inside Out (Walsh Gallery New Jersey) 2011, Inner and Out Landscapes: Contemporary Self-Portraiture (A.D. Gallery North Carolina) 2011, The Artist's Studio (Royal Scottish Academy Edinburgh) 2012, The Royal Hibernian Academy Dublin 2012, Terra Incognita (The Castle Gallery NY) 2013, Outwin Boochever National Portrait Exhibition (National Portrait Gallery Washington DC) 2013, Skin Over Bone (with James Hardie and Amy Hardie, Stirling University Scotland) 2013, Push/Pull (Rag and Bone NY) 2013, Skin: An Artistic Atlas (with Marlene Dumas, John Coplans and others, Royal Hibernian Academy Dublin) 2013, Borderline, Depictions of Skin (with Cynthia Lin, Diana Schmertz, Garis & Hahn, NY) 2013, The Art of Healing (Attic Salt Gallery Edinburgh Festival) 2014, Reality: Modern and Contemporary Painting (with Lucien Freud, Cecily Brown, Peter Doig and others, Sainsbury Centre Norwich) 2014; *Work in Collections* Br Cncl London, Contemporary Art Soc London, Scottish Nat Gallery of Modern Art Edinburgh, City Art Collection Edinburgh, Met Museum NYC, Gulbenkian Collection Lisbon, Scottish Arts Cncl Edinburgh, Glaxo Group Research Ltd London, Manchester Museum of Modern

Art, Elaina Richardson NY, Miriama Young Sydney Australia, Dominique Mancellon Scotland, Jeanne Dorsey NY, Claire Colebrook USA, Logan MacWatt Hong Kong, The Grace of the Birch (New Stobhill Hospital), Reiach & Hall Architects Glasgow, David Cohen NY, Sherry Roush USA, Jayne Anne Phillips USA, Gail Tsukiyama California, Kasen Summer Collection Connecticut, Gulbenkian Collection Lisbon, Scottish Arts Cncl Edinburgh, Glaxo Group Research Ltd London, Manchester City Galleries, Kirklees Museum and Galleries, Leicestershire County Cncl Artworks Collection, City of Edinburgh Cncl, Aberdeen Art Gallery and Museums, Highland Cncl, New Hall Art Collection, Univ of Cambridge, Univ of Edinburgh Fine Art Collection; *Recreations* travel; *Clubs* Chelsea Arts; *Style—* Ms Gwen Hardie; ✉ website www.gwenhardie.com

HARDIE, Prof Philip Russell; s of late Miles Clayton Hardie, and Pauline Le Gros, *née* Clark; *b* 13 July 1952; *Educ* St Paul's, CCC Oxford (BA), Warburg Inst Univ of London (MPhil); *Partner* Susan Elizabeth Griffith; 2 s (Hugh Andrew, David Robert (twins) b 12 Aug 1989); *Career* editorial asst OED 1977–80, P S Allen jr res fell in classics CCC Oxford 1980–84, fell and coll lectr in classics Magdalene Coll Cambridge 1986–90, fell New Hall Cambridge 1990–2002, reader in Latin lit Univ of Cambridge 1998–2002, Corpus Christi prof of Latin Univ of Oxford 2002–06, sr research fell Trinity Coll Cambridge 2006–; FBA 2000; *Books* Virgil's Aeneid: Cosmos and Imperium (1986), The Epic Successors of Virgil (1993), Ovid's Poetics of Illusion (2002), Lucretian Receptions (2009), Rumour and Renown (2012), The Last Trojan Hero (2014); *Recreations* walking, cooking; *Style—* Prof Philip Hardie; ✉ 5 Stretten Avenue, Cambridge CB4 3ES (☎ 01223 513020); Trinity College, Cambridge CB2 1TQ (☎ 01223 338400)

HARDIE, Sean; s of late Ven A G Hardie, and late Shelagh, *née* Jacob; *b* 4 March 1947, Hexham; *Educ* Trinity Coll Glenalmond, Trinity Coll Cambridge (MA); *m* 1, 1973 (m dis 1979), Janet, *née* Hall; 1 s (William); m 2, Kerry Jolley; *Career* prodr and dir current affairs BBC TV 1969–79 (incl 24 Hours, Panorama, Midweek), prodr light entertainment BBC TV 1979–81 (incl Not the Nine O'Clock News, later Spitting Image), contract writer and dir Video Arts Ltd; prodns incl: The Signal Box (RTE) 1995, Rory Bremner – Who Else? (Channel 4) 2003; TV awards incl: BAFTA, Silver Rose Montreux, Writers' Guild, US Emmy; chair Duiske Concerts; *Books* Not!, Not the Royal Wedding (1981), Not 1982 (1982), The Last Supper (1990), Right Connections (1991), Till The Fat Lady Sings (1993), Falling Off a Log (1994), Moldova (play, 2006), Burning Your Boots (play, 2007), God's Hairdresser (play, 2008), The Life of Wiley (play, 2010), Ken and Margaret and the End of the World (play, 2012); *Recreations* reading; *Clubs* Ballytighlea Social; *Style—* Sean Hardie, Esq; ✉ Milltown, Skeoghvosteen, Co Kilkenny, Eire (☎ 00 353 599 73194, e-mail seanhardie@gmail.com); agent: Alexandra Cann, 14 Water Lane, Camden, London NW1 8NZ (☎ 020 7584 9047, e-mail alex@alexandracann.co.uk)

HARDING, Daniel; s of John and Caroline Harding, of Oxford; *b* 31 August 1975; *Career* asst to Sir Simon Rattle, *qv*, 1993–94; professional debut CBSO (won Royal Philharmonic Soc Best Debut Award) 1994; asst to Claudio Abbado Berlin Philharmonic 1995–96, youngest conductor BBC Proms conducting two programmes 1996, debut Berlin Philharmonic Berlin Festival 1996, conductor Scharoun Ensemble (incl members of Berlin Philharmonic) Salzburg Festival 1997, princ conductor Trondheim Symphony Orch Norway 1997–2000; princ guest conductor: Norrkoping Symphony Orch Sweden 1997–2003, London Symphony Orch 2007–; music dir Die Deutsche Kammerphilharmonie Bremen 1997–2003, music dir Mahler Chamber Orch 2003–, music dir Swedish Radio Orch 2007–, artistic ptnr New Japan Philharmonic 2010–; conducted new opera productions 1998: Don Giovanni (dir by Peter Brook Aix-en-Provence Festival with Mahler Chamber Orch, toured Lyon, Milan, Brussels and Tokyo 1998–99), Janacek's Jenufa (Katie Mitchell prodn for WNO), Aix-en-Prevence Festival (Turn of the Screw, Eugene Onegin, La Traviata, Die Zauberflöte, Le nozze di Figaro), La Scala Milan (Idomeneo, Salome); orchs conducted incl: London Philharmonic, Leipzig Gewandhausorchester, Houston Symphony Orch, Rotterdam Philharmonic, Los Angeles Philharmonic, Oslo Philharmonic, Berlin Philharmonic, Oslo Philharmonic, Frankfurt Radio Orch, Orchestre des Champs Elysees, Bayerische Staatsoper Orch, Vienna Philharmonic, Dreden Staatskapelle, Philadelphia Orch, LA Philharmonic, Chicago, Bayerische Rundfunk; *Recordings* works by Lutoslawski with soprano Solveig Kringelborn and the Norwegian Chamber Orch, works by Britten with Ian Bostridge and the Britten Sinofonia (awarded Choc de L'Annee 198), Beethoven Overtures, Brahms' Symphonies 3 and 4, with Deutsche Kammerphilharmonie, Mozart's Don Giovanni, Mahler Symphony 4 with Mahler Chamber Orch recorded live at Aix-en-Provence Festival, Mahler's Symphony no 10 with Vienna Philharmonic Orchestra, Mozart, Gluck and Haydn arias with Patricia Petibon and Concerto Köln for Deutsche Grammophon, Billy Budd with LSO for Virign/EMI, Tchaikovsky Violin Concerto with MCO and Janine Jansen for DG; *Style—* Daniel Harding, Esq; ✉ c/o Askonas Holt, Lincoln House, 300 High Holborn, London WC1V 7JH (☎ 020 7400 1700, fax 020 7400 1799, e-mail info@askonasholt.co.uk)

HARDING, Frank Alexander; s of Eric Harding (d 1981), and Elsie, *née* Alexander (d 2004); *b* 20 September 1937; *Educ* Malvern Coll, Ecole de Commerce de Neuchâtel; *m* 30 Aug 1960, Belinda Ruth; 2 s (David b 1961, Thomas b 1968), 2 da (Kate b 1963, Amanda b 1967); *Career* CA 1961, ptnr KPMG (formerly KMG Thomson McLintock) 1967–96 (joined 1955); chm: Provalis plc 1998–2006, KLM Cityhopper UK Ltd 1998–2016; memb Cncl: ICAS 1980–85, ICAEW 1990–93; Int Fedn of Accountants: memb Cncl (UK rep) 1987–97, pres 1997–2000; memb Exec Ctee Union of European Accountants 1983–86, memb Int Accounting Standards Advsy Cncl 1995–2000; Officier de l'Ordre National de Mérite (France); *Recreations* golf, opera, bridge; *Style—* Mr Frank Harding; ✉ 11 Pilgrim's Lane, London NW3 1SJ (☎ 020 7435 3728, fax 020 7431 8689, e-mail frankaharding@btinternet.com)

HARDING, Dr Geoffrey Wright; s of Jack Harding (d 1989), of Gravesend, Kent, and Ethel Florence, *née* Wilkinson (d 1997); *Educ* KCL (LLB, AKC), Northwestern Univ Sch of Law Chicago (LLM), QMC London (PhD); *m* 7 Oct 1972, Margaret June, da of Eric Oscar Danger; 1 da (Kate Joanna b 1978), 1 s (Peter James John b 1980); *Career* Nat Serv RAF 1951–53; called to the Bar Gray's Inn 1957; asst sec FCEC 1958–60, legal advsr Br Insurance (Atomic Energy) Ctee 1960–63, exchange lawyer under Harvard Law Sch Prog Isham Lincoln and Beale Attorneys Chicago 1963–64, asst slr Joynson Hicks 1965–67, ptnr Wilde Sapte London and Brussels (specialising in banking, consumer, competition, IT and Euro Union law) 1967–94, ind legal conslt 1994–; legal advsr Competition Cmmn 2001–02; visiting prof in commercial law Univ of Greenwich 1995–98, external examiner Bd of Examiners Univ of London and UWE; former patient govr and former lead govr Membership Cncl Royal Marsden Hosp NHS Fndn Tst; memb Alumni Ctee KCL; Gen Electric Fndn fell Northwestern Univ Sch of Law Chicago; Freeman City of London 1986, memb Guild of Freemen of City of London; *Books* Banking Act 1987 – Current Law Annotated (1987), Encyclopaedia of Competition Law (contrib ed, 1987–2002), Consumer Credit and Consumer Hire Law (1995); *Recreations* family, mountain biking, scuba diving, trying to understand autism, avoiding domestic DIY; *Style—* Dr Geoffrey Harding; ✉ SNR Denton, 1 Fleet Place, London EC4M 7WS (☎ 020 7246 7000, fax 020 7246 7777)

HARDING, Prof Graham Frederick Anthony; s of Frederick William Harding (d 1991), of Shenstone, and Elizabeth Louise Harding (d 1991); *b* 19 March 1937; *Educ* Torquay GS, UCL (BSc), Univ of Birmingham (PhD), Aston Univ (DSc); *m* 1, 4 March 1961 (m dis 1990), Margaret; 2 da (Catherine Louise b 25 Oct 1965, Laura Jane b 14 Aug 1969); m 2, 20 Sept 1991, Pamela Frances, da of Peter Frederick Evans, of Solihull; 1 s (Anthony Gray b 20 May 1993); *Career* hon conslt electroencephalographer Wolverhampton AHA 1974–, hon conslt neuropsychologist Birmingham AHA 1974–, hon conslt clinical neurophysiologist Royal Wolverhampton Hosps Tst 1995–, hon sr research fell Med Sch Univ of Birmingham; Aston Univ: reader in neuropsychology 1973–78, head of neuropsychology unit 1969–78, prof of clinical neurophysiology 1978–2004 (emeritus prof 2004–), head of Clinical Neurophysiology Unit 1979–, head of Vision Sciences 1981–89, head of psychology and biology 1997–99; pres Br Soc for Clinical Neurophysiology (formerly Electroencephalographic Soc) 1996–99 (memb 1963–, memb Cncl 1971–75), sec Int Fedn of Clinical Neurophysiology 2001–06, dir Neurosciences Research Inst 1999–2002; memb: Ctee on Clinical Neurophysiology W Midlands RHA 1975–2004, Midland Opthalmological Soc 1985–, Int League Against Epilepsy 1983–, Int Soc for Clinical Electrophysiology of Vision 1973–2004 (vice-pres 2001–03), Birmingham Medico-Legal Soc 1992–2004; tstee Birmingham Eye Fndn 1989–2004, patron Birmingham Royal Inst for the Blind Appeal 1990–2004, patron Queen Alexandra Coll Birmingham; FRSM 1996–2004 (memb Cncl for Neurosciences 1997), Hon FRCP 2006 (Hon MRCP 1998), FBPsS, CPsychol; *Books* Photosensitive Epilepsy (1975 and 1994); over 300 chapters and papers on electroencephalography, visual evoked responses, Alzheimer's disease, psychiatry, prematurity, ophthalmology and neuromagnetism; *Recreations* railways, model railways; *Style—* Prof Graham Harding; ✉ Electro Diagnostic Centre, Greenfields, Upton Snodsbury, Worcestershire WR7 4NR (☎ and fax 01905 381335, e-mail gharding@wyenet.co.uk)

HARDING, Ian John; s of Reginald Harding, of Basildon, Essex, and Sheila, *née* Felton; *b* 19 March 1964; *Educ* St Nicholas Basildon, Southend Coll of Technol (Design Dip, HND Graphic Design, SIAD Award); *m* 30 July 1988, Nicola, da of Antony George; 2 da (Emma b 1990, Jessica b 2001), 1 s (Joe b 1993); *Career* former creative appts: MWA Advertising, Moorgate fin advtg & mktg, FCB Impact (sr art dir), FCA (jt creative dir); founding ptnr Heresy, owner and founder The Complete Image Ltd, owner and fndr Complete Creative Communication; recipient over 78 awards across all mktg disciplines since 1992 incl: D&AD Silver Award 1993, 12 DMA Gold Awards, ISP Grand Prix, Campaign Poster Award; memb D&AD 1993 (SIAD 1984); *Recreations* gym, golf, squash, painting; *Style—* Mr Ian Harding; ✉ 43 Elmhurst Avenue, Benfleet, Essex SS7 5RY (☎ 01268 565171, fax 01268 565171, e-mail ianharding@blueyonder.co.uk)

HARDING, Prof John Edmond; s of William Gordon Harding (d 1987), and Alice Eleanor Harding (d 1985); *b* 22 November 1948; *Educ* St Joseph's Coll Beulah Hill, Imperial Coll London (BSc(Eng), MSc, DIC, PhD); *m* 7 Jan 1978, Patricia Anne, da of late Henry Wigfull; 2 da (Emma Philippa b 18 Aug 1980, Laura Anne b 20 July 1982); *Career* lectr in structural engrg Imperial Coll London 1978–85 (research asst/research fell 1971–78); Univ of Surrey: prof of structural engrg 1985–, pro-vice-chllr 1991–2001, head Dept of Civil Engrg 1997–2002, dir of external academic relationships 2002–; memb US Structural Stability Research Cncl 1988–; ed Int Jl of Constructional Steel Research 1980–, hon ed Structures and Buildings proceedings Instn of Civil Engrs until 1996; memb Bd of Govrs: Farnborough Coll of Technol, NE Surrey Coll of Technol, Reigate Sixth Form Coll, St Mary's Coll Strawberry Hill, Tormead Sch Guildford, Wimbledon Sch of Art; awarded Trevithick Premium Instn of Civil Engrs 1977; CEng, FIStructE 1986 (MIStructE 1980), FICE 1993 (MICE 1989); *Books* Bridge Management – Inspection, Maintenance, Assessment and Repair (ed 3 vols, 1990, 1993 and 1996), Traversely Stiffened Girder Webs Subject to Combined Loading (1991), Constructional Steel Design – an International Guide (ed, 1992), World Developments in Constructional Steel Design (ed, 1993), Manual of Bridge Engineering (ed, 2000); also author of numerous conference papers, and contribs to learned jls; *Style—* Prof John Harding; ✉ University of Surrey, Guildford, Surrey GU2 5XH (☎ 01483 689119, fax 01483 572454, e-mail j.harding@surrey.ac.uk)

HARDING, Prof John James; s of George James Harding, and Mary Edith, *née* Simmons; *b* 2 June 1938, London; *Educ* Trinity Coll Cambridge (BA), Univ of London (PhD); *m* 1962, Ruth, *née* Taylor; 2 s (Paul b 9 Nov 1969, Daniel b 20 March 1971); *Career* Nuffield Lab of Ophthalmology Univ of Oxford: sr research scientist 1986–96, reader in ophthalmology 1996–97, prof of ocular biochemistry 1997–; head of ophthalmology Univ of Oxford 2003–05; visiting prof Tangdu Hosp Fourth Military Medical Univ (FMMU) Xi'an China; memb Biochemical Soc; chm Tackley and Dist Field Paths Gp, sec Tackley Local History Gp, chm Science Discussion Gp of U3A Woodstock; *Books* Cataract: Biochemistry, Epidemiology and Pharmacology (1991); *Recreations* walking, grandchildren, local history, painting, music; *Style—* Prof John J Harding; ✉ 55 St John's Road, Tackley, Oxfordshire OX5 3AR; Nuffield Laboratory of Ophthalmology, University of Oxford, West Wing, John Radcliffe Hospital, Oxford

HARDING, Dr (Leslie) Keith; s of Leslie Charles Harding (d 1964), of West Bromwich, and Priscilla Olive, *née* Mason (d 1984); *b* 3 February 1939; *Educ* Handsworth GS, Univ of Birmingham Med Sch (BSc, MB ChB); *m* 18 Aug 1962, Carol Margaret, da of Dr Colin Starkie, of Kidderminster; 1 s (Nicholas b 1969), 1 da (Victoria b 1972); *Career* lectr in med Queen Elizabeth Hosp Birmingham, conslt in nuclear med Dudley Rd Hosp Birmingham 1982– (conslt physician in gen and nuclear med 1972–82), clinical sr lectr in med Univ of Birmingham 1982–, med dir/conslt in nuclear med City Hosp NHS Tst Birmingham 1994–2000, hon reader in med Univ of Birmingham 1999–; author of chapters on gastric emptying and bile reflux; papers on: gastro intestinal motility, the lung, radiation safety in nuclear med depts; former memb Advsy Cncl European Assoc of Nuclear Med, Int Cmmn radiological prot and sec Ctee 3, memb Article 31 Ctee (advising EC), memb Ionizing and Radiation Ctee Health and Safety Cmmn; former chm: Regnl Med Advsy Ctee, Med Exec Ctee W Birmingham Health Authy (also dep dist gen mangr), Admin of Radioactive Substances Advsy Ctee, Euro Task Gp exploring risks; past treas and pres Br Nuclear Med Soc; bailiff and fndn govr King Edward VI Schs Birmingham, vice-chm of govrs Five Ways Sch; FRCP, FRCR, FSRP; *Recreations* music, King Edward VI School; *Clubs* Lunar Soc; *Style—* Dr Keith Harding; ✉ Huntroyd, 27 Manor Road North, Edgbaston, Birmingham B16 9JS (☎ 0121 242 2497, e-mail keith@huntroyd.freeserve.co.uk)

HARDING, Nigel; *b* 1 May 1976, Manchester; *Educ* Univ of East Anglia (BA); *Partner* Brad Hunner (civil partnership 15 Jan 2006); *Career* music promotions Alan James PR 1996–2002, radio programmer XFM 2002–06, music policy exec BBC Radio 1 2006–15, dir Nothing Else Matters Records 2015–; *Recreations* electronic music production; *Style—* Nigel Harding, Esq; ✉ Nothing Else Matters Records, Sony Music Entertainment, 99 Derry Street, London W8 5HY

HARDING, Philip; s of Douglas Harding, and Leonora, *née* Browne; *b* 28 April 1947; *Educ* Univ of York (BA), Wharton Business Sch; *m* 1979, Margo; 1 da (Laura); *Career* dep ed Nationwide 1980–81, dep ed Panorama 1981–83 (sr prodr 1978–80), ed London Plus 1984–86, asst head current affrs BBC TV 1986–87 (prodr 1972–78), ed Today BBC Radio Four 1987–93, project dir Radio Five Live, ed Five Live News Progs 1993, BBC chief political advsr 1995–96, controller Editorial Policy 1996–2001, dir English Networks and News BBC World Service 2001–07, journalist and media conslt 2007–; tstee: Press Assoc 2008–, One World Media 2008, CPU 2010–; memb Cncl Media Soc 2010; fell Radio Acad 1999 (memb Cncl 1995–2001), FRSA 1999, fell Soc of Eds 2007; *Awards* Emmy Award for Best Documentary Who Killed Georgi Markov? (Panorama) 1980; Sony Awards: Best Current Affrs Prog 1989 (for Today), Best Response to a News Event 1989 (for Today), Best Daily News Prog 1990 (for Today), Best Response To A News Event 1990 (for Today), Best Breakfast Prog 1992 (for Today), Best Coverage Breaking News 2005 (for BBC World Service), Best News Feature 2006 (for BBC World Service); BPG Award

H

1992; *Recreations* thinking, walking, watching football and supporting QPR; *Style*— Philip Harding, Esq; ✉ e-mail phil@hardingmedia.com

HARDING OF WINSCOMBE, Baroness (Life Peer UK 2014) of Nether Compton in the County of Dorset; Diana (Dido) Harding; da of 2 Baron Harding of Petherton; *Educ* Univ of Oxford, Harvard Business Sch (MBA); *m* John Penrose, MP, *qv*; *Career* formerly: mktg dir Thomas Cook Gp, commercial dir Woolworths Gp, commercial dir then int support dir Tesco plc, convenience dir Sainsbury's; ceo Talktalk Gp 2010–; non-exec dir Br Land plc 2010–; *Style*— Baroness Harding of Winscombe; ✉ TalkTalk Telecom Group plc, 11 Evesham Street, London W11 4AR

HARDINGE OF PENSHURST, 4 Baron (UK 1910); Julian Alexander Hardinge; s of 3 Baron (d 1997); *b* 23 August 1945; *Educ* Eton, Trinity Coll Cambridge; *m* 1, 1972 (m dis 1993), Anthea June, da of Harold Mills West; 2 da (Frances Melanie b 1973, Sophie Jane b 1974); *m* 2, 2001, Ulrike, da of Heinz Adolph, of Jestetten, Germany; *Career* chm and chief exec Mallory Int Ltd 2002–, chm Batch.co.uk 2002–07 (dir 1998–2007); dir: Book Tokens Ltd 1984–2004, Hardinge Simpole Publishing 2002–12, EQSN Ltd 2002–12; former chair Export Gp and Coll and Univ Gp Booksellers Assoc, chm Baobab Ebook Services 2013–; memb Int Bd Publishers Assoc; *Style*— The Rt Hon Lord Hardinge of Penshurst; ✉ website www.malloryint.co.uk

HARDINGHAM, Michael; s of Edmund Arthur Hardingham, and Winifred, *née* Leeding; *b* 16 October 1939; *Educ* West House Sch, Solihull Sch, St Mary's Hosp Univ of London (MB BS); *m* 25 Sept 1982, Ellen, da of William McCafferty, of Pennsylvania, USA; 1 s (Henry b 1984), 1 da (Isabel b 1986); *Career* postgrad med trg London, Edinburgh and Sweden, trg in otorhinolaryngology St Mary's Royal Marsden Hosp, conslt ENT surgn Cheltenham Gen Hosp and Gloucestershire Royal Hosp 1974– (special interest head and neck oncology), pres Glos Div BMA 2003–04, former hon sec Br Assoc of Head and Neck Oncologists, foreign corresponding memb American Soc of Head and Neck Surgns; past pres SW Laryngolical Assoc; vice-pres Nursing Assoc of Midland Inst of Otology, past pres Midland Inst Otorhinolaryngology; contrib pubns to otolaryngolical clinics N America; FRCSEd, FRCS 1973, FRSM, fell BMA 2006; *Recreations* theatre, opera, scuba diving; *Style*— Michael Hardingham, Esq; ✉ Winfield Hospital, Tewkesbury Road, Gloucester GL2 9EE (☎ 01452 337279, fax 01452 331200, e-mail hardinghamcheltorl@hotmail.com)

HARDWICK, Nicholas Lionel (Nick); CBE (2010); s of Herbert Lionel Hardwick (d 1987), and Nancy Enid, *née* Nightingale (d 1990); *b* 19 July 1957; *Educ* Epsom Coll, Univ of Hull (BA); *Children* 1 da (Sophie b 1979); *m*, Susan, *née* Heaven; 1 s (Jack b 1992); *Career* chief exec: Centrepoint 1985–95, Refugee Cncl 1995–2003; special advsr to DOE 1990, memb Social Security Advsy Ctee 1994–99; chm: Euro Cncl on Refugees and Exiles (ECRE) 1999–2003, Independent Police Complaints Cmmn 2003–10, Housing Ombudsman Service 2010–13, Parole Bd 2016–; HM chief inspector of prisons 2010–16; prof of criminal justice Sch of Law Royal Holloway Univ of London 2016–; hon visiting fell Criminology Dept Univ of Leicester; Hon DSSc Univ of Wolverhampton 2002, Hon DLitt Univ of Hull 2011, Hon DLaw Leeds Beckett Univ 2016; *Recreations* family; *Clubs* RSA; *Style*— Nick Hardwick, CBE; ✉ The School of Law, Royal Holloway University of London, Egham, Surrey TW20 0EX (☎ 07808 208785, e-mail nicholas.hardwick@rhul.ac.uk)

HARDY, Amanda; QC (2015); *b* 12 December 1969; *Educ* City of London Sch for Girls, KCL (LLB, LLM, AKC); *m* 2 April 1994, Matthew; 3 da (Megan May b 30 March 2000, Phoebe June b 12 Aug 2002, Ella April b 30 March 2006); *Career* called to the Bar (Middle Temple) 1993 (Queen Mother's Scholar); hon sec Chancery Bar Assoc, chair Pro Bono Sub-Ctee Chancery Bar Assoc, memb Revenue Bar Assoc; visiting lectr Law of Trusts KCL 1993–98; Liveryman Worshipful Co of Tax Advisors, Freedom of the City of London 2011; *Recreations* cinema, fashion, reading, travel; *Style*— Ms Amanda Hardy, QC

HARDY, David Gordon; s of Gordon Patrick Hardy, of Auchtermuchty, Fife, and Margaret Maud, *née* Cunningham; *b* 5 July 1940; *Educ* Daniel Stewart's Coll Edinburgh, Univ of Edinburgh (BSc, MB ChB), Univ of Cambridge (MA); *m* 8 Aug 1967, Maria Rosa (Rosemary), da of Johann Breu (d 1965), of Appenzell, Switzerland; 1 da (Ruth Maria b 10 Oct 1969), 1 s (James Patrick b 5 Oct 1971); *Career* Fulbright Hayes scholar Univ of Florida 1977–78, sr lectr in neurosurgery London Hosp Med Coll 1979–80, conslt neurosurgn Addenbrooke's Hosp Cambridge 1980–2005, med dir Addenbrooke's Hosp NHS Tst, supervisor in anatomy Gonville & Caius Coll Cambridge (assoc lectr faculty of clinical med); visiting conslt Norfolk and Norwich Hosp; chm Medical Advsy Panel The Evelyn Tst 2003–14, tstee Addenbrooke's Charitable Tst 2005–09 (chm of tstees 2009–14); contrib various chapters and papers on various neurosurgical and anatomical subjects; memb Section of Neurology RSM; pres Soc of Br Neurosurgeons 2002–04 (vice-pres 2001–02 and 2004–05); FRCSEd 1970, FRCS 1971, FRSM; *Recreations* gardening, walking; *Style*— David Hardy, Esq; ✉ 20 High Street, Great Wilbraham, Cambridge CB21 5JD (☎ 01223 881347)

HARDY, Edward Thomas (Tom); s of Edward John Hardy, and Elizabeth Ann, *née* Barrett; *b* 15 September 1977, Hammersmith, London; *Educ* Reeds Sch Oxshott, Duff Miller Tutorial Coll London, Central St Martin's; *Career* actor; artistic dir Shotgun Theatre Co (with Robert Delamere and Brett C Leonard); *Theatre* Man of Mode (Nat Theatre), In Arabia We Would All Be Kings (Hampstead Theatre), Blood (Royal Court), Festen (Almeida), The Modernists (Sheffield), Roger and Vanessa (Shotgun at 503 Theatre), Two Storm Wood (Shotgun at 503 Theatre), Blue on Blue (Shotgun at 503 Theatre); *Television* Cape Wrath, Colditz, Stuart: A Life Backwards, The Virgin Queen, Oliver Twist, Wuthering Heights, The Take; *Film* Band of Brothers, Black Hawk Down, Star Trek, The Reckoning, The Code, Deserter, Scenes of a Sexual Nature, Layer Cake, Bronson, Thick as Thieves, Inception, Tinker Tailor Soldier Spy, Warrior, This Means War, Lawless, The Dark Knight Rises, Locke, Legend 2015; *Awards* Most Promising Newcomer Evening Standard Awards 2003, nominee Best Newcomer Olivier Awards 2007, nominee Best Breakthrough TV Southbank Awards 2007, Orange Rising Star Award BAFTA 2011; *Clubs* Groucho, Union; *Style*— Tom Hardy, Esq; ✉ c/o Lindy King, United Agents Limited, 12–26 Lexington Street, London W1F 0LE (☎ 020 3214 0800, fax 020 3214 0801)

HARDY, Col James Howard; s of Kenneth William Hardy, and Sheila Kathleen, *née* Hurst; *b* 14 May 1944, Borden, Kent; *Educ* King's Sch Canterbury, London Dental Sch UCH (BDS, MSc, LDS RCS(Eng)); Diploma in Forensic Human Identification (Dip FHID), Diploma in Forensic Odontology (Dip F Od); *m* 10 Aug 1985, Jean Rosemary, *née* Reid; 1 da (Olivia b 6 June 1991); *Career* general dental practitioner with specialist interests in periodontology and forensic odontology; Br Army: served UK and NI, Germany, Brunei and Belize, dir Sch of Dental Hygiene and clinical advsr in periodontology and preventive dentistry Aldershot 1980–83; RADC: dep commandant HQ and Training Centre 1991, cdr 9 Dental Gp (NI) 1993–96, cdr 5 Dental Gp 1996, estab and led DDA Postgrad Inst RAF Halton 1996–99, ret RADC 2001; civilian dental practitioner MOD 2001–10; currently lead forensic odontologist LGC Forensics and lectr in forensic odontology; memb UK Disaster Victim Identification Team; memb: BDA 1966, RSM 1971, Br Soc for General Dental Surgery (1985), Br Assoc for Forensic Odontology (past pres) 1987; past examiner and ctee memb Nat Examining Bd for Dental Nurses; tstee Army Medical Services Museum; Liveryman Soc of Apothecaries; MGDS RCS(Eng), MGDS RCS(Ed); OStJ (Brother) 2001; *Publications* chapters in: Forensic Human Identification (2006), Forensic and Legal Dentistry (2013); *Recreations* cinema, gardening, music, opera, skiing, travel, walking, photography, keep fit and gym training; *Clubs*

Candlewick Ward; *Style*— Col J H Hardy, OStJ; ✉ 6 Trebor Avenue, Farnham, Surrey GU9 8JH (☎ 01252 721026, mobile 07714 381029, e-mail jojhardy@gmail.com)

HARDY, Timothy (Tim); s of Robert Norman Hardy (d 1992), and Patricia Margaret May, *née* Keen (d 1985); *b* 17 February 1956; *Educ* Royal GS High Wycombe, Balliol Coll Oxford (MA); *m* 29 April 2000, Angela, *née* Spencer; *Career* admitted slr 1982; ptnr Barlow Lyde & Gilbert 1987–2008 (slr 1982–87); asst sec-gen (admin) and presidential cncl memb Association Internationale de Droit des Assurances (AIDA) and chm AIDA Climate Change Working Party 2010–, treas and memb Ctee AIDA Europe 2012–; Br Insurance Law Assoc (BILA): memb Ctee 1993–, chm 1996–98, vice-pres 2004–; CEDR accredited mediator 1998; memb: AIDA Reinsurance & Insurance Arbitration Soc; vice-chair BILA Charitable Tst, tstee Stagetext 2013– (vice-chair Bd 2015–), mentor City Disabilities 2015–; MCII; *Publications* Reinsurance Practice and the Law (co-author, 1993); also author of various journal articles, conference papers and presentations; *Recreations* reading, theatre, sports, travel; *Clubs* Nepotists Cricket, MCC, Hampstead Golf; *Style*— Tim Hardy, Esq; ✉ 16 Chalcot Crescent, Primrose Hill, London NW1 8YD (☎ 020 7722 6981, e-mail t_hardy@btconnect.com)

HARE, Christopher Peter; s of Reginald Charles Hare (d 1980), and Mary Euphemia, *née* Lefroy (d 1988); *b* 6 November 1947; *Educ* Dover Coll; *m* (Dorothy) Jane, da of Richard Gough Dowell (d 1996), of Middleton-on-Sea, W Sussex; 1 da (Rebecca Anne b 14 Feb 1975), 2 s (Nicholas Anthony b 28 May 1977, Julian Charles b 17 Nov 1981); *Career* John Dickenson & Co 1966–68, Lyon Trail Attenborough (formerly Lyon Lohr & Sly) 1968–85; dir: Lyon Lohr Group Services 1979 (gp admin 1979–85), Lyon Lohr Int 1980; md Aberdeen Underwriting Advisers (formerly Minories Underwriting Agencies) 1997–99 (joined 1985, dir 1986–99); dir: Hampden Agencies Ltd 1999–2001, PRO Syndicate Mgmnt 2001–05, RITC Syndicate Mgmnt Ltd 2007–12; non-exec dir Lloyd's Members Agency Services Ltd (LMAS) 1998–2012, ind non-exec dir Resolute Management Ltd 2016–; govr Dover Coll 1982– (memb Cncl and Fin Ctee 1982–2007, vice-chm 1991–94, chm 1994–2007), pres Old Dovorian Club 2003–05 (memb 1975–96, chm 1984–90), govr Merchant Taylors' Sch 1993–2005 (chm of govrs 2011); Freeman City of London, memb Ct of Assts Worshipful Co of Merchant Taylors (Master 2009–10); *Recreations* cricket, tennis, squash, golf; *Clubs* MCC, RAC, Roehampton; *Style*— Christopher Hare, Esq; ✉ 40 Doneraile Street, London SW6 6EP (☎ 020 7736 4218, e-mail chris@hare100.co.uk)

HARE, Sir David; kt (1998); s of Clifford Theodore Rippon, and Agnes Cockburn Hare; *b* 5 June 1947; *Educ* Lancing, Jesus Coll Cambridge (MA); *m* 1 (m dis), Margaret Matheson; 2 s, 1 da; *m* 2, Nicole Farhi; *Career* playwright and director; fndr Portable Theatre 1968, literary mangr and resident dramatist Royal Court Theatre 1969–71, resident dramatist Nottingham Playhouse 1973, fndr Joint Stock Theatre Gp 1975, fndr Greenpoint Films 1982, assoc dir Royal Nat Theatre 1985–98; Officier de l'ordre des Art et des Lettres 1997; US/UK Bicentennial fell 1976; FRSL 1985; *Plays* writer: Slag (Royal Court and NY Shakespeare Festival 1971), The Great Exhibition (Hampstead 1972), Brassneck (also dir, Nottingham Playhouse 1973, televised 1974), Knuckle (Comedy Theatre 1974, televised 1989), Fanshen (Joint Stock, ICA and Hampstead 1975, televised 1975, NT 1992), Teeth'n'Smiles (also dir, Royal Ct 1975, Wyndhams 1976), Plenty (also dir, NT 1978 and NYSF 1982, Albery 1999), A Map of the World (Adelaide Festival 1982, NT 1983, NYSF 1985), Pravda (also dir, with Howard Brenton, NT 1985), The Bay at Nice (also dir NT 1986), The Secret Rapture (NT 1988, and dir NYSF & Broadway 1989), Racing Demon (NT 1990 and 1993, Broadway 1995), Murmuring Judges (NT 1992 and 1993), The Absence of War (NT 1993, televised 1995, Headlong tour 2015), Skylight (NT 1995, Wyndhams and Broadway 1996, Vaudeville 1997, Wyndhams 2014, Broadway 2015), Amy's View (NT 1997, Aldwych 1998, Broadway 1999 and Garrick 2006), The Judas Kiss (Almeida Playhouse and Broadway 1998, Hampstead 2012 and Duke of York's 2013), The Blue Room (from Schnitzler, Donmar and Broadway 1998, Theatre Royal Haymarket 2000), Via Dolorosa (also performed, Duke of York's 1998, Almeida and Broadway 1999, Duchess Theatre 2002, Melbourne Festival 2004), My Zinc Bed (also dir, Royal Court 2000, televised 2008), The Breath of Life (Theatre Royal Haymarket 2002), The Permanent Way (Out of Joint 2003 and 2005, NT 2004), Stuff Happens (NT 2004, NYSF 2006), The Vertical Hour (Music Box Theatre NY 2006, Royal Court Theatre 2008, Park Theatre 2014), Gethsemane (NT 2008), Berlin/Wall (also performed, NT, Royal Court and NYSF 2009), The Power of Yes (NT 2009), South Downs (Chichester Festival Theatre 2011, Harold Pinter Theatre 2012), Behind the Beautiful Forevers (NT 2014), The Moderate Soprano (2015), The Red Barn (from Simenon, 2016); dir: Christie in Love (Portable Theatre, 1969), Fruit (Portable Theatre, 1970), Blowjob (Portable Theatre, 1971), England's Ireland (co-dir, Portable Theatre, 1972), The Provoked Wife (Palace Theatre Watford, 1973), The Pleasure Principle (Theatre Upstairs, 1973), The Party (NT, 1974), Weapons of Happiness (NT, 1976), Devil's Island (Joint Stock, 1977), Total Eclipse (Lyric Hammersmith, 1981), King Lear (NT, 1986), The Designated Mourner (NT, 1996), Heartbreak House (Almeida, 1997), The Year of Magical Thinking (Broadway 2007, NT 2008); wrote libretto for The Knife (with Nick Bicat and Tim Rose Price, NY 1988); *Adaptations* The Rules of the Game (from Pirandello, NT 1971 and Almeida 1992), The Life of Galileo (from Brecht, Almeida 1994), Mother Courage and Her Children (from Brecht, NT 1995), Ivanov (from Chekhov, Almeida 1997, Broadway 1998, Chichester 2015), Platonov (from Chekov, Almeida 2001, Chichester 2015), The House of Bernarda Alba (from Lorca, NT 2005), Enemies (from Gorky, Almeida 2006), The Seagull (from Chekhov, Chichester 2015), The Master Builder (from Ibsen, 2015); *Television* Man Above Men (BBC, 1973), Licking Hitler (also dir 1978, BAFTA Award), Dreams of Leaving (BBC, also dir, 1979), Saigon: Year of the Cat (also assoc prodr, 1983), Heading Home (BBC, also dir, 1991), Page Eight (BBC and NBC Universal, also dir, 2011), Turks and Caicos (BBC and NBC Universal, also dir, 2014), Salting the Battlefield (BBC and NBC Universal, also dir, 2014); *Films* writer and dir: Wetherby (1985, Golden Bear Award Berlin), Paris By Night (1989), Strapless (1990); writer only: Plenty (1985), Damage (adapted from Josephine Hart novel, 1992), The Secret Rapture (also assoc prodr, 1993), The Hours (adapted from Michael Cunningham novel, 2002), The Reader (from the novel by Bernard Schlink, 2008), Wall (also performed, 2016), Denial (2016), The White Crow (2017); *Radio* Murder in Samarkand (BBC, 2010); *Books* Writing Lefthanded (1991), Asking Around (1993), Acting Up (1999), Obedience, Struggle and Revolt (2005), The Blue Touch Paper (2015); *Style*— Sir David Hare, FRSL; ✉ c/o Casarrotto Ramsay Ltd, 7–12 Noel Street, London W1F 8GQ (☎ 020 7287 4450, fax 020 7287 9128)

HARE, John Neville; s of late Capt Lancelot Geldart Hare, MC (d 1957), and Esther Maria, *née* Whales (d 1969); *b* 11 December 1934; *Educ* St Edward's Sch Oxford; *m* 17 Sept 1966, Pippa, da of Harding McGregor Dunnett (d 2000); 3 da (Charlotte b 1968, Henrietta b 1970, Emily b 1974); *Career* Lt Oxford and Bucks LI, Royal W Africa Frontier Force 1954–55; sr dist offr Colonial Serv Northern Nigeria 1957–64; dir Macmillan Education Publishers 1966–74, author and conslt Hodder and Stoughton Publishers 1980–89; UN Environment Prog 1989–96; memb: Scientific Expdn to the Mongolian Gobi 1993 and 2005, Xinjiang Environment Protection Inst Expdn to the Gobi to survey the wild camel population 1995 and to Lop Nur 1996, 1997, 1999, 2005 and 2011; ldr Trans-Sahara Camel Expedition 2001–02, Lake Turkana 2006; fndr Wild Camel Protection Fndn 1997; Ness Award RGS 2004, Lawrence of Arabia Meml Medal RSAA 2004, Mungo Park Medal RSGS 2006, Lowell Thomas Award Explorers Club 2010; FRGS; *Books* The Lost Camels of Tartary (1998), Shadows Across the Sahara (2003), Mysteries of the Gobi (2009), Last Man In (2013), and 38 other books; *Recreations* hunting, travel, writing; *Clubs* Travellers; *Style*— John Hare, Esq; ✉ School Farm, Benenden, Kent TN17 4EU

(☎ 01580 241132, e-mail harecamel@aol.com, website www.wildcamels.com and www.johnhare.org.uk)

HAREN, Dr Sir Patrick Hugh; kt (2008); *Educ* Queen's Univ Belfast; *Career* Viridian Gp Ltd (formerly NI Electricity plc): gp chief exec 1992–2007, dep chm 2007–; formerly dir of new business investment Electricity Supply Bd; former research fell European Centre for Nuclear Research Geneva; memb Bd Invest NI; FREng 1998; *Style—* Dr Sir Patrick Haren, FREng; ✉ Viridian Group Ltd, 120 Malone Road, Belfast BT9 5HT

HAREWOOD, David Michael; MBE (2012); s of Romeo Cornelius Harewood, and Mayleen Coppin; *b* 8 December 1965, Birmingham; *Educ* Washwood Heath Comprehensive Birmingham, RADA; *Career* actor; *Television* incl: Spatz 1991–93, Agony Again 1995, Macbeth on the Estate 1997, Always and Everyone 1999–2001, The Vice 1999–2003, Silent Witness 2004, Fat Friends 2004–05, New Street Law 2006, The Palace 2008, The Last Enemy 2008, Criminal Justice 2008, Robin Hood 2009, Mrs Mandela 2010, Strike Back 2010, Hustle 2011, Homeland 2011–12, Treasure Island 2012, Playhouse Presents 2013; *Film* incl: Mad Dogs and Englishmen 1995, I Wonder Who's Kissing You Now 1998, The Merchant of Venice 2004, Separate Lies 2005, Blood Diamond 2006, Victim 2011, The Man Inside 2012; *Theatre* incl: Romeo and Juliet, Anthony and Cleopatra (David Papp Public Theater NY) 1997; NT: Othello 1997, Henry IV 2005, His Dark Materials 2004, Welcome to Thebes 2010; The Mountaintop (Theatre503) 2009, A Midsummer Night's Dream (Polonsky Shakespeare Center NY) 2013; Best Actor Award Screen Nations, Best Actor Award EMMA; ambass Princes Tst, Anthony Nolan Leukaemia Tst; *Recreations* cinema, motorsport, reading, tennis, travel; *Clubs* Groucho; *Style—* David Harewood, Esq, MBE; ✉ c/o Conway van Gelder Grant, Third floor, 8/12 Broadwick Street, London W1F 8HW

HARGRAVE, David Grant; s of late (Frank) Edward Hargrave, of Cyncoed, Cardiff, and late Margaret Constance Mabel, *née* Grant; *b* 11 April 1951; *Educ* Howardian HS Cardiff, Univ of Birmingham (BCom, MSc); *m* 13 Dec 1969, Celia, da of Harry Hawksworth (d 1963); 1 da (Emma Louise b 17 June 1970), 1 s (Neil David b 30 July 1974); *Career* actuary Duncan C Fraser & Co (later Mercer Human Resource Consulting Ltd) 1973–79; ptnr and head of employee benefits Aon Hewitt (formerly TG Arthur Hargrave then Hewitt Bacon & Woodrow) 1979–95, chm and non-exec dir engage Mutual Assurance (formerly Homeowners Friendly Soc Ltd) 1982–2011; non-exec dir NHP plc 1996–2001; chm and non-exec dir Deutsche Asset Management Life & Pensions Ltd 1998–2006; non-exec dir MetLife Assurance Ltd 2007–14; tstee: Melton Medes (Fletchers) Pension Fund 1996–2009, Alstom Pension Scheme 1998–2005, Wiggins Teape Pension Scheme 2000–08, Kalamazoo Pension & Life Assurance Plan 2002–06, TKM Gp Pension Scheme 2006–; chm of tstees: Royal Mail Sr Executives Pension Plan 2001–, Antalis Pension Scheme 2008–; FIA 1977; *Recreations* long distance running, swimming, windsurfing, rugby; *Style—* David Hargrave, Esq; ✉ Trench Hill, Painswick, Stroud, Gloucestershire GL6 6TZ (e-mail d.hargrave@btconnect.com)

HARGRAVE, Dr Philip John; s of Edward James Anthony Hargrave (d 1963), and Doris Elsie, *née* Jackson (d 1995); *b* 21 June 1950; *Educ* Hinchley Wood Sch, Univ of Bristol (BSc), Cavendish Laboratory Univ of Cambridge (PhD); *m* 5 Oct 1985, Maureen Joyce, da of Alfred James Brook (d 2013); 1 s (David John b 13 Dec 1990); *Career* Sci Research Cncl research fell Cavendish Laboratory Cambridge 1975–77; Standard Telecommunications Laboratories (STL, part of STC UK R&D Lab for ITT): joined 1977, successively research engr, sr research engr, princ research engr and sr princ research engr 1977–84, departmental mangr Adaptive Antenna Systems 1984–86, successively chief research fell, mangr tech strategy and asst dir 1986–92; Harlow Laboratories (following acquisition of STC by Nortel): dir Govt and External Progs then dir Radio and High Integrity Communications 1992–94, dir Next Generation Architecture 1994–95, dir Next Generation Products 1995–98, dir Next Generation Network Technology 1998–99, dir Next Generation Networks 1999–2000; chief scientist EMEA/Nortel 2000–06, ind conslt 2006–08, ceo and network dir Digial Communications KTN 2008–11, ICT KTN 2011–14 (ind conslt 2014–); IET: memb Professional Gp Ctee E15 (Radar, Sonar and Navigation) 1986–92 (chm 1990–92), memb Electronics Divnl Bd 1992–95, memb Schs Educn and Liaison Ctee 1993–96 and 1997–2001, chm Engrg and Technol Educn Editorial Advsy Bd 1997–2011; memb: Global Research Award Steering Gp Royal Acad of Engrg 1999–2002, Standing Ctee for Research and Secondment Schemes Royal Acad of Engrg 2003–08, Standing Ctee for Engrg Policy Royal Acad of Engrg 2005–08, Engrg and Technol Strategic Panel BCS 2005–10 (chm 2007–10), Forward Looking Steering Panel Irish Cmmn for Communication Regulation (ComReg) 2003–08, Bd IT Telecommunications and Electronics Industry Association (Intellect, now techUK) 2001–06, Bd EICTA (European Industry Association for Information Systems, Communication Techologies and Consumer Electronics, now DIGITALEUROPE) 2001–05, Exec Bd UK Broadband Stakeholder Gp 2003–06, Engrg and Sci Bd BCS 2010–13; chm and sec Friends of St James the Great Thorley, chm Governing Cncl Bishop's Stortford Coll; FRAS 1976, CEng 1983, CPhys 1987, FInstP 1987, FIET 1995 (MIET 1983), FREng 1996, CSci 2005, CITP 2007, FBCS 2007; *Publications* Observations of Cygnus A with the 5-km Radio Telescope (with Sir Martin Ryle, 1974), Design and Performance Evaluation of a Five Channel Navstar Receiver (jtly, 1982), Application of a Systolic Array to Adaptive Beamforming (jtly, 1984), A Novel Algorithm and Architecture for Adaptive Digital Beamforming (jtly, 1986), Adaptive Antennas for Modern Electronic Systems (1989), Systolic Beamforming – from Theory to Practice (1991), Next Generation Networks: Design for Reliability (2005); *Recreations* genealogy, local history; *Style—* Dr Philip Hargrave, FREng; ✉ 60 The Paddock, Bishop's Stortford, Hertfordshire CM23 4JW (☎ 01279 657273, e-mail philip.hargrave@btinternet.com)

HARGREAVE, Dr Timothy Bruce; s of Cdr John Michael Hargreave, VRD, and Margaret Isobel Hargreave; *b* 23 March 1944; *Educ* Harrow, Univ of London (MB BS, MS); *m* 27 March 1971, Molly; 2 da (Alison Lucinda b 1972, Sophie Louise b 1976); *Career* sr fell Dept of Surgery Univ of Edinburgh; former: conslt urological surgn, clinical dir Surgical Services Directorate Western General Hosp NHS Tst; corresponding memb German Urological Soc; former chair: Scientific and Ethical Review Gp UNDP, UNFPA, WHO, World Bank Special Prog of Research Devpt And Research Trg in Human Reproduction; co-chair Devices and Innovations Technical Advsy Gp Male Circumcision HIV Prevention Dept of HIV WHO Geneva, former memb Research Review Gp HRP WHO Geneva; former: memb Steering Ctee WHO Infertility Task Force, chm Br Andrology Soc, memb Cncl Br Assoc of Urological Surgns, sec Scot Urological Soc, pres Scottish Urological Assoc; hon memb: Hellenic Urology Soc, Columbian Urology Soc; korrespondierende mitglieder Deutsche Gesellshaft für Urologie; FRCS, FRCSEd, FEB (Urol), FRCPEd; *Books* Practical Urological Endoscopy (1988), Management of Male Infertility (1990), Male Infertility (2 edn, 1994), Andrology for the Clinician (2006), WHO Manual for Male Circumcision Under Local Anaesthesia (2008); *Recreations* skiing; *Style—* Dr Timothy Hargreave; ✉ 20 Cumin Place, Edinburgh EH9 2JX

HARGREAVES, Andrew Raikes; s of Col and Mrs David William Hargreaves; *b* 15 May 1955; *Educ* Eton, St Edmund Hall Oxford (MA); *m* 1978, Fiona Susan, o da of Guy William Dottridge; 2 s (William b 1985, Thomas b 1986); *Career* auctioneer and valuer Christies 1977–81, exec Hill Samuel 1981–83; asst dir: Sawwa International 1983–85, Schroders 1985–87 (conslt 1987–1992); MP (Cons) Birmingham Hall Green 1987–97; former PPS to 4 FO Mins and vice-chm Cons Backbench Def Ctee; memb: House of Commons Parly Cmmr for Admin, Information Technol Select Ctee 1992–97, Armed Forces Parly Scheme RN 1994–95; UK md DaimlerChrysler Aerospace 1997–2000; Euro Aeronautics Defence and Space Co: UK chm 2000–04, sr advsr and gp dir govt affrs 2004–; conslt Midlands Electricity plc 1989–97; sec: back bench Urban and Inner Cities Ctee 1987–91 (chm 1992–94), Defence Ctee 1992–94 (vice-chm 1994–97); memb Bow Gp; *Recreations* fishing, gardening, walking, antiques, art; *Clubs* Boodle's; *Style—* Andrew Hargreaves, Esq

HARGREAVES, Prof Ian Richard; CBE (2012); s of Ronald Hargreaves (d 1988), and Edna, *née* Cheetham (d 2006); *b* 18 June 1951; *Educ* Burnley GS, Altrincham GS, Queens' Coll Cambridge; *m* 1, 20 May 1972 (m dis 1991), Elizabeth Anne, da of Charles Crago, of Cornwall; 1 s (Ben b 20 Oct 1975), 1 da (Kelda b 23 June 1977); m 2, 13 Feb 1993, Adele Blakebrough; 2 da (Zola Grace b Jan 1996, Yoko May b May 1998); *Career* Bradford & District Newspapers 1973–76, Financial Times 1976–87, dir BBC News and Current Affrs 1987–90, dep ed Financial Times 1990–94, ed The Independent 1994–95, ed New Statesman 1996–98, prof of journalism Univ of Wales Cardiff 1998–2010, dir corp and public affrs BAA plc 2003–07, sr ptnr Ofcom 2007–08 (memb Bd 2003–08), seconded as strategic communications dir FCO 2008–10; prof of digital economy Cardiff Univ 2010–; chm Demos 1997–2002; memb Bd: Greenpeace UK 1997–2002, S London and Maudsley NHS Tst 2000–03, Nat Theatre Wales 2013–, Alacrity Fndn 2013–; memb Editorial Ctee Reuters Inst for Journalism 2011–; tstee: Centre Forum 2011–15, Wincott Fndn 2011–, Wales Millennium Centre 2015–; research fell NESTA 2012–14, sr fell Lisbon Cncl 2013–; *Books* Journalism: Truth or Dare (2003), Journalism: A Very Short Introduction (2005, revised 2014), The Heart of Digital Wales: Welsh Assembly Government (2010), Digital Opportunity: review of intellectual property and growth (2011), Manifesto for the Creative Economy (2013), Text and Data Mining: Expert Review for European Commission (2014), The Creative Citizen Unbound (ed, 2016); *Style—* Prof Ian Hargreaves, CBE; ✉ Cardiff University, Bute Building, King Edward VII Avenue, Cardiff CF10 3NB (e-mail hargreavesi@cardiff.ac.uk)

HARINGTON, His Hon Judge Michael Kenneth; s of Kenneth Douglas Evelyn Herbert Harington, and Maureen Helen, *née* McCalmont; *b* 9 August 1951; *Educ* Eton, ChCh Oxford (MA); *m* 1984, Deirdre Christine Kehoe; 1 s, 2 da; *Career* called to the Bar Inner Temple 1974; recorder 1998, circuit judge (Western Circuit) 2000–; *Recreations* golf, shooting; *Clubs* MCC; *Style—* His Hon Judge Harington; ✉ Gloucester County Court, Kimbrose Way, Gloucester GL1 2DE (☎ 01452 834900)

HARKIN, Marian; TD, MEP; da of James Gilmartin, and Annie Gilmartin; *b* 26 November 1953, Ballintogher, Co Sligo; *Educ* UC Dublin (BSc, HDipEd); *m* 28 July 1978, Sean Harkin (d 1996); 2 s (James 3 June 1979, John 28 July 1983); *Career* mathematics teacher Mercy Coll Sligo 1977–2002; TD (Ind) Sligo-Leitrim 2002–, MEP (Ind) N and W Ireland 2004–; European Parl: memb Ctee on Regnl Devpt, memb Delgn for Rels with Canada; chair Cncl for the West; memb: Nat Statistics Bd, Western Devpt Partnership Bd, Ulster Community Investment Tst; *Style—* Mrs Marian Harkin, TD, MEP; ✉ European Parliament, 60 rue Wiertz, B-1047 Brussels, Belgium; Office of the Houses of the Oireachtas, Leinster House, Dublin 2, Ireland

HARKNESS, Very Rev Dr James; KCVO (2005), CB (1993), OBE (1978); s of James Harkness, of Dumfries, and Jane McMorn, *née* Thomson; *b* 20 October 1935; *Educ* Dumfries Acad, Univ of Edinburgh (MA), Univ of Aberdeen (DD); *m* 1960, Elizabeth Anne, da of George Tolmie (d 1959); 1 da (Jane b 1962), 1 s (Paul b 1965); *Career* joined RAChD 1961; DACG: NI 1974–75, 4 Div 1975–78; staff chaplain HQ BAOR 1978–80, asst chaplain gen Scotland 1980–81; sr chaplain: 1 (Br) Corps 1981–82, BAOR 1982–84; dep chaplain gen 1985–86, chaplain gen 1987–95; Moderator of the Gen Assembly of the Church of Scotland 1995–96; Dean of the Chapel Royal in Scotland 1996–2006; extra chaplain to HM The Queen 1995–96 and 2006–, chaplain in ordinary to HM The Queen 1996–2006; chm Bd of Dirs Carberry 1998–2001; chm Veterans Scotland 2002–06; memb: Scottish Advsy Ctee ICRF 1995–2000, Exec Ctee Anglo Israel Assoc 1995–2001, Bd Mercy Corps Scotland 2001–09; patron: Napier Univ Craighouse Appeal 1995–2000, St Mary's Music Sch Appeal 1995–2000; nat chaplain: Br Limbless Ex-Servicemen's Assoc 1995–2002, Royal Br Legion Scotland 1995–2002 (pres 2001–06); dean Order of St John in Scotland 2005–11; gen tstee Church of Scotland 1996–2011; tstee: The Liberating Scots Tst, Scottish Nat War Meml 2003–15; pres: Army Cadet Force Assoc Scotland 1996–2004, Friends of St Andrew's Jerusalem 1996–2005, Earl Haig Fund Scotland 2001–06; govr Fettes Coll 1999–2009; QHC 1982–95; FRSA 1992; KStJ 2012 (OStJ 1988, ChStJ 1999); *Recreations* walking, reading, watching sport; *Clubs* New (Edinburgh), Royal Scots; *Style—* The Very Rev Dr James Harkness, KCVO, CB, OBE, DD; ✉ 13 Saxe Coburg Place, Edinburgh EH3 5BR (☎ 0131 343 1297)

HARLE, John Crofton; s of Jack Harle, and Joyce, *née* Crofton; *b* 20 September 1956; *Educ* Royal GS Newcastle upon Tyne, Royal Coll of Music (Fndn scholar, ARCM); *m* 1985, Julia Jane Eisner; 2 s; *Career* saxophonist, composer, conductor; ldr Myrha Saxophone Quartet 1977–82, formed duo with pianist John Lenehan 1979, saxophone soloist 1980–; appeared at numerous int venues incl: Carnegie Hall, South Bank Centre, BBC Proms, Germany, Switzerland, Far East; soloist Last Night of the Proms 1995 (world premiere of Sir Harrison Birtwistle's saxophone concerto Panic written for him); composer: Terror and Magnificence performed by Elvis Costello and Sarah Leonard, Little Death Machine performed by Orchestra of St John's Proms 2002; premiered Nyman Double Concerto with Julian Lloyd Webber, *qv*, James Judd, *qv*, and the Philharmonia; performer world premiere of Total Eclipse by John Tavener, *qv*, The Fall of Jerusalem by Dominic Muldowney and The Same Dog Joby Talbot 2000; conducted Film Music programme with the Winterthur Orch 2000–02; played with: LSO, English Chamber Orch, Basel Chamber Orch, London Sinfonietta, Northern Sinfonia, BBC orchs; princ saxophone London Sinfonietta 1987–, prof of saxophone Guildhall Sch of Music and Drama 1988–; composer of music for feature films (Butterfly Kiss, Breed of Heroes), TV (Love Lies Bleeding, Silent Witness, History of Britain) and advertising (Nissan, Harveys, Sony); regular broadcaster on BBC Radio, featured in One Man and his Sax BBC 2 TV 1988; EMI Classics artist 1990–; Decca recording artist 1991–; collaborations with Ute Lemper, Paul McCartney, *qv*, Willard White, the Brodsky Quartet and Lesley Garrett, *qv*; Dannreuther Concerto Prize Royal Coll of Music 1980, GLAA Young Musician 1979 and 1980, Best Artistic Achievement in a Feature Film Cannes Fim Festival 1988, RTS Award for Best Original Music 1996; FGSM 1990; *Books* John Harle's Saxophone Album (1986); *Recreations* family life, travel; *Style—* John Harle, Esq; ✉ www.johnharle.com

HARLEN, Prof Wynne; OBE (1991); da of Arthur Mitchell, and Edith, *née* Radcliffe; *b* 12 January 1937; *Educ* Pate's GS for Girls Cheltenham, Univ of Oxford (MA), Univ of Bristol (MA, PhD); *m* 14 Aug 1958, Frank Harlen (d 1987); 1 s (Oliver b 1 Jan 1965), 1 da (Juliet b 9 July 1967); *Career* teacher Cheltenham 1958–60; lectr: St Mary's Coll Cheltenham 1960–64, Glos Coll of Art 1965–66; res fell: Univ of Bristol 1966–73, Univ of Reading 1973–77; sr res fell Univ of London 1977–84, Sidney Jones prof of sci educn Univ of Liverpool 1985–90, dir Scottish Cncl for Res in Educn 1990–99, visiting prof Univ of Bristol 1999–; pres BERA 1993–94; ed Primary Science Review 1999–2004, exec ed Assessment in Educn 1999–2013; chm Science Expert Group OECD/PISA Project 1998–2003; pres BA Educn section 2001–02, dir ASF project Univ of Cambridge 2003–06; chm Int Oversight Ctee IAP 2006–10; chair Working Gp Royal Soc 2009–10; memb: Sec of State's Working Gp For Devpt of the Nat Sci Curriculum, Teaching Educn Ctee CNAA until 1991, ASE (pres 2009), AEA-Europe, ESERA, BERA, Int Advsy Bd IAP SEP (global network of science acads science educn prog), AAAS; Purkwa Prize Academies of Science of France 2008, Special Award ASE 2009, Mexican Miny of Educn and Innovation on Science Educn (INNOVEC) Award 2011; *Books* incl: Science 5 to 13: A

Formative Evaluation (1975), Guides to Assessment in Education: Science (1983), Teaching and Learning Primary Science (1985, 3 edn 2000), Primary Science: Taking the Plunge (1985, revised 2001), Developing Primary Science (with S Jelly, 1989, 2 edn 1997), Environmental Science in the Primary Curriculum (with Elstgeest, 1990), The Teaching of Science (1992, 4 edn 2004), UNESCO Sourcebook for Science in the Primary School (1992), Enhancing Quality in Assessment (1994), Effective Teaching of Science: A Review of Research (1999), Setting and Streaming: A Research Review (revised, 1999), Making Progress in Primary Science (with C Macro et al, 2003), Teaching, Learning and Assessing Science 5–12 (4 edn 2006), ASE Guide to Primary Education (ed, 2006, revised 2011), Assessment of Learning (2007), Student Assessement and Testing (ed, 4 vols, 2008), Developing Teacher Assessment (with J Gardner, L Hayward and G Sotbart, 2010), Principles and Big Ideas of Science Education (2010), Assessment and Inquiry-based Science (ed, 2013), The Teaching of Science in Primary Schools (with A Qualter, 6 edn 2014), Working Towards Big Ideas of Science Education (2015), Teaching Science for Understanding (2015), Inquiry-based Learning in Science: Assessment and Content Implications (2015); *Recreations* listening to music, walking; *Style—* Prof Wynne Harlen, OBE; ✉ Haymount Coach House, Bridgend, Duns, Berwickshire TD11 3DJ (☎ 01361 884710, e-mail wynne@torphin.freeserve.co.uk)

HARLEY, Ian; *Educ* Falkirk HS, Univ of Edinburgh (MA); *m*; 3 s; *Career* articled clerk Touche Ross & Co 1972, later in Corp Planning Dept Morgan Crucible Ltd; Abbey National plc: joined Abbey National Building Society as financial analyst 1977, SE regnl mangr Retail Ops Div 1984–86, commercial mangr for business devpt 1986, gp financial controller 1986–88, asst gen mangr fin 1988–91, fin dir retail ops 1991–92, ops dir 1992, gp treas 1992–93, memb main bd 1993–2002, gp fin dir 1993–98, chief exec 1998–2002; dir Dah Sing Financial Holdings Ltd 1998–2002; non-exec dir: Rentokil Initial plc 1999–, British Energy plc 2002–, Remploy 2004–; pres CIB 2001–02 (dep pres 2000–01); memb Ct of Govrs Whitgift Fndn 2002–, a vice-pres Nat Deaf Children's Soc; MICAS, FCA, FCIB; *Clubs* Oriental; *Style—* Ian Harley, Esq

HARLEY, Sophie Elizabeth; da of Dr Clifford Elliot Harley, and Anne Maureen, *née* Phillips; *b* 14 January 1965; *Educ* Bryanston, W Surrey Coll of Art & Design (BA), RCA (MA); *Children* 1 da (Millie Mercedes Harley Holdsworth b 31 Jan 1998); *m* 12 Feb 2011, John Andrew James Hutton; *Career* jewellery designer 1990–, fndr memb The New RenaisCAnce (multi media co specialising in fashion and accessory design, display, styling and video prodn) 1991–; creative dir Sophie Harley London Ltd; gp and solo exhbns incl: Taxidermy, Love and Letters (Southbank Crafts Gallery) 1990, Six of the Best (Barbican Centre) 1990, The Art Machine (McLellan Gallery Glasgow) 1990, Triennale Européenne du Bijou (Musee du Luxembourg Paris) 1990, From the Heart (Fouts & Fowler Gallery) 1991, The Evening Standard Art Machine (Barbican) 1991, Celebration of Gold (Mappin & Webb London) 1991, De Beers Diamond Showcase (David Thomas London) 1991, Four Play – The World of New RenaisCAnce (Royal Festival Hall and Parco Gallery Tokyo) 1992, Decorative Arts Today (Bonhams Knightsbridge) 1992, Court Couture 1992 (Kensington Palace) 1992, The World of New RenaisCAnce (Tokyo) 1992, Dazzle (NT) 1992, Decorative Arts Today (Bonhams Knightsbridge) 1993, Crafts in Performance (Crafts Cncl touring exhbn) 1993; New Generation catwalk show as part of London Fashion Week (with The New RenaisCAnce) 1994; cmmnd by De Beers Diamonds to make prize (18 carat yellow and white gold and diamond brooch) for King George VI and Queen Elizabeth Diamond Stakes Royal Ascot 2002, designed jewellery for Bond films Casino Royale 2006 and Quantum of Solace 2008; *Awards* Greater London Arts Award 1992, UK Jewellery Designer of the Year 2013; lectr various colls of art nationwide incl RCA (actg conslt on course structure); memb: Nat Assoc of Jewellers 2013, The Goldsmiths Directory 2016; *Recreations* cinema, fashion, gardening, music, reading, travel, walking; *Style—* Ms Sophie Harley; ✉ Sophie Harley London Ltd, Studio 122 Westbourne Studios, 242 Acklam Road, London W10 5JJ (☎ 020 7430 2070, e-mail sophie@sophieharley.com, website www.sophieharley.com, Twitter @SophieHarleyUK)

HARMAN, Claire Patricia; da of John Edward Harman, of the Isle of Skye, and Patricia Josephine, *née* Mullins; *b* 21 September 1957; *Educ* Farnborough Hill Convent, Univ of Manchester (BA, Samuel James Woodall Prize); *m* 1, 1979 (m dis 1989), Michael Norton Schmidt, s of Carl Bernhardt Schmidt; 2 s (Charles b 21 March 1980, Benedict b 19 Oct 1985), 1 da (Isabel b 12 July 1982); m 2, Paul Holzworth Strohm; *Career* with Carcanet Press Manchester 1979–81, co-ordinating ed PN Review Manchester 1981–84; adjunct prof Sch of the Arts Columbia Univ 2003–11; Wingate scholar 1996–98; John Llewellyn Rhys Prize 1990, Writers' Award Arts Cncl 2003; memb Soc of Authors 1990; FRSL 2006; *Books* Sylvia Townsend Warner: Collected Poems (ed, 1982), Sylvia Townsend Warner: A Biography (1989), Robert Louis Stevenson: Essays and Poems (ed, 1992), Robert Louis Stevenson: Selected Stories (ed, 1992), Sylvia Townsend Warner: Diaries (ed, 1994), Fanny Burney: A Biography (2000), Robert Louis Stevenson: A Biography (2005), Sylvia Townsend Warner: New Collected Poems (ed, 2008), Jane's Fame: How Jane Austen Conquered the World (2009); *Clubs* Univ Women's; *Style—* Claire Harman; ✉ c/o Zoë Waldie, Rogers, Coleridge and White, 20 Powis Mews, London (website www.claireharman.com)

HARMAN, Rt Hon Harriet; PC (1997), QC, MP; da of Dr John Bishop Harman (d 1994), and Anna Charlotte Malcolm Spicer; *b* 20 July 1950; *Educ* St Paul's Girls' Sch, Univ of York; *m* Jack Dromey, MP; 2 s, 1 da; *Career* lawyer, memb Liberty (formerly Nat Cncl for Civil Liberties); MP (Lab): Peckham 1982–97, Camberwell and Peckham 1997–; oppn front bench spokesperson: on health and social servs 1984–89, on health 1989–92; shadow chief sec to the Treasy 1992–94; chief oppn spokesperson on: employment 1994–95, health 1995–96, social security 1996–97; sec of state for social security and min for women 1997–98, slr gen 2001–05, min of state DCA 2005–06, ldr House of Commons 2007–10, min for women 2007–10, dep ldr Lab Pty 2007–15 (acting ldr Lab Pty and HM Oppn 2010), shadow sec of state for int devpt 2010–11, shadow sec of state for culture, media and sport 2011–15; elected to Lab NEC 1993–; *Books* The Century Gap (1993); *Style—* The Rt Hon Harriet Harman, QC, MP; ✉ House of Commons, London SW1A 0AA

HARMAN, Sir John; kt (1997), DL (W Yorks 2012); s of John Edward Harman, of Dunvegan, Isle of Skye, and Patricia Josephine, *née* Mullins; *b* 30 July 1950, Leeds; *Educ* St George's Coll Weybridge, Univ of Manchester (BSc), Huddersfield Coll of Educn (PGCE); *m* 4 Dec 1971, Susan Elizabeth, *née* Crowther; 1 s (Christopher b 24 Dec 1974), 3 da (Ruth b 4 Feb 1977, Catherine b 20 June 1979, Alison b 14 Dec 1981); *Career* teacher of mathematics 1974–97; chm Environment Agency 2000–08 (memb Bd 1995–, dep chm 1999), memb Bd Energy Saving Tst 1997–2012, tstee Forum for the Future 2006–14; chm Kirklees Stadium Devpt Ltd 1992–2016; cncllr W Yorks CC 1981–86, ldr Kirklees Met Cncl 1986–99, ldr Yorks and Humber Regnl Assembly 1999, lead cmmr Doncaster MBC 2010–12; chm Steering Gp Univ of Warwick Inst of Governance and Public Mgmnt 2001–08, memb Bd Nat Sch of Govt 2006–08; memb Advsy Cncl RSA 2006–09; tstee Nat Coal Mining Museum 2004–, chm One Community Fndn 2010–, dir Centre for Low Carbon Futures 2010–14; dir Aldersgate Gp 2007–15, tstee Inst for European Environmental Policy 2008– (chm 2010–), memb Bd Nat House Builders Cncl 2009–; memb Huddersfield Choral Soc 2008– (tstee 2014–); Hon DCL Univ of Huddersfield; memb Mathematical Assoc 1968, Hon FICE 2000, Hon FCIWEM 2002, Hon FIWM 2002, Hon FSE 2005; *Publications* The Green Crunch (2009); *Recreations* reading, music, gardening, Huddersfield Town AFC, choral singing; *Clubs* Farmers; *Style—* Sir John Harman, DL; ✉ e-mail john_harman2003@yahoo.co.uk

HARMAN, Nigel Derek; *b* 11 August 1973; *Educ* Dulwich Coll; *Career* actor; *Radio* Friday Night is Music Night (BBC Radio 2), The Big Broadcast (BBC Radio 4); *Theatre* incl: Tommy (Shaftesbury Theatre), Damn Yankees (Adelphi Theatre), Mamma Mia (Prince Edward Theatre), Signing Off (Jermyn Street Theatre), Pirates of Penzance (Regent's Park Open Air Theatre), A Midsummer Night's Dream (Regent's Park Open Air Theatre), Much Ado About Nothing (Regent's Park Open Air Theatre), Lady in the Van (Birmingham Repertory Theatre), My One and Only (Chichester Festival Theatre), Three Sisters (Chichester Festival Theatre), Privates on Parade (Donmar Warehouse), The Exonerated (Riverside Studios), Guys and Dolls (ATG/Donmar Warehouse), The Caretaker (Tricycle Theatre, Sheffield Theatre and tour), The Common Pursuit (Menier Chocolate Factory), Three Days of Rain (CMP & Neal Street Prodns for Apollo Theatre), Public Property (Trafalgar Studios), True West (Sheffield Crucible), Celebration (Gate Theatre Dublin), Shrek – The Musical (Theatre Royal Drury Lane) 2011–12 (Best Supporting Performance in a Musical Olivier Award, Best Supporting Actor in a Musical Theatregoers' Choice Award), The School for Scandal (Theatre Royal Bath) 2012, A Chorus of Disapproval (Harold Pinter Theatre) 2012–13, I Can't Sing! 2014; *Television* incl: Doctors (BBC), Red Cap (BBC), EastEnders (BBC 1) 2003–05, The Outsiders 2006, City of Vice, Plus One (Channel 4) 2009, Lark Rise to Candleford (BBC), Hotel Babylon (BBC 1) 2009, Miss Marple: The Mirror Crack'd (ITV) 2010, Mount Pleasant, Downton Abbey 2013; *Film* incl Blood Diamond 2006, Telstar 2008, Patience; *Style—* Mr Nigel Harman; ✉ c/o United Agents, 12–26 Lexington Street, London W1F 0LE

HARMAN, Richard Stuart; s of late Donald George Harman, and Jean Patricia, *née* Harrison; *b* 11 March 1959; *Educ* King's Sch Worcester (King's scholar), Trinity Coll Cambridge (MA), Univ of Exeter (PGCE); *m* 22 July 1989, Karin Lee, da of Rev Stanley Milton Voth; 1 da (Olivia Ruth b 13 Nov 1991); *Career* sales exec HBJ Academic Press 1981–83, asst master Marlborough Coll 1984–88, head of dept, housemaster and memb sr mgmnt team Eastbourne Coll 1988–2000, headmaster Aldenham Sch 2000–06, headmaster Uppingham Sch 2006–16; chm Boarding Schools' Assoc 2011–12; memb: HMC 2000 (chm 2014–15), ASCL 2000; *Recreations* sports, theatre, travel; *Style—* Richard Harman, Esq; ✉ Association of Governing Bodies of Independent Schools (AGBIS), 3 Codicote Road, Welwyn, Hertfordshire AL6 9LY (☎ 01438 840730, e-mail gensec@agbis.org.uk, website www.agbis.org.uk)

HARMAR-NICHOLLS, Hon Susan Frances; *see:* Nicholls, Susan

HARMER, Dr Clive Lucas; s of Cecil Norman Harmer (d 1986), and Elizabeth Mary, *née* Lucas (d 1989); *b* 18 August 1940; *Educ* Westminster Hosp Med Sch (state scholarship, MB BS); *m* 9 Nov 1993, Pauline Ann Cattell; 2 da from prev m (Kasha b 1968, Victoria b 1971); *Career* instr Dept of Radiation Oncology Stanford Univ Calif 1970; conslt in radiotherapy and oncology: St Luke's Hosp Guildford 1970–73, St George's Hosp London 1973–2005; former head Thyroid Unit Royal Marsden Hosp London, ret; chair Thyroid Cancer Clinical Studies Gp Nat Cancer Research Inst 2003–05; life fell RSM; FRCR 1968, FRCP 1992 (MRCP 1968); *Publications* author of over 200 pubns on treatment of cancer, in particular thyroid cancer and management of soft tissue sarcomas; *Recreations* wildlife photography; *Style—* Dr Clive Harmer; ✉ Apartment 97, 55 Ebury Street, Belgravia, London SW1W 0PB (☎ 020 7730 8330, e-mail cliveharmer@fsmail.net)

HARMSWORTH, 3 Baron (UK 1939); Thomas Harold Raymond Harmsworth; o s of Hon Eric Beauchamp Northcliffe Harmsworth (d 1988), and Hélène Marie, *née* Dehove (d 1962); suc uncle, 2 Baron Harmsworth, 1990; *b* 20 July 1939; *Educ* Eton, ChCh Oxford; *m* 26 June 1971, Patricia Palmer, da of Michael Palmer Horsley, of Waltham House, Brough, N Humberside; 2 s (Hon Dominic Michael Eric b 18 Sept 1973, Hon Timothy Thomas John b 6 April 1979), 3 da (Hon Philomena Hélène Olivia b 10 Feb 1975, Hon Abigail Patricia Thérèse (now Mrs Valentin Stefan) b 14 June 1977, Hon Pollyanna Mary Clare (now Mrs Timothy Montagu) b 8 Sept 1981); *Heir* s, Hon Dominic Harmsworth; *Career* Nat Serv 2 Lt Royal Horse Gds 1957–59; in the City 1962–74, Civil Serv 1974–88, publisher 1988–; chm Dr Johnson's House Gough Square London; *Publications* Gastronomic Dictionaries: French-English (2003), Spanish-English (2004), Italian-English (2005), Portuguese-English (2008); *Clubs* Carlton, Brooks's; *Style—* The Lord Harmsworth; ✉ The Old Rectory, Stoke Abbott, Beaminster, Dorset DT8 3JT

HARPER, Alexander James Christopher; s of late Lt-Col Alexander Forrest Harper, DSO, of W Sussex, and Rosemary Helen Margaret, *née* Hayward; *b* 16 March 1948; *Educ* Winchester; *m* 1, 1972 (m dis 1977), Peta Seccombe; 1 da (Eugénie Rose b 16 Nov 1973), 1 s (Alexander Forrest (Tom) b 17 Sept 1975); m 2, 1978 (m dis 1998), Suzy Kendall; 1 da (Elodie Lauren Geraldine b 1 July 1979); m 3, Susana Maria Tubio; 2 s (José Benito Christopher b 11 Nov 2003, Juan Bautista William b 12 May 2008); *Career* sugar trader Rionda de Pass Ltd 1967–70, various posts rising to head of sugar dept Ralli Merrill Lynch 1970–74, md Lambourn (UK) Ltd 1974, various appointments incl int commodity trader UK, Africa and S America 1975–97, co-fndr Cia Minera el Desquite (brought together Brancote Holdings plc and MB Holdings SA) Argentina 1996–, co-fndr Patagonia Organic Meat Co SA Argentina 2006–10; dir Golden Santa Cruz SA Argentina 2006–14; memb Bd and Audit Ctee Quinsa SA 2004–06; hon consul for Repub of Guinea 1987–; int polo player 1967–89, memb Young Eng Polo Team 1972, 1975 and 1976, Young Player of the Year 1972; *Recreations* polo, sailing, t'ai chi ch'uan, fishing, exploring, travel in third world, writing, reading, music, bio-energetic healing; *Clubs* La Cañada Polo, Whites; *Style—* Alexander Harper, Esq; ✉ Poste Restante, Av del Libertador 498-P27, C1001ABR Buenos Aires, Argentina (e-mail aharper@mbh.com.ar)

HARPER, Dr Caroline; CBE (2016, OBE 2002); da of Douglas Harper, and Barbara Harper; *b* 4 May 1960, Almondsbury, S Glos; *Educ* Univ of Bristol (BSc), Energy Research Gp Cambridge (PhD); *Career* various roles Br Gas 1985–89, transportation mangr Br Gas Iransco 1989–91, md Amerada Hess Gas Ltd 1991–2002, Harper & Assocs 2002–05, ceo Sightsavers 2005–; Hon DSc 2013; *Recreations* cricket, horse racing, music, opera, tennis, travel; *Style—* Dr Caroline Harper, CBE; ✉ Sightsavers, 2a Halifax Road, Melksham SN12 6YY

HARPER, David Finlay; s of Muir Harper, of Eaglesham Strathclyde, and Margaret; *b* 15 July 1956; *Educ* Kelvinside Acad Glasgow, Mackintosh Sch of Art (BArch), Univ of Glasgow (DipArch); *m* 20 July 1985 (m dis 2007), Katharine, *née* MacCarthy; 4 s (Aidan Muir b 24 April 1991, Connal David b 12 Aug 1992, Finlay Peader b 20 Oct 1996, Rory Stuart b 19 Oct 1999); *Career* architect; projects incl: St Martins Lane and the Sanderson Hotels, the Trafalgar, Butlers Wharf, the Whitefriars devpt; founding dr Harper Downie; regular contrib to many newspapers and jls; *Awards* incl: Heritage Award 1987, European Heritage Awards 1987, Electricity Cncl Awards 1988, Civil Tst Awards 1989, Patent Glazing Awards 1989, Design Week Awards 1991, 1994, 1997 and 1998, D&AD Awards 1994 and 2001, Minerva Awards 1994 and 1995, Carpenters Award 1994, Hilight Awards 1995, Br Cncl for Offices award 1998, FX Awards 2001 and 2002; RIBA 1983, RIAS 1983, FCSD 1991; *Recreations* benign exaggeration; *Clubs* Groucho; *Style—* David Harper, Esq; ✉ Harper_Downie Limited, Gate House, No 1 St John's Square, London EC1M 4DH (☎ 020 7490 7674, fax 020 7490 4941, mobile 07767 348811, e-mail david.harper@harperdownie.com)

HARPER, Prof David Ross; CBE (2002); s of Frank Harper (d 1998), and Louise, *née* Mason (d 2006); *b* 6 June 1955, Wolverhampton, W Midlands; *Educ* Univ of Dundee (BSc), Univ of Birmingham (PhD); *m* 24 June 1978, Lorraine, *née* Chadwick; 1 da (Laura b 4 Feb 1987), 2 s (Ross b 3 Nov 1989, Edmund b 9 Sept 1993); *Career* Dept of Health: chief scientist and head of profession for scientists 1996–, DG of health protection, int health and scientific devpt 2003–08, DG for health improvement and protection 2008–; hon prof Univ of Dundee; Hon DSc Cranfield Univ 2010; FIBiol 1995, FFPH 2006; *Recreations* music, sport, motorcycles; *Style*— Prof David R Harper, CBE; ✉ Department of Health, Richmond House, 79 Whitehall, London SW1A 2NS (☎ 020 7210 5522, e-mail david.harper@dh.gsi.gov.uk)

HARPER, Ewan; kt 2003, CBE 1997, JP (Northants, 1973); s of Leonard Robert Harper, and Enid, *née* Redman; *b* 21 June 1939; *Educ* Marlborough Coll, Trinity Hall Cambridge (MA, Open Exhibitioner); *m* 1965, Jeniffer Margaret, *née* Hoare-Scott; 1 s, 3 da; *Career* vice chm Bd of Visitors Wellingborough Borstal 1970–82, md Harper and Tunstall Ltd 1972–87 (chm 1985–87), dir Restoration of Lambeth Palace Chapel 1987–88, sec Archbishop's Cmmn on Rural Areas 1988–90, memb Hurd Cmmn on Office of Archbishop of Canterbury 2000; chief exec United Church Schs Tst 1990–2011, ceo and govr The United Learning Tst 2002–11, lay memb Chapter of Peterborough Cathedral 2002–07, chm Education Fellowship Ltd 2011–14; govr: Benenden Sch 1983–92 (chm Benenden Sch Tst), Oundle Sch 1992–2003, Maidwell Hall 1993–2000, UC Northampton 1997–2002; tstee: Lambeth Fund 1983–2014 (chm 2011–14), Maurice and Hilda Laing Tst 1997–, Academy Sponsors Tst 2004–06, Oundle Music Tst 2014–; hon fell Trinity Hall Cambridge 2013; Knight Cdr Order of King Francis II 2012; *Recreations* gardening, golf, tennis, watercolours, history; *Clubs* Athenaeum, MCC; *Style*— Sir Ewan Harper, CBE; ✉ Titchmarsh House, Titchmarsh, Northamptonshire NN14 3DA

HARPER, Prof John Martin; s of late Geoffrey Martin Harper, and late Kathleen, *née* Birks; *b* 11 July 1947, Wednesbury; *Educ* King's Coll Sch Cambridge, Clifton, Selwyn Coll Cambridge (MA), Univ of Birmingham (PhD), DMus Lambeth; *m* 1, 1 July 1970 (m dis), Cynthia Margaret, da of late George Dean; 3 s (Edward John b 1976, William George b 1978, Joseph Martin b 1985); m 2, 21 Dec 1991, Sally Elizabeth, da of late John Stephen Roper; *Career* lectr in music Univ of Birmingham 1974–75 and 1976–81, asst dir of music King Edward's Sch Birmingham 1975–76, fell and tutor in music Magdalen Coll Oxford (also organist and informator choristarum) 1981–90; Bangor Univ: prof of music 1991–98, research prof 1998–2014, emeritus prof 2015–; hon prof Univ of Birmingham 2014–; Leverhulme fell 1997–98; DG Royal Sch of Church Music 1998–2007 (emeritus dir 2008–); visiting scholar Sarum Coll 2005–; dir Edington Music Festival 1971–78, dir of music St Chad's Cathedral Birmingham 1972–78; fndr ed Welsh Music History 1996–99; fndr dir Centre for Advanced Welsh Music Studies 1994–2003, dir Int Centre for Sacred Music Studies 2008–; chm Early English Organ Project 2000–05 (tstee 1999–2005), vice-pres Plainsong and Medieval Music Soc 2008– (memb Cncl 1994–2008, chm 1998–2006); Benemerenti Papal Award 1978; DMus (Lambeth) 2010; FRCO (CHM), Hon FGCM 1996, FRSCM 2007, FLSW 2012; *Books* Orlando Gibbons: Consort Music (Musica Britannica 48, ed, 1982), The Forms and Orders of Western Liturgy (1991), Hymns for Prayer and Praise (ed, 1996 and 2011–12), Music for Common Worship (7 vols, ed, 2000–07), The Light of Life (2002), The Spirit of the Lord (2004), Psallam (ed, 2007); *Recordings* The English Carol (1984), The English Anthem (5 vols, 1990), The Victorian Carol (1990); *Web Resources* Sarum Customary Online (www.sarumcustomary.org.uk, project dir and ed, 2013), The Experience of Worship in Late Medieval Cathedral and Parish Church (www.experienceofworship.org.uk, project dir 2013); *Recreations* ecclesiastical architecture, canals; *Style*— Prof John Harper; ✉ Bethania, Llangoed, Beaumaris, Anglesey LL58 8PH

HARPER, Mark; MP; *b* 1970; *Educ* Headlands Sch Swindon, Swindon Coll, BNC Oxford (MA); *Career* CA 1995; auditor KPMG 1991–95, Intel Corp 1995–2002, own chartered accountancy practice 2003–05; MP (Cons) Forest of Dean 2005– (Parly candidate (Cons) Forest of Dean 2001); parly under-sec of state Cabinet Office 2010–12, min for immigration Home Office 2012–14, min of state for disabled people 2014–15, chief whip 2015–; South Swindon Cons Assoc: treas 1993–98, dep chair 1998; govr Newent Community Sch 2000–05; *Style*— Mark Harper, Esq, MP; ✉ House of Commons, London SW1A 0AA (e-mail mark.harper.mp@parliament.uk, website www.markharper.org, Twitter @Mark_J_Harper)

HARPER, Dr Peter George; s of Frederick Charles Harper (d 1965), of Bath, and Catherine Tryphosa, *née* Judah; *b* 30 August 1945; *Educ* UCH and UCL (MB BS, LRCP); *m* 21 June 1971, Saga Margaret Elizabeth (d 1996), da of Peter Guise Tyndale; 3 s (Benjamin b 1974, Sebastian b 1976, Maximillian b 1988), 1 da (Harriet b 1980); *Career* house offr then SHO UCH and Addenbrooke's Hosp Cambridge 1969–71, SHO and med registrar St Mary's Hosp 1972–76, sr med registrar UCH 1976–82, conslt physician and med oncologist Guy's Hosp 1982–; MRC: memb Lung Cancer Ctee, memb Gynaecological Malignancies Ctee, memb Genito-Urinary Malignancies Ctee; memb: UK Central Co-ordinating Cancer Ctee, Br Prostate Gp, Hampstead Med Soc; FRCP 1987 (MRCP), MRCS; Chevalier de la Légion d'Honneur (France) 2003; *Books* numerous papers on aspects of cancer treatment; contrib chapters: The Treatment of Urological Tumours (1985), A Textbook of Unusual Tumours (1988); *Recreations* music (especially opera), walking, fly fishing, shooting; *Style*— Dr Peter Harper; ✉ London Oncology Clinic, 95 Harley Street, London W1G 6AF (☎ 020 7317 2530, fax 020 7009 4230)

HARPER, Rev Roger; s of Albert William Harper (d 1979), of Peel, IOM, and Joyce, *née* Griffiths (d 1990); *b* 10 January 1943; *Educ* Merchant Taylors', UMIST (BSc); *m* 1, 26 July 1966 (m dis 2008), Joan, da of John Worthington, of Freckleton, Lancs; 2 da (Charlotte b 1967, Camilla b 1969); m 2, 2008, June, *née* O'Neill; *Career* CA; ordained priest 1988 (diocese of Sodor and Man), chm Diocesan Bd of Fin 1984–2007; dir: Manx Industrial Trust 1973–, dir Renewable Energy Hldgs plc 2010–13; FCA; *Recreations* sailing; *Style*— Rev Roger Harper; ✉ The Barns, Strawberry Fields, Croit-e-Caley, Colby, Isle of Man IM9 4BZ (☎ 01624 834940, e-mail roger.harper@mcb.net)

HARPER, Prof (John) Ross; CBE (1986); s of Rev Thomas Harper (d 1960), and Margaret Simpson, *née* Ross; *b* 20 March 1935; *Educ* Hutchesons' Boys' GS, Univ of Glasgow (MA, LLB); *m* 26 Sept 1963, Ursula Helga Renate, da of Hans Gathmann (d 1966), of Zimerstrasse, Darmstadt; 2 s (Robin b 1964, Michael b 1969), 1 da (Susan b 1966); *Career* slr Scotland; conslt Harper Macleod; formerly pt/t prof of law Univ of Strathclyde (now emeritus); former pres: Law Soc of Scotland, Scottish Cons and Unionist Assoc, Glasgow Bar Assoc; former chm Tory Reform Gp Scotland; former pres Int Bar Assoc 1994–96 (former chm Gen Practice Section); former chm: Mining (Scotland) Ltd, Scottish Coal Company Ltd, European Scanning Centre Ltd, Scottish Biopower Ltd; chm: Alarm Protection Ltd, Admiralty Resources NL; conslt Makanyane Safari Lodge SA; Parly candidate (Cons) Hamilton and W Renfrewshire 1970s; Hon DUniv Glasgow 2002; *Books* Practitioners' Guide to Criminal Procedure, A Guide to the Courts, The Glasgow Rape Case, Fingertip Guide to Criminal Law, Rates Reform, Devolution, New Unionism, My Client My Lord, Scotland 97, Referendums are Dangerous, Global Law in Practice; *Recreations* angling, bridge; *Clubs* Caledonian; *Style*— Prof J Ross Harper, CBE; ✉ Flat 1, 67 Cadogan Square, London SW1X 0DY (☎ 020 7245 0078, e-mail jross.harper@btopenworld.com); Ca 'd'oro, 45 Gordon Street, Glasgow G1 3PE

HARPHAM, Prof Trudy; *b* 24 October 1956; *Educ* PhD; *Career* prof of urban devpt and policy London South Bank Univ 1994–; hon prof London Sch of Hygiene and Tropical Medicine 1998–; chair Cwlth Scholarship Cmmn in the UK; *Style*— Prof Trudy Harpham

HARPIN, Richard David; s of David Bryn Harpin (d 2007), of Northumberland, and Philippa Judith, *née* Barr; *b* 10 September 1964, Huddersfield; *Educ* Royal GS Newcastle upon Tyne, Univ of York (BA), Univ of Northumbria (Dip); *m* July 1997, Kate, *née* Dawes; 1 da (Jemima b 19 June 2000), 2 s (Tom b 15 Feb 2002, William b 28 Nov 2004); *Career* fndr and owner nat mail order fishing tackle business 1981–86, fndr earring mfrg business 1984–85, brand mangr Procter and Gamble 1986–90, fndr Harpin Ltd 1988–, sr conslt Deloitte 1990–91, franchisee The Mortgage Advice Shop 1991–92, co-fndr and md Homeserve GB Ltd 1993–99, chief exec Homeserve plc 1999–; non-exec chm: Heating Components and Equipment Ltd 1998–2004, Amsys Rapid Prototyping and Tooling Limited 1999–2001; non-exec dir: Professional Properties Ltd 1990–99, Baker Tilly Consulting 1992–97, Mortgage Advice Bureau 1997–2000; launched nat student magazine 1988; fndr Enterprise Tst 2009; created Scouting Entrepreneur Badge with the Scout Assoc 2010; memb: Nat Exec Grad Industrial Soc 1986–88, Nat Apprenticeship Ambassadors Network, Ldrs Gp Cons Pty; chair W Midlands Apprenticeship Network; Make It In Business Award 1984, regnl winner Livewire Business Competition 1985, Ernst & Young Entrepreneur of the Year 2008, Entrepreneur of the Year PLC Award 2011; *Books* A Mind for Business (2009); *Recreations* off-piste and heliskiing, swimming, squash, private pilots license and helicopter license; *Style*— Richard Harpin, Esq; ✉ Homeserve plc, Cable Drive, Walsall WS2 7BN (☎ 01922 659701, fax 01922 659785, e-mail richard.harpin@homeserve.com)

HARPUR, Oonagh Mary; da of late Dr William Ware Harpur, and Patricia Elizabeth, *née* Coote; *b* 26 September 1953, Belfast; *Educ* Keele Univ (BA); *m* 1974 (m dis 1991), Peter Edward Clamp, s of late Owen Gregory Edward Clamp; 1 da (Jennifer Sarah b 23 Nov 1978); *Career* various posts in strategy and operational research NCB 1976–85, ldr Professional Practices Consulting Gp Spicer & Pegler (now Deloittes) 1985–87, assoc Strategic Planning Assoc Washington DC 1987–88, princ exec Berwin Leighton 1988–94, princ tutor Centre for Law Firm Management Nottingham Law Sch 1994–2004; chief exec: The HUB Initiative 1997–2001, Enterprise Insight 2001–02; partnership sec and dir corp responsibility Linklaters 2002–11, sr advsr Tomorrow's Co 2011–; memb: City Values Forum, Advsy Working Gp 21st Century Leadership, Financial Skills Cncl; non-exec dir Hillingdon HA 1992–96; memb IWF London, tstee Scientific and Med Network; chm The Love and Integrity in Business Network 1995–2000; FRSA (lifetime fell); *Publications* The Economist Guide to Business Ethics (contrib, 2001); *Recreations* opera, swimming; *Clubs* Int Women's Forum; *Style*— Ms Oonagh Harpur; ✉ website www.oonaghharpur.com

H

HARRABIN, Roger; s of Hubert Harrabin, and Sylvia Harrabin; *Educ* King Henry VIII Sch Coventry, St Catharine's Cambridge (JCR pres); *m* Anne; 2 s (James, Hugo), 1 da (Jessica); *Career* reporter and sub ed Coventry Evening Telegraph 1976–83, freelance News of the World and Sunday Mirror 1983–84, prodr Thames TV News 1984–86, environment journalist BBC 1986–2006, environment analyst BBC 2006–; progs incl: Today, Ten O'Clock News, Panorama, Newsnight, Assignment, World at One, Costing the Earth; co-dir Cambridge Media Environment Prog; assoc press fell Wolfson Coll Cambridge, visiting fell Green Coll Oxford; *Publications* King's Fund Risk & Media report (co-author); *Recreations* family, friends, sport, architecture, Coventry City FC; *Style*— Roger Harrabin, Esq; ✉ c/o BBC Broadcasting House, Portland Place, London W1A 1AA (☎ 020 8624 9644, e-mail roger.harrabin@bbc.co.uk)

HARREL, David T D; *b* 23 June 1948; *m* Julia Mary;1 da (Rebecca b 1977), 2 s (Tom b 1979, Charlie b 1983); *Career* admitted slr 1974, asst slr then ptnr Messrs William Charles Crocker 1974–79, ptnr Messrs Burton & Ramsden 1979–82, former sr ptnr SJ Berwin (co-fndr and ptnr 1982, currently conslt); non-exec dir Rathbone Bros plc 2007–, chm Fairpoint plc; tstee Clore Duffield Fndn; *Recreations* golf, tennis, music, theatre; *Clubs* Royal St George's Golf, Swinley Forest Golf; *Style*— David Harrel, Esq; ✉ e-mail david.harrel@btinternet.com

HARRHY, Eiddwen Mair; *b* 14 April 1949; *Educ* St Winifred's Convent Swansea, Royal Manchester Coll of Music; *m* 23 Jan 1988, Gregory Strange; 1 da; *Career* soprano; debut: Royal Opera House Covent Garden 1974, English Nat Opera 1975; performances incl: Glyndebourne Festival, Scottish Opera, Welsh National Opera, Opera North, Teatro Colon Buenos Aires, Philharmonie St Petersburg, La Scala Milan, Amsterdam Concertgebouw, Sydney Opera House, Hong Kong, NZ, LA, BBC Promenade concerts; recordings: EMI, Harmonia Mundi, Erato, Deutsche Grammophon, Virgin Classics; prof of singing Royal Coll of Music 2001–; Imperial League of Opera Prize Gold Medal, Miriam Licette Prize; fndr convenor The Trust for Young Musicians; fell Royal Welsh Coll of Music and Drama; FRSA; *Recreations* playing golf, watching rugby in Wales, skiing; *Clubs* Friends of the Musicians' Benevolent Fund; *Style*— Miss Eiddwen Harrhy; ✉ c/o Allan Beavis, Phoenix Artists Management, 4th Floor, 6 Windmill Street, London W1P 1HF (☎ 020 7636 5021, fax 020 7631 4631, e-mail allan@phoenixartists.co.uk)

HARRI, Guto; s of Harri Pritchard-Jones, and Lenna Pritchard-Jones; *b* 8 July 1966, Cardiff; *Educ* Queen's Coll Oxford (BA), Centre for Journalism Studies (Dip); *m* 27 Oct 2000, Shireen; 2 s (Calum Dewi, Benjamin Aled b 27 Dec 2001 (twins)), 1 da (Amelia Nansi b 6 June 2009); *Career* corr Westminster, Rome, NY BBC until 2008, conslt Fleishman Hillard 2008, dir of communications London Mayor's Office 2008–12, dir of communications News UK 2012–; hon fell Bangor Univ; *Style*— Guto Harri, Esq; ✉ News UK, 3 Thomas More Square, London E98 1XY

HARRIES, Andy; *Career* television prodr, dir and exec prodr; scriptwriter/researcher/presenter Granada Television Manchester and London 1976–81, freelance prodr and dir 1982–92, controller of entertainment and comedy Granada Television 1994–2000 (head of comedy 1992–94), head of drama, comedy and film ITV Prodns 2000–06, co-fndr Left Bank Pictures 2007–; *Style*— Andy Harries, Esq

HARRIES, Kathryn Gwynne; da of Stanley George Harries, of St Davids, and Gwynneth Rosemary, *née* Hubbard, of Pembroke; *b* 15 February 1951; *Educ* Surbiton HS, Royal Acad of Music (jr exhibitioner, then at Sr Acad), Univ of London (BMus); *m* 30 July 1977 (m dis 1998), Christopher Charles Lane, s of Charles Victor Lane; 1 da (Victoria Jessica Gwynne b 27 Dec 1979), 1 s (William Stanley Gwynne b 21 Sept 1981); *Career* opera singer; lectr Kingston Poly 1969–82, prof Jr Dept RAM 1976–82, presenter BBC Schools TV series Music Time 1977–83, also various concerts, oratorios and recitals 1969–83; Wigmore Hall debut 1972, Royal Festival Hall debut 1977, operatic debut as a Flower Maiden in Parsifal (with WNO under Reginald Goodall) 1983; estab Coverwood Concerts Surrey 1991; Olivier Award nomination for Sieglinde and Gutrune in WNO's full Ring Cycle 1986; walked from John O'Groats to Lands End, with seven concerts and various impromptu concerts en route, to raise money for Speakability 2001; Hon DMus Kingston Univ 2001; FRAM 1991 (ARAM 1988); *Performances* incl: Leonora in Fidelio (with WNO in Liverpool 1983, Scottish Opera 1984, Teatro Colon Buenos Aires 1988, ENO 1996), Sylvie in La Colombe (Buxton Festival) 1983, Irene in Rienzi (ENO debut) 1983, Sieglinde in Die Walküre (WNO 1984, Nice Opera and Théâtre Champs Elysée 1988), Eva in Die Meistersinger (ENO) 1984, Female Chorus in The Rape of Lucretia (ENO) 1984, Adalgisa in Norma (WNO) 1985, title role in Hedda Gabler (Scottish Opera) 1985, Gutrune in Götterdämmerung (WNO 1985, Met Opera NY 1988 and 1989), Kundry in Parsifal (Met Opera debut 1986, Netherlands Opera 1990), Donna Elvira in Don Giovanni (Opera North 1986, Stuttgart debut 1992), Sieglinde and Gutrune in WNO's full Ring Cycle (Covent Garden) 1986, Senta in Der Fliegende Holländer (Scottish Opera, Paris Opera debut Palais Garnier) 1987, Donna Anna in The Stone Guest (ENO) 1987, Didon in Les Troyens (Berlioz Festival) 1987, title role in The Merry Widow (Opera North) 1988, Protaganista in Un Re in Ascolto (Covent Garden debut 1989, Opèra Bastille debut 1991), The Composer in Ariadne auf Naxos (WNO) 1989, title role in Katya Kabanova (ENO) 1989, Arianne in Arianne et Barbe Bleu (Netherlands Opera debut) 1989, Jocasta in Oedipus Rex (Los Angeles debut) 1989, Judith in Bluebeard's Castle

(Scottish Opera) 1990, Didon in Les Troyens (Scottish Opera and Covent Garden 1990, La Monnaie Brussels debut 1992), title role in Cléopatre (Massenet Festival debut) 1990, Giulietta in The Tales of Hoffmann (Théâtre du Châtalet debut) 1991, Die Frau in 'Intolleranza 1960' (Stuttgart) 1992, title role in Carmen (Orange Festival debut) 1992, Principessa di Bouillon in Adriana Lecouvreur (St Etienne) 1992, The Lady Macbeth of Mtensk (Stuttgart) 1995, Geschwitz in Berg's Lulu (BBC Proms) 1996, Jenufa in Kostelnika (Amsterdam, Chicago and San Francisco) 2001, Marco Polo (Netherlands Opera) 2001, title role in Herodiade (Liege) 2002, Countess Geschwitz in Berg's Lulu (BBC Proms and Glyndebourne); other roles incl: Flower Maiden and Voice from Above in Wagner's Parsifal, The Mother in Janácek's Osud, Fevronia in Rimsky-Korsakov's The Invisible City of Kitezh, Clairon (Glyndebourne and NY Met) 1998, Kundry in Parsifal (Bastille) 1997, Kostelnicka in Jenufa (Israel 1993, Amsterdam 1997, San Francisco 2001, Chicago 2000, Genoa 2003), Marie in Wozzeck (Chicago) 1993, Madame de Croisy in Poulenc's Dialogues des Carmelites (Hamburg) 2003; other credits incl: Chicago 1996, David Sawyer's From Morning to Midnight (world premiere) 2001, Waiting (Almeida Theatre) 2002, Carousel (Royal Festival Hall) 2002; *Recreations* riding and competing on own horses, reading, gardening, travelling, long-distance walking; *Clubs* Abinger Forest Riding; *Style—* Ms Kathryn Harries; ✉ c/o Ingpen & Williams Ltd, 7 St George's Court, 131 Putney Bridge Road, London SW15 2PA (☎ 020 8874 3222, fax 020 8877 3113, e-mail kathrynharries@hotmail.com)

HARRIES OF PENTREGARTH, Baron (Life Peer UK 2006), of Pentregarth of Ceinewydd in the County of Dyfed; Rt Rev Prof Richard Douglas Harries; s of Brig William Douglas Jameson Harries, CBE (d 1991), and Greta Miriam, da of A Bathurst Brown, MB, LRCP; *b* 2 June 1936; *Educ* Wellington, RMA Sandhurst, Selwyn Coll Cambridge (MA), Cuddesdon Theol Coll; *m* 1963, Josephine Bottomley, MA, MB BChir, DCH; 1 s, 1 da; *Career* Lt RCS 1955–58; curate Hampstead Parish Church 1963–69, chaplain Westfield Coll 1966–69, lectr Wells Theol Coll 1969–72, warden Wells, Salisbury and Wells Theol Coll 1971–72, vicar All Saints' Fulham 1972–81, dean KCL 1981–87, bishop of Oxford 1987–2006, Gresham prof of divinity 2008–12; conslt to Archbishop on Jewish Christian Relations 1986–92; chm Cncl of Christians and Jews 1992–2001 (vice-pres 2001–), chm C of E Bd of Social Responsibility 1996–2001; memb House of Lords 1993–, memb Ctee into reform of House of Lords 1999, chm House of Lords Select Ctee on Stem Cell Research 2001; chm The Johnson Soc 1988; memb Nuffield Cncl on Bioethics 2002–08, memb HFEA 2002–09; Sir Sigmund Sternberg award 1987, President's Medal Br Acad 2012; hon fell Selwyn Coll Cambridge; hon fell St Anne's Coll Oxford 2006, hon prof of theology KCL 2006; Hon DD London; Hon DUniv: Oxford Brookes, Open Univ 2006; Hon DCL Huddersfield Univ, Hon DD Grad Theological Fndn 2012; FKC, FRSL, Hon FMedSci 2005, hon fell Inst of Biology 2009, FLSW 2012; *Books* Prayers of Hope (1975), Turning to Prayer (1978), Prayers of Grief and Glory (1979), Being a Christian (1981), Should Christians Support Guerrillas? (1982), The Authority of Divine Love (1983), Praying Round the Clock (1983), Seasons of the Spirit (1984), Prayer and the Pursuit of Happiness (1985), Morning has Broken (1985), Christianity and War in a Nuclear Age (1986), C S Lewis – The Man and his God (1987), The One Genius (1987), Christ has Risen (1988), Is There a Gospel for the Rich? (1992), Art and the Beauty of God (1993), The Real God (1994), Questioning Belief (1995), A Gallery of Reflections: The Nativity of Christ (1995), In the Gladness of Today (1999), God outside the Box: Why Spiritual People Object to Christianity (2002), After the Evil – Christianity and Judaism in the Shadow of the Holocaust (2003), The Passion in Art (2004), Praying the Eucharist (2004), The Re-enchantment of Morality (2008), Faith in Politics? Rediscovering the Christian Roots of our Political Values (2010 and 2014), Issues of Life and Death: Christian Faith and Medical Intervention (2010), The Image of Christ in Modern Art (2013); contrib: What Hope in an Armed World (and ed, 1982), Reinhold Niebuhr and the issues of our Time (and ed, 1986), Stewards and the Mysteries of God (1975), Unholy Warfare (1983), The Cross and the Bomb (1985), Julian, Woman of our Time (1985), The Reality of God (1986), Two Cheers for Secularism (and ed, 1998), Christianity: Two Thousand Years (and ed, 2001), Reinhold Niebuhr and Contemporary Politics. God and Power (and ed, 2010), Religion, Society and God (2013), The Beauty and the Horror: searching for God in a suffering world (2016); *Recreations* theatre, literature, sport, walking; *Style—* The Rt Rev Prof the Lord Harries of Pentregarth; ✉ House of Lords, London SW1A 0PW

HARRIMAN, (Joseph) William Fletcher (Bill); TD (1989); s of Flt-Lt Joseph Fletcher Harriman, MBE (d 1974), and Kathleen Harriman, *née* Robinson; *b* 27 April 1956; *Educ* Oakham Sch, Trent Poly Nottingham (BSc); *m* 25 June 1991, Janet, da of Albert Benson, of Nottingham; 2 da (Annabel b 30 May 1996, Caroline b 17 Sept 1998); *Career* S Notts Hussars Yeomanry RHA TA 1974–, troop commander 1986–88, seconded Royal Yeomanry as artillery advsr 1989–91, Army reserve 1992–2006; head of Catalogue Dept and princ valuer Weller and Dufty Auctioneers 1984–90 (conslt 1987–91), ind conslt valuer and identifier of firearms 1987–, expert witness in court cases for firearms and ballistics 1987–; head of firearms Br Assoc for Shooting and Conservation 1991– (dir 2001–); forensic ballistics Cranfield Univ 2002–; pres Muzzle Loaders Assoc of GB 2011–; memb: Panel of Experts Antiques Roadshow, Home Office Working Gp reviewing Firearms Rules 1993–, Home Office Working Gp on Firearms Licensing by Category 1995, Home Office Working Gp Firearms Rules 1998, Home Office Working Gp Firearms Law – Guidance to the Police 2001–, Cncl Historical Breechloading Smallarms Assoc 1995–2001, Govt Firearms Consultative Ctee 1998–2004, Home Office Panel for Section 7 (3) Historic Handguns 2002–, Forensic Science Soc 2003–, Registrant Cncl for the Registration of Forensic Practitioners 2006–09, Home Office Working Gp Fees 2013, Home Office Working Gp Antique Firearms 2013; hon historical conslt Royal Armouries Museum 2011; ed Classic Arms and Militaria 2005, columnist Shooting Times; treas Br Shooting Sports Cncl 1993–96; assoc ISVA 1982–92 (memb Fine Arts and Chattels Ctee 1991–92); MAE 1999, FSA 2006, professional memb Chartered Soc of Forensic Science 2016; *Books* Experts on Antiques (contrib, 1987), Tiaras, Tallboys and Teddy Bears (contrib, 1990), Royal Armouries Yearbook 3 (contrib, 1998), Judith Miller: The Dictionary of Antiques (contrib, 2000), the Antiques Roadshow A-Z of Antiques and Collectables (contrib, 2008), The Mosin-Nagant Rifle (2016), BASC: Law and Licensing (2016); *Recreations* shooting, toxophily, wine, music, miniature figurines; *Clubs* Chester City, Sloane; *Style—* Bill Harriman, Esq, TD, FSA; ✉ Pistyll Bank, Springfield Lane, Marford, Wrexham LL12 8TF (☎ and fax 01244 570027, e-mail billharriman@btopenworld.com and jwfharriman@gmail.com); British Association for Shooting and Conservation, Marford Mill, Rossett, Wrexham LL12 0HL (☎ 01244 573010, fax 01244 573013, e-mail bill.harriman@basc.org.uk)

HARRINGTON, Jessica; da of Mary Fowler; *b* 25 February 1947, London; *Educ* Hatherop Castle Sch; *m* John Harrington; 1 s (James Lloyd), 3 da (Emma (Mrs Galway), Kate, Tara (Mrs O'Donoghue)); *Career* racehorse trainer 1991–; horses trained incl Moscow Flyer, Spirit Leader, Cork Allstar, Macs Joy, Jezki, Dragon Pulse and Pathfork; *Style—* Mrs Jessica Harrington; ✉ Commonstown Racing Stables, Moone, County Kildare, Ireland (☎ 00 353 598 624153, fax 00 353 598 624292, e-mail jessica@jessicaharringtonracing.com)

HARRINGTON, Prof (John) Malcolm; CBE (1992); s of John Roy Harrington, of Newport, Gwent, and Veda Naomi, *née* Harris; *b* 6 April 1942; *Educ* Newport HS, King's Coll, Westminster Med Sch London (BSc, MB BS, MSc, MD); *m* 20 May 1967, Madeline Mary, da of Brinley Hunter Davies (d 1971); 1 da (Kate b 27 Sept 1975); *Career* various hosp appts 1966–69, visiting scientist US Public Health Serv 1975–77, sr lectr in occupational med London Sch of Hygiene and Tropical Med 1977–80 (lectr 1969–75), fndn prof of occupational health Univ of Birmingham 1981–2001 (emeritus prof 2001–); chm Industrial Injuries Advsy Cncl 1984–96, head Ind Review Work Capability Assessment Dept for Work and Pensions 2010–13, specialist advsr House of Lords and House of Commons select ctees; vice-pres Int Cmmn on Occupational Health 1998–2003; memb: Nat Radiological Protection Bd 1992–2000, Soc of Occupational Med, Soc of Epidemiological Res, Int Epidemiology Assoc, Br Occupational Hygiene Soc; govr Royal Devon & Exeter NHS Fndn Tst 2007–10; FFPH, FRCP (MRCP, LRCP), MRCS, FFOM (MFOM), FFOM(I), FACE USA, FMedSci, Hon FRSM 2004; *Books* Occupational Health (with F S Gill, 1983, 6 edn 2016), Recent Advances in Occupational Health (ed vol 2, 1984, ed vol 3, 1987), Occupational Hygiene (with K Gardiner, 3 edn 2005); Hunter's Diseases of Occupation (10 edn 2010); over 200 scientific papers published; *Recreations* music, theatre, gardening, cricket; *Clubs* Athenaeum, RSM; *Style—* Prof Malcolm Harrington, CBE; ✉ 1 The Cliff, Budleigh Salterton, Devon EX9 6JU (e-mail jmharri6@aol.com)

HARRINGTON, Richard; MP; s of John Harrington (d 2008), and Alma, *née* Feldstein; *b* 4 November 1957, Leeds; *Educ* Leeds GS, Keble Coll Oxford; *m* 31 Dec 1982, Jessie, *née* Benardette; 2 s (James b 23 Dec 1989, Daniel b 14 Sept 1993); *Career* MP (Cons) Watford 2010–; govr Univ Coll Sch; *Clubs* Oriental; *Style—* Richard Harrington, Esq, MP; ✉ House of Commons, London SW1A 0AA (☎ 020 7219 7180, e-mail richard.harrington.mp@parliament.uk, website www.richardharrington.org.uk, Twitter @richard4watford)

HARRIOTT, Ainsley; s of Chester Leroy Harriott, of Manchester, and Peppy Petrona, *née* Strudwick (d 1993); *b* 28 February 1957; *Educ* Wandsworth Boys Sch, Westminster Catering Coll; *m* 3 Jan 1992, Clare Judy, da of Derek Fellows; 1 s (James Reuben b 24 June 1990), 1 da (Madeleine Joan Adaisma b 18 July 1993); *Career* trainee chef rising to commis chef Verreys Restaurant London 1975–78, demi chef de partie rising to chef tournant Strand Palace Hotel 1978–80, jr sous chef rising to sr sous chef Westbury Hotel 1980–85, chef de partie George V Paris, freelance chef and owner catering co 1985–95; head chef Long Room Lord's Cricket Ground 1985–95, head chef various ODC Cos; pres TRIC 2005–06; charity work incl: Help the Aged, Childline, Imperial Cancer Research, Children with Leukemia, Comic Relief, Barnardo's, Children in Need, Lord Taverners, MS Soc, Children's Tst, patron Kasiisi Porridge Project; *Television* presenter: Ainsley Harriott's Barbecue Bible, Can't Cook Won't Cook, Ready Steady Cook 1994–2010 (longest running cookery show ever), Nat Lottery Live, Holiday Memories, Party of a Lifetime, Hidden Camera Show, Celeb Ready Steady Cook, Meals in Minutes, Ainsley's Big Cookout, Gourmet Express, 50 Things to Eat Before You Die, Who Do You Think You Are?, GMTV, Take on the Takeaway, The Great British Food Revival (2 series), The Alan Titchmarsh Show, The One Show, Ainsley Harriott's Street Food, Strictlly Come Dancing, Len and Ainsley's Big Food Adventure; Television in USA incl: The Ainsley Harriott Show, The Tonight Show, Live with Regis & Kathie Lee, Rosie O'Donnell Show, Ready Set Cook; Off the Menu (two series, South Africa); *Theatre* narrator Rocky Horror Picture Show (tour) 2009–10; *Awards* winner various team medals Westbury Hotel, BBC Good Food Award for Best TV/Radio Personality 1997 and 1998, TV Quick Award for Best TV Cook 1997, 1998 and 1999, Birmingham Evening Mail Readers' Award for Top TV Chef 1997, PASTA Personality of the Year 1998, Satellite TV Personality of the Year 1998, Tric Awards, UKTV Favourite TV Presenter 2003–04, Best Cookery Show Good Housekeeping Award (for Ready Steady Cook) 2005, Screen Nation Film and TV Award TV Presenter 2007, TV Personality of the Year Michael Elliott Tst Award, Silver Medal Best Soup Grocer Award 2010, Carribean Tourism Orgn Journalism Award 2015 (for Ainsley Harriott's Street Food); *Books* In the Kitchen with Ainsley Harriott (1996), Ainsley Harriott's Barbecue Bible (1997), Can't Cook Won't Cook (1997), Ready Steady Cook IV (1997), Meals in Minutes (1998), Ainsley's Big Cookout (1998), Gourmet Express (2000), Gourmet Express 2 (2001), All New Meals in Minutes (2003), Low Fat Meals in Minutes (2004), Friends and Family Cookbook (2004), Ultimate Barbeque Bible (2005), Feel-good Cookbook (2006), Fresh and Fabulous Meals in Minutes (2008), Just Five Ingredients (2009), My Kitchen Table (series, 2010 and 2012), Great British Food Revival (2011 and 2012); *Clubs* Harbour, Soho House; *Style—* Ainsley Harriott, Esq; ✉ c/o Jeremy Hicks Associates Ltd, 3 Stedham Place, London WC1A 1HU

HARRIS, Prof Adrian Llewellyn; s of Luke Harris, and Julia Harris; *b* 10 August 1950; *Educ* Liverpool Collegiate Sch, Univ of Liverpool (BSc, MB), Univ of Oxford (DPhil); *m* 7 July 1975, Margaret Susan, da of Rev Ronald Denman; *Career* clinical scientist Clinical Pharmacology Unit MRC Oxford 1975–78, lectr in med oncology Royal Marsden Hosp London 1978–80, visiting fell ICRF London 1981, prof of clinical oncology Univ of Newcastle 1981–88, prof of medical oncology and dir of Molecular Oncology Lab Univ of Oxford 1988– (fell St Hugh's Coll); FRCP; *Recreations* swimming, walking, films and theatre; *Style—* Prof Adrian L Harris; ✉ Cancer and Haematology Centre, Level 2, Churchill Hospital, Oxford OX3 7LJ (☎ 01865 235310, fax 01865 235985)

HARRIS, Benedick Aron (Ben); s of Ansel Zev Harris (d 2001), and Toba Elisabeth, *née* Zaiman (d 2002); *b* 20 February 1962, London; *Educ* St Paul's, Wadham Coll Oxford (BA), Univ of Reading (MA); *m* 1992, Ramona, *née* Harman; 1 s (Benyamin Alexander b 7 July 2000); *Career* Br Cncl: teacher Kuala Lumpur 1987–91, asst dir of studies Budapest 1992–96, mangr teaching centre Beijing 1996–98, mangr teaching centre Bandar Seri Begawan 1998–99, dir Bandar Seri Begawan 1999–2001, various posts incl acting dir corp planning and acting dir commissioning support London 2001–06, dir Netherlands 2006–; memb Bd of Tstees Active Training and Educn (ATE), memb Assoc of the Br Sch of the Netherlands, memb Bd of Govrs Br Sch in Amsterdam; *Recreations* theatre, music, sport; *Style—* Ben Harris, Esq; ✉ British Council, Weteringschans 85A, 1017 RZ Amsterdam, Netherlands (☎ 00 31 20 550 6061, fax 00 31 20 620 7389, e-mail ben.harris@britishcouncil.nl)

HARRIS, Brian Nicholas; s of Claude Harris (d 1976), and Dorothy, *née* Harris (d 1982); *b* 12 December 1931; *Educ* Coll of Estate Mgmnt London; *m* 18 March 1961, Rosalyn Marion, da of Geoffrey Alfred Caines (d 1982); 2 da (Suzanne (Mrs Richard Thompson) b 1961, Jennifer (Mrs Frederick Batt) b 1965); *Career* chartered surveyor; Richard Ellis: ptnr 1961–96, chm 1984–93; conslt C B Richard Ellis 1996–; chm: Priority Sites Ltd 2001–03, Bann System Ltd 2004–11; non-exec dir EDI plc 2003–06; vice-chm: RICS Bldg Surveying Div 1976–77, RICS Continental Gp 1977–78; chm City Branch RICS 1984–85; London C of C: memb Cncl 1985–, memb Bd 1989–96, dep pres 1990–92, pres 1992–94; memb: Cncl Aust and NZ C of C (UK) 1988–2000 (chm 1996–98), Aust and NZ Trade Advsy Ctee 1988–98; first chm London Heathrow Support Gp 1993–99, chm Southern Region Assoc of Br C of Cs 1994–96, memb Bd Br C of C 1994–98 (dep pres 1996–98), memb Ct of Common Cncl Corp of London 1996– (chm Property Sub-Ctee 2002–04; memb London Int Ct of Arbitration Jt Consultative Ctee 1996–99; tstee Commercial Educn Tst Ctee 1990–96 (chm 2000–06); memb Bd Britain Aust Soc (chm 2002, dep chm 1999, vice-pres 2000–); chm Cook Soc 2001; Lay Sheriff City of London 1998–99; hon property advsr Order of St John of Jerusalem 1996–2001; memb Co of World Traders 1989–; Liveryman and memb Ct of Assts Worshipful Co of Glaziers and Painters of Glass 1975 (Upper Warden 2002, Master 2003); *Recreations* fly fishing, gardening, golf, opera; *Clubs* Carlton, Flyfishers', City of London, MCC; *Style—* Brian Harris, Esq; ✉ Grants Paddock, Grants Lane, Limpsfield, Surrey RH8 0RQ (☎ 01883 723215); CBRE, St Martins Court, 10 Paternoster Row, London EC4M 7HD (☎ 020 7182 2000)

HARRIS, Carolyn; MP; da of Donald Marvelly, of Swansea, and Pauline Marvelly (d 2014); *b* Jan 1954, Swansea; *Educ* BA; *m* David Harris; 2 s (Stuart b 4 Oct 1986, Tomas b 25

Aug 2001); *Career* MP (Lab) Swansea E 2015–; *Recreations* reading, walking; *Style—* Mrs Carolyn Harris, MP; ✉ Constituency Office, 485 Llangyfelach Road, Brynhyfryd, Swansea SA5 9EA (✆ 01792 462054); House of Commons, London SW1A 0AA

HARRIS, His Hon Judge (Geoffrey) Charles Wesson; QC (1989); s of Geoffrey Hardy-Harris (d 1994), and Joan, *née* Wesson (d 1979); *b* 17 January 1945; *Educ* Repton, Univ of Birmingham (LLB); *m* 25 July 1970, Carol Ann, da of J D Alston, CBE, of Norfolk; 2 s (Roger, Hugh), 1 da (Kate); *Career* called to the Bar Inner Temple 1967 (bencher 2009), in practice (common law) London and Midlands 1968–93, recorder 1990–93, circuit judge (Midland & Oxford Circuit) 1993– (sr circuit judge 2014–); designated civil judge (DCJ): Oxford and Northampton 1998–2001, Oxford and Thames Valley 2001–13, Oxon, Bucks, Berks, Beds and Herts 2014–; memb: Parole Bd 1995–2000, Crown Court Rules Ctee 1997–2005, Cncl of HM's Circuit Judges 2002– (pres 2010); Parly candidate (Cons) Penistone 1974; govr St Clement Danes C of E Primary Sch 1976–79; *Books* contrib Halsbury's Laws of England; author of various magazine articles; *Recreations* history, deer stalking, skiing, architecture, travel, fireworks; *Style—* His Hon Judge Charles Harris, QC; ✉ c/o Oxford Combined Court, St Aldates, Oxford OX1 1TL

HARRIS, Emeritus Prof Christopher John; s of George Henry Harris, BEM, and Hilda Winifred, *née* Ward; *b* 23 December 1945; *Educ* Portsmouth NGS, Univ of Leicester (BSc), Univ of Oxford (MA), Univ of Southampton (PhD, DSc); *m* 10 Sept 1965, (Ruth) Joy, da of Robert Garrod (d 1983); 2 da (Caroline Louise b 1968, Kathryn Ruth b 1978), 1 s (Philip Jonathan b 1971); *Career* lectr in electronics Univ of Hull 1969–72, lectr in control engrg and maths UMIST 1972–75, lectr and fell in engrg sci Univ of Oxford and St Edmund Hall 1976–80, prof and dep chief scientist MOD 1980–84, prof and chm of sch Cranfield Inst of Technol 1984–87, prof of computational intelligence Univ of Southampton 1987–, research prof ICSTM 2003–08, emeritus prof univ of Southampton 2014–; dir Nat Research Centre in Data of Information Fusion; author of over 450 scientific papers; IEE Senior Achievement Medallist 1998, IEE Faraday Medallist 2001; CEng 1972, FIMA 1975, FIEE 1976, FREng 1996; *Books* Mathematical Modelling of Turbulent Diffusion in the Environment (1979), Stability of Linear Systems (1980), Self Tuning and Adaptive Control (1981), The Stability of Input/Output Dynamic Systems (1983), Advances in Command, Control and Communication Systems (1987), Application of Artificial Intelligence to Command and Control Systems (1988), Intelligent Control: aspects of fuzzy logic and neural nets (1993), Neurofuzzy Adaptive Modelling and Control (1994), Advances in Intelligent Control (1994), Advances and Adaptive Control (1995), Neutral Network Control of Robotic Manipulators (1998), Data Based Modelling, Control and Estimation (2002); *Recreations* gardening, sailing, wildlife photography; *Style—* Emeritus Prof Christopher Harris, FREng; ✉ Department of Electronics & Computer Sciences, University of Southampton, Highfield, Southampton S017 1BJ (✆ 023 8047 2363, e-mail cjh@ecs.soton.ac.uk)

HARRIS, Prof Christopher John; s of Colin Christopher Harris, and Barbara Kay, *née* Hall; *b* 22 September 1960; *Educ* Oundle, CCC Oxford (BA), Nuffield Coll Oxford (MPhil, DPhil); *m* 1993, Qun Li; 1 s (Alexander Sheng b 26 May 1998); *Career* Univ of Oxford: prize research fell in economics Nuffield Coll 1983–84, lectr in economics 1984–94, fell Nuffield Coll 1984–94; prof of mathematical economics Univ of Cambridge 1995–, fell King's Coll Cambridge 1995–; visiting prof MIT 1990–91, Br Acad research prof 2000–03, visiting fell Princeton 2000–01 (Richard B Fisher memb Inst for Advanced Study 2001–02); *Publications* author of articles in academic journals; *Style—* Prof C J Harris; ✉ Faculty of Economics and Politics, University of Cambridge, Austin Robinson Building, Sidgwick Avenue, Cambridge CB3 9DD (✆ 01223 335706, fax 01223 335475)

HARRIS, David Anthony; s of Dr Samuel Harris (d 1996), and Joan, *née* Pegler (d 2014); *b* 31 March 1954; *Educ* King Edward's Sch Birmingham, Univ of London (LLB); *m* 1, 7 Nov 1987, Penelope Anne (d 1998), da of Alfred Dalton, CB (d 2012); 1 da (Sophie Olivia b 30 Sept 1988), 1 s (Edward Robert b 15 Dec 1991); m 2, 17 July 1999, Margaret Evelyn; *Career* admitted slr 1979; Field Fisher & Martineau 1977–82; Hogan Lovells: (formerly Lovells) slr 1982–86, ptnr 1986–2014, managing ptnr 2005–10, co-ceo 2010–14, ret; currently exec coach, non-exec and advsy servs in professional servs sector; business mentor Mentore Consulting LLP; memb Int Advsy Panel Mosaic charity; memb Law Soc; Liveryman Worshipful Co of Slrs; *Recreations* polo, music, skiing; *Style—* David Harris, Esq; ✉ e-mail david@burrowshill.com

HARRIS, Col David Keith; OBE (1987, MBE 1983), TD (1978), DL (Lincs 1993); s of Edwin Harris (d 1974), of Epworth, Doncaster, and Mona Doreen, *née* Sleight (d 2001); *b* 27 January 1945; *Educ* Worksop Coll, KCL (LLB); *m* 25 Jan 1975, Veronica Mary, da of Arthur Vernon Harrison (d 1983), of Finningley, S Yorks; *Career* Univ of London OTC 1963–67, cmmnd Royal Lincolnshire Regt TA 1967; served: 5 Royal Anglian 1967–78, 7 Royal Anglian 1978–80, SO2 G3 7 Field Force 1980–82, SO2 G3 49 Inf Bde 1982; cmd 7 R Anglian 1984–87, dep cdr 49 Inf Bde 1987–90, TA Col RMAS 1991–94, Dep Col The Royal Anglian Regt 1992–97; admitted slr 1969, sr ptnr HSR Law (Hayes, Son & Richmond, formerly Richmonds) 1989–2014 (co dir), currently conslt slr Jones & Co Bawtry S Yorks; non-exec memb Doncaster HA 2000–02; Parly candidate (Cons) Bassetlaw: Oct 1974, 1979; memb Law Soc 1967; ADC 1990–93; *Recreations* rugby union, old motor cars, shooting, gardening, good food and wine; *Style—* Col David Harris, OBE, TD, DL; ✉ Green Hill House, Haxey, Doncaster, South Yorkshire DN9 2JU (✆ 01427 752794); Jones & Co, 48 High Street, Bawtrey, Doncaster, South Yorkshire DN10 6JB (✆ 01302 710555, fax 01302 711742, e-mail david.harris@jonessolicitors.co.uk)

HARRIS, Graham Derek; s of late Philip Henry Harris, of 16 Hardwick Rd, Folkestone, Kent, and May Dorothy, *née* Perovich; *b* 28 September 1956; *Educ* King's Sch Canterbury, Oriel Coll Oxford (MA); *m* 14 Feb 1987, Katarine Maria, da of Boris Stanislaus Brandl (d 1955), of Garstang, Lancs; 1 da (Philippa Josephine Brandl b 28 Sept 1989); *Career* slr; articled clerk Norton Rose Botterell & Roche 1979–83, admitted 1981, ptnr Richards Butler 1988–2001 (joined 1983), ptnr Thomas Cooper 2001–11, ptnr Squire Sanders (UK) LLP 2011–; SSC; *Style—* Graham Harris, Esq; ✉ Squire Patton Boggs (UK) LLP, 7 Devonshire Square, London EC2M 4YH (✆ 020 7655 1000, fax 020 7460 2844)

HARRIS, Harry; s of Jack Harris, and Sara, *née* Cohen; *b* 30 May 1952; *Educ* Davenant Fndn GS (soccer capt), Harlow Coll; *m* 1, (m dis); 1 s (Simon Paul b 16 Nov 1975), 1 da (Jordanna b 17 Aug 1980); m 2, Linda; 1 da (Poppy Georgina b 2 July 2001); *Career* journalist; Express & Independent 1971–72, North London Weekly Herald 1972–79, Newcastle Journal 1979–80, London Evening News 1980–81, Daily Mail 1981–85, The Mirror 1985–2001 (latterly chief soccer writer), Daily Express 2002–08; currently head of communications and media Football Nights, inventor of Football40, head of media Hinchc.as; co-fndr: H&H Sport & Media (zapsportz.com/Football30 Legends), Fleetstreetfc.co.uk, Fleet Street Sport & Media; football conslt Barratt; memb Sports Journalists Assoc; GB's Sports Journalist of the Year 1993 (runner-up 1996), Sports Reporter of the Year (jtly) Sports Cncl 1993 (runner up 1998), highly commended Race in the Media Awards 1993, shortlisted Br Sports Reporter of the Year 1994, Sports Reporter of the Year British Press Awards 1998, Sports Story of the Year Sport England 1999 and 2002 (highly commended Sports News Reporter of the Year 2000), Silver Heart for contribution to sports journalism Variety Club of GB 2004, highly commended Sports Story and Sports News Reporter of the Year 2005, highly commended Sports Scoop 2010; *Books* incl: Spurred to Success (with Glenn Hoddle), The Inside Story (Terry Venables), Rock Bottom (with Paul Merson), Against All the Odds (with Gary Mabbutt), Macca Can (with Steve McMahon), Revelations of a Football Manager (with Terry Neill); also Bill Nicholson's autobiography (co-author), Jurgen Klinsman's Diary of a Season, Portrait of a Genius (Ruud Gullit's biography), Ruud Gullit: The Chelsea Diary, My Autobiography: Ruud Guillit, The Road to France: World Cup Masterpieces, The Fergie Factor (Alex Ferguson biography), Vialli: A Diary of His Season, Pele: The Authorised Biography, Jose Mourinho: Simply the Best, The Vodafone Champions League Yearbook, Martin Jol: The Inside Story, Down Memory Lane: 50 Years Supporting Spurs (2009), The Roman Conquest, 19: The Remarkable Story of United's League Championship Record, Mancini: Diary of Title Season, Josè Mourinho: The King is Back, England Centurions, The Roman Conquest – Chelsea Kings of Europe (2012), A Tribute to Sir Alex Ferguson, José – Farewell to the King (2016), Up Front: My Autobiography (with Kerry Dixon, 2016); *Recreations* tennis; *Clubs* Wentworth; *Style—* Harry Harris, Esq; ✆ 07710 613939, e-mail harry.harris1@mac.com

HARRIS, Hugh Christopher Emlyn; CBE (2009); s of T E Harris, CB, CBE (d 1955), and M A Harris (d 1980); *b* 25 March 1936; *Educ* The Leys Sch Cambridge, Trinity Coll Cambridge (MA); *m* 7 Sept 1968, Pamela Susan, da of R A Woollard (d 1980); 1 da (Kate b 1970), 1 s (William b 1972); *Career* Nat Serv Lt RA 1954–56; dir: BE Services Ltd 1979–94, Houblon Nominees 1988–94, The Securities Mgmnt Tst Ltd 1988–94; Bank of England 1959–94: chief of corp servs 1984–88, assoc dir 1988–94; dir London First Global Network 1999–2012 (gen mangr London First Centre 1995, dir of ops London First 1995–99, conslt 2012–); dep chm Cmmn for Racial Equality 1996–2000 (cmmr 1995); special advsr City and Inner London NTEC (CILNTEC) 1994–97, dir London Film Cmmn 1996–2000; vice-pres Bankers Benevolent Fund 1990–2012; memb Cncl London Civic Forum 2001–09; memb Bd of Govrs Newham Coll of FE 2005–14; hon treas Kemsing Branch Royal Br Legion 1972–2014, churchwarden St Margaret Lothbury 1988–94, chm Solefield Sch Educnl Tst Ltd 1993–2000, chm Broad St Ward Club 2002–03, tstee Learning Revolution Tst 2014–; memb HAC; Liveryman Worshipful Co of Turners; FCIPD, FRSA; *Recreations* rugby, tennis, films, opera, ballet; *Style—* Hugh Harris, Esq, CBE; ✉ London First, Middlesex House, 34–42 Cleveland Street, London W1T 4JE (✆ 020 7665 1570, fax 020 7665 1501, e-mail hharris@londonfirst.co.uk)

HARRIS, Jeffery Francis (Jeff); *b* 8 April 1948; *Educ* Rendcomb Coll Cirencester, Univ of Southampton (BSc); *Career* early career with Barton Mayhew & Co and Ernst & Young; UniChem plc: joined as chief accountant 1985, memb Bd 1986, finance dir 1986–91, dep chief exec 1991–92, chief exec 1992–97; Alliance UniChem plc: chief exec 1997–2001, exec chm 2001–03, non-exec chm 2003–05; chm Filtrona (following demerger from Bunzl) 2005–10, chm Cookson Gp plc 2010–; non-exec dir: Associated British Foods plc 2003–, Bunzl plc 2000–10, W H Smith plc 2011–; chm Br Assoc of Pharmaceutical Wholesalers 1996–98; Hon DBA Kingston Univ; FCA 1979; *Style—* Jeff Harris, Esq; ✉ Cookson Group plc, 165 Fleet Street, London EC4A 2AE (✆ 020 7822 0000, fax 020 7822 0100, website www.cooksongroup.co.uk)

HARRIS, Joanne Michèle Sylvie; MBE (2013); da of Robert Ian Short, and Jeannette, *née* Payen; *b* 3 July 1964, Barnsley; *Educ* Wakefield Girls' HS, Barnsley Sixth Form Coll, St Catharine's Coll Cambridge (MA), Univ of Sheffield (PGCE); *m* 1988, Kevin Steven Harris; 1 da (Anouchka Fleur b 1 June 1993); *Career* writer; Hon DLitt: Univ of Huddersfield 2003, Univ of Sheffield 2004; *Books* The Evil Seed (1989), Sleep, Pale Sister (1993), Chocolat (1999, Creative Freedom Award 2000, Whittaker Gold 2001; shortlisted: Whitbread Novel of the Year Award 2000, Scripter Award 2001; film version nominated for 8 BAFTAs and 5 Oscars), Blackberry Wine (2000, winner Foreign and Int categories Salon du Livre Gourmand), Five Quarters of the Orange (2001; shortlisted: RNA Novel of the Year, Author of the Year 2002, WHSmith Award 2002), Coastliners (2002), The French Kitchen: A Cookbook (with Fran Warde, 2002), Holy Fools (2003), Jigs and Reels (2004), The French Market: A Cookbook (with Fran Warde, 2005), Gentlemen and Players (2005, shortlisted Edgar Award USA 2007), The Lollipop Shoes (2007), Runemarks (2007), Blueeyedboy (2010), Runelight (2011), Peaches for Monsieur le Curé (2012), A Cat, a Hat and a Piece of String (2012), The Gospel of Loki (2014), The Little Book of Chocolat (with Fran Warde, 2014), Different Class (2016); *Style—* Mrs Joanne Harris, MBE; ✉ c/o Eldon House, Sharp Lane, Almondbury, Huddersfield HD5 8XL (website www.joanne-harris.co.uk)

HARRIS, Prof John Buchanan; s of John Benjamin Sargent Harris (d 1971), of Adelaide, Aust, and Mary Isobel, *née* Pratt; *b* 18 January 1940; *Educ* Tiffin Sch Kingston upon Thames, Univ of London (BPharm), Univ of Bradford (PhD); *m* 6 Sept 1965, Christine Margaret, da of Clifford Morton Holt (d 1983), of Bradford, W Yorks; 2 s (Joel b and d 1972, Jolyon Leo b 1974), 1 da (Danica Mathilde b 1981); *Career* res asst Univ of Bradford 1963–67; Univ of Newcastle: sr res asst 1967–72, princ res assoc 1972–74, sr lectr 1974–80, prof 1980–2007, emeritus prof 2007–; res fell Univ of Lund Sweden 1970–71, UCLA America 1977–78, Monash Univ Aust 1980; FSB, CBiol, MRPharmS; *Books* Muscular Dystrophy and other Inherited Diseases of Muscle in Animals (1979), Natural Toxins (1986), Muscle Metabolism (with D M Turnbull, 1990), Medical Neurotoxicology (with P G Blain, 1999); *Recreations* reading, walking, riding horses; *Style—* Prof John Harris; ✉ Medical Toxicology Centre, Newcastle University Medical School, Newcastle upon Tyne NE2 4HH (✆ 0191 222 6977, e-mail j.b.harris@ncl.ac.uk)

HARRIS, John Charles; CBE (2007), DL (S Yorks 1986); s of Sir Charles Joseph William Harris, KBE (d 1986), and Lady Emily Kyle, *née* Thompson (d 1992); *b* 25 April 1936; *Educ* Dulwich Coll (LCC scholar), Clare Coll Cambridge (MA, LLM); *m* 1 April 1961, Alison Beryl, da of Dr Kenneth Reginald Sturley, and Beryl Marion Sturley; 1 da (Susan Alison b 15 Sept 1966), 1 s (Edward John Charles b 16 June 1968); *Career* Nat Serv 2 Lt Intelligence Corps 1954–56 (Lt 1957); with UKAEA (seconded to OECD) 1959–63, Poole BC 1963–67, admitted slr 1966, dep town clerk Bournemouth CB 1971–73 (offr 1967–73); S Yorks CC 1973–86: co sec 1973–83, chief exec and co clerk 1983–86, dir SY Resid Body 1985–86, non-exec dir S Yorks Passenger Tport Exec, clerk to Lord-Lieut S Yorks 1983–86; legal, mgmnt and recruitment conslt (incl for PA Conslt Group and Daniels Bates Partnership) 1986–; exec dir: Solace International Ltd 1992–2000, Solace International (Southern Africa) Pty Ltd 1993–2000; non-exec dir Pontefract HA 1990–93, dir Stray Services Ltd 2010–, dir Hatfield Colliery EBT Co Ltd 2014–15; chm: Bd Northern Counties Housing Assoc 1994–2000 (memb 1990–2009, vice-chm 1994 and 2002–03), Bd Northern Counties (Specialised) Housing Assoc Ltd 1994–07, Coal Authy 1999–2007, Audit Ctee MOD Police and Guarding Agency 2004–12, Coal Forum 2007–, Mid Yorks Hosps NHS Tst 2008–09 (non-exec dir 2007–08), Little Red Bus (HDCT) Ltd 2011–13; ind memb Police Ctee MOD 2003–07; memb Bd Guinness Tst Partnership 2007–08, ind memb MDPGA Mgmnt Bd 2011–13; memb: Rampton Special Hosp Ctee 1989–96, Arts Cncl Touring Advsy Bd 1988–92, Ctee Ackworth Gp Riding for the Disabled Assoc 1976–96; fndr memb and sec Barnsley-Rockley Rotary Club 1976–79, vice-chm and sec Friends of Opera North 1978–87; Opera North plc: memb Cncl 1979–88, memb Devpt Ctee 1987–94; tstee, dir and memb Mgmnt Cncl Homeless Int 1998–2000; dir South Africa Housing Support Network Tst 1998–2001; nat chm Soc of Co Secs 1983, Hon PRO S Yorks and Humberside Region RDA 1983–92; memb: Cncl Soc of Local Authorities Chief Exec 1984–86, RDA Nat Pubns Ctee 1988–90, W Yorks Police Authy (ind) 1994–99; tstee: Housing Assocs Charitable Tst 1995–96, The Art House 2009– (chm 2009–15, dep chm 2015–), Harrogate (White Rose) Theatre Tst 2011–, Royal Hall Restoration Tst 2013– (administrator 2014–), Harrogate Homeless Project 2015– (dep chm 2016–); chair Friends of Harrogate Theatre 2011–15; chm of govrs: Felkirk (formerly Ackworth Moor Top) Community Special Sch 1998–2005 (govr 1996), Wakefield Dist Community Sch (incorporating former Felkirk Community Special Sch) 2005–09; jt chair Ivory Park Township Johannesburg SA/Wakefield Educn Partnership 2002–08 (co-ordinator UK

H

imports to community devpt 1995–2008); memb European Movement (Britain Stronger IN Europe referendum campaign, N Yorks/ Harrogate coordinator) 2016; memb Law Soc; Freeman City of London 1957; FRSA 1984; *Recreations* foreign travel, opera, family and friends; *Clubs* Harrogate; *Style—* John Harris, Esq, CBE, DL; ✉ 7 Stray Towers, Victoria Road, Harrogate HG2 0LJ (☎ 01423 398847, mobile 07710 110407, e-mail jcharris7stray@gmail.com)

HARRIS, John Clement; s of Norman Rees, and Leah Eastwood, *née* Clement; *b* 9 July 1936; *Educ* Seaford Coll, Petworth; *m* 19 Sept 1962, Shirley, *née* Anderson; 1 s (Jonathan b 17 May 1964); *Career* Nat Serv RAF 1955–57; own business: nursing homes 1957–62, furnishing and interior design 1962–84, commercial property devpt/mgmnt 1978–; Fedn of Small Businesses: fndr memb 1975, branch and vice-chm, region and vice-chm, nat cncllr and exec memb Bd of Dirs, policy chm, hon nat chm; chm Southern Water Consumer Consultative Ctee; dir Southern Water; *Recreations* building, walking, travelling (particularily USA); *Style—* John Harris, Esq; ✉ 32a Lansdowne Road, Worthing, West Sussex BN11 5HB (☎ 01903 609308); Federation of Small Businesses, Parliamentary Office, 2 Catherine Place, Westminster, London SW1E 6HF (☎ 020 7233 7900, fax 020 7233 7899, e-mail jch@jcharris.net)

HARRIS, Prof Jose Ferial; da of Leonard and Freda Chambers; *Educ* Univ of Cambridge (MA, PhD); *Career* research fell Nuffield Coll Oxford 1966–69, lectr LSE 1969–74 (sr lectr 1974–78); Univ of Oxford: fell St Catherine's Coll 1978–, lectr in modern history 1978–83, reader 1983–87, prof 1997–, Leverhulme research prof 1998–2002, prof of modern history 2002–, vice-master St Catherine's Coll 2003–05; Br Acad Res Readership 1989–91; memb Social History Soc, memb Past and Present Soc; FRHistS 1974, FBA 1994; *Books* Unemployment and Politics 1886–1914 (1972, 2 edn 1982), William Beveridge: a Biography (1977, 2 edn 1997), Private Lives Public Spirit 1870–1914 (1994, 2 edn 1995), Ferdinand Tönnies: Gemeinschaft und Gesellschaft (2000), Civil Society in British History (2003); *Recreations* long-distance walking, river boats, the lesser arts, family life; *Clubs* Oxford and Cambridge, Freemen; *Style—* Prof Jose Harris; ✉ 5 Belbroughton Road, Oxford OX2 6UZ; St Catherine's College, Oxford OX1 3UJ (e-mail jose.harris@stcatz.ox.ac.uk); Faculty of Modern History, Broad Street, Oxford OX1 3BD

HARRIS, Joseph Hugh; DL (1984); s of John Frederick Harris (d 1990); *b* 3 June 1932; *Educ* Harrow, RAC Cirencester (DipAg); *m* 1957, Anne, da of Brig L H McRobert (d 1981); 3 s; *Career* Lt 11 Hussars PAO; chm Cumbrian Newspapers Ltd 1987–2002 (formerly dir); farmer, landowner; memb Miny of Agric Northern Regnl Panel 1977–83; RASE: sr steward 1957–77, hon dir Royal Show 1978–82, vice-pres 1980–92, dep pres 1986–87, tstee 1992–2007; High Sheriff Cumbria 1976–77; chm: govrs Aysgarth Sch 1975–85, Grasmere Sports 1977–97 (dir 1997–2008), Penrith and Alston Magistrates Bench 1991–96; memb Cumbria Rural Devpt Cmmn 1990–95; Liveryman Worshipful Co of Farmers; Vice Lord-Lt Cumbria 1994–2007; JP Penrith 1971–2002; *Recreations* shooting and field sports; *Style—* Joseph Harris, Esq, DL; ✉ West View, Bowscar, Penrith, Cumbria CA11 9PG (☎ 01768 885661)

HARRIS, Malcolm Robert; *Career* Bovis Homes: joined 1974, memb Bd 1978, chief exec 1996–2008, non-exec chm 2008–; non-exec dir: House Builders Fedn Ltd, Nat House Building Cncl; FCMA; *Style—* Malcolm Harris, Esq; ✉ Bovis Homes Group plc, The Manor House, North Ash Road, New Ash Green, Longfield, Kent DA3 8HQ

HARRIS, Mark Philip Allen; s of Roy Allen Harris, of Bishop's Stortford, Herts, and Vivienne Harris; *b* 29 July 1961, London; *Educ* Bishop's Stortford Coll, Univ of Nottingham (LLB); *m* 17 April 1993, Patricia Mary Allen; 1 da (Annabel b 24 Feb 1996), 1 s (Sean b 30 Nov 1998); *Career* Dist Audit Serv 1983–94, assoc controller Audit Cmmn 1994–97, exec conslt Hammersmith Hosps NHS Tst 1997–98, assoc dir (strategic devpt) Audit Cmmn 1998–99, chief exec and cmmr Nat Lottery Cmmn 1999–2013, dir Gambling Cmmn 2013–; chair Ashridge Alumni Cncl 2008–10; tstee: Responsibility in Gambling Tst 2007–09, Responsible Gambling Fund 2009–11; CIPFA 1987, CCMI 2011; *Recreations* family, driving, hill walking, photography, mountaineering literature; *Clubs* Cwlth, IOD; *Style—* Mark Harris, Esq; ✉ National Lottery Commission, 4th Floor, Victoria Square House, Victoria Square, Birmingham B2 4BP (☎ 0121 230 6703, e-mail m.harris@gamblingcommission.gov.uk)

HARRIS, Prof Sir Martin Best; kt (2000), CBE (1992), DL; s of William Best Harris (d 1987), of Plymouth, and Betty Evelyn, *née* Martin; *b* 28 June 1944; *Educ* Devonport HS for Boys Plymouth, Queens' Coll Cambridge (MA), Univ of London (PhD); *m* 10 Sept 1966, Barbara Mary, da of Joseph Daniels (d 1971); 2 s (Robert b 1 July 1968, Paul b 13 June 1970); *Career* lectr in French linguistics Univ of Leicester 1967–72; Univ of Salford: sr lectr in French linguistics 1972–76, prof of Romance linguistics 1976–87, dean social science and arts 1978–81, pro-vice-chllr 1981–87; vice-chllr: Univ of Essex 1987–92, Univ of Manchester 1992–2004; dir Office of Fair Access Dept for Business, Innovation and Skills 2004–12; pres Clare Hall Cambridge 2008–13; memb UGC 1984–87 (chm NI sub ctee 1985–89); chm: UFC NI Ctee 1989–91, Nat Curriculum Working Party on Modern Languages 1989–90, Govrs Centre for Information on Language Teaching 1990–96, Africa Ctee CICHE 1991–93, HEFCE Review of Postgraduate Educn 1995–96 (memb Libraries Review Ctee 1992–93), Clinical Standards Advsy Gp 1996–99, DfEE Review of Univ Careers Services 2000; memb Cmmn for Health Improvement 1999–2002; dir Investment NW Trust Ltd 1998–2001, dep chair NW Devpt Agency Bd 2002–08 (memb 2001–09), chair Manchester: Knowledge Capital 2003–08; chm: CVCP 1997–99 (vice-chm 1995–97), NW Univs Assoc 1999–2001, USS (Universities Superannuation Scheme) Ltd 2006–15 (dir 1991–15, dep chair 2004–06); dep chair Governing Body SOAS Univ of London 2014–; govr: Parrs Wood HS 1982–87, Anglia Poly 1989–92, SOAS 1990–93, Colchester Sixth Form Coll 1987–92, European Univ Inst 1992–97, Univ of Plymouth 2004–10; memb: Cncl Philological Soc 1985–92, Academia Europaea 1991–; hon fell: Queens' Coll Cambridge 1992, Bolton Inst 1996, Univ of Central Lancashire 1999; Hon LLD Queen's Univ Belfast 1992; Hon DUniv: Essex 1993, Keele 2007; Hon DLitt: Univ of Salford 1995, Manchester Met Univ 2000, Univ of Leicester 2003, Univ of Lincoln 2003, Univ of Ulster 2004, Univ of Manchester 2004, UMIST 2004, Univ of Exeter 2008, Univ of Plymouth 2009, SOAS Univ of London 2013; Hon FRCP 2005, Hon FRSE 2005; *Books* Evolution of French Syntax (1978), The Romance Verb (with N Vincent, 1983), The Romance Languages (with N Vincent, 1988, 2 edn 1990); *Recreations* walking, gardening, wine; *Style—* Prof Sir Martin Harris, CBE, DL; ✉ Director's Office, SOAS University of London, Thornhaugh Street, Russell Square, London WC1H 0XG (☎ 07899 061114)

HARRIS, Martin Fergus; OBE (2010); *b* 1969, Edinburgh; *Educ* Glenalmond Coll, Univ of Cambridge, Open Univ; *m* Linda MacLachlan; 3 da (Catriona b 2001, Tabitha b 2003, Flora b 2006); *Career* diplomat; joined FCO 1991, second sec UK Del to OSCE Vienna 1992–96, head Pakistan and Afghanistan Section FCO 1997–98, Br Embassy Moscow 1999–2003, consul gen and dep head of mission Kiev 2003–08; dep dir Cabinet Office 2008–10, ambass to Romania 2010–14, min and dep head of mission Moscow 2014–; *Style—* Mr Martin Harris, OBE

HARRIS, Matthew Edwin Charles; s of Lewis Martin Harris, of Hove, E Sussex, and Gaye, *née* Lloyd; *b* 31 May 1965; *Educ* Charterhouse, Brighton & Hove Tech Coll, Ecole le Nôtre Paris; *m* 4 May 1996, Donna Lynette, da of Donald Davies; *Career* chef Geneva 1984–85, Patisserie Sch Paris 1985–86, chef Hilaire Restaurant London 1986–87, exec head chef Bibendum Restaurant London 1995– (sous chef 1987–95); *Recreations* travel, eating out, cinema, swimming; *Style—* Matthew Harris, Esq; ✉ Bibendum, Michelin House, 81 Fulham Road, London SW3 6RD (☎ 020 7589 1481, fax 020 7823 7925)

HARRIS, Naomie Melanie; da of Carmen Harris; *b* 6 September 1976, London; *Educ* Pembroke Coll Cambridge, Bristol Old Vic Theatre Sch; *Career* actress; *Television* incl: White Teeth 2002, The Project 2002, Poppy Shakespeare 2008, Small Island 2009 (Best Actress RTS Award 2010), Blood & Oil 2010; *Film* incl: 28 Days Later 2002, Trauma 2004, After the Sunset 2004, Pirates of the Caribbean: Dead Man's Chest 2006, Miami Vice 2006, A Cock and Bull Story 2006, Pirates of the Caribbean: At World's End 2007, Street Kings 2008, August 2008, Street Kings 2008, Ninja Assassin 2009, Sex & Drugs & Rock & Roll 2010, The First Grader 2010, Skyfall 2012, Spectre 2015, Southpaw 2015, Mandela: Long Walk to Freedom 2013, Our Kind of Traitor 2016, Moonlight 2016, Collateral Beauty 2016, Jungle Book 2017; *Style—* Ms Naomie Harris; ✉ c/o Tavistock Wood, 45 Conduit Street, London W1S 2YN; c/o Untitled Management, Untitled Entertainment, 162 Fifth Avenue, 7th Floor, New York NY 10010

HARRIS, Nicholas Richard; s of Sidney George Harris, and Jean Elliott (d 1986); *b* 24 September 1941; *Educ* KHS and Nautical Coll General Botha South Africa, BRNC Dartmouth, Royal Naval Coll Greenwich, Royal Coll of Defence Studies; *m* 31 Dec 1966 (m dis 2006); 2 s (Rupert b 20 Oct 1967, Giles b 16 July 1973), 2 da (Jessica b 24 April 1971, Milly b 9 July 1983); *Career* qualified fixed wing pilot in Fleet Air Arm 1964–65; HMS Eagle 899 Sqdn (Sea Vixens) 1965–66, 766 Sqdn RNAS Yeovilton 1967–68, air warfare instr 764 Sqdn RNAS Lossiemouth 1969–70, USN VF121 and Topgun NAS Mirimar California 1971–72, HMS Devonshire 1973–74, Directorate of Naval Air Warfare MOD (Sea Harrier) 1975–76, CO 892 Sqdn (Phantoms) 1977, Air Warfare Course RAF Cranwell 1978, RN presentation team 1979, Directorate of Naval Manpower Planning MOD 1980–81, HMS Bristol (Falklands Campaign) 1982–84, Dep Sec Chief of Staff Ctee MOD 1986, Naval Attaché Rome 1987–89, Dir Mgmnt Strategy (Naval Personnel) MOD 1990–91, Asst Dir (AD1) Naval Staff MOD 1992–93, Dir Defence Staff MOD 1994–96, ret 1996; chm Farringdon Harris Group 1996–2007, special advsr to Guy's and St Thomas' Hosp Tst 1997–2004; dir: Bonvoyages SA 1998–2007, Spearhead Exhibitions (Central Europe) Ltd 1999–2000, Maiden Bower Ltd 2000–, Cyclotec Advanced Medical Technologies Inc 2001–06, Cyclotec International Ltd 2005–08, Depro (GVB) Inc 2005–10, Dart Technical Services Inc 2007; chm Sea Cadet Assoc (E Anglia) 1998–2005, special advsr to Sea Cadet Assoc 2000–05; MRUSI; *Recreations* sailing, most country pursuits, tennis, watching cricket; *Clubs* MCC, Lansdowne, Royal Naval Sailing Assoc; *Style—* Nicholas Harris, Esq; ✉ Coutts & Co, 440 Strand, London WC2R 0QS (☎ 020 7753 1000, e-mail nick.harris@maiden-bower.com)

HARRIS, Prof Paul Lansley; s of late Joseph Harris, and Betty, *née* Lansley; *b* 14 May 1946; *Educ* Chippenham GS, Univ of Sussex (BA), Univ of Oxford (DPhil); *m* Pascale, da of Claude Torracinta; 3 s (Simon b 5 May 1991, Rémi b 23 Sept 1993, Louis b 9 Sept 1998); *Career* research fell: Center for Cognitive Studies Harvard Univ 1971–72, Dept of Experimental Psychology Univ of Oxford 1972–73; lectr Dept of Psychology Lancaster Univ 1973–76, reader in psychology Free Univ Amserdam 1976–79, lectr in psychology LSE 1979–81; Univ of Oxford: lectr in experimental psychology 1981–96, reader in experimental psychology 1996–98, prof of developmental psychology 1998–2001; prof of educn Harvard Univ 2001–, Victor S Thomas prof of educn Harvard Univ 2005–; fell St John's Coll Oxford 1981–2001 (emeritus fell 2001–), fell Center for Advanced Study in the Behavioural Scis Stanford 1992–93, Guggenheim fell 2005–; FBA 1998, FAcSS 2015; *Books* Children and Emotion (1989), The Work of the Imagination (2000), Trusting What You're Told: How Children Learn from Others (2012); also former ed British Jl of Developmental Psychology; *Recreations* cooking, writing; *Style—* Prof Paul Harris, FBA; ✉ Larsen Hall, Appian Way, Cambridge, MA 02138, USA (e-mail paul_harris@gse.harvard.edu)

HARRIS, Philip Ian; s of Raymond Harris, of Hucknall, Nottinghamshire, and Cynthia, *née* Bunt; *b* 3 June 1965; *Educ* Friesland Comp Sch Sandiacre, Mansfield Coll of Art & Design (DATEC dipl), Bradford Coll of Art & Design (BA); *m* Louise Hooker; *Career* artist; *Solo Exhibitions* Tricycle Gallery London 1990, Merz Contemporary Art London 1990 and 1992, Paintings Drawings and Etchings Woodlands Art Gallery London 1991, Ghent International Art Fair Belgium 1991, Beaux Arts Gallery London 1997; *Group Exhibitions* Works on Paper (Central Space Gallery London) 1988, The Spectator Art Award (Spink & Son London) Portobello Open (Taberncale London) 1989, BP Portrait Award Exhbn (Nat Portrait Gallery London) 1990 and 1993, 20th Century Art Fair (RCA London) 1995, Ghent Int Art Fair Belgium 1995, The Discerning Eye (Mall Galleries London) 1995, Small Picture Show (Beaux Arts London) 1996, Art 96 London Contemporary Art Fair 1996, Artists of Fame and Promise (Beaux Arts London) 1996, Art 97 London Contemporary Art Fair 1997, Re-presenting Representation – 11 (Arnot Art Museum NY) 1997, Art 98 London Contemporary Art Fair 1998, Take 3 (Beaux Arts London) 1998, 20th Century Art Fair (RCA London) 1998, Art 99 London Contemporary Art Fair 1999, Simmer (Beaux Arts London) 1999; Portrait of Sir Anthony Dowell (Nat Portrait Gallery), In Focus (Plus One Gallery London); *Awards* BP Portrait Award 3rd Prize 1990, BP Portrait Award 1st Prize 1993; *Style—* Philip Harris, Esq; ✉ Plus One Gallery, 89–91 Pimlico Road, London SW1W 8PH (☎ 020 7730 7656, fax 020 7730 7664, e-mail philip_harris1@btinternet.com, website www.philip-harris.com)

HARRIS, Dame Philippa Jill Olivier (Pippa); DBE (2015); da of Dr A D Harris (d 1995), and Angela M O, *née* Richards (d 1982); *b* 27 March 1967, Oxford; *Educ* Oxford HS, Robinson Coll Cambridge (BA); *m* 17 May 1997, Richard John McBrien; 1 da (Ella b 24 Jan 2004); *Career* prodn asst Jacaranda Prodns 1989–91, drama ed Carlton TV 1993–97; BBC: devpt exec BBC Films 1997–99, exec prodr BBC Drama Serials 1999–2001, head of drama commissioning BBC TV 2001–03 (prodr/exec prodr: Warriors 1999 (BAFTA and RTS Awards), Care 2000 (BAFTA and Prix Italia Awards), Other People's Children 2000, The Sleeper 2000, Love in a Cold Climate 2001, The Cazalets 2001, The Way We Live Now 2001 (BAFTA and BPG Awards), The Inspector Lynley Mysteries 2001–02, The Key 2003, The Young Visitors 2003); co-fndr (with Sam Mendes, CBE, and Caro Newling, *qqv*) Neal Street Prodns 2003– (prodr: Jarhead 2005, Starter for Ten 2006, Stuart A Life Backwards 2007 (Banff World TV and RTS Awards, Best TV Film Reims Int TV Festival), On Blood 2013; exec prodr: Things We Lost in the Fire 2007, Revolutionary Road 2008, Away We Go 2009, Call the Midwife 2012– (TRIC Best Drama Prog of the Year, TV Choice Best New Drama, Christopher Award, TV Choice Best Family Drama), The Hollow Crown 2012 (Best Single Drama RTS, Best Single Drama Broadcasting Press Guilds Awards), Penny Dreadful 2014–, We Are Many 2015; tstee The Creative Soc 2009–, memb Charleston Appeal Ctee 2013–, tstee The Charleston Tst 2016–; memb BAFTA Cncl 2008–, memb BAFTA Film Ctee 2008– (chair 2015–); govr Central Sch of Speech and Drama 2010–; *Publications* Song of Love: The Letters of Rupert Brooke and Noel Olivier (1991); *Recreations* theatre, cinema, contemporary art; *Style—* Dame Pippa Harris, DBE; ✉ Neal Street Productions, 26–28 Neal Street, London WC2H 9QQ (☎ 020 7240 8890, e-mail post@nealstreetproductions.com)

HARRIS, Rebecca Elizabeth; MP; *m* Frank Harris; 1 s; *Career* mktg dir Phillimore & Co 1997–2007; MP (Cons) Castle Point 2010–; *Style—* Mrs Rebecca Harris, MP; ✉ Castle Point Conservatives, Bernard Braine House, 8 Green Road, Benfleet, Essex SS7 5JT; House of Commons, London SW1A 0AA

HARRIS, Prof (Ivor) Rex; s of John Fredrick Harris (d 1977), and Margaret Emily Harris (d 1980); *b* 27 July 1939; *Educ* Larkfield GS Chepstow, Univ of Birmingham (BSc, PhD, DSc); *m* Vera Winifred, da of Leslie Boylin; 2 s (Christopher John Edward b 9 June 1966, David James Andrew b 22 Aug 1968), 1 da (Margaret Jane b 13 July 1972); *Career* University of Birmingham: ICI research fell 1964–66, lectr Dept of Physical Metallurgy

1966–74, sr lectr of metallurgy and materials 1974–87, prof of materials science 1988–, head of sch of metallurgy and materials 1996–2001 (actg head 1989–90); lectr NATO Summer Sch Italy 1990, visiting lectr various univs worldwide; memb: Editorial Advsy Bd Jl of Alloys and Compounds, Int Steering Ctee Metal Hydride Conf Series; gp co-ordinator Concerted Euro Action on Magnets (CEAM), mission ldr Overseas Tech Experts Mission (OSTEM) USA 1987; chm: UK Magnetics Club 1988–90, Euro Material Research Soc (Strasbourg) 1988, Magnetism and Magnetic Materials Initiative SERC 1992–94, 13th Int Workshop on Rare Earth Magnets and their Application 1994, 8th Int Symposium on Magnetic Anisotropy and Coercivity in Rare-earth Metal Alloys 1994; memb: Metals and Magnetic Materials Ctee SERC 1991–94, EPSRC Functional Materials Coll; pres Birmingham Metallurgical Assoc 1992, Magnetics Panel Inst of Physics 1999–; foreign memb Nat Acad of Sci Ukraine 2000; Marie Curie individual fell 2000; FIM 1992, MIEEE 1992, FREng 1994, FInstP 2003; *Books* Hydrogen in Metals (ed with J P G Farr, 1976), Rare Earth Permanent Magnets (ed, 1989), Concerted European Action on Magnets (co-ed, 1989), Magnet Processing: Rare-earth Iron Permanent Magnets (contrib, 1996), Grain Boundaries: Their Character, Characterisation and Influence on Properties (co-ed, 2001); also author of over 500 scientific papers; *Style—* Prof Rex Harris, FREng; ✉ School of Metallurgy & Materials, The University of Birmingham, Edgbaston, Birmingham B15 2TT (☎ 0121 414 5165, fax 0121 414 5247, e-mail i.r.harris@bham.ac.uk)

HARRIS, Robert Brinley Joseph (Bob); OBE (2011); s of William Brinley Harris, of Hunstanton, Norfolk, and Doria Katherine, *née* Dow; *b* 11 April 1946; *Educ* Northampton Trinity GS; *m* 1; 3 da (Mirelle b 23 Nov 1970, Emily b 2 Feb 1973, Charlotte b 30 Sept 1977), 2 s (Benjamin Brinley Howard b 17 Sept 1982, James David b 19 Nov 1986); m 2, 24 April 1991, Trudie Myerscough-Harris, da of Simon Myerscough-Walker; 2 s (Miles Simon b 2 June 1992, Dylan Joseph b 2 Sept 1994), 1 da (Florence Jayne b 21 May 1997); *Career* broadcaster and writer; fndr Time Out magazine 1968, commenced broadcasting BBC Radio 1 1970, presenter Old Grey Whistle Test (weekly rock show) BBC 2 1972–79, Radio Luxembourg 1975, Radio 210 1977, BBC Radio Oxford 1981, LBC London 1985, rejoined BBC Radio 1 1989–93, currently broadcasting: BBC Radio 2, BFBS; film debut Made 1971, prodr records for EMI and Atlantic 1973–74, released Best of The Test LP compilation 1991; estab ind prodn co WBBC 2005; hon fell Univ of Northampton 2007; *Books* Rock and Pop Mastermind (1985), Bob Harris Rockdates (1992), The Whispering Years (autobiography, 2001); *Recreations* music, my family, watching Man Utd, fitness; *Style—* Bob Harris, Esq, OBE; ✉ c/o BBC Radio 2, London W1A 4WW (☎ 020 7580 4468, e-mail bob.harris@bbc.co.uk, website www.bobharris.org, Twitter @whisperingbob)

HARRIS, Robert Dennis; s of late Dennis Harris, and Audrey, *née* Hardy; *b* 7 March 1957; *Educ* King Edward VII Sch Melton Mowbray, Selwyn Coll Cambridge (BA, chm Cambridge Fabian Soc, pres Cambridge Union); *m* 1988, Gillian, da of Sir Derek Hornby, *qv*; 2 da (Holly Miranda b 21 July 1990, Matilda Felicity b 5 Oct 1996), 2 s (Charlie Robert Nicholas b 17 April 1992, Samuel Orlando Hornby b 15 Nov 2000); *Career* res and film dir Current Affairs Dept BBC TV (progs incl Tonight, Nationwide and Panorama) 1978–81; reporter: Newsnight 1981–85, Panorama 1985–87; political ed Observer 1987–89, political reporter This Week (Thames TV) 1988–89, political columnist Sunday Times 1989–92 and 1996–97; commended Columnist of the Year Br Press Awards 1992; FRSL 1996; *Books* A Higher Form of Killing – The History of Gas and Germ Warfare (with Jeremy Paxman, 1982), Gotcha! – The Media, The Government and The Falklands Crisis (1983), The Making of Neil Kinnock (1984), Selling Hitler – The Story of the Hitler Diaries (1986, televised 1991), Good and Faithful Servant – The Unauthorised Biography of Bernard Ingham (1990), Fatherland (novel, 1992, filmed 1994), Enigma (novel, 1995, filmed 2001), Archangel (novel, 1998), Pompeii (novel, 2003), The Ghost (novel, 2007); *Style—* Robert Harris, Esq; ✉ The Old Vicarage, Kintbury, Berkshire RG17 9TR

HARRIS, Robert Frederick (Bob); s of Frederick Cecil Harris (d 1972), of Ipswich, Suffolk, and Ellen Rose Mary, *née* Damant (d 2008); *b* 8 September 1943; *Educ* Northgate GS Ipswich, Kingston Coll of Art (BA); *m* 26 July 1969, Jayne Susan, da of Frederick Gibson; 1 da (Eleanor Volante Harris b 2 April 1977); *Career* art dir (advtg agencies): Collett Dickenson Pearce 1968–73, Sharps Advertising 1974–76, Geers Gross 1976–77, Marsteller 1977–78, Davidson Pearce 1978–85; freelance photographer 1985– (various clients incl Tesco, Sainsbury, Waitrose, King & Barnes Brewery and Northern Rock Building Society); Pilots and their Favourite Aircraft (solus exhbn) Biggin Hill Aerodrome, Goodwood; Freeman City of London 1987, Liveryman Worshipful Co of Loriners 1987 (memb Ct of Assts 2002, Master 2009), Freeman Hon Co of Air Pilots; memb Assoc of Photographers (chm 1991, 1992 and 1993, chm Awards Ctee 1992, 1993 and 1994); *Recreations* gardening, aviation; *Clubs* Aldersgate Ward, RAF; *Style—* Bob Harris, Esq; ✉ 26 Albany Park Road, Kingston upon Thames, Surrey KT2 5SW (☎ 020 8546 4018)

HARRIS, Prof Robert James; s of Charles William Harris (d 1996), of Sanderstead, Surrey, and Lucy Dorothea Emily, *née* Weller (d 2000); *b* 10 March 1947; *Educ* The GS Enfield, Univ of Leeds (BA), McMaster Univ (MA), Univ of Hull (PhD); *m* 1, 23 Feb 1974 (m dis 2000), Janet Nuttall, da of James Nuttall Horne (d 1987), of Ewell, Surrey; 2 da (Ruth b 1978, Amelia b 1979), 1 s (George b 1982); m 2, 20 July 2002, Josephine Yee-kei, da of Chun-yau Tsang, of Tuen Mun, Hong Kong; *Career* probation offr Middx 1973–75; lectr: Brunel Univ 1975–77, Univ of Leicester 1977–87; Univ of Hull: prof 1987–2004, pro-vice-chllr 1993–98; govr and pro-chllr DeMontfort Univ 2011–, asst dir Quality Assurance Agency for HE 2004–; *Books* Welfare, Power and Juvenile Justice (1987), Crime, Criminal Justice and the Probation Service (1992), Secure Accommodation in Child Care (1993), Probation Round the World (1995), Overseas Students in Higher Education (1997), Mentally Disordered Offenders (1999), Political Corruption (2003), The Politics and Economics of Drug Production on the Pakistan-Afghanistan Border (2003); *Recreations* antiquarian book collecting, travelling, talking, working; *Style—* Prof Robert Harris; ✉ 31 Sutherland Square, London SE17 3EQ (☎ and fax 020 7701 6534); The Quality Assurance Agency for Higher Education, Southgate House, Gloucester GL1 1UB (☎ 01452 557000, e-mail r.harris@qaa.ac.uk)

HARRIS, Robert William (Bob); s of Frank Harris (d 1992), of Birmingham, and Joan, *née* Lee (d 1995); *b* 9 November 1944; *Educ* George Dixon GS Edgbaston; *m* 1, Carol Lillian; 1 da (Zoë b 1971); m 2, Carol Ann; 2 s (Dominic b 1976, Adam b 1985); *Career* sports writer and sports ed: Birmingham Planet 1963–66, Thomson Regional Newspapers 1966–86; sports writer and chief football writer Today 1986–89, exec sports ed Sunday Mirror 1993–95 (sports ed 1989–93), ed dir and ed-in-chief Sport First 1997–99 (ed 1996–97), sports ed Optimist World website; columnist Le Weekend Mauritius for 23 years; contrib: The Sun, News of the World, Talksport, Radio Five, Skysport, BBC News 24; major events covered incl: 10 Olympic Games 1972–2012, 7 football World Cups, 9 Cwlth Games, World Athletics Championships, Wimbledon 1969–93 and 2005–14, various world title fights, cricket World Cup; *Books* No Half Measures (with Graeme Souness, 1985), Touch and Go (with Steve Coppell, 1985), More Than Somewhat (with Bruce Grobbelaar, 1986), World Cup Diary (with Bobby Robson, 1986), Bring on the Clown (with Bruce Grobbelaar, 1988), Against the Odds (with Bobby Robson, 1990), Kevin Keegan Autobiography (co-author, 1997), An Englishman Abroad (with Bobby Robson, 1998), Sweet FA (with Graham Kelly, 1999), Sir Viv (with Sir Vivian Richards, 2000), Psycho (with Stuart Pearce, 2000), Sir Garfield Sobers (co-author, 2002), Dennis Lillee: the Autobiography (2003), King John (with John Charles, 2003), The King (with Denis Law, 2003), Sir Bobby Robson: Living the Game (2003), Butcher! (with Terry Butcher, 2005), Pure Gold (with David Gold, 2006), Sir Bobby Robson: A Life in Football (2010), The Boxer's Story (with Nathan Shapow, 2012); *Style—* Bob Harris, Esq; ✉ 25 Broadheath Drive, Chislehurst, Kent BR7 6EU (☎ 020 8289 3000, mobile 07702 480995, e-mail bobharrissport@hotmail.com)

HARRIS, Prof Robin Kingsley; s of Alfred William Harris (d 1964), of Hornchurch, Essex, and Nellie, *née* Missen (d 1987); *b* 23 December 1936, Romford, Essex; *Educ* Royal Liberty GS Romford, Magdalene Coll Cambridge (MA, PhD, ScD); *m* 6 Aug 1960, Maureen Elizabeth, da of James Samuel Reardon (d 1968), of Langley, Berks; 1 s (Nigel b 1962); *Career* fell in independent res Mellon Inst Pittsburgh 1962–64; prof of chemistry UEA 1980–84 (lectr 1964–70, sr lectr 1970–73, reader 1973–80), emeritus prof of chemistry Univ of Durham 2002– (prof 1984–2002); chm Instrumentation Panel SERC 1986–89, sec-gen Int Soc of Magnetic Resonance 1986–92; author and co-author of 530 research publications; Royal Soc of Chemistry Medals: Chem Instrumentation 1985, Analytical Spectroscopy 1998; FRSC, CChem; *Books* Nuclear Magnetic Resonance Spectroscopy: A Physicochemical View (1983), Encyclopedia of Nuclear Magnetic Resonance (9 vols, jt ed-in-chief with D M Grant, 2002, continuation online 2008), Solid-state NMR: Basic Principles and Practice (2012); *Recreations* gardening; *Style—* Prof Robin K Harris; ✉ Department of Chemistry, University of Durham, South Road, Durham DH1 3LE (☎ 0191 334 2021, fax 0191 384 4737, e-mail r.k.harris@durham.ac.uk)

HARRIS, Rosemary; da of Gp Capt Stafford Berkeley Harris, DFC, AFC, RAF (d 1952), and Enid Maud, *née* Campion (d 1942); *Educ* St Helen's Sch Abingdon, All Hallows' Sch Ditchingham, RADA; *m* 1, 1960 (m dis 1967), Ellis Rabb; m 2, 1967, John Marsden Ehle; 1 da (Jennifer Anne b 1969); *Career* actress; Hon Dr: Smith Coll 1968, Wake Forest Univ 1976, North Carolina Sch of the Arts 1980; *Theatre* incl: Climate of Eden (Broadway, Theatre World Award) 1952, The Seven Year Itch (London) 1953–54, Hamlet and Uncle Vanya (NT) 1964–65, The Lion in Winter (Broadway, Tony Award) 1966, Plaza Suite (London, Evening Standard Award) 1969, The Merchant of Venice (Broadway) 1973, A Streetcar Named Desire (Broadway) 1973, All my Sons (London) 1980, Heartbreak House (London and Broadway) 1983, A Pack of Lies (Broadway) 1984, Hayfever (Broadway) 1985, Best of Friends (London) 1989, Steel Magnolias (London) 1990, Lost in Yonkers (Broadway) 1991, Arsenic and Old Lace (Chichester) 1991, Preserving Mr Panmure (Chichester) 1991, Lost in Yonkers (London) 1992, In the Summer House (Lyric Hammersmith) 1993, An Inspector Calls (Broadway) 1994, Women of Troy (RNT) 1995, A Delicate Balance (Broadway) 1996, Waiting in the Wings (Broadway) 1999, All Over (Off Broadway) 2002 (Obie Award), Oscar and the Lady in Pink (Old Globe Theatre San Diego) 2007 and (George St Playhouse New Brunswick) 2008 and (off Broadway) 2009, The Royal Family (Broadway) 2009, The Road to Mecca (Broadway) 2012, Indian Ink (Off Broadway) 2014; *Television* incl: Twelfth Night, A Tale of Two Cities, Dial M For Murder, Wuthering Heights, Notorious Woman (Emmy Award), The Holocaust (Golden Globe Award), To The Lighthouse, The Camomile Lawn, Summers Day Dream, Death of a Salesman, Belonging; *Film* incl: The Shiralee, Beau Brummel, The Boys From Brazil, The Ploughman's Lunch, Crossing Delancey, The Bridge, Tom and Viv (Academy Award nomination), Hamlet, My Life So Far, Sunshine, Blow Dry, Spiderman, Spiderman 2, Spiderman 3, Before the Devil Knows You're Dead, The Trapp Family – A Life of Music 2015; *Style—* Ms Rosemary Harris; ✉ c/o Independent Talent, Oxford House, 40 Whitfield Street, London W1T 2RH (☎ 020 7636 6565, fax 020 7323 0101)

HARRIS, Russell James; QC (2003); s of Donald Harris, and Jean, *née* Hall; *b* Tredegar, Gwent; *Educ* Heolddu Comp Sch Bargoed, St John's Coll Cambridge (MA, Larmour Award, MacMahon scholar); *m* 7 Aug 1999, Nicola, *née* Richards; 2 da (Elinor Catrin b 26 Oct 2000, Nia Rhiannon b 7 July 2007), 1 s (Huw Meredydd b 2 Dec 2003); *Career* barr specialising in public and planning law 1986–; memb Planning and Environment Law Assoc; *Books* Environmental Law (2000); *Recreations* rugby football, the sea around Ramsey Island St David's; *Clubs* London Welsh RFC, St Davids RFC (vice-pres); *Style—* Russell Harris, Esq, QC; ✉ Landmark Chambers, 180 Fleet Street, London EC4A 2HG (☎ 020 7430 1221)

HARRIS, Stephen Francis; s of Michael Harris, and Audrie, *née* Beresford-Webb (d 1987); *b* 25 August 1961, London; *Educ* Queen Elizabeth's Sch Faversham, KCL (BA); *Partner* Emma Read; 1 s (Stanley Harris b 2013); *Career* chef-owner The Sportsman 1999– (Catey Award 2003, Michelin Star 2008, 12th Best Restaurant in UK Nat Restaurant Award 2009, runner up Best Restaurant UK Observer Food Monthly Award 2009, runner up Nat Restaurant Awards 2015, Gastropub of the Year 2015 and 2016, winner Nat Restaurant Awards 2016, GQ Pub of the Year 2016); food writer Daily Telegraph 2015–; Good Food Guide Chef of the Year 2010, Chef's Chef of the Year Nat Restaurant Awards 2013; *Style—* Stephen Harris, Esq; ✉ The Sportsman, Faversham Road, Seasalter, Whitstable, Kent CT5 4BP (☎ 01227 273370, e-mail stephen.harris61@virgin.net)

HARRIS, Stewart; *Career* chief exec sportscotland; *Style—* Stewart Harris, Esq; ✉ sportscotland, Doges, Templeton on the Green, 62 Templeton Street, Glasgow G40 1DA

HARRIS, Sir Thomas George; KBE (2002), CMG (1995); s of Kenneth James Harris (d 1995), and Dorothy, *née* Barrett, of Worcester; *b* 6 February 1945, London; *Educ* Mercers' Sch, Haberdashers' Aske's, Gonville & Caius Coll Cambridge; *m* 21 Oct 1967, Mei-Ling, da of Kono Hwang (d 1976), of Kobe, Japan; 3 s (Ian Kenneth b 1969, Paul David b 1970, Simon Christopher b 1984); *Career* asst princ Bd of Trade 1966–68, third sec Br Embassy Tokyo 1969–71, asst private sec to Min for Aerospace 1971–72, princ Dept of Trade and Indust 1972–76, Cabinet Office 1976–78, princ private sec to Sec of State for Trade and Indust 1978–79, asst sec Civil Aviation Policy DTI 1979–83, commercial cnsllr Br Embassy Washington 1983–88, head of chancery Br High Cmmn Lagos 1988–90, Br dep high cmmr Nigeria 1990–91, head African Dept (Equatorial) FCO 1991–94, ambass Korea 1994–97, DG for Export Promotion DTI 1997–99, DG Trade and Investment in USA and HM consul-gen NY 1999–2004; vice-chm Standard Chartered Bank 2004–14; non-exec dir: Biocompatibles Int plc 2005–11, IFSL Ltd 2007–10, SC Bank Korea 2007–14, Johnson Matthey plc 2009–12, City UK plc 2010–14; chm: Taiwan Br Business Cncl 2007–13, Pakistan Britain Trade and Investment Forum 2007–12, Trade Policy Ctee Br Bankers' Assoc 2007–13, European Services Forum Brussels 2013–; memb Int Advsy Cncl of Br American Business 2004–16; dir Imperial War Museum 2004–09, dir IWM Devpt Tst 2012–; tstee: Asia House 2004–10, Confucius Business Centre 2011–14; *Recreations* reading, travel; *Clubs* Oxford and Cambridge; *Style—* Sir Thomas Harris, KBE, CMG; ✉ 8 Oakeshott Avenue, Highgate, London N6 6NS (☎ 020 8348 5907)

HARRIS, Tom; s of Tom Harris, and Rita Ralston; *Educ* Garnock Acad Ayrshire, Napier Coll (HND Journalism); *m* 1998; *Career* trainee reporter East Kilbride News 1986–88, reporter Paisley Daily Express 1988–90, press offr Lab Pty in Scot 1990–92, press offr Strathclyde Regnl Cncl 1993–96, PR mangr E Ayrshire Cncl 1996–98, chief PR and mktg offr Strathclyde Passenger Tport Exec 1998–2001; MP (Lab): Glagow Cathcart 2001–05, Glasgow S 2005–15; Parly under sec of state for transport 2006–08, shadow min for environment, food and rural affrs 2012–13; memb: Administration Ctee 2013–15, Tport Select Ctee 2014–15; chair Cathcart Lab Pty 1998–2000; *Books* Why I'm Right and Everyone Else Is Wrong (2011); *Recreations* tennis, cinema, astronomy; *Style—* Tom Harris, Esq; ✉ House of Commons, London SW1A 0AA (e-mail tomharrismp@parliament.uk, website www.tomharris.com); Constituency Office ☎ 0141 637 1962

HARRIS, Wil; s of John Harris, and Glenys Harris; *b* 20 September 1982, Hereford; *Educ* Keble Coll Oxford (MA); *Career* ed in chief Bit-Tech.net 2004–07, co-fndr and md

ChannelFlip Media 2007–14 (acquired by 21st Century Fox 2012), dir of digital Condé Nast Publications 2014–; *Style—* Wil Harris, Esq; ✉ Vogue House, Hanover Square, London W1S 1NX (Twitter @wilharris)

HARRIS OF HARINGEY, Baron (Life Peer UK 1998), of Hornsey in the London Borough of Haringey; (Jonathan) Toby Harris; s of Prof Harry Harris, FRS (d 1994), and Muriel Harris (d 2009); *b* 11 October 1953, London; *Educ* Haberdashers' Aske's, Trinity Coll Cambridge (BA); *m* 7 April 1979, Ann Sarah, da of Stephen Austen Herbert (d 1988); 2 s (Hon James Phillip b 1981, Hon Matthew Anthony b 1984), 1 da (Hon Francesca Rebekah Bryony Herbert b 1999); *Career* Econ Div Bank of England 1975–79, dep dir Electricity Consumers' Cncl 1983–86 (joined 1979), dir Assoc of Community Health Cncls for Eng and Wales 1987–98, chm Toby Harris Associates 1998–; cncllr (Lab) Haringey BC 1978–2002 (chm Social Servs Ctee 1982–87, ldr 1987–1999), memb London Assembly (Lab) Brent and Harrow 2000–04 (memb Mayor's Advsy Cabinet 2000–04, ldr Lab Gp 2000–04); memb Home Office Advsy Cncl on Race Rels 1993–97, memb Human Rights Act Task Force 1999–2001, chair All-Pty Parly Gp on Policing 2005–, treas Parly Info and Communications Technol Forum (formerly PITCOM) 2005–16, vice-chair All-Party Parly Gp on Road Safety 2006–10, memb House of Lords Select Ctee Inquiry on Personal Internet Security 2006–07, chair Ind Advsy Panel on Deaths in Custody (reporting to Miny of Justice, Dept of Heath and Home Office) 2009–15, memb Parly Jt Ctee on the Nat Security Strategy 2010–14, chm House of Lords Olympics and Paralympics Legacy Ctee 2013, chair Harris Review (ind review into self-inflicted deaths in NOMS Custody since 2007) 2014–15; chm Univ of Cambridge Lab Club 1973, pres Cambridge Union Soc 1974, nat chm Young Fabian Gp 1976–77, chm Hornsey Lab Pty 1978, 1979 and 1980, memb Lab Pty Nat Policy Forum 1992–2004, co-opted memb Lab Pty Local Govt Policy Ctee 1993–2004; Local Govt Assoc: chm Lab Gp 1996–2004, memb Exec 1999–2004, vice-pres 2005–10, memb Community Safety Panel 1997–98, memb Social Exclusion Panel 1998–99, chair Lab Peers' Gp 2012– (vice-chair 2008–12); chm: Assoc of London Authorities 1993–95 (chm Social Servs Ctee 1984–88, dep chm 1990–93), Assoc of London Govt 1995–2000, Local Govt Anti-Poverty Unit 1994–96, Nat Trading Standards Bd 2013–; memb: Ctee of the Regions of the EU 1994–2002, Public Sector Advsy Cncl Anite 2005–06; jt chm London Pride Partnership 1995–98, jt chm London Waste Action 1997–2000, chm Wembley National Stadium Tst 1997–; memb: London Drug Policy Forum 1990–98, Nat Nursery Examination Bd 1992–94, Bd London First 1993–2002, Jt London Advsy Panel (Cabinet sub-ctee for London) 1996–97, London Pension Funds Authy 1998–2000, London Devpt Partnership Bd 1998–2000; special advsr Bd Transport for London 2004–08; memb Met Police Ctee 1998–2000, chm Metropolitan Police Authy 2000–04 (memb (representing Home Sec) 2004–12), vice-pres Assoc of Police Authorities 2007–12 (memb Exec 2000–06), memb Police Counter-Terrorism Bd 2007–12, memb Police Counter-Terrorism Ministerial Advsy Gp 2008–10, memb Advsy Bd Info Systems Security Assocs UK 2008–, chm Audit Panel Met Police 2012; memb NHS Charter Advisors' Gp 1997–98, memb Ctee on the Med Effects of Air Pollution 1997–2002, non-exec dir London Ambulance Services NHS Tst 1998–2005; trg advsr Infolog Ltd 1998–2005, conslt Harrogate Mgmnt Centre 1998–2004, sr advsr KPMG 1999–2013; dep chm AMA 1991–96 (chm Social Servs Ctee 1986–93); chm LBTC - Trg for Care 1986–94; sr assoc The King's Fund 1999–2004; dep chm Nat Fuel Poverty Forum 1981–86, pres Haringey Foster Care Assoc 1982–87, memb Exec Cncl RNIB 1993–94, memb Exec Ctee Royal Assoc for Disability and Rehabilitation 1990–93; tstee: Evening Standard Blitz Meml Appeal 1995–99, Help for Health Tst 1995–97, Learning Agency 1996–97; chm of tstees Freedom Charity 2011–15; govr: St Mary's Jr and Infants Schs 1978–96, Sch of St David and St Katharine 1978–96, Nat Inst for Social Work 1986–94; patron The Larches 2002–04, vice-patron Vocal Eyes 2004, vice-patron Artificial Heart Fund 2004; memb Advsy Bd Three Faiths Forum 2003–08; memb Ct Univ of Middx 1995–; Hon Dr Univ of Middlesex 1999; Freeman City of London 1998; FRSA 1993, FBCS 2011; *Books* Why Vote Labour? (with Nick Butler and Neil Kinnock, 1979), The Economics of Prosperity (contrib, 1980), Energy and Social Policy (ed with Jonathan Bradshaw, 1983), Rationing in Action (contrib, 1993), Whistleblowing in the Health Service: Accountability, Law and Professional Practice (contrib, 1994); *Style—* The Rt Hon the Lord Harris of Haringey; ✉ House of Lords, London SW1A 0PW (website www.lordtobyharris.org.uk, Twitter @lordtobysays)

HARRIS OF PECKHAM, Baron (Life Peer UK 1996), of Peckham in the London Borough of Southwark; Sir Philip Charles Harris; kt (1985); s of Charles William Harris, MC, and Ruth Ellen, *née* Ward; *b* 15 September 1942; *Educ* Streatham GS; *m* 1960, Dame Pauline Norma, *née* Chumley; 3 s, 1 da; *Career* Harris Queensway plc: chm 1964–88, chief exec 1987–88; chm: Harris Ventures Ltd 1988–, C W Harris Properties Ltd 1988–97, Carpetright plc 1993–2014 (dir 1988–93); dir Harveys Holdings plc 1986–99; non-exec dir: Fisons plc 1986–94, Great Universal Stores plc 1986–2004, Molyneux Estates plc 1990–95, Matalan 2004–, Arsenal FC; chm Guy's and Lewisham NHS Tst 1991–93, vice-chm Lewisham Hosp NHS Tst 1993–97; memb: Cncl of Govrs UMDS 1984–98 (hon fell 1992), Ct of Patrons RCOG 1984–, conslt TAPI Carpets and Floors Ltd 2015–; chm Generation Tst 1984–, dep chm Cons Pty Treasurers 1993–97; memb Br Show Jumping Assoc 1974–, memb Westminster Abbey Campaign Development Bd 2011–; Hambro Business Man of the Year 1983, Ernst & Young Entrepreneur of the Year 2007; Freeman City of London 1992; fell Goldsmiths Coll London 1995, hon fell Oriel Coll Oxford 1989; Beacon Award 2015;Hon FRCR 1992; FGCL 1995, FKC 1998; *Recreations* football, cricket, show jumping, tennis; *Clubs* Mark's, Mosimann's; *Style—* The Rt Hon Lord Harris of Peckham; ✉ c/o Judy Willett (executive PA), Harris Ventures Ltd, Philip Harris House, 1a Spur Road, Orpington, Kent BR6 0PH

HARRIS OF RICHMOND, Baroness (Life Peer UK 1999), of Richmond in the County of North Yorkshire; Angela Felicity Harris; DL (N Yorks) 1994; *née* Richards; da of Rev George Henry Hamilton Richards, and Eva, *née* Lindley; *b* 4 January 1944, St Annes on Sea, Lancs; *Educ* Canon Slade GS Bolton, Ealing Hotel Catering Coll; *m* 1, 1965 (m dis 1974), Philip Martin Bowles; 1 s (Mark John Hamilton Bowles); m 2, 1976, John Philip Roger Harris; *Career* memb N Yorks CC 1981–2001 (first woman chair 1991–92), chm N Yorks Police Authy 1994–2001, dep chm Assoc of Police Authorities 1997–2001; dep speaker House of Lords, chair Industry and Parliament Tst 2010–14, chair Ind Reference Gp to the Police Fedn of England and Wales 2015–; former JP N Yorks, mayor of Richmond 1993–94; pres Nat Assoc of Chaplains to the Police 2002–, vice-pres Local Govt Assoc 2002–05 and 2006–12; patron Herriot Hospice Homecare; memb Ct Univ of York 1996–, memb Nominations Ctee Univ of York; High Steward Ripon Cathedral 2010–; *Recreations* music, reading political biographies; *Clubs* RAF, Civil Service (London); *Style—* The Baroness Harris of Richmond, DL; ✉ House of Lords, London SW1A 0PW (☎ 020 7219 6709)

HARRIS-JENKINS, His Hon Judge Philip Leigh; s of Geraint Jenkins, and Ann, *née* Davies; *b* 15 August 1968, Cardiff; *Educ* Aberystwyth Univ (LLB); *m* 21 Oct 1995, Rebecca, *née* Saunders; 2 da (Manon b 4 Oct 1998, Siwan b 12 Jan 2004); *Career* called to the Bar 1990; recorder 2008, circuit judge (Wales Circuit) 2015–; *Recreations* cinema, horse racing, reading, walking; *Style—* His Hon Judge Harris-Jenkins; ✉ Caernarfon Crown Court, Caernarfon, Llanberis Road, Caernarfon LL55 2DF (☎ 01286 669700)

HARRISON, (William) Alistair; CMG (2012), CVO (1996); s of late William K Harrison, and late (Alice) Rita Harrison; *b* 14 November 1954, Guisborough, N Yorks; *Educ* Royal GS Newcastle upon Tyne, UC Oxford, Birkbeck Coll London (Dip Economics); *m* 1, 1981 (m dis 1991), Theresa Mary, *née* Morrison; m 2, 1996, Sarah Judith, *née* Wood; 2 da (Matilda b 1999, Eliza b 2003), 1 s (Ralph (twin) b 2003); *Career* diplomat; entered HM Dip Serv 1977, desk offr NATO Section Defence Dept FCO 1977–78, Polish language trg 1978–79, third then second sec (Chancery) Warsaw 1979–82, first sec FCO 1982–84, private sec to Parly Under Sec FCO 1984–86, first sec (economic) UK Mission to UN NY 1987–92, dep head Middle East Dept FCO 1992–95, cnsllr and dep head of mission Warsaw 1995–98, seconded as foreign policy advsr European Cmmn Brussels 1998–2000, cnsllr (political) UK Mission to UN NY 2000–03, head UN Dept (later Int Orgns Dept) FCO 2003–05, high cmmr to Zambia 2005–08, head Zimbabwe Unit FCO 2008–09, govr Anguilla 2009–13; HM Marshal Diplomatic Corps; *Recreations* music (especially opera), bridge, golf, skiing; *Style—* Alistair Harrison, Esq, CMG, CVO

HARRISON, Prof Andrew; s of Prof Martin Harrison, of Keele, Staffs, and Wendy Hanford, *née* Hindle; *b* 3 October 1959, Oxford; *Educ* Newcastle-under-Lyme Sch, St John's Coll Oxford (MA, DPhil, Gibbs Prize); *m* 10 Dec 1988, Alison Charlotte, *née* Ironside-Smith; 3 da (Catriona Charlotte b 10 Aug 2002, Eleanor Elizabeth b 9 Feb 2004, Rebecca Rachel b 29 Dec 2005); *Career* Fereday fell St John's Coll Oxford 1985–88, res fell McMaster Univ Canada 1988–89, Royal Soc univ research fell 1990–92; Univ of Edinburgh: lectr Chemistry Dept 1992–96, reader 1996–99, prof of solid state chemistry 1999–, dir Centre for Science at Extreme Conditions 2001–05, seconded as assoc dir Institut Laue-Langevin Grenoble 2006– (DG 2011–13), ceo Diamond Light Source Ltd 2014–; Nuffield research fell 1997–98, Eminent Scientist Award Riken Japan 2000–03; CChem, MRSC 1995, FRSE 2002; *Publications* Fractals in Chemistry (1995); author of over 100 reports and pubns in scientific jls; *Recreations* hill walking, skiing, cycling on and off road, drinking British beer and French wine; *Style—* Prof Andrew Harrison; ✉ Diamond Light Source Ltd, Harmell Science and Innovation Campus, Didcot, Oxon O11 0DE (☎ 01235 778811, e-mail andrew.harrison@diamond.ac.uk)

HARRISON, Andrew John; s of David Harrison, of Nottingham, and Mary, *née* Brodie (d 1996); *b* 28 October 1964, Derby; *Educ* Trent Coll Nottingham, Univ of Durham (BA); *m* 1, Pamela; 1 s (Jack b 24 Oct 1994) 1 da (Katie b 3 Jan 1997); m 2, 3 Nov 2007, Gillian, *née* Ross; 2 s (Ross b 1 March 2004, Lewis b 2 Oct 2005); *Career* mktg dir: Procter & Gamble 1987–98, Coca Cola 1998–2000, Nestlé Rowntree 2000–03; ceo Müller Dairy UK 2004–05, fndr The Zentist 2005–, ceo RadioCentre 2006–13, chief operating offr Asia Pacific Brand Union 2013–; chm Radioplayer Ltd 2010–13; non-exec dir The Brand Cellar 2008–13; chm Mktg Gp of GB 2007–08, chm Radio Advertising Bureau 2007–09; Marketer of the Year 2003; FCIM 2001, fell Mktg Soc 2004, FRSA 2008, fell Radio Acad 2011; *Recreations* sport, radio; *Clubs* Century, Lansdowne, Newcastle United FC; *Style—* Andrew Harrison, Esq; ✉ Brand Union, 23/F The Center, 99 Queen's Road Central, Hong Kong (☎ 00 852 9132 0855, e-mail andrew.harrison@brandunion.com)

HARRISON, Prof Brian David Walter; s of Joseph Harrison (d 1955), and Constance Jennings, *née* Horsfall (d 1994), of Lytham St Annes; *b* 24 April 1943; *Educ* Shrewsbury, St John's Coll Cambridge (MA, MB BChir), Guy's Hosp Med Sch London (LRCP, MRCS); *m* 13 July 1968, Jennifer Anne, da of Dr John Fisher Stokes, of Stoke Row, Oxfordshire; 1 s (Ben b 1970), 1 da (Nicola b 1974); *Career* house physician Guy's Hosp 1967–68, house surgn Bolingbroke Hosp London 1968–69, SHO New Cross Hosp London 1969, jr registrar cardiology and gen med Guy's Hosp 1969–70, hon clinical lectr in physiology Brompton Hosp 1971–72 (house physician 1970–71), registrar to Med Professorial Unit Westminster Hosp 1971–72, clinical lectr in physiology Brompton Hosp 1973, sr med registrar Ahmadu Bello Univ Hosp Zaria Nigeria 1973–74, lectr and sr registrar in thoracic and gen med Middlesex Hosp 1974–77; conslt physician: Norfolk and Norwich Univ Hosp 1978–2005, West Norwich Hosp 1978–2001; hon prof UEA 2005– (hon sr lectr 1997–2005); memb Cncl ASH 1983–2000 (fndr and first chm Norfolk ASH 1979); British Thoracic Soc: memb Research Ctee 1980–86, clinical coordinator Nat Pneumonia Study 1981–87, memb Educn Ctee 1986–89 and 1994–98, chm Pneumonia Standing Sub Ctee 1987–89, chm Standards of Care Ctee 1989–93, memb Cncl and Exec 1989–93 and 2002–04, coordinator confs to produce guidelines on the mgmnt of asthma in Britain 1990, 1992 and 1995, memb Manpower and Trg Ctee 1996–2003, memb Professional Standards Ctee 1999–2004 (chm 2002–04); memb Mortality and Severe Morbidity Working Gp Nat Asthma Task Force 1991–2002 (chm 1994–98); pres East Anglian Thoracic Soc 1982–84, tstee Br Lung Fndn 2001–04; FRCP 1987 (MRCP 1970), FCCP 1990, FRCPEd 1998; *Publications* author of numerous med pubns on pneumonia, smoking, asthma, pulmonary function, respiratory failure, secondary polycythemia, chronic airflow obstruction, lung biopsy, sarcoidosis; *Recreations* gardening, sailing, theatre, travel; *Clubs* Stranger's (Norwich); *Style—* Prof Brian Harrison; ✉ The White House, Church Avenue East, Norwich NR2 2AF (☎ 01603 456508)

HARRISON, Prof Sir Brian Howard; kt (2005); s of Howard Harrison (d 1966), and Mary Elizabeth, *née* Savill (d 2001); *b* 9 July 1937; *Educ* Alcuin House Sch, Stanmore, Middx; Merchant Taylors' Sch Northwood; St John's Coll Oxford (MA, DPhil); *m* 1967, Anne Victoria, da of Lawrence and Isabel Greggain; *Career* Nat Serv 2 Lieut Malta Signal Sqdn 1956–58; Univ of Oxford: sr scholar St Antony's Coll 1961–64, jr res fell Nuffield Coll 1964–67, reader 1990–2000, titular prof of modern British history 1996–2004 (emeritus 2004–); CCC Oxford: tutorial fell 1967–2000, sr tutor 1984–86 and 1988–90, vice-pres 1992, 1993, and 1996–98, official fell 2000–04, emeritus fell 2004–; visiting prof: Univ of Michigan 1970–71, Harvard Univ 1973–74; visiting fell: Univ of Melbourne 1975, ANU 1995; hon fell St John's Coll Oxford 2010; ed Oxford DNB 2000–04; FRHistS 1973, FBA 2005; *Books* Drink and the Victorians (1971, 2 edn 1994), Separate Spheres: the opposition to women's suffrage in Britain (1978), Robert Lowery: Chartist and lecturer (ed with P Hollis, 1979), Peaceable Kingdom: stability and change in modern Britain (1982), A Hundred Years Ago: Britain in the 1880s in words and photographs (with C Ford, 1983), Prudent Revolutionaries: portraits of British feminists between the wars (1987), The History of the University of Oxford Vol 8: The Twentieth Century (ed and contrib, 1994), Corpuscles: a History of Corpus Christi College in the twentieth century (ed, 1994), The Transformation of British Politics 1860–1995 (1996), Civil Histories: Essays presented to Sir Keith Thomas (ed with P Burke and P Slack, and contrib, 2000), two volumes in New Oxford History of England (Seeking a Role: The United Kingdom 1951–1970 (2009) and Finding a Role? The United Kingdom 1970–1990 (2010)); *Recreations* looking at architecture, listening to classical music, cooking; *Style—* Prof Sir Brian Harrison; ✉ The Book House, Yarnells Hill, Oxford, OX2 9BG

HARRISON, Prof Bryan Desmond; CBE (1990); s of John William Harrison (d 1963), and Norah, *née* Webster (d 1998); *b* 16 June 1931; *Educ* Whitgift Sch, Univ of Reading (Wantage scholar, BSc), Rothamsted Experimental Station Harpenden, Univ of London (PhD); *m* 13 Jan 1968, Elizabeth Ann, da of Vivian Francis Latham-Warde (d 1981); 2 s (Peter William b 1969, Robert Anthony b 1972), 1 da (Claire Janet b 1977); *Career* res scientist: Virology Section Scot Horticultural Research Inst Dundee 1954–57, Plant Pathology Dept Rothamsted Experimental Station Harpenden 1957–66; James Hutton Inst (formerly Scot Horticultural Research Inst then Scot Crop Research Inst Dundee): research scientist and head Virology Dept 1966–91, sr pso 1969, dep chief scientific offr 1981, hon research prof 1996–2006, hon research fell 2006–; Univ of Dundee: hon visiting prof 1988–91, prof of plant virology 1991–96, prof emeritus 1997–; hon prof Univ of St Andrews 1986–98, hon visiting prof Univ of Zhejiang PRC 2001–; Hon Doctorate in Agriculture and Forestry Univ of Helsinki 1990; hon memb: Assoc of Applied Biologists 1989, Soc for Gen Microbiology 1990, Phytopathological Soc of Japan 1992; foreign assoc US Nat Acad of Sciences 1998; FRSE 1979, FRS 1987; *Publications* Plant Virology: the Principles (with A J Gibbs, 1976, translated into Russian and Chinese), over 200 research papers and reviews on plant viruses; *Recreations* gardening; *Style*— Prof Bryan Harrison, CBE, FRS, FRSE; ✉ The James Hutton Institute, Invergowrie, Dundee DD2 5DA (☎ 01382 562731, e-mail bryan.harrison@hutton.ac.uk)

HARRISON, Clive Fiske; s of William Henry Harrison (d 1992), and Evelyn, *née* Stubbs (d 1990); *b* 23 November 1939, Colchester, Essex; *Educ* Felsted, Trinity Hall Cambridge (MA); *m* 1965, Barbara Gail, *née* Horne; 3 s (Byron b 1967, Jules b 1969, Alexander b 1976); *Career* Panmure Gordon 1961, Hodgson & Baker 1965, fndr Fiske plc 1973 (currently chm and ceo); memb: London Stock Exchange 1965, Securities Inst 1990; *Clubs* Garrick; *Style*— Clive Harrison, Esq; ✉ Fiske plc, Salisbury House, London Wall, London EC2M 5QS (☎ 020 7448 4700)

HARRISON, Sir (Robert) Colin; 4 Bt (UK 1922), of Eaglescliffe, Co Durham; s of late Sir John Fowler Harrison, 2 Bt, and late Kathleen, *née* Livingston; suc bro, Sir (John) Wyndham Harrison, 3 Bt, 1955; *b* 25 May 1938; *Educ* Radley, St John's Coll Cambridge; *m* 1963, Maureen Marie, da of late E Leonard Chiverton, of Langley House, Lanchester, Co Durham; 2 da (Rachel Deborah (Mrs Waddell) b 1966, Dr Claire Grace (Mrs Caesar) b 1974), 1 s (John Wyndham Fowler b 1972); *Heir* s, John Harrison; *Career* Nat Serv cmmnd 5 Royal Northumberland Fusiliers 1957–59; general cmmr of income tax; chm Young Master Printers Nat Ctee 1972–73; *Style*— Sir Colin Harrison, Bt; ✉ Dinsdale House, 6 Uppleby, Easingwold, York YO61 3BB (☎ 01347 824471)

HARRISON, David; s of Robert Stanley Harrison, of Liverpool, and Jean, *née* Edmondson; *b* 9 April 1957; *Educ* Alsop Comp Sch Liverpool, Pembroke Coll Oxford (exhibitioner, MA, Football blue); *m* 17 Aug 1985, Linda Elizabeth, da of Thomas Ellis; 2 s (Matthew David b 29 Aug 1986, Alexander James b 14 Feb 1989); *Career* news, sports and feature writer Liverpool Daily Post and Echo 1980–83 (team award for coverage of Toxteth riots Nat Press Awards 1981), conslt China Daily Beijing 1983–84, asst foreign ed Daily Telegraph 1985–90 (also home and foreign news sub-ed), news ed The European 1990–91, sr reporter (home and foreign) then environment and tport ed The Observer 1991–98, environment and tport ed, war corr (incl Kosovo, Afghanistan and Iraq), sr corr Sunday Telegraph 1999–2011; Amnesty Int Press Award 1997, Paul Foot Award for Investigative Journalism 2006, shortlisted for various awards; writer, broadcaster and media conslt 2011–15, investigative TV reporter Al-Jazeera Int 2015–; conslt Thomson Fndn; conference and literary festival chair and speaker; former memb sch, regnl and coll teams in various sports, former semi-professional footballer England and France; *Recreations* travel, reading, cinema, theatre, supporting Liverpool FC, swimming, playing cricket, football and tennis, languages (French, Spanish and Mandarin); *Style*— David Harrison, Esq; ✉ e-mail davidw.harrison@hotmail.co.uk

HARRISON, Douglas Hamilton; s of Stewart Hamilton Harrison (d 2011), and Phyllis May, *née* Eustace (d 2006); *b* 31 August 1944, Glasgow; *Educ* Haileybury, Middlesex Hosp Med Sch (MB, BS); *m* 1, 1975 (m dis 1999); 1 da (Fiona b 16 July 1977), 1 s (Stewart b 7 March 1980); m 2, 13 June 2010, Nina; *Career* Radcliffe Infirmary 1970, registrar in surgery Queen Elizabeth Hosp Barbados 1971, surgn registrar Plastic Surgery Unit Mt Vernon Hosp 1973, surgn registrar Edinburgh and Mt Vernon Hosp 1975, conslt plastic surgn Mt Vernon Hosp and Edgware Gen Hosp Barnet 1979–; Hunterian prof RCS 1988, visiting prof Mayo Clinic Minnesota US 1994, fndn lectr Royal Aust Coll Surgns 1997, Maliniac lectr 1999; author of numerous articles in scientific jls; memb: Br Assoc of Plastic Reconstructive and Aesthetic Surgns, Br Assoc of Aesthetic Plastic Surgns (BAAPS); FRCS 1972; *Recreations* golf, sailing, running; *Clubs* Royal Ocean Racing, Berks Golf, Moor Park Golf; *Style*— Douglas Harrison, Esq; ✉ Suite 2, 14 Queen Anne Street, London W1G 9LG (☎ 020 7580 7555, fax 020 7636 6669, e-mail dhharrison@hotmail.co.uk)

HARRISON, Dr Edward Peter Graham (Ted); s of Rev Peter Graham Harrison (d 1998), of Bishops Lydeard, Somerset, and (Eleanor) Joan, *née* Rowland (d 2005); *b* 14 April 1948; *Educ* Grenville Coll Bideford, Univ of Kent at Canterbury (BA, PhD), Univ of Creative Arts (MA); *m* 1968, Helen Grace, da of Ronald Percy Waters (d 1986); 1 s (David Edward Graham b 1969), 1 da (Caroline Helen b 1971); *Career* writer, artist, broadcaster, television prodr and cartoonist; trainee journalist Kent Messenger and Evening Post 1968–72; reporter: Morgan-Grampian Magazines 1972, Southern TV 1970–73, You and Yours (BBC Radio 4) 1972–80, Sunday (Radio 4) 1972–90 (presenter 1986–88), BBC Scotland News and Current Affrs 1980–85 (also presenter), World Tonight (Radio 4) 1981–83, World at One and PM (Radio 4) 1983–87; presenter: numerous radio documentaries in Profile and Soundings series (Radio 4), Opinions (Radio 4) 1986–87, The Human Factor (ITV) 1986–92, Does he take Sugar? (Radio 4) 1991–95; series ed Ultimate Questions (ITV); dir: Redcoats (ITV), Essentials of Faith (ITV), Mosque (ITV) 2005; religious affrs corr BBC 1988–89, currently writer and artist; dir Pilgrim Productions Canterbury, fndr Unst Animation Studio Shetland; Parly candidate (Lib) Bexley 1970 and Maidstone Feb 1974; exhibitions: London 1977 (caricatures), Oxford and Canterbury 1981 (watercolours), St Martin's Acrise Kent 2010 (paintings), Rutherford Coll Univ of Kent 2010–11 (paintings and cartoons), Innocence Betrayed (St Paul's Cathedral) 2011, Stations of the Cross – Forces of Creation (Norwich Cathedral) 2013, North, South-East (Georges House Gallery Folkestone) 2013, Twelve Apostles (St David's Cathedral Wales) 2014, Llandaff Cathedral 2015, Cherry Tree (public art work in Atrium 2 Guy's Hospital London) 2015, Holy Wells of Wales (St David's Cathedral) 2016; *Books* Modern Elizabethans (1977), McIndoe's Army (with Peter Williams, 1979), Marks of the Cross (1981), Commissioner Catherine (1983), Much Beloved Daughter (1985), The Durham Phenomenon (1986), Living with Kidney Failure (1990), Kriss Akabusi – On Track (1991), Elvis People (1992), Members Only (1994), Stigmata (1994), Letters to a Friend I Never Knew (1995), Disability – Rights and Wrongs (1995), Defender of the Faith (1996), Tanni (1996), Diana – Icon and Sacrifice (1998), Beyond Dying (2000), Will the Next Archbishop Please Stand Up (2002), Diana: Myth and Reality (2006), King Clone (2010), Apocalypse When? (2012), Remembrance (2012), Improbable Saints (with Richard Coles, 2013), Tales of Three Popes (2014), The Death and Resurrection of Elvis Presley (2016); *Recreations* visiting old churches and empty beaches; *Style*— Dr Ted Harrison; ✉ website www.tedharrison.co.uk

HARRISON, Frank Ronald; s of Ronald Charles Gully Harrison, of Helensburgh, Dumbartonshire, and Eva Luise Johanne, *née* Hornäffer; *b* 11 July 1962, Glasgow; *Educ* Eton, Oxford Poly (now Oxford Brookes Univ) (BA); *m* Caroline Elizabeth, da of Malcolm B C Ward; 1 da (Emma Louise Elizabeth b 19 Feb 1990), 2 s (William Frank Ion b 20 April 1992, Oliver Frederick Charles b 16 April 1997); *Career* media research dir/bd dir Saatchi & Saatchi Advertising 1987–91; ZenithOptimedia: dir media research 1992–94, dir worldwide media info systems 1994–95, dir worldwide strategic resources 1995–; speaker at numerous indust confs, author of various papers published on media; memb IPA/ISBA/AFVPA Working Pty on Equity Repeat Fee Agreement 1992 and 1996; memb MRS 1985 (DipMRS), FIPA 1996 (MIPA 1989), memb Mktg Soc 2000–; *Books* UK Media Yearbook (annually 1987–), UK Television Forecasts (annually 1988–), Interactive Media (1995), Television in Asia Pacific to 2000 (1995), Television in Europe to 2005 (1996), Digital Media (1997); *Recreations* music, family, travel; *Style*— Frank Harrison, Esq; ✉ The Forge, Golden Ball Lane, Pinkneys Green, Berkshire SL6 6NW (☎ 01628 634110); ZenithOptimedia, 24 Percy Street, London W1T 2BS (☎ 020 7961 1038, fax 020 7961 1113, e-mail frank.harrison@zenithoptimedia.com)

HARRISON, Howard Michael; s of Michael Amyas Harrison, and Yvonne Betty Harrison; *Educ* Central Sch of Speech and Drama; *Career* lighting designer; memb Cncl of Nat Youth Theatre of GB; nomination Best Lighting Designer Olivier Awards 1998, 2000, 2001, 2002 and 2008 (for Macbeth); *Theatre* credits incl: Nabucco and the Makropulos Case (Met Opera), Il Trovatore (ROH and Teatro Real Madrid), Privates on Parade (Donmar Warehouse), Tales from Hollywood (Donmar Warehouse), To the Green Fields and Beyond (Donmar Warehouse), Creditors (Donmar Warehouse), The Tempest (RSC), As You Like It (RSC), The Prisoners Dilemma (RSC), Finding the Sun/The Marriage Play (RNT), Look Back in Anger (RNT), Private Lives (RNT), Swan Lake (English Nat Ballet), Romeo and Juliet (English Nat Ballet), Nutcracker! (Sadler's Wells and US tour), Edward Scissorhands (Sadler's Wells and US tour), Putting it Together (Broadway), Cat on a Hot Tin Roof (West End), The Witches of Eastwick (West End), Mammia Mia (West End, Broadway, Toronto, Las Vegas, Hamburg, Japan, Stockholm, Aust and US tour), Mary Poppins (West End, Holland, UK tour, Broadway and US tour), Hay Fever, House of Special Purpose, The Circle and The Music Man (all Chichester Festival Theatre), King Lear (Young Vic), Complicit (Old Vic), Macbeth (West End and Broadway), Rock 'n' Roll (West End and Broadway), Glengarry Glen Ross, Love Song, Guys and Dolls, Donkeys' Years and Heroes (all West End), In a Dark House, The Last Days of Judas Iscariot (Almeida), King Lear (Young Vic), Grasses of a Thousand Colours (Royal Court), Inherit the Wind, Complicit (Old Vic), Creditors (Donmar Theatre and Broadway), Back Beat (Citizens Theatre), Love Story (Chichester); *Clubs* Groucho; *Style*— Howard Harrison, Esq; ✉ c/o David Bingham, Simpson Fox Associate, 6 Beauchamp Place, London SW3 1NG (☎ 020 7434 9167, e-mail david.bingham@simpson-fox.com)

HARRISON, John; s of Kenneth Ridley Harrison (d 1960), of Stockton-on-Tees, and Margaret, *née* Calvert (d 1998); *b* 12 November 1944; *Educ* Grangefield GS, Univ of Sheffield (BA); *m* 4 June 1969, Patricia Alice Bridget (d 2014), da of Dr Harry Raymond Alban (d 1974), of London; 2 da (Rachel b 1971, Philippa b 1973), 1 s (Joseph b 1979); *Career* articled clerk Coopers & Lybrand 1966–70, Tillotson corp planner 1970–72; Deloitte Consulting: mgmnt conslt 1972–2001, ptnr 1981–2001, ptnr i/c Corp Special Servs 1992–94, ptnr i/c Financial Institutions Consulting; chm: Erinaceous Property Maintenance Ltd 2001–07, Portal Ltd 2002–08; fin dir Marchpole plc 2006–07, non-exec dir Crown Northcorp Inc 2007–14, non-exec dir Crown Mortgage Mgmnt Ltd 2013–14; administrator Ely Cathedral 2010–13; FCA 1969, FIMC 1973, FRSA 1991; *Recreations* fly fishing, sailing, shooting; *Style*— John Harrison, Esq; ✉ The Coach House, 69A High Street, Wilburton, Ely, Cambridgeshire CB6 3RA (☎ 01353 740770, e-mail john@the-coach-house.co.uk)

HARRISON, John; s of John Henry Jordan (d 1995), of Grantham, Lincs, and Margaret, *née* Harrison; *b* 20 February 1944; *Educ* Silverdale Secdy Modern Sch, Sheffield Tech Coll; *m* 13 July 1968, Vivien Ann Eveline, da of Frederick Charles Hardisty (d 1988), of Brighton; 1 s (Mark b 31 July 1976); *Career* lighting designer Theatre Projects Ltd 1964–68, prodn mangr and tech dir ENO 1968–74, theatre conslt John Wyckham Associates 1975–76; tech dir: WNO 1976–88, Vancouver Opera Canada 1984–88; md Cardiff Theatrical Services Ltd 1984–88; ROH: developed live outdoor screened performances of opera and ballet to venues in the UK and worldwide 1989–, tech dir 1989–98, admin dir 1998–2000, commercial dir 1999–2004; exec prodr Creative Entertainment Gp 2004–07; conslt: Creative Entertainment Gp UK/USA 1999–2009, Palau de les Arts Reina Sofia Valencia 2002–09, Viva Arts Poland 2005–, Breakthru Films London 2006–09; tstee English Bach Festival 2004–09, memb Tech Ctee Opera America 2004–09, fndr Opera Latin America Sao Paulo 2007–12; Carl Alan Award for outstanding service to dance 2001; *Recreations* travel, gardening; *Style*— John Harrison, Esq; ☎ and fax 020 8668 9481, e-mail harrisonjordan@btinternet.com

HARRISON, Baron (Life Peer UK 1999), of Chester in the County of Cheshire; Lyndon Henry Arthur; s of late Charles William Harrison, and late Edith Harrison, *née* Johnson; *b* 28 September 1947; *Educ* Oxford Sch, Univ of Warwick (BA), Univ of Sussex (MA), Keele Univ (MA); *m* 1980, Hilary Anne, *née* Plank; 1 s (Adam b 1982), 1 da (Sara b 1985); *Career* mangr Students' Union NE Wales Inst of HE Wrexham; MEP (Lab): Cheshire W 1989–94, Cheshire W and Wirral 1994–99; Euro Parl: memb Transport and Tourism Ctee, memb Economic and Monetary Ctee, socialist spokesperson Monetary Sub-Ctee, sec European Parly Lab Pty (EPLP) 1991–94, socialist spokesperson Delegation for ASEAN and Korea, vice-pres Intergroup for Small Business, pres Tourism Intergroup; memb House of Lords Ctee: on Foreign and Security Policy 2000–04, Delegated Powers and Regulatory Reform 2003–, on Social Policy and Consumer Affrs 2004–, on The Equality Act 2010 and the Disabled 2015–16, on Financial Exclusion 2016–17; chm House of Lords Ctee on EU Economic and Financial Affrs 2010–15; cncllr Cheshire CC 1981–90 (formerly chm Libraries and Countryside and Tourism Ctees); *Recreations* chess, music, sport, House of Lords bridge team; *Style*— The Rt Hon the Lord Harrison; ✉ House of Lords, London SW1A 0PW (☎ 020 7219 3000)

HARRISON, Dr Michael; JP (Birmingham 1980); s of Frank Harrison (d 1973), of Leamington Spa, and Ruby Wilhelmina, *née* Proctor (d 1981); *b* 1 March 1939, Leamington Spa, Warks; *Educ* Leamington Coll, St Mary's Hosp Med Sch London (MB BS, LRCP, MRCS), Univ of Bristol (DPH), Open Univ (BA); *m* 23 April 1962, Ann, da of Eric Bertram Haiser (d 1963), of Leamington Spa; 2 da (Mary Jane b 1965, Susan Elizabeth b 1967); *Career* hosp med appts 1964–66, Public Health Dept City of Birmingham 1966–70, princ asst SMO Birmingham RHB 1971–74, specialist in community med West Midlands RHA 1974–76; Sandwell Health Authy: area med offr 1976–83, dist med offr 1983–88, gen mangr 1985–88; asst md and regnl dir of public health West Midlands RHA 1988–93, public health conslt 1993–96, med dir and chm Midlands Health Consultancy Network Ltd 1996–; sr clinical lectr Univ of Birmingham 1988–, visiting fell Business Sch Aston Univ 1988–, conslt advsr WHO 1989–; pres: Lichfield Sci and Engrg Soc 1991, Assoc for Industrial Archaeology 1998–99; pres Droitwich Spa Saltway Rotary Club 2001; FRSH 1978, FFPHM 1980, FIMgt 1984, LHSM 1985, FRSM 1989; SBStJ 1977; *Recreations* sailing, photography, industrial archaeology; *Style*— Dr Michael Harrison, JP; ✉ 19 Sandles Close, The Ridings, Droitwich Spa WR9 8RB (☎ 01905 798308, e-mail michael65@harrison-online.co.uk)

HARRISON, Sir Michael James Harwood; 2 Bt (UK 1961), of Bugbrooke, Co Northampton, JP (1993); s of Col Sir (James) Harwood Harrison, 1 Bt, TD (d 1980), MP (Cons) Eye 1951–79, of Hasketon, Suffolk, and Peggy Alberta Mary, *née* Stenhouse (d 1993); *b* 28 March 1936; *Educ* Rugby; *m* 1967, (Rosamund) Louise, da of Edward Buxton Clive (d 1975), of Swanmore, Hants; 2 da ((Auriol) Davina (Mrs Benet Northcote) b 1968, Priscilla Caroline (Mrs Stephen Howell) b 1971), 2 s (Edwin Michael Harwood b 1981, Tristan John b 1986); *Heir* s, Edwin Harrison; *Career* Nat Serv 17/21 Lancers 1955–56; insurance broker Lloyd's 1958–92; dir of various private cos 1980–; dep chm STA Tall Ships Ltd 1996–2000; memb Cncl Sail Training Assoc 1968–2003; Assoc of Combined Youth Clubs: vice-pres 1983–2000, chm Mgmnt Ctee 1987–95; Freeman City of London 1964, Master Worshipful Co of Mercers 1986 (Liveryman 1967); *Recreations* sailing (yacht 'Falcon'), sudoku; *Clubs* Boodle's; *Style*— Sir Michael Harrison, Bt; ✉ Rise Cottage, Hasketon, nr Woodbridge, Suffolk IP13 6JA (*E-mail* sirmharrison@hotmail.com)

HARRISON, Paul; s of Ronald Harrison, and Maureen Harrison; *Educ* Wednesfield HS Wolverhampton, Mid Cheshire Coll of FE, Bath Coll of HE (BA); *Career* artist; in partnership with John Wood, *qv*; *Exhibitions* incl: The British Art Show 5 2000, Twenty Six (Drawing and Falling Things) (Chisenhale Gallery London) 2002, Sudden Glory (CCAC Inst Calif) 2002, Gwangju Biennale Korea 2002, Monitor: Volume One (Gagosian Gallery NY) 2002, Performing Bodies (Tate Modern London) 2002, Selected Works (MOMA NY) 2004, Art Now (Tate Britain) 2004, Irreducible (CCA Inst Calif) 2005; *Style*— Paul Harrison, Esq

H

HARRISON, (Walter) Paul; s of Walter Harrison, of Morecambe, and Margaret Hildred, *née* Buttery; *b* 19 March 1955; *Educ* Skerton Co Boys' Sch Lancaster, Univ of Lancs (OND, HNC), De Montfort Univ (BA, DipArch); *m* Josephine Mary Winwood; *Career* architect; Cassidy & Ashton Partnership Preston 1973–75, W E Moore & Sons Leicester 1978–79, ptnr Robert Davies John West & Assocs Crawley 1987–90, md RDJW Architects Ltd 1990–; RIBA, ARCUK; *Recreations* squash, badminton, cars, horse riding, property devpt and rental market, travel; *Clubs* Maserati Drivers; *Style*— Paul Harrison, Esq; ✉ Denholme, Crawley Road, Horsham, West Sussex (☎ 01403 262224); RDJW Architects Ltd, Quoin House, 11 East Park, Crawley RH10 6AN (☎ 01293 404300, fax 01293 404299, e-mail architecture@rdjwa.co.uk)

HARRISON, Philippa Mary; da of Charles Kershaw Whitfield (d 1972), and Alexina Margaret, *née* Dykes; *b* 25 November 1942; *Educ* Walthamstow Hall, Univ of Bristol (BA), Courtauld Inst; *m* July 1967 (m dis), James Fraser Harrison; *Career* jt ed-in-chief Penguin Books 1979–80, editorial dir Michael Joseph 1980–85, md and publisher Macmillan London 1986–88, md V and A Enterprises 1990–91, chief exec and publisher Little Brown & Co (UK) 1996–2001 (md 1992–96), editorial dir Ed Victor Ltd 2002–; dir Book Tokens Ltd 1996–; pres Publishers Assoc 1998–99 (vice-pres 1997–98); memb: Bd of Book Marketing Cncl 1983–88, Literature Panel Arts Cncl 1988–92, Cncl Publishers Assoc 1995–; tstee Eric & Salome Estorick Fndn 1996–; CIMgt 1987, FRSA 1992; *Books* Publishing: The Future (contrib, 1988); *Recreations* walking, theatre, reading, the arts; *Clubs* Groucho; *Style*— Mrs Philippa Harrison

HARRISON, Prof Robert Graham; s of Robert Graham Harrison, of Essex, and Constance May, *née* Scott; *b* 26 February 1944; *Educ* Wanstead Co HS, Univ of London (BSc, PhD); *m* Rowena Indrania; 1 s (Samuel Scott b 1972), 1 da (Sophia Victoria b 1982); *Career* research fell Univ of London/Culham Lab UKAEA 1970–72, lectr Dept of Physics Univ of Bath 1972–76; Dept of Physics Heriot-Watt Univ: lectr then sr lectr 1976–83, reader 1983–87, prof 1987–2005, emeritus prof 2005–; dir of several confs and advanced workshops; FRSE 1987, FInstP; *Publications* author of over 350 pubns in int scientific jls and ed of 5 books in the fields of laser physics, nonlinear optics, chaos and complexity; *Style*— Prof Robert Harrison, FRSE; ✉ School of Engineering and Physical Sciences, Heriot-Watt University, Riccarton, Edinburgh EH14 4AS (☎ 0131 337 3412)

HARRISON, (Desmond) Roger Wingate; s of Maj-Gen Desmond Harrison, CB, DSO, and Kathleen, *née* Hazley; *b* 9 April 1933; *Educ* Rugby, Worcester Coll Oxford (MA), Harvard Business Sch; *m* 1965, Victoria Harrison, MVO, da of late Rear Adm John Lee-Barber; 1 s (decd), 4 da (1 decd); *Career* The Times 1957–67 (freelance writer 1955–57); The Observer: joined 1967, dir 1970–92, jt md 1977–84, chief exec 1984–87; non-exec dir: LWT Holdings plc 1976–94, Trinity Mirror plc 1991–2003, SPG Media Gp plc (formerly Sterling Publishing Group plc) 1993–2004 (chm 1993–96); dir Sableknight 1981–; dep chm Capital Radio plc 1991–2000 (dir 1975–2000); exec dir The Oak Fndn (UK) Ltd 1987–89; memb Bd Ashoka Innovators for the Public 2006–; chm: Toynbee Hall 1989–2002, Asylum Aid 1990–97, Royal Acad of Dancing 1992–2006; govr Sadler's Wells Theatre 1984–95; *Recreations* theatre, country pursuits, tennis; *Clubs* Beefsteak, Flyfishers'; *Style*— Roger Harrison, Esq; ✉ Itchen Stoke Mill, Alresford, Hampshire SO24 0RA

HARRISON, Timothy David Blair (Tim); s of Blair Wilfred Wortley Harrison (d 1999), of Banwell, Avon, and Sheelagh Margurite Hildergarde, *née* Woolford (d 1972); *b* 13 December 1944; *Educ* Blundell's; *m* 2 Nov 1991, Beverley, da of George William Brindle, of Bahrain; 2 s (Blair Edward Charles b 1976, Thomas George b 1992), 1 da (Paige-Elise b 1996); *Career* UBM/MAC Group Bristol 1963–73, GKN Mills Building Services Ltd 1973–76, Norplant/Witpalm International Ltd 1976–79, Mallinson-Denny Group 1979–86 (sales and mktg dir Formwood Ltd, md Bushboard Ltd), md GA Harvey Office Furniture Ltd 1986–88, Trafalgar House Building & Civil Engineering Holdings Ltd 1988–89 (dir, sector md), gp chief exec The Company of Designers plc 1989–92; 1992–96: dir CAMAS UK Ltd (formerly part of English China Clays), md CAMAS Building Materials Ltd, pres Prefabricados de Hormigon Lurgain SA Spain, dir SMMO France; divnl md Luxfer Group Holdings plc 1996–98, md Apollo Logistics Ltd 1999–2001, divnl md Corton Gp Holdings Ltd 2001–; chm Corton Management Servs Ltd, Generation Metals Int Ltd, Norcot Engrg Ltd; Freeman City of London, memb Worshipful Co of Builders Merchants; FInstD; *Recreations* hunting, boating; *Clubs* Royal Dart Yacht; *Style*— Tim Harrison, Esq; ✉ Shiningford Farm, Carsington, Derbyshire DE4 4DD

HARRISON, Tony; s of Harry Ashton Harrison (d 1980), and Florence Horner, *née* Wilkinson (d 1976); *b* 30 April 1937; *Educ* Leeds GS, Univ of Leeds (BA); *Partner* Sian Thomas; *Career* poet and dramatist; Wilfred Owen Award for Poetry 2006, Pen Pinter Prize 2009, European Prize for Literature (Strasbourg) 2011, David Cohen Prize for Literature 2015; FRSL; *Television* The Oresteia (Channel 4 1982), The Big H (BBC 1984), The Mysteries (Channel 4 1985), Yan Tan Tethera (Channel 4 1986), Loving Memory (BBC 1986), V (Channel 4 1987, Royal Television Soc Award), The Blasphemers' Banquet, The Gaze of the Gorgon (1992), Black Daisies for the Bride (1993, Prix Italia 1994), A Maybe Day in Kazakhstan (1994), The Shadow of Hiroshima (Channel 4 1995), Metamorpheus (BBC 2000), Crossings (LWT 2002); *Films* Prometheus (1999); *Books and Plays* Earthworks (1964), Aikin Mata (1965), Newcastle is Peru (1969), The Loiners (1970), The Misanthrope (1973), Phaedra Britannica (1975), Palladas: Poems (1975), The Passion (1977), Bow Down (1977), from The School of Eloquence (1978), Continuous (1981), A Kumquat for John Keats (1981), US Martial (1981), The Oresteia (1981), Selected Poems (1984), The Mysteries (1985), V (1985), Dramatic Verse 1973–85 (1985), The Fire-Gap (1985), Theatre Works 1973–85 (1986), Selected Poems (augmented edn 1987), The Trackers of Oxyrhynchus (performed ancient stadium of Delphi 1988, NT 1990), A Cold Coming – Gulf War Poems (1991), The Common Chorus (1992), The Gaze of the Gorgon and other poems (Whitbread poetry award, 1992), Square Rounds (1992), Poetry or Bust (1993), The Kaisers of Carnuntum (1995), Permanently Bard (1995), The Labourers of Herakles (1995), The Shadow of Hiroshima and other film/poems (1995), The Prince's Play (1996), Prometheus (1998), Laureate's Block and Other Poems (2000), Under the Clock (2005), Hecuba (2005), Fram (2008); *Collections* Tony Harrison Plays Three (1996), Tony Harrison Plays One (1999), Tony Harrison Plays Two (2002), Tony Harrison Plays Four (2002), Plays Five (2004), Collected Film Poetry (2007), Collected Poems (2007); *Style*— Tony Harrison

HARRISON-CRIPPS, William Lawrence; s of William Harrison Harrison-Cripps (d 1998), and Anne Elizabeth, *née* Graham Smith (d 1959); *b* 25 January 1950; *Educ* Marlborough; *m* 4 Nov 1977, Elizabeth Joy, da of Kenneth Henry Cornwell; 2 s (William Henry b 17 Aug 1979, Thomas Peter Seddon b 24 Oct 1987), 1 da (Alexandra Elizabeth b 9 April 1981); *Career* PricewaterhouseCoopers (formerly Price Waterhouse): articled clerk 1968–72, mangr 1976, ptnr 1982–, chm M/A Tax Servs (Europe) 1989, memb European Tax Bd and European Corp Fin Exec 1990, ptnr i/c Int Corp Tax Services Gp 1991, UK Tax Service Exec 1992, chm UK Tax Servs 1993, World Tax Service Exec 1993, managing ptnr Tax & Legal Servs EMEA 1998–2003, global markets ldr Tax and Legal Servs 2003–05, dep global ldr Tax Servs 2005–06, conslt 2006–10; chm H C Consulting Ltd, dir Giftsearch Ltd, dir InterResolve Hldgs Ltd 2009–12; memb Addington Soc 1992–; FCA 1973, ATII 1975, assoc Inst for Ind Business (AInstIB) 2008; *Books* Mergers and Acquisitions – The Complete Guide To Principles and Practice (contrib, 1986); *Recreations* sailing, photography; *Clubs* Royal Southern Yacht; *Style*— William Harrison-Cripps, Esq; ✉ Giftsearch Limited, 15 Tunsgate, Guildford GU1 3QT (☎ 01483 202315)

HARRISS, David James Bernard; s of Henry James Harriss (d 1975), and Jessie May, *née* Bright; *b* 18 April 1947; *Educ* Handsworth Tech Sch Birmingham, Architectural Assoc of Architecture (AADipl); *m* 1985, Patricia Anne; 1 da (Sarah Louise b 11 November 1987); *Career* architect; Foster Assocs 1972–75, Rock Townsend 1975–77, Michael Hopkins 1977–81; Nicholas Grimshaw & Partners Ltd (latterly Grimshaw Architects LLP): joined 1981, assoc 1983, dir 1992–2007, conslt 2007–; projects incl: R&D Facility Rank Xerox, Homebase Brentford, Gillingham Business Park, Pier 4A Heathrow, Lord's Grandstand, Terminal 1 Devpt Manchester Airport, Rolls Royce Goodwood; winner of RIBA Portfolio Prize 1970; RIBA 1974; *Books* The Pattern of Technological Innovation (1972), Building Design – Cladding Special Report (1990), Computers in Architecture (contrib chapter, 1992); *Recreations* classic cars, motor sport; *Clubs* Lotus 7, Club Lotus; *Style*— David J B Harriss, Esq; ✉ 2B The Chase, London SW4 0NH; Grimshaw Architects LLP, 57 Clerkenwell Road, London EC1M 5NG (☎ 020 7291 4137, e-mail david.harriss@grimshaw-architects.com)

HARRISS-WHITE, Prof Barbara; da of Philip Beeham, and Betty, *née* Browning; *b* 1946, Westminster; *Educ* Univ of Cambridge (MA, Dip Agric Sci), Univ of Oxford (MA), UEA (PhD), Trinity Coll of Music London (ATCL); *Career* lectr Cambs Coll of Arts and Technol 1969–72, res offr Centre for S Asian Studies Univ of Cambridge 1972–77, res fell ODI London 1977–80, res fell LSHTM 1980–87; Univ of Oxford: lectr in agric econs 1987–96, fell Wolfson Coll 1987–2011 (emeritus fell 2011–), special lectureship 1994–95, prof of devpt studies 1998– (reader 1996–98); Directrice d'Etudes MSH Paris 2004, dir Queen Elizabeth House Oxford 2004–07, dir Contemporary S Asian Studies Prog Univ of Oxford 2007–11, professeur invite IEDES Paris 2008–12; Smuts lectureship Univ of Cambridge 1999; memb Cncl Devpt Studies Assoc 1987–90, 1994–97 and 2004–10, memb South Asia Panel Br Acad 2009–13; chair Devpt Studies Sub-Panel Research Assessment Exercise 2008; tstee: Action Aid 1988–94 and 1998–2005, Int Food Policy Research Inst Washington 2006–12; memb Lab Pty 1976–98; memb: Bd of Govrs Sch of Oriental and African Studies Univ of London, Bd of Dirs South Asia Inst Heidelberg Univ, Research Advsy Gp DFID 2010–; Membre Le Comité d'Orientation Stratégique de L'IEDES (Paris-1, Sorbonne) 2011–, Membre College International Conseil National de Développement et la Solidarité Internationale (French Govt) 2016–; FAcSS 2013–; *Publications* author, co-author and ed of 40 books and major reports incl: Globalisation and Insecurity (2001), Outcast from Social Welfare: Adult Disability and Incapacity in Rural South India (2002), India Working (2003), Rural India facing the 21st Century (2004), India's Market Society (2005), Coming to Terms with Nature (2006), Trade Liberalization and India's Informal Economy (2007), Defining Poverty in Developing Countries (2007), Rural Commercial Capital: Agricultural Markets in West Bengal (2008, jt winner Edgar Graham Prize for Original Scholarship in Devpt 2008), The Comparative Political Economy of Development: Africa and S Asia (2010), Dalits and Adivasis in India's Business Economy: Three Essays and an Atlas (with Elisabetta Basile, Anita Dixit, Pinaki Joddar, Aseem Prakash and Kaushal Vidyarthee, 2014), China-India: Pathways of Economic and Social Development (ed, with Delia Davin, 2014), Indian Capitalism in Development (ed, with Judith Heyer, 2015), Middle India and Urban-Rural Development: Four Decades of Change (2015), Mapping India's Capitalism: Old and New Regions (with Elisabetta Basile and Christine Lutringer, 2015); over 250 published papers and chapters, 80 working papers on aspects of devpt particularly in S Asia; *Recreations* music, swimming, walking, novels, craft enamelling, France; *Clubs* Alpine; *Style*— Prof Barbara Harriss-White; ✉ Wolfson College, Oxford OX2 6UD (☎ 01865 274100, e-mail barbara.harriss-white@qeh.ox.ac.uk)

HARRISSON, Tim; *b* 1952; *Educ* Hammersmith Coll of Art, Norwich Coll of Art (BA), Byam Shaw Sch of Fine Art, Sir John Cass Sch of Art; *Career* sculptor; *One and Two Person Exhibitions* Salisbury Art Centre 1984, The Showroom Gallery London 1986, Exhibition of Prints and Drawings (Halesworth Gallery Suffolk) 1987, South Hill Park Art Centre Bracknell 1988, The Flaxman Gallery Stoke on Trent 1988, Purdy-Pomeroy Gallery London 1988, Artsite Gallery Bath 1989, Recent Sculpture (New Art Centre London) 1991, Four Stone Sculptures (New Art Centre London) 1993, Winchester Cathedral 1997, Stone Works (Galerie Sebastians Kapelle Germany) 1999, New Stone Carvings (New Art Centre Roche Court) 2001, Eagle Gallery London 2007, Rabley Drawing Centre Marlborough 2009, Salisbury Museum 2010, Land/Stone/Colour (Canary Wharf London) 2015; *Group Exhibitions* incl: Salisbury Library 1981, RIBA Sculpture Ct Winter Exhbn 1984, Still Life a New Life (Harris Museum Preston) 1985, Art for the Garden (Hannah Peschar Gallery Surrey) 1986–87, Coastlines (The Towner Museum Eastbourne) 1987, a winner in int art competition organised by Metro Art NYC 1987, Sculpture Open (The Minories Colchester) 1989, The Salisbury Festival 1991, The Economist Bldg Plaza London 1991, London Contemporary Art Fair 1991, Art 23 '92 Basel Switzerland 1992, Art on the Waterfront (Southampton Civic Centre) 1992; *Commissions* incl: Roche Ct Sculpture Garden 1989, The Millfield Cmmn (Millfield Sch with Artsite Gallery Bath) 1989, James Kirkham in Sussex 1989, Ivor Braka in Norfolk 1990, Russell Cotes Museum Bournemouth 1995, new terminal building Southampton Airport for BAA 1995, The Liverpool Victoria Friendly Soc Building Southampton 1996, Winchester Cathedral 1999, 'Reflection' in Epsom Coll 2000, Pegasus for Chatsworth Estate Derbys 2001, Ring for Wingfield Arts Suffolk 2002, Column I Woodford Valley Salisbury 2005; *Style*— Tim Harrisson; ✉ 4 Beckford Cottages, Hindon, Salisbury, Wiltshire SP3 6ED (website www.timharrisson.com)

HARROD, Henry Mark; s of Sir (Henry) Roy Forbes Harrod (d 1978), and Wilhelmine Margaret Eve, *née* Cresswell (d 2005); *b* 6 January 1939; *Educ* Eton, ChCh Oxford (MA); *m* 1, 1965 (m dis 1973); 2 s ((Henry) Barnaby b 1965, Huckleberry Nathaniel b 1967); m 2, 1977, Tanya Olivia Ledger, PhD, da of Dr Peter Ledger, MD (d 2003); 1 s (Hugo Roy Francis b 1979), 1 da (Horatia Mary b 1983); *Career* called to the Bar Lincoln's Inn 1963 (bencher 1991); pupil of Conrad Dehn 2 Crown Office Row Temple 1963; memb chambers of David Fenwick 46 Grainger St Newcastle upon Tyne 1964–68, chambers of Quintin Hogg 4 Paper Bldgs Temple 1968; chambers of John Brightman and others 2 New Sq Lincoln's Inn (chambers moved to 5 Stone Bldgs 1993): joined 1969, head of chambers 1990–; recorder 1993–2004 (asst recorder 1989–93), conveyancing counsel of the Court 1991–; *Clubs* Garrick; *Style*— Henry Harrod, Esq; ✉ 5 Stone Buildings, Lincoln's Inn, London WC2A 3XT (☎ 020 7242 6201)

HARROP, Andrew Jonathan Gilbert; s of Sir Peter Harrop, and Margaret, *née* Elliott Binns; *Educ* Gonville and Caius Coll Cambridge (BA), LSE (MSc), London Business Sch (MBA); *Partner* Katie Ghose; 1 da; *Career* head of policy Age Concern 2006–09, dir of policy and public affairs Age UK 2009–11, gen sec Fabian Soc 2011–; *Style*— Andrew Harrop, Esq; ✉ Fabian Society, 61 Petty France, Westminster, London SW1H 9EU (☎ 020 7227 4900, e-mail andrew.harrop@fabians.org.uk, website www.fabians.org.uk)

HARROP, Prof Stuart Reginald; s of Reginald Harrop, of E Yorkshire, and Valerie Mary, *née* Hotham; *b* 11 January 1956; *Educ* Beverley GS, Univ of Leeds (LLB); *m* 30 April 1983, Tracy Ann, da of Dennis Roy Green; 3 s (Lee Stuart b 11 May 1986, Joel William b 3 Feb 1990, Christian Sean b 7 Aug 1993); *Career* admitted slr 1980; slr Costain Group plc 1982–84, co slr Albright & Wilson Ltd 1984–86, ICI plc 1986–88; dir legal servs: Stock Exchange 1988–91, RSPCA 1991–96; prof of wildlife mgmnt law and dep head Dept of Anthropology Univ of Kent at Canterbury 1996–13, prof of environmental law Univ of Sussex 2013–; tstee: Global Diversity Fndn, Kent Wildlife Tst, Gilchrist Educnl Tst; memb Law Soc; *Recreations* freelance photography (natural history); *Style*— Prof

Stuart Harrop; ✉ School of Law, Politics and Sociology, University of Sussex, Sussex House, Brighton BN1 9RH

HARROW, Prof Martyn; *Educ* Univ of Bath; *Career* formerly dir of information services Cardiff Univ, chief exec Jisc until 2015; currently chair Pension Fund Investment Ctee ICI Specialty Chemicals; *Style—* Prof Martyn Harrow

HARROWBY, 8 Earl of (UK 1809); (Dudley Adrian) Conroy Ryder; also Baron Harrowby (GB 1776) and Viscount Sandon (UK 1809); o s of 7 Earl of Harrowby, TD (d 2007); *b* 18 March 1951, London; *Educ* Eton, Univ of Newcastle upon Tyne, Magdalene Coll Cambridge (MA); *m* 1, 1977, Sarah Nichola Hobhouse (d 1994), o da of Capt Anthony Denys Phillpotts Payne, of Carraway Barn, Marnhull, Dorset; 3 s (Hon Dudley Anthony Hugo Coventry (Viscount Sandon) b 5 Sept 1981, Hon Frederick Whitmore Dudley b 6 Feb 1984, Hon Henry Mansell Dudley b 13 July 1985), 1 da (Lady Emily Georgina Hobhouse b 13 Jan 1992); m 2, 1998, Mrs Caroline Jane Coram James, o da of Geoffrey Marks (d 2000); *Career* commercial property devpt; exec dir Compton St Securities Ltd 1988–; memb NFU 1975–, vice pres Staffs branch Cncl for the Protection of Rural England 1988–95, govr John Archer Sch Wandsworth 1986–88, patron The Guild of Handicraft Tst 1991–, pres The Staffordshire Soc 1995–97, memb Governing Cncl Goldsmiths Univ of London 2003–09 (memb Finance and Resources Ctee 2004–09, memb Audit Ctee 2009–14), govr Dean Close Sch Cheltenham 2004–, pres Stafford Historical and Civil Soc 2008–, vice-pres Glos County Branch CPRE 2008–, patron N Staffs County Branch Royal Br Legion 2008–13, memb Assoc of Cons Peers 2009–, memb Ctee Glos County Branch CLA 2011–; tstee Bathtub 2 Boardroom 2010–, patron Oak Tree Farm Rural Project 2014–; Liveryman Co of Goldsmiths 1997; FRICS 1992; *Recreations* fell-walking, music, study of fine art and architecture; *Clubs* Pratt's, Boodle's; *Style—* The Earl of Harrowby; ✉ Sandon Estate Office, Sandon, Stafford ST18 0DA (e-mail conroy.harrowby@harrowbyestates.co.uk)

HARSENT, Prof David; s of Albert Edward Harsent (d 1990), and Mary Dorothy May Harsent (d 2004); *b* 1942, Bovey Tracey, Devon; *m* 1988, Julia Watson; 1 da (Hannah b 1990); 3 c from previous m (Ysanne, Simon, Barnaby); *Career* author; distinguished writing fell Sheffield Hallam Univ 2005–08, visiting prof Sheffield Hallam Univ 2008–11; prof of creative writing: Bath Spa Univ, Univ of Roehampton 2013–; Geoffrey Faber Meml Award, Cheltenham Festival Prize, two bursaries Arts Cncl, travel fellowship Soc of Authors, Forward Prize 2005, Cholmondeley Award 2008, Griffin Internation Poetry Prize 2012, T S Eliot Prize 2015; Hon DLitt Univ of Roehampton 2013; FRSL 2000, FEA 2011, FHEA 2015; *Publications* poetry: Tonight's Lover (1968), Poetry Introduction 1 (contrib, 1968), A Violent Country (1969), Truce (1973), After Dark (1973), Dreams of the Dead (1977), Mister Punch (1984), Selected Poems (1989), Storybook Hero (1992), News from the Front (1993), The Sorrow of Sarajevo (trans, poems by Goran Simic, 1996), The Potted Priest (1997), Sprinting from the Graveyard (trans, poems by Goran Simic, 1997), A Bird's Idea of Flight (1998), Marriage (2002, shortlisted T S Eliot Prize and Forward Prize 2002), Legion (2005, Forward Prize 2005, shortlisted Whitbread Poetry Prize and T S Eliot Prize 2005), Selected Poems 1969–2005 (2007, shortlisted Griffin Int Poetry Prize 2008), Night (2011, Griffin Int Poetry Prize, shortlisted TS Eliot Prize, Costa Prize and Forward Prize), In Secret (trans, poems by Yannis Ritsos), Songs from the Same Earth (2013), Fire Songs (2014, Winner T. S. Eliot Prize); fiction: From an Inland Sea (1985); as ed: Savramena Britanska Poezija (poetry anthology, with Mario Susko), Another Round at the Pillars: A Festschrift for Ian Hamilton (1999), Raising the Iron: Poems for the Palace Theatre Watford (2004); music theatre: Serenade the Silkie (music by Julian Grant, 1994), Gawain (opera, music by Sir Harrison Birtwistle, *qv*, 1991), The Woman and the Hare (song cycle, music by Sir Harrison Birtwistle, 1999), When She Died (TV opera, music by Jonathan Dove, 2002), The Ring Dance of the Nazarene (music by Sir Harrison Birtwistle, 2003), The Minotaur (music by Sir Harrion Birtwistle, 2008), Crime Fiction (music by Huw Watkins, 2009), The Corridor (music by Harrison Birtwistle, 2009), In the Locked Room (music by Huw Watkins, 2012), Songs from the Same Earth (music by Sir Harrison Birtwistle), The Cure (music by Harrison Birtwistle, 2015); *Recreations* reinventing the past for future use; *Style—* Professor David Harsent; ✉ c/o United Agents, 12–26 Lexington Street, London W1F 0LE (✆ 020 3214 0800, fax 020 3214 0801, website www.unitedagents.co.uk)

HARSTON, Julian John Robert Clive; s of Lt-Col Clive Harston, ERD (d 1993), of Surrey, and Kathleen Mary, *née* Grace (d 2008); *b* 20 October 1942, Kenya; *Educ* King's Sch Canterbury, Univ of London (BSc); *m* 1, 1966 (m dis 2000), Karen Howard Oake, da of Col T E Longfield (ka 1941); 1 s (Alexander b 1978); m 2, 2008, Marina Vasic; 2 step-da (Ana b 1983, Marija b 1988); *Career* mangr Br Tourist Authy Copenhagen and Vancouver 1965–71; FCO: joined 1971, first sec/consul Hanoi 1973–74, first sec Blantyre 1975–79, first sec Lisbon 1982–84, cnsllr Harare 1984–88, cnsllr UN Geneva 1991–95; political advsr to Special Rep of Sec-Gen for former Yugoslavia 1995, dir UN Liaison Office Belgrade 1996–98, special rep of Sec-Gen and chief of mission Haiti 1998–99, dep special rep of Sec-Gen Bosnia and Herzegovina 1999–2001, dir Asia and ME Div Dept of Peace-Keeping NY 2001–04, dir UN Office Belgrade 2004–07, asst sec-gen UN Sec-Gen for Western Sahara 2007, special rep of Sec-Gen Western Sahara and head of mission Referendum in Western Sahara (MINURSO) 2007–09, rep of Sec-Gen Belgrade 2009, dir Harston Consulting Belgrade 2009, rep UN Sec-Gen Belgrade 2009–10, ret; dir Harston Consulting 2010–; *Publications* Responding to Crises: Are Present Policies & Practices the Answer? (2001), The Experience of East Timor (2002), What Makes a Peacekeeping Success Story? (2003), The United Nations as Government: Eastern Slavonia, Kosovo and East Timor (2005), Adapting the UN to the Post-Modern Era – the Case of Haiti (2005), Peacekeeping in 2007–2010, Kosovo and Metohija: Living in the Enclaves (contrib, 2008), Peacekeeping in 2011, Risk Analysis and Intelligence Assessment in Peacekeeping: A Necessity (2009, 2 edn 2010); *Recreations* travel, photography, Switzerland; *Clubs* East India, Gremio Literario (Lisbon), Harare, Goodwood Aero, Special Forces London; *Style—* Julian Harston, Esq; ✉ Topolin Venac 19, Apartment 19, 11000 Belgrade, Serbia (website www.harstonconsulting.rs)

HART, Alan; s of Reginald Thomas Hart (d 1980), of Haddenham, Bucks, and Lilian Clara, *née* Hanson (d 1992); *b* 17 April 1935; *Educ* UCS Hampstead; *m* 16 Dec 1961, Celia Mary, *née* Vine, da of Raglan Keough; 2 s (David Alan b 31 Oct 1962, Andrew Dominic b 6 May 1965), 1 da (Gabrielle Louise b 13 Nov 1975); *Career* reporter: Willesden Chronicle and Kilburn Times 1952–58, Newcastle Evening Chronicle 1958, London Evening News 1958–59; editorial asst BBC Sportsview 1959–61, TV sports prodr BBC Manchester 1962–64, ed BBC Sportsview 1965–68 (asst ed 1964–65), ed Grandstand 1968–77, head of sport BBC TV 1977–81, controller BBC 1 1981–84, special asst to DG BBC 1985, controller Int Rels BBC 1986–91, broadcasting conslt 1991–, chm Eurosport UK 1997–99 (memb Bd 1991–97), advsr to Euro Broadcasting Union on East European broadcasting 1991–93, exec dir Eurosport Consortium 1993–2005, dir Global Amg 1995–2001, dir Give Them A Sporting Chance 2003–, chm Inventure Tst 2003–07; govr S Devon Coll 2005–13, chm Friends of S Devon Coll 2008–; Hon DEd Univ of Plymouth 2014; FRTS; *Recreations* sport, walking, music; *Style—* Alan Hart, Esq; ✉ Cutwellwalls, Avonwick, Near South Brent, South Devon TQ10 9HA (✆ 01364 72552)

HART, Andrew Michael; s of Stanley Hart, of London, and Diana, *née* Godfrey; *b* 9 August 1966, London; *Educ* Univ of Manchester (BA); *Partner* Jodie Belman; 1 s from previous m (Max b 2 March 1998); *Career* Delaney Slaymaker Fletcher Delaney, 20/20 Media, Media Star, IDG 1995–99, Ask Jeeves 1999–2001, Diageo 2001–02, Daily Mail and General Tst 2002–; Online Publisher of the Year 2006; *Recreations* watching Arsenal, dance music and clubbing, composing music, playing guitar; *Clubs* Groucho, Arts; *Style—* Andrew Hart, Esq; ✉ Daily Mail and General Trust, Northcliffe House, 2 Derry Street, London W8 5TT (✆ 020 7752 8675, fax 020 7752 8453)

HART, Charles; s of George Hart, of Cookham, and Juliet, *née* Baddeley; *b* 6 June 1967; *Educ* Desborough Sch Maidenhead, Guildhall Sch of Music and Drama; *Career* lyricist; works incl: The Phantom of the Opera (musical), Aspects of Love (musical), The Vampyr (opera), The Kissing-Dance (musical), The Dreaming (musical), misc songs; *Style—* Charles Hart

HART, Prof George; eld s of George Hart, of Golborne, Lancs, and Mary, *née* Britton (d 2011); *b* 7 June 1951, Grappenhall, Cheshire; *Educ* Boteler GS, Churchill Coll Cambridge (MA), Trinity Coll Oxford and Oxford Univ Clinical Sch (MA, BM BCh), St Peter's Coll Oxford (DM); *m* 19 Jan 1980, Dr Judy Hart, da of Alfred Alan Reynolds (d 1988), of Bognor Regis, W Sussex; 1 da (Alice b 1982), 2 s (Samuel b 1985, Joseph b 1986); *Career* jr hosp posts 1975–77; registrar: cardiology Papworth Hosp 1977–78, med Addenbrooke's Hosp 1978–79; lectr in physiology Balliol Coll Oxford 1979–80, MRC research trg fell Univ Laboratory of Physiology Oxford 1979–82, Sidney Perry jr research fell St Peter's Coll Oxford 1979–82, sr registrar in cardiology Yorkshire Regnl HA 1982–86, BHF clinical reader in cardiovascular med Univ of Oxford 1986–98, hon conslt physician and cardiologist John Radcliffe Hosp Oxford 1986–98, supernumerary fell Lady Margaret Hall Oxford 1986–98, David A Price Evans chair of med Univ of Liverpool 1998–2011, hon conslt physician Royal Liverpool Univ Hosp 1998–2011, hon research fell Lady Margaret Hall Oxford 1999–; research prof Univ of Manchester 2012–; memb: Br Cardiac Soc, Physiological Soc, Soc of Expert Witnesses, Assoc of Physicians of GB and Ireland, Br Soc for Cardiovascular Research (chm 1990–93), Int Soc for Heart Research; FRCP 1990 (MRCP 1977), FACC 1999; *Recreations* photography, walking; *Style—* Prof George Hart; ✉ Institute of Cardiovascular Sciences, Core Technology Facility, 46 Grafton Street, Manchester M13 9NT (✆ 0161 275 1223/1202, fax 0161 275 1183, e-mail george.hart@manchester.ac.uk)

HART, Gerry; s of Tom Hart (d 1993), and Sylvia, *née* Robinson; *Educ* Dartford GS; *m* 31 March 1973 (sep 1997), Pamela Elizabeth; 1 da (Jane b 6 Dec 1976), 2 s (Robert Edwin b 6 Oct 1979, Jonathan William b 30 Dec 1990); *Career* tax trainee Nat West Bank 1963–66, tax mangr Temple Gothard 1970–73, gp tax asst Guthrie Corporation 1973–74, own tax practice 1980–, md The Tax Team 1994–97, head of UK ops The Tax Team (H&R Block UK Ltd) 1997–2002; fndr UK Tax Congress (held 1981–87); popular lectr in tax; memb Editorial Bd The Tax Jl; Chartered Inst of Taxation: assoc 1968, fell 1970, nat pres 1995–96, fndr chm Sussex branch; *Books* Dictionary of Taxation (Butterworths, 1983), Tolley's Tax Planning For Family Companies (1995); *Recreations* jazz, horse riding, watching most sports, travel; *Clubs* Morton's; *Style—* Gerry Hart, Esq

HART, Joanne; *Educ* Univ of Cambridge (MA); *Career* Evening Standard 1992–2002 (dep City ed 1996–2002), financial journalist The Times 2002–03, ed Bridgepoint magazine 2002–, investments ed Mail on Sunday 2006–; dir Joanne Hart Ltd 2003–; *Recreations* food, travel, cinema, spinning; *Style—* Ms Joanne Hart; ✉ e-mail joanne@joanne-hart.com, website www.joanne-hart.com, Twitter @joannemidas

HART, Matthew Jason; s of Colin Dennis Hart, and Susan Jean, *née* Ranson; *b* 13 July 1972; *Educ* Arts Educnl Sch London, Royal Ballet Upper Sch; *Career* dancer/choreographer and singer/actor; Royal Ballet: artist 1991–93, first artist 1993–95, soloist 1995–96; with Rambert Dance Co 1996–2000, with George Piper Dances 2001–03, freelance artist 2003–; dance analyst and expert Strictly Dance Fever (BBC1 and BBC3) 2006; *Roles* with Royal Ballet incl: The Trepak in The Nutcracker, head Fakir in La Bayadère, Bratfisch in Mayerling, Jester in Cinderella, Squirrel Nutkin in Tales of Beatrix Potter, Solo Boy in Dances Concertantes, Beggar Chief in Manon, Neopolitan Dance, lead Czardas, lead waltz in Swan Lake, 3rd movement, Symphony in C, Rhapsody, Stravinsky Violin Concerto, Les Noces, Petrouchka, Bryaxis in Daphnis and Chloë, cr role in Forsythe's Firstext, Forsythe's Steptext, Macmillans The Judas Tree; with Rambert Dance Co incl: Cruel Garden (The Poet), Four Scenes (cr role), Ghost Dances (Tie Dance, Ghost), Axioma 7, The Golden Section, Greymatter (cr role), Rooster (Rooster Man), Stream (Duet, Men's Dance), God's Plenty (cr roles), Quicksilver, No More Play, Petit Mort, Airs, August Pace; with George Piper Dances incl: Steptext, Sigue, Tangoid, Moments of Plastic Jubilation, Truely Great Thing, Red or White, Dearest Love; with ROH2 incl: Toad in Wind in the Willows 2003, The Devil in The Soldier's Tale 2004, 2005 and 2010, Asyla 2004, Anatomy of a Storyteller 2004, Oswald in Ghosts 2005, Pinocchio in Pinocchio 2005, King of the Mountains in The Thief of Baghdad 2008, Tom Rakewell in Pleasure's Progress 2010; others incl: Sidney Cohn in On Your Toes (musical) 2004, Frank Lawson in Mrs Henderson Presents (film) 2005, Menshikov in Riot at the Rite (film, BBC2) 2006, Betrothal in a Monastery (opera, Glyndebourne) 2006, The Prince in Matthew Bourne's Swan Lake (Paris and London) 2006, Gus Fielding in Babes in Arms (musical, Chichester Festival Theatre) 2007, guest artist in Viva la Diva 2007, Puck in A Midsummer Night's Dream and Sampson in Romeo and Juliet (both Regent's Park Open Air Theatre) 2008, Michael Somes in Margot (film, BBC 2) 2009; *Choreography* The Dream of the Cherry Blossom (Birds Gala Royal Opera House) 1991, Simple Symphony (Royal Ballet Sch) 1992, Forbidden Fruit (Royal Ballet) 1992, Solo (Royal Ballet) 1992, Street (Birmingham Royal Ballet) 1993, Fanfare (Royal Ballet) 1993, Caught Dance (Royal Ballet) 1994, Tusk (Royal Ballet) 1994, Peter and the Wolf (Royal Ballet Sch) 1995, 1997 and 2010, Cinderella (London City Ballet) 1995, Sleepers (Royal Acad of Dancing 70 Anniversary) 1995, Dances with Death (Royal Ballet) 1996, Blitz (Eng Nat Ballet) 1996, Cry Baby Kreisler (Royal Ballet) 1996, Physical Propery (Jerwood Fndn) 1996, Highly Strung (RADA Gala and Royal Ballet 1997), The Golden Vanity (Royal Ballet Sch) 1998, Sonate au Chocolat (Eng Nat Ballet Sch) 1999, Revenge (solo) 1999, Girl Band (Deutche Oper Am Rhein Düsseldorf Germany) 2000, Acheron's Dream (Royal Ballet) 2000, Mulan (Hong Kong Ballet) 2001, Images of Mulan (London Studio Centre) 2002, Other Men's Wives (George Piper Dances) 2002, Meet in the Middle (K Ballet Co) 2003, Young Persons Guide to the Orchestra (London Studio Centre) 2007, Whodunnit (Central Sch of Ballet) 2009 and 2012, Ballet Shoes (London Children's Ballet) 2010, Tchaikovsky's Ballet Fantasy (London Studio Centre and Sarasota Ballet) 2011, My First Sleeping Beauty (English Nat Ballet) 2012, Games for Gods (Royal Ballet Sch) 2012, The Nutcracker (Sarasota Ballet) 2012, 2013, 2015, Young Apollo, Super Ap! (New English Ballet Theatre) 2015; *Awards* Cosmopolitan/C & A Dance Award 1988, winner Ursula Moreton Choreographic Competition 1991, winner Frederick Ashton Choreographic Award 1994, Jerwood Fndn Award for Choreographers 1996; *Style—* Matthew Hart, Esq

HART, Miranda; da of Capt David Hart Dyke, CBE, LVO, RN, and Diana Margaret, *née* Luce; n of The Lord Luce, KG, GCVO, PC, DL (Life Peer), *qv*; *b* 14 December 1972, Torquay, Devon; *Educ* Downe House, UWE, Acad of Live and Recorded Arts; *Career* comedy writer and actress; *Television* incl: Smack the Pony 2001, Nighty Night 2005, My Family and Other Animals 2005, Hyperdrive 2006–07, Not Going Out 2006–09, Miranda 2009– (also writer and asst prodr, Best Comedy Performance RTS Award 2010, Best New Br TV Comedy, Best TV Comedy Actress and People's Choice Award Br Comedy Awards 2010, Best Scripted Comedy and Best Comedy Performance RTS Awards 2011, Best TV Comedy Actress Br Comedy Award 2011), Call the Midwife 2012– (Best Female Drama Performance Nat Television Award 2013); *Film* incl: Spy 2015; first woman to do stand-up arena tour, My, What I Call, Live Show; *Books* Is It Just Me? (2012), The Best of Miranda (2014), Peggy and Me (2016); *Recreations* tennis, travel, cycling, dancing and singing badly; *Style—* Ms Miranda Hart; ✉ c/o

Rachael Clarke, Troika Talent, 10a Christina Street, London EC2A 4PA (website www.mirandahart.com, Twitter @mermhart)

HART, Prof Oliver Simon D'Arcy; s of Philip Montagu D'Arcy Hart (d 2006), and Ruth Hart (d 2007); *b* 9 October 1948; *Educ* Univ Coll Sch, King's Coll Cambridge (BA), Univ of Warwick (MA), Princeton Univ (PhD); *m* 1974, Rita Goldberg; 2 s; *Career* lectr in economics Univ of Essex 1974–75, asst lectr then lectr in economics Univ of Cambridge 1975–81, fell Churchill Coll Cambridge 1975–81; prof of economics: LSE 1981–85 (centennial visiting prof 1997–), MIT 1985–93, Harvard Univ 1993– (Andrew E Furer prof of economics 1997–); visiting Scholar Harvard Law Sch 1987–88, Marvin Bower fell Harvard Business Sch 1988–89; memb: Coordinating Ctee Social Sci Res Cncl Econ Theory Study Gp UK 1975–79, Prog Ctee Fourth World Congress of the Econometric Soc 1980, Editorial Advsy Bd Review of Econ Studies 1975–88, Editorial Advsy Bd Cambridge Surveys of Economic Literature Cup 1984–90, Cncl Econometric Soc 1983–89 (memb Exec Ctee at large 1984–87), Nat Sci Fndn Economics Panel 1987–, Advsy Cncl Princeton Univ Economics Dept 1989–97, vice-pres American Economic Assoc 2006, pres American Law and Economics Assoc 2006–07; assoc ed: Jl of Economic Theory 1976–79, Econometrica 1984–87, Games and Economic Behaviour 1988–, Jl of Accounting Auditing and Finance 1989–; ed Review of Economic Studies 1979–83 (asst ed 1978–79), prog dir Centre for Econ Policy Res London 1983–84, res assoc Nat Bureau of Econ Res 1990–; sec-treas American Law and Economics Assoc 2004–05; Dr (hc): Free Univ of Brussels 1992, Univ of Basel 1994, Univ of Paris-Dauphine 2009, Copenhagen Business Sch 2009; Hon DSc London Business Sch 2011, Hon LLD Univ of Warwick 2012; fell: Econometric Soc 1979, American Acad of Arts and Scis 1988, American Finance Assoc 2016; corresponding FBA 2000; *Books* Firms, Contracts, and Financial Structure (1995); also author of numerous articles and chapters in various books; *Recreations* playing and watching tennis, swimming, playing the piano; *Style*— Prof Oliver Hart; ✉ Littauer 220, Department of Economics, Harvard University, Cambridge, Mass 02138, USA

HART, Simon Anthony; MP; *b* 15 August 1963; *m* Abigail; 2 c; *Career* chief exec Countryside Alliance 2003–10; MP (Cons) Carmarthen W and Pembrokeshire S 2010–; *Style*— Simon Hart, MP; ✉ House of Commons, London SW1A 0AA

HART, Stefa Belitis; da of Vladimir Georgief Daskaloff (d 1995), and Helen Brookes, *née* Bremner (d 1968); *b* 10 March 1949, Gibraltar; *Educ* Convent of the Sacred Heart Hove, Branston Coll, V&A (Dip); *m* 17 April 1974, Timothy Frederick Hart, *qv*; 3 s (Sam Kinsford, Edward George, James Harry); *Career* interior designer; sec to librarian Royal Instn 1969, sec to Christopher Selmes and Richard Jacobs 1969–70, asst to Marcel d'Argy Smith (as ed The Antiques Year Book) 1971–72, Galerie Altman Paris 1972–73; dir and interior designer Hambleton Hall Hotel Rutland 1980–, estab Hambleton Decorating 1988, dir and interior designer Hart's Hotel Nottingham 2003–, dir Fino's Restaurant London 2003–; former pres Rutland Macmillan Cancer Support, pres For Rutland in Rutland 2014; *Recreations* painting, walking, stalking, fishing, gardening, music; *Style*— Mrs Stefa Hart

HART, Timothy Frederick (Tim); DL (Rutland 2013); s of Louis Albert Hart (d 1977), of Dynes Hall, Halstead, Essex, and Theresa Elsie Hart (d 1994); *b* 7 December 1947; *Educ* Westminster, Jesus Coll Cambridge (MA); *m* Stefa Belitis, *qv*, da of Vladimir Daskaloff; 3 s (Samuel b Sept 1974, Edward b Aug 1976, James b March 1982); *Career* Henry Ansbacher and Co 1969–73, Lehman Brothers Inc 1974–79; purchased Hambleton Hall 1979 (opened as Country House Hotel 1980); fndr chm and chief exec Hart Hambleton Ltd 1986, purchased and redeveloped Ram Jam Inn 1986, opened Hart's restaurant Nottingham 1997, opened Hart's Hotel 2003, opened Hambleton Bakery 2008; chm Br Section of Relais et Chateaux 1987–90; govr Oakham Sch 1990–; *Recreations* shooting, fishing, gastronomy, oenology, literature, gardening, deer stalking, tree climbing; *Style*— Tim Hart, Esq, DL; ✉ Hart Hambleton plc, Hambleton Hall, Hambleton, Oakham, Rutland LE15 8TH (☎ 01572 756991, fax 01572 724721)

HART OF CHILTON, Baron (Life Peer UK 2004), of Chilton in the County of Suffolk; Garry Richard Rushby Hart; s of Dennis George Hart (d 1984), and Evelyn Mary, *née* Rushby; *b* 29 June 1940; *Educ* Northgate GS Ipswich, UCL (LLB); *m* 1, 24 March 1966 (m dis 1986), Paula Lesley, da of Leslie Shepherd; 2 s (Hon Alexander, Hon Jonathan), 1 da (Hon Kaley); m 2, 1986, Valerie Elen Mary, da of Cledwyn Wilson Davies; 2 da (Hon Sarah, Hon Stephanie (twins)); *Career* slr; ptnr Herbert Smith 1970–98 (head Property Dept 1988–98); special advsr to: Lord Chllr 1998–2003, Sec of State for Constitutional Affrs and Lord Chllr 2003–07, Sec of State for Justice 2007; memb Jt Ctee of the House of Lords and the House of Commons on the Draft Constitutional Renewal Bill Session 2007–08, memb House of Lords Select Ctee on the Merits of Statutory Instruments 2008–13, memb House of Lords Select Ctee on the Constitution 2009–14, memb House of Lords Ldrs Gp on the Conduct for Members of the House of Lords 2009, memb House of Lords Appointments Cmmn 2010–, memb Select Ctee on Extradition 2014–15; chllr Univ of Greenwich 2008–14; memb Building Strategy Ctee V&A 2007–; dep chm of tstees Architecture Fndn 1997–2005, tstee Almeida Theatre Islington 1997–2005 (chm 1997–2002), tstee Br Architectural Library Tst 2001–10, vice-patron Ipswich Soc for the Blind; fell UCL (memb Cncl 2004–10); Freeman City of London, Liveryman Worshipful Co of Slrs; Hon LLD Univ of Greenwich 2014; memb Law Soc 1966; FRSA, Hon FRIBA; *Books* Blundell and Dobrys Planning Applications Appeals and Proceedings (jtly, 5 edn); *Recreations* conservation, theatre, talking and travel; *Clubs* Beefsteak, Garrick; *Style*— The Rt Hon the Lord Hart of Chilton; ✉ 36 Alwyne Road, London N1 2HW

HART-DAVIS, (Peter) Duff; s of Sir Rupert Hart-Davis (d 1999), of Marske-in-Swaledale, N Yorks, and Comfort Borden, *née* Turner (d 1970); *b* 3 June 1936; *Educ* Eton, Univ of Oxford (BA); *m* 1961, Phyllida, da of Col John Barstow; 1 s (Guy b 1965), 1 da (Alice b 1963); *Career* journalist and author; graduate trainee Western Mail Cardiff 1960; Sunday Telegraph: asst to Literary Ed 1961–63, ed Close-Up (news background) team 1968–70, literary ed 1976–77, asst ed 1977–78, editorial advsr 1980–85; contrib Country Matters column The Independent 1986–2001; *Novels* The Megacull (1968), The Gold of St Matthew (1970), Spider in the Morning (1972), The Heights of Rimring (1980), Level Five (1982), Fire Falcon (1983), The Man-Eater of Jassapur (1985), Horses of War (1991); *Non-fiction* Peter Fleming (1974), Ascension (1976), Monarchs of the Glen (1978), Hitler's Games (1986), The Letters and Journals of Sir Alan Lascelles (ed 2 vols, 1986 and 1988), Armada (1988), Country Matters (1989), The House the Berrys Built (1990), Wildings: the Secret Garden of Eileen Soper (1991), Further Country Matters (1992), When the Country Went to Town (1997), Raoul Millais (1998), Fauna Britannica (2002), Audubon's Elephant (2003), Pavilions of Splendour (ed, 2004), Honorary Tiger (2006), King's Counsellor: Abdication and War – the Diaries of Tommy Lascelles (ed, 2006), Philip de László: His Life and Art (2010), The War That Never Was (2011), Among the Deer (2011), Man of War (2012), Our Land at War (2015); *Recreations* opera, gardening, deer, splitting wood; *Style*— Duff Hart-Davis, Esq

HARTILL, Edward Theodore (Ted); OBE (2004); s of Clement Augustus Hartill (d 2001), of Salop, and Florence Margarita, *née* Ford (d 1989); *b* 23 January 1943, Stoke on Trent; *Educ* Priory Sch for Boys Shrewsbury, Coll of Estate Mgmnt, Univ of London (BSc); *m* 1, 2 s (Jeremy Alexander b 1969, Richard Marcus b 1972); m 2, 4 April 1975, Gillian Ruth, da of Harold Todd (d 1963); 2 s (Andrew Julius b 1977, Giles Simeon b 1981); *Career* joined Messrs Burd and Evans Land Agents Shrewsbury 1963; Estates Dept Legal and Gen Assurance Society 1964–73, Property Investment Dept Guardian Royal Exchange Assurance Gp 1973–85, The City Surveyor City of London Corp 1985–2008, business devpt advsr Corderoy (int chartered quantity surveyors and cost conslts) 2008 (subsequently conslt); visiting lectr in law of town planning and compulsory purchase Hammersmith and West London Coll of Advanced Business Studies 1968–78; memb Govt Study Team on Professional Liability 1988–89; RICS: memb Gen Practice Divnl Cncl 1989–97, memb Governing Cncl 1990–2004, pres Gen Practice Div 1992–93, hon treas 2000–04; Construction Industry Standing Conference (CISC): memb Steering Ctee 1992–99, chm Property Services Sub-Gp; chm Property Services Nat Trg Organisation 1999–2004; Asset Skills: chm 2003–04, vice-chm 2004–07; Univ of London: memb Cncl 2004–08, memb Estates Ctee 2004–08 (dep chm 2006–08), chm Senate House Project Bd 2006–15, memb Bd of Tstees 2008–15, memb Investments Ctee 2008–15 (dep chm 2009–15), memb Bd of Tstees Univ Marine Biological Station 2008–13 (dep chm 2009–13), chm Safety Ctee 2009–15, memb Estates Sub-Gp Univ of London 2014– (actg chm 2014–15); hon memb Assoc of Chief Estates Surveyors and Property Managers in Local Govt 2007– (memb 1985–2007, memb Nat Cncl 1988–2007, pres 1996–97); govr and tstee Coram 2006–14 (vice-chm 2007–08, chm 2008–14, hon vice pres 2014–); memb Br Schs Exploring Soc; hon assoc Czech Chamber of Appraisers; former hon memb Investment Property Forum; Master Worshipful Company of Chartered Surveyors 2003–04 (Liveryman 1985–, memb Ct of Assts 1991–2009); FRICS, life fell RSA; *Recreations* travel, watching GT racing; *Style*— E T Hartill Esq, OBE; ✉ 215 Sheen Lane, East Sheen, London SW14 8LE (☎ 020 8878 4494, e-mail ted.hartill23@gmail.com)

HARTILL, Rosemary Jane; da of Clement Augustus Hartill (d 2001), of Salop, and Florence Margarita, *née* Ford (d 1989); *b* 11 August 1949; *Educ* Wellington Girls' HS, Univ of Bristol (BA); *Career* ed Tom Stacey Ltd 1970–73, jr ed David & Charles 1973–75, sr non-fiction ed Hamish Hamilton Children's Books 1975–76, freelance dance and book reviewer Times Education Supplement 1976–79, BBC religious affrs corr 1982–88 (reporter 1979–82), reporter Human Factor (ITV) 1988–92; presenter of progs incl: Woman's Hour (BBC Radio 4, NE editions) 1989–91, Meridian Books (BBC World Service); independent broadcaster and writer; co-fndr Voyager Television Ltd 1997, fndr Rosemary Hartill and Assoc independent radio productions 1996–; series for BBC World Service incl: Wisdom of the World 1997, Stories from the Afterlife 1998, Practical Peacemaking 1998, Just Business? 1999, Dreamtime Dreams 1999, Write Inside 2001, Healing the Wounds of War 2002; occasional presenter Something Understood (BBC Radio 4) 2004–08; Sony Award nominations for: Best Radio Reporter of the Year 1988, Best Arts Feature 1990; Sandford St Martin Tst prizes 1992, 1994 and 1998 (incl personal award for outstanding contrib to religious broadcasting 1994), various other awards and nominations; dir: Ethical Investment Research and Information Service 1996–2001, Shared Interest 1997–2005; memb Bd: Nat Probation Serv Northumberland 2001–07, Northumberland Tyne & Wear SHA 2002–05; memb: Courts Bd Northumbria 2004–07, Youth Justice Bd for England and Wales 2004–08; ldr Barter Books Bookgroups 2003–, memb Mgmnt Gp Newcastle Conflict Resolution Network 2008–15; tstee Alternatives to Violence Project 1998–2001 (facilitator 1996–); memb Soc of Friends; Hon DLitt: Univ of Hull 1995, Univ of Bristol 2000; FRSA 2001; *Books* Wild Animals, Emily Brontë – Poems (ed), In Perspective, Writers Revealed, Were You There?, Florence Nightingale: Letters and Reflections (ed); *Recreations* wildlife, walking, theatre, art exhibitions, being in Northumberland; *Style*— Rosemary Hartill

HARTLAND, Michael; *see:* James, Michael Leonard

HARTLEY, Dr David Fielding; s of Robert Maude Hartley (d 1980), of Hebden Bridge, W Yorks, and Sheila Ellen, *née* Crabtree (d 1977); *b* 14 September 1937, Halifax, Yorks; *Educ* Rydal Sch, Clare Coll Cambridge (MA, PhD); *m* 23 April 1960, Joanna Mary (d 1998), da of John Stanley Bolton (d 1988), of Halifax; 2 da (Caroline (Mrs Eatough) b 1963, Rosalind (Mrs Fell) b 1968), 1 s (Timothy b 1965); *Career* Univ of Cambridge: sr asst in res 1964–65, jr res fell Churchill Coll 1964–67, asst dir of res 1966–67, lectr Mathematical Laboratory 1967–70, dir computing serv 1970–94, fell Darwin Coll 1969–86, fell Clare Coll 1987–; chief exec UK Educn and Research Networking Assoc 1994–97, exec dir Cambridge Crystallographic Data Centre 1997–2002, steward Clare Coll Cambridge 2002–05; dir: NAG Ltd 1979–2006 (chm 1986–97), Lynxvale Ltd 1982–94, CAD Centre Ltd 1983–94; memb: Computer Bd for Univs and Res Cncls 1979–83, PM's Info Technol Advsy Panel 1981–86, BBC Sci Consultative Gp 1984–87, pres Br Computer Soc 1999–2000 (vice-pres 1984–90, dep pres 1998–99), chm Computer Conservation Soc 2007–11, museum dir Nat Museum of Computing 2012–13; Freeman: City of London 1988, Co of Info Technologists 1988; FBCS 1967, CEng 1990; Medal of Merits Nicholas Copernicus Univ Poland 1984; *Style*— Dr David Hartley; ✉ Clare College, Cambridge CB2 1TL (☎ 01223 333200, e-mail david.hartley@clare.cam.ac.uk)

HARTLEY, Prof Frank Robinson; DL (Beds 2005); s of Sir Frank Hartley, CBE (d 1997), and Lydia May, *née* England (d 1996); *b* 29 January 1942; *Educ* KCS Wimbledon, Magdalen Coll Oxford (MA, DPhil, DSc); *m* 1, 12 Dec 1964, Valerie (d 2005), da of George Peel (d 1984); 3 da (Susan b 1967, Judith b 1971, Elizabeth b 1974); m 2, 23 Sept 2009, Charmaine, da of Norman Thrift (d 1994); *Career* res fell Div of Protein Chem CSIRO (Aust) 1966–69, ICI res fell and tutor in chem UCL 1969–70, lectr in chem Univ of Southampton 1970–75, princ and dean RMCS 1982–89 (prof of chem 1975–82), vice-chllr Cranfield Univ 1989–2006 (emeritus prof 2007–); chm: CIM Technology Ltd 1990–2006, CIT Holdings Ltd 1990–2006; md Cranfield Ventures Ltd 1990–2006; dir: Beds TEC 1994–96, Shuttleworth Tst 1994–97; non-exec dir: T & N plc 1989–98, Eastern Regnl Bd National Westminster Bank plc 1990–92, Kalon plc 1994–99, Kenwood Appliances plc 1995–99, Hunting-BRAE Ltd 1999–2000; special advsr to PM on Defence Systems 1988–90, memb Parly Scientific Ctee 1987–2006 (Cncl 1992–98, vice-pres 1996–98), memb Cncl IOD 2000–09, memb Eastern Region Bd CBI 2000–06; Sr Cncl for Devon 2008–14; chm: Lorch Fndn 1995–2006, Teignmouth branch Devon Sr Voice 2008–13, Teignmouth and Dawlish Ramblers; Oxon Soc of Rugby Football Referees; RFU touch judge; fell KCS Wimbledon 2003; FRSC 1977, FRSA 1988, CIMgt 1991, FRAeS 1996; *Books* Chemistry of Platinum and Palladium (1973), Elements of Organometallic Chemistry (1974), Solution Equilibria (1980), Supported Metal Complexes (1985), Chemistry of the Metal-Carbon Bond (vol 1 1983, vol 2 1984, vol 3 1985, vol 4 1987, vol 5 1989), Chemistry of Organphosphorus Compounds (vol 1 1990, vol 2 1992, vol 3 1994, vol 4 1996), Chemistry of the Platinum Group Metals (1991); *Recreations* swimming, walking, reading, gardening; *Clubs* Shrivenham; *Style*— Prof Frank Hartley, DL; ✉ 7 St Scholasticas, Abbey Mount, New Road, Teignmouth, Devon TQ14 8FF (e-mail f.r.hartley@cranfield.ac.uk)

HARTLEY, Julian Matthew Frederick; s of Max Hartley, of Bingley, W Yorks, and Rosalind, *née* Gill; *b* 24 February 1967, Keighley, W Yorks; *Educ* Bingley GS, Univ of Durham (BA, MBA), Univ of Cambridge (PGCE), Open Univ, Nuffield Inst Univ of Leeds (Cert); *m* 24 May 1997, Karina, *née* Wood; 1 da (Lydia b 22 Nov 1999), 1 s (Max Peter b 4 Oct 2002); *Career* teacher King Edward VI Sch Morpeth 1989–91, nat trainee NHS general mgmt training scheme 1991–93, planning mangr South Durham HA 1993–94, planning and mktg mangr South Tees Acute Hosps NHS Tst 1994–95, dep head of devpt Northern and Yorks regnl office NHS Exec 1995–99, asst dir planning and devpt Newcastle upon Tyne Hosps NHS Tst 1999–2000, dir of acute servs, planning and devpt North Tees and Hartlepool NHS Tst 2000–02, chief exec Tameside and Glossop PCT 2002–05, chief exec Blackpool Fylde and Wyre Hosps NHS Tst 2005–09, chief exec Univ Hosp of South Manchester NHS Fndn Tst 2009–12, md NHS Improving Quality 2012–, chief exec Leeds Teaching Hosps 2013–; *Recreations* Manchester United FC, theatre, literature, film; *Style*— Julian Hartley, Esq; ✉ Leeds Teaching Hospitals, St James Hospital, Leeds (e-mail julianhartley@nhs.uk)

HARTLEY, Keith; s of Albert Hartley, MBE (d 1991), and Joan Winifred, *née* Dixson (d 1973); *b* 11 October 1956; *Educ* Chislehurst & Sidcup GS for Boys, KCL (LLB), Coll of Law; *m* 1986, Barbara Elizabeth Rundle-Smith, da of Capt Arthur Edmund Smith; 1 s (Dominic Edward b 23 Nov 1993), 1 da (Elena Joan b 28 Dec 1997); *Career* admitted slr 1982; Masons (now Pinsent Masons): articled clerk 1980–82, slr London 1982–84, Hong Kong office 1984–95 (ptnr 1986–2010), Leeds office 1995–2010; ptnr Reed Smith LLP 2010–; memb: Law Soc Hong Kong 1984, Inst of Arbitrators 1987, Asia Pacific Lawyers Assoc 1990; *Recreations* history, computing, family; *Style*— Keith Hartley, Esq

HARTLEY, Prof Keith; s of W Hartley, of Leeds, and Ivy, *née* Stead; *b* 14 July 1940; *Educ* Univ of Hull (BA, PhD); *m* 12 April 1966, Winifred; 1 s (Adam b 27 Feb 1969), 2 da (Lucy b 18 Oct 1970, Cecilia b 20 July 1975); *Career* Univ of York: dir Inst for Research in Social Scis 1982–94, prof of economics 1987–2008, fndr dir Centre for Defence Economics 1990–2008, emeritus prof 2008–; visiting prof: Univ of Illinois, Univ of Malaysia, Univ of NSW; *Books* Economics of Defency Policy (2011), Economics of Conflict (jtly, 2011), The Political Economy of Aerospace Industries (2014); *Recreations* angling, football, walking, reading; *Style*— Prof Keith Hartley; ✉ Economics Department, University of York, York YO10 5DD (☎ 01904 433784, telex 01904 433759, e-mail kh2@york.ac.uk)

HARTMANN, Dr Reinhard Rudolf Karl; s of Walther Eduard Hartmann, of Vienna, Austria, and Gerta Emilia Stanislawa, *née* Müllner; *b* 8 April 1938; *Educ* Vienna GS, Vienna Sch of Economics (BSc and Doctorate), Univ of Vienna (Dip Translation), Southern Illinois Univ (MA); *m* 22 June 1965, Lynn, da of Kingston Vernon Warren, of Droylsden, Manchester; 1 da (Nasim b 1965), 1 s (Stefan b 1967); *Career* lectr in modern languages UMIST 1964–68, lectr in applied linguistics Univ of Nottingham 1968–74; Univ of Exeter: sr lectr in applied linguistics 1974–91, dir Language Centre 1974–92, dir Dictionary Res Centre 1984–2001, reader in applied linguistics 1991– (Sch of English 1996–2001), head Dept of Applied Linguistics 1992–96; hon prof Dept of English Univ of Birmingham 2000–12, visiting prof and hon univ fell Sch of English Univ of Exeter 2001–09; memb: Br Assoc for Applied Linguistics (BAAL) 1967, Euro Assoc for Lexicography (EURALEX) 1983 (fndr memb, former sec and pres, hon life memb 1994), Dictionary Soc of N America (DSNA) 1984, Asian Assoc for Lexicography (ASIALEX) 1997; *Books* Dictionary of Language and Linguistics (jtly, 1972), Contrastive Textology (1980), Lexicography Principles and Practice (ed, 1983), LEXeter '83 Proceedings (ed, 1984), The History of Lexicography (ed, 1986), Lexicography in Africa (ed, 1990), The English Language in Europe (ed, 1996), Solving Language Problems (ed, 1996), Dictionary of Lexicography (jtly, 1998 and 2001, Chinese translation 2000, Japanese translation 2003), Oxford Dictionary of National Biography (assoc ed 1998–2004), Annotated Bibliography for English Studies (assoc ed 1998–2004), Dictionaries in Language Learning (ed, 1999), Teaching and Researching Lexicography (2001), Lexicography – Critical Concepts (ed, 2003), Dictionaries across Cultures (2004), Interlingual Lexicography (2007); *Recreations* listening to music, yoga, table tennis; *Style*— Dr Reinhard Hartmann; ✉ 40 Velwell Road, Exeter EX4 4LD (e-mail r.r.k.hartmann@exeter.ac.uk)

HARTNELL, Dr George Gordon; s of Francis George Hartnell (d 1996), and Margaret, *née* Gordon; *b* 19 July 1952; *Educ* Abingdon Sch, Univ of Bristol (BSc, MB ChB); *m* 1998, Dr Julia Gates; *Career* registrar in cardiology Harefield Hosp 1979–81, registrar and sr registrar Royal Postgrad Med Sch Hammersmith Hosp London 1983–87, formerly dir of cardiovascular and interventional radiology Beth Israel Deaconess Medical Center Boston and assoc prof Harvard Med Sch, head of cardiovascular and interventional radiology Baystate Medical Center and prof of radiology Tufts Univ Sch of Med 2000–08, dir of vascular and special interventions Cooley Dickinson Hospital MA 2008–; author of over 400 original papers, book chapters and review articles; FRCR 1987, fell American Coll of Cardiology 1992, fell Soc of Interventional Radiology 1992, FRCP 2008 (MRCP 1982); *Publications* Film Viewing – Cardiovascular System (1990), SCVIR Syllabus 8: Noninvasive Vascular Imaging with Ultrasound, Computed Tomography and Magnetic Resonance (jt ed, 1997); *Recreations* sailing, skiing; *Style*— Dr George Hartnell; ✉ Vascular and Special Interventions, Cooley Dickinson Hospital, 30 Locust Street, Northampton MA 01061, USA (☎ 00 1 413 582 2554)

HARTNETT, Angela; MBE (2007); *b* 5 September 1968; *Educ* Cambridge Poly (BA); *Career* chef; Midsummer House Cambridge 1991–93, Tamarind Cove Barbados 1993–94, Aubergine London 1994–95, L'Oranger London 1996–98, Pétrus London 1999–2001, Verre Dubai Creek Hilton 2001–02; chef and patron: Angela Hartnett at The Connaught 2002–07 (winner Best New Restaurant BMW Square Meal Award 2003, Michelin Star 2004), Murano 2008– (Michelin Star), York and Albany 2008–; *Recreations* cinema, reading, gym; *Style*— Ms Angela Hartnett, MBE

HARTY, Bernard Peter; CBE (1998); s of William Harty (d 1975), and Eileen Nora, *née* Canavan; *b* 1 May 1943; *Educ* St Richard's Coll Droitwich, Ullathorne GS Coventry; *m* 12 Aug 1965, Glenys Elaine, da of Ernest Simpson (d 1969); 1 da (Sarah Jane b 1970); *Career* accountant Coventry City Cncl 1961–69; forward budget planning offr Derbys CC 1969–72, chief accountant Bradford City Cncl 1972–73, chief fin offr Bradford Met DC 1973–76, co treas Oxfordshire CC 1976–83, Chamberlain Corp of London 1983–95, md Barbican Centre 1994–95, town clerk and chamberlain Corp of London 1996–99; chm and non-exec dir Dexia Municipal Bank 1993–2000; chm: London Pension Fund Authy 1999–2001, Imerys (UK) Pension Fund 1999–2008, London Processing Centre Retirement and Death Benefit Scheme 2000–03; sometime chm: Fndn for IT in Local Govt, Superannuation Investment Panel and Treasy Mgmnt Panel Chartered Inst of Public Fin Accountants; parish cncllr Charlton Kings Cheltenham 2006–10; Liveryman Worshipful Co of Tallow Chandlers, fndr memb and Hon Liveryman Worshipful Co of Information Technologists; Hon PhD London Guildhall Univ 1997; CPFA 1966; Cdr Order of Merit (France) 1996; *Recreations* National Trust, music, cricket, theatre; *Style*— Bernard Harty, Esq, CBE; ✉ e-mail bernardharty@aol.com

HARVARD TAYLOR, Nicholas; s of Paul Harvard Taylor (d 1980), and Esmèe Mary, *née* Biggs (d 1980); *b* 4 December 1952; *Educ* Haileybury and ISC; *m* Tessa Ann Harvard Taylor, JP, *née* Morris; 2 c (Jack Alfred, Katie Esmée (twins) b 3 Oct 1989); *Career* chm and ceo Harvard Marketing Services 1981– (fndr 1979); chm: Harvard Public Relations Ltd 1982–; memb British Red Cross Soc; Freeman City of London, Liveryman Worshipful Co of Merchant Taylors; FRSA; *Recreations* classic cars, tennis, keeping a lawn, favourite outdoor sport is the same as indoor sport but with his coat on; *Clubs* Foxhills Country; *Style*— Nicholas Harvard Taylor, Esq; ✉ Kenwolde Manor, Callow Hill, Virginia Water, Surrey GU25 4LF

HARVERSON, Paddy; LVO (2013); *Educ* LSE; *Career* FT: stock market reporter 1988–89, economics staff writer 1989–90, NY corr 1990–95, business reporter 1995–97, sports corr 1997–2000; dir of communications Manchester United FC 2000–04, communications sec to TRH The Prince of Wales and The Duchess of Cornwall 2004–12, co-fndr and managing ptnr Milltown Ptnrs 2013–; *Style*— Paddy Harverson, Esq, LVO; ✉ Milltown Partners, 22 Cross Keys Close, London W1U 2DW

HARVEY, Prof Andrew Charles; *b* 10 September 1947; *Educ* Leeds Modern Sch, Univ of York (BA), LSE (MSc); *Career* economist/statistician Central Bureau of Statistics Kenya 1969–71, lectr in economic and social statistics Univ of Kent 1971–77; LSE: sr lectr 1978–80, reader 1980–84, prof 1984–96; prof of econometrics Univ of Cambridge and fell Corpus Christi Coll Cambridge 1996–; fell Econometric Soc 1985, FBA 1999; *Books* The Econometric Analysis of Time Series (1981), Time Series Models (1981), Forecasting, Structural Time Series Models and the Kalman Filter (1989), Dynamic Models for Volatility and Heavy Tails (2013); *Recreations* football, opera, walking; *Style*— Prof Andrew Harvey; ✉ Corpus Christi College, Cambridge CB2 1RH (☎ 01223 335228, fax 01223 335475, e-mail ach34@cam.ac.uk)

HARVEY, Andrew Quested; s of David Quested Harvey, of Nottingham, and Merle Roslyn Harvey (d 2002); *b* 29 May 1962, Stourbridge, W Midlands; *Educ* Annie Holgate Technical GS Nottingham, Manchester Business Sch; 25 June 2011, Sean Brian Harvey, *né* Rodgerson (civil partnership converted); *Career* mktg dir Dickinson Dees LLP 2009–13; chair Chartered Inst of Mktg 2012–14 (memb Bd 2007–14, vice-chair 2008–12), chm European Mktg Confederation 2013– (memb Bd 2008–, vice-chair 2008–13); mktg dir Vail Williams LLP 2014–16; chair Queen's Hall Arts 2016– (memb Bd 2015–); memb Bd Northumbria Students' Union 2016–; FCIM, FRSA; *Recreations* cinema, music, reading, travel; *Style*— Andrew Harvey, Esq; ✉ 1 Bingfield Cottages, Bingfield, Hexham NE46 4HT (e-mail aharvey@emc.be, Twitter @questedh)

HARVEY, Caroline; *see:* Trollope, Joanna

HARVEY, Prof David Robertson; s of Capt John Harvey (d 1983), of New Milton, Hants, and Ann, *née* Dodgson; *b* 24 October 1947; *Educ* Berkhamsted Sch, Univ of Newcastle upon Tyne (BSc), Univ of Manchester (MA, PhD); *m* 1 (m dis 1984), Cathryn, *née* Whitehead; 2 s (Daniel b 1975, James b 1977); m 2, 9 April 1985, Joan, da of John Hayward, of Ripon, N Yorks; 1 s (John b 1985); *Career* asst lectr Univ of Manchester 1972–73, sr agric economist Agriculture Canada (Ottawa) 1977–79 (agric economist 1973–76), lectr Univ of Newcastle 1979–83; prof: Univ of Reading 1984–86, Univ of Newcastle 1986– (head Dept of Agric Economics and Food Mktg 1992–97); memb Nat Ctee SDP 1983–87; pres Agricultural Economics Soc 2004; *Books* Costs of The Common Agricultural Policy (1982), The CAP and the World Economy (1 ed 1991, 2 ed 1997); *Style*— Prof David Harvey; ✉ School of Agriculture, Food and Rural Development, The University, Newcastle upon Tyne NE1 7RU (☎ 0191 222 6872, fax 0191 222 6720, e-mail david.harvey@ncl.ac.uk)

HARVEY, Gillian Elizabeth (Gill); da of Albert George Harvey (d 1995), and Phyllis Maria, *née* Howell (d 2016); *b* 5 April 1957, Swansea; *Educ* Central St Martin's Sch of Art (BA, Queen Mary's Award for Design), RCA (MDes, Babycham Sparkle Costume Design Prize); *Partner* Adam Sweeting; *Career* fashion designer; head designer Medici Collections LIM Int Ltd 1981–92, design dir Medici 1992–; ranges incl: Decisions, Medici, Medici Sport, Gina, After Six International, Invite, Medici Casual, Devout Denim, After Six OK Red Carpet Collection, Eliza Jane Howell Bridal Collection 2012–, Gill Harvey Collection 2012–; Best Mother of the Bride Collection Bridal Buyer Awards 2014, Best Designer British Wedding Awards 2016, Best Bridal Designer UK Wedding Awards 2016; *Recreations* cooking, cats, opera, theatre, St Barts in hurricane season, marathon running (ran first London marathon in 4 hours 19 minutes and 53 seconds, in 2009), cricket; *Style*— Miss Gill Harvey; ✉ website www.gillharvey.com; Eliza Jane Howell, 15 Connaught Street, London W2 2AY (☎ 020 7436 2882, e-mail info@gillharvey.com, website www.gillharvey.com); Medici Ltd (☎ 020 7436 2882, fax 020 7436 3113, e-mail mediciltd@aol.com, website www.medicigroup.co.uk, www.aftersixcollection.com, www.aftersixokredcarpet.com, www.mediciboutique.com and www.elizajanehowell.com)

HARVEY, Guy Landor; s of Paul William Harvey, of Chichester, W Sussex, and Elizabeth Jonet, *née* Roberts (d 2003); *b* 26 February 1951, Harpenden, Herts; *Educ* Stowe (open scholar), Trinity Coll Cambridge (BA); *m* 27 Sept 1980, Henrietta Jane Almond, *née* Gibson; 1 da (Celia b 7 Feb 1984), 1 s (George b 15 July 1987); *Career* slr Simpson Curtis Leeds 1976–96 (ptnr 1978), ptnr Dickinson Dees 1997–2009, ptnr Shepherd and Wedderburn LLP 2009–; dir Landor Records Ltd 2004–, dir Landor Prodns Ltd 2007–13, dir CMF Records Ltd 2014–; memb Law Soc 1976, FRSA; *Recreations* music, arts, France; *Style*— Guy Harvey, Esq; ✉ Shepherd and Wedderburn LLP, Condor House, 10 St Paul's Churchyard, London EC4M 8AL (☎ 020 7429 4900, fax 020 7329 5939, e-mail guy.harvey@shepwedd.co.uk)

HARVEY, Ian Alexander; s of Dr Alexander Harvey (d 1987), and Mona (d 2004), *née* Anderson; *b* 2 February 1945; *Educ* Cardiff HS, Univ of Cambridge (MA), Harvard Business Sch (MBA); *m* 21 Nov 1976, Dr DeAnne Julius, CBE, *qv*, da of Prof Marvin Julius, of Ames, Iowa, USA; 1 da (Megan b 1979), 1 s (Ross b 1980); *Career* apprentice mech engr Vickers Ltd 1963–69, project engr Laporte Industries 1969–73, sr loan offr World Bank 1975–82, ptnr Logan Associates Inc 1984–85, dir Process Automative and Computer Systems (PACS) 1985–92, chief exec BTG plc (formerly British Technology Group Ltd) 1985–2004; dir Primaxis Technol Ventures Inc 1999–2004, advsr NTEM Tianjin China 2005–, memb Global Advsy Bd Innoveas AG 2009–; chm: Intellectual Property Inst 1999–2011, Intellectual Property Advsy Ctee 2001–05; memb: PM's Advsy Cncl on Sci and Technol 1989–93, Research and Mfrg Ctee CBI 1986–92, Advsy Bd Science Policy Research Unit Univ of Sussex 1988–2003, PPARC Cncl Appointments Ctee 1999–2008, CCMI Companions Bd 1999–, Air Products & Chemicals Inc European Advsy Cncl 1999–2005, Centre for Intellectual Property Chalmers Univ Gothenberg, Advsy Bd Int Intellectual Property Inst Washington DC 2004–, Policy Ctee Cancer Research UK 2004–06, Bd London Bioscience Innovation Centre 2007–; chm Advsy Bd Tsinghua Univ IP Center Beijing; fell Univ of Nottingham 1994, adjunct prof Imperial Coll Business Sch London 2004–; Hon LLD Univ of Wolverhampton 2006; CCMI 1987–2013; FRSA 1997–2008; *Publications* China Dialogue (2008), Myths and Legends (2008), Technology in a Warming World, Technology and IP- Problems and Solutions, IP and a Low-carbon Economy, Do intellectual property rights stimulate or threaten innovation? Europe's World (2014), Intellectual Property: China in the global economy- myth and reality (2014), Breaking the Climate Deadlock (2014), Briefing Paper: Intellectual Property Rights – The Catalyst to Deliver Low Carbon Technologies (2014) Tony Blair and The Climate Group (2014); numerous articles and book chapters related to IP, innovation and China; *Recreations* piano, skiing, sailing, kayaking, scuba diving, mountain walking; *Style*— Ian Harvey

HARVEY, Prof Jake; *b* 3 June 1948; *Educ* Edinburgh Coll of Art (DA); *Career* sculptor; currently head of sculpture Edinburgh Coll of Art; memb: Scottish Soc of Artists 1975, Fedn of Scottish Sculptors 1983; tstee Scottish Sculpture Tst 1984–87; RSA 1989 (ARSA 1977); *Solo Exhibitions* incl: NORTH (Pier Arts Centre, Stromness Artspace and Peacock Printmakers Aberdeen) 1993, Scottish Gallery Edinburgh 1993, Retrospective (Talbot Rice Gallery Univ of Edinburgh) 1993, Recent Works (Christopher Boyd Gallery Galashiels) 1994, Ground (Crystal Gallery Japan) 1998, Residency (Iwate Art Festival Japan) 1998, The Early Imagist Works (Motherwell Heritage Centre) 1998, Nat Museum of Scotland 1999, Signifier (Art First London) 1999; *Group Exhibitions* incl: RSA Award Winners (Artspace Aberdeen) 1980, Built in Scotland (Third Eye Centre, City Arts Centre Edinburgh and Camden Arts Centre London) 1983, Putting Sculpture on the Map (Talbot Rice Art Centre) 1984, Dublin/Edinburgh (Edinburgh Coll of Art) 1985, Works on Paper (RSA Edinburgh) 1990, Scottish Art in the 20th Century (Royal W of England Acad Bristol) 1990, Scottish Scupture Open (Kildrummy Castle Aberdeen) 1991, Virtue and Vision Festival Exhbn (Nat Gallery of Scotland) 1991, William Gillies Bursary Exhbn (RSA) 1992, A Collection of Self-Portraits (Pier Art Centre Stromness) 1994, The Art of the Garden (Greywalls, Scottish Gallery) 1994, Scandex (Aberdeen Art Gallery and Norway, Sweden and Finland) 1995, Jake Harvey Sculpture (Aikwood Tower Selkirk) 1995, A Battle for Hearts and Minds (Robson Gallery Selkirk) 1995, Art First (London) 1996, Transistors (Hashimoto Art Museum Japan) 1998 (Edinburgh and Trondheim Norway 1999), Celtic Connections (Yorozu Tetsugoro Museum Japan) 1998, ECA Sculptors (Arizona State Univ and Tucson Gallery USA) 1999, Scotland's Art (Edinburgh

H

Int Festival Exhbn) 1999, Edinburgh Artists (Odapark Sculpture Park The Netherlands and Sudbahnhoff Gallery Krefeld Germany) 2000, Marie R (Bourne Fine Art Edinburgh) 2000, Leabhar Morna Gaidhlig (Proiseact Nan Ealan) 2001; *Major Commissions* incl: Hugh McDiarmid Memorial Langholmn 1985, Charles Mackintosh Scupture Glasgow 1985, Compaq Computers Glasgow 1988, Poacher's Tree (Maclay Murray & Spens Edinburgh) 1991, Tools for the Shaman (Hunterian Museum Glasgow) 1996, Shift (granite sculpture, Aberdeen) 1999; *Public Collections* Scottish Arts Cncl, Edinburgh Museums and Galleries, Univ of Edinburgh, Contemporary Art Soc, Borders Educn Authy, Kelvingrove Museum Glasgow, Aberdeen Art Gallery, Motherwell DC, Kulturtoget Collection Lulea Sweden, Hunterian Museum Collection, Eda Garden Museum Tokyo Japan; *Awards* incl: Helen Rose Bequest 1971, Latimer award RSA 1975, Benno Schotz Sculpture prize RSA 1976, William Gillies bursary 1989; *Style*— Prof Jake Harvey, RSA

HARVEY, Jonathan Nigel Vigurs; OBE (2014); *b* 1949, Cornwall; *Educ* Univ of Reading, Chelsea Sch of Art, City Univ; *Career* co-fndr and chief exec Acme Studios 1972–; *Style*— Jonathan Harvey, Esq, OBE; ✉ Acme Studios, 44 Copperfield Road, Bow, London E3 4RR

HARVEY, Jonathan Paul; s of Brian Harvey, of Liverpool, and Maureen, *née* Pratt; *b* 13 June 1968; *Educ* Blue Coat Sch Liverpool, Univ of Hull (BSc); *Partner* Paul Hunt; *Career* writer; special needs teacher Abbey Wood Comp London 1990–93, writer in residence Bush Theatre 1993–94; memb Writers' Guild; *Awards* National Girobank/Liverpool Playhouse Young Writer of the Year 1987, Royal Court/Rank Xerox Young Writers Award 1988, George Devine Award 1993 (for Babies), Thames TV Bursary Award 1993, John Whiting Award 1994 (for Beautiful Thing), Evening Standard Most Promising Playwright 1994 (for Babies), London Lesbian & Gay Film Festival Best Film 1996 (for Beautiful Thing), Norway Film Festival Audience Award 1996 (for Beautiful Thing), Mike Rhodes Award for furthering the understanding of lesbian and gay life 1996, Manchester Evening News Award for Best Play 1996 (for Rupert Street Lonely Hearts Club), Fort Lauderdale International Film Festival President's Award Best Screenplay 1996 (for Beautiful Thing), GLAAD Outstanding Film Award 1997 (for Beautiful Thing), Best Live Entertainment Manchester Evening News Award 2011 (for Corrie!), Best Sitcom BAFTA 2011 (for Rev); *Plays* The Cherry Blossom Tree (1987), Mohair (1988), Tripping and Falling (1989), Catch (1990), Lady Snogs The Blues (1991), Wildfire (1992), Babies (1993), Beautiful Thing (1993, released as film 1996), Boom Bang A Bang (1995), Rupert Street Lonely Hearts Club (1995), Swan Song (1997), Guiding Star (RNT, 1998), Hushabye Mountain (English Touring Theatre, 1999), Out in the Open (Hampstead Theatre, 2001), Closer to Heaven (Arts Theatre, 2001), Jack and the Beanstalk (Barbican, 2007), Corrie! (Lowry Theatre Manchester and nat tour, 2010), Canary (Liverpool Playhouse, Hampstead Theatre and English Touring Theatre, 2010), Tomorrow I'll Be Happy (RNT) 2013; *Television* West End Girls 1993, Gimme Gimme Gimme (3 series BBC2) 1999, 2000 and 2001, Murder Most Horrid (BBC2) 1999, Birthday Girl (ITV) 2002, At Home With the Braithwaites (ITV) 2003, Margo: Life Beyond the Box (BBC 2) 2003, Coronation Street (ITV1) 2004–, Von Trapped! (ITV1) 2004, Charlie's Angels (BBC3), Love For Sale (BBC3), The Catherine Tate Show (BBC), Lilies (BBC), Beautiful People (two series, BBC) 2008 and 2009, Britannia High (ITV1) 2008, Rev (BBC) 2011, Panto! (ITV) 2012, Great Night Out (ITV) 2013, You Me and Them (Gold), The Tracey Ullman Show (BBC); *Novels* All She Wants (2012), The Confusion of Karen Carpenter (2013), The Girl Who Just Appeared (2014), The Secrets We Keep (2015); *Clubs* The Club at the Ivy; *Style*— Jonathan Harvey, Esq; ✉ c/o Michael McCoy, Independent Talent Group, Oxford House, 76 Oxford Street, London W1N 0AX (☎ 020 7636 6565, fax 020 7323 0101)

HARVEY, Mark Andrew; s of late Laurence Harvey, and Sheila, *née* Holland; *b* 2 September 1962, Chiswick, London; *Educ* Gunnersbury RC Sch for Boys, Coll of Law Guildford; *m* 24 April 1993 (sep), Karen, *née* Welton; 1 da (Rebecca Myfanwy b 11 May 1995), 1 s (Jonathan David 20 Dec 1997); *Career* slr; Owen White 1981–89, Lawford & Co 1990–94, Smith Llewellyn Partnership 1994–2001, Hugh James 2001–; former tstee and chm Carmarthen CAB, former memb Civil Justice Cncl, UK govr American Assoc for Justice, past pres Cardiff Law Soc, tstee and treas Reaching Justice Wales (Cyrraedd Cyfiawnder Cymru); memb Law Soc 1990; fell Inst of Legal Execs 1987; *Publications* APIL Guide to Conditional Fees (2004 and 2008), APIL Personal Injury (contrib, 2006–), Jl of Personal Injury Law (memb Ed Bd and contrib, 2007–), APIL Guide to Costs and Funding (jtly, 2014), Kemp & Kemp: Personal Injury Law, Practice and Procedure (memb Ed Bd and contrib, 2014); *Recreations* wine appreciation, skiing, golf, cookery; *Clubs* Cottrell Park Golf; *Style*— Mark Harvey, Esq; ✉ Hugh James, Hodge House, 114–116 St Mary Street, Cardiff CF10 1DY

HARVEY, Michael Llewellyn Tucker; QC (1982); s of Rev Victor Llewellyn Tucker Harvey, of Suffolk, and Pauline, *née* Wybrow; *b* 22 May 1943; *Educ* St John's Sch Leatherhead, Christ's Coll Cambridge (BA, LLB, MA); *m* 2 Sept 1972, Denise Madeleine, da of Leonard Walter Neary, of London; 1 s (Julian b 19 June 1976), 1 da (Alexandra b 30 June 1973); *Career* called to the Bar Gray's Inn 1966 (bencher 1991); recorder 1986; memb Review Bd Cncl of Legal Educn 1993–94, additional memb Bar Cncl 1994–; *Books* Damages (jtly, in Halsbury's Laws of England 4 edn, 1975); *Recreations* shooting, golf; *Clubs* Athenaeum, Hawks' (Cambridge); *Style*— Michael Harvey, Esq, QC

HARVEY, Nicholas (Nick); kt (2012); s of Frederick Harvey, and Christine Harvey; *b* 3 August 1961; *Educ* Queen's Coll Taunton, Middx Poly; *m* Kate, *née* Fox; 1 da, 1 s; *Career* pres Middx Poly Students' Union 1981–82, nat vice-chm Union of Liberal Students 1981–82, communications and marketing exec Profile PR Ltd 1984–86, Dewe Rogerson Ltd 1986–91, communications conslt 1991–92; Parly candidate (Alliance) Enfield Southgate 1987, MP (Lib Dem) N Devon 1992–2015; Lib Dem spokesman: on Tport 1992–94, on Trade and Industry 1994–97, on English Regions 1997–99, on Health 1999–2001, on Culture, Media and Sport 2001–03, on Def 2006–; min of state for the Armed Forces 2010–; chair of campaigns and communications 1994–99; *Recreations* travel, football, walking, music; *Style*— Sir Nick Harvey; ✉ House of Commons, London SW1A 0AA (☎ 020 7219 6232, e-mail mail@nickharveymp.com, website www.nickharveymp.com)

HARVEY, Prof Paul H; CBE (2008); s of Edward Walter Harvey, of Kidderminster, Worcs, and Eileen Joan, *née* Pagett; *b* 19 January 1947; *Educ* Queen Elizabeth GS Hartlebury, Univ of York (BA, DPhil), Univ of Oxford (MA, DSc); *Children* 2 s (Joseph Edward b 2 April 1980, Benjamin Mark b 18 March 1982); *Career* lectr in biology Univ of Wales Swansea 1971–73, reader in biology Univ of Sussex 1984–85 (lectr 1973–84); Univ of Oxford: lectr in zoology 1985–89, fell and tutor in biology Merton Coll 1985–96, reader in biology 1989–96, professorial fell Jesus Coll 1996–2014 (emeritus professorial fell 2014–), estab prof in zoology 1996–2014, head Dept of Zoology 1998–2011, emeritus prof in zoology 2014–; visiting lectr Harvard Univ 1978–79; visiting prof: Harvard Univ 1980, Univ of Washington Seattle 1982, Princeton Univ 1984–85, Imperial Coll London 1995–; sec Zoological Soc of London 2000–10; Scientific medal Zoological Soc 1986, US Nat Acad of Sciences J Murray Luck Award 1997, Frink Medal Zoological Soc 2011; FRS 1992 (memb Cncl 2000–02); *Books* The Comparative Method in Evolutionary Biology (with M D Pagel, 1991); *Style*— Prof Paul H Harvey, CBE, FRS; ✉ University of Oxford, Department of Zoology, South Parks Road, Oxford OX1 3PS (e-mail paul.harvey@zoo.ox.ac.uk)

HARVEY, Peter Derek Charles; s of Norman Charles Harvey (d 1991), and Sheila June, *née* Curtis, of Stanmore, Middx; *b* 21 December 1958; *Educ* Haberdashers' Aske's, Magdalen Coll Oxford, Guildhall Sch of Music and Drama (BP opera scholarship, Schubert Lieder prize); *Career* baritone soloist; Lieder recitals; dir Magdalena Consort; regularly appears with other ensembles and choirs incl: Monteverdi Choir, London Baroque, Gabrieli Consort, Purcell Quartet, The Sixteen, The Kings Consort, Orch of the Age of Enlightenment, Stuttgart Chamber Choir, Netherlands Bach Soc, L'ensemble Vocal de Lausanne, Collegium Vocale (Ghent), Tafelmusik (Canada), many symphony orchs and cathedral choirs; numerous appearances in UK and Europe, also Japan, Israel and N America; major soloist Sir John Eliot Gardiner's Bach Cantata Pilgrimage in the celebrations marking the 250 year anniversary of Bach's Death 2000 and Boston Symphony Orch with Bernard Haitink 2008; *Recordings* over one hundred incl: Schubert's Die Winterreise 2009, a great many works by J S Bach (passions, cantatas, etc), C P E Bach Die Auferstehung, Handel (Messiah, Solomon), many Purcell works incl Dido and Aeneas and King Arthur, the Requiums by Fauré and Duruflé, Rossini's opera La Cambiale di Matrimonio, numerous works from French Baroque by Charpentier, Lully, Du Mont, Campra, Gilles incl a solo recording of secular cantatas by Rameau with London Baroque, Buxtehude and early Bach cantatas with the Purcell Quartet, many other baroque and classical recordings; *Recreations* attempting foreign languages when on tour, making and fixing things; *Style*— Peter Harvey, Esq; ✉ e-mail enquire@peterharvey.com, website www.peterharvey.com and www.magdalenaconsort.com

HARVEY, Dr Peter Kenneth Philip; s of late Philip Harvey, of London, and Leah Harvey; *b* 22 January 1942; *Educ* Emanuel Sch, Gonville & Caius Coll Cambridge (MA, MB BChir); *m* 5 June 1971, Lesley MacGregor, da of late George Henderson; 2 s (Alan b 24 May 1978, Johnny b 26 July 1980), 1 da (Zehra b 4 March 1984); *Career* successively: pre-registration posts Middx Hosp Mortimer St and Queen Elizabeth II Hosp Welwyn Garden City, post-registration house posts Middx, Brompton and Nat Heart Hosps, further studies Imperial Coll London, neurological trg Middx Hosp and Nat Hosp for Nervous Diseases Queen Sq; lately conslt neurologist: Royal Free Hampstead NHS Tst (med dir 1991–93, chm Med Advsy Ctee 1991–94, ret 1997), Chase Farm Hosp NHS Tst Enfield; currently hon and emeritus conslt neurologist Royal Free Hosp; author of articles on neurological topics incl epilepsy in various learned jls; memb: Acad of Experts, BMA, RSM (memb Section Cncl 1980–90, hon sec for overseas affrs 1985–90); FRCP; *Recreations* cooking, wining, dining, opera, France; *Style*— Dr Peter Harvey; ✉ 134 Harley Street, London W1G 7JY (☎ 020 7486 8005, fax 020 7224 3905)

HARVEY, Polly Jean (PJ); MBE (2013); *b* 9 October 1969, Corscombe, Dorset; *Career* singer/songwriter; with band PJ Harvey 1991–93, solo artist and collaborator 1993–; contrib to records by: Pascal Comelade, Nick Cave, Tricky, Sparklehorse, Giant Sand, John Parish, Josh Homme's Desert sessions; wrote songs and produced music for Marianne Faithfull; Best Songwriter and Best New Female Singer Rolling Stone magazine 1992; *Albums* Dry 1992, Rid Of Me 1993 (nominated Mercury Music Prize), 4-Track Demos 1993, To Bring You My Love 1995 (nominated Mercury Music Prize and 2 Grammys), Dance Hall At Louse Point (with John Parish) 1996, Is This Desire? 1998 (nominated Mercury Music Prize, Grammys and Brit Awards), Stories From The City, Stories From The Sea 2000 (Mercury Music Prize 2001), Uh Huh Her 2004 (nominated Grammy Award), Peel Sessions 2006, White Chalk 2007, A Woman A Man Walked By (with John Parish) 2009, Let England Shake 2011 (Mercury Music Prize 2011, Ivor Novello Album Award 2012); *Singles* incl: Dress 1992, Sheela-na-Gig 1992, 50 Foot Queenie 1993, Man-Size 1993, C'mon Billy 1995, Down By The Water 1995, Send His Love To Me 1995, That Was My Veil 1996, Good Fortune 2000, A Place Called Home 2001, This Is Love 2001, The Letter 2004, When Under Ether 2007, The Piano 2007, The Devil 2008, Black Hearted Love (with John Parish) 2009; *DVD* PJ Harvey on Tour: Please Leave Quietly 2006. PJ Harvey Let England Shake – 12 Short Films by Seaumus Murphy; *Style*— Ms P J Harvey, MBE; ✉ c/o Sumit Bothra, ATC Management, The Hat Factory, 166–168 Camden Street, London NW1 9PT (e-mail sumit@atcmanagement.com)

HARVEY, Sarah Anne; *see:* Percy-Davis, Sarah

HARVEY WOOD, (Elizabeth) Harriet; OBE (1993); da of Henry Harvey Wood, OBE, FRSE (d 1977), and Lily, *née* Terry (d 2005); *b* 1 October 1934; *Educ* Cranley Sch for Girls, Univ of Edinburgh (MA, PhD); *Career* mangr Philomusica of London Orchestra 1959–66, sec Faculty of Music KCL 1966–68, head Literature Dept British Cncl 1980–94 (joined British Cncl 1973); dir The Harvill Press 1995–2002; memb: Bibliographical Soc 1970–94, English PEN 1985–2007 (memb Exec Ctee 1994–99), Panel of Judges Booker Prize for Fiction 1992, Wingate Scholarship Ctee 1992–2012, Booker Prize Mgmnt Ctee 2000–03; tstee: Stephen Spender Meml Tst Ctee 1997–, Golsoncott Fndn 1997–, Asham Literary Endowment Tst 1999–2011; *Books* James Watson's Choice Collection of Comic and Serious Scots Poems Vol I (1977), The Percy Letters: The Correspondence of Thomas Percy and John Pinkerton (1985), James Watson's Choice Collection of Comic and Serious Scots Poems Vol II (1991), Banned Poetry (with Peter Porter, 1997), Selected Poems of William Dunbar (1999), Sightlines (with P D James, 2001), Sir Walter Scott (2006), Memory (with A S Byatt, 2008), The Battle of Hastings (2008); *Recreations* reading, music, gardening, cooking; *Clubs* Oxford and Cambridge; *Style*— Miss Harriet Harvey Wood, OBE; ✉ 158 Coleherne Court, Redcliffe Gardens, London SW5 0DX (☎ 020 7373 2113/9658, e-mail harriet@harveywood.com)

HARVIE, Patrick; s of David Harvie, of Dumbarton, and Rose, *née* Radford; *b* 18 March 1973, Dumbarton; *Educ* Dumbarton Acad, Manchester Met Univ; *Career* youth worker, sexual health project worker and devpt worker Phace Scotland 1997–2003; MSP (Green Party) Glasgow 2003–; supporter: Amnesty, CND, Friends of the Earth, Greenpeace, Humanist Soc of Scot, Nat Secular Soc; Pride Award for Lesbian Gay Bisexual and Transgender Activism 2003; Scot Politician of the Year Awards: Election Campaign of the Year 2003 (jtly), One to Watch 2004, Progress in Politics 2006 (jtly); *Recreations* science fiction, computing, food and drink; *Style*— Patrick Harvie, Esq, MSP; ✉ Room MG.05, Scottish Parliament, Horse Wynd, Edinburgh EH99 1SP (☎ 0131 348 6363, e-mail patrick.harvie.msp@scottish.parliament.uk)

HARVIE-WATT, Sir James; 2 Bt (UK 1945), of Bathgate, Co Linlithgow; er s of Sir George Steven Harvie-Watt, 1 Bt, TD, QC (d 1989), and Jane, *née* Taylor (d 2003); *b* 25 August 1940; *Educ* Eton, ChCh Oxford (MA); *m* 28 May 1966, Roseline Gladys Virginia, da of Baron Louis de Chollet (d 1972); 1 da (Isabelle Frances b 19 March 1967), 1 s (Mark Louis b 19 Aug 1969); *Heir* s, Mark Harvie-Watt; *Career* Lt London Scottish (TA) 1959–67; with Coopers and Lybrand 1962–70, exec Br Electric Traction Co Ltd and dir of subsid cos 1970–78, md Wembley Stadium Ltd 1973–78, chm Crystal Palace Nat Sports Centre 1984–88, dir Lake & Elliot Industries Ltd 1988–93; memb: Exec Ctee London Tourist Bd 1977–80, Sports Cncl 1980–88 (vice-chm 1985–88); chm: Cannons Sports & Leisure Ltd 1990–93, Medi@Invest plc 1995–2002, Oliver & Saunders Group Ltd 1997–2011; dir various other cos incl: Weststar Holidays Ltd 1993–2005, Penna Consulting plc 1995–2013 (chm 2004–05), US Smaller Companies Investment Trust plc 1998–2001, Wellington Management Portfolios (Ireland) plc 2000–02; memb Mgmnt Ctee: The Nat Coaching Fndn 1984–88, The Nat Water Sports Centre Holme Pierrepont 1985–88; memb: Sports Cncl Enquiries into Financing of Athletics in UK 1983, Karate 1986, Cncl NPFA 1985–90; dir Int Tennis Hall of Fame 1996–2005 and 2006–14 (chm Exec Ctee 2001–05, chm Int Ctee 2006–11); FCA 1975 (ACA 1965), FRSA 1978; OStJ 1964 (memb London Cncl of the Order 1975–84); *Recreations* tennis, golf, shooting, photography, walking, philately; *Clubs* White's, Pratt's, Queen's (vice-chm 1987–90, chm 1990–93, dir 1987–2006), Swinley Forest, All England Lawn Tennis and Croquet; *Style*— Sir James Harvie-Watt, Bt; ☎ 020 7602 7353, e-mail harviewattjames@gmail.com

HARWOOD, Prof John Leander; s of Capt Leslie James Harwood, of Tunbridge Wells, and Lt Beatrice, *née* Hutchinson; *b* 5 February 1946; *Educ* King Edward's GS Aston, Univ of Birmingham (BSc, PhD, DSc); *m* 1, 27 Aug 1967, Gail (d 1991), da of Harry Burgess (d 1968); 1 s (Nicholas James b 27 Feb 1969); m 2, 14 April 1993, Bernice Adele (d 1994), da of Brian Alfred Andrews (d 1971); m 3, 17 Sept 2000, Marilyn Joan, da of David Emrys Evans (d 1970); *Career* postdoctoral res: Univ of Calif Davis 1969–71, Univ of Leeds 1971–73; UC Cardiff: lectr 1973–80, reader 1980–84, personal chair 1984–, head of research 2001–, dep dir 2003–, head Sch of Biosciences 2004–10 (dep dir 2010–); author of over 590 scientific pubns; guide book writer for S Wales Mountaineering Club and The Climbers Club; Supelco Award 2010, Chevreul Medal 2014; memb: Biochemical Soc, Phytochemical Soc, Soc of Experimental Biology; hon fell Hungarian Acad of Sciences 2010, FLSW 2011, fell Int Soc of Biocatalysis and Agricultural Biotechnology 2013, fell American Oil Chemists Soc 2014; *Books* South East Wales – A Rock Climber's Guide (ed, 1977), Lipids of Plants and Microbes (1984), The Lipid Handbook (jt ed, 1986, 2 edn 1994, 3 edn 2007), Plant Membranes (jt ed, 1988), Methods in Plant Biochemistry (Vol 4, jt ed, 1990), Plant Lipid Biochemistry, Structure and Utilization (jt ed, 1990), Lipid Biochemistry (jt author, 1991, 5 edn 2002), Climbers Guide to Pembroke, 2 Vols (jt ed, 1995), Plant Lipid Biosynthesis (ed, 1998), Handbook of Olive Oil (jt ed, 2000, 2 edn 2013); *Style—* Prof John Harwood; ✉ School of Biosciences, Cardiff University, Cardiff CF1 3AX (☏ 029 2087 4108, fax 029 2087 4116, e-mail harwood@cardiff.ac.uk)

HARWOOD, John Warwick; DL (Oxon 2001); s of late Denis George Harwood, of Dorchester, Dorset, and Winifred, *née* Hoatson; *b* 10 December 1946; *Educ* Catford Sch, Univ of Kent (BA), Univ of London (MA); *m* 1967; 1 s, 1 da; *Career* admin offr GLC 1968–73, private sec to Sir Ashley Bramall as Ldr ILEA 1973–77, asst chief exec London Borough of Hammersmith and Fulham 1979–82 (head Chief Exec's Office 1977–79); chief exec Lewisham Borough Cncl 1982–88, chief exec Oxfordshire CC 1989–2000, chief exec Learning and Skills Cncl 2000–04; clerk of the lieutenancy for Oxfordshire 1989–2001; chm CfBT Educn Tst 2004–11, chief exec Food Standards Agency 2006–08, cmmr Care Quality Cmmn 2010–14; dir: N Oxfordshire Business Venture Ltd 1989–97, Heart of Eng TEC (chm 1999–2001), Thames Business Advice Centre, Oxfordshire Ethnic Minorities Enterprise Developments Ltd, Thames Valley Economic Partnership 1997–98; associate fell Warwick Univ Business Sch 2004–08; memb: Exec Ctee Town and Country Planning Assoc 1981–89, Nat Cmmn on Future of Voluntary Sector 1995–96, Business Link Accreditation Bd 1996–2000, Ct Oxford Brookes Univ 1999–2010; clerk S London Consortium 1983–89; pres CPRE Oxon 2013–; tstee: Oxfordshire Community Fndn 1997–2003, Oxfordshire VCH Tst and Appeal 1997–, Cogges Heritage Trust 2012–; tstee and chm Northmoor Tst 2004–10, tstee Oxfordshire Youth (formerly Oxfordshire Assoc for Young People) 2011–, tstee Marriott Tst 2013–, tstee Young Dementia Care Homes 2013–; govr Marlborough Sch 2002–12; Vice Lord-Lt Oxon 2009–; Hon MA Univ of Kent 1995; *Publications* contrib: The Renaissance of Local Government (1995), Understanding British Institutions (1998); *Recreations* walking, cooking, gardening; *Clubs* Reform; *Style—* John Harwood, Esq, DL; ✉ Lieutenancy Office, County Hall, Oxford OX1 1ND

HARWOOD, Michael John; CB (2012), CBE (2004, MBE 1995); s of Alan Harwood (d 1984), and Mavis, *née* Thompson; *b* 29 October 1958, Buenos Aires, Argentina; *Educ* Merchant Taylors' Sch Northwood, KCL (MA); *m* 6 June 1981, Cheryl, *née* South; 2 da (Sophie b 15 July 1984, Nina b 12 Dec 1985); *Career* cmmnd RAF 1978, instr RAF Valley and RAF Chivenor 1980–84, IV(AC) Sqdn RAF Gütersloh 1984–88, Harrier trials pilot then staff offr Strike Attack Operational Evaluation Unit Boscombe Down 1988–92, OC Night then Dep OC 1(F) Sqdn RAF Wittering 1992–95, staff offr MOD PR Directorate and Perm Jt HQ 1996–98, cmd 20 Sqdn 1998–2000, Gp Capt 2000, Cdr Br Forces UK ops Southern Iraq 2000, Higher Cmd and Staff Course 2001, Station Cdr RAF Cottesmore 2001–03, Air Cdre HQ Strike Cmd RAF High Wycombe 2003–05, Asst Cmdt (Air) and dir Higher Cmd and Staff Course JSCSC Shrivenham 2005–07, UK air component cdr UK ACC and air offr commanding AOC 83 Expeditionary Air Gp ME 2008, head of Br def staff US and def attaché 2008–12, dir Matrix Blue Ltd 2012– (including non-exec dir The Military Mutual), staff pilot with 8 Air Experience Flight RAF Cosford 2014–, staff pilot with 3 Air Experience Flight Colerne 2015–; memb United Nations Assoc (UNA-UK); Arthur Barratt Meml Prize 1994; QCVSA; *Publications* Thoughts from a 34-year Career (2012), Michael Harwood considers the future evolution of UN peacekeeping (2013), Reassessing the UK's potential role in UN peacekeeping (2014), The Conceptual Component – Would Socrates have had a tattoo? (2014), Harrier Boys (Vol 1, chapter, 2015), Harrier Boys (Vol 2, chapter, 2016); *Recreations* reading, conversation, walking (for fitness and inspiration); *Clubs* RAF; *Style—* Mr Michael Harwood, CB, CBE; ✉ e-mail mjh.cyber@gmail.com

HARWOOD, Richard Francis Wilson; s of Gerald Wilson Harwood, of Sutton Coldfield, and Ellen Margaret, *née* Small; *b* 7 September 1944; *Educ* Wycliffe Coll; *m* 8 Sept 1967, Kathleen Janet, da of Edward Charles Shelley; 1 s (Charles Richard Louis b 23 Oct 1973); *Career* articled to C Herbert Smith & Russell 1961–66; subsequent positions with: Thos Bourne & Co 1967, Kenneth Hayes & Co 1967–68, Deloitte & Co 1968–81; ptnr Hart Harwood 1981–98, princ Harwoods CAs 1998–; pres Birmingham and W Midlands CAs 1991–92; ICAEW: Birmingham and W Midlands rep Nat Cncl 1992–, chm Trg Standards Ctee 1995–97 (dep chm 1993–95), dep chm Educn & Trg Directorate 1995–97, chm Investigation Ctee 1999–2000 (vice-chm 1997–1999), memb Exec Ctee 2000–02, chm Professional Standards Bd 2007–13, memb Bd 2007–13; chm Canwell Estate Agricultural Soc 2010–13; former dep chm of govrs Bishop Vesey's GS Sutton Coldfield (ret 1999); churchwarden St Mary, St Giles and All Saints Canwell 1997–2005; memb Nat Tst; Liveryman Worshipful Co of Chartered Accountants; FCA; *Recreations* gardening, music, cricket umpiring; *Style—* Richard F W Harwood, Esq; ✉ The Old Dairy, Bangley Lane, Tamworth, Staffordshire B78 3EA (☏ 0121 308 1715, e-mail richard@bangang.co.uk); Harwoods, 1 Trinity Place, Midland Drive, Sutton Coldfield B72 1TX (☏ 0121 355 0901, e-mail rfwh@harwoods-account.co.uk, website www.harwoods-account.co.uk)

HARWOOD, Richard John; OBE (2014), QC (2013); *Educ* Nottingham HS, Jesus Coll Cambridge (MA, LLM); *Career* called to the Bar 1993; barr specialising in planning and environment law, memb 39 Essex Chambers; case ed Jl of Planning and Environment Law 2000–; *Books* Planning Enforcement (1996, 2 edn 2013), Historic Environment Law (2012), Planning Permission (2016); *Style—* Richard Harwood, Esq, OBE, QC; ✉ 81 Chancery Lane, London WC2A 1DD

HARWOOD, Sir Ronald; kt (2010), CBE (1999); s of Isaac Horwitz (d 1950), and Isobel, *née* Pepper (d 1985); *b* 9 November 1934, Cape Town, SA; *Educ* Sea Point Boys' HS Cape Town, RADA; *m* 1959, Natasha (d 2013), da of William Charles Riehle, MBE (d 1979); 1 s (Antony), 2 da (Deborah, Alexandra); *Career* actor 1953–60; writer 1960–; artistic dir Cheltenham Festival of Lit 1975; chm Writers' Guild of GB 1969; memb Lit Panel Arts Cncl of GB 1973–78; visitor in theatre Balliol Coll Oxford 1986; pres: PEN (Eng) 1989–93, PEN (Int) 1993–97 (vice-pres 1997), Royal Literary Fund 2005–; Nat Jewish Theatre Fndn Lifetime Achievement 2014; Hon DLitt Keele Univ, Hon Dr Krastyo Sarafov Nat Acad for Theatre and Film Arts Sofia Bulgaria 2007, Hon DLit Univ of Aberdeen 2013; hon fell Royal Central Sch of Speech and Drama 2007, hon fell Univ of Chichester 2009; FRSL (chm 2001–04); Chevalier de l'Ordre des Arts et des Lettres (France); *Television* presenter: Kaleidoscope (BBC) 1973, Read All About It (BBC) 1978–79, All The World's A Stage (also writer, BBC); *Television Plays* incl: The Barber of Stamford Hill (1960), Private Potter (1961), The Guests (1972), Breakthrough at Reykjavik (1987), Countdown to War (1989); *Screenplays* incl: A High Wind in Jamaica (1965), One Day in the Life of Ivan Denisovich (1971), Evita Peron (1981), The Dresser (1983), Mandela (1987), The Browning Version (1994), Cry The Beloved Country (1995), Taking Sides (2002), The Pianist (2002, winner Academy Award 2002), The Statement (2003), Being Julia (2004), Oliver Twist (2005), The Diving Bell and the Butterfly (2007, BAFTA Award 2008), Love in the Time of Cholera (2007); *Books* All the Same Shadows (1961), The Guilt Merchants (1963), The Girl in Melanie Klein (1969), Articles of Faith (1973), The Genoa Ferry (1976), César and Augusta (1978), Home (Jewish Quarterly Prize for Fiction, 1993); short stories: One Interior Day (adventures in the film trade 1978), New Stories 3 (ed, 1978); biography: Sir Donald Wolfit, CBE – his life and work in the unfashionable theatre (1971); essays: A Night at the Theatre (ed, 1983), The Ages of Gielgud (1984), Dear Alec (ed, 1989); others: All The World's A Stage (1984), The Faber Book of Theatre (ed, 1993); *Plays* Country Matters (1969), The Ordeal of Gilbert Pinfold (from Evelyn Waugh, 1977), A Family (1978), The Dresser (New Standard Drama Award, Drama Critics' Award, 1986), After the Lions (1982), Tramway Road (1984), The Deliberate Death of a Polish Priest (1985), Interpreters (1985), J J Farr (1987), Ivanov (from Chekov 1989), Another Time (1989), Reflected Glory (1992), Poison Pen (1993), Taking Sides (1995), The Handyman (1996), Equally Divided (1998), Quartet (1999), Mahler's Conversion (2001), An English Tragedy (2008), Collaboration (2008); *Musical Libretto* The Good Companions (1974); *Recreations* watching cricket; *Clubs* Garrick, MCC; *Style—* Sir Ronald Harwood, CBE, FRSL; ✉ c/o Judy Daish Associates, 2 St Charles Place, London W10 6EG (☏ 020 8964 8811, fax 020 8964 8966)

HARWOOD, Rosalind Jane (Ros); da of Dr John Harwood, of Wiltshire, and Frances, *née* Lee; *b* 20 May 1965, Welwyn Garden City, Herts; *Educ* Bath HS GDST, Churcher's Coll Petersfield, Univ of Birmingham (Longman professional prize, LLB), Coll of Law Guildford; *Career* slr specialising in charity law; Lee Bolton & Lee 1987–97, Speechly Bircham 1997–2000, Rollits 2001–05, ptnr Dickinson Dees 2005–12, ptnr Gordons LLP 2012–14, ret; memb Law Soc 1987; FRSA 2006; *Recreations* gardening, cycling, hockey, travel; *Clubs* Lansdowne; *Style—* Ms Ros Harwood

HASAN, (Syed) Salmaan; s of Arshad Hasan, and Waheeda Hasan; *b* 24 December 1964, London; *Educ* Univ of London (BA), City Univ Business Sch (MBA); *m* 1989, Farida, *née* Huda; 1 da (Amira b 29 Sept 1993), 2 s (Anis b 27 Jan 1997, Ismail b 25 Feb 2000); *Career* property finance Samuel Montagu & Co 1988–92, property finance IBJ London 1992–94, head of property finance Deutsche Postbank/BHF 1994–2005, chief exec Minerva plc 2005–; MInstD 2005; *Recreations* running, cinema; *Clubs* Walbrook; *Style—* Salmaan Hasan, Esq; ✉ Minerva plc, 42 Wigmore Street, London W1U 2RY (☏ 020 7535 1000, fax 020 7725 0125, e-mail shasan@minervaplc.co.uk)

HASELER, Prof Stephen Michael Alan; s of Maj Cyril Percival Haseler (d 1973); *b* 9 January 1942; *Educ* Westcliff HS for Boys, LSE (BSc, PhD); *m* 24 Feb 1968, Roberta Berenice Haseler; *Career* prof of govt: London Guildhall Univ (formerly City of London Poly) 1968–, Univ of Maryland 1982–; visiting prof: Georgetown Univ Washington DC 1978, Johns Hopkins Univ 1984; chm Gen Purposes Ctee GLC 1973–75 (memb 1973–77), fndr memb SDP 1981, chm Radical Soc 1987– (fndr memb); Parly candidate (Lab): Saffron Walden 1966, Maldon 1970; hon prof Univ of Maryland 1986–; *Books* The Gaitskellites (1969), The Tragedy of Labour (1976), Eurocommunism (1978), Thatcher & The New Liberals (1989); *Clubs* IOD; *Style—* Prof Stephen Haseler; ✉ 2 Thackeray House, Ansdell Street, Kensington, London W8 (☏ 020 7937 3976)

HASELHURST, Rt Hon Sir Alan Gordon Barraclough; kt (1995), PC (1999), MP; s of late John Haselhurst, and late Alice, *née* Barraclough; *b* 23 June 1937; *Educ* Cheltenham Coll, Oriel Coll Oxford; *m* 1977, Angela, da of late John Bailey; 2 s, 1 da; *Career* MP (Cons): Middleton and Prestwich 1970–74, Saffron Walden 1977–; PPS to sec of state for Educn 1979–81; chm of tstees Community Devpt Fndn 1986–97, chm Ways and Means 1997–2010; dep speaker 1997–2010; hon sec All-Pty Parly Cricket Gp 1993–2010 (chm 2010–), memo House of Commons Finance Ctee 1997–, chm House of Commons Admin Ctee 2010–15, chm Exec Ctee Cwlth Parly Assoc 2011– (chm UK Branch 2010–15), memb Exec Ctee Essex CCC 1996–2008; *Publications* Occasionally Cricket, Eventually Cricket, Incidentally Cricket, Accidentally Cricket (2009), Unusually Cricket (2010), Fatally Cricket (2013), Politically Cricket (2016); *Recreations* music, gardening, watching cricket; *Style—* The Rt Hon Sir Alan Haselhurst, MP; ✉ House of Commons, London SW1A 0AA (e-mail alan.haselhurst.mp@parliament.uk, website www.siralanhaselhurst.net)

HASHEMI, Kambiz; s of Hussain Hashemi, of Tehran, Iran, and Aghdas, *née* Tehrani; *b* 13 August 1948; *Educ* Greenmore Coll Birmingham, Univ of Birmingham (MB ChB, MD); *m* 11 Sept 1974, Elahe, da of Dr Abbas Hashemi-Nejad, of Tehran, Iran; 1 s (Nima b 14 Nov 1978), 1 da (Neda b 14 May 1989); *Career* surgical registrar United Birmingham Hosp 1974–82, sr registrar in accident and emergency med Dudley Rd and East Birmingham Hosp 1982–85, dir of accident and emergency serv Mayday Univ Hosp 1985–, conslt in hand surgery Mayday Univ Hosp Croydon 1985–; author of numerous scientific pubns in med jls; regnl tutor in A/E med SW Thames RHA, SW Thames speciality rep to RCS; chm: Medical Cmmn for Accident Prevention, STC A/E Medicine; memb: Manpower Advsy Ctee, Bd of Examiners RCS, Dist Child Accident Prevention Gp, Academic Ctee BAEM, BMA, BAEM, BSSH, Emergency Med Res Soc, Iran Soc; FRCS, FRSM; *Books* Hazards of Forklift Truck (1989); *Recreations* squash, tennis, photography, theatre and opera; *Style—* Kambiz Hashemi, Esq; ✉ 16 Rose Walk, Purley, Surrey CR8 3LG (☏ 020 8668 8127); Accident and Emergency Unit, Mayday University Hospital, Mayday Road, Thornton Heath, Surrey CR7 7YE (☏ 020 8401 3000, fax 020 8401 3092)

HASKEL, Prof (the Hon) Jonathan Edward; s of Baron Haskel (Life Peer), *qv*, and Carole, *née* Lewis; *b* 1963; *Educ* Univ of Bristol (BSc), LSE (MSc, PhD); *m* 1997, Sue Alexander; 2 da; *Career* lectr Univ of Bristol 1987–88, research offr Centre for Business Strategy London Business Sch 1988–90; Queen Mary & Westfield Coll (now Queen Mary, Univ of London): joined 1990, prof 2000–08, head Economics Dept 2003–07; prof of economics Imperial Coll Business Sch Imperial Coll London 2008–; fndr and dir Centre for Research into Business Activity (CeRiBA) 2001–; non-exec dir UK Statistics Authy 2015–; visiting research scholar ANU 1995, visiting asst prof Stern Sch of Business NYU 1997, research fell Centre for Economic Policy Research, external fell Centre for Research on Globalisation and Labour Markets Univ of Nottingham, research assoc Inst for the Study of Labor (IZA) Bonn; memb Reporting Panel Competition Cmmn 2002–09, visiting academic conslt HM Treasy 2000–; author of numerous articles in refereed jls and conf papers; memb Editorial Bd Economica; *Recreations* cycling; *Style—* Prof Jonathan Haskel; ✉ Imperial College Business School, Tanaka Building, Room 296, South Kensington Campus, London SW7 2AZ (☏ 020 7594 8563, fax 020 7594 5915, e-mail j.haskel@ic.ac.uk, website www.imperial.ac.uk/people/j.haskel)

HASKEL, Baron (Life Peer UK 1993), of Higher Broughton in the County of Greater Manchester; Simon Haskel; s of Isaac Haskel, of Kaunas, Lithuania; *b* 8 October 1934; *Educ* Sedbergh, Salford Coll of Advanced Technol (BSc); *m* 1962, Carole, da of Wilbur Lewis, of New York, USA; 1 s (Hon Jonathan Edward, *qv*, b 1963), 1 da (Hon Lisa Frances b 1965); *Career* chief exec Perrotts Gp plc 1970–89 (joined Perrotts Ltd as technician 1961); sits as Lab peer in House of Lords, oppn whip 1994, front bench spokesman on trade and industry 1994–97, Lord in Waiting (Govt whip) and Govt spokesperson on trade and industry, pensions Treasy 1997–99, liaison peer DTI 2000–05, dep speaker and dep chm of ctees 2002–; memb Select Ctee on Science and Technol 1994–97, 1999–2001 and 2007–10; fndr memb Labour Fin and Industry Gp 1972 (sec later chm 1976–95); chm of tstees Smith Inst 1999–2009, pres Inst for Jewish Policy Research 2007–15, tstee Haskel Family Fndn; hon pres: Environmental Industry Cmmn, Materials UK; *Style*— The Rt Hon the Lord Haskel; ✉ House of Lords, London SW1A 0PW

HASKELL, James Andrew Welbon; s of Jonathan Haskell, and Susie Haskell; *b* 2 April 1985, Windsor, Berks; *Educ* Papplewick Sch Ascot, Wellington Coll; *Career* rugby union player; clubs: London Wasps 2003–09 and 2012–, Stade Français 2009–11, Ricoh Black Rams 2011–12, Otago Highlanders 2012; England: 71 caps, debut v Wales 2007; ambass: Landrover, Musto, RNLI, Sebastian's Action Tst; *Recreations* shooting, reading, UFC, DJ-ing; *Clubs* East India, Ivy, Soho House; *Style*— Mr James Haskell; ✉ c/o Jonathan Haskell (✆ 07971 404125, e-mail jh@jhhf.co.uk, website www.jameshaskell.com)

HASKINS, Baron (Life Peer UK 1998), of Skidby in the East Riding of Yorkshire; Christopher Robin Haskins; s of Robin Haskins, and Margaret Haskins, of Wicklow; *b* 30 May 1937; *Educ* Trinity Coll Dublin (BA); *m* 1959, Gilda, da of Alec Horsley, of Hessle, E Yorks; 3 s (Hon Paul b 1961, Hon Daniel b 1962, Hon David b 1966), 2 da (Hon Gina (Hon Mrs Hocking) b 1964, Hon Kate (Hon Mrs Campbell) b 1967); *Career* with Ford Motor Co 1960–62; chm Northern Foods 1986–2002 (joined 1962), chm Better Regulation Task Force 1997–2002, chm Express Dairies plc 1998–2002, rural recovery co-ordinator 2001–, chm European Movement 2004–06; pro-chllr Open Univ 2004–14; chair Humber Local Enterprise Partnership 2011–; memb: Runnymede Tst 1989–98, Culliton Irish Industry Policy Review Gp 1991–92, Cmmn for Social Justice 1992–94, Demos 1993–2000, UK Round Table on Sustainable Devpt 1995–98, Hampel Ctee on Corp Governance 1996–97, Civil Liberties Tst 1996–2001, Bd Yorks and Humber RDA 1998–2008, Legal Assistance Tst 1998–2004, Lawes Agricultural Tst 1999–2016, Advsy Bd Nat Assoc of Citizens Advice Bureaux 2000–04, New Deal Task Force 1997–2001; Hon LLD: Univ of Hull, Univ of Dublin, Univ of Nottingham, Univ of Huddersfield; Hon DUniv: Essex, Leeds Metropolitan, Lincoln, Bradford; Hon DSc Cranfield Univ; *Recreations* writing, weekend farm relief man, cricket; *Style*— The Rt Hon the Lord Haskins; ✉ Quarryside Farm, Main Street, Skidby, Cottingham, East Yorkshire HU16 5TG (✆ 01482 842692)

HASLAM, Prof David Antony; CBE (2004); *b* 4 July 1949; *Educ* Monkton Combe Sch, Univ of Birmingham Med Sch (MB ChB, DObstRCOG, DFFP); *m* 1974, Barbara Flannery; 1 da, 1 s; *Career* house physician Warneford Hosp Leamington Spa 1972–73, house surgn N Staffs Royal Infirmary 1973; SHO: (obstetrics) Birmingham Maternity Hosp 1973–74, (paediatrics) Birmingham Children's Hosp 1974, (psychiatry) Midland Nerve Hosp 1974–75, (gen med) Birmingham Gen Hosp 1975; trainee GP 1975–76, GP in partnership Ramsey Health Centre Huntingdon 1976–2011; nat clinical advsr to Healthcare Cmmn 2005–09, nat clinical advsr Care Quality Cmmn 2009–13; visiting prof of primary healthcare De Montfort Univ (hon reader 1999), prof of general practice Univ of Nicosia 2014–; RCGP: memb Cncl 1987–2009 (chm 2001–04), pres 2006–09; memb Postgrad Med Educn Trg Bd (PMETB) 2003–08, co-chair MMC Prog Bd for England, chair NICE (Nat Inst for Health and Care Excellence) (chair Evidence Advsy Bd 2008–13), memb Medical Educn England (MEE) 2009, memb Nat Quality Bd 2009–14, pres BMA 2011–12, chair Scientic Ctee Int Inst for Compassionate Healthcare; patron Crysis (Parents' Self Help Gp); hon dr Univ of Birmingham 2014; FRCGP 1989 (MRCGP), FFPH 2003, FRCP 2004, FRSM 2004, hon FAcadMEd 2010; *Books* Sleepless Children (1984), Eat it Up (1986), Travelling with Children (1987), ParentStress (1989), The Expectant Father (1990), Bulimia – A Guide for Sufferers and Their Families (1994), Your Child's Symptoms Explained (1997), Stress-free Parenting (1998); author of numerous articles and reg contrib various academic and non-academic jls, numerous appearances on local and nat radio and on TV; *Recreations* running (incl London marathon 2006), photography, skiing; *Style*— Prof David Haslam, CBE; ✉ Purbeck House, Martinstown, Dorchester DT2 9LB (✆ 01305 889125, e-mail davidhaslam@hotmail.com)

HASLAM, Jonathan; CBE (1997); s of Arthur S Fish, and Irene Florence Fish; *b* 2 October 1952; *Educ* Cowbridge GS, Plymouth Poly, Croydon Coll of Art and Technol, Univ of London (BSc); *m* 1982, Dawn Rachel; 2 s (James Samuel Charles b 25 July 1991, George Michael Anthony 27 July 1994); *Career* with National Westminster Bank 1975–79; information offr: COI 1979–82, DTI 1982–84; sr information offr Home Office 1984–86, dep head of information and dep press sec to sec of state Dept of Employment 1988–89 (princ information offr 1986–88), dep dir of information, dep press sec to Sec of State and head of news Home Office 1989–91, dep press sec to PM 1991–95, head of information and press sec to min for Agric, Fisheries and Food 1995, chief press sec to PM 10 Downing Street 1996–97, dir of communications Dept for Educn and Employment (DFEE) 1997, first dir of corp affrs London Metal Exchange 1997–2003, dir of gp communications Jarvis plc 2003–05, chief exec Haslamedia Ltd 2005–; sr advsr Smith Square Ptnrs LLP 2010–; chm: The Spokesmen 2003–06, Friends of Dulwich Coll 2007–10 (dep chm 2006–07); Bishop Challoner Sch: govr 2007–14, tstee 2014–16; MCIPR 2005, FRGS 2010; *Recreations* golf, music, cinema, reading; *Style*— Jonathan Haslam, Esq, CBE

HASLAM, Prof Jonathan George; s of E A Haslam, and M M G Haslam; *b* 15 January 1951, Copthorne, Sussex; *Educ* Wellington, LSE (BSc), Trinity Coll Cambridge (MLitt); *m* 28 April 2006, Dr Karina Urbach; *Career* lectr Univ of Birmingham 1975–84, assoc prof John Hopkins Univ 1984–86; visiting assoc prof: Stanford 1986–87, Berkeley 1987–88; sr research fell King's Coll Cambridge 1988–92, Univ of Cambridge 1992– (currently prof of the history of int rels), fell CCC Cambridge 1994–; specialist advsr House of Lords EU Ctee Sub-Ctee C 2002; FRHistS 1985; *Publications* The Vices of Integrity: E H Carr, 1892–1982 (1999), No Virtue Like Necessity: Realist Thought in International Relations Since Machiavelli (2002), The Nixon Administration and the Death of Allende's Chile (2005); *Recreations* travel, languages, music; *Clubs* Athenaeum; *Style*— Prof Jonathan Haslam; ✉ Corpus Christi College, Cambridge CB2 1RH (✆ 01223 338000, fax 01223 338057, e-mail jgh1001@cam.ac.uk)

HASLAM, Mark Stanley Culloden; s of Nigel Haslam (d 1994), and Daphne, *née* Low (d 1991); *b* 16 June 1957, Nairobi, Kenya; *Educ* Wellington Coll, Pembroke Coll Cambridge (MA); *m* 24 Sept 1996, Helen Fiona, *née* Lambert; 3 step s (James b 25 May 1985, Andrew b 24 March 1988, Ian b 13 Sept 1989); *Career* admitted slr 1981; Claude Hornby & Cox 1979–93, Magrath & Co 1993–97, BCL Burton Copeland 1998– (ptnr Criminal Litigation Dept); memb Criminal Law Solicitors' Assoc; past pres London Criminal Courts Solicitors' Assoc, past chm Forces Law; *Recreations* cricket, horse racing, theatre, rugby; *Clubs* Brook CC, Sandown Park, Jersey RFC, Esher RFC; *Style*— Mark Haslam, Esq; ✉ Brook Place, 23 Brook Farm Road, Cobham, Surrey KT11 3AX (mobile 07976 294270); BCL Burton Copeland, 51 Lincoln's Inn Fields, London WC2A 3LZ (✆ 020 7430 2277, fax 020 7430 1101, e-mail mhaslam@bcl.com)

HASLAM, Nicholas Ponsonby (Nicky); s of William Heywood Haslam, and Diana Ponsonby; *b* 27 September 1939, Bucks; *Educ* Eton; *Career* interior designer; prop NH Design; clientele incl: Rod Stewart, Rupert Everett, Bryan Ferry, Charles Saatchi, *qqv*, Ringo Starr, Mick Jagger; *Publications* Sheer Opulence: Modern Glamour for Today's Interiors (2002); *Style*— Nicky Haslam, Esq; ✉ NH Design, 76–78 Holland Park Avenue, London W11 3RB

HASLEHURST, Peter Joseph Kinder; s of Col Arthur Kinder Haslehurst, TD (d 1987), and Beatrice Elizabeth, *née* Birkinshaw (d 1998); *b* 4 March 1941, Derby; *Educ* Repton, Loughborough Univ (BSc); *m* 29 Oct 1977, Susan Marilyn, da of Mr and Mrs Geoffrey W Y Heath; 1 s (Thomas William Kinder b 22 May 1983), 2 step s (Matthew, Adam); *Career* md Wellman Mech Engrg Ltd 1969–81, chief-exec Flexibox Int Ltd 1981–86 (chm 1986–98), dep chm and chief exec EIS Gp plc 1985–98; dir M&G Income Investment Tst plc 1994–2004; chm: Br Metalworking Plant Makers Assoc 1974 and 1980, VA Tech UK 1999–2002, Brunner Mond Gp plc 2000–08, Magadi Rail Co Ltd Kenya 2002–08, Magadi Soda Ltd Kenya 2002–08, IMAGO at Loughborough Ltd 2003–09, Luxfer plc 2006– (dir 2003–); dir ECGD 2006–11; founding chm Br Metallurgical Plant Constructors Assoc (BMPCA) 1980–81, dep chm VAI Industries UK Ltd 1999–2004 (pres emeritus 2004); ldr Industry Missions to E Europe and Latin America; industrial advsr to Min of State on official visit to Czechoslovakia 1978, ldr Metals Soc Team NE China 1979; memb: Jt Trade Cmmn with Czechoslovakia 1978–80, Anglo-Soviet Econ Conf 1978–88, Materials Chemicals and Vehicles Requirement Bd Dept of Industry 1981–84, Br Hydromechanics Research Assoc Cncl 1984–89, Cncl Inst of Materials 1991–2003 (vice-pres 1997–2000, hon treas 2000–03, chm Audit Ctee 2003–); Inst of Mgmnt: memb Bd of Companions 1996–2002, chm Manufacturing Sector Review Panel 2011–; pres Macclesfield Cons Assoc 2011–; chm Leonard Cheshire Hill House Appeal 2008–; memb: Cncl Loughborough Univ 1999–2008, Mensa, WOW Advsy Bd Liverpool John Moores Univ 2009–, Ct Univ of Reading 2010–; Eisenhower fell 1980, hon chief of the Maasai 2008; Freeman City of London 1992, Liveryman Worshipful Co of Engrs 1993; Hon DSc Loughborough Univ 2008; CEng, FIMechE, FIEE, FIMMM, CCMI, FRSA; *Recreations* sailing and the countryside; *Clubs* Royal Thames Yacht (Rear Cdre 1994–96, tstee 2005–, chm and Vice Cdre 2008–11); *Style*— Peter Haslehurst, Esq; ✉ e-mail pjkh@phtechnology.com

HASLETT, Prof Christopher; OBE (2004); s of James Haslett, of Bebington, Wirral; *b* 2 April 1953; *Educ* Wirral GS, Univ of Edinburgh (BSc, MB ChB, Ettles scholar and Leslie Gold medal); *m* Jean Margaret, da of Thomas Hale; 1 da (Kate b 29 Jan 1983), 1 s (Andrew b 4 March 1990); *Career* house physician and surgn Edinburgh Royal Infirmary 1977–78, SHO Dept of Respiratory Med City Hosp Edinburgh 1978–79, res fell and hon med registrar Eastern General Hosp Edinburgh 1980 (SHO in general med 1979–80), general med registrar Ealing Hosp and Dept of Med RPMS 1980–82, res assoc F L Bryant Jr Research Lab for the Study of the Mechanisms of Lung Disease and instr Dept of Med Nat Jewish Hosp and Research Centre/Nat Asthma Centre Denver 1982–85, sr registrar in respiratory med Dept of Med RPMS Hammersmith Hosp 1982–85, sr lectr Respiratory Div Dept of Med RPMS and conslt physician Hammersmith Hosp 1985–90, prof of respiratory med and dir of The Rayne Laboratories Univ of Edinburgh 1990–, chm Dept of Med Royal Infirmary Edinburgh 1995–98, assoc dean (research) Univ of Edinburgh 1996–, head Div of Med Sci and Community Health Edinburgh 1996–; visiting prof RPMS 1990–; sec Working Gp on Lung Injury Euro Respiratory Soc 1991–, memb Cell and Molecular Med Bd MRC 1992–, vice-chm Res Ctee Nat Asthma Campaign; Dorothy Temple Cross Award MRC 1982, George Simon Meml Fell Award Fleischner Soc 1985, sr clinical fell MRC 1986; memb: Fleischner Soc, Assoc of Physicians (memb Cncl for Scotland 1993–), Assoc of Clinical Profs, Br Thoracic Soc, MRS, American Thoracic Soc, Int Soc for Leukocyte Biology; FRCP(Edin) 1988, FRCP(London) 1991, Fndr FMedSci 1998, FRSE 2000; author of numerous medical pubns; *Style*— Prof Christopher Haslett, OBE; ✉ Respiratory Medicine Unit, Department of Medicine, The Royal Infirmary, 1 Lauriston Place, Edinburgh EH3 9YW (✆ 0131 536 2263)

HASSALL, Antony David; s of Frank Hassall, and Marlene Hassall; *Educ* Britannia HS, Rewley Regis Sixth Form Coll, Open Univ; *Career* mangr J Sainsbury 1982–90; prison offr 1990–92, princ offr Feltham YOI 1993–94 (staff offr to dir of custody 1994–95), govr 5/4 Wormwood Scrubs 1995–97, team ldr Area Mangrs Support Team 1997–99, govr HMP Bullwood Hall 2002–05 (dep govr 2000–02), govr HMP Holloway 2006–; memb: Howard League, Lab Pty, Fabian Soc; *Recreations* holidays, reading, current affairs; *Style*— Antony Hassall, Esq; ✉ HMP Holloway, Parkhurst Road, London N7 0NU

HASSELL, Barry Frank; s of Edgar Frank Hassell (d 1990), and Rosetta Ethel Hassell (d 2010); *b* 26 September 1944; *Educ* Swanscombe Co Secdy Sch, London Business Sch (LEP); *m* 29 Dec 1971, Sylvia Booth (wid); 2 step s (Stephen, Richard); *Career* various accounting and mktg appts incl periods in Scandinavia and Africa 1959–73, mgmnt conslt 1973–85, special projects exec Scope (formerly The Spastics Soc) 1980–85, chief exec The Children's Tst (formerly Tadworth Court Tst) 1983–92 (memb 1992–), dir Project Bombay 1983–88, chief exec Independent Healthcare Assoc 1992–2003, chief exec Ind Healthcare Conslts Ltd 2004–; hon sec Union of Euro Private Hosps (UEHP) 1993–97 (vice-pres 1997–2000); memb Tadworth Court Children's Hosp Appeal Fund 1984–2003; govr Nat Inst for Social Work 1998–2004; led concordat negotiations between Ind Healthcare Assoc and Dept of Health 2000; MInstD, FCMI, FRGS; *Recreations* travel, photography, skiing; *Style*— Barry Hassell

HASSELL, Prof Michael Patrick; CBE; s of Maj Albert Marmaduke Hassell, MC, of Clench, Wilts, and Gertrude, *née* Loeser (d 1973); *b* 2 August 1942; *Educ* Whitgift Sch, Clare Coll Cambridge (MA), Oriel Coll Oxford (DPhil); *m* 1, 7 Oct 1966 (m dis), Glynis Mary Ethel, da of John Everett; 2 s (Adrian Michael b 6 Feb 1971, David Charles b 2 April 1973); m 2, Victoria Anne, da of Reginald Taylor (d 1984); 1 s (James Mark b 10 June 1986), 1 da (Kate Helen b 18 April 1988); *Career* Imperial Coll London: lectr Dept of Zoology and Applied Entomology 1970–75, reader in insect ecology Dept of Zoology and Applied Entomology 1975–79, prof of insect ecology Dept of Pure and Applied Biology 1979–, dep head Dept of Biology 1984–93, dir Silwood Park 1988– (head Dept of Biology 1993–2001), princ Faculty of Life Scis 2001–04, campus dean 2004–07; tstee Natural History Museum 1999–2008, chm Nat Biodiversity Network Tst 2013–; pres Royal Entomological Soc 2016–18; FRS 1986, fell Academia Europaea 1998; *Books* The Dynamics of Competition and Predation (1976), The Dynamics of Arthropod and Predator-Prey Systems (1978), The Spatial and Temporal Dynamics of Arthropod Predator-Prey Systems (2000); *Recreations* walking, natural history, croquet; *Style*— Prof Michael Hassell, CBE, FRS; ✉ Barnside, Buckland Brewer, Bideford, Devon EX39 5NF; Imperial College at Silwood Park, Department of Biology, Ascot, Berkshire SL5 7PY (✆ 01344 294207, fax 01344 874957, e-mail m.hassell@imperial.ac.uk)

HASTE, Cate Mary; da of Eric L Haste, of Almondsbury, nr Bristol, and J Margaret, *née* Hodge; *b* 6 August 1945; *Educ* Thornbury GS Bristol, Univ of Sussex (BA), Univ of Manchester (Dip Adult Ed); *m* 1973, Baron Bragg (Life Peer), *qv*; 1 da (Hon Alice b 1977), 1 s (Hon Tom b 1980); *Career* freelance television documentary producer and director, writer and broadcaster; memb: Directors UK 1988–, BAFTA 1995–, English PEN 1998–, WGGB 2014; *Television* The Secret War (BBC), End of Empire (Granada), Writing on the Wall (Channel 4), Munich – The Peace of Paper (Thames), Secret History – Death of a Democrat (Channel 4), The Churchills (ITV), Cold War (CNN), Millennium (CNN), Nazi Women (Channel 4), Married to the Prime Minister (Channel 4); *Books* Keep The Home Fires Burning – Propaganda in the First World War (1977), Rules of Desire – Sex in Britain WWI to the Present (1992), Nazi Women (2001), The Goldfish Bowl – Married to the Prime Minister 1955–97 (with Cherie Booth, 2004), Clarissa Eden: A Memoir from Churchill to Eden (ed, 2007), Sheila Fell: A Passion for Paint (2010), Craigie Aitchison: A Life in Colour (2014); *Recreations* reading, designing, gardening; *Style*— Ms Cate Haste; ✉ 12 Hampstead Hill Gardens, London NW3 2PL (✆ 020 7794 0473)

HASTE, Prof Helen Elizabeth; da of Eric Leighton Haste (d 2000), and Joan Margaret, *née* Hodge (d 2010); *b* 17 March 1943, Devizes, Wilts; *Educ* Univ of London (BA), Univ of Sussex (MPhil), Univ of Bath (PhD); *m* 1, (m dis 1978), 6 April 1963, Peter Weinreich; 1 da (Joanna Rachel b 10 Aug 1963); m 2, 30 June 1980 (m dis 1986), Paul Mosley; partner, Beverly Halstead (d 1991); *Career* Univ of Bath: lectr in psychology 1971–83, sr lectr in psychology 1983–92, reader in psychology 1992–1998, prof of psychology 1998–2008, prof emeritus 2008–; Harvard Univ: assoc Center for Moral Educn 1980, visiting prof Grad Sch of Educn 1998 and 2003–; visiting prof Univ of Exeter 2010–, visiting prof

Univ of Jinan China 2013–; co-ordinator Moral and Social Action Interdisciplinary Colloquium 1977–2001; research dir Nestlé Social Research Prog 2004–06; BAAS: pres Psychology Section 1991, vice-pres 2002–07, chair Cncl 2004–05; pres Int Soc for Political Psychology (ISPP) 2002 (memb 1981); Leverhulme research fell 2003–04, Nevitt Sanford Award ISPP 2005, Kuhmerker Lifetime Achievement Award Assoc for Moral Educn 2011, sr research fell Hong Kong Inst of Educn 2013–; FBPsS (memb 1965), FRSA 2002, hon fell BAAS 2002, FAcSS 2006; *Publications* Half The Sky: An Introduction to Women's Studies (co-author, 1979), Morality in the Making: Thought, Action and Social Context (co-author, 1983), Making Sense: The Child's Construction of the World (co-author, 1987), The Development of Political Understanding (co-author, 1992), The Sexual Metaphor (1993); *Recreations* photography; *Style—* Prof Helen Haste; ✉ 10 Belgrave Crescent, Bath BA1 5JU (☎ 01225 420230, e-mail helhaste@aol.com); Harvard Graduate School of Education, 613 Larsen Hall, Appian Way, Cambridge, MA 02138, USA (☎ 00 1 617 354 1544)

HASTE, Norman David; OBE (1997); s of Jack Haste (d 1959), of Cleethorpe, Lincs, and Edith Eleanor, *née* Jarvis (d 1961); *b* 4 November 1944; *Educ* Humberstone Fndn Sch Cleethorpes, N Lindsey Tech Coll (ONC Mechanical Engrg), Royal Coll of Advanced Technol (now Univ of Salford, Associate); *Career* graduate engr rising to project mangr John Laing Construction Ltd 1966–73, section mangr Humber Bridge 1973–75, marine works mangr Littlebrook D Power Station Construction 1976–78, project mangr Long Sea Outfall Construction Gosport 1978–81, divnl chief engr Laing Civil Engineering 1981–82, contracts mangr McConnell Dowell SE Asia Singapore 1982–84, dir special projects John Laing Construction Ltd 1984–85; project dir: Civil Engrg Works Sizewell B Power Station 1985–90, Second Severn Crossing 1990–95, Terminal 5 Heathrow 1996–2002; chm Severn River Crossing plc 2000–06, chief exec Cross London Rail Links 2002–06, chief operating offr Middle East and South Asia Laing O'Rourke 2006–09, chief exec Aldar Laing O'Rourke JV 2006–09; dir Transnet South Africa 2006–; memb Cncl ICE 1994–97 and 1999–; James Prescott Joule Medal ICE 1970, Gold Medal ICE 1996, Highways and Transportation Award Instn of Highways and Transportation 1996; Hon DEng UWE 1997, Hon DSc Univ of Salford 1998; MASCE 1983, MIE Aust 1983, FICE 1984 (MICE 1970), FREng 1996, FIHT 1996; *Recreations* golf, music; *Style—* Norman Haste, Esq, OBE, FREng

HASTIE-SMITH, Rev Timothy Maybury; s of Richard Maybury Hastie-Smith, of London, and Bridget Noel, *née* Cox; *b* 8 March 1962, London; *Educ* Cranleigh Sch, Magdalene Coll Cambridge (MA), Wycliffe Hall Oxford (CertTheol); *m* 20 June 1987, Joanne Elizabeth, *née* Ide; 2 da (Emily Caroline Catherine b 7 Nov 1988, Alice Bridget Grace b 23 May 2000), 1 s (Edward Frederick Maybury b 5 Feb 1991); *Career* curate St Ebbe's Oxford 1988–91, chaplain and admissions tutor Stowe Sch 1991–98, headmaster Dean Close Cheltenham 1998–2008; chm Ind Schs Christian Alliance 2002–08; tstee David Ross Educn Tst 2009–15; vicar Kempsford 2009–15, vicar Bibury with Winson and Barnsley 2015–; sr conslt Perret Laver 2009–10; nat dir Scripture Union 2010–; *Recreations* reading, politics, theatre, cinema, chicken husbandry; *Clubs* Coningsby, East India; *Style—* The Rev Timothy Hastie-Smith; ✉ The Vicarage, Bibury, Cirencester, Gloucestershire GL7 5NT (☎ 01285 740301, mobile 07515 984887, e-mail tim.hastie-smith@hotmail.com); Scripture Union, 207–209 Queensway, Bletchley, Milton Keynes MK2 2GB (☎ 01908 856118, e-mail timhs@scriptureunion.org.uk)

HASTINGS, Christine Anne (Mrs John Gambles); da of Peter Edwards Hastings, and Anne Fauvel, *née* Picot; *b* 15 February 1956; *Educ* Whyteleafe GS; *m* 1, 5 May 1985 (m dis 1988), Lawrie Lewis; m 2, 7 June 1991, John Gambles; *Career* dir: Pact Ltd (PR Consultancy) 1980–86, Biss Lancaster plc 1986–88; founding dir (currently ptnr) Quadrangle Gp Ltd 1988–; FRSA; *Style—* Ms Christine Hastings; ✉ Quadrangle, The Butlers Wharf Building, 36 Shad Thames, London SE1 2YE (☎ 020 7357 9919, fax 020 7357 9773, e-mail christine.hastings@quadrangle.com)

HASTINGS, Sir Max Macdonald; kt (2002); s of Douglas Macdonald Hastings (d 1982), and Anne Scott-James (Lady Lancaster, d 2009); *b* 28 December 1945; *Educ* Charterhouse (scholar), UC Oxford (exhibitioner); *m* 1, 1972 (m dis 1994), Patricia Mary, da of Tom Edmondson, of Leics; 1s (and 1 s decd), 1 da; m 2, 1999, Penny Grade; *Career* researcher Great War Series BBC TV 1963–64, reporter Evening Standard 1965–67, fell US World Press Inst 1967–68, roving corr Evening Standard 1968–70, reporter Current Affairs BBC TV 1970–73, ed Evening Standard Londoner's Diary 1976–77, columnist Daily Express 1981–83, contrib Sunday Times 1985–86; ed The Daily Telegraph 1986–95; dir: The Daily Telegraph plc 1989–95 (ed-in-chief 1990–95), Evening Standard Ltd 1996–2002, Associated Newspapers plc 1996–; ed Evening Standard 1996–2002, contrib Daily Mail 2002–; as war corr covered: Middle East, Indochina, Angola, India-Pakistan, Cyprus, Rhodesia, S Atlantic; documentaries for BBC and ITV; memb PCC 1991–92; pres CPRE 2002–07, vice-pres Game Conservancy 1992–; tstee Nat Portrait Gallery 1995–2004; Liddell-Hart lectr KCL 1994, Mountbatten lectr Univ of Edinburgh 2004; Journalist of the Year Br Press Awards 1982 (cited 1973 and 1980); What the Papers Say (Granada TV) awards: Reporter of the Year 1982, Ed of the Year 1988; Pritzker Literature Award for Lifetime Achievement 2012, Friuladria Prize 2014; Hon DLitt Univ of Leicester 1992; hon fell KCL 2004, Churchill fell Westminster Coll Fulton 2011; FRHistS 1988, FRSL 1996; *Books* America 1968: The Fire This Time (1968), Ulster 1969: The Struggle for Civil Rights in Northern Ireland (1970), Montrose: The King's Champion (1977), Yoni: The Hero of Entebbe (1979), Bomber Command (1979, Somerset Maugham Prize for Non-Fiction 1980), The Battle of Britain (with Len Deighton, 1980), Das Reich (1981), The Battle for The Falklands (with Simon Jenkins, 1983, Yorkshire Post Book of the Year Award), Overlord: D-Day and the Battle for Normandy (1984, 2 edn 1989, Yorkshire Post Book of the Year Award), Victory in Europe (1985), The Oxford Book of Military Anecdotes (ed, 1985), The Korean War (1987, shortlisted NCR Prize), Outside Days (1989), Scattered Shots (1999), Going to the Wars (2000), Editor: A Memoir (2002), Armageddon (2004), Warriors (2005), Country Fair (2005), Nemesis (2007), Finest Years (2009), Did You Really Shoot the Television? (2010), All Hell Let Loose: The World At War 1939–45 (2011), Catastrophe: Europe Goes to War 1914 (2013), The Secret War: Spies, Codes and Guerillas 1939–45 (2015); *Recreations* shooting, fishing; *Clubs* Brooks's; *Style—* Sir Max Hastings, FRSL; ✉ Northcliffe House, 2 Derry Street, London W8 5TT; secretary (☎ 01380 720894)

HASTINGS, Lady Selina Shirley; da of 16 Earl of Huntingdon (d 1990), and his 2 w, Margaret Lane (d 1994); *b* 5 March 1945; *Educ* St Paul's Girls' Sch, St Hugh's Coll Oxford (MA); *Career* writer and journalist; FRSL; *Books* incl: Nancy Mitford, Evelyn Waugh, Rosamond Lehmann, The Secret Lives of Somerset Maugham, The Red Earl; *Style—* The Lady Selina Hastings; ✉ c/o Rogers, Coleridge & White, 20 Powis Mews, London W11 1JN

HASTINGS, Steven Alan; s of Thomas Alan Hastings, OBE, of Beckenham, Kent, and Margaret Elizabeth, *née* Webber (d 2009); *b* 18 September 1957; *Educ* Dulwich Coll, Univ of Bristol (BSocSci); *m* 1, 19 July 1987 (m dis 2003), Teresa Lynne Eugenie, da of John Wimbourne, of Esher, Surrey; 1 s (Thomas Magna b 1 April 1989), 2 da (Rosie Beatrice b 14 April 1991, Flora Isabella b 15 Dec 1993); m 2, 27 March 2004, Penelope Ann, da of Donald Chilvers, of Brightwell Balwdin, Oxon; 2 step da (Maria-Africa b 28 Feb 1990, Gemma Mercedes b 18 Sept 1992); *Career* planner Leagas Delaney 1980–83, planner D'Arcy McManus & Masius 1983–84, sr planner Lowe Howard-Spink 1984–88, planning dir BBDO UK Ltd 1988–91, dir The Planning Group 1991–92, managing ptnr Banks Hoggins O'Shea FCB 1992–2003, fndr partner isobel (advtg agency) 2003–; memb: MRS, Account Planning Gp; *Recreations* classic cars, golf, football, running; *Clubs* Serpentine Running, OAPs (sec), Solus; *Style—* Steven Hastings, Esq; ✉ 15 Stoneleigh Street, London W11 4DU (mobile 07770 785445, e-mail steve@isobel.com)

HASTINGS OF SCARISBRICK, Baron (Life Peer UK 2005), of Scarisbrick in the County of Lancs; Michael John Hastings; CBE (2002); *b* 29 January 1958; *Educ* Scarisbrick Hall Sch, London Bible Coll (BA), Westminster Coll Oxford (PGCE); *m* 1990, Jane Mellor; 1 s, 2 da; *Career* teacher 1981–85, TV presenter and reporter 1990–94; BBC: head Public Affrs 1995–2003, head Corporate Social Responsibility 2003–06; global head of corp citizenship and diversity KPMG Int 2006–; dir Responsible Business Bd BT; former cmmr Cmmn for Racial Equality, tstee Crime Concern (chm 1995–2008), tstee Vodafone Cuba Fndn, chm Millenium Promise UK, vice-pres UNICEF UK, pres Zane; *Style—* Lord Hastings of Scarisbrick, CBE; ✉ House of Lords, London SW1A 0PW

HATCH, Lionel; s of Douglas Hatch (d 2012), and Clarice, *née* Aldred (d 1985), of Bolton, Lancs; *b* 20 August 1949, Bolton, Lancs; *Educ* Cast Hill County Secdy Sch, Bolt Coll of Art and Design; *m* Vivien, *née* Smith (m dis 1984); 1 s (Benjamin b 1974); *Career* jr art dir Royds 1970–71; art dir: Rileys 1971–72, Cogent Elliott 1972–73, Stowe Bowden 1973–75, McDonalds 1975–77, Yeoward Taylor Bonner 1977–79; creative gp head J Walter Thompson 1979–80, graphic design conslt 1980–86, co-fndr and dir The Chase 1986–; Twelve Lettering Artists 1983, New York Type Directors Club 1984, Br Design & Art Dirs Club Annual 1986–; Best In Show The Roses Awards 1987, Bronze Award Donside Annual 1989, Grand Global Award New York Advertising Festival 1994, Effectiveness Award Design Business Assoc 2003, Gold Lion Cannes Festival 2010; drawings, projects and design effectiveness studies exhibited internationally, occasional visiting lectures and workshops at UK schs and univs; *Books* The Chase by The Chase: How a design consultancy thinks it thinks (1993); *Recreations* cinema, gardening, music, reading, walking, pondering; *Style—* Lionel Hatch, Esq; ✉ 53 Lindley Drive, Parbold, West Lancs WN8 7ED (e-mail line.thepod@yahoo.co.uk); The Chase, 2 Commercial Street, Manchester M15 4RQ (☎ 0161 832 5575, e-mail lionel.hatch@thechase.co.uk, website www.thechase.co.uk)

HATCHARD, Michael Edward; s of Kenneth Edward William Hatchard (d 1997), and Diana Margaret Suzanne, *née* McMullin (d 2014); *b* 21 November 1955, Wilts; *Educ* Sherborne, Univ of Reading (LLB), Coll of Law; *m* 1, 4 June 1983, Erica Aminta Mary Bourdon Smith; 1 s (Augustus Edward Percy b Sept 1991); m 2, 24 Feb 1994, Pia Lucinda Bruna Lucia, *née* Gabriele; 1 s (George William Salvatore b July 1996); m 3, 30 Dec 2015, Anna Newsam, *née* Gardner; *Career* admitted slr 1980; ptnr: Theodore Goddard 1985–94 (joined 1978), Skadden Arps Slate Meagher & Flom 1994–; contrib to various legal pubs; memb Law Soc 1980; *Recreations* fishing, collecting variously, rowing; *Clubs* George, 51, RAC, KYC, Leander; *Style—* Michael Hatchard Esq; ✉ Skadden, Arps, Slate, Meagher & Flom (UK) LLP, 40 Bank Street, Canary Wharf, London E14 5DS (☎ 020 7519 7020, fax 020 7072 7020, e-mail michael.hatchard@skadden.com)

HATCHER, Prof (Melvyn) John; s of John Edward Hatcher (d 1960), and Lilian Florence, *née* Lepper (d 1981); *b* 7 January 1942; *Educ* Owens GS Islington London, LSE (BSc, PhD), Univ of Cambridge (LittD); *m* 16 Dec 1967, Janice Miriam, da of Herbert John Ranson; 2 da (Melissa Ann b 12 Sept 1978, Zara Sophie b 29 June 1982); *Career* research fell Inst of Historical Research Univ of London 1966–67, sr lectr in history Univ of Kent at Canterbury 1973–75 (lectr 1967–73); Univ of Cambridge: lectr in history 1976–86, reader in economic and social history 1986–95, prof of economic and social history 1995–; fell Corpus Christi Coll Cambridge 1976– (vice-master 2001–06); visiting prof Univ of Colorado at Boulder USA 1975–76, visiting fell Huntington Library Calif USA 1986–87, visiting fell Humanities Center Stanford Univ USA 2008–09; memb SSRC Econ and Social History Ctee 1979–82; ESRC: vice-chm Econ Affrs Ctee 1982–84, memb (jtly with UGC) New Blood Ctee, dir research initiative on history of prices and incomes 1984–86, Postgrad Awards Ctee 1988–90; memb Cncl Economic History Soc 1980–; ed Economic History Review 1995–2001; FRHistS 1974, AcSS 2001; *Books* Rural Economy and Society in the Duchy of Cornwall, 1300–1500 (1970), English Tin Production and Trade before 1550 (1973), A History of British Pewter (with T C Barker, 1974), Plague, Population and the English Economy, 1348–1530 (1977), Medieval England: rural society and economic change 1086–1348 (with E Miller, 1978), The History of the British Coal Industry: Before 1700 (1993, Wadsworth Prize 1993), Medieval England: towns, commerce and crafts, 1086–1348 (with E Miller, 1995), Modelling the Middle Ages (with M Bailey, 2001), The Black Death: an intimate history (2008); also author of book chapters and articles in learned jls; *Recreations* football, jazz; *Style—* Prof John Hatcher; ✉ Corpus Christi College, Cambridge CB2 1RH (☎ 01223 338000, fax 01223 338061)

HATCHER, Rev Mark; s of Peter Thomas Hatcher (d 1995), of Great Bookham, Surrey, and Joan Beatrice, *née* Crisp; *b* 16 October 1954; *Educ* Sutton Valence, Exeter Coll Oxford (Winter Williams law prize, MA); *m* 9 July 1988, Clare Helen, eld da of Prof Hugh Lawrence, FSA, of London; 1 da (Sophie b 13 Nov 1990); *Career* called to the Bar Middle Temple 1978 (Astbury scholar, bencher 2013), ad eundem Lincoln's Inn; in private practice 1978–80, with Law Cmmn 1980–83, with Legislation Gp Lord Chancellor's Dept 1983–88, Courts and Legal Servs Gp 1988; mgmnt conslt Deloitte Haskins & Sells 1988–90; PricewaterhouseCoopers (formerly Coopers & Lybrand before merger 1998): head of public affrs 1990–2000, public affrs counsel Coopers & Lybrand (UK) 1996–98, memb Global Regulatory and Professional Affrs Bd 2000–03, head of public affrs consulting 2000–03; dir and head of public affrs Cubitt Consulting 2004–06, dir of representation and policy Bar Cncl 2006–13, special advsr to the chm of the Bar Bar Cncl 2013–; rapporteur for European Services Forum 2000–06; memb Advsy Bd: Centre for Corp and Public Affrs Manchester Met Univ, Centre on Migration, Policy and Society Univ of Oxford 2002–07; special advsr European Economic and Social Ctee 2003–05; dir Bar Services Co Ltd 2006–, dir Nat Pro Bono Centre 2013–15; memb Editorial Bd: Jl of Communication Mgmnt, Jl of Public Affrs; contrib to various jls; ordained: deacon 2012, priest (SSM) 2013; hon asst curate St Saviour Brockley Hill 2012–15; Reader of the Temple Church 2015–; govr Sutton Valence Sch 2005–10, tstee United Westminster Schs 2011–; corp fell Industry and Parl Tst 1994, Euro fell 1995; memb: Ecclesiastical Law Soc, Greenwich Soc (conservation); FRSA 1994, MCIPR 2010; *Books* New Activism and the Corporate Response (with S John and S Thomson, 2003), Moving People to Deliver Services (ed A Mattoo and A Carzaniga, 2003); *Recreations* exploring churches, second-hand books, cooking; *Clubs* Reform; *Style—* The Rev Mark Hatcher; ✉ Bar Council, 289–293 High Holborn, London WC1V 7HZ (☎ 020 7611 1369, fax 020 7831 9217, e-mail mhatcherdrp@barcouncil.org.uk); The Temple Church Office, 2 King's Bench Walk, Temple, London EC4Y 7DE (e-mail reader@templechurch.com); 41 Gloucester Circus, Greenwich, London SE10 8RY (☎ 020 8293 4969, fax 020 8305 9601)

HATELEY, Linzi; da of Raymond William Hateley, and Margery, *née* Hammond; *b* 23 October 1970; *Educ* Wilnecote HS Tamworth, Italia Conti Acad of Theatre Arts London; *Career* actress; *Theatre* incl: title role in RSC's Carrie, Eponine in RSC's Les Miserables, Kolakola Bird in Cameron Mackintosh's Just So, narrator in Andrew Lloyd Webber's Joseph And The Amazing Technicolor Dreamcoat, Shakers – The Musical, Peter Pan, The Rise and Fall of Little Voice, Rizzo in Grease, Romance, Romance, Divorce Me Darling, Into the Woods, The Rink, Oliver, The Secret Garden, On Your Toes, Roxie Hart in Chicago, Mrs Banks in Mary Poppins, Donna in Mamma Mia, London Road (NT), Barnum; *Television* The Day The Music Died (Channel 4 documentary film), Children's Variety Performances 1992 and 1993, Brucie's Guest Night, Pebble Mill, Going Live, Children in Need, Win Lose or Draw, Des O'Connor Show; *Film* London Road (NT film) 2015 *Awards*

H

incl: Theatre World Award for Most Promising Newcomer on Broadway 1988, Olivier Award nomination for Best Actress in a Musical/Entertainment 1992; *Recordings* Joseph (cast recording), Divorce Me Darling (cast recording), Secret Garden (cast recording), Mary Poppins (cast recording); 3 solo albums; *Style—* Ms Linzi Hateley; ✉ Burnett Crowther Ltd, 3 Clifford Street, London W15 2LF (✆ 020 7787 3239)

HATHORN, (Alexander) Michael; s of Douglas Stuart Hathorn, and Elizabeth, *née* Snowdon; *b* 5 June 1948; *Educ* Stranraer HS Sedbergh; *m* 1, 14 Oct 1972 (m dis 2010), Deborah Christian, da of Hamish Gordon Farquhar; 2 s (Iain Fergus b 30 April 1977, Andrew Alexander b 4 Aug 1984), 1 da (Emma Louise b 4 Sept 1979); m 2, Jan 2011, Carol Lyn; *Career* ptnr Scott-Moncrieff, CAs (formerly Scott-Moncrieff Thomson & Shiells) 1974–2003 (apprentice 1967–72); dir: Baillie Gifford Shin Nippon plc 1994–2009, Companies House 2001–07; chm Moore Stephens UK Ltd 1989–2003, ptnr Moore Stephens London 2003–, chief operating offr Moore Stephens Int 2013–; assoc dir (Fin) Edinburgh International Festival 1989–90; chm: Local Authy (Scotland) Accounts Advsy Ctee 1991–93, LASAAC/CIPFA Jt Ctee 1992–94; memb ASB Public Sector and Not-for-Profit Ctee 1994–2010; memb IFAC Int Public Sector Accounting Standards Bd 1999–2009 (chm 2007–09); memb: CIPFA 1993 (Capital Accounting Gp 1991–93, Tech Ctee 1995–2002, chair Accounting and Auditing Standards Panel), ICAS 1972 (chm Members Services Ctee 1990–99, chm Public Sector Ctee 1995–2001, memb Cncl 1999–2006, pres 2005–06); *Recreations* music, visual arts; *Clubs* Hon Co of Golfers; *Style—* Michael Hathorn, Esq; ✉ Moore Stephens LLP, 150 Aldersgate Street, London EC1A 4AB (✆ 020 7248 4499, e-mail mike.hathorn@moorestephens.com)

HATOUM, Mona; da of Joseph Salim Hatoum, MBE (d 1986), of Beirut, and Claire Indrawes Eid; *b* 11 February 1952; *Educ* Beirut UC, The Byam Shaw Sch of Art (Leverhulme Tst Fund bursary), Slade Sch of Art London; *Career* artist; Gtr London Arts Assoc grant 1982, Arts Cncl of GB bursary 1985; artist-in-residence: Western Front Art Center Vancouver 1984 and 1988, Chisenhale Dance Space London 1986–87, Capp Street Project San Francisco 1996; pt/t lectr St Martin's Sch of Art 1986–89, visual arts advsr Gtr London Arts 1986–88, sr fell in fine art Cardiff Inst of HE 1989–92, pt/t lectr Jan Van Eyck Akademie Maastricht 1992–97; nominated for Turner Prize 1995; awarded hon fell Dartington Coll of Arts 1997; *Important Works* incl: The Light at the End (installation work with electric heating elements in the collection of Arts Cncl of GB) 1989, Light Sentence (installation work with wire-mesh lockers and moving lightbulb in the collection of FNAC Paris) 1993, Corps Étranger (video projection inside a cylindrical structure in the collection of Centre Georges Pompidou); *Exhibitions* incl: The British Art Show (McLellan Galleries Glasgow and tour) 1990, Pour la Suite du Monde (Musée d'Art Contemporair de Montréal) 1992, Arnolfini Gallery Bristol 1993, Centre Georges Pompidou (solo exhbn) 1994, Sense and Sensibility: Women Artists and Minimalism in the Nineties (MOMA NY) 1994, Cocido y Crudo (Centro de Arte Reina Sofia Madrid) 1994/95, Heart of Darkness (Kröller Müller Holland) 1994/95, Corps Étranger (Venice Biennale) 1995, Rites of Passage: Art for the End of the Century (Tate Art Gallery) 1995, 4th International Istanbul Biennial 1995, The British Sch at Rome (solo exhbn) 1995, Distemper: Dissonant Themes in the Art of the 1990s (Hirshhorn Museum and Sculpture Garden Washington) 1996, Life/Live la Scène artistique au Royaume-Uni en 1996, de nouvelles aventures (Musée d'art moderne de la Ville de Paris) 1996, A Quality of Light (St Ives Cornwall) 1997, De-Genderism: détruire dit-elle/il (Setagaya Art Museum Tokyo) 1997, Chicago Museum of Contemporary Art (solo exhbn) 1997, The New Museum of Contemporary Art NY (solo exhbn) 1997, Sensation (Royal Academy of Art London) 1997, MOMA Oxford (solo exhbn) 1998; *Style—* Ms Mona Hatoum

HATT, Paul William David; s of William Oliver Hatt (d 1989), and Henrietta, *née* McGregor (d 2012); *b* 21 November 1949; *Educ* Sir Joseph Williamson's Sch Rochester, Lincoln Coll Oxford (scholar, MA, PGCE), Nat Defence Coll; *m* 1975, Cecilia Anne, *née* Freeman; 2 s (James b 1978, Robert b 1980), 2 da (Mary b 1983, Elinor b 1985); *Career* MOD: joined 1973, princ 1980–85, on secondment to FCO as first sec UK Delgn to NATO 1985–89, asst sec 1990, head Defence Lands 1990–92, dir Proliferation and Arms Control Secretariat 1992–97, head Resources and Progs (Army) 1997–98, asst under sec 1998; command sec RAF Logistics Command 1998–2000, command sec to Second Sea Lord and C-in-C Naval Home Command and asst under sec of state (Naval personnel) MOD 2001–06; sec Royal Hosp Chelsea 2007–16; fell Center for Int Affrs Harvard Univ 2000–01; *Recreations* sedentary pursuits, incl family, literature and music; *Style—* P W D Hatt, Esq; ✉ 313 Ewell Road, Surbiton, Surrey, KT6 7 BX

HATT-COOK, Mark Edward; OBE (1996), RD (and Bar); s of Lt-Col John Edward Hatt-Cook, MC (d 1999), of Stoke Farthing, Wilts, and Lavender Helen, *née* Covernton (d 2008); *b* 18 December 1942; *Educ* Bradfield Coll; *m* 18 Oct 1969, Susan Georgina, da of Lt-Col Ronald John Henry Kaulback, OBE (d 1995), of Hoarwithy, Herefords; 2 da (Catherine Emma b 13 Aug 1974, Georgina Alice b 13 June 1977); *Career* cmmnd RMR 1963, 45 Commando S Arabia 1963 (active serv), 42 Commando Malaysia 1969, 41 Commando N Ireland 1970, qualified Arctic survival instr 1980, TAVR staff course Camberley 1981, USMC staff course Quantico 1984, Lt-Col CO RMR City of London 1990–92, RMR Col 1992–95; chm City RFCA 1999–2002; vice-chm: Eastern Wessex TAVRA 1991–99, Cncl TAVRA 1992–95, Gtr London RFCA 1998–2007; Lord Mayor's Marshal 1980–; ADC to HM The Queen 1992–95; HM Cmmr of Lieutenancy for City of London 1999–; articled with Hunters and with Bischoffs, admitted slr 1970, asst slr Deacons Hong Kong, ptnr Wilsons Salisbury (sr ptnr 1997–2002); memb regnl Br Olympic Ctee 1988, pres Salisbury Slrs Assoc 1989; tstee Salisbury Museum 1998–2007, pres Salisbury Sea Cadets 2001–, chm Ulysses Tst 1999–2006, chm RFCA Pension Fund 2001–08; Freeman City of London 1981, Liveryman Worshipful Co of Turners 1995, Hon Col RMR City of London 2012–; memb Law Soc; FRNS; *Recreations* shooting, skiing, sailing, deer management; *Clubs* Army and Navy; *Style—* Col Mark Hatt-Cook, OBE, RD*; ✉ Mascalls, Broadchalke, Salisbury, Wiltshire SP5 5HP (✆ 01722 780480); Alexandra House, St John Street, Salisbury SP1 2SB (✆ 01722 412412, e-mail mark.hatt-cook@wilsonslaw.com)

HATTERSLEY, Baron (Life Peer UK 1997), of Sparkbrook in the County of West Midlands; Rt Hon Roy Sydney George Hattersley; PC (1975); s of late Frederick Hattersley, and Enid Hattersley (Lord Mayor Sheffield 1981–82, d 2001); *b* 28 December 1932; *Educ* Sheffield City GS, Univ of Hull (BScEcon); *m* 1956, Edith Mary (Molly), da of Michael Loughran; *Career* joined Lab Pty 1949, memb Sheffield City Cncl 1957–65, Parly candidate (Lab) Sutton Coldfield 1959; MP (Lab) Birmingham Sparkbrook 1964–97, PPS to Min of Pensions and Nat Insurance 1964–67, jt Parly sec of state for employment and productivity 1967–69, min of defence for admin 1969–70; oppn spokesman on: defence 1972, educn and science 1972–74; min of state FCO 1974–76, sec of state for prices and consumer protection 1976–79; chief oppn spokesman on: environment 1979–80, home affairs 1981–83, Treasy and econ affairs 1983–87, home affairs 1987–92; dep ldr Lab Pty Oct 1983–1992; pres Local Govt Gp for Europe 1998–; journalist; named columnist of the year What the Papers Say (Granada TV) 1982; *Books* Nelson (1974), Goodbye to Yorkshire (essays, 1976), Politics Apart (1982), Press Gang (1983), A Yorkshire Boyhood (1983), Choose Freedom – The Future for Democratic Socialism (1987), Economic Priorities for a Labour Government (1987), The Maker's Mark (novel, 1990), In That Quiet Earth (novel, 1991), Skylark's Song (novel, 1993), Who Goes Home? Scenes from a Political Life (1995), Fifty Years On: A Prejudiced History of Britain Since The War (1997), Buster's Diaries: As told to Roy Hattersley (1998), John Wesley: A Brand from the Burning (2002), The Edwardians: Biography of the Edwardian Age (2004), Buster's Secret Diaries (2007), David Lloyd George: The Great Outsider (2010); *Recreations* writing, watching football and cricket; *Style—* The Rt Hon Lord Hattersley, PC; ✉ House of Lords, London SW1A 0PW

HATTON, His Hon Judge Andrew John; *b* 1964, Bolton, Lancashire; *Educ* Bolton Sch, Leeds Met Univ (LLB), Inns of Court Sch of Law, Liverpool John Moores Univ (LLM); *m* 1990, Caroline, *née* Headley; 1 da (Annabel), 1 s (Rupert); *Career* called to the Bar Gray's Inn 1987; dep district judge Magistrates Ct 2005–12, recorder 2009–12, int criminal judge EULEX Mission Kosovo 2011–12, circuit judge (Northern Circuit) 2012–, UN appointed judge Residual Special Court Sierra Leone 2013–; *Style—* His Hon Judge Andrew Hatton; ✉ The Queen Elizabeth II Law Courts, Derby Square, Liverpool L2 1XA

HATTON, His Hon Judge David William; QC (1996); s of Thomas William Hatton, of Bolton, and Margery, *née* Greenhalgh; *b* 29 May 1953; *Educ* Bolton Sch, Univ of Bristol (LLB); *Children* 1 da (Charlotte Rose b 6 Nov 1995), 1 s (David Jack Terence b 14 Sept 1997); *Career* called to the Bar Gray's Inn 1976, recorder of the Crown Court 1995–, bencher 2005–, circuit judge (North Eastern Circuit) 2012–; *Recreations* music, history, cooking, dining; *Clubs* Bradford, Bolton Wanderers; *Style—* His Hon Judge Hatton, QC

HATTON, Humphry; s of Dr Joseph Hatton, and Gwyneth Hatton; *b* 18 January 1962; *Educ* St Edward's Sch Oxford, Imperial Coll London (BSc, ARSM); *m* Ruth; 1 s (Thomas), 1 da (Lucy); *Career* ptnr i/c forensic and dispute servs Deloitte 2000–; FCA 1988; *Recreations* rowing, wine and food, music, tennis; *Clubs* Univ of London Tyrian, Leander, Crabtree, Bantham Sailing; *Style—* Humphry Hatton, Esq; ✉ Deloitte & Touche LLP, Stonecutter Court, 1 Stonecutter Street, London EC4A 4TR

HATTON, Richard John (Ricky); MBE (2007); s of Raymond Hatton, of Gee Cross, Hyde, and Carol, *née* Slann; *b* 6 October 1978, Stockport; *Educ* Hattersley Comp Hyde; *Partner* Jennifer Dooley; 1 s (Campbell b 9 Jan 2001), 2 da (Millie Meg b 17 Sept 2011, Fearne b 31 July 2013); *Career* former professional boxer; ABA Champion 1997, Bronze medalist World Boxing Games 1997, WBU Light Welterweight World Champion 2001, IBF and WBA Light Welterweight World Champion 2005, WBA Welterweight World Champion 2006, IBF and IBO Light Welterweight World Champion 2007; memb British Boxing Bd of Control; British Boxer of the Year 2003 and 2005, American Boxing Writers' Fighter of the Year 2005; owner/dir: Hatton Promotions 2009–, Hatton Health and Fitness, Hatton Acad, Hatton Clothing; currently boxing mangr and trainer; dir/owner: Hatton Health and Finess Centre, Hatton Clothing; patron: Genesis Charity, Manchester Kids Charity, Willow Wood Hospice, Barnabus charity for homeless people Manchester; *Books* Ricky Hatton, The Hitman: My Story (2006), Ricky Hatton: War and Peace (2013), Ricky Hatton's Vegas Tales (2015); *Recreations* boxing, football (season ticket holder at Manchester City FC), music (Oasis); *Style—* Ricky Hatton, Esq, MBE; ✉ Hatton House, Market Street, Hyde; c/o Paul Speak, PO Box 76, Manchester M26 3YW (✆ 07932 001309 or 01204 397259, fax 0161 723 4862, e-mail speak3536@aol.com, website www.hattonboxing.tv, Twitter @hitmanhatton)

HAUGHEY, Edward Enda; *see:* Lord Ballyedmond, OBE

HAUGHEY, Baron (Life Peer UK 2013), of Hutchesontown in the City of Glasgow; Sir William Haughey; kt (2012), OBE (2003); s of Thomas Haughey, and Margaret, *née* Morton; *b* 2 July 1956, Glasgow; *Educ* Holyrood Sr Secdy Sch Glasgow, Springburn Coll Glasgow (C&G); *m* 30 Sept 1978, Susan, *née* Moore; 1 s (Kenneth b 17 April 1980); *Career* engrg supervisor Turner Refrigeration Ltd 1973–83, head of engrg in UAE UTS Carrier 1983–85, jt owner and md (with Susan Haughey) City Refrigeration Hldgs (UK) Ltd 1985–; chm: Scottish Enterprise Glasgow, Asset Skills; non-exec dir: Dunedin Enterprise Tst, Glasgow Culture and Leisure; charter memb Duke of Edinburgh Awards Scheme, memb Growth Fund Panel Prince's Scottish Youth Business Tst, patron CSV; Entrepreneur of the Year Entrepreneurial Exchange 2000 (finalist 1999), Business to Business section and Masterclass winner Ernst & Young Awards 2000, Refrigeration Industry Business of the Year 2000, Lanarkshire Business of the Year 2002, Business Man of the Year Award Insider Pubns 2003, Bighearted Business Person of the Year 2004, Excellence in Public Service Award 2004, Business Award Great Scot 2005, Awards Sunday Mail 2005; Loving Cup from Lord Provost of Glasgow for charity work 2001, St Mungo Prize for distinguished serv to the City of Glasgow 2007; Hon DTech Glasgow Caledonian Univ 2005; *Recreations* golf, reading, football; *Clubs* Celtic FC (ambass); *Style—* The Lord Haughey, OBE; ✉ City Refrigeration Holdings (UK) Ltd, Caledonia House, Lawmoor Street, Glasgow G5 0US (✆ 0141 418 9117, fax 0141 418 9317, e-mail willie.haughey@city-holdings.co.uk)

HAUSER, Dr Hermann Maria; Hon CBE (2001); s of Hermann Hauser (d 1979), and Gerti Hauser; *b* 23 October 1948, Vienna; *Educ* Vienna Univ (MA), Univ of Cambridge (PhD); *Career* co-fndr and later chm Acorn Computers 1978 (led devpt of Acorn system 1 and Acorn ATOM, and BBC Basic and BBC Micro Computer), fndr dir IQ (Bio) 1982, vice-pres research Olivetti 1986, fndr dir Harlequin 1986, fndr dir IXI Ltd 1987, co-fndr Active Book Co 1988, co-chm and chief technical offr EO Incorporated 1991, fndr dir Vocalis 1992, fndr dir SynGenix 1993, fndr dir Advanced Displays Ltd 1993, fndr dir Electronic Share Infomation Ltd 1993, fndr and chm Advanced Telecommunications Modules Ltd (now Virata Corp) 1993, fndr Net Products Ltd 1996, fndr NetChannel 1996, co-fndr Amadeus Capital Ptnrs Ltd 1997, co-fndr Cambridge Network Ltd 1998; memb: Esprit Advsy Bd 1986, Foresight Panel 1994, Cncl for Science and Technol 2004–; Computer Personality of the Year 1984; Hon Dr: Univ of Bath 1990, Loughborough Univ 1998, Anglia Poly Univ 2001; hon fell King's Coll Cambridge 1999; FInstP 1998, FREng 2002; *Style—* Dr Hermann Hauser, CBE; ✉ Amadeus Capital Partners Ltd, Mount Pleasant House, 2 Mount Pleasant, Cambridge CB3 0RN (✆ 01223 707000, fax 01223 707070, e-mail hhauser@amadeuscapital.com)

HAVARD, Dai; MP; s of Edward (Ted) Havard (d 1989), and Eileen Havard (d 2006); *b* 7 February 1950, Quakers Yard, Merthyr Tydfil; *Educ* Secdy Modern Treharris, Grammar Tech Quakers Yard, Edwardsville Comp Afon Taf, St Peter's Coll Birmingham (CertEd), Univ of Warwick (MA); *m* 1986 (m dis), Julia Watts; *Career* MSF: studies tutor 1971–75, researcher 1975–79, educn 1975–82, official 1988–, delgn ldr, Wales sec; MP (Lab) Merthyr Tydfil and Rhymney 2001–, memb Deregulation and Reform Ctee 2001–, memb Regulatory Reform Select Ctee 2001–, memb Defence Select Ctee 2003–; memb Armed Forces Parly Scheme 2001–02 (attached to Army); memb: Co-operative Pty 1996–, Constituency Lab Pty 2001–, Jt Policy Ctee Wales Lab Pty 2001–, MSF Section AMICUS, Merthyr Tydfil Credit Union; *Publications* contrib to academic pubns on trade union and economic devpt; *Recreations* hill walking, horse riding, bird watching, Commons and Lords Rugby Team; *Style—* Dai Havard, Esq, MP; ✉ House of Commons, London SW1A 0AA

HAVARD, (Michael) Robin; s of Capt Cyril Havard, of St Nicholas, Cardiff, and Elizabeth Mary Morgan Havard, JP, *née* Williams; *b* 7 May 1957; *Educ* Epsom Coll, UC Cardiff (BSc); *m* 4 Dec 1982, Ann, da of Kenneth John Evans (d 1976); 2 da (Abigail Tanya b 31 May 1987, Clare Elizabeth Orla b 7 April 1990); *Career* slr; ptnr: Loosemore 1981–83, Watkin Jones & Co 1984–85, Morgan Bruce 1985–98, Morgan Cole 1998– (chm 2003–); pt/t chm Employment Tbnls Eng and Wales; memb Law Soc 1981; *Recreations* watching rugby, sailing, golf, cycling; *Clubs* Bridgend, London Welsh, Swansea, Newport, Glamorgan County, WRU Presidents XV; *Style—* Robin Havard, Esq

HAVELOCK-ALLAN, His Hon Judge; Sir (Anthony) Mark David; 5 Bt (UK 1858), of Lucknow; QC (1993); s of Sir Anthony James Allan Havelock-Allan, 4 Bt (d 2003), and Valerie Babette Louise Hobson (d 1998) (later married to John Profumo, CBE (d 2006)); *b* 4 April 1951; *Educ* Eton, Univ of Durham (BA), Trinity Coll Cambridge (LLB, Dip Int Law); *m* 1, 1976 (m dis 1984), Lucy Clare; yr da of Alexander Plantagenet Mitchell-Innes;

m 2, 1986, Alison Lee Caroline, da of Leslie Francis Foster; 2 da (Miranda Antonia Louise b 29 July 1993, Hannah Marie Josephine b 18 Oct 1997), 1 s (Henry Caspar Francis (Harry) b 6 Oct 1994); *Heir* s, Harry Havelock-Allan; *Career* called to the Bar Inner Temple 1974 (bencher 1995); recorder of the Crown Court 1997–2001 (asst recorder 1993–97), sr circuit judge (Bristol Mercantile Court) 2001–; pres Br Assoc for Cemeteries in S Asia (BACSA) 2016–; FCIArb 1991; *Recreations* salmon fishing, foreign travel; *Clubs* Garrick, RAC; *Style*— His Hon Judge Havelock-Allan, QC; ✉ The Bristol Civil Justice Centre, 2 Redcliff Street, Bristol BS1 6GR (☎ 0117 366 4861, fax 0117 366 4801)

HAVENHAND, Martin; *Educ* Sheffield Hallam Univ (MSc, DMS); *Family* 3 c; *Career* formerly: asst chief offr with S Yorks Met CC, dir of leisure and environment Trafford MBC, chief exec Bassetlaw DC; chief exec Yorkshire Forward 1999–, currently chm NAMTEC (Nat Metals Technol Centre); memb IOD; FISRM, FRSA; *Recreations* golf, gardening, reading; *Style*— Martin Havenhand, Esq

HAVERS, Hon Nigel Allan; yr s of Baron Havers, PC, QC (Life Peer, d 1992), and Carol Elizabeth, *née* Lay (now Mrs Charles Hughesdon); *b* 6 November 1951; *m* 1, 1974 (m dis 1989), Carolyn Gillian, da of Vincent Cox; 1 da (Katharine b 1977); m 2, 1989, Mrs Polly Bloomfield (d 2004); m 3, 2007, Mrs Georgiana Bronfman; *Career* actor; *Theatre* incl: Importance of Being Earnest, Ricochet, Art, See You Next Tuesday, Rebecca; *Television* incl: A Horseman Riding By, Upstairs Downstairs, Nancy Astor, Strangers and Brothers, Don't Wait Up, The Charmer, A Perfect Hero, Sleepers, The Good Guys, The Heart Surgeon, Brothers and Sisters, Coronation Street; *Film* incl: Chariots of Fire, A Passage to India, Burke and Wills, The Whistle Blower, Empire of the Sun, Farewell to the King, Burning Season, Paradise Lost; *Recreations* keeping fit, reading, gardening; *Clubs* Garrick; *Style*— The Hon Nigel Havers

HAVERS, Hon Philip Nigel; QC (1995); er s of Baron Havers, PC, QC (Life Peer, d 1992), and Carol Elizabeth, *née* Lay (now Mrs Charles Hughesdon); *b* 16 June 1950; *Educ* Eton, CCC Cambridge; *m* 20 March 1976, Patricia Frances, *née* Searle; *Career* called to the Bar Inner Temple 1974; *Books* An Introduction to Human Rights and the Common Law (jt ed); *Recreations* tennis, music; *Clubs* Garrick; *Style*— The Hon Philip Havers, QC; ✉ 1 Crown Office Row, Temple, London EC4Y 7HH (☎ 020 7797 7500, fax 020 7797 7550, e-mail philip.havers@1cor.com)

HAVILLE, Robert William; s of James Haville (d 1983), and Eileen Haville; *b* 27 July 1955; *Educ* Marlborough GS, Lancaster Univ (BA), Univ of Bradford (MBA); *m* 18 Oct 1980, Hazel Dawn, da of George Burke (d 2011), of London; 2 da (Rosalind b 1986, Sarah b 1990), 2 s (James b 1988, Ralph b 1995); *Career* fin analyst Kimberley Clark 1976–77; investment analyst: McAnally Montgomery 1978–81, James Capel 1982–87, Morgan Stanley 1988–91, Smith New Court/Merrill Lynch 1991–99, West LB Panmure 1999–2002, College Hill Associates 2003–04, Financial Dynamics 2005–07, Town End Conslts 2007–; md OSR Wealth Mgmnt 2010–; memb Assoc of Business Graduates (AMBA); FCSI, MIRS; *Clubs* RAC, Sutton & Epsom Rugby; *Style*— Robert Haville, Esq

HAW, Jonathan Stopford; s of Denis Stopford Haw (d 1979), of Sidcup, Kent, and Elisabeth Mary Dorothy, *née* Mack (d 1998); *b* 16 March 1945, St Paul's Cray, Kent; *Educ* Radley Coll, Keble Coll Oxford (MA), Coll of Law; *m* 20 Dec 1969, Hélène Lucie, da of Louis Lacuve, Chevalier de l'Ordre National du Mérite, of Perpignan, France; 1 s (Alexander b 1973), 1 da (Katherine b 1976); *Career* slr; Slaughter and May: ptnr 1977–2002, first ptnr NY 1984–87, exec ptnr 1996–2001; dep chm Coll of Law 2005–12; Juvenile Diabetes Research Fndn: dir 1990–99 and 2003–10, chm 1996–99, memb Int Lay Review Ctee 2004–08; tstee Mary Kinross Charitable Tst 2003–, tstee Novo Nordisk UK Research Fndn 2013–; Freeman City of London 1970, Master Worshipful Co of Armourers and Brasiers 2008–09 and 2013–14; *Recreations* gardening, art, wine; *Clubs* Leander; *Style*— Jonathan S Haw, Esq

HAWES, Ven Arthur John; s of late John Beadnell Hawes, and late Sylvia Mary Lilian, *née* Taylor; *b* 31 August 1943, Oxford; *Educ* City of Oxford HS for Boys, Chichester Theol Coll, Richmond Fellowship Coll (Cert Human Rels), Univ of Birmingham (Dip Pastoral Studies, Dip Liturgy and Architecture), UEA (BA); *m* 1969, Melanie Gay, da of late John Harris, and late Gay Harris; 1 da (Emma (Mrs Matthew Morrall) b 13 July 1971), 1 s (Luke John b 6 June 1973); *Career* curate St John the Baptist Kidderminster 1968–72, priest-in-charge St Richard Droitwich 1972–76, rector of Alderford with Attlebridge and Swannington 1976–92, chaplain Hellesdon and David Rice Hosps and Yare Clinic 1976–92, rural dean of Sparham 1981–91, canon of Norwich Cathedral 1988–95, chm Norwich Diocesan Bd for Social Responsibility 1990–95, rector St Faith's Gaywood King's Lynn 1992–95, archdeacon of Lincoln and canon and prebendary of Lincoln Cathedral 1995–2008 (archdeacon emeritus 2008–); visiting fell Staffs Univ 2009–13; memb: Gen Synod of the C of E 2000–08, Mission and Public Affairs Cncl 2000–11; Mental Health Act cmmr for England and Wales 1986–94, chm E Midlands Regnl Devpt Centre 2003–05; non-exec dir S Lincs Healthcare NHS Tst 1998–2001, non-exec dir Lincs Partnership NHS Tst 2002–06, memb NHS Confederation Mental Health Policy Ctee 2003–07, jt chm Nat Spirituality and Mental Health Forum 2009–11 (vice-chm 2006–09), Mental Health Act advsr Lincs Partnership Tst 2006–08, trg conslt Lincs partnership Fndn Tst 2008–12, patron Nat Assoc for Mental Health (MIND), pres Purfleet Tst 1995–2007, pres Lincs Rural Housing Assoc 1997–2007, vice-pres Br Assoc for the Study of Spirituality 2010–, pres Reepham Rotary Cub 2016–17; The Archbishop of Canterbury's Langton Award for Community Service; *Publications* Anne French Meml Lectures (ed, 1996), Creating Accepting Communities (contrib), Spirituality, Values and Mental Health – Jewels for the Journey (contrib), Handbook on Spirituality and Mental Health (contrib), Spirituality and End of Life Care (contrib, 2013), Crossing the River – The Contribution of Spirituality to Humanity and its Future (ed); co-author of C of E responses to amendments to 1983 Mental Health Act and to the Bradley Report, author of pubns on mental health and allied community issues in Crucible and Pastoral Studies Jl, and of papers for Gen Synod's debates on mental health 2003 and 2008; *Recreations* golf, theatre, music, medieval art and architecture; *Clubs* Reepham Rotary, Royal Norwich Golf; *Style*— The Venerable Arthur Hawes; ✉ e-mail arthur.hawes@yahoo.co.uk

HAWKER, Eur Ing Geoffrey Fort; TD; s of Albert Hawker (d 1975), and Florence Lilian, *née* Fort (d 1978); bro of Ven Alan Hawker, *qv*; *Educ* Univ of London (BSc Eng); *m*; 2 da; *Career* Nat Serv Royal Engrs 1951–52; chartered civil engr 1956; called to the Bar Gray's Inn 1970; with: Aston Construction Co 1945–50, Sir William Halcrow & Ptnrs 1953–59, Mitchel Construction Co 1960–61, Rendel Palmer & Tritton 1961–63, Chadwick, O'Heocha and Assocs 1963–64; in practice as: engrg conslt 1964–, arbitrator 1970–; head of barristers' chambers 1990–2003; formerly: pres Soc of Construction Arbitrators, memb Cncl ICE (chm Arbitration Advsy Bd), memb Cncl CIArb; memb: Soc of Construction Law, Int Bar Assoc, Dispute Review Bd Fndn USA, Adjudication Soc; Liveryman: Worshipful Co of Arbitrators, Worshipful Co of Engrs; FREng 1988, FICE, CEng, FIEI, FIStructE, FConsE, MSocIS (France), FCIArb; *Books* A Guide to Commercial Arbitration under the 1979 Act (with R Gibson-Jarvis, 1980), The ICE Arbitration Practice (with Uff and Timms, 1986), The ICE Conditions of Contract for Minor Works – A User's Guide and Commentary (with G Cottam, 1992); *Style*— Eur Ing Geoffrey Hawker, TD, FREng; ✉ 2nd Floor Flat North, 10/11 Gray's Inn Square, Gray's Inn, London WC1R 5JD (☎ 020 7405 1953, fax 020 7405 7553, e-mail geoffreyhawker@cuthbertlake.co.uk); c/o Russell Burton-Lawrence, PO Box 180, Edenbridge, Kent TN8 9DN (☎ 01732 866562, e-mail russell@thebarristerbroker.com)

HAWKES, Prof David John; s of Roy Hawkes, of Teignmouth, Devon, and Joyce, *née* Davey; *b* 16 January 1953; *Educ* Portsmouth GS, ChCh Oxford (BA, Keasbey Bursary, Allen Award), Univ of Birmingham (MSc), Univ of Surrey (PhD); *m* 8 July 1978, Elizabeth Anne, da of John Nicholson; 2 da (Sarah Joanne b 20 August 1983, Rosie Louise b 12 Oct 1986); *Career* basic grade physicist in nuclear med Southampton Gen Hosp 1976–78, research assoc Univ of Surrey and Royal Marsden Hosp 1978–81, WHO conslt in medical physics and nuclear medicine Philippines 1982; St George's Hosp London: sr physicist 1981–84, princ physicist and head of imaging section Dept of Medical Physics and Bio-Engrg 1984–88; reader in radiological scis UMDS 1993–98 (Leverhulme fell 1988–91, sr lectr 1988–93); KCL: prof in computational imaging sci 1998–2004, chm Div of Imaging Scis 2002–04; UCL: prof of computational imaging sci 2005–, dir Centre of Medical Image Computing 2005–; dir Med Images and Signals IRC 2003–07; sr investigator Nat Inst for Health Research 2010; Royal Soc visiting fell Montreal Neurological Inst Canada 1991, visiting prof Johns Hopkins Univ USA 1999, Willhelm Conrad Roentgen hon lectr European Congress of Radiology 2006; Coorkshank Lecture and Medal RCR 2008; fell Inst of Physics and Engrg in Medicine 1993, FInstP 1997, CPhys 1997, FBIR 2007, FMedSci 2011; *Style*— Prof David Hawkes

HAWKESFORD, John Ernest; s of Ernest Hawkesford (d 1965), of Rushwick, Worcs, and Sarah Elizabeth, *née* Jones (d 1992); *b* 29 November 1946; *Educ* Warwick Sch, UC Med Sch London; *m* 29 June 1974, Barbara, da of Alexander Howe, of Gateshead, Tyne & Wear; 3 da (Abigail Lisa b 1976, Julia Marie b 1979, Rachel Chloe b 1989); *Career* registrar in oral maxillofacial surgery Stoke Mandeville Hosp Bucks 1973–76, sr registrar in oral maxillofacial surgery W of Scotland Plastic Surgery Unit Canniesburn Hosp Bearsden Glasgow, hon clinical lectr in oral surgery and oral med Univ of Glasgow 1976–79, hon clinical teacher in oral and maxillofacial surgery Univ of Newcastle upon Tyne 1979–2007; conslt in oral maxillofacial surgery: Newcastle Nuffield Hosp 1979–, Newcastle upon Tyne Hosps NHS Fndn Tst 1979–2007 (clinical dir of oral and maxillofacial surgery 1991–95), Ramsey Health 2007–12; chm Specialist Sub-Ctee Dentistry Northern Regnl Med Ctee 1987–95, chm Regnl Ctee for Hosp Dental Servs 1990–96, memb Northern Regnl Med Ctee 1987–95, memb Central Ctee for Hosp Dental Services 2000–04; pres BDA Hosp Gp 1993–94 (vice-chm 2000–), pres N of England Odontological Soc 2001–02, tstee BDA Benevolent Fund 2000–04; Liveryman The Worshipful Co of Tin Plate Workers Alias Wire Workers 2012–, Freeman City of London 2012; memb: BDA, RSM, Br Assoc of Oral Maxillofacial Surgery, Oral Surgery Club of GB (pres 2006–07), Euro Assoc for Cranio-Maxillofacial Surgery; *Books* Maxillofacial and Dental Emergencies (1994); *Recreations* squash, skiing, swimming; *Style*— Mr John Hawkesford; ✉ The Quarry, 31 Batt House Road, Stocksfield, Northumberland NE43 7RA (☎ 01661 842338, e-mail john@hawkesford.onyxnet.co.uk)

H

HAWKHEAD, Sir Anthony Gerard (Tony); kt (2011), CBE (2003); s of Harry Cheltenham (d 2010), and Mary, *née* Geary; *b* 7 October 1957, Bedford; *Educ* Whitefriars Sch Cheltenham; *m* 31 Aug 1981, Marion, *née* Small; 1 da (Laura b 19 April 1988), 1 s (James b 13 Feb 1991 d 1991); *Career* MOD 1978–87, Inner Cities Unit DTI 1987–88, leader Govt Task Force N Peckham 1988–89, head of business and econ devpt LDDC 1989–91; chief exec: E London Partnership 1991–96, Groundwork 1996–2014, Action for Children 2014–; non-exec memb Bd Defra 2011–15, memb UK Nat Advsy Bd on Social Investment 2016–; FRSA, hon fell Inst of Employment Professionals; *Publications* DWP/ACEVO Third Sector Welfare to Work Taskforce Report (2009); *Recreations* sport, music, wine, France; *Clubs* Mandarins' CC, West Warks Sports; *Style*— Sir Tony Hawkhead, CBE; ✉ Action for Children, 10 Great Queen Street, London WC2B 5DG (☎ 020 3124 0660, e-mail beth.munby@actionforchildren.org.uk)

HAWKINS, Andrew John; s of Austen Ralph Hawkins, of Bournemouth, and May, *née* O'Donnell; *b* 24 September 1958; *Educ* Bedford Modern Sch, Lancaster Univ (BA), Kellogg Graduate Sch of Mgmnt Northwestern Univ Evanston (MBA); *m* 16 Nov 1990 (m dis 2008), Karen, da of Gerald Edward Pursey; 2 s (Jack b 2 May 1992, Ned b 14 Sept 1994), 1 da (Martha (twin) b 14 Sept 1994); *Career* graduate trainee Ogilvy and Mather advtg 1982, account dir Publicis 1985 (account mangr 1983); GGK London: joined Bd 1988, dep md Jan 1990, md Nov 1990–93, jt chm and ceo 1993–95; md Doner Cardwell Hawkins 1995–; *Recreations* water-skiing, running, movies; *Style*— Andrew Hawkins, Esq; ✉ 30 Honeywell Road, London SW11 6EG; DCH, 60 Charlotte Street, London W1T 2NU

HAWKINS, Prof Anthony Donald; CBE (2000); s of Kenneth St David Hawkins, and Marjorie, *née* Jackson; *b* 25 March 1942; *Educ* Poole GS, Univ of Bristol (BSc, PhD); *m* 31 July 1966, Susan Mary; 1 s (David Andrew b 23 Feb 1973); *Career* dir of Fisheries Res Scotland 1987–2002, chief scientific offr SO 1987–2002, prof Univ of Aberdeen 2002–, research assoc Environmental Research Inst Thurso; md Loughine Ltd 2002–; dir NAFC Marine Centre 2008–09; FRSE 1988; *Publications* The Effects of Noise on Aquatic Life Vol I (with Arthur Popper, 2012), The Effects of Noise on Aquatic Life Vol II (with Arthur Popper, 2016); *Recreations* whippet racing; *Clubs* Royal Soc of Edinburgh; *Style*— Prof Anthony Hawkins, CBE, FRSE; ✉ Kincraig, Blairs, Aberdeen AB12 5YT (☎ 01224 868984, e-mail a.hawkins@btconnect.com)

HAWKINS, Helen Amanda Jacqueline; da of Edwin John Hawkins (d 2001), and Peggy Norah, *née* Bysouth; *b* 19 December 1950, Enfield, Middx; *Educ* Stonar House Sch Wilts, Millfield, Univ of Kent at Canterbury (BA), Univ of Colorado (MA); *Career* instructor and researcher English Dept Univ of Colorado 1977–81, freelance journalist 1981–87, Sunday Times 1987– (culture ed 1996–); memb Bd Between the Notes; Supplement of the Year Br Press Awards 2003; *Recreations* arts-going; *Clubs* Groucho, Adam Street; *Style*— Miss Helen Hawkins; ✉ Culture, The Sunday Times, 1 London Bridge Street, London SE1 9GF (☎ 020 7782 5771, e-mail helen.hawkins@sunday-times.co.uk)

HAWKINS, James Bruce (Jim); s of Philip J C Hawkins (d 2014), and José P, *née* Thorneloe; *b* 10 December 1965, Crawley, Sussex; *Educ* King Edward VI Camp Hill Sch for Boys Birmingham, Brasenose Coll Oxford (MA, PGCE); *m* 17 July 1999, Zoe A, *née* Neeves; 1 da (Raphaella b 12 Sept 2004); *Career* teacher Radley 1988–92, head of mathematics Forest School 1992–97, dep head Chigwell Sch 1997–2002, head master Norwich Sch 2002–11, head master Harrow 2011–; govr: Aysgarth Prep Sch, Wellesley House Prep Sch, Orley Farm Prep Sch, Francis Holland Schs Tst; tstee: W London Zone, The Harrow Mission; *Recreations* cinema, music, reading, shooting, cafés; *Clubs* East India, Lansdowne; *Style*— Jim Hawkins, Esq; ✉ Harrow School, 5 High Street, Harrow on the Hill, Middlesex HA1 3HP (☎ 020 8872 8003)

HAWKINS, Keith John; *b* 19 November 1947; *m* 1 (m dis 1985), 23 April 1977, Linda Claire; 1 s (Richard b 1979), 1 da (Philippa b 1982); m 2, 30 Aug 1991, Anthea Frances Hedley; *Career* admitted slr 1974; ptnr Dutton Gregory; memb Law Soc 1974; *Style*— Keith Hawkins, Esq; ✉ St Just, Red Lane, West Tytherley, Salisbury, Wiltshire SP5 1NY (☎ 01794 340689); Dutton Gregory, Trussell House, 23 St Peter Street, Winchester, Hampshire SO23 8BT (☎ 01962 844333, fax 01962 863582, e-mail k.hawkins@duttongregory.co.uk)

HAWKINS, Prof Keith Owen; s of (Lewis) Cyril Hawkins (d 1989), and (Lillian) Grace Hawkins (d 1974); *b* 8 September 1941, Chinnor, Oxford; *Educ* Univ of Birmingham (LLB), Univ of Cambridge (Dip Criminology, MA, PhD), Univ of Oxford (MA, DPhil); *m* 1 July 1978, Susan Jillian, *née* Lock; 3 s (Alexander James Owen b 3 May 1981, Nicholas Guy Lewis b 9 Feb 1984, Edmund Charles Stuart b 28 Sept 1985); *Career* W M Tapp research fell Gonville & Caius Coll Cambridge 1970–73; Centre for Socio-Legal Studies Univ of Oxford: research fell 1972–75, sr research fell 1975–93, dep dir 1985–93, actg dir 1999; Univ of Oxford: research fell Wolfson Coll 1972–93, reader in law and society 1993–2004, tutorial fell Oriel Coll 1993–2006 (tutor for graduates 2001–06 and 2012–13, emeritus 2006–), research assoc Centre for Criminological Research 2002–06, prof of law and society 2004–06, emeritus prof of law and society 2006–; visiting prof: Law Sch Univ of Texas at Austin 1985, Coll of Law Ohio State Univ 1989, LSE 2006–10; visiting fell: Nat Inst of Justice US Dept of Justice 1979–80, Gonville & Caius Coll Cambridge 1987–88; Ford Fndn fell Columbia Law Sch NY 1967–68, Inter-Univ Cncl visiting lectr Univ of Singapore 1973, Rockefeller Fndn collaborative residency Bellagio 2000; delivered papers at legal confs and symposia worldwide; memb: Parole Bd for England and Wales 1977–79 and 1983–86, Research Ctee American Bar Fndn 1986–2009, Socio-Legal Task Force Campaign for Oxford 1990–93; former memb Research Ctee on the Sociology of Law Int Sociological Soc; memb Advsy Ctee: Centre for Law, Policy and Social Science Ohio State Univ, Mannheim Centre for Criminal Justice and Criminal Justice Policy LSE; US Law and Society Assoc: memb Bd of Tstees 1981–84 and 2008–11, memb 25th Anniversary Prog Ctee 1988–89, memb Didactic Workshops Ctee 1998–99, memb Kalven Prize Ctee 2005–07, memb Prog Ctee 2007–08, memb Best Article Prize Ctee 2010–11, memb Jacob Prize Ctee 2011–12, memb Wheeler Mentor Award Ctee 2013–14; founding co-ed Law in Social Context Univ of Pennsylvania Press 1984–93, ed Law and Policy 1987–2006 (memb Editorial Bd 1981–83 and 2006–, memb Sr Editorial Bd 1983–86), gen ed Oxford Socio-Legal Studies OUP (formerly Macmillan) 1993–2010 (memb Editorial Bd 1979–93); memb Editorial Bd: Law and Society Review 1982–83, Jl of Financial Regulation and Compliance 1988–95, The Justice System Jl, Jl of Regulation and Governance 2006–; reviewer for numerous jls incl: Br Jl of Criminology, Jl of Law and Society, Justice Quarterly, Law and Policy, Oxford Jl of Legal Studies; memb US Law and Society Assoc; *Publications* Psychology, Law and Legal Processes (co-ed, 1979), Enforcing Regulation: policy and practice (co-ed, 1984), Environment and Enforcement. Regulation and the social definition of pollution (1984, reprinted 1993), Making Regulatory Policy (co-ed, 1989), The Uses of Discretion (ed, 1992), The Regulation of Occupational Health and Safety: a socio-legal perspective (1993), Law as Last Resort: prosecution decision-making in a regulatory agency (2002, Herbert Jacob Prize American Law and Society Assoc 2003); author of numerous essays, monographs and papers; *Recreations* music, wine, food, sport, travel; *Style*— Prof Keith Hawkins; ✉ Oriel College, Oxford OX1 4EW (☎ 01865 276555, e-mail keith.hawkins@oriel.ox.ac.uk)

HAWKINS, Kit; s of Anthony Van Laast, MBE, and Angela Thomas, *née* Kean; *b* 24 May 1977; *Educ* Univ Coll Sch; *m* 26 April 2014, Jade, *née* Anderson; 2 s (Bodhi b 23 Oct 2012, Indio b 22 Sept 2015); *Career* co-fndr Tudhope Hawkins Mgmnt 2003, co-fndr Everybody's (music mgmnt co with clients incl Mumford & Sons) 2006, head of entertainment Mother 2009–12, co-fndr and ceo The Sunshine Company 2012–; nominated Best Short Film BAFTA 2006; *Recreations* cinema, music, reading, tennis, travel; *Clubs* Soho House; *Style*— Mr Kit Hawkins; ✉ Sunshine, 8 Shepherdess Walk, London N1 7LB (☎ 020 3725 8950, e-mail kit@thesunshinecompany.com, website www.thesunshinecompany.com

HAWKINS, Richard Ingpen Shayle; s of Vice Adm Sir Raymond Hawkins, KCB (d 1987), and Rosalind Constance Lucy, *née* Ingpen (d 1990); *b* 20 June 1944; *Educ* Bedford Sch; *m* 26 July 1969, Amanda Louise, da of Rear Adm E F Gueritz, CB, OBE, DSC (d 2008); 2 s (William b 1973, George b 1976); *Career* cmmnd 2 Lt RM 1962, Lt 42 Commando Far East 1964–65, 43 Commando UK 1965–66, 45 Commando Aden and UK 1967–69, Capt 40 Commando Far East 1970–71, GSO3 HQ Commando Forces 1971–73, Adj RMR Tyne 1973–75, Army Staff Coll Camberley 1976, Co Cdr 45 Commando UK 1977–78, Maj Instr Sch of Inf 1978–80, GSO2 Dept of Cmdt Gen RM MOD 1980–82, ret 1982; insurance broking 1982–2016; md Marsh Inc 1999–2001; dir: Bowring Marsh & McLennan Ltd 1994–97, Marsh UK Ltd 1997–2001, AIG 2002–04; *Recreations* sailing, field sports; *Clubs* Royal Yacht Sqdn, Boodle's; *Style*— Richard Hawkins, Esq; ✉ The Old Forge, Upton, Andover, Hampshire SP11 0JS (☎ 01264 736269)

HAWKINS, Prof Robert Edward; *b* 10 November 1955; *Educ* Trinity Coll Cambridge (open and sr scholar, MA Maths 1981, MB 1981), UCH London (MB BS 1984, Magrath and Fellowes Gold Medal 1984), MRC Lab of Molecular Biology Cambridge (PhD 1992); *Career* actuarial trainee Prudential Assurance Co 1977–79; house offr: in gen surgery Basingstoke Dist Hosp 1984–85, in med with oncology and haematology UCH London 1985; SHO: rotation in gen med Whittington Hosp London 1985–86, in thoracic med Brompton Hosp London 1986–87, in med oncology and radiotherapy Royal Marsden Hosp London 1987; St George's Hosp med registrar rotation: registrar in gen med and endocrinology St Helier Hosp Carshalton 1987–88, registrar in med oncology/haematology and palliative care Royal Marsden Hosp 1988–89; MRC recombinant DNA trg fellowship MRC Lab of Molecular Biology Cambridge 1989–92; MRC Centre and Addenbrooke's Hosp Cambridge: CRC sr clinical research fell and hon sr registrar in med oncology 1992–94, CRC sr clinical research fell and hon conslt in med oncology 1994–96; prof and head Dept of Oncology Univ of Bristol 1996–98, hon conslt in med oncology Bristol Oncology Centre 1996–98, CRC prof and dir of med oncology Univ of Manchester 1998–, hon conslt in med oncology Christie Hosp NHS Tst 1998–, head Cancer Studies Univ of Manchester 1998–2004; co-ordinator: EU project www.attack-cancer.org 2005–11, EU integrated trg network ATTRACT 2009–, EU FP7 Clinical Trials Network ATTACT 2005–; memb MRC Molecular and Cellular Medicine Bd 2012–; conslt to Biotech, dir Cellulartherapeutics Ltd; clinical ed Br Jl of Cancer 1997–2005; author of numerous articles in learned jls, invited lectures at home and abroad; FRCP 1999 (MRCP 1987); *Recreations* golf; *Style*— Prof R E Hawkins; ✉ Paterson Institute of Cancer Research, Wilmslow Road, Manchester M20 4BX (☎ 0161 446 3208, fax 0161 446 3269, e-mail rhawkins@picr.man.ac.uk)

HAWKINS, Sally; da of Colin Hawkins, and Jacqui Hawkins; *b* 27 April 1976; *Educ* James Allen Girls' Sch, RADA; *Career* actress; Film Actress of the Year Glamour Awards 2014; *Theatre* As You Like It (Buckingham Palace Gala), The Whore of Babylon (Globe Educational Centre), Accidental Death of an Anarchist (BAC), Svejk (Gate Theatre), The Dybukk (BAC), Romeo and Juliet (Theatre Royal York), The Cherry Orchard (Theatre Royal York), Perapalas (NT Studio), Much Ado About Nothing (Regents Park), Midsummer's Night's Dream (Regent's Park), Misconceptions (Octagon), The Way of The World (Wilton Music Hall), Country Music (Royal Court), House of Bernada Alba (RNT), The Winterling (RNT), Mrs Warren's Profession (Roundabout Theatre NY) 2010, Constellations (Royal Court and West End) 2012–13; *Television* Tipping the Velvet 2002, Promoted to Glory 2003, Byron 2003, The Young Visitors 2003, Little Britain 2003–05, Bunk Bed Boys 2004, Fingersmith 2005, 20,000 Streets Under the Sky 2005, Shiny Shiny Bright New Hole In My Heart 2006, Man to Man with Dean Learner 2006, Persuasion 2007 (Golden Nymph Award Best Actress Monte Carlo Television Festival 2007, RTS Award for Best Actress 2008), Little Crackers 2011, Room on the Broom 2012, How & Why 2014, The Hollow Crown II (Henry VI 1 & 2) 2015, Stick Man 2015; *Film* All or Nothing 2002, Layer Cake 2004, Vera Drake 2004, The Painted Veil 2006, Waz 2007, Cassandra's Dream 2007, An Education 2008, Desert Flower 2008, Happy Ever Afters 2008, Happy Go Lucky 2008 (Silver Bear Award Best Actress Berlin Film Festival 2008, Peter Sellers Award for Comedy Evening Standard Br Film Award 2009, Best Actress in a Comedy or Musical Golden Globes, Breakthrough Award Hollywood Film Festival, Best Actress Award LA Film Critics Awards, NY Film Critics Awards, NYFC Online, Boston Critics Awards and American Nat Soc of Film Critics Awards), It's a Wonderful Afterlife 2009, Never Let Me Go 2010, Made in Dagenham 2010, Submarine 2010, Love Birds 2010, Jane Eyre 2011, Great Expectations 2012, Almost Christmas 2013, The Double 2013, Blue Jasmine 2013 (Best Supporting Actress Empire Awards), The Phone Call 2013 (Golden Horseman of the Audience Int Award FilmFest Dresden), Godzilla 2014, Paddington 2014, X+Y 2014, Maudie 2016, The Shape of Water 2016; *Style*— Ms Sally Hawkins; ✉ c/o Conway Van Gelder Grant, 8–12 Broadwick Street, London W1F 8HW (☎ 020 7287 0077, e-mail vena@conwayvg.co.uk); c/o PA, Vanessa Green (e-mail vgreen@dsl.pipex.com)

HAWKINS, Dr Stanley Arthur; s of Canon John Henry Hawkins, of Dublin; *b* 2 March 1948; *Educ* Belfast Royal Acad, Queen's Univ Belfast (BSc, MB BCh, BAO, MD); *Career* registrar rising to sr registrar NI Neurology Serv 1974–79, res registrar Nat Hosp Queen Sq London 1979–81, conslt neurologist and sr lectr Queen's Univ Belfast and Royal Victoria Hosp Belfast 1981–97 (hon archivist 2012–), conslt neurologist and reader in neurology Queen's Univ Belfast 1997–2012, ret; part-time work Belfast Health and Social Care Tst 2012–; visiting prof UCLA 1984; pres Ulster Med Soc 2005–06, pres Irish Neurological Assoc 2010; former chair Res Ctee Multiple Sclerosis (MS) Ireland, memb Scientist Panel on Neuroimmunology Euro Fedn of Neurological Socs 1996–2005, medical advsr Multiple Sclerosis Soc of GB & I 2007–; Euro Ctee on Treatment and Res in Multiple Sclerosis (ECTRIMS): memb Cncl 1996–2008, memb Scientific Organising Ctee Basel 1999, Toulouse 2000, Dublin 2001 and Vienna 2004; session chair World Fedn of Neurology Delhi 1989, chair scientific session Int Fedn of Multiple Sclerosis Socs Dublin 1990, delivered numerous lectures in Europe and USA; memb Int Editorial Bd Multiple Sclerosis Clinical and Laboratory Research 1994–2013; FRCP 1990 (MRCP 1975); *Publications* over 100 full papers in peer-review jls; articles reviewed for numerous jls; *Recreations* gardening; *Style*— Dr Stanley Hawkins; ✉ Queen's University, Belfast BT12 6BJ (☎ 028 9024 0503, fax 028 9032 9899)

HAWKSWORTH, Prof David Leslie; CBE (1996); s of Leslie Hawksworth (d 1992), and Freda Mary, *née* Dolamore (d 1992); *b* 5 June 1946; *Educ* Univ of Leicester (BSc, PhD, DSc); *m* 1, 1968 (m dis 1998), Madeleine Una, *née* Ford; 1s, 1 da; m 2, 1999 (m dis 2008); m 3, 2009, Patricia E J, *née* Wiltshire; *Career* mycologist Cwlth Mycological Inst Kew 1969–81 (princ taxonomist 1980–81), scientific asst to exec dir Cwlth Agric Bureaux Farnham Royal Slough 1981–83, dir Int Mycological Inst Kew and Egham 1983–97, dir MycoNova 1998–2001; Universidad Complutense de Madrid: visiting prof 2000–01, Ramón y Cajal res prof 2001–06, prof contratado doctorado indefinido 2006–16; scientific assoc: Natural History Museum London 2006–, Royal Botanic Gardens Kew 2013–14 (hon research assoc 2014–); prof of biology Univ of Glos 2007–09, prof of ecology Univ of Gloucestershire 2013–14; memb Cncl (Govt appointee) English Nature 1996–99; visiting prof: Univ of Reading 1984–, Univ of Kent 1990–, Royal Holloway Coll London 1992–, Birkbeck Coll London 2013– (research fell 2008–13); chm: Int Cmmn on the Taxonomy of Fungi 1982–2002, Int Cmmn on Bionomenclature 1995–2012; pres Br Lichen Soc 1986–87 (memb 1964–), pres Br Mycological Soc 1990 (memb 1969–), pres Int Union of Biological Sciences 1994–97, hon pres Int Mycological Assoc 1994– (sec gen 1977–90, pres 1990–94); Int Assoc for Plant Taxonomy: memb 1967–, memb Ctee for Fungi 1981–93 and 2005–11, memb Gen Ctee 1987–, memb Editorial Ctee 1987–, Admin Finances 1993–99; Systematics Assoc: memb 1969–, treas 1972–81, ed-in-chief 1981–84 and 1986, memb Cncl 1970–72, 1986–95 and 2010–12; ed: The Lichenologist 1970–90, Mycopathologia 1984–87, Plant Systematics and Evolution 1986–98, Systema Ascomycetum 1986–98, Mycosystema 1986–, Mycological Research 1999–2009 (sr ed 2000–08), Biodiversity and Conservation (ed-in-chief 2006–, memb Editorial Bd 1991–2005); ed-in-chief IMA Fungus 2010–; memb Editorial Bd: Field Studies 1975–80, Nat History Book Reviews 1976–80, Plant Pathology 1985–91, Cryptogamic Botany 1988–90, Fungal Diversity 1999–, Taxon 2006–10, MycoKeys 2011–; memb: Field Studies Cncl 1965–2005, Int Assoc for Lichenology 1967– (awarded Acharius Medal 2002), Botany Sub-Ctee Royal Soc Nat Ctee for Biology 1975–82, Tropical Agric Assoc 1982–98, Ct Univ of Surrey 1983–98, Ruislip Woods Mgmnt Advsy Gp 1983–2001, American Phytopathological Soc 1986–98, Exec Bd World Fedn of Culture Collections 1988–96, Standing Ctee on Nomenclature Int Union of Biological Scis 1988–94, Int Relations Ctee Royal Soc 1994–95, Chartered Soc of Forensic Science (formerly Forensic Science Soc) 2011–, Int Soc for Human and Animal Mycology 2012–, Chartered Soc of Forensic Scientists 2011–; cncllr (Ashtead Independents) Mole Valley District Cncl 2016–; Josef Adolf von Arx Award 2011, Ainsworth Medal 2014, Founders' Award European Mycological Assoc 2015; Dr (hc) Univ of Umeå 1996; hon memb: Società Lichenologica Italiana 1989, Ukrainian Botanical Soc 1992, Mycological Soc of America 1994, Latin American Mycological Assoc 1996, Br Mycological Soc (Centenary fell) 1996, Br Lichen Soc 1997, Japanese Soc for Lichenology 2002; FLS 1969 (Bicentenary Medal 1978, vice-pres 1985–88), FIBiol 1982 (FSB 2011, FRSB 2015), CBiol 1986, FRSA 1997; *Publications* numerous books, articles, papers and book reviews in learned jls mainly on fungi (incl lichens), biological diversity and bionomenclature; *Recreations* gardening, natural history, museums, history of biology; *Style*— Prof David L Hawksworth, CBE; ✉ Milford House, The Mead, Ashtead, Surrey KT21 2LZ (☎ 01372 272087, e-mail d.hawksworth@nhm.ac.uk)

HAWLEY, Prof Christine Elizabeth; CBE (2008); da of John and Margaret Hawley; *b* 3 August 1949, Shrewsbury; *Educ* City of London Sch for Girls, AA Sch of Arch London (AADipl); *m* 1974, Clyde Watson; 1 da (Lucy b 1982), 2 s (Samuel b 1984, Joseph b 1991); *Career* asst R&D Unit Dept of the Environment 1972; asst architect: Renton Howard Wood and Levin Architects London 1972–73, De Soissons Partnership London 1974–77, YRM (Yorke Rosenberg and Madell) London 1977, Pearson International London 1978; ptnr Cook and Hawley Architects London 1974–; unit master AA Sch of Architecture London 1980–88 (tutor 1979–80), head Univ of E London (formerly Poly of E London) Sch of Architecture 1987–93; prof of architectural studies Bartlett Sch of Architecture UCL 1993–, dean Bartlett Faculty of the Built Environment UCL 1999–; visiting prof: Western Aust Inst of Technol Perth 1985, Oslo Sch of Architecture 1987, Tech Univ Vienna 1993 and 1996–97; Hyde prof Lincoln Univ Nebraska 1987; lectures at numerous instns at home and abroad incl: Rhode Island Sch of Design 1978, AA 1979–87, Berkeley Calif 1980–91, Aarhus Sch of Architecture 1985–93, UCLA 1993, Hong Kong Univ 1994, RIBA 1995, UCL (inaugural lecture) 1996; subject of numerous articles in architectural/design pubns; Br Cncl Award Rome 1977, Yamagiwa Art Fndn Award Tokyo 1979, Br Cncl Award Helsinki and Stockholm 1980; ARCUK 1978, RIBA 1982, FRSA 1983; *Projects* incl: limited int competition for social housing and exhbn centre W Berlin 1991, Stadel Acad Frankfurt 1992, competition in Lower Austria for a museum, belvedere, external amphitheatre and gallery 1993, participation of urban devpt forum on int workshops and symposium Hamburg 1993, Strathclyde Visions Centre Glasgow 1993, Elbberg Offices Hamburg 1993, Kitagata social housing Gifu 1994–, Shanghai planning study for social housing 1996; *Exhibitions* incl: Graham Fndn Chicago (Three Architects) 1982, Manspace London and NY 1982, Aedes Gallery Berlin 1994 and 1995, Venice Biennale 1996, Sagacho Gallery Tokyo 1997; *Recreations* swimming, reading, badminton; *Style*— Prof Christine Hawley; ✉ The Bartlett School of Architecture, University College London, 22 Gordon Street, London WC1H 0QB (☎ 020 7380 7504, fax 020 7380 7453, e-mail c.hawley@ucl.ac.uk)

HAWLEY, Dr Robert; CBE (1997); s of William Hawley (d 1960), and Eva, *née* Dawson; *b* 23 July 1936; *Educ* Wallasey GS, Wallasey Tech Coll, Birkenhead Tech Coll, King's Coll Durham (BSc, PhD), Univ of Newcastle upon Tyne (DSc); *m* 1, 1962 (m dis), Valerie, da of Colin Clarke; 1 da (Fiona Jane b 10 Dec 1966), 1 s (Nicholas Richard b 30 July 1968); m 2, 2002, Pamela Elizabeth, da of John Neesham; *Career* C A Parsons: head of research team 1961–64, electrical designer Generators 1964–66, dep chief generator engr 1966–70, dir and chief electrical engr 1973–74 (chief electrical engr 1970–73), dir of prodn and engrg 1974–76; NEI plc: md NEI Parsons Ltd (following t/o of C A Parsons) 1976–84, md Power Engineering Gp 1984–88, dir 1984–88, md Ops 1989–92; chm Engrg Cncl 1999–2002; chief exec: Rolls-Royce 1992 (main bd dir 1989–92), Nuclear Electric plc 1992–96, British Energy plc 1995–97; non-exec chm: Rotork plc 1996–98, INBIS plc 1997–2000, Taylor Woodrow plc 1999–2003, Rocktron 2001–04, Berkeley Resources Ltd 2006–11, Lister Petter Investment Hldgs Ltd 2006–, Welsh Power Gp Ltd 2007–10; non-exec dir: W S Atkins plc 1994–97, Colt Telecommunications plc 1998–2010, Tricorder Technology plc 1997–2001, Rutland Tst plc 2000–06; conslt SEMA 1994–96; chm Hawley Ctee on Corp Governance and Information Mgmnt 1993–98; pres IEE 1996–97, chm Engrg Cncl 1998–2002, memb Cncl Fellowship of Engrg (now Royal Acad of Engrg) 1981–84; vice-chllr World Nuclear Univ 2006–; author of numerous scientific papers; C A Parsons meml lectr IEE and Royal Soc 1977, Hunter meml lectr IEE 1990, Blackadder lectr NE Coast Instn of Engrs and Shipbuilders 1992, Wilson Campbell meml lectr 1994, Bowden lectr 1994, John Collier lectr 1997; IEE Achievement Medal 1989; pres Energy Industries Club 1989–91; memb Boat and Shoreworks Ctee RNLI 1992–97; chm Anglo-Korean Soc 2002– (pres 2002); memb Ct Univ of Newcastle upon Tyne 1979–, chm Cncl Univ of Durham 1997–2002, memb Ct Loughborough Univ 2003; Freeman City of London, Master Worshipful Co of Engrgs 2005–06; Hon DSc: Univ of Durham 1996, City Univ 1998, Cranfield Univ 2002; Hon DEng: South Bank Univ 1997, UWE 1997, Univ of Newcastle upon Tyne 2002, UMIST 2002; Hon DTech: Staffordshire Univ 2000, Univ of Abertay 2001, Robert Gordon Univ 2002; Hon DUniv Surrey Univ; hon fell Inst of Nuclear Engrs 1994, hon fell Liverpool John Moores Univ 2002; fell City and Guilds of London Inst 2003; FIEE 1970, FInstP 1970, FREng 1979, FIMechE 1987, FRSE 1997, Hon FIEE 2003, Hon FIIE 2003, FCGI 2003, Hon FIET 2006; Order of Diplomatic Serv Gwanghwa Medal Korea 1999; *Recreations* gardening, philately; *Clubs* Athenaeum; *Style—* Dr Robert Hawley, CBE, FREng, FRSE

HAWORTH, Baron (Life Peer UK 2004), of Fisherfield in Ross and Cromarty; Alan Robert Haworth; s of John Haworth (d 1991), and Hilma, *née* Westhead (d 1990); *b* 26 April 1948, Blackburn, Lancs; *Educ* Blackburn Tech and GS, Univ of St Andrews, Barking Regnl Coll of Technol (BSc); *m* 1, 1973 (m dis), Gill Cole; m 2, 1991, Maggie Rae; *Career* N E London Poly: registrar Faculty of Art & Design 1972–73, asst to Dir of Course Devpt 1973–75; PLP: ctee offr 1975–85, sr ctee offr 1985–92, sec 1992–2004; memb: John Muir Tst, Ramblers, Munro Soc, Scottish Wild Land Gp, Mountain Bothies Assoc, Nat Tst for Scotland, Marine Conservation Soc, Scottish Rights of Way Soc; *Publications* Men Who Made Labour (co-ed, 2006); *Recreations* hill walking, mountaineering (completion of the Munros 2001), foreign travel; *Style—* The Lord Haworth; ✉ House of Lords, London SW1A 0PW (e-mail harwortha@parliament.uk)

HAWORTH, Jane Victoria, née Wright; da of Peter Donald Wright (decd), and Barbera Anne, *née* Haworth; *b* 8 April 1964; *Educ* White Lodge, Royal Ballet Sch; *Career* ballerina; English Nat Ballet (formerly London Festival Ballet): joined 1983, sr soloist 1990–, artistic co-ordinator 2002–; *Performances* princ and soloist roles incl: title roles in La Sylphide and Carmen, Sugar Plum Fairy in The Nutcracker, Teresina in Napoli, Olga/Tsarina in Anastasia, Prelude and Waltz in Les Sylphides, Persian Princess in Prince Igor, Good Girl in Graduation Ball, Flower Festival pas de deux, Pink Lady in Sanguine Fan, Livia in Romeo and Juliet, Polyhymnia in Apollo, Fairy Godmother and Winter Fairy in Cinderella, Pas de Deux in Petrouchka Variations, Dawn in Coppélia, first solo in Raymonda, second solo in La Bayadere, Pas de Quatre, Pas de Trois and Lead Swans in Swan Lake; created roles: Woman in Stranger I Came, Symphony in 3, Countess in Sleeping Beauty, Cook in Alice in Wonderland, Stepmother in Cinderella, Batilde in Giselle, Lady Capulet in Romeo and Juliet, Clara's Mother in The Nutcracker; guest appearance in La Sylphide (with Peter Shaufuss, Vienna State Opera Ballet) 1990; character roles incl: Queen in Swan Lake, Lady Capulet and Nurse in Romeo and Juliet, Berthe in Giselle, Queen and Countess in Sleeping Beauty; *Television* Young Indiana Chronicles 1992, Live and Kicking 1995, Boxing Academy 2004, Don't Just Dream It 2005; *Recreations* horse riding, gardening, collecting antiques; *Style—* Miss Jane Haworth; ✉ c/o English National Ballet, Markova House, 39 Jay Mews, London SW7 2ES (☎ 020 7581 1245, fax 020 7225 0827, e-mail jane.haworth@ballet.org.uk)

HAWORTH, Nigel; s of Harry Haworth (d 2001), and Constance, *née* Southern; *b* 11 July 1958; *Educ* St Christopher's C of E Secdy Mod, Accrington & Rossendale Coll of FE; *m* 2006, Katherine, *née* Brooks; 1 da (Keeley Emma b 20 May 1985), 1 s (Kirk James b 26 July 1987); *Career* chef; lectr in catering Accrington & Rossendale Coll 1981–84; chef patron Northcote (one Michelin star) 1984–; jt md: Northcope Gp of Companies, Ribble Valley Inns; finalist Great British Menu (BBC 2) 2009; Egon Ronay Chef of the Year 1995, winner Wedgwood Chef & Potter Top 100 Chefs 2000; memb Acad of Culinary Arts, former memb Master Chefs of GB; sponsor: Lady Taverners, NSPCC; Prince Philip Medal C&G; hon prof Lancaster and Morecombe Coll; *Recreations* running, football, golf; *Clubs* Blackburn Rovers; *Style—* Nigel Haworth, Esq; ✉ Northcote, Northcote Road, Langho, Blackburn, Lancashire BB6 8BE (☎ 01254 240555, fax 01254 246568, mobile 07787 537824, e-mail reception@northcote.com)

HAWORTH, Richard Anthony; s of George Ralph Haworth (d 1995), and Joan Kershaw, *née* Taylor (d 2014); *b* 3 September 1955; *Educ* Oundle, Univ of Leeds (LLB); *m* 18 March 1994, Sara Kay (d 2009), da of Dr Ian Smith (d 2015); 1 s (George Frederick b 1 Jan 1996); *Career* called to the Bar Inner Temple 1978; in practice Northern Circuit; jr counsel Crown Provincial Panel; *Recreations* shooting, salmon fishing, growing sweet peas, stalking, working gundogs; *Clubs* East India, Yorkshire Flyfishers'; *Style—* Richard Haworth, Esq; ✉ 15 Winckley Square, Preston, Lancashire (☎ 01772 252828, fax 01772 258520, e-mail haworth@15wsq.co.uk)

HAWTON, Prof Keith Edward; s of Lesley William Hawton (d 1988), and Eliza, *née* Davies (d 1999); *b* 23 December 1942, Barnet, Herts; *Educ* Univ of Cambridge (MB BChir, MA), Univ of Oxford (DM, DSc); *m* 1978, late Joan; 2 da (Jane b 17 May 1981, Katherine b 1 Oct 1983); *Career* trg in psychiatry 1969–74, research psychiatrist 1974–76; Dept of Psychiatry Univ of Oxford: lectr 1976–79, clinical tutor 1979–84, prof of psychiatry 1996–, dir Centre for Suicide Research; conslt psychiatrist Oxfordshire Mental Healthcare Tst 1984–; Erwin Stengel Research Award Int Assoc for Suicide Prevention 1995, Louis I Dublin Award American Assoc of Suicidology 2001, Research Award American Fndn for Suicide Prevention 2002, Morselli Medal Int Acad for Suicide Research 2013; fell Governing Body Green Templeton Coll Oxford 1985–; fell Acad of Medical Sciences 2013; FRCPsych 1972; *Books* Attempted Suicide: A Practical Guide to its Nature and Management (with José Catalán, 1982), Sex Therapy: A Practical Guide (1985), Suicide and Attempted Suicide among Children and Adolescents (1986), Cognitive Behaviour Therapy for Psychiatric Problems: A Practical Guide (1989), Dilemmas and Difficulties in the Management of Psychiatric Patients (ed with Philip Cowen, 1990), Practical Problems in Clinical Psychiatry (ed with Philip Cowen, 1992), Suicide and Stress in Farmers (1998), The International Handbook of Suicide and Attempted Suicide (ed with Kees van Heeringen, 2000), Deliberate Self-Harm in Adolescence (with Claudine Fox, 2004), Prevention and Treatment of Suicidal Behaviour: From Science to Practice (ed, 2005), By Their Own Young Hand: Deliberate Self-Harm and Suicidal Ideas in Adolescents (with Karen Rodham, 2006), Suicide (with Rory O'Connor, 2013); *Recreations* golf, fishing, cricket, wine; *Style—* Prof Keith Hawton; ✉ Centre for Suicide Research, Warneford Hospital, Oxford OX3 7JX (e-mail keith.hawton@psych.ox.ac.uk)

HAY, Alexander Douglas; s of Lt-Col George Harold Hay, DSO (d 1967), and Patricia Mary, *née* Hugonin (d 1998); *b* 2 August 1948; *Educ* Rugby, Univ of Edinburgh (BSc); *m* 20 Jan 1973, Aline Mary, da of Robert Rankine Macdougall; 1 s (Robert Alexander b 29 July 1976), 1 da (Caroline Laura b 9 July 1978); *Career* ptnr Greaves West & Ayre CAs Berwick-upon-Tweed 1978–2005 (joined 1975); chm: Scottish Episcopal Church Widows & Orphans Fund Corp Ltd 1980–89, Roxburgh & Berwickshire Cons & Unionist Assoc 1989–92, Berwickshire Housing Assoc 1994–2000, Historic Houses Assoc for Scotland 2009–15; MICAS 1975; *Recreations* golf; *Clubs* Hon Co Edinburgh Golfers; *Style—* Alexander Hay, Esq; ✉ Duns Castle, Duns, Berwickshire (☎ 01361 883211)

HAY, David John MacKenzie; s of Ian Gordon McHattie Hay, of Inverness, and Ishbel Jean Hay, *née* MacKenzie; *b* 30 June 1952; *Educ* Inverness Royal Acad, Univ of Edinburgh (MA), Magdalene Coll Cambridge (MA, LLM); *Career* called to the Bar Inner Temple 1977, joined Butterworth & Co (Publishers) Ltd 1979, managing ed Atkin's Encyclopaedia of Court Forms 1984–85, ed R&D 1985–86, managing ed Electronic Forms Publishing 1986–88; gen ed: Halsbury's Laws of England (reissue) 1995–96 (ed 1989–96), Words and Phrases Legally Defined 1993–, Halsbury's Laws of Hong Kong 1995–, Major Works Butterworths Asia 1996–; *Recreations* music, enjoying the countryside, reading, travel; *Style—* David Hay, Esq; ✉ The Cottage, School Lane, Barley, Royston, Hertfordshire SG8 8JZ; E3–02–4 Pantai Hill Park Phase 1, Jalan Pantai Dalam, 59200 Kuala Lumpur Malaysia; Malayan Law Journal Sdn Bhd, 3 Floor, Wisma Bandar, No 18 Jalan Tuanku Abdul Rahman, 50100 Kuala Lumpur, Malaysia (☎ 00 60 3 291 7273, fax 00 60 3 291 6471)

HAY, Prof Frank Charles; s of Edward Frank Hay, of London, and Doris Irene, *née* Webber; *b* 8 October 1944, Chelmsford, Essex; *Educ* Sir George Monoux GS, Brunel Univ (BTech), Univ of London (PhD); *m* 2 Aug 1969, Frances Margaret, da of Prof George Baron; 1 da (Rebecca b 28 March 1974), 1 s (Thomas b 9 Feb 1977); *Career* Middx Hosp Med Sch: res assoc 1972–77, lectr in immunology 1977–78, sr lectr 1978–84, reader 1984–89; currently prof of immunology Centre for Medical and Healthcare Educn St George's Univ of London (chm Div of Immunology 1989, head Dept of Cellular and Molecular Scis 1991, vice-princ 1993) and visiting prof Inst Medicine Universiti Brunei Darussalam; vice-chm Salops Geological Soc; memb: Br Soc for Immunology 1970, Royal Soc of Med 1982; *Books* Epitope Mapping (2001), Practical Immunology (4 edn, 2002), How to Assess Students and Trainees in Medicine and Health (2013); *Recreations* swimming, mountain walking, pre-cambrian rocks and fossils, playing the lute; *Style—* Prof Frank Hay; ✉ 5 Long Mynd Place, Church Stretton, Shropshire SY6 6HX

HAY, Ian Wood; s of John William Hay (d 1977), of Harwich, Essex, and Winifred May, *née* Fox (d 1975); *b* 25 January 1940; *Educ* Colchester Sch of Art (NDD), RCA; *m* 26 March 1968, Teresa Mary, da of Stanislav Antoni Sliski, of Harwich, Essex; 2 s (James b 1978, Rupert b 1982); *Career* artist known for pastel paintings of London and The Thames; visiting lectr: St Martin's Sch of Art 1963–77, Norwich Sch of Art 1971–75; sr lectr in drawing Sch of Art Colchester Inst 1978–2001 (sch gall named The Hay Gallery in his honour); RCA prize for landscape painting 1963; many one man and group shows in Essex and London in The Minories and Phoenix Art Gallery; works in private and public collections incl: Guildhall Art Gallery, Sheffield Art Gallery, Doncaster City Art Gallery, Univ of Essex; chm of selectors Colchester Art Soc 2002–; major retrospective exhibition A Life Drawing (Minories Art Gallery Colchester) 2010; memb North Countryman's Club Colchester 2002–; hon doctorate Univ of Essex 2009; ARCA (1963); *Recreations* travel; *Style—* Ian Hay, Esq; ✉ 32 Tall Trees, Mile End, Colchester, Essex CO4 5DU (☎ 01206 852510, e-mail innwoodhay@hotmail.co.uk)

HAY, Lady Olga; *see:* Maitland, Lady Olga

HAY, Peter Laurence; s of Norman Leslie Stephen Hay (d 1979); *b* 7 March 1950; *Educ* St Paul's, Brunel Univ, London Business Sch; *m* 1, 19 July 1985 (m dis 1992) , Perdita Sarah Amanda Lucie Rogers; m 2, 29 Aug 1996, Caroline Mary Buchanan-Jones; *Career* chm: Norman Hay plc and subsidiary cos 1977–; dir: Ultraseal Ltd, Applied Precision Coatings Ltd, Advanced Surface Treatments, Surface Technol plc, Armourcote East Kilbride, Armourcote Suface Treatments, Norman Hay Int, Plasticraft Ltd, Lancy Technol Ltd, Pollshare, MX Systems, Advanced Coating Initiative; *Style—* Peter Hay, Esq; ✉ Windlesham Grange, Kennel Lane, Windlesham, Surrey GU20 6AA (☎ 01276 472980); Treviskey House, Treviskey, Portloe, Cornwall TR2 5PN (☎ 01872 501625); Norman Hay plc, Lyons Park, Coventry CV5 9PF (☎ 024 7622 9373, e-mail peter.hay@normanhay.com and peter.hay@gmail.com)

HAY, Peter Rossant; s of Vincent Hay, and Marie Winifred, *née* Chase; *b* 11 October 1948; *Educ* Clifton Coll, The Coll of Law Guildford; *m* 14 April 1973, Christine Maria; 1 da (Nicola Marie b 8 March 1975), 2 s (Alexander William Rossant b 11 Feb 1978, James Vincent Rossant b 10 Aug 1985); *Career* admitted slr 1973; ptnr: Ward Bowie 1973–86, Penningtons 1986–92, Perry Hay & Co 1993–; accredited mediator CEDR 1993; hon slr The Royal Scot Corp 1985–; chm Richmond Athletic Association Ltd 1986–91; non-exec dir: Meat Trade Suppliers plc 1988–89, West London TEC 1996–97, London Scottish Rugby Ltd 1996–98; vice-pres Richmond Chamber of Commerce 1994–98, vice-pres London Scottish FC; govr and vice-chm Corp of Richmond-upon-Thames Coll 1999–2005; tstee Richmond Parish Lands Charity 2005–08; memb Law Soc; *Recreations* golf, skiing, swimming, ex-rugby and rowing; *Clubs* Caledonian, Sunningdale Golf (captain 2014); *Style—* Peter R Hay, Esq; ✉ Perry Hay & Co, 25 The Green, Richmond, Surrey TW9 1LY (☎ 020 8332 7532, fax 020 8948 8013, e-mail peterhay@perryhay.co.uk)

HAY, Robin William Patrick Hamilton; s of William Reginald Hay (d 1975), of Nottingham, and (Mary Constance) Dora, *née* Bray; *b* 1 November 1939; *Educ* Eltham Coll, Selwyn Coll Cambridge (MA, LLB); *m* 18 April 1969, Lady Olga Maitland, *qv*, er da of 17 Earl of Lauderdale, *qv*; 2 s (Alastair b 18 Aug 1972, Fergus b 22 April 1981), 1 da (Camilla b 25 June 1975); *Career* called to the Bar Inner Temple 1964, recorder of Crown Court 1985–2005; legal assessor GMC 2002–, memb Research Ethics Ctee Nat Neurological Hosp 2002–13, chm Appeal Panel Postgrad Medical and Education and Training Bd 2005–09, legal advsr Faculty and Inst of Actuaries 2006–, legal advsr Royal Pharmaceutical Soc Statutory Ctees 2006–, legal assessor Nursing and Midwifery Cncl 2007–, legal assessor Gen Chiropractic Cncl 2009–, legal advsr GDC 2010–, memb Regulatory Panel Assoc of Chartered Certified Accountants 2010–, legal assessor Health and Care Professionals Cncl 2012–; ILEA candidate (Cons) Islington S and Finsbury 1986, chm Young Musicians Symphony Orch 1990–2001; *Recreations* gastronomy, church tasting, choral singing; *Clubs* Garrick; *Style—* Robin Hay, Esq; ✉ Lamb Chambers, Lamb Building, Temple, London EC4Y 7AS (☎ 020 7797 8300, fax 020 7797 8308, e-mail robinhay@lambchambers.co.uk)

HAY, Prof Roderick James; s of Kenneth Stuart Hay (d 1992), and Margery Geidt, *née* Winterbotham (d 1983); *b* 13 April 1947; *Educ* Wellington, Merton Coll Oxford, Guy's Hosp Med Sch London (MA, BM BCh, DM); *m* 18 August 1973, Delyth, *née* Price; 2 da (Lucy Arianwen b 6 March 1976, Harriet Alexandra b 20 August 1979); *Career* former registrar Guy's Hosp, lectr, sr lectr then reader LSHTM 1977–89, Mary Dunhill prof of cutaneous med GKT 1989–2002 (dean for external affrs 1995–2002), dean and clinical dir St John's Inst of Dermatology St Thomas' Hosp 1996–2002, dir Centre for Caribbean Med (UK) 1997–2002, head Sch of Med and Dentistry Queen's Univ Belfast 2005– (dean Faculty of Med and Health Sciences 2002–05); Dowling orator 1989, Avery Chan meml lectr 1997; pres: St John's Dermatology Soc, Br Soc for Med Mycology, Euro Confedn for Med Mycology, Br Assoc of Dermatologists 2001; non-exec dir EHSSB, chm Int Fndn for Dermatology; FRCP 1984, FRCPath 1992, FMedSci 2000; *Recreations* music,

H

gardening, walking; *Style*— Prof Roderick Hay; ✉ School of Medicine and Dentistry, Queens University Belfast, 71 University , Belfast BT7 1NN (✆ 028 9097 2186, e-mail r.hay@qub.ac.uk)

HAY, Prof Simon Iain; s of Robert Iain Hay, of Grantham, and Julia Allyson Perry, *née* Harmsworth; *b* 15 January 1971, Rinteln, Germany; *Educ* The Richard Aldworth Sch Basingstoke, Univ of Bristol (BSc), Univ of Oxford (DSc, DPhil, MA); *m* 1 June 2002, Sarah Judith, *née* Tomlin; 1 s (Maximilian Geoffrey b 4 May 2009), 1 da (Florence Julia Elinor b 4 Sep 2012); *Career* Univ of Oxford: postgrad research asst 1993–96, postdoctoral research offr 1996–99, sr research fell 1999–2008, reader of infectious disease epidemiology 2008–12, prof of epidemiology 2012–, research fell St John's Coll 2012–; sr research fell Wellcome Tst 2006–, dir of geospatial science and prof of global health Inst for Health Metrics and Evaluation Dept of Global Health Univ of Washington 2015–; author of over 250 peer-reviewed works, speaker at over 150 conferences and other scientific mettings; pres Royal Soc of Tropical Medicine and Hygiene 2013–; Scientific Medal ZSL 2008, Back Award RGS 2012, Bailey K Ashford Medal American Soc of Tropical Medicine and Hygiene 2013, Chalmers Memorial Medal Royal Soc of Tropical Medicine and Hygiene 2015; fell Remote Sensing and Photogrammetry Soc, CBiol, FRSB 2007, FRGS 2007, FLS 2013, FRCPEd 2014, FRSA 2014, fell American Soc of Tropical Medicine and Hygiene 2014, FMedSci 2015; *Recreations* gardening, music, reading, travel, natural history; *Style*— Prof Simon I Hay; ✉ Institute for Health Metrics and Evaluation, Department of Global Health, University of Washington, 2301 Fifth Avenue, Suite 600, Seattle WA 98121 USA (✆ 001 206 8972878, e-mail sihay@uw.edu); The Wellcome Trust Centre for Human Genetics, University of Oxford, Roosevelt Drive, Oxford OX3 7BN (✆ 01865 287854, e-mail simon.hay@well.ox.ac.uk, website www.simonhay.well.ox.ac.uk)

HAY, William; MLA; *b* 1950, Co Donegal; *Educ* Faughan Valley HS Londonderry; *Career* cncllr Derry City Council 1981–2010 (dep mayor 1992, mayor 1993), MLA (DUP) Foyle 1998–, speaker NI Assembly 2007–; nominated Life Peer 2014; *Recreations* walking, reading, enjoying the company of my family; *Style*— William Hay, Esq, MLA; ✉ Northern Ireland Assembly, Parliament Buildings, Belfast BT4 3XX

HAYASHI, HE Keiichi; *Career* Japanese diplomat; ambass to the Ct of St James's 2011–16; *Style*— HE Mr Keiichi Hayashi; ✉ Embassy of Japan, 101–104 Piccadilly, London W1J 7JT

HAYCOCKS, Richard John; s of Roy Terence Haycocks (d 1988), of Wilts, and Barbara Alice, *née* Rons; *b* 8 June 1949; *Educ* City of Westminster Coll, Dartford GS; *m* 30 June 1986, Myra Anne, da of Alan Douglas Kinghorn; 2 s (Thomas Richard Henry b 20 May 1987, James Richard John b 20 Aug 1990); *Career* Allfields 1969–74, Deloitte Haskins & Sells 1974–80, dir Baker Energy Holdings Ltd (part of Baker Hughes) 1980–83; Ernst & Young: joined 1984, ptnr 1989, ptnr corp fin 1990–2001; ptnr Baker Tilly 2002–06, dir Consensus Business Gp 2007–11, ptnr Bishop's Rock Capital Ltd; portfolio of non-exec directorships; Liveryman Worshipful Co of Coachmakers and Coach Harness Makers; FCSI (ACA 1971), MSI; *Clubs* RAC; *Style*— Richard Haycocks, Esq; ✆ 020 8658 4330, e-mail richardhaycocks@hotmail.com

HAYDAY, Terence John (Terry); s of John Alfred Hayday (d 1978), and Annie Dorothy Hayday (d 2004); *b* 23 June 1947, Bexhill-on-Sea, Sussex; *Educ* Hampton GS, Univ of Sussex (BA), City Univ (MBA); *m* 9 June 1973, Susan Pamela, da of Gordon Grenville Dean (d 1997); 2 s (Nicholas b 1977, Christopher b 1979), 1 da (Annabel b 1987); *Career* Lloyd's broker Leslie & Godwin Ltd 1965–67, Lloyd's underwriting asst R W Sturge & Co 1967–69, reinsurance underwriter Slater Walker Insurance Co Ltd 1972–76; Holmes Hayday (Underwriting Agencies) Ltd (formerly Holmes Kingsley Carritt Ltd): dep Lloyd's underwriter and dir 1976–79, md 1980–88, chm 1988–92; active underwriter Lloyd's Syndicate 694 1980–91, dir and chief exec Sturge Holdings plc (which acquired Holmes Hayday in 1990) 1991–94, co sec and dir Owen & Wilby Underwriting Agency Ltd 1995–99, co sec Gerling Corporate Capital Ltd 1998–99, dir and compliance offr Gerling at Lloyd's Ltd (which acquired Owen & Wilby Underwriting Agency in 1999) 1999–2003, co sec Gerling UK Ltd 2002–03, tech exec Lloyd's Market Assoc 2004–07; Professional Standards Lloyd's Market Assoc: mangr 2007–09, head 2009–12; chm Optimum Consultants Ltd 1994–, non-exec chm Pembroke Managing Agency Ltd (acquired by Ironshore 2008) 2007–09, non-exec chm Antares Managing Agency Ltd 2010–13; memb sr mgmnt team GIS UK (German Industrial Insurer), memb Bd of Mgmnt GCSA LLC (USA) 2013–15; dir: Highgate Managing Agencies Ltd 1994–96, Apex Professional Education Programme at Lloyd's 1995–98, Mitchell McLure Ltd 1995–2007, Pembroke JV Ltd 2007–08; non-exec dir: Newman & Stuchbery Ltd 1988–93, LIMNET Bd (London Insurance Market Network) 1992– The Channel Managing Agency Ltd 2014–; vice-pres Insurance Inst of London (memb Cncl 2008–12); memb: Advsy Bd of Exec Educn Saïd Business Sch Univ of Oxford 2007–12, Advsy Bd Centre for Risk & Insurance Studies Univ of Nottingham 2008–12, Advsy Bd CII London Market Faculty 2009–12, CII London Market Educn Gp 2011–12; dir and tstee Joshua Hayday Helping Hand Tst 2010–; Distinguished Serv Medal CII 2004, Pres's Award Insurance Inst of London 2007; Liveryman Worshipful Co of Insurers 2007 (chm Insurance Non-Exec Dir Forum, court asst 2013, chm Insurance Non-Exec Dir Ctee), Freedom of City of London 2008; FCII 1976 (vice-pres CII 2013); *Publications* Insurance Institute of London Centenary Publication First 100 Years (co-author and ed, 2007), Online iNED Information Bank: Worshipful Company of Insurers website (lead author and ed, 2014); *Recreations* sailing, rugby, theatre, literature, European painting, opera; *Clubs* Lloyd's Yacht, Twickenham Yacht, Harlequins FC, Three Rooms, Lloyd's; *Style*— Terry Hayday, Esq; ✉ e-mail terryhayday@gmail.com, terry.hayday@optimumconsultants.co.uk; website www.wci.org.uk; Lloyd's, One Lime Street, London EC3M 7HA

HAYDEN, Prof Jacqueline (Jacky); CBE (2013); da of Robert Leslie James Hayden, of Majorca, Spain, and Dorothy Blanche, *née* Cowell (d 1986); *b* 4 December 1950; *Educ* Croydon HS, KCL, St George's Hosp Med Sch (MB BS, LRCP, MRCS); *m* 11 Dec 1976, Edward Milne Dunbar, s of David Milne Dunbar; 2 s (Alexander James b 10 July 1980, Benjamin David b 20 Jan 1984); *Career* gen practice trg scheme Oxford 1976–79, princ in gen practice Unsworth Med Centre Bury Lancs 1979–, dean of postgrad med studies Univ of Manchester and NHS North West 1997– (assoc advsr in gen practice 1990–91, regional advsr in gen practice 1991–96), civil conslt in gen practice RAF 1998–2002; memb: Cncl RCGP 1985– (chm NW England Bd 1994–96), Jt Ctee on Postgraduate Trg for Gen Practice 1986–2006, Chief Med Offr's Working Pty on Specialist Trg 1993–94; chm Ctee of Regional Advsrs in Gen Practice in England 1994–97, vice chm Conf of Postgrad Med Deans (COPMED) 2006–, chm English Deans Ctee 2008–; FRCP, FRCGP, DCH, DRCOG; *Books* A Guide for New Principals (1996); contrib: The Medical Annual (1987), Practice Information Booklets (1987), The Practice Receptionist (1989), Change and Teamwork in Primary Care (1993), The Child Surveillance Handbook (1994), Professional Development in General Practice (series ed, 1990–99); *Recreations* my family, the house and garden; *Style*— Prof Jacky Hayden, CBE; ✉ North Western Deanery, 4th Floor, Barlow House, Minshull Street, Manchester M1 3DZ (✆ 0161 237 6168, fax 0161 237 3774)

HAYDEN, Richard Michael; s of Richard Taylor Hayden, and Cecelia Hayden; *b* 31 July 1945; *Educ* Georgetown Univ (BA), Wharton Grad Sch of Business (MBA); *m* 1978, Susan Margolies; 1 s, 1 da; *Career* Goldman Sachs & Co: assoc 1969–73, vice-pres 1973–80, ptnr/md 1980–98; Goldman Sachs International: dep chm 1995–98, vice-chm 1999; ptnr and chm GSC Partners Europe Ltd 2000–09, vice-chm GSC Gp 2000–09, chm GSC Investment Corp 2007–09; currently: non-exec chm Haymarket Financial LLP, chm Riverstone Energy Ltd; memb Bd: Compton & Knowles 1988–2000, Cortefiel SA 1994–96, Abbey National Gp 1999–2004, Perry Capital 2002–04, Cofra Holding AG 2003–07, Deutsche Börse 2005–; chm Advsy Bd TowerBrook Capital Ptnrs; non-exec dir CQS Capital; *Recreations* golf, tennis; *Clubs* Queenwood, RAC, Queen's, Hurlingham, Links (NYC), Union (NYC), Campden Hill Lawn & Tennis, Sebonack Golf (NYC); *Style*— Mr Richard Hayden; ✉ TowerBrook Capital Partners, 1 Pall Mall East, London SW1Y 5AU (✆ 020 7451 2056, e-mail richard.hayden@towerbrook.com)

HAYDON, Christopher; *Educ* Univ of Cambridge, Central Sch of Speech and Drama; *Career* assoc dir Bush Theatre 2008–11, artistic dir Gate Theatre 2011– (prodns incl: Wittenberg 2011, The Prophet 2012, The Trojan Women 2012, Purple Heart 2013, Grounded 2013, The Edge of Our Bodies 2014, Image of an Unkown Woman 2015, The Christians 2015); Twelve Angry Men (as freelance dir, West End) 2013–14; journalist: The Scotsman, Financial Times, Prospect Magazine, Guardian, Independent, New Statesman, The Stage; *Books* Conversations on Religion, Conversations on Truth, Identity and Identification; *Style*— Christopher Haydon, Esq; ✉ The Gate Theatre, 11 Pembridge Road, Notting Hill, London W11 3HQ; c/o Giles Smart, United Agents, 12–26 Lexington Street, London W1F OLE

HAYES, Helen; MP; *Career* MP (Lab) Dulwich and W Norwood 2015–; *Style*— Ms Helen Hayes, MP; ✉ House of Commons, London SW1A 0AA

HAYES, John Forbes Raymond; s of (George) Forbes Raymond Hayes (d 1995), of Brocastle, Mid Glamorgan, and Jean Hayes, OBE, *née* Cory (d 2007); *b* 21 October 1948; *Educ* Harrow, Trinity Hall Cambridge (MA); *m* 1 May 1976, Nicola Anne, da of Brian Thomas Reilly (d 1988); 4 s (Charles, Hugh, Matthew, Benjamin); *Career* mgmnt conslt; PricewaterhouseCoopers: accounting articles 1971, consltt 1980, dir Nigerian firm 1982–84, ptnr UK firm 1986–2002, chm UK Investment Gp 1990; ptnr IBM Business Consulting Services Europe 2002–; memb Fin Ctee RUSI 1999–2005 (memb Cncl 1999–2003); govr Harrow Sch 2000–, govr John Lyon Sch 2005; Freeman City of London 1970, memb Worshipful Co of Tin Plate Workers 1970 (Master 1992); FCA 1980 (ACA 1975); *Recreations* music, sailing, golf; *Clubs* Leander; *Style*— John Hayes, Esq; ✉ Wood End, Beech Lane, Jordans, Buckinghamshire HP9 2SZ (✆ 01494 872419); IBM United Kingdom Ltd, 76/78 Upper Ground, South Bank, London SE1 9PZ (✆ 020 7021 8758, mobile 07710 045150)

HAYES, Rt Hon John Henry; CBE (2016), PC (2013), MP; *b* 23 June 1958, Woolwich, London; *Educ* Colfe's GS, Univ of Nottingham (BA, PGCE); *m* 12 July 1997, Susan, *née* Hopewell; 2 s (William b 24 Nov 2000, Edward b 11 June 2004); *Career* dir The Database (Nottingham) Ltd 1986–99; cncllr Nottingham CC 1983–98 (party spokesman on educn 1988–96); MP (Cons) S Holland and The Deepings 1997– (Parly candidate (Cons) Derbyshire NE 1987 and 1992); vice-chm Cons Pty 1999–2000, actg head Political Section Office of the Ldr of the Oppn 2000, frontbench spokesman on educn and employment (shadow schs min) 2000–01, oppn pairing whip 2001–02, shadow min for agriculture and fisheries 2002–03, shadow min for housing and planning 2003–05, shadow min for tport 2005, shadow min for vocational educn and skills 2005–07, shadow min for lifelong learning, FE and HE 2007–10, min of state Dept for Business, Innovation and Skills and Dept of Educn 2010–12, min of state Dept for Energy and Climate Change 2012–13, min of state Cabinet Office and sr Parly advsr to the PM 2013–14, min of state at Dept for Transport 2014–15, min of state at the Home Office 2015–; memb: Agriculture Select Ctee 1997–99, Educn Employment Select Ctee 1998–99, Admin Select Ctee 2001–02, Ctee of the Selection 2001–02; vice-chm Cons Backbench Educn Ctee 1997–99, jt chm All-Pty Disablement Gp 1998–2009, sec All-Pty Acquired Brain Injury Ctee; author of various articles and pamphlets; adjunct assoc prof Richmond the American Int Univ in London 2002–10; former chm: Univ of Nottingham Cons Assoc, E Midlands Regnl Cons Students, Young Conservatives; memb: Countryside Alliance, countryside NFU, SPUC; chm Br Caribbean Assoc; patron Headway Cambs; *Recreations* the arts (particularly English painting, poetry and prose), good wine and food, many sports (incl darts and boxing), painting, history, making jam, antiques, architecture and aesthetics; *Clubs* Carlton, Spalding, Spalding Gentleman's Soc (Lincs); *Style*— The Rt Hon John Hayes, CBE, MP; ✉ House of Commons, London SW1A 0AA (✆ 020 7219 1389, e-mail hayesj@parliament.uk)

HAYES, Josephine Mary (Jo); da of Reginald Francis Hayes, DFC (d 1977), and Eileen, *née* Bass (d 2005); *b* 26 June 1955; *Educ* Colchester Co HS for Girls, Lady Margaret Hall Oxford, City Univ (Dip Law), Yale Law Sch (alumni fell, LLM); *Career* called to the Bar 1980; chair Assoc of Women Barristers 1996–98; memb SDP 1983–87, fndr memb Lib Dems 1987–; *Clubs* Reform; *Style*— Miss Jo Hayes; ✉ 2 Greens Yard, Colchester, Essex CO1 1QP (✆ 01206 543463); Gough Square Chambers, 6–7 Gough Square, London EC4A 3DE (✆ 020 7353 0924, e-mail josephine.hayes@goughsq.co.uk)

HAYES, HE Kirsty Isobel; da of Robert Colin Paton, and Rowena Antoinette, *née* Liesching; *b* 2 February 1977, Aberdeen; *m* Dr Peter Richard Hayes, *qv*; 1 da (Liberty Paton b 2004), 1 s (Jasper William b 2006); *Career* diplomat; desk offr (Biodiversity) Environment Policy Dept FCO 1999–2000, vice-consul (Political/Economic) Hong Kong 2000–01, second sec (Economic) Washington (Temp) 2001–02, private sec to HM ambass Washington 2002–04, head Institutions/France Team Common Foreign and Security Policy Gp FCO 2005–06, head HR (Diversity and Devpt Team) FCO 2007, dep head HR (Training, Recruitment and Devpt Section) FCO 2007–08, int contractor to UN Devpt Prog Regional Centre Colombo 2008–09, head Corp Communications Dept FCO 2010–11, 2012 Unit FCO 2011, head Int Orgns Dept FCO 2011–, ambass to Portugal 2014–; *Books* Reinventing International Food Architecture (2008); *Recreations* eventing, yoga; *Clubs* Farmers; ✉ c/o FCO (Lisbon), King Charles Street, London SW1A 2AH (Twitter @KirstyHayesFCO)

HAYES, Malcolm Lionel Fitzroy; s of Vice Adm Sir John Hayes, KCB, OBE (d 1998), and Hon Rosalind Mary Finlay (d 2002); *b* 22 August 1951; *Educ* St George's Sch Windsor, Eton, Univ of St Andrews, Univ of Edinburgh (BMus, Tovey Prize for Composition); *Career* formerly involved in weaving indust Lewis Outer Hebrides until 1981; music critic: The Times 1985–86, The Sunday Telegraph 1986–89, The Daily Telegraph 1989–95; contrib 1982–: Tempo, The Independent, Musical Times, The Listener, Classical Music, Opera Now, BBC Music Magazine, Classic FM Magazine, BBC Radio 4, BBC Radio 3, BBC World Service, Classic FM; memb Critics' Circle 1988–; compositions incl: 3 Songs on Chinese Poems (1972), Cantata for flute and chamber group (1983), Into the Night for unaccompanied choir (1984), Stabat Mater for soloists and orchestra (2001), Odysseus remembers for soloists and orchestra (2004), From the Paradiso of Dante for solo piano (2006), The Wild Swans of Coole for unaccompanied choir (2009), May Magnificat for unaccompanied choir (2010), Byzantium for orchestra (2012); *Books* New Music 88 (co-ed, 1988), Anton von Webern (1995), 20th Century Music (2001), Selected Letters of William Walton (ed, 2002), Liszt: His Life and Music (2009); *Recreations* skiing, photography; *Clubs* Surrey CCC; *Style*— Malcolm Hayes, Esq; ✉ e-mail malcolmhayes@btinternet.com, website www.malcolmhayes.co.uk

HAYES, Dr Peter Richard; s of Jasper Terence Hayes (d 1997), and Greta Louvaine, *née* Sharman; *b* 11 April 1963, Ashford, Surrey; *Educ* County Sch Ashford Surrey, Univ of Surrey (BSc), KCL (PhD); *m* 26 Oct 2002, Christine Isobel (Kirsty), *née* Paton; 1 da (Liberty Paton b 31 Aug 2004), 1 s (Jasper William b 24 April 2006); *Career* diplomat; post-doctoral res assoc KCL 1989–90, sr scientific offr Nat Physical Lab 1990–93, DTI 1993–94, Office of Sci and Technol Cabinet Office1994–98; dep head Environment, Sci and Energy Gp FCO 1998–2000, dir nuclear decommissioning DTI 2000–01, cnsllr then consul gen Br Embassy Washington DC 2001–05, princ private sec to Sec of State for Foreign and Cwlth Affrs 2005–07, high cmmr to Sri Lanka and non-resident high cmmr to Maldives 2008–10, head of public affrs London Stock Exchange Gp 2011–12, dir overseas territories FCO 2012–, cmmr Br Antarctic Territory 2012–, cmmr Br Indian Ocean Territory 2012–; contrib to various scientific jls; MInstP, CPhys 1990; *Recreations* family; *Clubs* Farmers; *Style—* Dr Peter Hayes; ✉ Foreign and Commonwealth Office, King Charles Street, London SW1A 2AH

HAYES, Dr Roger Peter; s of Peter Hall, and Patricia Mary, *née* Lacey; *b* 15 February 1945; *Educ* Isleworth GS, Univ of London, Univ of Southern Calif (BSc, MA), Henley Business Sch (DBA); *m* 15 Feb 1974, Margaret Jean Hayes; 1 s (Nicolas Alexander b 25 Nov 1983); *Career* corr Reuters Paris 1967–72, dir and vice-pres Burson Marsteller 1972–79, PA Management Consultants 1979–83, dir of corp communications Thorn EMI plc 1985–88, dir IT World 1985–, chm Hayes Macleod International and Investor Corporate Communications 1988–91, non-exec dir Echo Communications Research Gp 1989–99; pres Int PR Assoc 1997; vice-pres Public Affrs and Govt Rels Ford of Europe 1991–93, DG British Nuclear Industry Forum 1993–97, dir Int Inst of Communications 1998–2003; sr cnsllr APCO Worldwide; memb Bd of Regents Potomac Inst Washington DC; assoc Euro Centre for Public Affrs; visiting lectr Greenwich Univ Business Sch 2014–, visiting fell Henley Business Sch 2015–17; FIPRA 1987, FIPR 1988 (memb emeritus 2006); *Books* Corporate Revolution (jtly, 1986), Experts in Action (jtly, 1988), Systematic Networking (1996), Reframing the Leadership Landscape (2015); *Recreations* tennis, travel, movies and music; *Clubs* Reform, Hurlingham, IOD; *Style—* Dr Roger Hayes; ✉ 75 Ellerby Street, London SW6 6EU (☎ 020 7731 1255, e-mail roger_p_hayes@yahoo.co.uk)

HAYES, Simon John; s of John Hayes, and Bridget Hayes; *b* London; *Partner* Melissa Cliff; *Career* production sound mixer 1993–; film projects incl: Lock Stock and Two Smoking Barrels 1997, Snatch 2000 (Best Sound Gold Reel Award 2000), Mean Machine 2001, Collusion 2001, Swept Away 2001, I'll Be There 2002, Calcium Kid 2002, Shaun of the Dead 2003, Layer Cake 2003, Bridget Jones: The Edge of Reason 2004, Nanny McPhee 2004, Revolver 2004, Stardust 2006, 28 Weeks Later 2006, The Bank Job 2006, Mamma Mia 2007, Green Zone 2008, Kick Ass 2008, Harry Brown 2009, Nanny McPhee and the Big Bang 2009, Bel Ami 2010, X-Men: First Class 2010, Prometheus 2011, Les Misérables 2012 (Best Sound Editing and Mixing Satellite Award 2013, Best Sound BAFTA 2013, Best Sound Mixing Acad Award 2013, Best Sound Mixing Cinema Audio Soc Award 2013), Kick Ass 2 2012; UK Screen Assoc Conch Award for Prodn Sound Mixer of the Year 2008, 2009 and 2012; memb: Assoc of Motion Picture Sound 1999–, Acad of Motion Picture Arts and Sciences 2013–, Cinema Audio Soc 2013–, BAFTA 2013–; *Recreations* judo (blackbelt 2nd dan); *Clubs* Budokwai (Chelsea); *Style—* Simon Hayes, Esq; ✉ c/o Sue Greenleaves, Independent Talent Group, Oxford House, 76 Oxford Street, London W1D 1BS (☎ 020 7034 2141, e-mail suegreenleaves@independenttalent.com, website www.simon-hayes.com)

HAYES, Dr William; s of Robert Hayes (d 1986), and Eileen, *née* Tobin (d 1985); *b* 12 November 1930; *Educ* UC Dublin (BSc, PhD), Univ of Oxford (MA, DPhil); *m* 28 Aug 1962, Joan Mary (d 1996), da of John Ferriss (d 1986); 1 da (Julia b 1970), 2 s (Robert b 1973, Stephen b 1974); *Career* official fell and tutor in physics St John's Coll Oxford 1960–78, 1851 overseas scholar 1955–57, sr fell American Nat Sci Fndn Purdue Univ 1963–64, visiting prof Univ of Illinois 1971, princ bursar St John's Coll Oxford 1977–87, Oxford Univ prof, dir and head Clarendon Lab Oxford 1985–87, pres St John's Coll Oxford 1987–2001, pro-vice-chllr Univ of Oxford 1990–2001, delg of OUP 1991–2001, chm of curators Oxford Univ Chest 1992–2000, currently sr research fell Clarendon Lab Oxford; hon fell St John's Coll Oxford 2001; Hon DSc: Nat Univ of Ireland 1988, Purdue Univ 1996; fell American Physical Soc 1990, Hon MRIA 1998; *Books* Scattering of Light by Crystals (with R Loudon, 1978), Defects and Defect Processes in Non-Metallic Solids (with A M Stoneham, 1985); *Recreations* walking, reading, listening to music; *Style—* Dr William Hayes; ✉ St Johns College, Oxford OX1 3JP (☎ 01865 277300, e-mail w.hayes1@physics.ox.ac.uk)

HAYES, William (Billy); s of William Hayes, and Margaret, *née* Ellis; *b* 8 June 1953; *Educ* St Swithins RC Sch, Univ of Liverpool (Dip); *m* 1995, Dian Lee; 1 s (Niall William b 7 Feb 2000), 1 da (Melissa Clare b 15 April 2002); *Career* former welder JJ Howards Fabrication Steel then John West Foods; joined Post Office 1974; Communication Workers Union: memb 1974–, former positions incl magazine ed, TUC youth conf delg, union conf delg and branch sec, memb Nat Exec 1992–, nat offr 1992–2001, gen sec 2001–; world pres of post and logistics UNI Global; memb Lab Pty, memb Lab Pty Policy Forum, memb Lab Campaign for Electoral Reform, regular delg to Lab Pty Conf; memb: Greenpeace, Gen Cncl TUC; vol Simon Community; *Publications* All Around the World (1998); *Recreations* films, books, music, Liverpool FC; *Style—* Billy Hayes, Esq; ✉ Communication Workers Union, 150 The Broadway, Wimbledon, London SW19 1RX (☎ 020 8971 7251, fax 020 8971 7430, e-mail bhayes@cwu.org)

HAYLER, Clive Reginald; s of Reginald Hayler (d 1985), and Dorothy Edith Hayler (d 2001); *b* 11 August 1955; *Educ* Steyning GS, Univ of Liverpool (BSc), Univ of Exeter; *m* Heather Jayne, da of Derek John Roberts (d 2002); 2 s (Richard Mark b 1984, Christopher James b 1985); *Career* mktg mangr Beckman RIIC Ltd 1979–83 (UK Sales Person of the Year 1981); md: Hawksley & Sons Ltd 1985–91 (gen mangr 1983–85), Marco Scientific Ltd 1991–98; dir AIS Cleanroom Products Ltd 1998–2000; md Primarius Ltd 2000–; memb Ctee: BSI Cleanroom Standards Working Gp, UK/Ireland Chapter of Parental Drug Assoc (chm Biotech Gp), Soc of Environmental Engrgs; memb: Int Soc for Pharmaceutical Engrg, Inst of Environmental Sciences and Technol, Int Soc for Cellular Therapy, Br Fertility Soc, S2C2; FInstD, CBiol, FSEE, MPS; *Recreations* running, surfing, martial arts, tropical horticulture, travel; *Clubs* IOD, HMC; *Style—* Clive Hayler, Esq; ✉ Primarius Ltd, 66 Roman Road, Steyning, West Sussex BN44 3FN (e-mail chayler@primarius.co.uk)

HAYMAN, (Anne) Carolyn; OBE; da of Prof W K Hayman, FRS, *qv*, and Margaret Riley, *née* Crann (d 1994); *b* 1951; *Educ* Univ of Cambridge (BA), SOAS (MSc); *Career* chief exec: Foyer Federation 1996–2004, Peace Direct 2004–14 (co-fndr); chair Preventable Surprises 2015–; *Style—* Ms Carolyn Hayman, OBE; ✉ 36a Lawford Road, London NW5 2LN

HAYMAN, Baroness (Life Peer UK 1995), of Dartmouth Park in the London Borough of Camden; Dame Helene Valerie Hayman; GBE (2012), PC (2000); da of Maurice Middleweek (decd); *b* 26 March 1949; *Educ* Wolverhampton Girls' HS, Newnham Coll Cambridge (MA, pres Cambridge Union); *m* 1974, Martin Hayman, *qv*, s of Ronald Hayman (decd); 4 s (Hon Ben b 1976, Hon Joseph b 1980, Hon Jacob b 1982, Hon David b 1985); *Career* worked successively with SHELTER (nat campaign for homeless), Camden Social Servs Dept then Nat Cncl for One Parent Families (dep dir) 1969–74, MP (Lab) Welwyn and Hatfield 1974–79, fndr memb Maternity Alliance and broadcaster 1979–85, vice-chm Bloomsbury HA 1985–92, chm Whittington Hosp NHS Tst 1992–97, chm Cancer Research UK 2001–04; sat as Lab peer House of Lords 1995–2006, Parly under-sec of state DETR 1997–98, Parly under-sec of state Dept of Health 1998–99, min of state MAFF 1999–2001, Lord Speaker House of Lords 2006–; chair Human Tissue Authy 2005–06, memb Human Fertilisation and Embryology Authy 2005–06, memb GMC 2013–, chair Cambridge Univ Health Partners 2014–, chair Ethics and Governance Cncl UK Biobank 2015–; former lay memb UCL Cncl; former chair of govrs Brookfield Sch; tstee: Royal Botanic Gardens Kew 2002–06, Sabin Vaccine Inst 2011–15, Malaria Consortium 2013–16, DEC 2014–; patron Anne Frank Tst UK 2009–; hon degree: Univ of N London 1995, Univ of Middlesex 1996, Univ of Herts 1999, Univ of Wolverhampton 2007, Brunel Univ 2012; fell Newnham Coll Cambridge 2008; *Style—* The Rt Hon the Baroness Hayman, GBE; ✉ House of Lords, London SW1A 0PW (e-mail haymanh@parliament.uk)

HAYMAN, Martin Heathcote; *b* 20 December 1942; *Educ* Highgate Sch, Univ of Cambridge (MA); *m* 1974, Baroness Hayman, PC (Life Peer), *qv*; 4 s (Hon Ben, Hon Joseph, Hon Jacob, Hon David); *Career* slr 1964–69; successively co slr: Plessey Co, ITT and Pullman Kellogg; sec and chief legal advsr Cadbury Schweppes 1985–88 (chief legal advsr 1978–88), gp sec and head of gp legal servs Standard Chartered Bank 1988–2000; chm Mediation UK 2001–03; non-exec dir Fin Objects plc 2002–08; memb Mgmnt Bd Standard Chartered's Seeing is Believing, memb Bd of Tstees Care Int UK 2002–09, memb Bd of Tstees Nat Family Mediation 2008–12, chair Restless Devpt 2010–; former memb Bd CEDR, former dir Inst of Business Ethics; former chair of govrs William Ellis Sch NW London; *Recreations* family; *Style—* Mr Martin Hayman; ☎ 07813 662974, e-mail martinhayman@yahoo.co.uk

HAYMAN, Michael; MBE (2014); *b* 1970; *Educ* Millfield, Queen Mary Coll London (BA), LSE (MSc); *m* Claire Hayman; 2 da (Alexandra b 13 May 2011, Aurelia b 19 April 2013); *Career* co-fndr Seven Hills 2010–; non-exec dir Creative Sheffield 2005–; chm of entrepreneurs Coutts & Co 2009–; co-fndr StartUp Britain, co-fndr E20, chm MADE: The Entrepreneur Festival; memb: Advsy Bd Nat Business Awards 2013, Bd Duke of York's iDEA, Advsy Bd MassChallenge UK; fell Br American Project; hon fell Judge Business Sch Univ of Cambridge; one of GQ's 100 Most Connected Men 2014; Freeman Guild of Public Relations Practitioners 2011; Freeman City of London; FCIPR, FRSA 2011; *Publications* Face Value: Your Reputation As A Business Asset (2008), Disruptive Influence: The Entrepreneur Report (2010), Growth Britannia: Britain's Breakthrough Opportunity (2014), Mission: How the Best in Business Break Through (with Nick Giles, 2015), Growth Britannia: Trading Places (2015); *Clubs* RAC, The Clubhouse, The Addison, The Club at the Ivy; *Style—* Michael Hayman, MBE; ✉ 104 Chapelier House, London SW18 1LR (☎ 020 7199 2201, mobile 07957 243986, e-mail michael.hayman@wearesevenhills.com, Linkedin michael hayman)

HAYMAN, Sue; MP; da of John Bentley, of Seaton, Devon, and Rita, *née* Williams (d 1982); *b* 28 July 1962, Upper Bucklebury, Berks; *Educ* St Bartholomew's Comp Newbury Berks, Anglia Ruskin Univ (BA); *m* 1997, Ross Hayman; *Career* communications conslt: Copper Consultancy 2005–14, self-employed 2014–15; memb Assoc of the Consultation Inst; cncllr Cumbria CC 2013–15, MP (Lab) Workington 2015–; *Style—* Mrs Sue Hayman, MP; ✉ House of Commons, London SW1A 0AA (e-mail sue.hayman.mp@parliament.uk, Twitter @SueHayman1)

HAYMAN-JOYCE, James Leslie; s of Maj Thomas F Hayman-Joyce, RA (d 1946), and Betty Christine, *née* Bruford (d 1995); *b* 12 May 1945; *Educ* Radley, RAC Cirencester; *m* 3 March 1973, Charlotte Alexandra Mary, da of J P Crump, DFC (d 1998); 2 s (Thomas Leslie b 12 April 1981, Simon Patrick b 10 Nov 1983); *Career* chartered surveyor; ptnr Blinkhorn & Co 1983–88, dir Sandoes Nationwide Anglia Estate Agents 1988–91, princ Hayman-Joyce Chartered Surveyors 1991–; FRICS 1970; *Style—* James Hayman-Joyce, Esq; ✉ Bakers Farmhouse, Barton-on-the-Heath, Moreton-in-Marsh, Gloucestershire GL56 0PN (☎ 01608 674170, e-mail hj@haymanjoyce.co.uk)

HAYMAN-JOYCE, Lt-Gen Sir Robert John; KCB (1996), CBE (1989, OBE 1979), DL (Monmouthshire 1996); s of Maj Thomas Fancourt Hayman-Joyce (d 1946), and Betty Christine, *née* Bruford (d 1995); *b* 16 October 1940; *Educ* Radley, Magdalene Coll Cambridge (MA); *m* 19 Oct 1968, Diana, da of Maj Neil Livingstone-Bussell (d 2005), of Sydling St Nicholas, Dorset; 2 s (Richard Livingstone b 21 Oct 1973, Alexander Robert b 11 Dec 1976); *Career* cmmnd 11 Hussars (PAO) 1963, Cmd Royal Hussars (PWO) 1980–82, Cdr RAC BAOR 1983–85, Dep Cmdt RMCS 1987, Dir UK Tank Prog 1988, DG Fighting Vehicles MOD(PE) 1989, DG Land Fighting Systems MOD (PE) 1990–92, Dir Royal Armoured Corps 1992–94, Mil Sec 1994–95, Master Gen of the Ordnance 1995–98, dep chief of def procurement (Ops) 1997–98; Col Cmdt Royal Armoured Corps 1995–99; non-exec dir Alvis plc 1999–2004; non-exec chm: Raytheon Systems Ltd 2000–12, March Security Ltd 2007–09; Col The Royal Yeomanry 2002–10; chm: tstees Tank Museum 1995–2002, Monmouthshire Hunt 1998–2002, London Int Horse Show 2010–16 (vice-pres 2016–); patron: Retired Offrs Assoc 2000–09, Soc for Welfare of Horses and Ponies 2003– (chm of tstees 2015–), Museum of the Welsh Regiments 2010–; project dir St Mary's Winston Appeal 2012–; Hon DSc Cranfield Univ 1998; *Recreations* skiing, horses, reading, music; *Clubs* Cavalry and Guards', Leander, Monmouthshire Hunt (chm 2009–); *Style—* Sir Robert Hayman-Joyce, KCB, CBE, DL; ✉ Ty Isha, Mamhilad, Pontypool, Gwent NP4 0JE (☎ 01495 785507, e-mail robert@frengis.com)

HAYNES, Anthony Robert; s of Robert Haynes (d 1976), and Joan Haynes; *b* 1959; *Educ* Trinity Coll Cambridge (MA, PGCE), Univ of Malta (Cert), Open Univ (Cert); *m* 1985, Karen, *née* Turner; 1 da (Frances Rachel), 2 s (Jonty Gower, Simon Walcott); *Career* various teaching jobs 1983–96; various publishing jobs incl Continuum International Publishing Gp Ltd (editorial dir 2002–03, publishing dir 2003–06); ptnr The Professional and Higher Partnership Ltd 2006–, dir Frontinus Ltd (formerly The Professional and Higher Partnership Ltd) 2014–; visiting prof: Beijing Normal Univ 2005–10, Hiroshima Univ 2010–11; *Publications* Writing Successful Textbooks (2001), 100 Ideas for Lesson Planning (2007), 100 Ideas for Teaching Writing (2007), Writing Successful Academic Books (2010), Complete Guide to Lesson Planning and Preparation (2010); *Recreations* beach-hutting; *Clubs* Burrough Green CC, IOD; *Style—* Anthony Haynes, Esq; ✉ c/o Frontinus Ltd, 4 The Links, Cambridge Road, Newmarket, Suffolk CB8 0TG (☎ 01638 663456, e-mail anthony@frontinus.org.uk, website frontinus.org.uk)

HAYNES, Derek Leslie; s of Frederick Leslie Haynes, North Walsham, Norfolk, and Doreen Florence, *née* Saville; *b* 13 June 1950; *Educ* Dagenham Co HS; *m* Julie Iris, da of Iris Maskell; 1 s (Kieren Stephen b 20 Jan 1992); *Career* qualified CA 1975; articled clerk Rowley, Pemberton, Roberts 1968–74, mangr Deloitte Haskins & Sells 1974–80; Clark Whitehill: sr audit mangr 1980–82, tech ptnr 1982–92; ptnr and head of audit Mazars & Guerard 1993–98, ptnr Mazars Neville Russell 1998–2002, dep gp fin dir Pinnacle Insurance plc 2002–05, principle KPMG 2005–; memb ICAEW Nat Tech Advsy Ctee (chm); chm Investment and Life Assurance Gp (ILAG) Fin Reporting Standards Practitioner Gp; memb Worshipful Co of Insurers 2002; Freedom of The City of London 1985, memb Worshipful Co of Glass Sellers of London 1985; FCA; *Recreations* jazz and classical music; *Style—* Derek L Haynes, Esq; ☎ 020 7311 6025, mobile 07880 558666

HAYNES, John Harold; OBE (1995); *b* 25 March 1938; *Educ* Sutton Valence; *m* Annette Constance; 3 s (John b 1967, Marc b 1968, Christopher b 1972); *Career* wrote and published first book 1956, ret from RAF as Flt-Lt 1967 to take up full-time publishing, having founded J H Haynes and Co 1960; dir Haynes Publishing Gp plc; dir: J H Haynes and Co Ltd 1960–, Haynes Publications Inc (USA) 1974, GT Foulis and Co Ltd 1977–, Haynes Developments Ltd 1979–, J H Haynes (Overseas) Ltd 1979–, John H Haynes Developments Inc (USA) 1979–, Oxford Illustrated Press Ltd 1981–, Gentry Books Ltd, Camway Autographics Ltd 1984–, Oxford Publishing Co 1988–, Patrick Stephens Ltd 1990–; *Recreations* cycling, walking, veteran and vintage cars, reading; *Clubs* Southern Milestone Motor (pres), Guild of Motoring Writers; *Style—* John H Haynes, Esq, OBE; ✉ Haynes Publishing Group plc, Sparkford, Somerset BA22 7JJ (☎ 01963 440635, e-mail smackinnon@haynes.co.uk); 861 Lawrence Drive, Newbury Park, Ca 91320, USA (☎ 00 1 818 889 5400)

HAYNES, Keith Anthony; s of Ernest Haynes (d 1996), and Mary, *née* McElroy (d 1980); *b* 2 March 1958; *Educ* St Peter's GS, Univ of Hull (LLB), Manchester Poly (MSc); *m* 3 Sept 1986, Louise Mary, *née* Jackson; *Career* gen mangr Booth Hall Children's Hosp 1984–87, gen mangr Maternity and Paediatric Servs Gtr Glasgow Health Bd 1988–90; chief exec: Liverpool Obstetric and Gynaecology Servs NHS Tst 1990–94, Royal Liverpool Univ Hosp Tst 1994–95; Med Protection Soc: gen mangr Clinical Negligence Scheme for NHS Tsts 1995–98, dir MPS Risk Consulting 1998–2008, dir Healthcare Risk Consulting Ltd 2008–; memb Bd Family Housing Assoc Manchester 1997–2002; visiting lectr York St John Univ 1996–2012, visiting sr lectr Dept of Health Sciences Univ of York 1999–2005; hon fell Faculty of Med Univ of Manchester 2003–06, hon sr lectr Faculty of Med Univ of Leeds 2006–08; MHSM; *Publications* Clinical Risk Management in Primary Care (2005); *Recreations* walking, political biography, fine wine; *Style*— Keith Haynes, Esq; ✉ Healthcare Risk Consulting, Main Street, Sutton on the Forest, York YO61 1DP (☎ 07789 505937, e-mail kh@healthcareriskconsulting.co.uk)

HAYNES, Lawrence John (Lawrie); s of Donald H Haynes, of Eastoft, Lincs, and Irene, *née* Langford; *b* 6 December 1952; *Educ* North Axholme Comp Sch Crowle, Stevenson Coll of FE, Heriot-Watt Univ (BA); *m* Carol Anne, *née* Nelson; 1 da (Liberty Rose b 26 Aug 1981), 2 step da (Natasha Jane b 15 March 1969, Victoria Louise b 21 July 1970); *Career* apprentice RAF (Halton) 1968–71, RAF Sqdn Serv 1971–78, Stevenson Coll 1978–79, Heriot-Watt Univ 1979–83, contracts offr rising to contracts exec British Aerospace (Space Systems) Ltd 1983–88, legal dir then md Microtel Communications Ltd (now Orange) 1988–91, projects dir British Aerospace plc 1991–94, chief exec Highways Agency 1994–99, md Lattice Group Telecommunications 2000–02, ceo British Nuclear Gp and memb Bd BNFL plc 2003–07, ceo White Young Green plc 2007–09, pres – nuclear Rolls Royce 2009–; tstee RAF Benevolent Fund 2006; FRSA 1994, FIHT 1995, FCIT 1997; *Recreations* sailing, cricket, skiing; *Style*— Lawrie Haynes, Esq

HAYNES, Timothy Hugh Penzer; s of Denzil Barry Penzer Haynes (d 1992), of Hampton-in-Arden, and Felicia Ann, *née* Nettlefold; *b* 2 April 1955; *Educ* Shrewsbury, Univ of Reading (BA), Pembroke Coll Cambridge (PGCE); *Children* 2 s (Theo Robert Penzer b 12 May 1994, Joseph Edward Penzer b 4 Dec 1995); *Career* stockbroker 1979–80; teacher: Queen Elizabeth's GS Blackburn 1980, Hampton Sch 1980–82; St Paul's Sch: teacher 1982–88, undermaster 1988–92, surmaster 1992–95; headmaster: Monmouth Sch 1995–2005, Tonbridge Sch 2005–; *Style*— Tim Haynes, Esq; ✉ Tonbridge School, Tonbridge, Kent TN9 1JP (☎ 01732 365555)

HAYTER, Baroness (Life Peer UK 2010), of Kentish Town in the London Borough of Camden; Dr Dianne Hayter; da of Flt Lt Alec Bristow Hayter (d 1972), and Nancy, *née* Evans (d 1959); *b* 7 September 1949; *Educ* Penrhos Coll, Aylesbury HS, Trevelyan Coll Durham (BA), Queen Mary Univ of London (PhD); *m* Prof Anthony David Caplin; *Career* research asst GMWU 1970–72, research offr European Trade Union Confedn Brussels 1973, research offr Trade Union Advsy Ctee to OECD Paris 1973–74, gen sec Fabian Soc 1976–82 (asst gen sec 1974–76), journalist Channel 4's A Week in Politics 1982–83, dir Alcohol Concern 1983–90, chief exec EPLP 1990–96, dir corp affrs Wellcome Trust 1996–99, chief exec Pelican Centre 1999–2001; memb: Royal Cmmn on Criminal Procedure 1978–81, Exec Ctee NCVO 1987–90, Financial Services Consumer Panel 2001–05 (vice-chm), Bd Nat Consumer Cncl 2001–08, Bd Nat Patient Safety Agency 2001–04, Determinations Panel Pension Regulator 2005–10, Bd of Actuarial Standards Financial Reporting Cncl 2006–11, Insolvency Practices Cncl 2006–10; chair: Consumer Panel Bar Standards Bd 2006–09, Property Standards Bd 2008–10, Legal Services Consumer Panel 2009–11; memb: London Lab Party Exec 1976–82, Exec Ctee Fabian Soc 1986–95 (chair 1992–93), Lab Party Nat Constitutional Ctee 1987–98, Lab Party NEC 1998–2010 (vice-chair 2006–07, chair 2007–08); Lab whip and shadow min Cabinet Office and Dept for Business, Innovation and Skills 2012–; visiting prof Univ of Westminster 2012–; JP Inner London 1976–90; *Publications* Fightback! (2005), Men Who Made Labour (co-ed, 2006); *Style*— The Baroness Hayter of Kentish Town; ✉ House of Lords, London SW1A 0PW

HAYTER, Sir Paul David Grenville; KCB (2007), LVO (1992); s of Rev Canon Michael George Hayter, and Katherine Patricia, *née* Schofield; *b* 4 November 1942; *Educ* Eton (King's scholar), ChCh Oxford (MA); *m* 1973, Hon Deborah Gervaise, da of Baron Maude of Stratford-upon-Avon; 2 s, 1 da; *Career* House of Lords: clerk Parliament Office 1964, seconded as private sec to Ldr of the House and Chief Whip 1974–77, clerk of ctees 1977, princ clerk of ctees 1985–90, reading clerk 1991–97, princ fin offr 1991–94, clerk of legislation 1994–2003, clerk asst 1997–2003, Clerk of the Parliaments 2003–07; sec Assoc of Lord-Lieuts 1977–91; chm CPRE Northants 2007–; *Recreations* music, gardening, botanising, local history, archery, painting; *Style*— Sir Paul Hayter, KCB, LVO; ✉ Walnut House, Charlton, Banbury, Oxfordshire OX17 3DR

HAYTER, Peter; s of Reginald James Hayter (d 1994), of Bushey, Herts and Lucy Gertrude Gray (d 2004); *b* 13 March 1959; *Educ* Aldenham, Goldsmiths Coll London (BA); *m* 28 Nov 1987, Mary Ann (d 2013), da of late Geoffrey William Hamlyn; 1 s (Maximilian Geoffrey Reginald Hamlyn b 28 Dec 1990), 1 da (Sophie Grace b 9 July 1995); *Career* journalist; Hayter's Sports Reporting Agency 1982–86 (office boy, jr reporter, reporter, managing ed), football corr Sportsweek Magazine 1986–87, freelance writer 1987–88 (football diarist, writer and cricket writer Independent, football writer Observer, features ed Allsport Photographic), editorial prodr Running Late (Channel 4 sports discussion prog) 1988, cricket corr Mail on Sunday 1989–2014, chief corr The Cricket Paper 2012–; *Theatre* as actor: Greatest Show on Legs 1977–78, Twelfth Night (as Orsino, Two Score Theatre Co) 2014, Aladdin (as Nobby the Naughty Panda, Regal Theatre Tenbury Wells) 2014, Henry V (as Pistol, Rooftop Theatre Co The Brewery Ludlow) 2015, Jack and the Beanstalk (as King Bertie the Brave, Regal Theatre Tenbury Wells) 2015; as dir: Macbeth (Two Score Theatre Co Ludlow Assembly Rooms) 2015; *Books* Visions of Sport (1988), The Ashes – Highlights since 1948 (with BBC Test Match Special Team, 1989), Cricket Heroes (1990), Great Tests Recalled (1991), England v West Indies – Highlights since 1948 (with BBC Test Match Special Team, 1991), Botham – My Autobiography (Don't Tell Kath) (with Ian Botham, 1994), The Botham Report (with Ian Botham, 1997), Postcards from The Beach (with Phil Tufnell, 1998), Tufnell – My Autobiography (What Now?) (with Phil Tufnell, 1999), Botham's Century – My 100 great cricketing characters (with Ian Botham, 2001), Ashes Victory (with the England cricket team, 2005), Coming Back To Me: the autobiography of Marcus Trescothick (with Marcus Trescothick, 2008), England's Ashes (with the England team, 2009); *Video* Botham Hits Back (interview, 1992), Ashes Fever (2005); *Recreations* cricket, theatre, cinema, hard liquor; *Clubs* MCC, The Cricketers Club of London, Stanmore Cricket, Elvino's Cricket, Incogniti Cricket, Fleet St Strollers Cricket, The Lord's Taverners, Bunbury's Cricket, Cricket Writers'; *Style*— Peter Hayter, Esq

HAYTER, 4 Baron (UK 1927); Sir (George) William Michael Chubb; 4 Bt (UK 1909); s of 3 Baron Hayter, KCVO, CBE (d 2003), and Elizabeth Anne, *née* Rumbold; *b* 9 October 1943; *Educ* Marlborough, Univ of Nottingham (BSc); *m* 8 Jan 1983, Waltraud, yr da of J Flackl, of Sydney, Aust; 1 s (Hon Thomas Frederik Flackl Chubb b 23 July 1986); *Heir* s, Hon Thomas Frederik Flackl Chubb; *Career* md Chubb Malaysia 1972–79, md Chubb Aust 1979–82, dir Business Devpt Chubb plc 1982–89, dir William Chubb Associates 1991–2005, dir UELS Ltd 1996–; Liveryman Worshipful Co of Weavers (Upper Bailiff 1999); *Style*— The Rt Hon the Lord Hayter; ✉ Rookery Cottage, Monk Sherborne, Hampshire RG26 5HS

HAYTHORNTHWAITE, Richard Neil; s of Christopher Haythornthwaite (d 1984), and Angela, *née* Painter (d 1967); *b* 17 December 1956, Chatham, Kent; *Educ* Colston's Sch Bristol, Queen's Coll Oxford (MA), MIT (SM); *m* 7 April 1979, Janeen, *née* Dennis; 1 s (Alisdair b 27 Sept 1981), 1 da (Sophia b 21 May 1986); *Career* Br Petroleum 1975–95, commercial dir Premier Oil 1995–97, gp ceo Blue Circle Industries 1999–2001 (ceo Europe and Asia 1997–99), ceo Invensys plc 2001–05, advsr Star Capital Partners 2006–12; chm: Mastercard Inc 2006–, Network Rail 2009–12, Centrica plc 2014–, Arc International 2015–, QIO Technologies 2015–; non-exec dir: ICI 2001–08, Land Securities 2008–09; advsr PSI (UK) Ltd 2008–14; chm: Better Regulation Cmmn, Almeida Theatre, Corp Advsy Gp Tate Gallery, Risk and Regulatory Advsy Cncl 2008–09, Southbank Centre 2008–15, World Wide Web Fndn 2013–16; *Recreations* cycling; *Clubs* RAC, 67 Pall Mall, 5 Hertford Street; *Style*— Richard Haythornthwaite, Esq; ✉ RH Management, 1 Curzon Street, London W1J 5HD (☎ 020 7514 0103, fax 020 7514 0178)

HAYTON, Brian John; s of John Edward Hayton, of Ardrossan, Ayrshire, and Williamina Boden Cairns, *née* Tipper; *b* 1 May 1953; *Educ* Ardrossan Acad, Univ of Glasgow (MA), Univ of London (Dip), Museums Assoc (Dip), Univ of Bradford (MBA), CIM (DipM); *m* 23 July 1976, Fiona Mary-Ellen, da of John Murray Innes; 1 da (Pamela Jane b 21 July 1979), 1 s (Ian Brian b 8 June 1981); *Career* volunteer N Ayrshire Museum 1967–74, trainee Glasgow Museums and Art Galleries 1975–78, dist curator Moray DC 1978–80, dep dir NW Museums and Art Gallery Serv 1981–87 (asst dir 1980–81), county museum offr N Yorks Co Cncl 1987–95, museum advsr ACC 1990–95, dir Compton Verney House Tst 1996–98, project dir Nat Railway Museum 1998–2000; museum conslt 1998–2000; Kingston upon Hull City Cncl: head of museums 2000–03, head of cultural services 2003–06, head of cultural, leisure and sports services 2006–; pres NW Fedn of Museums and Art Galls 1987–88, pres elect Midlands Fedn of Museums and Art Galls 1997; chm: Soc of County Museum Officers 1994–95, Museums Benevolent Fund 2000–; dir Humber Sports Partnership 2006–, hon treas Museums Assoc 1996–2002; tstee: Beecroft Bequest 1996–2002, Trevor Walden Tst 2000–; memb: Registration Ctee Museums and Galleries Cmmn 1992–2000, Museums Assoc Cncl 1996–2002 and 2003–; chm MA Pension Fund 2001–; Chartered Marketer; FMA 1988, FRSA 1996, FCIM 2006 (MCIM 1998); *Recreations* walking, swimming, exploring towns; *Style*— Brian J Hayton, Esq; ✉ Ferens Art Gallery, Queen Victoria Square, Hull HU1 3RA (☎ 01482 613900, e-mail brian.hayton@hullcc.gov.uk)

HAYTON, Hon Mr Justice David John; s of Flt Lt Arthur Hayton (d 2001), and Beatrice, *née* Thompson (d 1999); *b* 13 July 1944; *Educ* Royal GS Newcastle upon Tyne, Univ of Newcastle upon Tyne (LLB, LLD), Jesus Coll Cambridge (MA, LLD); *m* 17 March 1979, Linda Patricia, da of James David Rae (d 1974); 1 s (John James b 28 July 1990); *Career* called to the Bar Inner Temple 1968; in practice Lincoln's Inn 1970–2005 (bencher 2004), recorder Co Court 1984–2000, acting justice Supreme Court of the Bahamas 2000–01, justice of Caribbean Ct of Justice Trinidad 2005–; lectr Univ of Sheffield 1968–69 (asst lectr 1966–68), fell Jesus Coll Cambridge 1973–87, prof of law KCL 1987–2005 (dean Faculty of Law 1988–90); head of UK delgn to Hague Conf On Private Int Law 1988 (1984), dep chm English Trust Law Ctee 1994–2005; memb Law Panel for Higher Education Funding Cncl Research Assessment Exercise 2001; coach Cambridge RFC I XV 1980–83; *Publications* books: Registered Land (1973, 3 edn 1981), Cases and Commentary on Law of Trusts (6–12 edns 1975–2005), Law of Trusts and Trustees (13–19 edns 1979–2016), Law of Trusts (1989, 4 edn 2003), European Succession Laws (1991, 2 edn 2002), Modern International Developments in Trust Law (1999), Extending the Boundaries of Trusts and Similar Ring-Fenced Funds (2002), The International Trust (2011); author of Hayton Report on Financial Services and Trust Law for SIB and IMRO (1990); *Recreations* playing tennis, watching rugby, health club; *Clubs* Queen's Park Oval (Trinidad), Tranquility Tennis (Trinidad), MCC, Athenaeum; *Style*— Hon Mr Justice David Hayton; ✉ Caribbean Court of Justice, 134 Henry Street, Port of Spain, Trinidad and Tobago (☎ 00 1 868 625 9118, fax 00 1 868 627 0238, e-mail davidhayton@caribbeancourtofjustice.org or david.hayton@gmail.com)

HAYWARD, Debra; *Career* film producer; Working Title Films: joined as prodr's asst 1989, rising to devpt exec, head of film until 2011; fndr Monumental Pictures 2011–; *Film* incl: The Guru 2002, Thunderbirds 2004, Wimbledon 2004, Bridget Jones: The Edge of Reason 2004, Pride & Prejudice 2005, Nanny McPhee 2005, United 93 2006, Atonement 2007, Elizabeth: The Golden Age 2007, Frost/Nixon 2008, The Boat That Rocked 2009, State of Play 2009, Green Zone 2010, Nanny McPhee and the Big Bang 2010, Senna 2010, Paul 2011, Tinker Tailor Soldier Spy 2011, Johnny English Reborn 2011, Le Misérables 2012 (Best Picture Musical/Comedy Golden Globe 2013), I Give It A Year 2013; *Style*— Ms Debra Hayward

HAYWARD, Prof Jack Ernest Shalom; s of Menachem Hayward (d 1961), of Vancouver, Canada, and Stella, *née* Isaac (d 1959); *Educ* Horsley Hall, LSE (BSc, PhD); *m* 10 Dec 1965, Margaret Joy, da of Harold Clow Glenn (d 1985), of Adelaide, Aust; 1 da (Clare b 1971), 1 s (Alan b 1973); *Career* Nat Serv flying offr RAF 1956–58; asst lectr and lectr Univ of Sheffield 1959–63, lectr and sr lectr Keele Univ 1963–73, sr research fell Nuffield Coll Oxford 1968–69, prof of politics Univ of Hull 1973–92, dir Oxford Univ European Studies Inst and professorial fell St Antony's Coll 1993–98, research prof Univ of Hull 1999–; visiting prof: Univ of Paris III 1979–80, Inst d'Études Politiques Paris 1990–91; vice-pres Political Studies Assoc of the UK 1981– (chm 1975–77, pres 1979–81); Award for Lifetime Achievement in Political Studies 2003, Political Studies Assoc of the UK Sir Isaiah Berlin Prize for Lifetime Achievement 2011; Hon DLitt Univ of Hull 2013; FBA 1990; Chevalier de l'Ordre Nat du Mérite (France) 1980, Chevalier de la Légion d'Honneur (France) 1996; *Books* Private Interests and Public Policy, The Experience of the French Economic and Social Council (1966), The One and Indivisible French Republic (1973), Planning Politics and Public Policy: The British French and Italian Experience (jtly, 1975), Planning in Europe (jtly, 1978), State and Society in Contemporary Europe (jtly, 1979), The Political Science of British Politics (jtly, 1986), The State and the Market Economy: Industrial Patriotism and Economic Intervention in France (1986), Developments in French Politics (jtly, 1990 and 1994), After the French Revolution: Six Critics of Democracy and Nationalism (1991), De Gaulle to Mitterrand (1993), Industrial Enterprise and European Integration (1995), Governing the New Europe (jtly, 1995), The Crisis of Representation in Europe (1995), Elitism, Populism and European Politics (1996), The British Study of Politics in the Twentieth Century (jtly, 1999), Developments in French Politics (jtly, 2001), Governing from the Centre (jtly, 2002), Governing Europe (jtly, 2003), Fragmented France: Two Centuries of Disputed Identity (2007), Leaderless Europe (jtly, 2008), The Withering of the Welfare State (jtly, 2012), European Disunion: Between Sovereignty and Solidarity (jtly, 2012); *Recreations* music, books, walking; *Style*— Prof Jack Hayward, FBA; ✉ School of Politics, University of Hull, Hull HU6 7RX (☎ 01482 655027, fax 01482 466208)

HAYWARD, Paul; *Career* jt managing ptnr and head of private equity Gateley LLP; *Style*— Paul Hayward, Esq; ✉ Gateley LLP, 111 Edmund Street, Birmingham B3 2HJ (e-mail phayward@gateleyuk.com)

HAYWARD, Paul; s of Dennis Hayward, and Shirley Hayward; *Educ* Ringmer Comp Sch, Eastbourne Coll of FE, Univ of Bristol (BA); *Children* 1 s (Lewis b 27 Nov 1995), 1 da (Martha b 7 Feb 1999); *Career* journalist; chief reporter Racing Post, racing corr The Independent, chief sports feature writer Daily Telegraph, chief sports writer Daily Telegraph, chief sports writer The Guardian, chief sports writer Daily Telegraph until 2005, columnist Daily Mail 2005–08, chief sports writer The Observer 2008–11, chief sports writer The Telegraph 2011–; Sports Cncl Sports Writers' Assoc Br Sports Journalist of the Year 1996, Sky Sports Writer of the Year 1997, 1999 and 2001, Br Press

Awards Sports Writer of the Year 2002 and 2003; *Recreations* post-war American fiction, tennis, Brighton and Hove Albion, the South Downs, the National Trust; *Style*— Paul Hayward, Esq

HAYWARD, His Hon Judge Richard Michael; s of George Michael Hayward (d 1993), of Winchelsea, E Sussex, and Esmè Mary Florence, *née* Howard (d 1985); *b* 12 July 1946; *Educ* Highgate Sch, Inns of Court Sch of Law; *m* 1969, Laura Louise, da of E M Buchan; 2 s (Nicholas Richard b 20 Feb 1971, Anthony Pascoe b 17 Oct 1972), 1 da (Emily Alexandra b 23 Sept 1977); *Career* called to the Bar Middle Temple 1969, recorder 1994–96 (asst recorder 1990), circuit judge (SE Circuit) 1996–; *Recreations* golf, painting, gardening, horses; *Clubs* R&A, Rye Golf; *Style*— His Hon Judge Hayward; ✉ Lewes Combined Court, High Street, Lewes, East Sussex BN7 1YB

HAYWARD, Baron (Life Peer UK 2015), of Cumnor in the County of Oxfordshire Robert Antony Hayward; OBE (1991); s of late Ralph Hayward, of Eynsham, Oxon, and Mary Patricia, *née* Franklin; *b* 11 March 1949; *Educ* Maidenhead GS, Univ of Rhodesia (BSc); *Career* vice-chm Nat Young Cons 1976–77, cncllr Coventry City Cncl 1976–78, MP (Cons) Kingswood 1983–92; PPS: to under sec of state for Trade and Industry 1985–87, to min for Industry 1986–87, to sec of state for Transport 1987–92; memb Select Ctee on Energy 1983–85, jt sec Back Bench Aviation Ctee 1991–92, advsr to Chm Cons Pty 2009–12; co-fndr and jt co-ordinator Gulf Support Gp 1990–91; DG Br Soft Drinks Assoc 1993–99, chief exec Br Beer and Pub Assoc 1999–2009, dir Portcullis Public Affrs 2011–; chm CBI Trade Assoc Forum 2007–; dir Stonewall 1997–2003; chm/pres Kingscross Steelers RFC 1999–2003; tstee Community YMCA 2010–; *Recreations* former national level rugby official, psephology; *Style*— The Lord Hayward, OBE; ✉ 11 Grosvenor Park, London SE5 0NQ

HAYWOOD, Nigel Robert; CVO (2006); s of Leslie Haywood (d 1965), and Peggy, *née* Webb (d 2009); *b* 17 March 1955, Betchworth, Surrey; *Educ* Truro Sch, New Coll Oxford (MA, MPhil), Univ of Bournemouth (MSc); *m* 1979, (Mary) Louise, da of Robert Smith (d 2007), of Bedworth, Warks; 3 s (Christopher b 1984, Thomas b 1985, Peter b 1991); *Career* Lt RAEC 1977–80; entered HM Dip Serv 1983, second later first sec Budapest 1985–89, FCO 1989–92, dep consul-gen Johannesburg 1992–96, cnsllr and dep head of delgn UK Delgn to OSCE Vienna 1996–2000, FCO 2000–03, ambass to Estonia 2003–07, HM consul-gen Basra 2008–09, govr Falkland Islands and cmmr South Georgia and South Sandwich Islands 2010–; hon pres Golden Scale Club 2002– (memb 1982–); Bard of the Cornish Gorseth 1976; memb Philological Soc 1981, memb Br Ecological Soc 2009; MCIL (MIL 1988); *Publications* The One That Got Away (contrib, 1991); various articles in the angling press; *Recreations* fishing (especially saltwater fly fishing), running, renaissance lute, recorders, archery, butterfly conservation; *Clubs* Oxford and Cambridge, Purbeck Runners; *Style*— Nigel Haywood, Esq, CVO; ✉ c/o Foreign & Commonwealth Office, King Charles Street, London SW1A 2AH (e-mail nigelhaywood@mac.com)

HAYWOOD, Roger; s of Maj George Haywood, of Norwich, and Ethel Florence, *née* Reynolds; *b* 24 July 1939; *Educ* Westcliff Sch; *m* 30 June 1962, Sandra Leonora, da of George Yenson (d 1972); 2 da (Sarah b 1963, Laura b 1971), 2 s (Ian b 1965, Mark b 1966); *Career* mktg positions with Dunlop, Dexion and in various advertising agencies, Euro PR mangr Air Products 1970–72; md: Haywood Hood & Associates Ltd 1972–75, Tibbenham Group 1975–82; chm: Roger Haywood Associates Ltd 1982–92, Worldcom Inc 1989–91, Kestrel Communications Ltd 1992–2001; chief exec Issues Analysis Ltd 2001–; pres Inst of PR 1991; chm: Chartered Inst of Mktg 1992, Worldcom Europe 1997–98, PR Standards Cncl 1998–; vice-chm PR Conslts Assoc 1982–92; Freeman City of London, memb Worshipful Co of Marketers; FCIM, ABC, FCAM, FIPR, FRSA; *Books* All About Public Relations (1985, 3 edn 1994), Managing Your Reputation (1994), Public Relations for Marketing Professionals (1997); *Recreations* economics, the media, motoring, music, politics and sport; *Clubs* Reform, Capital; *Style*— Roger Haywood, Esq; ✉ 34 The Cloisters, Folgate Street, London E1 6EB (☎ and fax 020 7247 4670); Barron Lodge Farm, Happisburgh, Norfolk NR12 0QZ (☎ 01692 651494, fax 01692 651573)

HAYWOOD, Timothy Paul (Tim); s of Ron Haywood, of Walsall, West Midlands, and Marilyn, *née* Farmer; *b* 2 June 1963, Walsall, West Midlands; *Educ* Queen Mary's GS Walsall, St Edmund Hall Oxford (MA); *m* 7 June 1986, Beverley, *née* Bird; 1 s (Chris b 8 Sept 1990), 1 da (Daisy b 9 April 1992); *Career* Arthur Andersen & Co 1985–91, Williams Holdings 1991–97 (finance dir of subsids Larch Lap and Swish), chief financial offr Hagemeyer UK Ltd 1997–2003, finance dir St Modwen Properties plc 2003–10, gp finance dir Interserve plc 2010–; treas and tstee Areley Kings Village Hall 1999–2005, chm The Hive 2009–12; FCA; *Recreations* rowing, gardening; *Clubs* Stourport Boat; *Style*— Tim Haywood, Esq; ✉ e-mail tim.haywood@interserve.com

HAZEEL, Francis Ida McCulloch; s of late Capt Harry Hazeel, of Dunoon, Argyllshire, and late Eliane, *née* Parascou, of Chelsea; *b* 13 February 1945; *Educ* George Watson's Coll Edinburgh, King's Sch Canterbury, Pembroke Coll Oxford (Cleobury scholar); *m* 1985, Carolyn Robin, da of late Hon Robin Warrender; 2 s (Jamie, Geordie); *Career* successively asst mangr Charterhouse Japhet, mangr Spencer Thornton Brussels, mangr corp fin and export credits Nordic Bank, mangr property and project fin Banque Indosuez London, gen mangr Aareal Bank (formerly DePfa Bank) London branch 1993–2004; pres Assoc of Property Bankers 1994–95; dir Asset & Infrastructure Mgmnt Solutions Ltd (AIMS) 2004–08, non-exec chm Wolsey Residential Finance plc 2005–12; govr, sr fell and visiting prof De Montfort Univ Leicester 1997–2004; memb: Advsy Bd Royal Acad of Arts Tst 1986–98, Sadlers Wells Appeal Ctee, Keats-Shelley Memorial Assoc Devpt Gp, Cncl Oxon Historic Churches Tst, Business Mentor Start-up Loans Co; tstee: Public Arts Devpt Tst, Our Right to Read 2005–07, Guild of Educators Tst Fund, Friends of Round Square UK; fell Round Square; *Recreations* art, opera, architecture; *Style*— Francis Hazeel, Esq; ✉ e-mail francis@hazeel.co.uk

HAZELL, Peter Frank; s of Frank Henry Hazell (d 1977), and Kathleen, *née* Rowland (d 2009); *b* 4 August 1948, Kent; *Educ* Hertford Coll Oxford (MA, MPhil); *m* 11 Aug 1972, Maureen Pamela, *née* Church; 1 da (Lucy Alexandra b 11 April 1979), 1 s (Rupert Peter James b 4 Sept 1983); *Career* econs asst Home Office 1971–72; Deloitte Haskins & Sells: conslt, mangr then ptnr Mgmnt Consultancy Div and memb Mgmnt Ctee 1972–85, nat corp fin ptnr 1985–89; Coopers & Lybrand (following merger): ptnr 1989–91, seconded as business strategy dir Nat Grid Co 1991–92, memb Partnership Bd 1992–98, head of ops London Central 1992–94, managing ptnr London office 1994–96, memb Mgmnt Ctee 1994–98, managing ptnr HR 1996–98, managing ptnr audit practice 1996–98; UK managing ptnr PricewaterhouseCoopers (following merger) 1998–2000, chm Argent Gp plc 2001–14; non-exec dir: UK Coal plc 2003–11, Smith & Williamson Holdings 2004–, BRIT Insur Holdings plc 2004–12, Axa UK 2013–, Canopius Managing Agents 2014–, Axa Ireland 2014–; memb Competition Cmmn 2002–10, memb Cncl and chm Audit Ctee NERC 2004–11; memb Ct Univ of Greenwich 2010–; *Recreations* opera, ballet, theatre, cinema, hill walking, all sports (especially cricket and rugby), reading; *Clubs* MCC; *Style*— Peter Hazell, Esq; ✉ Axa UK, 5 Old Broad Street, London EC2N 1AD

HAZELL, Prof Robert John Davidge; CBE (2006); s of Peter Hazell, of Cheltenham, Glos, and Elizabeth Complin, *née* Fowler; *b* 30 April 1948; *Educ* Eton, Wadham Coll Oxford (MA); *m* 27 June 1981, Alison Sophia Mordaunt, da of Arthur Hubert Mordaunt Richards (d 1982); 2 s (Alexander Robert Mordaunt b 5 May 1982, Jonathan William Joshua b 4 Jan 1985); *Career* barr 1973–75; bencher Middle Temple 2012; numerous depts of Home Office 1975–89, Nuffield and Leverhulme travelling fellowship to study freedom of info in Aust, Canada and NZ 1986–87, dir Nuffield Fndn 1989–95, dir Constitution Unit UCL 1995–2015, prof of govt and the constitution UCL 1998–; magistrate 1978–96; vice-chm Assoc of Charitable Fndns 1990–92; tstee Citizenship Fndn 1991–2000; vice-chm Ind Cmmn to Review Britain's Experience of PR 2002–03; memb: Cncl JUSTICE 1995, Cncl Hansard Soc 1997 (vice-chm Cmmn on Scrutiny Role of Parliament 2000–01); sr fell Inst for Govt 2010; FRSA 1991, AcSS 2011; *Books* Conspiracy and Civil Liberties (1974), The Bar on Trial (1978), Constitutional Futures (1999), The State and the Nations: the first year of devolution in the United Kingdom (ed, 2000), The State and the Nations: the third year of devolution in the United Kingdom (ed, 2003), Devolution, Law Making and the Constitution (ed, 2005), The English Question (ed, 2006), Constitutional Futures Revisited (ed, 2008), Does Freedom of Information Work? The Impact of FOI on Central Government in the UK (2010), The Politics of Coalition: How the Conservative-Liberal Democrat Coalition Works (2012), Special Advisers: Who They Are, What They Do, and Why They Matter (2014), The Politics of Judicial Independence in Britain's Changing Constitution (2015), Magna Carta and its Modern Legacy (ed, 2015); *Recreations* opera, badgers, bird watching, canoeing, sailing; *Style*— Prof Robert Hazell, CBE; ✉ 94 Constantine Road, London NW3 2LS (☎ 020 7267 4881); Constitution Unit, School of Public Policy, University College London, 29 Tavistock Square, London WC1H 9QU (☎ 020 7679 4977, fax 020 7679 4978, e-mail constitution@ucl.ac.uk)

HAZLEHURST, Dr (George) Cameron Lee; s of George Henry Hazlehurst (d 1985), and Eileen Leonie, *née* Carmody (d 2001); *b* 12 October 1941, Harrogate, N Yorks; *Educ* Footscray HS, Melbourne HS, Univ of Melbourne (BA), Balliol Coll and Nuffield Coll Oxford (DPhil); *m* 2, 7 May 1983, Dr Kayleen M Hazlehurst, *née* Morrison; 3 c from previous m (David b 1969, Peter b 1972, Jane b 1974); *Career* jr research fell Nuffield Coll Oxford 1968–70, The Queen's Coll Oxford 1970–72, sr fell Research Sch of Social Sciences ANU 1988–92 (fell 1972–88), fndn prof and head Sch of Humanities Queensland Univ of Technol 1992–97, adjunct prof of govt Hawke Inst Univ of South Australia 2002–05, adjunct prof Humanities Research Centre ANU 2006–; asst sec Dept of Urban and Regnl Devpt 1973–75, first asst sec Dept of Communications 1984–86, nat campaign dir AIDS Educn and Info 1988–89, chm NSW Pesticides Implementation Ctee 2000–04, memb NSW Radiation Advsy Cncl 2005–11, chm NSW Environmental Tst Environmental Hazards Sub-Ctee 2014–; md Flaxton Mill House 1997–, princ Ethicos Gp 2003–; archives by-fell Churchill Coll 2015, Sassoon visiting fell Bodleian Libraries 2016; FRHistS 1971, FRSL 1973; *Publications* Politicians at War (1971), Menzies Observed (1979), Gordon Chalk (1987), A Liberal Chronicle (ed with Christine Woodland, 1995), A Guide to the Papers of British Cabinet Ministers 1900–1964 (with Sally Whitehead and Christine Woodland, 1996), Gangs & Youth Subcultures (ed with Kayleen Hazlehurst, 1998), Public Sector Ethics Resource Series (CD-ROMs, with Howard Whitton, 1999), Ten Journeys to Cameron's Farm (2013); *Recreations* watching television, cricket, soccer; *Clubs* Univ House (Canberra); *Style*— Dr Cameron Hazlehurst; ✉ PO Box 60, Mapleton, Queensland 4560, Australia (☎ 00 61 7 5445 7708, e-mail cameron.hazlehurst@gmail.com, website www.ethicos.net)

HAZLITT, Anne Frances (Fru); da of Rodney Hazlitt (d 2009), and Sheena, *née* Scott; *b* Guildford, Surrey; *Educ* Downe House, Goldsmiths Coll Univ of London (BA); *m* 19 Jan 2008, Charlie Porter; 2 da (Annie b 22 Aug 2002, Mary b 18 Jan 2005 (twin)), 1 s (Josh b 18 Jan 2005 (twin)); *Career* European sales dir Yahoo then md Yahoo UK & Ireland; chief exec: Virgin Radio until 2007, GCAP Media plc 2007–08; md of commercial and online ITV 2010–; non-exec dir Merlin Entertainments; chair Women's Leadership Gp Prince's Tst, memb 30 Club, govr Downe House; vice-chair Advertising Assoc, fndr emeritus memb Marketing Gp of GB; *Recreations* cinema, music, running, history; *Clubs* Soho House; *Style*— Ms Fru Hazlitt; ✉ ITV plc, The London Television Centre, Upper Ground, London, SE1 9LT.

HAZZARD, Charles Walker; s of Frank Hazzard, of Droitwich, and Margaret, *née* Harris (d 1980); *Educ* Bournville Sch of Art and Design, Glos Coll of Arts and Technol (BA), Sir Henry Doulton Sch of Sculpture 1988–90, London Art Sch (postgrad higher dip); *Career* sculptor; Bro Art Workers Guild 1996–, memb Art and Architecture Soc 1998; Grants for Individuals Award Arts Cncl 2003 and 2007, Emley Fndn Art Award 2007; fell Henry Moore Fndn (sponsored fell in sculpture at Loughbrough Univ Sch of Art and Design) 1996–99, FRBS 1998 (ARBS 1992–98, memb Cncl 1994–97); *Selected Exhibitions* The London Gp Barbican London 1992, Whitechapel Open Atlantis Gall London 1994, Royal West of England Acad Autumn Show 1994, Royal West of England Acad 2nd Sculpture 1996, Loughborough Univ 1999, Woodlands Art Gall London 1999; selected solo exhbns: Worthing Museum and Art Gall 2014–15, Worthing Museum and Art Gallery 2017–18; selected commissions incl: figure sculpture, portraits, wooden assemblies; *Recreations* running, cycling; *Clubs* British Cycling; *Style*— Charles Hazzard, Esq; ✉ 6 Clydesdale Road, Droitwich, Worcestershire WR9 7SA (e-mail c.w.hazzard@charleswalkerhazzard.com, website www.charleswalkerhazzard.com)

HAZZARD, (Lawrence) Gordon; s of Frederick Hazzard, and Minnie Hazzard; *b* 1925; *Educ* Waverley GS Birmingham; *m* 1, 1956 (m dis), Margery Elizabeth Charles; 1 da (Clare); m 2, 1985 (m dis), Miyuki Sedohara; *Career* served WWII, RAF 1943–47; gp md MK Electric Holdings until 1980; dep chm then chm Grosvenor Gp plc 1981–86; chm: Gordon Hazzard Ltd Business Advsrs 1980–2005, Wigfalls plc 1981–88, HB Electronic Components plc 1983–85, Toby Lane Ltd 1984–89, Waingate Insurance Ltd 1985–88, Green Park Health Care plc 1989–94, Opera Hldgs Ltd 1992–2004, Fleet International plc 1994–99, Fleet Electronics 1996–99, DataNet Gp plc 2000–; former: pres London Handel Festival, dep pres Br Electric and Allied Mfrs Assoc, vice-chm EIEMA, memb Cncl and Industrial Policy Ctee CBI, memb Bd ASTA; memb Japan-Br Soc of Hiroshima; CIMgt, FInstD; *Recreations* music; *Clubs* Annabel's, George; *Style*— Gordon Hazzard, Esq; ✉ 5 Balfour Place, Mayfair, London W1K 2AU (☎ 020 7408 0626, e-mail hazzard@btclick.com)

HB, Sarah (née Sarah HB Mastronardi); da of Giovanni Mastronardi, and Susan, *née* Hill; *b* 28 October 1967, Wimbledon, London; *Educ* The Study Wimbledon, Chelsea Art Sch; *Children* 2 s (Harry Wingate b 26 Oct 1998, Archie Wingate b 24 Jan 2003); *Career* DJ; runner Thames News 1985–87, ed Avatar Films 1987–88, ed Worldwide Pictures 1988–90; DJ/broadcaster: Kiss 100 FM 1990–98; host Ministry of Sound 1996–98, Galaxy 1998–99, BBC Radio 1 1999–2003; label mngr Freetown Inc. records 1994–96; freelance DJ/broadcaster BBC Radio and internationally; int club DJ (currently Ibiza and London); columnist Blues and Soul magazine 1992–95; fndr memb SoundWomen; *Recreations* music, art, walking, travel, horses, gardening, festivals, classic cars, saving the sealyam terrier breed from extinction; *Clubs* Mark Hix's LATE at Hix Soho, Groucho; *Style*— Ms Sarah HB; ✉ e-mail (for bookings) sarah@hashbar.com, website www.mixcloud.com/sarahHB (music mixes and biography), Facebook www.facebook.com/DJSarahHB, Twitter @DJSHB; c/o Guy Wingate, Paradise Productions Ltd, PO Box 989, London NW3 1SQ (☎ 020 3369 6933, fax 020 3369 6977, e-mail guy@paradise.org)

HEAD, Anthony Stewart; s of Seafield L S M Head (d 2009), and Helen Shingler; *b* 20 February 1954, London; *Children* 2 da; *Career* actor; *Theatre* incl: Henry V (Ludlow Festival) 1977, Joseph and the Amazing Technicolor Dreamcoat (Everyman Theatre Cheltenham) 1977–79, Godspell (UK nat tour) 1978 and 1981, The Winslow Boy (Everyman Theatre Cheltenham) 1978, The Confidential Clerk (Everyman Theatre Cheltenham) 1978, See How They Run (Everyman Theatre Cheltenham) 1978, Alphabetical Order (Everyman Theatre Cheltenham) 1978, Teeth 'N' Smiles (Nottingham Playhouse) 1979, Julius Caesar (Riverside Studios London) 1980, Maske: Scene from the Heroic Life of the Middle Classes (Gate Theatre London) 1981, Prince of Homburg (Nat

H

Theatre) 1982, Danton's Death (Nat Theatre) 1982–83, A Patriot For Me (Chichester Festival Theatre) 1983, Yonadab (Nat Theatre) 1985–86, Chess (Prince Edward Theatre London) 1988–89, Anatol in Love (Theatre Clwyd) 1989, Lady Windermere's Fan (Bristol Old Vic) 1990, Around the World in Eighty Days (Boxton Opera House) 1990, The Rocky Horror Show (Piccadilly Theatre London) 1990–91, The Heiress (UK nat tour) 1992, Rope (Minerva Theatre Chichester) 1993 and (UK nat tour) 1994, Peter Pan (Savoy Theatre) 2003–04, The Pirates of Penzance (Savoy Theatre) 2004, Otherwise Engaged (UK nat tour) 2005–06, Little Britain Live (Blackpool Opera House, Birmingham NIA, Hammersmith Apollo Theatre and Carling Acad Brixton) 2006 and (Hordern Pavilion Sydney, Vodafone Arena Melbourne) 2007, The Tempset (City Hall Theatre Hamilton Bermuda) 2009, Six Degrees of Separation (Old Vic London) 2010; *Television* incl: The Mallens 1978, Enemy at the Door 1978, Lillie 1978, Love in a Cold Climate 1980, The Grudge Fight 1981, Howard's Way 1985, Royce 1994, VR5 1995–97, Roger Roger 1996, Buffy the Vampire Slayer 1997–2003, Best Actress 2000, Manchild 2002–03, And Starring Pancho Villa as Himself 2003, Reversals 2003, Little Britain 2003–06, Him and Us 2006, Pursuasion 2007, Free Agents 2007 and 2009, Sold 2007, The Invisibles 2008, Merlin 2008–09; *Film* incl: Lady Chatterley's Lover 1981, I'll Be There 2003, Fat Slags 2004, Framing Frankie 2005, Imagine Me & You 2005, Sparkle 2007, Amelia & Michael 2007, Macbeth 2009, The Iron Lady 2011; *Style*— Mr Anthony Head; ✉ c/o Gordon and French, 12–13 Poland Street, London W1F 8QB

HEAD, Byron Preston; DL (W Midlands); s of late Samuel Preston Head, of Hollybush, Gwent, and Edith Florence Head; *b* 18 April 1941, Wales; *Educ* Pontllanfraith Tech Sch, Newport and Monmouthshire Coll of Technol (HNC), Sir John Cass Coll London (Dip), Univ of Surrey (BMet), Henley Business Sch; *m* Janet; 2 s (Alastair Edward Byron, Richard Preston); *Career* Br Steel Corp 1958–78, md William Mitchell 1978–82; Rical Ltd: md 1982–87, chm 1987–; High Sheriff W Midlands 2008–09; Freeman City of London, memb Worshipful Co of Gunmakers; *Recreations* Victorian paintings, golf, L S Lowry paintings; *Style*— Byron Head, Esq, DL; ✉ mobile 07968 184640, e-mail byron@byronhead.com

HEAD, His Hon Judge John Philip Trevelyan; s of Walter Raleigh Trevelyan Head (d 1996), and Rosemary Constance Beatrice, *née* Borwick; *b* 6 July 1953, Bombay; *Educ* Marlborough, Merton Coll Oxford (MA, Hockey blue), Univ of Virginia (LLM, Fulbright scholar, univ grad fell); *m* 26 March 1983, Erica Lesley, *née* Cox; 1 da (Eleanor Beatrice b 29 Sept 1985), 1 s (Lawrence James Trevelyan b 31 July 1989); *Career* called to the Bar Middle Temple 1976; recorder 2000–04 (asst recorder 1996–2000), circuit judge 2004–; memb Hon Artillery Co 1978–85; *Recreations* travel, books; *Clubs* Saville, Sette of Odd Volumes; *Style*— His Hon Judge Head; ✉ The Crown Court, 90 Wellington Street, Leicester LE1 6HG

HEAD, Miguel; *b* 7 September 1977, Braga, Portugal; *Educ* Bancroft's Sch Essex, Univ of Nottingham (BA); *Partner* Robert Smith (civil partnership 19 Nov 2011); *Career* with MOD 2003–08, press sec to TRH The Duke and Duchess of Cambridge and Prince Harry 2008–13–, private sec to HRH The Duke of Cambridge 2013–; *Style*— Miguel Head, Esq; ✉ Kensington Palace, Palace Green, London W8 4PU

HEAD, Prof Peter; CBE (2011, OBE 1998); s of Robert Cyril Head (d 1974), and Vera Alice, *née* Kent; *b* 27 February 1947; *Educ* Tiffin Sch Kingston upon Thames, Imperial Coll London (BSc); *m* 1970, Susan, da of Edmund East; 1 s (Andre b 3 Feb 1975), 1 da (Melody b 30 Oct 1976); *Career* engr: Geo Wimpey & Co 1965–66, Freeman Fox & Partners 1969–80; Maunsell Group: sr engr 1980–84, assoc 1985–89, tech dir 1989–93, dir 1993–95, md 1995–97, chief exec 1997–2001; also dir Maunsell Structural Plastics Ltd 1983–97; corp devpt dir FaberMaunsell / AECOM 2001–04, dir ARUP 2004–11, exec chm Ecological Sequestration Tst 2011–14, chief exec Ecological Sequestration Tst 2014–; maj projects incl: Avonmouth Bridge Bristol 1970–74, Friarton Bridge Perth 1975–78, Myton Bridge Hull 1973–79, Second Severn Crossing 1984–96, Aberfeldy Bridge (world's first major advanced composite bridge) 1992, Kap Shui Mun Bridge Hong Kong 1993–97, Bonds Mill Bridge (world's first advanced composite road bridge) 1994, Rion-Antiron Bridge Greece 1998–2004, Tsing Lung Bridge Hong Kong 2000–03, Dongtan Eco-city Shanghai 2005–, Wanzhuang Eco-city Lang Fang 2006–; inventor of the advanced composite construction system and the SPACES bridge concept; cmmr GLA Sustainable Devpt Cmmn 2003–09, ICE Waste Mgmnt Bd 2003–07, chm SCI 2003–06; ICE Brunel lectr 2008–09, visiting prof in sustainable systems engrg Univ of Bristol 2011–, visiting prof in eco-cities Univ of Westminster 2012–14; chair Bd Inst of Sustainability 2010–15; author and deliverer of numerous papers UK and overseas; nominated as one of 30 global eco-heros Time Magazine 2008; Hon Doctorate Univ of Bristol 2008; FICE 1977, FIHT 1981, FIStructE 1983, FREng 1996, FCGI 2001, FRSA 2006; *Awards* John Howard Structural Challenge Award SE ICE 1984, Gold Medal BPF Congress 1986 and 1990, Premier Gold Award Plastics and Rubber Weekly Awards for Excellence in Design 1993, Personal Award for Best Presentation and Best Paper Euro Pultrusion Technol Assoc 1994, Royal Acad of Engrg Silver Medal for Outstanding Contrib to Br Engrg 1995, Prince Philip Award for Polymers in the Serv of Mankind 1996, Coopers Hill Meml Prize ICE 1997, laureate IABSE Award of Merit for Outstanding Contrib to Structural Engrg 1998 (first Br engr to receive honour since 1979), Telford Medal ICE 2005, Frank Whittle Medal RAE 2008, CNN Principle Voice 2008; *Recreations* gardening, painting, hill walking; *Style*— Prof Peter Head, CBE, FREng; ✉ e-mail peter.head@ecosequestrust.org, website www.ecosequestrust.org, Twitter @peterheadcbe

HEAD, 2 Viscount (UK 1960); Richard Antony Head; s of 1 Viscount Head, GCMG, CBE, MC, PC (d 1983), and Lady Dorothea Louise (d 1987), da of 9 Earl of Shaftesbury, KP, PC, GCVO, CBE; *b* 27 February 1937; *Educ* Eton, RMA Sandhurst; *m* 1974, Alicia Brigid, da of Julian John William Salmond, of Tetbury, Glos; 2 s (Hon Henry Julian b 30 March 1980, Hon George Richard b 20 July 1982), 1 da (Hon Sarah Georgiana b 26 Nov 1984); *Heir* s, Hon Henry Head; *Career* served The Life Guards 1957–66, ret Capt; trainer of racehorses 1968–83; farmer; *Recreations* shooting, golf; *Style*— The Rt Hon the Viscount Head; ✉ Throope Manor, Bishopstone, Salisbury, Wiltshire SP5 4BA (☎ 01722 718318)

HEAD, Sarah Daphne (Sally); da of Richard George Head, of Helston, Cornwall, and Daphne Grace, *née* Henderson; *b* 20 February 1951; *Educ* Ancaster House Sussex, St Maurs Convent Weybridge; *m* 25 Sept 1975 (m dis 1987), Francis Vincent Keating, s of Bryan Keating; *Career* Sally Head Poetry Corner Radio London 1969, story ed of Warner Bros (Europe) 1972–75, script ed BBC and Thames TV 1976–84; prodr BBC Drama 1984–88: First Born, Marksman, Life and Loves of a She Devil, Breaking Up, The Detective, Inside Out; head then controller of drama Granada TV 1988–95 (credits incl Prime Suspect, Cracker and Band of Gold), controller of drama London Weekend Television 1995–97 (credits incl Jane Eyre and Tess of D'Urbervilles), fndr Sally Head Productions 1997– (prodr Four Fathers, Plastic Man, The Cry, The Mayor of Casterbridge, Tipping the Velvet, Fingersmith); *Recreations* gardening sailing, theatre, pubs, ceramic painting; *Clubs* Helford River Sailing, Strand-on-the-Green Sailing; *Style*— Miss Sally Head; ✉ The Dutch House, 60 Strand-on-the-Green, Chiswick, London W4 3PE (☎ 020 8994 8650); Sally Head Productions Ltd, Twickenham Film Studios, The Barons, St Margarets Twickenham, Middlesex TW1 2AW (☎ 020 8607 8730, fax 020 8607 8964, e-mail sally@shpl.demon.co.uk)

HEAL, Jeremy Philip Winteringham; s of Philip William Dunstan Heal (d 1997), and Elizabeth, *née* Winteringham (d 1995); *b* 18 September 1942; *Educ* Marlborough (scholar), Queens' Coll Cambridge (MA, LLM), Coll of Law; *m* 22 Oct 1971, Joanna Sylvia, *née* Bromley-Martin; 3 da (Robin Mary, Charlotte Mary, Bibi Doyle (aka Bibi Heal, the soprano)), 1 s (Dominic Philip); *Career* business mangr Cambridge Footlights 1963–64; admitted slr 1967; slr specialising in tax, tsts, estate planning, private client, agric and devpt; ptnr: E Edwards Son and Noice 1969–70, Turner Martin and Symes 1970–88, Howes Percival 1988–; author of articles in pubns incl: Taxation, Farmers Weekly, Private Client Business; tstee Mrs L D Rope Third Charitable Settlement 1986–; memb: Law Soc 1987, Soc of Tst and Estate Practitioners (past chm Norfolk and Norwich branch), Agricultural Law Assoc, Royal Norfolk Agicultural Assoc, Country Land and Business Assoc; ACIArb; *Recreations* music, sailing, gliding, playing tenor saxophone; *Style*— Mr Jeremy Heal; ✉ Knoll Cottage, 30 Knoll Road, Dorking, Surrey RH4 3EP (☎ 01306 882629, e-mail jeremyheal@aol.com); Howes Percival, The Guildyard, 51 Colegate, Norwich NR3 1DD (☎ 01603 762103, fax 01603 766212, e-mail jeremy.heal@howespercival.com)

HEALD, Prof Richard John; CBE (2012, OBE 1998); s of late John Eric Heald, and late Muriel Heald; *b* 11 May 1936; *Educ* Berkhamsted Sch, Gonville & Caius Coll Cambridge, Guy's Hosp Med Sch (MA, MB MChir); *m* 6 Aug 1969, Denise Christine, *née* Boncey; *Children* 3 da (Sara, Lucy, Anna); *Career* ships surgn Union Castle Line; conslt surgn Basingstoke Dist Hosp, currently prof of surgery North Hampshire Hosp and surgical dir Pelican Cancer Fndn; hon prof Univ of Leiden Holland, hon prof Univ of Belgrade; European Cancer ORG Clinical Research Award 2009, B V Petrovsky hon prof Nat Research Centre of Surgery 2011; author of books and papers on surgery of rectal cancer; former vice-pres RCS, pres Sections of Surgery and Coloproctology RSM, pres Assoc of Coloproctology of GB, pres Colostomy Assoc 2008; Sir Peter Freyer Medal Galway Ireland 2011, Hungarian Coloproctology Herczel Award (Bronze Placket) 2011; Hon DUniv Linköping Sweden; FRCS, FRCSEd, Hon FRSM; hon fell Surgical Assocs of: Austria, France, Germany, Israel, Poland, Rome, Sweden, Switzerland; hon fell: American Soc of Colon and Rectal Surgeons, American Coll of Surgeons, RCSI; hon memb Polish Soc of Surgical Oncology (Gold Medal), memb d'honneur de l'Association Francaise de Chirurgie; *Recreations* sailing; *Style*— Prof Richard Heald, CBE

HEALD, Sir Sir Oliver; kt (2014), QC, MP; s of John Anthony Heald (d 2000), and Joyce, *née* Pemberton (d 2009); *b* 15 December 1954; *Educ* Reading Sch, Pembroke Coll Cambridge (MA); *m* 18 Aug 1979, Christine Janice, da of Eric Arthur Whittle (d 1980), of Eastbourne; 2 da (Sarah b 1985, Victoria b 1989), 1 s (William b 1987); *Career* called to the Bar Middle Temple 1977 (bencher 2013), SE Circuit; MP (Cons): Herts N 1992–97, Herts NE 1997–; PPS: to Rt Hon Sir Peter Lloyd, MP 1994, to Rt Hon William Waldegrave, MP 1994–95; Parly under-sec of state DSS 1995–97; oppn whip 1997–2000, shadow police min 2000–01, oppn frontbench spokesman on health 2001–02, shadow min for work and pensions 2002–03, shadow ldr of the House of Commons 2003–05, shadow sec of state for constitutional affrs 2004–07, shadow chllr of the Duchy of Lancaster 2005–07, slr gen 2012–14; memb: Employment Select Ctee 1992–94, Admin Select Ctee 1998–2000, Modernisation Ctee 2003–05, Work and Pensions Select Ctee 2007–12, Ctee on Standards in Public Life 2008–12, Standards and Privilages Ctee 2010–12, Ecclesiastical Ctee 2010–12, Select Ctee on Governance of the House of Commons 2014–15; vice-chm Backbench Employment Ctee 1992–94; sponsor Private Members Bill Insurance Companies (Reserves) Act 1995; exec chm Soc of Cons Lawyers 2008–12; patron Southwark and Bermondsey Cons Assoc; *Recreations* travel, gardening, sports; *Style*— Sir Oliver Heald, QC, MP; ✉ House of Commons, London SW1A 0AA

HEALD, Timothy Villiers; s of Col Villiers Archer John Heald, CVO, DSO, MBE, MC (d 1972), and Catherine Eleanor Jean, *née* Vaughan (d 2011); *b* 28 January 1944, Dorchester, Dorset; *Educ* Sherborne, Balliol Coll Oxford (MA); *m* 1, 1968 (m dis 1999), Alison Martina, da of Norman Alexander Leslie, of Bucks; 2 da (Emma b 1970, Lucy b 1973), 2 s (Alexander b 1971, Tristram b 1977); *m* 2, 1999, Penelope, *née* Byrne; *Career* author; contrib to various newspapers and magazines, writer Atticus Column Sunday Times 1965–67; features ed: Town Magazine 1967, Daily Express 1967–72; assoc ed Weekend Magazine Toronto 1977–78, thriller reviewer The Times 1983–89, Pendennis (The Observer) 1990; visiting fell: Jane Franklin Hall Univ of Tasmania 1997 and 1999, St John's Coll Univ of Sydney 2007; Evelyn Wrench lectr English Speaking Union USA 2010; guest speaker QE2, etc 1998–, writer in residence Univ of South Aust 2001; FRSL 2000; *Books* Simon Bognor Mystery Novels (1973–, televised by Thames TV), Networks (1983), Class Distinctions (1984), Red Herrings (1985), The Character of Cricket (1986), Brought to Book (1988), The Newest London Spy (ed, 1988), The Rigby File (ed, 1989), Business Unusual (1989), 150 Years of The Royal Warrant and Its Holders (by appt, 1989), My Lord's (ed, 1990), A Classic English Crime (ed, 1990), The Duke: A Portrait of Prince Philip (1991), Honourable Estates: The English and Their Country Houses (1992), Barbara Cartland – A Life of Love (1994), Denis – The Authorised Biography of the Incomparable Compton (1994), Brian Johnston – The Authorised Biography, A Classic Christmas Crime (ed, 1995), Beating Retreat – Hong Kong under the Last Governor (1997), Stop Press (1998), A Peerage for Trade: A History of the Royal Warrant (2001), The Best After-Dinner Stories (ed, 2003), Village Cricket (2004), Death and the Visiting Fellow (2004), Death and the D'Urbervilles (2005), Denis Compton: The Life of a Sporting Hero (2006), Princess Margaret: A Life Unravelled (2007), A Death on the Ocean Wave (2007), Palmers: the story of a Dorset brewer (2008), Tomfoolery – Writings of Thomas Braun (jt ed, 2010), Death in the Opening Chapter (2011), Poison in the Pueblo (2011), My Dear Hugh – letters of Richard Cobb (ed, 2011), Yet Another Death in Venice (2014); *Recreations* spectator sports, lunch; *Clubs* MCC, Hyde Tennis (Dorset), Crime Writers' Assoc (chm 1987–88), PEN (int co-ordinator Writers-in-Prison Ctee 1986–89), Soc of Authors, Groucho, Detection, Frontline; *Style*— Timothy Heald, Esq, FRSL; ✉ Roselands, Blind Lane, Bower Hinton, Martock, Somerset TA12 6LG (☎ 01935 826059, e-mail tim@timheald.com, website www.timheald.co.uk)

HEALE, Simon John Newton; s of James Newton Heale (d 1999), and Ruth Elizabeth, *née* Max; *b* 27 April 1953; *Educ* Winchester, Oriel Coll Oxford (exhibitioner, BA); *m* 16 Oct 1982, Catriona Jean, da of Lt-Gen Sir Robin Carnegie, KCB, OBE, DL; 1 s (James Newton b 16 Aug 1985), 2 da (Charlotte Esme Serena b 17 May 1987, Anna Frances b 15 April 1989); *Career* Price Waterhouse 1975–79; Swire Gp: joined 1979, fin dir Swire Japan 1982–85, pres Ocean Routes Inc 1985–88, gen mangr cargo Cathay Pacific 1988–90, chief operating offr Dragon Air 1990–94, dep md Cathay Pacific 1994–97; Jardine Fleming Ltd: gp fin dir 1997–99, chief operating offr 1999–2001; chief exec London Metal Exchange 2001–06, dir London Clearing House 2001–06, chief exec China Now 2007–08; non-exec dir: Morgan Crucible Co 2005–14, Panmure Gordon & Co plc 2007–11, Kaz Minerals plc (formerly Kazakhmys) 2007– (chm 2013–), PZ Cussons 2008–13, Marex Spectron plc 2008– (chm 2016–), Coats plc 2011–14; chm Gulf Marine Services plc 2014–; dir Hong Kong Tourism Assoc 1994–97, chm Jt Cncl of the Tourism Industry Hong Kong 1995–97; tstee and treas Macmillan Cancer Support 2010–16; Aviation Week and Space Technology Laurel Award 1993; ACA 1978; *Recreations* travel, reading, walking dogs; *Style*— Simon Heale, Esq

HEALEY, Rt Hon John; PC (2008), MP; *Career* MP (Lab): Wentworth 1997–10, Wentworth and Dearne 2010–; PPS to Chancellor of the Exchequer 1999–2001, Parly under-sec of state Dept of Educn and Skills 2001–02, economic sec to HM Treasy 2002–05, financial sec to HM Treasy 2005–07, min of state (local govt) Dept for Communities and Local Govt 2007–09, min of state for housing Dept for Communities and Local Govt 2009–10, shadow sec for health 2010–11, shadow min for housing and planning 2015–; *Style*— The Rt Hon John Healey, MP; ✉ House of Commons, London SW1A 0AA

HEALEY, Dr Norman John; s of Dr Ronald Jack Healey (d 2008), of Launceston, Cornwall, and Monica Mary Patricia Healey, JP, *née* Gibbins (d 1995); *b* 2 September 1940; *Educ* Mount House Sch Tavistock, Epsom Coll, Guy's Hosp Med Sch London (Kitchener scholarship 1959, MRCS, LRCP, DA, DObstRCOG, 1st XV Rugby); *m* 24 June 1978, Maureen Anne, da of Clarence Meadows Brock; 3 da (Rebecca Jane b 10 Feb 1980, Alicia June, Nicola Joy (twins) b 13 Sept 1981); *Career* Surgn Lt RN 1965–71; RN Hosp Haslar: Dept of Orthopaedics 1966, Dept of Anaesthetics 1967, HMS Albion serv in Far East 1968–69, RM Depot Deal 1970–71; SHO Obstetrics and Gynaecology Royal Bucks Hosp Aylesbury 1972, London Coll of Osteopathic Med 1973–74; clinical asst Dept of Rheumatology and Rehabilitation St Mary's Hosp London 1975–82; full time private practice as conslt physician and medical osteopath 1975–2015; hon conslt St Luke's Hosp London 1987–; hon sec Br Osteopathic Assoc 1976–82, memb Cncl Br Assoc of Manipulative Med 1980–83; MRO 1975, FLCOM 1979, FRSM 1985, ND 1994; memb: Br Soc for Rheumatology 1982, Br Inst of Manual Med 1992, Br Natural Hygiene 1994; *Recreations* Madeira seaside, chamber music, flowers and shrubs; *Clubs* RSM; *Style—* Dr Norman J Healey; ✉ 6 Upper Montagu Street, London W1H 2PA (✆ 01296 681394, e-mail healeyma@aol.com, website www.healeyclinic.co.uk)

HEALEY, Prof Patsy; OBE (1999); *née* Ingold; da of late Prof C T Ingold, CMG, (who d 2010), and L M Ingold, *née* Kemp; *b* 1 January 1940; *Educ* Walthamstow Hall Sevenoaks, UCL (BA), LSE (PhD), Regents St Poly (DipTP), Univ of Wales (DipEd); *m* 1, 25 June 1961, Dr Ian Nevill Healey (d 1972), s of Douglas Healey (d 1978); m 2, 9 July 1977, David Reiach Hunter (d 1979), s of David Reiach (d 1919); *Career* sch teacher 1962–65, planning offr London Borough of Lewisham GLC 1965–69, sr res fell LSE 1970–72, lectr in planning Kingston Poly 1969–70 and 1972–74, lectr then head of dept and dean Oxford Poly 1974–87; Univ of Newcastle upon Tyne: prof and head of Dept of Town and Country Planning 1988–92, prof and dir Centre for Research in European Urban Environments 1992–2002, emeritus prof 2002–; memb: various ctees CNAA 1976–81, Cncl and various ctees RTPI 1987–92, various ctees ESRC, Bd Tyne & Wear Devpt Corp 1998, JRF Housing and Neighbourhoods Ctee 1999–2003, RTPI Knowledge and Res Ctee 2003–, Newcastle Conflict Resolution Network 2009–12, Bd Glendale Gateway Tst Mgmnt Gp 2010–; pres Assoc of European Schs of Planning 1994–96; Gold Medal RTPI 2006; *Books* Professional Ideals and Planning Practice (with J Underwood, 1979), Planning Theory – Prospects for the 1980s (ed with G McDougall and M Thomas, 1982), Local Plans in British Land Use Planning (1983), Land Policy: Problems and Alternatives (ed with S M Barrett, 1985), A Political Economy of Land (with A Gilbert, 1985), Land Use Planning and the Mediation of Urban Change (with P F McNamara, M J Elson and A J Doak, 1988), Land and Property Development in a Changing Context (ed with R Nabarro, 1990), Dilemmas of Planning Practice (with H Thomas, 1991), Rebuilding the City (with S Davoudi, M O'Toole, S Tavsanoglu and D Usher, 1992), Managing the City (with S Cameron, S Davoudi and S Graham, 1995), Collaborative Planning (1997), Making Strategic Spatial Plans (with A Khakee, A Motte and B Needham, 1997), Planning, Governance and Spatial Strategy in Britain (with G Vigar, A Hull and S Davoudi, 2000), Urban Governance, Institutional Capacity and Social Milieux (jtly, 2002), Urban Complexity and Strategic Spatial Planning (2007), Crossing Borders: international exchange and planning practices (co-ed with Robert Upton, 2010), Making Better Places (2010); *Recreations* reading, walking, gardening, swimming, travelling; *Style—* Prof Patsy Healey, OBE; ✉ School of Architecture, Planning and Landscape, University of Newcastle upon Tyne, Newcastle upon Tyne NE1 7RU (✆ 0191 222 8810, fax 0191 222 5709, telex UNINEW 953654)

HEALY, Sheila Elizabeth; *b* 20 October 1954, Dublin, Repub of Ireland; *Educ* TCD (BA, MA); *m* 29 Sept 2007, Richard Harvey; 1 s (Owain b 18 Dec 1986), 1 step s (Tristan b 4 July 1979), 1 step da (Tamsin b 20 Oct 1982); *Career* residential social worker Brent London BC 1978–80, community worker Pensions UNK 1980–83, policy offr GLC 1983–85, head of urban prog and head of policy and performance Wolverhampton MBC 1985–90, asst city sec Quality and Business Servs Nottingham City Cncl 1990–92, chief exec City Challenges and dir of Environ Walsall MBC 1992–97, corp dir of environment and econ Telford and Wrekin Cncl 1997–2000, dir community covernance Telford and Wrekin Cncl 2000–03, regnl assoc West Midlands Improvement and Devpt Agency (IDeA) 2003–04, regnl dir local govt ODPM 2004–06, chief exec Cornwall CC 2006–08, interim chief exec Salops CC 2008–09; dir H & H Horizons Ltd 2009–; dir and vice-chair Ikon Gallery Birmingham 2000–04, chair Audiences Central 2000–06, dir Arts Cncl England, chair SW Regnl Arts Cncl 2010–; memb: Advsy Cncl Tate St Ives 2006–, Bd of Tstees Royal Cornwall Hosp Tst 2009–10, Leading Museums Gp 2009–, Bd Kneehigh Theatre Co 2011–; memb SOLACE 1998–, FInstD; *Recreations* walking, theatre, reading, cinema, travel, contemporary and modern art; *Style—* Ms Sheila Healy; ✉ Lanhethians, Porth Kea, Truro, Cornwall TR3 6AL (e-mail sheila@porthkea.myzen.co.uk)

HEALY, Prof Thomas Edward John (Tom); s of Thomas Healy (d 1977), and Gladys May, *née* Paulger (d 1998); *b* 11 December 1935, Doncaster, S Yorks; *Educ* St Brendans Coll Bristol, Guy's Hosp Med Sch Univ of London (Bristol City sr scholarship, BSc, MBBS, MD), Univ of Cardiff (LLM), Univ of Manchester (MSc); *m* 3 Nov 1966, Lesley Edwina, *née* Sheppard; 3 da (Maria Edwina b 23 March 1968, Michaela Louise b 8 Dec 1970, Laura Jayne b 28 Jan 1975), 1 s (Thomas Frederick b 19 April 1979); *Career* Nat Serv Royal Corps of Signals; conslt anaesthetist and conslt i/c intensive care Nottingham 1971– (planned and commissioned Intensive Care Unit for opening of Queens Medical Centre Nottingham 1978), reader in anaesthesia Univ of Nottingham 1974–81, prof of anaesthesia Univ of Manchester 1981–97 (chm Sch of Surgical Sciences 1992–94); int visiting prof incl: Univs of Arizona (Tuscon and Phoenix), Michigan, Philadelphia, Vancouver, Cluj-Napoca, Bucharest, Mahidol Univ Thailand, Univs in China, Egypt, Turkey, Hong Kong, South Africa, France and Germany; invited to join Eisenhower People to People Citizen Ambass Prog 1988 (visit incl hospitals and medical meetings in Nanjing, Hong Kong, Beijing and Shanhai (Shanghai Second Military Hosp and Shanghai Children's Hosp)); memb S Manchester DHA 1981–89; ed Monographs in Anaesthesiology, ed-in-chief European Jl of Anaesthesiology 1995–2000, author of over 142 published papers; expert witness in court cases UK and Canada for the Crown, GMC, defendants and claimants; memb Cncl: Assoc of Anaesthetists 1973–76, Anaesthetic Research Soc Cncl 1978–80, RSM (hon sec 1986–88, pres Section of Anaesthetics 1996–97), Royal Coll of Anaesthetists 1989–97 (estab Professional Standards Ctee (chm 1994–97)), Postgrad Medical Fellowship 1990–94; memb Advisory Bd Medical Litigation 1999–; memb Bd of Govrs: Becket Sch Nottingham 1973–75, Linacre Centre for Health Care Ethics 1999–2005; memb SW Notts Cncls Ctee and Planning Ctee Parish Cncl Stanton-on-th-Wolds 1979; Freeman: Worshipful Soc of Apothecaries, City of London; academician and memb of Senate and Exec Ctee European Acad of Anaesthesiology, hon memb Romanian Soc of Anaesthesia, special visitor Shanghai Univ 1993; FRCA, MRCS; *Books* Aids to Anaesthesia Book 1: Basic Science, Aids to Anaesthesia Book 2: Clinical Practice, Anaesthesia for Day Case Surgery, A Practice of Anaesthesia (6 edn, 1st Prize BMA Book Competition, 9 edn 2003); chapters in 12 books incl: Encyclopedia of Forensic Medicine (contrib, 2005), Medicine for Lawyers (contrib, 2005); *Recreations* cycling, reading, skiing, travel, walking; *Clubs* RSM; *Style—* Prof Tom Healy; ✉ 15 South Park, Sevenoaks, Kent TN13 1EN; Department of Anaesthesia, Manchester Royal Infirmary, Oxford Road, Manchester M13 9WL (✆ 01424 883243, e-mail prof_healy@yahoo.co.uk)

HEALY OF PRIMROSE HILL, Baroness (Life Peer UK 2010), of Primrose Hill in the London Borough of Camden; Anna Healy; da of Martin Healy (d 1992), and Kathleen, née Lally; *b* 10 May 1955, London; *Educ* St Aloysius Convent Grammar London; Univ of London: Royal Holloway Coll, Birkbeck Coll, City Univ; *m* 1992, Jon Cruddas, MP, *qv*; 1 s; *Career* special advsr to: Sec of State for NI 1997–98, Min of Transport 2000–01, Min to the Cabinet Office 2001–03, Ldr of the House of Commons 2007–10; COS to Actg Ldr of the Oppn House of Commons 2010; memb: HIV and AIDS Ctee in the UK House of Lords, Parly Privilege Jt Ctee House of Lords 2013, Communications Ctee House of Lords 2013–; *Recreations* cinema, music, reading, walking; *Style—* The Baroness Healy of Primrose Hill; ✉ House of Lords, London SW1A 0PW

HEANEY, Kevin; s of Patrick Heaney, and Carol Hicks; *b* 20 March 1963, London; *m* 17 Feb 2001, Marina; 1 s (Sean b 8 Jan 2002), 1 da (Grace b 5 June 2004); *Career* owner cornishhomes.co.uk (now Cornish Properties Ltd); chm and owner Truro City FC; Cornwall memb Panel Prince's Tst, memb Panel Lord Lt's Tst Fund for Youth; *Recreations* football, international travel; *Style—* Kevin Heaney, Esq

HEAPPEY, Maj James Stephen; MP; s of Stephen Heappey, of Bedford, and Anita, *née* Winters, of Nailsea, N Somerset; *b* 30 January 1981, Nuneaton; *Educ* Queen Elizabeth's Hosp Bristol, Univ of Birmingham (BA); *m* 14 Sept 2009, Kate Heappey; 1 s (Charles b 18 June 2012), 1 da (Matilda b 26 July 2014); *Career* Br Army 2003–12; MP (Cons) Wells 2015–; *Recreations* cricket, golf, sailing, skiing, tennis, travel; *Style—* Major James Heappey, MP; ✉ House of Commons, London SW1A 0AA (✆ 020 7219 4289, e-mail james.heappey.mp@parliament.uk, website www.jamesheappey.org.uk)

HEAPS, Christopher Seymour; s of Capt Christopher Robert Milner Heaps, TD (d 1962), and Peggy Margaret Catherine, *née* Mill (d 1984); *b* 15 November 1942; *Educ* Dorking GS, Univ of Exeter (LLB); *m* 14 March 1970, Ann Mary, da of Capt Peter Dudley Frederick Mays (d 1994), of Dorking; 2 da (Grace b 1973, Elizabeth b 1975); *Career* admitted slr 1967; ptnr Eversheds (formerly Jaques & Lewis) 1971–96 (conslt 1996–98); traffic cmmr Western Traffic Area 1997–2000, traffic cmmr South Eastern and Metropolitan Area 2000–07; dir Porterbrook Leasing Co Ltd 2000–02, dir UK Bus Driver of the Year Assoc Ltd 2004–, dir Road Operator Safety Cncl 2012–, chm Bus Appeals Body 2014–; pres Holborn Law Soc 1983–84, memb Cncl Law Soc 1985–97, memb Cncl on Tbnls 1991–97; chm Law Soc: Planning & Environmental Law Ctee 1988–91 and 1995–96, Adjudication and Appeals Ctee (Slrs' Complaints Bureau) 1992–95; memb: Transport Users' Consultative Ctee for London 1981–84, London Regnl Passengers Ctee 1984–92 (dep chm 1985–92), Advsy Panel Railway Heritage Tst 1985–, Advsy Bd First Great Western 2009–14; chm Railway Study Assoc 1997–2003; chm Dorking Round Table 1978–79, pres Dorking Deepdene Rotary Club 1986–87; memb Cncl of Mgmnt PDSA 1996–2011 (dep chm 2007–09); hon steward Helston Furry Dance 1996–, vice-pres Helston Railway Preservation Soc 2010–, tstee Transport Tst 2011–, chm London Bus Preservation Tst London Bus Museum 2015–; Liveryman Worshipful Co of Curriers 1976 (Master 1997–98), Liveryman Worshipful Co of Coachmakers and Coach Harness Makers 1985; FCIT 1996 (MCIT 1988); *Books* London Transport Railways Album (1978), Western Region in the 1960's (1981), This is Southern Region Central Division (1982), BR Diary 1968–1977 (1988), The Helston Railway (2012); *Recreations* transport and transport history; *Style—* Christopher Heaps, Esq; ✉ Pinecroft, Ridgeway Road, Dorking, Surrey RH4 3AP (✆ 01306 881752, e-mail heaps@waitrose.com); 33 Wendron Street, Helston, Cornwall TR13 8PT

HEAPS, John Robert; s of Dennis Heaps (d 1986), and Madeleine, *née* Coburn; *b* 8 July 1953, Ilkley, W Yorks; *Educ* Ratcliffe Coll, Univ of Liverpool (LLB); *m* 6 June 1981, Vivienne Anne, *née* Smith; 2 s (Robert b 11 Jul 1984, Timothy b 2 Aug 1987); *Career* admitted slr 1978; slr Freshfields 1978–84, ptnr Eversheds LLP 1985–2015 (chm 2010–14); chm Yorkshire Building Soc 2015–; memb Cncl Section on Public and Professional Interest (SPPI) of Int Bar Assoc 2011–, memb Bd CPR Inst USA 2013–, memb Bd Business and Oversight Law Soc 2014–; memb Bd of Tstees Garden Bridge Tst 2013–; FCIArb 1991–; *Books* IBA Guide to the Law of Privilege and Confidentiality (co-author); *Recreations* cricket, golf, music, opera, skiing, fishing; *Clubs* Reform, Pannal Golf, Senior Golfing Soc; *Style—* John Heaps, Esq; ✉ Yorkshire Building Society, Broad Gate, The Headrow, Leeds LS1 8EQ (e-mail Heapsj@btinternet)

HEARING, Roger; s of Terence Hearing, and Margaret, *née* Standley; *b* 20 September 1960, London; *Educ* Hardye's Sch Dorchester, Downing Coll Cambridge (MA), City Univ (Dip Journalism); *m* 1994 (m dis 2013), Emma, *née* Garfit; 1 da, 1 s; *Career* reporter Birmingham Post 1984–87, corr BBC World Serv Zambia 1988–89, reporter and presenter The World at One (BBC Radio 4) 1990–93, reporter Newsnight (BBC 2) 1993, E Africa corr BBC 1993–96, presenter The World Tonight (BBC Radio 4/BBC World Serv) 1998–, presenter Business Matters (BBC Radio 4/BBC World Serv) 2013–; owner Hearing Things Ltd 2009–; *Recreations* genealogy, walking, fishing (unsuccessfully); *Style—* Roger Hearing, Esq; ✉ BBC New Broadcasting House, Portland Place, London W1A 1AA (✆ 020 7240 3456, mobile 07939 176801, e-mail roger.hearing@bbc.co.uk)

HEARLEY, Timothy Michael; s of Maurice James Goodwin Hearley, CBE (d 1975); *b* 10 March 1942; *Educ* Malvern Coll, Lincoln Coll Oxford (MA); *m* 1966, Pauline Muriel, *née* Dunn; 3 s (Philip Michael b 1967, James Paul b 1970, Richard Matthew b 1973); *Career* currently chm: Rolfe & Nolan plc, Securitex Investments Ltd, Vail Corporation Ltd, Virgin Cars UK Ltd, C4 Group Ltd, Vicorp Group Ltd, Binns & Co PR Ltd; currently dir: Nyne plc, Green Cone Ltd, Oakdene Homes plc; AIIMR, MSI; *Recreations* tennis, piano, ballet, theatre; *Clubs* Fox; *Style—* Timothy Hearley, Esq; ✉ Rush Leys, 4 Birds Hill Rise, Oxshott, Surrey KT22 0SW (✆ 01372 842506); Vail Corporation Ltd, 58 Grosvenor Street, London W1K 3JB (✆ 020 7240 6090, fax 020 7240 6091)

HEARN, Andrew; *b* 23 July 1957; *Educ* UC Sch London, St John's Coll Oxford (BA); *m* Sarah; 3 s (Luke, Adam, Matthew); *Career* Dechert: articled clerk (qualified 1982), litigation ptnr and slr-advocate (Higher Courts Civil) 1986–, specialising in intellectual property, defamation and gen commercial litigation; recorder London and South Eastern Circuit; accredited mediator CEDR and mediator World Intellectual Property Orgn; former memb Litigation Sub-Ctee City of London Law Soc; author of various pubns and articles in the press; memb: City of London Law Co, Law Soc; FCIArb; *Recreations* skiing, the arts, trying to keep fit; *Clubs* Campden Hill Lawn Tennis, Old Gowers; *Style—* Andrew Hearn, Esq; ✉ Dechert LLP, 160 Queen Victoria Street, London EC4V 4QQ (✆ 020 7184 7000, e-mail andrew.hearn@dechert.com)

HEARN, Barry Maurice William; *m* Susan; 1 da (Katie), 1 s (Edward); *Career* sports promoter; qualified CA 1970, spent several years at int accountancy firm before becoming fin dir Kensal House Investments, chm Lucania Snooker Clubs 1974–82, currently prop and chm Matchroom Ltd; clients incl Steve Davis; *Recreations* fishing, cricket, golf; *Style—* Barry Hearn, Esq

HEARN, Prof John Patrick; s of Lt-Col Hugh Patrick Hearn, and Cynthia Ellen, *née* Nicholson; *b* 24 February 1943; *Educ* Crusaders Sch Headley, St Mary's Sch Nairobi, UC Dublin (MSc, BSc), ANU (PhD); *m* 30 Sept 1967, Margaret Ruth Patricia, *née* McNair; 4 s (Shaun Robin b 1968, Bruce Edward b 1973, Adrian Hugh b 1975, Nicholas Gordon b 1984), 1 da (Karina Anne b 1970); *Career* lectr in zoology Strathmore Coll Nairobi 1967–69, research scholar Dept of Zoology Aust Nat Univ Canberra 1969–72, scientist MRC Reproductive Biology Unit Univ of Edinburgh 1972–79 (hon fell 1974–79), conslt scientist WHO Geneva 1978–79; Zoological Soc of London: dir Wellcome Laboratories of Comparative Physiology 1979–80, dir of science 1980–87, dir Inst of Zoology 1980–87; dep sec AFRC 1987–90 (dir MRC/AFRC Comparative Physiology Research Gp 1983–89),

H

prof Dept of Physiology Univ of Wisconsin Med Sch 1990–96, dir Wisconsin Regnl Primate Research Center 1990–96, sr scientist WHO Research Prog in Reproductive Health Geneva 1996–98, dir Research Sch of Biological Sciences ANU Canberra 1998–2001, dep vice-chllr (research) ANU Canberra 2001–04, prof of physiology Univ of Sydney 2004–, dep vice-chllr (int) Univ of Sydney 2004–13; chief exec Worldwide Univ Network 2009–, chm Australia Africa Univs Network (AAUN) 2010–; visiting prof in reproductive biology Dept of Biology UCL 1979–94; chm Hearn Int Pty Ltd 2013–; memb Bd: Sports Knowledge Aust 2005–11, OECD Bioeconomy 2030 2006–13, Aust Nuclear Sci and Technol Orgn 2008–13, memb Educn Advsy Gp Br Cncl 2014–, advsr Swedish Int Sci and Tech Gp (STINT) 2014–, memb Australian Govt Advsy Gp for Australia Africa Relations 2015–; chm Sydney Confucius Inst 2008–13; author of 210 research papers and editor of 6 books; Scientific Medal Zoological Soc of London 1983, Osman Hill Medal Primate Soc of GB 1986, Aust Centenary Medal 2003; memb: Soc for Reproductive Biology (chm 2000–04), Int Primatological Soc (pres 1984–88); DSc (hc) UC Dublin 2015; scientific fell Zoological Soc of London; *Recreations* swimming, running, conservation, seven grandchildren; *Clubs* Athenaeum, Bronte Surf and Lifesaving Sydney; *Style*— Prof John Hearn; ✉ The Worldwide Universities Network, Room 207, The Old Teachers College A22, The University of Sydney, NSW 2006, Australia (e-mail john.hearn@sydney.edu.au)

HEARNDEN, Dr Arthur George; OBE (1990); s of Hugh William Hearnden (d 1985), of Bangor, Co Down, and Violet May, *née* Frazer (d 1971); *b* 15 December 1931; *Educ* Methodist Coll Belfast, Christ's Coll Cambridge (MA), Wadham Coll Oxford (DPhil); *m* 25 August 1962, Josephine Honor, da of Joseph Cuthbert McNeill; 1 s (Barney Hugh b 11 June 1963), 2 da (Katharine Louisa (Mrs Farrow) b 21 Nov 1964, Anna Mary (Mrs Hummerston) b 4 Jan 1968); *Career* former schoolmaster and univ lectr; sec Standing Conf on Univ Entrance 1975–84, gen sec ISC 1985–97, memb Sch Exams and Assessment Cncl 1988–91, memb Funding Agency for Schs 1994–97, memb Press Complaints Cmmn 1999–2005; pres Ind Schs Assoc 1997–2002, vice-pres Cncl of Br Int Schs (formerly Cncl of Br Ind Schs in the European Communities) 1997–2010; chm: Worldwide Volunteering for Young People 1995–2000, HSBC Bursary Fund 1998–2002, The Hall Sch Charitable Tst 1997–2009, Millwood Education Tst 2007–11; *Books* Paths to University (1973), Education in the Two Germanies (1974), Education, Culture and Politics in West Germany (1974), The British in Germany (ed, 1978), Red Robert, A Life of Robert Birley (1984), A Flying Start: The Story of The Manor (2007); *Recreations* family, theatre, coarse gardening; *Clubs* Athenaeum; *Style*— Dr Arthur Hearnden, OBE; ✉ Eversleigh, Middle Street, Islip, Oxfordshire OX5 2SF (☎ 07702 408155, e-mail arthurandjo@clara.co.uk)

HEARNE, Sir Graham James; kt (1998), CBE (1990); s of Frank Hearne, and Emily, *née* Shakespeare; *b* 23 November 1937; *Educ* George Dixon GS Birmingham; *m* 1961, Carol Jean, *née* Brown; 1 s, 3 da; *Career* admitted slr 1959, Pinsent & Co Slrs 1959–63, attorney NYC Fried Frank Harris Shriver & Jacobson 1963–66, Herbert Smith & Co Slrs 1966–67, Industrial Reorganisation Corp 1967–68, N M Rothschild & Sons Ltd 1968–77 (non-exec dir 1977–2010), fin dir Courtaulds Ltd 1977–81, chief exec Tricentrol plc 1981–83, gp md Carless Capel & Leonard plc 1983–84, chief exec Enterprise Oil plc 1984–91 (chm 1991–2002); non-exec dir Rowan Companies Inc 2004– (chm 2016–); High Sheriff Gtr London 1995; *Clubs* Reform, MCC, Brooks's; *Style*— Sir Graham Hearne, CBE; ✉ 5 Crescent Place, London SW3 2EA

HEARNE, Dr John Michael; s of Reginald Hearne (d 1974), of Ipplepen, Devon, and Mary Rachel, *née* Rees (d 2001); *b* 19 September 1937; *Educ* Torquay GS, St Luke's Coll Exeter, UC Wales Aberystwyth (BMus, MMus), Univ of Wales (DMus); *m* 1, 6 July 1974, Margaret Gillespie, da of Archibald Jarvie (d 2006), of Glasgow; m 2, Margaret (Pearl, d 2016); *Career* teacher Tónlistarskóli Borgarfjardar (Rural Music Sch) Iceland 1968–69, lectr Aberdeen Coll of Educn 1970–87; composer, singer (bass-baritone) and conductor; compositions incl: Piano Sonata 1968, Piano Trio 1981, Songs and Choral Music, String Quartet 1971, Triduum (Festival Oratorio) 1982, Channel Firing 1979, The Four Horsemen (brass, percussion) 1985, Trumpet Concerto (BBC Cmmn) 1990, Laetatus Sum for Chorus (jt winner Gregynog Composers Award of Wales 1992), De Profundis for wind band (Aberdeen University Quincentenary cmmn) 1995, A Legend of Margaret for Sch Choirs and Ensemble (St Margaret's Sch Aberdeen cmmn for 150th anniversary) 1996, Quintet for Alto Saxophone and String Quartet 1997, Solemn and Strange Music (for piano duet) 1998 (Gregynog Composers' Award for Wales 1998), Into Uncharted Seas (overture for orch, Dundee Orch Soc cmmn for centenary of launch of RRS Discovery) 2001, The Ben (cantata for soloists, choirs and orch, Gordon Forum for the Arts Cmmn) 2001, Echoes of Inchcolm (for voices and instruments) 2002, Thus Scorning all the Cares (for voices) 2002, Songs for All Seasons (for girls' choir) 2004, Mo Chasan dubh (for chorus or strings) 2005, Pictograms (for piano) 2007, Kishmul's Galley (Nat Youth Choirs GB cmmn to commemorate 25th anniversary of NYCBG) 2008, Crux Fidelis (for chorus) 2009, Exultate Deo (for chorus) 2010, Dream Riders (for chorus and chamber orchestra or piano duet) 2014, Violin Sonata 2016; performances incl: reader in Sincerely Edvard Grieg (compilation of Grieg's letters, songs, piano music), regular concert appearances in Scotland; conductor: Stonehaven and Dist Choral Soc 1989–2014 (conductor emeritus 2014–), Inverurie Choral Soc 1998–2003; self publishing Longship Music; chm: Gordon Forum for the Arts 1991–94, Scot Music Advsy Ctee BBC 1986–90; memb Bd Enterprise Music Scotland 2006–; dist cncllr (E Scotland) Inc Soc of Musicians 1992–98; warden Performers & Composers Section Inc Soc Musicians 1999–2000; Caledonian Hilton Audience Prize in Waverley Care Carol Competition 2010; memb: Exec Ctee Composers' Guild of GB 1994–98, Bd Nat Youth Choir of Scotland 1996–2003, Bd Aberdeen Sound Festival 2010–; *Publications* numerous vocal, choral and instrumental works; *Recreations* classic motoring – 1954 Daimler Conquest Roadster, 1991 SAAB 900s Aero Classic; *Style*— Dr John Hearne; ✉ Longship Music, Smidskot, Fawells, Keithhall, Inverurie AB51 0LN (☎ and fax 01651 882274, website www.impulse-music.co.uk/johnhearne)

HEARSE, Prof David James; s of James Read Hearse (d 1974), of Holt, Wilts, and Irene Annetta, *née* Nokes (d 1982); *b* 3 July 1943; *Educ* John Willmott GS, Univ of Wales (BSc, PhD, DSc); *Career* instr in pharmacology New York Univ Med Centre 1968–70, res fell Br Heart Fndn Imperial Coll London 1970–76, hon sr lectr St Thomas' Hosp Med Sch 1976–86, prof of cardiovascular biochemistry United Med and Dental Schs Guy's Hosp and St Thomas' Hosp, currently cardiovascular research The Rayne Inst Guy's and St Thomas' Hosp; author of 8 books and over 500 scientific papers in areas of res into heart disease; fell American Coll of Cardiology 1980; memb: RSM, Br Cardiac Soc; *Recreations* furniture, house restoration, photography, carpentry; *Clubs* RSM; *Style*— Prof David Hearse; ✉ Cardiovascular Research, The Rayne Institute, St Thomas' Hospital, London SE1 7EH (☎ 020 7188 1101)

HEATH, Prof Anthony Francis; CBE (2013); s of Ronald John Heath (decd), of Bampton, Oxon, and Cicely Florence, *née* Roberts; *b* 15 December 1942; *Educ* Merchant Taylors', Trinity Coll Cambridge (sr scholar, BA, Cross-Country half blue); *m* Mary-Jane, da of David Lionel Pearce; 2 s (Oliver Francis b 17 Oct 1975, Ralph Francis b 18 April 1987), 1 da (Eleanor b 13 Nov 1984); *Career* asst lectr Univ of Cambridge 1968–70; Univ of Oxford: lectr and fell Jesus Coll 1970–87, fell Nuffield Coll 1987–2010 (emeritus fell 2010–), prof of sociology 1999–2010 (emeritus prof 2010–), dir Centre for Social Investigation Nuffield Coll 2014–; prof of sociology Univ of Manchester 2010–; FBA 1992; *Books* Rational Choice and Social Exchange (1976), Origins and Destinations (with A Halsey and J Ridge, 1980), Social Mobility (1981), How Britain Votes (with R Jowell and J Curtice, 1985), Understanding Political Change (jtly, 1991), The Rise of New Labour (with Jowell and Curtice, 2001), Unequal Chances (with Cheung, 2007), The Political Integration of Ethnic Minorities in Britain (with Fisher, Rosenblatt, Sanders and Sobolewska, 2013), Unequal Attainments: Ethnic Educational Inequalities in Ten Western Countries (with Brinbaum, 2014), Hard Times: The Divisive Toll of the Economic Slump (with Clark, 2014); *Recreations* running, climbing, piano; *Clubs* Achilles; *Style*— Prof Anthony Heath, CBE, FBA; ✉ Nuffield College, Oxford OX1 1NF (☎ 01865 278669, e-mail anthony.heath@nuffield.ox.ac.uk)

HEATH, Christopher John; s of Lt-Gen Sir Lewis Macclesfield Heath (d 1954), of Bath, and Katherine Margaret, *née* Lonergan (d 1984); *b* 26 September 1946; *Educ* Ampleforth; *m* 14 June 1979, Margaret Joan, da of Col Richard Arthur Wiggin, TD, JP, DL (d 1977), of Ombersley, Worcs; 1 s (William Henry Christopher b 29 April 1983); *Career* commercial asst ICI 1964–69; sales exec George Henderson & Co 1969–75; ptnr Henderson Crosthwaite & Co 1975–84; ceo Baring Securities Ltd 1984–93, dir Baring Bros & Co Ltd 1986–93, dir Barings plc 1992–93; fndr investment bank Caspian Securities Ltd 1995, joined as md Optima Fund Mgmnt NY 1998; FSI, memb SFA; *Recreations* fishing; *Clubs* Boodle's, Pratt's, Turf, The Brook (NY); *Style*— Christopher Heath, Esq; ✉ 230 East 67th Street, New York, NY 10065, USA

HEATH, David William St John; CBE (1989); s of Eric William Heath, of Street, Somerset, and Pamela Joan, *née* Bennett; *b* 16 March 1954; *Educ* Millfield, St John's Coll Oxford (MA), City Univ; *m* 15 May 1987, Caroline Marie Therese, da of Harry Page Netherton, of Alicante, Spain; 1 da (Bethany b 31 March 1988), 1 s (Thomas b 2 May 1991); *Career* optician; memb Somerset CC 1985–97 (ldr 1985–89), Nat Exec Lib Pty 1986–87, Fed Exec Lib Democrats 1989–92 and 1994–96, Audit Cmmn 1995–97; vice-chm and ldr Lib Democrats Assoc of CCs 1994–97; chm Avon & Somerset Police Authy 1993–96 (dep chm 1996–97), vice-chm Ctee of Local Police Authorities 1995–97; MP (Lib Dem) Somerton and Frome 1997–2015; Lib Dem spokesman on: European affrs 1997–98, foreign affrs 1997–99, agric, rural affrs and fisheries 1999–2001, work and pensions 2001–02, science 2001–04, constitutional affrs 2002–06, Home Office 2002–05, Cabinet Office 2006–10; shadow to Ldr of the House 2005–10, dep ldr of the House of Commons 2010–; memb Foreign Affrs Select Ctee 1997–; Parly conslt to Worldwide Fund for Nature 1990; head of fund raising Nat Meningitis Tst 1992–93; *Recreations* rugby football, cricket, pig breeding; *Clubs* Nat Lib; *Style*— David Heath, Esq, CBE; ✉ 34 The Yard, Witham Friary, Frome, Somerset BA11 5HF; House of Commons, London SW1A 0AA (☎ 020 7219 6245)

HEATH, (Barrie) Duncan; s of Sir Barrie Heath (d 1988), and Joy Heath (d 1980); *b* 30 June 1946, Leamington Spa, Warks; *Educ* St Peters Court Sch Broadstairs, Wrekin Coll; *m* 1, (m dis 1989) Hilary Dwyer; 1 s (Daniel), 1 da (Laura); m 2, Alexandra Harries; 1 s (Jacob), 1 da (Edie); *Career* agent William Morris 1970–72, chm Duncan Heath Associates 1972–88, chm Independent Talent Ltd (named International Creative Management until 2002, incorporating Duncan Heath Assocs) 1988– (led MBO from US owners 2002), co-fndr ICM Models (now TESS Mgmnt) 2003; supporter of various animal and medical charities; memb BAFTA 1984; *Recreations* sailing, horse racing, motorbikes, ballroom dancing; *Clubs* Royal London Yacht, RAC, Hurlingham; *Style*— Duncan Heath, Esq; ✉ ITG Ltd, 40 Whitfield Street, London W1T 2RH (☎ 020 7636 6565, fax 020 7323 0101)

HEATH, His Hon Judge Michael John; s of Norman Heath (d 2006), of Grimsby, Lincs, and Dorothy, *née* Fryman (d 2000); *b* 12 June 1948, Grimsby, Lincs; *Educ* Wintringham GS Grimsby, Univ of Leeds (LLB); *m* 5 Aug 1972, Heather, *née* Croft; 2 s (John Alexander b 1 June 1978, Duncan Robert b 6 Nov 1981); *Career* ptnr RAC Symes & Co 1977–95 (asst slr 1975–77), dep dist judge 1987–95, recorder 1993–95 (asst recorder 1989–93), circuit judge (Midland Circuit) 1995–, ethnic minorities liaison judge for Lincs 1995–2009, youth justice liaison judge for Lincs 2000–, magistrates' liaison judge for Lincs 2000–10, hon recorder City of Lincoln 2001–10, resident judge Lincoln Crown Court 2000–10; memb: Lincs Courts Bd 2004–06, Lincs Probation Bd 2004–06; FCIArb 1993; *Recreations* strolling, weight-training, foreign languages; *Style*— His Hon Judge Heath; ✉ Lincoln Crown Court, The Castle, Lincoln, LN1 3GA (☎ 01522 525222)

HEATH, Stephen Christopher; s of George Albert Heath, of Knottingley, W Yorks, and Patricia Anne, *née* Miller (d 1989); *b* 18 April 1959; *Educ* Knottingley HS, Wakefield Coll of Art, Teesside Poly (BA), Leicester Poly (MA); *m* 31 May 2001, Trisha Andee Theodore-Heath, *née* Theodore; *Career* commercial design conslt; site mangr Space Planning and Coordinated Environmental Services Ltd (Spaces) 1985–86 (designer/planner 1983–85), assoc David Leon Partnership 1989–94 (joined 1986, design team ldr 1988–94), design assoc BDG/McColl 1994–96, dir and princ conslt Special Projects Bureau 1996–, dir and company sec HxR Special Projects 1999, sr ptnr SPB3 2002–04; work covers the professions, professional instns, healthcare, science and technol, financial instns; clients incl: Unilever Research Ltd, Borax Consolidated Ltd, National Trust, V&A, Russell Reynolds Associates Inc, BMW (GB) Ltd; FCSD 1993; *Recreations* fitness training, travelling, writing; *Style*— Stephen Heath, Esq

HEATH-BROWN, Prof David Rodney (Roger); s of Basil Heath-Brown, of Welwyn Garden City, Herts, and Phyllis Joan, *née* Watson; *b* 12 October 1952; *Educ* Welwyn Garden City GS, Trinity Coll Cambridge (BA, PhD, Smith's essay prize); *m* 11 July 1992, Ann Louise, da of William Sharpley; 2 da (Jennifer Louisa b 5 Oct 1993, Phoebe Clare Eleanor b 24 June 1997); *Career* research fell Trinity Coll Cambridge 1977–79; Univ of Oxford: tutor in pure mathematics Magdalen Coll 1979–98; reader in pure mathematics 1990–98, prof of pure mathematics 1999–, professorial fell Worcester Coll 1999–; corresponding memb Göttingen Acad of Science 1999–; memb London Mathematical Soc 1979 (Jr Berwick Prize 1981, Sr Berwick Prize 1996, Polya Prize 2010); FRS 1993; *Recreations* British field botany, gardening, bridge; *Style*— Prof Roger Heath-Brown, FRS; ✉ Mathematical Institute, Radcliffe Observatory Quarter, Woodstock Road, Oxford, OX2 6GG (☎ 01865 273535, e-mail rhb@maths.ox.ac.uk)

HEATH-WELCH, Anne; da of late L R Welch, and Le Noir Rabb Welch; *b* Shreveport, Louisiana, USA; *Educ* Centenary Coll of Louisiana USA (BMus), Univ of Texas at Austin (MM), Vienna Conservatory of Music; *m* 28 April 2006, Gottfried Schiller; *Career* princ ENO 1995–98, artistic dir Kingwood Summer Opera 2008–15; stage direction: The Crucible, Carmen, Cavalleria Rusticana, La Boheme (Kingwood Summer Opera), Ariadne auf Naxos (Kingswood Summer Opera); adjunct prof of voice Sam Houston State Univ Texas 2006–09, adjunct prof of voice, diction and opera Lone Star Coll Kingwood 2008–15, private voice studio 2005–; memb Nat Assoc of Teachers of Singing (NATS) USA; *Roles* Minnie in La Fanciulla del West (WNO), title role in Tosca (WNO and ENO), title role in Madam Butterfly (ENO), title role in Turandot (ENO), title role in Manon Lescaut (Kentish Opera Gp), Mimi in La Bohème, Iphigenie in Iphigenie en Tauride (WNO), Foreign Princess in Rusalka (ENO), Leonore in Fidelio (ENO), Brangaene in Tristan und Isolde (Scottish Opera), Sieglinde, Freia and Gutruene in Der Ring (reduced version for Pocket Opera Nurenberg), title role in Aida (Nonsuch Opera & Kentish Opera Gp), Violetta in La Traviata, Lady Macbeth in Macbeth (WNO), Leonora in La Forza del Destino (ENO), Santuzza in Cavalleria Rusticana (Kentish Opera Gp), Tatyana in Eugene Onegin (Kentish Opera Gp and (as cover) WNO), Laura in La Gioconda (Hull), Erste Dame in Magic Flute (ENO), Donna Elvira in Don Giovanni (ENO), Minnie in La Fanciulla Del West (Opera Zuid Maastricht and (as cover) ROH), Amelia in Un Ballo in Maschera (Opera Zuid Maastricht); *Recreations* gardening, sailing; *Style*— Ms Anne Heath-Welch; ✉ e-mail anneheathwelch@gmail.com, website www.anneheathwelch.com

HEATHCOAT AMORY, (Ian) Mark; *see:* Amory, Mark

HEATHCOTE, Capt Alastair; s of Mark Heathcote, and Susan Heathcote; grand s of Brig Sir Gilbert Heathcote, Bt, CBE, *qv*; *b* 18 August 1977, Athens, Greece; *Educ* Eton, Newcastle Univ, Oxford Brookes Univ; *Career* army offr and rower; cmmnd Blues and Royals 2002 (tours incl Basra Iraq 2004–05), Capt 2005; achievements as rower incl: Bronze medal eights World Rowing Championships 2007, Silver medal eights Olympic Games Beijing 2008; *Recreations* dancing; *Clubs* Army Rowing; *Style*— Capt Alastair Heathcote; ✉ 8 Beeches Road, London SW17 7LZ

HEATHCOTE, Paul; MBE (2009); s of Ken Heathcote, of Bolton, Lancs, and Brenda, *née* Walsh; *b* 3 October 1960; *Educ* Turton HS Bromley Cross Bolton, Bolton Catering Coll; *Career* chef/restaurateur; apprenticeship Holdsworth House Halifax 1979–80, Hotel Sternen Bern Switzerland 1980–81, Sharrow Bay Hotel Ullswater 1981–83, The Connaught Mayfair London 1983–85, Le Manoir aux Quat'Saisons Oxford 1985–87, Broughton Park Hotel Preston 1987–90, chef/prop Paul Heathcote's Restaurant Preston 1990–, prop Heathcote's Brasserie 1995–, prop Simply Heathcote's 1996–, fndr Heathcote's Sch of Excellence 1997–; 1 Egon Ronay star 1990, 1 Michelin star 1990, Good Food Guide Co Restaurant of Year 1990, Catey Newcomer of Year 1992, 2 Michelin stars 1994, Egon Ronay Chef of Year 1994, 2 Egon Ronay stars 1994, 4/5 Good Food Guide (Paul Heathcote's Restaurant) 1996 and 1997, Good Food Guide Lancashire Newcomer Restaurant of the Year (Heathcote's Brasserie) 1996, Catey Restaurateur of the Year 1997; hon fell: Univ of Lancs 1995, Bolton Inst 2001; *Style*— Paul Heathcote, Esq, MBE; ✉ Paul Heathcote's Restaurant, 104–106 Higher Road, Longridge, Preston, Lancashire PR3 3SY (☎ 01772 784969, fax 01772 785713, e-mail longridge@heathcotes.co.uk)

HEATHERINGTON, Stuart; JP (1998); s of Harold Heatherington (d 1992), and Olive Watson, *née* Marr (d 2012); *b* 25 September 1949; *Educ* Dame Allan's Boys' Sch Newcastle upon Tyne, Univ of Wales Aberystwyth (BSc), Univ of Durham (MSc), Open Univ (BA); *m* 1980, Pauline Elizabeth, da of John Alderson Holt (d 1983); 1 da (Rachel Anne b 18 Sept 1984); *Career* princ mathematician Durham County Cncl 1971–83, major shareholder and tech dir Moss Systems Ltd 1983–97, dir Euromoss BV 1991–97, jt md Euromoss GMBH 1995–97, chm Worthing Priority Care NHS Tst 1998–2000, chm Worthing and Southlands Hosps NHS Tst 2000–06 (non-exec dir 1998); lay memb: GMC 2003–09, GOC 2007–09 (memb Statutory Ctee 2009–); ind memb Mgmnt Bd RICS 2009–11; involved with: Tyneside Samaritans 1972–83 (dir 1981–83), British Red Cross 1997–98; FIMA 1981, MBCS 1983, CEng 1983, CMath 1993, CSc 2005; *Recreations* art history, running, walking, cycling, genealogy, Cumbrian local history; *Style*— Stuart Heatherington, Esq; ✉ 3 The Gables, Nightingale Lane, Storrington, West Sussex RH20 4TB (☎ 01903 740840)

HEATHERWICK, Thomas Alexander; CBE (2013); s of Hugh Heatherwick, and Stefany, *née* Tomalin; *b* 17 February 1970; *Career* designer; estab Heatherwick Studio 1994–; visiting lectr: Manchester Met Univ 2000, RCA 2000 and 2002, Bartlett Sch of Architecture 2001, Kingston Univ 2001; artist consIt St Hellier Waterfront for Jersey Govt 2000, consIt Milton Keynes Cncl 2001; sr research fell V&A Museum; memb Panel Farrell Review of Architecture and the Built Environment 2014; hon doctorates: RCA, Univ of Dundee, Univ of Manchester, Univ of Brighton, Sheffield Hallam Univ; Hon FRIBA, RA 2013; current projects incl: Maggie's Centre Yorkshire, Zeitz Museum of Contemporary Art Africa (Zeitz MOCCA), Al Fayah Park Abu Dhabi, two large scale devpts in Shanghai, Google Campus Mountain View California, Pier55 NY, Garden Bridge London; other architectural projects incl: sitooterie for English Heritage Northumberland 2003, kiosk for Royal Borough of Kensington and Chelsea, temple for Shingon-Shu Sect Kagoshima Japan, cultural centre for St Francis Initiative Hereford, Longchamp world flagship store NY, Pacific Place Hong Kong, East Beach café Littlehampton, pavillion for World Expo Shanghai 2010, Bombay Sapphire Distillery Laverstoke Mill, Learning Hub Nanyang Technological Univ Singapore; sculpture projects incl: Harvey Nichols Autumn Intrusion 1997, Guastavino's for Sir Terence Conran NY 2000, Bleigiessen for The Wellcome Tst London 2004; infrastructure projects incl: Paternoster Vents for MEC / Stanhope plc Paternoster Square London 2002, King's Cross Glass Bridge, Rolling Bridge for Paddington Basin Devpts Ltd London 2004, Teesside Power Station in Stockton; planning and urban design projects incl: Arts Cncl 2002, Milton Keynes (lead artist for the city 2004–05), Edgware Road, Guy's Approaches Guy's Hosp London, design for New Bus for London; RDI 2004; other projects incl: Spun Chairs 2007, Extrusion Benches 2009, London 2012 Olympic cauldron 2012; *Awards* Edward Marshall Prize 1994, Crafts Cncl Setting-up Award 1995, Gold D&AD Awards 1998 (Silver 2003), Sustainable Furniture Competition Earth Centre Doncaster 2000, Design Week Awards 2001, Paviors Award for Excellence 2002, Bombay Sapphire Awards 2003 and 2004, International Footbridge Awards 2005, Structural Steel Design Awards 2005, Walpole Award for Design 2005, Art and Work Awards 2006, Prince Philip Designer's Prize 2006, Lubetkin Prize RIBA 2010, London Design Medal 2010, Designer of the Year Wallpaper Design Awards 2011, Visual Arts South Bank Award 2013 (for Olympic cauldron), Critics' Circle Visual Arts and Architecture Award 2013, Champion for London London First Awards 2013; *Books* Thomas Heatherwick: Making (2012); *Style*— Thomas Heatherwick, Esq, CBE, RDI; ✉ Heatherwick Studio, 356–364 Grays Inn Road, London WC1X 8BH (☎ 020 7833 8800, e-mail studio@heatherwick.com)

HEATLEY, Dr (Richard) Val; s of Walter Russell Heatley, of Bridport, Dorset, and Constance Marjorie, *née* Davis; *b* 11 October 1947; *Educ* Latymer Upper Sch, Welsh Nat Sch of Med (MB BCh, MD); *m* 5 May 1979, Ruth Mary, da of William Elderkin, of Leics; 2 da (Kirsteen Ruth b 1980, Francine Mary b 1982), 2 s (Richard Piers b 1986, Matthew Connel b 1988); *Career* clinical fell Sr Res Dept of Med Univ of McMaster Hamilton Ontario 1978–80, sr lectr in med WNSM and consIt physician Univ Hosp of Wales 1981–82, sr lectr in med Univ of Leeds 1982–, consIt physician and gastroenterologist St James's Univ Hosp Leeds 1982–; ed Int Jl of Gastroenterology; memb: Br Soc of Gastroenterology and Immunology, Bd Aliment Pharmacology and Therapeutics, Ctee on Gastroenterology RCP; FRCP; *Books* The Helicobacter pylori Handbook (1998), Clinical Economics in Gastroenterology (1999), Dyspepsia: The Clinical Consequences (2000), Medicine and Myths (2003); *Recreations* children, music, travel, walking; *Style*— Dr Val Heatley; ✉ Department of Medicine, St James's University Hospital, Leeds LS9 7TF (☎ 07522 804237, e-mail rheatley@medicineandmyths.com)

HEATON; *see also:* Henniker-Heaton

HEATON, His Hon Judge Clive William; QC (2006); s of William Heaton, and Dilys, *née* Eley; *b* 20 July 1957, Manchester; *Educ* Huddersfield New Coll, Keble Coll Oxford, Chester Coll of Law; *m* 1, 1980, Susan Margaret, *née* Taylor (d 2007); 2 s (David James William b 25 Sept 1987, Richard John b 13 Feb 1990); m 2, 11 Feb 2012, Her Hon Judge Finnerty, *qv*; *Career* slr 1982–92; called to the Bar 1992; dep district judge 2000, recorder 2003, circuit judge (North Eastern Circuit) 2011–; *Publications* Adoption: The Modern Practice (with Her Hon Judge Swindells, QC, 2006), Forced Marriage (gen ed, 2009); *Style*— His Hon Judge Heaton, QC; ✉ Leeds Combined Court Centre, The Courthouse, 1 Oxford Row, Leeds LS1 3BG

HEATON, Frances Anne; *née* Whidborne; da of John Ferris Whidborne (d 1985), and Marjorie Annie, *née* Maltby (d 1989); *b* 11 August 1944, Winchester, Hants; *Educ* Queen Anne's Sch Caversham, Trinity Coll Dublin (BA, LLB); *m* 26 April 1969, Martin Christopher Crispin Heaton; 2 s (Mark Christopher Francis b 14 April 1972, Andrew John Ralph b 9 Nov 1974); *Career* called to the Bar Inner Temple 1967; Dept of Econ Affrs 1967–70, HM Treasy 1970–80 (seconded S G Warburg & Co Ltd 1977–79), dir of corp fin Lazard Brothers & Co Ltd 1986–2001 (joined 1980); non-exec dir: W S Atkins 1990–2003 (dep chm 1996–2003), Commercial Union 1994–98, Elementis plc (formerly Harrisons & Crosfield) 1994–99, BUPA 1998–2001, Worldpay Ltd 2000–02, Legal & General Gp plc 2001–10, AWG plc 2002–07, Jupiter Primadona Growth Tst 2005–14, BMT Gp Ltd 2007–14; chm: Lazard London Directors Pension Scheme 2006–15, Schroder Pension Tstee Ltd 2008–14; DG Takeovers and Mergers Panel 1992–94, memb Ct Bank of England 1993–2001, memb Ctee on Standards in Public Life 1998–2003; *Recreations* riding, gardening, bridge; *Style*— Mrs Frances Heaton; ✉ e-mail fah@carillon.co.uk

HEATON, Naomi Claire Helen; da of Dr Boaz Antony Jarrett (d 2003), of Chiswick, London, and Patricia Evelyn, *née* White (d 2008); *b* 11 September 1955; *Educ* Walthamstow Hall Sch for Girls, St Hilda's Coll Oxford (BA); *m* 1, 18 March 1988 (m dis 2010), Mark Frederick Heaton; m 2, 14 Dec 2013, Prof Jonathan Hugh Waxman; *Career* Leo Burnett Advertising 1977–82; main bd dir: Saatchi & Saatchi Advertising 1984 (joined 1982), Young & Rubicam 1985–86; chief exec London Central Portfolio Ltd (specialists in residential investment asset mgmnt, estab 1989) 1999– (md 1994–99); dir: London Central Portfolio Property Fund Ltd 2005–, London Central Residential Recovery Fund Ltd 2009–, London Central Apartments Ltd 2012–, London Central Apartments II Ltd 2014–, London Central Apartments III Ltd 2015–; *Recreations* skiing, country pursuits, interior design; *Clubs* Ivy; *Style*— Mrs Naomi Heaton; ✉ 116 Seymour Place, London W1H 1NW (☎ 020 7723 1733, e-mail naomi.heaton@londoncentralportfolio.com, website www.londoncentralportfolio.com)

HEATON, Richard Nicholas; CB (2011); *Career* called to the Bar Inner Temple 1988 (bencher 2013); various roles in the Govt legal service 1991–2005, dir for legal services Dept for Constitutional Affrs (now Miny of Justice) 2005–07; Dept for Work and Pensions: DG Legal Gp 2007–09, DG for strategy, info and pensions 2009–12; perm sec Cabinet Office and first parly counsel 2012–; chair of tstees United St Saviour's Charity Southwark; *Style*— Richard Heaton, Esq, CB; ✉ Cabinet Office, 1 Horse Guards Road, London SW1A 2HQ (Twitter @rhcabinetoffice)

HEATON-ARMSTRONG, Anthony Eustace John; s of William Henry Dunamace Heaton-Armstrong, of Berks, and Idonea, *née* Chance; *b* 27 September 1950, Bromsgrove, Worcs; *Educ* Ampleforth, Univ of Bristol (LLB); *m* 1, 10 Feb 1973 (m dis 1977), Susan, *née* Allnutt; m 2, 20 May 1982, Anne Frances, da of late Ethel Robigo; 1 s (John William b 15 Feb 1983), 2 da (Eleanor b 8 May 1985, Celestine b 3 Sept 1988); *Career* called to the Bar Gray's Inn 1972, in practice 1973–; expert on police evidence, Int Cmmn of Jurists' observer at trials overseas involving alleged human rights abuses, memb team appointed by Home Office to conduct fundamental review of death certification and Coronial Inquest systems 2001–03; tstee Aldo Tst, chm Witness Confident; *Books* Confession Evidence (with David Wolchover, 1996), Analysing Witness Testimony (with Eric Shepherd and David Wolchover, 1999), Witness Testimony: Psychological, Investigative and Evidential Perspectives (with Eric Shepherd, Gisli Gudjonsson and David Wolchover, 2006), Witness Testimony in Sexual Cases (with Pamela Radcliffe, Gisli Gudjonsson, CBE and David Wolchover, 2016); also author of numerous legal articles in learned jls; *Recreations* prisoners' welfare, gardening, dry fly fishing, wildlife and the countryside; *Clubs* Garrick; *Style*— Anthony Heaton-Armstrong, Esq; ✉ 9–12 Bell Yard, London WC2A 2JR (☎ 020 7400 1800, fax 020 7404 1405, e-mail anthonyha123@btinternet.com)

HEATON-HARRIS, Chris; MP; s of David Barry Heaton-Harris, of Esher, Surrey, and Ann Geraldine, *née* Cox; *b* 28 November 1967; *Educ* Tiffin Boys GS; *m* 30 June 1990, Jayne Yvonne, da of Gregory Harold Spencer Carlow; 2 da (Megan Elizabeth Tate b 5 May 1996, Tess Alexandra Jayne b 1 April 2000); *Career* MEP (Cons) E Midlands 1999–2009, MP (Cons) Daventry 2010– (Parly candidate Leicester S 1997 and 2004 (by-election)); memb various Euro Parl Ctees; *Recreations* Grade 5 soccer referee; *Style*— Chris Heaton-Harris, MP; ✉ Danventry Conservative Association, 78 St George's Avenue, Northampton NN2 6JF (☎ 01604 859721, website www.heatonharris.com)

HEATON-JONES, Peter; MP; *Career* MP (Cons) N Devon 2015–; *Style*— Peter Heaton-Jones, Esq, MP; ✉ House of Commons, London SW1A 0AA

HEBER-PERCY, Sir Algernon Eustace Hugh; KCVO (2014), JP; s of Brig Algernon George William Heber-Percy, DSO (d 1961), of Hodnet Hall, and Daphne Wilma Kenyon, *née* Parker Bowles; *b* 2 January 1944; *Educ* Harrow; *m* 6 July 1966, Hon Margaret Jane, *née* Lever, yst da of 3 Viscount Leverhulme, KG, TD; 3 da (Emily Jane b 19 Feb 1969, Lucy Ann b 29 Dec 1970, Sophie Daphne b 22 Jan 1979), 1 s ((Algernon) Thomas Lever b 29 Jan 1984); *Career* Lt Grenadier Gds 1962–66; farmer; memb Exec Ctee and chm Mercia Regnl Ctee Nat Tst 1990–99, tstee Nat Gardens Scheme 1990–2005; govr Shrewsbury Sch 2004–13; Hon Col 5 LI (Shropshire and Herefordshire Regt) 1998–99, Hon Col (W Midlands Regt) 1999–2005; High Sheriff Shropshire 1987, HM Lord-Lt Shropshire 1996– (DL 1986, Vice Lord-Lt 1990); *Recreations* gardening, country sports; *Clubs* Cavalry and Guards'; *Style*— Sir Algernon Heber-Percy, KCVO; ✉ Hodnet Hall, Hodnet, Market Drayton, Shropshire TF9 3NN (☎ 01630 685202)

HEDDEN, Robert; s of Frederick Hedden (d 1982), of Okehampton, Devon, and Winifred Elizabeth, *née* Trenaman (d 1996); *b* 22 February 1948; *Educ* Okehampton GS, KCL (LLB, AKC); *m* 10 Sept 1977 (m dis 1996), Jean Mary, da of Walter John Worboyes (d 1982), of London; 1 da (Rachel Louise), 1 s (Oliver Michael Ward); partner, Mustakeem Shariff (civil partnership 7 July 2007), of Penang, Malaysia; *Career* admitted slr 1972 (Clifford's Inn prizeman), ptnr Herbert Smith 1980–93 (consIt 1993–94), gp slr Freshwater Group of Companies 1993–2014 (special advsr 2015–); memb: Ctee Br-Polish Legal Assoc 1989–93, Planning and Environmental Law Sub-Ctee City of London Law Soc 1991–93; memb Law Soc; assoc memb Dirs' Guild of GB 1990–96; Freeman City of London, Liveryman Worshipful Co of Slrs; *Recreations* theatre, music, tennis, skiing, cruising, powerboating, swimming, homes in Ibiza and Malaysia and other travel; *Clubs* Athenaeum; *Style*— Robert Hedden, Esq; ✉ Freshwater House, 158–162 Shaftesbury Avenue, London WC2H 8HR (☎ 020 7836 1555, fax 020 7240 9770)

HEDGES, Dr Anthony John; s of Sidney George Hedges (d 1974), and Mary, *née* Dixon; *b* 5 March 1931; *Educ* Bicester GS, Keble Coll Oxford (MA, BMus, DipEd); *m* 28 Aug 1957, (Delia) Joy, da of Maj Albert Marsden (d 1971); 2 da (Fiona b 25 Feb 1959, Deborah b 4 March 1961), 2 s (Nicholas b 28 Oct 1964, Simon b 10 May 1966); *Career* Nat Serv Royal Signals Band 1955–57; teacher and lectr Royal Scottish Acad of Music 1957–63; Univ of Hull: lectr 1963, sr lectr 1968, reader in composition 1978–95; princ compositions incl; orchestral: Comedy Overture 1962 (revised 1967), Overture Oct '62 1962 (revised 1968), Variations on a Theme of Rameau 1969, Festival Dances 1976, Four Breton Sketches 1980, Sinfonia Concertante 1980, Scenes from the Humber 1981, Symphony 1 1972–73, A Cleveland Overture 1984, Concertino for Horn and String Orchestra 1987, Sinfonia Giovanile 1991, Symphony 2 1998, Fiddlers Green 2001, West Oxford Walks 2002, Three Concert Miniatures 2004, Serenade for Strings 2013; choral: Epithalamium 1969, Psalm 104 1973, The Temple of Solomon 1979, I Sing the Birth (Canticles for Christmas) 1985, I'll Make Me a World 1990, The Lamp of Liberty 2006; chamber music: String Quartets 1970 and 1990, Piano Trio 1977, Flute Trios 1985 and 1989, Clarinet Quintet 1988; Sonatas for Piano 1974, Flute 1989, Cello 1982, Viola 1982, Wind Quintet 1984, Bassoon Quintet 1991, Piano Quartet 1992, Piano Duets 1993, Ten Bagatelles 2005, Three Humours 2010, Trialogues 2011; opera: Shadows in the Sun 1976; musical: Minotaur 1978; miscellaneous: song cycles, anthems, partsongs music for TV, film and stage, complete archive in Hull Central Library; memb Cncl The Composers' Guild of GB (memb Exec Ctee 1969–73 and 1977–81, chm 1972–73); memb: Cncl Central Music Library Westminster 1970–91, SPNM Cncl 1974–81; memb Music Panels: Yorkshire Arts 1974–

75, Lincs and Humberside Arts 1975–78; memb Music Bd CNNA 1974–77; Hon DMus Univ of Hull 1977; LRAM; *Books* Basic Tonal Harmony (1988), An Introduction to Counterpoint (1988); also many CD recordings; *Recreations* reading, playing chamber music; *Style—* Dr Anthony Hedges; ✉ Malt Shovel Cottage, 76 Walkergate, Beverley, East Yorkshire HU17 9ER (☎ 01482 860580, e-mail ahedges@westfieldmusic.karoo.co.uk, website www.westfieldmusic-anthonyhedges.co.uk)

HEDGES, Mike; AM; *Educ* Swansea Univ, Cardiff Univ; *m* Anne; 1 da (Catrin); *Career* memb Nat Assembly for Wales (Lab) Swansea E 2011–; *Style—* Mike Hedges, Esq, AM; ✉ National Assembly for Wales, Cardiff Bay, Cardiff CF99 1NA

HEDGES, Neil Francis; s of Kenneth Francis Chevalier, of Walmer, Kent, and Peggy, *née* Best; *b* 12 December 1956; *Educ* Watford Boys' GS, Univ of Sheffield (BA); *m* 19 Sept 1981, Katherine Anne, da of Trevor Noel Louis, of Bushey Heath, Herts; 2 da (Frances b 13 Feb 1986, Alexandra b 18 March 1989); *Career* md Valin Pollen Ltd 1988–90 (asst md 1985, account exec 1980), co-fndr and chm Fishburn Hedges (formerly Fishburn Hedges Boys Williams) until 2011; *Recreations* music, cinema, walking, family; *Style—* Neil Hedges, Esq

HEDLEY, Sir Mark; kt (2002); s of late Peter Hedley, of Windsor, and late Eve, *née* Morley; *b* 23 August 1946; *Educ* Framlingham Coll, Univ of Liverpool (LLB); *m* 14 April 1973, Erica Rosemary, da of late John Capel Britton, of Ashbourne; 3 s (Michael b 1975, Steven b 1981, Peter b 1982), 1 da (Anna b 1978); *Career* called to the Bar Gray's Inn 1969 (bencher 2002); recorder of the Crown Court 1988; circuit judge (Northern Circuit) 1992–2002, judge of the High Court of Justice (Family Div) 2002–13, ret; visiting prof of law Liverpool Hope Univ 2013–; reader C of E; chllr Diocese of Liverpool 2002–; Hon LLD Univ of Liverpool 2003, hon fell Liverpool John Moores Univ 2005; *Recreations* cricket, railways; *Style—* Sir Mark Hedley; ✉ 55 Everton Road, Liverpool L6 2EH

HEDLEY LEWIS, Vincent Richard; s of John Hedley Lewis (d 1976), of Birkholme Manor, Corby Glen, Lincs, and Sheelagh Alice Valentine, *née* De Paravicini (d 1990); *b* 24 May 1941; *Educ* Wellesley House, Harrow; *m* 17 June 1978, Penelope Ann, da of A C Hobson, MC; 3 da (Selena Priscilla b 27 Sept 1980, Melissa Sheelagh b 12 Sept 1982, Amanda Jane b 28 Jan 1985); *Career* articled to H R Crouch, Crouch Chapman & Co 1960–68, CA 1966; ptnr Agribusiness Div Deloitte & Touche 1968–2000; memb: Lincolnshire Jt Devpt Ctee 1981–97, Econ Advsy Panel Rural Devpt Cmmn 1989–99, Country Landowners' Cncl 1994–2003; dir: Peterborough Devpt Agency 1987–94, JSR Farms Ltd 2000–14, Farmacy plc 2000–14, Strutt & Parker Farms 2001–14, Oxford Farming Conference 2007–11; tstee NIAB 2007–11; farmer of 1700 acres Corby Glen Lincs; chm CLA Game Fair Bd 2005–11; govr Harper Adams Univ 2000–07; memb SCGB (Gold medallist), ran London Marathon 1989; *Books* Contract Farming (1976); *Recreations* cricket, skiing, tennis, golf, shooting; *Clubs* Farmers', MCC, Free Foresters Cricket, Luffenham Heath Golf, Lincolnshire; *Style—* Vincent Hedley Lewis, Esq; ✉ mobile 07836 759553, e-mail vincent@birkholme.co.uk

HEDLEY-MILLER, Rosalind; da of Roger Latham Hedley-Miller (d 2004), and Dame Mary Elizabeth Hedley-Miller, DCVO, CB (d 2010); *b* 25 November 1954, London; *Educ* St Paul's Girls' Sch, St Hugh's Coll Oxford (MA), Harvard Univ; *Career* Investment Dept J Henry Schroder Wagg & Co Ltd 1977–79; Kleinwort Benson (now Commerzbank): Corp Fin Dept 1979–, dir 1987–, jt head Corp Fin Dept 1994–96, gp dir 1996–2001, vice-chm 2001–14; non-exec dir: Bejam Group plc 1987–89, TV-am plc 1990–93; memb: Fin Ctee Oxford University Press 1995–2009, Industrial Devpt Advsy Bd DTI 1997–2005, Competition & Markets Authy 2013–; Rhodes Tstee 1999–2011; *Recreations* music, bridge, golf; *Clubs* Chelsea Arts; *Style—* Miss Rosalind Hedley-Miller; ✉ 48 Elms Road, London SW4 9EX

HEDWORTH, (Alan) Toby; QC (1996); s of John William Swaddle Hedworth (d 1998), and Margaret Ena, *née* Dodds (d 2004); *b* 23 April 1952; *Educ* King's Sch Tynemouth, Royal GS Newcastle upon Tyne, St Catharine's Coll Cambridge (MA); *m* 12 Dec 1987, Kathleen Mary, da of Gordon Luke; 2 da (Anna Charlotte Pettinger b 2 July 1979, Alice Lucinda Marie b 6 May 1989); *Career* called to the Bar Inner Temple 1975, called to the Bar of NI 2012; recorder 1995– (asst recorder 1991), head of chambers Trinity Chambers Newcastle upon Tyne 1999–; memb Criminal Bar Assoc; vice-chm Northumberland & Newcastle Soc; *Recreations* Newcastle United FC, English Lake District, motoring, the built environment; *Clubs* Northern Counties (Newcastle upon Tyne); *Style—* Toby Hedworth, Esq, QC; ✉ Trinity Chambers, The Custom House, Quayside, Newcastle upon Tyne NE1 3DE (☎ 0191 232 1927, fax 0191 232 7975)

HEEREMA, Eric; s of Pieter Heerema (d 1981), and Erna, *née* Kühnen (d 1999); *b* 31 December 1960, Sherbrooke, Canada; *Educ* American Coll Paris (BA), Utrecht Univ The Netherlands (Law degree); *m* 5 Oct 2013, Hannah Heerema; 2 da (Genevieve b 29 Aug 2014, Vivienne b 5 Nov 2015); *Children* from a previous relationship: 2 s (Paul b 17 Dec 1991, Alexander b 11 Aug 1993), 1 da (Laurine b 9 Nov 1998); *Career* lawyer Nauta Dutilh Rotterdam 1990–91, fndr and md Finadco Antwerp 1992–99, advsr on investment projects 1998–2006, owner and ceo Nyetimber 2006–; memb Bd English Wine Producers 2016–; JM Compagie Endowment Fund 2003–12; memb Bd Mauritshaus Museum The Hague; *Recreations* motorsport, sailing, skiing; *Clubs* RAC, Royal Thames Yacht, 5 Hertford Street; ✉ Nyetimber, Broughton House, 6–8 Sackville Street, London W1S 3DG (Twitter @Nyetimber)

HEFFER, Dr Simon James; s of James Heffer (d 1971), of Woodham Ferrers, Essex, and Joyce Mary, *née* Clements; *b* 18 July 1960; *Educ* King Edward VI Sch Chelmsford, CCC Cambridge (MA, PhD); *m* 31 July 1987, Diana Caroline, da of Sqdn Ldr P A Clee, of Marlow, Bucks; 2 s (James William Frederick b 3 Sept 1993, Charles Hubert John b 5 July 1996); *Career* med journalist 1983–85, freelance journalist 1985–86; Daily Telegraph: leader writer 1986–91, dep political corr 1987–88, political sketch writer 1988–91, political columnist 1990–91; dep ed: The Spectator 1991–94, Daily Telegraph 1994–95; columnist: Evening Standard 1991–93, Daily Mail 1993–94 and 1995–2005; assoc ed Daily Telegraph 2005–11, political columnist Daily Mail 2011–15; columnist Daily and Sunday Telegraphs 2015–; memb Bd: Britten Sinfonia 2005–09, Elgar Fndn 2009–, New Queen's Hall Orchestra 2012–; fell commoner CCC Cambridge 2010; *Books* A Century of County Cricket (ed, 1990), A Tory Seer (jt ed with C Moore, 1989), Moral Desperado: a Life of Thomas Carlyle (1995), Power and Place: The Political Consequences of King Edward VII (1998), Like the Roman: The Life of Enoch Powell (1998), Nor Shall My Sword: The Reinvention of England (1999), Vaughan Williams (2000), Great British Speeches (ed, 2007), Strictly English (2010), A Short History of Power (2011), High Minds: The Victorians and the Birth of Modern Britain (2013), Simply English (2014); *Recreations* cricket, music, ecclesiology, bibliophily, my wife and children; *Clubs* Beefsteak, Garrick, MCC, Pratt's; *Style—* Dr Simon Heffer; ✉ The Daily Telegraph, 111 Buckingham Palace Road, London SW1W 0DT (e-mail simon.heffer@telegraph.co.uk)

HEFFERNAN, Patrick Benedict; s of Dr Daniel Anthony Heffernan (d 2000), of Reading, Berks, and Margaret, *née* Donovan (d 1996); *b* 17 March 1948; *Educ* Wimbledon Coll, Jesus Coll Cambridge (MA); *m* 5 May 1973, Elizabeth, da of Robert Essery (d 1966), of Huddersfield and Melbourne; 2 s (Thomas b 1984, Rory Patrick b 1993), 1 da (Miranda b 1987); *Career* slr 1974; ptnr: Clyde & Co 1988–97, Mishcon de Reya 1997–99, Halliwell Landau 1999–2002, Orchard Brayton Graham LLP 2002–08, OBG Cameron Banfill LLP 2008–09, Smithfield Partners Ltd 2009–; Liveryman Worshipful Company of Farriers 1994; *Recreations* Times crossword, sport, reading; *Style—* Patrick Heffernan, Esq; ✉ 3 Cholmeley Crescent, Highgate, London N6 5EZ; Smithfield Partners Ltd, 107 Cannon Street, London EC4N 5AF (☎ 0845 539 1000, fax 0845 652 0775, e-mail paddy.heffernan@smithfieldpartners.com)

HEGARTY, Sir John Kevin; kt (2007); *Career* jr art dir Benton and Bowles 1965, briefly with John Collings & Ptnrs; Cramer Saatchi (later Saatchi & Saatchi): joined 1967, founding shareholder Saatchi & Saatchi 1970, dep creative dir 1971–73; TBWA London: co-fndr 1973, creative dir 1973–82; Bartle Bogle Hegarty (BBH): fndr 1982, currently worldwide creative dir; Hon Dr Univ of Middx 2006, Hon Dr New Univ Bucks 2006; hon fell Central St Martins 1998; *Awards* Campaign Agency of Year for TBWA 1980; for BBH: Campaign Agency of Year 2003, 2004 and 2005, Cannes Advtg Festival Agency of Year 1993 and 1994; 2 Gold and 6 Silver D&AD Awards, Cannes Golds and Silvers, Br TV Gold and Silvers, D&AD President's Award for outstanding achievement in advtg industry, inducted into One Club Creative Hall of Fame (US) 2005, Lifetime Achievement Award Clio Awards 2005; *Style—* Sir John Hegarty; ✉ Bartle Bogle Hegarty, 60 Kingly Street, London W1B 5DS (☎ 020 7734 1677, fax 020 7437 3666)

HEGGESSEY, Lorraine; *Career* jr reporter Acton Gazette 1978–79; BBC TV: news trainee 1979–81, news sub-ed 1981–82, asst prodr Current Affrs Dept (Newsnight, Panorama, 60 Minutes) 1982–83, prodr Current Affrs Dept (60 Minutes, Panorama) 1983–86; prodr Thames TV (This Week) 1986–90; Channel 4 TV: dep ed Hard News 1990–91, prodr and reporter Dispatches 1991, prodr As It Happens 1991; BBC TV: ed Biteback 1991, series prodr The Underworld 1992–94, exec prodr Minders, Animal Hospital Live and States of Mind 1994, exec prodr Animal Hospital 1994–96, series ed QED 1994–96, exec prodr The Human Body 1996–97, head of Children's Progs 1997–99, dir of programmes BBC Production 1999–2000, jt dir BBC Factual and Learning 2000, controller BBC1 2000–05, chief exec talkbackTHAMES 2005–10; *Recreations* skiing; *Style—* Ms Lorraine Heggessey

HEGLEY, John Richard; s of René Hegley, and Joan, *née* Harris; *b* 1 October 1953, Islington, London; *Educ* Univ of Bradford (BSc); *Children* 1 da (Isabella b 1995); *Career* performance poet; began career in children's theatre with Interaction and Soapbox 1980 then at Comedy Store 1981 and John Peel sessions with The Popticians 1983–84 (previously employed as bus conductor); numerous tours; regular presenter BBC Radio 4; performed in The Pyjama Game (musical) 1999; Hon Dr of Arts Univ of Luton 2000; *Poetry* Poems for Pleasure (1989), Glad to Wear Glasses (1990), Can I Come Down Now, Dad? (1991), Five Sugars Please (1993), Saint and Blurry (audio recording, poetry and songs, 1993), These Were Your Father's (1994), Love Cuts (1995), The Family Pack (collection, 1996), Beyond Our Kennel (1998), Dog (2000), My Dog is a Carrot (for children, 2002), The Sound of Paint Drying (2003); *Clubs* Islington Folk; *Style—* John Hegley, Esq; ✉ c/o Will Darlow, Torika Management, 74 Clarenwell Road, London EC1M 5QA (☎ 020 7336 7868)

HEILBRON, Hilary Nora Burstein; QC (1987); da of Dr Nathaniel Burstein, and Dame Rose Heilbron, DBE; *b* 2 January 1949; *Educ* Huyton Coll, LMH Oxford (MA); *Career* called to the Bar: Gray's Inn 1971 (bencher 1995), NSW Aust 1996 (SC 1997); dep chm City Disputes Panel, DTI inspr into the affairs of Blue Arrow plc 1989; chm: Jt Ctee on Civil Cts Gen Cncl of the Bar and Law Soc, London Common Law and Commercial Bar Assoc 1992–93; memb: Gen Cncl of the Bar 1991–98, Advsy Cncl CEDR; vice-chm Marshall Aid Commemoration Cmmn 1998–2002; *Style—* Hilary Heilbron, QC; ✉ Brick Court Chambers, 7–8 Essex Street, London WC2R 3LD (☎ 020 7379 3550, fax 020 7379 3558)

HEILBRON, Jonathan; *Career* Pricewaterhouse 1982–86, Nat West 1986–97, Thomas Pink: finance dir 1997–2004, pres and ceo 2004–; chair Walpole Brands of Tomorrow Prog; *Style—* Jonathan Heilbron, Esq; ✉ Thomas Pink Ltd, 1 Palmerston Court, Palmerston Way, London SW8 4AJ (website www.thomaspink.com)

HEIN, Prof Jotun John; *b* 19 July 1956, Denmark; *Educ* Aarhus Univ; *Career* grad asst Aarhus Univ 1981–84, visiting assoc Nat Inst of Environmental Health Sciences (NIEHS) NC 1985–87, conslt Harvard Med Sch 1987, research assoc Inst of Mathematics Univ of Southern Calif 1987–1988, post-doctoral fell Center for Molecular Genetics Univ of Calif San Diego 1988–89, visiting appt Univ of Washington Seattle 1989, post-doctoral work Centre Recherche Mathematiquee Montreal 1989–90, Japanese Soc for the Promotion of Sci fell Nat Inst of Genetics Mishima and Japanese DNA Database 1990–91; Aarhus Univ: sr stipend 1991–, assoc prof 1994–, dir Bioinformatics Research Centre 2001–; prof of bioinformatics Dept of Statistics Univ of Oxford 2001–; visiting Miller research prof UC Berkeley Calif 2011; invited stay Newton Inst for Mathematical Sciences Cambridge 1998, Erskine Award to stay at Dept of Mathematics Massey Univ Christchurch 1999; assoc ed Genetics 2001–03, author of numerous articles and reviews in learned jls; memb Royal Soc of Sci Denmark; *Style—* Prof Jotun Hein; ✉ Department of Statistics, University of Oxford, 1 South Parks Road, Oxford OX1 3TG (☎ 01865 285387, fax 01865 272595)

HEINDORFF, Michael; *b* 1949; *Educ* Art Coll and Univ of Braunschweig, RCA London; *Children* 1 s (b 13 Sept 1984), 1 da (b 15 June 1988); *Career* artist; teacher RCA London 1980–99; work in the collections of: RCA, Univ of Liverpool, V&A, Vicaria di Santiago de Chile, Herzog Anton Ulrich-Museum Braunschweig, State of Niedersachsen Germany, Arts Cncl of GB, The Br Cncl, Bank of America LA, Security Pacific Bank LA, MOMA NY, The Bank of Montreal London, Bradford Municipal Museum, Green Coll Oxford, Imperial War Museum, Nat Gallery Washington USA; *Solo Exhibitions* Galerie Axiom Cologne 1977, Bernard Jacobson Gallery London 1978–1992, Bernard Jacobson Gallery NY 1983–89, Bernard Jacobson Gallery LA 1981, 1982 and 1984, Jacobson/Hochman Gallery NY 1981 and 1982, Mathildenhöhe Darmstadt Germany 1983, Villa Massimo Rome 1984, Northern Centre for Contemporary Art Sunderland 1987, Royal Coll of Art 1993 and 1995, NORD/LB Galerie (Braunschweig) 1998, NORD/LB Forum (Dessau) 1998, Schlossmuseum (Furstenberg) 1998, touring show of drawings (museums in northern Germany) 1999–2001, Guildhall Art Gallery 2002, Deutsche Bank London 2003; *Group Exhibitions* incl: John Moore's Liverpool Exhibition 1976, Air Gallery 1977, Royal Coll of Art London (Annual Exhibitions) 1977, Whitechapel Art Gallery London 1979, Serpentine Gallery London (Summer show 1) 1980, Anne Berthand Gallery London 1981, Herzog Anton Ulrich-Museum Braunschweig 1981 and 2004, Bradford Print Biennale 1982, Paton Gallery London (Alternative Tate) 1982, Ashmolean Museum Oxford (Innovations in Contemporary Printmaking) 1982, Third Biennale of European Graphic Art Baden-Baden 1983, Bruecke Museum Berlin 1984, MOMA NY 1984, Univ of Maryland USA 1985, Bank of America San Francisco 1985, V&A Museum London 1986, Sunderland Arts Centre & Laing Art Gallery Newcastle 1987, Royal Acad of Arts London 1988–, RCA 150th Anniversary Show 1988, Imperial War Museum London (On Commission) 1989, Nat Gallery Washington USA 1989, Bernard Jacobson Gallery London 1990 and 1991, Flowers East Gallery London 1992, 1994, 1997 and 1998, Royal Acad Summer Exhibition 1995, V&A Museum London 1996, Museum of London 1997 and 2001; *Awards*: German Nat Scholarship Fndn scholar 1972–76, DAAD scholarship for London 1976–77, John Moore's Liverpool award 1976, State of Niedersachsen scholarship 1980, Schmidt-Rotluff prize 1981, Rome prize Villa Massimo 1981; hon fell RCA; *Recreations* travelling, learning; *Clubs* Chelsea Arts (life memb); *Style—* Michael Heindorff, Esq; ✉ e-mail heindorff@aol.com

HELLAWELL, Keith; QPM (1990); s of Douglas Hellawell (d 1986), and Ada Alice, *née* Battye; *b* 18 May 1942; *Educ* Kirkburton Secdy Modern Sch, Dewsbury Tech Coll, Barnsley Coll of Mining, Univ of London (LLB), Cranfield Inst of Technol (MSc); *m* 1963, Brenda, da of late Percy Hey; 2 da (Samantha Louise b 26 Sept 1965, Alexandra Jane b 18 May 1967), 1 s (Charles Justin Spencer b 17 May 1970); *Career* Huddersfield Borough Police: joined 1962, Sgt 1965, Inspr 1967; W Yorks Police (later W Yorks Metropolitan Police): joined 1968, Chief Inspr 1972, Supt 1975, Chief Supt 1979, Asst Chief Constable 1983;

Dep Chief Constable Humberside 1985–90, Chief Constable Cleveland Constabulary 1990–93, Chief Constable W Yorks Police 1993–98; UK Anti-Drugs co-ordinator 1998–2001, Govt advsr on int drug issues 2001–02; runs private consulting co KHMTC; non-exec dir: Evans plc 1998–, Universal Vehicles Gp plc 2001, Catapult Presentations plc 2001, Dalkia plc 2002–06, Mortice plc 2008–; chm smart witness vehicle camera company 2015–; non-exec chm: Sterience Ltd 2003–06, Howells Assocs 2005–06, Goldshield Gp plc 2006–09, Dynamic Change 2006–10, Sports Direct Int 2009–; chm Airshelter Ltd 2009–10; memb Bd of Tstees NSPCC; exec dir Huddersfield Giants (rugby league); newspaper columnist and broadcaster; Dr (hc): Leeds Metropolitan Univ 1997, Bradford Univ 1998, Huddersfield Univ 1998; Officer Brother StJ 1995; *Books* The Outsider (autobiography, 2002); *Recreations* reading, design, gardening, sport; *Style—* Dr Keith Hellawell, QPM

HELLER, John A; *Career* chief exec London & Associated Properties plc 2001–; *Style—* John Heller, Esq; ✉ London & Associated Properties plc, 24 Bruton Place, London W1J 6NE

HELLER, Lawrance (Laurie); *b* 14 April 1934; *Educ* Battersea GS, Sidney Sussex Coll Cambridge (scholar, MA); *m* Lilian Patricia Heller; 1 da (Charlotte b 9 April 1964); *Career* articled Silkin & Silkin 1956–59, jr ptnr Titmuss Sainer & Webb 1962–63 (asst slr 1959–62), ptnr Leighton & Co 1964–70, a fndr and sr ptnr Berwin Leighton (now Berwin Leighton Paisner) 1970–99, conslt Berwin Leighton Paisner LLP 1999–2013; memb Law Soc Conveyancing and Land Law Ctee, hon memb City of London Law Soc Property Sub-Ctee; *Books* Practical Commercial Precedents (contrib, 1987), Commercial Property Development Precedents (gen ed and maj contrib, 1993); *Recreations* teaching law, writing articles, skiing, gardening; *Style—* Laurie Heller, Esq

HELLER, Lucy; *Educ* Hampstead Comp, Univ of Oxford; *Career* exec chm Verso 1995–97, gen mangr The Observer 1998–99, jt md TSL Educn 2000–03, md educn ARK Schs 2004–, chief exec ARK 2012–; *Style—* Ms Lucy Heller; ✉ ARK, 65 Kingsway, London WC2B 6TD

HELLER, Sir Michael Aron; kt (2013); s of Simon Heller (d 1989), of Harrogate, N Yorks, and Nettie, *née* Gordon (d 1997); *Educ* Harrogate GS, St Catharine's Coll Cambridge (MA); *m* 1965, Morven, da of Dr Julius Livingstone; 2 s (John b 1966, Andrew b 1968), 1 da (Nicola b 1981); *Career* chm: London & Associated Properties plc, Bisichi Mining plc, Electronic Data Processing plc; dep chm Centre for Policy Studies; FCA; *Recreations* opera, walking, collecting twentieth century art; *Clubs* RAC; *Style—* Sir Michael Heller; ✉ London & Associated Properties plc, 24 Bruton Place, London W1J 6NE

HELLICAR, Michael William; s of Jonathan Ernest Hellicar (d 1991), of London, and Eileen May, *née* Williams (d 1983); *b* 3 April 1941; *m* 1962, June Betty, da of Charles Edward Pitcher; 3 da (Nicola Jane b 24 May 1965, Justine Louise b 28 July 1966, Charlotte Laura b 18 April 1979); *Career* journalist; apprentice reporter South London Observer 1956–60, asst news ed and feature writer New Musical Express 1960–63, news ed Rave Magazine 1963–64, feature writer Daily Sketch 1964–67; Daily Mirror: feature and leader writer 1967–72, ed Inside Page 1972–73, features ed 1973–76, sr writer 1976–81; asst ed Daily Star 1989–99 (chief feature writer 1982–89), freelance writer and ed 1999–; regular contrib: Daily Mail 2001–, Weekend magazine 2001–, Hello magazine 2006–; *Recreations* snowboarding; *Style—* Michael Hellicar, Esq; ✉ 13 Charlecote Grove, Sydenham, London SE26 4BW (☎ 020 8699 8289, mobile 07957 939482, e-mail michael.hellicar@tiscali.co.uk)

HELLIKER, Adam Andrew Alexander; s of Maurice William Helliker, DFC, AFC (d 1984), and Jane Olivia, *née* Blunt (d 2005); *b* 13 September 1958; *Educ* King's Sch Bruton, Somerset Coll of Arts and Technol; *m* 2003, Lucy Alice Elizabeth, da of John Naylor; 1 da (Marina b 24 May 2006); *Career* reporter: Western Times Co Ltd 1978–81, Daily Mail 1981–86; dep diary ed: Daily Mail 1986–98, Mail on Sunday 1988–98; diary ed Sunday Telegraph 1998–2002; diary ed Mail on Sunday 2002–04, columnist Sunday Express 2004– (also ed Crossbencher column); contrib to several nat magazines; vice-chm London Diarists' Club; Freeman: City of London 1989, Worshipful Co of Wheelwrights 1989; memb Royal Soc of Lit; FRGS, FRSA; *Books* The Debrett Season (ed, 1981), The English Season (contrib, 1988); *Recreations* shooting, collecting leather luggage; *Clubs* Carlton, St James's, Mosimann's, Morton's, RAC, Hurlingham, Century; *Style—* Adam Helliker, Esq; ✉ Sunday Express, 10 Lower Thames Street, London EC3R 6EN (☎ 020 7098 2750, e-mail adamhelliker@aol.com)

HELLMAN, Louis Mario; MBE (1993); s of late Mario Biselli, and Monalda, *née* Caraffi; *b* 19 March 1936; *Educ* Cardinal Vaughan GS, William Ellis GS, UCL (BArch), Ecole des Beaux-Arts Paris; *m* Maria Anna, da of late Sabin Popkiewicz; 1 da (Katherine Monalda b 31 Aug 1963), 1 s (Nicholas Sabin b 5 Sept 1964); *Career* architect; work incl: Spastics Soc (now Scope), GLC, YRM; cartoonist Architects Jl 1967–92 and 1997–, Building Design 1992–97, Design Week 1995–2010; cartoons published in: The Observer, Sunday Times, The Guardian, Evening Standard, Architectural Review, Design Week, Punch, Private Eye; lectr: UK, USA, Australia; Exhibitions incl: AA 1979, Interbuild 1991, RIBA 1989–, Sir John Soane's Museum 2000, Barcelona 2001, Shrewsbury 2006; subject of biography – Seven Ages of the Architect: The Very Best of Louis Hellman 1967–92 (1991); memb: Assoc of Architect Artists, ARB, Br Cartoonists' Assoc; Hon Dr Oxford Brookes Univ 2002; *Publications* A Is for Architect (1974), All Hellman Breaks Loose (1980), Architecture for Beginners (1986), Archi-têtes (1999), Do it with an Architect (1999), Architecture A to Z: A Rough Guide (2001); author of numerous articles in architectural magazines; *Recreations* music, cinema, travel, art; *Style—* Dr Louis Hellman, MBE; ☎ 020 8992 8318, e-mail info@louishellman.co.uk, website www.louishellman.co.uk

HELME, Patrick Ian (Tom); s of Anthony Helme, and Pauline, *née* Lancaster; *b* 17 January 1956; *Educ* Charterhouse, Brighton Coll of Art, UEA (BA); *m* 9 Aug 1984, Hon Mirabel Guinness, da of 2 Baron Moyne (d 1992); 3 da (Alice Mirabel b 15 May 1987, Tyga Elizabeth b 12 Feb 1990, Lily Pauline b 17 March 1994), 1 s (Toby Antony b 17 July 1992); *Career* apprentice (with restorer and decorator John Sutcliffe) 1978–80, studied restoration Soc for the Preservation of New England Antiquities 1980, asst to David Mlinaric 1981, co-fndr Silvergate Papers 1982, fndr interior design business 1982–91, official advsr on decoration National Trust 1991–98 (advsr 1982–91), organised and originated National Trust Paints (jtly with The National Trust Enterprises Ltd and Farrow & Ball Ltd) 1991, dir Farrow & Ball Ltd mfrs of paint and wallpaper 1992–2006 (with Martin Ephson, *qv*), co-fndr Fermoie (fine fabrics co) 2011–; interior design projects 1982– incl: HM Ambassadors' residences (in The Hague, Rome, Cairo, Paris, Prague and Lisbon), Hoares Bank, Linton Park plc, King's Lynn Town Hall, Duncombe Park, Ashridge Mgmnt Coll, Madame Tussauds, Luton Hoo, St John's Coll Cambridge, Brooks's Club, Magdalen Coll Oxford, John Murray Publishers Ltd, Wadham Coll Oxford, The Medical Soc; ptnr Carskiey (beef farm and lettings enterprise); winner Queen's Award 2004; *Publications* Paint and Colour in Decoration (2003); *Recreations* salmon fishing; *Clubs* Piscatorial Soc, Georgian Gp, Old Carthusian Art Soc (OCAS, chm); *Style—* Tom Helme, Esq; ✉ e-mail tom@mount-orleans.com

HELMER, Roger; MEP; *Educ* King Edward VI GS Southampton (state scholarship), Churchill Coll Cambridge (MA); *m* Sara; 3 c; *Career* MEP (Cons) E Midlands 1999–; md Donisthorpe & Co Ltd 1996–98; formerly mktg and mgmnt roles with Procter & Gamble, Nat Semiconductor, United Distillers; vice-chm Br C of C Seoul 1992–93, memb Bd Euro Chamber Seoul 1992–93; hon chm Freedom Assoc 2007–; memb: Countryside Alliance, NFU, Lutyens Tst; *Style—* Roger Helmer, Esq, MEP; ✉ website www.rogerhelmermep.co.uk

HELMS, Prof Peter Joseph; s of Joseph Helms (d 1966), and Eileen Dorothea, *née* Macfarlane (d 2003), of Geelong, Aust; *b* 26 June 1947; *Educ* Wimbledon Coll, Royal Free Hosp Sch of Med London (MB BS), Univ of London (PhD); *m* 7 Nov 1970, Kathleen Mary, da of Reginald Woodward; 3 da (Rachel Anne b 19 March 1973, Joanna Catherine b 23 April 1974, Laura Jane b 1 Oct 1980 d 2008), 1 s (Matthew John b 12 May 1977); *Career* house offr posts Royal Free Hosp, London Hosp, Royal Brompton Hosp, Hammersmith Hosp and Hosp for Sick Children Great Ormond St 1973–76, lectr Charing Cross Hosp 1977–78, research fell Inst of Child Health and Cardiothoracic Inst Univ of London 1978–83, sr lectr Inst of Child Health London 1983–92, prof of child health and head of dept Univ of Aberdeen 1992–2013; Donald Patterson Prize Br Paediatric Assoc 1983; FRCPEd 1992, FRCPCH 1996; over 250 scientific pubns and book chapters on paediatric respiratory health and disease and pharmacology; co-ed on paediatric undergraduate and postgraduate texts; *Recreations* hill walking, music; *Style—* Prof Peter Helms; ✉ Department of Child Health, University of Aberdeen, Foresterhill, Aberdeen AB25 2ZD (☎ 01224 438468, e-mail p.j.helms@abdn.ac.uk)

HELPS, Dominic David Wycliffe; s of Dr (Edmund) Peter Wycliffe Helps, of Coleshill, Bucks, and Heather, *née* Hood; *b* 8 July 1956, London; *Educ* Radley, Downing Coll Cambridge (scholar, BA, CPE); *m* 2005, Serena Elizabeth Chandler, *née* Cobley; *Career* staff writer Management Today and Engineering Today 1978–79, articled clerk then asst slr Linklaters & Paines 1980–84, sr asst slr Lovell White and King (latterly LWD then Lovells) 1984–96, ptnr Shadbolt & Co LLP 1996–2010, conslt Corbett & Co; co-ed Construction Law Jl, regular contrib of articles to Building magazine and various construction law pubns; memb Construction Umbrella Bodies Adjudication Task Gp 2004–; social sec Technol and Construction Slrs Assoc (TeCSA), chm Law Courts Branch Arbitration Club; memb: Soc of Construction Law 1980–, Law Soc 1982–; TeSCA accredited adjudicator, TeSCA and CEDR trained mediator; memb Worshipful Co of Arbitrators 2007; *Recreations* sports (especially football and cricket), gardening, reading (literature, history, arts); *Clubs* Deerhound; *Style—* Dominic Helps, Esq; ✉ Sungai Lalu, Frogmill, Hurley, Berkshire SL6 5NL (☎ 01628 290493, e-mail dominichelps@gmail.com)

HELSBY, Richard John Stephens (Rick); s of John Michael Helsby (d 1972), and Margaret Stella, *née* Andrews; *b* 10 January 1949; *Educ* Magdalen Coll Sch Oxford, Univ of Warwick (BA), Univ of Oxford (DipEd); *Children* 4 s (James b 1968, Nathan b 1972, William b 1986, Joseph 1993); *Career* HM inspr of Taxes Oxford 1972–78, sr inspr of Taxes Inland Revenue Enquiry Branch 1978–84, sr tax mangr Deloitte Haskins & Sells 1984–87; PricewaterhouseCoopers (formerly Coopers & Lybrand before merger): nat ptnr Fraud and Investigations Gp 1987–93, ptnr in charge Forensic Accountancy 1993–2000, head Forensic Invesitgations (Europe, Middle East and Africa) 2000–; *Books* Trouble with the Taxman (1985), Offshore Survival (with Jim McMahon, Bernard McCarthy 1988); *Recreations* squash, football, theatre, cinema, snooker; *Style—* Rick Helsby, Esq; ✉ Questa, 25 Polstead Rd, Oxford OX2 6TW

HELY HUTCHINSON, Hon Timothy Mark; 2 s of 8 Earl of Donoughmore, *qv*; *b* 26 October 1953, London; *Educ* Eton (Oppidan scholar), Univ of Oxford (William Doncaster scholar); *Partner* 2007, Sean Eliot Swallow (civil partnership); *Career* md: Macdonald & Co (Publishers) Ltd 1982–86, Headline Book Publishing plc 1986–93; gp chief exec Hodder Headline Ltd 1993–2004, chm WHSmith News Ltd 2001–04, chief exec Hachette UK Ltd 2004–; dir: WHSmith Gp plc 1999–2004, Inflexion plc 2000–03, Hachette Book Gp Inc 2006–; *Recreations* horse racing, opera, skiing, bridge; *Clubs* Athenaeum, Groucho; *Style—* The Hon Timothy Hely Hutchinson; ✉ Hachette UK Ltd, Carmelite House, 50 Victoria Embankment, London EC4Y 0D2 (☎ 020 7873 6000)

HELYAR, Mark Andrew Jonathan; s of Barry Robert Helyar (d 2004), and Constance, *née* West; *b* 15 March 1968, Guernsey; *Educ* Elizabeth Coll Guernsey, UEA (BSc), Nottingham Trent Univ (PGDL), Univ of Caen (Cert); *m* 20 Jan 2012, Corin Kate Miller-Helyar; 1 s (Charlie Gordon Barry b 17 March 2011), 1 da (Liliana Jennifer Constance Helyar b 12 Oct 2012); 2 da from a previous relationship (Natascha May b 2 Sept 1996, Aimee Adele b 10 June 2000); *Career* called to the Bar: Gray's Inn 2000, Guernsey 2001; NP Guernsey; States of Guernsey Civil Service 1991–96, Babbe le Pelley Tostevin Advocates 1996–2006 (ptnr 2003–06), managing ptnr Bedell Cristin Guernsey and ptnr Bedell Gp 2006–; sec Condor Gp, chm Culture Guernsey; memb Performing Rights Soc; *Recreations* golf, scuba, motor sport; *Clubs* Guernsey Sporting; *Style—* Mark Helyar, Esq; ✉ Bedell Group, 3rd Floor, La Plaiderie House, La Plaiderie, St Peter Port, Guernsey GY1 1ND (☎ 01481 812812, fax 01481 812813, e-mail mark.helyar@bedellgroup.com)

HEMBLADE, Christopher Mark Andrew; s of late Bernard Hemblade, of Sussex, and late Jennie, *née* Howard; *b* 1 May 1970; *Educ* Cardinal Newman Sch, KCL (BA), Central St Martin's Sch of Art (MA); *Career* freelance journalist: Arena, The Face, ID, Interview, BBC Radio, The Observer and The Guardian 1994–96; ed Student Guide Time Out 1994–96, London ed Marie Claire 1994–97, asst ed Empire Magazine 1996–98, ed Sky Magazine 1998–99, sr ed Scene Magazine 1999, features ed Time Out Magazine 2000–04 (latterly actg ed, nominated (entertainment category) BSME Awards 2004), exec ed and entertainment dir Elle magazine 2005–08, VIP and celebrity mangr Macmillan Cancer Support 2008–; freeelance contrib ed 2008–, sr contrib ed Harper's Bazaar 2008–; memb Panel Opinion Leader Research 2003–09, memb Art and Dance Ctee Whitechapel Art Gallery 2005–06; Vogue talent contest honourable mention 2003–04; *Recreations* theatre, film, travel, yoga, dance, cycling; *Clubs* Century; *Style—* Christopher Hemblade, Esq; ✉ c/o HomeL, 22 Thomas Hollywood House, Approach Road, London E2 0NB (Twitter @chrishemblade)

HEMINGWAY, Ann Elizabeth; CBE (2003); *née* Cherrill; da of Robert Cherrill (d 1973), and (Nora) Betty, *née* Kingsley (d 1967); *b* 17 July 1947, Beckenham, Kent; *m* 9 Sept 1981, Anthony John Hemingway (d 2002); *Career* lectr Flour Advsy Bureau 1968–1970, jr posts SE Gas Bd (Home Service) 1970–73; British Gas Trading Ltd (formerly British Gas plc): regnl chief home service advsr SE Region 1973–77, project mangr HQ 1977–78, marketing devpt mangr NW Region 1978–88, IT mangr NE Region 1988–89, dir of personnel British Gas Wales 1989–91, project mangr IS Personnel Policy Devpt 1991–92, dir of personnel NW Region 1992–93, HR leader and memb Devpt Strategy Team 1993–94, business dir Public Gas Supply 1994–96, head of sales Home Energy 1996–99; memb Bd and chm Advsy Ctee Wales Food Standards Agency 2000–06; Driver Vehicle Licence Agency: memb Advsy Bd 1993–2002, chm Audit Ctee 2003–05 (memb 1997–2003); Dept for Tport: non-exec memb Driver and Vehicle Operators Strategic Review 1998–2003, memb Bd DVO 2003–07, memb Bd 2003–08; memb: Cncl CBI Wales 1994–98, Bd Business in the Community in Wales 1994–98, Advsy Bd Cardiff Common Purpose 1995–98, Bd and Audit Ctee Strategic Rail Authy 2000–02, Advsy Bd Highways Agency 2002–05, Bd Local Better Regulation Office Dept for Business, Innovation and Skills (formerly Dept for Business and Regulatory Reform) 2007–12; tstee Sports Aid Wales 1994–2000, chm Steering Gp Opportunity 2000 in Wales 1995–99, ind assessor Nat Assembly for Wales 1997–2002, chm Fair Trade Wales 2009–11; dir Uskbridge Mgmnt Co Ltd 1999–2013 (sec 1996–99), ind memb Audit Ctee RCUK SSC Ltd 2008–13; FCIPD, FCIM (DipM); *Recreations* walking, cookery, entertaining; *Style—* Mrs Ann Hemingway, CBE; ✉ e-mail ae.hemingway@btconnect.com

HEMINGWAY, Gerardine Mary; MBE (2006); da of Thomas Kenneth Astin, and Mary Patricia Astin; *b* 1961, Padiham, Lancs; *m* Wayne Andrew Hemingway , *qv*, s of Chief Billy Two Rivers; 2 s (Jack b 1986, Beck b 1997), 2 da (Tilly b 1987, Corey b 1990); *Career* designer; co-fndr (with husband) Red or Dead 1982 (winner Street Style category

H

British Fashion Cncl Awards 1996, 1997 and 1998), prop Hemingway Design (interior, product and building design consultancy) 2000–, co-fndr Vintage Festival; building design: Home 1997, Workplace offices 2000, mass-market housing estate for Taylor Wimpey Homes, new wing for IoD; projects incl: carpet design for Milliken, wall coverings for Graham and Brown; Hon DDes Univ of Plymouth 2006, Hon Dr Lancaster Univ 2008, Hon DDes Stafford Univ 2008; *Recreations* gardening, cooking, travelling; *Style*— Mrs Gerardine Hemingway, MBE; ✉ websites www.hemingwaydesign.co.uk and www.vintagefestival.co.uk

HEMINGWAY, Prof Janet; CBE (2012); *Educ* BSc, PhD; *Career* prof of insect molecular biology and dir of medical scis Liverpool Sch of Tropical Medicine; Hon DSc Univ of Sheffield 2009, Hon DSc Univ of Warwick 2015; foreign assoc Nat Acad of Scientists USA 2010, fell American Acad of Microbiology 2011; FMedSci 2006, FRCP 2008, FRS 2011; *Style*— Prof Janet Hemingway, CBE; ✉ Liverpool School of Tropical Medicine, Pembroke Place, Liverpool L3 5QA

HEMINGWAY, Michael Patrick; s of John Allman Hemingway, and Helen Bridget Barbara, *née* Prowse; *b* 28 August 1951; *Educ* Oundle; *m* 17 Dec 1977, Annamaria, da of John David Fitness; 2 s (Jay Matthew John Allman b 15 May 1980, Toby Michael Christopher Allman b 28 May 1983); *Career* account mangr Leo Burnett advtg agency 1976 (joined Invoice Control Dept 1975), account dir Michael Bungey and Partners 1977–82, Collett Dickenson Pearce 1982–85; bd dir: Boase Massimi Pollitt 1985–88, DDB Needham 1989; Grey Communications Group: joined as bd dir 1989, vice-chm Grey London 1991, subsequently sr vice-pres Grey Europe, latterly exec vice-pres Grey International (i/c Mars Confectionery); fndr brandhunger; *Recreations* watching sport, travel, popular music; *Clubs* Tramp; *Style*— Michael Hemingway, Esq

HEMINGWAY, Wayne Andrew; MBE (2006); s of Chief Billy Two Rivers (chief of Khanawake Tribe (Mohawk) Quebec), and Maureen, *née* Hemingway; *b* 19 January 1961; *Educ* Queen Elizabeth's GS Blackburn, UCL (BSc); *m* Gerardine Mary Hemingway , *qv*, da of Ken Astin; 2 s (Jack b 22 June 1986, Beck b 11 June 1997), 2 da (Tilly b 23 July 1987, Corey b Aug 1990); *Career* fashion designer; Red or Dead: founded as design co retailing from Camden Market stall 1982, entered jt venture with Pentland Gp plc 1996, currently non-exec chm, winners of Street Style Category British Fashion Awards 1995, 1996 and 1997; md Dr Martens Clothing 1992–94; dir Br Fashion Cncl 1999–; designer Hemingway Design (projects incl IoD club, George Wimpey Homes devpt), co-fndr Vintage Festival; tstee: Bd Design Cncl, Cmmn for Achitecture and Built Environment; prof of built environment Univ of Northumbria 2004; regular speaker to housing industry on housing and urban regeneration, and to fashion colls and footwear assocs on shoe, clothing and interior design; work shown in numerous exhibitions of Br design incl: Boymans Museum Rotterdam, Orange County California, V&A London; second place Young Business Person of the Year 1990; Hon MA Surrey Inst 2002, Hon DDes Univ of Wolverhampton 2005, Hon Dr Univ of Lancaster 2008, DDes Univ of Stafford 2008; FRSA; *Recreations* football, cricket, tennis; *Style*— Wayne Hemingway, Esq, MBE; ✉ Hemingway Design, 15 Wembley Park Drive, Wembley, Middlesex HA9 8HD (☏ 020 8903 1074, fax 020 8903 1076, e-mail info@hemingwaydesign.co.uk, websites www.hemingwaydesign.co.uk and www.vintagefestival.co.uk)

HEMINSLEY, Alexandra; da of Lt Col W J Heminsley, OBE, of Salisbury, Wilts, and Katherine, *née* Ganteaume; *b* 14 February 1976, Chipping Norton, Oxon; *Educ* Univ of Bristol (BA); *m* 2014, David Humphreys; *Career* writer, broadcaster, book reviewer and author of titles and journalism on women in sports; former books ed Elle UK, currently books ed thedebrief.co.uk; regular contrib: BBC Radio 2 Arts Show (BBC Radio 2), BBC Radio 4 Today Programme, Woman's Hour, Simon Mayo Books Panel (BBC Radio 5 Live), Richard Bacon Show (BBC Radio 5 Live), The Times, Sunday Times, Independent on Sunday, Grazia, Red magazine, the-pool.co.uk; event host for clients incl: Waterstones, PanMacmillan, Jonathan Cape, the Bookseller, Hachette Gp; judge Costa Novel of the Year Award 2012; *Books* Ex and the City: You're Nobody Till Somebody Dumps You (2007), Hang the DJ: An Alternative Book of Music Lists (contrib, 2008), Running Like a Girl (2013), Knowing the Score (co-author with Judy Murray, 2017), Leap In (2017); *Style*— Ms Alexandra Heminsley; ✉ Twitter @hemmo, Facebook AlexandraHeminsley, Instagram @hemmograms; c/o United Agents, 12–26 Lexington Street, London W1F OLE

HEMMING, John; *Educ* King Edwards Sch Edgbaston, Magdalen Coll Oxford (MA); *Career* fndr John Hemming & Co (now JHC plc) 1983, fndr MarketNet 1994, fndr Music Mercia Int (MMI) 1997, fndr The Purchasing Agency (SafeSimple.com) 2000, fndr Phoenix Consortium 2000; cncllr (Lib Dem) South Yeardley City Cncl 1990–, ldr Birmingham City Cncl Lib Dem Gp; Parly candidate (Lib Dem): Birmingham Hall Green 1983, Birmingham Yardley 1992, 1997 and 2001; MP (Lib Dem) Birmingham Yardley 2005–15; *Style*— John Hemming, Esq; ✉ House of Commons, London SW1A 0AA

HEMMING, Dr John Henry; CMG (1994); s of Lt-Col Henry Harold Hemming, OBE, MC (d 1977), and Alice Louisa, OBE, *née* Weaver (d 1994); *b* 5 January 1935; *Educ* Eton, McGill Univ Montreal, Univ of Oxford (MA, DLitt); *m* 19 Jan 1979, Sukie Mary, da of Brig Michael J Babington-Smith, CBE (d 1984), and Lady Jean Babington-Smith; 1 s (Henry Sebastian b 1979), 1 da (Beatrice Margaret Louisa b 1981); *Career* charity dir Royal Geographical Soc 1975–96; publisher; chm: Hemming Gp Ltd (formerly Municipal JI Ltd) 1976–2015 (dir 1962–, dep chm 1967–2011); chm: Brintex Ltd 1979–2015 (md 1962–71, dir 2015–), Newman Books Ltd 1979–; ldr Maracá Rainforest Project Brazil 1987–89; fndr tstee and sponsor Survival Int; memb Cncl/Ctee: Br Cncl 1992–2002, John Ellerman Fndn 1997–2010, Rainforest Fndn, Gilchrist Educnl Tst, Hakluyt Soc, Global Diversity Fndn, Cusichaca Tst, Earthwatch Tst; chm Anglo-Peruvian Soc 1997–2009, chm Amazon Charitable Tst; dep chm LEPRA 1992–2012; Pitman Literary Prize 1971, Christopher Medal NY 1972, Founders Medal RGS 1990, Mungo Park Medal Royal Scottish Geographical Soc 1988, Washburn Medal Boston Museum of Sci 1990; Rolex Award for Enterprise citation 1988, Explorers' Club NY citation of merit 1997; Hon DUniv: Univ of Warwick 1989, Univ of Stirling 1991; hon fell Magdalen Coll Oxford 2004; FRGS 1961, FSA 2001, FRSL 2013; hon corresponding memb Academia Nacional de Historia Venezuela, special award Instituto Nacional de Cultura Peru 1996, Ordem do Cruzeiro do Sul (Brazil) 1998, Grand Cross Orden al Mérito (Peru) 2007, El Sol del Peru 2010; *Books* The Conquest of the Incas (1970, revised 1993, 2012), Tribes of the Amazon Basin in Brazil (1973), Red Gold (1978, revised 1995), The Search for El Dorado (1978), Machu Picchu (1981), Monuments of the Incas (1982, rewritten 2010), Change in the Amazon Basin (1985), Amazon Frontier (1987, revised 1995), Maracá (1988), Roraima, Brazil's northernmost frontier (1990), The Rainforest Edge (1993), The Golden Age of Discovery (1998), Die If You Must (2003), Tree of Rivers: The Story of the Amazon (2008), Naturalists in Paradise: Wallace, Bates and Spruce in the Amazon (2015); *Recreations* writing, travel; *Clubs* Beefsteak (chm 2002–05), Boodle's, Geographical; *Style*— Dr John Hemming, CMG; ✉ 10 Edwardes Square, London W8 6HE (☏ 020 7602 6697); e-mail j.hemming@hgluk.com, website www.johnhemming.co.uk

HEMMING, Susan (Sue); OBE (2005); *Educ* Univ Coll Cardiff (LLB); *Career* called to the Bar 1988; CPS Cambs 1988–2000, branch crown prosecutor Casework Directorate 2000–05; CPS: head Counter Terrorism Div 2005–11, head Special Crime and Counter Terrorism Div 2011–; Attorney Gen's Excellence Award 2009, Special Achievement Award Int Assoc of Prosecutors 2010; *Publications* Chatham House – International Affairs (2010); *Style*— Ms Sue Hemming, OBE; ✉ Special Crime and Counter Terrorism Division, Crown Prosecution Service, Rose Court, 2 Southwark Bridge, London SE1 9HS

HEMMINGS, Richard; *Career* slr; controller of admin and slr to Cncl London Borough of Croydon 1984–89, county sec Kent CC 1989–97, currently chief exec and clerk Br Transport Police Authy; *Style*— Richard Hemmings, Esq

HEMMINK, Wilhelmus Hubertus Matheus Maria (Wim); s of late Matheus Hemmink, and late Maria Hemmink Van Den Brink; *Educ* Fashion Dept Koninklijke Academie voor Beeldende Kunst S'Gravenhage, Rotterdamse Snijschool, Rundshau, Constance Wilbaut's Sch Amsterdam, Chambre Syndicale de la Couture Parisienne; *Career* fashion designer; recipient Cotton Inst award Holland, subsequent experience with Madeleine de Rauch (haute couture house) Paris, Kay Selig Inc NY, Michael of Carlos Place (couture house) London; latterly estab own label Wim Hemmink (retailed worldwide and with extensive private clientele); *Style*— Wim Hemmink, Esq; ✉ 106 Crawford Street, London W1H 2HY (☏ 020 7935 1755, fax 020 7224 0573)

HEMPHILL, 6 Baron (UK 1906); Charles Andrew Martyn Martyn-Hemphill; s of 5 Baron Hemphill (d 2012), and Anne, *née* Ruttledge; *b* 8 October 1954; *Educ* Downside, St Benet's Hall Oxford; *m* 1 June 1985, Sarah J F, eld da of Richard Edward Walter Lumley, of Windlesham, Surrey; 3 da (Dr Clarissa Mary b 31 May 1986, Amelia Rose b 31 March 1988, Marina Olivia Astrid b 22 Oct 1992), 2 s (Richard Patrick Lumley b 17 May 1990, Oliver Francis Robert b 10 Dec 1998); *Heir* s, Hon Richard Martyn-Hemphill; *Career* md Morgan Grenfell Deutsche Asset Mgmnt and Waverton Investment Mgmnt 1979–2005, ptnr Spencer House Capital Mgmnt 2006–11, dir Jo Hambro Investment Mgmnt 2011–; tstee Dulverton Tst and various other charities, chm of govrs St Mary's Sch Ascot; *Recreations* skiing, family, golf; *Clubs* White's, NZ Golf, Hurlingham; *Style*— The Lord Hemphill; ✉ 66 Manville Road, London SW17 8JL; 21 St James's Square, London SW1Y 4HB

HEMSLEY, Jasmine; *Career* co-fndr (with sis Melissa Hemsley and Nick Hopper, *qqv*) Hemsley + Hemsley 2010–, estab Hemsley + Hemsley café at Selfridges; *Television* Eating Well with Hemsley and Hemsley (Channel 4) 2016; *Books* The Art of Eating Well (2014), Good + Simple (2016); *Style*— Ms Jasmine Hemsley

HEMSLEY, Melissa; da of Jack Rupert Hemsley (d 2014), and Evangelina Garcia, of London; *b* 17 September 1985, London; *Educ* Surbiton HS, Tiffin Girls Sch; *Career* sales and mktg dir The Columbo Gp 2008–10, co-fndr (with sis, Jasmine Hemsley and Nick Hopper, *qqv*) Hemsley + Hemsley 2010–, estab Hemsley + Hemsley café at Selfridges; food blogger Vogue 2012–16; judge: YBFs 2016, Nat Cookery Sch Guide 2016; *Television* Eating Well with Hemsley and Hemsley (Channel 4, sold internationally) 2016; *Books* The Art of Eating Well (2014), Good + Simple (2016); *Recreations* music, reading, travel, my dog Nelly; *Style*— Ms Melissa Hemsley; ✉ website www.hemsleyandhemsley.com, Twitter @HemsleyHemsley

HEMSLEY, Michael Stuart; s of Alan Fraser Hemsley, of Totton, Hants, and Janet Enid, *née* Taylor; *b* 13 July 1957; *Educ* Beverley Boys' Sch New Malden, Salisbury Coll of Art; *m* 30 May 1981, Catherine Bernadette Hemsley, da of Thomas Oswald O'Keeffe; 2 s (Thomas Joseph b 26 Sept 1986, Robert Michael b 19 Oct 1988); *Career* professional photographer; Colt International Ltd Havant: Photographic Dept 1974, photographed industrial sites for advtg and promotional use until 1981; industrial and commercial photographer Walter Gardiner Photography Worthing 1981–2008; currently digital imaging technician Norwich Univ of the Arts; photographic assignments in UK and abroad incl: magazine illustration, corporate video, report and accounts, public relations, managerial portraits; specialisms incl: 3D imaging, advertising photography, book illustration, digital imaging technology; FBIPP 1986; *Awards* Bausch and Lomb Young Photographer of the Year 1982, Ilford Photographer of the Year 1985 and 1989 (highly commended 1992), Peter Grugeon Award for best fellowship application 1986, BIPP Gold Award 1996, 2004 and 2006, Creativematch folio winner 2006 and 2007; *Books* Digital Photography (author and illustrator, 2006); *Recreations* walking Norfolk countryside, volunteering in community village shop, staying in Landmark Trust properties; *Style*— Michael Hemsley, Esq; ✉ Sweerbriar Cottage, The Street, Oulton, Norfolk NR11 6AF (e-mail mike@wgphoto.co.uk)

HEMSLEY, Oliver; *Children* 3 c; *Career* fndr and ceo Numis Corp plc; non-exec dir: Quoted Companies Alliance, ECU Gp plc; *Recreations* gardening, opera, skiing, kite surfing; *Clubs* Garrick; *Style*— Oliver Hemsley, Esq; ✉ Numis Securities Ltd, The London Stock Exchange Building, 10 Paternoster Square, London EC4M 7LT

HEMSLEY, Stephen Glen; *b* 3 August 1957; *Career* qualified CA 1982; Domino's Pizza UK & IRL plc: joined as fin dir 1998, chief exec 2001–08, exec chm 2008–; *Style*— Stephen Hemsley, Esq; ✉ Franchise Brands, Edwin Avenue, Hoo Farm Industrial Estate, Kidderminster DY11 7RA

HENCKE, David Robert; s of late Charles Ewald Hencke, of London, and Enid, *née* Rose; *b* 26 April 1947; *Educ* Tulse Hill Comp Sch, Univ of Warwick (BA); *m* 5 July 1969, Margaret Mary, da of late Laurie Langrick; 1 da (Anne Margaret b 14 Aug 1979); *Career* jr reporter Northamptonshire Evening Telegraph 1968–71; reporter: Western Mail 1971–73, Times Higher Educational Supplement 1973–76; The Guardian: reporter 1976–79, planning corr 1979–81, social servs corr 1981–86, Westminster corr 1986–2009; freelance lobby and TV journalist 2009–, Westminster corr The Tribune, assoc ed and memb Bd Exaro News 2016; memb Ld Chllr's Advsy Gp on Implementing Freedom of Information, memb Gosport Ind Panel (set up by Dept of Health to investigate unexplained deaths at a local hosp) 2014; Reporter of the Year: E Midlands Allied Press 1971, Br Press Awards 1989 (specialist writer of the year 1981) and 1993 (reporter of the year), Journalist of the Year What the Papers Say 1994, Scoop of the Year (Peter Mandelson's Home Loan) What The Papers Say 1998, London Press Club Scoop of the Year Award 1998, Best Environmental Campaign Br Environment and Media Awards 2001, Political Journalist of the Year 2012, longlisted Orwell Prize 2013; dir Brown Envelope TV Ltd 2000–13; FRSA; *Books* Colleges in Crisis (1976), The Blairs and their Court (jtly, 2004), Marching to the Fault Line (jtly, 2009), Blair Inc: The Man Behind the Mask (co-author, 2015); *Recreations* theatre, walking, gardening, cooking, riding; *Style*— David Hencke, Esq; ☏ 07887 833931, e-mail david.hencke@gmail.com, website www.davidhencke.wordpress.com

HENDERSON, Alan Brodie; yr s of Neil Brodie Henderson (d 1982), of Buntingford, Herts, and Conn, *née* Madden (d 1979); *b* 30 July 1933; *Educ* Eton; *m* 1, 25 April 1956 (m dis), Antonia, only da of James McMullen, of 63 Eaton Square, London; 2 s (Bryan Brodie b 1960, Gavin Brodie b 1963), 1 da (Kerena Brodie b 1958); m 2, 9 June 1969, Fiona Douglas, er da of Maj Thomas Douglas Pilkington of Reay; 2 s (David Brodie b 1970, Thomas Brodie b 1976); m 3, 30 Sept 1992, Hon Diana Cara, da of 3 Baron Fairhaven, *qv*; m 4, 18 April 2008, Beryl, *née* Gibbs; *Career* Capt Welsh Gds 1952–59; with James Capel stockbrokers 1959–63, md Henderson Administration Ltd 1965–77 (joined 1963), Greenfrar Investment Tst 1968–98, chm Henderson Unit Trust Co Ltd 1974–77; dir: Ranger Oil Ltd 1972–92, Mackay Shields Financial Corporation NY 1974–77, Schlesinger Investment Management Services Ltd 1977–81; md Schlesinger Trust Managers Ltd 1979–81; non-exec chm: Newmarket Venture Capital plc 1972–90, Ranger Oil (UK) Ltd 1982– (dir 1972–2000, chm 1995–2000), Aberdeen Emerging Economies Investment Trust plc 1990–2001, Forum Energy plc 1994–2004 (chm 2005–09), Aberdeen New Thai Investment Trust plc 1989–2006, Aberdeen New Dawn Investment Trust plc 2000–12 (dir 1991–2012); chm Smart Matrix Ltd 2012–; dir Energy Capital Investment Company plc 1994–2004 (chm 1998–2004), dir Global Energy Development plc 2001–, dir and chm Public Service Properties Investments Ltd 2005–09; chm and tstee Sea Change Tst 1991–2007, dep chm RAFT 1996–2009; dir: North One Garden Centre 2011–, West Six Garden

Centre 2011–; *Clubs* White's, City of London; *Style*— Alan Henderson, Esq; ✉ Old Pound Farm, Pound Lane, Framfield, East Sussex TN22 5RT (☎ 01825 890386, mobile 07973 257633, e-mail alanhenderson37@gmail.com)

HENDERSON, Charles Edward; CB (1992); s of David Henderson (d 1972), and Georgiana Leggatt, *née* Mackie (d 2000); *b* 19 September 1939; *Educ* Charterhouse, Univ of Cambridge; *m* 1966, Rachel, da of Dr A S Hall, of Bucks; 1 da (Catherine b 1970), 1 s (Luke b 1971); *Career* asst investment sec Equity and Law Life Assurance Soc Ltd 1966–70, princ Export Credits Guarantee Dept DTI 1971–73; Dept of Energy: princ 1974–75, asst sec 1976–82, head Atomic Energy Div 1982–84, head Oil Div 1984–85, princ estab and fin offr 1985–88; head Office of Arts and Libraries 1989–92, dep sec DTI 1992–96, chm Total Holdings UK and Total Exploration and Production UK 1998–2005; memb Competition Commn 1998–2007; pres Soc for Underwater Technol 1999–2001, pres Inst of Petroleum 2000–02; FIA; *Recreations* music (listening and playing), golf, reading, mountain walking; *Style*— Charles Henderson, Esq, CB; ✉ 17 Sydney House, Woodstock Road, London W4 1DP

HENDERSON, Fergus; MBE (2005); s of Brian Henderson, of Wilts, and Elizabeth, *née* Evans; *b* 31 July 1963, London; *Educ* King Alfred Sch London; *m* 20 Feb 1993, Margot, *née* Clayton; 1 s (Hector b 21 Feb 1994), 2 da (Owen b 6 Oct 1995, Frances b 8 June 1999); *Career* chef and dir: St John London 1994–, St John Bread and Wine 2003–, H G Wines 2003–, St John Bakery 2010–; memb Architectural Assoc; *Books* Nose to Tail Eating (1999), Beyond Nose to Tail (2007), Complete Nose to Tail (2012); *Recreations* cooking, eating; *Clubs* Groucho; *Style*— Fergus Henderson, Esq, MBE; ✉ St. John, 26 St John Street, London EC1M 4AY (☎ 020 7553 9842, fax 020 7251 4090, e-mail kitty@stjohnrestaurant.com)

HENDERSON, Prof Gavin Douglas; CBE (2004); s of Magnus Reginald Henderson (d 1975), and Sybil Nancy, *née* Horton, of Brighton; *b* 3 February 1948; *Educ* Brighton Coll (music and art scholar), Brighton Coll of Art, Kingston Coll of Art (BA), Slade Sch of Fine Art (Goldsmith's travelling scholarship to USA); *m* 1, 1973, Jane Williams; m 2, 1984, Carole Becker; 2 s (Piers b 1980, Caspar b 1985); m 3, 1992, Mary Jane Walsh; *Career* solo trumpet St Bartholomew's Church & Orchestra 1963–2014, front of house and publicity mangr Victoria Theatre Stoke on Trent 1970–71, princ trumpet Worthing Municipal Orch 1970–72; artistic dir: Crawley Festival 1972–73, York Festival and Mystery Plays 1973–76, Portsmouth Festival 1974–76, Brighton Festival 1984–94, Bournemouth Festival 1995–97; chief exec Philharmonia Orch 1975–79, dir South Hill Park Arts Centre and fndr Wilde Theatre Bracknell 1979–85, dir Dartington Int Summer Sch 1985–2010, princ Trinity Coll of Music 1994–2002, princ Trinity Laban 2003–05, princ Royal Central Sch of Speech and Drama 2007–; chm: Music Panel Arts Cncl of England 1994–2003, Brighton Youth Orch 1998–2003, Nat Fndn for Youth Music 1998–2008, Regency Soc of Brighton and Hove 2000–06; pres Nat Piers Soc, pres Bournemouth Festival, vice-pres Euro Festivals Assoc, vice-pres Br Arts Festivals Assoc (chm 1992–99); memb Bd Corps of Army Music 2001–08; tstee West Pier Tst 2000–05; patron: Chiddingly Festival, A Very Moving Festival, Farnham Maltings; chm Arts Worldwide; hon fell Brimingham Conservatoire 2010; memb: Musicians' Union 1964, ISM 1994 (pres 2010–11), RSM 1996; Liveryman Worshipful Co of Musicians 1996, Freeman City of London 1997; Hon MA Univ of Sussex 1999; FRSA, Hon FTCL 1998, Hon FRCM 2003, Hon FRNCM 2005, hon companion Trinity Laban 2007; *Recreations* cooking seafood, baroque trumpet, vintage motoring; *Clubs* Garrick, Savile, Royal Over-Seas League (hon memb), Beefsteak, VSCC, Acad, Club for Acts and Actors; *Style*— Prof Gavin Henderson, CBE; ✉ The Royal Central School of Speech and Drama, Embassy Theatre, Eton Avenue, London NW3 3HY (☎ 020 7559 3904, e-mail gavin.henderson@ccsd.ac.uk, website www.cssd.ac.uk)

HENDERSON, Giles Ian; CBE (1992); s of Charles David Henderson (d 1980), of Henfield, W Sussex, and Joan, *née* Firmin (d 1994); *b* 20 April 1942; *Educ* Michaelhouse Natal, Univ of the Witwatersrand (BA), Magdalen Coll Oxford (sr Mackinnon scholar, MA, BCL); *m* 21 Aug 1971, Lynne, da of Charles William Fyfield, OBE (d 1997), of Alnmouth, Northumberland; 2 s (Mark b 1974, Simon b 1975), 1 da (Clare b 1978); *Career* memb Law Faculty Univ of Calif Berkeley (Fulbright Award 1966–67); admitted slr 1970, sr ptnr Slaughter and May 1993–2001 (ptnr 1975–2001); master Pembroke Coll Oxford 2001–13, chm Conf of Oxford Colls 2007–09, memb Cncl Univ of Oxford 2007–13; memb: Hampel Ctee on Corp Governance, Fin Reporting Cncl 1998–2001, chm Law Gp UK/China Forum 1997–2000, Takeover Appeal Bd 2016–; non-exec dir: Land Securities plc 2000–02, The Standard Life Assurance Co 2001–03; chm Nuffield Medical Tst 2003–15, dir Cumberland Lodge 2007–08; tstee Tanaka UK Japan Educnl Fndn Ltd 2014–; *Recreations* sport, opera, ballet; *Style*— Giles Henderson, Esq, CBE; ✉ The Old Rectory, Fifield, Chipping Norton, Oxfordshire OX7 6HF

HENDERSON, Gordon; MP; s of William John Butler Henderson, and Pauline, *née* Pullen (d 1953); *Educ* Fort Luton Secdy Sch for Boys; *m* 1, 1971 (m dis), Marilyn; 1 da (Tamara b 1972); m 2, 1979 (m dis), Benita; m 3, 1993, Louise; 1 step-da (Jo-Anne b 1972), 1 step-s (Christopher b 1974); *Career* Woolworths 1964–79, restaurateur 1979–83, agent Cons Pty 1983–85, GEC Marconi 1985–93, Unwins Wine Gp 1993–2003, Beams UK Ltd 2003–08, mgmnt conslt 2008–10; cncllr: Swale Borough Cncl 1985–94, Kent CC 1989–93; MP (Cons) Sittingbourne & Sheppey 2010–; *Books* Pigeon Pie and Other Tasty Tales (2014); *Style*— Gordon Henderson, Esq, MP; ✉ House of Commons, London SW1A 0AA

HENDERSON, Prof Graham; CBE (2011), DL (N Yorks 2012); s of Thomas Henderson (d 2014), and Elizabeth Henderson (d 1989); *b* 23 August 1952, Newcastle upon Tyne; *Educ* Heaton GS Newcastle upon Tyne, Lanchester Poly (BSc), City Univ London (MSc), Nene Coll Northampton (FE Teachers' Cert); *m* 15 Dec 1987, Joan, *née* Younger; 1 da (Nicola b 22 March 1981), 2 s (Robert b 26 June 1986, Michael b 4 Aug 1988); *Career* lectr Nene Coll Northampton 1975–79, lectr rising to princ lectr Newcastle Business Sch Northumbria Univ 1980–89, asst dir Newcastle Business Sch Northumbria Univ 1989–97, dir Sunderland Business Sch Univ of Sunderland 1997–99, vice-chllr Univ of Teesside 2003–2015 (dep vice-chllr 1999–2003); dir Univs Vocational Awards Cncl 2002–06; nat exec memb Million+; chair: Univs for the NE Bd until 2009, Regnl Cncl of the NE Higher Skills Network until 2009, NE Rgnly STEM Bd, Tees Valley Common Purpose Advsy Gp 2009–12, Leadership Fndn for HE Membership Advsy Gp 2010–15, NE Common Purpose Advsy Gp 2012–13; vice-chair TRAC Devpt Gp (formerly TRAC Devpt and Implementation Gp) 2008–14; dir Middlesbrough Town Centre Co 2003–06; memb: Corp Bd Darlington Coll of Technol 1999–2006, NE Assembly 2003, Strategic Leadership Bd Tees Valley Unlimited (LEP, formerly Tees Valley Partnership) 2003–15, CBI Regnl Cncl 2003–09 and 2012–15, City Region Leadership Bd Tees Valley Unlimited 2007–15, Bd Durham and Tees Valley LSC 2007–08, Student Policy Network (and its predecessors) Univs UK 2007–, Innovation and Growth Policy Network (and its predecessors) Univs UK 2007–, Bd NE Regnl LSC 2008–10, Bd Public Health NE, HEFCE Leadership Governance and Mgmnt Strategy Gp 2008–15, Bd Cncl for Industry and HE 2010–12, Cncl NE C of C 2010–15, Bd Univs UK 2010–15, Bd Univ Alliance 2011–15, Leadership Cncl Nat Centre for Univs and Businesses 2012–, Int Academic Advsy Panel Southern Univ Coll Malaysia 2013–, Bd Univ of Birmingham 2013–, York St John Univ 2016–; chair: Redcar & Cleveland Fndn for Jobs 2014–, Tees Valley Arts and Culture Task Gp 2014–15; tstee: Captain Cook Birthplace Tst 2003 (chair 2015–), Trincomalee Tst 2003–07; patron: Middlesbrough Older Persons' Partnership 2012–, patron Community Campus 2013–, patron Theatre Hullabaloo in Darlington 2015–; memb Arete Learning Tst 2015–; pres Guisborough RUFC 2014–; hon fell Nat Centre for Entrepreneurship in Educn (NCEE) 2015–; FSS 1977–2016, FRSA 2000, CCMI 2009; *Recreations* rugby union (spectator), football (spectator), walking, golf, ballroom dancing; *Style*— Prof Graham Henderson, CBE, DL; ☎ 01287 631335, e-mail grahamhendersoncbe@outlook.com

HENDERSON, Henry Merton (Harry); s of John Ronald Henderson, CVO, OBE, and Katherine Sarah, *née* Beckwith-Smith (d 1972); *b* 25 April 1952; *Educ* Eton; *m* 4 Feb 1977, Sarah Charlotte Margaret, *née* Lowther; 1 s (Harry Oliver b 24 March 1979), 1 da (Katie Sarah b 7 April 1981); *Career* Cazenove & Co: joined 1975, ptnr 1982–2002, md Cazenove Unit Tst Mgmnt Ltd 1988–98, md Cazenove Fund Mgmnt Ltd 1996–2000, md Cazenove Private Wealth Services 2000–02; chm: Witan Investment Tst plc 2003– (dir 1988–), Witan Investment Services Ltd; dir: Updown Investment Co plc 1982–99, Cadogan Settled Estates Ltd; High Sheriff Berkshire 2007–08; MSI; *Recreations* skiing, shooting, squash, golf; *Clubs* White's; *Style*— Harry Henderson, Esq; ✉ West Woodhay House, Newbury, Berkshire RG20 0BS

HENDERSON, Hugh Peter; s of Dr Peter Wallace Henderson (d 1984), and Dr Stella Dolores Henderson (d 2006); *b* 23 October 1945; *Educ* Radley, St Catharine's Coll Cambridge, St Thomas' Hosp (MB BChir); *m* 11 Dec 1971, Elizabeth Anne Lynette, da of Hon Mr Justice Arthur Douglas Davidson (d 1977), of Johannesburg, South Africa; 1 da (Fiona Elizabeth b 28 Sept 1984); *Career* trg as plastic surgn 1975–82, conslt plastic surgn 1982– (NHS practice until 2006, private practice 2006–); author of over 12,000 medico-legal reports in the past 30 years and articles in plastic surgery on subjects incl: thermography, hypospadias, palate fistulae, anti-drooling operation, use of turbinates as graft material; former chm: Research and Educn Sub-Ctee Br Assoc of Plastic Surgns, Leicester Royal Infirmary Pressure Sore Working Party; memb Cncl Br Assoc of Aesthetic Plastic Surgns; church warden 1990–; FRCS 1975; *Books* Questions and Answers in General Surgery, Questions and Answers in Surgery for Students; *Recreations* music, opera, shooting, travel; *Style*— Hugh Henderson, Esq; ✉ Nether Hall, Snows Lane, Keyham, Leicestershire LE7 9JS (☎ 01162 595214, e-mail hugh.h@home.gb.com); The Spire Hospital, Gartree Road, Oadby, Leicester LE2 2FF (☎ 0116 265 3043, fax 0116 265 3600)

HENDERSON, Iain Stirling; s of Michael Henderson, of Lamberhurst, Kent, and Anita, *née* Skidmore; *b* 2 August 1965, Oxted, Surrey; *Educ* Tonbridge, CCC Cambridge (open exhibitioner, Adam Fox exhibitioner, Manners scholar, BA); *m* 1 (m dis), Heloise, *née* Stevenson; 2 s (Maximilian b 23 March 1997, Charles b 6 Nov 1999); m 2, Amanda Grygelis; *Career* Accenture (UK) Ltd (formerly Arthur Andersen and Andersen Consulting): joined 1988, assoc ptnr 1998, ptnr 2000–12, head UK Delivery Centre 2002–08, head UK Solutions Workforce 2002–08, memb Bd Accenture UK and I 2003–08, head UK People Advocates 2004–06, md Systems Integration & Technol UK and I 2005–08, memb CEO Advsy Cncl 2006–08, communications and high tech client account lead 2008–, sr md 2012–, technol lead for communications, media and technol in Europe, Africa and Latin America 2014–; Accenture sponsor Inst of Electronics and Technol, alliance ptnr Microsoft/Avanade UK 2005–08; changemaker Working Families; FBCS 2006; *Recreations* guitar collector, guitarist in band (President Reagan is Clever 1985–97, Uncle Keith's Disco Champion 2004–08 and Straight Outta Brompton 2015–), film investment; *Style*— Iain Henderson, Esq; ✉ Accenture Ltd, 1 Plantation Place, 30 Fenchurch Street, London EC3M 3BD (☎ 020 7844 2689, e-mail iain.henderson@accenture.com)

HENDERSON, Ian James; CBE (2001); s of Robert Henderson, and Sheila, *née* Macpherson; *Educ* Coll of Estate Mgmnt London (BSc); *m* Sheila Sturrock; 1 da, 1 s; *Career* Hillier Parker May & Rowden 1966–71; Land Securities Group plc: joined 1971, exec dir 1987, gp chief exec 1997–2004; conslt Quintain Estates and Devpt plc 2005–13, dep chm Capital & Counties Properties plc 2010–16; pres New West End Co until 2008, non-exec chm Dawnay Day Treveria 2005–09; non-exec dir: Capital Shopping Centres Gp plc (formerly Liberty International) 2005–12, Evans Property Group 2006–12; non-exec chm Ishaan Real Estate plc 2006–13, chm Circle Property plc 2016–; pres Br Property Fedn 2002–03, vice-pres Central and Cecil Housing Tst, chm Devpt Tst for the Renewal of the Buildings of St-Martin-in-the-Fields 2004–11; currently farming in Surrey and Moray; tstee Nat History Museum 2005–13, memb Cncl Royal Albert Hall 2005–16, memb President's Ctee London First, cmmr Cwlth War Graves Cmmn 2002–10; chm of the govrs Dolphin Square Fndn 2005–16; FRICS; *Style*— Ian Henderson, Esq, CBE

HENDERSON, Ian Ramsay; s of David Hope Henderson (d 1977), of New Galloway, Kirkcudbrightshire, and Eleanora A Henderson, *née* Spence (d 2006); *Educ* Eton, Univ of Edinburgh (MA, LLB); *m* 28 Oct 1978, Virginia Theresa, da of Lt-Col John E B Freeman (d 1986), and Lady Winefride Freeman (d 2006); 3 s (Alexander b 1982, Charles b 1984, George b 1987); *Career* Peat Marwick Mitchell & Co 1972–76, Morgan Grenfell & Co 1977–82; md Wardley Marine International Investment Management Ltd 1985 (dir 1982), dir Wardley Investment Services International Ltd 1987–91, dir Fleming Investment Management Ltd 1991–2001, md JP Morgan Fleming Asset Management Ltd 2006– (md (investments) 2001–13), non-exec dir Endeavour Mining 2013–, non-exec dir Bank of Montreal Capital Markets Ltd 2015–; FCA 1980 (ACA 1975), MSI 1992; *Recreations* golf, tennis; *Clubs* Brooks's, St James's; *Style*— Ian Henderson, Esq; ✉ 20 Westbourne Park Road, London W2 5PH (☎ 020 7221 7515, e-mail ianrhenderson@hotmail.co.uk)

HENDERSON, Hon Mr Justice; Hon Sir Launcelot Dinadan James; kt (2007); er s of late Baron Henderson of Brompton (Life Peer), and Susan Mary, *née* Dartford; *b* 20 November 1951; *Educ* Westminster, Balliol Coll Oxford; *m* 1989, Elaine Elizabeth, er da of late Kenneth Frank Webb, of Dringhouses, York; 2 s (Peter George Galahad b 12 Aug 1990, Arthur Frank Gabriel b 18 Feb 1994), 1 da (Matilda Jane b 29 Aug 1992); *Career* called to the Bar Lincoln's Inn 1977 (bencher 2004); appointed standing jr counsel Chancery to the Inland Revenue 1987, standing jr counsel to Inland Revenue 1991–95, QC 1995, judge of the High Court of Justice (Chancery Div) 2007– (dep High Ct judge 2001); fell All Souls Coll Oxford 1974–81, 1982–89 and 2008–; tstee Samuel Courtauld Tst 2005–13; *Recreations* botany, art, music, books; *Style*— The Hon Mr Justice Henderson; ✉ c/o Royal Courts of Justice, 7 Rolls Building, Fetter Lane, London EC4A 1NL

HENDERSON, Mark; s of Gordon Henderson, of Mansfield, and Margaret Eileen, *née* Moakes; *b* 26 September 1957; *Educ* Sherwood Hall Tech GS Mansfield; *m* Julie; 2 s (Sam b 8 Nov 1993, Charlie b 1 Aug 1995), 2 da (Holly b 21 Sept 2003, Daisy b 16 July 2006); *Children* 2 s (Sam b 8 Nov 1993, Charlie b 1 Aug 1995); *Career* lighting designer; started career as lighting technician Newark Notts 1975; subsequently chief electrician for: Kent Opera, English Music Theatre, London Contemporary Dance, Sadler's Wells, Opera North; assoc RNT, lighting advsr Almeida Theatre; *Theatre* has lit over 80 West End shows incl: Funny Girl, Gypsy, The Bodyguard, Grease, Follies, Girlfriends, Mutiny, Kiss me Kate, Carmen Jones, Becket, The Merchant of Venice, A Patriot for Me, The Dresser, Gasping, Heartbreak House, No Man's Land, The Deep Blue Sea, Rowan Atkinson in Revue, Neville's Island, Indian Ink, Design for Living, Passion, Sweeney Todd; RNT prodns incl: History Boys (also Broadway), The Shaugraun, Cat on a Hot Tin Roof (also Broadway), Hamlet, The Changeling, Racing Demon, Long Day's Journey into Night, Napoli Millionaria, Murmuring Judges, Pygmalion, The Absence of War, The Birthday Party, Les Parent Terribles (Indiscretions, Broadway) Sweet Bird of Youth, Le Cid, Absolute Hell, La Grande Magia, A Little Night Music, John Gabriel Borkman, Oedipus Plays, The Cripple of Inishmaan, Marat/Sade, Amy's View, Copenhagen, Antony and Cleopatra; RSC prodns incl: Macbeth, The Tempest, Kiss Me Kate, Measure for Measure, General from America; Almeida prodns incl: The Deep Blue Sea, Rules of the Game, No Man's Land, Life of Galileo, Hamlet, Tartuffe, Britannicus, Judas Kiss, Naked, Iceman Cometh; other prodns incl: Hamlet (Broadway), Rowan Atkinson Tours (Aust,

H

NZ, USA), The Seagull (Old Vic); *Opera* numerous prodns incl: The Flying Dutchman, Tosca and Manon Lescaut (Royal Opera), The Makropulos Case, The Fairy Queen, Hippolyte et Arice (Glyndebourne Festival Opera), Tosca (Welsh Nat Opera), Anna Karenina, Sweeney Todd, Sunset Boulevard and The Flying Dutchman (ENO); *Dance* prodns incl: Agora, Shadows in the Sun (both London Contemporary Dance Theatre), Swan of Tuonela (Sadler's Wells Royal Ballet), Quicksilver (Rambert Dance Co); for Royal Ballet: The Tales of Beatrix Potter, The Planets, Don Quixote, The Judas Tree, Daphnis and Chloë, Swan Lake, The Nutcracker; *Films* incl: The Tall Guy (Working Title Prodn), Under Milk Wood (Imagination Entertainment), Rowan Atkinson in Boston USA; *Other Work* Madame Tussaud's: 200 Years Exhibition, Garden Party Exhibition, Spirit of London Dark Ride, Rock Circus Entrance, Planetarium Foyer, Royal Court redevelopment; *Awards* incl: Olivier Award for Lighting Designer of the Year 1992, 1995, 2000, 2002, 2010 and 2016, Olivier Award for Best Lighting Designer 1995, Tony Award nomination Best Lighting Designer 1995, Olivier Award nomination for Best Lighting Designer 1996, 1997, 1999 and 2001, Tony Award nominations 1996, 1999, 2005 and 2006 (for Faith Healer), Tony Award for Best Lighting Design (Play) 2006 (for History Boys), Welsh BAFTA; *Style*— Mark Henderson, Esq; ✉ c/o PBJ Management Ltd, 22 Rathbone Street London, W1T 1LG (☎ 020 7287 1112, fax 020 7287 1191)

HENDERSON, Michael John Glidden; s of William Glidden Henderson (d 1946), and Aileen Judith, *née* Malloy (d 1996); *b* 19 August 1938; *Educ* St Benedict's Sch Ealing; *m* 29 Sept 1965, Stephanie Maria, da of John Dyer, of Hampton Court, Surrey; 4 s (Nicholas b 1966, Simon b 1968, Angus b 1972, Giles b 1976); *Career* chm and chief exec Cookson Group plc 1978–90; chm Henderson Crosthwaite Ltd 1995–2000, vice-chm Quexco Inc (USA) 2002; dir: Pennymead Sports Ground Ltd 1980– (chm 1991–), Guinness Mahon Holdings plc 1988–2000, Sweett Gp plc (formerly Cyril Sweett plc) 1998–2015 (chm 2010–15), Eco-Bat Technolgies plc 1999–2002, Wisley Golf Club plc 2002–08 (dep chm 2003–08); memb DTI Innovation Advsy Bd 1988–93; tstee Natural History Museum Devpt Tst 1990–2000; govr: St George's Coll Weybridge 1990–2011 (chm Fin and Gen Purposes Ctee 1991–2011, dep chm 2002–11), Cranmore Sch West Horsley 1991 (chm Fin and Gen Purposes Ctee 1992–2013, dep chm 1998–2013, chm 2013–), St Teresa's Convent Effingham 2002–14 (chm Fin and Gen Purposes Ctee 2002–11, dep chm 2010–14); memb Cncl St Augustines Soc 2006, memb Catholic Union of GB 2008 (memb Cncl 2010–, chm Membership and Communication Ctee 2012–), tstee Catholic Union Charitable Tst 2013– (chm exec ctee 2013–), memb Investment Ctee Handicapped Children Pilgrimage Tst 2014–; FCA 1961, FRSA 1989; Knight Cdr of the Holy Sepulchre 2011 (Knight 2005); *Publications* book review of Just Money: how Catholic social teaching can redeem capitalism by Clifford Longley; *Recreations* tennis, golf; *Clubs* MCC, Wisley Golf, Horsley Sports, Queen's, Thurlestone Golf, Salcombe Yacht, Knightsbridge Tennis; *Style*— Michael Henderson, Esq; ✉ Langdale, Woodland Drive, East Horsley, Surrey KT24 5AN (☎ 01483 283844, e-mail mike.henderson3@btopenworld.com)

HENDERSON, Nicholas John; s of John Ronald Henderson, CVO, OBE, of Newbury, Berks, and Katherine Sarah, *née* Beckwith-Smith (d 1972); *b* 10 December 1950; *Educ* Eton; *m* 10 June 1978, Diana Amanda, da of John Thorne; 3 da (Sarah Lucy b 5 Dec 1981, Tessa Jane b 8 Dec 1983, Camilla Penny b 3 Nov 1987); *Career* national hunt racehorse trainer; asst trainer to Fred Winter 1973–78, amateur rider 1970–78 (rode 75 winners incl The Imperial Cup Sandown and Liverpool Foxhunters); trainer 1978–; trained over 2500 winners incl 53 Cheltenham Festival winners (incl 5 Champion Hurdles, 2 Gold Cups, 3 Queen Mother Champion Chases), 2 King George VI Chases (Kempton), 2 Hennessy Gold Cups (Newbury), 4 Tote Gold Trophies (Newbury); Champion Trainer 1986/87, 1987–88 and 2013–14; *Recreations* golf, shooting, fishing; *Style*— Nicholas Henderson, Esq; ✉ Seven Barrows, Lambourn, Hungerford, Berkshire RG17 8UH (☎ 01488 72259, fax 01488 72596, e-mail nj.henderson@virgin.net)

HENDERSON, Prof Paul; CBE (2003); s of Thomas William Henderson (d 1988), and Dorothy Violet, *née* Marriner; *b* 7 November 1940; *Educ* KCS Wimbledon, Univ of London (BSc), Univ of Oxford (DPhil); *m* Aug 1966, Elizabeth Kathryn, da of William Albert Ankerson; 1 s (Gideon Mark b 29 July 1968), 1 da (Laura Kate b 19 Jan 1972); *Career* asst lectr in chemistry Univ of Glasgow 1966–67, lectr in geochemistry Chelsea Coll London 1968–76; Br Museum (Natural History): head Rock and Mineral Chemistry Div 1977–87, dep keeper of Mineralogy Natural History Museum (name change) 1987–89, keeper of Mineralogy 1989–95, also assoc dir for Earth Scis 1992–95, dir of Sci 1995–2003; UCL: visiting prof in mineral scis 1990–98, hon prof 1998–; Muséum National d'Histoire Naturelle Paris: memb Sci Advsy Ctee 2000–01, memb Conseil Scientifique 2003–06; pres Mineralogical Soc of GB and Ireland 1989–91, vice-pres Geological Soc London 2002–08; tstee Horniman Museum and Public Park Tst 2004–12; Fourmarier Medal Belgian Geological Soc 1989; FGS 1990, chartered geologist; *Books* Inorganic Geochemistry (1982), Rare Earth Element Geochemistry (1984), Cambridge Handbook of Earth Science Data (jtly, 2009), James Sowerby: The Enlightenment's Natural Historian (2015); *Recreations* history, music, Paris, wine; *Clubs* Oxford and Cambridge; *Style*— Prof Paul Henderson, CBE; ✉ UCL Earth Sciences, University College London, Gower Street, London WC1E 6BT (e-mail p.henderson@ucl.ac.uk)

HENDERSON, Dr Richard; *b* 19 July 1945; *Educ* Hawick HS and Boroughmuir Secdy Sch, Univ of Edinburgh (Isaac Newton scholar, Neil Arnott scholar, BSc), Univ of Cambridge (MRC scholar, PhD); *Career* research staff MRC Lab of Molecular Biology Cambridge 1969–70, Helen Hay Whitney postdoctoral fell Yale Univ 1970–73; MRC Lab of Molecular Biology Cambridge: research staff 1973–79, sr research staff 1979–84, special appts grade research staff 1984–86, jt head Div of Structural Studies 1986–95, dep dir 1995–96, dir 1996–2006; fell Darwin Coll Cambridge 1982–, hon fell Corpus Christi Coll Cambridge 2003–; memb EMBO 1981; William Bate Hardy Prize Cambridge Philosophical Soc 1978, Ernst-Ruska Prize for electron microscopy 1980, Rosenstiel Award 1991, Louis Jeantet Award 1993, Gregori Aminoff Award 1999, Alexander Hollaender Award Nat Acad of Sci USA 2016; foreign assoc Nat Acad of Scis USA 1998; FRS 1983; *Style*— Dr Richard Henderson, FRS; ✉ MRC Laboratory of Molecular Biology, Francis Crick Avenue, Cambridge CB2 0QH (☎ 01223 267065, fax 01223 268305, e-mail rh15@mrc-lmb.cam.ac.uk)

HENDERSON, Roger Anthony; QC (1980); s of Dr Peter Wallace Henderson (d 1984), and Dr Stella Dolores, *née* Morton (d 2006); *b* 21 April 1943; *Educ* Radley, St Catharine's Coll Cambridge; *m* 1968, Catherine Margaret (d 2013); 3 da (Camilla (Mrs William Gray Muir), Antonia (Mrs Andrew Dalmahoy), Venetia); *Career* called to the Bar Inner Temple 1964 (bencher 1985); recorder 1983–2012, dep judge of the High Court 1987–2012, head of chambers 1989–2007; pres Br Acad of Forensic Sci 1986; chm: Public Affrs Ctee of the Bar 1989 and 1990, Special Ctee of St Peter's Hosps Gp 1989–92, Civil Serv Arbitration Tbnl 1994–; chm Assoc of Regulatory and Disciplinary Lawyers 2002–09; chm London Hosp Med Coll 1993–95 (govr 1989–95), chm Medical Coll of St Bartholemew's Hosp Tst 2012–; hon fell Queen Mary Univ of London; *Publications* Medicine Science and the Law (contrib, 2008); *Recreations* fly fishing, gardening, shooting; *Clubs* Boodle's; *Style*— R A Henderson, Esq, QC; ✉ 7A Berkeley Gardens, London W8 4AP (e-mail rogerhqc@gmail.com); Holbury Mill, Lockerley, Hampshire SO51 0JR

HENDERSON, Simon Charles; s of Giles Henderson, and Lynne, *née* Fifield; *b* 16 December 1975, London; *Educ* Winchester, Brasenose Coll Oxford (MA, PGCE); *m* 31 March 2007, Alison, *née* Cochrane; 2 s (Charlie b 25 May 2008, Jack b 26 Oct 2011), 2 da (Mary b 1 Jan 2010, Rosie b 30 March 2013); *Career* history teacher The Windsor Boys' Sch 1999–2001, history teacher Eton Coll 2001–09 (head of History 2005–09), dep head (Academic) Sherborne 2009–11, head Bradfield Coll 2011–15, headmaster Eton Coll 2015–; govr: Theale Green Sch 2011–16, Holyport Coll 2015–, London Acad of Excellence 2015–, Wycombe Abbey 2016–; memb: HMC 2011, ASCL 2011; *Recreations* cricket, golf, music, reading, skiing, travel; *Clubs* Lansdowne, East India; *Style*— Simon Henderson, Esq; ✉ Eton College, Windsor, Berkshire SL4 6DW (☎ 01753 370800, e-mail headmaster@etoncollege.org.uk, website www.etoncollege.com)

HENDRICK, Prof David John; *b* 18 October 1941, Reading, Berks; *Educ* Maidstone GS, Guy's Hosp Med Sch London (pre-clinical entrance scholar, MB BS, MD), McGill Univ Montreal (MSc); *m* Alex Margaret; 2 da (Vicki, Shona); *Career* house physician (gen med and cardiology) and house surgn Guy's Hosp 1966–67, SHO (neurology) Royal Victoria Infirmary Newcastle upon Tyne 1968, jr med registrar Guy's Hosp 1968, med registrar Greenwich Hosp and clinical asst Brompton Hosp 1968–70, sr med registrar Sydney Hosp 1970–72, research asst (clinical immunology) Brompton Hosp 1972–73, sr registar (chest and gen med) Churchill Hosp and Radcliffe Infirmary Oxford 1973–76, asst prof of pulmonary and internal med West Virginia Univ Morgantown 1976–79, assoc prof of pulmonary and internal med Tulane Univ New Orleans 1979–82, conslt physician (chest and gen med) and head Dept of Respiratory Med Newcastle Gen Hosp 1982–94, conslt physician (respiratory and gen med) Royal Victoria Infirmary NHS Tst 1994– (head Dept of Respiratory Med 1994–98), sabbatical year McGill Univ Montreal 1998–99; Univ of Newcastle upon Tyne Med Sch: hon lectr then hon sr lectr 1982–97, sr lectr then prof of occupational respiratory med 1997–; memb: Ctee on Thoracic Med RCP 1988–92, Steering Ctee SWORD (Surveillance of Work-related and Occupational Respiratory Diseases) Project 1988–, Grants Ctee Br Lung Fndn 1991–95, Med Appeals Tbnl 1992–, Advsy Gp on Respiratory Sensitizers Dept of Employment 1993–96, Nat Asthma Taskforce Mortality and Severe Morbidity Working Gp 1994–98, Grants Ctee North of England Cancer Research Campaign 1996–98; memb Editorial Bd Thorax 1988–91, co-ordinating ed Thorax – Year in Review Annual Supplement 1994–98; MRCS 1966, FRCP 1985 (LRCP 1966, MRCP 1969), FFOM 1994; *Publications* Occupational Disorders of the Lung: recognition, management and prevention (jt ed, 2002); jl articles and book chapters chiefly related to asthma, allergic alveolitis, and occupational diseases of the lung; *Recreations* family, coarse golfing, even coarser sailing; *Style*— Prof David Hendrick; ✉ Department of Respiratory Medicine, Royal Victoria Infirmary, Queen Victoria Road, Newcastle upon Tyne NE1 4LP (☎ 0191 282 0140, fax 0191 282 0112)

HENDRICK, Mark; MP; *b* 2 November 1958; *Educ* Univ of Manchester (MSc, CertEd), Liverpool Poly (BSc); *Career* design engr for six years SERC (Daresbury Lab); Lab Pty: memb 1982–, memb (and former branch sec) Salford Co-op Pty 1984–1994, chm Weaste and Seedley Branch 1987–94, chm Eccles Constituency 1990–94; MEP (Lab Co-op) Lancashire Central 1994–99; Euro Parly Lab Pty spokesperson on economic and monetary affrs, memb Euro Parl Economic and Monetary Affrs Ctee, sec NW Gp of Lab MEPs 1994–98; MP (Lab Co-op) Preston (by-election) 2000–; memb Salford City Cncl 1987–95 (served on Policy, Planning, Educn Ctees and Management Services Ctee (vice-chm)); alternate dir representing City of Salford Manchester Airport plc 1985–94; memb GMB; *Style*— Mark Hendrick, Esq, MP; ✉ PTMC, Marsh Lane, Preston PR1 8UQ (☎ 01772 883575, e-mail mark.hendrick.mp@parliament.uk)

HENDRICKS, Rt Rev Paul Joseph; s of Gerald St Alban Hendricks, of Southampton, and Grace Rose, *née* Deacon (d 1994); *b* 18 March 1956, Beckenham, Kent; *Educ* St Mary's RC GS Sidcup, CCC Oxford (MA), English Coll Rome and Gregorian Univ Rome (BTh, MPhil); *Career* microwave engr GEC Hirst Research Centre Wembley 1977–79; ordained: deacon Rome 1983, priest Orpington 1984; asst priest St Boniface Parish Tooting 1985–89, philosophy lectr and bursar St John's Seminary Wonersh 1989–99, parish priest Our Lady of Sorrows Peckham 1999–2006, auxiliary bishop (RC) SW Area Archdiocese of Southwark 2006–; chm Catholic Truth Soc, patron Inform, co-chair Christian-Muslim Forum; memb Jane Austen Soc; *Recreations* walking, reading, model flying, cats; *Style*— The Rt Rev Paul Hendricks; ✉ 95 Carshalton Road, Sutton SM1 4LL; Archbishop's House, 150 St George's Rd, Southwark, London SE1 6HX (☎ 020 8643 8007, e-mail bishop.hendricks@gmail.com)

HENDRY, Rt Hon Prof Charles; PC (2015); s of late Charles W R Hendry, and late Peggy Hendry; *b* 6 May 1959, E Grinstead, W Sussex; *Educ* Rugby, Univ of Edinburgh (BComm); *m* 20 July 1995, Sallie A Moores, yr da of Stuart Smith; 2 s (Charles Stuart Benjamin b 3 Sept 1996, James William Ruairidh b 13 May 1998); *Career* account dir Ogilvy & Mather PR Ltd then assoc dir Burson-Marsteller Ltd PR conslts 1982–88; political advsr: to Rt Hon John Moore MP (as Sec of State for Social Servs) 1988, to Rt Hon Tony Newton MP (as Min for Trade and Industry then Sec of State for Social Security) 1988–90; MP (Cons): High Peak 1992–97, Wealden 2001–2015 (Parly candidate (Cons): Clackmannan 1983, Mansfield 1987); PPS: to Rt Hon William Hague, MP, *qv* (as Min for Disabled People) 1994–95, to Rt Hon Gillian Shephard, DL, *qv* (as Sec of State for Educn) 1995; COS Office of the Ldr of the Oppn 1997, oppn pairing whip 2001–02, shadow min for young people 2002–05, dep chm Cons Pty 2003–05 (vice-chm 1995–97), shadow min for industry and enterprise 2005–07, shadow min for energy, industry and postal affrs 2007–08, shadow min for energy 2008–10, min of state Dept of Energy and Climate Change 2010–12, PM's trade envoy to Azerbaijan, Kazakhstan and Turkmenistan 2012–15; chm All-Pty Parly Gp on Homelessness 1992–95, memb Culture, Media and Sport Select Ctee 2004, memb Select Ctee on Energy and Climate Change 2009–; sec Cons Backbench: Social Security Ctee 1992–94, Inner Cities and Urban Affairs Ctee 1994–95; sec E Midlands Cons MPs 1992–97, chair Br-Swiss Parly Gp 2007–; head of business liaison Cons Pty 1997–99; The Agenda Gp Ltd: dir 1999–2005, chief exec 1999–2001, non-exec chm 2001–05; non-exec dir IncrediBull Ideas Ltd 2003–04; chm Forewind Ltd 2013–15, chm Eurasia Ptnrs 2015–; visiting prof Univ of Edinburgh 2012–; pres Edinburgh Univ Cons Assoc 1979–80, vice-chm Scot Fedn of Cons Students 1980–81, vice-chm Battersea Cons Assoc 1981–83; pres: Nat Energy Action 2013–15, Br Inst of Energy Economics 2014–, Advsy Bd Russo-Br Chamber of Commerce 2013–, Br Chamber of Commerce in Kazakhstan 2015–; cmmr-gen UK Pavilion Expo 2017 Kazakhstan 2015–; tstee Drive for Youth 1989–99, hon pres Br Youth Cncl 1992–97, patron The Big Issue Fndn 1997– (tstee 1996–97), tstee UK Youth Parl 2004–, tstee Burrell Collection 2016–; patron Nuclear Inst 2015–; Hon FEI 2013–; *Recreations* tennis, skiing, opera, Scottish heritage; *Style*— The Rt Hon Prof Charles Hendry; ✉ House of Commons, London SW1A 0AA (☎ 020 7219 3000, e-mail hendryc@parliament.uk)

HENDRY, Charles Donald (Charlie); CBE (2009), QFSM; s of Donald Hendry, of Worthing, W Sussex, and Angela, *née* Pullen; *b* 9 September 1960, St Albans, Herts; *Educ* St George's Sch Harpenden, Solihull Sixth Form Coll, Univ of York (BA), London South Bank Univ (MSc); *m* 2003, Sandra, *née* Briggs-Watson; *Career* asst chief fire offr London Fire Brigade 1997–2000; Kent Fire & Rescue Service: dep chief fire offr 2000–05, chief fire offr and chief exec 2005–; pres UK Chief Fire Officers' Assoc 2008–09, non-exec dir Fire Protection Assoc; memb Ctee Fairbridge Kent; fell Instn of Fire Engrs 2009; *Recreations* gardening, reading, walking, film and music; *Style*— Charlie Hendry, Esq, CBE, QFSM; ✉ Kent Fire & Rescue Service Headquarters, The Godlands, Straw Mill Hill, Tovil, Maidstone, Kent ME15 6XB

HENDRY, Sir David Forbes; kt (2009); s of Robert Ernest Hendry (d 2010), and Catherine Helen Forbes, *née* Mackenzie (d 2014); *b* 6 March 1944, Nottingham, UK; *Educ* Glasgow HS, Univ of Aberdeen (MA), LSE (MSc, PhD); *m* 7 Oct 1966, Evelyn Rosemary, da of Rev John Vass (d 1974), of Aberdeen; 1 da (Vivien Louise b 1977); *Career* LSE: lectr 1969–73, reader 1973–77, prof of economics 1977–81; Univ of Oxford: prof of economics

1982–, fell Nuffield Coll 1982–, Leverhulme personal research prof 1995–2000, chm Economics Dept 2001–07, ESRC professorial fell 2003–06, dir Prog in Economic Modelling Inst for New Economic Thinking Oxford Martin Sch (INET at Oxford); visiting prof: Yale Univ 1975, Univ of Calif Berkeley 1976, Catholic Univ of Louvain-la-Neuve 1980, Univ of Calif San Diego 1981 and 1989–90; special advsr House of Commons Select Ctee on the Treasy and Civil Serv 1979–80 and 1991, memb Academic Panel of HM Treasy 1976–89, chm Research Assessment Panel in Economics 1995–96, memb Advsy Panel on Foresight for Chief Scientific Advsr to HM Govt 2008–12; Royal Economic Soc: pres 1992–95, hon vice-pres 1995–; pres Section F BAAS 1999–2000; foreign hon memb: American Econ Assoc 1991, American Acad of Arts and Sciences 1994; Guy medal in Bronze of the Royal Statistical Soc 1986, Isaac Kerstenetzky Scholarly Achievement Award 2012, Thomson Reuters Citation Laureate 2013, Lifetime Achievement Award Economic and Social Research Cncl 2014; chartered statistician 1992; Hon LLD Univ of Aberdeen 1987, Hon DSc Univ of Nottingham 1998, Hon DPhil Norwegian Univ of Sci and Technol, Hon Dr Univ of St Gallen, Hon LLD Univ of St Andrews 2002, Hon DPhil Univ of Lund 2006, Hon Dr Carlos III Univ Madrid 2009, hon doctorate Aarhus Univ 2013; hon fell Int Inst of Forecasters 2001; fell Econometric Soc 1976, FBA 1987, FRSE 2002, FAcSS 2012; *Books* Econometrics and Quantitative Economics (with K F Wallis, 1984), Pc-Give: An Interactive Econometric Modelling System (1989, with J A Doornik 1992, 1994, 1997, 2001, 2006 and 2013), Pc-Naive: An Interactive Program for Monte Carlo Experimentation in Econometrics (with A J Neale and N R Ericsson, 1991, with J A Doornik 2001 and 2006), Econometrics: Alchemy or Science (1993, 2 edn 2000), Cointegration, Error Correction and the Econometric Analysis of Non-stationary Data (with A Banerjee, J J Dolado and J W Galbraith, 1993), Dynamic Econometrics (1995), The Foundations of Econometric Analysis (with M S Morgan, 1995), Forecasting Economic Time Series (with M P Clements, 1998), Forecasting Non-stationary Economic Time Series (with M P Clements, 1999), Understanding Economic Forecasts (ed with N R Ericsson, 2001), Automatic Econometric Model Selection Using PcGets (with H M Krolzig, 2001), Companion to Economic Forecasting (ed with M P Clements, 2002), General to Specific Modelling (ed with J Campos and N R Ericsson, 2005), Econometric Modelling (with B Nielsen, 2007), Oxford Handbook of Economic Forecasting (ed with M P Clements, 2011), Empirical Model Discovery and Theory Evaluation (with J A Doornik, 2015), Introductory Macro-econometrics: A New Approach (2015); *Recreations* golf; *Style*— Sir David F Hendry, FBA, FRSE; ✉ 26 Northmoor Road, Oxford OX2 6UR (☎ 01865 515588); Nuffield College, Oxford OX1 1NF (☎ 01865 278654, fax 01865 278621)

HENDRY, Diana Lois; da of Leslie Gordon McConomy (d 1964), and Amelia, *née* Kesler (d 1993); *b* 2 October 1941; *Educ* W Kirby Co GS for Girls, Filton Tech Coll, Univ of Bristol (BA, MLitt), privately (LLCM); *m* 1965 (m dis 1981), George Alexander Forbes Hendry; 1 s (Hamish b 1966), 1 da (Kate b 1970); *Career* reporter/feature writer The Western Mail Cardiff 1960–65, freelance journalist and writer 1965–; Eng teacher Clifton Coll 1987–90, tutor Bristol Poly 1987–93, tutor in lit Open Univ 1990–91, tutor in creative writing Univ of Bristol 1995–97, writer in residence Dumfries and Galloway Royal Infirmary 1997–98, co-ed New Writing Scotland 2015–; Robert Louis Stevenson Fell 2007, Royal Literary Fund Fell Univ of Edinburgh 2008–10; first prize Stroud Int Poetry Competition 1976, second prize Peterloo Poetry Competition 1993 (third prize 1991), Whitbread Award (for children's novel) 1991, first prize Housman Soc Poetry Competition 1996, Scottish Arts Cncl Children's Book Award 2001, shortlisted Costa Award, shortlisted Scottish Children's Book Award 2013; memb Soc of Authors 1987, memb PEN 1993; *Books* incl: Fiona Finds Her Tongue (1985, short-listed Smartie Award), Double Vision (1990), Harvey Angell (1991), Peterloo Preview 3 (1993), Making Blue (Peterloo Poets) (1995), The Awesome Bird (1995), Harvey Angell and the Ghost Child (1997), Minders (1998), Harvey Angell Beats Time (2000), Borderers (Peterloo Poets, 2001), You Can't Kiss It Better (2003), Twelve Lilts: Psalms and Responses (2003), Sparks (with Tom Pow, 2005), Late Love & Other Whodunnits (2008), The Seeing (2012), The Seed-Box Lantern: New & Selected Poems (2013), libretto for The Pied Piper, cantata for soprano, baritone, choir and orchestra (composer John Glenesk Mortimer, 2013), Second Wind (with Douglas Dunn and Vicki Feaver, 2015), Out of the Clouds (2016); numerous poems published in leading jls and anthologies; contrib book reviews The Spectator; *Recreations* playing the piano; *Style*— Diana Hendry; ✉ c/o Fraser Ross Associates, 6 Wellington Place, Edinburgh EH6 7EQ (☎ 0131 553 2759 / 0131 657 4412, e-mail kjross@tiscali.co.uk, lindsey.fraser@tiscali.co.uk)

HENDRY, Drew; MP; *Career* MP (SNP) Inverness, Nairn, Badenoch and Strathspey 2015–; *Style*— Drew Hendry, Esq, MP; ✉ House of Commons, London SW1A 0AA

HENDRY, Gerry; s of James Hendry (d 1995), and Phaneulina, *née* Webster (d 2000); *b* 5 May 1948, Leeds; *Educ* Fraserburgh Acad, Buchan Coll, Univ of Leeds; *m* 1, 1973 (m dis); 1 s (Craig b 18 July 1973), 1 da (Emma b 7 Nov 1975); m 2, 1993, Geraldine, *née* Hamer; 2 da (Alexandra b 4 Oct 1996, Antonia b 13 Nov 1997); *Career* engr Consolidated Pneumatic 1968, civil servant MOD 1970–, joined Prison Serv as prison offr Northallerton 1980, past positions incl head of residence, head of regimes, head of security, head of personnel and planning, head of secretariat and dep govr, govr Shrewsbury Prison 2005–; memb Hambleton DC 1978, dep mayor Northallerton 1979, Northallerton parish cncllr; involved with UN Mission in Kosovo (UNMIK) as head of team evacuating refugees from Macedonia and Albania during Kosovo Conflict; supporter NE Aid to Orphans Lithuania; memb Inst of Mgmnt 1994; *Recreations* golf, folk music, freemasonry; *Clubs* Brancepeth Golf; *Style*— Gerry Hendry, Esq; ✉ HMP Shrewsbury, The Dana, Shrewsbury SY1 2HR (☎ 01743 273101, fax 01743 273002, e-mail gerry.hendry@hmps.gsi.gov.uk)

HENDY, John; QC (1987); s of late Jack Hendy, of Penzance, and Mary, *née* Best; *b* 11 April 1948; *Educ* Univ of London (LLB), Queen's Univ Belfast (LLM); *m*; 3 c; *Career* memb Hon Soc of Gray's Inn 1966; called to the Bar 1972 (bencher 1995), admitted to the Bar NSW 1998; visiting prof KCL 1999–2005, hon prof UCL 2014–; chm Inst Employment Rights 1989–, pres Int Centre for Trade Union Rights, chair Employment Law Bar Assoc 2003–05; fell Inst of Advanced Legal Studies; FRSM; *Publications* Does the new Disciplinary Procedure improve on HC(90)9? (2009), The Dramatic Implications of Demir and Baykara (with K D Ewing, 2010), Days of Action: the legality of protest strikes against government cuts (with K D Ewing, 2011), Reserving the right to change terms and conditions: how far can the employer go? (with F Reynold, 2012), Unfair dismissal law: unfair (with K D Ewing, 2012), Giving Life to the ILO- Two Cheers for the SCC (with K D Ewing, in Constitutional Labour Rights in Canada: Farm Workers and the Fraser Case, 2012), Reconstruction after the crisis: a manifesto for collective bargaining (with K D Ewing, 2013), ECtHR Procedure (chapter in The European convention on Human Rights and the Employment Relation, 2013), A Personal Viewpoint: 42 Years of Employment Law (2014), International Litigation Possibilities in European Collective Labour Law: ECHR (with K D Ewing in The Economic and Financial Crisis and Collective Labour Law in Europe, 2014); *Clubs* Groucho; *Style*— John Hendy, Esq, QC; ✉ 10–11 Bedford Row, London WC1R 4BU (☎ 020 7269 0300, fax 020 7405 1387, e-mail hendyqc@oldsquarechambers.co.uk)

HENDY, Sir Peter; kt (2013), CBE (2006); *Educ* Univ of Leeds (BA); *Career* London Transport 1975–89 (joined as grad trainee, latterly sr mangr personnel and ops), md CentreWest London Buses Ltd 1989–97 (led mgmnt buyout 1994), divnl dir for London and SE then dep dir UK bus FirstGroup plc 1997–2001; Transport for London: md of surface transport 2001–06, cmmr 2006–15; chair Network Rail 2015–; memb Cncl Confedn of Passenger Transport 1994–2000, chair Cmmn for Integrated Transport 2005–10 (memb 2004–), pres UITP (International Association of Public Transport) 2013–15; Hon DSc City Univ 2010, Hon DEng Univ of Bath 2014, Hon LLD Univ of Leeds 2015; FCILT (pres 2011–12), FCIHT, FICE; *Style*— Sir Peter Hendy, CBE; ✉ Network Rail, Waterloo General Office, Suite 2, Floor 2, London SE1 8SW

HENIG, Baroness (Life Peer UK 2004), of Lancaster in the County of Lancashire; Ruth Beatrice Henig; CBE (2000), JP (1984), DL (Lancs 2002); da of Kurt Munzer, of Leicester; *b* 10 November 1943, Leicester; *Educ* Bedford Coll London, Univ of London, Lancaster Univ (PhD); *m* 1, 1966 (m dis 1993), Stanley Henig, s of Sir Mark Henig (d 1978), of Leicester; 2 s (Hon Simon Anthony b 1969, Hon Harold David b 1972); m 2, 1994, Jack Johnstone (d 2013); *Career* Lancaster Univ: lectr History Dept 1968–93, sr lectr 1993–, dean of arts and humanities 1997–2000; elected cncllr Lancaster E Lancs CC 1981; chair: Lancs Police Authy 1995–2005, Nat Assoc of Police Authorities 1997–2005, Security Industry Authy 2007–13; memb: Lawrence Steering Gp Home Office 2000–05, Nat Criminal Justice Bd 2002–2005; chair Bd Duke's Playhouse Lancaster; Infologue Building the Future Award 2012, ASC Imbert Prize 2013; memb Worshipful Co of Security Professionals 2007–; *Books* The League of Nations (1973), Versailles and After (1984), Origins of the Second World War (1985), Origins of the First World War (1989), The Weimar Republic (1998), Women and Political Power (with Simon Henig, 2000), Modern Europe, 1870–1945 (with Chris Culpin, 1997), History of the League of Nations (2010); *Recreations* fell walking, bridge, gardening, wine appreciation; *Clubs* Young Chelsea Bridge; *Style*— The Rt Hon the Lady Henig, CBE, DL; ✉ House of Lords, London SW1A 0PW (☎ 020 7219 5133, mobile 07768 526210, e-mail ruthhenig@gmail.com)

HENKE, Malcolm; s of Donald Henke, of Spain, and Berry, *née* Entwisle (d 2003); *b* 27 January 1959, Coventry, West Midlands; *Educ* Holy Trinity Sch Crawley; *partner* Jane Hall; 4 da (Alexis, Ashley, Lydia, India), 1 s (Oliver); *Career* slr: Hextall Erskine & Co 1977–90, Davies Arnold Cooper 1990–2000, Barlow Lyde & Gilbert 2000–02, Greenwoods 2002–; memb Master of the Rolls Working Party on Structured Settlements, memb Clinical Disputes Forum; *Recreations* golf, motor racing; *Style*— Malcolm Henke, Esq; ✉ Greenwoods Solicitors, Plantation Place South, 60 Great Tower Street, London EC3R 5AZ (☎ 020 7323 4632)

H

HENLEY, Darren Richard; OBE (2013); *b* 16 February 1973; *Educ* St Edmund's Sch Canterbury, Univ of Hull (BA); *Career* freelance radio journalist for stations incl Invicta, LBC, IRN, Classic FM and BBC GLR 1989–92, sr broadcast journalist ITN Radio 1992–95; Classic FM: prog ed Classic Newsnight 1995–96, news mangr 1996–99, news and prog mangr 1999–2000, managing ed 2000–04, station mangr 2004–, md 2006–15; CEO Arts Cncl Eng 2015–; md: theJazz 2006–08, Xfm and Choice FM 2008; memb: Bd of Judges and Advsrs NY Int Radio Festival 2001–03, Bd DCSF/DCMS Music Prog 2007–10, Devpt Ctee Philharmonia Orch Business 2007–11, Steering Gp In Harmony 2009–11, Nat Year of Music Steering Gp 2009–10, Creative and Cultural Industries Task Force 2009–10, Nat Plan for Music Educn Monitoring Bd 2012–13; chm: Music Manifesto Partnership and Advocacy Gp 2007–10, Dept for Educn/DCMS Henley Review of Music Educn in England 2010–11, DFE/DCMS Henley Review of Cultural Educn in England 2011–12, DCLG Communities in Tune Advsy Gp 2012–15, Mayor of London's Music Education Steering Gp 2013–15; dir Bd Canterbury Festival and Theatre Tst 2001–15, memb SE Regnl Cncl Arts Cncl England 2002–05, tstee Future Talent 2006–10, memb Media Bd Prince's Fndn for Children and the Arts 2007–15, patron Mayor of London's Fund for Young Musicians 2011–, memb Cultural Advsy Gp Birmingham City Univ 2012–15, memb Advsy Bd City Music Fndn 2012–15, co-chair DfE/DCMS Cultural Education Bd 2013–15, memb Scottish Govt Instrumental Music Gp 2013, memb Warwick Cmmn on the Future of Cultural Value Univ of Warwick 2013–15, tstee ABRSM 2013–15, tstee Global Charities 2013–15; UN Gold medal 2000, Gold medal Arts and Culture Catgory NY Int Radio Festival 2000, UK Station of the Year Sony Radio Acad Awards 2007, Gold medal Best Music Prog NY Int Radio Festival 2007, Chm's Award Arqiva Commercial Radio Awards 2007, Arqiva Commercial Radio Programmer of the Year 2009, Gold Award Music Programming Sony Radio Acad Awards 2009, Station of the Year Arqiva Commercial Radio Award 2011, Making Music/Sir Charles Groves Prize for Outstanding Contribution to Br Music 2012, Gold Arqiva Commercial Radio Award 2012, UK Radio Brand of the Year Sony Radio Acad Award 2013, Creative Communication Award Royal Philharmonic Soc 2013, Presidents Medal Br Acad 2015; Hon DLitt Univ of Hull 2014, Hon DUniv Birmingham City Univ 2014, Hon DUniv Buckinghamshire New Univ 2014, Hon MA Univ for the Creative Arts 2016; hon fell: Canterbury Christ Church Univ 2010, Trinity Laban Conservatoire of Music and Dance 2011, Liverpool John Moores Univ 2014, Guildhall Sch of Music and Drama 2015; hon memb RNCM 2012, fell London Coll of Music 2012, hon memb Incorporated Soc of Musicians 2013, hon memb Royal Coll of Music 2016, companion Liverpool Inst for the Performing Arts 2016; FRSA 1998, CCMI 2010, fell Radio Acad 2011; *Publications* The Classic FM Pocket Book of Music (2003), The Classic FM Pocket Book of Quotes (2004), The Story of Classical Music (audio, 2004, Best Original Audio Book American Audio Publishers Awards, Radio Times Readers' Choice Award Br Spoken Word Awards 2005, nominated Grammy Award 2005), The Classic FM Pocket Book of Trivia (2004), Aled – The Autobiography (with Aled Jones, 2005), Classic Ephemera (2005), Famous Composers (audio, 2005, Best Original Audio Book Audio Publishers Awards 2006), G4 – The Official Book (2005), The Classic FM Friendly Guide to Mozart (2005), The Classic FM Friendly Guide to Beethoven (with John Suchet, 2006), The Classic FM Friendly Guide to Music (2006), More Famous Composers (2007), The Classic FM Friendly Guide to Elgar (2007), Hayley Westenra – In Her Own Voice (with Hayley Westenra, 2007), The Classic FM Friendly Music Quiz Book (2007), 101 Q&A About Classical Music (2008), The Incredible Story of Classical Music (2008), The Original Liverpool Sound: The Official History of the Royal Liverpool Philharmonic (2009), Classic Ephemera – A Classic FM Miscellany (2009), The A-Z of Classic FM Music (2010), The Classic FM Hall of Fame (2011), Everything You Ever Wanted To Know About Classical Music...But Were Too Afraid To Ask (2012), The Classic FM Quiz Book (2012), The Big Book of Classic FM (2014), 50 Moments that Rocked the Classical Music World (2014), Charting the Classics (2014), The Virtuous Circle: Why Creative and Cultural Education Matter (2014), The Classic FM Handy Guide to the Orchestra (2015), The Classic FM Handy Guide to Everything You Ever Wanted to Know About Classical Music (2015), The Arts Dividend: Why Investment in Culture Pays (2016); *Recreations* horse racing, classical music, food, train travel, arts and culture; *Clubs* Gillingham FC; *Style*— Darren Henley, Esq, OBE; ✉ Arts Council England, 21 Bloomsbury Street, London WC1B 3HF (☎ 08453 006200, e-mail chief.executive@artscouncil.org.uk)

HENLEY, Prof Jeremy Martin; s of Brian Henley, and Brenda Mavis Gillette, *née* Colley; *b* 10 September 1958, Worcester; *Educ* Queen Elizabeth's GS Hartlebury, Aston Univ (BSc), KCL (PhD); *m* 1984, Kathrine Jean, *née* Garvey; 2 s (Samuel Edward, Benjamin Seth), 1 da (Sophie Annabelle); *Career* Cornell Univ 1984–86, MRC Cambridge 1986–89, Univ of Birmingham 1990–94, Univ of Bristol 1995– (head Dept of Anatomy and asst dir MRC Centre for Synaptic Plasticity); sabbatical Kyoto Univ 1996; *Publications* over 180 peer-reviewed pubns in scientific jls, and ed and/or contrib to several academic books; *Recreations* building stone walls, reading, travel; *Style*— Prof Jeremy Henley; ✉ Department of Biochemistry, School of Medical Sciences, Bristol BS8 1TD (☎ 0117 954 6449, fax 0117 929 1687, e-mail j.m.henley@bris.ac.uk)

HENLEY, 8 Baron (I 1799); Oliver Michael Robert Eden; also (and sits as) Baron Northington (UK 1885); s of 7 Baron (d 1977) by his 2 w Nancy, da of late S Walton, of Gilsland, Cumbria; *b* 22 November 1953; *Educ* Clifton, Univ of Durham; *m* 11 Oct 1984, Caroline Patricia, da of late A G Sharp, of Mackney, Oxon; 3 s (Hon John Michael Oliver b 30 June 1988, Hon Patrick Francis b 23 Nov 1993, Hon Edward Andrew b 16 July 1996), 1 da (Hon Elizabeth Caroline b 26 Feb 1991); *Heir* s, Hon John Eden; *Career* sits as Cons in House of Lords; called to the Bar Middle Temple 1977; memb Cumbria CC 1986–89, chm Penrith and The Border Cons Assoc 1987–89 (pres 1989–94); Lord in Waiting 1989; Parly under sec of state: Dept of Social Security 1989–93, Dept of Employment 1993–94, MOD 1994–95; min of state Dept for Education and Employment 1995–97, oppn spokesman on home affrs House of Lords 1997–98, oppn chief whip House of Lords 1998–2001, Parly under-sec of state Dept for Environment, Food and Rural Affrs 2010–11, min of state Home Office 2011–12; *Clubs* Brooks's, Pratt's, Northern Counties (Newcastle); *Style*— The Rt Hon the Lord Henley; ✉ Scaleby Castle, Carlisle, Cumbria CA6 4LN

HENLEY, Peter; *b* 28 November 1964, London; *Educ* Dauntsey's Sch Wilts, Univ of Leicester (BA), Falmouth Sch of Art (MA); *m* 27 Aug 1988, Samantha Jane, *née* Reed; 3 s (Ben b 19 Oct 1991, Harry b 3 Sept 1993, Toby b 2 Nov 1996); *Career* political corr; formerly: BBC Radio Leicester, reporter and newsreader Pennine Radio, Radio 210 Reading, reporter Television South, political corr Meridian until 2001; health corr then political ed BBC South 2001–; Medical Journalism Assoc Broadcast Journalist 2003, Journalist of the Year RTS South 2010; *Clubs* Waterside Archers, Ashlett, Ashlett Sailing; *Style*— Peter Henley, Esq; ✉ website www.bbc.co.uk/peterhenley, Twitter @BBCPeterH

HENMAN, Tim; OBE (2004); *b* 6 September 1974; *m* Lucy; 2 da (Rose Elizabeth b 2002, Olivia Susan b 2004); *Career* tennis player; turned professional 1993, highest ATP Tour ranking no 4 in the world 2004; semi-finalist: Wimbledon Championships 1998, 1999 and 2001, French Open 2004, US Open 2004; Silver medal men's doubles (with Neil Broad) Olympic Games Atlanta 1996; winner: Br Nat Championships 1995, 1996 and 1997, (singles and doubles) Seoul ATP Challenger 1995, Reunion ATP Challenger 1995, Sydney Int ATP Tour Event 1997, President's Cup Tashkent 1997 and 1998, Swiss Indoor Championships Basle 1998, CA Trophy Vienna 2000, Samsung Open Brighton 2000, Copenhagen Open 2001, Australian Hardcourt Championships Adelaide 2002, Legg Mason Classic Washington 2003, BNP Paribas Masters Paris 2003; memb Br Davis Cup Team 1995–2007; ret 2007; voted 2nd in BBC Sports Personality of the Year 1997; *Style*— Tim Henman, Esq, OBE; ✉ c/o IMG, The Pier House, Strand on the Green, Chiswick, London W4 3NN (☎ 020 8233 5000)

HENNESSY OF NYMPSFIELD, Baron (UK Life Peer 2010), of Nympsfield in the County of Gloucestershire; Prof Peter John Hennessey; s of William Gerald Hennessy (d 2001), and Edith, *née* Wood-Johnson (d 1986); *b* 28 March 1947; *Educ* Marling Sch Stroud, St John's Coll Cambridge (BA, PhD), LSE, Harvard Univ; *m* 14 June 1969, Enid Mary, *née* Candler; 2 da (Cecily b 1976, Polly b 1979); *Career* lobby corr Financial Times 1976, reporter Br Section The Economist 1982; The Times: reporter Higher Educn Supplement 1972–74, reporter 1974–76, Whitehall corr 1976–82, ldr writer 1982–84; columnist: New Statesman 1986–87, Whitehall Watch The Independent 1987–91, Director Magazine 1989–93; presenter Analysis BBC Radio Four 1986–92; dir and columnist The Tablet 2003–; co fndr and co dir Inst of Contemporary Br History 1986–89 (memb Bd 1989–98, hon fell 1995–2003), ptnr Intellectual R&D 1990–, prof of contemporary history Queen Mary & Westfield Coll London 1992–2000, Gresham prof of rhetoric Gresham Coll 1994–97 (fell 1997–), Attlee prof of contemporary British history Queen Mary Univ of London 2001–; visiting prof of govt Univ of Strathclyde 1989–, visiting scholar Griffith Univ Brisbane 1991; memb Cncl Policy Studies Inst 1992–97; visiting fell: Policy Studies Inst 1986–92, Dept of Politics Univ of Reading 1988–94, Politics Dept Univ of Nottingham 1989–94, RIPA 1989–92; hon res fell Birkbeck Coll London 1990–91; chair Advsy Ctee Inst of Contemporary British History 2001–03, memb Advsy Ctee Sharman Inquiry into Parly Audit and Accountability 2000–01; govr Ditchley Fndn 2001–, chm Kennedy Meml Tst 1995–2000, tstee Attlee Fndn 1986–98, tstee Geffrye Museum 2001–; Hon DLitt: UWE 1995, Univ of Westminster 1996, Kingston Univ 1998; hon fell LSE 2000; FRSA 1992, FRHistS 1993 (vice-pres 1996–2000), FBA 2003; *Books* States of Emergency (jtly, 1983), Sources Close to the Prime Minister (jtly, 1984), What the Papers Never Said (1985), Cabinet (1986), Ruling Performance (jt ed, 1987), Whitehall (1989), Never Again – Britain 1945–51 (1992, Duff Cooper prize 1993, NCR award for non-fiction 1993), The Hidden Wiring – Unearthing the British Constitution (1995), Muddling Through – Power, Politics and the Quality of Government in Post War Britain (1996), The Prime Minister: The Office and its Holders Since 1945 (2000), The Secret State: Whitehall and the Cold War (2002); *Recreations* watching West Ham, listening to music; *Clubs* Savile, Attlee Meml Runners; *Style*— The Lord Hennessy of Nympsfield; ✉ Department of History, Queen Mary, University of London, Mile End Road, London E1 4NS (☎ 020 7882 5016)

HENNEY, Dr Jane; *Career* non-exec dir AstraZeneca plc; *Style*— Dr Jane Henney

HENNING, Matthew Clive Cunningham; s of Matthew Henning (d 1982), of Co Londonderry, and Olivia Mary, *née* Cunningham (d 1990); *b* 4 January 1934; *Educ* St Andrew's Coll Dublin, Coll of Architecture Oxford (DipArch); *m* 27 Sept 1972, Vivien Margaret, da of David Ernest Walker (d 1971), of Armagh; 1 s (Daniel Clive Walker b 1978), 1 da (Kate Louise b 1982); *Career* conslt architect in private practice; princ architect for the Southern Educn and Library Bd 1966–78; ARIBA, MRIAI, MRSUA (memb Royal Soc of Ulster Architects); *Recreations* Golf; *Clubs* Bushfoot Golf; *Style*— Matthew C C Henning, Esq; ✉ Carraboo, Upper Church Lane, Portadown, Craigavon, Co Armagh BT63 5JE (☎ 028 3833 3066); Clive Henning Architects, Savoy Building, 16 West Street, Portadown, Co Armagh BT62 3PD (☎ 028 3833 8811, e-mail architecture@charc.co.uk)

HENRY, Anthony Patrick Joseph; s of Patrick Joseph Henry (d 1944), of Nottingham, and Helen Alethea, *née* Green; *b* 19 April 1939; *Educ* Epsom Coll Surrey, St Thomas' Hosp Med Sch London (MB BS); *m* 1973, Patricia Mary, da of Kenneth Spiby, of Packington, nr Ashby De La Zouch, Leics; 2 s (Joseph Patrick b 1974, George Michael b 1981), 1 da (Sarah Louise b 1977); *Career* TA Artists Rifles 21 SAS 1959–61; lectr in anatomy Univ of Alberta Canada 1966–67, res in surgery Durban South Africa 1968–70, sr registrar in orthopaedics Nottingham 1972–76, conslt orthopaedic surgn Derby 1976–2015; lectr in anatomy Derby Sch of Occupational Therapy 1974–88; examiner in surgery Br Assoc of Occupational Therapists 1976–88, pres Naughton-Dunn Club (orthopaedic club of the Midlands) 1993–94, pres Br Orthopaedic Foot Surgery Soc 1998; memb Int Ed Bd Foot and Ankle Surgery 1996–; govr St Wynstans Sch Repton 1980–86; memb BMA 1963; author of numerous papers in orthopaedic jls; FRCS 1971, FBOA 1976 (memb Cncl 2000–03); *Recreations* sailing, tennis, cricket; *Style*— Anthony Henry, Esq; ✉ Four Winds, Wagon Lane, Bretby, Derbyshire DE15 0QF (☎ 01283 217358)

HENRY, Clare; *née* Jenkinson; da of Walter Price Jenkinson (d 1989), and Marjorie Amy, *née* Bratley (d 1997); *b* 21 February 1942; *Educ* Queen Elizabeth GS, Univ of Reading (BA); *Children* 1 s (Damian b 25 Dec 1969), 1 da (Zara b 29 Nov 1976); m, 2 Mar 2002, Phillip A Bruno, of New York; *Career* researcher Paul Mellon Fndn of Br Art 1968–70, art critic The Herald 1980–2000, art critic FT NY 2000–, ed-at-large State of Art USA 2005–; Scot ed: Artline 1984–90, Arts Review 1984–93, Scottish TV 1984–87; arts contrib: Sculpture Magazine 1999–, ARTNews 1999–, The Scotsman 2000–, Photoicon 2008, The Herald, The Art Newspaper and BBC radio and TV; contrib to various magazines and exhbn catalogues incl: Victoria Crowe 1999, Hugh O'Donnell 203, Patricia Leighton 2004, RT Houben 2005, Julie Spiedel 2006, Polly Hope 2007, John Cunningham 2010, Adrian Wiszniewski 2010; exhbn curator: New Scottish Prints (NY) 1983, London's Serpentine Summer Show 1985, Artists at Work (Edinburgh Festival) 1986, The Vigorous Imagination (Nat Gallery of Scot, Edinburgh Festival) 1987, Scotland at the Venice Biennale 1990, Critics Choice London 1992, Critics Choice Glasgow 1994, Glasgow Sch of Art Choice 1994, Illinois Women Artists Nat Museum of Women Washington 2000, Illinois Millennium Artists 2004; tstee Scot Sculpture Tst 1986–89; memb: Glasgow Print Studio 1973–80 (also chm), NUJ, AICA, Visiting Arts Br Cncl; fndr memb: SALVO, Glasgow Print Studio; FRSA; *Publications* Francis d'Haene, architect (2010); *Clubs* Chelsea Arts; *Style*— Clare Henry; ✉ Sculpture Magazine (e-mail isc@sculpture.org); website http://clarehenry-artjournal.blogspot.com

HENRY, Hugh; MSP; *b* 12 February 1952, Glasgow; *Educ* St Mirin's Acad Paisley, Univ of Glasgow (BAcc), Jordanhill Coll of Educn Glasgow; *m* ; 2 da, 1 s; *Career* Strathclyde Regnl Cncl: teacher Educn Dept 1976–79, welfare rights offr then sr welfare rights offr Social Work Dept 1979–93; community care mangr Community Enterprise Strathclyde 1993–96; MSP (Lab): Paisley South 1999–2011, Renfrewshire S 2011–; Scot Parl dep min for health and community care 2001–02, dep min for justice 2002–06, min for educn and young people 2006–07; *Style*— Hugh Henry, Esq, MSP; ✉ The Scottish Parliament, Edinburgh EH99 1SP

HENRY, Julie; da of Mrs A M Hood, of Cambridge; *b* 1959, Cambridge; *Educ* N Herts Coll, London Coll of Fashion, Mornington Centre Art Fndn, Central St Martins Sch of Art (BA); *Partner* Jim Chynoweth; 1 da (Emma); *Career* artist; *Solo Exhibitions* Anthony Wilkinson Gallery London 2000 and 2003, Impressions Gallery York 2002, BCA Gallery Bedford 2003, Millais Gallery Southampton 2004, Metroploe Gallery Folkstone 2004, Northern Gallery Sunderland 2004, Presentation Gallery Vancouver 2005, Great Eastern Hotel London 2006; *Group Exhibitions* Six British Artists (Ars Locus Gallery Tokyo)) 1996, Zone Multi-media Festival (Maidstone Kent) 1996, Arts Alive Festival (Dorking) 1997, WorldCup 98, The Final (London Printworks Tst) 1998, Volcano Festival (The Oval House London) 1998, Going Down (Croydon Clocktower 1998, Edinburgh City Gallery 1999, Oldham Museum and Gallery 2000, Dynamo Kiev 2001), My Eyes My Eyes (Milch Gallery London, The Silo Greenwich) 1998, New Contemporaries 99 (South London Gallery, Exchange Flags Liverpool) 1999, The Fantastic Recurrence of Certain Situations: Recent British Art and Photography (Sala de Exposiciones del Canal de Isabel II Madrid) 2001, Record Collection (VTO Gallery London) 2001, Sport in der zeitgenossischen Kunst (Kunsthalle Nurnberg) 2001, Tirana Biennale (Tirana Nat Gallery) 2001, Predator (KX auf Kampnagel Hamburg) 2001, Sense of Wonder (Herzliya Museum of Art Israel) 2001, Cornerhouse Gallery Manchester 2002, Galeria Arsenal Blalystok Poland 2002, Velan Centre for Contemporary Arts Torino 2002, Intervention (John Hansard Gallery Southampton) 2003, Strangers (Int Centre of Photography) 2003, Somewhere Better Than This Place (Contemporary Arts Centre Cincinnati) 2003, Sport in Art (The Israel Museum Jeruslaem, Contemporary Arts Centre Cincinnati) 2004, Brittania Works (Br Cncl Athens) 2004, Going Down (John Hansard Gallery Southampton) 2004, Divine Heroes (Minoritten Galerien Graz) 2004, Belgrade Biennale (Galerija Zvomo) 2004, Ready Steady Go (Three Colts Gallery London) 2004, Only a Game (Impressions Gallery York) 2004, Upon Further Review (Hunters Gallery NY) 2005, Star Star (Contemporary Arts Center Cincinnati) 2005, Episode (Temporary Contemporary London) 2005, Celebrations (Pumphouse Gallery London) 2005, Rundlederwelten (Martin Gropius Bau Berlin) 2005, X (Millais Gallery Southampton) 2006, You'll Never Walk Alone (OK Centre for Contemporary Art Austia) 2006, The Beautiful Game: Contemporary ARt and Fùtbol (Brooklyn Inst of Contemporary Art) 2006, Human Game (Stazione Leopolda Florence) 2006; *Publications* Dyed In The Wool: Julie Hendry (2004); *Recreations* Liverpool FC supporter, keen breakdancer; *Style*— Ms Julie Henry; ✉ c/o Anthony Wilkinson Gallery, 242 Cambridge Heath Road, London E2 9DA (☎ 020 8980 2662, fax 020 8980 0028, website www.anthonywilkinsongallery.co.uk)

HENRY, Keith Nicholas; s of Kenneth George Henry (d 1999), and Barbara, *née* Benns (d 1989); *b* 3 March 1945; *Educ* Bedford Sch, Univ of London (BSc), Univ of Birmingham (MSc); *m* 1974, Susan Mary, da of Roy Horsburgh; 2 da (Lucy Elizabeth b 1976, Claire Susanne b 1978); *Career* engr mangr Brown & Root de France SA 1975–77, md Far East area Brown & Root (Singapore) Ltd 1977–80; Brown & Root (UK) Ltd: sr mangr 1980–83, chief engr 1983–85, commercial dir 1985–87; md Brown & Root Vickers Ltd 1987–89, pres Brown & Root Marine 1989–90; chief exec: Brown & Root Ltd 1990–95, National Power plc 1995–99, Kvaerner E&C plc 2000–03; chm: Burren Energy plc 2006–08 (non-exec dir 2005–08), Petrojarl ASA 2006, Regal Petroleum plc 2008–, Mediterranean Oil & Gas plc 2012–14, Greenko Gp plc 2012–; dep chm PGS ASA 2003–06; non-exec dir: Enterprise Oil plc 1995–2002, Emerald Energy plc 2004–09, South-East Water Ltd 2005–07, High Point Rendel Hldgs Ltd 2006–15, First Calgary Petroleums Ltd 2007–08, Reynolds Partners Ltd 2007–10, Aegis Defence Services Ltd 2007–10, Sterling Energy plc 2009–, KSK Power Ventur plc 2014–; memb Cncl on Science and Technol 1990–96, memb Cncl DERA 1992–2001, memb Cncl Royal Acad of Engrg 1998–2001; FREng, FICE; *Recreations* shooting; *Clubs* RAC; *Style*— Keith Henry, Esq, FREng; ✉ e-mail keithhenry@btinternet.com

HENRY, Sir Lenny; kt (2015), CBE (1999); *b* 29 August 1958; *m* (m dis 2010), Dawn French; *Career* comedian and actor; numerous tours incl Loud! 1994, Australia 1995, Large! (Aust) 1998, Large'99 (UK) 1999, Have You Seen This Man (UK) 2001, So Much Things to Say (UK, Aust and NZ) 2003–04, Where You From? (UK) 2007; Monaco Red Cross Award, TRIC Award for BBC Personality of the Year 1993, Inspiration Award BFM Awards 2002, Lifetime Achievement Award (Performance) British Comedy Awards 2003, Lifetime Achievement Award Black Entertainment Comedy Awards 2003; *Television* incl: New Faces (debut), Tiswas, Three of a Kind (BBC) 1981–83, The Lenny Henry Show, Alive and Kicking (BBC) 1991 (Golden Nymph Award), Bernard & the Genie (BBC) 1991, In Dreams (BBC) 1992, The Real McCoy (BBC) 1992, Gareth Blackstock in Chef (3 series, BBC), Lenny Hunts the Funk (South Bank Special), New Soul Nation (Channel 4), White Goods (ITV) 1994, Funky Black Shorts 1994, The Lenny Henry Show (BBC) 1995, Comic Relief 1996–, Lenny Go Home (Channel 4) 1996, host The British Academy Awards 1997, Lenny's Big Amazon Adventure (BBC) 1997, Lenny Goes to Town (BBC) 1998, Ian George in Hope & Glory (BBC) 1999–2000, The Man 1999, Lenny Henry in Pieces Christmas Special 2000, Lenny's Atlantic Adventure (BBC 1) 2000, Goodbye Mr Steadman Roy (ITV) 2001, Lenny Henry in Pieces Special 2001 (Golden Rose of Montreux 2001), Lenny Henry in Pieces (series) 2002 and 2003, Little Robots (BBC) 2003, Lenny Henry: This is My Life (BBC) 2003, The Lenny Henry Show (BBC 1) 2004–05, Lenny Henry's Comedy Heroes (Channel 5) 2005, Lenny's Perfect Night In (Channel 4) 2007, Lenny's Britain (BBC 1) 2007, Lennyhenry.tv (BBC1) 2006 and 2008; *Films* incl: True Identity 1991, Harry Potter and the Prisoner of Azkaban 2004, Penelope 2006, The Pirates! In an Adventure with Scientists! 2012; *Video* Lenny Henry Live and Unleashed 1989, Lenny Henry Live and Loud 1994; *Radio* presenter: Talking Comedy (BBC Radio 2) 2004, Lenny and Will (BBC Radio 4) 2006; *Theatre* Othello 2009 (Outstanding Newcomer Evening Standard Theatre Award 2009), Comedy of Errors (NT) 2011; *Books* The Quest for the Big Woof (1991), Charlie and the Big Chill (children's book, 1995); *Style*— Sir Lenny Henry, CBE; ✉ c/o PBJ and JBJ Management, 22 Rathbone Street, London W1T 1LA (☎ 020 7287 1112, fax 020 7287 1191, e-mail general@pbjmgt.co.uk); website www.lennyhenry.com

HENRY, Richard Charles; TD (1976); s of John Richard Henry, OBE, JP (d 1993), and Blanche Catherine, *née* Barrett; *b* 26 February 1941; *Educ* Sherborne; *m* 15 April 1976, Judy Ann Massey; 1 s (Charles b 1977), 3 da (Belinda b 1979, Jane b 1979, Margaret b 1983); *Career* articled Deloittes 1960; fin dir and sec Press Association 1984–96 (tstee pension fund 2010–), gp fin dir Nation Media Gp 1996–2004, gp fin dir Credit Reference Bureau 2004–07; Capt HAC (TA) 1961–76; memb Ct of Assts HAC 1975–96 (treas 1990–93, vice-pres 1994–96); steward Jockey Club of Kenya 1998–2007; memb Bd Kenya Hosp Assoc 1999–2005; Freeman City of London 1986, Liveryman Worshipful Co of Barbers 1989; FCA 1966; *Recreations* racing, bridge, fishing; *Clubs* Army and Navy, Muthaiga; *Style—* Richard Henry, Esq, TD; ✉ Bailiff's Farm House, Ibworth, Hampshire RG26 5TJ

HENRY, Stephen James Bartholomew (Steve); s of John Keith Maxwell Henry (d 1979), and Jose Isobel Prendergast, *née* Bartholomew (d 1975); *b* 21 September 1955; *Educ* Cranleigh Sch, St Catherine's Coll Oxford (BA, Shelley-Mills prize); *m* 18 Oct 1986, Angela Marie, da of Michael Coates; 2 da (Sophia Dominique Marie b 19 Nov 1989, Bryony Christabel b 24 Dec 1992); *Career* copywriter: Crawfords 1979–81, Gold Greenlees Trott 1981–85; copywriter and creative gp head Wight Collins Rutherford Scott 1985–87, fndr and creative ptnr HHCL and Partners (formerly Howell Henry Chaldecott Lury) 1987–2004, chm HHCL/Red Cell 2004–06, exec creative dir TBWA/London 2006–; agency of year Campaign magazine 1989 and 1993, agency of the decade Campaign magazine 2000, winner of awards for various advertising campaigns; FIPA; *Recreations* swimming, reading, writing, being with my daughters; *Style—* Steve Henry, Esq; ✉ HHCL/Red Cell, Kent House, 14–17 Market Place, Great Titchfield Street, London W1N 7AJ (☎ 020 7436 3333, fax 020 7436 2677)

HENSHALL, John Mark; s of John Henshall (d 1996), of Stockport, and Margaret Winifred, *née* Passmore (d 1989); *b* 6 January 1942; *Educ* Queen Elizabeth GS Wakefield, Stockport GS; *m* 21 Sept 1979 (m dis 2003), Paulien, da of Dr Pieter Roorda (d 1991), of Haarlem, Netherlands, and Jeanette Pauline, *née* Volkmaars; 2 da (Annelies b 11 Jan 1981, Martien b 13 July 1984), 1 s (John Pieter b 12 May 1987); *Career* BBC cameraman and lighting 1961–76; dir of photography and lighting in film and TV 1978–, dir Electronic Photo-Imaging 1993–; conslt, writer and lectr on digital imaging – photography without film 1991–, professional photographer; Guild of TV Cameramen: vice-chm 1974–78 and 2008–11, hon life memb 1978, hon fell 1984, hon vice-pres 2011–; memb Ctee Soc of Tv Lighting Dirs 1986–93, memb Cncl RPS 1988–94, chm Film and Video Associateship and Fellowship Distinctions Ctee 1992–2008, memb Applied and Professional Distinctions Ctee 2006–11; BIPP: chm Admissions and Qualifications in motion picture, TV, video and electronic imaging, memb Cncl 1986–94, pres 1991–92; Br Imaging and Photographic Assoc: memb Cncl 1991–97, chm Digital Imaging Ctee 1993–98; pres Guild of Television Cameramen 2015–; Hon MA Univ for the Creative Arts 2009; FRGS 1967, FRPS 1985, FBIPP 1985, fell Br Professional Photographer Assocs (FBPPA) 2005; *Books* Dealers in Coins (1969), Sir H George Fordham, Cartobibliographer (1969), Photographic Qualifications for Professionals (1992 and 1997), Wedding and Portrait Photography (co-author, 2003); ed Digital Imaging Plus; contributing ed digital imaging The Photographer; author of numerous articles on digital imaging, photography, film and TV; *Recreations* freelance philosopher; *Style—* John Henshall; ✉ 6 Divinity Close, Wanborough, Swindon, Wiltshire SN4 0EH (☎ 01793 790333, website tinyurl.com/jhalamy)

HENSHALL, Keith Rodney; s of Bernard Henry Henshall, and Doris Lilian Henshall, of London; *b* 15 August 1947; *Educ* Henry Thornton Sch London, Univ of Manchester (LLB, MBA); *m* 9 Dec 1967, Maureen, da of George Pascoe; 1 s (Carl Matthew b 10 July 1968), 1 da (Sharon Marie b 9 Sept 1970); *Career* md Charles Barker Public Relations Ltd 1985–88; chm: The Henshall Centre Ltd 1988–, Cutting Edge Software Ltd 1988–, One Clear Voice Ltd 1997–; IPR: memb Nat Cncl 1984–89, nat educn chm 1988 and 1989, pres-elect 1994, pres 1995; founding external examiner to PR degrees Bournemouth and Stirling Univs, fndr chm Professional Advsy Ctee to PR masters degree Manchester Metropolitan Univ; MIPR 1984, FInstD 1986; *Recreations* basketball; *Style—* Keith Henshall, Esq

HENSHALL, Ruthie; da of David Henshall, of Stutton, Suffolk, and Gloria Diana Mary, *née* Wilson; *b* 7 March 1967; *Educ* Bullerswood GS Chislehurst, Laine Theatre Arts Coll Epsom; *Career* actress and singer; Theatregoers Award for Most Popular Musical Actress of the Last 21 Years; FRSA; *Theatre* work incl: Mitzi in the Pied Piper of Hamlyn (Churchill Theatre Bromley) 1985, Ethel Dobbs in Fainettes (Bromley) 1985, lead role in Celluloid City, Dandini in Cinderella (Aldershot) 1986, Maggie in A Chorus Line (nat tour) 1987, Jemima/Demeter/Grizabella/Griddlebone in Cats (New London Theatre) 1987–89, Ellen in Miss Saigon (Theatre Royal London) 1989–90, Aphra in Children of Eden (The Prince Edward Theatre) 1990–91, season at Chichester Festival Theatre 1991 and 1997, Ellen in Miss Saigon (NY) 2001; singer and dancer: Mack and Mabel (charity performance for Theatre Royal), Fantine in Les Miserables, Polly Baker in Crazy for You (Prince Edward) 1993 (Olivier nomination for Best Actress in a Musical), Amalia Balash in She Loves Me (Savoy Theatre) 1995 (Olivier Award for Best Actress in a Musical), Nancy in Oliver! (London Palladium) 1996, Polly in Divorce Me Darling (Chichester Festival Theatre) 1997, Roxie Hart in Chicago (Adelphi Theatre) 1997 (Olivier nomination for Best Actress in a Musical), Zigfield Follies 1936 (New York City Centre), Velma Kelly in Chicago (Shubert Theatre NY) 1999, Putting it Together (NY) 1999, Peggy Sue in Peggy Sue Got Married (Shaftesbury Theatre) 2001 (Olivier nomination for Best Actress in a Musical), Velma Kelly in Chicago (West End) 2003, The Woman in White (Palace Theatre) 2005, The Other Woman (Ensemble Studio Theatre NYC); other credits incl: singer in Andrew Lloyd Webber's concert in Spain for Expo 92, Ruthie Henshall in Concert (Royal Festival Hall), opening solo performance Olivier Awards 1994, solo concert Crazy for Musicals (nat tour) 1997, solo appearance Hey Mr Producer! (tribute to Cameron Mackintosh, Lyceum Theatre) 1998; *Television* Law and Order 2000, Mysteries of 71st Street 2000, The Sound of Musicals (BBC 1); *Recordings* original London cast albums of: Miss Saigon (also sang role of Ellen on int recording), Children of Eden, Crazy for You, She Loves Me, Chicago, Fantine in 10th anniversary concert of Les Miserables (Royal Albert Hall) 1996 (also on video); solo albums: Love is Here to Stay, Ruthie Henshall Sings Gershwin, The Ruthie Henshall Album, Pilgrim; *Style—* Ms Ruthie Henshall

HENSHALL, (Alastair) Scott; s of Nigel Henshall, and Mavis *née* Smith; *b* 15 November 1975, York; *Educ* Scorton Boys Sch, Richmond Assumption Sch, Univ of Northumbria (BA, British Fashion Cncl Best Womenswear Award 1997); *Career* Scott Henshall main line 1998–, Revisitation by Scott Henshall Japan 1999–, creative dir Mulberry 2000–02, Core Jeans by Scott Henshall 2006–; Vidal Sassoon London Fashion Week Award for cutting edge talent 2001; ambass: Prince's Tst 2002–, Happy Hearts Fndn 2005–; *Recreations* travelling, painting, living life to the full; *Style—* Scott Henshall, Esq

HENSHER, Robert; s of Walter Hensher, and Elsie Alice *née* Wright; *b* 26 August 1948, London; *Educ* Newham Coll, Univ of Liverpool (Henry Briggs Gold Medal, BDS, MB ChB); *m* 1987, Judy, *née* Candy; 1 s (Charles b 17 July 1993); *Career* registrar Westminster Hosp 1981–83, employed at Charity Hosp New Orleans; sr registrar 1984–86: UCH, Gt Ormond St Hosp, ZMK Clinic Münster, conslt Cheltenham and Gloucester hosps 1986–2000, currently conslt maxillo-facial surgn King Edward VII Hosp (pioneering TMJ (jaw) joint surgery, especially prosthetic replacement, practice includes dental implantology and facial osteotomy (orthognathic) surgery); conslt British Assoc for Performing Arts Med; memb American Soc of Temporomandibular Joint Surgns 1988; FDSRCS 1981, FRCS 1985; *Publications* various papers in jls, 2 chapters in Operative Maxillofacial Surgery (2 vols); *Recreations* music, historic car restoration, equestrianism; *Clubs* Savage, Garrick; *Style—* Robert Hensher, Esq; ✉ King Edward VII Hospital for Officers, Beaumont Street, London W1G 6AA (☎ 020 7467 3232, e-mail oralsurgeon@kingedwardvii.co.uk or roberthensher@aol.com, website www.roberthensher.org)

HENSON, Her Hon Judge Christine Ruth; QC (2015); *Educ* Univ of Warwick (BA); *Career* called to the Bar (Middle Temple) 1994; recorder Crown Court 2013, circuit judge (South Eastern Circuit) 2015–; *Style—* Her Hon Judge Henson, QC

HENSON, Michael Brian; s of Patrick Henson (d 2005), and Irene Henson; *b* 3 May 1961; *Educ* Collyers Sch Horsham, Univ of Sheffield (BMus), Univ of Leicester (MPhil), scholarship to study in Vienna; *m* 1993, Helen; 2 s (Luke, Zachary), 1 da (Corinne); *Career* research fell Huddersfield Poly 1985–88, educn and community dir Bournemouth Orchestras 1988–92, chief exec Ulster Orch 1992–99, md and ceo Bournemouth Symphony Orchestra 1999–2008, pres and ceo Minnesota Orchestral Assoc 2008–; memb: Bd of Sonorities Contemporary Music Festival of Ireland 1995–99, Bd of Assoc of British Orchestras 1999–2007 (chair 2004–07); govr Arts Inst of Bournemouth 2003–08; *Books* Musical Awareness (with G Pratt), Proceedings of Musical Awareness (ed); also author of 20 articles; *Clubs* Minneapolis, Woodhill; *Style—* Michael Henson, Esq; ✉ Minnesota Orchestra, Orchestra Hall, 1111 Nicollet Mall, Minneapolis, MN 55403, USA (website www.minnesotaorchestra.org)

HENSON, Nicholas Victor Leslie (Nicky); s of Leslie Lincoln Henson, and Billie Dell, *née* Collins; *b* 12 May 1945; *Educ* St Bede's Eastbourne, Charterhouse, RADA; *m* 1, 1968 (m dis 1975), Una Stubbs; 2 s (Christian b 25 Dec 1971, Joe b 18 Sept 1973); m 2, 1 Aug 1986, Marguerite Ann Porter, *qv*; 1 s (Keaton b 24 March 1988); *Career* actor; former popular song writer incl 3 year writing contract with The Shadows and Cliff Richard, fndr memb Young Vic Co 1970; *Theatre* incl: All Square (Vaudeville) 1963, Camelot (Drury Lane) 1964, Passion Flower Hotel (Prince of Wales) 1965, London Laughs (Palladium) 1966, Canterbury Tales (Phoenix) 1968, The Ride Across Lake Constance (Hampstead and Mayfair) 1973, Hamlet (Greenwich) 1973, Mind Your Head (Shaw) 1973, A Midsummer Night's Dream (Open Air) 1973, Taming of the Shrew (Shaw) 1973, Cinderella (Casino) 1973, Mardi Gras (Prince of Wales) 1976, Rookery Nook (Her Majesty's) 1979, Noises Off (Lyric and Savoy) 1982, The Relapse (Lyric) 1983, Sufficient Carbohydrate (Hampstead and Albery) 1983, Journeys End (Whitehall) 1988, Ivanov (Strand) 1989, Much Ado About Nothing (Strand) 1989, Three Sisters (Royal Court) 1990, Reflected Glory (Vaudeville) 1992, An Ideal Husband (Globe, Broadway and Australia) 1993, Rage (Bush) 1994, Enter the Guardsman (Donmar) 1997, Alarms and Excursions (Gielgud) 1998, Passion Play (Donmar at Comedy) 2000, Frame 312 (Donmar) 2002, Jumpers (Piccadilly London and Broadway NY) 2004; Young Vic incl: Waiting for Godot, Scapino, The Soldier's Tale, She Stoops to Conquer, Measure for Measure, Oedipus, Wakefield Nativity Plays, Romeo and Juliet, The Maids, Deathwatch, Look Back in Anger, Rosencrantz and Guildenstern are Dead, Charley's Aunt; NT incl: The Cherry Orchard, Macbeth, The Woman, The Double Dealer, A Fair Quarrel, The Browning Version, Harlequinade, The Provok'd Wife, The Elephant Man, Mandragola, Long Time Gone; RSC incl: Man and Superman 1977, As You Like It 1985–86, The Merry Wives of Windsor 1985–86, Twelfth Night 2005; *Television* incl: A Midsummer Night's Dream, Absurd Person Singular, Seasons Greetings, Love After Lunch, Thin Air, Startrap 1988, Inspector Morse 1988, Boon 1989, After Henry 1990, The Upper Hand 1990, The Green Man 1990, The Healer 1994, Preston Front 1994, Shine On Harvey Moon 1994, Blue Dove 2001, NCS Manhunt 2002, Downton Abbey 2010; *Film* appearances in over 30 incl: There's A Girl in My Soup, Witch Finder General, Tom Jones, Number One of The Street Service, Vera Drake, Syriana, Blitz; *Recreations* snooker; *Style—* Nicky Henson, Esq; ✉ c/o Richard Stone Partnership, Suite 3, De Walden Court, 85 New Cavendish Street, London W1W 6XD (☎ 020 7497 0849, fax 020 7497 0869)

HENWOOD, John Philip; MBE (1998); s of Snowdon William Henwood (d 1980), and Amy Doris, *née* Stickley (d 1979); *b* 27 August 1945, Jersey; *Educ* St Lawrence Sch Jersey, Victoria Coll Jersey; *Career* Channel Television: joined as trainee 1962, rising to chief exec 1987, ret 2000; chm: Byerley Ltd 1999–, Jersey Telecom Ltd 2002–09, G4S Secure Solutions (Jersey) Ltd 2010–, Visit Jersey Ltd 2014–; dir: Jersey Finance Ltd 2001–09 (dep chm), Flying Brands Ltd 2007–12, Kleinwort Benson Channel Islands Hldgs, Kleinwort Benson Bank 2004–12, Bailiwick Investments Ltd 2009–, LFH Int Ltd 2009–; memb Horserace Writers' Assoc, past pres Jersey Race Club, past sr steward Channel Islands Racing & Hunt Club; pres Jersey CIM; tstee: Durrell Wildlife Conservation Tst 2006–12, St John Youth & Community Tst; MInstD (past pres Jersey Branch (chm 2001–02)); *Recreations* the turf and the thoroughbred, writing, skiing, travel; *Clubs* Channel Islands Racing and Hunt; *Style—* John Henwood, MBE; ✉ e-mail john.henwood@jerseymail.co.uk

HENWOOD, Roderick Waldemar Lisle (Rod); s of Noel Gordon Lisle Henwood (d 1972), and Daphne Muirhead, *née* Schroeder; *b* 29 November 1963; *Educ* Dollar Acad, Univ of Geneva, New Coll Oxford (BA); *m* 22 June 1996, Amanda Penelope, da of Michael Stacey, of Blakedown, Worcs; *Career* controller of prog business affrs Central Independent TV plc 1988–90; Central Broadcasting: dir of legal and business affrs 1990–93, dir of broadcasting 1993–94, md 1994–96; md Fox Kids 1997–99, fndr dir Prism Entertainment Ltd 1999–2001 (non-exec dir 2001–), dir of TV NTL 2001–02, chief exec PTV 2003–05, new business dir Channel 4 2005–14, CEO Zodiak UK 2014–; *Recreations* tennis, running; *Style—* Rod Henwood, Esq; ✉ Zodiak Media, Gloucester Building, Kensington Village, Avonmore Road, London W14 8RF

HEPBURN, James Douglas (Jamie); MSP; *b* 21 May 1979, Glasgow; *Educ* Hyndland Secdy Sch Glasgow, Univ of Glasgow (MA); *Career* front of house asst Citizen's Theatre Glasgow 2001–02, temp data processor Scottish Power 2002, research asst to Alex Neil, MSP, *qv*, 2002–07; MSP (SNP): Central Scotland 2007–11, Cumbernauld & Kilsyth 2011–; memb NUJ; *Style—* Jamie Hepburn, MSP

HEPBURN, Robin; *b* 1961; *Educ* Milton Abbey, Arnewood Sch, Brockenhurst Coll; *m* 1989, Emma; 2 s, 3 da; *Career* Barclays Bank plc 1979–88, Dewe Rogerson 1988–94, dir Shandwick Consultants 1994–96, chief exec Ludgate Communications 1996–2001, fndr Waughton 2002; memb Worshipful Co of Parish Clerks, Freeman City of London; ACIB, MIPR; *Recreations* piano, organ, flyfishing, shooting; *Clubs* Athenaeum; *Style—* Robin Hepburn, Esq

HEPBURN, Stephen; MP; s of late Peter Hepburn, and Margaret, *née* Pollock; *b* 6 December 1959; *Educ* Springfield Comp Jarrow, Univ of Newcastle upon Tyne (BA); *Career* dep ldr S Tyneside Cncl 1990–97 (cncllr 1985–97); MP (Lab) Jarrow 1997–, chair All-Pty Shipbuilding Shiprepair Gp, memb NI Affrs Select Ctee; chm Tyne & Wear Pensions Cmmn 1989–97; memb Union of Construction, Allied Trades and Technicians (UCATT); *Recreations* sport, music; *Clubs* Iona Catholic, Jarrovians RFC, Jarrow FC; *Style—* Stephen Hepburn, Esq, MP; ✉ House of Commons, London SW1A 0AA (☎ 020 7219 4134, fax 020 7219 1111)

HEPHER, Michael Leslie; s of Leslie Hepher, and Edna Hepher; *b* 17 January 1944; *Educ* Kingston GS; *m* 1, 1971 (m dis 2004), Janice Morton; 2 da (Kelly b 1973, Erin b 1975), 1 s (Daniel b 1980); m 2, 2006, Raissa Chtcherbakova; *Career* former chm and chief exec Lloyds Abbey Life plc, former dir Lloyds Bank, former pres and chief exec Maritime Life Assurance Co of Canada; gp md British Telecommunications plc until 1995, chm and chief exec Charterhouse plc 1996–98; non-exec chm TeleCity 2000–05, chm Lane, Clark and Peacock LLP 2003–05, non-exec chm Cardpoint plc 2005–06; non-exec dir: Kingfisher plc 1997–2010, Canada Life 1999–, Catlin Gp Ltd 2003–10, Great West Life

H

Co 2006–, Chartis (UK) 2010–12; memb Int Advsy Cncl CGI Gp 2004–08; Liveryman Worshipful Co of Actuaries; FIA, FCIA, ASA, FLIA; *Recreations* golf, reading; *Style*— Michael Hepher, Esq; ✉ 35 Piccadilly, London W1J 0DW (☎ 020 7734 3399, e-mail michael.hepher@btconnect.com)

HEPPLE, Prof Sir Bob Alexander; kt (2004), Hon QC (1996); s of Alexander Hepple (d 1983), of Canterbury, and Josephine, *née* Zwarenstein (d 1992); *b* 11 August 1934; *Educ* Univ of the Witwatersrand (BA, LLB), Univ of Cambridge (LLD, MA); *m* 1, 1960 (m dis 1993), Shirley Rona, da of Morris Goldsmith (d 1972), of London; 1 da (Brenda (Mrs Henson) *b* 7 July 1961), 1 s (Paul Alexander *b* 11 Dec 1962); *m* 2, 1994, Mary Coussey, da of Rev Stanley Dowding; *Career* practising attorney Johannesburg 1958, lectr in law Univ of the Witwatersrand 1959–62, practising advocate Johannesburg 1962–63, called to the Bar Gray's Inn 1966 (bencher 1996), practising barr 1972–2007; lectr in law Univ of Nottingham 1966–68, fell Clare Coll and lectr law Cambridge 1968–76, prof of comparative social and labour law Univ of Kent 1976–77, chm Industrial Tbnls England and Wales 1977–82 (pt/t chm 1974–77 and 1982–93); UCL: prof of English law 1982–93, dean Faculty of Laws and head Dept of Laws 1989–93; master Clare Coll Cambridge 1993–2003 (emeritus master 2003–), prof of law Univ of Cambridge 1995–2001 (emeritus prof 2001–); chm Univ of Cambridge: Local Exams Syndicate 1994–97, Septemviri 1995–98 and 2002–03, Cncl 1998–99; chm Managers Smuts Meml Fund 1994–2003; chair European Roma Rights Centre 2001–07, judge UN Administrative Tbnl 2007–09, chm Appointing Authy for Phase 1 Ethics Ctees 2007–09; memb: Cmmn for Racial Equality 1986–90, Tbnls Ctee Judicial Studies Bd 1988–93, Lord Chllr's Advsy Ctee on Legal Educn and Conduct 1994–99, Legal Services Consultative Panel 2000–01, Nuffield Cncl on Bioethics 2000–07 (chm 2003–07), Bd Int Centre for Protection of Human Rights 2005–07; chm Equal Rights Tst 2006–14; tstee Canon Collins Educnl Tst for South Africa 1990–2007; Leverhulme emeritus fell 2003–05, Nuffield Fndn New Career Devt Fellowship (with Dr J Browne) 2003–06, fell Stellenbosch Institute for Advanced Study 2011; Lifetime Achievement Award Labour Law Research Network 2013; Hon LLD: Univ of the Witwatersrand 1996, UCL 2005, Univ of Cape Town 2006, Università degli studi di Bari 2009, Univ of Kent 2015; hon prof Univ of Cape Town 1999–2005; FBA 2003; South African Order of Luthuli (Gold, for exceptional contribution to the struggle for democracy and human rights) 2014; *Publications* The Making of Labour Law in Europe (1986), Independent Review of Anti-Discrimination Legislation (with M Coussey, 2000), Labour Laws and Global Trade (2005), Rights at Work (Hamlyn Lectrs 2005), The Transformation of Labour Law in Europe (2009), Equality: the new legal framework (2011, 2 edn 2014), Young Man with a Red Tie: a memoir of Mandela and the Failed Revolution 1960–1963 (2013); numerous books and articles on labour law and industrial relations, race relations and discrimination and legal obligations in general; *Recreations* theatre, music, reading, walking, gardening; *Style*— Prof Sir Bob Hepple, QC, FBA; ✉ Clare College, Queens' Road, Cambridge CB3 9AJ (☎ 01223 333200)

HEPWORTH, David; s of Ernest Hepworth (d 1981), of Ossett, W Yorks, and Sarah Marjorie, *née* Rollinson; *b* 27 July 1950; *Educ* Queen Elizabeth GS Wakefield, Trent Park Coll of Educn Barnet (BEd); *m* 5 Sept 1979, Alyson, da of Ronald Elliott, of Hove, E Sussex; 2 da (Clare *b* 1982, Imogen *b* 1992), 1 s (Henry *b* 1987); *Career* freelance journalist 1975–79; presenter: The Old Grey Whistle Test (later just Whistle Test, BBC TV) 1980–86, BBC Radio GLR; ed: Smash Hits 1980–82, Just Seventeen 1983–85; editorial dir Emap Metro 1984–94, former editorial dir Emap Consumer Magazines (launched Q 1985, Empire 1988, Mojo 1997, Heat 1999), co-fndr Development Hell Ltd 2002 (launched Word magazine 2003); contrib Front Row BBC Radio 4; Periodical Publishers' Assoc: Ed of the Year 1985, Writer of the Year 1988; Mark Boxer Award British Soc of Magazine Editors 1993; *Books* The Secret History of Entertainment (2004); *Recreations* books, tennis, music; *Style*— David Hepworth, Esq; ✉ Development Hell Ltd, 90–92 Pentonville Road, London N1 9HS (☎ 020 7520 8625, e-mail mail@davidhepworth.com, website www.davidhepworth.com)

HERBERT, Rt Rev Christopher William; s of Walter Meredith Herbert, of Coleford, Glos, and Hilda Lucy, *née* Dibbin (d 1948); *b* 7 January 1944; *Educ* Monmouth, St David's UC Lampeter (BA, Badminton colours), Univ of Bristol (PGCE), Wells Theological Coll, Univ of Leicester (MPhil, PhD); *m* 27 July 1968, Janet Elizabeth, da of Eric Turner, of Headingley, Leeds; 2 s (Robin William *b* 1970, James Kimbell *b* 1973); *Career* curate St Paul's Tupsley and asst master Bishop's Sch Hereford 1967–71, dir of educn Diocese of Hereford 1976–81 (advsr in religious educn 1971–76), prebendary Hereford Cathedral 1977–81, vicar St Thomas on the Bourne Farham Surrey 1981–90, dir of post-ordination trg Diocese of Guildford 1983–90, hon canon Guildford Cathedral 1985–95, archdeacon of Dorking 1990–95, bishop of St Albans 1995–2009; memb House of Lords 1999–2009; visiting prof in Christian Ethics Univ of Surrey 2016; Hon DLitt Univ of Hertfordshire 2003, Hon DA Univ of Bedfordshire 2008; hon citizen Fano Italy 2008; *Books* The New Creation (1971), A Place to Dream (1976), St Paul's: a Place to Dream (1981), The Edge of Wonder (1981), Listening to Children (1983), On the Road (1984), Be Thou My Vision (1985), This Most Amazing Day (1986), Ways Into Prayer (1987), The Question of Jesus (1987), Alive to God (1987), Help in Your Bereavement (1988), Prayers for Children (1993), Pocket Prayers (1993), The Prayer Garden (1994), Words of Comfort (1994), Pocket Prayers for Children (1999), Pocket Words of Comfort (2004), Seeing and Believing (2008), Pocket Prayers for Commuters (2009), Health (2012); *Recreations* walking, music, cycling, gardening; *Style*— The Rt Rev Christopher Herbert; ✉ e-mail cwherbert7@gmail.com, website www.threeabbeys.me.uk

HERBERT, 19 Baron (E 1461); David John Seyfried Herbert; s of Capt John Beeton Seyfried, RHG (d 2008), of Warks, and Lady Cathleen Hudson, *née* Eliot (d 1994); suc on termination of abeyance 2002; assumed the additional surname of Herbert; co-heir to Barony of Botetourt (E 1305); *b* 3 March 1952, London; *Educ* Harrow; *m* 29 Aug 1975, Jane, *née* Bishop; 1 s (Dr the Hon Oliver Richard *b* 17 June 1976), 1 da (Hon Charlotte Sophia Caroline (Hon Mrs Collett) *b* 27 Oct 1977); *Career* dir David Seyfried Ltd; *Style*— The Lord Herbert; ✉ David Seyfried Ltd, 1/5 Chelsea Harbour Design Centre, London SW10 0XE (☎ 020 7823 3848, e-mail info@davidseyfried.com)

HERBERT, James; OBE (2010); s of H Herbert, of London, and Catherine, *née* Riley; *b* 8 April 1943; *Educ* Our Lady of the Assumption Sch Bethnal Green, St Aloysius Coll Highgate, Hornsey Coll of Art Highgate; *m* August 1967, Eileen; 3 da (Kerry Jo *b* 22 July 1968, Emma Jane *b* 21 April 1972, Casey Lee *b* 31 Oct 1983); *Career* author; typographer John Collings Advertising 1962, successively art dir, gp head then assoc dir Charles Barker Advertising 1965–77; World Grand Master of Horror 2010; *Films* The Rats, The Survivor, Fluke (1995), Haunted (1995); *Television* The Secret of Crickley Hall (BBC) 2012; *Books* The Rats (1974), The Fog (1975), The Survivor (1976, Avoriaz Grand Prix for Literature Fantastique 1977), Fluke (1977), The Spear (1978), Lair (1979), The Dark (1980), The Jonah (1981), Shrine (1983), Domain (1984), Moon (1985), The Magic Cottage (1986), Sepulchre (1987), Haunted (1988), Creed (1990), Portent (1992), James Herbert: by Horror Haunted (ed by Stephen Jones, 1992), James Herbert's Dark Places (photographs by Paul Barkshire, 1993), The City (graphic novel, illustrated by Ian Miller, 1993), The Ghosts of Sleath (1993), '48 (1996), Others (1999), Once (2001), Nobody True (2003), James Herbert: Terror in the Dark (2003), The Secret of Crickley Hall (2006), Ash (2012); *Recreations* guitar, painting, book design, wildlife conservation; *Style*— James Herbert, Esq, OBE; ✉ c/o David Higham Associates, 5–8 Lower John Street, Golden Square, London W1R 4HA (☎ 020 7437 7888, fax 020 7437 1072)

HERBERT, Dr Jeffrey William; *b* 21 July 1942; *Educ* Loughborough Univ (DTech), Cranfield Business Sch; *m*; 2 da, 1 s; *Career* grad trainee rising to mfrg dir Perkins Engines Ltd/ Massey Ferguson Gp Ltd 1965–76, md Rover Triumph Cars Ltd 1976–81, md GEC Diesels Ltd 1981–85; Charter plc: exec dir industry 1985–89, chief exec 1990–96, chm 1996–2001; chm: Cape plc 1985–96, Anderson Group plc 1987–95, Esab AB 1994–2001, British South Africa Co 1996–2001, Howden Gp plc 1997–2001, Claverham Ltd 1998–2000, Concentric Gp plc 1999–; dep chm House of Fraser plc 2001–06; non-exec dir: Vickers plc 1991– (dep chm 1997–2000), M&G Recovery Investment Trust plc 1992–2002, F T Everard & Sons 2002–, Tendring Hundred Water Services Ltd 2003–12, Affinity Water Ltd 2012–15; memb Cncl Royal Acad of Engrg 1995– (hon treas 1997–2003); dir Thrombosis Research Inst 2005–; memb Worshipful Co of Wheelwrights; CEng, FIMechE, MIEE, MIMfgE, MInstD, MIMgt, FREng 1993; *Style*— Dr Jeffrey Herbert, FREng

HERBERT, Prof Joe; s of Dr Benjamin Herbert (d 1972), of Birmingham, and Elizabeth, *née* Leek (d 1983); *b* 8 April 1936; *Educ* Bromsgrove Sch, Univ of Birmingham (scholar, BSc, MB ChB), Univ of London (PhD); *m* 1980, Rachel Meller; 2 s (Daniel Meller-Herbert *b* 21 Jan 1982, Oliver Meller-Herbert *b* 15 Dec 1983); *Career* Gonville & Caius Coll Cambridge: fell 1976, dir of studies in med 1993; Univ of Cambridge: reader in neuroendocrinology Dept of Anatomy 1987, dir of trg 1992, dir of res, prof of neuroscience 1999, dir of trg Dept of Clinical Neuroscience; *Publications* The Minder Brain (2007), Testosterone, Sex, Power and the Will to Win (2015); papers in learned jls on reproduction, stress, brain function, financial decision-making and depression; *Recreations* classic cars; *Clubs* Bentley Drivers; *Style*— Prof Joe Herbert; ✉ Cambridge Centre for Brain Repair, University of Cambridge, Cambridge CB2 0PY (☎ 01223 331160, e-mail jh24@cam.ac.uk)

HERBERT, John Paul (Johnny); s of Robert Ernest Trevor Herbert, and Georgina Jane Herbert; *b* 25 June 1964; *Educ* Forest Lodge Comp Sch; *m* 10 Dec 1990, Rebecca May, da of Michael Francis and Pauline Ann Cross; 2 da (Chloe Ann *b* 31 Jan 1990, Aimelia Jane *b* 21 July 1992); *Career* motor racing driver; go-karts: began racing aged 10, memb Br team 1978–82, Br jr champion 1979, Br sr champion 1982; Formula Ford 1600 1983–85 (Formula Ford Festival winner 1985), Formula Ford 2000 and Formula 3 1986, Br Formula 3 champion 1987, Formula 3000 1988 (won first race then injured in crash at Brands Hatch), Formula 3000 Japan 1990–91 (winner Le Mans with Mazda 1991); Formula One: Benetton 1989 (fourth in debut race Brazil), Lotus 1991–94, Benetton 1995, Sauber team 1996–98, Jaguar (formerly Stewart-Ford) 1999–2000 (winner British Grand Prix 1995, Italian Grand Prix 1995 and European Grand Prix, 1st win for Stewart); devpt driver Arrows F1 Team; driver: Le Mans 24 hour 2001 (Champion Racing), 2002 (Audi Works, second place), 2003 (Bentley, second place), 2004 (Audi Works, second place) and 2007 (Aston Martin), Road Atlanta USA 2001, American Le Mans Series 2002, 2003 (Champion Racing, second place) and 2007 (Porsche), Sebring 12 hour 2002 (winner), 2003 (Bentley, third place) and 2004 (Audi, third place), Sears Point USA 2002 (second place), Elms at Monza (Audi works team, winner), Speedcar series Asia 2007, Speedcar Series Champion 2007; Formula One career: 130 races, 3 wins; Cellnet Award 1986; PR mangr MFI Formula One team 2005–06, presenter Sky F1 2012, 2013 and 2014; *Recreations* golf; *Style*— Johnny Herbert, Esq; ✉ c/o Mark Perkins, 31 Avenue Princesse Grace, Monaco 98000 (☎ 00 377 97 700525, fax 00 377 93 305159, e-mail csm@csm.mc)

HERBERT, Mark Jeremy; QC (1995); s of Kenneth Faulkner Herbert (d 1993), and Kathleen Ellis, *née* Robertson (d 2010); *b* 12 November 1948; *Educ* Lancing, KCL (BA); *m* 1977, Shulanjini Shiranikha, da of late Dr Sefton Pullenayegum; *Career* called to the Bar Lincoln's Inn 1974 (bencher 2004), in practice Chancery Bar 1975–2016; mediator 2002, dep high court judge Chancery Division 2004–2015, cmmr Royal Court Jersey 2013–; *Books* Whiteman on Capital Gains Tax (contrib, 1988), Drafting and Variation of Wills (1989), Arbitration of Trust Disputes (contrib, ed S I Strong, 2016); *Recreations* bell-ringing, theatre, travel, Italy; *Style*— Mark Herbert, Esq, QC; ✉ 3 Milner Place, London N1 1TN (☎ 020 7226 2693, e-mail mherbert8@sky.com)

HERBERT, Mary Therese; da of James Ewart Herbert (d 1984), and Anne Josephine, *née* Blee; *b* 30 March 1954, Omagh, Co Tyrone; *Educ* Univ of Leeds (BSc); *Partner* Prof Julian Anthony Pearce; 1 s (Simon Alexander *b* 9 Aug 1992); *Career* admitted slr 1988; Ingledew Botterell 1988–90, ptnr Eversheds LLP 1993– (slr 1990–93); memb Law Soc 1988; FFB 2002; *Recreations* art, gardening; *Style*— Ms Mary Herbert; ✉ Eversheds LLP, 1 Callaghan Square, Cardiff CF10 5BT (☎ 029 2047 7905, e-mail maryherbert@eversheds.com)

HERBERT, Nicholas; *see:* Hemingford, 3 Baron

HERBERT, Rt Hon Nick; CBE (2016), PC (2010), MP; *b* 1963; *Educ* Haileybury, Magdalene Coll Cambridge (MA); *Partner* Jason Eades (civil partnership 2008); *Career* dir political affrs Br Field Sports Soc 1992–96 (co-fndr Countryside Movement), chief exec Business for Sterling 1998–2000 (fndr 'No' Campaign), dir Reform 2002–05, MP (Cons) Arundel and S Downs 2005– (Parly candidate (Cons) Berwick upon Tweed 1997), shadow min for police reform 2005–07, shadow sec of state for justice 2007–09, shadow sec of state for environment, food and rural affrs 2009–10, min for policing and criminal justice 2010–12; co-chm All Pty Parly Gp on Global TB 2006–10 and 2013–, co-chm GovernUp 2014–, co-chm Global TB Caucus 2014–; *Books* Why Vote Conservative (2015); *Style*— The Rt Hon Nick Herbert, CBE, MP; ✉ House of Commons, London SW1A 0AA (☎ 020 7219 4080, e-mail nick@nickherbert.com, website www.nickherbert.com)

HERBERTSON, (Robert) Ian; yr s of Robert Hopkirk Herbertson (d 1969), and Winifred Rose, *née* Rawlinson (d 1994); *b* 30 December 1953; *Educ* Selhurst GS, Birkbeck Coll London (BA), Univ of East London (MA), Univ of London (MA); *m* 22 March 1985 (m dis 2001), Joanna Hazel, da of Reginald Bernard North, of Gwent; 3 da (Rebecca Elizabeth *b* 1987, Emma Louise *b* 1990, Amy Ellen *b* 1992); *Career* Bank of England: joined 1985, an audit mangr 1990–92, official Banking Supervision 1992–93, Legal Unit 1993, Monetary and Fin Statistics Div 1994–96, Business Fin Div 1996–97, head of IT Audit 1997–99, dep head Internal Audit 1999–2003; VocaLink Ltd (formerly BACS Ltd): head of risk and compliance 2003–08; dir Claridge Press 1987–88; memb: Convocation Univ of London 1984, Ctee Ct of Electors Birkbeck Coll London 1987–90; chm IIA Professional Issues Gp 2000–02, chm Bd of Tstees Voca Final Salary Scheme 2006–15, chm Ian Herbertson Tstees Ltd, chair G10 Central Banks IT Audit Gp 2002–03; Freeman of City of London, Liveryman Worshipful Co of Chartered Secs and Admins, memb Incorporation of Maltmen 2010, Burgess and Freeman City of Glasgow 2010; memb: Lithic Studies Soc (memb Ctee 2000–09, treas 2002–09), Cambridge Antiquarian Soc, Prehistoric Soc; author of articles on archaeology; memb Caledonian Soc of London 2009, memb Ctee Old Croydonians Soc (chm designate); CDipAF 1985, FIAP (Inst of Analysts and Programmers) 1986–92, FCIS 1995 (ACIS 1991), fell Royal Statistical Soc 1995–2011, CFIIA 2000 (MIIA 1998), memb Inst of Risk Mgmnt (MIRM) 2004, fell Royal Anthropological Inst 2006 (sec Environment and Anthropology Ctee), memb NY Acad of Science 2006, FLS 2008, fell Royal Asiatic Soc 2015; Lay Dominican 2009 (vice-pres Cambridge and Laxton); *Recreations* philosophy, prehistoric archaeology, palaeoanthropology, literature; *Clubs* City Univ; *Style*— Ian Herbertson, Esq; ✉ 18 Weir Close, Buckden, Cambridgeshire PE19 5TH (☎ 01480 810929, e-mail ianherbertson@aol.com)

HERD, Christopher John (Chris); s of Robin Herd, CBE, and Eve Herd; *b* 19 June 1967; *Educ* Abingdon Sch, Aston Univ (BSc); *Career* WCRS: grad trainee 1990–91, account mangr 1991–93, account dir 1993–95; account dir Leagas Delaney 1995–97; WCRS: gp dir 1997–

2001, head of e-brands 2000–01; md Bates UK 2001–03, exec dir Branded 2004–; nominated as a 'face to watch' Campaign magazine 1995; *Recreations* golf (handicap 4, competed in English Amateur Golf Championship 1987), skiing, Oxford United FC; *Style—* Chris Herd, Esq; ✉ Branded Ltd, Albert Bridge House, 127 Albert Bridge Road, London SW11 4PL (☎ 020 7978 7780, website www.branded.co.uk)

HERDAN, Bernard Laurence; CB (2007); s of Gustav Herdan (d 1969), and Innes, *née* Jackson (d 2008); *b* 23 November 1947; *Educ* Univ of Cambridge (MA), Univ of Bath (Dip Mgmnt); *m* 1971, Janet Elizabeth, *née* Hughes; 2 da (Charlotte Lucy b 13 May 1974, Emma Jane b 10 March 1976 d 27 Oct 1988); *Career* gp ldr Space Systems Div Br Aerospace 1969–73, prog mangr Euro Space Agency The Netherlands 1973–84, divisional mangr BIS-Macintosh 1984–85, md Defence Technol Enterprises Ltd (DTE) 1985–1990, dir of commercial services Met Office 1990–95, chief exec Driving Standards Agency 1995–99, chief exec Passport and Records Agency 1999–2003, chief exec UK Passport Service 2003–06, exec dir of service delivery Identity and Passport Serv 2006–08, chief exec Security Industry Authy 2008–09, chief exec Nat Fraud Authy 2009–11; non-exec dir: Lazards Defence Fund Ltd 1988–90, MIKROS Corp New Jersey 1989–91, JRA Aerospace 1990–2003; conslt Renaissance Venture Capital Fund 1989–91; bd advsr: BSB 1986–89, Scott Instruments Texas 1989–91; advsr City of London Police 2011–14; non-exec dir: MOD Carrier Strike Prog 2012–13, Disclosure and Barring Service 2012–, Legal Ombudsman 2015–; dep chm Bedford Hosp NHS Tst 2005–09, chm Fitness to Practise Panel GMC 2011–, memb Disciplinary Panel Bar Standards Bd 2013–15; tstee: Victim Support 2010–15, Bedford Citizens Advice Bureau 2010–12, Corporate Alliance Against Domestic Violence 2011–13, The Fostering Network 2011–13, Alzheimer's Society 2013–; chm Supporting the Educn of Disadvantaged Children in Uganda (SEDCU) 2013–; Hon DBA Univ of Beds; *Publications* conceived quarterly jl Space Communications (ed-in-chief until 1987, currently ed emeritus); *Recreations* horse riding, charity work, foreign travel, theatre, the Arts; *Clubs* Oxford and Cambridge; *Style—* Dr Bernard Herdan, CB; ✉ e-mail blherdan@yahoo.co.uk

HERDMAN, Dr John Macmillan; s of William Morrison Herdman (d 1975), of Edinburgh, and Catherine, *née* Macmillan (d 1991); *b* 20 July 1941; *Educ* Merchiston Castle Sch Edinburgh, Magdalene Coll Cambridge (MA, PhD); *m* 1, 30 July 1983 (m dis 1993), Dolina, da of Angus Maclennan (d 1950), of Marvig, Isle of Lewis; m 2, 17 Aug 2002, Mary Ellen Watson, da of late JGR Robertson, of Cupar, Fife; *Career* writer; awarded Scottish Arts Cncl bursaries 1976, 1982, 1998 and 2004, creative writing fell Univ of Edinburgh 1977–79, winner book awards 1978 and 1993, Hawthornden Writer's fellowship 1989 and 1995, William Soutar Writer's fellowship 1990–91, writer in residence Champlain Coll Trent Univ Canada 1998; *Books* Descent (1968), A Truth Lover (1973), Clapperton (1974), Pagan's Pilgrimage (1978), Stories Short and Tall (1979), Voice without Restraint: Bob Dylan's Lyrics and their Background (1982), Three Novellas (1987), The Double in Nineteenth Century Fiction (1990), Imelda and Other Stories (1993), Ghostwriting (1996), Cruising: A Play (1997), Poets, Pubs, Polls and Pillar-Boxes (1999), Four Tales (2000), The Sinister Cabaret (2001), Triptych (2004), My Wife's Lovers (2007), Some Renaissance Culture Wars (2010), Another Country (2013); *Recreations* reading, walking, listening to music, medieval church history; *Style—* Dr John Herdman; ✉ Flat 8, 25 Ashwood Gait, Edinburgh EH12 8PE (website www.johnherdman.co.uk)

HEREFORD, Archdeacon of; *see:* Colmer, Ven Malcolm John

HEREFORD, Bishop of 2014–; Rt Rev Richard Michael Cokayne Frith; s of Canon Roger Cokayne Frith (d 1989), and Joan Agnes, *née* Pearson; *b* 8 April 1949; *Educ* Marlborough, Fitzwilliam Coll Cambridge (MA), St John's Coll Nottingham; *m* 1, 1975 (m dis 2000), Jill, da of Norman Richardson; 2 s (James b 1977, Timothy b 1982), 2 da (Rachel b 1979, Elizabeth b 1985); m 2, 2006, Kay Gledhill.; *Career* ordained: deacon 1974, priest 1975; curate Mortlake with E Sheen (Dio of Southwark) 1974–78, team vicar Thamesmead (Dio of Southwark) 1978–83, team rector Keynsham (Dio of Bath and Wells) 1983–92, archdeacon of Taunton 1992–98, bishop of Hull 1998–2014; *Recreations* cricket, theatre; *Clubs* MCC; *Style—* The Rt Rev the Bishop of Hereford

HEREFORD, 19 Viscount (E 1550); Sir (Charles) Robin de Bohun Devereux; 16 Bt (E 1611); Premier Viscount in the Peerage of England; s of 18 Viscount Hereford (d 2004), and Susan Mary, *née* Godley; *b* 11 August 1975, London; *Educ* Stowe, UEA (BA); *m* 12 June 2010, Louisa Jane, yst da of William Knight, of Holland Park, London; 1 da (Hon Sophia Emily Florence Devereux b 12 Jan 2013), 1 s (Hon Henry Walter de Bohun Devereux b 11 Feb 2015); *Heir* son, Hon Henry Walter de Bohun Devereux; *Career* Bonhams Auctioneers: gen valuer 1998–, dir Valuations 2007–, dir Bonhams UK 2010; *Recreations* fishing, the arts, wine and old cars (but not together), childcare; *Clubs* White's; *Style—* The Rt Hon the Viscount Hereford; ✉ 98 Elms Crescent, London SW4 8QT

HERFORD, (Richard) Henry; s of Philip Henry Herford (d 1982), of Glasgow, and Elisabeth Jean, *née* Hawkins; *b* 24 February 1947; *Educ* Trinity Coll Glenalmond, King's Coll Cambridge, Univ of York, Royal Manchester Coll of Music; *m* 14 Feb 1982, Jane Lindsay, da of Peter John; 2 s (Thomas Hal b 31 Oct 1982, John Peter b 19 Jan 1985), 1 da (Alice Jane b 5 March 1988); *Career* opera and concert singer; performances incl operas with Covent Garden, Glyndebourne, Scottish Opera and throughout Europe, concerts, recitals, broadcasts and recordings throughout Britain, Europe and the USA, and in Canada, S America and China; co-fndr and dir Abingdon Summer Sch for Solo Singers 1998–; tutor Sch of Vocal Studies: Royal Northern Coll of Music 1994–, Royal Coll of Music 1998–2004, Birmingham Conservatoire 1998–; examiner and adjudicator in all principal British conservatoires; Curtis Gold Medal for singing Royal Northern Coll of Music 1976, Benson and Hedges Gold Award 1980, first prize Int American Music Competition 1982; *Recordings* incl: Rameau Castor et Pollux (Erato), Bridge The Christmas Rose (Pearl), Handel Messiah (excerpts, Contour), Peter Dickinson Dylan Thomas Song Cycle (Conifer), Britten A Midsummer Night's Dream (Virgin) Charles Ives Song Recital I and II (Unicorn-Kanchana, Music Retailers' Assoc Record of the Year), Charles Ives songs with instrumental ensemble (Ensemble Modern, EMI), George Lloyd Iernin (Albany), Stravinsky Pulcinella (Naxos), Edward Gregson Missa Brevis Pacem, Handel Israel in Egypt (Decca), John Joubert The Instant Moment (Naxos), Arthur Bliss: Complete Songs (Hyperion), Sir John Manduell: Renaissance Songs (ASC); *Recreations* family, garden, beekeeping, churchwarden of village church, chamber music (cello), reading, walking, badminton; *Style—* Henry Herford; ✉ Pencots, Northmoor, Oxfordshire OX29 5AX (☎ 01865 300884, e-mail herfords@gmail.com)

HERMAN, Daniel James; s of Kenneth Joseph Herman (d 2006), and Miroslava, *née* Radi?; *b* 12 August 1974, Manchester; *Educ* Bury GS for Boys, Univ of Warwick (LLB), Coll of Law Chester (DipLP); *m* 2 July 2005, Rebecca, *née* Such; *Career* slr; Graham Leigh Pfeffer & Co 1996–98, Kingsford Stacey Blackwell 1998–2000, Stewarts Slrs 2000–08 (ptnr 2003–08), Stewarts Law LLP 2008–; memb Law Soc 1999; *Recreations* football, tennis, relaxing in Croatia; *Style—* Daniel Herman, Esq; ✉ e-mail dherman@stewartslaw.com

HERMAN, Dr Stephen Sydney; s of Maurice Herman (d 1975), and Deborah, *née* Dutkevitch (d 1980); *b* 7 July 1942; *Educ* Central Foundation Boys GS, King's Coll London, St George's Hosp Med Sch (MB BS); *m* 21 June 1966, Yvette Hannah, da of Isaac Solomons (d 1964); 1 s (Simon b 13 March 1969), 2 da (Rachel b 31 July 1970, Ruth b 5 May 1973); *Career* hon conslt paediatrician Royal National Orthopaedic Hosp, conslt paediatrician Central Middx Hosp 1974–93; memb: Neonatal Soc 1972; FRCP 1981, FRCPCH 1997; *Recreations* amateur radio (call sign M0SSH); *Style—* Dr Stephen Herman; ✉ Barbary House, California Lane, Bushey Heath, Hertfordshire WD23 1EX (☎ 020 8950 1006, e-mail stephen_herman@hotmail.com)

HERMER, Richard; QC (2009); *b* 1968; *Career* called to the Bar 1993; practising barr specialising in human rights and tort law, currently memb Doughty Street Chambers; human rights practitioner in residence Columbia Univ NY 2000–; *Style—* Richard Hermer

HERMON, Lady; Sylvia; MP; da of Samuel Robert Paisley, and Mary Eileen, *née* McMinn (d 1959); *b* 11 August 1955, Co Tyrone; *Educ* Dungannon HS for Girls, Univ of Aberystwyth (LLB); *m* Sir John Charles Hermon; 2 s (Robert Paisley b 21 Oct 1989, Thomas Rowan b 11 April 1992); *Career* lectr in law Queen's Univ Belfast 1978–88; MP (UUP then Ind) Down N 2001–; *Publications* incl: A Guide to European Community Law in Northern Ireland, The UUP Response to the Patten Report; *Recreations* ornithology, swimming; *Style—* Lady Hermon, MP; ✉ House of Commons, London SW1A 0AA

HERON, David Leslie Norton; s of late Edward Wallace Heron, and Eunice Cecilia, *née* Mott; *b* 5 October 1941; *Educ* Christ's Coll Finchley; *m* 25 July 1965, Margaret Ann, *née* Berry, da of Leonard Kenneth Berry; 3 s (Simon Alexander b 6 Sept 1968, Daniel Mark b 17 April 1970, Luke Nicholas b 20 Sept 1978), 1 da (Kathryn Alice b 29 Dec 1973); *Career* trainee chartered accountant 1957–59; James Capel & Co: accountant asst 1959–61, investment analyst asst 1961–66, stockbroker 1966–, fund mgmnt 1966–68, institutional sales 1968–72 and 1976–83, head of Far East sales 1972–76, head of derivatives 1983–94, dir 1987–94; head of derivatives Smith New Court 1994, dep chm LIFFE 1992–94; chm: Premier Radio 1995–2008, CCP Ltd (magazine publishing) 1998–; tstee Mildmay Hospital, tstee Shere Jesus Int; church warden St Michael and All Angels Lyndhurst; *Recreations* tennis, active church member; *Style—* David L N Heron, Esq; ✉ Whinwood, Beaulieu Road, Lyndhurst, Hampshire SO43 7DA (☎ 02380 283154)

HERRING, Timothy Stephen; s of Cdr Philip Maurice Herring, RNVR (d 1982), and Flora Pepita Herring (d 1985); *b* 25 May 1936; *Educ* Bishop's Stortford Coll; *m* 22 April 1960, Cathleen Elizabeth, da of Thomas Stephen Nevin (d 1972); 2 s (Stephen Ashley b 26 Nov 1960, Andrew Philip b 15 March 1963); *Career* Lamson Engineering 1956–66; proprietor: Julie's Restaurant 1969–, Portobello Hotel 1970–, Ark Restaurant USA 1983–93; yachtsman; winner: Britannia Cup, Queen's Cup, Queen Victoria Cup; Freeman City of London 1961, Prime Warden Worshipful Co of Blacksmiths 1997–98 (memb 1961), Liveryman Worshipful Co of Turners; *Recreations* yachting; *Clubs* Royal Burnham Yacht, Royal Thames Yacht; *Style—* Timothy Herring, Esq; ✉ 133 Portland Road, London W11 4LW (☎ 020 7727 2776); Quaycote, Burnham-on-Crouch, Essex CM0 8AS

H

HERRINGTON, Timothy John (Tim); s of John Herrington (d 2014), and Barbara Jean Margaret, *née* Toon (d 1996); *b* 22 April 1954; *Educ* Queen Mary's GS Basingstoke, Univ of Bristol (LLB); *m* 20 Feb 1982 (m dis 2007), Kathleen Mary, da of Peter Loy Chetwynd Pigott, of Bulawayo, Zimbabwe; 1 s (James b 1987); m 2, 30 July 2013, Maria Fenton, *qv*; *Career* admitted slr 1978; ptnr: Coward Chance 1985–87 (joined 1976), Clifford Chance 1987–2005; chm: Law Soc Standing Ctee on Co Law 1996–99 (memb 1988–2004), Investment Funds Ctee Int Bar Assoc 2000–02, Regulatory Decisions Ctee Financial Servs Authy 2005–12; judge Upper Tbnl Tax and Chancery Chamber 2012–; memb Advsy Bd Financial Servs Lawyers' Assoc 2007–; Freeman: City of London 1977, Worshipful Co of Slrs 1985; memb Law Soc; *Books* Life After Big Bang (contrib, 1987), Insider Dealing in Europe (contrib, 1994), Law Making, Law Finding and Law Shaping (contrib, 1997), Capital Guide to Offshore Funds (contrib, 1999), Legal Aspects of Investment Management (contrib, 1999); *Recreations* cricket, travel, walking, gardening, numismatics, wine, English countryside; *Clubs* Hampshire CCC, National Liberal; *Style—* Tim Herrington, Esq; ✉ Upper Tribunal, Royal Courts of Justice, Strand London WC2A 2LL (☎ 020 7612 9666, e-mail uppertribunaljudge.herrington@judiciary.net)

HERSOV, Gregory Adam (Greg); s of Dr Lionel Hersov, and Zoe, *née* Menell; *b* 4 May 1956; *Educ* Bryanston, Mansfield Coll Oxford (MA); *Career* theatre dir; Thames TV regnl dirs trainee Redgrave Theatre Farnham 1976–78, involved with Royal Exchange Theatre 1979– (artistic dir 1987–); *Theatre* Royal Exchange prodns incl: The Tempest, King Lear, One Flew Over the Cuckoo's Nest, Blues for Mister Charlie, All My Sons, Death of a Salesman, The Crucible, Ghosts, A Doll's House, The Alchemist, The Beggar's Opera, Look Back in Anger, The Homecoming, Venice Preserv'd, The Voysey Inheritance, Uncle Vanya, The Seagull; Royal Exchange on tour prodns: Romeo and Juliet, A View From the Bridge (TMA Best Dir); premieres: Prize Night, Woundings, Behind Heaven, Winding the Ball, Misfits; other credits incl: Les Blancs (co-dir European premiere), Animal Crackers (Royal Exchange, Barbican Int Festival and West End), Look Back in Anger (RNT), Palace of the End (RET Studio, Galway and Edinburgh Festivals, Amnesty Int Freedom of Expression Award 2009); *Style—* Greg Hersov, Esq; ✉ Royal Exchange Theatre, St Ann's Square, Manchester M2 7DH (☎ 0161 615 6704)

HERTFORD, Archdeacon of; *see:* Jones, Ven Trevor Pryce

HERZBERG, Prof Joseph Larry; s of Adolf Heinrich Herzberg (d 2008), and Pearl, *née* Mesh; *b* 10 May 1953, London; *Educ* Carmel Coll, Hasmonean Sch, The London Hosp Med Coll (BSc, MB BS, MPhil); *m* 13 Feb 1977, Helene Ruth, da of Harry Gordon, of London; 1 s (Laurence b 1982); *Career* SHO and registrar in pyschiatry London Hosp 1980–84 (house physician 1979–80); sr registrar in psychiatry: St Mary's Hosp London 1984–85, The Bethlem Royal and Maudsley Hosps London 1986–87; conslt psychogeriatrician Lewisham & Guy's Mental Health and NHS Tst (formerly Guy's Hosp) and sr lectr UMDS Guy's Campus 1987–96; conslt old age psychiatrist E London Fndn HNS Tst 1996–2010 (assoc med dir 1998–2008), assoc dean of postgrad med London Deanery Univ of London 1996–2008, emeritus prof of postgraduate medical educn Queen Mary Univ of London 1998–, NHS prof of postgraduate medical educn Barts and the London Sch of Med and Dentistry and Queen Mary Univ of London 2006–08 (hon reader in postgraduate medical educn 2002–06, now emeritus prof); second opinion doctor Care Quality Cmmn 2010–13; freelance executive coach, mentor and medical educationalist 2013–; author of various scientific papers on: social psychiatry, neuropsychiatry, psychogeriatrics, audit and med educn; former memb Exec Assoc for the Study of Medical Education ASME (RCPsych representative, treas 2002–06); tstee Francon Tst; Worshipful Soc of Apothecaries, Guild Asst Guild of Freemen of the City of London; FRSM, FRCPsych 1995 (MRCPsych 1983); *Recreations* music (particularly opera), theatre, travel; *Style—* Prof J L Herzberg

HESELTINE, Baron (Life Peer UK 2001), of Thenford in the County of Northamptonshire; Michael Ray Dibdin Heseltine; CH (1997), PC (1979); s of late Col R D Heseltine, of Swansea, Glamorgan; *b* 21 March 1933; *Educ* Shrewsbury, Pembroke Coll Oxford (BA, pres Oxford Union); *m* 1962, Anne Harding Williams; 1 s, 2 da; *Career* Nat Serv cmmnd Welsh Gds 1959; dir Bow Publications 1961–65, chm Haymarket Press 1966–70, chm Haymarket Group plc 1999–; Parly candidate (Cons): Gower 1959, Coventry North 1964; MP (Cons): Tavistock 1966–74, Henley 1974–2001; vice-chm Cons Parly Tport Ctee 1968, oppn spokesman on Tport 1969, Parly sec Miny of Tport June-Oct 1970, Parly under-sec for the Environment 1970–72, min for Aerospace and Shipping DTI 1972–74, oppn spokesman on Indust 1974–76, oppn spokesman on the Environment 1976–79, sec of state for the Environment 1979–83, sec of state for Defence 1983–86 (resigned over Westland affair), contested leadership of Cons Party Nov 1990, sec of state for the Environment Nov 1990–92, pres Bd of Trade (sec of state for Trade and Industry) 1992–95, dep PM 1995–97; pres: Assoc of Cons Clubs 1978–79, Nat Young Conservatives 1982–84 (vice-pres 1978); chm UK-China Forum 1998–2001, chm Regnl Growth Fund Advsy Ctee 2010–; pres: Quoted Companies Alliance 2000–05, Chartered Inst of Mktg 2005–08; memb Cncl Zoological Soc of London 1987–90, vice-pres RHS 2009; hon fell: Pembroke Coll Oxford 1986, Leeds Met Univ 1989, UC Swansea 2001, John Moore Univ Liverpool 2013, Univ of Northampton 2013; Freeman: City of Liverpool 2012, City of London 2012,

Hon Liveryman Worshipful Co of Marketors, Hon Liveryman Livery Co Masters' Assoc 2015; Hon LLD Univ of Liverpool 1990, Hon DBA Beds Univ 2003, hon degree Aston Univ 2013, hon doctorate Univ of S Wales 2013, hon doctorate Birmingham City Univ 2014; *Publications* Reviving the Inner Cities (1983), Where There's A Will (1987), The Challenge of Europe, Can Britain Win? (1989), Life in the Jungle (autobiography, 2000), No Stone Unturned (2012); *Clubs* Carlton, Beefsteak, Brooks's, Pratts, Whites; *Style*— The Rt Hon the Lord Heseltine, CH

HESELTINE, Hon Rupert; s of Lord Heseltine, CH, PC, *qv*, and Anne Harding Williams; *b* 9 July 1967, London; *m* Sarah; 2 s, 1 da; *Career* Haymarket Media Gp: joined 1994, dir 2001–, dep chm Haymarket Exhibitions 2004–05, dep chm 2005–09, exec chm 2009–; *Style*— The Hon Rupert Heseltine; ✉ Haymarket Media Group, Bridge House, 69 London Road, Twickenham, Middlesex TW1 3SP (website www.haymarket.com)

HESKETH, 3 Baron (UK 1935); Sir Thomas Alexander Fermor-Hesketh; 10 Bt (GB 1761), KBE (1997), PC (1991); s of 2 Baron Hesketh (d 1955), and Dowager Lady Hesketh; *b* 28 October 1950; *Educ* Ampleforth; *m* 1977, Hon Claire, da of 3 Baron Manton; 1 s, 2 da; *Heir* s, Hon Frederick Fermor-Hesketh; *Career* a govt whip House of Lords 1986–91, Parly under sec of state DOE 1989–90, min of state DTI 1990–91, Capt Hon Corps of Gentlemen-at-Arms (govt chief whip House of Lords) 1991–93; exec chm British Mediterranean Airways 1994–2007; vice-chm Freestream Aircraft Ltd 2010–; non-exec dir: Babcock International Gp plc 1993–2010 (dep chm 1996–2010), British Aerospace plc 1993–2005; ind dir Air Astana JSC 2007–; Hon FSE 1979, Hon FIET 1982; *Clubs* Turf, White's; *Style*— The Rt Hon the Lord Hesketh, KBE, PC; ✉ Towcester Racecourse Limited, London Road, Towcester, Northamptonshire NN12 6LB (☎ 01327 353414, fax 01327 358534)

HESKETH-READ, Carly; da of John Haydn Davies (d 1993), and Ethel Beryl, *née* Blackmore (d 2010); *b* Swansea; *Educ* Ystalyfera GS (head girl), Bristol Poly; *m* 13 Aug 2006, James Barrie Hesketh; 1 da (Emma b 13 April 1976), 1 s (Tom Haydn b 17 Oct 1980); *Career* sec to Chief Economist, computer programmer and O&M analyst Esso Petroleum 1969–75, fndr and md Match Mktg 1975–2001, fndr and md Icon Live 2002–; third place Women Mean Business Award 1983, Sussex Business Small Business Award 1993; MInstD 2003; *Recreations* tennis, music, opera, theatre; *Style*— Mrs Carly Hesketh-Read; ✉ 82 Dyke Road Avenue, Brighton, East Sussex BN1 5LF (☎ 01273 262689); Icon Live Limited, Icon House, Unit 2, York Road, Victoria Business Park, Burgess Hill, West Sussex RH15 9TT (☎ 01444 240000, fax 01444 240001, e-mail carly.read@iconlive.com)

HESKIA, Samantha; da of Mansour Heskia, and Patricia Heskia; *Educ* Francis Holland Sch, Chelsea Sch of Art; *Career* designer; Ofner Associates 1991–93 (projects incl Boeing 757 private aircraft); set up own accessories business 1995, collection designer Debenhams plc 1999–; work featured in The Handbag by Carmel Allen (1999); asst art dir on British films incl Second Best and Princess Caraboo 1993–2003; costume asst: Love Actually 2003, Ferrero Rocher commercial; patron Gilda's Club, patron Red Cross; memb Guild of Master Craftsmen 1998; *Recreations* playing the piano, Far Eastern travel, tennis, yoga; *Style*— Miss Samantha Heskia; ✉ 53A Moreton Street, London SW1V 2NY (☎ 020 7931 7604, e-mail enq@samanthaheskia.co.uk, website www.samanthaheskia.com)

HESLOP, Martin Sydney; QC (1995); s of Sydney Heslop, and Patricia Mary, *née* Day; *b* 6 August 1948; *Educ* St George's Coll Weybridge, Univ of Bristol; *m* 11 March 1994, Aurea Jane (Jenny), *née* Boyle; *Career* called to the Bar Lincoln's Inn 1972, first jr Treasy counsel Central Criminal Court 1992 (jr Treasy counsel 1987), sr Treasy counsel Central Criminal Court and recorder of the Crown Court 1993– (asst recorder 1989–93); *Recreations* sailing, travel, photography, swimming, wine and food, sport generally; *Clubs* Royal London Yacht, Bar Yacht; *Style*— Martin Heslop, Esq, QC; ✉ 2 Hare Court, Temple, London EC4Y 7BE (☎ 020 7353 5324, fax 020 7353 0667)

HESLOP, Sean Martin; s of Roy Heslop (d 1990), and Eileen Carroll; *b* 31 October 1967, Huntingdon, Cambs; *Educ* Neale Wade Community Coll March, Queens' Coll Cambridge (MA), KCL (PGCE), Inst of Educn London (MA), London Leadership Centre (NPQH); *m* 6 Aug 2005, Céline Gagnon; *Career* English teacher Queen Elizabeth's Sch Barnet 1994–97, head of English St Olave's GS Orpington 1997–2000, dep head Ravens Wood Sch Bromley 2000–04, headteacher Tiffin Sch Kingston upon Thames 2004–09, princ Folkestone Acad 2009– (exec princ 2014–), exec princ Marlowe Acad 2014–; research assoc Nat Coll of Sch Leadership; FRSA; *Publications* The Challenge of Change: The effect on knowledge capital and social capital in times of turbulence (2005); *Recreations* walking, reading, wine; *Style*— Sean Heslop, Esq; ✉ Folkestone Academy, Academy Lane, Folkestone, Kent CT19 5FP

HESS, Nigel John; s of John Hess, of Weston-super-Mare, Somerset, and Sheila, *née* Merrick; *b* 22 July 1953; *Educ* Weston-super-Mare GS for Boys, St Catharine's Coll Cambridge (MA); *m* 1996, Lisa Claire, da of Raymond Telford; 1 da (Alice Elizabeth b 31 Aug 1990); *Career* composer for TV, theatre and film; music scores for TV incl: A Woman of Substance, Vanity Fair, Campion, Summer's Lease (TV and Radio Industries Club Award for Best TV Theme), Testament (Novello Award for Best TV Theme), Titmuss Regained, Maigret, Wycliffe, Just William, Dangerfield, Hetty Wainthropp Investigates (Novello Award for Best TV Theme); film scores incl Ladies in Lavender (nominated Classical Brit Award 2005);Royal Shakespeare Company scores incl: Troilus and Cressida, Much Ado About Nothing, Julius Caesar, Cyrano de Bergerac (NY Drama Desk Award for Outstanding Music in a Play on Broadway), Comedy of Errors, Hamlet, Love's Labour's Lost, Love's Labour's Won, Othello, The Winter's Tale, The Swan Down Gloves, A Christmas Carol, Twelfth Night; other theatre incl: The Merry Wives of Windsor, Romeo and Juliet, Henry VIII, Knight of the Burning Pestle (all Shakespeare's Globe), Nell Gwynn, The Secret of Sherlock Holmes (West End); composer many concert works incl Piano Concerto (cmmnd by HRH The Prince of Wales, nominated Classical Brit Award 2009); commercial recordings incl: TV Themes (television compilation), The Winds of Power & New London Pictures (works for Symphonic Wind Band), Chameleon (MRA award for Best MOR Album), Piano Concerto (performed by Lang Lang), Ladies in Lavender (performed by Joshua Bell), Silent Nights; *Recreations* travel and photography; *Clubs* Br Acad of Songwriters, Composers and Authors, BAFTA; *Style*— Nigel Hess, Esq; ✉ c/o Bucks Music Ltd, Roundhouse, 212 Regents Park Road Entrance, London NW1 8AW (☎ 020 7221 4275, fax 020 7229 6893, e-mail nigel@myramusic.co.uk, website www.myramusic.co.uk)

HESSAYON, Dr David Gerald; OBE (2007); s of Jack Hessayon (d 1958), and Lena Hessayon (d 1933); *b* 13 February 1928; *Educ* Univ of Leeds, Univ of Manchester; *m* 1951, Joan Parker (d 2001), da of Weeden T Gray, of USA; 2 da; *Career* chm: Turbair 1970–93, Pan Britannica Industries Ltd 1972–93, pbi Publications 1988–93, Expert Publications 1988–, Hessayon Books Ltd 1993–; dir Orion Publishing Group 1992–93; chm Br Agrochemicals Assoc 1980–81; Lifetime Achievement Trophy Nat British Book Awards 1992, Veitch Gold Meml Medal RHS 1992, Lifetime Achievement Award Garden Writers Guild 2005; hon vice-pres Capel Manor; Freeman City of London; *Books* The Tree and Shrub Expert, The Armchair Book of the Garden, The Indoor Plant Spotter, The Garden Expert, The Home Expert, The Gold Plated House Plant Expert, Rose Jotter, House Plant Jotter, Vegetable Jotter, Be Your Own Greenhouse Expert, The Bio Friendly Gardening Guide, The Fruit Expert, The House Plant Expert, The Garden DIY Expert, The Rock and Water Garden Expert, The Greenhouse Expert, The Flowering Shrub Expert, The Flower Arranging Expert, The Container Expert, The Bulb Expert, The Easy-care Gardening Expert, The Bedding Plant Expert, The Rose Expert, The Lawn Expert, The Vegetable and Herb Expert, The Evergreen Expert, The Flower Expert, The Pocket Flower Expert, The Pocket Tree and Shrub Expert, The Pocket Garden Troubles Expert, The Pocket House Plant Expert, The Pocket Vegetable Expert, The Home DIY Expert, The Garden Revival Expert, The House Plant Expert: Book Two, The Pest and Weed Expert, The Orchid Expert, The Bedside Book of the Garden, The Green Garden Expert, The Expert Vegetable Notebook, The Complete Garden Expert, The New Vegetable and Herb Expert; *Recreations* Times crossword, history research; *Style*— Dr David Hessayon, OBE; ✉ c/o Transworld Publishers Ltd, 61–63 Uxbridge Road, London W5 5SA (☎ 020 8579 2652, fax 020 8231 6666)

HESTER, Stephen A M; *b* 14 December 1960; *Educ* Univ of Oxford (MA); *Career* Credit Suisse First Boston: joined 1982, co-head European Investment Banking 1993–96, memb Exec Bd 1996, chief financial offr 1996–2000, head Fixed Invome Div 2000–01; Abbey National plc: finance dir 2002–03, chief operating offr 2003–04; ceo British Land Company plc 2004–08, chief exec RBS Gp 2008–13, ceo RSA Insurance Gp 2014–; non-exec dep chm Northern Rock 2008, non-exec dir Centrica plc 2016–; *Style*— Stephen Hester, Esq

HETHERINGTON, John William; s of John Albert Hetherington, of Doncaster, S Yorks, and Eva Mary, *née* Reed; *b* 9 July 1951; *Educ* Sir Percy Jackson GS Doncaster, Univ of Birmingham Med Sch (MB ChB); *m* 9 Jan 1991, Kim, *née* Dawes; *Career* house surgn Birmingham Gen Hosp 1974–75, house physician Dudley Rd Hosp Birmingham 1975, SHO (orthopaedics) Nottingham Gen Hosp 1975–76 (concurrently anatomy demonstrator Nottingham Med Sch), surgical trg scheme United Birmingham Hosps 1976–81, registrar in paediatric urology Alder Hay Children's Hosp Liverpool 1981–92, univ tutor in urology St James's Univ Hosp Leeds 1982–85, research fell in prostate cancer Unit for Cancer Research Univ of Leeds 1985–86, sr registrar in urology St Mary's Hosp London 1986–87, lectr and sr registrar in urology Charing Cross Hosp London 1987–88, sr registrar in urology Royal Marsden Hosp London 1988–89, conslt and head Dept of Urology Castle Hill Hosp Cottingham 1989–2013 (clinical co-ordinator for urology 1993–2013); chm: Yorks Urological Cancer Research Gp 1991–95, Humber & East Coast Urology Cancer Network; memb: Genito-Urinary Gp European Orgn for the Research and Treatment of Cancer (EORTC) 1989–, MRC Superficial Bladder Cancer Working Pty 1991–2001, Yorks Urology Trg Ctee 1992–2001, Med Advsy Gp Yorkshire Cancer Orgn 1995–2000, Scientific Ctee Br Prostate Gp 1996–2002; author of numerous articles in urological jls; cmmnd RAMC (TA) 202 Gen Hosp Birmingham 1978–1992; memb: BMA, Br Prostate Gp 1985, EORTC 1989; FRCS 1979, FRCSEd 1979; *Recreations* fell walking, photography; *Style*— John Hetherington, Esq; ✉ Spire Hull & East Riding Hospital, Lowfield Road, Anlaby, Hull HU10 7AZ

HETTIARATCHY, Dr Pearl Daisy Jebaranee; OBE (2002), DL (Hants 2009); *née* Muttiah; da of Solomon Vinnasitamby Muttiah (d 1952), and Grace Constance Manonmanie, *née* Sittampalam (d 1977); *b* 4 February 1942, Colombo, Sri Lanka; *Educ* Holy Family Convent Bambalipittya Sri Lanka, Univ of Colombo Sri Lanka (MB BS), Univ of London (DPM); *m* 2 Jan 1967, Dr Sidney Walter Hettiaratchy, s of Cornelius Peter Hettiaratchy; 2 da (Ashanti Suvendrini (Mrs Dickson) b 25 Jan 1968, Chemaine Natasha (Mrs Bravery) b 25 May 1975), 1 s (Dr Shehan Peter Hettiaratchy b 5 Nov 1969); *Career* pre-registration Kandy Gen Hosp Sri Lanka 1965–66, women's med offr Akurana Sri Lanka 1966–68; conslt psychiatrist (old age psychiatry): St James' Hosp Portsmouth 1975–84 (trg in psychiatry 1968–75), Winchester and Eastleigh Healthcare NHS Tst (formerly Winchester DHA) 1984–2001, W Hampshire Tst 2001–02 (emeritus conslt until 2010); clinical teacher Univ of Southampton 1985–2002, memb Exec Ctee Age Concern Hampshire 1985–93, Mental Health Act cmmr (Sec of State appt) 1989–98, second opinion appt dr (Sec of State appt) 1989–2003 and 2005–; hon conslt St Luke's Hosp for the Clergy London 1990–2003, selector Med Faculty Univ of Southampton 1990–94, conslt advsr Samaritans Winchester and Dist Branch 1990–2002; RCPsych: memb Special Ctee on Unethical Psychiatric Practice 1990–94, vice-pres 1995–97, memb Mental Health Law Sub-Ctee 2000–01, College rep for Southern Region for High Awards 1999–2001; elected memb GMC 1994–2003 (assoc memb 2003–13, screener for conduct and performance, memb Overseas Review Bd, Ctee on Professional Performance, Race Equality and Diversity Ctee and Interim Orders Panel); memb Mental Health Review Tbnl (Miny of Justice appt) 1994–2014; vice-patron: BASE (Br Assoc for Services to the Elderly) 2006–, Abbeyfield 2008–, Smile Support & Care 2012–; postgrad dean's rep Wessex Deanery 2002–07, govr Univ of Winchester 2008–14; memb: BMA, Southern Region Awards Ctee 1997–2000; Hon FRCPsych 2003 (FRCPsych 1986, MRCPsych 1972); *Publications* Care in the Community (contrib chapter, 1982), Psychotherapy Supporting the Carers of Mentally Ill People (contrib chapter, 1992), International Review of Psychiatry (contrib chapter, 1993), Clinical Governance in Mental Health and Learning Disabilities, a practical guide (contrib chapter, 2005); *Recreations* gardening, religious music, spending time with my children and grandchildren; *Style*— Dr Pearl Hettiaratchy, OBE, DL, FRCPsych; ✉ Robin's Hill, 2 Oliver's Battery Road North, Winchester, Hampshire SO22 4JA (☎ 01962 861287, e-mail pearl.hetti@sky.com)

HEUVEL, Christopher John; s of Desmond John Heuvel, of Lower Earley, and Joan Margaret, *née* Hooper; *b* 22 October 1953; *Educ* Douai Sch Woolhampton, Univ of Newcastle upon Tyne (BA, BArch), Poly of Central London (DipTP), Huddersfield Poly (CertEd), Anglia Poly Univ (DMS, MBA), Nottingham Trent Univ (PGCHE); *m* 7 March 1986, Diana Crystal, da of James William Joseph Collis (d 1981), of Ipswich; 1 s (Benjamin b 1985), 1 da (Beatrice b 1986); *Career* architect and teacher; princ in one-man private practice 1980–98, princ architect Carter Design Gp 1999–2004, sr assoc LSI Architects LLP 2005–10, dir 2hD Architects Ltd; sr lectr in environmental science City Coll Norwich 1985–98, sr lectr in architecture and professional studies advsr Nottingham Trent Univ 2010–; memb Cncl RIBA 1998–2004; FRSA 1994, FHEA 2012; *Recreations* the arts, landscape; *Clubs* RIBA, Norfolk Punt, Norfolk Contemporary Art Soc; *Style*— Christopher J Heuvel, Esq; ✉ Chris Heuvel Architect, 9 Earlham Road, Norwich NR2 3RA (☎ 01603 629746, mobile 07598 239263, e-mail chris@2hd.co.uk)

HEWITT, Charles Edward James; s of Sir Nicholas Hewitt, 3 Bt, *qv*, and Pamela, *née* Hunt; *b* Yorks; *Educ* Rugby (received Sword of Honour as CCF senior cadet, 1st XV), Kingston Business Sch (BA); *m* 18 May 2002, Alison Brown; 1 s (Freddie George Charles b 29 Dec 2005); *Career* account mangr Riley Advtg 1993–96; Pen & Sword Books Ltd: publishing mangr 1996–98, chief exec 1998–99, md 1999–; dir: Tours With Experts Ltd 2000–, Barnsley Chronicle 2003–, Script Media 2003–, Acredula Gp 2003–; prop Resolution Vineyard 2007–; memb Young Newspaper Persons Executives Assoc (YNA) 1996; MInstD 1999; *Recreations* pigeon racing, Barnsley FC supporter, viticulture and wine collecting, salmon fishing; *Clubs* Kings; *Style*— Charles Hewitt, Esq; ✉ The Hollies, Huttons Ambo, York YO60 7HF; Resolution Vineyard, Sunnybanks Road, Middleton, Tasmania, Australia (website www.theresolutionvineyard.com); Pen & Sword Books Ltd, 47 Church Street, Barnsley, South Yorkshire S70 2AS (☎ 01226 734222, fax 01226 734438, e-mail charles@pen-and-sword.co.uk)

HEWITT, Gavin James; s of Thomas Hewitt (d 1964), and Daffodil Anne Hewitt (d 2007); *Educ* St John's Sch Leatherhead, Univ of Durham (BA); *m* Sally Jane, da of Norman Lacey; 1 da (Rebecca Jane), 1 s (Daniel James); *Career* reporter BBC TV News 1976–81, corr The Journal (CBC Canada) and documentary maker McNeil-Lehrer Newshour USA 1981–84, corr Panorama (BBC1) 1985–98, special corr BBC News 1999–; *Awards* Broadcast Award 2001, RTS Award 2002, BAFTA Award for Ten O'Clock News coverage of London bombings; *Books* Terry Waite and Oliver North (1991), Soul On Ice

(2005), The Lost Continent (2013); *Style—* Gavin Hewitt, Esq; ✉ BBC, IPC Building, 1 Boulevard Charlegmagne, 1041 Brussels, Belgium (e-mail gavin.hewitt@bbc.co.uk)

HEWITT, Gavin Wallace; CMG (1995); s of Rev George Burrill Hewitt, TD, FEIS (d 1976), and Elisabeth Murray, *née* Wallace (d 1976); *b* 19 October 1944; *Educ* George Watson's Coll Edinburgh, Univ of Edinburgh (MA); *m* 1, 6 Oct 1973 (m dis 2009), Heather Mary, da of Trevor Shaw Clayton, of Whaley Bridge, Derbys; 2 da (Claire Rebecca b 20 March 1975, Mary Elisabeth Courtney b 29 Sept 1979), 2 s (Alexander Francis Reid b 3 Nov 1977, Peter James Clayton b 26 Jan 1982); m 2, 14 Aug 2015, Amanda Harvie; *Career* asst princ Miny of Tport 1967–70, second sec UK delegation to the Euro Communities Brussels 1970–72, first sec Br High Cmmn Canberra 1973–78, first sec and head of Chancery Br Embassy Belgrade 1981–84, head of liaison staff NI Office Belfast 1984–87, dep permanent rep UK mission UN Geneva 1987–92, cnsllr FCO 1992–94; ambass: Croatia 1994–97, Finland 1997–2000, Belgium 2001–03; chief exec Scotch Whisky Assoc 2003–13, dir Spirits Energy Efficiency Co 2003–14; non-exec dir Artisanal Spirits Co Ltd; memb: CBI Trade Assoc Cncl 2003–13, Scottish Cncl for Devpt and Industry 2003–13, Exec Gp Scotland Food and Drink 2008–13, Int Advsy Bd Scotland-Asia Inst 2013–, Advsy Bd Pure Scot; dir UK Bladnoch Distillery Ltd; vice-chm Bd of Govrs Geneva English Sch 1989–92, patron Br Sch of Brussels 2001–03; Global Scot 2001–, Keeper of the Quaich 2009, Liveryman Worshipful Co of Distillers 2014–; *Style—* Gavin Hewitt, Esq, CMG; ✉ 27 Chester Street, Edinburgh EH3 7EN (☎ 0131 226 3909, e-mail gavinhewitt2@googlemail.com)

HEWITT, Prof Geoffrey Frederick (Geoff); s of Frederick Hewitt (d 1961), and Elaine, *née* Ellam (d 1975); *b* 3 January 1934; *Educ* Boteler GS, UMIST (BScTech, PhD); *m* 11 Aug 1956, Shirley Hodges (d 2014), da of Stanley Foulds; 2 da (Karen Louise b 4 April 1958, Alison Jane b 29 Oct 1959); *Career* scientist UKAEA Harwell 1957–90 (div head 1976); fndr and head Heat Transfer and Fluid Flow Service 1968–82; pres: Heat Transfer Soc 1977 and 2000, Inst of Chem Engrs 1989; Courtaulds prof of chem engrg Imperial Coll London 1985–99 (emeritus prof 1999–); foreign assoc US Nat Acad of Engrg 1998; Hon DSc Univ of Louvain, Hon DEng Heriot-Watt Univ 1995, Hon DEng UMIST 1998; FIChemE, FRSC, FIMechE, FCGI, FREng 1985, FRS 1989; *Awards* Donald Q Kern award American Inst of Chem Engrs 1981; Int Centre for Heat and Mass Transfer: fellowship award 1982, Cncl medal Inst of Chem Engrs 1984, Luikov Medal 1996, Arnold Greene Medal Inst of Chem Engrs 2000; Max Jacob award American Soc of Mechanical Engrs 1994, Nusselt-Reynolds Prize 1997, Sr Multiphase Flow Award 2007, Global Int Energy Prize 2007, Imperial Coll Medal 2016; *Books* Annular Two-Phase Flow (with N S Hall Taylor, 1970), Measurement of Two-Phase Flow Parameters (1978), Two-Phase Flow and Heat Transfer in the Power and Process Industries (with J G Collier, A E Bergles, J M Delhaye and F Mayinger, 1981), Introduction to Nuclear Power (with J G Collier, 1987), Process Heat Transfer (with G L Shires and T R Bott, 1994), Encyclopedia of Heat and Mass Transfer (1998), Prediction of Turbulent Flows (with C Vassilicos, 2005), Multiphase Flow Metering (with G Falcone), Crude Oil Fouling (with F Coletti, 2015); *Recreations* music, bridge; *Style—* Prof Geoffrey Hewitt, FRS, FREng; ✉ Department of Chemical Engineering, Imperial College London, Prince Consort Road, London SW7 2BY (☎ 020 7594 5562, e-mail g.hewitt@imperial.ac.uk)

HEWITT, Prof (Brian) George; s of Thomas Douglas Hewitt (d 1991), and Joan, *née* Cousins (d 1991); *b* 11 November 1949; *Educ* Doncaster GS for Boys, St John's Coll Cambridge (open Henry Arthur Thomas scholarship, John Stewart of Rannoch univ scholarship, coll Graves' Prize, MA, Warr classical studentship, Dip Linguistics, PhD, Br Cncl exchange postgrad (to Tbilisi), Marjory Wardrop scholarship); *m* 1976, Zaira Kiazimovna, *née* Khiba; 2 da (Amra Shukia b 18 Nov 1977, Gunda Amza-Natia b 2 Sept 1984); *Career* lectr in linguistics Univ of Hull 1981–88; SOAS Univ of London: lectr in linguistics and Caucasian languages 1988–92, reader in Caucasian languages 1992–96, prof of Caucasian languages 1996–2015; first pres Societas Caucasologica Europaea 1986–88 and 1988–90, memb Philological Soc 1973–; memb Bd of Mgmnt Marjory Wardrop Fund 1983–; one-time tstee: North Caucasus Tst (NCT), Med Aid and Relief for the Children of Chechnya (MARCCH); memb Writers' Union of Abkhazia 2003; hon memb: Int Circassian Acad of Sciences 1997, Acad of Sciences of Abkhazia 1997; hon prof Abkhazia State Univ 1995; FBA 1997; Abkhazian Order of Honour and Glory (Axjdz-Apsha) 2004, Medal of Abkhazia's Miny of Foreign Affrs 2013, Medal of Abkhazia's Miny of Defence 2015; *Books* Lingua Descriptive Studies 2: Abkhaz (1979), Typology of Subordination in Georgian and Abkhaz (1987), Georgian – A Learner's Grammar (1995, 2 edn 2005), Structural Reference Grammar of Georgian (1995), A Georgian Reader (1996), An Abkhaz Newspaper Reader (with Zaira Khiba, 1998), The Abkhazians – A Handbook (ed, 1998), The Languages of the Caucasus – Scope for Study and Survival (1998), Introduction to the Study of the Languages of the Caucasus (2004), Abkhaz Folk-tales (2005), Pages from Abkhazian Folklore (with Zurab Dzhapua, 2008), Abkhaz: A Comprehensive Self-Tutor (2010), Discordant Neighbours: A Reassessment of the Georgian-Abkhazian and Georgian-South Ossetian Conflicts (2013); *Recreations* classical music; *Style—* Prof George Hewitt, FBA; ✉ School of Oriental and African Studies, Thornhaugh Street, Russell Square, London WC1H 0XG (☎ 01302 784735, e-mail gh2@soas.ac.uk)

HEWITT, Jamie Neil Terry; s of Peart Derek Hewitt, and Leanne, *née* Vallely; *b* 3 January 1959; *Educ* Rugby, City of London Poly (BA); *m* Roslyn Joyce, da of Thomas Russell Lennon; 2 da (Eleanor Joy b 21 July 1990, Madeleine Victoria b 3 Oct 1998), 1 s (Harry Moutray b 6 March 1992); *Career* articled clerk Peat Marwick Mitchell CAs 1980–83, co sec Zetland Advertising Ltd 1983–86, chief accountant Conran Design Group Ltd 1986–88; fin dir: Brewer Jones Ltd 1988–89, Butterfield Day Devito Hockney Ltd 1989–95, Collett Dickenson Pearce & Partners Ltd advtg agency 1995–97, McCann-Erickson Advertising Ltd 1997–2000, Hat Pin plc 2001–2003, WCRS Ltd 2003–04, M&C Saatchi UK 2004–10, M&C Saatchi Worldwide 2010–; ACA 1983; *Recreations* rugby, running, dogs, riding in Richmond Park; *Style—* Jamie Hewitt, Esq; ✉ M&C Saatchi Ltd, 36 Golden Square, London W1F 9EE (☎ 020 7543 4500)

HEWITT, Jeffrey Lindsay; s of Enoch Reginald Hewitt, of Stoke-on-Trent, Staffs, and Brenda Elizabeth, *née* Mason; *b* 6 September 1947, Stoke-on-Trent; *Educ* Longton Sixth Form Coll Stoke-on-Trent, St Catherine's Coll Oxford (MA, Gibbs prize), Stanford Univ (MBA); *m* 6 July 1968, Pauline Margaret, da of Reginald Rezin; 1 s (Richard Lindsay b 11 Jan 1975), 1 da (Karen Faye b 9 March 1977); *Career* with Arthur Andersen & Co 1969–72, The Boston Consulting Gp 1974–80, strategy dir Coats Viyella plc 1980–90, fin dir Unitech plc 1990–96, dep chm and fin dir Electrocomponents plc 1996–2005, chm Plasmon plc 2006–07, chm Regenersis plc 2007–11; dep chm: Dialight plc 2001–07, ZincOx Resources plc 2008–11; non-exec dir: Cookson Gp plc 2005–, TDG plc 2006–08, Whatman plc 2007–08, Cenkos Securities plc 2008–, Foreign & Colonial Investment Tst 2010–, Cyril Sweett Gp 2010–; external chm Audit Ctee John Lewis Partnership 2005–; memb DTI Industrial Devpt Advsy Bd 1985–95; memb Advsy Bd Oxford Philomusica Orch, former memb Business Forum Saïd Business Sch Univ of Oxford; ICAEW Gold Medal 1972; memb Ct of Assts Worshipful Co of Glovers; FCA 1974, CCMI, MRSC; *Recreations* theatre, concerts, tennis, antique maps; *Clubs* Royal Over-Seas League; *Style—* Jeffrey Hewitt, Esq; ✉ Palo Alto, 6 College Way, Northwood, Middlesex HA6 2BL (☎ 01923 821190, mobile 07767 887186)

HEWITT, Michael Geoffrey; s of Geoffrey Hewitt, of Bradmore, Wolverhampton, and Edna, *née* Sharples; *b* 6 September 1962; *Educ* Wolverhampton Sch, Univ of Stirling (BA); *m* 21 April 1990, Sara da of Ian Bryant; 1 s (Max b 17 April 1994), 2 da (Susanna b 21 May 1996, Matilda b 7 Jan 2000); *Career* ed The Publisher 1987–89, ed Journalist's Week 1989–91; Haymarket Publishing: ed Marketing 1993–96, publisher Marketing 1998–2000, Planning 1998–, new media dir Haymarket Business Publications Ltd 2000–03; publishing dir: World Business 2003–, Management Today 2003–; pres and ceo gtnews; Freeman City of London 1993, Liveryman Worshipful Co of Stationers and Newspapermakers 1994; *Recreations* travel, books, military history, food; *Clubs* Arts, Royal Over-Seas League; *Style—* Michael Hewitt, Esq

HEWITT, Rt Hon Patricia Hope; PC (2001); da of Sir (Cyrus) Lenox Simson Hewitt, OBE, of Canberra, Aust, and (Alison) Hope Hewitt (d 2011); *b* 2 December 1948, Canberra, Australia; *Educ* Girls' GS Canberra, Aust Nat Univ Canberra, Newnham Coll Cambridge (MA), Univ of Sydney (AMusA); *m* 1, 8 Aug 1970 (m dis 1978), (David) Julian Gibson-Watt, s of Baron Gibson-Watt (Life Peer, d 2002); m 2, 17 Dec 1981, His Hon Judge William Jack Birtles, *qv*, s of William George Birtles (d 1976), of Shepperton, Middx; 1 da (Alexandra b 1986), 1 s (Nicholas b 1988); *Career* gen sec NCCL 1974–83, policy coordinator to Ldr of the Opposition 1988–89 (press and broadcasting sec 1983–88), dep dir and sr res fell Inst for Public Policy Research 1989–94, dir of research Andersen Consulting (now Accenture) 1994–97; MP (Lab) Leicester W 1997–2010; economic sec to the Treasy 1998–99, min of state for e-commerce and small business DTI 1999–2001, sec of state for trade and industry and cabinet min for women 2001–05, sec of state for health 2005–07; sr ind dir BT Gp plc 2009–14, non-exec dir Eurotunnel Gp 2010–, non-exec dir Bupa 2013–14, memb Global Advsy Bd Sutherland Global Servs 2012–, sr advsr FTI Consulting 2015–; chair UK India Business Cncl 2009–; assoc Newnham Coll Cambridge 1989–97 (hon assoc 2012–), visiting fell Nuffield Coll Oxford until 1992; tstee Inst for Public Policy Research 1995–98; memb: Bd Int League for Human Rights 1979–1997, Sec of State's Advsy Ctee on the Employment of Women 1977–83, vice-chm Bd Br Cncl 1997–98; dep chair Cmmn for Social Justice 1992–94; Parly candidate Leicester East 1983; FRSA; *Books* The Abuse of Power: Civil Liberties in the United Kingdom (1983), Your Second Baby (with Wendy Rose-Neil, 1990), About Time: The Revolution in Work and Family Life (1993); *Recreations* gardening, music, theatre, cooking; *Style—* The Rt Hon Patricia Hewitt; ✉ UKIBC, 12th Floor, Millbank Tower, London SW1P 4QP (e-mail patricia.hewitt@ukibc.com)

HEWITT, Dr Penelope Boulton; da of Leslie Frank Hewitt (d 1967), of Cheam, Surrey, and Beryl Boulton (d 1978); *b* 23 July 1938, Cheam, Surrey; *Educ* Sutton HS GPDST, Guy's Hosp, Univ of London (MB BS); *Career* res anaesthetist Guy's Hosp 1962–63; registrar in anaesthetics 1963–67: Nat Hosp for Nervous Diseases Queen Square London, St Mary's Hosp, Guy's Hosp; Guy's Hosp: sr registrar 1967–72, conslt anaesthetist 1972–2001, hon sr lectr in anaesthetics 1992–, emeritus conslt anaesthetist 2001–; recognised teacher in anaesthetics Univ of London 1974–2001; approved lectr: Central Midwives Bd 1979–83, English Nat Bd 1983–2001, combined Guy's and St Thomas' Hosp Schs of Midwifery, King's Coll 1994–2001; anaesthetics tutor Faculty of Anaesthetists RCS Guy's Hosp 1980–87, regnl assessor in anaesthetics for confidential enquiries into maternal deaths SE Thames Region Dept of Health 1981–2000, hon sec and treas SE Thames Soc of Anaesthetists 1984–87 (pres 1991–93), anaesthetic assessor confidential enquiry into perioperative deaths Nuffield Prov Hosp Tst 1985–87, examiner for fellowship examination of the Royal Coll of Anaesthetists 1986–97, examiner for European Dip in Anaesthesia and Intensive Care 1992–2003, chm OSCE Working Pty Royal Coll of Anaesthetists 1994–96, memb Cncl Anaesthetics Section RSM (hon sec 1987–89, pres elect 1996–97, pres 1997–98, immediate past pres 1998–99, vice-pres 1999–2002, membership offr 2001–04), hon life memb Assoc of Dental Anaesthetists 2002– (hon asst sec and ed of proceedings 1989–92, hon sec 1992–95, pres 1995–97), memb Cncl European Soc of Anaesthesiology 2005–06, memb Cncl Medical Soc of London 2011–; Sutton and District Medical Soc: memb Ctee 2008, asst hon sec 2008–10, hon sec 2010–15, pres 2015–; examiner GMC 1997–2008; assoc ed European Jl of Anaesthesiology 2000–04; senator European Acad of Anaesthesiology 2001–05; hon memb Anaesthetic Research Soc 2002–; LRCP, MRCS, FFARCS (FRCA) 1966; *Books* Emergency Anaesthesia (1986, 2 edn 1998); *Recreations* golf, gardening; *Clubs* Addington Golf, RAC; *Style—* Dr Penelope B Hewitt; ✉ Hillcrest, 150 Burdon Lane, Cheam, Sutton, Surrey SM2 7DQ (☎ 020 8642 2993)

HEWITT, Peter John; CBE (2008); s of Charles Rowland Hewitt (d 1993), and Eunice, *née* Nixon (d 2004); *b* 17 November 1951; *Educ* Barnard Castle Sch, Univ of Leeds (BA, MA); *m* 1 (m dis), Joan, *née* Coventry; 3 da (Laura b 26 March 1978, Anna b 29 July 1980, Kate b 23 Jan 1984); m 2, Dr Judith Bell; *Career* Inter-Action Trust 1976–77, arts offr N Tyneside BC 1977–82; Northern Arts 1982–97: community arts and gen arts offr, asst dir Local Devpt, dep dir, chief exec 1992–97; corp affrs dir Tees HA 1997–98, chief exec Arts Cncl of England (latterly Arts Cncl England) 1998–2009, chief exec Guy's and St Thomas' Charity 2009–16; *Recreations* the arts, walking, cycling; *Style—* Peter Hewitt, Esq, CBE; ✉ Guy's and St Thomas' Charity, Francis House, 9 King's Head Yard, London SE1 1NA (☎ 020 7089 4550, website www.gsttcharity.org.uk)

HEWITT, Peter William Hughes (Pete); s of David Claud Hughes Hewitt (d 1981), and Eileen Winifred, *née* Chambers; *b* 9 October 1962, Brighton, E Sussex; *Educ* Christ's Hosp, London Coll of Printing, Nat Film Sch; *m* 14 June 1994, Sophie Jane, da of George Ringrose (d 2003); 3 da (Molly Rose b 18 March 1992, Elsie Rose b 5 March 1996, Dora Unity Rose b 1 Jan 2001); *Career* filmmaker; feature films incl: Bill and Ted's Bogus Journey 1991, Tom and Huck 1995, The Borrowers 1997, Whatever Happened to Harold Smith 1999, Thunderpants 2001, Garfield 2004, Zoom 2006; TV incl: Wild Palms (miniseries, ABC US) 1992, Princess of Thieves (ABC US) 2000; BAFTA Award for Best Short Film (for The Candy Show) 1990; *Style—* Pete Hewitt

HEWLETT, David; *b* 2 October 1954; *Educ* Forest Sch Winnersh, Univ of Birmingham (BA); *Career* lecteur d'Anglais Univ of Montpellier 1978–80, regnl examiner Languedoc-Rousillon Univ of Cambridge 1978–80, researcher and lectr Univ of Cambridge 1981–86; with Dept of Social Security 1986–87, dep mangr Benefits Office Stoke Newington 1987–88, with Dept of Health 1988–90, head Family Health Servs Mgmnt Unit Dept of Health 1990–91; NHS Exec: head NHS Performance Mgmnt Central Unit 1991–93, head GP Fundholding and Prescribing 1993–95, head NHS Purchasing and Commissioning 1995–97, head NHS Quality Strategy 1997; Dept of Health: head Health Servs Branch 1 1997–2000, head Specialist Health Servs 2000–; *Recreations* current affairs, modern lit, modern art, motorcycling; *Style—* David Hewlett, Esq

HEWLETT, Hon Thomas Anthony; s of Baron Hewlett, CBE (Life Peer, d 1979), and Millicent, *née* Taylor (d 1991); *b* 31 March 1952; *Educ* Oundle, Magdalene Coll Cambridge (MA); *m* 2 Oct 1980, Jane Elizabeth, da of Brian A Dawson, of Aldeburgh, Suffolk; 2 da (Emily b 14 Feb 1983, Georgina b 24 July 1984), 2 s (Harry, Charles (twins) b 30 Dec 1986); *Career* dir: Anchor Chemical Gp plc 1976–88, V Berg & Sons Ltd 1986–91; vice-pres Morgan Guaranty Tst 1974–84; owner Portland Gallery 1985–; Freeman City of London, Liveryman Worshipful Co of Tin Plate Workers; *Books* Cadell – A Scottish Colourist (1988); *Recreations* golf, tennis; *Clubs* Aldeburgh Golf, Royal St Georges Golf, Chelsea Arts; *Style—* The Hon Thomas Hewlett; ✉ Kyson House, Woodbridge, Suffolk IP12 4DN (☎ 0139438 3441); Portland Gallery, 3 Bennet Street, London SW1A 1RP

HEWSON, Paul; *see:* Bono

HEY, Prof John Denis; s of George Brian Hey (d 1991), of Adlington, Cheshire, and Elizabeth Hamilton, *née* Burns; *b* 26 September 1944; *Educ* Manchester Grammar, Univ of Cambridge (BA), Univ of Edinburgh (MSc); *m* 18 Oct 1968 (m dis 1998), Marlene Robertson, da of Thomas Bissett (d 1958), of Perth; 2 da (Clare b 1979, Rebecca b 1984), 1 s (Thomas b 1981); *Career* econometrician Hoare & Co Stockbrokers 1968–69; lectr in econs: Univ of Durham 1969–73, Univ of St Andrews 1974–75; Univ of York: lectr in social and econ statistics 1975–81, sr lectr 1981–84, prof of econs and statistics 1984–98 (part-time 1998), co-dir Centre for Experimental Econs 1986–; professore ordinario Universita di Bari Italy 1998–2006, professore ordinario LUISS Rome Italy 2006–10; ed Economic Journal 1986–96, author of articles for numerous jls; memb: RES, AEA; *Books* Statistics in Economics (1974), Uncertainty in Microeconomics (1979), Britain in Context (1979), Economics in Disequilibrium (1981), Data in Doubt (1984), A Century of Economics (ed, 1990), Experiments in Economics (1991), Recent Developments in Experimental Economics (ed, 1993), The Economics of Risk and Uncertainty (ed, 1996), Intermediate Microeconomics (2003), Microeconomia (2007); *Recreations* cycling, walking, eating; *Style*— Prof John Hey; ✉ Department of Economics, University of York, York YO1 5DD (☎ 01904 433786, fax 01904 433759, e-mail jdh1@york.ac.uk)

HEYES, David; *b* 2 April 1946, Manchester; *Educ* Blackley Tech HS, Open Univ; *Career* dep dist mangr Manchester CAB; cncllr (Lab) Oldham MBC 1992– (sec Lab Gp 1994–2000, chair Personnel Ctee 1994–2000), MP (Lab) Ashton-under-Lyne 2001–15; vice-chair Ashton-under-Lyne Lab Pty; memb Unison; *Style*— David Heyes, Esq; ✉ House of Commons, London SW1A 0AA

HEYGATE, Sir Richard John Gage; 6 Bt (UK 1831), of Southend, Essex; s of Sir John Edward Nourse Heygate, 4 Bt (d 1976), suc bro, Sir George Lloyd Heygate, 5 Bt (d 1991); *b* 30 January 1940; *Educ* Repton, Balliol Coll Oxford; *m* 1, 1968 (m dis 1972), Carol Rosemary, da of late Cdr Richard Michell, RN, of Amberley, W Sussex; m 2, 1974 (m dis 1988), Jong-Ja Hyun, da of In Suk, of Seoul, South Korea; 1 da (Eun-Hee Isobella Gage b 1977); m 3, 1988, Susan Fiona, da of late Robert Buckley, of Peasmarsh, E Sussex; 2 s (Frederick Carysfort Gage b 1988, Robert George Liam b 1991); *Heir* s, Frederick Heygate; *Career* IBM (United Kingdom) Ltd 1967–70, McKinsey & Co Inc 1970–77; dir: Olaf Foods Ltd 1977–85, Index Group 1985–86; princ McKinsey & Co Inc 1986–98, ceo Sophron Partners 1998–2005, managing ptnr Oneida Assocs 2008–; chm: Mouse Smart Software 2004–09, Birgate Partnership 2006–07, Welford Technol Ptnrs 2006–10, Red Unida 2011–, Anglo Cathay Enterprises 2013–; dir: Isis Technology 1999–, Web Connectivity 2008–11, Global Project Partners 2013–15, Horizon Software Solutions 2013–, Macromac plc 2015–; fndr and dir The 88 Initiative 2013–; memb Advsy Bd Fortone Gp 2015–, advsr China Rail Construction Gp 3 2015–; FRSA 2008; *Books* Endangered Species (2008), The Book of English Magic (2009); *Recreations* rowing, motorcycling; *Clubs* RSA; *Style*— Sir Richard Heygate, Bt; ✉ e-mail rheygate@yahoo.co.uk

HEYHOE FLINT, Baroness (Life Peer UK 2011), of Wolverhampton in the County of West Midlands; Rachael Heyhoe Flint; OBE (2008, MBE 1971), DL (W Midlands 1997); da of Geoffrey Heyhoe (d 1972), of Penn, Wolverhampton, and Roma Kathleen, *née* Crocker (d 1978); *b* 11 June 1939; *Educ* Wolverhampton Girls' HS, Dartford Coll of PE (DipPhysEd); *m* 1 Nov 1971, Derrick Flint, s of Benjamin Flint, of Underwood, Notts; 1 s (Benjamin b 8 June 1974); *Career* women's cricket int England 1960–83 (capt 1966–77, scored 179 v Aust (Oval) 1976 (world's fifth highest score by woman in tests)); hon life memb MCC (first lady appointed) 1999– (memb Cricket Ctee 2003–10, memb Main Ctee 2004–11, tstee 2011–13), pres: Lady Taverners 2001–11, England and Wales Cricket Bd 2011–16; tstee England and Wales Cricket Tst; women's hockey int England 1964; journalist; ambass La Manga Club Spain, vice-pres Wolverhampton Wanderers FC; Best After Dinner Speaker Guild of Professional Toastmasters 1972; hon fell Univ of Wolverhampton 2002; Freeman City of Wolverhampton 2011; Hon DUniv Bradford 2002, Hon DSc Univ of Greenwich 2003, Hon Dr in Sports Science Leeds Met Univ 2006; *Books* Fair Play, History of Women's Cricket (1976), Heyhoe (autobiography, 1978); *Recreations* watching football and cricket, golf; *Clubs* South Staffs Golf (Wolverhampton), La Manga Club Resort (Spain), Patshull Park Golf and Country (Wolverhampton); *Style*— The Baroness Heyhoe Flint, OBE, DL; ✉ c/o House of Lords, London SW1A 0PW

HEYLIN, Angela Christine Mary (Mrs Maurice Minzly); LVO (2008), OBE (1997); da of Bernard Heylin (d 1985), and Ruth Victoria, *née* D'Arcy (d 1997); *b* 17 September 1943, London; *Educ* Apsley GS, Watford Coll; *m* 13 March 1971, Maurice Minzly, s of Solomon Minzly (d 1974); 1 s (James b 1982); *Career* chief exec Charles Barker Lyons 1984 (formerly dir F J Lyons, dir 1976, jt md 1980), chm and chief exec Charles Barker Gp 1988 (dir 1984), chm Charles Barker BSMG (formerly Charles Barker plc) 1996–98 (chief exec 1992–96), UK pres Charles Barker BSMG Worldwide 1999–2001; non-exec dir: Mothercare plc 1997–2004, Provident Financial plc 1998–2003, Austin Reed plc 2001–06; tstee Historic Royal Palaces 1998–2007 (chm Campaign Bd 2003–08); chm The House of St Barnabas 2001–04, chm PRCA 1990–92; memb Citizen's Charter Advsy Panel 1993–97; FCIPR 1987, FPRCA 2010; *Publications* Putting It Across (1991); *Recreations* theatre, gardening; *Style*— Miss Angela Heylin, LVO, OBE; ✉ 46 St Augustine's Road, London NW1 9RN (☎ 020 7485 4815, mobile 07767 491508, e-mail angela@heylin.com)

HEYMAN, Norma Frances; *b* Liverpool; *Career* film and TV prodr; former actress; memb Cncl BAFTA, fndr memb Bd Women in Film and TV, memb American Acad, memb Advsy Ctee Br Ind Film Awards; Women in Film Business Award 1992, Special Jury Prize British Ind Film Awards 2004, 25th Anniversary Award London Critics' Circle Film Awards 2005, Women in Film and Television Lifetime Achievement Award 2006; *Films* credits incl: The Honorary Consul (first woman in Br to produce a solo independent prodn) 1983, Burning Secret 1987, Buster (Oscar nomination) 1988, Dangerous Liaisons 1989 (3 Oscars, 7 Academy Award nominations, 10 BAFTA's, César Best Foreign Film), Clothes in the Wardrobe (for BBC, theatrical release in the USA as The Summer House (film won Writers' Guild Award, BAFTA nomination)) 1992, Sister My Sister 1993–94, The Secret Agent 1995–96, Gangster No 1 2000, Kiss Kiss (Bang Bang) 2000, Mrs Henderson Presents (winner: Ensemble Award Nat Bd of Review, London Film Critics' Circle Award; nominated for: 2 Oscars, 3 Golden Globes, 4 BAFTAs) 2006; *Style*— Mrs Norma Heyman; ✉ c/o NFH Ltd & Heyman-Hoskins, 37 Ovington Square, London SW3 1LJ (☎ 020 7584 3355, fax 020 7589 1863)

HEYS, Prof Steven Darryll; s of Keith Heys, and Alice, *née* McNamee; *Educ* St Mary's Coll Blackburn, Univ of Aberdeen (BMedBiol, MB ChB, MD, PhD); *m*; 3 c; *Career* Capt RAMC (V) 252 Highland Field Ambulance 51 Highland Bde 1985–89; SHO Aberdeen Royal Infirmary 1982–84 (house offr 1981–92), memb Health Bd Aberdeen 1984–87, registrar (neurosurgery, orthopaedics, plastic surgery and gen and vascular surgery) Aberdeen Royal Infirmary 1984–86, registrar (gen surgery (gastroenterology)) Woodend Hosp Aberdeen 1985–86, registrar (gen, paediatric and urology) Dr Grays Dist Gen Hosp Elgin 1986–87, Wellcome research trg fell and hon research assoc Rowett Research Inst and Dept of Surgery Univ of Aberdeen 1987–89, hon sr registrar Grampian Health Bd 1989–92; locum conslt surgn: Dr Grays Hosp Elgin 1988, 1989 and 1990, Balfour Hosp Orkney 1990, 1992, 1993 and 1994; hon conslt surgn Aberdeen Royal Hosps NHS Tst 1992–; Univ of Aberdeen: tutor in surgery 1984–87, lectr 1989–92, sr lectr 1992–96, dir Surgical Nutrition and Metabolism Unit Dept of Surgery 1995–, reader 1996–99, prof of surgical oncology 1999–, specialist assessor readership appointments, memb Strategic Planning Gp for Med Sch 1991, memb Med Sch Curriculum Steering Gp 1995–, memb Dean's Advsy Research Ctee Faculty of Med 1996–, cancer research program ldr 2004–, head Div of Applied Medicine and co-dir Inst of Medical Sciences Sch of Medicine and Dentisty 2011–, dean Sch of Medicine, Med Sciences and Nutrition; clinical tutor in minimal access therapy (gen surgery) Minimal Access Therapy Trg Unit for Scotland Scottish Royal Colls 1994–97; hon professorial research fell Rowett Research Inst 1992–; external examiner: Queen's Univ Belfast, RCS, Univ of Southampton, Univ of Dundee, Univ of Belfast, St Georges Coll London; examiner in surgery for fellowship RCPSGlas, external assessor for Francis Mitchell Caird Prize in Surgery RCS(Ed), assessor Scottish Mortality Study; specialist assessor for professorial appointments Queen's Univ Belfast; reviewer: NHS R&D prof, Health Technol Bd for Scotland; chm: Aberdeen Breast Res Gp 1998–, Symptomatic Breast Service Grampian Univ Hosps NHS Tst 2000–03; vice-chm NE of Scotland Clinical and Audit Focus Gp Breast Cancer; Br Assoc of Surgical Oncology memb Surgical Advsy Bd RCS(Ed) 2001–07, Br Assoc of Surgical Oncology Scottish Rep UK Ctee for Breast Surgery 2001–08, memb Scientific Advsy Bd Breast Cancer Campaign UK 2009–; GMC inspr new med sch UEA 2000–, memb QABME teams GMC 2000–; ptnr PMETB 2007–, chair SIGN Guidelines for Breast Cancer Treatment 2011–; memb Editorial Bd World Jl of Surgical Oncology; assessor and reviewer for pubns incl: Clinical Immunotherapeutics, Br Jl of Surgery, The Cancer Jl, Br Jl of Nutrition, Clinical Science, Nutrition and Cancer, Jl of the Royal Coll of Surgns of Edinburgh, BMA Annual Book Competition, Euro Jl of Applied Physiology and Occupational Med, Br Jl of Cancer, Surgical Oncology; memb: Surgical Res Soc, Br Assoc of Surgical Oncology, Nutrition Soc, BMA; FRCSGlas 1985, FRCS (ad eundem) 1998, FRCSEd (without examination) 1999, fell HE Acad 2007; *Awards* as student: Alexander Smith Cardno Prize 1976, George Thomson Bursary 1976, Durno Prize 1977, MRC Trg Award 1977–78, Scot Prize 1979, Russel Gold Medal 1979, Ogston Prize 1979, Munday and Venn Prize 1980, Dyce Davison Medal 1981, McQuibban Prize 1981 (dux in surgery), McQuibban Prize 1981 (dux in med), Smith Davidson Prize 1981, Lyon Prize 1981, David Tomory Prize 1981, Murray Medal and Scholarship 1981; travelling fellowships: Chest, Heart and Stroke Assoc 1980 (at Northwestern Univ Chicago), Wellcome Travelling fell 1988 (at Huddinge Univ Hosp Karolinska Inst Stockholm), Br Jl of Surgery Soc 1993 (at oncological centres of excellence in Europe); *Publications* War Surgery 1914–18 (jtly, 2012), War, Pestilence and the Surgeon's Blade (2014), Understanding the Somme 1916 – an illuminating battlefield guide (jtly, 2014); author of over 200 scientific papers, 450 presentations to learned societies and 35 book chapters; *Recreations* karate, cycling, bagpiping; *Style*— Prof Steven Heys; ✉ University of Aberdeen, Medical School Buildings, Foresterhill, Aberdeen AB9 2ZD (☎ 01224 552105, e-mail s.d.heys@abdn.ac.uk)

HEYWOOD, Sir Jeremy; KCB (2012, CB 2008), CVO (1999); *Career* sr roles incl princ private sec to Norman Lamont and Kenneth Clarke (as Chllrs of the Exchequer), head of securities and markets policy and head of corp and mgmnt change HM Treasy until 1997, princ private sec to PM 1999–2003, md and co-head UK Investment Banking Div Morgan Stanley 2004–07, head of domestic policy and strategy Cabinet Office 2007–08, perm sec to the PM 2008–12, sec to the Cabinet 2012–, head Civil Service 2014–; *Style*— Sir Jeremy Heywood, KCB, CVO; ✉ Cabinet Office, 70 Whitehall, London SW1A 2PS

HEYWOOD, John Kenneth; s of Samuel George Heywood (d 1987), of Devon, and Hilda Kathleen, *née* Lamey (d 1985); *b* 29 January 1947; *Educ* Shebbear Coll, UCL (LLB), INSEAD Fontainebleau (Advanced Mgmnt Course); *m* 1976, Susan Ann Heywood; 2 s (James Samuel b 15 Nov 1980, William John b 27 Oct 1983), 1 da (Sophie Elizabeth b 2 May 1990); *Career* PricewaterhouseCoopers (formerly Price Waterhouse before merger 1998): joined 1968, ptnr 1980–2006, dir London office and memb UK Exec 1991–95, chm E European firm 1993–2006, memb European Mgmnt Bd 1993–98, dir PricewaterhouseCoopers China 1996–98; chair Exemplas Holdings Ltd 2015–; non-exec dir Home Office 2007–12 (chair Audit Ctee), ind memb Audit Ctee Evraz Gp SA; tstee UCL Friends Tst, govr and memb Ct Herts Univ 2007–15; fell UCL 2007; FCA; *Recreations* golf, tennis, opera, history; *Style*— John Heywood, Esq

HEYWOOD, Matthew David; s of David Main Heywood (d 1999), and Patricia Ann, *née* Robinson; *b* 26 December 1970, Derby; *Educ* Dunfermline HS, Duncan of Jordanstone Coll of Art Univ of Dundee (BSc, BArch); *m* 10 Aug 2002, Sarah Elizabeth, *née* Casemore; 2 s (Noah David b 20 Sept 2005, Jonah Luke b 21 March 2008); *Career* architect; J R Wilks & G R Vaughen-Ellis Architects 1991–92, T P Bennett Partnership 1994–96; assoc dir Future Systems 2000–03 (joined 1996, projects incl Media Centre Lord's Cricket Ground 1996–99, Selfridges Birmingham 1999–2003), dir Matthew Heywood Architecture 2003–15 (projects incl Trish House Yalding 2011–13), Foster + Ptnrs 2015–; RIBA 1995, memb ARB 1995; *Style*— Matthew Heywood, Esq; ✉ Matthew Heywood Limited, 23 Berber Road, London SW11 6RZ (☎ 020 7352 7583, e-mail email@matthewheywood.com)

HEYWOOD, Sir Peter; 6 Bt (UK 1838), of Claremont, Lancashire; s of Sir Oliver Kerr Heywood, 5 Bt (d 1992), and Denise, *née* Godefroi; *b* 10 December 1947; *Educ* Bryanston, Keble Coll Oxford (MA); *m* 1970, Jacqueline Anne, da of Sir Robert Frederick Hunt, CBE (d 2004); 2 da (Vanessa Jane (Mrs Paul Fewell) b 1975, Annabel Sarah (Mrs Ian Gallifant) b 1976); *Heir* bro, Michael Heywood; *Career* company director; chair of Genesis Tst Bath; *Style*— Sir Peter Heywood, Bt

HEYWOOD, Victoria Mary Taylor (Vikki); CBE (2012); da of late Kenneth Heywood Taylor and Gillian Dorothea, *née* Black; sis of Lord Taylor of Goss Moor, *qv*; *b* 25 June 1956, London; *Educ* Truro HS, Fortismere Sch London, Central Sch of Speech and Drama (Dip); *m* 1, 1988, Christopher Wright; 1 s (Thomas b 11 Feb 1992); m 2, 2004, Clive Jones, CBE, *qv*; *Career* stage mangr 1977–84, gen mangr London Bubble Theatre Co 1986–89, exec dir Contact Theatre Manchester 1989–93, gen mangr London Int Festival 1994, exec dir Royal Court Theatre 1994–2001, exec dir RSC 2003–12 (govr 2006–12); chm: RSA 2012–, Mountview Acad of Theatre Arts 2012–; vice-chm: Lyric Theatre Hammersmith 1999–2004, Young Vic Theatre 2002–06; tstee Shakespeare Birthplace Tst 2004–12; memb Cncl Univ of Warwick 2008–14, chm Warwick Cmmn 2015; chm 18–14 Now 2013–; Hon DLitt Univ of Birmingham 2009; FRSA 2005, CCMI 2007; *Recreations* sleeping, eating, reading, walking; *Clubs* Reform; *Style*— Mrs Vikki Heywood, CBE

HIBBERD, Dr Alan Ronald; s of George Peter Hibberd (d 1946), of Bendigo, Victoria, Aust, and Flora Gertrude, *née* Dainty (d 1973); *b* 25 October 1931, Bendigo, Victoria, Australia; *Educ* High Sch Bendigo (Alexander Rushall scholarship), Ridley Coll Melbourne, Victorian Coll of Pharmacy Melbourne (PhC), Chelsea Coll Univ of London (DCC, PhD); *m* 1, 1954, Doreen Imilda, da of James Collier; 2 s (David b 1954, Andrew b 1957), 2 da (Wendy b 1959, Christine b 1962); m 2, 1974, Lois, da of Howard Kenneth Stratton; *Career* specialist in clinical ecology/clinical toxicology; community pharmacy practice Melbourne 1953–73; dir: ARH Pharmaceuticals 1959–74, Pressels Laboratories 1959–74; pt/t demonstrator in practical pharmaceutics Victorian Coll of Pharmacy 1961–64; Victorian Branch Aust Dental Assoc 1966–74: lectr to postgrads in pharmacology and therapeutics, conslt in dental therapeutics and prescribing; i/c of Drug Info Dept and Ward Pharmacy Services Hackney Hosp London 1975, res fell Pharmacy Dept Chelsea Coll London 1976–79, lectr Sch of Pharmacy Univ of London 1980–81, tutor and in charge clinical pharmacy Northwick Park Hosp Harrow and NW Thames Regional Health Authy 1980–81, first course organiser and supervisor MSc course in clinical pharmacy Univ of London (first clinical pharmacy degree course in SE England) 1980–81, dir Hibbro Research Hereford 1981–84, private practice in clinical ecology and toxicology London 1985–2009, conslt in clinical pharmacology and toxicology Biocare Ltd 1989–, conslt in clinical biochem/pharmacology to Soc for Promotion of Nutritional Therapy (UK) 1992–2001, scientific advsr to Register of Nutritional Therapists (UK) 1993–2009, private consultancy in clinical ecology, clinical toxicology and nutrition 2009–; author of numerous articles and scientific papers on the metabolism of nicotine and related compounds, mercury toxicity, and relating to specialist field and contrib to many learned pubns; vice-pres The Int Acad of Oral Med and Toxicology (UK) 1994–98; memb: Pharmaceutical Soc of Victoria 1953 (fell (by examination) 1961), Royal Soc of Victoria

1968–74 and 2010–, Br Dental Soc for Clinical Nutrition 1985–98, Nutrition Assoc 1987–, Environmental Dental Association USA 1991–98, British Soc for Ecological Medicine (BSEM, formerly British Soc for Allergy, Environmental and Nutritional Medicine) 1993–, Br Assoc for Nutritional Therapy 2001–; FRSH 1971, MRPharmS 1974–2005, fell Pharmaceutical Soc of Aust 1983 (life fell 1991), FRSM 2003; *Recreations* golf, flying light aircraft, bridge, travelling, languages, music, theatre; *Clubs* Ross-on-Wye Golf, Herefordshire Flying, Greenacres Golf (Melbourne); *Style*— Dr Alan Hibberd; ✉ c/o 42 Kendal Street, London W2 2BU (e-mail ar.hibberd@gmail.com)

HIBBERT, William John; s of Sir Reginald Hibbert, GCMG (d 2002), of Machynlleth, Powys, and Ann Alun, *née* Pugh; *b* 23 February 1957; *Educ* Charterhouse, Worcester Coll Oxford (MA); *m* 1, (Caroline) Maria, da of Sir John Lucas-Tooth, 2 Bt, *qv*; m 2, Julia Mair Wheldon, da of Anthony Smith, QC; 3 da (Cosima Mary b 1984, Clover Frances b 1988, Saffron Lucy b 2005); *Career* called to the Bar Inner Temple 1979; *Style*— William Hibbert, Esq; ✉ Gough Square Chambers, 6/7 Gough Square, London EC4A 3DE (☎ 020 7353 0924, fax 020 7353 2221, e-mail william.hibbert@goughsq.co.uk)

HIBBIN, Sally; da of Eric Hibbin (d 2001), and Nina, *née* Masel (d 2004); *b* 3 July 1953; *Educ* Tottenham Sch, Keele Univ (BA), Open Univ (MA); *Career* journalist and producer; memb: BAFTA, WFTV; *Films* as documentary film-maker for Channel 4 incl: Live A Life 1982, The Road to Gdansk 1985 and Great Britain United 1991; as prodr credits incl: A Very British Coup 1988, Riff-Raff 1991 (European Film of the Year and Cannes Critics' Award), Raining Stones 1992 (Cannes Jury Prize and Evening Standard Award for Best Film), Ladybird Ladybird 1993, i.d. 1994, Carla's Song 1995, Stand and Deliver 1998, Hold Back the Night 1999, Dockers; as exec prodr credits incl: Bad Behaviour 1992 (Evening Standard Award – Peter Sellers Best Comedy), London South-West (short) 1992, Tomorrow Calling (short) 1993, Land and Freedom 1994, The Englishman Who Went Up A Hill But Came Down A Mountain 1994, The Governess, Liam 2000, The Intended, Blind Flight 2003, Yasmin 2004, Almost Adult 2006, I Know You Know 2008; *Publications* The Making of Licence to Kill, The Making of Back to the Future; *Recreations* walking, Spurs FC, cooking, bridge; *Clubs* The Union; *Style*— Ms Sally Hibbin; ✉ Parallax East Ltd, Victoria Chambers, St Runwald Street, Colchester CO1 1HF

HICHENS, Antony Peverell; RD (1969); s of Lt Cdr Robert Peverell Hichens, DSO and bar, DSC and two bars, RNVR, and Catherine Gilbert Enys; *b* 10 September 1936; *Educ* Stowe, Magdalen Coll Oxford, Univ of Pennsylvania; *m* 1963, Sczerina Neomi, da of Dr F T J Hobday; 1 da (Tamsin); *Career* Nat Serv Midshipman RNVR 1954–56, ret as Lt Cdr RNR 1969; called to the Bar Inner Temple, dep md Redland Ltd 1979 (fin dir 1972), md fin Consolidated Gold Fields plc 1981–89; chm: Caradon plc 1987–89, Y J Lovell (Holdings) plc 1990–93, Caradon plc 1990–98, LASMO plc 2000–01 (dep chm 1995–2000), DS Smith plc 1999–2006, WaterRower (UK) Ltd 2007–11; dir: Greenfriar Investment Co plc 1985–98, Candover Investments plc 1989–2010 (dep chm 1991–2004), J P Morgan Income & Capital Tst 1989–2013, South Western Electricity plc 1990–95, Courtaulds Textiles plc (dep chm) 1990–99, British Coal Corporation 1992–96, Limit plc (formerly London Insurance Market Investment Trust) 1993–2000, Global Stone Corp 1994–98; memb: Takeover Panel 2002–10, Oxford Ct of Benefactors; Waynflete fell Magdalen Coll Oxford 1996; *Books* Gunboat Command: The Biography of Lieutenant Commander Robert Hichens, DSO*, DSC**, RNVR; *Recreations* travel, shooting, marine paintings, wine; *Clubs* Brooks's, Naval; *Style*— Antony Hichens, Esq; ✉ Slape Manor, Netherbury, Bridport, Dorset DT6 5LH

HICKEY, Christopher John; CMG (2009); s of William Hickey (d 1971), and Mary, *née* Watkins (d 1995); *b* 8 November 1951; *Educ* Monmouth, Univ of Sheffield (BA), Univ of Leeds (PGCE), RSA (Dip TEFL), UCL (MPhil), London Business Sch (Sr Exec Prog); *m* Dec 1984, Pauline; 1 da (Caroline b 1986), 1 s (Michael b 1988); *Career* British Cncl: first sec (educn) Ivory Coast 1986–90, English language offr Barcelona 1990–93, head Educn Enterprises Spain 1993–95, dir Educn Enterprises 1999–2000 (dep dir 1996–99), dir Greece 2000–03, dir Spain 2003–09, dir France 2009–13, dir British Cncl Schs 2013–; chair British Nat Ctee for Cultural Olympiad 2001–04; *Books* The Influence of Malraux on Camus (1986); *Recreations* literature, language, the arts, watching football, restaurants; *Style*— Christopher Hickey, Esq, CMG; ✉ British Council, 10 Spring Gardens, London SW1A 2BN (☎ 020 7389 4143, e-mail chrishickey@britishcouncil.org)

HICKEY, His Hon Judge Simon Roger Greenwood; *Career* called to the Bar 1985; recorder 2002, dep district judge Maigstrates Courts 2006, district judge Magistrates Courts 2009, circuit judge (North Eastern Circuit) 2012–; *Recreations* cycling, reading, writing; *Clubs* RAF; *Style*— His Hon Judge Hickey; ✉ Durham Crown Court, Old Elvet, Durham DH1 3HW

HICKEY, Dr Stephen Harald Frederick; *née* Hickinbotham; s of Rev Dr James Peter Hickinbotham (d 1990), and Ingeborg Alice Lydia, *née* Manger; *b* 10 July 1949; *Educ* St Lawrence Coll, Corpus Christi Coll Oxford (BA), St Antony's Coll Oxford (DPhil); *m* 1976, Janet Elizabeth, *née* Hunter; 3 s (James b 1979, Thomas b 1982, Edward b 1985); *Career* admin trainee and higher exec offr (admin) DHSS 1974–79, asst private sec to Sec of State Social Services 1978–79 and 1984–85, princ/asst sec DHSS 1979–89, seconded to Rank Xerox (UK) Ltd 1989–90, asst sec Benefits Agency/DSS 1990–94; chief exec Civil Serv Coll Cabinet Office 1994–98; princ fin offr DSS 1998–2000, DG corp servs DSS/DWP 2000–02, acting chief exec Highways Agency 2003, DG Dept for Tport 2003–08; non-exec dir NHS Wandsworth Primary Care Tst 2009–13 (vice-chair 2011–13), lay memb NHS Wandsworth Clinical Commissioning Gp 2012–; chair Community Tport Assoc 2010–, memb Ind Tport Cmmn 2011–; tstee: St George's Hosp Charity 2008– (chair 2012–), Disabled Living Fndn 2009–14; memb RSA; *Books* Workers in Imperial Germany: The Miners of the Ruhr (1985); *Recreations* music, walking, tennis, history; *Style*— Dr Stephen Hickey; ✉ 21 Stanley Road, London SW19 8RE (e-mail shfhickey@gmail.com)

HICKINBOTTOM, Hon Mr Justice; Sir Gary Robert Hickinbottom; kt (2009); s of Samuel Geoffrey Hickinbottom, and Jean Irene, *née* Greaney; *b* 22 December 1955, Birmingham; *Educ* Queen Mary's GS Walsall, UC Oxford (MA); *m* Caroline Hamilton; *Career* lectr: PCL 1980–82, UC Oxford 1987–89; admitted solicitor 1981, ptnr CMS Cameron McKenna (formerly McKenna & Co) 1986–2000, admitted solicitor-advocate (all courts) 1997, asst recorder 1994–98, recorder 1998–2000, circuit judge 2000–09, dep High Court judge 2001–09, chief social security and child support cmmr 2003–09, chief pensions appeal cmmr 2005–09, designated civil judge for Wales 2005–07, judge Supreme Court of the Falkland Islands 2005–, dep sr pres of tbnls 2008–09, pres Admin Apps Chamber of Upper Tbnl 2008–09, bencher Middle Temple 2009, judge of the High Court 2009–, Queens Bench Div liaison judge for Northern and North Eastern Circuits 2012–13 and for Midland, Wales and Western Circuits 2013–16, sr liaison judge for diversity 2012–15; pres Slrs' Assoc of Higher Court Advocates 2010–; memb: Gen Bar Cncl and Law Soc working pty on the civil courts 1992–93, Law Soc working pty on group actions 1994–2000, Central London County Court Mediators Panel 1996–98, Acad of Experts' Disciplinary Ctee 1996–2000, Judicial Technol Bd 2004–05 and 2010–12; parking adjudicator Parking Appeals Service (London) and Nat Parking Adjudication Serv 1994–2000, asst cmmr Boundary Cmmn for England 2000; author of various articles and contributions to books on law and legal procedure; registered mediator; Liveryman Worshipful Co of Arbitrators 2009 (Ct Asst 2011–, Warden 2016–), Freeman City of London 2009, Liveryman Worshipful Co of Bakers 2012; fell Soc of Advanced Legal Studies; FCIArb (DipCIArb); *Recreations* choral singing, opera and ballet, sport; *Clubs* London Welsh, Reform; *Style*— The Hon Mr Justice Hickinbottom; ✉ The Royal Court of Justice, Strand, London WC2A 2LL

HICKISH, Dr Tamas Frederick Gordon; s of Gordon Walter Hickish, and Aileen, *née* Key; *Educ* Brockenhurst Coll, KCL, The Queen's Coll Oxford (MA), Westminster Med Sch (MB BS), Univ of London (MD); *Career* conslt med oncologist Poole and Royal Bournemouth Hosps 1995–; visiting prof Bournemouth Univ; author and co-author of publications on oncology; tstee Youth Cancer Tst; FRCP (2000), MRCP (1988); *Recreations* marathon running; *Style*— Dr Tamas Hickish

HICKMAN, James; s of Derek Hickman (d 1999), and Sue, *née* Peacock; *b* 2 February 1976; *Educ* William Hulmes GS, Univ of Manchester; *m* 7 Nov 2009, Sophy, *née* White; 1 s (Jack James b 25 July 2011), 1 da (Amelie Bliss 8 June 2013); *Career* swimmer; memb: Stockport Metro Swimming Club, City of Manchester Aquatics Club, City of Leeds Swimming Club; pres Manchester Univ XXI Club (Elite Sports Alumni) 2013–; 100m butterfly: finalist Olympic Games 1996, finalist World Championships 1997, European record holder 1997 and 1998, world record holder 1998, third World Short-Course Championships 1999, fourth Cwlth Games 2002, second World Short-Course Championships 2004; 200m butterfly: Br record holder 1993, Gold medal European Jr Championships 1993, Bronze medal Cwlth Games 1994, finalist Olympic Games Atlanta 1996, Gold medal World Short-Course Championships 1997, 1999, 2000, 2002 and 2004, finalist World Championships 1998, Gold medal Cwlth Games (championship record) 1998, world record holder 1998, Bronze medal Cwlth Games 2002; 4x100m medley: Gold medal European Junior Championships 1993, Bronze medal Cwlth Games 1994, Bronze medal World Short-Course Championships 1997, Silver medal Cwlth Games 1998, Bronze medal World Championships 1999, Silver medal Cwlth Games 2002; 200m individual medley: Silver medal Cwlth Games 1998, Gold medal European Short-Course Championships 1998, Silver medal World Short-Course Championships 1999; Silver medal 400m individual medley Cwlth Games 1998, Br record holder 200m Backstroke 1998 (Br junior record holder 1991), Cwlth record holder 100m and 200m individual medley 1998; ret 2004; dir Made in Manchester Prodns (PR for the 2008 World Swimming Championships Manchester 2006–08 and World Lacrosse Championships 2010, also prodns for ITV and BBC Radio 2, 4 and World Serv), dir Enjoy Swimming 2008–, dir Greater Sport (Manchester) 2008–, global sports mktg mangr Speedo Int 2011–; Young Mancunian of the Year 1994 and 1996, Mancunian of the Year 1998; *Style*— James Hickman, Esq; ✉ e-mail james@jameshickman.com, website www.jameshickman.com, Twitter @jh_5wim

HICKMAN, Dep District Judge Neil Edward; s of late Tony (Albert Frederick William) Hickman, and Nellie Elizabeth Hickman; *b* 13 May 1951; *Educ* King Edward's Sch Birmingham, Worcester Coll Oxford (MA); *m* 1973, Susan Mary, da of late William Charles Tucker, and Mary Elayne Tucker; 1 da (Jo), 1 s (Ben); *Career* admitted slr 1976, appointed dep registrar/district judge 1986, sr ptnr Batcheldors 1997–98, district judge (SE (Provincial) Circuit) 2000–16 (dep district judge 2016–); pres Bedfordshire Law Soc 1994–95; chm Bedford Divnl Liberal Assoc 1978–79, hon slr Bedfordshire Housing Aid Centre 1985–2000; author of various articles in legal periodicals, contrib Family Court Practice, former gen ed Civil Court Service; *Books* May it Please You, Madam... A Little Book of Legal Whimsy (2016); *Recreations* chess, singing, bellringing, family and ecclesiastical history; *Style*— Dep District Judge Hickman; ✉ Milton Keynes County Court, 351 Silbury Boulevard, Central Milton Keynes MK9 2DT (☎ 01908 302800)

HICKS, Dr Colin Peter; CB (2007); s of George Stephen Frederick Hicks (d 1976), and Irene Maud, *née* Hargrave; *b* 1 May 1946, Wimbledon, Surrey; *Educ* Rutlish Sch Merton, Univ of Bristol (BSc, PhD); *m* Elizabeth Joan, da of Rev Sidney Eric Escourt Payne, of Birmingham; 2 da (Rachel Heather b 1970, Joanna Katharine b 1972); *Career* lectr in chemistry Univ of the West Indies 1970–73, ICI research fell Univ of Exeter 1973–75, researcher Nat Physical Laboratory 1975–80, various research positions DTI 1980–83, tech advsr Barclays Bank 1983–84, dep dir Laboratory of the Govt Chemist 1984–87, sec Industrial Devpt Advsy Bd 1988–90, under sec i/c res and technol policy DTI 1990–94, under sec i/c environment and energy technologies DTI 1994–96, dir Environment Directorate DTI 1996–99, dir of space DTI and DG British National Space Centre 1999–2006, pres Eurisy 2006–15; sec Teddington Baptist Church 1979–1990, memb London Baptist Assoc Cncl 1986–2001, memb London Baptist Assoc Bd 2002–12, tstee Baptist Union of GB 2009–13 (memb Cncl 2006–13); FRSC 1985; *Recreations* computing; *Style*— Dr Colin Hicks, CB

HICKS, Nicola Katherine; MBE (1995); da of Philip Lionel Shalto Hicks, of Radcot House Bampton Oxfordshire, and Jill Tweed; *b* 3 May 1960, London; *Educ* Frensham Heights Sch, Chelsea Sch of Art (BA), RCA (MA); *m* 1 (m dis); m 2, 28 Feb 1992, Daniel Flowers; 1 s (William Gabriel Sholto b 31 March 1992), 1 da (Edith Lilly b 13 September 1994); *Career* artist; RWA, FRBS; *Solo Exhibitions* incl: Angela Flowers Gallery London 1985 and 1986, Angela Flowers Co Cork 1986, Beaux Arts Gallery Bath 1987, Flowers East London 1988, 1989, 1992, 1994, 1995, 1996 and 1998, Tegnerforbundet Oslo 1991, Fire and Brimstone (Flowers East and Watermans Art Centre Brentford) 1991, Peter Scott Gallery Lancaster Univ 1993, Castlefield Gallery Manchester 1993, Djanogly Art Gallery Univ of Nottingham 1995, Furtive Imagination at Whitworth Art Gallery Manchester and Yorkshire Sculpture Park 1996, Riverside Studios London 1997, Galerie de Bellefeuille Quebec 1997, Outrageous Fortune (Flowers East London) 1998, Flowers West Santa Monica CA 1999, Galerie Rachlin Lemarié Beaubourg Paris 1999, Outrageous Fortune (Ferens Art Gallery Hull) 1999, Flowers Central London 2002, New Grafton Gallery London 2003, Newby Hall Yorks 2003, Schoenthal Monastery Langenbuck 2003, Monuments to Love (Flowers East London) 2003, Flowers NY 2004, Abbot Hall Kendal 2005, Drawings (Flowers Central London) 2006; *Work in Collections* incl: Arthur Andersen, Contemporary Arts Soc, Chase Manhattan Bank, Castle Museum Norwich, Coopers & Lybrand, Govt Art Collection, Huddersfield Art Gallery, Hakone Open Air Museum, Ipswich Cncl; cmmn for monument in Battersea Park; artist in residence Brentwood HS; *Recreations* poker, backgammon, dice, dog and horse racing, travelling, searching for horned rhino on elephantback and white water surfing, gardening and gaming; *Clubs* Chelsea Arts; *Style*— Nicola Hicks, MBE; ✉ c/o Flowers East, 82 Kingsland Road, London E2 8DP (☎ 020 8985 3333, fax 020 8985 0067, e-mail gallery@flowerseast.co.uk, website www.flowerseast.co.uk)

HICKS, Philip; s of Brig Philip Hugh Whitby Hicks, CBE, DSO, MC (d 1967), and Patty, *née* Fanshawe (d 1985); *b* 11 October 1928; *Educ* Winchester, RMA Sandhurst, Royal Acad Schs (Dip RAS); *m* 22 July 1952, Jill, da of Maj Jack Tweed (d 1979); 1 da (Nicola b 1960), 1 s (David b 1971); *Career* Irish Gds 1946–47, 2 Lt Royal Warwicks Regt 1948–49; artist (represented by David Messum Fine Art Cork St); pt/t teacher various art schs 1960–85, concentrated full time on painting 1986–; solo exhibitions incl: Camden Arts Centre 1971, Richard Demarco Gallery Edinburgh 1971, Robert Self Gallery London 1971, Imperial War Museum 1975, Galerie VFCU Antwerp 1977–79, Battersea Arts Centre 1977, Gallery 22 Dublin 1980, New Art Centre (London) 1980–82, Galleri Engstrom Stockholm 1985, Gallery 10 London 1986–91, Bohun Gall Henley 1986–90, Heffer Gallery Cambridge 1992, Courcoux and Courcoux Fine Art Salisbury 1992, David Messum Fine Art London 1996, 1997, 1998, 2000, 2001, 2003, 2006, 2009, 2011 and 2013; mixed exhibitions incl: Tate Gallery London 1976, Mall Galleries London 1980, Israel Israel Museum Jerusalem 1980–81, Serpentine Gallery London 1982, Angela Flowers Gallery 1985, Art '89 London 1989; works in public collections incl: Tate Gallery, Contemporary Art Soc, V&A, Imperial War Museum; Br Cncl award 1977; also performed professionally

H

as a jazz pianist; past chm and vice-pres Artists Gen Benevolent Inst; *Books* Philip Hicks (monograph by John Russell Taylor, 2013); *Recreations* music; *Clubs* Chelsea Arts, Royal Over-Seas League; *Style*— Philip Hicks, Esq; ✉ Radcot House, Buckland Road, Bampton, Oxfordshire OX18 2AA (☎ 01993 850347); c/o Messum's, 8 Cork Street, London W1X 1PB

HICKS, Sophie; da of late Richard Hicks, and Joan Hicks; *b* 18 September 1960; *Educ* AA Sch of Architecture (AADipl), RIBA; *m* 1988 (m dis 2008), Roderick Campbell; 1 s (Arthur b 1988), 2 da (Edie b 1990, Olympia b 1995); *Career* fashion ed British Vogue and Tatler magazines 1977–86, acted in the film L'Intervista (dir Federico Fellini) 1986, stylist with Azzedine Alaïa 1986–88, student AA 1987–93, in private practice SH Ltd Architects 1990–; projects: various private house designs 1991–98, architect for Paul Smith's Westbourne House and int shops 1997–2001, architect for Royal Acad exhbns (Sensation – Young British Artists from the Saatchi Collection 1997, Picasso – Painter and Sculptor in Clay 1998, Maeght Fndn 2008), concept for Chloe Stores Worldwide 2001–07 (architect of flagship stores in London, Paris, Tokyo and Hong Kong, plus 100 other stores worldwide), architect Yohji Yamamoto flagship store Paris 2008–; property developments in London 2010; memb Cncl AA 1993–99 (vice-pres 1997–99); *Recreations* travelling; *Style*— Ms Sophie Hicks; ✉ SH Architects Limited, 17 Powis Mews, London W11 1JN (☎ 020 7792 2631, fax 020 7727 3328, e-mail sophie@sophiehicks.com, website www.sophiehicks.com)

HICKS, William David Anthony; QC (1995); s of Maj-Gen (William) Michael Ellis Hicks (d 2008), and Jean Hillary, *née* Duncan; *b* 11 June 1951; *Educ* Eton, Magdalene Coll Cambridge (MA); *m* 1982, Jennifer Caroline, da of Dr Louis Ross; 2 da (Julia Rebecca b 6 June 1986, Olivia Clare b 4 May 1988), 1 s (George David Alexander b 1 March 1990); *Career* called to the Bar Inner Temple 1975; memb Atlantic Salmon Tst, tstee Salmon and Trout Conservation UK; Liveryman Worshipful Co of Fishmongers; *Recreations* painting, fishing, bee keeping, walking; *Clubs* Flyfishers'; *Style*— William Hicks, Esq, QC; ✉ Landmark Chambers, 180 Fleet Street, London EC4A 2HG (☎ 020 7430 1221, fax 020 7421 1399, e-mail clerks@landmarkchambers.co.uk)

HICKSON, Peter Charles Fletcher; s of Geoffrey Fletcher Hickson (d 1978), of Cambridge, and Jane Margaret Amy, *née* Cazenove (d 1993); *b* 30 May 1945; *Educ* Uppingham, Fitzwilliam Coll Cambridge (MA); *m* Rosemary, da of Hugh and Margaret Dawson, of Newport, Gwent; 1 da (Sally b 1978), 3 s (Richard b 1979, David b 1981, James b 1983); *Career* articled clerk Chalmers Impey 1967–71, chief accountant Doulton Glass Industries 1971–78, fin dir Wimpey Asphalt 1978–80, fin dir Tarmac Building Products 1980–85, dep chief exec United Scientific Holdings 1986–89, fin dir MAI plc 1991–96, fin dir PowerGen plc 1996–2002; chm: Anglian Water Gp Ltd (formerly AWG plc) 2003–09, Communisis plc 2007–, Chemring Gp plc 2010–16; non-exec dir: Meridian Broadcasting Ltd 1991–95, Intrum Justitia NV 1993–97, Anglia Television 1993–95, RAC plc 1994–2002, Telent plc (formerly Marconi Corp) 2004–07, Scottish Power 2006–07, London & Continental Railways Ltd 2007–11, Kazakhmys 2009–11; sr ind dir Harworth Gp plc (formerly UK Coal plc) 2011–16; memb Bd Orbis UK 2008– (chm 2015–), treas Orbis Int 2010–13; govr St John's Sch Leatherhead 2003–14 (chm 2006–14); FCA 1970; *Recreations* cricket, reading, golf, music; *Clubs* Oxford and Cambridge, City of London, MCC, Royal Wimbledon Golf, Wimbledon Park Golf, Real Club de Golf Las Brisas, Isle of Harris Golf; *Style*— Peter Hickson, Esq; ✉ Communisis plc, Longbow House, 14–20 Chiswell Street, London EC1Y 4TW (☎ 020 7382 8950, e-mail peter.hickson@communisis.com)

HIDDLESTON, Thomas William (Tom); *b* 9 February 1981; *Educ* Pembroke Coll Cambridge, RADA; *Career* actor; Breakthrough South Bank Award 2013; *Film* incl: Unrelated 2008, Archipelago 2010, Thor 2011, Midnight in Paris 2011, The Deep Blue Sea 2011, War Horse 2011, Avengers Assemble 2012, Only Lovers Left Alive 2013, Thor: The Dark World 2013, Exhibition 2013, Muppets Most Wanted 2014, I Saw the Light 2015, Crimson Peak 2015, High-Rise 2016; *Theatre* incl: Yorgjin Oxo: The Man (Theatre 503 The Latchmere Battersea) 2005, The Changeling (Barbican and European tour) 2006, Cymbeline (Barbican and world tour, Best Newcomer Laurence Olivier Award 2008) 2007, Othello (Donmar Warehouse) 2008 (third prize Ian Charleson Award 2008, Whatsonstage.com Theatregoers' Award for Best Supporting Actor in a Play 2008), Ivanov (Wyndham's Theatre) 2008 (Whatsonstage.com Theatregoers' Award for Best Supporting Actor in a Play 2008), Coriolanus (Donmar Warehouse and NT) 2013–14; *Television* incl: Nicholas Nickleby (ITV) 2001, Conspiracy (HBO) 2001, Armadillo (BBC) 2001, The Gathering Storm (HBO) 2002, A Waste of Shame (BBC) 2005, Suburban Shootout (Channel 5) 2006–07, Miss Austen Regrets (BBC) 2008, Cranford (BBC) 2009, Wallander (BBC) 2008–10, Henry IV Part 1 (BBC) 2012, Henry IV Part 2 (BBC) 2012, Henry V (BBC) 2012, The Night Manager (BBC) 2016; *Style*— Mr Tom Hiddleston; ✉ c/o Christian Hodell, Hamilton Hodell, 20 Golden Square, London W1F 9JL

HIDER, (Kenneth) Mark; s of Maj Kenneth George Hider, RA, of Hampstead, London, and Marian, *née* Richards; *b* 18 September 1953; *Educ* Sir William Borlase's Sch Marlow, Trinity Coll Oxford (MA); *m* 20 June 1981, Nicola Louise, da of John Haigh; 3 s (Tom, Ben, George); *Career* former media res controller Scottish Television, subsequently analyst rising to a sr planner Masius advtg; Ogilvy & Mather: joined London office 1982, initially sr planner, successively UK planning dir, Ford of Europe planning dir and UK business devpt dir, estab strategic planning consultancy 1995, strategy dir for Ford account 1995–97, global head of client servs Jaguar account 1997–2000; chief exec NY office Imagination Gp 2000–06, exec vice-pres and dir of engagement strategy Publicis USA 2006–; memb: Mktg Soc, Market Res Soc; MIPA; *Recreations* cricket, soccer, theatre, walking the dog, supporting Manchester United FC, travel; *Style*— Mark Hider, Esq; ✉ Publicis USA, 4 Herald Square, 950 6th Avenue, New York NY 10001, USA (website www.publicis-usa.com)

HIGGINS, Dr Andrew James; s of Edward James Higgins (d 1966), and Gabrielle Joy, da of Sir John Kelland; *b* 7 December 1948; *Educ* St Michael's Coll Leeds, RVC, Univ of London (BVetMed, PhD), Centre for Tropical Veterinary Med Univ of Edinburgh (MSc); *m* 19 Dec 1981, Nicola Lynn, da of Peter Rex Eliot (d 1980); 1 s (Benjamin b 1982), 3 da (Amelia b 1984, Joanna b 1986, Venetia b 1993); *Career* cmmnd RAVC 1973, Capt, served Dhofar War 1974; veterinary offr HM The Sultan of Oman 1975–76, veterinary advsr The Wellcome Fndn 1977–82, conslt FAO 1981–86, scientific dir and chief exec Animal Health Tst 1988–99, chm Strata Technol Ltd 2001–11, managing conslt Compton Fundraising Conslts 1999–2014; hon vet advsr to Jockey Club 1988–99, hon scientific advsr Fédération Equestre Internationale 1991–2010 (memb Veterinary Ctee, chair Medication Advsy Gp 1990–2010); Greyhound Bd of GB: ind doping and medication advsr 2009–13, memb Disciplinary Ctee and Impartiality Ctee 2009–, chair Ind Anti-doping and Medication Control Review 2009–10, chair Doping and Medication Advsy Panel 2010–12, ind doping and medication advsr 2012–14; memb: Welfare and Ethics Ctees ZSL 1987–2014, Govt Advsy Ctee on Quarantine 1997–98, Lord Chancellor's Advsy Sub-Ctee for W Suffolk 1999–2008; chair Veterinary Panel Br Equestrian Fedn 2004–09; ed-in-chief The Veterinary Jl 1991–2015 (dep ed 1990–91, hon ed-in-chief 2016–); chm Retired Greyhound Tst 2008–15; tstee: Pet Plan Charitable Tst 1995–2000, Soc for the Protection of Animals Abroad (SPANA) 1985–98 (vice-chair 1986–98), Dogs Trust and chair Canine Welfare Grants Ctee 1999–2009, RCVS Tst 2001–06, Animals in War Meml Fund 2001–08; tstee and memb Cncl World Horse Welfare 1999–2006 (hon scientific advsr 2006–), hon life memb: Dogs Trust, SPANA, IVSA; Univ of London Laurel 1971, Equine Veterinary Jl Open Award 1986, Central Veterinary Soc Centenary Prize 1986, Br Veterinary Jl George Fleming Prize 1987, Ciba-Geigy Prize for Research in Animal Health 1985, Pres's Medal Veterinary Mktg Assoc 1997; Liveryman Worshipful Co of Farriers; FBS, scientific fell Zoological Soc of London, MRCVS; *Books* An Anatomy of Veterinary Europe (contrib, 1972), The Camel in Health and Disease (ed and contrib, 1986), The Equine Manual (ed, 1995, 2 edn 2005), With the SAS and Other Animals (2011, pbk 2015); papers in scientific and general pubns and communications to learned societies; *Recreations* skiing, countryside, opera; *Clubs* Kennel (hon memb 2015, tstee Kennel Club Charitable Tst 2016–), RSM; *Style*— Dr Andrew Higgins; ✉ e-mail tvj@aht.org.uk

HIGGINS, Benny; *Educ* Univ of Glasgow (Football blue); *Career* Standard Life: joined 1983 (qualified actuary 1986), various sr appts, appointed gen mangr (sales) 1996; Royal Bank of Scotland: joined 1997, chief operating offr Tesco Personal Finance 1997–98 (memb Bd), appointed md Retail Banking 1998, chief exec Retail Banking 1999–2006, chm Royal Scottish & Nat West Life, chm RBSG Independent Financial Services; head of retail businesses HBOS plc 2006–07, ceo Tesco Personal Finance 2008–; memb Bd Citizens in the USA; *Recreations* reading, art, music, sport – particularly football (former capt Celtic Youth Team); *Style*— Benny Higgins, Esq

HIGGINS, Prof Christopher Francis; s of Prof Philip John Higgins, of Durham, and Betty Ann, *née* Edmonds; *b* 24 June 1955; *Educ* Raynes Park Grammar/Comp Sch, Univ of Durham (scholar, BSc, PhD, W E Foster prize), Royal Coll of Music (exhibitioner, Hugh Bean prize), Univ of Oxford (MA); *m* 1, 1978 (m dis), Elizabeth Mary Joy; 2 da (Alison Elizabeth b 1982, Julia Katherine b 1984); m 2, 1994 (m dis), Suzanne, *née* Wilson; 3 da (Katherine Ann b 1989, Jennifer Dorothy b 1992, Emily Frances b 1995); *Career* SERC/NATO fell Univ of Calif Berkeley 1979–81, prof of molecular genetics Univ of Dundee 1988–89 (lectr 1981–87, reader 1987–88); Univ of Oxford: princ scientist Imperial Cancer Res Fund 1989–93, dep dir Inst of Molecular Med; prof and head Nuffield Dept of Clinical Biochemistry 1993–97; fell: Keble Coll Oxford 1989–93, Hertford Coll Oxford 1993–97; dir MRC Clinical Sciences Centre and prof and head of Div of Clinical Sciences Imperial Coll London 1998–2007, vice-chllr and warden Durham Univ 2007–14, pro-chllr Durham Univ 2014–15; res fell Lister Inst 1983–89, Howard Hughes int res scholar 1993–98; chair Spongiform Encephalopathy Advsy Ctee (SEAC) 2004–11; memb: Cncl BBSRC 1997–2000, Cncl Acad Med Sci 2001–03, Human Genetics Cmmn 2006–09, Exec Ctee Assoc of Medical Research Charities; specialist advsr House of Commons Select Ctee on Stem Cells 2004–06; memb Bd Regnl Devpt Agency (ONE) 2007–11, chair of tstees Nat Youth Choirs of GB 2011–; tstee: 2Higher Ground 2001–04, Future Harvest UK 2001–05, Kennedy Inst for Rheumatology 2004–07, Suffolk Acads Tst 2015–; govr W Suffolk Coll 2015–; DL (Durham) 2010–15; Fleming award Soc for General Microbiology 1987, CIBA medal and prize Biochemical Soc 1994; fell European Molecular Biology Orgn 1989; FRSE 1990, FMedSci 1998, FRSA 2006; *Recreations* daughters, medieval house, opera, classical music; *Style*— Prof Christopher Higgins, FRSE, FRSA, FMedSci; ✉ e-mail chris.higgins@durham.ac.uk

HIGGINS, Clare Frances Elizabeth; da of James Stephen Higgins, and Paula Cecilia, *née* Murphy; *Educ* St Philomena's Convent Sch, Ecclesbourne Sch, LAMDA; *Career* actress; *Theatre* Royal Exchange: Isabella in Measure for Measure, Alexis in Rollo, Judith in Blood Black and Gold, The Deep Man; Greenwich: Kay in Time and the Conways, Julie in The Rivals, Stella in A Street Car Named Desire; RSC: Titania in A Midsummers Night's Dream 1989–90, Gertrude in Hamlet 1989–90, Cleopatra in Antony and Cleopatra 1992–93; RNT: Lili Brik in The Futurists 1986, Katherine in The Secret Rapture 1988, Queen Elizabeth in Richard III 1990–91, Regan in King Lear 1990–91, Amelia in Napoli Milionaria 1991, Lyndsey Fontaine in The Absence of War 1993–94, Princess Kosmanopolis in Sweet Bird of Youth 1995 (Best Actress: Olivier Award, Critics' Circle Award and Time Out Reader's Award 1995), Martha Dobie in The Children's Hour 1995 (Critics' Circle Best Actress Award 1995), Stella in The Walls 2001, Ursula in Vincent in Brixton (also at Wyndam's Theatre, Golden Theatre, Broadway, The Playhouse Theatre) 2002 (Best Actress Olivier Award, Critics' Circle Award, Evening Standard Award, Tony Nomination), Major Barbara 2008, A Slight Ache 2008, Oedipus 2008, All's Well That Ends Well 2009; other credits incl: A View from the Bridge (Harrogate), The White Devil (Oxford Playhouse), Beethoven's Tenth (Vaudeville), Jenkin's Ear (Royal Court), The Ride Down Mt Morgan (Wyndhams, world premiere), A Letter of Resignation (Comedy Theatre) 1998, Arkadina in The Seagull, Liz in Private Lives (West Yorkshire Playhouse) 1998–99, Hesione Hushabye in Heartbreak House (Chichester) 2000, Martha in Who's Afraid of Virginia Woolf (Bristol Old Vic) 2002, Hecuba (Donmar Warehouse) 2004 (Best Actress Olivier Award), Death of a Salesman (Lyric Theatre) 2005, Night of the Iguana (Lyric) 2006, Phaedra (Donmar Warehouse) 2006; *Television* incl: Pride and Prejudice, Unity, Byron, The Concubine, Mitch, The Citadel, Cover Her Face, Foreign Body, Beautiful Lies, After the War, Downtown Lagos, Boon, Inspector Alleyn, Circle of Deceit, Men of the Month, Absence of War, Kavanagh QC, Silent Witness; *Film* incl: 1919, Hellraiser, Hellbound, The Fruit Machine, Bad Behaviour, Small Faces, The House of Mirth, Caught in the Act, The Libertine, The Golden Compass; *Recreations* yoga, being in the country, reading, theatre-going, seeing friends, cats; *Style*— Miss Clare Higgins

HIGGINS, David Charles; s of Prof Peter Higgins, and Jean Margaret Lindsey, *née* Currie; *b* 23 June 1958, Birmingham; *Educ* St Bedes Sch Bishton, Ampleforth, Oxford Brookes Univ (BSc); *m* 18 Oct 2014, Kristina Jurgenson; *Career* VNU Business Pubns 1982–85, Lloyd Chapham Assoc 1985–87, ceo Harvey Nash plc 1987–2009 (Best Small Business Deloitte 1996), currently chm Inception Partners; chm/non-exec dir: Arrow Gp, Lawrence Harvey Ltd, RP Int Ltd, Intuition Ltd, Empiric Ltd, Portland Resources Ltd, JAM Ltd, Inception Mktg Recruitment Ltd; dir EG360 Consulting; RSA 2006; *Recreations* cricket, rugby, golf, travel, supporting entrepreneurship; *Style*— David Higgins, Esq

HIGGINS, Prof James; s of Peter Higgins (d 1998), and Annie, *née* McShane (d 2002); *b* 28 May 1939; *Educ* Our Lady's HS Motherwell, Univ of Glasgow (MA), Univ of Lyons (Licence-ès-lettres), Univ of Liverpool (PhD); *m* 1962, Kirstine Anne, da of John Atwell; 2 s (Anthony James b 1964 d 2001, Graham b 1967); *Career* Univ of Liverpool: asst lectr in Latin American Studies 1964–67, lectr 1967–73, sr lectr 1973–83, reader 1983–88, prof of Latin American literature 1988–2004, emeritus prof 2004–; visiting prof: Univ of Pittsburgh PA 1968, Univ of Waterloo Ontario 1974, Univ of WI Trinidad 1979, Univ of Wisconsin-Madison 1990; hon prof: Universidad Nacional Mayor de San Marcos Lima 1984, Univ of Stirling 2006; corresponding fell Peruvian Acad 2002; FBA 1999; Comendador de la Orden al Mérito (Peru) 1988; *Books* César Vallejo: An Anthology of His Poetry (1970), Visión del hombre y de la vida en las últimas obras poéticas de César Vallejo (1970), The Poet in Peru (1982), A History of Peruvian Literature (1987), César Vallejo: A Selection of His Poetry (1987), César Vallejo en su poesía (1990), Cambio social y constantes humanas. La narrativa corta de J R Ribeyro (1991), Hitos de la poesía peruana (1993), Myths of the Emergent. Social Mobility in Contemporary Peruvian Fiction (1994), The Literary Representation of Peru (2002), Lima: A Cultural and Literary History (2005), Historia de la Literatura Peruana (2006), John Barbour's The Bruce, A Free Translation in Verse (2013), The Emancipation of Peru: British Eyewitness Accounts (2014); *Recreations* reading, walking, gardening, whisky, Celtic FC, early Scottish literature; *Style*— Prof James Higgins; ✉ 6 Carlton House, 15 Snowdon Place, Stirling FK8 2NR (☎ 01786 470641, e-mail jameshig@talktalk.net)

HIGGINS, John; MBE (2008); s of John and Josephine Higgins; *b* 18 May 1975; *Educ* St Aiden's HS Wishaw; *Career* professional snooker player 1992–; tournament winner: Australian Open 1994, Grand Prix 1994, 1999 and 2005, British Open 1995 and 1998,

German Open 1995 and 1997, International Open 1995 and 1996, Castrol/Honda World Team Cup 1996, European Open 1997, Liverpool Victoria Charity Challenge 1997 and 1999, Embassy World Championship 1998 and 2007, Liverpool Victoria UK Championship 1999 and 2000, Benson & Hedges Masters 1999 (runner-up 1995 and 2005), Regal China International 1999, Riley Premier Snooker League 1999, Benson & Hedges Irish Masters 2000, Regal Welsh 2000, Nations Cup 2001, Champions Cup 2001, Scottish Regal Masters 2001, British Open Championship 2001 and 2004, Irish Masters 2002, Saga Masters 2006, Shanghai Masters 2007, Betfred World Champion 2009, Welsh Open 2010; memb Br Inst for Brain Injured Children; *Recreations* golf, football; *Clubs* Wishaw Golf, Southerness Golf; *Style*— John Higgins, Esq, MBE

HIGGINS, Prof Dame Julia Stretton; DBE (2001, CBE); da of George Stretton Downes, and Sheilah, *née* Gavigan; *Educ* Somerville Coll Oxford (BA), Univ of Oxford (DPhil), Univ of London; *Career* SRC research student Physical Chem Lab Oxford 1964–66, physics teacher Mexborough GS 1966–68, SRC research fell Dept of Chem Univ of Manchester 1968–72, research fell Centre de Recherche Macromoleculaire CNRS Strasbourg 1972–73, physicist Institut Laue-Langevin Grenoble 1973–76; Imperial Coll London: lectr 1976–85, reader in polymer sci 1985–89, postgraduate tutor 1989–94, prof of polymer sci Dept of Chem Engrg 1989–, princ Faculty of Engrg 2006–07, coll tutor 1990–93, pt/t dean City and Guilds Coll 1993–97; chm Neutron Scattering Gp of Inst of Physics and RSC 1980–84; RSC: memb Faraday Cncl 1984–87 and 1996–98, chm Research Fund Ctee 1991–96, memb Faraday Ed Bd 1994–97, chm Sci Advsy Bd 1998–99; memb SERC: Neutron Beam Res Ctee 1979–83 and 1988–91, Sci Planning Gp for Spallation Neutron Source 1977–85, Chem Sub-Ctee ILL Grenoble 1978–81, Polymers and Composites Ctee 1989–94, Materials Cmmn 1991–94; chm EPSRC 2003–07 (memb Cncl 1994–2000); memb: Instrument Sub-Ctee ILL Grenoble 1986–89, Sci Advsy Cncl of Br Cncl 1993–98, Materials Sector Panel Technol Foresight Prog 1994–98, Cncl for the Central Laboratories of the Research Cncls 1995–2000, Editorial Advsy Bd Jl of Polymer Sci, Cncl for Sci and Technol 1998–, Research Ctee HEFCE 1998–2002; foreign memb Ed Advsy Bd of Macromolecules ACS Jl 1984–87, tstee Daphne Jackson Meml Fellowships 1994–2010; hon fell Somerville Coll Oxford; Hon DSc: Univ of Nottingham 1999, Univ of Oxford 2003, Univ of Sheffield 2003; Hon DEng Heriot-Watt Univ 2000; MACS, CChem, FRSC, FCGI, FIM (memb Cncl 1996–99), FInstP (memb Polymer Physics Ctee 1987–93, pres-elect 2015–17), FIChemE, CEng, FREng, FRS (memb Cncl 1998 and 1999, foreign sec 2001–06); *Publications* over 200 articles in jls; *Recreations* opera, theatre, travel; *Style*— Prof Dame Julia Higgins, DBE, FRS, FREng; ✉ Department of Chemical Engineering, Imperial College, London SW7 2AZ

HIGGINS, Mark; s of Andrew Higgins (d 1991), and Kathleen, *née* Monaghan; *b* 31 January 1970, Glasgow; *Educ* Univ of Glasgow (LLB, DipLP); *m* 5 Sept 1997, Rachel, *née* Macleod; 2 da (Leah b 19 July 2001, Amy b 20 May 2003); *Career* admitted slr 1993; ptnr Irwin Mitchell Slrs 1999–; memb Law Soc of Scotland 1993; *Publications* Scottish Repossessions (2002), The Enforcement of Heritable Securities (2010, 2 edn 2016); *Recreations* reading, astronomy, football; *Style*— Mark Higgins, Esq; ✉ 5 Drymen Wynd, Bearsden, Glasgow G61 2UB (☎ 0141 942 2866); Irwin Mitchell Solicitors, Stewart House, 123 Elderslie Street, Glasgow G3 7AR (☎ 0370 150 0100, e-mail mark.higgins@irwinmitchell.com)

HIGGINS, Dame Rosalyn; DBE (1995), QC (1986); da of Lewis Cohen, and Fay, *née* Inberg; *b* 2 June 1937; *Educ* Burlington GS London, Girton Coll Cambridge (minor and major scholar, Campell scholar, Bryce-Tebbs scholar, BA, MA, LLB, Montefiore award), Yale Univ (JSD); *m* 1961, Baron Higgins, KBE, PC, DL (Life Peer), *qv*; 1 s, 1 da; *Career* UK intern Office of Legal Affairs UN 1958, Cwlth Fund fell 1959, visiting fell Brookings Inst Washington DC 1960, jr fell in int studies LSE 1961–63, staff specialist in int law RIIA 1963–74, visiting lectr in law Yale Law Sch 1966 and 1975, visiting fell LSE 1974–78; visiting prof of law: Stanford Law Sch 1975, Yale Law Sch 1977; prof of int law: Univ of Kent Canterbury 1978–81, Univ of London 1981–95; judge Int Court of Justice 1995–2009 (pres 2006–09); bencher Inner Temple 1989; memb: UN Ctee on Human Rights 1984–95, Gen Course in Public Int Law Hague Acad of Int Law 1991; pres British Inst of Int and Comparative Law (vice-pres and chm Advsy Cncl); guest lectr at numerous univs in Europe and America, memb Bd of Eds American Jl of Int Law 1975–85; Hon Doctorate: Univ of Paris 1980, Univ of Dundee 1992, Univ of Durham 1995, Univ of London 1995, Univ of Greenwich 1996, City Univ London 1996, Univ of Essex 1996, Univ of Cambridge 1996, Univ of Kent 1996, Univ of Sussex 1996, Univ of Birmingham 1997, Univ of Leicester 1997, Univ of Glasgow 1997, Univ of Nottingham 1999, Univ of Bath 2001, Univ of Paris II 2001, Univ of Oxford 2002, Univ of Reading 2003; Yale Univ Medal of Merit 1997; Manley Hudson Medal ASIL 1998; memb Int Law Assoc; hon pres American Soc of Int Law (hon life memb), hon memb American Acad of Arts and Sciences; memb Int Law Assoc, memb Institut de Droit International 1991 (assoc 1987); Ordre des Palmes Académiques; *Books* The Development of International Law Through the Political Organs of the United Nations (1963), Conflict of Interests: International Law in a Divided World (1965), The Administration of the United Kingdom Foreign Policy Through the United Nations (1966), UN Peacekeeping: Documents and Commentary (Vol I ME 1969, Vol II Asia 1970, Vol III Africa 1980, Vol IV Europe 1981), Law in Movement-Essays in Memory of John McMahon (jt ed with James Fawcett, 1974), The Taking of Property by the State (1983), International Law and the Avoidance, Containment and Resolution of Disputes (General Course on Public International Law), Vol 230 Recueil des cours (Martinus Nijhoff, 1991), Problems and Process: International Law and How We Use It (1994), Themes and Theories (2009); author of numerous articles for law jls and jls of int relations; *Recreations* golf, cooking, eating; *Style*— Dame Rosalyn Higgins, DBE, QC

HIGGINSON, Lucy Amanda; da of late Keith Higginson, of Bowdon, Cheshire, and Judith Rosemary Britain, *née* Godber; *b* 13 March 1970, Gothenberg, Sweden; *Educ* Manchester HS for Girls, Coll of St Hild and St Bede Durham (BA); *m* 27 March 1999, Dr Alexis Warnes; 1 da (Madeleine Charlotte b 4 Sept 2005), 1 s (Alexander Max Wilfred b 22 Oct 2008); *Career* journalist; sub ed rising to dep ed The Field, ed Horse & Hound 2002–14 (first female ed and last person to hold the title); owner Lucy Higginson Ltd (consulting, editing, writing, event devpt and PR in equestrian sector); memb Advsy Panel Riding Club London, memb Selection Panel Br Horse Soc Hall of Fame; *Recreations* riding, hunting, dog walking, rowing; *Style*— Ms Lucy Higginson; ✉ Villiers, Common Lane, Eton, Windsor, Berkshire SL4 6EG (☎ 01753 671490, e-mail lucy@lucyhigginson.co.uk, Twitter @HigginsonLucy)

HIGGS, Prof Roger Hubert; MBE (1987); s of Rt Rev Hubert Lawrence Higgs, Bishop of Hull (d 1992), and Elizabeth Higgs (d 2006), of Chediston, Suffolk; *b* 10 December 1943; *Educ* Marlborough (fndn scholar), Christ's Coll Cambridge (Classics and Tancred scholar, MA, MB BChir, pres JCR, Coll 1st VIII Boat), Westminster Med Sch (Hart prize); *m* 9 Jan 1971, Susan, da of Prof Tom Hewer, and Anne Hewer, of Henbury, Bristol; 1 s (Ben b 18 Dec 1971), 1 da (Jessie b 2 July 1975); *Career* VSO Starehe Boys' Centre Nairobi Kenya 1961–62; house offr posts: Westminster Hosp 1969–70, W Middx Hosp 1970, Whittington Hosp 1970–71; resident med offr Whittington Hosp 1971–72, med registrar St George's Hosp 1972–74, gen practice trainee Dr McEwan and Partners 1974–75, princ in gen practice partnership Drs Higgs, Haigh, Herzmark, Nixon, Maycock and Osonuga Walworth London 1975–2004 (founded as solo practice 1975); ldr Lambeth Community Care Centre Devpt Gp 1979–85; King's Coll Sch of Med (now GKT): lectr in gen practice 1978–81, sr lectr and head of dept 1981–89, prof and chair Dept of Gen Practice and Primary Care 1989–2004, dep head Division of Primary Care and Public Health 1998–2004; emeritus prof of gen practice and primary care KCL 2004–; fndr Jl of Med Ethics, chair Editorial Bd and consltg ed Case Conference 2001– (ed 1974–96); memb CND; memb Worshipful Soc of Apothecaries 1978; FRCGP 1986, FRCP 1993; *Books* In That Case (with Alastair Campbell, 1982), A Case Study in Developing Primary Care: The Camberwell Report (1991), Mental Health and Primary Care: A Changing Agenda (1993), New Dictionary of Medical Ethics (1997); also author of papers on medical ethics, medical educn, devpt and psychosocial issues in primary healthcare; *Recreations* playing oboe, planting trees, listening to classical music and jazz, print-making; *Style*— Prof Roger Higgs, MBE; ✉ 81 Brixton Water Lane, London SW2 1PH

HIGHAM, John Arthur; QC (1992); s of Frank Greenhouse Higham (d 1988), and Muriel, *née* King; *b* 11 August 1952; *Educ* Shrewsbury, Churchill Coll Cambridge (scholar, MA, LLM); *m* 1, 1982, Francesca Mary Antonietta, *née* Ronan (d 1988); 2 da (Miranda Elizabeth Francesca b 9 April 1983, Charlotte Daisy Emilia b 14 August 1984), 1 s (John) Christian Alexander b 3 March 1987); m 2, 1988, Catherine Ennis, *qv*; 2 s (Patrick Rupert James b 14 Sept 1989, Edmund George Christopher b 24 March 1992), 1 da (Cecily Mary Catherine b 17 Jan 1994); *Career* called to the Bar Lincoln's Inn 1976 and Gray's Inn (ad eundem) 1989, asst recorder 1998–2000, recorder 2000–10; admitted slr and authorised slr advocate 1999, ptnr Stephenson Harwood 2000–04, ptnr White & Case 2004–15 (conslt 2016–); *Books* Loose on Liquidators (jt ed, 1981), A Practitioner's Guide to Corporate Insolvency and Corporate Rescues (contrib, 1991), Corporate Administrations and Rescue Procedures (jt ed, 2004); *Recreations* opera, gardening, cricket; *Clubs* Lancashire CCC; *Style*— John Higham, Esq, QC; ✉ White & Case, 5 Old Broad Street, London EC2N 1DW (☎ 020 7532 1000, fax 020 7532 1001, e-mail jhigham@whitecase.com)

HIGHAM, Nicholas Geoffrey (Nick); s of Geoffrey Arthur Higham, of Abingdon, Berks, Audrey Mary, *née* Hill; *b* 1 June 1954; *Educ* Bradfield, St Catharine's Coll Cambridge (BA); *m* 1981, Deborah Joan, da of Brig J G Starling, CBE, MC; 1 s (William b 12 May 1987), 1 da (Catherine b 10 July 1989); *Career* freelance journalist 1978–88; BBC News: media corr 1988–93, arts and media corr 1993–2003; analyst BBC News 24 2003–07, corr BBC News 2007–; pres Meet the Author 2010–16; *Style*— Nick Higham, Esq; ✉ BBC News and Current Affairs, Broadcasting House, Portland Place, London W1A 1AA (☎ 020 3614 1414, e-mail nick.higham@bbc.co.uk)

HIGHFIELD, Ashley; s of Roy Highfield, and Sheila, *née* Whitmore; *b* 3 October 1965; *Educ* City Univ Business Sch London; *m* 2005, Charlotte Payter; 1 da (b 2008); *Career* media and IT consIt Coopers & Lybrand 1988–94 (participated in launch of Vodacom in South Africa), head of IT and new media NBC 1995–96, md Flextech Interactive 1996–2000, dir New Media and Technol Div BBC 2000–08, ceo Project Kangaroo 2008, md and vice-pres consumer and online Microsoft 2008–11, ceo Johnston Press 2011–; FRSA, FRTS; *Clubs* Soho House, Ivy; *Style*— Ashley Highfield, Esq

HIGHFIELD, Dr Roger; s of Ronald Albert Highfield, of Enfield, Middx, and Dorothea Helene, *née* Depta; *b* 11 July 1958; *Educ* Christ's Hosp, Pembroke Coll Oxford (Domus scholar, MA, DPhil), Queen Elizabeth House Oxford (Leverhulme fell), Balliol Coll Oxford (sabbatical fell); *m* Julia Brookes; 1 da (Holly Elizabeth), 1 s (Rory James Charles); *Career* news/clinical reporter Pulse 1983–84 (dep features ed), news ed Nuclear Engineering International 1984–86; The Daily Telegraph: technol corr 1986, technol ed 1987, science ed 1988–2008; ed New Scientist 2008–11, dir of external affrs Science Museum Gp; memb Advsy Ctee Science Museum; former memb: Bioscience Futures Forum, Health Protection and Soc Advsy Gp, Communications and Public Enjoyment Ctee, Royal Acad of Engineering; former organiser of Live Lab nat experiments; organiser: Science Writer Awards, Visions of Science Awards; advsr Cheltenham Sci Festival; co-curator TEDxLondon 2016; judge: Samuel Johnson Prize 2010, Wellcome Tst Book Prize 2011, Hippocrates Prize for Poetry and Medicine 2013, ABSW Award 2013, Eurostem Cell Non Fiction Writing Competition, Br Press Awards 2013, 2014 and 2015, Royal Soc Insight Investment Science Book Prize 2016; memb Longitude Prize Ctee, memb Royal Acad of Engrg Communcations and Public Engagement Ctee, memb Advsy Ctee Mosaic Douglas Adams Memorial Lecture 2014, memb Royal Soc Sci Policy Advsy Gp *Awards* Medical Journalist Assoc Award 1987 and 1999 (runner-up 2001), Assoc of Br Sci Writers Awards 1988, 1995, 1997 and 1998, Br Press Awards Specialist Corr of the Year 1989 (commended 1991 and 2001), cited by Save British Science as Campaigning Journalist of the Year, Cwlth Media Award 1994, Chemical Industries Assoc Award 1997, Royal Soc Wilkins-Bernal-Medawar Prize, shortlisted New Consumer Ed of the Year 2009 and 2010 Br Soc of Magazine Eds, shortlisted Current Affrs Magazine of the Year Br Soc of Magazine Eds 2011; FRSB; *Books* The Arrow of Time (1990), The Private Lives of Albert Einstein (1993), Frontiers of Complexity (1995), Can Reindeer Fly? (1998), The Science of Harry Potter: How Magic Really Works (2002), After Dolly (2006), A Life Decoded (ed, 2007), SuperCooperators: Evolution, Altruism and Human Behaviour, or Why We Need Each Other to Succeed (2011), Life at the Speed of Light (ed, 2013); *Recreations* writing books, children; *Style*— Dr Roger Highfield; ✉ website www.rogerhighfield.com; Science Museum Group, Exhibition Road, London SW7 2DD (website www.sciencemuseum.org.uk)

HIGHTON, David Peter; s of Allan Peter Highton, of Sittingbourne, Kent, and May Highton; *b* 22 May 1954; *Educ* Borden GS, Univ of Bristol (BSc); *m* Wendy Ann; 1 da (Emily Katherine Highton b 7 May 1990); *Career* Turquands Barton Mayhew (now Ernst & Young): articled clerk 1975–78, qualified CA 1978, audit sr 1978–79, audit supr 1979; fin accountant Tunnel Avebe Starches Ltd 1979–81, London controller R P Martin plc 1981–83, fin planning and analysis mangr Watney Mann & Truman Ltd 1986–87 (fin controller (central staffs and Cos) 1983–86), regnl fin dir SE Region Prudential Property Services 1987–89, md Property Mail 1989–90, chief exec Ealing HA 1991–92 (dir of fin and purchasing 1990–92), dir of fin and business devpt Riverside Hosps 1992–94; chief exec: Chelsea and Westminster Healthcare NHS Tst 1994–2000, St Mary's Hosp NHS Tst 1998–99 (on secondment), Oxford Radcliffe Hospitals NHS Trust 2000–03; chm Healthwork UK 2001–05, chm Skills for Health 2002–03 (non-exec dir 2007–11), md Clinicenta Ltd 2003–10, head of business devpt MediHome Ltd 2010–11, exec dir Hamad Medical Corp Qatar 2011–, chm Sussex Health Care Audiology Ltd 2011–; vice-pres Sittingbourne RUFC 2008– (treas 1976–90, chm 1991–94 and 1997–99, pres 1999–2008), vice-pres Imperial Medical RFC 1999–, fin sec Gore Court Cricket Club 1994–97; FCA 1989; *Recreations* rugby, cricket, reading; *Clubs* Sittingbourne RFC; *Style*— David Highton, Esq; ✉ PO Box 63162, Doha, Qatar (e-mail david@hyperium.co.uk)

HIGLETT, Simon Ian; s of John Higlett, of Allesley, Coventry, and Patricia Anne, *née* Such; *b* 30 May 1959; *Educ* Wimbledon Sch of Art (BA), Slade Sch of Fine Art (Higher Dip Fine Art, Leslie Hurry Prize for Theatre Design); *m* 21 Aug 1988, Isobel, da of Alan Arnett, of Tuffley, Gloucester; 2 da (Charlotte Hope b 27 Sept 1994, Emily Georgina b 9 June 1997); *Career* theatre designer; asst to Tim Goodchild 1982–84, head of design New Shakespeare Co 1986–89; bd dir: Arundel Festival, Soc of Br Theatre Designers; artistic assoc (design) Chichester Festival Theatre; *Productions* West End: The Prisoner of Second Avenue (with Richard Dreyfuss and Marsha Mason), A Song at Twilight, Antony and Cleopatra, The Taming of the Shrew (all with Vanessa Redgrave), Blithe Spirit, Man and Boy, The Dresser, The Witches; Comedy Theatre: Talking Heads (with Maggie Smith), Kean (dir Sam Mendes, with Derek Jacobi), Medea (with Eileen Atkins); RSC: Singer (dir Terry Hands, with Antony Sher), The Chiltern Hundreds, A Russian In The Woods, A Long Days Journey Into Night (with Jessica Lange), Thomas More; Chichester: Our Betters (with Kathleen Turner), Beethoven's Tenth (with Peter Ustinov), Mansfield Park, The Miser, A Doll's House, Three Sisters, Scenes from a Marriage;

H

Houston Grand Opera: Resurrection, The Barber of Seville, The Rake's Progress, Don Giovanni, La Traviata, La Cenerentola, The Marriage of Figaro, The Magic Flute; regional tours: The Lion in Winter (with David McCallum), Peer Gynt, The Ride Down Mount Morgan; other credits incl: The Magistrate (Savoy), Lady Windermere's Fan (Haymarket), In a Little World of Our Own (Donmar), The Force of Change (Royal Court), The Country Wife (Shakespeare Theater Washington DC), Three Sisters: Elizabeth Rex: Accidental Death of an Anarchist (Donmar Warehouse, TMA Designer of the Year Award 2002), Whistling Psyche (Almeida), Of Mice and Men (Savoy), Hay Fever (Haymarket) 2006, Albert Herring (Darmsdadt) 2006, Barber of Seville (Scottish Opera) 2007, Merry Wives of Windsor (Royal Dramatic Theatre Stockholm), School of Night (Marc Tapor Forum LA), Marriage of Figaro (Scottish Opera), Rozencrantz and Guildenstern Are Dead (Haymarket Theatre), Singin' In The Rain (Palace Theatre) 2012, The Magic Flute (Scottish Opera) 2012, A Marvellous Year For Plums (Chichester Festival Theatre) 2012, Arturo Ui (Chichester Festival Theatre) 2012, Don Giovanni (Scottish Opera) 2013, Blithe Spirit (Stratford Festival Ontario), Derren Brown Infamous (Palace Theatre) 2013, The Importance of Being Earnest (Shakespeare Theatre DC) 2014, Blithe Spirit (London and LA) 2014, Amadeus, Stevie, An Ideal Husband (all Chichester Festival Theatre) 2014, Love's Labours Lost and Much Ado About Nothing (RSC) 2014–15 and (Chichester Festival Theatre and Haymarket Theatre) 2016, The Tempest (Singapore) 2015, Derren Brown Miracle (London) 2015, Chitty Chitty Bang Bang (UK tour) 2016, Hobson's Choice (Vaudeville Theatre) 2016, Big the Musical (Ireland and West End) 2016; *Recreations* reading, drawing, theatre; *Style*— Simon Higlett, Esq; ✉ Oak Tree House, 16 Torton Hill Road, Arundel, West Sussex BN18 9HE (☎ 01903 882586)

HIGSON, Charlie; *b* 1958; *Career* writer and comedian; lead vocalist The Higsons 1980–86; *Television* as writer, prodr and actor incl: The Fast Show 1994, Ted & Ralph 1998, Swiss Tony 2003; as writer, prodr and dir: Randall & Hopkirk (Deceased) 2000; *Publications* as Charles Higson: King of the Ants (1992), Happy Now (1993), Full Whack (1995), Getting Rid Of Mister Kitchen (1996); as Charlie Higson: SilverFin: A James Bond Adventure (2005), Blood Fever (2006), Hurricane Gold (2007); *Style*— Charlie Higson; ✉ c/o Curtis Brown Agency, 5th Floor, Haymarket House, 28–29 Haymarket, London SW1Y 4SP (☎ 020 7393 4400, fax 020 7393 4401)

HIGSON, Prof Helen Elisabeth; OBE (2011); *née* Kettle; da of Kenneth Barry Kettle (d 1995), and Margaret Grace, *née* Spicer; *b* 14 May 1960, Winchester; *Educ* Newnham Coll Cambridge, Open Univ (MA), Birkbeck Coll London (PhD); *m* Oct 1982, Richard Higson; *Career* dep vice-chllr Aston Univ and prof of HE learning and mgmnt Aston Business Sch 2010– (joined 1988); fndr and convenor Centre for HE Learning and Mgmnt 2003; Princ FHEA, NFTS, FRSA, FAUA, fell Assoc of Univ Administrators; *Recreations* cricket, opera, reading; *Clubs* Univ Women's; *Style*— Prof Helen Higson, OBE; ✉ Aston University, Aston Triangle, Birmingham B4 7ET

HILDITCH, David; MLA; s of David Hilditch, and Agnes, *née* Smith (d 2003); *b* 23 July 1963, Larne, Co Antrim; *Educ* Carrickfergus GS, E Antrim Inst of Further and Higher Educn; *m* 23 July 1987, Wilma; 2 s (Stuart b 1 Aug 1981, Michael b 13 Oct 1989); *Career* worked in building and construction industry 1980–87, with Royal Mail 1987–2004, MLA (DUP) E Antrim 1998– (vice-chair Dept of Educn 2010); memb NI Assembly 1999–; memb Carrickfergus BC 1991– (memb numerous ctees), mayor Carrickfergus 1997–98 and 2005–06 (dep mayor 1995–96); memb: Carrickfergus Dist Policing Partnership, NE Gp Building Control, Ulster Tourist Devpt Assoc, Antrim Coast and Glens Tourist Orgn; RUC Bravery Award 1997; *Style*— David Hilditch, Esq, MLA; ✉ Constituency Office, 31 Lancasterian Street, Carrickfergus, Co Antrim BT38 7AB (☎ 028 9332 9980, fax 028 9332 9979, e-mail david.hilditch@btconnect.com); Northern Ireland Assembly, Parliament Buildings, Stormont Estate, Belfast BT4 3XX

HILDYARD, Hon Mr Justice; Sir Robert Henry Thoroton Hildyard; kt (2011), QC (1994), DL (Notts 2014); s of Sir David Henry Thoroton Hildyard, KCMG, DFC (d 1997), of London, and Millicent, *née* Baron (d 1998); *b* 10 October 1952; *Educ* Eton, ChCh Oxford (MA); *m* 1, 9 Aug 1980 (m dis 2010), Isabella Jane, da of James Rennie (d 1964); 3 da (Catherine b 31 Oct 1983, Camilla b 15 May 1985 d 1987, Alexandra b 15 Sept 1988); m 2, 2 June 2012, Janet Lucy Gibson; 1 da (Charlotte b 11 April 2012); *Career* called to the Bar: Inner Temple 1977, Lincoln's Inn (ad eundem) 1994 (bencher 2005); jr counsel to the Crown (Chancery) 1992–94, dep judge of the High Court 2001–11, attorney-gen to Duchy of Lancaster 2006–11, judge of the High Court of Justice (Chancery Div) 2011–; memb Fin Reporting Review Panel 2002–06; conslt ed Annotated Companies Act; *Books* Annotated Companies Legislation (conslt ed); *Recreations* tennis, shooting; *Clubs* Garrick; *Style*— The Hon Mr Justice Hildyard, DL; ✉ Royal Courts of Justice, Strand, London WC2A 2LL

HILHORST, Rosemary; OBE (2003); da of Raymond Bowditch (d 2002), of Portesham, Dorset, and June, *née* Ebdon; *b* 10 April 1954; *Educ* Woodroffe Sch Lyme Regis, UCL (BSc), Chelsea Coll (PGCE); *m* 10 April 1981, Francis Hilhorst, s of Henk Hilhorst (d 1991); 1 da (Malaika b 5 April 1982), 1 s (Sean b 6 Jan 1985); *Career* physics/integrated science teacher: Portslade Community Coll 1976–80, Int Sch of Tanganyika Dar es Salaam 1980–82, American Cultural Assoc Turin 1982–83, Portesham CE Primary Sch (pt/t) 1983–84; British Council: science advsr 1985–86, asst rep Khartoum 1986–88, head Exchanges Unit Khartoum 1988–89, head Project Devpt Dept (asst dir 1989–90), dir Bratislava 1991–93, dir Slovakia 1993–95, UK 1995–97, dir Tanzania 1997–2000, UK 2000–03, dir Portugal 2003–08, dir Russia 2008–; memb Governing Body Br Assoc for Central and Eastern Europe 2000–02; *Recreations* family, literature, walking, running and cycling; *Style*— Mrs Rosemary Hilhorst, OBE; ✉ c/o British Council, Ulitsa Nikoloyamskaya 1, Moscow 109189, Russia (☎ 00 7 495 782 0200)

HILL, Andrew Thomas Gray; s of Thomas Gray (Tim) Hill (d 1998), and Judith Ann, *née* Crook, of Cheshire; *b* 28 December 1964, Bolton, Lancs; *Educ* Shrewsbury Sch, Trinity Coll Cambridge (MA); *m* 29 April 1995, Jimena Adriana Rebeca López-Menchero Cartujo; 1 s (Tomás Gray b 22 Oct 1997), 1 da (Ana María-Teresa b 12 July 2001); *Career* Financial Times: UK companies reporter 1988–91, Brussels corr 1991–94, Milan corr 1994–96, foreign news ed 1996–99, NY bureau chief 1999–2003, comment and analysis ed 2003–05, fin ed 2005–06, City ed 2006–10, assoc ed 2006–, mgmnt ed 2011–; Best Commentator and Decade of Excellence Business Journalist of the Year Awards 2009, Towers Watson HR Journalist of the Year (National Media) 2012; chair Cambridge Alumni Advsy Bd Communications Working Gp; memb Cambridge Alumni Advsy Bd; tstee: Ruskin Fndn, Blueprint Tst; memb NUJ 1988; companion Guild of St George 2010; FRSA; The Best Business Stories of the Year (contrib, 2004), Unto This Last (by John Ruskin, intro, 2010), Leadership in the Headlines (2016); *Recreations* playing the piano, reading, theatre, tennis, cricket; *Clubs* Lancs CCC; *Style*— Andrew Hill, Esq; ✉ c/o Financial Times, 1 Southwark Bridge, London SE1 9HL (☎ 020 7873 4954, e-mail andrew.hill@ft.com, Twitter @andrewtghill)

HILL, Prof (Norman) Berkeley; s of Ewart Edward Wesley Hill (d 1984), and Doris May, *née* Nelson; *b* 6 May 1944; *Educ* Univ of Nottingham (BSc), Univ of Reading (PhD); *m* 1970, Hilarie Angela, *née* Scott; 2 da (Deborah b 1966, Emily b 1974), 1 s (Timothy b 1972); *Career* lectr, sr lectr and reader in agricultural economics Wye Coll Univ of London 1970–99, prof of policy analysis Dept of Agricultural Sciences Imperial Coll London (formerly Wye Coll) 1999–2005 (emeritus prof 2005–); conslt/advsr: Eurostat, European Cmmn, NAO, Defra, OECD, UNECE; memb Agricultural Economics Soc 1967; *Books* incl: Size and Efficiency in Farming (with D K Britton, 1975), An Introduction to Economics for Students of Agriculture (1980, 3 edn 2006), Farm Tenure and Performance (with Ruth Gasson, 1984), Economics for Agriculture: Food, Farming and the Rural Economy (with Derek Ray, 1987), Farm Incomes, Wealth and Agricultural Policy (1989, 3 edn 2000), Policy Reform and Adjustment in the Agricultural Sectors of Developed Countries (with David Blandford, 2006); *Recreations* choral conductor and organist; *Style*— Prof Berkeley Hill; ✉ 1 Brockhill Road, Hythe, Kent CT21 4AB (☎ 01303 265312, fax 01303 237381, e-mail b.hill@imperial.ac.uk)

HILL, Bernard; *b* 17 December 1944; *Career* actor; *Theatre* incl: John Lennon in John, Paul, George, Ringo... and Bert (West End), Toby Belch in Twelfth Night, title role in Macbeth (Leicester Haymarket), Lopakhin in The Cherry Orchard (Aldwych), Eddie in A View From the Bridge (Bristol Old Vic and Strand Theatre); *Television* for BBC: Boys from the Blackstuff, John Lennon – A Journey in the Life, The Burston Rebellion, New World, Permanent Red, The Lawlord, Olly's Prison – Edward Bond Trilogy Once Upon a Time in the North; for Channel 4: Squaring the Circle, Lipstick on your Collar, Without Walls – The Art of Tripping; other credits incl: The Mill on the Floss, Great Expectations; *Film* incl: The Bounty, Gandhi, The Chain, Restless Natives, No Surrender, Bellman and True (and TV series), Drowning By Numbers, Shirley Valentine, Mountains of the Moon, Skallagrigg (also TV release), The Wind in the Willows, The Ghost and the Darkness, Titanic, Short Stories, True Crime, A Midsummer Night's Dream, The Loss of Sexual Innocence, Blessed Art Thou, The Criminal, The Lord of the Rings – The Two Towers, The Lord of the Rings – The Return of the King, The Scorpion King, The Boys from County Clare, Gothika; *Recreations* skiing, squash, tennis, swimming, fishing, Apple Macintosh; *Style*— Bernard Hill, Esq; ✉ c/o ARG Talent, 4 Great Portland Street, London W1W 8PA

HILL, Sir Brian John; s of Gerald A Hill, OBE (d 1974); *b* 19 December 1932; *Educ* Stowe, Emmanuel Coll Cambridge (MA); *m* 1959, Janet Joyce, da of Alfred S Newman, OBE; 2 s (William b 1960, Peter b 1962), 1 da (Sarah b 1964); *Career* Nat Serv Army; gp md Higgs and Hill Ltd 1972–83, exec chm Higgs and Hill plc 1989–92 (chm and chief exec 1983–89); chm Goldsborough Holdings 1993–97, chm Longmartin Properties Ltd 2008–15; dir: Building Centre 1981–85, Lazard Property Unit Trust 1982–98, Sackville Property Unit Tst 1998–2005, Property Services Agency 1986–88, Southern Regnl Bd National Westminster Bank 1990–92, London Docklands Development Corp 1994–98; memb Advsy Bd Property Services Agency 1981–86; pres Bldg Employers' Confedn 1992–95 (pres London Region 1981–82, chm Nat Contractors Gp 1983–84), pres Chartered Inst of Building 1987–88, chm Vauxhall Coll of Bldg and Further Educn 1976–86; dir Gt Ormond Street Hosp for Children NHS Tst 1984– (chm 1992–97, special tstee 1997–2000), chm Children's Tst 1998–2008; govr: Aberdour Sch Tadworth 1987–2007, Pangbourne Coll 2000–04; external examiner Univ of Reading 1993–97; tstee Falklands Islands Meml Chapel 1997–2007; Hon DSc, Hon LLB; memb Ct of Assts Worshipful Co of Chartered Surveyors (Master 1994–95); FRICS, FCIOB, Hon FIStructE, Hon FCGI; *Recreations* travelling, tennis, gardening, amateur dramatics; *Clubs* RAC; *Style*— Sir Brian Hill; ✉ Corner Oak, 5 Glen Close, Kingswood, Surrey KT20 6NT

HILL, Bronwyn; CBE (2001); *Career* DG city and regnl networks, DG major projects and London Dept for Transport 2007–11, perm sec DEFRA 2011–; *Style*— Ms Bronwyn Hill, CBE; ✉ Department for Environment, Food and Rural Affairs, Area 6C, Nobel House, 17 Smith Square, London SW1P 3JR

HILL, Rt Rev Christopher John; *see:* Guildford, Bishop of

HILL, Damon Graham Devereux; OBE (1997); s of (Norman) Graham Hill, OBE (d 1975, twice Formula 1 world champion 1962 and 1968), and Bette Hill; *b* 17 September 1960; *Educ* Haberdashers' Aske's; *m* 21 Oct 1988, Georgie; 2 s, 2 da; *Career* Formula 1 racing driver; Williams test driver 1991 and 1992, first Grand Prix (Silverstone) 1992 (driving for Brabham team); driver with: Canon Williams team 1993, Rothmans Williams Renault team 1994, 1995 and 1996, Danka Arrows Yamaha team 1997, Benson and Hedges Jordan team 1998–99, ret; winner: Hungarian Grand Prix 1993 and 1995, Belgian Grand Prix 1993, 1994 and 1998, Italian Grand Prix 1993 and 1994, Spanish Grand Prix 1994, British Grand Prix 1994, Portuguese Grand Prix 1994, Japanese Grand Prix 1994 and 1996, Argentinian Grand Prix 1995 and 1996, San Marino Grand Prix 1995 and 1996, Australian Grand Prix 1995 and 1996, Brazilian Grand Prix 1996, Canadian Grand Prix 1996, French Grand Prix 1996, German Grand Prix 1996; Formula 1 World Drivers' Championship: third place 1993, second place 1994 and 1995, world champion 1996; 84 Grand Prix starts, 21 wins, 20 pole positions, 19 fastest laps, 41 podium finishes; pres British Racing Drivers' Club 2006–; chm: Damon Hill BMW, P1 International Ltd; *Awards* Sportsman of the Year Daily Express 1993, Newsround's Sportsman of the Year 1994, RAC Trophy 1994, Gold Star Award for Courage Daily Star 1994, International Racing Driver of the Year Autosport Awards 1994 and 1996, British Competition Driver of the Year Autosport Awards 1995 and 1996, Driver of the Year Guild of Motoring Writers 1994, BBC Sports Personality of the Year 1994 and 1996, sixteen awards (incl Gold Stars 1993, 1994, 1995 and 1996) British Racing Drivers' Club 1993, 1994, 1995 and 1996, Abbey National RADAR People of the Year Award 1996, Autosprint Golden Helmet Award 1996, l'Automobile Magazine Trophy 1996, Daily Mirror Sports Personality of the Year 1996, Barclaycard Daily Telegraph Champion of British Sport 1996, Bluebird Trophy for British Achievement 1996, Blue Peter Gold Badge 1996, Sunshine Award The Sun 1997; *Books* Damon Hill Grand Prix Year (1994), Damon Hill My Championship Year (1996); *Video* Damon Hill The Fight for Victory (1996); *Recreations* golf, music, motorcycles, skiing, playing the guitar, training; *Style*— Damon Hill, Esq, OBE

HILL, David Neil; *b* 13 May 1957; *Educ* Chetham's Sch Manchester, St John's Coll Cambridge (organ scholar); *m* 3 Dec 1994, Alice Mary; *Career* asst to Dr George Guest St John's Coll Cambridge, studied under Gillian Weir and Peter Hurford; sub-organist Durham Cathedral, master of music Westminster Cathedral 1982–87, dir of music Winchester Cathedral 1987–2002; artistic dir Philharmonia Chorus 1992–98, dir Waynflete Singers 1987–2002, music dir Bach Choir 1998–, organist and dir of music St John's Coll Cambridge 2003–07, chief conductor BBC Singers 2007–; princ conductor: Southern Sinfonia 2003, Leeds Philharmonic 2004; assoc guest conductor Bournemouth Symphony Orch 2009, adjunct prof of choral conducting Yale Inst of Sacred Music and princ conductor Yale Schola Cantorum 2013–; dir numerous choral workshops and summer schs UK, USA, Australasia; choral advsr to Music Sales Ltd, regular contrib to Choir and Organ Magazine; Hon DMus Univ of Southampton 2002; FRCO 1974; *Performances* organ recitals: NY, Chester Cathedral, Colston Hall Bristol, Lincoln Cathedral, Truro Cathedral, Bridgewater Hall Manchester, Royal Festival Hall, St Alban's, Westminster Cathedral, Westminster Abbey, St Paul's Cathedral; *Recordings* incl: William Byrd and John Blow Anthems (works by Stanford), Rachmaninov Vespers (with Philharmonia Chorus), Fauré's Requiem, Elgar's The Dream of Gerontius (with Bournemouth Symphony Orch), works by Mendelssohn, Bairstow and Jongen (with Choir of St John's Coll), works by Howells and Handel (with Bach Choir), works by Finzi (with Bournemouth Symphony Orch and Chorus); as conductor of: Bournemouth Symphony Orch, Brandenburg Consort, City of London Sinfonia, Parley of Instruments, Philharmonia Orch, English Chamber Orch, Royal Liverpool Philharmonic Orch, BBC Philharmonic Orch, London Philharmonic Orch, Florilegium, Britten Sinfonia, Ulster Orch, Opera North, Northern Sinfonia, BBC Nat Orch of Wales, Orch of the Age of Enlightenment, Westminster Cathedral Choir, Winchester Cathedral Choir, The Bach Choir, Waynflete Singers, Choir of St John's Coll; *Books* Giving Voice (jtly); *Clubs* Athenaeum; *Style*— David Hill, Esq; ✉ Rayfield Allied, Southbank House, Black Prince Road, London SE1 7SJ (☎ 020 3176 5500, Twitter @davidhconductor)

HILL, Dominic; *b* 22 April 1969, Wimbledon; *Educ* Douai Sch, Lincoln Coll Oxford (BA); *Career* dir The Room Orange Tree Studio Theatre 1993–94, asst dir Perth Theatre 1994–96, asst dir RSC 1997, assoc dir Orange Tree Theatre 1998–99, artistic dir Dundee Rep Theatre 2003–07 (previously assoc dir, nomination best dir TMA/Barclays Theatre Awards for The Winter's Tale 2001, best dir Scottish Critics Awards for Scenes from an Execution 2004, best dir Scottish Critics Awards 2008), artistic dir Traverse Theatre Edinburgh 2008–11, artistic dir Citizens Theatre Glasgow 2011–; prodns as freelance dir at Mercury Theatre Colchester, Salisbury Playhouse, Greenwich Theatre, Derby Playhouse, Northcott Theatre Exeter, Cotteloe Theatre RNT, Nuffield Theatre Southampton, Bath Theatre Royal, Bush Theatre, Open Air Theatre Regent's Park; *Style—* Dominic Hill, Esq

HILL, Prof (Anthony) Edward (Ed); OBE; s of Anthony Sidney Hill, and Philomena Ward; *b* 30 December 1959, Coventry; *Educ* Bishop Wulstan RC HS Rugby, Univ of Sheffield (BSc), UCNW Bangor (MSc, PhD); *m* 1989, Jacqueline Patricia, *née* Caukwell; 2 s (Oliver b 1991, Patrick b 1993); *Career* lectr then sr lectr in oceanography UCNW Bangor (latterly Univ of Wales Bangor) 1986–99, dir Proudman Oceanographic Lab NERC 1999–2005, hon visting prof Univ of Liverpool 1999–2004, dir Nat Oceanography Centre Southampton 2005–10, dir Nat Oceanography Centre 2010–, interim dir Br Antarctic Survey 2012; memb Exec Bd NERC 2001–, chm Bd Nat Centre for Ocean Forecasting 2005–07, memb Science and Innovation Strategy Bd NERC 2008–11; author of numerous pubns on shelf sea oceanography in learned jls; Hon DSc Univ of Sheffield 2011, hon fell Bangor Univ 2014; memb Challenger Soc for Marine Sci; FIMarEst, chartered marine scientist 2006; *Recreations* oil painting, visiting historic monuments, walking; *Style—* Prof Ed Hill, OBE; ✉ National Oceanography Centre, University of Southampton, Waterfront Campus, European Way, Southampton SO14 3ZH (✆ 023 8059 5106)

HILL, Emma Rhian; CBE (2012); da of Keith Hill (d 2005), and Valerie Christine, *née* Edwards (d 1996); *b* 5 August 1969, Kingston, Surrey; *Educ* Putney HS, Kingston Coll of FE, Wimbledon Sch of Art (Dip), Ravensbourne Coll of Design (BA); *Children* 1 s (Hudson Hill Eckart b 29 June 2006); *Career* Calvin Klein 1997–99, Marc Jacobs 1999–2002, vice-pres Accessories Gap 2002–05, creative dir Mulberry 2008–13; hon fell Univ of the Arts London 2014; *Clubs* Soho House; *Style—* Ms Emma Hill, CBE

HILL, Prof Sir Geoffrey William; kt (2012); *b* 18 June 1932, Bromsgrove, Worcs; *Educ* Co HS Bromsgrove, Keble Coll Oxford (MA); *Career* poet and critic; prof of English lit Univ of Leeds 1976–80, univ lectr in English Univ of Cambridge and fell Emmanuel Coll Cambridge 1981–88; Boston Univ: prof of lit and religion 1988–2006, co-dir Editorial Inst 1998–2004, univ prof emeritus and prof emeritus of lit and religion, prof of poetry Univ of Oxford 2010–15; Churchill fell Univ of Bristol 1980, hon fell Keble Coll Oxford 1981–, hon fell Emmanuel Coll Cambridge 1990–, assoc fell Centre for Research in Philosophy and Lit Univ of Warwick 2004–08; Joseph Bard meml lectr RSL 1979, Judith Wilson lectr Univ of Cambridge 1980, F W Bateson meml lectr Univ of Oxford 1984, Clark lectr Trinity Coll Cambridge 1986, T S Eliot centenary lectr Univ of Leeds 1988, Warton lectr Br Acad 1998, Morris Gray lectr Harvard Univ 1998, Tanner lectr BNC Oxford 2000, Ward-Phillips lectr Univ of Notre Dame 2000, President's lectr Univ of Montana 2000, TS Eliot meml lectr St Louis 2001, Charles Rosenthal lectr Brown Univ 2004, Empson lectr Cambridge Univ 2005, Goldsmith lectr Univ of Leeds 2006, Wolfson lectr Univ of Oxford 2010; MA by incorporation Univ of Cambridge 1984; DLitt (hc): Univ of Leeds 1988, Univ of Warwick 2007, Univ of Bristol 2009, Univ of Oxford 2010; LittD (hc) Univ of Cambridge 2010; FRSL 1972–2012, FAAAS 1996; *Awards* Gregory Award for Poetry 1961, Hawthornden Prize 1969, Geoffrey Faber Meml Prize 1970, Whitbread Award 1971, Heinemann Award 1971 and 1999, Alice Hunt Bartlett Award 1971, Duff Cooper Meml Prize 1979, Loines Award American Acad and Inst of Arts and Letters 1983, Ingram Merrill Fndn Award in Lit 1985, Kahn Award 1998, Cholmondeley Award Soc of Authors 1999, T S Eliot Prize Ingersoll Fndn 2000, Truman Capote Award for Literary Criticism 2009, Horst-Bienek Preis Für Lyrik Bavarian Acad of Fine Arts 2014; *Publications* Henrik Ibsen's Brand: A Version for the Stage (1978, 3 edn 1996), The Lords of Limit: Essays on Literature and Ideas (1984), The Enemy's Country: Words, Contexture and other Circumstances of Language (1994), Style and Faith (2003), Collected Critical Writings (2008); *Poetry* For the Unfallen (1959), King Log (1968), Mercian Hymns (1971), Somewhere is Such a Kingdom: Poems 1952–1971 (1975), Tenebrae (1978), The Mystery of the Charity of Charles Péguy (1983), Collected Poems (1985), New and Collected Poems 1952–1992 (1994), Canaan (1996), The Triumph of Love (1998), Speech! Speech! (2000), The Orchards of Syon (2002), Scenes from Comus (2005), Without Title (2006), Selected Poems (2006), A Treatise of Civil Power (2007), Oraclau/Oracles (2010), Clavics (2011), Odi Barbare (2012), Broken Hierarchies: Poems 1952–2012 (2013); *Style—* Prof Sir Geoffrey Hill; ✉ The Rectory, 2 Apthorpe Street, Fulbourn, Cambridgeshire CB21 5EY (✆ 01223 880337)

HILL, Harry Douglas; s of Jack Hill, of S Yorks, and Katheline Francis, *née* Curran; *b* 4 April 1948; *Educ* Holgate GS Barnsley; *m* 1 (m dis 1979), Glenis Margaret, *née* Brown; 2 s (Jonathan b 1973, Matthew b 1975); m 2, 23 Nov 1985, Mandy Elizabeth, da of Frederick Aldred, of Downham Market, Norfolk; 3 s (William b 1986, Joshua b 1987, Rupert b 1992); *Career* surveyor; articles A E Wilby & Son Barnsley 1964–67, various surveying appts 1967–74; ptnr: David Bedford Norfolk 1974–82, Hill Nash Pointen 1982–84, James Abbott Partnership 1984–86; dir Mann & Co 1986–87; Countrywide Assured Gp plc: dir 1987–88, md 1988–2006, chm 2007–08; non-exec dir Rightmove 2003–08; *Style—* Harry Hill, Esq

HILL, (Michael) Hedley; s of late Kenneth Wilson Hill, and Dorothy, *née* Etchells (d 1984); *b* 3 February 1945, Huddersfield; *Educ* Rydal Sch Colwyn Bay, St John's Coll Cambridge; *Career* admitted slr 1969; NP; ptnr Weightmans Liverpool 1971–95 (conslt 1995–97); gen cmmr for Income Tax 1996–; pres Liverpool Law Soc 1992–93 (vice-pres 1991–92), former chm Liverpool Young Slrs Gp; dir: Slrs' Benevolent Assoc 1999–2006, Liver Housing Assoc (chm 2001); memb Bd Arena Housing Gp 2006–08; former pres Old Rydalian Club; dep chm Arena Housing Assoc 2001–05; memb: Law Soc, Liverpool Law Soc; *Recreations* canal boating, oenology, freemasonry; *Clubs* Union Soc Cambridge; *Style—* Hedley Hill, Esq; ✉ Fulwood Park Lodge, Liverpool L17 5AA (✆ 0151 727 3411, mobile 07932 437382, e-mail michael@hedleyhill.com)

HILL, Sir James Frederick; 4 Bt (UK 1916), of Bradford; OBE (2000), DL (W Yorks 1994); s of Sir James Hill, 3 Bt (d 1976), and Marjory, *née* Croft (d 2006); *b* 5 December 1943; *Educ* Wrekin Coll, Univ of Bradford; *m* 1966, Sandra Elizabeth, da of late J C Ingram, of Ilkley, W Yorks; 3 da (Juliet Clare (Mrs Wells) b 1969, Georgina Margaret b 1971, Josephine Valerie b 1976), 1 s (James Laurence Ingram b 1973); *Heir* s, James Hill; *Career* chm Sir James Hill (Wool) Ltd; Hon DUniv 1997; *Recreations* walking, sailing; *Clubs* RAC, Bradford, St Enodoc; *Style—* Sir James F Hill, Bt, OBE, DL; ✉ Roseville, Moor Lane, Menston, Ilkley, West Yorkshire LS29 6AP (✆ 01943 874624)

HILL, Prof (William) John; s of Rowan Jardine Hill, and Dorothy Isobel Hill; *b* 15 February 1954; *Educ* The Acad Annan, Univ of Glasgow (MA), Univ of York (PhD); *Career* Univ of Ulster: lectr 1978–88, sr lectr 1988–98, prof of media studies 1998–2004; prof of media Royal Holloway Univ of London 2004–; visiting prof of film Hochschule für Fernsehen und Film Munich 1994–95, visiting prof of media studies Aichi Shukutoku Univ Nagoya 1997–98, sr res fell AHRB Centre for Br Film and Television Studies 2001–02; dir UK Film Cncl 1999–2004 (chair Working Pty on Specialised Exhbn and Distribution 2001–02), chair NI Film Cncl 1994–97, govr BFI 1994–97; chair Working Gp on the Film Industry in Europe European Inst for the Media 1998–2004, princ investigator research project The History of Forgotten Television Drama in the UK (AHRC funded) 2013–; memb Communications, Cultural and Media Studies Panel HEFCE Res Assessment Exercise 1996; founding chair Foyle Film Festival 1987; FRSA; *Books* Sex, Class and Realism: British Cinema 1956–63 (1986), Cinema and Ireland (jtly, 1987), Border Crossing: Film in Ireland, Britain and Europe (co-ed, 1994), Big Picture, Small Screen: The Relations Between Film and Television (co-ed, 1996), The Oxford Guide to Film Studies (co-ed, 1998), British Cinema in the 1980s (1999), Film Studies (co-ed, 2000), American Cinema and Hollywood (co-ed, 2000), World Cinema (co-ed, 2000), National Cinema and Beyond (co-ed, 2004), Film History and National Cinema (co-ed, 2005), Cinema and Northern Ireland (2006), National Cinemas and World Cinema (2006), Ken Loach: The Politics of Film and Television (2011); *Style—* Prof John Hill; ✉ Department of Media Arts, Royal Holloway, University of London, Egham, Surrey TW20 0EX (✆ 01784 414684, e-mail john.hill@rhul.ac.uk)

HILL, Judith Lynne; LVO (1995); da of Dr Michael James Raymond (d 1996), and Joan, *née* Chivers; *b* 8 October 1949; *Educ* Brighton and Hove HS, Univ of Cambridge (MA); *m* 1, 9 Oct 1976 (m dis 1986), Brent Arthur Hill; 1 da (Olivia b 1981); m 2, 6 March 1987, Edward Richard Regenye, s of Edward Joseph Regenye (d 1987), of New Jersey, USA; *Career* admitted slr 1975, ptnr Farrer and Co 1986; former chm: Ctee 20 Int Bar Assoc, Charity Law Assoc; memb Law Soc; *Recreations* travel, gardening; *Clubs* Reform; *Style—* Mrs Judith Hill, LVO; ✉ Messrs Farrer & Co, 66 Lincoln's Inn Fields, London WC2A 3LH (✆ 020 7242 2022, fax 020 7831 9748, e-mail jlh@farrer.co.uk)

HILL, Kenneth Leslie (Ken); s of William Leslie Hill (d 1965), of Great Barr, Birmingham, and Doris Agnes, *née* Clarke (d 1975); *b* 13 May 1941; *Educ* West Bromwich Tech HS, West Bromwich Tech Coll, Wolverhampton Poly, Alban & Lamb Coll, Harvard Business Sch; *m* 2 Sept 1964, Wendy, da of George Somerville; 2 da (Suzanne Marie b 8 Aug 1965, Lisa Joanne b 28 Nov 1971), 2 s (Christopher David, Richard Anthony (twins) b 28 July 1966); *Career* accountant West Bromwich CBC 1957–62, sr accountant Walsall CBC 1962–67, chief accountant Harlow Development Corp 1967–69, chief fin offr Essex River Authy 1969–72, chief fin offr Glamorgan River Authy 1972–73, dir of fin Severn Trent Water 1973–89, gp dir of fin Pennon Group plc (formerly South West Water plc) 1989–2002; chm: Eden Project Ltd 1999–, Vocalis plc 2000–04; chm Westcountry Rivers Tst; CIPFA 1963; *Recreations* golf; *Clubs* Harvard Business, Isle of Purbeck Golf; *Style—* Ken Hill, Esq; ✉ Eden Project Ltd, Bodelva, Cornwall PL24 2SG (✆ 01726 811918, fax 01726 811959)

H

HILL, Max Benjamin Rowland; QC (2008); s of Rowland Hill, of Oxfordshire and Shirley, *née* Reeve; *b* 10 January 1964, Hatfield; *Educ* Royal GS Newcastle, St Peter's Coll Oxford (BA); *m* 25 July 1993, Heather Coombs; 2 da (Natasha b 22 Aug 2000, Amber b 8 Nov 2004); *Career* called to the Bar 1987; recorder 2005, memb Red Lion Chambers (head of chambers 2012–); chm: Criminal Bar Assoc 2011–12 Kalisher Tst 2014–; ldr SE Circuit 2014–16; patron Scene and Heard, academic advsr Curriculum for Cohesion 2015–; FRSA; *Style—* Max Hill, Esq, QC; ✉ Red Lion Chambers, 18 Red Lion Court, London EC4A 3EB

HILL, Rt Rev Michael Arthur; *see:* Bristol, Bishop of

HILL, Prof Peter David; s of Derryck Albert Hill (d 1988), and Phyllis Mary, *née* Carn (d 2008); *b* 16 March 1945; *Educ* Leighton Park Sch Reading, Univ of Cambridge and St Bartholomew's Hosp London (MA, MB BChir); *m* 10 June 1972, Christine Margaret, da of Stanley William Seed (d 1996), of Seaton, Devon; 2 s (Gulliver b 1974, Luke b 1976), 1 da (Jessica b 1981); *Career* registrar then sr registrar Maudsley Hosp 1972–79, sr lectr then prof of child mental health, head of section and conslt in child and adolescent psychiatry St George's Hosp and Med Sch Univ of London 1979–98, hon conslt St Thomas' Hosp 1981–89, conslt Tadworth Court Children's Hosp 1987–, conslt, departmental head and prof Great Ormond St Hosp for Children 1998–2003 (hon conslt 2003–10), emeritus prof Univ of London 1998–, visiting prof St George's Hosp 1999–; conslt advsr British Army 1995–2007, conslt advsr Huntercombe Manor Hosp 1998–, med advsr Tourettes Action, advsr Select Ctee on Health 1995–97, specialist advsr Health Advisory Serv 1999–2003; currently ind medical practitioner; pres Union Européene des Médecins Spécialistes (Child and Adolescent Psychiatry) (UEMS-CAPP) 2002–06; chm Child and Adolescent Specialist Section RCPsych 1993–97; partner UK ADHD Partnership (UKAP) 2013–; memb Professional Bd ADDISS; FRCPsych 1987 (MRCPsych 1975), FRCP 1994 (MRCP 1972), FRCPCH 1997 (MRCPCH 1996); *Books* Essentials of Postgraduate Psychiatry (jtly, 1979, 1986 and 1997), A Manual of Practical Psychiatry (jtly, 1986), Adolescent Psychiatry (1989), The Child Surveillance Handbook (jtly, 1990 and 1994), The Child with a Disability (jtly, 1996), Child Mental Health in Primary Care (jtly, 2001), A Perfect Start (jtly, 2007), A Handbook for the Assessment of Children's Behaviours (jtly, 2012); numerous publications on child and adolescent mental health services development and psychopharmacology; *Recreations* jazz trumpet, house restoration; *Style—* Prof Peter Hill; ✉ Strand End, 78 Grove Park Road, London W4 3QA; 127 Harley Street, London W1G 6AZ (✆ 020 7486 2332, website www.prof-peter-hill.org)

HILL, Phelan; *b* 21 July 1979; *Educ* Bedford Sch, Univ of Leicester; *Career* rower (cox); achievements incl: Silver medal (eights) World Championships 2010 and 2011, Bronze medal (eights) Olympic Games 2012; *Clubs* Leander; *Style—* Phelan Hill, Esq

HILL, Robin Arthur; s of Paul Colin Hill, and Ellen, *née* Barclay-Moore (d 1993); *b* 2 January 1956; *Educ* Victoria Univ of Manchester (BA (Arch), BArch); *m* 1985, Dawn Rebecca Teago; 1 da (Tamsin b 1992), 1 s (Tobias b 1998); *Career* architect in private practice 1988–; expert witness 1992–; memb Nat Cncl RIBA 1997–2003; MAE, corp memb RIBA 1985; *Style—* Robin Hill, Esq; ✉ Robin Hill Chartered Architects Ltd, 93 Ashley Road, Altrincham, Cheshire WA14 2LX (✆ 0161 928 7143, e-mail robinhillrhca@btinternet.com)

HILL, Dr Rosemary; da of Edward Hill (d 2003), and Barbara, *née* Pegler (d 1982); *b* London; *Educ* Newnham Coll Cambridge (MA), Univ of London (PhD); *m* 1985, Christopher Logue, CBE (d 2011); m 2, 2014, Gavin Stamp; *Career* writer and historian; contrib ed: Jl of Modern Craft 2008–, London Review of Books 2012–; tstee: London Library 1999–2002, Victorian Soc 2003–15; memb English Heritage Blue Plaques Panel 2014–; quondam fell All Souls Coll Oxford (visiting fell 2004–05), hon research prof Univ of York; tstee Pugin Soc; FRSL, FSA; *Books* God's Architect: Pugin and the Building of Romantic Britain (James Tait Black Meml Prize, Wolfson History Prize, Elizabeth Longford Prize for Historical Biography, Marsh Biography Award), Stonehenge (Historians of British Art Prize), Unicorn: the poetry of Angela Carter; *Clubs* Cocked Hat, Groucho; *Style—* Dr Rosemary Hill; ✉ All Souls College, Oxford OX1 4AL; c/o David Godwin, DGA, 55 Monmouth Street, London WC2H 9DG (✆ 020 7240 9992, website www.rosemaryhill.co.uk)

HILL, Selima; da of James Wood, and Elisabeth, *née* Robertson (d 1991); *b* 13 October 1945; *Educ* New Hall Cambridge; *m* 1968, Roderic Hill; 1 da (Maisie b 1970), 2 s (Moby 1972, Albert 1977); *Career* author; writer in residence: Royal Festival Hall 1992, Science Museum London 1996; writing fell UEA 1991, tutor Exeter and Devon Arts Centre 1990–96, tutor South Bank Centre 2001, Royal Literary Fund fell 2003; exhibitor Imperial War Museum 1996; judge T S Eliot Prize 1999; memb Assoc Faculty Schumacher Coll 19920, cultural exchange visit to Mongolia 1993 and 1994; winner: Cholmondeley Award for Lit 1989, Arvon Observer Int Poetry Competiton 1989, Arts Cncl writers bursary 1993; shortlisted: T S Eliot Prize, Forward Prize and Whitbread Poetry Award 1997; FRSL 2016; *Books* Saying Hello at the Station (1984), My Darling Camel (1987), The Accumulation of Small Acts of Kindness (1988), Point of Entry (multimedia work

Imperial War Museum, 1990), A Little Book of Meat (1993), Trembling Hearts in the Bodies of Dogs (1994), Violet (1996), Bunny (2001, winner Whitbread Poetry Book of the Year 2001), Portrait of My Lover as a Horse (2002), Lou Lou (2004), Red Roses (2006), The Hat (2008), Fruitcake (2009), People who Like Meatballs (2012), The Sparkling Jewel of Naturism (2014), Jutland (2015), The Magnitude of my Sublime Existence (2016), Splash Like Jesus (2017); *Recreations* swimming, learning Mongolian; *Style*— Ms Selima Hill; ✉ c/o Bloodaxe Books, Eastburn, South Park, Hexham, Northumberland NE46 1BS

HILL, Shaun Donovan; s of George Herbert Hill (d 1969), and Molly, *née* Cunningham, of London; *b* 11 April 1947; *Educ* The London Oratory, St Marylebone GS; *m* 11 June 1966, Anja Irmeli, da of Martti Toivonen, of Lahti, Finland; 1 s ((Kim) Dominic b 18 Jan 1967), 2 da (Maija b 9 April 1972, Minna b 10 June 1975); *Career* cook: Carrier's Restaurant London 1968–71, The Gay Hussar London 1972–74, Intercontinental Hotel London 1975–76; head chef: Capital Hotel Knightsbridge 1976–77, Blakes Chelsea 1978–80, Lygon Arms Broadway 1981–82; chef and patron Hill's Stratford-upon-Avon 1983–85, chef and md Gidleigh Park Chagford 1985–94, chef and prop Merchant House Ludlow 1995–2004 (8 out of 10 Good Food Guide 1999 and 2000), chef patron Walnut Tree Abergavenny 2007–; memb Académie Culinaire de France 1982, elected master chef by Master Chef's Inst 1983, Egon Ronay Guide Chef of the Year 1992, Catey Chef Award 1993; research fell Dept of Classics Univ of Exeter; *Books* Shaun Hill's Gidleigh Park Cookery Book, Quick and Easy Vegetables, Masterclass, Cooking at the Merchant House (2000), How To Cook Better (2004), The Cook's Book (jtly, 2005), Food in Ancient World (jtly, 2006), Salt is Essential (2016); *Recreations* eating and drinking (not necessarily in that order); *Style*— Shaun Hill, Esq; ✉ 24 Droitwich Road, Worcester WR3 7LH

HILL, Stephen Guy; s of Michael Lawrence Hill, and Joan Florence, *née* Luce; *b* 19 July 1960; *Educ* King Edward VII Sch Lytham, St John's Coll Cambridge (MA, Whitehead Scholar, Wright Prize), Harvard Grad Sch of Business (Prog for Mgmnt Devpt); *Career* conslt Boston Consulting Gp 1982–85, exec asst to ceo Guinness plc 1985–87, various positions (incl ceo Financial Times Gp 1998–2002, memb Pearson Mgmnt Bd 1998–2002 and chm Interactive Data 2000–02) Pearson plc 1987–2002, ceo Betfair Ltd 2003–05; chm and ceo D'Aval Ltd 2002–; non-exec dir: Royal & SunAlliance plc 2000–04, Psion plc 2003–06, Channel 4 2006–11, IG Gp plc 2011–, SandAire Ltd 2013–, Aztec Ltd 2014–, Ofcom 2014–16; tstee and hon treas RNID 2008– (dep chair 2012–), chm RNID Action on Hearing Loss 2013–17, chm Alzheimer's Soc 2016–; memb Advsy Bd Judge Business Sch Univ of Cambridge 2008–17; *Recreations* triathlon, gardening, travel; *Clubs* RAC; *Style*— Stephen Hill, Esq

HILL, Susan Elizabeth (Mrs Stanley Wells); CBE (2012); da of R H Hill, and Doris, *née* Bailey; *b* 5 February 1942, Scarborough; *Educ* Scarborough Convent, Barr's Hill Sch Coventry, KCL (BA); *m* Prof Stanley Wells, CBE, *qv*; 3 da (Jessica b 1977, Imogen b 1984 d 1984, Clemency b 1985); *Career* novelist, playwright, book reviewer; *Novels* The Enclosure (1961), Do Me A Favour (1963), Gentleman and Ladies (1968), A Change for the Better (1969), I'm the King of the Castle (1970), Strange Meeting (1971), The Bird of Night (1972), In the Springtime of the Year (1974), The Woman in Black (1983), Air and Angels (1991), The Mist in the Mirror (1992), Mrs de Winter (1993), The Service of Clouds (1997), The Various Haunts of Men (2004), The Pure in Heart (2005), The Risk of Darkness (2006), The Man in the Picture (2007), The Vows of Silence (2008), The Beacon (2008), The Small Hand (2010); *Non-Fiction* The Magic Apple Tree (autobiography, 1982), People (ed, 1983), Through the Kitchen Window (1984), Through the Garden Gate (1986), The Lighting of the Lamps (1987), Shakespeare Country (1987), The Spirit of the Cotswolds (1988), Family (autobiography, 1989), Reflections from a Garden (1995); *Children's Books* One Night at a Time (1984), Mother's (1985), Can it be True? (1987), Susie's Shoes (1989), I've Forgotten Edward (1990), I Won't Go There Again (1990), Pirate Poll (1991), The Glass Angels (1991), Beware, Beware (1993), King of King's (1994), The Christmas Collection: An Anthology (1995); *Short Stories* The Albatross (1970), A Bit of Singing and Dancing (1973), The Penguin Book of Modern Women's Short Stories (ed, 1991), The Penguin Book of Contemporary Women's Short Stories (ed, 1995), The Second Penguin Book of Women's Short Stories (ed, 1997), Listening to the Orchestra (1997), The Boy Who Taught the Beekeper to Read (2003); *Style*— Miss Susan Hill, CBE; ✉ website www.susan-hill.com

HILL, Vernon W; s of Vernon W Hill; *b* 18 August 1945, San Francisco; *Educ* Wharton Sch Univ of Pennsylvania (BSc); *m* 22 Dec 1973, Shirley Hill; 4 c; *Career* fndr Commerce Bank 1973 (chm and ceo until 2007); fndr and chm Metro Bank 2010–; chm Fetch Inc; *Books* Fans Not Customers: How to Create Growth Companies in a No Growth World (2012); *Recreations* golf; *Style*— Mr Vernon W Hill, II; ✉ Metro Bank plc, One Southampton Row, London WC1B 5HA (☎ 020 3402 8382, e-mail vernon.hill@metrobank.plc.uk)

HILL, Prof William George; OBE (2004); s of William Hill (d 1984), of Hemel Hempstead, Herts, and Margaret Paterson, *née* Hamilton (d 1987); *b* 7 August 1940, Hemel Hempstead, Herts; *Educ* St Albans Sch, Wye Coll London (BSc), Univ of Calif Davis (MS), Iowa State Univ, Univ of Edinburgh (PhD, DSc); *m* 1 July 1971, (Christine) Rosemary, da of John Walter Austin (d 2002), of Kingskerswell, Devon; 2 da (Louise b 1973, Rachel b 1974), 1 s (Alastair b 1977); *Career* Univ of Edinburgh: lectr 1965–74, reader 1974–83, prof of animal genetics 1983–2002 (emeritus prof 2003–), head Inst of Cell, Animal and Population Biology 1990–93, head Div of Biological Sciences 1993–98, dean and provost Faculty of Sci and Engrg 1999–2002; visiting prof and visiting research assoc: Univ of Minnesota 1966, Iowa State Univ 1967–78, N Carolina State Univ 1979, 1985 and 1988–2005; ed: Animal Production 1971–78, Livestock Production Science 1994–95, Genetical Research 1996–2007, Genetics Research 2008–12; ed-in-chief Proceedings of the Royal Soc B 2005–08; memb: Sci Study Gp Meat and Livestock Cmmn 1969–72, AFRC Animals Res Grant Bd 1986–92, Dir's Advsy Gp AFRC Animal Breeding Res Orgn 1983–87, AFRC Inst of Animal Physiology and Genetics Res 1987–93, Bd of Govrs Roslin Inst 1994–2002 (dep chair 1998–2002), Cncl Royal Soc 1993–94, RAE Biological Scis Panel 1995–96 and 1999–2001 (chair 1999–2001); chair Nat Ctee Conservation Animal Genetic Resources 2001–02; pres: Br Soc of Animal Sci 1999–2000 (vice-pres 1997–99), Cwlth Scholarships Cmmn 1998–2004 (dep chair 2002–04); vice-pres Genetics Soc 2004–08; Hon DSc N Carolina State Univ 2003, Dr (hc) Univ of Edinburgh 2005; FRSE 1979, FRS 1985; *Books* Benchmark Papers on Quantitative Genetics (1984), Evolution and Animal Breeding (1989); many papers in scientific jls; *Recreations* farming, bridge; *Clubs* Farmers'; *Style*— Prof William Hill, OBE, FRS, FRSE; ✉ 4 Gordon Terrace, Edinburgh EH16 5QH (☎ 0131 667 3680); Institute of Evolutionary Biology, School of Biological Sciences, University of Edinburgh, West Mains Road, Edinburgh EH9 3JT (☎ 0131 650 5705, fax 0131 650 6564, e-mail w.g.hill@ed.ac.uk)

HILL ABRAHAMS, Rosalind Margaret; da of Brian Percival Hill (d 1992), and Joan Barbara Warren, *née* Rollinson (d 2004); *b* 18 April 1955; *Educ* St Margaret's Convent Sussex, Univ of Exeter (BA); *m* 7 June 1997, David Jacques Abrahams; *Career* Ernst & Young 1977, J Henry Schroder Wagg & Co Ltd 1986, dir corporate fin P&P plc 1988–92; dir: Warren Hill Assocs Ltd 1992–, Strand Partners Ltd 1993–, Beaumont Cornish Ltd 2000–; vice-chm Grosvenor Chapel 2011–13; memb: The Pilgrims, Int Fundraising Ctee Br Red Cross, RIIA; Liveryman: Worshipful Co of Glaziers and Painters of Glass, Worshipful Co of Gardeners; ACA 1981, FRSA 2001; *Recreations* travel, entertaining, the arts; *Style*— Mrs Rosalind Hill Abrahams; ✉ Warren Hill Associates Ltd, 93 Cheyne Walk, London SW10 0DQ (e-mail warrenhillco@aol.com)

HILL OF OAREFORD, Baron (Life Peer UK 2010), of Oareford in the County of Somerset; Jonathan Hopkin Hill; CBE (1995); s of Rowland Louis Hill, and Paddy Marguerite, *née* Henwood; *b* 24 July 1960; *Educ* Highgate Sch, Trinity Coll Cambridge (MA); *m* 3 Sept 1988, Alexandra Jane, da of John Nettelfield, MC; 2 da (Georgia Elizabeth b 9 Oct 1991, Harriet Victoria b 10 Jan 1993), 1 s (Archie William Augustus b 1 June 1995); *Career* RIT & Northern 1983, Hamish Hamilton 1984–85, Cons Research Dept 1985–86, special advsr to Rt Hon Kenneth Clarke at Dept of Employment, DTI and Dept of Health 1986–89, Lowe Bell Communications 1989–91, No 10 Policy Unit 1991–92, political sec to PM 1992–94, sr conslt Bell Pottinger Communications (formerly Lowe Bell Communications) 1994–98, dir Quiller Consultants 1998–2010; Parly under-sec of state Dept for Educn 2010–13, ldr of the House of Lords and Chllr of the Duchy of Lancaster 2013–14; cmmr Financial Stability, Financial Services and Capital Markets Union EC 2014–16; *Books* Too Close to Call (with Sarah Hogg, 1995); *Recreations* reading, gardening, walking; *Style*— The Lord Hill of Oareford, CBE; ✉ European Commission, 200 Rue de la Loi, Brussels, 1040, Belgium

HILL SMITH, Marilyn; da of George Francis Smith, and Irene Charlotte, *née* Clarke; *b* 9 February 1952; *Educ* Nonsuch HS For Girls Ewell Surrey, Guildhall Sch of Music & Drama; *Career* opera singer; soprano soloist: Viennese Gala Performances Southbank and touring 1975–80, Gilbert & Sullivan For All touring England Australasia (1974) USA/Canada (1975–76) 1969–75; debut: BBC Radio 1975, princ soprano ENO 1978 (memb co 1978–84), Royal Opera House 1981, New Sadler's Wells Opera 1981, Canadian Opera 1984, Welsh Nat Opera 1987, Scottish Opera 1988, New D'Oyly Carte Opera 1990, Singapore Opera 1992 and 1993; festivals incl: Aldeburgh, Henley, Versailles, Nurenburg, Cologne, Athens, Granada, Bologna, Siena, Rome, Zimbabwe, Hong Kong; TV incl: Top C's and Tiaras (C4) 1983, Queen Mother's 90 Birthday Celebration 1990, Sound of Music 2010–11; recordings incl: Dixit Dominus (CBS Masterworks) 1977, The Songwriters (BBC) 1978, Christopher Columbus (Opera Rara) 1978, La Princesse de Navarre (Erato) 1980, Dinorah (Opera Rara) 1980, Robinson Crusoe (Opera Rara) 1981, Count of Luxembourg and Countess Maritza (New Sadler's Wells Opera) 1983, Vienna Premiere Vol I (Chandos, Music Retailers Assoc award 1984) 1983, Friday Night is Music Night (BBC Records) 1985, Treasures of Operetta Vol I (Chandos Retailers Assoc award 1985) 1985, Vienna Premiere Vol II (Chandos) 1987, Ruddigore (New Sadler's Wells) 1987, Candide (Bernstein, Scottish Opera) 1988, Treasures of Operetta Vol III (Chandos) 1989, Pirates of Penzance (New D'Oyly Carte, Music Retailers Assoc) 1990, Student Prince (TER) 1990, Marilyn Hill Smith sings Kálmán and Lehár (Chandos) 1991, Is It Really Me? (TER) 1991, Edwardian Echoes (Chandos) 1992, Novello Centenary (Chandos) 1992, Celebrating the Musicals (BBC) 1998, Friday Night is Music Night (BBC) 1998, The Rose of Persia (BBC) 1999, It Is Really Me! (TER) 2011; patron: Epsom Light Opera 1998, Central Festival Opera 1999, Ivor Novello Appreciation Bureau 2001, Bromley OEcumenical Singers 2005, Sinfonia Britannia 2006; teacher and adjudicator Fedn of Music Festivals; *Recreations* cooking, reading, sleeping; *Style*— Ms Marilyn Hill Smith; ✉ c/o Music International, 13 Ardilaun Road, Highbury, London N5 2QR (☎ 020 7359 5183, fax 020 7226 9792)

HILL WILLIAMS, Dr Christina Bernadette Thérèse; DL (Berks 2005); da of Howard E Hill (d 1971), and Elsie, *née* Punnett-Beale (later Mrs Robert L Hall, d 2003); *Educ* Univ of Wales (BA), Univ of Birmingham (MA, PhD); *m* (David) Clive Harries Williams, OBE; 1 step da (Rebecca b 1975), 1 step s (Robert b 1977); *Career* Tidy Britain Gp: field offr 1977, dir Midlands 1977–81, dir Devpt and Trg 1981–88, head of research and legislation 1988; dir of public affrs Aviation Environment Fedn & Tst 1988–89, nat dir Sch & Gp Travel Assoc (SAGTA) 1988–94; environmental and educnl conslt 1988–; UK Environmental Law Assoc (UKELA): hon dir of conferences and hon annual conference organiser 1989–93, memb Cncl of Mgmnt 1989–95, memb Noise Working Pty 1989–96, co sec 1995–96, gen sec 1996–2006, life memb 2006; co sec TecKnow Ltd 1995–98; lay interviewer Ind Tribunal Service 1999, census enumerator 2001; vice-chm Berks Environment Tst 1990–92 (memb Exec Ctee 1989–92); Berks Healthcare Tst: non-exec dir 2001–07, co-convenor 2002–04, chair Clinical Effectiveness Ctee 2002–04, chair Improving Working Lives Steering Gp 2004–07; lead govr Berks Healthcare NHS Fndn Tst 2007–08 (govr 2007–09); Mental Health Act mangr 2001–, Mental Health Act hosp mangr Priory Gp Ltd (Thatcham) 2007– and (Southampton) 2011–15; memb Lord Chllr's Advsy Ctee on JPs and Appointments Panel (Berks) 1998–2010 (chm Appointments Panel 2001–10, chm W Berks Advsy Sub-Ctee 2007–10 (memb 2001–10)), chm Berks Gen Cmmrs of Income Tax 2004–09 (gen cmmr 1998–2009, divnl vice-chm 2001–03, chm South Central gen cmmrs 2007–09), presenter and facilitator Nat Training Prog for Gen Cmmrs 2004–08, memb Berks Advsy Ctee for Gen Cmmrs of Income Tax 2006–09, tax memb finance and tax Tribunals Service 2009–; YWCA: chair Steering Gp for Major Appeal Ctee 1993, acting chair Appeal Ctee 1994, chair Open The Door Appeal Ctee 1994–95, chair Special Events Ctee 1996, memb YWCA Incorporated Co 1996–, YWCA Bd of Govrs and Audit Ctee 1996–99; advsr Bd of Tstees Prisoners Abroad 1990–95 (vice-chair Fundraising Ctee 1988, memb Fundraising Working Gp 1990–93), vice-pres SPISE (Sane Planning in the SE) 2008– (memb Exec Ctee 1989–2008, memb Working Gp 1989–91, memb Policy Gp 1991–93), vice-patron Abbeyfield House Reading 2000– (vice-patron Appeal 1998–2000); CPRE Berks: memb Exec Ctee 2002–09, vice-chm 2003–06, chm 2006–09, vice-pres 2009–; author various pubns for Tidy Britain Gp and SAGTA, ed SAGTA News 1989–92; Berks Gardens Tst: co-fndr 2008, chm 2008–13, vice-pres 2013–; tstee and memb Exec Ctee League of Friends Royal Berks Hosp 2011– (vice-chm 2012–), tstee Catholic Nat Library 2012–16, vice-patron Appeal Thumbs Up Club 2012, life memb Indo-Br Scholars' Assoc 2012, ind memb Exec Bd Berks Local Nature Partnership 2015–; govr Oratory Schs 2010– (govr for child protection 2013–, memb Finance and Gen Purpose Ctee 2014–); High Sheriff Berks 2009–10; Freeman City of London 2010 (life memb Guild of Freemen of City of London 2013); affiliate memb Chartered Inst of Wastes Mgmnt 1994– (assoc memb 1981–94), assoc memb Chartered Inst of Environmental Health 1988; FIPD 1985–96, FRGS 1989, FRSA 1989; *Recreations* reading, theatre, music, walking, skiing, gardening; *Clubs* Phyllis Court; *Style*— Dr Christina Hill Williams, DL; ✉ Honeycroft House, Pangbourne Road, Upper Basildon, Berkshire RG8 8LP (☎ and fax 01491 671631, e-mail clive@clivewilliams.orangehome.co.uk); Railway Cottage, Throop Road, Templecombe, Somerset BA8 0HR

HILL-ARCHER, Clive; s of late Malcolm Hill-Archer, and late Agnes Keech, *née* Harrison; *b* 23 March 1946, London; *Educ* Duke of York Sch Nairobi, Dulwich Coll, SW London Tech Coll (HND Business Studies), DipM (CIM), Univ of Strathclyde (MSc); *m* 2 April 1966, Valerie Frances, *née* Balchin; 2 da (Maxine Louise b 6 Feb 1969, Naomi Angelina b 29 Aug 1970); *Career* account mangr/dir with several advtg agencies incl Garland Compton, Dorland Grey (Paris) and Allen Brady & Marsh 1967–80, Univ of Strathclyde 1980–82, new technol mangr Thames Television Ltd 1982–84, mktg dir Thorn EMI Cable Television Ltd 1984–86, mktg devpt dir Tupperware UK and Ireland 1986–87, mangr mktg consultancy Pannell Kerr Forster Associates 1987–92, non-exec dir International Weather Productions 1990–93, owner/managing conslt Niche Marketing & Communications 1992–97 and 2011–, head of mktg Hempsons 1997–2011; interim exec mktg mangr The Wine Soc 1996; memb Nat Cncl CIM 1990–97 (Pres's Award 1993), regulated memb CIM Global Delivery Framework 2014–; visiting lectr in mktg London Guildhall Univ 1988–95; external examiner: Univ of E London 1995–98, South Bank Univ 1999–2002; memb: Wine Soc, BASC; memb: PCC St Bride's 2005–16, Guild of St Bride 2006–; lay memb City Deanery Synod 2008–16; Freeman City of London 1991, Liveryman Worshipful Co of Marketors 1991–2013; FCIM 1990 (MCIM 1969), chartered marketer 1995, MIMC 1997, certified mgmnt conslt 1997; *Recreations* walking, driving (follower of F1), travelling, wine, the Arts (ballet, music, theatre and art); *Style—* Clive Hill-Archer, Esq; ✉ 127 Turney Road, Dulwich Village, London SE21 7JB (☎ 020 7274 5235, mobile 07947 738786, e-mail chillarcher@aol.com)

HILL-WOOD, Peter Denis; s of Denis John Charles Hill Hill-Wood, MC (d 1982), of Hartley Wintney, Hants, and Mary Cecilia, *née* Martin Smith (d 1997); *b* 25 February 1936; *Educ* Eton; *m* 1971, Sarah, *née* Andrews; 1 da (Sarah Frances b 5 July 1972), 2 s (Julian Peter b 16 Jan 1974, Charles Denis b 21 April 1976); *Career* with David A Bevan Simpson & Co (later de Zoete & Bevan) stockbrokers 1956–60; Hambros Bank Ltd: joined 1960, exec dir i/c fund mgmnt 1968, vice-chm 1987, non-exec dir 1994–96, ret; chm: Arsenal Football Club plc, Top Technology Ltd; dir Peter Hambro Mining plc 2003–, non-exec dir Delphi Group plc 1996–98; *Recreations* association football, golf, country pursuits; *Clubs* White's, Pratt's; *Style—* Peter Hill-Wood, Esq

HILLER, Susan; *b* 1942; *Educ* Smith Coll US (AB), Tulane Univ (MA); *Career* artist; lectr Maidstone Coll of Art and tutor St Martin's Sch of Art 1975–80, postgrad tutor Slade Sch of Fine Art 1980–91, assoc prof of art Dept of Fine and Applied Arts Univ of Ulster 1991–, Baltic chair in contemporary art Univ of Newcastle upon Tyne 2000–; distinguished visiting prof Dept of Art Calif State Univ Long Beach 1988, visiting prof of new genres UCLA 1991, visiting Art Cncl chair Dept of Fine Art UCLA 1992; external examiner CNAA (various BA and MA Fine Art courses); curator Dream Machines Arts Cncl touring exhbn 2000–01, selector Bienale of Sydney 2002; memb Visual Arts Panel Greater London Arts Assoc 1976–81; memb Visual Arts Panel Arts Cncl of England 1997–99; artist in residence Univ of Sussex 1975, Visual Artist's Award GB (Gulbenkian Fndn) 1976 and 1977, Nat Endowment for the Arts fell (USA) 1982, Guggenheim fell (USA) 1998; work in public collections incl: Arts Cncl of GB, Tate Gallery, V&A, Contemporary Arts Soc; *Works* incl: Belshazzar's Feast (video installation), Monument (photography and audio), From the Freud Museum 1991–97 (mixed media installation), An Entertainment (video installation), Wild Talents (video installation), Psi Girls (video installation), Witness (audio sculpture); *Exhibitions* solo incl: Gallery House 1973, Hester van Royen 1976 and 1978, Serpentine Gallery 1976, MOMA Oxford 1978, Gimpel Fils London (various 1980–95), A Space Toronto 1981, Akumulatory Warsaw 1982, Roslyn Oxley Gallery Sydney 1982, Interim Art 1984, ICA 1986, Pat Hearn NY 1988–90, Kettle's Yard Cambridge 1989, Mappin Gallery Sheffield 1990, Matt's Gallery London 1991, Pat Hearn Gallery NY 1991, Nicole Klagsbrun NY 1991, Third Eye Centre Glasgow 1991, Tate Gallery Liverpool 1996, Art Angel cmmn 2000, Testa Konsthalle Stockholm 2000, Gagosin Gallery NY 2001, Tate Modern monograph room 2000–01, Gagosian Gallery NY 2001, Fondacion Mendoza Caracas Venezuela 2001, Museet for Samtidskunst Roskilde Denmark 2002, Galerie Volker Diehl Berlin 2003, Baltic Centre for Contemporary Art Newcastle England 2004, Museu Seralves Porto Portugal 2004, Kunsthalle Basle Switzerland 2004; group incl: From Britain 75 (Taidehall Helsinki) 1975, Hayward Annual 1978, The British Art Show (Arts Cncl of GB) 1984, Kunst mit Eigen-Sinn (Museum Moderner Kunst Vienna) 1985, Staging the Self (Nat Portrait Gallery) 1986, Towards a Bigger Picture (V&A) 1987, 100 Years of Art in Britain (Leeds City Museum) 1988, Lifelines (Br Cncl, BASF, Tate, Ludwigshafen and Liverpool) 1989–90, Great British Art (Maclellon Galleries Glasgow) 1990, Ten Artists (Ceibu Caison Tokyo) 1990, Now for the Future (Hayward Gallery London) 1990, At One/At War with Nature (Pratt Inst Galleries NY) 1991, In Vitro (Joan Miro Fndn Barcelona), Rites of Passage (Tate Gallery London) 1995, Sydney Biennale 1996, Inside the Visual (ICA Boston) 1996, Material culture: the object in British art of the 1980s and 90s (Hayward Gallery London) 1997, Now/Here (Louisiana Museum, Humlebaek Denmark) 1997, The Object of Performance (Museum of Contemporary Art LA) 1998, The Muse in the Museum (MOMA NY) 1998, Amateur/Eksdal (Gothenburg Museum) 2000, Intelligence (Tate Britain) 2000, The British Art Show 2000–01, Memory (Br Museum) 2003, Dream Extensions (SMAK Ghent) 2004; *Books* Dreams – Visions of the Night (co-author), The Myth of Primitivism (ed), After the Freud Museum (1996), Thinking About Art: Conversations with Susan Hiller (1997); various artists books and monographs; *Style—* Ms Susan Hiller

HILLIARD, Spenser Rodney; s of Alfred Hilliard (d 1982), of London, and Kathleen Claribelle Hilliard (d 2006); *b* 14 March 1952; *Educ* City of London Sch, QMC, Univ of London (LLB); *m* 1 May 1993, Rachel Frances, *née* Hindle; 4 c (Daisy Isobel b 2 April 1994, Chloë Valentine b 14 Feb 1996 d 1998, Cora Columbine b 31 March 1999, Digby Easter b 15 April 2001); *Career* called to the Bar Middle Temple 1975, practising barr; memb Hon Soc of Middle Temple; *Recreations* wine; *Style—* Spenser Hilliard, Esq; ✉ Lamb Building, Temple, London EC4Y 7AS (☎ 020 7797 7788, fax 020 7353 0535)

HILLIER, Dr Bevis; s of late Jack Ronald Hillier, and late Mary Louise, *née* Palmer; *b* 28 March 1940, Redhill, Surrey; *Educ* Reigate GS, Magdalen Coll Oxford (Demy, Gladstone prizeman); *Career* editorial staff The Times 1963–68, ed British Museum Society Bulletin 1968–70, antiques corr The Times 1970–84, guest curator Minneapolis Inst of Arts 1971, ed The Connoisseur 1973–76, dep literary ed The Times 1980–82, features ed Sunday Telegraph magazine 1983–84 (exec ed 1982–83), columnist and assoc ed Los Angeles Times 1984–88, ed Sotheby's Preview 1990–93; freelance work incl: TV critic New Statesman (as Garry Reffell), restaurant critic Vogue (Corning Glass Award 1980), antiques columnist Punch, Country Living and Harpers & Queen; frequent broadcaster on radio and TV; presenter: Collecting on a Shoestring (TV series), and Trash or Treasure? (TV series); co-fndr and first chm The Thirties Soc (now The Twentieth-Century Soc) 1979, pres Betjeman Soc 2006– (vice-pres 1988–2006); Hon DLitt Univ of Winchester 2009; FRSA 1967, FRSL 1997; Commedatore Order of Merit Republic of Italy 1976; *Publications* Master Potters of the Industrial Revolution: The Turners of Lane End (1965), Pottery and Porcelain 1700–1914 (1968), Art Deco of the 1920s and 30s (1968), Posters (1969), Cartoons and Caricatures (1970), The World of Art Deco (1971), 100 Years of Posters (1972), Travel Posters (1973), Victorian Studio Photographs (1974), Façade (jtly, 1974), Austerity/Binge: Decorative Arts of the 1940s and 1950s (1975), Punorama (1975), Dead Funny (1975), A Tonic to the Nation: The Festival of Britain, 1951 (jt ed, 1976), The New Antiques (1977), Fougasse (1978), Ealing Film Posters (1981), Bevis Hillier's Pocket Guide to Antiques (1981), John Betjeman, Uncollected Poems (ed, 1982), The Style of the Century 1900–1980 (1983), John Betjeman: A Life in Pictures (1984), Mickey Mouse Memorabilia (1986), Young Betjeman (1988), Early English Porcelain (1992), Art Deco Style (jtly, 1997), John Betjeman: New Fame, New Love (2002), Betjeman: The Bonus of Laughter (2004), The Wit and Wisdom of G K Chesterton (2010), The Virgin's Baby: The Battle of the Ampthill Succession (2013), Going for a Song: An Anthology of Poems About Antiques (2014); author of numerous articles in newspapers and learned jls; *Recreations* piano, collecting; *Clubs* Garrick; *Style—* Dr Bevis Hillier; ✉ Flat 23, The Hospital of St Cross, St Cross Road, Winchester, Hampshire SO23 9SD

HILLIER, Katie; *Educ* Univ of Westminster; *Career* accessory designer; launched design consultancy 2002, consulted for and collaborated with: Marc by Marc Jacobs, Jonathan Saunders, Giles, Stella McCartney, House of Holland, Luella Bartley, Hogan, Salvatore Ferragamo, Loewe – Madrid, Victoria Beckham, Asprey; launched own collection 2010; Accessory Designer of the Year Br Fashion Cncl Award 2009; *Style—* Miss Katie Hillier; ✉ c/o Chenelle Hall, Hall London Ltd, 30 Gresse Street, London W1T 1QR

HILLIER, Meg; MP; *Educ* St Hilda's Coll Oxford, City Univ; *Career* freelance journalist 1998–2000; mayor of Islington 1998–99; memb London Assembly 2000–04, former chair Culture, Sport and Tourism Ctee; MP (Lab/Co-op) Hackney S and Shoreditch 2005–; shadow sec for energy and climate change 2010–11; tstee War Memorials Tst; memb: Unite, Co-op Pty; *Style—* Ms Meg Hillier, MP; ✉ House of Commons, London SW1A 0AA

HILLIER, Prof Sheila Mary Bernadette; da of John Francis Kelleher, of Penwortham, Lancs, and Bridget Cecilia, *née* O'Riordan; *b* 5 October 1944; *Educ* Convent of the Holy Child Jesus Preston, LSE (BSc), Bedford Coll London (MSc(Econ)), Renmin Daxue (People's Univ) Beijing (Dip Chinese), London Hospital Medical Coll, Univ of London (PhD), Univ of Lancaster (MA); *m* William Robert George Hillier, s of late Reginald Hillier; 1 da (Martha Tamar Riordan b 6 Sept 1975); *Career* research asst Dept of Social Admin LSE 1965–66, researcher Dept of Social Med Guy's Med Sch 1966–68, research asst Statistical Research Unit DHSS 1968–70; Bedford Coll London: research offr Social Research Unit 1971–73, lectr in med sociology 1973–74; St Bartholomew's and The London Queen Mary's Sch of Med and Dentistry: lectr in med sociology 1974–86, sr lectr 1986–94, head Dept of Human Science and Med Ethics 1990–, prof 1994–, head Div of Community Sciences 1998–2001, emeritus prof 2006; tstee Nilgaris Adivasi Tst 2009, memb Friends of Christ Church Spitalfields, memb Barbican Residents Assoc; Hamish Canham Poetry Prize 2009; memb: Br Sociological Assoc 1984, RSM 1987, RHS 1991, Poetry Soc 2004; *Books* Health-Care and Traditional Medicine in China 1800–1982 (with J A Jewell, 1983), Researching Cultural Differences in Health (with D Kelleher, 1995), A Quechua Confession Manuel – Poems (2010), Hotel Moonmilk (Poems) 2013; *Recreations* early music, cookery, gardening, choral singing; *Style—* Professor Sheila Hillier; ✉ 409 Mountjoy House, Barbican, London EC2Y 8BP; Les Bastides de St Veran 84220, Goult, France; Blizard Inst of Cell and Molecular Science, St Bartholomew's and The London Hospital School of Medicine and Dentistry, Queen Mary, London E1 2AD (☎ 020 7628 1339, e-mail s.m.hillier@qmul.ac.uk)

HILLIER, Air Chief Marshal Sir Stephen John; KCB (2014), CBE (2005), DFC (1999), ADC (2006); *Career* cmmnd RAF 1980, flying offr 1982, sqdn ldr 1991, wing cdr 1996, gp capt 2000, Station Cdr RAF Lossiemouth 2002, Head Theatre Airspace Capability MOD 2005, Air Offr Commanding No 2 Gp 2008, Dir Information Superiority MOD 2010, Dep Chief of the Defence Staff (Capability) 2012, Chief of the Air Staff 2016–; ADC to HM the Queen 2016–; *Style—* Air Chief Marshal Sir Stephen Hillier, KCB, CBE, DFC, ADC

H

HILLMAN, David; s of Leslie Hillman (d 1969), and Margery Joan, *née* Nash (d 1988); *b* 12 February 1943, Oxford; *Educ* Aristotle Central Sch, London Sch of Printing (Graphic Art NDD); *m* 1, 27 Oct 1963 (m dis 1983), Eileen Margaret, *née* Griffin; 1 da (Jane b 1965), 1 s (Stephen b 1968); m 2, 2 July 1983, Jennie Diana, da of Max David Keith Burns, of Burley, Hants; 2 s (James Daniel b 3 July 1992, Thomas David b 3 July 1995); *Career* asst Sunday Times Magazine 1962–65; art ed: London Life 1965–66, Sunday Times 1966–68; ed Design for Living Section Sunday Times Magazine 1968–75, art dir and dep ed Nova Magazine 1968–75, freelance practice London 1975–76; art dir: Wolff Olins Ltd 1976–77, Le Matin de Paris 1977–78; ptnr Pentagram Design 1978–2007; estab Studio David Hillman 2007; exhibition Hillman in Print 2009; sr fell RCA 2004; D&AD: Gold Award for Design 1973, Silver Award 1972–73, 1975, 1983, 1984, 1989, 1994 and 2001, Most Awarded Designer of All Time 2013; NY Art Dirs Int Silver Award 1992, Critics Award Critique Magazine USA 2000; memb AGI (int pres 2003–04), FCSD, RDI 1997, FRSA 1998; *Books* Ideas on Design (co-ed, 1986), Puzzlegrams (1989), Pentagames (1990), Phantasmagrams (1992), Pentagram, The Compendium (co-ed 1993), Nova 1965–75 (co-author, 1993), Puzzlegrams Too! (1994), Century Makers (co-author, 1999), Pentagram Book 5 (co-author, 1999), Terence Donovan. The Photographs (co-author, 2000), Terence Donovan Fashion (co-author, 2012); *Style—* David Hillman, Esq; ✉ Studio David Hillman Limited, Glebe Wood House, Bodmin Street, Holsworthy EX22 6BH (☎ 01453 842810, e-mail hillman@studiodavidhillman.com, website www.studiodavidhillman.com)

HILLMAN, Prof John Richard; s of Robert Hillman (d 1990), of Farnborough, Kent, and Emily Irene, *née* Barrett; *b* 21 July 1944; *Educ* Chislehurst and Sidcup GS, UC Wales (BSc, PhD); *m* 23 Sept 1967, Sandra Kathleen, da of George Palmer (d 1997), of Luton, Beds; 2 s (Robert George b 1968, Edmund John b 1969); *Career* lectr in physiology and environmental studies Univ of Nottingham 1969–71 (asst lectr 1968–69); Univ of Glasgow: lectr in botany 1971–77, sr lectr 1977–80, reader 1980–82, prof and head of dept 1982–86; dir Scottish Crop Research Inst 1986–2005, dep chm and fndr Mylnefield Research Services Ltd 1989–2005; visiting prof: Univ of Dundee 1986–, Univ of Strathclyde 1986–97, Univ of Edinburgh 1988–, Univ of Glasgow 1991–; adjunct prof Petra Univ Jordan 2015; author of papers in scientific jls and books on plant physiology, agriculture and horticulture, plant biochemistry and biotechnology; chm and memb numerous ctees and panels; Bawden lectr 1993; chm Technology Foresight Panel: on Agric, Natural Resources and Environment 1994–95, on Agric, Horticulture and Forestry 1995–97; pres Agric and Food Section BAAS 2001–02; memb: Bd BioIndustry Assoc 1998–2004 (chair Industrial Applications Ctee), Ct Univ of Abertay Dundee 1998–2005; dir: The Mylnefield Tst 2000–05, Mylnefield Holdings Ltd 2000–05; advsr Arab Acad of Sciences 2002–, tstee Jl of Horticultural Science and Biotechnology 2003–, tstee Scottish Soc of Crop Research 2006–, pres Scotia Agricultural Soc 2006–10, chair Angus Cons and Unionist Assoc 2008–10–; Br Potato Industry Award 1999, World Potato Industry Award 2000, Scottish Horticultural Medal 2003; Hon DSc: Univ of Strathclyde 1994, Univ of Abertay Dundee 1996; FSB, CBiol 1985, FLS 1982, FRSE 1985, MInstD 1995, FRSA 1997, FIHort 1998, FCMI (FIMgt 1987), FRAgS 2004; *Books* ed: Isolation of Plant Growth Substances (1978), Biosynthesis and Metabolism of Plant Hormones (with A Crozier, 1984), Biochemistry of Plant Cell Walls (with C T Brett, 1985), Opportunities and Problems in Plant Biotechnology (with W Powell, 1992); *Recreations* landscaping, building renovations, horology, reading, Arab affairs, cricket; *Clubs* Farmers'; *Style—* Prof John Hillman, FRSE; ✉ The James Hutton Institute, Invergowrie, Dundee DD2 5DA (☎ 01382 562731, fax 01382 561412, e-mail jrhillman@tiscali.co.uk)

HILLS, Barrington William (Barry); s of William George (d 1967), of Upton upon Severn, Worcs, and Phyllis, *née* Biddle; *b* 2 April 1937; *Educ* Ribston Hall Gloucester, St Mary's Convent Newmarket, Mr Whittaker's Worcester; *m* 1, 21 Nov 1959 (m dis 1977), Maureen, da of late Patrick Newson; 3 s (John b 1960, Michael b 1963, Richard b 1963); m 2, 1 Sept 1977, Penelope Elizabeth May, da of John Richard Woodhouse; 2 s (Charles b 1978, George b 1983); *Career* Nat Serv King's Troop RHA, racehorse trainer 1969–; won: Prix de L'Arc de Triomphe, Budweiser Irish Derby, Irish 1000 Guineas (twice), Irish Oaks (twice), Prix Royal-Oak, 2000 Guineas Newmarket (twice), 1000 Guineas Newmarket (twice), St Leger, Prix de l'Abbaye; second place Epsom Derby three times; *Recreations* hunting, shooting, golf; *Clubs* Turf; *Style—* Barry W Hills, Esq; ✉ B W Hills Southbank Ltd, Wetherdown House, Lambourn, Hungerford, Berkshire RG17 8UB (☎ 01488 71548)

HILLS, Prof Sir John Robert; kt (2013), CBE; s of Derrick Walter Hills (d 1979), and Valerie Jean, *née* Gribble; *b* 29 July 1954, Luton, Beds; *Educ* Univ of Cambridge (BA), Univ of Birmingham (MSocSc); *m* 1989, Prof Anne Power; *Career* Dept of the Environment 1979–80, House of Commons Treasy Ctee 1980–82, Inst for Fiscal Studies 1982–84, Cmmn of Inquiry into Taxation in Zimbabwe 1984–86, Welfare State Prog LSE 1986–97, dir Centre for Analysis of Social Exclusion and prof of social policy LSE 1997–, LSE Richard Titmuss Prof of social Policy 2015–, co-dir LSE Int Inequalities Inst 2015–; memb Pensions Cmmn 2003–06, chair Nat Equality Panel 2008–10; ind review of fuel poverty 2011–12; FBA 2002, AcSS 2009; *Publications* New Inequalities (ed, 1996), The State of Welfare (co-ed, 1998), Understanding Social Exclusion (co-ed, 2002), Inequality and the State (2004), A more equal society? New Labour, poverty, inequality and exclusion (co-ed, 2005), Towards a More Equal Society? Poverty, Inequality and Policy since 1997 (co-ed, 2009), An Anatomy of Economic Inequality: The report of the National Equality Panel (2010), Getting the Measure of Fuel Poverty (2012), Wealth in the UK: Distribution, Accumulation and Policy (jtly, 2013), Good Times, Bad Times: The Welfare Myth of Them and Us (2015), Social Policy in a Cold Climate: Policies and their consequences since the crisis (co-ed, 2016); *Recreations* fell walking; *Style*— Prof Sir John Hills, CBE; ✉ Centre for Analysis of Social Exclusion, London School of Economics and Political Science, Houghton Street, London WC2A 3AE (☎ 020 7955 6562, fax 020 7955 6951, e-mail j.hills@lse.ac.uk)

HILLS, Prof Paul; *Educ* Univ of Cambridge, Courtauld Inst of Art London (MA, PhD); *Career* lectr Univ of Warwick 1976–98, Andrew Mellon visting prof Courtauld Inst of Art London 2003, prof Courtauld Inst of Art London 2004–; sometime visiting prof: Inst of Fine Arts NY, Villa I Tatti, Harvard Center for Renaissance Studies, RCA; *Books* incl: David Jones (1981), The Light of Early Italian Painting (1987), David Jones: Artist and Poet (ed, 1997), Venetian Colour: Marble, Mosaic, Painting and Glass, 1250–1550 (1999); *Style*— Prof Paul Hills; ✉ Courtauld Institute of Art, Somerset House, Strand, London WC2R 0RN

HILTON, Anthony Victor; s of Dr Raymond W Hilton (d 1975), and Miriam Eileen Norah, *née* Kydd (d 2003); *b* 26 August 1946; *Educ* Woodhouse Grove Sch Bradford, Aberdeen Univ (MA); *m* 1 (m dis); 1 s (Steven b 1969); m 2, Cyndy Miles; 2 s (Michael b 1985, Peter b 1987), 1 da (Emily b 1991); *Career* city ed The Times 1982–83; Evening Standard: city ed 1984–89 and 1996–2002, md 1989–95, fin ed 2002–; dir Associated Newspapers plc 1989–95, chm Newsdesk Communications Ltd 2003–; Wincott Journalist of the Year 2003, London Press Club Business Journalist of the Year 2005, World Leadership Forum Decade of Excellence Award 2007; visiting prof London Met Univ 2011; memb Stock Exchange Ctee on Private Share Ownership (Weinberg Ctee) 1995–96; dir: London Forum 1993–96, London First 1993–96, St John's Ambulance Nat Fundraising Appeal 1993–95; vice-pres Children's Film Unit 1993–95; hon degree Univ of Aberdeen 2010; *Books* Employee Reports (1978), City within a State (1987); *Recreations* after dinner speaking; *Clubs* Lansdowne, Reform; *Style*— Anthony Hilton, Esq; ✉ Evening Standard, Northcliffe House, Derry Street, London W8 5EE (☎ 020 7938 6000)

HILTON, Isabel N; OBE; da of Dr Raymond W Hilton (d 1975), and Miriam Evelyn, *née* Kydd (d 2003); *b* 25 November 1947; *Educ* Bradford Girls' GS, Walnut Hills HS Ohio, Univ of Edinburgh (MA), Peking Languages Inst, Univ of Fudan Shanghai (scholar); *m* 1 (m dis 1975), John Armstrong Black; m 2, Charles Neal Ascherson; 1 s, 1 da; *Career* journalist; teaching asst Chinese Dept Univ of Edinburgh 1972–73, Scottish TV 1976–77, Sunday Times 1977–86 (special corr China, feature writer, news reporter, Latin America ed, asst foreign ed); The Independent: Latin America ed 1986, European Affrs ed 1989, chief feature writer 1991–95; presenter The World Tonight (BBC radio) 1995–99, presenter Night Waves (BBC Radio 3) 1999–; corr (BBC2); columnist The Guardian, staff writer The New Yorker, ed chinadialogue.net; reg contrib: New Statesman, Time Magazine, El Pais, New York Times; memb: Bd Free Word, Advsy Bd Bureau of Investigative Journalism, Advsy Bd Inst of Human Rights and Business; tstee Br American Project; memb: Chatham House (RIIA) 1977, Br Assoc of China Studies 1978; Hon DLitt: Univ of Bradford 2003, Univ of Stirling 2009; IISS 1989, FRSA 2007, fell Soc of Women Geographers; *Books* The Falklands War (jtly, 1982), The Fourth Reich (jtly, 1984), Betrayed (contrib, 1988), The General (1990), The Search for the Panchen Lama (1999), The Thinking Man's Guide to the World Cup (contrib, 2006), Eating Mud Crabs in Kandahar (contrib, 2011); *Recreations* family, gardening; *Style*— Ms Isabel Hilton, OBE; ✉ c/o Gillon Aitken Associates Ltd, 18–21 Cavaye Place, London SW10 9PT (e-mail isabelhilton@mac.com, website www.chinadialogue.net and www.thethirdpole.net)

HILTON, Jane Elizabeth Anne; da of Derek George Ernest Hilton, and Anne Kathleen, *née* Stacy; *b* 3 November 1962; *Educ* Beaconsfield HS, Lancaster Univ (BA); *Career* professional photographer and film maker (specializes in people, quirky situations and the USA); clients incl: Nescafe, BT, Next, Sunday Times Magazine, Telegraph Magazine, BBC; work incl The Brothel (10-part documentary series for BBC); *Style*— Jane Hilton; ✉ mobile 07785 795158, e-mail jane@janehilton.com, website www.janehilton.com

HILTON, (Alan) John Howard; QC (1990); s of Alan Howard Hilton, (d 1986), of Bowdon, and Barbara Mary Campbell, *née* Chambers, (d 1958); *b* 21 August 1942; *Educ* Haileybury, Univ of Manchester (LLB); *m* 21 Dec 1978, Nicola Mary, da of Percy Harold Bayley (d 1977), of Brighton; 1 s (Felix b 24 Dec 1983); *Career* called to the Bar Middle Temple 1964; in practice 1964–, recorder 1985–; *Books* Fish Cookery (1981), Opera Today (1985); *Recreations* opera, conjuring, 19th century females in oils, cooking; *Clubs* Garrick, Les Six; *Style*— John Hilton, Esq, QC; ✉ Queen Elizabeth Building, Temple EC4Y 9BS (☎ 020 7583 5766, fax 020 7353 0339, e-mail john.hilton@holliswhiteman.co.uk)

HILTON, Prof Julian; s of R K Hilton; *b* 11 September 1952; *Educ* Canford Sch, BNC Oxford, Univs of Grenoble, Munich and Salamanca (BA, MA, DPhil); *m* 1, 10 July 1976, Hanne, da of H J Boenisch; 1 da (Ruth b 18 Feb 1978); m 2, 29 Aug 1996, Malika, da of B Moussaid; 1 da (Nermeen b 11 Nov 1996), 1 s (Kenz b 24 May 2002); *Career* res fell Alexander van Humboldt Stiftung 1976, fell Stiftung Maximilianeum Munich 1977, prof of drama and communications UEA 1988–91 (lectr 1977, sr lectr 1987, dir Audio-visual Centre 1987–91); fndr and ptnr Technol Arts Info 1985–98, project mangr AIM prog EC 1989–91, dir AVC Multimedia Ltd 1991–92, md Telos Consulting Ltd 1992–95, pres Telos Gp 1995–98, chm Aleff Gp Ltd 1999–; jt project mangr COMETT proj EC 1991–94, dir Value Project EC DGXIII; conslt: IAEA Vienna 1991–, WHO 1995–, FAO Rome 1997–, OCP Gp 2008–; memb Bd Global Assoc of Clinical Res Professionals Washington DC 1998–2000, memb UNECE Geneva Expert Working Gp on Resources Classification 2012–; dir Advanced Veterinary Information System (AVIS) project FAO 1992–2006, princ investigator Milo Project Florida Inst of Phosphate Res 1999–, princ investigator Beneficial Uses of Phosphogypsum 2006–11; chm Artificial Intelligence and Interactive Systems Gp, chm IAEA/NEA-OECD UxP Expert Working Gp 2011–; memb Bd Theatre Royal Norwich, vice-chm Norfolk Arts Forum; fell Swedish Center for Working Life; visiting prof Tech Univ Vienna; dean Inst ACRP 2000–02; *Books* Georg Buchner (1982), Performance (1987), New Directions in Theatre (1992), IAEA Phosphate Industry Safety Report (2013); plays incl: The Enchanted Bird's Nest (1985), Broken Ground (1986), The Marriage of Panurge (1986), Courage (1989); *Recreations* opera, walking, shopping; *Style*— Prof Julian Hilton; ✉ Cross Keys Centre, 36 Erith High Street, Erith DA8 1QY (☎ 020 7515 9009, fax 020 7515 8842, e-mail jhilton@aleffgroup.com, website www.aleffgroup.com)

HILTON, Mark William; s of Peter Entwistle Hilton, of Ripley, N Yorks, and Monica, *née* Smith; *b* 15 July 1958, Bradford; *Educ* Wrekin Coll, Univ of Leeds (LLB); *m* 25 April 1987, Catharine, da of George Canavan, of Ripon; 1 da (Camilla b 21 July 1991), 1 s (Thomas b 26 March 1994); *Career* admitted slr 1982; Last Suddards Bradford 1980–82, Barlow Lyde & Gilbert London 1982–85, ptnr Last Suddards Leeds 1986–88 (joined 1982, rejoined 1985), ptnr and head of construction and engrg Hammond Suddards Leeds 1988–2000, Hammond Suddards Edge 2001–03, Hammonds 2003–05, ptnr Addleshaw Goddard 2005–13, ptnr DLA Piper London 2013–; memb Law Soc 1979–; FCIArb 1995, CEDR accredited mediator 2000; *Recreations* skiing, scuba diving, tennis; *Clubs* RAC; *Style*— Mark Hilton, Esq; ✉ DLA Piper, 3 Noble Street, London EC2V 7EE (☎ 020 7796 6675, mobile 07968 559035, e-mail mark.hilton@dlapiper.com)

HILTON, Nicholas David; s of John David Hilton, and Dorothy Gwendoline, *née* Eastham; *b* 27 June 1952; *Educ* Marlborough; *m* 14 July 1984, Vanessa Jane, da of late Brig W John Reed; 2 da (Lucy Vanessa b 1989, Emma Rachel b 1992); *Career* CA 1974; Moore Stephens 1979–; 2020 Practice Exchange 2013–; FCA 1979; *Recreations* golf, bridge, mah-jong, entertaining; *Style*— Nicholas Hilton, Esq; ✉ Moore Stephens, 150 Aldersgate Street, London EC1A 4AB (☎ 020 7334 9191, fax 020 7248 3408, e-mail nick.hilton@moorestephens.com)

HILTON OF EGGARDON, Baroness (Life Peer UK 1991), of Eggardon in the County of Dorset; Jennifer Hilton; QPM (1989); da of late John Robert Hilton, CMG, of London; *b* 12 January 1936; *Educ* Bedales, Univ of Manchester (MA); *Career* police offr Met Police Serv 1956–90 (Cdr 1984–90); opposition whip 1991–95, spokesman on the environment 1991–97; tstee Police Rehabilitation Tst; tstee Life in Fresh Waters; *Style*— The Baroness Hilton of Eggardon; ✉ House of Lords, London SW1A 0PW

HILTON-BARBER, Miles Anthony; s of Lt-Col Maurice Clinton Hilton-Barber, OBE, DFC, and Moira Yvonne Hilton-Barber; *m* 1976, Stephanie Evans; 2 da (Deborah, Abigail), 1 s (David); *Career* adventurer, marathon runner and author; achievements incl: London Marathon 1998, Marathon des Sables (250km ultra-marathon in Sahara Desert) 1999, climbed 17,500 feet in Himalayas 2000, reached summit of Kilimanjaro 2000, Highest and Deepest Project Mont Blanc 2000, first blind person to manhaul a sledge 400km across Antarctica 2000 (frostbite prevented continutation of bid to be first blind person to reach S Pole), 11-day 200km ultra-marathon across parts of ancient Silk Road in China 2001, climbed Ben Nevis 2001, abseiled down several tower blocks for charity 2001, Siberian Ice Marathon 2002, memb 5-man team which set new world record for non-stop unsupported 200km crossing of Qatar Desert 2002, Around the World in 80 Ways Project 2002 (part of team of 3 people with disabilities circumnavigating the globe using at least 80 of the most challenging forms of transport), first blind person to fly English Channel in a microlight 2003, set new world high-altitude record (20,300ft) in tandem microlight 2004, did wing-walk on Boeing Steerman 2004, first blind person to do solo kamakazi skeleton run down 5G Olympic bobsleigh track Lillehammer 2005, participated in Bad Water Ultra-Marathon across Death Valley 2005, cage-diving with great white sharks 2006, first blind person to abseil 350 feet down Table Mountain 2006, competed in 3 day int canoe race Atlantic to Pacific via Panama Canal 2006, co-piloted 3 engined 1932 Dornier float plane Austrian air display 2006, set Malaysian Grand Prix lap record for a blind driver in a 230kph Lotus, first blind pilot to undertake a sortie of extreme aerobatics in a 600 mph Hawker Hunter fighter jet with an ex-Red Arrows co-pilot, first blind person to drive a 340 bhp performance rated Zap Cat power boat in ocean time trials, set three new aviation speed/altitude/acceleration records for blind pilot (first blind aviator to break sound barrier); also competed in tandem cycling marathons, hot-air ballooning, para-sailing, and made 40 sky-diving jumps; qualified scuba diver, Grade 5 Zambesi white water rafting, Scottish Grade 3 technical ice climbing; subject of TV documentaries: Against All Odds (Carlton, three int film festival Gold Awards), Blind Faith (Carlton, int film festival Gold Award), National Geographic Channel Antarctica documentary; int motivational speaker and writer; hon freedom of the Borough of Amber Valley; hon master Univ of Derby 2003; *Books* Living Your Dreams (audio book); *Style*— Miles Hilton-Barber, Esq; ✉ 10 Ferrers Crescent, Duffield, Belper, Derbyshire DE56 4DH (☎ 01332 843590, mobile 07973 360470, e-mail miles@mhb.demon.co.uk)

HINCH, Prof (Edward) John; s of Joseph Edward Hinch (d 2010), and Mary Grace, *née* Chandler (d 2010); *b* 4 March 1947; *Educ* Edmonton County GS, Trinity Coll Cambridge (BA, PhD); *m* 28 June 1969, Christine Bridges; 1 da (Clare b 9 Dec 1975), 1 s (Robert b 22 Aug 1977); *Career* Univ of Cambridge: asst lectr in mathematics 1972–75, lectr in mathematics 1975–94, reader in fluid mechanics 1994–98, prof in fluid mechanics 1998–; fell Trinity Coll Cambridge 1971–; European Mechanics Soc Fluid Dynamics Prize 2010, American Physical Soc Fluid Dynamics Prize 2010; memb Academia Europeae 2011, foreign assoc Nat Acad of Engrg USA 2012; FRS 1997; Chevalier de l'Ordre Nationale du Mérite (France) 1997; *Books* Perturbation Methods (1991); *Style*— Prof John Hinch, FRS; ✉ Trinity College, Cambridge CB2 1TQ (☎ 01223 338427, fax 01223 337918, e-mail e.j.hinch@damtp.cam.ac.uk)

HINCHCLIFFE, Christian; *b* 7 March 1973, London; *Educ* Eton, Univ of Bristol; *Career* started career in advtg at Ogilvy Gp 1996; Euro RSCG: joined as account mangr 1998, rising to account dir, new business dir and bd memb 2002–04; mktg dir McCann Erickson 2004–; Top 10 New Business Director Campaign Magazines 2002; memb: Cncl IPA, Mktg Soc; *Recreations* golf, tennis; *Clubs* The Berkshire, Queen's, RAC, Soho House; *Style*— Christian Hinchcliffe, Esq; ✉ McCann Erickson Advertising Limited, 7–11 Herbrand Street, London WC1N 1EX (☎ 020 7961 2267)

HIND, Andrew; CB (2011); *b* 29 September 1955, Portsmouth, Hants; *Educ* Portsmouth GS, Univ of Southampton (BSc); *m* 1985, Christina; 3 s; *Career* Ernst & Young 1976–80, Pannell Kerr Forster Kenya 1980–83, divnl financial controller Balfour Beatty Ltd 1983–86; ActionAid: dir of fin 1986–89, dep chief exec 1989–91; dir of fin and corporate servs Barnardo's 1992–95; BBC World Serv: dir of finance and business devpt 1995–2002, chief operating offr 2002–04; chief exec Charity Cmmn for England and Wales 2004–; FCA 1979; *Publications* Charity Managers and Charity Trustees: Meeting the challenges of the 1990s (jt ed, 1993), The Charity Finance Handbook (ed, 1994), The Governance and Management of Charities (1995); *Recreations* running, golf, travel, collecting old books on Africa; *Style*— Andrew Hind, Esq, CB; ✉ 11 Byng Road, High Barnet, Hertfordshire EN5 4NW; Charity Commission for England and Wales, Harmsworth House, 13–15 Bouverie Street, London EC4Y 8DP (☎ 020 7674 2473, fax 020 7674 2309, e-mail andrew.hind@charitycommission.gsi.gov.uk)

HIND, Dr Charles Robert Keith; s of Col (Robert) Keith Hind, of Derby, and Dorothy, *née* Kinsey; *b* 7 June 1953; *Educ* King's Coll Taunton, Univ of London Med Sch (BSc, MB BS, MD); *m* 21 July 1985, Fiona, da of Maj Alexander Hugh Fraser, of Cradley, Worcs; 2 s (James b 1986, Alexander b 1992), 1 da (Eleanor b 1989); *Career* conslt physician gen and respiratory med: Liverpool Heart and Chest Hosp 1987– (med dir 2000–04), Royal Liverpool Hosp 1987–2001; censor and dir of publications RCP 1997–2000, ed Postgraduate Medical Jl 1994–98; pres Int Soc of Internal Med 2002–04; FRCP, FRCPE, FACP; *Books* X-Ray Interpretation for the MRCP (1983), Short Cases for the MRCP (1984), Amyloidosis and Amyloid P Component (1986), Communication Skills in Medicine (1997); *Style*— Dr Charles Hind; ✉ 47 Rodney Street, Liverpool L1 9EW (☎ 0151 327 5107, e-mail crkh@btopenworld.com); Liverpool Heart and Chest Hospital, Liverpool L14 3PE (☎ 0151 600 1675)

HIND, Kenneth Harvard; CBE (1995); *b* 15 September 1949; *Educ* Woodhouse Grove Sch Bradford, Univ of Leeds; *m* Sue, *née* Hall; 1 step-da; 1 s, 1 da from previous m; *Career* called to the Bar Gray's Inn 1973; practising barr: Leeds 1973–83, Temple 1992–2000; Oriel Chambers Liverpool and Preston 2006–; MP (Cons) Lancs W 1983–92 (Parly candidate 1992); PPS to: Lord Trefgarne MOD 1986–87, John Cope as Min of State DOE 1987–90, Rt Hon Peter Brooke as Sec of State for NI 1990–92; memb Soc of Cons Lawyers 1983–, chm Assoc of Conservative Parly Candidates 1997–2002 (offr 1995–97), chm Ribble Valley Cons Assoc 2006–09 (sr vice-chm 2009–); *Recreations* sailing, skiing; *Style*— Kenneth Hind, Esq, CBE

HINDE, David Richard; s of Walter Stanley Hinde (d 1952), and Marjorie Jewell Grieg, *née* Butcher (d 1970); *b* 16 August 1938; *Educ* Marlborough, Univ of Cambridge; *m* 1963, Rosemary Jill, da of Malcolm Hartree Young (d 1965); 3 da (Sasha Karen b 1966 d 2009, Rachel Olivia b 1968, Anna-Louise b 1972); *Career* asst slr Slaughter and May 1961–69;

exec dir: Wallace Bros Group 1969–77, Wardley Ltd 1977–81, Samuel Montagu and Co Ltd 1981–95, Dah Sing Financial Hong Kong 1995–2004; chm: Invesco Asia Tst plc 2005–13, Macau Property Opportunities Fund Ltd 2006–15; Liveryman Emeritus Worshipful Co of Woolmen; *Recreations* skiing, tennis, cricket, shooting, reading, walking, travel; *Clubs* MCC, City of London, Hong Kong, Oriental; *Style*— David Hinde, Esq; ✉ The Martins, High Street, Chipping Campden, Gloucestershire GL55 6AG (☎ and fax 01386 841328, e-mail david.hinde@yahoo.com)

HINDE, Thomas; *see:* Chitty, Sir Thomas

HINDLEY, Her Hon Judge Estella Jacqueline; QC (1992); da of Arthur John Hindley, of Sutton Coldfield, and Olive Maud, *née* Stanley; *b* 11 October 1948; *Educ* Sutton Coldfield Girls GS, Univ of Hull (LLB); *m* 1, Timothy Raggatt, QC; 1 s (Andrew Timothy Hindley b 14 May 1977); m 2, John Gilbert Harvey (d 2015); *Career* called to the Bar Gray's Inn 1971; recorder of the Crown Court 1989–97, circuit judge (Midland & Oxford Circuit) 1997–, designated family judge for Birmingham 2008–14; former memb Parole Bd; chm and non-exec dir Birmingham Children's Hosp NHS Tst 1993–2003; pres Birmingham Medico-Legal Soc 1999–2001, sec UK Assoc of Women Judges 2006–13; *Recreations* book collecting, painting, music; *Style*— Her Hon Judge E Hindley, QC; ✉ Birmingham Civil Justice Combined Court Centre, 33 Bull Street, Birmingham B4 6DS (☎ 0121 681 4441)

HINDMARCH, Anya (Mrs James Seymour); MBE (2009); da of Michael Hindmarch, and Susan Hindmarch; *b* 7 May 1968; *m* 1996, James Seymour; 4 s (Hugo, Bert, Felix, Otto), 1 da (Octavia); *Career* fashion designer; Anya Hindmarch (own label specialising in bags): fndr, chm and chief creative offr, first store opened London 1993, subsequent stores in NY, LA, Tokyo and Hong Kong, concessions worldwide, launched Blue Label 1999, launched Be a Bag (charity promotion) 2001, launched shoe range 2002; conslt Br Airways (designer First Class amenity kit); non-exec dir Br Fashion Cncl; UK trade ambass, memb Birthday Honours Ctee; tstee: RA, Design Museum; patron Blue Sky, tstee Mothers for Children; Best British Accessories Designer Br Fashion Cncl 2001, Veuve Clicquot Business Woman of the Year Award 2012, BFC Accessory Designer of the Year 2016, Elle Style Award 2016, Glamour Woman of the Year 2016; DArts (hc) Anglia Ruskin Univ; *Clubs* Chelsea Arts; *Style*— Ms Anya Hindmarch, MBE; ✉ The Stable Block, Plough Brewery, 516 Wandsworth Road, London SW8 3JX (☎ 020 7501 0177, fax 020 7501 0170, website www.anyahindmarch.com)

HINDS, Damian Patrick George; MP; *b* 27 November 1969; *Educ* St Ambrose Coll Altrincham, Univ of Oxford; *Career* MP (Cons) Hants E 2010–; *Style*— Damian Hinds, Esq, MP; ✉ House of Commons, London SW1A 0AA

HINE, Dame Deirdre Joan; DBE (1997); *née* Curran; da of David Alban Curran (d 1987), and Noreen Mary, *née* Cliffe; *b* 16 September 1937; *Educ* Charlton Park Sch Cheltenham, WNSM (DPH, MB BCh); *m* 12 Sept 1963, Raymond Hine; 2 s (Jonathan David b 2 Feb 1966, Andrew James b 17 Sept 1967); *Career* house physician and surgn Cardiff Royal Infirmary 1961–62, MO Glamorgan CC 1964–74 (asst MO 1962–64), specialist in community med S Glamorgan HA 1974–82, sr lectr in geriatric med Univ of Wales Coll of Med 1982–84, dep chief MO Welsh Office 1984–87, dir Breast Cancer Screening Serv Breast Test Wales 1987–90, chief MO Welsh Office 1990–97; pres: RSM 2000–02, BMA 2005–06, Royal Medical Benevolent Fund 2008–13, Age Cymru 2011–; vice-pres: Marie Curie Cancer Care, Br Lung Fndn; chm: No Smoking Day Bd 1999–2001, Cmmn for Health Improvement 1999–2004, BUPA Fndn 2004–11, Press Bd RSM 2004–08; ind memb House of Lords Appts Cmmn 2000–05, non-exec dir Glas Cymru 2001–10; Hon FRCS, Hon FRCA, Hon FRCGP, FRCP, FFPHM; *Recreations* reading, walking, canal cruising, classical music; *Style*— Dame Deirdre Hine, DBE; ✉ The Red House, Mill Road, Lisvane, Cardiff (☎ 029 2076 6729, e-mail dj.hine@btinternet.com)

HINE, John; s of late Leonard John Hine, and Elizabeth Jane, *née* Jenkins; *b* 21 January 1946; *Educ* Taunton Sch, Univ of Bristol (LLB); *m* 14 Dec 1974, Margaret Alice Stuart, *née* Morton; 3 c; *Career* articled clerk Dodson & Pulman Taunton 1968–70; asst slr: Wragge & Co Birmingham 1970–73, Lovell White & King 1974–80; ptnr Slaughter and May 1983–2000 (joined 1980); CEDR registered mediator 1997; tstee Royal Courts of Justice Advice Bureau; Freeman Worshipful Co of Slrs 1974; FIArb 1994; *Recreations* theatre, opera, architecture, railway history, occasional cycling; *Style*— John Hine, Esq; ✉ 50 Blackheath Park, London SE3 9SJ (e-mail john.hine@50bhp.co.uk)

HINE, Rear Adm Nicholas William; *Educ* City Univ (BSc), King's Coll (MA); *Career* joned RN 1984; trg 1984–89, various submarine appts 1989–99, CO HMS Talent 1999–2000, various staff appts MOD 2000–07, asst dir Maritime Change prog 2007–08, dir Iraq Maritime and Trg 2009, team ldr Warfare Officers and Ratings 2010–11, CO and Capt Anti-Submarine Warfare HMS Westminster 2011–12, def policy advsr to HM Treasy 2012–15, Asst Chief of the Naval Staff 2015; Howard Johnstone Meml Sword; memb IOD, memb RSA; *Style*— Rear Adm Nicholas Hine

HINES, Prof Peter; *b* 8 August 1962; *Educ* Univ of Cambridge (MA, William Vaughan Lewis Prize), Cardiff Business Sch (MBA, Alexander Duckhams Meml Trophy, PhD, Euro Fedn of Quality Mgmnt Bronze Plate); *m*; 2 c; *Career* purchasing mangr Madison Cycles 1985–88, supply chain manager Spong Housewares 1988–91, freelance conslt 1991–92; Cardiff Business Sch Wales: co-ordinator Materials Mgmnt Unit 1992–94, prof of supply chain mgmnt 1997–, chm Lean Enterprise Res Centre 2008–10 (dep dir 1994–97, co-dir 1997–2000, dir 2000–07); conslt ed Casebook, ed Lean Logistics, ed Int Jl of Logistics: Res & Applications 1998–; chm SA Partners 2000–; memb Ed Advsy Bd: Euro Jl of Purchasing & Supply Mgmnt, Int Jl of Logistics Mgmnt, Supply Chain Forum; chm of nat and int conferences on mgmnt and logistics; fndr ctee chm Logistics Res Network 1996–2001; Euro Best Practice Benchmarking Award 1998; *Books* Creating World Class Suppliers: Unlocking Mutual Competitive Advantage (1994), Selected Readings in Purchasing & Supply (jt ed, 1994), Selected Readings in Supply Chain Management (jt ed, 1996), The Lean Enterprise: Designing and Managing Strategic Processes for Customer Winning Performance (jtly, 1997), Advanced Supply Management: The Best Practice Debate (jt ed, 1997), Value Stream Management: Strategy and Excellence in the Supply Chain (jtly, 2000), Staying Lean (jtly, 2008, Shingo Research Award 2009), Creating a Lean and Green Business System (jtly, 2013, Shingo Research Award 2014); also author of numerous res papers; *Style*— Professor Peter Hines

HINETT, Karl; s of Darren Hinett, of Tipton, W Midlands, and Jennifer, *née* Ashfield; *b* 5 January 1987, Sandwell, W Midlands; *m* Beth Louise, *née* Platts; *Career* Br Armed Forces (Staffs Regt) 2004–08; mountaineer and fundraiser Walking With The Wounded 2011–12, motivational speaker 2014–; charity ambass Queen Elizabeth Hosp Birmingham 2011–, charity-based fundraising running 100 official marathons in two years, patron Rugby 4 Heroes 2014–; Olympic torchbearer 2012, Paralympic torchbearer 2012; Best Recruit (awarded for infantry trg within Br Armed Forces) 2004, W Midlands Local Hero 2011, Beacon Radio's Hero Award 2011, Outstanding Achievement Award Univ Hosps Birmingham NHS Fndn Tst's Best in Care Awards 2011, Sporting Endeavour Award Soldiering on Through Life Tst 2013, Pooleys Aviator of the Year 2013, Pride of Birmingham Outstanding Bravery Award 2014, Pride of Britain Regnl Fundraiser Award 2014, Pride of Tipton Succeeding in the Face of Adversity Award 2015; *Recreations* marathon/ultra runner, mountaineer, adventure sports; *Clubs* UK 100 Marathon; *Style*— Karl Hinett, Esq; ✉ 18 Hall Lane, Tipton, West Midlands DY4 0XN (☎ 07792 490162, e-mail karl7807@msn.com); agent Lily Newman (☎ 01606 883383, e-mail lily@morganjamesconsulting.co.uk)

HINKES, Alan Charles; OBE (2006); *b* 26 April 1954, N Yorks; *Children* 1 da (Fiona); *Career* mountaineer and author; first Briton and thirteenth person to climb the world's highest mountains, the fourteen peaks over 8000m: Shisha Pangma 1987, Manaslu 1989, Cho Oyu 1990, Broad Peak 1991, K2 1995, Everest 1996, Gasherbrum I 1996, Gasherbrum II 1996, Lhotse 1997, Nanga Parbat 1998, Makalu 1999, Annapurna 2002, Dhaulagiri 2004, Kangchenjunga 2005; int mountain guide Int Fedn of Mountain Guides Assocs (UIAGM), writer, inspirational/motivational speaker, columnist Trail magazine, produced 11 documentaries for ITV; currently works with Br Mountaineering Cncl; environmental and organic supporter, charity work with Water Aid (Pres's Award for outstanding vol contribution to Water Aid), Cystic Fibrosis Tst, Duke of Edinburgh's Award Scheme, Outward Bound, Mountain Rescue and Diabetes UK, ambass YHA; Olympic torch bearer 2012; Yorkshireman of the Year 2005–06, Yorkshireman of the Year Dalesman Award 2011; Hon Dr Univ of York, Hon Dr Univ of Teesside; hon citizen Northallerton N Yorks, hon fell Univ of Sunderland; *Publications* Alan Hinkes 8000 Metres Climbing the World's Highest Mountains (2013); *Recreations* regularly seen in Yorkshire or the Lake District, tramping the fells and moors, clinging to a rock face or in winter climbing a frozen waterfall; *Style*— Alan Hinkes, OBE; ☎ 07802 202128, Twitter @alanhinkes; c/o Outdoor-ambition.co.uk (☎ 07801 444495)

HINKS, Frank Peter; QC (2000); s of Henry John Hinks, and Patricia May, *née* Adams; *b* 8 July 1950; *Educ* Bromley GS, St Catherine's Coll Oxford (MA, BCL); *m* 31 July 1982, Susan Mary, da of Col John Arthur Haire; 3 s (Julius b 1984, Alexander b 1985, Benjamin b 1987); *Career* called to the Bar Lincoln's Inn 1973, Chancery Bar 1974–, bencher Lincoln's Inn 2008; writer, illustrator and publisher of children's stories 1992–, exhbns incl The Chapel Gallery Hall Place Bexley 2002; churchwarden Shoreham PC 1995–2005 and 2010–; Liveryman Worshipful Co of Innholders 1991; *Books* The Land of Lost Hair and The Vicar's Chickens (2003, originally published as part of Shoreham Festival of Music 1992), The Crystal Key (2003), Creatures of the Forest (2003), Ramion (2003), The Dim Daft Dwarves (2004), The Bands of Evil (2004), The Magic Magpie (2004), The Cruel Count (2004), Realm of Ramion (2004), The Seven Stones of Iliana (2005), The Black Marchesa (2005), Gary the Frog Prince (2005), The Embodiment of Evil (2005), Swords of Ramion (2005), The Kingdom of the Deep (2009), The Blizzard Wizard (2010), The Body Collector (2012), Boris and the Dumb Skulls (2014), Seas of Ramion (2015); *Recreations* gardening, collecting jugs; *Clubs* Knole; *Style*— Frank Hinks, Esq, QC; ✉ Serle Court, 6 New Square, Lincoln's Inn, London WC2A 3QS (☎ 020 7242 6105, fax 020 7405 4004)

H

HINNELLS, Prof John Russell; s of William Hinnells (d 1978), and Lilian, *née* Jackson; *b* 27 August 1941; *Educ* Derby Coll of Art, KCL (BD, AKC), SOAS Univ of London; *m* 24 June 1965, Marianne Grace, da of William Bushell (d 1973); 2 s (Mark b 11 June 1966, Duncan b 9 Oct 1968); *Career* lectr Univ of Newcastle 1967–70; Univ of Manchester: joined 1970, prof 1985–93, dean Faculty of Theology 1987–88; prof of comparative religion SOAS Univ of London 1993–98; res prof of comparative religion Derby Univ 1999–2002, prof of comparative religion Liverpool Hope Univ 2002 (currently prof emeritus); visiting appts: sr lectr Open Univ 1975–77, govt res fellowship lectr Bombay 1975, Shann lectr Univ of Hong Kong 1986, Ratanbai Katrak lectr Univ of Oxford 1986; visiting prof: Univ of London 1998–, Univ of Stirling 1998–; hon research prof in the study of religions SOAS; author of numerous articles on religious and theological topics published in books and jls; series ed: Library of Religious Beliefs and Practices, Sources for the Study of Religion, Religion and the Arts, Sherman Studies on Judaism in Modern Times; advsr on religion: Penguin Books (Penguin Classics on Religion), Routledge; sec gen Soc for Mithraic Studies, fndr and first sec Shap Working Pty on world Religions in Educn 1968–75; memb: Governing Cncl Br Inst of Persian Studies 1982–86, Cncl of the Br Acad Soc of South Asian Studies 1996–; convenor Int Congress of Mithraic Studies Manchester (first) 1971, Tehran (second) 1975, Rome (Fourth) 1990, chm UNESCO Int Symposium on the Conception of Human Rights in World Religions Inter-Univ Centre Dubrovnik 1985, chief speaker American Acad of Religious Conference LA USA 1985; pres Assoc of Univ Depts of Theology and Religious Studies 1997–2000; life memb Clare Hall Cambridge 1998, sr memb Robinson Coll Cambridge 1999; FSA, FRAS; *Books* incl: Comparative Religion in Education (1970), Hinduism (ed, 1972), Persian Mythology (1974), Mithraic Studies (2 vols, ed, 1975), Spanning East and West (1978), Zoroastrianism and Parsis (1981), Penguin Dictionary of Religions (ed, 1984), Handbook of Living Religions (ed, 1985), Who's Who of World Religions (1991), Studies in Mithraism (1993), New Dictionary of Religions (ed, 1995), Zoroastrians in Britain (1996), Religion, Health and Suffering (jt ed, 1999), The South Asian Religious Diaspora in Britain, Canada and the United States (jt ed, 2000), Zorastrian and Parsi Studies: Selected Works of John R Hinnells (2000), The Zoroastrian Diaspora (2005), Sufism in the West (jt ed, 2006), The Routledge Companion to the Study of Religion (ed, 2006, 2 edn 2010), Religion and Violence in South Asia: Theory and practice (jt ed, 2007), Handbook of Ancient Religion (ed, 2007), Religious Reconstruction in the South Asia Diasporas (ed, 2007), Parsis in India and the Diaspora (jt ed, 2007), The Penguin Handbook of the World's Living Religions (ed, 2010); *Recreations* drawing, painting, photography; *Style*— Prof John Hinnells, FSA; ✉ e-mail jhinnells@btinternet.com

HINTON, Kevin Leslie; s of Ernest Leslie Hinton, of Oxford, and Diana, *née* Churchill; *b* 27 November 1955; *Educ* Oxford Sch, Newcastle upon Tyne Poly (BA); *m* 7 May 1988, Carolyn, da of Robert Ian Tricker; 2 da (Lauren Kay b 12 Nov 1990, Fern Elise b 24 July 1998), 1 s (Jack Samuel b 16 May 1993); *Career* design asst Hancock Museum Newcastle upon Tyne 1977–78, graphic designer VAP Kidlington 1978–80, sr designer The Medicine Group Abingdon 1980–89, fndr ptnr The Hinton Chaundy Design Partnership 1989–98 (ind conslt 1998–2000), fndr dir The Blake Project Ltd 2000–09, dir Kevin Hinton Design Ltd 2010–; MCSD 1988 (chm S of England Region 1994–97 and 1999, memb Cncl 2001–03); *Recreations* reading, writing, drawing, painting; *Style*— Kevin Hinton, Esq; ✉ Mill Lane House, Cassington, Oxfordshire OX29 4DL

HINTON, Wendy Pamela; da of Norman George Hinton (d 1991), and Jean Clarise, *née* Swain (d 1999); *b* 14 July 1962; *Educ* Benedictine Convent Sch Dumfries, Emerson Park Sch Hornchurch, Havering Tech Coll Hornchurch, London C of C and Industry; *m* 18 Sept 1987 (m dis 2008), Paul Doherty, s of Llewellyn Patrick John Doherty; 1 da (Jasmine Anne b 4 July 1991), 1 s (Jordan Llewellyn George b 13 Nov 1996); *Career* Woman's Journal magazine 1981–86, Signature magazine 1986–87, picture ed ES Magazine 1987–2001, picture dir InStyle UK magazine 2001–12, photography bookings ed Harrods Publishing and Creative 2013–; judge: Assoc of Photographers Twelfth Awards 1995, London Photographic Awards 1998, 2003 and 2008, Assoc of Photographers' Assistants Awards 2001; Newspaper Supplement of the Year Br Picture Eds Award (for ES) 2000, highly commended Picture Ed of the Year IPC Media Editorial Awards 2004, Best Commissioned Photography IPC Media Editorial Awards 2008; *Recreations* photography exhibitions, being a mother; *Style*— Ms Wendy Hinton; ✉ Harrods Publishing and Creative, 7th Floor, 68 Hammersmith Road, London W14 8YW (☎ 020 3626 7955, e-mail wendy.hinton@harrods.com)

HINTON COOK, Gavin; s of Ronald Edward William Cook, and Gwendolin Bessie Hinton; *b* 9 April 1947; *Educ* Kingsbury GS, Architectural Assoc Sch of Architecture (AA Dipl); *m* 11 Sept 1971, Janine Dewar, da of Wing Cdr William Charles Ramsay (d 1979); *Career* chartered architect: WF Johnson and Assoc, Melvin and Lansley, London Borough of Lambeth, Philip Mercer RIBA; project architect Milton Keynes Devpt Corp 1976–79 (chief architect 1979–85, completed 2400 houses and co-ordinated Energy World at MK); prop Hinton Cook Architects 1986–; lectr in architectural studies Univ of Birmingham; awards: Arch Design Magazines, Best of Br Architecture Design Award Commendation, RIBA

S Regn Energy Award; ARIBA; *Recreations* sailing, squash, cycling; *Style—* Gavin Hinton Cook, Esq

HIORNS, Roger; *b* 1975, Birmingham; *Educ* Bournville Coll Birmingham, Goldsmiths Coll London (BA); *Career* artist; founding chair Artists Advsy Ctee Inst of Contemporary Art London 2011; Turner Prize 2009; *Solo Shows* incl: Corvi-Mora London 2001, 2003, 2006 and 2008, Marc Foxx LA 2003, 2007 and 2009, Galerie Nathalie Obadia Paris 2006, Milton Keynes Gallery 2006, Cubitt Gallery London 2006, Glittering Ground (Camden Arts Centre) 2007, Church of St Paulinus Richmond N Yorks 2007, Seizure (Harper Road London) 2008, Art Inst of Chicago 2010, Aspen Art Museum 2010, Annet Gelink Gallery Amsterdam 2011, Untitled, class (Wide Open School Hayward Gallery London Corvi-Mora), MIMA Middlesborough 2012, De Hallen Haarlem Netherlands 2012, The Hepworth Wakefield 2013, Firstsite Colchester 2013, Luhring Augustine NY 2014, Kunsthalle Wien Vienna 2014, Kunsthaus CentrePasquArt, Biel 2015, Corvi-Mora London 2015, Galerie Rudolfinum, Prague 2015, IKON Birmingham 2016; *Group Exhibitions* incl: Still Life (Museo Alejandro Otero Caracas, Buenos Aires, Centro Cultural Parque de España, Rosario, Biblioteca Luis Angel Arango, Bogotá) 2003, (Museo de Arte Contemporáneo Rio de Janeiro) 2004, (Museo de Arte de Lima) 2005 and (Meadow Gallery Hanbury Hall W Midlands) 2007, Marc Foxx LA 2005 and 2009, Jaybird (Galleria Zero Milan) 2005, British Art Show 6 (BALTIC Centre for Contemporary Art Gateshead) 2005, The Way We Work Now (Camden Arts Centre) 2005, ETC (Le Consortium Dijon) 2005, Le Voyage Interieur Paris-London (Espace EDF Electra Paris) 2005, Sculpture new spirit (Galerie Nathalie Obadia Paris) 2005, Sculptures d'Appartement (Musee Departemental d'Art Contemporain Rochechouart France) 2005, Water Event (Migros Museum für Gegenwartskunst Zürich) 2005, Corvi-Mora London 2006, How to improve the World: 60 Years of British Art (Hayward Gallery London) 2006, Le Retour de la Colonne Durutti (Isabella Bortolozzi Berlin) 2006, Refract (Marc Foxx LA) 2006, If Everybody And an Ocean Brian Wilson an Art Exhibition (CAPC Musée d'art Contemporain Bordeaux) and (Tate St Ives) 2007, Fusion Now! More Light, More Power, More People (Rokeby London) 2007, Grit and Vigor (Licht & Sie Dallas) 2007, Destroy Athens (1st Athens Biennial Athens) 2007, Insubstantial Pageant Faded (Western Bridge Washington) 2007, Ultramoderne (Espace Paul Wurth Luxembourg) 2007, Good Morning Midnight (Casey Kaplan NY) 2007, Sculpture Biennale Jesus Coll Cambridge 2007, You Have Not Been Honest (MADRE Naples) 2007, Echo Room (Alcalá 31 Madrid) 2007, A Life of Their Own (Lismore Castle Arts Ireland) 2008, Galerie Diana Stigter Amsterdam 2008, Busan Biennale Korea 2008, Legende (Centre d'Art Contemporain France) 2008, Run Run (The Collins Gallery Univ of Strathclyde) 2008, Thyssen-Bornemisza Art Contemporary as Aleph (Kunsthaus Graz) 2008, Stain Pattern (Annet Gelink Gallery Amsterdam) 2008, The Knight's Tour (De Hallen Haarlem Netherlands) 2009, The Quick and the Dead (Walker Art Centre Minneapolis) 2009, The Richter Scale (Fondazione Palazzo Strozzi Firenze) 2010, Crash (Gagosian Gallery) 2010, Br Art Show 7 (London and tour) 2010–11, Gerhard Richter (Centro di Cultura Contemporanea Florence) 2010, Dystopia (CAPC Musée d'Art Contemporain Bordeaux) 2011, Dread fear in the age of technological acceleration (De Hallen Haarlem) 2013, Folk Devil (David Zwirner NY) 2013, do it 2013 (Manchester Int Festival Manchester Art Gallery) 2013, The Encyclopaedic Palace (55th Venice Biennale) 2013, The World is Almost Six Thousand Years Old: Contemporary Art and Archaeology from the Stone Age to the Present (Lincoln Cathedral) 2013, Days in Lieu (David Zwirner London) 2013, The Universal Addressability of Dumb Things (Bluecoat Liverpool, Nottingham Contemporary and De La Warr Pavilion Bexhill-On-Sea) 2013, The Great Acceleration (Taipei Biennial 2014 Taipei Fine Arts Museum Taiwan) 2014, Making Colour (National Gallery London) 2014, Quiz (Galeries Poirel Nancy) 2014, Body and Void: Echoes of Henry Moore in Contemporary Art (Henry Moore Fndn, Perry Green UK) 2014, Private Utopia: Contemporary Works from the British Collection (Tokyo Station Gallery, Itami City Museum of Art Japan, Kochi Museum of Art Japan and Okayama Museum of Art Japan) 2014, Strange Pilgrims (The Contemporary, Texas) 2015, Lustwarande 15 Rapture and Pain (park De Oude Warande, Tilburg) 2015, Sculpture in the Close (Jesus Coll, Cambridge) 2015, Artists for Ikon (Ikon Gallery, Birmingham) 2015, Private Utopia (Dunedin Public Art Gallery) 2015, Rare Earth (Thyssen-Bornemisza Art Contemporary, Vienna) 2015, History is Now (Hayward Gallery, London) 2015, Birmingham Show (Birmingham) 2015, The Nothing Uv It (Bergen) 2015; *Books* Roger Hiorns – Untitled (2012), Roger Hiorns: Seizure 2008/2013 (2013), Roger Hijorns (2015; *Style—* Roger Hiorns, Esq; ✉ c/o Corvi Mora, 1A Kempsford Road (off Wincott Street), London SE11 4NU

HIRST, Chris; s of R C C Hirst, and P Hirst, *née* Snell; *b* 4 April 1971, Cannock, W Midlands; *Educ* Haydon Bridge Co HS, BNC Oxford (MEng), Harvard Business Sch (AMP); *m* 27 May 2000, Ann, *née* Jenkins; 2 s (Dylan b 28 March 2003, Sam b 18 Dec 2004); *Career* Bartle Bogle Hegarty 1995–99, client servs dir Fallon London 1999–2003, md Grey London 2003–; FRSA; *Recreations* lots of tennis, a little golf, running, reading, writing, the kids; *Clubs* Groucho; *Style—* Chris Hirst, Esq; ✉ Grey London, 77 Hatton Garden, London EC1N 8JS (☎ 020 3037 3030, e-mail chris.hirst@greyeu.com)

HIRST, Damien; *b* 1965, Bristol; *Educ* Goldsmiths Coll London; *Career* artist; guest ed The Big Issue 1997; co fndr and owner Pharmacy 1998–2003, prop The White Hart Bar Ifracombe Devon 2004–; Prix Eliette von Karajan 1995, Turner Prize 1995; *Solo Exhibitions* incl: In & Out of Love (Woodstock Street London) 1991, When Logics Die (Emmanuel Perrotin Paris) 1991, Internal Affairs (ICA London) 1991, Where's God Now? (Jay & Donatella Chiat NY) 1992, Marianne, Hildegard (Unfair/ Jay Jopling Cologne) 1992, Pharmacy (Cohen Gall NY) 1992, Visual Candy (Regen Projects LA) 1993, Damien Hirst (Galerie Jablonka Cologne) 1993, Making Beautiful Drawings (Bruno Brunnet Fine Arts Berlin) 1994, Currents 23 (Milwaukee Art Museum) 1994, A Bad Environment for White Monochrome Paintings (Mattress Factory Pittsburgh) 1994, A Good Environment for Coloured Monochrome Paintings (DAAD Gall Berlin) 1994, Pharmacy (Dallas Museum) 1994, Pharmacy (Kukje Gall Seoul) 1995, Still (White Cube/Jay Jopling London) 1995, Prix Eliette von Karajan '95 (Max Gandolph-Bibliothek Salzburg) No Sense of Absolute Corruption (Gagosian Gall NY) 1996, The Beautiful Afterlife (Bruno Bischofberger Zürich) 1997, Damien Hirst (Astrup Fearnley Museum Oslo) 1997, Damien Hirst (Southampton City Art Gall) 1998, Pharmacy (Tate Gall London) 1999, Damien Hirst (Sadler's Wells London) 2000, Theories, Models, Methods, Approaches, Assumptions, Results and Findings (Gagosian Gall NY) 2000, Damien Hirst's art education (The Reliance Leeds) 2002, Damien Hirst in a Spin; The Action of the World on Things (Galerie Aurel Scheibler) 2003, Damien Hirst (The Saatchi Gall London) 2003, From the Cradle to the Grave: Selected Drawings (25th Int Biennale of Graphic Arts Ljubljana and The Marble Palace St Petersburg) 2003, Romance in the Age of Uncertainty (White Cube London) 2003, The Agony and The Ecstasy: Selected works 1989–2004 (Archaeological Museum Naples) 2004, A Selection of Works by Damien Hirst from Various Collections (MFA Boston) 2005, Damien Hirst – Works on Paper (Andipa Gall London) 2005, Damien Hirst. In a Spin (Gascoigne Gall Harrogate) 2005, The Elusive Truth! (Gagosian Gall NY) 2005, Damien Hirst (Static Gall Liverpool 2005), Damien Hirst (Astrup Fearnley Museet fur Moderne Kunst Oslo) 2005, In the darkest hour there may be light: works from Damien Hirst's murderme collection (Serpentine Gall London) 2006; *Group Exhibitions* incl: Freeze (Surrey Docks London) 1988, New Contemporaries (ICA London) 1989, Third Eye Centre Glasgow 1989, Modern Medicine (Building One London) 1990, Broken English (Serpentine Gall London) 1991, Young British Artists (Saatchi Collection London) 1992, British Art (Barbara Gladstone Gall NY) 1992, Turner Prize Exhbn (Tate Gall London) 1992, The 21st Century (Kunsthalle Basel) 1993, Aperto: Venice Biennial (Aperto Section Venice) 1993, Some Went Mad, Some Ran Away (Serpentine Gall London and tour) 1994, Virtual Reality (Nat Gall of Aust Canberra) 1994, Art Unlimited (Centre for Contemporary Art Glasgow and tour) 1994, Drawing the Line (Southampton City Art Gall, Manchester City Art Gall, Ferens Art Gall Hull, Whitechapel Art Gall London) 1995, Turner Prize Exhbn (Tate Gall London) 1995, British Art Show 4 (touring exhbn) 1995, Spellbound (Art and Film exhbn, Hayward Gall London) 1996, A Small Shifting Sphere of Serious Culture (ICA London) 1996, Dimensions Variable (British Cncl touring exhbn) 1997, Sensation (Royal Acad of Arts London) 1997, Picture Britannica: Art from Britain (Museum of Contemporary Art Sydney, Art Gall of S Aust Adelaide, Te Papa Wellington) 1997, Wall Projects (Museum of Contemporary Art Chicago) 1998, London Calling (British Sch of Rome/Galleria Nazionale d'Art Moderne Guarene) 1998, Damien Hirst, Jeff Koons, Charles Ray (11 Duke Street London) 1998, Modern British Art (Tate Gall Liverpool) 1998, On the Sublime (Rooseum Center for Contemporary Art Malmö) 1999, Examining Pictures (Whitechapel Art Gall London, Museum of Contemporary Art Chicago) 1999, Fourth Wall (South Bank London) 1999, The History of the Turner Prize (ArtSway Sway) 1999, Sincerely Yours: British Art from the 90's (Astrup Fearnley MOMA Oslo) 2000, Art in Sacred Spaces (St Stephen's Church London) 2000, Out There (White Cube 2 London) 2000, Ant Noises (Saatchi Gall London) 2000, Video Vibe: Art, Music and Video in the UK (British Sch of Rome) 2000, The History of the Turner Prize 1983–1999 and People's Show 2: Pictures selected by the public (Victoria Art Gall Bath) 2000, Peter Blake: About Collage (Tate Gall Liverpool) 2000, Century City (Tate Modern London) 2001, Breaking the Mould: 20th Century British Sculpture from Tate (Norwich Castle Museum and Art Gall) 2001, Public Offerings (Museum of Contemporary Arts LA) 2001, Warhol/Koons/Hirst: Cult and Culture Selections from the Vicki and Kent Logan Collection (Aspen Art Museum Colorado) 2001, Beautiful Productions. Art to play, art to wear, art to own (Whitechapel Art Gall London) 2001, Art > Music, Rock Pop Techno (MOMA Sydney) 2001, Artist's London: Holbein to Hirst (Museum of London) 2001,The Rowan Collection. Contemporary British & Irish Art (Irish MOMA Dublin) 2002, Le Part de l'Autre (Carre d'Art Musée d'aer Contemporaine Nimes) 2002, In Good Form: Recent Sculpture from the Arts Cncl Collection (Yorkshire Sculpture Park Wakefield) 2003, Dreams and conflicts: the Dictatorship of the Viewer (50th Venice Biennale) 2003, In-A-Gadda-Da-Vida (Tate Britain London) 2004, Singular Forms (Sometimes Repeated) (Solomon R Guggenheim Museum NY) 2004, The Stations of the Cross (Gagosian Gall London) 2004, Summer Exhibition (Royal Acad of Arts London) 2004, Den Haag Sculpture Project 2004, Imageless Icons: Abstract Thoughts (Gagosian Gall London) 2005, Logical Conclusions (Pacewildenstein NY) 2005, An International Legacy: Selections from Carnegie Museum of Art (Columbus Museum of Art) 2005, Figure It Out (Hudson Valley Center for Contemporary Art NY) 2005; *Works in Collections* incl: Saatchi Gall London, Tate Gall London, Br Cncl, Arts Cncl, Contemporary Art Museum Kanazawa, Denver Art Museum, Deste Fndn for Contemporary Art Athens, Deutsche Bank London, Fondazione Prada Milan, Hirshhorn Museum Washington, MOMA NY, Samsung Museum Seoul, San Diego Museum of Contemporary Art, San Francisco MOMA, Scottish Nat Gall of Modern Art Edinburgh, Stedelijk Museum Amsterdam, Weltkunst Fndn Dublin, Yale Center for British Art New Haven; *Film* dir Breath (Beckett on Film Channel 4 and RTÉ) 2001; *Books* I Want to Spend the Rest of My Life Everywhere, with Everyone, One to One, Always, Forever, Now (1997), On the Way to Work (with Gordon Burn, 2001); *Style—* Damien Hirst, Esq; ✉ White Cube, 144–152 Bermondsey St, London SE1 3TQ (☎ 020 7930 5373, fax 020 7749 7480)

HIRST, (Nathania) Gemma Louise; da of Peter John Hirst, of Surrey, and Anne Jennifer, *née* Steele; *b* 1 September 1970, Cuckfield, Sussex; *Educ* Croham Hurst Sch Croydon (scholar, head girl), Newnham Coll Cambridge (MA); *Career* foreign rights asst Kingfisher Larousse plc 1993–94, asst agent Deborah Owen Ltd 1994–97, media agent David Higham Assocs Ltd 1997–; affiliate memb of Writers' Guild; memb Bafta Children's Jury 2005; *Recreations* film, books, theatre, travel, gourmet cuisine; *Style—* Miss Gemma Hirst; ✉ David Hingham Associates Ltd, 7th Floor, Waverley House, 712 Noel Street, London W1F 8GQ (☎ 020 7434 5900, fax 020 7437 1072, e-mail gemmahirst@davidhigham.co.uk)

HIRST, Jonathan William; QC (1990); s of Rt Hon Sir David Hirst, and Pamela Elizabeth Molesworth, *née* Bevan; *b* 2 July 1953; *Educ* Eton, Trinity Coll Cambridge (MA); *m* 20 July 1974, Fiona Christine Mary, da of Dr Peter Anthony Tyser; 2 s (Thomas James b and d 1991, Charles John b 1993); *Career* called to the Bar Inner Temple 1975 (bencher 1994, reader 2011, treas 2012); in practice at commercial bar SE Circuit, recorder 1997– (asst recorder 1993–97), dep High Court judge 2002–, jt head Brick Court Chambers 2005–; memb Gen Cncl of Bar 1986–2000 (vice-chm 1999, chm 2000); chm: Univ of Cambridge Cons Assoc 1974, Law Reform Ctee 1992–94, Professional Standards Ctee 1996–98; govr Taverham Hall Sch Norfolk 1990–95, govr Goodenough Coll London 2001– (memb Bd 2006–, chm Bd 2008–); *Recreations* shooting, gardening, music; *Clubs* Boodle's, Norfolk, Hurlingham; *Style—* Jonathan Hirst, Esq, QC; ✉ Brick Court Chambers, 7–8 Essex Street, London WC2R 3LD (☎ 020 7379 3550, fax 020 7379 3558, e-mail jonathan.hirst@brickcourt.co.uk)

HIRST, Sir Michael William; kt (1992); s of John Melville Hirst (d 1969), and Christina Binning, *née* Torrance (d 2002); *b* 2 January 1946; *Educ* Glasgow Acad, Univ of Glasgow (LLB), Univ of Iceland (exchange student); *m* 1, 21 Sept 1972, Naomi Ferguson, da of Robert Morgan Wilson (d 1977); 2 da (Sarah b 1974, Kate b 1979), 1 s (John b 1976); *Career* qualified CA 1970, ptnr Peat Marwick Mitchell & Co 1977–83, conslt KPMG Peat Marwick 1983–92, Michael Hirst Assocs 1987–; MP (Cons) Strathkelvin and Bearsden 1983–87, PPS Dept of Energy 1985–87; company director; chm: Millstream Assocs Ltd 2000–, Pagoda Public Rels Ltd 2000–; pres Scottish Cons and Unionist Assoc 1989–92, chm Scottish Cons and Unionist Pty 1993–97 (vice-chm 1987–89), pres Stirling and Clackmannanshire Cons Assoc 1999–; Diabetes UK: tstee 1988–2006, hon sec 1993–98, vice-chm 1998–2001, chm 2001–06, vice-pres 2006–; pres Int Diabetes Fedn 2012–15 (vice-pres 2006–09, pres-elect 2009–12, hon pres 2016–); chm The Park Sch Educn Tst 1986–2009; dir: Erskine Hosp Ltd 1979–2011, Weavers Soc of Anderston 1981–, Childrens Hospice Assoc Scotland 1993–2005; memb Ct Glasgow Caledonian Univ (chm Audit Ctee 1992–98), memb Cncl Imperial Soc of Knights Bachelor 2002– (chm Scottish Div); elder: Kelvinside Hillhead Parish Church 1975–98, Kippen Parish Church 1999–; chm Friends of Kippen Kirk Tst 2004–; Hon DLitt Glasgow Caledonian Univ 2004; FRSA 1993, MCIPR 2003, FRCPEd 2012; *Recreations* golf, hill walking, theatre, skiing; *Clubs* Carlton, Western (Glasgow); *Style—* Sir Michael Hirst; ✉ Glentirran, Kippen, Stirlingshire FK8 3DY (☎ 01786 870283, e-mail smh@glentirran.co.uk)

HIRST, Rachel Joy; da of late Rt Hon Sir David Hirst, and Pamela Elizabeth Molesworth, *née* Bevan; *b* 14 November 1960; *Educ* Cranborne Chase Sch; *m* 1998, Leslie Johnston; *Career* PR exec; with Good Relations 1982–85; dir: Valin Pollen 1990 (joined 1985), Gavin Anderson & Co 1991–94, Shandwick Consultants 1994–97; fndr ptnr The Hogarth Partnership 1997, currently md MHP Communications; *Style—* Ms Rachel Hirst

HISCOCK, David Miles; s of Jeffrey Hiscock, of Coombe Bissett, Wilts and Rosalind Mary, *née* Marshall; *b* 20 September 1956; *Educ* Bishop Wordsworths GS, Salisbury Art Sch, St Martin's Sch of Art (BA), RCA (MA); *m* Anna Maria Russell; 1 s (Hunter Mannix Russell-Hiscock b 24 March 2000); *Career* freelance photographer and artist; editorial, advertising cmmns and commercials dir 1985–; Pentax bursaries 1983–85, Vogue Award for photography 1985, Madame Tussaud's Award for figurative work 1985, official VISA

Olympic artist 1992; FRCA 1996; *Solo Exhibitions* incl: RPS Bath 1987, Pomeroy Purdey Gallery London 1988, 1990 and 1992, Parco Gallery Tokyo 1990, Norwich Arts Centre Norwich 1990, The Chateau d'Eau Gallery Toulouse 1991, Olympic Works (Zelda Cheatle Gallery London) 1992, Zelda Cheatle Gallery London 1993 and 1995, Transmutations (Purdy Hicks Gallery London) 1994, Strokes (Purdy Hicks Gallery and Focal Point Gallery Southend on Sea) 1997; *Selected Group Exhibitions* 1990: Identities (Philadephia Art Alliance USA), Rencontres Photographiques (Carcassonne France), Face On (Zelda Cheatle Gallery London), David Hiscock and Calum Colvin (Seagate Gallery), Dundee and Theatre Clwyd (Mold), Works by 54 Master Printers (John Jones Gallery London) 1992, The Figure Laid Bare (Pomeroy Purdy Gallery London) 1992, Print Center Editions (Pomeroy Purdy Gallery London) 1992, Fictions of the Self (Weatherspoon Art Gallery USA and tour) 1993, Time Machine (British Museum London) 1994, Little Boxes (Photofusion Gallery London and Cambridge Dark Room) 1997, Wait and See What's for Dinner (Towner Art Gallery Eastbourne) 1997, History the Mag Collection (Ferens Art Gallery Hull and Fruit Market Gallery Edinburgh), In To The Light (RPS Bath) 1999, Revelation (Purdy Hicks Gallery London) 1999, Revelation (Tullie House City Museum Carlisle) 2000, Visual Arts Scotland Annual Exhbn Edinburgh 2000, Bittersweet (Danielle Arnaud Gallery London) 2001; *Work in Collections* incl: Madame Tussauds's London, Nat Portrait Gallery, Haggerty Museum USA, Chateau D'Eau, Toulouse, Leeds City Art Gallery, Deutsche Bank, Mag Collection Ferens Art Gallery Hull, P&O Oriana Collection, RPS Bath, Tullie House City Museum Carlisle; *Books* David Hiscock – Work from 1982–90 (SKOOB Books, 1992), David Hiscock (Zelda Cheatle Press, 1994); *Style*— David Hiscock, Esq

HISCOCK, (Nicholas) Toby; s of late David Hiscock, of Cheltenham, Glos, and Anne Kathleen Audrey Mary Elizabeth, *née* Clark; *b* 8 January 1960, Chelmsford, Essex; *Educ* Sexey's GS Blackford, Wells Cathedral Sch, Hertford Coll Oxford (MA); *m* 21 Aug 1982, Gail Shirley, *née* Audley-Miller; 1 da (Camilla Anne Ismay b 29 May 1990, Charles Cosmo Hugh b 11 March 1993); *Career* Binder Hamlyn Chartered Accountants 1981–88, sr audit mangr Midland Bank plc 1988–92; Henderson Group plc: joined 1992, dir of finance 1996, chief financial officer 2003–09; non-exec dir: Henderson Family of Hedge Funds 2008, John Laing Gp plc 2009; FCA 1996 (ACA 1986); *Recreations* the arts, cycling, travel, motorsport; *Style*— Toby Hiscock, Esq; ✉ 49 Burlington Avenue, Kew, Surrey TW9 4DG (e-mail tobyhiscock@blueyonder.co.uk)

HISCOX, Robert Ralph Scrymgeour; DL (Wilts 2013); s of Ralph Hiscox, CBE (d 1970), and Louisa Jeanie Hiscox (d 2002); *b* 4 January 1943; *Educ* Rugby, CCC Cambridge (MA); *m* 1, 1966 (m dis 1978), Lucy (d 1996), da of Charles Henry Mills; 2 s (Renshaw b 5 June 1968, Frederick b 5 June 1972); m 2, 1985, Lady Julia Elizabeth, da of 6 Earl of Clanwilliam (d 1989); 3 s (Milo Edmund b 4 Jan 1987, Henry Charles b 23 Sept 1989, Sidney John b 24 Jan 1993); *Career* chm Hiscox Ltd 1973–2013 (hon pres 2013–); dep chm Lloyd's of London 1993–95, memb Lloyd's 1967–98, founder chm Lloyd's Market Assoc 1999–2000; memb Bd Business for Britain 2013–; dir Grainger Tst plc 2002–12; treas: Friends of the Tate Gallery 1990–93, Museums and Galleries Cmmn 1996–2000; tstee: Campaign for Museums 1998–2004, Wilts Bobby Van Tst 1998– (chm 2002–), 24 Hour Museum 2000–01, Kenneth Armitage Fndn 2005 (chm 2011–), Paolozzi Fndn 2009 (chm 2011–), Marlborough Brandt Gp 2012–14 (patron 2014–); patron Friends of Erlestoke Prison 2013–, chm Swindon Museum and Art Gallery Tst 2015–; High Sheriff Wilts 2011–12; Lloyd's Gold Medal 2013; *Recreations* family life, country life, art, changing things; *Clubs* White's, Queen's, Shakar; *Style*— Robert Hiscox, Esq, DL; ✉ Rainscombe Park, Oare, Marlborough, Wiltshire SN8 4HZ (☎ 01672 563491); Hiscox Ltd, 1 Great St Helen's, London EC3A 6HX (☎ 020 7488 6011, e-mail robert.hiscox@hiscox.com)

HISKEY, Rex Arthur; s of Harry Charles Hiskey (d 2013), and Gwynneth, *née* Bush (d 1999); *b* 9 March 1947; *Educ* Chelmsford Tech HS, Univ of Birmingham (LLB); *m* 2 Oct 1971, Christine Elizabeth, da of Maurice Henry Cobbold (d 1997); 1 s (Thomas b 1981), 2 da (Florence b 1986, Clara b 1990); *Career* slr (ret); holding various local appts, formerly ptnr Hayes & Storr; *Recreations* reading, gardening, cooking; *Style*— Rex Hiskey, Esq; ☎ 01328 710328

HISLOP, Ian David; s of late David Atholl Hislop, and Helen Hislop; *b* 13 July 1960; *Educ* Ardingly, Magdalen Coll Oxford (BA, Underhill exhibition, Violet Vaughan Morgan scholarship); *m* 16 April 1988, Victoria, *née* Hamson; 1 da (Emily Helen b 3 Oct 1990), 1 s (William David b 26 June 1993); *Career* ed Private Eye 1986– (joined 1981, dep ed 1985–86); scriptwriter Spitting Image 1984–89, columnist The Listener 1985–89, TV critic The Spectator 1994–96, columnist Sunday Telegraph 1996–2003; regular book reviewer and contrib to various newspapers and magazines; writer and broadcaster for radio and TV; radio: The News Quiz 1985–90, 4th Column 1992–96, Lent Talk 1994, Words on Words 1999, The Hislop Vote (BBC Radio 2) 2000; team capt Have I Got News For You (BBC 2) 1990–; presenter: Canterbury Tales (Channel 4) 1996, School Rules (Channel 4) 1997, Pennies from Bevan (Channel 4) 1998, Great Railway Journeys East to West 1999, A Revolution in 5 Acts (BBC Radio 4) 2001, The Real Patron Saints (BBC Radio 4) 2002, A Brief History of Tax (BBC Radio 4) 2003, The Choir Invisible (BBC Radio 4) 2003, There'll be Blue Birds over the White Cliffs of Dover (BBC Radio 4) 2004, Are we being offensive enough? (BBC Radio 4) 2004, Who do you think you are? (BBC 2) 2004, Not Forgotten (Channel 4) 2005, Looking For Middle England (BBC Radio 4) 2006, Not Forgotten: Shot at Dawn (Channel 4) 2007, Scouting for Boys (BBC 4) 2007; TV plays (all co-written with Nick Newman): The Stone Age (BBC 2) 1989, Briefcase Encounter (ITV) 1991, He Died a Death (BBC 2) 1991, The Case of the Missing (BBC 2) 1991, Mangez Merveillac (BBC 2) 1993, Dead on Time (BBC 2) 1995, Gobble (BBC 2) 1996, Confessions of a Murderer 1999, My Dad's The Prime Minister (BBC 1) 2003 and 2004; scriptwriter Sermon from St Albions (ITV) 1998; scriptwriter (with Nick Newman): The Programme 1990–92, Gush (BBC Radio 4) 1994, Harry Enfield and Chums 1994–98, Songs and Praise from St Albions (ITV) 1999; *Awards* BAFTA (for Have I Got News For You) 1991, Editor's Editor Br Soc of Magazine Eds 1991, Magazine of the Year 1991, Editor of the Year Br Soc of Magazine Eds 1998, Channel 4 Political Award for Political Satire 2004, Channel 4 Political Award for Political Comedy 2006; *Publications* incl various Private Eye compilations; *Style*— Ian Hislop, Esq; ✉ Private Eye, 6 Carlisle Street, London W1V 5RG (☎ 020 7437 4017, fax 020 7437 0705)

HITCHCOCK, Alfred; QPM (2008); *Career* joined Lancs Constabulary 1977, Met Police Service 2003–09 (roles incl Cdr Specialist Crime Directorate 2003–04 and Dep Asst Cmmr (operational services) 2007–09), Dep Chief Constable Police Coll Bramshill 2009–10, Chief Constable Beds Police 2011–13, Chief Constable MOD Police 2013–; *Style*— Alfred Hitchcock, Esq, QPM; ✉ Ministry of Defence Police, Wethersfield, Braintree, Essex CM7 4AZ

HITCHCOCK, Teresa Caroline; *b* 22 January 1960; *Educ* Ripley Tech Sch, Trent Poly (Dip), Nottingham Trent Univ (LLB, Dip); *m* 15 Aug 1981, Michael Hitchcock; *Career* admitted slr 1993; Erewash BC: dist environmental health offr 1981–84, sr grade environmental health offr 1984–86; princ grade environmental health offr NW Leics DC 1986–90, ptnr DLA Piper Slrs 1996–; memb: Chartered Inst of Environmental Health, Law Soc, UK Environmental Law Assoc; *Publications* A Guide to the Food Safety Act 1990 (1989–90), Department of Environment Liability from Methane Generation (jt paper, 1994), DTI Sequestration of CO2: Onshore Actvities (2002); *Recreations* equestrian pursuits, netball, walking; *Style*— Mrs Teresa Hitchcock; ✉ DLA Piper UK LLP, 1 St Paul's Place, Sheffield S1 2JX (☎ 0114 283 3302, fax 0114 276 6720, e-mail teresa.hitchcock@dlapiper.com)

HITCHCOX, John; s of Brian Hitchcox, OBE, and Jean Hitchcox; *b* 14 September 1961, Sussex; *Educ* Michael Hall Sch; *m* 12 June 2014, Phoebe, *née* Vela; *Career* property developer; co-fndr (with Harry Handlesman) Manhattan Loft Corp 1992–99, co-creator (with Philippe Starck) and dir YOO 1999–; memb The Prince's Youth Business Tst, supporter Amnesty Int; *Recreations* playing music, sailing, yoga, tennis, skiing, travel, kite surfing, spending time with his children; *Style*— John Hitchcox, Esq; ✉ 167 Westbourne Grove, London W11 2RS; YOO, 2 Bentinck Street, London W1U 2FA (☎ 020 7009 0100, website www.yoo.com)

HITCHENS, Peter Jonathan; s of Eric Hitchens (d 1987), and Yvonne, *née* Hickman (d 1974); *b* 28 October 1951, Sliema, Malta; *Educ* The Leys Sch Cambridge, Oxford Coll of FE, Univ of York (BA); *m* 1983, Eve, da of David and Tamara Ross; 1 da, 2 s; *Career* journalist; with: Socialist Worker 1972, Swindon Evening Advertiser 1973–76, Coventry Evening Telegraph 1976; Daily Express: joined 1977, sometime industrial reporter, educn reporter, labour corr, dep political ed, diplomatic corr, Moscow corr 1990–92, Washington corr 1993–95, asst ed 1995–2001, columnist 1997–2001; Mail on Sunday 2001–; Orwell Prize for Journalism 2010; *Books* The Abolition of Britain (1999), The Rape of the Constitution (contrib, 2000), Monday Morning Blues (2000), A Brief History of Crime (2003), The Abolition of Liberty (2004), The Broken Compass (2009), The Rage Against God (2010), The War We Never Fought (2012), Short Breaks In Mordor (2014); *Recreations* long train journeys, second-hand bookshops; *Style*— Peter Hitchens; ✉ Mail on Sunday, 2 Derry Street, London W8 5TS (☎ 020 3615 3258, e-mail peter.hitchens@mailonsunday.co.uk)

HITCHENS, HE Timothy Mark; CMG, LVO; *m* Sara Kubra; 1 da, 1 s; *Career* diplomat; East African Dept FCO 1983–84, second sec Tokyo 1985–89, first sec European Community Dept 1989–91; FCO: private sec to Min for Europe 1991–94, speechwriter to Foreign Sec 1994–95; head Political Dept Islamabad 1995–97, dep head SE Asian Dept FCO 1997–98, asst private sec to HM The Queen 1998–2002, head Africa Dept (Equatorial) FCO 2002–05, dep head of mission Paris 2005–08; FCO: dir European political affairs 2008–10, Africa dir 2010–12; ambass to Japan 2012–; *Style*— HE Mr Timothy Hitchens, CMG, LVO; ✉ c/o Foreign & Commonwealth Office (Tokyo), King Charles Street, London SW1A 2AH

HITCHIN, Prof Nigel James; s of Eric Wilfred Hitchin (d 1987), and Bessie, *née* Blood (d 1993); *b* 2 August 1946; *Educ* Jesus Coll Oxford (jr mathematical prize, BA), Wolfson Coll Oxford (DPhil); *m* 17 Aug 1973, Nedda Vejarano Bernal, da of Luis Vejarano; 1 da (Gloria Louise b 1977), 1 s (Julian James b 1981); *Career* research asst Inst for Advanced Study Princeton 1971–73, instructor Courant Inst NYU 1973–74; Univ of Oxford: successively research asst, jr research fell, research fell Wolfson Coll 1974–79, fell and tutor in mathematics St Catherine's Coll 1979–90; prof of mathematics Univ of Warwick 1990–94, Rouse Ball prof of mathematics Univ of Cambridge and professorial fell Gonville & Caius Coll Cambridge 1994–97, Savilian prof of geometry Univ of Oxford and professorial fell New Coll Oxford 1997–2016; visiting appts: Institut des Hautes Etudes Scientifiques 1975, 1979, 1987, 1990, 1994, 1997, École Normale Superieure Paris 1979, Univ of Bonn 1979, Inst for Advanced Study Princeton 1982, SUNY 1983–84, École Polytechnique 1988; pres London Mathematical Soc 1995–96 (memb Cncl 1992–96); memb: SERC Mathematics Panel 1991–94, Cncl Royal Soc 2002–04; memb Academia Europaea; jr Whitehead Prize London Mathematical Soc 1981, sr Berwick Prize London Mathematical Soc 1990, Royal Soc Sylvester Medal 2000, Polya Prize London Mathematical Soc 2002, Shaw Prize in Mathematics 2016; hon fell Jesus Coll Oxford 1998, hon fell Gonville & Caius Coll Cambridge 2008, hon fell St Catherine's Coll Oxford 2014; Hon DSc Univ of Bath 2003, Hon DSc Univ of Warwick 2014; FRS 1991; *Publications* author of over 90 learned articles in scientific jls; *Style*— Prof Nigel Hitchin, FRS; ✉ Mathematical Institute, Radcliffe Observatory Quarter, Woodstock Road, Oxford OX2 6GG (☎ 01865 273515, e-mail hitchin@maths.ox.ac.uk)

HITCHMAN, Prof Michael L; s of Leslie S Hitchman (d 1993), and Grace H Hitchman, *née* Callaghan (d 1991); *b* 17 August 1941; *Educ* Stratton GS Biggleswade, QMC London (BSc), King's Coll London (PGCE), UC Oxford (DPhil); *Family* 2 da (Natasha M b 8 July 1971, Fiona E b 17 May 1977), 1 s (Timothy S b 8 Feb 1973); m 21 Aug 2007, Dr Migeun Park; 2 step da (Seunghi b 12 Feb 1987, Taegyeong b 6 June 1990); *Career* asst lectr in chemistry Leicester Regnl Coll of Technol 1963–65, jr res fell Wolfson Coll Oxford 1968–70, ICI postdoctoral res fell Physical Chemistry Laboratory Oxford 1968–70, chief scientist Orbisphere Corporation Geneva 1970–73, staff scientist Laboratories RCA Ltd Zurich 1973–79, lectr then sr lectr Univ of Salford 1979–84; Univ of Strathclyde: Young prof of chemical technol 1984–2004, chm Dept of Pure and Applied Chemistry 1986–89, vice-dean Faculty of Sci 1989–92; hon prof Taiyuan Univ of Technol China 1994–; treas Electrochemistry Gp RSC 1984–90, chm Electroanalytical Gp RSC 1985–88; memb Advsy Bd EUROCVD 1985– (chm 1989–92); memb SERC ctees on: chemistry 1987–90, semiconductors 1988–90, non-metallic materials 1986–88; dir: Jinju Consultancies Ltd, Innovative Coating Technologies Ltd; co-chm W Scotland Sci Park Advsy Ctee 1988–92; memb: Electrochemical Soc, Int Soc of Electrochemistry, Br Assoc of Crystal Growth, Materials Research Soc; visiting prof Univ of the West of Scotland 2005–; British Vacuum Cncl medal and prize 1992; CSci, CChem, FRSC, FRSA, FRSE; *Publications* Ring Disk Electrodes (jtly, 1971), Measurement of Dissolved Oxygen (1978), Proceedings of the Eighth European Conference on Chemical Vapour Deposition (ed, 1991), Chemical Vapour Deposition (ed, 1992), Advanced Materials Chemical Vapour Deposition (ed, 1995–), Proceedings of the Fifteenth International Symposium on Chemical Vapour Deposition (jt ed, 2000), Proceedings of EUROCVD 15 (jt ed, 2005), Chemical Vapour Deposition – Precursors, Processes and Applications (jt ed, 2009); *Recreations* humour, cooking, eating, walking, losing weight; *Style*— Prof Michael L Hitchman; ✉ Jinju Consultancies Ltd, 67 Montrose Drive, Bearsden G61 3LF

HITMAN, Prof Graham Alec; s of Maxwell Hitman (d 1987), and Annette Hitman (d 1968); *b* 19 January 1953; *Educ* Bromley GS, UCH Med Sch (MB BS), Univ of London (MD); *m* Avril Froma, da of Ivor Sevitt, of Chislehurst; 1 da (Nadia b 1978), 1 s (Oliver b 1980); *Career* formerly: SHO and registrar KCH London, RD Lawrence res fell Bart's; Bart's and The London Sch of Med and Dentistry: successively lectr Med Unit, asst dir, then reader, currently prof of molecular med and diabetes, hon conslt, dep dir Blizard Inst of Cell and Molecular Sci; chief ed Diabetic Medicine; memb Br Diabetic Assoc; FRCP; *Recreations* windsurfing, tennis, running; *Style*— Prof Graham Hitman; ✉ 2 Yester Road, Chislehurst, Kent BR6 5LT (☎ 020 8467 3331); Department of Diabetes and Metabolic Medicine, 7th Floor, John Harrison House, Royal London Hospital, Whitechapel, London E1 1BB (☎ 020 7377 7111, fax 020 7377 7636, e-mail g.a.hitman@qmul.ac.uk)

HIX, Mark Ernest; s of Ernest Hix, and Gillian, *née* Ward; *b* 10 December 1962, Dorset; *Educ* Colfox Sch Bridport, South Dorset Tech Coll Weymouth; *m* 1, (m dis) Suzie; 3 da (Lydia, Ellie (twins) b 2 Nov 1994, Isla b 15 June 2012); *Career* chef; Grosvenor House Park Lane 1981, Park Lane W1 1983, Dorchester Hotel Grill Room 1983, Park Lane W1 1984; Mr Pontac's Candlewick Restaurant: sous chef 1985, head chef 1985, exec chef 1986; head chef Le Caprice 1990, exec chef Le Caprice and The Ivy 1993, chef dir Caprice Holdings Ltd 2000–07, restaurant conslt Brown's Hotel London 2008–; prop: Hix Oyster & Chophouse London 2008, Hix Oyster & Fish House Dorset 2008, Hix Soho 2009, Hix Restaurant and Champagne Bar Selfridges London 2010, HIX Belgravia 2012, Tramshed

H

London 2012, Hixter City 2013, Hixter Bankside 2013; currently cookery writer Independent on Saturday magazine and Esquire Magazine; memb: Mutton Renaissance, Leuka, Acad of Culinary Arts, Serpentine Gallery, Guild of Food Writers; Glenfiddich Award Newspaper Cookery Writer of the Year 2003, Guild of Food Writers Best Cookery Writer 2005, Andre Simon Special Commendation for British Rgnl Food 2006, Guild of Food Writers Michael Smith Award for Work on British Food in British Rgnl Food 2007, Outstanding Contrib to London Restaurants London Restaurant Award 2008, GQ Chef of the Year 2008, Tatler Restaurateur of the Year 2009, Chef of the Year Catey's 2010, Guild of Food Writers Cookery Journalist of the Year 2011; *Publications* The Ivy: The restaurant and its recipes (1997), Le Caprice (1999), Eat Up (2000), British (2003), Fish Etc (2004), The Simple Art of Marrying Food and Wine (2005), British Regional Food (2006), British Seasonal Food (2008), Hix Oyster and Chop House (2010), HIX Collection (2013); *Recreations* fishing, foraging, golf, shooting; *Clubs* Groucho, Stoke Park, Soho House; *Style*— Mark Hix, Esq

HOARE, Alexander; *Educ* Univ of Edinburgh (BComm); *m* 6 Jan 2012, Claudia Martin; 1 s; *Career* C Hoare & Co Ptnrs: joined 1987, chief exec 2001–09, currently ptnr; former non-exec dir Jupiter Green Investment Tst; former pres Groupement European de Banques, memb Westminster Abbey Finance and Advsy Cncl; former tstee: Training for Life, Trinity Hospice; ACIB; *Style*— Alexander Hoare, Esq; ✉ C Hoare & Co, 37 Fleet Street, London EC4P 4DQ

HOARE, Prof Sir (Charles) Antony Richard (Tony); kt (2000); s of late Henry Samuel Malortie Hoare, and Marjorie Francis, *née* Villiers; *b* 11 January 1934; *Educ* King's Sch Canterbury, Merton Coll Oxford (MA), Moscow State Univ; *m* 13 Jan 1962, Jill, da of late John Pym, of Brasted Chart, Kent; 2 s (Thomas b 1964, Matthew b 1967 d 1981), 1 da (Joanna b 1965); *Career* Nat Serv RN 1956–58, Lt RNR 1958; Elliot Bros Ltd 1960–68: programmer, chief engr, tech mangr, chief scientist; prof of computer sci Queen's Univ Belfast 1968–77, prof of computation Univ of Oxford 1977–93, James Martin prof of software engrg Univ of Oxford 1993–99 (fell Wolfson Coll 1977–); Microsoft: princ researcher 1999–2013, conslt 2013–15, visitor 2015–17; Turing award 1980, Faraday medal 1985, Kyoto prize 2000; Hon DSc: Univ of Southern Calif 1979, Univ of Warwick 1985, Univ of Pennsylvania 1986, Queen's Univ Belfast 1987, Univ of York 1989; Hon DUniv: Essex 1991, Bath 1993, Oxford Brookes 2000, Queen Mary Coll 2005, Heriot Watt Univ 2007, Athens Univ of Economics and Business 2007; hon doctorate: Univ of Warsaw 2012, Complutense Univ Madrid 2013, Nat Reasearch Univ (ITMO) St Petersburg 2013; hon fell: Kellogg Coll Oxford 1998, Darwin Coll Cambridge 2001, Merton Coll Oxford 2004; Soc Stran Accad dei Lincei 1988, corresponding memb Bayerische Akad der Wissenschaften 1997, foreign assoc US Nat Acad Egrg 2006, Einstein prof Chinese Academy of Science 2006 Distinguished FBCS 1978, FRS 1982, FREng 2005; *Books* Structured Programming (1972), Communicating Sequential Processes (1985), Essays in Computing Science (1988), Unifying Theories of Programming (1998); *Recreations* reading, walking, music, travel; *Style*— Prof Sir Tony Hoare, FRS, FREng; ✉ Microsoft Research Ltd, 21 Station Road, Cambridge CB1 2FB (☎ 01223 479800, e-mail t_tohoar@microsoft.com)

HOARE, Christopher Henry St John (Toby); s of J Michael Hoare, and Ann St John, *née* Kingham; *b* 2 February 1960; *Educ* Harrow; *m* 2 Aug 1986, Hon Sarah Jane, da of Baron Dixon-Smith (Life Peer), *qv*; 2 s (Oscar b 16 July 1988, Giles b 22 June 1990); 1 da (Camilla b 18 Nov 1994); *Career* mgmnt trainee Distillers Co Ltd 1979–80, Express Newspapers 1980–84, Centaur Communications 1984–85, Dorland Advertising Ltd 1985–87; Young & Rubicam Ltd: joined 1987, dir 1989, business devpt dir 1991–94, md 1994–96, chief exec 1996–99; gp chief exec Bates UK Gp 1999–2002, chm Bates Gp Europe 2002–; global client leader (ceo Team HSBC) WPP plc 2004–, head of UK ops JWT 2005–, chm and ceo JWT Europe 2007–; chm Geometry Global 2013–; govr Harrow Sch 2001; Liveryman Worshipful Co of Distillers 1982, Freeman City of London 1987; *Recreations* shooting, golf, music, wine, following Arsenal FC; *Clubs* Garrick, Royal Worlington Golf, Swinley Forest Golf; *Style*— Toby Hoare, Esq; ✉ 17 Stanley Crescent, London W11 2NA (e-mail thoare@wpp.com)

HOARE, David; *b* 31 January 1950, Dublin; *Educ* Univ of Birmingham (BSc), Stanford Univ (MBA); *m* 30 Aug 1975, Jammy; 2 s (Nicholas, Alexander), 1 da (Katherine); *Career* co-fndr Talisman 1987, chair Ofsted 2014–; chm Teenage Cancer Tst 2010–; *Clubs* Queen's London; *Style*— David Hoare, Esq; ✉ Ofsted, Aviation House, 125 Kingsway, London WC2B 6SE

HOARE, Sir David John; 9 Bt (GB 1786), of Barn Elms, Surrey; s of Sir Peter William Hoare, 7 Bt (d 1973); suc bro, Sir Peter Richard David Hoare, 8 Bt (d 2004); *b* 8 October 1935; *Educ* Eton; *m* 1, 1965, Mary Vanessa, yr da of Peter Cardew, of Westhanger, Cleeve, Bristol; 1 s (Simon Merrik b 1967); m 2, 1984, Virginia Victoria Labes, da of Michael Menzies, of Long Island, NY; *Heir* s, Simon Hoare; *Career* banker; chm C Hoare & Co 2001–06 (managing ptnr 1964–); *Recreations* fishing, skiing; *Clubs* White's, Royal St George's Golf, Swinley; *Style*— Sir David Hoare, Bt; ✉ Luscombe Castle, Dawlish, Devon; C Hoare & Co, 37 Fleet Street, London EC4P 4DQ (☎ 020 7353 4522)

HOARE, Henry Cadogan; s of Henry Peregrine Rennie Hoare (d 1981), and Lady Beatrix Lilian Ethel Cadogan (d 1999); *b* 23 November 1931; *Educ* Eton, Trinity Coll Cambridge (MA); *m* 1, 30 May 1959 (m dis 1970), Pamela Saxon, da of late Col G F Bunbury, OBE; 2 s (Timothy b 1960, Nicholas b 1964), 1 da (Arabella b 1968); m 2, 16 June 1977, Caromy Maxwell Macdonald, da of Robert Jenkins, CBE, JP; *Career* banker; sr ptnr C Hoare & Co 2001– (managing ptnr 1959–, chm 1988–2001); *Style*— Henry Hoare, Esq; ✉ C Hoare & Co, 37 Fleet Street, London EC4P 4DQ (☎ 020 7353 4522, fax 020 7353 4521)

HOARE, Jonathan Michael Douro; s of Capt Michael Douro Hoare, of Downsland Court, Ditchling, E Sussex, and Valerie Ann, *née* James; *b* 21 October 1953; *Educ* Eton, Oriel Coll Oxford (MA); *m* 7 Aug 1982, Clare Elizabeth, da of Peter Parsons, of Stocklinch, Somerset; 1 da (Natasha Ruth b 1 June 1984), 2 s (Timothy Jonathan b 4 Oct 1986, Sebastian Michael b 18 Dec 1989); *Career* advertising mangr The Economist 1977–83, business devpt mangr Valin Pollen 1983–85, chief exec BMP Business 1985–91, chief exec Hoare Wilkins Advertising Ltd 1991–94; TBWA: md (following merger) 1994–96, chm 1996–97; chm TBWA Simons Palmer (following merger with Simons Palmer Clemmow Johnson) 1997–98, md Griffin Bacal 1998–2000, md Burkitt DDB (following merger) 2000–03, md DDB Healthcare 2003–; Freeman City of London, Liveryman Worshipful Co of Marketors; memb: IAA, IPA, Inst of Mktg, Mktg Soc; *Books* The Third Crusade (1974), Racial Tension in the Twelfth Century in the Holylands (1975); *Recreations* tennis, cricket, real tennis, golf, shooting; *Clubs* RAC, Queen's, Hurlingham, White's, MCC, Wentworth Golf, Piltdown Golf; *Style*— Jonathan Hoare, Esq

HOARE, Prof Michael; s of Ernest Charles Hoare (d 1992), and Pat, *née* Morgan; *b* 28 February 1950; *Educ* Penarth County GS, UCL (BSc, MSc, PhD); *m* 16 April 1983, Deborah, da of Derek Heywood-Waddington (d 1996); 2 s (Benjamin David b 11 June 1986, Simon Gareth b 18 May 1988), 1 da (Megan Kathleen Mary b 7 March 1991); *Career* scientist/mangr Unilever Research Lab Colworth House Beds 1971–74, biochemical engr UCL/UKAEA Harwell 1974–78; UCL: lectr 1978, reader 1984, prof of biochemical engrg 1991–, head of Dept of Biochemical Engrg 1998–, dir Advanced Centre for Biochemical Engrg; memb Editorial Bd: Trends in Biotechnology, Pharmaceutical Technology International, Jl of Biotechnology; Donald Medal for Contributions to Biochemical Engineering; FIChemE, FREng 1997; *Recreations* Wales, chamber music; *Style*— Prof Michael Hoare, FREng; ✉ Department of Biochemical Engineering, University College London, Torrington Place, London WC1E 7JE

HOARE, Richard John; s of Wing Cdr Charles Frederick Hoare, of Fleet, Hants, and Joyce Mary, *née* Stamp; *b* 5 October 1952; *Educ* Mill Hill Sch; *m* 1993, Jennifer Grace Agnes, da of William Thomas Patrick Donohue, of Marlborough, Wilts; 1 da (Héloïse Trafalgar Agnès Archer b 30 Nov 1996), 1 s (Lancelot Theodore Richard Falconer b 25 Aug 1998); *Career* ptnr: Barlow Lyde and Gilbert 1983–93 (joined 1973), Wilkinson Maughan 1993–95; slr to Hinduja Group 1995–, gen counsel Gulf Oil Int Ltd 1995–; Freeman City of London 1984; memb Law Soc 1978; *Publications* Personal Injury Precedents and Pleadings; *Recreations* gardening, sport, fine arts; *Style*— Richard Hoare, Esq; ✉ 18 Woodseer Street, London E1 5HD (☎ 020 7375 2856); Chateau de Villeneuve Les Montreal, Villeneuve Les Montreal, 11290, Aude, France; Richard Hoare, 4th Floor, 16 Charles II Street, London SW1Y 4QU (☎ 020 7321 5530, fax 020 7839 2399, e-mail richard@gulfoilltd.com)

HOARE, Richard Quintin; OBE (2007), DL (Hants 1997); s of Quintin Vincent Hoare, OBE, and Lucy Florence, *née* Selwyn; *b* 30 January 1943; *Educ* Eton; *m* 19 Oct 1970, Hon Frances Evelyn Hogg, da of Baron Hailsham of St Marylebone, KG, CH, PC (d 2001); 2 s (Alexander b 1973, Charles b 1976), 1 da (Elizabeth b 1978); *Career* HAC 1963–68, Home Serv Force HAC Detachment 1985–88; managing ptnr C Hoare & Co Bankers 1969– (also dep chm); chm: Bulldog Holdings Ltd 1986– (dir 1964), The Bulldog Trust 1983–2008 (fndr tstee); dir Placehill Ltd 1992–; govr Westminster Med Sch 1972–76, memb Cncl Univ of Buckingham 1999–2001; treas Old Etonian Assoc 1984–95, hon tstee African Med Research Fndn (memb Cncl 1977–84), pres Interbank Athletics Assoc 1980, chm Meridian Tst 2004–06; Hon DBA Univ of Winchester 2009; *Recreations* travel, walking, stalking, reading, collecting antiques; *Clubs* Boodle's, HAC, Pratts, RGS; *Style*— Richard Hoare, Esq, OBE; ✉ Oakland House, Ramsdell, Hampshire RG26 5SJ (☎ 01256 889368); C Hoare & Co, 37 Fleet Street, London EC4P 4DQ (☎ 020 7353 4522)

HOARE, SaraJane; da of Jeff Hoare, of Strand on the Green, London, and late Elizabeth Jane Hoare; *b* 27 June 1955; *Educ* Univ of Warwick (BA); *Career* fashion dir Observer newspaper 1984–86, fashion dir British Vogue 1986–92, ed-at-large Harpers Bazaar NYC 1992–2001, fashion ed Vanity Fair NYC 2001–10 (contributing ed 2010–), fashion dir Town and Country 2010–; contributor int edns of Vogue; *Books* Talking Fashion (2001); *Style*— Miss SaraJane Hoare

HOARE, Simon James; MP; s of Colin Hoare, and Maria *née* Trialonas; *b* 28 June 1969, Cardiff; *Educ* Bishop Hannon HS Cardiff, Greyfriars Coll Oxford Univ (BA); *m* 20 May 2000, Kate *née* Lund; 3 da (Imogen 22 April 2008, Jessica 2 March 2010, Laura 1 Aug 2012); *Career* conslt and advsr to property and development businesses, md Community Connect Ltd 2002–15; MP (Cons) Dorset North 2015–; membr Country Alliance; *Recreations* Gardening, Opera, Horse Racing, Reading; *Clubs* Garrick, Royal Over-Seas League, Newport (Pembroke) Boat, Blandford Constitutional, United and Cecil; *Style*— Simon Hoare, Esq, MP; ✉ Stroud Farmhouse, Stock Gaylard Estate, Lydlinch Common, DT10 2JD (☎ 02072 195697 e-mail simon.hoare.mp@parliament.co.uk, Twitter simon4dorset, www.ndca.org.uk), House of Commons, London SW1A 0AA

HOBAN, Mark; s of Tom Hoban, of Durham, and Maureen, *née* Orchard; *b* 31 March 1964; *Educ* LSE (BSc); *m* 6 Aug 1994, Fiona Jane, da of Peter and Sally Barrett; *Career* chartered accountant with PricewaterhouseCoopers and predecessor firms 1985–2001 (mangr 1990–92, sr mangr 1992–2001); MP (Cons) Fareham 2001–15, oppn whip 2002–03, shadow min for educn 2003–05, shadow financial sec to the Treasy 2005–10, financial sec to the Treasy 2010–12, min of state for work and pensions 2012–13; House of Commons: Select Ctee on Sci and Technol 2001–03, All Pty Local Hosp Gp, All Pty Small Business Gp; chair Flood Re 2015–; hon vice-pres Soc of Maritime Industries 2003–; sr advsr Markit 2014–, non-exec dir London Stock Exchange plc 2015–; Freeman City of London 2003, Liveryman Worshipful Co of Fruiterers 2003–; FCA 2014 (ACA 1988); *Recreations* cooking, reading, travel, entertaining; *Style*— Mark Hoban, Esq; ✉ 20 The Vale, Locks Heath, Southampton SO31 6NL (e-mail markhoban@btinternet.com)

HOBBS, HE Dr Jeremy Alexander; *m* Ana Maria Eréndira Granados de Hobbs; 1 s, 1 da; *Career* diplomat; research analyst for Cuba, Central America, Argentina, Uruguay and the S Atlantic overseas territories Americas Research Unit Research and Analysis Dept FCO 1991–95, second sec Political and Tech Cooperation Bogotá 1995–99, research analyst for Andean Repubs Americas Research Gp FCO 1999–2003, first sec political Mexico City 2003–06, head Americas Research Gp 2006–12 (also dep head of research analysts 2010–12), chargé d'affaires Quito 2012, research analyst for Mexico and Andean Repubs Americas Research Gp FCO 2012–13, ambass to Paraguay 2013–; *Style*— HE Dr Jeremy Hobbs; ✉ c/o FCO (Asunción), King Charles Street, London SW1A 2AH

HOBBS, Prof Kenneth Edward Frederick (Ken); s of Thomas Edward Ernest Hobbs (d 1951), of Suffolk, and Gladys May, *née* Neave (d 1986); *b* 28 December 1936; *Educ* W Suffolk Co GS Bury St Edmunds, Guy's Hosp Med Sch Univ of London (MB BS), Univ of Bristol (ChM); *Partner* Kenneth Charles Marshall (civil partnership 24 Dec 2005); *Career* surgical res fell Harvard Univ 1968–69, sr lectr in surgery Univ of Bristol 1970–73 (lectr 1966–70), prof of surgery Royal Free Hosp Sch of Med 1973–98 (now Royal Free and Univ Coll Sch of Med), hon conslt surgn Royal Free Hosp Hampstead (now Royal Free Hampstead NHS Tst) 1973–98, dean Faculty of Med Univ of London 1994–98, (elected memb of Senate 1985–98, memb Cncl 1985–98), emeritus prof of surgery Royal Free and Univ Coll Sch of Med 1998–; memb MRC Ctee Systems Bd 1982–86, chm MRC Grants Ctee A 1984–86; memb: UGC Med Sub Ctee (now Univ Funding Cncl) 1986–89, UFC Med Ctee 1991–93, GMC 1996–2001 (dep chm Professional Conduct Ctee 1999–2001); chm Mason Medical Fndn 1993–98, pres Stanley Thomas Johnson Fndn 1996–2004 (memb 1976–96), lead govr Norfolk & Norwich Univ Hosp Fndn Tst 2008–14; professional memb: GMC Fitness to Practice Ctees 2002–06, GMC Fitness to Practice Panel 2009–; Int Master Surgeon Int Coll of Surgeons 1994; hon fell The Sri Lanka Coll of Surgeons 1995; hon fell Chinese Univ Hong Kong 2002; memb RSM; FRCS 1964; *Books* contrib: Surgical Techniques Illustrated (1985), Operative Surgery and Management (1987), Surgery of the Liver and Biliary Tract (1988), Oxford Textbook of Hepatology (1991), Liver and Biliary Disease (1992), General Surgical Operations (1994), Oxford Textbook of Hepatology (1998); *Recreations* gourmet dining, the countryside; *Style*— Prof Ken Hobbs; ✉ e-mail profkenhobbs@aol.com

HOBBS, Philip John; s of Anthony Lewis Hobbs, and Barbara, *née* Thomas; *b* 26 July 1955; *Educ* King's Coll Taunton, Univ of Reading (BSc); *m* 12 June 1982, Sarah Louise, da of Albert Edwin Hill; 3 da (Caroline Elizabeth, Katherine Louise, Diana Margaret); *Career* professional jockey for 10 years (160 winners); racehorse trainer 1985–: currently trg 100 horses, over 1,000 winners incl Mackenson Gold Cup, Queen Mother Champion Chase, Hennesy Gold Cup, County Hurdle, Racing Post Chase (twice), Champion Hurdle and Scottish Champion Hurdle; *Recreations* shooting, skiing; *Clubs* Sportsman; *Style*— Philip Hobbs; ✉ Sandhill, Bilbrook, Minehead, Somerset (☎ 01984 640366, fax 01984 641124, website and e-mail www.pjhobbs.co.uk)

HOBBY, Russell; *b* 22 January 1972, Abingdon, Oxon; *Educ* Univ of Oxford; *Career* Damascus Technology Ltd 1993–95, Second Sight Ltd 1995–98, asst dir Hay Gp 1998–2010, gen sec NAHT 2010–; *Style*— Russell Hobby, Esq; ✉ NAHT, 1 Heath Square, Boltro Road, Haywards Heath, West Sussex RH16 1BL

HOBHOUSE, Penelope (Mrs Malins); da of Capt James Jackson Lenox-Conyngham Chichester-Clark, DSO, RN (d 1933), and Marion Caroline Dehra, *née* Chichester (d 1976); sis of Sir Robin Chichester-Clark, *qv*; *b* 20 November 1929; *Educ* North Foreland Lodge, Girton Coll Cambridge (BA); *m* 1, 17 May 1952 (m dis 1983), Paul Rodbard Hobhouse (d 1994), s of Sir Arthur Hobhouse (d 1965), of Castle Cary, Somerset; 1 da (Georgina

Dehra Catherine b 9 March 1953), 2 s (Niall Alexander b 29 Aug 1954, David Paul b 9 Sept 1957); m 2, 1983, Prof John Melville Malins (d 1992); *Career* writer and garden designer; Victoria Medal of Honour RHS 1996; Hon DLitt: Univ of Birmingham, Writtle Coll Univ of Essex; *Books* incl: The Country Gardener (1976), The Smaller Garden (1981), Gertrude Jekyll on Gardening (1983), Colour in Your Garden (1985), The National Trust: A Book of Gardening (1986), Private Gardens of England (1986), Garden Style (1988), Borders (1989), The Gardens of Europe (1990), Flower Gardens (1991), Plants in Garden History (1992), Penelope Hobhouse on Gardening (1994), Penelope Hobhouse's Garden Designs (1997), Penelope Hobhouse's Natural Planting (1997), Gardens of Italy (1998), The Story of Gardening (2002), The Gardens of Persia (2003); *Style*— Ms Penelope Hobhouse; ✉ The Clock House, Hadspen House, Castle Cary, Somerset BA7 7NG (☎ 01963 350987, e-mail p.malins560@btinternet.com)

HOBLEY, Mary Elizabeth Agnes; da of George Frederick Hobley (d 1992), Maria Wilhelmina, *née* Meiresonne (d 2010); *b* 9 December 1961; *Educ* Sacred Heart HS for Girls, UCNW Bangor (BSc), Australian Nat Univ Canberra (PhD); *m* 18 July 1987, (Michael) Mark Agnew; 1 s (Alexander Michael Hobley Agnew b 28 June 2000); *Career* rural devpt forestry res fell ODI 1987–95, ptnr in local governance, nat resource mgmnt and planning consultancy 1995–; worldwide consultancies for IUCN, DFID, SDC, World Bank and ODI; extensive res in India, Nepal, Vietnam and Australia; devpt of teaching modules for masters, diplomas and short courses for foresters, agric lectures and rural devpt professionals; Westoby mem lectr ANU 2007; memb numerous forestry ctees, review panels and gps on forestry issues; tstee bd Centre for Int Forestry Res; Cwlth Scholarship 1984, Amy Rustomjee Scholarship 1985; memb: Cwlth Forestry Assoc, RFS; *Publications* Participatory Forestry: The Process of Change in India and Nepal (1996), Where in the World is there Pro-Poor Forest Policy and Tenure Reform? (2007), Everyone is Leaving – Who Will Sow Our Fields? The effects of migration from Nepal to the Gulf and Malaysia (2013), Persistence and Change: thirty years of community forestry in Nepal (2013); also numerous learned papers, courses, reports and chapters on forestry, poverty and organisational change; *Recreations* walking, swimming, antiquarian book collecting; *Style*— Dr Mary Hobley; ✉ Mary Hobley & Associates Ltd, Glebe House, Thorncombe, Dorset TA20 4NE (☎ 01460 30385, e-mail mary@maryhobley.co.uk)

HOBLEY, Tina; *b* 20 May 1971; *Educ* Webber Douglas Sch of Drama London; *m* 16 Dec 2006, Oliver Wheeler, *qv*; 2 da (Isabella b 9 April 1999, Olivia Kitty Alice b 18 April 2008), 1 s (Orson Henry Attwood b 1 March 2010); *Career* actress; *Theatre* View from a Bridge (Colchester), Only When I Laugh (Bath, World Tour), The Taming of the Shrew (Chichester); *Television* Coronation Street (Granada) 1996–98, Harbour Lights (BBC) 1998–99, Holby City (BBC) 2000–13; *Style*— Ms Tina Hobley; ✉ c/o Paul Lyon-Maris, ICM, Oxford House, 76 Oxford Street, London W1N 0AX (☎ 020 7636 6565)

HOBMAN, Anthony (Tony); s of late David Burton Hobman, CBE, and Erica Agatha, *née* Irwin; *b* 5 July 1955; *Educ* De La Salle Coll, Cardinal Newman Sch Hove, N Staffs Poly (BA); *m* 1, 1978 (m dis 1994), Catherine Fenton; 1 s, 2 da; m 2, 2001, Victoria Richards *née* Maynard; 1 da, 2 step s; *Career* Barclays Bank plc: joined as grad mgmnt trainee 1976–81, various roles in mktg, project, change and serv mgmnt 1982–95; ProShare Ltd: head of investor servs 1996–99, ceo 1999–2000; ceo: Money Channel plc 2000–01, Occupational Pensions Regulatory Authy 2002–05, Pensions Regulator, Money Advice Service; memb: Consultative Ctee Co Law Review DTI 1999–2000, Advsy Gp Employer Task Force on Pensions DWP 2003–04; tstee David Hobman Charitable Tst 1987–96; *Clubs* Reform; *Style*— Tony Hobman, Esq

HOBSBAWM, Julia Nathalie; OBE (2015); da of Eric Hobsbawm (d 2012), and Marlene, *née* Schwarz; *b* 15 August 1964, London; *Educ* Camden Sch for Girls, Univ of Westminster; *m* 1 May 2004, Alaric Bamping; 2 s (Roman b 31 Oct 1998, Wolfgang Jim b 20 Feb 2005), 1 da (Anoushka b 1 Jan 2001); *Career* fndr Editorial Intelligence Ltd 2005–; memb Global Agenda Cncl World Economic Forum 2012–14, memb Diplomatic Excellence Panel FCO 2014; winner First Business Media Woman of the Year 2012; hon visiting prof: Cass Business Sch 2011–, Univ Campus Suffolk 2013–; *Books* The See-Saw: 100 Ideas for Work-Life Balance (2009, e-book 2013), Fully Connected: Working & Networking in 2020 (2014); *Recreations* reading, walking, conversation; *Clubs* Groucho, Soho House, eiClub; *Style*— Ms Julia Hobsbawm, OBE; ✉ e-mail julia@editorialintelligence.com, website www.editorialintelligence.com and www.namesnotnumbers.com, Twitter @juliahobsbawm

HOBSON, David Llewelyn (Daf); s of Alan Hobson, and Mary Ellen, *née* Roberts; *Educ* Caernarfon GS, Jacob Kramer Coll of Art and Design Leeds, Leeds Coll of Art and Design (DipAD); *Career* cinematographer; asst cameraman World in Action Granada 1974–75, dir film and TV 1974–81, estab Woodthrush Ltd 1981, dir of photography S4C 1981–92, dir of photography and facilities supply BBC, ITV and Channel 4 features 1992–; inventor Wonkycam; memb BSC 1998–; *Television* Family (BBC 1) 1993 (Best Photography and Lighting BAFTA Awards 1994), Bramwell (ITV) 1994 (Best Photography and Lighting RTS Awards 1995), Y Wisg Sidan (S4C) 1995 (nomination BAFTA Cymru Awards 1996), The Tenant of Wildfell Hall (BBC 1) 1996 (Best Camera RTS Awards 1997, nomination Best Photography and Lighting BAFTA Awards 1997), The Lakes (BBC 1) 1997 (nomination Best Photography and Lighting BAFTA Awards 1998), Births Marriages and Deaths (BBC 2) 1998, Spoonface Steinberg (BBC 2) 1998, Eureka Street (BBC 2) 1999 (Best Photography and Lighting Irish Film and TV Acad 1999), Sword of Honour (Channel 4) 2000, Swallow (Channel 4) 2001, Othello (ITV) 2001 (winner Best Photography and Lighting BAFTA Awards 2002, Best Photography and Lighting RTS Awards 2002), Early Doors (BBC) 2003 and 2004, The Street (Granada TV) 2005, Fallout (Channel 4) 2008, Café (SKY 1) 2011, After Hours (SKY 1) 2014, Broken Biscuits (BBC) 2015, Rovers (SKY 1) 2016; *Film* Welcome to Sarajevo 1996, Tatoo (short film) 2002 (Kodak Swan Award, nomination BAFTA Awards 2002); *Recreations* sailing, invention; *Style*— Daf Hobson, BSC; ✉ e-mail wetinwales@gmail.com

HOCHGREB, Prof Simone; *Educ* Princeton Univ (PhD); *Career* assoc prof MIT 1999, princ investigator Combustion Research Facility Sandia Nat Labs 2000, managing engr Exponent Failure Analysis Assocs 2002, prof of experimental combustion Univ of Cambridge 2002–; *Style*— Prof Simone Hochgreb; ✉ Department of Engineering, Trumpington Street, Cambridge CB2 1PZ

HOCHHAUSER, Andrew Romain; QC (1997); s of Jerome Romain Hochhauser, MD, FRCSE (d 1978), and Ruth, *née* Binks (d 2002); *b* 16 March 1955; *Educ* Highgate Sch, Univ of Bristol (LLB), LSE (LLM), Courtauld Inst of Art (MA); *Career* called to the Bar Middle Temple 1977 (Harmsworth scholar, bencher 2000); recorder 2004–, dep judge of the High Court of Justice 2013; hon counsel to Westminster Abbey 2004–; pt/t memb Law Sch LSE 1979–86; chm Dance Umbrella 2007–14, tstee V&A Museum 2011–, tstee Propeller Theatre Co 2012–15, vice-chm Paintings in Hospitals 2013–, govr Central Sch of Ballet 2015–; FCIArb 1995, FRSA 2013; *Recreations* collecting paintings, swimming with sharks, contemporary dance; *Clubs* Garrick; *Style*— Andrew Hochhauser, QC; ✉ Essex Court Chambers, 24 Lincoln's Inn Fields, London WC2A 3ED (☎ 020 7813 8000, fax 020 7813 8080)

HOCKLEY, Rear Adm Chris J; CBE (2014); s of Peter Hockley (d 1986), and Valerie, *née* Oades; *b* 24 August 1959, Orpington, London; *Educ* Dulwich Coll, RN Engrg Coll (BSc, MSc); *m* 10 Sept 2005, Kate, *née* Henderson; 4 s (Tom b 1975, Luke b 1977, Oliver b 1979, Peter b 1986), 1 da (Jennifer b 1984); *Career* dep IPTL Future Aircraft Carrier Project 1999–2002, military asst to Chief of Defence Procurement 2002–04, through life support dir Defence Logistic Orgn 2005–07, naval base Cdr HMNB Clyde 2007–10, flag offr Scotland Northern England and NI and flag offr Reserves 2011–14; ceo The MacRobert Tst 2014–; ADC 2008–10; CEng 1988, FIMarEst 2008 (MIMarEst 1987, CMarEng 2007), FCMI 2010; *Recreations* walking, sailing; *Style*— Rear Adm Chris Hockley, CBE

HOCKMAN, Stephen Alexander; QC (1990); s of late Dr Nathaniel Hockman, of London, and Trude, *née* Schlossman; *b* 4 January 1947; *Educ* Eltham Coll, Jesus Coll Cambridge; *m* August 1998, Elizabeth St Hill Davies; *Career* called to the Bar Middle Temple 1970 (treas 2015); recorder of the Crown Court 1987, dep judge of the High Court 1998–, ldr SE Circuit 2001–03, head of chambers 6 Pump Court; chair Bar Cncl 2006 (vice-chair 2005); *Clubs* Garrick, RAC; *Style*— Stephen Hockman, Esq, QC; ✉ 6 Pump Court, Temple, London EC4Y 7AR (☎ 020 7797 8400, fax 020 7797 8401, e-mail stephenhockmanqc@6pumpcourt.co.uk)

HOCKNEY, David; OM (2012), CH (1997); s of Kenneth and Laura Hockney; *b* 9 July 1937, Bradford, Yorks; *Educ* Bradford GS, Bradford Coll of Art, RCA, Univ of Aberdeen; *Career* artist; Hon Dr RCA; RA 1991 (ARA 1985); *Solo Exhibitions* incl: Kasmin Gallery London 1963–89, Museum of Modern Art NY 1964 and 1968, Stedelijk Museum Amsterdam 1966, Whitechapel Gallery London 1970, Andre Emmerich Gallery NY 1972–96, Musée des ArtsDecoratifs Paris 1974, Museo Tamayo Mexico City 1984, LA Louver CA 1986, 1989, 1995, 1998 and 2005, Nishimura Gallery Tokyo 1986, 1989, 1990 and 1994, Met Museum of Art 1988, LA County Museum of Art 1988, 1996 and 2006, Tate Gallery London 1988, 1992 and 2007, Royal Acad of Arts London 1995 and 1999, Hamburger Kunsthalle 1995, Nat Museum of American Art WA 1997 and 1998, Museum Ludwig Cologne 1997, MFA Boston 1998 and 2006, Centre Georges Pompidou Paris 1999, Musée Picasso Paris 1999, Museum of Contemporary Art LA 2001, Kunst-Und Ausstellung Halle Bonn 2001, La Museum of Modern Art Copenhagen 2001, Annely Juda Fine Art London 1997, 1999, 2003 and 2006, Richard Gray Gallery Chicago and NY 1992, 1999, 2002 and 2004, Nat Portrait Galley London 2003 and 2006, Whitney Biennial NY 2004; designer Rake's Progress (Glyndebourne UK) 1975; set designer for: Magic Flute (Glyndebourne) 1978, Parade Triple Bill, Stravinsky Triple Bill (Met Opera House) 1980–81, Tristan und Isolde (LA Music Opera) 1987, Turnadot (Lyric Opera Chicago and San Francisco Opera) 1992–, Die Frau Ohne Schatten (Covent Garden London) 1992; *Awards* Guinness Award first prize for etching 1961, Gold Medal Royal Coll of Art 1962, Graphic Prize Paris Biennale 1963, first prize 8th Int Exhibition Drawings Lugano Italy 1964, first prize John Moores Exhibition Liverpool 1967, German Award for Excellence 1983, Praemium Inperiale Japan Art Assoc 1989, fifth annual Govt CA Visual Arts Award 1994, Charles Wollaston Award Royal Acad of Arts 1999; *Books* Six Fairy Tales of the Brothers Grimm (illustrator, 1969), David Hockney by David Hockney (1976), The Blue Guitar (illustrator, 1977), David Hockney: Travels with Pen, Pencil and Ink (1978), Paper Pools (1980), David Hockney Photographs (1982), Cameraworks (1983, Kodak Photography Book Award 1984), David Hockney: A Retrospective (1988), Hockney Paints the Stage (1983), Hockney's Alphabet (illustrator, 1991), That's the Way I See It (1993), David Hockney's Dog Days (1998), Hockney on Art (1999), Secret Knowledge: Rediscovering the Lost Techniques of the Old Masters (2001), Hockney's Portaits and People (2003), Hockney's Pictures (2004), David Hockney: Portraits; *Style*— David Hockney, OM, CH, RA; ✉ 7508 Santa Monica Boulevard, Los Angeles, CA 90046–6407, USA

H

HOCKNEY, Michael Brett; MBE (2011); s of Stanley Waller Hockney (d 2009), and Jean, *née* Duston; *b* 29 July 1949, Liverpool, Lancs; *Educ* Beechenhurst Sch Liverpool, King Edward Sch Lytham, Univ of Manchester, LSE; *m* 30 July 1983, Dr Elizabeth Anne Hockney, da of Bruce Cryer, of Richmond, Surrey; *Career* account planner J Walter Thompson 1972–75, account mangr then assoc dir Boase Massimi Pollitt Partnership 1975–80, bd dir and memb Exec Ctee BMP plc 1980–87, gp chm and md BDDH Gp plc 1987–93, global mktg dir and memb Mgmnt Bd Christie's International 1993–95, advsr to MOD 1995–99, interim exec dir ICAEW 1999–2001, chief exec D&AD 2003–07; non-exec dir: Adjutant Gen's Mgmnt Bd 1996–99, BCMG Ltd 1996–2005, Souk Hldgs Ltd 2010–13; memb Cncl: Inst of Practitioners in Advtg 1981–93 (chm UK Advtg Effectiveness Awards 1984–94), Advtg Assoc 1989–93; memb Cncl and tstee Royal Sch of Church Music 1986–2004 (chm Nat Headquarters Devpt Ctee 1990–2000, chm Gen Purposes Ctee 1998–2000, dep chm Cncl 2000–04), memb Royal Hosp Chelsea Bd of Commissioners' Estates Ctee 2010–; vice-chm Berkeley Square Ball Charitable Trust 1986–90; memb Bd and tstee: English Chamber Orchestra 1994– (dep chm 2012–), ABF The Soldiers' Charity 1998–2010 (chm Devpt Ctee 2001–10, fndr Lord Mayor's Big Curry Lunch 2007, chm Lord Mayor's Big Curry Lunch Ctee 2007–), Christian Aid 1995–2001 (chm Corporate Fundraising Ctee 1998–2001); memb Cncl and tstee Cncl of Christians and Jews 2012– (memb Advsy Bd 2010–11); memb Gtr London RFCA 1999–2007; memb Min for Veterans' Affrs Working Party 2000–03, memb Nikaeans 2004–, memb Bd of Govrs Univ of Berlin Sch of Creative Leadership 2006–11, memb Gen Assembly (Ct) Univ of Manchester 2011–, memb Pilgrims 2012–; govr Army Fndn Coll 1999–2003; organist and choir master All Saints Church London 1976–98; chm All Saints Concert Series 2002–09; memb Worshipful Co of Musicians (Freeman 2006, Liveryman 2009, Steward to the Ct 2015–), Freeman City of London 2007; MIPA 1978, FIPA 1984, FCIM 1985, FCMI 1986, FRSA 2002, FRSCM 2004, CCMI 2011, FSA; *Recreations* the organ, baroque opera, early music, 18th century Worcester porcelain, French wine, English furniture, architecture, biography; *Clubs* Athenaeum; *Style*— Michael B Hockney, Esq, MBE; ✉ c/o The Athenaeum, Pall Mall, London SW1Y 5ER

HODDER, Prof Ian Richard; s of Bramwell William (Dick) Hodder, and Noreen Victoria Hodder; *b* 23 November 1948; *Educ* Magdalen Coll Sch Oxford, Inst of Archaeology Univ of London (BA), Univ of Cambridge (PhD); *m* 1, (m dis), Françoise Hivernel; 2 s (Christophe b 1976, Gregoire b 1979); m 2, Christine Hastorf; 2 s (Kyle, Nicholas (twins) b 1991); *Career* lectr Dept of Archaeology Univ of Leeds 1974–77; Univ of Cambridge: asst lectr Dept of Archaeology 1977–81, lectr Dept of Archaeology 1981–90, reader in prehistory 1990–96, prof of archaeology 1996–2000, fell McDonald Inst 2001–; fell Darwin Coll Cambridge 1990–2000; Stanford Univ: co-dir Archaeology Center 1999–2002, prof Dept of Cultural and Social Anthropology 1999–, Dunlevie Family prof Sch of Humanities and Sciences 2002–; adjunct asst prof of anthropology SUNY 1984–89, adjunct prof and visiting prof Dept of Anthropology Univ of Minnesota 1986–; visiting prof: Van Giffen Inst for Pre- and Proto-history Amsterdam 1980, Univ of Paris I Sorbonne 1985; fell Center for Advanced Study in the Behavioural Scis Stanford CA 1987; dir gen Cambridge Archaeological Unit 1990–2000; memb Ed Bd: New Directions in Archaeology 1978–89, Anthropology Today, Archeologia e Calcolatori, Cambridge Archaeological Jl, Jl of European Archaeology; memb Advsy Bd: Rural History: Economy, Society, Culture, Jl of Material Culture; Gordon Childe prize Inst of Archaeology; memb Founding Ctee Euro Assoc of Archaeologists 1991–95; memb Prehistoric Soc, Associate Inst of Field Archaeologists (memb Cncl 1986–89); FRAI (memb Cncl 1985–88), FSA, FBA 1996; *Publications* authored volumes: Spatial analysis in archaeology (with C Orton, 1976), Symbols in action. Ethnoarchaeological studies of material culture (1982), The Present Past. An Introduction to anthropology for archaeologists (1982), Reading the Past. Current approaches to interpretation in archaeology (1986, revised edn, 1991), The domestication of Europe: structure and contingency in Neolithic societies (1990), Theory and practice in archaeology (1992), The archaeological process (1999), Archaeology beyond dialogue (2003), The Leopard's Tale (2006); edited volumes incl: The Archaeology of contextual meanings (1987), Archaeology as long term history (1987), The meanings of things: material culture and symbolic expression (1989), Archaeological Theory in Europe. The last three decades (1991), Interpreting Archaeology (with M Shanks, 1994), Archaeology in Theory. A Reader (with R Preucel, 1996); also author of numerous articles and reviews in learned jls; *Recreations* playing piano and violin, sports especially tennis, sailing and golf; *Style—* Prof Ian Hodder, FBA, FSA; ✉ Department of Anthropology, Stanford University, Stanford, CA 94305, USA (☎ 00 1 650 723 1197, e-mail ihodder@stanford.edu)

HODDER-WILLIAMS, Richard; s of Paul Hodder-Williams (d 2008), and Felicity, *née* Blagden (d 1985); *b* 18 March 1943; *Educ* Rugby (mathematics scholar), CCC Oxford (MA, Coll prize); *m* 1972, Rhiain Rhys, *née* Morgan; 2 s (Matthew b 1 June 1975, John-Paul b 27 Jan 1979); *Career* scholar Miny of Overseas Devpt UC of Rhodesia and Nyasaland 1965–67; Univ of Bristol: lectr in politics 1967–81, reader 1981–91, prof of politics 1991–, dean Faculty of Social Sciences 1996–99, pro-vice-chllr 1999–2004; visiting lectr: Univ of South Africa 1976, Univ of Cape Town 1980 and 1981, Univ of Nairobi 1981, chllr Coll Univ of Malawi 1981; visiting prof of political science Univ of Calif Berkeley 1984–85, visiting fell ANU 1988, dep to Mellon chair of American politics Univ of Oxford 1990, visiting scholar Inst of Governmental Studies Univ of Calif Berkeley 1996; co-ed Jl of Southern African Studies 1973–76; memb Editorial Bd: Jl of American Studies 1985–88, African Affrs 1987–2007 (jt ed 1977–87), Politikon 1991–99; memb: Exec Ctee VSO 1979–82, Royal African Soc (memb Cncl 1978–98, vice-pres 1998–2011), African Studies Assoc of the UK (pres 1994–96, treas 1999–2008), Political Studies Assoc, American Political Gp (chm 1975–78); govr: Sherborne Sch 1979– (vice-chm 2001–07, chm 2007–13), Cheltenham Coll 1991–98, Fairfield Sch 1981–99 (chm 1985–99), Badminton Sch 1994–2016 (chm 1998–2007); vice-chm Sherborne Qatar 2009–16, pro-chllr Univ of Bristol 2014–; tstee African Educnl Tst 2004– (treas 2008–); High Sheriff City of Bristol 2008–09; distinguished fell Rottermere American Inst 2010, Distinguished Africanist Award 2016; *Books* Public Opinion Polls and British Politics (1971), The Politics of the US Supreme Court (1983), An Introduction to the Politics of Tropical Africa (1984), White Farmers in Rhodesia (1984), USA and UK: a comparative study (ed with James Ceaser, 1986), From Churchill to Major: the British Prime Ministership (ed with Donald Shell, 1995), Directory of Africanists in Britain (ed, 3 edns), Judges and Politics in the Contemporary Age (1997); *Recreations* cricket, golf, listening to classical music, playing the piano; *Clubs* Vincent's (Oxford), Château des Vigiers GC, Eymetois de Cricket (vice-pres 2001–04, treas 2004–08), Clifton; *Style—* Prof Richard Hodder-Williams; ✉ e-mail hodderw@wanadoo.fr

HODGE, Andrew; *see:* Triggs-Hodge, Andrew

HODGE, His Hon Judge David Ralph; QC (1997); s of Ralph Noel Hodge, CBE, and late Jean Margaret Hodge; *b* 13 July 1956, Prestatyn, N Wales; *Educ* St Margaret's Sch Liverpool, UC Oxford (scholar, BA, BCL); *m* 2003, Jane, yst da of Tom and Mabel Woosey; *Career* called to the Bar Inner Temple 1979, admitted to Lincoln's Inn 1980 (bencher 2000); practising barr and memb of chambers: 9 Old Square 1980–2004, Maitland Chambers 2004–05; recorder 2000–05 (asst recorder 1998–2000), dep judge of the High Court 2004–05, specialist chancery circuit judge (Northern Circuit) 2005–, pt/t judge of the Court of Protection 2007–, p/t judge of the Upper Tribunal (Tax & Chancery Chamber) 2013–, p/t judge of the Upper Tribunal (Lands Chamber) 2014–; chm Lincoln's Inn Bar Representation Ctee 1997–98, memb Cncl of Circuit Judges 2007– (sec Civil Sub-ctee 2014–), jt chm Student Activities Ctee Lincoln's Inn 2008–14, memb Incorporated Cncl of Law Reporting 2010–, memb Costs Ctee Civil Justice Cncl 2013–; civil tutor (specialist jurisdictions) Judicial Coll 2010–; dep-chllr Dio of Blackburn 2016–, memb Legal Advsy Cmmn Gen Synod 2016–; *Publications* contrib chapter on Chancery matters to The Law and Practice of Compromise (4 edn 1996– 8 edn, 2015), Rectification: The Modern Law and Practice Governing Claims for Rectification for Mistake (1 edn 2010, 2 edn 2015); contrib titles on Compromise & Settlement (2013), Declaratory Judgments (2014), Injunctions (2014) and Interim Remedies (2014) to Atkin's Court Forms; *Recreations* wife, theatre and wine; *Clubs* Garrick, Athenaeum (Liverpool); *Style—* His Hon Judge Hodge, QC; ✉ c/o Manchester Civil Justice Centre, 1 Bridge Street West, Manchester M60 9DJ (☎ 0161 240 5307, e-mail manchester.chancery@hmcts.gsi.gov.uk)

HODGE, Prof Ian David; s of Robert Hodge (d 1982), and Georgina, *née* Padfield (d 2013); *b* 1952, Chelmsford, Essex; *Educ* Univ of Reading (BSc), Wye Coll London (PhD); *m* 1979, Bridget, *née* Palmer; 3 da (Rebecca b 1982, Susannah b 1987, Louisa b 1990), 1 s (David b 1984); *Career* research assoc and lectr Univ of Newcastle upon Tyne 1976–78, lectr in agric economics Univ of Queensland 1979–83; Dept of Land Economy Univ of Cambridge: Gilbey lectr 1983–2000, univ sr lectr 2000–01, reader in rural economy 2001–05, head of dept 2002–11, prof of rural economy 2005–; fell Hughes Hall Cambridge 2004–; govr: Macaulay Land Use Research Inst 1998–2003, Cambridge Int Land Inst 2002–11; pres Agricultural Economics Soc 2007–08; memb: Socio Economic Advsy Gp English Nature 1994–2006, Broads Research Advsy Panel 1999–2003, MAFF/DEFRA Academic Economist Panel 1999–2012, MAFF Task Force for the Hills 2000–01, Bd Cambridge Inst for Sustainability Leadership 2010–14, Economic Advsy Panel DEFRA 2012–; tech assessor Salmon and Freshwater Fisheries Legislation Review Gp 1999; memb Cncl of Chiefs Essodo community Enugu state Nigeria, memb Bd of Tstees Nene Park Tst 2012–; FRICS 2004; *Publications* Rural Employment: Trends, Options, Choices (with Martin Whitby, 1981), Environmental Economics: Individual Incentives and Public Choice (1995), Countryside in Trust: Land Management by Conservation, Recreation and Amenity Organisations (with Janet Dwyer, 1996), Governance of the Countryside (2016); also author of articles in academic jls and other professional pubns; *Recreations* gardening, walking; *Style—* Prof Ian Hodge; ✉ Department of Land Economy, University of Cambridge, 19 Silver Street, Cambridge CB3 9EP (☎ 01223 337134, fax 01223 337132, e-mail idh3@cam.ac.uk)

HODGE, Sir James William; KCVO (1996), CMG (1996); s of William Hodge (d 1994), of Edinburgh, and Catherine, *née* Carden (d 1977); *b* 24 December 1943, Edinburgh; *Educ* Holy Cross Acad Edinburgh, Univ of Edinburgh (MA), Royal Coll of Defence Studies (Defence Acad UK); *m* 20 June 1970, Frances Margaret, da of Michael Coyne (d 1995), and Theresa, *née* Walsh (d 1993); 3 da (Catherine b 1973, Fiona b 1975, Claire b 1979); *Career* HM Dip Serv 1966, third sec Tokyo 1967–69, second sec Tokyo 1970–72, FCO 1972–75, first sec Lagos 1975–78, FCO 1978–81, first sec Tokyo 1981–82, cnsllr (commercial) Tokyo 1982–86, cnsllr and head of Chancery Copenhagen 1986–90, cnsllr FCO 1990–93, RCDS 1994, min Peking 1995–96, ambass to Thailand 1996–2000 (concurrently non-resident ambass to Laos), consul-gen Hong Kong 2000–03 (concurrently non-resident consul-gen Macao); chm: Soc of Pension Professionals 2007–, FCO Assoc 2009–15; Hon DLitt Univ of Ulster 2003, Hon LLD Univ of Liverpool 2004; MCIL 1990, FRSA 2009; Knight Grand Cross Order of the White Elephant (Thailand) 1996; *Recreations* books, music; *Clubs* MCC, Oriental, Royal Scots (Edinburgh), Hong Kong, Foreign Correspondents' (Hong Kong), China (Hong Kong), Macao Jockey, Number Twenty (London); *Style—* Sir James Hodge, KCVO, CMG

HODGE, Rt Hon Dame Margaret Eve; DBE (2015, MBE 1978), PC (2003), MP; da of Hans and Lisbeth Oppenheimer; *b* 8 September 1944; *Educ* Bromley HS, Oxford HS, LSE (BSc(Econ)); *m* 1, 1968 (m dis 1978), Andrew Watson; 1 s (Nick), 1 da (Lizzi); m 2, 1978, Sir Henry Hodge (d 2009); 2 da (Anna, Amy); *Career* teacher and int market research 1966–73; London Borough of Islington: cncllr 1973–94, chm Housing Ctee 1975–79, dep ldr 1981, ldr 1982–92; sr conslt Price Waterhouse 1992–94, MP (Lab) Barking 1994–; chm: Lab Pty's inquiry team on early years educn 1994–97, London Gp of Lab MPs, Educn and Employment Select Ctee 1997–98, Public Accounts Ctee 2011–; Parly under sec Dept for Educn and Employment 1998–2001, min of state for lifelong learning and HE DfES 2001–03, min of state for children, young people and families DfES 2003–05, min of state for work DWP 2005–06, min of state DTI 2006–07, min of state for culture and creative industries 2007–08, min of state for culture 2009–10; fndr and chm Assoc of London Authorities 1984–92, vice-chm AMA 1991–92, chm Circle 33 Housing Assoc 1993–96; dir CILNTEC 1990–92, non-exec dir London First 1992–94, former memb Cncl Univ of London; govr LSE 1990–2001; chm Fabian Soc 1997–98 (memb Exec Ctee 1990–99); visiting fell Inst of Public Policy Research 1992–, hon fell Univ of North London, Hon DCL City Univ; *Publications* Quality, Equality and Democracy: Improving Public Services (1991), Beyond the Town Hall – Reinventing Local Democracy (1994), More than the Flower Show: elected mayors and democracy (1997); contrib chapters to: Reinventing the Left (ed David Miliband), Making Gender Work (ed Jenny Shaw); *Recreations* family, cooking, cycling, theatre and opera; *Style—* The Rt Hon Dame Margaret Hodge, DBE, MP; ✉ House of Commons, London SW1A 0AA (☎ 020 7219 6666, fax 020 7219 3640)

HODGE, Patricia Ann; da of Eric Hodge (d 1988), and Marion, *née* Phillips (d 2011); *b* 29 September 1946; *Educ* Grimsby Wintringham Girls' GS, St Helen's Sch for Girls Northwood, Maria Grey Teachers' Training Coll Isleworth, LAMDA (Eveline Evans Award for Best Actress on graduating); *m* 31 July 1976, Peter Douglas Owen; 2 s (Alexander Richard Charles b 18 Feb 1989, Edward Frederick James b 27 Dec 1991); *Career* actress; Hon DLitt Univ of Hull, Hon DLitt Brunel Univ, Hon DLitt Univ of Leicester; *Theatre* incl: Popkiss (Globe) 1972, Pippin (dir Bob Fosse, Her Majesty's Theatre) 1973, Two Gentlemen of Verona (musical, dir Mel Shapiro, Phoenix) 1993, Hair (dir Rufus Collins, Queen's) 1974, The Beggar's Opera (dir Max Stafford-Clarke, Nottingham Playhouse) 1975, Pal Joey, Look Back In Anger (dir Phillip Hedley, Oxford Playhouse) 1976, Then and Now (Hampstead) 1979, The Mitford Girls (Chichester Festival Theatre) 1981 and (Globe) 1982, Noel and Gertie (Comedy Theatre) 1989/90, Separate Tables 1993, The Prime of Miss Jean Brodie (Strand) 1994, A Little Night Music (RNT) 1995, Heartbreak House (Almeida) 1997, Money (RNT0 1999, Summerfolk (RNT) 1999, Noises Off (RNT) 2000, His Dark Materials (NT, 2004), The Country Wife 2007, Calendar Girls (Noel Coward Theatre) 2009, Dandy Dick 2012, Relative Values (Harold Pinter Theatre) 2014; *Television* for BBC incl: Valentine (series) 1973, The Girls of Slender of Means 1975, Jackanory Playhouse 1977, Act of Rape 1977, Crimewriters 1978, Hotel du Lac 1985, The Life and Loves of a She Devil 1986, The Legacy of Reginald Perrin 1996, The Moonstone 1996, Miranda 2009–10 (2 series); for Thames incl: The Naked Civil Servant 1975, Rumpole of the Bailey (various) 1978–90, Edward and Mrs Simpson 1978, Jemima Shore Investigates 1982; other credits incl: The Professionals (Mark 1 Prodns) 1979, Holding the Fort (LWT, 3 series) 1979–82, Robin of Sherwood (HTV) 1985, Time for Murder (Granada) 1985, Inspector Morse (Central) 1988, The Shell Seekers (ABC/Central) 1989, The Secret Life of Ian Fleming (Turner Entertainment) 1989, Rich Tea and Sympathy (Yorkshire) 1991, The Cloning of Joanna May (Granada) 1991, The Falklands Play 2002, Sweet Medicine 2003, Marple 2004, Maxwell 2007, Poirot 2013; *Films* incl: The Disappearance (dir Stuart Cooper) 1977, The Elephant Man 1979, Betrayal (dir David Jones) 1982, Sunset (dir Blake Edwards) 1987, Just Ask for Diamond (dir Stephen Bayly) 1988, The Leading Man 1996, Jilting Joe 1997, Before You Go 2002; *Awards* Olivier Award Best Supporting Actress (for Money) 1999, Female Performer of the Year Spoken Word Award 2003; nominations for: 2 Olivier Awards, 1 Br Acad Award, 1 Ace Award (USA); *Style—* Miss Patricia Hodge; ✉ c/o Independent Ltd, 40 Whitfield Street London, W1T 2RH (☎ 020 7636 6565, fax 020 7323 0101)

HODGE, Stephen Murley Garfield; s of Raymond G Hodge (d 1960), and Ruth Egar (d 1997); *b* 11 March 1942, Peterborough; *Educ* Univ of Oxford; *m* 5 Aug 1967, Leila; 1 s (Thomas b 7 Aug 1975); *Career* admitted slr 1966; early career in various financial roles UK, Venezuela, Argentina, the Netherlands and Australia, treas then finance dir Shell Australia 1979–86, dep gp treas then gp treas Shell Int Petroleum Co, dir of finance Royal Dutch/Shell Gp of Cos until 2001, chm Shell Pensions Tst 2001–08, non-exec dep chm O2 plc 2005–06 (non-exec dir 2001–06), dep chm Franchise Bd Lloyd's of London 2002–08, memb Financial Reporting Review Panel 2005–08; pres Highgate Literary & Scientific Instn 2010–14; MCT; *Clubs* Athenaeum; *Style—* Stephen Hodge, Esq; ✉ 12 Highgate Close, London N6 4SD (e-mail hoj@sloth.demon.co.uk)

HODGES, Prof Christopher John Stratford; s of John Henderson Hodges, and Norah, *née* Stratford; *b* 19 March 1954; *Educ* King Edward's Sch Birmingham, RMA Sandhurst, New Coll Oxford (MA), KCL (PhD); *m* Fiona Mary, *née* Ewart; 3 da; *Career* admitted slr 1979; slr Slaughter and May 1979–85 (articled clerk 1977–79), slr Clifford Chance 1986–89, ptnr McKenna & Co (now CMS Cameron McKenna) 1990–2005; visiting lectr Univ of Surrey 1994–97; Centre for Socio-Legal Studies Univ of Oxford: visiting research fell 2003–04, assoc fell 2005–, head CMS Research Prog on Civil Justice Systems 2008–; Erasmus prof of the fundamentals of private law Erasmus Univ Rotterdam 2010–13, prof of justice systems Univ of Oxford 2014; visiting prof Catholic Univ of Leuven 2013, hon prof China Univ of Political Science and Law Beijing 2013–16, guest prof Wuhan Univ China 2013–16, visiting fell Australian Nat Univ Canberra 2014, supernumerary fell Wolfson Coll Oxford 2015; memb Editorial Bd: Consumer Law Jl 1993–98, Int Business Law 2001–03; memb Editorial Advsy Bd The Regulatory Affrs Jl (Devices) 1993–; contrib: Law Quarterly Review, Common Market Law Review, European Business Law Review, Int Business Lawyer, Jl of Personal Injury Litigation; chair Legal Issues Ctee European Confedn of Med Devices Assocs (EUCOMED)/European Diagnostic Mfrs Assoc (EDMA) 2000–, vice-chair Cncl Assoc of Br Health-Care Industries (memb 1992–2008, chair Legal Ctee 1995–2008, chair Tech Policy Gp 2005–08), co-chair Health Industries Task Force Working Gps on Regulation and Communications 2002–07, chair Pharmaceutical Services Negotiating Ctee 2007–11; memb: Consumer Affrs Panel CBI 1992– (chair Working Ptys: Product Liability 1998–, Representative Claims 2000–), Academic Advsy Panel on Consumer Law DTI 2001–, Med Res Ethics Ctee Harrow HA 1990–97 (vice-chair 1992–97), Bd UK Research Integrity Office 2008–; tstee and dir The Sixteen 1989–2007, chair Bampton Classical Opera 2005–13; memb Equity 1980–, memb RHS 1998–; Freeman: City of London 1982, City of London Slrs Co 1982; Liveryman Worshipful Soc of Apothecaries 2009; hon res assoc New Coll Oxford 2001–04; memb: Int Bar Assoc 1993–2003 (chair Ctee on Product Liability, Advtg, Unfair Competition and Consumer Affrs 2001–03), Int Assoc of Def Counsel, Def Res Inst, Soc of Legal Scolars 2005–; fell Inst of Continuous Professional Devpt 1998, fell Soc of Advanced Legal Studies 2000; *Publications* Product Liability: European Laws and Practice (1993), Product Safety (jtly, 1995), Multi-Party Actions (2001), European Regulation of Consumer Product Safety (2005), The Reform of Class and Representative Actions in Europe: A New Approach to Collective Redress (2008), The Costs and Funding of Civil Litigation (jtly, 2010), Law and Corporate Behaviour: Integrating Theories of Regulation, Enforcement, Compliance, Culture and Ethics (2015); also author of various book chapters and numerous articles; *Recreations* singing and conducting classical music, horticulture; *Clubs* Oxford and Cambridge; *Style—* Prof Christopher Hodges; ✉ Centre for Socio-Legal Studies, Manor Road, Oxford OX1 3UQ (☎ 01869 284245, e-mail christopher.hodges@csls.ox.ac.uk)

HODGES, Dan Pearce Jackson; s of Roy Hodges, and Glenda Jackson, CBE, MP, *qv*; *b* 7 March 1969; *Career* columnist Daily Telegraph; *Style—* Dan Hodges, Esq; ✉ The Telegraph, 111 Buckingham Palace Road, London SW1W 0DT

HODGES, Prof Richard Andrew; OBE (1995); s of Roy Clarence Hodges, of Box, Wilts, and Joan Mary, *née* Hartnell; *b* 29 September 1952; *Educ* City of Bath Boys' Sch, Univ of Southampton (BA, PhD); *m* 1, (m dis 1998), Deborah, da of F C P Peters; 1 s (William b 15 March 1984), 1 da (Charlotte b 25 Oct 1986); m 2, Kim Bowes, da of C V Bowes; 1 s (Raphael b 12 Dec 2009); *Career* archaeologist; Univ of Sheffield: lectr 1976–86, sr lectr 1986–88, prof 1993–95; prof UEA 1995–2014; visiting prof: SUNY-Binghamton 1983, Univ of Siena 1984–87, Univ of Copenhagen 1987–88; dir Br Sch at Rome 1988–95, dir Prince of Wales' Inst of Architecture 1996–98; princ advsr Min of Culture Albania 1999, princ advsr Packard Humanities Inst Albania 2000–09, dir Univ of Pennsylvania Museum 2007–12, pres American Univ of Rome 2012–; maj archaeological excavations: Roystone Grange Derbyshire 1978–88, San Vincenzo al Volturno 1980–98, Montarrenti Siena 1982–87, Butrint Albania 1994–12, Maremma project ERC 2015–20; memb Packard Humanities Bd 2003–; FSA 1984; *Books* The Hamwih Pottery (1981), Dark Age Economics (1982), Mohammed, Charlemagne and Origins of Europe (1983), Primitive and Peasant Markets (1988), The Anglo-Saxon Achievement (1989), Wall-to-Wall History (1991), San Vincenzo al Volturno I (1993), San Vincenzo al Volturno 2 (1995), Light in the Dark Ages (1997), Towns and Trade in the Age of Charlemagne (2000), Visions of Rome: Thomas Ashby, Archaeologist (2000), Villa to Village (with R Francovich, 2003), Byzantine Butrint (ed, 2004), Goodbye to the Vikings (2006), Eternal Butrint (2006), Roman Butrint (ed, 2007), Rise and Fall of Byzantine Butrint (2008), The Triconch Palace (with Will Bowden, 2011), San Vincenzo Maggiore (2011), Dark Age Economics (2012), The Archaeology and Histories of an Ionian Port (ed, 2012), New Directions in Early Medieval Archaeology (ed, 2015); *Recreations* hill walking, listening to classical music; *Clubs* LoveItaly! (pres); *Style—* Prof Richard Hodges, OBE, FSA; ✉ American University of Rome, Via Pietro Roselli 4, Rome 00153, Italy (☎ 0039 06 5833 0919)

HODGES, Stephen Richard; *b* 23 May 1954; *Educ* Latymer Upper Sch, Trinity Hall Cambridge (MA); *m* 1980, Felice; 1 s, 1 da; *Career* barr-at-law 1976; Close Brothers Ltd: joined 1985, md 1990–2002, ceo 2002–; md Close Brothers Group plc 2002– (dir 1995–2002); *Recreations* fishing, walking, bridge, rare books; *Clubs* Flyfishers'; *Style—* Stephen Hodges, Esq; ✉ Close Brothers Group plc, 10 Crown Place, London EC2A 4FT (☎ 020 7655 3100, fax 020 7247 1203)

HODGKIN, Sir (Gordon) Howard Eliot; kt (1992), CH (2003), CBE (1977); s of Eliot Hodgkin, and Hon Katherine Mary Hodgkin, *née* Hewart; *b* 6 August 1932, London; *Educ* Camberwell Sch of Art London, Bath Acad of Art Corsham; *m* 16 April 1955, Julia Hazel Ann, da of Albert Ernest Lane; 2 s (Louis b 23 Oct 1957, Sam b 20 Feb 1960); *Career* artist (represented by Gagosian Gallery and Galleria Lawrence Rubin Milan); teacher: Charterhouse 1954–56, Bath Acad of Art Corsham 1956–66, Chelsea Sch of Art 1966–72; visiting lectr Slade and Chelsea Schs of Art London 1976–77, artist in residence BNC Oxford 1976–77; tstee: Tate Gallery London 1970–76, Nat Gallery London 1978–85; memb Exec Ctee Nat Art Collections Fund 1988–; second prize John Moore's Liverpool Exhibition 1976 and 1980, Turner Prize Tate Gallery London 1985, Shakespeare Prize 1997; hon fell BNC Oxford 1988; Hon DLitt Univ of London 1985, Hon DLitt Univ of Oxford 2000 *Collections* incl: Arts Cncl of GB, Br Cncl London, Govt Picture Collection London, Contemporary Art Soc London, Tate Gallery London, V&A London, Br Museum London, Scottish Nat Gallery of Modern Art Edinburgh, MOMA NY, Met Museum of Art NY, Museum of Art Carnegie Inst, Nat Gallery of Washington, Fogg Art Museum Cambridge Mass, Louisiana Museum Denmark, Modern Art Museum Fort Worth, Oldham Art Gallery, São Paulo Museum Brazil, St Louis Art Museum, Walker Art Center Minneapolis, S Aust Art Gallery Adelaide; *One Man Exhibitions* incl: Arthur Tooth and Sons London 1962, 1964 and 1967, Kasmin Gallery London 1969 and 1971, Arnolfini Gallery Bristol 1970, Galerie Muller Cologne 1971, Kornblee Gallery New York 1973, Serpentine Gallery London 1976, Waddington/Kasmin Galleries London 1976, MOMA Oxford 1976 and 1977, Andre Emmerich New York and Zurich 1977, Br Cncl exhbn touring India 1978 (graphics), Bernard Jacobson NY 1980 and 1981, LA 1981 and London 1982 (graphics), M Knoedler & Co New York 1981, 1982, 1984, 1986, 1988, 1990 and 1993–94, Waddington Galleries London 1980, 1988 and 1991 (graphics), Macquarie Galleries Sydney 1981, Tate Gallery London 1982, Br Pavilion Venice Biennale 1984, Phillips Collection Washington DC 1984, Yale Center for Br Art 1985, Kestner-Gesellschaft Hanover 1985, Whitechapel Art Gallery London 1985, Tate Gallery London 1985 (graphics), Michael Werner Gallery Cologne 1990, Anthony d'Offay Gallery London 1993 and 1999–2000, retrospective exhbn Metropolitan Museum of Art NY to Modern Art Museum Fort Worth then Der Kunstverein Düsseldorf and Hayward Gallery 1995–97, Galerie Lawrence Rubin Zurich 1997, Gagosian Gallery New York 1998 and 2003, Haas and Fuchs Galerie Berlin 1998, Galleria Lawrence Rubin Milan 2001, Dulwich Picture Gallery London 2001, Scottish Nat Gallery of Modern Art Edinburgh 2002, Gagosian Gallery LA 2004, Irish Museum of Modern Art Dublin (major retrospective touring to Tate Britain London and Reina Sofia Madrid) 2006, Howard Hodgkin Prints 2006, Cross Street Gallery London, Barbican Int Exhibitions tour, Laing Art Gallery Newcastle-upon-Tyne 2006, Abbott Hall Art Gallery Cumbria 2007, Ormeau Art Gallery Belfast 2007, Howeard Hodgkin Paintings 1992–2007 (Yale Centre for Br Art and Fitzwilliam Museum Cambridge) 2007, Howard Hodgkin Paintings (Gagosian Gallery) 2008, Winchester Discovery Gallery 2008, Turnpike Gallery Leigh 2008, PM Gallery and House Ealing 2009, Howard Hodgkin Seven New Paintings (Gagosian Gallery) 2009, As Time Goes By Print Show (Alan Cristea Gallery London) 2009 and (Southampton City Art Gallery) 2010, Time and Place (Modern Art Oxford and De Pont Museum of Contemporary Art Tilburg Netherlands) 2010 and (San Diego Museum of Art) 2011, Scarborough Art Gallery 2011; *Style—* Sir Howard Hodgkin, CH, CBE; ✉ c/o Gagosian Gallery, 6–24 Britannia Street, London, WC1X 9JD (☎ 020 7841 9960)

HODGKINSON, (James) Andrew; s of Peter George Hodgkinson (d 1986), of Lincoln, and Gwyneth Anne, *née* Evans (d 1984); *b* 22 January 1952; *Educ* City Sch Lincoln, Brighton Poly (BA); *m* 6 Sept 1996, Mariann Halkjaer; *Career* dir John Michael Design Consultants 1975–80, fndr and md Simons Design 1980–94, Main Bd dir and shareholder of The Simons Gp, fndr and md Hodgkinson & Co 1994; MInstD, MCSD 1989; *Recreations* design, art, polo and numerous sports, ethnography, natural history; *Clubs* Guards Polo; *Style—* Andrew Hodgkinson, Esq; ✉ Hodgkinson & Co, 29 Alexander Street, London W2 5NU

HODGKINSON, Sir Michael Stewart; kt (2003); s of Stewart Hodgkinson (d 2006), and Ruth, *née* Pentelow; *b* 7 April 1944, Berkhamsted; *Educ* Hornchurch GS, Univ of Nottingham; *m* April 1988, Elspeth, *née* Cherry; 1 s (Andrew b 1971), 2 da (Jessica Ridd Jones b 1974, Julia Needham b 1976); *Career* Ford Motor Co 1965–69, British Leyland 1969–83 (md Land Rover Ltd 1978–83), md UK Ops Express Dairy Gp, chief exec European Foods Div Grand Metropolitan plc 1983–92; chief exec BAA plc 1999–2003 (gp airports dir 1992–99); non-exec chm: Post Office Ltd 2003–07, First Choice Holidays plc 2004–; non-exec dir: FKI plc 2000–, Royal Mail plc 2003–; currently chm Keolis UK Ltd and dep chm TUI AG; memb Ct of Directors Bank of Ireland 2004–; chm Airports Advsy Cncl, memb Advsy Bd AviAlliance GmbH; memb Bd: Cmmn for Integrated Transport, Transport for London, Dublin Airport Authority; assoc memb Cost and Mgmnt Accountants; *Recreations* cinema, gardening, opera, travel, walking, theatre; *Style—* Sir Michael Hodgkinson

HODGKINSON, Paul Richard; CBE (2001); s of Peter George Hodgkinson, DL (d 1986), of St Georges House, Lincoln, and Gwyneth Anne, *née* Evans (d 1984); *b* 9 March 1956; *Educ* Lincoln GS, Oxford Poly (BA, DipArch); *m* 13 Oct 1984, Catherine Ann, da of George Giangrande, of New Vernon, NJ, USA; 2 s (Christopher Peter, Alexander George); *Career* Shepherd Epstein & Hunter 1975–76, Capital and Counties plc 1979–81, Simons Design Conslts 1981–86, chm and chief exec Simons Group Ltd 1986–; chm E Midlands Regional Ctee CBI 1997–98, chm Lincolnshire Training and Enterprise Cncl 1989–94, chm Notting Hill Housing Tst 2009–; tstee Mental Health Fndn 2013–; RIBA 1980, ARCUK; *Recreations* tennis, reading, golf, food; *Style—* Paul Hodgkinson, Esq, CBE; ✉ Simons Group Ltd, 991 Doddington Road, Lincoln LN6 3AA (☎ 01522 505000, fax 01522 525 500, e-mail paul.hodgkinson@simonsgroup.com)

HODGSON, Prof Emeritus Carole; *b* 1940, London; *Educ* Wimbledon Sch of Art, Slade Sch of Fine Art; *Career* artist; visiting prof of sculpture and painting Univ of Wisconsin 1968 and 1980, pt/t lectr Univ of Reading 1964–71, lectr in art Univ of London Inst of Educn 1975–79, visiting lectr Norwich Sch of Art 1979–87, visiting tutor RCA Painting Sch 1981–86; currently emeritus prof of sculpture and fine art Kingston Univ; appears in Br Sculptors of the Twentieth Century; fell RBS 1997; *Solo Exhibitions* Angela Flowers Gallery London 1973, 1977, 1979, 1984, 1989, 1994, 2005 and Flowers East London 1992, 1997, 2000 and 2005, UCW 1973, Royal Shakespeare Theatre Stratford 1975, Welsh Arts Cncl 1976, The Fine Arts Galleries Univ of Wisconsin 1980, The Wustum Museum Racine 1981, Lawrence Univ Appleton 1981, The Bedford Way Gallery Univ of London 1981, Llanelli Festival 1984, Christie's Fine Arts Courses London 1986, Whitefriars Museum Coventry 1991, New Ashgate Gallery Farnham 1991, Centro Cultural Recoleta Buenos Aires 1995, GEC Mgmnt Coll Rugby 1995, Sudbury bronzes in garden Gainsborough's house 1996, Patrick & Beatrice Haggerty Museum of Art Milwaukee 1999, Flowers West Santa Monica 1999, Flowers East Graphics Monoprints 2001, Monoprints (Wingfield Arts Suffolk) 2002, New Hall Cambridge 2014, Cardigan Ceredigion 2014, Journeys From Here 1968–2014 (Coach House Gallery St Dogmaels Abbey) 2014, Retrospective (Flowers Central London) 2015; *Group Exhibitions* incl: Br Art Show (Arts Cncl of GB touring Sheffield, Newcastle and Bristol) 1979, Probity of Art (Welsh Arts Cncl touring Wales, England, Spain and Turkey) 1980–82, RCA Painting Staff Exhibition 1981, City Gallery Arts Tst Milton Keynes 1984, Int Contemporary Art Fair London 1986, The Artist Day Book (Smiths Gallery London) 1987, Chicago Art Fair 1989, Bath Contemporary Print Fair 1990, Royal Acad Summer Exhibition 1990, Print of the Month (Flowers East London) 1990, Royal Acad Print Fair 1991, Islington Business Centre Art Fair 1991, Chelsea Harbour Sculpture 1993, Downeen Decade (Angela Flowers Ireland) 1994, Instituto Chileno-Britancio de Cultura Santiago1995, Grafica International Museo de Arte Contemporánea Santiago 1995, The Gallery Garden Broughton Stockbridge 1996, New Ashgate Gallery Farnham 1997 and 1998, Grand Valley State Univ 1999, Landscape (Angela Flowers) 1999, Gallery Artist Flowers Central 2000 and 2001, Palazzo Vendramin dei Carnini Venice 2000, Royal British Soc of Sculptors 2001, Oxford Brookes Univ 2001, FIDEM Paris 2002, Flowers East 2002, Flowers Central 2002, Pitshanger Manor 2003, Drawing as Process 2003, Martini Arte Internazionale Manufactured in the UK Turin 2003, Contemporary Br Sculpture (Gallery Chesterfield) 2005, 1979 Br Art Show Revisited (Bloomberg Space) 2005, Leinster Gallery Dublin 2006, New Works (Flowers Gallery) 2007, FIDEM Medal Exhibition USA 2008, 40 Year (Flowers East) 2010, Prints (Flowers Gallery London) 2012; *Commissions* incl: bronze sculpture for British Aerospace Kingston upon Thames 1986–87, medal for Br Medal Soc (commemorating' Bogman' exhibition Br Museum) 1987, bronze 'River Celebration' cmmnd by Royal Borough of Kingston upon Thames 1988–90, still life bronze cmmnd by Knee Surgery Unit Wellington Hosp 1996, wall sculpture cmmnd by Wingfield Arts Suffolk 2002, 8 wall-based sculptures cmmnd by Marie Curie Hospice Hampstead 2008 and 2009; *Work in Collections* Cardiff Museum, Reading Museum and Art Gallery, Arts Cncl of GB, Dept of the Environment, Br Cncl, Contemporary Arts Soc, Univ of London, Unilever House, Welsh Contemporary Arts Soc, Pontevedra Museum, Bello Piñeiro Museum Ferrol, La Escuelo Nacional de Bellas Artes Buenos Aires, Universidad Católica Santiago, Manpower, private collections in Europe, USA, Mexico and Aust; *Awards* Univ of Reading res grant to travel Mexico 1968, Arts Cncl of GB Award 1973, Br Cncl Award 1978 and 1980, The Elephant Tst Award 1979 and 1986, Grocers' Co bursary Br Sch at Rome 1982, Kingston Univ res grant to travel to China 1993 and to Chile and Argentina 1995, Br Cncl USA Exhibitions 1998, Kingston Univ res grant 1999, Humanity Medal (Honorarium Prize) RBS/Worshipful Co of Goldsmiths 1993, Purchase Prize X Premio de Grabado Maximo Ramos Ferrol Spain; *Publications* Vietnam (2009); contrib TES: Women Artist (1978), Sculpture a Missing Dimension in School Art (1980), From the Sea to the Wall (1995), Monograph (1999), From City to Lake (2005); *Style—* Prof Emeritus Carole Hodgson; ✉ c/o Flowers East, 82 Kingsland Road, London E2 8DP (website www.flowerseast.co.uk and www.flowersgalleries.com)

HODGSON, Charles Christopher (Charlie); s of Christopher Hodgson, and Christine Hodgson; *b* 12 November 1980, Halifax, Yorks; *Educ* Bradford GS, Univ of Durham; *m* 23 June 2007, Daisy, *née* Hartley; 1 s (Henry Charles b 1 April 2008), 1 da (Anastasia Christina b 22 Sept 2009); *Career* rugby union player; Sale Sharks 2000–11 (150 caps, winners European Challenge Cup 2005, winners Guinness Premiership 2006), Saracens 2011–; England: 34 caps, full debut v Romania 2001 (highest English individual point scorer with 44 points), also represented Under 18s and Under 21s (incl World Championships Australia 2001); memb squad Br & I Lions tour to NZ 2005; patron Yorkshire Air Ambulance Charity; *Recreations* listening to music, tennis, golf; *Clubs* West End Golf Halifax; *Style—* Charlie Hodgson, Esq; ✉ c/o Saracens, Kingsley House, Unit 3, Sandridge Park, Porters Wood, St Albans AL3 6PH

HODGSON, Christine Mary; da of Anthony Pickles, and Audrey, *née* Bingham; *b* 17 November 1964, Preston, Lancs; *Educ* Elmslie Girls' Sch Blackpool, Loughborough Univ (BSc Hons); *m* 3 Sep 1999, Howard Hodgson; 1 s (George b 24 Nov 2006); *Career* Coopers & Lybrand 1985–94, Ronson plc 1994–97, Capgemini UK plc 1997– (exec chm 2011–); non-exec dir Ladbrokes plc 2012–, non-exec dir Standard Chartered Bank 2013–; memb Prof Services Business Cncl; memb Bd: Prince of Wales's Business in the Community, The Tech Partnership; chm The Careers & Enterprise Company 2015–; First Women Award for Finance 2008, Woman of the Year CWT Everywoman in Technol Awards 2011, Distinguished Alumni Award Loughborough Univ 2012; FCA; *Style—* Ms Christine Hodgson; ✉ Capgemini UK plc, 40 Holborn Viaduct, London EC1N 2PB

HODGSON, HE George Wilson; *Career* diplomat; desk offr EU Enlargement Team FCO 2002–03, second sec Kabul 2004, second sec Brussels UK Representation to the EU 2005–06, first sec Islamabad 2008–10, political cnsllr 2010–11, sr advsr Office of the Special Rep for Afghanistan and Pakistan US Dept of State 2011–12, head Europe Parly and Comms Dept FCO 2012–14, head Ebola Taskforce FCO 2014–15, ambass to Repub of Senegal and non-resident ambass to Repub of Cabo Verde and to Repub of Guinea Bissau 2015–; *Style—* HE Mr George Hodgson

HODGSON, Godfrey Michael Talbot; s of Arthur Benjamin Hodgson (d 1962), of York, and Jessica, *née* Hill (d 1947); *b* Horsham, Sussex, England; *Educ* Winchester (open scholar, Goddard leaving scholarship, cricket first XI), Magdalen Coll Oxford (Demy open scholar, MA), Univ of Pennsylvania (MA); *m* 1, 1958 (m dis 1970), Alice Anne Simone, da of Jacques Vidal, Légion d'Honneur, MM; 2 s (Pierre Thomas Godfrey b 1959, Francis James Samuel b 1960); m 2, 1970, Hilary Mary (d 2015), da of Brian F C Lamb; 2 da (Jessica b 1971, Laura b 1974); *Career* reporter TES 1956, reporter The Times 1958; The Observer: wrote Mammon column 1960, Washington corr 1962–65; reporter This Week (ITV) 1965–67; ed Insight Sunday Times 1967–71, foreign features ed 1971; freelance 1972–90, presenter The London Programme (LWT) 1976–81, presenter of progs incl The

Great Depression (ITV) 1981 and Reagan on Reagan (Channel 4) 1988; foreign ed The Independent and The Independent on Sunday 1990–92, dir Reuter Fndn Prog Univ of Oxford 1992–2001; fell Green Coll Oxford 1993–2001, distinguished fell Rothermere American Inst Univ of Oxford, sr memb St Antony's Coll Oxford; contrib articles and reviews to numerous pubns incl: Sunday Times, The Economist, New Statesman, NY Times, FT, Washington Post, The Independent, and various academic jls; Sarah Tryphena Phillips lectr Br Acad 1999; Hon DHL Univ of the South TN 2009; memb Soc of American Historians; *Books* incl: Carpetbaggers et Ku-Klux Klan (in French, 1965), An American Melodrama (with L Chester and B Page, 1969), Do You Sincerely Want to Be Rich? (with B Page and C Raw, 1970), In Our Time (1976), All Things to All Men (1980), Lloyd's of London (1986), The Colonel (1990), A New Grand Tour (1995), People's Century (1995), The World Turned Right Side Up (1996), The Gentleman from New York (2000), More Equal Than Others (2004), Woodrow Wilson's Right Hand: The Life of Colonel Edward M House (2006), A Great and Godly Adventure (2006), Sweet Evenlode (2008), The Myth of American Exceptionalism (2009), JFK and LBJ (2015); *Recreations* travelling, reading, listening to classical music, watching cricket; *Style*— Godfrey Hodgson, Esq; ✉ 32 The Playing Close, Charlbury OX7 3RJ (☎ 01608 811067, e-mail godfrey.hodgson@dsl.pipex.com)

HODGSON, Prof Humphrey Julian Francis; s of Harold Robinson Hodgson (d 1985), and Celia Frances Hodgson; *b* 5 May 1945; *Educ* Westminster (Queen's scholar), ChCh Oxford (scholar, MA, BSc, Martin Wronker Prize), St Thomas' Hosp Med Sch London (BM BCh, DM, Charles Box Prize in Med); *m* Shirley Victoria, da of Prof Lionel Penrose; 1 s (Julian b 1973), 1 da (Anna b 1974); *Career* research fell Massachusetts Gen Hosp Boston 1976–77, conslt physician Hammersmith Hosp 1978–99; Imperial Coll Sch of Med Hammersmith Hosp (Royal Postgraduate Med Sch until merger 1997): vice-dean 1989–97, prof of gastroenterology 1990–95, prof of med 1995–99; prof of med (Sheila Sherlock Chair) Royal Free and Univ Coll School of Med 1999–2011 (emeritus prof UCL 2012–), prof of medicine Univ of Namibia 2011–; vice-dean Royal Free and Univ Coll Medical Sch 2001–09; non-exec dir Royal Free Hampstead NHS Tst 2002–09; Radcliffe travelling fell UC Oxford 1976, Humphrey Davy Rolleston lectr RCP London 1991, Fitzgerald Peel lectr Scot Soc of Physicians 1993, Croonian lectr RCP London 2002; academic vice-pres RCP London 2008–11 (academic registrar 1993–97); ed Clinical Medicine 2011–, author of books and original articles on gastrointestinal and liver disease; pres Br Assoc of Study of the Liver 2003–05; chm: Liver Group Charity 1993–, Scientific Co-ordinating Ctee Arthritis Res Campaign 1996–2003; FMedSci; FRCP 1982 (MRCP 1972); *Recreations* walking, reading; *Style*— Prof Humphrey Hodgson; ✉ 40 Onslow Gardens, London N10 3JU (☎ 020 8883 8297); University College, Rowland Hill Street, London NW3 2PF (☎ 020 7433 2851, fax 020 7433 2852, e-mail h.hodgson@ucl.ac.uk)

HODGSON, James Simon; s of Simon Hodgson, and Victoria Hodgson; *b* 30 April 1969, Guildford, Surrey; *Educ* Wellington, Durham Univ (BA), Univ of Cambridge (PGCE, Cricket Blue); *m* 21 July 1994, Rachel Hodgson; 3 da (Henrietta b 30 March 1998, Juliet b 12 Oct 1999, Penelope b 5 Feb 2003), 1 s (Edward b 1 May 2001); *Career* with Ernst & Young 1991–93. Trinity GS Sydney Aust 1994–2000, Tonbridge Sch 2000–11, sr dep head Magdalen Coll Sch Oxford 2011–14, headmaster Bedford Sch 2014–; memb: ASCL, HMC; *Recreations* cricket, sailing, golf; *Clubs* MCC; *Style*— James Hodgson, Esq; ✉ Bedford School, De Parys Ave, Bedford MK40 2TU

HODGSON, Jonathan James; s of John Hodgson, of Sutton Coldfield, and Barbara, *née* Middlemiss; *b* 6 May 1960; *Educ* Park Hall Comp, Solihull Coll of Technol, Liverpool Poly (BA), RCA (MA); *Career* animation director, musician and soundtrack composer; co fndr Unicorn Productions 1985; freelance dir: Barry Joll Associates 1985–88, Practical Pictures 1985–88, Felix Films 1988–90, Bermuda Shorts 1991–93, Mojo Working 1993–94, Speedy Films 1995; co-fndr (with Jonathan Bairstow) Sherbet Ltd 1996; commercials, title sequences and short films for clients incl: UN, Brooke Bond, McVities, MTV, BBC, Channel Four, Lambie-Nairn, English-Markell-Pockett, Thames TV, SAAB USA, Prince Matchabelli, Initial TV, Bank of Switzerland, Bell Atlantic, Unilever; films credits incl: An Unseen Flight 1980, Dogs (first prize Stuttgart Trickfilmtage) 1981, Experiments In Movement and Line 1981, Night Club (6 int awards) 1983, Menagerie 1984, Train of Thought 1985, The Doomsday Clock (cmmnd by UN) 1987, Feeling My Way 1997 (5 int awards), The Man with the Beautiful Eyes 1999 (BAFTA award for Best Short Animation 2000 and 10 int awards), Camouflage 2001; art work published in European Illustration 1981–; *Recreations* digging; *Style*— Jonathan Hodgson, Esq

HODGSON, Mark Thomas; s of Thomas Hodgson (d 1975), and Joyce, *née* Page; *b* 2 December 1957, Bishop Auckland, Co Durham; *Educ* Barnard Castle Sch, Emmanuel Coll Cambridge (MA); *m* 5 June 1982, Janet, *née* Annas; 2 s (James b 30 July 1987, Edward b 13 Jan 1991), 1 da (Louise b 10 March 1993); *Career* slr; Woodham Smith 1981–84, ptnr Simmons & Simmons 1994–99 (joined 1984), ptnr and head Life Sciences Gp Taylor Wessing 1999–2007, London managing ptnr Howrey LLP 2007–10, ptnr Field Fisher Waterhouse LLP 2011–; chm Intellectual Property Lawyers Assoc; memb: Intellectual Property Court Users Ctee, Int Assoc for the Protection of Intellectual Property (AIPPI), Intellectual Property Owners Assoc (IPO), City of London Slrs' Co; *Recreations* sport, travel, gardening; *Style*— Mark Hodgson, Esq; ✉ Field Fisher Waterhouse LLP, 35 Vine Street, London EC3N 2AA (☎ 020 7861 4703, fax 020 7488 0084, e-mail mark.hodgson@ffw.com)

HODGSON, Dame Patricia Anne; DBE (2004, CBE 1995); da of Harold Hodgson, of Brentwood, Essex, and Lilian Mary, *née* Smith; *b* 19 January 1947; *Educ* Brentwood Co HS, Newnham Coll Cambridge (MA); *m* 23 July 1979, George Edward Donaldson, s of Edward George Donaldson, of Donington-le-Heath, Leics; 1 s; *Career* Cons Research Dept 1968–70, prodr BBC Open Univ (specialising in history and philosophy) 1970–82 (TV series incl: English Urban History 1978, Conflict in Modern Europe 1980, Rome in the Age of Augustus 1981), broadcaster and freelance journalist in UK and USA, ed Crossbow 1976–80; BBC: dep sec 1982–85, the sec 1985–87, head Policy and Planning Unit 1987–92, dir Policy and Planning 1993–99, dir Public Policy 2000; chief exec ITC 2000–03; chm Bow Group 1975–76; dir BARB 1987–98; chair HE Regulatory Review Gp 2004–06, chair Sch Teachers' Review Body 2012–14; memb: Monopolies & Mergers Cmmn 1993–99, London Arts Bd 1991–96, Statistics Cmmn 2000–06, Cncl Competition Cmmn 2004–11, Ctee on Standards in Public Life 2004–08, Bd HEFCE 2005–11, BBC Tst 2006–11, Ind Cmmn on Freedom of Information 2015–16; Ofcom: non-exec dir 2011–, dep chair 2012–14, chm 2014; govr Wellcome Tst 2004–08; non-exec dir GCap Media Gp plc 2004–06; Parly candidate (Cons) Islington 1974; princ Newnham Coll Cambridge 2006–12 (assoc fell 1994–96, visiting bye-fell 2004, hon fell 2013–); *Recreations* quietness; *Clubs* Oxford and Cambridge; *Style*— Dame Patricia Hodgson, DBE; ✉ Ofcom, 2A Southwark Bridge Road, London SE1 9HA (☎ 020 7981 3513)

HODGSON, Peter Barrie; s of Clive Ward (d 1980), and Gladys Stewart, *née* Ross (d 1983); *b* 12 March 1942; *Educ* Clayesmore Sch, St Peter's Coll Oxford (BA); *m* 10 Feb 1973, Audrone Ona, da of Jonas Grudzinskas (d 1992), formerly of Kretinga, Lithuania, and Ona Grudzinskiene (d 2007); 1 s (Lindsay Matthew Oliver b 3 Aug 1977); *Career* dir: Opinion Research Centre 1973–75, Professional Studies Ltd 1975–77; md: Professional Studies Ireland 1977–79, Action Research Ltd 1977–78; chm and md Travel and Tourism Research Ltd 1978–2010; dir: City Research Associates Ltd 1981–89, Quay Management (Waterside) Ltd 1999–2015; head of mktg Midsummer Opera 2012–; chm: Assoc of Br Market Research Cos 1987–89, Alliance of Int Market Research Insts 1991–94; memb Editorial Bd Jl of Consumer Research 2000–08; memb: Cncl Market Research Soc 1978–81, Cncl Tourism Soc 1981–84, Market Research Soc, Euro Soc for Opinion & Marketing Res; fndr memb Social Research Assoc; dep chm and memb Cncl Br Market Research Assoc 1998–2004; fell Tourism Soc 1980, FInstTT 1989; *Publications* author of articles in: Espaces (Paris), Imprints (Canada), Marketing, Jl of the Market Res Soc, Jl of the Professional Market Res Soc of Canada, Research Magazine, Research Plus, Jl of Travel Research (US), Survey, Tourism Management; *Recreations* opera, wine, travel, cats; *Style*— Peter Hodgson, Esq; ✉ 5 Park Vista, London SE10 9LZ (☎ 020 8853 1903, e-mail hodgsonpeter@yahoo.co.uk)

HODGSON, Peter John Dixon; CBE (1992, OBE 1979), DL (Cornwall 2006); s of John Dixon Hodgson (d 1998), of Manaton, Launceston, Cornwall, and Dorothy Blanche, *née* Saunders (d 1991); *b* 21 March 1947; *Educ* Charterhouse; *m* 18 July 1970, Cecilia Anne, da of Brig Arnold de Lerisson Cazenove, CBE, DSO, MVO (d 1969); 2 s (James b 1973, Timothy b 1975), 1 da (Charlotte b 1977); *Career* chartered accountant, sr ptnr Hodgsons 1972–2014; chm: Fin Ctee Red Cross Cornwall 1988–95, Western Area Nat Union of Cons and Unionist Assocs 1991–94, SRC Nat Union of Cons and Unionists Assocs 1995–98; chm of govrs: UC Falmouth (formerly Falmouth Coll of Arts) 1999–2007 (govr 1997–2007), Mount House Sch 2000–06 (govr 1993–2006); govr Sutton's Hosp Charterhouse; hon fell Falmouth Univ 2011; High Sheriff Cornwall 2005–06; FCA 1970; *Recreations* gardening, fishing; *Style*— Peter Hodgson, Esq, CBE, DL; ✉ Manaton, Launceston, Cornwall PL15 9JE (☎ 01566 772880); Hodgsons, 12 Southgate Street, Launceston, Cornwall PL15 9DP (☎ 01566 772177)

HODGSON, Roy; *b* 9 August 1947, Croydon; *Educ* John Ruskin GS; *Career* football mangr: Halmstads BK 1976–80 (Swedish champions 1976 and 1979), Bristol City 1980–82, Örebro SK 1983–85, Malmö FF 1985–90 (winners Svenska Cupen 1986 and 1989, Swedish League champions 1985, 1986, 1987, 1988 and 1989), Neuchâtel Xamax 1990–92, Switzerland nat team 1992–95, Internazionale 1995–97 (UEFA Cup finalists 1997) and 1999, Blackburn Rovers 1997–98, Grasshoppers 1999–2000, FC Copenhagen 2000–01 (winners Danish Superliga 2001), Udinese 2001, UAE nat team 2002–04, Viking FK 2004–06, Finland nat team 2006–07, Fulham 2007–10, Liverpool 2010–11, West Bromwich Albion 2011–12, England nat team 2012–16; *Style*— Roy Hodgson, Esq

HODGSON, Sharon; MP; *b* 1 April 1966; *Educ* Heathfield Sr HS, Newcastle Coll; *m* Alan; 2 c; *Career* Lab Pty organiser; Lab link co-ordinator Unison; MP (Lab): Gateshead E and Washington W 2005–10, Washington and Sunderland W 2010–; PPS to Dawn Primarolo, MP (as Min for Public Heath), PPS to Liam Byrne, MP (as Min of State for Immigration, Nationality and Citizenship), PPS to Bob Ainsworth, MP (as Armed Forces Min MOD), asst whip HM Treasy 2009–10, oppn whip House of Commons 2010, shadow min for educn 2010–13, shadow women and equalities min 2013–15, shadow education min 2015–16; Select Ctee membership: Regulatory Reform 2005–10, Ecclesiastical Ctee 2005, European Scrutiny Ctee 2005–06, Children, Schs and Families 2007–10, NE Regnl 2009–10, Ecclesiastical (Jt Ctee) 2010–, memb: Fabian Soc, Christian Socialist Movement, Communication Workers Union; *Style*— Mrs Sharon Hodgson, MP; ✉ House of Commons, London SW1A 0AA

HODGSON, Prof Shirley Victoria; da of Lionel Sharples Penrose, and Margaret, *née* Leathes; *b* 22 February 1945; *Educ* Hendon Co GS, UCL (BSc), Somerville Coll Oxford (BM BCh), Univ of Oxford (DM, DCH); *Career* house surgn Churchill Hosp Oxford 1969–70, house physician Cowley Rd Hosp Oxford 1970, house surgn (obstetrics and gynaecology) N Middx Hosp London 1970–71, registrar (paediatrics and med) Saadi and Pahlavi Hosps Shiraz Iran 1971–72, SHO (paediatrics) St Stephen's Hosp Chelsea 1972–73, registrar (paediatrics) Whittington Hosp London 1973–74, paediatric offr Islington Local HA 1974–75, trainee GP 1975–76, fell in paediatrics Psychosomatic Unit Children's Hosp Boston Mass 1976–77, asst GP Canonbury 1977–79, locum registrar S Thames (E) Regnl Genetics Centre Guy's 1979–80, registrar (paediatrics) Chase Farm Hosp Enfield 1980–83, sr registrar (clinical genetics) S Thames (E) Regnl Genetics Centre Guy's 1983–88, conslt clinical geneticist E Anglian Regnl Genetics Centre Addenbrooke's Hosp Cambridge 1988–90, dir Family Cancer Clinic St Mark's Hosp Northwick Park 1990–96, hon conslt clinical geneticist S Thames (E) Regnl Genetics Centre Guy's and St Thomas' NHS Tst Guy's 1990–2003, sr lectr in clinical genetics St Mark's Hosp and Bart's 1990–96, sr lectr in clinical genetics Div of Med and Molecular Genetics UMDS 1990–98, reader in clinical genetics GKT 1998–2003, prof of cancer genetics St George's Hospital London 2003– (now emeritus); part-time prof UNAM Medical Sch Namibia 2011–; currently locum conslt of cancer genetics Leicester; external examiner in genomic med MSc Univ of Birmingham; memb Public and Professional Policy Ctee Soc for Human Genetics 2001–13; D(Obst)RCOG 1970; FRCP 1993 (MRCP 1982), FSB; *Publications* A Practical Guide to Human Cancer Genetics (jt ed, 1993, 4 edn 2014), Inherited Susceptibility to Cancer: Clinical, Predictive and Ethical Perspectives (jt ed, 1998), Familial Breast and Ovarian Cancer (jt ed, 2002); numerous book chapters and jl papers; *Recreations* cycling, walking, painting, classical music; *Style*— Prof Shirley Hodgson; ✉ Department of Clinical Genetics, St George's University of London, Jenner Wing, Cranmer Terrace, London SW17 0RE (☎ 020 8725 5279, fax 020 8266 6410, e-mail shodgson@sgul.ac.uk)

HODGSON, Simon; *Career* chief exec Forest Enterprise England; *Style*— Simon Hodgson, Esq; ✉ Forest Enterprise England, 340 Bristol Business Park, Coldharbour Lane, Bristol BS16 1EJ

HODGSON OF ABINGER, Baroness (Life Peer UK 2013), of Abinger in the County of Surrey; Fiona Ferelith Hodgson; CBE (2012); da of Keith Storr Allom; *Educ* Queen Anne's Sch Berks, Guildford HS; *m* 8 May 1982, Robin Hodgson (now Lord Hodgson of Astley Abbotts, CBE, *qv*); 4 s (Barnaby Peter Granville b 1986, James Maxwell Gower (twin) b and d 1986, Toby Henry Storr b 1988, Hugo Edward Valentine b 1992), 1 da (Poppy Ferelith Alice b 1990); *Career* dir Johnson Bros & Co 1989–; Cons Pty: hon vice-pres Cons Women's Orgn 1992– (dep chm 2002–05, chm 2005–08, pres 2008–11), memb Cons Human Rights Cmmn 2009–, vice chm Cons Policy Forum, elected rep sitting on pty bd Nat Cons Convention 2009–12 (vice-pres 2009–11, pres 2011–12), patron Cons Friends of Int Devpt 2012–; delegate Cmmn on Status of Women at UN in NY 2008–15; memb: Advsy Bd Widows for Peace Through Democracy 2008–, All-Pty Parly Gp on Women, Peace and Security 2008– (co-chair 2015–), UN Women UK 2009–, Leadership Circle of Women for Women 2009–13, Assoc of Oxfam 2009–15, Steering Bd Preventing Sexual Violence Initiative 2012–, Select Ctee on Sexual Violence in Conflict 2015–; chm Advsy Bd Gender Action for Peace & Security (GAPS) 2009–, tstee Chalker Fndn 2010–, patron Afghan Connection 2011–, fndr memb Afghan Women's Support Forum 2012–; memb: Nat Cncl of Women's Animal Welfare Ctee 1984–86, Nat Birthday Tst Fund 1989–93, Farm Animal Welfare Cncl 1989–97, Gen Cncl and Appeals Ctee of Wellbeing 1993–2006, APPROP 1997–2001, Advsy Ctee on Animal Foodstuffs Food Standards Agency 2001–04, Cncl of Int Social Services UK 2003–04, Ind Health Forum 2003–04, European Union of Women 2006–, Ind Sector Working Gp 2006–09, Ind Doctors Fedn (ISAAC) Gp 2010–14, Women's Justice Taskforce 2010–; non-exec dir Barnet District Health Authy 1992–94, chm PTA Thomas's Sch Kensington 1999–2001, chair Governance Gp ISCAS (Ind Health Advsy Services Complaints and Adjudication Service) 2012–; FRGS 2011 (memb 2005); *Recreations* travel, riding, walking, cookery; *Style*— Baroness Hodgson of Abinger, CBE; ✉ House of Lords, London SW1A 0PW

HODGSON OF ASTLEY ABBOTTS, Baron (Life Peer UK 2000), of Nash in the County of Shropshire; Robin Granville; CBE (1992); s of late Henry Edward Hodgson, of Astley Abbotts, Salop, and Natalie Beatrice, *née* Davidson; *b* 25 April 1942; *Educ* Shrewsbury, Univ of Oxford (BA), Wharton Sch Univ of Pennsylvania (MBA); *m* 8 May 1982, Fiona

Ferelith, da of Keith Storr Allom; 4 s (Barnaby Peter Granville b 1986, James Maxwell Gower (twin) b and d 1986, Toby Henry Storr b 1988, Hugo Edward Valentine b 1992), 1 da (Poppy Ferelith Alice b 1990); *Career* Lt 4 Bn Kings Shrops LI TA 1960–64; chm: Granville Baird Gp (investment bankers) 1972–2003 (also former gp chief exec), Nasdim 1979–85, Rostrum Gp 2000–08, Nova Capital Gp 2002–, RFIB Gp Ltd 2007–; non-exec chm: Spotlaunch plc, Walter Alexander plc 1990–92; dir: Dominic Hunter plc 1992–2002, Community Hospital plc 1995–2001, Staffordshire Building Society 1995–2004; non-exec dir Marston's plc (formerly Wolverhampton and Dudley Breweries plc) 2002–; memb West Midland Industrial Devpt Bd 1988–96; dir: Securities and Investment Bd 1985–89, Securities and Futures Authy 1991–2002; MP (Cons) Walsall N 1976–79, chm Cons Party W Midlands Area 1991–94 (treas 1985–91); Nat Union of Cons Assocs: memb Exec Ctee 1988–98, vice-pres 1995–96, chm 1996–98; dep chm Cons Pty 1998–2000, chm Nat Cons Convention 1998–2000; chm Red Tape Task Force 2010–11, official reviewer Charities Act 2011–12; Liveryman Worshipful Co of Goldsmiths; tstee and hon fell St Peter's Coll Oxford; *Style*— The Rt Hon the Lord Hodgson of Astley Abbotts, CBE; ✉ House of Lords, London SW1A 0PW (☎ 020 7219 8256); Nova Capital Management Ltd, 1st Floor, Cayzer House, 30 Buckingham Gate, London SW1E 6NN (☎ 020 7901 1760)

HODKINSON, James Clifford (Jim); s of John Eric Thomas Hodkinson (d 1985), of Ferndown, Dorset, and Edith Lilian, *née* Lord; *b* 21 April 1944; *Educ* Salesian Coll Farnborough; *m* 8 Feb 1969, Janet Patricia, da of George William Lee (d 1941); 1 da (Justine b 30 April 1970); *Career* trainee mangr F W Woolworth 1962–71; B & Q plc: mangr Bournemouth Store 1971–74, sales mangr in South 1974–79, ops dir 1979–84, ops and personnel dir 1984–86, chief exec 1986–92, int devpt dir 1992–94, chm and chief exec 1994–1998; chm (DIY) Kingfisher plc 1994–1998; chief exec New Look plc 1998–2000; non-exec chm: Furniture Village plc 2002–, Ideal Shopping Direct 2004–07, Wyevale Garden Centres 2005–08; non-exec dir: Hamleys plc 1994–2003, Provident Financial plc 1998–2000, B&Q Int Ltd 2002–03, Polymer Logistics Hldgs Ltd 2002–06, Big Ideas Mgmnt Ltd 2002–05, Edinburgh Woollen Mill plc 2004–05, Ultimate Products 2007–, IMO 2010–; FInstD, CIMgt; *Recreations* golf, shooting; *Style*— Jim Hodkinson, Esq

HODSON, Beverley; OBE (2003); da of Clifford Vernon Hodson (d 1984), of London, and Frances Jeanne Hodson, *née* Cox (d 1971), of London; *b* 14 June 1951, Brenchley, Tunbridge Wells, Kent; *Educ* Univ of Cambridge (BA, Women's Lawn Tennis capt and blue); *m* Peter John Cottingham; 1 s (Thomas Hodson Cottingham b 14 April 1988), 3 step-da; *Career* business gen mangr Boots The Chemist 1989–95 (various positions 1978–89); md: Childrens World 1995–96, Dolcis Cable 1996–97, WH Smith 1997–2004; non-exec dir: Trent FM GWR Radio 1990–97, M&G (Fin Services/Unit Tst) 1998–99, Legal & General 2000–07, First Milk 2005–, Robert Wiseman Dairies 2005–10, Vedior NV 2006–08, Randstad 2008–15, NFU Mutual 2008–12; hon sec AT Med Research Tst; memb Regnl Devpt Agency Yorks and N Humberside 1990–97; memb Nat Coll of Sch Leadership 1999–2005, hon assoc Newnham Coll Cambridge 2012– (vice-pres Newnham Coll Associates 1998–2008), memb Cncl Univ of Glos, chair F&GP Employment Ctees; memb: RSA, WACL, Int Women's Forum (IWF) 1995–; *Recreations* tennis, skiing, walking, swimming, reading, theatre, music, cinema, gardening, cookery; *Clubs* RSA, WACL, Forum UK; *Style*— Beverley Hodson, OBE

HODSON, Prof Howard Peter; s of Edward Hodson, and late Kathleen Janette Hodson; *b* 18 February 1957; *Educ* Churchill Coll Cambridge (MA, PhD); *m* 1978, Dr Jane Hodson; *Career* engr Perkins Engine Co Ltd 1978–79; Dept of Engrg Univ of Cambridge: res asst Whittle Lab 1982–85, sr asst in res 1985–89, lectr 1989–98, reader in thermofluid engrg 1998–2000, prof of aerothermal technol 2000–12; Girton Coll Cambridge: res fell 1984–85, dir of studies 1985–2000, lectr 1985–, professorial fell 2000–12 (official fell 1985–2000), life fell 2012–; dir and sec CTC Ltd 1983–2005; CEng 1999, FRAeS 1999, FASME 2002, FREng 2005; *Publications* author of papers published in transactions of: ASME, American Inst of Aeronautics and Astronautics, IMechE; *Recreations* gardening, veteran motor vehicles; *Style*— Prof Howard Hodson; ✉ Whittle Laboratory, Department of Engineering, University of Cambridge, Madingley Road, Cambridge CB3 0DY (☎ 01223 337588, fax 01223 337596, e-mail hph1000@cam.ac.uk)

HODSON, Phillip I; *Educ* Univ of Oxford; *Partner* Anne Hooper; 1 s (Alexander), 2 step s (Barnaby, Joel); *Career* psychotherapist, broadcaster, lecturer and writer; ed Forum (int jl of human rels) 1972–79; problem page columnist: Psychology Today, SHE Magazine (columnist of the year 1984), Woman's World, Family Circle, TV Quick, Today newspaper, Daily Star, OK Weekly, Woman's Journal; contributing ed Cosmopolitan Magazine 1994–96, regular contrib The Times 2003– and Woman & Home Magazine 2007–10; host LBC Radio problem phone-in 1976–91, agony columnist News of the World 1992–94, counsellor BBC Radio 2 1995–99, counsellor Talk Radio 1996–98; numerous appearances on TV incl own shows for TVS, LWT, and as presenter of BBC1's Daytime UK, Going Live! and Channel 4's Sex Box, prodr-presenter of award winning films on counselling skills; author of numerous books on related subjects and also on opera; past chm and tstee Impotence Assoc; fell and former head of media relations British Assoc for Counselling and Psychotherapy, spokesperson UK Cncl for Psychotherapy; past pres Tetbury CC; FRSA; *Books* Wagner (1984), Men: An Investigation into the Emotional Male (1984), Cosmopolitan Guide to Love, Sex and Relationships (1997), How to Make Great Love to a Man/Woman (2000), How 'Perfect' is your Partner? (2004); *Recreations* watching cricket, playing piano, opera, mending broken objects and machines; *Clubs* Groucho; *Style*— Phillip Hodson, Esq; ✉ website www.philliphodson.co.uk

HOERNER, John Lee; s of Robert Lee Hoerner (d 1990), and Lulu Alice, *née* Stone, of St Louis, MO; *b* 23 September 1939, Lincoln, Nebraska; *Educ* Univ of Nebraska (BS, BA); *m* 1, 9 Aug 1959 (m dis 1971), Susan Kay, da of Fred W Morgan, of Lincoln, NE; 1 s (John Scott b 30 May 1960), 1 da (Joanne Lynne b 21 Sept 1962); m 2, 16 Feb 1973, Anna Lea, da of Leonard O Thomas, of Kansas City, MO; *Career* Hovland-Swanson Lincoln NE 1959–68, Woolf Brothers Kansas City MO 1968–72, Hahnes NJ 1972–73, pres and ceo First 21st Century Corp McLean VA, Hahnes NJ 1974–81; Associated Dry Goods Corp/May Co: chm and chief exec H & S Pogue Co Cincinnati OH 1981–82, chm and chief exec L S Ayres & Co Indianapolis IN 1982–87; The Burton Gp plc: chm Debenhams 1987–92, chm Harvey Nichols 1988–91, gp chief exec 1992–98; chief exec Arcadia Gp plc 1998–2000; Tesco plc: chief exec clothing 2001–05, ceo Central Europe Clothing 2005–08, conslt 2008–; non-exec dir BAA plc 1998–2004; chm British Fashion Cncl 1997–2000; chm The Dogs' Home Battersea 2002–06 (vice-chm 1995–2002); *Books* Ayres Adages (1983), The Director's Handbook (1991), Recipes for Retailers (2015); *Recreations* dogs, flying; *Clubs* The Air Squadron, Groucho, Travellers; *Style*— John Hoerner, Esq; ✉ Hawling Lodge, Hawling, Cheltenham, Gloucestershire GL54 5SY (☎ 01451 850223, fax 01451 850741, e-mail john.hoerner@btinternet.com); ☎ 07802 771043, e-mail john.hoerner.uk.tesco.com

HOEY, Catharine Letitia (Kate); MP; da of Thomas Hoey, and Letitia Hoey; *b* 21 June 1946; *Educ* Belfast Royal Acad, Ulster Coll of Physical Educn, City of London Coll (BSc); *Career* lectr Southwark Coll 1972–76, sr lectr Kingsway Coll 1976–85, educnl advsr to London Football Clubs 1985–89; memb Hackney Borough Cncl 1978–82, Parly candidate (Lab) Dulwich 1987, MP (Lab) Vauxhall June 1989–, shadow min for Citizens Rights and Equality 1992–93; memb: Select Ctee on Broadcasting, Political Ctee South East CWS 1984–, Select Ctee on Social Security 1994–97; PPS to Rt Hon Frank Field, MP as min of state for Welfare Reform DSS 1997–98, Parly under sec Home Office 1998–99, Parly under-sec of state Dept of Culture, Media and Sport (sport) 1999–2001; chm Countryside Alliance 2005–; author of various articles on sport; *Recreations* watching soccer, keeping fit; *Style*— Kate Hoey, MP; ✉ House of Commons, London SW1A 0AA

HOFFMAN, Anthony Edward; s of late Geoffrey and late Jean Hoffman; *b* 21 February 1937; *Educ* City of London Sch; *Career* admitted slr 1960; slr advocate (Higher Courts Civil); sole practitioner 1960–62, former sr ptnr and head of litigation Hamlin Slowe, conslt slr Edwin Coe Slrs; former dep costs judge, dep Chancery master and dep Queen's Bench master Supreme Court, dep dist judge Princ Registry Family Div, dep dist judge County Court, dep adjudicator to HM Land Registry; chm Friends of St Pancras Housing 1995–2001, vice-chm St Pancras Properties Ltd 1995–2001, chm Gear 2009–13, vice-chm Glos Housing Assoc 2010–12, dir/tstee Age UK Glos 2015–; *Books* Civil Costs Cases: Taxation Handbook (1997, 3 edn 2003); *Recreations* game shooting, hill walking, theatre, arts, architecture; *Clubs* Circolo Unione Venezia; *Style*— Anthony E Hoffman, Esq

HOFFMAN, Gary Andrew; s of Dennis Hoffman, of Coventry, Warks, and Joyce, *née* Watkins; *Educ* Bablake Sch Coventry, Queens' Coll Cambridge (BA), Henley Mgmnt Coll; *m* 2003, Nicola; 1 s (Nathan b 22 March 2003); *Career* Barclays Bank plc: joined 1982, chief exec UK retail banking 1998, md mktg and distribution 1999–2001, chief exec Barclaycard 2001–06, gp vice-chm 2006–; non-exec dir Trinity Mirror plc 2005–; *Recreations* Coventry City FC, golf; *Clubs* Coventry Sch Former Pupils Assoc; *Style*— Gary Hoffman, Esq; ✉ Barclays Bank plc, 54 Lombard Street, London EC3P 2AH

HOFFMAN, George Henry; s of George Hoffman (d 1993), and Anna Cecilia, *née* Hojnowski (d 2004); *b* 30 October 1939; *Educ* Cornell Univ (BA), Columbia Univ (MA); *m* 1961 (m dis 1998); 2 da (Erika b 1962, Bridgit b 1965), 1 s (Philip b 1968); *Career* banker 1962–88, chm and chief exec GHH Mgmnt Conslts 1988–; memb Ad Hoc Cncl Euro Govt Business Relations Cncl 1979–; former dir American C of C UK; Massive Open Online Courses (MOOC) certificates of achievement: Univ of Edinburgh, Univ of Toronto, Harvard Univ, Univ of Pennsylvania, Cornell Univ, Univ of Valencia; *Recreations* theatre, reading, tennis, travel; *Clubs* Cornell, Columbia; *Style*— George Hoffman; ✉ c/o GHH Management Consultants, PO Box 71, Guildford, Surrey GU3 3XY (☎ 01483 306820, mobile 07810 104238, e-mail ghhoffman@gmail.com, website www.georgehhoffman.com)

HOFFMAN, Mark; s of Dr Mark Hoffman (d 1975), of USA; *b* 14 December 1938; *Educ* Harvard Univ (AB), Trinity Coll Cambridge (MA), Harvard Business Sch (MBA); *m* 1968, Mary Jo, da of John C Pyles, of Washington DC, USA; 3 s (Nicholas b 1969, John b 1972, James b 1978); *Career* E African Common Services Orgn/MIT (Africa/USA) 1964–66, World Bank's International Finance Corp (Washington) 1966–68, Olympic Investment Gp (Paris) 1968–69; dir: Hambros Bank (UK) 1970–74, Millipore Corp (USA) 1975–2010, George Weston Ltd (Canada) 1975–2008 (fin dir 1975–80, pres Weston Resources 1980–82), Guinness Peat Group plc (UK) 1982–84 (gp md 1982–83), LAC Minerals (Canada) 1984–86, Guinness Flight Global Asset Management Ltd (UK) 1989–97, Glenhuron Bank Ltd (Barbados) 1989–, Glenmaple Reinsurance Ltd (Barbados) 1989–, Advent International Inc (Boston) 1989–; chm: International Financial Markets Trading Ltd (UK) 1984–93, Cambridge Research Group Ltd 1990–2009, Guinness Flight Venture Capital Trust plc 1997–2008, Hermes Focus Asset Management Ltd 1998–2001 (dir 2002–09); int dir Harvard Alumni Assoc 1989–92, vice-pres United World Colls Int and Exec Bds 1999– (chm 1993–99); chm Oxford and Cambridge Rowing Fndn 1990–94; *Clubs* Boodle's, Leander (chm 1989–93), Oxford and Cambridge, Hawks' (Cambridge), Guards Polo, Toronto, Harvard (UK pres 1988–93); *Style*— Mark Hoffman, Esq; ✉ 14 Barrington House, Cambridge CB2 7TY (e-mail markhoffman1@aol.com); Cambridge Research Group Ltd, Salisbury House, Station Road, Cambridge CB1 2LA

HOFFMAN, Maxine; da of Philip Porter (d 2002), and Beatrice, *née* Sims; *b* 5 January 1951, London; *m* 9 Jan 1972, Anthony Hoffman; 1 s (Nick b 17 Sept 1976), 1 da (Zoë b 18 Dec 1979); *Career* with Citizens Advice Bureau 1983–87, with J M Associates 1992–94, agent London Management 1994–2002, agent Curtis Brown Gp 2002–; *Recreations* theatre, cinema, reading; *Style*— Mrs Maxine Hoffman; ✉ Curtis Brown Group Ltd, Haymarket House, 28–29 Haymarket, London SW1Y 4SP (☎ 020 7393 4470, fax 020 7393 4401, e-mail hoffman@curtisbrown.co.uk)

HOFFMAN, Tom; s of Dirk Hoffman (d 1986), of Cambridge, and Marie-Luise, *née* Leyser (d 1999); *b* 9 August 1945, Cambridge; *Educ* St John's Coll Sch Cambridge, The Leys Sch Cambridge, Univ of Exeter (LLB); *m* June 1971, Verena; 1 s (Alexander b 1975); *Career* Spicer & Pegler 1963–70, Arthur Andersen 1970–71, Williams & Glyn's Bank 1971–76, Hill Samuel & Co 1976–78, dir of capital markets Lloyds Bank International 1978–84, dep md Fuji International Finance 1984–89, head of corporate banking in UK Algemene Bank Nederland NV 1989–91, gen mangr UK and Ireland Banco Espírito Santo 1991–2003, dir Espírito Santo plc 1999–2005; sr advsr Bd Banif Financial Gp 2004–12; Bd Guildhall Sch of Music and Drama 2003–12 (chm 2009–12), Bd London Festival Orch 1996–2008 (chm 2004–08), Advsy Bd The Sixteen Choir and Orch 2001–08 (chm 2004–08); tstee: Maryport Heritage Tst Cumbria 1989–96, Portuguese Arts Tst 1992–2001, City Arts Tst and City of London Festival 2003–16, Stour Festival Company 2008 (chm 2014–), Corp of the Sons and Friends of the Clergy 1996–, Cncl of Almoners Christ's Hospital Fndn 2006–10 (chm Finance Ctee 2006–08); Univ of Exeter: memb Audit Ctee 1999–2005 (chm 2003–05), memb Univ Cncl 2003–06; govr: City of London Sch for Girls 2002– (chm 2003–06), Birkbeck Univ of London 2004–11, KCH NHS Fndn Tst 2004–11, Guy's and St Thomas' NHS Fndn Tst 2012–; memb Cncl UK-Portuguese C of C 1993–2003 (chm 1998–2001, hon vice-pres 2003–); memb City of London Corp: Ct of Common Cncl 2002–, Community Servs Ctee 2002–04, Markets Ctee 2002–, Planning and Transportation Ctee 2002–12, City Lands and Bridge House Estates Ctee 2004–06, Port Health and Environmental Servs Ctee 2004–10, Livery Ctee 2005–11, Gresham Ctee 2005– (chm 2011–14), Finance Ctee 2006–, Culture, Heritage and Libraries Ctee 2011–; Bd of Govrs: Museum of London 2008–, Barbican Centre 2009–; Cncl Gresham Coll 2009– (vice-chm 2013–14), tstee Guildhall Sch Tst 2007–12; hon treas: Ward of Cordwainer Club London 1985– (chm 1993–94), Vintry and Dowgate Wards Club (chm 2001–02); memb Ct Hon Irish Soc 2004–12 (dep govr 2009–10); hon treas Guildhall Historical Assoc 2008–; Ct Worshipful Co of Tylers and Bricklayers 1979– (Master 2006–07); memb Royal Soc for Asian Affrs 1985–; fell Birkbeck Univ of London 2012–; FCA 1981 (ACA 1971), FRSA 1990; *Publications* various articles in banking, finance and accountancy journals, and on histories of guilds outside London, bibliography on guilds of Great Britain and Ireland published on Birkbeck College website; *Recreations* gardening, listening to music, eating crab and drinking fine wine, collecting and reading histories of medieval guilds, collection of 1800 books on rowing from 34 countries donated to Leander in 2012; *Clubs* City Livery, Leander; *Style*— Tom Hoffman; ✉ Old Curteis, Biddenden, Kent TN27 8JN; 72 Gainsford Street, Tower Bridge Square, London SE1 2NB

HOFFMANN, Baron (Life Peer UK 1995), of Chedworth in the County of Gloucestershire; Sir Leonard Hoffmann; kt (1985), PC (1992); s of B W Hoffmann, of South Africa; *b* 8 May 1934; *Educ* South African Coll Sch Cape Town, Univ of Cape Town (BA), The Queen's Coll Oxford (Vinerian Law scholar, MA, BCL); *m* 1957, Gillian Lorna, *née* Sterner; 2 da; *Career* advocate Supreme Court of South Africa 1958–60, called to the Bar Gray's Inn 1964 (bencher 1984), QC 1977, judge Courts of Appeal Jersey and Guernsey 1980–85, judge of the High Court of Justice (Chancery Div) 1988–92, a Lord Justice of Appeal 1992–95, a Lord of Appeal in Ordinary 1995–2009; non-permanent judge Hong Kong Court of Final Appeal 1998–; Stowell civil law fell UC Oxford 1961–73; memb: Royal Cmmnon Gambling 1976–78, Cncl of Legal Educn 1983–92; pres Br-German Jurists Assoc 1991–2009; dir ENO 1985–94; Hon DCL: City Univ 1992, UWE 1995, Univ of Glos

2003; hon fell The Queen's Coll Oxford 1992, hon fell Chartered Inst of Taxation 2006; *Style*— The Rt Hon Lord Hoffmann, PC; ✉ House of Lords, London SW1A 0PW

HOFMEYR, Stephen Murray; QC (2000); s of late Jan Murray Hofmeyr, of Cape Town, and Stella Mary, *née* Mills; *b* 10 February 1956; *Educ* Diocesan Coll Rondebosch, Univ of Cape Town (BCom, LLB), UC Oxford (MA); *m* 28 June 1980, Audrey Frances, da of late James Murray Cannan, of Cape Town; 3 c (Timothy, Paul, Rebecca (triplets) b 6 July 1986); *Career* called to the Bar Gray's Inn 1982, recorder 2005, dep judge of the High Ct (Queen's Bench Div); *Recreations* photography, bird watching, golf; *Clubs* Vincent's (Oxford), Clandon Regis; *Style*— Stephen Hofmeyr, Esq, QC; ✉ Acre Holt, One Tree Hill Road, Guildford GU4 8PJ; 7 King's Bench Walk, Temple, London EC4Y 7DS (☎ 020 910 8300, fax 020 910 8400, e-mail shofmeyr@7kbw.co.uk)

HOGAN, Prof Eileen Mary; da of Thomas Matthew Hogan (d 1996), and Marjorie Coyle (d 1982); *b* 1 March 1946; *Educ* Streatham Hill and Clapham HS, Camberwell Sch of Arts and Crafts, Royal Acad Schs, Br Sch of Archaeology Athens, RCA (BA, MA); *m* (m dis) Kenneth Ersser; *Career* artist; princ lectr and dir Camberwell Press 1985, dean Sch of Applied and Graphic Arts 1989–98, currently research prof University of the Arts London; currently exhibiting with Browse & Darby; represented by The Fine Art Soc 1979; numerous work in public collections; artist-in-residence Garden Museum 2016; *Solo Exhibitions* incl: Br Cncl Athens 1971 and 1983, New Grafton Gallery 1972, RCA 1974 and 1977, The Fine Art Soc London 1980, 1982, 1984, 1985, 1986, 1988, 1992, 1997, 2000 and 2006, The Imperial War Museum 1984, Bankside Gallery 1999, NewArtCentre Roche Court 2013, Browse and Darby 2015; *Commissions* incl: Women at Work in the Royal Navy (for Artistic Records Ctee of Imperial War Museum) 1983–84, The Queen presenting Colours to the Portsmouth Fleet (for HMS Nelson) 1986, stamps for Royal Mail 1989, 1990, 1993 and 2001, artist-in-residence Wimbledon Championships 2009, Olympic artist (tennis) 2010; *Publications* A Selection of Poems by C P Cavafy (1985), On Common Ground (1987), Anaskaphes (1989), All Over the Place (1993), Under the Influence (1997), A Day Out For Mehment Erbil by Louis de Bernieres (1999), A Green Place (1999), Early Japanese Stories by Kazuo Ishiguro (2000), Murder in Triplicate by PD James (2001), Three Easy Pieces by Peter Carey, Bountiful UL238, Sweet Promise FH 172, Golden Gain FR 59, Paintings and Drawings by Eileen Hogan (2013); *Clubs* Chelsea Arts; *Style*— Prof Eileen Hogan; ✉ 13 Wythburn Place, London W1H 7BU (website www.eileenhogan.co.uk)

HOGAN, James; s of Reg Hogan, of Mornington, Victoria, Aust, and Lorna, *née* Thomson (d 1988); *b* 28 November 1956, Melbourne, Aust; *Educ* Ivanhoe GS Victoria Aust; *m* 28 Nov 1981, Heather, *née* Debney; 2 s (Mark b 24 March 1985, Andrew b 27 Nov 1987), 1 da (Nicole b 21 April 1990); *Career* formerly: vice-pres mktg/sales Europe Hertz Corp, worldwide sales dir Forte Hotels Ltd, chief operating offr bmi British Midland, former non-exec dir and memb of audit cmmn Gallaher plc; pres and chief exec Gulf Air 2002–06; ceo Etihad Airways 2006–, vice-chair Bahrain Hotels Corp; fell: Aust Mktg Inst, RAeS; *Clubs* Melbourne CC, Sydney CC; *Style*— James Hogan, Esq; ✉ Etihad Airways, PO Box 35566, New Airport Road, Abu Dhabi, United Arab Emirates (☎ 00 9 712 505 8300 fax 00 9 712 505 8333)

HOGAN, James V J; s of Thomas Joseph Hogan, and Bridget, née Lemon; *b* 12 September 1951; *Educ* Lancaster Univ (BA), St Edmund Hall Oxford (MLitt); *m* Jane Eveline, née Kinnock; 1 da (Cassandra Jane Eveline b 1983), 1 s (Alexander James William b 1987); *Career* BBC TV News and Current Affrs 1978–91: asst prodr/researcher Nationwide, Westminster, and Tonight 1978–80, prodr Newsweek, The Pursuit of Power, and 20th Century Remembered 1980–84, sr prodr Panorama and Newsnight 1984–88, ed This Week Next Week 1987–88, ed BBC News Event Unit (exec prodr of Gen Election progs, Party Political Confs and major current affrs documentaries on domestic and foreign topics) 1988–90, ed BBC Question Time 1990–91, md subsid of Zenith Prodns 1992–94, dir subsid of SelecTV plc 1994–96, ptnr Brunswick Group Ltd 1996–; memb Cncl Britain in Europe; Robert McKenzie fell LSE 1993–94, memb Advsy Bd Oxford Business Sch; MInstD, MIPR; memb: RTS, BAFTA, Media Soc Cncl, Br in Europe; fell LSE; *Publications* BBC Review of the Year (ed, 1990 and 1991), From Demigods to Democrats? the Television Revolution 1976–96 (1997), LSE working papers; *Recreations* writing, classical music, opera, food, fine wine, post-war English abstract art, horse racing, sport; *Clubs* Savile, Mosimann's; *Style*— James Hogan, Esq; ✉ Brunswick Group Ltd, 16 Lincoln's Inn Fields, London WC2A 3ED (☎ 020 7404 5959, fax 020 7831 2823)

HOGAN, John Anthony; s of John and Margaret Hogan; *b* 14 April 1953; *Educ* KCL (BA); *m* 1977, Jane, da of Frederick J Ford; 2 da (Jennifer b 23 March 1980, Katherine b 7 June 1982), 1 s (James b 19 Feb 1985); *Career* exploration geologist Elf UK, BNOC and Shell 1974–81, regnl explorationist LASMO plc 1981–84, sr vice-pres LASMO Energy Corp USA 1984–89, md LASMO North Sea plc 1989–93, chief operating offr LASMO plc 1993–2001, chm Acteon Gp 2001–, dir Caledonia Oil and Gas 2003–, chief exec Argos Resources 2005–, dir Noreco AS 2005–; *Recreations* walking, reading, clay pigeon shooting, rugby; *Style*— John Hogan, Esq

HOGAN, William Patrick (Bill); s of William Daniel Hogan (d 1983), of Laindon, Essex, and Lilian, *née* Morley (d 2003); *b* 7 September 1943, London; *Educ* Christ's Hosp; *m* 20 March 1971, Audrey Margaret, da of Arthur Willber; 2 c (Neil b 28 May 1975, Natalie b 15 Dec 1982); *Career* qualified chartered accountant 1966, int tax specialist, writer, lectr and consultant, now dir of taxation Baker Tilly Int; FCA 1976 (ACA 1966); *Recreations* travel, biographies, theatre, bridge; *Clubs* Old Blues, Royal Over-Seas League; *Style*— Bill Hogan, Esq; ✉ 216 Stock Road, Billericay, Essex, CM12 0SH (☎ 01277622817, e-mail bill.hogan@hotmail.co.uk)

HOGAN-HOWE, Sir Bernard; kt (2013), QPM (2004); Bernard Howe (d 2000), and Cecilia Teresa, *née* Hogan; *b* 25 October 1957; *Educ* Sheffield Poly (HNC), Merton Coll Oxford (MA), Fitzwilliam Coll Cambridge (Dip), Univ of Sheffield (MBA); *m* Marion White; *Career* Supt S Yorks Police 1994–97, Asst Chief Constable Mersyside Police 1997–2001, Asst Cmmr Met Police 2001–04, Chief Constable Merseyside Police 2004–09, HM Inspector of Constabulary 2009–11, Cmmr Met Police 2011–; hon fell: Liverpool John Moores Univ, Merton Coll Oxford 2013; hon doctorate: Sheffield Hallam Univ 2012, Univ of Sheffield 2013; *Recreations* horse riding, opera, Sheffield Wednesday FC, playing football; *Style*— Sir Bernard Hogan-Howe, QPM; ✉ Metropolitan Police, New Scotland Yard, Broadway, London SW1H 0BG

HOGARTH, Adrian John; s of Prof Cyril Alfred Hogarth (d 2006), and Audrey, *née* Jones (d 2010); *b* 7 July 1960; *Educ* St Paul's, Magdalene Coll Cambridge (MA, LLM), Inns of Court Sch of Law; *m* 20 July 1996, Archana, da of K P Singh; 1 da (Emily b 3 Oct 2008), 1 s (Thomas b 2 April 2010); *Career* called to the Bar Inner Temple 1983; joined Office of the Parly Counsel 1985, on secondment to Law Cmmn 1992–94, on secondment as sr Parly counsel Law Cmmn 2011–15; memb Cncl Cwlth Assoc of Legislative Counsel 2015–; memb Hon Soc of the Inner Temple; FRSA; *Recreations* travel, cricket, tennis, reeling; *Clubs* Cypos CC, Lansdowne; *Style*— Adrian Hogarth, Esq; ✉ Office of the Parliamentary Counsel, 1 Horseguards Road, London SW1A 2HQ

HOGG, Sir Christopher; kt (1985); *b* 2 August 1936; *Educ* Marlborough, Trinity Coll Oxford (MA), Harvard Univ (MBA); *m* (m dis); 2 da; *Career* Nat Serv 1955–57; IMEDE Business Sch Lausanne 1962, Philip Hill Higginson Erlangers Ltd (now Hill Samuel & Co Ltd) 1963–66, Industrial Reorganisation Corporation 1966–68; Courtaulds plc: joined 1968, dir 1973–, dep chm 1978, chief exec and chm designate 1979, chm and chief exec 1980–91, non-exec chm until July 1996; non-exec chm: Reuters Gp plc 1985–2004 (non-exec dir 1984), Courtaulds Textiles plc 1990–95, Allied Domecq plc 1996–2002 (dep chm 1995–96), GlaxoSmithKline plc 2002–04 (memb Bd: Smithkline Beecham 1993–2000, GlaxoSmithKline 2000–04); memb International Cncl J P Morgan 1988–2003; non-exec dir Bank of England 1992–96, chm Financial Reporting Cncl 2006–10; memb: Bd of Tstees Ford Fndn 1987–99, Dept of Industry's Industrial Advsy Bd 1976–80; chm Royal National Theatre 1995–2004; Centenary medal Soc Chem Indust 1989, Alumni Achievement award Harvard Business Sch 1989, Gold medal BIM 1986; Hon DSc Cranfield Inst of Technol 1986, Hon DSc Aston Univ 1988; hon fell Trinity Coll Oxford 1982; Hon FCSD, Hon FCGI; *Recreations* theatre, reading, skiing, walking; *Style*— Sir Christopher Hogg

HOGG, Douglas; *see:* Hailsham, 3 Viscount

HOGG, Dame Mary Claire Hogg; DBE (1995); eld da of Baron Hailsham of St Marylebone, KG, CH, PC (d 2001), and Mary Evelyn, *née* Martin (d 1978); *b* 15 January 1947; *Educ* St Paul's Girls' Sch; *m* 11 Sept 1987, Eric Koops, *qv*, s of late Lendeert Koops; 1 da (Katharine Mary b 17 March 1989), 1 s (William Quintin Eric b 21 Dec 1991); *Career* called to the Bar: Lincoln's Inn 1968 (bencher 1995), NI 1993; QC 1989, recorder of the Crown Court 1990–95 (asst recorder 1986–90), judge of the High Court of Justice (Family Div) 1995–2016; govr Univ of Westminster 1992– (govr Poly of Central London 1982–92), tstee The Harrison Homes 1983–2010; memb Cncl Church of England's Children's Soc 1990–95; Hon LLD Univ of Westminster 1995; Freeman City of London 1981; FRSA; *Style*— Dame Mary Hogg, DBE

HOGG, Baroness (Life Peer UK 1995), of Kettlethorpe in the County of Lincolnshire; Sarah Elizabeth Mary Hogg; yr da of Baron Boyd-Carpenter, PC, DL (Life Peer) (d 1998); *b* 14 May 1946, 1946; *Educ* St Mary's Convent Ascot, Lady Margaret Hall Oxford; *m* 6 June 1968, Rt Hon Douglas Hogg, QC, 3 Viscount Hailsham, *qv*; 1 s, 1 da; *Career* Economist Newspaper 1968–81; economics ed: Sunday Times 1981–82, The Times 1983–86; presenter and economics ed Channel 4 News 1982–83, dir London Broadcasting Co 1985–90, govr Centre for Economic Policy Research 1985–90, asst ed, business and fin ed The Independent 1986–89, dir National Theatre 1987–90, economics ed The Daily Telegraph and The Sunday Telegraph 1989–90, head of Policy Unit No 10 Downing St with rank of second permanent sec 1990–95; govr of the BBC 2000–04; chm: London Economics 1997–99, Foreign and Colonial Small Companies 1997–2002 (dir 1995–2002), Frontier Economics 1999–2013, 3i Group 2002–10; non-exec dir: GKN plc 1996–2006 (dep chm and sr ind dir 2003–06), National Provident Institution 1996–99, P&O 1999–2000, P&O Princess 2000–03, Carnival Corp and Carnival plc 2003–08, BG Gp 2005–16; dir John Lewis plc 2011–; memb: Cncl Hansard Soc 1995–98, House of Lords Select Ctee on Sci and Technol 1996–99, Inst of Fiscal Studies 1996–2005, Select Ctee on Monetary Policy 2000–03, Financial Reporting Cncl 2005–14 (chm 2010–14), Cncl London Business Sch 2005–10, The Takeover Panel 2011–; Martin Curie Portfolio Tst 1999–2002, tstee Historic Lincoln Tst 2013–, tstee Queen Elizabeth Diamond Jubilee Tst 2013–; lead ind dir HM Treasy 2010–, non-exec dir FCA 2016–; Wincott Fndn Fin Journalist of the Year 1985; fell Eton Coll 1996–2009, hon fell LMH Oxford; Hon MA Open Univ 1987, Hon DLitt Loughborough Univ 1992, Hon DL Univ of Lincoln 2001, Hon DSc City Univ 2002; *Books* Too Close to Call (with Jonathan Hill, 1995); *Style*— The Baroness Hogg; ✉ House of Lords, London SW1A 0PW

HOGGARD, Matthew James; MBE (2006); *b* 31 December 1976, Leeds; *Educ* Pudsey Grangefield Sch Leeds; *m* Sarah; *Career* cricketer (bowler); Yorkshire CCC 1996– (more than 100 first class appearances); England: 64 test caps, 26 one day appearances, test debut v West Indies Lord's 2000, one day debut v Zimbabwe 2001, best bowling 7–61 v SA Johannesburg 2005 (12–205 in the match), memb Ashes-winning team 2005; ranked 4th best Test match bowler in the world 2006; NBC Denis Compton Award 1998, Wisden Cricketer of the Year 2006; *Style*— Mr Matthew Hoggard, MBE; ✉ c/o Jim Souter, 117 Oslo Court, Prince Albert Road, London NW8 7EP (☎ 07769 906295)

HOGGETT, Brenda Marjorie; *see:* Hale of Richmond, Baroness

HOGWOOD, Paul Arthur; s of Robert Thomas Hogwood, of Forest Hill, and Hilda Jesse, *née* Marshall; *b* 18 July 1949; *Educ* Haberdashers' Aske's, Univ of Hull (BSc); *m* 30 Oct 1971, Sylvia Ann, da of Gordon McCulloch (d 1971); 2 s (James b 1978, Christopher b 1980); *Career* CA; audit mangr Coopers & Lybrand 1970–78, project fin asst dir Morgan Grenfell & Co Ltd 1983–86 (chief internal auditor 1978–83); co sec: Morgan Grenfell Securities Holdings Ltd 1986–88, Anglo & Overseas Trust plc 1989–, The Overseas Investment Trust plc 1989–99, Deutsche Equity Income Trust plc 1991–; dir DWS Investment Funds Ltd 1993–; co sec: Deutsche Latin American Companies Trust plc 1994–2005, Deutsche Asset Management Gp Ltd 1996–; FCA 1974; *Recreations* travel, theatre; *Style*— Paul Hogwood, Esq; ✉ 15 Ambleside, Epping, Essex CM16 4PT (☎ 01992 570264); Deutsche Asset Management Group Ltd, One Appold Street, London EC2A 2UU (☎ 020 7545 0036, fax 020 7547 1042, telex 920286 MGAM G)

HOLBROOK, Rt Rev John Edward; *see:* Brixworth, Bishop of

HOLDEN, Anthony Ivan; s of John Holden (d 1985), of Southport, Lancs, and Margaret Lois, *née* Sharpe (d 1985); *b* 22 May 1947; *Educ* Oundle, Merton Coll Oxford (MA); *m* 1, 1 May 1971 (m dis 1988), Amanda Juliet, da of Sir Brian Warren; 3 s (Sam b 1975, Joe b 1977, Ben b 1979); m 2, 21 July 1990, Cynthia Blake, da of Mrs Rosemary Blake; *Career* trainee reporter Evening Echo Hemel Hempstead 1970–73; The Sunday Times: home and foreign corr 1973–77, Atticus column 1977–79; Washington and chief US corr The Observer 1979–81, Transatlantic Cables columnist Punch 1979–81, features ed and asst ed The Times 1981–82, exec ed Sunday Today 1985–86, classical music critic The Observer 2002–08; fell Center for Scholars and Writers NY Public Library 1999–2000; Br Press Awards: Young Journalist of the Year 1972, Reporter of the Year 1976, Columnist of the Year 1977; freelance journalist and author: Holden At Large column Sunday Express magazine 1982–85, presenter In the Air BBC Radio 4 1982–83; TV documentaries: The Men who Would be King 1982, Charles at Forty 1988, Anthony Holden on Poker 1992, Who Killed Tchaikovsky? 1993; opera translations (with Amanda Holden): Don Giovanni ENO 1985, La Boheme Opera North 1986, The Barber of Seville ENO 1987; memb Bd of Govrs South Bank Centre 2002–08, tstee Shakespeare North, pres Int Fedn of Poker 2009–13; *Books* Aeschylus' Agamemnon (translated and ed, 1969), The Greek Anthology (contrib, 1973), Greek Pastoral Poetry (translated and ed, 1974), The St Albans Poisoner (1974), Charles, Prince of Wales (1979), Their Royal Highnesses (1981), Anthony Holden's Royal Quiz – The Penguin Masterquiz (1983), Of Presidents, Prime Ministers and Princes (1984), The Queen Mother (1985, revised edns 1990 and 1993), Don Giovanni (1987), Olivier, A Biography (1988, new edn 2007), Charles, A Biography (1989), Big Deal: A Year as a Professional Poker Player (1990), The Last Paragraph: The Journalism of David Blundy (ed, 1990), The Oscars: A Secret History of Hollywood's Academy Awards (1993), The Tarnished Crown: Crisis in the House of Windsor (1993), Power and the Throne (contrib, 1994), Tchaikovsky (1995), Diana: A Life and a Legacy (1997), Charles (1998), William Shakespeare (1999), The Mind Has Mountains (co-ed with Sir Frank Kermode, *qv*, 1999), There are Kermodians (co-ed with Ursula Owen, 1999), The Drama of Love, Life and Death in Shakespeare (2000), William Shakespeare: An Illustrated Biography (2002), The Wit in the Dungeon: A Life of Leigh Hunt (2005), All In: Poker As Seen on Late-Night TV (2005), The Man Who Wrote Mozart: A Life of Lorenzo Da Ponte (2006), Bigger Deal: A Year Inside the Poker Boom (2007), Holden on Hold'em (2008), Poems That Make Grown Men Cry (co-ed with Ben Holden, 2014), Poems That Make Grown Women Cry (co-ed with Ben Holden, 2016); *Recreations* poker, Arsenal FC, Lancashire CCC; *Clubs* Victoria Casino; *Style*— Anthony

Holden, Esq; ✉ c/o Rogers Coleridge & White Ltd, Literary Agents, 20 Powis Mews, London W11 1JN (✆ 020 7221 3717, fax 020 7229 9084)

HOLDEN, Lawrence; DL (1992); s of Trevor Holden, of Liverpool (d 1983), and Alice Mary Christine, *née* Roper (d 1991); *b* 19 September 1940, Liverpool; *Educ* Liverpool Coll, Univ of Liverpool (LLB), Coll of Law; *m* 17 Sep 1966, Rosemary Anne, *née* Sutton; 2 s (Rupert b 2 Nov 1967, Timothy b 1 Oct 1969), 1 da (Alison Rebecca b 14 Dec 1971); *Career* admitted slr 1965; ptnr Duncan Oakshott & Co 1966; Brabner Holden Banks Wilson (following merger): managing ptnr 1989, sr ptnr 1994; conslt Brabners Chaffe Street LLP 2001–07; pres Liverpool Law Soc 1990–91; memb: Cncl Soc for Computers and Law 1982–87, Law Office Mgmnt and Technology Ctee Law Soc 1983–88, National Inquiry into Governance of Housing Assocs 1994–95, Liverpool City Cncl Advsy Panel on Urban Design and Conservation 1999–2009; Univ of Liverpool: memb Cncl 1982–2004, pres 1993–99, pro-chllr 1999–2004; vice-pres Liverpool Cncl of Charity and Voluntary Service 1992– (treas 1983–92); tstee Reader Orgn 2011–15, chair Friends of the Williamson Art Gallery and Wirral Museums 2015–; Hon LLD Univ of Liverpool 2005; memb Law Soc 1965; *Recreations* mountain walking, painting, sculpture; *Style*— Lawrence Holden, Esq; ✉ Hollybank, 12 Pine Walks, Birkenhead, Merseyside CH42 8LQ (✆ 0151 608 2884, e-mail lawrence.holden@me.com)

HOLDEN, Patrick Brian; s of Reginald John Holden (d 2005), and Winifred Isabel Holden (d 2003); *b* 16 June 1937, Exmouth, Devon; *Educ* All Hallows Sch (major scholar), St Catharine's Coll Cambridge (MA); *m* 1972, Dr Jennifer Ruth (m dis 2001), da of Francis Meddings (d 1985); *Career* served Royal Hampshire Regt 1955–57, seconded 1 Ghana Regt RWAFF; Fine Fare Group 1960–69 (legal and property dir 1965–69), Pye Telecom 1969–74 (int dir 1971–74), sec New Towns Assoc 1974–75, Oriel Foods Group 1975–81 (sec 1975, dir 1979); chm: Steak Away Foods Ltd 1982–, Holden Homes (Southern) Ltd 1985–, Ainsfield plc 1991–; tstee Cartoon Art Tst 2012–; FCIS; *Publications* Map of Tewin and its Rights of Way (1991), The Ultimate Golden Retriever (contrib, 1997), A-Z of Dog Training & Behaviour (1999, Chinese version 2001), The Old School House, A Dickensian School (1999), Agility: A Step by Step Guide (2001, German translation 2002), The History of Tewin (contrib, 2009), Lively Limericks (2015); *Recreations* walking, bridge, cartoons, travel, dog training; *Clubs* Naval and Military; *Style*— Patrick Holden, Esq; ✉ The Old School House, Lower Green, Tewin, Welwyn, Hertfordshire AL6 0LD (✆ 01438 717573)

HOLDEN, Sue; *b* 13 May 1966, Morden; *Educ* Univ of Cambridge (MA); *Career* early career with Shell Int and Shell UK; various operational roles rising to business admin dir National Tst 1996–2005, chief exec Woodland Tst 2005–13, exec dir Earthwatch Inst 2014–; *Style*— Ms Sue Holden; ✉ Earthwatch Institute, Mayfield House, 256 Banbury Road, Oxford OX2 7DE (✆ 01865 311383)

HOLDEN, Wendy; da of Anthony Holden, and Elaine, *née* Murgatroyd; *Educ* Whitcliffe Mount Sch Cleckheaton, Girton Coll Cambridge (MA); *m* Jonathan McLeod; 1 s (Andrew Arthur b 2002), 1 da (Isabella b 2004); *Career* writer and journalist; dep ed Style section Sunday Times 1996–97, dep ed Tatler 1997–98, sr ed You magazine Mail on Sunday 1998–2000; Hon DLitt Univ of Derby 2015; *Books* Simply Divine (1999), Bad Heir Day (2000), Pastures Nouveaux (2001), Fame Fatale (2002), Azur Like It (2003), The Wives of Bath (2005), The School for Husbands (2006), Filthy Rich (2008), Beautiful People (2009), Gallery Girl (2010), Marrying Up (2011), Gifted and Talented (2013), Wild and Free (2015), Honeymoon Suite (2016); *Style*— Miss Wendy Holden; ✉ c/o Jonathan Lloyd, Curtis Brown, 4th Floor, Haymarket House, 28–29 Haymarket, London SW1Y 4SP (✆ 020 7393 4400, e-mail jonathan@curtisbrown.co.uk, website www.wendyholden.net, Twitter @wendy_holden, Facebook wendyholdenauthor)

HOLDEN-BROWN, Heather; da of Sir Derrick Holden-Brown, and Patricia, *née* Mackenzie (d 2001); *b* 13 August 1951, Cuckfield, W Sussex; *Educ* Hampden House, Tudor Hall, QMC London (BA); *Career* The Economist 1975–81, Waterstone's Firethorn Press 1985–86, Harrap 1986–87, BBC Books 1988–97, non-fiction publisher and dir Headline Book Publishing Ltd 1997–2003, dir HHB Agency Ltd 2005–; govr Tudor Hall Sch 1988–2015, tstee Sparrow Schs Fndn 2005–; *Recreations* reading, exploring London and the Thames, visiting historic houses and churches, theatre, cooking for friends; *Clubs* Royal Lymington Yacht, Boodle's; *Style*— Ms Heather Holden-Brown; ✉ HHB Agency Ltd, 6 Warwick Court, London WC1R 5DJ (✆ 020 7405 5525, e-mail heather@hhbagency.com)

HOLDER, Kevin John; s of K Holder, of Bracknell, Berks, and L Holder, *née* Warboys; *b* 6 November 1958; *Educ* Windsor GS, RMA Sandhurst; *m* (m dis); 1 da (Katherine Anne b 22 Dec 1988), 2 s (Michael Anthony, James Simon (twins) b 18 Nov 1992); *Career* cmmnd RAPC 1981, left Army as Maj 1994; dir of corp affrs Lincs HA 1994, dir of ops Community Healthcare Serv (CHS) Southern Derbys 1998, chief exec NE Derbys PCT 2001–; assoc ICSA 1993; *Recreations* golf, skiing, photography, travel; *Style*— Kevin Holder, Esq; ✉ North Eastern Derbyshire Primary Care Trust, St Mary's Court, St Mary's Gate, Chesterfield, Derbyshire S41 7TD (✆ 01246 544610, fax 01246 544689, e-mail kevin.holder@nederbypct.nhs.uk)

HOLDER, Nicholas Paul; TD (1982); s of late Air Marshal Sir Paul Holder, KBE, CB, DSO, DFC, of Hindhead, Surrey, and Mary Elizabeth, *née* Kidd; *b* 10 November 1942; *Educ* Sherborne; *Career* Royal Scots Greys (2 Dragoons) 1963–71, Royal Scots Dragoon Gds Reserve of Offrs 1971–82; cmmnd Inns of Court and City Yeo Home Service Force 1987–91; assoc dir Kleinwort Benson Ltd 1984–87, dir Fuji International Finance (merchant banking subsid of Fuji Bank Tokyo) 1987–94, dir Silverdale Investment Management Ltd 1994–, md Party-Time.co.uk Ltd 2000–; cncllr (Cons) Waverley BC 2007–; memb: Br Jostedhals Glacier Expedition 1967, Br White Nile Hovercraft Expedition 1969; treas Br Ski Mountaineering Assoc; Freeman City of London 1999, Liveryman Worshipful Co of Fanmakers 1999; *Recreations* mountaineering, skiing, gardening, walking, shooting; *Clubs* Boodle's, Alpine, Lloyd's, Pratt's; *Style*— Nicholas Holder, Esq, TD; ✉ Winkford House, Witley, Godalming, Surrey GU8 5PR

HOLDERNESS, Sir Martin William; 4 Bt (UK 1920), of Tadworth, Surrey; s of Sir Richard William Holderness, 3 Bt (d 1998), and Pamela, *née* Chapman; *b* 24 May 1957; *m* 2 Oct 1984, Elizabeth D, da of Dr W Thornton; 1 s (Matthew William Thornton b 23 May 1990), 1 da (Tessa Elizabeth Mary b 8 Sept 1992); *Heir* s, Matthew Holderness; *Career* CA 1983; articled clerk KPMG Peat Marwick until 1983, ind financial advsr MH Financial Servs Ltd 1984–, currently md MH Financial Management Ltd; *Style*— Sir Martin Holderness, Bt; ✉ website www.mhfm.ifanetsite.com

HOLDSWORTH, Brian John; s of Reginald Hugh Holdsworth (d 1996), of Long Eaton, Derbys, and Dorothy, *née* Ellis (d 2012); *b* 27 January 1950; *Educ* Southwell Minster GS, Guy's Hosp Med Sch (BSc, MB BS); *m* 21 Sept 1974 (m dis 2012), Ursula Jean, da of Victor Robert Lees (d 1974); 3 s (Matthew b 1978, Thomas b 1982, Christopher b 1989); *Career* house jobs Guy's Gp of Hosps 1973–76, registrar in surgery Royal Infirmary Sheffield 1976–78, sr orthopaedic registrar Nottingham Hosps 1981–86 (orthopaedic registrar 1978–81); conslt orthopaedic surgn: Harlow Wood Orthopaedic Hosp nr Mansfield 1986–95, Univ Hosp Nottingham 1986–2015, ret; in practice p/t Nottingham Woodhorpe and BMI Park Hosps 2015–; FRCS 1978, FBOA 1987; *Publications* Frontiers of Fracture Management (contrib, 1989), Principles of Fracture Management (contrib, 2000), Oxford Book of Trauma (contrib, 2002); author various papers on traumatic conditions of the elbow joint; *Recreations* photography, picture framing; *Style*— Brian Holdsworth, Esq; ✉ 2 Nottingham Road, Lowdham NG14 7AP (✆ 0115 966 4861); c/o Janet Boulton, Sherwood Business Centre, 616a-618a Mansfield Road, Nottingham NG5 2GA (✆ and fax 0115 960 6091)

HOLE, Max; CBE (2015); s of Anthony Frederick Hole (d 1975), of London, and Barbara Mary Hole; *b* 26 May 1951; *Educ* Haileybury, Univ of Kent at Canterbury; *m* 1 (m dis), Cynthia; 2 s (Jamie b 23 June 1979, Mark b 24 Jan 1984); m 2, Jan Ravens, *qv* (actress); 1 s (Louis b 20 May 1998); *Career* fndr (with Geoff Jukes): Gemini Artists 1972 (clients incl Camel, Mungo Jerry, Arthur Brown), Criminal Records 1976 (signings incl Bram Tchaikovsky, Robin Williamson, Susan Fassbender); mangr: Chris Hughes, Ross Cullum; WEA: A&R mangr 1982–83, dir of A&R 1983–87, md UK div 1987–90; md East West Records (following splitting of WEA into 2 cos) 1990–98; Universal Music Gp Int: sr vice-pres of mktg and A&R 1998–2004, pres Asia Pacific and then exec vice-pres 2005–10, chief operating offr 2010–12, currently chm and ceo; memb Bd ENO; tstee EMI Sound Fndn; *Recreations* walking and boating at my house in Cornwall, watching cricket; *Clubs* MCC, Groucho; *Style*— Max Hole, Esq, CBE; ✉ Universal Music Group International , 364–366 Kensington High Street, London W14 8NS (✆ 020 7471 5603, fax 020 7471 5605)

HOLES, Prof Clive Douglas; s of Douglas John Holes, and Kathryn Mary, *née* Grafton; *b* 29 September 1948; *Educ* Trinity Hall Cambridge (MA), Univ of Birmingham (MA), Wolfson Coll Cambridge (PhD); *m* 8 March 1980 (m dis 2003), Gillian Diane, da of late James Herbert Pountain; 2 s (Timothy Peter b 23 March 1984, Michael James b 21 March 1988); m 2, 7 Aug 2004, Deidre Margaret, da of Charles William Allen; *Career* British Cncl offr Bahrain, Kuwait, Algeria, Iraq and Thailand 1971–83, lectr then sr lectr in applied linguistics Univ of Salford 1983–85, dir Language Centre Sultan Qaboos Univ Oman 1985–87; Univ of Cambridge: lectr in Islamic Studies 1987–96, reader in Arabic 1996, fell Trinity Hall 1989–96; Khalid Bin Abdallah Al-Saud prof for the study of the contemporary Arab world Univ of Oxford 1997–2014, fell Magdalen Coll; memb: Philological Soc 1985, Br Soc for Middle Eastern Studies 1985; FBA 2002, FRSA 2008; *Books* Colloquial Arabic of the Gulf & Saudi Arabia (1984, 2 edn 2010), Language Variation and Change in a Modernising Arab State (1987), Gulf Arabic (1990), Modern Arabic (1995), Dialect, Culture and Society in Eastern Arabia (Vol I 2001, Vol II 2005, Vol III 2015), Poetry and Politics in Contemporary Bedouin Society (2009), The Nabati Poetry of the United Arab Emirates (2011); also author of numerous professional jl articles on the Arabic language and Arabic literature; *Recreations* long distance walking, watching soccer and rugby, travel, cooking; *Style*— Prof Clive Holes; ✉ Magdalen College, Oxford OX1 4AU; Oriental Institute, Pusey Lane, Oxford OX1 2LE (e-mail clive.holes@orinst.ox.ac.uk)

HOLGATE, Andrew; *Career* literary ed Sunday Times; *Style*— Andrew Holgate, Esq; ✉ The Sunday Times, 1 London Bridge Street, London SE1 9GF

HOLGATE, Hon Mr Justice; Sir David John Holgate; kt (2014), QC (1997); s of John Charles Holgate (d 2007), and Catherine Philbin, *née* Rooney; *b* 3 August 1956; *Educ* Davenant Fndn GS, Exeter Coll Oxford (BA); *Partner* Alexander Nicholas Constantine (civil partnership 2006); *Career* called to the Bar Middle Temple 1978 (bencher 2004); recorder of the Crown Court 2002–14, dep judge of the High Court of Justice 2008–14, judge of the High Court of Justice (Queen's Bench Div) 2014–; pres Upper Tribunal (Lands Chamber) 2016–; memb Supplementary Panel of Jr Counsel to the Crown (Common Law) 1986–97, Standing Jr Counsel to the Inland Revenue in Rating and Valuation Matters 1990–97; admitted Hong Kong Bar 2000; *Recreations* music (particularly opera), travel, reading; *Clubs* Travellers; *Style*— The Hon Mr Justice Holgate; ✉ Royal Courts of Justice, Strand, London WC2A 2LL (✆ 020 7073 2681, website www.judiciary.gov.uk)

HOLGATE, Prof Peter Alan; s of Harold Holgate, of Leeds, and Ivy, *née* Instrell; *b* Leeds; *Educ* West Leeds Boys HS, Univ of Bradford (MSc), City Univ (BMus); *m* 1980, Dr Nelda Elizabeth Frater; 1 s (Andrew b 25 Nov 1985); *Career* articled clerk John Gordon Walton & Co CAs Leeds 1970–74, audit sr and asst mangr Coopers & Lybrand London and Nairobi 1975–78, fin controller Mitchell Cotts Kenya Ltd 1978–79, business planning mangr Hertz Europe Ltd London 1979–81; under sec then sec Accounting Standards Ctee 1981–86; sr tech mangr Deloitte Haskins & Sells 1986–90, sr accounting tech ptnr PricewaterhouseCoopers (formerly Coopers & Lybrand before merger) 1990–2013, sr accounting advsr FTI Consltg 2014–; author of numerous articles in professional jls, frequent speaker at accounting confs, expert witness on accountancy matters; visiting prof of accounting LSE 2012–; chm Research Advsy Bd ICAEW 2006–12; memb: Fin Reporting Ctee ICAEW 1990–98, Main Ctee and Tech Ctee LSCA 1990–93 (chm Tech Ctee 1991–93), Accounting Standards Bd's Urgent Issues Task Force 1994–2012, Int Accounting Ctee CCAB 1996–2000, Advsy Bd Fin Reporting Faculty ICAEW 2008–14; dir The Frater Clinic Ltd; FCA; *Books* A Guide to Accounting Standards – Accounting For Goodwill (1985, updated 1990), A Guide To Accounting Standards – SSAP 23 Accounting For Acquisitions and Mergers (1986), A Guide to Accounting Standards – SSAP 12 revised Accounting for Depreciation (1987), Goodwill, Acquisitions & Mergers (1990), Operating and Financial Review (1994), The Coopers & Lybrand Manual of Accounting (princ author, 1995, 1996, 1997 and 1998), The PricewaterhouseCoopers Manual of Accounting- UK GAAP (princ author, 1999–2012), The PricewaterhouseCoopers Manual of Accounting – IFRS for the UK (princ author, annually 2005–13), Accounting Principles for Lawyers (2006), Accounting Principles for Non-executive Directors (2009); *Recreations* music, jazz pianist, accompanist, tennis, reading; *Style*— Prof Peter Holgate; ✉ e-mail peteralanholgate@gmail.com

HOLLADAY, Norman Charles; s of Reginald George Holladay, BEM (d 2009), and Gladys Doreen, *née* Couldry (d 2007); *b* 15 December 1951, Croydon, Surrey; *Educ* Hove GS for Boys, UCL (BSc (Eng)); *m* 7 Sept 1974, Carol Ann Foulkes; 2 s (James Richard b 1977, Andrew Charles b 1980), 2 da (Laura Jane b 1979, Sarah Lucy b 1981); *Career* formerly with Binnie & Ptnrs, md Dee Valley Gp plc 2009–; CEng, FCIWEM, MICE; *Recreations* rowing, fishing, golf; *Clubs* Rex Boat; *Style*— Norman Holladay, Esq; ✉ Dee Valley Group plc, Packsaddle, Wrexham Road, Rhostyllen, Wrexham LL14 4EH

HOLLAND, Sir (John) Anthony; kt (2003); s of late Maj John Holland, of Yelverton, Devon, and late Dorothy Rita, *née* George; *b* 9 November 1938; *Educ* Ratcliffe Coll, Univ of Nottingham (LLB), Univ of the West of England (MPhil), Univ of London (MA); *m* 1 June 1963, Kathleen Margaret (Kay), da of John Smellie Anderson (d 1978); 3 s (Andrew John, Christopher Iain, Nicholas Alexander); *Career* admitted slr 1962, sr ptnr Foot & Bowden Plymouth 1980–97, princ ombudsman PIA 1997–2000; chm: Regnl Advsy Cncl BBC SW 1984–87, Social Security Appeals Tbnl 1991–97, Plymouth C of C and Industry 1994–96, Exec Bd Justice 1997–2000 (memb Cncl 1991–2003), Jt Insolvency Monitoring Unit 2000–04, NI Parades Cmmn 2000–05, Standards Bd for England 2001–08, Access Dispute Ctee 2002–10, NI Legal Servs Cmmn 2004–07; chm (jtly) Securities and Futures Authy 1993–2001; dep chm Regulatory Decisions Ctee FSA 2002–04, complaints cmmr to FSA 2004–14; govr Coll of Law 1991–97; memb: Cncl Howard League for Penal Reform, Marre Ctee, Criminal Injuries Compensation Appeals Panel 2000–05, Bd Pensions Protection Fund 2006–13, Investigatory Powers Tbnl 2009–14, Speakers Ctee Ind Parly Standards Ctee 2011–14; pres: Plymouth Law Soc 1986, Cornwall Law Soc 1988; hon memb Soc of Legal Slrs 1992; memb Law Soc 1962 (elected to Cncl 1976, vice-pres 1989, pres 1990); Hon LLD Plymouth Univ 2013; *Books* Principles of Registered Land Conveyancing (1968), Landlord and Tenant (1970), Mines and Quarries Section Butterworths Encyclopedia of Forms and Precedents (jt consulting ed, 1989–2005), Cordery on Solicitors (gen ed, 9 edn); *Recreations* opera, travel, sailing; *Clubs* Royal Western Yacht of England, Athenaeum; *Style*— Sir Anthony Holland; ✉ 262 Lauderdale Tower, Barbican, London EC2Y 8BY (✆ 020 7638 5044, mobile 07779 600249, e-mail holland46@btinternet.com)

HOLLAND, Darryll; s of Lenord Holland, and Anne, *née* Tynan; *b* 14 June 1972, Manchester; *m* 16 Sept 2001, Jacqueline Elizabeth, *née* Merchant; *Career* jockey (flat racing); ridden in UK, Europe, Asia and N America; Group 1 wins incl: Yorkshire Oaks, Singapore Derby, July Cup, St James Palace Stakes, Juddmonte Int, Queen Elizabeth II Stakes, Dewhurst Stakes, Gran Criterium, Italian Oaks, Coronation Cup, Coral Eclipse (twice), Pretty Polly, Fillies Mile; other wins incl: Goodwood Cup, Doncaster Cup, Italian 2000 Guineas, German 2000 Guineas; *Recreations* golf, football, tennis, skiing; *Clubs* Links Golf (Newmarket); *Style—* Darryll Holland, Esq; ✉ c/o Peter Merchant, Baden Lodge, 184 High Street, Cheveley, Newmarket CB8 9DG (☎ and fax 01638 731050, e-mail petermerchant@lineone.net)

HOLLAND, Henry; *b* 26 May 1983; *Educ* London Coll of Printing (BA); *Career* fashion designer; fndr House of Holland 2006–; H! by Henry Holland on sale in Debenhams 2010–; *Style—* Henry Holland, Esq; ✉ website www.houseofholland.co.uk, www.twitter.com/houseofholland and www.twitter.com/henryholland; c/o Caroline Adams, The Communications Store, 2 Kensington Square, London W8 5EP

HOLLAND, Julian Miles (Jools); OBE (2003); s of Derek Holland, of London, and June Rose, *née* Lane; *b* 24 January 1958; *Educ* Park Walk Sch, Invicta Sherington Sch, Shooters' Hill Sch; *Partner* (until 1986), Mary Leahy; 2 c (George Soloman b 14 April 1984, Rosie Areatha Mae b 1 Oct 1985); m, Aug 2005, Christabel Durham; 1 da (Mabel Ray Brittania b 22 Nov 1990); *Career* pianist 1975–78; keyboard player Squeeze 1978–80 (hits incl Take Me I'm Yours, Cool for Cats, Up The Junction, Hourglass, Annie Get Your Gun, Pulling Mussels from a Shell, Tempted, Slap and Tickle), regularly tours UK, concerts at Royal Albert Hall; solo albums: A World of His Own 1990, Full Compliment 1991, A-Z Of Piano 1993, Live Performance 1995, Solo Piano 1995, Sex, Jazz & Rock and Roll 1996, Lift The Lid 1997, Best of 1998, As The Sun Sets Over London 1999, Hop the Wag 2000, Small World Big Band 2001, Small World Big Band Vol II – More Friends 2002, Small World Big Band Friends III 2003; band leader Rythm & Blues Orchestra 1993–; extensive touring and guest performances with numerous artists incl: BB King (duet Deuces Wild CD), Elvis Costello, Sting, Al Green, Dr John, The The, Fine Young Cannibals, George Harrison; TV Presenter: The Tube (Channel 4) 1981–86, Juke Box Jury (BBC2) 1989, Sunday Night (with David Sanborn, NBC) 1990, The Happening (BSB) 1990, Later With Jools Holland (series, BBC2) 1993–; presenter The Jools Holland Show (Radio 2); writer The Groovy Fellers (Channel 4) 1988; wrote and produced films: Walking To New Orleans 1985, Mr Roadrunner (Channel 4) 1991, Spiceworld The Movie (cameo) 1997, Beat Route 1998, Jools Meets The Saint 1999; wrote film score for feature film Milk 1999; Music Broadcaster of the Year Sony Radio Acad Gold Award 2012; *Books* Barefaced Lies & Boogie-Woogie Boasts (autobiography, 2007); *Recreations* sketching, architecture; *Style—* Jools Holland, Esq, OBE; ✉ Jools Holland, BBC Radio 2, London W1A 1AA

HOLLAND, Katharine Jane; QC (2010); da of Wilfred Holland, and Margaret Holland; *Educ* Lady Manners Sch, Hertford Coll Oxford (BA, BCL); *Career* called to the Bar 1989; memb: Hon Soc of Middle Temple, Hon Soc of Lincoln's Inn, Chancery Bar Assoc, Professional Negligence Assoc; DipICArb 2010, FCIA 2010; *Style—* Ms Katharine Holland, QC; ✉ Landmark Chambers, 180 Fleet Street, London EC4A 2HG

HOLLAND, Prof Peter William Harold; s of late William Harold Bolton, and Mrs Christine Holland, *née* Bartrop; step-s of Franklin Holland; *b* 17 August 1963, Hyde; *Educ* Marple Hall Sch, The Queen's Coll Oxford (MA), Nat Inst for Med Research and Univ of London (PhD), Univ of Reading (DSc); *m* 1996, Amanda Susan, *née* Horsfall; 2 s; *Career* demonstrator in zoology Univ of Oxford 1987–91, Browne research fell The Queen's Coll Oxford 1988–91, Royal Soc univ research fell Univ of Oxford 1991–94, prof of zoology Univ of Reading 1994–2002, Linacre prof of zoology Univ of Oxford 2002– (head Dept of Zoology 2011–16), fell Merton Coll Oxford 2002–; Scientific Medal Zoological Soc of London 1996, De Snoo Medal 1999, Genetics Soc Medal 2004, Blaise Pascal Medal 2005, Kowalevsky Medal 2006, Linnean Medal 2012, Frink Medal 2015; FLS 2002, FRS 2003, fell Marine Biology Assoc 2014; *Publications* Essential Development Biology (jt ed, 1993), The Evolution of Developmental Mechanisms (jt ed, 1994), Swifter than the Arrow (2009), The Animal Kingdom (2011); *Recreations* entomology, angling, table tennis, sporting history; *Style—* Prof Peter Holland; ✉ Department of Zoology, University of Oxford, South Parks Road, Oxford OX1 3PS (☎ 01865 271185, fax 01865 271184)

HOLLAND, Tom; s of Martin Holland, and Janet Holland; *b* 5 January 1968, Oxford; *Educ* Queens' Coll Cambridge; *m* Sadie Holland; 2 da (Katy, Eliza); *Career* author; presenter Making History (BBC Radio 4), presenter and writer: The Letters of Saint Paul (Channel 4) 2010, Dinosaurs, Myths and Monsters (BBC 4) 2011, Islam: The Untold Story (Channel 4) 2012; former chair Soc of Authors; *Books* novels: Attis (1995), The Vampyre: Being the True Pilgrimage of George Gordon, Sixth Lord Byron (1995), Supping with Panthers (1996), Deliver Us from Evil (1997), The Sleeper in the Sands (1998), The Bonehunter (2001); non-fiction: Rubicon: The Triumph and Tragedy of the Roman Republic (2003, Hessell-Tiltman Prize 2004), Persian Fire: The First World Empire and the Battle for the West (2005), Millennium: The End of the World and the Forging of Christendom (2008), In the Shadow of the Sword: The Battle for Global Empire and the End of the Ancient World (2012), Herodotus: The Histories (translation, 2013), Dynasty: The Rise and Fall of the House of Caesar (2015); *Recreations* cricket, walking ancient roads, caring for hedgehogs; *Clubs* Literary Soc, Beefsteak; *Style—* Tom Holland, Esq; ✉ c/o Conville & Walsh, 2 Ganton Street, London W1F 7QL

HOLLAND, Prof Walter Werner; CBE (1992); s of Henry H Holland (d 1959), of London, and Hertha, *née* Zentner; *b* 5 March 1929, Teplice-Sanov; *Educ* Rugby, Univ of London, St Thomas' Hospital Med Sch (BSc, MB BS, MD); *m* 29 Oct 1964, Fiona, da of Douglas C Love (d 1976), of Bristol; 3 s (Peter b 1965, Richard b 1967, Michael b 1970); *Career* Flying Offr and Flt Lt RAF 1956–58; res fell: MRC 1959–61, Johns Hopkins Univ 1961–62; prof (former sr lectr and reader) St Thomas' Hosp 1962–94 (casualty offr 1955–56), visiting professor LSE Health London Sch of Economics 1995–, chm Euro Health Policy Network 1996–; author of over 315 articles and books; inaugural lectr Johns Hopkins Univ 1977 (elected lifetime memb Soc of Scholars 1970), Fogarty Scholar-in-Residence NIH Bethesda USA 1984–85, Theodore Badger visiting prof Harvard Univ 1984, first Sawyer Scholar in Res Case Western Reserve Med Sch Cleveland USA 1985, Europe et Médecine Prize Institut des Sciences de la Santé 1994, Queen Elizabeth The Queen Mother lectr Faculty of Public Health Med RCP 1995, Harben lectr Royal Inst of Public Health 1995, Cruickshank lectr Int Epidemiological Assoc 1996, Rock Carling lectr Nuffield Provincial Hosps Tst 1996/97; pres Int Epidemiological Assoc 1987–90, pres Faculty of Public Health Med 1989–92, vice-chm W Lambeth HA 1983–86, hon memb American Epidemiological Soc 1985; hon fell Italian Soc of Hygiene, Preventative Medicine and Public Health 2005; Hon DUniv Bordeaux Univ 1981, Hon DUniv Free Univ of Berlin 1990; memb: RSM, Soc for Social Med, Royal Statistical Soc, Int Epidemiological Assoc; FFPHM, FRCPE, FRCPath, FRCP, FRCGP, FFPHMI; *Books* Improving Health Services (2013); *Clubs* Athenaeum; *Style—* Prof Walter Holland, CBE; ✉ South End Cottage, Orleans Road, Twickenham, Middlesex TW1 3BL

HOLLAND, Will; s of John Holland, and Helen, *née* Gell; *b* 17 November 1979, Bristol; *Career* Homewood Park Hotel Bath (under Gary Jones)1998–2001, Gravetye Manor Hotel W Sussex (under Mark Raffan, *qqv*) 2001–04, L'ortolan Berks 2004–07 (under Alan Murchison), chef patron La Bécasse Ludlow 2007– (three AA Rosettes 2007–, Michelin Star 2009–11, Acorn Award 2009, 19th Best Restaurant in the UK Sunday Times 2010); television appearances incl: Saturday Kitchen, Hairy Bikers, Great British Menu; *Books* Yes Chef (contrib, 2009), Good Food Guide Recipes (contrib, 2010); *Style—* Will Holland, Esq; ✉ La Bécasse, 17 Corve Street, Ludlow, Shropshire SY8 1DA (☎ 01584 872325, website www.labecasse.co.uk)

HOLLAND-MARTIN, Robert George (Robin); s of Cyril Holland-Martin (d 1983), and Rosa, *née* Chadwyck-Healey (d 1997); *b* 6 July 1939; *Educ* Eton; *m* 1976, Dominique, da of Maurice Fromaget; 2 da; *Career* Cazenove & Co 1960–74 (ptnr 1968–74), fin dir Paterson Products Ltd 1976–86, conslt Newmarket Venture Capital plc 1982–94, dir Henderson plc 1983–98; non-exec dir: Dorling Kindersley Holdings plc 1992–2000, The Fine Art Soc plc 1995–, Service Point Solutions SA (formerly Grupo Picking Pack SA) 1998–2006, Grapes Direct Ltd 2000–06; conslt Investindustrial Group of Companies 1997–2013; memb: Met Hosp-Sunday Fund 1964–2002 (chm 1977–2002), Homoeopathic Tst 1970–90 (vice-chm 1975–90), Advsy Cncl V&A 1972–83, Assocs of V&A Ctee 1976–85 (chm 1981–85), Visiting Ctee RCA 1982–93 (chm 1984–93); tstee V&A 1983–85 (dep chm); hon dep treas Cons and Unionist Pty 1979–82; pres Blackie Fndn Tst 1998– (tstee 1971–96, chm 1987–96), tstee King's Med Res Tst 2000–, tstee City & Guilds of London Art Sch 2001– (chm 2002–); memb Ct of Assts Worshipful Co of Fishmongers 1999– (Prime Warden 2010–11); *Clubs* White's; *Style—* Robin Holland-Martin, Esq; ✉ 94 Old Church Street, London SW3 6EP (☎ 020 7352 7871)

HOLLANDER, Charles Simon; QC (1999); s of Paul Hollander, of London, and Eileen, *née* Flanagan; *b* 1 December 1955; *Educ* UCS Hampstead (nat schoolboy bridge champion, rep Univ of Cambridge, Cambs and Hunts), King's Coll Cambridge (Douton entrance scholar, sr scholar, MA); *m* 1986, Heather, da of Trevor Pilley; 2 da (Jennifer b 19 April 1990, Hilary b 15 Jan 2000), 2 s (Andrew b 11 May 1993, Ian b 1 Nov 1997); *Career* called to the Bar: Gray's Inn 1978, Gibraltar, Brunei; in private practice specialising in commercial litigation 1978–, recorder of the Crown Court 2000–; chm Bar Standards Ctee 2006–07, memb Bar Standards Bd 2006–07; CEDR accredited mediator; *Books* Documentary Evidence (1 edn 1985, 7 edn 2000), Conflicts of Evidence and Chinese Walls (2000), Phipson on Evidence (contrib and ed, 15 edn 1999); *Recreations* tennis, food, wine; *Style—* Charles Hollander, Esq, QC; ✉ Brick Court Chambers, 7–8 Essex Street, London WC2R 3LD (☎ 020 7379 3550, fax 020 7379 3558, website www.brickcourt.co.uk)

HOLLENS, Jerry Robert; s of Robert Hollens, of Northwich, Cheshire, and Rita, *née* Burrows; *b* 17 August 1964, Northwich, Cheshire; *Educ* Sir John Deane's GS Northwich, Warrington Coll of Art, Maidstone Coll of Art (BA); *m* 16 May 1992, Mariabella, *née* Weightman; 2 s (Wilkie F b 2 Dec 1993, Mischa H b 23 July 1996); *Career* Saatchi & Saatchi 1986–94 (Saatchi & Saatchi NY 1990–91), BMP DDB 1994–98, Rainey Kelly Campbell Roalfe 1998–99, RKCR/Y&R 1999–2014, Jerry Hollens Ltd 2014–; awards at most major advertising festivals incl D&AD, Cannes Lions, Clio, British Arrows, Campaign Press and Poster Awards, Creative Circle Award, Big and Promax; *Recreations* cycling, motorcycling, photography, art, film, Liverpool FC, playing the guitar badly; *Clubs* VCC, SRAA; *Style—* Jerry Hollens, Esq; ✉ RKCR/Y&R, Greater London House, Hampstead Road, London NW1 7QP (☎ 020 7611 6614, e-mail jerry_hollens@uk.yr.com, website www.mikeandjerry.com)

HOLLERN, Kate; MP; *b* 12 April 1955, Dunbarton, Dunbartonshire; *m* ; 2 da (Donna, Katrina); *Career* MP (Lab) Blackburn 2015–; *Style—* Ms Kate Hollern, MP; ✉ House of Commons, London SW1A 0AA

HOLLICK, Baron (Life Peer UK 1991), of Notting Hill in the Royal Borough of Kensington and Chelsea; Clive Richard Hollick; *Educ* Taunton's Sch, Univ of Nottingham; *m*; 3 da; *Career* dir various United Business Media plc subsids, chief exec United Business Media plc until 2005; Kohlberg Kravis Roberts: ptnr 2005–08, sr advsr 2008–10; dir: Hambros Bank 1973–96, Diageo plc, TRW Inc 2000–02, Honeywell Inc, Pro Sieben Gp AG, BMG Music Rights Mgmnt; special advsr to Pres Bd of Trade 1997–98; chm House of Lords Econ Affrs Ctee 2014–, PM's trade and investment envoy 2014–; chm South Bank Bd 2002–08; fndr tstee IPPR; *Style—* The Rt Hon Lord Hollick

HOLLIDAY, Raymond (Ray); OBE (1999); s of Ronald Holliday (d 1992), and Mary Louisa, *née* Cowen; *b* 30 May 1949; *Educ* Boteler GS Warrington, Univ of Newcastle upon Tyne (BA, PGCE, MEd), Newcastle upon Tyne Poly (TEFL Dip (RSA)); *m* 1, 1975 (m dis 2003), Régine, da of Gérard Leclerc; 4 da (Kristelle b 6 May 1981, Chloé b 13 April 1985, Loriane b 19 April 1987, Géraldine b 8 Aug 1992), 1 s (Marc Alexandre b 20 Feb 1988); m 2, 2004, Cécile, da of Roland Bonnin; 1 da (Océane Cécilia b 9 Feb 2004); *Career* teacher of French and English Seaton Sluice Middle Sch Northumberland 1975–80, dep head Blyth Wensleydale Middle Sch Northumberland 1982–87(year ldr 1980–82); British Council School of Madrid: dep head 1987–93, actg head 1993–94, head 1994–2001; head French American Int Sch of Boston 2001–06, dir American Int Sch of Budapest 2006–; *Recreations* reading, music, theatre, cycling, a wide variety of sports with no great level in any; *Style—* Ray Holliday, Esq, OBE; ✉ American International School of Budapest, PO Box 53, 1525 Budapest, Hungary (☎ +36 26 556000, fax +36 26 556003, e-mail rhollidayb@nk.aisb.hu)

HOLLIDAY, Steven John; *b* 26 October 1956; *Educ* Univ of Nottingham; *Career* early career with Exxon Gp (latterly sr positions in int gas business, refining and shipping), exec dir British Borneo Oil and Gas 1997–2000; Nat Grid plc: exec dir UK and Europe 2001–02, exec dir for UK gas distribution 2002–06, dep chief exec 2006–07, chief exec 2007–; chm Crisis 2011–, vice-chm Business in the Community 2014–, vice-chair The Careers and Enterprise Co 2015–; non-exec dir Marks & Spencer 2004–14; memb Bd Electricity Assoc 2001–03; hon degree: Univ of Nottingham, Strathclyde Univ; *Style—* Mr Steven Holliday; ✉ National Grid plc, 1–3 Strand, London WC2N 5EH

HOLLINGBERY, George Michael Edward; MP; *Educ* Radley, Lady Margaret Hall Oxford (BA), Univ of Philadelphia (MBA); *Career* stockbroker 1985–89, Private Venture Capital Investments 1991–94, chm and fndr Pet Depot Ltd 1994–99, chm and fndr Companion Care Ltd 1997–2002, Thompson Sowerbutts 2005–; cncllr Alresford Town Cncl 1999–2003 (chm 2001–02), cncllr Winchester City Cncl 1999– (dep ldr and portfolio holder for communications and performance mgmnt 2006–08); MP (Cons) Meon Valley 2010–; *Style—* George Hollingbery, Esq, MP

HOLLINGHURST, Alan James; s of James Kenneth Hollinghurst (d 1991), and Elizabeth Lilian, *née* Keevil; *b* 26 May 1954; *Educ* Canford Sch Dorset, Magdalen Coll Oxford (BA, MLitt); *Career* dep ed Times Literary Supplement 1985–90 (on staff 1982–95); hon fell Magdalen Coll Oxford; Hon DLit UCL; FRSL; *Books* The Swimming-Pool Library (1988, Somerset Maugham Award, American Acad of Arts and Letters E M Forster Award), The Folding Star (1994, James Tait Black Memorial Prize, shortlisted Booker Prize), The Spell (1998), The Line of Beauty (2004, Man Booker Prize), The Stranger's Child (2011); *Recreations* listening to music, looking at buildings; *Style—* Alan Hollinghurst, Esq, FRSL; ✉ Antony Harwood Ltd, 103 Walton Street, Oxford OX2 6EB (☎ 01865 559615, fax 01865 310660, e-mail mail@antonyharwood.com)

HOLLINGSWORTH, Timothy Philip (Tim); s of Michael Hollingsworth, and Marjorie, *née* Whittaker; *b* 10 April 1967, Farnborough, Kent; *Educ* Sevenoaks Sch, Univ of Exeter (BA, MA); *m* 8 July 2000, Emma, *née* Houston; 2 s (Thomas b 26 Aug 2002, Oliver b 13 Jan 2005); *Career* head of media relations CBI 1995–2000, head of communications Granada plc 2000–01, dir HBL Media 2001–05; UK Sport: dir of policy and communications 2005–10, chief operating offr 2010–11; chief exec British Paralympic Assoc 2011–; tstee and Bd dir Youth Sport Tst, tstee Nat Parlympic Heritage Tst; Hon LLD: Univ of Exeter 2014, Univ of Bath 2014; *Recreations* music, reading, theatre, current affrs, all sport; *Style—* Tim Hollingsworth, Esq; ✉ British Paralympic Association, 60

Charlotte Street, London W1T 2NU (☎ 020 7842 5789, e-mail tim.hollingsworth@paralympics.org.uk, website www.paralympics.org.uk, Twitter @timhparagb)

HOLLINRAKE, Kevin; MP; s of Geoffrey Hollinrake, and Muriel, *née* Lee; *Educ* Easingwold Sch, Sheffield Hallam Univ; *m* 16 April 1994, Nicola, *née* Thompson; 1 s (Charles b 22 Oct 1996), 3 da (Madeleine b 13 Oct 1998, Arabella b 27 Dec 2002, Gabriella 18 Oct 2007); *Career* co-fndr Hunters Property plc 1992 (chm 2015–); MP (Cons) Thirsk and Malton 2015–; *Recreations* cricket, golf, horse racing, reading, skiing; *Style*— Kevin Hollinrake, Esq, MP; ✉ House of Commons, London, SW1A 0AA (Twitter @kevinhollinrake)

HOLLINS, Christopher Jonathan (Chris); s of John William Hollins, MBE, and Linda Kay, *née* Barnes; *b* 20 March 1971, Bromley; *Educ* Tonbridge Sch, Univ of Durham, Keble Coll Oxford (cricket and football blues); *m* 3 March 2012, Sarah Louise *née* Alexander; 1 s (George John Alexander); *Career* early career as footballer with Charlton and Aldershot Town 1994; began media career with Channel One TV, Meridian and Five TV, joined BBC 1999, sports presenter BBC Breakfast 2005–12 (also regular co-host), co-presenter Watchdog (BBC 1) 2010–, presenter BT Sport; other television appearances incl: Celebrity MasterChef, Royal Wedding, Strictly Come Dancing (winner); *Recreations* cricket, tennis, golf; *Clubs* MCC, The Oxfordshire; *Style*— Mr Chris Hollins; ✉ c/o Jo Carlton, Talent4 Media Limited, Studio LG16, Shepherds Building Central, Charecroft Way, London W14 0EH (☎ 020 7183 4330)

HOLLINS, Peter; *Educ* East Barnet GS, Hertford Coll Oxford (BA); *Career* ICI 1973–1992, chief operating offr European Vinyls Corp 1992–98, ceo British Energy 1998–2001, various roles as chm and non-exec dir 2001–03, chief exec British Heart Fndn 2003–13, ret; *Recreations* music (especially opera), European history; *Style*— Peter Hollins, Esq; ✉ British Heart Foundation, 180 Hampstead Road, London NW1 7AW (☎ 020 7935 0185, fax 020 7486 5820)

HOLLINS, Baroness (Life Peer UK 2010), of Wimbledon in the London Borough of Merton and of Grenoside in the County of South Yorkshire; Prof Sheila Clare Hollins; *née* Kelly; da of Capt Adrian M Kelly (d 1995), of Bristol, and Monica Dallas, *née* Edwards (d 2005); *b* 22 June 1946; *Educ* Notre Dame HS Sheffield, St Thomas' Hosp Med Sch London (MB BS); *m* 7 June 1969, Martin Prior Hollins, s of Harry Pryor Hollins (d 1985), of Cheadle Hulme; 3 da (Kathryn b 1971, Emily b 1976, Abigail b 1978), 1 s (Nigel b 1973); *Career* sr registrar in child psychiatry Earls Court Child Guidance Unit and Westminster Children's Hosp 1979–81; St George's Hosp Med Sch London: sr lectr in the psychiatry of learning disability St George's Hosp Med Sch 1981– (prof 1990–), head Dept of Psychiatry of Disability 1986–2002, head Div of Mental Health 2002–05; hon conslt Wandsworth Community Health Tst and Richmond Twickenham and Roehampton Healthcare Tst 1981–99, hon conslt SW London and St George's Mental Health Tst 2002–11; Dept of Health: seconded to Policy Div as pt/t sr policy advsr on learning disability 1993–94 and 2001–03; memb: Minister's Advsy Gp on Learning Disability 1999–2001, Nat Learning Disabilty Taskforce 2001–04, Independent Inquiry into Access to Healthcare for People with Learning Disabilities 2007; chair NHS Working Party on Breast and Cervical Screening in Learning Disability 1999–2000, chair External Advsy Gp Nat Confidential Inquiry into Suicides and Homicides 2007–10, chair Expert Reference Gp on Workforce Trg for Learning Disability Servs Health Educn England 2015–; RCPsych: chair Exec Ctee Psychiatry of Learning Disability Faculty 1994–98, memb Ct of Electors 1999, vice-pres 2003–04, pres 2005–08; vice-pres Inst of Psychiatry and Disability 2001–; hon memb World Psychiatric Assoc 2011–; memb lay community St Benedict; memb Pontifical Cmmn for the Protection of Minors 2014–; Winston Churchill fell 1993; Hon DD Univ of London, Hon MD Univ of Sheffield, Hon LLD Univ of Bath, Hon DSc Univ of Worcester, Hon DLitt Univ of Durham 2016; FRCPsych 1988 (MRCPsych 1978), FRCPCH, hon FRCP, FRSM, fell HE Acad, fell Coll of Medicine SA, fell Medical Women's Fedn, fell Inst of Psycotherapy and Disability, Hon memb Tavistock Centre for Couple Relationships; Twickenham and roehampton Healthcare Tst 1981–99; Hon Conslt SW; *Books* Mental Handicap: A Multi Disciplinary Approach (ed with M Craft, J Bicknell, 1985), Going Somewhere – Pastoral Care for People with Mental Handicap (with M Grimer, 1988), Understanding Depression in People with Learning Disabilities (with J Curran, 1996), Understanding Grief (with L Sireling, 1999); ed and co-author of 50 titles in Books Beyond Words series incl: When Dad Died and When Mum Died (2 books with L Sireling, 1990), Jenny Speaks Out (with V Sinason, 1992), Bob Tells All (with V Sinason, 1992), Hug Me, Touch Me (Best Author Read Easy Awards Book Tst and Joseph Rowntree Fndn 1994), Getting on With Epilepsy (with J Bernal, 1999), George Gets Smart (with M Flynn and P Russell, 2001), Mugged (with V Sinason, 2002), You and Your Child: Making Sense of Learning Disability (with M Hollins, 2005), Am I Going to Die? (with I Tuffrey, 2009), The Drama Group (with M Hollins and Hugh Grant, 2015), When Dad Hurts Mum (with Patricia Scotland and Noelle Blackman), Finding a Safe Place from Abuse (with Patricia Scotland and Noelle Blackman); author of numerous peer reviewed papers and chapters on mental health and learning disability; *Recreations* family, walking, music; *Style*— The Baroness Hollins; ✉ (☎ 020 7219 0520)

HOLLIS, Prof Malcolm Richard Arthur; s of Arthur Edwin Hollis (d 1970), of Southport, Merseyside, and Esmé Muriel, *née* Pettit (d 2002); *b* 17 March 1944; *Educ* King George V GS Southport, Univ of South Wales and Monmouth, Univ of London (BSc); *m* 11 Sept 1965, Andrea Joan, da of Sqdn Ldr John Edward Fuller (d 1989), of West Chiltington, W Sussex; 2 s (Richard b 1969, Gavin b 1976), 1 da (Tricia b 1970); *Career* chartered building surveyor; ptnr Best Gapp & Ptnrs 1969, princ Malcolm Hollis Associates 1972–80, ptnr Baxter Payne & Lepper (incl Malcolm Hollis Associates) 1980–91 (dep chm 1986–88), sr ptnr Malcolm Hollis & Partners 1991–95; chm Acutec UK 1995–; Surveyor to the Fabric Worshipful Co of Skinners 1982–, mangr professional servs Nationwide Anglia Estate Agents 1987–91, memb Cncl RICS Bldg Surveyors 1988–92 and 1998–2001; over 100 appearances on TV and radio 1984–; prof Univ of Reading 1989–, visiting prof Univ of Malaya Malaysia 2006–, visiting prof Politecnic of Bari Italy 2007–; ed Jl of Building Appraisal 2002–; cncllr London Borough of Lambeth 1977–81; govr Woodmansterne Sch 1978–81 (chm 1979–81), cncllr Strete PC 2011– (chm 2015–), ed Stretewise website 2012–; tstee Upkeep (incl The Upkeep Building Museum); Freeman City of London 1983, Freeman Worshipful Co of Chartered Surveyors 1982; FSVA 1969, FBEng 1969, FRICS 1970, MCIArb 1974, MAE 1997; *Books* Surveying Buildings (1983, 5 edn 2003), Householders Action Guide (1984), Model Survey Reports (1985, 2 edn 1989), Surveying for Dilapidations (1988), Cavity Wall Tie Failure (1990), Dilapidations (1992, 2 edn 1996), Introduction to Dilapidations (1999, 3 edn 2009), Surveyors Fact Book (2001, revised edns 2007, 2008 and 2009), Surveying Buildings Pocket Book (2002, 3 edn 2015); *Recreations* writing, photography, skiing, thinking; *Clubs* Dartmouth Golf; *Style*— Prof Malcolm Hollis; ✉ 6 Rydal Road, London SW16 1QN (☎ 020 8769 9927, fax 020 8769 2670, e-mail mh@malcolmhollis.org)

HOLLIS OF HEIGHAM, Baroness (Life Peer UK 1990), of Heigham in the City of Norwich; Patricia Lesley Hollis; PC (1999), DL (Norfolk 1994); da of H L G Wells, of Norwich, and (Queenie) Rosalyn, *née* Clayforth; *b* 24 May 1941; *Educ* Plympton GS, Univ of Cambridge (MA), Univ of Calif Berkeley, Columbia Univ NY, Nuffield Coll Oxford (MA, DPhil); *m* 18 Sept 1965, Prof (James) Martin Hollis (d 1998), s of (Hugh) Mark Noel Hollis, of Oxted, Surrey; 2 s (Hon Simon b 1969, Hon Matthew b 1971); *Career* Harkness fell 1962–64, Nuffield scholar 1964–67; UEA: lectr in modern history 1967–79, sr lectr 1979–85, reader 1985–90, dean Sch of English and American Studies 1988–90; oppn whip 1990–97, oppn spokesperson on social security, disability, local govt and housing 1992–97, Parly under sec of state DSS 1997–2001, min for children and the family Dept of Work and Pensions 2001–05; cncllr: Norwich City Cncl 1968–91 (ldr 1983–88), Norfolk CC 1981–85; Parly candidate Great Yarmouth 1974 and 1979; memb: E Anglia Economic Planning Cncl 1975–79, Govt Cmmn on Housing 1975–77, RHA 1979–83, BBC Regnl Advsy Ctee 1979–83, Press Cncl 1989–91, Bd Pensions Advsy Serv 2006–; chair Broadland Housing Assoc 2009–; dir Radio Broadland 1983–95; nat cmmr English Heritage 1988–91; tstee History of Parl Tst 2005–, Sainsbury tstee UEA 2006–; hon fell Girton Coll Cambridge 2000; Hon DLitt: Anglia Poly Univ 1995, London Guildhall Univ 2001; Hon DUniv Open 2000; FRHistS; *Books* The Pauper Press (1970), Class and Class Conflict 1815–50 (1973), Women in Public 1850–1900 (1979), Pressure from Without (1974), Ladies Elect: Women in English Local Govt 1865–1914 (1987), Jennie Lee, A Life (1997, Orwell Prize for political biography 1998, Wolfson Prize for history 1998); *Recreations* singing, boating on the broads, domesticity; *Style*— The Rt Hon Baroness Hollis of Heigham, PC, DL; ✉ House of Lords, London SW1A 0PW (☎ 020 7219 3000)

HOLLOBONE, Philip; MP; *b* 7 November 1964; *Educ* Lady Margaret Hall Oxford; *Career* industry research analyst 1987–2004; cncllr (Cons): Bromley BC 1990–94, Kettering BC 2003–; Parly candidate (Cons) Kettering 2001, MP (Cons) Kettering 2005–; *Style*— Philip Hollobone, Esq, MP; ✉ House of Commons, London SW1A 0AA (☎ 020 7219 8373, fax 020 7219 8802, e-mail philip.hollobone.mp@parliament.uk)

HOLLOWAY, Adam; MP; *Educ* Univ of Cambridge (MA), Imperial Coll London (MBA); *Career* former offr Grenadier Guards; TV reporter and undercover reporter, Bosnia reporter ITN; worked on programs incl: Newsnight, World in Action, News At Ten; MP (Cons) Gravesham 2005–, memb House of Commons Defence Select Ctee 2006–10, PPS to FCO 2010–11, memb House of Commons Foreign Affrs Select Ctee 2015–; former chm Cncl for Arab British Understanding, dep chm Cons Middle East Cncl; former memb Bd Christian Aid; *Style*— Adam Holloway, Esq, MP; ✉ House of Commons, London SW1A 0AA (☎ 020 7219 8402, e-mail hollowaya@parliament.uk, website www.adamholloway.co.uk)

HOLLOWAY, Prof John Henry; OBE (2000); s of William Henry Holloway (d 1983), of Coalville, and Ivy May, *née* Sarson (d 1997); *b* 20 December 1938, Ashby-de-la-Zouch. Leics; *Educ* Ashby-de-la-Zouch Boys' GS, Univ of Birmingham (BSc, PhD, DSc); *m* 14 April 1962, Jennifer, da of Albert Burne (d 1993); 2 da (Sarah b 1964, Amanda b 1965), 1 s (Mark b 1969); *Career* Univ of Aberdeen: asst lectr 1963–64, lectr 1964–70; Univ of Leicester: lectr 1971–78, sr lectr 1978–87, prof and head of chemistry 1987–96, dean of science 1997–99, pro-vice-chllr 1999–2001, sr pro-vice-chllr 2001–03, prof emeritus 2004; Royal Soc of Chemistry: memb Disciplinary Ctee, memb Applied Materials Chemistry Gp; Univ of Leicester: chm of tstees PAS Pension Scheme, memb Haldane Soc Ctee; meetings sec Uppingham Probus Ctee, memb Rutland Reminders Ctee; author of over 300 papers on fluorine chemistry; past chm HE Chemistry Conf; Hon LLD Univ of Leicester; CChem, FRSC; *Books* Noble Gas Chemistry (1968); *Recreations* painting, drawing, sailing, classic car restoration; *Style*— Prof John Holloway, OBE; ✉ 5 Hall Gardens, High Street East, Uppingham, Rutland LE15 9HG (☎ 01572 820276, e-mail jhh2@le.ac.uk)

H

HOLLOWAY, Julian Pendrill Warner; s of Adrian George Warner Holloway, JP, of Minchinhampton, Glos, and Helen Pendrill, *née* Charles; *b* 6 May 1954; *Educ* Winchester, Univ of Durham (BA); *m* 4 Oct 1980 (m dis 1998), Emma Jane Caroline, da of Col Peter Charles Ormrod, MC, JP, DL, of Pen-y-Lan Ruabon, Clwyd; 1 da (Lavinia b 28 April 1984), 3 s (James b 29 June 1986, Thomas b 14 March 1988, Alexander b 29 Aug 1991); m 2, 1999, Sarah Louise Balfe, da of Jeremy Bennett, Esq, OBE, of Sherborne, Dorset; *Career* articled clerk Denton Hall & Burgin 1979–81, admitted slr to the Supreme Ct 1981, asst slr Brecher & Co 1981–83, ptnr McKenna & Co 1988–92 (asst slr 1984–88), ptnr Greenwoods 1993–2000, ptnr Berwin Leighton Paisner 2001–08, ptnr Speechly Bircham 2008–10, owner Julian Holloway Dispute Resolution Services 2010–; case-notes ed Construction Law Jl; memb Law Soc; *Recreations* tennis, skiing, shooting; *Clubs* Hurlingham; *Style*— Julian Holloway, Esq; ✉ 64 Alderbrook Road, London SW12 8AB (☎ 020 8675 0308)

HOLLOWAY, Laurence (Laurie); MBE (2013); s of Marcus Holloway (d 1978), of Oldham, Lancs, and Annie, *née* Gillespie (d 1992); *b* 31 March 1938; *Educ* Oldham GS; *m* 1, 31 March 1956, Julia Planck, da of Rufus Macdonald (d 1975), of Rothesay, Isle of Bute; 1 da (Karon Julie b 9 Jan 1957); m 2, 16 June 1965, Marian Montgomery (d 2002), singer, da of Forrest Marion Runnels (d 1966), of Atlanta, Georgia; 1 da (Abigail Ann Montgomery Hellens b 31 Jan 1967); m 3 27 July 2014, Maryann Lallyette; *Career* pianist, composer, arranger; studio musician 1959–69; compositions incl: A Dream of Alice (BBC TV), pop preludes, About Time (C5 Records); musical dir: Engelbert Humperdinck 1969–74, Dame Edna Everage 1980– (currently md), Elaine Paige 1992–, Piaf (musical) 1992, Bob Monkhouse, Lily Savage TV Special, Bob Downe TV Special, Bob Holness radio series, Parkinson TV series 1998–, Strictly Come Dancing (BBC TV) 2004–05; pianist for: Judy Garland and Liza Minnelli London Palladium 1964, Dame Kiri Te Kanawa on Popular Recordings (special guest at concert); composer TV signature tunes incl Blind Date, occasional guest conductor London Symphony Orch; tstee Montgomery-Holloway Music Tst; subject of This is your Life 2000; *Recreations* golf, music, shooting, fishing; *Clubs* Temple Golf; *Style*— Laurie Holloway, Esq, MBE; ✉ Elgin, Fishery Road, Bray-on-Thames, Berkshire SL6 1UP (☎ 07711 671557, e-mail piano@laurieholloway.com)

HOLLOWAY, Neil; *Educ* Univ of Bath (BSc), Univ of Cambridge (MPhil); *Career* md Migent UK until 1990; Microsoft Corporation: joined 1990, md Microsoft Ltd 1998–2000, vice-pres for sales, mktg and servs EMEA 2000–05, pres EMEA 2005, corporate vice-pres 2003–; *Recreations* football, swimming, golf, family; *Style*— Neil Holloway, Esq; ✉ Microsoft Ltd, Microsoft Campus, Thames Valley Park, Reading RG6 1WG

HOLLOWAY, Prof Robin Greville; s of Robert Charles Holloway (d 1986), and Pamela Mary, *née* Jacob (d 1996); *b* 19 October 1943; *Educ* St Paul's Cathedral Choir Sch, KCS Wimbledon, King's Coll Cambridge, New Coll Oxford; *Career* composer; Univ of Cambridge: lectr in music 1975–, prof of musical composition 2001–; compositions incl: Scenes from Schumann (Cheltenham) 1970, Domination of Black (London) 1974, Second Concerto for Orchestra (Glasgow) 1979, Seascape and Harvest (Birmingham) 1986, Clarissa (ENO) 1990, The Spacious Firmament (Birmingham) 1992, Violin Concerto (Manchester) 1992, Frost at Midnight (Bournemouth) 1994, Third Concerto for Orchestra (London) 1996, Clarinet Concerto (Canterbury) 1997, Scenes from Antwerp (Antwerp) 1998, Clarissa – Sequence (San Francisco) 1998, Double Bass Concerto 1999, Symphony (London) 2000, Fourth Concerto for Orchestra 2001–06, Missa Caiensis 2002, String Quartet No 1 2003, String Quartet No 2 2004, Fifth Concerto for Orchestra (London) 2009–10, Reliquary 2010, Gold on Bronze 2010, Trio for Oboe, Violin and Piano 2011, String Quartets Nos 2–5 2007–15, Blooms of Passion 2012, In China (Beijing) 2013, Autumn Music 2014, The Day's Deep Midnight 2015; *Books* Debussy and Wagner (1978), On Music: Essays and Diversions (2003), Essays and Diversions II (2008), Poems of Richard Crashaw (selected and introduced, 2013); *Style*— Prof Robin Holloway; ✉ Gonville & Caius College, Cambridge CB2 1TA (☎ 01223 335424, e-mail rgh1000@cam.ac.uk); 531 Caledonian Road, London N7 9RH (☎ 020 7607 2550)

HOLM, Sir Ian; kt (1998), CBE (1990); *b* 12 September 1931; *Educ* RADA; *m* 2003, Sophie de Stempel, *qv*; *Career* actor; *Theatre* debut in Othello (Shakespeare Memorial Theatre) 1954, Worthing Rep 1956, at Stratford 1957–60: roles incl Verges, Puck, The Fool in King Lear, Lorenzio and Gremio; with RSC (Aldwych) until 1967: Ondine, The Devils,

Becket, The Taming of the Shrew, The Cherry Orchard; other RSC prodns until 1967: Troilus and Cressida (Stratford), The Tempest, Edward IV, Richard III, Henry IV and Henry V (Evening Standard for Best Actor) 1964, Edward IV 1964, Richard III 1964, The Homecoming (Aldwych) 1965 and (Music Box NY) 1967 (Tony Award for Best Supporting Actor in a Drama), Henry IV (I and II) 1966, Henry V 1966, Twelfth Night 1966, Romeo and Juliet 1967; other prodns incl: The Friends (Roundhouse) 1970, A Bequest to the Nation (Haymarket) 1970, Caravaggio Buddy (Traverse Theatre, Edinburgh) 1972, Hatch in the Sea (Royal Court), Other People (Hampstead) 1974, The Iceman Cometh (Aldwych) 1976, The Devil's Disciple (Aldwych) 1976, Uncle Vanya (Hampstead) 1979, The Room (Pinter benefit, Haymarket) 1989, Moonlight (Almeida) 1993 (Evening Standard Award for Best Actor), Moonlight and Landscape (Pinter Festival Gate Theatre Dublin) 1994, Landscape (RNT) 1994, King Lear (RNT) 1997 (Evening Standard Award for Best Actor, Olivier Award for Best Actor), The Homecoming (Comedy Theatre) 2001; *Television* for BBC: Flayed, The Lost Boys, The Misanthrope, Lloyd George, We The Accused, The Bell, After The Party, The Browning Version, Mr and Mrs Edgehill, Uncle Vanya, The Last Romantics, The Borrowers, Landscape, King Lear; for Granada: Night School, Strike, Game Set and Match, Mirage; other credits incl: Napoleon in Love, Jesus of Nazareth, The Road From Mandalay, SOS Titanic, All Quiet on the Western Front, Inside The Third Reich, Death Can Add (Anglia TV), The Endless Game (HTV), Taylor of Gloucester (Thames), Alice Through The Looking Glass (Channel 4); *Film* A Midsummer Night's Dream, The Fixer, The Bofors Gun (BAFTA for Best Supporting Actor), The Homecoming, Juggernaut, Shout at the Devil, The Man in the Iron Mask, March or Die, Thief of Baghdad, Alien, Chariots of Fire (BAFTA for Best Supporting Actor, Cannes Film Festival Best Supporting Actor, Oscar nomination), The Time Bandits, The Return of the Soldier, Dead as they Come, Greystoke, Brazil, Laughterhouse, Dance with a Stranger, Wetherby, Dreamchild, Another Woman, Henry V, Michaelangelo, Hamlet, Kafka, The Naked Lunch, Blue Ice, The Hour of the Pig, Frankenstein, Dr Willis in The Madness of King George 1994 (BAFTA nomination), Loch Ness 1995, Big Night 1995, Night Falls on Manhattan 1995, The Fifth Element 1996, A Life Less Ordinary 1996, The Sweet Hereafter 1996, Simon Magus 1998, Existenz 1998, The Match 1998, Beautiful Joe 1999, Bless the Child 1999, Joe Gould's Secret 1999, Esther Kahn 1999, Lord of the Rings: The Fellowship of the Ring 2001, From Hell 2002, Lord of the Rings: the Return of the King 2003, Garden State 2004, The Day After Tomorrow 2004, The Aviator 2004, The Treatment 2005, Lord of War 2005, Chromophobia 2005, Beyond Friendship 2005, Ratatouille 2007; *Style*— Sir Ian Holm, CBE

HOLM, Dr Jessica Lynn; da of Sir Ian Holm, CBE, *qv*, and Lynn Mary, *née* Shaw; *b* 29 March 1960; *Educ* Putney HS for Girls, Royal Holloway Coll London (BSc, PhD); *m* 27 Feb 1988 (m dis 2012), Gavin Bernard Chappell, s of Lt-Col Robin Chappell, OBE; 2 c (Tierney Brook b 15 Oct 1997, Karris Layne b 27 Sept 2000); *Career* zoologist and broadcaster BBC Natural History Unit and others; BBC Natural History Unit films: The Case of the Vanishing Squirrel 1987, Daylight Robbery 1988, Badger Watch 1990, Daylight Robbery II 1991, Nightshift 1993; presenter: Natural History Progamme (BBC Radio 4) 1988–93, Wild about the West (TSW) 1988, Up Country (Tyne Tees TV) 1990, 1991, 1992 and 1993, Crufts (BBC TV then More 4) 1991–, Wild West Country (WCTV) 1994, 1995 and 1996, Cross Country (HTV) 1999, Changing Places (BBC Radio 4) 2001–02; commentator The Underdog Show (BBC 2) 2007; regular columnist and cartoonist Dog World newspaper; painter; Slipper Thief (first limited edn print, Greenwich Workshop) 1996, I Spy Summer (second limited edn print, Greenwich Workshop) 1997, Five Persians (third limited edn print) 1998, The Sentry (fourth limited edn print) 1998, solo exhibition The Kennel Club 1997; *Publications* Squirrels (1987), The Red Squirrel (1989); contrib various articles to wildlife and conservation magazines; *Recreations* my children, my dogs, my vegetable garden; *Clubs* Kennel, Soc of Equestrian Artists; *Style*— Dr Jessica Holm; ✉ c/o Rachel Daniels, Berlin Associates, 14 Floral Street, London WC2E 9DH (☎ 020 7836 1112, e-mail jessica.holm@btinternet.com)

HOLMAN, Hon Mr Justice; Sir (Edward) James Holman; kt (1995); s of Edward Theodore Holman (d 2001), and Mary Megan, *née* Morris, MBE (d 2006), formerly of Ringwood, Hants and Manaccan, Cornwall; *b* 21 August 1947; *Educ* Dauntsey's Sch, Exeter Coll Oxford (MA); *m* 14 July 1979, Fiona Elisabeth, da of late Dr Ronald Cathcart Roxburgh, of Wiggenhall St Mary, Norfolk; 1 da (Charlotte b 1984), 2 s (Edward b 1988, Henry b 1991); *Career* called to the Bar Middle Temple 1971 (bencher 1995); memb Western Circuit, QC 1991, recorder of the Crown Court 1993–95, judge of the High Court of Justice (Family Div) 1995–, Family Div liaison judge for Western Circuit 1995–2002; standing counsel to the Treasury (Queen's Proctor) 1980–91, legal assessor UK Central Cncl for Nursing Midwifery and Health Visiting 1983–95; Family Law Bar Assoc: sec 1988–92, chm 1992–95; ex officio memb Gen Cncl of the Bar 1992–95; memb: Family Proceedings Rules Ctee 1991–95, Supreme Court Procedure Ctee 1992–95; memb: Cncl RYA 1980–83, 1984–87 and 1988–91, Ctee Royal Ocean Racing Club 1984–87; *Recreations* sailing, skiing, music; *Clubs* Royal Yacht Sqdn, Royal Ocean Racing, Ocean Cruising; *Style*— The Hon Mr Justice Holman; ✉ Royal Courts of Justice, Strand, London WC2A 2LL

HOLMES, Prof Andrew Bruce; AM (2004); s of late Bruce Morell Holmes, and Frances Henty Graham Holmes; *b* 5 September 1943; *Educ* Scotch Coll Melbourne, Ormond Coll Univ of Melbourne (BSc, MSc), UCL (PhD), Univ of Cambridge (ScD), Univ of Oxford (MA, DSc); *m* 1971, Jennifer Lesley, *née* Hodson; 3 s; *Career* Royal Soc European postdoctoral fell ETH-Zürich 1971–72; Univ of Cambridge: demonstrator 1972–77, lectr 1977–94, dir Melville Lab for Polymer Synthesis 1994–2004, reader in organic and polymer chemistry 1995–98, prof of organic and polymer chemistry 1998–2004; fell Clare Coll Cambridge 1973–; ARC Fedn and VESKI fell and prof of chemistry Univ of Melbourne/CSIRO Molecular and Health Technologies 2004–09, prof of chemistry Imperial Coll London 2004–09 (emeritus prof and distinguished research fell 2009–), CSIRO fell CSIRO Materials Science and Engrg 2008–14 (fell emeritus 2014–), laureate prof Univ of Melbourne 2009–14 (Univ laureate prof emeritus 2014–); foreign sec Australian Acad Science 2010–14; princ ed Jl of Materials Research 1994–99, chm Editorial Bd Chemical Communications 2000–03, assoc ed Organic Letters 2006–; memb: Bd of Editors Organic Syntheses Inc 1996–2001, Editorial Bd New Jl of Chemistry 2000–03, Publishing Bd RSC 2003–06, Publishing Advsy Ctee CSIRO 2006–14; memb Int Advsy Bd: Macromolecular Chemistry and Physics 1999–2006, Jl of Materials Chemistry 1996–2006, Chemical Communications 2004–12, Chemistry World 2004–, Australian Jl of Chemistry 2004–, Bulletin of the Chemical Society of Japan 2004–, Beilstein Jl Organic Chemistry 2005–, Angewandte Chemie 2006–13; visiting fell La Trobe Univ 1977; visiting prof: Univ of Calif Berkeley 1984, Univ of Calif Irvine 1991; Hans Kupczyk Fndn guest prof Univ of Ulm 2009, Newton Abraham visiting prof and fell Lincoln Coll Oxford 2011–12; Royal Soc Leverhulme sr research fell 1993–94, Wilsmore fell Univ of Melbourne 2002–03, hon fell UCL 2012; memb: Cncl Australian Acad of Science 2007–10, Int Science Advsy Bd A*-STAR Inst of Material Science and Engrg Singapore 2008–11, External Review Panel Int Cncl for Science 2013–14; lectures: W G Dauben Univ of Calif Berkeley 1999–2000, Aggarwal Cornell Univ 2002, Tilden RSC 2003, Merck-Karl Pfister MIT 2005, W Heinlen Hall Bowling Green State Univ 2006, Merck Researcher RSC 2008, Merck Univ of Cambridge 2009, Robert Robinson Univ of Oxford 2010, Ta-shue Chou Meml Academia Sinica Taiwan 2010, H Dudley Wright Fndn Colloquium Univ Geneva 2012; Chemical Record lectr Chemical Soc Japan 2013, Nozoe lectr Int Symposium on Novel Aromatic Compounds Taipei 2013, C N R Rao Lecture Chemical Research Soc of India Mumbai 2014, McRae Lecture Queen's Univ Ontario 2014; Alfred Bader Award 1994, Materials Chemistry Award 1995, RSC Descartes Prize EU 2003, Macro Gp Medal UK for Outstanding Achievement 2003, Royal Medal Royal Soc 2012, RA Glenn Award American Chemical Soc Energy and Fuels Div 2015; dir Cambridge Quantum Fund 1995–2004, memb CUP Syndicate 2000–04; Dr (hc) Univ Hasselt 2010; FAA 2006 (pres 2014–), FTSE 2006, hon fell Chemical Research Soc of India 2013, fell Materials Research Soc 2013, Hon FRSC 2013, fell Royal Australian Chemical Inst 2014, pres Australian Acad of Science 2014–, pres Australian Cncl of Learned Acads (ACOLA) 2016, fell Nat Acad of Inventors 2016; *Publications* contrib to various learned chemistry, physics and materials science jls on the subject of synthesis of polymeric materials and of natural products; *Recreations* music appreciation, walking; *Clubs* Athenaeum; *Style*— Prof Andrew Holmes, AM, FRS, PresAA, FTSE; ✉ Bio21 Institute, University of Melbourne, 30 Flemington Road, Victoria 3010, Australia (☎ 00 61 3 8344 2344, fax 00 61 3 8344 2384, e-mail aholmes@unimelb.edu.au); Department of Chemistry, Imperial College, South Kensington, London SW7 2AZ

HOLMES, David Frederick Cecil; s of Norman Holmes (d 1995), and Kathleen Alice, *née* Bennett (d 1983); *b* 10 September 1933; *Educ* Little Ealing Sr Boys' Sch, Ealing Coll of Art, Shrewsbury Coll of Art, Central Sch of Art (pt/t); *m* 16 April 1960, Marie Lily Theresa, da of James Frederick Wilkinson; 2 s (Toby John b 20 Oct 1962, Rupert James b 20 May 1964), 1 da (Polly Victoria b 18 Nov 1967); *Career* joined Colman Prentis & Varley as junior 1950–52; Nat Serv RAOC 1952–54; jr creative Colman Prentis & Varley 1954–55, jr art dir W S Crawford Advertising 1955–58, art dir Mather & Crowther 1958–63, gp head of art Colman Prentis & Varley 1963–65, sr art dir (later ptnr and head of art) Kingsley Manton & Palmer Partnership 1965–71, dir and art dir The Television Department Ltd 1971–75, prop David Holmes & Partners (creative consultants) 1975–77, jt fndr dir and creative dir Holmes Knight Keeley Ltd (later Holmes Knight Ritchie WRG Ltd) 1977–92, exec creative dir TBWA/Holmes Knight Ritchie Ltd 1990–92, freelance artist, art dir and film maker 1992–, jt fndr dir Messrs Holmes & Watson Ltd 1994–; winner: numerous D&AD awards 1966–, Campaign Poster award for The Macallan 1986, Clio award for the Macallan poster 1988, D&AD Silver medal for Singapore Brochure design 1988 (also Gold award Aust Art Dirs' and Writers' Club 1988), shortlist certificate for The Long Sleep (The Macallan Malt Whisky cinema commercial) 1990 (also winner The One Show merit award 1990, Clio award 1990 and Oscar Br Animation awards 1990), 4 Gold awards Scotmedia Advertising Awards 1991; paintings accepted for RA Summer Exhibition 2010, 2011 and 2013; 6 illustrations for Royal Mail Christmas postage stamps 2015; memb: D & AD 1967– (memb Ctee 1971–72), The Advertising Creative Circle 1967– (memb Cncl and sec 1979–81); *Publications* David's Book (2016); also created books for Pan Books: My First Watch (Timex), My First Torch (Duracell), My First Toothbrush (Wisdom), My First Fountain Pen (Platignum), My First Crayons (Platignum); *Clubs* Arts; *Style*— David Holmes, Esq; ✉ Studio, 5 Calvert Street, Primrose Hill, London NW1 8NE (☎ 020 7586 0363, e-mail david@cecilholmes.demon.co.uk, website www.davidcecilholmes.com)

HOLMES, Dr Geoffrey Kenneth Towndrow; s of Kenneth Geoffrey Holmes (d 1974), and Majorie, *née* Towndrow; *b* 15 February 1942; *Educ* Tupton Hall GS, Univ of Birmingham (BSc, MB ChB, MD), DRCOG, PhD; *m* 4 May 1970, Rosemary, da of Stanley Alfred Guy, MBE (d 1997); 2 da (Rachel b 1971, Emma b 1976), 1 s (Simon b 1973); *Career* res fell Birmingham Gen Hosp and Dept of Experimental Pathology Univ of Birmingham 1971–74, sr med registrar United Birmingham Hosps 1974–78, conslt physician and gastroenterologist Derbyshire Royal Infirmary 1978–, clinical teacher Univ of Nottingham 1980–; examiner RCP 1990; author various research papers on gastrointestinal disorders particularly coeliac disease; memb Br Soc of Gastroenterology 1973, med advsr Derby and Dist Coeliac Soc 1980–, memb Medical Advsy Cncl Coeliac UK; pres: Derby and Burton Ileostomy Assoc 1986, Midland Gastroenterological Soc 2002–03; memb BMA 1966; FRCP (MRCP); *Books* Coeliac Disease Inflammatory Bowel Disease and Food Intolerance in Clinical Reactions to Food (1983), Coeliac Disease (1984), Coeliac Disease in Bockus Gastroenterology (1985), Coeliac Disease (2000); *Recreations* gardening, reading, theology; *Style*— Dr Geoffrey Holmes; ✉ Derbyshire Royal Infirmary, London Road, Derby (☎ 01332 347141)

HOLMES, James Christopher (Jim); s of Herbert Frederick Holmes (d 1978), and Dorothy Gladys, *née* Thomas (d 2001); *b* 21 November 1948; *Educ* Tottenham Co GS, Univ of Sheffield (BA), London Opera Centre; *Children* 2 s (Edward b 1983, Robert b 1985); *Career* conductor and arranger; ENO: chorus master 1973–78, princ coach 1978–96, resident conductor 1985–96; head of music/asst music dir Opera North 1996–2008; princ coach Glyndebourne Festival 1986–94; seasonal music staff: Met Opera NY 2010–, Salzburg Festival 2011–; memb Editorial Advsy Bd Kurt Weill Edn 1994–, memb Bd of Tstees Kurt Weill Fndn 2012–, artist-in-res Kurt Weill Festival Dessau 2013, regular contributor of reviews and articles to Kurt Weill newsletter, concert and theatre programmes etc; *Repertoire* incl: Orpheus in the Underworld, The Magic Flute, Mikado, Princess Ida, Die Fledermaus, Hänsel and Gretel, Peter Grimes, Turn of the Screw, Falstaff, Oedipus Rex, Pacific Overtures, La Belle Vivette, Fidelio, Mahagonny, Katya Kabanova, The Cunning Little Vixen, Paradise Moscow, Pelleas and Melisande, Marriage of Figaro, Gloriana, Sweeney Todd, One Touch of Venus, Seven Deadly Sins, Arms and the Cow, Tannhäuser, Cosi Fan Tutte, Don Giovanni, Peter Grimes, Albert Herring; other prodns incl: assoc music dir Carousel RNT 1993, I'm A Stranger Here Myself – Kurt Weill in America (BBC TV/Hessischer Rundfunk), Street Scene (Theater des Westens Berlin, Theater im Pfalzbau Ludwigshafen) 1994–95, debut Montreal Symphony Orch 1995, City of Birmingham Symphony Orch 2002, Norwegian Radio Orch 2002, Almeida Festival 2003, Hallé Orchestra 2005, BBC Nat Orchestra of Wales 2006, RLPO 2007, Into the Woods (ROH) 2008, LSO 2008, The Girl I Left Behind Me, Pat Kirkwood Is Angry (London and tour), Songs From A Hotel Bedroom (ROH) 2010, One Touch of Venus Dessau 2010, Zaubernacht (ROH) 2011, Carousel (Opera North) 2012/2015, debut with Ensemble Modern 2014, The King and I (Théâtre du Châtelet Paris) 2014, Sweeney Todd (WNO) 2015; *Recordings* Pacific Overtures (Grammy Award nomination 1989), Soprano in Red (with Lesley Garrett, Gramophone Award) 1996, Porgy and Bess (musical asst to Sir Simon Rattle), Something Wonderful / If Ever I Would Leave You (with Bryn Terfel, arranger/musical asst), Mercy and Grand (Gavin Bryars/Opera North) 2012, One Touch of Venus (first complete recording, 2014); *Recreations* reading, crosswords, cinema, lifelong Spurs fan; *Style*— Jim Holmes, Esq; ☎ 07534 940802, e-mail jim@james-holmes.co.uk, website www.james-holmes.co.uk

HOLMES, Sir John Eaton; GCVO (2004, CVO 1998), KBE (1999), CMG (1997); s of Leslie Howard Holmes, of Preston, Lancs, and Joyce Mary, *née* Stone; *b* 29 April 1951; *Educ* Preston GS, Balliol Coll Oxford (MA); *m* 1976, Penelope, da of Lt Col Rev E I Morris; 3 da (Sarah Victoria b 21 Jan 1981, Lucy Alexandra Mary b 22 Sept 1982, Emilie Catherine b 27 Nov 1985); *Career* FCO: joined 1973, third then second sec Moscow 1976–78, Near East and North Africa Dept 1978–82, private sec to Foreign Sec 1982–84, first sec Paris 1984–87, dep head Soviet Dept 1987–89, seconded to Thomas de la Rue plc 1989–91, cnsllr (econ and commercial) New Delhi 1991–95, head EU Dept (external) FCO 1995, princ private sec (overseas affairs) 10 Downing St 1997–99 (private sec 1996–97), ambass to Portugal 1999–2001, ambass to France 2001–07; under sec-gen for humanitarian affrs and emergency relief co-ordinator UN 2007–10, dir Ditchley Fndn 2010–, chair Int Rescue Ctee 2011–; *Recreations* golf, tennis, music; *Style*— Sir John Holmes, GCVO, KBE, CMG

HOLMES, Jon; *Educ* Christ Church Coll Univ of Kent Canterbury; *m*; *Career* writer, comedian and presenter; columnist and travel writer Sunday Times; *Television* Stop The World (BBC Choice) 1998, Footage and Mouth (Play UK) 1998, Wish We Were There (BBC Choice) 1999, The Way It Is (TV pilot, BBC1) 2000, The 11 O'Clock Show (Channel 4) 2000, I Love... (BBC2) 2000, Dead Ringers (BBC2) 2000–, The State We're In (BBC3) 2002–03, Gash (Channel 4) 2003, Jon Culshaw Show (BBC 1) 2009, Horrible Histories (BBC 1) 2009 and 2010; writer, script ed and actor The Impressionable Jon Culshaw (BBC) 2004; writer: V Graham Norton (prog conslt, Channel 4), Spitting Image (ITV), Patrick Keilty Almost Live (BBC1), Jim Tavare In Cabaret (five), Have I Got News For You (BBC1), Harry Hill (Channel 4), Comedy Nation (BBC2), Br Acad Film Awards 2005, Br Acad Television Craft Awards 2005, Horrible Histories (BBC, BAFTA and British Comedy Award); voice artist: Crash Test Danny (Discovery Kids), 7 Days (BBC 3); *Radio* comedy for Radio 4: Grievous Bodily Radio 1997, The Way It Is 1998–2002, The Now Show 1998–, Dead Ringers 2000– (Best Radio Prog Broadcasting Press Guild Awards 2001, Gold Comedy Award Sony Radio Awards 2001), Concrete Cow 2002, The 99p Challenge, The Armando Iannucci Show 2004, Armando Iannucci's Charm Offensive (presenter) 2005; writer for Radio 4: Yes Sir, I Can Boogie, The Very World of Milton Jones (Bronze Comedy Award Sony Radio Awards 2000), Harry Hill's Fruit Corner, Big Town All Stars, This is Your Life (also script ed); music radio: Jon & Andy on 106 CTFM 1997–98 (Presentation Newcomer of the Year KPMG Awards 1999), Jon & Andy on Power FM 1999–2000 (Gold Entertainment Award Sony Radio Awards 2000), TFI Galaxy Celebrity Pantomime (Galaxy Network) 1999, Jon Holmes on Xfm 2000, Jon Holmes on Virgin Radio 2001–02, Jon Holmes on LBC 97.3 2003–, presenter BBC6 Music 2003–, The Day the Music Died (Radio 2) 2003–, Jon Holmes on Radio One 2005, Jon Holmes on BBC6 (6Music) 2006–, Listen Against (Radio 4) 2007 and 2008 (Radio Acad Sony Award 2009), The Secret World (Radio 4) 2009, creator and writer I'm Spartacus (Radio 2) 2009, cover presenter Chris Evans Breakfast Show (BBC Radio 2), cover presenter Graham Norton (BBC Radio 2), Jon Holmes and Miranda Hart (BBC Radio 2), presenter XFM Breakfast Show 2013–16, presenter Radio X 2015–16, presenter talkRADIO 2016–; *Books* Status Quo and the Kangaroo (2007), Rock Star Babylon (2008), The Now Show Book of World Records (2009), The History of the World on Twitter (2009), A Portrait of an Idiot as a Young Man: Part Memoir, Part Explanation As To Why Men Are So Rubbish (2015); *Style—* Jon Holmes, Esq; ✉ c/o The Richard Stone Partnership, 2 Henrietta Street, London WC2E 8PS (✆ 020 7497 0849, fax 020 7497 0869)

HOLMES, Katherine; *née* Humphrey; da of late Idwal Humphrey, and late Agnes, *née* Richard; *b* 10 May 1952, Porchester, Hants; *Educ* Coll of Law London; *m* 20 July 1985, Christopher Holmes; *Career* called to the Bar 1973; barr in private practice 1973–76, head of commercial law CBI 1976–81, lawyer Distillers Co Ltd 1981–87, head of competition law Guinness plc 1987–89; Reed Smith (merged with Richards Butler 1989): assoc 1989–91, ptnr 1991–2009, conslt 2009–12; memb UK Competition and Markets Authy 2009–; memb: Senate Inns of Court and Bar 1979–83, Senate/Bar Cncl 1985–86 and 1987 (memb various sub-ctees 1979–90); Bar Assoc for Finance and Industry: chm 1986–87, sr vice-chm 1987–88, vice-pres 1988–90; vice-chm ICC Cmmn on Competition 1989–93, chm Jt Working Party of the Bars and Law Socs of the UK of Competition Law 1998–2005; tstee Guinness Gp Pension Fund 1988–89; dir Scotch Whisky Assoc 1987–89; memb Law Soc 1990; *Publications* Fiscal Frontiers (1993), Guide to Competition Act 1988 (1988), Guide to Competition Law in the UK (2002), European Community Law of State Aid (contrib, 2009); *Recreations* sailing, skiing, entertaining, music; *Style—* Mrs Katherine Holmes

HOLMES, Dame Kelly; DBE (2005, MBE 1998); da of Pamela, *née* Norman; *b* 19 April 1970; *Educ* Hugh Christie Comp Sch; *Career* athlete; memb Ealing Southall and Middx Athletics Club; English Schs winner 1,500m 1983 and 1987, Gold medal 800m Mini Youth Olympics 1987, Gold medal 1,500m GB Int Germany and Ipswich 1987, semi-finalist World Championships 1993, Silver medal 1,500m European Championships 1994, Gold medal 1,500m Cwlth Games Victoria 1994, Silver medal 1,500m and Bronze medal 800m World Championships 1995, Silver medal 1,500m Cwlth Games Kuala Lumpur 1998, Bronze medal 800m Olympic Games Sydney 2000, Silver medal 800m Goodwill Games 2001, Gold medal 1,500m Cwlth Games Manchester 2002, Bronze medal 800m European Championships 2002, Silver medal 1,500m World Indoor Championships 2003, Silver medal 800m World Championships 2003, Gold medal 800m and Gold medal 1,500m Olympic Games Athens 2004; English and Br record holder 800m, Br and Cwlth record holder 1000m and 1,500m, Br record holder 1500m indoors; ranked no 1 in world for 1,500m 1997 and 2004, ranked no 3 in the world for 800m 2001; Army judo champion, Army volleyball player; Army Athlete of the Year 1989–97, Combined Servs Sports Woman of the Year 1993 and 1994, Middx County Sports Woman of the Year 1994 and 1995, Athlete of the Year Sports Writers' Assoc 1995, nominated Mover & Shakers Award Company magazine 1995, Br Athletics Female Athlete of the Year 1995, 3rd place Carlton TV Sports Personality of the Year 1997, BBC Sports Personality of the Year 2004, European Athlete of the Year 2004, IAAF Female Performance of the Year 2004, Int Athlete of the Year 2004, Sports Writers Assoc Sports Woman of the Year 2004, Br Athletic Writers Assoc Female Athlete of the Year 2004, Laureus World Sportswoman of the Year 2005; non-sporting career: nursing asst 1986–87, Sgt (HGV driver then army physical trg instr) HM Forces 1988–97, md Double Gold Enterprises Ltd 1997–, currently owner Café 1809; fndr and dir On Camp with Kelly 2004–, fndr Believe to Achieve with Kelly, nat sch sport champion 2005–08, motivational speaker; Hon Dr in Sports Science Leeds Met Univ 2005, Hon DCL Univ of Kent 2005, Hon Dr Univ of Hull, Hon Dr Univ of Birmingham; *Books* My Olympic 10 Days (2005), Black, White and Gold, Just Go For It; *Recreations* duathlon, keeping fit; *Style—* Dame Kelly Holmes, DBE; ✆ 01732 838800, e-mail info@doublegold.co.uk, websites www.doublegold.co.uk and www.cafe1809.co.uk, Twitter @damekellyholmes and @cafe1809

HOLMES, Dr (Janet) Martha Lee; da of Sir Peter Holmes (d 2002), and Judith Holmes (d 2003); *Educ* Bryanston, Univ of Bristol (BSc), Univ of York (DPhil); *Career* broadcaster and prodr with BBC Natural History Unit; presenter: Reefwatch 1988, Sea Trek 1991, The Blue Planet Deep Trouble 2001; asst prodr Life in the Freezer 1993; prodr: Wildlife Special Polar Bear 1997, The Blue Planet 2001; series prodr: The Nile 2004, Man Hunters 2005; RGS Cherry Kearton Medal and Award 1999; Sea Trek (1991), Wildlife Specials (1997), The Blue (1999), The Blue Planet (2001), Nile (2004); *Style—* Dr Martha Holmes; ✉ BBC-NHU, Whiteladies Road, Bristol BS8 2LR (✆ 0117 974 7677)

HOLMES OF RICHMOND, Baron (Life Peer UK), of Richmond in the London Borough of Richmond upon Thames; Christopher Holmes; MBE (1993); *b* 15 October 1971, Peterborough; *Educ* Harry Cheshire Comp Sch Kidderminster, King's Coll Cambridge (MA), BPP Law Sch (Dip); *Career* swimmer, memb GB swimming team 1985–2001 (capt for 5 years), competed in 4 Paralympic Games (9 Paralympic Gold Medals), 2 World Championships and 7 European Championships, held 7 world records, 10 European records and 12 GB records; freelance journalist 1994–2000, slr specialising in employment and pensions law Ashurst London 2002–09, dir of paralympic integration 2012 Olympic and Paralympic Games 2009–13; cmmr Disability Rights Cmmn 2002–07; memb: Implementation Bd UK Sports Inst 1999–2000, Panel UK Sport Awards 2001–04, Bd UK Sport 2005–13; ambass London 2012 Olympic bid 2003–05; sporting patron Youth Sport Tst 1994–, patron Br Paralympic Assoc 2005–; patron Help for Heroes 2008–, ambass Queen Elizabeth Diamond Jubilee Trust, supporter Duke of Edinburgh Awards 2013–; public speaker 1990–; diversity advsr Civil Service 2015, chair Channel 4's Year of Disability Advsrs 2016; memb: House of Lords Select Ctee on Digital Skills 2014–15, House of Lords Select Ctee on Social Mobility 2015–16, House of Lords Select Ctee on Financial Exclusion 2016–; dep-chllr BPP Univ 2015–; Sports Personality of the Year 1992, Bass Midlander of the Year 1992, SAF Paul Zetter Award 1996, Sports Personality of the Year Variety Club of GB 1997; Hon LLD Univ of Bath 2012, Hon LLD BPP 2015; *Style—* The Lord Holmes of Richmond, MBE; ✉ House of Lords, London SW1A 0PW (website: www.chrisholmes.co.uk, twitter: @LordCholmes)

HOLROYD, (William) Andrew Myers; CBE (2009, OBE 2003); s of William Holroyd (d 1992), of Bradford, and Joan, *née* Myers (d 1993); *b* 13 April 1948; *Educ* Bradford GS, Univ of Nottingham (BA); *m* 26 July 1975, Caroline Irene, da of Jack Skerry, of Southport; 2 da (Emma b 1 Feb 1977, Clare b 5 Dec 1979); *Career* VSO Indonesia 1970–72, articled clerk Alsop Wilkinson 1972–74, managing ptnr Jackson & Canter Liverpool (ptnr 1977–); Law Soc: memb 1974–, memb Cncl 1996–2009, dep vice-pres 2005–06, vice-pres 2006–07, pres 2007–08; Liverpool Law Soc: memb Ctee 1983–95, vice-pres 1993, pres 1994; lay canon Liverpool Cathedral 2009–, memb Bd Liverpool John Moores Univ 2010– (fell 2008, govr 2009–); hon doctorate Univ of Nottingham 2009; *Recreations* music, walking; *Style—* Andrew Holroyd, Esq, CBE; ✉ Jackson Canter, 3rd Floor Walker House, Exchange Flags, Liverpool L2 3YL (✆ 0151 282 1700, fax 0151 282 1715, e-mail aholroyd@jacksoncanter.co.uk)

HOLROYD, Air Marshal Sir Frank Martyn; KBE (1989), CB (1985); s of George Lumb Holroyd (d 1987), and Winifred Hetty (d 2009); *b* 30 August 1935; *Educ* Southend-on-Sea GS, RAF, Cranfield Univ (MSc), RCDS; *m* 1 Feb 1958, Veronica Christine (d 2001), da of Arthur George Booth (d 1984); 2 s (Martyn Paul b 26 Jan 1959, Myles Justin b 9 Nov 1966), 1 da (Bryony Jane b 4 June 1961); *Career* joined RAF 1956, appt Fighter Stations RAF Leconfield and RAF Leeming, No 14 Grad Course RAF Tech Coll 1959, Blind Landing Experimental Unit RAE Bedford 1960–63, HQ Fighter Cmd 1965–67, OC Electrical Engrg Sqdn RAF Changi Singapore 1967–69, Wing Cdr Staff Coll RAF Bracknell 1970, MOD 1970–72, OC Engrg Wing RAF Brize Norton 1972, Gp Capt 1974, Station Cdr No 1 Radio Sch RAF Locking 1974–76, sr engrg offr HQ 38 Gp 1976, Air Cdre dir Aircraft Engrg MOD 1977, RCDS 1981, dir Weapons and Support Engrg 1982, Air Vice Marshal dir gen Strategic Electronic Engrg MOD (PE) 1982, air offr engrg HQ Strike Cmd 1986, Air Marshal chief engr RAF 1988–91, chief Logistics Support RAF 1989–91; chm: AVR Communications Ltd 1991–95, Composite Technology Ltd 1992–2004, Electronica (UK) Ltd 1992–95, Military Aircraft Spares Ltd 2004–06 (dep chm 1999–2004), Troy Court Mgmnt Ltd 2004–07, Military Asset Services Ltd 2007–; dir: Admiral plc 1992–2000, REW Communications Services plc 1995–96, Ultra Electronics plc 1995–2003, Airinmar Ltd 1996–2001; memb: BBC Engrg Advsy Bd 1984–90, Advsy Cncl RMCS 1988–91, Cncl Cranfield Univ 1988–2005 (memb Ct 1988–, dep chm Cncl 1997–2005), Cncl (now Senate) Engrg Cncl 1990–2000 (chm Fin & Audit Ctee), BIM Bd of Companions 1991–99 (chm 1998–99), Tribology Tst Ctee 1997–; pres RAeS 1992–93, life vice-pres Chelmsford RAFA 1992; MacRobert Award tstee Royal Acad of Engrg 1992–97, chm tstees Eng Cncl Pension Fund 2000–09; memb Ct Cranfield Univ 1997–; Hon DSc Cranfield Univ 2006; CEng, FREng 1992, FIEE; *Recreations* shooting, gardening, maintaining 14th century house, travel; *Clubs* RAF; *Style—* Air Marshal Sir Frank Holroyd, KBE, CB, FREng; ✉ c/o RAF Club, 128 Piccadilly, London W1V 0PY

HOLROYD, Sir Michael de Courcy Fraser; kt (2007), CBE (1989); s of Basil de Courcy Fraser Holroyd, of Surrey, and Ulla, *née* Hall; *b* 27 August 1935; *Educ* Eton; *m* 1982, Margaret Drabble, *qv*, da of John Frederick Drabble, QC (d 1983), of Suffolk; *Career* biographer; chm: Soc of Authors 1973–74, Nat Book League 1976–78; pres: English PEN 1985–8, Royal Soc of Literature 2003–10 (chm 1997–2001, currently pres emeritus); chm: Arts Cncl Literature Panel 1992–95, Public Lending Right Ctee 1997–2000; memb Arts Cncl of GB 1992–95; David Cohen Prize for Literature 2005, James Tait Black Meml Prize 2009; Hon DLitt: Univ of Ulster 1992, Univ of Sheffield 1993, Univ of Warwick 1993, UEA 1994, LSE 1998, Univ of Sussex 2009; CLit (FRSL 1968), FRHistS; *Books* Lytton Strachey (1967–68 and 1994), A Dog's Life (1969, 2 edn 2014), Augustus John (1974–75 and 1996), Bernard Shaw (1988–92 and 1997), Basil Street Blues (1999), Works on Paper (2002), Mosaic: Portraits in Fragments (2004), A Strange Eventful History (2008), A Book of Secrets (2010), On Wheels (2012); *Recreations* listening to music and stories, watching people dance; *Style—* Sir Michael Holroyd, CBE, CLit; ✉ 85 St Mark's Road, London W10 6JS (✆ 020 8960 4891, e-mail michael.holroyd@hotmail.com)

HOLROYD, Richard Norton; s of Maj C I P Holroyd (d 1976), and Lady Sheila Holroyd, *née* Cairns (d 2001, da of 4 Earl Cairns); *b* 25 December 1946, Bath; *Educ* Marlborough, Selwyn Coll Cambridge, Indiana Univ Grad Sch of Business; *m* 12 Nov 1977, Karine Phèlip; 3 s (Wilfrid Andrew b 15 Nov 1980, Alistair Hugo b 15 April 1985, Alexander Ivor b 17 May 1987), 1 da (Annabel Juliette b 19 July 1983); *Career* European dir Reckitt & Colman 1988–91, ceo Colman's of Norwich 1991–95, sr mangr Shell Int 1995–2001; non-exec dir: OW AG 1988–2011, Cantrell & Cochrane plc 2001–, AMRO/DSG (MOD trading fund) 2003–08; memb Competition Cmmn 2001–10; *Recreations* opera, history, skiing; *Clubs* Naval and Military; *Style—* Richard Holroyd, Esq; ✉ Chemin des Clochettes 2, Geneva 1206, Switzerland (✆ 0041 22 346 6500, e-mail rnholroyd@aol.com)

HOLROYD, Robert; *Educ* Birkenhead Sch, ChCh Oxford (scholar, MA, PGCE); *Career* asst master Oakham Sch 1985–86, Colegio Anglo Colombiano Bógota 1986–88, head of dept and housemaster Radley Coll 1989–2003, headmaster Repton Sch 2003–15; *Style—* R A Holroyd, Esq; ✉ The Hall, Repton, Derbyshire DE65 6FH (✆ 01283 559220, fax 01283 559223, e-mail headmaster@repton.org.uk, website www.repton.org.uk)

HOLROYDE, Hon Mr Justice; Sir Timothy Victor (Tim) Holroyde; kt (2009), QC (1996); s of Frank Holroyde, and Doreen, *née* Bell; *b* 18 August 1955, Liverpool; *Educ* Bristol GS, Wadham Coll Oxford (BA); *m* 1980, Miranda Elisabeth, da of Alex Stone; 2 da (Caroline Louise, Imogen Sarah); *Career* called to the Bar Middle Temple 1977 (bencher), judge of the High Court 2009–, a presiding judge Northern Circuit 2012–15; memb Sentencing Cncl 2015–; *Recreations* tennis; *Style—* The Hon Mr Justice Holroyde; ✉ Royal Courts of Justice, Strand, London WC2A 2LL (✆ 020 7947 7323)

HOLT, Dame Denise Mary; DCMG (2009, CMG 2002); *née* Mills; da of William Dennis Mills (d 1971), and Mary Joanna, *née* Shea (d 2009); *b* 1 October 1949; *Educ* New Hall Sch Chelmsford, Univ of Bristol (BA); *m* John David Fletcher Holt; 1 s (Patrick David Mills Holt b 1987); *Career* diplomat; joined FCO 1970, res analyst for Iberia 1970–83, first sec (political) Dublin 1984–87, head of section FCO 1988–90, first sec (political) Brasilia 1991–93, dep head Eastern Dept FCO 1993–94, asst dir (personnel) FCO 1996–98, dep head of mission Dublin 1998–99, dir (personnel) FCO 1999–2001, ambass to Mexico 2002–05, dir (migration) FCO 2005–07, ambass to Spain 2007–09 (concurrently non-resident ambass to Andorra); non-exec dir: HSBC Bank plc 2011–, Scottish Power Renewable Energy Ltd 2011–12, Scottish Power Energy Networks Hldgs Ltd 2012–14, Nuffield Health 2013– (also govr), Iberdrola SA 2014–; chm and non-exec dir M&S Bank plc 2013–; memb Bd Ofqual 2010–13, memb NHS Pay Review Body 2010, chair Anglo-Spanish Soc 2010–13, memb Governing Cncl Canada Blanch Centre for Contemporary Spanish Studies 2010–, ind chair of nominations Alzheimer's Soc 2011–, chair Inst for Latin American Studies Univ of London 2012–15, tstee FCO Library, memb Wilton Park Advsy Cncl 2013–16, tstee Univ of Bristol 2013–; Hon LLD Univ of Bristol 2012; *Recreations* reading, theatre; *Clubs* RAC; *Style—* Dame Denise Holt, DCMG; ✉ e-mail ddpholt@aol.com

HOLT, (Roma) Hazel Kathryn; da of Charles Douglas Young (d 1986), of Clearwell, Glos, and Roma, *née* Simpson; *b* 3 September 1928; *Educ* King Edward VI HS Birmingham,

H

Newnham Coll Cambridge (BA); *m* Geoffrey Louis Holt; 1 s (Thomas Charles Louis Holt, *qv*, b 13 Sept 1961); *Career* editorial asst International African Institute 1950–79, feature writer and reviewer Stage and Television Today 1979–82; *Books* edited for posthumous publication the novels of Barbara Pym (literary executor); A Very Private Eye (with Hilary Pym, 1984), Gone Away (1989), A Lot to Ask: A Life of Barbara Pym (1990), The Cruellest Month (1991), The Shortest Journey (1992), Uncertain Death (1993), Murder on Campus (1994), Superfluous Death (1995), Death of a Dean (1996), The Only Good Lawyer... (1997), Dead and Buried (1998), Fatal Legacy (1999), Lilies That Fester (2000), Delay of Execution (2001), Leonora (2002), Death in Practice (2003), The Silent Killer (2004), Death in Practice (2005), A Death in the Family (2006), A Time to Die (2008), Any Man's Death (2009), My Dear Charlotte (2009), A Necessary End (2012), Death is a Word (2014); *Recreations* reading, writing and watching cats; *Style*— Mrs Hazel Holt; ✉ 7 Kinforde Chard, Somerset TA20 1DT (☎ 01460 64414, e-mail holt369@btinternet.com)

HOLT, Jeremy Martin; s of Cdr Graham John Holt, RN, of Brampton, Cambs, and Doreen Marie Holt; *b* 1956, London; *Educ* Sexey's Sch Bruton, Exeter Coll Oxford (MA); *m* Dr Antonia Newell; 2 da (Georgina b 1988, Katharine b 1991); *Career* admitted slr 1980; articled clerk Macfarlanes 1978–80, slr Herbert Oppenheimer, Nathan & Vandyk 1980–83, slr Compton Carr 1983–84, ptnr Peake & Co 1986–89 (slr 1984–86), ptnr Charles Russell 1989–95, co-fndr and ptnr Clark Holt Commercial Slrs 1995–; chm Swindon Computer Museum; memb Tylers and Bricklayers Livery Co; *Publications* A Manager's Guide to IT Law (2004, 2 edn 2011); author of numerous magazine articles on law and IT; *Recreations* military history, long-distance running, China, outdoor swimming, parkour; *Clubs* Hon Artillery Co (veteran memb); *Style*— Jeremy Holt, Esq; ✉ 14 Belmont Crescent, Swindon, Wiltshire SN1 4EY; Clark Holt Commercial Solicitors, Hardwick House, Prospect Place, Swindon, Wiltshire SN1 3LJ (☎ 01793 617444, e-mail jeremyh@clarkholt.com)

HOLT, John Antony; *b* 31 March 1938; *Educ* Imperial Coll London (BSc(Eng), ACGI, Dip Imperial Coll, MSc), Henley Mgmnt Centre; *m*; 2 c; *Career* sr industrial fell Univ of Leeds 1969–71, chief systems engr (space) and head of New Space Technol Electronic and Space Systems Guided Weapons Div British Aircraft Corporation 1971–76 (joined 1960), gen mgmnt course Henley Mgmnt Centre 1976; British Aerospace: head of Guided Weapons New Projects British Aerospace Dynamics Gp (Bristol) 1976–80, engrg dir 1980–82, tech dir British Aerospace Dynamics Gp 1982–85, md British Aerospace Space and Communications Ltd 1985–92; fndr dir McLaurin-Holt Associates Ltd 1993–2002; chm Surrey Satellite Technology Ltd 2005–06 (non-exec dir 1994–2005); non-exec dir: Orion Network Systems Inc 1989–92, Arthur C Clarke Fndn USA 2003–08; visiting prof RMCS 1985; chm: Euro MESH consortium for collaboration on space projects 1987–92, UK Electronic Industry Component Policy Cncl 1987–91, UK Industrial Space Ctee 1988–90, UK Electronic Components Policy Cncl 1993–, ESYS Ltd 1997–2001 and 2003–08 (non-exec dir 1995–97 and 2001–03); memb Advsy Bd: Inst of Engrg Survey and Space Geodesy Univ of Nottingham 1990–94, Centre for Space Engrg Research Univ of Surrey 1991–97; Hon DSc Capitol Coll Maryland 1992; FRAeS, FREng 1985; *Style*— John Holt, Esq, FREng; ☎ 01462 436626, fax 01462 452885, e-mail holtja@compuserve.com

HOLT, His Hon Judge John Frederick; s of Edward Basil Holt (d 1984), and Monica, *née* Taylor; *b* 7 October 1947; *Educ* Ampleforth, Univ of Bristol (LLB); *m* 26 Sept 1970, Stephanie Ann, da of Peter Watson, of Belaugh, Norfolk; 3 s (Samuel John b 16 June 1973, Benjamin Alexander b 2 Sept 1974, Edward Daniel b 11 Oct 1980); *Career* called to the Bar Lincoln's Inn 1970 (former head of East Anglian Chambers), asst recorder 1988–92, recorder of the Crown Court 1992–98, circuit judge (SE Circuit) 1998–; memb Co Court Rules Ctee 1981–85; *Recreations* cricket, restoring vintage motor cars; *Clubs* Twinstead Cricket, Strangers (Norwich), MG Car, Octagon Car, Jaguar Driving; *Style*— His Hon Judge Holt; ✉ Ipswich Crown Court, Civic Drive, Ipswich, Suffolk IP1 2DX (☎ 01473 213841)

HOLT, Nicholas John; s of Eric Holt and Eileen Patricia, *née* Macritchee; *b* 2 April 1958; *Educ* Manchester Grammar, Fitzwilliam Coll Cambridge (BA, MA); *m* 14 April 1984, Georgina Mary, da of Dr William Mann; 2 s (William James Edward b 1987, Frederick Nicholas Jack b 1993), 1 da (Alexandra Olivia b 1989); *Career* articled clerk then asst slr Coward Chance 1980–84, asst slr then mangr Corp Legal Dept Jardine Matheson & Co Hong Kong 1984–87, legal and compliance dir Smith New Court plc 1989–92 (gp legal advsr 1987–89), chief exec Smith New Court Far East Ltd 1992–94, dir Merrill Lynch International Ltd 1994–95, ptnr Weil Gotshal & Manges 1995–2000, managing ptnr McGrigors London (formerly KLegal) 2000–04, ptnr Global Legal Search 2004–09, ptnr SR Search 2009–; memb Law Soc; *Recreations* football, cricket; *Clubs* Reform; *Style*— Nicholas Holt, Esq; ✉ e-mail nickholt@srsearch.com

HOLT, Robert (Bob); OBE (2016); s of Jim Howard (d 1985), and Alice, *née* Smith (d 2010); *b* 20 September 1954, Littleborough, Lancs; *Educ* Counthill Oldham; *m* (m dis 2006); *Children* 3 s (Robert b 1985, James b 1988, Willam b 1992); *Career* chm: Mears Gp plc 1996–, Inspired Energy plc 2011–, DX (Gp) plc 2014–, Totally plc 2015–; involved with: Footprints Fndn, Holt Tst; *Recreations* cricket, horse racing, travel, walking; *Clubs* Marks, Harry's; *Style*— Bob Holt, Esq, OBE; ✉ 68 Vincent Square, London SW1P 2NU (☎ 07778 798816, Twitter @BobHolt1954 or @BobFootprints); Mears Group plc, 1390 Montpellier Court, Gloucester Business Park, Brockworth, Gloucestershire GL3 4AH

HOLT, Thelma Mary Bernadette; CBE (1994); da of David Holt (d 1941), and Ellan, *née* Finnagh Doyle (d 1969); *b* 4 January 1932; *Educ* St Anne's Coll for Girls, RADA; *m* 1, 31 March 1957 (m dis), Patrick Graucob; m 2, 6 Oct 1968 (m dis), David Pressman; m 3, 9 Aug 2011 (remarried), Patrick Graucob; *Career* producer; actress 1955–68; jt art dir Open Space Theatre 1968–77, art dir Round House Theatre 1977–83, exec prodr Theatre of Comedy 1983–85, head of touring and commercial exploitation Nat Theatre 1985–88, exec prodr Peter Hall Co 1988; prodr Int Theatre, Nat Theatre 1989–, assoc prodr RSC 2004–; Cameron Mackintosh prof of contemporary theatre Univ of Oxford 1998; emeritus fell St Catherine's Coll Oxford 2003; dir: Thelma Holt Ltd, Stage One, Almeida Theatre 2001–09; chm Yvonne Arnaud Theatre 2002–05; vice-pres Citizens' Theatre Glasgow; Observer Award for Special Achievement in Theatre 1987; memb Cncl: RADA 1986–2011, Arts Cncl of England 1993–98 (chm Drama Advisory Panel); Special Award for Individual Achievement TMA Awards 2006; patron Oxford Univ Dramatic Soc, tstee Rose Theatre Kingston; Hon DUniv Middx 1994, Hon DLitt UEA 2003; companion Liverpool Inst for Performing Arts 2002, distinguished friend Univ of Oxford 2006; Order of the Rising Sun (Japan) 2004; *Style*— Miss Thelma Holt, CBE; ✉ Thelma Holt Ltd, Noel Coward Theatre, 85 St Martin's Lane, London WC2N 4AU (☎ 020 7812 7455, fax 020 7812 7550, e-mail thelma@dircon.co.uk)

HOLT, Thomas Charles Louis; s of Geoffrey Louis Holt, and (Roma) Hazel Kathryn Holt, *qv*, *née* Young; *b* 13 September 1961; *Educ* Westminster, Wadham Coll Oxford, Coll of Law Chancery Lane; *m* 6 Aug 1988, Kim Nicola, da of John Clifford Foster; 1 da (Natalie Alicia Alexandria b 12 March 1992); *Career* author; *Publications* incl: Poems by Tom Holt 1973, Lucia in Wartime (1985, US 1986), Lucia Triumphant (1986, US 1986), Expecting Someone Taller (1987, US 1988), Who's Afraid of Beowulf? (1988, US 1989), Goatsong (1989, US 1990), I Margaret (with Steve Nallon, 1989), The Walled Orchard 1990, Flying Dutch (1991, US 1992), Ye Gods! (1992), Overtime (1993), Here Comes The Sun (1993), Grailblazers (1994), Faust Among Equals (1994), Odds and Gods (1995), Djinn Rummy (1995), My Hero (1996), Paint Your Dragon (1996), Open Sesame (1997), Wish You Were Here (1998), Valhalla (1998), Only Human (1998), Snow White & The Seven Samurai (1999), Nothing But Blue Skies (2000), Falling Sideways (2001), Little People (2002), The Portable Door (2003), A Song For Nero (2003); *Recreations* engineering; *Style*— Thomas Holt, Esq; ✉ c/o James Hale, 47 Peckham Rye, London SE15 3NX (☎ and fax 020 7732 6338)

HOLTBY, HE Christopher Bruce; OBE; *m* Polly Jane; 1 s, 2 da; *Career* diplomat; desk offr NATO and European Policy Dept MOD 1992–93, desk offr Navy Resources and Progs Dept MOD 1993–94, second sec UK Delgn to NATO and the Western European Union Brussels 1994–98, head Policy and Operations Section Balkans Dept MOD 1998–99, head Kosovo Review Team MOD 1999–2000, head Kosovo Section FCO 2000–02, policy advsr on Asia and the Pacific to EU High Rep Javier Solana and his UK Liaison Offr EU Cncl Secretariat Brussels 2002–07, dep head Security Policy Dept FCO 2007–12, ambass to Estonia 2012–; *Style*— HE Mr Christopher Holtby, OBE; ✉ c/o FCO (Tallinn), King Charles Street, London SW1A 2AH

HOLTEN, Kasper; *b* 1973, Copenhagen, Denmark; *Career* artistic dir Royal Danish Opera 2000–2011, dir of opera ROH 2011–; *Style*— Kasper Holten, Esq; ✉ Royal Opera House, Bow Street, Covent Garden, London WC2E 9DD

HOLTHAM, Gerald Hubert; s of Denis Arthur Holtham (d 1995), of Quinton, Birmingham, and Dilys Maud, *née* Bull (d 1999); *b* 28 June 1944, Aberdare, Glamorgan; *Educ* King Edward's Sch Birmingham, Jesus Coll Oxford (BA), Nuffield Coll Oxford (MPhil); *m* 1, 1969 (m dis), Patricia Mary, *née* Blythin; 1 da (Clare Miriam b 1971); m 2, 1979, Edith, *née* Hodgkinson; 1 da (Sophie Maud b 1976), 1 s (Rhodri Huw b 1982); *Career* journalist 1962–66 and 1969–70, at Oxford 1967–69 and 1971–73, res offr Overseas Devpt Inst London 1973–75, head Gen Econs Div Econs Dept Orgn for Econ Co-operation and Devpt (OECD) Paris 1982–85 (economist 1975–81), visiting fell Brookings Instn Washington DC 1985–87, chief int economist Credit Suisse First Boston London 1987–88, chief international economist Shearson Lehman Hutton London 1988–91, fell and tutor in econs Magdalen Coll Oxford 1991–92, chief economist Europe Lehman Brothers London 1992–94, dir IPPR 1994–98, head of global strategy Norwich Union Investment Mgmnt 1998–2000, chief investment offr Morley Fund Mgmnt 2000–04, managing ptnr Cadwyn Capital LLP; chm Ind Cmmn on Financing the Welsh Assembly Govt 2008–10; visiting prof Univ of Strathclyde 1990–93, affiliated prof London Business Sch 1993–99, hon prof Cardiff Univ Business Sch 2004, hon fell Univ of Swansea 2010, Hodge Foundation prof of regnl economy Cardiff Met Univ 2016–; FLSW 2015; *Publications* several books on economic topics, one novel and numerous articles in learned jls; *Recreations* gardening, windsurfing, listening to jazz; *Style*— Gerald Holtham, Esq; ✉ 13 Lansdowne Gardens, London SW8 2EQ (☎ 020 7622 8673, e-mail ghholtham@gmail.com)

HOM, Ken; Hon OBE (2009); s of Thomas Hom (d 1950), and Ying Fong Hom (d 2010); *b* 3 May 1949; *Educ* Univ of Calif Berkeley; *Career* chef, TV presenter and food writer; Oriental Restaurant Gp: conslt 1993–99, gp conslt chef 1999–2004; consulting chef Maison Chin Restaurant Bangkok 2008–12, currently exec consulting chef MEE Copacabana Palace Hotel Rio de Janeiro 2014 (1 Michelin star); Ken Hom brands incl: Ken Hom Wok and Accessories, Ken Hom Ready-Cooked Meals; contrib: NY Times, The Financial Times; hon chairperson Inst for the Advancement of the Science and Art of Chinese Cuisine 1993; patron Oxford Gastronomica: the Centre for Food, Drink and Culture; supporter of various charities incl: Action Against Hunger, Barnardo's, NSPCC, Prostate Cancer UK; inducted into the Who's Who of Food and Beverage in America 1990; hon doctorate Oxford Brookes Univ 2007; *Television* credits incl: Ken Hom's Chinese Cookery (BBC series), Ken Hom's Hot Wok (BBC series), Ken Hom Travels with a Hot Wok (BBC series), Exploring China: A Culinary Adventure (BBC series) 2012 (Food Broadcast of the Year Guild of Food Writers Award 2013); *Books* Ken Hom's Encyclopaedia of Chinese Cookery Techniques (1984), Ken Hom's Chinese Cookery (1984, 25th anniversary edn 2009), Ken Hom's East Meets West Cuisine (1987), Ken Hom's Vegetable & Pasta Book (1987), Ken Hom's Quick & Easy Chinese Cookery (1989), The Taste of China (1990), Fragrant Harbour Taste (1991), Cooking of China (1993), Ken Hom's Illustrated Chinese Cookery (1993), Ken Hom's Chinese Kitchen (1994), Chinese Recipes (1994), Ken Hom's Vegetarian Cookery (1995), Ken Hom Cooks Chinese (1996), Ken Hom's Hot Wok (1996), Ken Hom Travels with a Hot Wok (1998), Easy Family Dishes: A Memoir with Recipes (1998, Andre Simon Meml Book of the Year), Ken Hom Cooks Thai (1999), Ken Hom's Foolproof Chinese Cookery (2000), Ken Hom's Quick Wok (2001), Ken Hom's Foolproof Thai Cookery (2002), Ken Hom's Foolproof Asian Cookery (2003), 100 Top Stir Fries (2004), Simple Chinese Cookery (2005, Simple Thai Cookery (2005), Simple Asian Cookery (2006), The Ken Hom Nutri Wok Kit Recipe Book (with Wynnie Chan, 2008), My Kitchen Table – 100 Quick Stir-fry Recipes (2011), Classic Chinese Recipes (2011), Ken Hom Complete Chinese Cookbook (2011), Asian (2011), My Kitchen Table – 100 Easy Chinese Suppers (2012), Exploring China: A Culinary Adventure (with Ching HE Huang, 2012), Truffles (with Pierre-Jean Pebeyre, 2014); *Recreations* wines (claret), swimming, cycling; *Clubs* 48 Group; *Style*— Ken Hom, OBE; ✉ c/o Luisa Vogliolo-Welch, I-Mage Communications Ltd, 1–7 Woburn Walk, London WC1H 0JJ (☎ 020 7631 3116 or 020 7387 0828, mobile 07774 234899, e-mail luisawelch@i-magepr.com)

HOMA, Peter Michael; CBE (2000); *b* 1957; *Educ* Ernest Bevin Sch Tooting, Univ of Sussex (BA), Univ of Hull (MBA), IHSM (DipHSM), Brunel Univ (DBA); *m* 1; 1 s (b 1988), 1 da (b 1990); m 2, 16 July 2006, Deborah Hallas; *Career* health serv mangr; self-employed 1979–81, nat admin trainee SW Thames RHA 1981–82, operational servs administrator St George's Hosp London 1982–84, dep unit administrator Bristol Children's and Maternity Hosps 1984–86, dep unit gen mangr Acute Servs Unit Bromsgrove and Redditch HA 1986–89; The Leicester Royal Infirmary: assoc gen mangr 1989–90, unit gen mangr 1990–93, chief exec The Leicester Royal Infirmary NHS Tst 1993–98; head of National Patients' Access Team NHS Exec 1998–99, chief exec Cmmn for Health Improvement 1999–2003, chief exec St George's Healthcare NHS Tst 2003–06, chief exec Nottingham Univ Hosps NHS Tst 2006–; visiting prof: LSE 2000–03, Univ of Lincoln 2007, Univ of Nottingham 2008; IHSM: vice-chm 1996–97, chm 1997–98, pres 1998–99; pres Infirmary Drama and Operative and Literary Soc (IDOLS) 1990–98; companion Inst of Health Mgmnt 2003; *Recreations* running, cycling, photography, writing, reading; *Style*— Dr Peter Homa, CBE; ✉ Nottingham University Hospitals NHS Trust, Trust Headquarters, City Hospital Campus, Hucknall Road, Nottingham NG5 1PB (☎ 0115 969 1169 x 76007, e-mail peter.homa@nuh.nhs.uk)

HOMAN, Prof Roger Edward; s of Edward Alfred Homan (d 1997), and Olive Florence, *née* Dent (d 1988); *b* 25 June 1944; *Educ* Varndean GS Brighton, Univ of Sussex (BA), Lancaster Univ (PhD), LSE (MSc), Heythrop Coll Univ of London (MA); *Career* Brighton Coll of Educn: lectr in religious studies 1971–73, lectr in educn 1973–76; University of Brighton (formerly Brighton Poly): lectr in religious educn 1976–85, princ lectr in religious studies 1985–, prof of religious studies 1998–2009 (emeritus prof 2009–); memb: Prayer Book Soc (current vice-pres), Victorian Soc; fell Victoria Coll of Music 1994; *Recreations* sweet peas and auriculas, church music, chapel hunting, poetry, aesthetics; *Style*— Prof Roger Homan; ✉ University of Brighton, Falmer, East Sussex BN1 9PH (☎ 01273 643405)

HOME, Anna Margaret; OBE (1993); da of James Douglas Home (d 1989), and Janet Mary, *née* Wheeler (d 1974); *b* 13 January 1938; *Educ* Convent of Our Lady St Leonards-on-Sea, St Anne's Coll Oxford (MA); *Career* joined: BBC Radio 1961, BBC TV 1964; researcher, dir and prodr Children's Programmes 1964–70, exec prodr Children's Drama 1970–81; controller of programmes (later dep dir programmes) TVS 1981–86, head of

Children's Programmes BBC TV 1986–97, chief exec Children's Film and Television Fndn (CFTF) 1998–2012; chair: Second World Summit on Television for Children 1998, Cinemagic 1999–2005, Eurokidnet 2002–06, Showcomotion Children's Media Conf 2004–09, Kidnet 2006–, Save Kid's TV 2006–11, Children's Media Conf 2010–; chair Children's Media Fndn 2012–; memb Bd: Screen South 2002–, Unicorn Children's Theatre 2004–11; tstee Prince of Wales Fndn for Children and the Arts (formerly Prince of Wales Arts and Kids Fndn) 2006–14; Women in Film and Television Lifetime Achievement Award 1996, BAFTA Special Award for Lifetime Achievement 1997; FRTS, FRSA; *Recreations* reading, theatre, gardening; *Style*— Ms Anna Home, OBE; ✉ 3 Liberia Road, London N5 1JP

HOME, 15 Earl of (S 1605); Sir David Alexander Cospatrick Douglas-Home; KT (2014), CVO (1997), CBE (1991); also Lord Dunglass (S 1605), Lord Home (S 1473), and Baron Douglas (UK 1875); only s of Baron Home of the Hirsel, KT, PC, who disclaimed the Earldom of Home for life 1963 (d 1995), and Elizabeth Hester, *née* Alington (d 1990); *b* 20 November 1943; *Educ* Eton, ChCh Oxford; *m* 1972, Jane Margaret, yr da of Col John Williams-Wynne, CBE, DSO, JP (d 1998); 2 da (Lady Iona Katherine b 1980, Lady Mary Elizabeth b 1982), 1 s (Michael David Alexander, Lord Dunglass b 1987); *Heir* s, Lord Dunglass; *Career* dir Morgan Grenfell & Co Ltd 1974–99, chm Deutsche Export Services Ltd 1984–99, chm Deutsche (Scotland) Ltd 1986–99 (dir 1978–99), chm Morgan Grenfell International Ltd 1987–98, dir Deutsche Morgan Grenfell Hong Kong Ltd 1989–99, dir Deutsche Morgan Grenfell Asia Pacific Holdings Pte Ltd 1989–99, pres cmmr PT Deutsche Morgan Grenfell Indonesia 1993–99, dir Deutsche Morgan Grenfell Group plc 1996–99 (chm 1999); chm: Tandem Group plc (formerly EFG plc) 1991–96 (dir 1981–96), Cegelec Controls Ltd 1991–94, Coutts & Co 1999–2013, MAN Ltd 2000–09, Coutts (Switzerland) Ltd 2000–04, Bank von Ernst 2003–04, Coutts & Co Ltd (formerly RBS Coutts and Coutts Bank von Ernst) 2004–; dir: Douglas and Angus Estates 1966–, Agricultural Mortgage Corporation 1979–93, Credit for Exports plc 1984–94, K & N Kenanga Holdings Bhd (formerly K & N Kenanga Sdn Bhd until 1996) 1993–99, Kenanga Deutsche Futures Sdn Bhd 1995–99; tstee Grosvenor Estate 1993–2010, non-exec dir Grosvenor Estate Holdings 1993–2000, chm Grosvenor Gp Ltd 2007–10 (non-exec dir 2005–10); govr The Ditchley Fndn 1976–2010 (memb Cncl of Mgmnt 1976–2003); chm Ctee for ME Trade 1986–92, memb Export Guarantee Advsy Cncl ECGD 1988–93, govr Cwlth Inst 1988–98; memb: Offshore Industry Export Advsy Gp 1989–93, Cncl RASE 1990–2005, Bd Dubai FSA 2005–12; pres Old Etonian Assoc 2002–03; sits as Cons House of Lords, oppn front bench spokesman on trade and industry 1997–98; *Recreations* outdoor sports; *Clubs* Turf; *Style*— The Rt Hon the Earl of Home, KT, CVO, CBE; ✉ 43 Chelsea Towers, Chelsea Manor Gardens, London SW3 5PN (☎ 020 3730 1690); The Hirsel, Coldstream, Berwickshire TD12 4LP (☎ 01890 882345); Castlemains, Douglas, Lanarkshire ML11 0RX (☎ 01555 851241); Coutts & Co, 440 Strand, London WC2R 0QS (☎ 020 7753 1000, fax 020 7753 1066)

HOME, Prof Philip David; s of Philip Henry Home, and Kathleen Margaret, *née* Young; *b* 11 January 1948; *Educ* Birkenhead Sch, Univ of Oxford (MA, DM, DPhil), Guy's Hosp (BM BCh); *m* 28 Aug 1971, Elizabeth Mary, da of Sidney Thomas Broad; 1 s (Jonathan Paul b 1979), 1 da (Deborah Mary b 1976); *Career* Wellcome Tst sr res fell in clinical sci 1982–86, prof Univ of Newcastle upon Tyne 1993– (reader 1986–93); conslt physician Newcastle Hospitals 1986–2011; ed Diabetic Medicine 1987–91, ed Diabetes Voice 2002–04; author of over 400 articles on aspects of diabetes med; vice-pres Int Diabetes Fedn 1997–2003; FRCP 1989; *Recreations* gardening, travel, work; *Style*— Prof Philip Home; ✉ ICM-Diabetes, Framlington Place, Newcastle upon Tyne NE2 4HH (☎ 0191 208 7154, fax 0191 208 0723, e-mail philip.home@ncl.ac.uk)

HOME, Sir William Dundas; 14 Bt (NS 1671), of Blackadder, Co Berwick; o s of John Home (d 1988, er s of Sir David George Home, 13 Bt), and Nancy Helen, *née* Elliott (now Lady Gorton); suc gf 1992; *b* 19 February 1968; *Educ* Cranbrook Sch Sydney; *m* 30 Sept 1995, Dominique Meryl, da of Sydney Fischer, OBE; 1 s (Thomas John b 29 Nov 1996), 1 da (Petra Sydney b 23 June 1998); *Heir* s, Thomas Home; *Career* horticulturalist and arboriculturalist; memb: Int Soc of Arboriculture, Aust Inst of Horticulture, Nat Arborist Assoc; *Recreations* tennis, golf, fly fishing; *Clubs* Royal Sydney Golf; *Style*— Sir William Home, Bt

HOMER, Andy; s of Charles Henry Homer (d 1982), and Kathleen Homer, *née* Welch (d 2004); *b* 2 March 1953; *Educ* St Chad's Coll Wolverhampton, Becket GS Nottingham, Wharton Sch Univ of Philadelphia; *m* 1971, Maria; 2 s (Oliver Charles b 1980, Alexander Charles b 1983); *Career* Commercial Union plc: dep corp fin and planning mangr 1992–93, dir of fin UK 1994–96, gen mangr UK General Insurance 1996–98; chief exec Axa Insurance plc 1998–, exec dir AXA UK plc 1999–2001; chief exec Folgate Partnership 2001–05, chief exec Towergate Partnership 2005–11; non-exec dir Towergate Insurance and Open GI 2011–, mentor Merryck & Co 2012–, chm Utility Aid 2014–; chm Motor Insurers Bureau UK 1998–2001, pres CII 2003 (vice-pres 1999–2003), chm Br Insurance Brokers Assoc 2012–13; Freeman City of London Co of Firefighters 1997; FCII 1976; *Recreations* aerobics, raquet ball, jogging; *Clubs* Worcestershire CC, West Bromwich Albion FC; *Style*— Andy Homer, Esq

HOMER, Dame Linda Margaret (Lin); DCB (2016, CB 2008); *b* 4 March 1957, Norfolk; *Educ* UCL (LLB); *Career* Herts CC 1982–98, chief exec Suffolk CC 1998–2002, chief exec Birmingham City Cncl 2002–05, DG Immigration and Nationality Directorate Home Office 2005–08, chief exec Border and Immigration Agency (later UK Border Agency) 2008–10, perm sec Dept for Transport 2010–12, perm sec and chief exec HMRC 2012–; hon doctorate Univ of Birmingham 2011; *Style*— Dame Lin Homer, DCB; ✉ HM Revenue & Customs, 100 Parliament Street, London SW1A 2BQ

HON, Prof (Kwok Keung) Bernard; s of Chung Ki Hon, and Yuet Seen, *née* Shaw; *b* 16 January 1950; *Educ* Hong Kong Tech Coll, Univ of Birmingham (MSc, PhD); *m* 18 Dec 1976, Yuk Ching Metis, da of late Yat Chow Hui; 2 s (Chen Yue (Daniel) b 1979, Wai Yue (Adrian) b 1982); *Career* lectr: Univ of Bath 1979–81, Univ of Birmingham 1981–87, prof of mfrg systems Univ of Dundee 1987–90; Univ of Liverpool: prof of mfrg systems 1990–, head Dept of Industrial Studies 1990–97, dep dean of engrg 1997–2000; dir: Merseyside Innovation Centre 1992–96, Rapid Prototyping Centre 1994–, Product Innovation and Development Centre 1995–2003, Merseyside TCS Centre 1995–2003; memb Technology Foresight Manufacturing Production and Business Processes Panel 1994–98; academic advsr: Hong Kong Poly Univ 1996–2001, Hong Kong Univ of Science and Technology 2001–03; visiting lectr Univ of Hong Kong 2004; founding chm Int Conference on Design and Manufacture for Sustainable Devpt; Outstanding PolyU Alumni Award Hong Kong Poly Univ 2007; fell CIRP (Int Acad for Production Engrg) 2001; FIEE 1990; *Publications* Design and Manufacture for Sustainable Development (2003); *Recreations* badminton, music; *Style*— Prof Bernard Hon; ✉ Department of Engineering, Harrison Hughes Building, University of Liverpool, Liverpool L69 3GH (☎ 0151 794 4680, fax 0151 794 9364, e-mail hon@liv.ac.uk)

HONAN, Corinna Jeannette; da of Prof Park Honan, of Burley, Leeds, and Jeannette, *née* Colin; *b* 7 May 1953, St Germain-en-Laye, France; *Educ* Classical HS RI USA, King Edward VI HS for Girls Birmingham, St Hugh's Coll Oxford (BA), NCTJ; *m* 21 July 1984, Nicholas Inge, s of Edward Inge; 2 da (Anabel India Kitty b 20 June 1985, Sophie Georgia Rachelle b 12 April 1989); *Career* news reporter Newcastle Journal 1975–78, staff feature writer Woman magazine 1978–81; Daily Mail: news reporter 1981–83, TV and foreign correspondent 1984–87, showbusiness ed 1987–91, feature writer and personality interviewer 1991–95; Daily Telegraph: features ed 1995–97, asst ed (features) 1997–2005, asst ed 2005–07, dep ed Saturday paper 2003–05; conslt ed (features) Daily Mail 2007, assoc ed News Review Sunday Times 2008–10, book serialiser Daily Mail and freelance ed/writer 2010–; *Recreations* reading, hunting for antiques, going to France; *Style*— Ms Corinna Honan; ✉ e-mail corinnahonan@yahoo.com

HONDERICH, Prof Edgar Dawn Ross (Ted); s of John William Honderich (d 1956), and Rae Laura, *née* Armstrong (d 1952); *b* 30 January 1933; *Educ* Univ of Toronto (BA), UCL (PhD); *m* 1, 22 Aug 1964 (m dis 1976), Pauline da of Paul Goodwin (d 1976), of Dunlavin; 1 da (Kiaran Aeveen b 1960), 1 s (John Ruan b 1962); m 2, 8 Dec 1989, Jane, da of Maj Robert O'Grady, MC, of Midford Place, Bath; m 3, 4 July 2003, Ingrid Coggin Purkiss, da of Maurice Coggin, of Cambridge; *Career* lectr in philosophy Univ of Sussex 1962–64; UCL: lectr 1964–72, reader 1972–83, prof 1983–88, Grote prof of philosophy of mind and logic 1988–; visiting prof: Yale Univ 1970, City Univ of NY 1971, Univ of Bath 2005–; chm Royal Inst of Philosophy 2006– ed: International Library of Philosophy And Scientific Method 1965–, The Arguments of the Philosophers 1970–, The Problems of Philosophy 1983–; advsy ed Penguin Philosophy 1965–; memb: Mind Assoc, Aristotelian Soc; memb Lab Pty; *Books* Punishment: The Supposed Justifications (1969), Essays on Freedom of Action (ed, 1973), Social Ends and Political Means (ed, 1976), Philosophy As It Is (ed with M Burnyeat, 1979), Violence for Equality: Inquiries in Political Philosophy (1980), Philosophy Through its Past (ed, 1984), Morality and Objectivity (ed, 1985), A Theory of Determinism: The Mind, Neuroscience and Life-Hopes (1988), Conservatism (1990, revised edn 2004), How Free are You? The Determinism Problem (1993, 2 edn 2002), The Oxford Companion to Philosophy (ed, 1995, new edn 2005), Philosopher: a Kind of Life (2000), After the Terror (2002), On Political Means and Social Ends (2003), Terrorism for Humanity: Inquiries in Political Philosophy (2003), On Consciousness (2004), On Political Means and Social Ends (2004), On Determinism and Freedom (2005), Punishment: The Supposed Justifications Reconsidered (2005), Humanity, Terrorism, Terrorist War: Palestine, 9/11, Iraq, 7/7... (2006), Radical Externalism: Honderich's Theory of Consciousness Discussed (contrib, 2006), Actual Consciousness (2014, paperback edn 2016), Philosophers of Our Times (2015); *Recreations* wine, music, Queen's Wood, Highgate Wood; *Clubs* Garrick; *Style*— Prof Ted Honderich; ✉ 66 Muswell Hill Road, London N10 3JR (☎ 020 8350 4936)

H

HONE, His Hon Judge Richard Michael; QC (1997); s of late Maj-Gen Sir (Herbert) Ralph Hone, KCMG, KBE, GCStJ, MC, TD, QC, and Sybil Mary, *née* Collins; *b* 15 February 1947; *Educ* St Paul's (scholar), UC Oxford (MA); *m* 1, Sarah Nicholl-Carne; 2 s (Nathaniel b 1987, Rufus b 1989); m 2, Diana Pavel; 2 s (Adam b 1995, Charles b 1997); *Career* called to the Bar Middle Temple 1970 (bencher 1994); recorder of the Crown Court 1987–2004, circuit judge (SE Circuit) 2004–, sr circuit judge Central Criminal Court 2005–; Cocks' referee 1988–94; chm Jt Regulations Ctee 1995–2000; memb Professional Conduct Ctee of the Bar 1993–97, legal memb MHRT 2000–; pres Freemasons' Grand Charity 2012–16, pres Masonic Charitable Fndn 2016–; Liveryman Worshipful Co of Ironmongers 2008; KStJ 2000 (CStJ 1993, OStJ 1972); *Recreations* wine, reading, travel; *Clubs* Boodle's, Pratt's, Beefsteak; *Style*— His Hon Judge Hone, QC; ✉ Central Criminal Court, Old Bailey, London EC4M 7EH (☎ 020 7248 3277)

HONER, Julian Anthony; s of John David Honer, of Cambridge, and Shirley, *née* Gerrish; *b* 19 February 1961; *Educ* Lewes Priory Sch, Univ of Stirling (BA), Univ of Birmingham, Barber Inst of Fine Arts (MPhil); *m* 1997, Alison, *née* Starling; 1 da (Charlotte Miranda b 22 March 2005); *Career* researcher and cataloguer Dept of Modern Br Pictures Bonhams Fine Art Auctioneers 1986–88, fine art insurance underwriter Eagle Star (Star Assurance Soc Ltd) 1988–89, account exec Frizzell Fine Art Insurance 1989–90; ed: The Art Directory 1990–93, The Dictionary of Art 1992–95; Macmillan: managing ed 1995–97, sr commissioning ed 1997–98; Merrell Publishers Ltd: ed 1998–99, editorial dir 1999–2008; Thames & Hudson: head of editorial 2009–11, dir 2011–; author of a number of articles; *Recreations* travel, art, architecture, photography, music; *Clubs* The Book Soc; *Style*— Julian Honer, Esq; ✉ Thames & Hudson, 181A High Holborn, London WC1V 7QX (☎ 020 7845 5067, e-mail j.honer@thameshudson.co.uk)

HONEYBALL, Mary Hilda Rosamund; MEP (Lab) London; da of late Stanley James Honeyball, and late Betty Gath, *née* Tandy; *b* 12 November 1952; *Educ* Pate's GS for Girls Cheltenham, Somerville Coll Oxford (MA); *Career* administrative offr GLC 1975–77, negotiations offr Soc of Civil and Public Servants 1977–83, political organiser Royal Arsenal Co-operative Soc 1983–85, gen sec Newham Voluntary Agencies Cncl 1986–90, service mangr Spastics Soc 1990–91, chief exec Gingerbread (lone parents' support orgn) 1992–94, gen sec Assoc of Chief Offrs of Probation 1994–98, MEP (Lab) London 2000–; cncllr Barnet BC 1978–86; chair Women's Ctee Gtr London Lab Pty 1983–85, memb Nat Alliance of Women's Orgns 1992–94; chair Docklands Forum 1987–90; govr: Grahame Park Sch London 1978–84, Deptford Green Sch London 1986–95, Sir Francis Drake Primary Sch London 1986–95; *Books* Parliamentary Pioneers – Labour Women MPs 1918–1945 (2015); *Recreations* reading, art; *Clubs* RSA; *Style*— Ms Mary Honeyball, MEP; ✉ 4G Shirland Mews, London W9 3DY (☎ 020 8964 9815, fax 020 8960 0150, e-mail mary@maryhoneyball.net)

HONEYBORNE, Dr Christopher Henry Bruce; s of Henry Thomas Honeyborne (d 1998), and Lily Margaret, *née* Fox (d 1991); *b* 5 December 1940, Richmond, N Yorks; *Educ* Cambs HS for Boys, St Catharine's Coll Cambridge (MA, DipAgSci), Univ of Reading (PhD); *m* 12 Oct 1968, (Anne) Veronica, da of Stephen Sullivan (d 2003), of Guernsey; 1 s (James, *qv* b 1970), 2 da (Clare b 1975, Katharine b 1986); *Career* res demonstrator Univ of Reading 1964–68, res scientist ARC Univ of Bristol 1968–70, mangr Cuprinol Ltd 1971–72, sr mangr Lazard Bros & Co Ltd 1972–77 (seconded to Dalgety Ltd 1976–77), Banque Paribas 1977–89 (dep gen mangr London Branch 1977–86, chief exec Quilter Goodison Co Ltd 1986–88); chief exec Bank of N T Butterfield & Son Ltd London Branch and Seymour Pierce Butterfield Ltd 1993–94; chm: Finotel plc 1989–98 (dir 1983), Cameron Richard and Smith (Holdings) Ltd 1989–2007, Gremlin Group plc 1997–99, Aerosol Products Ltd 1999–2004, Aspect Internet Hldgs Ltd 2003–04, Dyson Gp plc 2006–10, ZOO Digital Group plc (formerly KAZOO3D plc) 2006–10 (dir 2000–); dir: Cartier Ltd 1979–97, Secure Retirement plc 1991–93, Yorkshire Water plc 1993–98, Kunick plc 1995–2002, BWDAimVCT plc (now Rensburg Aim VCT plc) 1999–2005, Coolbeans Productions Ltd 1999–2001, ukphonebook.com ltd (now Simunix Ltd) 1999–2005, Bede plc 2000–08, Birse Group plc 2000–06, Bannatyne Fitness Ltd 2001–03, LBIconAB(publ) 2005–06, Matica plc 2007–10, Prime Focus London plc 2012–14; Freeman Cutlers' Co (Sheffield) 2008–; MIBiol, MSI; *Recreations* gardening, shooting, viewing art; *Clubs* Oxford and Cambridge; *Style*— Dr Christopher Honeyborne; ✉ Scawton Croft, Rievaulx, York YO62 5LE (☎ 01439 770392); office (☎ 01439 771900, e-mail chbhoneyborne@aol.com)

HONEYBORNE, James; *b* 7 August 1970, Bristol; *Educ* Ampleforth, Newcastle Univ; *Career* wildlife filmmaker; researcher 1991–96, prodr/dir 1996–2006, co-presenter Wildest Dreams 2009, currently exec prodr BBC Nat History Unit; hon patron Dublin Univ Zoological Soc 2013; *Television* incl: Supernatural (BBC 1) 1999, Weird Nature (BBC 1) 2002, Pelican (Wildlife on One, BBC 1) 2001, Peregrine (Wildlife on One, BBC 1) 2004, Dragonfly (Wildlife on One, BBC 1) 2004, Diving with Whales (BBC 2) 2005, Dive Galapagos (BBC 2) 2005, Natural World (BBC 2) 2006, Africa (as series prodr, BBC 1) 2013, 24 Hours on Earth (BBC 1) 2014, Autumnwatch (BBC 2) 2014, Wonders of the Monsoon (BBC 2) 2014, Alaska: Earth's Frozen Kingdom (BBC 2) 2015, Japan: Earth's Enchanted Islands (BBC 2) 2015, Big Blue Live (BBC 1) 2015, Patagonia (BBC 2) 2015; *Film* incl: (as feature dir) Meerkats the Movie 2007; *Style*— James Honeyborne, Esq;

✉ BBC Natural History Unit, Whiteladies Road, Bristol, Somerset BS8 2LR (☎ 0117 973 2211)

HONEYBOURNE, Dr David; *b* 26 March 1951; *Educ* Redditch HS, Univ of Bristol Med Sch (MB ChB, MD), Coll of Medicine Univ of Wales (MSc); *Career* house physician Bristol Gen Hosp 1974; SHO: Southmead Hosp Bristol 1975–76 (house surgn 1975), Brook Hosp London 1976–77; registrar in med KCH London 1977–78, res fell KCH Med Sch London 1978–80, sr registrar in med Manchester 1980–85; conslt physician specialising in chest diseases: City Hosp Birmingham 1985–98, Birmingham Heartlands Hosp 1998–2011 (hon conslt physician 2011–); sr clinical lectr in med Univ of Birmingham; author of books and pubns on chest diseases; memb: Br Thoracic Soc; FRCP 1993 (MRCP 1977); *Recreations* golf, photography, beekeeping; *Clubs* Goodwood Golf; *Style—* Dr David Honeybourne; ✉ Priory Hospital, Priory Road, Edgbaston, Birmingham B5 7UG (☎ 0121 446 1670); Department of Respiratory Medicine, Birmingham Heartlands, Birmingham B9 5SS (☎ 0121 424 2261, fax 0121 424 1661, e-mail davidhoneybourne@aol.com)

HONEYMAN BROWN, Christopher; s of Edward Honeyman Brown (d 1981), of St Mawes, and Nancy Elisabeth Ellen Odgers, *née* Hall (d 1991); *b* 2 June 1948, Whitechapel, London; *Educ* Stowe; *m* 7 Sept 1973, Rosamund, da of late Peter Bluett Winch; 1 da (Emma b 15 Sept 1976), 1 s (Thomas b 2 Nov 1978); *Career* ptnr: Croydon & Co (chartered accountants) 1977–85, Binder Hamlyn (chartered accountants) 1986–96, chief exec Alsop Wilkinson (slrs) 1996, dir of ops Dibb Lupton Alsop (slrs) 1996–98, ptnr Horwath Clark Whitehill (chartered accountants) 1998–2001, chief exec asb law (slrs) 2001–06; dir Winmark Ltd, dir Hennik Gp Ltd; govr Stowe Sch 1993–2007, chm of govrs Stowe Sch 2007–16, chm Acad Cncl The Littlehampton Acad; FCA 1979 (ACA 1973), FRSA; *Recreations* music, gardening, golf; *Style—* Christopher Honeyman Brown, Esq; ✉ 31 Old Glebe, Fernhurst, Haslemere, Surrey GU27 3HT (☎ 01428 645911, e-mail honeymanbrown@gmail.com)

HOOD, Dr Alison Sinclair; da of Alexander B Hood (d 1986), and Agnes Prise, *née* Edgar (d 1989); *b* 21 January 1952; *Educ* Univ of Glasgow (PhD); *Career* princ Lipton Orthoptic Inst Sch of Orthoptics Glasgow and head Lipton Orthoptic Inst Glasgow 1979–84, head Sch of Orthoptics The Queen's Coll Glasgow 1984–90, sr lectr in orthoptics Dept of Vision Sciences Glasgow Caledonian Univ 1990–92, md Eye Scan (UK) 1993–2012; head of research Guide Dogs UK 2010–; Scottish memb Orthoptists' Bd Cncl for Professions Supplementary to Med (CPSM) 1979–93; memb Br Orthoptic Soc 1973–; *Recreations* art, golf; *Style—* Dr Alison Hood; ✉ Eye Scan (UK), 30 Lanton Road, Lanton Park, Newlands, Glasgow G43 2SR (☎ 0141 637 7503, mobile 07860 735911, e-mail alison.eyescan@talk21.com)

HOOD, Prof Christopher Cropper; CBE (2011); s of David White Hood (d 2003), and Margaret, *née* Cropper (d 1985); *b* 5 March 1947; *Educ* Univ of York (BA, DLitt), Univ of Glasgow (BLitt); *m* 1979, Gillian Thackwray White; 2 da; *Career* jr research fell Carnegie Corporation Project 1970–72, lectr Dept of Politics Univ of Glasgow 1972–77, research fell SSRC Machinery of Govt Project Univ of York 1977–79, lectr Dept of Politics Univ of Glasgow 1979–86, sr teaching fell Faculty of Law Nat Univ of Singapore 1984–85, prof of govt and public admin Univ of Sydney 1986–89, prof of public admin and public policy LSE 1989–2000, Gladstone prof of government and fell All Souls Coll Oxford 2001–14 (emeritus prof 2014–); chair Section S5 (Politics and Int Relations) Br Acad 2002–05, chair Nuffield Cncl on Bioethics Working Party on Medical Profiling and Online Healthcare 2008–10; FBA 1996, AcSS 2001, FRSA 2007; *Books* The Limits of Administration (1976), Bureaumetrics (with Prof A Dunsire, 1981), Big Government in Hard Times (ed with Prof M Wright, 1981), The Tools of Government (1983), Administrative Analysis: An Introduction to Rules, Enforcement and Organization (1986), Delivering Public Services: Sharing Western European Experience (1988), Cutback Management in Public Bureaucracies (with Prof A Dunsire, 1989), Administrative Argument (with Prof M W Jackson, 1991), Rewards at the Top (ed with Prof Guy Peters, 1994), Explaining Economic Policy Reversals (1994), The Art of the State (1998), Regulation inside Government (with Colin Scott and others, 1999), The Government of Risk: Understanding Risk Regulation Regimes (with Henry Rothstein and Robert Baldwin, 2001), Reward for High Public Office: Asian and Pacific Rim States (ed with Prof Guy Peters, 2003), Controlling Modern Government (jt ed, 2004), The Politics of Public Service Bargains (with Martin Lodge, 2006), The Tools of Government in the Digital Age (with Helen Margetts, 2007), Transparency: The Key to Better Governance (jt ed, 2006), The Blame Game (2011), Forging a Discipline: A Critical Assessment of Oxford's Development of the Study of Politics and International Relations in Comparative Perspective (jt ed, 2014), When the Party's Over: The Politics of Fiscal Squeeze in Perspective (jt ed, 2014), A Government that Worked Better and Cost Less? Evaluating Three Decades of Reform and Change in UK Central Government (with Ruth Dixon, 2015); also author of numerous book chapters and articles in learned jls; *Style—* Prof Christopher Hood, CBE, FBA; ✉ All Souls College, Oxford OX1 4AL

HOOD, (Hilary) David Richard; s of Hilary Ollyett Dupuis Hood (d 1982), and Mrs Patrick Reid, *née* Sampson (d 2004); *b* 6 February 1955, Oxford; *Educ* Radley, Millfield, KCL (LLB); *Career* called to the Bar Inner Temple 1980; *Style—* David Hood, Esq; ✉ 26 The Gateways, Sprimont Place, London SW3 3JA (e-mail dhoodesq@aol.com)

HOOD, 8 Viscount (GB 1796); Sir Henry Lyttelton Alexander; 8 Bt (GB 1778); also Baron Hood (I 1782 and GB 1795); s of 7 Viscount Hood (d 1999); Lord Hood is seventh in descent from 1 Viscount, the naval hero who captured Corsica 1793; *b* 16 March 1958; *m* 5 Oct 1991, Flora, yr da of Cdr Michael Bernard Casement, OBE, RN, of Dene Cottage, West Harting, Petersfield, Hants; 3 s (Archibald Lyttelton Samuel b 16 May 1993, Atticus Michael Alexander b 20 Oct 1995, Willoughby Henry Caspar b 11 Nov 1998); 2 da (Edith Clementine Matilda (twin) b 11 Nov 1998, Darcy Ellen Fynvola b 8 July 2002); *Career* slr; a Personal Lord-in-Waiting to HM The Queen 2008–; *Style—* The Rt Hon Viscount Hood; ✉ 29 Lansdowne Road, London W11 2LQ

HOOD, James (Jim); *m* Marion; 1 s, 1da; *Career* cncllr Newark and Sherwood DC 1979–87; MP (Lab): Clydesdale 1987–2005, Lanark and Hamilton E 2005–15; House of Commons: fndr chm All-Pty Gp on ME 1987–92, memb Defence Select Ctee 1997–2001, memb Liaison Ctee 1992–2006, chm European Scrutiny Select Ctee 1998–2006, memb Speaker's Panel of Chm 1997–; memb: NATO UK Parly Assembly 2005–10, Parly Assembly of the Cncl of Europe 2008–, Assembly WEU 2008–; ldr Nottingham striking miners 1984–85; fell Industry and Parl Tst, memb Armed Forces Parly Scheme; *Style—* Jim Hood, Esq; ✉ House of Commons, London SW1A 0AA (☎ 020 7219 4585, fax 020 7219 5872, e-mail hoodj@parliament.uk, website www.jimhoodmp.org.uk); Constituency Office: Council Offices, South Vennel, Lanark ML11 7JT (☎ 01555 673177, fax 01555 673188)

HOOD, (William) Nicholas (Nick); CVO (2012), CBE (1991); s of Sir Tom Hood, KBE, CB, TD, and Joan, *née* Helyar; *b* 3 December 1935; *Educ* Clifton; *m* 1, 1963 (m dis 1990), Angela, *née* Robinson; 1 s, 1 da; m 2, 1994 (m dis 2003), Ann E H Reynolds; m 3, 2006, Patricia Lang; *Career* served DCLI 1955–57; NEM General Insurance Association Ltd and Credit Insurance Association Ltd 1958–64, G B Britton UK Ltd 1964–70 (rising to sales and mktg dir); UBM Group plc: various positions rising to dir Central Region 1970–84, md UBM Overseas Ltd 1972–82; dir HAT Group Ltd 1984–86; chm: Wessex Water Authy 1987–89, Winterthur Life plc 1988–2007, Wessex Water plc 1989–98, Wessex Water Ltd 1998–99, MHIT plc 1998–2003, Frogmat International Ltd 2004–09, Winterthur Life (UK) Ltd 2002–07, Wessex Water Services Ltd, Wessex Water Commercial Ltd, Wessex Waste Management Ltd; vice-chm Azurix Ltd 1998–99; dir: QHIT plc 1998–2004, Clifton College Services Ltd 1997–2014, Royal United Hospital Bath 2012–; non-exec dir: Bremhill Industries plc 1987–93, Commercial Union Environmental Trust plc 1992–98, APV plc 1994–97, Brewin Dolphin Holdings plc 2000–13 (dep chm); cncl memb Water Trg Cncl 1987–99, Fndn for Water Research 1989–99, chm WaterAid 1990–95 (memb Cncl 1989–96), pres International Water Services Assoc 1997–99 (vice-pres 1993–97), life vice-pres American Waterworks Assoc 1998, life vice-pres Int Water Assoc 2002, memb Cncl Water Servs Assoc (vice-chm 1994, chm 1995), tstee West Country Rivers Tst 2000–15; memb Advsy Cncl for Business and the Environment 1990–93, memb Advsy Bd Great Western Railway 2001–; dep chm Business in the Community 1993–2007; chm @Bristol 1994–2002 (life vice-pres 2002); dir: The Harbourside Centre 1995–2001, The Harbourside Foundation 1996–2001, West of England Philharmonic Orch 2003–07; chm of tstees: Bristol Cancer Help Centre 2000–07, Walk the Walk charity 2005–2013; memb The Prince of Wales' Duchy of Cornwall Cncl 1992–2011; govr Merchant's Acad; Master Soc of Merchant Venturers 2007–08, Liveryman Worshipful Co of Plumbers; Hon MBA UWE 2000; fell WWF 1989–2016; *Recreations* music, fishing, cricket, painting; *Clubs* Army and Navy, MCC, Boodle's; *Style—* Nick Hood, Esq, CVO, CBE; ✉ One Queen's Parade, Bath BA1 2NJ (☎ 01225 334423)

HOOD, Prof Roger Grahame; CBE (1995); s of Ronald Hugo Frederick Hood (d 1996), of Aldridge, W Midlands, and Phyllis Eileen, *née* Murphy (d 1991); *b* 12 June 1936; *Educ* King Edward's Sch Five Ways Birmingham, LSE (BSc), Downing Coll Cambridge (PhD), Univ of Oxford (DCL); *m* 1, 15 June 1963 (m dis 1985), Barbara, da of Donald Waldo Smith (d 1979), of Washington, IL; 1 da (Catharine b 1964); m 2, 5 Oct 1985, Nancy Colquitt, da of Maj John Heyward Lynah (d 1984), of Charleston, SC; 2 step da (Clare b 1964, Zoe b 1969); *Career* research offr LSE 1961–63, lectr in social admin Univ of Durham 1963–67, asst dir of research Inst of Criminology Univ of Cambridge 1967–73, fell Clare Hall Cambridge 1969–73; Univ of Oxford: reader in criminology 1973–96, dir Centre for Criminological Res 1973–2003, prof of criminology 1996–2003; fell All Souls Coll Oxford 1973–2003 (sub-warden 1994–96, emeritus fell 2003–); distinguished visiting prof Univ of Hong Kong 2003–04, visiting prof Univ of Virginia Law Sch 2005–11; adjunct prof Law Sch City Univ Hong Kong 2007–11; Sellin-Glueck Award for Int Contribs to Criminology 1986; memb: Parole Bd 1973, SSRC Ctee on Social Science and Law 1975–79, Judicial Studies Bd 1979–85, Dept Ctee to Review the Parole System 1987–88; expert conslt UN Ctee on Crime Prevention and Control 1988–95, 1999–2001 and 2004–05, memb Foreign Sec's Death Penalty Panel 1998–, pres Br Soc of Criminology 1986–89; Cesare Beccaria Medal Int Soc of Social Defence and Humane Criminal Policy 2011, European Soc of Criminology Award for a Lifetime Contrib as a European Criminologist 2012; Hon LLD Univ of Birmingham 2008, Hon LLD Edinburgh Napier Univ 2011; hon QC 2000; FBA 1992; *Books* Sentencing in Magistrates Courts (1962), Borstal Re-Assessed (1965), Key Issues in Criminology (jtly, 1970), Sentencing the Motoring Offender (1972), Crime, Criminology and Public Policy – Essays in Honour of Sir Leon Radzinowicz (ed, 1974), A History of English Criminal Law – Vol 5, The Emergence of Penal Policy (jtly, 1986), The Death Penalty – A Worldwide Perspective (1989, 5 edn jtly 2015), Race and Sentencing (1992), The Parole System at Work (jtly, 2000), Differences or Discrimination? Minority ethnic young people in the youth justice system (jtly, 2004), A Fair Hearing? Ethnic Minorities in the Criminal Courts (jtly, 2005), Public Opinion on the Mandatory Death Penalty in Trinidad (jtly, 2011), The Death Penalty in Malaysia (2013), Confronting Capital Punishment in Asia (jt ed, 2013); *Recreations* travel, cooking; *Style—* Prof Roger Hood, CBE, QC, DCL, FBA; ✉ 36 The Stream Edge, Fisher Row, Oxford OX1 1HT (☎ and fax 01865 243140); All Souls College, Oxford OX1 4AL (☎ 01865 279379, mobile 07528 116429, e-mail roger.hood@all-souls.ox.ac.uk)

HOOD, Stephen John; s of Leslie Gilbert Hood, of Australia, and Margaret, *née* Vinnicombe; *b* 12 February 1947; *Educ* Brisbane Boys Coll, Univ of Queensland, Univ of London (LLM); *Children* 5 s (Ludovic b 1973, William b 1974, Roderick b 1978, Frederick b 1980 d 2008, Anthony b 2004), 1 da (Victoria b 1985); *Career* ptnr: Clifford Chance 1978–2007, Mayer Brown 2007–11; David Polk 2011–; chm: Royal Cwlth Soc in Hong Kong 1983–86, Exec Ctee Sir Robert Menzies Meml Tst 1988–98, Latin American Advsy Gp British Invisibles 1999–; Freeman City of London, Liveryman City of London Solicitors' Co; *Books* Equity Joint Ventures in The People's Republic of China, Technology Transfer in The People's Republic of China; *Recreations* viticulture, cocoa production, fly fishing, skiing, contemporary art; *Clubs* Garrick, Oriental, Union (NY), NY Anglers; *Style—* Stephen Hood, Esq

HOODLESS, Dame Elisabeth Anne Marian Frost; DBE (2004, CBE 1992); *née* Plummer; da of late Maj Raymond Evelyn Plummer, TD, of Shoreham, Kent, and late Maureen Grace, *née* Frost; *b* 11 February 1941; *Educ* Redland HS Bristol, Univ of Durham (BA), LSE (Dip); *m* 28 Aug 1965, Donald Bentley Hoodless, s of late Ernest William Hoodless, of Ticehurst, E Sussex; 2 s (Christopher, Mark); *Career* Community Service Volunteers: asst dir 1963, dep dir 1975, exec dir 1986–2011; cncllr London Borough of Islington 1964–68, JP Inner London 1969; chm Juvenile Court 1985–2011; memb Inst of Med Social Work 1963, Churchill fellowship 1966, Sec of State's nominee to Personal Social Services Cncl 1973–80, Cwlth Youth fellowship to Jamaica 1974, pres Volonteurope 1988–2011; dep chm Speaker's Cmmn on Citizenship 1987–90; memb: Home Sec's Ctee on Volunteering 1994–96, Dept of Health Working Gp on Volunteering in the NHS 1994–96, DfEE Advsy Bd on Citizenship 1997–98; dir The Experience Corps 2001–03; memb: Community Advsy Bd IBM 1988–91, Bd Innovation in Civic Participation USA 2001–11, Bd Attend (formerly Nat Assoc of Hosp Friends) 2002–05 (vice-pres 2006–); chm Int Assoc for Nat Youth Service 2006–11; tstee UK Disaster Relief 2010–12; chm of govrs Barnsbury Sch 1971–89; govr: Reeves Fndn 1981–2003, Elizabeth Garrett Anderson Sch 1985–98, Sevenoaks Sch 1991–2000, Redland HS Bristol 2011–16; Third Sector Lifetime Achievement Award 2006; Freedom City of London 1992; Hon Dr Sheffield Hallam Univ 2004; *Publications* Getting Money from Central Government (1981), Managing Innovation (1997), Any Volunteers for a Good Society? (2002), Citoyenneté Active: Intégrer la Théorie à la Pratique par le Volontariat (2002), Senior Volunteers: Solutions Waiting to Happen (2003); *Recreations* ballet, grandchildren, travel, volunteering; *Style—* Dame Elisabeth Hoodless, DBE; ✉ Flat 10, The Eclipse, 26 Laycock Street, London N1 1AH (☎ 020 7359 0231); 2 Shoreham House, Shoreham, Sevenoaks, Kent TN14 7RY (☎ 01959 525672, e-mail donald@hoodless.org)

HOOK, Prof Andrew; s of Wilfred Thomas Hook (d 1964), and Jessie, *née* Dunnett (d 1984); *b* 21 December 1932; *Educ* Wick HS, Daniel Stewart's Coll Edinburgh, Univ of Edinburgh (MA), Princeton Univ (PhD); *m* 18 July 1966, Judith Ann (d 1984), da of George Hibberd, of Comberton, Cambridge; 1 da (Sarah b 1964 d 1995), 2 s (Caspar b 1968 d 2006, Nathaniel b 1975); *Career* Nat Serv NCO Intelligence Corps 1954–56; lectr in American lit Univ of Edinburgh 1961–70, sr lectr in English Univ of Aberdeen 1970–79, Bradley prof of English lit Univ of Glasgow 1979–98; visiting prof: English Dept Princeton Univ 1999–2000, Dartmouth Coll 2003, 2006 and 2007, Univ of St Thomas Minnesota 2005; Gillespie visiting prof Coll of Wooster Ohio 2001–02; CNAA: chm Ctee on Humanities, memb Ctee on Academic Affrs 1986–92; chm: English Panel Scottish Univ Cncl on Entrance, English Panel (Scotland) UCAS 1994–98; memb: Scottish Exam Bd 1986–92, English Panel Scottish Qualifications Authy 1997–99; pres Eighteenth Century Scottish Studies Soc 1990–92; FRSE 2000, FBA 2002; *Books* ed: Scott's Waverley (1972), Charlotte Brontë's Shirley (with Judith Hook, 1974), John Dos Passos Twentieth Century Views (1974); Scotland and America – A Study of Cultural Relations 1750–1835 (1975, 2 edn

2008), American Literature in Context 1865–1900 (1983, 2 edn 2016), History of Scottish Literature Vol II 1660–1800 (1987), Scott Fitzgerald (1992), The Glasgow Enlightenment (with Richard Sher, 1995), From Goosecreek to Gandercleugh: Studies in Scottish-American Literary and Cultural History (1999), Scott's The Fair Maid of Perth (with Donald Mackenzie, 1999), F Scott Fitzgerald: A Literary Life (2002), Francis Jeffrey's American Journal: New York to Washington 1813 (with Clare Elliott, 2011), Eliza Oddy's A Mississippi Diary: From St Paul, Minnesota to Alton, Illinois, October 1894 to May 1895 (ed, 2013); *Recreations* theatre, opera, reading; *Style*— Prof Andrew Hook, FBA, FRSE; ✉ 5 Rosslyn Terrace, Glasgow G12 9NB (☎ 0141 334 0113, e-mail nassau@palio2.vianw.co.uk)

HOOK, Brian Laurence; s of Laurence Hook (d 2002), and Joan Brooks, *née* Read (d 2011); *b* 31 December 1934; *Educ* Christ's Hosp, Oxford Sch of Architecture (DipArch), Oxford Brookes Univ (MSc); *m* 26 March 1960, (Thelma) Jill, da of Morton Griffiths Mathias (d 1974), of Deddington, Oxford; 3 da (Caroline Sanderson, Dr Sarah Hall, Philippa Rothwell); *Career* Nat Serv 2 Lt RE served Malta and N Africa 1958–60, Lt RE (TA) 1961–64; architect; assoc Peter Bosanquet & Partners Oxford 1966–70, princ in own practice Brian Hook & Partners Wantage and Oxford 1970–2014; cncllr Berks CC 1971–74; Oxfordshire CC: cncllr 1973–81 and 1989–2005, chm Environmental Ctee 1979–81, chm 1998–99; chm: Wantage Constituency Cons Assoc 1987–91, Wilts Cons European Constituency Cncl 1991–93, Soldiers of Oxfordshire Tst 2000–07; memb Oxford Regnl Health Authy 1977–79; chm of govrs Sch of St Helen and St Katharine Abingdon 1985–90; memb Ct Oxford Brookes Univ 1999–2007; hon alderman Oxon CC 2009–; ARIBA 1959, FRSA 1995–2014; *Recreations* sailing, travel, water colour painting; *Clubs* Frewen (Oxford); *Style*— Brian Hook, Esq; ✉ Green Farm, 1 The Green, Charney Bassett, Wantage, Oxfordshire OX12 0EU (☎ 01235 868477, e-mail bhbrianhook@aol.co.uk)

HOOKE, James; *Educ* Hampton GS, Univ of Leeds (BSc, PGCE); *Career* Tullet Tokyo 1986–90, St John's Sch Buenos Aires 1992–94, The Harrodian Sch 1995– (headmaster 1999–); *Style*— James Hooke, Esq; ✉ The Harrodian School, Lonsdale Road, London SW13 9QN (☎ 020 8748 6117, fax 020 8563 7327, e-mail admin@harrodian.com)

HOOKER, David Symonds; s of Cdr John Joseph Symonds Hooker, RN, and Pamela Bowring, *née* Toms; *b* 9 October 1942; *Educ* Radley, Magdalene Coll Cambridge (MA), Royal Sch of Mines (MSc); *m* 16 Jan 1965, (Catharine) Sandra, da of Maurice Hilary Thornely Hodgson (d 1986); 1 da (Samantha b 1966), 2 s (Benjamin b 1969, Joshua b 1979); *Career* Pennzoil Co 1965–73, Edward Bates & Sons Ltd 1973–75; md: Candecca Resources plc 1978–82, Plascom Ltd 1982–85, Hurricane International Ltd 1985–87, Aberdeen Petroleum plc 1987–93: chm: Bakyrchic Gold plc 1993–96, Goshawk Insurance Holdings plc 1996–2003; currently chm Avoco Secure Ltd; *Style*— David Hooker, Esq; ✉ 12 Lindsay Square, London SW1V 3SB; Ardura, Isle of Mull PA65 6BD

HOOKER, Prof Morna Dorothy; da of Percy Francis Hooker (d 1975), of High Salvington, W Sussex, and Lily, *née* Riley (d 1988); *b* 19 May 1931; *Educ* Univ of Bristol (BA, MA), Univ of Manchester (PhD), Univ of Cambridge (DD); *m* 30 March 1978, Rev Dr (Walter) David Stacey (d 1993), s of Walter Stacey (d 1957); *Career* res fell Univ of Durham 1959–61, lectr in New Testament King's Coll London 1961–70; Univ of Oxford: lectr in theology 1970–76, fell Linacre Coll 1970–76, lectr in theology Keble Coll 1972–76; Lady Margaret's prof of divinity Univ of Cambridge 1976–98 (now emeritus); visiting prof: McGill Univ Montreal 1968, Duke Univ N Carolina 1987 and 1989; visiting fell Clare Hall Cambridge 1974; jt ed Jl of Theological Studies 1985–2005; fell: Robinson Coll Cambridge 1977–, King's Coll 1979–; hon fell: Linacre Coll Oxford 1980–, Westminster Coll Oxford 1996–; pres Studiorum Novi Testamenti Societas 1988–89 (memb 1959–); Burkitt Medal for Biblical Studies 2004; Hon DLitt Univ of Bristol 1994, Hon DD Univ of Edinburgh 1997; *Books* Jesus and The Servant (1959), The Son of Man in Mark (1967), What about The New Testament? (ed, 1975), Pauline Pieces (1979), Studying The New Testament (1979), Paul and Paulinism (ed, 1982), The Message of Mark (1983), Continuity and Discontinuity (1986), From Adam to Christ (1990), A Commentary on the Gospel According to St Mark (1991), Not Ashamed of the Gospel (1994), The Signs of a Prophet (1997), Beginnings: Keys that Open the Gospels (1997), Paul: A Short Introduction (2003), Endings: Invitations to Discipleship (2003), Not in Word Alone (ed, 2003), Holiness and Mission (jtly, 2010); *Recreations* molinology, music, walking; *Style*— Prof Morna Hooker; ✉ Robinson College, Cambridge CB3 9AN (☎ 01223 339100, fax 01223 351794, e-mail mdh1000@cam.ac.uk)

HOOLE, John George Aldick; s of John Aldick Hoole (d 1992), and Pamela Betty, *née* Coleman (d 2003); *b* 3 February 1951; *Educ* Canford Sch, Lawrenceville Sch NJ, Southampton Coll of Technol, UEA (BA); *m* 1975, Lindsey Gladstone, *née* Rushworth; 1 da (Poppy Imogen b 9 Nov 1983), 1 s (Theodore Edmund Inigo b 23 June 1990); *Career* asst keeper of art Southampton Art Gallery 1974–78, asst dir MOMA Oxford 1978–82, dir Barbican Art Gallery 1982–2001, Arts and Culture worker Oxford Brookes Univ 2003–08; *Exhibitions curated* James Dickson Innes (Southampton Art Gallery) 1977, John Piper (MOMA) 1980, The Young Ones (Saïd Business Sch Univ of Oxford) 2005; Barbican Art Gallery: Matthew Smith 1983, Patrick Heron 1985, The Edwardian Era 1987, Stanley Spencer 1991, The Cutting Edge 1992, Alphonse Mucha 1993; *Books* James Dickson Innes 1887–1914 (with Margaret Simons, 2013); *Recreations* house renovation, horticulture; *Style*— John Hoole, Esq; ✉ e-mail jhoole@appleinter.net

HOOPER, Baroness (Life Peer UK 1985), of Liverpool and St James's in the City of Westminster; Gloria Hooper; CMG (2002); da of Frederick Hooper (d 1977), of Shawford, Hants, and Frances, *née* Maloney (d 1984); *b* 25 May 1939; *Educ* Univ of Southampton (BA); *Career* slr 1973, ptnr Taylor & Humbert 1974–85; MEP (Cons) Liverpool 1979–84; baroness-in-waiting and govt whip House of Lords 1985–87; Parly under sec of state: Dept for Educn and Science 1987–88, Dept of Energy 1988–89, Dept of Health 1989–92; dep speaker House of Lords 1993–, memb Parly Delgn to Cncl of Europe and WEU 1992–97 and 2002–08; govr Centre for Global Energy Studies; vice-pres Hispanic and Luso Brazilian Cncl (Canning House) 1996–99; chm: Dance Teachers' Benevolent Fund 2007–15, Advsy Cncl UCL Inst of the Americas 2012–; tstee: Industry and Parl Tst 1993–2013, The Tablet 1999–, St George's House Windsor Castle 2006–13; Hon LLD Univ of Southampton 2009; memb Law Soc 1972; *Recreations* gardening, opera, walking, ballet; *Clubs* In & Out (Naval and Military); *Style*— The Rt Hon Baroness Hooper, CMG; ✉ House of Lords, London SW1A 0PW

HOOPER, Dr John David; s of Wilfred John Hooper (d 1976), and Vera, *née* Bradbury (d 2005); *b* 22 March 1947; *Educ* Univ of Bath (BSc), Univ of Salford (MSc), Columbia Pacific Univ Calif (PhD); *m* Veronica Jane; 1 s (Robert b 1972), 1 da (Suzanne b 1983); *Career* apprentice engr UK Atomic Energy 1964–69, project engr United Glass Ltd 1969–74, sr project engr Cadbury Schweppes Ltd 1974–78, sales mangr, gp energy mangr, dep gp chief engr Glaxo Pharmaceuticals plc 1978–85; chief exec Chartered Inst of Building 1985–87, dir of Pan-European Ops Carlson Mktg Gp Inc 1987–90, business strategy mangr Scottish Hydro-Electric plc 1990–94, chief exec Br Sports and Allied Industries Fedn 1994–97, chief exec RoSPA 1997–2004, chief exec Inst of Clinical Research 2004–09, chief exec Br Polo Fellowship 2009–11, chief exec Chartered Assoc of Building Engrs (formerly Assoc of Building Engrs) 2011–; dir Science Cncl; chartered dir 2001, memb IOD Examinations Bd, chartered dir interviewer; non-exec dir Thera Tst 2012–; patron: Lifeskills, Learning for Living; advsr to Business in the Arts; ambass to Highlands and Islands of Scotland; tstee RIPH (memb Qualifications Bd); CEng 1980, FCMI 1985, FInstD 1986 (memb Examination Bd), FRSA 2000, FRIPH 2002, Hon FCABE 2016; *Publications* Heat Energy Recovery in the Pharmaceutical Industry (1982), Energy Management and Marketing in the UK Pharmaceutical Industry (1985); monthly article in Building Engineer since 2011; *Recreations* flying light aircraft, DIY; *Style*— Dr John Hooper

HOOPER, John Edward; s of William John Henry Hooper (d 1996), and Noëlle Patricia Thérèse, *née* Lang (d 1979); *b* 17 July 1950; *Educ* St Benedict's Abbey London, St Catharine's Coll Cambridge (BA); *m* 19 July 1980, Hon Lucinda Mary Evans, da of 2 Baron Mountevans (d 1974); *Career* reporter BBC Current Affrs 1971–73, dip corr Independent Radio News 1973–74, Cyprus corr BBC, Guardian and Economist 1974–76; Guardian: corr Spain and Portugal 1976–79, London staff 1979–88; presenter Twenty Four Hours BBC World Service 1984–88; Madrid corr The Guardian, The Economist and The Observer 1988–94; Guardian: Southern Europe corr 1994–99, Central Europe corr 1999–2003, Rome corr 2003–12, Southern Europe ed 2012–15, contributing ed 2015–; Rome corr Economist 2003–; winner Allen Lane award best first work of history or lit 1987; memb Soc of Authors; *Books* The Spaniards: portrait of the new Spain (1986 and 1987), The New Spaniards (1995 and 2006), Fatal Voyage (2012), Alien Landing (2013), The Italians (2015); *Recreations* reading, contemporary art, motor boating; *Clubs* Frontline; *Style*— John Hooper, Esq; ✉ Presso Corriere della Sera, Via Campania 59c, 00187 Roma, Italy; c/o Lucy Luck, Aitken Alexander Associates, 18–21 Cavaye Place, London SW10 9PT (☎ 020 7373 8672, e-mail lucyluck@aitkenalexander.co.uk)

HOPE, Christopher David Tully; s of Dudley Mitford Hope, and Kathleen Mary, *née* McKenna; *b* 26 February 1944; *Educ* Christian Brothers Coll Pretoria, Univ of the Witwatersrand (BA, MA), Univ of Natal (BA); *m* 18 Feb 1967, Eleanor Marilyn Margaret, da of Hans Richard Klein (d 1977); 2 s (Jasper Antony b 1969, Daniel Clement b 1973); *Career* author and poet; fndr Franschhoek Literary Festival Cape SA 2007 (dir 2007–10), co-fndr Fynarts Festival Hermanus Cape SA 2013; FRSL 1990; *Publications* A Separate Development (1981), The King, the Cat and the Fiddle (with Yehudi Menuhin, 1983), Kruger's Alp (1984), The Dragon Wore Pink (1985), The Hottentot Room (1986), Black Swan (1987), White Boy Running (1988), My Chocolate Redeemer (1989), Learning to Fly and Other Tales (1990; originally published as Private Parts, 1982), Moscow! Moscow! (1990), Serenity House (1992, shortlisted Booker Prize 1992), The Love Songs of Nathan J Swirsky (1993), Darkest England (1996), Me, The Moon and Elvis Presley (1997), Signs of the Heart: Love and Death in Languedoc (1999), Heaven Forbid (2002), Brothers Under The Skin (Travels in Tyranny) (2003), My Mother's Lovers (2006), The Garden of Bad Dreams (2008), Shooting Angels (2011), A Distant Drum (librettist, US premiere commissioned by Carnegie Hall 2014), Jimfish (2015); *Poetry* Cape Drives (1974), In the Country of the Black Pig (1981), Englishmen (1985); *Awards* Cholmondeley Award 1972, David Higham Award 1981, Whitbread Prize for Fiction (for Kruger's Alp) 1985, CNA Literary Award (South Africa) 1989, Travelex Travel Writer Award 1997; *Recreations* getting lost; *Style*— Christopher Hope, Esq, FRSL; ✉ c/o Rogers, Coleridge & White, 20 Powis Mews, London W11 1JN (☎ 020 7221 3717, fax 020 7229 9084)

H

HOPE, Daniel; *b* 17 August 1973; *Educ* Highgate Sch, Royal Acad of Music; *Career* soloist violinist; performing with orchestras incl Boston, Chicago, Toronto and Atlanta Symphony Orchestras, as well as orchestras of Berlin, Birmingham, Dallas, Detroit, Dresden, Israel, London, Los Angeles, Moscow, Oslo, Paris, Stockholm and Vienna; music dir Zurich Chamber Orchestra 2016/2017 season; *Style*— Daniel Hope, Esq; ✉ c/o International Classical Artists, Dunstan House, 14a St Cross Street, London EC1N 8XA

HOPE, His Hon (Antony) Derwin; *b* 22 August 1944; *Educ* King's Coll Taunton, Leighton Park Sch Reading, Coll of Estate Mgmnt London (BSc), Coll of Law; *m* 5 May 1979, Heidi; 1 s (Matthew b 3 June 1983), 1 da (Zoe b 18 Oct 1985); *Career* called to the Bar 1970; in practice 3 Paper Buildings, London, Winchester, Oxford and Bournemouth 1970–2002, circuit judge (Northern Circuit) 2002–04, circuit judge (Western Circuit) 2004–14, ret, resident judge Southampton Combined Court; UK rep Int Assoc of Judges; *Publications* The 1990–91 Planning Acts, Charles Dickens: From Portsmouth to Pickwick (2012); *Recreations* walking, cricket, travelling, historical studies; *Style*— His Hon Derwin Hope

HOPE, Emma Mary Constance; MBE (2012); da of Capt John David Hope, RN, and Margaret Daphne, *née* Boutwood; *Educ* Reigate Co Sch for Girls, Sevenoaks Sch, Cordwainers Coll (SIAD Dip); *Career* shoe designer; fndr own business, 2 shops in London (Notting Hill and Sloane Square); has designed for: Laura Ashley, Betty Jackson, Jean Muir, Nicole Farhi, Anna Sui, Paul Smith; speaker Oxford Union against 'High Fashion: Does this house think we pay too high a price?' 2004; hon fell Univ of the Arts London 2011; FRSA 1993; *Awards* 5 Design Cncl Awards for Footwear 1987–88, Martini Style Award 1988, Harpers and Queens Award for Excellence 1988, DTI/Clothes Show Award for Best Accessories 1996; *Recreations* surfing, hunting, golf, shopping; *Style*— Miss Emma Hope, MBE; ✉ Emma Hope's Shoes, 207 Westbourne Grove, London W11 1RQ (☎ 020 7792 7800, fax 020 7792 5351, e-mail mail@emmahope.co.uk)

HOPE, Prof Ronald Anthony (Tony); s of Ronald Sidney Hope (d 2014), and Marion Nuttall, *née* Whittaker (2014); *b* 16 March 1951, London; *Educ* Dulwich Coll, New Coll Oxford (Bosanquet open scholarship, MA), Univ of London (PhD), Univ of Oxford (BM BCh); *m* 4 July 1981, Sally Louise, *née* Hirsh; 2 da (Katherine Anna b 1 Sept 1988, Elizabeth Eleanor b 6 March 1991); *Career* SHO and registrar trg in psychiatry Oxford 1981–85, Wellcome Tst trg fell 1985–87, clincal lectr in psychiatry 1987–90; Univ of Oxford: fell St Cross Coll 1990–2012 (emeritus fell 2012–), lectr in practice skills 1995–2000, prof of med ethics 2000–12 (emeritus prof 2012–); ldr Oxford Practice Skills Project 1990–95; Research Prize and Medal RCPsych 1989; memb Inst of Med Ethics (memb Governing Body 1998–2008); FRCPsych 1997 (MRCPsych 1985), FRCP 2011; *Publications* Oxford Handbook of Clinical Medicine (1985, 4 edn 1998), Manage Your Mind (1995, 2 edn 2007), Medical Ethics: a very short introduction (2004); numerous articles and papers in med ethics and Alzheimer's Disease; *Recreations* family, literature, wine and food; *Style*— Prof Tony Hope; ✉ St Cross College, 61 St Giles, Oxford OX1 3LZ (e-mail tonyhope@doctors.org.uk)

HOPE, Sean; s of Barry Colin Hope (d 1999), and Shirley Anne, *née* Goldsmith; *b* 21 September 1969, Portsmouth, Hants; *Educ* Casterton Community Coll; *m* 29 Sept 2000, Victoria Anne, *née* Webster; 2 da (Lydia Anne b 24 March 2004, Annabel May b 4 May 2006); *Career* chef; co-prop and chef The Olive Branch Clipsham Leics 1999– (2 AA Rosettes 2001–, 1 Michelin Star 2002–, Gold Award for Best Pub East Midlands Tourism Enjoy England Excellence Awards 2007, Good Pub Guide Inn of the Year 2008), co-prop The Beech House Clipsham Leics 2006–; Full English (2006); *Recreations* diving, motorcycling, dining, cooking, family; *Style*— Sean Hope, Esq; ✉ The Olive Branch, Main Street, Clipsham, Leicestershire LE15 7SE (☎ 01780 410355, fax 01780 410000, e-mail sean@theolivebranchpub.com)

HOPE, Simon Richard; s of Richard Hope, and Carole, *née* Byrom; *b* 1 July 1964, Congleton, Cheshire; *Educ* King Edward VI GS Macclesfield, RAC Cirencester, Univ of Reading (MBA); *m* 1994, Margaret, *née* Carnell; 4 da (Camilla, Laura, Eleanor, Georgina); *Career* Savills plc: RICS qualification 1986–88, West End office 1989–, dir 1992–, memb Bd 1999–; chm Dinton and Ford Cons Assoc, memb Bd Charities Property Fund; MRICS; *Recreations* golf, racing, tennis, hunting, shooting (chm Kimblewick Hunt); *Clubs* Oxfordshire Golf, Turf, Lansdowne, Vale of Aylesbury Hunt; *Style*— Simon Hope, Esq; ✉ Aston Mullins Farm, Chapel Road, Ford, Aylesbury, Buckinghamshire HP17 8XG (☎ 01296 748400, fax 01296 748110, e-mail s.r.hope@btinternet.com); Savills plc, 20 Grosvenor Hill, Berkeley Square, London W1K 3HQ (☎ 020 7409 8725, e-mail shope@savills.com)

HOPE, Prof (David) Terence; s of George Charles Oswald Hope (d 1988), and Lucy, *née* Bollom (d 1970); *b* 2 April 1946; *Educ* Rutherford GS Newcastle upon Tyne, Univ of Liverpool (MB ChB, ChM); *Children* 1 s ((Charles) Benjamin b 1976), 2 da (Lucy Alexandra b 1979, Victoria Mary b 1983); m, August 2003, Alexandra Frances, *née* Crabbie; *Career* served in RNR; conslt neurosurgeon: Aberdeen 1982, Univ Hosp of Nottingham 1985–, teacher in clinical neurosciences Univ of Nottingham Hosps; prof of neurosurgery: Bir Hosp Kathmandhu Nepal, Nepal Inst of Neurosciences Bansbari Kathmandu; author of chapters in books on vascular neurosurgery; examiner: RCS, Intercollegiate Bd of Examiners in Neurosurgery; sec Intercollegiate Bd of Neurosurgery 1999; memb: Soc of British Neurological Surgeons, Ct of Examiners RCS; FRCS 1985; *Recreations* fishing, shooting, gardening; *Clubs* Athenaeum, Osler (London); *Style*— Prof Terence Hope; ✉ The Nunnery, Hemington, Derby DE74 2SQ (☎ 01332 811724, fax 01332 811724, e-mail terencehope@btinternet.com); Department of Neurosurgery, University Hospital, Queen's Medical Centre, Nottingham NG7 2UH (☎ 0115 970 9102)

HOPE OF CRAIGHEAD, Baron (Life Peer UK 1995), of Bamff in the District of Perth and Kinross; Sir (James Arthur) David Hope; KT (2009), PC (1989); s of Arthur Henry Cecil Hope OBE, TD, WS (d 1986), of Edinburgh, and Muriel Ann Neilson, *née* Collie; *b* 27 June 1938; *Educ* Edinburgh Acad, Rugby, St John's Coll Cambridge (MA), Univ of Edinburgh (LLB); *m* 11 April 1966, (Katharine) Mary, da of William Mark Kerr, WS (d 1985), of Edinburgh; 2 s (Hon William Thomas Arthur, Hon James David Louis (twins) b 1969), 1 da (Hon Lucy Charlotte Mary b 1971); *Career* Nat Serv cmmnd Seaforth Highlanders 1957, Lt 1959; admitted Faculty of Advocates 1965, standing jr counsel in Scotland to Bd of Inland Revenue 1974–78, QC (Scot 1978), advocate depute 1978–82, chm Med Appeal Tbnls 1985–86, legal chm Pensions Appeal Tbnl 1985–86; memb Scottish Ctee on Law of Arbitration 1986–89; elected dean Faculty of Advocates 1986, senator of the Coll of Justice, a Lord of Session with the title of Lord Hope, Lord Justice General of Scotland and Lord President of the Court of Session 1989–96, a Lord of Appeal in Ordinary 1996–2009, Second Sr Law Lord 2009, dep pres Supreme Court of the UK 2009–13; convenor Crossbench Peers 2015–; chm Sub-Ctee E House of Commons Select Ctee on EU 1998–2001; chllr Univ of Strathclyde 1998–2013; pres: The Stair Soc 1993–2013, Int Criminal Lawyers Assoc 2000–13, Cwlth Magistrates' and Judges' Assoc 2003–06; hon prof of law Univ of Aberdeen; hon fell: St John's Coll Cambridge 1995, American Coll of Trial Lawyers 2000; hon memb: Canadian Bar Assoc 1987, Soc of Public Teachers of Law 1991; hon bencher: Gray's Inn 1989, Inn of Court of N Ireland 1995; Hon LLD: Univ of Aberdeen 1991, Univ of Strathclyde 1993, Univ of Edinburgh 1995, Univ of Glasgow 2013, BPP Univ London 2014, Abertay Univ Dundee 2014; Hon DUniv Strathclyde 2013; fell Univ of Strathclyde 2000; FRSE 2003; *Books* Gloag and Henderson's Introduction to the Law of Scotland (jt ed 7 edn 1968, asst ed 8 edn 1980 and 9 edn 1987, contrib ed 11 edn 2001), Armour on Valuation for Rating (jt ed 4 edn 1971, 5 edn 1985), Court of Session Practice (contrib); *Recreations* walking, music, ornithology; *Clubs* New (Edinburgh); *Style*— The Rt Hon Lord Hope of Craighead, KT, PC, FRSE; ✉ 34 India Street, Edinburgh EH3 6HB (0131 225 8245); House of Lords, London SW1A 0PW (e-mail hopejad@parliament.uk)

HOPE-DUNBAR, Sir David; 8 Bt (NS 1664), of Baldoon; o s of Maj Sir Basil Douglas Hope-Dunbar, 7 Bt (d 1961), and Edith Maude Maclaren, *née* Cross; *b* 13 July 1941; *Educ* Eton, RAC Cirencester; *m* 1971, Kathleen Ruth, yr da of late J Timothy Kenrick; 2 da (Philippa b 1973, Juliet Antonia b 1976), 1 s (Charles b 1975); *Heir* s, Charles Hope-Dunbar; *Career* founded Dunbar & Co (now Allied Dunbar) 1962, chartered surveyor; ARICS; *Recreations* fishing, tennis, shooting; *Style*— Sir David Hope-Dunbar, Bt; ✉ Banks House, Kirkcudbright DG6 4XF (☎ 01557 330424)

HOPE-FALKNER, Patrick Miles; s of Robert E Hope-Falkner (d 1991), and Diana, *née* Hazlerigg (d 1977); *b* 1 December 1949; *Educ* Wellington; *m* 1972 (m dis 1994), Wendy Margaret, *née* Mallinson; 2 s (Timothy Douglas b 1980, James Edward b 1982); *Career* articles 1968–73, admitted slr 1973, Freshfields 1973–84, Lazard Brothers & Co Ltd 1985–90; dir: Lazard Investors Ltd 1985–90, Lazard Brothers & Co (Jersey) Ltd 1985–89; ptnr Crossman Block 1991–94; sr dir: American Express Bank 1995–2005; memb Law Soc; *Clubs* Royal Cornwall Yacht; *Style*— Patrick Hope-Falkner, Esq

HOPEWELL, Martin; s of late Tom Clifford Hopewell, and Joan, *née* Walker; *b* 27 May 1951; *Educ* Nottingham HS for Boys, Univ of Reading (BA); *m* 1 (m dis); 1 da (Kate Laura b 1981), 1 s (Tom Martin b 1984); m 2, Patsy Politoff; *Career* music agent and conf organiser; agent Noel Gay Orgn 1972, agent Chrysalis Gp (successively Chrysalis Agency, Cowbell Agency and World Service Agency); former clients incl: The Jam, The Cure, The Eurythmics, The Pretenders, Fine Young Cannibals, Bronski Beat, The Style Council, The Sex Pistols, Marc Almond, Peter Gabriel; former chm Primary Talent International Ltd, chm International Live Music Conference Ltd; memb: Cncl Agents Assoc of GB, UK Govt's Live Music Forum; inducted Br Music Roll of Honour 1999; *Recreations* clay target shooting, astronomy, gliding, archery; *Style*— Martin Hopewell, Esq; ✉ Primary Talent International, The Primary Building, 10–11 Jockey's Fields, London WC1R 4BN (☎ 020 7400 4500, fax 020 7400 4501, website www.primary.uk.com)

HOPKIN, Professor Sir Deian Rhys; kt (2009); s of Islwyn Hopkin (d 1951), of Llanelli, and Charlotte, *née* Rees (d 1969); *b* 1 March 1944; *Educ* Llandovery Coll, Univ of Wales Aberystwyth (BA, PhD); *m* 1, 11 June 1966 (m dis 1989), Orian, da of Edryd Jones; 2 da (Elinor Mair b 1970, Gwenno Eleri b 1974); m 2, 23 Sept 1989, Lynne, da of Richard Hurley; 2 s (Kieran, Liam (twins) b 1981); *Career* tutor QMC London 1966–67, lectr in modern history Univ of Wales Aberystwyth 1967–84, staff tutor in arts (secondment) Open Univ 1974–76, sr lectr Dept of History Univ of Wales Aberystwyth 1984–91 (head of dept 1990–91), dean of human sciences City of London Poly (later London Guildhall Univ) 1992–96, vice-provost London Guildhall Univ 1996–2001, vice-chllr and chief exec London South Bank Univ 2001–09, interim vice-chllr Univ of E London 2009–10; emeritus prof: London South Bank Univ 2009–, Univ of E London 2010–; chm and tstee UNIAID 2004–08, chair Univs UK Skills Task Gp 2006–09, chm Student Loans Co 2010; vice-chm London Higher 2006–08; jt chair HE Engagement Bd DfES 2006–10; memb: Exec Ctee UK Arts and Humanities Data Serv 1997–2002, Bd Learning and Skills Cncl 2007–09, Editorial Bd Times Higher Educn 2008–, HE Cmmn 2011–; chm Cityside Regeneration Ltd 1996–2002; memb: Bd Central London Partnership 2001–08, Bd South Bank Employers' Gp 2004–06, Bd Skills for Health UK 2004–09, Cncl for Industry and HE 2006–09, Bd Fndn Degree Forward 2007–11, London Skills and Employment Bd 2007–08, Cncl City and Guilds Inst 2009–, Cncl and Ct Univ of Essex 2011–14 (hon prof of History 2014–), Educn Honours Ctee 2011–; govr: Hackney Community Coll Corp 1999–2001, Lambeth Coll Corp 2001–05; govr and tstee Bishopsgate Fndn and Inst 1997–2003 (patron 2007–); tstee: Cncl for Academics at-Risk 2003–, Campaign for Learning 2009–, Inst of Historical Research Univ of London 2009–14, North-West Univ SA 2010–; patron Hillcroft Coll Surrey 2009–; memb Gen Advsy Cncl BBC 1988–96; Nat Library of Wales: govr and memb Cncl 1975–90, pres 2011–15; Freeman City of London 1999, Freeman Worshipful Co of Information Technologists 1999, Liveryman Worshipful Co of Educators 2014 (Freeman 2004); Hon DLitt Univ of Glamorgan 2008, Hon LLD McGill Univ Montreal 2010, Hon DUniv Open Univ 2012; hon fell Univ of Wales Aberystwyth 2003, FCGI 2010, hon fell Univ of Wales Trinity St Davids 2012; FRHistS 1978, FRSA 1996, Hon FCIBSE 2008; *Publications* incl: History and Computing (jt ed, 1987), Class, Community and the Labour Movement: Wales and Canada, 1880–1930 (jt ed, 1989), The Labour Party in Wales, 1900–2000 (jt ed, 2000), The Role of Universities in the Modern Economy (2002); also author of numerous book chapters and articles, reviews and features in jls incl: Int Review of Social History, Jl of Contemporary History, English Historical Review, Welsh History Review, Anglo-Welsh Review, History, Times Higher Educn Supplement, Educn Guardian, Taliesin; *Recreations* music (especially jazz), writing, broadcasting; *Clubs* Athenaeum; *Style*— Professor Sir Deian Hopkin; ✉ 4 Eversleigh Place, Beckenham BR3 1DF

HOPKIN, Prof Julian; CBE (2011); s of Meurglyn Hopkin, and Mair, *née* Watkins; *b* 30 August 1948, Ystradgynlais; *Educ* Maesydderwen Sch Ystradgynlais, WNSM Univ of Wales (MB BCh, MD), Univ of Edinburgh (MSc); *m* 1, 1973, Janina, *née* Maczak (d 2009); 3 c (Gruffydd, William, Kathryn); m 2, 2011, Amanda Louise Moorhouse, *née* Barfoot; *Career* clinical scientist MRC 1978–79, conslt physician Oxford 1984–99, sr clinical lectr Univ of Oxford 1984–99, fell BNC Oxford 1992–99; Univ of Wales Swansea: prof of med 1999–2010, head Sch of Med 2004–08, rector Med and Health 2008–10, chair Advsy Bd Coll of Med 2012–, prof of experimental med 2012–; visiting prof: Osaka 1994, Rome 2001, Kyoto 2002; exec ed Quarterly Jl of Med 1992–2000; dir Allerna Therapeutics Ltd 2007–11; chair of tstees St David's Medical Fndn 2007–; Daiwa-Adrian Prize in Med 2001; hon fell Swansea Univ 2011; FRCP 1988, FRCPEd 1999, FMedSci 2005, FLSW 2011; Derwydd er Anrhydedd (druid Bardic Circle of the Isle of Britain) 2008; *Publications* Pneumocystis Carinii (monograph, 1991); author of over 150 medical and scientific papers and articles; *Recreations* the outdoors; *Style*— Prof Julian Hopkin, CBE; ✉ College of Medicine, Swansea University, Swansea SA2 8PP

HOPKINS, Sir (Philip) Anthony; kt (1993), CBE (1987); s of Richard Arthur Hopkins (d 1981), and Muriel Annie Yeates; *b* 31 December 1937; *Educ* Cowbridge GS, Welsh Coll of Music and Drama, RADA; *m* 1, 1968 (m dis), Petronella; 1 da (Abigail b 1968); m 2, 1973 (m dis), Jennifer Ann, da of Ronald Arthur Lynton; m 3, 2003, Stella Arroyave; *Career* actor and director; first joined Nat Theatre 1965, Broadway debut Equus 1974 (NY Drama Desk Award for Best Actor, Outer Critics' Circle Award, American Authors and Celebrities Forum Award, LA Drama Critics' Award); lived and worked in USA 1975–84, returned to England 1984, took US citizenship 2000; Hon DLitt Univ of Wales 1988, hon fell St David's Coll Lampeter Wales, FBA 2008; Commandeur de l'Ordre des Arts et des Lettres (France) 1996; *Theatre* incl: Julius Caesar (debut) 1964, A Flea in Her Ear (NT) 1966, The Three Sisters, Dance of Death (NT) 1967, As You Like It 1967, The Architect and The Emperor of Assyria, A Woman Killed with Kindness, Coriolanus (NT) 1971, The Taming of the Shrew (Chichester) 1972, Macbeth (NT) 1972, Equus (Plymouth Theatre NY) 1974–75 and (Huntington Hartford Theatre LA) 1977, The Tempest (The Mark Taper Forum Theatre LA) 1979, Old Times (Roundabout Theatre NY) 1983, The Lonely Road (Old Vic) 1985, Pravda (NT) 1985 (Variety Club Stage Actor Award, Br Theatre Assoc Best Actor Award, The Observer Award for Outstanding Achievement (Olivier Awards)), King Lear 1986, Antony and Cleopatra 1987, M Butterfly (Shaftesbury) 1989, August (also dir) 1994; *Television* incl: A Heritage and Its History (ATV) 1968, A Company of Five (ATV) 1968, The Three Sisters (BBC) 1969, The Peasants Revolt (ITV) 1969, Dickens (BBC) 1970, Danton (BBC) 1970, The Poet Game (BBC) 1970, Uncle Vanya (BBC), Hearts and Flowers (BBC), Decision to Burn (Yorkshire) 1970, War and Peace (BBC) 1971 & 1972 (BAFTA Best Television Actor Award), Cuculus Canorus (BBC) 1972, Lloyd George (BBC) 1972, QB VII (ABC) 1973, Find Me (BBC) 1973, A Childhood Friend (BBC) 1974, Possessions (Granada) 1974, All Creatures Great and Small (NBC) 1974, The Arcata Promise (Yorkshire) 1974, Dark Victory (NBC) 1975, The Lindbergh Kidnapping Case (NBC) 1975 (Emmy Award for Best Actor), Victory at Entebbe (ABC) 1976, Kean (BBC) 1978, The Voyage of the Mayflower (CBS) 1979, The Bunker (CBS) 1980 (Emmy Award for Best Actor), Peter and Paul (CBS) 1980, Othello (BBC) 1981, Little Eyolf (BBC) 1981, The Hunchback of Notre Dame (CBS) 1981, A Married Man (LWT/ Channel 4) 1982, Strangers and Brothers (BBC) 1983, The Arch of Triumph (CBS) 1984, Mussolini and I (RAI Italy) 1984 (Ace Award), Hollywood Wives (ABC) 1984, Guilty Conscience (CBS) 1984, Blunt (BBC) 1985, Across the Lake (BBC) 1988, Heartland (BBC) 1988, The Tenth Man (CBS) 1988, Magwitch in Great Expectations (Disney Primetime TV USA) 1988, To Be The Best (USA mini series) 1990, Big Cats (wildlife documentary) 1993; *Films* The Lion in Winter (debut) 1967, The Looking Glass War 1968, Hamlet 1969, When Eight Bells Toll 1969, Young Winston 1971, A Doll's House 1972, The Girl from Petrovka 1973, Juggernaut 1974, A Bridge Too Far 1976, Audrey Rose 1976, International Velvet 1977, Magic 1978, The Elephant Man 1979, A Change of Seasons 1980, The Bounty 1983 (Variety Club Film Actor of 1983 Award), The Good Father 1985, 84 Charing Cross Road 1986 (Moscow Film Festival Best Actor Award), The Dawning 1987, A Chorus of Disapproval 1988, The Desperate Hours 1989, The Silence of the Lambs 1990 (Academy Award for Best Actor, BAFTA Award for Best Film Actor, NY Film Critics' Circle Award for Best Actor, Chicago Film Critics' Award for Best Actor, Boston Film Critic's Award for Best Actor), Spotswood 1990, One Man's War 1990, Howard's End 1991, Freejack 1992, Chaplin 1992, Bram Stoker's Dracula 1992, The Trial 1993, Remains of the Day 1993 (BAFTA Award for Best Film Actor, Guild of Regnl Film Writers Award for Best Actor, LA Film Critics' Assoc Award for Best Actor, Variety Club Film Actor of 1993 Award, Japan Critics' Awards Best Actor in a Foreign Film), Shadowlands 1993 (US Nat Bd of Review Best Actor Award, LA Film Critic's Assoc Best Actor Award, Mexican Int Film Festival Best Actor Award), Legends of the Fall 1994, The Road to Welville 1994, August (also dir) 1994, Nixon 1995, Surviving Picasso 1995, The Edge 1996, Amistad 1997 (Oscar nomination for Best Supporting Actor), The Mask of Zorro 1997, Meet Joe Black 1997, Instinct 1998, Titus 1999, The Grinch (voice) 2000, Mission: Impossible II 2000, Hannibal 2001, Hearts in Atlantis 2001, The Devil and Daniel Webster 2001, Bad Company 2002, Red Dragon 2002, The Human Stain 2003, Alexander 2004, Proof 2005, The World's Fastest Indian 2005, Bobby 2006, All the King's Men 2006, Slipstream 2007, Fracture 2007, Beowulf 2007, Immutable Dream of Snow Lion 2008, Bare Knuckles 2009, The Wolfman 2010, You Will Meet a Tall Dark Stranger 2010; *Awards* Award for Career Excellence (Montreal Film Festival) 1991, Evening Standard Film Awards' Special Award for UK Body of Work 1994, The US Film Advisory Bd Special Career Achievement Award for US Body of Work 1994, US BAFTA The Britannia Award for Outstanding Contribution to the Int Film and TV Industry 1995, Spencer Tracy Award for Excellence on Stage and Screen 1996, Donostia Award 1998; *Recreations* piano, reading; *Style*— Sir Anthony Hopkins, CBE

HOPKINS, Emma Kate; OBE (2014); HE; *née* Brown; *b* Bolton, Lancashire; *Educ* Fitzwilliam Coll Cambridge (BA); *m* 2 Dec 2006, Steven; 2 da; *Career* diplomat; called to the Bar Middle Temple, barr Chambers of Kieran Coonan QC 1996–2001, sr advsy lawyer Home Office Legal Adviser's Branch 2001–06, head of organised immigration crime Organised and Fin Crime Unit Home Office 2006–08, sr legal advsr UK Border Agency 2009, head EU/Int Team Legal Advsr's Branch 2009–12, head Preventing Sexual Violence Initiative FCO 2012–15, ambass to Bulgaria 2015–; *Style*— HE Mrs Emma Hopkins, OBE; ✉ c/o FCO (Sofia), King Charles Street, London SW1A 2AH

HOPKINS, Brig Graham Owen; s of Ivor Hopkins (d 1978), and Sarah Elizabeth, *née* Owen (d 1999); *b* 16 December 1943; *Educ* Llanelli GS, Newton le Willows GS, Bart's Med Coll (MB BS); *m* 1, 1970, Rita Janis, *née* Howlett; 2 s (Simon Owen b 1973, Peter Edward b 1981); m 2, 2003, Vanessa Maria, *née* Cartmell; 1 step da (Eleanor Jayne b 1992); *Career* cmmnd 1966; MO 23 Parachute Field Ambulance 1970, MO 16 Parachute Bde 1970–71, MO 3 Bn Parachute Regt 1971, trainee specialist Jt Servs Med Rehabilitation Unit (JSMRU) Chessington 1974, SHO and registrar Cambridge Mil Hosp 1977, sr specialist in rheumatology and rehabilitation JSMRU, conslt in rheumatology and rehabilitation

Queen Elizabeth Mil Hosp 1982, conslt rheumatology and rehabilitation Cambridge Mil Hosp Aldershot 1985, QHP 1999–2005, conslt dir of defence rehabilitation and Cdr Defence Services Med Rehabilitation Centre Headley Ct 2002–05; hosp appointments: house surgn (orthopaedics) Bart's 1969, house physician (gen med) Brook Hosp 1970, SHO (gen surgery) 1970, clinical asst sr registrar post Middx Hosp 1980, hon conslt St Thomas' Hosp London; RCM rep and memb Investigation Ctee Ctee for Professions Supplementary to Med (CPSM) 1994–97, examiner Intercollegiate Academic Bd for Sport and Exercise Med 2000–; memb: Br Soc for Rheumatology 1980–, Br Rehabilitation Soc 1980–, Br Assoc of Sport and Exercise Science 1982–; ed Jl of the RAMC 1992–99; fndr chm Army Martial Arts 1995–99 (pres 1999–2006), chm Combined Servs Martial Arts, 6th Dan Black Belt Wado Ryu Karate, English Karate Governing Body Reg Coach; LTA Intermediate Tennis Coach, memb Professional Tennis Coaches Assoc 1982–95; FRCPEd 1991, fell Inst of Sports Med 1993, FRCP 1997 (MRCP 1978), FFSEM(I) 2003, FFSEM (UK) 2006; OStJ 2006; *Publications* articles: Snake Bite in Cyprus (1974), A Co-location System for the Management of Brain Damaged Patients (jtly, 1981), Muscle Changes in Ankylosing Spondylitis (jtly, 1983), Multiple Joint Tuberculosis Presenting as HLA B27 Disease (1983), Food Antibodies in Palindromic Rheumatism (jtly), Lone Axillary Nerve Injury due to Non Dislocating Injury of the Shoulder (jtly), Double Blind Cross Over Trial of Infra Red Laser in the Treatment of Tennis Elbow (1985), Osteoarticular Tuberculosis – A Review (1986), Stress Fractures in Parachute Regiment Recruits (jtly, 1988); *Recreations* walking, karate, music, sketching; *Style*— Brig Graham Hopkins; ✉ DSMRC, Headley Court, Epsom, Surrey KT18 6JN (☎ 01372 381000, fax 01372 363849, e-mail grahamowen.hopkins672@mod.uk)

HOPKINS, Joel; s of Sir Michael John Hopkins, and Patricia Ann, *née* Wainwright; *b* 6 September 1970; *Educ* Highgate Sch, Christ Church Coll Canterbury (BA), New York Univ (MA); *Partner* Nicola Usborne; 3 s (Jesse, Caspar, Maximilian); *Career* filmmaker; *Films* The South Bank – A Day in the Life (documentary) 1994, Just William (documentary) 1995, Belt (short) 1995, Growth (short) 1996, Jorge (short) 1998, The Independent (short) 1999, Jump Tomorrow 2001, Last Chance Harvey 2008, The Love Punch 2014, Hampstead 2016; *Awards* for Growth: Craft Award for Outstanding Acting, Craft Award for Outstanding Directing; for Jorge: Best Dramatic Film BBC British Short Film Festival, Wasserman Award, Best Short Minneaolis Film Festival, Best Short USA Film Festival, Official Selection Sundance Film Festival; for Jump Tomorrow: BAFTA Carl Foreman Award Most Promising Newcomer to British Film, Audience Award Deauville American Film Festival, Richard Vague Production Grant, one of Festival Directors Best of Festival Edinburgh Film Festival, official selection Sundance Film Festival, finalist Perrier Award, nominated five BIFA Awards (Best British Independent Film, Best Screenplay, Douglas Hicock Award Best Feature Debut, Best Music, Most Promising Newcomer); Best Actor and Best Actress Golden Globe nominations for Last Chance Harvey; *Style*— Joel Hopkins, Esq; ✉ c/o Katie Haines, The Agency, 24 Pottery Lane, London W11 4LZ (☎ 020 7727 1346)

HOPKINS, Kelvin Peter; MP; s of Prof Harold Horace Hopkins, FRS (d 1994), and Joan Avery Frost; *b* 22 August 1941; *Educ* Queen Elizabeth's GS Barnet, Univ of Nottingham (BA); *m* 1965, Patricia, da of Alfred Thomas Langley; 1 s (Daniel Robert b 29 Sept 1969), 1 da (Rachel Louise b 30 March 1972); *Career* with Econ Dept TUC 1969–70 and 1973–77, lectr St Alban's Coll of FE 1971–73, policy and research offr Nalgo/Unison 1977–94, MP (Lab) Luton N 1997–; shadow sec of state for culture, media and sport 2016–; chm of govrs Luton Coll of HE (now Luton Univ) 1985–89; hon fell Univ of Luton 1993; *Recreations* music, theatre, photography, sailing on the Norfolk Broads; *Clubs* Luton Socialist, Lansdowne (Luton); *Style*— Kelvin Hopkins, Esq, MP; ✉ House of Commons, London SW1A 0AA (☎ 020 7219 6670)

HOPKINS, Sir Michael John; kt (1995), CBE (1989); s of late Gerald Hopkins, and Barbara Hopkins; *b* 7 May 1935; *Educ* Sherborne, Architectural Assoc (AADipl); *m* 1962, Patricia Ann, *née* Wainwright; 1 s, 2 da; *Career* architect: worked in offices of Sir Basil Spence, Leonard Manasseh and Tom Hancock; partnership with: Norman Foster 1969–75, Patricia Hopkins 1976–; fndr ptnr Michael Hopkins and Partners 1976–; projects incl: own house and studio Hampstead 1976 (RIBA Award, Civic Tst Award), Greene King brewery bldg 1979 (RIBA Award, FT Award), Patera Bldg System 1984, research centre for Schlumberger Cambridge 1984 (FT Award, RIBA Award, Civic Tst Award), infants sch Hants 1986 (RIBA Award, Civic Tst Award), Bicentenary Stand Lord's Cricket Ground 1987 (RIBA Award, Civic Tst Award), R&D centre Solid State Logic 1988 (RIBA Award, Civic Tst Award), London Office and country workshop for David Mellor 1989 and 1991 (FT Award, two RIBA Awards, Civic Tst Award), redevelopment of Bracken House St Paul's for Ohbayashi Corp 1992 (RIBA Award, FT Award, Civic Tst Award), offices at New Square Bedfont Lakes 1992 (FT Award), Glyndebourne Opera House 1994 (RIBA Award, Royal Fine Art Cmmn Award, Civic Tst Award, FT Award), Inland Revenue Centre Nottingham 1995 (Civic Tst Award), Queen's Bldg Emmanuel Coll Cambridge 1995 (RIBA Award, Royal Fine Art Cmmn Award), Jewish Care residential home for the elderly 1996, Saga Gp HQ 1999, Jubilee Campus Univ of Nottingham 1999 (Br Construction Industry Award, RIBA Award), Dynamic Earth Edinburgh 1999 (Civic Tst Award, RIBA Award), Westminster Underground Station 1999 (Br Construction Industry Award, Royal Fine Art Cmmn Award), Portcullis House Westminster 2000 (Civic Tst Award, RIBA Award, Concrete Award), Wildscreen Bristol 2000 (Civic Tst Award, DTLR Urban Design Award), Pilkington Labs Sherborne Sch 2000, housing at Charterhouse 2000, Goodwood Racecourse 2001, (Ind Fabric Assoc Award) 2001, Manchester Art Gall 2002, The Forum Norwich 2002, Haberdashers' Hall London 2002, Nat Coll of Sch Leadership Univ of Nottingham 2002, London Olympics VeloPark Stratford; pres Architectural Assoc 1997–99 (vice-pres 1987–93); cmmr Royal Fine Art Cmmn; memb: Architecture Advsy Panel Arts Cncl, Cncl Architecture Assoc, Cncl RIBA, London Advsy Ctee English Heritage; hon memb Bund Architekten 1996; tstee: British Museum 1993–, Thomas Cubitt Tst; Royal Gold Medal for Architecture 1994, Prince Philip Prize for Designer of the Year 1994; Dr (hc) RCA 1994, Hon DLitt Univ of Nottingham 1995, Hon DTech London Guildhall Univ 1996; RIBA 1966, RWEA 1989, RA 1992, Hon FAIA 1996, Hon FRIAS 1996; *Recreations* Blackheath, sailing, Catureglio; *Style*— Sir Michael Hopkins, CBE, RA; ✉ 49A Downshire Hill, London NW3 1NX (☎ 020 7435 1109); Hopkins Architects, 27 Broadley Terrace, London NW1 6LG (☎ 020 7724 1751)

HOPKINS, Rowland Rhys; s of David Verdun Hopkins, of Ammanford, Carmarthenshire, and Phyllis, *née* Dyson; *b* 19 December 1948; *Educ* Lawrence Sheriff Sch Rugby, UCL (LLB); *m* 12 Dec 1987, Elizabeth Ann, da of Ronald Williams (d 1980), of Church Stretton, Salop; 1 da (Sarah Elizabeth b 24 Oct 1989); *Career* called to the Bar Inner Temple 1970; barr 1984–; pt/t immigration adjudicator 2001–05, pt/t immigration judge 2005–10, pt/t judge (immigration and asylum) First Tier Tbnl 2010–; memb Gen Synod C of E 1985–90, chm House of Laity of Birmingham Diocesan Synod C of E 1988–94; *Recreations* skiing, fell walking; *Style*— Rowland Hopkins, Esq; ✉ 108 Stanmore Road, Birmingham B16 0SX

HOPKINSON, Jeremy Stephen Frederick; s of John Gordon Hopkinson, of Kensworth, Dunstable, and Edith, *née* Lord; *b* 28 August 1943, Southport, Lancs; *Educ* Berkhamsted Sch; *m* 14 Sept 1968, Helle, da of Alfred Holter, of Brevik, Norway; 1 s (Peter John b 18 Nov 1969), 2 da (Cecilia Ann b 22 Feb 1972, Theresa Janet b 19 July 1974); *Career* articled clerk Robert H Marsh & Co CA 1961–68, qualified 1966, Hillier Hills Frary & Co 1968–70; ptnr Marsh Wood Drew & Co 1972–78 (joined 1970), ptnr Dearden Farrow 1978–88 (chm Tax Ctee 1983–86), joined Binder Hamlyn 1988, ptnr (following merger) Arthur Andersen from Oct 1994 (ret); princ Jeremy Hopkinson & Co 1999–2013; tstee Milton Keynes City Counselling Centre until 2012, tstee Assoc of Church Accountants and Treasurers London (chm 1999–2004), consIt numerous charities; reader C of E 2003–, memb local church and treas Mursley Deanery Synod; FCA 1976 (ACA 1966); Freemason (Gadebourne Lodge, King Henry VIII Chapter and Berkhamsted Rose Croix); *Recreations* golf, choir singing, marquetry; *Clubs* Woburn Golf & Country; *Style*— Jeremy Hopkinson, Esq; ✉ Lynghouse, 12 Heath Road, Great Brickhill, Milton Keynes, Buckinghamshire MK17 9AL (☎ 01525 261674, fax 0709 200 8274)

HOPKINSON, Simon Charles; s of Frederick Bruce Hopkinson, of Pembrokeshire, and Anne Dorothie Mary, *née* Whitworth; *b* 5 June 1954; *Educ* St John's Coll Cambridge (chorister), Trent Coll; *Career* Normandie Hotel Birtle 1970–71, Hat & Feather Knutsford 1971–72, St Non's Hotel St Davids 1972–74, Druidstone Hotel Little Haven 1974–75; chef and proprietor: Shed Restaurant Dinas 1975–77, Hoppy's Restaurant 1977–78; inspr Egon Ronay 1978–80; chef: private house 1980–83, Hilaire London 1983–87; founding chef and co-prop Bibendum 1987–95; former cookery writer The Independent (winner Glenfiddich Award for Cookery writing (three times)); *Books* Roast Chicken and Other Stories (1994, Andre Simon Award 1995, Glenfiddich Award 1995, Most Useful Cookery Book Ever Waitrose Food Illustrated 2005), The Prawn Cocktail Years (1997), Gammon and Spinach and Other Recipes (1998), Roast Chicken and Other Stories: Second Helpings (2001), Week in Week Out (2007); *Recreations* dining; *Clubs* The Groucho, Colony Room; *Style*— Simon Hopkinson, Esq

HOPKINSON, (George) William; s of William Hartley Hopkinson (d 1971), and Mary, *née* Ashmore (d 2003); *b* 13 September 1943; *Educ* Tupton Hall GS, Pembroke Coll Cambridge (MA); *m* 1, (m dis 1997), Mary Agnes, *née* Coverdale; 1 s (William St John b 9 Nov 1974); m 2, Virginia Frances Dewhurst; *Career* Inland Revenue: joined 1965, Civil Serv Dept 1973–76, private sec to Min of State 1976–77, asst sec 1978–81; HM Treasy 1981–86; MOD: head Defence Arms Control Unit 1988–92, head Defence Lands Serv 1992–93, asst under sec of state (Policy) 1993–97; dep dir and dir of studies RIIA 1999–2000 (head of int security prog 1997–99, assoc fell); visiting fell Univ of Cambridge 1991, sr visiting fell WEU Inst Paris 2001; contrib to pubns on security policy, writer and speaker on int relations; *Publications* The Making of British Defence Policy (2000), Enlargement: A New NATO (2001), Sizing and Shaping European Armed Forces (2004), International Organizations in the 21st Century: Challenges Facing the International System in the Europa Directory of International Organizations 1999 to 2004, La Fin de l'Atlantique Nord Critique Internationale no 15, The Atlantic Crises: Britain, Europe and Parting from the United States (2005); *Recreations* walking, reading; *Clubs* Oxford and Cambridge; *Style*— William Hopkinson, Esq; ✉ Gloucester House, The Southend, Ledbury, Herefordshire HR8 2HD (☎ 01531 631546, e-mail g.w.hopkinson@btinternet.com)

HOPKIRK, (Margaret) Joyce; da of late Walter Nicholson, of Newcastle, and late Veronica, *née* Keelan; *Educ* Middle St Secdy Sch Newcastle; *m* 1, 1964, Peter Hopkirk; 1 da (Victoria b 11 April 1966); m 2, 9 Aug 1974, William James (Bill) Lear, s of Maj Cyril James Lear (d 1988), of Newick, E Sussex; 1 s (Nicholas b 22 Nov 1975); *Career* women's ed (launch) Sun Newspaper 1969, ed (launch) Br Cosmopolitan 1970, asst ed Daily Mirror 1972–78, women's ed Sunday Times 1986, ed dir (launch) Br Elle 1987, ed She magazine 1987–89, ed Chic magazine 1993–94 (fndr ed), conslt to ed Sunday Express 1992–; co-chm PPA Awards; media memb Competition Cmmn 2001–06; FRSA; *Books* Splash (co-author, 1995), Best of Enemies (1996), Double Trouble (1997), Unfinished Business (1998), Relative Strangers (1999), The Affair (2000); *Style*— Mrs Joyce Hopkirk

HOPMEIER, George Alan Richard; JP (Inner London); s of Dr Lucian Hopmeier (d 1981), and Yolanda Hopmeier; *b* Oldham, Gtr Manchester; *Educ* Dulwich Coll, UCL (BA); *Chidren* 1 da (Charlotte b 29 March 1981); *Career* chief exec: First Trade Ltd 2003–, Safe Beauty Ltd; dir Photo Therapeutics Ltd; *Recreations* boating, reading, flying; *Clubs* RAC, Citrus (USA); *Style*— George Hopmeier, Esq; ✉ Unit 1, Kingfisher House, Juniper Drive, London SW18 1TX (☎ 020 7350 2020, fax 020 7350 2545, e-mail hopmeier@msn.com)

HOPMEIER, His Hon Judge Michael Andrew Philip; *b* 25 October 1950, Oldham, Lancs; *Career* called to the Bar 1974, bencher Middle Temple (Master of the Bench); recorder 1994, circuit judge (South Eastern Circuit) 2009–; visiting prof City Univ London, hon prof Univ of the West Indies Jamaica 2016; *Publications* Millington and Sutherland Williams on the Proceeds of Crime (jt ed, 4 edn); *Recreations* sailing, skiing; *Clubs* Emsworth Sailing, Bar Yacht; *Style*— His Hon Judge Hopmeier; ✉ c/o The South Eastern Circuit, 289–293 High Holborn, London WC1V 7HZ

HOPPÉ, Benjamin Finley; OBE (2004); s of Benjamin Finley Hoppé, and Gwendoline May, *née* Evans; *b* 7 May 1933, Swansea; *Educ* Swansea GS; *m* 10 June 1957, Valerie, *née* Rowe; 2 s (Andrew Finley b 7 Oct 1958, Ian David b 18 Dec 1963), 1 da (Angela Gillian b 31 Jan 1960); *Career* apprentice structural draughtsman Dawnays Ltd 1950–54, cmmnd Nat Serv Royal Engrs Sch of Mil Engrg Chatham 1955–57, site engr Braithwaite Engrs Ltd 1957–59, site agent Metal Construction Ltd 1959–61, area agent Rees and Kirby Ltd 1961–68, fndr Rowecord Engrg Ltd 1968, currently chm Rowecord Holdings Ltd; pres Br Constructional Steelwork Assoc 1996–98, chm Newport Successful City Status Bid 2003, chm Newport Gwent Enterprises Agency 1993–2005; hon fell Univ of Wales Newport 2002; Wales Business Achiever of the Year 2003; *Clubs* Newport Fugitives CC (pres), Newport Golf; *Style*— Benjamin Hoppé, Esq, OBE; ✉ Newholme, Glasllwch Lane, Newport, Gwent NP20 3PT (☎ 01633 258527, fax 01633 267253); Rowecord Holdings Ltd, Neptune Works, Uskway, Newport NP20 2SS (☎ 01633 250511, fax 01633 253219, e-mail benhoppe@rowecord.com)

HOPPEN, Kelly Elaine; MBE (2009); *b* South Africa; *Career* interior designer; owner Kelly Hoppen Interiors; panel memb Dragons' Den (BBC 2) 2013–; author of 8 books; ambass Prince's Tst; Andrew Martin Interior Design Award 1996, European Woman of Achievement 2007; *Style*— Ms Kelly Hoppen, MBE; ✉ Kelly Hoppen Interiors, Unit 5, 3 Vencourt Place, London W6 9NU

HOPPER, Prof Andrew (Andy); CBE (2007); *b* 9 May 1953, Warsaw, Poland; *Educ* Univ of Wales Swansea (BSc), Univ of Cambridge (PhD); *m*; 2 c; *Career* Univ of Cambridge: research asst Computer Laboratory 1977–79, asst lectr Computer Laboratory 1979–93, dir of studies in computer science CCC Cambridge 1981–93, (fell 1981–2011), lectr Computer Laboratory 1983–92, reader in computer technol Computer Laboratory 1992–97, prof of communications Dept of Engrg 1997–2004, prof of computer technol and head Computer Laboratory 2004–, tstee Cncl 2011–, memb Finance Ctee 2011–; dir Orbis Ltd 1978–81, research dir Acorn Computer plc 1979–85 (dir 1996–99), fndr Olivetti Research 1986, md AT&T Laboratories Cambridge 1986–2002 (vice-pres 1994–2002); chm: Cambridge Broadband Ltd 2000–05, Adventiq Ltd 2005–09, VNC Gp Ltd 2002–; dir: Qudos Ltd 1985–89, Virata Inc 1993–2001, Adaptive Broadband Ltd 1998–2001, Telemedia Systems Ltd 2000–03 (chm 1995–2003), Level 5 Networks Ltd 2002–08, Ubisense plc 2003–06 (chm 2003–), TxtEz Ltd 2013–; memb Advsy Bd: Amadeus Capital Partners 2001–05, Cambridge Gateway Fund 2001–06, Queen's Univ Belfast Inst of Electronics Communications and IT 2005–, CRFS Ltd 2007–10, Univ of Oxford Dept of Computer Science 2008–, École Polytechnique Fédérale de Lausanne Sch of Computer and Communication Sciences 2011–, Univ of Cambridge Centre for Business Research 2013–; dir Cambridge Wireless 2005–08, tstee Fraser Research 2003–, chm Emerging Technologies and Industries Steering Gp Technol Strategy Bd 2009–12, memb Techical Advsy Cncl BP plc 2011–; Royal Soc Clifford Paterson Lecture 1999, Royal Acad of

H

Engrg Silver Medal 2003, Royal Assoc of Computing Machinery SIGMOBILE Outstanding Contribution Award 2004, IEE Mountbatten Medal 2004; hon fell Swansea Univ 2005, hon fell Trinity Hall Cambridge 2011, hon fell CCC Cambridge 2013; hon degree Queen's Univ Belfast 2010; FIET 1993 (MIET 1981, memb IT Sector Panel 2002–07 (chm 2005–07), tstee 2003–06 and 2009–, pres 2012–), FREng 1996 (memb Panel 5 2002–07, memb Awards Ctee 2006–08, tstee Cncl 2007–10, memb Int Ctee 2007–11, memb Enterprise Ctee 2013–), FRS 2006 (memb Innovation Panel 2006–08, memb Sectional Ctee 4 2006–08, tstee Cncl 2009–11, memb Awards Nominations Ctee 2012–); *Recreations* flying; *Style*— Prof Andy Hopper, CBE; ✉ University of Cambridge Computer Laboratory, William Gates Building, 15 J J Thomson Avenue, Cambridge CB3 0FD

HOPPER, Nick; *Career* photographer, creative director, actor and model; co-fndr (with Jasmine Hemsley and Melissa Hemsley, *qqv*) and creative dir Hemsley + Hemsley; contrib: British Vogue, Vogue.co.uk, marie claire, Red, House & Garden, The Telegraph, Stella, Stylist, BBC Good Food, BBC Worldwide; *Books* photographer: The Art of Eating Well (2014), Good + Simple (2016); *Style*— Nick Hopper, Esq; ☎ 07859 055876, e-mail nickhopperphoto@gmail.com, website www.nickhopper.com

HOPPER, Prof Stephen Donald; s of Donald Arthur Hopper, and Patricia Love, *née* Wilson; *b* 18 June 1951, Bangalow, NSW; *Educ* Univ of Western Aust (BSc, PhD); *m* 1975, Christine, *née* Ridgen; 2 s (Luke b 1 July 1979, Jonathan b 23 June 1982), 1 da (Claire b 4 June 1985); *Career* pt/t music teacher (guitar and mandolin) Zenith Music WA 1970–75, botany lab demonstrator Univ of Western Aust 1973–77, contractual botanist Western Australian Herbarium Dept of Agriculture 1977, res offr (flora conservation) Dept of Fisheries and Wildlife 1977–85; Western Australian Wildlife Reseach Centre Dept of Conservation and Land Mgmnt: sr res scientist (flora conservation) 1985–88, sr princ res scientist and OIC 1988–92; dir Kings Park and Botanic Garden Perth WA 1992–99, ceo Botanic Gardens and Parks Authy 1999–2004, fndn prof of plant conservation biology Univ of Western Australia 2004–06, dir Royal Botanic Gardens Kew 2006–12, prof of biodiversity Univ of Western Aust 2012–; visiting prof: Univ of Reading, Univ of Western Aust; visiting sr res scholar Kings Park and Botanic Garden Perth WA; CSIRO Visiting Scientist Award 1984, Fulbright Senior Scholar's Award 1990, Cwlth Centenary Medal 2003, inductee Western Australian Science Hall of Fame 2012, Australian Research Cncl Discovery Outstanding Researcher 2014–16; corresponding memb Botanical Soc of America, memb Royal Soc of Western Aust; Hon DSc: Univ of Western Australia 2010, Univ of Sussex; FLS 2007, fell Australian Acad of Technological Sciences and Engrg 2011; AC; *Publications* Leaf and Branch: Trees and Tall Shrubs of Perth (contrib, 1990), Western Australia's Endangered Flora (jtly, 1990), The Banksia Atlas (jtly, 1991), Kangaroo Paws and Catspaws: a Natural History and Field Guide (1993), Gondwanan Heritage: Past, present and future of the Western Australian Biota (jt ed, 1996), Conservation Biology for the Coming Decade (contrib, 1997), Western Australia's Threatened Flora (contrib, 1998), Managing our Bushland: Proceedings of a conference about the protection and management of urban bushland (contrib, 1999), Life on the Rocks: The Art of Survival (jtly, 1999, 2 edn 2008), Soul of the Desert (jtly, 2005), Australian Seeds: A Guide to their collection, identification and biology (contrib, 2006), Orchids of Western Australia (jtly, 2008), OCBIL theory: towards an integrated understanding of the evolution, ecology and conservation of biodiversity on old, climatically-buffered, infertile landscapes (in Plant & Soil 322: 49–86, 2009); more than 200 additional scientific pubns; *Recreations* music, walking, photography, travelling; *Style*— Prof Stephen D Hopper; ✉ Centre of Excellence in Natural Resource Management and School of Plant Biology, The University of Western Australia, Foreshore House, Proudlove Parade, Albany 6630, Western Australia (☎ 00 61 8 9842 0842, fax 00 61 8 9842 8499, e-mail steve.hopper@uwa.edu.au, website www.cenrm.uwa.edu.au)

HOPPER, William Joseph; s of late Isaac Vance Hopper, and late Jennie Josephine Black; *b* 9 August 1929; *Educ* Queen's Park Secdy Sch, Univ of Glasgow (MA); *m* 1 (m dis); 1 da (Catherine b 1962); m 2, 1987 (m dis), Marjorie Orr; *Career* Pilot Offr RAF 1952–55; fin analyst W R Grace and Co New York 1956–59, London office mangr H Hentz and Co (memb NYSE) 1960–66, gen mangr S G Warburg and Co Ltd 1966–69; dir: Hill Samuel and Co Ltd 1969–74, Morgan Grenfell and Co Ltd 1975–79 (advsr 1979–86); MEP (Cons) Greater Manchester W 1979–84; dir: Wharf Resources Ltd (Calgary) 1984–87, Manchester Ship Canal Co 1985–87; exec chm Shire Trust Ltd 1986–91, chm Robust Mouldings Ltd 1986–90, exec chm W J Hopper & Co Ltd (investment bankers)1996–2012; fndr chm (now memb Exec Ctee) Inst for Fiscal Studies 1969–2014, treas Action Resource Centre 1985–94, tstee Nat Hosp for Nervous Diseases Devpt Fndn 1986–90, tstee Hampstead Wells and Campden Tst 1989–99; memb Ctee of Mgmnt Rosslyn Hill Unitarian Chapel 1995–2000 (chm 1995–98) and 2004–06; *Publications* The Puritan Gift: Triumph, Collapse and Revival of an American Dream (co-author, 2007, published in paperback as The Puritan Gift: Reclaiming the American Dream amidst Global Financial Chaos 2009, published in Chinese trans 2013); *Recreations* listening to music, gardening; *Clubs* Garrick; *Style*— W J Hopper; ✉ 9A Flask Walk, London NW3 1HJ (☎ 020 7435 6414, e-mail will@puritangift.com)

HOPPS, Stuart Gary; s of Alec Hopps (d 1973), of London, and Lucie, *née* Dombek; *b* 2 December 1942; *Educ* Stratford GS, KCL (BA), MFA Sarah Lawrence Coll; *Career* choreographer; Dance Dept Dartington Coll of Art 1970–71, assoc dir Scottish Ballet 1971–76, fndr dir SB's movable Workshop, fndr chm Dance Panel Gr London Arts, chm Br Assoc of Choreographers, memb Dance Panel Arts Cncl of GB 1976–80, dir MA Studies Laban Centre 1986–89, memb Accreditation Ctee Cncl for Dance Educn & Training; fndr chm Br Assoc of Choreographers; *Theatre* incl: Elizabeth (Ginza Saison Theatre Tokyo), Medea (Barcelona Cultural Olympics), A Midsummer Night's Dream, Salome, Candide (Edinburgh Festival), The Oresteia, Animal Farm (NT), Henry VIII, As You Like It and Beauty and the Beast (RSC), Oliver (Nat Youth Music Theatre), Chips With Everything (NT), Galileo (NT), The Entertainer (Manchester Royal Exchange); theatre in West End: Pal Joey, Girl Friends, The Rocky Horror Show, Carmen Jones, The Betrayal of Laura Blake; *Opera* incl: The Cunning Little Vixen, The Silver Tassie and Christmas Eve (ENO), Orfeo ed Euridice (Glyndebourne), Carmen, Idomeneo, Onegin and The Merry Widow (WNO), HMS Pinafore and The Merry Widow (Sadler's Wells), The Cunning Little Vixen and Carmen (Royal Opera), Macbeth (Metropolitan Opera), Peter Grimes (Kent Opera); *Television* The Passion (BBC 2); *Film* incl: Sense and Sensibility, Twelfth Night, Kenneth Branagh's Much Ado About Nothing, Hamlet and Love's Labour's Lost, A Knight's Tale, The Magic Flute, The Nutcracker, Mrs Henderson Presents, Your Highness; Hon Dr of Arts City Univ 2007, Citation of Hon for Lifetime Achievement in Choreography USA 2009; *Style*— Stuart Hopps, Esq; ✉ c/o Simpson Fox Associates, 6 Beauchamp Place, London SW3 1NG (☎ 020 7434 9167, fax 020 7494 2887, e-mail david.bingham@simpson-fox.com)

HOPSON, Christopher Ian (Chris); s of David Joseph Hopson (d 2001), of Newbury, Berks, and Susan, *née* Buckingham; *b* 9 April 1963; *Educ* Marlborough, St Andrews Sch Middletown Delaware USA (ESU Scholarship), Univ of Sussex (BA), Cranfield Sch of Mgmnt (MBA); *m* May 1994, Charlotte, da of Keith Gascoigne (d 2013); 2 s (Matthew James b 14 July 1998, Nicholas Henry b 1 Sept 2000); *Career* SDP 1985–90: sometime constituency agent, Pty researcher (Rosie Barnes), dir elections and campaigns and chief exec; communications conslt Corporate Communications Strategy 1990–91, political adviser to David Mellor (then Sec of State for National Heritage) 1992, corporate affrs dir Granada Media Group 1993–2000, md Result educn serv 1999–2002, conslt DfES 2002–04; HMRC: communications and mktg dir 2005–07, memb Bd 2006–08, change and capability dir 2007–08, customer contact dir 2008–12; chief exec NHS providers (previously Foundation Trust Network) 2012–; chm Foyer Fedn 2004–11 (memb Bd 2001–11); memb Cncl RTS 1995–98; *Recreations* walking, travel, reading, theatre, good food and wine (not necessarily in that order); *Style*— Chris Hopson, Esq; ✉ NHS Providers, One Birdcage walk, London SW1H 9JJ (e-mail chris.hopson@nhsproviders.org)

HOPTON, Nicholas Dunster; s of David Hopton, and Janet Dunster; *b* 8 October 1965, Manchester; *Educ* St Peter's Sch York, Magdalene Coll Cambridge (Peskett Prize for Modern Languages/Literature); *m* 1993, Alexandra Echenique de Hopton; 2 da (Sophia b 1998, Angelica b 2000), 3 s (Gabriel b 2002, Louis b 2003, Sebastian b 2006); *Career* diplomat; asst desk offr ME Dept FCO 1989–90, asst desk offr European Community Dept FCO 1990–91, political and information second sec Rabat 1991–95, press offr News Dept and Resource Planning Dept FCO 1995–97, Agenda 2000 section head EU Dept FCO 1997–98, private sec to Min for Europe FCO 1998–2000, foreign and security policy first sec Rome 2000–03, EU and economic counsellor Paris 2003–07, Nat Security Strategy Team Cabinet Office 2007–08, Policy Unit No 10 Downing St 2008, head Int Orgns Dept FCO 2008–11, acting dir Int Security and Instns Directorate FCO 2011, ambass to Yemen 2012–13, ambass to Qatar 2013–15, Chargé d'Affaires to Iran 2015–16, ambass to Iran 2016–; visiting academic St Antony's Coll Oxford 2013–14; *Publications* In Pieces (1999); *Recreations* music, writing, hill walking, sailing, squash; *Clubs* RAC, Hawks; *Style*— Mr Nicholas Hopton; ✉ c/o FCO, King Charles Street, London SW1A 2AH (e-mail nicolas.hopton@fco.gov.uk, Twitter @nicholashopton)

HOPWOOD, Prof Sir David Alan; kt (1994); s of Herbert Hopwood (d 1963), of Lymm, Cheshire, and Dora, *née* Grant (d 1972); *b* 19 August 1933, Kinver, Staffs; *Educ* Purbrook Park Co HS, Lymm GS, Univ of Cambridge (MA, PhD), Univ of Glasgow (DSc); *m* 15 Sept 1962, Joyce Lilian, da of Isaac Bloom (d 1964), of Hove, E Sussex; 2 s (Nicholas Duncan b 1964, John Andrew b 1965), 1 da (Rebecca Jane b 1967); *Career* John Stothert bye-fell Magdalene Coll Cambridge 1956–58, univ demonstrator and asst lectr in botany Univ of Cambridge 1957–61, res fell St John's Coll Cambridge 1958–61, lectr in genetics Univ of Glasgow 1961–68, John Innes prof of genetics UEA 1968–98 (emeritus prof 1998–); formerly head Genetics Dept John Innes Centre (emeritus fell 1998–); hon prof: Chinese Acad Med Sciences 1987, Chinese Acad of Sciences (Insts of Microbiology and Plant Physiology) 1987, Huazhong Agric Univ Wuhan China 1989, Guangxi Univ Nanning China 2004, Jaio Tong Univ Shanghai China 2004, Wuhan Univ China 2013; hon fell: UMIST 1990, Magdalene Coll Cambridge 1992, St John's Coll Cambridge 2008; memb: Genetics Soc of GB 1957 (pres 1984–87), Euro Molecular Biology Orgn 1984, Academia Europaea 1988; hon memb: Spanish Microbiological Soc 1985, Hungarian Acad of Sciences 1990, Soc Gen Microbiology (pres 2000–03); foreign fell Indian Nat Sci Acad 1987; Hon DSc: ETH Zürich 1989, UEA 1998, Athens 2012; Hon FIBiol 2001, FRS 1979; *Publications* Streptomyces in Nature and Medicine: the Antibiotic Makers (2007); author of over 270 articles in scientific jls and books; *Recreations* cooking, gardening, natural history; *Style*— Prof Sir David Hopwood, FRS; ✉ John Innes Centre, Norwich Research Park, Colney, Norwich NR4 7UH (☎ 01603 450000, fax 01603 450778, e-mail david.hopwood@jic.ac.uk); 244 Unthank Road, Norwich NR2 2AH (☎ 01603 453488)

HORAM, Baron (Life Peer UK 2013), of Grimsargh in the County of Lancashire; John Rhodes Horam; s of Sydney Horam, of Preston, Lancs, and Catherine Horam; *b* 7 March 1939; *Educ* Silcoates Sch Wakefield, St Catharine's Coll Cambridge; *m* 1, 1977, Iris Crawley; m 2, 1987, Judith Margaret Jackson; *Career* former fin journalist: Financial Times, The Economist; MP (Lab 1970–81, SDP 1981–83) Gateshead West 1970–83, joined Cons Pty Feb 1987, MP (Cons) Orpington 1992–2010; Parly under sec for Tport 1976–79, memb Public Accounts Ctee 1992–95, Parly sec Office of Public Service 1995, Parly under sec Dept of Health 1995–97; chm Environmental Audit Ctee 1997–2003; memb: Exec 1922 Ctee of Cons MPs 2004–08, Foreign Affrs Ctee 2005–10, House of Lords EU Ctee (External Affrs Sub-Ctee); electoral cmmr 2012–; CRU International Ltd: md 1968–70 and 1983–92, dep chm 1992–95, non-exec dir 1997–; fell commoner St Catharine's Coll Cambridge 2010–; memb Royal Inst of Int Affrs 2011–; *Style*— The Lord Horam

HORGAN, Sharon; da of John Horgan, of Co Meath, Ireland, and Ursula, *née* Campbell; *b* 13 July 1970, London; *Educ* English and American Studies Brunel Univ (BA); *m* 16 Oct 2004, Jeremy Rainbird; 2 da (Sadhbh b 18 Jan 2004, Amer b 16 June 2008); *Career* actress, comedienne and writer; Best New Comedy Writer Edinburgh Festival 2001, Best Comedy Actress Br Comedy Award 2009, 2 BAFTA nominations; memb WEA; *Television* performer: Annually Retentive (Series 1 and 2), Broken News 2005, The Friday Night Project (Series 1) 2005; writer and performer: Pulling 2006–10 (2 series and a Christmas special), Angelos 2007, Free Agents 2009, Catastrophe 2015; *Film* Imagine Me and You, Valiant; *Style*— Ms Sharon Horgan; ✉ c/o Duncan Hayes, United Agents Ltd, 12–26 Lexington Street, London W1F 0LE (☎ 020 3214 0800, fax 020 3214 0801, website www.unitedagents.co.uk, Twitter @realsharhorgan)

HORLEY, Sandra; CBE (2011, OBE 1999); *Educ* BA; *m* Julian Nieman; 1 da (Samantha); *Career* former dir Haven Project, ceo Refuge 1983–; memb Judging Panel The Guardian Public Service Awards 2010; Voluntary Sector Achiever of the Year and Outstanding Achiever of the Year Dods and Scottish Widows Women in Public Life Awards 2008, Cosmopolitan Ultimate Woman's Woman Award 2008, named one of Evening Standard's 1000 most influential people in London 2007, named one of Nat Magazine Co and Hearst UK's 1000 most influential women in the UK today 2010, nominated Top Public Sector Innovator by Helen Lewis (Dep Ed New Statesman) 2012; hon fell London South Bank Univ 2006; *Books* Power and Control, Love and Pain; numerous articles for the nat press and professional jls; *Style*— Ms Sandra Horley, CBE; ✉ Refuge, 4th Floor, International House, 1 St Katharine's Way, London E1W 1UN

HORLICK, Nicola Karina Christina; da of Michael Robert Dudley Gayford (d 1997), of Chichester, W Sussex, and Suzanna Christina Victoria, *née* Czyzewska; *b* 28 December 1960; *Educ* Cheltenham Ladies' Coll, Birkenhead HS GPDST, Phillips Exeter Acad (USA), Balliol Coll Oxford (BA); *m* 1, 23 June 1984 (m dis 2005), Timothy Piers Horlick, s of Vice-Adm Sir Ted Horlick, KBE, FREng; 4 da (Georgina b 19 Oct 1986 d 27 Nov 1998, Alice b 17 Nov 1988, Serena b 2 Nov 1990, Antonia b 10 June 1996), 2 s (Rupert b 1 Dec 1993, Benjamin b 18 Sept 1999); m 2, 8 Sept 2006, Martin Francis Damian Baker; *Career* Mercury Asset Management 1983–91, md Morgan Grenfell Investment Management (UK Institutional Business) Morgan Grenfell Asset Management 1991–97 (resigned), md SG Asset Management 1997–2003, fndr and chief exec Bramdean Asset Mgmnt Gp LLP 2004–12, chief exec Money&Co 2013–; chm Rockpool Investments LLP 2011–15; *Books* Can You Have It All? (1997); *Recreations* music, theatre, skiing; *Style*— Mrs Nicola Horlick

HORLOCK, Timothy John; QC (1997); s of John Harold Horlock, and Sheila, *née* Stuteley; *b* 4 January 1958; *Educ* Manchester Grammar, St John's Coll Cambridge (BA); *m* (m dis); 3 s (Matthew b 1985, Alex b 1987, Guy b 1991); *Career* called to the Bar Middle Temple 1981, in practice Northern Circuit, asst recorder 1997–; *Recreations* football, tennis, cricket; *Style*— Tim Horlock, QC

HORN, Bernard P; *Educ* Catholic Coll Preston, John Dalton Faculty of Technol Manchester (DMS), Harvard Business Sch (Exec Prog); *m*; *Career* National Westminster Bank plc: joined 1965, in retail banking in N of England 1965–70, joined International Div 1972, dir of corp and institutional fin 1988–89, gen mangr Gp Chief Exec's Office 1989–90, gen mangr i/c gp strategy and communications 1990–91, chief exec NatWest Gp Int

Businesses 1991–96, gp main bd dir 1995–2000, exec dir Gp Ops 1996–2000; chm: Rock Consulting 2001–07, Netik Holdings Ltd 2002–10, Eontec Ltd (Dublin) 2003–04, E-Box 2004–15, Econiq (Ireland) 2007, Social Finance Ltd 2007–16; sr advsr investcloud llc; cmmr on unclaimed assets 2005–; chm Magic Bus (UK), vice-pres EnhamTrust 2015–; Freeman City of London 2002; *Recreations* theatre, music; *Clubs* RAC, Hurlingham; *Style—* Bernard P Horn, Esq; ✉ e-mail bph@bernardhorn.com

HORN, Trevor; CBE (2011); s of Robert Horn, of Durham, and Elizabeth, *née* Lambton; *b* 15 July 1949; *Educ* Johnson GS; *m* 1980, Jill, da of David Sinclair; 1 s (Aaron b 15 Dec 1983), 3 da (Alexandra b 24 April 1982, Rebecca b 25 March 1990, Gabriella b 17 April 1995); *Career* record prodr; formerly vocalist of pop bands Buggles and Yes, fndr memb and innovator The Art of Noise, fndr ZTT records, dir SPZ Group, estab Perfect Songs; past prodn credits incl: Buggles' The Age of Plastic (1980, gold disc), ABC's Lexicon of Love (1982, platinum), Malcolm McClaren's Duck Rock (1983, gold), Yes' 90125 (multi platinum), Frankie Goes To Hollywood's Welcome To The Pleasure Dome (multi platinum), Simple Minds' Street Fighting Years (platinum), Seal (multi platinum), Mike Oldfield's Tubular Bells II, Pet Shop Boys' Fundamental; prodr of many other artists incl: Grace Jones, Spandau Ballet, Foreigner, Godley and Creme, Paul McCartney, Rod Stewart, Pet Shop Boys, Propaganda, Dollar, Tina Turner, Tom Jones, Tatu, Robbie Williams, Gary Barlow, Estelle, Olly Murs, Kelly Rowland; writer Pass the Flame (Official Olympics 2004 song); songwriter for film and TV incl: Toys, Coyote Ugly, Mona Lisa Smile, The Glam Metal Detectives; Prince's Tst charity concert at Wembley Arena celebrating 25 years as record prodr 2004; memb band The Producers; BPI Br Prodr of the Year 1983, 1985 and 1991 (nominated 1983, 1984, 1985, 1986, 1987, 1988 and 1994), Radio 1 Award for contribution to pop music 1984; Ivor Novello Awards: best recorded record for Owner of a Lonely Heart 1983, best contemporary song for Relax 1984, most performed work for Two Tribes 1984; 49 Grammy Award nominations incl: winner Best Instrumental (Cinema 90125), nomination Best Prodr 1994, Best Record (for Kiss From a Rose by Seal) 1996, Best Dance Song (I'm with Stupid by the Pet Shop Boys); Brit Award Best Br Prodr 1982, 1983 and 1992, BMI Award for Owner of A Lonely Heart 1984, Q Magazine Best Prodr Award 1991, Music Week Best Prodr Award 1991, Music Week Prodr of the Year Award 2004, Ivor Novello Award for Outstanding Contribution to Br Music 2010; *Style—* Trevor Horn, Esq, CBE; ✉ Sarm Music Village, 105 Ladbroke Grove, London W11 1PG (☎ 020 3741 9033)

HORN-SMITH, Sir Julian; kt (2004); *b* 14 December 1948, London; *Educ* Univ of London (BSc), Univ of Bath (MSc); *Career* Rediffusion 1972–78, Philips 1978–82, Mars GB 1982–84; Vodafone Gp plc: joined 1984, memb Bd 1996–2006, chief exec Vodafone AirTouch International Limited and exec dir Vodafone AirTouch plc 1999–2001, gp chief operating offr 2001–05, dep chief exec 2005–06, chm Supervisory Bd Vodafone Deutschland GmbH; chm Sage Gp plc 2006–07; non-exec dir: Smiths Gp plc 2000–06, Lloyds TSB Gp 2005–12; dir Acer Gp Taiwan; memb: Bd Digicel Gp 2006–, Advsy Bd Alpha Gp Russia 2006–; sr advsr: UBS Investment Bank 2007–, Etisalat UAE, Media/Telecoms CVC; chm: Turkish Br Business Cncl 2007–12, Advsy Bd Sch of Mgmnt Univ of Bath 2008–; pro-chllr Univ of Bath; co-chair Turkish/British Forum 2010; Hon DLL Univ of Bath; *Clubs* Army and Navy, Royal Ascot Racing; *Style—* Sir Julian Horn-Smith

HORNBY, John Fleet; s of John Fleet Hornby, of Cumbria (d 1997), and Marion, *née* Charnley (d 1981); *b* 23 December 1945; *Educ* Dowdales Sch Cumbria; *m* 1976, Elizabeth, da of John Chorley, of Cumbria (d 1988); 1 s (Paul b 1978); *Career* chartered accountant; audit mangr R F Miller & Co 1968–69 (articled clerk 1963–68); James Fisher & Sons plc (shipowners and port operators): accountant special duties 1969, asst co sec 1969–70, PA to md 1970–71, group accountant 1971–78, divnl dir of fin 1978–81, fin dir 1981–86, commercial dir 1986–88, md 1988–89, chm and md 1989–93; princ J F Hornby Ltd Chartered Accountants 1994– (dir 2014–), business conslt 1994–, assoc conslt Armstrong Watson & Co Chartered Accountants 1994–99; former dir/chm numerous other companies; dir Chamber of Shipping 1991–94, memb Gen Ctee Lloyd's Register of Shipping 1992–94; chm: Cumbria Christian Crusade Tst 1990–2000, Mgmnt Ctee The Sea Cadet Corps Barrow-in-Furness Unit 23 TS Sovereign 1997–2014; pres Barrow Chrysanthemum Soc 1989–2007, dep chm Governing Body Dowdales Sch 1995–2000; hon consul of Norway at Barrow-in-Furness; Freeman City of London, Liveryman Worshipful Co of Shipwrights; FCA 1968, FInstD, FRSA; Knight First Class Royal Norwegian Order of Merit; *Recreations* fell walking, fitness, running, travelling, reading; *Style—* John Hornby, Esq; ✉ Hillside, Guards Road, Lindal, Ulverston, Cumbria LA12 0TN (☎ 01229 465614, fax 01229 588061, e-mail jfh@jfhornby.com)

HORNBY, John Hugh; s of Richard Phipps Hornby (d 2007), and Stella, *née* Hichens, of Bowerchalke, Wilts; *b* 23 January 1954; *Educ* Winchester, Univ of Exeter (BSc); *m* 18 June 1983, Anne Elizabeth Meredydd, da of George Hugh Kenefick Rae (d 1989); 3 s (David Hugh b 1988, Edward John b 1990, Julian Patrick b 1992); *Career* admitted slr 1980, Macfarlanes: joined 1977, ptnr 1987–2014, specialised in private client property (housing, leisure and agric); formed and ran Private Client Property Gp 1994–2014 (grad recruitment ptnr 2005–13); conslt business coach The Professional Career Partnership 2014–; *Recreations* ball game sports, vocal classical music, oak wood planting in the Gironde; *Clubs* Hurlingham; *Style—* John Hornby, Esq; ✉ The Professional Career Partnership, 52 Cornhill, London EC3V 3PD (☎ 020 7398 6644, e-mail info@thepcp.com)

HORNBY, Jonathan Peter; s of Sir Derek Hornby (d 2013), and Sonia Margaret, *née* Beesley; *b* 29 March 1967; *Educ* Marlborough, Univ of Edinburgh (MA); *m* 1; 2 s (Benedict b 1994, Joseph b 1997), 1 da (Arabella b 1995); m 2, Clare, née Griffiths; 2 da (Madeleine b 2004, Grace b 2005); *Career* account dir Ogilvy & Mather Advertising 1993–94 (joined as graduate trainee 1990), client servs dir Collett Dickenson Pearce & Partners 1996–98 (bd account dir 1995–96), jt md TBWA GGT Simons Palmer 1998–2001; fndr Clemmow Hornby Inge 2001; assoc memb D&AD; *Recreations* real tennis (Br Open Handicap champion 1986), lawn tennis; *Clubs* Thirty, Marketing Group of GB, 5 Hertford St, George, Soho House; *Style—* Johnny Hornby, Esq; ✉ CHI & Partners, 7 Rathbone Street, London W1T 1LY (☎ 020 7462 8514, e-mail johnny.hornby@chiandpartners.com)

HORNBY, His Hon Judge Keith Anthony Delgado; s of James Lawrence Hornby (d 1993), of Heathfield, E Sussex, and Naomi Ruth, *née* Delgado (d 2003); *b* 18 February 1947; *Educ* Oratory Sch, Trinity Coll Dublin (BA); *m* 14 Feb 1970, Judith Constance, da of Patrick Yelverton Fairbairn; 1 da (Katya Eugenie b 13 Dec 1973), 2 s (Jamie Alexander Fairbairn b 11 Oct 1976, Nicholas Thomas Fairbairn b 11 May 1980); *Career* lectr in commercial law 1969–70; called to the Bar Gray's Inn 1970; recorder of the Crown Court 1992–95 (asst recorder 1988–92), circuit judge (SE Circuit) 1995–; *Recreations* art, theatre, music, golf, tennis, squash; *Clubs* Hurlingham; *Style—* His Hon Judge Keith Hornby; ✉ Bow County Court, 96 Romford Road, Stratford, London E15 4EG (☎ 020 8536 5200)

HORNBY, Nicholas Peter John (Nick); s of Sir Derek Hornby, *qv*, and Margaret Withers; *b* 17 April 1957, Maidenhead, Berks; *Educ* Maidenhead GS, Univ of Cambridge; *m* 1, 1993 (m dis), Virginia Bovell; 1 s (Danny b 1993); m 2, 2006, Amanda Posey; 2 s (Lowell b 2002, Jesse b 2004); *Career* author, screenwriter and freelance journalist; former teacher; co-fndr TreeHouse (nat educnl charity for children with autism), co-fndr Miny of Stories (literacy centre in E London); E M Forster Award American Acad of Arts and Letters 1999, W H Smith Award for Fiction 2002, Writers' Writer Award Orange Word Int Writers Festival 2003; FRSL; *Novels* High Fidelity (1995, film adaptation 2000), About a Boy (1998, film adaptation 2002), How to be Good (2001), A Long Way Down (2005, shortlisted Whitbread Novel of the Year 2005), Slam (2007), Juliet, Naked (2009); *Non-Fiction* Fever Pitch (1992, film adaptations 1997 and 2005), 31 Songs (2003), The Complete Polysyllabic Spree (2006); *Anthologies* My Favourite Year (ed, 1993), Speaking with the Angel (ed, 2000); *Screenplays* Fever Pitch (1997), An Education (2009, nominated for BAFTA and Acad Award); *Recreations* Arsenal FC; *Style—* Nick Hornby, Esq; ✉ c/o Georgia Garrett, Rogers, Coleridge and White

HORNE, Alex; *b* 13 July 1972, Cambridge; *Career* qualifed CA PricewaterhouseCoopers; The FA: joined as finance dir 2003, md Wembley Stadium 2006–08, chief operating offr 2008–10, ceo 2010–15; sports conslt 2015–; *Style—* Alex Horne, Esq; ✉ e-mail horne.aj@gmail.com

HORNE, Christopher Malcolm; CVO (1996); s of Gerald Fitzlait Horne (d 1970), and Dora, *née* Hartley (d 1995); *b* 14 June 1941; *Educ* King Edward VI Chelmsford; *m* 12 Sept 1964, Christine Ann, da of Reginald Arthur Fradley (d 1985); 2 s (Darren James b 7 Feb 1968, Alec Gerald b 20 Jan 1970); *Career* Coutts & Co 1958–97: head of personnel 1980–88, assoc dir 1980–89, sec of Bank 1988–, sr assoc dir 1989–97, co sec Coutts & Co Group 1991–97; memb Vines Rochester United Reformed Church, chm of tstees Vines Centre Tst 1998–2001; *Recreations* golf, gardening, interest in most sports; *Clubs* Rochester & Cobham Park Golf (vice-pres); *Style—* Christopher Horne, Esq, CVO; ✉ Silver Birches, 151 Maidstone Road, Chatham, Kent ME4 6JE (☎ 01634 847594, e-mail chrishorne@blueyonder.co.uk)

HORNE, James Hayward Neale; s of John Horne, and Bridget, *née* Neale; *b* 20 November 1957, Limpsfield, Surrey; *Educ* Shrewsbury, Ealing Coll, Kingston Univ; *m* 11 July 2005, Alison, *née* Cole; 1 s (Christopher), 2 da (Zoë, Megan); *Career* md CCL Foods plc 1994–2003, chief exec GunsonPegs.com 2007–14, chief exec GunDealer.nET 2011–4, chief exec RodsOnRivers 2012–14; dir Bretteston Ltd 2007–12, chm ITap Gp Ltd 2014–, chm James Purdey and Sons Ltd 2014–; memb: Game and Wildlife Conservation Trust (GWCT), Br Assoc for Shooting and Conservation (BASC); *Recreations* gardening, motorsport, shooting; *Clubs* Forum; *Style—* James Horne, Esq; ✉ Lansdowne House, Calverley Park Gardens, Tunbridge Wells, Kent TN1 2JN; James Purdey & Sons Ltd, Audley House, 57–58 South Audley Street, Mayfair, London W1K 2ED (☎ 020 7499 1801, e-mail james.horne@purdey.com, website www.purdey.com)

HORNE, Prof (Charles Hugh) Wilson; MBE; s of Charles Hugh Wilson Horne (d 1977), and Jean, *née* Wells; *b* 13 September 1938; *Educ* Ardrossan Acad, Univ of Glasgow (MB ChB, MD), Univ of Aberdeen (DSc); *m* 5 Sept 1964, Agnes Irvine, da of Joseph Scott (d 1977); 1 da (Glenda May b 16 Nov 1966), 1 s ((Charles Hugh) Wilson b 25 Oct 1969); *Career* lectr in pathology Univ of Glasgow 1966–73; Univ of Aberdeen: sr lectr in pathology 1973–80, prof of immunopathology 1980–84; Univ of Newcastle upon Tyne: prof of pathology 1984–97, head Sch of Pathological Sciences 1988–95; chm Novocastra Labs Newcastle upon Tyne 1989–2005, conslt Vision Biosystems 2005–06; author of numerous pubns on immunology and pathology; FRCPEd, FRCPath; *Recreations* philately, rugby union; *Clubs* Northern Counties; *Style—* Prof Wilson Horne, MBE; ✉ 12 Adderstone Crescent, Jesmond, Newcastle upon Tyne NE2 2HH (☎ 0191 281 3695, e-mail chw.horne@btinternet.com)

HORNE-ROBERTS, Jennifer; *née* Horne; da of Frederick William Horne (d 1969), and Daisy Jessie Elizabeth, *née* Norman (d 2007); *b* 15 February 1949; *Educ* State Schs NW London, Univ of Perugia (Dip Italian), Univ of London (BA), Cncl of Legal Educn London, Coll of Law London; *m* Keith Michael Peter Roberts, s of Gerald Roberts (d 1962); 1 s (Harry Alexander (d 2009)), 1 da (Francesca Elizabeth); *Career* called to the Bar Middle Temple 1976, ad eundem memb Inner Temple; UK counsel for claimants in US Omnibus proceedings (vaccine/autism links); dir of family co; contrib pubns on: political issues, family law, employment law, human rights, literature; Parly candidate: (Lab) Fareham 1974, (Alliance) Medway 1987, (Lib Dem) Holborn and St Pancras 1992; cncllr (Lab) Camden 1971–74; founder and first chair Assoc of Women Barristers; memb: Bar Assocs, Family Law Bar Assoc, Bar European Gp, Human Rights Lawyers Assoc, Personal Injury Bar Assoc, Lib Dem Lawyer Assoc; former memb Young Bar Ctee; fndr Alliance for Govt of National Unity 1994; memb: Tate Gallery, Royal Acad of Arts, Highgate Literary and Scientific Inst, Highgate Soc; tstee and co-chair Harington Charity Highgate, dir Tst for Autism, campaigner Campaign for Fairer Votes; former govr Parliament Hill Secdy Sch London; *Books* Trade Unionists and the Law (1984), Justice for Children (1992), New Frontiers in Family Law (1998), Labour's True Way Forward (2000), Labour's Agenda (2002), Selected Poems (2002), In Harm's Way: The MMRIO Story (co-author, 2006), Access to Justice (co-author, 2006), Harry's Story – A Brilliant Boy's Short Life (2010), Harry's Inquest – A Brilliant Boy's Short Life (2012), The Gates (novel, 2012), Harry's Art Book (2012), Lament for Harry (2013), Jennifer Horne-Roberts: A Memoir (2015); *Recreations* art, writing, visual and literary arts, politics, family; *Clubs* Highgate Golf, Arts; *Style—* Mrs Jennifer Horne-Roberts; ✉ Goldsmith Chambers, Temple, London EC4Y 7BL (☎ 020 7272 2245, mobile 07753 680678, e-mail keith@horne-roberts.co.uk, website www.horne-roberts.co.uk)

HORNER, Christian; OBE (2013); *b* 16 November 1973, Leamington Spa, Warks; *Educ* Warwick Sch, Arnold Lodge Sch Leamington Spa; *Career* driving career: Br Formula Renault Championship 1992 (Formula Renault scholarship 1991), Br Formula Three 1994–96, Br Formula Two 1996–97, Formula 3000 1997–98; fndr Arden team 1997, team princ Red Bull Racing 2005–; *Style—* Christian Horner, Esq, OBE; ✉ Red Bull Racing, Bradbourne Drive, Tilbrook, Milton Keynes MK7 8BJ

HORNER, John Patrick Francis; s of Arthur William Horner, CMG, TD (d 1999), and Patsy Denise, *née* Campbell (d 1993); *b* 20 September 1946; *Educ* St Mary's Sch Nairobi, Stafford House Tutorial Coll London; *m* 1, 1964 (m dis 1973), Diana Pring; 1 s (Jeremy b 20 Sept 1964), 2 da (Geraldine b 4 Oct 1968, Annelise b 16 Aug 1980); m 2, 1974 (m dis 1982), Nicola Bates; 2 da (Sophie b 4 June 1985, Clio b 17 June 1988); m 3, 1999, Penelope, da of late Christopher Grey; *Career* in advtg: Dorland 1965–68, Leo Burnett 1968–73, Kirkwood Co 1973–83 (md 1981–83); fndr Horner, Collis and Kirvan 1983 (subsequently sold to Eurocom Gp), joined Conzept Strategic Systems 1993, headhunted by J Walter Thompson to set up Blue Logic (strategic brand and new product devpt consultancy) 1997; chief exec Models 1 1999– (led MBO), non-exec chm Mint Design Ltd (led MBO); small business mentor Prince's Tst; tstee: Jaipur Heritage, Engaged Events, Palfest Charity; memb Cncl Assoc of Model Agencies 1999; FIPA 1992; *Recreations* classical music, travel, cooking, reading, business; *Style—* John Horner, Esq; ✉ Models 1 Ltd, 12 Macklin Street, London WC2B 5SZ (e-mail jh@johnhorner.com)

HORNER, Prof (Robert) Malcolm Wigglesworth; s of James William Horner (d 1986), and Emma Mary, *née* Wigglesworth (d 1977); *b* 27 July 1942; *Educ* Bolton Sch, UCL (BSc, PhD); *m* 21 March 1970, Beverley Anne, *née* Wesley, da of Ewart Alexander (d 1986); 1 da (Victoria b 10 Sept 1977), 1 s (Jonathan b 3 Oct 1980); *Career* Taylor Woodrow Construction Ltd: civil engr 1966–72, engrg rep W Germany 1972–74, site agent 1974–77; Univ of Dundee: lectr Dept of Civil Engrg 1977–83, sr lectr 1983–86, head of dept 1985–91, prof of engrg mgmnt 1986–2006 (emeritus prof of engrg mgmnt 2006–), chair Sch of Engrg and Physical Sciences 1997–99, dir of enterprise mgmnt 2000–05, dep princ 2002–06, vice-princ 2012; dir Atlantic Power and Gas Ltd 1993–99, dir Objective 3 Partnership 2000–03 (dep chair 2002–03); chm Winton Caledonian Ltd 1995–97, md International Maintenance Management 1996–97, fndr chair Whole Life Consultants Ltd 2004–, dir CXR Biosciences Ltd 2008–15, chair Daviot Gp Ltd 2015–; dir Scottish Enterprise Tayside 2003–08 (chair 2005–08), fndr chm Tayside branch Opening Windows on Engrg 1980–85, chm ICE Scotland Mgmnt Bd 2007–09, dir Scottish Construction Centre 2009–10, chair Constuction Skills Labour Market Intelligence

Technical Reference Gp 2011–14; memb: ICE Working Pty on Strategy Construction Mgmnt Res 1987–89, Technol Foresight Construction Sector Panel 1994–98, Science and Engrg Advsy Ctee Br Cncl 1992–2005, Editorial Bd Construction Mgmnt and Economics 1991–94, Bd and Mgmnt Exec Scottish Inst for Enterprise 2000–05 (chair Mgmnt Exec 2003–05), Tayside and Central Scotland Transport Partnership (TACTRAN) 2006–10, Cncl Construction Industry Training Bd (CITB) 2014–, ICE Expert Mgmnt Panel 2014–, Scottish Advsy Ctee CITB 2015–; govr Duncan of Jordanstone Coll of Art 1990–92; chm: Educn Ctee Engrg Cncl Regnl Orgn Mgmnt Ctee (E Scotland) 1988–91, Scottish Int Resource Project Steering Gp 1993–95, Friends of St Paul's Cathedral 1993–95; dir: Dundee Repertory Theatre Ltd 1991–2006, CAB Dundee 2003–05; memb Cncl Nat Conf of Univ Profs 1989–93; CEng, FRSE, FICE, Hon FRIAS; *Publications* over 100 pubns in conf proceedings and academic jls; *Recreations* gardening, amateur dramatics; *Clubs* Rotary, Bonnetmakers of Dundee, Guildry of Dundee; *Style—* Prof Malcolm Horner; ✉ Westfield Cottage, 11 Westfield Place, Dundee DD1 4JU (☎ 01382 225933, fax 01382 229721); Division of Civil Engineering, The University, Dundee DD1 4HN (☎ 01382 344350, fax 01382 344816, telex 76293, e-mail r.m.w.horner@dundee.ac.uk)

HORNSBY, Guy Philip; s of Norman Dalton Hornsby (d 1971), and Yvonne Betty Hornsby (d 1997), of Twickenham, Middx; *b* 24 March 1958, London; *Educ* Emanuel Sch; *m* in The Netherlands 8 July 2006, Michael Clement Charles Gray, s of Robert Arnold Gray (d 2005), and Dolores Ameé Alexandra Gray; *Career* computer programmer and company liaison supervisor Head Office Honda (UK) Ltd 1978–79; BBC Radio London: joined 1979 as reporter and prodn asst on daily arts prog, variously asst prodr Robbie Vincent Telephone Prog, prodr Tony Blackburn Show, presenter/prodr London Today and London This Week, exec prodr Radio London Unemployment Festival of Music, prodr BBC Children in Need prog, prodr daily afternoon music prog; outside broadcast presenter Saturday Superstore BBC TV 1984, prodr Popular Music Unit BBC World Service 1984–85, continuity announcer TVS Southampton 1986–90; Southern Radio plc (formerly Ocean Sound plc): presenter breakfast show then prodr and presenter afternoon prog 1986–90, prog mangr Ocean Sound and South Coast Radio 1990–92, gp prog controller Southern Radio plc 1992–94; md Kiss 102 Manchester 1994–96, gp chief exec Kiss 102 Manchester and Kiss 105 Yorkshire 1996–97; dir: IT Computer Systems Ltd 1999–, Out UK 2000–, Out Europe 2000–; exec dir Riverside Studios and Riverside TV Studios Hammersmith 2006–; md Assembly Theatre 2006–, dir Showcatcher Ltd 2011–, dir London 8 Ltd 2012–16; International Radio Award for Sweet Soul Music series BBC World Service 1985 (prodr and writer); memb: BFI, Edinburgh Fringe Soc, Stonewall, Amnesty Int, Albert Kennedy Tst; *Recreations* web design, music, cinema, swimming; *Style—* Guy Hornsby; ✉ Schoolenaerlaan 2, 2034 KA, Haarlem, Amsterdam, The Netherlands (☎ 00 31 23 844 4738); 1928 Willow Wood Drive, Kissimmee, Florida 34746, USA (☎ 00 1 407 933 1928, e-mail guyhornsby@consultant.com, website www.guyhornsby.com)

HORNSBY, Timothy Richard; CBE (2008); s of Harker William Hornsby (d 1973), and Agnes Nora Phillips (d 1992); *b* 22 September 1940; *Educ* Bradfield Coll, ChCh Oxford (MA); *m* 1971, Charmian Rosemary, da of Frederick Cleland Newton (d 2001), of Weybridge, Surrey; 1 da (Gabrielle b 1975), 1 s (Adrian b 1977); *Career* Harkness fell 1961–63, res lectr ChCh Oxford 1964–65, HM Treasy 1971–73, various posts then dir ancient monuments historic bldgs and rural affrs DOE 1973–88, DG Nature Conservancy Cncl 1988–91; chief exec: Royal Borough of Kingston upon Thames 1991–95, National Lottery Charities Board 1995–2001; cmmr and chair National Lottery Cmmn 2001–08; chair Harkness Fellows Assoc 2002–; chair Horniman Museum 2004–14, chair Int Tree Fndn 2014–; tstee: Castle Howard Arboretum 2008–, Royal Botanical Gardens Kew 2008–14, Field Lane Charity 2014–, Bd Br Architectural Tst 2015–, King's Hosp Charity 2016–; memb Bd Audience Agency 2014–; *Recreations* conservation, skiing, opera, conversation; *Clubs* Athenaeum; *Style—* Timothy Hornsby, Esq, CBE; ✉ mobile 07785 376172, email thornsby@timothyhornsby.freeserve.co.uk

HORNYOLD-STRICKLAND, 8 Count Della Catena (Malta 1745); Henry Charles; s of Lt Cdr Thomas Henry Hornyold-Strickland, DSC, RN, 7 Count della Catena (d 1983), of Sizergh Castle, Kendal, Cumbria, and Angela Mary, *née* Engleheart (d 2015); *b* 15 December 1951; *Educ* Ampleforth, Exeter Coll Oxford (BA), INSEAD Fontainebleau (MBA); *m* 1979, Claudine Thérèse, da of Clovis Poumirau, of Hossegor, France; 2 s (Hugo b 1979, Thomas b 1985); *Heir* s, Hugo; *Career* engr Rolls Royce Ltd 1970–76, mgmnt conslt Arthur D Little Ltd 1977–84, ind mgmnt conslt 1984–; dir: Allied Newspapers Ltd (Malta) 1988–, Progress Press (Malta) 1988–, Allied Insurance Agency (Malta) 1991–2002, Logical Processes Ltd 1997–98, Oxford Creativity Ltd 2000–06, Media Maker Ltd (Malta) 2004–, Catena Solutions Ltd 2014–; Knight of Honour and Devotion SMOM 1977; *Publications* Defence Acquisition for the Twenty-first Century (contrib, 2015); *Clubs* IOD; *Style—* Henry Hornyold-Strickland, Esq (Count della Catena); ✉ Sizergh Castle, Kendal, Cumbria LA8 8AE (fax 07053 660408, mobile 07775 894650, e-mail hstrickland@uk2.net)

HOROVITZ, Joseph; s of Dr Bela Horovitz (d 1955), and Lotte Horovitz (d 2003); *b* 26 May 1926; *Educ* City of Oxford HS, New Coll Oxford (MA, BMus); *m* 16 Aug 1956, Anna Naomi, da of Frederic Moses Landau, of London; 2 da; *Career* WWII Army Educn Corps 1943–44; music dir Bristol Old Vic 1949–51, conductor Ballets Russes 1952, music staff Glyndebourne Opera 1956, prof of composition RCM 1961–2016, dir Performing Rights Soc 1969–96, pres Conseil International des Auteurs de Musique 1981–89; compositions incl: 12 ballets incl Alice in Wonderland, Ninotchka (opera), two one act operas, five string quartets, eleven concertos, works for orchestra, brass band, wind band and choirs incl Capt Noah and his Floating Zoo; Son et Lumière incl: St Paul's Cathedral, Canterbury Cathedral, Royal Pavilion Brighton, Chartwell, Bodiam Castle, English Harbour Antigua; numerous TV scores incl: Search for the Nile, Lillie, The Tempest, Twelfth Night, Agatha Christie Series, Dorothy L Sayers Series, Rumpole of the Bailey; memb: Royal Soc of Musicians 1968, Cncl Composers Guild of GB 1970–99; Cwlth Medal for Composition 1959, Ivor Novello Award 1976 and 1979, Nino Rota Prize Italy 2002, Cobbett Medal Worshipful Co of Musicians 2008; FRCM 1981; Gold Order of Merit of Vienna 1996, Cross of Honour for Science and Arts First Class Austria 2007; *Recreations* books; *Style—* Joseph Horovitz, Esq; ✉ The Royal College of Music, Prince Consort Road, London SW7

HOROWITZ, Anthony; OBE (2014); *b* 1955, Stanmore, Middx; *Educ* Rugby, Univ of York (BA); *m* Jill Green, *qv*; 2 s (Nicholas b 1989, Cassian b 1991); *Career* novelist, children's author and scriptwriter; early career as advtg copywriter with McCann Erickson; *Theatre* Dinner with Saddam, Mindgame; *Television* Foyle's War (ITV), Midsomer Murders (ITV), Murder in Mind (BBC), Agatha Christie's Poirot (ITV), Murder Most Horrid (BBC), Crime Traveller (BBC), Anna Lee (ITV), The Last Englishman (BBC), Robin of Sherwood (ITV), New Blood (BBC), Collision (ITV), Injustice (ITV); *Film* The Gathering, Just Ask For Diamond, Stormbreaker; *Awards* Red House Children's Book Award 2003 (for Skeleton Key), Lew Grade Audience Award 2003 (for Foyle's War); *Books* The Alex Rider series, Raven's Gate, The Killing Joke, Granny, The Switch, Groosham Grange, Return to Groosham Grange, Horowitz Horror, More Horowitz Horror, Myths and Legends, The Sinister Secret of Frederick K Bower, Misha, The Magician and the Mysterious Amulet, The Devil's Doorbell, The Night of The Scorpion, The Silver Citadel, The Day of the Dragon, Evil Star, Magpie Murders, Trigger Mortis, Moriarty, The House of Silk; *Recreations* scuba diving, cinema; *Style—* Anthony Horowitz, Esq, OBE; ✉ c/o United Agents Limited, 12–26 Lexington Street, London W1F 0LE (☎ 020 3214 0800, fax 020 3214 0801, website www.unitedagents.co.uk)

HORRIDGE, Chris P; s of Colin Horridge, of Lincoln, and Carol Ann, *née* Blain; *b* 2 June 1970, RAF Nocton Hall, Lincs; *Educ* Castle Hills Sch Gainsborough, Gainsborough Coll of FE, Tidworth Coll; *Career* RAF 1988–97; vocational training and qualifications in catering and hospitality (City & Guild qualifications incl 705, 706/1, 706/2, 707), vocational training in manufacturing business mgmnt; sr chef de partie Le Petit Blanc restaurant Oxford 1997–98, demi chef de partie to Sr Sous Chef Le Manoir aux Quat'Saisons Great Milton 1998–2003, Gordon Ramsay Holdings (Petrus, Gordon Ramsay at Royal Hospital Road, Marcus Wareing at The Savoy) 2003, private chef to Canadian entrepreneur 2003–05, head chef The Bath Priory 2005–09 (1 Michelin Star, Good Food Guide Top 40 2008, Conde Nast Traveller Gold List Award 2008), exec head chef Cliveden Country House Hotel 2009–10, chef/dir Fine Dining Acad 2010–; founding memb Nutrition Research Gp; *Recreations* flying historic aircraft, cycling TT; *Clubs* Arts; *Style—* Mr C Horridge

HORROCKS, (Barbara) Jane; da of John Horrocks, of Rossendale, Lancs, and Barbara, *née* Ashworth; *b* 18 January 1964; *Educ* Fearns Co Secdy Sch, Oldham Coll of Technol, RADA (Bronze medal); *Career* actress; *Theatre* RSC (joined 1985) incl: Hetty in The Dillon, Flo in Mary After the Queen, Phoebe in As You Like It; other roles incl: Fanny in Ask For The Moon (Hampstead) 1986, various parts in Road (Royal Court) 1987, Beatrice in A Colliers Friday Night (Greenwich) 1987, Sherry in Valued Friends (Hampstead) 1989, Teddy in The Debutante Ball (Hampstead) 1989, Sylvie in Our Own Kind (Bush) 1991, Little Voice in The Rise and Fall of Little Voice (RNT and Aldwych) 1992, Sally Bowles in Cabaret (Donmar) 1994, Lady Macbeth in Macbeth (Greenwich) 1995, Mrs Trevel in Sweet Panic (Duke of York's) 2003–04, Jane in Absurd Person Singular (Garrick Theatre) 2007–08, Shen Te and Shui Ta in The Good Soul of Szechuan (Young Vic) 2008, Lemon in Aunt Dan and Lemon (Royal Court), Annie in Annie Get Your Gun (Young Vic), Ella in East is East (Trafalgar Studios) 2014–15, If You Kiss Me, Kiss Me (Young Vic) 2016; *Television* BBC incl: Road 1987, Heartland 1988, Nona 1990, Alive and Kicking 1991, Came Out, It Rained, Went Back In Again 1991, Roots 1991, Absolutely Fabulous 1992–94, 2001–03 and 2011, Bad Girl 1992, Suffer the Little Children 1994, Nightlife (BBC Scotland) 1995, Henry IV (parts I and II) 1995, Mirrorball 2000, Linda Green 2002, The Street 2005, The Amazing Mrs Pritchard 2006, Gracie!, The Road to Coronation Street 2010, True Love 2012, Inside No. 9 (BBC 2) 2015; Channel 4 incl: Storyteller 1988, Self Catering (TV film) 1993, Never Mind the Horrocks 1996; other credits incl: Cabaret (Carlton) 1994, Some Kind of Life (Granada) 1995, Tales from the Crypt (HBO) 1996, Hunting Venus 1998, The Flint Street Nativity (ITV) 1998, Jericho (ITV) 2005, This is Jinsy (Sky Atlantic) 2011, Trollied (Sky One) 2011, The Cruise (Sky Arts) 2013; *Film* incl: The Dressmaker 1987, The Wolves of Willoughby Chase 1988, Witches 1988, Getting It Right 1988, Memphis Belle 1989, Life Is Sweet 1990, Deadly Advice 1993, Second Best 1993, Bring Me the Head of Mavis Davis 1996, Little Voice 1997, Born Romantic 2000, Chicken Run 2000, Feathers (short) 2002, Corpse Bride 2006, Sunshine on Leith 2012, Bubble in Ab Fab the Movie 2015; *Awards* LA Film Critics' Award and American Nat Soc of Film Critics' Award for Best Supporting Actress 1991 (for Life Is Sweet); Royal Television Soc Award for Best Actress and Banff Television Festival Special Jury Award (for Suffer the Little Children); *Recordings* The Further Adventures of Little Voice (2000), Swing When You're Winning by Robbie Williams (2001), If You Kiss Me, Kiss Me sessions (2016); *Style—* Ms Jane Horrocks

HORROCKS, Peter Leslie; s of (Arthur Edward) Leslie Horrocks (d 2005), of Beaconsfield, Bucks, and Phillis Margaret Chiene, *née* Bartholomew (d 2008); *b* 31 January 1955; *Educ* Winchester, Trinity Hall Cambridge (MA); *m* 15 Sept 1995, Catherine Alicia Brinsley, er da of Dr (Moryd) Brinsley Sheridan; 1 s (Edward Leslie Sheridan b 26 March 1997); *Career* called to the Bar Middle Temple 1977 and Lincoln's Inn 1987, in private practice 1978–; memb Cncl Royal Stuart Soc 1987–, pres Covent Garden Minuet Co 2004–10, chm Sherlock Holmes Soc of London 1999–2003; Freeman City of London 1982; FRAS 1984; *Recreations* travel, real tennis, cricket, Sherlock Holmes, opera, collecting books, dancing the minuet; *Clubs* MCC, Travellers, Royal Tennis Court, City Pickwick; *Style—* Peter Horrocks, Esq; ✉ 1 Garden Court, Temple, London EC4Y 9BJ (☎ 020 7797 7900, fax 020 7797 7929)

HORROX, Prof Alan; s of Stanley Horrox, and Gudrun Jonsdottir; *b* 3 January 1947; *Educ* St John's Sch Leatherhead, Christ's Coll Cambridge; *m* Viveka Britt Inger, da of Torsten Nyberg, of Föllinge, Sweden; 2 da (Anna Helga b 1981, Katarina b 1983); *Career* prodr-dir of children's progs BBC, educn progs, dramas and documentaries Thames TV (controller Children's and Educn Dept 1986–92), md Tetra Films 1992–, prof of film and media Univ of Hertfordshire 2006–; *Television* incl: Our People, Small World, Accidental Death of an Anarchist, A Foreign Body, Voices in the Dark, The Belle of Amherst, Rose, The Gemini Factor, Catherine, Ingmar Bergman-The Magic Lantern, The Thief, Young Charlie Chaplin, The Green Eyed Monster, Brief Lives, Rosie The Great, Somewhere to Run, Handle with Care, Spatz, Lorna Doone, Forget About Me, Long Way Home, The Strangers, Sea Dragon, A Small Dance, Time Riders, Pirate Prince, Romeo and Juliet, Tomorrow People, The Merchant of Venice, Delta Wave, Treasure Seekers, Canterville Ghost, The Gift, Bill's New Frock, Magic with Everything, What Katy Did; *Film* London Film Festival Screenings: Forget About Me 1990, A Small Dance 1991, Under The Sun 1992, Faith 1996; *Awards* Int Emmy 1987, Special Jury Award at the San Francisco Film Festival 1988, Valladolid Int Film Festival Award 1988, Special Prize for Fiction Prix Europa 1988, 1989 and 1991, Prime Time Emmy Nomination 1989, BAFTA Nominations 1989, 1990, 1991, 1995, 1996, 1997 and 1998 Chicago Int Film Festival Special Live Action Award 1990, RTS Enid Love Award Nomination 1990 and 1991, Writers' Guild Award B&B 1992 (nomination 1995), Japan Prize 1996, runner up BFI Children's Award 1995, Special FX Monitor Award 1996, RTS Award 1996, 1997 and 1998, Houston Gold Award 1997 and 1998, Best TV Movie Monte Carlo 1999; *Style—* Prof Alan Horrox; ✉ Tetra Films Ltd, 24 Stormont Road, London N6 4NP

HORSHAM, Bishop of 2009–; Rt Rev Mark Crispin Rake Sowerby; s of Geoffrey Nigel Rake Sowerby, of Bedale, N Yorks, and Hilary Gwyneth, *née* Evans; *b* 28 October 1963, Ripon, Yorks; *Educ* Barnard Castle Sch, St Aidan's and St John Fisher's VI Form Harrogate, KCL (BD), Univ of Lancaster (MA), Coll of the Resurrection Mirfield; *m* 1 Aug 1989, Ruth Mary, *née* Jones; 3 da (Bethan Ruth b 10 Sept 1990, Philippa Sandry b 9 Aug 1992, Anna Daisy b 3 June 1996); *Career* curate Knaresborough 1987–90, curate St Cuthbert Darwen with St Stephen Tockholes 1990–92, vicar Accrington St Mary Magdalen 1992–97, vocations offr and selection sec Archbishop's Cncl 1997–2001, rector St Wilfrid Harrogate 2001–07, asst bishop of Guildford 2011, asst bishop of Oxford 2011; KCL Jelf Medal 1985; AKC; *Recreations* theatre, fishing; *Style—* The Rt Rev the Bishop of Horsham; ✉ Bishop's House, 21 Guildford Road, Horsham, West Sussex RH12 1LU (☎ 01403 211139, e-mail bishop.horsham@chichester.anglican.org, website www.chichester.anglican.org)

HORSLEY, Adrian Mark; JP, DL (E Riding of Yorks 2013); s of (Ian) Mark Horsley (d 1999) and Patricia Horsley, JP, *née* Farrell (d 1994); *b* 12 April 1949; *Educ* Ampleforth, Leicester Sch of Architecture (DipArch); *m* 28 Sept 1974, Louise Jane, da of Peter Bentham Oughtred, JP (d 1999); 2 s (Adam b 1979, Luke b 1982); *Career* architect; Gelder & Kitchen: joined 1974, ptnr 1978–2004, managing ptnr 1994–2004, conslt 2004–09; Adrian Horsley Architect Expert Witness 2009–14; former pres N Humberside Soc of Architects, former chm Yorks Region RIBA; memb: Magistrates' Assoc of E Yorks, Hull Civic Soc, Georgian Soc of E Yorks; chm of tstees Hull and E Riding Charitable Tst; tstee: Lees Rest Homes, Hearing Dogs for Deaf People, Hull Street Angels Trinity; High Sheriff E

Riding of Yorks 2010–11; Govr Co of Merchant Adventurers of the City of York 2004 (joined 1978); RIBA 1976; *Recreations* shooting, tennis, croquet, gardening; *Style—* Adrian M Horsley, Esq, JP, DL; ✉ Wheels, 42 Station Road, South Cave, East Yorkshire HU15 2AA (☎ 01430 422562, mobile 07710 919873, e-mail adrian.horsley@architectexpert.co.uk)

HORSLEY, William Frederick Moreton; s of Harold Cecil Moreton Horsley (d 1969), and Lady Angela Horsley, *née* Leslie Courtenay (d 2008); *b* 28 January 1949, Macau; *Educ* St Edward's Sch Oxford, Pembroke Coll Oxford (exhibitioner, MA); *m* 1979, Noriko, *née* Makuuchi; *Career* prodr BBC Far Eastern Serv External Servs 1971–74, BBC secondee to Radio Japan (Japan Broadcasting Co Tokyo 1974–76, prodr Special Current Affairs unit BBC and The World Tonight 1977–80, prodr and news presenter Newsnight BBC TV 1981, reporter The World Tonight and BBC Radio News 1981–83, Tokyo corr and bureau chief BBC Tokyo 1983–90, corr for radio and TV BBC Bonn 1991–97, BBC European Affairs corr 1997–2007; chm Foreign Press 1984–88; chm Br branch AEJ 2002–, media freedom rep of Int AEJ 2007–, int dir Sheffield Univ Centre for Freedom of the Media (ptnr orgn of UNESCO for implementation of UN action plan on safety of Journalists and the issue of impunity) 2012–; memb: Advsy Bd Index on Censorship 2008–, Int News Safety Inst 2014–, Ctee on Safety of Journalists and Protection of Journalism Cncl of Europe 2014–; visiting fell City Univ Centre for Law, Justice and Journalism 2011–; Assoc of Euro Journalists Euro Journalism Prize 2000; *Publications* Newspapers and Democracy (contrib, 1980), Nippon – New Superpower (with Roger Buckley, 1990), Goodbye to Freedom? A Survey of Media Freedom in Europe (2007 and 2008), OSCE Safety of Journalists Guidebook (edns 2012 and 2014); expert reports for Parly Assembly Cncl of Europe: The State of Media Freedom in Europe (2009 and 2012), The Protection of Media Freedom in Europe (2014); author of numerous articles on Japan, Europe, int affairs and media in The Listener, The World Today, International Herald Tribune, BBC News Online, BBC College of Journalism, Open Democracy, Standpoint, euractiv and other jls and websites; *Clubs* Frontline, Roehampton; *Style—* William Horsley, Esq; ✉ Flat 1, 30 Bina Gardens, London SW5 0LA (☎ 07711 912499, e-mail wh@williamhorsley.com, websites www.aej-uk.org, www.cfom.org.uk and www.williamhorsley.com)

HORSMAN, Michael John; s of late Graham Joseph Vivian Horsman, of Dollar, Scotland, and late Ruth, *née* Guest; *b* 3 March 1949; *Educ* Dollar Acad, Univ of Glasgow (MA), Balliol Coll Oxford (Snell exhibitioner, Brackenbury scholar); *m* 1977, Anne Margaret, da of late John Marley; 3 s (Graham John b 10 Dec 1979, Ian Michael b 17 Feb 1982, William David b 27 April 1986); *Career* Dept of Employment: joined 1974, sec to Chm of Manpower Services Cmmn 1978–79, area mangr 1982–84, dir Professional and Exec Recruitment 1984–85, head of MSC Fin Policy and resource controller 1985–87, head of Employment Serv Ops Branch 1987–89, regnl dir Employment Serv London and SE 1989–92, dir Office of Manpower Economics 1992–2003; ind memb House of Commons Sr Pay Panel 2003–16; special prof Nottingham Univ Business Sch 2003–06; *Recreations* reading, historical research, cycling; *Clubs* Cyclist Touring; *Style—* Prof Michael Horsman; ✉ e-mail professormhorsman@hotmail.com

HORTA-OSÓRIO, António; *b* 28 January 1964, Lisbon; *Educ* Colegio do São João de Brito Lisbon, Universidade Católica Portuguesa (Licenciatura em Management and doctoral degree in Business Admin), INSEAD (MBA, Henry Ford II Prize), Harvard Business Sch (AMP); *Career* asst prof in finance and econometrics Universidade Católica Portuguesa 1985–90 (guest prof MBA in Financial Strategic Planning 1992–96), vice-pres and head Capital Markets Citibank Portugal 1987–90, Corp Finance Goldman Sachs Int NY and London 1991–93; Banco Santander SA 1993–2010: ceo Banco Santander de Negócios Portugal 1993–2000, ceo Banco Santander Brasil 1997–2000, ceo Santander Totta Portugal 2000–06 (exec vice pres and memb Mgmnt Ctee 2000–10, chm 2006–10), ceo Santander UK plc 2006–10; ceo Lloyds Banking Gp 2011–; non-exec dir: Bank of England 2009–11, Champalimaud Fndn 2011–, Sociedade Francisco Manuel dos Santos BV 2011, Exor 2015–; memb Governing Body: Universidade Católica Portuguesa 2007–10, London Business Sch 2010–15; memb Advsy Cncl: Saïd Business Sch Univ of Oxford 2008–12, Judge Business Sch Univ of Cambridge 2009–11, CityUK 2010–12; chm Wallace Collection 2015; Hon Dr: Univ of Edinburgh 2011, Univ of Bath 2012, Univ of Warwick 2015; Cdr Order of Civil Merit Spain 1998, Order of Southern Cross Brazil 1998, Encomienda de Numero Orden de Isabella Católica Spain 2009, Order of Merit Grã-Cruz Portugal 2014; *Recreations* tennis, scuba diving, skiing; *Clubs* Queen's, Clube VII (Lisbon); *Style—* Mr António Horta-Osório; ✉ Lloyds TSB Group plc, 25 Gresham Street, London EC2V 7HN

HORTON, Chantelle; *Career* asst ed then dep ed Bliss until 2007; More!: dep ed 2007–09, ed 2009–13; *Style—* Ms Chantelle Horton

HORTON, Geoffrey; s of Leonard Horton (d 1987), and Joan, *née* Bissell (d 1997); *b* 23 July 1951; *Educ* Bristol GS, Exeter Coll Oxford (MA), UCL (MSc); *m* 1991, Dianne Alexandra (Alex), da of Dr Eric Craker; 2 da (Camilla b 1993, Beatrice b 1996); *Career* econ asst HM Treasy 1974–76, lectr in econ UC Swansea 1976–78, econ advsr HM Treasy 1978–85, chief economist DRI (Europe) Ltd 1985–88, sr econ advsr Dept of Energy 1988–90, pt/t sr conslt Nat Econ Research Assocs 1990–92, pt/t dir of regulation and business affairs Office of Electricity Regulation (GB) 1990–95, pt/t DG (electricity supply) Office of Electricity Regulation (NI) 1992–95, dir of consumer affairs OFT 1995–98, dir Horton 4 Consulting 1998–; memb: Panel of Experts for the Reform of the Water Serv in NI 2003–06, Climate and Energy Security Panel Dept of Energy and Climate Change 2007–10; Award for Gallantry Br Humane Soc 2005; *Publications* working papers: Modelling the World Economy (1984), The Economic Effects of Lower Oil Prices (with Stephen Powell, 1984); Links between Environmental and International Trade Policies: A Study on the Implications of Greenhouse Gas Emissions Control Policies for Trade (with James Rollo and Alistair Ulph, 1992), British Electricity Privatisation: The Customer's Standpoint (proceedings of BIEE conf, 1995); contrib various reports for EC, articles in economic jls and seminar papers; *Recreations* sailing, reading, cooking; *Style—* Geoffrey Horton; ✉ 84 Berglen Court, 7 Branch Road, London E14 7JX (☎ 020 7001 1677, e-mail geoff@horton4.co.uk)

HORTON, Matthew Bethell; QC; s of Albert Leslie Horton, of Tunbridge Wells, Kent, and Gladys Rose Ellen, *née* Harding; *b* 23 September 1946; *Educ* Sevenoaks, Trinity Hall Cambridge (MA, LLM); *m* 1, 22 May 1972 (m dis 1983), Liliane, da of Henri Boleslawski, of Nice, France; 1 s (Jerome b 1971), 1 da (Vanessa b 1973); m 2, 10 Oct 1999, Jane Louise Pendower, da of John Pendower FRCS, of Purley, Surrey; 1 da (Ursula b 1998), 1 s (Jonas b 2001); *Career* called to the Bar Middle Temple 1969; in private practice specialising in: commercial property law, planning, environmental and local govt law, admin law, Parly law; *Recreations* tennis, skiing, windsurfing; *Style—* Matthew Horton, Esq, QC; ✉ 39 Essex Street, London WC2R 3AT (☎ 020 7832 1111, fax 020 7353 3978, e-mail clerks@39essex.com, DX 298 London/Chancery Lane)

HORTON, (John) Philip (Phil); s of Frank Horton (d 1982), and Elsie, *née* Gill; *b* 19 January 1956; *Educ* Bournemouth Boys' Sch, Univ of Southampton (BA); *m* 1997; *Career* various positions in sales and mktg Ford of Britain 1977–85, Mktg Dept Ford of Europe 1985–90, dir of communications (i/c advtg, promotions and PR activities) Renault UK 1990–97, mktg dir BMW (GB) 1997–; *Recreations* motorcycling, skiing, tennis; *Style—* Phil Horton; ✉ BMW (GB) Ltd, Ellesfield Avenue, Bracknell, Berkshire RG12 8TA (☎ 01344 426565)

HORTON, (Gavin) Tobias Alexander Winterbottom (Toby); s of late Alistair Winterbottom (bro of late Lord Winterbottom), and Maria Kersti; *b* 18 February 1947; *Educ* Westminster, ChCh Oxford (MA); *m* 1977, Hon Fiona Catherine Peake, da of 2 Viscount Ingleby; 2 da (Alice Emily Rose (Mrs Robert Procopé) b 1978, Violet Constance Lily b 1980), 2 s (George William Arthur b 1983, Thomas Henry Ralph b 1985); *Career* md Sound Broadcasting (Teesside) 1979–83, dir and head Corp Fin Dept Minster Trust Ltd 1984–90; md Heritage Media Ltd 1993–2014, dir Divine Art Ltd 2008–, dir Ingleby Water Co Ltd 2014–; Parly candidate (Cons) Sedgefield 1983, Parly agent (Cons) Bethnal Green and Stepney 1987, Euro Parly candidate (Cons) Yorkshire SW 1989, Parly candidate (Cons) Rother Valley 1992, chm Richmond Cons Assoc 1996–99; Parly candidate (UKIP): Sedgefield 2007, Thirsk & Malton 2010 and 2015; *Books* Going to Market: New Policy for the Farming Industry (1985), Programme for Reform: a New Agenda for Broadcasting (1987); *Recreations* radio, country pursuits; *Clubs* Royal Over-Seas League, English Speaking Union; *Style—* Toby Horton, Esq; ✉ Snilesworth Lodge, Osmotherley, Northallerton, North Yorkshire DL6 3QD (☎ 01609 883296); Flat 1, 61 Onslow Square, London SW7 3LS (☎ 020 7589 0609)

HORWICH, Prof Alan; s of late William Horwich, and late Audrey Miriam Lindley, *née* Rigby; *b* 1 June 1948; *Educ* William Hulme's GS, UCL, UCH Med Sch (MB BS, PhD); *m* 1981, Pauline Amanda, da of A R Barnes; 2 s (Oscar Samuel b 18 May 1985, Barnaby James b 24 March 1987), 1 da (Florence Harriet b 27 April 1989); *Career* house physician/surgn UCH 1972–73, house physician Royal N Hosp London 1973, SHO Hammersmith Hosp 1974, fell in oncology Harvard Med Sch Boston 1974–75, res fell ICRF 1975–78, registrar The Royal Marsden Hosp 1979–81, lectr Inst of Cancer Res 1981–83, MRC sr grade scientist MRC Radiobiology Unit 1983–84; Inst of Cancer Res and Royal Marsden Hosp: sr lectr 1984–86, prof of radiotherapy 1986– (head of section 1992–2012), dean 1993–97 and 2005–12, dir of clinical res 1994–2005; memb European Soc for Medical Oncology Educational Ctee 2013–; Warden RCR 1998–2002; memb RSM; FRCR (MRCR), FRCP (MRCP); *Books* Testicular Cancer (1991, 2 edn, 1996), Combined Radiotherapy and Chemotherapy in Clinical Oncology (1992), Oncology: A Multidisciplinary Textbook (1995), Systemic Treatment of Prostate Cancer (2010); *Recreations* golf, opera; *Style—* Prof Alan Horwich; ✉ The Royal Marsden Hospital, Downs Road, Sutton, Surrey SM2 5PT (☎ 020 8661 3274, fax 020 8643 8809, e-mail alan.horwich@icr.ac.uk)

HORWOOD, Martin; s of Don Horwood, ISO, and Nina, *née* Edge; *b* 12 October 1962, Cheltenham, Glos; *Educ* Cheltenham Coll, The Queen's Coll Oxford (BA); *m* 1995, Dr Shona Arora; 2 c; *Career* joined Cheltenham Young Liberals 1979; account exec Ted Bates Advtg 1985–86, dir of devpt Br Humanist Assoc 1986–88, creative co-ordinator Help the Aged 1988–90, donor mktg mangr Oxfam 1990–95, dir of communications and fundraising Oxfam India 1995–96, dir of fundraising Alzheimer's Soc 1996–2001, sr conslt then head of consultancy Target Direct 2001–05; MP (Lib Dem) Cheltenham 2005–15 (Parly candidate (Lib Dem): Oxford E 1992, Cities of London and Westminster 2001); Lib Dem spokesperson for: charities bill 2005–06, environment 2006–10; memb Select Ctee on Communities and Local Govt (formerly ODPM) 2005–07, memb Environmental Audit Ctee 2007–10, sec All Pty Corp Responsibility Gp 2005–, chm All Pty Gp for Tribal Peoples 2007–, co-chair Lib Dem Parly Ctee on Transport 2010–11, co-chair Lib Dem Parly Ctee on Int Affrs 2011–15; cncllr Vale of White Horse DC 1991–95 (dep ldr Lib Dem Gp 1993–95) memb: Global Justice Now (formerly World Devpt Movement) 1988–, Alzheimer's Soc 1996–, Amnesty Int 1999–; memb Inst of Fundraising 1996; *Style—* Martin Horwood; ✉ Liberal Democrat Office, 16 Hewlett Road, Cheltenham, Gloucestershire GL52 6AA (e-mail martin@martinhorwood.net, website www.martinhorwood.net)

HORWOOD, Air Cdre Raymond James; CBE (2001, OBE 1991); *b* 1949; *Educ* Abbs Cross Sch Hornchurch, trg RAF Gaydon/Stradishall, RAF Staff Coll Bracknell, Canadian Nat Defence Coll; *m* 1972, Gwyneth Mary Bridge; 3 c (Andrew, Emma, Anna); *Career* Navigator 6 Sqdn (Phantom) RAF Coningsby 1970–73, 17 and 31 Sqdn (Phantom) RAF Brüggen Germany 1973–76, instr Navigation Sch RAF Finningley 1976–79, 16 Strike/Attack Sqdn (Buccaneer) RAF Laarbruch Germany 1979–84, mgmnt Offensive Weapons MOD 1984–85, HQ STC 1985–87, OC Ops Wing RAF Marham 1987–90, Wing Cdr Strike/Attack Gp Upavon 1990–92, Head of Ops Muharraq Bahrain (Gulf War), Air Warfare Centre 1993–96, Cdr Br Forces Riyadh Saudi Arabia 1994, Detachment Cdr Jaguar/Harrier Ops Gioia Del Colle S Italy 1997, Air Cdr and Jt Force Cdr UK tri-service evacuation of Br Nationals Albania, Station Cdr RAF Waddington 1998, Cmdt Air Warfare Centre/Defence EW Centre 1998–2000, Dep Force Cdr/COS NATO Airborne Early Warning and Control Force 2000–04; chief exec Nat Fedn of Roofing Contractors and Competent Roofers 2004–15; dep-chm Construction Products Assoc 2013–16, non-exec dir Langley Gp 2016–; Liveryman Worshipful Co of Tylers and Bricklayers; QCVSA 1973; FRAeS 1998; Order of Bahrain 1991; *Recreations* golf; *Clubs* RAF; *Style—* Air Commodore Raymond Horwood, CBE, FRAeS; ✉ Langley House, Lamport Drive, Heartlands Business Park, Daventry NN11 8YH

HORWOOD-SMART, Rosamund; QC (1996); da of John Horwood-Smart (d 1997), of Cheveley, Cambs, and Sylvia, *née* Nutt (d 2015); *b* 21 September 1951; *Educ* Felixstowe Coll, Cambridgeshire HS for Girls, Inns of Court Sch of Law; *m* 1, 16 July 1983 (m dis 1994), Richard Clive Blackford; 1 s (Frederick John b 3 Sept 1986), 1 da (Eleanor Kate b 30 Aug 1989); m 2, 22 Feb 1996, Richard Oliver Bernays, *qv*; *Career* called to the Bar Inner Temple 1974 (bencher 1998), recorder 1995–; memb: S Eastern Circuit, Criminal Bar Assoc; vice-pres Int Students House, patron Prisoner of Conscience Appeal Fund; tstee: Temple Music Fndn 2006–, Handel House Tst 2008–, Longborough Festival Opera 2014–; patron New English Ballet Theatre 2010–; *Recreations* music, gardening, theatre; *Clubs* Ivy; *Style—* Miss Rosamund Horwood-Smart, QC; ✉ 18 Red Lion Court, London EC4A 3EB (e-mail rosamund@bernays.net)

HOSFORD, David Jeremy; s of Desmond James Hosford, of Belfast, and Heather, *née* Wallace; *b* 21 March 1969, Londonderry; *Educ* Royal Belfast Academical Instn, Univ of Warwick (LLB), Coll of Law Chester; *m* 8 Sept 2001, Sarah Elizabeth, *née* Hallam; 2 da (Elizabeth Laura b 17 Oct 2002, Chloe Imogen b 1 Aug 2004); *Career* slr; Burges Salmon 1993–2001, Pitmans 2001–; memb: Assoc of Pension Lawyers, Ind Tstee Gp; assoc Pensions Mgmnt Inst; *Recreations* windsurfing, walking; *Style—* David Hosford, Esq; ✉ Pitmans, 47 Castle Street, Reading RG1 7SR (☎ 0118 957 0393, fax 0118 957 0372, e-mail dhosford@pitmans.com)

HOSFORD-TANNER, (Joseph) Michael; s of late Dr Hubert Hosford-Tanner, of London, and Betty, *née* Bryce; *b* 8 August 1951; *Educ* Midleton Coll, Trinity Coll Dublin (BA, LLB); *Career* called to the Bar Inner Temple 1974; legal assessor: Farriers Registration Cncl 1985–, Nursing and Midwifery Cncl Panel 2003–, Gen Dental Cncl 2010–, Inst of Financial Accountants 2013–; *Recreations* horses, cricket, motorcycles; *Clubs* Chelsea Arts, Kildare Street and Univ; *Style—* Michael Hosford-Tanner, Esq; ✉ Queen Elizabeth Building, Temple, London EC4Y 9BS (☎ 020 7797 7837, fax 020 7353 5422)

HOSIE, Stewart; MP; *b* 1963, Dundee; *Educ* Carnoustie HS, Bell Street Tech Coll; *Career* former IT conslt Scottish Telecom; SNP: nat sec 1999–2003, orgn convener 2003–05; MP (SNP) Dundee E 2005– (Parly candidate (SNP) Dundee E 2001); *Style—* Stewart Hosie, Esq, MP; ✉ House of Commons, London SW1A 0AA

HOSKING, Prof Geoffrey Alan; OBE (2015); s of late Stuart William Steggall Hosking, and late Jean Ross *née* Smillie; *b* 28 April 1942; *Educ* Maidstone GS, King's Coll Cambridge (BA), Moscow State Univ, St Antony's Coll Oxford, Univ of Cambridge (MA, PhD); *m* 19 Dec 1970, Anne Lloyd Hirst; 2 da (Katya b 1974, Janet b 1978); *Career* Univ of Essex:

H

lectr Dept of Govt 1966–71, lectr Dept of History 1972–76, reader Dept of History 1976–80 and 1981–84; SSEES Univ of London: prof of Russian history 1984–99 and 2004–07, dep dir 1996–98, Leverhulme personal research prof 1999–2004, emeritus prof 2007–; visiting prof: Dept of Political Science Univ of Wisconsin 1971–72, Slavisches Inst Univ of Cologne 1980–81; Reith lectr BBC 1988, memb jury Booker Prize for Russian Fiction 1993; memb: Cncl of Writers and Scholars Int 1985–2007, Cncl Moscow Sch of Political Studies 1992–2000, Br Univs Assoc for Soviet and E Euro Studies, Royal Inst for Int Affrs, Exec Ctee Britain-Russia Centre 1992–2000, Acad Cncl Museum of Contemporary History Moscow, Inst for Advanced Study Princeton Univ 2006–07, Public Policy Ctee Br Acad 2009–12, Int Engagement Ctee Br Acad 2011–14; memb Editorial Bd: Nations and Nationalism, Ab Imperio, Rossiiskaia Istoriia; Hon Doctorate Russian Acad of Scis 2000; FBA 1993, FRHistS 1995; *Books* The Russian Constitutional Experiment: Government & Duma 1907–14 (1973), Beyond Socialist Realism: Soviet Fiction since Ivan Denisovich (1980), A History of The Soviet Union (1985, 3 edn 1992, Los Angeles Times History Book Prize 1986), The Awakening of The Soviet Union (1990, 2 edn 1991), The Road to Post-Communism: independent political movements in the Soviet Union 1985–91 (with J Aves and P Duncan, 1992), Russia: People and Empire 1552–1917 (1997), Myths & Nationhood (ed with G Schöpflin, 1998), Russian Nationalism Past and Present (ed with R Service, 1998), Reinterpreting Russia (ed with R Service, 1999), Russia and the Russians: A History (2001, American Independent Publishers' History Book Prize 2002, 2 edn 2012), Rulers and Victims: The Russians in the Soviet Union (2006, Alexander Nove Prize 2008), Trust: Money, Markets and Society (2010), Very Short Introduction to Russian History (2012), Trust: a History (2014); *Recreations* walking, music, chess; *Style—* Prof Geoffrey Hosking, FBA, FRHistS, OBE; ✉ Flat 15 Julian Court, 150 Camden Road, London NW1 9HU (e-mail geoffreyhosking@mac.com); School of Slavonic & East European Studies, University College London, Gower Street, London WC1E 6BT

HOSKING, Patrick Anthony James; s of Roger Michael Hosking, and Mollie June, *née* Allen; *b* 8 February 1960; *Educ* Rugby, Pembroke Coll Cambridge; *m* Amanda Clare, *née* Lindsay; *Career* asst ed Inst for Int Research 1981–83, newsletter ed Stonehart Publications 1983–86, business reporter then banking corr The Independent 1986–90; business corr: The Age Melbourne 1990–91, The Independent 1991–93; The Independent on Sunday: sr business writer 1993–94, dep City ed then City ed 1994–96; dep business ed The Age Australia 1996–97, City Office Evening Standard 1997–2000, City head Express Newspapers and City ed Daily Express 2000–01, columnist Investors Chronicle 2002–04, columnist New Statesman 2002–05, dep City ed Evening Standard 2002–04 (freelance contrib 2001–02), investment ed then banking and finance ed then financial ed The Times 2004–; tstee News Int Pension Plan 2006–10; *Style—* Patrick Hosking, Esq; ☎ 020 7782 5040, e-mail patrick.hosking@thetimes.co.uk

HOSKING, Sophie; MBE (2013); *b* 25 January 1986, Edinburgh; *Educ* Kingston GS, Durham Univ; *Career* rower; achievements incl: Bronze medal (lightweight quad sculls) World Championships 2006, Silver medal (lightweight quad sculls) World Championships 2007, Bronze medal (lightweight double sculls) World Championships 2009 and 2011, Gold medal (lightweight double sculls) Olympic Games 2012; *Clubs* London Rowing; *Style—* Ms Sophie Hosking, MBE

HOSKINS, Prof Sir Brian John; kt (2007), CBE (1998); s of George Frederick Hoskins (d 1979), and Kathleen Matilda Louise, *née* Rattue; *b* 17 May 1945; *Educ* Bristol GS, Trinity Hall Cambridge (MA, PhD); *m* 25 May 1968, Jacqueline, *née* Holmes; 2 da (Brooke b 22 Sept 1972, Bryony b 7 Oct 1974); *Career* prof of meteorology Univ of Reading 1981– (reader in atmospheric modelling 1976–81, head of dept 1990–96), dir Grantham Inst for Climate Change Imperial Coll London 2008–14 (chair 2014–); Rothschild visiting prof Isaac Newton Math Inst Cambridge 1996, Royal Soc research prof 2001–10; special advsr to Sec of State for Tport 1989–90; memb Cncl NERC 1988–94, pres Int Assoc for Meteorology and Atmospheric Physics 1991–95; Starr Meml lectr MIT 1989, Br Geological Survey distinguished lectr 1992, Haurwitz lectr American Meteorological Soc 1995, Welsh lectr Univ of Toronto 2006; Royal Meteorological Soc: L F Richardson prize 1972, Buchan prize 1976, Symons Meml lecture 1982, pres 1998–2000, hon fell 2007; memb Royal Commission for Environmental Pollution 1998–2005; vice-chm Jt Scientific Ctee Climate Res Programme, memb UK Ctee on Climate Change 2008–; non-exec dir Met Office 2004–13; memb Cncl Royal Soc 1999–2001; Charles Chree Silver medal Inst of Physics 1987, Carl-Gustaf Rossby Res medal American Meteorological Soc 1988, Geophysical Soc Bjerknes prize 1997, Symons medal RMS 2007, Buys Ballot Medal Royal Netherlands Acad for Arts and Sciences 2014, Gold Medal Int Union of Geology and Geophysics 2015; hon prof Chinese Acad of Sciences 1998, hon fell Trinity Hall 2011; Hon DSc Univ of Bristol 2008, Hon DSc UEA 2009; foreign assoc US Nat Acad of Sciences 2002, foreign memb Chinese Acad of Sciences 2002, fell American Assoc for Advancement of Science 2012, hon fell American Meteor Soc 2014; FRMetS 1970, FRS 1988, fell Academia Europaea 1990, Hon FRMetS 2001, FCGI 2011, FEI 2012; *Books* Large-Scale Dynamical Processes in the Atmosphere (1982), Fluid Dynamics of the Mid-Latitude Atmosphere (2014), author of 180 papers in learned jls; *Recreations* singing, gardening; *Style—* Prof Sir Brian Hoskins, CBE, FRS; ✉ Grantham Institute for Climate Change, Imperial College London SW7 2AZ (☎ 020 7594 9666, fax 020 7594 9668, e-mail b.hoskins@imperial.ac.uk)

HOSSAIN, Ajmalul; QC (1998); s of Asrarul Hossain, Barrister and Sr Advocate Supreme Ct of Bangladesh (d 2002), and Rabia *née* Ahmed (d 1992); *b* 18 October 1950, Dhaka, Bangladesh; *Educ* King's Coll London (LLB, LLM); *m* Nasreen, da of Prof M U Ahmed (decd); 2 c (Syed Ahrarul b 8 June 1979, Syed Afsar b 14 Nov 1981); *Career* called to the Bar Lincoln's Inn 1976 (Buchanan Prize); bencher Hon Soc of Lincoln's Inn; Supreme Ct of Bangladesh: High Ct Div 1977, Appellate Div 1986, Senior Advocate 1998; pt/t chm Employment Tbnls 1995–2005; memb: SE Circuit, Chancery Bar Assoc, Supreme Ct Bar Assoc Bangladesh, Int C of C Int Ct of Arbitration 2006–09, Int C of C Cmmn on Arbitration 2010–; memb Int Cricket Cncl Code of Conduct Cmmn 2006–15; fell Soc of Advanced Legal Studies, FCIArb 1994; *Recreations* travel, bridge; *Style—* Ajmalul Hossain, Esq, QC; ✉ Selborne Chambers, 10 Essex Street, London WC2R 3AA (☎ 020 7420 9500, fax 020 7420 9555)

HOSTOMBE, Roger Eric; s of late Eric Rudolf Hostombe, of Sheffield, and late Irene, *née* Baxter; *b* 22 December 1942; *Educ* Sedbergh; *m* 20 Sept 1975, Susan Mary, da of late Frank Ian Cobb, of Sheffield; 5 da (Clare b 1976, Natalie b 1979, Annabel b 1982, Lucinda b 1982, Sophie b 1989); *Career* CA 1968; Hostombe Group Ltd: exec chm 1975–2013, non-exec chm 2013; underwriter Lloyd's 1975–; regnl cncllr CBI Yorkshire and Humberside branch 1981–87; *Recreations* tennis, skiing, gardening; *Style—* Roger E Hostombe, Esq; ✉ Fullwood Hall, Sheffield S10 4PA (☎ 0114 230 2148); Hostombe Group Ltd (e-mail roger.hostombe@hostombe.co.uk)

HOTUNG, Eric Edward; CBE (2001); s of Edward Sai Kim Hotung (d 1957), and Mordia Alice, *née* O'Shea (d 1992); gs of Sir Robert Hotung; *b* 8 June 1926; dual Anglo-Chinese nationality; *Educ* St Francis Xavier Coll Shanghai, Georgetown Univ Washington DC (BSS), NY Inst of Finance NYC; *m* 17 Jan 1959, Patricia Anne, da of Michael Shea (d 1938); 4 s (Michael Eric b 1960, Robert Eric 1961, Eric Shea-kim b 1963, Sean Eric b 1965), 3 da (Mara Tegwen b 1967, Gabrielle Marie b 1971, Sheridan Patricia b 1972); *Career* security analyst Henry Hentz & Co NY 1951, admin asst to dir Pacific Area Foreign Distributors Div General Motors 1953–58, dir Hong Kong & Kowloon Entertainment Co 1958, chm Hotung Int Ltd 1960, fndr chm Hong Kong Devpt Ltd and Cosmopolitan Properties & Securities Ltd 1970–, chm Hotung Int Devpt; memb Hong Kong Stock Exchange and Hong Kong Gold and Silver Exchange 1958; special advsr on Chinese affrs Centre for Strategic and Int Studies Washington DC 1975, dir US Nat Ctee on US-China Relations 1986, US Senate-China Trade Caucus 'In the decade ahead' 1987, econ and fin advsr to Tianjin Govt of China 1990, fin advsr Municipal Govt of Xuzhou 1999, advsr to Wai Hai Operation Res Museum 1999, special econ and fin advsr to the Nat Cncl of Timorese Resistance East Timor 1999, memb Advsy Cncl Bd of Fundacao Luso-Americana Lisboa 2000, sr advsr Korea Int C of C 2009; fndr Hotung Inst; fndr/sponsor numerous philanthropical, charitable and other projects incl: Convent of Santa Rosa de Lima Macáu 1962, Low Cost Home Ownership and Financing Schemes Hong Kong 1964–93, Eric Hotung Tst Fund for Secdy Educn 1965, initial funding for restoration of Castle Mailberg and Church of St John the Baptist 1974, radio stations for marginados (underprivileged youth) Costa Rica 1975, Georgetown Univ Trauma Team for Vietnamese refugees in Cambodia and other projects 1978, Intercultural Centre Georgetown Univ (jt sponsor with US Govt) 1980, Brathay Expdn and Operation Drake 1980, visit of Cardinal Sin of the Philippines to China 1984, US-China Trade Confs at US Senate (advocating unconditional renewal of China's Most Favoured Nation trading status) 1987, SES Expdn to Mt Xixibangma Tibet 1987, co-sponsor (with US-China Business Cncl) conf on Reassessing US-China Ties: Economic Policy and the Role of Business at US State Dept 1990, co-host (with US Nat Ctee on US-China Relations) to Chinese Mayors' Delgn at US Senate and State Dept 1990, founding benefactor East Timor Good Samaritan Fndn 2000, funding and construction of accomodation for East Timorese students 2002, estab Eric Hotung Research Fellowship to promote research and enhance the research profile of the Sch of Law Univ of Canterbury NZ 2005; co-host (with China Inst for Int Stategic Studies) an Int Symposium on: 'Asia-Pacific Security Situation' 2002, 'Sino-US-European Relations in the New Century: Opportunities and Challenges' 2003, 'Int Counter-Terrorism Situation and Cooperation' 2004, 'Non-traditional Security: Challenges and Responses' 2005; tstee Marine Mil Acad Harlingen TX 1978; vice-pres: Operation Drake 1979, Operation Raleigh 1984; dir Soong Ching Ling Fndn for Children 1987, patron Hotung Tech Sch for Girls 1988; hon memb 22nd Special Service Regt 1985, chm Non-Combatants Pacific War 1937–45 Assoc Inc 1994, chm China AIDS Fund Inc 2003; patron: Royal British Legion, Hong Kong Ex-Serviceman's Assoc, WWII Veterans Assoc 1998; tstee: Spirit of Normandy Int Appeal 1994, Spirit of Normandy Tst 2000, Soc for Aid and Rehabilitation of Drug Abusers Hong Kong 2000, Bd of China Inst in America 2001; sponsor: Hotung Pavilion, Shanghai Museum 1996, Cathedra Basilica of the Sacred Heart NJ 1998–2006, hosp ship East Timor 1999; donation of plaques to the Wai Hai Cemetery 1999, donation to Chinese Scholar's Garden Staten Island NY 1999 (fndr memb Scholar's Soc of NY Chinese Scholar's Garden 1999), donation incl the former RAN vessel HMAS Moresby (renamed as 'MV Patricia Anne Hotung') to East Timor 1999, donation to Eye Hosp China Acad of Traditional Chinese Med Beijing 2000, donation to Georgetown Univ Law Center (building named Eric Hotung Int Law Center) 2000; memb Bd of Dirs Community Chest Hong Kong 2000; established free clinic in Dili East Timor 2000; ambass at large of the Democratic Republic of East Timor 2002–, hon ambass at large Govt of the Federated States of Micronesia 2010; hon pres China Soc for People's Friendship Studies 2005; Scientific Exploration Soc: hon memb 1980, hon vice-pres 2005; memb Frank Hogan Soc Georgetown Univ 2004; life memb: Hong Kong Arts Centre 1984, RPO 1984; companion St George's Chapel Windsor 2006 (friend 1984); Charter Award from Bd of Dirs Georgetown Univ 1985, charter memb 1789 Soc Georgetown Univ 1997, John Carroll Award Georgetown Univ 1997; sr assoc memb St Antony's Coll Oxford 1999, fndn fell St Antony's Coll Oxford 1999, memb Chllr's Ct of Benefactors Univ of Oxford 2000; The Path to Peace Fndn Servitor Pacis Award 2003 (Vatican Award) 2003, Court Leadership of the King's Presence Chamber 2008; Freeman City of San Francisco 1972, Hon Citizen Pyongyang City N Korea 2002; Hon Dr Georgetown Univ 1984; fell Hong Kong IOD 2000; Knight of Malta Grand Cross with Star Pro Merito Meletensi 1974, Cruz de Caballero de la Orde de Isabel la Católica 1973, Das Kommitur Cruz Mit Stern Leichtenstein 1974, Knight of St Sylvester 1984, Grand Cross of the Order of NS DA Conceicao de Vila Vicosa Portugal 1985, CStJ 1995 (OStJ 1966), Marquez de Baucau de Timor 1997, Cert of Friendship Order N Korea 2002, Medalha de Ouro da Resistenca das Falintil 2002; *Recreations* game fishing, calligraphy; *Clubs* Carlton, Metropolitan (Washington DC), Chinese (Hong Kong), China (Beijing), American (Hong Kong), Foreign Correspondents' (Hong Kong), Hong Kong Country, Jockey, Hong Kong Golf; *Style—* Eric Hotung, Esq, CBE; ✉ c/o Hotung International Development Ltd, PO Box 72826, Kowloon Central Post Office, 405 Nathan Road, Kowloon, Hong Kong

HOUBEN, Francine; *b* Sittard, Netherlands; *Educ* Delft Univ of Technol; *Career* architect; founding ptnr and creative dir Mecanoo; *Style—* Ms Francine Houben; ✉ Mecanoo, CUBE, 113–115 Portland Street, Manchester M1 6DW

HOUGH, Robert Eric; CBE (2015), DL (Gtr Manchester 1997); s of Gordon Hough, and Joyce, *née* Davies; *b* 18 July 1945; *Educ* William Hulme's GS Manchester, Univ of Bristol (LLB); *m* 14 June 1975, Pauline Elizabeth, da of Austin David Gilbert Arch, and Amy Jean, *née* Watt; 2 s (Mark Ian b 11 Oct 1979, Christopher James b 21 Feb 1985); *Career* admitted slr 1970, NP; ptnr Slater Heelis (slrs) Manchester 1974–89; exec chm The Manchester Ship Canal Co 1989–2002 (chm 1987–2002); Peel Holdings plc: dir 1986–, exec dep chm 1989–2002, non-exec dep chm 2002–09; chm: Liverpool Airport Ltd 1997–2009 and 2014–, Doncaster Sheffield Airport 1999–2009 and 2012–, Durham Tees Valley Airport 2002–09 and 2012–, Northwest Rgnl Devpt Agency 2009–12 (dir 2007–09), New East Manchester Ltd 2002–10 (non-exec chm), Cheshire Building Soc 2006–08 (non exec dir 2002–08), Turley Associates Ltd 2008–14 (non-exec dir 2003–14); non-exec dir: Brammer plc 1993–2003 (non-exec dep chm 1998–2003), Alfred McAlpine plc 2003–08, Styles & Wood Gp plc 2006–, Provident Financial plc 2007–13; dir PJ Kennedy Investments Ltd 1997–2011; pres Manchester C of C 1994–95, memb NW Regnl Assembly 2000–04 (memb Exec Bd 2006–07, memb N W Regnl Ldrs Bd 2013–), chm NW Business Leadership Team 2000–03, former vice-pres and former chm Manchester Cwlth Games 1995–99 and 2002, memb Learning and Skills Nat Cncl 2009–10, chm Liverpool City Regnl Local Enterprise Partnership 2012–, memb Advsy Cncl Tate Liverpool 2013–, memb Transport for the North Partnership Bd 2015–; govr Univ of Manchester 2005– (dep chm of govrs 2012–), memb Transport for the North Ptnrship bd 2015–; High Sheriff Gtr Manchester 2004; Hon DBA Manchester Metropolitan Univ 1996, Hon DLitt Univ of Salford 1996; memb Law Soc, fell CILT; *Recreations* golf, gardening, walking; *Clubs* Hale Golf; *Style—* Robert Hough, Esq, CBE, DL

HOUGH, Stephen; CBE (2014); *b* 1961, Heswall, Cheshire; *Educ* RNCM, Juilliard Sch NY; *Career* concert pianist; performed with orchs incl: Philharmonia, Royal Philharmonic, LSO, London Philharmonic, BBC Symphony, Eng Chamber, City of Birmingham Symphony, NY Philharmonic, Cleveland, Chicago Symphony, Detroit Symphony, Hong Kong Philharmonic, Toronto Symphony, Monte Carlo Philharmonic, Philadelphia, LA Philharmonic, Lausanne Chamber, Orch of St Cecilia Rome, Deutsche Symphonie Orch Berlin, Orchestre National de France, Berlin Philharmonic, NHK Symphony, Tonhalle Orch; worked with conductors incl: Claudio Abbado, Klaus Tennstedt, Mstislav Rostropovich, James Levine, Simon Rattle, Lorin Maazel, Charles Dutoit, Esa-Pekka Salonen, Christoph von Dohnányi, Yuri Temirkanov, Jeffrey Tate, Gustavo Dudamel, Christoph Eschenbach, Mikhail Pletnev; performed at festivals incl: Ravinia, Blossom, Spoleto, NY Mostly Mozart, Sorrento, Tivoli, Bath, Cheltenham, La Grange de Meslay, BBC Promenade Concerts, Edinburgh, Salzburg, Aldeburgh, Sapporo; Terence Judd award 1982, first prize Naumburg Int Piano Competition 1983, awarded MacArthur Fellowship 2001, Jean Gimbel Lane Prize Northwestern Univ 2008, Gramophone Gold Disc Award 2008, Instrumentalist Award Royal Philharmonic Soc 2010; hon doctorate Univ of Liverpool 2011; memb RAM 2003; FRNCM 1996; *Recordings* incl: Hummel piano concertos (with the Eng Chamber Orch, Gramophone magazine best concerto record 1987), The Piano Album (collection of favourite encores), Brahms piano concerto no 1 and no 2 (with the BBC Symphony Orch and Andrew Davis, various works by Britten, Schumann and Liszt (awarded Deutsche Schallplattenpreis), Scharwenka and Sauer piano concertos (Gramophone Record of the Year 1996), York Bowen piano music (awarded Diapason d'Or), Franck piano music (awarded Deutsche Schallplattenpreis), Mompou piano music (Gramaphone magazine Best Instrumental Record 1998), Mendelssohn complete works for piano and orch, Liebermann piano concertos, New York Variations recital (Grammy nomination), Schubert piano sonatas, new piano album, complete works for piano and orch by Saint-Saens (Grammy nomination, Gramophone Record of the Year 2002), English Piano Album, Liszt sonata (Grammy nomination), Brahms F minor sonata, Rachmaninoff and Franck cello sonatas (with Steven Isserlis), Liszt Années de Pèlerimage, Hummel piano sonatas, Chopin Ballades and Scherzos, complete Rachmaninov piano concertos 2005, A Spanish Album 2006, A Mozart Album 2007, Stephen Hough in Recital, complete Tchaikovsky works for piano and orchestra 2009, Chopin complete Waltzes 2011 (winner Diapason d'or de l'annee), Liszt and Grieg piano concertos 2011, Broken Branches (compositions by Stephen Hough) 2011, Piano Sonata no 2 (Notturno Luminoso), Sonata for cello and piano (Les Adieux), Brahms Piano Concertos 2013, In The Night 2014, Grieg Lyric Pieces 2015, Janá?ek and Scriabin recital 2015, Dvo?ák and Schumann Concertos 2016; *Publications* incl The Bible as Prayer, Nosing Around (2014), five volumes of solo pieces and transcriptions; other compositions incl: Other Love Songs, Sonata for piano (broken branches), Herbstlieder (Rilke settings), Bridgewater (bassoon and piano), Un Piccolo Sonatina, Loneliest Wilderness (elegy for cello and orchestra), Misssa Mirabilis (chorus and orchestra), Piano Sonata No 2 (Notturno Luminoso), Sonata for cello and piano (Les Adieux), Mass of Innocence and Experience, Piano Sonata III (Trinitas); *Recreations* reading, writing, painting; *Style—* Stephen Hough, Esq, CBE; ✉ website www.stephenhough.com, blog http://blogs.telegraph.co.uk/culture/author/stephenhough/

HOUGHTON, Frances; *b* 19 September 1980; *Educ* King's Sch Canterbury, KCL (BA, Jelf Medal, Sir Douglas Logan Award); *Career* amateur rower; achievements incl: Bronze medal double sculls World Jr Championships 1998, Gold medal double sculls World Under 23 Championships 1999, Silver medal double sculls and Silver medal quadruple sculls Cwlth Regatta 1999, ninth place double sculls Olympic Games Sydney 2000, winner double sculls World Cup 2002, winner quadruple sculls World Cup 2004 and 2005, Silver medal quadruple sculls Olympic Games Athens 2004, Gold medal quadruple sculls World Championships 2005, 2006 and 2007, Silver medal quadruple sculls Olympic Games Beijing 2008; jr champion World Indoor Rowing Championships 1999; ITV Sporting Midlander of the Year 2004; hon life memb Univ of London Union 2005; *Style—* Miss Frances Houghton

HOUGHTON, Sir John Theodore; kt (1991), CBE (1983); s of Sidney Maurice Houghton (d 1987), of Abingdon, Oxon, and Miriam, *née* Yarwood (d 1974); *b* 30 December 1931; *Educ* Rhyl GS, Jesus Coll Oxford (MA, DPhil); *m* 1, 1962, Margaret Edith (d 1986), da of Neville Broughton, of Colne, Lancs; 1 da (Janet b 1964), 1 s (Peter b 1966); m 2, 1988, Sheila, da of Sydney Thompson, of Bradford, W Yorks; *Career* res fell Royal Aircraft Estab, lectr in atmospheric physics Univ of Oxford 1958 (reader 1962, prof 1976), official fell and tutor in physics Jesus Coll Oxford 1960–73 (prof fell 1973, hon fell 1983), visiting prof UCLA 1969; dir Appleton Sci and Engrg Res Cncl 1979–83, DG (later chief exec) Meteorological Office 1983–91, hon scientist Rutherford Appleton Lab 1991–; developed: Selective Chopper Radiometer (for the Nimbus 4 and 5 satellites), Pressure Modulator Radiometer (flown on Nimbus 6) 1975, Stratospheric and Mesopheric Sounder (flown on Nimbus 7) 1978; chm: Jt Scientific Ctee for World Climate Res Programmes 1981–84, Scientific Assessment Intergovernmental Panel on Climate Change 1988–2002, Jt Scientific and Technical Ctee Global Climate Observing System 1992–95, Royal Cmmn on Environmental Pollution 1992–98; vice-pres World Meteorological Orgn 1987–91; pres John Ray Initiative 2006– (chm 1997–2006); tstee Shell Fndn 2000–10; Darton Prize (RMS) 1954, Buchan Prize (RMS) 1966, Charles Chree Medal Inst of Physics 1979, Glazebrook Medal Inst of Physics 1989, Rank Prize for opto electronics 1989 (jtly), Symons Gold Medal Royal Meteorological Soc 1991, Bakerian lectr Royal Soc 1991, Global 500 Award UN Environment Prog 1994, Gold Medal Royal Astronomical Society 1995, Int Meterological Orgn Prize 1998, Japan Prize 2006, Albert Einstein Science Award World Cultural Cncl 2009; Hon DUniv Stirling 1992; Hon DSc: Univ of Wales 1991, UEA 1993, Univ of Leeds 1995, Heriot-Watt Univ 1997, Univ of Greenwich 1997, Univ of Glamorgan 1998, Univ of Reading 1999, Univ of Birmingham 2000, Univ of Glos 2001, Univ of Hull 2002, Univ of Oxford 2006; Hon DL Dalhousie Univ Canada 2010; hon memb American Meteorological Soc; fell Optical Soc of America; FRS, FInstP, FRMetS (pres 1976–78, hon memb), Hon FRIBA 2001; *Books* Infra Red Physics (with S D Smith, 1966), The Physics of Atmospheres (1977, ed 1986, 3 edn 2002), Remote Sensing of Atmospheres (with F W Taylor and C D Rodgers, 1984), The Global Climate (ed, 1984), Does God Play Dice? (1988), Global Warming: The Complete Briefing (1994, 5 edn 2014), The Search for God: Can science help? (1995), In The Eye of the Storm, the Autobiography of Sir John Houghton (with Gill Tavner, 2013); *Style—* Sir John Houghton, CBE, FRS

HOUGHTON, Gen Sir (John) Nicholas Reynolds; GCB (2011, KCB 2008), CBE (2000, OBE 1993); *b* 18 October 1954; *Educ* St Peter's Coll Oxford (MA), RMA Sandhurst; *Career* cmmd Green Howards 1974, subsequently Military Asst to COS Br Army of the Rhine then memb Directing Staff Royal Military Coll of Science Shrivenham, Commanding Offr 1st Battalion Green Howards 1993–94, Dep Asst COS HQ Land Command 1994, Cdr 39 Infantry Brigade NI 1997, Dir of Military Operations MOD 1999–2002, COS Allied Rapid Reaction Corps 2002–04, Asst Chief of Defence Staff 2004–05, Sr Br Military Rep Iraq and Dep Commanding Gen Multi-National Foce Iraq 2005–06, Chief of Jt Operations Perm Jt HQ 2006–09, Vice-Chief of the Defence Staff 2009–13, Chief of the Defence Staff 2013–16; Constable of the Tower of London 2016–; *Style—* Gen Sir Nicholas Houghton, GCB, CBE, ADC Gen; ✉ HM Tower of London, London EC3N 4AB

HOULDER, Bruce Fiddes; CB (2014), QC (1994), DL (Gtr London 2010, rep DL London Borough of Hillingdon 2014); s of Dr Charles Alexander Houlder (d 1993), and Jessie, *née* Fiddes; *b* 27 September 1947; *Educ* Felsted; *m* 1974, Stella Catherine, da of Dr Michael Mattinson, and Barbara, *née* Wilkins; 2 da (Diana Elizabeth b 3 March 1981, Francesca Maria b 20 Aug 1983); *Career* called to the Bar Gray's Inn 1969 (bencher 2001); recorder 1991–; dir of service prosecutions Service Prosecuting Authy Miny of Defence 2009–13; tutor judge Judicial Coll 2002–; memb General Cncl of the Bar 1995–2000 and 2003–05, vice-chm Professional Standards Ctee 1995–2000, chm Public Affairs Ctee Bar Cncl 1998–2000 and 2004–05 (vice-chm 1996–98), vice-chm IT Panel Bar Cncl 2004–, chm Bar Quality Advsy Panel 2007–, Bar Cncl memb responsible for criminal justice modernisation prog; chm Criminal Bar Assoc of England and Wales 2001–02 (vice-chm 2000–01), memb Criminal Ctee Judicial Studies Bd 2001–04; dir Bar Services Co Ltd 2003–; vice-chm Millennium Bar Conference 2000; Hon DUniv Sheffield Hallam Univ 2015; *Recreations* painting, walking, theatre, cycling, opera; *Clubs* Garrick, Winchester House (Putney); *Style—* Bruce Houlder, Esq, CB, QC, DL; ✉ e-mail bhqc@aol.com

HOULDSWORTH, Philippa Caroline (Pippy); da of Maj Ian George Henry Houldsworth, TD, JP (d 1963), of Dallas, Moray, and Clodagh Houldsworth, JP, *née* Murray; *b* 17 August 1957; *m* 18 Aug 1995 (m dis 2004), Matthew Julius Radford; 2 s (Frederick b 1994, Cosmo b 1996); *Career* head buyer Children's Book Centre 1978–80, ed Children's Book News 1981–82, New Art Centre 1986–87, proprietor Houldsworth Gallery 1987–; patron of new art Tate Gallery 1992–2001, memb Exec Ctee Soc of London Art Dealers 2000–02; *Recreations* reading, visiting galleries, photography; *Style—* Pippy Houldsworth; ✉ Pippy Houldsworth Gallery, 6 Heddon Street, London W1B 4BT

HOULIHAN, Michael Patrick; s of Michael Houlihan, and Kathleen, *née* Small (d 2007); *b* 27 September 1948; *Educ* St Francis Xavier's Coll Liverpool, Univ of Bristol (BA); *m* 1969, Jane, *née* Hibbert; 1 s (Sean b 11 May 1970), 1 da (Sarah b 7 Sept 1974); *Career* Imperial War Museum: research asst 1971–75, dep keeper Dept of Exhibits 1975–76, keeper Dept of Permanent Exhbns 1976–84; dir Horniman Museum and Gardens 1994–98 (dep dir 1984–94), chief exec Nat Museums and Galleries of NI 1998–2003, dir Amgueddfa Cymru-Nat Museum Wales 2003–10, chief exec Museum of NZ Te Papa Tongarewa; chm Collections Tst 2003–09; memb: Br Cmmn for Military History 1982–, NI Ctee Br Cncl 1998, Bd NI Museum Cncl 1998, Advsy Cncl CyMAL; visiting prof Univ of Ulster 1999–2005; tstee: Nat Self-Portrait Collection of Ireland 1998–2003, Nat Coal Mining Museum 2004–10; memb Cncl Goldsmiths Coll London 1997–98; *Publications* Trench Warfare 1914–18 (1974), No Man's Land (jtly, 1984); *Recreations* military history, cycling, Romanesque architecture, battlefields; *Style—* Michael Houlihan, Esq; ✉ Reevoo, Friars Bridge Court, 41–45 Blackfriars Road, London SE1 8NZ

HOULSBY, Prof Guy Tinmouth; s of Thomas Tinmouth Houlsby (d 1998), of South Shields, and Vivienne May, *née* Ford; *b* 28 March 1954; *Educ* Trinity Coll Glenalmond (War Meml scholar), St John's Coll Cambridge (Whytehead open scholar, MA, PhD, Rex Moir prize, Roscoe prize, Archibald Denny prize); *m* 28 March 1985, Jenny Lucy Damaris, da of Dr Ronald M Nedderman; 2 s (Neil Matthew Tinmouth b 16 Oct 1987, Ian Thomas Tinmouth b 13 Oct 1990); *Career* civil engr: Binnie & Partners 1975–76, Babtie Shaw & Morton 1976–77; Univ of Oxford: jr res fell Balliol Coll 1980–83, lectr in engrg and fell Keble Coll 1983–91, prof of civil engrg and fell Brasenose Coll 1991–, head Dept of Engrg Science 2009–14; Br Geotechnical Soc prize 1985, Geotechnical Res medal ICE 1989, Telford Prize ICE 2001; Rankine Lecture 2014; DSc Univ of Oxford 2003; CEng 1983, FICE 1997 (MICE 1983), FREng 1999; *Books* Basic Soil Mechanics (with G W E Milligan, 1984), Predictive Soil Mechanics – Proceedings of the Wroth Memorial Symposium (ed), Principles of Hyperplasticity (with A M Puzrin, 2006); *Recreations* ornithology, woodwork, Northumbrian small pipes, rowing; *Style—* Prof Guy Houlsby; ✉ 25 Purcell Road, Marston, Oxford OX3 0HB (☎ 01865 722128); Department of Engineering Science, Parks Road, Oxford OX1 3PJ (☎ 01865 273138, e-mail guy.houlsby@eng.ox.ac.uk)

HOULT, David; s of Percy Frederick Hoult, of Exmouth, Devon, and Flora, *née* Macdonald; *b* 18 April 1948; *Educ* Univ of Manchester (MusB), Royal Manchester Coll of Music (GRSM, ARMCM), Lancaster Univ (MPhil); *m* 21 Aug 1971, Mary Agnes, da of Richard Percy Fentiman; 1 da (Alice Agnes b 6 April 1982), 2 s (Thomas William b 7 Oct 1985, George Frederick b 6 Feb 1990); *Career* dir of music Cheadle Hulme Sch 1974–79, head of music UC Salford 1988–93 (sr lectr 1984–87), princ Leeds Coll of Music 1993–; also: horn player, singer, teacher, broadcaster, conductor and adjudicator; ISM 1993; *Recreations* brewing, walking; *Style—* David Hoult, Esq; ✉ Leeds College of Music, 3 Quarry Hill, Leeds LS2 7PD (☎ 0113 222 3456, fax 0113 222 3455, e-mail d.hoult@lcm.ac.uk)

HOULT, Nicholas Caradoc; s of Roger Hoult, and Glenis Hoult; *b* 7 December 1989, Wokingham, Berks; *Educ* Ranelagh C of E Sch Bracknell, Sylvia Young Stage Sch; *Career* actor; *Film* incl: About a Boy 2002, The Weather Man 2005, Kidulthood 2006, A Single Man 2009, Clash of the Titans 2010, X-Men: First Class 2011, Warm Bodies 2013, Jack the Giant Slayer 2013, X-Men: Days of Future Past 2014, Kill Your Friends 2015, Dark Places 2015, Mad Max Fury Road 2015, Collide 2016, X-Men Apocalypse 2016, Equals 2016; *Television* incl: Skins 2007–08, Wallander 2008; *Theatre* New Boy (Trafalgar Studios) 2009; *Style—* Mr Nicholas Hoult

HOUSDEN, Sir Peter James; KCB (2010); *b* 7 December 1950, Hereford; *Educ* Grove Comp Market Drayton Salop, Univ of Essex (BA); *Career* teacher Madeley Ct Comp Sch 1975–79, Humberside LEA 1979–82, Notts LEA 1982–86, Lancs LEA 1986–88; Notts CC: dep chief educational offr 1988–91, dir of educn 1991–94, chief exec 1994–2001; DG (schs) DfES 2001–05, perm sec Office of the Dep PM 2005–06, perm sec Dept for Communities and Local Govt 2006–10, perm sec Scottish Govt 2010–15; currently public servs conslt; tstee RNLI; *Publications* Bucking the Market: LEA and Special Needs (1996), Local Statesmen (2000), This Is Us (2013), So The New Could Be Born – The Passing of a County Grammar School (2015); *Style—* Sir Peter Housden, KCB

HOUSE, James Michael; QC (2015); *Career* called to the Bar 1995; memb Criminal Bar Assoc; *Style—* James House, Esq, QC; ✉ 7 Bedford Row, London WC1R 4BS

HOUSE, Keren Ruth (Mrs John Hookway); da of Alan Sidney House, of Purley, Surrey, and Maureen Elizabeth Evelyn, *née* Atkinson; *b* 1 June 1951; *Educ* Purley Co GS for Girls, London Coll of Printing (BA), RCA (MA); *m* 9 Feb 1980, John Hookway, s of Leslie Hookway; 3 da (Jessica Rose b 27 Aug 1984, Eleanor Kate b 22 Oct 1987, Meredith Anne b 17 June 1992); *Career* lectr in graphic design Pennsylvania State Univ 1976–78; graphic designer: Bloomfield/Travis London 1978–79, Pentagram London 1979–81; pt/t lectr in graphic design Harrow Sch of Art 1981–82, fndr ptnr (with David Stuart) The Partnership 1981–83, fndr ptnr and dir The Partners 1983–87, art dir Glenn Travis Associates 1988–90; creative dir: Design Bridge 1990–98, Siebert Head 1998–2003, Ziggurat Brands 2011–13; owner and creative dir Aricot Vert 2009–; external assessor on BA and MA courses in graphic design; work accepted: D&AD Annual and exhbn 1979, 1981, 1983, 1985, 1987 and 1989, Communication Arts Annual (USA) 1982, 1986 and 1989, Design Effectiveness Awards 1995, 1997, 2001 and 2005, Brand Design Awards 2002; memb D&AD 1978 (memb Exec Ctee 2000–03); FRSA 1999; *Recreations* everything I can't do at work; *Style—* Ms Keren House; ✉ e-mail keren@aricotvert.co.uk

HOUSE, Rachael Laura; da of Terence House (d 2008), of Maidstone, Kent, and Margaret, *née* Mannering; *b* 19 September 1961, Maidstone, Kent; *Educ* Univ of Kent, Camberwell Sch of Art, Central St Martins Sch of Art; *Partner* Jo David, *qv*; *Career* youth worker Southwark 1990–2001, client participation worker 1996–2001; co-dir and curator Space Station Sixty-Five (with Jo David); artist: various work exhibited since 2001, including Peckham Pet-Tastic 2004, Peckham Pet-Tastic 2 2005, HÅ Pet-Tastic Norway 2006, Bexhill Bow-Wow De La Warr Pavilion 2006, Lewisham Pet-Tastic 2007, Peckham Pet-Tastic 3 2007; Red Hanky Panky comic books (1991–2001), DIY Culture (by Amy Lou Spencer, 2005), Picture This: The artist as illustrator (ed Sylvia Blackemeyer, 2005), Event (by Stephen Hollingshead, 2007), Freeplay Exhibition Catalogue (2006); *Recreations* contemporary art, punk, comics, collecting photo opportunities, walking and swimming in Whitstable, science fiction; *Clubs* World of Flimsy; *Style—* Ms Rachael House; ✉ Space Station Sixty-Five, 65 Northcross Road, London SE22 9ET (☎ 020 8299 5036, e-mail info@spacestationsixtyfive.com)

HOUSHIARY, Shirazeh; *b* 10 January 1955, Iran; *Educ* Chelsea Sch of Art London; *Career* artist/sculptor; work subject of numerous exhibition catalogues, articles and reviews; jr fell Cardiff Coll of Art 1979–80; prof London Inst 1997–; *Solo Exhibitions*: Chapter Arts Centre 1980, Kettle's Yard Gallery Cambridge 1982, Centro d'Arte Contemporanea Siracusa Italy 1983, Galleria Massimo Minini Milan 1983, Galerie Grita Insam Vienna

1983, Lisson Gallery London 1984, Galerie Paul Andriesse Amsterdam 1986, Breath (Lisson Gallery London) 1987, Centre d'Art Contemporain Musée Rath Geneva (travelling to MOMA Oxford) 1988–89, Valentina Moncada Rome 1992, Lisson Gallery London 1992, Camden Arts Centre London (travelling to Douglas Hyde Gallery Dublin), Fine Arts Centre Univ of Massachusetts (travelling to Art Gallery of York Univ Canada) 1993–94, The Sense of Unity (Lisson Gallery London) 1994, Isthmus (Le Magasin Centre National d'Art Contemporain Grenoble, travelling to Munich, Maastricht and Vienna) 1995–96, Islamic Gallery British Museum 1997; *Group Exhibitions* incl: London/New York 1982 (Lisson Gallery London) 1982, The Sculpture Show (Arts Cncl of GB, Hayward Gallery and Serpentine Gallery London) 1983, New Art (Tate Gallery London) 1983, British Art Show – Old Allegiances and New Directions 1979–84 (Arts Cncl of GB, travelling to Birmingham Museum and Art Gallery, Ikon Gallery Birmingham, Royal Scottish Acad Edinburgh, Mappin Art Gallery Sheffield and Southampton Art Gallery) 1984, Galerie Montenay-Delsol Paris 1985, The British Show (Art Gallery of NSW Sydney and Br Cncl, travelling to Art Gallery of Western Aust Perth, Art Gallery of NSW Sydney, Queensland Art Gallery Brisbane, The Exhibition Hall Melbourne and Nat Art Gallery Wellington NZ) 1985, Jack Shainman Gallery NY 1987, Walk out to Winter (Bess Cutler Gallery NY) 1988, Magiciens de la Terre (Centre Georges Pompidou Paris) 1989, Terskel II/Threshold II (Museet for samtidskunst Oslo Norway) 1990, Studies on Paper – Contemporary British Sculptors (Connaught Brown London) 1990, Now for the Future (Arts Cncl of GB, Hayward Gallery London) 1990, Dujourie, Fortuyn/O'Brien, Kapoor, Houshiary (Rijksmuseum Kröller-Müller Otterlo Holland) 1990, Rhizome (Haags Gemeentemuseum Netherlands) 1991, Misure e Misurazioni (Naples) 1992, Bruges La Morte Gallery Belgium 1992, II Tyne Int Newcastle 1993, Venic Biennale 1993, Travellers Treasures (Mechitarist Monastery Venice) 1993, Int Biennale of Obidos Portugal 1993, Sculptors' Drawings The Body of Drawing (Univ of Warwick Coventry and The Mead Gallery) 1993, Sculptors' Drawings presented by the Weltkunst Fndn (Tate Gallery London) 1994, Turner Prize Shortlist Artists' Exhibition (Tate Gallery London) 1994, Sculpture at Goodwood (The Hat Hill Sculpture Fndn Goodwood) 1994 and 1997, Contemporary British Art in Print (Scottish Nat Gallery of Modern Art Edinburgh touring to Yale Center for British Art New Haven) 1995, Dialogues of Peace (Palais de Nations Geneva) 1995, A Changing World – 50 Years of Sculpture from the British Council Collection (Castle Riding Hall Prague) 1995, Negotiating Rapture (Museum of Contemporary Art Chicago) 1996, 23rd Bienal Internacioal de Sao Paolo 1996, Meditation (Madras Ibn Youssef Marakesh) 1997, Follow Me – Britische Kunst an der Unterelbe (Schloss Agathenburg) 1997; *Style*— Ms Shirazeh Houshiary; ✉ Lisson Gallery London Ltd, 67 Lisson Street, London NW1 5DA (✆ 020 7724 2739, fax 020 7724 7124)

HOUSLAY, Prof Miles Douglas; s of (Edwin) Douglas Houslay, of Wolverhampton, and Georgina Marie (Molly) Houslay; *b* 25 June 1950; *Educ* The Grammar Sch Brewood, UC Cardiff (BSc), King's Coll Cambridge (PhD); *m* Rhian Houslay; 1 da (Emma b 1978), 2 s (Thomas b 1981, Daniel b 1988); *Career* res fell Queens' Coll Cambridge 1975–76 (ICI postdoctoral res fell Dept of Biochemistry 1974–76), reader in biochemistry UMIST 1982–84 (lectr 1976–82), Gardiner prof of biochemistry Univ of Glasgow 1984–2011 (chair Neuroscience and Molecular Pharmacology 2009–11, co-dir Inst of Psychology and Neuroscience 2010–11, emeritus prof of biochemistry 2011–); ceo/md BioGryffe Consulting Ltd 2011–; pt/t prof of pharmacological innovation KCL 2011–, pt/t prof of pharmacology Univ of Strathclyde 2011–15; co-fndr and chair Scientific Advsy Bd BioTheryX Inc 2008–14, co-fndr and CSO Mironid Ltd 2014–; memb: Res Ctee British Diabetic Assoc 1986–91, MRC Cell Biology & Disorders Bd 1990–94 (memb Grant Ctee A 1989–93 (chm 1990–93)), Clinical Biomedical Res Ctee Scottish Office Home & Health Dept 1991–93, AFRC Cell Signalling Initiative Grant Ctee 1992–97, HEFC Res Assessment Panel (Basic Medical and Dental Sciences) 1992 and 1996, Cell and Biochemistry Grant Panel Wellcome Trust 1996–2002, Advsy Bd for External Appts Univ of London 1990–97, Ctee of the Biochemical Soc of GB 1983–86; external assessor Univ of Malaysia 1991–97; ed-in-chief Cellular Signalling 1987–; Br Heart Fndn: tstee 1997–99, chm Projects Grant Ctee 1997–99, memb Chairs and Programme Grants Ctee 1997–99; memb Editorial Bd: Biochemical Jl 1981–88 (dep chm 1985–88), Biochem Biophys Acta 1982–93, Biochemical Pharmacology 1988–90, Progress in Growth Factor Res 1988–93; hon sr res fell: California Metabolic Res Fndn 1982–94, Hannah Res Inst 1988–2004, Celgene Corp 2000– (memb Scientific Advsy Bd 2002–05); memb Scientific Advsy Bd: Fission Pharmaceuticals 2007–10, BioTheryX 2008–14; Selby fell Australian Acad of Sci 1984; Colworth Medal Biochemical Soc GB 1985, Most Cited Scientist in Scotland 1992 (period 1986–91), Joshua Lederberg Prize Celgene Corp USA 2012; FRSE 1986, FIBiol 1988, fndr fell Acad Med Sci 1998, CBiol, FMedSci, FRSB 2015; *Books* Dynamics of Biological Membranes (with K K Stanley, 1983); author of over 510 res pubns (H-Index 81, RG Score 49.6); *Recreations* photography, driving, walking, reading, travel, cooking, music; *Style*— Prof Miles Houslay, FRSE, FRSB, FMedSci; ✉ Institute of Pharmaceutical Science, King's College London, 5th Floor, Franklin-Wilkins Building, 150 Stamford Street, London SE1 9NH (e-mail miles.houslay@kcl.ac.uk)

HOUSTON, Robert Ian; s of Ivan Thomas Houston (d 1985), of Gloucester, and Joy, *née* Meehan (d 1986); *b* 18 October 1950; *Educ* Sebright Sch, Nottingham Trent Univ (BSc); *m* Gillian Duret, da of Frederick John Floyd; 2 s (Ian David b 8 July 1979, Andrew Robert b 6 May 1983), 1 da (Claire Alexandra b 10 March 1981); *Career* chartered surveyor; Richard Ellis 1972–80, chief exec Rowe & Pitman Property Services 1980–84, chm ING Real Estate Investment Management Ltd (formerly Baring, Houston & Saunders) 1984–2009, princ St Bride's Strategic Advsrs and St Bride's Mangrs 2009–; chm: Boost Charitable Tst, Guildford Rugby Club; Liveryman Worshipful Co of Chartered Surveyors; FRICS; *Recreations* cricket; *Style*— Robert Houston, Esq; ✉ Winkford Lodge, Church Lane, Witley, Godalming, Surrey GU8 5PR (✆ 01428 683016); St Bride's Strategic Advisers, 5 St Bride Street, London EC4A 4AS (✆ 020 7078 1950)

HOUTEN, Peter Charles; CB (2011); s of John Joseph Houten (d 2001), and Celia Houten (d 1995); *b* 5 April 1956, Fleetwood, Lancs; *Educ* St Joseph's Coll Blackpool, Univ of Salford (BSc); *Partner* Rema Laver; 1 s (Adam b 1991), 1 da (Kim b 1994); *Career* Dept for Employment: joined 1978, positions in Jobcentres and regnl office in NW until 1986, fndr memb Govt Office for Merseyside 1994, working on aspects of nat skills and educn policy since 1996, dir Academies Policy and Schs Orgn Gp Dept for Educn 2006–12; tstee and memb Audit Ctee Priory Academies Tst 2012–; *Recreations* sports, reading; *Style*— Peter Houten, Esq, CB

HOUVENAGHEL, Wendy Louise; *née* McLean; da of Joseph Philip McLean, and Mary Rachel, *née* McIvor; *b* 27 November 1974, Magherafelt, Co Londonderry, NI; *Educ* Rainey Endowed GS Magherafelt, Univ of Dundee (BDS, Dip, LLB); *m* 5 Aug 2000, Ian Houvenaghel; *Career* cyclist; early career as dentist RAF 1998–2004 (rising to Sqdn Ldr 2003), Grosvenor Dental Practice 2004–06, The Old Carriageworks Dental Practice 2013–; first cycling race 2002, memb GB cycling road squad 2003, int track competition debut 2005, ft/t track cyclist 2006–; achievements incl: winner Br Nat Time Trial Championships 2003 (second place 2004), winner Br Nat 10 mile and 25 mile time trials 2004, 2005 and 2006, winner 3 km pursuit Br Nat Track Championships 2005 and 2006, champion UCI Women's Pursuit World Cup 2005–06, 2006–07 and 2009–10, winner Br Nat Time Trial Championships 2007 (second place 2006), Gold medal team pursuit World Track Championships Manchester 2008, Silver medal individual pursuit Olympic Games Beijing 2008, Silver medal pursuit and Gold medal team pursuit World Track Championships Poland 2009, Silver medals individual pursuit and team pursuit World Track Championships Denmark 2010, Gold medal individual pursuit Br Nat Track Championships 2010, Silver medal individual pursuit Cwlth Games Delhi 2010, Gold medal team pursuit European Championships 2010, gold medal team pursuit World Championships Holland 2011, Gold medal Br Nat Time Trial Championships 2011, world no 1 ranking women's team pursuit 2011, Silver medal individual pursuit World Championships 2012, Gold medal Br Nat Time Trial Championships 2012; Hon LLD Univ of Dundee; *Style*— Mrs Wendy Houvenaghel

HOW, Peter Cecil; s of Cecil P How (d 1995, aged 100), of Rugeley, Staffs, and Dora, *née* Marshall (d 1960); *b* 27 June 1931; *Educ* Oundle, Open Univ (BA); *m* 21 Sept 1951, Jane, da of Thomas Erickson (d 1936); 2 s (Neil b 1952, Adam b 1954); *Career* dir Froggatt & Prior Ltd 1955–63; chm: How Group Ltd and assoc cos 1974–86 (dir 1963), H & V Welfare Ltd 1974–90, How Group plc 1986–97, Hansgross Estates plc 1986–97; non-exec dir Hazard Chase Ltd 2000–; pres Genie Climatique International 1986–88 (hon pres 1994–); memb W Midlands Regnl Cncl CBI 1979–85; pres Heating and Ventilating Contractors' Assoc 1975–76; memb Chm's Circle Symphony Hall Birmingham 2002–06; Liveryman Worshipful Co of Fan Makers 1975; *Recreations* travel, theatre, opera, music, books, memb Magic Circle; *Clubs* East India; *Style*— Peter How, Esq; ✉ 11 The Regents, Norfolk Road, Edgbaston, Birmingham B15 3PP (✆ 0121 454 4777, fax 0121 246 1572, e-mail phownow@gmail.com)

HOW, Timothy; s of Mervyn How and Margaret How, of Norwich; *b* 29 December 1950; *Educ* Churchill Coll Cambridge (MA), London Business Sch (MSc); *m* Elizabeth; 4 da (Jennifer, Rachel, Caroline, Susan); *Career* gen mangr Polaroid (UK) Ltd 1979–83; Bejam Freezer Food Centres Ltd: mktg dir 1983–85, trading dir 1985–87, managing dir 1987–89; chief exec Majestic Wine plc 1989–; non-exec chm Framlington AIM VCT plc, non-exec dep chm Austin Reed Gp plc; *Recreations* dinghy racing; *Clubs* Oxford and Cambridge Sailing Soc, Brancaster Staithe Sailing; *Style*— Timothy How, Esq; ✉ 47 Battlefield Road, St Albans AL1 4DB (✆ 01727 857884); Majestic Wine Warehouses Ltd, Majestic House, Otterspool Way, Watford WD25 8WW (✆ 01923 298200, fax 01923 819105)

HOWARD; *see also:* Fitzalan Howard

HOWARD, Anthony John; s of Peter Dunsmore Howard (d 1965, former Capt England Rugby Team), of Sudbury, Suffolk, and Doris Emily, *née* Metaxas (former winner Wimbledon Ladies Doubles); *b* 31 December 1937; *Educ* Eton, Trinity Coll Oxford; *m* 12 Oct 1963, Elisabeth Ann, da of Capt Roddie Casement, OBE, RN (d 1987); 1 s (Tom), 2 da (Katie, Emma); *Career* film researcher, producer, dir and writer for TV; 2500 films and progs for TV incl: Greece – The Hidden War, A Passage to Britain, A Full Life, Dick Barton – Special Agent, Country Ways (25 series), Every Night Something Awful, The Missa Luba, The Cathedrals of Britain, Country Faces, Great House Cookery, Pub People, Land Girls, Michael Barry's Undiscovered Cooks, Reflections on Science, Tool Box, Coastal Ways (11 series), Famous Foods of the South (2 series); fndr chief exec Countrywide Films Ltd 1989–2005 (taken over by da Katie Macey); currently freelance writer, prodr and dir; *Books* Milly and Me – One Dog and her Man(2013); thirteen books published on the English countryside; *Recreations* walking, talking, shepherding and shearing, teaching at junior school, reading, wood clearing, tennis, golf, prison visiting, church bell ringing; *Style*— Anthony Howard, Esq; ✉ Drove Cottage, Newbridge, Cadnam, Southampton, Hampshire SO40 2NW (✆ 023 8081 3233); Countrywide Films Ltd, Production Office, Tatchbury House, Loperwood, Calmore, Southampton, Hampshire SO40 2RN (✆ 023 8066 9006)

HOWARD, Charles Anthony Frederick; QC (1999); s of John Howard (d 1970), of London, and Mrs Naida Royal, formerly Howard, *née* Guest (d 1997); *b* 7 March 1951; *Educ* Sherborne, St John's Coll Cambridge (open history scholarship, McMahon studentship); *m* 1, (m dis), Geraldine Howard; 1 s (Alexander b 27 April 1981), 1 da (Francesca b 22 Dec 1982); m 2, Rosie Boycott, *qv*, da of Maj Charles Boycott; 1 step da (Daisy Leitch b 9 Aug 1983); *Career* called to the Bar 1975; barrister in private practice 1975–; memb Family Law Bar Assoc; *Recreations* cricket, tennis, films, gardening, breeding pigs and walking; *Clubs* Groucho, Somerset CCC; *Style*— Charles Howard, Esq, QC; ✉ 1 King's Bench Walk, Temple, London EC4Y 7DB (✆ 020 7936 1500, fax 020 7936 1590)

HOWARD, Sir David Howarth Seymour; 3 Bt (UK 1955), of Great Rissington, Co Gloucester; s of Sir (Hamilton) Edward de Coucey Howard, 2 Bt, GBE (d 2001); *b* 29 December 1945; *Educ* Radley, Worcester Coll Oxford (MA); *m* 15 June 1968, Valerie Picton, o da of late Derek Weatherly Crosse, of Broadstairs, Kent; 2 da (Caroline Picton Seymour (Mrs Dore) b 1970, Victoria Picton Seymour (Mrs Turner) b 1975), 2 s (Robert Picton Seymour b 1971, James Picton Seymour b 1979); *Heir* s, Robert Howard; *Career* chm Charles Stanley & Co Ltd (Stockbrokers) 1999– (md 1971–2014); dir: Wealth Management Association (WMA) 2001–, Chartered Inst for Securities and Investment 2002–14 (chm Examination Bd 2003–14); pres Chartered Mgmnt Inst 2008–10 (pres City of London Branch 2002–); pro-chllr and chm of Cncl City Univ 2003–08; Alderman City of London 1986–2015, Common Councilman City of London 1972–86, Sheriff City of London 1997–98, Lord Mayor of London 2000–01; councillor London Borough of Sutton 1974–78; chm London Gardens Soc 1996–; Master Worshipful Co of Gardeners 1990–91; Hon FSI; KStJ 2000, Grand Cordon (First Class) of the Order of Independence (Jordan) 2001; *Style*— Sir David Howard, Bt; ✉ 25 Luke Street, London EC2A 4AR

HOWARD, Prof David Martin; s of Jack Bruere Howard, of Rochester, Kent, and Philis Joan, *née* Probert; *b* 13 April 1956, Chatham, Kent; *Educ* Throwley House Sch, King's Sch Rochester, UCL (BSc((Eng)), Clinton prize, PhD); *m* 3 October 1981, Clare, da of Robert Hilton Wake; 1 s (Joseph Leo b 11 March 1993), 1 da (Antonia Elizabeth b 11 June 1996); *Career* trainee offr RN BRNC Dartmouth 1974–78; lectr in experimental phonetics UCL 1979–90; Univ of York: lectr in music technol 1990–93, sr lectr 1993–96, prof 1996–, head Dept of Electronics 1996–2000 and 2011–15; founding head Dept of Electronics Royal Holloway Univ of London 2016–; fndr ed Voice 1992–95; ed-in-chief Logopedics Phoniatrics Vocology 2002–15; chm Engrg Professors' Cncl 1999–2001, vice-pres and tstee Instn of Engrg and Technol 2004–07; memb Editorial Bd: Forensic Linguistics Int Jl of Speech Language and the Law 1999–, Organised Sound 2001–, Jl of Voice 2012–, Logopedics Phoniatrics Vocology 2015–; memb: Br Assoc of Academic Phoneticians 1988–, Br Voice Assoc 1990–, Int Assoc of Forensic Phoneticians 1991–; musical dir: The Beningbrough Singers 2004–11, Vale of York Voices 2004–13; dep tenor songman York Minster 2004–11; Ferens Inst of Otolaryngology Prize 1989, Design Cncl/BAe Engrg Design Award 1992, Ken Brodie Award 1993, Thorn EMI Prize 1994; memb and dir Audio Engrg Soc; CEng 1995, FIEE (now FIET) 1998, sr memb IEEE 2013; *Publications* A Student's Guide to Music Technology for AS an A2 (jtly, 2005), Penguin Dictionary of Electronics (ed, 4 edn, 2005, Japanese edn, 2009), Music Techonology: Acoustics and Psychoacoustics (jtly, 3 edn, 2006, Chinese edn, 2010), Voice Science, Acoustics and Recording (jtly, 2008), Choral Singing and Healthy Voice Production (2015); contrib to several book chapters and research pubns; *Recreations* organist, keyboard playing, choral direction, choir singing, sailing, skiing, walking; *Clubs* Victory; *Style*— Prof David M Howard; ✉ Department of Electronics, Royal Holloway Univ of London, Egham, Surrey TW20 0EX (✆ 01784 443655, e-mail david.howard@rhul.ac.uk, website www.davidmhoward.com)

HOWARD, Prof Deborah Janet; da of Thomas Were Howard (d 1997), and Isobel, *née* Brewer (d 1990); *b* 26 February 1946, Westminster, London; *Educ* Loughton HS for Girls, Newnham Coll Cambridge (MA), Courtauld Inst of Art (MA, PhD); *m* 26 Sept 1975, Prof Malcolm Sim Longair, s of James Longair; 1 s (Mark Howard b 13 Sept 1976), 1 da

(Sarah Charlotte b 7 March 1979); *Career* Leverhulme fell in history of art Clare Hall Cambridge 1972–73, lectr in history of art UCL 1973–76, visiting lectr Yale Univ 1977 and 1980, pt/t lectr, sr lectr then reader Dept of Architecture Univ of Edinburgh 1982–91, pt/t lectr Courtauld Inst of Art 1991–92; Univ of Cambridge: librarian to Faculty of Architecture and History of Art 1992–96, fell St John's Coll 1992–, reader in architectural history 1996–2001, prof of architectural history 2001–13, ret, head Dept of History of Art 2002–05 and 2007–09, prof emerita of architectural history and dir of research 2014–; Kennedy prof of Renaissance studies Smith Coll Massachusetts 2006, visiting prof Harvard Univ Center for Italian Renaissance Studies Florence 2007, Robert Janson-La Palme visiting prof Princeton Univ 2009, MacGeorge fell Univ of Melbourne 2012, Daphne Mayo visiting scholar Univ of Queensland 2012; cmmr: Royal Fine Art Cmmn for Scotland 1985–95, Royal Cmmn on Ancient and Historic Monuments of Scotland 1989–99, chm Soc of Architectural Historians of GB 1997–2000; Hon LittD UCD 2014; FSA 1984, FSA Scot 1991, Hon FRIAS 1996, FRSE 2004, FBA 2010; *Books* Jacopo Sansovino: Architecture & Patronage in Renaissance Venice (1975, 2 edn 1987), The Architectural History of Venice (1980, revised edn 2002), William Adam (Architectural Heritage I, ed 1990), Scottish Architects Abroad (Architectural Heritage II, ed 1991, Glenfiddich Award), Scottish Architecture from the Reformation to the Restoration (1995), La Scuola Grande della Misericordia di Venezia (co-author, 1999), Venice and the East: The Impact of the Islamic World on Venetian Architecture 1100–1500 (2000), Architettura e musica nella Venezia del Rinascimento (co-ed, 2006), Sound and Space in Renaissance Venice: Architecture, Music, Acoustics (with L Moretti, 2009), Venice Disputed: Marc' Antonio Barbaro and Venetian Architecture (1550–1600) (2011), The Music Room in Early Modern France and Italy (ed with L Moretti, 2012), Architecture and Pilgrimage 1000–1500: Southern Europe and Beyond (ed with P Davies and W Pullan 2013), The Image of Venice: Fialetti's View and Sir Henry Wotton (ed with Henrietta McBurney 2014), Santa Maria Gloriosa dei Frari: Immagini di Devozione, Spazi della Fede (ed with Carlo Corsato); *Recreations* music (especially opera and chamber music), hill walking (completed the Scottish Munros 2011), gardening, photography; *Style*— Prof Deborah Howard, FBA, FSA, FRSE; ✉ Faculty of Architecture and History of Art, University of Cambridge, 1 Scroope Terrace, Cambridge CB2 1PX (☎ 01223 332975, fax 01223 332960); St John's College, Cambridge CB2 1TP (☎ 01223 339360, fax 01223 740399, e-mail djh1000@cam.ac.uk)

HOWARD, Prof Ian; s of Harold Geoffrey Howard, of Aberdeen, and Violet, *née* Kelly; *b* 7 November 1952; *Educ* Aberdeen GS, Univ of Edinburgh, Edinburgh Coll of Art; *m* 1977, Ruth, da of Henry D'Arcy; 2 da (Francesca b 21 April 1982, Annabelle b 25 Jan 1986); *Career* artist; travelling scholarship Italy 1976, lectr in painting Grays Sch of Art Aberdeen 1977–86, head of painting Duncan of Jordanstone Coll of Art and Design Dundee 1986–95, prof of fine art Univ of Dundee 1995–2001, dean of faculty Duncan of Jordanstone Coll of Art Univ of Dundee 1999–2001, princ Edinburgh Coll of Art 2001–11 (ret); William Gillies Bequest Scholarship 1990 (travelled in India and Thailand); over 80 exhibitions incl: Different Realists (Talbot-Rice Art Centre Edinburgh) 1973, Edinburgh Int Film Festival 1976, Recent Acquisitions Scot Arts Cncl Gallery 1979 and 1981, Grease & Water (Scot Arts Cncl touring) 1982, Dunbar & Howard (Glasgow Arts Centre) 1984, Contemporary Scottish Printmakers (Mercury Gallery London) 1984, Sculptors' Drawings (Arts Cncl touring) 1984–85, New Drawings (Compass Gallery Glasgow) 1985, The Human Touch (Fischer Fine Art London) 1986, Br Cncl British/Malaysian Exhibition Kuala Lumpur 1986, Br Cncl touring exhibition (Bangkok, Singapore, Hong Kong) 1987, Scottish Contemporary Art (Clare Hall Cambridge) 1987, Scottish Art in Yugoslavia 1988, Fine Art Soc (Edinburgh and Glasgow) 1990, Print Works Chicago 1996, Dubrovnik Festival 1997, Iwate Festival Japan 1998, John David Mooney Fndn Chicago 2000; work in collections incl: Edinburgh Coll of Art, Scot Arts Cncl, Contemporary Arts Soc, Hunterian Gallery Glasgow, Unilever plc, Arts Cncl of England, ICI plc, Clare Coll Cambridge, City Arts Centre Edinburgh, Aberdeen Hosps Art Project, Fleming's Bank Collection; awards incl: Guthrie award Royal Scot Acad 1978, Scot Arts Cncl award 1979, Scot Arts Cncl major bursary 1984–85, first prize Scot Open Drawing competition 1985, Shell Premier award 1985, prizewinner Tolly-Cobbold Eastern Arts Nat competition 1985, Chicago prize 2000; Royal Scot Acad: associate 1984–, academician 1998–, treas 2008–; dir: ALBA magazine 1989–, Dundee Contemporary Arts (DCA) 1998–; memb Scot Arts Cncl Awards Panel and Purchasing Ctee 1990–96, memb Faculty of Fine Art Br Sch at Rome 1995–2001; *Style*— Prof Ian Howard

HOWARD, John; s of Henry Vivian Howard, and Florence Elizabeth, *née* Pulley; *b* 11 February 1951; *Educ* Strode's Sch Egham; *m* Angela Margaret; 2 da (Sasha Sophie, Tamzin Alice); *Career* admitted slr 1979; presenter: You and Yours (Radio 4) 1980–95, Nature (BBC TV) 1988–89, The Leading Edge (Radio 5), An Unfortunate Turn of Events (Radio 4) 1995, BBC World TV 1996–99; dir Sharp End Productions, dir Idea Films 1985–; dir Mortgage Code Compliance Bd 2000–05; non-exec dir Financial Ombudsman Service 2008–10; cmmr ind cmmn Equitable Life Payments 2010–11; non-exec dir nat counties building soc 2008–; non-exec dir Ofgem 2009–15; memb Fin Servs Consumer Panel 2000 (chm 2005–08); advsr Lloyds Banking Gp 2012–; tstee Thalidomide Tst 2009–; Soc of Authors/Pye Radio Award Best Light Entertainment Programme Radio 1979, RICS Radio Award Best Investigative Programme Radio 1983, Argus Consumer Journalist Award Radio 1985, Sony Award for Best Social Affairs Programme Radio 1989; *Style*— John Howard, Esq; ✉ e mail: johnhoward@consumer-insights.co.uk

HOWARD, Prof (James) Ken; OBE (2010); s of Frank Howard (d 1974), of Mousehole, Cornwall, and Elizabeth Crawford, *née* Meikle (d 1987); *b* 26 December 1932; *Educ* Kilburn GS, Hornsey Coll of Art, RCA (ARCA); *m* 1, 1961 (m dis 1974), Margaret Ann, da of Philip Popham, of Ickenham, Middx; *m* 2, 1991, Christa Gaa, *née* Koehler, ARWS (d 1992), formerly wife of Hartmut Gaa; 2 step da; *m* 3, 2000, Dora Bertolutti, formerly wife of Bruno Di Giorgio; *Career* Nat Serv RM 1953–55; artist; Br Cncl scholarship Florence 1958–59, taught at various London art schs 1959–73, official artist Imperial War Museum NI 1973 and 1978; painted for Br Army: NI, Germany, Cyprus, Hong Kong, Brunei, Nepal, Belize, Norway, Lebanon; Hon RBA 1988, Hon ROI 1988 (hon fell 2007), hon Soc of Graphic Fine Art 2008; past pres New English Art Club (PPNEAC); Freeman City of London 2007, Liveryman Worshipful Co of Painter Stainers 2007; NEAC 1962 (pres 1998), RWA 1981, RWS 1983, RBSA 1991, RA 1992 (ARA 1983); *Solo Exhibitions* Plymouth Art Centre 1955, John Whibley Gallery 1966–68, New Grafton Gallery 1971–2000, Hong Kong 1979, Jersey 1980, Nicosia 1982, Delhi 1983, Oscar J Peter Johnson 1986–92, Duncalfe Gallery Harrogate 1987–, Sinfield Gallery 1991, 1993 and 1995, Hollis Taggart Inc Washington DC 1993, Everard Reed Gallery Johannesburg 1998 and Cape Town 2001, Richard Green Gallery 2002, 2003, 2004, 2005, 2006, 2007 and 2009, Royal Acad Friends Room 2009, Richard Green Gallery 2010 and 2012; *Work in Collections* Plymouth Art Gallery, Imperial War Museum, Guildhall Art Gallery, Ulster Museum, Nat Army Museum, Southend Art Gallery, HNC Art Gallery, Sheffield Art Gallery, Bankside Gallery; *Portraits* incl: Gerald Durrell, Gen Sir Martin Farndale; *Commissions* Drapers' Co, Haberdashers' Co, States of Jersey, HQ Br Army of the Rhine, HM Forces in Cyprus, The Stock Exchange, Lloyd's of London, Royal Hosp Chelsea, Banque Paribas, *Video* Inspired by Light 1996, Vision of Venice in Watercolour 1998, Vision of Venice in Oils 2000; *Books* The War Artists (1986), Art Class (1989), Venice – The Artist's Vision (1990), Visions of Venice (1990), The Paintings of Ken Howard (1992), Ken Howard – a Personal View (1998), Light and Dark (autobiography, 2011), Ken Howard in the Footsteps of Turner (2012); *Style*— Prof Ken Howard, Esq, OBE, RA; ✉ 8 South Bolton Gardens, London SW5 0DH (☎ 020 7373 2912, fax 020 7244 6246); St Clements Studio, Paul Lane, Mousehole, Cornwall TR19 6TR (☎ 01736 731596); Cannaregio 6262, Venice, Italy (☎ 0039 041 5202277)

HOWARD, Dr Laurence; OBE (2003); s of Henry Lovering Howard (d 1990), of Surrey, and Beryl Cicely Howard; *b* 29 March 1943, Woking, Surrey; *Educ* Strode's Sch Egham, Univ of Nottingham (BSc), Univ of Leicester (PhD); *m* 1966, Christine Mary, da of William Kinver; 1 da (Anna b 16 July 1972), 1 s (Stephen b 29 May 1974); *Career* Wolfson research fell Univ of Leeds 1970–73, lectr in physiology Univ of Leicester 1974–90, sub dean Leicester Med Sch 1990–2003; author of various articles in physiological jls; chm: Rutland Bench 1991–97, Central Cncl of Magistrates' Courts Ctees 2002–03; memb Bd Unified Courts Admin Prog 2003–04; pres: Leicester and Rutland Magistrates' Assoc, Leicester and Rutland Headway, Leics and Rutland Community Fndn 2010–; patron Leicester Charity Link 2010–, chm Rutland Sinfonia; HM Lord-Lt Rutland 2003–; fell UC Northampton, hon Air Cdre 504 (County of Notts) Squadron 2008; Hon LLD Univ of Leicester 2013; memb Physiological Soc 1980; *Recreations* horses and music; *Style*— Dr Laurence Howard, OBE; ✉ Daventry House, Main Street, Whissendine, Rutland LE15 7ET (☎ 01664 474662)

HOWARD, Margaret; da of John Bernard Howard (d 1969), and Ellen Corwena, *née* Roberts (d 2009); *b* 29 March 1938; *Educ* St Mary's Convent Rhyl, St Teresa's Convent Sunbury-on-Thames, Guildhall Sch of Music and Drama (LGSM), Univ of Indiana, LRAM, Open Univ (BA); *Career* BBC announcer 1966–69, reporter World This Weekend 1971–74, presenter Pick of the Week 1974–91, radio columnist Sunday Express 1991–92; Classic FM: presenter Classic Reports 1992–94, ed and presenter Howard's Week 1994–97, presenter Masterclass 1994–98, presenter Hot Ticket Hour, Vienna City of Dreams and Classic Discoveries 1997–99; radio critic The Tablet 1991–2001, columnist The Universe 1973–79, classical CD reviewer Chic Magazine 1995–98; presenter: Viva Verdi GB Concert Tour with Opera Nazionale Italiana 2001, Haydn's Seven Last Words From The Cross with the Medici Quartet Geneva and London 2001 and 2002, Coverwood Farm Concert 2002; conslt and recording artist Classical Communications Ltd 2003–07, interviewer Appreciating Great Music CD series for Haysbridge (UK) Ltd 2003–; female UK Personality of the Year Sony Awards 1984, Sony Radio Awards Roll of Honour 1988, Voice of the Listener Award for Excellence 1991, Radio Personality of the Year Television and Radio Industries Club Awards 1996; *Books* Margaret Howard's Pick of the Week (1984), Court Jesting (1986); *Recreations* swimming, dog walking, wine tasting; *Clubs* South London Swimming (Tooting Bec Lido); *Style*— Miss Margaret Howard; ✉ 215 Cavendish Road, London SW12 0BP (☎ 020 8673 7336, e-mail margaret.howard@virgin.net)

H

HOWARD, Dr Mary Elizabeth; da of William Joseph Howard (d 1974), and Mary, *née* Breaden (d 1979); *b* 17 April 1953; *Educ* Notre Dame HS Glasgow, Univ of Glasgow (MB ChB); *m* 14 July 1976, John Hilary Higgins, s of John Joseph Higgins, MBE (d 1972); 1 da (Louise Mary Anne b 1985); *Career* sr registrar in histopathology Gtr Glasgow Health Bd 1980–83 (house surgn and house physician 1976–77, registrar 1977–80), conslt histopathologist Wishaw General Hosp (now part of Lanarkshire Acute Hospitals Tst) 1983–; memb: BMA, Assoc of Clinical Pathologists, Mensa; FRCPath 1994 (MRCPath 1982); *Recreations* music, arts and crafts, reading; *Style*— Dr Mary Howard; ✉ Department of Histopathology, Wishaw General Hospital, 50 Netherton Street, Carluke, Lanarkshire ML2 0DP (☎ 01698 366325, fax 01698 366333, e-mail mary.howard@laht.scot.nhs.uk)

HOWARD, Michael Newman; QC (1986); s of late Henry Ian Howard, and Tilly Celia, *née* Newman; *b* 10 June 1947; *Educ* Clifton, Magdalen Coll Oxford (MA, BCL); *Career* lectr in law LSE 1970–74; called to the Bar Gray's Inn 1971 (bencher 1995); in practice at the Bar 1972–, recorder of the Crown Court 1993– (asst recorder 1989–93); ldr Admiralty Bar 2000–; visiting prof: of law Univ of Essex 1987–92, of maritime law UCL 1996–99, of marine law Tulane Univ New Orleans 2011–; panel memb Lloyds Salvage Arbitrators 1988–2009; *Books* Phipson on Evidence (jt ed, 12 edn 1976, 13 edn 1982, 14 edn 1990, 15 edn 2000), Force Majeure and Frustration of Contract (contrib, 1991, 2 edn 1994), Halsbury's Laws of England (4 edn, contrib Damages), Consensus ad idem: Essays on Contract in Honour of Guenter Treitel (contrib, 1996), Butterworth's Commercial Court and Arbitration Pleadings (contrib, 2005), Palmer on Bailment (contrib, 3 edn 2010), Foreign Currency: Claims, Judgments, Damages (with J A Knott and J A Kimbell, 2016); *Recreations* books, music, sport; *Clubs* Oxford and Cambridge, RAC, Garrick; *Style*— M N Howard, Esq, QC; ✉ Quadrant Chambers, Quadrant House, 10 Fleet Street, London EC4Y 1AU (☎ 020 7583 4444, fax 020 7583 4455, e-mail michael.howard@quadrantchambers.com)

HOWARD, Nigel; *Educ* BSc; *Career* dir Morgan Crucible plc 1992–2003, chm Zotefoams plc 2007– (memb Bd 2006–); non-exec dir Alliance One Int Inc 2005–; ARCS; *Style*— Nigel Howard, Esq; ✉ Zotefoams plc, 675 Mitcham Road, Croydon, Surrey CR9 3AL

HOWARD, Philip Ewen; s of Francis John Adrian Howard, of London, and Lynnette, *née* Maider; *b* 5 June 1966; *Educ* Bradfield Coll, Univ of Kent at Canterbury (BSc); *m* 15 Dec 1990, Jennifer Elizabeth, da of Robert Collier; 1 da (Amelia Mae b 7 July 1995), 1 s (Alexander Gregory Robert b 1 Feb 1999); *Career* trg/apprenticeship: with Roux Restaurants Ltd 1988–89, under Marco Pierre White Harvey's Restaurant 1989–90, under Simon Hopkinson Bibendum 1990–91; head chef/jt owner The Square 1991– (8 out of 10 Good Food Guide 1999–2015, second Michelin star 1998– (first 1994)), jt owner The Ledbury 2005– (second Michelin star 2010 (first 2007)), jt owner Kitchen W8 2009– (Michelin star 2011–), jt owner Sonny's Kitchen 2013–; television appearances incl Great British Menu (BBC 2) 2012 (winner, cooked fish course for the Olympic Banquet); *Books* The Square, The Cookbook: Vols 1 and 2, Savoury and Sweet; *Recreations* skiing; *Style*— Mr Philip Howard; ✉ 84 Madrid Road, Barnes, London SW13 9PG; The Square, 6–10 Bruton Street, Mayfair, London W1J 6PU (☎ 020 7495 7100, fax 020 7495 7150, e-mail phil@squarerestaurant.com, website www.squarerestaurant.com)

HOWARD, Philip Nicholas Charles; s of Peter Dunsmore Howard (d 1965), and Doris Emily Metaxa; *b* 2 November 1933; *Educ* Eton, Trinity Coll Oxford (MA); *m* 1959, Myrtle Janet Mary, da of Sir Reginald Houldsworth, 5 Bt, *qv*; 2 s, 1 da; *Career* Nat Serv Lt Black Watch; newspaper reporter, columnist and author; Glasgow Herald 1959–64, columnist, ldr writer and composer of Word Watching and Modern Manners Lost Words and Word Routes The Times 1990– (joined 1964, literary ed 1978–90), London ed Verbatim 1977–; pres Classical Assoc 2001–, fndr patron Friends of the Classics; Liveryman Worshipful Co of Wheelwrights; FRSL; *Books* The Black Watch (1968), The Royal Palaces (1970), London's River (1975), New Words for Old (1977), The British Monarchy (1977), Weasel Words (1978), Words Fail Me (1980), A Word in Your Ear (1983), The State of the Language (1984), We Thundered Out, 200 Years of The Times 1785–1985 (1985), Winged Words (1988), Word-Watching (1988), A Word in Time (1990), The Times Bedside Book (ed, 1990 and 1992), The British Library: A Treasure House of Knowledge (2008), Lost Words, A Feast of Forgotten Words, Their Origin and Their Meanings (2012); *Recreations* reading, walking, talking; *Style*— Philip Howard, Esq; ✉ Flat 1, 47 Ladbroke Grove, London W11 3AR (☎ 020 7727 1077, fax 020 7221 7626, e-mail philip.howard@the-times.co.uk)

HOWARD, Russell Joseph; *b* 23 March 1980, Bristol; *Educ* Bedford Modern Sch, Perins Sch New Alresford, Univ of the West of England; *Career* comedian; stand-up tours incl: Wandering 2006–07, Adventures 2007–08, Dingledodies 2008–09, Big Rooms and Belly Laughs 2009, Right Here, Right Now 2011, Wonderbox 2014, Round the World 2017;

television appearances incl: Never Mind the Buzzcocks (BBC2) 2006 and 2007, regular panellist Mock The Week (BBC2) 2007–, Would I Lie To You? (BBC1) 2007, Live at the Apollo (BBC1) 2007 and 2009, 8 Out of 10 Cats (Channel 4) 2008, Room 101 2015; presenter: Russell Howard's Good News (BBC3) 2009–, Russell Howard's Stand-Up Central 2015–; Best Compère Chortle Comedy Award 2006, Best Theatre Show Chortle Comedy Award 2009; *DVDs* Live (2008), Live 2 (2009), Right Here Right Now (2011), Wonderbox (2014); *Style*— Mr Russell Howard; ✉ c/o Avalon Management, 4a Exmoor Street, London W10 6BD

HOWARD, Hon Simon Bartholomew Geoffrey; 3 s of Baron Howard of Henderskelfe (Life Peer; d 1984); *b* 26 January 1956; *Educ* Eton, RAC Cirencester, Study Centre for Fine and Decorative Arts; *m* 1, 1983 (m dis 2000), Annette Marie, Countess Compton, er da of Charles Antony Russell Smallwood, and formerly 2 w (m dis 1977), of Earl Compton (now 7 Marquess of Northampton); m 2, 2001, Rebecca Verassana, da of Jonathan and Angela Sieff; 2 c (Merlin, Octavia (twins) b 2002); *Career* chm of estate co 1984–2015; landowner (10,000 acres); chm Yorkshire Regnl HHA 1986–97, dir HHA 1996–2016 (chm Tourism and Commercial Devpt Ctee 1995–2005); chm Treasure Houses of England 1995–2014, dir Assoc of Leading Visitor Attractions 2012–15; conslt Sotheby's 1998–; High Sheriff North Yorks 1995–96; *Recreations* photography, wine, country sports; *Style*— The Hon Simon Howard; ✉ Castle Howard, York YO60 7DA (☎ 01653 648444)

HOWARD OF LYMPNE, Baron (Life Peer UK 2010), of Lympne in the County of Kent; Rt Hon Michael Howard; CH (2011), PC (1990), QC (1982); s of late Bernard Howard, and Hilda Howard; *b* 7 July 1941; *Educ* Llanelli GS, Peterhouse Cambridge; *m* 1975, Sandra Clare, da of Wing Cdr Saville Paul; 1 s, 1 da, 1 step s (Sholto Douglas-Home, *qv*); *Career* pres Cambridge Union 1962, called to the Bar Inner Temple 1964, chm Bow Group 1970; Parly candidate (Cons) Liverpool Edge Hill 1966 and 1970, MP (Cons) Folkestone and Hythe 1983–2010; memb: Cons Gp for Europe, Euro Movement Exec Ctee 1970–73; PPS to Slr-Gen 1984–85, Parly under sec of state for Consumer and Corporate Affrs 1985–87, min for Local Govt 1987–88, min for Water and Planning 1988–90, sec of state for Employment 1990–92, sec of state for the Environment 1992–93, home sec 1993–97; shadow foreign sec 1997–99, shadow Chllr of the Exchequer 2001–03, ldr Cons Pty and HM Oppn 2003–05 (Cons Pty leadership challenger 1997); memb Cons Pty Policy Bd 2001–03; chm: Coningsby Club 1972–73, Atlantic Partnership 2000–03, Entré Gold Inc, Soma Oil & Gas Ltd; memb Advsy Bd: Orca Exploration Inc, Tetronics Ltd; chm Hospice UK; Parliamentarian of the Year Spectator Awards 2003; *Recreations* watching sport, reading; *Clubs* Carlton, Pratt's; *Style*— The Rt Hon the Lord Howard of Lympne, CH, QC; ✉ House of Lords, London SW1A 0PW (☎ 020 7219 3964, fax 020 7219 4551, e-mail howardm@parliament.uk)

HOWARD OF RISING, Baron (Life Peer UK 2004), of Castle Rising in the County of Norfolk; Greville Patrick Charles Howard; s of Col Henry Redvers Greville Howard (d 1978), and Patience Nichol (d 1987); *b* 22 April 1941; *Educ* Eton; *m* 1, 1968 (m dis 1972), Zoe Rosaleen, da of Douglas Walker; m 2, 1978, Mary Rose (d 1980), da of Sir (Edward) John Chichester, 11 Bt (d 2007); m 3, 1981, Mary Cortlandt, da of Robert Veitch Culverwell; 2 s (Hon Thomas Henry Greville b 1983 (page of honour to HM The Queen 1995–98), Hon Charles Edward John b 1986), 1 da (Hon Annabel Rosemary Diana b 1984); *Career* landowner; Liveryman Worshipful Co of Mercers; *Recreations* reading; *Style*— The Rt Hon the Lord Howard of Rising; ✉ Castle Rising, Kings Lynn, Norfolk PE31 6AF

HOWARTH, Prof David; s of George Albert Howarth, and Jean, *née* Rowbotham; *b* 10 November 1958, Wednesbury, Staffs; *Educ* Queen Mary's GS, Univ of Cambridge (MA), Yale Univ (LLM, MA, MPhil); *m* Edna Helen Murphy; 2 s (Joseph (Joe), Jacob (Jake)); *Career* Univ of Cambridge: lectr 1988–2005, reader in law 2005–15, dir MPhil in Public Policy 2012–, prof of law and public policy 2015–; Cambridge CC: cncllr 1987–2004, ldr Lib Dems 1990–2003, ldr oppn 1992–2000, ldr 2000–03; Parly candidate (Lib Dem): Cambridge 1992 and 2001, Peterborough 1997; MP (Lib Dem) Cambridge 2005–10, shadow min for legal affrs and justice 2007–10; memb: Lib Dem Federal Policy Ctee 1989–2000, European Lib Dem Cncl; former chair Lib Dem Economic Policy Working Gp; writer of numerous jl articles and book chapters; Butterworth Prize Best New Legal Textbook 1995; fell Clare Coll Cambridge 1985–; *Books* Textbook on Tort (1995), Hepple and Matthews, Tort: Cases and Materials (co-ed from 5 edn), Reinventing the State (co-ed, 2007), Law as Engineering: Thinking about what lawyers do (2013); numerous articles in learned jls and book chapters; *Style*— Professor David Howarth; ✉ Clare College, Cambridge CB2 1TL

HOWARTH, George; PC (2005), MP; Rt Hon; *Career* MP (Lab): Knowsley N 1986–97, Knowsley N and Sefton E 1997–2010, Knowsley 2010–; Parly under-sec of state: Home Office 1997–99, NI 1999–2001; memb Intelligence and Security Ctee 2005–; *Style*— The Rt Hon George Howarth, MP; ✉ House of Commons, London SW1A 0AA (☎ 020 7219 3000)

HOWARTH, Sir (James) Gerald Douglas; kt (2012), MP; s of late James Howarth, and late Mary Howarth; *b* 12 September 1947; *Educ* Bloxham Sch, Univ of Southampton; *m* 1973, Elizabeth; 1 da, 2 s; *Career* gen sec Soc for Individual Freedom 1969–71, Bank of America International 1971–76, European Arab Bank 1976–81, Standard Chartered Bank plc 1981–83 (loan syndication mangr); MP (Cons): Cannock and Burntwood 1983–92, Aldershot 1997–; PPS to: Michael Spicer at the Dept of Energy 1987–90, Sir George Young at the DOE 1990–91, Rt Hon Margaret Thatcher 1991–92; shadow def min 2002–10, Parly under-sec of state Miny of Defence 2010–12; memb Home Affairs Select Ctee 1997–2001, memb Defence Select Ctee 2001–03; chm Parly Aerospace Gp 1998–99 (vice-chm 1997–98 and 1999–2000), vice-chm Cons Parly Environment, Tport and the Regions Ctee 1997–99, vice-chm Cons Home Affairs Ctee 1999–2002, chm Lords and Commons Family and Child Protection Gp, hon sec Cons Parly Aviation Ctee 1983–87, memb Exec 1922 Ctee 1999–2002; jt md Taskforce Communications Ltd 1993–95; pres British Air Display Assoc, memb Cncl Air League 2004–10 and 2012–; chm 92 Gp 2001–07 and 2013–; cncllr London Borough of Hounslow 1982–83; tstee: Vulcan to the Sky Tst 2006–, Br Forces Fndn 2009–; jt patron Br Disabled Flying Assoc; Liveryman Hon Co of Air Pilots; fell Industry and Parly Tst; *Publications* No Turning Back (1985) and other publications of the No Turning Back Group; *Recreations* flying (Britannia Airways Parly Pilot of the Year 1988), photography, walking, DIY; *Clubs* Royal Air Force; *Style*— Sir Gerald Howarth, MP; ✉ House of Commons, London SW1A 0AA (☎ 020 7219 5650, fax 020 7219 1198, e-mail geraldhowarth@parliament.uk, website www.geraldhowarth.org)

HOWARTH OF BRECKLAND, Baroness (Life Peer UK 2001), of Parson Cross in the County of South Yorkshire; Valerie Georgina Howarth; OBE (1999); da of George Howarth, and Edith Elizabeth Steele; *b* 5 September 1940; *Educ* Abbeydale Girls' GS, Univ of Leicester (Sheila McKay Meml Prize), Henley Business Sch; *Career* mgmnt trainee Walsh's Ltd 1959–60, family caseworker Family Welfare Assoc 1963–68; London Borough of Lambeth: sr child care worker and trg offr 1968–70, area co-ordinator 1970–72, chief co-ordinator of social work 1972–76, asst dir of personal services 1976–82; dir of social services London Borough of Brent 1982–86, chief exec ChildLine 1987–2001; chair: Lambeth and Brent Area Review Ctee, London Directors' Child Care Gp; advsr to: London Boroughs' Regnl Planning Ctee, Women's Refuges; conslt to: John Grooms Assoc for Disabled People 1987 (tstee 1988–2007), Thomas Coram Fndn 1987, Ind Ctee for the Supervision of Telephone Information Systems (ICSTIS) 1988–2001; tstee: National Cncl for Voluntary Child Care Orgns 1990–95 (vice-chair), Lucy Faithfull Fndn 1992– (vice-chm), National Children's Bureau 1993–94; UK rep Euro Forum for Child Welfare 1994–97; fndr memb: Telephone Helplines Assoc 1995–96 (first chair), King's Cross Homelessness Project (first chair), London Homelessness Forum, NCH Commn considering Children as Abusers 1991–92, NSPCC Professional Advsy Panel 1993–95, Working Gp on Children and the Law (resulting in Child Witness Pack 1991–94 and trg video for judges 1997), Home Office Steering Gp on Child Witnesses; bd memb Food Standards Agency 2000–07; tstee Sieff Fndn 1992–2006; memb Br Assoc of Social Workers (BASW), Nat Care Standards Cmmn 2001–05, tstee Little Hearts Matter 2002–16, patron Little Hearts Matter 2002–, chair Child Helplines Int 2003–07, memb Select Ctee House of Lords 2005– (chair Sub-Ctee G 2007–10, memb Sub-Ctee D 2010–15, memb Ecclesiastic Ctee 2015–), memb Bd Children and Family Courts and Support Services 2002–08 (chair 2008–12), patron NYAS 2003–16, chair/pres John Grooms Shaftesbury (now Livability) 2007–, chair Stop It Now Steering Gp 2009–12, vice-pres LGA 2008–, patron TRACKS (autism) 2010–; Children's Champion Dods Charity Champion Award 2012; hon doctorate Open Univ 2007; assoc memb Assoc of Directors of Adult Social Services; *Style*— The Baroness Howarth of Breckland, OBE; ✉ House of Lords, London SW1A 0PW

HOWARTH OF NEWPORT, Baron (Life Peer UK 2005), of Newport in the County of Gwent; Alan Thomas Howarth; CBE (1982), PC (2000); *b* 11 June 1944; *Educ* Rugby, King's Coll Cambridge; *m* 1967 (m dis 1996), Gillian Martha, da of Arthur Chance, of Dublin; 2 s, 2 da; *Career* former head Chm's Office CCO (private sec to Rt Hon William Whitelaw and Rt Hon Lord Thorneycroft as Pty Chm), dir Cons Res Dept 1979–81, vice-chm Cons Pty Orgn 1980–81; MP: Stratford-upon-Avon 1983–97 (resigned Cons Pty 1995, memb Lab Pty 1995–), (Lab) Newport E 1997–2005; PPS to Dr Rhodes Boyson 1985–87, asst Govt whip 1987, a Lord Cmmr of HM Treasy (Govt whip) 1988, min for Schools 1989–92, min for HE and Sci 1990–92, Employment min and min for Disabled People 1997–98, min for the Arts 1998–2001, memb Intelligence and Security Ctee 2001–05; memb: Nat Heritage Select Ctee 1992–93, Social Security Select Ctee 1996–97; *Books* Changing Charity (jtly, 1984), Monty At Close Quarters (jtly, 1985), Save Our Schools (jtly, 1987), Arts: The Next Move Forward (jtly, 1987), Cities of Pride (jtly, 1994); *Recreations* books, arts, hill walking; *Style*— The Rt Hon the Lord Howarth of Newport, CBE, PC; ✉ House of Lords, London SW1A 0PW (☎ 020 7219 3000/5077)

HOWDEN, Alan Percival; s of C P Howden (d 1986), and Marian, *née* Grindell (d 1980); *b* 28 August 1936; *Educ* Sale GS, UMIST (BSc Tech); *m* Judith, da of Edward L South; 1 da (Charlotte b 1981); *Career* BBC TV: exec Purchased Progs 1964–77, head of Purchased Progs 1977–83, gen mangr Prog Acquisition 1983–91, Bd memb BBC Enterprises 1989–94, controller Prog Acquisition 1991–99, conslt Prog Acquisition 1999–2000; dir Picturedrome Media Ltd 2000–, non-exec dir UK Film and Television Prodns Ltd 2001–; Br Fedn of Film Socs: vice-chm 1965–80, chm 1980–82, vice-pres 1982–; govr BFI 1994–2001; chm BFI Film Educn Working Gp 1998–99; memb: BAFTA 1990, Br Kinematograph Sound and Television Soc (BKSTS) 1988, RTS 1995; *Recreations* theatre, early music, English countryside; *Style*— Alan Howden; ✉ 31 Thornton Road, London SW19 4NG (☎ 020 8944 1921, e-mail alanhowden@btconnect.com)

HOWE, Alison; da of Fred Howe (d 1996), and Gladys, *née* Luck (d 2000); *b* 19 September 1969, Northampton; *Educ* Weston Favell Upper Sch Northampton, Northampton Coll of FE; *m* Nick Draper; *Career* prodr BBC Radio 1 (John Peel, Andy Kershaw, Annie Nightingale and Jo Whiley) 1994–98, exec prod BBC Music Entertainment (progs incl: Later...with Jools Holland, Jools' Annual Hootenanny, Glastonbury Festival, Reading Festival and other live music shows) 1998–; RTS nominee 2008, winner multiple Broadcast Awards, nominee BAFTA TV Awards 2014; *Style*— Ms Alison Howe; ✉ BBC Broadcasting House, Portland Place, London W1A 1AA

HOWE, Prof Christopher Barry; MBE (1997); s of Charles Roderick Howe, and Patricia, *née* Creeden; *b* 3 November 1937; *Educ* William Ellis Sch Highgate, St Catharine's Coll Cambridge (MA), Univ of London (PhD); *m* 2 Dec 1967, Patricia Anne, da of L G Giles; 1 da (Emma Claire (Mrs Dominic Soares) b 1968), 1 s (Roderick Giles b 1972); *Career* Econ Directorate Fedn Br Industries 1961–63; SOAS Univ of London: res fell and lectr 1963–72, reader in the economics of Asia 1972–79, prof 1979–, prof of Chinese business mgmnt 2001 (prof emeritus 2003); head Contemporary China Inst 1972–78; memb: Hong Kong Univ and Poly Grants Ctee 1974–93, UGC 1979–84, Hong Kong RGC 1991–; fell 48 Gp Club; FBA 2001; *Books* Employment and Economic Growth in Urban China (1971), Wage Patterns and Wage Policies in Modern China (1973), China's Economy: A Basic Guide (1978), Shanghai (1980), Foundations of the Chinese Planned Economy (1989), The Origins of Japanese Trade Supremacy (1995), China and Japan (1996), Chinese Technology Transfer in the 1990s (1997), China's Economic Reform (2003), China and the Global Energy Crisis (jtly, 2007); *Recreations* walking, swimming, cycling, antiquarian books, France, music, photography; *Style*— Prof Christopher Howe, MBE; ✉ School of Oriental and African Studies, Thornaugh Street, Russell Square, London WC1A 0XG (☎ 020 7637 2388)

HOWE, Darren; QC (2015); *Educ* Univ of Hull; *Career* called to the Bar (Gray's Inn) 1992; recorder; memb: Family Law Bar Assoc, Coll of Mediators; *Style*— Darren Howe, Esq, QC; ✉ 1 Garden Court, Temple, London EC4Y 9BJ

HOWE, Elizabeth; OBE (2008); da of Allen Howe (d 1998), and Katherine, *née* Davies; *b* 22 March 1956; *Educ* Howell's Sch Llandaff, Univ of Exeter (LLB); *m* 11 Oct 1986, Patrick; 1 da (Emily b 2 April 1991), 1 s (David b 2 July 1994); *Career* admitted slr 1980; higher court advocate; chief crown prosecutor Kent 1999–2007, gen counsel Int Assoc of Prosecutors 2007–15, chair Int Legal Assistance Consortium (ILAC) 2015–; chair Kent Criminal Justice Bd 2003–05; memb: Kent Law Soc (pres 2006–07), Law Soc, Int Bar Assoc, American Bar Assoc, Int Assoc of Prosecutors; Hon LLD Univ of Kent 2015; *Recreations* riding, tennis, swimming, theatre; *Style*— Miss Elizabeth Howe, OBE; ✉ e-mail elizabeth.howe@ilacnet.org

HOWE, 7 Earl (UK 1821); Frederick Richard Penn Curzon; PC (2013); also Baron Howe of Langar (GB 1788), Baron Curzon of Penn (GB 1794) and Viscount Curzon of Penn (UK 1802); s of Cdr (Chambré) George William Penn Curzon, RN (d 1976), and Enid Jane Victoria (d 1997), da of late Malcolm Mackenzie Fergusson; suc cous, 6 Earl Howe, CBE (d 1984); *b* 29 January 1951; *Educ* Rugby, ChCh Oxford (MA); *m* 1983, Elizabeth Helen (DL Bucks 1995), elder da of late Capt Burleigh Edward St Lawrence Stuart, of Ickford, Bucks; 3 da (Lady Anna Elizabeth b 19 Jan 1987, Lady Flora Grace b 12 June 1989, Lady Lucinda Rose b 12 Oct 1991), 1 s (Thomas, Viscount Curzon b 22 Oct 1994); *Heir* s, Viscount Curzon; *Career* banker and farmer; dir: Adam & Co plc 1987–90, Provident Life Assoc Ltd 1988–91, Andry Montgomery Ltd 2000–10; Lord-in-Waiting to HM The Queen (Govt Whip) 1991–92; Govt spokesman: on Employment and Transport 1991, on Environment and Def 1992; Parly sec: MAFF 1992–95, MOD 1995–97; oppn spokesman on health House of Lords 1997–2010, Parly under-sec of state Dept of Health 2010–15, min of state MOD and dep ldr House of Lords 2015–; chm LAPADA 1999–2010; pres: Nat Soc for Epilepsy 1985–2010, RNLI (Chilterns Branch), South Bucks Assoc for The Disabled, LAPADA 2010–; vice-pres RNLI 2014–; memb: Cncl RNLI, RAFT 2000–10; govr: King William IV Naval Fndn, Milton's Cottage Tst 1985–2011; patron: DEMAND 2000–10, The Chiltern Soc; ACIB 1976, Hon FRCP 2008; *Recreations* musical composition, music, cinema, gardening, reading; *Style*— The Rt Hon the Earl Howe, PC; ✉ House of Lords, London SW1A 0PW (☎ 020 7219 5353, e-mail howef@parliament.uk)

HOWE, Geoffrey Michael Thomas; s of Michael Edward Howe, and Susan Dorothy, *née* Allan; *b* 3 September 1949; *Educ* Manchester Grammar, St John's Coll Cambridge (MA); *Career* admitted slr 1973; ptnr Co Dept Clifford-Turner 1980 (joined 1975), managing ptnr Clifford Chance 1989–97, general counsel and dir Robert Fleming Holdings Ltd 1998–2000; chm: Railtrack Gp plc 2002, Jardine Lloyd Thompson plc 2006– (non-exec dir 2002–), Nationwide Building Soc 2007–15 (non-exec dir 2005–); non-exec dir: Gateway Electronic Components Ltd 2000–, Investec plc 2003–10, Close Brothers Gp plc 2011–; Freeman Worshipful Co of Slrs; memb Law Soc 1973; *Recreations* wine, antiques, opera; *Style*— Geoffrey Howe, Esq

HOWE, Ven George Alexander; s of Eugene Howe (d 2009), and Olivia Lydia Caroline, *née* Denroche (d 2011); *b* 22 January 1952; *Educ* Liverpool Inst HS, St John's Coll Durham (BA), Westcott House Cambridge; *m* 3 Oct 1980, Jane, da of Allen Corbould (decd); 1 da (Katharine Rachel b 19 May 1982), 1 s (Simon Andrew 22 Feb 1984); *Career* curate St Cuthbert Peterlee 1975–79, curate St Mary Norton Stockton-on-Tees 1979–81, vicar Hart with Elwick Hall 1981–85, rector St Edmund Sedgefield 1985–91, rural dean of Sedgefield 1988–91, vicar Holy Trinity Kendal 1991–2000, rural dean of Kendal 1994–99, hon canon of Carlisle Cathedral 1994–, archdeacon of Westmorland and Furness 2000–11, archdeacon emeritus, Bishop's COS and diocesean dir of ordinands 2011–15, ret; chm Church and Community Fund 2007–13; *Style*— The Ven George A Howe; ✉ 1 St John's Gate, Threlkeld, Keswick, Cumbria CA12 4TZ

HOWE, Graham Edward; *b* 23 May 1961, St Albans, Herts; *Educ* St Albans Boys' GS, Univ of Birmingham (BCom); *m* Caroline Jane; 3 s; *Career* formerly with: Hutchison Telecom, First Pacific Company, Touche Ross Mgmnt Consltș; co-fndr Orange 1992, chief financial offr Orange 1996, dep ceo Orange plc 1996–2003; currently chm Promethean; non-exec dir Cable and Wireless plc 2003–06; ACA; *Recreations* charity fundraising (cycled Land's End to John O'Groats 2003, NY Marathon 2005, North Pole 2006); *Style*— Graham Howe, Esq; ✉ e-mail gh@grahamhowe.com

HOWE, John Francis; CB (1996), OBE (1974); s of late Frank Howe, OBE, of Devon, and Marjorie Alice, *née* Hubball; *b* 29 January 1944; *Educ* Shrewsbury, Balliol Coll Oxford (MA); *m* 1981, Angela Ephrosini, da of Charalambos Nicolaides (d 1973), of Alicante and London; 1 da (Alexandra b 1983), 1 step da (Caroline b 1973); *Career* Civil Serv: princ MOD 1972 (asst princ 1967), civil advsr GOC NI 1972–73, private sec to Perm Under Sec 1975–78, asst sec MOD 1979, seconded FCO, cnsllr UK Delgn to NATO 1981–84, head Def Arms Control Unit 1985–86, private sec to Sec of State for Def 1986–87, asst under sec of state (personnel and logistics) 1988–91, dep under sec of state (civilian mgmnt) 1992–96, dep chief of defence procurement (support) 1996–2000, seconded as exec dir to Thales plc (formerly Thomson-CSF Racal plc) 2000–02; vice-chm Thales UK 2002–09 (non-exec memb Advsy Bd 2009–), pres EuroDefense UK 2010–; chm Citylink Telecommunications 2004–; chm Frederick Bonnart-Braunthal Tst 2014–16; *Books* International Security and Arms Control (contrib); *Recreations* travel, gardening, pictures; *Clubs* Athenaeum; *Style*— John Howe, Esq, CB, OBE; ✉ Thales UK, 2 Dashwood Lang Road, Addlestone, Weybridge, Surrey KT15 2NX (☎ 01932 824809)

HOWE, Leslie Clive; s of Alexander Leslie Howe, of Cheshunt, Herts, and Patricia Ann, *née* Lord; *b* 21 April 1955; *Educ* Cheshunt GS, Royal Dental Hosp Univ of London (BDS); *Career* house surgn Royal Dental Hosp 1979, sr house surgn London Hosp 1979–80; lectr in conservative dentistry: Royal Dental Hosp 1980–85, Guy's Dental Sch 1985–; conslt in restorative dentistry Guy's Hospital 1993–; currently head Dept of Conservative Dentistry KCL Dental Sch; Lunt prize, Sounders scholar, Baron Cornelius ver Heyden de Lancey award; memb: Br Soc for Restorative Dentistry, Br Soc for Dental Res; Accreditation in Restorative Dentistry 1989; FDSRCS 1983; *Books* Inlays, Crowns and Bridges (1993), Implants in Clinical Dentistry (2000), Planning and Making Crowns and Bridges (2007); *Style*— Leslie Howe, Esq; ✉ Conservation Department, KCL (Guys) Dental Institute, Floor 25, Guys Tower, London Bridge, London SE1 9RT (☎ 020 7188 1582, e-mail leslie.howe@kcl.ac.uk); 21 Wimpole Street, London W1G 8GG (☎ 020 7636 3101, fax 020 7735 8810, e-mail admin@trdp.co.uk)

HOWE, Martin Russell Thomson; QC (1996); s of Colin Thomson Howe, FRCS (d 1988), of Kenley, Surrey, and Dr Angela Mary, *née* Brock (d 1977), da of Baron Brock (Life Peer; d 1979); *b* 26 June 1955; *Educ* Trinity Hall Cambridge (MA); *m* 30 Dec 1989, Lynda, *née* Barnett; 1 s (Philip Anthony Russell b 19 Oct 1990), 3 da (Julia Angela b 13 Nov 1992, Jennifer Rosalind b 19 Feb 1996, Elizabeth Florence b 6 Nov 1999); *Career* called to the Bar Middle Temple 1978 (bencher 2013); specialising in EU law and intellectual property; jt ed Halsbury's Laws of England section on Trade Marks, Trade Names and Designs; Parly candidate (Cons) Neath 1987, memb Hammersmith and Fulham Borough Cncl 1982–86 (chm Planning Ctee), memb Coalition Govt Cmmn on a Bill of Rights for the UK 2011–12, appointed person for hearing designs appeals 2015–; chm Lawyers for Britain 2016–; *Publications* Russell-Clarke and Howe on the Legal Protection of Industrial Designs (6 edn 1998, 9 edn 2016), EU Renegotiation from Zero Plus (2014); author of other pubns on EU constitutional law and human rights reformn and a Bill of Rights for the UK; *Recreations* sailing; *Style*— Martin Howe, Esq, QC; ✉ 8 New Square, Lincoln's Inn, London WC2A 3QP (☎ 020 7405 4321, website www.martinhowe.co.uk)

HOWE OF IDLICOTE, Baroness (Life Peer UK 2001), of Shipston on Stour in the County of Warwickshire; Elspeth Rosamund Morton Howe; CBE (1999), JP (Inner London 1964); da of late Philip Morton Shand, and Sybil Mary, *née* Sissons; *b* 8 February 1932; *Educ* Bath HS, Wycombe Abbey, LSE (BSc); *m* Aug 1953, Baron Howe of Aberavon (Life Peer), *qv*; 2 da (Hon Caroline b 1955, Hon Amanda b 1959), 1 s (Hon Alexander (twin) b 1959); *Career* sec to princ of AA Sch of Architecture 1952–55, dep chm Equal Opportunities Cmmn Manchester (chm Legal Ctee) 1975–79; chm Inner London Juvenile Cts: Southwark 1970–80, Greenwich 1980–83, Lambeth 1983–86, Wandsworth 1987–90; non-exec dir: Kingfisher (Holdings) plc (formerly Woolworth Holdings plc) 1986–2000, United Biscuits (Holdings) Ltd 1988–94, Legal and General Group plc 1989–97; chm BOC Foundation 1990–2003; pres: Peckham Settlement 1976–2012, Fedn of Recruitment and Employment Servs 1980–94, UNICEF UK 1993–2002, Nat Govrs' Assoc 2007–; chm: Business in the Community Opportunity 2000 Initiative 1991–98, NACRO Working Pty on Fine Enforcement 1980–81, NACRO Drugs Advsy Gp 1988–93, Local Govt Mgmnt Bd Inquiry and Report 'The Quality of Care' 1991–92, The Archbishops' Cmmn on Cathedrals 1992–94, Broadcasting Standards Cmmn 1993–99; vice-pres Pre-School Playgroups Assoc 1978–83; vice-chm Cncl Open Univ 2001–03 (memb Cncl 1996–2003); memb: Lord Chllr's Advsy Ctee on Legal Aid 1971–75, Parole Bd For England and Wales 1972–75, Advsy Cncl Inst of Business Ethics 1990– (vice-pres 2002–), The Justice Ctee on the English Judiciary 1992; tstee: The Westminster Fndn for Democracy 1992–96, St Andrews' Prize for the Environment 1999–; govr LSE 1985–2007; memb Cncl St George's House Windsor 1989–93; contrib articles to: The Times, FT, The Guardian, New Society; Hon LLD Univ of London 1990, Hon DUniv Open Univ 1993; Hon DLitt: Univ of Bradford 1993, Univ of Aberdeen 1994, Univ of Liverpool 1994, Univ of Sunderland 1995, South Bank Univ 1995; hon fell LSE 2001; *Style*— The Baroness Howe of Idlicote, CBE; ✉ House of Lords, London SW1A 0PW (☎ 020 7219 6581, e-mail howee@parliament.uk)

HOWELL, Gwynne Richard; CBE (1998); s of Gilbert Lewis Howell (d 1991), and Ellaline, *née* Richards (d 1986); *b* 13 June 1938; *Educ* Pontardawe GS, Univ Coll Swansea (BSc), Univ of Manchester (DipTP); *m* 26 Oct 1968, Mary Edwina, da of Edward Morris (d 1988); 2 s (Richard b 23 May 1970, Peter b 31 May 1972); *Career* bass; sr planning offr Corporation of Manchester 1965–68; commenced professional music career 1968; with Sadler's Wells Opera (now ENO) 1968–72, Royal Opera 1972; given concerts with numerous leading conductors incl: Claudio Abbado, Daniel Barenboim, Pierre Boulez, Leonard Bernstein, Sir Colin Davis, Sir Bernard Haitink, James Levine, Zubin Mehta, Riccardo Muti, Tadaaki Ozawa and Sir Georg Solti; *Performances* notable operatic roles incl: First Nazarene in Salome (Covent Garden debut) 1969, Arkell in Pelleas and Melisande (Glyndebourne and Covent Garden 1969 and 1982), Otello (Met Opera NY debut) 1985, Hans Sachs in Die Meistersinger (ENO), Bluebeard in Bluebeard's Castle (ENO) 1991, Phillip II in Don Carlos (ENO) 1992, Boris Godunov (San Francisco Opera) 1992, Iolanta (Opera North) 1993, Fidelio (ENO) 1996, King Marke in Tristan und Isolde (ENO) 1996, King in Ariodante (ENO) 1996, The Croucher Silver Tassie (ENO premier) 2000, Thomas Adé's The Tempest (world premier Covent Garden) 2004; concert performances incl: St Matthew Passion (US debut, with Chicago Symphony Orch) 1974, Oedipus Rex (with Chicago Symphony Orch under Solti and with NY Philharmonic), numerous others at festivals incl Salzburg and Edinburgh; *Recordings* incl: Mahler's 8th Symphony (with Boston Symphony Orch under Ozawa), Un Ballo in Maschera, Luisa Miller and Rossini's Stabat Mater (all under Muti), Handel's Messiah (under Solti), Beethoven's 9th Symphony (under Kurt Masur); fell Welsh Coll of Music and Drama 1994; *Recreations* tennis, golf, gardening, good wine, walking; *Style*— Gwynne Howell, Esq, CBE; ✉ 197 Fox Lane, London N13 4BB

HOWELL, Dr John Frederick; s of Frederick Howell (d 1996), and Glenys Griffiths (d 1990); *b* 16 July 1941; *Educ* Welwyn Garden City GS, UC Swansea (BA), Univ of Manchester (MA), Univ of Reading (PhD); *m* 1993, Paula Wade; 2 s, 1 step s; *Career* lectr Univ of Khartoum 1966–73, sr lectr Univ of Zambia 1973–77, dir ODI 1987–97 (res fell 1977–87), advsr to Min for Agric and Land Affairs Govt of South Africa 1997–2001, sr res fell ODI 2001–; visiting prof Wye Coll London 1988–96; pres UK Chapter Soc for Int Devpt, advsr All-Pty Parly Gp on Overseas Devpt; *Style*— Dr John Howell; ✉ Overseas Development Institute, 203 Blackfriars Road, London SE1 8NJ (e-mail j.howell@odi.org.uk)

HOWELL, John Michael; OBE (2000), MP; *Educ* Univ of Edinburgh (MA), St John's Coll Oxford (DPhil); *Career* former ptnr Ernst & Young; MP (Cons) Henley 2008–; *Style*— John Howell, Esq, OBE, MP; ✉ House of Commons, London SW1A 0AA

HOWELL, Lee Thomas; QFSM (2014); s of Howard Ungoed Howell, and Linda Annette Howell; *b* 13 September 1969, Hants; *Educ* Shoeburyness HS, Univ of Reading (MBA), South Bank Univ (BEng), CII (Dip, London Market); *m* 20 July 2002, Fiona Catherine, *née* Holland; 1 da (Jemima Jane), 1 s (Barnaby Thomas); *Career* Fire Service: jr ranks 1988–98, sr ranks 1998–2003; chief fire offr and corp dir of public protection Suffolk CC 2004–09, chief fire offr/chief exec Devon & Somerset Fire & Rescue Service 2009–; chief fire and rescue advsr Welsh Govt and Inspector for Wales 2013–15; pres Chief Fire Offrs Assoc 2011–12, ind chm Nat Arson Prevention Forum 2011–; advsr UK Trade and Investment 2016–; dep chm and tstee Firefighters Meml Tst 2008–; Queen's Golden Jubilee Medal 2002, Fire Service Long Service and Good Conduct Medal 2008, Queen's Diamond Jubilee Medal 2012, Queen's Fire Service Medal for distinguished service 2014; FIFireE 2000, FRSA 2012; *Recreations* rugby union (qualified coach and referee), reading, Polar travel; *Style*— Lee Howell, Esq, QFSM, FRSA; ✉ Devon & Somerset Fire & Rescue Service Headquarters, The Knowle, Clyst St George, Exeter, Devon

HOWELL, Lisbeth Edna (Lis); da of Frederick Baynes, and Jessica Edna Baynes; *b* 23 March 1951; *Educ* Liverpool Inst HS for Girls, Univ of Bristol (BA); *Partner* Ian Prowiewicz; 1 da (Alexandra b 19 Sept 1984); *Career* reporter BBC local radio 1973–77; reporter/presenter: Border TV 1977–79, Granada TV 1978–80, Tyne Tees TV 1981–84; Border TV: head of news 1986–88, dep dir of progs 1988–89; managing ed Sky News 1990–91, dir of progs GMTV 1991–93, conslt United Artists Programming 1993, dir of progs UK Living satellite and cable channel 1993–97, vice-pres Flextech Programming 1997–; *Books* After the Break (novel, 1995), The Director's Cut (novel, 1996), A Job to Die For (novel, 1997); *Style*— Ms Lis Howell

HOWELL, Margaret; CBE (2007); *b* 5 September 1946; *Educ* Goldsmiths Coll London; *Children* 2 c; *Career* first of new Br fashion designers to modernise the classics of Br clothing using traditional fabrics; postgrad experience mfrg accessories 1969, expanded to produce clothing collections (wholesaled internationally) from own studio 1970–, shops on Wigmore St and Fulham London, in Richmond Surrey, Place de la Madeleine Paris and Florence Italy (2015), jt venture with Anglobal Tokyo 1990, currently produces mens and womenswear with 65 retail outlets worldwide incl UK, Japan, France; outfits donated to Costume Museum Bath and Costume Dept V&A; engaged in promoting post-war Br modern design and architecture; hon doctorate Univ of Arts London 2010, hon professorship Univ for the Creative Arts (UCA) 2013, hon fell Goldsmiths Univ 2015; Royal Designer for Industry 2007; *Recreations* walking, art exhibitions, films and photography; *Style*— Ms Margaret Howell; ✉ Margaret Howell Ltd, 6 Welbeck Way, London W1G 9RZ

HOWELL, Michael William Davis; s of Air Vice Marshal Evelyn Michael Thomas Howell, CBE (d 2008), and Helen Joan, *née* Hayes (d 1976); *b* 11 June 1947; *Educ* Charterhouse, Trinity Coll Cambridge, INSEAD and Harvard Business Sch (MBA); *m* 1975, Susan Wanda, da of Andrew Adie (d 1986); 2 s (William b 1982, Andrew b 1988), 1 da (Anna b 1990); *Career* BL Truck & Bus Div 1969–74, vice-pres Cummins Engine Co Inc 1976–88; gen mangr Gen Electric Co (US) Inc 1988–91; dir: Arlington Capital Partners Ltd 1991–2009, Fenner plc 1993–96; commercial dir Railtrack Group plc 1996–97, exec chm FPT Group Ltd 1998–2002, chief exec Transport Initiatives Edinburgh Ltd 2002–06; chm: City and Guilds Inst 2006–12 (treas 2001–06), Evo Electric Ltd 2007–12; dir: Westinghouse Airbrake Technology Corp 2003–, Hutchison China Meditech Ltd 2006–; Court Asst Worshipful Co of Clothworkers (Master 2014–15); *Recreations* walking, travel; *Clubs* Oxford and Cambridge; *Style*— Michael Howell, Esq; ✉ Clothworkers' Hall, Mincing Lane, London EC3R 7AH ☎ 020 7623 7041

HOWELL, Robert Stuart (Rob); s of Stuart Henry Howell, and Doreen Marjorie Howell; *Educ* Birmingham Poly (BA); *m* Gail; 2 s (Oscar, Dexter); *Career* theatre designer; res design asst RSC 1990–92, freelance set and costume designer 1992–; Hon DUniv Birmingham City 2009; *Theatre* credits incl: Relative Values (Chichester Festival Theatre and UK tour) 1993, Eurovision (Sydmonton Festival and Vaudeville Theatre) 1993, Oliver (Crucible Theatre Sheffield) 1993, Private Lives (Dalateatern Sweden) 1994, Julius Caesar (Royal Exchange Theatre) 1994, The Shakespeare Revue (RSC) 1994, True West (Donmar Warehouse) 1994, Simpatico (Royal Court Theatre) 1995, The Painter of Dishonour (RSC) 1995, The Glass Menagerie (Donmar Warehouse) 1995 (nominated for Olivier Award Best Set Designer 1996), Tartuffe (Almeida Theatre) 1996, The Loves of Cass Maguire (Druid Theatre Co) 1996, Habeas Corpus (Donmar Warehouse) 1996, Peter Pan (W Yorks Playhouse) 1996, Little Eyolf (RSC) 1996, Tom and Clem (Aldwych Theatre) 1997, Chips with Everything (RNT) 1997 (nominated for Olivier Award for Best Set Designer 1997), Entertaining Mr Sloane (Theatre Clwyd) 1997, The Government Inspector (Almeida Theatre) 1997, Eddie Izzard – Glorious (tour) 1997, How I Learned to Drive (Donmar Warehouse) 1998, Richard III (RSC) 1998 (Olivier Award Best Set Designer 2000), Real Classy Affair (Royal Court Theatre) 1998, Vassa (Almeida Theatre) 1999 (Olivier Award Best Set Designer 2000), Troilus and Cressida (RNT) 1999 (Olivier Award Best Set Designer 2000, nominated for Olivier Award for Best Costume Design 2000), Money (RNT) 1999 (nominated for Olivier Award for Best Costume Design 2000), Family Reunion (RSC) 1999, Betrayal (Theatre d'Atelier Paris) 1999, Battle Royal (RNT) 1999, Eddie Izzard – UK Tour 1999–2000, Hard Fruit (Royal Court Theatre) 2000, Turn of the Screw (WNO) 2000, Conversations after a Burial (Almeida Theatre) 2000, The Caretaker (Comedy Theatre) 2000 (nominated for Olivier Award for Best Set Designer 2001), Lulu (Almeida Theatre and Kennedy Center Washington) 2001, Howard Katz (RNT) 2001,

H

Sunset Boulevard (UK tour) 2001, Faith Healer (Almeida Theatre) 2001, The Graduate (Gielgud Theatre and Broadway) 2002, Proof (Donmar Warehouse) 2002, Our House (Cambridge Theatre) 2002 and (UK tour) 2008, Sophie's Choice (Royal Opera House) 2002, Simply Heavenly (Young Vic Theatre) 2003, Tell Me on a Sunday (Gielgud Theatre) 2003, The Lady fron the Sea (Almeida Theatre) 2003, Endgame (Albery Theatre) 2004, Buried Child (RNT) 2004, Hedda Gabler (Almeida) 2005 (Best Set Design Olivier Awards 2006 (nominated Best Costume Design)), Lord of the Rings (Toronto) 2006 (Best Costume Design Dora Mavor Award 2006 (nominated Best Set Design)), Bash (The Trafalgar Studios) 2007, Boeing Boeing (The Comedy Theatre) 2007 and (Broadway) 2008, The Reporter (RNT) 2007, Lord of the Rings (Theatre Royal Drury Lane) 2007 (nominated Best Costume Design and Best Set Design Olivier Awards 2008), Speed The Plow (Old Vic) 2008, Her Naked Skin (RNT) 2008, The Norman Conquests (Old Vic) 2008 (nominated Best Design Evening Standard Award, Best Costume Design Olivier Award 2009) and (Broadway) 2009 (nominated Best Set Design Drama Desk Award, Best Set Design Tony Award 2009), Boeing Boeing (UK tour) 2009, Complicit (Old Vic) 2009, The Last Cigarette (Chichester and West End) 2009, The Observer (RNT) 2009, Matilda The Musical (Cambridge Theatre) 2011 (Best Set Designer Olivier Award 2012), (Shubert Theatre NY) 2013 (Tony Award, Best set Design, Tony Nomination, Best Costume Design) 2013, (Outer Critics Circle Award, Best Set Design 2013), Drama Desk Award, (Best Set Design) 2013, US tour, Australian Tour, Metropolitan Opera NY: Carmen, Werther, The Marriage of Figaro, Manon Lescaut (co-production with Baden Baden, US tour, Australian tour) 2011 (best set design); *Style*— Rob Howell, Esq; ✉ c/o Judy Daish Associates, 2 St Charles Place, London W10 6EG (☎ 020 8964 8811, fax 020 8964 8966)

HOWELL, Rupert Cortlandt Spencer; s of Lt-Col F R Howell, of Seaview, IOW, and Sheila Dorothy Lorne McCallum; *b* 6 February 1957; *Educ* Wellington, Univ of Warwick (BSc); *m* 4 Sept 1987, Claire Jane, da of Dr Nigel Ashworth; 1 da (Amy Jane b 8 Aug 1991), 1 s (Dominic James Spencer b 4 Feb 1995); *Career* account exec Mathers Advertising (now Ogilvy and Mather Partners) 1979–80, account supervisor Grey Advertising 1982–83 (account mangr 1981); Young and Rubicam: account dir 1983–84, dir 1984–87, jt head of Account Mgmnt 1987; fndr ptnr HHCL and Partners (formerly Howell Henry Chaldecott Lury) 1987–97 (UK Agency of the Decade Campaign magazine), jt ceo Chime Communications plc 1998–2002, pres EMEA and chm UK and I McCann Erickson 2003–07, md brand and commerical ITV plc 2007–10; pres IPA 2000–01; memb Govt Communications Review Gp; memb Advsy Bd Warwick Business Sch; FIPA 1995 (MIPA 1989); *Recreations* cricket, golf, tennis (playing and spectating), rugby and soccer (spectating only!); *Clubs* MCC, London Rugby, Sandown & Shanklin Golf, Seaview Yacht; *Style*— Rupert Howell, Esq; ☎ 020 7961 2301, mobile 07770 381300

HOWELL, Prof Simon Laurence; s of Laurence James Howell (d 2007), of Eastbourne, E Sussex, and Rosemary, *née* Wheelwright (d 1984); *b* 29 June 1943; *Educ* St John's Sch Leatherhead, Chelsea Coll London (BSc), KCL (PhD), Univ of London (DSc); *m* 1969 (m dis 2012), Linda Margaret, *née* Chapman; 1 da (Tessa Louise); *Career* research fell Univ of Sussex 1968–78, lectr Charing Cross Hosp Med Sch 1978–80; KCL: reader then prof of endocrine physiology 1980–, head Div of Biomedical Scis 1988–98, head Sch of Biomedical Scis 1998–2003, research dean Sch of Biomedical Scis 2003–06, dir of research devpt 2007–, exec dean Faculty of Life Sciences and Medicine 2014–15; chair Diabetes UK 2006–09 (vice-chair 2002–06), chair Lord Brock Meml Tst 2011–; memb Cncl: Br Diabetic Assoc 1985–91 (chm Research Ctee 1987–90), Assoc of Medical Research Charities 1989–92, European Assoc for the Study of Diabetes 1992–95, KCL 1992–96 and 2006–08; R D Lawrence Lecture Br Diabetic Assoc 1976, Minkowski Prize European Assoc for the Study of Diabetes 1983; *Books* Biochemistry of the Polypeptide Hormones (with M Wallis and K W Taylor, 1985), Diabetes and its Management (with P Watkins and P Drury, 1996 and 2003), Biology of the Pancreatic Beta Cell (1999); *Recreations* gardening, opera; *Style*— Prof Simon Howell; ✉ Faculty of Life Sciences and Medicine, King's College London, Hodgkin Building, Guys Campus, London SE1 9UL (☎ 020 7848 6390, fax 020 7848 6394, e-mail simon.howell@kcl.ac.uk)

HOWELL OF GUILDFORD, Baron (Life Peer UK 1997), of Penton Mewsey in the County of Hampshire; David Arthur Russell Howell; PC (1979); s of Col Arthur Howard Eckford Howell, DSO, TD, DL (d 1980), and Beryl Stuart, *née* Bowater; *b* 18 January 1936; *Educ* Eton, King's Coll Cambridge (MA); *m* 1967, (Cary) Davina, da of Maj David Wallace (ka 1944); 2 da (Hon Frances Victoria (Mrs George Osborne) b 1969, Hon Kate Davina b 1970), 1 s (Hon Toby David b 1975); *Career* serv Coldstream Gds 1954–56, 2 Lt; worked in Econ Section Treasy 1959–60, ldr writer Daily Telegraph 1960–64, chm Bow Gp 1961–62, ed Crossbow 1962–64, Parly candidate (Cons) Dudley 1964, dir Cons Political Centre 1964–66, MP (Cons) Guildford 1966–97, lord cmmr Treasy 1970–71, Parly sec CSD 1970–72; Parly under sec: Employment 1971–72, NI March-Nov 1972; min of state: NI 1972–74, Energy 1974; oppn spokesman on: Treasy and financial affrs 1974–77, home affrs 1977–79, sec of state for: Energy 1979–81, Transport 1981–83; chm: House of Commons Foreign Affrs Ctee 1987–97, House of Lords European Sub-Ctee on Common Foreign and Security Policy 1999–2000; House of Lords: oppn spokesman on foreign and Cwlth affrs 2001–10, dep ldr of the Oppn 2005–10, min of state FCO 2010–12; chm UK Japan 21st Century Gp 1989–2001; non-exec dir: Queens Moat Hotels plc 1989–93, Trafalgar House plc 1990–96, Monks Investment Trust 1993–2004, Jardine Insurance Brokers 1994–97, John Laing plc 2000–03; advsr: Wood Mackenzie 1976–79, Merck, Sharp and Dohme 1976–79; conslt: Savory Milln plc 1983–86, Coopers and Lybrand 1984–89; memb Int Advsy Bd Swiss Bank Corporation 1987–96, advsy dir Warburg Dillon Read 1997–2000, sr advsr Japan Central Railway Co 2001–, European adsvsr Mitsubishi Electric BV 2003–, memb Financial Advsy Bd Kuwait Investment Authority 2003–; pres Br Inst of Energy Economists 2003–13, chm Windsor Energy Gp, memb Governing Bd Centre for Global Energy Studies 2006–13, chm Cncl for Cwlth Societies 2013–, pres Royal Cwlth Soc 2013–, pres Energy Industries Cncl 2013–; columnist Japan Times 1983–; govr Sadlers Wells Fndn 1998–2000, tstee Shakespeare's Globe Theatre 2000–10, tstee Duke of Edinburgh's Cwlth Conference 2007–10; visiting fell: Policy Studies Inst 1983–85, Nuffield Coll Oxford 1983–2001; Liveryman Worshipful Co of Clothworkers; *Publications* A New Style of Government (1970), Time to Move On (1976), Freedom and Capital (1981), Blind Victory (1986), The Edge of Now (2000), Out of the Energy Labyrinth (2007), Old Link and New Ties (2013), Empires in Collision (2016); *Recreations* writing, travel; *Clubs* Beefsteak; *Style*— The Rt Hon Lord Howell of Guildford, PC; ✉ House of Lords, London SW1A 0PW (e-mail howelld@parliament.uk, website www.lordhowell.com)

HOWELL-RICHARDSON, Phillip Lort; s of Graham Howell-Richardson (d 1980), and Jean, *née* McDonald (d 2012); *b* 21 June 1950, Cardiff; *Educ* Univ of Kent at Canterbury (BA), Coll of Law Guildford; *m* 20 May 1978, Sally Anne, *née* Chamberlin; 1 s (James b 14 May 1980), 2 da (Victoria b 13 March 1982, Charlotte b 5 Oct 1983); *Career* admitted slr 1975; asst slr Osborne Clarke Bristol 1976–81; Morgan Cole: ptnr London Thames Valley and Wales 1982–2005, head of commercial litigation 1985–98, memb Bd 1998–2000; conslt in alternative dispute resolution S J Berwin 2005–13, mediator and memb Independent Mediators 2010–; fndr memb Panel of Ind Mediators 1995, co-chm ADR Gp 1995–2008; memb: Panel of Ct of Appeal Mediators, Mediation Panel Hong Kong Arbitration Cncl, CMAP Paris, Exec Advsy Bd CPR NY; conslt ed Inst of Advanced Legal Studies; visiting prof Univ of Hong Kong; govr Clifton Coll Bristol; memb Law Soc 1975, accredited mediator ADR Gp 1990, fell Inst of Professional Devpt 1999, mediation fell CIArb 2008, fell Int Acad of Mediators; *Publications* Mediators on Mediations, many articles in periodicals; *Recreations* sailing, mountain biking, modern art; *Style*— Phillip Howell-Richardson, Esq; ✉ Flat 7, 198 St John Street, London EC1V 4JY (☎ 07720 700228, e-mail phillip@howell-richardson.com)

HOWELLS, Prof Christina; *née* Mitchell; da of John Mitchell, of Frimley, Surrey, and Elizabeth, *née* Johnson; *b* 13 April 1950; *Educ* Merrow Grange Covent Sch Guildford, KCL (BA, PhD); *m* 21 July 1973, Bernard Howells; 1 da (Marie-Elise b 1 Feb 1984), 1 s (Dominic b 2 March 1986); *Career* temporary posts Philippa Fawcett Coll, Stockwell Coll and KCL 1975–79; fell in French Wadham Coll Oxford 1979–; Univ of Oxford: CUF lectr 1979, reader 1996, prof of French 1999–; delivered numerous lectures and papers and chaired sessions at colloquia and confs in GB, Europe and USA; fndr memb and Br rep Groupe d'Etudes Sartriennes (also co-ed jl), assoc memb Conseil National des Programmes (CNP) 2001–; memb: Int Assoc of Philosophy and Literature (IAPL), Forum for European Philosophy; co-ed Sartre Studies International 1995–; Commandeur dans l'Ordre des Palmes Académiques (France); *Publications* Sartre's Theory of Literature (1979), Sartre: The Necessity of Freedom (1988), Sartre: A Companion (ed and contrib, 1992), Sartre (ed and contrib, 1995), Derrida: Deconstruction from Phenomenology to Ethics (1998), French Women Philosophers: Subjectivity, Identity, Alterity (2004), Mortal Subjects: Passions of the Soul in Late Twentieth-Century French Thought (2011); also author of numerous essays, chapters and reviews; *Recreations* theatre, opera, cinema, reading, travel, friends; *Style*— Prof Christina Howells; ✉ Wadham College, Oxford OX1 3PN (☎ 01865 277985, e-mail christina.howells@wadh.ox.ac.uk)

HOWELLS, David John; Lord of the Manor of Carnwyllon; s of Ivor Mervyn Howells, of Shrewsbury, and Veronica Carey, *née* Jones; *b* 14 March 1953; *Educ* London Hosp Med Coll (BDS), Univ Hosp of Wales (MScD); *Family* 2 da (Lowri b 1989, Ffion b 1991); *Career* postgrad training in orthodontics Welsh Nat Sch of Med, registrar Queen Alexandra Hosp Portsmouth 1982–84, sr registrar Birmingham Dental Hosp 1984–87, conslt orthodontist to Morriston Hosp Swansea and Prince Phillip Hosp Llanelli 1987–, clinical dir Morriston Hosp 1990–95, chm W Glam Dist Dental Ctee 1991–96, chm Iechyd Morgannwg Dist Dental Ctee 1996–2002, chm Dyfed Powys Local Dental Ctee 2004–; also in private orthodontic practice in Llanelli and Carmarthen; author of several academic papers in specialist jls; LDS, DOrth, MOrth, FDSRCS (Eng); *Recreations* nature conservation, hiking, photography; *Style*— Dr David Howells; ✉ Pencastell Orthodontics, 1 Murray Street, Llanelli (☎ 01554 777799, fax 01554 776699, e-mail dai_dant@yahoo.co.uk)

HOWELLS, Michael Sandbrook; s of Benjamin George Howells (d 1971), of Pembroke Dock, and Blodwen, *née* Francis (d 1978); *b* 29 May 1939; *Educ* Dean Close Sch Cheltenham, UCL; *m* 18 June 1966, Pamela Vivian, da of Gordon Harry Francis, of Clandon, Surrey; 2 s (Luke b 1970, Toby b 1972); *Career* admitted slr 1966; sr ptnr Price and Kelway Slrs 1980–95 (ptnr 1971), princ Michael S Howells Slrs 1995–2003; HM coroner Pembrokeshire 1980–2009; conducted inquests into: Richard and Helen Thomas (double murder), 1985, explosion on tanker Pointsman 1985, Peter and Gwenda Dixon (double murder) 1989, loss of fishing vessel Inspire 1990, ferry Norrona fire 1991, the Tregwynt Hoard (last Treasure Trove inquest in Wales) 1997; memb: Cncl Law Soc 1983–99 (dep treas 1992–95, treas 1995–96), Supreme Court Rules Ctee 1985–88, Cncl of Coroners' Soc of England and Wales 1986– (vice-pres 1997–98, pres 1998–99, conf sec 2002–08), Dyfed-Powys Local Resilience Forum 2001–09, Lord Chancellor's Standing Ctee for the Welsh Language 2003–09, Wales Fatalities Gp 2006–12 (chair 2010–11), Wales Drug Related Deaths Forum 2006–09; High Ct costs assessor 1988–2003, Llanstadwell Community Cncl 2012– (vice-chair 2014–16, chair 2016–), Pembroke Power Station LLC 2013–; author of columns and articles in Pembrokeshire Life incl monthly essay; pres Pembrokeshire C of C 1995–96, pres Milford Haven Rotary Club 1997–98, volunteer advsr Pembs CAB 2011–; chm West Wales Decorative & Fine Arts Soc 2016–; *Recreations* theatre, messing about in boats; *Clubs* Naval & Military, Neyland Yacht; *Style*— Michael Howells, Esq; ✉ Glenowen, Mastlebridge, Milford Haven, Pembrokeshire SA73 1QS (☎ 01646 600208, e-mail mike_howells8@btinternet.com)

HOWES, Sir Christopher Kingston; KCVO (1999, CVO 1997), CB (1993); s of Leonard Arthur Howes, OBE (d 1999), of Norfolk, and Marion Amy, *née* Bussey (d 1999); *b* 30 January 1942; *Educ* Gresham's, Univ of London, Coll of Estate Mgmnt (BSc), Univ of Reading (MPhil); *m* 1967, Clare, da of Gordon Edward Cunliffe (d 1987), of Sussex; 2 da (Catherine b 1973, Rosalind b 1975 (decd)), 2 s (Robert b 1976, Michael b 1977 (decd)); *Career* GLC Planning and Valuation Depts 1965–67; ptnr (later sr ptnr) Chartered Surveyors & Planning Conslts 1967–79, dep dir Land Economy Directorate DOE 1979–80 (dir Land Economy 1981–84), dir Land and Property 1985–89, second Crown Estate cmmr and chief exec Crown Estate 1989–2001, advsr Operational Effeciency Unit HM Treasy 2008–09; non-exec dir: Norwich & Peterborough Building Society 1998–2005, Howard de Walden Estates Ltd 2002– (dep chm 2012), Compco Hldgs 2004–16; memb Advsy Bd Barclays Private Bank Ltd 2001–, non-exec chm Property Finance Team Barclays Bank 2005–; memb Advsy Bd Three Delta LLP 2005–11; visiting lectr Univs of London, E Anglia (sr visiting fell 1973), Cambridge, Reading and Aberdeen 1966–, UCLA and Univ of Calif South LA 1983, Harvard 1985, North Carolina Chapel Hill 1985; visiting prof UCL 1985–; dir RIBA Tst 2010–; memb Norwich Cncl 1970–74, steward and hon surveyor to Dean and Chapter Norwich Cathedral 1972–79, magistrate for Norfolk 1973–79, memb Ct of Advsrs St Paul's Cathedral 1980–; RICS: memb Policy Review Ctee 1979–81, memb Planning & Devpt Divnl Cncl 1984–92; memb Cncl Duchy of Lancaster 1993–2004, memb Sec of State for the Environment's Thames Advsy Gp 1995–98; hon memb Cambridge Univ Land Soc 1989; jt chm World Land Policy Congress 1986; memb: OECD Urban Policy Gp 1985–87, HRH Prince of Wales's Cncl 1990–, Cncl Br Property Fedn 1992–2001, Ct UEA 1992–; tstee: HRH Prince of Wales's Inst of Architecture 1991–99, Br Architectural Library Tst 1997–2012, Suffolk Historic Churches Tst 2009–14, Britten-Pears Fndn 2016–; patron Heatherley Sch of Fine Arts Chelsea 2008–, vice-patron Suffolk Fndn 2007; memb Bd British Architecture Tst 2011–16; first hon fell Local Authy Valuers' Assoc 1990, Hon DLitt UEA 2000; Hon FRIBA 1995; *Books* Value Maps: Aspects of Land and Property Values (1980), Economic Regeneration (1988), Urban Revitalization (1988); contributor to many books and articles in learned journals; *Recreations* architecture, music, painting, sailing; *Clubs* Athenaeum, Garrick, Norfolk (Norwich), Aldeburgh Yacht; *Style*— Sir Christopher Howes, KCVO, CB; ✉ Westerly House, Aldeburgh, Suffolk IP15 5EL (☎ 01728 453826)

HOWGEGO, Charles; s of David Howgego, of Wild Hill, Herts, and Sybil, *née* Jones; *b* 8 January 1971, Welwyn Garden City, Herts; *Educ* St Albans Sch, Sheffield Hallam Univ; *m* Carolyn, *née* Fearn; 2 s (Evan, Jonah), 1 da (Yasmin); *Career* ed The Big Issue; memb CAMRA; *Style*— Charles Howgego, Esq

HOWICK OF GLENDALE, 2 Baron (UK 1960); Charles Evelyn Baring; s of 1 Baron Howick of Glendale, KG, GCMG, KCVO (d 1973; formerly Hon Sir Evelyn Baring, sometime govr Kenya and yst s of 1 Earl of Cromer), and Lady Mary Grey (d 2002), da of 5 Earl Grey; *b* 30 December 1937; *Educ* Eton, New Coll Oxford; *m* 1964, Clare, yr da of Col Cyril Darby, MC, of Kemerton Court, Tewkesbury; 3 da (Hon Rachel Monica (Hon Mrs Lane Fox) b 1967, Hon Jessica Mary Clare (Hon Mrs Laithwaite) b 1969, Hon Alice Olivia (Hon Mrs Ward-Thomas) b 1971), 1 s (Hon David Evelyn Charles b 1975); *Heir* s, Hon David Baring; *Career* md Baring Bros & Co 1969–82, dir London Life Assoc 1972–82, dir Northern Rock plc 1988–2001; memb: Exec Ctee Art Collections Fund 1973–88, Cncl Baring Fndn 1982–99; tstee: Chelsea Physic Garden 1994–2012, Northern Rock Fndn 1997–2007, Royal Botanic Garden Edinburgh 2001–09; chm Botanics Fndn 2009–12, pres NE Div Plant Heritage 2009–; memb Advsy Cncl Nat Arboreta 1999–, memb Advsy Bd

Quarryhill Botanical Garden Calif 2000–; *Style*— The Lord Howick of Glendale; ✉ Howick, Alnwick, Northumberland NE66 3LB (☎ 01665 577624)

HOWIE, Prof Archibald; CBE (1998); s of Robert Howie (d 1992), of Grange, Kirkcaldy, Fife, and Margaret Marshall, *née* McDonald (d 1971); *b* 8 March 1934; *Educ* Kirkcaldy HS, Univ of Edinburgh (BSc), Caltech (MS), Univ of Cambridge (PhD); *m* 15 Aug 1964, Melva Jean, da of Ernest Scott (d 1959), of Tynemouth, Northumberland; 1 s (David Robert b 9 Oct 1965, d 1986), 1 da (Helena Margaret b 14 July 1971); *Career* Univ of Cambridge: ICI fell 1960–61, demonstrator in physics 1962–65, lectr 1965–78, reader 1978–86, prof 1986–2001, head Dept of Physics 1989–97; Churchill Coll Cambridge: fell 1960–, res fell 1960–61, teaching fell in physics 1962–86; visiting prof of physics: Aarhus 1974, Bologna 1984; NPL Management Ltd 1995–2001; pres: Royal Microscopical Soc 1984–86, Int Fedn of Societies for Electron Micoscopy 1999–2002; Hughes Medal Royal Soc (with Dr M J Whelan) 1988, Royal Medal Royal Soc 1999; Hon Dr of Physics: Bologna 1989, Thessaloniki 1995, York 2011; FRS 1978, FInstP 1978 (Hon FInstP 2015), Hon FRMS 1978, Hon FRSE 1995; *Books* Electron Microscopy of Thin Crystals (jtly 1965, revised 1977), Electron Optical Imaging of Surfaces (jtly); *Recreations* winemaking; *Style*— Prof Archibald Howie, CBE, FRS; ✉ 194 Huntingdon Road, Cambridge CB3 0LB (☎ 01223 570977); Cavendish Laboratory, Madingley Road, Cambridge CB3 0HE (☎ 01223 337335, fax 01223 363263, e-mail ah30@cam.ac.uk)

HOWITT, Richard; MEP (Lab) East England; *Educ* Lady Margaret Hall Oxford (BA), Univ of Hertfordshire (Dip Mgmnt Studies); *Career* co-ordinator Harlow Cncl for Voluntary Service 1982–86, specialist in community care for the disabled Waltham Forest Social Services 1986–94; chm South-East Economic Devpt Strategy (SEEDS) 1986–94, memb Bd Centre for Local Economic Strategies (CLES) 1988–91, UK rep Helios Prog 1988–91; Harlow DC: cncllr 1984–94, chm Planning and Economic Devpt Ctee 1985–91, leader 1991–94; MEP (Lab): Essex South 1994–99, E England 1999–; pres All-Pty Disability Gp of MEPs; vice-pres Regional Affrs Ctee; memb: Devpt Ctee, Delgn with S America; sec Lab Gp of MEPs in South East; *Recreations* photography, travel, opera and cricket; *Style*— Richard Howitt, MEP; ✉ Labour European Office, Unit 3, Frohock House, 222 Mill Road, Cambridge CB1 3NF (☎ 01223 240202, fax 01223 241900, e-mail richard@richardhowittmep.com, website www.richardhowittmep.com)

HOWKINS, Ben Walter; s of Col Walter Ashby (Tim) Howkins (d 1977), and Lesley, *née* Stops (d 2003), of Olney, Bucks; *b* 19 August 1942; *Educ* Rugby, Amherst Coll Massachusetts; *m* 6 Nov 1976, Clarissa Jane, da of Thomas John Fairbank, of Cambridge; 1 s (James b 1980), 1 da (Lucy b 1981); *Career* Vintners scholar 1963, Lt Northants Yeo TA 1964–69; brand mangr IDV UK 1968–70, int sales and mktg dir Croft & Co 1970–80, md Morgan Furze 1980–89, dir Taylor Fladgate & Yeatman 1989–90, chm Wine Promotion Bd 1990–93, wine conslt Waddesdon Manor 1991–, co-fndr and dir Royal Tokaji Wine Co 1993–; dir: Last Drop Distillers 2009–, Wine Cellar Consultants 2013–; memb Cncl Wine Guild of UK 1995–2003, tstee Wine and Spirit Educn Tst 2000–04, chm Northants Yeomanry Assoc 2009–; Freeman City of London 1986, Liveryman Worshipful Co of Vintners 1986; *Books* Rich, Rare and Red – A Guide to Port (1982, paperback edn 1987, 4 edn 2014), Tokaji – A Classic Lost and Found (1999), Real Men Drink Port...and Ladies Too (2011); *Recreations* skiing, tennis, shooting; *Clubs* Brooks's; *Style*— Ben Howkins, Esq; ✉ Staverton Manor, Staverton, Northamptonshire NN11 6JD (☎ 01327 703600, mobile 07949 203480, e-mail benhowkins@royal-tokaji.com)

HOWKINS, John Anthony; s of Col Ashby (Tim) Howkins (d 1977), and Lesley, *née* Stops (d 2003); *b* 3 August 1945, Northampton; *Educ* Rugby, Keele Univ (BA), AA Sch of Architecture (AADipl); *m* 1, 1971, Jill, da of Ian Liddington; m 2, 1977, Annabel, da of John Whittet; *Career* mktg mangr Lever Bros 1968–70, TV ed Time Out 1971–74, fndr TV4 Gp 1971, ed InterMedia 1974–84, dir Whittet Books 1976–84, chm Pool Video Graz Austria 1976, ed Vision 1977–79, chm London Film Sch 1979–84, TV columnist Illustrated London News 1981–83, exec ed Nat Electronics Review 1981–90, exec dir Int Inst of Communications 1984–89, conslt and dir ITR & Co 1989–, assoc Coopers & Lybrand Deloitte 1990–91, chm Createc 1996–2001, dir Equator Gp plc 1999–2006, chm Tornado Productions Ltd 2000–04, chm BOP Consulting Ltd 2007–11; dir: Handmade plc 2006–10, Hotbed Media Ltd 2006–15; memb: Interim Action Ctee on the Film Industry DTI 1980–85, Exec Ctee Broadcasting Research Unit 1981–90; European advsr HBO Time Warner 1981–96, specialist advsr Select Ctee on European Communities House of Lords 1985, advsr Polish Radio and TV 1989–95, advsr Min for Film Poland 1991–93; vice-chm Assoc of Ind Prodrs 1984–85, dep chm Br Screen Advsy Cncl 1991–2013 (memb 1985–); project dir World Learning Network 1996–2002, dir Adelphi Charter on Creativity, Innovation and Intellectual Property 2005–07; co-ordinator European Audiovisual Conf 1998; visiting prof: Lincoln Univ 2004–15, Shanghai Theatre Acad China 2006–09, City Univ London 2009–; exec in residence Drucker Sch of Mgmnt 2014–15; *Books* Understanding Television (1977), Mass Communications in China (1982), New Technologies, New Policies (1982), Satellites International (1987), Four Global Senarios on Information and Communication (1997), The Creative Economy (2001), CODE (2002), Duffy's Dare (2009), Creative Ecologies (2009); *Style*— John Howkins, Esq; ✉ E6 Albany, Piccadilly, London W1J 0AR (☎ 020 7434 1400, e-mail john@johnhowkins.com)

HOWKINS, John David; s of Gordon Arthur Howkins, and Olga Annie, *née* King; *b* 4 February 1955; *Educ* Windsor GS, Univ of Exeter (BSc); *m* 14 April 1984, Susan, da of Richard Andreas Oakley; 2 da (Lily May b 23 May 1988, Scarlett Hannah b 20 Feb 1991); *Career* media trainee rising to dep media dir D'Arcy McManus Masius advtg agency 1976–82, assoc dir of planning DMB&B 1982–84, planning dir Lowe Howard-Spink 1984–88, ptnr Elgie Stewart Smith 1988–90, md Planning Consultancy 1990–91, md DDM Advertising 1991–93, strategic planning dir McCann-Erickson 1993–97, planning ptnr Rainey Kelly Campbell Roalfe/Y&R Ltd 1997–2005, consumer planning dir HTW Ltd 2005–07, fndr The Nub Consultancy 2007–; memb Market Res Soc 1982; *Recreations* media journalism, campanology; *Clubs* Royal Scottish Automobile; *Style*— John Howkins, Esq; ✉ Hermongers Barn, Rudgwick, West Sussex RH12 3AL (☎ 01403 822476, mobile 07845 048725); The Nub Consultancy (☎ 07845 048725, e-mail john@thenubconsultancy.com, website www.thenubconsultancy.co.uk)

HOWLETT, Ben; MP; *Career* MP (Cons) Bath 2015–; *Style*— Ben Howlett, Esq, MP; ✉ House of Commons, London SW1A 0AA

HOWLETT, Stephen William; s of Ivan William Howlett (d 1955), and Marjorie Elsie Howlett (d 1997); *b* 18 November 1951, Sudbury, Suffolk; *Educ* King Edward VI Sch Bury St Edmunds, West Suffolk Coll of Further Educn, Thames Poly (BA); *m* 1989, Jane Elizabeth, *née* Everton, CBE; 2 s (William b 1 Aug 1989, George b 16 April 1994), 1 da (Emma b 1 July 1996); *Career* admin offr Housing Corporation 1975–76, housing offr Warden Housing Assoc 1976–78, London regnl offr Nat Fedn of Housing Assocs 1978–82, dir Croydon Churches Housing Assoc 1982–88, dir Notting Hill Housing Tst 1988–92, chief exec Swale Housing Assoc 1992–99, chief exec Amicus Gp Ltd 1999–2004, chief exec Peabody Tst 2004–; chair G15 Gp of Major London Housing Assoc 2009–11; memb Bd Asset Skills 2004–13; former memb Bd: Nat Housing Fedn, New Islington and Hackney Housing Assoc; memb Bd Canterbury Coll 1995–2004 (vice-chair 1999–2004), memb Ct Univ of Greenwich 2008– (vice-chair 2010–13, chair and pro-chllr 2013–), tstee Open City 2013–; *Recreations* cinema, opera, watching sport; *Clubs* MCC, Blackheath FC; *Style*— Stephen Howlett, Esq; ✉ Peabody Trust, 45 Westminster Bridge Road, London SE1 7JB (☎ 020 7021 4230, fax 020 7021 4070, e-mail stephen.howlett@peabody.org.uk)

HOWLETT, Dr Trevor Anthony; s of Ivan William Howlett, of Cambridge, and Daphne May, *née* Long; *b* 20 July 1952; *Educ* Perse Sch Cambridge, Gonville & Caius Coll Cambridge (MA, MB BChir, MD), KCH Med Sch London; *Career* house physician KCH 1977–78, SHO Central Middx Hosp London 1978–79, med registrar Frimley Park Hosp Surrey 1980–81, lectr in endocrinology Dept of Endocrinology Bart's 1985–88 (MRC trg fell 1981–85), conslt physician and endocrinologist Leicester Royal Infirmary 1988–2015, dir of R&D Leicester Royal Infirmary NHS Tst 1996–2001, head Specialty Sch of Medicine East Midlands Deanery (South) 2007–10; sec Endocrine Section RSM 1992–96, UK rep Euro Bd Endocrinology 1994–2011, regnl advsr RCP 2002–06; chair Specialist Working Gp in Endocrinology to the Clinical Terms Project (NHS Mgmnt Exec Info Mgmnt Gp); numerous scientific articles on clinical endocrinology and endogenous opioid peptides; memb Soc for Endocrinology; FRCP; *Recreations* gardening, skiing; *Style*— Dr Trevor Howlett; ✉ Leicester Royal Infirmary, Leicester LE1 5WW (☎ 0116 254 1414)

HOWORTH, Prof Jolyon Michael; s of Joseph Alfred Howorth (d 1966), and Constance, *née* Styles (d 2006); *b* 4 May 1945; *Educ* Rossall and Henry Box Schs, Univ of Manchester (BA), Univ of Reading (PhD), Univs of Lausanne and Geneva; *m* 1, 27 Aug 1966 (m dis 1982), Pauline, *née* Macqueen; 1 da (Stephanie Jeanne b 1974); m, 6 Oct 2001, Prof Vivien, *née* Schmidt; 1 da (Emily Kirstine b 1988) and 1 s (Alexander Boris b 1989) by previous m; *Career* lectr: Univ of Paris III (Sorbonne Nouvelle) 1969–76, sr lectr Aston Univ 1979–85 (lectr 1976–79); Univ of Bath: prof of French civilisation 1985–2004, Jean Monnet prof of European politics 1992–, emeritus prof of European studies 2010–; visiting scholar Harvard Univ 1981–82, 1983–84, 1985 and 2002–03, visiting fell Institut Français des Relations Internationales (IFRI) Paris 1999–2000 (res assoc 2000–), sr res fell Inst for Security Studies WEU Paris 2000, Marshall Monnet distinguished scholar in residence Univ of Washington Seattle 2001; visiting prof: Univ of Wisconsin Madison 1974–75, NYU 2002, Columbia Univ 2002, Yale 2003–, Luiss Univ Rome 2009–, Hebrew Univ of Jerusalem 2012; dir: EU/US Transatlantic Studies Prog, Language Conslts for Industry Bath 1986–91; conslt: Univs Funding Cncl, FCO, RIIA, EU, US State Dept, Govt of Canada, Boeing, Thales, BAES, UEFA, European Defence Agency; European def analyst Oxford Analytica; memb: Centre National Jean Jaurès, Mgmnt Bd Centre for Def Studies 1996–2002, Advsy Bd Centre for the Study of Security and Diplomacy 1999–, Scientific Advsy Ctee European Inst for Public Admin Maastricht 2002–, Conseil Scientifique Centre National Jean Jaures, Conseil Scientifiques IRSEM (Paris), Advsy Ctee European Policy Centre; fndr memb Assoc for Study of Modern and Contemporary France, pres Br Assoc for the Study of European Languages and Socs 1993–96; memb: RIIA, IISS, Soc for French Hist Studies, Institut Français d'Histoire Sociale; Chev dans l'Ordre des Palmes Académiques; *Books* Elites in France: Origins, Reproduction and Power (with P Cerny, 1981), Edouard Vaillant et La Création de l'Unité Socialiste en France (1982), France: The Politics of Peace (1984), Defence and Dissent in Contemporary France (with P Chilton, 1984), Contemporary France: A Review of Interdisciplinary Studies (with George Ross, vol 1 1987, vol 2 1988, vol 3 1989), Europeans on Europe: Transnational Visions of a New Continent (with M Maclean, 1992), The European Union and National Defence Policy (with A Menon, 1997), Language, Politics and Society (co-ed, 2000), European Integration and Defence: The Ultimate Challenge (2000), Defending Europe: NATO and the Quest for European Autonomy (2003), Security and Defence Policy in the European Union (2007, 2nd edn 2014); *Recreations* travel, skiing, numismatics, ballet, opera; *Style*— Prof Jolyon Howorth; ✉ 126 Amory Street, Brookline, Ma 02446, USA (e-mail jolyon.howorth@yale.edu)

HOWSE, Dr Michael Gilbert James William; CBE (2011, OBE 2000); *b* 20 June 1942; *Educ* Witney GS, Univ of Reading (BSc, PhD); *m* Valerie; *Career* Rolls Royce plc: res engr 1968, asst chief engr 1981–83, chief devpt engr 1983–84, chief engr RB211 In-service Engines 1984–87, chief engr RB211 Devpts 1987–89, head of advanced engrg Aerospace Gp 1989–91, dir of engrg Military Engine Gp 1991–95, dir of engrg Rolls Royce Commercial Aero Engines Ltd (now Airlines, Rolls Royce plc) 1995–2000, dir of engrg & technol Civil Aerospace 2000–01, dep dir Engrg & Technol 2001, dir Engrg & Technol 2001–, exec dir 2001–; memb: Tech Bd SBAC 1991–99 (chm 1996–98), Technology Strategy Bd DTI 2004–; visiting prof Sch of Mech Engrg Cranfield Univ 1996–; Sir Roy Fedden Lecture RAeS 1998; FRAeS 1998, CEng 1998, FREng 2000; *Style*— Dr Michael Howse, CBE, FREng; ✉ Rolls-Royce plc, PO Box 31, Derby DE24 8BJ (☎ 01332 248216, e-mail mike.howse@rolls-royce.com)

HOWSON, Prof Cncllr John; JP (1990); s of Harold Howson (d 1998), and Joan, *née* Boxall (d 1991); *b* 16 May 1947, London; *Educ* Tottenham Co Sch, LSE (Westminster Bank exhibitioner, BSc), Worcester Coll Oxford (MSc); *Career* dep head Sch of Educn Oxford Brookes Univ 1987–96, chief professional advsr Teacher Training Agency 1996–97, dir Education Data Surveys Ltd 1997–2011, dir DataforEducation.info 2011–; dir Masabi US 2013–; author: Senior Staff in Schools Workforce Surveys (26 edns) 1984–2011, various reports on teacher supply for govt bodies, professional assocs and other groups; vice-pres Magistrates' Assoc 2010, vice-pres Lib Dems Educn Assoc 2011, co-fndr Supply and Training of Teachers Advsy Gp, chm TeachVac; county cncllr St Margaret's Div Oxon 2013–; *Publications* Teacher Training Places in England (with C Waterman, 2013); *Recreations* reading, walking, railways; *Clubs* National Liberal; *Style*— Prof Cncllr John Howson; ✉ Data for Education, 70 Rewley Road, Oxford OX1 2RQ (☎ 01865 203270, e-mail dataforeducation@gmail.com)

HOWSON, Peter John; OBE (2009); s of Tom William Howson, of Prestwick, Scotland, and Janet Rosemary, *née* Smith; *b* 27 March 1958; *Educ* Prestwick Acad, Glasgow Sch of Art (BA); *m* 1, 1983 (m dis 1984), Francis, *née* Nevay; m 2, 1989, Terry Jane, da of James Peter Cullen; 1 da (Lucie Elizabeth b 19 May 1986); *Career* artist; RHF 1977, warehouseman Tesco Stores Ltd 1978, bouncer Caledonian Hotel 1978, shelf filler Safeway plc 1983, labourer 1983; official Br war artist Bosnia 1993, The London Times war artist in Kosovo 1999; painter; Hon Doctorate Strathclyde Univ 1996; *Exhibitions* incl: Flowers East London 1993, 1994, 1996, 1997, 1999 and 2003, McLellan Galleries Glasgow 1993, Imperial War Museum (series of paintings of Bosnia) 1994, The Drawing and Art Assoc of Norway Oslo 1996, Galleri Christian Dam Copenhagen 1997, Flowers West LA 2001, Maclaurin Gallery Ayr 2002; *Public Collections*: BBC, Br Cncl, Br Museum, Cartwright Hall Bradford, Christie's Corporate Collection, Contemporary Art Soc, Fitzwilliam Museum Cambridge, Glasgow Art Gallery and Museum, Glasgow Royal Concert Hall, Gulbenkian Collection Lisbon, Hunterian Museum Glasgow, Imperial War Museum London, Library of Congress Washington DC, Metropolitan Museum of Art NY, MOD London, MOMA NY, National Gallery of Norway Oslo, NY Library, Arts Cncl of GB, Scot Arts Cncl, Scot National Gallery of Modern Art Edinburgh, STV, Tate Gallery London, V&A, Aberdeen Art Gallery, City Art Centre Edinburgh, Dundee Art Gallery, Paul Mellon Centre, Yale Univ, Scottish Television, Flemings Bank; *Awards* Scottish Drawing Prize 1985, Edwin Morgan Prize 1987, First Prize European Painters Sofia Bulgaria 1989, Henry Moore Prize Bradford International Print Biennia, Lord Provost's Medal Glasgow 1995, Lord Provost's Prize Glasgow 1998; *Recreations* walking, reading; *Clubs* Caledonian, Glasgow Art; *Style*— Peter Howson, Esq, OBE; ✉ c/o Matthew Flowers, Flowers East, 82 Kingsland Road, London E2 8DP (☎ 020 8985 3333)

HOY, Sir Chris; kt (2009), MBE (2005); s of David Hoy, and Carol Hoy, MBE; *b* 23 March 1976, Edinburgh; *Educ* George Watson's Coll Edinburgh (rep Scotland at rowing), Univ of St Andrews (Sportsman of the Year), Univ of Edinburgh (BSc); *Career* cyclist; memb GB nat cycling squad specialising in track sprint 1996–2013, ret; memb: GT Factory BMX Team 1986–91, Dunedin Cycling Club 1992–94, City of Edinburgh Racing Club 1994–2001, Team Athena 2001–03, Team Persil 2004, Team Wolfson Microelectronics / Miller 2005–07; achievements incl: Silver medal team sprint World Championships 1999

H

and 2000, Silver medal team sprint Olympic Games Sydney 2000, Bronze medal team sprint World Championships 2001, Gold medal kilometre and Bronze medal team sprint Cwlth Games 2002, Gold medal kilometre and Gold medal team sprint World Championships 2002, Bronze medal team sprint World Championships 2003, Gold medal kilometre and Bronze medal team sprint World Championships 2004, Gold medal kilometre Olympic Games Athens 2004, Gold medal team sprint and Bronze medal kilometre World Championships 2005, Gold medals track team sprint, keirin and individual sprint Olympic Games Beijing 2008, 2 Gold medals team sprint and keirin Olympic Games London 2012, numerous Gold medals and podium finishes in World Cup series races; Team of the Year (jtly) BBC Sports Personality of the Year Awards 2000, Glenfiddich Scottish Sports Personality 2002, Scottish Sports Personality Award Cwlth Games Cncl 2003, 2004, 2005 and 2007, BBC Scottish Sports Personality of the Year 2003, Track Cyclist of the Year Cyclingnews.com 2005, Glasgow Sportsperson of the Year 2007, BBC Sports Personality of the Year 2008, BBC Sports Personality of the Year Lifetime Achievement Award 2014; Hon Dr: Univ of Edinburgh 2005, Heriot Watt Univ 2005; *Style*— Sir Chris Hoy, MBE; ✉ website www.chrishoy.com

HOY, David Forrest; s of Peter Harold Hoy, of Epsom, Surrey, and Helena Muriel, *née* Blackshaw; *b* 7 April 1946, Wallasey, Cheshire; *Educ* Leeds GS, Merchant Taylors'; *m* 11 Sept 1971, Angela, da of John Piddock; 1 da (Susanne Mary b 4 April 1976); *Career* asst internal auditor Dunlop Co Ltd 1964–67, accountant Redwood Press Ltd 1967–68, gen mangr Guinness Superlatives Ltd 1974–76 (co accountant 1968–74), md Guinness Publishing Ltd 1976–88, project dir Guinness Enterprises Ltd 1989–90; vice-pres: Gleneagles Group Inc, Champneys Group Inc 1991–92; commercial dir Guinness Nigeria plc 1992–95, fin dir Guinness Brewing Worldwide Ltd (Africa) 1995–96, strategic and devpt dir Park Royal Partnership 1996–97, dir Strategic Devpt Guinness Ltd 1997–2000, facilities and devpt dir Guinness UDV 2000–01, property devpt dir Diageo plc 2001–06; non-exec dir: Metropolitan Housing Tst, Metropolitan Living Ltd, Clapham Park Devpt Ltd 2008–13; FCCA, FRSA; *Recreations* powerboating, photography, philately, travel; *Style*— David Hoy, Esq; ✉ Laurel House, Maltmans Lane, Gerrards Cross, Buckinghamshire SL9 8RS

HOYLAND, Prof Daniel Victor (Vic); s of Frank Hoyland (d 2000), of Yorks, and Nanette, *née* Tingle; *b* 11 December 1945; *Educ* Univ of Hull (BA), Univ of York (PhD); *Career* composer; commnd by UK ensembles incl: Lontano, Birmingham Contemporary Music Gp, BBC Symphony Orch, Arditti Quartet, Vocem, Lindsay Quartet; cmmnd by UK festivals incl: Aldeburgh, Almeida, Bath, Cheltenham, Huddersfield, South Bank, York; visiting composer in residence Univ of Calif San Diego, Hayward fell Barber Inst of Fine Art Univ of Birmingham 1980–83, visiting lectr Univ of York, currently prof in composition Univ of Birmingham (sometime lectr); dir Northern Music Theatre (NMT); involved with SPNM and Royal Philharmonic Soc; *Compositions* incl: Em 1970, Es 1971, Jeux thème 1973, Ariel 1974–75, Esem 1975, Seranade 1979, Xingu 1979, Andacht zum Kleinen 1980, Reel 1980, Michelagniolo 1981, Quartet movement 1982, Fox 1983, Head and 2 Tails 1983–84, Quintet of Brass 1984, Seneca – Medea 1985, String Quartet 1985, In Transit 1987, Work-out 1987, Hoquetus David 1987, Crazy Rosa – La Madre 1988, Work-out 1988, Of Phantasy, of Dreams and Ceremonies 1989, Trio 1989, Quintet 1990, The Other Side of Air 1991–92, November 2nd P.P.P. 1992, Chamber Concerto 1993, String Quartet No 3 (Bagatelles) 1995, Vixen (A-vixen-A) 1996, Shadow-Show 2002, Qibti 2003, The Attraction of Opposites 2003, Sicilian Vespas 2006, Phoenix 2007, Pierrot 2008, Hey Presto! 2009, Token 2009; *Recordings* incl: The Other Side of the Air (piano solo) 1994, In Transit and Vixen (conducted by Martyn Brabbins, *qv*) 2002, Token 2010; *Recreations* travel, archaeology, mediterranean food and wine; *Style*— Prof Vic Hoyland; ✉ c/o Michael Hooper, University of York Music Press (UYMP) (☎ 01904 430000 or 01904 432434, mobile 07516 132628, fax 01904 432450)

HOYLE, Baron (Life Peer 1997), of Warrington in the County of Cheshire; (Eric) Douglas Harvey Hoyle; JP (1958); s of late William Hoyle, of Adlington, Lancs, and Leah Ellen Hoyle; *b* 17 February 1930; *Educ* Adlington Sch, Horwich and Bolton Tech Colls (HNC); *m* 1953, Pauline (d 1991), da of William Spencer, of Blackrod, Lancs; 1 s (Lindsay Hoyle, MP, *qv*); *Career* sales engr; Parly candidate (Lab) Clitheroe 1964; MP (Lab): Nelson and Colne 1974–79 (contested same 1970 and 1974), Warrington (by-election) July 1981–83, Warrington N 1983–97; chm PLP 1992–97, memb shadow cabinet 1992–97; a Lord in Waiting (Govt whip) 1997–99; memb Manchester Regnl Hosp Bd 1968–74, pres ASTMS 1985–88 (memb 1958, vice-pres 1981–85), pres MSF 1990–91 (jt pres 1988–90), memb Lab Pty NEC 1978–82 and 1983–85 (chm Home Policy Ctee 1983), chm PLP Trade and Industry Ctee 1987–92; memb: House of Commons Trade and Industry Select Ctee 1985–92, House of Lords Select Ctee on Procedure 2003–; chm Warrington Wolves RLFC 1999–2009 (pres 2009–); Freedom of Gibraltar 2004, Freedom of Warrington 2005; Hon DLitt Univ of Chester 2010; *Style*— The Lord Hoyle; ✉ House of Lords, London SW1A 0PW

HOYLE, Jonathan Wilson; CBE (2005); s of Walter Hoyle (d 2002), and Barbara, *née* Wilson (d 2009); *b* 5 December 1960; *Educ* Baines GS, Univ of Hull (BA), Cranfield Univ (MBA); *m* 27 Oct 1991, Amanda, *née* Catlow; *Career* civil servant 1982–2014, COS Def Equipment and Support MOD until 2009, DG commercial MOD 2009, DG Govt and industry cyber security GCHQ 2010–14, vice-pres Europe and Latin America Lockheed Martin 2014–; *Recreations* golf, theatre, hiking; *Style*— Jonathan Hoyle, Esq, CBE

HOYLE, Rt Hon Lindsay; MP, PC (2013); *Career* Chorley BC: cncllr 1980–98, dep ldr 1994–97; mayor of Chorley 1997–98; MP (Lab) Chorley 1997–; dep speaker, chm of ways and means 2011–; memb Catering Ctee 1997–; memb Trade and Industry Select Ctee 1998–, vice-chair All-Pty Rugby League Gp, treas All-Pty Parly Cricket Gp, chair All-Pty Gibraltar Gp 2000, chair All-Pty Br Vigin Island Gp, memb European Scrutiny Ctee, chair Unite Parly Gp; *Style*— The Rt Hon Lindsay Hoyle, MP; ✉ House of Commons, London SW1A 0AA (☎ 020 7219 3515, fax 020 7219 3831)

HOYLE, Susan (Sue); OBE (2011); da of Roland Hoyle, and Joan, *née* Dickson; *b* 7 April 1953; *Educ* Nottingham HS for Girls, Univ of Bristol; *m* 2005, Graham Devlin; *Career* educn offr Eng Nat Ballet (formerly London Festival Ballet) 1980–83, admin Extemporary Dance Theatre 1983–86; Arts Cncl: dance and mime offr 1986–89, dance dir 1989–94, dep sec-gen 1994–97; head of arts Br Cncl France 1997–98, exec dir The Place 1998–2003; Clore Leadership Prog: dep dir 2003–08, dir 2008–; visiting research assoc KCL 2008–10; lead advsr (dance) Arts Cncl 2003–08, chair CreateKX 2003–06, chair DV8 Physical Theatre 2004–09; memb Franco-Br Cncl 2000–06, tstee Br Cncl 2008–14; hon fell Falmouth Univ 2014; Chevalier dans l'Ordre des Palmes Académiques 2010; *Style*— Ms Sue Hoyle, OBE; ✉ Clore Leadership Programme, Somerset House, Strand, London WC2R 1LA (☎ 020 7420 9430, e-mail sue.hoyle@cloreleadership.org)

HOYLES, Prof Dame Celia Mary; DBE (2014, OBE 2004); da of Harold Gainsford French, of Loughton, Essex, and Elsie Florence, *née* Last; *b* 18 May 1946; *Educ* Univ of Manchester (BSc), Univ of London (MEd, PhD); *m* 1, (m dis); m 2, 1996, Prof Richard Noss; *Career* mathematics teacher in secdy schs 1967–72, sr lectr then princ lectr Poly of N London 1972–84, prof of mathematics educn Univ of London 1984–; chair Jt Mathematical Cncl of the UK 1999–2003, Govt chief advsr for mathematics 2004–07, dir Nat Centre for Excellence in the Teaching of Mathematics 2007–13; presenter Fun and Games YTV 1987–90; first recipient Hans Freudenthal Medal 2003, Royal Soc Kavli Medal 2011; *Books* Learning Mathematics and Logo (with R Noss, 1992), Windows on Mathematical Meanings: Learning Cultures and Computers (with R Noss, 1996), Mathematics Education and Technology: Rethinking the Terrain (2009), Improving Mathematics at Work (2010); *Recreations* tennis, swimming, theatre, film, travel; *Style*— Prof Dame Celia Hoyles, DBE; ✉ e-mail c.hoyles@ioe.ac.uk

HRUSKA, Dr Jan; s of Prof Ivan Hruska (d 1998), and Bozena Bozicek-Ferrari (d 1983); *b* 22 April 1957, Zagreb, Croatia; *Educ* Downing Coll Cambridge (MA), Magdalen Coll Oxford (DPhil); *m* 2000, Regula Voellm; *Career* co-fndr and jt ceo (with Peter Lammer, *qv*) Sophos plc 1985–2005 (non-exec dir 2006–15), md LogicIQ Ltd 2006–; *Publications* The PC Security Guide (jtly, 1988), Data Security Solutions (jtly, 1990), Computer Viruses and Anti-Virus Warfare (1990, 2 edn 1992), Computer Security Reference Book (jtly, 1992); *Recreations* sub-aqua diving, running, piano, skiing, lock-picking; *Style*— Dr Jan Hruska; ✉ Sophos Ltd, The Pentagon, Abingdon Science Park, Abingdon, Oxfordshire OX14 3YP (☎ 01235 559933, fax 01235 559935, e-mail jh@sophos.com)

HUBBARD, Michael Joseph; QC (1985); s of Joseph Thomas Hubbard, of Sussex, and Gwendoline Phyllis, *née* Bird (d 1957); *b* 16 June 1942; *Educ* Lancing; *m* 1967, Ruth Ann, *née* Logan; 5 s (Mark b 1968, Duncan b 1970, Lucian b 1972, Angus b 1974, Quinten b 1976); *Career* slr 1966–72, called to the Bar Gray's Inn 1972, initially in practice Western Circuit; prosecuting counsel to Inland Revenue Western Circuit 1983–85; recorder of the Crown Ct 1984–; *Recreations* sailing – yacht 'Wild Confusion'; *Style*— Michael Hubbard, QC; ✉ 1 Paper Buildings, Temple, London EC4Y 7EP (☎ 020 7353 3728, fax 020 7353 2911)

HUCK, Prof Steffen; s of Jochen Huck, of Mainhausen, Germany, and Waltrand Huck; *b* 2 October 1968, Seligenstadt, Germany; *Educ* Goethe Univ Frankfurt, Humboldt Univ Berlin; *Partner* Heike Harmgart; *Career* sr lectr Royal Holloway Univ of London 2000–01; UCL: reader in economics 2002–03, prof of economics 2003–, head of dept 2008–11; dir Economics of Change WZB Berlin 2012–; Philip Leverhulme Prize 2004; *Publications* contrib to numerous jls incl: American Economic Review, American Political Science Review, Jl of Theoretical Biology, Cambridge Opera Jl; ed first German edn of Wilfred Owen's war poems (published 1993); *Recreations* opera and more opera, TV binge watching; *Style*— Prof Steffen Huck; ✉ University College London, Department of Economics, Gower Street, London WC1E 6BT (☎ 020 7679 5895, e-mail s.huck@ucl.ac.uk, website www.ucl.ac.uk/~uctpshu/)

HUDD, Dr Nicholas Payne (Nick); s of Harold Payne Hudd (d 1977), of Essex, and Marguerita Eva, *née* Clarke (d 2012); *b* 11 October 1945, Romford, Essex; *Educ* Palmer's Sch, Sidney Sussex Coll Cambridge (MA, MB BChir, first boat colours), Westminster Hosp; *m* 11 Oct 1969, Gwendeleen Mary, da of John Johnstone, of Glasgow; 2 s (Alastair Payne b 28 Dec 1973, Robert Nicholas Harold b 23 June 1984), 1 da (Anne Marguerita Jane b 10 Dec 1976); *Career* house surgn Westminster Children's Hosp 1970, house physician Princess Alexandra Hosp Harlow 1971, SHO Orsett Hosp 1972, med registrar St Andrew's Hosp Billericay and Basildon Hosp 1972–74, haematology registrar Orsett Hosp 1974–76; sr med registrar: Withington Hosp and Manchester Royal Infirmary 1976–78, Benenden Hosp 1978–79; conslt physician Benenden Hosp 1980–2004; memb: BMA, Br Diabetic Assoc, Historical Assoc, Royal Nat Rose Soc, Canterbury Diocesan Synod; chm: Romney Marsh Historic Churches Tst 1988–96 (vice-chm 1982–88), Tenterden & District Local History Soc; pres The Rising Mercury Soc (Benenden Ex-Patients) 1993–2004; FRCP 1995; *Recreations* golf, music (singing and conducting), rose-growing, history, astronomy, talking; *Clubs* Tenterden Golf, RSM; *Style*— Dr N P Hudd; ✉ 13 Elmfield, Tenterden, Kent TN30 6RE (☎ 01580 763704, e-mail nphudd@cantab.net, website www.nphudd.com)

HUDD, Roy; OBE (2004); s of Harold Hudd, of London, and Evalina, *née* Barham; *b* 16 May 1936; *Educ* Croydon Secdy Tech Sch; *m* 25 Sept 1988, Deborah Ruth, da of Gordon Flitcroft (d 1986), of Lytham, Lancs; *Career* comedian, playwright, author and actor; commercial artist 1952–55, Nat Serv RAF 1955–57, entered show business 1958; tstee Br Actors Equity; pres: Br Music Hall Soc, Max Miller Appreciation Soc; Hon DLitt Univ of Westminster 2010; Centenary King Rat of The Grand Order of Water Rats 1989 and 2000; twice monthly column Yours magazine; Hon DCL UEA 2007; *Theatre* incl: seasons at Richmond Theatre and The Young Vic, the clown in The Birth of Merlin (Theatr Clwyd), Fagin in Oliver!, Stanley Gardner in Run For Your Wife (Whitehall and Criterion), The Fantasticks (Open Air Theatre) 1990, Babes in the Wood (Ashcroft Theatre Croydon 1990, Theatre Royal Plymouth 1991, New Theatre Cardiff 1992, Pavilion Theatre Bournemouth 1993, Sadler's Wells 1994), Midsummer Night's Dream (Open Air Theatre) 1991, George Pigden in Two into One 1993, A Funny Thing Happened on the Way to the Forum (Open Air Theatre) 1999, Hard Times (Theatre Royal Haymarket) 2000, Theft (nat tour) 2001, The Solid Gold Cadillac (Garrick Theatre) 2005, The Merry Widow (London Coliseum) 2008, Wizard of Oz (Royal Festival Hall) 2008, When We Are Married (Garrick Theatre) 2010–11, Roy Hudd's Exeedingly Entertaining Evening (nat tour); writer of stage prodns: The Victorian Christmas, Roy Hudd's very own Music Hall, Just a Verse and Chorus, Beautiful Dreamer, While London Sleeps, Underneath the Arches (winner Best Actor in a Musical from Soc of West End Theatre), numerous pantomimes and music hall shows; *Radio* incl: Workers' Playtime, The News Huddlines, Like They've Never Been Gone, disc jockey Radio 2; *Television* incl: Not So Much a Programme More a Way of Life, The Maladjusted Busker (winner Montreaux Press Prize), Hudd, The Illustrated Weekly Hudd, Comedy Tonight, The 607080 Show, Movie Memories, Halls of Fame, The Puppet Man, Hometown, regular panelist on What's My Line?, Lipstick on Your Collar, Common as Muck, Karaoke, Cold Lararus, Common as Muck 2, The Quest, Coronation Street, The Quest Two, The Quest Three, Hollyoaks in the City, Casualty, Doctors, New Tricks, The Unusual Miss Nightingale, Little Dorritt, Ashes to Ashes, Missing, Coronation Street, Call the Midwife, Law & Order UK, Midsomer Murders, Our Robot Overlords, Holby City; *Awards* incl: Sony Gold Award 1990 for outstanding contrib to radio, LWT Lifetime Achievement for Radio Comedy Award 1990, Variety Club BBC Radio Personality 1979 and 1993, Columnist of the Year EMAP 1994, Roy Castle Award for Outstanding Services to Variety 2003; *Books* Music Hall (1970), Roy Hudd's Book of Music Hall, Variety and Showbiz Anecdotes (1993), Roy Hudd's Cavalcade of Variety Acts (1997), A Fart in a Colander (autobiography, 2009); *Recreations* walking, singing, napping; *Clubs* Garrick; *Style*— Roy Hudd, Esq, OBE; ✉ Roy Hudd Enterprises, PO Box 604, Ipswich IP6 9WZ

HUDDLESTON, Nigel; MP; s of Alan Huddleston (d 2015), and Pauline, *née* Franklin, of Lincoln; *b* 13 October 1970, Lincoln; *Educ* Robert Pattinson Comp Lincs, Univ of Oxford (BA, MA), The Anderson Sch of Mgmnt UCLA (MBA, Dean's List); *m* 24 Sept 1999, Melissa, *née* Peters; 1 s (Tyler Joseph b 25 March 2006), 1 da (Mackenzie Grace b 18 Nov 2008); *Career* Arthur Andersen 1993–2001, Deloitte 2001–11, Google 2011–15; MP (Cons) Mid Worcestershire 2015–; *Recreations* cinema, travel, walking, history and heritage; *Style*— Nigel Huddleston, Esq, MP; ✉ House of Commons, London SW1A 0AA (☎ 020 7219 5814, e-mail nigel.huddleston.mp@parliament.uk, website www.nigelhuddleston.com)

HUDSON, Andrew Peter; CB (2012); s of John Thomas David Hudson (d 1986), and Margaret Hudson; *Educ* King Edward's Sch Birmingham, New Coll Oxford; *m* 2002, Judith Simpson; *Career* Inland Revenue 1980–82 and 1984–86, HM Treasy 1982–84 and 1986–99 (press sec to Chancellor of the Exchequer 1992–96); Essex CC: asst chief exec 1999–2002, dep chief exec (fin and performance) 2002–04; chief exec Valuation Office Agency 2004–09, md Public Services and Growth Directorate HM Treasy 2009–; hon RICS 2008; *Recreations* running, walking, watching sport; *Style*— Andrew Hudson, Esq, CB

HUDSON, Gaye; *née* Emery; da of late Rt Hon Sir Peter Emery, and Elizabeth, *née* Nicholson; *b* 14 February 1957; *Educ* Westonbirt Sch, Eastbourne Coll, Coll of Distributive Trade, London Business Sch, Global Business Consortium; *m* 2 Oct 1982, Jonathan Michael Hudson; 1 da (Holly Elizabeth b 13 Feb 1988), 1 s (Charles Peter Meadows b 22 Dec 1989); *Career* Young and Rubicam 1977–79, dir Burson-Marsteller 1979–89, main bd dir and head of mktg Hill and Knowlton 1989–95, Oracle Corporation 1997– (currently vice-pres corp communications EMEA); *Recreations* skiing, family, fine cuisine; *Style—* Mrs Gaye Hudson; ✉ The Tree House, Station Road, Wargrave, Berkshire RG10 8EU

HUDSON, Gillian Grace (Gill); da of Brian Hudson (d 1985), of East Grinstead, W Sussex, and Grace Iris, *née* Hill; *b* 23 March 1955; *Educ* Univ of Sussex (BA); *Children* 1 da (Alexia b 15 Jan 1994); *Career* press offr Eng Tourist Bd 1978–81, ed Home and Country Magazine 1981–83, dep ed then ed Fitness Magazine 1984–85, ed Cook's Weekly 1986, dep ed then ed Company Magazine 1987–92, ed New Woman 1992–95; editorial dir: Maxim 1995–99, Stuff 1996–99, Eve 1999–2002; editorial dir (new devpts) BBC Magazines 2002, ed Radio Times 2002–09, ed in chief Reader's Digest 2009–12, currently writer and editorial conslt; BSME: memb 1981, memb Ctee 1993–96, chm 1993, memb Periodicals Trg Ctee 2001–12; memb Complaints Ctee IPSO 2014–; PPA Campaign of the Year Award 1991 and 1993, BSME Men's Magazine Ed of the Year 1997, BSME Entertainment Magazine Ed of the Year 2003, BBC Magazines Ed of the Year 2005, PPA Ed of the Year 2006 and 2011, Mark Boxer Award 2011; *Clubs* Groucho; *Style—* Ms Gill Hudson

HUDSON, Hugh; s of Michael Donaldson-Hudson (d 1965), and Jacynth Mary, *née* Ellerton (later Lady Lawrence, d 1987); *b* 25 August 1936; *Educ* Eton; *m* 25 Aug 1977, Susan Caroline, *née* Michie; 1 s (Thomas John b 8 May 1978); *Career* director and film maker; memb: Exec Ctee Cinema 100, 2nd Decade Cncl of AFI, BAFTA, Acad of Motion Picture, Arts and Sci (USA); Liveryman Worshipful Co of Haberdashers; *Films* incl: Chariots of Fire 1980 (5 BAFTA Awards, 4 Oscars, Golden Globe Award for Best Foreign Film, Best Picture UK & USA 1982), Greystoke – Legend of Tarzan 1983 (6 BAFTA & 5 Oscar nominations, BFI Technical Achievement Award), Revolution 1985 (BFI Anthony Asquith Award for Music), Lost Angels 1989, Lumière and Company (multi-directional participation in film to celebrate cinema's centenary) 1992, A Life So Far 1997, I Dreamed of Africa 1998; *Documentary* incl: A is for Apple (BAFTA nomination for Best Short Film 1963, Screenwriters' Guild Award), Tortoise & Hare (BAFTA nomination, Venice Festival Documentary Award), Fangio; *Political Films* Labour Party Election Broadcasts 1987–92 (incl Kinnock the Movie); *Advertising* over 600 commercials produced 1968–92 for clients incl: Levis, Coty, Benson & Hedges, Fiat Strada, Courage (Gercha), British Airways (Island and Face); *Theatre* co-prodr Chariots of Fire 2012; *Awards* incl: 3 times D&AD Gold & Best Dir Awards, 5 Gold and 6 Silver Cannes Awards 1975–85, Cannes Grand Prix, Venice Grand Prix; *Style—* Hugh Hudson, Esq; ✉ Hudson Film Ltd, 24 St Leonards Terrace, London SW3 4QG (☎ 020 7730 0002, fax 020 7730 8033, e-mail hudsonfilm@mac.com, website www.hudsonfilmltd.co.uk/home)

HUDSON, Ian; s of Allen Hudson, and Ivy, *née* Angell; *Educ* Queen Elizabeth GS Gainsborough, Univ of Derby, Henley Mgmnt Coll; *m* Nicola; 2 s (Elliot, Tom), 1 da (Georgia); *Career* Marshall Cavendish Ltd: fin controller 1988–90, Euro dir 1990–92; The Random House Gp (now Penguin Random House): dep gp fin dir 1992–96, md Random House Children's Books 1996–97, gp commercial dir 1997–98, gp md 1998–2005, dep gp ceo 2005–, ceo Penguin Random House Int; memb Supervisory Bd Bertelsmann AG; chm Trade Publishers' Cncl, pres Publishers' Assoc; memb Young Presidents Org; FCMA 1987 (memb 1985); *Recreations* family life, reading, football, skiing, music, travel, surfing; *Clubs* Soho House, Hogarth; *Style—* Ian Hudson, Esq; ✉ Penguin Random House, Random House, 20 Vauxhall Bridge Road, London SW1V 2SA (☎ 020 7840 8876, e-mail ihudson@randomhouse.co.uk)

HUDSON, John; s of Don Hudson, of Barnsley, S Yorks, and Joyce, *née* Winterbottom (d 1995); *b* 16 February 1961; *Educ* Worsborough HS Barnsley, Gravnille Art Coll Sheffield, GSM; *m* Claire Elizabeth Olwen, da of Richard John Foulkes Taylor; *Career* tenor; memb chorus Welsh Nat Opera 1992–93, co princ ENO 1993–; performances incl: Paris, Auckland, Ireland, Canada, Barbican, Kenwood, Birmingham Symphony Orch, Royal Albert Hall; appeared with Lesley Garratt Viva La Diva (BBC 2) 1996; subject of various articles in magazines and newspapers; *Recreations* tennis, painting, cooking, playing cricket; *Clubs* Savage, London Sketch; *Style—* John Hudson, Esq

HUDSON, John Lewis; OBE (2003), DL (W Midlands 2010); s of Wilfred Hudson, and Edith Hudson; *Educ* Aston Univ (MSc), Birmingham City Univ (DUniv); *m* 22 Sept 1973, Eileen Cornelia; 1 s (Mark Standring b 7 Feb 1975), 1 da (Samantha Vicki b 24 Sept 1977); *Career* BSA Motorcycles Ltd 1960–71, Chrysler (UK) Ltd 1971–72, md Morphy Richards Ltd 1972–78; Delta Group plc: md Sperryn & Co Ltd 1978–82, divnl dir and gen mangr Gas Controls and Engrg Div Delta Group 1982–84, divnl md Fluid Controls Div 1984–86, gp chief exec Wagon Industrial Holdings 1986–97; chm and chief exec Calder Industrial Materials Ltd 1998–2006; chm: Birmingham International Airport 1997–, Metal Castings Ltd 1998–2006, Whittan Group Ltd 2002–06, Bromford Industries Ltd 2009–14, Acenta Gp Ltd 2011–13; non-exec dir: Senior Engineering Group plc 1991–2001, Temple Bar Investment Trust plc 1991–2005; pres Birmingham C of C 1999–2000, chm W Midlands Industrial Devpt Bd 1999–2001; memb Cncl Aston Univ 1992–97; Hon DUniv Birmingham City Univ 2014; CEng, FIET, FIMechE; *Recreations* walking; *Style—* John Hudson, Esq, OBE, DL; ✉ Birmingham Airport, Birmingham B26 3QJ (☎ 0121 767 7100, fax 0121 767 7310)

HUDSON, Lucian; *b* 5 July 1960; *Educ* Lycee Francais de Londres, St Catherine's Coll Oxford (MA); *m* 1982, Margaret Prythergch; *Career* trainee journalist Central TV 1983–84, asst prodr Newsnight BBC 1984–85, sr researcher TVS 1985–88, prodr then sr prodr BBC Nine O'Clock News and Weekends 1988–93, night ed BBC Breakfast News 1993–94, chief asst to controller Radio 5 Live 1994, ed party confs BBC TV News 1994, ed Newsdesk, News Hour, Live Events and Breaking News BBC World 1994–97, head of programming (int channels) BBC Worldwide 1997–99, editorial dir Armstrong International, Skillcapital and Justpeople.com 2000, dir of e-communications Cabinet Office 2000–01; dir of communications: DEFRA (also chief knowledge offr) 2001–04, Dept for Constitutional Affrs 2004–06, FCO 2006–08; dir Miny of Justice 2008–09, ptnr and md Cornerstone Global Assocs 2009–11, dir of communications Open Univ 2011–; praxis ed Annual Review of Social Partnerships 2014–; chm Tavistock Inst of Human Relations 2003–07; chm: Rory Peck Tst 1998–2000, Liberal Judaism 2009–15; *Publications* The Enabling State: Collaborating for Success (2009); *Recreations* travel, reading, music, swimming, watching rugby; *Style—* Lucian Hudson, Esq; ✉ The Open University, Walton Hall, Milton Keynes MK7 6AA

HUDSON, (Anthony) Maxwell; s of Peter John Hudson, CB (d 2012), and Joan Howard Hudson, *née* Fitzgerald (d 1998); *b* 12 April 1955; *Educ* St Paul's, New Coll Oxford (MA); *m* 14 Sept 1991, Cordelia Jennifer, da of Nigel Roberts, of Haslemere; 1 s (James Nicholas Maxwell b 10 Sept 1994), 1 da (Katharine Jennifer Sophie b 27 March 1997); *Career* admitted slr 1980; ptnr: Frere Cholmeley 1987–95, Payne Hicks Beach 1995–; *Recreations* history, wine, architecture; *Clubs* Oxford and Cambridge; *Style—* Maxwell Hudson, Esq; ✉ Payne Hicks Beach, 10 New Square, Lincoln's Inn, London WC2A 3QG (☎ 020 7465 4300, fax 020 7465 4400, e-mail mhudson@phb.co.uk, website www.phb.co.uk)

HUDSON, Prof Ray; s of Jack Hudson (d 1977), and Jean, *née* Macfarlane (d 1982); *b* 7 March 1948, Alnwick, Northumberland; *Educ* Alnwick Dukes GS, Univ of Bristol (BA, PhD, DSc), Univ of Durham (DLitt); *m* 2 Aug 1975, Geraldine, *née* Holder Jones; 1 s (Matthew b 23 March 1979), 1 da (Anna b 28 May 1981); *Career* Univ of Durham: lectr 1972, sr lectr 1984, reader 1987, prof of geography 1990–2016, dir Wolfson Research Inst 2003–, pro-vice-chllr 2007–12, dep vice-chllr 2012–14, actg vice-chllr 2014–15, emeritus prof of geography 2016–; various visiting appts incl prof Copenhagen Business Sch 1984 and visiting prof of geography Univ Coll Dublin 2016–; tstee County Durham Community Fndn 2016; Edward Heath Award RGS 1988, Victoria Medal RGS 2005, Sir Peter Hall Award Regional Studies Assoc 2014; Hon DSc Roskilde Univ 1987; FRGS 1989, FAcSS 2002, FBA 2006, memb Academia Europaea 2007; FRSA 2009, FeRSA 2012; *Books* Wrecking a Region (1989), Producing Places (2001), Placing the Social Economy (2002), Economic Geographies: Circuits, Flows and Spaces (2005), Digging up Trouble: The Environment, Protest and Opencast Coal Mining (2000), Approaches to Economic Geography: Towards a Geographical Political Economy (2016); *Recreations* travel, walking, sport, reading; *Style—* Prof Ray Hudson; ✉ University of Durham, Department of Geography, Durham DH1 3LE (☎ 0191 334 6045, mobile 07793 903351, fax 0191 334 6087, e-mail ray.hudson@durham.ac.uk)

HUDSON, Richard Bayliss; *b* 9 June 1954; *Educ* Peterhouse Sch Zimbabwe, Wimbledon Sch of Art (BA); *Career* set and costume designer for theatre and opera 1980–; Olivier Award 1988, Tony Award for The Lion King on Broadway 1998, Critics Choice Award NY 1998 and London 2000, Gold Medal for Set Design Prague Quadreniale 2003; fell Liverpool Inst for Performing Arts 2009, companion Royal Welsh Coll of Music and Drama 2010; Hon Dr Univ of Surrey 2005; RDI 1999, FRSA; *Theatre* RSC: The Master Builder, A Clockwork Orange, Travesties, The Cherry Orchard, Women Beware Women, Coriolanus; RNT: The Misanthrope, Volpone, Blue Remembered Hills, The Ends of the Earth; Old Vic: Andromache, One Way Pendulum, Too Clever by Half, Bussy d'Ambois, The Tempest, Candide; Young Vic: 'Tis Pity She's a Whore, The Skin of our Teeth, Doctor Faustus; other credits incl: The Emperor (Royal Court), Desire (Almeida), Hippolytos (Almeida), La Bete (NY and London), The Lion King (NY, Tokyo, Osaka, London, Toronto, Los Angeles and Hamburg); *Opera* Glyndebourne Festival Opera: The Queen of Spades, Eugene Onegin, Ermione, Manon Lescaut, Le Nozze di Figaro, Don Giovanni, Cosi Fan Tutte; ENO: Figaro's Wedding, The Force of Destiny, The Ring of the Nibelung; Scottish Opera: La Vie Parisienne, Candide, The Vanishing Bridegroom, Maria Stuarda; Vienna State Opera: Ernani, Guillaume Tell, Les Contes d'Hoffmann; other credits incl: Die Meistersinger von Nurnberg (Royal Opera), Samson et Dalila (Met Opera NY), The Rake's Progress (Chicago Lyric Opera and Saito Kinen Festival Japan) I Puritani (Gran Teatro la Fenice Venice), L'Inganno Felice (Rossini Opera Festival Pesaro), Lucia di Lammermoor (Zurich and Bayerisches Staatsoper Munich), A Night at the Chinese Opera (Kent Opera), Count Ory (Kent Opera), The Queen of Spades (Chicago), Idomeneo (Florence), Tamerlano (Florence), Of Mice and Men (Bregenz, Houston and Washington), Khovanshchina (Paris Opera), Benvenuto Cellini (Zurich), Les vêpres siciliennes (Paris), The Makropulos Case (Copenhagen), Fall of the House of Usher (Bregenz), La Forza del Destino (Vienna and Brussels), La Boheme (Athens), Rushes (Royal Ballet), Divozio all'Italiana (Opéra de Nancy), Kafka's Monkey and Pictures from an Exhibition (Young Vic), Armida (Met Opera NY), Ruddigore (Opera North), Die Entfürung aus dem Serail (Rome Opera), Das Rhinegold and Die Walküre (Teatro Massimo Palermo); *Ballet* Rushes, Goldberg, Invitus Invitam (all Royal Ballet), The Nutcracker, Dunbarton (both American Ballet Theatre), Romeo and Juliet (Nat Ballet of Canada), La Bayadère, Le Coq d'Or (both Royal Danish Ballet); *Style—* Richard Hudson, Esq; ✉ c/o Judy Daish Associates, 2 St Charles Place, London W10 6EG (☎ 020 8964 8811)

HUDSON-WILKIN, Rev Prebendary Rose Josephine; *née* Hudson; da of Joseph Hudson (d 1994), of Jamaica, and Eunice, *née* Desporte; *b* 19 January 1961, Montego Bay, Jamaica; *Educ* Montego Bay HS, Queen's Theol Coll, Univ of Birmingham (BPhil); *m* 23 April 1983, Kenneth Wilkin, s of Matthew Wilkin; 2 da (Amanda b 1986, Hannah b 1988), 1 s (Jamie b 1990); *Career* Christian educn offr Dioc of Jamaica 1982–85, asst curate St Matthew's Wolverhampton 1991–95, diocesan offr Lichfield and assoc priest Church of the Good Shepherd West Bromwich 1995–98, vicar Holy Trinity Dalston and All Saints Haggerston 1998–; Broadcasting Standards cmmr 1998–2003; chaplain to HM The Queen 2007–, chaplain to Speaker of the House of Commons 2010; hon canon St Paul's Cathedral 2013; chair: Nat Ctee for Minority Ethnic Anglicans 1999–2009, Worldwide Ctee SPCK until 2004; tstee Trusthouse Charitable Fndn 2010; *Recreations* cooking, reading, entertaining, tennis, Scrabble, travelling; *Style—* The Rev Prebendary Rose Hudson-Wilkin; ✉ The Vicarage, Livermere Road, London E8 4EZ (☎ 020 7254 5062, fax 020 7249 7028, e-mail revdrose@aol.com)

HUDSPETH, Neil; *Educ* UCLA (BA); *Career* md Lloyd Northover until 2006, ceo Asia Pacific The Brand Union (formerly Enterprise IG) 2006–; dir: Design Business Assoc, Bd Int Design in Business Assoc; memb Writers' Guild of America; *Style—* Neil Hudspeth, Esq

HUE WILLIAMS, Charles James; s of Charles Anthony Hue Williams (d 1969), and Joan, *née* Winfindale (d 1991); *b* 28 September 1942; *Educ* Harrow; *m* 14 March 1964, Joey Oriel Marie-Lou, da of Charles George Clover, of South Stoke; 1 da (Sarah b 27 June 1966), 1 s (Mark b 29 Oct 1968); *Career* ptnr Wedd Durlacher Mordaunt & Co 1970–85; dir: Kleinwort Benson Ltd 1986–90, Kleinwort Benson Securities 1986–90 (md 1989–90), Kleinwort Benson Holdings plc 1989–90, Henderson Crosthwaite Institutional Brokers Ltd 1992–99, Investec Securities (formerly Investec Henderson Crosthwaite Securities) 1999–2002, Lambert Energy Advisory Ltd 2002–, Endeavour Int Corp 2007–14; *Recreations* rackets, lawn tennis, real tennis, golf; *Clubs* Tennis and Rackets Assoc, Racquet and Tennis (NY), Queen's, Turf, Swinley, Prestwick, Royal St George's Sandwich, Royal & Ancient, Berkshire, MCC; *Style—* Charles Hue Williams, Esq; ✉ Headley Meadows, The Hanger, Headley, Hampshire GU35 8SQ (☎ 01428 713970); Lambert Energy Advisory Ltd, 17 Hill Street, London W1J 5LJ (☎ 020 7491 4473)

HUEY EVANS, Gay; OBE (2016); da of C Calvin Huey (d 1989), and Frances, *née* Wismar; *b* 17 July 1954, USA; *Educ* Bucknell Univ Lewisburg PA (BA); *Children* 1 da (Alexandra Evans b 12 Nov 1986); *Career* with Bankers Tst Co 1984–98 (sr md of risk mgmnt servs); FSA: dir of markets and exchanges 1998–2003, dir of markets 2003–05, capital markets sector ldr 2004–05; pres Tribeca Global Mgmnt (Europe) Ltd 2005–07, head of governance Citi Alternative Investments 2007–08, vice-chm investment banking and investment mgmnt Barclays 2008–10; dep chm Financial Reporting Cncl; non-exec dir: ConocoPhillips, Standard Chartered plc; chair: Int Swaps and Derivatives Assoc (ISDA) 1994–98, Jt Forum 2003–05; chair Beacon Awards; former co-opted tstee Tate Audit Ctee, former tstee Wigmore Hall, tstee Wellbeing of Women; *Recreations* tennis, reading, walking, piano playing; *Style—* Ms Gay Huey Evans, OBE

HUGGETT, Monica Elizabeth; da of Victor Lewis Huggett (d 1983), of Epsom, and Monica Germaine, *née* May; *b* 16 May 1953; *Educ* Green Sch for Girls, Isleworth, RAM London; *Career* violinist; ldr Amsterdam Baroque Orchestra 1979–87, ldr/dir The Hanover Bond 1983–86 (recordings incl Beethoven Symphonies), dir Sonnerie (baroque ensemble), first violin of Hausmusik (romantic chamber ensemble), currently artistic dir Irish Baroque Orchestra and Portland Baroque Orchestra USA, teacher of baroque and classical violin RAM London; guest dir: Seville Baroque Orchestra, Kristiansand Symphony Norway, Arion Baroque Orchestra Montreal, Tafelmusik Toronto, LA Chamber Orchestra, Philharmonia Baroque San Francisco, Norwegian Chamber Orchestra, Concerto Copenhagen; recordings incl: J S Bach solo sonatas and partitas (Editor's Choice Award Gramophone Magazine 1997), Bach sonatas with Ton Koopman, Vivaldi concertos with

H

The Academy of Ancient Music, Mozart concertos, Beethoven concerto and Mendelssohn concerto with the Orchestra of the Age of Enlightenment, Heinrich Biber's Violin Sonatas 2002 (Best Instrumental Recording Award Gramophone Magazine), Music for a Young Prize (early versions of the J S Bach Four Orchestral Suites, Diapason d'Or 2009, nominated Grammy Award); Vantaa Baroque Energy Prize (Finland) 2005; memb Musicians' Union; fell RAM London 1994; *Recreations* gardening, cycling, narrow-boating; *Style*— Ms Monica Huggett

HUGGETT, Nicola Anne; da of Stuart Chambers, and Susan McGrath, *née* Mudford; *b* 4 April 1969, Chesterfield; *Educ* St Gabriel's Sch, Marlborough Coll, St Hugh's Coll Oxford (MA), Wolfson Coll Oxford (PGCE); *m* 27 July 1996, Spencer Hugget; 2 da (India *b* 19 June 1998, Honor *b* 6 March 2004 (twin)), 2 s (Joshua *b* 23 Dec 2000, Harry *b* 6 March 2004 (twin)); *Career* acct exec J Walter Thompson 1991–93, housemistress and head of boarding Haileybury Coll 1996–2007, dep head Downe House Sch 2007–13, head Blundell's 2013–; *govr*: Cranleigh Sch, Godolphin and Latymer; former *govr*: Orwell Park Sch, Mount House Sch; memb: HMC, Assoc of Teachers and Lecturers; *Recreations* eventing, skiing, travel; *Clubs* Lansdowne; *Style*— Mrs Nicola Huggett

HUGHES, Prof Alan; s of Benjamin Redshaw Hughes (d 1957), and Lilias, *née* Eyre; *b* 1 August 1946, Sunderland; *Educ* King's Coll Cambridge (BA); *m* 17 Aug 1968, Jean, *née* Braddock; 1 da (Rachel Sarah *b* 29 June 1979), 2 s (John Redshaw, Robert Benjamin (twins) *b* 17 Dec 1981); *Career* sr economic asst NEDO 1971–73, fell Sidney Sussex Coll Cambridge 1973–; Univ of Cambridge: univ asst lectr then lectr in economics 1973–94, chm Faculty Bd of Economics and Politics 1983–88, dir ESRC Small Business Research Centre Dept of Applied Economics 1989–93, dir Centre for Business Research 1994–, Margaret Thatcher prof of enterprise studies Judge Business Sch 1999–, dir of research Judge Business Sch 2001–04, dir Nat Competitiveness Network Prog Cambridge-MIT Inst 2002–03; visiting prof: Coll of Business Florida State Univ 1983, Univ of Social Sciences Toulouse 1993–95 and 1998, Doshisha Univ Kyoto 2005, Univ of Queensland Business Sch Brisbane 2006; memb: Cmmn on Public Policy and Br Business 1995–96, Advsy Bd Centre for Research on Innovation and Competition 1997–, Expert Panel on Educn, Learning and Lifelong Skills DfES 2000–05, Cncl for Science and Technol 2004–; sometime advsr to UK and Dutch Govts on business support policies and and German Govt on science educn; *Books* incl: Finance and the Small Firm (jtly, 1994), The Changing State of British Enterprise: Growth Innovation and Competitive Advantage in SMEs 1986–95 (jt ed, 1996), Enterprise and Community: New Directions in Corporate Governance (jt ed, 1997), Enterprise Challenged: Policy and Performance in the British SME Sector 1999–2002 (jt ed, 2003), UK Plc: Just How Innovative Are We? (jtly, 2006), British Enterprise: Thriving or surviving? SME growth, innovation and public policy 2001–2004 (jt ed, 2007); author of 200 other pubns; *Recreations* photography, walking, golf, gardening, watching football and rugby; *Style*— Prof Alan Hughes; ✉ Centre for Business Research, Judge Business School, University of Cambridge, Trumpington Street, Cambridge CB2 1AG (✆ 01223 765335, fax 01223 765338, e-mail a.hughes@cbr.cam.ac.uk)

HUGHES, Alan Renatus Frederick; s of Wilfred Alan Hughes, and Lily Hughes; *Educ* Arnold Sch Blackpool, Henley Mgmnt Coll (MBA); *m* Dr Sandy Hewitt; 1 da, 1 s (from previous m); *Career* HSBC 1969–2004: memb Exec Bd 1997–2004, ceo First Direct Bank 1999–2004, chair First Direct Investments (UK) Ltd 2001–04; dir: Forward Tst Gp Ltd 1997–2000, Capital One Bank (Europe) plc 2008–10, NewDay Gp 2012–; chair: Ffrees Family Finance 2013–, RateSetter 2014–, Unity Trust Bank plc 2015–; vice-chair: Factors Chain Int Amsterdam 1994–97, Hampden & Co plc 2014–; dir Bd Banking Ombudsman 1997–99, chair Ind Assurance Panel Govt Identity Card Scheme 2005–09, dir Identity and Passport Service 2006–09; memb: Home Office 2005–09, Cabinet Office Delivery Cncl 2005–09; chair Advsy Bd Univ of Leeds Business Sch 2002–13, hon treas and memb Cncl Loughborough Univ 2011–; FRSA, FCIB; *Recreations* family, reading, hill walking, old cars; *Clubs* Sloane; *Style*— Alan Hughes, Esq; ✉ website www.renatus.net

HUGHES, Anthony (Tony); s of Richard Hughes (d 1944), and Lucy Cotton, *née* Sproule (d 1989); *b* 24 September 1944; *Educ* Blackfriars Sch, UCL, Univ of Edinburgh (MA); *m* 1975, Marie-Estelle, da of Jean Dufournier; 1 da (Chantal Madeleine Lucy *b* 26 Sept 1980), 2 s (Timothy Anthony Jean *b* 16 March 1983, Christopher François Wilfrid *b* 27 Aug 1986); *Career* film ed BBC 1970–74; called to the Bar Inner Temple 1975 (scholar 1973), barr 1975–77; tax mangr Peat Marwick Mitchell 1978–82; PricewaterhouseCoopers (formerly Deloitte Haskins & Sells then Coopers & Lybrand): tax mangr 1982–86, ptnr 1986–; memb Dell Ctee 1982; contrib to Financial Times and professional jls; ATII 1979; *Books* International Tax Planning for UK Companies (1984, 1990 and 1994); *Recreations* music, theatre, bridge, tennis; *Clubs* Wimbledon Lakeside; *Style*— Tony Hughes, Esq; ✉ PricewaterhouseCoopers, 1 Embankment Place, London WC2N 6NN (e-mail hughesapc@hotmail.com)

HUGHES, His Hon Judge (Michael) Antony; s of late Joseph Frederick Hughes, and Doris Anne Hughes, MBE; *b* 26 May 1953, Moshi, Tanzania; *Educ* King's Sch Canterbury, Coll of Law; *m* 1977, Ann Holdsworth; 3 da; *Career* admitted slr 1977; recorder 2000–06, circuit judge (South Eastern Circuit) 2006–, dep High Court judge 2007–, hon recorder Milton Keynes 2012–; designated family judge for Milton Keynes, Northampton and Oxford 2014–; *Recreations* walking, vegetable gardening, family, fly fishing, family life; *Clubs* Lansdowne; *Style*— His Hon Judge Hughes; ✉ c/o Milton Keynes County Court, 351 Silbury Boulevard, Central Milton Keynes, MK9 2DT

HUGHES, Benjamin Mark; s of Ewart Wythan Hughes (d 2003), and Jane Yates Stewart, *née* Murrow; *b* 4 October 1955, Marlborough,Wilts; *Educ* St Edward's Sch Oxford, Jesus College Oxford (MA), Univ of Oxford (CertEd); *m* 7 Sept 1991, Chantal, *née* Smyth; 2 s (Julien *b* 26 March 1986, Joshua 29 Oct 1992 (twin)), 1 da (Kelly *b* 29 Oct 1992 (twin)); *Career* teacher of French, German and business studies Radley Coll Abingdon 1979–81, lectr Sorbonne Univ Paris 1981–83, European advtg sales exec Playboy and Media Networks 1981–83; FT: sales and mktg mangr (France) Financial Times (Europe) Ltd 1983–87, publishing dir Financial Times (France) Ltd 1987–91, European advertisement dir 1991–93, project dir Financial Izvestia 1992–94, advertisement and mktg dir (continental Europe) 1993–94, memb Newspaper Mgmnt Bd 1994–, worldwide advertisement sales dir 1995–97, memb Mgmnt Bd Business Day Financial Mail (South Africa) and Vedomosti (Russia) 1996, md Central Europe, Rest of the World and Asia Pacific 1997–2003, worldwide advtg dir 2003–06, global commercial dir and dep chief exec 2006–; chm: Walpole Br Luxury, Superskills, Rolley Golf Ltd; memb Friendly Forces Ctee Help for Heroes; *Recreations* cinema, theatre, all sports, writing children's books (English/French); *Style*— Benjamin Hughes, Esq; ✉ Financial Times, 1 Southwark Bridge, London SE1 9HL (✆ 020 7873 4797, fax 020 7775 6842, e-mail ben.hughes@ft.com)

HUGHES, Charles Edward; s of Frank Hughes (d 1967), and Irene, *née* Holt (d 1970); *b* 15 September 1946, Manchester; *Educ* Stockport GS, Univ of Manchester (BSc); *m* 5 May 1973, Beverley Dawn, da of Maurice Kennerley Humphreys, of Grimsby; 1 s (Daniel Charles *b* 14 March 1977), 1 da (Samantha Louise *b* 29 Jan 1979); *Career* ICL 1967–99 (dir 1985), seconded as project dir DTI 1995–97, fndr and ceo eManagement Ltd 1999–; chm: European Computer Res Centre GmbH 1988–91, Sherwood-CFM Ltd 1996–97, Outsource UK Ltd 2013–; non-exec dir: PERQ Systems Corp 1984–85, ICL Australia pty 1989–90, Screen plc 2000–02; memb Cncl Parly IT Ctee 2000–11; pres BCS (Chartered Inst for IT) 2005–06 (vice-pres 2001–04, dep pres 2004–05), memb Cncl Inst for the Mgmnt of Information Systems 2000–03, memb Spectrum Mgmnt Advsy Bd 2001–03,

chm Int Professional Practice Partnership (IP3) Int Fedn for Info Processing (IFIP) 2006–09, vice-pres Strategic Relations 2010–12; chm and cncllr Smallwood Parish Cncl 1987–93; IFIP Outstanding Service Award 2009; Freeman City of London, past Master Worshipful Co of Information Technologists (Warden 2007–09, Master 2009–10); MCMI 1974, MCIPS 1991, fell Inst for the Mgmnt of Information Systems (FIMIS), FBCS, CEng, CITP; *Publications* International Professional Practice Partnership (IP3) – Overview (2008), The IFIP IP3: Transforming and Informing IT Professional Practice (2008); *Recreations* sport, travel, gardening, family enjoyment, philately; *Clubs* Real Time (past chm), Goring and Streatley Tennis; *Style*— Charles Hughes, Esq; ✉ eManagement Ltd, The Ridge, Lower Basildon, Berkshire RG8 9NX

HUGHES, Christopher Wyndham; OBE (2012); s of Dr John Philip Wyndham Hughes (d 1981), and Christine, *née* Jolley (d 1947); *b* 22 November 1941; *Educ* Manchester Grammar, King Edward's Sch Birmingham, UCL (LLB); *m* 31 Dec 1966, Gail, da of Percival Eric Ward (d 1957); 3 s (Christian Wyndham, Marcus Wyndham (twins) *b* 29 Feb 1968, Dominic Wyndham *b* 20 June 1974); *Career* admitted slr 1966; Wragge & Co Birmingham: articled clerk and slr until 1970, ptnr 1970–2005, managing ptnr 1994–95, head of int 2005–09; NP; memb Bd Severn Trent Water Authy 1982–84, non-exec chm Newman Tonks Group plc 1995–97; non-exec dir Pension Protection Fund 2004–11; memb and later chm Solihull Ctee of Cancer Research Campaign 1972–85; govr The Schs of King Edward VI Birmingham 1984–; memb: Law Soc 1966, Birmingham Law Soc 1966 (memb Cncl 1977–91, jt hon sec 1977–84, vice-pres 1988–89, pres 1989–90), The Notaries Soc 1979, Polish Bar 2009; *Recreations* travel, theatre, sport, languages, old buildings; *Style*— Christopher Hughes, Esq, OBE; ✉ Cuttle Pool Farm, Cuttle Pool Lane, Knowle, Solihull, West Midlands B93 0AP (✆ 01564 772611)

HUGHES, Prof Colin; s of Joseph Hughes (d 2000), and May, *née* Roberts; *b* 14 March 1953, St Asaph; *Educ* Univ of Kent (PhD), Univ of Cambridge (ScD); *Career* research fell: Sandoz Research Inst Vienna 1977–80, Univ of Wurzburg 1980–84, SmithKline Research Philadelphia 1984–85; Univ of Cambridge: lectr 1985–96, reader 1996–2001, prof of microbiology 2001–; fell Trinity Coll Cambridge 1997–; author of ca 130 publications in molecular microbiology in learned jls; FLSW 2012; *Style*— Prof Colin Hughes; ✉ Trinity College, Cambridge CB2 1TQ (✆ 01223 338538)

HUGHES, David Campbell; yr s of Trevor George Hughes (d 1988), of Herefordshire, and Flora Jean, *née* Britton; *b* 13 December 1953; *Educ* Millfield, KCL (LLB, pres Union 1975–76); *m* 1992, Claire Margaret, da of Ian Mitchell Bennet (d 1990), and Doreen Margaret, *née* Wilson, of Cheshire; 2 da, 1 s; *Career* admitted slr 1979, admitted slr Hong Kong 1992; ptnr Allen & Overy 1985–2003; md DC Hughes Falmouth Ltd; Parly candidate (Cons) Bow and Poplar 1987; memb Law Soc, MInstD; *Recreations* golf; *Clubs* Oriental, Falmouth Golf; *Style*— David C Hughes, Esq; ✉ DC Hughes Falmouth Limited, Kingham, Oxfordshire OX7 6YD (✆ 01608 659505, fax 01608 659745)

HUGHES, David John; s of John David Hughes (d 1994), of Wendover, Bucks, and Mary Deirdre, *née* Lowen; *Educ* St Paul's, Univ of Southampton (BA, pres Students' Union 1975–76); *m* 21 Oct 1995 (m dis 2003), Jane Wynsome Katherine, *née* Anstiss; 2 da (Alice *b* 1 Aug 1996, Lucy *b* 22 Sept 2000), 1 s (Harry *b* 5 July 1999); *Career* mktg exec Express Newspapers 1979–82, Parly and external affrs offr Fedn of Civil Engrg Contractors 1982–85, exec sec Cncl for Environmental Conservation 1985–88, sr conslt then bd dir Shandwick Public Affairs 1988–93, dir of govt rels and public affrs The Communication Gp plc 1993–95, jt md The Rowland Co and md Rowland Sallingbury Casey 1995–97, fndr Cothelstone Consulting Ltd 1996–, dir Precise Communications Gp 1998–2001, dir Burlington Entertainment Ltd 1999–, md Palliser Public Counsel Ltd 2002–; conslt ESL & Network SA (Paris) 1998–; nat chm Lib Students 1976–77; Parly candidate: (Lib) Southampton Test 1979, (Lib-SDP Alliance) Westbury 1983 and 1987; nat chm Parly Candidates Assoc 1984–87, vice-chm Lib Pty 1985–88; memb: Hansard Soc for Parly Govt 1991, Int Assoc of Political Conslts 1995, Political Studies Assoc 2001; MInstD 1996; *Books* Liberals and Social Democrats: the Case for an Alliance (1981), Guide to Westminster and Whitehall (1994), Marketing in the Voluntary Sector (2001); various articles in New Statesman, PR Week and other pubns; *Recreations* historical and political biography, theatre and cinema; *Clubs* National Liberal; *Style*— David Hughes, Esq

HUGHES, Prof David John; *b* 5 May 1947, London; *Educ* Royal GS High Wycombe, Aston Univ (MSc); *m* 7 Nov 1970, Dawn Anne, *née* Newman; 2 da (Rachel Sarah *b* 8 Oct 1972, Elizabeth Jane *b* 30 July 1975); *Career* Ford Motor Co Ltd 1970–91 (latterly head of electrical/electronic systems Ford of Europe), dir advanced vehicle systems Lucas plc (then Lucas Varity plc) 1991–97, exec vice-pres technol mgmnt GEC-Marconi plc 1997–2001, special projects dir avionics BAE Systems plc 2002, DG Innovation Gp and chief scientific advsr DTI 2002–06, md The Business Innovation Gp LLP 2006–; visiting prof of engrg mgmnt City Univ 2006–; author of numerous articles for various jls and conferences; chm Industrial Partnership Panel City Univ 2008–12, chm Mgmnt Bd EPSRC Centre in Additive Manufacturing 2011–14; memb: Technol and Innovation Ctee CBI 1999–2003, EPSRC 2003–06, Innovation and Engagement Bd Cardiff Univ 2005–11, Innovation Advsy Bd Univ of Surrey 2006–11; Hon DTech Loughborough Univ 2008; CEng 1975, FIMechE 1996, MIEEE 2000, FREng 2000, CDir 2005, FInstD 2015; *Recreations* walking, 20th century British art, antique metalware, African tribal art; *Style*— Prof David Hughes, FREng, CDir; ✉ School of Engineering and Mathematical Sciences, City University, Northampton Square, London EC1V 0HB (✆ 07801 712139, e-mail david.hughes@thebigpartnership.com)

HUGHES, Dr David Treharne Dillon; s of Maj-Gen W D Hughes, CB, CBE (d 1999), of Farnham, Surrey, and Kathleen Linda Elizabeth, *née* Thomas (d 1976); *b* 31 October 1931; *Educ* Cheltenham Coll, Trinity Coll Oxford (BSc, MA), London Hosp Med Coll (BM BCh); *m* 14 Nov 1959, Gloria Anna; 2 da (Carly Anna *b* 22 Sept 1960, Mandy Lou *b* 19 Oct 1962), 1 s (David Edward Treharne *b* 29 March 1974); *Career* Capt RAMC 1959–61 (jr med specialist BMH Hong Kong); jr research fell MRC Univ of Oxford 1953–54, research fell Univ of Calif 1963–64, conslt physician Royal London Hosp 1970–96 (jr appts 1957–68), head Dept of Clinical Investigation Wellcome Research Laboratories 1978–93; tstee Hunterian Soc (former pres); memb Int Soc of Internal Med (former pres), memb GMC 1993–96; chm Bd of Govrs Moving Theatre Tst 1994–2000, memb Bd of Dirs King's Head Theatre Islington 2008–10; Freeman City of London, past Master Worshipful Soc of Apothecaries (memb Court of Assts 1981); memb RSM, FRCP; *Books* Tropical Health Science (1967), Human Biology and Hygiene (1969), Lung Function for the Clinician (1981); *Recreations* cricket, horseracing, theatre, film, rowing; *Clubs* Savage, Garrick, Leander (Henley); *Style*— Dr David Hughes; ✉ 94 Overbury Avenue, Beckenham, Kent BR3 6PY (✆ 020 8650 3983)

HUGHES, Frances Mary Theresa; da of Noel Hughes, and Joanna, *née* Cartledge; *b* 15 June 1954, Richmond, Surrey; *Educ* Ursuline Convent Wimbledon, St Anne's Coll Oxford (BA, MA); *m* 5 August 2003, Jonathan Buckeridge, s of Paul Buckeridge; 1 da (Florence *b* 28 Nov 1987), 2 s (Sydney *b* 18 Feb 1989, Nathaniel *b* 3 Feb 1993); *Career* admitted slr 1981; Theodore Goddard: articled clerk 1979–81, slr 1981–83; ptnr and head Family Dept Bates Wells & Braithwaite 1983–2001, fndr and sr ptnr Hughes Fowler Carruthers 2001–; vice-pres Int Acad of Matrimonial Lawyers (European Chapter) 2003–09; memb Law Soc, memb Slr's Family Law Assoc; govr Hanover Primary School 1993–98, co-fndr Poet in the City 1999 (memb Steering Ctee 1999–2002), memb Bd Poetry Soc 2001–05, tstee Shelter from the Storm 2009–11, memb Bd Complicité 2014–; fell and govr-at-large Int Acad of Matrimonial Lawyers 2005–11; FRSA; *Recreations* opera, theatre, poetry, Hampstead Ladies Pond, gardening, playing the viola (both orchestral and in string quartets); *Style*— Ms Frances Hughes; ✉ Hughes Fowler Carruthers, Academy Court, 94 Chancery Lane, London WC2A 1DT (☎ 020 7421 8383, fax 020 7421 8384)

HUGHES, Gary William; s of William Muir Hughes, of Paisley, and Frances, *née* Carruthers; *b* 23 April 1962; *Educ* Castlehead HS Paisley, Univ of Strathclyde (BA); *m* July 1990, Margaret Frances, da of Frank Swallow; 2 s (Gavin Andrew b June 1996, Scott William b Nov 1999); *Career* accountant Ernst & Whinney 1985–89 (articled clerk 1985–87); Guinness plc/United Distillers: gp accountant 1989–90, controller mergers and acquisitions Guinness plc 1990–92, vice-pres fin United Distillers N America 1992–94; dir of financial control Forte plc 1994–96, commercial dir Forte Hotels Div Granada plc Feb-May 1996, finance dir Scottish Media Group plc (formerly Scottish Television plc) 1996–2000, finance dir Emap plc 2000–04, chm Emap Performance 2004–05, chief exec CMP Information 2006–08, chief financial offr Gala Coral Gp 2008–11, chm Getmemedia 2012–; FCA 1997 (ACA 1987); *Recreations* golf, tennis, cooking, running, reading, football; *Style*— Gary Hughes, Esq

HUGHES, Geoffrey; s of Ceredig (Ceri) Hughes (d 1985), and Megan, *née* Jones (d 2000); *b* 4 August 1950, Usk, Monmouthshire; *Educ* Monmouth, Cardiff Coll of Educn (CertEd), Open Univ (BA, MBA), Univ of Wales (MEd); *m* 18 Aug 1973, Susan Janet, *née* Carthey; 1 s (Rhys John b 1 April 1976), 1 da (Bethan Jane b 3 Feb 1978); *Career* PE teacher 1972–81; joined HM Prison Serv as asst govr 1981, asst govr HM Young Offenders Instn Onley, HMP Wandsworth and HM Young Offenders Instn Feltham, dep govr HMP Brixton 1991–94, govr HMP Drake Hall 1994–98, team ldr HM Inspectorate of Prisons 1998–2002, govr HMP Belmarsh 2002–05, head of security gp HM Prison Serv 2005–06, govr HMP Cardiff 2006–07, head Prison Serv Wales 2007–08, ret 2008; dir Int Custodial Consultancy and Training (ICCT) 2009–, memb Independent Restraint Advsy Panel 2012–; currently int prisons conslt; memb Bd of Dirs Inside Time 2009, memb Standards Ctee South Wales Fire and Rescue Service 2010– (chm 2016–); memb Lord Chllr's Advsy Ctee for Gwent; Winston Churchill travelling fell 1999, visiting lectr Univ of Wales 2008–, assoc Int Centre for Prison Studies KCL 2008–; memb Worshipful Livery Co of Wales; *Recreations* rugby union football, skiing, travel; *Clubs* Usk RFC, Newport (Salop) RFC; *Style*— Geoffrey Hughes, Esq; ✉ Geneva Cottage, Llansoy, Usk, Monmouthshire NP15 1DE

HUGHES, Rev Dr Gerard J; *b* 6 June 1934; *Educ* St Aloysius Coll Glasgow, Inst of Educn Univ of London (DipEd), Campion Hall Oxford (MA), Univ of Michigan (PhD), Univ of London (DLit); *Career* Soc of Jesus: entered 1951, ordained priest 1967, vice-provincial with responsibility for the trg of Jesuits in the British Province 1982–88; Heythrop Coll London: lectr in philosophy 1970–98, head Dept of Philosophy 1974–95, vice-princ 1983–98; Campion Hall Oxford: master 1998–2006, tutor in philosophy 2006–; memb Academic Cncl and Senate Univ of London 1986–94; Austin Fagothey/Bannan visiting prof Univ of Santa Clara Calif 1988, 1992 and 1996; author of numerous articles for learned jls incl The Heythrop Jl, Religious Studies and Philosophical Quarterly; *Books* Authority in Morals: An Essay in Christian Ethics (1978), Moral Decisions (1980), The Philosophical Assessment of Theology: Essays in Honour of Frederick C Copleston (ed and contrib, 1987), The Nature of God (1995), Aristotle on Ethics (2000, 2 edn 2013), Is God to Blame? (2007), Fidelity without Fundamentalism: A dialogue with tradition (2010); *Style*— The Rev Dr Gerard J Hughes, SJ; ✉ Campion Hall, Oxford OX1 1QS

HUGHES, Prof Graham Robert Vivian; s of Robert Arthur Hughes, and Emily Elizabeth Hughes (d 1989); *b* 26 November 1940; *Educ* Cardiff HS For Boys, London Hosp Med Coll (MD); *m* 2 March 1966, Monica Ann; 1 da (Sarah Imogen b 19 Oct 1967), 1 s (Richard John Vivian b 7 July 1971); *Career* rheumatologist; trained London Hosp; successively: res fell Columbia Presbyterian Hosp, reader in med and head of Dept of Rheumatology Royal Postgrad Med Sch London; currently head London Lupus Centre London Bridge Hosp and emeritus conslt physician and emeritus prof of med St Thomas' Hosp London (formerly head Lupus Arthritis Research Unit); conslt rheumatologist RAF, 900 pubns on arthritis res; Ciba Geigy ILAR int res prize for rheumatology res 1993; ed LUPUS, life pres LUPUS UK, tstee St Thomas' Lupus Tst, patron Hughes' Syndrome Fndn, patron Arthritis Research UK; master American Coll of Rheumatology 2006; hon memb: Aust Rheumatology Soc, Scandinavian Rheumatology Soc, Hong Kong Rheumatology Soc, Portugese Rheumatology Soc, Turkish Rheumatology Soc, memb: American Lupus Hall of Fame, Assoc of Physicians of GB & I; AESKU Lifetime Achievement Award Int Soc for Immunology 2006, Graham Hughes Autoimmune Diseases Centre opened in Madeira Portugal 2016, Graham Hughes Annual Lecture (opening lecture of Argentine Med Soc); Dr (hc): Université de la Méditerranée 2001, Barcelona Univ 2004; FRCP; *Books* Connective Tissue Diseases (1971, 4 edn, 1994), Modern Topics in Rheumatology (1978), Systemic Lupus Erythematosus (1982), Lecture Notes in Rheumatology (1987), Problems in The Rheumatic Diseases (1988), SLE: A Guide for Patients (1988), Phospholipid Binding Antibodies (1991), Understanding Lupus (1996), Hughes' Syndrome: a patient's guide to the Antiphospholipid Syndrome (1997), Lupus. The Facts (2000), Hughes Syndrome. A Patient's Guide (2001), Lupus, Your First 100 Questions (2001), Observations on Lupus (2006), Hughes Syndrome: Past, Present and Future (2006), The Brain and Other Animals (2008), The London Lupus Centre – A Patient's Guide to Lupus (2008), Understanding Hughes Syndrome (2009), Top 20 in Rheumatology (2011), Tales of a Flying Doctor (2011), Clinician's Manual on Lupus (2012), Hughes Syndrome: The Antiphospholipid Syndrome (2012), Clinical Case Studies (2013), Hughes Syndrome: Highways and Byways (2013), Sjogren's Syndrome in Clinical Practice (2014); *Recreations* golf, piano; *Style*— Prof Graham Hughes; ✉ London Lupus Centre, London Bridge Hospital, London SE1 2PR (☎ 020 7234 2155 or 020 7188 3570, fax 020 7633 9422, e-mail graham.hughes@hcaconsultant.co.uk, website www.thelondonlupuscentre.com)

HUGHES, HE Ian Noel; *m* Teresa June; 2 s, 1 da; *Career* diplomat; vice-consul Kabul 1976–80, vice-consul Warsaw 1980–82, Australia desk offr FCO 1982–85, dep head of mission Tegucigalpa 1985–88, 1 sec political Berne 1988–90, desk offr ME Dept FCO 1990–91, press offr News Dept FCO 1991–93, 1 sec press and public affrs New Delhi 1993–97, dep head Near East and North Africa Dept FCO 1997–2000, dep head of mission Mexico City 2000–03, dep high cmmr Mumbai 2003–05, ambass to Guatemala 2005–08, high cmmr to Sierra Leone and non-resident ambass to Liberia 2009–13, ambass to S Sudan 2013–15; *Style*— HE Mr Ian Hughes; ✉ c/o FCO (Juba), King Charles Street, London SW1A 2AH

HUGHES, Prof Ieuan Arwel; s of Arwel Hughes, OBE (d 1988), of Cardiff, and Enid Phillips, *née* Thomas (d 1995); bro of Owain Arwel Hughes, CBE, *qv*; *b* 9 November 1944, Cardiff; *Educ* Univ of Wales Coll of Med (MB BCh, MD), Univ of Cambridge (MA); *m* 26 July 1969, Margaret Maureen (Mac), da of William Edgar Davies; 2 s (Gareth Arwel, William Arwel), 1 da (Mari Jones, *née* Arwel); *Career* reader in child health Univ of Wales Coll of Med 1985–89 (sr lectr 1979–85), prof of paediatrics Univ of Cambridge 1989–2012 (emeritus prof of paediatrics 2012–); life memb Clare Hall Cambridge, fell Fitzwilliam Coll Cambridge; chm Ctee on Toxicity of Chemicals in Food, Consumer Products and the Environment 2002–08; advsr Science Media Centre 2009–, advsr Sense About Science 2009–, assoc advsr Intelligent Insights 2013–; pres: Endocrine Section RSM, Euro Soc of Paediatric Endocrinology 1993 (sec 1987–92, Andrea Pradar Prize 2006), Assoc of Clinical Professors of Paediatrics 1995–99; tstee Newlife Fndn for Disabled Children 2011–; fndr fell Acad of Med Scis 1998, hon fell Royal Coll of Paediatrics and Child Health 2013, visiting fell Public Health Genetics (PHG) Cambridge 2014; memb Advsy Bd Cambridge in Africa 2014–; FRCP(C) 1975, FRCP 1984, FRCPCH 1997 (James Spence Medallist 2014), FLSW 2011 (chm Medical and Biomedical Sciences Scrutiny Ctee); *Publications* Handbook of Endocrine Tests In Children (1989), Doctor to the Genome (ed, 1999); also author of 300 papers and 70 chapters in standard endocrine textbooks; *Recreations* music (memb Ralph Vaughan Williams Soc and Wager Soc), travel, cycling, hill walking; *Clubs* RSM; *Style*— Prof Ieuan Hughes; ✉ 4 Latham Road, Cambridge CB2 7EQ; University of Cambridge, Department of Paediatrics, Addenbrooke's Hospital, Hills Road, Cambridge CB2 2QQ (e-mail iah1000@cam.ac.uk)

HUGHES, Jeremy Michael; CBE (2015); s of Martyn Lawrence Hughes (d 2010), and Mary Dorothea, *née* Kempe (d 2008); *b* 15 August 1957, Oakham, Rutland; *Educ* Harrow, St Edmund Hall Oxford (MA); *m* 2 Sept 1989, Caroline Anne; 2 s (Edward Fauchon b 31 Jan 1991, Alistair John b 13 March 1993); *Career* md LMS PR 1983–89, assoc dir policy and info NCH Action for Children 1989–92, mktg and communications dir Muscular Dystrophy Gp 1992–93, dir of public affrs Leonard Cheshire 1994–99, dir of mktg and income generation Br Red Cross 1999–2003, head external rels and communications Int Fedn of Red Cross and Red Crescent Socs 2003–05, chief exec Breakthrough Breast Cancer 2005–10, chief exec Alzheimer's Soc 2010–; *Style*— Jeremy Hughes, Esq, CBE; ✉ Alzheimer's Society, Devon House, 58 St Katharine's Way, London E1W 1LB (☎ 020 7423 3507)

HUGHES, Prof John; s of Joseph Henry Hughes (d 1956), and Edith Annie Hughes; *b* 6 January 1942; *Educ* Mitcham Co GS, Chelsea Coll London (BSc), King's Coll London (PhD), Univ of Cambridge (MA); *m* 1, (m dis 1981), Madeleine Carol; 1 da (Katherine b 1967); m 2, 1997, Ann Rosemary Elizabeth Mutti; 4 c by previous partner (Georgina Anne b 1984, Joseph Francis b 1986, John Stephen b 1988, Tomas James b 1990); *Career* sr lectr and dep dir Unit for Res on Addictive Drugs Univ of Aberdeen 1973–77 (lectr in pharmacology 1969–73), prof in pharmacological biochemistry Imperial Coll London 1979–83 (reader in biochemistry 1977–79), dir Parke-Davis Res Centre Cambridge 1983–2000, fell Wolfson Coll Cambridge 1983–2010 (emeritus fell 2010–), vice-pres of res Parke-Davis (Warner-Lambert Corp) 1988–2000, chm and co-fndr Cambridge Biotechnology Ltd 2000–03; hon prof of: neuropharmacology Univ of Cambridge 1989–, pharmacology Univ of Aberdeen 1998–; jt chief ed Neuropeptides 1980–; chm Persistent Viral Disease Res Fndn; memb Substance Abuse Ctee Mental Health Fndn; sch govr Local Educn Authy Swaffham Prior Community Sch; Hon Dr of Med Univ of Liège 1978, Hon DSc Univ of Aberdeen 2011; memb of honour Romanian Acad of Sciences, memb Biochemical Soc, MPS, FRS 1993; *Books* Centrally Acting Peptides (1978), Opioid Peptides (1983), Opioids Past Present and Future (1984), The Neuropeptide Cholecystokinin (1989); *Recreations* gardening, golf; *Style*— Prof John Hughes, FRS; ✉ e-mail john@sbulbeck.com

HUGHES, Dr (Edgar) John; s of late William Hughes, and late Martha Hughes; *b* 1947, Pengam, Wales; *Educ* LSE, Lehigh Univ Bethlehem PA, Pembroke Coll Cambridge; *m* Lynne; 2 s; *Career* diplomat; entered HM Dip Serv 1973, posted Washington DC 1976–77, Research Dept FCO then on loan to Cabinet Office 1977–79, first sec (conf offr) Madrid 1981–82, first sec (political) Santiago 1983–95, first sec (info) Washington DC 1985–88, dep head rising to head Aviation and Maritime Dept FCO 1989–92, dep head of mission Oslo 1993–97, change mangr FCO 1997–99, seconded to BAE Systems 1999, ambass to Venezuela 2000–03, vice-pres int relations (on secondment) Shell 2003–04, ambass to Argentina 2004–08 and concurrently non-resident ambass to Paraguay 2005–08; cmmr Marshall Scholarships, cmmr then chair Marshall Aid Commemoration Cmmn 2012–; dir LatAmConsult, chm Canning House 2012–; Robin Humphreys fell Inst for the Study of the Americas Univ of London 2009–10, sr visiting fell LSE 2011–12; *Publications* The Historian As Diplomat (jtly); *Recreations* sport, reading, travelling; *Clubs* Rhymney RFC, RSA; *Style*— Dr John Hughes; ✉ c/o Marshall Aid Commemoration Commission ACU, Woburn House, 20–24 Tavistock Square, London WC1H 9HF (e-mail john.hughes@marshallscholarship.org)

HUGHES, Dr John Llewellyn Mostyn; CBE (2011); s of late Hugh Mostyn Hughes, and late Marion, *née* Trohear; *b* 20 July 1951, Bolton, Lancs; *Educ* Univ of Herts (BSc); *Career* Cossor Electronics 1969–75, UK Computer Agency 1975–77, Gould Inc 1977–83, vice-pres worldwide sales mktg and serv Metheus Corp 1983–87, pres and ceo Numerix Corp 1987–90; Hewlett-Packard Co: vice-pres and md Convex Computer Corp EMEA 1991–95, dir Convex Worldwide Field Organisation 1995–97; Lucent Technologies: region pres Microelectronics Gp 1997–99, pres GSM/UMTS Wireless Networks 1999–2000; Thales Gp: ceo IT&S Business Area and chm Thales Venture Capital 2000–04, exec vice-pres, gp chief operating offr and ceo Aerospace Business Area 2002–04; Parity Gp plc: exec chm 2005–07, dep chm 2007–10; chm: Citylink plc 2001–04, Intec Telecom Systems plc 2005–10, Telecity Gp plc 2007–16, Spectris plc 2008– (memb Bd 2007–08), Aircom Int 2010–13, Sepura plc 2010–15, Just Eat Gp 2012–; memb: Supervisory Bd FACEO 2001–04, Mgmnt Bd ACSS Inc 2002–04, Supervisory Bd ERTICO 2003–05 (vice-chm 2004–05), Bd Global Crossing UK Ltd 2005–07, Bd Nice Systems Inc 2002–11, Bd Barco NV 2006–09, Bd Chloride Gp plc 2009–10, Bd Vitec Gp plc 2011–12, Bd CSGSystems Int Inc 2011–, Bd Equinix Inc 2016–; pres Historic Motor Sport Cmmn FIA 2006–13; Hon DSc Univ of Hertfordshire 2014; *Recreations* historic and modern motor sport, golf, shooting, boating; *Clubs* RAC, Automobile Club de Monaco, Automobile Club de France, Soho House; *Style*— Dr John Hughes, CBE; ✉ e-mail boards@johnlmhughes.com

HUGHES, Her Hon Judge Judith Caroline Anne; QC (1994); 3 da of William Frank Hughes, and Eva-Ruth, *née* Meier; *b* 13 October 1950; *Educ* Woodhouse GS Finchley, Univ of Leeds (LLB); *m* 1, 27 Aug 1977 (m dis 1998), Mark G Warwick; 2 da (Sarah b 1981, Lucy b 1985); m 2, 31 March 2004, His Hon Inigo Bing, *qv*; *Career* called to the Bar Inner Temple 1974 (bencher 1994); recorder of the Crown Court 1995 (asst recorder 1991–95), dep judge of the High Court of Justice 1997, circuit judge (SE Circuit) 2001–; vice-chair Legal Service Ctee Bar Cncl 1999, judicial memb Parole Bd 2002–09; memb: SE Circuit 1974–2001, Family Bar Assoc 1983–2001; tstee: Gilbert Place Centre 1995–98, The Children's Soc 1996–2003, HASTE 1998– (chair 2000–); memb Ctee Bottoms Up 2001–03; memb PTA S Hampstead HS 1997–98; *Publications* Butterworth's Guide to Family Law (jt author, 1996); *Recreations* reading, theatre, philately, gardening, handicrafts; *Style*— Her Hon Judge Judith Hughes, QC; ✉ Principal Registry of the Family Division, First Avenue House, London WC1V 6NP

HUGHES, Katherine; BEM (2015); da of William Frank Hughes, and Eva Ruth Hughes; *b* 24 July 1949; *Educ* Woodhouse GS Finchley, UEA (BA), Univ of Wales (MSc); *m* 2014, D R Thomas; *Career* res assoc Univ of Wales 1973–75, asst planning offr Mid Glamorgan CC 1975–77, dir Welsh Consumer Cncl 1978–94 (res offr 1977–78); acting head Wales office Nat Fedn of Women's Institutes 1994–95, md Katherine Hughes Assocs 1994–; chair Planning Aid Wales 2004–07 (dir 1995–2001 and 2007–12); memb: Welsh Ctee Buttle Tst 1996–2003, Bd Tai Cymru/Housing for Wales 1997–98, Ct and Cncl Nat Library of Wales 1997–2003; tstee: Rhondda Housing Assoc 1999–2009, Encams Cymru 2000–05; ed Int Jl of Consumer Studies (formerly Jl of Consumer Studies and Home Economics) 1998–; chair Keep Wales Tidy 2005–11, co sec Caerphilly Miners Centre for the Community 2011–; MRTPI; *Recreations* walking, photography, friends, singing, writing; *Style*— Katherine Hughes, BEM; ✉ Katherine Hughes Associates, 26 Bryngwyn, Caerphilly CF83 1ET (☎ 029 2088 6569, mobile 07989 938833, e-mail katherine.hughes@btconnect.com)

HUGHES, Lee Terence; CBE (2004); s of Thomas John Hughes (d 1989), and Joyce Ellen, *née* Lee (d 1984); *b* 16 January 1951; *Educ* Surbiton Co GS, Middx Poly (BA), Univ of Birmingham (Postgrad Cert Public Sector Mgmnt); *Career* civil servant; sec Police Nat Computer Bd 1986–89, sec Advsy Bd on Restricted Patients 1990–93, memb Cncl of Europe Ctee on Corruption (chm criminal law working gp) 1995–97, head of bill team

H

Protection from Harrassment Act 1997; head Freedom of Information Unit (Constitutional and Community Policy Directorate) Home Office 1998–2001, head Freedom of Information and Data Protection Div Lord Chllr's Dept 2001–03, sec Hutton Inquiry 2003–04, dir (courts appts) Judicial Appts Cmmn 2004–07, sec Inquests into the deaths of Diana, Princess of Wales and Dodi Al Fayed 2007–08, sec Baha Mousa Inquiry 2008–11, sec Al Sweady Inquiry 2009–12, sec Inquest into the Death of Alexander Litvinenko (conslt to Asst Dep Coroner) 2012–14, sec Litvinenko Inquiry 2014–16; conslt Leederm Ltd 2011–; *Style*— Lee Hughes, Esq, CBE; ✉ Leederm Ltd, 7 St Pauls Yard, Silver Street, Newport Pagnell MK16 0EG

HUGHES, Melvyn; s of Evan Llewellyn Hughes, of Newcastle upon Tyne, and Irene Kathleen, *née* Spires; *b* 18 November 1950; *Educ* Royal GS Newcastle upon Tyne, St Catherine's Coll Oxford (MA); *m* 6 July 1974, Diane, da of Percival Moffett (d 1987); 1 da (Alexandra b 28 Oct 1980), 2 s (Richard b 2 Nov 1983, David b 9 March 1990); *Career* Slaughter and May: articled clerk 1974–76, asst slr 1976–83, ptnr 1983–, exec ptnr 1989–; memb: City of London Slrs' Co, Law Soc; Freeman City of London; *Recreations* reading, cars, sport; *Clubs* RAC; *Style*— Melvyn Hughes, Esq; ✉ Slaughter and May, 1 Bunhill Row, London EC1Y 8YY (☎ 020 7600 1200, fax 020 7600 0289/1455)

HUGHES, His Hon (Thomas) Merfyn; QC (1994); s of John Medwyn Hughes (d 2001), of Beaumaris, Anglesey, and Jane Blodwen, *née* Roberts (d 2014); *b* 8 April 1949; *Educ* Rydal Sch Colwyn Bay, Univ of Liverpool (LLB); *m* 16 April 1977, Patricia Joan Hughes, DL (High Sheriff Gwynedd 2002–03), da of John Edmund Talbot (d 1982), of Brentwood, Essex; 1 da (Caitlin Mary b 19 Feb 1980), 2 s (Thomas Jenkin Edmund b 14 Sept 1982, Joshua Edward Talbot b 7 Dec 1987); *Career* called to the Bar Inner Temple 1971; in practice Wales & Chester Circuit, recorder 1991–2001 (asst recorder 1987–91), circuit judge (Wales & Chester Circuit) 2001–14, resident judge N Wales 2010–14, dep circuit judge 2014–; pres Restricted Patients Panel of Mental Health Review Tbnl 1999–2011, chm Sports Dispute Resolution Panel 2000–01; memb: Parole Bd for England and Wales 2004–11, N Wales Courts Bd 2005–10, N Wales Probation Bd 2005–10; Lab Pty candidate Caernarfon 1979; *Recreations* sailing, watching rugby, golf; *Clubs* Royal Anglesey Yacht, Bangor RFC; *Style*— His Hon Merfyn Hughes, QC; ✉ c/o The Crown Court, Shirehall, Mold, Flintshire CH7 1AE

HUGHES, Michael; CBE (1998); s of Leonard Hughes (d 1998), of Clwyd, and Gwyneth Mair, *née* Edwards (d 1997); *b* 26 February 1951; *Educ* Rhyl GS, Univ of Manchester (BA), LSE (MSc); *m* 11 Feb 1978, Jane Ann (d 2016), da of Percival Frederick Gosham (d 1977), of Ipswich, Suffolk; 2 da (Sophie b 1979, Harriet b 1981); *Career* economist BP Pension Fund 1973–75, chief economist and ptnr de Zoete and Bevan 1976–86, dir Barclays de Zoete Wedd Securities Ltd; BZW: Capital Markets 1986, exec dir Gilts Ltd 1986–89, md Economics and Strategy 1989–97, chm BZW Pensions Ltd 1996; gp economic advsr Barclays Capital 1997–98; chief investment offr Baring Asset Management 2000–07 (dir and memb strategic policy gp 1998–2000); investment conslt Guide Dogs for the Blind 1995–; sr ind dir JP Morgan UK Mid Cap Investment Tst 2008–, non-exec dir T Bailey 2009–; memb: ESRC 1995–98, Cncl Univ of Essex 1997–2006; chm Fin Panel Foresight Prog DTI 1994–97; ASIP 1977, FSI, FRSA 2005; *Recreations* horses, gardens; *Clubs* National Liberal; *Style*— Michael Hughes, Esq, CBE; ✉ e-mail michael@dedham.uk.com

HUGHES, Prof (John) Michael Barton; s of Dr Stanley Barton Hughes (d 1963), of Helen's Bay, Co Down, and Dorothy Jane Augusta, *née* Tornblad (d 1990); *Educ* Lancing, Trinity Coll Oxford (BM BCh, MA, DM); *m* 22 Feb 1963, Shirley Ann, da of Hedley Frank Stenning (d 1977); 2 da (Penelope Barton b 1971, Caroline Barton b 1975); *Career* house physician med unit London Hosp 1963–64, house physician and res fell Hammersmith Hosp 1965–68, MRC travelling fell Harvard Sch of Public Health 1968; conslt physician Hammersmith Hosp 1974–97 (Cournand lectr 1975, Fleischner lectr 1989–, E S Garnett lectr 2000, Ludwig Engel lectr 2004); Imperial Coll Sch of Med at Hammersmith Hosp (Royal Postgrad Med Sch until merger 1997): lectr, sr lectr then reader 1969–93, prof of thoracic med 1993–97, emeritus prof 1997; author of chapters on lung gas exchange, pulmonary circulation, radioisotopes and lung function, over 150 sci articles on pulmonary physiology, pharmacology and lung disease; memb: Med Res Soc, Assoc Physicians, Physiological Soc, American Physiological Soc, British Thoracic Soc, Euro Resp Soc; FRCP 1979; *Books* Pulmonary Function Tests (with N B Pride, 1999), Pulmonary Circulation (with N W Morrell, 2001), Physiology and Practice of Pulmonary Function (2009); *Recreations* golf, ornithology, round tower churches; *Clubs* Royal West Norfolk Golf, Hunstanton Golf; *Style*— Prof Michael Hughes; ✉ Respiratory Medicine, NHLI, Imperial College, Hammersmith Hospital, London W12 0HS (☎ 020 8383 3269, e-mail mike.hughes@imperial.ac.uk)

HUGHES, Nerys (Mrs Turley); da of Roger Edward Kerfoot Hughes (d 1974), of Rhyl, N Wales, and Annie Myfanwy, *née* Roberts; *b* 8 November 1941; *Educ* Howells Sch Denbigh, Rose Bruford Coll; *m* 13 May 1972, (James) Patrick Turley, s of James Turley (d 1983), of Wednesbury, Staffs; 1 s (Ben b 1974), 1 da (Mari-Claire b 1978); *Career* actress; vice-pres Nat Children's Home, hon fell Univ of Wales; *Theatre* work incl: BBC Rep Co, RSC, English Stage Co Royal Court Theatre, RNT (Under Milk Wood 1995); *Television* series incl: Diary of a Young Man, The Liver Birds (revival 1996), The District Nurse, How Green was my Valley, Alphabet Zoo (children's TV), Bazaar (BBC) 1990, With A Little Help (BBC Wales) 1995, Capital Woman 1997, Molly 1997, Queen's Nose (BBC)1998, Liverpool Mums (Channel Five) 1998 and 1999, Labour of Love (BBC Wales) 1999, Labour of Love (BBC Wales) 2000, Fun in the Funeral Parlour (BBC) 2002, The Secret (BBC) 2002, Promenade Rock 2003, Hospital (BBC Cardiff) 2004, 2005, 2008 and 2009, Torchwood (BBC) 2008; *Film* Second Best 1993, Handmade Moon (for TV) 1993, Swing 1999, Hospital (BBC Wales) 2003, Autumn Girls (BBC Wales) 2004, CBeebies (BBC) 2004; *Awards* incl: Pye Female Comedy Star Award 1974, Variety Club TV Actress of the Year 1984; *Recreations* gardening, reading; *Style*— Miss Nerys Hughes; ✉ c/o Barry Burnett Organisation Ltd, 3 Clifford Street, London W1S 2LF (☎ 020 7437 8008, fax 020 7257 3239)

HUGHES, Nicholas Maxwell Lloyd; s of late Glyn Hughes, of Brighton, E Sussex, and late (Muriel) Joyce, *née* Hardaker; *b* 10 October 1955; *Educ* Univ of Sheffield (BA); *m* 8 June 1985, (Margaret) Ruth, da of late Prof David Cornelius Morley, CBE; 2 da (Olivia Emily b 3 July 1990, Eleanor Joyce b 27 July 1993), 1 s (Russell David Glyn b 12 Jan 1997); *Career* admitted slr 1981; ptnr Barlow Lyde & Gilbert 1984–2011, ptnr Holman Fenwick Willan 2011–; dir AIRMIC 1992–; author of articles on aviation and space law; Freeman City of London, Liveryman City of London Slrs' Co (Senior Warden 2015/16), Freeman Worshipful Co of Insurers 2015–; memb City of London Law Soc (treas 2007–), MRAeS; *Publications* Contracts for the Carriage of Goods by Land, Sea and Air (gen ed, 1993); *Recreations* wine, antique furniture, golf, opera, rugby, football; *Clubs* City of London; *Style*— Nick Hughes; ✉ Friary Court, 65 Crutched Friars, London EC3N 2AE (☎ 020 7264 8555, e-mail nick.hughes@hfw.com)

HUGHES, Nigel; *Career* head Southbank Int Sch London 2001–; *Style*— Nigel Hughes, Esq; ✉ Southbank International School, 36–38 Kensington Park Road, London W11 3BU

HUGHES, Owain Arwel; CBE (2009, OBE 2004); s of Arwel Hughes, OBE (d 1988), of Cardiff, and Enid Phillips, *née* Thomas (d 1995); bro of Prof Ieuan Hughes, *qv*; *b* 21 March 1942; *Educ* Howardian HS Cardiff, Univ Coll Cardiff, RCM London; *m* 23 July 1966, Jean Bowen, da of William Emlyn Lewis; 1 da (Lisa Margaret b 25 Dec 1970), 1 s (Geraint John b 15 Feb 1974); *Career* conductor; since 1970 has conducted all the UK symphony orchs and their respective choirs, in particular The Hallé, London Philharmonic and The Royal Philharmonic; assoc conductor: BBC Welsh Symphony Orch 1980–86, Philharmonia Orch London 1985–90; musical dir Huddersfield Choral Soc 1980–86, fndr, artistic dir and conductor the Annual Welsh Proms 1986–, creator and musical dir The World Choir (10,000 male voices) 1992, princ conductor Aalborg Symphony Orch Denmark 1995–2000, princ assoc conductor Royal Philharmonic Orch 2003–, musical dir Nat Youth Orch of Wales 2003–10, music dir Camerata Wales 2005–; prof of performance Univ of Wales Trinity St David's 2015–; performances in Norway, Sweden, Finland, Iceland, Luxembourg, France, Germany, Portugal, Hong Kong, Japan and NZ; many TV appearances in concert or special projects incl Mahler Symphony No 8, Requiem series, Holy Week series, Much Loved Music series, 40 anniversary concert of Granada TV (with Hallé and Royal Liverpool Philharmonic Orchs); memb Inst of Advanced Motorists, vice-pres Nat Children's Home; hon bard Royal Nat Eisteddfod of Wales; fell: UC Cardiff, Univ of Glamorgan, Royal Welsh Coll of Music and Drama, Trinity Coll Carmarthen, Lampeter Univ, Univ of Bangor; Hon DMus: CNAA London, Univ of Wales; *Recordings* incl: Music of Delius (Philharmonia Orch), London Symphony by Vaughan Williams (Philharmonia Orch), Music of Paul Patterson (London Philharmonic), Much Loved Music Vols I and II (Hallé Orch), Carols Album and Hymns Album (Huddersfield Choral Soc), St David by Arwel Hughes (BBC Welsh Orch and Choir), African Sanctus by David Fanshawe (Ambrosian Chorus and Instrumentalists), complete cycle of Holmboe twelve symphonies (with Aarhus Symphony Orch), Handel Messiah (with RPO and Royal Choral Soc), Verdi Requiem (with RPO, Royal Choral Soc and Brighton Festival Chorus), Sullivan Irish Symphony (with BBC Concert Orch), Holmboe Symphony No 13 & Koppel Oratorio Moses da Capo (with Danish Radio Symhony Orch), Ludolf Nielsen Oratorio Tower of Babel (with Danish Radio Symhony Orch), Sibelius Symphony No 1 (with BBC Concert Orch), Rachmaninov Piano Concertos 1, 2, 3 and 4 and Paganini Variations (with Malmo Symphony Orch), Holmboe Orchestral Tone Poems, Brass and Woodwind Concertos, and Chamber Symphonies (with Aalborg Symphony Orch), Borresen Symphony No 1 (Aalborg Symphony Orch), Borresen Violin Concerto (Aalborg Symphony Orch), Borresen Symphonies 2 and 3 (Aalborg Symphony Orch), Horniman Theatre Music (Aalborg Symphony Orch), Norby Orchestral Music (Aalborg Symphony Orch), Rachmaninov Symphonies 1, 2 and 3 (Youth Symphony and Royal Scottish Nat Orch), Tchaikovsky Piano Concertos 1, 2 and 3 (Aalborg Symphony Orch), Choral Classics (Royal Philharmonic Orch), Opera Classics (Royal Philarmonic Orch), Through Gold and Silver Clouds (Camerata Wales), Elgar Symphony No 2 (Nat Youth Orchestra of Wales) and Vaughan Williams (London Symphony Orch), Holst Planets (Royal Philharmonic Orch), Schnittke Symphony 9 and Oratorio Nagasaki Symphony '01 (Cape Philharmonic Orch), Brahms Symphonies 1–4 (Stuttgart Philharmonic Orch), Riisager Benzin (Danish Nat Symphony Orch), Walton Symphonies 1 and 2 (Orchestre National de Lille), Arwel Hughes Orchestral Works (Royal Philharmonic Orch), Holmboe Kairos (Camerata Wales); *Awards* Gold medal Welsh Tourist Bd, Communicator of the Year, 2 Gold Discs BPI, Jubilee Award Welsh Music Guild, Guild of Welsh Music Sir Geraint Evans Meml Award 2011; *Books* Owain Arwel Hughes, My Life In Music (autobiography, 2012); *Recreations* rugby, cricket, golf, motoring, travel; *Clubs* London Welsh Assoc, London Welsh Rugby, Lord's Taverners; *Style*— Owain Arwel Hughes, Esq, CBE; ✉ 2A, Byron Hill Road, Harrow-on-the-Hill, Middlesex HA2 0HY

HUGHES, Paul; s of James Henry Hughes (d 1986), of Dublin, and Mary, *née* O'Hanlon; family in wool business handed down some 200 years; *b* 22 June 1956, Dublin; *m* 24 June 1983, Liliane Niederer; 1 s (Kean b 11 Sept 1990); *Career* studied knitwear design Antwerp 1973–76, fndr and knitwear designer Cachaca (later Liberated Lady) shop King's Road 1976–79, travel through Latin America and Africa (studying and collecting ethnic textiles) 1979, subsequently studied textile collections at Met Museum of Art NY, Br Museum, Washington Textile Museum and V&A whilst serving an internship handling conservation co-ordination and customer serv at Artweave Textile Gallery NY, opened own textile gallery NY 1980, relocated to San Francisco 1981, fndr/proprietor Paul Hughes Gallery London 1983–; exhbns co-ordinated and curated in London 1983–91: Pre-Columbian Andean Textile Art & 2,000 Years of Andean Textile Art (both Wilson Hale Gallery London), European Textiles 15th-20th Century (Centre for Embroidery, Fashion and Textile Studies London), Kuba Raffia Textiles from Zaïre, 17th Century English Embroideries, Textiles of Africa & Pre-Columbian and Coptic Textiles (all Paul Hughes Gallery London); int and travelling exhbns co-ordinated and curated 1989–96: Pre-Columbian Textile Art (Grasse Austria, 1989, Milan Italy 1991), Tiger Rugs of Tibet (Milan) 1992, African Majesty (Antwerp Belgium) 1992, Rediscovery of Pre-Columbian Textiles (Antwerp) 1993, Time Warps (Sammlung, Hauser & Wirth Zurich, Gallerie Asbek Copenhagen, Le Monde d'Art Paris, Paul Kasmin Gallery NY) 1995, Andean Textile Art (Kasmin Gallery NY, also Japan) 1996; author of exhibition catalogues and contribs to magazines; *Style*— Paul Hughes, Esq; ✉ The Gallery, 3A Pembridge Square, London W2 4EW (☎ 020 7243 8598, fax 020 7221 8785)

HUGHES, His Hon Judge Peter Thomas; QC (1993); s of Peter Hughes, JP (d 1991), and Jane Blakemore, *née* Woodward (d 2002); *b* 16 June 1949; *Educ* Bolton Sch, Univ of Bristol; *m* 20 July 1974, Christine Stuart, da of Rex Taylor, of West Kirby, Wirral; 1 da (Rosemary b 27 May 1982), 1 s (Richard b 12 July 1985); *Career* called to the Bar Gray's Inn 1971 (bencher 2001);asst recorder Wales & Chester Circuit 1988–92, recorder 1992–2007, dep judge of the High Court 2001–, circuit judge (Northern Circuit) 2007–; chm: Med Appeal Tbnl 1988–93, Registered Homes Tbnl 1993–2002 (lead chm 2000–2002), Mental Health Review Tbnl 1999–; memb: Gen Cncl of the Bar 1993–98, Cncl of Circuit Judges 2011–; circuit jr 1991, circuit treas 1999–2000; tutor judge Judicial Studies Bd 2008–12; chm: City of Chester Cons Assoc 1983–86, Euro Constituency Cncl 1984–87; Freeman City of London 2014, Liveryman Worshipful Co of Clockmakers 2015 (Freeman 2005); *Recreations* fell walking, book collecting, taming an unruly garden; *Style*— Peter Hughes, Esq, QC; ✉ Carlisle Combined Court Centre, Earl Street, Carlisle CA1 1DJ (☎ 01228 590588)

HUGHES, Peter Travers; OBE (1993); *b* 24 December 1946; *Educ* Wishaw HS Lanarkshire, Tech Coll Coatbridge (HNC Metallurgy), Univ of Strathclyde (DMS), Univ of Dundee (MBA); *m* 1; 2 s (Alan, William); m 2, (m dis); 1 s (Alexander); m 3, 2007, Neena, *née* Barr; *Career* trainee metallurgist Clyde Alloy (latterly British Steel), foundry metallurgist rising to foundry mangr North British Steel Gp 1968–76, gen mangr Lake & Elliot Essex 1976–80 (also dir 1977–80), md National Steel Foundry (1914) Ltd (subsid of Lake & Elliot) 1980–83, initiated MBO forming Glencast Ltd 1983 (co sold to NACO Inc Illinois USA 1994), chm and md Glencast Ltd 1983–98 (winners Queen's Award for Technological Achievement 1990), chief exec Scottish Engineering 1998–2013 (pres 1993), ret; chm: Steel Castings Research and Trade Assoc 1988–92 (chm Research Ctee 1985–88), DTI Steering Ctee on UK Devpt of Solidification Simulation Prog for Castings 1988–89; guest lectr at various confs UK and abroad; UK pres Inst of Br Foundrymen 1994–95 (pres Scottish Branch 1984–85), former chm Scottish Steel Founders' Assoc; former govr and memb Ct Univ of Abertay (formerly Dundee Inst of Technol), memb Ct Univ of Strathclyde; chm Bd New Park Preparatory Sch 1998–2001; elder Church of Scotland 1976; Hon Dr Univ of Paisley 2001, Hon DUniv W of Scotland Univ 2001, Hon DSc Univ of Strathclyde 2006, Hon DEng Napier Univ 2006; fell Univ of Abertay 2001 FIMgt 1986, FIBF 1988, FIM 1993, CEng 1994, FREng 1995; *Recreations* soccer, golf, tennis, curling, music, church, after dinner speaking; *Style*— Dr Peter T Hughes, OBE, FREng, FIMMM

HUGHES, Philip Arthur Booley; CBE (1982); s of Leslie Booley Hughes, and Elizabeth Alice, *née* Whyte; *b* 30 January 1936; *Educ* Bedford Sch, Univ of Cambridge (BA); *m* 21 Aug 1964, Psiche Maria Anna Claudia, da of Bertino Bertini (d 1971); 2 da (Francesca b 1966, Simona b 1968), 2 step da (Pauline b 1952, Carole b 1954); *Career* engr Shell International Petroleum Co 1957–61, computer consIt Scicon (formerly CEIR) 1961–69, dir Logica plc 1990–95 (co-fndr, chm and md 1969–72, chm 1972–90); artist; official visiting artist Br Antartica Survey to Antartica 2001–02; chm Bd of Tstees National Gallery London 1996–2000 (tstee 2000–02); dir Thames & Hudson Ltd; *Solo Exhibitions* Parkway Focus Gallery London 1976, Angela Flowers Gallery London 1977, Gallery Cance Manguin Vaucluse 1979, 1985 and 2000, Francis Kyle Gallery London 1979, 1982, 1984, 1987, 1989, 1992, 1994, 1997, 2000, 2003, 2007, 2010 and 2012, Inverness Museum 1990, Lesley Craze Gallery London 1992, Galerie Le Tour des Cardinaux Vaucluse France 1993, L'Ambassade de l'Australie Paris 1995, Museo Marco Monterrey Mexico 1997, Museo Tameyo Mexico 1998, Drill Hall Gallery Canberra 1998, 2002 and 2008, Volvo Gallery Sydney 1999, George Adams Gallery Melbourne 1999, Tate Gallery St Ives 2000, Victoria and Albert Museum 2001, Musée Chatillonais Chatillon-sur-Seine France 2002, Star Gallery Lewes 2004, Chateau La Nerthe Vaucluse 2004, Watermill Gallery Aberfeldy 2005, 2012 and 2016, Rex Irwin Gallery Sydney 2005 and 2008, Maison de la Truffe et du Vin Ménerbes France 2007, Gallerie Pascal Lainé Ménerbes France 2007, 2010 and 2014, Charleston Gallery Sussex 2008, Pier Arts Centre Orkney 2008, Galerie Gimpel Múller 2011, Brighton Museum and Gallery 2012, Cromarty Arts Centre 2012, Univ of Stirling 2012, Museum of Salisbury and South Wiltshire 2012, Jerwood Gallery Hastings 2014, Keynes Coll Univ of Kent, Studio 3 Gallery Univ of Kent; *Group Exhibitions* incl: Monks Gallery Sussex (with Beryl Bainbridge) 1972, Contemporary Br Painting (Madrid) 1983, Contemporary Painters (Ridgeway Gallery Swindon) 1986, Sherman Gallery Sydney (with Philip Wolfhagen) 2002, Churchill Coll Cambridge (with Keith Grant) 2003, Landscapes of Exploration (Peninsula Arts Gallery Plymouth) 2012 and (Scott Polar Institute Cambridge) 2013, Antarctica (Drill Hall Gallery ANU Canberra) 2012; *Publications* Patterns in the Landscape: The Notebooks of Philip Hughes (1998), Tracks: walking the ancient landscapes of Britain (2012); *Style*— Philip Hughes, Esq, CBE

HUGHES, Robert Charles; s of Clifford Gibson Hughes, of Walton-On-The-Hill, Surrey, and Elizabeth Joan, *née* Goodwin; *b* 20 January 1949; *Educ* Westminster, Emmanuel Coll Cambridge (MA); *m* 1, 1973 Cindy *née* Kirby-Turner (m dis 1998); 3 da (Zoe b 1975, Emma b 1976, Sophie b 1980); m 2, 2000, Annie *née* Bennett; *Career* Ernst & Young (formerly Barton Mayhew & Co): joined 1970, ptnr London 1978–81, ptnr Dubai UAE 1981–86, London 1986–; FCA; *Recreations* golf, puzzles; *Clubs* RAC, Sutton Tennis and Squash, Cuddington Golf; *Style*— Robert Hughes, Esq; ✉ Crazes, Heather Close, Kingswood, Surrey KT20 6NY (☏ 01737 832 256); Ernst & Young, Becket House, 1 Lambeth Palace Road, London SE1 7EU (☏ 020 7951 2000, fax 020 7951 1345, e-mail rhughes1@cc.ernsty.co.uk)

HUGHES, Rodger Grant; s of Eric Hughes, of Rhyl, Clwyd, and Doreen, *née* Barnes; *b* 24 August 1948; *Educ* Rhyl GS, Queens' Coll Cambridge (MA); *m* 9 June 1973, Joan Clare, da of James Barker; 2 s (Marcus, Oliver); *Career* PricewaterhouseCoopers (formerly Price Waterhouse before merger): joined 1970, ptnr 1982–2007, ptnr i/c Ind Business Gp 1988–91, ptnr i/c NW Region 1991–95, memb Supervisory Ctee 1991–95, UK dir Audit and Business Advisory Services (ABS) 1995–97, ABS dir UK, Scandinavia and Netherlands 1997–98, UK head ABAS, memb Euro and ME ABAS Exec and Global ABAS Mgmnt Team 1998–2002, UK managing ptnr 2002–07; auditor to Duchy of Cornwall 1998–2007, sr ind dir Chime Communications plc 2007–15, non-exec dir Friends Provident 2009, non-exec memb Bd Bell Pottinger Communications USA LLC 2010–12, chm Nat Counties Building Soc 2015– (non-exec memb Bd and chm Audit Ctee 2013–); memb Educn Leadership Team Business in the Community 2005–08, memb Steering Bd and chm Audit Ctee Companies House 2008–10, non-exec memb Bd and chm Audit Ctee Simmons & Simmons 2008–; FCA 1973; *Style*— Rodger Hughes, Esq; ✉ National Counties Building Society, Ebbisham House, 30 Church Street, Epsom, Surrey KT17 4NL

HUGHES, Dr Roger Llewellyn; s of Flt-Lt Clifford John Silke Hughes (d 1963), and Jean Christine Roger, *née* Stewart (d 1999); *b* 2 June 1947; *Educ* The HS of Glasgow, Univ of Glasgow (MB ChB, MD); *m* 14 Oct 1971, Pamela Jane, da of Dr Finlay Finlayson (d 1983); 4 da (Vivienne b 1972, Caroline b 1974, Zoe b 1979, Jennifer b 1981); *Career* sr registrar Glasgow Royal Infirmary 1975 (sr house offr 1971–72, registrar of anaesthesia 1972–75), consIt in anaesthesia Stobhill Hosp Glasgow 1980–2011, currently hon clinical sr lectr Univ of Glasgow (lectr in anaesthesia 1975–80); author of papers on liver blood flow and baroreceptor reflex; chm of jr gp Assoc of Anaesthetists of GB and I 1977–79; memb: BMA, Intensive Care Soc; FRCP, FRCA, fell Faculty of Intensive Care Medicine; *Recreations* gardening, walking; *Style*— Dr Roger Hughes; ✉ 7 Ballaig Avenue, Bearsden, Glasgow G61 4HA (☏ and fax 0141 942 5626, e-mail llewellynroger@ntlworld.com); Glasgow Royal Infirmary (☏ 0141 211 4620); Glasgow Nuffield Hospital, Glasgow G12

HUGHES, Sean; *Career* comedian, writer and actor; stand up comic London clubs 1987; performances incl: Edinburgh Fringe, A One Night Stand with Sean Hughes (Int tour, Perrier Award 1990), Patrick's Day (Edinburgh Critics' Award 1991), nat UK and Eire tour 1994, Melbourne Comedy Festival 1994, live tour Aust 1995, Thirtysomehow (nat tour, also TV) 1995, The Montreal Comedy Festival 1997, Edinburgh 1997, Alibis for Life (nat tour, Aust, NZ) 1997, The World Comedy Tour – Melbourne 2001, The Right Side of Wrong (UK tour) 2007, Sean Hughes Live (Aust tour) 2007; *Theatre* with Owen O'Neill: Dehydrated, Travellin' Light; Art (Wyndhams Theatre) 2000; *Radio* own show GLR 1997, own show London Live 2000, The Sunday Lie-in (BBC), 6 Music (BBC); *Television* incl: Sean's Show (Channel Four), Sean's Shorts (BBC), Aaaah Sean (Channel Four), The Signal Box (Parallel Films) 1995, Never Mind The Buzzcocks (team captain, 10 series and various specials, BBC) 1996–2002, The Greatest Store in the World (BBC) 1999, Inside Tracks (BBC Choice) 2000, Gormenghast (BBC/WGBH) 2000, Turn The World Down (Channel 4) 2001, Celebrity Blind Man's Bluff (Channel 4) 2001, The Last Detective (ITV) 2002, The Last Detective (second series, ITV) 2004, Friday Night Hijack (Sky Arts) 2007; *Films* incl: The Commitments (debut) 1991, Snakes and Ladders (Livia Films) 1995, The Butcher Boy (Warner Bros) 1997, Fast Food (Twin Pictures) 1998, Puckoon (Insight Pictures) 2001; *Video* Sean Hughes Live and Seriously Funny; winner for Outstanding Production of New Work Fringe First award Edinburgh Festival 1999; *Books* Sean's Book (1993), The Grey Area (1995), The Detainees (1997), It's What He Would Have Wanted (1999); *Style*— Sean Hughes, Esq

HUGHES, Prof Sean Patrick Francis; s of Dr Patrick Hughes (d 1995), and Kathleen Ethel, *née* Bigg (d 2001); *b* 2 December 1941; *Educ* Downside, St Mary's Hosp Med Sch Univ of London (MB BS, MS); *m* 22 Jan 1972, Dr Felicity Mary Anderson; 2 da (Sarah Jane (Mrs Kristian Glynn) b 28 Nov 1972, Emily Anne (Mrs Andrew Hills) b 25 July 1974), 1 s (John Patrick b 3 Feb 1977); *Career* successively: MO Save the Children Fund Nigeria, sr registrar in orthopaedics The Middx Hosp and Royal Nat Orthopaedic Hosp London, res fell Mayo Clinic USA, sr lectr/hon consIt orthopaedic surgn Royal Postgrad Med Sch Hammersmith Hosp London, prof and head Dept of Orthopaedic Surgery Univ of Edinburgh, hon consIt orthopaedic surgn Royal Infirmary Edinburgh and Princess Margaret Rose Orthopaedic Hosp Edinburgh, prof and head of orthopaedic surgery Royal Postgrad Med Sch Univ of London, prof of orthopaedic surgery Imperial Coll London (following merger with Royal Postgrad Med Sch), head of surgery and anaesthetics Imperial Coll London, dir Inst of Musculoskeletal Surgery Ravenscourt Park Hospital Hammersmith Hosps NHS Tst; currently emeritus prof of orthopaedic surgery Imperial Coll London; hon consIt Nat Hosp for Neurology and Neurosurgery Queen's Square 1995–2008; non-exec dir W Middx Univ Hosp 2001–05; pres Br Orthopaedic Res Soc 1996–98; vice-pres RCSEd 1995–97; memb Int Soc for Study of the Lumbar Spine; chm DISCS Medical Charity; civilian advsr RN 1995–2012; DHMSA, DPMSA 2015; FRCS, FRCSI, FRCSEd Orth, FRSA; *Books* Short Textbook of Orthopaedics and Traumatology (5 edn), Orthopaedics: The Principles and Practice of Musculoskeletal Surgery (1987); *Recreations* walking, music, opera; *Clubs* Athenaeum; *Style*— Prof Sean Hughes; ✉ 5 Meadow Place, Edensor Road, London W4 25Y (e-mail seanfrancishughes@imperial.ac.uk)

HUGHES, (Winifred) Shirley; OBE (1999); da of Thomas James Hughes (d 1933), of Liverpool, and Kathleen, *née* Dowling (d 1971); *b* 16 July 1927, West Kirby, Wirral; *Educ* West Kirby HS for Girls, Liverpool Sch of Art, Ruskin Sch of Fine Art Oxford; *m* 26 April 1952, John S P Vulliamy, s of C E Vulliamy; 2 s (Edward b 1954, Thomas b 1956), 1 da (Clara b 1962); *Career* author and freelance illustrator; total sales over 11.5 million by 2006; exhbns of artwork at Ashmolean Museum Oxford 2002 and Walker Art Gallery Liverpool 2003; Eleanor Farjeon Award for Services to Children's Literature 1984, UK nominee Hans Anderson Award 1997; Hon DLitt: UEA 2004, Univ of Liverpool 2004; hon fell Liverpool John Moores Univ 2004; hon fell CILIP 1997, FRSL 2000; *Books* for the very young: Lucy and Tom's Day Out, Lucy and Tom Go to School, Lucy and Tom's Christmas, Lucy and Tom at the Seaside, Lucy and Tom's ABC, Lucy and Tom's 123, Out and About, Giving, Bouncing, Chatting, Hiding, Noisy, Colours, Bathwater's Hot, All Shapes and Sizes, Two Shoes New Shoes, When We Went to the Park, Olly and Me, Alfie's Alphabet, Alfie's Numbers, Rhymes for Annie Rose, Annie Rose is My Little Sister; story picture books: Dogger (Kate Greenaway Medal 1977, Greenaway of Greenaways Medal 2007), Moving Molly, The Trouble with Jack, Stories by Firelight, Enchantment in the Garden, The Lion and the Unicorn, Alfie Wins a Prize, Alfie Gets In First, Alfie Gives a Hand, An Evening at Alfie's, Alfie's Feet, Alfie and the Birthday Surprise, Alfie Weather, Alfie and the Big Boys, The Big Alfie and Annie Rose Story Book, The Big Alfie Out of Doors Story Book, Alfie's World, Helpers (The Other Award 1976), Sally's Secret, Up and Up, Abel's Moon, Ella's Big Chance (Kate Greenaway Medal 2004), The Shirley Hughes Collection; to read alone: Chips and Jessie, Another Helping of Chips, Here Comes Charlie Moon, Charlie Moon and the Big Bonanza Bust Up, Angel Mae, The Big Concrete Lorry, Wheels, The Snow Lady, It's Too Frightening for Me, Jonodab and Rita (2008), Don't Want To Go! (2010), The Christmas Eve Ghost (2010), All About Alfie (2011), Alfie's Christmas (2013), Alfie's Garden (2014); A Life Drawing (illustrated memoir), A Brush with the Past 1900–1950 (memoir), Bye Bye Birdie (wordless adult strip cartoon, 2009), Hero on a Bicycle (teenage novel), Whistling in the Dark (teenage novel, 2015); poems: Out and About A First Book of Poems (2014); *Recreations* looking at paintings, sewing, wandering about with a sketchbook; *Style*— Ms Shirley Hughes, OBE; ✉ c/o Random House Children's Books, 61–63 Uxbridge Road, Ealing, London W5 5SA (☏ 020 8231 6800, fax 020 8231 6737)

HUGHES, Rt Hon Sir Simon Henry Ward; kt (2015), PC (2010); s of James Henry Annesley Hughes (d 1976), and Sylvia, *née* Ward; *b* 17 May 1951; *Educ* Llandaff Cathedral Sch Cardiff, Christ Coll Brecon, Selwyn Coll Cambridge (MA), Inns of Court Sch of Law, Coll of Europe Bruges (Cert Higher Euro Studies); *Career* called to the Bar Inner Temple 1974, trainee EEC Brussels 1975–76, trainee and memb Secretariat, Directorate and Cmmn on Human Rights Cncl of Europe Strasbourg 1976–77, in practice as barr 1978–; MP (Lib 1983–88, Lib Dem 1988–2015): Southwark, Bermondsey 1983–97, Southwark N and Bermondsey 1997–2010, Bermondsey & Old Southwark 2010–15; Parly spokesman: (Lib) on Environment 1983–87 and 1987–88, (Alliance) on Health 1987, (Lib Dem) on Environment 1988, on Educn, Sci and Trg 1988–90, on Environment 1988–94, on Community & Urban Affrs and Young People and on the C of E 1994–95, on Health & Social Welfare 1995–97, Health 1997–99; Lib Dem dep whip 1989–97, Lib Dem shadow home sec 1999–2003, Office of the Dep PM 2005, shadow AG 2005–07, shadow sec of state for energy and climate change 2009–10, dep ldr Lib Dems 2010–14; co-chair until 2013 APPGs on conflict issues, Islamophobia and youth affrs, Lib Dem federal pres 2004–08; HM's govt advocate Access to Educn 2010–11; memb: Accommodation and Works Ctee House of Commons 1992–97, Jt Ecclesiastical Ctee 2002–05 and 2010–14, Modernisation Ctee House of Commons 2007–10, Jt Ctee on Human Rights 2012–14; pres Southwark C of C 1984–87, 2004–07 and 2013– (memb 1983–); patron: Bermondsey and Rotherhithe Choral Soc, Southwark Playhouse, Surrey Docks Farm, Dockland Ringers; chair London Bubble Theatre, chair of govrs St James C of E Sch Bermondsey; tstee: Bacon's Coll Rotherhithe, Bermondsey and Rotherhite Outdoors, Rose Theatre Tst; former tstee: Social Mobility Fndn, Salmon Centre Bermondsey; The Spectator Highland Park Member to Watch Award 1985, Nat Motivation Week's Most Motivated MP Award 1989, Green MP of the Year 1992, Epolitix Environment Champion 2005, Govnet Communications Alternative Parliamentarian of the Year 2010; hon fell South Bank Univ; Hon Freeman London Borough of Southwark 2013–; *Publications* jtly: Human Rights in Western Europe – The Next Thirty Years (1981), The Prosecutorial Process in England and Wales (1981), Across the Divide – Liberal Values for Defence and Disarmament (1986), Pathways to Power (1992), Asylum – Opportunity not Crisis (2002), Beyond Blair (2006); *Recreations* books, music, theatre, sport (Millwall and Hereford FC, Glamorgan CCC and Wales RFU), the open air, sleeping; *Clubs* London Cab Drivers (hon memb); *Style*— The Rt Hon Sir Simon Hughes; ✉ House of Commons, London SW1A 0AA (☏ 020 7219 6256, e-mail simon@simonhughes.org.uk, website www.simonhughes.org.uk)

HUGHES, Tim; *Career* chef dir Caprice Holdings; *Style*— Tim Hughes, Esq; ✉ Caprice Holdings Ltd, 2nd Floor, 3–5 Rathbone Place, London W1T 1HJ

HUGHES, William (Bill); s of Kathy Hughes (d 2006); *b* 21 July 1941, Ireland; *m* 1; 1 s (Brendan b 11 June 1975), 1 da (Colleen b 3 March 1977); m 2, 28 May 2005 (m dis); 2 da (Laura Jane b 20 April 1995, Tara Louise b 23 Nov 1997), 1 s (Matthew b 28 Feb 2000); *Career* emigrated to England 1960, subsequently worked as construction worker; chm B&M Care 1972–; *Recreations* collector of veteran and vintage cars; *Style*— Bill Hughes, Esq; ✉ B&M Investments, B&M Care, Old Town Court, 70 Queens Way, Hemel Hempstead, Hertfordshire HP2 5HD (fax 01442 215584, e-mail info@bmcare.co.uk)

HUGHES, William Young; CBE (1987); s of Hugh Prentice Hughes, and Mary Henderson Hughes; *b* 12 April 1940; *Educ* Firth Park GS Sheffield, Univ of Glasgow (BSc), Univ of Strathclyde; *m* 1964, Anne MacDonald Richardson; 2 s, 1 da; *Career* lectr in Dept of Pharmacy Heriot-Watt Univ 1964–66, ptnr R Gordon Drummond Retail Chemists 1966–70, md MSJ Securities Ltd 1970–76, chm and chief exec Grampian Holdings plc 1976–98; chm: Aberforth Smaller Companies Trust plc 1990–2005, Fairfaxis plc 2005–13, Palm Tree Technol plc 2007–14; dir: Cashbox plc 2007–10, Frenkel Topping plc 2007–10; chm: Scottish Churches Industrial Mission Tst 2000–06, The Princes Scottish Youth Business Tst 2000–07, The Princes Tst Scot 2003–07; tstee The Princes Tst UK 2003–07; dir Royal Scottish Nat Hosp and Community NHS Tst 1992–95, Central Scotland NHS Tst 1995–98; dep chm Scottish Conservative Party 1989–92 (treas 1993–96), chm Euro Summer Special Olympic Games 1990, chm CBI Scotland 1987–89; memb Murrayfield Parish Church Edinburgh; *Style*— William Hughes, Esq, CBE; ✉ Flat 7, 1 Succoth Avenue, Edinburgh EH12 6BE

HUGHES HALLETT, Prof Andrew Jonathan; s of Vice Adm Sir Charles Hughes Hallett, KCB, CBE (d 1985), of Salisbury, Wilts, and Joyce Plumer, *née* Cobbold (d 1996); *b* 1 November 1947; *Educ* Radley, Univ of Warwick (BA), LSE (MSc), Nuffield Coll Oxford

H

(DPhil); *m* 22 July 1982, Claudia Ilse Luise, da of Karl Becker (d 1988), of Kassel, W Germany; 2 s (David b 1983, James b 1986), 1 da (Nicola b 1990); *Career* lectr in economics Univ of Bristol 1973–77, assoc prof of economics Erasmus Univ Rotterdam 1977–85, David Dale prof of economics Univ of Newcastle upon Tyne 1985–89, Jean Monnet prof of economics Univ of Strathclyde 1989–2001, prof of economics Vanderbilt Univ 2001–06, prof of economics and public policy George Mason Univ 2006–, prof of economics and public policy St Andrews Univ 2007–; prof of economics: Harvard Univ, Princeton Univ, Univs of Rome, Berlin, Frankfurt; author of papers on: theory of economic policy, int economic policy, (european) economic integration, commodity markets and economic devpt, game theory, numerical analysis; reg broadcasts on economic affairs; conslt to: IMF, UN, World Bank, EEC Cmmn, OECD, UNESCO, various govts; memb Cncl of Economic Advsrs to Scottish Govt; cmmr Scottish Fiscal cmmn; advsr Econ and Monetary affrs, Euro Parl; memb: Royal Econ Soc 1975, Euro Econ Assoc 1985, Scot Econ Assoc 1998, American Econ Assoc 1998, American Mathematical Soc 2000; fell Centre for Econ Policy Res; FRSE (convenor Econ Ctee); *Books* Quantitative Economic Policies and Interactive Planning (1983), Stabilising Speculative Commodity Markets (1987), Optimal Control, Expectations and Uncertainty (1989), Fiscal Aspects of European Monetary Integration (1999), Theory of Economic Policy in a Strategic Context (2012), Macroeconomic Paradigms (2016); over 220 papers in professional jls; *Recreations* hill walking, beer, blues, history; *Style—* Prof Andrew Hughes Hallett; ✉ e-mail ahughesh@gmu.edu

HUGHES OF OMBERSLEY, Lord, of Ombersley, in the County of Worcestershire; Rt Hon Sir Anthony Philip Gilson Hughes; kt (1997), PC (2006); s of late Patrick and Patricia Hughes; *b* 11 August 1948; *Educ* Tettenhall Coll, Univ of Durham (BA); *m* 1972, Susan Elizabeth March; 1 s, 1 da; *Career* lectr in law Univ of Durham and QMC 1969–71; called to the Bar Inner Temple 1970, recorder of the Crown Court 1985–97, head of chambers until 1997, QC 1990; judge of the High Court of Justice: (Family Div) 1997–2003, (Queen's Bench Div) 2004–06; Lord Justice of Appeal 2006–13, a Justice of the Supreme Court 2013–; presiding judge Midland circuit 2000–04; vice-pres Criminal Div Court of Appeal 2009–13; Hon LLD Univ of Birmingham 2008, Hon DLitt Univ of Worcester 2014; *Style—* Lord Hughes of Ombersley, PC; ✉ The Supreme Court of the United Kingdom, Parliament Square, London SW1P 3BD

HUGHES OF STRETFORD, Baroness (Life Peer UK 2010), of Ellesmere Port in the County of Cheshire; Rt Hon Beverley June (Bev) Hughes; PC (2004); da of Norman Hughes (d 1987), and Doris, *née* Gillard (d 2010); *b* 30 March 1950; *Educ* Ellesmere Port Girls' GS, Univ of Manchester (BSc), Univ of Liverpool (DSA), Univ of Manchester (MSc); *m* 1973, Thomas Kevin McDonald; 2 da (Anna 1979, Sarah b 1980), 1 s (Michael b 1984); *Career* probation offr Merseyside 1971–76; Univ of Manchester: research assoc 1976–81, lectr 1981–94, sr lectr and head Dept of Social Policy and Social Work 1994–97; MP (Lab) Stretford and Urmston 1997–2010; Parly under sec of state DETR 1999–2001, Parly under sec of state Home Office 2001–02, min of state Home Office 2002–04, min of state DfES 2006–07, min of state for Children and Youth Justice 2007–09; memb EU Justice Sub Ctee House of Lords; ldr Trafford MBC 1995–97 (cncllr 1986–97); non-exec dir: Trafford Park Devpt Corporation 1992–97, Manchester Airport plc 1995–97, Gr Manchester C of C; non-exec dir and tstee The Lowry, chair Governing Cncl Univ of Salford; *Books* Older People and Community Care (1995); also author of numerous academic journal and conference papers; *Recreations* jazz, walking, reading, gardening; *Style—* The Rt Hon the Baroness Hughes of Stretford; ✉ House of Lords, London SW1A 0PW

HUGHES-D'AETH, (Wyndham) Jonathan; TD (1999); s of (Wyndham) Peter Hughes-D'Aeth, TD (d 2004), and (Gertrude Marion) Joy, *née* Hird; *Educ* Haileybury (head of sch), Univ of Liverpool (BA), Queens' Coll Cambridge (PGCE); *Career* asst master Rugby Sch 1979, asst master (on exchange) Melbourne GS Aust 1987, housemaster Rugby Sch 1990, headmaster Milton Abbey Sch 1995–2010; memb: Ctee Bloxham Project 1994, SHMIS 1995 (memb Exec Ctee 2001), Ctee Boarding Schools Assoc 2001 (chm 2004–05), inf offr TA 5 Bn Royal Regt of Fusiliers 1978–91; *Recreations* family, field sports, military history; *Clubs* East India, Public Schools; *Style—* Jonathan Hughes-D'Aeth, Esq, TD

HUGHES-HALLETT, James Wyndham John; CMG (2012); s of late Michael Hughes-Hallett, and late Penelope, *née* Fairbairn; bro of Lucy Hughes-Hallett and Sir Tom Hughes-Hallett, *qqv*; *b* 10 September 1949; *Educ* Eton, Merton Coll Oxford; *m* 1991 (m dis), Lizabeth Louise Hall; 2 da; *Career* articled clerk Dixon Wilson Tubbs & Gillett 1970–73, with Swire Gp 1976–; chm: Cathay Pacific Ltd 1999–2005, Swire Pacific Ltd 1999–2005, John Swire & Sons (Hong Kong) Ltd 1999–2005, John Swire & Sons Ltd 2005–14, dir 2005–; dir HSBC Holdings Ltd 2005–14; chm Esmée Fairbairn Fndn 2013–, chm Clarkson PLC 2015–; govr SOAS 2005–10, chm Courtauld Inst of Art 2013–; FCA 1973; Silver Bauhinia Star (Hong Kong) 2004; *Style—* James Hughes-Hallett, Esq, CMG; ✉ John Swire & Sons Ltd, Swire House, 59 Buckingham Gate, London SW1E 6AJ

HUGHES-HALLETT, Lucy Angela; da of Michael Hughes-Hallett, of Glos, and late Penelope, *née* Fairbairn; sis of James Hughes-Hallett and Sir Tom Hughes-Hallett, *qqv*; *b* 7 December 1951; *Educ* St Mary's Calne, Bedford Coll London (BA); *m* 1985, Dan J Franklin, s of Michael Franklin, of Much Hadham, Herts; 2 da (Lettice, Mary (twins) 1 March 1990); *Career* writer and critic 1973–; *Books and Publications* Cleopatra: Histories, Dreams and Distortions (1990), Heroes (2004), The Pike: Gabriele D'Annunzio (2013); *Awards* Catherine Pakenham Award 1980, Emily Toth Award 1990, Fawcett Book Prize 1992, Samuel Johnson Prize for Non-Fiction 2013, Costa Biography Award 2014, Duff Cooper Prize 2014, Paddy Power Political Biography of the Year 2014; *Style—* Lucy Hughes-Hallett; ✉ c/o Lutyens & Rubinstein Literary Agency, 21 Kensington Park Road, London W11 2EU (☎ 020 7792 4855, e-mail info@lutyensrubinstein.co.uk)

HUGHES-HALLETT, Sir Thomas Michael Sydney; kt (2012); s of Michael Hughes-Hallett, and late Penelope, *née* Fairbairn; bro of James Hughes-Hallett and Lucy Hughes-Hallett, *qqv*; *b* 28 August 1954; *Educ* Eton, Univ of Oxford (MA), Coll of Law; *m* Juliet, da of Col Anthony Rugge-Price, and Joy Rugge-Price; 2 s, 1 da; *Career* Robert Fleming & Co Ltd: chm Robert Fleming Securities 1993–99, chm Fleming Private Asset Mgmnt, memb Bd Fleming Asset Mgmnt and chm Flemings Private Bank 1999–2000; chief exec Marie Curie Cancer Care 2000–; chm: Palliative Care Funding Review, Philanthropy Review, End of Life Care Implementation Advsy Bd, Kings Fund Gen Advsy Cncl; tstee Esmée Fairbairn Fndn 2008–; *Recreations* music, tennis, cooking, walking; *Style—* Sir Thomas Hughes-Hallett; ✉ 10 Stanley Gardens, Notting Hill, London, W11 2NG

HUGHES-ONSLOW, James Andrew; s of Andrew Hughes-Onslow (d 1979), and Betty Lee (later Mrs David Crichton, d 2017), half-sister of Lord Rossmore; gs of Capt Oliver Hughes-Onslow (d 1972), of Ayrshire; *b* 27 August 1945; *Educ* Castle Park Dublin, Eton; *m* 1982, Christina Louise, da of Peter Henry Hay, bro of Sir David Hay, of Aust; 1 s (Andrew b 21 March 1985), 3 da (Flora b 7 Sep 1988, Marina b 29 July 1990, Harriet b 4 May 1993); *Career* sub ed and feature writer The Field 1968–70; reporter: Sunday Telegraph 1970–71, Daily Express 1971–73; columnist: The Spectator 1974–75, What's On in London 1976–82; columnist and feature writer: Evening Standard 1983–96 and 1999–2013, The Express (Beachcomber Column) 1996–98, The Oldie 2007–, Daily Mail 2014–; articles and reviews in: Punch, The Times, The Field, Books and Bookmen, Business Traveller, The Spectator, Tatler, Country Times, The Illustrated London News, Country Living, The Melbourne Age, Sydney Morning Herald, The Lady; *Clubs* Boodle's; *Style—* James Hughes-Onslow, Esq; ✉ 42 Knatchbull Road, Camberwell, London SE5 9QY (☎ 020 7274 9347)

HUGHES-PARRY, Thomas Antony; s of Maj Thomas Garrard Hughes-Parry (d 1987), of Llangollen, Denbighshire, and Rachael Constance Luz, *née* Boger (d 2000); *b* 9 February 1949, Port Dickson, Malaysia; *Educ* Canford Sch, Univ of Exeter; *m* 1 May 1976, Rosemary Constance, da of Robert James Foster; 2 s (Thomas David b 9 Sept 1981, Philip John b 19 Sept 1983); *Career* articled clerk Harmood Banner 1969–73, chartered accountant Investigation Dept Deloitte Haskins & Sells 1974–78, ptnr Beer Aplin 1979–2004, ptnr Thomas Westcott 2004–06 (conslt 2006–); memb SW Soc Chartered Accountants: Tech Advsy Ctee 1979–91 (del to London Ctee 1988–91), GP Panel 1991– (del to London Ctee); chm ICAEW Charity and Voluntary Sector Gp 1999–2004; Exeter District Soc of Chartered Accountants: careers advsr 1980–84, vice-chm 1989–90, chm 1990–91; vice-treas Exeter Cncl for Voluntary Service 1980–88, various offices Dawlish Round Table 1980–89, bursar and sec to the govrs Maynard Sch 1981–2012, sec to the govrs Exeter Royal Acad for Deaf Educn (formerly Royal West of England Residential Sch for the Deaf) 1986–2008 (tstee 2008–10), adult educn lectr 1986–, chm Exeter Voluntary Trading Enterprizes 1988–2004, chm Devon & Exeter Deaf Soc 2005–13; tstee CAs Benevolents Assoc 2003–15, tstee and treasurer Hospiscare 2013–; FCA; *Recreations* swimming, walking, gardening, yoga, boating, classical music, reading, Open Univ; *Clubs* Devon and Exeter Instn; *Style—* Tom Hughes-Parry, Esq; ✉ 8 Cavendish Close, Dawlish EX7 9ED (☎ 01626 863653, e-mail tomhparry@talktalk.net)

HUISMANS, Sipko; s of Jouko Huismans, and Roeloffina Huismans; *b* 28 December 1940; *Educ* Univ of Stellenbosch (BA); *m* 1969, Janet, *née* Durston; 2 s (Jake, Nicholas), 1 da (Emma); *Career* Usutu Pulp Co Swaziland 1961–68; Courtaulds plc: sales mangr 1968, gen mangr Springwood Cellulose Co Ltd 1968, md Courtaulds Central Trading (formerly Lustre Fibres Ltd) 1973, md Fibres Bd 1982, main bd dir 1984–96, non-exec dir BCL 1985–86, ldr Chem and Industry Task Force 1986–88, chm International Paint 1986–96, chm Chemical and Industrial Executive 1988–90, gp md 1990, chief exec 1991–96; non-exec dir: Vickers plc 1994–99, Imperial Tobacco plc 1996–; ceo Volharding (UK) Ltd; *Recreations* motor racing, sailing; *Style—* Sipko Huismans, Esq

HULL, Janet Elizabeth; OBE (2014); da of Thomas Edward Lacy (d 1989), of Southport, and Marjorie, *née* Forster (d 2003); *b* 20 March 1955; *Educ* Southport HS for Girls, St Anne's Coll Oxford (MA), Napier Coll Edinburgh (DEML), Inst of Direct Mktg (DipIDM); *Children* 1 s (Archibald Campbell b 19 Dec 1991), 1 da (Florence Campbell b 2 March 1998); *Career* Ted Bates 1979–80, Abbott Mead Vickers 1980–85, Young & Rubicam 1985–89, Burson-Marsteller 1992–93, IPA 1993–99, Lewis Moberly 2000–02, IPA 2003–; memb: The Marketing Soc, Women's Advtg Club of London (WACL), RHS; memb Worshipful Co of Marketors; *Recreations* piano, art, travel; *Style—* Ms Janet Hull, OBE; ✉ 4 Edith Grove, London SW10 0NW

HULME, Cdr Laon Stuart Grant; OBE (1999); s of Capt James Edmund Hulme (d 2013), and Dorothea Valentia, *née* Valless (d 2000); *b* 2 November 1944; *Educ* Hardye's Dorchester, BRNC Dartmouth; *m* 1968, Karen Mary, *née* Welch; 2 da (Sara-Louise b 9 May 1970, Anna-Marie b 21 July 1972); *Career* RN 1963–98; qualified aircraft control/air direction; memb trg staff: RNAS Yeovilton (fighter control), FOST (operational sea trg), SMOPS (i/c ops trg); specialised in NATO Command systems/data links; cmd: HMS Hubberston (minehunter), HMS Galatea (frigate); exec offr HMS Brilliant (Falklands War, mentioned in dispatches); seagoing flag staff Ops Offr, head Warfare Branch Implementation Team; ed Broadsheet (RN annual magazine, BACB awards) MOD, ret as Cdr 1998; sec/chief exec Insurance Inst of London 1998–2009, ed New London Jl (Insurance Inst of London magazine) 2000–09; vice-pres Insurance Orch 2000–09, vice-pres Insurance Charities 2000–04; memb Worshipful Insurers Golf Soc; Freeman City of London 1999, memb Worshipful Co of Insurers 1999; MInstD 1996 (memb Business Panel); *Recreations* golf, being with family and friends; *Clubs* Royal Navy of 1765 and 1795, City Livery, Anchorites, Lime Street and Bassishaw Ward, Rowlands Castle Golf; *Style—* Cdr Laon Hulme, OBE; ✉ 147 Portsmouth Road, Horndean, Hampshire PO8 9LQ (☎ 02392 593968, e-mail laon.hulme@sky.com)

HULME, Prof Mike; s of Ralph Hulme (d 1989), and Shelagh Mary, *née* Close; *b* 23 July 1960, London; *Educ* Madras Coll St Andrews, Univ of Durham (BSc), Univ of Swansea (PhD); *m* 1987, Gillian Margaret, *née* Walker; 1 da (Emma Jane b 1992); *Career* lectr in physical geography Univ of Salford 1984–88; Sch of Environmental Sciences UEA: sr research assoc Climatic Research Unit (CRU) 1988–98, reader CRU 1998–2000, founding dir Tyndall Centre for Climate Change Research 2000–07, prof of climate change 2002–13; prof of climate and culture Dept of Geography KCL 2013–; ed: Climate Research 1997–2000, Global Environmental Change 2003–10; ed-in-chief Wiley's Interdisciplinary Review of Climate Change 2008–; memb Editing Ctee Int Jl of Climatology 1994–99, editorial advsr Progress in Physical Geography 1999–2002; memb Editorial Bd: Climate Policy 2005–12, Environmental Science & Policy 2009–, Global Evironmental Change 2010–, Transactions Inst of Br Geography 2013–; contrib The Guardian 1988–2001 (monthly climate summaries); Hugh Robert Mill Prize Royal Meteorological Soc 1995, Queen's lecture Berlin 2005, Nobel Peace Prize 2007 (jtly as a significant memb of the Intergovernmental Panel on Climate Change); Carson fell Rachel Carson Center LMU Munich 2014; *Books* incl: An Annotated Bibliography of the Climate of Sudan (1987), Climate Change, Desertification and Desiccation, with Particular Emphasis on the African Sahel (with Mick Kelly, 1993), Climate Change and Southern Africa (ed, 1996), Climate of the British Isles: Present, Past and Future (ed with Elaine Barrow, 1997), Climate Change Scenarios for the UK (ed, 1998, 2 edn 2002), Imagined Memories and the Seductive Quest for a Family History (2008), Why We Disagree About Climate Change: Understanding Controversy, Inaction and Opportunity (2009, Gerald L Young Human Ecology Book of the Year Award 2010), Making Climate Change Work for Us: European Perspectives on Adaptation and Mitigation Strategies (jt ed, 2010), Exploring Climate Change Through Science and in Society: An Anthology of Mike Hulme's Essays, Interviews and Speeches (2013), Can Science Fix Climate Change? (2014), Climates and Cultures (ed, 2015), Weathered: Cultures of Climate (2016); also many other academic and popular articles and book chapters; *Recreations* cricket, genealogy, modern history; *Style—* Prof Mike Hulme; ✉ Department of Geography, King's College London, Strand, London WC2R 2LS (website www.mikehulme.org)

HULSTONE, Simon; s of Roger Raymond Hulstone, and Lorraine Elizabeth Anne, *née* Wild; *b* 2 November 1974, Stoke-on-Trent, Staffs; *Educ* Paignton Community Coll, Westminster Coll; *m* 7 Aug 2005, Katy, *née* Cale; 3 da (Tansy Etoile b 11 Feb 2006, Cicely Anais b 1 June 2007, Betony Melisse b 6 Jan 2012); *Career* apprentice chef Selsdon Park Hotel Croydon 1991–92, commis chef Hanbury Manor Hotel Hertford 1992–93, commis chef Ston Easton Park Hotel Bath 1993–94, chef de partie Swallow Royal Hotel Bristol 1994–96, chef de partie Regent Hotel Auckland NZ 1996–97; head chef: Mirabelle Restaurant Eastbourne 1997–99, Hotel on the Park Cheltenham 1999–2001, Cotswold House Cotswolds 2001–04; chef and proprietor Elephant Restaurant Torquay 2004–; memb: Br Culinary Fndn 2000, Craft Guild of Chefs, Acad of Culinary Arts; *Awards* Youth Skill Olympics Gold 1995, World Jr Champion 1996, New Zealand Chef 1997, Chef of the Year 1999, Roux Scholar 2003, Michelin Star 2006–, Nat Chef of the Year 2008–10, Bocuse D'Or UK Representative 2009 and 2011, over 30 int gold medals Br team of chefs (capt); *Recreations* classic scooter restoration; *Style—* Simon Hulstone, Esq; ✉ e-mail simonhulstone@aol.com, Twitter @hulstone; The Elephant Restaurant, 3 & 4 Beacon Terrace, Torquay, Devon TQ1 2BH (☎ 01803 200044, fax 01803 202717, e-mail info@elephantrestaurant.co.uk, website www.elephantrestaurant.co.uk, Twitter @elephantrest); c/o Koyah PR (☎ 07814 028664)

HUM, Sir Christopher Owen; KCMG (2003, CMG 1996); s of Norman Charles Hum (d 1950), and Muriel Kathleen, *née* Hines (d 2001); *b* 27 January 1946, Southend-on-Sea, Essex; *Educ* Berkhamsted Sch, Pembroke Coll Cambridge (MA), Univ of Hong Kong, SOAS Univ of London (PGDip); *m* 31 Oct 1970, Julia Mary, da of Hon Sir Hugh Park (d 2001), of London and Cornwall; 1 da (Olivia b 1974), 1 s (Jonathan b 1976); *Career* FCO: joined 1967, Hong Kong 1968–70, Peking 1971–73, office of UK Perm Rep to the EEC Brussels 1973–75, FCO 1975–79, Peking 1979–81, Paris 1981–83, head Hong Kong Dept 1986–89 (asst head 1983, cnsllr 1985), dep head Falkland Islands Dept 1985–86, cnsllr and head of Chancery UK Mission to the UN NYC 1989–92, asst under sec of state (Northern Asia) 1992–94, asst under sec of state (Northern Asia and Pacific) 1994–95, ambass Poland 1996–98, dep under-sec and chief clerk 1998–2001, ambass to China 2002–05; master Gonville and Caius Coll Cambridge 2006–12 (life fell 2012–); non-exec dir Laird plc 2004–16; memb GB China Centre 2006– (vice-chm 2012–), hon pres China Assoc 2014–; govr SOAS Univ of London 1998–2001, chm Cambridge Assessment 2010–12, syndic (tstee) Fitzwilliam Museum Univ of Cambridge 2006–14, tstee Young Classical Artists Tst 2006–14; hon fell Pembroke Coll Cambridge 2004; Hon LLD Univ of Nottingham 2006, Hon PhD London Met Univ 2006; *Recreations* all the arts, Asia, walking; *Clubs* Athenaeum; *Style—* Sir Christopher Hum, KCMG; ✉ Gonville & Caius College, Trinity Street, Cambridge CB2 1TA (e-mail ch407@cam.ac.uk)

HUMBLE, James Kenneth; OBE (1996); s of Joseph Humble (d 1993), and Alice, *née* Rhodes (d 1992); *b* 8 May 1936; *m* 1962, Freda, da of George Frederick Holden, OBE (d 1964); 3 da (Josephine Clare b 1964, Rebecca Jane b 1965, Sarah Louise b 1966); *Career* Nat Serv RN 1954–56; Weights and Measures Oldham 1956–62, asst supt metrology Nigeria 1962–66, chief dep trading standards offr Croydon 1966–73, asst dir of consumer affrs Office of Fair Trading 1973–78, dir of Metrication Bd 1978–80, chief exec Local Authorities Co-ordinating Body on Food and Trading Standards (LACOTS) 1980–98; dir Nat Metrological Co-ordinating Unit 1980–88; vice-pres Inst of Trading Standards 1998–, dir National Consumer Cncl 1998–2002, non-exec dir Wine Standards Bd 1999–2003, memb Exec Ctee Consumer Congress 1995–99; memb: Methven Ctee 1976, Eden Ctee 1987, Forum of Euro Food Law Enforcement Practitioners (FLEP) 1990–98, Western Euro Legal Metrologists Cooperative (WELMEC) 1989–98, Euro Product Safety Enforcement Gp (PROSAFE) 1991–98, Cars Ctee 1984–96; chm (various) Euro Ctee of Experts 1976–82; tstee Golden Leaves 2002–, memb Bd Dignity in Dying 2007–13; orator TSi Coll of Fells 1999–2012; sport: capt Oldham RU 1957–59, professional rugby league Leigh RFC 1959–65; chm Addiscombe and Shirley Round Table 1980–81; *Books* A Grandad's Life (2008), The History of Trading Standards (2014), History of the Trading Standards Institute (jtly, 2014); *Recreations* golf, bridge, opera; *Style—* James K Humble, Esq, OBE; ✉ 153 Upper Selsdon Road, Croydon, Surrey (☎ 020 8657 6170)

HUME, Jim; MSP; s of Walter Jardine Hume, of Yarrow, Selkirk, and Marion Joyce, DL, *née* Anderson; *b* 4 November 1962, Peebles, Tweeddale; *Educ* DipAg, MBA; *m* 5 June 1986, Lynne; 2 s (Duncan b 23 Feb 1988, Callum b 26 Sept 1989), 1 da (Julia b 24 March 1994); *Career* ptnr John Hume & Son (farming) 1983–; MSP (Lib Dem): S of Scotland 2007–11, S Scotland 2011–; pty spokesperson on rural affrs, tport and housing until 2013, pty spokesperson for housing and health 2013–; memb Rural Affrs, Climate Change and Environment Ctee Scottish Parliament; chair Borders Fndn for Rural Sustainability 2001–07; dir: Scottish Enterprise Borders 2002–07, NFU Scotland 2004–06 and 2007; tstee Borders Forest Tst 1999–2005; *Publications* Shepherds (jtly); *Recreations* amateur radio, gardening; *Style—* Jim Hume, Esq, MSP; ✉ The Scottish Parliament, Edinburgh EH99 1SP (☎ 0131 348 6703, fax 0131 348 6705, e-mail jim.hume.msp@scottish.parliament.uk)

HUME, Dr Robert; *b* 6 January 1928; *Educ* Ayr Acad, Bellahouston Acad, Univ of Glasgow (MB ChB, MD, DSc); *m* 1 June 1959, Kathleen Ann Ogilvie; 2 s (Robert, David), 1 da (Morag); *Career* Nat Serv Intelligence Corps, cmmnd Gordon Highlanders India and Germany 1946–48; Univ of Glasgow: Hutcheson res scholar 1955–56, Hall fellowship 1956–59, hon clinical lectr 1965, hon sub dean Faculty of Med 1988; conslt physician Southern Gen Hosp Glasgow 1965–93, ret 1993; author of numerous pubns on haematological and vascular disorders; memb BMA 1954, memb Scot Soc for Experimental Med 1955–, memb Br Soc for Haematology 1960, memb Res Support Gp Gtr Glasgow Health Bd 1978–90, memb Intercollegiate Standing Ctee on Nuclear Med UK 1980–83, memb Scot Cncl BMA 1980–83, chm Sub-Ctee in Med Gtr Glasgow Health Bd 1985–90, memb Bd of Dirs HCI (Scotland) Clydebank 1995–2003; RCPS: hon registrar for examinations 1971–83, visitor and pres elect 1988, pres 1990–92; chm: Conf of Scot Royal Colls and Faculties 1991–92, Jt Ctee on Higher Med Trg of Royal Colls of UK 1990–93; memb Scot Soc of Physicians 1965, FRCPS 1968, FRCPE 1969, hon memb Assoc of Physicians of GB and Ireland 1971, Hon FACP 1991, Hon RACP 1991, memb Acad of Med of Malaysia 1991, Hon FCM (SA), Hon FRCPS (Canada), FRCPath, FRCSEd 1992, FRCPI 1993; *Recreations* hill walking, reading, opera, TV; *Clubs* Glasgow Antiques and Fine Arts Soc, Royal Philospophical Soc of Glasgow, Nat Tst for Scotland, Buchanan Castle Golf; *Style—* Dr Robert Hume; ✉ 6 Rubislaw Drive, Bearsden, Glasgow G61 1PR (☎ 0141 586 5249)

HUMM, Roger Frederick; s of Leonard Edward Humm, MBE (d 1964), and Gladys, *née* Prevotat (d 1986); *b* 7 March 1937; *Educ* Hampton Sch, Univ of Sheffield (BA); *m* 1966 (m dis), Marion Frances, *née* Czechman; *Career* md Ford Motor Co Ltd 1986–90 (dir 1980–90); dir: Ford Motor Credit Co Ltd 1980–90, Imperial Hospitals Ltd 1991–2001; vice-chm and chief exec Alexanders Holdings plc 1992–2000 (non-exec dir 2000–02), dir Andrew Macdonald (London) Ltd 2002–, Mount Securities Ltd 2005, St James and Country Estates Ltd 2005; Freeman City of London 1986, Liveryman Worshipful Co of Carmen; FIMI, FInstD, FRSA; *Recreations* golf, scuba diving, writing; *Clubs* RAC, Variety Club of GB, Lord's Taverners, Wentworth; *Style—* Roger F Humm, Esq; ✉ c/o The Clock House, Kelvedon, Essex CO5 9DG

HUMPHREY, Jacob John (Jake); *b* 7 October 1978, Peterborough, Cambs; *Educ* Framingham Earl HS, The Hewett Sch Norwich; *m* Harriet; *Career* presenter; *Television* incl: G@mers (Rapture TV) 1999–2000, Against All Odds 2001–04, Rule the School 2001–05, CBBC 2002–07, CBBC At The Fame Academy (BBC) 2002–07, The Saturday Show (BBC) 2004–05, BAMZOOKi (BBC) 2004–06; for BBC Sport: Sportsround 2005–08, Sport Relief 2005–, Football Focus 2006–, Final Score 2006–, Match of the Day 2007–, NFL International Series at Wembley Stadium 2007–, 2008 African Cup of Nations highlights 2008–, Super Bowl XLII 2008, Newsround 2008, UEFA Euro 2008 coverage 2008, 2008 Summer Olympics coverage 2008, BBC Sports Personality of the Year 2008–, Super Bowl XLIII 2009, Formula One 2009–, Super Bowl XLIV 2010, Commonwealth Games coverage 2010, Super Bowl XLV 2011; *Radio* incl BBC Radio 5 Live 2005–; *Style—* Mr Jake Humphrey

HUMPHREY, Dr Peter Ronald David; *b* 19 March 1946; *Educ* Merchant Taylors', St John's Coll Oxford (scholar, MA), Univ of Oxford Med Sch (BM BCh, DM); *m*; 2 c; *Career* house physician Radcliffe Infirmary Oxford 1973, house surgn Royal S Hants Hosp Southampton 1973–74, SHO rotation Knowle Hosp, Southampton Gen Hosp, Wessex Neurological Centre and Royal S Hants Hosp Southampton 1974–75, med registrar Southampton Gen Hosp 1975–76, registrar in neurology Wessex Neurological Centre 1977–78; Nat Hosps for Nervous Diseases London: SHO (neurology) 1976–77, cerebral blood flow res registrar 1978–80, locum registrar in neurophysiology 1980, sr registrar 1980–83; sr registrar Bart's 1980–83, hon reader in neurology Univ of Liverpool 1983–, conslt neurologist Walton Centre for Neurology and Neurosurgery (WCNN) Liverpool 1983–2009 (neurology dir 1994–99, res and educn dir WCNN Tst Bd 1999–2005, med dir WCNN Tst Bd 2005–06, emeritus conslt neurologist 2009–, non-exec dir 2015–); pres N of Eng Neurological Assoc 2006 (memb Cncl 1988–91), pres Br Assoc of Stroke Physicians 2007–09, memb Cncl Assoc of Br Neurologists 1994– (sec 1995–2001, memb Servs Ctee 1986–93 (sec 1989–94)); membs rep Neurology Standing Ctee RCP 1980–83; memb: RCP Ctee on Neurology 1989–, R&D Ctee Stroke Assoc 1995–99, Stroke Task Force, Stroke Project Gp, Organizing Ctee and Scietific Panel World Congress of Neurology Meeting London 2001; neurological rep S Sefton Ethical Med Ctee 1987–93; participant in numerous clinical trials incl European Carotid Artery Surgery Trial 1983–96; medicolegal practice with extensive experience of plaintiff, defendent and jt reports; memb Editorial Bd Jl of Neurology, Neurosurgery and Psychiatry 1995–98; hon reader Univ of Liverpool; FRCP 1989; *Publications* numerous pubns on strokes in learned jls; *Recreations* sailing, golf; *Style—* Dr Peter Humphrey; ✉ Walton Centre for Neurology and Neurosurgery, Lower Lane, Liverpool L9 7LJ (☎ 0151 529 5717, fax 0151 529 5512); 88 Rodney Street, Liverpool L1 9AR (☎ 0151 709 7066, e-mail humphreyprd@talktalk.net)

HUMPHREY, Rachel; *Career* Le Gavroche: apprentice 1996–98, first commis chef 1998–99, chef de partie 1999–2000; RAF chef 2000–03; Le Gavroche: chef de partie 2003–04, sous chef 2004–08, head chef 2008– (2 Michelin stars); *Style—* Ms Rachel Humphrey; ✉ Le Gavroche, 43 Upper Brook Street, London W1K 7QR

HUMPHREY OF DINNET, (James Malcolm) Marcus; CBE (1993), DL (Aberdeenshire 1989); s of Lt Col James McGivern Humphrey, MC (d 1979), and Violet Joan (d 1999), da of Col Sir Malcolm Barclay-Harvey of Dinnet, Govr of S Aust 1939–44 and for many years MP for Kincardine and W Aberdeenshire; *b* 1 May 1938; *Educ* Eton, ChCh Oxford (MA); *m* 15 Oct 1963, Sabrina Margaret, da of Lt Cdr Thomas Edward Pooley, RN (ret); 2 s (Edward b 1965, Simon b 1978), 2 da (Tania b 1966, Natasha b 1972); *Heir* s, Edward; *Career* chartered surveyor; landowner; chm N of Scotland Bd Eagle Star Group 1971–91; memb: NFU of Scotland HQ Cncl 1968–73, Grampian Regnl Cncl 1974–94 (chm of fin 1974–78); non-exec dir Grampian Healthcare NHS Tst 1993–99; alternate memb UK Delegation Euro Ctee of the Regions 1994–2002; Parly candidate (Cons): N Aberdeen 1966, Kincardine and Deeside By-election 1991; chm of fin Aberdeen CC 1973–75, memb Aberdeenshire Cncl 1995–2012 (ldr Cons Gp 1999–2012, dep provost 2007–12); memb Bd Cairngorms Nat Park Authy 2004–12, chm NE Scotland Preservation Tst 2005–; Grand Master Mason of Scotland 1983–88, chm Ct of the Convention of the Baronage of Scotland 2007–, memb Queen's Body Guard for Scotland (Royal Co of Archers) 1969–; OStJ 1970; *Recreations* fishing, shooting, photography, philately; *Clubs* Royal Northern and Univ (Aberdeen); *Style—* Marcus Humphrey of Dinnet, CBE, DL; ✉ Estate Office, Dinnet, Aboyne AB34 5LL (☎ 01339 885341)

HUMPHREYS, Prof Sir Colin John; kt (2010), CBE (2003); s of Arthur William Humphreys (d 1994), of Syston, Leics, and Olive Annie Harton (d 1965); *b* 24 May 1941; *Educ* Luton GS, Imperial Coll London (BSc), Churchill Coll Cambridge (PhD), Jesus Coll Oxford (MA); *m* 30 July 1966, Sarah Jane, da of Henry Matthews, of Cottingham, N Humberside; 2 da (Katherine Jane b 1968, Elizabeth Mary Louise b 1971); *Career* Univ of Oxford: sr research offr 1971–80, sr research fell Jesus Coll 1974–85, lectr in metallurgy and science of materials 1980–85; Henry Bell Wortley prof of materials engrg and head Dept of Materials Science and Engrg Univ of Liverpool 1985–89; Univ of Cambridge: prof of materials science 1990–92, professorial fell Selwyn Coll 1990–, head Dept of Materials Science and Metallurgy 1991–95, Goldsmiths' prof of materials science 1992–; prof of experimental physics Royal Instn of GB 1999–; visiting prof: Arizona State Univ 1979, Univ of Illinois 1982–86; dir Rolls Royce Univ Technol Centre 1994–; hon pres Canadian Coll for Chinese Studies 1996–; chm: Cmmn on Electron Diffraction Int Union of Crystallography 1984–87 (memb Cmmn on Int Tables), Materials Science and Engrg Cmmn SERC 1988–92; pres Inst of Materials, Minerals and Mining 2002–03 (memb Cncl 2002–, chm Managing Bd 2004–05); sr vice-pres Inst of Materials 2000– (memb Cncl 2000–), vice-pres Inst of Metals 1993–96 (memb Cncl 1992–96); memb Cncl: SERC 1988–92, Inst of Metals 1989–92; vice-chm Technol Foresight Ctee on Materials DTI 1994–99, memb Nat Advsy Ctee on Electronic Materials and Devices 1999–; chm Int Advisory Bd Nat Inst for Materials Science Tsukuba Japan 2003–, memb Int Advsy Panel Etisalat Univ UAE 2003–, chm Int Review Panel Dept of Materials The Technion Israel 2004; Inst of Physics fell in the public understanding of physics 1997–99; pres Physics Section BAAS 1998–99; RSA Medal 1963, Reginald Mitchell Medal 1989, Rosenhain Medal and Prize 1989, Templeton Award 1994, Elegant Work Prize Inst of Materials 1996, Kelvin Medal and Prize Inst of Physics 1999, Euro Materials Gold Medal Fedn of Euro Materials Socs 2001, Robert Franklin Mehl Gold Medal Minerals Metals and Materials Soc USA 2003; D K C MacDonald meml lectr Canada 1993, Hume-Rothery meml lectr Oxford 1997, Gladstone lectr London 1999, Hatfield meml lectr Sheffield 2000, Sterling lectr Singapore and Malaysia 2001, John Matthews meml lectr Durban South Africa 2002, Robert Warner lectr London 2002; memb: Ct Univ of Bradford 1990–94, Ct Cranfield Univ 1997–, John Templeton Fndn 1994–, BBC Panel on Engrg and Technol progs 1995–96; tstee Link House 1994–; Freeman City of London 1994, Liveryman Worshipful Co of Goldsmiths 1997, Liveryman Worshipful Co of Armourers and Brasiers 2001 (Freeman 1998, memb Ct of Assts 2004); Hon DSc Univ of Leicester 2001; CEng 1980, FIM 1985, FInstP 1985, memb Academia Europaea 1991, FREng 1996, Selby fell Australian Acad of Science 1997; *Books* High Voltage Electron Microscopy (ed, 1974), Electron Diffraction 1927–77 (ed, 1978), Creation and Evolution (1985, translated into Chinese 1988), Understanding Materials (ed, 2002), The Miracles of Exodus (2003); *Recreations* chronology of biblical events, contemplating gardening; *Style—* Prof Sir Colin Humphreys, CBE, FREng; ✉ 8 Diamond Close, Cambridge CB2 2AU; Department of Materials Science and Metallurgy, University of Cambridge, Pembroke Street, Cambridge CB2 3QZ (☎ 01223 334457, fax 01223 334437, e-mail colin.humphreys@msm.cam.ac.uk)

HUMPHREYS, Stephen Alan; *b* 12 March 1959; *Educ* Open Univ (BA); *m* 3 Sept 1994, Elizabeth, *née* Goode; *Career* Miny of Justice (formerly Lord Chllr's Dept then Dept for Constitutional Affrs): joined 1978, head Remuneration and Costs Branch Legal Aid Div 1993–99, dep sec of cmmns 1999–2002, sec to Corp Bd 2002–03, chief exec Law Cmmn 2004–07, interim dir Judicial Offices of England and Wales 2008–09; exec dir Judicial Office for Scotland 2010–; *Recreations* numismatics, photography, theatre, eating out and music; *Clubs* Middlesex CCC; *Style—* Stephen Humphreys, Esq; ✉ Judicial Office for Scotland, +1/R14, Parliament House, 11 Parliament Square, Edinburgh EH1 1RQ (☎ 0131 240 6664, e-mail shumphreys@scotcourts.gov.uk)

HUMPHRIES, (John) Barry; AO (1982), CBE (2007); *b* 17 February 1934; *Career* actor and writer; stage characters incl: Dame Edna Everage, Sir Les Patterson, Sandy Stone; Hon DUniv Griffith Aust 1994, Hon LLD Univ of Melbourne 2003; *Theatre* incl: Estragon in Waiting for Godot (Melbourne), Fagin in Oliver (Piccadilly and Palladium), Maggie May (Adelphi), Bed-Sitting Room (Comedy Theatre), Long John Silver in Treasure Island (Mermaid), Just A Show (one man show, Australia and Fortune Theatre), Housewife Superstar (Apollo and Globe), A Night with Dame Edna (Piccadilly), An Evening's Intercourse (Drury Lane), Song for Australia (Albert Hall), Back with A Vengeance (Strand, Royal and tour), Edna, The Spectacle (Haymarket), Edna, The Royal Tour (San Francisco and Broadway), Remember You're Out (Australia/New York), Royal Tour (Broadway and N America tour), Last Night of the Proms (Albert Hall and nat tour) 2009, All About Me (Broadway) 2010, Eat, Pray, Laugh (Australia and London Palladium), numerous one man shows in Aust; *Television* incl: The Bunyip (Channel 7), The Barry Humphries Scandals (BBC), The Dame Edna Experience (LWT), Audience

H

With Dame Edna (LWT), A Profile of Barry Humphries (LWT), Single Voices (BBC), Selling Hitler (Euston Films), Dame Edna's Hollywood (NBC), Dame Edna's Neighbourhood Watch (series of 12, LWT), Dame Edna's Work Experience (BBC), Flashbacks with Barry Humphries, The Talk Show Story, Heroes of Comedy (Thames Television), Biography (ABC News Productions), Chickens (Sky), Jack Irish (ABC1 and ZDF); *Film* incl: Bedazzled, Bliss of Mrs Blossom, The Adventures of Barry McKenzie, Barry McKenzie Holds His Own, Sir Les Saves the World, The Getting of Wisdom, The Hobbit; *Awards* SWET Award Best Comedy of the Year (for A Night with Dame Edna) 1979, BAFTA Award nomination Best Arts Programme (for A Profile of Barry Humphries), TV Personality of the Year 1990, Golden Rose of Montreux Award (for A Night with Dame Edna) 1991, JR Ackerley Prize 1994 (for More Please), Bay Area Theatre Critics Outstanding Achievement Award 1998, Tony Award 2000 (nomination 2005), Drama Desk Award 2000, Outer Critics Circle Award 2000, League of American Theatres Award 2001, Sydney Theatre Lifetime Achievement Award 2013, Aardman Animations and Slapstick Festival Comedy Legend Award 2014; *Books* incl: Bizarre (1965), The Wonderful World of Barry McKenzie (1970), Dame Edna's Coffee Table Book (1976), Les Patterson's Australia (1979), The Traveller's Tool (1985), My Gorgeous Life: The Autobiography of Dame Edna Everage (1989), More Please (autobiography, 1992), Women in the Background (debut novel, 1995), My Life As Me: A Memoir (2002), Handling Edna (2009); *Style*— Barry Humphries, Esq, AO, CBE

HUMPHRIES, Chris; CBE (1998); s of John Joseph Humphries, and Berenice Mary Lee; *b* 31 August 1948; *Educ* Univ of NSW (BA); *m* Hazel Maxwell, *née* Cross; 1 s (Jesse b 28 Jan 1977), 2 da (Samantha b 11 Feb 1987, Katie b 10 April 1989); *Career* media resources offr ILEA 1975–79, prodr Promedia 1979–82; Cncl for Educnl Technol (CET): IT prog mangr 1982–84, asst dir 1984–87; prodn mangr ICL Interactive Learning Services 1987–88, educn business unit mangr Acorn Computers Ltd 1988–91, chief exec Herts TEC 1991–94, dir then chief exec TEC Nat Cncl 1994–98, DG Br Chambers of Commerce 1998–2001, DG City & Guilds of London Inst 2001–07, chief exec UK Cmmn for Employment and Skills 2007–2010, ret; chm: Nat Skills Task Force 1998–2000, UK Skills 2000–12, Nat Numeracy 2012–14; memb: Nat Learning and Skills Cncl 2000–02, Nat Adult Learning Ctee 2000–07, Cncl for Excellence in Leadership and Mgmnt 2001–02, Educn Advsy Gp BBC 2002–, Skills Strategy Steering Gp 2002–04; memb: Bd NHSU Tst 2003–05, Cncl Gresham Coll 2003–08; chair Bd of Govrs Univ of W London 2010–; *Style*— Chris Humphries, Esq, CBE

HUMPHRIES, Prof (Katherine) Jane; *b* 1948; *Educ* Univ of Cambridge (BA), Cornell Univ (MA, PhD); *Career* prof of economic history Univ of Oxford, fell All Souls Coll Oxford; presenter The Child Who Built Victorian Britain (BBC4) 2011; *Publications* Gender and Economics (ed, 1995), The Economics of Equal Opportunities (ed with Jill Rubery, 1995), Childhood and Child Labour in the British Industrial Revolution (2010); also other edited collections and many articles in social science history jls; *Style*— Prof Jane Humphries; ✉ All Souls College, Oxford OX1 4AL; Faculty of Modern History, Broad Street, Oxford OX1 3BD

HUMPHRISS, Dr David Bryan; s of Bryan Eric Humphriss, and Jean Beverley Humphriss; *b* 30 March 1962, Liverpool; *Educ* Liverpool Coll (scholar), Univ of Liverpool (BSc, MB ChB); *m*; 2 c; *Career* house offr Royal Liverpool Hosp 1985–86, SHO Fazakerley and Walton Hosps 1986–88, med registrar Merseyside rotation 1988–90, med registrar Freeman Hosp Newcastle upon Tyne 1990–91, res registrar Univ of Newcastle upon Tyne 1991–94, sr registrar Newcastle upon Tyne 1994–96, conslt physician specialising in gen med, diabetes and endocrinology Scarborough Hosp 1996–, clinical dir Acute and General Med Scarborough Hosp 2013–; hon sr lectr Hull York Med Sch 2005–; immediate care practitioner and motorsport dr 1990–, instructor in major incident mgmnt 2000–10, advanced trauma life support (ATLS) instructor 2015–; author of numerous papers and abstracts; memb: Diabetes UK 1990–, UK Prospective Diabetes Study Gp 1996–2002, Br Assoc for Immediate Care (BASICS); chm Hosp Arts for NE Yorks 1999–; MRCP 1988, FRCPEd 2006; *Recreations* gardening, reading, cycling, MTBO, juggling, trying to keep up with the teenagers and the dog; *Style*— Dr David Humphriss; ✉ Scarborough Hospital, Woodlands Drive, Scarborough, North Yorkshire YO12 6QL (☎ 01723 368111)

HUMPHRYS, John Desmond; s of Edward George Humphrys, and Winifred May Humphrys (d 1988); *b* 17 August 1943, Cardiff; *Educ* Cardiff HS; *m* 5 Sept 1964 (m dis), Edna Wilding (d 1997); 1 s (Christopher b 30 April 1967), 1 da (Catherine b 21 July 1969); 1 s (with Valerie Sanderson, Owen b 2000); *Career* BBC TV: joined as reporter Liverpool 1966, northern industrial corr 1967, foreign corr USA and SA 1970–80, dip corr 1980–81, presenter 9 O'Clock News 1981–86; presenter: Today Programme (BBC Radio 4) 1987–, On the Record (BBC TV) 1993–2002, BBC TV News, Mastermind; Journalist of the Year House Magazine/Channel 4 2000, Gold Sony Radio Award 2003, Radio Journalism of the Year Sony Radio Award 2013; *Books* Devil's Advocate (1998), The Great Food Gamble (2001), Lost for Words (2004), Beyond Words (2007), In God We Doubt (2008), The Welcome Visitor (2009), Blue Skies and Black Olives (2009); *Recreations* music, walking; *Style*— John Humphrys, Esq; ✉ BBC Broadcasting House, Portland Place, London W1A 1AA

HUNGERFORD, John Leonard; s of Leonard Harold Hungerford (d 1979), and Violet Miriam, *née* Bickerstaff (d 2004); *b* 12 October 1944; *Educ* The Glyn Sch Epsom, Gonville & Caius Coll Cambridge, Charing Cross Hosp Med Sch (MA, MB BChir, DO); *m* 16 July 1987, Yvonne Carole, da of Sydney George Rayment (d 1962); 1 da (Miranda b 1988); *Career* Moorfields Eye Hosp: conslt surgn 1983–, dir Oncology Serv; conslt ophthalmic surgn St Bartholomew's Hosp 1983–, lately conslt ophthalmic surgn Royal London Hosp; author of over 250 scientific articles and chapters in books on cancer of the eye in children and adults; vice-pres Int Soc for Ocular Oncology 2001; FRCS 1978, FRCOphth 1988; Knight of the Order of the Falcon Iceland, Officer's Cross of the Order of Merit Republic of Poland; *Recreations* travel, gardening, architecture; *Style*— John Hungerford, Esq; ✉ Kingswood Hanger, Colekitchen Lane, Gorismall, Surrey GU5 9PB (☎ 01483 202212, mobile 07792 727860, e-mail john.hungerford@btopenworld.com)

HUNNIFORD, Gloria; *b* 10 April 1940; *Career* TV and radio personality; started singing at age of 9 in NI (appearing on 3 TV networks and releasing 4 records), own weekly TV and radio music request show Ontario Canada 1969, worked on own 2 1/2 hour daily radio programme and weekly World Serv programme on Irish music for BBC NI, appeared on TV programmes such as Songs of Praise, Big Band specials and Queen's Jubilee Celebrations culminating in own daily one hour TV programme for Ulster TV, weekly broadcast for Br Forces Broadcasting to Germany 1969–81; host own daily radio show for BBC Radio 2 (first woman to do so) 1982–95, host chat show Sunday Sunday (LWT) 1982–91, host Gloria Live (Monday to Friday, BBC) 1990–93, stand in for Terry Wogan 1991, co-hosted (with Kenny Everett) That's Showbusiness (BBC), family affairs prog (with da Caron Keating, BBC) 1992–, reports for Holiday (BBC) 1993; other TV shows hosted: We Love TV (LWT), The Newly Wed Game (LWT), Gloria Plus (Saturday night chat show, UTV), Saturday Night Live (BBC), 6 O'Clock Show (LWT), BBC Pebble Mill Lunchtime Show, Good Fortune (BBC 1) 1994, Sunday Live (YTV) 1995–97, Sunday (LWT) 1995–, 'Time Off With.... 1997– (BBC), Open House with Gloria Hunniford 1998–2002 (Open House Specials (Five) 2003), Heaven and Earth (BBC) 1998–2007, Rip Off Britain (BBC 1) 2009–11, Angels (Sky Real Lives) 2009–10 (2 series), Glorious Grandparenting 2010, This Morning (ITV) 2011 (co-presenter), The Travelling Picture Show 2012–13, Rip Off Britain – Food (BBC) 2013–14, Rip Off Britain – Holidays (BBC) 2013–14, Rip Off Britain – Consumer (BBC) 2013–14; appeared in Strictly Come Dancing 2005, Cash in the Attic (BBC) 2008, 2009 and 2010, Castle in the Country (BBC) 2008, Alan Titchmarsh Show (ITV) 2008 and 2010, Celebrity Cash in the Attic 2009 and 2010, Angels (Sky Real Lives) 2009; guest appearances: Loose Women (ITV), Paul O'Grady Show (Channel 4), Countdown (Channel 4), One Show (BBC 1, also co-presenter); guest presenter This Morning (ITV) 2004, presenter and prodr Biography Channel (series of profiles) 2004–05; other TV credits (as singer): ten Royal Variety Performances, Val Doonican Show, Les Dawson Show, Children in Need Appeal, Paul Daniels Magic Show, Paul McKenna Show, Des O'Connor Show, Cannon & Ball Show, Bruce Forsyth's Show, Noel Edmonds' Saturday Night Live Show, Noel's House Party and Xmas Presents, Freddie Starr Show; pres TRIC 1999–2000 (first woman pres), runs family fndn in memory of da Caron Keating; *Awards* incl: Variety Club Radio Personality of the Year 1982 and 1992, TRIC Radio Personality of the Year 1983 and 1992, Panavista Britain's Best Dressed Woman 1985, TV Times TV Personality of the Year 1987, Spectacle Wearer of the Year 1991, Top Radio Personality (voted by readers of Chat magazine) 1991, Neighbour of the Year 1993, Comic Heritage Radio Personality 1997, Lifetime Achievement Award TRIC 2002, Irish World awards 2002, Variety Club Pride of Eirean Award 2008, Lifetime Inspirational Woman Award 2012; *Books* Gloria (autobiography, 1994), Gloria Hunniford's Family Cookbook (1995), Feel Fabulous Over Fifty (with Yan de Fries, 2000), Next to You (2005), Always With You (2008), Glorious Grandparenting (2010); *Style*— Miss Gloria Hunniford

HUNSDON OF HUNSDON; *see:* Aldenham (and Hunsdon of Hunsdon), Rt Hon Lord

HUNT, Dr Anthony Blair (Tony); s of Norman Blair Hunt, and Dorothy Gaskell Mottershead; *b* 21 March 1944, Bebington, Cheshire; *Educ* Birkenhead Sch, Worcester Coll Oxford (MA, BLitt), Univ of St Andrews (DLitt); *Career* reader in French Univ of St Andrews 1979–90 (temp lectr 1968–72, lectr 1972–79); Univ of Oxford: faculty lectr in medieval French lit 1990–2009, fell St Peter's Coll 1990–2011 (vice-master 2007–09, sr research fell 2009–11, emeritus fell 2011–), lectr Worcester Coll 1993–2009, lectr Pembroke Coll 1995–2009; visiting prof of medieval studies Westfield Coll London 1986–88, R N Coe distinguished visitor Univ of Warwick 1987; research reader Br Acad 1986–88; dep warden Southgait Hall Univ of St Andrews 1975–79, dep warden John Burnet Hall 1979–80, warden Hamilton Hall 1980–90; advsy ed Arthurian Lit 1981–92, memb Advsy Bd Westfield Medieval Studies, former memb Editorial Bd Rhetorica and Cambridge Studies in Medieval Lit; memb Drama Panel Soc of West End Theatre Lawrence Olivier Awards London 1986–87; hon treas Anglo-Norman Text Soc 1976–2011 (jt pres 2011–); foreign memb Norwegian Acad of Sci Letters 1999; FSA 1986, FBA 1999; Officier dans l'Ordre des Palmes Académiques 2009; *Books* Rauf de Linham: Kalender (1983), Chrétien de Troyes: Yvain (Le Chevalier au Lion) (1986), Les Giupartiz des Eschez (1986), Plant Names of Medieval England (1989), Popular Medicine in Thirteenth-Century England: Introduction and Texts (1990), Teaching and Learning Latin in Thirteenth-Century England (1991), The Medieval Surgery (1992), Anglo-Norman Medicine 1 (1994), Le Livre de Catun (1994), Villon's Last Will: Language and Authority in the Testament (1996), Anglo-Norman Medicine 2 (1997), Anglo-Norman Sermons on Joshua (1998), Three Receptaria from Medieval England (2001), Les Paraboles Maistre Alain en François (2005), Les Cantiques Salemon: The Song of Songs in MS Paris BNF fr 14966 (2006), Les Proverbez d'Alain (2007), Miraculous Rhymes: the Writing of Gautier de Coinci (2007), Ovide: Du remede d'amours (2008), An Old French Herbal (2008), Three Anglo-Norman Treatises on Falconry (2009), 'Cher Alme': Texts of Anglo-Norman Piety (2010), Four Old French Medical Texts (2011), Les Paroles Salomun (2012), Writing the Future: Prognostic texts and practices in Anglo-Norman England (2013), An Anglo-Norman Medical Compendium (2014); *Recreations* playing the double bass, opera, fell walking; *Style*— Dr Tony Hunt; ✉ St Peter's College, Oxford OX1 2DL (e-mail anthony.hunt@spc.ox.ac.uk)

HUNT, Dr Anthony James (Tony); s of James Edward Hunt (d 1976), and Joan Margaret, *née* Cassidy (d 2002); *b* 22 June 1932; *Educ* Salesian Coll Farnborough, Westminster Tech Coll; *m* 1, 1957 (m dis 1972), Patricia, *née* Daniels; 1 s (Julian b 12 Sept 1959), 1 da (Polly Leah b 27 July 1961); m 2, 1975 (m dis 1982), Patricia, *née* Daniels; m 3, 1985 (m dis 2007), Diana Joyce, *née* Collett; m 4, 2013, Helene Josephine Marguerite Moore, *née* Etchats; *Career* articled pupil Worshipful Co of Founders 1948–51, engr F J Samuely & Ptnrs 1951–59, engr Morton Lupton Architects 1960–62; Anthony Hunt Associates conslt engrs: fndr 1962, chm 1988–2002, conslt 2002–; chm YRM plc 1993–94; Graham Willis visiting prof Sch of Architecture Sheffield 1993–2009, Graham prof of architecture Univ of Pensylvania 2002, visiting prof Sch of Architecture Chinese Univ of Hong Kong 2004–05, visiting prof Instituto Superior Téchnico (IST) Lisbon, Velux visiting prof KAA Copenhagen 2009–11; projects incl: Hilton Hotel Heathrow, Waterloo Int Station, The Law Faculty Cambridge, West India Quay Bridge; recent projects incl: New HQ for Lloyds Register of Shipping, National Botanic Garden of Wales, Blackfriars Station for Thameslink, The Eden Project Cornwall, Barajas Airport Madrid; subject of a book by Angus MacDonald: Anthony Hunt – The Engineer's Contribution to Contemporary Architecture; visiting prof Sch of Architecture Royal Danish Acad of Fine Arts 2009–11; Gold medal IStructE 1995; Hon DLitt Univ of Sheffield 1999, Hon DEng Univ of Leeds 2003, hon doctorate RCA 2012; CEng, Hon FRIBA 1989, FIStructE, FRSA; *Awards* for: The Reliance Controls Factory Swindon, Willis Faber HQ Ipswich, Sainsbury Centre for the Visual Arts Norwich, Inmos Micro-electronics Factory Newport, Schlumberger Research Facility Cambridge, Don Valley Athletics Stadium Sheffield, Museum of Scotland, Nat Botanic Garden of Wales, Lloyds Register of Shipping, J C Decaux, Eden Project, Barajas Airport; *Books* Tony Hunt's Structures Notebook, Tony Hunt's Sketchbook and Second Sketchbook, Engineering Timelines (biography, 2008), subject of The Engineer's Contribution to Contemporary Architecture: Anthony Hunt (by Angus Macdonald, 2000), Connexions: The Unseen Hand of Tony Hunt (biography, by Nigel Dale, 2011), Connexions (2012); *Recreations* music, sailing, food, wine, painting; *Clubs* Chelsea Arts, Oriental; *Style*— Dr Tony Hunt; ✉ Dolphin House, Vicarage Street, Painswick, Gloucestershire GL6 6XR (☎ 07770 655151, e-mail tony@huntprojects.co.uk)

HUNT, Bernard Andrew Paul; s of Sir Joseph (Anthony) Hunt (d 1982), and Hilde, *née* Pollitzer (d 2004); *b* 24 March 1944; *Educ* Oundle, Magdalene Coll Cambridge (MA); *m* 1973, Florence, da of Alan White, of W Sussex; 1 da (Susanna b 1975), 1 s (Andrew b 1977); *Career* architect; ptnr Hunt Thompson Assocs 1969–98, md HTA Architects Ltd 1999–2003, chm HTA Architects Ltd 2004–13, conslt HTA Design LLP 2013–; memb Cncl NHBC 1995–2015 (dir 1995–2001); chm: Housing Gp RIBA 1995–99, 2000 Homes 1997–2001, Architects in Housing 1999–2001, NHBC Services Ltd 1999–2001, Design for Homes 2001–07; Coll of Estate Mgmnt Property Award 2001; FRSA, RIBA 1969; *Recreations* cinema, theatre, reading, swimming, travel; *Clubs* Reform; *Style*— Bernard Hunt, Esq; ✉ HTA, 106–110 Kentish Town Road, London NW1 9PX

HUNT, David Maitland; s of Bernard Wallis Hunt, and Doreen Margeret, *née* Shipp (d 1985); *b* 8 August 1948; *Educ* Radley, Guy's Hosp Med Sch London (MB BS); *m*; 2 s, 2 da; *Career* conslt orthopaedic surgn St Mary's Hosp 1983–; Oppenheimer travel award 1969, St Mary's Hosp short paper prize 1981 and 1982; pres Orthopaedic Section RSM 2001–02; pres Br Soc for Children's Orthopaedic Surgery 2004–; memb: BMA, Hunterian Soc, Br Orthopaedic Res Soc, Br Assoc for Surgery of the Knee, Med Defence Union; FRCS 1978, FRCSEd 1978, fell Br Orthopaedic Assoc; *Publications* Minimal Access Surgery (contrib chapters, ed R Rosin), Minimal Access Orthopaedics (ed), author of papers in various learned jls; *Recreations* fishing, sailing; *Clubs* RSM; *Style*— David M Hunt, Esq; ✉ 106 Harley Street, London W1N 1AF (☎ 020 7935 6347, fax 020 7935 2788)

HUNT, David Roderic Notley; QC (1987); s of Dr Geoffrey Notley Hunt (d 1982), of Pembury, Kent, and Deborah Katharine Rosamund, *née* Clapham; *b* 22 June 1947; *Educ* Charterhouse, Trinity Coll Cambridge (MA); *m* 27 April 1974, Alison Connell, da of Lt-Col Arthur George Jelf (d 1958); 2 s (Thomas b 8 Feb 1976, Robert b 20 Feb 1979); *Career* called to the Bar Gray's Inn 1969 (bencher 1995, treas 2016); recorder 1991–; cmmr Royal Court of Jersey 2012–; *Recreations* sailing, golf, skiing; *Clubs* Bar Yacht, Nevill Golf, Old Carthusian Yacht, Jr Offshore Gp; *Style*— David Hunt, Esq, QC; ✉ Blackstone Chambers, Blackstone House, Temple, London EC4Y 9BW (☎ 020 7583 1770)

HUNT, James; s of Robert and Cynthia Hunt; *b* 19 October 1957; *Educ* Oakham Sch, Leicester Sch of Fine Art (BA); *m* 1985, Bryony Margaret, da of Robin Sellick; 1 da (Holly b 17 April 1986), 2 s (Freddie b 30 Sept 1987, Arthur b 11 June 1989); *Career* with Leicester Mercury 1980–85, journalist News Service Leicester 1985–87, prodr Central TV 1987–89; Granada TV: prodr This Morning 1989–92, ed This Morning 1992–94, exec prodr This Morning 1994–96, head of features Granada TV 1994–96; exec prodr Granada Sky Broadcasting 1996–97; controller: Granada Sky Broadcasting 1997–98, Lifestyle Progs GTV 1998–2001, Daytime and Lifestyle Progs Granada Content 2001–04; currently head of programming Sky Arts; dir: channel programming GTP 1998–, Moving Image Devpt Agency; memb RTS; *Awards* Team of the Year Award for This Morning RTS 1994, Outstanding Technical Achievement for Granada Sky Broadcasting 1997; *Style*— James Hunt, Esq

HUNT, Jay; *Career* dir of progs Five 2007–08, controller BBC 1 2008–10, chief creative offr Channel 4 2010–; *Style*— Ms Jay Hunt; ✉ Channel Four Television, 124 Horseferry Road, London SW1P 2TX

HUNT, Rt Hon Jeremy; PC (2010), MP; s of Adm Sir Nicholas Hunt, GCB, LVO, and Meriel Eve, *née* Cooke Givan; *b* 1 November 1966; *Educ* Charterhouse, Magdalen Coll Oxford; *m* Lucia; 1 s (Jack), 2 da (Anna, Eleanor); *Career* mgmnt conslt 1988–89, English teacher Japan 1990–91, fndr Profile PR, jt chief exec and co-fndr Hotcourses, fndr Hotcourses Fndn; MP (Cons) Surrey SW 2005–, shadow min for disabled people 2005–07, shadow sec of state for culture, media and sport 2007–10, sec for culture, Olympics, media and sport 2010–12, sec of state for health 2012–; *Style*— The Rt Hon Jeremy Hunt, MP; ✉ 2 Royal Parade, Tilford Road, Hindhead, Surrey GU26 6TD; House of Commons, London SW1A 0AA (website www.jeremyhunt.org)

HUNT, John Brian; s of Peter Douglas Hunt, of Croxley Green, Herts, and Cynthia Mary, *née* Weatherilt; *b* 19 April 1951; *Educ* Rickmansworth GS, Harlow Tech Coll, Open Univ (BA); *m* 7 Feb 1986, Christine Elizabeth, da of Ronald Arthur Curl; 1 step s (Dean Keith Halls b 18 Feb 1970), 1 step da (Candice Margaret Halls b 30 Nov 1971); *Career* trainee journalist Doncaster Newspapers 1970–73, Sheffield Morning Telegraph 1973–79, dep chief sub ed Oracle Teletext 1979–84, scriptwriter and dep news ed 1984–89, sr news ed Channel Four News 1989–95, head ITN Resources ITN 1997– (resource mangr 1995–97); memb NUJ Nat Exec 1979, vice-chm NUJ Broadcasting Industrial Cncl 1988–89, chm ITN Jt Shops' Ctee 1989–93, tstee ITN Pension Fund 1989–95; *Recreations* cricket, football, photography, travel; *Clubs* Watford FC, Surrey CCC; *Style*— John Hunt, Esq; ✉ ITN, 200 Gray's Inn Road, London WC1X 8XZ (☎ 020 7833 3000, e-mail john.hunt@itn.co.uk)

HUNT, Jonathan Charles Vivian; OBE (1983), TD (1977, 3 clasps 1983, 1990 and 1994), DL (S Yorks 1981); s of Col George Vivian Hunt, OBE, TD (d 1979), and Sylvia Ann, *née* Tyzack (d 1985); *b* 6 March 1943; *Educ* Stowe; *m* 17 July 1971, Susan Aline, eld da of Francis Rawdon Crozier (d 2003); 2 s (James b 14 Sept 1973, Edward 6 June 1976); *Career* sr ptnr Wake Smith Slrs Sheffield 1988–2006 (ptnr 1967, conslt 2006–09); dir Sheffield Training and Enterprise Cncl 1990–2001; chm: Sheffield Enterprise Agency Ltd 1986–2002, S Yorks Community Fndn 2005–15, S Yorks branch SSAFA 2011– (memb 1982–); dir: Key Fund Investments Ltd 2005–16; memb Cncl Sheffield C of C 1999–2008; TA: cmmnd Queen's Own Yorks Yeo 1963, transferred B (Sherwood Rangers Yeo) Sqdn Royal Yeo (OC 1975–78), cmd Royal Yeo 1979–82, Dep Cdr 49 Inf Bde 1983–87, ADC (TA) to HM The Queen 1984–87, Project Offr Fast Track (TA compact commissioning course) 1987–91, TA Col RMA Sandhurst 1988–91, TA Col Ind Units MOD 1991–92, TA Col (Combat Arms) HQ UKLF 1992–95, Hon Col Sherwood Rangers Yeo 1994–2004; chef de delegation Br Team for the Saumur Challenge 1999–2004; High Sheriff S Yorks 2007–08; *Publications* Unicorns: A History of the Sherwood Rangers Yeomanry 1794–1899 (2012), Hard Fighting: A History of the Sherwood Rangers Yeomanry 1900–1946 (2016); *Recreations* sailing, the countryside, golf, military history, TA; *Clubs* Aldeburgh Yacht, Lindrick Golf, Sheffield; *Style*— Jonathan C V Hunt, Esq, OBE, TD, DL; ☎ 01709 812431, e-mail jonathan_hunt@btinternet.com

HUNT, Rev Canon Dr Judith Mary (Judy); da of Norman Thornley Hunt, and Constance Mary, *née* Fielding; *b* 16 April 1957, Darwen, Lancs; *Educ* Univ of Bristol (BVSc), Royal Vet Coll Univ of London (PhD), Univ of Cambridge (MA), Univ of Liverpool (postgrad dip); *Career* house surgeon Royal Vet Coll 1980–82, research scholar Royal Vet Coll 1982–85, lectr in equine vet science Univ of Liverpool 1985–88, ordinand 1988–91, deacon and curate Heswall Wirral 1991–95, priest in charge Tilston and Shocklach Cheshire 1995–2002, dir of mission and miny and cathedral res canon Cheshire 2002–09, archdeacon of Suffolk 2009–12; memb Windsor Leadership Tst; Cambridge Church History Prize 1990; MRCVS 1980, FRSM 1998; *Recreations* labrador dogs, flute; *Style*— The Rev Canon Dr Judith Hunt; ✉ Glebe House, The Street, Ashfield-cum-Thorpe, Stowmarket, Suffolk IP14 6LX (☎ 01728 685497, e-mail archdeacon.judy@stedmundsbury.anglican.org); Diocese of St Edmundsbury and Ipswich, Diocesan Office, St Nicholas Centre, 4 Cutler Street, Ipswich IP1 1UQ (☎ 01473 298500, website www.stedmundsbury.anglican.org)

HUNT, Neil Philip; s of Keith Hunt, of Devon, and Doreen Hunt; *b* 2 May 1954, London; *Educ* Univ of Sussex (BA), Goldsmiths Coll London (PGCE), Croydon Coll (CQSW); *Partner* Tracey Hassell; 2 s (Thomas, Oliver (twins) b 17 May 2001); *Career* sometime dir of child protection NSPCC, formerly with Home Office and Dept of Educn and Skills; chief exec Alzheimer's Soc 2003–11, chief exec Royal Coll of General Practitioners 2011–; *Style*— Neil Hunt, Esq; ✉ Royal College of General Practitioners, 30 Euston Square, London NW1 2FB (e-mail neil.hunt@rcgp.org.uk)

HUNT, His Hon Judge (David) Peter; *b* 25 April 1951; *Educ* Grangefield GS Stockton, Keble Coll Oxford (MA); *m* 1 June 1984, Cherryl Janet, da of Alexander Hubert Nicholson, of Pinner, Middx; 2 s (James b 1985, Nicholas b 1987); *Career* called to the Bar Gray's Inn 1974; memb Bar Cncl 1981–84, jr NE circuit 1982, recorder 1993–97, circuit judge 1997–, designated family judge Leeds 2000–; memb Family Proceedings Rules Ctee 2001–; *Books* Distribution of Matrimonial Assets on Divorce (1990); *Style*— His Hon Judge Hunt; ✉ Leeds Combined Court, The Courthouse, 1 Oxford Row, Leeds LS1 3BG

HUNT, Peter Roland; MBE (1998); s of Roland George Hunt (d 1974), and Violet Hunt (d 1998); *Educ* Taunton's Sch Southampton; *m* 1955, Mary Elizabeth, da of late Arthur Davis, and late Henrietta Davis; 1 s (Roger Ian b 1958); *Career* successively reporter, feature writer then air reporter Southern Daily Echo Southampton 1944–53; Nat Serv RAF India/UK 1945–48; account exec John Webb Press Services London 1954–55, PR mangr Downtons Ltd Fleet St 1955–58; The Coca-Cola Company: joined Coca-Cola Export Corp London as PR mangr UK and Ireland 1958, subsequently head of PR Coca-Cola Northern Europe, dir of PR Coca-Cola Europe, dir of public affrs Coca-Cola Northwest Europe, exec asst to the Pres and dir of Govt and industry affrs, external affrs advsr Coca-Cola GB 1988–2007; co-fndr Dolphin Trophy Learn to Swim Awards Scheme (sponsored by Coca-Cola GB) 1963, author of first research paper on sports sponsorship for IPR 1966, recipient Olympic medal (awarded by Pres of Austria for originating the company-sponsored film Olympic Harmony) 1976, memb Ctee of Enquiry into Sports Sponsorship for CCPR (The Howell Report) 1981–83; IPR (now CIPR): chm Int Ctee 1974–77, pres IPR 1978, chm Benevolent Fund Tstees (now Iprovision) 1992–2002, chm Fellows' Forum Working Pty 1994–97, memb Govt Affrs Gp; BSDA: chm PR Ctee 1987–93, memb Exec Cncl and Bd 1987–95, pres 1988–90, chm Publishing Panel 1993–99, memb Europe Gp until 1995, hon life memb 1996; tstee Br Soft Drinks Industry Fndn (formerly The Soft Drinks Industry Benevolent Soc) 1987–; Union of Euro Soft Drinks Assocs (UNESDA) Brussels: memb Nominations Ctee 1990, vice-chm Communications Ctee 1991–95; fndr and chm Coca-Cola Civil Serv/Industry Prog 1982–2007; memb: Mgmnt Ctee and Cncl Industry Cncl for Packaging and the Environment 1983–88, Food and Drink Fedn Key Issues Forum 1992–96; Tree Cncl: memb Fin and Gen Purposes Ctee 1990–2002, memb Funding Review Ctee 1992–94; chm Charing Cross Club 1991–2007 (fndr memb 1975), co-fndr Caxton Gp1984; Freeman City of London 2000; fndr memb Guild of PR Practitioners 2001; MCAM (DipCAM), Hon FCIPR (MIPR 1959, FIPR 1977, Hon FIPR 1998); *Recreations* family, home, garden, watercolour painting; *Clubs* Travellers; *Style*— Peter R Hunt, Esq, MBE

HUNT, Sharon; da of Terry Hunt, and Janice, *née* Collier; *b* 11 October 1977, Bury St Edmunds, Suffolk; *Educ* Culford Sch Suffolk, Perse Sch Cambridge; *Career* three-day eventer; 5th then 6th place Badminton Horse Trials, 6th place World Equestrian Games 2006, Bronze medal team eventing Olympic Games Beijing 2008, winner CCI**** Luhmühlen 2010; UK CC Level 3 coach BS and BE, Under 18 BE coach for eastern region; *Recreations* skiing, water skiing, tennis, cycling, music, travel; *Style*— Miss Sharon Hunt; ✉ e-mail sharonhuntpa@gmail.com, website www.sharonhunteventing.com, Twitter @SHEventing, Facebook Sharon Hunt Eventing

HUNT, Simon; *Career* global mktg Diageo plc 1994–98, vice-pres Global Mktg Diageo plc 1998–2000, sr vice-pres Global Innovation Allied Domecq plc 2000–03, sr vice-pres Mktg N America Allied Domecq plc 2003–05, ceo Malibu Kahlua Int 2005–07; William Grant & Sons: pres N America 2007–13, chief commercial offr 2013–16, ceo 2016–; *Style*— Simon Hunt, Esq

HUNT, Simon Hugh d'Aquilar (Sam); s of Prof Hugh Hunt, CBE, of Criccieth, Gwynedd, and Janet Mary, *née* Gordon; *b* 4 January 1948; *Educ* Cranbrook Sch Australia, Abbotsholme Sch, Univ of Manchester (BA, post grad dip); *m* Anne, *née* Please; *Career* asst keeper Salford Museum and Art Gall 1972–73, sr curator Royal Albert Meml Museum Exeter 1975–78 (curator of decorative art 1973–75), curator Bath Museum Serv 1978–83, curator and asst dir of leisure Bath 1983–88, dir Area Museum Cncl for the SW 1988–2000, chief exec SW Museums Cncl 2000–05, assoc and sr conslt Kingshurst Gp 2005–; dir Assoc of Ind Museums 2011–; sec Bath Archaeological Trust 1978–88, tstee Dorset Archaeology and Natural History Soc, tstee Nat Maritime Museum Cornwall, memb SW Ctee Heritage Lottery Fund; FMA; *Books* Bath Camera (1987), West Country Silversmiths (1977); *Recreations* fly fishing, sketching, walking; *Style*— Sam Hunt, Esq; ✉ Henley Manor, Crewkerne TA18 8PQ (☎ 01460 75222, mobile 07833 366624, e-mail henleymanor@btinternet.com)

HUNT, Terence William (Terry); s of William Herbert Hunt, (d 1983), and Audrey, *née* Austen; *b* 8 June 1955; *Educ* Royal Liberty GS, UEA (BA); *Career* teacher N Africa 1977–78, graduate trainee Macmillan Publishers 1978–79, copywriter Smith Bundy Partners 1979–83, bd dir DDM Advertising 1986 (creative dir 1983–86), chm Evans Hunt Scott 1990 (founding ptnr 1986), chm EHSrealtime 2000–, chm EHS Brann 2002–08, dir Leaders in Football Ltd 2009–11, fndr Customer & Co Ltd 2011–, fndr ptnr Future Customer 2012–; chm Adpoints; memb Advsy Bd Aimia; winner: over 50 creative and mktg awards, Most Creative Direct Marketer Campaign Poll 1989, Direct Marketer of the Year 1996, top of Marketing Direct Magazine Power 100 League 2005; pres Inst of Direct Mktg 2010– (also pres and memb Ctee); memb Bd World Child Cancer Fndn; FIDM; *Books* Nationwide Book of Literary Quizzes (1979), Scoring Points: How Tesco Wins Customer Loyalty (2002); *Recreations* family, AFC Wimbledon, fishing, running, collecting books; *Clubs* Groucho, Shoreditch House, RSA; *Style*— Terry Hunt, Esq; ✉ 11 Granard Road, London SW12 8UJ (☎ 020 7488 5585, e-mail terry@customerandco.co.uk)

HUNT, Terry; CBE (1996), Knight's Cross of the Order of the Falcon (Iceland, 2001); s of Thomas John Hunt (d 1976), of Taunton, Somerset, and Marie Louise, *née* Potter (d 2002); *b* 8 August 1943, Monkton Heathfield, Somerset; *Educ* Huish's GS Taunton; *m* 7 Jan 1967, Wendy Graeme, da of Dr Aldwyn Morgan George, MC (d 2000), of Perranwell Cornwall; 1 s (Philip Benjamin (Ben) b 1968), 1 da (Nicola Jane b 1969); *Career* hosp admin: Tone Vale Hosp 1963–65, NE Somerset Hosps 1965–67, Winchester Hosps 1967–69, Lincoln Co Hosp 1969–70; hosp sec Wycombe Gen Hosp 1970–73, dep gp sec Hillingdon Hosps 1973–74, area gen admin Kensington & Chelsea and Westminster AHA (T) 1974–76, dist admin NW Kensington & Chelsea and Westminster 1976–82, dist admin Paddington & N Kensington Health Authy 1982–84; gen mangr NE Thames RHA 1984–91; nat dir NHS Supplies Authy 1991– (chief exec 1996–2000); memb: Cncl of Govrs The London Hosp Med Coll 1985–91, Cncl UCL 1985–91, Steering Gp on Undergraduate Med and Dental Educn and Res 1987–91, Med Ctee Universities Funding Cncl 1989–93, Hosp Ctee of the EEC 1991–93, NHS Central R&D Ctee 1991–96; memb: Twyford & Dist Round Table 1975–84 (chm 1980–81, pres 1988), Ctee Reading Town Regatta 1983–93 (treas 1984–86, chm 1989), Rotary Club of Reading Maiden Erlegh 2004–13; church warden St Andrew's Church Sonning on Thames Berks 2010–; memb Inst of Health Serv Mgmnt; Liveryman Worshipful Co of Barbers 1998; CIMgt, memb RSM; Knight's Cross Order of the Falcon Iceland 2001; *Recreations* clock making, model engineering; *Style*— Terry Hunt, Esq, CBE; ✉ 36 Old Bath Road, Charvil, Reading, Berkshire RG10 9QR (☎ 01189 341062, e-mail terry@oldbathroad.com)

HUNT, Sir Tim; kt (2006); s of Richard Hunt (d 1979), and Kit, *née* Rowland (d 1977); *b* 19 February 1943; *Educ* Magdalen Coll Sch Oxford, Clare Coll Cambridge (MA, PhD); *m* Dr Mary Collins; 2 da (Celia Daisy b 27 Nov 1994, Agnes Beatrix b 7 May 1998); *Career* postdoctoral fell Dept of Med Albert Einstein Coll of Med 1968–70; Dept of Biochemistry Univ of Cambridge: joined as research fell 1971, Beit meml fell 1972–75, MRC sr asst in research 1975–76, Royal Soc research fell 1976–81, univ lectr 1981–90; Clare Coll Cambridge: research fell 1967–74, official fell 1975–2002, hon fell 2002–, princ scientist Cancer Research UK Clare Hall Labs South Mimms 1991–2010 (ret); jr proctor Univ of Cambridge 1982–83; summer course instr Marine Biological Lab Woods Hole: in embryology 1977 and 1979, in physiology 1980–83; chair Cncl EMBO 2006–; memb: EMBO Fund Ctee 1990–94, Cncl John Innes Inst 1991–93, BBSRC Cell and Molecular Biology Panel 1995–97, Scientific Advsy Bd IMP Vienna 1995–2001, Cncl Royal Soc 1996–97, Scientific Cncl European Research Cncl 2011–; tstee Brit Meml Fellowships 2004–; author of numerous articles in learned jls; memb Editorial Bd: Jl of Cell Sci, Molecular Biology of the Cell, Genes to Cells; Nina C Werblow lecture Cornell Univ Med Coll NY 1993; Abraham White Scientific Achievement Award George Washington Univ Dept of Biochemistry and Molecular Biology Washington DC 1993, Nobel Prize in Physiology or Medicine 2001 (jtly with Leland H Hartwell and Dr Sir Paul Nurse, FRS, *qv*); foreign hon memb American Acad of Arts and Sciences 1997, foreign assoc memb US Nat Acad of Sciences 1999, memb Academia Europaea 1999, memb EMBO 1979, FRS 1991, FMedSci 1998; offr Légion d'Honneur (France) 2002; *Publications* Molecular Biology of the Cell: The Problems Book (with John Wilson, 5 edn 2014); *Recreations*

H

photography, cooking; *Clubs* Athenaeum; *Style*— Sir Tim Hunt, FRS; ✉ Cancer Research UK, Clare Hall Laboratories, South Mimms, Hertfordshire EN6 3LD (☎ 07595 037171, e-mail rtimhunt@gmail.com)

HUNT, Vivian; *Educ* Harvard Univ (AB, MBA); *Career* Senegal regnl supervisor US Peace Corps 1989–91, healthcare project dir LEAP Inc 1993, previously head Pharmaceuticals and Medical Products Practice (EMEA) McKinsey & Co, currently managing ptnr (UK and I) McKinsey & Co; chair Cncl CBI London; memb Bd: Henry Smith Charity, Action on Addiction, Br American Business; memb Advsy Cncl Tate Modern; *Style*— Ms Vivian Hunt; ✉ McKinsey & Company, No. 1 Jermyn Street, London SW1Y 4UH

HUNT, William George; TD (1988, and Clasp 1994); s of late Frank Williams Hunt, TD, and late Mary Elizabeth Leyland Hunt, JP, *née* Orton; *b* 8 December 1946; *Educ* Liverpool Coll, Univ of Southampton (BA), Constance, Lausanne and Caen (Dip); *m* 26 Sept 1998, Michaela, da of Werner Wedel; 2 s; *Career* mentor Salem Sch 1967–69, audit mangr Arthur Young McClelland Moores 1970–83, fin controller and partnership sec Frere Cholmeley 1983–92, fin dir Hopkins & Wood 1993–95; Portcullis Pursuivant of Arms 1992–99, Windsor Herald of Arms 1999–; registrar Coll of Arms 2007–14, genealogist Order of St John 2010–; clerk HM Cmmn of Lieutenancy for the City of London 1990–2013, one of HM Lts for the City of London 2012–; dir Heraldry Soc 1997–2006 and 2016–; Maj and memb Ct of Assts HAC 1988–2000, treas HAC Biographical Dictionary (1537–1914) Tst 1993–; dep clerk City Livery Club 1998–2003 (clerk 1996–98), memb Ct of Common Cncl City of London 2004–13, memb RFCA 1990, exec memb City of London Assoc 2007–15; fndr memb Soc of Young Freemen of the City of London (treas 1976–78, chm 1978–79); govr City of London Sch 2009–13; Freeman City of London, Master Worshipful Co of Makers of Playing Cards 2000–01 (memb Ct of Assts 1996–); FCA; SBStJ 1999, CStJ 2011; *Books* Guide to the Honourable Artillery Company (1987), Dictionary of British Arms vol I (asst ed, 1992); *Recreations* orders and decorations; *Style*— William Hunt, Esq, TD*, Windsor Herald; ✉ College of Arms, 130 Queen Victoria Street, London EC4V 4BT (☎ 020 7329 8755)

HUNT OF CHESTERTON, Baron (Life Peer UK 2000), of Chesterton in the County of Cambridgeshire; Prof Julian Charles Roland Hunt; CB (1998); s of Roland Charles Colin Hunt, CMG (d 1999), and Pauline, *née* Garnett (d 1989); *b* 5 September 1941; *Educ* Westminster, Trinity Coll Cambridge (BA, PhD); *m* 1965, Marylla, *née* Shephard; 3 c (Jemima, Matilda, Tristram); *Career* res offr Fluid Dynamics Section Central Electricity Res Laboratories 1968–70; Univ of Cambridge: lectr in applied mathematics and engrg 1970–78, reader in fluid mechanics 1978, prof of fluid mechanics 1990–91, hon prof 1992–; chief exec Meteorological Office 1992–97, prof Arizona State Univ 1997–98 and 2007–, sr research fell Trinity Coll Cambridge 1998–99, visiting prof Delft Univ of Technol 1998–, prof of climate modelling UCL 1999–2008, dir Lighthill Inst for Mathematical Sciences UCL and Univ of London 2003–06; pt/t lectr in fluid mechanics Lanchester Coll of Technol 1965, visiting lectr Univ of Cape Town 1967, res assoc Dept of Theoretical and Applied Mechanics Cornell Univ 1967, teaching fell Trinity Coll Cambridge 1970 (res fell 1966), visiting prof Dept of Civil Engrg Colorado State Univ 1975, visiting assoc prof Dept of Geosciences N Carolina State Univ 1977–79, visiting scientist CIRES Univ of Colorado Boulder 1980–86, memb UK Atmospheric Dispersion Working Gp 1980, visiting scientist Nat Center for Atmospheric Res Boulder Colorado 1983, distinguished visiting prof Hong Kong Univ 2011–14, visiting fell Malaysian Cwlth Studies Centre Univ of Cambridge 2008–; asst (later assoc) ed Jl of Fluid Mechanics 1978–99; Inst of Mathematics and its Applications: chm Environmental Mathematics Gp 1978, hon sec and chm Prog Ctee and memb Cncl Fin and Gen Purposes Ctees 1983–, chair Prog Ctee of Int Congress of Industrial and Applied Mathematics 1986–, pres 1993–95; visiting lectr and res advsr Indian Inst of Technol Delhi 1984 and 1986, chm Turbulence Sub-Ctee Euro Mechanics Ctee 1984–92, memb Advsy Panel on Environmental Research Central Electricity Generating Bd 1985–91, visiting scientist Stanford Univ and NASA Ames 1987–90, gen sec Euro Res Community for Flow Turbulence and Combustion 1988 (chm Steering Ctee 1987–88), visiting scientist Japanese Soc for Visiting Scholars 1988; chm Cambridge Environmental Research Consultants Ltd 2000– (dir 1986–91), memb Stakeholder Advsy Gp EDF Energy 2006–08; cncllr Cambridge City Cncl 1971–74 (ldr Lab Gp 1972–73); memb House of Lords Select Ctees on: Animals in Scientific Procedures, Int Treaties in Sci, EU and Climate Change, the Arctic; vice-pres Globe All Pty Parly Gp 2007–, memb House of Lords Pre-legislative Ctee for Marine Environment Bill 2008; govr: Chesterton Secdy Sch 1971–85 (chm 1979–85), Westminster Sch 2003–; L F Richardson medal Euro Geophysics Soc 2001; Hon Dr: Univ of Salford, Univ of Bath, UEA, Univ of Warwick, Univ of Grenoble, Univ of Uppsala, Western Univ Canada; tstee RI 2012; FRS 1989, Hon FIMA 2003, Hon FICE 2004; *Style*— The Lord Hunt of Chesterton, CB, FRS; ✉ Department of Earth Sciences, University College London, Gower Street, London WC1E 6BT

HUNT OF KINGS HEATH, Baron (Life Peer UK 1997), of Birmingham in the County of West Midlands; Philip Alexander Hunt; OBE, PC (2009); *b* 19 May 1949; *Educ* City of Oxford HS, Univ of Leeds (BA); *m* 1, 1974 (m dis); 1 da; m 2, 1988, Selina Ruth Helen, da of Prof John Stewart, *qv*; 3 s, 1 da; *Career* catering asst Mount Newman W Aust 1971–72, work study offr Oxford RHB 1972–74, hosp admin Nuffield Orthopaedic Centre 1974–75, sec Edgware/Hendon Community Health Cncl 1975–78; National Association of Health Authorities: asst sec 1978–79, asst dir 1979–84, dir 1984–90; dir National Association of Health Authorities and Trusts 1990–97, chief exec NHS Confedn 1997; Lord in Waiting (Govt whip) 1998–99, Parly under sec of state for health 1999–2003, Parly under sec of state Dept for Work and Pensions 2005–07, min of state Dept of Health 2007, Parly sec of state Miny of Justice 2007–08, min of state DEFRA and Dept of Energy and Climate Change 2008–09, dep ldr House of Lords 2008–10, min of state Dept of Energy and Climate Change 2009–10, shadow dep ldr House of Lords 2010–, oppn home affrs spokesman 2010–; co-chair Assoc for Public Health 1994–97 (memb Cncl 1992–94), chair Nat Patient Safety Agy 2004–, chm Heart of England NHS Fndn Tst 2011–; pres Family Planning Assoc 1997–98; memb: Oxford City Cncl 1973–79, Oxon AHA 1975–77, Bd Volunteer Centre 1979–83, Birmingham City Cncl 1980–82, Home Office Devpt Gp on Voluntary Action 1980–82, Cncl Flouridation Soc 1981–93, Nat Advsy Ctee World Assembly on Ageing 1981–83, Cncl Int Hosp Fedn 1986–91, NHS Exec Advsy Gp on Patient's Charter 1992–93, Working Gp on Induction and Devpt of Chm and Bd Dirs NHS Exec 1993–94, Rail Users' Consultative Ctee (Midlands) 1994, External Advsy Study of Probity in the NHS Audit Cmmn 1994; *Publications* The Authority Member (with W E Hall, 1978), The Quango Debate (contrib), various articles in Health Service pubns (incl regular column in Health Services Jl); *Recreations* City of Birmingham Symphony Orchestra, cycling, swimming, football (Birmingham City), cricket (Warks CCC); *Style*— The Rt Hon the Lord Hunt of Kings Heath, OBE; ✉ House of Lords, London SW1A 0PW

HUNT OF WIRRAL, Baron (Life Peer UK 1997), of Wirral in the County of Merseyside; Rt Hon David James Fletcher Hunt; MBE (1973), PC (1990); s of late Alan Hunt, OBE; *b* 21 May 1942; *Educ* Liverpool Coll, Montpellier Univ, Univ of Bristol, Guildford Coll of Law; *m* 1973, Patricia Margery (Paddy), *née* Orchard; 2 s, 2 da; *Career* slr; Beachcroft Wansbroughs (now DAC Beachcroft LLP): ptnr (also in predecessor firms) 1968–, sr ptnr 1996–2005, chm Financial Servs Div 2005–; chm YC Nat Advsy Ctee 1972–73, vice-chm Nat Union of Cons and Unionist Assocs 1974–76, oppn spokesman on shipping 1977–79, vice-chm Parly Youth Lobby 1978–80, pres Br Youth Cncl 1978–81 (chm 1971–74), chm Cons Gp for Europe 1981–82; MP (Cons): Wirral 1976–83, Wirral W 1983–97 (Parly candidate: Bristol S 1970, Kingswood 1974); PPS to: Trade Sec 1979–81, Def Sec 1981; jr Cons whip 1981–83, a Lord Cmmr of the Treasy (govt whip) 1983–84, vice-chm Cons Party 1983–85, Parly under-sec of state Dept of Energy 1984–87, treas HM Household (dep Govt chief whip) 1987–89, min for Local Govt and Inner Cities 1989–90, sec of state for Wales 1990–93, sec of state for Employment 1993–94, Chancellor of the Duchy of Lancaster (with responsibility for Public Service and Science) 1994–95, shadow min for business, enterprise and regulatory reform 2008–10; chair Press Compaints Cmmn 2011–14; pres Tory Reform Gp 1991–97, pres All-Pty Parly Gp on Occupational Safety and Health 1999–; chair Lending Standards Bd 2011–; pres CMS UK 2005– (chm 2001–05); dir Slrs Indemnity Mutual Insurance Assoc Ltd 2000–06, chm Assoc of Ind Fin Advsrs 2000–03, pres CII 2007–08 (dep pres 2006–07, chm Professional Standards Bd 2004–06), chm McDonald's Educn Co Ltd 2009–, chm Br Insurance Brokers' Assoc 2014–; memb Cncl CBI; govr and chm ESU 2006–11 (dep chm 1999–2006); vice-pres Holocaust Educnl Tst 2011– (tstee 1998–2011); churchwarden Parish St Mary Magdalene Chewton Mendip 2007–14; *Recreations* football, cricket, walking; *Clubs* Hurlingham, Rotary; *Style*— The Rt Hon the Lord Hunt of Wirral, MBE, PC; ✉ DAC Beachcroft LLP, 100 Fetter Lane, London EC4A 1BN (☎ 020 7242 1011, fax 020 7894 6240, e-mail lordhunt@dacbeachcroft.com)

HUNT-DAVIS, Brig Sir Miles Garth; GCVO 2010 (KCVO 2003, CVO 1998), CBE (1990, MBE 1977); 2 s of Lt-Col Eric Hunt Davis, OBE, ED (d 1977), of Johannesburg, South Africa, and Mary Eleanor Turnbull, *née* Boyce (d 1964); *b* 7 November 1938; *Educ* St Andrew's Coll Grahamstown; *m* 11 Jan 1965, (Anita) Gay, da of Francis James Ridsdale; 1 da (Joanna b 2 June 1968), 2 s (Justin b 11 Sept 1970, Benedict b 15 March 1972); *Career* cmmnd 6 Queen Elizabeth's Own Gurkha Rifles 1962, active serv Borneo and Malaya 1964–66, student Canadian Land Forces Cmd and Staff Coll 1969–70, Brig Maj 48 Gurkha Infantry Brigade 1974–76, Cmdt 7 Duke of Edinburgh's Own Gurkha Rifles 1976–79, Instr Staff Coll Camberley 1982–83; Cdr: Br Gurkhas Nepal 1985–87, Bde of Gurkhas 1987–90 (ret 1991); private sec and treas to HRH The Prince Philip, Duke of Edinburgh 1991–10 (asst private sec 1991–92, private sec 1993–2010), Col 7 Duke of Edinburgh's Own Gurkha Rifles 1991–94; chm Gurkha Brigade Assoc 1991–2003; govr Sutton's Hosp at Charterhouse 2009–13; yr bro Trinity House 2004; Hon MA Univ of Cambridge 2009, hon doctorate Univ of Edinburgh 2010; *Clubs* RSA; *Style*— Brig Sir Miles Hunt-Davis, GCVO, CBE; ✉ 25 Pound Street, Warminster, Wiltshire BA12 8NL (☎ 01985 216445)

HUNTER, Andrew Reid; s of John Horatio Hunter, and Irene, *née* Fish; *b* 28 September 1958, Nairobi, Kenya; *Educ* Kenton Coll Nairobi, Aldenham Sch Herts, St Luke's Coll Exeter (BEd), Univ of Manchester (BA), Manchester Poly (PGCE); *m* 22 Aug 1981, Barbara Gandy, *née* Bradford; 2 s (Edward, Oliver), 1 da (Laura); *Career* gap teacher Westbrook Hay Prep Sch Herts 1978–79, Worksop Coll Notts 1983–91, English and religious studies teacher Bradfield Coll Berks 1991–98, headmaster Merchiston Castle Sch Edinburgh 1998–; govr: Ardvreck Prep Sch Crieff 2008–, Laidlaw Schools Tst (formerly Excelsior Acad) Newcastle-upon-Tyne 2009–; advsy bd Springboard Bursary Fdn 2012–; *Recreations* reading, cinema, travel, sport (spectator these days), international cuisine and culture; *Clubs* New (Edinburgh), Nottingham Hockey (vice-pres), Western (Glasgow); *Style*— Andrew Hunter, Esq; ✉ Merchiston Castle School, Colinton Road, Edinburgh EH13 0PU (☎ 0131 312 2202)

HUNTER, Dr Anthony Rex (Tony); s of late Ranulph Rex Hunter, and Nellie Ruby Elsie, *née* Hitchcock (d 2014); *b* 23 August 1943, Ashford, Kent; *Educ* Felsted, Gonville & Caius Coll Cambridge (MA, PhD); *m* 1, 1969 (m dis 1974), Philippa Charlotte Marrack; m 2, 1992, Jennifer Ann Maureen Price; 2 s (Sean Alexander Brocas Price Hunter b 17 Dec 1990, James Samuel Alan Hunter b 21 Dec 1996); *Career* research fell Christ's Coll Cambridge 1968–71 and 1973–75; Salk Inst La Jolla California: research assoc 1971–73, asst prof 1975–78, assoc prof 1978–82, prof 1982–, dir Salk Inst Cancer Center 2008–16; adjunct prof Univ of Calif San Diego 1983– (adjunct assoc prof 1979–83), research prof American Cancer Soc 1992–2008, Renato Dulbecco chair in cancer research 2011–, Einstein prof Chinese Acad of Sciences 2013, hon fell Christ's Coll Cambridge 2016; memb Editorial Bd: Molecular and Cellular Biology 1982–88 (ed 1989–93), Jl of Virology 1982–98, Molecular Endocrinology 1987–91, Cancer Cells 1989–91, Current Biology 1991–2001, Jl of Cell Biology 1997–2003; assoc ed: Cell 1980–, Virology 1982–93, Molecular Biology of the Cell 1996–2004, Molecular Cell 1997–, Proceedings Nat Acad of Sci 1999–, EMBO Jl 1999–, eLife 2012–; Thomson-Reuters Citation Laureate 2012; Einstein prof Chinese Acad of Sciences 2013; author of over 500 scientific pubns; memb Melbourne Branch Ludwig Inst for Cancer Research Scientific Review Ctee 1983–96, memb Sci Advsy Bd Burnham Inst 1984–2009, Scientific Advsy Bd Sanford-Burnham-Prebys Medical Discovery Inst (formerly Sanford-Burnham Medical Research Inst) Cancer Center 2003– (chair 2011–); vice-chm Animal Cells and Viruses Gordon Conf 1988; dir Fndn for Advanced Cancer Studies 1989–2014; memb: Advsy Ctee Frederick Cancer Research Facility 1985–89, Scientific Review Bd Howard Hughes Med Inst 1989–97 and 2003–06, Ciba Novartis Fndn Scientific Advsy Panel 1994–2007, Bd Scientific Counselors Nat Cancer Inst 1996–99, Med Advsy Bd Howard Hughes Med Inst 1999–2002, Bd of Scientific Advsrs Van Andel Research Inst 1999–, Vollum Inst 2000–02, Biology Panel AAAS Project 2061, External Advsy Bd Beth Israel Deaconess Cancer Center 2008–13; assoc memb European Molecular Biology Orgn 1992; foreign assoc National Acad of Scis (USA) 1998, memb Nat Acad of Med (formerly Inst of Med) 2004–; American Business Fndn for Cancer Research Award 1988, Katharine Berkan Judd Award, Meml Sloan-Kettering Cancer Center 1992, General Motors Cancer Research Fndn Mott Prize 1994, Gairdner Fndn International Award 1994, Biochemical Soc Hopkins Meml Medal 1994, Bristol-Myers Squibb Cancer Grant Award 1997, Feodor Lynen Medal 1999, J Allyn Taylor Int Prize in Med 2000, Keio Med Sci Prize 2001, Sergio Lombroso Award in Cancer Research 2003, Medal of Honour American Cancer Soc 2004, Kirk A Landon American Assoc for Cancer Research Prize 2004, Louisa Gross Horowitz Prize 2004, Wolf Prize in Med 2005, Daniel Nathans Meml Award 2005, Pasarow Award in Cancer Research 2006, Clifford Prize for Cancer Research 2007, ASBMB Herbert Tabor Award 2007, Benvenuto Meml Award 2009, Signal Transduction Soc Honorary Medal 2011, Thompson Reuters Citation Laureate 2012, Royal Medal Royal Soc of London 2014, BBVA Fndn Frontiers of Knowledge Biomedicine Award 2014; memb American Philosophical Soc 2006; FRS 1987, FRSA 1989, FAAAS 1992, fell American Assoc for Cancer Research Acad 2013; *Publications* Signal Transduction: Principles, Pathways and Processes (ed, with Lewis C Cantley, Richard Sever and Jeremy Thorner 2014); *Recreations* white water rafting, exploring Baja peninsula; *Style*— Dr Tony Hunter, FRS; ✉ Molecular and Cell Biology Laboratory, The Salk Institute,10010 North Torrey Pines Road, La Jolla, California, USA (☎ 00 1 858 453 4100, fax 00 1 858 457 4765, e-mail hunter@salk.edu, websites pingu.salk.edu/hunter and www.salk.edu/faculty/hunter)

HUNTER, Archibald Sinclair (Archie); DL (Renfrewshire, 1995); s of John Lockhart Hunter (d 1986), and Elizabeth Hastings, *née* Sinclair (d 1998); *b* 20 August 1943, Glasgow; *Educ* Queens' Park Sch Glasgow; *m* 6 March 1969, Patricia Ann; 1 da (Claire Patricia b 4 Feb 1973), 2 s (Stephen John b 4 July 1974, Craig Robertson b 25 Oct 1977); *Career* CA Mackie & Clark Glasgow 1966; Thomson McLintock: joined 1966, ptnr 1974, managing ptnr Glasgow Office 1983; KPMG: managing ptnr 1987, Scottish sr ptnr 1992–99, memb UK Bd 1992–96; memb Bd: Macfarlane Group plc 1998–2012 (chm 2003–12), Clydeport plc 1999–2003, North American Income Tst (formerly Edinburgh US Tracker Tst) 2003–, Royal Bank of Scotland 2004–10, The Beatson Inst for Cancer Res; treas Scottish Cancer Fndn 2005–; Chm of Ct Univ of Strathclyde 2002–07; pres ICAS 1997–98; Hon Dr Univ of Strathclyde 2006; fell Univ of Strathclyde 2008; *Recreations* golf, swimming, hill walking; *Clubs* Williamwood Golf (former capt), Western Gailes Golf; *Style*— A S Hunter, Esq; ✉ ASH Business Services, 21 Newton Place, Glasgow G3 7PY

HUNTER, Dr Colin M; OBE (2000); s of Robert S Hunter (d 2002), and Elizabeth G, *née* Moffat; *b* 28 April 1958, Stirling; *Educ* HS of Stirling, Univ of Aberdeen (MB ChB); *m* 9 Sep 2000, Fiona S, *née* McKenzie; 1 da (Joanne b 6 Dec 1981), 1 s (Rory b 5 June 1984); *Career* princ gen medical practitioner Skene Med Gp 1986–; chm RCGP Scot 1996–2000, chair of tstees RCGP (UK) 2012– (hon treas 2003–12); nat coordinator primary care NHS Educn for Scot 1999–2005; Marinker Prize for Innovation in Primary Care 2000; memb: BMA 1981, RCGP Scot 1986; hon fell IHM 1996, FRCPEd 2000; *Recreations* singing, hill walking; *Style*— Dr Colin Hunter, OBE; ✉ 1 Craigston Gardens, Westhill, Aberdeenshire AB32 6NL; Skene Medical Group, Discovery Drive, Westhill, Aberdeenshire, AB32 6FG (☎ 01224 849400, e-mail colin.hunter@nhs.net)

HUNTER, Ian Gerald Adamson; QC (1980); s of Gerald Oliver Hunter (d 1995), and June, *née* Brown (d 1979); *b* 3 October 1944; *Educ* Reading Sch, Pembroke Coll Cambridge (open scholar, Squire Univ law scholar, Trevelyan scholar, BA, MA, LLB), Harvard Law Sch (Kennedy Meml scholar, LLM); *m* 1, 22 March 1975 (m dis 1999), Maggie, da of Herbert Reed (d 1984); 2 s (James Elyot b 1977, Edward Iain b 1981); m 2, 8 July 2000, Jill van Vliet; *Career* called to the Bar Inner Temple 1967 (bencher 1986); sr counsel New South Wales 1994, avocat au barreau de Paris 1995–2010; Bar Cncl: memb Int Rels Ctee 1982–90, memb Exec Ctee 1985–86; chm Consolidated Regulations and Transfer Ctee Senate of the Inns of Court 1986–87; Union Internationale des Avocats: pres 1989–90, dir of studies 1990–91; pres Anglo-Australian Lawyers Soc 1997–, memb CPR Panel of Distinguished International Mediators 1996–; accredited mediator CEDR 1998, accredited arbitrator 1998; hon memb Canadian Bar Assoc 1990, treas Bar Pro Bono Unit 1995, vice-pres Franco-Br Lawyers Soc 1996, pres Anglo-Australasian Lawyers Soc 1998; FCIArb; *Recreations* be-bop, French cuisine; *Clubs* Boodle's; *Style*— Ian Hunter, Esq, QC; ✉ Essex Court Chambers, 24 Lincoln's Inn Fields, London WC2A 3ED (☎ 020 7813 8000, fax 020 7813 8080)

HUNTER, Ian William; s of William Gurnham Hunter, and Anna-Maria, *née* Faliescewska; *b* 17 March 1955, London; *Educ* Alleyn's Sch Dulwich, Univ of Surrey; *m* 1, 8 Nov 1986, Susan, da of James Edward Morris; m 2, 7 July 2006, Davina, da of Michael Lester; 1 s (Oscar b 2 Jan 2009 (twin)), 1 da (Tallulah b 2 Jan 2009 (twin)); *Career* economist Bank of England 1975–79, fund mangr Swiss Bank Corp 1979–81, sr investment mangr Lazard Bros 1981–87, exec dir Far E div Midland Montagu Asset Mgmnt 1987–92, dir Martin Currie Investment Management 1992–94, dep md Daishin International (Europe) Ltd 1994–98, exec dir LG Securities Ltd 1998–99, dir and head of North Asian sales Nomura International plc 1999–2003, dir and head of sales LG Securites/Woori Investment Bank 2004–07, chief investment offr active strategies Sabre Fund Mgmnt 2007–08, chief investment offr Westhall Capital Mgmnt 2009–10, investment dir Fabien Pictet Ptnrs Asset Mgmnt 2010–; MSI, ACA; *Recreations* skiing, motor racing, cinema, music, opera, tennis, travel; *Clubs* 190, AMOC; *Style*— Ian Hunter, Esq; ✉ Lagness, 31 Keswick Road, London SW15 2JA (e-mail ianwilliamhunter@hotmail.com)

HUNTER, Prof John Angus Alexander; OBE (1997); s of Dr John Craig Alexander Hunter (d 1992), of Holbeach, Lincs, and Alison Hay Shand, *née* Alexander, MBE (d 1998); *b* 16 June 1939; *Educ* Loretto, Pembroke Coll Cambridge (BA), Univ of Edinburgh (MB ChB, MD); *m* 26 Oct 1968, Ruth Mary, da of Douglas Verdun Farrow (d 1998), of Spalding, Lincs; 2 da (Rebecca Jean Alexander b 13 Sept 1970, Abigail Ruth Alexander b 24 Jan 1972), 1 s (Hamish John Alexander b 2 July 1973); *Career* med posts: Royal Infirmary Edinburgh, Inst of Dermatology London 1967, Univ of Minnesota 1968–69; Grant prof of dermatology Univ of Edinburgh 1981–99 (ret), prof emeritus Univ of Edinburgh 2000–; author dermatological papers in scientific jls; memb Med Appeal Tbnl 1981–89; memb: BMA, Assoc of Physicians of GB and Ireland, Br Assoc of Dermatologists (pres 1998–99), Scottish Dermatological Soc (pres 1994–96); FRSM, FRCPE 1978; *Books* Common Diseases of the Skin (jtly, 1983), Clinical Dermatology (jtly, 1989, latest edn 2008), Skin Signs in Clinical Medicine (jtly, 1996), Davidson's Principles and Practice of Medicine (jtly, 1999, latest edn 2006), Davidson's 100 Clinical Cases (jtly, 2008, latest edn 2012); *Recreations* gardening, music, golf; *Clubs* Hon Co of Edinburgh Golfers, Hawks' (Cambridge); *Style*— Prof John Hunter, OBE; ✉ Sandy Lodge, Nisbet Road, Gullane, East Lothian EH31 2BQ (☎ 01620 842 220, e-mail jaa.hunter@virgin.net)

HUNTER, John Garvin; CB (2004); s of Garvin Hunter (d 1970), and Martha, *née* McCracken (d 1976); *b* 9 August 1947; *Educ* Merchant Taylors', Queen's Univ Belfast (BA), Cornell Univ (MBA); *m* 20 March 1976, Rosemary Alison, *née* Haire; 2 da (Laurie Helen b 8 July 1979, Fiona Aileen b 14 May 1983), 1 s (Michael Garvin b 18 June 1981); *Career* asst princ N Ireland Office 1970–72, dep princ DHSS 1972–77, Harkness fell Cornell Univ 1977–79; asst sec: DHSS 1982–86 (princ offr 1979–82), Dept of Fin and Personnel 1986–89; dir General International Fund for Ireland 1987–89, under sec DHSS 1989–90, chief exec Health and Personal Social Servs Mgmnt Exec 1990–96, dir of personnel NI Civil Service 1997–99; perm sec Dept for Social Devpt 1999–2003, perm sec Dept for Finance and Personnel 2003–07; chair Chief Executives' Forum 2008–14; pro-chllr Ulster Univ 2015; *Recreations* singing, camping, hill walking; *Style*— John Hunter, Esq, CB

HUNTER, Kathryn; née Aikaterini Hadjipateras; *b* 1957, NY; *Educ* RADA; *m* Marcello Magni; *Career* actress and dir; assoc RADA, artistic asst RSC 2008; *Theatre* as actress incl: The Visit (Olivier Award 1990), King Lear, Richard III (The Globe) 2003, The Bee (Soho Theatre) 2006, Fragments (int tour), Kafka's Monkey (Young Vic) 2009; dir Othello (Warwick Arts Centre, Hackney Empire, Northern Stage, Oxford Playhouse and Liverpool Playhouse) 2009; *Television* incl Rome; *Film* incl: All or Nothing 2002, Harry Potter and the Order of the Phoenix 2007; *Style*— Ms Kathryn Hunter

HUNTER, Prof Sir Laurence Colvin; kt (1995), CBE (1987); s of late Laurence O Hunter, and late Jessie P, *née* Colvin; *b* 8 August 1934; *Educ* Hillhead HS Glasgow, Univ of Glasgow (MA), UC Oxford (DPhil); *m* 1958, Evelyn Margaret, *née* Green; 3 s (David Stuart b 1962, Niall Laurence b 1964, Martin Alan b 1967), 1 da (Jennifer Ann b 1973); *Career* asst lectr Univ of Manchester 1958–59; 2 Lt RAEC Nat Serv 1959–61; Walgreen post doctoral fell Univ of Chicago 1961–62; Univ of Glasgow: lectr 1962–66, sr lectr 1966–70, prof of applied economics 1970–2003, vice-princ 1982–86, dir of external relations 1987–92, dir Business Sch 1996–99, emeritus prof and hon sr research fell; treas Royal Soc of Edinburgh 1999–2004; visiting prof: Industry and Labour Relations Sch Cornell Univ 1973, Univ of Melbourne 2002 and 2004; memb: Cncl ACAS 1974–86, Scottish Economic Soc (pres 1993–96); chm Police Negotiating Bd 1986–2000 (dep chm 1979–86), ed Scottish Jl of Political Economy 1966–97; Hon DUniv Paisley 1999; FRSE, FRSA; *Recreations* golf, painting; *Style*— Prof Sir Laurence Hunter, CBE, FRSE; ✉ (e-mail l.c.hunter@ntlworld.com)

HUNTER, Margaret Steele; da of Thomas Hunter (d 2001), of Irvine, Ayrshire, and Norma, *née* Botley (d 1986); *b* 20 January 1948; *Educ* Irvine Royal Acad, James Watt Coll, Glasgow Sch of Art (1981–85), Hochschule der Künste Berlin (1985–87); *m* 1, 1969 (m dis 1982); 1 s (Thomas b 1969), 1 da (Alana b 1970); m 2, Joachim Gross (d 2003); partner Roger Webb; *Career* artist; drawing office tracer/jr draughtswoman Skefko Ball Bearing Co 1964–68, masterclass Edinburgh Coll of Art Summer Sch 1996–2000; memb: Berufsverband bildender Künstler Berlins eV, Brandenburgischer Verband bildender Künstlerinnen und Künstler eV, Atelierhaus Panzerhalle eV, Artists Initiative East Side Gallery eV; patron Edinburgh Sculpture Workshop; *Solo Exhibitions* incl: Rozelle House Gallery Ayr 1986, Berlin-Scotland-Transfer (Galerie IX Atelier) 1988, 369 Gallery Edinburgh 1988, Vanessa Devereux Gallery London 1988, touring exhbn (Maclaurin Gallery Ayr, 369 Gallery, Vanessa Devereux Gallery) 1990, Deutsche Industrie Bank Berlin 1990, touring exhbn Changing Places (Collins Gallery Univ of Strathclyde, Galerie M Berlin, Talbot Rice Gallery Univ of Edinburgh, Kunstverein Weinheim Germany, Vanessa Devereux London, Darlington Art Centre) 1992–93, Scratching the Surface (Rebecca Hossack Gallery) 1994, Portal Gallery Bremen 1995, Signs of Life (Art First London) 1995, Between the Lines (ATP-Expo 2000 Hanover) 1996, Vital Patterns (Art First, London) 1998, Tangents (International Cultural Centre, Cracow, Poland) 1998, Jean Bauscher's Vineyard Germany 1999, 10th Anniversary of the Fall of the Berlin Wall (Pentagon Centre Glasgow) 1999, Elemental Traces (Art First London) 2000, Paintings and Sculptures (Galerie im Gerstenboden, Hof, Germany), Holding Together (Paisley Museums and Art Gallery) 2001, Intercessions (Stathclyde Univ Glasgow, cat) 2001, Natural Adaptations (Art First NY) 2002, Lines of Continuity (Art First London) 2002, Malerei and Grafik (Kronacher Kunstverein eV Kronach Germany) 2003, Intonations (Art First London) 2004, Thinking Through the Body (Galerie der Umweltbundesamt Berlin) 2004, Paintings and Sculptures (Galerie Wichtendahl) 2006, Exerpts (Remise DEGEWO) 2006, Bunch of Person (Art First London) 2006, Atachments (Wichtenahl Galerie Berlin) 2008, Awaiting (Art First London) 2009, re:STATEMENT (Galerie aquabitART Berlin) 2011, Ports of Call (Sa Taronja Mallorca) 2013, Stepping Places (Art First London) 2013; *Group Exhibitions* incl: Art in Exile (Mackintosh Museum Glasgow Sch of Art) 1987, The Franciscan Monastery Przemysl Poland 1988, jt venture at East Side Gallery painted on remainder of Berlin Wall 1990, Scottish Art Since 1900 (Scottish Nat Gallery of Modern Art and Barbican London) 1989–90, EAST Nat Open Art Expdn Norwich 1991, Festival Fourteen – Scottish Women Artists Exhbn (Dunfermline Museum) 1992, Through Women's Eyes (City Art Centre Edinburgh) 1992–93, Pendant Perdu (Gallery Dr Christiane Muller Berlin), Thursday's Child (Roger Billcliffe Gallery Glasgow) 1994, Paths of the Spirit The Artist as Shaman (Isis Gallery Leigh-on-Sea) 1995, The Continuing Tradition 75 Years of Painting at Glasgow Sch of Art 1920–95 (GSA Glasgow) 1995, Ausländische Kunstlerinnen in Berlin (Rote Rathaus Alexander Platz Berlin) 1997, REPERCUSSIONS – German Identities, Elastic Borders (Axiom Centre for the Arts Int Festival of Music Cheltenham) 1997, Ein Schöner Blick in dieser Zeit (Panzerhalle, Gross Glienicke, Germany) 1997, Great Britain in Brandenburg (Galerie Bauscher, Potsdam, Germany) 1997, Back to Nyk (Goethe Institute, Helsinki and the Gallery of Modern Art, Vaasa, Finland) 1998, Footsteps (initiated and coordinated artists exchange between Berlin Brandenburg and Scotland, Panzerhalle Gross Glienicke, Germany) 1998, 7 dones am Kunstmann (Galeria d'Art Joanna Kunstmann Santanyi, Mallorca) 1998, Restoration of Joint Venture (East Side Gallery on remaining part of the Berlin Wall) 2000, Bodies of Substance (Talbot Rice Gallery Univ of Edinburgh, cat) 2002, Skulptur Pur (Panzerhalle Gross Glinicke Germany) 2002, Between the 3rd and the 5th (Universitaet der Kuenste Berlin) 2002, Blue Hall Marktplatz Europa (Kunsthalle Arnstadt Gernamy), Sektor Panzerhalle (Atelier Panzerhalle Gross Glienicke Germany) 2005, Neue Mitglieder 2005 (BVBK Postdam) 2005, 12 x 12 Gallery Artists (Art First London) 2005, Scots Abroad (Open Eye Gallery Edinburgh) 2006, Thirty by Thirty (MacLaurin Gallery Ayr) 2006, Summer Exhibition Millstream Sculpture Garden 2008, Der Fixiete Augenblick (Produzentengalerie M Potsdam) 2009, Der Geschmack von Wolken (Der Kunstraum Postdam) 2009, invited artist RSA 184th Annual 2010, Fleming-Wyfold Fndn 10th Anniversary Summer Exhbn Fleming Gallery London 2010, JUST FAIR Gallery Weekend Berlin (aquabitArt und WHITECONCEPTS) 2014; *Public Collections* Scottish Nat Gallery of Modern Art Edinburgh, Graphothek Kunstamt Charlottenburg Berlin, Scottish Arts Cncl, Städtische Kunstsammlung Görlitz Germany, Niederschlesische Sparkasse Görlitz Germany, Univ of Strathclyde, Robert Fleming plc London, Harry and Margery Bosswell Art Collection, Beriner Hypo-Pfandbrief Bank AG Berlin, Chelsea and Westminster Hosp London, Evangelische Gesundbrunnen eV Steinbach Germany, Marienstift Arnstadt Germany, Hengeler Mueller Berlin Germany, St George's Hosp Tst London, The Fleming Wyfold Art Collection London, Duncan of Jordonstone Sch of Art Dundee, Paisley Museum and Art Gallery, Carla and Hugo Brown Collection, Univ of Stirling; *Awards and Residencies* Cargill Travel Scholarship 1985, Scottish Int Educn Tst 1985, Wilforge Fndn 1985, American Express Travel Prize 1985, Artists Bursary Scottish Arts Cncl 1987, prizewinner for painting exhbn Franciscan Monastery Przemysl Poland 1988, scholarship The Karl Hofer Gesellschaft Berlin 1993, artist-in-residence The Swedish Sch of Art Vaasa Finland 1997, artist-in-residence Atelier de Nigorra, Santanyi, Mallorca 1998, winner Arts Category European Woman of Achievement European Union of Women 1998, sculpture residency Lorbottle Hall Northumberland 2001, 2006 and 2008, ceramics summer workshop Verein Gebrannte Erde e V Glindow Germany 2002, Kunstbuch-Buchkunst artists and writers collaboration Brigitte-Reimann-Literaturhaus Neubrandenburg; *Publications* Changing Places (1992), Scratching the Surface (1994), Margaret Hunter (1998), Vital Patterns (1998), Elemental Traces (2000), Intercessions (2001), Lines of Continuity (2002), Bunch of Person (2006); *Style*— Ms Margaret Hunter; ✉ 22 Castlepark Drive, Fairlie, Largs KA29 0DF (☎ 01475 568861 or 00 49 30 302 7354, e-mail margaret.hunter@gmx.de, website www.margaret-hunter.com)

HUNTER, Mark James; s of Arthur Brian Hunter (d 2014), and Betty Elizabeth Mary Hunter (d 2009); *b* 25 July 1957, Manchester; *Educ* Audenshaw GS; *m* 25 July 1997, Lesley, *née* Graham (d 2013); 1 da (Francesca b 29 Aug 1987), 1 s (Robert b 10 June 1989); *Career* ldr Stockport Cncl 2002–05 (dep ldr 2001–02), MP (Lib Dem) Cheadle (by-election) 2005–15 (Parly candidate (Lib Dem) Stockport 2001), cncllr Stockport Cncl 2016–; Lib Dem spokesman on ODPM 2005–06, Lib Dem spokesman on home affrs 2006–07, Lib Dem dep shadow min for foreign affrs 2007–08, PPS to Lib Dem Ldr and Lib Dem Shadow Transport Min 2008–10, Lib Dem dep chief whip and Govt whip 2010–14, currently dep ldr Lib Dem Gp; involved with: Nat Tst, CAMRA, Amnesty Int; *Recreations* Manchester City FC, cinema, reading, travel, walking; *Style*— Mark Hunter, Esq; ✉ 7 Hillbury Road, Bramhall, Stockport SK7 3AF (0161 439 1870, e-mail mark.hunter2507@yahoo.co.uk)

HUNTER, Mark John; MBE (2009); s of Terence Hunter, and Joan, *née* Pye; *b* 1 July 1978, Forest Gate, London; *Educ* Bower Park Sch Havering, Havering Sixth Form Coll; *Career* rower; Bronze medal lightweight double sculls World Rowing Championships 2007, Gold medal lightweight double sculls Olympic Games Beijing 2008, lightweight double scull world champion 2010 and 2011, Silver medal lightweight double sculls Olympic Games London 2012; waterman and lighterman 2002–, Freeman of the Thames; *Clubs* Leander; *Style*— Mark Hunter, Esq, MBE; ✉ e-mail mark@markhuntergb.com, website www.markhuntergb.com, Twitter @markhuntergb

HUNTER, Prof (J) Martin Hugh; s of Colin Boorer Garrett Hunter (d 1958), of IOW, and Barbara Anne Crawford, *née* Cavendish (d 1962); *b* 23 March 1937; *Educ* Shrewsbury, Pembroke Coll Cambridge (MA), Coll of Law London; *m* 21 Jan 1972, Linda Mary, da of Francis Kenneth Ernest Gamble (d 1971); *Career* admitted slr 1964, ptnr Freshfields 1967–94 (asst slr 1964); called to the Bar Lincoln's Inn 1994, barr in private practice Essex Court Chambers 1994–; prof of int dispute resolution Nottingham Trent Univ 1995–2010 (emeritus prof 2015–); hon dean of postgraduate studies Asser Inst The Hague 1991–, hon visiting fell Faculty of Law Univ of Edinburgh 1992–; visiting prof: Victoria Univ of Wellington NZ 1999, KCL 2003– (hon prof 2015–), Univ of Miami Law Sch 2010–, Central European Univ 2008–; visiting lectr: Harvard Law Sch 2000, Columbia Law Sch 2003, Univ of Cologne Summer Acad 2003–11; chm Dubai Int Arbitration Centre 2004–, vice-chm DTI Ctee on Arbitration Law 1990–97; memb Editorial Bd: Arbitration

International 1985–1997, American Review of International Arbitration 1989–, International Arbitration Law Review 1998–, Vindebona Jl 1999–; memb: Int Cncl for Commercial Arbitration 1988–, London Court of Int Arbitration 1985–2003, Int C of C Court of Arbitration 1988–90; Freeman: City of London, Worshipful Co of Arbitrators; FCIArb; *Books* The Freshfields Guide to Arbitration and ADR Clauses in International Contracts (with others, 1991), Arbitration Title, Butterworths Encyclopedia of Forms & Precedents (ed), The Internationalisation of International Arbitration (ed with others, 1995), The English Arbitration Act 1996: Text and Notes (with Toby Landau, 1998), Arbitration Title, Halsbury's Laws of England (ed with Ben Pilling, 2003), Redfern & Hunter on International Commercial Arbitration (ed with others, 6 edn 2015); *Recreations* motor boat cruising, golf; *Clubs* Royal Cruising, Sunningdale Golf; *Style*— Prof Martin Hunter; ✉ Essex Court Chambers, 24 Lincoln's Inn Fields, London WC2A 3EG (☎ 020 7813 8000, fax 020 7813 8080); Nottingham Law School, Belgrave Centre, Chancer Street, Nottingham NG1 5LP

HUNTER, Prof Richard Lawrence; s of John Lawrence Hunter, and Ruth Munro Hunter; *b* 30 October 1953; *Educ* Cranbrook Sch Sydney, Univ of Sydney (BA, univ medal), Pembroke Coll Cambridge (PhD); *m*; 1 s (b 22 July 1985), 1 da (b 12 March 1988); *Career* pt/t lectr Univ of Sydney 1975, actg asst prof of classics Univ of Virginia 1979 and 1984, acad dir Univ of Calif Cambridge programme 1982–85; Pembroke Coll Cambridge: fell 1977–2001, dir of studies in classics 1979–99 (coll lectr in classics 1981–87), asst tutor 1985–87, tutor for admissions (arts and social sciences) 1987–93; Univ of Cambridge: actg dir of studies in classics Girton Coll 1982–83, 1986 and 1993–94 (coll lectr in classics 1982–87), univ lectr in classics 1987–97, actg dir of studies New Hall 1996 and 1999, reader in Greek and Latin lit 1997–2001, regius prof of Greek 2001–, fell Trinity Coll 2001–, chm Faculty Bd of Classics 2003–04, chm Sch of Arts and Humanities 2007–08; pres Cncl Aristotle Univ of Thessaloniki 2013–; visiting sr fell Cncl of the Humanities and Old Dominion fell in classics Princeton Univ 1991–92 and 2012, Brittingham visiting scholar Univ of Wisconsin 1998; T B L Webster meml lectr Stanford Univ 1999; jt ed Proceedings of the Cambridge Philological Soc 1985–93, ed Jl of Hellenic Studies 1995–2000, jt ed Cambridge Greek and Latin Classics 1999–; memb: Comitato Scientifico Materali e discussioni per l'analisi dei testi classici 1994–, Advsy Bd Hellenistica Groningana 1997–, Editorial Advsy Ctee and Mgmnt Ctee New Greek Lexicon Project 1998–, Comitato Scientifico Seminari Romani di Cultura Greca 1998–, Editorial Bd Cambridge Classical Studies 2001–; advsr in Greek lit and culture Int Visiting Ctee Centro de Estudos Clássicos Lisbon 1997–2003; memb Cncl Soc for the Promotion of Hellenic Studies 1980–82, 1989–91 and 1994–96, pres Classical Assoc Cambridge 1997–2002 (memb Cncl 1992–95, chair Jls Bd 2001–); jt sec Cambridge Greek Play Ctee 1987–95; memb Ctee Dover Fund 1995–; Hon PhD Univ of Thessaloniki; foreign fell Acad of Athens, fell Australian Acad of the Humanities, Premio Anassilaos Regio Calabria 2006; FBA; *Books* Eubulus: The Fragments (1983), A Study of Daphnis & Chloe (1983), The New Comedy of Greece and Rome (1985), Apollonius of Rhodes: Argonautica III (1989), The 'Argonautica' of Apollonius: literary studies (1993), Jason and the Golden Fleece (The Argonautica) (trans, 1993), Theocritus and the Archaeology of Greek Poetry (1996), Studies in Heliodorus (ed, 1998), Theocritus – A Selection (1999), Theocritus – Encomium of Ptolemy Philadelphus (2003), Tradition and Innovation in Hellenistic Poetry (jtly, 2004), Plato's Symposium (2004), The Hesiodic Catalogue of Women (ed, 2005), The Shadow of Callimachus (2006), On Coming After: Studies in Post-Classical Greek Literature and its Reception (2008), Critical Moments in Classical Literature (2009), Wandering Poets in Ancient Greek Culture (ed, 2009), Plutarch How to Study Poetry (jtly, 2011), Plato and the Traditions of Ancient Literature (2012), Hesiodic Voices (2014); author of numerous articles in learned jls; *Recreations* sport, travel; *Style*— Prof Richard Hunter; ✉ Trinity College, Cambridge CB2 1TQ (☎ 01223 338400, e-mail rlh10@cam.ac.uk)

HUNTER, Prof Robert; *b* Glasgow; *Educ* Univ of Glasgow (BSc, MB ChB, MD), Marine Biological Lab Mass USA; *m* Eleanor Campbell; 1 s, 1 da; *Career* registrar in psychiatry West Scotland Psychiatric Trg Scheme 1982–85, clinical research scientist MRC Brain Metabolism Unit Dept of Pharmacology Univ of Edinburgh 1985–90, conslt psychiatrist Gartnavel Royal Hosp Glasgow 1990– (clinical servs mangr 1992–95), dir R&D NHS Gtr Glasgow and Clyde 1995– (chair R&D Mgmnt Gp 2003–08), clinical dir Psychiatric Research Inst of Neuroscience Univ of Glasgow 2007–, chair Glasgow Biomedicine Regulatory Affrs Gp 2008–; hon prof of psychiatry Univ of Glasgow 2004–, hon sr research fell Faculty of Biomedical and Life Sciences Univ of Glasgow 2009–12, visiting prof Univ of Strathclyde Strathclyde Inst of Pharmacy and Biomedical Sciences 2010–; assoc R&D dir research governance Glasgow Biomedicine 2007–; research advsr Alzheimer's Scotland – Action on Dementia 1989–99, medical memb Mental Health Tbnl for Scotland 2013–; memb: various ctees RCPsych 1986–88, Working Gp on Mental Illness Clinical Resource and Audit Gp (CRAG) Scottish Office 1992–96, Panel Scot Health Advsy Service (SHAS) 1995–2002, Nat Projects Ctee CRAG 1997–98, Outcomes Measures in Mental Health Working Gp Scottish Exec 1997–2000, Clinical Effectiveness Sub-Gp CRAG 1998–2000, Mental Health Scoping Gp 1999–2000, Coll of Experts NHS R&D Nat Coordinating Centre for Health Technol Assessment 1999–, Scot R&D Dirs Gp 2000–, Examinations Bd RCPsych 2000–12, Exec Ctee Nat Assoc of Psychiatric Intensive Care Units 2002–04, NHS R&D Advsy Gp of Chief Scientist Office 2002–, Int Gp for the Devpt and Use of HoNOS (Health of the Nation Outcome Scales) RCPsych 2003–12, Scot Ethics Implementation Gp Chief Scientist Office 2006–10; chair Scot Mental Health Research Network Steering Gp 1999–2002, chair Working Gp to Review the Avon Mental Health Measure for NHS Quality Improvement Scotland 2008–12; second opinion doctor Mental Welfare Cmmn for Scotland 1995–2002, reviewer Cochrane Schizophrenia Gp Univ of Leeds 1996–; assoc ed Jl of Medical Case Reports 2007–; non-exec dir Bd of Mgmnt Scot Assoc for Mental Health 2000–15 (tstee 2015–); memb: European Coll of Neuro-Psychopharmacology (ECNP) 1995–, Assoc of European Psychiatrists 2000–, Soc for Int Research on Schizophrenia (SIRS) 2005–, Soc for Biological Psychiatry 2006–, Corp of the Marine Biological Laboratory Mass USA 2007–, Int Soc for Psychiatric Genetics 2007–; fell Collegium Internationalle Neuropsycho Pharmacologium 1997; FRCPsych 2002 (MRCPsych 1985); *Publications* Report on The Scottish Schizophrenia Outcomes Study (with R Cameron, 2006), Treatment of Schizophrenia in the 21st Century: towards a more personalized approach (2012); author of over 160 scientific papers and contrib to numerous professional jls; *Recreations* Scotland, skiing, golf; *Clubs* Inverary Golf, Ross Priory; *Style*— Prof Robert Hunter; ✉ Gartnavel Royal Hospital, 1055 Great Western Road, Glasgow G12 0XH (☎ 0141 211 3600, e-mail robert.hunter@glasgow.ac.uk, website www.bobhunter.tel and uk.linkedin.com/in/RobertHunterMD)

HUNTER, Robert John; s of Dr Henry Hunter, and Nora, *née* Sheehy (d 1993); *b* Bunbury, Western Aust; *Educ* Univ of York (BA), UCL (LLM); *m* 28 March 1987, Julie Raven; 2 s (Matthew Henry b 1991, Michael David b 1994); *Career* admitted slr 1984; Allen & Overy: slr 1984–90 then ptnr and head Trust, Asset Tracing and Fraud Gp; currently ptnr Herbert Smith Freehills LLP; sec and fndr memb Assoc of Contentious Tst and Probate Specialists (ACTAPS); *Recreations* flying, fishing; *Clubs* Reform; *Style*— Robert Hunter, Esq

HUNTER, Ross Buchanan; s of Ronald James McKinlay Hunter, and Agnes Rose, *née* Musk; *Educ* Dollar Acad, Alva Acad, Mackintosh Sch of Architecture (BArch, DipArch); *m* Prof Janice Kirkpatrick, *qv*; *Career* designer; fndr Graven Images Ltd 1986; involved in graphic, interior and exhbn design; dir: Merchant City Tourism and Marketing Co-operative Ltd 2009, 3Fold; ARCUK 1987, memb RIAS 1990; *Recreations* motorcycling; *Style*— Ross Hunter, Esq; ✉ Graven Images Ltd, 175 Albion Street, Glasgow G1 1RU (☎ 0141 552 6626, fax 0141 552 0433, e-mail ross@graven.co.uk)

HUNTER, Sally Elizabeth; *née* Andrews; da of Edward Ison Andrews (d 1986), of Woodbridge, Suffolk, and Elizabeth Margaret, *née* Hutchison (d 1992); *b* 20 March 1947; *Educ* Queenswood Sch, Cambridge Coll of Arts and Technol; *m* 1, 1970 (m dis 1978), Ian Hunter; m 2, 1990, Ian Richard Posgate; *Career* ptnr Wills Lane Gallery St Ives Cornwall 1971–74, with Patrick Seale Gallery London 1978–83, fndr Sally Hunter Fine Art London (specialising in mid 20th Century Br paintings) 1984; *Recreations* theatre; *Style*— Ms Sally Hunter; ✉ Sally Hunter Fine Art, 54 Clarendon Road, London W11 2HJ (☎ 0845 367 0887, e-mail sallyhunter.fineart@btconnect.com)

HUNTER, Tom; s of Ian Hunter, of Somerset, and Sheelagh, *née* Wilson; *b* 30 July 1965, Bournemouth; *Educ* London Coll of Printing (BA), RCA (MA); *Career* photographer and artist; solo exhbns incl: Life and Death in Hackney (White Cube London) 2000, (Green on Red Gallery Dublin) 2001 and (Yancey Richardson Gallery) 2003, Photographs (Contemporary Art Centre Vilnius) 2002, Thoughts of Life and Death (Manchester City Art Gallery) 2002, Frans Hals Museum Haarlem 2003, Digital Landscapes (Lighthouse Poole) 2003, Irish MOMA Dublin 2003–04, Centro de Fotographia Salamanca 2004, Galeria Visor Valencia 2005, Living In Hell and Other Stories (Nat Gallery) 2005; numerous gp exhbns; John Kobal Portrait Award 1997; *Publications* Tom Hunter (2004), Living in Hell (2005); *Style*— Tom Hunter, Esq; ✉ e-mail info@tomhunter.org, website www.tomhunter.org

HUNTER, Sir Tom; kt (2005); *m* Marion; *Career* md Sports Division until 1998, co-fndr The Hunter Foundation 1998–, fndr West Coast Capital 2001–; memb Rwanda Presidential Advsy Cncl; former chm Entrepreneurial Exchange, tstee Carnegie Tst; bequested Hunter Centre for Entrepreneurship Univ of Strathclyde; Carnegie Medal of Philanthropy 2013; Hon Dr: Univ of Strathclyde 2001, Univ of Glasgow 2006, Univ of Aberdeen 2006, Univ of W Scotland (UWS) 2007, Univ of Edinburgh 2009; *Style*— Sir Tom Hunter; ✉ The Hunter Foundation, Marathon House, Olympic Business Park, Drybridge Road, Dundonald, Ayrshire KA2 9AE

HUNTER GORDON, Christopher Neil (Kit); s of Maj Patrick Hunter Gordon, CBE, MC, JP, DL (d 1978), of Beauly, Inverness, and Valerie Margaret Frances, *née* de Ferranti; *b* 8 June 1958; *Educ* Ampleforth, Trinity Hall Cambridge (MA); *m* 29 Sept 1984, Georgina Mary, da of Capt Owen Varney, of Dedham, Essex; 2 s (Sam William b 5 March 1988, Ivan b 20 Sept 1989), 2 da (Ione Mary b 18 July 1992, Hebe Elizabeth b 9 Aug 1996); *Career* Morgan Guaranty 1979–83, J Rothschild Holdings plc, md Aurit Serv 1983–85, md and co fndr The Summit Group 1985–, dir Comcap plc 1986–89, ceo Anglo Leasing Holdings 1993–95, chm Seraphim Capital 2006–; chm Resources for Autism 2004–; *Recreations* painting, architecture, tennis; *Clubs* Brooks's, White's, Chelsea Arts, Beefsteak; *Style*— Kit Hunter Gordon, Esq; ✉ The Summit Group Limited, 10 Cloisters House, 8 Battersea Park Road, London SW8 4BG (☎ 020 77204262, fax 020 7627 1218)

HUNTER GORDON, Nigel; s of Maj Patrick Hunter Gordon, CBE, MC, JP (d 1978), of Beauly, Inverness-shire, and Valerie Margaret Frances, *née* de Ferranti; *b* 2 September 1947; *Educ* Ampleforth, Univ of St Andrews (MA); *m* 16 April 1977, Linda Anne, da of Brendan Robert Magill, of Eastbourne; 2 s (Kim b 23 March 1981, Bret b 19 March 1983); *Career* trained as CA Coopers & Lybrand 1970–76, James C Pringle & Co CA Inverness 1977–79; Ernst & Young: joined 1979, tax ptnr 1983–92, managing ptnr Highlands & Islands 1992–2000; dir Kinloch Damph Ltd 2001–04, dir Dunrobin Castle Ltd 2002–; Highland Area rep on Tax Practices Ctee, chm Highland Area Tax Ctee 1985–91 (memb Tech Sub Ctee); sec CBI Highland Area Gp, memb CBI Scotland Cncl, memb Chm's Ctee CBI Scotland 1992–98, memb IoD Scottish Ctee 1996–2000; FCA 1975 (ACA 1973), CTA 1979; *Recreations* skiing, gardens; *Style*— Nigel Hunter Gordon, Esq; ✉ Killearnan House, Muir of Ord, Ross-shire IV6 7SQ (☎ 01463 870002)

HUNTER-PEASE, Charles E; OBE (2013); *b* 1946; *m* 1984, Susan; 1 da (Alison b 1986), 1 s (Henry b 1988); *Career* articled clerk 1964–68, asst accountant in bldg industry 1968–69, branch mangr Autohall 1969–70, operational auditor, agency mangr then dist mangr Avis 1970–72, internal auditor Continental Oil 1972–73; Volvo 1973–: business mgmnt conslt 1973–75, dist planning mangr 1975, dealer representation mangr 1976–78, regnl mangr 1978–83, nat sales mangr 1983, field ops mangr 1984–86, UK bd dir 1986–97, dir of dealer ops 1986, sales and mktg dir 1987–92, dep chief exec 1990–92, chm VOCS Finance Ltd 1991–97, md Volvo Car UK Ltd 1992–96, sr vice-pres Volvo Car Corp Sweden 1993–98, chief exec Volvo Car UK Ltd 1996–98, vice-pres Network Volvo Cars Europe Mktg 1996–98, chm Benelux/UK Region 1996–98, sr advsr Volvo 1999–2006; ind business advsr 1999–; RNLI: memb Fundraising Ctee 1991–2001, non-exec dir RNLI Sales 1995–2004, memb Cncl 1996–, chm Resources Ctee 1998–2008, tstee 1998–2008 and 2009–13, vice-chm 2013, chm 2013–; *Recreations* sailing, antiques; *Style*— Charles Hunter-Pease, Esq, OBE; ✉ e-mail chunterp@hotmail.com

HUNTING, Richard Hugh; CBE (2010); s of Charles Patrick Maule Hunting, CBE (d 1993), and Diana Margaret, *née* Pereira (d 1995); *b* 30 July 1946; *Educ* Rugby, Univ of Sheffield (BEng), Univ of Manchester (MBA); *m* 31 Oct 1970, Penelope Susan, da of Col L L Fleming, MBE, MC (d 2010); 1 s (Rupert b 1974), 2 da (Joanna b 1976, Chloë b 1979); *Career* Hunting Group 1972–: Hunting Surveys and Consultants, Field Aviation, E A Gibson Shipbrokers, Hunting Oilfield Services, Hunting Engineering, chm Hunting Associated Industries 1989 (dir 1986–89), chm Hunting plc 1991– (dir 1989–), dir Yule Catto & Co plc 2000–09; memb Cncl CBI 1992–97; chm: Geffrye Museum 2000–09 (tstee 1995–2009), Battle of Britain Meml Tst 2000– (tstee 1998–); cmmr Royal Hosp Chelsea 2002–08, non-exec dir Royal Brompton and Harefield NHS Fndn Tst 2007–15, chm Royal Brompton and Harefield Hosps Charity 2012–; memb Worshipful Co of Ironmongers (Master 1996–97); *Recreations* skiing, family history, arts; *Clubs* Boodle's, Chelsea Arts, Hurlingham; *Style*— Richard Hunting, Esq, CBE; ✉ Hunting plc, 5 Hanover Square, London W1S 1HQ (☎ 020 7321 0123, fax 020 7839 2072)

HUNTINGFORD, Richard Norman Legh; *b* 14 May 1956; *Educ* Radley; *m* 10 May 1996, Nicky, *née* Rice; 2 da, 1 s; *Career* with KPMG 1975–87; ceo Chrysalis Gp plc 1987–2007; chm: Virgin Radio 2007–08, UTV Media plc 2012–; FCA 1979; *Recreations* tennis, cricket, rugby, travel, restaurants; *Clubs* MCC, Queen's; *Style*— Richard Huntingford, Esq; ✉ UTV, Ormeau Road, Belfast BT7 1EB

HUNTON, Christopher John (Chris); s of Thomas Hunton, of Bishop's Stortford, Herts, and Elsie, *née* Smith; *b* 12 August 1961, Enfield, Middx; *Educ* Univ of London (BA), Univ of Cambridge (PGCE); *m* 6 June 1992, Sara, da of Eric Finch; 1 s (Samuel George b 22 Nov 1992), 1 da (Amelie Louisa b 10 Jan 1995); *Career* teacher Knox Sch NY 1984–85, asst housemaster Wellingborough Sch 1985–86, account mangr Foote, Cone & Belding 1986–88, account dir Ayer Barker 1988–90, bd account dir Young & Rubicam 1990–94, gp account dir Lowe Howard-Spink 1994–98, chief exec McCann Erickson 1998–2004, md Lowe London 2005–06, ceo Team Land Rover WPP 2007–15, global team ldr WPP 2015–; MIPA (elected to Cncl 2003), FRGS; *Recreations* family, sport, musical theatre, fishing; *Style*— Chris Hunton, Esq

HUNWICKS, Trevor Alec; s of Alec Alfred Hunwicks (d 2011), and Jean, *née* Brazier (d 2009); *b* 22 September 1943, Fairlie, Ayrshire; *Educ* Chislehurst and Sidcup GS, Braintree County HS, Univ of Greenwich (MA); *m* 14 Dec 1968, Zara, da of late Peter John Harris, and Valerie, *née* Harris (d 1998); 1 da (Victoria Louise b 21 August 1971), 1 s (William George b 7 Oct 1974); *Career* Nationwide Anglia Building Soc (formerly Anglia Building Soc) 1968–90: branch mangr 1968, London mangr 1971, London regnl mangr 1975, gen mangr mktg 1985, gen mangr corp devpt 1987; dir Benton Int (retail banking conslts) 1991–95, managing ptnr (UK) Strategic Futures Int (strategic forecasting and policy analysts) 1995–; strategy and mktg dir First Security 2007–10, chm Nat Centre for Strategic Leadership 2010–; chm of govrs Northampton Coll 1990–2005 (govr 2005–); FCIB 1977, FCIM 1981; *Recreations* theatre, music, painting, tennis; *Clubs* Royal Fowey Yacht; *Style*— Trevor Hunwicks, Esq; ✉ e-mail trevor.hunwicks@btinternet.com

HUPPERT, Prof Herbert Eric; s of Leo Huppert (d 1957), and Alice, *née* Neuman (d 1967); *b* 26 November 1943; *Educ* Sydney Boys' HS, Univ of Sydney (BSc), Aust Nat Univ (MSc), Univ of Calif San Diego (MS, PhD), Univ of Cambridge (MA, ScD); *m* 20 April 1966, Felicia Adina, da of Bernard David Ferster (d 1993), of Bellevue Hill, NSW; 2 s (Julian b 1978, Rowan b 1982); *Career* Univ of Cambridge: fell King's Coll 1970–, asst dir of research 1970–81, lectr 1981–88, reader in geophysical dynamics 1988–89, prof of theoretical geophysics and dir Inst of Theoretical Geophysics 1989–; prof of mathematics Univ of NSW 1991–96; assoc ed Jl of Fluid Mechanics 1971–90; memb Editorial Bd: Philosophical Transactions of the Royal Soc 1994–99, Reports on Progress in Physics 1997–2003; sr res fell BP Venture Unit 1983–89; co-chm Scientists for the Release of Soviet Refusniks 1987–91; memb Cncl: NERC 1993–99, Royal Soc 2001–03; Arthur L Day Prize and Lectureship US Nat Acad 2005, Israel Pollak distinguished lectr Technion (Israel Inst of Technol) 2005, William Hopkins Prize Cambridge Philosophical Soc 2005, Murchison Medal Geological Soc of London 2007; fell American Geographical Union 2002, fell American Physical Soc 2004; FRS 1987; *Recreations* my children, playing squash and tennis, walking, mountaineering, dreaming of a less hassled life in the sunshine; *Style*— Prof Herbert Huppert, FRS; ✉ 46 De Freville Avenue, Cambridge CB4 1HT (☎ 01223 356071); Institute of Theoretical Geophysics, Department of Applied Mathematics & Theoretical Physics and Department of Earth Sciences, CMS, Wilberforce Road, Cambridge CB3 0WA (☎ 01223 337853, fax 01223 765900, e-mail hehl1@esc.cam.ac.uk)

HUPPERT, Dr Julian; *b* 21 July 1978; *Educ* Perse Sch Cambridge, Trinity Coll Cambridge (BA, MSci, PhD); *Career* MP (Lib Dem) Cambridge 2010–15; univ lectr Univ of Cambridge 2012–; fell Trinity Coll Cambridge 2004–08, RCUK fell Cavendish Lab Cambridge 2007–12, fell Clare Coll Cambridge 2009–; *Style*— Dr Julian Huppert; ✉ House of Commons, London SW1A 0AA

HURD, Martyn Roy; s of late (Bernard) Roy Hurd, and Marjorie Sheila, *née* Burton; *b* 28 September 1948; *Educ* Blatchington Court, Open Univ (BA); *m* 31 Aug 1976, Philippa Helen, da of late (John) Angus Beckett, CB, CMG; 2 da (Jane b 6 May 1979, Helen b 21 July 1981); *Career* production planning offr Central Independent TV until 1983; ITN: mangr of prodn planning 1983–91, head of studios programme and resource planning 1991–94, dir of human resources 1994–96, dir of resources 1996–2003; co sec Broadcast Journalism Trg Cncl (BJTC) until 2016; dir: GR Communications until 2015, Martyn Hurd & Assocs Ltd; govr Ravensbourne Coll of Design and Communication until 2016; currently managing tstee ITN Pension Scheme Ltd; memb: BAFTA, RTS; fell Ravensbourne Coll of Design and Communication; fell and past pres Moving Image Soc (BKSTS); *Recreations* walking, swimming, reading; *Style*— Martyn Hurd, Esq; ✉ 9 Roy Road, Northwood, Middlesex HA6 1EQ (☎ 01923 826868, e-mail martyn.hurd@blueyonder.co.uk)

HURD, (Hon) Nicholas Richard (Nick); MP; s of Baron Hurd of Westwell, CH, CBE, PC (Life Peer), *qv*, and Tatiana Elizabeth Michelle, *née* Eyre; *b* 13 May 1962; *Educ* Univ of Oxford; *m* 1, 1998 (m dis), Kim; 2 s, 2 da; m 2, 2010, Lady Clare; *Career* business dir, formerly COS to Tim Yeo MP, *qv*, MP (Cons) Ruislip-Northwood 2005–, oppn whip 2007–08, shadow min for charities, volunteering and social enterprise 2008–10, min for civil soc (parly sec) Cabinet Office 2010–14; memb Environmental Audit Ctee House of Commons 2005–10; dir Band-X Ltd; *Style*— Nick Hurd, Esq, MP; ✉ House of Commons, London SW1A 0AA (☎ 020 7219 1053, e-mail nick.hurd.mp@parliament.uk, website www.nickhurd.com, Twitter @nickhurdmp)

HURD OF WESTWELL, Baron (Life Peer UK 1997), of Westwell in the County of Oxfordshire; Douglas Richard Hurd; CH (1996), CBE (1974), PC (1982); eld s of Baron Hurd, sometime MP Newbury and agric corr The Times (Life Peer, d 1966; himself er s of Sir Percy Angier Hurd, sometime MP Frome and Devizes, ed Canadian Gazette and London ed Montreal Star; Sir Percy was er bro of Sir Archibald Hurd, also a journalist (Daily Telegraph) and formerly chm Shipping World Co), and Stephanie Frances, *née* Corner (d 1985); *b* 8 March 1930; *Educ* Eton, Trinity Coll Cambridge (MA); *m* 1, 1960 (m dis 1982), Tatiana Elizabeth Michelle, o da of (Arthur Charles) Benedict Eyre, MBE, of Bury, W Sussex; 3 s (Hon Nicholas Richard, *qv*, b 13 May 1962, Hon Thomas Robert Benedict b 20 Sept 1964, Hon Alexander Paul Anthony b 7 June 1969); m 2, 1982, Judy J (d 2008), 2 da of Sidney Smart (d 2008), of Chaddleworth, Berks; 1 s (Hon Philip Arthur b 1983), 1 da (Hon Jessica Stephanie b 1985); *Career* Dip Serv 1952–66 (Peking, UK Mission to UN, Rome, also private sec to perm under sec FO); CRD 1966–68 (head Foreign Affrs Section 1968); MP (Cons): Mid Oxon Feb 1974–1983, Witney 1983–97; private sec to Rt Hon Edward Heath as ldr of Oppn 1968–70, political sec to PM 1970–74, oppn spokesman on foreign affrs (with special responsibility for EEC) 1976–79; min of state: FCO 1979–83, Home Office 1983–84; sec of state for NI 1984–85, home sec 1985–89, sec of state for foreign and Cwlth affrs 1989–95; dir National Westminster Bank plc 1995–99, dep chm NatWest Markets 1995–98, chm British Invisibles 1997–2000 (dep chm 1996–97), dep chm Coutts & Co 1998–2010; chm: Prison Reform Tst 1997–2001 (hon pres 2001–), CEDR 2000–04 (currently chm Advsy Cncl), Canterbury Review Gp 2000; memb: Royal Cmmn on reform of House of Lords 1999, Appointments Cmmn 2000–10; visiting fell Nuffield Coll Oxford 1978, fell Eton Coll 1981–96; chm of judges Booker Prize 1998; high steward Westminster Abbey 2000–10; chm German-Br Forum 2000–05; co-pres RIIA 2001–09; *Books* The Arrow War (1967), Truth Game (1972), Vote to Kill (1975), An End to Promises (1979); with Andrew Osmond: Send Him Victorious (1968), The Smile on The Face of the Tiger (1969), Scotch on the Rocks (1971), War Without Frontiers (1982); Palace of Enchantments (with Stephen Lamport, *qv*, 1985), Search for Peace (1997), Shape of Ice (1998), Ten Minutes to Turn the Devil (1999), Image in the Water (2001), Memoirs (2003), Sir Robert Peel (2007), Choose Your Weapons (with Edward Young, 2010), Disraeli (with Edward Young, 2013), Elizabeth II: The Steadfast (2015); *Clubs* Travellers, Pratt's, Beefsteak; *Style*— The Rt Hon Lord Hurd of Westwell, CH, CBE, PC; ✉ Elizabeth Steadfast, House of Lords, London SW1A 0PW

HURDLE, Michael William Frederick; s of Maurice Frederick Hurdle (d 1994), of Burton-on-Trent, and Mary Murielle Morton Wilson (d 1997); *b* 3 June 1941; *Educ* Uppingham, Keele Univ (BA); *Career* chm Marston Thompson and Evershed plc (Brewers); Liveryman Worshipful Co of Brewers; *Recreations* shooting, fishing, golf, horseracing; *Clubs* The Burton, The Oriental, Lloyds; *Style*— Michael Hurdle, Esq; ✉ Marston Thompson & Evershed plc, PO Box 26, Shobnall Road, Burton-on-Trent, Staffordshire DE14 2BW

HURFORD, Prof James Raymond (Jim); *b* 16 July 1941; *Educ* Exeter Sch, St John's Coll Cambridge (BA), UCL (PhD); *Career* assoc Dept of Germanic Languages UCLA 1963–64, postdoctoral res fell System Development Corporation Calif 1967–68, asst prof Dept of English Univ of Calif Davis 1968–71, sr lectr Dept of Linguistics Lancaster Univ 1976–79 (lectr 1972–76), prof of general linguistics Univ of Edinburgh 1979–; visiting res fell Univ of Melbourne 1989–90; visiting prof: Cairo Univ 1976, Univ of Calif 1982; memb of Faculty Linguistic Inst Linguistic Soc of America 1995; *Books* The Linguistic Theory of Numerals (1975), Semantics: A Coursebook (with B Heasley, 1983), Language and Number: The emergence of a cognitive system (1987), Grammar: A Student's Guide (1994), The Origins of Meaning (2007), The Origins of Grammar (2011), The Origins of Language (2014); *Style*— Prof Jim Hurford; ✉ Department of Linguistics, University of Edinburgh, Dugald Stewart Building, Edinburgh EH8 9LL (☎ 0131 650 3959/3960)

HURLEY, Elizabeth Jane; da of late Roy Leonard Hurley, and Angela Mary Hurley; *b* 10 June 1965; *Children* 1 s (Damian Charles b 4 April 2002); *Career* actress, prodr and model; spokeswoman and model for Estée Lauder; creative dir Elizabeth Hurley Beach; prodr Simian Films; Best Supporting Actress ShoWest Award 1997, Entrepreneur of the Year Glamour Magazine 2006; *Theatre* incl: The Cherry Orchard – A Jubilee (Russian & Soviet Arts Festival), The Man Most Likely To (Middle East tour); *Television* incl: title role in Christabel (BBC), The Orchid House (Channel 4), Rumpole (Thames), Inspector Morse (Zenith), The Young Indiana Jones Chronicles (Lucas Films Ltd), Sharpe's Enemy (Sharpe Films), The Job (ABC), The Human Face (BBC), Gossip Girl, presenter Project Catwalk (Sky One); *Film* incl: Aria, Rowing in the Wind, The Long Winter of 39, Passenger 57, Mad Dogs and Englishmen, Dangerous Ground, Samson and Delilah, Austin Powers: International Man of Mystery, Permanent Midnight, My Favourite Martian, Ed TV, Austin Powers: The Spy Who Shagged Me, Bedazzled, The Weight Of Water, Double Whammy, Serving Sara, Method; prodr: Extreme Measures, Mickey Blue Eyes; *Style*— Miss Elizabeth Hurley

HURN, David; s of Stanley Hurn, of Cardiff, and Joan, *née* Maynard; *b* 21 July 1934, Redhill, Surrey; *Educ* Dorchester GS, RMA Sandhurst; *m* 1964 (m dis 1971), Alita Naughton; 1 da (Siân); *Career* photographer; asst photographer Reflex Agency London 1955–57, freelance for pubns incl The Observer, Sunday Times, Look and Life 1957–70, memb Magnum Photos 1967–; editorial advsr Album photographic magazine 1971; head Sch of Documentary Photography Gwent Coll of HE Newport 1973–90, distinguished visiting artist and adjunct prof Arizona State Univ Tempe 1979–80; memb: Photographic Ctee 1972–77, Arts Panel 1975–77, Cncl for Nat Academic Awards 1978–87, Arts Cncl of GB; Welsh Arts Cncl Award 1971, Kodak Special Photographic Bursary 1975, UK/USA Bicentennial Fellowship 1979–80, Imperial War Museum Arts Award 1987–88, Bradford Fellowship 1993–94, Arts Cncl Wales Bursary 1995; hon fell Univ of Wales Coll Newport; *Selected Solo Exhibitions* Serpentine Gallery London 1971, Bibliotheque Nationale Paris 1973, Nat Museum of Wales Cardiff 1974, The Photographers' Gallery London 1974, Recontres Internationales de Photographie Arles 1976, Centre d'Animation Culturelle Dovai 1976, Ecole Municipale des Arts Decoratifs Strasbourg 1976, FNAC Etoile Gallery Paris 1977, Arnolfini Gallery Bristol 1977, Ecole des Beaux Arts Angers 1977, Musée du Chateau d'Eau Toulouse 1977, Rheinisches Landesmuseum Bonn 1977, Rathaus Augsburg 1977, Stadtbucherei Stuttgart 1977, Stadtisches Museum Bochum 1978, Northlight Gallery Arizona State Univ Tempe 1978, Gemeentekijke Van Reekum Galerij Apeldoorn 1978, Culturele Raad Leeuwarden 1978, Openbare Bibliotheek Arnhem 1978, Culturee Centrum Winterswijk 1978, Canon Photo Galerij Amsterdam 1978, Univ of Idaho Moscow 1978, Galeria Spectrum Barcelona 1978, Galeria Spectrum Zaragosa 1978, San Carlos Opera House Lisbon 1979, Univ of Idaho Museum Moscow 1979, Univ of New Mexico Albuquerque 1979, Texas Christian Univ Fort Worth 1979, Midland Gp Gallery Nottingham 1979, Fifth Ave Gallery Scotsdale 1980, Sterling Coll of Art 1980, Les Recontres D'Olympus Paris 1981, Contrasts Gallery London 1982, Olympus Gallery London 1982, Malmo Museum 1982, Palais des Congres Lorient 1982, Olympus Gallery Tokyo 1983, Palais des Beaux Arts Charlerois 1983, Olympus Gallery Hamburg 1984, Ffotogalley Cardiff 1984, The Photographers' Gallery London 1985, Nat Museum of Photography Bradford 1985 and 1994, Cambridge Darkroom 1986, Axiom Gallery Cheltenham 1986, Stills Gallery Edinburgh 1986, Newport Museum 1994, Nat Museum and Gallery Cardiff 2000, Nat Library of Wales Aberystwyth 2000, Hay Literary Festival 2000, Int Eisteddfod Llangollen 2000, Aberystwyth Arts Centre 2007, Jersey Arts Centre 2007, Newport Museum and Arts Centre 2008, Third Floor Gallery Cardiff 2012, Sture Hof Stockholm 2012; *Selected Group Exhibitions* Personal Views 1850–1970 (touring) 1972, Images des Hommes (touring) 1978, Visitors to Arizona 1846–1980 (Phoenix Museum Arizona) 1980, British Photography 1955–1965 (The Photographers' Gallery London) 1983, Images of Sport (Ffotogallery Cardiff) 1983, Autographs (Cambridge Darkroom) 1983, Quelques Anglais (Centre National de la Photographie Paris) 1985, The Miners World (touring) 1985, Take One: British Film Stills (touring) 1985, Through the Looking Glass: Photographic Art in Britain 1945–89 (Barbican London) 1989, In Our Time: The world as seen by Magnum Photographers (touring) 1989, Distinguished visiting artists (Northlight Gallery Arizona State Univ Tempe) 1991, Revelations. Male and Female Nudes (John Jones Gallery London) 1994, A Positive View (The Saatchi Gallery London) 1994; *Work in Public Collections* incl: Welsh Arts Cncl, Contemporary Arts Soc for Wales, Arts Cncl of GB, Br Cncl, Bibliotheque Nationale Paris, FNAC Paris, Musée du Chateau d'Eau Toulouse, Int Center of Photography NY, Centre for Creative Photography Univ of Arizona Tucson, Univ of New Mexico Albuquerque, San Francisco MOMA, Calif Museum of Photography Univ of Calif Riverside, Int Museum of Photography George Eastman House Rochester, Nat Library of Wales, Nat Museum and Gallery Cardiff, Multimedia Art Museum Moscow 2014; *Books* David Hurn: Photographs 1956–76 (1979), A Day in the Life of London (1984), One Moment of The World (1984), Ireland. A week in the life of a nation (1986), History of Photography (1987), Bons Baisers (1987), In Our Time (1989), Music (1990), A L'Est de Magnum (1991), The Circle of Life (1991), L'Argot d'Eros (1992), Il Medico e il reportage (1992), Magnum Cinema (1994), Contemporary Photographers (1995), Magnum Landscape (1996), The Photo Book (1997), Magnum Photos, Photo Poche (1997), On being a photographer (with Bill Jay, 1997), 1968 Magnum throughout the world (1998), Young Meteors (1998), Hugs and Kisses (1998), On looking at pictures (with Bill Jay, 2000), Wales: Land of My Father (2000), Magnum (2000), Living in Wales (2003), Cardiff: Rebirth of a Capital (2005), Writing the Picture (with John Fuller, 2010); *Recreations* exchanging photographs, gardening; *Style*— David Hurn, Esq; ✉ Prospect Cottage, Tintern, Gwent NP16 6SG (☎ 01291 689358, e-mail hurn@tintern.u-net.com); Magnum Photos, Ground Floor, 63 Gee Street, Lonndon EC1V 3RS (☎ 020 7490 1771, e-mail hurn@magnum.co.uk)

HURN, Sir (F) Roger; kt (1996); s of Francis James Hurn, and Joyce Elsa, *née* Bennett; *b* 9 June 1938; *Educ* Marlborough; *m* 1980, Rosalind Jackson; 1 da; *Career* Nat Serv 1959–61; engrg apprentice Rolls-Royce Motors 1956–58; Smiths Industries plc: export rep Automotive Business Europe and N America 1958–59 and 1961–65, export dir Motor Accessory Div 1969 (export mangr 1965–69), corp staff dir Overseas Ops 1969–74, md Int Ops 1974–76, exec dir 1976–78, md 1978–81, chief exec and md 1981–91, chm and chief exec 1991–96, chm 1991–98; chm: Marconi (formerly GEC) plc 1998–2001, Prudential plc 2000–02; non-exec dir: ICI plc 1993–2001, GlaxoSmithKline plc until 2003 (dep chm 1997–2003), Cazenove Group plc 2001–; chm of govrs Henley Management Coll until 2004; Liveryman Worshipful Co of Coachmakers and Coach Harness Makers 1979; *Style*— Sir Roger Hurn

HURST, Sir Geoffrey Charles (Geoff); kt (1998), MBE (1977); s of Charles Hurst, of Chelmsford, Essex, and Evelyn May, *née* Hopkins; *b* 8 December 1941; *Educ* Rainsford Secdy Modern Chelmsford; *m* 13 Oct 1964, Judith Helen, da of Jack Henry Harries; 3 da (Claire Helen b 30 Oct 1965, Joanne Louise b 16 March 1969, Charlotte Jane b 13 Feb 1977); *Career* former professional footballer and mangr; clubs: West Ham (500 appearances, 250 goals scored), Stoke City 1972–75 (128 appearances, 37 goals scored), West Bromwich Albion 1975–76 (12 appearances, 2 goals scored); player mangr Telford United 1976–79; mangr: Chelsea 1979–81, Kuwait 1982–84; England: debut v W Germany

H

1966, scored hat-trick in World Cup final 4–2 defeat of W Germany Wembley 1966, 49 caps, 24 goals, coach 1977–82; sales dir Motor-Plan Limited 1984–90, new business support mangr Ryan Insurance Group Europe 1992–93, dir i/c acquisitions London General Insurance 1998 (md Appliance Warranty Div 1993–98), latterly conslt AON Warranty Gp; *Books* World Game (1967), 1966 and All That (2001); *Recreations* golf; *Clubs* Reform; *Style*— Sir Geoff Hurst, MBE

HURST, John Edward; s of Edward Gostling Hurst (d 1964), of Weston Longville, Norwich, and Grace, *née* Holder (d 2000); *b* 10 October 1947; *Educ* Gresham's, Univ of London (LLB), Univ of Amsterdam (Post Grad Dip); *m* 19 Dec 1972, Julia, da of Hendrik Jan Engelbert van Beuningen, of Cothen (U), The Netherlands; 1 s (Robert Adriaan b 13 April 1979), 2 da (Olivia b 8 Sept 1974, Annette b 16 April 1977); *Career* admitted slr 1976; ptnr: Hurst van Beuningen (Farms) 1982–, Daynes Hill & Perks 1987–92, Eversheds Daynes Hill & Perks 1992–95, Eversheds 1995–2001; conslt Eversheds 2001–05, conslt Birketts LLP 2005–12; nat chm Law Soc's Slr's Euro Gp 1987–88, lay chm Sparham Deanery Synod C of E 1987–96; dir Briningham Farms Ltd 1998–2006, ptnr Green Farm Elsing 2006–; govr Taverham Hall Prep Sch 1996–2010; memb: Law Soc 1976, NFU 1982; *Books* Legal Issues of European Integration: Harmonisation of Company Law in the EEC (1974); *Recreations* swimming, stalking and country pursuits; *Clubs* Norfolk; *Style*— John Hurst, Esq; ✉ Rectory Farm, Morton-on-the-Hill, Norwich NR9 5JR (☎ 01603 860225)

HURST, Kim Barbara; da of late Norman Campbell Hurst, of Sheffield, and late Elsie, *née* Hands; *b* 8 August 1956; *Educ* Ecclesfield Sch, Univ of Leicester (BA); *Career* trainee Grant Thornton 1978–81, Griffin Stone Moscrop 1982–83, under sec to the Auditing Practices Ctee ICAEW 1983–85, risk mgmnt and standards ptnr Mazars 1990– (joined 1985); chm Audit Registration Ctee ICAEW; tstee Vineyard Churches in UK and Ireland; FCA 1992 (ACA 1982); *Recreations* theatre, charity work, cycling, skiing; *Clubs* David Lloyd; *Style*— Ms Kim Hurst; ✉ Mazars LLP, Tower Bridge House, 1 St Katharine's Way, London E1W 1DD (☎ 020 7063 4369, fax 020 7063 4001, e-mail kim.hurst@mazars.co.uk)

HURST, Lilla; da of John Hurst, of Petworth, West Sussex, and Anne, *née* Pendlebury; *b* 16 February 1973, Beaconsfield, Bucks; *Educ* Holy Cross Convent for Girls Chalfont St Peter, Framlingham Coll, De Montfort Univ (BA); *m* 16 Sept 2006, Jonathan Benton-Hughes; 1 s (Bertram b 16 Feb 2006); *Career* sales and devpt exec British Pathé 1997–1999, dir TVF Int 1999–2001, dir of acquisitions and co-production RDF Media 2001–04, head of co-prodn Channel Five 2004–; *Recreations* cooking, design, walking in the British countryside; *Clubs* Century; *Style*— Miss Lilla Hurst; ✉ Channel Five, 22 Long Acre, London WC2E 9LY (☎ 020 7550 5674, fax 020 7550 5554)

HURST, Nigel; s of George Edward Hurst, and Ivy Lawton, *née* Evans; *b* 21 February 1965, Lichfield, Staffs; *Educ* Friary Grange Sch Lichfield, Goldsmiths Coll London (BA); *m* 7 Oct 1995, Samantha, *née* Colborne; 2 s (Jed Rowan b 1 June 1999, Finley John b 23 May 2002); *Career* curator and exhbn organiser 1986–1997; Saatchi Gall London: asst curator 1997–2000, assoc dir 2000–02, dir 2002–, chief exec 2007–; memb Royal Borough of Kensington & Chelsea Public Art Advy Bd 2009–, memb Chelsea and Westminster Health Charity Arts Advsy Bd 2013–; memb Devpt Cncl Univ of the Arts London 2013–; *Style*— Nigel Hurst, Esq; ✉ Saatchi Gallery, Duke of York's HQ, King's Road, Chelsea, London SW3 4RY (☎ 020 7811 3070, website www.saatchigallery.com)

HURT, Sir John Vincent; kt (2015), CBE (2004); s of Rev Father Arnould Herbert Hurt, and Phyllis, *née* Massey (d 1975); *b* 22 January 1940; *Educ* Lincoln Sch, St Martin's Sch of Art, RADA; *m* 1, 1984 (m dis 1990), Donna Lynn Peacock, da of Don Wesley Laurence (d 1986), of Texas USA; m 2, 1990 (m dis 1996), Jo Dalton; 2 s; m 3, 2005, Anwen Rees-Myers; *Career* actor; debut Arts Theatre London 1962; Outstanding Contribution to Cinema BAFTA 2012, Alexander Walker Special Award Evening Standard Br Film Award 2012; *Theatre* incl: Chips with Everything (Vaudeville) 1962, The Dwarfs (Arts, Critics Award for Most Promising Actor 1963) 1962, Inadmissible Evidence (Wyndhams) 1965, Little Malcolm and His Struggle Against The Eunuchs (Garrick) 1966, Belcher's Luck (Aldwych, RSC) 1966, The Caretaker (Mermaid) 1971, Travesties (Aldwych, RSC) 1973, The Shadow of a Gunman (Nottingham Playhouse) 1978, The Seagull (Lyric Hammersmith) 1985, London Vertigo (Gate Dublin) 1991, A Month in the Country (Albery) 1994, Krapps Last Tape (Barbican) 1999 and (Gate Theatre Dublin) 2001, Afterplay (Gate Theatre Dublin) 2002, Heroes (Wyndhams) 2005, Krapps Last Tape (Gate Theatre Dublin and Barbican) 2006; *Television* incl: The Playboy of the Western World (BBC) 1971, The Naked Civil Servant (Thames TV) 1975 (Br Acad Award for Best Actor 1978), I Claudius (BBC) 1976, Treats (YTV) 1977, Crime and Punishment (BBC) 1978, Fool in King Lear (with Olivier) 1982, The Storyteller (35 episodes) 1986, Poison Candy (BBC) 1987, Deadline 1988, Who Bombed Birmingham? (Granada) 1989, Journey to Knock 1991, Red Fox (LWT) 1991, Six Characters in Search of an Author (BBC) 1992, Enemy Within (BBC) 1995, Prisoner in Time (BBC) 1995, Krapp's Last Tape 2000, Bait 2001, The Alan Clark Diaries 2004, Merlin (BBC) 2008–11, The Confession 2011; *Films* incl: A Man for All Seasons 1966, 10 Rillington Place 1970, East of Elephant Rock 1976, Spectre 1977, The Disappearance 1977, The Shout 1977, Watership Down 1977, Midnight Express 1977 (Oscar nomination 1978, Br Acad Award 1978, Golden Globe Award 1978, Variety Club Award 1978), Alien 1978, Heaven's Gate 1979, The Elephant Man 1980 (Oscar nomination, Br Acad Award, Variety Club Award), Night Crossing 1980, History of the World Part I 1982, Champions 1983 (Evening Standard Award for Best Actor 1984), Nineteen Eighty-Four 1984, The Hit 1984, Jake Speed 1986, Rocinante 1986, Aria 1987, White Mischief 1987, Bengali Night 1988, Scandal 1988, La Dame aux Chats 1988, Windprints 1989, Frankenstein Unbound 1989, The Field 1990, King Ralph 1990, Memory 1990, Dark at Noon 1991, Lapse of Memory 1991, Even Cowgirls get the Blues 1992, Great Moments in Aviation 1992, Crime & Punishment 1993, Wild Bill 1994, Rob Roy 1995, Saigon Baby 1995, Love and Death on Long Island 1998, The Commissioner 1998, All the Little Animals 1998, Night Train 1998, You're Dead 1998, New Blood 1999, Lost Souls 2000, Crime and Punishment 2000, Captain Corelli's Mandolin 2001, Harry Potter and the Philospher's Stone 2001, Tabloid 2001, Miranda 2002, Owning Mahowny 2003, Dogville 2003, Hellboy 2004, The Proposition 2004, Skeleton Key 2004, Shooting Dogs 2005, V for Vendetta 2005, Outlander 2006, Oxford Murders 2007, Lecture 21 2007, Indiana Jones IV 2007, Hellboy II 2007, 44 Inch Chest 2007, An Englishman in New York 2008, The Limits of Control 2008, 44 Inch Chest 2009, Lou 2009, Harry Potter and the Deathly Hallows: Part 1 2010, Brighton Rock 2010, Melancholia 2011, Harry Potter and the Deathly Hallows: Part 2 2011, Tinker Tailor Soldier Spy 2011, Snowpiercer 2012, Only Lovers Left Alive 2012; *Recreations* painting, charity work; *Clubs* MCC, Garrick; *Style*— Sir John Hurt, CBE; ✉ c/o Independent Talent Group Ltd, 40 Whitfield Street, London W1T 2RH

HURTLEY, Richard; *Educ* Hurstpierpoint Coll, Univ of Exeter (BA); *Career* fndr and md Lions Rampant Ltd 2007–; *Style*— Richard Hurtley, Esq; ✉ Lions Rampant Limited, 497 Safron Lane, Leicester LE2 6UG (website www.lionsrampant.com)

HUSBAND, Prof Dame Janet Elizabeth Siarey; DBE (2007, OBE 2002); *née* Siarey; da of Ronald Howard Siarey (d 1982), of Chinnor, Oxon, and Clarissa Marian Siarey (d 1987); *b* 1 April 1940; *Educ* Headington Sch, Guy's Hosp Med Sch (MB BS); *m* 1963, Peter Husband; 3 s (Matthew Bernard, Andrew Charles, Timothy Edward); *Career* prof of diagnostic radiology Inst of Cancer Res 1976–2007 (currently emerita prof), conslt radiologist Royal Marsden Hospital 1980–2007, med dir Royal Marsden NHS Fndn Tst 2003–06; pres: BIR 2003–04, RCR 2004–07; vice-chair Acad of Med Royal Colls 2005–07; Gold medal EACR 2006, Gold medal ICIS 2009, Gold medal RCR 2009; Hon DSc Univ of London 2013; FMedSci 2001, Hon FRCSI 2005, Hon FRCSGlas 2008; hon memb: Belgian Radiological Soc 1994, European Soc of Therapeutic and Radiation Oncology 1999, Radiological Soc of North America 2006; hon fell: Hong Kong CR 2007, Acad of Med Singapore 2007; *Publications* Imaging in Oncology (jt ed, 2 vols 2004, 3 edn 2009), author of over 300 pubns on imaging in oncology; *Recreations* walking, opera; *Clubs* Sloane; *Style*— Prof Dame Janet Husband, DBE

HUSBAND, John; s of John Husband (d 1986), of Edgware, and Bridget Agnes Leahy; *b* 21 April 1945; *Educ* St Vincent's RC Sch Mill Hill, St James' RC HS Edgware, Univ of Hull (BSc); *Career* Daily Mirror: trainee reporter 1966–68, fin reporter 1968–74, dep City ed 1974–90 (and Sunday Mirror 1975–90), City ed 1990–93, Personal Finance ed 1993–, tstee Mirror Gp Newspaper Pension Scheme; memb: ABI Code Monitoring Ctee 1990–2001, FSA Treating Customers Fairly Consultative Ctee 2006–; Personal Fin Journalist of The Year 1990, Wincott Business Jl of the Year (for Sunday Mirror City column) 1991; ABI Lifetime Award for Achievements in Personal Finance, Bradford & Bingley Lifetime Award for Achievement in Personal Finance; chair of govrs: St Margaret Clitherow RC Primary Sch, St Catherine's RC Sch for Girls; *Books* Money Mirror (1980), Daily Mirror Guide to Money (1993), Managing Your Money (1998); *Recreations* music, record collecting, walking, history; *Style*— John Husband, Esq; ✉ Mirror Group Newspapers, 1 Canada Square, Canary Wharf, London E14 5AP (☎ 020 7293 3323, e-mail j.husband@mgn.co.uk)

HUSBANDS, Prof Chris; *Educ* MA, PhD, PGCE; *Career* formerly: prof of educn and head Sch of Educn and Lifelong Learning Univ of East Anglia, dir Inst of Educn Univ of Warwick; Inst of Educn Univ of London: prof of educn and dean Faculty of Culture and Pedagogy 2007–11, dir 2011–16; vice-chllr Sheffield Hallam Univ 2016–; *Style*— Prof Chris Husbands

HUSKINSON, His Hon Judge (George) Nicholas Nevil; s of Thomas Leonard Bousfield Huskinson (d 1974), of Triscombe House, Somerset, and Helen Margaret, *née* Hales (d 1983); *b* 7 December 1948; *Educ* Eton, King's Coll Cambridge (MA); *m* 20 Dec 1972, Pennant Elfrida Lascelles, da of Thomas Lascelles Isa Shandon Valiant Iremonger (d 1998), of Milbourne Manor, Malmesbury, Wilts; 2 s (Thomas b 1978, Charles b 1981); *Career* called to the Bar Gray's Inn 1971 (Arden scholar 1972); in practice 1971–2003, recorder 1999–2003, circuit judge (SE Circuit) 2003–; a vice-pres Immigration Appeal Tbnl and subsequently sr immigration judge Asylum and Immigration Tbnl 2003–05, memb Lands Tbnl and subsequently memb Upper Tbnl (Lands Chamber) 2006–; *Books* Woodfall's Law of Landlord and Tenant (asst ed 28 edn, 1978); *Recreations* tennis, cooking, family life, wine and food; *Clubs* MCC, Garrick; *Style*— His Hon Judge Huskinson; ✉ Snaresbrook Crown Court, 75 Hollybush Hill, Wanstead, London E11 1QW (☎ 020 8530 0000)

HUSSAIN, Mukhtar; QC (1992); s of Karam Dad (d 1991), and Rehmi Bi (d 1955); *b* 22 March 1950; *Educ* William Temple Secdy Sch Preston; *m* 1972, Shamim Akhtar, *née* Ali; 3 da (Rukhshanda Jabeen b 30 March 1974, Farakhanda Jabeen b 12 Dec 1975, Mariam Sophia Rahmi b 20 May 1985); *Career* called to the Bar Middle Temple 1971 (bencher 2000), asst recorder 1987–90, recorder 1990–, head of chambers 1992–; Police Discipline Tbnl 1997–; memb: Criminal Injuries Compensation Bd (CICB) 1999, Mental Health Review Tbnl 2000, Bar Cncl 2000–01; *Recreations* reading, cricket, squash, bridge, golf; *Style*— Mukhtar Hussain, Esq, QC; ✉ Lincoln House Chambers, Tower 12, The Avenue South, Springfields, Manchester M3 3BZ (☎ 0161 832 5701)

HUSSAIN, Baron (Life Peer UK 2011), of Luton in the County of Bedfordshire; Qurban Hussain; *b* Kashmir; *Career* sec Luton TUC 1994–96; memb Lib Dem Pty 2003–, cncllr Luton Borough Cncl (dep ldr 2005–07), Parly candidate (Lib Dem) Luton S 2005 and 2010, EU Parly candidate (Lib Dem) E of England 2009; *Style*— The Lord Hussain; ✉ House of Lords, London SW1A 0PW

HUSSEIN, Leyla; da of Sirad Elmi, and Ahmed Sheikh; *b* 1980, Somalia; *Educ* Thames Valley Univ; *Children* 1 da (Feyrus Ali b 8 Aug 2002); *Career* psychotherapist and fndr Dahlia Project (counselling services for FGM survivors), fndr (with Nimco Ali and Sainab Abdi) Daughters of Eve 2010–, chief-exec Hawa's Haven; ind training conslt; community facilitator Manor Garden Health Advocacy Project, sr conslt The Girl Generation Programme; presented documentary The Cruel Cut (Channel 4) 2013 (nominated: BAFTA 2014, Amnesty Media Awards 2014, Best Onscreen Talent CDN Awards 2014, Broadcaster Award 2015); blogger: The Guardian, Huffington Post, Cosmopolitan Magazine; *Awards* Cosmopolitan Ultimate Campaigner Women of the Year Award 2010, Emma Humphrey Award 2011, Lin Groves Special Award 2011, True Honour Award Iranian and Kurdish Women's Rights Orgn 2012, World Peace and Prosperity Fndn Award 2013, BBC 100 Women List 2013, RedLine Magazine Woman of the Year 2014, Woman's Hour Power List 2014, Debrett's 500 2015; *Recreations* cinema, fashion, music, reading, travel, walking, cooking; *Style*— Ms Leyla Hussein; ✉ website www.leylahussein.com, Twitter @LeylaHussein

HUSSEIN-ECE, Baroness (Life Peer UK 2010), of Highbury in the London Borough of Islington; Meral Hussein Ece; OBE (2009); da of late Hasan Nihat Hussein, and Ayshe Cuma Abdullah; *b* 10 October 1953, Islington, London; *Career* cncllr: Hackney Cncl 1994–2002 (dep ldr 1995–96), Islington Cncl 2002–10; cmmr Equality and Human Rights Cmmn 2009; *Style*— The Baroness Hussein-Ece, OBE; ✉ House of Lords, London SW1A 0PW

HUSSEY, Derek Robert; s of Robert Sydney Hussey, and Rachel *née* Maguire; *b* 12 September 1948, Padstow, Cornwall; *Educ* Omagh Acad, Stranmillis Coll Belfast (CertEd); *m* Karen, *née* Vaughan; 2 s (Robert Samuel b 3 May 1984, Craig David Michael b 12 Jan 2003), 1 da (Rachel Rebecca Kate b 6 April 2000); *Career* head of business studies Castlederg HS 1972–98, publican 1992–; cncllr Strabane DC 1989–2015, memb NI Forum 1996–98, alderman Derry City and Strabane DC 2015–; MLA (UUP) W Tyrone 1998–2007; memb: Educn and Library Bd 2001–11, UUP, Castlederg C of C, Orange Order, Apprentice Boys of Derry, Royal Black Inst, Castlederg Young Loyalists Old Boys' Flute Band; *Recreations* football, rugby, country and western music, church choir, skiing; *Clubs* Leeds United Supporters, NI Supporters, Dergview Football; *Style*— Derek R Hussey

HUSSEY, Mike; *Career* assoc dir Edward Erdman 1987–93, ptnr Knight Frank 1993–97, head of leasing and mktg Canary Wharf Gp 1997–2002, exec dir London portfolio Land Securities plc 2002–09, chief exec Almacantar 2009–; *Style*— Mike Hussey, Esq; ✉ Almacantar, 3 Quebec Mews, London W1H 7NX

HUSSEY, Ross Michael; MLA; s of Sydney Robert Hussey (d 1972), and Rachel, *née* Maguire (d 2015); *b* 25 February 1959, Omagh; *Educ* Open Univ (BA), Nat Univ of Ireland Galway (Dip), Queens Univ Belfast (Cert); *Career* district mangr (Omagh) Pearl Assurance plc 1976–2002, pt/t police offr Royal Ulster Constabulary GC 1977–2003; MLA (UUP) W Tyrone 2011–; chair Royal Ulster Constabulary GC Assoc Part Time Offrs Welfare Gp; memb NI Policing Bd 2011; sec: W Tyrone Constituency Assoc UUP, Kevlin Community and Devpt Assoc; tstee: Assembly Members Pension Scheme 2011–, Royal Ulster Constabulary GC Fndn 2014–; *Recreations* collector of masonic, military and police memorabilia; *Style*— Ross Hussey, Esq, MLA; ✉ Northern Ireland Assembly, Parliament Buildings, Belfast BT4 3XX; 64 Market Street, Omagh, Co Tyrone BT78 1EN (☎ 028 8224 5568, e-mail westtyroneuup@gmail.com, website www.rosshusseymla.com)

HUSSEY, Lady Susan Katharine; GCVO (2013, DCVO 1984, CVO 1971); 5 da of 12 Earl Waldegrave, KG, GCVO, TD (d 1995); *b* 1 May 1939; *m* 25 April 1959, Baron Hussey of North Bradley (d 2006); 1 s (Hon James Arthur b 1961, Page of Honour to HM The Queen 1975–76), 1 da (Hon Katharine Elizabeth (Hon Lady Brooke) b 1964); *Career* Lady-in-Waiting to HM The Queen 1960–; *Style*— Lady Susan Hussey, GCVO; ✉ 18 Lochmore House, Cundy Street, London SW1W 9JX (☎ 020 7730 7406)

HUSTLER, John Randolph; s of William Mostyn Collingwood Hustler (d 1976), and Angela Joan, *née* Hanson (d 1983); *b* 21 August 1946, Newbury, Berks; *Educ* Eton; *m* 23 Sept 1978, Elizabeth Mary, da of Andrew George Hughes-Onslow (d 1979); 2 s (Charles b 1982, Frederick b 1986), 1 da (Willa b 1983); *Career* chartered accountant; ptnr KPMG Peat Marwick 1983–93 (joined 1965); chm: Hustler Venture Partners Ltd 1993–, Northern Venture Tst plc 1995–2014, Octopus Titan VCT 2007–, RenaissanceRe Syndicate Mgmnt Ltd 2007–; dir Hygea VCT 2001–; FCA 1975; *Recreations* golf, tennis, gardening; *Clubs* Boodle's; *Style*— John Hustler, Esq; ✉ Acklam, Itchenor Road, West Itchenor, Chichester, West Sussex PO20 7DD (☎ 01243 513681, e-mail john.hustler@btconnect.com)

HUTCHEON, Dr Andrew William; s of George Hutcheon (d 1989), of Aberdeen, and Elsie Sophia, *née* Murison (d 1983); *b* 21 May 1943; *Educ* Robert Gordon's Coll, Univ of Aberdeen (MB ChB, MD); *m* 14 July 1966, Christine Gray, da of Francis Gray Cusiter, of Kirkwall, Orkney; 2 da (Louise b 1967, Wendy b 1973), 1 s (Barry b 1970); *Career* house offr med and surgery Aberdeen Royal Infirmary 1968–69, SHO and registrar gen med Glasgow Western 1969–72, research fell Western Infirmary Glasgow 1972–75, sr registrar Western Infirmary Glasgow and Royal Marsden London 1975–78, conslt physician and conslt med oncologist Aberdeen Hosps 1978–2016 (ret), sr lectr in med Univ of Aberdeen 1978–2016; memb: Cancer Research Campaign, ICRF, Br Assoc for Cancer Research; FRCP, FRCPEd, MRCP; *Books* Textbook of Medical Treatment (contrib, 1987); *Recreations* skiing, curling; *Clubs* Rubislaw Curling, Aberdeen; *Style*— Dr Andrew Hutcheon; ✉ Moreseat, 159 Midstocket Road, Aberdeen AB15 5LU (☎ 01224 637204); Ward 17, Aberdeen Royal Infirmary, Foresterhill, Aberdeen AB25 2ZN (☎ 01224 681818)

HUTCHINGS, Graham Derek; s of William Hutchings, of Upper Beeding, W Sussex, and Beryl, *née* Bedwell; *b* 2 November 1951; *Educ* Imberhorne Co Secdy Modern Sch, Hatfield Poly, Ealing Coll of HE; *m* Elisabeth Marion, da of Cyril Leslie Judd (d 1987); 1 s (Nicholas Graham b 1978), 1 da (Anna Elisabeth b 1981); *Career* int affrs analyst; office jr JLP Denny Ltd fruit importers 1968–69, shop asst Forrest Stores 1969–70, telephone engr 1970–76, lectr in modern history Hatfield Poly 1983–85, research ed China Business Report 1985–86, dep ed Asian Electricity 1986–87; Daily Telegraph: China specialist 1987–89, Peking corr 1989–93, China corr 1993–98; writer on Chinese Affairs 1998–2000, managing ed Oxford Analytica Daily Brief 2000–10, dir Analysis 2010–13, md Oxford Analytica 2013– (chm 2015–16); chair Advsy Bd China Policy Inst Univ of Nottingham, assoc Univ of Oxford China Centre; *Books* Modern China: A Companion To A Rising Power (2000); *Recreations* music, walking, history; *Clubs* Foreign Correspondents', Hong Kong; *Style*— Graham Hutchings, Esq; ✉ Oxford Analytica, 5 Alfred Street, Oxford OX1 4EH (☎ 01865 261600, e-mail ghutchings@oxford-analytica.com)

HUTCHINGS, Prof Ian Michael; s of Douglas Gilbert Hutchings, and Sheila Margaret Hutchings; *b* 6 May 1950, Barnet, Herts; *Educ* Rugby, Trinity Coll Cambridge (MA, PhD); *m* 1973, Jennifer Rosemary; 4 c; *Career* St John's Coll Cambridge: research fell 1975–78 (working in Cavendish Lab 1975–77), fell 1975–, coll lectr 1978–2001, tutor with responsibility for engrg students 1983–86, admissions tutor 1988–90, dir of studies in materials science and metallurgy 1990–2000; Dept of Materials Science and Metallurgy Univ of Cambridge: univ demonstrator 1977–82, univ lectr 1982–97, reader in tribology 1997–2000, dep head of dept 1998–2000; Dept of Engrg Univ of Cambridge: GKN prof of mfrg engrg 2001–, dep head of dept 2002–05; visiting research scientist Lawrence Berkeley Lab Univ of Calif 1980, visiting research scientist German Federal Materials Research Estab (BAM) Berlin 1992, visiting prof Xi'an Jiaotong Univ 2004; jt course ldr Annual Course on Tribology 1993–; pres Int Research Gp on Wear of Engrg Materials (IRG-OECD) 2007– (UK nat rep 1993–97) chm: Tribology Gp Inst of Physics 1993–95 (memb Ctee 1987–97, hon treas 1989–91), Prog and Pubns Ctee World Tribology Congress IMechE 1997, 2nd Int Conf on Erosive and Abrasive Wear Cambridge 2003, Int Conf on Abrasive Processess 2008; jt chm: 8th Int Conf on Erosion by Liquid and Solid Impact 1994, Int Conf on Abrasive and Erosive Wear 1998; memb: Peer Review Coll EPSRC 1995–, Ctee G2 on Friction Wear American Soc for Testing and Materials 1998–2004, Surface Engrg Divnl Bd Inst of Materials 1999–; memb Editorial Bd: Tribology Int 1992–, Wear 1993–98 (ed-in-chief 1998–2012), Tribology Letters 1994–; chm St John's Innovation Centre Ltd 1996– (memb Bd of Dirs 1993–); Toshiba/Design Cncl Year of Invention Award 1989, IMechE Tribology Silver Medal 1994, Univ of Cambridge Pilkington Teaching Prize 1996, Inst of Materials NPL Award for Materials Metrology 2000, IMechE Donald Julius Groen Prize 2000, ETH Zürich Staudinger-Durrer Prize 2007; hon prof China Univ of Mining and Technol Beijing 1999; CEng, CPhys, FIM 1993 (MIM 1981), FInstP 1994 (MInstP 1978), FREng 2002; *Publications* Tribology: Friction and Wear of Engineering Materials (1992), Inkjet Technology for Digital Fabrication (jt ed, 2012); more than 350 papers on tribology, surface engrg, manufacturing engrg, inkjet printing and related subjects; *Style*— Prof Ian Hutchings; ✉ University of Cambridge, Institute for Manufacturing, 17 Charles Babbage Road, Cambridge CB3 0FS

HUTCHINGS, Michael Balfour; OBE (2005); s of Benjamin Legh Balfour Hutchings (d 1981), and Ann, *née* Carter; *b* 8 November 1948; *Educ* Marlborough, Coll of William and Mary VA (BA); *m* m 1, 29 June 1974 (m dis 1987), Jane Elizabeth, *née* Bristow; 1 da (Anna b 4 July 1978), 1 s (William b 9 Jan 1981); m 2, 8 April 1992, Victoria, da of Arthur Trollope; 3 step s (Robin b 6 March 1979, Sholto b 16 Nov 1981, Dominic b 11 Aug 1985); *Career* articled clerk McKenna & Co 1970–72, admitted slr 1973, ptnr Lovell White Durrant 1981–95 (asst slr 1974–81); EU law conslt 1996–; memb: Law Soc 1973, Br Inst of Int and Comparative Law, Competition and Markets Authy 2013–; Liveryman Worshipful Co of Drapers; *Recreations* golf, tennis, walking, cabinet-making; *Clubs* Travellers, St Enodoc Golf; *Style*— Michael Hutchings, Esq, OBE; ✉ Lesters, Maperton Road, Charlton Horethorne, Sherborne, Dorset DT9 4NT (☎ 07768 105777, e-mail mbh@dircon.co.uk)

HUTCHINSON, Anne-Marie; OBE (2002); da of Samuel Gerald Hutchinson, and Catherine, *née* Fitzgerald; *b* 1 January 1958, Ireland; *Educ* Univ of Leeds (BA), Nottingham Trent Law Sch; *children* 1 da (Catherine Louise b 1987), 1 s (Samuel Gerald b 1995); *Career* admitted slr 1985; slr specialising in matters relating to children (incl int custody disputes, child abduction and int adoption); ptnr Beckman & Beckman 1988–98, head Children's Law Dept Dawson Cornwell 1998–; memb Nat Cmmn on Forced Marriage House of Lords; int corr Int Family Law; chair Bd of Tstees Reunite Int Child Abduction Centre, founding fell Int Surrogacy Forum; UNICEF Child Rights Lawyer of the Year 1999, Legal Aid Lawyer of the Year 2004, Outstanding Int Woman Lawyer Int Bar Assoc 2010, IKWRO (Iranian and Kurdish Womens Rights Orgn) True Honour Award 2011, Albert KennedyTst Award 2011, Jordans Int Family Lawyer of the Year 2012, Int Acad of Matrimonial Lawyers Pres's Medal 2014; memb: Law Soc 1985, Int Soc of Family Law, Int Bar Assoc, Int Centre for Missing and Exploited Children; fell Int Acad of Matrimonial Lawyers; *Books* International Parental Child Abduction (jtly, 2003); *Publications* Children Law and Practice (conslt ed), International Parental Child Abduction (jt author); *Recreations* film, charitable work; *Style*— Miss Anne-Marie Hutchinson, OBE; ✉ Dawson Cornwell, 15 Red Lion Square, London WC1R 4QT (☎ 020 7242 2556, fax 020 7539 4841, e-mail amh@dawsoncornwell.co.uk)

HUTCHINSON, Colman Joseph; s of William Joseph Hutchinson (d 2000), and Eileen Patricia, *née* Hogan (d 1985); *b* 10 July 1953, Dublin; *Educ* Christian Brothers' Coll Monkstown Park Dublin; *m* 3 June 1977, Sharon Elizabeth, *née* Leahy; 2 s (Aaron Patrick b 21 May 1978, Adam Joseph b 22 Dec 1979), 1 da (Ava Jean b 30 March 1983); *Career* researcher Gay Byrne's Late Late Show RTE Ireland 1977–85, prodr LWT 1985–95 (programmes incl Blind Date and Surprise Surprise); head of entertainment: Hat Trick Productions 1995–98, Celador 1998–2008 (responsible for Who Wants to Be a Millionaire, nominee BAFTA Award 2000); fndr Prime Suspects prodn co (subsid of 2way traffic) 2008–, fndr and creative dir Boxatricks 2010–; memb Advsy Bd Entertainment Masterclass; *Style*— Colman Hutchinson, Esq; ✉ mobile 07768 037473

HUTCHINSON, Prof Gregory Owen; s of Rev J O Hutchinson, and Mrs D Hutchinson; *Educ* City of London Sch, Balliol Coll Oxford (scholar, MA, DPhil); *Career* Univ of Oxford: res lectr ChCh 1981–84, fell and tutor in classics Exeter Coll 1984–2015, reader in classical lit 1996–98, prof of Greek and Latin languages and lit 1998–2015, regius prof of Greek 2015–; *Books* Aeschylus, Septem Contra Thebas (1985), Hellenistic Poetry (1988), Latin Literature from Seneca to Juvenal: A Critical Study (1993), Cicero's Correspondence: A Literary Study (1998), Greek Lyric Poetry: A Commentary on Selected Larger Pieces (2001), Propertius: Elegies Book IV (2006), Talking Books: Readings in Hellenistic and Latin Poetry-Books (2008), Greek to Latin: Frameworks and Contexts for Intertextuality (2013); *Recreations* playing the piano, reading literature (mostly English, French, German, Italian, Russian, Sanskrit, Spanish); *Style*— Prof Gregory Hutchinson; ✉ Christ Church, Oxford OX1 1DP (☎ 01865 279600, e-mail gregory.hutchinson@classics.ox.ac.uk)

HUTCHINSON, (John) Maxwell; s of Frank Maxwell Hutchinson (d 1977), and Elizabeth Ross Muir, *née* Wright (d 1987); *b* 3 December 1948; *Educ* Oundle, Scott Sutherland Sch of Architecture Aberdeen, AA Sch of Architecture (AADipl); *m* 2008, Georgina Burrell; *Career* chm: The Permarock Group Loughborough 1985–95, Hutchinson and Ptnrs Architects Ltd 1972–92, The Hutchinson Studio Architects 1992–2000; RIBA: memb Cncl 1978–93, sr vice-pres 1988–89, pres 1989–91; visiting prof of architecture Queen's Univ Belfast 1989–93, special prof of architectural design Univ of Nottingham 1992–96, visiting prof of architecture Univ of Westminster 1997–2001; chm: Industrial Building Bureau 1986–88, Br Architectural Library Tst 1991–, Schools of Architecture Validation Panel 1991–96, E Midlands Arts Bd 1991–94; vice-chm Construction Industry Cncl 1989–91; radio and TV broadcaster, compositions incl: The Kibbo Kift (Edinburgh Festival) 1976, The Ascent of Wilberforce III (Lyric Hammersmith) 1982, Requiem 1988, Christmas Cantata 1990; memb Cncl Royal Sch of Church Music 1997–2000; tstee Article 25 (humanitarian architecture charity) 2006; Freeman City of London 1980, Freeman Worshipful Co of Chartered Architects 1988; Hon DDes Robert Gordon Univ Aberdeen; hon fell Univ of Greenwich; hon fell Royal Soc of Ulster Architects, assoc memb PRS 1988; *Books* The Prince of Wales Right or Wrong? (1989), Number 57 – The Story of a House (2003); *Recreations* playing jazz piano, travel; *Clubs* Athenaeum, Blacks, Groucho; *Style*— Maxwell Hutchinson, Esq; ✉ e-mail maxwell@hutchinsonstudio.co.uk

HUTCHINSON, Prof Philip; DL (Oxfordshire 2003); s of George Hutchinson, of Bishop Auckland, Co Durham, and Edna Hutchinson; *b* 26 July 1938; *Educ* King James I GS Bishop Auckland, King's Coll Durham (BSc), Univ of Newcastle upon Tyne (PhD); *m* 1960, Joyce Harrison, da of Fred Harrison, of Bishop Auckland, Co Durham; 1 da (Barbara Helen b 1967), 1 s (John Paul b 1972); *Career* AERE Harwell: scientific offr rising to princ scientific offr Theoretical Physics Div 1962–69 and 1970–75, head Thermodynamics and Fluid Mechanics Gp Engrg Scis Div 1975–80, head Combustion Centre 1980–87, head Engrg Physics Branch Engrg Scis Div 1980–85, head Engrg Scis Div 1985–87; Cranfield Univ: head Sch of Mech Engrg 1987–2000, dep vice-chllr 1996–2003, pro-vice-chllr 1996–99, head Sch of Engrg 2000–02; princ Royal Mil Coll of Sci 1996–2006; visiting fell Dept of Chem Engrg Univ of Houston Texas 1969–70; visiting prof: Imperial Coll London 1980–85, Univ of Leeds 1985–; formerly chm: Exec Ctee on Fundamental Research in Combustion Int Energy Agency (1977–81), Combustion Physics Gp Inst of Physics (1985–89), Computational Fluid Dynamics Advsy Gp SERC; chm Bd European Research Community on Flow Turbulence and Combustion 1994–2000 (fndr memb, treas 2000–02); non-exec dir NUMECA Belgium 1998–2002; formerly Inst of Physics rep then Combustion Inst (Br Section) rep on Watt Ctee Inst of Energy, memb Energy Panel Foresight Survey, UK memb COST (Co-operation in Sci and Technol) F1 Gp of CEC, Ed Advsy Bd Experiments in Fluids jl; Hon Dr Technol Univ of Lund Sweden 1999; MRI 1989, CPhys, CEng, FInstP, FREng 1997; *Publications* author of numerous articles in learned jls on statistical mechanics, fluid mechanics, spray and particle cloud disperson and combustion; *Recreations* music, reading, Go, gadgets; *Style*— Prof Philip Hutchinson, DL, FREng; ✉ Long Barn, Letcombe Regis, Wantage, Oxfordshire OX12 9JD (☎ 01235 770302)

HUTCHINSON OF LULLINGTON, Baron (Life Peer UK 1978), of Lullington in the County of East Sussex; Jeremy Nicolas Hutchinson; QC (1961); o s of St John Hutchinson, KC (d 1943), and Mary, o da of Sir Hugh Barnes, KCSI, KCVO; *b* 28 March 1915; *Educ* Stowe, Magdalen Coll Oxford (MA); *m* 1, 1940 (m dis 1966), Dame Peggy Ashcroft, DBE (d 1991); 1 da (Hon Eliza b 1941), 1 s (Hon Nicholas St John b 1946); m 2, 1966, June (d 2006), yr da of Capt Arthur Edward Capel, CBE (d 1919), and formerly wife of Franz Osborn; *Career* served RNVR 1939–46; called to the Bar Middle Temple 1939; recorder: Bath 1962–72, Crown Court 1972–76; sits as Lib Dem Peer in House of Lords (sat as Lab Peer until joining SDP 1981); vice-chm Arts Cncl 1977–79; tstee: Tate Gallery 1977–84 (chm 1980–84); prof of law RA 1988; *Clubs* MCC; *Style*— The Rt Hon Lord Hutchinson of Lullington, QC; ✉ House of Lords, London SW1A 0PW

HUTCHISON, David Alan; MBE (1976); s of Hector Donald Hutchison (d 1948), of Enfield, Middx, and Winifred, *née* Middlehurst (d 1986); *b* 13 January 1937; *Educ* Royal Masonic Sch Bushey, Bartlett Sch of Architecture UCL (BA); *m* 3 April 1961 (m dis 1989), Helen Elizabeth, da of Arthur George Penn (d 1981), of Pembury, Kent; 2 da (Gillian b 21 Jan 1962, Christine b 9 Aug 1965), 2 s (Michael b 1 Nov 1963, Peter b 24 Dec 1966); m 2, 18 May 1990, Audrey, da of Horace Scott, of Tolworth, Surrey; *Career* architect; worked with Powell & Moya 1960–64: chm: HLM (formerly Hutchison Locke & Monk) 1988–92 (fndr ptnr 1964), HLM Architects Ltd, HLM Planning Ltd, HLM Landscape Ltd; fndr and sr dir Moloney O'Beirne Hutchison Partnership Dublin 1977–, fndr and sr ptnr David Hutchison Partnership 1992– (architect St James Hosp Dublin, Royal London Hosp redevelopment, Barry Hosp, Chepstow Hosp, Hammersmith Hosp, Sixth Form Coll Farnborough, St John's Sch Marlborough, Broomfield Hosp Chelmsford, Royal London Hosp redevelopment, Royal Marsden Hosp, Princess Alexandra Hosp Harlow, Aldershot Hosp, Frenchay Hosp, Weston Hosp, Torbay Hosp, Nevill Hall Hosp, Monmouth Hosp); architect for major public sector cmmns in health and civic authorities 1964–88; health projects (hosps) incl: Bournemouth, Cheltenham, Ealing, Whipps Cross, Lister, Northern Gen Sheffield, Medway, Dunfermline West Fife, Liverpool Maternity, Royal Brompton London, Nottingham City, Guy's, N Middx; civic projects: Surrey Heath BC, Broxbourne BC, Daventry DC, Colchester BC, Waltham Forest Cncl, Macclesfield Cncl, Epsom and Ewell Cncl, Reigate and Banstead Cncl, Stoke-on-Trent Cncl, Stroud Cncl, North Staffs Cncl, schs in Redditch, Bristol and Bath; cmmns: Univs of Reading and Surrey, Smithfield Market Corp of London; winner: int competition (architecture) Paisley Civic Centre 1964, 7 Civic Tst Awards DOE Good Housing Award, RIBA Architecture Commendation, Redland Roof Tile Award, RIBA Energy Award, Concrete Soc Architecture Award; nat seat on Cncl RIBA 1987–93, assessor Civic Tst; Freeman: City of London 1977 (Liveryman 1990), Worshipful Co of Constructors 1977 (Master 2000), Worshipful Co of Arbitrators 1987; RIBA, ARIAS, FIA, FFB, AInst(Hosp)E, FIE, FRSA 1989; *Recreations* amateur theatre, local amenity soc; *Clubs* Arts (London), Camberley Soc (chm), Farnborough and RAE Operatic Soc, Camus Productions, Bath Light Operatic Gp,

Gilbert and Sullivan Soc; *Style*— David Hutchison, Esq, MBE; ✉ 7 St Michael's Court, Monkton Combe, Bath BA2 7HA (mobile 07901 716866); Whittaker House, 2 Whittaker Avenue, Richmond upon Thames, Surrey TW9 1EH (☎ 020 8822 6907)

HUTCHISON, Sir Peter Craft; 2 Bt (UK 1956), of Rossie, Co Perth, CBE (1992); s of Sir James Riley Holt Hutchison, 1 Bt, DSO, TD (d 1979), and Winefryde Eleanor Mary (Anne) (d 1988); *b* 5 June 1935; *Educ* Eton, Magdalene Coll Cambridge (BA); *m* 1966, Virginia, da of John Millar Colville, of Gribloch, Kippen, Stirlingshire; 1 s; *Heir* s James Colville Hutchison; *Career* former Lt Royal Scots Greys; chm Hutchison and Craft Ltd, former dir Stakis plc and other cos; memb Bd: Scottish Tourist Bd 1981–87, Deacon Incorporation of Hammermen 1984–85; Scottish Natural Heritage June-Dec 1994; chm Forestry Cmmn 1994–2001; vice-chm Bd Br Waterways Bd (memb 1987–98); chm of tstees Royal Botanic Garden Edinburgh 1985–94, dep convenor Loch Lomond and the Trossachs Nat Park 2002–; FRSE 1997; *Publications* Seeds of Adventure (with P Cox); *Style*— Sir Peter Hutchison, Bt, CBE, FRSE; ✉ Broich, Kippen, Stirlingshire FK8 3EN

HUTCHON, Dr David James Riddell; s of James Hutchon (d 1971), and Alice Mary Hutchon; *b* 17 April 1945; *Educ* George Watson's Boys Coll Edinburgh, Univ of Edinburgh (BSc, MB ChB); *m* 12 June 1971, Rosemary Elizabeth; 2 s (Christopher b 1978 d 2015, Andrew b 1995), 1 da (Fiona b 1979); *Career* govt med offr Grand Cayman BWI 1972–74, SHO Simpson Memorial Hosp Edinburgh 1974–76, registrar in obstetrics and gynaecology Ninewells Hosp Dundee 1976–78, res registrar Northwick Park Hosp London 1978–79, sr registrar in obstetrics and gynaecology Eastern Gen Hosp Edinburgh and clinical tutor Univ of Edinburgh 1979–81, conslt obstetrician and gynaecologist Darlington Health Authy 1981–; co-inventor BASICS neonatal resuscitation trolley (now marketed as LifeStart trolley); launched Stop Cord Clamping at Birth 2003; considered a world expert in the question of cord clamping at birth and invited speaker at many conferences; FRCOG 1995; *Publications* incl: Resuscitate with the Placental Circulation Intact (with I Thakur, 2008), Immediate or Early Cord Clamping vs Delayed Clamping (2012), Early vs Delayed Cord Clamping at Birth; in Sickness and in Health (2013), Cutting the Cord: An International Conference (2013), The Broader Implications of Early Cord Clamping at Birth (2015), Ventilation, Chest Compression and Placental Circulation at Neonatal Resuscitation (2015), The normal range of heart rate at birth in a healthy term neonate: a critical review of the evidence (2016); *Recreations* skiing, sailing, flying; *Clubs* Blackwell Grange Golf; *Style*— Dr David Hutchon; ✉ 9 Farr Holme, Blackwell, Darlington, Co Durham DL3 8QZ (e-mail djrhutchon@hotmail.co.uk)

HUTH, Angela Maureen; da of Harold Edward Strachan Huth (d 1967), and Bridget, *née* Nickols (d 2004); *b* 29 August 1938, London; *Educ* Guilsborough Lodge Sch, Lawnside Great Malvern, Beaux Arts Sch of Art Paris, Annigoni's Sch of Art Florence, Byam Shaw Art Sch London; *m* 1, 1961 (m dis 1970), Quentin Crewe (d 1998); 1 da (Candida Crewe, *qv*, b 1964); *m* 2, 1978, Dr James Howard-Johnston, s of late Rear Adm C D Howard-Johnston, CB, DSO, DSC; 1 da (Eugenie b 1981); *Career* memb Art Dept J Walter Thompson Advertising 1958–59, travel ed Queen Magazine 1959–61, woman's page Sunday Express 1962–63, reporter Man Alive (BBC) 1965–68, presenter How It Is (BBC) 1969–70, freelance journalist and reviewer 1965– (incl The Times, Sunday Times, Telegraph, Sunday Telegraph, Spectator, Guardian, Observer); FRSL 1975; *Publications* novels: Nowhere Girl (1970), Virginia Fly is Drowning (1972), Sun Child (1975), South of the Lights (1977), Monday Lunch in Fairyland and Other Stories (1978), Wanting (1984), Such Visitors (1989), Invitation to the Married Life (1991), Land Girls (1994), Another Kind of Cinderella and other stories (1996), Wives of the Fishermen (1998), Easy Silence (1999), Of Love and Slaughter (2002), The Collected Stories of Angela Huth (2003), Once a Land Girl (2010), Colouring In (2015); non fiction: The English Woman's Wardrobe (1987), Island of the Children (ed, poetry anthology, 1987), Casting a Spell (ed, poetry anthology, 1991), Well Remembered Friends (ed, anthology of eulogies, 2004); stage plays: The Understanding (first performed 1981), The Trouble with Old Lovers (first performed 1995); TV plays incl: The Summer House (BBC, 1969), The Emperor's New Hat (BBC, 1971), Virginia Fly is Drowning (adaptation, BBC, 1975), The Understanding (YTV, 1987), Sun Child (YTV, 1988); radio plays incl Past Forgetting (2001); *Recreations* tap dancing, buying and selling paste jewellery; *Style*— Miss Angela Huth

HUTH, Johannes Peter; s of Prof Karl Huth, of Frankfurt, Germany, and Dr Brigitte, *née* Soergel; *b* 27 May 1960, Heidelberg, Germany; *Educ* LSE (BSc), Univ of Chicago (MBA); *m* 20 July 1991 (m dis), Leili, *née* Persson; 2 s (Christopher b 18 April 1992, Nikolas b 7 Jan 1997), 3 da (Elisabeth b 1 June 1994, Susanna, Katrina (twins) b 5 April 1998); *Career* a vice-pres M&A Dept Salomon Brothers 1986–1991, memb Mgmnt Ctee Investcorp until 1999, with Kohlberg Kravis Roberts & Co 1999– (currently md and head London office); *Style*— Johannes Huth, Esq; ✉ Kohlberg Kravis Roberts & Co Limited, Stirling Square, 7 Carlton Gardens, London SW1Y 5AD (☎ 020 7839 9800, fax 020 7839 9832)

HUTSON, Maurice Arthur; MBE (1998); s of William Arthur Hutson (d 1980), of S Yorks, and Ivy, *née* Roberts (d 1989); *b* 27 January 1934; *Educ* Gainsborough Tech Coll, Leeds Coll of Technol; *m* 1959, Janet, da of Arthur Edward Parkin, of S Yorks; 2 s (Mark Andrew b 1961, Jonathan Peter b 1970), 1 da (Helen Claire b 1963); *Career* chartered engr; apprentice Newell Ltd 1949–57, Nat Serv RAF 1957–59, design engr Pegson Ltd 1959–63, devpt engr Tarmac Roadstone Ltd 1963–71 (prodn and engrg mangr 1965, staff offr 1970); chm and md: Seaham Harbour Dock Co 1971–81 (dir 1981–87), Transport and Aggregates Ltd 1972–81, Mahcon Construction (Services) Ltd 1972–, Wath Quarries Ltd 1977–, Allerton Engrg Ltd 1983–2000, Naylor Sportscars Ltd 1986–93, Hutson Motor Co Ltd 1986–; exec chm: Parker Plant Ltd (chm and chief exec 1990–97 and 2003–08), Templars of Rothley; chm: E Type Cars Ltd 1997, Canon Street Properties Ltd 1997, Park Hill Golf and Leisure Ltd 2000–; exec chm Universal Conveyors Co Ltd 1998–2008; dir: Necoast Ltd 1980–90, The Sundial Hotel Ltd Northallerton until 1996, Modern Air Systems Ltd 1992–2008, Leicestershire Engrg Trg Gp 1996–2008; memb: Round Table Gainsborough 1967–74, Rotary Int Seaham 1970–80, Ctee Seaham RNLI 1971–76, Rotary Int Stokesley 1980–90, Cncl and vice-pres Fedn of Mfrs of Construction Equipment and Cranes (FMCEC) 1992–96, Lighthouse Club 1990–2008, Br Thai Business Gp, Asia Europe Meeting (ASEM); pres Seaham Sea Angling Club 1972–81; advsr Prince's Tst until 1997; fndr Yarm Boys Sch 1971; CEng, MIMechE, MIEE, FIQ; *Recreations* grandchildren, advising people on new ventures and business set ups, motor sport, travel and walking, gardening, steam engines and vintage vehicles, collecting antiques, cycling, water colour painting, writing my life story (second edition); *Clubs* 41 (Guisborough); *Style*— Maurice A Hutson, Esq, MBE; ✉ West Acre, 25 The Ridgeway, Rothley, Leicestershire LE7 7LE (☎ 0116 230 3230, fax 0116 230 2868, e-mail maurice.hutson@hotmail.co.uk); Canon Street Properties Limited, Moorland House, 4/5 Woodgate, Rothley, Leicestershire LE7 7LE (☎ 0116 237 6863)

HUTSON, Robin; s of Derek Charles Hutson, of Fordingbridge, Hants, and Eileen Hilda, *née* Juniper; *b* 9 January 1957; *Educ* Haberdashers' Aske's Hatcham, Godalming GS, Brookland Tech Coll (OND); *m* 25 June 1983, Judith Alison, da of Douglas Hill; 2 s (Oliver Charles Westley b 10 Oct 1985, William Charles Westley b 3 Nov 1988); *Career* trainee Savoy Hotels Ltd 1975–81, front office mangr The Berkeley Hotel 1981–84, ops mangr Elbow Beach Hotel Bermuda 1984–86, md Chewton Glen Hotel Ltd 1990–94 (gen mangr 1986–90), md and chm Hotel du Vin Ltd 1994–2004; chm and dir Limewood Gp Ltd 2009–, chm and ceo Home Grown Hotels 2011–; non-exec dir Richmond FC 1996–99, dir Soho House Ltd 1997–2008; memb: Bd of Patrons Academy of Culinary Arts 2004–, Champagne Acad; Caterer and Hotelkeeper Hotelier of the Year 2003, Hotel Catey

Outstanding Contribution Award 2014, The AA Lifetime Achievement Award 2015, memb Hospitality Hall of Fame 2016; Hon DBA Southampton Solent Univ 2015; MHCIMA 1990; *Recreations* wine, fly fishing, motorcycling, food, travel; *Clubs* Soho House, Groucho; *Style*— Robin Hutson, Esq; ✉ Home Grown Hotels Ltd, Clayhill, Beechen Lane, Lyndhurst, Hampshire SO43 7DD

HUTT, Ven David Handley; s of late Frank Handley Hutt, and Evelyn Violet Catherine, *née* Faarup; *b* 24 August 1938; *Educ* Brentwood Sch, RMA Sandhurst, KCL (AKC, Hanson Prize for Christian Ethics, Barry Prize for Theology); *Career* Reg Army 1957–64; ordained: deacon 1969, priest 1970; curate: Bedford Park London 1969–70, St Matthew Westminster 1970–73; priest vicar and succentor Southwark Cathedral 1973–78, sr chaplain King's Coll Taunton 1978–82; vicar: St Alban and St Patrick Birmingham 1982–86, All Saints' St Marylebone 1986–95, canon and steward Westminster Abbey 1995–2005 (canon emeritus 2005–), sub dean and archdeacon of Westminster 1999–2005, memb Bd Assoc of Leading Visitor Attractions (representing The Cathedrals' Gp) 2001 (memb Cncl 2000–05); fell Sion Coll 2007– (pres 1996–97, memb Ct 2005–07), fndr ed Affirming Catholicism; govr Westminster City Sch 1995–2005, patron London Parks and Gardens Tst 2003–, tstee United Westminster Schs Fndn 2006–14, govr Sutton Valence Sch 2007–12; MA (Lambeth) 2005; *Recreations* reading, travel, the enjoyment of fine wines; *Style*— The Ven David Hutt; ✉ 14 The Quadrangle, Morden College, Blackheath, London SE3 0PW

HUTT, Sir Dexter Walter; kt (2004); Walter Hutt, of West Palm Beach, FL, and Binks Hutt (d 1948); *b* 25 July 1948, Georgetown, Guyana; *Educ* Mackenzie HS, Greenmore Coll, Univ of Birmingham (BSocSci); *m* Aug 1976, Rosemary Lyn; 1 da (Elizabeth b 23 June 1979), 2 s (Andrew b 7 Aug 1981, Steven b 16 July 1987); *Career* former teacher Handsworth and Coventry; head Ninestiles Sch Birmingham 1998–2004, chief exec Ninestiles Plus, exec ldr Hastings Schs' Fedn; cmmr Cmmn for Racial Equality 2004–; *Recreations* current affairs, reading, golf and most sports; *Style*— Sir Dexter Hutt; ✉ Ninestiles School, Hartfield Crescent, Acocks Green, Birmingham B27 7QG (☎ 0121 693 1642, fax 0121 778 4234)

HUTT, Jane Elizabeth; AM; da of late Prof Michael S R Hutt, and Elizabeth, *née* Newton-Jones, of Crickhowell, Powys; *Educ* Highlands Sch Eldoret Kenya, Rosemead Sch Littlehampton, Univ of Kent (BA), LSE (CQSW), Univ of Bristol (MSc); *m* 14 July 1984, Michael John Hilary Trickey; 2 da (Jessica, Rachel); *Career* community worker: Impact (town planners and architects) 1972–74, Polypill Community Project Fndn 1975–77; co-ordinator Welsh Women's Aid 1975–88; dir: Tenant Participation Advsy Serv 1988–92, Chwarae Teg (equal opportunities) 1992–99; vice-chair Wales Cncl for Voluntary Action; memb: Common Purpose Advsy Ctee 1989–99, New Deal Wales Advsy Task Force 1996–99, New Opportunities Fund 1998–99; memb Nat Assembly for Wales (Lab) Vale of Glamorgan 1999–, min for health and social servs 1999–2005, min for assembly business and budget 2005–07 and 2009–11, min for children, educn, lifelong learning and skills 2007–09, min for finance and ldr of the house 2011–; hon fell Cardiff Met Univ 1996; *Books* Opening the Town Hall: An Introduction to Local Government (2 edn, 1989), Making Opportunities: A Guide for Women and Employers (1992); *Recreations* reading, music; *Style*— Ms Jane Hutt, AM; ✉ National Assembly for Wales, Cardiff Bay, Cardiff CF99 1NA (☎ 02920 898469, fax 02920 898537, e-mail jane.hutt@wales.gov.uk)

HUTT, Peter Morrice; s of late Sqdn Ldr Harry Morrice Hutt, of Caversham, Berks, and late Joan Ethel Ludlow, *née* Whitmore; *b* 15 April 1945; *Educ* Leighton Park Sch Reading, Univ of Southampton (LLB); *m* 23 March 1974, Cynthia Anne, da of John Gauntlett Gubb (d 1988), of Uitenhage, South Africa; 1 s (Stephen b 1977); *Career* admitted slr 1969, Notary Public 1978; ptnr Brain & Brain 1973–97, conslt Field Seymour Parkes 1997–2010; dep master Supreme Court Queen's Bench Div 1992–99; Rotherfield Peppard: chm Parish Cncl 1987–90, lay chm All Saints Parochial Church Cncl 1986–90, churchwarden All Saints Church 2005–09; clerk Polehampton Charities Twyford 1981–2010, former memb Caversham Round Table; memb: Law Soc 1967, Slr's Benevolent Assoc 1969, Notaries Soc 1978; *Recreations* music, walking, arts, reading, travel, bridge; *Style*— Peter Hutt, Esq; ✉ 6 Tidmarsh Grange, The Street, Tidmarsh, Reading, Berkshire RG8 8FD (☎ 0118 984 1061, e-mail pchutt16@btinternet.com)

HUTTON, Baron (Life Peer UK 1997), of Bresagh in the County of Down; (James) Brian Edward Hutton; kt (1988), PC (1988); s of late James Hutton, and Mabel Hutton, of Belfast; *b* 29 June 1931; *Educ* Shrewsbury, Balliol Coll Oxford (BA), Queen's Univ Belfast; *m* 1, 1975, Mary Gillian (d 2000), da of James Murland, of Saintfield, Co Down; 2 da (Hon Louise b 1976, Hon Helen b 1978); *m* 2, 2001, Rosalind Anne Nickols, wid of Christopher Nickols; 2 step s (James b 1975, Hugo b 1981), 1 step da (Annabel b 1977); *Career* called to the Bar NI 1954, jr counsel to Attorney Gen NI 1969, QC (NI) 1970, sr crown counsel NI 1973–79, judge of the High Court of Justice (NI) 1979–88, Lord Chief Justice of NI 1988–97, a Lord of Appeal in Ordinary 1997–2004; chm Hutton Inquiry 2003–04; memb Jt Law Enforcement Cmmn 1974, dep chm Boundary Cmmn for NI 1985–88; pres NI Assoc for Mental Health 1983–90; visitor Univ of Ulster 1999–2004; *Style*— The Rt Hon the Lord Hutton, PC; ✉ House of Lords, London SW1A 0PW

HUTTON, Dame Deirdre Mary; DBE (2004, CBE 1998); *née* Cassels; da of Kenneth Alexander Home Cassels, of Wimbish Green, Essex, and Barbara Kathleen, *née* Alington; *b* 15 March 1949; *Educ* Sherborne Sch for Girls, Hartwell House; *m* 1 Nov 1975 (m dis 2010), Alasdair Henry Hutton, s of late Alexander Hutton; 2 s (Thomas Kennedy b 28 June 1978, Nicholas Alasdair b 27 Feb 1982); *Career* Anchor Housing Assoc Oxford 1973–75, res asst Glasgow C of C 1975–82; pro-chllr Cranfield Univ 2012–; chm: Scot Consumer Cncl 1991–99 (memb 1986–90, vice-chm 1990–91), Rural Forum (Scotland) Ltd 1992–99, Ombudsman Cncl Personal Investment Authy 1997–2000 (chm 1994–96), Nat Consumer Cncl 2001–05 (memb Cncl 1991–2005, vice-chm 1997–2001), Steering Gp Food Chain Centre 2002–05, Food Standards Agency 2005–09, Civil Aviation Authy 2009–; vice-chm Scottish Environmental Protection Agency 1999–2002; memb: Scot Consultative Cncl on the Curriculum 1987–91, Ctee on Reporting 1989–91, Parole Bd for Scot 1993–96, Cabinet Office Better Regulation Task Force 1999–2005, Sustainable Devpt Cmmn 2000–01, Curry Cmmn on the Future of Agric and Food 2001; non-exec dir: FSA 1997–2007 (dep chm 2004–07), Edinburgh City Theatres Tst 1998–99, Thames Water Utilities Ltd 2010–, HM Treasy 2008–13, Castle Tst 2012–; lay memb for Scot of Gen Dental Cncl and memb Professional Misconduct Ctee 1988–94, memb Ctee to Review Curriculum Examinations in Fifth and Sixth Years of Scot Educn (Howie Ctee) 1990–92; memb, treas and chm Broomlands Sch Bd 1984–91, memb Music Ctee Scot Arts Cncl 1985–91, hon sec Kelso Music Soc 1985–95, chm Enterprise Music Scotland Ltd 1993–95; vice-chm Borders Local Health Cncl 1991–95, memb Bd Borders Health Bd 1996–2002; pro-chllr Cranfield Univ 2012–; Hon DUniv Stirling 2000, Hon DSc Loughborough Univ 2005, Hon DSc Cranfield Univ 2007; *Recreations* gardening, music; *Style*— Dame Deirdre Hutton, DBE; ✉ Civil Aviation Authority, CAA House, 45–59 Kingsway, London WC2B 6TE

HUTTON, John Christopher; s of John Francis Hutton (d 1997), of Cardiff, and Elizabeth Margery Ethel, *née* Pugh (d 1998); *b* 7 June 1937; *Educ* Monmouth Sch, Kingswood Sch Bath, ChCh Oxford (MA), Coll of Advanced Technology Aston (DMS), Coll of Aeronautics Cranfield; *m* 5 Aug 1963, Elizabeth Ann, da of Prof Eric Evans (d 1967); 2 da (Catrin b 1965, Bethan b 1968); *Career* Nat Serv RA Cyprus 1956–58; methods engr Tube Investments 1963–64 (graduate trainee 1961–63); Bristol and West Building Society: PA to Gen Mangr 1964–67, res mangr 1967–76, asst gen mangr 1976–88 (mktg and res 1976–86, corporate info and analysis 1986–88); fin mktg conslt 1988–2005; dir:

Bristol & West Personal Pensions Ltd 1988–89, Wildscreen Trading Ltd 1991–94; conslt Money Which? 1971–2005; chm Housing Fin Panel Bldg Socs Assoc 1973–84 (memb 1967–), co-chm Tech Sub-Ctee of Jt Advsy Ctee on Mortgage Fin 1973–82; memb: Construction Industries Jt Forecasting Ctee NEDO 1978–89 (Housing Strategy Ctee 1975–77), Cncl Sub-Ctee on Reserves and Liquidity BSA 1981, Fin Advertising Sub-Ctee Advertising Standards Authy 1982–92; ldr BSA Netherlands Res Gp 1979; dir: Bristol Bldgs Preservation Tst Ltd 1984–2003, The Wildscreen Tst 1987–94; chm Kingsweston Preservation Soc 1993–97; FSS 1968, assoc IMS 1968; *Publications* author of many articles for the nat press; *Recreations* antiques, wine, countryside, journalism; *Style—* John Hutton, Esq; ✉ Ferns Hill, Kingsweston Road, Bristol BS11 0UX (✆ 0117 982 4324); Wyevern, Aberedw, Builth Wells, Powys LD2 3UN (✆ 01982 560439)

HUTTON, Prof Ronald Edmund; s of Geoffrey Edmund Hutton (d 1955), and Elsa Edwina, *née* Hansen (d 1978); *b* 19 December 1953, Ootacamund, India; *Educ* Ilford County HS for Boys, Pembroke Coll Cambridge (MA), St John's Coll Oxford (DPhil); *m* 1988, Lisa Radulovic; 1 da (Sophia Elisabeth b 19 March 1993); partner, Ana Adnan; *Career* Prize fell Magdalen College Oxford 1979–81; Univ of Bristol: lectr in history 1981–88, reader 1988–96, prof of history 1996–; cmmr English Heritage 2009–13, tstee English Heritage 2015–; Benjamin Franklin Prize Booksellers Assoc of America 1993; FRHistS 1981, FSA 1994, FLSW 2011, FBA 2014; *Publications* author of 15 books, jt author of 2 books, author of 75 essays; *Recreations* travel with a view to adventure; *Style—* Prof Ronald Hutton; ✉ Department of Historical Studies, University of Bristol, 13 Woodland Road, Bristol BS8 1TB (✆ 0117 928 7595, fax 0117 331 7933, e-mail r.hutton@bristol.co.uk)

HUTTON, Stuart Michael Colman; s of David S Hutton (d 1985), and Marjorie, *née* Colman; *b* Kent; *Educ* King's Sch Gloucester, Guildford and Lancaster Gate Colls of Law; *m* 25 July 1992, Clare Patricia, *née* Strowbridge; 1 da (Emelie Clare b 8 May 1993), 1 s (William Stuart b 11 April 1995); *Career* admitted slr 1975, slr advocate 1999; articled to E W Sankey at Ingledew & Sons slrs Cardiff, ptnr Edwards Geldard (now Geldards) 1977–86, fndr Hutton's Slrs Cardiff 1986–; fndr memb Child Care Panel Law Soc, pt/t chm Social Securities Appeal Tbnl 1986–89, past dir Slrs' Benevolent Assoc; former lectr in professional legal studies and examiner Police and Criminal Evidence Act Centre for Professional Legal Studies Cardiff Univ; regular contrib on law and current affrs to radio and TV; pres Cardiff and District Law Soc 2009–10; memb Law Soc 1975; *Publications* Jordan's Criminal Transaction Pack (1996); *Recreations* 16mm film collecting; *Style—* Stuart Hutton, Esq; ✉ The Old Parsonage, Colwinston, Vale of Glamorgan CF71 7NL (e-mail smch300@o2icloud.com); Hutton's Solicitors, 16 St Andrew's Crescent, Cardiff CF10 3DD (✆ 029 2037 8621, fax 029 2038 8450, e-mail stuart.hutton@huttons-solicitors.co.uk)

HUTTON, Will; s of late William Thomas Hutton, and Dorothy Anne, *née* Haynes; *b* 21 May 1950; *Educ* Chislehurst & Sidcup GS, Univ of Bristol (BSocSci), INSEAD Fontainebleau (MBA); *Career* institutional account exec Phillips and Drew 1971–77; BBC: presenter various Panoramas, BBC2 series and radio documentaries, sr prodr The Financial World Tonight (Radio 4) 1978–81, prodr and dir The Money Programme (BBC2) 1981–83, economics corr Newsnight (BBC2) 1983–88; ed-in-chief European Business Channel Zürich 1988–90, economics ed The Guardian 1990–96 (asst ed 1995–96); The Observer: ed 1996–98, ed-in-chief 1998–99, contributing ed and columnist 2000–; memb Scott Tst 2004–; presenter: series on the City (Radio 4) 1995, series on The State We're In (Channel 4) 1996; chief exec The Work Fndn 2000–08 (exec vice-chair 2008–11), princ elect Hertford Coll Oxford 2011–; memb: Editorial Bd New Economy, Bd LSE, New Life for Health ACHCEW Cmmn on NHS accountability; led Fair Play Review 2011, chair Ownership Cmmn; sr assoc memb St Antony's Coll Oxford summer 1993, hon fell Mansfield Coll Oxford 1997, visiting prof Manchester Univ Business Sch; Political Journalist of the Year What the Papers Say Awards 1993; govr LSE 1996–; Hon DLitt: Univ of Central England, Univ of Strathclyde, Kingston Univ 1995, De Montfort Univ 1996, Univ of Stafford 1999, Open Univ 2001, Univ of Bristol 2003, Univ of Glasgow 2003; *Books* The Revolution That Never Was (1986), The State We're In (1994), The State to Come (1997), The Stakeholding Society (1998), On the Edge (ed with A Gidden, 2000), The World We're In (2002), The Writing on the Wall: China and the West in the 21st Century (2007), Them & Us (2010); *Style—* Will Hutton, Esq; ✉ The Guardian, Kings Place, 90 York Way, London N1 9GU (✆ 020 7713 4284, fax 020 7713 4794); The Work Foundation, 21 Palmer Square, London SW1H 0AD

HUTTON OF FURNESS, Baron (Life Peer UK 2010), of Aldingham in the County of Cumbria; Rt Hon John Matthew Patrick Hutton; PC (2001); s of late George Hutton, and Rosemary Hutton; *b* 6 May 1955; *Educ* Westcliff HS Southend, Magdalen Coll Oxford (MA, BCL); *m* 1, 28 April 1978 (m dis 1993), Rosemary Caroline, *née* Little; 3 s (and 1 s decd), 1 da; m 2, 24 July 2004, Heather Rogers; *Career* legal asst CBI 1978–80, res fell Templeton Coll Oxford 1980–81, sr lectr in law Newcastle Poly 1981–92; Parly candidate (Lab) Penrith and the Border 1987, Euro Parly candidate Cumbria and N Lancs 1989, MP (Lab) Barrow and Furness 1992–2010; PPS: to Sec of State for Trade and Industry 1998, to Ldr of the House 1998; Parly under-sec of state Dept of Health 1998–99, min of state Dept of Health 1999–2005, Chllr of the Duchy of Lancaster 2005, sec of state for work and pensions 2005–07, sec of state for business and enterprise 2007–08, sec of state for defence 2008–09; chair All-Pty Gp: Welfare of Park Home Owners 1995–97, Br Latin Americal Gp 1997; memb: Select Ctee on Home Affrs 1994–97, Select Ctee on Unopposed Bills 1994–97; tstee Furness Animal Refuge; *Recreations* football, cricket, films, music, First World War history; *Clubs* Cemetary Cottages Working Men's (Barrow-in-Furness); *Style—* The Lord Hutton of Furness, PC; ✉ House of Lords, London SW1A 0PW

HUXLEY, Prof George Leonard; s of late Sir Leonard G H Huxley, and late Lady (Molly) Huxley; *b* 23 September 1932; *Educ* Blundell's, Magdalen Coll Oxford (BA); *m* 1957, Davina, da of L W H D Best, OBE, IPS; 3 da; *Career* Mil Serv cmmnd RE 1951, Actg Ops Supt Longmoor Mil Rly 1951; fell All Souls Coll Oxford 1955–61, asst dir Br Sch at Athens 1956–58, visiting lectr Harvard Univ 1958–59 and 1961–62, prof of Greek Queen's Univ Belfast 1962–83, temp asst lectr St Patrick's Coll Maynooth 1984–85, hon research assoc TCD 1984–89, dir Gennadius Library American Sch of Classical Studies Athens 1986–89, hon prof of Greek Trinity Coll Dublin 1989–, adjunct prof of classics and mathematics NUI Maynooth Ireland 2008–; vice-pres Great Central Railway Assoc 1966; memb: Exec NI Civil Rights Assoc 1971–72, Royal Irish Acad Dublin 1971– (sec for polite literature and antiquities 1979–86, sr vice-pres 1984–85 and 1999–2000, hon librarian 1990–94, special envoy 1994–97, vice-pres 1997–98), Irish Advsy Bd Inst of Irish Studies Univ of Liverpool 1996–2004, chm Organising Ctee 8th Int Congress of Classical Studies Dublin 1984, keynote speaker XVI Int Congress of Classical Archaeology Boston 2003; sr vice-pres Fédération Internationale des Sociétés d'Études Classiques 1984–89, Irish memb Standing Ctee for the Humanities Euro Sci Fndn Strasbourg 1978–86, memb: Managing Ctee American Sch of Classical Studies Athens 1990–, Int Komm Thesaurus Linguae Latinae (Munich) 1999–2001; visiting prof of history Univ of Calif San Diego 1990; hon pres Classical Assoc of Ireland 1999; Cromer Greek Prize 1963; Hon LittD Dublin 1984, Hon DLitt Belfast 1996, Hon DLitt NUI Maynooth 2013; patron Irish Inst of Hellenic Studies Athens 1998–; memb Academia Europaea 1990 (chm Classics subject gp 1995–96); FSA, MRIA; Hon Freeman of Kythera 2012; *Books* Achaeans and Hittites (1960), Early Sparta (1962), The Early Ionians (1966), Greek Epic Poetry from Eumelos to Panyassis (1969), Kythera, Excavations and Studies (ed with J N Coldstream, 1972), Pindar's Vision of the Past (1975), On Aristotle and Greek Society (1979), Homer and the Travellers (1988), author of various articles on Hellenic, Byzantine, and railway subjects; *Recreations* siderodromophilia; *Clubs* Athenaeum; *Style—* Prof G L Huxley; ✉ Forge Cottage, Church Enstone, Oxfordshire OX7 4NN (✆ 01608 677595); c/o School of Classics, Trinity College, Dublin 2, Ireland

HUXLEY, Prof Paul; s of late Ernest William Huxley, of London, and Winifred Mary, *née* Hunt; *b* 12 May 1938; *Educ* Harrow Sch of Art, Royal Acad Sch; *m* 1, Sept 1957 (m dis 1972), Margaret Doris, *née* Perryman; 2 s (Mark b 1961, Nelson b 1963); m 2, 18 May 1990, Susie Allen, *qv*, da of late Henry Francis Metcalfe; *Career* artist; prof of painting RCA 1986–98 (prof emeritus 1998–); memb Ctee Serpentine Gallery 1971–74, memb Arts Panel Arts Cncl GB 1972–76, tstee Tate Gallery 1975–82, treas Royal Acad 2000–14; Harkness fell 1965–67, Lindbury Tst award 1977, Athena Arts award 1985, Nat Arts Collections Fund award 1989; RA 1991 (ARA 1987); *Group Exhibitions* incl: Whitechapel Gallery London 1964, Marlborough Gerson NY 1965, Galerie Milano Milan 1965, Pittsburgh Int Carnegie Inst Pittsburgh 1967, UCLA Art Galleries Los Angeles 1968, Tate Gallery London 1968, MOMA NY 1968, Museum am Ostwall Hanover 1969, Walker Art Gallery Liverpool 1973, Hayward Gallery London 1974, Royal Acad London 1977, Museo Municipal Madrid 1983, RCA London 1988, Mappin Art Gallery Sheffield 1988, Kettle's Yard Cambridge 1999; *Solo Exhibitions* Rowan Gallery London, Gillian Jason Gallery London, Galerie zur Alten Deutchen Schule Switzerland, Kornblee Gallery NY, Galleria da Emenda Lisbon, Forum Kunst Rotweil, Gardner Arts Centre Univ of Sussex, Jason & Rhodes Gallery London, Rhodes & Mann London, Pallant House Gall Chichester, Watergate Gallery Seoul, Chang Art Gallery Beijing; *Commissions* incl: London Tport to design 22 ceramic murals for King's Cross Underground Station 1984, Rambert Dance Co to design sets and costumes for Cats Eye 1992; *Work in Public Collections* incl: Albright-Knox Gallery Buffalo NY, Art Gallery of NSW Aust, Leeds City Art Gallery, MOMA NY, Tate Gallery, V&A Museum, Whitworth Art Gallery Manchester, Ulster Museum Belfast, Art Gallery of Ontario Toronto, Arts Cncl of GB, Museum of Contemporary Art Sydney; *Books* Exhibition Road – Painters at The Royal College of Art (1988); *Style—* Prof Paul Huxley, RA; ✉ 2 Dalling Road, London W6 0JB (✆ 020 8563 9660, e-mail paul@paulhuxley.com)

HYDE, Dame Helen; DBE (2013); da of Henry Seligman, and Tilly Seligman; *b* 11 May 1947, Johannesburg, SA; *Educ* Parktown Girls' HS Johannesburg, Univ of the Witwatersrand (BA 1965–67, BA 1969), Transvaal Teachers' Trg Coll (Dip), KCL (MA); *m* 4 Jan 1968, John Hyde; 2 da (Liza b 1 Aug 1973, Nicole b 27 Sept 1978); *Career* Acland Burghley Sch London: asst teacher 1970, second i/c Languages Dept 1972, head of modern languages 1978, primary liaison and PR offr 1979; dep head (pastoral) then dep head (curriculum) Highgate Wood Sch London 1983–87, headmistress Watford GS for Girls 1987–2016; tstee Freedom and Autonomy Nat Schs Assoc (FASNA) 2006 (hon treas 2000–06); currently external educnl advsr; co-dir Refugees to Recovery, chair Nat Holocaust Educn and Training Cmmn, tstee Holocaust Educn Tst, patron Rwandan Sisterhood, patron Nat Religious Educn Ctee, memb Mgmnt Ctee European Union of Progressive Jews; *Books* Moving on Up (2003); *Recreations* reading, exercise, visiting art galleries, walking; *Clubs* David Lloyd; *Style—* Dame Helen Hyde, DBE; ✉ e-mail hyde.h@ntlworld.com

HYDE, Matthew Thomas (Matt); s of Richard Hyde, and Diana Hyde, of Ramsey, Cambridgeshire; *b* 22 February 1975, Peterborough; *Educ* QMC (BA), Univ of Westminster (MA, MBA); *m* 9 April 2005, Laura, *née* Bates; 1 s (Reuben b 16 March 2008); *Career* dep gen mangr KCL Students' Union 1999–2001, gen mangr Goldsmiths Coll Students' Union 2001–06, gp chief exec NUS 2006–13, chief exec The Scout Assoc 2013–; patron Unlock (Nat Assoc of Reformed Offenders), tstee and vice-chair NCVO 2011–, tstee Step Up to Serve 2014–; hon fell QMC 2012; *Recreations* football (support Peterborough United), food, family, cinema, cricket, travel; *Clubs* House of St Barnabas; *Style—* Matt Hyde, Esq; ✉ Twitter @matthyde

HYDE, Peter John; s of late Arthur Albert Hyde, of Harpenden, Herts, and Eileen, *née* Smith; *b* 21 July 1941; *Educ* Aldenham; *m* 19 Feb 1971, Jennifer Anne, da of Anne Gavina Venables, of Maresfield Park, Uckfield, E Sussex; 2 da (Henrietta b 24 May 1973, Gemma b 7 Nov 1979), 1 s (Nicholas b 5 Jan 1976); *Career* WS Crawford Ltd 1960–64; Hyde and Partners Ltd: dir 1966, md 1971, chm and chief exec 1976–95; md Hyde Marketing Services Ltd 1995–97, ptnr Hyde Business Partnership 1998–; vice-chm Arc Gp of Cos 1996–99; memb: Cncl Inst of Practitioners in Advertising 1974–2000, Membership Ctee Inst of Dirs 1977–88; pres Solus Club 1989 (hon treas 1983–2001), chm Bd of Govrs Epsom Sch of Art and Design 1989–94 (govr 1980), govr Surrey Inst of Art and Design 1994–2006; MCAM 1966, FIPA 1977 (MIPA 1966); *Recreations* golf, offshore sailing, skiing, scuba diving, swimming; *Clubs* Buck's; *Style—* Peter Hyde, Esq; ✉ Treverran Barton, Par, Cornwall PL24 2TZ (✆ 01208 872048); Hyde Business Partnership (✆ 01208 873978, e-mail pjh@hydebusiness.co.uk)

HYETT, Paul David Etheridge; s of Derek James Hyett (d 2014), of Breinton Common, Hereford, and Josephine Mable, *née* Sparks (d 1990); *b* 18 March 1952; *Educ* Hereford Cathedral Sch, AA Sch of Architecture (AADipl), Bartlett Sch of Planning (MPhil); *m* 1976, Susan Margaret, da of Richard Harry Beavan; 3 s (James b 1981, Benjamin b 1983, Peter b 1986); *Career* asst: Cedric Price Architects 1974–78, Alan Baxter Assocs 1978–80; ptnr: Arno Jobst and Paul Hyett Architects 1981–82, Nicholas Lacey Jobst and Hyett Architects 1982–87, Paul Hyett Architects 1987–97, Hyett Salisbury Whiteley Architects 1997–2000; chm: Ryder 2000–04, Ryder HKS Int 2005–08, HKS Architects Ltd 2008–; teacher: Canterbury Sch of Architecture 1986–87, Düsseldorf Sch of Architecture 1987–89, Bartlett Sch of Architecture and Planning 1994–; visiting prof Univ of Lincoln Sch of Architecture 2004–; columnist: Architects' Jl 1995–2000, RIBA Jl 2001–03; memb Governing Body AA Sch (hon treas 1993–98, vice-pres 1999–); tstee: Br Architectural Library Tst (BALT) 2003–07, Civic Tst 2004–07; dir Building Centre 2004–09, chm Carbon Vision (Carbon Tst) 2004–09; memb Expert Witness Inst; Hon DArt Univ of Lincoln; memb AA 1972, RIBA 1979 (vice-pres 1998–2000, pres 2001–03), MRTPI 1992, Hon FAIA, Royal Soc of Architects in Wales (RSAW); *Publications* In Practice (2000), Rough Guide to Sustainability (co-author, 2001), Architecture in the Anti-Machine Age (co-author, 2001); *Style—* Paul Hyett, Esq; ✉ HKS Architects Limited, 82 Dean Street, London W1D 3SP (✆ 020 7292 9494)

HYLAND, Paul Robert; s of Kenneth George Hyland (d 1979), and Hetta Grace, *née* Tilsley (d 2000); *b* 15 September 1947, Poole, Dorset; *Educ* Canford Sch, Univ of Bristol (BSc); *m* 1, 21 Aug 1971 (m dis 1988), Noëlle Jean, da of James Houston Angus; m 2, 8 Dec 1990 (m dis 1998), Margaret Ann, da of Thomas William Ware; m 3, 27 Oct 2001 (m dis 2008), Susan Margaret, da of William Arthur Wilson, MBE; m 4, 6 Aug 2015, Jana Collins Bundy, da of James Linwood Collins III; *Career* writer, broadcaster, teacher of creative writing, magician; memb: Dorset Natural History and Archaeological Soc, Poetry Soc, Soc of Authors, PEN, Int Brotherhood of Magicians, Magic Circle; broadcast work incl: plays, drama-documentaries, features, poetry; *Awards*: Eric Gregory Award for Poetry, Alice Hunt Bartlett Award, Authors' Fndn Award; *Books* Domingus (1978), Riddles for Jack (1978), Purbeck: The Ingrained Island (1978), Poems of Z (1982), Wight: Biography of an Island (1984), The Stubborn Forest (1984), The Black Heart: A Voyage into Central Africa (1988), Getting Into Poetry (1992), Indian Balm: Travels in the Southern Subcontinent (1994), Kicking Sawdust (1995), Backwards out of the Big World: a Voyage into Portugal (1996), Discover Dorset: Isle of Purbeck (1998), Ralegh's Last Journey (2003), Art of the Impossible (2004); *Style—* Paul Hyland, Esq; ✉ c/o David Higham Associates Ltd, 7th Floor, Waverley House, 712 Noel Street, London W1F 8GQ

H

HYLTON, 5 Baron (UK 1866); Sir Raymond Hervey Jolliffe; 5 Bt (UK 1821); s of Lt-Col 4 Baron Hylton (d 1967, whose mother was Lady Alice Hervey, da of 3 Marquess of Bristol), and Lady Perdita Asquith (d 1996), sis of 2 Earl of Oxford and Asquith and gda of 1 Earl, better known as HH Asquith, the Lib PM, by his 1 w); *b* 13 June 1932; *Educ* Eton, Trinity Coll Oxford (MA); *m* 1966, Joanna, da of Andrew de Bertodano, himself eldest s of 8 Marques de Moral (cr by King Charles III of Spain 1765), by Andrew's m to Lady Sylvia Savile (3 da of late 6 Earl of Mexborough, and sis of late Lady Agnes Eyston and late Lady Sarah Cumming-Bruce); 4 s (Hon William b 1967, Hon Andrew b 1969, Hon Alexander b 1973, Hon John b 1977), 1 da (Hon Emily b 1975); *Heir* s, Hon William Jolliffe; *Career* Lt Coldstream Gds Reserve; landowner, organic farmer and forester; asst private sec to Govr-Gen Canada 1960–62; sits as independent peer in House of Lords (elected in 1999); memb All-Pty Parly Gps on: Human Rights, Penal Affairs, British-Palestinian, British-Russian, British-Philippines; former pres NIACRO; chm MICOM re Moldova; tstee Forward Thinking re Peace in the Middle East, chm Advsy Cncl Fndn for Reconciliation and Relief in the Middle East; former chm: Catholic Housing Aid Soc, Nat Federation of Housing Associations, Housing Assoc Charitable Tst, Help the Aged Housing Tst; formerly tstee: Acorn Christian Healing Tst, ABCD (a tst for Palestinian children with disabilities); govr Ammerdown Study Center, patron The Soul of Europe (working for reconciliation in SE Europe); Hon DSocSc Univ of Southampton 1994; ARICS; *Publications* articles and letters in the press; *Style—* The Lord Hylton; ✉ House of Lords, London SW1A 0PW (☎ 020 7219 5353, fax 020 7219 5979)

HYMAN, Howard Jonathan; s of late Joe Hyman, of London, and late Corrine Irene, *née* Abrahams; *b* 23 October 1949, Manchester; *Educ* Bedales, Univ of Manchester (BA), Beijing Normal Univ; *m* 21 Sept 1972, Anne Moira, da of late Capt Harry Sowden; 2 s (Daniel b 1977, Sam b 1979), 1 da (Hannah b 1982); *Career* Price Waterhouse: ptnr 1984–94, specialist advsr on privatisation HM Treasy 1984–87, head Corporate Fin Europe 1990–94, memb E European Jt Venture Bd 1990–94, memb China Bd 1991–94, memb Euro Mgmnt Bd 1991–94, memb World Gen Cncl 1992–94, world head Corporate Fin 1994; dep chm Charterhouse Bank 1994–96, md Charterhouse plc 1994–96; chm: Hyman Associates 1996–, VinoVeritas Asia 2012–; dir Kingstream Steel 2000–02; FCA; *Books* Privatisation: The Facts (1988), The Implications of Privatisation for Nationalised Industries (1988); *Recreations* Chinese culture, walking, classical music, watching cricket, gardening; *Clubs* Reform, MCC, Minchinhampton Golf; *Style—* Howard Hyman, Esq; ✉ 1 Cato Street, London W1H 5HG (☎ 020 7258 0404, fax 020 7258 1424, e-mail howard@hyman.eu)

HYMAN, Robin Philip; s of Leonard Albert Hyman (d 1964), of London, and Helen Josephine, *née* Mautner (d 1991); *b* 9 September 1931; *Educ* Henley GS, Univ of Birmingham (BA); *m* 17 April 1966, Inge, *née* Neufeld; 2 s (James b 29 May 1967, Peter b 23 Nov 1968), 1 da (Philippa 13 March 1971); *Career* Nat Serv RAF 1949–51; ed Mermaid 1953–54, md Evans Bros Ltd 1972–77 (dep md 1967, dir 1964), chm Bell and Hyman Ltd 1977–86, chm and chief exec Unwin Hyman Ltd 1989–90 (md 1986–88), chm Laurence King Publishing Ltd (formerly Calmann & King Ltd) 1991–2004, dir Spiro Inst 1991–98, memb BBC Gen Advsy Cncl 1992–97; tstee ADAPT 1997–2006; memb Editorial Bd World Yearbook of Educn 1969–73, treas Educnl Publishers' Cncl 1972–75 (memb Exec Ctee 1971–76), memb first Br Publishers' Delgn to China 1978, pres Publishers' Assoc 1989–91 (memb Cncl 1975–92, treas 1982–84, vice-pres 1988–89 and 1991–92), chm Samuel Pepys Award Tst 2007–15; FRSA; *Books* A Dictionary of Famous Quotations (1962), Boys and Girls First Dictionary (with John Trevaskis 1967); 11 children's books with Inge Hyman incl: Barnabas Ball at the Circus (1967), Runaway James and the Night Owl (1968), The Hippo Who Wanted to Fly (1973), The Greatest Explorers in the World (1978), The Treasure Box (1980); *Clubs* Garrick, MCC, Samuel Pepys; *Style—* Robin Hyman, Esq; ✉ 101 Hampstead Way, London NW11 7LR (☎ 020 8455 7055)

HYMAN, Timothy; s of Alan Hyman, and Noreen, *née* Gypson, of London; *b* 17 April 1946, Hove, Sussex; *Educ* Charterhouse, Slade Sch of Fine Art; *m* 1982, Judith, *née* Ravenscroft; *Career* painter and curator; curator Narrative Paintings (ICA and Arnolfini) 1979–80, co-curator Carinvalesque (Hayward Gallery touring) 2000, lead curator Stanley Spencer (Tate) 2001, co-curator British Vision (Ghent) 2007–08; artist in residence Maggies Cancer Caring Centres 2011–12; chm The Powys Soc; Nat Portrait Gallery Travel Prize 2007; elected Royal Academician 2011; *Solo Exhibitions* incl: Blond Fine Art London 1981, 1983 and 1985, Austin/Desmond Fine Art London 1990, 2000, 2003, 2006 and 2009, Castlefield Gallery Manchester 1993, Gallery Chemould Bombay India 1994, Flowers East London 1994, Gallery of the Artists Studios Tel Aviv 2006, A Year with Maggie's (Royal Academy of Arts London) 2015; *Publications* Bhupen Khakhar (1998), Bonnard (monograph, 1998), Sienese Painting (monograph, 2003), The World New Made: Reshaping Figurative Painting in the Twentieth Century (2016); approx 40 articles and reviews in the TLS; *Recreations* cinema, reading, travel, walking, the novels of John Cowper Powys; *Style—* Timothy Hyman, Esq, RA; ✉ 62 Myddelton Square, London EC1R 1XX (☎ 020 7837 1933, e-mail timothy.hyman@virgin.net)

HYMAS, Charles Southern Albert; s of Peter David Hymas, of Northampton, and Margaret, *née* Southern; *b* 7 January 1961; *Educ* Harrow, Univ of Durham (BA), UC Cardiff (Postgrad Dip Journalism); *m* Sarah Elizabeth, da of Prof Michael Barbour; 1 da (Katharine Anna), 2 s (Tom, Luke); *Career* trainee journalist South Wales Argus Newport 1983–84 (educn corr 1984–85); Western Mail Cardiff: gen news reporter 1985–86, educn corr 1986–87, political corr 1987–88; political reporter Yorkshire Post 1988–90; The Sunday Times: educn corr 1990–95, dep ed Insight 1995–96, dep news ed 1996–97, news ed 1997–99, ed Focus 1999–2000, news ed 2000–08, managing ed (news) 2008–; *Books* Guide to the National Curriculum (1992); *Recreations* swimming, tennis and cooking; *Style—* Charles Hymas, Esq; ✉ The Sunday Times, 1 London Bridge Street, London SE1 9GF

HYND, Ronald; s of William John Hens (d 1991), of London, and Alice Louisa, *née* Griffiths (d 1994); *b* 22 April 1931; *Educ* Holloway Co Sch, Rambert Sch of Ballet; *m* 24 June 1957, Annette, da of James Lees Page (d 1979); 1 da (Louise b 20 April 1968); *Career* former ballet dancer, now dir and choreographer; Ballet Rambert 1949–51, Royal Ballet 1951–70 (princ dancer 1959), danced all major classical roles and many dramatic and romantic ballets; dir Bavarian State Ballet 1970–73 and 1984–86; choreographed full length ballets: The Nutcracker (London Festival Ballet, L'Opera de Nice) 1976 and (La Scala) 2000, Rosalinda (Johannesburg Ballet, Festival Ballet, Houston, Ljubljana, Santiago, Cincinnati, Bonn, Salt Lake City, Tulsa, Deutsche Oper Berlin) 1978 and (Tallinn) 2011, Papillon (Houston, Sadlers Wells Royal Ballet, Johannesburg, Munich, Santiago) 1979, Le Diable a Quatre (Johannesburg, Santiago) 1984, Coppélia (Festival Ballet) 1985, (Santiago and Berlin) 2000, (Hong Kong) 2008 and (Tallinn) 2010, The Merry Widow (Aust) 1975, (Canada) 1986, (Johannesburg) 1993, (Vienna) 1994, (Santiago and Houston) 1995, (La Scala Milan) 1996, (American Ballet Theatre) 1997, (Royal Danish Ballet) 1998, (Maggio Musicale Florence) 2001, (Pacific NW) 2002, (Hong Kong Ballet) 2007, (Joffrey Ballet Chicago and Tulsa Ballet) 2011, (Montevideo) 2012, (Budapest) 2014 and (Dallas) 2015, Ludwig II (Munich) 1986, Hunchback of Notre Dame (Houston) 1988, The Sleeping Beauty (English Nat Ballet) 1993 and (Pacific N W) 2001; one act ballets incl: Dvorák Variations, Le Baiser de la Fee, Mozartiana, Pasiphaë, La Chatte, Wendekreise, Das Telefon, Charlotte Brontë, Liaisons Amoureuses, Marco Polo, Scherzo Capriccioso, The Seasons, The Sanguine Fan, Les Valses, In a Summer Garden, Fanfare, Valse Glacé and Winter 1850 for John Curry, Sylvia for Diana, Princess of Wales's 30 birthday; *Television* prodns incl: The Nutcracker (BBC), The Sanguine Fan (BBC), The Merry Widow (Canadian TV and Aust TV), Rosalinda (Slovenian TV), Coppelia Tallinn; *Recreations* music, travel, gardens; *Style—* Ronald Hynd, Esq

HYND, Sam; s of Darrell Hynd, of Kirkby in Ashfield, and Helen, *née* Stewart; *b* 3 July 1991, Mansfield, Notts; *Career* Paralympic swimmer; achievements incl: Gold medal 400m freestyle Paralympics Beijing 2008, Bronze medal 200m Paralympics Beijing 2008, Gold medal 400m freestyle Br Championships 2008 and 2009, 2 Bronze medals (100m freestyle and 200m) Br Championships 2008, Gold 400m freestyle Paralympic World Cup 2008 and 2009, Gold medal 400m freestyle and Bronze medal 200m individual medley European Championships 2011, Bronze medal (400m freestyle) Paralympic Games 2012, world record holder 400m freestyle (long and short course), European record holder 200m (long and short course), world record holder 50m and 200m breaststroke (short course), world record holder 100m (shortcourse); BBC East Midland Junior Disabled Sportsperson of the Year 2006 and 2008, Notts Junior Disabled Sportsperson of hte Year 2006, 2007 and 2008; *Recreations* music; *Clubs* Nova Centurion Swimming; *Style—* Sam Hynd, Esq; ✉ c/o British Paralympic Association, 40 Bernard Street, London WC1N 1ST

HYNES, (Tallulah) Jessica Elina; *née* Stevenson; *Educ* Kingston Coll; *m* Adam Hynes; 3 c; *Career* actress and writer; supporter of various charities incl Breast Cancer Res and Romanian Orphanage Fund; *Theatre* Night Heron (Royal Court) 2003; *Television* credits incl: Alice in Staying Alive 1995, Daisy in Spaced 1997–2000 (co-writer), Cheryl in The Royle Family 1998–2009, Holly in Bob and Rose 2001, According to Bex 2005, Pinochet in Suburbia 2006, Doctor Who 2007, Learners 2007, Twenty Twelve 2011–12 (Best Comedy Performance RTS Award 2013); *Film* credits incl: Swing Kids 1992, Baby of Macon 1992, Tomorrow La Scala! 2002, Shaun of the Dead 2004, Bridget Jones: The Edge of Reason 2004, Confetti 2006, Four Last Songs 2007, Son of Rambow 2007, Magicians 2007; *Awards* Best Comedy Female Newcomer 1999, Best Comedy Actress 2001; nominated: Olivier Award 2003, BAFTA Award 2003; *Recreations* walking, church; *Style—* Mrs Jessica Hynes; ✉ c/o United Agents Limited, 12–26 Lexington Street, London W1F 0LE (☎ 020 3214 0800, fax 020 3214 0801, website www.unitedagents.co.uk)

HYPHER, David Charles; OBE (2012), DL (Surrey 2007); s of Harold Eldric Hypher, MBE (d 1971), of Byfleet, Surrey, and Marcia Evelyn, *née* Spalding (d 1992); *b* 24 July 1941; *Educ* Brooklands Coll, Open Univ (BSc); *m* 1, March 1966 (m dis 1971), Jennifer, da of Robert Ingle; m 2, July 1978, Pamela Alison, da of Peter Rowland Craddock; 2 da (Nicola, Emma); *Career* stockbroker 1958–82; dir: INVESCO Asset Management Ltd (Britannia Asset Management) 1983–98, INVESCO Fund Managers Ltd 1984–98, various INVESCO International (offshore) Jersey and Luxembourg fund cos 1985–96, MIM International Management 1987–92, London Wall Britannia 1989–2002, INVESCO Luxembourg SA 1993–96, AMVESCAP Management Ltd 1998–99, David Hypher Consulting Ltd 1998–2002, Groupe Du Savoy 1998–2007; chm Surrey Youth Focus 2006–14 (vice-pres 2014–); tstee: Rydes Hill Prep Sch Guildford 1989–2007, Transform Housing & Support (formerly Surrey Community Devpt Tst) 2000–11 (chair 2004–07, patron 2014–), High Sheriff of Surrey Youth Award Scheme 2005–11; Queen Elizabeth's Fndn: govr 2006–15, tstee 2007–15, tstee Pension Scheme 2010–, vice-pres 2015–; patron: Surrey Care Tst 2007–, Lifetrain Tst 2007–; High Sheriff Surrey 2005–06; memb IIMR 1965–2005, memb Stock Exchange 1972–83; *Recreations* collecting antiques and cars; *Style—* David Hypher, Esq, OBE, DL, BSc (Hons); ☎ 01483 234938, e-mail dhypher@aol.com

HYTNER, Jim; *b* 22 July 1964; *Educ* Oxford Poly (BSc); *Children* 2 da (Molly, Lucy); *Career* marketeer; formerly: asst brand mangr on Bird's Trifle and Angel Delight, brand mangr on Lilt, Fanta and Sprite, mktg mangr Coca-Cola, Euro mktg mangr Sega, mktg dir BSkyB; dir of mktg and new business Channel 5 1998–2001, mktg and commerical dir ITV 2001–04, mktg dir Barclays 2004–07, commercial dir Top Up TV 2007–09, pres EMEA Universal McCann 2009–12, worldwide ceo Initiative 2012–13, ceo G14 and pres global clients IPG Mediabrands 2013–; lectr Wharton Business Sch; tstee Comic Relief; nominated Marketeer of the Year by Marketing Week 1999; *Recreations* cajoling brother into journeys up the M6 to see their beloved reds; *Style—* Jim Hytner, Esq

HYTNER, Joyce Anita; OBE (2004); da of Bernard Myers (d 1979), of Altrincham, Cheshire, and Vera Myers, *née* Classick (d 1974); *b* 9 December 1935; *Educ* Withington Girls' Sch Manchester; *m* 19 Dec 1954, Benet Hytner, QC; 3 s (Sir Nicholas Hytner, *qv*, b 1956, Richard b 1959, James b 1964), 1 da (Jennifer b 1958); *Career* dir Act IV; memb Bd: Royal Court Theatre 2002–, Old Vic Theatre Tst 2000–, Criterion Theatre 2006–, Manchester Int Festival 2010–, Quintessentially Fndn 2012–; memb bd Charterhouse 2013–; *Recreations* theatre, music; *Style—* Joyce Hytner, OBE; ✉ Act IV, 47 Frith Street, London W1D 4SE

HYTNER, Nicholas Robert; kt (2010); s of Benet Alan Hytner, QC, of London, and Joyce Hytner, OBE, *qv*, *née* Myers; *b* 7 May 1956; *Educ* Manchester Grammar, Trinity Hall Cambridge (MA); *Career* theatre, opera and film dir; prodns at Northcott Theatre Exeter and Leeds Playhouse; assoc dir Royal Exchange Theatre Manchester 1985–88, assoc dir NT 1989–2003, dir NT 2003–; *Theatre* dir: Measure for Measure (RSC) 1987, The Tempest (RSC) 1988, King Lear (RSC) 1990, Miss Saigon (Drury Lane Theatre and Broadway) 1989–91, The Importance of Being Earnest (Aldwych) 1993; prodns for NT incl: Ghetto 1989, Wind in the Willows 1990, The Madness of George III 1991, Carousel 1993 (Best Musical Direction Olivier Award 1993, Best Director of a Musical Tony Awards 1994), The Cripple of Inishmaan 1997, Mother Clap's Molly House 2001, Henry V 2003, The History Boys 2004 (Best Dir Olivier Award 2005, also Broadway NY (Best Dir Tony Awards 2006)), Henry IV Parts One and Two 2005, Southwark Fair 2006, One Man, Two Guvnors 2011; *Opera* prodns incl: King Priam (Kent Opera) 1984, Rienzi (ENO) 1983, Xerxes (ENO) 1985, The Magic Flute (ENO) 1988, Julius Caesar (Paris Opéra) 1987, Le Nozze di Figaro (Opéra de Genève) 1989, La Clemenza di Tito (Glyndebourne) 1991, The Force of Destiny 1992, Xerxes (ENO) 2002 (Olivier Award for Best Opera Prodn, Evening Standard Opera Award); *Film* dir The Madness of King George 1995, The Crucible 1995, The History Boys 2006; *Style—* Sir Nicholas Hytner; ✉ National Theatre, Upper Ground, South Bank, London SE1 9PX (☎ 020 7452 3333)

I

IACOBESCU, Sir George; kt (2012), CBE (2003); *b* 9 November 1945, Bucharest; *Educ* Lyceum D. Cantemir (BSc), Univ of Civil & Industrial Engrg Bucharest (MSc); *m* 1976, Gabriela Iacobescu; 1 da; *Career* construction dir Homeco Invst Montreal and Toronto 1975–78, project dir Olympia Center and Neiman Marcus Bldgs Chicago 1981–84, vice-pres Devpt and Construction World Financial Center 1984–87, vice-pres Construction 1987–92, dir CWL 1993–95; Canary Wharf Gp: dep ceo 1995–97, memb Bd 1995–, ceo 1997–, chm 2011–; dir: London First, Gateway to London, Wood Wharf (Gen Ptnrs) Ltd; memb: Advsy Bd UK Acad of Finance, Defence Reform Unit MOD 2010–, Advsy Bd City UK; co-chm Teach First, tstee Br Museum 2007–15, cmmr Govt's Thames Estuary Growth Cmmn 2016; hon DBA East London 2007; CCMI; *Recreations* jazz, opera, antiques, football, tennis, impressionist and modern painting; *Style*— Sir George Iacobescu, CBE; ✉ Canary Wharf Group plc, One Canada Square, Canary Wharf, London E14 5AB (☎ 020 7418 2209)

IAN, David; professional name of David Ian Lane; s of Reg Lane, of Loughton, Essex, and Jean, *née* Wiens (d 1997); *b* 15 February 1961, Ilford, Essex; *Educ* Ilford Co High GS for Boys; *m* 17 Sept 1994, Tracy, *née* Carter; 1 s (James William), 1 da (Emily Grace); *Career* actor until 1991, ind theatre prodr 1991–2000, joined Clear Channel Entertainment 2000, chm global theatre Live Nation (formerly Clear Channel Entertainment) 2005–07 (previously ceo), currently chm David Ian Prodns; memb Bd Soc of London Theatre 1997–; credits as theatre prodr internationally incl: Grease, Saturday Night Fever, The King and I , West Side Story, Singin' in the Rain, Ain't Misbehavin', Anything Goes, The Producers, Defending the Caveman, Guys and Dolls, Daisy Pulls it Off, The Sound of Music, La Cage Aux Folles, Sweet Charity, Flashdance, Gypsy, The Shawshank Redemption, The Phantom of the Opera (Las Vegas), My Fair Lady, Jesus Christ Superstar, Evita, Chess, The Rocky Horror Show, Cats, Chicago, Dr Doolittle, Starlight Express, Seminar, Steel Magnolias, Ghost the Musical, Priscilla Queen of the Desert, The Bodyguard, Jersey Boys, Annie, Xanadu, Show Boat; winner 5 Olivier Awards, nominee 2 Tony Awards; *Recreations* theatre, running (5 marathons); *Style*— David Ian, Esq; ✉ David Ian Productions, Fifth Floor, 53 Parker Street, London WC2B 5PT (☎ 020 7427 8380, e-mail jo@davidianproductions.com, website www.davidianproductions.com)

IANNUCCI, Armando; OBE (2012); s of Armando Iannucci (d 1982), and Gina, *née* Mignano; *b* 28 November 1963, Glasgow; *Educ* St Aloysius Coll Glasgow, Univ of Glasgow, UC Oxford (BA, DPhil); *m* 25 Aug 1990, Rachael, *née* Jones; 2 s (Emilio b 20 Jan 1994, Marcello b 1 July 1999), 1 da (Carmella b 23 Aug 2002); *Career* writer, producer, director, presenter; prodr BBC Radio Light Entertainment 1988–91; columnist: Daily Telegraph 2000–06, The Observer 2006–, Gramophone 2006–; memb BAFTA 2006; Award for Special Contribution to Comedy Br Comedy Award 1995, The Writers' Guild of GB Award Br Comedy Award 2011; *Radio* BBC Radio 4 shows incl: On The Hour 1991–92 (Best Radio Comedy British Comedy Awards 1992), Knowing Me, Knowing You 1992–93 (Best Comedy Sony Radio Awards 1993, Best Radio Comedy British Comedy Awards 1993), Armando Iannucci Show (presenter) 1993–97, News Quiz (regular panellist); *Television* incl: The Day Today (BBC 2) 1994, Knowing Me, Knowing You With Alan Partridge (writer and prodr, BBC 2) 1994 (Best New TV Comedy British Comedy Awards 1995), Saturday Night Armistice (BBC 2) 1995, The Friday Night Armistice (BBC 2) 1996–99 (Bronze Rose of Montreux 1996), I'm Alan Partridge (writer and prodr, BBC 2) 1997 (Best Comedy BAFTA 1998, British Comedy Award 1998), The Armando Iannucci Shows (presenter and dir, Channel 4) 2001, The Thick of It (BBC 4) 2005–09 (Best Comedy BAFTA 2005, Best Comedy RTS 2005, Best Scripted Comedy RTS 2010), Time Trumpet (BBC 2) 2006, Veep 2012; *Film* In The Loop 2009 (Best Screenplay Evening Standard Br Film Award 2010, Screenwriter of the Year London Film Critics' Circle Award 2010); *Publications* Facts and Fancies (1999); *Recreations* astronomy, classical music; *Style*— Armando Iannucci, Esq, OBE; ✉ c/o PBJ Management, 22 Rathbone Street, London W1T 1LA (☎ 020 7287 1112)

IDLE, Eric; *b* 29 March 1943, South Shields, Co Durham; *Educ* Royal Sch Wolverhampton, Pembroke Coll Cambridge (BA, pres Footlights); *m* 1 (m dis), Lyn Ashley; 1 s (Carey b 1973); m 2, Tania Kosevich; 1 da (Lily b 1990); *Career* actor, writer and film director; pres Prominent Features film co; *Stage* performances incl: Footlights '63 and '64 (Edinburgh Festival), I'm Just Wild About Harry (Edinburgh Festival) 1963, One For the Pot (Leicester Phoenix) 1965, First Farewell Tour (UK and Canada) 1973, Monty Python Live at Drury Lane 1974, Monty Python Live at City Centre 1976, Monty Python Live at the Hollywood Bowl 1980; writing incl: Pass the Butler (Globe) 1981, The Frog Prince (also dir, Faerie Tale Theatre), Seussical: A new musical based on the books of Dr Seuss 1998, Monty Python's Spamalot (Shubert Theater NY) 2005 (Best Broadway Musical Outer Critics Circle Awards, Best Musical Tony Awards); *Opera* Ko-Ko in Jonathan Miller's prodn of The Mikado (ENO 1987, Houston Opera House 1989); *Television* acting/performing incl: We Have Ways of Making You Laugh (LWT) 1968, Do Not Adjust Your Set (two series, BBC) 1968–69, Monty Python's Flying Circus (also writer, four series, BBC, winner Silver Rose Montreux) 1969–74, Monty Python's Fliegende Zirkus (Bavaria TV) 1971–72, Rutland Weekend Television (also writer, two series, BBC) 1975–76, Laverne and Shirley (ABC), Saturday Night Live (guest star twice, host four times, NBC), The Mikado (Thames TV) 1987, Nearly Departed (Lorimar Productions for NBC) 1989, Parrot Sketch Not Included (BBC) 1989, Suddenly Susan 1999–2000, House of Mouse 2001, The Scream Team 2002; writing also incl: Twice a Fortnight (BBC) 1967, The Frost Report (BBC, winner Golden Rose Montreux) 1967, The Two Ronnies (BBC), Marty Feldman (BBC) 1968–69; *Radio* performing incl: Radio Five (also writer, two series, BBC Radio 1) 1975, Behind the Crease (also writer, musical, BBC) 1990; writing also incl I'm Sorry I'll Read That Again (BBC); *Films* acting incl: Isadora The Biggest Dancer in the World (dir Ken Russell, BBC TV film) 1966, Alice in Wonderland (dir Jonathan Miller, BBC TV film) 1966, And Now For Something Completely Different (also writer) 1971, Monty Python and the Holy Grail (also writer) 1974, The Rutles – All You Need is Cash (also writer and dir, NBC TV film) 1978, Monty Python's Life of Brian (also writer) 1979, Monty Python Live at the Hollywood Bowl (also writer) 1980, Monty Python's The Meaning of Life (also writer, winner Cannes Jury Prize) 1983, Yellowbeard 1983, The Adventures of Baron Munchausen 1988, Nuns on the Run 1990, Too Much Sun 1990, Missing Pieces 1991, Splitting Heirs (also writer and prodr) 1993, Casper 1995, Burn Hollywood Burn 1998, The Quest for Camelot (voice of Devon) 1998, Dudley Do-Right 1999, South Park: Bigger Longer & Uncut 1999, Journey Into Your Imagination 1999, 102 Dalmatians 2000, Brightness 2000, Ella Enchanted 2004; *Recordings* incl: Monty Python's Flying Circus 1970, Another Monty Python Record 1970, Monty Python's Previous Record 1972, Matching Tie and Handkerchief 1973, Live at Drury Lane 1974, Monty Python's Instant Record Collection 1977, Monty Python's Contractual Obligation Album (prodr) 1980, The Final Ripoff Album 1987, Monty Python Sings 1989, Nearly Departed (theme song for TV series) 1989, One Foot in the Grave (theme song for TV series) 1990, Always Look on the Bright Side of Life (single, reached No2) 1991, The Quite Remarkable Adventures of The Owl and the Pussycat 1997; *Books* Monty Python's Big Red Book (contrib and ed, 1971), The Brand New Monty Python Bok (contrib and ed, 1973), The Monty Python Paperbok (1974), Hello Sailor (novel, 1975), The Rutland Dirty Weekend Book (1976), Monty Python and the Holy Grail (1977), Monty Python's Scrapbook/Life of Brian (contrib and ed, 1979), Pass the Butler (1981), Monty Python's Flying Circus – Just the Words (1989), The Road to Mars 1999; *Style*— Eric Idle, Esq

ILEY, Malcolm; s of Thomas Iley (d 1980), and Barbara, *née* David; *b* 12 April 1949, Bradninch, Devon; *m* 29 May 1971, Joy, *née* Sharpe; 1 s (Lawson-Thomas b 1974), 1 da (Rachel Alexandra b 1978); *Career* slr; various sr lawyer and exec positions in local govt (culminating in city slr and chief exec Plymouth City Cncl) and advsr to nat assocs 1970–94, head Public Sector Projects Dept Nabarro Nathanson 1997–2004, head Public Sector Commercial Gp Trowers and Hamlyns 2004–; chm and advsr Devon Environmental Business Tst 1992–95, dir BURA 1997–2001, non-exec dir and advsr Sutton Harbour plc 1989–2004, non-exec dir Sheffield Urban Regeneration Co, dir Prospects Ltd 1998–; memb Ministerial Advsy Gp DETR 2001–03; memb Bd and advsr: Plymouth Coll, Plymouth Arts Coll, Hammersmith and West London FE Corporation; chm Local Govt Chronicle regeneration awards; memb New Local Govt Network Ltd; advsr to Central Govt and leading major contractors; Thomas Edis Prize Law Soc 1976; memb Law Soc; *Publications* incl: Local Government Act 1999: Best Value and Contracting, Local Government Contracting (contrib); author of articles in various public sector magazines; *Recreations* sport, golf, skiing, tennis, walking on Dartmoor, music (listening and playing trumpet); *Style*— Malcolm Iley, Esq; ✉ Trowers & Hamlins, Sceptre Court, 40 Tower Hill, London EC3N 4DX (☎ 020 7423 8345, e-mail miley@trowers.com)

ILIFFE, 3 Baron (UK 1933); Robert Peter Richard Iliffe; DL (Berks 2007); s of Hon William Henry Richard Iliffe (d 1959; yr s of 1 Baron Iliffe, GBE); suc uncle, 2 Baron Iliffe (d 1996); *b* 22 November 1944, Oxford; *Educ* Eton, ChCh Oxford; *m* 1966, Rosemary Anne, da of late Cdr Arthur Grey Skipwith, RN; 3 s (Hon Edward Richard b 1968, Hon George Langton b 1970, Hon Thomas Arthur b 1973), 1 da (Hon Florence Clare (twin) b 1973); *Heir* s, Hon Edward Iliffe; *Career* chm: Yattendon Gp (formerly Investment Tst) plc 1984– (subsidiary cos: Marina Developments Ltd, Iliffe News & Media Ltd, Yattendon Estates Ltd); dir Scottish Provincial Press; former chm: Birmingham Post and Mail Ltd, West Midlands Press Ltd, Dillons Newsagents, Coventry Newspapers Ltd, Cambridge Newspapers Ltd, Herts and Essex Newspapers Ltd, Staffordshire Newspapers Ltd; memb Cncl RASE 1972– (chm 1994–98); pres Rare Breeds Survival Tst 1999–2003, memb Governing Body Bradfield Coll 1996–2008 (warden 2001–06); High Sheriff Warks 1983–84; *Recreations* yachting, shooting, fishing, old motor cars; *Clubs* Royal Yacht Sqdn (Cdre 2005–09), Royal Motor Yacht (Vice-Adm 2013–), Boodles; *Style*— The Rt Hon the Lord Iliffe, DL; ✉ Barn Close, Yattendon, Thatcham, Berkshire RG18 0UX

ILLING, Amanda Marguerite; da of Ronald Illing, of Wickham Market, Suffolk, and Cass, *née* Price; *b* 19 October 1968, Dartford, Kent; *Educ* Bullerswood Sch for Girls Chislehurst (head girl), Cambridge Judge Business Sch; *m* 27 June 2009, David Frederick Harris Wolfe, QC; 2 step-da (Katie Harris Wolfe Clark, Megan Harris Wolfe Clark b 11 Jan 1997 (twins)); *Career* private sec to Dir of Public Prosecutions1993–99, practice dir Matrix until 2000–09, chief exec Hardwicke 2009–; tstee: Public Law Project, London Legal Support Tst; memb Legal Practice Mangrs' Assoc; FCIPD 2015; *Recreations* golf, skiing, walking, friends and festivals, gardening; *Clubs* Scottish Malt Whisky Soc; *Style*— Ms Amanda Illing; ✉ Hardwicke, Hardwicke Building, New Square, Lincoln's Inn, London WC2A 3SB (☎ 020 7242 2523, website www.hardwicke.co.uk, Twitter @amandailling)

ILLMAN, (Charles) John; s of Henry Alfred Charles Illman (d 2005), of Kirkby Fleetham, N Yorks, and Margaret Moorhouse (d 1975); *b* 22 September 1944; *Educ* King's Sch Ely; *m* 1975, Elizabeth Mary, da of Ronald Stamp; 2 s (James David Charles b 21 Dec 1979, Christopher George John b 12 June 1982); *Career* student actor Nottingham Playhouse 1963, asst stage mangr Southwold Repertory Company 1963; trainee reporter Hertfordshire Express 1964, reporter The Journal Newcastle upon Tyne 1968, features ed General Practitioner 1971; ed: New Psychiatry 1974, General Practitioner 1975; freelance journalist 1976–83, med corr Daily Mail 1983–88, health ed The Guardian 1989–96, med corr The Observer 1996–98; chm Med Journalists Assoc 1996–2003; Family Planning Assoc Award for reporting on women's health 1993, first prize Norwich Union Healthcare/Med Journalists' Assoc Awards 1994, Tony Thistlewaite Medical Journalists' Assoc Book Award 2005, Feature of the Year (specialist audience) Medical Journalists' Association 2016; md JIC Productions Ltd 2003; memb RSM 1987; *Books* Body Machine (jtly, 1981), Use Your Brain to Beat Depression (2004), Use Your Brain to Beat Panic and Anxiety (2005), Beat Panic and Anxiety (2006), Politics, Protest and Progress: 100 Years of Animal Research (2008), Beyond the Patient (2009), Handling the Media: Communication Skills for Healthcare Professionals (2011), The MJA Guide to Clinical Trials (2014); *Recreations* family, cricket, running, reading; *Style*— John Illman, Esq; ✉ e-mail john@jicmedia.co.uk

IMESON, Michael David; s of Terence Imeson, of Bradford, W Yorks, and Marian, *née* Glasby; *b* 26 October 1955; *Educ* Hanson GS Bradford, Univ of Bradford (BSc), LSE (MPhil); *m* 14 May 1988, Joanne Edwina, da of John Edward Simpson; 2 da (Sophia Rose b 8 June 1992, Olivia Mary b 12 Dec 1996), 1 s (Theodore David Robert b 27 Dec 2001); *Career* ed Export Times 1983–84 (reporter 1980–83); reporter: The Times 1984–86, London Daily News 1987; ed Maxwell Consumer Publishing and Communications 1987–92, publisher Financial and Business Publications 1992–, ed: Financial World (formerly Chartered Banker, Chartered Inst of Bankers magazine) 1995–2000, The Paper (Barclays Bank staff newspaper) 2000–01, Eclectic (Inst of Fin Servs magazine) 2000–05, Business Money Int 2005–07; contributing ed The Banker 2003–, assoc ed FT Live; memb: Inst of Internal Communication, Advsy Bd Inst for Regulations and Ethics QMUL, CPRE, CAMRA; affiliate CISI; *Books* Finance for Growth (ed, 1989), The Future of Building

Societies (1999), Dangers in E-Banking (2001); *Recreations* running, skiing, renovating old houses, antiques, cycling, photography, travel; *Style*— Michael Imeson, Esq; ✉ The Old Post House, Stanton, Broadway, Worcestershire WR12 7NE (☎ 01386 584978, e-mail imeson@fbp.co.uk)

IMOMOH, Egbert; *Career* various positions with Shell Gp (incl latterly dep md Shell Petroleum Devpt Co (Nigeria)); chm Afren Nigeria 2006, chm Afren plc 2010; memb Soc of Petroleum Engrs (pres 2013); *Recreations* golf; *Clubs* Ikoyi (Lagos); *Style*— Egbert Imomoh, Esq; ✉ Afren plc, Kinnaird House, 1 Pall Mall East, London SW1Y 5AU

IMPALLOMENI, Dr Mario Giuseppe; s of Prof Col Rosario Impallomeni (d 1983), and Ada, *née* Ascarelli (d 1994); *b* 19 July 1937; *Educ* Scuole Pie Fiorentine Florence, Faculty of Med Univ of Florence (MD); *m* 1, 10 March 1973 (m dis 2005), Madeleine Clare, da of Hugh Edward Blackburn (d 1964); 1 s (Tommaso Fergus b 11 Oct 1979), 1 da (Laura Chiara b 18 July 1982); m 2, 17 July 2009, Beatrice Anne, da of Harben Bouturline-Young (d 1982); *Career* jr lectr Dept of Clinical Med Univ of Florence 1961–66, registrar Queen's Hosp Croydon 1966–69, conslt physician Italian Hospital London 1969–90, sr registrar Central Middx Hosp & St Thomas' Hosp 1969–71, consl geriatrician N Middx Hosp & St Anne's Hosp 1972–78, consl gen and geriatric med and sr lectr Imperial Coll Sch of Med (formerly Royal Post Grad Med Sch) 1978–2002, consl emeritus and hon sr lectr Dept of Med B Imperial Coll Sch of Med 2002–; hon physician Saracens RUFC 1992–2005; fndr memb and pres Italian Med Soc of GB 2002–04; contrib to several books on geriatric med, memb editorial bd of several med jls; chm NW Branch Br Geriatrics Soc 1985–89; FRCP 1985 (MRCP 1969); Commendatore dell'Ordine al Merito della Repubblica Italiana 2002; *Books* Textbook of Diagnostic Imaging in the Elderly (2002); *Recreations* history, chess, cycling, fell walking, classic music; *Style*— Dr Mario Impallomeni; ✉ Department of Medicine B, Faculty of Medicine, Imperial College, Hammersmith Hospital Campus, Du Cane Road, London W12 0HS (☎ 020 8383 4290, fax 020 8383 3056, e-mail mario.impallomeni@gmail.com)

IMRAY, Sir Colin Henry; KBE (1992), CMG (1983); s of Henry Gibbon Imray (d 1936), and Frances Olive, *née* Badman (d 1992); *b* 21 September 1933, Newport, Monmouthshire; *Educ* Highgate and Hotchkiss USA, Balliol Coll Oxford (MA); *m* 1957, Shirley Margaret, da of Ernest Matthews (d 1972); 1 s (Christopher), 3 da (Frances (Mrs King), *qv*, Elizabeth, Alison); *Career* Nat Serv 2 Lt Seaforth Highlanders (Royal W African Force) 1952–54; CRO 1957, third (later second) sec UK High Cmmn Canberra 1958–61, first sec Nairobi 1963–66, Br Trade Cmmn Montreal 1970–73, cnsllr, head of Chancery and consul gen Islamabad 1973–77, RCDS 1977, commercial cnsllr Tel Aviv 1977–80, dep high cmmr Bombay 1980–84, dep chief clerk and chief inspr FCO 1984–85, high cmmr to the United Republic of Tanzania 1986–89, high cmmr to the People's Republic of Bangladesh 1989–93; sec-gen Order of St John 1993–97 (dir of overseas rels 1997–98); patron Chameleon Arts Wallingford 2011– (chm 2008–11); High Steward Wallingford 2002–15; Freeman City of London 1994; KStJ 1993; *Publications* Remember and Be Glad (2009); *Recreations* gardening, watching the career of Professor Christopher Imray, Phd, FRCS, FRCP, FRGS; *Clubs* Royal Over-Seas League (memb Central Cncl 1998–2005, memb Exec Cncl 1999–2005, chm 2000–05, vice-pres 2005–); *Style*— Sir Colin Imray, KBE, CMG; ✉ 1 A St Johns' Road, Wallingford, Oxford OX10 9AD

IMRIE, Celia Diana Savile; *b* Guildford, Surrey; *Educ* Guildford HS; *Children* 1 s (Angus); *Career* actress; *Television* incl: Bergerac 1983, Victoria Wood: As Seen on TV 1985–86, Acorn Antiques 1986–87, Oranges Are Not the Only Fruit 1989, Victoria Wood 1989, Thacker 1992, Absolutely Fabulous 1995 and 2001, Blackhearts in Battersea 1995–96, The Canterville Ghost 1997, Wokenwell 1997, The History of Tom Jones, a Foundling 1997, Dinnerladies 1998–2000, A Christmas Carol 1999, Gormenghast 2000, Love in a Cold Climate 2001, A is for Acid 2002, Doctor Zhivago 2002, Daniel Deronda 2002, Agatha Christie Marple: 4.50 from Paddington 2004, The Lavender List 2006, The Commander: The Devil You Know 2007, After You've Gone 2007–08, Kingdom 2007–09, The Road to Coronation Street 2010, The Bleak Old Shop of Stuff 2011, Titanic 2012, Love and Marriage 2013, Blandings 2014, Our Zoo 2014; *Film* incl: Highlander 1986, Frankenstein 1994, In the Bleak Midwinter 1995, The Borrowers 1997, Bridget Jones's Diary 2001, Thunderpants 2002, Calendar Girls 2003, Wimbledon 2004, Bridget Jones: The Edge of Reason 2004, Wah-Wah 2005, Imagine Me & You 2005, Nanny McPhee 2005, St Trinian's 2007, St Trinian's 2: The Legend of Fritton's Gold 2009, The Best Exotic Marigold Hotel 2011, Love Punch 2014, What We Did On Our Holidays 2014, Molly Moon: The Incredible Hypnotist 2014, Nativity 3: Dude Where's My Donkey 2014, The Second Best Exotic Marigold Hotel 2015; *Theatre* incl: The Sea 1991 (Best Supporting Actress Clarence Derwent Award 1992), The School for Scandal 1998, Unsuspecting Susan 2005, Acorn Antiques: The Musical! 2005 (Best Performance in a Supporting Role in a Musical Laurence Olivier Award 2006), Plague Over England 2009, Mixed Up North 2009, The Rivals 2010, Polar Bears 2010, Hay Fever 2010, Drama at Inish 2011, Noises Off 2011, Laughing Matters 2014; *Books* The Happy Hoofer (2011), Not Quite Nice (2015); *Style*— Ms Celia Imrie; ✉ c/o Dallas Smith (acting agent), United Agents, 12–26 Lexington Street, London W1F 0LE (☎ 020 3214 0800; c/o Robert Caskie at PFD (literary agent), c/o Alexa Pearson at Public Eye Communications (publicist)

INCHCAPE, 4 Earl of (UK 1929); (Kenneth) Peter Lyle Mackay; also Baron Inchcape (UK 1911), Viscount Inchcape (UK 1924), and Viscount Glenapp (UK 1929); s of 3 Earl of Inchcape (d 1994), and his 1 w, Aline Thorn, *née* Pease; *b* 23 January 1943; *Educ* Eton; *m* 7 June 1966, Georgina, da of Sidney Cresswell Nisbet; 2 da (Lady Elspeth Pease (Lady Elspeth Hordern) b 1972, Lady Ailsa Fiona (Lady Ailsa Stonor) b 1977), 1 s (Fergus James Kenneth, Viscount Glenapp b 1979); *Heir* s, Viscount Glenapp; *Career* Lt 9/12 Royal Lancers served: Aden, Arabian Gulf, BAOR; formerly with Inchcape plc (20 years); chm: Inchcape Family Estates Ltd, The Glenapp Estate Co Ltd; dir: Gray Dawes Travel Ltd, Assam Oil and Gas Co Ltd, Duncan Macneill & Co Ltd; pres Royal Alfred Seafarers Soc 1992–2015; memb Ct of Assts: Worshipful Co of Grocers (Master 1993–94), Worshipful Co of Shipwrights (Prime Warden 1998–99); Liveryman Worshipful Co of Fishmongers; AIB; *Recreations* shooting, fishing, golf, skiing, travel, farming; *Clubs* White's, Oriental, Pratt's, New, Prestwick, Royal Sydney Golf; *Style*— The Earl of Inchcape; ✉ Manor Farm, Clyffe Pypard, Wiltshire SN4 7PY

IND, Dr Philip Waterloo; s of John Waterloo Ind, of San Juan, Spain, and Marjorie, *née* Hesketh; *b* 17 February 1950; *Educ* Haberdashers' Aske's, Gonville & Caius Coll Cambridge (BA, MA), UCH (MB BChir); *m* 30 June 1973, Dr Sally Ind, da of Dr Charles Hutcheon Thomson (d 1962), of Low Fell, Durham; 1 s (Robert b 3 Oct 1977), 2 da (Sarah b 25 April 1980, Kathryn b 28 Oct 1982); *Career* med registrar Edgware Gen Hosp 1975, hon sr registrar Hammersmith Hosp 1981 (registrar 1977), hon sr lectr and consl physician Hammersmith and Ealing Hosp 1985–, currently sr lectr and actg head Dept of Respiratory Med NHLI Hammersmith Hosp; multiple academic papers and book chapters; FRCP 1991 (MRCP); *Recreations* reading, windsurfing, bridge, squash, tennis; *Style*— Dr Philip Ind; ✉ Respiratory Medicine, Clinical Investigation Unit, Imperial College School of Medicine at Hammersmith Hospital, Du Cane Road, London W12 0HS (☎ 020 8740 3077, fax 020 8743 9733, e-mail p.ind@imperial.ac.uk)

INESON, Dr Nigel Richard; s of Jeffrey Ineson, of Milton Keynes, and late Eileen, *née* Wood; *Educ* Watford GS, Guy's Hosp Med Sch London (MB BS, DRCOG, DFFP); *Children* 2 s (James Richard Mannakee b 8 Dec 1984, Andrew Nicholas Mannakee b 23 July 1986); *Career* various house jobs Hillingdon Hosp (med) and Wycombe Gen Hosp (surgical), subsequently on staff A&E Dept Hillingdon Hosp then SHO (gen surgical and orthopaedics rotation) Medway Hosp Gp Kent, SHO posts in med/geriatrics, psychiatry, paediatrics & obstetrics and gynaecology then gen practice trainee (vocational trg scheme) Watford 1981–84, ptnr in teaching practice Watford 1984–; princ Herts FHSA, company med offr DDD Ltd (mfr of ethical pharmaceuticals), med offr Watford FC; MAE, memb Expert Witness Inst, chm Beds & Herts Faculty RCGP; FRCGP; *Style*— Dr Nigel Ineson; ✉ Wentworth, 30 Green Lane, Oxhey, Hertfordshire WD1 4NH (☎ 01923 233992); The Callowland Surgery, 141a Leavesden Road, Watford, Hertfordshire WD2 5EP (fax 01923 443143, mobile 078 3168 6531)

INFIELD, Paul Louis; s of Gordon Mark Infield, and Roda Molca, *née* Lincoln; *b* 1 July 1957; *Educ* Haberdashers' Aske's, The Peddie Sch Hightstown NJ, Univ of Sheffield (LLB); *m* 6 Feb 1987, Catharine Grace, da of Ancrum Francis Evans, of Clifton on Teme, Worcs, 1 s (Samuel b 1988), 1 da (Margery b 1991); *Career* called to the Bar Inner Temple 1980; memb Bd of Visitors HM Prison Wandsworth 1992–2000 (chm 1996–98), memb Exec Ctee Assoc of Membs of Bds of Visitors 1997–2000, memb Duke Corporate Educn Non-Traditional Global Learning Resource Network; treas 36 Bedford Row Ltd 2014–; tstee: The Suzy Lamplugh Tst 1999–2016 (chm 2009–16), Prisoners' Educn Tst 1999–2000, Network for Surviving Stalking 2001–05; memb Ed Bd Community Safety Jl 2002–05; chm S London Liberal Synagogue 2002–07, offr Liberal Judaism 2005–08; Freeman City of London 1979, Liveryman Worshipful Co of Plaisterers 1979; MCIArb 2013; *Publications* The Prisons Handbook (contrib, 1997 and 1998), The Law of Harassment and Stalking (with Graham Platford, 2000), Stalking and Psychosexual Obsession (contrib, 2002); *Recreations* running, theatre, cricket; *Style*— Paul Infield; ✉ 34 Hillier Road, London SW11 6AU; 36 Bedford Row, London WC1R 4JH (☎ 020 7421 8019, e-mail pinfield@36family.co.uk, website www.36group.co.uk, Twitter @Leagality)

INGALL, Mike; *Educ* Univ of Greenwich; *Career* fndr, chm and ceo Allied London 2000–; developments incl: Spinningfields Manchester, Sky Park Glasgow, The Brunswick Centre, St John's Manchester; over 60 awards incl Developer of the Decade Property Week 2000; FRIBA; *Style*— Mike Ingall, Esq; ✉ Allied London, 49 Grosvenor Street, London W1K 3HP

INGE, Charles; *b* 9 June 1961, Rugby, Warks; *Educ* Univ of Oxford (MA); *m* Jane; 3 da (Sarah, Emma, Laura); *Career* Lowe: joined 1986, various positions rising to creative dir 1999–2001; co-fndr Clemmow Hornby Inge 2001; winner numerous advtg industry awards incl: Cannes Grand Prix (for The Independent TV campaign) 1999, Cannes Grand Prix (for Stella Artois press campaign) 2000, IPA Effectiveness Grand Prix (for Tesco campaign) 2000; for Lowe: Campaign Agency of the Year 2000, Ad Age European Agency of the Year 2000, Br TV Advtg Agency of the Year 2001; for Clemmow Hornby Inge: Br TV Advtg Agency of the Year 2004, Creative Agency of the Year Marketing magazine 2004; *Clubs* Groucho; *Style*— Charles Inge, Esq; ✉ CHI & Partners, 7 Rathbone Street, London W1T 1LY (☎ 020 7462 8514, fax 020 7462 8501, website www.chiandpartners.com)

INGE, Baron (Life Peer UK 1997), of Richmond in the County of North Yorkshire; Field Marshal The Rt Hon Peter Anthony Inge; KG (2001), GCB (1992, KCB 1988), PC (2004), DL (N Yorks 1994); s of Raymond Inge (d 1995), and Grace Maud Caroline, *née* Du Rose (d 1962); *b* 5 August 1935; *Educ* Wrekin Coll, RMA Sandhurst; *m* 26 Nov 1960, Letitia Marion, da of Trevor Thornton Berry (d 1967); 2 da (Hon Antonia b 17 May 1962, Hon Verity b 12 Oct 1965); *Career* cmmnd Green Howards 1954; served: Hong Kong, Malaya, Germany, Libya and N Ireland, ADC to GOC 4 Div 1960–61, Adj 1 Green Howards 1963–64, student Staff Coll 1966, MOD 1967–69, Co Comd 1 Green Howards 1969–70, student JSSC 1971, BM 11 Armd Bde 1972, instr Staff Coll 1973–74, CO 1 Green Howards 1974–77, Comdt Jr Div Staff Coll 1977–79, Comd 4 Armd Bde 1979–81, Chief of Staff HQ 1 (BR) Corps 1982–83, GOC NE Dist and Comd 2 Inf Div 1984–86, DGLP (A) MOD 1986–87, Comd 1 (BR) Corps 1987–89, C-in-C BAOR and Comd NORTHAG 1989–91, Col Comdt RMP 1987–92, ADC (Gen) to HM The Queen 1991–94; CGS 1992–94, CDS 1994–97, Field Marshal 1994; Constable HM Tower of London 1996–2001, pres Army Benevolent Fund 1997–2002, Pilgrims 2003–10; Col The Green Howards 1982–94, Col Comdt APTC 1988–96; non-exec chm Aegis 2006–10 (memb Advsy Bd 2010); non-exec dir: Racal Electronics plc 1997–2000, Greenlys plc 1998–99; chm Cncl King Edward VII's Hosp Sister Agnes 2003–12; memb: Cncl Marborough Coll 1998–2006, Cncl St George's House Windsor Castle 1999–2006 and 2011–; tstee: Royal Amouries 1996–2000, Historical Royal Palaces 1998–2006; Hon DCL Univ of Newcastle upon Tyne 1995; CIMgt 1993; *Recreations* cricket, walking, music, reading (especially military history); *Clubs* Army and Navy, MCC, Boodle's, Beefsteak, Travellers; *Style*— Field Marshal the Lord Inge, KG, GCB, PC, DL; ✉ House of Lords, London SW1A 0PW

INGE, Rt Rev Dr John; *see:* Bishop of Worcester

INGHAM, Sir Bernard; kt (1990); s of Garnet Ingham (d 1974); *b* 21 June 1932; *Educ* Hebden Bridge GS; *m* 1956, Nancy Hilda, da of Ernest Hoyle (d 1944), of Halifax, W Yorks; 1 s (Dr John Bernard Ingham, *qv* b 16 Feb 1958); *Career* journalist: Hebden Bridge Times 1948–52, The Yorkshire Post and Yorkshire Evening Post 1952–59, The Yorkshire Post (northern industrial corr) 1959–62, The Guardian 1962–67 (Leeds 1962–65, Lab Staff London 1965–67); press advsr Nat Bd for Prices and Incomes 1967–68, head of info Dept of Employment and Productivity 1968–72; dir of info: Dept of Employment 1973, Dept of Energy 1974–78; under sec (Energy Conservation Div) Dept of Energy 1978–79, chief press sec to Prime Minister 1979–90; chm Bernard Ingham Communications 1991–2011; columnist: The Express 1991–98, PR Week 1994–2001 (winner Business and Professional Magazines Columnist of the Year PPA Awards 1995), The Yorkshire Post 2004–; non-exec dir Hill and Knowlton 1991–2001, non-exec dir McDonald's Restaurants Ltd 1991–2005, memb Advsy Bd McDonald's UK 2005–09; pres Br Franchise Assoc 1993–2012; sec Supporters of Nuclear Energy 1998–2014; visiting fell Dept of Politics Univ of Newcastle upon Tyne 1989–2003, visiting prof Univ of Middlesex Business Sch 1998–2006; memb Cncl Univ of Huddersfield 1994–2000; hon fell Communication, Advertising and Marketing Educn Fndn 1998; Hon DLitt Univ of Buckingham 1997, Hon DUniv Middlesex 1999, Hon DUniv Bradford 2004; Hon FINucE 1998; *Books* Kill the Messenger (1991), Yorkshire Millennium (1999), Yorkshire Castles (2001), Yorkshire Villages (2001), The Wages of Spin (2003), Yorkshire Greats (2005); *Recreations* writing, reading; *Clubs* Reform, Midgehole Working Men's, Pennine, Hebden Bridge; *Style*— Sir Bernard Ingham; ✉ 9 Monahan Avenue, Purley, Surrey CR8 3BB (☎ 020 8660 8970, e-mail bernardinghamcom@aol.com)

INGHAM, Prof Derek Binns; *b* 7 August 1942; *Educ* Univ of Leeds (BSc, PhD, DSc); *m* 22 Aug 1964, Jean; 1 da (Catherine Gail b 30 Dec 1965), 1 s (Mark Andrew b 10 July 1967); *Career* Univ of Leeds: lectr in mathematics 1968–78 (1964–66), sr lectr 1978–83, reader 1983–86, prof 1986–2015, head Dept of Applied Mathematical Studies 1988–91, emeritus prof 2007–; prof of applied mathematics Univ of Sheffield 2015–; CLE Moore instr MIT 1966–68; hon grad Univ of Cluj Romania 2000; FIMA 1988; *Books* incl: Boundary Integral Equation Analyses of Singular, Potential and Biharmonic Problems (1984), The Mathematics of Blunt Body Sampling (1988), The Boundary Element Method for Solving Improperly Posed Problems (with Y Yuan, 1994), Boundary Element Methods in Fluid Dynamics II (ed with C A Brebbia and H Power, 1994), Boundary Elements XVIII (ed with C A Brebbia, J A Martins, M H Aliabadi, N Haie and M Power, 1996), Enhanced Sedimentation in Inclined Fracture Channels (with L Elliott and S McCaffery, 1997), Boundary Integral Formulations for Inverse Analysis (with L C Wrobel, 1997), Transport Phenomena in Porous Media (with I Pop, 1998, vol 2 2002), Convective Heat Transfer (with I Pop, 2001), Inverse Problems and Experimental Design in Thermal and Mechanical Engineering (ed with D Petit, Y Jarny and F Plourde, 2002), Proceedings of the First UK Conference on Boundary Integral Methods (ed with L Elliott and D Lesnic); *Style*— Prof Derek Ingham; ✉ Department of Mechanical Engineering, University of Sheffield, Sheffield S10 2TN (✆ 0114 215715, e-mail d.ingham@sheffield.ac.uk or d.b.ingham@leeds.ac.uk)

INGHAM, Graham; s of late Alan Ingham, and Marjorie, *née* White; *b* 30 September 1953; *Educ* Bacup and Rawtenstall GS, Thames Poly (BA), LSE (MSc), Birkbeck Coll London (MA); *Partner* Jonathan Birt (civil partnership June 2009); *Career* HM Treasy 1975–84: private sec to Sir Kenneth Couzens 1978–80, princ monetary policy 1980–81, princ Euro monetary affrs 1982–84; visiting fell and Fulbright scholar Princeton Univ 1981–82, economics specialist BBC World Serv 1984–88, economics corr BBC TV News and Current Affrs 1988–96, Guardian research fell Nuffield Coll Oxford 1995–96 (on leave from BBC), freelance broadcaster and journalist 1996–2000, with The Economist 2000–03, speechwriter and advsr (to Anne Krueger) Int Monetary Fund Washington DC 2003–06, advsr to the Pres Federal Reserve Bank of NY 2006–08, freelance writer and broadcaster 2008–; dir Sutton Belmont Ltd 2014–; presenter Greenback: How the Dollar Came to Rule the World (BBC Radio 4) 2013; visiting prof of economics Univ of Greenwich 1992–93, visiting reader in economics Royal Holloway Coll London 1995–97, dir of public affairs Centre for Economic Performance LSE 1995–2000; ed CentrePiece 1995–2001; *Books* Romance of the Three Empires (contrib, 1988), Managing Change: a guide to British economic policy (2000); author of articles in The Guardian, The Independent, etc; *Recreations* opera, travel, reading, playing the piano; *Style*— Graham Ingham, Esq; ✉ e-mail grahamingham@hotmail.com

INGHAM, John Bernard; s of Sir Bernard Ingham, *qv*, of Purley, Surrey, and Nancy Hilda, *née* Hoyle; *b* 16 February 1958; *Educ* Univ of Durham (BA, Fulbright scholar, PhD), Bowling Green State Univ of Ohio (MA); *m* 7 Sept 1985, Christine, da of James Yendley; 1 da (b 21 Sept 1991), 1 s (b 16 Sept 1994); *Career* visiting researcher Georgetown Univ Washington DC 1982–83, dep ed BNFL News 1984–87, ed Sellascene 1986–87, freelance sports reporter Sunday Express 1986–89; Northern Correspondent, Building Magazine, Chartered Surveyor Weekly 1987–89; news reporter Daily Express Manchester 1989–90; Daily Express: def and dip corr 1990–94, political corr 1994–96, environment corr 1996–99, environment and tport ed 1999–2002, environment, tport and def ed 2002–, columnist 2005–; RSPCA Nat Media Award 2000, Dilys Breese Medal Br Tst for Ornithology 2013; *Recreations* travel, birdwatching, following cricket and soccer; *Style*— Mr John Ingham; ✉ Daily Express, The Northern & Shell Building, 10 Lower Thames Street, London EC3R 6EN (✆ 020 8612 7108, fax 020 7098 2723, e-mail john.ingham@express.co.uk)

INGHAM, Mike; MBE (2010); *Career* BBC Radio 5 Live: football corr 1991–2004, chief football corr 2004– (commentator on all major football tournaments incl numerous World Cups, European Championships, Champions League and FA Cup finals and Premier League seasons); *Style*— Mike Ingham, Esq, MBE; ✉ BBC Radio 5 Live, MediaCityUK, Salford M50 2EQ

INGHAM, Prof Philip William; s of George Philip Ingham (d 1980), and Dorothy, *née* Wensley (d 2012); *b* 19 March 1955, Liverpool; *Educ* Univ of Cambridge (MA), Univ of Sussex (DPhil); *m* 1993, Anita, *née* Taylor; 2 da (Madeleine Philippa b 20 April 1994, Isabella Alexandria b 15 Sept 1998), 1 s (James William b 18 Sept 1995); *Career* research trg: Laboratoire de Génètique Molèculaire CNRS Gif-sur Yvette 1979, Laboratoire de Génètique Molèculaire des Eukaryotes Faculté de Médecine Strasbourg 1981–82, Developmental Genetics Laboratory ICRF London 1982–85; research scientist MRC Laboratory of Molecular Biology Univ of Cambridge 1986, research scientist rising to sr scientist ICRF Developmental Biology Unit Univ of Oxford 1986–94, princ scientist ICRF London 1994–96, prof of developmental genetics Univ of Sheffield 1996–2009 (dir MRC Centre for Developmental and Biomedical Genetics 2006–09); visiting prof Nat Univ of Singapore 2005; dep dir Inst of Molecular and Cell Biology Singapore 2006–13, prof of developmental biology, Toh Kian Chui distinguished prof and vice-dean of research Lee Kong Chian Sch of Medicine Imperial Coll London-Nanyang Technological Univ Singapore 2014–16, prof of developmental biology and inaugural dir The Living Systems Inst Univ of Exeter 2016–; chm Br Soc for Developmental Biology 1999–2004 (pubns sec 1991–95), vice-chm MRC/Wellcome Tst Human Developmental Biology Resource Steering Ctee 2000–02; memb Ctee: Br Soc for Developmental Biology 1987–95, Genetics Soc of GB 1993–97; memb Scientific Advsy Bd Ontogeny Inc 1995–99; memb: Fellowship Review Panel Human Frontiers Science Prog 1996–98, Molecular and Cell Review Panel Wellcome Tst 1997–2001, Review Panel Yorks Cancer Research 1997–2001, Int Scientific Advsy Bd Max-Planck-Institut für Entwicklungsbiologie Tübingen 1999–2008, EMBO Courses and Workshops Ctee 2002–05, Wellcome Tst Sanger Inst 2008–11, Hong Kong Research Grants Ctee 2010–12, Wellcome Tst Investigator Awards Panel 2012–14, Max Planck Inst for Heart and Lung Resarch Bad Nauheim 2012–; assoc ed: Developmental Biology 1995–2002, Molecular Cell 1999–2001; reviews ed Developmental Cell 2001–03; memb Editorial Advsy Bd: Current Topics in Developmental Biology 1990–, Genetical Research 1991–96, Development 1991–98, Genes & Development 1991–2005, Mechanisms of Development 1991–, Current Biology 1993–2008, EMBO Jl 1999–2008, Genome Biology 1999–2011, Comparative and Functional Genomics 1999–2005, EMBO Reports 2000–08, Developmental Cell 2003–, Development 2014–; author of 160 papers published in scientific jls; Balfour Meml Prize Genetical Soc of GB 1991, Genetics Soc Medal 2005, Waddington Medal Br Soc for Developmental Biology 2014; Royal Soc European exchange fell 1980, EMBO long-term fell 1981, hon research lectr Univ of Oxford 1992; MA (by incorporation) Univ of Oxford 1987; memb EMBO 1995, FIBiol 2000, FMedSci 2001, FRS 2002, Hon FRCP 2007, memb Academia Europaea 2014; *Recreations* tennis, skiing, music, photography; *Clubs* British (Singapore); *Style*— Prof Philip Ingham; ✉ Living Systems Institute, University of Exeter, Stocker Road, Exeter EX4 4QD

INGHAM, Tim; s of Michael Ingham (d 2009), and Carol, *née* Rimington; *b* 28 November 1982, Norwich; *m* 31 Aug 2013, Rebecca, *née* Almond; *Career* reporter Metro/Evening Standard 2002–06, assoc ed MCV 2006–10, ed CVG 2010–11, ed Music Week 2011–; freelance writer: The Independent 2008–11, The Observer 2012–; Future Publishing Ed of the Year 2010; *Recreations* cinema, music, reading; *Style*— Tim Ingham, Esq; ✉ Music Week, Suncourt House, 18–26 Essex Road, Islington, London N1 8LN (Twitter @tsingham)

INGILBY, Sir Thomas Colvin William; 6 Bt (UK 1866), of Ripley Castle, Yorkshire; s of Maj Sir Joslan William Vivian Ingilby, 5 Bt, JP, DL (d 1974), and Diana, *née* Colvin (d 2013); *b* 17 July 1955; *Educ* Eton, RAC Cirencester (MRAC); *m* 25 Feb 1984, Emma Clare Roebuck, da of Maj Richard R Thompson, of Whinfield, W Yorks; 4 s (James William Francis b 1985, Joslan Richard Ryland b 1986, Jack Henry Thomas b 1990, Richard Joseph Frederick b 1994), 1 da (Eleanor Jane Pamela b 1989); *Heir* s, James Ingilby; *Career* teacher Springvale Sch Rhodesia 1973–74; asst land agent: Stephenson & Son York 1978–80, Strutt and Parker Harrogate 1981–83; mangr Ripley Castle Estates 1983– (Best Tourist Devpt RICS White Rose Awards, Silver Award for Best Small Visitor Attraction VisitBritain Enjoy Excellence in England Awards 2007 and 2010); pres Nidderdale Amateur Cricket League 1979–; dir: N York TEC 1989–93, Yorkshire Tourist Bd 1997–2009 (vice-chm 2005–09), Welcome to Yorkshire 2014–; chm: Yorkshire's Great Houses, Castles and Gardens 1994–, The Great Inns of Britain 1996–2013, bd of govrs Cundall Manor Sch 2007–; festival dir Golden Oldies World Cricket Festival 2010; hotelier Boar's Head Ripley; Lifetime Achievement Award Harrogate Business Award 2011; int hon citizen New Orleans 1979; ARICS, FAAV, FBII; *Books* Yorkshire's Great Houses – Behind the Scenes (2005); *Recreations* tennis, cricket, reading, shooting, walking; *Style*— Sir Thomas Ingilby, Bt; ✉ Ripley Castle, Ripley, Harrogate, North Yorkshire HG3 3AY (✆ 01423 770152, e-mail enquiries@ripleycastle.co.uk, website www.ripleycastle.co.uk)

INGLE, Prof Stephen James; s of James Ingle (d 1991), and Violet Grace, *née* Stephenson (d 1997); *b* 6 November 1940; *Educ* The Roan Sch, Univ of Sheffield (BA, MA Econ, DipEd), Victoria Univ of Wellington NZ (PhD); *m* 5 Aug 1964, Margaret Anne, da of Henry James Hubert Farmer (d 1979), of Sutton Bridge, Lincs; 2 s (Jonathan James Stuart b 11 Oct 1970, Benedict John Stephen b 13 April 1972), 1 da (Cassie Louise b 8 June 1979); *Career* Cwlth scholar in NZ 1964–67, head of dept Univ of Hull 1985–90 (lectr in politics 1967–80, sr lectr 1980); Univ of Stirling: prof and head of Dept of Politics 1991–2002, vice-dean Faculty of Arts 1996–2002, emeritus prof 2006–; visiting research fell Victoria Univ of Wellington NZ 1993; sec Political Studies Assoc UK 1987–88, chief examiner in politics Oxford, Cambridge and RSA Examinations Syndicate 1987–2002; memb AHRC Peer Review Coll 2005–; memb E Yorks HA 1985–90; acadamic fell and int scholar Open Soc Inst 2005–08; panel memb and assessor AHRC 2009–14, res assessor Carnegie Tst 2014–; *Books* Socialist Thought in Imaginative Literature (1979), Parliament and Health Policy (1981), George Orwell: A Political Life (1993), Narratives of British Socialism (2002), The Social and Political Thought of George Orwell: A Reappraisal (2006), British Party System (4 edn 2008); *Recreations* music, theatre, travelling; *Clubs* Soc of Authors, Orwell Soc; *Style*— Prof Stephen Ingle; ✉ University of Stirling, Stirling FK9 4LA (✆ 01786 467593, e-mail s.j.ingle@stir.ac.uk)

INGLE-FINCH, Sydney; *m* Charles Finch, *qv*; *Career* fashion and brand conslt; advsr on special projects Prada; *Style*— Ms Sydney Ingle-Finch; ✉ Finch & Partners, Top Floor, 35 Heddon Street, London W1 (✆ 020 7851 7140, e-mail sydney@finchandpartners.com, website www.finchandpartners.com)

INGLEBY, Richard William; s of late William Ingleby, and Elizabeth Blackwood, *née* Craig; *b* 29 January 1967, Glasgow; *Educ* Trinity Coll Glenalmond, Univ of Durham (BA); *m* 22 Dec 1994, Florence; 3 da (Molly b 18 March 1996, Edie b 31 Oct 1997, Esme b 21 July 2002); *Career* Fine Art Soc 1990–97 (dir 1995–97), dir and prop Ingleby Gallery Edinburgh 1998–; art critic and columnist for various pubns 1996–2002; tstee: Arts Tst for Scotland, Edinburgh Art Festival, Little Sparta Tst; *Publications* Christopher Wood: An English Painter (1994), C R W Nevinson (1998), Alfred Wallis and James Dixon (1999), To the North: Jon Schueler (2003), I Look to You: Callum Innes (2009), Iona: Sean Scully (2010), Modern Richard Forster (2014); *Recreations* arts, books, food, drink; *Clubs* Soho House; *Style*— Richard Ingleby, Esq

INGLESE, Anthony Michael Christopher; CB (2008); s of Angelo Inglese, and Dora, *née* Di Paola; *b* 19 December 1951; *Educ* Salvatorian Coll Harrow Weald, Fitzwilliam Coll Cambridge (MA, LLB); *m* 1974, Jane Elizabeth Kerry, *née* Bailes; 1 s, 1 da; *Career* called to the Bar Gray's Inn 1976, bencher 2003, Legal Adviser's Branch Home Office 1975–86, legal secretariat to Law Offrs 1986–88, Legal Adviser's Branch Home Office 1988–91, legal dir Office of Fair Trading 1991–95, legal advsr Treasy Slr's Dept Min of Defence 1995–97, dep Treasy slr 1997–2002, slr to DTI 2002–08, gen counsel and slr to HM Revenue and Customs 2008–14; *Style*— Anthony Inglese, Esq, CB; ✉ e-mail anthony.inglese@btinternet.com

INGLEWOOD, 2 Baron (UK 1964); (William) Richard (Fletcher-) Vane; s of 1 Baron Inglewood, TD, DL (d 1989); *b* 31 July 1951, Carlisle, Cumbria; *Educ* Eton, Trinity Coll Cambridge (MA), Cumbria Coll of Agric and Forestry; *m* 29 Aug 1986, Cressida Rosa, yst da of late (Alan) Desmond Frederick Pemberton-Pigott, CMG, of Fawe Park, Keswick; 2 da (Hon Miranda Mary b 19 May 1987, Hon Rosa Katharine b 25 July 1989), 1 s (Hon Henry William Frederick b 24 Dec 1990); *Heir* s, Hon Henry Vane; *Career* called to the Bar Lincoln's Inn 1975; MEP (Cons): Cumbria and Lancs N 1989–94, NW England 1999–2004; Parly candidate (Cons): Houghton and Washington Gen Election 1983, Durham European election 1984; Cons spokesman on legal affrs European Parl 1989–94 and 1999–2004, Cons spokesman on constitutional affrs 2001–04, Cons chief whip European Parl 1994 (dep whip 1992–94), Lord in Waiting 1994–95; Capt Yeomen of the Guard 1995, Parly under sec of state Dept of National Heritage 1995–97, oppn spokesman on the environment House of Lords 1997–98, memb Sub-Ctee F European Communities Ctee of House of Lords 1997–99, elected memb House of Lords 1999–, memb Sub-Ctee A House of Lords 2004–07, memb Communcations Ctee House of Lords 2007–10, memb Sub-Ctee G House of Lords 2008–10, chm Communications Ctee House of Lords 2011–14; memb Parly Delgn to the Cncl of Europe 2010–11; chm Reviewing Ctee on the Export of Works of Art 2003–13, chm House of Lords Select Ctee on Extradition Law 2014–15, memb House of Lords Select Ctee on Nat Policy for the Built Environment 2015–; chm: C N Gp 2002– (dir 1997–), Carr's Milling Industries 2005–13 (dir 2004–13); pres Br Art Market Fedn 2014–; pres Cumbria Tourism (formerly Cumbria Tourist Bd) 2004–, chm Cumbria Local Nature Partnership 2013–, pres Uplands Alliance 2015–; memb: Lake Dist Special Planning Bd 1984–90, NWWA 1987–89 (memb Regnl Land Drainage Ctee 1985–89); memb Ct Lancaster Univ 1985–2008, memb Advsy Bd Reuters Inst Univ of Oxford 2015–; visiting parly fell St Antony's Coll Oxford 2014–15; Vice-Lord-Lt Cumbria; Liveryman Worshipful Co of Skinners; MRICS, FSA; *Clubs* Travellers, Pratt's; *Style*— The Rt Hon Lord Inglewood; ✉ Hutton-in-the-Forest, Penrith, Cumbria CA11 9TH (✆ 017684 84500, fax 017684 84571, e-mail inglewood@hutton-in-the-forest.co.uk or inglewoodw@parliament.uk)

INGLIS, Craig; *Educ* Napier Univ (BA); *Career* product mangr Thomson Holidays 1992–96, sales and mktg dir Virgin Trains 1997–2007; John Lewis: head of brand communications 2008–10, mktg dir 2010–; Mktg Soc Marketer of the Year 2011; *Style*— Craig Inglis, Esq; ✉ John Lewis, 171 Victoria Street, London SW1E 5NN

INGLIS, Dr Stephen; s of John Reid Inglis, and Joan, *née* De Vear; *b* 1 September 1952, Aberdeen; *Educ* Univ of Aberdeen (BSc), Univ of Cambridge (PhD); *m* 26 July 1975, Moira, *née* Hunter; 2 s (Jamie b 11 Sept 1983, David b 22 May 1986), 1 da (Alison b 23 Feb 1992); *Career* Univ of Cambridge: res fell Churchill Coll 1977–80, univ lectr 1979–90, vice-pres molecular sciences and res dir pharmaceuticals 1995–2002; dir Nat Inst for Biological Standards and Control 2002–16, dir WHO Collaborating Laboratory for Standards 2002–16; author of 60 scientific publications on viruses and vaccines; FRSB; *Recreations* music, skiing, watersports, walking; *Style*— Dr Stephen Inglis; ✆ 07733 106080, e-mail stephen.inglis@cantab.net

INGOLD, Prof Timothy; s of Cecil Terence Ingold (d 2010), and Leonora Mary, *née* Kemp (d 1998); *b* 1 November 1948; *Educ* Leighton Park Sch Reading, Churchill Coll Cambridge (BA, PhD); *m* 30 Dec 1972, Anna Kaarina, *née* Väli-Kivistö; 3 s (Christopher b 1975, Nicholas b 1977, Jonathan b 1981), 1 da (Susanna b 1994); *Career* Dept of Social Anthropology Univ of Manchester: lectr 1974–85, sr lectr 1985–90, prof 1990–95; Max Gluckman prof of social anthropology Univ of Manchester 1995–99, prof of social anthropology Univ of Aberdeen 1999– (head Sch of Social Science 2008–11); pres Section H (Anthropology and Archaeology) BAAS 1998–99, chair of tstees Esperanza Tst RAI 1997–2007; Rivers Meml Medal RAI 1989, Award of Jean-Marie Delwart Fndn Royal Belgian Acad of Sciences 1994, Anders Retzius Gold Medal Swedish Soc for Anthropology and Geography 2004, Huxley Meml Medal Royal Anthropological Inst 2014; Hon DPhil Leuphana Univ 2015; FBA 1997, FRSE 2000; Knight (1st Class) of the Order of the White Rose of Finland 2014; *Books* The Skolt Lapps Today (1976), Hunters, Pastoralists and Ranchers (1980), Evolution and Social Life (1986), The Appropriation of Nature (1986), The Perception of the Environment (2000), Lines (2007), Being Alive (2011), Making (2013), The Life of Lines (2015); *Recreations* music (playing cello and piano); *Style*— Prof Timothy Ingold; ✉ Department of Anthropology, School of Social Science,

I

University of Aberdeen, Aberdeen AB24 3QY (☎ 01224 274350, fax 01224 272552, e-mail tim.ingold@abdn.ac.uk)

INGRAM, Adam; MSP; *b* 1 May 1951, Kilmarnock, Ayrshire; *Educ* Kilmarnock Acad, Univ of Glasgow, Paisley Coll (BA); *Career* mangr A H Ingram & Son (family firm) 1971–76, sr econ asst Manpower Servs Cmmn 1985–86, researcher and lectr Paisley Coll 1987–88, Devpt Options Ltd 1989–91, EES Conslts Ltd 1991–95, freelance econ conslt 1995–99; MSP (SNP): South of Scotland 1999–2011, Carrick Cumnock & Doon Valley 2011–; Scot Parl: shadow dep 2000–07, min for children and early years 2007–; *Style*— Adam Ingram, Esq, MSP; ✉ The Scottish Parliament, Edinburgh EH99 1SP

INGRAM, Christopher John (Chris); s of late Thomas Frank Ingram, of Southwick, W Sussex, and late Gladys Agnes, *née* Louttid; *b* 9 June 1943; *Educ* Woking GS; *m* 10 Oct 1964, Janet Elizabeth, da of late Charles Rye; 1 da (Kathryn Elizabeth b 30 March 1967), 1 s (Jonathan Devereux b 25 June 1969); *Career* md TMD 1972–76, fndr Chris Ingram Assocs 1976; Tempus Gp plc (formerly CIA Gp plc): chm and chief exec 1989–97, chm 1997–2002; ptnr Genesis Investments 2002–06, chm Ingram Partnership 2003–07, fndr Ingram Enterprise Investors LLP 2007–; chm Sports Revolution 2009–13; tstee Ingram Tst 1989–, chm Woking FC Holdings (now KCS) 2002–, fell WWF, hon fell London Business Sch, enterprise fell Princes Tst; *Recreations* modern British art, theatre, travel in cold climates, eating out, football; *Clubs* Enterprise 100, Surrey 100, Marketing Group, Pi Capital; *Style*— Mr Chris Ingram; ✉ Ingram Enterprise Investors LLP, 2nd Floor, 17–18 Margaret Street, London W1W 8RP (☎ 020 3828 8880, e-mail chris@ingramenterprise.com)

INGRAM, Prof David Stanley; OBE (1999), VMH (2004); s of Stanley Arthur Ingram, of Birmingham, and Vera May, *née* Mansfield (d 1973); *b* 10 October 1941; *Educ* Yardley GS Birmingham, Univ of Hull (BSc, PhD), Univ of Cambridge (MA, ScD); *m* 28 July 1965, Alison Winifred, da of Spencer Thomas Graham (d 1975); 2 s (Michael b 27 Aug 1967, Jonathan b 14 Aug 1969); *Career* res fell: Univ of Glasgow 1966–68, Univ of Cambridge 1968–69; sr scientific offr Agric Res Cncl Cambridge 1969–74; Univ of Cambridge: lectr in botany 1974–88, fell Downing Coll 1974–90 (dean, tutor and dir of studies in biology, hon fell 2000–), reader in plant pathology 1988–90, master St Catharine's Coll 2000–06, chm Colls Ctee 2003–05, memb Cncl 2003–05; regius keeper (dir) Royal Botanic Garden Edinburgh 1990–98 (hon fell 1998), hon prof Univ of Edinburgh 1991– (advsr on Public Engagement with Science 1998–2012), visiting prof of plant pathology Univ of Glasgow 1991–2012, prof of horticulture RHS 1995–2000, visiting prof of environmental biology and horticulture Napier Univ 1998–2005, hon prof Univ of Lancaster 2009–, hon prof of science, technology and innovation studies Univ of Edinburgh 2012–, visiting prof Glynd?r Univ 2012–; pres Br Soc of Plant Pathology 1998; chm Sci Ctee RHS 1994–2000; memb Bd Scot Nat Heritage 1998–2000; chm: Scot Sci and Plants for Schools Project 1990–98, Advsy Ctee on the Darwin Initiative for the Survival of Species DETR 1999–2005; memb Bd Jt Nature Conservation Ctee (JNCC) 1999 and 2002–08 (actg chair 2004, dep chair 2006–08); memb Advsy Ctee ESRC Genomics Forum 2005–; RSE: prog convenor 2005–09, chair Science and Soc Steering Gp 2006; tstee: Dynamic Earth 1998–2000, World Conservation Monitoring Centre 2000–04; hon pres Int Congress of Plant Pathology 1998; hon fell: Scot Geographical Soc 1998, Downing Coll Cambridge 2000, Myerscough Coll 2001, Worcester Coll Oxford 2003, St Catharine's Coll Cambridge 2006; Companion Guild of St George 2015–; Hon DUniv Open Univ 2000; hon prof Univ of Glasgow 2005; hon memb Br Soc for Plant Pathology 2008; CBiol, FRSB 1988, FRSE 1993, FCIHort 1997, FRCPEd 1998; VMH 2004; *Books* Plant Tissue Culture (1974), Tissue Culture Methods for Plant Pathologists (1980), Advances in Plant Pathology (vols I-IX, 1982–93), Cambridge Encyclopaedia of Life Sciences (1985), Shape and Form in Plants and Fungi (1994), Molecular Tools for Screening Biodiversity: Plants and Animals (1997), Plant Disease: A Natural History (1999), Science and the Garden (2002, 3 edn 2015), The Flora of Blackwell (2011), Painting Flowers – Fantin-Latour & the Impressionists (2011), Ruskin's Flora: The Botanical Drawings of John Ruskin (2011), The Gardens at Brentwood – Evolution of John Ruskin's Lakeland Paradise (2014); numerous articles in academic journals and other publications concerning botany, plant pathology, conservation of biodiversity, public engagement with science, systematics, horticulture, sociology and history of art; *Recreations* music, art, ceramics, gardening, travel, strolling around cities; *Clubs* New (Edinburgh); *Style*— Prof David Ingram, OBE, VMH, FRSE; ✉ c/o Royal Society of Edinburgh, 22–26 George Street, Edinburgh (☎ 0131 240 5000)

INGRAM, Julian Andrew; s of Ernest Alfred Ingram, of Dawlish Warren, Devon and June Jamieson, *née* Ralph; *b* 17 April 1956, Carshalton, Surrey; *Educ* Worthing GS for Boys, Worthing Sixth Form Coll, LSE (BSc, London Univ laurel); *m* 1, 19 July 1980 (m dis 1987), Jane, *née* Brockliss; m 2, 1 Oct 1994, Jennifer Lorraine, *née* Smith; 1 da (Alicia Imogen b 1 Sept 1995), 1 s (Edward Henry Alfred b 2 Oct 1997); *Career* bd dir and chair London Student Travel Ltd 1978–80, Saatchi & Saatchi Advertising 1980–86; Abbott Mead Vickers BBDO 1986–95; BBDO Europe: dir 1995–2003, ceo The Brewery 2004–05, European dir and managing ptnr McCann Worldgroup 2005–09 (worldwide dir 2008–09), md Momentum UK Ltd 2009–11 (regnl dir EMEA and memb Worldwide Bd 2011), exec vice-pres and dir corporate devpt Europe McCann Worldgroup 2012–; Party candidate (Lib Dem) 1983 and 1987 gen elections; memb Bd EACA 2000–03; memb: Lib Dems 1974, LSE Soc 1982, Mensa 1992, Mktg Soc 1994; FIPA 2000; *Recreations* films, military history, cooking, gym; *Style*— Julian Ingram, Esq; ✉ mobile 07850 741834, e-mail ingram.julian@btinternet.com; McCann Worldgroup, 7–11 Herbrand Street, London WC1N 1EX (☎ 020 7961 2004, e-mail julian.ingram@mccann.com)

INGRAM, Kevin; s of Leonard Ingram, and Jennifer, *née* Lewis; *b* 7 August 1966, Cardiff; *Educ* St Cyres Comp Sch Penarth, UC Oxford (BA, BCL, Football blue); *m* 2 Sept 1995, Caroline Ingram, MBE, *née* Baggs; 1 s (James b 7 Feb 1998), 1 da (Katie b 26 July 1999); *Career* admitted slr 1991; Clifford Chance: trainee slr 1989–91, assoc slr 1991–98, ptnr 1998–, London head of securitisation 2003–; *Recreations* football, squash, cricket, writing poetry; *Clubs* Walton Casuals Jrs Football, East Molesey Cricket; *Style*— Kevin Ingram, Esq; ✉ Clifford Chance, 10 Upper Bank Street, London E14 5JJ (e-mail kevin.ingram@cliffordchance.com)

INGRAM, Tamara; OBE (2011); da of John Ingram, and Sonia, *née* Bolson; *b* 1 October 1960; *Educ* Queen's Coll Harley St London, UEA (BA); *m* Andrew Millington; 1 s (Max b 4 April 1991), 1 da (Anya Eve b 31 Dec 1992); *Career* prodr's asst working on various films incl A Private Function (with Dame Maggie Smith and Michael Palin) 1982–85; Saatchi & Saatchi: jt ceo 1995–99, chief exec 1999–2001, exec chm 2001; ceo and chm McCann-Erickson UK & Ireland Gp 2001–03, pres Added Value, Fusion 5 and Henley Centre (all part of Kantar Gp) 2003–05, UK gp ceo Grey Gp 2005–07, exec vice-pres Grey Global Gp 2007–, pres team Proctor & Gamble 2007–; non-exec dir The Sage Gp plc 2004–; chair VisitBritain, chair Devpt Bd Royal Court Theatre; finalist Veuve Clicquot Business Woman of the Year Awards 1998; memb Mktg Soc, memb Mktg Gp of GB; FIPA 1995 (memb Cncl); *Recreations* theatre, opera, family and friends; *Clubs* Women in Advertising and Communications in London; *Style*— Ms Tamara Ingram, OBE

INGRAM, Timothy Charles William; s of Stanley Ingram (d 2006), and Sheila, *née* Angliss (d 1996); *b* 18 June 1947; *Educ* Harrow, Univ of Cambridge (MA), INSEAD Business Sch (MBA); *m* 30 Aug 1975, Christine; 3 s (Christopher Charles Sebastian b 7 March 1977, Jonathan James Angliss b 4 July 1978, Nicholas David Oliver b 1 Jan 1986); *Career* ANZ Grindlays Bank: trainee 1969–71, planning mangr 1972–73, md Banque Grindlay Internationale au Zaïre 1975–77, gen mangr (2 branches in Greece) 1977–79, gen mangr (30 branches in Cyprus) 1979–81, dir Eurocurrency Dept 1981–83, regnl dir (8 countries in Far East) 1983–84, regnl dir (7 countries in Middle East) 1984–87, gen mangr (UK & Europe) 1987–89, gen mangr Business Banking Australia 1989–91; gp fin dir First National Corp plc 1992–94, chief exec First National Finance Corp 1994–2002, exec dir Abbey National 1995–2002, chief exec Caledonia Investments 2002–10, chm Collins Stewart plc 2010–; non-exec dir: Hogg Robinson 1999–2000, Sage plc 2002–11, Savills plc 2002–, ANZ Bank (Europe) Ltd 2004–10, Alliance Tst plc 2010–; chm Fulham Palace Tst 2010–; FCIB; *Recreations* opera, skiing; *Clubs* Reform, Hurlingham; *Style*— Timothy Ingram, Esq; ✉ Collins Stewart plc, 88 Wood Street, London EC2V 7QR (☎ 020 7523 8000)

INGRAMS, Richard Reid; s of Leonard St Clair Ingrams (s of Rev William Smith Ingrams, MA), and Victoria Susan Beatrice (d 1997), da of Sir James Reid, 1 Bt, GCVO, KCB, MD, LLD; *b* 19 August 1937; *Educ* Shrewsbury, UC Oxford; *m* 1962 (sep), Mary Joan Morgan; 1 s (1 s and 1 da decd); *Career* ed Private Eye 1963–86 (chm 1974–), columnist The Observer 1988–, fndr and ed The Oldie magazine 1992–; *Books* Muggeridge – the biography (1995), The Life and Adventures of William Cobbett (2005); *Style*— Richard Ingrams, Esq; ✉ The Oldie Magazine, 45/46 Poland Street, London W1V 4AU (☎ 020 7734 2225, fax 020 7734 2226)

INKSON, Prof John Christopher; s of George William Inkson, and Catherine Cynthia, *née* Laing (d 1988); *b* 18 February 1946; *Educ* Gateshead GS, Univ of Manchester (BSc), Univ of Cambridge (MA, PhD, ScD); *m* Pamela, da of William Henry Hepworth (d 1971); 1 s (Jonathan Allen), 2 da (Andrea Louisa, Beverley Jane); *Career* res physicist English Electric 1966–69, res fell Jesus Coll Cambridge 1972–85, demonstrator and lectr Univ of Cambridge 1975–85; Univ of Essex: prof of theoretical physics 1985–, head Dept of Physics 1989–, dep vice-chllr 1994–; memb PPARC 2002–; conslt to MOD; FInstP; *Publications* over 150 articles published on the theory of semiconductor physics; *Recreations* reading, walking; *Style*— Prof John Inkson; ✉ Department of Physics, University of Exeter, Exeter EX4 4QL (☎ 01392 264148, fax 01392 264111, telex 42894 EXUNIV G)

INMAN, Christopher (Chris); OBE (2012); s of Trevor Inman, and Molly, *née* Jones; *b* 2 May 1962, Scunthorpe, Lincs; *Educ* Univ of Sunderland (BA); *m* 16 Sept 1989, Elspeth Maye, *née* Blyth; 1 da (Sophie Laura b 13 Dec 1992), 1 s (Thomas Scott b 11 Aug 1995); *Career* finance dir Rubicon Retail Ltd 2001–05, dir Mint Velvet 2009–15; treas and non-exec dir Br Fashion Cncl 2006–15, non-exec dir Laurie Communications Ltd 2013–; tstee Rennie Grove Hospice Care 2016–; ACMA 1989; *Clubs* Gerrards Cross golf; *Style*— Chris Inman, Esq, OBE; ✉ Laurie Communications Ltd, 1&3 French Place, London E1 6JB

INMAN, Edward Oliver; OBE (1998); s of John Inman (d 2011), and Peggy Florence, *née* Beard (d 2015); *b* 12 August 1948, Oslo, Norway; *Educ* KCS Wimbledon, Gonville & Caius Coll Cambridge (MA), SSEES Univ of London (MA); *m* 1, 1971 (m dis 1982) Elizabeth *née* Douglas; 1 s, 1 da; m 2, 1984 (m dis 2005), Sherida Lesley, *née* Sturton; 1 da; m 3, 2009, Julia Suzanne, *née* Heasman; *Career* Imperial War Museum: joined as res asst 1972, asst keeper 1974, dir Duxford 1978–2004, chief exec South Bank Employers' Gp 2004–15; tstee American Air Museum 2004–, chair Jubilee Gardens Tst 2011–; FRAeS 1999; *Style*— Edward Inman, Esq, OBE, FRAeS; ✉ Jubilee Gardens Trust, Elizabeth House, 39 York Road, London SE1 7NQ (☎ 020 7202 6900, e-mail jubileegardens@southbanklondon.com)

INMAN, His Hon Judge Melbourne Donald; QC (1998); s of Melbourne Alfred Inman; and Norah Freda Inman, *née* Thompson; *b* 1 April 1957; *Educ* Bishop Vesey's GS, Univ of Oxford (MA); *Career* called to the Bar 1979; asst recorder 1996–98, recorder 1998–2007, head of advocacy, trg and continuing professional devpt 1998–2007, circuit judge 2007–, sr circuit judge and resident judge Birmingham Crown Court 2014–; *Recreations* skiing, listening to the piano; *Style*— His Hon Judge Melbourne Inman, QC; ✉ Birmingham Crown Court, Queen Elizabeth II Law Courts, 1 Newton Street, Birmingham B4 7NA

INNES, Callum; s of Donald Innes, of Edinburgh, and Christina Dow, *née* Charmichael (d 1968); *b* 5 March 1962; *m* 20 Sept 1990, Hyjdla Jadwiga Paula Kosaniuk; *Career* artist; *Solo Exhibitions* incl: Sean Kelly NY 1997, 1998, 2000, 2003 and 2006, Frith Street Gall London 1998 and 2001, Ingleby Gall Edinburgh 1999, 2001, 2004 and (with Hiroshi Sugimoto) 2008, Jensen Gall Auckland NZ 2000, 2002 and 2008, Kerlin Gall Dublin 2000, 2004 and 2008, The Pier Arts Centre Stromness Orkney 2000, Galerie Tschudi Switzerland 2004, 2006–07 and 2008, Tate St Ives 2005, Fruitmarket Gall Edinburgh 2006, Modern Art Oxford 2007, Kettle's Yard Cambridge 2007, Discourse (Frith Street Gall) 2007, From Memory (Museum of Contemporary Art Sydney) 2008, Jensen Gall 2009, I Look to You (Ingleby Gall Edinburgh) 2009, At One Remove (Sean Kelly Gall NY) 2010, Galeria Helga de Alvear Madrid 2010, Loock Gall Berlin 2010, Watercolour (Sean Kelly Gall NY) 2010, Fox (Jensen Auckland NZ) 2011, Jensen Gall Sydney (with Colm Toibin) 2011, New Paintings and Watercolours (Frith Street Gall) 2011, Fraser outside Ingleby Gall 2012, Callum Innes: Regent Bridge, public artwork created with Gavin 2012, Callum Innes: Works on Paper 1982–2012 (Ingleby Gall Edinburgh) 2012, Edouard Malingue Gall Hong Kong 2012, Unforeseen (Kerlin Gall Dublin) 2012, i8 Gall Reykjavik 2013, Callum Innes (Whitworth Art Gall Manchester) 2013, Watercolours (Galerie Tschudi Switzerland) 2013, Liminal (Sean Kelly Gall NY) 2013, Callum Innes (Neues Museum) Nuremberg 2013, Loock Gall Berlin 2014, Frith Street Gall 2015; *Group Exhibitions* incl: Melancholia (Jensen Gall 2005), Elements of Abstraction: Space, Line & Interval in Modern British Art (Southampton City Art Gall) 2005, Galerie Tschudi Switzerland 2005, Evergreen (Inverleith House Edinburgh) 2005, Whos Afraid of Red, Yellow & Blue? (Ingleby Gall Edinburgh) 2005, Edition (Ingleby Gall) 2005–06, Helga de Alvear Collection 2005, Lux (Jensen Gall) 2005, Niele Toroni (Galerie Tschudi) 2005, Resonance and Summer Exhibition (Frith Street Gall) 2006, The Collection: Selected Abstract Works (Mead Gall Warwick Arts Centre) 2006, Helga de Alvear Concepts for A Collection (Exhibition Centre of CentroCultural de Belem Brazil) 2006, Less is More, More or Less (Martin Weinstein Gall Minneapolis) 2006, Print Run: An Exhibition of Prints (Frith Street Gall) 2006, Everything (Dun and Prown Contemporary Dallas) 2007, PURE (Sean Kelly Gall) 2007, Jensen Gall 2007, Three: 3 Artists in solo displays (Irish Museum of Modern Art), Beziehungsweise Galeries Hubert 2007, Structures and Surfaces (Sean Kelly and R Gall NY) 2007, Cancelled, Erased & Removed (Sean Kelly) 2008, Conversations (Kettles Yard Cambridge) 2008, Callum Innes and Hiroshi Sugimoto (Ingleby Gall) 2008, Sometimes Making Something Leads to Nothing, (Ingleby Gall) 2009, Galerie Tschudi 2009, Jensen Gall 2009, Summer Exhibition RA 2010, La Pesanteur et la Grace (Le Collège des Bernardins Paris) 2010 and (Villa Medici Rome) 2010, What you see is where youre at (Scottish National Gall of Modern Art Edinburgh) 2010, Monochrome Reflections (Sammlung Haurbrok Berlin) 2010, Jensen Gall 2010, Watercolour (Tate Britain) 2011, Someone Elses Life (Kerlin Gall Dublin) 2011, E=MC2 (Jensen Gall Sydney) 2011, Artists For Kettles Yard (Kettles Yard) 2011, Conversations (John Berggruen Gall San Francisco) 2011, Within / Beyond Borders (Byzantine and Christian Museum Athens) 2011, The Architecture of Colour (Jensen Gall Sydney) 2012, HAUPTSACHE GRAU 03 Farbiges Grau (Mies Van Der Rohe Haus Berlin) 2013, The Art of the Present (Centro + Centro Palacio de Cibeles Madrid), Helga de Alvear Collection 2013, Florence and Daniel Guerlain Donation (Centre Pompidou Paris) 2013, Moving, Norman Foster on Art (Carré dArt Nimes France) 2013, Summer Show (John Berggruen Gall San Francisco) 2013, Silver (Frith Street Gall) 2014, GENERATION: 25 Years of Contemporary Art in Scotland (Scottish Nat Gall Edinburgh) 2014, Within/ Beyond Borders: Art from the European Investment Bank Collection (Banco de Portugal

Lisbon) 2014, Chromophobia (Gagosian Gall Geneva) 2015; *Works in Public Collections* incl: Auckland Art Gall NZ, Albright-Knox Art Gall NY, Arts Cncl of England, Birmingham City Museum & Art Gall UK, Birmingham Museum of Art USA, Bohen Foundation NY, Br Cncl UK, Centro de Arte Moderna José de Azeredo Perdigão – Fundação Calouste Gulbenkian Lisbon, City Art Centre Edinburgh, Contemporary Arts Museum Houston (USA), Contemporary Art Soc London, Centre Pompidou Paris, Deutsche Bank London, Deutsche Bank Australia, Govt Art Collection UK, Guggenheim Collection NY, HypoVereinsbank Germany, Irish Museum of Modern Art Dublin, Kunsthalle Bern Switzerland, Kunsthaus Zurich Switzerland, Kunstmuseum Nuremberg Germany, Modern Art Museum of Fort Worth USA, Musee des Beaux-Arts Switzerland, National Galleries of Australia Canberra, Neuberger & Berman, NY Progressive Corporation Cleveland Ohio, Philadelphia Museum of Art USA, Phillips Collection Washington DC, Royal Bank of Scotland UK, San Francisco Museum of Modern Art USA, Scottish Nat Gall of Modern Art Edinburgh, Guggenheim Museum NY, Southampton City Art Gall UK, Tang Teaching Museum/Art Gall, Skidmore College, Saratoga Springs USA, Tate Gall London, Scottish Parl, Toledo Museum of Art USA, Towner Art Gall and Museum UK, Univ of Colorado USA, Walker Art Gall Liverpool; *Books* work featured in: Scatter New Scottish Art (1989), Painting Alone (1990), From Here (1995), New Voices (1995), Callum Innes Watercolours (1997), Abstraction/ Abstraction Géométries Provisoires (1997), Abstract Painting Once Removed (1997), Callum Innes (1999), Callum Innes (1999), Callum Innes, Exposed Paintings (2001), 6 Degrees of Separation (2001), Sacha Craddock, Jerwood Painting Prize (2002), Callum Innes (2004), Callum Innes, Resonance (2005), Callum Innes: From Memory (2006), I look to you (2009), Water | colour (2010), Within / Beyond Borders (2011), Callum Innes (2012); *Style*— Callum Innes, Esq; ✉ c/o Frith Street Gallery, 17–18 Golden Square, London W1F 9JJ (☎ 020 7494 1550, fax 020 7287 3733)

INNES, Prof John Francis; s of Anthony Michael Innes, and Marguerite Mary, *née* Conway; *b* 7 February 1967, Walthamstow, London; *Educ* Ilford Co HS, Univ of Liverpool (BVSc), Univ of Bristol (PhD); *m* July 1995, Caroline, *née* Bell; 3 da (Claudia Caitlin, Gabriella Marilyn, Francesca Rose); *Career* lectr in vet surgery Univ of Bristol 1996–2001 (fell in vet surgery 1991–93), prof of vet surgery Univ of Liverpool 2001–13, referral dir CVS Gp plc 2013–; fndr and dir Veterinary Tissue Bank Ltd 2009; contrib to numerous papers published in academic jls; *Recreations* skiing; *Style*— Prof John Innes; ✉ CVS Vets, Chestergates Referral Hospital, Units E & F, Telford Court, Chestergates Road, Chester CH1 6LT (☎ 01244 853823, e-mail john.innes@cvsvets.com)

INNES OF EDINGIGHT, Sir Malcolm Rognvald; KCVO (1990, CVO 1981), WS (1964), Orkney Herald of Arms Extraordinary (2001); s of Sir Thomas Innes of Learney, GCVO, LLD (d 1971), and Lady Lucy Buchan, 3 da of 18 Earl of Caithness; *b* 25 May 1938; *Educ* The Edinburgh Acad, Univ of Edinburgh (MA, LLB); *m* 19 Oct 1963, Joan, da of Thomas D Hay, CA, of Edinburgh; 3 s (John Berowald Innes of Edingight, yr b 1965, Colin William Innes of Kinnairdy b 1967, Michael Thomas Innes of Crommey b 1970); *Career* Lord Lyon King of Arms 1981–2001 (Falkland Pursuivant Extraordinary 1957–58, Carrick Pursuivant 1958–71, Lyon Clerk and Keeper of the Records 1966–81, Marchmont Herald 1971–81); Orkney Herald of Arms Extraordinary 2001; sec to Order of Thistle 1981–2001; KStJ 1981, Grand Offr of Merit SMO Malta; memb Queen's Body Guard for Scotland (Royal Co of Archers); *Recreations* reading; *Clubs* New (Edinburgh); *Style*— Sir Malcolm Innes of Edingight, KCVO, WS, Orkney Herald of Arms Extraordinary

INNES OF KINNAIRDY, Colin William; s of Sir Malcolm Innes of Edingight, KCVO, WS, and Joan, *née* Hay; *b* 1 December 1967, Edinburgh; *Educ* Edinburgh Acad, Univ of Aberdeen (LLB, DipLP, LLM); *m* 19 June 1993, Joanna, *née* Judge; 2 s (Thomas Cosmo David b 19 Jan 1995, William James Maxim b 19 Jan 1997); *Career* slr; ptnr and head of planning and environmental law Shepherd and Wedderburn LLP 1998– (trainee then asst assoc 1992–97); memb WS Soc; memb Scottish Cncl Salmon & Trout Assoc, life memb Nat Tst for Scotland, pres Edinburgh Academical Club; memb Law Soc of Scotland 1993, memb Law Soc 1997, legal assoc RTPI 2000; *Publications* Scottish Planning Encyclopaedia (case right ed, 1997), Scottish Human Rights Service (planning and environment section, 2004); *Recreations* fishing, shooting, historic buildings; *Clubs* 1790; *Style*— Colin Innes of Kinnairdy; ✉ 2A Wester Coates Gardens, Edinburgh EH12 5LT (☎ 0131 337 2321); Shepherd and Wedderburn LLP, 1 Exchange Crescent, Conference Square, Edinburgh EH3 8UL (☎ 0131 473 5104, fax 0131 228 1222, e-mail colin.innes@shepwedd.co.uk)

INNES-HOPKINS, Robert; s of Colin Innes-Hopkins, of St Albans, Herts, and Judy, *née* Candy; *b* 4 May 1966, London; *Educ* Nottingham Trent Univ (BA); *m* 2008, Sophy Rickett; 1 da (Edith b 2004), 1 s (Marlowe b 2007); *Career* designer for theatre, opera, television and film; theatre designs for: RSC, RNT, West Yorkshire Playhouse, Actors Theatre NY, Chichester Festival, Royal Court, Abbey Theatre, Young Vic, Regents Park; opera designs for: Opera North, WNO, Santa Fe Opera, Glyndebourne, Lyric Opera of Chicago, Bolshoi Moscow, San Francisco Opera, Deutscher Oper Berlin, Zurich Oper, Geneva Opera, Ruhr Triennale; *Awards* Critics Circle Designer of the Year 1996, TMA Barclays Designer of the Year 1997, nomination TMA Barclays Outstanding Achievement in Opera 1999, TMA Designer of the Year 2006, Opernwelt Set Designer of the Year 2007; *Style*— Robert Innes-Hopkins, Esq

INNES-WILKIN, David; s of Charles Wilkin (d 1978), and Louisa Jane, *née* Innes; *b* 1 May 1946; *Educ* Lowestoft GS, Univ of Liverpool Sch of Architecture (BArch, MCD); *m* 1, 10 April 1968, Beryl; 1 da (Thomasine b 1971), 2 s (Dylan b 1972, Matthew b 1974); m 2, 25 April 1987, Sarah, da of Rev Prof Peter Runham Ackroyd; 1 da (Emma Jane Louisa b 1989), 1 s (James Ackroyd b 1991); *Career* chartered architect; princ Innes-Wilkin Associates; chm SW Housing Assoc 1986–87, pioneered tenant participation in new housing estates designed 1979–; memb: RIBA Regnl Ctee, Community Architecture Gp 1983–84; visiting lectr Univs of Liverpool, Cardiff, Manchester and Bristol; memb Int Congress of Architects; design awards: RTPI Commendation 1983, Housing Centre Tst Jubilee Award for Good Design in Housing 1983, Times/RIBA Community Enterprise Awards 1986/87 (three), Energy Action Award 1990, Civic Soc 1991, Housing Project Design Award DOE 1997, Carpenters Award 1999, Chepstow Bridgespace Design Competition Award 2009, Local Authy Building Control Award for Technical Excellence 2011; RIBA, MRTPI, MFB; *Publications* A Common Language (The Architects Jl, 1984), Among The Grass-Roots (RIBA Jl, 1983), Cuba: Universal Home Ownership (Roof, 1987), Shelter and Cities (Int Congress of Architects, 1987), Community Schools (Educn Research Unit, 1972); *Recreations* offshore sailing, painting, writing, the Renaissance; *Style*— David Innes-Wilkin; ✉ e-mail architects@inneswilkin.co.uk

INSKIP, Peter Thurston; MBE (2014); s of Geoffrey Inskip (d 1959), and Lily Ethel, *née* Thurston (d 1979); *b* 17 August 1944; *Educ* Bedford Sch, AA Sch of Architecture, Gonville & Caius Coll Cambridge (exhibitioner, scholar, Schuldham Plate, MA, DipArch); *Career* dir of studies in architecture Univ of Cambridge: Gonville & Caius Coll 1972–80, Newnham Coll 1973–82, Peterhouse 1975–82; jr bursar Newnham Coll Cambridge 1973–82; architect; fndr ptnr Peter Inskip + Peter Jenkins Architects 1972; princ works incl: restoration of Waddesdon Manor, Chastleton House, Stowe, Albert Meml, Somerset House, Moggerhanger House, Chatsworth, Emmanuel Coll Chapel, Strawberry Hill, Marshcourt, Castle Drogo; rep for Bedfordshire Nat Art Collections Fund 1992–2004; hon artistic advsr Cwlth War Graves Cmmn 2010–; memb: Architectural Panel Nat Tst 1993–96 and 2000–13, Expert Panel for Historic Buildings and Land Heritage Lottery Fund 1995–99, Architectural Panel World Monuments Fund in Britain 1996–, Historic Areas and Buildings Advsy Ctee English Heritage 1999–2001, Historic Built Environment Advsy Ctee English Heritage 2001–03; RIBA 1972, FSA 1996; *Publications* Edwin Lutyens (1979), Louis Kahn and the Yale Center for British Art (2011), Moggerhanger Park Bedfordshire (2012); *Recreations* historic landscapes and sketching; *Style*— Peter Inskip, Esq, MBE; ✉ Peter Inskip + Peter Jenkins Architects, 19–23 White Lion Street, London N1 9PD (☎ 020 7833 4002, fax 020 7278 5343)

INVERARITY, James Alexander (Sandy); CBE (1997, OBE); s of William Inverarity (d 1978), and Alexina, *née* Davidson (d 1978); *b* 17 September 1935; *Educ* Loretto; *m* 1, 8 March 1960, Jean Stewart (d 2006), da of James Rae Gellatly (d 1979); 2 da (Catherine b 1960, Alison b 1962), 1 s (Graeme b 1964); m 2, 4 July 2008, Frances Dorothy, da of Bernard Clifford Bowman (d 1993); *Career* farmer, CA and co dir; pres NFU of Scot 1970–71; memb: Eggs Authy 1971–74, Farm Animal Welfare Cncl 1978–88, Panel of Agric Arbiters 1983–2007, Governing Body Scot Crop Research Inst 1984–97 (chm 1989–90), Dairy Produce Quota Tbnl for Scot 1984–85; dir: Scottish Agricultural Securities Corporation plc 1983–2016 (chm 1987–2016), United Oilseeds Producers Ltd 1985–97 (chm 1987–97); chm Scottish Agric Coll 1990–98 (dir 1990–98); FRAgS, FInstD, FRSA; *Recreations* shooting, curling; *Clubs* Farmers'; *Style*— Sandy Inverarity, Esq, CBE; ✉ Cransley Fowlis, by Dundee DD2 5NP (☎ 01382 580327)

INVERDALE, John Ballantyne; s of Capt J B Inverdale, CBE, RN and Stella Norah Mary Westlake, *née* Richards; *b* 27 September 1957; *Educ* Clifton, Univ of Southampton; *m* Jackie; 2 da (Josie, Juliette); *Career* with: Lincolnshire Echo 1979–82, BBC Radio Lincolnshire 1982–86; radio reporter BBC (Today Prog Radio 4 and Radio 2) 1986–88; presenter: Sport on 5 (previously Sport on 2, BBC Radio) 1988–94, Drivetime (Radio 5 Live), Rugby Special (BBC TV) 1994–97, Onside (BBC TV) 1997–, Grandstand (BBC TV) 1999–; Broadcaster of the Year Sony Awards 1997, Radio Personality of the Year Variety Club Awards 1997; *Recreations* rugby (mangr of Esher RFC), tennis, Lincoln City (pres Lincoln City Supporters Club), gardening, music, pubs; *Style*— John Inverdale, Esq; ✉ c/o Mike Burton Management Ltd, Bastion House, Brunswick Road, Gloucester GL1 1JJ (☎ 01452 419666, fax 01452 309146)

IPSWICH, Archdeacon of; *see:* Gibson, Ven Terence Allen

IRANI, Dr Mehernoosh Sheriar; s of late Sheriar Ardeshir Irani, of London, and late Banoo Sheriar; *b* 24 August 1949; *Educ* Chiswick County GS for Boys, KCH (BSc, LRCP, MRCS, MB BS); *m* 19 Sept 1987, Susan Clare, da of late Air Cdre Philip David Mallalieu Moore, of Fowey, Cornwall; 1 da (Jasmine b 1989), 2 s (Matthew b 1991, Beyrom b 1993); *Career* house physician KCH 1974, house surgn Kent and Sussex Hosp Tunbridge Wells 1974, registrar in nephrology and gen med Kent and Canterbury Hosp Kent 1977 (SHO 1975–76), registrar in rheumatology and gen med Radcliffe Infirmary Oxford 1977–79, hon sr registrar and res fell Dept of Rheumatology and Biochemical Pharmacology KCH 1979–81, sr registrar Westminster and Charing Cross Hosp 1981–85, currently conslt rheumatologist Ashford and St Peter's Hosps Middx; visiting physician: Princess Margaret Hosp Windsor, Runnymede Hosp, Clementine Churchill, Syon Clinic; MO Br Olympic team: Los Angeles 1984, Calgary 1988, Seoul 1988, Barcelona 1992; Int Weightlifting Fedn duty dr: Olympic Games Atlanta 1996, Olympic Games Athens 2004, Olympic Games Beijing 2008, Olympic Games London 2012; MO England Cwlth games team: Edinburgh 1986, Auckland 1990, Victoria 1994; MO: Br Amateur Weightlifters Assoc 1986–, BCU 1986–, English Badminton Team World Championships Beijing China 1987, Br Dragon Boat Racing Assoc 1988–; dep MO Br Pistol & Rifle Assoc 1996–2002; sec-gen Int Assoc of Olympic MOs 1988–98; pres Med Ctee EWF 1994–99; memb: Med Ctee Int Weight Lifting (IWF) (memb Exec Bd and chm 2013–), Medical Cmmn on Accident Prevention RCS 1992–99, Br Soc for Rheumatology, BOA, Bd British Weight Lifting (BWL) 2014–; vice-chm Ethics Ctee NW Surrey, chm Ethics Ctee Ravenscourt 1997–2003, past med advsr Ind Tbnl Service; pres Sport Med Section RSM 2001–02 (sec 1996–98); examiner: RCS, RCP; hon sr lectr Charing Cross & Westminster Hospital Med Schs (recognised teacher in med Univ of London), lectr in basic sciences RCS; fell Inst of Sports Med 1996; Freeman City of London, Liveryman Worshipful Soc of Apothecaries; FRCP; *Books* contrib to Rheumatology and Rehabilitation (1984); *Recreations* family, cricket; *Clubs* Riverside; *Style*— Dr M S Irani; ✉ 20 Devonshire Gardens, Chiswick, London W4 3TN (☎ 020 8994 0119); Department of Rheumatology, Ashford Hospital, London Road, Ashford, Middlesex TW15 3AA (☎ 01784 884888, fax 01784 884240, e-mail mehernooshuk@hotmail.com)

IRBY, Charles Leonard Anthony; s of Hon Anthony P Irby (d 1986), and Mary, *née* Apponyi (d 1952); *b* 5 June 1945, London; *Educ* Eton; *m* 23 Sept 1971, Sarah Jane, da of Col David G Sutherland, MC, of London; 1 s (Nicholas Charles Anthony b 10 July 1975), 1 da (Caroline Sarah (Viscountess Combermere) b 21 May 1977); *Career* dir: Baring Brothers & Co Ltd 1984–95, Baring Brothers International Ltd 1995–99 (dep chm 1997–99), ING Baring Group Holdings Ltd 1995–98, E C Harris 2001–05, QBE Insurance Gp Ltd 2001–13, North Atlantic Smaller Companies Investment Tst plc 2002–, Great Portland Street Estates plc 2004–14, Gabelli Value Plus+ Trust plc 2015–; md ING Barings 1995–99, sr UK advsr ING Baring 1999–2001; chm Aberdeen Asset Management plc 2000–09; govr King Edward VII's Hosp Sister Agnes 2000– (tstee 2000–13); FCA; *Recreations* travel, photography, skiing; *Clubs* Boodle's, City of London; *Style*— Charles L A Irby, Esq; ✉ 125 Blenheim Crescent, London W11 2EQ (☎ 020 7221 2979); The Old Vicarage, Chieveley, Newbury, Berkshire RG20 8UX (☎ 01635 248117)

IREDALE, (John) Martin; s of John Leslie Iredale (d 1988), and Hilda, *née* Palfrey (d 1997); *b* 10 June 1939, Workington, Cumberland; *Educ* Abingdon Sch; *m* 14 Sept 1963, (Margaret) Anne, da of Reginald Walter Jewell (d 1968), of Reading; 3 s (Edward b 1 May 1965, Mathew b 3 Oct 1966, William b 18 May 1976), 1 da (Hannah b 30 March 1973); *Career* chartered accountant and licensed insolvency practitioner; ptnr: Cork Gully 1971–99, PricewaterhouseCoopers (formerly Coopers & Lybrand before merger) 1980–99; Royal Shakespeare Theatre: sec Tst 1970–91, memb Cncl of Mgmnt 1970–2008, govr 1981–2002 (hon govr 2002–), memb Bd 1991–2002, memb Audit Ctee 1997–2006; memb Hodgson Ctee on Profits from Crime and their Recovery 1981–82, memb ICAEW Investigation Ctee 1995–99; pres Old Abingdonian Club 1982–84, chm Cornhill Club 1985–86; Freemason 1973; Freeman City of London 1973; Liveryman Worshipful Co of Carmen 1978; FCA 1963–2005, FIPA 1985–2000; *Books* Receivership Manual (with C J Hughes, 1987); *Recreations* holidays, shooting clay and bird, Foden trucks, waiting on my family; *Clubs* Leander, Cornhill, Reading Abbey Rotary 1988–2006, Burghfield Gun (sec 2006–12), Phyllis Court; *Style*— Martin Iredale, Esq; ✉ 24 Philimore Road, Emmer Green, Reading RG4 8UR (☎ 0118 947 7378, mobile 07778 495490, e-mail martin@martiniredale.com)

IRELAND, John; s of Victor Edwin Ireland (d 1986), of Ipswich, Suffolk, and Mina Mary, *née*, Bugler; *b* 14 July 1942; *Educ* Ipswich Sch, Westminster Hosp Med Sch; *m* 24 Sept 1972, Shahla Monireh, da of General A Samsami; 2 s (Michael b 1973, David b 1978), 1 da (Roya b 1974); *Career* formerly: sr registrar Royal Nat Orthopaedic Hosp, conslt surgn Dept of Orthopaedics King George Hosp Ilford Essex; currently conslt orthopaedic surgn Knee Surgery Unit Holly House Hosp Buckhurst Hill Essex; fndr and organiser New Knee Golf Soc; memb Int, Euro and Br Assocs for Surgery of the Knee; FRCS 1971; *Publications* author of scientific papers on knee surgery and arthroscopy; *Recreations* golf, music, wine, gardening; *Clubs* RAC, New (Edinburgh), NZ Golf; *Style*— John Ireland, Esq; ✉ 17 Kings Avenue, Woodford Green, Essex IG8 0JD (☎ 020 8505 3211, fax 020 8559 1161, e-mail j.ireland@woodford.com, website

I

www.johnirelandkneesurgeon.org.uk); Royal National Orthopaedic Hospital, 45 Bolsover Street, London W1W 5AQ

IRONS, Jeremy John; s of Paul Dugan Irons (d 1983), and Barbara Anne Brereton Brymer, *née* Sharpe (decd); *b* 19 September 1948; *Educ* Sherborne, Bristol Old Vic Theatre Sch; *m* 23 March 1977, Sinead Cusack, *qv*, da of late Cyril Cusack; 2 s (Samuel b 16 Sept 1978, Maximilian b 17 Oct 1985); *Career* actor; joined Bristol Old Vic Theatre Co 1971; Officier des Artes et Lettres 1996; *Theatre* incl: What the Butler Saw, Hayfever, Godspell 1971, Simon Gray's Rear Column (Clarence Derwent Award) 1976, Embers 2006, Never So Good 2008; RSC incl: Wild Oats, A Winter's Tale, The Rover, Richard II, The Gods Weep 2009; Broadway: The Real Thing (Tony Award Best Actor, Drama League Distinguished Performance Award) 1984, Impressionism 2009; *Television* incl: Brideshead Revisited 1982 (TV Times Best Actor Award), Elizabeth 1 2005 (Best Supporting Actor in a Miniseries or TV Movie Golden Globe Awards 2007), The Borgias 2011; *Films* incl: French Lieutenant's Woman (Variety Club Best Actor Award), Moonlighting 1982, The Captain's Doll (BBC TV film) 1982, The Wild Duck (Aust film of Ibsen play) 1983, Betrayal 1983, Swann in Love 1983, The Mission 1985, Dead Ringers (Best Actor NY Critics Award, Best Actor Canada Genie Award) 1988, Chorus of Disapproval 1988, Danny Champion of the World 1988, Australia 1989, Reversal of Fortune (Golden Globe Best Actor Award, Academy Best Actor Award) 1990, Kafka 1991, Waterland 1992, Damage 1993, M Butterfly 1994, House of the Spirits 1994, voice of Scar in The Lion King 1994, Die Hard with a Vengeance 1995, Stealing Beauty 1995, The Man in the Iron Mask 1997, Lolita 1997, Longitude 1999, Dungeons & Dragons 2000, Fourth Angel 2000, And Now Ladies and Gentlemen 2001, Callas Forever 2001, Last Call 2001, Being Julia 2003, Merchant of Venice 2004, Kingdom of Heaven 2004, Casanova 2005, Eragon 2006; *Awards* European Film Acad Special Achievement Award 1998, French Cezar 2002; *Recreations* sailing, riding, skiing; *Clubs* West Carberry Hunt (jt MFH); *Style*— Mr Jeremy Irons; ✉ c/o Katy Riddell, 12 High Street, Watlington, Oxfordshire OX49 5PY

IRONSIDE, Gordon Douglas; s of Douglas William Ironside (d 2002), and Doreen Grant, *née* King (d 2011); *b* 11 August 1955, Workington, Cumbria; *Educ* Dame Allan's Sch Newcastle upon Tyne, Pembroke Coll Cambridge (open scholar, MA), UC Durham (PGCE); *m* 18 Aug 1979, Rachael Elizabeth Ann, *née* Golder; 2 s (Matthew Stuart b 8 June 1983, Christopher William b 2 May 1989), 1 da (Jennifer Rachael b 2 Feb 1986); *Career* teacher: Strathallan Sch 1978–79, Alleyn's Sch Dulwich 1979–83; headmaster Sutton GS 1990– (teacher 1983–90); pres Sutton Rotary Club 1998–2000, former tstee Learning Plus UK; CMath, FIMA 1990; *Style*— Gordon Ironside, Esq; ✉ Sutton Grammar School, Manor Lane, Sutton, Surrey SM1 4AS (☎ 020 8642 3821, fax 020 8661 4500, e-mail gironside@aol.com)

IRRANCA-DAVIES, (Ifor) Huw; AM; s of Gethin Davies, and Anne Teresa Davies; *b* 22 January 1963; *Educ* Crewe and Alsager Coll (BA), Swansea Inst of HE (MSc); *m* 1991, Joanna Teresa Irranca; 3 s; *Career* research asst then duty mangr Lliw Valley BC 1986–89, mangr CLM Ltd and Serco Ltd 1989–92, facilities mangr Swansea Coll 1994–96, sr lectr Swansea Inst of HE 1996–2002, MP (Lab) Ogmore 2002–16; asst Govt whip 2006–07, Parly Under-Sec of State for Wales 2007–08, Parly under-sec of state for marine and natural environment 2008–10, shadow min for energy 2010–11, shadow min for food, farming and rural affrs 2011–; memb Nat Assembly for Wales (Lab) Ogmore 2016–; *Recreations* hill walking, most sports, reading history and biographies; *Style*— Huw Irranca-Davies, Esq, AM; ✉ House of Commons, London SW1A 0AA (☎ 020 7219 4027)

IRVINE, Ian James; *b* 23 December 1957; *Educ* Robert Gordon's Coll Aberdeen, Pembroke Coll Oxford; *m* Sophie Brodie; 3 s, 2 da; *Career* journalist; reviews ed Vogue 1979–81, dep ed The Literary Review 1982, arts ed Sunday Today 1985–86, asst arts ed The Independent 1987–89, dep ed Punch 1990, arts ed Evening Standard 1991–92, arts ed Harpers & Queen 1993, dep ed Sunday Telegraph Review 1994–98, features ed The Independent 1998–99, arts ed The Independent 1999–2002, ed Talk of the Town (Independent on Sunday's London magazine) 2003, asst ed Independent on Sunday 2004, assoc ed The Independent 2005, ed ABC Magazine Independent on Sunday 2006–07, freelance writer and publisher Tacit Hill Edns 2007–, books ed New Statesman 2008–09, contrib ed Prospect 2009–, asst ed The Independent 2011–13, columnist Independent on Sunday 2013–16, ed The Day 2014, asst comment ed The Independent 2015–16, asst ed Prospect 2016–; *Clubs* Academy, Soho House; *Style*— Ian Irvine, Esq; ✉ e-mail ian.irvine@prospect-magazine.co.uk

IRVINE, Very Rev John Dudley; s of late Rt Hon Sir Arthur Irvine, QC, MP, and Lady Irvine; *b* 2 January 1949, Chelsea, London; *Educ* Haileybury (head boy), Univ of Sussex (BA), Univ of Oxford (MA); *m* 1972, Andrea, *née* Carr; 3 s, 1 da; *Career* called to the Bar Middle Temple 1973, in practice 1973–78; ordained: deacon 1981, priest 1982; curate Holy Trinity Brompton 1981–85, vicar St Barnabas Kensington 1985–2001, dean of Coventry 2001–; *Publications* Love from the Ruins (2007); *Recreations* walking, film, theatre; *Style*— The Very Rev the Dean of Coventry; ✉ The Deanery, 11 Priory Row, Coventry CV1 5EX; Coventry Cathedral, 1 Hill Top, Coventry CV1 5AB (☎ 024 7652 1227, fax 024 7652 1220, e-mail dean@coventrycathedral.org.uk)

IRVINE, Lady; Dr Sally Irvine; *née* Day; da of Stanley Arthur Day, of Bellingem, NSW, and Vera Marion, *née* Little; *b* 22 September 1944, Leicestershire; *Educ* Univ of Cambridge (MA), UEA (PhD); *m* 1, 1973 (m dis), Alan Fountain; m 2, 1986 (m dis), Sir Donald Hamilton Irvine, CBE, *qv*; 3 step-c; *Career* head Prog Office and asst to the DG GLC 1976–83; RCGP: gen admin 1983–94, conslt on mgmnt in gen practice 1994–97; ptnr Haman and Irvine Associates professional practice consultancy 1995–2008; non-exec dir Northern RHA 1993–94, non-exec chair Newcastle City Health (NHS) Tst 1994–99; pres Assoc of Health Centre and Practice Admins (now Inst of Health Mgmnt); tutor and examiner Dip in Advanced Gen Practice Univ of Newcastle upon Tyne 1993–99, dir Practice Consultancy Trg Prog 1994–96, dir Pinning Down Partnership Kindling Ltd 1998–2000, non-exec dir Colchester Hosp Univ NHS Fndn Tst 2010– (chair 2010–14); non-exec advsr Civil Serv Occupational Health Agency 1995–96; ptnr Galbraith & Irvine Quality Improvement & Trg for Mental Health Act 1999–2001; GDC: memb 1999–2009, chair Standards Ctee 2003–05; JP Highgate Sessional Div 1977–95 (dep chair Juvenile Bench 1990–95); memb: Cncl Law Soc 2001–05, Slrs Regulations Authy 2005–09, Ind Appt Selection Bd RICS 2007–12, Professional Standards Authy (formerly Cncl for Healthcare Regulatory Excellence) 2009–14; tstee Britten-Pears Fndn 2008–, dir Aldeburgh Cinema 2009–; govr Univ of Northumbria 2002–04, memb Ct Univ of Newcastle Upon Tyne 2005–10, memb Cncl Univ of Essex 2013–; arbitrator ACAS 1999–2001; vol guide Britten-Pears Library The Red House; Hon FRCGP, FAMGP, FRSA; *Books* Management Appreciation – the Book (with June Huntington, 1991), Balancing Dreams and Discipline – The Manager in Practice (1992), The Practice of Quality (with Donald Irvine, 1996), Making Sense of Personnel Management (with Hilary Haman, 2 edn 1997), Making Sense of Audit (ed jtly with Donald Irvine, 2 edn 1997), Spotlight on General Practice: reflections on quality management and governance in general practice (with Hilary Haman, 2001), Good Practice, Good People (with Hilary Haman, 2001), The Peer Appraisal Handbook for General Practitioners (with Hilary Haman and Di Jelley); also author of book chapters and published papers; *Recreations* travelling, cooking, walking, gardening; *Style*— Dr Sally Irvine; ✉ Fig Tree House, Church Walk, Aldeburgh IP15 5DU (☎ 01728 452510, e-mail sally.bkc@btinternet.com)

IRVINE OF LAIRG, Baron (Life Peer UK 1987), of Lairg in the District of Sutherland; Alexander Andrew Mackay Irvine; PC (1997); s of Alexander Irvine and Margaret Christina, da of late Alexander Macmillan; *b* 23 June 1940; *Educ* Inverness Royal Acad, Hutchesons' Boys' GS Glasgow, Univ of Glasgow (MA, LLB), Christ's Coll Cambridge (scholar, BA, LLB, George Long Prize in Jurisprudence); *m* 1974, Alison Mary, yst da of Dr James Shaw McNair, MD, and Agnes McNair, MA; 2 s (Hon David b 1974, Hon Alastair b 1976); *Career* lectr LSE 1965–69; contested (Lab) Hendon N (gen election) 1970; called to the Bar Inner Temple 1967 (bencher 1985); QC 1978, head of chambers 11 King's Bench Walk 1981–97, recorder 1985–88, dep judge of the High Court 1987–97, oppn spokesman on Legal and Home Affairs 1987–92, Lord Chllr 1997–2003 (shadow Lord Chllr 1992–97); pres Magistrates Assoc 1997–; jt pres: Industry and Parliament Tst 1997–, Br-American Parliament Gp 1997–, Inter-Parliamentary Union 1997–, Cwlth Parliamentary Assoc 1997–; church cmmr; memb Ctee Slade Sch of Fine Art 1990–; chm 2001 Ctee Univ of Glasgow 1998–; vice-patron World Fedn of Mental Health 1998–; fndn tstee Whitechapel Art Gallery 1990–97; tstee: John Smith Meml Tst 1992–97, Hunterian Collection 1997–; fell US Coll of Trial Lawyers 1998, hon bencher Inn of Court of NI 1998–, hon memb the Bar of Poland 2000; hon fell: Christ's Coll Cambridge 1996, Soc for Advanced Legal Studies 1997, LSE 2000–; Hon LLD Univ of Glasgow 1997, Hon Dr (Laurea hc) Univ of Siena 2000; *Recreations* collecting paintings, reading, theatre, cinema, travel; *Clubs* Garrick; *Style*— The Rt Hon Lord Irvine of Lairg, PC; ✉ House of Lords, London SW1A 0PW (☎ 020 7219 3232)

IRVING, Dorothy (Dotti); da of Alexander Irving (d 1984), and Sheila, *née* McCaig; *b* 18 May 1950, Annan, Dumfriesshire; *Educ* Esdaile and St George's Sch for Girls, Univ of Edinburgh (MA), Moray House Coll of Educn (DipEd); *m* 31 Aug 1981 (m dis 2004); 1 da (Tess Riley b 6 March 1985); *Career* Penguin Books 1974–86 (latterly PR dir), fndr and chief exec Colman Getty 1987–, chief exec Four Colman Getty 2012; *Clubs* Groucho; *Style*— Ms Dotti Irving; ✉ Four Colman Getty, 20 St Thomas Street, London SE1 9BF (☎ 020 3697 4240, e-mail dotti.irving@fourcolmangetty.com)

IRVING, Dr Henry Charles; s of Dr Gerald Ian Irving, of Leeds, and Sonia Carol, *née* Sinson; *b* 6 October 1950; *Educ* Leeds GS, King's Coll and Westminster Med Sch London (MB BS); *m* 8 July 1973, (Alison) Jane, da of Peter Brackup, of Leeds; 2 da (Juliet b 1975, Georgina b 1978); *Career* conslt radiologist St James's Univ Hosp Leeds 1979–2013, sr clinical lectr radiodiagnosis Univ of Leeds 1979–; RCR regional postgrad educn advsr 1996–99; pres Br Med Ultrasound Soc 1994–96, offr and treas Royal Coll of Radiologists 2000–05; memb Editorial Bd: British Jl of Radiology, Radiology Now, Radiography; author of 20 chapters in several textbooks of ultrasound and radiology and 67 published papers in peer-reviewed jls; RCR: memb Cncl, memb Examining Bd 1996–2000, treas 2000–05; FRCR 1978; *Recreations* golf, tennis, bridge, golf; *Clubs* Moor Allerton Golf, Hartsbourne Country, Leeds Bridge; *Style*— Dr Henry Irving; ✉ 24 Alwoodley Lane, Leeds LS17 7PX (☎ 0113 261 1820, e-mail henry.irving@ntlworld.com)

IRVING, Prof Sir Miles Horsfall; kt (1995); s of Frederick William Irving (d 1953), of Southport, Lancs, and Mabel, *née* Horsfall (d 1988); *b* 29 June 1935; *Educ* King George V Sch Southport, Univ of Liverpool (MB ChB, MD, ChM), Univ of Sydney; *m* 13 Nov 1965, Patricia Margaret, da of Dr Richard Alexander Blaiklock, late Capt RAMC, of Alnwick, Northumberland; 2 da (Katherine Susan b 1966, Jane Elizabeth b 1967), 2 s (Peter Miles b 1970, Simon Richard b 1974); *Career* house physician then house surgn Broadgreen Hosp Liverpool 1959–60, Robert Gee fell in human anatomy Univ of Liverpool Med Sch 1961–62, Phyllis Anderson surgical res fell Univ of Sydney Med Sch 1965–67, reader in surgery and asst dir Professorial Surgical Unit Bart's London 1972–74, prof and head Univ Dept of Surgery Hope Hosp Salford 1974–99, chm Sch of Surgical Scis Univ of Manchester 1974–92, head Univ Dept of Surgery Manchester Royal Infirmary 1992–95, emeritus prof Univ of Manchester 1999–; regnl dir of res and devpt North Western RHA 1992–94, non-exec memb Salford HA 1992–94, dir NHS Health Technol Prog 1994–99, chm Newcastle Hosps NHS Tst 1998–2006, chm NHS Innovations (North) 2004–10, chm Health Innovation and Educn Cluster (HIEC) for the NE 2010–12; visiting prof of surgery Newcastle Univ 1998– (memb Cncl 2003–11); hon conslt surgn to the Br Army; numerous guest lectureships and external examinerships since 1974; Royal Coll of Surgns: former memb Cncl, former chm External Affrs Bd; Dept of Health: former memb Expert Advsy Gp on AIDS, former memb Trauma Centre Evaluation Advsy Gp, chm Standing Gp on Health Technologies 1993–99; tstee Imperial War Museum 2006–14, dir Trading Co Imperial War Museum 2012–14; past pres: Ileostomy Assoc of GB and I, Int Surgical Gp, Assoc of Surgns of GB and I, Section of Coloproctology RSM, Assoc of Coloproctology; memb GMC (and its Overseas and Educn Ctees) 1990–92, James IV Assoc of Surgns; past chm Fedn of Surgical Speciality Assocs; chm Order of St John Northumbria 2007–13; Guthrie Medal RAMC 2005; Hon Col 201 (Northern) Field Hospital 1998–2006; Hon Freeman Worshipful Co of Barbers 2013; Hon DSc Univ of Salford 1996, Hon DUniv of Sibiu Romania 1997, Hon DCL Northumbria Univ 2007, Dr (hc) Univ of Medicine Ia?i Romania 2015; Hon FFAEM, hon fell Royal Coll of Emergency Med 2008, Hon FRCSGlas 1997, Hon FRCS (Canada) 1998, hon fell American Surgical Assoc 2000, Hon FACS 2000; fell Assocs of Surgeons of GB and I, fell Manchester Med Soc (hon fell 1995); FMedSci 1998; Serving Brother OStJ; *Publications* Gastroenterological Surgery (1983), Intestinal Fistulas (1985), A B C of Colo Rectal Diseases (1993), Minimal Access Surgery (1996), 100 Years of the Royal Victoria Infirmary (2006); author of over 250 articles in surgical and other med jls; *Recreations* reading the Spectator, mountain climbing, opera; *Style*— Sir Miles Irving; ✉ 12 Ashford Close, Woodstock, Oxfordshire OX20 1FF (e-mail m.h.irvingjuniper@gmail.com)

IRWIN, Lt-Gen Sir Alistair Stuart Hastings; KCB (2002), CBE (1994, OBE 1987); s of Brig Angus Digby Hastings Irwin, CBE, DSO, MC (d 1997), and Elizabeth Bryson, *née* Cumming; *b* 27 August 1948; *Educ* Wellington Coll, Univ of St Andrews (MA), RMCS Shrivenham, Pakistan Army Staff Coll Quetta; *m* 8 April 1982, Nicola Valentine Blomfield, *née* Williams; 2 da (Mary-Rose b 1975, Laura b 1978), 1 s (George b 1983); *Career* cmmnd Black Watch (RHR) 1970, Gen Staff Offr 2 (Weapons) MOD 1981–82, cmd mech inf co W Germany and NI 1982–83, second in command 1 Bn Black Watch 1983–84, promoted Lt-Col, Directorate of Command Control and Communications Systems (Army) MOD 1985, cmd 1 Bn Black Watch 1985–88 (despatches), tours of duty NI, Edinburgh and W Berlin, memb Directing Staff Camberley 1988–92, student then asst dir Higher Command and Staff Course Army Staff Coll Camberley, promoted Brig 1992, cmd 39 Inf Bde NI 1992–94, Dir Land Warfare 1994–95, project dir Procurement Exec 1996, promoted Maj-Gen, Cmdt RMCS Shrivenham 1996–99, Mil Sec 1999, promoted Lt-Gen, GOC NI 2000–03, Adj-Gen and memb Army Bd 2003–05, ret; Col The Black Watch 2003–06 (Rep Col The Black Watch 3 Bn Royal Regt of Scotland 2006–09), Hon Col Tayforth Univs OTC 1997–2009, Col Cmdt Scottish Div 1999–2004; offr (Brig) Queen's Body Guard for Scotland (Royal Co of Archers); pres: Army Angling Fedn 1997–2005, Tidworth Combined Services Polo Club 2003–05, Quetta Assoc 2003–, Royal Br Legion Scotland 2006–, Earl Haig Fund for Scotland 2006–, Offrs Assoc Scotland 2006–, Offrs Assoc 2006–15, Veterans Scotland 2006–11; memb Br Cmmn of Mil History; cmmr Cwlth War Graves Cmmn 2005–13 (vice-chm 2011–13), memb Scottish Govt Great War Commemoration Panel 2013–; author of numerous articles in military jls, book reviews in Spectator, War in History and Br Army Review; chm: Black Watch Tsts 2003–12, Black Watch Museum 2003–, Christina Mary Hendrie Tst 2005–12, Black Watch Heritage Appeal 2008–15; dir Queen Mother Meml Fund for Scotland 2003–08, memb Highland Soc of London 2003–, vice-pres Royal Caledonian EducnTst 2005–, memb Advsy Bd CPD Fndn, hon pres City of Dundee Ex Servicemen's Assoc 2010–; advsr Eruma plc 2008–13; Hon Keeper of the Quaich 2007, hon memb Incorporation of Dundee Weavers 2012; *Recreations* gardening, shooting, fishing; *Clubs* Boodle's, Royal Scots,

Highland and Lowland Bde; *Style*— Lt-Gen Sir Alistair Irwin, KCB, CBE; ✉ c/o Adam and Co plc, 25 St Andrew Square, Edinburgh EH2 1AF

IRWIN, Christopher Conran; s of John Conran Irwin (d 1997), and Helen Hermione, *née* Fletcher (d 2005); *b* 2 April 1948, London; *Educ* Bedales (scholar), Univ of Sussex (BA); *m* Stephanie Jane, da of Hilary Noble Ball (d 1972); 2 da (Bryony b 12 Jan 1972, Tamsin b 25 April 1974), 1 s (John Phineas Hilary b 20 June 1978); *Career* freelance broadcaster BBC Radio Brighton 1968–69, Fed Tst for Educn and Res 1969–75, sr visiting fell Univ of Sussex 1971–72, Secretariat N Atlantic Assembly Brussels 1973–74, current affrs prodr BBC World Service 1975–77, sr res assoc IISS 1977–78; various BBC appointments incl: sec of BBC Scot 1978–79, head of radio BBC Scot 1979–82, gen mangr Satellite devpt 1982–84, chief exec Satellite Broadcasting Bd 1984–85; sold concept for Br Satellite Broadcasting to Pearson plc 1985; gen mangr new media devpt Pearson plc 1986–88, controller of resources and admin BBC World Service 1989–90, chief exec BBC World Service Television Ltd 1990–94, md Guinness World Records Ltd 1994–2001; dir TravelWatch SouthWest 2005– (chair 2005–13), memb European Rail Research Advsy Cncl 2004–, memb for passengers European Railway Agency 2004–14 (chair 2012–14), European policy advsr Transport Focus 2005–, memb Tport Advsy Gp EC 2013–; head UK Delgn to and co-chair Channel Tunnel Intergovernmental Cmmn 2012–; hon doctorate Univ of Plymouth 2012; *Books* The Security of Western Europe (with Sir Bernard Burrows, 1972), Electing the European Parliament (1973), Towards a Peaceful Europe (1974); contrib to: International Affairs, Strategic Survey; *Recreations* gardening, historical topography, timetables; *Style*— Christopher Irwin, Esq; ✉ Bourton House, Bourton, Bishops Cannings, Devizes, Wiltshire SN10 2LQ (☎ 01380 860252, mobile 07900 218290, e-mail christophercirwin@hotmail.com)

IRWIN, Prof George William; s of Charles James Irwin (d 1988); *b* 19 September 1950; *Educ* Sullivan Upper Sch Holywood, Queen's Univ Belfast (BSc, PhD, DSc); *m* 1, 4 Aug 1976, Margaret Yvonne, *née* McFeeters (d 2009); 1 s (Robin Charles b 29 April 1981); m 2, 15 Jan 2011, Donna Anne, *née* Rowell; *Career* lectr Engrg Maths Dept Loughborough Univ of Technol 1976–80; Queen's Univ Belfast: lectr 1980–87, reader 1987–88, prof of control engrg (personal chair) Sch of Electrical and Electronic Engrg 1988–2013; emeritus prof Queens Univ Belfast 2013–; dir Virtual Engrg Centre 2001–06; non-exec dir Anex6 Ltd 1989–2004; author of 400 research pubns in the field of automatic control systems; chair UK Automatic Control Cncl; hon prof: Harbin Univ of Technol China 1999, Shanghai Univ China 2005, Shangfong Univ China 2005; IEE: Kelvin Premium 1985, Heaviside Premium 1987, Mather Premium 1991, Hartree Premium 1996; Inst of Measurement and Control: Honeywell Prize 1994, Honeywell Int Medal 2002, Outstanding Service Award Int Fedn of Automatic Control 2008; CEng 1992, FIEE 1992, FInstMC 1992, MRIA 2002, FREng 2002, FIEEE 2004, fell IFAC 2009; *Publications* 400 pubns, incl 5 books, 120 jl papers and almost 200 peer-reviewed conference papers; *Recreations* cottage in Portballintrae, swimming, reading, music, travel, popular culture, walking; *Style*— Prof George W Irwin; ✉ Rosnaree, 49 Magheralave Grange, Lisburn, Co Antrim BT28 3BZ (☎ 028 9258 6392, e-mail irwingw1@gmail.com)

IRWIN, Dr Gregor; CMG (2014); *b* 26 January 1972, Glasgow; *Educ* Univ of Glasgow (BAcc), Univ of Oxford (MPhil, DPhil); *Career* strategy conslt Marakon Assocs 1997–97, economics fell LMH Oxford 1997–2000, economics fell Univ Coll Oxford 2000–02, economic advsr HM Treasy 2002–04, sr mangr Bank of England 2004–08, dir of economics and chief economist FCO 2008–13, chief economist Global Counsel 2014–; *Style*— Dr Gregor Irwin, CMG; ✉ Global Counsel, 5 Welbeck Street, London W1G 9YQ (e-mail g.irwin@global-counsel.co.uk)

IRWIN, Dr Michael Henry Knox; s of William Knox Irwin, FRCS, MD (d 1973), of Watford Heath, Herts, and Edith Isabel Mary, *née* Collins; descendant of John Knox; *b* 5 June 1931; *Educ* Merchant Taylors' Sch, St Bartholomew's Hosp London (MB BS), Columbia Univ NY (MPH); *m* 1, 1958 (m dis 1982), Elizabeth, *née* Naumann; 3 da (Christina, Pamela, Diana); m 2, 1983 (m dis 1991), Frederica, *née* Harlow; m 3, 1994 (m dis 2000), Patricia, *née* Walters; partner Angela Farmer; *Career* physician; joined UN 1957, UN medical dir 1969–73, dir of personnel UN Devpt Programme 1973–76, UNICEF rep in Bangladesh 1977–80, sr advsr UNICEF 1980–82, medical dir UN, UNDP and UNICEF 1982–89, dir Health Servs Dept World Bank 1989–90; conslt American Assoc of Blood Banks 1984–90, advsr ActionAid 1990–91, dir Westside Action 1991–93, int health conslt 1993–95; treas World Fedn of Right-To-Die Socs 2008–12 (vice-pres 2000–02, pres 2002–04); chm UN Assoc 1996–98 (vice-chm 1995, vice-pres 1999–), chm Vol Euthanasia Soc 2002–04 (chm 1996–2000, vice-chm 2000–02), dir Doctors for Assisted Dying 1998–2001, co-ordinator Secular Medical Forum 2006–08, fndr and co-ordinator Soc for Old Age Rational Suicide 2009–15 (patron 2015–), hon assoc Nat Secular Soc 2011, dir Right-To-Die Europe 2011–13, patron Br Humanist Assoc 2015–; Parly candidate Kensington and Chelsea by-election (Living Will Campaign) 1999; initiated Secularist of the Year Award 2005, Tenrei Ohta Award 2014; Offr Cross Int Fedn of Blood Donor Organisations 1984; *Books* Overweight: A Problem for Millions (1964), What Do We Know About Allergies? (1972), Nuclear Energy: Good or Bad? (1984), The Cocaine Epidemic (1985), Can We Survive Nuclear War? (1985), Talpa (1990), Peace Museums (1991), Pro-Choice Living Will (2003), Psyche-Anima (2004), What Survives? (2005), Tilting at Windmills (2007), Irish Living Will (2008), Old Age Rational Suicide (2009), Approaching Old-Old (2014), I'll See Myself Out, Thank You (2015); *Recreations* politics, metaphysics, reading; *Style*— Dr Michael Irwin; ✉ 9 Waverleigh Road, Cranleigh, Surrey GU6 8BZ

IRWIN, Robert Graham; *b* 23 August 1946; *Educ* Epsom Coll, Merton Coll Oxford (postmaster, MA), SOAS; *m* 30 Sept 1972, Helen Elizabeth, *née* Taylor; 1 da (Felicity Anne); *Career* writer; lectr Dept of Mediaeval History Univ of St Andrews 1972–77; pt/t teacher 1977–: Arabic Dept Univ of Oxford, Arabic Dept Univ of Cambridge, History Dept SOAS, Islamic Art dip course Sotheby's, Morley Coll; dir Dedalus publishing, conslt ed TLS, conslt Time-Life Books History of the World; visiting lectr Arabic Dept Univ of St Andrews 1985, assoc Inst of Medieval Studies Univ of Nottingham 1991–, sr research assoc Dept of History SOAS 1997–; memb interview panel Wingate scholarships 2000–11; numerous radio and TV broadcasts; Br Cncl: tour of Germany 1997, rapporteur Arabic Literary Trans Conf 2000, tour of Syria 2001; attended literary festivals incl: Antwerp 1997, Bath 1998, Edinburgh 1998 and 2006, Turku Finland 2003, Lewes Live Literary Festival 2003, Prague Writers' Festival 2004, Hay-on-Wye Festival 2004 and 2006, Edinburgh Literary Festival 2004, Cheltenham 2006, Dubai 2009, Berlin 2011, Wigtown 2011; memb Inst of Historical Research Univ of London; patron Nat Acad of Writing; former fell London Coll of Pataphysics; FRAS (former memb Cncl), FSA, FRSL (memb Cncl); *Non-Fiction* books incl: The Middle East in the Middle Ages: The Early Mamluk Sultanate 1250–1382 (1986), The Arabian Nights: A Companion (1994, 2 edn 2003), Islamic Art (1997), Night and Horses and the Desert: An Anthology of Classical Arabic Literature (1999), The Alhambra (2004), For Lust of Knowing: The Orientalists and Their Enemies (2006), Camel (2010), Mamluks and Crusaders (2010), The New Cambridge History of Islam Vol 4 (ed, 2010), Visions of the Jinn: Illustrations of the Arabian Nights (2010), Memoirs of a Dervish (2011); author of numerous articles and reviews in books, newspapers and jls; *Fiction* novels: The Arabian Nightmare (1983, 5 edn 2002, trans into 14 other languages), The Limits of Vision (1986, 2 edn 1993), The Mysteries of Algiers (1988, 2 edn 1993), Exquisite Corpse (1995, nomination Best Novel Br Fantasy Soc 1995), Prayer-Cushions of the Flesh (novella, 1997, reprinted 2004), Satan Wants Me (1999); *Recreations* Times crossword; *Style*— Robert Irwin, Esq; ✉ c/o Juri Gabriel, 35 Camberwell Grove, London SE5 8JA (☎ 020 7703 6186, e-mail juri@jurigabriel.com)

IRWIN, Hon Mr Justice; Sir Stephen John; kt (2006); s of John McCaughey Irwin (d 1993), of Co Down, NI, and Norma Gordon, *née* Cosgrove; *b* 5 February 1953; *Educ* Methodist Coll Belfast, Jesus Coll Cambridge (BA); *m* 29 July 1978, Deborah Rose Ann, da of Lawrence Spring (decd), and Katherine, *née* Ferguson; 2 da (Rachel b 8 Sept 1983, Ruth b 13 July 1992), 1 s (William b 18 August 1985); *Career* called to the Bar Gray's Inn 1976; QC 1997, recorder 1999–2006, judge of the High Court of Justice (Queen's Bench Div) 2006–, presiding judge Northern Circuit 2008–12; chm Special Immigration Appeals Cmmn 2013–16; co-fndr Doughty St Chambers; memb Bar Cncl 1999–2004 (vice-chm 2003, chm 2004); specialist in medical and related litigation, currently Master of Finance Gray's Inn; chm Poetry Soc 2011–14; *Books* Medical Negligence: Practitioner's Guide (lead author, 1995); *Recreations* walking, reading, Irish history, verse; *Style*— The Hon Mr Justice Irwin; ✉ Royal Courts of Justice, Strand, London WC2A 2LL

ISAAC, David; CBE (2011); *b* Johannesburg, SA; *Educ* Trinity Hall Cambridge, Wolfson Coll Oxford; *Career* ptnr Strategic Business Services Gp and head Advanced Manufacturing and Technol Sector Pinsent Masons 2000–; chair: Stonewall 2003–12, Modern Art Oxford, British Future 2013–15; tstee Princess of Wales Meml Fund 2006–13, dir Big Lottery Fund 2014; *Recreations* visual arts, walking, bee-keeping; *Clubs* Home House; *Style*— David Isaac, Esq, CBE; ✉ Pinsent Masons, Crown Place, London EC2A 4ES

ISAACS, Jason; *b* 6 June 1963, Liverpool; *Educ* Haberdashers' Aske's, Univ of Bristol, Central Sch of Speech and Drama; *Partner* Emma Hewitt; 2 da (Lily, Ruby); *Career* actor; *Television* incl: Capital City 1989–90, Eye Contact 1991, Ashenden 1991, Civvies 1992, A Relative Stranger 1995, Loved Up 1995, The Fix 1997, The Last Don II 1998, The West Wing 2004, Avatar: The Last Airbender 2005, Scars 2006, The State Within 2006, Brotherhood 2006–08, The Curse of Steptoe 2008, Case Histories 2011, Awake 2012; *Film* incl: Dragonheart 1996, Event Horizon 1997, Armageddon 1998, Divorcing Jack 1998, The End of the Affair 1999, The Patriot 2000, Sweet November 2001, The Tag 2001, The Last Minute 2001, Black Hawk Down 2001, Windtalkers 2002, Passionada 2002, High Times Potluck 2002, The Tuxedo 2002, Mr Darling/Captain Hook in Peter Pan 2003, Nine Lives 2005, Tennis, Anyone..? 2005, Friends with Money 2006, Good 2008, Green Zone 2010, Cars 2 2011, Abduction 2011, Resident Evil: Retribution 2012; as Lucius Malfoy: Harry Potter and the Chamber of Secrets 2002, Harry Potter and the Goblet of Fire 2005, Harry Potter and the Order of the Phoenix 2007, Harry Potter and the Deathly Hallows: Part 1 2010, Harry Potter and the Deathly Hallows: Part 2 2011; *Style*— Jason Isaacs; ✉ c/o Independent Talent Group, 40 Whitfield Street, London W1T 2RH

ISAACS, Sir Jeremy Israel; kt (1996); s of Isidore Isaacs, and Sara, *née* Jacobs; *b* 28 September 1932; *Educ* Glasgow Acad, Merton Coll Oxford (MA, pres Oxford Union); *m* 1, 1958, Tamara (d 1986); 1 s, 1 da; m 2, 1988, Gillian Mary Widdicombe; *Career* TV prodr: Granada TV 1958–63 (progs incl What the Papers Say, All Our Yesterdays), Associated-Rediffusion 1963–65 (This Week), BBC 1965–67 (Panorama); Associated-Rediffusion (renamed Thames Television 1968): controller of features 1967–74, dir of progs 1974–78, prodr The World at War 1974, conslt Hollywood series; ind prodr: A Sense of Freedom (Scottish TV), Ireland – A Television History (13 part series BBC TV), Cold War (Turner Broadcasting) 1998, Millennium (Turner Broadcasting) 1999; chief exec Channel 4 1981–87, gen dir ROH 1988–97, chief exec Jeremy Isaacs Productions 1997–, chm Artsworld Channels Ltd 2000–03, chm DCMS Advsy Panel European Capital of Culture 2001–03; awarded: Desmond Davis Award for outstanding contrib to TV 1972, George Polk Meml Award 1973, Cyril Bennett Award for outstanding contrib to TV programming (RTS) 1982, Peabody Award, Prix Italia 1999; govr BFI 1979, BFI fellowship 1986; pres RTS 1999–2001; Hon DLitt: Univ of Strathclyde 1984, CNAA 1987, Univ of Bristol 1988, Univ of Manchester 1999; fell British Acad of Film and TV 1985; RTS Hall of Fame 1996; Cdr Order of Arts and Letters (France) 1988, L'Ordre National du Mérite (France) 1992; *Books* Storm Over Four (1988), Cold War (jtly, 1998), Never Mind the Moon (1999), Look Me in the Eye (2006); *Recreations* walking, reading; *Style*— Sir Jeremy Isaacs; ✉ c/o PFD, Drury House, 34 Russell Street, London WC2B 5HA

ISAACS, Jeremy M; CBE (2015); *Career* exec dir Goldman Sachs 1989–96; Lehman Brothers 1996–2008: co chief operating offr European Equities 1996, head of global equity derivative activities 1996, head of overall equity activities in Europe 1997, chief exec European activities 1999 (previously chief operating offr), responsible for Asian ops 2000–08, ceo Europe, Middle East and Asia-Pacific until 2008, founding partner JRJ Gp 2009, chm Marex Gp 2010; memb Advsy Bd Bridges Devpt Fund; non-exec dir Imperial Coll Healthcare NHS Tst; tstee The J Isaacs Charitable Tst, tstee Noah's Ark Children's Hospice; hon fell London Business Sch; *Style*— Jeremy M Isaacs, Esq, CBE

ISAACSON, Laurence Ivor; CBE (1998); s of Henry Isaacson (d 1980), and Dorothy Hannah, *née* Levitt (d 1976); *b* 1 July 1943, Southport; *Educ* Quarry Bank GS Liverpool, LSE (BSc), Northwestern Univ Chicago (summer business course); *Career* restaurateur; various business traineeships 1962–64 (Commercial Bank of Italy Milan, Shell Italiana Genoa, Manpower Inc Milwaukee), mgmnt trainee rising to account exec Unilever plc 1964–67, account mangr Doyle Dane Bernbach advtg 1967–70, sr int account mangr Foote Cone & Belding advtg 1970–72; The Creative Business Ltd: fndr md 1974–81, dep chm 1981–83, chm 1986–90; dir Amis du Vin Group Ltd and fndr ptnr/dir Café des Amis Ltd 1972–83 (sold to Kennedy Brookes plc 1983), bd dir i/c mktg and gourmet restaurant gp Kennedy Brookes plc 1983–86, fndr ptnr/dep chm Groupe Chez Gérard plc (Chez Gérard, Bertorelli's, Café Fish, St Quentin, Soho Soho, Scotts and Livebait) 1986–2003, dir and ptnr Paris Commune Restaurant NYC 2004–, chm L'Escargot Restaurant Ltd 2014–; non-exec dir: Cullens Holdings plc 1984–87, Lazard Food & Drink Fund Ltd 1987–90, Katie's Kitchen Ltd 1988–91, Metabolic Services Ltd 1991–94, London Tourist Board Ltd 1994–2002, CRUSAID 1996– (memb Bd 1996–), Bd Arts and Business 1989–2002 (memb Cncl 1985–), Transaction Television plc 1998–2000, Berkley Adam Ltd 1998–, Ambassador Theatre Gp 2000–; co-owner and dir Paris Commune Restaurant LLC (NY); Contemporary Dance Trust: tstee 1980–, govr 1982–, chm Fundraising Ctee 1983–88, chm Bd 1989–94; memb Bd Royal Shakespeare Co Fndn 1998–, chm Actors Circle RSC 2001–, Bd dir RSC 2003–10, dir RSC America Inc 2004–, memb Bd RSC Enterprises 2010–, memb Bd RSC Property 2010–, memb Bd World Cancer Research Fund Hong Kong, memb Bd RADA 2014–; memb Covent Garden Forum of Representatives 1976 (hon treas 1978–80), chm Covent Garden Festival 1993– (fndr/dep chm 1990–93), patron Int Festival of Musical Theatre Cardiff 2002, chm World Cancer Research Fund (UK) 2011 (tstee and dir 2003–11), patron PKD Charity 2011–; MIAA (memb UK Branch Ctee 1979–, chm Activities Ctee 1982–83), FHCIMA 1996, FRSA 1997; *Recreations* the arts, travel, food and drink; *Clubs* Groucho, Garrick, Home House, Norwood (USA); *Style*— Laurence Isaacson, Esq, CBE; ✉ 5 Chalcot Crescent, London NW1 8YE (☎ 020 7586 3793, e-mail laurencei@aol.com)

ISHERWOOD, Mark Allan; AM; s of Rodney Isherwood, and Pat McLean, *née* Curry; *b* 21 January 1959; *Educ* Stockport GS, Univ of Newcastle upon Tyne (BA); *m* 6 May 1985, Hilary, *née* Fleming; 4 da (Genevieve b 16 Nov 1985, Charlotte b 25 June 1987, Olivia b 24 Nov 1990, Meredith b 17 March 1993), 2 s (Myles b 13 Dec 1994, Henry b 17 June 1997); *Career* mgmnt trainee raising to branch mangr Cheshire Building Soc 1981–89, commercial business devpt mangr NWS Bank plc 1989–90, area mangr Cheshire Building Soc 1990–2003, memb Nat Assembly for Wales (Cons) N Wales 2003–; memb All Pty Gp on: Nat Assembly Sustainable Energy Gp (NASEG), Looked After Children,

I

Disablity Gp, Funerals and Bereavement, Deaf Issues, Autism; memb Energywatch; founding memb CHANT Cymru; community cncllr Treddyn 1999–2004; patron Tyddyn Bach Tst Respite Centre, vice-pres N Wales Play and Playing Fields Assoc, memb Venture Housing Assoc (former Bd memb), memb Conwy Citizens Advice Bureau, former sch govr and chm Ysgol Parc y Llan, ambass Clwyd Girl Guiding; ACIB 1997; *Recreations* sailing, family, house, garden; *Clubs* S Caernarvonshire Yacht, Mold Round Table, Ruthin Conservative (hon memb); *Style*— Mark Isherwood, Esq, AM; ✉ National Assembly for Wales, Cardiff Bay, Cardiff CF99 1NA (☎ 029 2089 8730, fax 029 2089 8323, e-mail mark.isherwood@wales.gov.uk)

ISHIGURO, Kazuo; OBE (1995); s of Shizuo Ishiguro, and Shizuko Michida; *b* 8 November 1954; *Educ* Woking Co GS, Univ of Kent (BA), UEA (MA); *m* Lorna Anne, da of Nicol Mackechnie MacDougall; 1 da (Naomi b 29 March 1992); *Career* author; work translated into 40 languages; memb: Soc of Authors 1989, PEN 1989, Writers' Guild of America 2013; Peggy V Helmerich Distinguished Author Award (USA) 2013, NY Public Library Lions Medal 2014, Sunday Times Award for Literary Excellence 2014; hon foreign memb American Acad of Arts and Sciences 1993; Hon DLitt: Univ of Kent 1990, UEA 1995, Univ of St Andrews 2003; FRSL 1989, FRSA 1990; Chevalier de l'Ordre des Arts et des Lettres (France) 1998; *Fiction* A Pale View of Hills (1982, Winifred Holtby Award 1983), An Artist of the Floating World (1986, Whitbread Book of the Year 1986, Premio Scanno (Italy) 1995, shortlisted Booker Prize 1986), The Remains of the Day (1989, Booker Prize 1989, Merchant-Ivory film 1993), The Unconsoled (1995, Cheltenham Prize 1995), When We Were Orphans (2000, shortlisted Man Booker Prize 2000), Never Let Me Go (2005, Corine Prize (Germany) 2006, Serono Prize (Italy) 2006, Casino de Santiago European Novel Prize (Spain) 2007, shortlisted Man Booker Prize 2005, film version 2010), Nocturnes: Five Stories of Music and Nightfall (2009, Guiseppe Tomasi di Lampedusa Int Literary Prize (Italy) 2009), The Buried Giant (2015); *Television Plays* A Profile of Arthur J Mason (broadcast 1984), The Gourmet (broadcast 1987); *Film* The Saddest Music in the World (screenplay co-writer, 2003), The White Countess (original screenplay, 2005), Never Let Me Go (exec prodr, 2010); *Songwriting* as lyricist: The Ice Hotel, I Wish I Could Go Travelling Again, Breakfast on the Morning Tram, So Romantic (all incl on Stacey Kent's album Breakfast on the Morning Tram 2007), Postcard Lovers (incl on Stacey Kent's album Dreamer – In Concert, 2011), The Changing Lights, The Summer We Crossed Europe in the Rain, Waiter Oh Waiter (all incl on Stacey Kent's album The Changing Lights 2013); *Recreations* playing musical instruments; *Style*— Kazuo Ishiguro, Esq, OBE, FRSL; ✉ c/o Rogers, Coleridge and White Ltd, 20 Powis Mews, London W11 1JN (☎ 020 7221 3717, fax 020 7229 9084)

ISHII, Yoshinori; *Career* sous chef Kyoto Kitcho Co Ltd 1990–98, head chef Japanese Embassy for UN Geneva then NY 1999–2004, chef Morimoto 2006–10, exec chef Umu Restaurant Mayfair 2010– (Michelin star); *Style*— Yoshinori Ishii, Esq; ✉ Umu Restaurant, 14–16 Bruton Place, Mayfair, London W1J 6LX

ISLAM, Aktar; *b* Birmingham; *Career* chef dir Lasan Restaurant Birmingham 2002–; television appearances incl: Market Kitchen (UKTV), Gordon Ramsay's F Word (Channel 4) 2010 (winner Best Local Restaurant), Great British Menu (BBC 2) 2011 (winner, cooked fish course for the People's Banquet); *Books* Spice for Life (2008), Simple Indian Home Cooking (2010); *Style*— Mr Aktar Islam; ✉ Lasan Restaurant, 3–4 Dakota Building, James Street, St Paul's Square, Birmingham B3 1SD

ISLAM, Runa; *b* 1970, Dhaka, Bangladesh; *Educ* Manchester Met Univ, Middx Univ, Rijksakademie van Beeldende Kunsten Amsterdam, Royal Coll of Art; *Career* artist; Campden Charities Scholarship 1997, NUFFIC Scholarship 1998, Univ of E London Richmix Cmmn 1999, Ford Motor Co and Breakthrough Nurture & Desire Cmmn 2000, Arena Sammling Fndn and NESTA Cmmn 2002–03, Public Art Strategy Artists Cmmn for Home Office Bldg 2004–2005; Fndn of Sports and Arts Award 1997, Rijksakademie van Beeldende Kunsten Acquistions Prize 1998, Amsterdam Fonds voor de Kunst Aanmoedigings Prijs '99 1999, Fondazione Sandretto Re Rebaudengo Premio Regione Piemonte 2000, London Arts Visual Arts Award 2001; *Solo Exhibitions* incl: Screen Test/ Unscript (Fig-1 London) 2000, Tschumi Pavillion Groningen 2000, Director's Cut (Fool for Love) (White Cube London) 2001, One day a day will come, when a day will not come any more (April in parking meters, Cologne) 2001, Rapid Eye Movement (MIT List Visual Arts Center Cambridge) 2003, Film and Video Works (Voralberger Kunstverein Bregenz) 2003, Director's Cut (Fool for Love) (Kunsthalle Wien Karlsplatz Project Space Vienna) 2003, Scale (1/16 inch = 1 foot) (ShugoArts Tokyo) 2004; *Group Exhibitions* Transit at Art Focus (Central Bus Station Tel Aviv) 1994, Lost Property (The Lost Goods Building London) 1995, Yerself is Steam (85 Charlotte Rd London) 1996, Big Blue (Coins London and Café Fix Berlin) 1997, The Road (Espace Culturel François Mitterand Beauvais) 1998, Martin (Catalyst Arts Belfast and Waygood Gallery Newcastle) 1998, The Vauxhall Gardens (Norwich Art Gallery) 1998, 000Zero, Zero, Zero (Whitechapel Art Gallery London) 1999, East International (Norwich Art Gallery) 1999, Dis-Locations (hARTware projekte Dortmund) 1999, And If There Were No Stories (Stephen Friedman Gallery London) 2000, The British Art Show 5 (Hayward Gallery touring exhbn) 2000, Haven Lodge (Haven Lodge Residential Home Ramsgate) 2000, Nurture and Desire (in aid of Breakthrough Breast Cancer, Hayward Gallery London) 2000, Century City (Tate Modern London) 2001, Whitechapel Centenary 1901–2001 (Whitechapel Art Gallery London) 2001, Please Disturb Me (Great Eastern Hotel London) 2001, Looking With/Out (Courtauld Inst London) 2001, A Haunted House of Art (Outline Amsterdam) 2002, Videodrome II (Zenith Media Lounge New Museum NY) 2002, Great Theatre of the World (Taipei Fine Arts Museum) 2002, Miradas Cómplices (Accomplished Glances) (Centro Galego de Arte Contemporanea Santiago de Compostela) 2003, Sharjah Int Biennial 6 2003, Poetic Justice (8th International Istanbul Biennial) 2003, Love/Hate, Attempts at the Grand Emotion Between Art and the Theatre (Ursula Blickle Fndn Kraichal) 2003, In Movement: UNESCO Salutes Women in Video Art (UNESCO HQ Paris) 2004, Britannia Works (Ileana Tounta Contemporary Art Centre Athens) 2004, Párpados y Labios (Eyelids and Lips) (Antigua Fábrica de Tabascos Madrid) 2004, Lilith (Mot London) 2004, Eclipse, Towards the Edge of the Visible (White Cube London) 2004; *Collaborations* Life/Live (with David Medalla, Adam Nakervis and Peter Lewis, Musée d'Art Moderne de la Ville de Paris) 1996, Curator's Arse (with Peter Lewis, Catalyst Arts Belfast and Waygood Gallery Newcastle) 1997, Plaats (with J Daf, P Fillingham and J Isaacs, W139 Amsterdam) 1998, 'Alice in Bed' by Susan Sontag (with HZT and NY Theatre Workshop) 2000, History Lessons at Kunst en der Stadt 2000 (with Peter Lewis, Korn Theatre Bregenz) 2000, What's Wrong (with Peter Lewis, Trade Apartment London) 2001, Cité (with Roger Cremers, Institut Néerlandais Paris and Inst Hollandaise Paris) 2001; *Festivals, Events and Screenings* Hit and Run 1–4 (Arch 53 and The Ministry of Sound London) 1994, 1995 and 1996, Scope 2 International Film Festival (Artists Space NY) 1998, Runa Islam at Impakt Film Festival (Begane Grond Utrecht) 1999, World Wide Video Festival (Uitmarkt Stedlijk Museum Amsterdam) 1999, Devil Eats Out (Flag London) 2000, Idea Festival Video in the City (Centrum Hedendaagse Kunst Maastricht) 2001, Film and Video (Danish Film Inst) 2002, Rapid Eye Movement (Camden Arts Centre Off Centre Event, Everyman Cinema London) 2003; *Style*— Ms Runa Islam; ✉ White Cube, 48 Hoxton Square, London N1 6PB (☎ 020 7930 5373, fax 020 7949 7480)

ISLE OF MAN, Archdeacon of the; *see:* Partington, Ven Brian Harold

ISSA, Caroline; *b* Canada; *Educ* Univ of Pennsylvania Wharton Sch; *Career* publisher and fashion dir TANK Magazine 2002–; *Style*— Ms Caroline Issa; ✉ TANK, 91–93 Great Portland Street, London W1W 7NX

ISSERLIS, Steven John; CBE (1998); s of George Isserlis, and Cynthia Saville; bro of Annette and Rachel Isserlis, musicians; gs of Julius Isserlis, Russian composer and pianist; *b* 19 December 1958; *Educ* City of London Sch, Int Cello Centre (with Jane Cowan), Oberlin Coll Ohio (with Richard Kapuscinski); *m* Pauline Ann Mara (d 2010); 1 s (Gabriel Mara b 26 April 1990); *Career* cellist; recitals and concerts all over Europe, N America, S America, Far East and Australia with maj worldwide orchs; worked with conductors incl: Sir Georg Solti, Christoph Eschenbach, Christopher Hogwood, Roger Norrington, Richard Hickox, John Eliot Gardiner, Gennadi Rozhdestvensky, Vladimir Ashkenazy, Mstislav Rostropovich, Philippe Herrweghe, Franz Brüggen, Ton Koopman, Lorin Maazel, Sakari Oramo, Daniel Harding, Simon Rattle, Zubin Mehta, Kurt Masur, Alan Gilbert, Robin Ticciati, Philippe Herrweghe, Paavo Jarvi; has played a leading role in many prestigious chamber music projects incl: own festival Schumann and his Circle (Wigmore Hall London) 1989, Mendelssohn Series Salzburg Festival 1997, Brahms Series Salzburg Festival 2000, Brahms Frühling Series London, Berlin, Vienna 2000–01, Taneyev Series London 2002, Saint-Saëns Series London 2004, Schumann series NY and Japan 2006, Russian Series (Wigmore Hall) 2008, Weber/Mendelssohn/Schumann series (Salzburg Festival) 2009, Voice and Cello series (Wigmore Hall) 2011–12, Czech Music (Wigmore Hall, Verbier and Salzburg festivals) 2012–15, Chamber Music in Time of War series (Wigmore Hall and Salzburg Festival) 2013–14; premiered many new works incl: John Tavener, Wolfgang Rihm, Thomas Adès; annual series of concerts for children 92nd St NY; several television films incl Channel 4 films on Saint-Saëns 1993 and Schumann 1997; Royal Philharmonic Award Piatgorsky Prize (1993), Schumann Preis City of Zwickau (2000); memb: Dvorâk Soc, Liszt Soc, Bloch Soc, Wilkie Collins Soc; Hon RAM, FRCM; *Recordings* incl: John Tavener The Protecting Veil and Threenos and Britten Suite no 3 (with LSO and Gennadi Rozhdestvensky, 1992, Gramophone Magazine Contemporary Music Award 1992, shortlisted for Mercury Prize and Grammy Award), Rachmaninov and Franck Cello Sonatas (with Stephen Hough, 2003), Brahms Sonatas, works by Dvorak and Suk (with Stephen Hough, 2005, Disc of the Year BBC Review), Children's Cello (with Stephen Hough, Simon Callow, 2006), Bach Cello Suites (2007, Instrumental Disc of the Year Gramophone Award, Disc of the Year BBC CD Review, Classical Brits Critics' Choice), Schumann Recital with Denis Varjon (2009), Revisions – works arranged for cello and chamber orchestra (2010), Thomas Ades Lieux Retrouvés (with Thomas Ades, 2012), Music in the Shadow of War (with the Dutch Symphony Orchestra and Hugh Wolff, 2012), Dvorak concertos (with the Mahler Chamber Orchestra and Daniel Harding, 2013), Beethoven Complete Works for cello and fortepiano (with Robert Levin, 2014), works by Martinu, Mustonen and Sibelius (with Olli Mustonen, 2014), Julius Isserlis Ballade (with Sam Haywood, 2014), Shostakovich/Prokofiev concertos (2015), Grieg/Mendelssohn/Hough Sonatas (with Stephen Hough, 2015), Bach Gamba Sonatas (with Richard Egarr) 2015; *Publications* music: Beethoven Mandolin Variations (arranged for cello and piano), Saint Saens – Complete Short Works for Cello and Piano, Steven Isserlis's Cello World, Unbeaten Tracks, Hummel Variations on God Save the King (arranged for violin and cello), various cello works for online sheet music; Why Beethoven Threw the Stew (children's book, 2001), Why Handel Waggled His Wig (children's book, 2006); Musical Stories for Children: Little Red Violin (music by Anne Dudley, 2008), Goldiepegs and his Three Cellos (music by Anne Dudley, 2009), Cindercella (music by Anne Dudley, 2010), Hummel arr Isserlis: Variations on God Save the Queen for violin and cello (2015); various articles for the Guardian etc.; *Recreations* reading, sleeping, eating, talking, jetlag, panicking, dropping names, generally wasting time (my own and others'), sitting at the computer, trying to get away from the computer, wondering why I don't have any interesting hobbies; *Style*— Steven Isserlis, Esq, CBE; ✉ website www.stevenisserlis.com; c/o IMG Artists – Europe, The Light Box, 111 Power Road, London W4 5PY (☎ 020 7957 5801, e-mail artistseurope@imgartists.com)

ITALY AND MALTA, Archdeacon of; *see:* Reid, Ven Gordon

IVE, Sir Jonathan; KBE (2012, CBE 2006); *b* 1967, London; *Educ* Newcastle Polytechnic (BA); *Career* designer; with Tangerine 1990–92; Apple Computer Inc: joined 1992, dir of design 1996, vice-pres of industrial design 1998, sr vice-pres of design 2005–, designer iMac, iBook, PowerBook G4, iPod, iPad, iPhone and iMac G5; Design Achievement Medal RSA 1999, Royal Designer for Industry RSA 2003, Designer of the Year Design Museum 2003, Benjamin Franklin Medal RSA 2004, Pres's Award D&AD 2005; Hon Dr RCA; RDI 2003; *Style*— Sir Jonathan Ive, KBE, RDI; ✉ Apple Computer Inc, 1 Infinite Loop, Cupertino, CA 95014, USA

IVEAGH, 4 Earl of (UK 1919); Sir Arthur Edward Rory Guinness; 4 Bt (UK 1885), DL; also Baron Iveagh (UK 1891), Viscount Iveagh (UK 1905), and Viscount Elveden (UK 1919); er s of 3 Earl of Iveagh (d 1992), and Miranda Daphne Jane, *née* Smiley; *b* 10 August 1969; *m* 27 Oct 2001, Clare Georgina Hazell; 2 s (Arthur Benjamin Jeffrey, Viscount Elveden b 6 Jan 2003, Rupert Bertram Ralph b 4 June 2005); *Heir* s, Viscount Elveden; *Career* pres Inst of Agricutural Mgmnt; fell Royal Agricultural Univ; patron Easton Otley Coll; *Style*— The Rt Hon the Earl of Iveagh, DL; ✉ The Estate Office, Elveden, Thetford, Norfolk IP24 3TQ

IVENS, Martin Paul; s of Michael Ivens, CBE (d 2001); *b* 29 August 1958, London; *Educ* St Peter's Coll Oxford; *m* 1994, Anne McElvoy; 2 s, 1 da; *Career* Sunday Times: dep ed 1996–2013, acting ed then ed 2013–; *Style*— Martin Ivens, Esq; ✉ Sunday Times, 1 London Bridge Street, London SE1 9GF

IVERSEN, Dr Leslie Lars; CBE (2013); s of Svend Iversen, and Anna Caia Iversen; *b* 31 October 1937; *Educ* Heles Sch, Trinity Coll Cambridge (BA, MA, PhD, prize fellowship); *m* 1961, Susan Diana; 1 s, 1 da (and 1 da decd); *Career* Nat Serv Educn Branch RN 1956–58; Harkness fell of the Cwlth Fund Nat Inst of Mental Health Harvard Med Sch 1964–66, res fell Trinity Coll and Dept of Pharmacology Univ of Cambridge 1966–71, Locke res fell Royal Soc London 1967–71, dir MRC Neurochemical Pharmacology Unit Cambridge 1971–83, vice-pres Neuroscience Research Centre Merck Sharp & Dohme Research Laboratories Harlow 1987–95 (exec dir 1983–87), visiting prof Dept of Pharmacology Univ of Oxford 1995–, prof of pharmacology and dir Wolfson Centre for Age Related Diseases KCL 1999–2004; assoc of neurosciences Res Prog MIT USA 1975–84, foreign hon memb American Acad of Arts and Sciences 1981, Rennebohm lectr Univ of Wisconsin 1984, visiting prof Inst of Psychiatry Univ of London 1985, assoc memb Royal Coll of Psychiatrists UK 1986, foreign assoc memb Nat Acad of Sciences USA 1986, hon prof Beijing Med Univ China 1988; chm Advsy Cncl on the Misuse of Drugs 2010–; memb: Academia Europaea, American Coll of Neuropsychopharmacology, Bayliss and Starling Soc, Biochemical Soc UK, Br Pharmacological Soc, Collegium Internationale Neuro-Psychopharmacologicum, Euro Molecular Biology Orgn, Int Brain Res Orgn, Int Soc for Neurochemistry, Physiological Soc UK, Royal Acad of Med Belgium, Royal Soc of Med London, Save Br Science, Soc for Drug Res UK, Soc for Neuroscience USA; pres Euro Neuroscience Assoc 1980–82 (vice-pres 1978–80); FRS 1980; *Books* The Uptake and Storage of Noradrenaline in Sympathetic Nerves (1967), Behavioural Pharmacology (with S D Iversen, 1975), The Science of Marijuana (2000), Speed, Ecstasy, Ritalin: The Science of Amphetamines (2006); author of numerous articles in learned jls; *Style*— Dr Leslie Iversen, CBE, FRS; ✉ University Department of Pharmacology, University of Oxford, Mansfield Road, Oxford OX1 3QT (☎ 01865 271850, fax 01865 271882, e-mail les.iversen@pharm.ox.ac.uk)

IVES, Kenneth Ainsworth; s of Lawrence George Ives (d 1956), and Margaret, *née* Walker (d 1978); *b* 26 March 1934; *Educ* Queen Mary's GS Walsall, Pembroke Coll Oxford (MA), RADA (Leverhulme scholar); *m* 1, Ann Brown; m 2, Imogen Hassall; m 3, 1985, Lynne

Shepherd (the comedienne Marti Caine (d 1995)); *Career* Mil Serv Lt RN; director: over fifty plays for BBC TV, NT and West End, seven plays by Harold Pinter; latest theatre work The Philanthropist (by Christopher Hampton); called to the Bar Middle Temple 1993; *Recreations* cricket, opera, reading, walking; *Clubs* Garrick, Oxford & Cambridge, MCC; *Style*— Kenneth Ives, Esq

IVES, William (Bill); *Career* fndr Rainham Steel Gp Ltd 1973 (currently chm); *Style*— Bill Ives, Esq; ✉ Rainham Steel Group Ltd, Kathryn House, Manor Way, Rainham RM13 8RE

IVORY, Sir Brian Gammell; kt (2006), CBE (1999); s of late Eric James Ivory, and late Alice Margaret Joan, da of late Sir Sydney Gammell; *b* 10 April 1949; *Educ* Eton, Magdalene Coll Cambridge (MA); *m* 21 Feb 1981, Oona Mairi Macphie Ivory, DL, *qv*, da of Archibald Ian Bell-MacDonald (d 1987); 1 s (Euan b 1986), 1 da (Roseanna b 1989); *Career* CA; The Highland Distilleries Co, subsequently Highland Distillers plc: dir 1978–99, md 1988–94, gp chief exec 1994–97, exec chm 1997–99; exec chm: Macallan Glenlivet plc 1996–99, Scottish American Investment Co plc 2001–16, Retec Digital plc 2006–13, Arcus European Infrastructure Fund 2010–; chm Marathon Asset Management LLP 2011–; dep chm Shawbrook Bank 2011–15; dir: Rémy Cointreau SA 1991–2015, HBOS plc 2001–07, Orpar SA 2003–13, Insight Investment Mgmnt Ltd 2003–, Synesis Life Ltd 2007–08; vice-chm Scottish Arts Cncl 1988–92, memb Arts Cncl of GB 1988–92, memb Scottish Economic Cncl 1996–98, chm of tstees Nat Galleries of Scotland 2001–09, chm of tstees Great Steward of Scotland's Dumfries House Tst 2011–; chair Governance and Nominations Ctee St Andrews Univ 2007–16; fndr and chm The Nat Piping Centre 1996–; memb Royal Co of Archers (Queen's Body Guard for Scotland) 1996; Paolozzi Gold Medal Nat Galleries of Scotland 2009; Freeman City of London 1996; FRSA 1993, FRSE 2001; *Recreations* the arts, travel and wild places; *Clubs* New (Edinburgh); *Style*— Sir Brian Ivory, CBE, FRSE; ✉ 12 Ann Street, Edinburgh EH4 1PJ (☎ 0131 311 6900, e-mail judy@enitar.co.uk)

IVORY, Lady Oona Mairi MacPhie; DL (Edinburgh 1998); da of Archibald Ian Bell-MacDonald (d 1987), and Mary Rae, *née* Macphee (d 1983); *b* 21 July 1954; *Educ* Royal Scottish Acad of Music & Drama, King's Coll Cambridge (MA), Royal Acad of Music (ARCM); *m* 21 Feb 1981, Sir Brian Gammell Ivory, CBE, *qv*; 1 s (Euan b 1986), 1 da (Roseanna b 1989); *Career* dir RSAMD 1989–2001, chm Scottish Ballet 1995–97 (dir 1988–), fndr dir The Nat Piping Centre 1996–; dir Glasgow Int Piping Festival 2004–; tstee: The Piping Tst 1996–, The Sri Lanka Reconciliation Music Tst 2010–; FRSA 1996; *Recreations* The Arts, sailing, wild places; *Style*— Lady Ivory, DL; ☎ 0131 311 6900, e-mail judy@enitar.co.uk

IWANIEC, Prof Stanis?awa Dorota; DL (Co Borough of Belfast 2007); *b* 20 April 1940; *Educ* Gimna?ium Oleandry Kraków, Jagiellonian Univ Kraków (MA, DipEd), Univ of Leicester (CQSW, PhD); *m* 1, 1960, Zygfryd Iwaniec, s of Aleksander Iwaniec; 2 c (Zygmunt Witold b 16 Oct 1961, Andrzej Jan b 12 July 1966); *m* 2, 1993, Prof James Stevens Curl, *qv*, s of George Stevens Curl (d 1974); *Career* teacher Liceum Sienkiewicza Kraków 1959–60, generic social worker Leicester Social Servs Dept 1971–75, therapist/

researcher Dept of Child Health Leicester Royal Infirmary and Univ of Leicester Med Sch 1977–82, dir Student Trg Unit Leicester 1982–89, team ldr Practice-Teaching Resource Centre Univ of Leicester/Social Servs Dept 1989–92; Queen's Univ Belfast: chair of Social Work 1992, head Sch of Social Work 1995–2002, dir Inst for Child-Care Res 1995–2005, currently emeritus prof; Science Award Women of Achievement Save the Children 2005; memb: Br Assoc of Behavioural and Cognitive Psychotherapists, Br Assoc of Social Workers; AcSS 2002, MRIA 2007; *Publications* Working with Children and Their Families (1987), Failure-to-thrive in Children, Emotional Abuse, Prediction of Child Abuse and Neglect (1989), The Emotionally Abused and Neglected Child: Identification, Assessment, and Intervention (1995), Making Research Work: Promoting Child-Care Policy and Practice (co-ed, 1998), Child and Welfare Policy Practice: Current Issues in Child-Care Research (co-ed, 2000), Emotional Abuse and Failure to Thrive: British and Polish Experiences (co-ed, 2003), Children Who Fail to Thrive: A Practice Guide (2004), The Emotionally Abused and Neglected Child – Identification, Assessment and Intervention: A Practice Handbook (2006), The Child's Journey through Care: Placement Stability, Care Planning, and Achieving Permanency (2006), Residential Care of Children (co-ed, 2009); *Recreations* walking, opera, theatre, food and wine, travel; *Style*— Prof Stanis?awa Dorota Iwaniec, DL; ✉ 15 Torgrange, Holywood, Co Down BT18 0NG (☎ and fax 028 9042 5141, mobile 07738 612184, e-mail d.iwaniec@btinternet.com, website www.dorotaiwaniec.com)

IZAT, (Alexander) John Rennie; OBE (2002), JP; s of Sir James Rennie Izat (d 1962), of Balliliesk, and Lady (Eva Mary Steen) Izat, *née* Cairns (d 1984); *b* 14 July 1932; *Educ* Trinity Coll Glenalmond, Oriel Coll Oxford (MA); *m* 12 April 1958, Frederica Ann, da of Colin Champness McNiel, of Hants; 2 da (Davina b 1959, Rosanna b 1963), 1 s (Alexander b 1960); *Career* stockbroker, farmer; ptnr Williams de Broë & Co London 1955–75; John Izat & Partners: Balliliesk and Naemoor 1961–87, High Cocklaw 1987–; former chm: Shires Income plc, Moredun Research Institute, U A Gp plc, U A Properties Ltd, U A Forestry Ltd, Fraser Tennant (Insurance Brokers) Ltd; former dir: Wiston Investment Co, Glasgow Investment Managers Ltd, Shires Smaller Companies plc, Cromlix Estates Ltd, C Champness & Co, College Valley Estates Ltd; past pres: Fife-Kinross NFU, Kinross Agric Assoc; dir Royal Highland Agric Soc 1985–97 (hon treas 1992–96); fell Glenalmond Coll (memb Cncl 1975–95, chm Ctee 1989–95); FRAgS 2001; *Recreations* shooting, Suffolk sheep; *Clubs* Caledonian; *Style*— John Izat, Esq, OBE; ✉ High Cocklaw, Berwick-upon-Tweed TD15 1UZ (☎ 01289 386591, fax 01289 386775)

IZZA, Michael; s of Salvatore Izza (d 2001), and Jean Izza; *b* 13 December 1960, Manchester; *Educ* Thornleigh Salesian Coll Bolton, St Cuthbert's Soc Durham; *m* 1991, Gillian, *née* Johnston; 1 s (Alexander), 1 da (Madeline); *Career* Coopers & Lybrand 1983–89, John Labatt Ltd 1989–96, Spring Gp plc 1997–2001; ICAEW: exec dir of finance 2002–04, chief operating offr 2004–06, ceo 2006–; FCA; *Recreations* gardening, walking, philately; *Style*— Michael Izza, Esq; ✉ Chartered Accountants' Hall, Moorgate Place, London (☎ 020 7920 8100, website www.icaew.com)

J

JABALÉ, Rt Rev Mark; *see:* Menevia, Bishop of (RC)

JABBARI, David; *Educ* Univ of Warwick, Univ of Oxford; *Career* former global head of knowledge mgmnt Allen & Overy; Barlow Lyde & Gilbert: joined as ptnr and chief operating offr 2009, ceo 2010–11; ptnr and chief operating offr Clyde & Co 2011–12, ceo Connect2Law and head Pannone Affinity 2012–13, ptnr Parabis LLP 2013–; *Style*— David Jabbari, Esq; ✉ Parabis Group, Peninsular House, 30–36 Monument Street, London EC3R 8NB

JACK, Dominic; s of David William Jack, and Alison, *née* Aitken; *b* 2 April 1975, Edinburgh; *Educ* Telford Coll Edinburgh; *m* 24 June 2006, Francine, *née* Maitre; 2 s (Oscar *b* 1 Nov 2008, Ruben *b* 17 Jan 2013); *Career* formerly: Gleneagles Hotel, Fleur de Sel Haslemere, l'Arpège Paris, trainee rising to sous chef Hotel Vernet-restaurant Les Elysées Paris, sous chef de cuisine Taillevent Paris; chef de cuisine Swissôtel Istanbul 2005–08, The Kitchin Edinburgh 2008–10, chef patron Castle Terrace Restaurant Edinburgh 2010– (Michelin star 2012–); *Style*— Dominic Jack, Esq; ✉ Castle Terrace Restaurant, 33/35 Castle Terrace, Edinburgh EH1 2EL (Twitter @dominicjack)

JACK, Prof (James) Julian Bennett; *b* 25 March 1936; *Educ* Hamilton HS, Univ of Otago (MMedSc, PhD), Univ of Oxford (Rhodes scholar, BM, BCh); *Career* house offr Radcliffe Infirmary 1963–64; Univ of Oxford: fell, demonstrator, univ lectr, reader, prof 1968–2003, visiting prof Wolfson Inst UCL 2003–10, visiting prof Centre for Age Related Diseases KCL 2012–; Physiological Soc: memb ctee 1982–90 and 1998–2002 (treas 1986–90); memb cncl Action Research 1988–91; Wellcome Tst: govr 1987–2004, dep chm 1994–99; chm Sci Advsy Bd SYNTAXIN plc 2005–14; Hon DSc Univ of Otago 1999; FRS 1997, FMedSci 1998, FRCP 1999, Hon MRCP 1994; FRSNZ (Hon) 1999; *Style*— Prof Julian Jack, FRS; ✉ 24 Claylands Road, London SW8 1NZ (☎ 020 7582 3085, e-mail julian.jack@dpag.ox.ac.uk)

JACK, Rt Hon (John) Michael; CBE (2015), PC (1997); s of Ralph Niven, of York, and Florence Edith, *née* Reed; mother's family Hewish of Devon said to have arrived with William the Conqueror; *b* 17 September 1946; *Educ* Bradford GS, Bradford Tech Coll, Univ of Leicester (BA, MPhil); *m* 1976, Alison Jane, da of Cncllr Brian Rhodes Musgrave; 2 s (Edmund *b* 1979, Oliver *b* 1981); *Career* formerly with Marks & Spencer and Procter & Gamble, sales dir L O Jeffs Ltd 1980–87; Parly candidate Newcastle Central Feb 1974, MP (Cons) Fylde 1987–2010, PPS to Rt Hon John Gummer as min of state for local govt then for agric fisheries and food 1988–90, Parly under sec Dept of Social Security 1990–92, min of state Home Office 1992–93, min of state MAFF 1993–95, fin sec to the Treasy 1995–97, shadow min MAFF 1997–98; former chm: House of Commons Select Ctee for Environment Food and Rural Affrs (formerly Select Ctee on Agriculture) until 2005, Tax Law re-write Steering Ctee, 1922 Ctee 2000–03; jt sec Cons Tport Ctee 1987–88, chm Cons NW Membs Gp (sec 1988–90), vice-pres Think Green 1989–90; chm Topps Tiles plc 2011–; *Recreations* motor sport, dinghy sailing, growing vegetables, running, playing Boules; *Style*— The Rt Hon Michael Jack, CBE; ✉ Topps Tiles plc, Thorpe Way Grove Park, Leicester LE19 1SU

JACK, Prof Ronald Dyce Sadler; s of Muirice Jack (d 1982), of Ayr, and Edith Emily Sadler (d 1984); *b* 3 April 1941; *Educ* Ayr Acad, Univ of Glasgow (MA, DLitt), Univ of Edinburgh (PhD); *m* (Christabel) Kirsty Margaret, da of Rev Maj Angus Macdonald Nicolson, TD (d 1975), of Ayr; 2 da (Fiona *b* 1968, Isla *b* 1972); *Career* Dept of English Lit Univ of Edinburgh: lectr 1965, reader 1978, assoc dean 1971–73, prof of Scot and medieval lit 1987–2004, prof emeritus 2004–; visiting prof: Univ of Virginia 1973–74, Univ of Strathclyde 1993; Beinecke research fell Yale Univ 1992, visiting distinguished prof Univ of Connecticut 1998; memb Scot Consultative Ctee on the Curriculum 1987–89, dir UCAS (formerly UCCA) 1989–94; govr Newbattle Abbey Coll 1984–88; co-dir Bibliography of Scottish Literature in Translation 2002–05, convenor Patients' Cncl Royal Edinburgh Hosp 2011–; fell English Assoc (FEA), FRSE; *Books* The Italian Influence on Scottish Literature (1972), Scottish Prose 1550–1700 (ed, 1978), Choice of Scottish Verse 1560–1660 (ed, 1978), The Art of Robert Burns (co-ed, 1982), Alexander Montgomerie (1985), Scottish Literature's Debt to Italy (1986, 2 edn 2010), Patterns of Divine Comedy (1989), The Road to the Never Land (1991, 2 edn 2010), William Dunbar (1996), The Mercat Anthology of Early Scottish Literature (sr ed, 1997, revised edn 2000), New Oxford Dictionary of National Biography (assoc ed, 2004), Scotland in Europe (co-ed, 2006), Myths and the Mythmaker (2010), J M Barrie's Early Plays (2013), Stories of Changing Lives (ed, 2015); *Recreations* golf; *Style*— Prof Ronald Jack; ✉ 54 Buckstone Road, Edinburgh EH10 6UN (☎ 0131 445 3498, e-mail r.d.s.jack@ed.ac.uk)

JACK, His Hon Judge Simon Michael; s of Donald Fingland Jack (d 2003), and Hilary, *née* Gresham (d 2000); *b* 29 October 1951, Indore, India; *Educ* Winchester (scholar, head boy), Trinity Coll Cambridge (exhibitioner, BA); *m* (sep), Christine; 2 da (Kirsten Sarah *b* 8 July 1980, Zoë Alexandra *b* 5 Jan 1985), 1 s (Caspar Simon *b* 6 May 1982); partner, Sarah Fearon; *Career* called to the Bar Middle Temple 1974 (Harmsworth exhibitioner), practising barr 1975–2004, recorder 1996–2004 (asst recorder 1992–96), circuit judge (North Eastern Circuit) 2004–; memb of chambers: 37 Park Square Leeds 1975–82, 38 Park Square (later Pearl Chambers then 9 Woodhouse Square) Leeds 1982–2001, Zenith Chambers Leeds 2001–04; *Recreations* skiing, flying (private pilot), cycling, running, sailing; *Clubs* Barracuda Triathlon; *Style*— His Hon Judge Jack; ✉ Kingston upon Hull Combined Court Centre, Lowgate, Hull HU1 2EZ (☎ 01482 586161, fax 01482 588527, sjack@lix.co.uk)

JACK, Stephen Andrew; OBE (2014); s of John Jack (d 1993), and Winifred, *née* Hawkins; *b* 21 March 1958, Coleshill, Warks; *Educ* King's Sch Worcester, Univ of Durham (BA); *m* 5 June 1982, Ann Thimont; 3 da (Helen, Madeline, Isobel); *Career* Price Waterhouse 1981–84, Midland Bank 1984–86, Kleinwort Benson 1986–99, chief fin offr ING Barings 1999–2001, gp fin dir Tullett & Tokyo plc (latterly Collins Stewart Tullett plc) 2001–06, chief fin offr Straumur Investment Bank 2007–; treas Gtr London Fund For The Blind 2001–, tstee Independent Living Funds 2003– (chm 2007–); CA 1984; *Recreations* squash, football, long-distance walking, choral singing, cookery; *Style*— Stephen Jack, Esq, OBE; ✉ Straumur, 21 Sackville Street, London W1S 3DN (☎ 020 7297 0872, e-mail stephen.jack@straumur.net)

JACK, Dr Timothy Michael (Tim); s of Michael Henry Fingland Jack (d 1990), of Teignmouth, Devon, and Margaret Joyce, *née* Baker (d 1978); *b* 5 July 1947; *Educ* King Edward's Sch Birmingham, Guy's Hosp (MB BS); *m* 20 Oct 1979, (Veronica) Jane, da of Richard Christopher Warde (d 1953), of Orpington, Kent; 2 s (Benjamin *b* 1983, Jonathan *b* 1986);

Career anaesthetist Shanta Bhawan Hosp Kathmandu 1974–76, sr registrar Nuffield Dept of Anaesthetics Radcliffe Infirmary Oxford 1978–82, conslt anaesthetist Leeds Gen Infirmary and hon lectr Univ of Leeds 1982–90, conslt in pain relief and clinical dir Oxford Regnl Pain Relief Unit Oxford 1990–2007; chm Cancer Clinical Centre Oxford Radcliffe Hosp 1995–2001; memb: Exec Ctee Christian Med Fellowship 1987–95, Personnel Ctee Interserve (UK) 1978–98, Cncl The Pain Soc 1993–96; FRCA 1992, founding fell Faculty of Pain Med Royal Coll of Anaesthetists 2007; *Recreations* sailing, mountain walking, cycling, bird watching, very amateur archaeology and theology; *Style*— Dr Tim Jack; ✉ 46 Eaton Road, Appleton, Abingdon, Oxfordshire OX13 5JH (☎ 01865 864900)

JACKLIN, Walter William (Bill); s of Harold Jacklin (d 1964), of London, and Alice Mary, *née* Jones (d 1988); *b* 1 January 1943; *Educ* Walthamstow Sch of Art, Royal Coll of Art (MA, ARA); *m* 1, 1979 (m dis 1992), Lesley Sarina, da of Monty Berman; *m* 2, Janet Ann, da of Frank Russo; *Career* artist; teaching at various art colls 1967–75, artist in residence Br Cncl Hong Kong 1993–94; RA 1991; *Solo Exhibitions* Nigel Greenwood Inc London 1970, 1971 and 1975, Hester Van Royen Gallery London 1973 and 1977, Marlborough Fine Art London 1980, 1983, 1988, 1992, 1997, 2000, 2004, 2008, 2013 and 2016, Marlborough Gallery New York 1985, 1987, 1990, 1997, 1999, 2002, 2003, 2007, 2012 and 2014, Urban Portraits 1985–99 (retrospective, MOMA Oxford 1992, touring to Santiago Compostela Spain 1992–93), Urban Portraits Hong Kong (British Cncl, Hong Kong Arts Centre) 1995, L'Ecole de Londres Musée Maillol Paris 1998–99, Univ Gall Newcastle 2008, Marlborough Monaco 2009, Marlborough Fine Art London 2016, Bill Jacklin RA, a survey of graphic work 1961–2016 RA 2016; included in numerous int gp exhibitions; *Work in Public Collections* Arts Cncl of GB, Br Cncl London, Br Museum, Govt Arts Collection GB, Metropolitan Museum of Art NY, Museum of Modern Art NY, Tate Gallery, V&A, Yale Center for Br Art; *Books* Monograph on Bill Jacklin (by John Russell-Taylor, 1997), Bill Jacklin's New York: New York Paintings 1985–2015 (monograph, foreword by Sting, interview by Michael Peppiatt 2016), Bill Jacklin Graphics 1961–2016 (monograph, introduction by Jill Lloyd, essay by Nancy Campbell 2016); *Recreations* walking, planting trees, yoga; *Clubs* Chelsea Arts; *Style*— Bill Jacklin, Esq, RA; ✉ c/o Marlborough Fine Art, 6 Albermarle Street, London W1 (☎ 020 7629 5161)

JACKMAN, Frederick Charles; s of Stanley Charles Jackman (d 1978), of Brentwood, Essex, and Lilian May, *née* Brassett (d 1991); *b* 29 February 1944; *Educ* Warren Sch Dagenham, Barking Coll of Technol, Borough Poly (HNC); *m* 14 June 1969, Zarene, da of Karim Gulam Husain (d 1973), of London; *Career* Stinton Jones & Ptnrs 1960–64, Costain Construction 1964–66, T P Bennett & Son 1966–69, Arup Assocs 1969–73, Upton Associates bldg servs consulting engrs 1973– (resident Dubai 1976, sr ptnr 1979–, Malaysia 1991); conslt to Scott Wilson Consulting Engrs 2007–11, dir Jackman Consultancy Ltd 2011–; memb Soc of Light and Lighting (MSLL); CEng, FCIBSE, FIHEEM; *Recreations* travel, walking, fishing; *Style*— Frederick Jackman, Esq; ✉ New House, Holyport Road, Maidenhead, Berkshire SL6 2EY; (☎ 07801 457360, e-mail fred.jackman@aecom.com)

JACKSON, Alison Mary; da of George Hulbert Mowbray Jackson, and Catherine Mary, *née* Harvey Kelly; *b* 15 May 1960; *Educ* Chelsea Coll of Art, RCA; *Career* artist, photographer, film maker; ambass Spinal Injuries Assoc; *Exhibitions* incl: Richard Salmon Gallery London 1999, 2000 and 2003, Art London 2000, Jerwood Space London 2001, La Musée de la Photographie à Charleroi Brussels 2002, Paris Photo (Louvre Paris) 2002–05, Le Musée de la Photo Montreal 2003, Int Center of Photography (ICP) NY 2003, Photo London 2004, Hayward Gallery London 2004, Julie Saul Gallery NY 2005, Kundst Forum Vienna 2005–06, M&B Gallery LA 2007, Hamiltons Gallery London 2008, Liverpool Biennial Tate 2008, Voyeurism (San Francisco Museum of Mordern Art and Tate) 2009 and (Pompedou Centre) 2014; *Television* DoubleTake (BBC2) 2001–03, Saturday Night Live USA 2004–05, The Royal Wedding (Channel 4) 2005, The Secret Election 2005, Tony Blair Rock Star 2005, Sven – The Coach, the Cash and his Lovers 2006, Blaired Vision (Channel 4) 2007, The South Bank Show, Alison Jackson on Andy Warhol (ITV) 2009, Celebrity Bitch Slap News (BBC 3) 2012; *Advertising* Schweppes Campaign 2001–03 and 2007; *Awards* Photographers' Gallery Award 1999, BAFTA Award for Innovation (for DoubleTake) 2002; for Schweppes: Creative Circle Award 2002, Campaign Awards 2002, Best of the Best Award IPA 2002 and 2003, Int Center of Photography Infinity Award 2004; *Publications* Private- Photographs (2003), Taschen – Photographs (2007), Stern Photographs (2013); *Recreations* tennis, cycling; *Style*— Alison Jackson; ✉ c/o Kevin Cooper, CAA, 2000 Avenue of the Stars, Los Angeles, CA 90212, USA (☎ 001 424 2884545)

JACKSON, Andrew Malcolm; s of Douglas MacGilchrist Jackson (decd), of Milford on Sea, Hants, and Mabel Pauline, *née* Brand; *b* 4 May 1945; *Educ* Marlborough, Middx Hosp Med Sch Univ of London (MB BS); *m* Anne Marie, da of Joseph Lucas, of Silksworth, Sunderland; 2 s (Charles *b* 1979, Adam Stuart *b* 1981); *Career* conslt orthopaedic surgn: UCH 1981–91, Hosp for Sick Children Gt Ormond St 1981–91, Queen Mary's Univ Hosp Roehampton 1991–94, St George's Hosp 1994–2001, King Edward VII Hosp 2000–; hon conslt Royal Nat Orthopaedic Hosp 1983; Freeman City of London 1981, Liveryman Worshipful Soc of Apothecaries; memb RSM, FRCS 1979; *Recreations* sailing, fishing; *Style*— Andrew Jackson, Esq; ✉ 107 Harley Street, London W1G 6AL (☎ 020 7935 9521, fax 020 7486 0956)

JACKSON, Ashley Norman; s of Norman Valentine Jackson (POW Malaya, executed 1944/45), and Dulcie Olga, *née* Scott (Mrs Haigh); *b* 22 October 1940; *Educ* St Joseph's Singapore, Holyrood Barnsley, Barnsley Coll of Art; *m* 22 Dec 1962, (Patricia) Anne, da of Donald Hutchinson, of Barnsley, S Yorks; 2 da (Heather *b* 11 Nov 1968, Claudia *b* 15 Sept 1970); *Career* artist; exhibited: RI, RBA, RWS, Britain in Watercolour, UA; one man shows: Upper Grosvenor Gallery, Mall Gallery, Christina Foyle Gallery, Spanish Inst of Culture, London, New York, Chicago, San Francisco, Washington, Dallas, one-man exhibition in Huddersfield opened by HRH The Prince of Wales 1987, Huddersfield Art Gallery 1990, My Way – Art to the People (Rotherham Art Gallery) 1994, My Mistress and I – The Yorkshire Moors (touring) 1995, Here's to You, Dad (touring) 1995, From Yorkshire...with Love (touring) 1996, Earth, Wind and Fire (Salford Art Gallery) 1997, Twilight of the Twentieth Century (Cartwright Hall Bradford) 2000, Dawn's a New Day (Royal Armouries Leeds) 2000, Victoria Quarter Leeds 2002, Ashley Jackson's Yorkshire

Moors: A Love Affair (Int Yorks Business Convention) 2003, Painting in the Open Air (Laing Gallery Newcastle) 2008, The Power and the Passion – Ashley Jackson's Yorkshire Love Affair (Mall Galleries) 2010 and (Temple Newsam) 2010–11; works in the collections of: MOD, RN, NCB, British Gas, NUM, NATO HQ Brussels (original of The Day the World Changed – September 11th 2001) late Harold Wilson, Edward Heath, John Major, Pres Bill Clinton, Rudi Giuliani, George Robertson (Rt Hon Lord Robertson of Port Ellen); train named Ashley Jackson – The Yorkshire Artist with carriages containing paintings 2010; own TV series on: Yorkshire TV (A Brush with Ashley 1990, 1992, 1993, 1994, 1995, 1997, 1998, 1999 and 2000, A View with Ashley 1997 and 1998, In A Different Light 2001), BBC1, Channel 4 and PBS in America; vice-pres Yorkshire Soc; Yorks Arts Personality of the Year 1996, Lifetime Achievement Award Yorks Awards 2006, Lifetime Achievement Award Huddersfield Examiner 2007, memb Hall of Fame Yorks Icons Award 2008, Yorks Man of the Year Dalesman Rural Award 2009; Freeman City of London 2005; hon doctorate Univ of Huddersfield 2013; FRSA 1964; *Books* My Own Flesh and Blood (1981), The Artist's Notebook (1985), Ashley Jackson's World of Art 1 and 2 (1988), Painting in the Open Air (1992), A Brush With Ashley (1993), Painting the British Isles – a watercolourist's journey (1994), Ashley Jackson's Yorkshire Moors – a love affair (2000), 50 Golden Years with my Mistress and I – Yorkshire (2006), Ashley Jackson – an artist's life (biography by Chris Bond, 2010), My Yorkshire Sketchbook (2012); *Style*— Ashley Jackson, Esq; ✉ Ashley Jackson Galleries, 13–15 Huddersfield Road, Holmfirth, Huddersfield HD9 2JR (✆ 01484 686460, fax 01484 681766, e-mail ashley@ashley-jackson.co.uk, website www.ashley-jackson.co.uk)

JACKSON, Prof Bernard Stuart; s of Leslie Jackson (d 1989), of Liverpool, and Isabelle, *née* Caplan (d 1944); *b* 16 November 1944; *Educ* Liverpool Collegiate Sch, Univ of Liverpool (LLB), Univ of Oxford (DPhil), Univ of Edinburgh (LLD); *m* 1967, Rosalyn, *née* Young; 1 s (Iain Charles b 1970), 1 da (Judith Deborah b 1973); *Career* called to the Bar Gray's Inn 1966; lectr Dept of Civil Law Univ of Edinburgh 1969–76, princ lectr Div of Law Preston Poly 1976, prof of law Liverpool Poly 1980–85 (head Dept of Law 1977–85), prof of law Univ of Kent at Canterbury 1985–89, Queen Victoria prof of law Univ of Liverpool 1989–97, Alliance prof of modern Jewish studies and co-dir Centre for Jewish Studies Univ of Manchester 1997–2009, prof of law and Jewish studies Liverpool Hope Univ 2009–15; sr assoc fell Oxford Centre for Hebrew and Jewish Studies 1984–, pres The Jewish Law Assoc 1984–88 (chm 1980–84 and 2008–14), sec-gen and treas Int Assoc for the Semiotics of Law 1987–93, chm BILETA Inquiry into Computer Provision in UK Law Schs 1989–91, pres Br Assoc for Jewish Studies 1993; memb Editorial Bd: Archivos Latinoamericanos de Metodologia y Filosofia, Int Jl for the Semiotics of Law, International Jl of the Legal Profession, Zeitschrift für altorientalische und biblische Rechtsgeschichte, Law and Critique, Liverpool Law Review, Legal Ethics, Res Publica, Semiotic Crossroads; ed The Jewish Law Annual 1978–97; memb: Conseil d'administration Association Européenne pour la philosophie du droit 1989–2000, Soc for Old Testament Study 1974–, Br Assoc for Jewish Studies 1974–, Société d'Histoire du Droit 1975–, Soc for the Study of Theology 1976–, Mgmnt Ctee Nat Centre for Cued Speech 1985–89, Mgmnt Ctee UK Law Tech Centre 1989–92, Northern Circuit Ctee on Computer Support for Litigation 1991, Lord Chllr's Area Criminal Justice Advsy Ctee 1992–97, Liverpool Branch Soc for Computers and Law, Academic Advsy Bd Jews' Coll 1996–99; visiting appts: visiting asst prof Univ of Georgia Law Sch 1968–69, assoc fell Oxford Centre for Postgrad Hebrew Studies 1974 (Littman fell 1977), Br Cncl lectr Univ of Rotterdam and Univ of Amsterdam 1975, faculty lectr Faculty of Theology Univ Coll of N Wales 1980, Lady Davis visiting prof Dept of Bible Hebrew Univ of Jerusalem 1981, speaker's lectr in Biblical studies Univ of Oxford 1984–86, professeur invité Université de Paris-X Nanterre 1987–88, professore a contratto Università di Bologna 1988, Caroline and Joseph Gruss visiting prof in Talmudic legal studies Harvard Law Sch 1992, Gastprofessor Rechtstheorie Katholieke Universitet Brussels 1992–93 and 1994–2008, assoc prof University of Paris I (Panthéon-Sorbonne) 1994, professeur associé Université de Genève 2002; hon fell Soc for Advanced Legal Studies 1997–; DHL (hc) Hebrew Union Coll Jewish Inst of Religion 1998; *Books* Theft in Early Jewish Law (1972), Essays in Jewish and Comparative Legal History (1975), Semiotics and Legal Theory (1985), Law, Fact and Narrative Coherence (1988), Making Sense in Law (1995), Making Sense in Jurisprudence (1996), Studies in the Semiotics of Biblical Law (2000), Wisdom-Laws: A Study of the Mishpatim of Exodus 21:1–22:16 (2006), Essays on Halakhah in the New Testament (2008), Agunah: The Manchester Analysis (2011); ed of numerous legal books and jls; *Style*— Prof Bernard Jackson; ✉ e-mail jacksob@hope.ac.uk

JACKSON, Betty (Mrs David Cohen); CBE (2007, MBE 1987); da of Arthur Jackson (d 1977), and Phyllis Gertrude, *née* Rains (d 1983); *b* 24 June 1949; *Educ* Bacup and Rawtenstall GS, Birmingham Coll Art and Design; *m* 14 Jan 1986, David Cohen, s of Mansour Cohen (d 1977), of Marseille, France; 1 da (Pascale Phyllis b 1985), 1 s (Oliver Mansour b 1986); *Career* chief designer Quorum 1975, fndr Betty Jackson Ltd 1981, launched Betty Jackson for Men 1986; visiting prof RCA 1998; Cotton Designer of the Year 1983, Br Designer of the Year 1985, Fil D'Or award by International Linen 1985 and 1989, Viyella award by Coates Viyella 1987, Contemporary Designer of the Year 1999; tstee V&A 2005, memb Bd Skillset 2011; hon fell: Univ of Birmingham 1988, RCA 1989 (memb Cncl 2008), Univ of Central Lancashire 1992; Hon Dr Univ of Huddersfield 2011; RDI 1988, Master Faculty of RDIs RSA 2015–17; *Clubs* Groucho, Soho House; *Style*— Miss Betty Jackson, CBE; ✉ Betty Jackson Ltd, 30 Ashchurch Park Villas, London W12 9SP (✆ 020 8354 0145, e-mail betty@bettyjackson.com, website www.bettyjackson.com)

JACKSON, Bryan Alan; s of Michael Jackson, and Mildred, *née* Segal; *b* 26 February 1956; *Educ* Hutchesons GS, Glasgow Coll of Technol (Scottish HND in Accountancy); *m* 12 Aug 1980, Frances Lauren, da of Ronnie Freedman; 3 da (Leigh Sarah b 28 Jan 1982, Dawn Michele b 24 March 1985, Kara Nicole b 3 Aug 1987); *Career* articled clerk Ernst and Whinney Glasgow 1977–81; Pannell Kerr Forster: insolvency mangr 1981–85, ptnr (insolvency) 1985–94, managing ptnr 1995–, sr ptnr 2006–; lectr ICAS, spokesperson in insolvency to media, speaker on insolvency to professionals, govt agencies, Fraud Squad, Consumer Credit Assoc and debt counselling bodies; appointed on Motherwell, Clyde and Clydebank football clubs 2003–06; examiner in Scotland of the personal insolvency paper for the Jt Insolvency Examinations; treas Children's Aid (Scotland) Ltd; MICAS 1981; memb: Inst of Credit Mgmnt 1989, Insolvency Practitioners' Assoc 1989, Soc of Practitioners of Insolvency 1992; fell Assoc of Business Recoveries Specialists 2000; *Recreations* squash (rep GB Maccabiah Games Israel 1993, rep Scotland (silver medal) Euro Maccabi Games 1995), karate, skiing, football; *Style*— Bryan Jackson, Esq; ✉ PKF, 78 Carlton Place, Glasgow G5 9TH (✆ 0141 429 5900, fax 0141 429 5901, mobile 07802 470 478)

JACKSON, Calvin Leigh Raphael; s of late Air Cdre John Arthur George Jackson, CBE, DFC, AFC, and Yolanda, *née* de Felice; *b* 13 August 1952; *Educ* Douai Sch, KCL (LLB, LLM), CCC Cambridge (MPhil), Inst of Advanced Studies (IALS) Sch of Advanced Study London Univ (LLM); *m* 14 Aug 1993, Caroline Mary, da of late Colin Herbert Clout; *Career* called to the Bar Lincoln's Inn 1975; in practice 1981–83, legal asst Office of the Dir of Public Prosecutions 1983–85, sr compensation conslt William M Mercer Ltd 1985–87, princ Coopers & Lybrand 1987–92, dir Consulting Services Towers Watson 1992–2010, in practice at Bar 2011–; memb: Hon Soc of Lincoln's Inn, Worshipful Co of Clockmakers; *Clubs* Oxford and Cambridge; *Style*— Calvin Jackson, Esq; ✉ Charter Chambers, 33 John Street, London WC1N 2AT (✆ 020 7618 4400)

JACKSON, Dr Caroline Frances; *b* 5 November 1946; *Educ* Sch of St Clare Penzance, St Hugh's Coll Oxford (MA), Nuffield Coll Oxford (DPhil); *m* 1975, Robert Victor Jackson (MP for Wantage 1983–2005); 1 s (decd); *Career* res fell St Hugh's Coll 1972, memb Oxford City Cncl 1970–73, Parly candidate (Cons) Birmingham Erdington 1974; MEP (Cons): Wilts 1984–94, Wilts N and Bath 1994–99, SW England 1999–2009; dep chm Cons MEPs 1997–99, chm European Parl Ctee on Environment, Consumer Protection and Public Health 1999–2004; chm Inst European Environment Policy 2006–10, pres Environmental Protection UK 2010–12; dir Peugeot UK Ltd 1987–99; memb Nat Consumer Cncl 1982–84; *Books* A Student's Guide to Europe (1985 and 1996), Europe's Environment: A Conservative Approach (1989), The End of the Throwaway Society (1998), Playing by the Green Rules (2000), Britain's Waste: The lessons we can learn from Europe (2006), EU Waste Law: the Challenge of Better Compliance (2012), The Diaries of Captain James Primrose 1851–53 (ed, 2016); *Recreations* golf, gardening, painting; *Style*— Dr Caroline Jackson; ✉ New House, Hanney Road, Southmoor OX13 5HR (website www.drcarolinejackson.com, email contactcfjackson@gmail.com)

JACKSON, Charles Vivian; s of Louis Charles Jackson, MC (d 2009), and Sylvia, *née* Kerr; *b* 2 July 1953, Kanpur, India; *Educ* Marlborough (scholar), Magdalen Coll Oxford (exhibitioner, MA), Stanford Univ (Arjay Miller scholar, Alexander Robichek Finance Prize, MBA); *m* 12 Feb 1982, Frances Miriam, da of Frederick Schwartzstein (d 1982), of NJ; 1 da (Rebecca (Viscountess Glenapp) b 1983), 1 s (David b 1985); *Career* Charter Consolidated 1974–76, Harkness fell 1976–78, NM Rothschild 1978–81, vice-pres Citibank 1981–85, md Mercury Asset Management Holdings 1987–90, dep chm Warburg Asset Management 1988–95, vice-chm Mercury Asset Management plc 1993–98, md Merrill Lynch Mercury Asset Management 1998–2000; dir: Warburg Investment Management 1985–87, Mercury Bond Fund 1985–98, Munich London 1986–90, Warburg Asset Management 1988–95, Mercury Asset Management plc 1990–98, Mercury Asset Management Group plc 1993–98, Govett European Enhanced Investment Tst 2003–04, Lux-Fix Ltd 2011–13; sec Projects Ctee Nat Art Collections Fund 1979–84; hon treas Action Med Research 2009– (tstee 2006–); jt vice-chm Cncl Univ of Buckingham 2015– (memb 2011–); *Publications* Active Investment Management (2003), Whither Active Management? (2005), Saving Savings: How to Promote Personal Investment (2005), Can alignment of active manager and investor interests ever be aligned? (2013); *Clubs* Brooks's; *Style*— Charles Jackson, Esq; ✉ Cottisford House, Brackley, Northamptonshire NN13 5SW (✆ 01280 847675)

JACKSON, Christopher Murray; s of Rev Howard Murray Jackson (d 1955), and Doris Bessie Jackson (d 1995); *b* 24 May 1935, Norwich; *Educ* Kingswood Sch Bath, Magdalen Coll Oxford (MA), Univ of Frankfurt, LSE; *m* 1971, Carlie Elizabeth, da of Bernard Sidney Keeling; 1 s (David Bernard Murray Jackson b 30 Oct 1972), 1 da (Catherine Anna Helen Jackson (Mrs Ivory) b 30 Nov 1974); *Career* Nat Serv cmmnd Pilot RAF; former: dir of corp devpt Spillers plc, sr mangr Unilever plc; parly candidate (Cons) E Ham S 1970 and Northants N 1974, MEP (Cons) Kent E 1979–94, Hon MEP 1994–; Cons Pty spokesman on: co-operation with developing countries 1981–86, agric 1987–89, foreign affrs and defence 1991, economics and monetary affrs and industrial policy 1992–94; dep chm and dep ldr Cons MEPs 1989–91; memb Cons Nat Union Exec 1995–98; dir: Westminster Communications Ltd 1988–95, Politics International Ltd 1995–98, David Jackson Consulting Ltd 2011–13; ptnr Christopher Jackson Associates 1994–; dir and chm European Broadcasting Network plc 1997–2001, dir CJA Consultants Ltd 1995–2015 (chm 1995–2003), dir and chm Natural Resources International Ltd 1997–2003; nat chm Cons Countryside Forum 1995–98; govr Ashford Sch 1998–2001, memb Cncl Bethany Sch Ltd 2009– (chm 1999–2009); memb RIIA (Chatham House) 1995–; *Books* Europe and the Third World (1985), Shaking the Foundations – Britain and the New Europe (1990), Your Watchdogs in Europe (1990), Careers in Europe (2 edn, 1991), The Maastricht Summit (with B Patterson, 1992), Whose Job Is It Anyway? – Subsidiarity in the EC (1992), Future of Industrial Property Rights in the European Union (ed, 1997), EU Referendum: Both Sides of the Coin. Arguments for and against UK membership of the EU (with B Patterson, 2016); *Recreations* music, tennis, travel, sailing, reading, opera, gardening, walking; *Clubs* Athenaeum, Rye Lawn Tennis; *Style*— Christopher Jackson, Hon MEP; ✉ Flackley Ash Farmhouse, Peasmarsh, Rye, East Sussex TN31 6TB (e-mail flackley.ash2@btinternet.com)

JACKSON, David John; *b* 25 January 1953; *Educ* Univ of Bristol (LLB); *Career* articled clerk Grey Lloyd & Co slrs 1975–77, asst slr Barlow Lyde and Gilbert 1977–79, slr The Nestlé Company Ltd 1979–81, asst gp legal advsr Chloride Group plc 1981–87, head of legal Matthew Hall plc 1987–89, gen counsel and co sec PowerGen plc 1989–2002, co sec BP plc 2003–;; *Recreations* rugby, tennis, sailing; *Clubs* Royal Ocean Racing, Seaview Yacht, Harlequins FC; *Style*— David Jackson, Esq

JACKSON, Prof Emily; da of Douglas Jackson, of Watford, Herts, and Lesley Jackson (d 1983); *b* 28 December 1966, London; *Educ* Univ of Oxford (MA); *Career* fell and lectr St Catharine's Coll Cambridge 1991–93, lectr Birkbeck Coll London 1993–98, sr lectr LSE 1998–2004, prof of medical law Queen Mary Univ of London 2004–07, prof of law LSE 2007–; judicial appointments cmmr 2014–; dep chair HFEA 2008–12; memb: Medical Ethics Ctee BMA, Regulation and Public Involvement Ctee MRC; *Publications* Regulating Reproduction (2001, Prize for Outstanding Legal Scholarship Soc for Legal Scholars 2002), Medical Law (2006, 4 edn 2016), Debating Euthanasia (2011), Law and the Regulation of Medicines (2012); *Style*— Prof Emily Jackson; ✉ Law Department, London School of Economics, Houghton Street, London WC2A 2AE

JACKSON, Glenda; CBE (1978); *b* 9 May 1936; *Educ* West Kirby Co GS for Girls, RADA; *Career* actress, former memb RSC; MP (Lab) Hampstead and Highgate 1992–2015; oppn spokesperson on tport 1996–97, Parly under sec of state DETR 1997–99; memb GLA Advsy Cabinet on Homelessness 2000; stood for mayor of London 2000; assoc memb RADA; *Theatre* incl: Marat/Sade 1966 (nominated Tony Award Best Supporting Actress), Rose 1981 (nominated Tony Award Best Actress), Strange Interlude 1985 (nominated Tony Award Best Actress), Macbeth 1988 (nominated Tony Award Best Actress); *Television* incl: Howards End 1970, Elizabeth R 1971, Strange Interlude 1988, A Murder of Quality 1991, The House of Bernarda Alba 1991, The Secret Life of Arnold Bax 1992, A Wave of Passion 1994; *Films* incl: Marat/Sade 1967, Women In Love 1969 (Oscar Best Actress), Mary, Queen of Scots 1971, Sunday Bloody Sunday 1971, A Bequest to the Nation 1973, A Touch of Class 1973 (Oscar Best Actress), Hedda 1975, Nasty Habits 1977, Stevie 1978, Lost and Found 1979, The Return of the Soldier 1982, Salome's Last Dance 1988, The Rainbow 1989; *Style*— Ms Glenda Jackson, CBE; ✉ House of Commons, London SW1A 0AA

JACKSON, Jane Therese (Tessa); OBE (2011); *b* 5 November 1955; *Educ* Univ of E Anglia (BA), Univ of Manchester (Dip Museum Studies), Univ of Bristol (MA); *Career* museum asst Art Dept Castle Museum Norwich 1977–78, art ed Oxford University Press 1978–80, exhbns organiser Soc for the Protection of Ancient Bldgs London 1981–82, curator Eyemouth Museum Berwickshire 1982, curator Collins Gallery Univ of Strathclyde Glasgow 1982–88, seconded as visual arts offr Glasgow 1990 1988–91, dir Arnolfini Bristol 1991–99; dir Scottish Arts Cncl 1999–2001, conslt Int Cultural Devpt 2001–, founding artistic dir and chief exec Artes Mundi Prize 2002–10, chair Edinburgh Art Festival 2005–10, chief exec Inst of Int Visual Arts (INIVA) 2009–15, ind conslt Int Cultural Devpt 2015–; tstee: Centre for Chinese Contemporary Art 2015–, Spike Island 2016–; FRSA; *Style*— Ms Tessa Jackson, OBE; ✉ e-mail tessajackson@aol.com

JACKSON, Joanne; da of Barry Jackson, and Gill, *née* Simpson; *b* 12 September 1986, Northallerton, Yorks; *Career* swimmer; debut GB jr squad 2001, debut GB sr squad 2003; achievements incl: Gold medal 400m freestyle (short course) European Championships 2003 (Silver medal 2005), Silver medal 400m freestyle (short course) World Cup 2003 (Bronze medal 2008), competed Olympic Games Athens 2004, Gold medals 200m freestyle and 400 m freestyle Br Championships 2006 (Silver medals 200m and 400m freestyle 2008), Silver medal 400m freestyle (long course) European Championships 2006 (Silver medal 4 x 200m relay 2008), Silver medals 400m freestyle and 4 x 200m freestyle relay Cwlth Games Melbourne 2006, Bronze medal 400m freestyle Olympic Games Beijing 2008, world record 400 freestyle 2009; *Style*— Ms Joanne Jackson; ✉ 2 Beechfield, Richmond, North Yorkshire DL10 4PN (e-mail joannejackson86@hotmail.com)

JACKSON, Kenneth A; *Educ* Cannock HS, Birmingham Coll of Commerce; *Career* trained with Cannock Advertiser and Northern Mail, asst news ed The Journal Newcastle on Tyne 1962–64, business desk Express & Star Wolverhampton 1964–66, dep business ed/property ed Birmingham Post 1966–68, PR mangr Reliant Motor Company 1968–70, industrial ed/property ed Birmingham Evening Mail 1970–77; Tarmac plc: divnl mktg advsr Housing Div 1977–80, gp press advsr 1980–83, head of press and public affrs 1983–90 (led Tarmac's successful Channel Tunnel PR and mktg campaign), dir of corp affrs 1990–93; fndr Jackson-Brown & Associates media rels, public rels and corp affrs conslts 1993– (appointed conslt to Govt Inner Cities Initiative, Wolverhampton City Challenge, DOE Award for best City Challenge community newspaper in GB 1994 and 1997); chm Community Forum to Fight Drugs Abuse; audit chair (non-exec) Cannock Chase PCT 1999; chm Chase Voluntary Services; fndr memb: Wolverhampton Business Initiative, Partners in Progress; involved in various charity work; patients ambass Patients Assoc 2011; FRSA, FCIPR; *Clubs* Birmingham Press; *Style*— Kenneth A Jackson, Esq; ✉ Sandy Leys Farm, Sandon, Stafford, Staffordshire ST18 0D2 (☎ 01889 508552)

JACKSON, Kenneth (Ken); s of Joseph Henry Jackson (d 1965), of Dewsbury, and Ada, *née* Smith (d 1981); *b* 23 September 1939; *Educ* Dewsbury Wheelwright GS, Batley Tech and Art Coll, Harvard Business Sch; *m* 25 Aug 1962, Elisabeth Joyce, da of David William Wilks (d 1975), of Dewsbury; 1 s ((Stephen) David b 8 Feb 1970); *Career* md Spencer & Halstead Ltd 1971 (personnel dir 1968–); vice-pres Bonded Abrasives Europe Carborundum & Co USA 1978, vice-pres (sales and mktg) Abrasives Carborundum Div Sohio 1981, gp md Carborundum Abrasives plc (became Carbo plc 1984), chief exec Carbo plc (formerly The Hopkinsons Gp plc) 1993–2002; non-exec chm: Ring plc 1997–2000, PMGroup plc 2002–06; non-exec dir: Nightfreight plc 1996–2000, Kelda Gp plc 2000–05; *Recreations* travel, gardening; *Style*— Ken Jackson, Esq; ✉ Savile Ings Farm, Holywell Green, Halifax, West Yorkshire HX4 9BS (☎ 01422 372608, fax 01422 313470, e-mail kenjsavileings@btinternet.com)

JACKSON, Len; OBE (2002); s of Eric Jackson (d 1981), and Katherine Jackson (d 1951); *b* 17 December 1948, Salford, Lancs; *m* Sept 1981, Angela Bayliss; 1 da (Elizabeth b Jan 1989); partner, Diana; 1 adopted s (Shaun b Oct 1975), 1 adopted da (Samantha b April 1978); *Career* md: Bowyers 1990–94, Pork Farms/Bowyers 1994–99, Amelca plc 2000–02; dep chair Ind Police Complaints Cmmn 2008–; memb Bd E Midlands Regnl Devpt Agency 1999–2001, chair E Midlands Regnl Sports Bd 2002–; chair: Nottingham Common Purpose 1994–98, Race for Opportunity E Midlands 1995–98, New Deal Employer Coalition 1997–98; chm East Bridgford Drama Gp; *Recreations* theatre, sport, bridge; *Style*— Len Jackson, Esq, OBE; ✉ IPCC, Independent House, Whitwick Business Park, Stenson Road, Coalville, Leicestershire LE67 4JP (☎ 01530 258751)

JACKSON, Dr Michael; s of Stanley Jackson, and Maisie Joan Jackson; *b* 12 March 1948; *Educ* St Nicholas GS Northwood, Univ of Salford (BSc); *m* 1, 21 July 1973, Jacqueline Yvonne Doreen, da of Jesse Hudson; 1 s (Robert b 5 May 1976), 1 da (Helen Sara b 17 Oct 1978); m 2, 12 Aug 2001, Lynn Susan Killion, da of Arthur Price; *Career* industrial engr Hawker Siddeley 1970–73, fin controller Citibank NA 1975–76 (expense controller 1973–75), chief of staff Citifin Finanziaria 1976–82, consumer banking dir Citibank Savings 1985–86 (customer servs dir 1982–85), head of EMEA ops Bank of America 1988–90 (head of consumer loans 1986–88), chief exec Birmingham Midshires Building Society 1990–98, chm Results Plus Ltd 1998–2005, md Salans 2003–05, fndr, ambass and past chm Shaping Tomorrow Ltd 2003–; non-exec dir Galliford Try plc 1997–2004; Hon DBA Univ of Wolverhampton 1997; FMS 1989, FRSA 1991, CIMgt 1993, FCIB 1994, FInstD 1995; *Books* Practical Foresight Guide (2011); *Recreations* model making, music, sport; *Clubs* Stafford; *Style*— Dr Michael Jackson; ✉ mobile 07966 155912, e-mail mike.jackson@shapingtomorrow.com

JACKSON, Gen Sir Michael David (Mike); GCB (2005, KCB 1998, CB 1996), CBE (1992, MBE 1979), DSO (1999), DL (2007); s of Maj George Michael Jackson (d 1982), of Camberley, Surrey, and Ivy, *née* Bower; *b* 21 March 1944; *Educ* Stamford Sch, RMA Sandhurst, Univ of Birmingham (BSocSc); *m* 2, 4 May 1985, Sarah Carolyn, da of Col Brian Jackson Coombe, GM; 2 s (Mark b 1973, Thomas b 1990), 1 da (Amanda b 1971); *Career* chief of staff Berlin Inf Bde 1977–78, Co Cdr 2 Para 1979–80, directing staff Staff Coll 1981–83, CO 1 Para 1984–86, sr directing staff Jt Serv Def Coll 1986–88, serv fell Wolfson Coll Cambridge 1989, Cdr 39 Inf Bde 1989–92, DG Personal Servs (Army) 1992–93, GOC 3 (UK) Div 1994–96, Cdr Multi-national Div South West (Bosnia) 1996, DG Development and Doctrine 1996–97, Cdr Allied Command Europe Rapid Reaction Corps 1997–2000, Cdr NATO Forces in Macedonia and Kosovo (KFOR) 1999, C-in-C UK Land Command 2000–03, CGS 2003–06; ADC Gen to HM The Queen 2001–06; dep chm Longhorn Ltd, dir ForceSelect; sr advsr PA Consulting Gp 2007–; Hon Dr: Univ of Birmingham, Univ of Sheffield; Freeman City of London 1988; *Books* Central Region vs Out-of-Area: Future Commitments (contrib, 1990), Soldier: The Autobiography (2007); *Recreations* skiing, tennis, music; *Clubs* Garrick, Bucks, St Moritz Tobogganing; *Style*— Gen Sir Mike Jackson, GCB, CBE, DSO, DL; ✉ c/o RHQ Para Regt, Merville Barracks, Colchester, Essex CO2 7UT

JACKSON, Michael Edward Wilson; s of Sqdn Ldr Edward Grosvenor Jackson, of East Rigton, N Yorks, and Yvonne Brenda Jackson, OBE, *née* Wilson; *b* 16 March 1950; *Educ* The Leys Sch, Univ of Cambridge (LLB); *m* 1, 19 April 1980 (m dis), Prudence Elizabeth Robinson, da of Michael John Boardman, of White Howe, Norfolk; m 2, 18 Nov 1989, Harriet Leigh, da of Air Cdre Denis Wilson; *Career* dir The Guidehouse Group plc 1983–90; chm: Elderstreet Investments Ltd 1990– (also fndr), Sage Group plc 2000–06 (dir 1984–2006), Party Gaming 2005–09, Access Intelligence plc, Netcall plc, Snacktime plc; FCA 1976; *Recreations* tennis; *Clubs* RAC, Annabel's; *Style*— Michael Jackson, Esq; ✉ Elderstreet Investments Ltd, 32 Bedford Row, London WC1R 4HE (☎ 020 7831 5088)

JACKSON, Most Rev Dr Michael Geoffrey St Aubyn; *see:* Dublin, Archbishop of

JACKSON, Michael Richard; s of Ernest Jackson, and Margaret, *née* Kearsley; *b* 11 February 1958; *Educ* King's Sch Macclesfield, Poly of Central London (BA); *Career* organiser Channel Four Gp (pressure gp campaigning for independent access to fourth channel) 1979–81, freelance prodr 1981–82, fndr Beat Productions (progs for C4 incl The Media Show, Open the Box and Whose Town Is It Anyway?) 1983–87; BBC Television: joined 1987, ed The Late Show BBC2 1988–90, ed Late Show Productions (incl Naked Hollywood, Moving Picture, The Lime Grove Story) 1990–91, head of music and arts 1991–93, controller BBC2 1993–96, dir of television and controller BBC1 1996–97; chief exec Channel Four Television Corporation 1997–2001, chm Universal Television Gp USA 2002–04, pres of programming IAC/InterActiveCorp 2006–; non-exec dir EMI Gp plc 1999–2002; chm Photographer's Gallery London 2001–02; *Recreations* reading, walking, cinema; *Style*— Michael Jackson, Esq

JACKSON, Prof Neville Stuart; s of David Jackson, and Sheila, *née* Smith; *b* 21 October 1959, Wickford, Essex; *Educ* Imperial Coll London (BSc), City Univ (DSc); *m* 16 Nov 1985, Claire Elizabeth, *née* Luckett; 2 s (Brendan Alec b 14 July 1992, Kieran Scott b 7 July 1998); *Career* Ricardo UK Ltd: mangr Powertrain and vehicle research 1992–95, sr mangr engine engrg 1995–98, chief engr technol 1998–2000, global product dir advanced technol 2000–10; chief technol and innovation offr Ricardo plc 2010–; chm UK Low Carbon Vehicle Partnership 2009–, dep chair UK Automative Cncl Technol Gp 2008–, vice-chair European Road Transport Research Advsy Cncl 2009–; visiting prof Univ of Brighton 2006–; author or jt author of over 120 technical papers and invited keynote presenations at int conferences; ACGI, FIMechE 2009, FREng 2011; *Recreations* motorsport, sailing, skiing; *Style*— Prof Neville Jackson; ✉ Ricardo, Shoreham Technical Centre, Shoreham-by-Sea, West Sussex BN43 5FG (☎ 01273 455611, website www.ricardo.com)

JACKSON, Sir Nicholas Fane St George; 3 Bt (UK 1913), of Eagle House, Wimbledon, Surrey; s of Sir Hugh Nicholas Jackson, 2 Bt (d 1979), and Violet Marguerite Loftus, *née* St George (d 2001); the 1 Bt, Sir Thomas Graham Jackson, was the architect responsible for many buildings in Oxford incl Examination Schools, Brasenose, Hertford and Trinity Colls; *b* 4 September 1934, London; *Educ* Radley, Wadham Coll Oxford, Royal Acad of Music; *m* 1, 1961 (m dis 1968), Jennifer Ann, da of F A Squire, of Marylebone St, London; m 2, 1972, Nadia Françoise Genevieve, da of Georges Michard, of St Etienne, France; 1 s (Thomas Graham St George b 1980); *Heir* s, Thomas Jackson; *Career* organist, harpsichordist and composer; organist: St Anne's Soho 1963–68, St James's Piccadilly 1971–74, St Lawrence Jewry 1974–77; organist and master of the choristers St David's Cathedral 1977–84, musical dir and fndr St David's Cathedral Bach Festival 1979–85; concert tours: USA, France, Germany, Spain, Belgium, Croatia; dir Festival Bach at Santes Creus Spain 1987–89; dir Concertante of London 1987–; hon fell Hertford Coll Oxford 1995 (hon patron Music Soc); memb Ct of Assts Worshipful Co of Drapers (Master 1994–95), Liveryman Worshipful Co of Musicians; LRAM, ARCM; *Recordings* own organ works Chartres Cathedral 2000, Bach's Christmas Organ Music 2001, Bach's organ and harpsichord music 2001, own organ music at St Antoine des Quinze Uinets Paris 2004, own choral music Eton 2006, Bach's A Musical Offering 2007, The Rose and the Ring (opera) 2016 (also performed); also organ and harpsichord recordings for Decca, RCA, Abbey, Oryx and Priory Records; CDs of organ works 2000 and choral works 2008, CD recordings for Naxos Somm Priory and Herald Records, CD of own instrumental and vocal works for Nimbus Records 2015; *Compositions* various (incl two operas) published by Boosey & Hawkes, Cardiff University Press and Anglo-American Publishers; *Publications* Recollections of Sir T G Jackson (edited and arranged, 2003), Bach's Musical Offering (CD, with Concertante of London, 2009); *Recreations* travel, architecture and lecturing on the architecture of Sir T G Jackson (incl Venice 2008), sketching; *Style*— Sir Nicholas Jackson, Bt; ✉ e-mail nicholas@jacksonmusic.co.uk

JACKSON, (Kevin) Paul; s of late T Leslie Jackson, of Ealing, London, and late Jo, *née* Spoonley, of Caersws, Powys; *b* 2 October 1947; *Educ* Gunnersbury GS, Univ of Exeter (BA); *m* 21 Aug 1981, Judith Elizabeth, da of John Charles Cain, DSO, of Cowden, Kent; 2 da (Amy b 1981, Katie b 1984); *Career* formerly stage mangr: Marlowe Theatre Canterbury 1970, Thorndike Theatre Leatherhead 1971; prodr BBC TV 1971–82 (progs incl The Two Ronnies, Three of a Kind, Carrott's Lib, The Young Ones and Happy Families), freelance prodr and dir 1982–84 (progs incl Cannon and Ball and Girls on Top), prodr and chm Paul Jackson Productions 1984–86 (progs incl Red Dwarf, Don't Miss Wax and Saturday Live), md NGTV 1987–91, md Carlton Television Ltd 1993–94 (dir of progs 1991–92), md Carlton UK Productions 1995–96, freelance prodr/dir 1996–97, controller of entertainment BBC 1998–2000 (head of entertainment BBC 1997–98), ceo Granada Productions Aust 2000–02, ceo Granada America 2002–06, dir of entertainment and comedy ITV plc 2006–08, ceo Eyeworks UK 2009–12, creative dir Houghton Street Media Beijing 2012–14; memb ITV Broadcast Bd 1993–94; exec prodr Appointments of Dennis Jennings (winner Oscar for Best Live Action Short 1989), BAFTA Awards 1983 and 1984; chm: Comic Relief 1985–98, Charity Projects 1993–98 (vice-chm 1990–92), RTS 1994–96; memb: Bd of Dirs Nat Assoc of Television Prog Execs (NATPE) 2004–06, Bd of Dirs Int Acad of Television Arts and Sciences 2004–08, Bd US Comedy Arts Festival Aspen 2004–10; patron TimeBank 2000– (chm of tstees 1999–2012), chm of tstees Pilotlight 1996–2000; Stanford Exec Prog 1993; visiting prof Univ of Exeter 1999–2010, Hon Dr Univ of Exeter 2004; FInstD 1992, FRTS 1993; *Recreations* theatre, rugby, travel, food and wine, friends and family; *Style*— Paul Jackson, Esq; ✉ c/o Capel and Land Ltd, 29 Wardour Street, London W1D 6PS

JACKSON, Paul Edward; s of George Edward Jackson, of Kington St Michael, Wilts, and Joan, *née* Barry; *b* 8 July 1953; *Educ* Taunton Sch, Watford Sch of Art, Canterbury Coll of Art (BA), Univ of Bradford; *m* 1, 8 May 1982, Jane Frances, da of Frank Haseler; 2 s (James Sims b 2 April 1980, Nicholas Edward Jackson b 16 Feb 1990); m 2, 4 Oct 2000, Elaine Claire, da of Bernard Adams; *Career* account exec Saatchi & Saatchi 1978–80, account exec Mathers 1980–81, account supr Fletcher Shelton Delaney 1981–83, account mangr Publicis 1983–85, bd dir BSB Dorland 1985–92, md Kevin Morley Marketing 1992–95, exec managing ptnr Ammirati Puris Lintas (following merger) 1995–97, client servs dir Citigate Dewe Rogerson (formerly Dewe Rogerson Ltd) 1997–99, chief exec Ogilvy & Mather London 2002–06 (exec mgmnt dir (Ford Europe) 1999–2002), md Int (American Express) Ogilvy Gp 2006–; non-exec dir Aga Foodservice 2006–; MInstD, MIPA, FRSA; *Recreations* sailing, painting, classical music, fly fishing; *Clubs* Little Ship; *Style*— Paul Jackson, Esq; ✉ Ogilvy & Mather, 10 Cabot Square, Canary Wharf, London E14 4QB (☎ 020 7345 3066, fax 020 7345 9027)

JACKSON, Sir (William) Roland Cedric; 9 Bt (UK 1869), of The Manor House, Birkenhead; s of Sir (William) Thomas Jackson, 8 Bt (d 2004); *b* 9 January 1954; *Educ* Wycliffe Coll, St Peter's Coll Oxford (MA), Exeter Coll Oxford (DPhil); *m* 1977, Nicola Mary, yr da of Prof Peter Reginald Davis, of St Mawes, Cornwall; 3 s (Adam William Roland b 1982, James Anthony Foljambe b 1984, Oliver Thomas Peter b 1990); *Heir* s, Adam Jackson; *Career* head of science Backwell Sch 1986–89, educn advsr ICI 1989–93, head of learning Science Museum 1993–2001 (actg head of museum 2001–02), chief exec BAAS 2002–13; exec chair Sciencewise 2012–16, memb Nuffield Council on Bioethics 2013–; Hon DSc Univ of Aston 2011, hon degree Univ of Aberdeen 2012; *Clubs* Athenaeum, Alpine; *Style*— Sir Roland Jackson, Bt

JACKSON, Rt Hon Lord Justice; Sir Rupert Matthew Jackson; kt (1999), PC (2008); s of George Henry Jackson (d 1981), and Nancy Barbara, *née* May (d 1999); *b* 7 March 1948; *Educ* Christ's Hosp, Jesus Coll Cambridge (MA, LLB, pres Cambridge Union); *m* 20 Sept 1975, Claire Corinne, da of Harry Potter (d 1979); 3 da (Corinne b 1981, Chloe b 1983, Tamsin b 1985); *Career* called to the Bar Middle Temple 1972; QC 1987, practising SE Circuit, recorder 1990–98, head of chambers 1994–96, judge of the High Court of Justice (Queen's Bench Div) 1999–2008, judge i/c Technology and Construction Court 2004–07, Lord Justice of Appeal 2008–; chm Professional Negligence Bar Assoc 1993–95; hon fell Jesus Coll Cambridge 2009–; *Publications* conslt ed Jackson and Powell on Professional Negligence 2000– (gen ed 1982–99), ed-in-chief Civil Procedure: The White Book 2010–; *Clubs* Reform; *Style*— The Rt Hon Sir Rupert Jackson; ✉ Royal Courts of Justice, The Strand, London WC2A 2LL

JACKSON, Prof Stephen Philip (Steve); s of late Philip George Jackson, and Marion Margaret, *née* Smith; *b* 17 July 1962; *Educ* Univ of Leeds (F Happold Prize, BSc), Univ of Edinburgh (PhD); *m* 21 Sept 1991, Teresa Margaret, *née* Clarke; 2 s (Alexander Stephen Jackson b 31 July 1997, Daniel Philip Jackson b 3 June 1999); *Career* postdoctoral res fell Univ of Calif 1987–91; Wellcome Tst/Cancer Research UK Gurdon Inst (formerly Wellcome/CRC Inst): gp ldr 1991–95, sr gp ldr 1996–, dep dir 2001–2004, head Cancer Research Laboratories 2004–; Frederick James Quick prof of biology: Dept of Zoology Univ of Cambridge 1995–2009, Dept of Biochemistry Univ of Cambridge 2009–; assoc faculty memb Sanger Inst 2012–; chief scientific offr KuDOS Pharmaceuticals Ltd 1996–2008, fndr and chief scientific offr Mission Therapeutics Ltd 2011–; Biochemical Soc: memb 1993–, memb Cncl 1996–2000, 34th Colworth Medal 1997, Biochemical Soc GlaxoSmithKline Award 2008; memb: Cambridge Philosophical Society 1993–, EMBO 1997–, Acad Med Sci 2001, Br Assoc for Cancer Research 2005–, European Assoc for Cancer Research 2005–; fell St John's Coll Cambridge 1995; Tenovus Medal Tenovus-Scotland Symposia Ctee Univ of Glasgow 1997; Euro Young Scientist of the Year Eppendorf-Gmbl 1995, Anthony Dipple Carcinogenesis Young Investigator Award 2002, BBSRC Innovator of the Year Award 2009, Royal Soc Buchanan Medal 2011, delivered Raymond and Beverly Sackler Distinguished Lecture 2015, Gagna A & Ch Van Heck Prize 2015, King Faisal Int Prize for Science 2016, John J Ryan Distinguished Medal Lecture RCSI 2016, J Gregor Mendel Medal Lecture Czech Repub 2016, Dr A H Heineken Prize for Med Royal Netherlands Acad of Arts and Scis 2016; fell European Acad of Cancer Scis 2014, fell Faculty of Medicine Imperial Coll 2014; FRS 2008; *Publications* author of over 200 primary scientific publications in international research jls, also various review articles and book chapters; *Recreations* my children, gardening, travel; *Style*— Prof Steve Jackson; ✉ Wellcome Trust/Cancer Research UK Gurdon Institute, University of Cambridge, Tennis Court Road, Cambridge CB2 1QN (✆ 01223 334102, fax 01223 334089, e-mail s.jackson@gurdon.cam.ac.uk)

JACKSON, Stewart James; MP; s of Raymond Thomas Jackson and Sylvia Alice Theresa Jackson *née* Woodman; *b* 31 January 1965, London; *Educ* Chatham House GS Ramsgate, Royal Holloway Coll London (BA), Thames Valley Univ (MA); *m* 31 July 1999, Sarah O'Grady; 1 da (Isabel Ruby b 3 March 2005); *Career* business and personal banking mangr Lloyds TSB plc 1993–96, branch mangr Lloyds TSB plc 1996–98, HR mangr AZTEC Training and Enterprise Cncl SW London 1998–2000, HR business advsr Business Link for London 2000–05; Parly candidate (Cons): Brent S 1997, Peterborough 2001; MP (Cons) Peterborough 2005–, memb House of Commons Public Accounts Ctee 2012–; memb London Borough of Ealing Cncl 1990–98, memb Bd of Tstees London City YMCA 1993–98; vice-pres Local Govt Assoc 2010–; memb Chartered Inst of Personnel and Devpt (MCIPD); *Recreations* family, biography, history, keep fit, travel; *Clubs* Carlton, Peterborough Cons; *Style*— Stewart Jackson, Esq, MP; ✉ House of Commons, London SW1A 0AA (✆ 020 7219 8286, e-mail jacksonsj@parliament.uk or mail@peterboroughconservatives.com, website www.stewartjackson.org.uk)

JACKSON, District Judge Susan; da of late Ronald Alfred Jackson, and late Sheila Jackson; *Educ* Orme Girls' Sch Newcastle-under-Lyme, KCL (LLB), Coll of Law; *Career* admitted slr 1984, ptnr in private practice 1984–91, dir of Legal Servs Royal Borough of Kingston 1991–2001, district judge (Central London County Court and Court of Protection) 2002–; memb: Law Soc, Assoc of District Judges; Rights of Audience Higher Ct 1996; foster carer providing respite care for disabled children; *Publications* Urgent Applications in the Court of Protection (jtly); *Recreations* travel, entertaining, media; *Style*— District Judge Jackson

JACOB, Nicholas Allen Swinton; s of Cdr John Jacob, and Rosemary Elizabeth Allen, *née* Shuter; *b* 25 June 1954; *Educ* Sherborne, Univ of Nottingham (BA, BArch); *m* 1979, Frederike Mathilde Maria Wilhelma, da of Theodorus Doreleijers; 1 s (Ian b 12 March 1983), 1 da (Philippa b 4 June 1985); *Career* Suffolk Co Architects' Dept 1979–81, joined Peter Cleverly (architect in Wetheringsett, Suffolk) 1981–84, ptnr Cleverly & Jacob Architects Stowmarket, ptnr Purcell Miller Tritton & Partners (following merger) 1985–96, established Nicholas Jacob Architects Ipswich 1996–; exec memb Ipswich Building Preservation Tst 1984– (chair 2009–), memb Ipswich Conservation Advsy Panel 1986–; dir Suffolk Architectural Heritage Tst 1997–; memb Diocesan Advsy Ctee Ipswich & St Edmundsbury Diocese 2009–; RIBA 1980 (chm Eastern Region Conservation Gp 1998–99), architect accredited in building conservation 2003–; *Recreations* choir of St Margaret's Church (Ipswich), walking, golf, sketching, painting; *Clubs* Rotary (Ipswich Wolsey); *Style*— Nicholas Jacob, Esq; ✉ Nicholas Jacob Architects, 89 Berners Street, Ipswich, Suffolk IP1 3LN (✆ 01473 221150, fax 01473 255550, e-mail nicholas.jacob@njarchitects.co.uk)

JACOB, Prof (John) Peter; s of William Thomas Jacob (d 1960), and Doris Olwen, *née* Llewellyn (d 1991); *b* 13 May 1942; *Educ* Sir William Borlase's Sch, Univ of Newcastle upon Tyne (BA), Durham Univ (BArch); *m* 21 July 1982, Lesley Diana, da of Alfred Charles Thomas James (d 1998); 1 da (Katharine b 1985); *Career* principal Peter Jacob Architect 1967–; Kingston Univ (formerly Kingston Poly) Sch of Architecture and Landscape: princ lectr 1972–83, dep head 1983–87, head of sch 1987–2002, prof 1993–; chm Kingston Chapter RIBA 1980–82, memb Cncl RIBA 1983–89, memb Bd Architectural Educn Architects' Registration Cncl 1987–97, memb RIBA/ARB Joint Validation Panel 1995–2002, chm RIBA Publications Ltd 1989–94, dir RIBA Companies Ltd 1990–93, lead examiner Architects' Registration Bd 2001–14, chm RIBA Educn Tst Funds Ctee 2003–10; RIBA 1967, FRSA 1988; *Recreations* reading, swimming, motoring; *Style*— Prof Peter Jacob; ✉ Benbow House, Hyde Hill, Upper Hyde, Chalford, Gloucestershire GL6 8PD (✆ 01453 889684, mobile 07770 266429, fax 01453 889685, e-mail peter.jacob1@btconnect.com)

JACOB, Rt Hon Prof Sir Robert Raphael Hayim (Robin); kt (1993), PC (2004); s of Sir Jack I H Jacob, of London, and Rose Mary, *née* Samwell; *b* 26 April 1941; *Educ* Mountgrace Comp Sch, St Paul's, Trinity Coll Cambridge, (MA), LSE (LLB); *m* 1967, Wendy, da of Leslie Huw Thomas Jones; 3 s (Sam b 1970, Matthew b 1972, Oliver b 1975); *Career* called to the Bar Gray's Inn 1965 (bencher 1989, treas 2007); jr counsel to Treasury in patent matters 1976–81, QC 1981, QC (NSW) 1989, judge of the High Court of Justice (Chancery Div) 1993–2003, Chancery supervising judge Birmingham, Bristol and Cardiff 1997–2001, judge in charge of the Patents List 1994–97 and 2002–03, a Lord Justice of Appeal 2003–11; dep chm Copyright Tbnl 1989–93, appointed to hear Trade Mark Appeals to Bd of Trade 1989–93; hon pres Assoc of Law Teachers 1999–; govr: LSE 1996–2016, Expert Witness Inst 1996–2006 and 2010–; hon fell St Peter's Coll Oxford 1998, hon prof Univ of Birmingham 1999–, distinguished judicial visitor UCL 2002–11, hon fell LSE 2005; Hon LLD Wolverhampton Univ 2009; *Style*— The Rt Hon Prof Sir Robin Jacob; ✉ UCL Faculty of Laws, Bentham House, Endsleigh Gardens, London WC1H 0BG (✆ 020 7679 1424, e-mail rjacob@ucl.ac.uk)

JACOB, Ven Dr William Mungo; s of John William Carey Jacob (d 1982), of Ringstead, Norfolk, and Mary Marsters, *née* Dewar (d 1959); *b* 15 November 1944; *Educ* King Edward VII Sch King's Lynn, Univ of Hull (LLB), Linacre Coll Oxford (MA), Univ of Edinburgh (Dip), Univ of Exeter (PhD); *Career* asst curate Wymondham 1970–73, asst chaplain Univ of Exeter 1973–75, dir of pastoral studies Salisbury and Wells Theol Coll 1975–80 (vice-princ 1977–80), sec Ctee for Theol Educn Advsy Cncl for Church's Miny 1980–86, warden Lincoln Theol Coll and prebendary of Gretton in Lincoln Cathedral 1986–96, archdeacon of Charing Cross 1996–2015 (archdeacon emeritus 2015–), rector St Giles-in-the-Fields 2000–15, priest-in-charge St John's E Dulwich 2015–16; FRHistS; *Style*— The Ven Dr William Jacob; ✉ 4 St Mary's Walk, London SE11 4HA (✆ 020 7582 2025, e-mail wmjacob15@gmail.com)

JACOBI, Sir Derek George; kt (1994), CBE (1985); *b* 22 October 1938; *Career* actor; artistic dir Chichester Festival Theatre 1995–; narrator of The Iliad (talking book) 1993; *Theatre* RSC: Benedick in Much Ado About Nothing (tour to NY and Washington, Tony Award), title role in Peer Gynt, Prospero in The Tempest, title role in Cyrano De Bergerac (tour to NY and Washington), Macbeth 1993; Old Vic: title role in Hamlet (tour), Thomas in The Lady's Not for Burning, title role in Ivanov; Haymarket Theatre: Breaking The Code 1987, To Know, title role in Becket (UK tour); Octavius in Antony and Cleopatra (Cambridge Theatre Co), Apimantus in Timon of Athens (New Shakespeare Co), Charles Dyer in Staircase (Oxford Playhouse), Byron in The Lunatic, The Lover and The Poet (Lyric Hammersmith), Semyon in The Suicide (Anta Theatre NY), Breaking The Code (Neil Simon Theatre, nominated for Tony Award) 1987–88, Richard II/Richard III (Phoenix Theatre) 1988–89, Narrator in The Wedding Bouquet (Royal Opera House), title role in Kean (Old Vic Toronto), Frederick William Rolfe in Hadrian VII (Chichester Festival Theatre) 1995; *Television* BBC: Man of Straw, The Pallisers, title role in I Claudius, Richard II, Hamlet, The Vision Thing, Breaking the Code (nominated for Best Actor Br Academy TV Awards 1998); other credits incl: Skin (Anglia), The Stranger Left No Card (Anglia), Philby, Burgess and MacLean (Granada), Budgie (LWT), The Strauss Family (ATV), My Pye (Channel 4), In My Defence (Oyster TV), Wolves Are Howling (Yorkshire), Cadfael (Central), Jason and the Argonauts, The Gathering Storm, Inquisition, Mr Ambassador, The Borgias, Titanic: Blood and Steel, Last Tango in Halifax, Vicious; *Films* incl: The Day of the Jackal, Blue Blood, The Odessa File, The Medusa Touch, The Human Factor, Charlotte, The Man Who Went Out In Smoke, The Hunchback of Notre Dame, Inside The Third Reich, Little Dorrit, The Tenth Man, Henry V, The Fool, Dead Again, Hamlet, Love is the Devil (Best Actor Evening Standard British Film Awards), Gladiator, Gosford Park, Two Men Who Went to War, Revengers Tragedy, Cloud Cuckoo Land, Nanny McPhee, Underworld: Evolution, The Golden Compass, The King's Speech, My Week With Marilyn; *Style*— Sir Derek Jacobi, CBE; ✉ c/o Independent Talent, 40 Whitfield Street, London W1T 2RH (✆ 020 7636 6565, fax 020 7323 0101)

JACOBI JEPHSON, Hon Mary Jo; da of L J Jacobi (d 1999), and D M L Jacobi (d 1993); *b* 7 February 1951, Bay St Louis, Mississippi; *Educ* Loyola Univ of New Orleans (BBA), George Washington Univ (MBA); *m* 31 Dec 2004, Patrick Jephson, LVO (former private sec to Diana, Princess of Wales); *Career* administrator US Senate Commerce Ctee 1973–76, public affrs Nat Assoc of Manufacturers 1977–79, public affrs 3M 1979–81, dir of business liaison US Dept of Commerce 1981–83, special asst to Pres Ronald Reagan 1983–85 (memb Advsy Ctee on Trade Negotiations 1986–90), public affrs Drexel Burnham Lambert 1985–90 (latterly exec dir), vice-pres gp public affrs USA Marine Midland Bank 1990–92, asst sec of commerce to Pres George Bush 1992–93; head of public affrs and advsr to the bd HSBC Hldgs 1993–2000, md Lehman Bros 2000–01, vice-pres Royal Dutch Shell 2001–05, exec vice-pres BP America 2010–11; non-exec dir: Tate & Lyle plc 1999–2004, Mulvaney Capital Mgmnt 2010–, The Weir Gp plc 2014–; UK Civil Serv cmmr 2005–10, chair Forensic Science Service Ind Advsy Gp 2008–12; memb Wilton Park Advsy Cncl FCO 2003–14, US-UK Fulbright cmmr 2003–10; memb Advsy Bd: Center for Global Philanthropy Hudson Inst, Business Sch Univ of Oxford, Business Sch George Washington Univ; memb Advsy Ctee on Business Appointments 2012–; visiting fell: Univ of Oxford, Univ of Leeds Business Sch; lectr Moscow Sch of Political Studies; tstee: Sir Heinz Koeppler Tst, Benjamin Franklin Hse 2008–10, Nat Youth Music Theatre; former memb Cncl: Congressional Mgmnt Fndn, Center for the Study of the Presidency, Industry and Parl Tst (also fell), Technol Colls Tst; non-exec dir American Cncl on Germany 1990–2012; non-exec dir Ladies European Golf Tour 1987–89, chair Ladies Professional Golf Assoc 1989–97; Good Housekeeping's 100 Young Women of Promise 1985, memb NY Acad of Women Achievers 1988–; memb: Forum UK, Worshipful Co of Int Bankers, Guild of PR Practitioners, Worshipful Co of Fuellers; FRSA, MRI; *Publications* America's New Women Entrepreneurs (contrib, 1986), Working with Americans (foreword, 2002); *Recreations* opera, golf, international affair; *Clubs* NY Economic, Sloane; *Style*— The Honorable Mary Jo Jacobi Jephson; ✉ e-mail maryjo@maryjojacobi.com

JACOBS, Brian David Lewis; s of late John Barry Lewis Jacobs, of Chobham, Surrey, and Elizabeth, *née* Mendes; *b* 14 December 1949; *Educ* Charterhouse; *m* 26 Nov 1983, Rosalind Mary, da of late Leslie Jory; 2 da (Katherine Alice (Katie) b 3 Sept 1985, Emily Rose b 13 Dec 1988); *Career* messenger rising to research asst Horniblow Cox-Freeman 1968–71, media and market research exec Southern TV 1971–74, market research exec Access 1974, media research mangr Davidson Pearce 1974–80; Leo Burnett Advertising: assoc media dir 1980, media dir 1985, exec media dir 1986, international media dir 1990–95; media devpt dir Aegis Group plc 1995–96, md Carat International 1996–2001, regnl dir EMEA and head of worldwide accounts Universal McCann 2001–03, exec vice-pres Global Media Practice Millward Brown 2003–06, fndr dir Brian Jacobs & Assocs 2006–; fndr dir Enreach Gp 2010–, fndr ptnr Optisca 2011–15; memb CAM, FIPA 1982; *Books* Spending Advertising Money (with Dr Simon Broadbent, 1984), Social Media Marketing (jtly, 2009); *Recreations* golf, family, reading, the media, travel, theatre; *Clubs* Sunningdale Golf, The Hospital; *Style*— Brian Jacobs, Esq; ✉ 4 Holroyd Road, London SW15 6LN (✆ 020 8785 1637, website www.bjanda.com)

JACOBS, Charles; *Career* Linklaters: articled clerk 1990–92, slr 1992–99, ptnr 1999–, sr ptnr 2016–; *Style*— Charles Jacobs, Esq; ✉ Linklaters LLP, One Silk Street, London EC2Y 8HQ

JACOBS, Michael Edward Hyman; s of Harry Ronald Jacobs, CC (d 1966), of London, and Edmonde, *née* London (d 1993); *b* 21 May 1948, London; *Educ* St Paul's, Univ of Birmingham (LLB); *m* 5 March 1973, Ruth; 2 s; *Career* admitted slr 1972; Nicholson Graham & Jones (now K & L Gates LLP): ptnr 1976–2004, head Tax Dept 1981–97, head Private Client Dept 1997–2004, conslt 2004–05; chm Jacobs Intrinsic Strategy 2005–; legal expert in charity law; ed Trust Law International (formerly Trust Law and Practice) 1989–95 (memb Editorial Bd 1986–89, conslt ed 1995–2008); author of articles on corporate and personal taxation; fndr memb and vice-chm Share Plan Lawyers Orgn 1989–2005, fndr memb Trust Law Ctee 1994– (sec 1994–97), chm Quoted Companies Alliance Share Schemes Ctee 1996–2002, dep chm Young Ctee on Investment and Corporate Governance for Voluntary Orgns ACEVO 2001–04; memb: Legal Ctee Br Friends of the Hebrew Univ of Jerusalem 1980–2007, Tax Working Pty ProShare 1992–96, Taxation Sub-ctee Quoted Companies Alliance 1993–97, VAT Practitioners Gp Trafalgar Chapter 1993–97, Private Tsts Ctee Assoc of Corp Tstees 1996–97, Exec Ctee Quoted Companies Alliance 1999–2002, Inland Revenue Ctee on the Simplification of Capital Gains Tax 2000–02, Int Acad of Estate and Trust Law 2002–04, Cncl Acad of Social Scis 2005–09 (hon sec 2006–08); tstee Kidasha (formerly Child Welfare Scheme) 2005–13 (chm 2005–11), tstee Taurus Fndn 2009–; chm Hall Sch Parents Assoc 1988–90 (memb Ctee 1984–90); memb: Law Soc 1972, Inst for Fiscal Studies 1984, Int Fiscal Assoc 1985–2002, Assoc of Pension Lawyers 1986–98, City of London Law Soc 1986, Charity Law Assoc 1992, Soc of Tst and Estate Practitioners 1993, Soc of Legal Scholars 2005–10; Freeman City of London 1983, Liveryman Worshipful Co of Slrs 1987; AcSS 1999; FRSA 1993, fell Soc for Advanced Advanced Legal Studies (FSALS) 1998; *Books* Tax on Takeovers (1989, 6 edn 1994), Tolley's Tax on Takeovers (1990), Tolley's Tax Planning (contrib 1989, 7 edn 1994–95), Tolley's VAT Planning (contrib, 2 edn 1994–

J

95), The Director's Guide to Employee Benefits (IOD, contrib 1991), Longman's Financial Precedents (contrib 1992), Rewarding Leadership (report on share schemes for key execs of smaller quoted cos, Quoted Companies Alliance, 1998); *Recreations* long distance trekking (Annapurna Base Camp 2006, Everest Base Camp 2008), photography, genealogy, travelling; *Style—* Michael Jacobs, Esq; ✉ 6 Constable Close, London NW11 6TY (☎ 020 8455 3243, e-mail mrjacobs@btinternet.com)

JACOBS, Michael Graham; kt (2016); s of Alan Jacobs, and Eva, *née* Rozenblum; *b* 18 January 1964, London; *Educ* St John's Coll Oxford (BA), St Bartholomew's Hosp London (MB BS), DTM&H, Univ of London (PhD); *m* 28 Aug 2010, Suzanne, *née* McBride; 1 s (Joe b 22 Oct 2000), 2 da (Rosie 8 Jan 2003, Sylvia b 6 Nov 2011); *Career* house physician Whipps Cross Hosp 1988–89, house surgeon St Bartholomew's Hosp 1989, SHO Infectious and Tropical Diseases Royal Free Hosp 1989–90, rotating med SHO Addenbrooke's Hosp and Hinchingbrooke Hosp 1990–91, med registrar rotation Ealing Hosp and Hammersmith Hosp 1991–94, Wellcome research trg fell Imperial Coll London 1994–98, specialist registrar in infectious and tropical diseases Northwick Park Hosp 1998–99, specialist registrar in infectious diseases and gen medicine Hammersmith Hosp 1999–2000, specialist registrar Dept of Infection Guy's and St Thomas's Hosps 2000, conslt lead in infectious diseases Royal Free Hosp London NHS Fndn Tst 2000–; Wellcome advanced fell 2001–04; FRCP; *Publications* incl numerous contribs to field of infectious diseases; *Recreations* cinema, reading, walking, fitness training; *Style—* Sir Michael Jacobs; ✉ Royal Free London NHS Foundation Trust, Pond Street, London NW3 2QG (☎ 020 7794 0500, e-mail michael.jacobs@ucl.ac.uk)

JACOBS, Michael Upton; s of Arthur Jacobs (d 1996), and Betty Upton Hughes (d 2002); *b* 3 December 1960, London; *Educ* Woodhouse Sch Finchley, Wadham Coll Oxford (BA), Middx Poly (postgrad dip); *m* 5 July 1997, Cathy McKenzie; 1 s (Calum b 22 Jan 1996), 2 da (Natasha b 10 Jan 1998, Lucienne b 23 Aug 2001); *Career* conslt dir and md CAG Conslts 1990–94, res fell Lancaster Univ and LSE 1994–97, gen sec Fabian Soc 1997–2003, memb Cncl of Economic Advsrs HM Treasy 2004–07, special advsr on climate change and the environment to The Rt Hon Gordon Brown, MP, *qv* (as PM) 2007–10; visiting prof Grantham Research Inst on Climate Change and the Environment LSE 2010–, visiting prof Dept of Political Science UCL 2011–; co-ed Political Quarterly 2012–14; memb: Advsy Bd Children's Investment Fund Fndn, Supervisory Bd European Climate Fndn 2011–13; tstee Action Aid 2004–07, assoc fell Inst of Public Policy Research 2011–; *Publications* The Green Economy: Environment, Sustainable Development and the Politics of the Future (1991), The Politics of the Real World (1996), Greening the Millennium: The New Politics of the Environment (ed, 1997), Paying for Progress: A New Politics of Tax for Public Spending (2000); *Recreations* sport, music, books, theatre; *Style—* Michael Jacobs, Esq; ✉ c/o New Climate Economy, Overseas Development Institute, 203 Blackfriars Road, London SE1 8NJ

JACOBS, Nicholas; *b* 8 September 1959; *Educ* Univ of Buenos Aires (DipArch), Cornell Univ USA (MA); *Career* Skidmore, Owings & Merrill: joined 1988, elected assoc 1993, assoc dir 1995, New York office 1996, design dir 1998–2003, dir Jacobs Webber 2003–13, vice-pres WATG 2014–; selected projects incl: St Giles Circus London 1989, Thames Poly Kent 1991, Sixt Hotel Germany 1992, Manchester Olympics 2000 1992, Olympia Halle Berlin 1992, Rehbrucke Germany 1993, Den Haag Central The Netherlands 1993, Apollo Museum Amsterdam 1993, Hilton Hotel Amsterdam 1994, Rembrandt Tower Amsterdam 1994, Broadgate Plaza London 1995, King's Hill Campus Greenwich Univ 1995, JFK Int Airport NY 1997, One Court Place Stanford Conn 1997, La Guardia Plaza Amsterdam 1998, Mahon Point Cork 1998, Torre Vasco de Gama Expo'98 1998, Atlantico Pavilion for Expo'98 Lisbon 1998 (winner of int design competitions), Shanakiel Residential Devpt Dublin 1999, Citibank Regnl HQ Bahrain 1999, Charrington Wharf London 2000, Arrowhead Quay London 2000, Paddington Basin St Mary's London 2000; Grand Offr Order of Merit Portugal 1999; *Style—* Nicholas Jacobs, Esq; ✉ WATG, Boston House, 36–38 Fitzroy Square, London W1T 6EY

JACOBS, Prof Patricia Ann; OBE (1999); da of Cyril Jacobs, and Sadie, *née* Jones; *b* 8 October 1934; *Educ* Univ of St Andrews (BSc, DSc, D'Arcy Thomson medal, Sykes medal); *m* 1972, Newton Ennis Morton; 3 step s, 2 step da; *Career* res asst Mount Holyoke Coll MA 1956–57, scientist MRC 1957–72, prof Dept of Anatomy and Reproductive Biology Univ of Hawaii Sch of Med 1972–85 (Regents medal 1983), prof and chief Div of Human Genetics Dept of Paediatrics Cornell Univ Med Coll NY 1985–87, dir Wessex Regional Genetics Lab 1988–2001; hon sr lectr Dept of Med Univ of Edinburgh 1966–72, hon prof of human genetics Univ of Southampton Med Sch 1988–; Allan Award American Soc of Human Genetics 1981, Premio Phoenix Anni-Verdi Award 1998, Euro Soc of Human Genetics Mauro Baschirotto Award 1999, March of Dimes Prize in Developmental Biology 2011; fndr memb American Bd of Med Genetics 1979–82; memb Cncl: RCPath 1991–94, Royal Soc 1993–95, Acad Med Sci 1998–2001; foreign assoc Nat Acad of Sciences of USA 2009; author of over 250 articles; Hon DSc Univ of St Andrews 2002; FRSE 1977, FRCPath 1987, FRS 1993, FMedSci 1998, Hon FRCPEd 1999, Hon FRCOG 1999; *Recreations* botany, gardening, walking; *Style—* Prof Patricia Jacobs, OBE, FRS; ✉ Wessex Regional Genetics Laboratory, Salisbury District Hospital, Salisbury SP2 8BJ (☎ 01722 429080, fax 01722 338095, e-mail wessex.genetics@salisbury.nhs.uk)

JACOBS, Paul Martin; s of Colin Alfred James Jacobs, of Ruthin, Clwyd, and Betty Mary, *née* Rowse; *b* 11 December 1951; *Educ* Oundle, The Queen's Coll Oxford (MA), Univ of Liverpool (MB ChB); *m* 1; m 2, 11 Feb 1989 (m dis 2001), Deborah Clare Josephine Smith; 1 s (Edmund Charles b 22 Nov 1991); m 3, 21 Feb 2004 (m dis 2012), Marie Colette McMahon; m 4, 21 June 2014, Ruth Ann Heatley; *Career* resident surgical offr Moorfields Eye Hosp 1982–85; conslt ophthalmic surgn: Univ Hosp Nottingham 1988–92, Borders Gen Hosp 1992–94, York Hosp 1995–; FRCPSGlas 1984, FRCOphth 1988, FRCSEd 2000; *Recreations* music, mountain running, bicycle frame building; *Clubs* RSM; *Style—* Paul Jacobs, Esq; ✉ Department of Ophthalmology, York Hospital, Wigginton Road, York YO31 8HE (☎ 01904 631313)

JACOBS, Peter Alan; s of Cyril Jacobs (d 1971), and Sadie, *née* Jones (d 1973); *b* 22 February 1943; *Educ* Univ of Glasgow (BSc), Aston Univ (Dip Mgmnt Studies); *m* 31 May 1966, Eileen Dorothy, da of Dr Leslie Naftalin; 2 s (Andrew, Michael (twins) b 4 Feb 1969), 1 da (Katrina b 14 July 1972); *Career* prodn controller Toy Div Tube Investments Ltd 1968–70 (graduate trainee 1965–67), prodn mangr Pedigree Petfoods Ltd 1970–83 (prodn shift mangr 1970–72, Purchasing Dept 1972–81), sales dir Mars Confectionery 1983–86, chief exec Berisford International plc and chm subsid British Sugar Ltd 1986–91, chief exec BUPA 1991–98; chm: Hillsdown Holdings plc 1998–99, Healthcall Ltd 1998–2001, WT Foods 2002–05, abc Media 2005–10, LA Fitness plc 1998–2005; non-exec dir: Allied Domecq plc 1998–2004, Bank Leumi UK plc 1998–2003, RAF Strike Command 2002–09; chm Cove Park 2000–13; *Recreations* reading, music, theatre, tennis, sailing; *Clubs* RAC; *Style—* Peter Jacobs, Esq; ✉ Garden Flat, 29 Daleham Gardens, London NW3 5BY (☎ 020 7435 2646, e-mail jacobs@peatonhouse.co.uk)

JACOBS, Richard David; QC (1998); s of Elliott Norman Jacobs (d 1998), and Ruth *née* Ellenbogen; *b* 21 December 1956; *Educ* Highgate Sch, Pembroke Coll Cambridge (MA); *m* 1990, Pamela, da of David and Joyce Fine; 2 da (Rebecca Maritza b 27 Dec 1991, Hannah Minnie b 14 May 1997), 1 s (Benjamin Alexander b 5 July 1994); *Career* called to the Bar Middle Temple 1979 (bencher 2011); recorder 2003–, co-head of chambers Essex Court Chambers 2013–; visiting fell LSE 2003–07; *Books* Liability Insurance in International Arbitration: The Bermuda Form (2004, 2 edn 2011); *Recreations* tennis, Arsenal FC, theatre, piano; *Clubs* MCC, RAC; *Style—* Richard Jacobs, Esq, QC; ✉ Essex Court Chambers, 24 Lincoln's Inn Fields, London WC2A 3ED (☎ 020 7813 8000, fax 020 7813 8080)

JACOBSON, Howard; s of Max Jacobson, of Manchester, and Anita, *née* Black; *b* 25 August 1942; *Educ* Stand GS Whitefield, Downing Coll Cambridge (MA, Table Tennis half blue); *m* 1, 1964 (m dis 1972), Barbara, *née* Starr; 1 s (Conrad b 1968); m 2, 1978 (m dis 2004), Rosalin Joy, da of Allan Sadler, of Balnarring, Aust; m 3, 2005, Jenny De Yong, da of Dena De Yong, of London; *Career* lectr in Eng lit Univ of Sydney 1965–67, Eng tutor Selwyn Coll Cambridge 1969–72, sr lectr Wolverhampton Poly 1974–81, novelist and critic 1981–; reg contrib Modern Painters 1988–, weekly columnist The Independent 1998–2016; visiting prof New Coll of the Humanities 2012; hon fell Downing Coll Cambridge 2012; FRSL 2011; *Books* Shakespeare's Magnanimity (with Wilbur Sanders, 1978), Coming From Behind (1983), Peeping Tom (1984), Redback (1986), In The Land of Oz (1987), The Very Model of a Man (1992), Roots Schmoots (1993), Seriously Funny: An Argument for Comedy (1997), No More Mister Nice Guy (1998), The Mighty Walzer (1999), Who's Sorry Now? (2002), The Making of Henry (2004), Kalooki Nights (2006), The Act of Love (2008), The Finkler Question (2010, Man Booker Prize for Fiction 2010), Whatever It Is I Don't Like It (2011), Zoo Time (2012, Bollinger Everyman Wodehouse Prize for Comic Writing 2013), J (2014), Shylock Is My Name (2016); *Television Films* Into the Land of Oz (1991), Yo, Mrs Askew (1991), Roots Schmoots (3 parts, 1993), Sorry, Judas (1993), Seriously Funny: An Argument for Comedy (5 parts, 1997), Howard Jacobson Takes on The Turner (2000), Why the Novel Matters (South Bank Show special, 2002), Jesus the Jew (2009), Creation (2010), Flesh (2010), The Rebels of Oz (2 parts, 2014); *Recreations* appearing on television; *Clubs* Chelsea Arts, Groucho; *Style—* Howard Jacobson, Esq; ✉ c/o Curtis Brown, Haymarket House, 28–29 Haymarket, London SW1Y 4SP (☎ 020 7393 4400, fax 020 7393 4401/02, e-mail cb@curtisbrown.co.uk)

JACOBSSON, Dr (Ivar) Måns Gösta; s of Gosta Jacobsson, and Anna-Lisa Jacobsson; *b* 14 January 1939; *Educ* Princeton Univ, Lund Univ Sweden; *m* Margareta; 1 da (Anna), 1 s (Marten); *Career* judge 1964–70, pres of div Stockholm Ct of Appeal 1985–2006; Swedish Miny of Justice: legal advsr 1970–81, head Dept for Int Civil Law 1982–84; dir and ceo Int Oil Pollution Compensation Funds 1985–2006, conslt in maritime and environmental matters 2007–14; visiting prof: World Maritime Univ Malmö Sweden, Shanghai Maritime Univ, Dalian Maritime Univ China; visiting fell: Int Maritime Law Inst Malta,Inst of Int Shipping and Trade Law Univ of Swansea; hon prof Univ of Nottingham; memb: Exec Cncl Comité Maritime Int 2007–14, Bd of Govrs World Maritime Univ, Advsy Bd Portius Int and EU Law Centre Antwerp; hon memb Cncl London Shipping Law Centre Maritime Business Forum, academic assoc Quadrant Chambers; head Swedish delgn to a number of int meetings (incl Int Maritime Orgn) 1970–1984; author of book on patent law and of numerous articles in various legal fields; Hon LLD Univ of Southampton; Gold Medal of the King of Sweden 2010; *Publications* author of book on maritime transport of environmentally hazardous substances international regimes on liability and compensation; *Clubs* Rotary Int; *Style—* Dr Måns Jacobsson; ✉ e-mail mans.jacobsson@me.com

JACOMB, Sir Martin Wakefield; kt (1985); s of Hilary Jacomb, and Félise Jacomb; *b* 11 November 1929; *Educ* Eton, Worcester Coll Oxford (MA); *m* 1960, Evelyn Helen, *née* Heathcoat Amory; 1 da, 2 s; *Career* called to the Bar Inner Temple 1955 (hon bencher), practised at bar 1955–68; with Kleinwort Benson 1968–85, Commercial Union Assurance Co plc 1984–93 (dep chm 1987–93), dep chm Barclays Bank plc 1985–93; chm: Barclays de Zoete Wedd 1986–91, Postel Investment Management Ltd 1991–95, The British Cncl 1992–98, Delta plc 1993–2004, Prudential plc 1995–2000 (non-exec dir 1994–), Share plc 2003–13; non-exec dir: Bank of England 1986–95, The Telegraph plc (formerly Daily Telegraph) 1986–95, Rio Tinto plc 1988–2000, Marks and Spencer plc 1991–2000, Canary Wharf Gp plc 1999– (actg chm 2003, chm 2004–11, special advsr 2011–); memb Nolan Ctee 1995–97; external memb Fin Ctee OUP 1971–95, tstee Nat Heritage Meml Fund 1982–97, chllr Univ of Buckingham 1998–2010; Liveryman Worshipful Co of Merchant Taylors; Hon Dr: Univ of Oxford, Univ of Buckingham, Humberside Univ; hon fell KCL; *Style—* Sir Martin Jacomb

JACQUES, Dr Martin; s of Dennis Arthur Jacques (d 1996), and Dorothy *née* Preston (d 1989); *b* 1 October 1945; *Educ* King Henry VIII Sch Coventry, Univ of Manchester (BA, MA), King's Coll Cambridge (scholar, PhD); *m* 1969 (m dis 1975), Brenda Simson; partner 1976–93, Philippa Anne, da of Sqdn Ldr Lloyd Norman Langton, RAF (decd); m 2, 1996, Harinder Kaur Veriah (d 2000); 1 s (Ravi Harinder b 1998); *Career* lectr in econ and social history Univ of Bristol 1971–77, ed Marxism Today 1977–91 (ed special issue 1998), dep ed The Independent 1994–96; writer for The Observer, The Guardian, The European and MSN online 1996–98; columnist: Sunday Times 1988–94, The Times 1990–91, L' Unità (Rome) 1990–93, The Guardian 2002–; also occasional contrib: The Independent, The Financial Times, Daily Mail, Daily Telegraph, The NY Times, Int Herald Tribune, Wall Street Journal, New Republic, South China Morning Post, Volkskrant, La Stampa, Corrière della Sera, Le Monde Diplomatique; writer and presenter of numerous TV progs incl The End of the Western World, Proud to Be Chinese, The Incredible Shrinking Politicians (BBC 2); visiting prof: Int Centre for Chinese Studies Aichi Univ Japan 2005, Ritsumeikan Univ Kyoto Japan 2005, Renmin Univ Beijing 2005–06, Tsinghua Univ Beijing 2011–, Lee Kuan Yew Sch of Public Policy Nat Univ of Singapore 2015; visiting research fell Asia Research Centre LSE 2003–08, visiting sr research fell Asia Research Inst Nat Univ of Singapore 2006, sr fell IDEAS LSE 2008–13, public policy fell Transatlantic Acad Washington DC 2010–11 (non-resident fell 2012–), sr fell Dept of Politics and Int Studies Univ of Cambridge 2014–, sr fell Inst of Modern Int Relations Tsinghua Univ 2015–; memb Cncl European Policy Forum 1992–98; Demos: fndr, chm Advsy Cncl 1992–98, tstee 1994–99; memb Exec Ctee Communist Pty 1967–90 (memb Political Ctee 1978–80 and 1982–90); memb Econ History Soc 1971–77, fndr and chair Harinder Veriah Tst 2003–; ambass for Coventry; winner (sports category) Race in the Media Award 2006; FRSA 1991; *Books* Forward March of Labour Halted (co-ed and contrib, 1981), The Politics of Thatcherism (co-ed and contrib, 1983), New Times (co-ed and contrib, 1989), When China Rules the World: The Rise of the Middle Kingdom and the End of the Western World (2009, trans into 15 languages, 2 edn 2012); contrib to many other books and publications; *Recreations* travel, Chinese language, tennis, skiing, running, motor racing, reading, cooking; *Style—* Dr Martin Jacques; ✉ 55 The Pryors, East Heath Road, London NW3 1BP (☎ and fax 020 7435 7142, e-mail martin@martinjacques.com, website www.martinjacques.com); c/o Andrew Wylie, The Wylie Agency, 250 West 57th Street, Suite 2114, New York, NY 10107, USA (☎ 001 212 246 0069, fax 001 212 586 8953, e-mail mail@wylieagency.com); 17 Bedford Square, London WC1B 3JA (☎ 020 7908 5900, fax 020 7908 5901, e-mail mail@wylieagency.co.uk)

JAFFA, Robert Harvey (Sam); s of Leslie Jaffa, and Dorothy, *née* Rakusen (d 1994); *b* 4 March 1953; *Educ* Allerton Grange Sch Leeds, Univ of Hull (BSc), Univ of Wales Coll of Cardiff (DipJour), Univ of London (pt/t MA); *m* 28 Aug 1988, Celia, da of Philip Barlow (d 1998); 2 s (Lewis b 28 Feb 1992, Torquil b 25 Oct 1996), 1 da (Lucy b 27 Jan 1995); *Career* trainee journalist Essex County Newspapers until 1980; BBC: reporter BBC Radio Humberside 1980–82, prodr BBC Radio Stoke 1982 (covered Ballykelly pub bombing while visiting N Ireland 1982), reporter National BBC Radio News 1984–91 (major assignments incl sinking of ferry Herald of Free Enterprise Zeebrugge, Bradford football stadium fire, Piper Alpha oil platform disaster), New York reporter 1991, reporter

Business & Economics Unit 1992–95, N American business corr 1995–97, London 1997; head of media relations PricewaterhouseCoopers Europe, Middle East, Africa (formerly Price Waterhouse before merger) 1997–; memb Media Tst; *Books* Maxwell Stories (1992), Safe As Houses (1997); *Style*— Sam Jaffa, Esq; ✉ e-mail sam.jaffa@uk.pwcglobal.com

JAGGARD, Anthony John Thorrold; JP (1976); s of Rev Arthur William Percival Jaggard (d 1967), of Guilsborough Vicarage, Northamptonshire, and Isabel Louise May, *née* Capell (d 1972); *b* 5 June 1936; *Educ* Bedford Sch, Liverpool Sch of Architecture Univ of Liverpool; *m* 29 April 1961, (Elizabeth) Jane Jaggard, DL (pres Br Red Cross Soc Dorset Branch 1988–99), da of Col Sir Joseph William Weld, OBE, TD (d 1992, Ld-Lt Dorset 1964–84), of Lulworth Castle, Dorset; 3 da (Victoria (Mrs Nigel Beer) b 14 Jan 1962, Charlotte (Mrs David Swann) b 27 Jan 1964, Sarah (Mrs Robin Price) b 5 March 1968), 2 s (Oliver b and d 3 April 1970, Simon (twin) b 3 April 1970); *Career* Cheshire (Earl of Chester's) Yeomanry 1958–67 (Capt 1964, Adj 1967), RARO 1967–86; sr ptnr John Stark and Partners architects 1965–99, conslt John Stark and Crickmay 1999–; projects incl consultation on: Callaly Castle Northumberland, Hoddam Castle Dumfries, Lulworth Castle Dorset, Wardour Castle Wiltshire, Roman Town House Dorchester (Dorset Archaeological Award 2000, shortlisted Br Millennium Archaeological Award 2000), Ivington Park Herefordshire; new or remodelled houses incl: Ince Castle Cornwall, Gaston Grange Bentworth Hants, Longford House Sydling St Nicholas Dorset, Lulworth Castle House Dorset, Holywell Swanmore Hants, Bellamont House Long Bredy Dorset (nominated Country Life House of the Year 2002), Hedsor Wharf Bucks; ecclesiastical work incl new Church of St Joseph Wool Dorset 1973 (awarded listed building status 2013); contrib: Archaeological Journal, Dorset Natural History and Archaeological Soc Proceedings, Jl of the British Archaeological Assoc; memb Cncl: Dorset Nat Hist and Archaeological Soc 1971–2006 (pres 1994–97), Dorset Cncl of St John 1978–81, Royal Archaeological Inst 1987–91, Salisbury Diocesan Re-use of Closed Churches Gp 1991– (chm 2009–), British Archaeological Assoc 1997–2000; dir Dorset Bldgs Preservation Tst 1984–89; judge CLA Farm Buildings Awards 1983, 1989 and 1995, adjudicator E C Raphael Fund Italy and Spain 1998–99; Liveryman Worshipful Co of Painter Stainers 1975; FRSA 1986; FSA 1990; *Recreations* old buildings, gardening, shooting; *Style*— Anthony Jaggard, Esq, JP, FSA; ✉ 2 The Old Green, Sherborne, Dorset DT9 3JY (☎ 01935 817695); John Stark and Crickmay Partnership, 13 and 14 Princes Street, Dorchester DT1 1TW (☎ 01305 262636, fax 01305 260960, e-mail jscp@johnstark.co.uk)

JAGGER, Denise; *Career* slr Slaughter and May 1982–88, gp legal advsr Scottish Heritable Tst 1988–91, gen cnsl and co sec Asda Gp plc 1992–2003, ptnr Eversheds LLP 2004–; non-exec dir: Redrow plc 2007–, Northern Ballet Theatre; tstee LawWorks, chm York Museums Tst; *Style*— Ms Denise Jagger, Esq

JAGGER, Ven Ian; *b* 17 April 1955; *Educ* Huddersfield New Coll, King's Coll Cambridge, St John's Coll Durham; *m* Ruth, *née* Green; 1 s (Aidan b 1994); *Career* ordained: deacon 1982, priest 1983; asst curate St Mary the Virgin Twickenham 1982–85, priest in charge Willen Milton Keynes 1985–87, chaplain Willen Hospice Milton Keynes 1985–94, dir Milton Keynes Christian Trg Scheme 1986–94, team vicar Willen Milton Keynes 1987–94, team ldr Stantonbury Ecumenical Parish 1990–94, diocesan ecumenical offr 1994–96, team rector Holy Trinity with St Columba Fareham 1994–98, rural dean of Fareham 1996–98, canon residentiary Portsmouth Cathedral 1998–2001, archdeacon of Auckland 2001–06, archdeacon of Durham and canon residentiary of Durham Cathedral 2006–; *Recreations* reading, exploring new places; *Style*— The Ven the Archdeacon of Durham; ✉ 15 The College, Durham DH1 3EQ (☎ 0191 384 7534, e-mail archdeacon.of.durham@durham.anglican.org)

JAGGER, Jade Jezebel; da of Sir Mick Jagger, and Bianca, *née* de Macias; *b* 21 October 1971, Paris; *Educ* St Mary's Sch Calne; *m* 2012, Adrian Fillary; 2 da (Assisi Jackson b 2 July 1992, Amba Jackson b 26 May 1995) from a previous relationship; *Career* artist and model 1990–95; fndr: Jade Inc 1995–2000, Jezebel; creative dir: Garrard 2000–06,Yoo 2005–; *Style*— Miss Jade Jagger

JAGPAL, Jagdip; da of late Darshan Singh Jagpal, and Jaswant Kaur; *b* 22 November 1964, London; *Educ* LSE (LLB), Coll of Law London, London Business Sch; *Career* managing ed Butterworths 1986–91, slr Rubinstein Callingham, Polden & Gale 1992–95, head of legal BBC Radio 1995–96, chief asst to Controller BBC Radio 4 1996–99, head of legal Television Div SMG 1999–2000, md of network prodn SMG plc 2000–02, assoc Franklin Rae Communications 2002–03, chief exec Cloisters 2004–07, exec search conslt 2007–09, md Anareva 2009–14, mangr Int Progs Tate 2014–15, freelance sr int arts and cultural programme mangr 2015–; non-exec dir Franklin Rae Communications 2004–; tstee Wallace Collection 2007–15, memb Bd Almeida Theatre 2009–14, memb Ct of Govrs LSE 2011–, memb Devpt Bd RCA 2014–; *Recreations* arts and heritage, swimming, cycling, opera, reading, theatre; *Clubs* Academicians' Room; *Style*— Miss Jagdip Jagpal; ✉ via Linkedin

JAGUSCH, Stephen Richard; QC (2016); s of Paul Franz Jagusch, of Auckland, NZ, and Eileen Marie, *née* Williamson (d 2003); *b* 1967, Auckland, NZ; *Educ* Auckland Univ (BCom, LLB, MComLaw); *m* (m dis); 3 da (Annabel Marie b 20 Dec 2005, Clara Louise b 1 May 2007, Miranda Grace b 28 April 2010); *Career* barr and slr NZ 1990, slr Eng and Wales 1995, slr advocate 1996; arbitrator specialising in int commercial and treaty arbitration; asst slr: Simpson Grierson Auckland 1989–94, Freshfields London 1994–96, Freshfields Paris 1996–2000; ptnr Allen & Overy LLP London 2002–12 (asst slr 2000–02), ptnr Quinn Emanuel 2013–; former sr special fell UN Inst for Trg and Res 1998, alternate memb for NZ of the ICC Cmmn on Arbitration; memb: Swiss Arbitration Assoc, Int Arbitration Club, Int Arbitration Inst, LCIA, Panel of Neutrals (Arbitrators), American Arbitration Assoc; FCIArb; *Publications* Arbitration World (contrib, 1st edn 2003, 2 edn 2005), Disputes (contrib, 2003), Towards a Uniform International Arbitration Law? (contrib, 2005), Pevasive Problems in International Arbitration (contrib, 2006), Investment Arbitration and the Energy Charter Treaty (contrib, 2006), Global Arbitration Review (contrib, 2006), Investment Treaty Arbitration and International Law (contrib, 2008), Electronic Disclosure in International Arbitration (contrib, 2008), Investment Protection and the Energy Charter Treaty (contrib, 2008), Jl of World Investment and Trade Vol 10 No 4 (contrib, 2009), The Backlash Against Investment Arbitration, Perceptions and Reality (contrib, 2010), The Art of Advocacy in International Arbitration (contrib, 2 edn 2010), The International Arbitration Review (contrib, 2010, 2 edn 2011); *Recreations* golf, skiing, holidaying in NZ; *Style*— Stephen Jagusch, Esq, QC

JAINE, Tom William Mahony; s of William Edwin Jaine (d 1970), and Aileen, *née* Mahony (d 1943); *b* 4 June 1943; *Educ* Kingswood Sch Bath, Balliol Coll Oxford (BA); *m* 1983, Sally Caroline, da of late Andrew Agnew, of Crowborough, E Sussex, and Hon Joyce Violet, *née* Godber; 4 da (Harriet b 1974, Elizabeth b 1976, Matilda b 1985, Frances b 1987); *Career* restaurateur 1973–84; ed: Good Food Guide 1989–93, Journal of the International Wine and Food Society 1989–91; publisher Prospect Books 1993–2014; freelance writer (Sunday Telegraph and others) 1993–; Glenfiddich Award Wine and Food Writer of the Year 2001, BBC Food and Farming Awards, Derek Cooper Lifetime Achievement Award 2014; *Books* Making Bread at Home, Building a Wood-Fired Oven for Bread and Pizza, Oxford Companion to Food (ed, 3 edn); *Recreations* baking; *Style*— Tom Jaine, Esq; ✉ Allaleigh House, Blackawton, Totnes, Devon TQ9 7DL (☎ 01803 712269)

JAMAL, Dr Goran Atallah; s of Atallah Jamal, of Iraq, and Nusrat Jamal (d 1987); *b* 19 July 1953; *Educ* Baghdad Univ (MB ChB), Univ of Glasgow (PhD, MD); *m* 15 Dec 1983, Nisan, da of Maj-Gen Mohamad Salih Anber (ret), of Iraq; 1 da (Lazia b 23 May 1986), 1 s (Arie b 3 June 1992); *Career* sr registrar in neurology Bart's Med Sch 1986–88, conslt Dept of Neurology and sr clinical lectr Univ of Glasgow 1988–98 (research fell in neurology 1981–86), sr lectr in neurosciences Dept of Educn Strathclyde Region 1988–98, conslt and sr lectr Div of Neuroscience and Psychological Med Imperial Coll Sch of Med Univ of London 1998–; memb: Assoc of Br Neurologists, EEG Soc, New York Acad of Science, American Assoc of Electrodiagnostic Med, American EEG Soc; fell Assoc of Lawyers, memb: Inst of Expert Witnesses, Acad of Expert Witnesses; FRCPGlas; *Publications* author of over 150 articles, papers and book chapters; *Style*— Dr G A Jamal; ✉ Department of Neurology, Central Middlesex Hospital, Acton Lane, London NW10 7NS (☎ 020 8453 2247, fax 020 8453 2246)

JAMES, Albert (Alby); s of Albert Samuel James (d 1982), of London, and Florence Cassetta Renalda, *née* Thomas (d 1989); *b* 24 May 1954, London; *Educ* St David's C of E Sch London, Southgate Tech Coll London, UEA (BA); *m* 5 Jan 1980, Vanessa Mary, da of Capt Christopher Simmonds; 2 s (William Marcus b 17 March 1980, Benjamin Andrew b 16 April 1982), 1 da (Eloïse Sarah b 4 Aug 1988); *Career* theatre dir, prodr/dir for radio, film and TV drama, trainer and conslt; Arts Cncl trainee asst dir English Stage Co 1979–80, asst dir RSC (Barbican) 1982–83, artistic dir and chief exec Temba Theatre Co 1984–93, radio drama prodr and dir 1994–96, radio and TV drama prodr, trainer an devpt conslt UK and S Africa 1996–99, head of screenwriting and external devpt Northern Film Sch Leeds Met Univ 1999–2006, academic ldr for media and performance London Met Univ 2006–07, head of devpt Eon Screenwriters' Workshop 2007–09, ind prodr and conslt 2009–; prodns incl: Meetings (Hampstead Theatre) 1982, Scrape off the Black (Temba) 1985, Pantomime (Temba and Leicester Haymarket) 1985, Woza Albert (Temba) 1986, Romeo and Juliet (Temba and Contact Theatre) 1988, Porgy and Bess (assoc dir, Glyndebourne Festival Opera) 1986 and 1987 (also ROH, BBC TV and Primetime TV 1992), Glory (Temba and Derby Playhouse) 1989, Fences (Liverpool Playhouse and Garrick Theatre London) 1990, Ghosts (Temba tour) 1991, My Children, My Africa (Watermill Theatre) 1993, The Ramayana (BBC Radio 4) 1994, The Roads to Freedom (BBC Radio 4) 1994, Taking Sides (BBC Radio 3, nominated Best Dramatisation) 1996, Aman (BBC World Service) 1997, Short Stories from Southern Africa (Ulwazi for SABC) 1996, three Wallace and Gromit audio books (Best Production Award for Wallace and Gromit in The Lost Slipper Sony Awards 1998), exec prodr Dramatic Encounters a series of short films for SABC 1998–99, creative prodr Thetha Mswawa (Speak Out, for SABC) 1999, Nothing But The Truth (BBC Radio 3) 2002, exec prodr Shakespeare in Mzanzi for TV, exec prodr 5 new original drama series for SABC 2006–07, exec prodr I'm Going to Change My Name (Anniko Films) 2009–10; consultancies incl revising commissioning procedures TV Div SABC 1998–99; report for Broadcasting Standards Cmmn (Cultural Diversity, Equality of Opportunity and Enterprise with Responsibility, for new regulatory structure for electronic media) 2003, plan for content-led industry devpt Nigerian Film Corp; training progs incl: SEDIBA training and devpt prog for NFVF SA 2005–, Triangle for Screen Yorkshire 2010–, Kultburo script lab Russia 2010–13; specialist advsr for performing arts CNAA 1989–92; memb: Gen Advsy Cncl BBC 1987–91, Bd Screen Yorks Ltd 2002–07, Bd First Light Movies Ltd 2004–14; jury memb Berlinale's World Cinema Fund 2007–11; memb BAFTA 2007–; *Publications* introduction to Death and the King's Horseman by Wole Soyinka (1997); *Recreations* listening to music, reading, photography, politics, foreign travel; *Style*— Alby James, Esq; ✉ 45 Cranworth Gardens, London SW9 0NR (☎ 020 7735 9776, mobile 07788 437198, e-mail albyjames@clara.co.uk)

JAMES, Clive Vivian Leopold; CBE (2012); s of late Albert Arthur James, and Minora May, *née* Darke; *b* 7 October 1939; *Educ* Sydney Tech HS, Univ of Sydney, Pembroke Coll Cambridge (pres Footlights); *Career* writer, TV presenter and entertainer; feature writer The Observer 1972– (TV critic 1972–82); fndr Watchmaker Productions 1994; *Television* presenter TV series: Cinema, Up Sunday, So It Goes, A Question of Sex, Saturday Night People, Clive James on Television, The Late Clive James, The Late Show with Clive James, Saturday Night Clive, The Talk Show with Clive James; TV documentaries: Shakespeare in Perspective – Hamlet 1980, The Clive James Paris Fashion Show 1981, Clive James and the Calendar Girls 1981, The Return of the Flash of Lightning 1982, Clive James in Las Vegas 1982, Clive James meets Roman Polanski 1984, The Clive James Great American Beauty Pageant 1984, Clive James in Dallas 1985, Clive James meets Katherine Hepburn 1986, Clive James on Safari 1986, Clive James and the Heroes of San Francisco 1987, Clive James in Japan 1987, Postcard from Rio 1989, Postcard from Chicago 1989, Postcard from Paris 1989, Clive James meets Jane Fonda, Clive James on the 80s 1989, Postcard from Miami 1990, Postcard from Rome 1990, Postcard from Shanghai 1990, Clive James meets Ronald Reagan 1990; *Music* record lyricist for Pete Atkin; albums incl: Beware of Beautiful Strangers, Driving through the Mythical America, A King at Nightfall, The Road of Silk, Secret Drinker, Live Lible, The Master of the Revels; song-book A First Folio (with Pete Atkin); *Non-fiction* incl: The Metropolitan Critic (1974), The Fate of Felicity Fark in the Land of the Media (1975), Peregrine Prykke's Pilgrimage through the London Literary World (1976), Britannia Bright's Bewilderment in the Wilderness of Westminster (1976), Visions Before Midnight (1977), At the Pillars of Hercules (1979), First Reactions (1980), Charles Charming's Challenges on the Pathway to the Throne (1981), Crystal Bucket (1981), From the Land of Shadows (1982), Glued to the Box (1982), Flying Visits (1984), Snakecharmers in Texas (1988), Even As We Speak (2001), Reliable Essays (2001), As of This Writing (2003), The Meaning of Recognition (2005), North Face of Soho (2006), Cultural Amnesia (2007); autobiographies: Unreliable Memoirs (1980), Falling Towards England: Unreliable Memoirs II (1985), May Week Was in June: Unreliable Memoirs III (1990); *Fiction* Brilliant Creatures (1983), The Remake (1987), Brrm! Brrm! (1992), The Silver Castle (1996); *Verse* Fan-mail (1977), Poem of the year (1983), Other Passports: poems 1958–85, The Book of My Enemy (2004); *Style*— Clive James, Esq, CBE; ✉ website www.clivejames.com

JAMES, David Benjamin; MBE (2012); *b* 1 August 1970, Welwyn Garden City, Herts; *Career* professional footballer; clubs: Watford 1990–92, Liverpool 1992–99, Aston Villa 1999–2001, West Ham United 2001–04, Manchester City 2004–06, Portsmouth 2006–10, Bristol City 2010–; England: 53 caps, debut v Mexico 1997, memb squad World Cup 2002, 2006 and 2010, memb squad European Championships 2004; columnist The Guardian; *Style*— Mr David James, MBE

JAMES, Prof David Edward; s of Charles Edward James (d 1982), of Eastleigh, Hants, and Dorothy Hilda, *née* Reeves (d 1984); *b* 31 July 1937; *Educ* Peter Symonds Coll Winchester, Univ of Reading (BSc), Univ of Oxford (DipEd), Univ of London (Dip FE), Univ of Durham (MEd); *m* 30 March 1963, Penelope Jane, da of Lt Cdr Edward J Murray, of Bradford-on-Avon, Wilts; 1 da (Lucy b 1964), 2 s (Philip b 1966, Christopher b 1969); *Career* lectr in zoology and psychology City of Bath Tech Coll 1961–63, lectr in science and psychology St Mary's Coll of Educn Newcastle upon Tyne 1963–64; Univ of Surrey: lectr in educnl psychology 1964–68, res lectr in educn 1968–69, dir of adult educn 1969–80, prof of adult educn 1980–, prof and head Dept of Educnl Studies 1981–93, dean of assoc instns 1996–2002, special advsr to vice-chllr on regnl academic affrs 2002–05; md: Interactive Educational Systems International Ltd, IV Epoch Productions Ltd 1989–93; non-exec dir: Transnational Satellite Education Co Ltd 1991–94, ICON Productions Ltd 1993–95; chm: Cncl of Science and Technol Regnl Orgn for Surrey 1983–93, Surrey Retirement Assoc 1984–2007 (pres 2007–12), Br Assoc for Educnl Gerontology 1986–99 (pres 1999–), High Coombe Tst for Midwife Educn 1990–2008, Moor Park Tst for Christian Adult Educn 1992–2009, Age Concern Waverley 1993–96; vice-chm: Br Assoc

J

for Servs to the Elderly 1991–94, Cncl of Assoc of Business Execs 1994–98; pres: Preretirement Assoc of GB and NI 1993–02, Cmmn for Social Service Users and Carers (Surrey) 1998–2002 and 2009 (chm 1994–99); memb: Bd of Educn RCN 1980–92, Educn Ctee Royal Coll of Midwives 1986–91, Governing Body Centre for Int Briefing 1975–02, Gen Nursing Cncl 1972–80, UK Central Cncl for Nursing Midwifery and Health Visiting 1980–83, English Nat Bd for Nursing, Midwifery and Health Visiting 1983–88, Exec Ctee Guildford Branch ESU 1985–; CBiol, CPsych, AFBPsS 1966, FRSH 1974, FRSA 1984, FITD 1991, FSB 2009 (MIBiol 1963); *Books* A Students Guide to Efficient Study (1966), Introduction to Psychology (1968); *Recreations* farming; *Style—* Prof David James; ✉ 30 Glendale Drive, Guildford, Surrey GU4 7HZ

JAMES, Dean; s of John James (d 1998), and Noreen, *née* Williams, of S Wales; *b* 10 September 1960, S Wales; *Educ* Ebbw Vale GS, Univ of Cardiff (LLB), UWE, Univ of Warwick (MBA); *m* 20 Aug 1988, Karen Elizabeth, *née* Edwards; 2 da (Hannah b 21 Sept 1990, Evie b 14 April 2002), 2 s (Tom b 13 Aug 1994, Joshua b 14 Dec 1996); *Career* slr 1985–88, commercial dir Module Gp plc 1988–90, dir of M&A Inchcape plc 1990–97, strategy conslt Ernst and Young 1998–2000, ceo Mean Fiddler plc 2000–05, co-ceo Mama Gp plc 2005–; Friend of Great Ormond Street; *Recreations* surfing, rugby, golf; *Clubs* Shoreditch House; *Style—* Dean James, Esq; ✉ Mama Group plc, 59–65 Worship Street, London EC2A 2DU (☎ 020 7688 9000, fax 020 7688 8999, e-mail dean@mamagroup.co.uk)

JAMES, Eirian; da of Dewi William James, of Cardigan, and Martha Ann, *née* Davies; *b* 7 September 1952; *Educ* Preseli Secdy Sch Crymych, Royal Coll of Music; *m* 29 Dec 1975 (m dis 1993), Alan Rowland Davies; 1 da (Sara Elen b 11 March 1990); *Career* soprano/mezzo-soprano; hosts own TV series on S4C featuring popular folk and operatic arias; Druid in Gorsedd y Beirdd 2001; memb Royal Soc of Musicians 2001; *Roles* with Kent Opera incl: Olga in Eugene Onegin, title role in L'Incoronazione di Poppea, Rosina in The Barber of Seville, Nero in Agrippina, Dido in Dido and Aeneas, Cherubino in The Marriage of Figaro, Meg Page in Falstaff, Man Friday in Robinson Crusoe; with other cos incl: title role in La Perichole (Singers Co), Dorabella in Cosi fan Tutte (Singers Co, Aix-en-Provence), title role in Ariodante (Buxton Festival), Medea in Cavalli's Jason (Buxton Festival), Hänsel in Hänsel and Gretel (Geneva), Second Lady in The Magic Flute (Geneva), Cupid in Orpheus in the Underworld (Houston, ENO), Siebel in Faust (Houston), Sextus in Julius Caesar (Houston, Scottish Opera), Annina in Der Rosenkavalier (Covent Garden), Smeaton in Anna Bolena (Covent Garden), Nancy in Albert Hering (Covent Garden), Hermia in A Midsummer Night's Dream (Aix-en-Provence), Isolier in Count Ory (Lyon), Orlofsky in Die Fledermaus (WNO), Olga in Eugene Onegin (Covent Garden), Zerlina in Don Giovanni (Parma, Amsterdam, Ludwigsburg, London), Cherubino in Marriage of Figaro (Bordeaux, Bastille Paris), Despina in Cosi Fan Tutte (Garnier Paris), Diane in Hippolyte et Aricie (Garnier Paris), Cherubino in Figaro (Dresden Semperoper 1997 and Madrid 1998), Theatergarderobiere, Gymnasiast and Groom in Lulu (Bastille 1998), Meg Page in Falstaff (with John Eliot Gardiner, 1998, and recording), Falsirena in La Catena d'Adone (Innsbruck); *Recordings* Reuben in Christmas Rose (conducted by Howard Williams), Second Lady in The Magic Flute (conducted by Roger Norrington) 1990, Despina in Cosi Fan Tutte (conducted by John Eliot Gardiner), Zerlina in Don Giovanni (conducted by John Eliot Gardiner), Sextus in Julius Caesar (conducted by Jean-Claude Malgoire), Diane in Hippolyte et Aricie (conducted by William Christie), title role in Teseo (conducted by Mark Minkovsky), Christus Apollo (cantata composed and conducted by Jerry Goldsmith); *Recreations* gardening; *Style—* Ms Eirian James; ✉ The Vicarage, Tremain, Cardigan SA43 1SJ (☎ and fax 01239 811 751, e-mail eirian.james1@btinternet.com)

JAMES, Elizabeth Sheila (Liz); (Mrs C Drummond Challis); da of Edward Leonard James, of Westerham, Kent, and Sheila Florence, *née* Jordan; *b* 24 August 1944; *Educ* Micklefield Sch for Girls Sussex, Ravensbourne Coll of Art and Design (BA); *m* 4 Oct 1984, (Christopher) Drummond Cremer Challis, s of Christopher George Joseph Challis; *Career* graphic designer: Crosby Fletcher Forbes 1965–66, Total Design Holland 1966–68, Pentagram 1968–74; freelance graphic designer Holland and London 1974–83, fndr ptnr Lambton Place Design 1983–87, design mangr Phaidon Press 1994–95, dir Liz James Design Consultancy 1987–; ret from graphic design, now practising in ceramics; memb Ctee W Country Potters Assoc 2004–; PPL 1977; memb: D&AD 1983, DBA 1983 (dir 1992–93); FCSD 1986 (memb Cncl 1992–95), FRSA 1992; *Style—* Mrs Elizabeth Challis; ✉ Old Crebor Farm, Gulworthy, Tavistock, Devon PL19 8HZ (☎ 01822 618814)

JAMES, Erica Jane; da of Peter Joseph Sullivan, and Marie Ruby Sullivan; *Career* novelist; Romantic Novel of the Year 2006 (five times shortlisted), finalist WH Smith Fresh Talent promotion 1996; *Books* A Breath of Fresh Air (1996), Time for a Change (1996), Airs & Graces (1997), A Sense of Belonging (1998), Act of Faith (1999), The Holiday (2000), Precious Time (2001), Hidden Talents (2002), Paradise House (2003), Love and Devotion (2004), Gardens of Delight (2005), Tell It to the Skies (2007), It's the Little Things (2009), The Queen of New Beginnings (2010), Promises, Promises (2010), The Real Katie Lavender (2011), The Hidden Cottage (2013); *Recreations* travelling, reading, learning Italian, following F1; *Style—* Miss Erica James; ✉ Curtis Brown, Haymarket House, 28/29 Haymarket, London SW1Y 4SP (☎ 020 7396 6600)

JAMES, Geraldine; OBE (2003); da of Gerald Thomas (d 1987), of Cornwall, and Annabella, *née* Doogan (d 1987); *b* 6 July 1950; *Educ* Downe House, Drama Centre London; *m* 28 June 1986, Joseph Sebastian Blatchley, s of John Blatchley (d 1994); 1 da (Eleanor b 20 June 1985); *Career* actress; worked in repertory theatre Chester, Exeter and Coventry 1972–75; numerous venues London Fringe; *Theatre* roles incl: Miss Julie, Desdemona, Raina, Annie Sullivan; other works incl: The White Devil (Oxford Playhouse) 1981, When I was a Girl I Used to Scream and Shout (Whitehall) 1987, Cymbeline (NT) 1988, Portia in The Merchant of Venice (Peter Hall Co London and Broadway, Drama Desk Award 1990, Tony Award nomination 1990) 1989, Death and the Maiden (Duke of York) 1992, Lysistrata (Old Vic) 1993, Hedda Gabler (Manchester Royal Exchange) 1993, Give Me Your Answer, Do (Hampstead Theatre) 1998, Faith Healer (Almeida Theatre) 2001, The Cherry Orchard (Oxford Stage Co) 2003, Home (Oxford Stage Co) 2004, The UN Inspector (NT) 2005, Victory (Arcola Theatre) 2009, Hamlet (Donmar on Broadway) 2009, Seagull (Arcola Theatre) 2011, 13 (NT) 2011; *Television* The Sweeney 1976, Dummy 1977 (Critics' Assoc Best Actress Award, BAFTA Best Actress nomination), Love Among The Artists 1978, The History Man 1980, The Jewel In The Crown (BAFTA Best Actress nomination), Blott on the Landscape 1984, Echoes 1987, Stanley and the Women 1991, A Doll's House 1991, Ex 1991, The Healer 1994, Band of Gold 1994 and 1995 (BAFTA Award nomination for Best Actress), Kavanagh QC 1994, 1995, 1997 and 1998, Over Here 1995, Rebecca 1996, Gold 1997, See Saw 1998, The Sins 2000 (BAFTA Best Actress nomination), Hans Christian Anderson 2001, Crime and Punishment 2001, White Teeth 2002, The Hound of the Baskervilles 2002, Hearts of Gold 2003, State of Play 2003, He Knew He Was Right 2003, Jane Hall's Big Bad Bus Ride 2004, Little Britain 2004, Poirot 2005, A Harlot's Tale 2006, The Amazing Mrs Pritchard 2006, The Heist 2007, City of Vice 2007, Rapunzel 2007, The Last Enemy 2008, Little Britian USA 2008, Caught in a Trap 2008, The Other Woman 2012, 13 Steps Down 2012, Utopia 2012, Utopia2 2014, Blackwork 2015, The Five 2015, Lawrence After Arabia (Hampstead Theatre) 2016; *Film* incl: Sweet William 1978, Night Cruiser 1978, Gandhi 1981, The Wolves of Willoughby Chase 1988, The Tall Guy 1988, She's Been Away 1989 (Venice Film Festival Best Actress Award), If Looks Could Kill 1990, The Bridge 1990, Beltenebros 1991, Losing Track 1991, No Worries 1992, Doggin' Around 1994, Moll Flanders, The Man Who Knew Too Little 1998, Lover's Prayer 1999, Testimony of Taliesin Jones 1999, The Luzhin Defence 1999, Tom and Thomas 2001, An Angel for May 2001, Odour of Chrysanthemums 2002, Calendar Girls 2002, Hex 2004, The Fever 2005, Alice in Wonderland 2009, Sherlock Holmes 2009, Made in Dagenham 2010, Arthur 2011, The Girl with the Dragon Tattoo 2011, Diana 2013, Our Robot Overlords 2014, 45 Years 2015, Alice Through the Looking Glass 2015; *Recreations* music; *Style—* Miss Geraldine James, OBE; ✉ c/o Julian Belfrage Associates, 9 Argyll Street, London W1F 7TG

JAMES, Glen William; s of Clifford Vizetelly James, of Long Ashton, Bristol, and Kathleen Mary Flora, *née* Doull; *b* 22 August 1952; *Educ* KCS Wimbledon, New Coll Oxford (MA); *m* 15 Aug 1987, Amanda Claire, da of Philip Dorrell, of Worcester; *Career* admitted slr 1976, ptnr Slaughter and May 1983–2012; Freeman Worshipful Co of Solicitors; govr King's Sch Wimbledon, tstee The Rhodes Tst Oxford; memb Law Soc; MSI; *Recreations* music, reading, various sports, involvement with various charitable and educational bodies; *Clubs* RAC; *Style—* Glen James, Esq; ✉ e-mail glenwjames@gmail.com

JAMES, Rt Rev Graham Richard; *see:* Norwich, Bishop of

JAMES, Helen; da of Peter Shaw, and Joan Mary, *née* Turner; *b* 29 March 1951; *Educ* Cheadle Hulme Sch, Girton Coll Cambridge (MA); *m* 30 August 1976, Allan James, s of Thomas Raymond James; 1 s (Peter Thomas b 26 March 1979), 2 da (Clare Elizabeth b 21 Oct 1980, Sarah Linda b 29 Sept 1985); *Career* actuary; Equity and Law (now Axa) 1972–74, ptnr Clay & Partners (now Aon Hewitt) 1977–97 (joined 1975), ptnr Watson Wyatt (now Willis Towers Watson) 1997–2006, dir of law Debenture Pension Tst Corp 2006–16 (pension scheme tstee); *Style—* Mrs Helen James; ✉ e-mail helenjames42@yahoo.co.uk; Law Debenture Pension Trust Corporation, 100 Wood Street, London (☎ 020 7696 5255 or 07972 179665)

JAMES, Prof Ioan Mackenzie; s of Reginald Douglas James (d 1966), of Heathfield, E Sussex, and Jessie Agnes, *née* Surridge (d 1982); *b* 23 May 1928; *Educ* St Paul's, The Queen's Coll Oxford; *m* 1 July 1961, Rosemary Gordon, da of William George Stewart (d 1953); *Career* Cwlth Fund fell (Princeton, Berkeley, Inst for Advanced Study) 1954–55, Tapp research fell Gonville & Caius Coll Cambridge 1956; Univ of Oxford: reader in pure mathematics 1957–69, sr research fell St John's Coll 1959–69, Savilian prof of geometry 1970–95 (emeritus prof 1995), hon fell St John's Coll 1987; New Coll Oxford: professorial fell 1987–95, hon fell, Leverhulme emeritus fell 1996–98; pres London Mathematical Soc 1985–86 (treas 1969–79), govr St Paul's Sch and St Paul's Girls' Sch 1970–99; hon prof Univ of Wales 1989; Hon DSc Univ of Aberdeen 1993; FRS 1968; *Books* The Topology of Stiefel Manifolds (1976), General Topology and Homotopy Theory (1984), Topological and Uniform Spaces (1987), Fibrewise Topology (1988), Introduction to Uniform Spaces (1990), Fibrewise Homotopy Theory (with Michael Crabb, 1998), Topologies and Uniformities (1998), History of Topology (1999), Remarkable Mathematicians (2002), Remarkable Physicists (2004), Asperger's Syndrome and High Achievement (2006), The Mind of the Mathematician (with Michael Fitzgerald, 2007), Driven to Innovate (2009), Remarkable Biologists (2009), Remarkable Engineers (2010); *Style—* Prof Ioan James, FRS; ✉ Mathematical Institute, Radcliffe Observatory Quarter, Woodstock Road, Oxford OX2 6GB (☎ 01865 735389)

JAMES, Jason Charles; s of Donald William James, of Dartington, Devon, and Lorna Constance, *née* Dunford; *b* 15 February 1965, Edinburgh; *Educ* King's Coll Sch Cambridge (chorister), Marlborough (scholar), King's Coll Cambridge (scholar, MA), Judge Business Sch Univ of Cambridge; *m* 10 Oct 1992, Kyoko, *née* Igarashi; 2 s (Tsutomu b 5 Feb 1994, Makoto b 29 Feb 1996), 1 da (Hannah b 8 April 2001); *Career* trainee analyst Nat Securities Tokyo 1985–86, Japanese equity fund mangr Robert Fleming Asset Mgmnt London 1987–89; HSBC: head of Japanese equity strategy Tokyo 1989–96, head of Japanese equity res Tokyo 1996–98, global strategist specialising in Asia London 1999, head of European equity strategy 1999–2002, head of global equity strategy 2002–04; Shimomura fell Devpt Bank of Japan 2004; supervisor Japanese Dept Univ of Cambridge 2004–07, md Cambridge Oriental Ltd 2007–, dir Japan Br Cncl 2007–11; DG Daiwa Anglo-Japanese Fndn 2011–; cncllr Ueno Gakuen Educational Fndn; Soc of Investment Analysts Extel Securities and Investment Prize 1989; *Publications* The Political Economy of Japanese Financial Markets (co-author, 1999); numerous jl articles and book chapters; *Recreations* Japan, music, reading, cryptic crosswords; *Clubs* Reform, Tokyo, Japan Soc (memb Bd); *Style—* Jason James, Esq; ✉ Daiwa Anglo-Japanese Foundation, 13–14 Cornwall Terrace, London NW1 4QP

JAMES, John Anthony; s of Charles Thomas James (d 1979), of Sutton Coldfield and Tenby, and Gwenith Aylwin, *née* Jones; *b* 15 July 1945; *Educ* King Edward VI GS Lichfield, Univ of Bristol (LLB); *m* 10 Sept 1973, Gwyneth Jane, da of Ambrose Elwyn Evans (d 1975), of Altrincham; 2 da (Harriet Lucy b 24 Sept 1975, Emily Jane b 22 Nov 1977); *Career* admitted slr 1969, ptnr Edge & Ellison 1974–93 (conslt 1993–), chief exec Birmingham City 2000, conslt Willis Corroon plc; dir: Remainders Ltd, Steel Plate and Sections Ltd, Quantum PR plc; sr jt hon sec Birmingham Law Soc 1987–91 (memb Cncl 1986–93), sec W Midlands Assoc of Law Socs 1991–93, memb Editorial Advsy Bd Law Soc Gazette; chm Lab Pty Fin and Industry Gp West Midlands; memb: Cncl Midlands Branch IOD, Ct Univ of Birmingham; dir Birmingham Repertory Theatre, chm Birmingham Press Club 1993–97; chm South Birmingham Coll 1998–; memb Law Soc 1970, FInstD 1985; *Recreations* reading, writing, theatre, jazz, opera; *Clubs* Solihull Sporting (chm), Moseley Rugby, Birmingham & Solihull Rugby, Avenue Bowling, Warwickshire Co Cricket; *Style—* John James, Esq; ✉ Birmingham City 2000, Rutland House, 148 Edmund Street, Birmingham B3 2JR (☎ 0121 214 2515, fax 0121 214 1855, e-mail info@birminghamcity2000.co.uk)

JAMES, John Arthur William; DL (Staffs) 2006; s of Dr Peter Michael James (d 1971), and Eileen Mary, *née* Walters (d 1993); *b* 7 January 1942; *Educ* Douai Sch Berks; *m* 5 Aug 1967, Barbara, da of Maj William Nicholls (d 1955); 2 da (Jessica b 1968, Alice b 1970), 1 s (John-Leo b 1982); *Career* admitted slr 1967, sr ptnr Hand Morgan & Owen Stafford 1988; under sheriff Staffs and W Midlands 1983–2008, adjudicator on immigration 1986–91, dep coroner S Staffs 1987–2012, clerk to Cmmrs of Taxes Stafford and Cannock 1987–2009; chm Mid Staffs NSPCC 1976–95; memb Bd Stafford Prison 1975–93 (chm 1983–86); Cdr St John Ambulance Staffs 1994–2005; CStJ 2002; *Publications* The James Report (1996), The Walsall Suicide Review (2002); *Recreations* walking, shooting; *Style—* John James, Esq, DL; ✉ Hand Morgan & Owen, 17 Martin Street, Stafford, Staffordshire ST16 2LF (☎ 01785 211411, fax 01785 248573)

JAMES, John Christopher Urmston; OBE (2003); s of John Urmston James (d 1964), of Llandeilo, Carmarthenshire, and Ellen Irene, *née* Walker (d 2000); *b* 22 June 1937; *Educ* Hereford Cathedral Sch; *m* 1 (m dis 1982), Gillian Mary, *née* Davies; *m* 2, 20 Nov 1982, Patricia Mary, da of Arthur Leslie Walter White (d 1983), of Sherborne, Dorset; 2 s (David Henry Urmston b 3 Feb 1960, Christopher Hammond Urmston b 1 Jan 1961); *Career* trainee buyer Harrods 1954; rep: Jaeger 1961, Pringle 1972; sec LTA 1981–2003 (asst sec 1973–81, vice-pres 2003–07, life vice-pres 2008–), pres European Tennis Fedn 2003–08 (hon life pres 2008–); memb Olympic Ctee Int Tennis Fedn 1989–2009, chm British Olympic Fndn; pres Middx Tennis Assoc 2003–; dir Torch Trophy, tstee Dan Maskell Tst; memb: Nat Tst, Friends of Osterley Park (chm 2012–), Ealing Nat Tst, Lib Dem Pty (pres Hounslow Lib Dem Pty); lay vice-chm St Mary's Church Osterley; lay memb: London Diocesan Synod, Hounslow Deanery Synod; *Recreations* tennis, rugby union, walking, architecture, topography, the countryside, gardening; *Clubs* All England Lawn Tennis and Croquet, Queen's, International Lawn Tennis Club of GB, Isleworth Probus, Cambridge Univ Tennis (vice-pres 2003–), London Welsh Rugby; *Style—* John

James, Esq, OBE; ✉ Parkfield Cottage, Osterley Road, Isleworth, Middlesex TW7 4PF (☎ 020 8232 8683)

JAMES, Julie; AM; da of Derek James, and Lorna, *née* Rees; *b* Swansea; *Educ* Univ of Sussex (BA), Univ of Central London (Dip); *m* 18 June 1988, David Flatt; *Career* called to the Bar Grays Inn 1983; memb Nat Assembly for Wales (Lab) Swansea W 2011–; *Style—* Ms Julie James, AM; ✉ 30/31 High Street, Swansea SA1 1LG (☎ and fax 01792 460836, e-mail julie.james@wales.gov.uk); National Assembly for Wales, Cardiff Bay, Cardiff CF99 1NA

JAMES, (David) Keith Marlais; OBE (2005); s of James Lewis James (d 1993), and Margaret Evelyn James (d 2001); *b* 16 August 1944; *Educ* Cardiff HS, W Monmouth Sch, Queens' Coll Cambridge (MA); *m* 4 Aug 1973, Kathleen Linda, da of Wilfred Lawson Marrs, OBE (d 1981), of Cyncoed, Cardiff; 2 da (Alys b 1978, Elizabeth b 1980), 1 s (Thomas b 1983); *Career* slr; ptnr Eversheds LLP 1969–2004 (chm 1995–2004); dir: various cos in Hamard Group 1977–86, Bank of Wales plc 1988–2001, AXA Insurance Co Ltd 1992–99, HTV Group 1997–98 and 1999–2006, Atlantic Venture Capital Ltd 2001–12, Julian Hodge Bank Ltd 2002– (chm 2012), Admiral Group plc 2002–12, International Greetings plc 2004–11; chm: Welsh Exec UN Assoc 1977–80, Welsh Centre for Int Affrs 1979–84, Editorial Bd Welsh Economic Review 1989–92; memb: UK Mgmnt Ctee Freedom from Hunger Campaign 1978–87, Welsh Mgmnt Ctee IOD 1985–94, Ct UWIST 1985–88, Cncl UWIST 1985–88, Advsy Panel Cardiff Business Sch 1986–94, Cncl Univ of Wales Coll of Cardiff 1988–94, Representative Body of the Church in Wales 1989–95, Gen Advsy Cncl BBC 1991–92; vice-pres Cardiff Business Club 1987–, dep chm Inst of Welsh Affrs 1987–2007, non-exec memb Welsh Health Common Servs Authy 1991–95; dir The Int Festival of Musical Theatre in Cardiff 2001–04; tstee Nat Tst 2011–14 (chm Wales Advsy Bd 2012–16), tstee Jane Hodge Fndn 2014–; memb Law Soc; *Recreations* hill walking; *Clubs* Cardiff and County, Oxford and Cambridge; *Style—* Keith James, Esq; ✉ Trehedyn Cottage, Peterston-Super-Ely, Vale of Glamorgan CF5 6LG

JAMES, Keith Royston; s of William Ewart Gladstone James (d 1990), of Birmingham, and Lilian Elizabeth James (d 1966); *b* 22 August 1930; *Educ* King Edward VI Camp Hill Sch Birmingham, Univ of Birmingham; *m* 6 May 1961, Venice Imogen, da of Maj Henry St John Murray Findlay (d 1954); 1 s (William b 1964), 3 da (Rohaise b 1966, Selina b 1968, April b 1971); *Career* admitted slr 1954; Needham & James: sr ptnr 1956–94, ptnr 1994–2001, conslt 2001–10; conslt Shakespeares 2010–15, conslt ShakespeareMartineau 2015–; dir Technology and Law 1980–97; chm Soc for Computers and Law 1988–90; pres Community Villacana Spain 2000–05, chm Michael Blanning Tst; *Books* A Guide to the Electronic Office for Practising Solicitors; author of articles on the application of technology to the law; *Recreations* shooting, walking, golf; *Clubs* St Pauls (Birmingham), Ingon Manor Golf, Welcombe Golf, El Paraiso Golf; *Style—* Keith R James, Esq; ✉ Welcombe House, 32 Avenue Road, Stratford-upon-Avon, Warwickshire CV37 6UN (☎ 01789 261810); ShakespearesMartineau, No. 1 Colmore Square, Birmingham B4 6AA (☎ 0121 631 5364, e-mail keith.james@shma.co.uk)

JAMES, Lesley; da of Albert Harry Showell (d 1978), of Birmingham, and Esme Kathleen, *née* Robinson; *b* 7 April 1949; *Educ* Lordswood Grammar Technical Sch, Open Univ (BA), Univ of Warwick (MA); *m* John William James; *Career* sec Joseph Lucas Ltd 1965–70, personnel mangr Delta Metal Co Ltd 1973–77 (PA 1970–73), personnel admin mangr Rank Hovis MacDougall Ltd 1977–79, mgmnt devpt mangr Sketchley Ltd 1979–80; Savacentre Ltd (subsid of J Sainsbury plc): personnel mangr 1980–83, checkout ops mangr 1983–85; Tesco Stores Ltd: regnl personnel mangr 1985–87, personnel dir (head office/distribution) 1987–89, personnel dir (retail) 1989–93, personnel and trg dir 1993–95; human resources dir Tesco plc 1995–99; non-exec dir: Selfridges plc 1998–2003, Care UK plc 2000–07, West Bromwich Building Society 2001–, Liberty International 2004–; memb: Insolvency Service Steering Bd DTI, Governing Cncl Nat Coll for Sch Leadership, Cncl Open Univ; CCIPD, FRSA; *Style—* Mrs Lesley James

JAMES, Lily Chloe Ninette; *Career* actress; *Film* Wrath of the Titans 2012, Fast Girls 2012, Cinderella 2015, Burnt 2015, Pride and Prejudice and Zombies 2016, Baby Driver 2016, The Exception 2016; *Television* Just William 2010, Secret Diary of a Call Girl 2011, Downton Abbey 2012–14, War and Peace 2015; *Style—* Ms Lily James

JAMES, Linda; *Educ* Univ of York; *Children* 1 da; *Career* television prodr; prodn asst TV commercials Sid Roberson Productions 1980, prodr Sgrin (82) Ltd (independent prodrs of progs for S4C) 1981–82 (prodr award-winning drama series Joni Jones with dir Stephen Bayly); Red Rooster Films Ltd (now subsid of Chrysalis plc): co-fndr with Stephen Bayly 1983, chief exec 1982–98; md Alibi Productions 1999–2003, md Sly Fox Films Ltd 2003–; investment fund mangr Wales Creative IP Fund 2005–11; non-exec dir Coolabi plc 1999–2012, non-exec dir Boomerang plc 2007–; govr: BFI 1991–95, Nat Film and TV Sch 1991–98 (tstee 1998–2004 and 2006–), Childrens' Media Fndn 1999–, Screen South 2001–; chair Edinburgh Int TV Festival 1992; memb: Br Screen Advsy Cncl 1993–96, Cncl BAFTA 2004–06, Kids' Ctee BAFTA, SE Media Network 2000–11; memb awards juries for BAFTA, RTS, Int Emmys and BFI; *Programmes* Red Rooster prodns incl: And Pigs Might Fly (feature-length film for S4C, prodr) 1983, The Works (feature-length film, English/Welsh versions for S4C and Channel 4, prodr) 1984, Coming Up Roses (feature-length comedy for S4C and cinema release, prodr) 1985–86, Homing (for S4C, exec prodr) 1986, Just Ask for Diamond (feature film for Coverstop, Children's Film Fndn and British Screen, prodr) 1987–88, The Gift (series for BBC, prodr) 1989–90, The Diamond Brothers – South by South East (series for TVS, exec prodr) 1990–91, The Life and Times of Henry Pratt (comedy drama series for Granada, exec prodr) 1992, Body and Soul (drama series for Carlton, exec prodr) 1992–93, Smokescreen (drama series for BBC, exec prodr) 1993, Crocodile Shoes (drama series for BBC, exec prodr) 1994, The Sculptress (drama series for BBC, prodr), Wilderness (drama series for ITV, exec prodr), Heaven on Earth (drama series for BBC, exec prodr); Alibi prodns incl: Without Motive (drama series for ITV, exec prodr), The Safe House (drama series for ITV, prodr) 2000–01, Dead (comedy film for ITV, prodr) 2000–01, Sir Gadabout (children's series for ITV, exec prodr) 2001–03; Wales Creative IP Fund incl: Big Nothing (feature film for Pathe, exec prodr), Hunger (feature film for Film 4, exec prodr), Mr Nice (feature film, exec prodr), Submarine (feature film, exec prodr), Hunky Dory (feature film, exec prodr); *Awards* numerous incl: Chicago Children's Awards (for Joni Jones and And Pigs Might Fly), official selection Cannes Film Festival (Coming Up Roses), Golden Pierrot (first prize) for Best First Feature Vevey Int Festival of Comedy Film and Special Jury Prize Golden Plaque Chicago Int Film Festival (for Coming Up Roses), Best Adventure Film Moscow Film Festival (for Just Ask for Diamond), Welsh BAFTA for Outstanding Contributions to Children's Programmes, Indie Award (for Sir Gadabout); BAFTA nominations (for Body and Soul, Crocodile Shoes, The Sculptress and Sir Gadabout); *Style—* Ms Linda James

JAMES, Dr Michael Leonard (Michael Hartland); MBE (2012); s of late Leonard James; *b* 7 February 1941; *Educ* Latymer Upper Sch, Christ's Coll Cambridge (Holland Rose and Wren prizes); *m* 1975 (m dis 1992), Jill, da of late George Tarján, OBE; 2 da (Ruth, Susanna); *Career* writer and broadcaster 1983–; entered Br Govt Serv (GCHQ) 1963, private sec to Rt Hon Jennie Lee MP as Min for the Arts 1966–68, DES 1968–71, planning unit of Rt Hon Margaret Thatcher MP as Sec of State for Educn & Sci 1971–73, asst sec 1973, DCSO 1974, dir Int Atomic Energy Agency Vienna 1978–83, advsr on int rels Cmmn of the Euro Union Brussels 1983–85; feature writer and book reviewer for: The Times (thriller critic 1990–91, travel corr 1993–2003), Sunday Times, The Guardian, Daily Telegraph (thriller critic 1993–2013); chm: Civil Serv Selection Bds 1983–93, GMC Professional Conduct Ctee 2000–06; memb: Asylum and Immigration Tbnl (formerly Immigration Appeal Tbnl) 1987–2013, Exec Ctee PEN 1997–2001; govr: Colyton GS 1985–90, Sidmouth Community Coll 1988–2004 (chm of govrs 1998–2001); chm Kennaway House Tst Devon 2001–11 (life pres 2011–); hon fell Univ of Exeter; FRSA; *Books* novels (as Michael Hartland): Down Among the Dead Men (1983), Seven Steps to Treason (1985, SW Arts Literary Award, dramatized for BBC Radio 4 1990), The Third Betrayal (1986), Frontier of Fear (1989), The Year of the Scorpion (1991), The Verdict of Us All (short stories, 2006), Masters of Crime: Lionel Davidson and Dick Francis (2006); (as Ruth Carrington) Dead Fish (1998); other publications (as M L James): Internationalization to Prevent the Spread of Nuclear Weapons (jtly, 1980); *Television and Radio* incl: Sonja's Report (ITV documentary, 1990), Masterspy (interviews with KGB defector Oleg Gordievsky, BBC Radio 4, 1991); *Clubs* Athenaeum, Detection, PEN; *Style—* Dr Michael James, MBE; ✉ Cotte Barton, Branscombe, Devon EX12 3BH

JAMES, Prof the Hon Oliver Francis Wintour; o s of Baron James of Rusholme (Life Peer, d 1992), and Cordelia Mary, *née* Wintour; *b* 23 September 1943; *Educ* Winchester, Balliol Coll Oxford (MA, BM BCh); *m* 4 Sept 1965, Rosanna, er da of Maj Gordon Bentley Foster (d 1963), of Sleightholme Dale, Fadmoor, York; 1 s (Patrick Esmond b 4 May 1967), 1 da (Helen b 26 Jan 1970); *Career* Univ of Newcastle upon Tyne: prof of geriatric med 1985–, head Dept of Med 1994–, head Sch of Clinical Med Sciences 1995–2004, pro-vice-chllr Faculty of Medical Sciences 2004–08; censor RCP, sr vice-pres RCP 1997–99, past pres Br Assoc for Study of the Liver; non-exec dir BUPA 1999–2008, non-exec chm e-therapeutics; sr med advsr Penrose Inquiry; chair Sir James Knott Tst 2004–, tstee Help the Aged 2002–06; landowner (170 acres); FRCP 1981, FMedSci 1999; *Books* Liver Disease in the Elderly, Oxford Textbook of Clinical Hepatology (ed, 1999), Oxford Textbook of Medicine (contrib chapters, 2003); *Recreations* golf, gardening; *Style—* Prof the Hon Oliver James; ✉ Department of Medicine, Floor 4, Clinical Block, Medical School, Framlington Place, Newcastle upon Tyne NE2 4HH; Sleightholmedale Lodge, Kirbymoorside, York YO62 7JG (e-mail o.f.w.james@ncl.ac.uk)

JAMES, Peter John; s of John Burnett James, and Cornelia, *née* Katz; *b* 22 August 1948, Brighton, E Sussex; *Educ* Charterhouse, Ravensbourne Film Sch; *m* 21 April 1979 (m dis 1999), Georgina Valerie James, da of T D Wilkin, of Hove, E Sussex; *Career* dir: Quadrant Films Toronto 1972–77, Yellowbill Ltd 1977–85; co-fndr Pavilion Internet plc, former md of Movision Entertainment Ltd; film prodr: Dead of Night 1973, Spanish Fly 1976, Biggles 1985, Five Moon Square 2002, Jericho Mansions 2002, A Different Loyalty 2003, Head in the Clouds 2003, The Bridge of San Luis Rey 2003, The Statement 2003, The Last Sign 2003, The Merchant of Venice 2004, Bailey's Billions 2004, The River King 2004, Perfect Creatures 2004; author; former Royal Warrant Holder Queen's Warrant for Glove Mfrs; chair Crime Writers' Assoc, memb Soc for Psychical Research; jt patron Sussex Crimestoppers; fell emeritus Hypnotherapy Soc; Freeman City of London 1980, Liveryman Worshipful Co of Glovers; Hon DLitt Univ of Brighton; *Books* Dead Letter Drop (1981), Atom Bomb Angel (1982), Billionaire (1983), Possession (1988), Dreamer (1989), Sweet Heart (1990), Twilight (1991), Prophecy (1992), Host (1993, floppy disk edn 1994, world's first electronic novel), Alchemist (1996), Getting Wired (1996), The Truth (1997), Denial (1998), Faith (2000), Dead Simple (2005), Looking Good Dead (2006), Not Dead Enough (2007), Dead Man's Footsteps (2008), Dead Tomorrow (2009), Dead Like You (2010), The Perfect Murder (2010), Dead Man's Grip (2011), Perfect People (2011); *Awards* Krimi Blitz (Crime Writer of the Year) Germany 2005, Le Prix Polar Int France 2006, Le Prix Coeur Noir France 2007, shortlisted Crime Thriller of the Year Br Galaxy Book Awards 2007, shortlisted ITV 3 Crime Novel of the Year Award 2008, Quick Reads Readers' Choice Award 2010; *Recreations* skiing, tennis, wine, motor racing, cars, restaurants; *Clubs* Groucho, Ivy, Annabels; *Style—* Peter James, Esq; ✉ c/o Carole Blake, Blake Friedmann, 122 Arlington Road, London NW1 7HP (☎ 020 7284 0408, e-mail scary@pavilion.co.uk, website www.peterjames.com)

J

JAMES, Prof (William) Philip Trehearne; CBE (1993); s of Jenkin William James (d 1944), and Lilian Mary, *née* Shaw (d 1992); *b* 27 June 1938, Liverpool; *Educ* Ackworth Sch Pontefract, UCL (BSc), UCH London (MB, BSc, MD), Univ of Cambridge (MA), Univ of London (DSc); *m* 1961, Jean Hamilton, da of James Lingford Moorhouse (d 1977); 1 s (Mark), 1 da (Claire); *Career* asst dir MRC Dunn Nutrition Unit Cambridge 1974–82, dir Rowett Res Inst Aberdeen 1982–99, hon prof London Sch of Hygiene and Tropical Medicine 2004–; former memb DHSS Ctees on Medical Aspects of Food Policy and Novel Foods; memb: EU Scientific Ctee for Food 1992–95, EU Sci Steering Ctee 1997–2000, BSE Ctee 2001–02; chm: FAO Expert Consultation on Nat Energy Needs 1987, UK Nat Food Alliance 1987–90 (pres 1990–98), Coronary Prevention Group 1988–96 (pres 1999–), Int Obesity Task Force 1996–2009, UN Cmmn on Future Global Food and Health Issues 1997–99; formerly chm Working Pty on Nat Advsy Ctee of Nutrition Educn, vice-chm FAO/WHO/UNU Expert Consultation on Energy and Protein Requirement of Man 1981–85, memb Cncl World Public Health Nutrition Assoc 2009–; memb Nutrition Advsy Ctee WHO Euro Region 1985–2007, chm Consultation on Nutrition and Health WHO 1989–91, special advsr to WHO DG 1989–, memb WHO Global Forum Noncommunicable Diseases 2010–; chm Scottish Working Pty on: Diet and Scottish Public Health 1992–93, Obesity Management 1994–98; chm Global Alliance for the Prevention of Chronic Diseases 2005–10, pres Int Assoc for the Study of Obesity (now World Obesity Fedn) 2009–14 (past pres 2014–16); lectures: Cuthbertson Meml Lecture 1979, Peter Beckett Lecture Dublin 1983, Ames Meml Lecture 1985, Mehta Oration India 1985, Middleton Meml Lecture 1986, Davidson Meml Lecture 1987, Minshull Meml Lecture 1989, Hallberg Oration 1994, Gopalan Oration 1994; Sir Alister McIntyre Distinguished Award Univ of WI 2002; Hon DSc: City Univ London 2004, Univ of Buckingham 2012, Univ of Aberdeen 2013; FRCP 1978, FRSE 1986, FIBiol 1987; *Books* incl: The Analysis of Dietary Fibre in Food (1981), Assessing Human Energy Requirements (1990), Human Nutrition and Dietetics for Doctors (10 edn, 1999); papers on nutrient absorption, energy and protein metabolism, health policy and food labelling incl: Food Standards Agency Report to PM, European Food Authority Report for EU Cmmn; author and chm UN ACC/SCN Millennium Cmmn on Ending Malnutrition by 2020, new sugar analyses to show clear link to dental caries (used by WHO to reduce sugar limits to below 5%); *Recreations* talking, writing government reports, eating; *Clubs* Athenaeum (London); *Style—* Prof Philip James, CBE, MD, FRSE; ✉ 1 Gatti's Wharf, 5 New Wharf Road, London N1 9RS (website www.worldobesity.org)

JAMES, Russell; *see:* Logan, Russell James Vincent Crickard

JAMES, Hon Sebastian Richard Edward Cuthbert; 3 and yst s of 5 Baron Northbourne, *qv*; *b* 11 March 1966; *Educ* Eton, Magdalen Coll Oxford (MA), INSEAD (MBA); *m* 22 Aug 1998, Anna; 3 s (Arthur b 20 Sept 1999, Alfred b 10 April 2001, Albert b 17 July 2006), 1 da (Alexandra b 18 Nov 2002); *Career* assoc Bain & co 1987–90, case ldr Boston Consulting Gp 1991–94, dir Longwall Hldgs 1995–2008, strategy dir Mothercare 2003–04, chief exec Synergy Insurance Services Ltd 2006–08, gp chief exec Dixons Carphone 2012– (joined 2008); non-exec dir Direct Line Insurance Gp 2014–; advsr Dept for Educn 2010–11; co-fndr Tablets for Schools 2012–; tstee Save the Children 2014–; *Publications* Review of Schools Capital Project (2011); *Recreations* skiing, scuba diving, playing guitar; *Clubs* Soho House; *Style—* The Hon Sebastian James; ✉ Dixons Carphone, 1 Portal Way, London W3 6RS (Twitter @DCSebJ)

JAMES, Siân; *b* 24 June 1959, Morriston; *m*; 2 c; *Career* MP (Lab) Swansea E 2005–15; dir Welsh Women's Aid; *Style—* Mrs Siân James; ✉ House of Commons, London SW1A 0AA (e-mail sianjamesmp@parliament.uk)

JAMES, His Hon Judge Simon John; s of Cdr David James, RN (Ret), and Anne, *née* Elder; *b* 24 January 1966, Plymouth, Devon; *Educ* Brookfield Comp Sch, Itchen Sixth Form Coll, Univ of Leeds (LLB), Inns of Court Sch of Law; *m* 19 Oct 1991, Dawn, *née* Hilditch; 1 s (Thomas b 1 Aug 2003), 1 da (Tabitha b 10 April 2007); *Career* circuit judge (South Eastern Circuit) 2010–; memb Lincolns Inn; *Style*— His Hon Judge Simon James; ✉ c/o The Law Courts, Chaucer Road, Canterbury, Kent CT1 1ZA

JAMES, Dr Simon Robert; s of Alan William James (d 1994), and Dorothy Denise James; *b* 1 April 1952; *Educ* LSE (BSc Econ, MSc), Open Univ (MBA, MA), Univ of Leicester (LLM), Leeds Metropolitan Univ (PhD), CDipAF DipM; *Career* res asst LSE 1974–76, reader in economics Univ of Exeter 1996– (lectr 1976–88, sr lectr 1988–96); visiting research fell Curtin Univ WA 1997 and 1999, visiting fell ANU 1998 and 2003; specialist conslt to New Shorter Oxford English Dictionary 1990–93; FRSA 1990, CTA (fell) (FTII 1992), ACIM 1996; *Books* incl: Self Assessment for Income Tax (with N A Barr and Prof A R Prest, 1977), The Economics of Taxation (with Prof C W Nobes, 1978, Chinese edn 1988, Japanese edn 1996, 7 edn 1998), A Dictionary of Economic Quotations (1981, 2 edn 1984), Pears Guide to Money and Investment (1982), A Dictionary of Sexist Quotations (1984), A Dictionary of Legal Quotations (1987, Indian edn 1994), The Comprehensibility of Taxation (1987), A Dictionary of Business Quotations (jtly, 1990), Chambers Sporting Quotations (1990), Collins Dictionary of Business Quotations (jtly, 1991), Trapped in Poverty? (jtly, 1992), Putting the Family First: Identities, Decisions, Citizenship (jtly, 1994), Self-Assessment and the UK Tax System (1995), A Dictionary of Taxation (1998), Taxation: Critical Perspectives on the World Economy (ed, 4 vols, 2002); *Recreations* distance learning, cooking, St John Ambulance, quotations; *Style*— Dr Simon James; ✉ School of Business and Economics, University of Exeter, Streatham Court, Rennes Drive, Exeter EX4 4PU (✆ 01392 263204, fax 01392 263242, e-mail s.r.james@exeter.ac.uk)

JAMES, Sue; *Educ* London Sch of Fashion; *Career* editorial dir: Woman and Home Magazine, womanandhome.com, Woman & Home SA; *Style*— Ms Sue James; ✉ Woman and Home, Timeinc (UK), Blue Fin Building, 110 Southwark Street, London SE1 0SU (✆ 020 3148 7836, e-mail sue.james@timeinc.com)

JAMES, Thomas (Tom); MBE (2009); *b* 11 March 1984, Cardiff; *Educ* King's Sch Chester, Trinity Hall Cambridge (rowing blue); *Career* rower; GB jr nat team debut 2001, GB sr nat team debut 2003; memb Cambridge team Oxford v Cambridge Boat Race 2003, 2005, 2006 and 2007, pres Univ of Cambridge Boat Club 2006–07; achievements incl: Bronze medal (eights) World Championships 2003, Bronze medal (eights) World Championships 2007, Gold medal coxless fours Olympic Games 2008, Gold medal (coxless four) World Championships 2011, Gold medal (coxless fours) Olympic Games 2012; *Clubs* Molesey Boat; *Style*— Tom James, Esq, MBE

JAMES, Valerie Mary; *née* Jacobs; da of Colin Alfred James Jacobs, of Llanbedr, Denbighshire, and late Betty Mary, *née* Rowse; *b* 9 November 1954, Plymouth; *Educ* Penrhos Coll Colwyn Bay (maj scholar), Somerville Coll Oxford (BA); *m* 12 May 1979, Michael Frank James; 2 s (Samuel Charles b 18 May 1983, Jeffrey William b 26 Oct 1985); *Career* slr; articled clerk Bond Pearce 1976–79, slr Coward Chance 1980–83, assoc Malcolm Lynch Slrs 1992–2000; Wrigleys Solicitors LLP (formerly Wrigleys): asst slr 2000–02, ptnr 2002–15, ret; govr: Penrhos Coll (later Rydal Penrhos) 1990–98, David Young Community Acad 2006–12; tstee LEAF Acad Tst 2013–15; memb: Law Soc 1980 (nat chm Trainee Slrs Gp 1977–78), Charity Law Assoc 1992, Ecclesiastical Law Soc 1995 (memb Gen Ctee 2010–16); *Publications* Charities, Governance and the Law: The way forward (contrib, 2003); *Recreations* cooking, classical music, tennis, reading; *Clubs* Farmers; *Style*— Mrs Valerie James; ✉ e-mail val.james@lineone.net

JAMES, Prof Vivian Hector Thomas; s of William Percy James (d 1970), of London, and Alice May James (d 1936); *b* 29 December 1924; *Educ* Latymer Upper Sch, Univ of London (BSc, PhD, DSc); *m* 20 April 1958, Betty Irene, da of Frederick Pike (d 1941), of London; *Career* joined RAF VR 1942, served as cmmnd pilot in UK and M East, released Flt Lt 1946; sci staff Nat Inst for Med Res 1952–56, reader in chemical pathology St Mary's Hosp Med Sch 1962–67 (lectr 1956–62), prof of chemical endocrinology Univ of London 1967–73, prof and head of Dept of Chemical Pathology St Mary's Hosp Med Sch Univ of London 1973–90 (currently emeritus prof of chemical pathology Imperial Coll Sch of Med at St Mary's Hosp following merger); chm Div of Pathology St Mary's Hosp 1981; ed Clinical Endocrinology 1972–74; memb Herts AHA 1967–72, sec Clinical Endocrinology Ctee MRC 1976–82, chm Human Pituitary Collection MRC, pres Section of Endocrinology RSM 1976–78, dep sec gen Int Soc of Endocrinology 1986–, sec gen Euro Fedn of Endocrine Socs 1987–94; hon memb Soc for Endocrinology 2003– (gen sec 1979–83, treas 1983–91); fndr ed Endocrine-related Cancer 1993–, editorial advsr Euro Jl of Endocrinology 1994–2003; chm UK Sport Expert Ctee 1999–2010, memb Review Bd Int Tennis Fedn 2007–12, memb Ind Review Bd Int Cricket Cncl 2009–12, memb Anti-Doping Gp 2012 London Olympics, chm Scientific Expert Gp UK Anti-Doping (UKAD) 2010–15; hon memb Italian Endocrine Soc 1980, Leverhulme emeritus fell 1991; Clinical Endocrinology Tst Medal 1990, Soc for Endocrinology Jubilee Medal 1992; Freedom of Haverfordwest, Fiorino D'Oro City of Florence 1977; hon memb Soc for Endocrinology; FRSM 1960, FRCPath, Hon MRCP; *Books* Hormones in Blood (1983), The Adrenal Gland (1979, 2 edn 1992); *Recreations* languages; *Style*— Prof Vivian James; ✉ Unit of Metabolic Medicine, Imperial College School of Medicine at St Mary's Hospital, London W2 1PG

JAMES, William Stirling; s of Wing Cdr Sir Archibald William Henry James, KBE, MC (d 1980), and Eugenia, *née* Morris (d 1991); *b* 20 November 1941; *Educ* St George's Coll Rhodesia, Stonyhurst, Magdalene Coll Cambridge (MA); *Career* Morgan Grenfell & Co Ltd 1964–65; Touche Ross & Co: London 1965–68, NY 1968–69; dir: Hill Samuel & Co Ltd 1980–96 (joined 1969), LCF Rothschild 1997–; farmer; external memb Lloyd's; FCA 1978 (ACA 1968); *Recreations* shooting, bridge; *Clubs* Boodle's, Pratt's, Annabel's; *Style*— William James, Esq; ✉ 14 Queensberry Mews West, London SW7 2DU (✆ 020 7584 6750); Champions Farm, Pulborough, West Sussex RH20 3EF

JAMESON, (David) Neil; CBE (2016); *b* 25 November 1946, Tynemouth, N Tyneside; *m* Jean Jameson; *Career* Somerset CC 1970–76, Coventry Cncl 1976–80, Save the Children Fund 1980–83, The Children's Soc 1983–89, exec dir Citizens UK (formerly Citizens Organising Fndn) 1989–; hon fell Queen Mary Univ London 2013; hon dr Open Univ 2014; *Style*— Neil Jameson, Esq, CBE; ✉ Citizens UK, 112 Cavell Street, London E1 2JA (website www.citizensuk.org)

JAMESON, His Hon Judge Rodney Mellor Maples; QC (2003); *Career* called to the Bar 1976; asst recorder 1998, recorder 2000, circuit judge (North Eastern Circuit) 2012–; *Style*— His Hon Judge Jameson, QC; ✉ Leeds Combined Court Centre, The Courthouse, 1 Oxford Row, Leeds, West Yorkshire LS1 3BG

JAMIESON, Prof Ian Miller; OBE (2010); s of James Miller Jamieson (d 1959), and Winifred Emma Jamieson (d 1980); *b* 10 November 1944; *Educ* Brockley County GS, Hastings GS, Univ of Surrey (BSc, PhD), Univ of Leicester (PGCE); *m* 1975, Anne Emmery, da of Aksel Pedersen; 1 s (Erik b 15 June 1976), 1 da (Claire b 27 Oct 1984); *Career* Ealing Coll of HE (now Thames Valley Univ): variously lectr, sr lectr, head of sociology 1969–77; evaluator then co-dir Schs Cncl industry project Schs Cncl London 1978–84, reader in business and mgmnt Thames Valley Univ 1984–85; Univ of Bath: lectr in educn and industry 1985–89, prof of educn 1989–, head Dept of Educn 1990–93, auditor Quality Assurance Agency, pro-vice-chllr 1994–97 and 2003–09, dean Faculty of Humanities and Social Sciences 1997–2005; dep chief exec HE Acad 2011–12; non-exec dir UCAS 1999–2001; ed Jl of Educn and Work 1987–2001; Hon LLD Univ of Bath; memb AcSS 2003; FRSA 1991; *Books* Capitalism and Culture (1980), Schools and Industry (1982), Industry and Education (1985), Mirrors of Work: Work Simulations in Schools (1988), Rethinking Work Experience (1991), School Effectiveness and School Improvement (1996); *Recreations* theatre, opera, golf, writing; *Clubs* Cumberwell Park Golf, Combe Grove Manor; *Style*— Prof Ian Jamieson, OBE; ✉ Heron, Summer Lane, Combe Down, Bath BA2 5JX; University of Bath, Claverton Down, Bath BA2 7AY (✆ 01225 386013, fax 01225 826113, e-mail I.M.Jamieson@bath.ac.uk)

JAMIL, Jameela; *b* 25 February 1986, Hampstead; *Career* former English as a foreign language teacher Callan Sch of English, former fashion model scout Premier Model Mgmnt, television and radio presenter; brand involvement with Pandora and Elegant Touch; *Television* incl: T4, Freshly Squeezed, T4 on the Beach, Koko Pop, Playing It Straight; *Radio* Request Show (BBC Radio 1) 2012, Chart Show (BBC Radio 1) 2013–15 (first solo female host); *Recreations* fashion; *Style*— Ms Jameela Jamil; ✉ c/o Money, 42A Berwick Street, London W1F 8RZ (✆ 020 7287 7490, e-mail megan@moneymanagementuk.com, website www.moneymanagementuk.com, Twitter @JameelaJamil)

JANKE, Baroness (Life Peer UK 2014) of Clifton in the City and Council of Bristol; Barbara Lilian Janke; *Career* formerly cncllr and dep ldr Lib Dem Gp Kingston-upon-Thames Cncl; Bristol City Cncl: cncllr (Clifton Ward) 1995–, ldr 2003–04, 2005–07 and 2009–12; ldr Lib Dem Gp 1997–2007 and 2008–; *Style*— Baroness Janke; ✉ House of Lords, London SW1A 0PW

JANKEL, Mark; s of Robert Jankel (d 2005), of Weybridge, Surrey, and Jennifer, *née* Loss; *b* 12 June 1974, London; *Educ* KCS Wimbledon, UEA (BSc), Butlers Wharf Chef Sch; *Career* chef de partie The Square Mayfair 1998–2000, chef de partie then sous chef QC Restaurant London 2000–02, head chef Notting Hill Brasserie London 2003–06, exec chef First Restaurant Gp (incl The Ebury, The Waterway, Notting Hill Brasserie, Taman Gang and The Running Horse) 2006–; memb Sherry Inst of Spain (involved in the promotion of sherry in the UK through various events and competitions); *Awards* Hardens Guide Remy Award 2004, International Copa Jerez (Sherry World Cup) 2005, nominated Harpers and Queen Chef of the Year 2005, 3 AA Rosettes 2006–; *Recreations* shopping at farmers' markets and finding new sustainable suppliers; *Style*— Mark Jankel, Esq; ✉ First Restaurant Group, 54 Formosa Street, London W9 2JU (✆ 020 7266 6320, e-mail info@frgroup.co.uk)

JANSON-SMITH, (Peter) Patrick; s of John Peter Janson-Smith, of London, and Diana Mary, *née* Whittaker, of Dinant, Belgium; *b* 28 July 1949; *Educ* Cathedral Sch Salisbury, Cokethorpe Park Sch Witney; *m* 1, 22 April 1972 (m dis), Lavinia Jane, da of Robert Hugh Priestley, MBE; 1 da (Emma Mary b 12 Dec 1975), 1 s (Mark Robert b 19 July 1978); m 2, 12 June 1987 (m dis), Pamela Jean, da of Cdr Anthony William Gossage, RN; 2 s (Oscar William Patrick b 9 Jan 1989, Daniel Alexander b 15 Jan 1991); m 3, 20 March 2006, Mrs Anne-Louise Fisher; *Career* publisher; asst to export publicity mangr University of London Press Ltd (Hodder & Stoughton) 1967–69; Granada Publishing: asst to publicity mangr Panther Books Ltd 1969–70, ed Mayflower Books 1970–71 and 1973–74, press offr 1971–72; publicity mangr Octopus Books 1972; Transworld Publishers: ed Corgi Books 1974–78, assoc editorial dir Corgi Books 1978–79, editorial dir Nationwide Book Serv 1979–81, publisher Corgi & Black Swan Books 1981–95, publisher Transworld Publishers Adult Trade Div 1995–99, dep md (publishing) 1999–2001, jt md and publisher 2001–03, publisher 2003–05; agent Christopher Little Literary Agency 2005–07, publisher Blue Door (HarperCollins) 2008–14; chm Kingsford Campbell Literary & Marketing Agency 2014–; memb: Ctee Soc of Young Publishers 1969–71, Whitefriars Soc 1992–, Bd Edinburgh Book Festival 1994–99, Soc of Bookmen 1998–; *Recreations* book collecting, late 19th and early 20th century illustrations, wine and food; *Clubs* Century, Beefsteak; *Style*— Patrick Janson-Smith, Esq; ✉ patrick@patrickjansonsmith.co.uk

JANSONS, Mariss; s of Arvid Jansons, conductor; *b* 1943; *Educ* Leningrad Conservatory, Second Vienna Acad; *Career* conductor; trained with Prof Hans Swarowsky in Vienna and with Herbert von Karajan in Salzburg (winner Herbert von Karajan Competition 1971); Leningrad (now St Petersburg) Philharmonic: assoc princ conductor 1985, conducted orch on numerous tours to Europe, N America and Japan; Oslo Philharmonic: music dir 1979–2000, conducted orch at numerous international venues incl Salzburg Festival and Edinburgh Festivals, Carnegie Hall NY, Suntory Hall Tokyo, Vienna Musikverein and BBC Proms; princ guest conductor LPO 1992–97, prof of conducting St Petersburg Conservatoire 1993–2000, music dir Pittsburgh Symphony Orch 1997–2004, chief conductor Symphony Orch of Bavarian Radio 2003–12, chief conductor Royal Concertgebouw Orch 2004–15; conducted numerous other orchs incl: Boston, Chicago, Baltimore and Pittsburg Symphonies, Cleveland Orch, Philadelphia Orch, Los Angeles Philharmonic, Toronto and Montreal Symphonies, Vienna Symphony and Philharmonic, Berlin Philharmonic, Royal Concertgebouw Amsterdam, NDR Symphony Germany, Israel Philharmonic, LSO, LPO, The Philharmonia; recorded TV series Jansons Conducts for BBC Wales 1991; hon dr Univs of Oslo and Riga; hon memb Royal Acad of Music; EMI Classics' Artist of the Year 1996; awarded Anders Jahre Norwegian Culture Prize, Cdr with Star Royal Norwegian Order of Merit 1995, Three Star Medal of Latvia, Golden Cross of Honour (Vienna) 2007, ECHO Klassik Award Conductor of the Year 2007, Bavarian Order of Merit 2007, Pro Europa Fndn European Conducting Prize 2007, Baltic Stars Award 2007, Austrian Cross of Honour 2009, Mertul Cultural Cavalier (Rumanian) 2009, Bavarian ORder of Maximilian 2010, IJ Award (Amsterdam) 2012, Ernst-von-Siemens-Musikpreis 2013, Medal of Merits of the Bayerischer Rundfunk 2013, Medal of Merit of St Petersburg 2013, German Federal Cross of Merit with Star 2013, Knight of the Lion of the Netherlands 2013, Comandeur des Arts et des Lettres 2015, Conductor of Honour of the Koniklijk Concertgebouworkest 2015, Latvian Great Music Award 2015; *Recordings* with St Petersburg Philharmonic incl Shostakovich's 7th Symphony 1989 (winner Eddison Award Holland 1989); with Oslo Philharmonic incl: complete Tchaikovsky Symphonies (Chandos), numerous for EMI incl Sibelius and Prokofiev violin concertos (with Frank-Peter Zimmerman), Wagner overtures, Dvořák's Symphonies 5 (winner Penguin Award), 8 and 9, Saint-Saens Symphony No 3 (winner Spellemannsprisen Norway), other works by Bartók, Mussorgsky, Ravel, Respighi, Shostakovich and Svendsen; complete symphones of Shostakovich (Grammy Award for Symphony No 13); *Style*— Mariss Jansons, Esq; ✉ c/o Radmila Schweitzer, Symphonieorchester des Bayerischen Rundfunks, Runfunkplatz 1, 80335 Munich, Germany (✆ 00 49 89 5900 4974)

JANVRIN, Baron (Life Peer UK 2007), of Chalford Hill in the County of Gloucestershire; Sir Robin Berry Janvrin; GCB (2007, KCB 2003, CB 1997), GCVO (2007, KCVO 1998, CVO 1994, LVO 1983), QSO (2008), PC (1998); s of Vice Adm Sir (Hugh) Richard Benest Janvrin, KCB, DSC (d 1993), and Nancy Edyth, *née* Fielding (d 1994); *b* 20 September 1946; *Educ* Marlborough, BNC Oxford; *m* 22 Oct 1977, Isabelle, da of Yann de Boissonneaux de Chevigny; 2 s, 2 da; *Career* RN: RNC Dartmouth 1964, HMS Devonshire 1965, HMS Lynx 1970, HMS Ganges 1973, HMS Royal Arthur 1974; Dip Serv: FCO 1975, 1978 and 1984, first sec UK Delgn NATO 1976, New Delhi 1981, cnsllr and dep head Personnel Dept 1985–87; private sec to HM The Queen 1999–2007 (press sec 1987–90, asst private sec 1990–95, dep private sec 1996–99); sr advsr HSBC Private Bank (UK) Ltd; tstee Nat Portrait Gallery; *Style*— The Lord Janvrin, GCB, GCVO, QSO

JARDINE, Sir Andrew Colin Douglas; 5 Bt (UK 1916), of Godalming, Surrey; er s of Brig Sir Ian Liddell Jardine, 4 Bt, OBE, MC (d 1982), and Priscilla, *née* Scott-Phillips (d 2012); *b* 30 November 1955; *Educ* Charterhouse, Royal Agric Coll/Univ of Reading 1993–96 (BSc); *m* 11 Oct 1997, Dr Claire Vyvien Griffith, da of Dr William Griffith, of Lyth Hill, Shrewsbury; 2 da (Iona Claire b 21 Feb 1999, Alexandra Scilla b 14 July 2001), 1 s (Guy Andrew b 15 March 2004); *Heir* s, Guy Jardine; *Career* served Royal Green Jackets 1975–78; C T Bowring & Co 1979–81, Henderson Administration Group plc 1981–92, dir Gartmore Investment Management Ltd 1992–93, Strutt & Parker 1996–99, resident land agent 2000–10; estates bursar and non-tutorial fell Worcester Coll Oxford 2010–14, property and charity conslt 2014–; MCSI 1993, MRICS 1998; *Style*— Sir Andrew Jardine, Bt; ✉ Caudle Farm, Caudle Green, Cheltenham, Gloucestershire GL53 9PR (☎ 01285 821895, e-mail andrewj@rdine.co.uk)

JARDINE, Prof Nicholas; s of Michael James Jardine (d 1988), and Jean Caroline, *née* Crook (d 1997); *b* 4 September 1943; *Educ* Monkton Combe, King's Coll Cambridge (Trevelyan scholar, BA, PhD); *m* 1992, Marina, da of Mario Frasca-Spada; 4 c by previous marriages; *Career* Royal Society research fell 1968–73, sr research fell King's Coll Cambridge 1971–75 (jr research fell 1967–71); Univ of Cambridge: univ lectr in history and philosophy of science 1975–85, reader 1985–91, prof of history and philosophy of the sciences 1991–; fell Darwin Coll Cambridge 1975–; ed: Studies in History and Philosophy of Science 1982–2011, Studies in History and Philosophy of Biological and Biomedical Sciences 1998–2012; FBA; *Books* Mathematical Taxonomy (with R Sibson, 1971), The Birth of History and Philosophy of Science (1984, revised edn 1988), The Fortunes of Inquiry (1986), Romanticism and the Sciences (ed with A Cunningham, 1990), The Scenes of Inquiry (1991, revised edn 2000), Cultures of Natural History (ed with J Secord and E Spary, 1996), Books and the Sciences in History (ed with M Frasca-Spada, 2000), La guerre des astronomes, Vols 1 and 2 (with A Segonds, 2008), Christoph Rothmann's Treatise on the Comet of 1585 (with M Granada and A Mosley, 2014); *Recreations* fungus hunting; *Style*— Prof Nicholas Jardine; ✉ Department of History and Philosophy of Science, University of Cambridge, Free School Lane, Cambridge CB2 3RH (☎ 01223 334546)

JARDINE, Prof Richard James; s of Maj David Jardine (d 1987), and Dorothy, *née* Whitbread (d 2009); *b* 15 May 1953; *Educ* Sir Roger Manwood's GS Sandwich, Imperial Coll London (BSc, MSc, DIC, PhD); *m* 1; 1 s (James Alexander b 5 Dec 1988), 1 da (Olivia Jane b 21 Jan 1991); m 2, Jayne Elizabeth, *née* Birch; 1 s (Alexander George b 2 Sept 2005); *Career* with Sir William Halcrow and Partners 1974–75, work on Thames tidal flood defences Southern Water Authy 1975–77, numerous major highways projects Kent CC 1977–81; Imperial Coll London: research asst 1981–84, lectr and reader 1984–98, prof of mechanics 1998–, head of geotechnics 2003–11, Coll consul for engrg 2012–; assoc Geotechnical Consulting Gp 1986–; ICE Telford Premium 1985, Unwin Prize Imperial Coll London 1985, Geotechnique Award 1988, American Soc for Testing Materials Hogentogler Award 1992, Japanese Ronbun Show Award 1993, Br Geotechnical Soc Prize 1996, Royal Acad of Engrg Medal 1998, ICE Geotechnical Research Medal 2007 and 2008, ICE Manby Prize 2010, Bishop Lecture 2013, Sowers Lecture 2014, Rankine Lecture 2016; FICE 2001 (MICE 1979), FREng 2002, FCGI 2007; *Publications* around 200 pubns on soil mechanics, geotechnics, fndns and offshore structures; *Recreations* tennis, diving, sailing, music; *Clubs* Iguales; *Style*— Prof Richard Jardine; ✉ Department of Civil and Environmental Engineering, Imperial College, London SW7 2BU (☎ 020 7594 6083, fax 020 7225 2716, e-mail r.jardine@imperial.ac.uk)

JARMAN, Andrew M; s of Basil Jarman (d 1999), of Petersfield, Hants, and Josephine Mary, *née* Lockyer (d 2000); *b* 16 May 1957; *Educ* Portsmouth GS, Hertford Coll Oxford (MA), Univ of Oxford (PGCE), NPQH; *m* 16 Aug 1980, Kerstin Maria, *née* Bailey; 1 s (Conrad William Anders b 24 April 1992), 2 da (Annika Elizabeth (twin) b 24 April 1992, Ella Louise b 15 June 1994); *Career* mathematics teacher: Aylesbury GS 1979–80, Portsmouth GS 1980–84, Haberdashers' Aske's Sch Elstree 1984–88; Cheltenham Coll: head of mathematics 1988–92, dir of studies 1992–2001; headmaster Lancaster Royal GS 2001–12, ret; memb ASCL, assoc memb HMC; memb Ct Lancaster Univ; Offr of Merit Mil and Hospitaller Order of St Lazarus of Jerusalem; *Recreations* golf, antique wineglasses; *Clubs* East India, Lansdowne; *Style*— Andrew Jarman, Esq; ✉ Lancaster Royal Grammar School, East Road, Lancaster LA1 3EF (☎ 01524 580600, fax 01524 847947, e-mail ajarman@lrgs.org.uk)

JARMAN, Prof Sir Brian; kt (1998), OBE (1988); *Educ* MB BS, MA, DIC, PhD; *Career* house physician St Mary's Hosp London 1969, house surgn St Bernard's Hosp Gibraltar 1970, resident in med Beth Israel Hosp Harvard Med Sch 1970, trainee GP London 1971, princ in GP Lisson Grove Health Centre London 1971–98, prof of primary health care and gen practice and head of dept Imperial Coll Sch of Med at St Mary's Hosp (St Mary's Med Sch until merger 1997)1984–98 (pt/t sr lectr 1973–83), head Primary Care and Population Health Sciences Div Imperial Coll Sch of Med 1997–98 (emeritus prof of primary health care 1998–); dir Dr Foster Unit Faculty of Medicine Imperial Coll London 2004–; memb: MRC Health Servs Research Ctee 1987–89, English Nat Bd 1988–90, Kensington Chelsea and Westminster FHSA 1990–96, King's Fund Mgmnt Ctee 1994–97, London Strategic Review Panel Dept of Health 1997–98; medical memb Bristol Royal Infirmary Inquiry 1998–2001, sr fell Inst for Healthcare Improvement Boston USA, pres BMA 2003–04; author of numerous papers in academic jls and research advsr to various bodies nationally and internationally; FRCGP 1984, FRCP 1988, FFPH 1999 (MFPHM 1994), FMedSci 1999; *Style*— Prof Sir Brian Jarman, OBE

JARMAN, Dr Paul Richard; s of Prof Sir Brian Jarman, OBE, *qv*; *b* 25 March 1964; *Educ* William Ellis Sch London, St Peter's Coll Oxford (exhibitioner, MA), UCL and Middx Hosp Sch of Med (MB BS), Inst of Neurology UCL (PhD); *Career* conslt neurologist Nat Hosp for Neurology and Neurosurgery, UC Hosps and Homerton Hosp London 2001–, hon sr lectr UCL 2001–; memb Fitness to Practice Ctee GMC; author of pubns on neurology and neurological genetics; *Style*— Dr Paul Jarman; ✉ National Hospital for Neurology and Neurosurgery, Queen Square, London WC1N 3BG (☎ 020 7837 3611)

JARMAN, Richard Neville; s of Dr Gwyn Jarman (d 1995), of Herts, and Pauline, *née* Lane (d 2002); *b* 24 April 1949; *Educ* King's Sch Canterbury, Trinity Coll Oxford (MA); *Career* ENO: mktg mangr 1971–74, asst to admin dir 1974–76; dance touring offr Arts Cncl of GB 1976–77; Edinburgh Int Festival: artistic asst 1978–82, festival admin 1982–84; general admin English Nat Ballet 1984–90, general dir Scottish Opera 1991–97, interim general mangr Arts Theatre Cambridge 1997–98, artistic dir Royal Opera House 1998–2000, DG Britten-Pears Fndn and The Britten Estate 2002–; dir Scottish Opera; FRSA; *Books* History of Sadler's Wells/English National Opera (1974), History of the London Coliseum (1976), History of the New Opera Company (1978); *Recreations* gardening, music, theatre, food and drink; *Style*— Richard Jarman, Esq; ✉ 78 Riversdale Road, Highbury, London N5 2JZ (☎ and fax 020 3227 0086, e-mail richard-jarman@btconnect.com)

JARVIS, Anthony (Tony); s of Donald Anthony Jarvis (d 1997), and Ida, *née* Allmond (d 1998); *b* 1945; *Educ* City of Oxford HS, Brighton Coll of Educn (CertEd), Univ of Sussex (BEd, MA); *m* Brigit Mary, da of Baillie Andrew and Elizabeth Convery; 1 s, 1 da; *Career* librarian, head of social studies and head of year Haywards Heath Co Sch 1971–74 (asst master and boarding housemaster 1968–72), head of social studies and curriculum co-ordinator Oathall Sch and PGCE tutor Univ of Sussex 1974–79, head of English Oathall Sch 1979–84, dep princ/headmaster secdy sch St George's Sch Rome 1984–90 (acting princ 1987), headmaster Sir Thomas Rich's Sch Gloucester 1990–94, headmaster St Olave's & St Saviour's GS Orpington 1994–2010; team inspr OFSTED 1996–2003; headteacher memb Army Scholarship Bd; govr Hurstpierpoint Coll 2001–, memb Sch Governing Body Christ's Hosp 2007–12, chm Cncl of Govrs Hurstpierpoint Coll 2013–; fell Woodward Corp 2006– (chm Educn Ctee and memb Bd of Dirs 2006–12); educn conslt UK and Europe; dir The Severals Freehold Ltd 2016; memb HMC 1996, registered on Nationally Recognised Outstanding Ldrs in Educn (NROLE) 2008, Chartered London Teacher 2008, Leadership Pathways coach NCSL 2009; FRSA 1993; *Recreations* books and newspapers, travel, restaurants, rugby union, Italy; *Clubs* East India and Public Schs (hon memb), Sir Thomas Rich's Bowling; *Style*— Mr Tony Jarvis; ✉ 19 The Severals, Bury Road, Newmarket, Suffolk, CB8 7YN

JARVIS, Daniel Owen Woolgar (Dan); MBE (2011), MP; *b* 30 November 1972, Nottingham; *Educ* Rushcliffe Sch Nottinghamshire, Univ of Wales, RMA Sandhurst; *Career* formerly Maj Parachute Regt Br Army; MP (Lab) Barnsley Central 2011–, shadow min for culture 2011–13, shadow min for justice 2013–15, shadow min for the Foreign Office 2015; *Style*— Dan Jarvis, Esq, MBE, MP; ✉ House of Commons, London SW1A 0AA

JARVIS, Dr John Herbert; s of Herbert Henry Wood Jarvis (d 1982), and Mabel, *née* Griffiths (d 2001); *b* 16 May 1947, Purfleet, Essex; *Educ* Univ of Wales Swansea (BSc, PhD); *m* 20 June 1970, Jean Elizabeth Levy; 1 da (Louise Hannah Mary b 5 Oct 1976), 1 s (Robin Alexander Levy b 14 Dec 1985); *Career* post-doctoral research fell WNSM 1972–75, post-doctoral fell Univ of Bristol 1975–77, medical ed Elsevier Publishers 1977–79, medical ed then publishing dir Wiley Publishers 1979–92, md John Wiley & Sons Ltd 1992–2007, sr vice-pres Wiley Europe 1996–2007; non-exec dir: Royal Pharmaceutical Soc Press; memb Publishers' Assoc Cncl 1999–2005, dir Int Assoc of Scientific, Technical and Medical Publishers (STM) 1999–2005; author of numerous scientific papers; tstee Weald and Downland Open Air Museum; Freeman Worshipful Co of Stationers; *Recreations* boating, walking, music, golf, daytrading; *Clubs* Groucho; *Style*— Dr John Jarvis; ☎ 07730 814152, e-mail johnhjarvis@btinternet.com)

JARVIS, John Manners; QC; s of Donald Edward Manners Jarvis, TD (d 1999), of Rockbourne, Hants, and Theodora Brixie, *née* Bryant (d 1991); *b* 20 November 1947; *Educ* KCS Wimbledon, Emmanuel Coll Cambridge (MA); *m* 5 May 1972, Janet Rona, da of Eric Cresswell Kitson, OBE (d 1975), of Mersham, Kent; 2 s (Christopher b 1974, Fergus b 1976); *Career* called to the Bar Lincoln's Inn 1970 (bencher); in practice at Commercial Bar, jt head of chambers 3 Verulam Buildings 1997–2009, recorder of the Crown Court, dep judge of the High Court; chm Commercial Bar Assoc 1995–97; int ed Jl of Banking and Finance Law and Practice, conslt ed Jl of Int Banking and Finance Law; chm of govrs KCS Wimbledon 2008–13; *Publications* Lender Liability (jtly, 1994), Banks, Liability and Risk (contrib 1991, 2 edn 1995); *Recreations* tennis, sailing, horse riding, skiing, cycling, music; *Clubs* Hurlingham; *Style*— John Jarvis, Esq, QC; ✉ 3 Verulam Buildings, Gray's Inn, London WC1R 5NT (☎ 020 7831 8441, fax 020 7831 8479, e-mail jjarvis@3vb.com)

J

JARVIS, Martin; OBE (2000); s of late Denys Jarvis, and Margot Jarvis; *b* 4 August 1941; *Educ* Whitgift Sch, RADA; *m* 1; 2 s; m 2, 23 Nov 1974, Rosalind Ayres, *qv*, da of Sam Johnson (d 1986); *Career* actor, dir and prodr; first appearance Nat Youth Theatre 1960–62 (played Henry V Sadler's Wells 1962); dir Children's Film Unit 1993–99, currently prodr and dir of dramas for BBC Radio 4; contrib Comic Relief and Children in Need; *Theatre* NT incl: Importance of Being Earnest 1982, Victoria Station 1983, The Trojan War Will Not Take Place 1983, An Audience with Martin Jarvis 2003; other credits incl: Manchester Library Theatre 1962–63, Poor Bitos (Duke of York's) 1963, Man and Superman (Vaudeville) 1966, The Bandwagon (Mermaid) 1970, The Rivals (USA) 1973, title role in Hamlet (Festival of Br Theatre) 1973, The Circle (Haymarket) 1976, She Stoops to Conquer (Canada and Hong Kong Arts Festivals) 1977, Caught in the Act (Garrick) 1981, Woman in Mind (Vaudeville) 1986, The Perfect Party (Greenwich) 1987, Jerome in Henceforward (Vaudeville) 1989, Viktor in Exchange (Vaudeville) 1990 (also LA 1992), Sir Andrew Aguecheek in Sir Peter Hall's revival of Twelfth Night (Playhouse) 1991, title role in Leo in Love (Nuffield Theatre and nat tour) 1992, Dennis in the revival of Ayckbourn's Just Between Ourselves (Greenwich) 1992, starred in Make and Break (LA) 1993, starred in On Approval (Playhouse) 1994, starred in Ayckbourn's Man of the Moment (LA) 1994 and Table Manners (LA Theatre Works) 1995, concert performance of Peter and The Wolf (narrator, Barbican) 1997, The Doctor's Dilemma (Almeida) 1998, David Hare's Skylight (USA) 1999, Passion Play (Donmar Warehouse Theatre) 2000, Shadowlands (USA) 2001, By Jeeves (USA) 2001, Gielgud Centenary Gala 2004, Twelfth Night (Open Air Theatre Regent's Park) 2005; *Television* incl: The Forsyte Saga 1967, Nicholas Nickleby 1968, David Copperfield 1975, Rings on their Fingers 1978, Breakaway 1980, The Black Tower 1985, Chelworth 1988, Rumpole of the Bailey 1988–89, Countdown 1989–95, all voices in children's animated series Huxley Pig 1989–90, You Say Potato (USA) 1990–, all voices on animation series Fourways Farm (series) 1993–95, Scarlet and Black (film series) 1993, Touch of Love 1994, starred as Brillat Savarin 1994; other credits incl: Inspector Morse (Greeks Bearing Gifts, feature length TV film) 1991, Maurice Howling in Murder Most Horrid 1991, Woof 1992, Charles Longmuir in The Good Guys 1992, Boon 1992, Casualty 1992, Library of Romance 1993, Countdown 1993, Pebble Mill 1993, House Party 1993, Lovejoy 1994, Murder She Wrote 1995, A Touch of Frost 1995, Fantastic Mr Fox 1995, Space – Above and Beyond (USA) 1996, Walker – Texas Ranger (USA) 1996, Nation's Favourite Children's Book 1997, Supply and Demand 1998, Space Island One 1999, Sex 'n' Death 2000, Lorna Doone 2000, Micawber 2001, By Jeeves 2001, Inspector Lynley Mysteries 2002, Bootleg 2003, Psi-Kix (series, USA) 2003, Doctors 2004, Much Ado About Nothing 2005, EastEnders 2010; commentaries for TV film documentaries and arts programmes; *Radio* numerous radio performances incl: Charles Dickens in The Best of Times, one-man series Jarvis' Frayn, Lord Illingworth in Wilde's A Woman of No Importance 1991, Speak After the Beep (also prodr), Dennis Potter Stories (also prodr) 1998, Colonel Clay (also prodr) 1998, M for Mother 1999, The Doctor's Dilemma (also prodr) 1999, Woman In Mind (also prodr) 2000, Spies 2001; as dir: Inappropriate Behaviour 2002, A Tribute to Finchie, Afternoons with Roger, The Trial of Walter Ralegh 2003, Forever Mine 2004, Teacher's Pet 2005; adapted and read over 120 of Richmal Crompton's William stories for radio, TV and CD; *Recordings* cassette recordings incl: Just William vols 1–5 (BBC), David Copperfield 1991, Jarvis's Frayn (CSA Telltapes) 1992, Tales From Shakespeare (LA) 1993, Honor Among Thieves (USA) 1993, narrator/host Concorde Playhouse 1994–95, Dick Francis series (Penguin) 1995–98, Oliver Twist 1996, Goodbye Mr Chips 1997, A Night to Remember 1997, The Third Man 1998, England Their England 1998, Hard Times 1998, Just William 6 1998, Jeffrey Archer Stories 1998, Ovid's Art of Love 1998, Fantastic Mr Fox 1998, A Tale of Two Cities 1999; *Film* incl: The Last Escape, Ike, The Bunker, Taste the Blood of Dracula, Buster, Emily's Ghost (CFU/Channel 4) 1993, Calliope 1993, Absence of War 1995, Titanic 1997, The X-Ray Kid 1998, Mrs Caldicot's Cabbage War 2001; *Awards* nominated Best Actor Sony Radio Awards 1991, NY Int Radio Award 1994, Peabody Award USA for Fourways Farm, Brit Talkies Award 1995, Audie Award (USA) 2001, Earphone Award 2002, Broadway Theatre World Award 2002; *Publications* Bright Boy (play, 1977), Just William Stories (ed, 1992), Meet Just William (1999), Acting Strangely (autobiography, 1999), Broadway, Jeeves? (2003); short stories for radio, articles in The Listener, Punch, Evening Standard, High Life, Daily Mail, Tatler, Sunday Telegraph; *Recreations* Beethoven, Mozart, people-watching, growing lemons; *Clubs* BBC; *Style*— Martin Jarvis, Esq, OBE; ✉ c/o Amanda Howard Associates, 21 Berwick Street, London W1F 0PZ (☎ 020 7287 9277)

JARVIS, His Hon (James) Roger; s of late Douglas Bernard Jarvis, DFC, of Poole, Dorset, and late Elsie Vanessa Jarvis; *b* 7 September 1944; *Educ* Latymer Upper Sch, Brockenhurst GS, Peter Symonds Coll Winchester; *m* 8 January 1972, Kerstin Marianne; 1 s (Simon Antony b 14 Sept 1973), 2 da (Marianne Susie b 23 Oct 1976, Sophie Emilia b 26 Dec 1981); *Career* admitted slr 1969; McQueen Yeoman (formerly Andrews McQueen): joined 1972, ptnr 1973–2000; circuit judge (Western Circuit) 2000–14, ret; *Recreations* jogging, walking, reading; *Style—* His Hon Roger Jarvis; ✉ e-mail jrogerjarvis@googlemail.com

JARVIS, Sian Elizabeth; CB (2010); da of Raymond Anthony Jarvis and Marjorie, *née* Owen; *b* 11 April 1963; *Educ* Chelmsford HS for Girls, Loughborough Univ (BA); *Children* 2 c (Georgina Lily, Jack William (twins) b 12 Jan 2006); *Career* trainee BBC News (regional) 1988–89, reporter/presenter BBC East 1989–92, political corr 1992–99, news presenter GMTV and Radio 5; DG of communication Dept of Health 1999–2011, dir of corporate affrs Asda 2012–13, Jarvis & Bo Strategic Communications Consultancy 2013–; PR Professional of the Year 2009; ptnr in African horseback safari business Botswana; *Recreations* opera, riding, yoga, playing piano; *Style—* Ms Sian Jarvis, CB; ✉ 31 Lansdowne Gardens, London SW8 2EQ (☎ 07867 538399, e-mail sianjarvis@btinternet.com)

JARVIS, William; s of W J Ryan Jarvis (d 1992), and Jean Marshall, *née* Hall (d 1984); *b* 14 October 1960; *Educ* Harrow; *m* (m dis); 2 s (Jack b 9 Nov 1988, Tom b 11 Sept 1990), 1 da (Lucinda b 16 May 1996); *Career* racehorse trainer Newmarket 1985–; trained winners at every English racecourse, trainer Grand Lodge (champion European 2 year old 1993 and winner of St James's Palace Stakes Royal Ascot 1994); vice-chm Newmarket Trainers Fedn; *Recreations* skiing and all sports; *Clubs* Turf, Jockey Club Rooms; *Style—* William Jarvis, Esq; ✉ Phantom House, Fordham Road, Newmarket, Suffolk CB8 7AA (☎ 01638 662677, fax 01638 667328)

JARY, Michael Keith; s of Keith Jary, and Jacqueline Ann, *née* Pogue (d 2004); *b* 15 June 1963, Cambridge; *Educ* Berkhamsted Sch (scholar), Merton Coll Oxford (postmaster, BA, MA), INSEAD France (Louis Franck scholar, Kitchener scholar, MBA, guest lectr), SOAS Univ of London (postgrad cert); *m* 2015, Jonathan Jimenez Ferrer; *Career* assoc Booz Allen & Hamilton 1985–87; OC&C Strategy Consultants: fndr memb 1987, ptnr London 1993–, managing ptnr London and head of worldwide retail practice 2000–05, worldwide managing ptnr and chm Int Exec Ctee 2005–11 (re-elected 2008); memb Investment Ctee Web-Angel plc 1999–2001; non-exec chm Duchy Originals Ltd 2008–, non-exec dir Nationwide Building Soc 2009–15; memb Advsy Bd World Retail Congress 2009–11, ambass The Retail Tst 2014–, memb Industry Advsy Ctee Fashion Retail Acad 2016–; non-exec chm The Prince's Social Enterprises 2010–15, memb Exec Sub-Ctee The Prince's Charities 2010–13, chm Fairtrade Fndn 2013–, chair Commercial Ctee The Prince of Wales's Charitable Fndn 2015–; FRAS 2011; *Publications* Retail Power Plays (co-author, 1997, US edn 1998), Markenpower (co-author, 1998), Brands the New Wealth Creators (co-author, 1998), Market Leader (contrib, 2009), In the Footsteps of a Himalayan Pilgrimage (2013); *Recreations* collecting Indian and South East Asian art and cultural artefacts, organic farming (pigs, sheep, poultry, bees and vegetables), opera going, playing croquet, classic cars, cooking, Himalayan trekking; *Style—* Michael Jary, Esq; ✉ OC&C Strategy Consultants, 6 New Street Square, London EC4A 3AT (☎ 020 7010 8024, fax 020 7010 8100)

JASON, Sir David; kt (2005), OBE (1993); s of Arthur White, and Olwen, *née* Jones; *b* 2 February 1940; *Educ* Northside Secdy Sch; *m* 2005, Gill Hinchcliffe; 1 da (Sophie Mae b 26 Feb 2001); *Career* actor; first professional job with Bromley Repertory 1965; early work incl: 3 months in Crossroads, tour with Ron Moody in Peter Pan, Summer seasons with Bob Monkhouse and Dick Emery; fell BAFTA 2003; *Theatre* incl: Under Milk Wood (Mayfair), Bob Acres in The Rivals (Sadler's Wells), No Sex Please...We're British! (Strand) 1972, Darling Mr London 1975–76, Fancourt Babberley in Charley's Aunt, Norman in The Norman Conquests (Oxford Playhouse) 1976, Lord Foppington in The Relapse (Cambridge Theatre Co), Buttons in Cinderella, Tom Bryce in The Unvarnished Truth (Middle and Far East) 1983, Look No Hans! (Strand Theatre and tour) 1985–86; *Television* incl: Do Not Adjust Your Set 1967, The Top Secret Life of Edgar Briggs (LWT) 1973–74, Mr Stabbs (Thames) 1974, Blanco in Porridge (BBC) 1975, Lucky Feller (LWT) 1975, A Sharp Intake of Breath (ATV) 1978, Granville in Open All Hours (with Ronnie Barker, several series, BBC), Del Trotter in Only Fools and Horses (several series, BBC), Skullion in Porterhouse Blue (C4) 1986, Ted Simcock in A Bit of a Do (2 series, YTV) 1988–89, Single Voices: The Chemist (monologue by Roy Clarke, BBC) 1989, George in Amongst Barbarians (screenplay, BBC) 1989, Pa Larkin in The Darling Buds of May (YTV) 1990–2002, Inspector Jack Frost in A Touch of Frost (YTV) 1992–2010, The Bullion Boys (1993, Int Emmy for Best Drama 1994), Frank Beck in All the King's Men (BBC), The Ghostboat 2006, The Hogfather 2006, The Colour of Magic 2008; voice of many cartoon characters incl Dangermouse and Count Duckula; dir The Quest 2002; *Film* Under Milk Wood, Royal Flash 1974, The Odd Job 1978, Only Fools and Horses (BBC), Toad in The Wind in the Willows; *Awards* Radio Times Funniest Actor, Variety Club Personality of the Year, Sony Radio Award, Water Rats Personality of the Year, TV Times Actor of the Year, TV Times Funniest Actor, BAFTA Award for Best Actor 1988, BAFTA Award for Best Light Entertainment Performer 1990, Nat Television Awards Special Recognition Award for Lifetime Achievement in Television 1996, Favourite Situation Comedy Performer at Aunties (BBC) 1996, BAFTA Award for Best Comedy Performance 1997, TV Quick Award for Best Actor 2000 and 2001, Nat TV Awards for Best Actor 2001, British Comedy Award for Lifetime Achievement 2001, BAFTA Fellowship Award 2003, Best Drama Performance Nat Television Award 2011; *Recreations* helicopter pilot, gliding, restoration of old machines, work; *Style—* Sir David Jason, OBE; ✉ c/o The Richard Stone Partnership, 2 Henrietta Street, London WC2E 8PS (☎ 020 7497 0849, fax 020 7497 0869)

JASON, Gillian Brett; da of A R F Bosworth (d 1963), of London, and Joan Lena, *née* Brett (d 2002); *b* 30 June 1941, Codsall, Staffs; *Educ* Dominican Covent Sch Brewood, Royal Ballet Sr Sch (Br Ballet Orgn award), London Opera Centre (with assistance from Vaughan Williams Tst); *m* 21 March 1961, Neville Abraham Jacobson; 1 da (Elli b 1967), 1 s (Alexander b 1970); *Career* art gallery director; visual arts work 1973–79, private dealer 1980–81, dir Gillian Jason Gallery London 1981–94 (represented estates of: David Bomberg, Frank Dobson, John Tunnard, Bryan Wynter), dir Jason & Rhodes London 1994–99 (artists represented: Ansel Krut, Eduardo Paolozzi, Michael Sandle, Paul Storey, John Virtue), dir Gillian Jason Modern and Contemporary Art London 1999–; memb Soc of London Art Dealers 1995–2014; *Awards* incl: Vaughan-Williams Tst Bursary, Countess of Munster Tst Award 1966, finalist Kathleen Ferrier Meml Scholarship RAM 1966; *Recreations* cinema, fashion, gardening, music, opera, reading, travel, walking, running; *Style—* Mrs Gillian Jason; ✉ (By appointment) Gillian Jason Modern & Contemporary Art, 3 Ormonde Terrace, London NW8 7LP (e-mail art@gillianjason.com, website www.gillianjason.com)

JASPAN, Andrew; s of Mervyn Aubrey Jaspan (d 1974), and Helen, *née* Wright; *b* 20 April 1953, Manchester; *Educ* Beverley GS, Marlborough, Univ of Manchester (BA); *m* 1990, Karen Grant; 2 s (Ewan b 1994, Calum b 1995); *Career* founding ed New Manchester Review 1975–77; sub ed: Daily Telegraph 1978–80, Daily Mirror 1981; reporter Journalists in Europe (Paris) 1982, sub ed and reporter The Times 1983–85, asst news ed The Sunday Times 1985–88; ed: The Sunday Times Scotland 1988, Scotland on Sunday 1989–94, The Scotsman 1994–95, The Observer 1995–96, The Sunday Herald 1998–2004, ed The Age (Aust) 2004–09; fndr, ed and exec dir The Conversation 2011; ed-in-chief: The Conversation UK 2013, The Conversation US 2014, The Conversation France 2015, The Conversation Africa 2015, The Conversation Global 2016, The Conversation Canada 2016; publisher and md The Big Issue 1996–98, business devpt exec Scottish Media Group plc 1997, conslt and Asia-Pacific dir Innovation Media 2009–; sr researcher Univ of Melbourne 2011–, adjunct prof RMIT Melbourne 2012–; *Recreations* reading, travelling, tennis; *Style—* Andrew Jaspan, Esq

JAVID, Rt Hon Sajid; PC (2014), MP; *Educ* Univ of Exeter; *Career* former vice-pres Chase Manhattan Bank, md Deutsche Bank until 2009; MP (Cons) Bromsgrove 2010–, financial sec to the Treasy 2013–14, sec for culture, media and sport and min for equalities 2014–15, sec of state for business, innovation and skills 2015–16, sec of state for communities and local govt 2016–; pres Bd of Trade, memb Nat Security Cncl; *Style—* The Rt Hon Sajid Javid, MP; ✉ House of Commons, London SW1A 0AA (☎ 020 7219 7027, e-mail sajid.javid.mp@parliament.uk, website www.sajidjavid.com)

JAY, Sir Antony Rupert; kt (1988), CVO (1993); s of Ernest Jay (d 1957), of London, and Catherine Mary, *née* Hay (d 1981); *b* 20 April 1930; *Educ* St Paul's (scholar), Magdalene Coll Cambridge (major scholar, MA); *m* 15 June 1957, Rosemary Jill, da of Leslie Watkins, of Stratford-upon-Avon, Warks; 2 s (Michael b 1959, David b 1972), 2 da (Ros b 1961, Kate b 1964); *Career* Nat Serv Royal Signals 1952–54 (2 Lt 1953), Lt TA 1954; BBC 1955–64: ed Tonight 1962–63, head talks features 1963–64; freelance writer and prodr 1964–; ed A Prime Minister on Prime Ministers 1977; writer: Royal Family (1969), Yes Minister (3 series with Jonathan Lynn, 1980–82), Yes Prime Minister (3 series, 1985, 1987 and 2013, and play (Gielgud Theatre) 2010–11), Elizabeth R (1992); chm Video Arts Ltd 1972–89; memb Annan Ctee on Future of Broadcasting 1974–77; BAFTA Writers' Award 1987; hon fell Magdalene Coll Cambridge 2001; Hon MA Univ of Sheffield 1987, Hon DBA Int Mgmnt Centre Buckingham 1988; FRSA, CIMgt 1991; *Books* Management and Machiavelli (1967), To England with Love (with David Frost, 1967), Effective Presentation (1970), Corporation Man (1972), The Complete Yes Minister (with Jonathan Lynn, 1984), Yes Prime Minister (1986, vol II 1987), Elizabeth R (1992), The Oxford Dictionary of Political Quotations (ed, 1996, 4 edn 2010), How to Beat Sir Humphrey (1997), Not In Our Back Yard (2005); *Style—* Sir Antony Jay, CVO; ✉ c/o Alan Brodie Representation Ltd, Paddock Suite, The Courtyard, 55 Charterhouse Street, London EC1M 6HA

JAY, John Philip Bromberg; s of Alec Jay (d 1993), and (Helena) June Jay (d 2005); *b* 1 April 1957; *Educ* UCS, Magdalen Coll Oxford (BA); *m* 1, 1987 (m dis 1992), Susy, *née* Streeter; m 2, 1992, Judi Bevan; 1 da (Josephine); *Career* reporter Western Mail 1979–81; city reporter: Thomson Regional Newspapers 1981–83, Sunday Telegraph 1984–86; city ed Sunday Times 1986 (dep business ed 1988), city and business ed Sunday Telegraph 1989–95, managing ed business news Sunday Times 1995–2001, devpt dir New Star Asset Management 2001–09, devpt ptnr Brompton Asset Mgmnt 2009–; *Recreations* skiing, reading, walking, cinema, theatre; *Style—* John Jay, Esq

JAY, Hon Martin; CBE (2000), DL; yr s of Baron Jay, PC (Life Peer, d 1996), and his 1 w, Margaret Christian, *née* Garnett; *Educ* Winchester, New Coll Oxford (MA); *m* 1969, Sandra, *née* Williams; 2 da (Claudia b 1971, Tabitha b 1972), 1 s (Adam b 1976); *Career* industrialist; with: GEC 1969–85 and 1987–89, Lewmar plc 1985; md and chief exec Vosper Thornycroft Holdings plc 1989–2002; chm: VT Gp plc 2002–05, Invensys plc 2003–09, EADS UK Ltd, Oxsensis Ltd 2010–; chm Tall Ships Youth Tst 2004–10; Hon LLD Univ of Portsmouth, Hon DBA Southampton Solent Inst; *Recreations* sailing, tennis, gardening; *Style—* The Hon Martin Jay, CBE, DL; ✉ Bishop's Court, Bishop's Sutton, Alresford, Hampshire SO24 0AN

JAY, (Hon) Peter; er s of Baron Jay, PC (Life Peer, d 1996), and his 1 w, Margaret Christian, *née* Garnett; *b* 7 February 1937; *Educ* Winchester, ChCh Oxford (MA); *m* 1, 1961 (m dis 1986), Hon Margaret Ann Callaghan (now Baroness Jay of Paddington, *qv*, Life Peer), er da of Baron Callaghan of Cardiff, KG, PC (Life Peer, d 2005); 2 da (Hon Tamsin Margaret b 1965, Hon Alice Katharine b 1968), 1 s (Hon Patrick James Peter b 1971); m 2, Emma Bettina, da of Peter Kai Thornton; 3 s (Thomas Hastings b 1987, Samuel Arthur Maxwell b 1988, James William Hagen Thornton b 1992); issue by Jane Tustian (Nicholas James Tustian b 1980); *Career* Midshipman and Sub Lt RNVR 1956–57; former pres Oxford Union; HM Treasy: asst princ 1961–64, private sec to Jt Perm Sec 1964, princ 1964–67; economics ed The Times 1967–77, assoc ed Times Business News 1969–77, presenter Weekend World (London Weekend Television) 1972–77, ambass to USA 1977–79, conslt Economist Group 1979–81, dir Economist Intelligence Unit 1979–83, chm and chief exec TV-am plc 1980–83, chm Nat Cncl for Voluntary Orgns 1981–86, presenter A Week in Politics (Channel Four) 1983–86, ed Banking World 1983–86, chief of staff to Robert Maxwell 1986–89, economics ed BBC 1990–2001, presenter The Road to Riches (BBC) 2000; non-exec dir Bank of England 2003–09, exec and prof of political economy Henley Business Sch 2006–; chm United Way (UK) Ltd 1982–83 and various United Way subsids; memb Cncl Cinema and TV Benevolent Fund 1982–83, govr Ditchley Fndn 1982–; dir New Nat Theatre Washington DC 1979–81; mayor of Woodstock 2008–10; holder of various broadcasting honours and TV awards; visiting scholar Brookings Inst 1979–80, Wincott Meml lectr 1975, Copland Meml lectr 1980; *Books* The Road to Riches, or The Wealth of Man (2000); *Clubs* Garrick; *Style—* Peter Jay; ✉ The Retreat, Woodstock, Oxfordshire OX20 1LJ

JAY, Hon Mr Justice; Sir Robert Maurice Jay; kt (2013), QC (1998); s of Prof Barrie Samuel Jay (d 2007), and Dr Marcelle Jay, *née* Byre; *b* 20 September 1959; *Educ* KCS Wimbledon (top scholarship), New Coll Oxford (open scholar, BA Jurisprudence); *m* Deborah, *née* Trenner; 1 da (Hannah b 17 Feb 2000); *Career* jr counsel to the Crown (common law) 1989–98, recorder 1999–, judge of the High Court of Justice (Queen's Bench Div) 2013–, former chm Administrative Law Bar Assoc; patron friend Wigmore Hall; *Recreations* opera, golf, cookery, politics, music; *Clubs* MCC (associate memb); *Style—* The Hon Mr Justice Jay; ✉ Royal Courts of Justice, Strand, London WC2A 2LL

JAY OF EWELME, Baron (Life Peer UK 2006), of Ewelme in the County of Oxfordshire; Sir Michael Hastings Jay; GCMG (2006, KCMG 1997, CMG 1993); s of Capt Alan David Hastings Jay, DSO, DSC, RN (d 1978), and Felicity, *née* Vickery, MBE (d 2011); *b* 19 June 1946; *Educ* Winchester, Magdalen Coll Oxford, SOAS Univ of London; *m* 1975, Sylvia, *née* Mylroie; *Career* Miny of Overseas Devpt 1969–73, UK delgn to IMF and World Bank Washington 1973–75, Miny of Overseas Devpt 1975–78, first sec Br High Cmmn New Delhi 1978–81, FCO London 1981–85, cnsllr Cabinet Office 1985–87, cnsllr Br Embassy Paris 1987–90, asst under sec for EC affrs FCO 1990–94, dep under sec for EU and economic affrs 1994–96, Br ambass Paris 1996–2001, perm sec FCO 2002–06; non-exec dir: Associated British Foods plc 2006–15 Valeo 2007–15, Credit Agricole 2007–11, Candover Investments plc 2008–14, EDF 2009–14; chm Merlin 2007–13; chm House of Lords Appointments Cmmn 2008–13, memb Advsy Cncl Br Library 2011–; sr assoc memb St Antony's Coll Oxford 1996; hon fell Magdalen Coll Oxford 2004; *Style—* The Lord Jay of Ewelme, GCMG; ✉ House of Lords, London SW1A 0PW (e-mail jaymh@parliament.uk)

JAY OF PADDINGTON, Baroness (Life Peer UK 1992), of Paddington in the City of Westminster; Margaret Ann Adler; PC (1998); er da of Baron Callaghan of Cardiff, KG, PC (Life Peer, d 2005); *b* 18 November 1939; *Educ* Blackheath HS, Somerville Coll Oxford (BA); *m* 1, 1961 (m dis 1986), as his 1 w, Hon Peter Jay; 2 da (Hon Tamsin Margaret b 1965, Hon Alice Katharine b 1968), 1 s (Hon Patrick James Peter b 1971); m 2, 26 March 1994, Prof Michael William Adler, *qv*; *Career* current and further educn depts BBC TV

1965–67, political res asst Senator John Tunney (Dem, Calif) 1969–70, freelance work for ABC TV and Nat Public Radio Washington DC 1977–82, memb Paddington and N Kensington DHA 1984–97, reporter Panorama and This Week BBC TV 1981–88, reporter and prodr Thames TV 1986–88, fndr dir Nat Aids Trust; oppn princ spokesperson on health House of Lords 1994–97, min of state Dept of Health 1997–98, Lord Privy Seal, ldr of the House of Lords and min for Women 1998–2001; House of Lords: chm Constitution Select Ctee 2010–14, memb Ctee on Extradition Law 2014–15, memb Ctee on Communications 2015–; tstee Hansard Soc 2013–; non-exec dir: Carlton Television 1996–97, Scottish Power 1996–97, Independent News and Media 2001–, BT 2002–08; non-exec memb Kensington Chelsea Westminster HA 1996–97; govr South Bank Univ 1995–97; chm Overseas Devpt Inst 2002–08 (memb Cncl 1994–97 and 2008–); memb Advsy Ctee Meteorological Office 1995–97; tstee Int Crisis Gp 1995–97; chm Nat Assoc of League of Hosp Friends 1994–97, chm Bringing Research to Life (Great Ormond Street Hosp Charity) 2010–; patron: Help the Aged, REACTION Tst; *Books* Battered – The Story of Child Abuse (co-author 1986); *Style*— The Rt Hon Baroness Jay of Paddington; ✉ House of Lords, London SW1A 0PW

JAYAWARDENA, Ranil Malcolm; MP; *b* London; *Educ* Robert May's Sch Odiham Hants, Alton Coll, LSE; *m* 29 Oct 2011, Alison Lyn, *née* Roberts; 1 da (Daisy Megan Mala b 2015); *Career* with Lloyds Banking Gp 2008–15; memb Basingstoke and Deane BC 2008–15 (dep ldr 2012–15); MP (Cons) NE Hants 2015–; memb House of Commons Home Affrs Ctee 2015–; FRSA; *Recreations* cinema, cricket, golf, reading, shooting, tennis, walking; *Style*— Ranil Jayawardena, Esq, MP; ✉ House of Commons, London SW1A 0AA

JAYSON, Prof Malcolm I V; *Educ* Middx Hosp Sch, Univ of London (MB BS), Univ of Bristol (MD); *m* 1 July 1962, Judith; 2 s (Gordon b 1963, Robert b 1966); *Career* lectr and sr lectr in med (rheumatology) Univ of Bristol and Royal Nat Hosp for Rheumatic Diseases Bath 1967–77, prof of rheumatology and dir of Rheumatism Res Laboratories Univ of Manchester 1977–99 (emeritus prof of rheumatology 1999–), dir Manchester and Salford Back Pain Centre 1993–2001; pres: Int Soc for Study of the Lumbar Spine, Section of Rheumatology and Rehabilitation RSM; sec gen Int Back Pain Soc; FRCP; *Books* Total Hip Replacement (1971), Stills Disease: Juvenile Chronic Polyarthritis (1976), Collagen In Health and Disease (1982), Locomotor Disability In General Practice (1983), Rheumatism and Arthritis (1991), Lumbar Spine and Back Pain (1992), Back Pain – The Facts (1992), Family Doctor Guide: Back Pain (2004); *Recreations* antiques, music, trout fishing; *Style*— Prof Malcolm I V Jayson; ✉ The Gate House, 8 Lancaster Road, Didsbury, Manchester M20 2TY (☎ 0161 445 1729, fax 0161 444 1729)

JEANS, Christopher James Marwood; QC (1997); s of David Marwood Jeans (d 1966), and Rosalie Jean, *née* Whittle (d 2003); *b* 24 January 1956; *Educ* Minchenden Comp Sch, King's Coll London (LLB, Hickling Prize in Industrial Law), St John's Coll Oxford (BCL), Inns of Court Sch of Law; *m* 1998, Judith Mary, *née* Laws; 1 da (b 19 Aug 1999); *Career* called to the Bar Gray's Inn 1980 (bencher 2007), lectr in law City of London Poly 1981–83, in practice (specialising in employment law) 1983–, pt/t chm/judge Employment Tbnls 1998–2008, recorder 2009–; memb The Times Law Panel 2005–08; memb Cwlth Secretariat Arbitral Tbnl 2009– (pres 2011–); FICPD 1998; *Recreations* football (Spurs), cricket, walking, swimming, theatre, cinema, Arctic and world travel; *Style*— Christopher Jeans, QC; ✉ 11 King's Bench Walk, Ground Floor, Temple, London EC4Y 7EQ (☎ 020 7632 8500, fax 020 7583 9123 and 020 7583 3690, e-mail jeans@11kbw.com)

JEANS, Michael Henry Vickery; MBE (2006); s of Henry Tendron Wilson Jeans (d 1997), of Walton-on-Thames, Surrey, and Joan Kathleen, *née* Vickery (d 2003); *b* 14 March 1943; *Educ* St Edward's Sch Oxford, Univ of Bristol (BA); *m* 1, 27 June 1970 (m dis 1981), Iris Carla, da of Franco Dell'Acqua, of Milan, Italy; m 2, 12 Jan 1987 (m dis 2004), Paula Wendy, da of David Arthur Spraggs, of Thorpe Bay, Essex; 2 c (James, Rebecca (twins) b 25 Aug 1987); *Career* trainee accountant KPMG (formerly Peat Marwick Mitchell) 1964–67, asst accountant Blue Circle Group 1967–70; KPMG: conslt 1970–81, ptnr 1981–94, memb Bd 1993–94, special advsr 1994–2003; ind mgmnt conslt 1994–; non-exec dir Ross Group plc 1995–2000; ind business advsr The Planning Inspectorate 1992–2003; lay memb Audit Ctee GMC 2004–13, chm Audit Ctee Bar Cncl 2013–; memb: St Matthew's Bayswater PCC 1990–2001 (church warden 2013–), Bd Bath Festivals Tst 2002–06 (vice-chair 2003–06), Bd Assoc of Governing Bodies of Ind Schs 2009–14; non-exec dir: Gemserv plc 2004–16, Bevan Brittan LLP 2004–08, Human Insight Ltd 2007–13; ind bd memb DTI Performance Monitoring Ctee 2005–07; memb VFM Ctee Univ of Oxford 2001–09; tstee: Br Sch of Brussels 2010–, Lib Dems 2010–16; memb Ct Cranfield Univ 2004–16, memb Ct Univ of Bristol 2007–; chair LGB Kensington Primary Acad 2016–, dir West London Free Schs Multi-Academy Tst 2016–; Freeman City of London 1965; fndr memb Worshipful Co of Mgmnt Conslts (Master 2001–02); Liveryman: Worshipful Co of Haberdashers 1965 (memb Ct of Assts 1985, Master 2007–08, chm Educn Ctee 2008–13), Worshipful Co of Chartered Accountants 1991 (memb Ct of Assts 2012, Master 2016–17); MBA (hc) Cranfield Univ 1996; FCA 1967, FCMC 1970 (pres 1990–91), FCMA 1971 (pres 2000–01), MMS 1984, FRSA 1990, CGMA 2012; contrib chapters to: Activity Based Management (1992), Management Consultancy, A Handbook for Best Practice (1998), Success in Sight, Visioning (1998), The International Guide to Management Consultancy (2001); *Recreations* opera, theatre, Italy; *Clubs* RAC, Henley Royal Regatta, Mensa, Soc of London Ragamuffins; *Style*— M H V Jeans, Esq, MBE; ✉ 512 Balmoral Apartments, 2 Praed Street, London W2 1AL (☎ 020 7087 4134, e-mail michael@quagon.co.uk); Via Lanza 56/2, Celle Ligure, 17015 Savona, Italy (☎ 00 390 19 993393)

JEANS, Royston (Roy); s of Ronald Henry Jeans, of Bordon, Hants, and Phyllis Margaret, *née* Kent; *b* 22 September 1956; *Educ* Heath End Sch, Farnham VI Form Coll, Univ of Sheffield (BA), Univ of Southern Calif (MA); *m* 15 Oct 1983, Amelia, da of Ubaldo Marini (d 1975); 2 da (Gabriella b 1993, Natasha b 1998), 1 s (Edward b 1996); *Career* teaching asst Univ of Southern Calif 1979–81, classified rep Farnham Herald 1982–83; advtg exec: Regional Newpaper Advertising Bureau (RNAB) 1983–86, Advertising Media Representation Agency (AMRA) 1986–87; Cordiant plc (formerly Saatchi & Saatchi Co plc): regnl media mangr Saatchi & Saatchi Advertising 1987–88, regnl media dir Zenith Media 1988–90, md Zenith Outdoor 1989–90, TV buying dir Zenith Media 1990–91, exec dir of press Zenith Media 1991–94, gen mangr Zenith Media 1994–95; md AMRA 1995–97, dir Initiative Media London 1997–2004 (md 1998–2000, chief operating offr 2001–04), dir Initiative Media Paris 1999–2004, md Unilever Europe at Initiative 2001–03, md Magna Global UK 2003–07; Rapport (formerly IPG Outdoor): ceo 2004–12, global ceo 2012–13; ceo Grey Scorpion 2013–; chm Symbiosis 2012–; memb Editorial Bd Headlines magazine 1989–97, chm Regnl Press Club 1995–97, elected memb IPA's Media Policy Gp 1999, elected dir Postar 2000–02, chm Face Gp 2005–08; winner Media Mind (jtly) 1991; FIPA 2007 (MIPA 1991); *Books* News from a Square World (with Alan Kamin, Unwin Paperbacks, 1986); *Recreations* travel, cinema, literature, modern art; *Style*— Roy Jeans, Esq; ✉ Grey Scorpion, Suite 602, Linen Hall, 162–168 Regent Street, London W1B 5TG (e-mail roy.jeans@greyscorpion.co.uk)

JEBENS, Ana; da of Klaus-Peter Jebens, and Leonore Jebens; *Educ* Rudolph Steiner Sch Kings Langley, Central St Martins Coll of Art and Design (BA); *Career* designer; former resident designer Swan Theatre Worcester, asst designer to Hildegard Bechtler, *qv*, and Chloe Obolensky 1993–99; visiting lectr Middx Poly 1975–90; *Productions* Half Moon Theatre: Wizard of Oz, Who's a Hero, On the High Road, Guys and Dolls; Swan Theatre Worcester: California Suite, Way Upstream, Female Parts; Stadttheater Essen: The Robbers, As You Like It, Pal Joey; costume design: The Changing Room (Royal Court), Madame Butterfly (Opera Zuid Maastricht) 1998, Rheingold (Scottish Opera) 2000, War and Peace (ENO) 2001; other credits incl: Breach of the Peace (Pain's Plough), Destry Rides Again (Donmar Warehouse), Puntilla (Nat Theatre Mannheim), Guys and Dolls (Nat Theatre Mannheim), As You Like It (Stadttheater Essen), Pal Joey (Stadttheater Essen), The Glass Menagerie (tour), Can't Pay Won't Pay (Habima Theatre Tel Aviv), Behind a Painted Smile (Finborough and tour), Munera and Think of a River (both Black Women's Touring Co), A Bright Room Called Day (Bush Theatre), The Bugger's Opera (Trent Park), Passion Killers (Mecklenburg Opera) 1995, Walküre (Scottish Opera) 2001, Siegfried (Scottish Opera) 2002, War and Peace (Minnesota) 2003, Götterdämmerung from The Ring Cycle (Scottish Opera) 2003, Flying Dutchman (Opera Suid Holland) 2004; TV credits: Burning Embers (Channel 4), Killing Time (Channel 4); *Recreations* yoga, interior design; *Clubs* Iyengar Inst; *Style*— Ms Ana Jebens; ✉ c/o Loesje Sanders, Pound Square, North Hill, Woodbridge, Suffolk IP12 1HH (☎ 01394 385260, fax 01394 388734, mobile 07747 603099)

JEENS, Robert Charles Hubert; s of John Rolfe Hinton Jeens (d 1982), and Mary Margaret, *née* Hubert (d 2004); *b* 16 December 1953; *Educ* Marlborough, Pembroke Coll Cambridge (MA); *m* 8 July 1978, Gillian Frances, da of (David) Gurney Arnold Thomas; 3 s (Richard b 6 Oct 1980, Henry b 2 May 1982, Edward b 15 Feb 1985); *Career* Touche Ross & Co 1975–87 (ptnr 1984–87), Kleinwort Benson Gp plc 1987–96 (gp finance dir 1992–96), finance dir Woolwich Building Society/Woolwich plc 1996–99; chm: Protx Group 2002–06, m.a.partners 2002–06, nCipher plc 2006–08, Allianz Technology Tst 2014–; non-exec dep chm Hepworth plc 1999–2001; non-exec dir: Dialight plc 2001–09, TR European Growth Tst plc 2002–14, The Royal London Mutual Insurance Society Ltd 2003–12, Bank Insinger de Beaufort NV 2005–08, Henderson Gp plc 2009–, JPMorgan Russian Securities plc 2011–; FCA 1978, FRSA 1997; *Recreations* family life, skiing, walking, music; *Style*— Robert Jeens, Esq; ✉ 7 Cambridge Road, London SW20 0SQ (☎ 020 8946 9304, e-mail robert@jeens.eu)

JEEVES, Prof Malcolm Alexander; CBE (1992); s of Alexander Frederic Thomas Jeeves (d 1977), and Helena May, *née* Hammond (d 1975); *b* 16 November 1926; *Educ* Stamford Sch, St John's Coll Cambridge (MA, PhD), Harvard Univ; *m* 7 April 1955, Ruth Elisabeth, da of Oscar Cecil Hartridge (d 1983); 2 da (Sarah b 1958, Joanna b 1961); *Career* Army 1945–48, cmmnd Royal Lincs Regt, served 1 Bn Sherwood Foresters BAOR; lectr Dept of Psychology Univ of Leeds 1956–59, fndn prof and head Dept of Psychology Univ of Adelaide S Aust 1959–69 (dean Faculty of Arts 1963–64); Univ of St Andrews: fndn prof of psychology 1969–93, vice-princ 1981–85, hon research prof 1993–; ed-in-chief Neuropsychologia 1990–93; pres: Int Neuropsychological Symposium 1985–91, Psychology Section BAAS 1988–89; memb: Cncl SERC 1985–89, Neuroscience and Mental Health Bd MRC 1985–89, Manpower Sub-Ctee ABRC 1990–93; pres RSE 1996–99 (vice-pres 1990–93, memb Cncl 1986–89); Hon Sheriff E Lothian and Tayside; memb Experimental Psychology Soc; Leverhulme emeritus fell 1994; Hon DSc: Univ of Edinburgh 1993, Univ of St Andrews 2000; Hon DUniv Stirling 1999; FRSE 1980, FBPsS 1958, FMedSci 1998; *Books* Thinking in Structures (with Z P Dienes, 1965), The Effects of Structural Relations upon Transfer (with Z P Dienes, 1968), The Scientific Enterprise and Christian Faith (1969), Experimental Psychology: an Introduction For Biologists (1974), Psychology and Christianity: the view both ways (1976), Analysis of Structural Learning (with G B Greer, 1983), Free to be Different (with R J Berry and D Atkinson, 1984), Behavioural Sciences: A Christian Perspective (1984), Psychology: Through the Eyes of Faith (with D G Myers, 1987, revised edn 2002), Mind Fields (1994), Callosal Agenesis: A Natural Split Brain? (with M Lassonde, 1994), Human Nature at the Millennium (1997), Science, Life and Christian Belief (with R J Berry, 1998), From Cells to Souls: and Beyond (ed and contrib, 2004), Human Nature (ed and contrib, 2006), Neuroscience, Psychology and Religion (co-author, 2009), Rethinking Human Nature (ed and contrib, 20011), Minds, Brains, Soul and Gods: A Conversation on Faith, Psychology and Neuroscience (2013), The Emergence of Personhood: A Quantum Leap? (ed and contrib, 2014); *Recreations* fly fishing, music, walking; *Style*— Prof Malcolm Jeeves, CBE, PPRSE; ✉ 7 Hepburn Gardens, St Andrews, Fife (☎ 01334 473545); School of Psychology and Neuroscience, University of St Andrews, St Andrews, Fife KY16 9JU (☎ 01334 462072, e-mail maj2@st-andrews.ac.uk)

JEFCOATE, Roger; CBE (1998), DL (Bucks 2011); s of A G Jefcoate (d 1986), of Amersham; *b* 22 November 1940; *Educ* UCS London; *m* 31 Aug 1963, Jean Hammond; *Career* helped develop the world's first electronic life support ventilator at Barnet Hosp 1960, developed assistive communication and mobility technol (with Paralympics fndr Sir Ludwig Guttmann) including the world's first remote control system for disabled people (still supplied by the NHS) Nat Spinal Injuries Centre Stoke Mandeville Hosp 1962; advsr on technology for disability 1973–2010; co-fndr: Possums Users' Assoc (now Sequal Tst, funding special needs technology) 1968, Mobility Tst (funding powered wheelchairs, vice-pres) 1972, Demand (design and manufacture for disability, patron) 1980, Canine Partners (training assistance dogs for disabled people, vice-patron) 1990, AbilityNet (adapted computers for disabled people, vice-pres) 1997, ME Research UK (patron) 1999, Medical Detection Dogs (patron until 2013 for Duchess of Cornwall to follow on) 2007; fndr: Aidis Tst (training and support for adapted computer users) 1975, Disability Aid Fund (supporting local, regional and nat healthcare charities) 1983; patron: Berks, Bucks and Oxon Wildlife Tst, Charity Search, MS Nat Therapy Centres, Raynaud's and Scleroderma Assoc, PACE Centre Bucks, CEDA (Community, Equality, Disability Action) Devon, Heart of Bucks (community fndn), WheelPower, Stoke Mandeville Stadium (birthplace of the paralympics); vice-pres Action4Youth, first chm Prince's Tst Bucks 1990–97; founding tstee John Lewis Partnership Golden Jubilee Tst 1999–; mangr Clare Milne Tst 2001–08 (then patron), Bucks ambass 2004; helped to develop: Arkell Dyslexia Centre Surrey, Compaid Tst Kent, Neuromuscular Centre Cheshire, Pield residential special sch London, St John's special sch Essex (oldest in UK), St Joseph's Pastoral Centre London; initiated various disability equipment and advice centres worldwide; Unsung Heroes Award Celebrities Guild of GB 1986; Hon MUniv Open Univ 1980, Hon DUniv Bucks New Univ 2005; Freedom City of London 1986, Liveryman Drapers' Co 1989; Order of St John 2010; *Recreations* conservation, planting trees especially female black poplars (Britain's rarest native timber tree); *Style*— Roger Jefcoate, CBE, DL; ✉ 2 Copse Gate, Winslow, Buckingham MK18 3HX (☎ 01296 715466)

JEFFCOAT, Rev Rupert Edward Elessing (baptised Robert); s of David Alan Jeffcoat, of Edinburgh, and Marilyn Annette, *née* Yeomans; *b* 23 June 1970; *Educ* St Mary's Music Sch Edinburgh (Episcopal Cathedral chorister), Glenalmond Coll (music scholar), St Catharine's Coll Cambridge (scholar and organ scholar, Ord travel grant), Royal Coll of Organists, Univ of Salford, Queen's Fndn for Ecumenical Theological Educn; *m* 22 June 2001, Catherine Jane, *née* Corrigan; 2 da (Anastasia Catherine Eudora b 3 Feb 2003, Euphemia Catherine Aurelia b 27 June 2005); *Career* composer, arranger, conductor, organist, pianist, accompanist and writer; acting asst organist Guildford Cathedral 1989, church appts Northampton 1992, London 1994 and Pickering 1995, music asst Edinburgh Int Festival 1992–95, music teacher and tutor Ampleforth Coll 1993–95, asst organist St Philip's Cathedral Birmingham 1995–97, accompanist Birmingham Bach Choir 1995–97, music teacher Bluecoat Sch Birmingham 1995–97, musical dir Bournemouth Sinfonietta Choir 1996–99, dir of music Coventry Cathedral 1997–2005, dir of music and organist St John's Cathedral Brisbane 2005–10, music staff St Luke's Chelsea 2011–, memb of staff Birmingham Conservatoire, accompanist Nat Youth Orch; performer: piano duet and two-piano recitals (with bro Richard) 1976–, organ recitals UK and Europe 1988–;

J

compositions incl: Missa Jacet Granum (for Canterbury Cathedral Choir) 1998, Here is my Servant 2000, The Prophet (words by Ted Hughes) 2000, Third Service 2000, Advent Calendar 2000 (words by Archbishop of Canterbury), Mass for Oakham 2001, Tabernacle of Peace 2001, Common Worship Psalter 2003–06, Poor World 2004, Four Corners 2006, The Disciples Awakening 2009, Toccatarama! 2009, A Barrel of Carols 2010, 1712 Overture (for organ) 2011, Etudiego 2012, Getting in the Doldrums (for orch) 2012, Les Marteaux sans Maitres (for 15 pianos) 2013, Muse-ings (for chamber ensemble) 2013, Chansons sans Chants 2013, Versuchung (for 2 pianos) 2013, Geige Counter (for string quartet) 2013, Synthony 2013, Johann Assassination Back 2014–, Te Deum Laudamus 2014–, The Scottish Play 2014–, Dunstable's Piano Concertino 2014–, Chaconne a son gout 2015–, The Emperor's New Concertoes 2015, Piano Triage 2015–; also composed music for nat, state and diocesan occasions in Australia; recitals in Australia and NZ 2005–; dir of music for various BBC progs, recorded and broadcast on BBC Radio 2, 3 and 4, appeared on German radio and Japanese and American TV, directed, played and produced several CDs; examiner Royal Sch of Church Music, tutor Guild of Church Musicians, leader cathedral choir tours and choral workshops, adjudicated at music festivals and sch competitions, pre-concert talks for Australian String Quartet 2007–, various organ-building consultancies, choral clinician Australia and NZ 2006–10; recitals, lectures and papers given throughout Australasia; memb: Cathedral Organists Assoc 1997–, Ctee ISM (Warks) 2001–, Performing Right Soc 2002–, Assoc of Ordinands 2002–, Coll of Preachers 2002–, Royal Philharmonic Soc 2003–, Anglican-Lutheran Soc 2003–, Fedn of Cathedral Old Choristers Assoc, Friends of Cathedral Music, Coventry and Warks Organists Assoc, Foleshill Multicultural Forum, Cncl for Music in Hospitals; fndr memb Mendelssohn on Mull Festival 1988; vice-patron EXPLORE, tstee Thomas Garratt Fund, involved with Live Music Now!; Prizewinner FRCO 1991; *Publications* Now Go In Peace (2003), The Edge of God (contrib, 2008); many other compositions, articles and papers for magazines, jls and instns; some 300 compositions, 400 sermons; *Recreations* most European languages and literature, travelling, cooking, translating, learning from my children, hill walking; *Clubs* Scottish Arts; *Style—* The Rev Rupert Jeffcoat; ✉ Arden House, 25 Saunders Avenue, Bedworth, Warwickshire, CV1 28J (✆ 02476 494099, mobile 07503 337301, e-mail ruperteejeffcoat@gmail.com, website www.rupertjeffcoat.co.uk)

JEFFCOATE, Prof William James; s of Prof Sir (Thomas) Norman Arthur Jeffcoate (d 1992), and Josephine, *née* Lindsay (d 1981); *b* 31 May 1947; *Educ* Liverpool Coll, St John's Coll Cambridge (MA), Middx Hosp Med Sch (MB BChir); *Career* conslt physician and endocrinologist City Hosp Nottingham 1979–; MRCP; *Publications* Lecture Notes on Endocrinology (5 edn, 1993), The Diabetic Foot: An Illustrated Guide to Management (with R M Macfarlane, 1995); author of papers on diabetes and endocrinology; *Recreations* sailing; *Style—* Prof William Jeffcoate; ✉ Nottingham University Hospitals, City Hospital Campus, Hucknall Road, Nottingham NG5 1PB (✆ 0115 969 1169, e-mail wjeffcoate@futu.co.uk)

JEFFCOTT, Prof Leo Broof; s of late Edward Ian Broof Jeffcott, and Pamela Mary, *née* Hull; *b* 19 June 1942; *Educ* Caius Sch Shoreham by Sea, Brighton Tech Coll, Royal Vet Coll Univ of London (BVetMed, PhD), Univ of Melbourne (DVSc), Univ of Cambridge (MA); *m* 14 June 1969, Tisza Jacqueline, *née* Hubbard; 2 da (Julie Marie b 9 Feb 1972, Michele Anne b 7 March 1978); *Career* Equine Res Station Animal Health Tst: asst pathologist 1967–71, radiologist and clinician 1972–77, head Clinical Dept 1977–82; prof of clinical radiology Vet Coll Swedish Univ of Agric Sciences 1981–82; Univ of Melbourne: prof of vet clinical sciences 1983–91, head Dept of Vet Clinical Sciences 1985–89, dep dean Faculty of Vet Science 1985, dir Vet Clinic and Hosp 1986–91; Univ of Cambridge: prof of vet clinical studies 1991–2004, dean Vet Sch 1992–2004, professorial fell Pembroke Coll 1993–2004; dean Faculty of Vet Science Univ of Sydney 2004–09 (prof of veterinary science 2010–); official veterinarian Int Equestrian Fedn at: Olympic Games Seoul 1988, World Equestrian Games Stockholm 1990, Olympic Games Barcelona 1992, World Equestrian Games The Hague 1994, Olympic Games Atlanta 1996, World Equestrian Games Rome 1998, Olympic Games Sydney 2000, World Equestrian Games Jerez 2002, Olympic Games Athens 2004, Olympic Games Beijing 2008, Kentucky Colonels 2011; chm Veterinary Ctee and memb Bureau of International Fedn (FEI) 1998–2006, int chm and convenor 5th Int Conf on Equine Exercise Physiology Japan 1998, chm Bd of Examiners Nat Veterinary Examination for Australian Veterinary Bds Cncl 2010–; Sir Frederick Hobday Meml Lecture 1977, Peter Hernquist Meml Lecture 1991, Share Jones Lectureship 1993, JD Stewart Address 2004, RR Pascoe Peroration 2005, John Hickman Meml Lecture at 50th Br Equine Veterinary Assoc Congress 2011; elected Univ of Kentucky Equine Res Hall of Fame 1991; G Norman Hall Medal 1978, Richard Hartley Clinical Prize 1980, Tierklinik Hochmoor Int Prize 1981, Open Award Equine Vet Jl 1982, John Hickman Orthopaedic Prize 1991, Animal Health Tst Outstanding Scientific Achievement Award 1994, Sefton Award for Servs to Equestrian Safety 1997, BVA Dalrymple-Champneys Cup and Medal 2001; memb: BVA, Br Equine Vet Assoc; hon memb: Societa Italiana di Ippologie 1977, Equine Section Swedish Soc for Vet Med 1992, Int Equestrian Fedn 2006, FEI Bureau 2006; Dr VetMed (hc) Swedish Agric Univ Uppsala; FRCVS 1978, Hon FRVC 1997; Hon Order of Kentucky Colonels in Fef 2011; *Publications* Comparative Clinical Haematology (jt ed, 1977), Equine Exercise Physiology 3 (jt ed, 1991), Osteochondrosis in the 90's (jt ed, 1993), On to Atlanta '96 (jt ed, 1994), Thermoregulatory Responses During Competitive Exercise in the Performing Horse (jt ed, Vol 1 1995, Vol 2 1996), Equine Exercise Physiology 5 (ed, 1999), Osteochondrosis and Musculoskeletal Devolpment in the Foal under the Influence of Exercise (jt ed, 1999), A Tribute to Colonel John Hickman (jt ed, 2001), Equine Juvenile Osteochondral Conditions (jt ed, 2013); author of over 350 articles in learned jls; *Recreations* photography, swimming, gardening; *Style—* Prof Emeritus Leo Jeffcott; ✉ University of Sydney, Faculty of Veterinary Science, Veterinary Teaching Hospital, 410 Werombi Road, Camden NSW 2570, Australia

JEFFERIES, Nicholas John (Nick); s of Peter Jefferies, of Ashtead, Surrey, and Lesley Jefferies; *b* 31 January 1966, Chichester, W Sussex; *m* Susan; *Career* global head of electronics Electrocomponents plc until 2009, gp chief exec Acal plc 2009–; *Recreations* golf, tennis, running; *Style—* Nick Jefferies, Esq; ✉ Acal plc, 2 Chancellor Court, Occam Road, Surrey Research Park, Guildford GU2 7AH

JEFFERIES, Stephen; s of George Frederick Jefferies, of Birmingham, and Kitty Barbara, *née* Salisbury; *b* 24 June 1951; *Educ* Turves Green Sch Birmingham, Royal Ballet Sch; *m* 1972, Rashna, da of Homi B Minocher Homji; 1 da (Lara b 1982), 1 s (Christopher b 1985); *Career* ballet dancer; joined Sadler's Wells Royal Ballet 1969, character princ dancer 1993, sr princ dancer Royal Ballet 1979–93 (princ dancer 1973–76 and 1977–79); all maj roles with the Royal Ballet and Nat Ballet of Canada, over 25 roles created; rehearsal dir Rambert Ballet 1995, artistic dir Hong Kong Ballet 1996 (prodns choreographed for the Hong Kong Ballet incl: Swan Lake 1996, Giselle and the Nutcracker 1997, Tango Ballet Tango 2000, Sleeping Beauty 2002, The Legend of the Great Archer (designer) 2004), choreographer of Suzie Wong 2006, artistic dir and choreographer Suzhou Dance Co Suzhou Science and Arts Cultural Centre Co Ltd 2007–; Hon ARAD; *Recreations* golf; *Style—* Stephen Jefferies, Esq

JEFFERIES, Timothy Nicolas (Tim); s of Richard Jefferies, and Hilary, *née* Tompkins; *b* 7 November 1961, Barnet, London; *m* 19 April 2008, Malin Johansson; 1 da (Coco), 1 s (Rex); *Career* princ Hamiltons Gallery London 1984–; *Style—* Tim Jefferies, Esq; ✉ Hamiltons Gallery, 13 Carlos Place, London W1K 2EU

JEFFERS, Raymond Jackson; s of George Dennis Jeffers, of Albany, Suffolk, and Jeannine, *née* Jacquier; *b* 5 August 1954; *Educ* Stanwell Sch Penarth, Aberystwyth UCW (LLB), Wadham Coll Oxford (BCL); *m* 4 Sept 1982, Carol Elizabeth, da of John Bernard Awty, of Freshwater, IOW; 3 da (Alice Elizabeth b 19 Aug 1994, Lara Victoria, Florence May (twins) b 27 Jan 1996); *Career* admitted slr 1980; Linklaters (formerly Linklaters & Paines): ptnr Corporate Dept 1986–, London head of employment 1990–2002, global head of employment 2002–; chm Employment and Industrial Rels Ctee Int Bar Assoc 2001–03; chm Employment Lawyers Assoc 2004–06 (dep chm 2003–04, chm Legislative and Policy Ctee 2000–03 (memb 1998–)); City of London Slrs' Co: memb Commercial Law Sub-Ctee 1986–89, chm Employment Law Sub-Ctee 2001– (memb 1987–); memb Law Soc 1980; *Recreations* ornithology, badminton, golf, tennis; *Style—* Raymond Jeffers, Esq

JEFFERSON, Prof Ann; *Career* fell New Coll Oxford 1987–2015 (emeritus fell 2015–), formerly prof in French Univ of Oxford; Leverhulme major research fell 2001–04; fell Inst of Advanced Study Paris 2016; FBA 2004; Commandeur dans l'Ordre des Palmes Académiques 2012 (Officière 2001); *Books* The Nouveau Roman and the Poetics of Fiction (1980), Modern Literary Theory: A Comparative Introduction (jtly, 1982, revised edn 1986), Reading Realism in Stendhal (1988), Nathalie Sarraute, Fiction and Theory: Questions of Difference (2000), Biography and the Question of Literature in France (2007), Genius in France: An Ideas and its Uses (2015); *Style—* Prof Ann Jefferson; ✉ New College, Oxford OX1 3BN

JEFFERSON, John Malcolm; s of George Arthur Jefferson, of Driffield, E Yorks, and Gladys Evelyn Jefferson; *b* 26 June 1945, Wold Newton, E Yorks; *Educ* Bridlington GS; *m* 30 March 1967, Gillian Mary; 2 s (Nathan b 28 Sept 1974, Daniel b 13 June 1978); *Career* news reporter Bridlington Free Press and Scarborough Evening News, chief reporter Redcar, industrial ed and dep news ed Evening Gazette Teesside; news prodr: BBC Radio Durham, BBC Radio Cleveland, BBC Radio Carlisle; prog organiser BBC Radio Humberside, station mangr and fndr BBC Radio York, managing ed BBC Radio Leeds 1988–95, memb BBC Ten Year Strategy Team 1995–96, media conslt and fndr JJ Media Projects 1996, dir em3media Ltd 2003–08, dir JJ Media Projects Ltd 2008–; conslt project co-ordinator BBC Public Space Broadcasting Project and London 2012 Olympics Live Sites Project; aid worker VSO Divine Word Univ Madang Papua New Guinea 1998; former memb: Carlisle Round Table, Holderness Rotary Club Hull; former chm York Branch Br Heart Fndn; memb: Radio Acad, Br Exec Services Oversea (voluntary work in Montenegro 1998, Moscow 1999, Nepal 2002 and Jasi Romania 2003 and 2004), Rotary Club of York Vikings; BBC Gillard Award for outstanding service to local broadcasting 2007; *Books* Disasters and the Media – Managing Crisis Communications (contrib, 1999), Connecting in a Crisis – Working with the BBC in an Emergency (2002); *Clubs* York Vikings Rotary; *Style—* John Jefferson, Esq; ✆ 01904 707026, mobile 07841 004391, fax 0871 2472441, e-mail john@jjmediaprojects.co.uk

JEFFERY, Prof Charles Adrian; CBE (2016); s of Frank Bertram Jeffery (d 1969), and June Dorothy Addington, *née* Rouse; *b* 27 July 1964, Holcot, Northants; *Educ* Univ of Loughborough (BA, PhD); *m* 22 Aug 1998, Elke Lieve Versmessen; 2 da (Mieke Dot b 12 March 2002, Elsie Paul b 19 Sept 2005), 1 s (Sid Albert b 19 Feb 2008); *Career* lectr: N Staffs Poly 1988–89, Univ of Leicester 1989–94; Inst for German Studies Univ of Birmingham: sr res fell 1994, reader 1996–99, prof of German politics 1999–2004; Univ of Edinburgh: prof of politics and co-dir Inst of Governance 2004–, head Sch of Social and Political Science 2009–; ESRC: dir Res Prog on Devolution and Constitutional Change 2000–06, memb Cncl and chm Strategic Res Bd 2005–11, dir Research Prog on the Future of the UK and Scotland 2013–15; advsr EU Ctee of the Regions 2002–05, advsr Ctee on Standards in Public Life 2002–07, specialist advsr House of Commons Select Ctee on the ODPM 2004–05, memb Ind Expert Gp on Finance Advising Cmmn on Scottish Devolution 2008–09, memb Cmmn on the Consequences of Devolution for the House of Commons 2011–13; AcSS 2004, FRSE 2007; German Federalism Today (co-ed, 1991), Federalism, Unification and European Integration (co-ed, 1993), Social Democracy in the Austrian Provinces, 1918–1934: Beyond Red Vienna (1995), The Regional Dimension of the European Union: Towards a 'Third' Level in Europe? (1997), Germany Today: A Student's Dictionary (co-ed, 1997), Recasting German Federalism: The Legacies of Unification (ed, 1998), Germany's European Diplomacy: Shaping the Regional Milieu (co-author, 2000), Verfassungspolitik und Verfassungswandel: Deutschland und Grossbritannien im Vergleich (co-ed, 2001), Devolution and Electoral Politics (co-ed, 2006), The Scottish Parliament 1999–2009: The First Decade (co-ed, 2009), Rethinking Germany and Europe: Democracy and Diplomacy in a Semi-Sovereign State (co-ed, 2010); *Style—* Prof Charles Jeffery, CBE; ✉ 9 West Savile Road, Edinburgh EH16 5NG (✆ 0131 478 0098); School of Social and Political Science, University of Edinburgh, Chrystal Macmillan Building, 15A George Square, Edinburgh EH8 9LD (✆ 0131 650 3941, e-mail charlie.jeffery@ed.ac.uk)

JEFFERY, Christopher Paul; s of Dr David Jeffery, and Jennifer, *née* Hartree; *b* 23 April 1962, Bristol; *Educ* Bristol GS, Univ of York (BA), Univ of Exeter (PGCE); *m* 12 March 1988, Carol, *née* Buckley; 2 s (Thomas b 5 June 1992, Matthew b 28 Jan 1995), 1 da (Kate b 16 Aug 2000); *Career* clerical asst Dept of Employment 1980–81, teacher St Peter's Sch York 1984–85, songwriter and singer Mimic Theatrical Co 1986–87, admin Univ of Bristol 1988, history teacher Bristol GS 1988–96 (housemaster 1990–96), history teacher Perse Sch for Boys Cambridge 1996–2004 (head of middle sch 1996–2001, dep head 2001–04), headmaster Grange Sch Hartford 2005–16, headmaster Bootham Sch York 2016–; memb HMC 2005–; FRSA 2007; *Recreations* family life, singer and songwriter, playing and watching sport, cinema, travelling, walking; *Style—* Christopher Jeffery, Esq; ✉ Bootham School, York YO30 7BU

JEFFERY, Jack; CBE (1995); s of Philip Jeffery (d 1973), and Elsie, *née* Carr (d 1999); *b* 10 March 1930; *Educ* Stanley GS Co Durham, King's Coll Durham (BSc, MSc); *m* 1 (m dis 1983); 3 da (Wyn b 1951, Carole b 1953, Jill b 1958); m 2, 1983, Deborah Mary (d 2009), da of Kenneth Hyde; m 3, 5 Aug 2013, Gillian Ann, *née* Thomson; *Career* scientist NCB 1953–61, chemist and bacteriologist Southwest Suburban Water Co 1961–73 (asst gen mangr 1968–73); North Surrey Water: water quality controller 1973–77, gen mangr 1977–87, md 1987–95, chm 1990–2001; chm: General Utilities Projects Ltd 1990–2000, Tendring Hundred Water Services Ltd 1995–2000, Northumbria Larder 2006–09, Durham County Waste Mgmnt Ltd 2012–13; dep chm Three Valleys Water plc 2000–01; dir: WRC plc 1989–99, Tendring Hundred Water Services Ltd 1992–2002, Durham County Waste Management Ltd 1992–, East Surrey Holdings plc 1995–2000, County Durham Environmental Tst 2006–12, Premier Waste Management 2008–; chm Water Cos Assoc 1987–90; pres: Freshwater Biological Assoc 1988–95, Instn of Water Offrs 1991; chm Cncl of RIPH 2002–06 (dep chm 1993–2002); chm: Surrey First 1993–96, Careers Advsy Bd Univ of Newcastle upon Tyne 1995–2000, Convocation Univ of Newcastle upon Tyne 1999–2009, World Humanity Action Tst 2000–03 (tstee 1993–); hon memb: Instn of Water Offrs 1992, American Waterworks Assoc 1994; tstee: Univ of Newcastle upon Tyne Devpt Tst 1999–2004 and 2005–11, Dementia North 2000–06; Distinguished Serv Certificate BSI 1995; author of various papers on water quality and treatment and water privatisation; hon fell Univ of Newcastle upon Tyne 2005; Freeman City of London 1980, Liveryman, memb Ct of Assts and past Master Worshipful Co of Plumbers; FCIWEM 1987, FRIPH 1987, FRSA 1989, CCMI (CIMgt 1994); A Pudding Full of Plums (2007); *Recreations* music, watching sport, books, wine; *Clubs* MCC, Forty, Durham CCC, Lord's Taverners; *Style—* Jack Jeffery, Esq, CBE; ✉ Laleham House, Hedley on the Hill,

Stocksfield, Northumberland NE43 7SW (☎ 01661 843729, e-mail jackjefferylaleham@gmail.com)

JEFFERY, Paul Francis; s of Arthur Felgate Sinclair Jeffery (d 1998), of Storrington, W Sussex, and Muriel Carmen, *née* Privett (d 1992); *b* 27 January 1946; *Educ* Eastbourne Coll; *m* 13 March 1971, Patricia Ann Jeffery, OBE, da of Edward Frederick Emes; 1 s (Edward Paul b 21 Oct 1972); *Career* CA; articled clerk: Harry Price & Co Eastbourne 1964–66, Jones Avens Worley & Piper Chichester 1966–68; Thomson McLintock & Co: London office 1969–77, ptnr Norwich office 1977–87 (managing ptnr 1986–87), memb Quality Review Gp 1981–84, UK dir of quality review 1984–86; ptnr specialising in insolvency and restructuring KPMG (following merger of Thomson McLintock and Peat Marwick Mitchell in 1987): London office 1991–94, St Albans office 1994–2001; ptnr The Jeffery Partnership (governance advsr and mentor to business) 2001–; founding ptnr The Governance Consultancy 2002–; pres Norfolk and Norwich Soc of CAs 1982–83, chm Norwich Enterprise Agency Tst 1989–92 (memb Bd 1986–92), treas Mid Norfolk Cons Assoc 1993–96, treas Norfolk Cons Euro Constituency Cncl 1994–99, asst area treas (Norfolk) Cons Pty 1994–98; tstee Norfolk Archeological Tst 2004–; govr Eastbourne Coll 1992–2005 (vice-chm 1999–2005); FCA 1979 (ACA 1969), Insolvency Licence (ICAEW) 1987, memb Soc of Practitioners in Insolvency 1990; *Recreations* golf, swimming, travelling, reading, walking; *Style—* Paul Jeffery, Esq; ✉ Bilney House, East Bilney, Dereham, Norfolk NR20 4HW (☎ 01362 860111)

JEFFERY, Timothy Arthur Rodney; s of Rodney Albert Jeffery, of Lymington, Hants, and Edith Rosina, *née* Meeks; *b* 13 June 1956; *Educ* Methodist Coll Belfast, Univ of Kent at Canterbury (BA); *m* 14 April 1984, (Margaret) Jennifer, da of Harold Gibson; 1 da (Kate Elizabeth Rosina b 4 Dec 1987); *Career* features ed Yachting World 1978–88, sailing corr The Daily Telegraph 1988–2008, communications dir ORACLE Racing, media and TV project dir and communications dir 34th America's Cup; winner 33rd America's Cup; former chm UKC Sports Fedn, memb Yachting Journalists' Assoc 1977; *Books* Sail of the Century (1983), Practical Sailing (1986), Sailing Year (1987), The Official History of The Champagne Mumm Admiral's Cup (1994), Beken of Cowes: Sailing Thoroughbreds (1998), Beken of Cowes: The America's Cup (1999), Alinghi America's Cup (2003); *Recreations* sailing, golf, skiing, tennis; *Clubs* Royal Thames Yacht, Royal Ocean Racing, Int Assoc of Cape Horners, Strangford Lough Yacht; *Style—* Timothy Jeffery, Esq; ✉ e-mail mail@timjeffery.com

JEFFORD, Nerys; QC (2008); *b* 25 December 1962; *Educ* Olchfa Comp Sch Swansea, Lady Margaret Hall Oxford (scholar, MA), Univ of Virginia (Fulbright scholar, LLM); *Career* called to the Bar Gray's Inn 1986 (Lord Justice Holker scholar, Karmel scholar, bencher); practising barr specialising in construction and engrg law and arbitration, memb Keating Chambers 1988–, recorder, dep judge of the High Court of Justice; memb Cncl Soc of Construction Law until 2009 (chm 2007–08); memb: Technology and Construction Bar Assoc, Commercial Bar Assoc, London Common Law and Commercial Bar Assoc; memb Advsy Cncl Lady Margaret Hall; memb: Gray's Inn Chapel Choir, London Welsh Chorale, The Harry Ensemble, Racehorse Owners Assoc; MCIArb 2006; *Publications* Keating on Construction Contracts (contrib, 10 edn 2016); *Recreations* singing; *Style—* Miss Nerys Jefford, QC; ✉ Keating Chambers, 15 Essex Street, London WC2R 3AA (☎ 020 7544 2600, fax 020 7544 2700, e-mail njefford@keatingchambers.com)

JEFFREY, Nicholas; s of Manfred Jeffrey (d 1995), and Doris MacKay, *née* Spouge (d 1997); *b* 6 June 1942; *Educ* Ecclesfield GS, Univ of Sheffield (LLB); *m* 1965, Dianne Michelle, da of Cyril Cantor (d 1985); 2 s (Alexander b 1966, David b 1969), 2 da (Danya b 1968, Miranda b 1971); *Career* chm: United Industries plc (formerly Neepsend plc) 1994–2002, Coffee Republic plc 1998–, Channel Holdings plc 1999–2000, Eurocity Properties plc 2000–02, Halcyon Internet plc 2000–03, Mountain Warehouse 2002–, Maccess Ltd 2002–, Nightspeed Holding Ltd 2003–, Sheffield Hallam Univ 2003–; Liveryman: Worshipful Co of Furniture Makers, Worshipful Co of Cutlers in Hallamshire; *Recreations* shooting, sailing; *Style—* Nicholas Jeffrey, Esq

JEFFREYS, Prof Sir Alec John; kt (1994); s of Sydney Victor Jeffreys, and Joan, *née* Knight (d 1994); *b* 9 January 1950; *Educ* Luton GS, Luton Sixth Form Coll, Merton Coll Oxford (MA, DPhil); *m* 28 Aug 1971, Susan, da of Frederick Charles Robert Miles (d 1975), of Luton, Beds; 2 da (Sarah Catherine b 1979, Elizabeth Jane b 1983); *Career* postdoctoral research fell European Molecular Biology Orgn Univ of Amsterdam 1975–77; Univ of Leicester: lectr 1977–82, Lister Inst research fell 1982–91, reader 1984–87, prof of genetics 1987–; Wolfson research prof of the Royal Soc 1991–; devpt of genetic fingerprinting system 1984–; memb: EMBO, Human Genome Orgn, Genetical Soc; hon memb: Int Soc for Forensic Haemogenetics 1997, American Acad of Forensic Sciences 1998, Biochemical Soc 2003; Hon DUniv Open Univ 1991; Hon DSc: Univ of St Andrews 1996, Univ of Strathclyde 1998, Univ of Hull 2004, Univ of Oxford 2004; hon fell: Merton Coll Oxford, Univ of Luton 1995; fell Forensic Sci Soc of India, fell Linnean Soc 1994, FRCPath 1991, Hon FRCP 1992, Hon FIBiol 1998, FMedSci 1998, Hon FRSM 2001, FRS; *Recreations* swimming, walking, postal history; *Style—* Prof Sir Alec Jeffreys, FRS; ✉ Department of Genetics, Adrian Building, University of Leicester, University Road, Leicester LE1 7RH (☎ 0116 252 3435, fax 0116 252 3378)

JEFFREYS, 3 Baron (UK 1952); Christopher Henry Mark Jeffreys; s of 2 Baron Jeffreys (d 1986), and Mrs Sarah Clarke, *née* Garnett (d 2014); *b* 22 May 1957; *Educ* Eton; *m* 22 Aug 1985, Anne Elisabeth, da of Antoine Denarie, of Johannesburg (d 2013), and Mrs Derek Johnson (d 2014); 1 da (Hon Alice Mary b 1986), 1 s (Hon Arthur Mark Henry b 1989); *Heir* s, Hon Arthur Jeffreys; *Career* futures broker; Johnson Matthey & Wallace Ltd 1976–85, GNI Ltd 1985–90, stockbroker Raphael Zorn Hemsley 1992–2000, stockbroker and dir Savoy Investment Mgmnt 2000–12 (ceo 2009–12); dir and ceo Ashcourt Rowan Asset Mgmnt Ltd 2011–12, investment mangr Ashcourt Rowan Asset Mgmnt Ltd 2012–15, investment mangr Towry Asset Mgmnt 2015–16; *Recreations* country sports, sailing, skiing; *Clubs* Pratt's, Inanda; *Style—* The Rt Hon the Lord Jeffreys

JEFFREYS, Prof Elizabeth Mary; da of Lawrence Brown (d 1995), of London, and Veronica, *née* Thompson (d 1987); *b* 22 July 1941; *Educ* Blackheath HS, Girton Coll Cambridge (MA), St Anne's Coll Oxford (BLitt); *m* 1965, Michael Jeffreys; 1 da (Katharine b 1974); *Career* res fell: Warburg Inst 1969–72, Dumbarton Oaks 1972–74, Univ of Ioannina 1974–76, Univ of Sydney 1976–95; Bywater and Sotheby prof of Byzantine and modern Greek language and literature Univ of Oxford 1996–2006 (emeritus prof 2006–); fell Aust Acad of the Humanities 1993; hon fell St Anne's Coll Oxford; *Books* Popular Literature in Late Byzantium (1983), The Chronicle of John Malalas (1986), Studies in John Malalas (1990), The War of Troy (1996), Digenis Akritis (1998), Through the Looking Glass (2000), Rhetoric in Byzantium (2003), The Age of the Dromon (2003), The Oxford Handbook of Byzantine Studies (2008), Iacobi Monachi Epistulae (2009), Four Byzantine Novels (2012); *Recreations* reading, walking; *Style—* Prof Elizabeth Jeffreys; ✉ Exeter College, Oxford OX1 3DP (☎ 01865 793358, fax 01865 279645, e-mail elizabeth.jeffreys@exeter.ox.ac.uk)

JEFFREYS, Prof Paul William; s of George Lewis Jeffreys (d 1995), and Naomi Emily, *née* Williams; *b* 4 July 1954; *Educ* Drayton Manor GS London, Univ of Manchester (BSc), Univ of Bristol (PhD); *m* 23 Feb 1985, Linda Christine, *née* Pay; 2 s (Simon Richard Lewis b 20 April 1990, Oliver Samuel Fields b 23 July 1994), 1 da (Eleanor Lucy Clare b 10 March 1992); *Career* CERN fell Experimental Physics Div CERN Geneva 1979–82; Rutherford Appleton Laboratory: physicist on Large Electron Positron Collider experiment 1982–87, head Particle Physics Dept Computing Gp 1987–94, head Computing and Resource Mgmnt Div 1995–2001, ldr CLRC e-Science Centre 2000–01; Univ of Oxford: dir Computing Services 2001–07, prof of computing 2003–, dir of IT 2007–12 (actg dir 2005–07), dir of IT risk mgmnt 2012–; professorial fell Keble Coll Oxford 2001– (tutor and hon memb SCR 1990–2001, vice-pres SCR 2013–); dir Oxford Regnl e-Science Centre (OeSC) 2001–06, dir Oxford e-Research Centre (OeRC) 2006–07; dir: Digitalspires 2004–08, e-Horizons Inst James Martin 21st Century Sch 2005–09; UK rep Plenary Ctee European Ctee for Future Accelerators 1996–2001, Research Cncl rep Jt Information Systems Ctee (JISC) for Networking 1997–2007, project ldr UK Particle Physics Grid 2000–01; chm IT Mgmnt Ctee Central Lab of the Research Cncls (CERN) 1999–2001, chair Proposal Mgmnt Bd UK Particle Physics Grid 2001; fndr memb: Int Ctee of Future Accelerators Networking Task Force 1997–2001, EU DataGrid Project 2000–02; memb: ESNet Working Ctee 1996–2001, Int Advsy Panel for Computing High Energy Physics Conf 1997 and 2000, High Energy Physics Central Computing Ctee 1999–2001, Int Advsy Ctee Topical Seminar on Global and Local Networks for Research and Educn Siena 2000, Informatics Ctee Office of Science and Technol 2000–01, Bioinfomatics Ctee Wellcome Tst 2000–01, Int Advsy Ctee for Computing High Energy Physics Conf 2001, Research Cncl Grid Opportunity Gp 2001, e-Science Steering Ctee ESPRC 2001, Dir of e-Science's Tech Advsy Gp 2001–06, e-Science Steering Ctee PPARC 2001–07, e-Oversight Panel PPARC 2001–07, e-Science Core Prog Grid Network Team 2001–03, Project Mgmnt Steering Ctee Nat Cancer Tissue Resource 2003–06, Bd Grid Ops Support Centre 2004, IBM World Community Grid Advsy Bd 2004–09, NCeSS Nodes Commissioning Panel 2007–08, UK Research Data Service Project Mgmnt Bd 2010, Ed Bd Br Jl of Interdisciplinary Studies 2014–, FCO academic expert network in support of HMG's int cyber security policy 2014–; fell Oxford e-Research Centre 2007–, research assoc Oxford Internet Inst 2007–10, tstee Jisc 2012–14; princ investigator: SUDAMIH Project 2010–11, VIDaaS Project 2011–12, DaMaRO Project 2012–; dir IT Risk Mgmnt; author of numerous papers and articles in learned jls; CPhys, MInstP; *Publications* Towards a Unified University Infratructure: The Data Management Roll-Out at the University of Oxford (with James A J Wilson in The Int Jl of Digital Curation Vol 8, No. 2, 2013), Diamonds and Paper Clips: Steps Needed to Make Your University Cybersecure (EDUCAUSE seminar, 2014), The Road to Institutional Information Security Management (with Peter Tinson and Anna Mathews, 2015); *Recreations* family, active church member, sport (mainly squash, skiing, real tennis and running), photography; *Clubs* Oxford and Cambridge Arcades; *Style—* Prof Paul Jeffreys; ✉ Keble College, Oxford OX1 3PG (☎ 01865 273229, fax 01865 283346, e-mail paul.jeffreys@it.ox.ac.uk)

JEFFRIES, Prof Donald James; CBE (2007); s of Edmond Frederick Jeffries (d 1976), and Eileen Elizabeth, *née* Elton (d 1993); *b* 29 August 1941; *Educ* William Ellis GS, Royal Free Hosp Sch of Med London (BSc, MB BS); *m* 11 Aug 1966, Mary Millicent, da of Eric James Bray; 1 da (Caroline Mary b 1967), 2 s (Paul James b 1969, Richard Anthony b 1973); *Career* St Mary's Hosp Med Sch: sr registrar in microbiology 1970–72, head Div of Virology 1982–90, dir of clinical studies 1985–90, reader and hon conslt in clinical virology 1987–90 (lectr 1972–74, sr lectr 1974–87); Bart's and Royal London Sch of Med and Dentistry QMC: prof and head of virology 1990–2006, head Dept of Med Microbiology 1998–2006, emeritus prof of virology 2006–; Barts and the London NHS Tst: clinical dir of virology 1994–98, head of Microbiology and Virology Services 1998–2006; conslt in virology St John Ambulance 1994–, sr examiner Univ of London 1993–2000; visiting prof Riyadh 1988, C T Huang lectr Hong Kong 1991, Wellcome visiting prof Coll of Med South Africa 1993; vice-pres RCPath 1999–2002; chm: Panel of Examiners in Virology RCPath 1995–2000, Examinations Ctee RCPath 1999–2002, SAC in Microbiology RCPath 1999–2002, Jt Ctee on Infection and Tropical Med RCP/RCPath 1999–2002, ACDP Working Gp on Transmissible Spongiform Encephalopathies 1999–, HPA Steering Gp on Healthcare Associated Infections 2004–07, ABI Expert Working Gp on HIV 2005–08, ABI Expert Advsy Gp on Health and Insurance 2008–; memb: Soc for General Microbiology 1970–, Hospital Infection Soc 1980– (memb Cncl 1980–83 and 1990–93), Advsy Ctee on Genetic Modification HSE 1988–99, Assoc of Profs of Med Microbiology 1991–2000, Expert Advsy Gp on AIDS 1992–2002 (actg chm 2003–05), UK Advsy Panel for Health Care Workers Infected with Blood Borne Viruses 1992–2002, Diagnostics and Imaging Panel Standing Gp on Health Technol NHS R&D Directorate 1993–98, Advsy Ctee on Dangerous Pathogens Dept of Health 1993–2002, Cncl RCPath 1996–2002, CJD Incidents Panel 2000– (actg chm 2003–05), Ctee on Safety of Med 2001–05 (memb Biologicals Sub-Ctee 1999–2005 (chm 2003–05)), Nat Expert Panel on New and Emerging Infections 2003–07; memb British HIV Assoc 1994–; Ellison Nash Prize 2001; FRCPath 1986 (MRCPath 1974), FRCP 2001; *Publications* Lecture Notes on Medical Virology (1987), Current Topics in AIDS (Vol I 1987, Vol II 1989), Antiviral Chemotherapy (1995), Viral Infections in Obstetrics and Gynaecology (1999); *Recreations* hill walking, fly fishing, gardening; *Style—* Prof Donald Jeffries, CBE; ✉ 63 Manor Park Avenue, Princes Risborough, Buckinghamshire HP27 9AS (e-mail d.j.jeffries@qmul.ac.uk)

JEFFRIES, (Richard) Mark; s of David Vincent Jeffries, of Cottingham, E Yorks, and Margaret, *née* Pritchards; *b* 26 June 1957, Horsforth, Leeds; *Educ* Hymers Coll Hull, St John's Coll Cambridge (Master's prize, MA); *m* 17 Sept 1983, Catherine, *née* Fowler; 1 s (Timothy Richard b 13 Aug 1986), 1 da (Alice Louise b 9 Feb 1989); *Career* admitted slr 1981; Mills & Reeve: articled clerk 1979–81, slr 1981–85, ptnr 1985–, managing ptnr Norwich 1990–96, head Corporate Servs Gp 1996–99, nat managing ptnr 2001–07, sr ptnr 2007–15; non-exec dir: Norfolk and Norwich Univ Hospitals NHS Fndn Tst, N W Brown Gp Ltd, R G Carter Hldgs Ltd; memb Law Soc; memb Cncl Norwich Univ of the Arts; *Recreations* skiing, cycling, horticulture; *Clubs* Cambridge Soc; *Style—* Mark Jeffries, Esq; ✉ 9 Judges Drive, Norwich NR4 7QQ (☎ 01603 454622); Mills & Reeve, 1 St James Court, Whitefriars, Norwich NR3 1RU (☎ 01603 693222, fax 01603 664670, e-mail mark.jeffries@mills-reeve.com)

JEFFRIES, Dr Michael Godfrey; *b* 16 April 1943; *Educ* Univ of Birmingham (BSc, MB ChB, DCCH), FRCGP; *m* 28 Aug 1965, Sheila; 2 s (Simon b 12 Dec 1967, Nick b 30 Dec 1975), 1 da (Clare b 28 Jan 1970); *Career* med dir Clwyd Community Care NHS Tst until 2000; RCGP: int devpt advsr UAE and rep on Kuwait Family Practice Examination Bd, former chm Welsh Cncl; memb: GP Educn Ctee Def Medical Servs, Fitness to Practice Ctee GMC; conslt advsr RAF, medical dir Br Forces Health Service Germany; *Style—* Dr Michael Jeffries; ✉ RCGP, 14 Princes Gate, Hyde Park, London SW7 1PU; HQ British Forces Germany Health Service, Haus Burgblick, Bethesda Weg, Gilead Complex, Bielefeld BFPO 39

JEFFRIES, Michael Makepeace Eugene; s of William Eugene Jeffries (d 1975), of Port of Spain, Trinidad, and Margaret, *née* Makepeace (d 1995); *b* 17 September 1944; *Educ* Queens Royal Coll Port of Spain, Poly of North London (Dip Arch); *m* 10 Sept 1966, Pamela Mary, da of Sir Gordon Booth, KCMG, CVO, of Poole, Dorset; 2 s (Andrew b 1969, Simon b 1973), 2 da (Kathryn b 1971, Victoria b 1975); *Career* John Laing and Sons Ltd 1963–67, Deeks Bousell Partnership 1968–73, Bradshaw Gass and Hope 1973–75; ASFA Ltd (WS Atkins Gp) 1975–: dir 1978, chm and md 1979; dir WS Atkins Conslts 1979, chm: W S Atkins plc 2001–05 (dir 1992–95, chief exec 1995–2001), Wembley National Stadium Ltd 2002–, VT Gp plc 2005–10, National Car Parks 2005–07, NSL Services Gp Ltd 2008–10, Civica plc 2010–, Priory Gp 2011–14; non-exec dir: De La Rue plc 2000–07, Mouchel Gp 2013–15; chm Banstead Round Table 1980; govr RNLI 2007–14, govr Canford Sch 2014–; RIBA 1973, FRSA 1987, FConsE 1998, FICE 2004; *Recreations* golf, sailing, skiing, water colours, antiquarian horology; *Clubs* Royal Motor Yacht (Poole); *Style—* Michael Jeffries, Esq; ✉ 1 The Whitehouse,

J

326 Sandbanks Road, Poole Dorset BH14 8HY (☎ 01202 706051, mobile 07860 366251, e-mail michaeljeffries@civica.co.uk)

JEFFRIES, Neil; *b* 1959, Bristol; *Educ* St Martin's Sch of Art, Slade Sch of Fine Art; *Career* artist; artist in residence Kingston Poly 1984–85, artist in Schools Project Whitechapel 1986; pt/t lectr: Slade Coll of Art 1985–, Ruskin Sch 1985–; sculpture cmmn Scott Tallon & Walker; *Solo exhibitions* Arnolfini 1985, Blond Fine Art 1986, Flowers East 1990, Angela Flowers Gall 1992, Flowers East at London Fields 1992, Galeria Ray Gun 1994, Stadt Tuttlingen Stadtische Galerie Tuttlingen Germany 1995, Flowers East 1996, Riverside Studios London 1997, Drumcoon Wigan 1997, Flowers West Santa Monica 1999; *Group exhibitions* incl: Stowells Trophy Exhbn (RA) 1982, The New Contemporaries (ICA) 1982, The Best of 1982 (Christies) 1982, New Directions in Sculpture (Blond Fine Art) 1984, Artist of the Day (Angela Flowers Gall) 1984, Home and Abroad (Serpentine Gall) 1984, Summer Show (Blond Fine Art) 1984, Contemporary Art Society Fair (Five Dials Gall) 1984, Monstrous Craws (Actors Inst) 1984, A View From My Window (Angela Flowers Gall) 1984, Ten Painters (St Martin's Sch of Art) 1985, International Contemporary Art Fair (Olympia) 1985, Group Show (Blond Fine Art) 1985, In Their Circumstances (Usher Gall) 1985, Art for Ethiopia (Bonham's) 1985, Newbury Arts Festival 1985, Proud and Prejudiced (Twining Gall NY) 1985, Figures and Figures (Manchester Arts Centre) 1985, Peter Moores Project (Walker Art Gall) 1986, Living Art (Ideal Home Exhbn) 1986, Britain in Vienna (Künstlerhaus) 1986, Modern Art? It's a Joke! (Cleveland Gall) 1986, State of the Nation (Herbert Art Gall) 1987, Small Is Beautiful (Angela Flowers Gall) 1987, The Big Fight (Vanessa Devereux Gall) 1987, London (Royal Festival Hall) 1987, Contemporary Portraits (Flowers East) 1988, Small Is Beautiful – Part 6 (Flowers East) 1988, A Personal View (Nigel Greenwood Gall) 1988, Big Paintings (Flowers East) 1989, Ingenious Inventions (Harris Art Gall) 1989, 30 Tage (Galerie Siegart) 1990, Academicians Choice (Mall Galls) 1990, Summer Exhbn (RA) 1990 and 1991, Flowers East at Watermans Art Centre 1991, Artist's Choice Exhbn (Angela Flowers Gall) 1992, Decouvertes (Grand Palais Paris) 1993, But Big is Better (Flowers East) 1993, Inner Visions (Flowers East) 1994, The Twenty Fifth Anniversary Exhibition (Flowers East London Fields) 1995, Wheels on Fire, Cars in Art 1950–96 (Wolverhampton Art Gallery) 1996, Angela Flowers Gallery (Ireland) Inc Co Cork, Small is Beautiful Part XIV: Sex (Flowers East at London Fields) 1996, Angela Flowers Gallery 1997 (Flowers East at London Fields) 1997, Small is Beautiful XV: Death (Flowers East at London Fields) 1997, British Figurative Art Part 2: Sculpture (Flowers East London) 1998, Comic? (Oldham Art Gallery) 1998, Small is Beautiful Part XVI: Music (Flowers East at London Fields), Angela Flowers Gallery 30th Anniversary Exhbn (Flowers East London) 2000, Carnivalesque (Brighton Museum and Art Gallery, Univ of Brighton Gallery, Nottingham Castle Museum, Djanogly Gallery, Univ of Nottingham) 2000, Artist's Choice (Flowers East London) 2000; *Public Collections* Arts Cncl of GB, British Cncl; *Awards* Boise Travelling Scholarship 1984, Wollaston Award Summer Exhibition RA 1991, Arts Fndn Award for Drawing 1997; *Style*— Neil Jeffries, Esq; ✉ c/o Flowers East, 82 Kingsland Road, London E2 8DP (☎ 020 8985 3333)

JEFFRIES, Tony; *b* 2 March 1985, CA; *Educ* Farringdon Comp Sch Sunderland; *Career* amateur boxer; memb Sunderland Amateur Boxing Club; achievements incl: Gold medal under 71kg European Cadet Championships 2001, Bronze medal under 81kg European Jr Championships 2003, Bronze medal under 81kg European Championships 2005, Gold medal light heavyweight ABA Championships 2005, Bronze medal light heavyweight Olympic Games Beijing 2008; owner Box 'n' Burn gyms Santa Monica CA and Brentwood LA; *Books* The Olympian (2009); *Style*— Tony Jeffries, Esq; ✉ Box 'n' Burn, 1654 Lincoln Boulevard, Santa Monica, CA 90404, USA (website www.tonyjeffries.com)

JEHU, Jeremy Charles Rhys; s of Thomas Colin Jehu, of Pyrford, Surrey, and Betty Burrows, *née* Wilson; *b* 31 August 1955; *Educ* Royal GS Guildford, Univ Coll Durham (BA); *Career* journalist; Surrey Daily Advertiser: joined 1976, chief reporter main area office 1978–79, sub ed 1979; The Stage and Television Today: joined 1979, news ed 1986, dep ed 1986–92, ed 1992–94; freelance journalist and conslt 1995–; book critic/columnist Teletext (ITV and Channel 4) 1997–2006, book critic/presenter Literary Heroes Talk Radio 1998–99, contrib Daily Telegraph books pages 2006–; fndr memb Arts Correspondent Gp 1981 (memb Ctee 1981–90), memb Broadcasting Press Guild 1989 (memb Ctee 1990–92); *Books* The Monday Lunchtime of the Living Dead (1999); *Recreations* shooting, classic car ownership, gossip, politics, all the usual cultural pursuits; *Clubs* Savage, Green Room (hon memb), London and Middx Rifle Assoc, Tennessee Squires Assoc, CAA (hon memb); *Style*— Jeremy Jehu, Esq; ✉ 11 Rita Road, London SW8 1JX (☎ 020 7587 0423)

JENAS, Jermaine Anthony; *b* 18 February 1983, Nottingham; *Career* professional footballer; clubs: Nottingham Forest 1999–2002, Newcastle United 2002–05, Tottenham Hotspur 2005–13, Queen's Park Rangers 2013–; England: 21 caps, 1 goal, debut v Australia 2003, memb squad World Cup 2006; PFA Young Player of the Year 2002; *Style*— Jermaine Jenas, Esq; ✉ c/o Queen's Park Rangers FC, Loftus Road Stadium, South Africa Road, London W12 7PJ

JENCKS, Charles Alexander; s of Gardner Platt Jencks (d 1989), *née* Pearl (d 1990); *b* 21 June 1939; *Educ* Brooks Sch, Harvard Univ (BA, MA), Univ of London (Fulbright scholar, PhD); *m* 1, Pamela Balding; 2 s (Ivor Cosimo b 1969, Justin Alexander b 1972); m 2, Maggie (d 1995), da of Sir John Henry Keswick, KCMG (d 1982); 1 s (John Keswick b 1979), 1 da (Lily Clare b 1980); m 3, Louisa Lane Fox; *Career* writer on architecture 1966–, lectr and prof 1969–, TV writer and sometime participant 1971–, architect and designer 1976–, writer on art 1985–, garden designer 1989–, writer on non-architectural subjects 1989–; author of numerous books and articles on the subject of modern architecture and its successors; furniture and drawings exhibited; cmmns incl: Centre for Life Newcastle 2000, Landform Scottish Gallery of Modern Art Edinburgh 2002 (Gulbenkian Prize 2004), Portello Park Milan 2003, DNA sculptures Cold Spring Harbor Labs Long Island and Kew Gardens London 2003, Cells of Life Jupiter Artland Edinburgh 2005, Fife Earth Project Kelty 2005, Northumberlandia Landform North of Newcastle 2004 and 2008, Crawick Artland Scotland 2006 and 2008; lectures at over 40 int univs; co-fndr Maggie Cancer Caring Centres 1995– (six completed, six underway); memb: AA, RSA; Nara Gold Medal for Architecture 1992, Country Life Gardener of the Year 1998; *Clubs* Groucho, Athenaeum, Chelsea Arts; *Style*— Charles Jencks, Esq; ✉ John Wiley and Sons, International House, Ealing Broadway Centre, London W5 5DB (☎ 020 8326 3800, fax 020 8326 3801); c/o Frances Lincoln Ltd, Torriano Mews, 4 Torriano Avenue, London NW5 2RZ (☎ 020 7284 4009, fax 020 7485 0490)

JENKALA, Adrian Aleksander; s of Georgius Ihorus Jenkala, and Olena, *née* Karpynec; *b* 21 May 1957; *Educ* Latymer Upper Sch, Univ of London (BSc, LLB); *Career* called to the Bar Middle Temple 1984; practising barr 1984–, lectr in law London Guildhall Univ 1985–92, instr Inns of Ct Sch of Law 1989–98; legal sec to Int Cmmn of Inquiry into 1932–33 Famine in Ukraine 1987–90 (report presented to UN in 1990); Sch of Slavonic and East European Studies (SSEES): chm Ukrainian Studies Tst Fund Ctee 1991–, hon res fell 1993–98; official international observer at the referendum and presidential elections in Ukraine 1991, advsr in legal affairs to the Ambass of Ukraine in GB 1998–; chm Assoc of Ukrainian Lawyers 1987–, memb Bd World Congress of Ukrainian Lawyers 1992– (vice-pres (Europe) 1994–2001); dep chm Br-Ukrainian Law Assoc 2001– (sec 1993–2001); visiting prof Cumberland Sch of Law Samford Univ Alabama 1994– (adjunct prof of law 2008–); memb: Bd of Foreign Advisers Ukrainian Legal Fndn Kiev, Central and E European Sub-Ctee of the Int Practice Ctee of Bar Cncl, Hon Soc of the

Middle Temple; Freeman City of London; ACIArb; *Books* Ukrainian Legal Dictionary (ed, 1994); *Recreations* squash, skiing, ski instructing; *Style*— Adrian Jenkala, Esq; ✉ Clarendon Chambers, 7 Stone Buildings, London WC2A 3SZ (☎ 020 7353 0003, fax 020 7353 9213)

JENKIN, Hon Bernard Christison; MP; yr son of Baron Jenkin of Roding, PC, *qv*; *b* 9 April 1959; *Educ* Highgate Sch, William Ellis Sch Highgate, CCC Cambridge (pres Cambridge Union 1982); *m* 24 Sept 1988, Anne Caroline (Baroness Jenkin of Kennington (Life Peer), *qv*), da of late Hon Charles Strutt, and sis of 6 Baron Rayleigh, *qv*; 2 s (Robert Patrick Christison b 13 May 1989, Peter Andrew Graham b 29 July 1991); *Career* sales and mktg exec Ford Motor Co Ltd 1983–86, with 3i plc 1986–88, mangr Legal and General Ventures Ltd until 1989–92, advsr Legal & General Group plc 1992–95; Parly candidate Glasgow Central 1987; MP (Cons): Colchester N 1992–97, Essex N 1997–2010, Harwich and Essex N 2010–; memb Social Security Select Ctee 1993–97, PPS to Rt Hon Michael Forsyth, MP (sec of state for Scotland) 1995–97; oppn frontbench spokesman on constitutional affrs 1997–98, shadow min for tport 1998–2001 and London 1999–2001, shadow sec of state for defence 2001–03, shadow sec of state for regions 2003–05, shadow min for energy 2005, dep chm Cons Pty 2005–06, memb Defence Select Ctee 2006–10, chm Public Admin Select Ctee 2010–15, chm Public Admin and Constitutional Affrs Ctee; memb St Paul's Cathedral Cncl London 2006–15; *Recreations* sailing, music (especially singing and opera), fishing, family, DIY; *Clubs* Colchester Cons; *Style*— The Hon Bernard Jenkin, MP; ✉ House of Commons, London SW1A 0AA (☎ 020 7219 4029, e-mail bernard.jenkin.mp@parliament.uk, website www.bernardjenkinmp.com)

JENKIN OF KENNINGTON, Baroness (Life Peer UK 2011), of Hatfield Peverel in the County of Essex; Anne Caroline Jenkin; *née* Strutt; da of late Hon Charles Strutt, and sis of 6 Baron Rayleigh, *qv*; *b* 8 December 1955; *m* 24 Sept 1988, Hon Bernard Jenkin, MP, *qv*; 2 s (Robert Patrick Christison b 13 May 1989, Peter Andrew Graham b 29 July 1991); *Career* PR conslt; *Style*— The Baroness Jenkin of Kennington; ✉ House of Lords, London SW1A 0PW

JENKINS, Alan Dominique; s of Ian Samuel Jenkins, of Dorset, and Jeannette Juliette Jenkins; *b* 27 May 1952; *Educ* Clifton, New Coll Oxford (BA); *m* 30 June 1979, Caroline, da of Paul Treverton Jones (d 1983), of Monmouthshire; 1 s (Mark b 30 May 1982), 3 da (Claire b 13 April 1984, Alice 17 Oct 1989, Emily b 9 Nov 1991); *Career* admitted slr 1977, ptnr Frere Cholmeley Bischoff 1983–98 (managing ptnr 1996–98), ptnr Eversheds (following merger) 1998–2011 (head of int 2002–09, chm 2004–10, chm of global markets 2010–11); non-exec dir: Financial Ombudsman Service 2011–, Gross Hill Properties Ltd 2011–, Sydney and London Properties Ltd 2011–; dir: GPS Malta Ltd, Northcourt Ltd, GPS Associates Ltd 2012–; head Advsy Bd Page Gp Ltd, memb Bd Roehampton Club Ltd 2016–; non-exec memb Bd: UK Trade & Investment 2009–15, CPS 2011–; tstee: Int Inst for Environment and Devpt (vice-chm 2006–14), Lattitude Global Volunteering Ltd 2005– (chm 2010–15), Mencap Tst Co Ltd 2009– (chm), London ME Inst, Kids for Kids 2015–; FInstD (memb Cncl 2007–); *Recreations* sport (rugby, golf, tennis, skiing), music, theatre, reading; *Clubs* MCC, Roehampton; *Style*— Alan Jenkins, Esq

JENKINS, (Thomas) Alun; QC (1996); s of Seward Thomas Jenkins, of Abergavenny, and Iris Jenkins; *b* 19 August 1948; *Educ* Ebbw Vale Tech Sch, Univ of Bristol (LLB); *m* 1971, Glenys Maureen, da of Maj John Constant, of Abergavenny; 2 da (Clare Elizabeth b 19 Sept 1976, Katie Jane b 19 Dec 1982), 1 s (Christopher Alun b 7 Nov 1985); *Career* called to the Bar Lincoln's Inn 1972, in practice in Bristol and London 1972–, recorder of the Crown Court 2000–; *Recreations* opera, Shakespeare, literature, riding, point-to-point, rugby, motor cars, reading; *Style*— T Alun Jenkins, Esq, QC; ✉ Queen Square Chambers, 56 Queen Square, Bristol BS1 4PR; (☎ 0117 921 1966, fax 0117 927 6493); 2 Bedford Row, London WC1R 4BU (☎ 020 7440 8888)

JENKINS, Anne; da of Roy Dudley, of Blackpool, Lancs, and Georgina Ledlie, *née* McKeen (d 1996); *Educ* Elmslie Girls' Sch Blackpool, Univ of Manchester (BA); *m* 24 Sept 1988, Peter Lewis Jenkins, s of David Jenkins (d 1994); 1 da (Victoria Anne b 14 June 1993), 1 s (William Dudley b 23 April 1996); *Career* Mazars Neville Russell CAs Stockport (formerly Neville Russell) 1980–84 (ACA 1983), Peat Marwick CAs London 1984–85, The Financial Training Co 1986–90, ind trg conslt in fin 1990–97; dir ATC (CPD) Ltd 1997–2000, dir demist.com 2000–; ICAEW: memb Cncl 1993–, chm Recruitment and Promotion Ctee 1994–96, memb Educn and Trg Directorate 1994–97, memb Post Qualification Ctee 1998–99; pres Women in Accountancy 1998–99 (memb Ctee 1994–98), memb Business Law Ctee 1996–98, ldr Student Taskforce 1999; awarded FCA 1994; *Recreations* swimming, running, cycling, skiing, London Triathlon (Olympic) 1999, theatre; *Clubs* LA Fitness (Isleworth); *Style*— Mrs Anne Jenkins; ✉ 50 Beaconsfield Road, St Margarets, Middlesex TW1 3HU (☎ 020 8287 4003, e-mail anne.jenkins@virgin.net)

JENKINS, Bethan Maeve; AM; da of Mike Jenkins, of Merthyr Tydfil, Glamorgan, and Marie, *née* Greagsby; *b* 9 December 1981, Aberdare, Glamorgan; *Educ* Ysgol Gyfun Gymraeg Rhydfelen Pontypridd, Univ of Wales Aberystwyth (BA); *Career* Aberystwyth Guild of Students: equal opportunities and campaigns sabbatical offr 2003–04, pres 2004–05; researcher for Leanne Woods, AM, *qv*, 2005–06, political asst to Jill Evans, MEP, *qv*, 2005–06, youth organiser Plaid Cymru 2005–07, AM (Plaid Cymru) S Wales West 2007–; memb: Aberystwyth Peace and Justice Network, CND Cymru, Welsh Language Soc, Friends of the Earth, Asylum Justice; *Recreations* playing the viola, sports, reading; *Clubs* Swansea Community Orch; *Style*— Ms Bethan Jenkins, AM; ✉ 75 Briton Ferry Road, Neath SA11 1AR (☎ 01639 643549, e-mail bethan.jenkins@wales.gov.uk)

JENKINS, Caroline Helen Clare; da of Daniel Jenkins, and Nell, *née* Cree; sis of Simon David Jenkins, *qv*; *b* 1952, Redhill, Surrey; *Educ* St Mary's Hall Brighton, KCL (BA); *m* 1975, Prof John Mack, *qv*; 1 da (Katherine Helen b 1985), 1 s (Samuel Thomas b 1989); *Career* admitted slr 1980; trainee slr Marcus Barnett, sr ptnr Parlett Kent 1986– (ptnr 1983–); memb: Clinical Negligence Panel Law Soc, Clinical Negligence Panel and Slrs Panel AVMA (Action against Medical Accidents); memb Assoc of Personal Injury Lawyers; *Publications* Medical Accidents Handbook (contrib, 1997); *Style*— Ms Caroline Jenkins; ✉ Parlett Kent, Ardenham House, Ardenham Lane, Aylesbury, Berkshire (☎ 01296 390009, e-mail cjenkins@parlettkent.co.uk)

JENKINS, Catrin Mary; da of late Charles Bryan Jenkins, and Anne, *née* Davies-Jones; *b* 22 December 1958; *Educ* Llanelli Girls GS, Univ Coll Cardiff (LLB); *m* 7 Sept 1996, Jonathan James; 1 s (Tomos b 19 Nov 1998); *Career* admitted slr 1983; ptnr: Eversheds Phillips & Buck 1988–95, Francis & Buck 1995–; *Style*— Ms Catrin Jenkins; ✉ 70 Ryder Street, Pontcanna, Cardiff; Francis & Buck, Celtic House, Cathedral Road, Cardiff CF11 9FB (☎ 029 2034 4995, fax 029 2039 9646, e-mail catrin@francisandbuck.co.uk)

JENKINS, Hon Charles Arthur Simon; s of Baron Jenkins of Hillhead (Life Peer, d 2003); *b* 25 March 1949; *Educ* Winchester, Holland Park Sch, New Coll Oxford; *m* 11 Sept 1971, Ivana Alexandra, da of Ing Ivo Vladimir Sertic (d 1986), of Zagreb, Croatia; 2 da (Alexandra Dorothea b 14 March 1986, Helena Harriet b 13 May 1988); *Career* European ed Economist Intelligence Unit 1975–, ed Euro Policy Analyst (quarterly magazine on European affairs); memb Exec Ctee Be Section European League for Economic Cooperation; memb Clapham Action on Tport; *Style*— The Hon Charles Jenkins

JENKINS, Dr David Anthony Lawson; s of Phillip Ronald Jenkins (d 1969), of Folkestone, Kent, and Olive Lilian, *née* Lear (d 2000); *b* 5 December 1938; *Educ* Dauntsey's Sch West Lavington, Clare Coll Cambridge (BA, DPhil); *m* 17 Feb 1963, Evanthia, da of Spirithonos Nicolopoulou, of Patras, Greece; 2 s (Charles David b 19 June 1969, Anthony Phillip b 8 Aug 1970); *Career* BP: joined 1961, chief geologist Exploration 1979–82, sr vice-pres

Exploration and Prodn Canada 1983–84, gen mangr Exploration 1985–88, chief exec Technol Exploration 1988–98, dir Exploration 1989–98, dir Canada 1989–91, ret 1998; dir: Chartwood Resources Ltd 1999–2016, Ranger Oil Ltd 1999–2000, GeoNet Energy Services Inc 1999–2001, BHP Billiton Ltd 2001–09, Mintaka Int (Oil & Gas) Ltd, Black Platinum Energy 2011–, President Energy Ltd 2012–15, Riverstone Hldgs 2012–, Hurricane Energy plc 2013–; chm Oil Industry Int Exploration and Prodn Forum 1991–95; memb Advsy Cncl: BP Amoco Technol 1998–2000, Landmark Co 1999–2002, Science Applications Int Corp 1999–05, Halliburton Co 2000–03, Consort Resources Ltd 2000–03, Celerant Conslt 2000–05, Temasck Hldgs 2009–15, Cuadrilla Resources 2010–15; FGS, AAPG; *Recreations* gardening, current affairs; *Style—* Dr David Jenkins; ✉ Ardennes, East Road, St George's Hill, Weybridge, Surrey KT13 0LB (☎ 01932 847377, fax 01932 821703, e-mail jenkins@chartwood.com)

JENKINS, David Hugh; DL (Dorset 2012); s of David Lyndhurst Jenkins (d 1985), and Charlotte Elizabeth, *née* Thomas (d 2003); *b* 28 April 1952, Barry, Glamorgan; *Educ* Barry Boys Comp Sch, Jesus Coll Oxford (open scholar, MA), Coll of Law Chester; *m* 1980, Ethna Geraldine, *née* Trafford; 1 da (Sarah Delia); *Career* admitted slr 1977; asst master Fairfield GS Bristol 1973–74, articled clerk then asst slr Oxon CC 1975–79, slr Cmmn for Local Admin in Wales 1979–84, asst county sec Hants CC 1984–89; Dorset CC: dep county slr 1989, asst chief exec 1991, county slr 1993, dir of corp servs 1996, chief exec 1999–2012; pres Dorset Law Soc 1993–94; clerk to Dorset Lieutenancy 1999–2012, clerk to Dorset Fire Authy 1999–2008, sec Dorset Probation Bd 1999–2009, memb Bd Bournemouth Symphony Orchestra, chm SW Regnl Improvement and Efficiency Partnership, chair Dorset Working Gp for the 2012 Games 2003–12, memb SW Bd for the 2012 Games 2011–12, dep chair Dorset NHS Clinical Commissioning Gp 2013–, ind chair Glos County Cncl Waste Working Gp 2013–14, chm Independent Inquiry into Infant Cremations in Shropshire 2014–15; memb Assoc of County Chief Execs (chm 2006–07), memb Bd Assoc of Drainage Authorities 2016–; patron Bridport Arts Centre 2009–, tstee Richard Ely Tst for Young Musicians 2013–15, chm Bournemouth Symphony Orchestra Endowment Tst 2013– (chm 2014–), Wessex Regional Flood and Coastal Ctee 2015–, tstee Minerva Learning Tst Bridport 2016–; FRSA 2009–15; *Recreations* theatre, music especially opera and choral singing, family; *Style—* David Jenkins, DL; ✉ Dorset NHS Clinical Commissioning Group, Vespasian House, Bridport Road, Dorchester, Dorset DT1 1TS

JENKINS, Derek William; s of William Jenkins (d 1961), of Burnley, Lancs, and Annie, *née* Haydock (d 1993); *b* 12 September 1934; *Educ* Burnley GS; *m* 3 June 1961, Hazel, da of late George Watson; 2 da (Fiona Louise (Mrs Fawcett) b 22 Dec 1962, Alison Helen (Mrs Winter) b 8 Feb 1966); *Career* articled clerk Proctor and Proctor CAs Burnley 1950–58 (Nat Serv 1952–54), various appts Binder Hamlyn & Co 1958–66, asst tax administrator Texaco UK Ltd 1966–68; RMC Gp plc: gp taxation mangr 1968–77, gp financial controller 1977–80, fin dir 1981–97; pres Cartophilic Soc of GB 2000–09 (pres emeritus 2009–); Freeman City of London 1982; FCA 1958, ATII 1962; *Recreations* cartophily, swimming, golf, family history, Burnley FC (past and present); *Clubs* Wentworth; *Style—* Derek W Jenkins, Esq; ✉ The Pines, Springfield Road, Camberley, Surrey GU15 1AB (☎ 01276 671700)

JENKINS, (John) Emyr; s of Llywelyn Jenkins (d 1957), of Machynlleth, Powys, and Mary Olwen, *née* Jones (d 1967); *b* 3 May 1938; *Educ* Machynlleth Co Sch, Univ of Wales Aberystwyth (BSc); *m* 1964, Myra Bonner, da of Brynley Samuel; 2 da (Manon Bonner (Mrs John Antoniazzi) b 1965, Ffion Llywelyn (Mrs William Hague) b 1968); *Career* BBC: trainee studio mangr BBC London 1961–62, asst studio mangr BBC Cardiff 1962–63, staff announcer and compere 1963–71, prog organiser BBC Wales 1971–77; dir Royal National Eisteddfod of Wales 1978–93, dir Welsh Arts Cncl 1993–94, chief exec Arts Cncl of Wales 1994–98; dep chm Royal Welsh Coll of Music and Drama 2000–06 (govr 1998–2000), chm Bd Univ of Wales Press 2003–06 (memb 1999–2003), chm Welsh Music Information Centre 2000–05, chm Sherman Cymru Theatre 2006–12; fndr chm MYM (Nat Assoc of Welsh-medium Playgroups) 1971–73; elder Crwys Welsh Presbyterian Church 1984– (treas 2009–); hon memb Gorsedd of Bards 1982–; Hon MA Univ of Wales 1993; FRSA 1992, FRWCMD 1997; *Recreations* music, theatre, sport, walking; *Style—* Emyr Jenkins, Esq

JENKINS, Graeme James Ewers; s of Kenneth Arthur Jenkins (d 2009), and Marjorie Joyce, *née* Ewers (d 1999); *b* 31 December 1958; *Educ* Dulwich Coll, Gonville & Caius Coll Cambridge (MA), Royal Coll of Music; *m* 19 July 1986, Joanna, da of Christopher Charles Cyprian Bridge, ERD, of E Sussex; 2 da (Martha Nancy b 18 May 1989, Isabella Dinah b 20 Dec 1991); *Career* conducted 183 opera prodns of over 117 different titles worldwide; music dir Glyndebourne Touring Opera 1985–91, music dir Dallas Opera 1993–2013, artistic dir Arundel Festival 1992–98, princ conductor Cologne Opera 1997–2002, opened Lord Foster's Winspear Opera House Dallas 2009; has conducted at: Glyndebourne Festival Opera, ENO, Scottish Opera, Kent Opera, Opera North, Geneva Opera, Netherlands Opera, Paris Opera, Glimmerglass Opera, Canadian Opera, Australian Opera, Cologne Opera, Deutsche Oper Berlin, Danish Opera, Vienna State Opera (Billy Budd, Jenufa, Flying Dutchman, Cav/Pag, Fanciulla del West, Ades the Tempest), Opera Theatre of St Louis, princ Br and several Dutch, German and French orchs (incl Orchestre de Lyon and Monte Carlo Philharmonique), Perth and Melbourne Symphony Orchs, Danish Radio Symphony Orch, Finnish Radio Symphony Orch, Göteborg Symphony Orch, Hungarian Radio Symphony Orch, Prague Symphony Orch, New Zealand Int Festival 2004, Swedish Opera, Bayerische Statsoper Debuts 2009, Bayerische Rundfunk Orch 2012, Theater an der Wien (Figaro), Vienna Symphony Orch; 2014/15 debuts: Korean Nat Opera (Otello), Hungarian Nat Opera (Jenufa), Bamberg Symphony Orch (recorded 2 symphonies of Paul Juon); conducted many American symphonic orchs: Utah, Houston, Dallas, San Antonio, Minnesota; recordings incl: Britten's Death in Venice, Picker's Therese Raquin; Freeman City of London 1989–, Freeman Worshipful Co of Goldsmiths 1989; ARCM; *Recreations* reading, cooking; *Style—* Graeme Jenkins, Esq; ✉ 21 Wendle Square, London SW11 4SS (☎ 020 7228 1317); c/o Hilbert Artists Management, Maximillianstrasse 22, 80539 Munich, Germany (website www.hilbert.de)

JENKINS, Dr John Gordon; CBE (2009); s of John Francis Jenkins (d 1992), and Eleanor Blair, *née* Gordon; *b* 30 November 1950; *Educ* Royal Belfast Academical Instn, Queen's Univ Belfast (Milroy Medal, MB BCh, BAO, MD); *m* 26 Oct 1974, Heather Caroline, *née* Harris; 2 s (Colin b 28 Nov 1976, Gareth b 17 Oct 1978), 1 da (Caroline b 9 Aug 1983); *Career* conslt paediatrician Northern Health and Social Services Bd NI (Waveney Hosp Ballymena then Antrim Hosp) 1982–2010, hon conslt paediatrician Royal Maternity Hosp Belfast 1999–2010, sr lectr in child health Queen's Univ Belfast 1999–2010, hon sr lectr in child health Queen's Univ Belfast 2011–; clinical dir Woman and Child Health Directorate United Hosps Gp 1994–96, med exec dir United Hosps Tst 1996–98; assessor GMC Performance Procedures 1998–2003, NI memb PMETB 2003–10, NI memb GMC 2003–; DHSSPS: memb Central Med Advsy Ctee 1992–2010 (chm 2003–10), chm Implemation Support Gp/Advsy Gp on Jr Doctors' Hours 2000–08; non-exec memb: Bd Regulation and Quality Improvement Authy 2013–, NI Medical and Dental Trg Agency 2013; pres Assoc for the Study of Medical Education 2013–; MRCP 1977, FRCPEd 1989, FRCPCH 1997, FRCPI 2003; *Style—* Dr J G Jenkins, CBE

JENKINS, Mark Andrew; s of Prof George C Jenkins, and Elizabeth, *née* Welch; *b* 15 November 1957; *Educ* Forest Sch, Chelmer Inst, Inns of Court Sch of Law; *m* 1986, Susan Hilary; 2 da (Eloise b 1989, Tabitha b 1993), 1 s (Oscar b 1995); *Career* practised at the Bar 1980–85; asst co-sec MK Electric Gp plc 1985–87; co-sec: SKF (UK) Ltd 1987–92, PEEK plc 1992–98; legal dir and co-sec COLT Telecom Gp plc 1998–2004, gp co sec Signet Gp plc 2004–; memb Bar Assoc for Commerce Fin and Industry; *Recreations* music, books, Napoleonic history; *Style—* Mark Jenkins, Esq; ✉ Elba House, Goosey, Faringdon, Oxfordshire SN7 8PA (☎ 01367 710156); Signet Jewelers Ltd, c/o Signet Group Ltd, 110 Cannon Street, London EC4N 6EU (☎ 020 7648 5203, fax 020 7621 0835, e-mail mark.jenkins@signet.co.uk)

JENKINS, Sir Michael Nicholas Howard; kt (1997), OBE (1991); s of Maj Cyril Norman Jenkins (d 1985), and Maud Evelyn Sophie, *née* Shorter; *b* 13 October 1932; *Educ* Tonbridge, Merton Coll Oxford (BA); *m* 28 Sept 1957, Jacqueline Frances, da of Francis Jones (d 1979); 3 s (Howard Michael Charles b 1958, (Edward) Hugo b 1961, Oliver John b 1966); *Career* Nat Serv 2 Lt RA 1951–53; Shell-Mex and BP 1956–61, IBM UK 1961–67, ptnr Robson Morrow Management Consultants 1967–71, tech dir The Stock Exchange 1971–77, md European Options Exchange Amsterdam 1977–80, chief exec London International Financial Futures Exchange (LIFFE) 1981–92, non-exec chm London Commodity Exchange 1992–96, chm Futures & Options Assoc 1993–99, chm The London Clearing House 1996–2003 (dir 1990–2003), chm E-Crossnet 1999–2005; dir: Tradepoint Investment Exchange 1995–99, British Invisibles 1998–2001, EasyScreen 1999–2005; govr Sevenoaks Sch 1993–2007; tstee Brain and Spine Fndn 1993–2010, pres Merton Soc 2007–10, tstee Success in Shortage Subjects 2007–; Liveryman: Worshipful Co of Information Technologists 2004, Worshipful Co of World Traders 2009; *Recreations* games, music, woodworking; *Clubs* Wilderness (Sevenoaks); *Style—* Sir Michael Jenkins, OBE

JENKINS, Neil Martin James; *b* 9 April 1945; *Educ* Westminster Abbey Choir Sch (chorister), Dean Close Sch Cheltenham (music scholar), King's Coll Cambridge (choral scholar, MA), RCM; *m* 1, 1969, Sandra, *née* Wilkes; m 2, 26 April 1982, Penny Maxwell, *née* Underwood; 5 c (Tom, Sam, Nicholas, Benjamin, Rosie); *Career* tenor; recital debut Kirckman Concert Series Purcell Rooms 1967, operatic debut Menotti's The Consul Israel Festival 1968; Geoffrey Tankard Lieder Prize 1967, Nat Fedn of Music Socs Award 1972; prof of singing RCM 1975–76, Cummins Harvey visiting fell Girton Coll Cambridge 2003; teacher various summer schs incl Dartington, Canford, Summer Music and Hereford 1989–; pres: Grange Choral Soc Hampshire, Haywards Heath Music Soc, Shoreham Oratorio Choir, Kent Chorus 2011–; vice-pres: Huntingdonshire Philharmonic, Brighton Competitive Music Festival; musical dir and conductor Sussex Chorus 2002–14; patron Goldsmiths Choral Union; *Roles* incl: Ottavio in Don Giovanni (Kent Opera) 1971, Fenton in Falstaff (BBC) 1972, Ferrando in Cosi fan Tutte (Kent Opera) 1974, Almaviva in The Barber of Seville (WNO) 1974, Quint in Turn of the Screw (Eng Music Theatre 1977, Kent Opera 1979), title role in Return of Ulysses (Kent Opera) 1978 and 1990, Nadir in The Pearl Fishers (Scottish Opera) 1981–82, title roles in Peter Grimes (New Sussex Opera) 1981 and Robinson Crusoe (Kent Opera) 1983, Cat/Milkman in Higglety Pigglety Pop (Glyndebourne Festival Opera), Junger Diener in Elektra (Geneva) 1986 and 1990, Herod in Salome (WNO) 1991 and (Scottish Opera) 1993, Valzacchi in Der Rosenkavalier (WNO) 1994 and 2000, Sellem in Stravinsky's The Rake's Progress (WNO) 1996, Berg's Lulu (BBC Proms) 1996, Sir Philip Wingrave Owen Wingrave (Glyndebourne) 1997, Arnalta in The Coronation of Poppea 1998, Almoner in The Carmelites (WNO) 1999, Vitek in The Makropulos (Glyndebourne) 2001, Irus in Il Ritorno d'Ulisses (WNO) 2006, Bardolph in Falstaff (WNO) 2008, Quint in The Turn of the Screw (Dartington) 2010, King Ouf in Chabrier's L'Etoile (New Sussex Opera) 2014; *Recordings* incl: Rossini's Elisabetta Regina D'Ingilterra, Mozart's Le Nozze di Figaro, Bernstein's Candide, White House Cantata, Purcell's St Cecilia's Day Ode, Bach's St Matthew Passion and Cantata 131, Handel's Wedding Anthem, Schumann's Scenes From Faust, Henze's Kammermusik, Britten's Peter Grimes, Vaughan Williams' Hugh the Drover, Maxwell Davies' Resurrection, Stephen Dodgson's London Lyrics, Finzi's A Young Man's Exhortation; *Film Soundtracks* incl: Chariots of Fire, Revenge of the Pink Panther, SOS Titanic, Lion of the Desert; *Books* Carol Singer's Handbook, O Praise God, O Holy Night, Sing Solo Sacred, Bach St Matthew Passion and St John Passion, Christmas Oratorio, Magnificat, B Minor Mass, Easter Oratorio, Ascension Oratorio, Schütz The Christmas Story, Haydn: The Creation, The Seasons, Haydn Society of Great Britain: The Text of Haydn's The Creation (2005), Handel (contrib, 2011), John Beard, Handel and Garrick's Favourite Tenor (2012), Haydn: The Seven Last Words, Handel: The Passion of Christ (Brockes Passion), Schutz The Resurrection Story; *Recreations* visiting ancient monuments, 18th century music research; *Style—* Neil Jenkins, Esq; ✉ agent for opera: c/o Music International, 13 Ardilaun Road, London N5 2QR (☎ 020 7359 5813); agent for concerts and oratorios: c/o Davies Music, 23 Church Street, Tewkesbury GL20 5PD (☎ 01684 850112)

JENKINS, Sir Paul Christopher; KCB (2012), Hon QC (2009); *Career* called to the Bar 1977; legal advsr Lord Chancellor's Dept then DG Legal and Int Gp Dept of Constitutional Affrs 1998–2004, DG Law, Governance and Special Policy Gp Dept for Work and Pensions, slr to Dept for Work and Pensions and Dept of Health until 2006, HM procurator gen and treasury slr, chief exec and perm sec Treasury Solicitor's Dept 2006–14; barr Matrix Chambers 2015–; *Style—* Sir Paul Jenkins, KCB, QC; ✉ Matrix Chambers, Griffin Building, Gray's Inn, London WC1R 5LN (e-mail pauljenkins@matrixlaw.co.uk, website www.matrixlaw.co.uk)

JENKINS, Peter Sefton; s of John Harry Sefton Jenkins (d 1978), of Brackley, Northants, and Helen Summers, *née* Staveley; *b* 9 February 1948; *Educ* King's Sch Canterbury, St Edmund Hall Oxford (MA); *m* 1, 8 June 1972 (m dis 1991), Jacqueline, da of John Mills (d 1976); 2 s (Benjamin b 13 June 1975, Christopher b 7 April 1979); m 2, 9 Jan 1998, Emma Anne Elizabeth, da of Christopher Howard; 2 s (Thomas Christopher Howard b 24 Dec 1998, George Peter William Howard b 15 Aug 2000); *Career* HM Customs and Excise 1969–86: private sec to chm 1972–74, Cabinet Office 1974–77, involved in EC negotiations on customs duty harmonisations 1977–79, private sec to Chllr of Exchequer 1979, asst sec VAT Admin 1983–86; nat head Indirect Tax Ernst & Young 1990–2001 (Ernst & Whinney 1986–90), global head of indirect tax Ernst & Young 2001–; memb VAT Practitioners' Gp; *Recreations* music, opera, walking, windsurfing; *Clubs* Reform; *Style—* Peter Jenkins, Esq; ✉ Ernst & Young LLP, Becket House, 1 Lambeth Palace Road, London SE1 7EU (☎ 020 7980 0477, e-mail pjenkins1@uk.ey.com)

JENKINS, Prof Rachel McDougall; da of Peter Osborne McDougall, of Durham, and Beryl, *née* Braddock; *b* 17 April 1949; *Educ* Monmouth Sch for Girls, St Paul's Girls' Sch, Girton Coll Cambridge (MA, MB BChir, MD); *m* 6 July 1974, (David) Keith Jenkins, s of Lt Cdr David Edward Jenkins, of Chesterfield; 1 da (Ruth b 1979), 1 s (Benjamin b 1983); *Career* registrar Maudsley Hosp 1975–77, conslt psychiatrist and sr lectr Bart's 1985–88, hon sr lectr Inst of Psychiatry 1985– (res worker and Wellcome fell 1977–82, sr lectr 1982–85), princ MO Mental Health, Elderly, Disability and Ethics Div Dept of Health 1988–96, dir WHO Collaborating Centre Inst of Psychiatry 1997–, prof of epidemiology and int mental health policy 2008–; 350 pubns in res jls; memb: Ctee of Mgmnt Inst of Psychiatry, Int Fedn of Psychiatric Epidemiologists, Cncl RCPsych; FRCPsych, FRIPHH, MFPH, FFOHM; distinguished fell American Psychiatric Assoc; *Books* Sex Differences in Minor Psychiatric Morbidity (1985), The Classification of Psychosocial Problems in Primary Care (1987), Post Viral Fatigue Syndrome (1991), Indicators of Mental Health in the Population (1991), Preventing Mental Ill Health at Work (1992), The Prevention of Depression and Anxiety – The Role of the Primary Care Team (1992), The Primary Care of Schizophrenia (1992), Promoting Mental Health Policies in the Workplace (1993), Prevention of Suicide (1994), Prevention in Psychiatry (1996), Mental Health Promotion and Prevention in Primary Care (1997), Management of Mental Disorders (2000),

J

Developing a Mental Health Policy (2002), Social Inequalities in Mental Health (2004), Implementing Mental Health Promotion (2007), Mental Capital and Wellbeing (2009); *Recreations* wild orchids, travel, walking, reading; *Clubs* Reform; *Style*— Prof Rachel McDougall Jenkins; ✉ Newhouse Farm, Moccas, Hereford HR2 9LA; WHO Collaborating Centre, Institute of Psychiatry, Denmark Hill, London SE5 8AF (e-mail rachel@olan.org)

JENKINS, His Hon Richard Peter Vellacott; s of Gwynne Jenkins (d 1988), and Irene Lillian, *née* Vellacott (d 2010); *b* 10 May 1943, Radlett, Herts; *Educ* Edge Grove Sch Aldenham, Radley, Trinity Hall Cambridge (MA); *m* 1, 5 April 1975, (Agnes) Anna Margaret, da of Howard Mullan (d 2003); 1 s (Daniel Gwynne b 1978), 1 da (Isobel Sarah b 1982); m 2, 9 Oct 2010, Jennifer Christine Kershaw (d 2012), *née* Heath (Her Hon Judge Kershaw, QC); *Career* called to the Bar Inner Temple 1966; memb: Midland Circuit 1968–71, Midland & Oxford Circuit 1972–89 (asst treas and remembrancer 1985–89); recorder 1988–89; circuit judge: Midland & Oxford Circuit 1989–2001, Midland Circuit 2001–11, North Eastern Circuit 2011–15; jt assigned judge: Lincs County Courts 1995–99, Humberside Probation Ctee 1996–2000, Lincs Probation Bd 2001–04; liaison judge Lincs Magistrates 1995–2005, designated family judge Lincoln Care Centre 1997–2007; pres Cncl HM Circuit Judges 2009, vice-pres Lincs Magistrates' Assoc 1995–2010, chm Lincs Criminal Justice Strategy Ctee 2000–03, hon pres Lincs Family Mediation Serv 2003–10 (chm 1997–2002); ctee memb Cncl of HM Circuit Judges 2000–09 (chm Family Sub-Ctee 2003–08, sr vice-pres 2008); chm Advsy Bd Lincoln Univ Law Sch 2006–10, memb Ct Univ of Lincoln 2011–; Freeman City of London, Liveryman Worshipful Co of Barbers 1967; Hon LLD Univ of Lincoln 2004; *Clubs* MCC, Lansdowne, Aula; *Style*— His Hon Richard Jenkins

JENKINS, (Sir) Simon David; kt (2004); s of Prof Daniel Jenkins (d 2002), and Agatha Helen Mary (Nell), *née* Cree (d 1992); bro of Caroline Helen Clare Jenkins, *qv*; *b* 10 June 1943; *Educ* Mill Hill Sch London, St John's Coll Oxford (BA); *m* 1, 1978 (m dis 2008), Gayle Hunnicutt; 1 s (Edward Lloyd b 24 Feb 1982), 1 step s (Nolan); m 2, 2014, Hannah Kaye; *Career* journalist; Country Life 1965, news ed Times Education Supplement 1966–68, columnist Evening Standard 1968–74, Insight ed Sunday Times 1974–75, ed Evening Standard 1976–78 (dep ed 1975–76), political ed The Economist 1979–86, columnist Sunday Times 1986–90 (ed Books Section 1988–89, Journalist of the Yr 1988); The Times: ed 1990–92, columnist 1992–2005 (Br Press Awards Columnist of the Year 1993); columnist: The Guardian 2005–, Sunday Times 2005–08, Evening Standard 2008–; memb: Bd BR 1979–90, Millennium Cmmn 1994–2000; dep chm English Heritage 1989–90, chm Buildings Books Tst 1995–, chm Nat Tst 2008–14; Hon Dr: UCE 1998, Univ of London 2000, City Univ 2001, Univ of Exeter 2002, Univ of Kent 2008; Hon RIBA, FRSL, FSA; *Books* A City at Risk (1971), Landlords of London (1974), Insight on Portugal (ed, 1975), Newspapers: The Power and The Money (1979), The Companion Guide to Outer London (1981), The Battle for the Falklands (with Max Hastings, 1983), Images of Hampstead (1983), With Respect Ambassador (with Anne Sloman, 1985), The Market for Glory (1986), The Selling of Mary Davies and Other Writings (1993), Accountable to None (1995), England's Thousand Best Churches (1999), England's Thousand Best Houses (2003), Thatcher & Sons: A Revolution in Three Acts (2006), Wales (2008), Short History of England (2011), England's 100 Best Views (2013); *Style*— Simon Jenkins

JENKINS, Thomas Islwyn David (Tom); s of David Jenkins, of Dyfed, and Elizabeth, *née* Davies (d 1976); *b* 17 October 1950; *Educ* Ardwyn GS Aberystwyth, Craft Design and Technol Coll London (HND advtg and mktg); *m* 1983, Bridget Anne Sellers, step da of John Saunders; 2 da (Katherine Alice Myfanwy b 19 Aug 1985, Lydia Branwen b 4 Aug 1987); *Career* began advtg career as copywriter J Walter Thompson, later joined Davidson Pearce until 1981 (winner D&AD, Cannes, Br TV and Campaign Silvers for The Observer), Abbott Mead Vickers 1981–85 (award-winning work on Volvo, Olympus Sports stores, Waterstone's Bookshops, Paul Masson Wine and Sainsbury's); subsequently creative dir: Colman's (D&AD and Cannes Silvers for work on Citroën), Horner Collis Kirvan (awards for Peugeot and Majestic Wine Warehouses), Weiden and Kennedy US; currently sr copywriter/bd dir Abbott Mead Vickers BBDO Ltd; memb D&AD (memb Ctee 1991–92); *Recreations* reading, writing, watching rugby; *Clubs* Chelsea Arts; *Style*— Tom Jenkins, Esq; ✉ Abbott Mead Vickers BBDO Ltd, 151 Marylebone Road, London NW1 5QE (☎ 020 7616 3500, fax 020 7616 3600)

JENKINSON, Carole Jeanne Marie; *b* 20 December 1955, Lebanon; *Educ* County GS for Girls Guildford, Univ of St Andrews (BSc), Inst of Educn (PGCE); *Children* 1 s (Harry b 12 Jan 1985), 1 da (Emily b 13 Dec 1987); *Career* Br Cncl 1981–87, Broomwood Hall Sch 1993– (head 2001–); memb IAPS 2007–; *Recreations* theatre, cinema, reading, crosswords, walking, skiing; *Style*— Mrs Carole Jenkinson; ✉ Broomwood Hall Upper School, 68–74 Nightingale Lane, London SW12 8NR (☎ 020 8682 8851, e-mail c.jenkinson@northwoodschools.com)

JENKINSON, Prof Crispin; *b* 1962; *Educ* Bedford Coll London (BA), Univ of Oxford (MA, MSc, DPhil); *Children* 1 s; *Career* Univ of Oxford: research fell Nuffield Coll until 1992, joined Health Services Research Unit 1992, currently prof of health services research, sr research fell Harris Manchester Coll; *Books* Measuring Health and Medical Outcomes (ed, 1994), Assessment and Evaluation of Health and Medical Care: A Methods Text (ed, 1997), Health Status Measurement: A Brief but Critical Introduction (with Hannah McGee, 1998), Health Status Measurement in Neurological Disorders (ed with Ray Fitzpatrick and Damian Jenkinson, 2000), The Parkinson's Disease Questionnaire User Manual (2 edn with Ray Fitzpatrick, Viv Peto, Robert Harris and Phillip Saunders, 2008, 3 edn with Ray Fitzpatrick, Viv Peto, Sarah Dummett, David Morley and Phillip Saunders, 2012), Quality of Life Measurement in Neurodegenerative and Related Conditions (ed with Michele Peters and Mark Bromberg, 2011), Evolutionary Thinking in Medicine: From Research to Policy and Practice (ed, with Alexandra Alvergne and Charlotte Faurie, 2016), Children and Young People's Response to Parental Illness: A Handbook of Assessment and Practice (ed, with David Morley and Xiaoming Li, 2016); *Style*— Prof Crispin Jenkinson; ✉ Nuffield Department of Population Health, Old Road Campus, Headington, Oxford OX3 7LF

JENKINSON, Dermot Julian; DL (Berwickshire); s of Julian Charles Lewis Jenkinson, and Diana Catherine, *née* Baird; *b* 2 December 1954; *Educ* Eton, Eurocentre (Lausanne and Cologne), Carnegie Mellon Univ Pittsburgh (GSIA); *m* 2 May 1979, Miranda Jane, da of John Maxwell Menzies (d 2007); 1 da (Emily Lavinia b 1981), 1 s (Oliver John Banks b 1984); *Career* dir: John Menzies plc 1985– (chm 2016–), Smith Hldgs 2003–11, Transcom SA; chm: beCogent Ltd 1999–2011, Ascensos Ltd; vice-chm Scottish Friendly Soc 2012–; *Clubs* White's, New (Edinburgh); *Style*— Dermot J Jenkinson, Esq, DL; ✉ Kames House, Duns, Berwickshire TD11 3RD (☎ 01890 840332, e-mail dermot.jenkinson@ascensos.com)

JENKINSON, Nigel; *b* 18 June 1955; *Educ* Univ of Birmingham (BSocSc), LSE (MSc); *m*; 2 s; *Career* Bank of England: joined 1977, past roles incl sr mangr reserves mgmnt Foreign Exchange Div and head Structural Economic Analysis Div, dep dir monetary analysis and statistics 1999–2003, exec dir financial stability 2003–08; asst dir Monetary and Capital Markets Dept Int Monetary Fund Washington DC 2014–; advsr Financial Stability Bd Bank for Int Settlements Basel 2009–; *Recreations* reading, theatre, football, cricket; *Style*— Mr Nigel Jenkinson

JENKS, Prof Chris; s of late Arthur Jenks, and Alice Elizabeth Jenks; *b* 12 June 1947; *Educ* Westminster City Sch, Univ of Surrey, Univ of London; *m* Barbara Read; 2 da; *Career* sociologist; Goldsmiths Coll London: lectr, sr lectr then reader in sociology 1971–94, prof of sociology 1995–2004, pro-warden 1995–2000; Brunel Univ: prof of sociology and pro-vice-chllr 2004–06, vice-chllr and princ 2006–12, emeritus prof 2012–; ed Childhood jl 1995–2005; fell Goldsmiths Coll London 2012; FRSA 2006, FRSM 2008, FCGI 2011, FAcSS 2014 (AcSS 2000); *Publications* Rationality, Education and the Social Organization of Knowledge (1976), Worlds Apart (1977), Towards a Sociology of Education (1977), The Sociology of Childhood (1982), Culture (1993, 2 edn 2005), Cultural Reproduction (1993), Visual Culture (1995), Childhood (1996, 2 edn 2005), Theorizing Childhood (1998), Core Sociological Dichotomies (1998), Images of Community: Durkheim, Social Systems and the Sociology of Art (2000), Aspects of Urban Culture (2001), Culture (4 vols, 2002), Transgression (2003), Urban Culture (4 vols, 2004), Subculture: The Fragmentation of the Social (2004), Childhood (3 vols, 2005), Qualitative Complexity (2006), Transgression (4 vols, 2006); author of articles in Br Jl of Sociology, Theory, Culture and Society, Cultural Values and others; *Recreations* cricket, art, literature; *Clubs* Athenaeum, Chelsea Arts, MCC; *Style*— Prof Chris Jenks; ✉ Brunel University, Uxbridge, Middlesex UB8 3PH

JENKYNS, Prof Richard Henry Austen; s of Henry Leigh Jenkyns, of Aldeburgh, Suffolk, and Rosalind Mary, *née* Home; *b* 18 March 1949; *Educ* Eton (King's scholar, Newcastle Scholar), Balliol Coll Oxford, CCC Oxford; *Career* writer and classicist; fell All Souls Oxford 1972–81, lectr in classics Univ of Bristol 1978–81, fell LMH Oxford 1981–2010; Univ of Oxford: lectr in classics 1981–96, reader in classical languages and literature 1996–99, prof of the classical tradition 1999–2010, public orator 2004–16; *Books* The Victorians and Ancient Greece (1980, Arts Cncl Nat Book Award 1981, Yorkshire Post Book Award 1981), Three Classical Poets (1982), Dignity and Decadence (1991), Classical Epic: Homer and Virgil (1992), The Legacy of Rome (ed, 1992), Virgil's Experience (1998), Westminster Abbey (2004), A Fine Brush on Ivory (2004), God, Space and City in the Roman Imagination (2013), Classical Literature (2015); *Recreations* playing the piano, looking at buildings, walking; *Clubs* Athenaeum; *Style*— Prof Richard Jenkyns; ✉ Lady Margaret Hall, Oxford OX2 6QA (☎ 01865 429241, e-mail richard.jenkyns@lmh.ox.ac.uk)

JENNER, Prof Peter George; s of George Edwin Jenner (d 1948), and Edith, *née* Hallett (d 1995); *b* 6 July 1946; *Educ* Gravesend GS, Chelsea Coll London (BPharm, PhD, DSc); *m* 1 Dec 1973 (m dis 2003), Katherine Mary Philomena, da of Hilary David Harrison Snell (d 1958); 1 s (Terence Martin b 19 Oct 1977); *Career* postdoctoral fell Dept of Pharmacy Chelsea Coll London 1970–72; Univ of London Dept of Neurology Inst of Psychiatry: lectr in biochemistry 1972–78, sr lectr 1978–85, hon sr lectr 1983–85, reader in neurochemical pharmacology 1985–89; reader in neurochemical pharmacology KCH Medical Sch 1985–89, hon sr lectr Inst of Neurology 1988–2000, prof of pharmacology and head of dept KCL 1989–98, dir Neurodegenerative Diseases Research Centre KCL 1993–, prof of pharmacology KCL Sch of Biomedical Sciences 2005– (head Div of Pharmacology and Therapeutics 1998–2004), emeritus prof of pharmacology KCL 2008–; European ed Synapsis 1990–, handling ed Neuropharmacology 2002–; dir Parkinson's Disease Soc Experimental Res Laboratories 1988–99, dir Proximagen Ltd 2005–10, memb Cncl Parkinson's Disease Soc 1993–99; vice-pres European Soc for Clinical Pharmacology 2001–08; The Spinout of the Year 2005; FRPharmS 1994, FBrPharmS 2005, FKC 2006, FRSM 2011; *Books* Dopamine Receptor Subtypes – From Basic Science to Clinical Application (co-ed with R Demirdamar, 1998), Beyond the Decade of the Brain – Neuroprotection in Parkinson's Disease Vol 3 (co-ed with C W Olanow, 1998), Cell Death and Neuroprotection in Parkinson's Disease (co-ed with M F Beal, 1998), Levodopa Induced Dyskinesias (co-ed with J Obeso, 2000); *Recreations* gardening, driving; *Clubs* Athenaeum; *Style*— Prof Peter Jenner; ✉ NDRC, School of Biomedical Sciences, Hodgkin Building, King's College, London SE1 1UL

JENNER, Air Marshal Sir Timothy Ivo (Tim); KCB (2000, CB 1996); s of Harold Ivo Jenner (d 2015), and Josephine Dorothy Jenner (d 2008); *b* 31 December 1945; *Educ* Maidstone GS, RAF Coll Cranwell; *m* 1968, Susan Lesley, da of Colin Stokes (d 1994); 2 da; *Career* with RAF; helicopter sqdn pilot UK, ME and Germany 1968–75, Puma pilot and instr 1976–78, desk offr Helicopter MOD 1979–80, Army Staff Coll Camberley 1981, OC 33 Sqdn 1982–84; mil asst to: ACDS (Commitments) 1985, DCDS (Progs & Personnel) 1986; OC RAF Shawbury 1987–88, RCDS 1989, dep dir Air Force Plans 1990–91, dir Def Progs 1992–93, AO Plans HQ Strike Cmd 1993, ACDS (Costs Review) 1993–95, Asst Chief of Air Staff 1995–98, COS and Dep C-in-C HQ Strike Command 1998–2000, NATO Cdr Combined Air Ops Centre 9 2000; dir European Air Gp 2000; strategic advsr Serco Gp 2001–03, chm Serco Def and Aerospace 2003–05 (sr mil advsr 2005–11), strategic advsr Atmaana 2006–10; non-exec dir NATS 1996–98; pres Coventry branch RAeS 2002–16; chm Thames Valley and Chiltern Air Ambulance Tst 2011–; FRAeS 1997; *Recreations* old cars, photography, mountain walking; *Clubs* RAF; *Style*— Air Marshal Sir Tim Jenner, KCB; ✉ Holly Bank, Beech Hill, Hellidon, Northamptonshire NN11 6LH (☎ 01327 261415)

JENNINGS, Alex Michael; s of Michael Thomas Jennings, of Shenfield, Essex, and Peggy Patricia, *née* Mahoney (d 2012); *b* 10 May 1957; *Educ* Abbs Cross Tech HS Hornchurch, Univ of Warwick (BA), Bristol Old Vic Theatre Sch; *Partner* Lesley Moors; 1 s (Ralph Jennings Moors b 23 March 1990), 1 da (Georgia Jennings Moors b 14 April 1992); *Career* actor; assoc actor RSC, assoc RNT; Hon DLitt Univ of Warwick 1999; *Theatre* incl: The Scarlet Pimpernel (Her Majesty's) 1985, The Country Wife (Royal Exchange Manchester) 1986, Too Clever By Half (Old Vic) 1988, The Liar (Old Vic) 1989, The Wild Duck (Peter Hall Co) 1990, The Importance of Being Earnest (Aldwych) 1993, My Fair Lady (RNT, Theatre Royal Drury Lane) 2002, Candide (ENO) 2008 and (Japan) 2010, My Fair Lady (Theatre du Chatelet Paris) 2010 and 2013, Charlie and the Chocolate Factory (Theatre Royal Drury Lane) 2013, My Fair Lady (Sydney Opera House) 2016 and (Chicago Lyric Opera) 2017; work for the RSC: Hyde Park, The Taming of the Shrew, Measure For Measure 1987–88, Richard II 1990–91, Peer Gynt (Young Vic), Oberon in A Midsummer Night's Dream (also US tour and Broadway) Measure for Measure 1995–96, Much Ado About Nothing, Hamlet (also US) 1996–98; work for RNT: Ghetto 1989, The Recruiting Officer 1992, Albert Speer 2000, The Winter's Tale 2001, The Relapse 2001, His Girl Friday 2003, Stuff Happens 2005, The Alchemist 2006, Present Laughter 2007, The Habit of Art 2009, Collaborators 2011, Cocktail Sticks 2012, Hymn 2012; *Television* BBC incl: Smiley's People, The Franchise Affair, Alfonso Bonzo, Ashenden (with Kelso Films), Inspector Alleyn, Dread Poet's Soc, Hard Times, Too Much Sun (with Talkback), Riot at the Rite, Waking the Dead, Spooks, State Within, Cranford, 10 Days to War, Hancock and Joan, The Last Days of Lehman Brothers, On Expenses, Silk, The Lady Vanishes, Castles in the Sky; other credits incl: Inspector Morse – Sins of the Fathers (Central), Bye Bye Columbus (Channel Four), Liberty!, The American Revolution, CSS Hunley (TNT TV movie), Bad Blood (Carlton), A Very Social Secretary, Poirot: Cards on the Table, Miss Marple: They Do It With Mirrors, Whitechapel, We'll Take Manhattan, Foyle's War, Churchill's Secret (ITV) 2016, Stan Lee's Lucky Man (Sky1) 2016, Victoria (ITV) 2016, The Crown (Netflix), The Halcyon (ITV); *Film* War Requiem, A Midsummer Night's Dream, The Wings of the Dove, Joseph and his Amazing Technicolor Dreamcoat, Four Feathers, Five Children and It, Bridget Jones: The Edge of Reason, Babel, The Queen, Trap for Cinderella, Belle, The Lady in the Van, Denial; *Awards* for Too Clever By Half: Drama Magazine Best Actor Award 1988, Plays and Players Actor of the Year Award 1988, Olivier Award for Comedy Performance of the Year 1988; Olivier Award for Best Actor (for Peer Gynt) 1996, Helen Hayes Award for Best Actor (for Hamlet) Washington DC 1999; Evening Standard Drama Award for Best Actor (for The Winter's

Tale and The Relapse) 2001, Olivier Award for Best Actor in a Musical (for My Fair Lady) 2002; *Style*— Alex Jennings; ✉ c/o Independent Talent, 40 Whitfield Street, London W1T 2RH (☎ 020 7636 6565)

JENNINGS, Colin Brian; s of Brian Jennings, of Salisbury, and Jean, *née* Thomas; *b* 27 November 1952; *Educ* Hereford Cathedral Sch, Univ of Leicester (BA, MA); *m* 1978, Jane, da of Stanley Barfield, and Joan Barfield; *Career* various posts incl NATO nuclear and conventional def policy MOD 1976–83; FCO: Policy Planning Staff 1983–86, first sec (econ) Lagos 1986–89, dep head Central and Southern Africa Dept 1990–92, dep high cmmr Nicosia 1992–96, chief exec Wilton Park 1996–2006, special prof of diplomacy Univ of Nottingham 2006–; vice-chair Diplomatic Serv Appeal Bd 2007–11; occassional lectr Inst of Policy Studies Rennes 2007–09, int advsr Electoral Reform Int Servs 2009–11; W Cornwall rep Cornwall Homeseekers Ltd 2011–; *Recreations* tennis, croquet, watching rugby, walking the fox terrier; *Style*— Colin Jennings, Esq; ✉ The Print Works, Market Place, Marazion, Cornwall TR17 0AR (☎ 01736 719123)

JENNINGS, Dr Kevin; s of Kevin Jennings, and Bridget, *née* Flynn; *b* 9 March 1947; *Educ* Downside, Bart's Med Sch (MB BS); *m* 24 June 1978, Heather Joanne, da of Ray Wolfenden; 2 s (Mark b 1979, Thomas b 1981), 1 da (Debra b 1987); *Career* registrar: KCL 1976–78, London Chest Hosp 1978–80; sr registrar Freeman Hosp Newcastle 1980–83, conslt cardiologist Aberdeen Royal Infirmary 1983–; vice-pres Br Cardiovascular Soc 2006–; memb Cncl: Br Heart Fndn, Br Cardiac Soc; FRCP 1988; *Publications* Acute Cardiac Care (1993), author of several articles on ischaemic heart disease and cardiac imaging; *Style*— Dr Kevin Jennings; ✉ Department of Cardiology, Royal Infirmary, Foresterhill, Aberdeen AB25 2ZN (☎ 01224 553548, fax 01224 550692)

JENNINGS, Nicholas David De Burgh; s of late Robin Jennings, and Diana, *née* Platt; *b* 28 November 1959, London; *Educ* Dulwich Coll, Haberdashers' Aske's Hatcham Boys' Sch, Keble Coll Oxford (MA); *m* 30 Oct 1999, Jane; *Career* Coopers & Lybrand 1982–87, Pentos plc 1987–88, Daily Mail and General Trust plc 1988–2012, co sec Close Brothers Gp plc 2013–; FCA; *Clubs* MCC; *Style*— Nicholas Jennings, Esq; ✉ Close Brothers Group plc, 10 Crown Place, London EC2A 4FT

JENNINGS, Prof Nicholas Robert (Nick); CB (2016); s of Robert George Jennings, of Dorchester, Dorset, and Valerie Ann Jennings; *b* 15 December 1966, London; *Educ* Univ of Exeter (BSc), QMC London (PhD); *m* 7 Aug 1993, Dr Joanne Marie, *née* Smith; 1 da (Anna Elizabeth b 25 June 1997), 1 s (Matthew James b 3 July 2000); *Career* Dept of Electronic Engrg QMC London: research asst 1988–89, lectr 1989–95, reader in intelligent systems 1995–98, prof of intelligent systems 1998–99; prof of computer science Univ of Southampton 1999–14 (regius prof 2014–); assoc dean (research and enterprise) Faculty of Engrg, Science and Maths 2008–10; chief scientific advsr to Govt in area of nat security 2010–15, regius prof of computer science Univ of Southampton 2014–16, vice-provost (Research) Imperial Coll London 2016–; founding dir Int Fndn on Multi-Agent Systems 1998–; fndr ed-in-chief Int Jl of Autonomous Agents and Multi-Agent Systems 1998–2002; chief scientific advsr Aerogility 2000–; memb Advsy Bd: German Research Centre for AI (DFKI) 2000–12, Frictionless Commerce Inc 2000–03, ISheads! 2001–05, IBM Autonomic Computing 2002–05, Defence Technology Centre on Systems Engrg and Integrated Systems for Defence 2005–; memb OST Foresight Panel on: Cognitive Systems 2002–03, CyberTrust 2003–04, Intelligent Infrastructure Systems 2004; memb: IT Computing Coll EPSRC 1997–, UK Computing Research Ctee (UKCRC) 2004, European Research Cncl Informatics Panel for Advanced Fellowships 2008–13, Research Appointments Panel Royal Soc 2011–13; Royal Acad of Engrg: chair Industrial Secondment Scheme, memb Membership Panel 2008–11, memb Research and Secondments Ctee 2008–11; memb steering ctee and chair of numerous confs; external examiner for numerous UK and int univs; Computers and Thought Award 1999, Achievement Medal IEE 2000, ACM: Autonomous Agents Research Award 2003; memb Academia Eurpaea 2008; CEng 2003, FBCS 2003, fell European Artificial Intelligence Assoc (ECCAI) 2003, CITP 2004, FIEE 2004 (sr memb 2003), FREng 2005, FIEEE 2008, fell Assoc for the Advancement of Artificial Intelligence (AAAI) 2010; *Books* Cooperation in Industrial Multi-Agent Systems (1994), Intelligent Agents (jt ed, 1995), Foundations of Distributed Artificial Intelligence (jt ed, 1996), Intelligent Agents III (jt ed, 1997), Agent Technology: Foundations, Applications and Markets (jt ed, 1998), Intelligent Agents IV (jt ed, 2000), Multi-Agent Systems for Manufacturing Control (jtly, 2004); contrib to numerous academic jls and conf proceedings; *Recreations* cricket, football (mangr Waltham Wolves youth soccer team), travelling; *Style*— Prof Nick Jennings, CB; ✉ Level 4 Faculty Building, Imperial College, South Kensington Campus, London SW7 2AZ (e-mail n.jennings@imperial.ac.uk)

JENNINGS, Patrick Thomas; s of Charles Thomas Jennings (d 1983), of Witham, Essex, and Helen Joan, *née* Scorer; *b* 23 February 1948; *Educ* Forest Sch; *m* Jayne, da of Ronald Stanley Green; 3 da (Victoria Anne b 3 June 1977, Joanna Emily b 6 Oct 1979, Charlotte Joy b 16 Oct 1983), 1 s (Edward Thomas Patrick b 16 Aug 1990); *Career* articled clerk H Kennard & Son 1967–72; Slaughter and May: joined 1973, ptnr 1979–, head of property group; chm Building Contracts Ctee of the Construction Law Ctee Int Bar Assoc 1985–89; memb: Law Soc, Anglo-American Real Property Inst, City of London Slrs Co; author of various articles and papers on construction law; *Style*— Patrick Jennings, Esq; ✉ Slaughter and May, 1 Bunhill Row, London EC1Y 8YY (☎ 020 7600 1200, fax 020 7090 5000)

JENSEN, Ashley; *b* 11 August 1969; *Educ* Queen Margaret Univ Edinburgh; *m* 29 Jan 2007, Terence Beesley; 1 s (Francis Jonathan b 2009); *Career* actress; *Television* incl: Extras 2005–07 (Best Actress and Best Newcomer Br Comedy Awards 2006, Best Sitcom Actress Rose D'Or Award 2006, Best Actress Monte Carlo Int Television Festival 2006), Ugly Betty 2006–09, Accidentally on Purpose 2009–10, Accidental Farmer 2010, The Reckoning 2011, Agatha Raisin 2014–, Catastrophe 2015–; *Film* Nativity! 2009, How to Train Your Dragon 2010, Gnomeo & Juliet 2011, Hysteria 2011, Arthur Christmas 2011, The Pirates! In an Adventure with Scientists! 2012, The Lobster 2015; *Theatre* incl: King Lear (Royal Exchange), A Chorus of Disapproval (Harold Pinter Theatre) 2012; *Style*— Ms Ashley Jensen; ✉ c/o Independent Talent Group, 40 Whitfield Street, London W1T 2RH

JEPSON, Martin Clive; s of Donald Jepson (d 2000), and Mildred, *née* Jones; *b* 6 April 1962, Leeds; *Educ* BSc; *m* Anne; 1 s (James), 1 da (Laura); *Career* dir Delancey 1995–2000, dir Taylor Woodrow Property Co 2000–03, chief exec Southside Capital 2003–05, UK md Howard Holdings 2005–08, md Hammerson plc 2008–11, pres and chief operating offr Brookfield Office Properties Europe 2011–; tstee Sparks children's medical health charity; FRICS 1999 (assoc 1985); *Recreations* cricket, golf, rugby, football, music, reading, travel, walking; *Clubs* Walton Heath Golf, Arts; *Style*— Martin Jepson, Esq; ✉ Brookfield Office Properties, 99 Bishopsgate, 2nd Floor, London EC2M 3XD (☎ 020 7408 8277, e-mail martin.jepson@brookfield.com, website www.brookfield.com)

JERMEY, HE Dominic; CVO (2010), OBE (2001); s of Kevin Jermey, of Kent, and Maureen Jermey, of Kent; *Educ* Univ of Cambridge; *m* Dr Clare Roberts; *Career* diplomat; formerly with Schroders; joined FCO 1993, first sec Islamabad 1994–97, UK rep to the warring factions Afghanistan 1997–99, UK rep to UN Transitional Admin in East Timor 2000, chargé d'affaires ad interim Kabul 2002; UKTI: dep ambass and dir Madrid 2004–07, md (sectors) 2007–10, head of defence and security orgn 2008, acting chief exec 2009, ceo 2014–; ambass to UAE 2010–14, ceo UKTI 2014–15, ambass to Afghanistan 2016–; tstee CAFOD 2008–; Liveryman Worshipful Co of Cutlers 2008; Hospitalier Hospitalité Notre Dame de Lourdes; *Style*— HE Mr Dominic Jermey, CVO, OBE; ✉ FCO, King Charles Street, London SW1A 2AH

JERMEY, Michael Francis; s of Clifford Jermey (d 2001), and Patience, *née* Hughes (d 2009); *b* 24 March 1964; *Educ* City of London Sch, BNC Oxford (MA); *m* 22 March 2003, Caroline, da of Dick Taverne; 1 s (Joseph b 2007); *Career* researcher Central Television 1985–86; ITN: grad trainee 1986–87, prodn journalist 1987–90, prog ed News at Ten 1990–91, head foreign news 1991–93, assoc ed ITV Progs 1993–95, dep ed ITN News on ITV 1995–99, exec prodr ITN progs for ITV2 1998–99, dir of development 1999–2004, launch managing dir ITN news channel 2000–01, md ITN International 2002–04, ed ITV Regnl News 2004–07, dir ITV Regions and Network News Ops 2007–09, dir ITV News, Current Affrs and Sport 2009–11, dir ITV News and Current Affrs 2011–; commissioning ed: The First Election Debate (ITV1) 2010, The Royal Wedding (ITV1) 2011, The ITV Leaders' Debate 2015, The ITV Referendum Debate 2016; non-exec dir Parly Broadcasting Unit Ltd 2007–11; memb Defence Press and Broadcasting Advsy Ctee 2007–15, memb Defence and Security Advsy Ctee 2015–; tstee Rory Peck Tst 2002–14 (chm 2011–14); *Recreations* family, reading, supporting Arsenal FC; *Style*— Michael Jermey, Esq; ✉ ITV plc, London Television Centre, Upper Ground, London SE1 9LT (☎ 020 7157 6425, e-mail michael.jermey@itv.com)

JERVIS, Simon Swynfen; s of Capt John Swynfen Jervis (ka 1944), and Diana Elizabeth, *née* Marriott (subsequently Mrs Christopher Parker) (d 2014); *b* 9 January 1943; *Educ* Downside, Corpus Christi Coll Cambridge; *m* 19 April 1969, Fionnuala, da of Dr John MacMahon (d 1961); 1 da (Thalia Swynfen b 5 Jan 1971), 1 s (John Swynfen b 25 June 1973); *Career* student asst, asst keeper of art Leicester Museum and Art Gallery 1964–66; Dept of Furniture V&A: asst keeper 1966–75, dep keeper 1975–89, acting keeper 1989, curator 1989–90; dir Fitzwilliam Museum Cambridge 1990–95; dir of historic buildings Nat Tst 1995–2002 (memb Arts Panel 1982–95 (chm 1987–95), memb Properties Ctee 1987–95); guest scholar J Paul Getty Museum 1988–89 and 2003, Ailsa Mellon Bruce sr fell Center for Advanced Study in the Visual Arts (CASVA) Nat Gall of Art Washington DC 2006–07; dir The Burlington Magazine 1993– (tstee 1997–); pres Soc of Antiquaries 1995–2001 (memb Cncl 1986–88, memb Exec Ctee 1987–90); chm: Furniture History Soc 1998–2013 (ed 1987–92), Walpole Soc 2003–13 (memb Cncl 1990–95), Leche Trust 2007–13 (tstee 1995–2013); tstee: The Royal Collection Tst 1993–2001, Emery Walker Tst 2003–12; chm of tstees Sir John Soane's Museum 2008–13 (tstee 1999–2002, life tstee 2002–13), memb: Advsy Cncl Nat Art Collections Fund 2002–, Reviewing Ctee on the Export of Works of Art 2007–15; Iris Fndn Award for outstanding contribution to the decorative arts 2003; FSA 1983; *Books* Victorian Furniture (1968), Printed Furniture Designs Before 1650 (1974), High Victorian Design (1983), Penguin Dictionary of Design and Designers (1984), Furniture from Austria and Hungary in the Victoria and Albert Museum (1986), British and Irish Inventories (2010), Roman Splendour, English Arcadia (with Dudley Dodd, 2015); *Recreations* churches; *Style*— Simon Swynfen Jervis, Esq, FSA; ✉ 45 Bedford Gardens, London W8 7EF (☎ 020 7727 8739, e-mail ss.jervis@btopenworld.com)

J

JESS, Dr Digby Charles; *b* 14 November 1953, Plymouth, Devon; *Educ* Plymouth Coll, Aston Univ (BSc), Univ of Manchester (LLM, PhD), Inns of Court Law Sch; *m* 4 Aug 1980, Bridie Connolly; 1 s (Piers b 1988), 1 da (Francesca b 1999); *Career* called to the Bar Gray's Inn 1978; in practice 1981–, treasy counsel Northern Region 1990–2003, lectr in law (pt/t) Univ of Manchester 1986–87; pres Manchester Liability Soc 2006–08; memb Ctee: NW Branch CIArb 1984–95 (chm 1992–93), Gtr Manchester and W Pennines Region BIIBA Liability Soc (dep chm 1992–93, chm 1993–99); legal assessor (pt/t) GMC/MPTS Fitness to Practise Panels 2002–, memb ACCA Disciplinary and Licensing Ctees 2002–12, legal advsr (pt/t) GDC Fitness to Practice Panels 2011–, legal assessor (pt/t) HCPC Fitness to Practise Panels 2012–; memb: Northern Circuit Commercial Bar Assoc, Northern Circuit, Assoc of Regulatory and Disciplinary Lawyers; Chartered Arbitrator 1999–2012, FCIArb 1992 (ACIArb 1981); *Books* The Insurance of Professional Negligence Risks: Law and Practice (1982, 2 edn 1989), The Insurance of Commercial Risks: Law and Practice (1986, 4 edn 2011), vol on Insurance in The Encyclopaedia of Forms and Precedents (vol 20, 1988), Butterworths Insurance Law Handbook (consulting ed, 3 edn 1992), Professional Indemnity Insurance Law (co-author, 2 edn 2007, BILA Book Prize 2008); numerous articles for various legal jls; *Recreations* family, walking, cinema; *Style*— Dr Digby C Jess; ✉ Exchange Chambers, 201 Deansgate, Manchester M3 3NW (☎ 0161 833 2722, fax 0161 833 2789, e-mail jess@exchangechambers.co.uk)

JESSEL, Sir Charles John; 3 Bt (UK 1883), of Ladham House, Goudhurst, Kent; s of Sir George Jessel, MC, 2 Bt (d 1977); *b* 29 December 1924; *Educ* Eton, Balliol Coll Oxford, Northampton Inst of Agric (dip), Inst for Optimum Nutrition (dip); *m* 1, 1956, Shirley Cornelia (d 1977), da of John Waters, of Northampton; 2 s (George Elphinstone b 1957, Alastair John b 1959), 1 da ((Cornelia) Sarah b 1963); *m* 2, 1979 (m dis 1983), Gwendoline Mary, da of late Laurence Devereux, OBE, and wid of Charles Langer; *Heir* s, George Jessel; *Career* Lt 15/19 Hussars (despatches) WWII; farmer 1953–85, farmer in partnership with son 1985–, nutrition consIt 1987–; JP Kent 1960–78; chm: Ashford NFU 1963–64, Canterbury Farmers' Club 1972; pres: Kent Branch Men of the Trees 1979–83 and 1996–2016, Br Soc of Dowsers 1987–93 (life vice-pres 1993–); pres Psionic Med Soc 1996–2002 (hon fell 1977, vice-pres 2003–); life memb Br Inst for Allergy and Environmental Therapy 2006– (memb 1990–2005); assoc memb Parly Gp for Alternative and Complementary Med 1991–2001, govr Inst for Optimum Nutrition 1994–98 (chm 1997–98), patron Nutritional Cancer Therapy Tst 1998–2005; hon fell Br Assoc of Nutritional Therapists 2008 (memb 1997–2008), hon memb Inst of Psionic Med (now Laurence Inst of Holistic Med) 2008; *Books* An Anthology of Inner Silence (1990), Memories by Request (2011); *Recreations* gardening, walking, planting trees, choral music, opera; *Clubs* Cavalry and Guards'; *Style*— Sir Charles Jessel, Bt; ✉ South Hill Farm, Hastingleigh, Ashford, Kent TN25 5HL (☎ 01233 750325)

JESSEL, Christopher Robert; s of Robert William Albert Jessel, and Audrey Agnes, *née* Warburg; *b* 16 March 1945, Much Hadham, Herts; *Educ* Bryanston, Balliol Coll Oxford (MA); *Career* ptnr Farrer & Co 1979–2008 (currently conslt); memb Law Soc 1970; *Books* The Law of the Manor (1998, 2 edn 2012), Farms and Estates – A Conveyancing Handbook (1999, 2 edn 2006), Development Land-Overage and Clawback (2001, 2 edn 2007), A Legal History of the English Landscape (2011), Private Rights of Way (contrib, 2012); *Style*— Christopher Jessel, Esq; ✉ Farrer & Co, 66 Lincoln's Inn Fields, London WC2A 3LH (☎ 020 3375 7000, fax 020 3375 7001, e-mail christopher.jessel@farrer.co.uk)

JESSON, Paul; s of Peter Jackson (d 1999), and Silvia, *née* Locke; *b* 6 July 1946, Hitchin, Herts; *Educ* Hitchin Boys' GS, Guildhall Sch of Music & Drama (LGSM, John Clifford Pettican & Walter Rose prizes), Manchester Poly Sch of Theatre; *m* 2008, Margaret Lunn; *Career* actor; bd memb Out of Joint; Manchester Library Theatre 1971–73, Northcott Theatre Exeter 1973–74, first London appearance as Wally in Bingo (Royal Court) 1974, Birmingham Rep 1975 and 1976, Prospect Theatre Co 1977, Liverpool Everyman 1977–79; *Theatre* credits incl: Dan Poots in Flying Blind, title role in Richard III (Liverpool Everyman), Comings and Goings (Hampstead) 1978, The House (Joint Stock) 1979, Irving Gammon in Goosepimples (Hampstead and Garrick) 1981, Falkland Sound/Voces de Malvinas (Royal Court) 1983, Richard in Rents (Hammersmith) 1984, Tesman in Hedda Gabler and Schuffenecker in Mrs Gauguin (Almeida) 1984, Deadlines (Joint Stock) 1985, Felix in The Normal Heart (Royal Court and Albery) 1986, Tusenbach in Three Sisters (Greenwich) 1987, Mike in A Lie of the Mind (Royal Court) 1987, Poppy in Slavs!

(Hampstead) 1994–95, Ryszard in The Flight into Egypt (Hampstead) 1996, Gayev in The Cherry Orchard, Camillo in The Winter's Tale (Brooklyn Acad and The Old Vic) 2009, F in Cock (Royal Court) 2010, Gloucester in King Lear (Donmar and Brooklyn Acad) 2011, Maurice Montgomery in Travelling Light (NT) 2012, Love and Information (Royal Court) 2012, Cardinal Wolsey in Wolf Hall and Bring Up the Bodies (RSC, The Aldwych and NY) 2013–15; RNT credits incl: Gooper in Cat on a Hot Tin Roof 1988, Alsemero in The Changeling 1988, Lovborg in Hedda Gabler 1989, Kruk in Ghetto 1989, Horatio in Hamlet 1989, Anderson in The Devil's Disciple 1994, Lord Burleigh in Mary Stuart 1996; RSC credits incl: Ulysses in Troilus and Cressida, John Ryder in Two Shakespearean Actors, Northumberland in Richard II 1990–91, Peachum in The Beggar's Opera, Oldrents in A Jovial Crew, Polixenes in The Winter's Tale, Enobarbus in Antony and Cleopatra 1992–93, Camillo in The Winter's Tale 1994, Prospero in The Tempest, Shakespeare in Bingo 1995–96, title role in Henry VIII 1996–98, First Gravedigger in Hamlet 1997–98; Cobett and Kell in Dreaming (Manchester Royal Exchange and the Queen's) 1999, Mr Braddock in The Graduate (Gielgud) 2000, Dad in Rita Sue and Bob Too 2001, Peter in A State Affair (Out Of Joint) 2001, Earl of Kent in King Lear (Almedia) 2002, Sir Toby Belch in Twelfth Night (Donmar and Brooklyn Acad) 2002–03, Sorin in The Seagull (Edinburgh Int Fest) 2003, Willy Loman in Death of a Salesman (Edinburgh Royal Lyceum) 2004, Leontes in The Winter's Tale (Shakespeare's Globe) 2005, Earl of Shrewsbury in Mary Stuart (Apollo) 2005–06, Pandarus in Troilus and Cressida (Edinburgh Int Festival and Stratford-upon-Avon) 2006, Shamrayev in The Seagull (Royal Court) 2007, Myron Berger in Awake and Sing! (Almeida) 2007, Fritz Busch in The Moderate Soprano (Hampstead) 2015; *Television and Film* numerous appearances incl: Clayhanger, The Winter's Tale, Richard III, Cymbeline, Widows, Love's Labour's Lost, Coriolanus, The Ploughman's Lunch, Pity in History, This Is History Gran, Interference, A Very Peculiar Practice, The Rivals, Quartermaine's Terms, Intimate Contact, War Poets of '39, The Gibraltar Inquest, Resnick, The Trial of Lord Lucan, Holding On, Midsomer Murders, A Touch of Frost, The Glass, All Or Nothing, Danielle Cable: Eyewitness, Vera Drake, Spooks, Rome, Slave Trader, Foyle's War, The Amazing Mrs Pritchard, Doctors, Talking to the Dead, The Devil's Whore, Margaret, Coriolanus, Closer to the Moon, Wall, Mr Turner, The Trials of Jimmy Rose, Chewing Gum; *Awards* Liverpool Actor of the Year 1978, Olivier Award for Best Supporting Actor (The Normal Heart) 1986; contrib Players of Shakespeare 4 (Cambridge Univ Press, 1998); *Style*— Paul Jesson, Esq; ✉ c/o Independent Talent Group, 40 Whitfield Street, London W1T 2RH (✆ 020 7636 6565, fax 020 7323 0101)

JEVANS, Debbie; CBE (2013); da of Reginald Jevans, and Leslie, *née* Adams; *b* 20 May 1960, London; *Partner* Kim Fraser; *Career* former tennis player; Int Tennis Fedn: dir of women's tennis 1987–91, gen sec 1991–2001; dir consultancy firm 2001–03, dir of sport London 2012 2003–12, chief exec England Rugby 2015 2012–15; non-exec dir Football League, vice-chair Sport England; memb various IOC cmmns and AELTC Club, former memb Women's Tennis Assoc Tour Bd, memb Bd AELTC 2005–15; tstee Invictus Games Fndn; *Clubs* All England; *Style*— Ms Debbie Jevans, CBE

JEWELL, Prof Derek Parry; s of late Ralph Parry Jewell, and late Eileen Rose, *née* Champion; *b* 14 June 1941; *Educ* Bristol GS, Pembroke Coll Oxford (MA, DPhil, BM BCh); *m* 6 July 1974, Barbara Margaret, da of late Leonard Pearson Lockwood; 1 s (Christopher b 1979), 1 da (Carolyn b 1981); *Career* visiting asst prof Stanford Univ Sch of Med 1973–74, sr lectr in med Royal Free Hosp 1974–80, conslt physician and prof in gastroenterology Univ of Oxford 1980–2008 (emeritus prof 2008–), fell Green Coll Oxford 1994–2008 (emeritus fell 2008–), sr tutor 2003–06; memb Res Ctee RCP 1978–87; memb Editorial Bds: Gut, Clinical Science, European Journal of Gastroenterology and Hepatology, Scandinavian Journal Gastroenterology, Canadian Journal of Gastroenterology; pres Br Soc of Gastroenterology 2001–02; ed Topics in Gastroenterology 1973 and 1984–89; FRCP 1979 (MRCP 1970), FMedSci 2000; *Books* Clinical Gastrointestinal Immunology (1979), Challenges in Inflammatory Bowel Disease (2000, 2 edn 2006); *Recreations* music, gardening; *Style*— Prof Derek Jewell; ✉ Madison, Brill Road, Horton-cum-Studley, Oxfordshire OX33 1BN (✆ 01865 351315, e-mail derek.jewell@ndm.ox.ac.uk)

JEWSON, Richard Wilson; JP (Norfolk 2004); s of Charles Boardman Jewson (d 1981), and Joyce Marjorie, *née* Laws (d 2008); *b* 5 August 1944, Carlisle; *Educ* Rugby, Pembroke Coll Cambridge (MA); *m* 1965, Sarah Rosemary, da of Henry Nevill Spencer, of Warks; 3 da (Henrietta b 1966, Charlotte b 1971, Camilla b 1977), 1 s (William b 1968); *Career* md Jewson Ltd 1974–86; Meyer International plc: dir 1984–93, md 1986, chm 1991–93; chm: InterX plc 1994–2002, Savills plc 1995–2004 (non-exec dir 1994), Archant Ltd (formerly Eastern Counties Newspaper Group Ltd) 1996–2014 (dir 1982–96), Anglian Housing Group Ltd 1996–2001, Octagon Healthcare 1998–2006, EastPort Great Yarmouth Ltd 2000–07, Queens Moat Houses plc 2002–03 (non-exec dir 1994), PFI Infrastructure plc 2004–07, Raven Russia plc 2007–, Tritax Big Box REIT plc 2014–; dir: Temple Bar Investment Tst plc 2001–; non-exec dir: AWG plc (previously Anglian Water plc) 1991–2002 (dep chm 1994–2002), Grafton Group plc 1995–2013, Anglian Water Services Ltd 2002–04, Jarrold and Sons Ltd 2003–13; chm East Anglia Art Fund; pro-chllr and chm Cncl UEA (memb Cncl 1980–2003); HM Lord-Lt Norfolk 2004–; *Recreations* golf, tennis, sailing, eventing, visual arts; *Clubs* Boodle's, Royal W Norfolk Golf, Newmarket Real Tennis; *Style*— R W Jewson, Esq, JP; ✉ Dades Farm, Barnham Broom, Norfolk NR9 4BT (✆ and fax 01603 757909 e-mail richard.jewson@icloud.com)

JIRICNA, Eva Magdalena; CBE (1994); da of Josef Jiricny (d 1973), and Eva, *née* Svata; *b* 3 March 1939; *Educ* Tech Univ of Prague, Prague Acad of Fine Arts; *Career* architect; GLC's Sch Division 1968–69, Louis de Soissons Partnership 1969–78 (assoc architect), in practice with David Hodges 1978–82, freelance working for Richard Rogers Partnership 1982–84, own practice 1984–86, reformed co as Eva Jiricna Architects 1986–; clients incl: Amec plc, Time Products, Boodles, Harrods, Dubai Festival City, Accenture (formerly Andersen Consulting), Jubilee Line Extension, Prague Castle, Royal Acad of Arts, V&A, Canary Wharf Gp plc, Canary Wharf Mgmnt PTE, Selfridges, Millennium Dome Faith Zone; conslt Sir John Soanes Museum; lectr various venues; pres AA 2003–04; formerly memb Cncl RIBA; prof of architecture and design Univ of Applied Arts Prague 2002; Jane Drew Prize for Women in Architecture 2013; Hon DTech Southampton Inst 2000, Hon DTech Technical Inst of Brno Czech Republic 2000, Hon DLitt Univ of Sheffield 2001, hon degree Univ of Nottingham 2008, hon degree London Met Univ, hon degree Univ of Bratislava 2009, hon degree De Montfort Univ 2010, hon doctorate for lifetime achievement Tomas Bata Univ Zlin 2011, hon doctorate RCA 2013; hon fell RCA 1990, Hon FSIA 1996, hon fell American Inst of Architects 2006, hon memb Architect's Assoc 2013; RDI 1991, RA 1997; *Style*— Ms Eva Jiricna, CBE, RA, RDI; ✉ Eva Jiricna Architects Ltd, 3rd floor, 38 Warren Street, London W1T 6AE (✆ 020 7544 2400, e-mail mail@ejal.com or gg@ejal.com (PA Gillian Gould), website www.ejal.com)

JOANNIDES, Professor Paul; s of Evdoros Joannides (d 1978), and Nancie, *née* Mayhew (d 2007); *b* 4 November 1945, London; *Educ* Haberdashers' Aske's, Trinity Coll Cambridge; *m* 1989, Marianne, *née* Sachs (d 2007); *Career* Dept of History of Art Univ of Cambridge: asst lectr 1973–78, lectr 1978–2002, reader in art history 2002–04, prof of art history 2004–13, emeritus prof of art history 2014–; chargé de mission Musée du Louvre 1991–92; memb Société de l'Histoire de l'Art Français; *Books* The Drawings of Raphael (1983), Masaccio and Masolino (1993), Titian to 1518 (2001), Michel-Ange, Ecole, Copistes (2003), Drawings by Michelangelo and his Followers in the Ashmolean Museum (2007); Exhibitions and their catalogues: Michaelangelo and his Influence, Drawings from Windsor Castle (touring exhbn USA and UK) 1997–98, Raphael and his Age, Drawings from the Palais des Beaux-Arts Lille (Cleveland Museum of Art and Palais des Beaux-Arts Lille) 2002–03, Late Raphael (in collaboration with Prof T Henry, Museo Nacional del Prado Madrid and Musée du Louvre Paris) 2012–13; *Recreations* cinema, theatre; *Style*— Professor Paul Joannides; ✉ Department of History of Art, 1–5 Scroope Terrace, Cambridge CB2 1PX (✆ 01223 332975, fax 01223 332976, e-mail pej1000@cam.ac.uk)

JOB, Sir Peter James Denton; kt (2001); s of Frederick Job (d 1944), and Marion Pickard; *b* 13 July 1941, Exeter, Devon; *Educ* Clifton, Exeter Coll Oxford (BA); *m* 1966, Christine, da of Frederick Cobley; 1 da (Laura (Mrs Christopher Braithwaite) b 21 May 1971), 1 s (Luke b 5 Sept 1973); *Career* Reuters: joined 1963, served as corr Paris, New Delhi, Kuala Lumpur, Jakarta 1963–71, mangr Buenos Aires 1971–73, mangr Reuters in Asia (mainly based Hong Kong) 1978–90, dir Reuters Holdings plc 1989–, chief exec 1991–2001; dir then chm Visnews Ltd 1989–92; non-exec dir: Grand Metropolitan plc 1994–97, Diageo plc (following merger between Grand Metropolitan plc and Guinness plc) 1997–99, Glaxo Wellcome plc 1997–2001, GlaxoSmithKline 2001–05, Schroders plc 1999–2010 (sr ind dir 2003–10), Shell Transport and Trading 2001–05, Instinet Inc NY 2001–05, Tibco Software Palo Alto 2001–14 (presiding dir 2007–14), Supervisory Bd Deutsche Bank 2001–11, Supervisory Bd Bertelsmann 2002–05, Royal Dutch Shell plc 2005–10; chm Int Advsy Cncl NASDAQ 1998–99; memb: INSEAD UK Nat Cncl 1993–2001, DTI Japan Trade Gp 1994, HM Treasy City Promotion Panel 1995–96; tstee Royal Nat Inst for Deaf People 2009–14; hon fell Green Coll Oxford 1995, Hon DLitt Univ of Kent 1998, Hon LLD Univ of Exeter 2007; Cdr Order of the Lion of Finland 2001; *Recreations* theatre, classical music, boating, golf, country sports, tennis, gardening; *Clubs* Garrick, Oriental; *Style*— Sir Peter Job; ✉ 701 Rowan House, 9 Greycoat Street, London SW1P 2QD

JOBSON, Anne Margaret; OBE (1992); *née* Bell; da of late Colin Thomas Figgins Bell, of Fareham, Hants, and Margaret, *née* Porter; *b* 12 January 1952; *Educ* Purbrook Park Co GS, City of London Poly (BA); *m* 10 July 1976, (Stephen) Andrew Jobson (decd), s of Norman Jobson, of Walkden, Manchester; *Career* called to the Bar Gray's Inn 1975; barr-at-law (in practice as Anne Bell), head of family team Rougemont Chambers; Parly candidate (Cons): Birmingham Yardley 1997, Exeter 2001, Chatham and Aylesford 2005; *Recreations* gardening, walking, theatre, watching cricket, keeping fit, falconry; *Style*— Mrs Anne Jobson, OBE; ✉ 26 Old Tiverton Road, Exeter, EX4 6LG (✆ 01392 421420, e-mail annejobson@hotmail.com); Rougemont Chambers, Victory House, Dean Clarke Gardens, Southernhay East, Exeter EX2 4AA

JOBSON, Timothy Akers; s of Maj E O A Jobson (d 1965), and Joan, *née* Webb (d 1991); *b* 16 July 1944; *Educ* Bromsgrove Sch, Keble Coll Oxford (MA); *m* 1, 27 July 1970 (m dis 1980), L Bazeley; 1 s (Simon b 1973), 1 da (Annie b 1974); m 2, 7 April 1982 (m dis 2001), S Jeavons; m 3, 27 Aug 2004, Janice Ashwood; *Career* admitted slr 1968; ptnr: Lyon Clark & Co West Bromwich 1970–84, Keely Smith & Jobson Lichfield 1985–95, Oldham Rust Jobson Stafford 1995–2005, ORJ Solicitors LLP Stafford 2005–11, Jobsons Solicitors Ltd Stafford 2011–; Techform Fine Chemicals Ltd; dir Stafford Chamber of Commerce Ltd, tstee Stafford Works, memb Bd Stafford Enterprise; winner Finance Monthly Dealmaker Award 2013; *Recreations* sailing, swimming, gardening, walking; *Clubs* Barnt Green Sailing, Oxford Univ Yacht, Old Bromsgrovians Expedition, Stafford Westminster; *Style*— Tim Jobson, Esq; ✉ Parkside Cottage, Ivetsey Road, Wheaton Aston, Stafford ST19 9QP (✆ 01785 841146, e-mail tim@jobsonssolicitors.co.uk)

JOFFE, Baron (Life Peer UK 2000), of Liddington in the County of Wiltshire; Joel Goodman Joffe; CBE (1999); s of Abraham Michael Joffe (d 1984), of Johannesburg, South Africa, and Dena, *née* Idelson (d 1984); *b* 12 May 1932, Johannesburg; *Educ* Univ of the Witwatersrand (BCom, LLB); *m* 1 Nov 1962, Vanetta, da of François Pretorius (d 1975), of Port Elizabeth, South Africa; 3 da (Hon Deborah b 11 June 1963, Hon Lisa b 13 Aug 1964, Hon Abigail b 4 Sept 1969); *Career* human rights lawyer SA 1954–65; admin dir Abbey Life Assurance plc 1966–70, dep chm (formerly dir and md) Allied Dunbar Assurance plc 1971–91; chm: Swindon Cncl of Voluntary Servs 1973–80, Oxfam 1980–2001 (tstee, hon sec and chm), Swindon HA and NHS Tst 1988–94, The Giving Campaign 2000–04, Assisted Dying Campaign House of Lords 2002–13; memb Royal Cmmn for the Care of the Elderly 1997–99; Order of the Grand Companions of O R Tambo SA 2010; *Books* The State vs Nelson Mandela (2007); *Recreations* tennis; *Style*— Lord Joffe, CBE; ✉ House of Lords, London SW1A 0PW, Tel/ 01793 790203, e-mail joel@lidmanor.co.uk

JOFFÉ, Roland Victor; *b* 17 November 1945, London; *m* 1, 1974 (m dis 1982), Jane Lapotaire, *qv*; 1 s (Rowan b 1973); m 2, (m dis) Cherie Lunghi, *qv*; 1 da (Nathalie-Kathleen b 26 Aug 1986); *Career* film dir and prodr; *Films* The Legion Hall Bombing 1978, The Spongers 1978, No Mama, No 1979, United Kingdom 1981, The Killing Fields 1984 (nomination Best Dir Academy Awards), The Mission 1986 (winner Palme D'Or Cannes Film Festival), Fat Man and Little Boy 1989, City of Joy 1992, Super Mario Bros 1993 (prodr), The Scarlet Letter 1995, Goodbye Lover 1997, Vatel 1999, Captivity 2007, You and I 2010, Singularity 2010, There Be Dragons 2011; *Style*— Roland Joffé, Esq

JOHANSON, Capt Philip; OBE (2002); s of Stanley Theodore Johanson (d 1991), and Betty Johanson (d 1984); *b* 10 April 1947, Hull; *Educ* Alderman Cogan C of E Sch Kingston upon Hull, Wilson Carlile Coll of Evangelism; *Career* Church Army: head of missions 1975–83, dir of evangelism 1983–90, chief sec 1990–2006, dir Bd, int sec Church Army International 2007–12; chaplain to the Mayor of Bournemouth 2014–15; patron African Pastor Fellowship 2000–12, chm of tstees Bournemouth Nightclub Outreach Work 2012–; *Recreations* theatre, music, travel, reading; *Clubs* Royal Cwlth, Nikaean, Boscome and Southbourne Rotary, Royal Overseas League; *Style*— Capt Philip Johanson, OBE; ✉ 10 Ditton Lodge, 8 Stourwood Avenue, Bournemouth BH6 3PN (✆ 01202 416917, e-mail p.johanson@btinternet.com)

JOHN, Daniel Howard; s of Michael Hanlon John, of London, and Patricia Ann, *née* Hawkes; *b* 6 June 1961; *Educ* Archbishop Tenison's GS London; *m* 1994, Tanya, *née* Allen; 2 s; *Career* trainee journalist West London Observer 1979–83, sr reporter West Kent Extra Series 1983–84, industrial reporter Kent Evening Post 1984–86, fin reporter Birmingham Post 1986–88, freelance reporter 1988–89 (The Guardian, Mail on Sunday, Daily Star), financial corr, tport corr and dep financial news ed The Guardian 1989, freelance Australian corr 1993, home news ed The Guardian 1993–96, managing ed (news) The Observer 1996–98, exec picture ed The Guardian and The Observer 1998–2001, exec ed Creative Dept Guardian 2001–02, picture ed The Sun-Herald Sydney Aust 2002–05, chief of staff photographic Sydney Morning Herald 2005–06, business reporter Sydney Morning Herald 2006–12; received Proficiency Test Cert from Nat Cncl for Trg of Journalists; NEC memb NUJ 1986–87; memb: Charter 88, Friends of the Earth; *Recreations* reading, current affairs, music, cooking, entertaining, cricket, golf; *Clubs* Ryde Hunters Hill Cricket; *Style*— Daniel John, Esq

JOHN, Sir David Glyndwr; KCMG (1999); s of William Glyndwr John (d 1967), of Pontypridd, Mid Glamorgan, and Marjorie, *née* Gaze (d 1985); *b* 20 July 1938; *Educ* Llandovery Coll (Thomas Phillips Fndn scholar, Johnes scholar), Christ's Coll Cambridge (MA), Columbia Univ NY (NATO Research Studentship, MBA), Harvard Business Sch (Int Sr Mgmnt Prog); *m* 22 Aug 1964, Gillian, da of Henry J Edwards; 1 da (Emma Victoria b 7 July 1967), 1 s (Ceri David b 30 July 1968); *Career* graduate trainee then shift mangr United Steel Companies Sheffield 1962–64, mgmnt conslt then mktg dir subsid Hardman and Holden Ltd RTZ Corporation 1966–73; Redland Group plc: gen mangr Land Reclamation Co 1973–77, regnl dir Middle E and Far E Redland Industrial Services 1977–80, md Redland Purle 1980, md Cleanaway Ltd 1980–81; Inchcape plc: chief exec subsid Gray Mackenzie & Co Ltd Bahrain 1986–87 (devpt dir 1981–85), chief exec Inchcape Berhad Singapore 1987–90, main bd dir 1988–95, chm Inchcape Berhad 1990–95, exec chm Inchcape Toyota Motors 1994–95; chm: The BOC Group plc 1996–2002 (non-exec dir 1993–), Premier Oil plc 1998–, BSI Group 2002– (non-exec dir 2002–), Balfour Beatty plc 2003–08 (non-exec dir 2000–08); non-exec dir: St Paul Cos Inc Minnesota USA 1996–2003, Welsh Development Agency 2001–02; chm External Funding Bd Dept Material Sciences Univ of Cambridge 1998–2001; memb CBI Int Advsy Bd 2002–; memb: CBI President's Ctee 1996–2002, Wilson Ctee on Review of Export Promotion, Cncl for Industry and Higher Educn 1996–2002, Panel 2000, Bd of Overseers Columbia Business Sch NY 1996–2001; govr SOAS Univ of London 1994–; *Recreations* sailing, skiing, reading; *Clubs* Oxford and Cambridge, Oriental, Travellers; *Style—* Sir David John, KCMG

JOHN, Sir Elton Hercules (né Reginald Kenneth Dwight); kt (1998), CBE (1996); s of Stanley Dwight, and Sheila, *née* Sewell; *b* 25 March 1947; *Educ* Pinner GS, Royal Acad of Music; 21 Dec 2005 David Furnish (civil partnership converted 21 Dec 2014); 2 s (Zachary b 2010, Elijah b 2013); *Career* pop singer, pianist and songwriter; keyboard player with R&B band Bluesology 1965, first album Empty Sky released 1969, US debut at Troubadour Club 1970, single Your Song first UK and US Top 10 record 1971, renowned during 1970s for outlandish costumes and ludicrous spectacles, albums Goodbye Yellow Brick Road, Captain Fantastic and The Brown Dirt Cowboy and Blue Moves confirmed worldwide stardom, toured Communist Bloc (played eight sell-out dates in Leningrad), album A Single Man 1978 and subsequent tour stripped away razzmatazz of early 1970s shows, album Two Low for Zero 1983 provided four worldwide hits, broadcast of Live in Australia album viewed by record Australian TV audience of six million 1987, stage costumes and memorabilia sold by Sotheby's 1988, 34th album Sleeping with the Past released 1989, No 1 in UK Album Charts July 1990, over 3 million copies sold worldwide, double A-Sided single Sacrifice/Healing Hands No 1 five weeks in UK (first UK No 1, all proceeds donated to AIDS related charities), No 1 double album The Very Best of Elton John released 1990 (over 9.5 million copies sold worldwide), album The One released 1992, album Duets released 1993, wrote music for film The Lion King (lyrics by Sir Tim Rice) 1994, album Made In England released 1995, album The Big Picture released 1997, single Candle in the Wind adapted as Candle in the Wind '97 (in memory of Diana, Princess of Wales, proceeds going to the Diana, Princess of Wales Memorial Fund) 1997, album Aida released 1999, album El Dorado released 2000, live album One Night Only released 2000, stage musical The Lion King playing at seven theatres worldwide and on tour in the USA 2010, two US productions of Aida 2001, album Songs from the West Coast released 2001, album Greatest Hits 1970–2002 released 2002, single Are You Ready for Love? UK No 1 2003, album Goodbye Yellow Brick Road re-released 2003, residency The Red Piano (241 shows) The Colosseum Las Vegas 2004–09, album Peachtree Road released 2004, composer Billy Elliot the Musical 2005; as actor cameo role in Spiceworld The Movie 1997; significant achievements: record number of shows (60) at Madison Square Garden, first artist to enter Billboard US Album chart at No 1, seven consecutive No 1 US albums, writer of over 600 songs and has released over 30 albums, more weeks spent in UK chart than any other recording artist during 1970s, biggest selling single of all time (Candle In The Wind 97, over 37,000,000 copies sold), 11 Ivor Novello Awards 1973–2000, five Grammy Awards 1986–2000 (incl Lifetime Achievement Award 2000), winner Best Male Artist BRIT Awards 1991, Lifetime Achievement award BRIT Awards 1995, Oscar for Can You Feel The Love Tonight? (from The Lion King) 1995, Polar Music Prize 1995, Freddie Mercury Award BRIT Awards 1998, Tony Award Best Original Score for Aida 2000, Kennedy Center Honor 2004; chm Watford FC 1979–90; tstee The Wallace Collection 1999; fndr The Elton John Aids Fndn 1992; involved in many charities incl: Nordoff Robbins Music Therapy, Terrence Higgins Tst, London Lighthouse; hon doctorate RAM 2002; fell Br Acad of Songwriters and Composers 2004; *Recreations* Watford FC (life pres); *Style—* Sir Elton John, CBE; ✉ website www.rocketmusic.com

JOHN, Geraint Morton; s of Frederick William John (d 1977), of Swansea, and Gwladys Mary John (d 1970); *b* 2 April 1938; *Educ* Swansea GS, Bartlett Sch of Architecture UCL (DipArch); *m* Jan 1959, Jane Doreen, da of William Aurelius Williams; 2 da (Catrin Elizabeth b 1959, Betsan Sarah b 1961), 1 s (Dylan William b 1964); *Career* architect; articled to Sir Percy Thomas 1954–58; Maxwell Fry and Jane Drew 1961–63, Denys Lasdun 1963–64, Arup Associates 1964–65, Parkin Associates Toronto Canada 1965–66, Herts CC 1966–69, Architects and Bldgs Branch DES 1969–72, head Tech Unit for Sport and chief architect to Sports Council 1975–96 (joined 1972), sr advsr HOK Sport 1998–2001, sr advsr HOK Sport Architecture 2001–09, sr advsr Populous 2009–; visiting prof of architecture (sports building design) Faculty of Creative Art & Technology Univ of Luton 1998– (sr lectr 1996–98), visiting prof Universidad Camilo Jose Cela Madrid, visiting prof Univ of Beds 2011–; corr on sports bldgs for Architects Jl 1978–82; memb: Arts Cncl Planning Bd 1988–93, Cncl Int Union of Architects 1990–93, RIBA Int Ctee 1985–93 and 2002–, Editorial Advsy Bd Crowd Management magazine Int Assoc of Auditorium Managers, ILAM, Football Stadia Advsy Design Cncl 1989–93, Tech Ctee Sports Ground Initiative 1995–, Panel Design Cmmn for Wales (DCfW) 2003–, Cncl RIBA 2004–10, DTI/UKTI Global Sports Projects Sector Advsy Gp 2007–; chm RIBA/UIA Co-ordinating Ctee 1987–93, hon life pres Sports and Leisure Prog Int Union of Architects 1996–, co-ordinator RIBA Client Forums on Spectator and Participation Facilities 1997–2015, hon advsr to Nat Playing Fields Assoc (NPFA) 1997–, client advsr RIBA 2007–; sec Sports and Leisure Work Gp Int Union of Architects 1985–96, chm Herts Assoc of Architects (HAA) 2004–07; RIBA part 3 examiner Univ of Cambridge and Univ of Westminster 2002– and Univ of Bath 2006–; pres: Old Albanians RFC 1983–85, St Albans Welsh Soc 1980–83 and 2000–02, St Albans Civic Soc 2007–; chm Old Albanian 948 Sports Fndn 2007–, chm Friends of Victoria Playing Field 2004–12 (current vice-pres); Pierre de Coubertin Medal for outstanding services to the Olympic movement IOC 2014 (first recipient from the UK), elected to inaugural Hall of Fame Int Assoc for Sport and Leisure (IAKS) 2015; Companion Inst of Sports and Recreation Management 1993–2012, Companion Chartered Inst for the Mgmnt of Sport and Physical Activity 2012–; hon memb Belgian Inst of Architects; RIBA (ARIBA 1962), FRSA; *Books* Handbook of Sports and Recreational Building Design (4 vols, jt ed 1981), Handbook of Sports and Recreation Design (revised edn, 3 vols, jt ed, 1994), Stadia Design (with Rod Sheard, *qv*, and Ben Vickery 1994, 5 edn 2013); *Recreations* water colours and sketching; *Style—* Prof Geraint John; ✉ 56 Fishpool Street, St Albans, Hertfordshire AL3 4RX (☎ 01727 844585); Populous, 14 Blades Court, Deodar Road, London SW15 2NU (fax 020 8874 7470, e-mail geraintmjohn@gmail.com)

JOHN, Philip David; s of David Alfred John, and Violet, *née* Quickenden; *b* 1 January 1955, London; *m* Kathryn; 1 da (Harriet b 1 Jan 1994), 1 s (Alexander b 16 May 1995); *Career* princ King Williams' Coll IOM 2000–08, headmaster Gresham's Sch 2008–14, ret; FIoD, FCMI; *Clubs* East India, Lansdowne; *Style—* Philip John; ✉ Gresham's School, Cromer Road, Holt, Norfolk NR25 6EA (website www.greshams.com)

JOHN, Simon; s of John Bedford, and Wendy Bedford; *b* 29 December 1966; *Educ* Mayfield Sch Portsmouth; *m* 22 July 1989, Victoria, da of John Richardson; 1 s (Charles b 6 Aug 1993), 1 da (Verity b 29 May 1996); *Career* photographer; prop Simon John Photographs Ltd; featured in exhbns at: Royal Albert Hall, Barbican, Dimbola Lodge; photography teacher, chm Br Professional Photography Awards 2008, judge Int Photographic Awards, memb Admissions and Qualifications Ctee BIPP; contrib to various books on improving social photography; FBIPP 1996, hon fell Master Photographers Assoc 2002; *Awards* 10 Kodak Gold Awards, Best Overall Portrait Face 2000 Portrait Competition, various int awards for portrait and wedding photography; *Recreations* fencing, running, exercise, travel, music; *Style—* Simon John, Esq; ✉ 2 Old Manor Cottages, Wickham Road, Fareham, Hampshire PO16 7BS (e-mail simon@simonjohn.co.uk)

JOHN, Stewart Morris; OBE (1992); s of Ivor Morgan John (d 1989), and Lilian, *née* Morris (d 1989); *b* 28 November 1938; *Educ* Porth Co GS, N Staffs Tech Coll, Southall Tech Coll (HNC); *m* 3 July 1961, Susan Anne, da of William Alfred Cody; 1 s (Philip Andrew b 23 May 1964), 1 da (Sarah Margaret b 10 Nov 1967); *Career* BOAC apprentice aeronautical engr 1955–60, seconded as station engr to Kuwait Airways 1961–65, seconded as chief engr Borneo to Malaysia-Singapore Airlines E Malaysia 1965–67 (gen inspr and project engr Singapore 1963–66), engr Avionics Devpt London Airport 1967–70, asst to Gen Manager Maintenance 1970–71, works supt Mechanical Workshops 1972–73, aircraft maintenance supt 1973–74, maintenance mangr American Aircraft 1975–77, engrg dir Cathay Pacific Airways 1980–93 (dep dir engrg and maintenance Hong Kong 1977–80); dep chm Hong Kong Aircraft Engineering 1987–93 (dir 1982–93), chm Assoc Engineers Ltd Hong Kong 1990–93, ret; tech dir Aviation Exposure Management Ltd 1995–; dir of quality and memb Cncl Aviation Trg Assoc; memb: Bd Commercial Aero Engine Rolls-Royce 1993–98, Bd British Aerospace Aviation Services 1993–98, Bd Taikoo Aircraft Engineering Co Xiamen 1993–2013, Bd of Tstees Brooklands Museum Tst 1994–, Bd Hong Kong Aero Engine Service Limited (HAESL) 1996–98, Bd British Midland Aviation Services 1997–2000, Bd Aerospace North America 2000–02, Advsy Bd Kingfisher Airlines (India) 2006–09; non-exec dir Green Dragon Gas (China) 2006–, non-exec dir Greka Drilling Ltd 2011–15; pres Int Fedn of Airworthiness 1993–96 (tstee 1997–), Selection Ctee François-Xavier Bagnond Aerospace Prize 2001–04; Gold medal Br Assoc of Aviation Conslts 1991; FREng 1990, FRAeS (pres 1997–98); *Recreations* golf, classic cars, rugger; *Clubs* The Hong Kong, Shek-o Country, Burhill Golf, Rolls Royce Enthusiast (pres Surrey section); *Style—* Stewart M John, Esq, OBE, FREng, FRAeS; ✉ Taipan, 5 Pond Close, Burwood Park, Hersham, Walton-on-Thames KT12 5DR (☎ 01932 253747, fax 01932 259467)

JOHNS, Prof Allan Thomas; s of William George Johns (d 1995), of Exeter, Devon, and Ivy Maud, *née* Camble (d 2007); *b* 14 April 1942; *Educ* St Luke's Sch Exeter, Dartington Coll for the Performing Arts, Univ of Bath (BSc, PhD, DSc); *m* 23 Sept 1972, Marion, da of Charles Franklin (d 1952); 2 da (Louisa Anne b 1979, Victoria Helen b 1981); *Career* professional singer: cathedral lay vicar and clerk 1960–63, p/t concert baritone 1963–; asst dist engr SW Electricity Bd 1963–68, reader in power systems Univ of Bath 1976–84 (res fell 1968–69, lectr in electrical engrg 1969–76), head of Electrical Electronic and Information Engrg Dept and dir of Power and Energy Systems Research Centre City Univ 1988–91 (prof of electrical and electronic engrg 1984–88), prof of electrical engrg Univ of Bath 1991–2001 (head Sch of Electronic and Electrical Engrg 1992–98, dir Overseas Devpt 1998–2001), emeritus prof of electrical and electronic engrg 2001–; non-exec chm Intalec Int Electrical Engrg Consulting Engrs 1995–2012; chm SERC Electricity Research Co-Funding Ctee 1989–94, memb SERC Electromechanical Engrg Ctee (chm Electrical Power Industries Gp 1991–94), memb numerous national and int ctees incl Br nat memb CIGRÉ 2000–04; conslt: GEC, NGC, British Technol Group; ed: IEE Power Engineering Series 1984–2005, IEE Power Engineering Jl 1989–99; govr Greendown Secdy Sch Swindon (sometime chm and vice-chm), ex-officio fndn govr Broad Hinton C of E Sch 2001–13 (chm 2003–13); ind memb Wilts Police Authy 2008–12 (chm Professional Standards Ctee and lead memb for custody and procurement), memb Miny of Justice Ind Monitoring Bd HMP Erlestoke, ind appeals and complaints investigator Office Wilts and Swindon Police Cmmnr 2013–; author of 4 books and over 200 res papers, awarded 4 learned soc premiums incl IEE Power Div and Crompton Awards (1968, 1982, 1988 and 1995); CEng, FIEE 1981, FRSA 1988, FIET 2006; *Recreations* ice-skating, bowls, walking, piano, singing (solo performer at major concerts), coaching promising young singers; *Clubs* Garrards; *Style—* Prof Allan T Johns; ✉ Faculty of Engineering and Design, University of Bath, Claverton Down, Bath (☎ 01225 826052, fax 01225 826865, e-mail a.t.johns@bath.ac.uk)

J

JOHNS, Derek; s of Oliver Johns, and Joan Johns; *Educ* Stratford GS Biggleswade; *Career* ed Random House NY 1983–86, publishing dir Harrap 1986–88, md The Bodley Head 1988–89, md Granta 1990–92, dir and literary agent A P Watt Ltd 1992– (jt md 1996–); pres Assoc of Authors 2003–06; tstee PEN; *Books* The Beatrice Mystery (1980), Wintering (2007); *Recreations* reading, music, walking; *Clubs* Soho House; *Style—* Derek Johns, Esq; ✉ A P Watt Ltd, 20 John Street, London WC1N 2DR (☎ 020 7405 6774, fax 020 7831 2154, e-mail djohns@apwatt.co.uk)

JOHNS, Michael Charles; s of Arthur Charles Johns (d 1998), of Crediton, Devon, and Margaret Mary Johns (d 1986); *b* 20 December 1947; *Educ* Tiffin Sch, St Edmund Hall Oxford (BA, Cross-Country blue 1967 and 1968), Law Soc Finals (New Inn prize); *m* Sept 1970, Lucy Mary; 2 da (Kathryn Helen b 23 Oct 1973, Clare Louise b 16 April 1976); *Career* ptnr: Withers 1974–87 (joined 1970), Ashurst 1987–2010; non-exec dir AerLingus plc 2006–11, non-exec dir Soco Int plc 2011–13; *Style—* Michael Johns, Esq; ☎ 07831 593100, e-mail michaeljohns20@aol.com

JOHNS, Michael Stephen Mackelcan; s of Jack Elliott Mackelcan Johns (d 1968), of Radlett, Herts, and Janet, *née* Price (d 1999); *b* 18 October 1943; *Educ* Marlborough; *m* 1, 20 Sept 1968 (m dis 1975), Joanna Turner, *née* Gilligan; 2 s (Alexander b 16 Sept 1971, Toby b 1 Sept 1973); m 2, 10 March 1979, Gillian, da of Geoffrey Duckett White (d 2004), of Perth, Western Aust; 1 da (Sophia b 2 Feb 1984); *Career* slr; sr ptnr K&L Gates (formerly Nicholson Graham & Jones) 2003– (ptnr 1973–); memb Law Soc; *Recreations* golf, cricket, gardening, theatre; *Clubs* MCC, St George's Hill Golf, Royal Sydney Golf Australia; *Style—* Michael Johns, Esq; ✉ 22 Bowerdean Street, London SW6 3TW (☎ 020 7731 7607); One New Change, London EC4M 9AF (☎ 020 7648 9000, fax 020 7648 9001, e-mail michael.johns@klgates.com)

JOHNS, Milton; né John Robert Milton; s of Arthur Wallace Milton (d 1956), and Olive Grace, *née* Trobridge (d 1968); *b* 13 May 1938; *Educ* Merrywood GS Bristol, Bristol Old Vic Theatre Sch; *m* 1961, Bella, da of Arthur Buckley Horsfield; 1 da (Leah b 1964), 1 s (Simeon Robert b 1969); *Career* actor; newspaper columnist The Stage 1992–95; Br Actors Equity: memb Cncl 1972–98, memb Exec 1972–92, hon treas 1975–92, hon life memb 2000; dir Equity Tst Fund 1988– (vice-chm 1995–2010, chm 2011–), chm Acting Accreditation Bd Nat Cncl for Drama Trg 1991–95; vice-pres The Actors' Benevolent Fund 2003 (memb Exec Cncl 1992–, hon treas 1997–); pt/t racecourse announcer and auctioneer; *Theatre* various repertory incl: Sheffield, Coventry, Leicester and Farnham (also dir); various seasons incl: Bristol Old Vic 1961–62, Chichester Festival Theatre and Royal Exchange Manchester; credits incl: She Stoops to Conquer (debut, Theatre Royal Bristol) 1960, Swiss Cheese in Mother Courage 1961, Czar Alexander II in War and Peace (West End debut, Old Vic and Phoenix) 1962, Peter Shirley in Major Barbara (RSC, Aldwych) 1970, The Woman in Black (Fortune) 1991; *Television* Shop at Sly Corner (debut, BBC) 1960; began by playing various unsavoury characters in detective series; roles since incl: Parker in Pickwick Papers (BBC), William Potter in Death of a Ghost (BBC), Kistiacowski in Oppenheimer (BBC), Rev Horsley in Horseman Riding By (BBC), Griffiths in The Florence Bravo Mystery (BBC), Cassidy in Murphy's Mob (Central), Fred Mitchell in South Riding (Yorkshire), Arnold Haithwaite in The Intruder (Granada), Brendan Scott in Coronation Street (Granada), Adolf Eichmann in War and Remembrance (USA), Ernest Gilles in Born and Bred (BBC); *Recreations* horse racing, reading, music, cricket (full memb Assoc of Cricket Umpires); *Clubs* Garrick, Lord's

Taverners, MCC; *Style—* Milton Johns, Esq; ✉ c/o Morwenna Preston Management, 49 Leithcote Gardens, London SW16 2UX (☎ 020 8835 8147)

JOHNS, Peter Andrew; s of Lt John Francis, DSC, RNVR, of Porthcawl, Mid Glamorgan, and Megan, *née* Isaac; *b* 31 December 1947; *Educ* Bridgend GS, UCL (BSc); *m* 12 Aug 1985, Rosanne Helen Josephine, da of Capt William John Howard Slayter, RA, of Oxted, Surrey; 3 s (Jack b 1987, Robert b 1989, Harry b 1994), 1 da (Megan b 1996); *Career* md and head of banking N M Rothschild & Sons Ltd 2006–08 (dir 1987–2008); chm: Upright Open MRI Ltd 2011–, Relendex Ltd 2012–15; vice-chm Autistica 2009–15; chm of govrs Terra Nova Sch 2005–12; ACIB 1975; *Recreations* rugby, cricket, football, current affairs, history, music; *Clubs* Lansdowne; *Style—* Peter Johns, Esq; ✉ Maple Bank, Macclesfield Road, Alderley Edge, Cheshire SK9 7BL (☎ 01625 586449, e-mail peterjohns@mac.com)

JOHNS, Air Chief Marshal Sir Richard Edward; GCB (1997, KCB 1994, CB 1991), KCVO (2007), CBE (1984, OBE 1977), LVO (1972); s of late Lt-Col Herbert Edward Johns, MBE, RM, of Emsworth, Hants, and Marjory Harley, *née* Everett; *b* 28 July 1939; *Educ* Portsmouth GS, RAF Coll Cranwell; *m* 23 Oct 1965, Elizabeth Naomi Anne, *née* Manning; 1 s, 2 da; *Career* cmmnd 1959; RAF, No 64 (F) Sqdn 1960–63, No 1417 (FR) Flt Aden 1965–67, flying instr duties 1968–71, Staff Coll 1972, PSO/AOC in C NEAF 1973, No 3 (F) Sqdn as CO 1975–77, MOD Air Staff 1978–81, Station Cdr and Harrier Force Cdr RAF Gütersloh 1982–84, ADC to HM the Queen 1983–84, RCDS 1985, SASO HQ RAF Germany 1986–88, SASO HQ Strike Cmd 1989–91 (incl Dir of Operations for Op Granby at JHQ High Wycombe), AOC No 1 Gp 1991–93, COS/Dep C-in-C HQ Strike Cmd 1993–94, AOC-in-C Strike Cmd 1994, C-in-C Allied Forces Northwestern Europe 1994–97, Chief of Air Staff and Air ADC to HM The Queen 1997–2000; Hon Col 73 Engr Regt (V) 1994–2002, Hon Air Cdre RAF Regt 2001–13; chm of tstees RAF Museum 2001–06, tstee Prince Philip Tst 2001–08, pres Windsor Festival 2001–08, vice-pres Royal Windsor Horse Show 2001–; Constable and Governor of Windsor Castle 2000–08; pres Hearing Dogs for Deaf People 2004–; govr: Portsmouth GS 1996–2010, Dauntsey's Sch 2008–; Freeman City of London 1999, Liveryman GAPAN 1999; FRAeS 1997; *Recreations* military history, rugby, cricket, equitation; *Clubs* RAF; *Style—* Air Chief Marshal Sir Richard Johns, GCB, KCVO, CBE, FRAeS; ✉ Dolphin House, Chitterne, Wiltshire BA12 0LH

JOHNSON, Rt Hon Alan Arthur; PC (2003), MP; s of Stephen Arthur Johnson and Lillian May Johnson; *b* 17 May 1950; *Educ* Sloane GS Chelsea; *m* 1 (m dis), Judith Elizabeth, *née* Cox; 1 s, 2 da; m 2 (m dis), 1991, Laura Jane, *née* Patient; 1 s; m 3, Carolyn Mary, *née* Burgess; *Career* postman 1968; UCW: branch official 1976, memb Exec Cncl 1981, nat offr 1987–93, gen sec 1993–95; jt gen sec Communication Workers Union (following merger with Nat Communication Union) 1995–97; MP (Lab) Hull West and Hessle 1997–; PPS to: fin sec to Treasury 1997–99, Paymaster General 1999; min for competitiveness DTI 1999–2001, min of state for Employment Relations, Industry and Regions 2001–03, min of state for Lifelong Learning, Further and Higher Educn 2003–04, sec of state for Work and Pensions 2004–05, sec of state for trade and industry 2005–06, sec of state for educn 2006–07, sec of state for health 2007–09, sec of state Home Office 2009–10, shadow chllr of the Exchequer 2010–11; memb: TUC Gen Cncl 1993–95, Nat Exec Lab Pty 1995–97, Postal, Telegraph & Telephone Int World Exec 1993–97; dir Unity Trust Bank plc 1992–97; govr Ruskin Coll 1991–97; Duke of Edinburgh Cwlth Study Conf 1992; *Recreations* music, tennis, reading, cooking, football, radio; *Style—* The Rt Hon Alan Johnson, MP; ✉ House of Commons, London SW1A 0AA (☎ 020 7219 3000)

JOHNSON, Alan Michael Borthwick; s of Dennis Daniel Borthwick Johnson, OBE (d 1976), of Calderstones, Liverpool, and Nora, *née* MacLeod (d 1992); *b* 7 June 1944; *Educ* Liverpool Coll 1951–63, CCC Oxford (MA); *Career* called to the Bar Middle Temple (Harmsworth scholar) 1971, ad eundem Gray's Inn 1973; *Clubs* Oxford Society; *Style—* Alan Johnson, Esq; ✉ 1 Farm Place, London W8 7SX

JOHNSON, Prof Dame Anne Mandall; DBE (2013); da of Dr Gordon Trevor Johnson (d 1979), of Hale, Cheshire, and Dr Helen Margaret Johnson, *née* Noble; *b* 30 January 1954; *Educ* Cheltenham Ladies' Coll, Newnham Coll Cambridge (MA), Univ of Newcastle upon Tyne (MB BS, MD), LSHTM (MSc); *m* 1996, Dr John Martin Watson, s of Robert Watson; 1 s (Oliver Mandall b 3 Aug 1993), 1 da (Sophie Mandall b 23 July 1995); *Career* various hosp posts and vocational trg in gen practice 1978–83, registrar in community med NE Thames Regnl HA 1983–84, lectr Middx Hosp Med Sch 1985–88; UCL Med Sch: sr lectr in epidemiology 1988–94, hon conslt in public health med 1998–, reader in epidemiology 1994–96; Royal Free and UCL Med Sch: prof of epidemiology 1996–, head Dept of Primary Care and Population Sciences 2002–, dir Div of Population Health 2007–10; co-dir UCL Inst for Global Health 2008–13; assoc Newnham Coll Cambridge 1996–2006, visiting prof LSHTM 1999–; dep chair Infection and Immunity Bd MRC 2004–06, chair Population and Health Sciences Gp MRC 2009–10; non-exec dir Whittington Hosp NHS Tst 2005–07; memb: Cncl Inst of Drug Dependency 1990–98, Physiological Med and Infections Bd MRC 2001–04, Specialist Advsy Ctee of Antimicrobial Resistance Dept of Health 2002–07, Nuffield Council on Bioethics Working Party on Ethics of Public Health 2006–07, Adaptation Sub-Ctee UK Climate Change Ctee 2010–; vice dean Int Faculty of Population Health Sciences 2014–; govr Wellcome Tst 2011– (memb Populations and Public Health Funding Ctee 2008–10); ed AIDS 1994–2000; Royal Instn Australian science scholar 1971, Terrence Higgins Tst Award for social research in HIV 2002; FFPH 1993, FMedSci 2001, FRCGP 2002 (MRCGP 1982), FRCP 2004 (MRCP 1998); *Publications* Sexual Attitudes and Lifestyles (1994); numerous scientific papers on HIV, sexually transmitted infections and infectious diseases; *Recreations* singing; *Style—* Prof Dame Anne Johnson, DBE; ✉ Division of Epidemiology and Health Care, Mortimer Market Centre, London WC1E 6AU (☎ 020 3108 2087, e-mail anne.johnson@ucl.ac.uk)

JOHNSON, Rt Hon (Alexander) Boris de Pfeffel; PC (2016), MP; s of Stanley Patrick Johnson, of Nethercote, Winsford, Minehead, Somerset, and Charlotte Mary Offlow, *née* Fawcett; bro of Jo Johnson, MP and Rachel Johnson, *qqv*; *b* 19 June 1964, NY; *Educ* Eton, Balliol Coll Oxford (Brackenbury scholar, BA); *m* 1, 1987 (m dis 1993), Allegra Mostyn-Owen; m 2, 1993, Marina, da of Charles Wheeler; 2 s, 2 da; *Career* reporter; LEK Management Consultants 1987; trainee reporter The Times 1987, reporter Wolverhampton Express & Star 1988; The Daily Telegraph: leader writer 1988, Euro community corr Brussels 1989–94, asst ed 1994–99, currently weekly columnist; ed The Spectator 1999–2005; MP (Cons): Henley 2001–08, Uxbridge & Ruislip South 2015–; vice-chm (i/c campaigning) Cons Pty 2003–04, shadow min for arts 2004, shadow spokesman for higher educn 2005–08; Mayor of London (Cons) 2008–16, chm Met Police Authy 2008–10; foreign sec 2016–; appearances on radio and TV; Political Commentator of the Year What The Papers Say Awards 1998, Nat Journalist of the Year Pagan Fedn of GB 1998, Eds' Ed of the Year 2003, Columnist of the Year British Press Awards 2004, Columnist of the Year What The Papers Say Awards 2005; Hon LLD Brunel Univ 2007; *Books* The Oxford Myth (contrib, 1988), Friends, Voters and Countrymen (2001), Lend Me Your Ears (2003), Seventy Two Virgins (2004), The Dream of Rome (2006), Have I Got Views For You (2006), The Perils of the Pushy Parents (2007), Life in the Fast Lane (2007), Johnson's Life of London (2011), The Churchill Factor (2014); *Recreations* painting; *Style—* The Rt Hon Boris Johnson, MP; ✉ House of Commons, London SW1A 0AA

JOHNSON, Brian Joseph; s of Joseph Johnson, of Billinge, nr Wigan, and Margary, *née* Nichson; *b* 12 October 1953; *Educ* Grange Park Tech Sch St Helens, Univ of Manchester Sch of Architecture (BA, BArch); *m* 1 Sept 1979, Marie, da of John O'Brien; 1 da (Emma b 19 Sept 1986); *Career* student architect Gearey Blair Weed Dickenson Partners Liverpool 1976–77, architect Weightman and Bullen Partnership Liverpool 1979–81; Holford Associates 1982–: assoc 1984–88, salaried ptnr 1988–92, equity ptnr (i/c educnl sector) 1992–1999, ptnr Abbey Holford (following merger of Holford Associates and Abbey Hawson Rowe) 1999–2002, dir AEDAS AHR Architects Ltd (formerly Abbey Holford) 2002–; Civic Tst Award (for Lincoln House Manchester) 1987; memb ARUCK, RIBA; *Recreations* travel, squash, skiing; *Style—* Brian Johnson, Esq

JOHNSON, Carlton (Carl); s of Ronald James Johnson (d 1990), and Margaret Ruth, *née* Vincent; *b* 3 November 1958; *Educ* Barton Peveril Coll Eastleigh Hampshire, Keble Coll Oxford (BA); *m* 29 Oct 1990, Linda Suzette; 4 s (Michael James b 16 Jan 1991, Christian Charles b 26 March 1993, Rory Alexander b 1 May 1995, Callum Luke b 1 Nov 1997); *Career* account exec Ogilvy & Mather advtg agency 1981–83, account mangr then dir Publicis 1983–85, account dir Gold Greenlees Trott 1985–88 (assoc bd dir 1987, bd dir 1988), gp md Simons Palmer Clemmow Johnson 1995–97 (md 1988–95), md TBWA Simons Palmer (following merger) 1997–98, chief exec TBWA GGT Simons Palmer (following merger) 1998–99, pres TBWA/Chiat/Day NY 1999–2002, chief operating officer TBWA Worldwide 2001–03, currently founding ptnr Anomaly; *Recreations* music, books, cinema, sport; *Style—* Carl Johnson, Esq

JOHNSON, Daniel Benedict; s of Paul Bede Johnson, and Marigold E G Hunt, MBE; bro of Luke Johnson, *qqv*; *b* 26 August 1957; *Educ* Langley GS, Magdalen Coll Oxford (BA); *m* 1988, Sarah Cynthia Charlotte, da of J W M Thompson, CBE; 2 s (Tycho b 1990, Leo b 1994), 2 da (Edith b 1992, Agatha b 1997); *Career* research student Peterhouse Cambridge 1978–81, Shakespeare scholar Berlin 1979–80, teaching asst in German history QMC London 1982–84, dir of pubns Centre for Policy Studies 1983–84; Daily Telegraph: leader writer 1986–87, Bonn corr 1987–89, Eastern Europe corr 1989–90, assoc ed 1998–2005; The Times: leader writer 1990–91, literary ed 1992–96, asst ed (comment) 1996–98; columnist New York Sun 2005–, ed Standpoint 2008–; contrib to pubns incl: The New Yorker, New Criterion, Commentary, American Spectator, TLS, Literary Review, Prospect, Wall St Jl; *Books* German Neo-Liberals and the Social Market Economy (co-ed, 1989), Death In Venice (Thomas Mann, introduction 1991), Collected Stories (introduction, 2001), White King and Red Queen: How the Cold War was fought on the chessboard (2007); *Recreations* chess, music, antiquarian books; *Style—* Daniel Johnson, Esq; ✉ 46 Aldbourne Road, London W12 0LN (☎ 020 8743 4995, e-mail danbjohn@aol.com)

JOHNSON, Darren; AM; s of late Alan Johnson, and Joyce Reynolds, *née* Abram; *Educ* Goldsmiths Coll London (BA); *Career* memb Green Pty 1987– (princ speaker 2001–03), election co-ordinator on Nat Exec 1993–95; memb London Assembly (Green) London (list) 2000–, chair London Assembly 2009–10 and 2013–14 (dep chair 2008–09 and 2012–13), dep chair London Assembly Environment Ctee 2009– (chair 2004–09), chair London Assembly Housing Ctee 2013–15 (dep chair 2015–), chair London Assembly Environment Ctee 2015–; cncllr (Green) London Borough of Lewisham 2002–14; *Recreations* walking, cycling; *Style—* Cncllr Darren Johnson, AM

JOHNSON, Prof David Edward; s of Ted Johnson. OBE, of Lymington, Hants, and Mary, *née* Wyatt; *b* 3 October 1957, Dar-es-Salaam, Tanzania; *Educ* Christchurch GS, Univ of Bristol (BSc), Univ of Reading (MSc), Nottingham Trent Univ (PhD); *m* 15 June 1985, Belinda, *née* Stavert; 2 s (William Edward b 25 Sept 1988, Henry Edward b 11 May 1991); *Career* Sub-Lt RN 1980–82, countryside conservation co-ordinator Surrey Vol Serv Cncl 1983–86, dir Owlfern Ltd 1986–92, sr lectr, princ lectr and course ldr Southampton Inst 1992–95, subject head Maritime Faculty Southampton Inst 1995–2003, prof of coastal mgmnt Southampton Solent Univ 2003–06 (latterly emeritus prof), exec sec OSPAR Cmmn 2006–12, dir Seascape Conslts Ltd; dir and tstee Surrey Wildlife Tst 1986–89, dir and tstee Countryside Venture 1989–2011 (chm 1998–2006), professional reviewer CIWEM 1998–, visiting prof World Maritime Univ 2003–; memb: Coastnet Int Ctee 1998–2002, Professional Review Mgmnt Bd Chartered Inst of Water and Enviromental Mgmnt 1998–2002, UK IDA LA21 Roundtable Guidance Panel on Sustainable Tourism 1999, Hants Coastal Biodiversity Working Gp 1999–2001, Military Educn Ctee 2001–05, WWF IMO Marine Environmental Protection Ctee Delegation 2002–06, Steering Ctee Global Ocean Forum 2007–, Editorial Bd Jl for Coastal Conservation 2007–; chair Advsy Ctee on the Protection of the Sea (ACOPS) 2015–; short-term Caird fell UK Nat Maritime Museum 2001–02; FRGS 1979, FCIWEM 1995; *Books* Coastal Recreation Management: The Sustainable Development of Maritime Lesiure (jt ed, 1996); *Recreations* photography, travel, kayaking; *Style—* Prof David Johnson; ✉ Seascape Consultants Ltd, Belbins Valley, Belbins, Romsey, Hampshire SO51 0PE (☎ 01794 367797, e-mail david.johnson@seascapeconsultants.co.uk)

JOHNSON, David Edward Dunn; DL (Staffs 1986); s of Frederick Shepard Johnson, CBE (d 1996), of Trentham, Staffs, and Barbara Crocker, *née* Dunn (d 1991); *b* 8 September 1937, Trentham, Staffs; *Educ* Stowe; *m* 22 May 1982, Virginia Wendy Hadden, *née* Todd; 1 da (Victoria Clare b 4 Nov 1972); *Career* cmmnd 7 Queen's Own Hussars Nat Serv 1956–58; joined family business Johnson Bros (later part of Wedgwood Gp) 1958 (rising to prodn dir 1968), md Midwinter Ltd 1975 (concurrently md: J&G Meakin 1976, Johnson Bros 1977), jt md Earthenware Div Wedgwood 1980, chm and owner Steelite Int plc (formerly Royal Doulton hotelware business) 1983–2002; chm of tstees Br Pottery Manufacturers' Fedn 1987–2009, pres Br Pottery Manufacturers' Fedn Club 1999–2002; chm: Willoughbridge Garden Tst 1986–99, Groundwork Stoke on Trent 1995–2005, Ptnrs Assuring a Safer Staffs 1999–2000, Fundraising Ctee for 30th Anniversary Douglas Macmillan Hospice 2001; High Sheriff Staffs 1999–2000; *Style—* David E D Johnson, Esq, DL; ✉ 4th Floor, Churchill House, 47 Regent Road, Stoke-on-Trent ST1 3RQ (☎ 01782 219903, fax 01782 219912, e-mail dedj@chartleyestates.co.uk)

JOHNSON, David Gordon; s of Sidney Burnup Johnson (d 2010), and Pearl, *née* Jenkinson; *b* 13 December 1951; *Educ* Dame Allan's Boys' Sch Newcastle upon Tyne, Univ of Manchester (BSc); *m* 1 (m dis 1986), Lesley Annis Johnson; 2 s (James Scott b 1981, Mark David b 1983); m 2, Judith Ann, da of Gerald Arthur Vernon Leaf, of Leeds; 2 s (Edward Matthew b 1989, William Charles b 1992), 1 da (Jessica Aimée b 1991); *Career* ptnr Duncan C Fraser and Co 1977, dir Mercer Human Resource Consulting Ltd 1986–2004, ceo Braybourne Associates Ltd 2007–; pres Soc of Pension Conslts 1990–92; dir Tstee GAAPS 2007–14; Freeman: City of London 1989, Worshipful Co of Actuaries 1989 (clerk 2007–), Guild of Air Pilots and Navigators 1991; FIA 1976; *Recreations* private aviation, motor racing, golf; *Clubs* Reform, City Livery; *Style—* David G Johnson, Esq; ✉ 17 Tilehouse Street, Hitchin, Hertfordshire SG5 2DU (e-mail david@braybourne.com)

JOHNSON, David Leonard; s of Richard Lewis Johnson, of Las Palmas, Canary Islands, and Olive Mary, *née* Bellamy; *b* 2 February 1956; *Educ* Wellington, Univ of Durham; *m* 13 Dec 1986, Susan, da of James Fitzjohn, of Worksop, Notts; 1 s (Edward James b 1988), 2 da (Caroline Francesca b 1990, Cordelia Sarah b 1996); *Career* admitted slr 1981; Rowe & Maw 1979–87, ptnr D J Freeman (latterly Kendall Freeman) 1988–2006, ptnr Boodle Hatfield LLP 2006–; memb: Law Soc, Soc for Construction Law, Adjudication Soc, City of London Law Soc; FCIArb; *Style—* David Johnson, Esq; ✉ Boodle Hatfield, 240 Blackfriars Road, London SE1 8NW (☎ 020 7629 7411, e-mail djohnson@boodlehatfield.com)

JOHNSON, Diana; MP; da of late Eric Johnson, and Ruth Johnson; *b* 25 July 1966; *Educ* Northwich Co GS for Girls, Sir John Deane's Sixth Form Coll Cheshire, QMC (LLB), Cncl for Legal Educn; *Career* vol/locum lawyer Tower Hamlets Law Centre 1991–94, employment, immigration and educn lawyer N Lewisham Law Centre 1995–99, employment lawyer Paddington Law Centre 1999–2002; cncllr London Borough of Tower Hamlets 1994–2002 (chair Social Services 1997–2000, chair Social Services and Health

Scrutiny Panel 2000–02), memb London Assembly (Lab) 2003–2004, MP (Lab) Hull N 2005– (Parly candidate (Lab) Brentwood and Ongar 2001); memb Public Accounts Select Ctee 2005, PPS to Rt Hon Stephen Timms, MP 2005–07, Govt asst whip 2007–10, Parly under-sec of state for schs 2009–10, shadow Home Office (crime and security) min 2010–15, shadow FCO min 2015–; legal visiting memb Mental Health Act Cmmn 1995–98; non-exec dir Tower Hamlets Primary Care Tst 2001–04, memb Met Police Authy 2003–04; nat offr FDA Trade Union 2002–03; memb: Co-operative Pty, Lab Women's Network, UNITE, Unison, Fawcett Soc, Amnesty Int, Fabian Soc; *Recreations* cinema, theatre, gardening, Hull City FC; *Style*— Ms Diana Johnson, MP; ✉ House of Commons, London SW1A 0AA (☎ 020 7219 5647, fax 020 7219 0959, e-mail johnsond@parliament.uk, website www.dianajohnson.co.uk, Twitter @dianajohnsonmp),Constituency Office, Sycamore Suite, The Community Enterprise Centre, Cottingham Road, Hull HU5 2DH (☎ 01482 319135, fax 01482 319137)

JOHNSON, Digby Mark; s of Raymond William Johnson (d 2005), and Ella Margaret, *née* Blanksby; *b* 17 April 1960, Chesterfield, Derbys; *Educ* Tapton Mt Sch for the Blind, Tapton Comp Sch Sheffield, Univ of Cambridge (MA); *children* 1 da (Ursula Grace Downes b 1 Feb 1994), 1 s (Alfred Gregory Downes b 2 June 1996); *Career* slr; trainee slr Emsley Collins 1982–84, asst slr, slr then ptnr Truman & Appleby 1984–90, founding ptnr Johnson Partnership 1990–; nat chm Trainee Slrs Gp Law Soc 1982–84; tstee Rothwell Lab Club; involved in Royal Soc for the Blind; Notts Law Soc Slr of the Year 2003–04; memb Notts Law Soc 1984–; *Recreations* Nottingham Forest FC, Derbys CCC, wine of any colour; *Clubs* Victoria (Nottingham), Oxford & Cambridge; *Style*— Digby Johnson, Esq; ✉ Cherry Tree House, 6 Caythorpe Road, Lowdham, Nottinghamshire NG14 7EA (☎ 07971 159003); The Johnson Partnership, Cannon Court Yard, Long Row, Nottingham NG1 6JE (☎ 0115 941 9141, fax 0115 947 0178, e-mail mail@thejohnsonpartnership.co.uk)

JOHNSON, Dr Donald Arthur Wheatley; s of Arthur Edwin Johnson (d 1982), of London, and Ellen Victoria, *née* Wheatley (d 1983); *b* 18 April 1934; *Educ* Nat Univ of Ireland (MD), Univ of Manchester (MSc(Med), MSc(Psych), DPM), Univ of London (DPM); *m* 3 Aug 1957, Dr Sheila MacDonald Johnson, da of Dr Hector MacDonald Walker (d 1969), of Manchester and Banff Scotland; 2 s (Ian James b 23 Nov 1960, Angus Howard b 9 June 1964); *Career* Capt RAMC 1960–63; lectr Univ of Manchester 1969–, res fell Univ of Oxford; conslt psychiatrist: N Manchester Gen Hosp 1971–72, Univ Hosp of S Manchester 1972–94, medico-legal practice 1994–; magistrate in Manchester 1977–88, chm NW Div RCPsych 1986–90 (past sec, convener and exec memb), regnl advsr in psychiatry N W Health Authy 1987–, advsr Dept of Health, chm N W Mental Health Advsy Ctee, clinical dir Dept of Psychiatry Univ Hosp of S Manchester, former chm of N Manchester Med Soc, former sec and pres Psychiatry Section Manchester Med Soc, fndr memb Br Assoc for Psychopharmacology, memb Collegum Internationale de Neuropharmacologie; Sir William Wheeler Medal RCSI 1959, Divnl Research Prize RCPsych 1976; MRCGP 1960, DRCOG 1963, FRCPsych 1977 (MRCPsych 1972); *Books* Therapeutics Today 2 (1982), New Perspectives in Treatment of Schizophrenia (1985), Causes and Management of Depression in Schizophrenia (1985), Maintenance Treatment of Chronic Schizophrenia (1989), Modern Trends in the Treatment of Schizophrenia (1991); over 200 jl pubns 1969–2010, 28 invited chapters; *Recreations* walking, shooting, fishing; *Clubs* Lancashire CCC, Mere Golf and Country; *Style*— Dr Donald Johnson; ✉ Lyndhurst, Warrington Road, Mere, Cheshire WA16 0TE (☎ 01565 830 188); Department of Psychiatry, University Hospital of South Manchester, West Didsbury, Manchester M20 8LR (☎ 0161 445 8111)

JOHNSON, Emma Louise; MBE (1996); da of Roger George Johnson, of Petts Wood, Kent, and Mary, *née* Froud; *b* 20 May 1966; *Educ* Newstead Wood Sch, Sevenoaks Sch, Pembroke Coll Cambridge; *m* 1997, Christopher West; 1 da (Georgina Mary West); *Career* clarinettist and conductor; visiting prof of clarinet Royal Coll of Music 1997–2002; debuts: London (Barbican Centre) 1985, Austria (Konzerthaus Vienna) 1985, France (Montpellier Festival with the Polish Chamber Orch) 1986, Africa (tour of Zimbabwe) 1988, USA (Newport Festival) 1989, Tokyo 1990, USSR 1990, Australia 1996; tours with: Royal Philharmonic Orch, Bournemouth Sinfonietta, English Chamber Orch; concerts with Royal Liverpool Philharmonic, City of London Sinfonia, Halle, New Japan Philharmonic; Netherlands Radio Symphony, Warsaw Sinfonia (with Sir Yehudi Menuhin), LSO, London Mozart Players, Schubert Festival Hohenems (with Arleen Auger); various TV appearances; composed Variations on a Hungarian Folk Tune (for solo clarinet) 1988; hon fell Pembroke Coll Cambridge 1999; *Recordings* for ASV: Mozart Clarinet Concerto with the Eng Chamber Orch under Leppard 1985, Crusell Clarinet Concerto number 2, Weber, Baermann, Rossini with the Eng Chamber Orch with Eco/Groves 1986, Weber Clarinet Concerto number 1, Crusell, Tartini, Debussy with the Eng Chamber Orch under Tortelier 1987, La Clarinette Française 1988, Weber Concerto no 2, Crusell Concerto no 3, Spohr Concerto no 1 with Eco/Schwartz, A Clarinet Celebration 1990, Emma Johnson plays Weber 1991, Crusell Concerto no 1, Krommer Concerto, Kozeluh Concerto with RPO under Gunther Herbig 1991, Finzi Concerto and Stanford Concerto with Sir Charles Groves 1992, Encores with Piano and Harp 1992, Michael Berkeley Concerto 1993, Pastoral – British Music for Clarinet and Piano 1994, Encores II 1994, Complete Clarinet Works of Sir Malcolm Arnold 1995, Mozart and Weber Clarinet Quintets 2000; for Universal: Voyage 2004, The Mozart Album 2005, Bernstein and Copland Sonatas 2009, Brahms Sonatas 2011, Brave New World 2014, Brahms/Zemlinsky 2015; *Awards* winner BBC Young Musician of the Year 1984, Eurovision Young Musician of the Year Bronze award 1984, Wavenden award 1986, USA Young Concert Artists award 1991; *Books* Encore!, First Repertoire, Concert Repertoire, The Emma Johnson Collection; *Recreations* learning languages, literature, theatre, writing about music; *Style*— Miss Emma Johnson, MBE; ✉ c/o Nick Curry, Clarion Seven Muses, 19 Whitehall Park, London N19 3TS (☎ 020 7272 8448, e-mail emma@emmajohnson.co.uk, website www.emmajohnson.co.uk)

JOHNSON, Dr Gordon; s of Robert Johnson (d 1960), of South Shields, Co Durham, and Bessie, *née* Hewson (d 1956); *b* 13 September 1943; *Educ* Richmond Sch, Trinity Coll Cambridge (MA, PhD, Thirlwall Prize, Seeley Medal, Royal Cwlth Soc Walter Frewen Lord Prize); *m* 1973, Faith, da of Wilfred Sargent Lewis, of New Haven, CT, and North Haven, ME; 3 s (Timothy Foy b 14 May 1975, Nathaniel James b 10 May 1977, Orlando Benedict b 19 Jan 1980); *Career* Univ of Cambridge: fell Trinity Coll 1966–74, fell Selwyn Coll 1974–93 (tutor 1975–93, hon fell 1994), univ lectr in history of S Asia 1974–2005, sr proctor 1977–78, dir Centre of S Asian Studies 1983–2001, pres Wolfson Coll 1993–2010, Sandars Reader in Bibliography 2010; Gates Cambridge Tst: provost 2000–10, dep vice-chllr 2002–10; chm Faculty of Oriental Studies 1984–87 (sec 1971–76); memb: Library Syndicate 1978–2008, Press Syndicate 1981–2010 (chm 1993–2009, chm Publishing Ctee 2009–10), Gen Bd of the Faculties 1979–82 and 1985–90, Cncl of the Senate 1985–92 and 1999–2002, Syndicate of the Govt of the Univ (The Wass Syndicate) 1988–89; chm Comberton Educn Tst 2008–, chm Comberton Acad Tst 2011–; tstee: Cambridge Cwlth Tst 1983–2013, Cambridge Overseas Tst 1989–2013, The Nehru Tst for Cambridge Univ, The Hinduja Tst for Cambridge Univ, Malaysian Commonwealth Studies Centre 1999–2012, Integrity Action 2011–, The Sir Ernest Cassel Educnl Tst 2011–, Cambridge Commonwealth, Int and European Tst 2013–; govr: Comberton Village Coll 1991–2002 (chm 1992–2001), Gresham's Sch Holt 2006–10, Stephen Perse Fndn 2012–; preacher The Lady Margaret's Cambridge 2006; Liveryman Worshipful Co of Stationers and Newspaper Makers; pres Royal Asiatic Soc 2009–12 and 2015–; *Books* Provincial Politics and Indian Nationalism (1973), University Politics: F M Cornford's Cambridge and his advice to the Young Academic Politician (1994), Cultural Atlas of India (1995), Printing and Publishing for the University, Three Hundred Years of the Press Syndicate (1999); The New Cambridge History of India (ed); ed Modern Asian Studies (CUP quarterly) 1971–2008; *Clubs* Oxford & Cambridge; *Style*— Dr Gordon Johnson; ✉ 59 Wimpole Road, Barton, Cambridge CB23 7AB (☎ 01223 264092, e-mail gj206@cam.ac.uk)

JOHNSON, Graham Lee; s of late Ronald Frank Johnson, and late June Rose Johnson; *b* 2 January 1953; *Educ* Ringmer Co Secdy Sch, Brighton Coll of FE, Weymouth Coll (Dip Mgmnt Studies); *m* Aline; 2 c (Lee, Sara); *Career* prison govr; joined Prison Serv HMP Wakefield 1977, Leyhill Trg Coll 1977, HMP Lewes 1977–88, HMP Aldington 1988–92, HMP Highdown 1992–96 (head of residence 1994–96), dep govr HM Holding Centre Haslar 1996–97, dep govr HMP Guys Marsh 1997–2001, area project and devpt mangr SW Area Office 2001, govr HMP Dartmoor 2001–2003, Prison Serv performance improvement mangr 2003–05, seconded to EU as residential twinning advsr to Bulgarian Prison Serv (in preparation for Bulgaria's entry to the EU) 2005–07, performance improvement lead HM Prison Service 2007–08, EU advsr (developing the penitentiary system) Miny of Justice Bulgaria 2008–10, EU Peer Review assessor on Justice and Home Affrs 2010, EU/CEB prison mgmnt conslt on FYR of Macedonia working on the design of the next generation of prisons 2011, advsr on the next generation of prisons to be constructed in Bulgaria 2012, EU Judicial Reform and Human Rights peer review inspector Croatia 2012, sr expert on justice, home affrs and human rights EU, EU conslt to Serbian and Latvian Govts on the design of new correctional facilities 2012–15, conslt to Libyan Govt on the evaluation of the prison and court system and the development of a strategic building programme of renewal 2014, EU sr prison expert Project Reform Project Moldova 2014, EU sr prison expert to Macedonia on prison design and operations 2015/16, Cncl of Europe sr prison expert Montenegro 2016; judicial reform conslt, owner Int Custodial Consultancy and Training (ICCT), assoc conslt G4S (Care and Justice UK); sr business conslt: Social Pioneers (UK), Agencia Consulting (UK) and SGT Export Bulgaria; Queen's Jubilee Medal 2004, Prison Service Long Service and Good Conduct Medal (LS&GCM) 2011; fell Inst of Leadership and Mgmnt (FInstLM), FCMI (MIMgt 2000); *Publications* Prison Senior Management Training Manual (Macedonia), Council of Europe Study on the Use of Electronic Monitoring of Offenders across the European Union (Moldova); *Recreations* golf, reading, restoring classic cars; *Style*— Graham Johnson, Esq; ✉ ICCT, Broadleigh, Old Totnes Road, Buckfastleigh, Devon TQ11 0BY (☎ 01364 642031, mobile 07917 451933, e-mail icctcorporate@gmail.com)

JOHNSON, Graham Rhodes; OBE (1994); s of John Edward Donald Johnson (d 1986), and Violet May, *née* Johnson; *b* 10 July 1950; *Educ* Hamilton HS Bulawayo, Royal Acad of Music; *Career* concert accompanist; accompanied Elisabeth Schwarzkopf, Victoria de Los Angeles, Peter Shreier, Dame Margaret Price, Dame Janet Baker, Dame Felicity Lott, Ann Murray, Sarah Walker, Anthony Rolfe Johnson, Brigitte Fassbaender, Philip Langridge, Elly Ameling, Thomas Hampson, Christine Schäfer, Matthias Goerne; appeared as accompanist at numerous festivals incl: Aldeburgh, Bath, Edinburgh, Schwarzenberg (Hohenems), Munich and Salzburg; has taught various classes worldwide, prof of accompaniment at Guildhall Sch of Music; fndr The Songmakers' Almanac 1976, writer of BBC series for TV and radio, song advsr to the Wigmore Hall London 1992, chm of jury Wigmore Hall Song Competition 1997–99; recordings incl: a complete Schubert Lieder series for Hyperion beginning 1988, completed 2000, Hyperion French Song Edn beginning 1993, Hyperion Schumann Edn beginning 1996; recipient of Royal Philharmonic Soc award for instrumentalist of 1998, Wigmore Hall Medal 2013, Hugo Wolf Medal Stuttgart 2014; elected hon memb Swedish Royal Acad of Music 2000, hon memb Royal Philharmonic Soc 2010; Hon DMus Durham Univ 2013, Hon DMus New England Conservatory of Music Boston MA 2013; FRAM 1985, FGSM 1988; Chevalier de l'Ordre des Arts et des Lettres (France) 2002; *Books* The Unashamed Accompanist by Gerald Moore (contrib, 1984), The Britten Companion (contrib, 1984), Song on Record (contrib, 1986), The Spanish Song Companion (contrib, 1992), The Songmakers Almanac 1976–96 (1996), A French Song Companion (2000), Britten, Voice and Piano (2003), Gabriel Fauré: The Songs and Their Poets (2009), Franz Schubert: The Complete Songs (3 volumes, 2014); *Recreations* book collecting, cats; *Style*— Graham Johnson, Esq, OBE; ✉ c/o Askonas Holt, Lincoln House, 300 High Holborn, London WC1V 7JH

JOHNSON, Hugh Eric Allan; OBE (2007); s of Maj Guy Francis Johnson, CBE (d 1969), of London, and Grace Enid Marian, *née* Kittel; *b* 10 March 1939, London; *Educ* Rugby, King's Coll Cambridge (MA); *m* 13 March 1965, Judith Eve, da of Col Antony Gibbons Grinling, MBE, MC (d 1982), of Dyrham, Glos; 2 da (Lucy b 1967, Kitty-Alice b 1973), 1 s (Redmond b 1970); *Career* staff writer Vogue and House & Garden 1960–63, ed Wine & Food (sec Wine & Food Soc 1963–65), travel ed Sunday Times 1967 (wine corr 1962–67), ed Queen 1968–70, wine ed Gourmet Magazine 1971–72, editorial dir The Garden 1975–90 (conslt 1990–2005), gardening corr New York Times 1985–86; chm The Hugh Johnson Collection Ltd 1985–2015; dir Société Civile de Château Latour 1986–2001; wine conslt: Jardines Wine Tokyo 1986–2002, The Royal Tokaji Wine Co 1989–; pres: Sunday Times Wine Club 1973–, The Circle of Wine Writers 1997–2007; hon pres The International Wine and Food Soc 2002–08, hon pres Wine and Spirit Educn Tst 2009–11, vice-chm Int Dendrology Soc 2014–; churchwarden St James Great Saling 1971–98, tstee St James's Conservation Tst 2005–15, pres Met Public Gardens Assoc 2012–, dir Exbury Gardens Ltd 2013–; fndr memb Tree Cncl 1974; Gold Veitch Meml Medal RHS 2000, Lifetime Achievement Award Inst of Masters of Wine 2015; corresponding memb Accademia dei Georgofili Florence 1996–; Hon Dr Univ of Essex 1998; fell commoner King's Coll Cambridge 2001; Chevalier de l'Ordre Nationale du Mérite 2004; *Films* How to Handle A Wine (video 1984), Wine – A Users Guide (with KQED San Francisco, 1986), Vintage – A History of Wine (with WGBH Boston and Channel 4, 1989), Return Voyage (for Star TV Hong Kong, 1992); *Books* Wine (1966, revised 1974), Frank Schoonmaker's Encyclopedia of Wine (ed, 1967), The World Atlas of Wine (1971, 7 edn (with Jancis Robinson) 2013), The International Book of Trees (1973, revised 1984 and 1993, reissued 2000), The California Wine Book (with Bob Thompson, 1976), Hugh Johnson's Pocket Wine Book (annually since 1977), The Principles of Gardening (1979, revised 1984, republished as Hugh Johnson's Gardening Companion 1996), Understanding Wine (1980), Hugh Johnson's Wine Companion (1983, 6 edn (with Stephen Brook) 2009), How to Enjoy Wine (1985, revised edn 1998), The Atlas of German Wines (1986, revised edn 1995), The Hugh Johnson Cellar Book (1986), The Wine Atlas of France (with Hubrecht Duijker, 1987, revised edn 1997), The Story of Wine (1989), The Art & Science of Wine (with James Halliday, 1992, revised edn 2007), Hugh Johnson on Gardening (1993), Tuscany and its Wines (2000), Wine: A Life Uncorked (2005), Hugh Johnson in The Garden (2009), Trees – A Lifetime's Journey through Forests, Woods and Gardens (2010); many articles on gastronomy, gardening and travel incl Tradescant's Diary in The Garden (monthly 1975–2006, now online and quarterly in Hortus magazine); *Recreations* gardening, forestry, the table, grandchildren; *Clubs* Garrick, Brooks's, Saintsbury, Beefsteak, Keyhaven Yacht; *Style*— Hugh Johnson, Esq, OBE; ✉ 70 Scarsdale Villas, London W8 6PP (website www.tradsdiary.com)

JOHNSON, Hugh Nicholas Tysilio; s of Basil Tysilio Johnson (d 1998), and Stella Gwendolen Johnson (d 1987); *b* 7 June 1958, Manila, Philippines; *Educ* Glengorse & Hydenye Preparatory Sch, Lancing Coll; *m* 21 Dec 1983, Hazel Frances, da of Ian Francis and Ann Digby; 1 da (Camilla Henrietta b 18 March 1985), 1 s (Frederick Charles Tysilio b 19 March 1989); *Career* photographer and film dir; advertising and editorial

J

photographer (specialising in still life, food, location, people, animals and cars) 1980–; clients incl: BP, Sony, BMW, VW, Volvo, IBM, Texaco, Br Govt, Bundesbank, Benson & Hedges, World of Interiors, Vogue, ICI, Carling, Coca Cola, Harrods, Lego, Landrover; numerous pictures in various books; recipient: Grand Prize at NY Festival of Arts and Advertising, Gold Award Internationaler Druckschriften Wettbewerb 1993 and 1994, Bronze Award Art Dirs' Club Germany 1994, Gold Award Art Dirs' Club NY 1994; Silver Awards Assoc of Photographers 2011/12/14, AOP Awards Best in Category for Moving Image and Innovation, Luerzers Archive top 200 photographers worldwide 2013 and 2014; other awards from Assoc of Photographers, Campaign Posters, Campaign Press, D&AD, Creative Circle, American Masters Cup 7th Photo Awards 2014, Pink Lady Photo Awards 2014/15/16; work selected for special mention by George Roger (fndr memb of Magnum photographic agency), only living English photographer selected for Photography Now (V&A exhibition celebrating 150 year anniversary of photography), 2 press campaigns selected in Campaign Annual Best Ads of 2011 and selected in Luezers Archive Top 200 Photographers World Wide, Best Moving Image AOP Awards 2011, 2 campaigns selected in Campaign Magazine Best Campaign 2012, Best listed in Archive Top 200 photographers worldwide, Luerzers Archive top 200 photographers worldwide 2013/14/15, winner Pink Lady Food Photographers of the Year Awards 2013/14, Best Commissioned Series AOP Awards 2013, 2 Awards American Masters Cup 2014/15, Best Still Life AOP Awards 2014, winner (Still Life) Int Colour Awards 2015 and 2016, Best Food Portraiture AOP Awards 2015 and 2016; memb AOP; *Books* Curry Cuisine; *Recreations* travelling, art, wildlife, sports; *Clubs* Chelsea Arts, Tottenham Hotspur FC, Sussex CCC,, Assoc of Photgraphers; *Style*— Hugh Johnson, Esq; ✉ Hugh Johnson Studio, 5 2a Byam Street, Fulham, London SW6 2RD (☎ 020 7731 3011, e-mail hugh@hughjohnson.co.uk, website www.hughjohnson.co.uk, blog www.hughjohnson.co.uk/blog, Twitter @hughntjohnson, Instagram HughNTJohnson)

JOHNSON, Ian Frederick; s of Alan Frederick Johnson, of Oswestry, Shropshire, and Betty, *née* Edwards; *b* 10 March 1960; *Educ* Oswestry Boys HS, Univ of Reading (LLB), Manchester Met Univ (PGCE), Liverpool John Moores Univ (LLM); *m* 18 March 1989, Hon Elizabeth Anne Cynlais, da of Baron Evans of Claughton (Life Peer, d 1992), of Claughton, Birkenhead; 2 da (Lucy Eva b 9 Oct 1995, Elise Claire b 19 April 1998); *Career* called to the Bar Gray's Inn 1982; memb Northern Circuit, barr at law 1983–; sr lectr in Law Manchester Metropolitan Univ 1998–; memb: Chancery Bar Assoc, Northern Chancery Bar Assoc; *Recreations* golf, sports cars, skiing; *Clubs* Allerton Park Golf (Liverpool); *Style*— Ian Johnson, Esq; ✉ 5 Stone Buildings, Lincoln's Inn, London WC2A 3XT (☎ 020 7242 6201, e-mail i.johnson@mmu.ac.uk)

JOHNSON, Prof Ian Richard; s of William Henry Johnson, of Eltham; *b* 14 July 1948; *Educ* Christ's Hosp, London Hosp Med Coll (BSc, MB BS), Univ of Nottingham (DM); *m* 1970, Jane, da of Frank Lewis Lockley (d 1984); *Career* sr house offr obstetrics and gynaecology Nottingham 1975–76 (house offr med and surgery 1974–75), registrar obstetrics and gynaecology Mansfield and Nottingham 1979–80, sr lectr and conslt North Staffs Med Centre Keele Univ 1983–87; Univ of Nottingham: lectr in physiology 1977–78, lectr in obstetrics and gynaecology 1980–83, prof of obstetrics and gynaecology 1987–2008, head Dept of Obstetrics and Gynaecology 1992–97 and 2002–08, head Sch of Human Devpt 1997–2002, emeritus prof of obstetrics and gynaecology 2008–; hon conslt: City Hosp Nottingham 1987–2008, Queen's Med Centre Nottingham 1987–2008; memb Gynaecological Visiting Soc; FRCOG 1988 (MRCOG 1978); *Books* MCQ's for Undergraduates in Obstetrics and Gynaecology (1985, 2 edn 1994), Obstetrics and Gynaecology Vade-Mecum (2000); *Recreations* gardening, antiques; *Style*— Prof Ian Johnson; ✉ Department of Obstetrics and Gynaecology, University of Nottingham, Queen's Medical Centre, Nottingham (☎ 0115 823 0702)

JOHNSON, James North; s of Edwin Johnson (d 1987), of Harpenden, Herts, and Elizabeth Marjorie, *née* North (d 2004); *b* 13 November 1946, Blackburn, Lancs; *Educ* Eastwood Sch Renfrewshire, Univ of Liverpool (MB ChB, MD); *m* 1, 1972 (m dis 2002), Dr Gillian Christine Markham, da of Harry Markham; 1 da (Katharine Sarah Markham b 2 Oct 1987), 1 s (Charles Henry North b 15 Jan 1990); m 2, 6 May 2006, Fiona Helen, da of Maj William Simpson (d 1970); *Career* visiting prof in anatomy Univ of Texas 1973; Univ of Liverpool: lectr in anatomy 1973–74, Merseyside Assoc for Kidney Research fell 1974, clinical lectr in surgery 1987–2010, assoc postgrad dean 1990–93; sr registrar in surgery Royal Liverpool Hosp 1980–85, conslt vascular surgn Halton Gen Hosp Runcorn 1985–2010 (dir of surgery 1993–97), hon conslt surgeon Guy's and St Thomas' NHS Tst 2009–10; BMA: memb Cncl 1975–80 and 1992–2007, chm Cncl 2003–07, chm Hosp Jr Staff Ctee 1979–80, chm Central Conslts and Specialists' Ctee 1994–98 (dep chm 1990–94), chm Jt Conslts' Ctee 1998–2003 (vice-chm 1994–98), memb Standing Medical Advsy Ctee 1998–2004; memb: Cncl Liverpool Med Instn 1988–90, Mgmnt Ctee Nat Counselling Serv for Sick Doctors 1985–2004; author of articles on surgical, vascular surgical and NHS topics in various jls; FRCS, FRCP, FDSRCS; *Recreations* travel, fine wine, modern languages; *Clubs* Athenaeum, Artists (Liverpool); *Style*— James N Johnson, Esq; ✉ Talgarth, 66 View Road, Rainhill, Prescot, Merseyside L35 0LS (☎ 0151 426 4306, mobile 07778 461492, fax 0151 426 6572, e-mail jnjohnson33@hotmail.com); 143 Wavertree Road, London SW2 3SN

JOHNSON, Jane; *see:* Johnson-Bakrim, (Helen) Jane

JOHNSON, Joseph Edmund (Jo); MP; s of Stanley Patrick Johnson, and Charlotte, *née* Fawcett; bro of Boris Johnson and Rachel Johnson, *qqv*; *Educ* European School Uccle, Hall Sch Hampstead, Ashdown House Sch E Sussex, Eton, Balliol Coll Oxford (Holloway scholar, Kington-Oliphant Prize), INSEAD (MBA), Institut d'Etudes Européennes Université Libre de Bruxelles; *m* Amelia, da of David Gentleman, *qv*; 1 da (Rose), 1 s (William); *Career* Investment Banking Div Deutsche Bank 1996–97; FT: joined 1997, Paris corr 2001–05, chief S Asia Bureau 2005–08, head Lex Column 2008–10; Foreign Journalist of the Year (Print) Indian Express Excellence in Journalism Award 2009; MP (Cons) Orpington 2010–, PPS to Mark Prisk, MP, *qv* (as Min of State for Business and Enterprise) 2012, asst Govt whip 2012, Parly sec to Cabinet Office, head Number 10 Policy Unit and chair Policy Advsy Bd 2013–15, min of state Cabinet Office 2014–15, min of state for univs and science 2015–; Wiener-Anspach fell Institut d'Etudes Européennes Université Libre de Bruxelles 1995; *Books* The Man Who Tried to Buy the World (2003); *Style*— Jo Johnson, Esq, MP; ✉ House of Commons, London SW1A 0AA (☎ 020 7219 7125, e-mail jo.johnson.mp@parliament.uk)

JOHNSON, Liz; da of Shane Johnson, and Yvonne, *née* East (d 2008); *b* 3 December 1985; *Educ* Univ of Wales Swansea; *Career* Paralympic swimmer; achievements incl: Bronze medal 200m Int Paralympic Ctee European Championships 2001, Silver medal 100m breaststroke Paralympics Athens 2004, 3 Gold medals (100m breaststroke, 4x50m freestyle relay and 4x50m medley relay) Int Paralympic Ctee World Championships 2006, Gold medal 100m breaststroke Br Championships 2008, Gold medal 100m breaststroke Paralympics Beijing 2008, Bronze medal 100m breaststroke Paralympics London 2012; *Style*— Ms Liz Johnson

JOHNSON, Luke Oliver; s of Paul Bede Johnson, and Marigold E G Hunt, MBE; bro of Daniel Johnson, *qqv*; *b* 2 February 1962; *Educ* Univ of Oxford; *Career* co-owner Pizza Express 1993–99; chm: Giraffe Restaurants, Patisserie Valerie, Risk Capital Partners Ltd 2000–, Channel 4 Television Corporation 2004–10; co-fndr InterQuest Gp plc, dir Dollar Financial Gp Inc 2004–06; columnist Financial Times; govr Univ of the Arts London 2000–06; chm-elect RSA 2008; *Books* The Maverick (2007), Start It Up (2011); *Style*— Luke Johnson, Esq; ✉ Risk Capital Partners LLP, 31 North Row, London W1K 6DA

JOHNSON, Prof Margaret Anne; da of Dr Frederick William Johnson, and Dr Margaret Rosemary Johnson, *née* Burke; *b* 7 February 1952; *Educ* Convent of the Sacred Heart Woldingham, Royal Free Hosp Med Sch London (MB BS, MD); *m* John William Winston Studd; 1 s (Thomas Joseph Benjamin b 16 Oct 1981), 2 da (Sarah Anne Victoria b 7 Dec 1984, Josephine Clare Francesca b 18 Feb 1992); *Career* house physician Royal Free Hosp 1976–77; SHO: postgrad trg scheme Whittington Hosp 1977–78, in thoracic med London Chest Hosp 1978, Nat Hosp for Nervous Diseases 1978–79; registrar rotation in gen med St Mary's Hosp Paddington 1979–81, research registrar Brompton Hosp 1981–83, sr registrar rotation in gen med and thoracic med Royal Free and Brompton Hosps 1983–89, conslt physician in gen med, HIV, AIDS and thoracic med Royal Free Hosp NHS Tst and hon sr lectr in virology Royal Free Hosp Sch of Med 1989–; med dir Royal Free NHS Tst; clinical dir Royal Free HIV/AIDS Unit; memb: Expert Advsy Gp on AIDS to the Dept of Health, AIDS Action Gp to Dept of Health, All Pty Parly Gp on AIDS, HIV Infection and AIDS Clinical Trials Working Pty MRC, Med Advsy Ctee to the Home Office on HIV/AIDS in Prisons, Med Advsy Ctee London Lighthouse; tstee, dir and memb Mgmnt Ctee Positively Women; FRCP 1993 (MRCP); *Books* HIV Infection in Women (jt ed with F Johnstone, 1993), An Atlas of HIV and AIDS: a Diagnostic Approach (with M C I Lipman and T A Gluck, 1994); numerous related articles in refereed jls; *Recreations* family, theatre, opera, tennis; *Style*— Prof Margaret Johnson; ✉ Medical Director, Royal Free Hospital, Pond Street, London NW3 2QG (☎ 020 7794 0500 ext 4701, fax 020 7830 2201)

JOHNSON, Margaret Pilar; OBE (2013); *née* Tulley; *b* Spain; *Educ* Univ of Edinburgh (BSc, MSc); *m* Quentin Johnson; *Career* gp ceo Leagas Delaney 2004–; non-exec dir Admiral Group plc 2006–; *Clubs* Tiffany Circle Red Cross; *Style*— Mrs Margaret Johnson, OBE; ✉ Leagas Delaney, 1 Alfred Place, London WC1E 7EB

JOHNSON, Marlene; da of James and Catherine Johnson; *Educ* City of London Business Sch; *Career* fin dir Macdonald & Co Publishers 1971–81, gp controller Fitch & Co Design Consultants 1982–84, fin controller Leo Burnett Advtg 1984–86, fin dir rising to md Watts Publishing Gp Ltd 1986–2005, md Hachette Children's Books 2005–; FCCA 1980; *Recreations* yoga, theatre, reading, travel; *Style*— Ms Marlene Johnson; ✉ Hachette Children's Books, 338 Euston Road, London NW1 3BH

JOHNSON, Martin; s of Basil Johnson (d 1993), of Shipston-on-Stour, Warks, and Bridget Natalie, *née* Wilde; *b* 23 June 1949; *Educ* Rougemont Sch Newport, St Julian's HS Newport, Monmouth; *m* 1985, Teresa Mary, da of Reginald Victor Wright; 1 s (Andrew Joseph b 25 Nov 1984), 1 da (Charlotte Elizabeth b 25 Dec 1986); *Career* sports writer; trainee RG French Ltd advtg agency Liverpool 1967–68, steelworks labourer 1968–69, trainee journalist South Wales Argus Newport 1969–72; Leicester Mercury: sports writer and sub ed 1973–86, cricket corr 1974–86, rugby corr 1979–86; cricket corr The Independent 1986–95, Daily Telegraph sports feature writer 1995–; highly commended Br Sports Journalism Awards 1993 and 1994, Sports Feature Writer of the Year 1998; *Books* The Independent Book of 1987 World Cup India and Pakistan (anthology, 1987), David Gower: the Autobiography (co-author, 1992), Rugby and All That (2000); *Recreations* golf; *Clubs* Cosby Golf (Leics); *Style*— Martin Johnson; ✉ The Daily Telegraph, 1 Canada Square, Canary Wharf, London E14 5DT (☎ 020 7538 5000, e-mail johnsonm@telegraph.co.uk)

JOHNSON, Prof Martin Hume; s of Reginald Hugh Ben Johnson, of Cheltenham, and Joyce Florence, *née* Redsell; *b* 19 December 1944, Bexleyheath, Kent; *Educ* Cheltenham GS, Christ's Coll Cambridge (scholar, MA, PhD); *m* 2006, Dr Francis Adrian Thomas Woodman, FSA; *Career* Univ of Cambridge: jr res fell Christ's Coll and MRC 1969–73, Elmore res studentship Physiological Lab 1973, sr res fell 1973–92 (professorial fell 1992–2014, life fell 2014–), lectr Dept of Anatomy 1974–84, reader 1984–91, prof of reproductive sciences 1992–2012 (now emeritus), head Dept of Anatomy 1995–99, vice-master Christ's Coll 2007–08, pres Christ's Coll 2009–10, tutor 2013–14; dir: Reproduction Research Information Service Ltd 1986–88, Company of Biologists Ltd 1986–94; co sec Cambridge Fertility Consultants 1989–91; inspr Human Fertilisation and Embryology Authy 1993– (memb 1994–99); Harkness fell Johns Hopkins Univ and Univ of Colorado 1971–73, Br Cncl fell Inst for Res in Reproduction Bombay and Indian Inst of Science 1979, Frank R Lillie fell Marine Biological Lab 1982, MRC res fell 1984–87, Albert Brachet Prize Belgian Royal Acad 1989, lectr CIBA Fndn Public Debate 1990, hon sr lectr UMDS 1991–95, Hammond lectr Soc for the Study of Fertility 1992, visiting fell La Trobe Univ Melbourne 1993 and 2006, annual public lectr Australasian Soc for Human Biology 1993, Halliburton lectr 1994, S T Huang meml lectr Hong Kong 1997, Anatomical Annual Review lectr 2000, Ver Heyden de Lancey lectr Law Faculty Univ of Cambridge 2007, A E Szulman lectr Univ of Pittsburg 2007, Nobel Symposium lectr 2010, R G Edwards Annual COGI Nobel lectr 2012, AE Szualman memorial lectr Univ of Pittsburgh 2015, RG Edwards lectr ACE Jaipur 2016; visiting prof Univ of Sydney 1999–2004, hon academic fell St Paul's Coll Sydney Univ 2005–; special advsr to Jt Lords and Commons Inquiry Ctee on the Human Tissue and Embryos (Draft) Bill 2007; ed: Reproductive BioMedicine Online 2010–, RBM and Society 2015–; memb: Br Soc for Developmental Biology, Soc for Reproduction and Fertility, Br Soc for Cell Biology, Euro Soc for Human Reproduction and Embryology, Soc of Scholars Johns Hopkins Univ 1993, Cambridge Philosophical Soc; chm Br Soc for Developmental Biology 1984–89, hon memb Stoke's Soc, hon sec Professional Advsy Gp for Infertility and Genetic Servs 1989–94; King's Fund prize for Innovation in Med Educn 1993, Marshall Medal Society for Reproduction and Fertility 2014; FRCOG (ad eundem) 2004, FSB 2011, FMedSci 2012, FRS 2014; *Publications* Immunobiology of Trophoblast (jt ed, 1975), Physiological Consequences of Immunity to Reproductive Hormones (jt ed, 1976), Development in Mammals (ed, Vol 1 1976, Vol 2 1977, Vol 3 1978, Vol 4 1980, Vol 5 1983), Immunobiology of Gametes (jt ed, 1977), Essential Reproduction (1980, 7 edn 2013, BMA Book Prize in Obstetrics and Gynaecology 2008), Sexuality Repositioned (jt ed, 2004), Death Rites and Rights (jt ed, 2007), Birth Rites and Rights (jt ed, 2011); author of over 300 papers on the science, medicine, ethics, law, teaching and history of reproduction and early development; *Recreations* opera, music, walking, theatre; *Style*— Prof Martin Johnson; ✉ Department of Physiology, Development and Neuroscience, Anatomy School, University of Cambridge, Downing Street, Cambridge CB2 3DY (☎ 01223 333777, fax 01223 333786, e-mail mhj21@cam.ac.uk, website www.pdn.cam.ac.uk/staff/johnson and www.christs.cam.ac.uk/college-life/people/academic-staff/tr_johnsonmh)

JOHNSON, Martin Osborne; CBE (2004, OBE 1998); *b* 9 March 1970, Solihull; *Educ* Welland Park Sch Market Harborough, Robert Smythe Upper Sch Market Harborough; *Career* rugby union coach and former player (lock); Leicester Tigers RUFC: capt 1997–2005, winners Pilkington Cup 1993, winners four successive Premiership titles 1999–2002, winners Heineken Cup 2001 and 2002, ret 2005; England: 84 caps, capt 1999–2003, debut v France 1993, winners Five Nations Championship 1995 (Grand Slam) and 1996, winners Six Nations Championship 2001 and 2003 (Grand Slam), memb squad World Cup 1995, 1999 and 2003 (champions 2003), ranked no 1 team in world 2003, ret as player 2004, mangr 2008–11; memb Br Lions touring squads to NZ 1993, South Africa 1997 and Aust 2001 (only player ever to have captained Br Lions on two tours 1997 and 2001); also represented England Under 18 and NZ Under 21; Allied Dunbar Premiership Player of the Season 1998/99; exec dir Rhino Rugby 2006–08; *Recreations* American football; *Style*— Martin Johnson, Esq, CBE

JOHNSON, Michael; s of Charles Beverley Johnson (d 1991), and Shirley Anne, *née* Fowler; *b* 26 April 1964; *Educ* Ecclesbourne Sch Duffield, Lancaster Univ (BA); *m* 1 July 1995,

Lizzie, da of Arthur Schoon; 1 s (Joe b 20 Aug 1996), 1 da (Molly b 4 June 1998); *Career* jr conslt Wolff Olins London 1985–86, designer The Billy Blue Gp Sydney 1986–87, freelance designer Tokyo 1987, designer Emery Vincent Design Melbourne and Sydney 1988, art dir Omon Advtg Sydney 1988, sr designer Sedley Place Design London 1988–89, gp art dir Smith and Milton London 1990–92, estab johnson banks 1992; D&AD: memb 1991–, memb Ctee 1991–, educn chm 2001–02, pres 2003; chm Design Week Awards 1998 and 1999; memb Re-validation Ctee RCA (communications course) 1998; external examiner: Glasgow Sch of Art 2001–04, Kingston Univ 2006–; visiting tutor Central St Martins; visiting lectr: Kingston Univ (and visiting tutor), Univ of Nottingham, Univ of Northumbria, Middlesex Univ, Falmouth Coll of Art, Glasgow Sch of Art; 25 posters and designs in perm design selection V&A London; *Exhibitions* The Power of the Poster (contrib curator, V&A) 1999, Rewind – 40 Years of Design and Advertising (co-curator, V&A) 2002, Somewhere Totally Else, European Design Biennial (Design Museum) 2003, Communicate, Independent Graphic Design since the Sixties (Barbican) 2004, Creation Gallery Tokyo 2004 (solo poster exhibition); *Awards* D&AD Silver Awards 1991, 1993, 1997, 1999, 2002, 2003 and 2004 (nominated 1995, 1997 (twice), 1999, commendation 1991), Design Week Awards 1995, 1996, 1997, 1998, 1999 (three), 2002, 2004, 2007, 2008 and best of show 2004, NY Art Dirs Gold Award 1991 and 2008, shortlisted BBC Design Awards 1996, D&AD Gold Award 2004, NY Art Dirs Silver Award 2004, ID Magazine Best of Category 2008; *Publications* Problem Solved: a primer in design and communication (2002), Rewind – 40 years of design and advertising (contrib, 2002), featured in numerous design books, dictionaries and annuals; *Recreations* guitar playing/collecting, music, rollerblading; *Style*— Michael Johnson, Esq; ✉ johnson banks, Crescent Works, Crescent Lane, London SW4 9RW (☎ 020 7587 6400, fax 020 7587 6411, e-mail michael@johnsonbanks.co.uk)

JOHNSON, Neil Anthony; OBE (Mil 1989), TD (1986), DL (Gtr London 1993, rep DL City of Westminster 1993–2007); s of Anthony Johnson, of Glamorganshire, and Dilys Mabel Vera, *née* Smith; *b* 13 April 1949; *Educ* Canton Sch Cardiff, RMA Sandhurst; *m* 1, 1971 (m dis 1996); 3 da (Sarah b 1973, Amanda b 1975, Victoria b 1977); m 2, 1996, Mrs Elizabeth Jane Hunter Johnston, *née* Robinson; 1 da (Charlotte b 1998), 3 step da (Katharine, Lucy, Alice); *Career* exec dir British Leyland Ltd 1977–82, dir Jaguar Cars Ltd 1982–86, CO 4 Bn The Royal Green Jackets 1986–89, dir Rover Gp plc 1989–92, DG Engrg Employers Fedn 1992–94, ceo Royal Automobile Club 1994–98, chief exec RAC Holdings Ltd 1998–2000; chm: Hornby plc 2000–13, Motability Finance Ltd 2001–08, Cybit plc 2001–10, Tenon plc 2003–06, Motability Operations plc 2008–, UMECO plc 2009–11, Synthomer plc (formerly Yule Catto plc) 2011–, e2v plc 2013–; sr ind dir Business Growth Fund 2011–; memb Royal Green Jackets TA Tst 1994–; Hon Col 157 Regt RLC (Pembroke Yeomanry) 1994–2001, Hon Col F Co (Royal Green Jackets) London Regt 2000–07; memb Nat Employers Advsy Bd MOD 2006–, ind memb Met Police Authy 2009–12; FIMI, FRSA, MInstM, CIMgt; *Recreations* country pursuits, fast British cars and slow Italian lunches; *Clubs* Army and Navy, Beefsteak, Cardiff & County, RAC, Royal Green Jackets, Arlberg Ski, Cavalry and Guards; *Style*— Neil Johnson, OBE, TD, DL; ✉ c/o Box 205, Royal Automobile Club, Pall Mall, London SW1Y 5HS

JOHNSON, Paula Joan; da of Grosvenor Marson Johnson (d 1981), and Diana Margery Joan, *née* Webb (d 1972); *b* 12 September 1953; *Educ* Atherley C of E Church Sch Southampton, Univ of Exeter (BA); *m* 20 April 1985, Lance Hamilton, s of John Harold Poynter, of Cowes, IOW; 1 s (Jago b 1994); *Career* currently organizer of literary prizes and awards and grants for Soc of Authors and RSL; literary ed Mail on Sunday 1983–1999; tstee Royal Literary Fund; assoc dir RSL 2015–; *Style*— Ms Paula Johnson

JOHNSON, Peter Charles; s of Dr William Arthur Johnson (d 1993), and Suzanne Renee, *née* Roubitschek; *b* 12 November 1950; *Educ* Merchant Taylors', Pembroke Coll Cambridge (MA); *m* 27 July 1974, Judith Anne, da of Vincent Larvan, of Southport; 2 s (Matthew b 1980, Elliot b 1982), 2 da (Charlotte, Sophie (twins) b 1987); *Career* articled clerk Herbert Smith and Co 1973–75, admitted slr 1975, currently sr ptnr Alexander JLO; Freeman City of London, Steward Worshipful Co of Distillers 1985; memb Law Soc; *Recreations* sailing; *Clubs* Oxford and Cambridge; *Style*— Peter Johnson, Esq; ✉ Alexander JLO, The Northern & Shell Tower, Selsdon Way, London E14 9GL (☎ 020 7537 7000, fax 020 7538 2442, e-mail peter@london-law.co.uk)

JOHNSON, Prof Peter Malcolm; s of Ronald John Johnson (d 1968), and Beryl Mary, *née* Donaldson; *b* 20 April 1950; *Educ* Dulwich Coll, Jesus Coll Oxford (MA, DSc), Univ of London (PhD); *Family* 2 da (Katherine b 1976, Nicole b 1978); *Career* Royal Soc visiting fell Rikshospitalet Univ Hosp Oslo 1975–76, prof and head Div of Immunology Univ of Liverpool 1985– (lectr 1977–80, sr lectr 1980–82, reader 1982–85), dean Univ of Liverpool Faculty of Med 1997–2001 (dep dean 1994–97); dep dir Cancer Tissue Bank Res Centre Univ of Liverpool 1995–2003 (dir 1992–95), memb Steering Ctee WHO Task Force for Birth Control Vaccines 1985–90; co-fndr and chm Br Materno-Fetal Immunology Gp 1978–86, cncllr and sec-gen Int Soc of Immunology of Reproduction 1986–95, vice-pres American Soc of Immunology of Reproduction 1991–93, vice-pres Liverpool Med Instn 2005–07; chm: Scientific Ctee of Br Soc for Rheumatology 1983–86 (memb Cncl 1981–86), Med Advsy Panel Nat Eczema Soc 1992–96, Cancer Res Ctee Univ of Liverpool 1992–96; memb: Ctee Br Soc of Immunology 1982–85, Ctee Br Transplantation Soc 1983–85, Cncl NW Cancer Res Fund 1992–96, Academic Ctee Univ of Liverpool 1991–2001, Liverpool HA 1997–2001, Cncl Euro Soc for Reproduction and Devpt Immunology 2000–07, MRC Coll of Experts 2004–09; chief ed Jl of Reproductive Immunology 1996–2009; author of over 200 papers and reviews concerning human immunology, notably the immunology of pregnancy; RYA nat umpire and nat judge 2002–, ISAF int judge 2005– (also int umpire 2007–), RYA NW regnl rules advsr 2007–; memb: Int Gp14 Class Ctee 1996–98, RYA Racing Rules Ctee 2002– (chm 2013–), RYA Judges and Umpires Gp 2003–11 (chm 2006–11), RYA Racing Ctee 2006–; hon pres Br Univs Sailing Assoc 2012–16; FRCPath 1993, Hon MRCP 2001; *Recreations* sailing, football, Sudoku; *Clubs* West Kirby Sailing, Oxford and Cambridge Society Sailing, Liverpool Artists; *Style*— Prof Peter Johnson; ✉ 8 Penrhos Road, Hoylake, Wirral CH47 1HU (☎ 0151 632 4179, mobile 07545 593341, e-mail mq22mq@gmail.com); Division of Immunology, University of Liverpool Medical School, Duncan Building, Daulby Street, Liverpool L69 3GA (☎ 0151 706 4354, fax 0151 706 5814, e-mail mq22@liv.ac.uk)

JOHNSON, Peter Michael; s of Joseph William Johnson, of Abingdon, Oxon, and Dorothy, *née* Woolley; *b* 21 December 1947, London; *Educ* Bec GS, Mansfield Coll Oxford (MA, CertEd, Rugby blue, Judo blue); *m* 31 August 1969, Christine Anne, *née* Rayment; 2 s (Tom b 3 July 1973, James b 17 Feb 1978); *Career* cmmnd Parachute Bde 1971; 7 Parachute Regt RHA 1971–76, gen serv in UK, Cyprus, Malaya, Canada, Germany, emergency tours in Northern Ireland 1972–74; Radley Coll: asst master 1976–91, housemaster 1983–91, dir lower sch studies, games coach; headmaster Wrekin Coll 1991–98, headmaster Millfield 1998–2008; educn advsr London Chamber Orch; capt Northampton Rugby Club 1978–79, Univ of Oxford rep RFU Cncl 1987–98, pres England Rugby Football Schs Union 2009–12; chm of tstees Wells Cathedral; govr: Blundell's Sch, Christ's Hosp; former govr Sherborne Girls; FRSA; *Recreations* sport, travel, music, oenology, cooking; *Clubs* East India, Vincent's (Oxford), Free Foresters; *Style*— Peter Johnson, Esq; ✉ e-mail pandcondart@btinternet.com

JOHNSON, Peter Michael; s of James Victor Johnson (d 1982), and Nancy Evelyn, *née* Taylorson (d 2001); *b* 3 July 1947; *Educ* Bromley GS, St Edmund Hall Oxford (Open exhibitioner, MA, BPhil); *m* 1972, Janet Esther, da of William Philip Ashman (d 2012); 2 s (Simon Christopher b 1976, Timothy Paul b 1979), 1 da (Sarah Elizabeth b 1983); *Career* Unilever plc 1970–73; Redland: joined 1973, gp treas 1978–81, dir of planning 1981–84, md Redland Bricks 1984–89, exec dir Redland plc 1988–96; chief exec: The Rugby Group plc 1996–2000, George Wimpey plc 2000–06; non-exec chm D S Smith plc 2007–12 (non-exec dir 1999–), non-exec dir SSL Int plc 2008–10, non-exec chm 2010–; dir Home Builders Fedn 2005–06; memb: Cncl Industry and Higher Educn (CIHE) 2001–06, Supervisory Bd Wienerberger AE 2005– (dep chm 2012–); pres: Tuiles et Briques Européennes (TBE) 1994–96, Nat Cncl of Bldg Material Prodrs 1998–2000; tstee Higher Studies Fund Univ of Oxford 2009–; *Recreations* tennis, music, cricket, sailing; *Style*— Peter Johnson, Esq

JOHNSON, Peter William; s of Alfred Johnson (d 1989), and Emily, *née* Hall (d 2013); *b* 2 November 1947; *Educ* Univ of Hull (BSc); *m* 10 Nov 1973, Ann Gillian, *née* Highley; 1 da (Rachael b 13 April 1974), 1 s (Simon b 19 March 1976); *Career* Rover Gp: mgmnt trainee 1969, sr mgmnt posts British Leyland 1970–79, sales dir Austin-Morris 1980–84, export dir Austin-Rover 1984–86, worldwide sales dir 1986–88; chief exec: Applied Chemicals 1988–90, Marshall Gp of Cos 1990–95; Inchcape plc: chief exec Inchcape Motor Retail 1995–96, chief exec Inchcape Motors Int 1996–98, main bd dir 1998–2009, gp chief exec 1999–2006 (gp chief exec designate 1998–99), non-exec chm 2006–09; non-exec chm Rank Gp plc 2007–11; non-exec dir: Wates Gp 2002–, Bunzl plc 2006–; vice-pres Inst of Motor Industry; Liveryman Worshipful Co of Coachmakers and Coach Harness Makers; FIMI 1984; *Recreations* golf, swimming, reading, travel; *Clubs* RAC, Redditch Golf; *Style*— Peter Johnson, Esq; ✉ Hillcrest, Little Inkberrow, Worcestershire WR7 4JQ

JOHNSON, Philip Robert; s of Robert Johnson, of Stockport, and Cicely, *née* Swalwell; *b* 12 October 1946; *Educ* Dialstone Sch Stockport; *m* 27 Aug 1969, Janette Anne, da of Arthur Gowling; 2 da (Clare Louise b 6 May 1976, (Nicola) Kate b 23 Sept 1978); *Career* articled clerk Pitt & Co Manchester 1964–69, qualified chartered accountant 1970; ptnr: Mann Judd 1977–79, Deloitte 1979–2007 (formerly Touche Ross); former head UK Audit Quality and Risk Mgmnt Gp Deloitte LLP; memb Deloitte UK Bd of Ptnrs 1988–93 and 1999–2004, chm Deloitte UK Audit Ctee 2002–04; chm and pres Fedn of European Accountants (FEE) 2010–12; memb: Audit Ctee Wellcome Tst 2008–, Scientific Ctee World Congress of Accountants 2014, Standing Advsy Gp Public Co Accounting Oversight Bd (PCAOB) 2014–, Technical Policy Bd ICAS 2015–; non-exec dir: Yorks Building Soc 2007–15 (chm Audit Ctee 2008–15), Lakeland Ltd 2013–; advsr on audit matters Treasy Select Ctee 2016–; chm of Bd of Govrs Cheadle Hulme Sch, govr The Manchester Coll 2015–; tstee Rugby Football Fndn 2014–; FCA 1979 (ACA 1970); *Recreations* travel, watching all forms of sport; *Style*— Mr Philip R Johnson; ✉ Arden House, Coppice Lane, Disley, Stockport SK12 2LT (☎ 01663 763566, mobile 07785 343240, e-mail prjohnsonuk@aol.com)

JOHNSON, Rachel; da of Stanley Patrick Johnson, and Charlotte, *née* Fawcett; sis of Boris Johnson, MP, and Jo Johnson, MP, *qqv*; *b* 3 September 1965, London; *Educ* Bryanston Sch Blandford, St Paul's Girls' Sch, New Coll Oxford; *m* 10 July 1992, Ivo N P Dawnay; 2 s (Ludovic, Oliver), 1 da (Charlotte); *Career* Financial Times 1989–94, BBC 1994–97, then columnist and freelance journalist writing for Sunday Telegraph, Daily Telegraph, Evening Standard, Easy Living magazine and Financial Times, contrib ed The Spectator, weekly columnist Daily Telegraph, Sunday Times and Evening Standard until 2009, ed The Lady 2009–12, currently columnist Mail on Sunday; *Books* fiction: The Mummy Diaries (2004), Notting Hell (2006), Shire Hell (2008, Bad Sex Prize 2008), Winter Games (2012); non-fiction: A Diary of The Lady, My First Year as Editor (2010), Fresh Hell (2015); *Recreations* reading, skiing, tennis, travel, walking; *Clubs* Campden Hill Lawn Tennis, Electric House; *Style*— Ms Rachel Johnson; ✉ 1 Rosmead Road, London W11 2JG (e-mail racheljohnson11@btinternet.com)

J

JOHNSON, Robert William Greenwood; s of Robert William Johnson (d 1960), and Susan, *née* Mills (d 1980); *b* 15 March 1942, Reigate, Surrey; *Educ* Licensed Victuallers' Sch Ascot, Univ of Durham (MB BS, MS); *m* 30 July 1966, Dr Carolyn Mary Johnson, da of Dr John Edmund Vooght (d 1997), of Newbury, Berks; 1 da (Melanie Jane b 16 June 1969), 1 s (Julian Robert Greenwood b 20 Aug 1972); *Career* asst prof of surgery Univ of Calif 1973–74 (Fulbright Scholar 1973), conslt surgn Manchester Royal Infirmary 1974–, hon conslt surgn Royal Manchester Children's Hosp; med dir Central Manchester and Manchester Children's Univ NHS Tst (CMMCT) 2000–02, former chm Med Exec Ctee Central Manchester Health Authy; hon reader in surgery Univ of Manchester, Hunterian prof RCS 1980; inter-collegiate examiner Royal Colleges of Surgery 1998–2003; pres: Br Transplant Soc 1996–99, Assoc of Surgeons of GB&I 2002–03, Fedn of Surgical Speciality Assoc 2003–; memb Senate of Surgery; Pybus Medal North of England Surgical Soc 1991, Hunterian Medal RCS; Freeman Worshipful Co of Innholders 1965; FRCS 1970, FRCSEd 1994; *Recreations* golf, tennis, skiing; *Clubs* Athenaeum, Royal Birkdale Golf; *Style*— Robert Johnson, Esq; ✉ Evergreen, Chapel Lane, Hale Barns, Cheshire WA15 0AJ (☎ 0161 980 8840, e-mail rwgj@hotmail.com); Calderbank Medical Chambers, 599 Wilmslow Road, Manchester M20 3QD (☎ 0161 434 2910, fax 0161 903 8452, e-mail rwgj@icloud.com)

JOHNSON, Roy Arthur; s of Leonard Arthur Johnson (d 1974), of Hove, E Sussex, and Cicely Elsie, *née* Turner (d 1995); *b* 3 March 1937; *Educ* Lancing; *m* 31 July 1965, Heather Campbell, da of Alfred John Heald, of Hove, E Sussex; 2 s (Mark b 1967, Paul b 1968); *Career* chartered accountant 1960; ptnr: Coopers & Lybrand 1966–92, Cork Gully 1981–92; ICAS: moderator of Examination Bd 1975–87, memb Cncl 1984–90, convenor Fin and Gen Purposes Ctee 1986–90; dir Glasgow C of C 1988–98; Univ of Strathclyde: memb Ct 1992–2003 (chm 1997–2002), treas 1994–97, hon fell 2003–; dir Strathclyde Grad Business Sch 1992–98, govr Glasgow Acad 1996–2000; chm Prince's Tst Volunteers W of Scotland 1991–2002; gen cmmr of Income Tax 1993–; Deacon Incorporation of Cordiners of Glasgow 1976 (memb 1968), Deacon Convener Trades House of Glasgow 1990; Freeman City of London 1992; Hon DUniv Strathclyde 1998; MIPA 1986; *Recreations* golf, photography, gardening; *Clubs* Western (Glasgow); *Style*— Roy Johnson, Esq; ✉ 8 Hillcrest Drive, Newton Mearns, Glasgow G77 5HH (☎ 0141 639 3800, fax 0141 616 0986, e-mail royjohnson@ntlworld.com)

JOHNSON, Stuart Peter; s of Brian Fredrick Nelson Johnson, of Twyford, Berks, and Yvonne Knowles, *née* Walker; *b* 17 May 1957; *Educ* Willink Sch Reading, Westminster Coll; *m* Penelope Linda, da of Hugh Anthony Valentine; 1 da (Lucy Victoria b March 1988), 1 s (Edward Rory b Feb 1991); *Career* mgmnt trg scheme Savoy Hotel plc 1974–78, asst banqueting mangr Claridges Hotel 1978–80, personnel and purchasing mangr The Connaught Hotel London 1982–86, res mangr Cliveden 1986–90, hotel mangr The Savoy 1990–94, dir/gen mangr Cliveden 1994–98, gen mangr Rocco Forte's Browns Hotel 2005–; publishing dir Johansens Hotel Guides 2002–; UK Hotelier of the Year 2012, European Hotelier of the Year 2013; Freeman City of London; Master Innholder 1995, chm Master Innholders 2011–13; Hon MSc 2014; FHCIMA 1995; *Recreations* riding, golf, squash, skiing; *Style*— Stuart Johnson, Esq

JOHNSON, Timothy James (Tim); s of Peter Johnson, of Tuddenham St Mary, Suffolk, and Shirley May, *née* Dickson; *b* 10 May 1967, Cambridge; *Educ* Westminster Kingsway College; *m* Faith Hawkins; *Career* chef-proprietor Restaurant Apicius Cranbrook (Michelin star); *Recreations* cycling; *Style*— Tim Johnson, Esq; ✉ Apicius, 23 Stone Street, Cranbrook, Kent TN17 3HE

JOHNSON-BAKRIM, (Helen) Jane; da of Donald Johnson, and Brenda Mary Johnson; *Educ* Liskeard GS, Goldsmiths Coll London (BA), Garnett Coll (Cert Higher and Further Educn), UCL (MA); *m* Abdellatif Bakrim; *Career* George Allen & Unwin Publishers 1984, Harper Collins Publishers 1990– (publishing dir 1996–); authors incl: J R R Tolkien, Clive

Barker, Brian Patten, David Eddings, Robin Hobb, George R R Martin, Raymond E Feist, Sam Bourne, Stuart MacBride, Michael Marshall, Dean Koontz; European Ed of the Year 1988; *Books* as Gabriel King: The Wild Road (1997), The Golden Cat (1998), The Knot Garden (1999), Nonesuch (2001), The Secret Country (2005), The Shadow World (2006), Dragon's Fire (2007), Crossed Bones (2008); as Jude Fisher: Visual Companions to Peter Jackson's Lord of the Rings movie trilogy, Sorcery Ring (2002), Wild Magic (2003), Rose World (2005); *Recreations* rock climbing, cinema, writing; *Style—* Ms Jane Johnson; ✉ Harper Collins Publishers, 77–85 Fulham Palace Road, London W6 8JB (☎ 020 8307 4701, fax 020 8307 4656, e-mail jane.johnson@harpercollins.co.uk, website www.janejohnsonbooks.com and www.janejohnson.eu)

JOHNSON-GILBERT, Christopher Ian; s of Thomas Ian Johnson-Gilbert (d 1998), and Gillian June, *née* Pool; *b* 28 January 1955; *Educ* Rugby, Worcester Coll Oxford (BA); *m* 25 July 1981, Hon Emma Davina Mary, da of Baron Terrington, DSO, OBE, FRSL (d 2001); 3 da (Cordelia b 14 June 1983, Jemima b 24 July 1985, Imogen b 11 Jan 1990), 1 s (Hugh b 22 Oct 1991); *Career* admitted slr 1980; ptnr Linklaters 1986–2002, ptnr Conyers Dill & Pearman 2008–; memb Int Bar Assoc; assoc Inst of Wine and Spirits; *Clubs* MCC, Hurlingham, Vincent's (Oxford), Rye Golf; *Style—* Christopher Johnson-Gilbert, Esq; ✉ 10 Dominion Street, London EC2M 2EE

JOHNSON-LAIRD, Dr Philip Nicholas; s of Frederick Ryberg Johnson-Laird (d 1962), of Middlesbrough, and Dorothy, *née* Blackett (d 1947); *b* 12 October 1936, Leeds, Yorks; *Educ* Culford Sch, UCL (BA, PhD); *m* 1 Aug 1959, Maureen Mary Bridget, da of John Henry Sullivan (d 1948); 1 s (Benjamin b 1966), 1 da (Dorothy b 1971); *Career* asst lectr in psychology UCL 1966–67 (lectr 1967–73), visiting memb Inst for Advanced Study Princeton 1971–72, reader in experimental pyschology Univ of Sussex 1973–78 (prof 1978–82), visiting fell Cognitive Science Prog Stanford Univ Spring 1980; visiting prof in psychology: Stanford Univ Spring 1985, Princeton Univ Spring 1986 and 1987; asst dir MRC Applied Psychology Unit Cambridge 1983–89 (fell Darwin Coll Cambridge 1986–89), emeritus prof of psychology Princeton Univ 2012 (Stuart prof 1994), visiting scholar psychology NYU 2012–; memb: Psychology Ctee SSRC 1975–79, Linguistics Panel SSRC 1980–82, Advsy Cncl Int Assoc for Study of Attention and Performance 1984; memb: Linguistics Assoc 1967, Experimental Psychology Soc 1968, Cognitive Sci Soc 1980, Assoc for Computational Linguistics 1981, Br Psychology Soc, American Philosophical Soc 2006, Nat Acad of Sci 2007; Fyssen Int Prize 2002; Hon DPhil Göteborg Sweden 1983, Hon Laurea (hc) Padua 1997, Hon DSc Trinity Coll Dublin 2000, Hon DPsych UNED Madrid 2000, Hon Dr Ghent 2002, Hon Laurea Univ of Palermo 2005, Hon DSc Univ of Sussex 2007, Hon Laurea Ca' Foscari Univ Venice 2008; FBA 1986, FRS 1991, fell Assoc of Psychological Sci 2007, memb American Philosophical Soc 2007, memb Nat Acad of Sciences 2007; *Books* Thinking and Reasoning (ed jtly, 1968), Psychology of Reasoning (with P C Wason, 1972), Language and Perception (with G A Miller, 1976), Thinking (ed jtly, 1977), Mental Models (1983), The Computer and the Mind (1988), Deduction (with R M J Byrne, 1991), Human and Machine Thinking (1993), How We Reason (2006); *Recreations* arguing, playing jazz piano, composing music; *Style—* Dr Philip Johnson-Laird, FRS, FBA; ✉ Department of Psychology, Princeton University, Princeton, NJ 08544, USA (e-mail phil@princeton.edu, websites http://mentalmodels.princeton.edu and https://pni.princeton.edu/faculty/philip-johnson-laird)

JOHNSTON, Alexander David; s of Sir Alexander Johnston, GCB, KBE (d 1994), and Betty Joan Johnston, CBE, *née* Harris (d 1994); *b* 3 September 1951; *Educ* Westminster, Corpus Christi Coll Cambridge (MA); *m* 1980, Jackie Barbara, da of Ernie Stephenson (d 2001); 2 s (Mark b 29 June 1987, George b 1 March 1990); *Career* Lazard London: joined 1973, dir 1986–2003, md 1999–2003, tstee Dirs Pension Scheme 2014–; sr advsr Lilja & Co AG 2006–; memb: Competition Cmmn and Utilities Panel Competition Cmmn 2005–14; external memb Fin Ctee Univ of Cambridge 2005–14, chm Syndicate for West and North West Cambridge 2006–15; non-exec dir BMS Associates Ltd 2005 (non-exec chm 2007–08); *Recreations* classical music, reading, skiing, walking; *Clubs* Reform; *Style—* Alexander Johnston

JOHNSTON, Alexander Dewar Kerr (Alistair); CMG (2011); s of Kerr Johnston (d 1999), and Elizabeth Alexandra Johnston; *b* 28 June 1952, Glasgow; *Educ* LSE (Stern scholarship, BSc); *Partner* Christina Maria Nijman; *Career* KPMG (formerly Peat Marwick Mitchell): joined 1973, sector specialist leasing and finance San Francisco 1977–79, US specialist Tech Advsy Gp 1979–83, departmental sr mangr 1983–86, ptnr 1986–2010, estab KPMG int HQ Amsterdam 1987–89, head of UK mktg 1990–94, head of UK insurance practice 1994–98, gen ptnr 1996, vice-chm UK Fin Servs Practice 1997–98, int managing ptnr Global Markets 1998–2003, fndr memb Int Exec 1998–2003, memb UK Bd 2002–07, vice-chm UK 2004–10, global vice chm 2007–10, chm China and Vietnam Oversight Ctees 2007–10; non-exec dir Prudential plc 2012–16; visiting prof Cass Business Sch; chair Devpt Cncl Create Arts 2012– (tstee 2014–); tstee: Design Museum 2012–, Kate's Home Nursing 2014–15, RA 2014–; memb Bd FCO 2005–10; chm Int Advsy Bd ICAEW 2006–08; FCA; *Recreations* art and design, restoration, music; *Clubs* Athenaeum; *Style—* Alistair Johnston, Esq, CMG; ✉ e-mail adkjohnston@gmail.com

JOHNSTON, Brendan; *Career* chief exec NI Social Care Cncl; *Style—* Brendan Johnston, Esq; ✉ NISCC, 7th Floor, Millennium House, 19–25 Great Victoria Street, Belfast BT2 7AQ

JOHNSTON, Catherine Elizabeth; CB (2000); da of Sir Alexander Johnston, GCB, KBE (d 1994), and Betty Johnston, CBE *née* Harris (d 1994); *b* 4 January 1953; *Educ* St Paul's Girls' Sch, St Hugh's Coll Oxford (scholar, BA); *m* 5 Aug 1989, Brendan Patrick Keith; 1 s, 1 da; *Career* with the office of the Parly Counsel 1980–2015 (seconded to Parly Counsel Office Canberra 1987–88), Parly counsel 1994–2015; *Style—* Miss Catherine Johnston, CB

JOHNSTON, Geoffrey Edward Forshaw; s of Ronald Douglas Graham Johnston (d 1985), of Fenwick, Ayrshire, and Nancy Forshaw, *née* Price; *b* 20 June 1940; *Educ* Loretto, Univ of St Andrews (LLB); *m* 21 Dec 1964, Elizabeth Anne, da of Maj William C Lockhart, of Irvine; 2 da (Susannah b 12 May 1968, Victoria b 14 Aug 1969); *Career* trained as CA Wilson Stirling & Co 1959–65; Arbuckle Smith Group: joined 1965, md 1972, MBO 1984, gp md 1984–99; vice-chm Scottish Friendly Assurance Society Ltd 2005–10; dir Glasgow C of C 1980–2001 (pres 1994–95), chm Scottish Chambers of Commerce 1996–2000, chm Central Coll of Commerce Glasgow 1999–2005; memb Scot Valuation Advsy Cncl 1982–2001; nat chm BIFA 1990–91; chm of tstees Roses Charitable Tst 2005–; memb Merchants' House City of Glasgow; hon Belgian consul for W of Scot 1988–94; FCIT, FILT; *Recreations* sailing, skiing, hill walking, golf; *Style—* Geoffrey Johnston, Esq; ✉ Upper Dunard, Station Road, Rhu, Dunbartonshire G84 8LW (e-mail geoffrey@dunard.demon.co.uk)

JOHNSTON, Lt-Col Grenville Shaw; OBE (1986), TD (1975), DL (Moray 1979); s of late William Dewar Johnston, and late Margaret Raynor Adeline, *née* Shaw; *b* 28 January 1945, Nairn; *Educ* Fettes; *m* 16 Sept 1972, Marylyn Jean, *née* Picken; 2 da (Heather Raynor b 25 Oct 1974, Maryanne Lucy 7 Feb 1977); *Career* TA: 2 Lt 540 Regt (Lovat Scouts) RA 1963–66, Capt 102 Ulster/Scottish Light Air Defence Regt RA 1966–70, Lt Col 2/51 Highland Vols 1970–86; apprentice CA Scott Moncrieff Thomson & Sheills Edinburgh 1963–68, Thomson McKlintock & Co Glasgow 1968–70; W D Johnston & Carmichael: joined 1970, ptnr 1971, sr ptnr 1975–2001, conslt 2001–05; chm: Caledonian Maritime Assets Ltd 2006–14, Cairngorm Mountain Ltd 2008–14, Highlands & Islands Airports Ltd 2009–16; district pres Moray Scouts 2005–, chm Homes for Heroes Moray District 2005–; Lord-Lt Moray 2005– (Vice Lord-Lt 1996–2005); JP 2005–07; hon memb Elgin Rotary Club 2008, pres Moray Soc 2009–; ICAS 1968; KCSG 1977, OStJ 2011; *Recreations* shooting, fishing, farming, skiing, tennis, singing (tenor); *Clubs* New (Edinburgh), Royal Scots; *Style—* Lt-Col Grenville Johnston, OBE, OStJ, TD; ✉ Spynie Kirk House, Elgin, Moray IV30 8XJ (☎ 01343 542578, mobile 07774 120202, e-mail gsj@spyniekirkhouse.co.uk)

JOHNSTON, Prof Ian Alistair; *b* 13 April 1949; *Educ* Univ of Hull (BSc, PhD); *Career* NERC postdoctoral research fell Univ of Bristol 1973–76; Univ of St Andrews: lectr 1976–84, reader in physiology 1984–85, dir Gatty Marine Lab 1985–2008, prof of comparative physiology (personal chair) 1985–97, Chandos prof of physiology 1997–2016, fndr chm Dept of Biological and Preclinical Med 1987–91, head Sch of Biological and Med Scis 1991–92, chm Research Div of Environmental and Evolutionary Biology 1992–97, head Sch (later Div) of Environmental and Evolutionary Biology 1997–2002, dir of research Sch of Biology 2002–06; dir Scottish Oceans Inst 2012–16, ceo and co-fndr Xelect Ltd 2012–; prof of biology 2016–; visiting scientist to various outside orgns, numerous research visits abroad; memb: Bd Scottish Assoc of Marine Scis 1991–97 (memb Cncl 1994–97), Antarctic Research Ctee Royal Soc 1993–96; pres Soc for Experimental Biology 2007–09, memb NERC (chm Marine Science and Technology Bd 1995–2000); Scientific Medal Zoological Soc of London 1984, Silver Medal 8th Plymouth Marine Sci lectr USA 1994; memb Physiological Soc 1982, scientific fell Zoological Soc of London 1985, FRSE 1987, FIBiol 1997; *Books* Essentials of Physiology (jtly, 3 edn 1991, trans Spanish 1987, Italian 1989, French 1990), Phenotypic and Evolutionary Adaptation of Animals to Temperature (jt ed, 1996), Environmental Physiology of Animals (2000); various book chapters, numerous reviews and original refereed papers; *Style—* Prof Ian Johnston, FRSE; ✉ Scottish Oceans Institute, School of Biology, University of St Andrews, St Andrews, Fife KY16 8LB (e-mail iaj@st-andrews.ac.uk)

JOHNSTON, Sir (William) Ian Ridley; kt (2009), CBE (2001), QPM (1993), DL (Gtr London 2008); s of late William Johnston, and late Alice, *née* Ridley; *b* 6 September 1945; *Educ* LSE (BSc); *m* 18 May 1968, Carol Ann, da of late George Smith; 2 s (Mark Daniel, Paul Matthew); *Career* Staff Offr to Cmmr Met Police 1988–89, Asst Chief Constable Kent 1989–92, Asst Cmmr Met Police 1994–2001, Chief Constable Br Tport Police 2001–09, dir of security London Organising Ctee for Olympic and Paralympic Games 2009–12; memb Bd SIA; chm Orpington Rovers Boys FC, memb Bd Canterbury Christchurch Univ, tstee Suzy Lamplugh Tst, memb Audit Ctee British Museum; Freeman City of London; *Recreations* jogging, football, tennis, squash, walking; *Clubs* Orpington Rovers FC; *Style—* Sir Ian Johnston, CBE, QPM, DL; ✉ e-mail carolian.johnston@me.com

JOHNSTON, Dr Leland Herries (Lee); s of Henry Johnston (d 1966), and Freda Johnston (d 2000); *b* 11 June 1944; *Educ* Milton HS Bulawayo, Univ of Cape Town (BSc, MSc), Univ of Oxford (Rhodes scholar, DPhil); *m* 19 Dec 1970, Margaret, *née* Caldwell; *Career* Damon Runyon cancer research fell Univ of Calif Berkeley 1971–73, Fulbright fell 1971–73, research fell Max Planck Soc Tubingen 1974–75, staff scientist Nat Inst for Med Research 1975–88, head Div of Yeast Genetics Nat Inst for Med Research 1988–; author of many papers in scientific jls; rep Rhodesia, All South African Univs and Univ of Oxford at waterpolo; FEMBO 1995, FMedSci 2000; *Recreations* reading, hiking, worrying, music, art, scuba diving; *Clubs* Bushey and Borehamwood Sub Aqua; *Style—* Dr Lee Johnston; ✉ Division of Genetics, National Institute for Medical Research, The Ridgeway, Mill Hill, London NW7 1AA (☎ 020 8816 2234, fax 020 8816 2523)

JOHNSTON, Mark Steven; s of Ronald Johnston, of Gartmore, by Stirling, Scotland, and Mary Woods, *née* Nicol; *b* 10 October 1959; *Educ* McLaren HS Calander, Univ of Glasgow; *m* 8 June 1985, Deirdre Munro, da of Dr Duncan Ferguson, of Bearsden, Glasgow; *Career* veterinary practice 1983–86; racehorse trainer 1987–; horses trained incl: Mister Baileys, Double Trigger, Bijon D'Inde, Princely Heir, Lend a Hand, Pearl of Love, Royal Rebel, Yavana's Pace, Attraction, Shamardal; races won incl: Two Thousand Guineas 1994, Ascot Gold Cup 1995, 2001 and 2002, St James Palace Stakes 1996, Phoenix Stakes 1997, Gran Criterium 1997 and 2003, Credit Suisse Private Banking Pokal 2002, One Thousand Guineas 2004, Irish One Guineas 2004, Coronation Stakes 2004, Sun Chariot Stakes 2004, Dewhurst Stakes 2004, Matron Stakes 2005; MRCVS 1983; *Style—* Mark Johnston, Esq; ✉ Kingsley House, Middleham, Leyburn, North Yorkshire DL8 4PH (☎ 01969 622237, fax 01969 622484, mobile 07802 339670)

JOHNSTON, HE Paul Charles; *m* Nicola, *née* Maskell; *Career* diplomat; MoD 1990–93; FCO: desk offr Bosnia Eastern Adriatic Gp 1993–95, head Kosovo Policy Team Eastern Adriatic Dept 1999–2001, dep head EU External Dept 2001–02, head Security Policy Dept 2002–04; head Political Section UKMIS NY 2005–08, dir int security FCO 2008, ambass to Sweden 2011–15, dep ambass to NATO 2015–; *Style—* HE Mr Paul Johnston; ✉ c/o FCO (UKDEL NATO), King Charles Street, London SW1A 2AH

JOHNSTON, Peter William; s of William Johnston (d 1974), and Louisa Alice, *née* Pritchard (d 2001); *b* 8 February 1943, Peebles, Tweeddale; *Educ* Larbert HS, Univ of Glasgow (MA, LLB); *m* 1967, Patricia Sandra, da of late Alexander Yates Macdonald; 1 da (Wendy Ann b 7 May 1969), 1 s (Alasdair Peter b 10 Dec 1970); *Career* ptnr MacArthur & Co Slrs 1971–76 (asst 1968–76), procurator fiscal Procurator Fiscal Service 1978–86 (sr legal asst 1976–78), Crown Office 1986–89 (latterly asst slr), chief exec and sec ICAS 1989–99, chief exec Int Fedn of Accountants (IFAC) 1999–2002 (conslt 2003–12), chm Risk Mgmnt Authority 2008– (memb Bd 2006–); FRSA 1990; *Recreations* music, languages; *Clubs* Banff Town and County; *Style—* Peter Johnston, Esq; ✉ 13 Scotstown, Banff, Aberdeenshire AB45 1LA (☎ 01261 818762)

JOHNSTON, Robert; s of F P M Johnston, of Edinburgh, and E A Jones; *b* 6 November 1964; *Educ* Edinburgh Acad, UEA (BA); *Career* journalist; ed Style Sunday Times 2000–2002 (dep ed 1999–2000), editorial conslt Evening Standard 2002, exec ed Wallpaper* 2003–07, exec style and business ed Esquire 2007–, assoc ed GQ 2008–; *Recreations* reading, travel, feuds and food; *Clubs* Soho House; *Style—* Robert Johnston, Esq; ✉ 16 West Square, London SE11 4SN (☎ 020 7771 1393)

JOHNSTON, Prof Ronald John (Ron); OBE (2011); s of Henry Louis Johnston (d 1989), and Phyllis Joyce, *née* Liddiard (d 2006); *b* 30 March 1941; *Educ* Commonweal Co GS Swindon, Univ of Manchester (BA, MA), Monash Univ (PhD); *m* 16 April 1963, Rita, *née* Brennan; 1 s (Christopher Martin b 18 Sept 1964), 1 da (Lucy Carolyn b 30 July 1966); *Career* Monash Univ: teaching fell 1964, sr teaching fell 1965, lectr 1966; Dept of Geography Univ of Canterbury: lectr 1967–69, sr lectr 1969–73, reader 1973–74; Univ of Sheffield: prof Dept of Geography 1974–92, pro-vice chllr for academic affairs 1989–92; vice-chllr Univ of Essex 1992–95, prof of geography Univ of Bristol 1995–; Inst of Br Geographers: sec 1982–85, vice-pres 1988–89, pres 1990; dep electoral cmmr and memb Boundary Ctee for England 2008–10; honors award for scholarly distinction Assoc of American Geographers 1991 (Lifetime Achievement Award 2010); Prix Vautrin Lud 1999; Hon DUniv Essex, Hon LLD Monash Univ, Hon DLitt Univ of Sheffield, Hon DLitt Univ of Bath; FRGS (Murchison award 1985, Victoria medal 1990), FBA 1999, Fellow Acad of Social Scis (FAcSS) 1999; *Publications* author of 50 and ed of over 40 books, author of 950 chapters and articles in jls; *Recreations* bell-ringing (pres Yorks Assoc of Change Ringers 1989–92, pres Central Cncl of Church Bellringers 1993–96 (vice-pres 1990–93)); *Style—* Prof Ron Johnston, OBE; ✉ School of Geographical Sciences, University of Bristol, Bristol BS8 1SS (☎ 0117 928 9116, fax 0117 928 7878, e-mail r.johnston@bristol.ac.uk)

JOHNSTONE, Dr Adrian Ivor Clive; *b* 14 January 1960; *Educ* St Dunstan's Coll London, Royal Holloway Coll London (BSc, PhD); *Career* Royal Holloway Coll London (now Royal

Holloway Univ of London): research fell 1984–86, lectr 1986–97, dean Faculty of Science 1994–97, sr lectr 1997–; visiting lectr in VLSI design: Curtin Univ of Technol Perth Australia 1991, King's Coll London 1991–92; tech dir Soroban Ltd 1987–91, visiting industrial fell Image Inspection Ltd 1990–93; memb/chm various Coll and Univ ctees and bds; assoc memb: Inst of Electrical and Electronic Engrs (USA), Assoc for Computing Machinery (USA); govr St Anne's Heath Junior Sch 1998–; MBCS, MIEE; *Books* LATEX, concisely (1992, revised edn and trans into Japanese 1994); also author of numerous articles and papers in learned jls; *Style*— Dr Adrian Johnstone; ✉ Faculty of Science, Royal Holloway, University of London, Egham, Surrey TW20 0EX (e-mail a.johnstone@rhul.ac.uk)

JOHNSTONE, Alexander; MSP; *b* 31 July 1961; *m* 7 Nov 1981, Linda; 1 s (Alexander b 21 March 1983), 1 da (Christine b 19 May 1987); *Career* self-employed farmer; MSP (Cons) Scotland NE 1999–; *Style*— Alex Johnstone, Esq, MSP; ✉ The Scottish Parliament, Edinburgh EH99 1SP (✆ 0131 348 5649, mobile 07802 190833); 25 Evan Street, Stonehaven, Kincardineshire AB39 2EQ (✆ and fax 01569 765826)

JOHNSTONE, Alison; MSP; *b* 11 October 1965, Edinburgh; *Educ* St Augustine's HS Edinburgh; *m*; 1 da; *Career* registrar Edinburgh Language Fndn 1988–95, registrar Basil Paterson Coll 1995–99, parly asst to Robin Harper, MSP 1999–2011, cncllr City of Edinburgh 2007–12, MSP (Green) Lothians 2011–; *Recreations* running, cycling, UKA licensed coach in endurance, speed and jumps; *Style*— Ms Alison Johnstone, MSP; ✉ The Scottish Parliament, Edinburgh EH99 1SP (✆ 0131 348 6421, e-mail alison.johnston.msp@scottish.parliament.uk)

JOHNSTONE, Patricia Anne (Pat); da of John Johnstone (d 2006), and Catherine (Kitty), *née* McGirr; *b* 17 March 1955, Dumfries; *Educ* Dumfries Acad, Univ of Glasgow (MA), Univ of Central Eng; *partner* Gilles Crawford; *Career* admitted slr 1986; Eversheds (formerly Evershed & Tomkinson): joined as trainee slr 1984, slr Corp Dept 1986, banking ptnr 1994–2011; MInstB; *Recreations* house renovation, riding, ballet, fencing; *Style*— Ms P A Johnstone; ✉ Long Marston Grounds, Long Marston, Stratford on Avon, Warwickshire CV37 8RP

JOHNSTONE, Shona Fay; da of Ronald George Sholto Douglas (d 1996), and Valerie Quarterman; *b* 13 May 1962, Birmingham; *Educ* Edgbaston C of E Coll for Girls Birmingham, Cambs Coll of Arts and Techol (BA); *m* 3 Sept 1983, Roderick McDiarmid; 2 s (Peter William Douglas b 6 Oct 1993, Tristan James Douglas b 19 July 1996), 1 da (Victoria Katharine b 22 Feb 1995); *Career* civil servant Home Office 1983–93; Cambs CC: cncllr 1993–2013, lead memb Environment and Transport 1998–2005, lead memb Children and Young People's Servs 2005–07, ldr 2007; non-exec dir Cambridge Univ Hosps NHS Fndn Tst 2002–09; cmmr Cmmn for Integrated Transport 2008–10; policy lead Future Roads Dept for Transport 2014–; memb: Economy and Transport Prog Bd Local Govt Assoc 2005–13, Cambs Police Authy 2007–12, Bd East of England Devpt Agency 2008–12; tstee Low Carbon Vehicle Partnership 2007–11; Bruce-Lockhart Member Scholarship 2012; *Publications* Delivering Localism in New Communities: the Role of the Elected Councillor (with Rosalyn Robison and Rachel Manning, 2013), Localism and New Communities (2014); *Recreations* music, gardening, reading; *Style*— Mrs Shona Johnstone; ✉ Highfield, 5 Lowburyholme Road, Over, Cambridge CB24 5NP (✆ 01954 230565, e-mail shonafj@googlemail.com)

JOHNSTONE-BURT, Vice Adm Charles Anthony (Tony); CB (2013), OBE; s of Cdr Charles Leonard Johnstone-Burt, OBE, RN, and Margaret Hilary, *née* Keir; *b* 1 February 1958, Helston, Cornwall; *Educ* Wellington, Univ of Durham (BA), US Naval War Coll RI (MA), Salve Regina Univ RI (MA); *m* Rachel Ann, *née* Persson; 3 s, 2 da; *Career* RN: HMS Brave 1994–96, Capt 6 Frigate Sqdn and HMS Montrose 2000–01, Cdre BRNC Dartmouth 2002–04, HMS Ocean 2004–05, Flag Offr Scot, Northern Eng, NI and Flag Offr Reserves 2006–08, Cdr Jt Helicopter Cmd 2008–11, dir of counter narcotics CJIATF Shafafiyat HQ ISAF Kabul 2011, COS NATO Supreme Allied Command Transformation Norfolk USA 2011–13; Master of the Royal Household Buckingham Palace 2013–; memb: Queen's Body Guard for Scotland, Royal Co of Archers; govr Haberdashers' Schs Elstree; Freeman Cities of Glasgow and London, Liveryman Worshipful Co of Haberdashers, Wright Trades House of Glasgow, Younger Brother Trinity House; CCMI, FCIPD, FRAeS; *Recreations* all sports, reading, hill walking, running; *Style*— Vice Adm Tony Johnstone-Burt, CB, OBE; ✉ Master of the Household, Buckingham Palace, London SW1A 1AA (✆ 020 7024 5832)

JOICEY-CECIL, James David Edward; s of Edward Wilfrid George Joicey-Cecil (d 1985), gs of 3 Marquess of Exeter, and Rosemary Lusia, *née* Bowes-Lyon (d 1989), gd of 14 Earl of Strathmore and Kinghorne, and of 5 Earl of Portarlington; *b* 24 September 1946; *Educ* Eton; *m* 1975, Jane Susanna Brydon, da of Capt P W B Adeley (d 1968); 2 da (Katherine Mary b 1978, Susanna Maud b 1981); *Career* Whinney Murray & Co (now Ernst & Young) 1965–72; James Capel & Co 1972–96 (pnr 1978–86), HSBC Investment Bank plc (formerly James Capel & Co) 1996–98; dir: HSBC Financial Services (Middle East) Ltd 1995–98, Sutherlands Ltd 1998–2000, Charterhouse Securities Ltd 2000; fund dir Cazenove 2000–02, Credit Suisse Private Banking 2004–08; memb London Stock Exchange 1978–92, dir Milton Abbey School Services Ltd 2010–; tstee Salisbury City Almshouse and Welfare Charities 2002–07, tstee Weldmar Hospicecare Tst 2008–, chm Turn2us Elizabeth Finn Fund Dorset 2012–, ambass Dorset Community Fndn 2015–; FCA 1979, FCSI 2001; *Clubs* Annabel's, Boodle's, City of London, HAC; *Style*— James Joicey-Cecil, Esq; ✉ 24 Clapham Mansions, Nightingale Lane, London SW4 9AQ (✆ 020 8675 0265); Keeper's Cottage, Delcombe, Milton Abbas, Blandford, Dorset DT11 0BT (✆ 01258 880292, e-mail jamiejoiceycecil@gmail.com)

JOLL, Christopher Andrew; s of Sqdn Ldr Ian K S Joll, DFC, AE, RAuxAF (d 1977), and Eileen Mary Sassoon Sykes (d 2014); *b* 16 October 1948, London; *Educ* Oundle, RMA Sandhurst (Armorers and Braziers Co young offrs prize), Mansfield Coll Oxford (MA); *Career* served Br Army: joined RMA Sandhurst 1966, cmmnd 2 Lieut Life Gds 1968, served NI 1969, 1970, 1972 and 1974, ret 1975; gen mangr Michael Peters & Partners Ltd 1978 (joined 1977), dir corp affrs United Scientific Holdings 1988 (joined 1978), chief exec Charles Barker City Ltd 1989 (dir 1988), dir Charles Barker Ltd 1989, chief exec Georgeson & Co Ltd 1991–93, dep chm GCI Financial Ltd (formerly GCI Focus Ltd) 1996–2001, chm MJ2 Ltd 2002–12, sr ptnr MJ2 Events LLP 2012–; dir: Kleinwort Benson Securities Ltd 1993–95, Butler Kelly Ltd 2001–12, Bisichi Mining plc 2001–, Dragon Retail Ltd 2002–; advsr Household Cavalry Operational Casualties Fund and Household Cavalry Museum Tst 2002–, advsr Household Div Beating Retreat; dir: Household Cavalry Pageant 2007, Chelsea Pageant 2008, Br Military Tournament 2010–13, Parade in the Park (Sainsbury Jubilee Family Festival) 2012, The Gurkha Pageant 2015, Waterloo 200 Service of Commemoration St Paul's Cathedral 2015, Shakespeare 400 Gala Concert 2016; tstee: Ironbridge Gorge Museum Tst 2008–14, Art Fund Prize for Museums and Galleries 2011–; *Publications* Uniquely British – The Speedicut Diaries (Books 1–18), The Spoils of War, Anecdotal Evidence; *Recreations* fine art collecting, military pageantry; *Clubs* Buck's, Garrick, Honourable Artillery Co; *Style*— Christopher Joll, Esq; ✉ The Old Vicarage, Richmond Road, Bath BA1 5PT; MJ2 Events LLP (✆ 07721 330730)

JOLLIFFE, John Anthony; s of Donald Norman Jolliffe (d 1967), of Dover, Kent, and Edith Constance Mary, *née* Lovegrove (d 1993); *b* 1 August 1937, Margate, Kent; *Educ* Dover Coll; *m* 1, 5 June 1965 (m dis 1983), Jacqueline Mary, *née* Smith, 1 da (Jenny b 1966), 1 s (Jeffrey b 1968); m 2, 3 Aug 1984 (m dis 1986), Irmgard Elizabeth, *née* Melville; 1 s (Andrew b 1985); m 3, 11 Aug 1990 (m dis 1994), Dorothy Jane, *née* Saul; *Career* Nat Serv RAF 1955–57; ptnr R Watson & Sons 1967–91 (joined 1957), princ J A Jolliffe & Co 1991–; examiner in pension funds Inst of Actuaries 1970–75 (tutor 1965–70), memb UK Steering Ctee for Local Govt Superannuation 1975–95, chm ACA Local Govt Superannuation Ctee 1975–95, treas Assoc of Consulting Actuaries 1980–84; dir: London Aerial Tours Ltd 1983–, Highverse Ltd 1991–; chm: Capital Pension Trustees Ltd 1992–99, Capital Cranfield Trustees Ltd 1999–2002, Pentrust Ltd 2002–, NuCurrencies Ltd 2012–15; memb Cncl Nat Assoc of Pension Funds 1983–91; chm: NAPF Int Ctee 1986–88, Euro Fedn of Retirement Provision 1988–91; Freeman City of London, Liveryman Worshipful Co of Actuaries; FIA 1964, FPMI 1977; *Books* The Independent Trustee (1992); *Recreations* flying, tennis, travel; *Style*— John Jolliffe, Esq; ✉ Hurst House, Clay Lane, Redhill, Surrey RH1 4EG (✆ 01737 779997, fax 01737 764598, e-mail john@jajolliffe.co.uk)

JOLLY, Baroness (Life Peer UK 2010), of Congdon's Shop in the County of Cornwall; Judith Anne Jolly; *b* Leamington Spa; *Educ* King's HS for Girls Warwick, Univ of Leeds (BSc), Univ of Nottingham (PGCE); *Career* mathematics teacher 1974–97, English as a foreign language teacher Br Cncl Oman 1990s; non-exec dir Mental Health and Learning Disability NHS Tst 1997–2007; memb Lib Dems 1984–; COS to Robin Teverson, MEP 1997–99, election agent to Paul Tyler, MP 1997 and Robin Teverson, MEP 1999; vice-chair Parly Candidates Assoc 1999–2008, memb Federal Policy Ctee 2002–10, chair Devon and Cornwall Regnl Exec 2007–10, memb English Cncl Exec 2007–10; Govt whip House of Lords 2013–15, Govt spokesperson for defence, health, women and equalities, culture, media and sport 2013–15, Lib Dem princ spokesperson for defence 2015–; memb: Ecclesiastical Ctee 2012–13, Jt Ctee on the Draft Care and Support Bill 2013; tstee: Focus on Labour Exploitations, Help Musicians UK; chair Hft (formerly known as Home Farm Tst); *Recreations* music, reading modern novels; *Style*— The Baroness Jolly; ✉ House of Lords, London SW1A 0PW (✆ 020 7219 1286, e-mail jollyj@parliament.uk, Twitter @jollyjudith)

JOLLY, (Robert) Miles; s of John Jolly (d 1990), and Lucy, *née* Bradley (d 1968); *b* 2 September 1937, Walton, Yorks; *Educ* Trent Coll; *m* 6 July 1963, Gillian, *née* Robson; 1 s (Marcus James Miles b 26 Sept 1967), 1 da (Fiona Claire b 31 Aug 1970); *Career* fin dir GEC Electronics 1969–71, md Britpack Ltd 1972–75, md Humberoak Group 1976–80, chm and md Limes Gp of Cos 1980–; lay canon emeritus Lincoln Cathedral (past memb Governing Chapter and chm of finance); FCA; *Style*— Miles Jolly, Esq; ✉ Limes House, Burton-by-Lincoln LN1 2RB

JOLLY, Nicholas John; s of Michael Harvey Jolly, and Anne Margaret, *née* Saunders; *b* 11 March 1962; *Educ* St Francis Xavier's Coll Liverpool, Worthing Sixth Form Coll, W Sussex Coll of Art, Glos Coll of Art (BA), Royal Acad Schs (postgrad dip); *Career* artist, co-fndr and art dir The Chap Magazine; television animator Jack Dee's Happy Hour; awarded Elizabeth Greenshields Fndn Grant 1989, Susan Kasen Travel Scholarship (6 Months in Connecticut) 1993, Pollock-Krasner Fndn Grant 1995 and 2009, Adolph and Esther Gottlieb Award 2010; *Solo Exhibitions* Paton Gallery London 1991 and 1993, Beaux Arts London 1996, 108 Gallery Harrogate 2009, The Age of Anxiety (Sarah Myerscough London) 2010; *Group Exhibitions* John Player Portrait Awards (Nat Portrait Gallery) 1984, Young Masters – Ten Young Painters (Solomon Gallery London) 1985, Young Masters (Kunsthaus im Welserhof Augsburg) 1988, New Faces II (Paton Gallery) 1989, Royal Over-Seas League Annual Exhbn 1989, 1990 and 1991, Threshold – Two Man Exhbn (Plymouth City Museum and Art Gallery) 1990, The Bridge Show (Lannon Gallery NY) 1994, The Kasen Summer Collection (touring exhbn Glasgow and London) 1994–95, Osaka Triennale (Japan) 1996, BP Portrait Awards (Nat Portrait Gallery) 1997, Arnot Art Museum Elmira NY 1997, René Magrite and Contemporary Art Ostend Belgium 1998, Figure Eight (Newarts Gallery CT) 1999; Hunting Art Prizes RCA 1998, Osaka Triennale 2001, Beasts Royale (Viktor Wynd Fine Art) 2010, The Art of Giving (Saatchi Gallery) 2010; *Public Collections* Metropolitan Museum of Art NY, Durban Museum of Art SA; *Books* The Chap Manifesto (2001), The Chap Almanac (2002), Around the World in Eighty Martinis (2003), The Lost Art of Travel (2006), The Gentleman's Guide to Motoring (2012), The Gentleman's Guide to Travel (2013); *Recreations* Rabelaisian high jinks, growing unusual facial hair; *Style*— Nicholas Jolly, Esq; ✉ Holmcroft, High Street, Findon, West Sussex BN14 0SZ (✆ 020 7916 1694, e-mail nick@artfink.demon.co.uk)

JOLLY, Sir (Arthur) Richard; KCMG (2001); s of late Arthur Jolly, and Flora Doris, *née* Leaver; *b* 30 June 1934; *Educ* Brighton Coll, Magdalene Coll Cambridge (BA, MA), Yale Univ (MA, PhD); *m* 1963, Alison Bishop (d 2014); 2 s, 2 da; *Career* community devpt offr Baringo Dist Kenya 1957–59, sec Br Alpine Hannibal Expedition 1959, research fell Makerere Coll Uganda 1963–64, research offr Dept of Applied Economics Univ of Cambridge 1964–68, advsr Parly Select Ctee on Overseas Aid and Devpt 1974–75; Univ of Sussex: professorial fell 1971–, dir Inst of Devpt Studies 1972–81; dep exec dir UNICEF 1982–95, special advsr UNDP 1996–2000; memb: Founding Ctee Euro Assoc of Devpt Insts 1973–75, Editorial Bd World Devpt 1973–90, UK Cncl on Int Devpt 1974–78, Triennial Review Gp Cwlth Fund for Tech Co-operation 1975–76, Governing Cncl for Society for Int Devpt 1976–85 (vice-pres 1982–85), UN Ctee for Devpt Planning 1978–81; chm North-South Round Table 1988–96 (memb 1978–2007); chm UNA-UK 2001–06, pres Br Assoc of Former UN Civil Servants 2007–11; tstee Oxfam 2001–06; Master Worshipful Co of Curriers 1977–78; Hon DLitt: UEA 1988, Univ of Sussex 1992; Hon Dr ISS The Hague 2007; *Publications* Cuba: The Economic and Social Revolution (jtly, 1964), Planning Education for African Development (1969), Redistribution with Growth (jtly, 1974), The Impact of World Recession on Children (ed jtly, 1984), Adjustment with a Human Face (ed jtly, 1987), Human Development Report (jtly, 1996–2000), UN Contributions to Development Thinking and Practice (2004), UN Ideas That Changed the World (2009), UNICEF: Global Governance that Works (2014); author various articles in professional jls; *Recreations* billiards, croquet, nearly missing trains and planes; *Style*— Sir Richard Jolly, KCMG; ✉ Institute of Development Studies, University of Sussex, Brighton, East Sussex BN1 9RE (✆ 01273 958561, e-mail r.jolly@ids.ac.uk)

JOLY, Simon Michael Bencraft; 2 s of Richard Bencraft Joly (d 1956), and Joan Letitia Brooke, *née* Parnell (d 1993); *b* 14 October 1952; *Educ* Christ's Hosp, CCC Cambridge (MA); *Career* conductor; music staff WNO 1974–78, asst then assoc chorus master ENO 1978–80, conductor BBC Singers 1989–95 (asst conductor 1980–89); asst to Pierre Boulez with BBC Singers Paris, Berlin and London; FRCO; *Performances* BBC Singers' concerts incl: 70th Anniversary Concert (music by Britten, Messiaen, Ligeti, Poulenc and Xenakis), Berio Coro (with London Sinfonietta, La Scala Milan); BBC Proms: Stravinsky Les Noces, Giles Swayne CRY, Steve Reich The Desert Music; work with BBC Symphony Orch incl: Hindemith Cello Concerto, Martinu Symphony No 6, Charles Ives Three Places in New England, Gavin Bryars The War in Heaven (premiere, Royal Festival Hall), Debussy La Damoiselle Élue and Le Martyre de St Sebastien, Stravinsky Canticum Sacrum, Messiaen Le Tombeau Resplendissant and L'Ascension, David Bedford 1st Symphony, Henze The Raft of the Medusa; work with other orchs incl: London Sinfonietta, Bournemouth Sinfonietta, City of London Sinfonia, BBC Philharmonic, Ulster Orch, Endymion Ensemble, New London Orch; *Operas* several Wexford Festivals, Smetana The Bartered Bride (ENO), Mozart Cosi Fan Tutte and Le Nozze di Figaro (Irish National Opera), Britten Peter Grimes (Irish and Royal Danish Opera), Gluck La Contesa de Numi (Royal Danish Opera), Bizet Carmen (with José Carreras, Berlin), rare operas by Max Brand, Wagner-Regeny and Weber (Radio 3); *Recordings* incl major choral music of Sir P Maxwell Davies, Sir John Tavener and Granville Bantock; *Recreations* theatre, films;

Style— Simon Joly, Esq, FRCO; ✉ 49B Disraeli Road, Putney, London SW15 2DR (☎ 020 8785 9617, e-mail simonjoly@tiscali.co.uk)

JONAS, Christopher William; CBE (1994); s of Philip Griffith Jonas, MC (d 1982), and Kathleen Marjory, *née* Ellis (d 2000); *b* 19 August 1941; *Educ* Charterhouse, Coll of Estate Mgmnt, London Business Sch; *m* 1, 1968 (m dis 1997), Penny, *née* Barker; 3 s ((Leslie) Peter b 16 April 1970, Toby Philip b 10 Nov 1971, Max Christopher b 2 Feb 1977), 1 da (Freya Josephine Wendy b 4 Feb 1981); m 2, 2003, Dame Judith Mayhew Jonas, DBE, *qv*; *Career* TA Inns of Court Regt 1959–66; Jones Lang Wootton 1959–67; Drivers Jonas: ptnr 1967–82, managing ptnr 1982–87, sr ptnr 1987–95; fndr Christopher Jonas/Strategy for Corporate Property 1995–2005; pres RICS 1992–93; property advsr Staffs CC 1982–2005; chm Economics Res Assoc (USA) 1987–93; fndr ProHelp 1989; dir: Securities and Futures Authy 1988–91, British Rail Property Bd 1991–94, Railtrack Group plc 1994–2001, Canary Wharf Gp plc 1994–2004, Sunrise Senior Living International 1998–2012, England Bd Bank of Scotland 1998–2000, Business in the Community 1999–2006, ECN Live 2010–14; memb: Port of London Authy 1985–99, Further Educn Funding Cncl 1992–98, Bd British Railways 1993–94; chm: Education Capital Finance 2000–, Glasgow Harbour 2001–03, Ethics Standards Bd Accountancy Fndn 2001–03, Henderson Global Property Companies Ltd 2006–11, Henderson Int Income Tst plc 2011–; sr advsr Lazard & Co 2007–13; tstee Westminster Abbey Pension Fund 2001–; chm: second stage devpt Tate Modern 2006– (chm original devpt 1997–2000), Contemporary Art Soc 2014–; dir ENO 1999–2007; govr: Charterhouse 1995–2006, UCL 1997–2005 (vice-chm 2000–04); chm Cncl: Roedean 2004–11, Goldsmiths Univ of London 2006–12; memb Counselors of Real Estate USA (Gold medal 2007); second career as street photographer (www.cwjpix.org); exhibitions of photographs: RA 2013, at Tate Modern 2013, Garsington Opera Wormsley 2013, National Churches Tst 2013, Canary Wharf Gp Atrium 2014, Peltz Gallery 2015; Hon DSc De Montfort Univ 1997; Liveryman Worshipful Co of Clothworkers (Master 2007–08); *Recreations* street photographer, walking, lieder, church music; *Clubs* Queen's; *Style*— Christopher William Jonas, Esq, CBE; ✉ 25 Victoria Square, London SW1W 0RB (☎ 020 7828 9977, e-mail cwj@kingslodge.com, website www.cwjpix.org)

JONAS, Sir Peter; kt (2000), CBE (1993); s of Walter Adolf Jonas (d 1965), and Hilda May, *née* Ziadie (d 2000); *b* 14 October 1946, London; *Educ* Worth Sch, Univ of Sussex (BA), Royal Northern Coll of Music (LRAM), Royal Coll of Music (CAMS), Eastman Sch of Music, Univ of Rochester; *m* 1, 22 Nov 1989 (m dis 2001), Lucy, da of Christopher Hull, and Cecilia, *née* Pollen; m 2, 1st June 2012, Barbara Burgdorf, da of Eckhard and Karin Burgdorf, of Stuttgart; *Career* Chicago Symphony Orch: asst to music dir 1974–76, artistic admin 1976–85; dir of artistic admin Orchestral Assoc of Chicago 1977–85 (Chicago Symphony Orch, Civil Orch of Chicago, Chicago Symphony Chorus, Allied Arts Assoc, Orchestra Hall), gen dir ENO 1985–93, Staatsintendant (gen dir) Bavarian State Opera Munich 1993–2006 (now hon life memb); lectr and faculty memb Univ of St Gallen 2003–, lectr Univ of Zürich 2004–, visiting lectr Bavarian Theatre Acad Munich; chm German Speaking Opera Intendants Conf 2001–05; memb: Bd of Mgmnt Nat Opera Studio 1985–93, Cncl of Mgmnt London Lighthouse 1990–93, Kuratorium Richard Strauss Gesellschaft 1993–2009, Beirat (Advsy Bd) Hypovereinsbank Munich 1994–2004, Rundfunkrat (Bd of Govrs) Bayerische Rundfunk (Bavarian Radio and TV) 1999–2006; memb: Assoc Internationale de Directeurs de L'Opera 1985–2006, Deutsche Bühnenverein 1993–2006, Bavarian Acad of Fine Arts 2005–, Deutsche Opernkonferenz 1993–2006, Stiftungsrat (Bd of Tstees) Berlin State Opera and Ballet cos 2005–12, Advsy Bd Carl Linde Acad Tech Univ Munich 2006–12, Governing Bd Netherlands Opera Amsterdam 2009–, Governing Bd Univ of Lucerne Switzerland 2009–16, Structural Cmmn State of Lower Saxony 2009–12, Governing Bd and Kuratorium Wissenschaftszentrum für Sozialforschung Berlin (WZB) 2015–; patron Stiftung Lebenspende Germany 2012–; memb and fell Bavarian Acad of Fine Arts 2005–; City of Munich Prize for the Arts and Culture 2004; Hon DMus Univ of Sussex 1994; fell Univ of Sussex 2012; FRCM 1989 (memb Cncl 1988–95), FRSA 1989, FRNCM 2000; Bavarian Constitutional Medal 2001, Bayerische Verdienstorden 2004, Maximiliansorden (Maximilian Order of Merit) Bavaria 2007; *Publications* Powerhouse, The English National Opera Experience (jtly, 1993), Eliten and Demokratie (jtly, 1999), Wenn Musik der Liebe Nahrung Ist (2006); *Recreations* mountain and long-distance hiking, cinema, cricket, 20th century architecture, old master paintings, epic TV series, yoga; *Clubs* Athenaeum, Surrey CCC, Munich CC; *Style*— Sir Peter Jonas, CBE; ✉ Scheuchzerstr 36, 8006 Zürich, Switzerland (☎ 0041 43 477 9871, fax 0041 43 477 9872, e-mail sirpeterjonas@gmail.com)

JONATHAN, Mark; s of John Francis Boyle (d 2009), and Josephine, *née* Harper (d 2000); *b* 2 January 1956; *Educ* Oxted Co Sch; *Career* lighting designer; chief electrician Nat Youth Theatre 1973–78, technical dir Nat Youth Theatre 1980–81, dep lighting mangr Glyndebourne Festival Opera 1978–92, head of lighting RNT 1993–2003, freelance lighting designer 2003–; external examiner MA in Collaborative Theatre Production and Design Guildhall Sch of Music and Drama; lighting designs incl prodns for: RNT, RSC, Royal Ballet, Birmingham Royal Ballet, LA Opera, Israeli Opera, Bavarian State Opera, Washington Nat Opera, Opera du Rhin, Vlammse Opera, Scottish Ballet, Berlin Staats Ballett, Scottish Opera, Northern Ballet Theatre, Stuttgart Ballet, American Ballet Theatre, Royal Court London, Chichester Festival, Finnish Nat Opera, Japanese Nat Ballet, Ballet Capitole de Toulouse, Spoleto Festival, Royal Exchange Theatre, Theater an der Wien, Opera Holland Park, Welsh National Opera, The Gate Dublin, Royal Swedish Opera, Royal Danish Opera, Teatro Real Madrid; various West End and Broadway prodns; lectr in lighting for dirs, designers and lighting designers on BA, postgrad and specialist courses; writer for Focus Magazine; designer memb and vice-chm Assoc of Lighting Designers; memb: United Scenic Artists, Br Actors Equity; nomination Outstanding Lighting Design Drama Desk NY 2007, nomination Knight of Illumination (opera) 2013, finalist World Stage Design 2013; ski teacher, memb Br Assoc of Snowsport Instructors; hon fell Guildhall Sch of Music and Drama 2014; *Recreations* classical music, theatre, winter sports, back country off-piste skiing; *Clubs* Ivy; *Style*— Mark Jonathan, Esq; ✉ 103 Bellenden Road, London SE15 4QY (☎ 020 7639 7815, mobile 07802 769376, e-mail mj@markjonathan.com, website www.markjonathan.com); c/o Clare Vidal-Hall, Clare Vidal Hall Agency, 57 Carthew Road, London W6 0DU (☎ 020 8741 7647)

JONES, Alec Norman; s of Norman Albert Jones, of Birmingham, and Iris Doreen, *née* Philips; *b* 23 December 1951; *Educ* West Bromwich GS, Univ of Nottingham (BA); *m* Mary Cherie; 2 da (Nicola Cherie b 21 July 1982, Sophie Elizabeth b 23 March 1984); *Career* ptnr PricewaterhouseCoopers (formerly Price Waterhouse before merger) 1981– (joined 1972); ACA 1975; *Recreations* all sports especially golf; *Style*— Alec Jones, Esq

JONES, (Charlotte) Alexandra (Alex); *b* Ammanford, Carmarthenshire; *Educ* Univ of Aberystwyth; *Career* television presenter: Tocyn (S4C), Chwa (S4C), The One Show (BBC 1) 2010–, Let's Dance For Comic Relief (BBC 1) 2011–; contestant Strictly Come Dancing (BBC 1) 2011; *Style*— Ms Alex Jones; ✉ c/o Independent Talent Group, 40 Whitfield Street, London W1T 2RH

JONES, Allen; s of William Jones, and Madeline, *née* Aveson; *b* 1 September 1937, Southampton; *Educ* Ealing GS for Boys, Hornsey Sch of Art, RCA; *m* 1, 1964 (m dis 1978), Janet, *née* Bowen; 2 da (Thea, Sarah (twins) b 1967); m 2, 1994, Deirdre Morrow; *Career* artist; teacher of lithography Croydon Coll of Art 1961–63, teacher of painting Chelsea Sch of Art 1966–68; tstee Br Museum 1990–99; first int exhbn Paris Biennale 1961; RA 1986 (ARA 1981); Hon Dr of Arts Southampton Solent Univ 2007; *Solo Exhibitions* incl: Crispolti Rome, Bischofberger Zurich, Ariadne Vienna, Von Wentzel Cologne, Springer Berlin, Thorden Wetterling Gothenburg, Heland Wetterling Stockholm, C Cowles NY, Richard Feigen Gallery NY, Chicago and LA, Marlborough Fine Art London, Waddington Galleries London, James Corcoran Gallery LA, Galerie Patrice Trigano Paris, Barbican Art Gallery London, Thomas Gibson Fine Art London, Br Cncl Print Retrospective Norway, Czechoslovakia, Cyprus and Brazil, Levy Hamburg, Trussardi Milan, Steinrötter Münster, Ars Nova Museum of Contemporary Art Turku, Forsblom Helsinki, Galleria d'Arte Maggiore Bologna, Galerie Terminus Munich, Palazzo dei Sette Orvieto, Nordeutscher Landesbank Hannover, Landeshauptstadt Schwerin, Galerie Hilger Vienna, Royal Acad of Arts London 2007–08, Tate Britain 2007–08, Alan Cristea Gall London 2007, Pop Art is... (Gagosian Gall London) 2007–08, Showtime (Marlborough Fine Arts London) 2008, Sculptures (Ludlow Castle Salops) 2009–10, Lorenzelli Arte Milan 2010, Playbill (Marlborough Fine Arts London) 2010, In Stages (Wetterling Gallery Stockholm and Gothenburg) 2011, Off the Wall (Kunsthalle Tübingen, UNESCO World Heritage Site Saarbrucken, State Art Collection Chemnitz Germany) 2012–13, Kaleidoscope (Pages Gallery Geneva, Galerie Levy Hamburg, Galerie Hilger Vienna) 2013, (Galerie Terminus Munich, Kunsthalle Hanover, Thomas Gibson Fine Art London, Galerie Forsblom Helsinki) 2014 and (Retrospective RA London) 2014–15, Art in the Park (Baur au Lac Zurich Switzerland) 2015; *Museum and Group Exhibitions* incl: 40 Years of Modern Art (Tate Gallery) 1986, British Art in the Twentieth Century (Royal Acad then Stuttgart) 1987, Pop Art (Tokyo) 1987, Picturing People (Br Cncl exhbn touring Hong Kong, Singapore and Kuala Lumpur) 1990, Br Art since 1930 (Waddington Gallery) 1991, Br Museum 1991 and 1997, Pop Art (Royal Acad, Museum Ludwig Cologne, Renia Sofia Madrid and Museum of Fine Arts Montreal) 1991–93, The Portrait Now (National Portrait Gallery) 1993, Treasure Island (Gulbenkian Fndn Lisbon) 1997, Augenlust (Kunsthaus Hannover) 1998–99, Pop Impressions (MOMA NY) 1999, Pop Art US/ UK Connections 1956–66 (Menil Foundation Houston) 2001, Les années pop (Centre Georges Pompidou Paris) 2001, Pop Art (Kunsthalle Villa Kobe Halle) 2002, Eurpa im Beeld (Den Haag Sculptur) 2002, Blast to Freeze (Wafsburg) 2002 (also at Les Abattoirs Toulouse 2003), Thinking Big: Concepts for 21st Century British Sculpture (The Peggy Guggenheim Collection Venice) 2002, Phantom der Lust (Stadtmuseum Graz) 2002, ...from little acorns... Early Works by Academicians (Royal Acad) 2002–03, Editions Alecto: A Fury for Prints (Whitworth Art Gallery Manchester and Bankside London) 2003, Mike Kelley – The Uncanny (Tate Liverpool) 2004, Art and the Sixties – This was Tomorrow (Tate Britain) 2004 (also at Birmingham Museum and Art Gallery 2004–05), The Human Figure in British Art from Moore to Gormley (Graves Art Gallery Sheffield) 2005, Small is Beautiful (Flowers Central) 2005, Newby Hall Sculpture Park 2005, British Pop Art Exhibition: The 1960s (Museum of the Arts Bilbao) 2005, Royal Academicians in China (China National Museum of the Arts Beijing) 2005 (also Shanghai 2006), Pop Art Portraits (Nat Gall London) 2007, True Romance (Vienna, Kiel and Rome) 2007, This is Pop (Rome) 2007, A Century of Olympic Posters (V&A and touring) 2008–12, DLA Piper Series: This is Sculpture (Tate Liverpool) 2009, Art Nouveau Revival (Musée D'Orsay Paris) 2009–10, WinterWaterColorland (Samuel Freeman Gallery LA) 2009, Crash (Gagosian Gallery London) 2010, Scultura Internazionale e Racconigi Turin 2010, 60s Design (Modelmuseum Vienna) 2012, Pop Art Design (Vitra Museum Weilam Rhein and Lousiana Museum Denmark) 2012–13, American Pop Art (Salzburg) 2012, Glam, The Art of Excess (Tate Liverpool) 2013, The Universal Addressability of Dumb Things (Liverpool, Nottingham and De La Warr Pavilion) 2012, The 60s in the Guggenheim Collections 2013, British Pop – The Founding Years (Christie's London) 2013, Beyond Limits (Sotheby's sculpture exhibition at Chatsworth) 2013, Pop Culture (MANDA Jersey USA) 2013, The Wish List (London Design Festival V&A) 2014, Pop to Popism (Art Gallery of NSW Sydney Australia) 2014–15, Pop Art Myth (Museo Thyssen Bornemisza Madrid) 2014, Pop Europe (Wolverhampton Art Gallery) 2014–15, Fighting History (Tate Britain) 2015; *Commissions* incl sculptures for: Cottons Atrium London Bridge City 1987, Heathrow Sterling Hotel 1990, Chelsea and Westminster Hosp 1993, LDDC 1994, Sir Terence Conran's Mezzo restaurant 1995, Swire Properties Hong Kong 1997 and 2002, Goodwood 1998, Chatsworth Derbys 2000 and 2007, GlaxoSmithKline London 2001, Yuzi Paradise Sculpture Parks Guilin and Shanghai 2005 and 2006, Chatsworth House Tst 2007–08; *Designs* designer of sets for TV and stage in UK and Germany (incl sets and costumes for Rambert Dance Co 1989 and Royal Ballet 1996); *Books* Allen Jones Figures (1969), Allen Jones Projects (1971), Waitress (1972), Sheer Magic (1979), Allen Jones (monograph, 1993), Allen Jones Prints (1995), Allen Jones (1997), Allen Jones Works (2005); *Recreations* gardening; *Clubs* Chelsea Arts, Garrick; *Style*— Allen Jones, Esq, RA; ✉ 41 Charterhouse Square, London EC1M 6EA (☎ 020 7606 2984, e-mail aj@allenjonestheartist.com)

JONES, (Robert) Alun; QC (1989); *Educ* Oldershaw GS Wallasey, Univ of Bristol (BSc); *Career* called to the Bar Gray's Inn 1972; recorder of the Crown Court 1992–96; memb: Bar Cncl, Criminal Bar Assoc; *Publications* Jones on Extradition and Mutual Assistance (2 edn, 2001); *Style*— Alun Jones, Esq, QC; ✉ 3 Raymond Buildings, Gray's Inn, London WC1R 5BH (☎ 020 7831 3833, fax 020 7242 4221)

JONES, Dr Alun Denry Wynn; OBE (2001); s of Thomas D Jones (d 1982), of Penygroes, Carmarthenshire, and Ray, *née* Morgan (d 1994); *b* 13 November 1939; *Educ* Amman Valley GS Ammanford, ChCh Oxford (MA, DPhil); *m* 22 Aug 1964, Ann, da of Brinley Edwards (d 1955), of Betws, Carmarthenshire; 2 da (Helen b 1966, Ingrid b 1969); *Career* sr student Cmmn for the Exhibition of 1851 1964–66, sr res fell UKAEA 1966–67, Lockheed Missiles and Space Co Calif 1967–70, tutor Open Univ 1971–82, dep ed Nature (Macmillan Journals) 1972–73 (joined 1971), BSC 1974–77, British Steel Overseas Services 1977–81, asst dir Tech Change Centre 1982–85, dir and sec Wolfson Fndn 1987–90 (dep dir 1986–87), chief exec Inst of Physics 1990–2002; BAAS: sec Working Pty on Social Concern and Biological Advances 1972–74, memb Section X Ctee 1981–92, memb Cncl 1999–2005, memb Exec Ctee 2001–05, memb Audit Ctee 2005–13; Br Library: memb Advsy Cncl 1983–85, Document Supply Centre Advsy Ctee 1986–89; memb Cncl Nat Library of Wales 1987–94 (govr 1986–94), govr UCW Aberystwyth 1990–92 and 2002–05 (memb Cncl 2002–05), govr City Univ 1991–2000; dir Science Cncl (formerly Cncl for Science and Technol Inst) 1990–2002, assessor Science Bd SERC 1991–94, chm Registration Authy Science Cncl 2005–09; memb Cncl Assoc for Schs Science Engrg and Technol (formerly Standing Conf on Schs' Science and Technol) 1992–2000 (dep chm 1997–2000), govr Sir William Perkins's Sch Chertsey 2003–12 (chm 2005–12); fell Univ of Wales Aberystwyth 2000; fell American Physical Soc 2003; FInstP 1973, CDipAF 1977; *Books* Our Future Inheritance: Choice or Chance (jtly, 1974); *Recreations* Welsh culture, gardening, theatre; *Clubs* Woking Welsh Soc (hon life memb 2006); *Style*— Dr Alun Jones, OBE; ✉ 4 Wheatsheaf Close, Woking, Surrey GU21 4BP

JONES, Alun Ffred; AM; *Educ* UCNW Bangor; *m* 1982, Alwen (d 2005); 2 s (Dafydd b 1984, Ifan b 1987), 1 da (Gwenllian b 1991); *Career* early career as Welsh teacher and head of dept Mold Alun Sch, journalist and presenter HTV Cardiff 1980–82, dir, prodr, author and co dir Nant Films 1982–2003; cncllr Arfon BC 1992, ldr Gwynedd Cncl 1996–2003; memb Nat Assembly for Wales (Plaid Cymru): Caernarfon 2003–07, Arfon 2007–; heritage min Welsh Assembly Govt 2008–11; past chair Environment Planning and Countryside Ctee, past chair Antur Nantlle regeneration non-profit co 1992–2007, chair Environment and Sustainability Ctee 2014–; chm Nantlle Vale FC; *Style*— Alun Ffred Jones, Esq, AM; ✉ National Assembly for Wales, Cardiff Bay, Cardiff CF99 1NA (e-mail alunffredjones@wales.gov.uk); 8 Stryd y Castell, Caernarfon, Gwynedd LL55 1SE (☎ 01286 672076); 70 Stryd Fawr, Bangor, Gwynedd LL57 1NR (☎ 01248 372948)

JONES, Alun Richard; s of Howell Jones (d 1993), and Olive Kathleen, *née* Williams (d 2012); *b* 9 March 1948; *Educ* Kingston GS, St Catharine's Coll Cambridge (British Steel scholar, MA); *m* 18 Sept 1971, Gail Felicity; 1 da (Hannah Clare Rhys b 2 June 1979); *Career* PricewaterhouseCoopers (formerly Price Waterhouse before merger): joined 1970, ptnr 1981, sr client ptnr 1993, memb UK and Global Supervisory Bds, ret 2006; chm Primary Health Properties plc 2014–; vice-chm Univ for the Creative Arts2012–; FCA 1973; *Recreations* golf, tennis, opera, concerts, living in France; *Clubs* Effingham Golf, RAC; *Style*— Alun Jones, Esq

JONES, Andrew Hanson; MP; *b* 28 November 1963, Yorks; *Educ* Bradford GS, Univ of Leeds; *Career* business career in mktg, chair Bow Gp 1999–2000; cncllr Harrogate Borough Cncl 2003–11, MP (Cons) Harrogate & Knaresborough 2010–; *Style*— Andrew Jones, Esq, MP; ✉ House of Commons, London SW1A 0AA

JONES, Andrew Philip David (Andy); s of Robert William Jones, of Woodlands, Hants, and Geraldine, *née* MacDonnell; *b* 1 June 1962, Taplow, Bucks; *Educ* Highcliffe Comp Sch Christchurch, Calday Grange GS Wirral, Univ of Bradford (BSc); *m* 29 July 1994, Catharine, *née* Pearson; 1 s (Alexander Robert b 12 Jan 1998), 1 da (Grace Elizabeth b 25 Feb 2000); *Career* sales admin TV SW 1983–84, sales exec Tyne-Tees TV 1985, media planner/buyer rising to media dir McCann-Erickson 1986–95, media dir rising to ceo Universal McCann London 1995–2013, ceo IPG Mediabrands 2013–; MIPA 2003 (memb Media Futures Bd 2005–); *Style*— Andy Jones, Esq; ✉ IPG Mediabrands, 42 St John's Square, London EC1M 4EA

JONES, Ann; AM; da of Charles Sadler (d 1978), and Helen (d 1999); *b* 4 November 1953; *Educ* Rhyl HS; *m* 1973, Adrian Jones; 1 da (Victoria b 1975), 1 s (Vincent b 1981); *Career* official Fire Brigades' Union Nat 1982–99, memb North Wales Fire Authy 1995–99; agent Lab Pty 1983–99, memb Nat Assembly for Wales (Lab) Vale of Clwyd 1999–; Rhyl: town cncllr 1991–99, mayor 1996–97; Denbighshire co cncllr 1995–99, local co-ordinator Jubilee 2000; *Style*— Ms Ann Jones, AM; ✉ National Assembly for Wales, Cardiff Bay, Cardiff CF99 1NA (☎ 029 2082 5111, e-mail ann.jones@wales.gov.uk); 25 Kinmel Street, Rhyl LL18 4AG (☎ 01745 332813, fax 01745 369038)

JONES, Prof Anne; da of Sydney Joseph Pickard (d 1987), and Hilda Everitt, *née* Bird (d 1999); *b* 8 April 1935; *Educ* Harrow Weald Co Sch, Westfield Coll London (BA), King's Coll London (PGCE), Univ of London (DipSoc); *m* 9 Aug 1958 (m dis 1988), Cyril Gareth Jones, s of Lyell Jones (d 1936); 1 s (Christopher Lyell b 24 July 1962), 2 da (Catherine Rachel (Mrs Spencer) b 8 Aug 1963 d 2015, Rebecca Madryn b 15 March 1966); *Career* asst mistress: Malvern Girls Coll 1957–58, Godolphin & Latymer Sch 1958–62, Dulwich Coll 1964; sch cnsllr Mayfield London 1965–71, dep head Thomas Calton Sch London 1971–74; head: Vauxhall Manor Sch 1974–81, Cranford Community Coll 1981–87; under sec (dir of educn) Employment Dept 1987–91, visiting prof of educn Univ of Sheffield, educn and training conslt 1991–; Brunel Univ: prof of continuing educn 1991–, dir Centre for Lifelong Learning 1995–2000, prof emeritus 2001–; ceo and dir Lifelong Learning Systems Ltd (LLS) 2001–09; advsr: European Trg Fndn, OECD, Br Cncl; dir: West London Leadership 1995–99, Business Link London NW 1995–99; chair: Assoc of Child Psychology and Psychiatry 1979–80, Area Manpower Bd for London South and West 1983–87; ind lay chair Complaints NHS 1996–2005; conslt EDGE 2005–07; former memb: Schools' Broadcasting Cncl, Home Office Advsy Ctees on Drugs and on Sexual Offences; former memb Cncl: UCL, CRAC, NICEC, Grubb Inst, W London Inst of HE, RSA; tstee: The Westfield Tst 1992–2005, Menerva Educnl Tst 1993–2004 (chair 1993–99); govr The Abbey Sch 2004–12; chm: Henley Choral Soc 2005–09, Boathouse Reach Mgmnt 2005–10; hon memb City and Guilds Inst; Hon FCP 1990; fell Queen Mary & Westfield Coll London 1992 (memb Cncl 1992–2002), FRSA (former memb Cncl 1992–2002), FCMI (chm Reading Branch 2004–08); *Books* Counselling Adolescents: School and After (1986), Leadership for Tomorrow's Schools (1987), The Education Roundabout (2015); *Recreations* walking, gardening, boating; *Clubs* Phyllis Court (Henley-on-Thames, dir 2009–15), Probus (chm); *Style*— Prof Anne Jones; ✉ 8 Boathouse Reach, Henley-on-Thames RG9 1TJ (☎ 01491 578672)

JONES, Arfon; *b* 21 April 1943; *Educ* Bristol GS, Clare Coll Cambridge (MA); *m* 27 Sept 1970, Janet Myra Hoskins Lloyd; 2 s (Rupert b 8 April 1971, Oliver b 18 April 1976), 1 da (Victoria b 28 Nov 1972); *Career* admitted slr 1968; sr corp ptnr CMS Cameron McKenna (formerly Cameron Markby Hewitt) (ptnr 1970–); non-exec dir Camford Engineering plc 1976–86; chm of govrs Rokeby Sch 1996–; memb: Law Soc 1968, City of London Slrs' Co; *Recreations* golf, skiing, hockey; *Clubs* Royal Wimbledon Golf; *Style*— Arfon Jones, Esq; ✉ CMS Cameron McKenna, Mitre House, 160 Aldersgate, London EC1A 4DD (☎ 020 7367 3000, fax 020 7367 2000, e-mail arfon.jones@cmck.com)

JONES, Prof (Norman) Barrie; s of Leslie Robert Jones, of Bebington, Merseyside, and Edith, *née* Morris; *b* 3 January 1941; *Educ* Liverpool Inst, Univ of Manchester (BSc), McMaster Univ (MEng), Univ of Sussex (DPhil); *m* 13 July 1963, Sandra Mary, da of George Albert Potts (d 1976), of Liverpool; 1 da (Victoria Mary b 21 Oct 1965), 1 s (Geoffrey Stephen b 7 May 1968); *Career* Univ of Sussex: lectr 1968–73, reader 1973–84, dir Centre for Med Res 1982–84; Univ of Leicester: prof of engrg 1985–, head Dept of Engrg 1988–95; recorder Med Sciences Section Br Assoc; CEng 1978, FIEE 1984; *Style*— Prof N Barrie Jones; ✉ Department of Engineering, The University, Leicester LE1 7RH (☎ 0116 223 1300, telex 347250, fax 0116 252 2619)

JONES, Prof Barry Edward; s of Frederick Edward Jones (d 1994), of Winchcombe, Glos, and Margaret Alice, *née* Redwood (d 1975); *b* 11 March 1940, Bristol; *Educ* Cheltenham GS, N Gloucestershire Tech Coll, Univ of Manchester (BSc, MSc, PhD, DSc); *m* 7 Dec 1963, Julie, da of William Pritchard (d 1993), of Torquay, Devon; 2 da (Ruth Gillian Sarah b 1966, Jennifer Claire b 1969); *Career* scientific asst Govt Communications Headquarters Cheltenham 1956–60, lectr in electrical engrg Univ of Manchester 1964–81, pt/t tutor Faculty of Technol Open Univ 1972–84, sr lectr Dept of Instrumentation and Analytical Sci UMIST 1981–86; Brunel Univ: dir The Brunel Centre for Mfrg Metrology (BCMM) 1986–2006, Hewlett Packard prof of mfrg metrology 1986–91, prof of mfrg metrology 1991–2003 (now emeritus); chm: IEE Professional Gp on Fundamental Aspects of Measurement 1980–81, IEE Professional Network Measurement, Sensors, Instrumentation and NDT 2001–04; vice-chm IEE Science Educn and Technol Div 1998–2000; dir: Advanced Acoustic Emission Systems Ltd 2003–07, Forcesensys Ltd 2005–11, AMAKA Beautiful Child Ltd 2006–07, Brunel Systems Ltd 2007–13; hon ed Jl of Physics E Sci Inst 1983–87, sensors series sr ed: Inst of Physics Publishing 1987–2005, CRC Press Taylor and Francis Gp 2005–; assoc ed Jl of Measurement and Control 2000–10; chm Awards and Prizes Ctee IET 2008–10; memb: CNAA 1983–85, DTI Measurement Advsy Ctee Working Parties 1992–2006, Cncl IEE 2004–06, Knowledge Services Bd IEE 2004–07, UK Sensors Forum Steering Bd, Lecture Ctee IET 2007–11, Knowledge Mgmnt Bd IET 2009–10; vice-pres and tstee IET 2010–13; Metrology award for World Class Manufacturing 1995; Dr (hc) Technical Univ of Sofia 2001; CEng 1970, FInstMC 1979, FInstP 1982, FIEE 1984, CPhys 1986, fell SPIE 1992, EurIng 1992, FRSA 1992; Methodist local preacher 1965–; *Books* Instrumentation, Measurement and Feedback (1977), Instrument Science and Technology (ed and contrib vol 1 1982, vol 2 1983, vol 3 1985), Current Advances in Sensors (ed and contrib, 1987); *Recreations* music, gardening; *Style*— Prof Barry E Jones; ✉ Stancombe House, 38 Moorlands Road, Great Malvern, Worcestershire WR14 2UA (☎ and fax 01684 893005, e-mail barryedwardjones@hotmail.com, website www.http://bedwardjones.com)

JONES, Baron (Life Peer UK 2001), of Deeside in the County of Clwyd; (Stephen) Barry Jones; PC (1999); s of Stephen Jones (d 1988), and Grace Jones (d 1944); *b* 1937; *m* Janet, da of F W Davies; 1 s (Hon Stephen); *Career* head Eng Dept Deeside Secdy Sch, regnl offr NUT, Parly candidate (Lab) Northwich Cheshire 1966; MP (Lab): Flint East 1970–83, Alyn and Deeside 1983–2001; PPS to the Rt Hon Denis Healey 1972–74, Parly Under Sec of State for Wales 1974–79, Oppn spokesman on employment 1980–83, chief Oppn spokesman on Wales 1983–92, memb Lab Shadow Cabinet 1983–87 and 1988–92; chm Political Parties Ctee 1999–2001; chm Welsh Grand Ctee; memb Intelligence and Security Ctee 1993–97 and 1997–2001; formerly memb Welsh Exec Ctee WEU and Cncl of Europe; memb Speaker's Panel of Chairmen, dep speaker Westminster Hall 2000–01; chm Diocesan Bd of Educn St Asaph; pres: Deeside Hosp 2001–, Dementia Champion Wales Flintshire Alzheimers Soc 2001–, Wrexham-Birkenhead Rail Users Assoc 2005, Chester and E Clwyd Advanced Motorists 2007, Neighbourhood Watch Flintshire 2008–, Flintshire Arthritis Care 2011, Welsh Assoc of ME and CFS Support (Wales Neurological Alliance) 2011, Deeside Industrial Park Forum 2012, Army Cadet Forces Wales 2013; pres NE Wales Inst of HE 2007, currently chllr Glynd?r Univ; govr: Nat Library of Wales, Nat Museum of Wales; life memb Royal Liverpool Philharmonic Soc, memb Bd Clwyd Theatre Cymru 2011; hon fell Gladstone's Library Flintshire, hon fell Bangor Univ 2012; fell Industry and Parliament Tst; friend: Royal Acad of Arts, Tate Gallery, Merseyside Museums & Galleries; tstee Bodelwyddan Castle Tst 2011; *Style*— The Rt Hon the Lord Jones

JONES, Barry Malcolm; s of Albert George Jones (d 1980), and Margaret Eileen, *née* Clark; *b* 4 April 1951; *Educ* Battersea GS, Charing Cross Hosp Med Sch Univ of London (MS, MB BS, LRCP); *m* 12 May 1973, Janine Diane, da of Laurence Henry Gilbey, of London; 1 s (Huw b 1984), 1 da (Georgina b 1986); *Career* sr registrar in plastic surgery Mount Vernon Hosp 1982–85, fell in craniofacial surgery Hôpital des Enfants Malades Paris 1985, currently conslt plastic and cranio-facial surgn The Hosp for Sick Children Gt Ormond St London; Hunterian prof RCS; memb: Br Assoc Plastic Surgns, Br Assoc Aesthetic Plastic Surgns (pres 1999–2001), Int Soc of Aesthetic Plastic Surgns, Int Soc of Craniomaxillofacial Surgns, Euro Craniofacial Soc, Euro Assoc Plastic Surgns, Craniofacial Soc of GB, Int Microsurgical Soc; Freeman: City of London 1982, Worshipful Soc of Apothecaries; FRCS; *Publications* Facial Rejuvenation Surgery (with DVD, 2007); *Recreations* exercise, golf, classical and contemporary guitar, literature, culinary arts, oenology; *Clubs* RAC, Moor Park Golf; *Style*— Barry M Jones, Esq; ✉ 14A Upper Wimpole Street, London W1G 6LR (e-mail bmj@barrymjones.co.uk)

JONES, Carey Frederick; s of Clifford William Jones (d 1990), of Bonvilston, S Glam, and Mary Gwendoline, *née* Thomas; *Educ* Llandovery Coll Univ of Wales Aberystwyth (BSc), Selwyn Coll Cambridge (MA); *m* 2 Dec 1979, Bernadette Marie, da of Anthony Fulgoni; 1 s (Alexander Anthony b 10 Feb 1985), 1 da (Mariclare Dominique b 2 July 1981); *Career* graduate surveyor MAFF 1975–79, surveyor Mid Glam CC 1979–80, sr surveyor Cardiff City Cncl 1980–82 (surveyor 1980–81), sole princ Crown & Co Chartered Surveyors 1982; chief exec Royal Life Estates West 1988–92, dir and gen mangr Crown and Company Estate Agents 1993–94, md Knights Chartered Surveyors 1994–; company sec Cardiff Aviation Ltd, dir Cardiff Aviation Training Ltd; FRICS 1991 (ARICS 1979); *Recreations* equine pursuits, classic cars; *Clubs* Pitt, Cardiff and County; *Style*— Carey Jones, Esq

JONES, Carwyn Howell; AM; s of Caron Wyn Jones, and Katherine Janice, *née* Howells, of Bridgend; *b* 21 March 1967; *Educ* Brynteg Comp Bridgend, Univ of Aberystwyth (LLB), Inns of Court Sch of Law (Judge Fricker Prize, Ede & Ravenscroft Prize); *m* 3 Dec 1994, Lisa Josephine, da of Edward Michael Murray, and Stella Therese; 1 da (Seren Hâf b 20 July 2000), 1 s (Ruairi Wyn b 18 Sept 2002); *Career* barrister; professional tutor Centre for Professional Legal Studies Cardiff 1997–99; cncllr (Lab) Bridgend Co BC 1995–2000, chair Bridgend County Borough Lab Gp 1998–99; memb Nat Assembly for Wales (Lab) Bridgend 1999–, min for Rural Affairs 2000–02, min for Open Govt 2002–03, min for Environment, Planning and the Countryside 2003–07, counsel gen and ldr of the House 2007–; memb: Amnesty Int, Fabian Soc; *Recreations* sport, travel, reading; *Clubs* Brynaman Rugby, Musselburgh Rugby, Bridgend Rugby; *Style*— Mr Carwyn Jones, AM; ✉ Constituency Office, 36 Caroline Street, Bridgend CF31 1DQ (☎ 01656 664320, e-mail carwyn.jones@wales.gov.uk)

JONES, Charlotte Elizabeth; da of Lindsey William Jones, of Worcester, and Carol, *née* O'Keefe; *b* 6 February 1968; *Educ* St Mary's Convent Worcester, Balliol Coll Oxford (BA); *m* 11 July 1998, Paul Bazely, s of Maurice Bazely, of Madras, India; 1 s (Daniel Sean b 22 July 2002), 1 da (Molly Gwendoline b 13 Feb 2005); *Career* playwright; stage plays: Airswimming (Battersea Arts Centre) 1998 (also broadcast on BBC Radio 4), In Flame (Bush Theatre, New Ambassador's Theatre) 1999–2000, Martha, Josie and the Chinese Elvis (Octagon Theatre Bolton, Everyman Theatre Liverpool and Palace Theatre Watford) 1999–2001 (Pearson TV Best New Play Award 1998, Best New Play Award Manchester Evening News 1999), Humble Boy (RNT, Gielgud Theatre, Manhattan Theatre Club NY) 2001–02 (Susan Smith Blackburn Award 2000, Critic's Circle Award for Best New Play 2001), The Dark (Donmar Warehouse), The Woman in White (book, Palace Theatre London and Marquis Theatre NY) 2005, The Lightning Play (Almeida Theatre) 2006; screenwriting for TV: Bessie and the Bell (Carlton) 2000, Mother's Ruin (Carlton) 2001, Without You (ITV) 2012; radio plays for BBC Radio 4: Mary Something Takes the Veil, Future Perfect, A Seer of Sorts, Sea Symphony for Piano and Child, Blue Air Love and Flowers, Pride and Prejudice, An American Rose 2013, What Would Elizabeth Bennett Do? 2014, The Henry Experiment 2015; writer Dogstar (film) 2000; Critics' Circle Most Promising Playwright Award 1999; *Style*— Ms Charlotte Jones; ✉ c/o St John Donald, United Agents Limited, 12–26 Lexington Street, London W1F 0LE (☎ 020 3214 0800, fax 020 3214 0801, website www.unitedagents.co.uk)

JONES, Chris; s of Phillip Jones, and Barbara Jones; *b* 15 July 1965, Woodley, Berks; *m* Judi, *née* Dixon; 1 s, 1 da; *Career* Reed Business Publishing and Emap plc 1986–96, gp dir FT Electronic Publishing 1997–99, sr vice-pres Lexis Nexis Gp 2000–01, ceo Lexis Nexis Risk Mgmnt Gp 2001–04, ceo Harcourt Educn Int Reed Elsevier 2004–08, DG City & Guilds 2008–; govr Activate Learning, memb Employment and Skills Leadership Team Business in the Community 2012–; *Clubs* Tallow Chandlers' Co; *Style*— Chris Jones, Esq; ✉ City & Guilds, 1 Giltspur Street, London EC1A 9DD (☎ 020 7294 2569, e-mail chris.jones@cityandguilds.com)

JONES, Christopher Kenneth; s of William Henry Jones (d 1942), and Dorothy Irene, *née* Tonge (d 1990); *b* 22 March 1939, Watford, Herts; *Educ* Sir Roger Manwood's GS Sandwich, Univ of Southampton Sch of Navigation; *m* 29 June 1963, (Moira) Jane, da of Gp Capt David Fowler McIntyre, AFC (d 1957), of Troon, Ayrshire; 2 s (Mark b 1964, Neil b 1965), 1 da (Amanda b 1967); *Career* third offr Union-Castle Mail SS Co Ltd 1957–62, merchandise dir Peter Robinson/Top Shop Ltd 1964–72, dep md Richard Shops Ltd 1972–76, md Bally London Shoe Co Ltd 1976–80, chief exec Lillywhites Ltd 1980–84, md retail activities Seaco Inc 1984–86, sr ptnr Sunningdale Marketing Management 1986–2008, dir Orebus Ltd 2000–03, dir Sport Retail Management Ltd 1993–2001; parish cncllr Grayshott; Freeman City of London; FRSA 1974; *Recreations* golf, travel, keep fit; *Clubs* Hindhead Golf, Grayshott Spa; *Style*— Christopher Jones, Esq; ✉ 2 The Brae, Glen Road, Grayshott, Hampshire GU26 6NF (e-mail chrisjones234@hotmail.com)

JONES, Christopher William; s of John Clayton Jones, and Ann, *née* Emsley; *b* 23 February 1953; *Educ* Fulneck Sch for Boys Pudsey, Univ of Nottingham, Chester Coll of Law (LLB); *m* 1975 (m dis), Caroline; 2 s (Oliver b 1980, Max b 2002), 1 da (Ava b 2007); *Career* admitted slr 1977; licensed insolvency practitioner; Sampson Wade & Co 1975–84 (slr and latterly ptnr), Hammond Suddards 1984–2006 (latterly managing ptnr),

J

managing ptnr Tourmalet Consulting 2005–; chm Clarity Credit Mgmnt Solutions Ltd 2004–06, chair Business Desk Ltd 2009–, chair Illius Properties Ltd; dir: Britannia Building Soc 2003–09, Agenda Mgmnt Servs Ltd 2003–, Co-operative Bank plc 2009–, CIS Insurance Ltd 2009–, Armitage Jones LLP and LPA Direct LLP 2009–; memb: Soc for Practitioners of Insolvency, Inst of Credit Mgmnt, Insolvency Lawyers Assoc, Insolvency Practitioners Assoc; fell Inst of Continuing Professional Devpt, FRSA, fell R3; *Recreations* family, football, cycling, wine, cars, rock music; *Clubs* Ilkley Rugby; *Style—* Christopher Jones, Esq

JONES, Clive William; CBE (2007); s of Kenneth David Llewellyn Jones, of Pontllanfraith, Gwent, S Wales, and Joan Muriel, *née* Withers; *b* 10 January 1949, Llanfrechfa, S Wales; *Educ* Newbridge GS, LSE (BSc Econ); *m* 1, 1971 (m dis 1987), Frances Jones; 2 s (Paul Dafydd b 24 Oct 1973, Samuel Alun b 7 Sept 1975), 1 da (Angharad Elizabeth Louisa b 7 May 1979); m 2, 12 Nov 1988 (m dis 2000), Fern Mary Philomena Britton, *qv*, da of Tony Britton, the actor, of London; 2 s (Harry, Jack (twins) b 14 Dec 1993), 1 da (Grace Alice Bluebell b 27 April 1997); m 3, 2004, Vikki Heywood, CBE, *qv*; *Career* journalist Yorkshire Post Group 1970–73, news ed and asst ed Morning Telegraph 1973–78, prodr Yorkshire TV 1978–82, managing ed then ed TV-am 1982–84; Television South: joined 1984, dep md and dir of regnl progs and dir TVS Entertainment Ltd and TVS Television Ltd until 1992; md London News Network 1992–94 (dir LNN Ltd 1992–), md Central Independent Television 1994–95 (dir 1994–2004), md Carlton UK Broadcasting (following t/o of Central by Carlton) 1995, chief exec Carlton Television 1996–2004 (dir 1994–2004), jt md ITV 2002–04, chief exec ITV News Gp 2004–07; chm: GMTV 2005–10, Energetic Communications NY 2007–, Mediabox 2007–11, Netplay TV 2009–14, Procam 2014–; dep chm ITV Pension Fund 2013–; chm: Skillset 2002–11, London Met Univ 2010–, Runnymede Tst 2010–, Disasters Emergency Ctee 2011–; dir: Young Vic 2005–, S4C Masnachol 2007–14, S4C 2007–14; tstee Thomson Fndn 2013–; FRSA, FRTS; *Recreations* books, films, rugby; *Clubs* Reform; *Style—* Clive Jones, Esq, CBE

JONES, Prof David Emrys Jeffreys; *b* 4 September 1963; *Educ* Bradford GS, Jesus Coll Oxford (BA, Jesus Coll Prize (twice)), Green Coll Oxford (BM BCh, Oxford Graduates' Med Club Essay Prize, George Pickering Prize), Univ of Newcastle upon Tyne (PhD); *Career* house surgn then house physician Freeman Hosp Newcastle upon Tyne 1988–89; SHO: Newcastle Gen Hosp 1989–90, Royal Victoria Infirmary Newcastle upon Tyne 1990 and 1991, Freeman Hosp Newcastle upon Tyne 1990–91; MRC trg fell Med Molecular Biology Gp Dept of Med Univ of Newcastle upon Tyne and hon registrar Liver Unit Freeman Hosp Newcastle upon Tyne 1991–94, registrar in gastroenterology Regnl Liver Unit Freeman Hosp Newcastle upon Tyne 1994, registrar in gen med and gastroenterology N Tyneside Gen Hosp 1995–96 (sr registrar 1996); Centre for Liver Research Univ of Newcastle upon Tyne: MRC clinician scientist 1996–99, hon lectr 1996–99, hon sr lectr 1999, sr lectr in hepatology 1999–2003; hon conslt hepatologist Freeman Hosp Newcastle upon Tyne 1999–; Univ of Newcastle upon Tyne: prof of liver immunology 2003–, postgrad tutor Sch of Clinical Med Sciences, memb Jt Research Exec Scientific Ctee, memb Sch Research Ctee, memb Sch Grad Ctee; sec NE Immunology Club, govr Liver North (memb Scientific Ctee); memb: Med Ctee Primary Biliary Cirrhosis (PBC) Fndn, Steering Ctee Euro-PBC Trial Gp, Refereeing Panel European Assoc for the Study of the Liver (EASL) Annual Meeting, Cncl Br Soc of Immunologists; memb Editorial Bd Jl of Hepatology; faculty lectureships: Netherlands Gastroenterological Assoc 2002, American Gastroenterological Assoc 2002 and 2003, Br Assoc for the Study of the Liver 2002, Falk Liver Week 2003; Mayo Fndn Travel Award 1994, Soc for Mucosal Immunology Travel Award 1995, finalist Med Research Soc Young Investigator Award 1996, Br Assoc for Study of the Liver Travel Award 1998, Br Assoc for the Study of the Liver Young Investigator Award 2001, RCP Goulstonian Lectureship 2002; memb Assoc of Physicians of GB and I; FRCP 2001 (MRCP 1991); *Publications* author of numerous book chapters, articles and peer-reviewed editorials; *Recreations* scuba diving, skiing, classic cars, Art Deco and Art Nouveau glassware and ceramics; *Style—* Prof David E J Jones; ✉ Centre for Liver Research, 4th Floor William Leach Building, The Medical School, Framlington Place, Newcastle upon Tyne NE2 4HH (☎ 0191 222 5784, fax 0191 222 0723, e-mail d.e.j.jones@ncl.ac.uk)

JONES, Rt Hon David Ian; PC (2012), MP; s of Brynley Jones, and Elspeth Savage Jones (*née* Williams); *b* 22 March 1952, London; *Educ* Ruabon GS, UCL; *m* Sara; 2 s; *Career* sr ptnr David Jones & Co 1985–2005; memb Nat Assembly for Wales 2002–03, MP (Cons) Clwyd W 2005– (Parly candidate (Cons): Conwy 1997, City of Chester 2001); parly under-sec of state for Wales 2010–12, sec of state for Wales 2012–14; memb Law Soc 1976; *Recreations* walking, travel, motoring; *Clubs* Carlton; *Style—* The Rt Hon David Jones, MP; ✉ House of Commons, London SW1A 0AA

JONES, Dr David Martin; s of John Trevor Jones (d 1971), and Mair Carno Jones (d 1962); *b* 14 August 1944, Prestbury, Cheshire; *Educ* Univ of London (BSc, BVetMed); *m* Janet Marian, *née* Woosley; 3 s (Mark Owen b 1976, Simon Wyn b 1978, Thomas Carno b 1980); *Career* The Zoological Soc of London: vet offr Whipsnade Park Zoo 1969–75, sr vet offr and head Dept of Vet Science 1975–84, asst dir of zoos 1981–84, dir of zoos 1984–91, gen dir 1991–92, dir Conservation & Consultancy 1992–94; dir North Carolina Zoological Park 1994–2015, ret (currently dir emeritus); overseas conslt, fund-raiser, author of scientific papers and articles; chm Bd: Central Park NC, Environmental Defense Fund NC, Brooke USA, Wild Welfare; MRCVS, CBiol, FRSB; *Recreations* travel, photography, gardening, hand coloured prints; *Style—* Dr David Jones; ✉ North Carolina Zoological Park, 4401 Zoo Parkway, Asheboro, NC 27205, USA (☎ 00 1 336 879 7100, website www.nczoo.org)

JONES, David Morris; s of Capt Morris Jones, MN (ka 1941), of Beaumaris, Anglesey, and Menna Lloyd, *née* Evans; *b* 24 March 1940; *Educ* Beaumaris GS, Univ Coll Bangor (BA, DipEd); *m* 3 Dec 1971, Patricia Jones; 2 da (Sian b 24 Nov 1976, Eira b 17 Feb 1980); *Career* journalist Liverpool Daily Post and Echo Ltd 1962–63; BBC News: journalist 1963–64, sr news asst 1964–67, chief news asst 1967–71, TV news prodr 1971–82, managing ed news and current affrs Wales 1982–85, head of news and current affrs BBC Wales 1985–89; controller of news and current affrs ITV South and South East 1989–92, head of prog devpt HTV plc 1994–96, currently md Merlin Broadcast Ltd, NewsNet UK Ltd; ed Wales Today (BBC); prodr and writer: Flight Deck (Discovery Channel), Friday Live with Eamonn Holmes (ITV), Friday Live with Simon Biagi (ITV), People (ITV), Trysorau (S4C), Seeing is Becoming (BBC), The Kane Programme (BBC), Business Week (BBC), Cutting Edge (BBC), Night Doctor (BBC), Air Beat (BBC), Enforcers (Channel Five); *Recreations* sailing, setting up local TV stations; *Clubs* English Speaking Union Dartmouth House; *Style—* David Morris Jones, Esq; ✉ 21 Uppercliff Close, Penarth, South Glamorgan CF64 1BE (☎ 029 2070 7018); Newsnet UK Ltd, Aquaplan House, Burt Street, Cardiff Bay CF10 5FZ (☎ 02920 488500, fax 02920 250703, e-mail dmj@newsnet.co.uk)

JONES, Della Louise Gething; da of Cyril Vincent Jones (d 1982), and Eileen Gething Jones; *Educ* Neath Girls' GS, Royal Coll of Music (LRAM, ARCM, GRSM); *m* 2 April 1988, Paul Anthony Hooper Vigars, s of Norman Vigars; 1 s (Raphael b 1989); *Career* mezzo-soprano; soloist ENO 1977–82, sung with all maj Br opera cos and at opera houses and concert halls throughout Europe, USA, USSR and Japan (specializing in Rossini, Handel and Mozart); Dido in Les Troyens (WNO) 1987, Ramiro in Finta Giardiniera and Cecilio in Lucio Silla (Mostly Mozart Festival NY), Sorceress in Dido and Aeneas (Buckingham Palace tercentenary celebration of William and Mary) 1988, Rosina in Il Barbier di Siviglia (Covent Garden) 1990, Handel's Riccardo Primo (in Cyprus and Covent Garden, to celebrate 800th anniversary of Richard I's arrival in Cyprus) 1991, Sesto in Mozart's La Clemenza de Tito (with Acad of Ancient Music, Japan) 1991; Laurence Olivier Award nomination for Rosina in The Barber of Seville ENO 1988; extensive recordings (incl Recital of Rossini arias 1990, and Spanish and French songs), frequent radio and TV broadcasts incl soloist Last Night of the Proms 1993 and Hong Kong Handover Celebrations; hon fell Welsh Coll of Music and Drama 1995, hon fell Univ of Wales Swansea 1999; *Recreations* collecting elephants, visiting Venice for Bellini, writing cadenzas, animal welfare, reading, writing; *Style—* Miss Della Jones; ✉ c/o Music International, 13 Ardilaun Road, Highbury, London N5 2QR (☎ 020 7359 5183)

JONES, Denis Raymond; s of Joseph David Jones (d 1981), of Marton, Cleveland, and Gladys Margaret, *née* Lennox; *b* 24 September 1950; *Educ* Eston Co Modern Sch; *m* 15 June 1990, Linda, da of Czeslaw Dworowski; 1 s (Samuel Joseph b 6 Feb 1989); *Career* press photographer; trainee marine engr 1966–70, maintenance engr London Zoo 1970–72, photographer Fleet St News Agency 1972–74, freelance photographer (Daily Express, Evening News, Sun) 1974–76; staff photographer: Evening News (mainly fashion assignments) 1976–80, Evening Standard 1985– (freelance 1980–85); *Recreations* video photography, collecting nostalgia, mountain trekking, country walks; *Clubs* Marylebone Rifle and Pistol; *Style—* Denis Jones, Esq; ✉ Evening Standard, Northcliffe House, 2 Derry Street, London W8 5EE (☎ 020 7938 7562 mobile 078 3624 1158)

JONES, Sir Derek William; KCB (2014, CB 2009); s of William Jones, and Patricia Mary, *née* Gill; *b* 8 December 1952; *Educ* Univ Coll Wales Cardiff (BA); *m* 1976, Fiona Christine Anne Laidlaw; 2 s; *Career* worked on regnl policy, company law and privatisation DTI 1977–82; HM Treasury: Public Expenditure Control 1982–84, head Financial Instns and Markets 1984–87; head Japan Desk and Overseas Trade Policy Div DTI 1987–89; Welsh Office: asst sec 1989, head Industrial Policy Div 1989–92; Finance Progs Div: head 1992–94, under sec 1994; dep sec dir of econ affrs 1999, sr dir Policy 2003; dir of business and strategic partnerships Univ of Cardiff 2008–12, permanent sec Welsh Govt 2012–; *Recreations* surfing, keeping fit, reading, blues guitar; *Clubs* Reform; *Style—* Sir Derek Jones, KCB; ✉ Welsh Government, Cathays Park, Cardiff CF10 3NQ (☎ 029 2082 3289)

JONES, Dylan; OBE (2013); s of Michael John Jones, and Audrey Joyce, *née* Wilshire; *Educ* Chelsea Sch of Art, St Martins Sch of Art; *Career* journalist; ed i-D 1984, contrib ed The Face 1987, ed Arena 1988, associate ed The Observer Magazine 1992, associate ed The Sunday Times Magazine 1993, gp ed The Face, Arena, Arena Homme Plus 1996, ed-at-large The Sunday Times 1997, ed GQ 1999–; *Books* Dark Star (1990), True Brit (1995), Meaty, Beaty, Big & Bouncy (1996), Sex, Power & Travel (1996), iPod, Therefore I Am (2004), Mr Jones' Rules (2006), Cameron on Cameron (2008); *Clubs* Groucho, George, Chelsea Arts; *Style—* Dylan Jones, Esq, OBE; ✉ GQ Magazine, Vogue House, Hanover Square, London W1S 1JU (☎ 020 7499 9080, e-mail dylan.jones@condenast.co.uk)

JONES, Eddie; *Career* rugby union coach and former player; played for: Randwick, New South Wales 1987–89; career as coach: Randwick 1994, Tokai Univ 1995–96, Japan (asst coach) 1996, Suntory Sungoliath 1997, Brumbies 1998–2001, Aust 2001–05, Saracens (conslt coach) 2006, Reds 2007, South Africa (asst coach) 2007, Saracens 2007–09, Suntory Sungoliath 2009–12, Japan 2012–15, England 2015–; *Style—* Mr Eddie Jones

JONES, Edward Bartley; QC (1997); s of Meurig Bartley Jones, of Yarnton, nr Oxford, and Ruby, *née* Morris; *b* 24 December 1952; *Educ* Cardiff HS, Balliol Coll Oxford (BA); *Career* called to the Bar Lincoln's Inn 1975, in practice Chancery and Commercial Bar in Liverpool 1976–, head Commercial Dept Exchange Chambers Liverpool 1994–, asst recorder 1997–; memb: Northern Circuit Commercial Bar Assoc, Chancery Bar Assoc, Northern Chancery Bar Assoc; pt/t lectr Univ of Liverpool 1977–81; *Recreations* opera, skiing, horses, golf; *Clubs* Oxford and Cambridge, Portal; *Style—* Edward Bartley Jones, Esq, QC; ✉ Exchange Chambers, 1st Floor, Pearl Assurance House, Derby Square, Liverpool L2 9XX (☎ 0151 236 7747, fax 0151 236 3433)

JONES, Prof Edward David Brynmor; CBE (2011); s of David Jones, and Margot, *née* Derricourt; *b* 20 October 1939; *Educ* Haileybury, AA Sch of Architecture (AADip); *m* 1 (m dis); 1 s, 2 da; m 2, Margot, *née* Griffin; 1 s, 2 da; *Career* architect; princ in private practice 1973–89, in partnership with Jeremy Dixon 1989–2003, Dixon Jones Ltd 2003–; cmmns incl: Royal Opera House 1983–99, Henry Moore Fndn Perry Green 1989–, Henry Moore Inst Leeds 1989–93, Darwin Coll Cambridge 1989–93, Robert Gordon Univ Aberdeen 1991–93, superstore for J Sainsbury plc Plymouth, Univ of Portsmouth 1993, housing New Delhi, Nat Portrait Gallery London 1994–2000, Saïd Business Sch Univ of Oxford 1996–2001, second phase Centre for Executive Educn 2007–12; master planners: Somerset House 1998–2001, Nat Gallery 1998–2006, Kensington and Chelsea Coll 2000–11, Chelsea apartments 2000–11, Magna Carta project Salisbury Cathedral 2001, Student Centre Queen's Univ Belfast 2001–, Panoptican building UCL 2001–, offices Kings Cross 2002, Portrait Gall of Canada 2003–, house in Provence 2003, Exhibition Road Project 2004, offices Regents Palace 2005, 5/6 St James's Square 2006, Chelsea Barracks 2009–; tutor AA, Poly of Central London and UC Dublin 1968–72, sr tutor RCA Sch of Environmental Design 1973–83, adjunct prof Univ of Toronto 1983–89 (visiting prof 1973–82); visiting prof: UC Dublin 1971–73, Cornell, Rice, Harvard, Yale, Princeton Univs USA and Syracuse (NY-based) Univ in Florence 1973–; RIBA external examiner: AA 1985, Kingston Univ, Univ of Portsmouth and Heriot-Watt Univ 1990–93, Univ of Wales 1994–97, Caribbean Sch of Arch 1997–2000, MacKintosh Sch Glasgow 2007–10; RIBA: memb President's Gold Medal Ctee 1993 and 1994, memb Stirling Prize Ctee 2003–08; memb jury for architectural competition: Laban Dance Centre Deptford 1998, Diana, Princess of Wales Meml Fountain London 2002, Barbara Hepworth Gallery Wakefield 2002, Parliamentary building Ottawa 2003, Univ Boulevard competition Univ of Br Columbia 2005, Victoria Embankment Competition 2005; chm Line of Site Competition 2009; vice-chair Quality Review Panel London Legacy Devpt Corp (LLDC) 2012–; memb Cncl AA 1993–99 (vice-pres 1995–97), memb Design Review Panel for 2012 Olympic Games 2006–; Hon DLitt Univ of Portsmouth 2001, hon fell Univ of Wales Cardiff 2001, hon prof Univ of Wales 2003; tstee Portsmouth Naval Base Property Tst 2005–08; fell RIAI 2011, RIBA, RAIC; *Awards* first prize: Northampton County Offices 1973, Mississauga City Hall Canada 1982 (Govr General's Award for Architecture 1988), Bus Station Venice 1990, Venice Biennale 1991; *Books* A Guide to the Architecture of London (with Christopher Woodward, 1983, 5 edn 2013), Jeremy Dixon and Edward Jones: Buildings and Projects 1959–2002; contrib to architectural jls; *Recreations* cooking, walking, drawing, looking out of the window, Staffordshire Bull Terriers; *Style—* Prof Edward Jones, CBE; ✉ Dixon Jones Ltd, 2–3 Hanover Yard, Noel Road, London N1 8YA (☎ 020 7483 8888, fax 020 7483 8899, e-mail edwardjones@dixonjones.co.uk)

JONES, Elin; AM; *Educ* Lampeter Comp Sch, Univ of Wales Cardiff (BSc), Univ of Wales Aberystwyth (MSc); *Career* devpt mangr Welsh Devpt Agency 1991–99; memb Nat Assembly for Wales (Plaid Cymru) Ceredigion 1999–, shadow agric min 1999–2002, shadow econ devpt min 2002–06, shadow environment min 2006–07, min for rural affrs 2007–11, shadow health min 2011–; memb Aberystwyth Town Cncl 1992–99, mayor of Aberystwyth 1997–98; dep ldr Plaid Cymru 2012– (chair 2000–02); *Style—* Ms Elin Jones, AM; ✉ National Assembly for Wales, Cardiff Bay, Cardiff CF99 1NA

JONES, Dr Emyr Wyn; s of Evan Walter Jones (d 2003), of Bodelen, Ffordd Caerdydd, Pwllheli, Gwynedd, and Buddug Morwenna Jones (d 2014); *b* 23 February 1950; *Educ* Pwllheli GS, Univ of Nottingham (DM), Univ of Liverpool (MB ChB); *m* 19 April 1974, Patricia Anne, da of Crowley Hammond (d 1989), of Walton-on-the-Naze, Essex; 3 da (Anne-Mair b 11 May 1976, Rhiannon Clare b 27 July 1978, Sioned Patricia b 17 March 1980), 1 s (Dafydd Benjamin b 28 Nov 1981); *Career* registrar in med Royal Liverpool

Hosp 1976–78, clinical res fell and hon sr registrar Dept of Med Univ Hosp Queen's Med Centre Nottingham 1979–86, conslt physician specialising in diabetes mellitus and endocrinology 1986–2010, clinical lead – nat implementation SCR Prog Health and Social Care Info Centre 2010–; secondary care doctor memb NHS Doncaster Clinical Commissioning Gp 2013–; clinical tutor Doncaster Postgrad Med Fedn (former), med dir Doncaster and Bassetlaw Hosps NHS Fndn Tst (former); chair UK Cncl Caldicott Guardians (former); former chair Bd and former tstee Br Assoc of Med Mangrs; author of papers on: platelets, thrombosis, diabetes; memb BMA; FRCP 1992 (MRCP 1978); *Publications* An Illustrated Guide for the Diabetic Clinic (1998); *Recreations* all sorts of music, ornithology; *Style—* Dr Emyr Jones; ✉ 16 St Eric's Road, Bessacarr, South Yorkshire DN4 6NG (☎ 01302 531059, e-mail emyr@winder-house.fsnet.co.uk); Summary Care Records Service, Health and Social Care Information Centre, 8th Floor, Bridgewater Place, Water Lane, Leeds LS11 5DR (☎ 0113 397 4338, e-mail emyrjones@hscic.gov.uk)

JONES, (David) Gareth; *m*; 1 s, 1 da; *Career* Abbey National plc: joined as asst gen mangr and treas 1989, dir of retail ops until 1993, exec dir and treas 1993–2001, also i/c Europe 1994–95, md Wholesale Banking 1996–2001; chm Paterson Enterprises Ltd; advsr Terra Firma Capital Ptnrs; non-exec dir Kensington Gp plc 2002–, non-exec dir and ptnr Prytania LLC 2005– ; formerly dir: Somerfield plc, TBI plc, Management Consulting Gp plc, Orbis Capital Ltd, Marley plc; former chm Assoc of Corporate Treasurers; memb: ESRC Centre for Business Research, Accountancy Review Bd; FCA, FCT; *Recreations* steam engines, model engineering, politics, opera, reading; *Clubs* RAC; *Style—* D Gareth Jones, Esq

JONES, Gary David; s of Charles William Jones (d 1997), and Myra Elizabeth, *née* Walton; *b* 14 August 1965; *Educ* Pensby Secdy Sch for Boys Wirral, Carlett Park Catering Coll Wirral, Oxford Coll of FE; *m* 8 Dec 1996, Caroline, da of Cdre John Burton Hall; 3 da (Holly Louise Isobel b 8 March 1999, Charlotte Annabel Lucy b 5 May 2001, Isobel Rose Clemmie b 15 March 2003); *Career* chef de partie saucier rising to jr sous chef Mountbatten Hotel Seven Dials 1986–88, chef de partie poissonier and saucier Waterside Inn 1988–90, sous chef Le Manoir aux Quat'Saisons 1990–93, resident exec chef to Richard Branson Necker Island Br Virgin Islands 1993–95, chef conslt Soneva Fushi Resort BAA ATOL Maldives 1995, head chef Homewood Park Hotel Hinton Charterhouse 1996–98 (four AA Rosettes 1997, first Michelin Star 1998, 7 out of 10 Good Food Guide 1998), head chef Cliveden House's Waldos Restaurant 1998–99 (four AA Rosettes 1998, 8 out of 10 Good Food Guide 1999, Michelin Star 1999), exec head chef Le Manoir aux Quat'Saisons 1999– (5 AA Rosettes 1999–, 2 Michelin Stars 2000–, 9 out of 10 Good Food Guide 2000–, RAC Guide Gold Ribbon and 4 Stars 1999, Zagat Guide Best Restaurant In and Around London 2000, 19 out of 20 Gault Millau and 4 Toques 2000, Readers' First Choice Restaurant Caterer and Hotelkeeper 2000, Best Restaurant in the UK with Rooms Tatler magazine 2000, placed 28th in Restaurant magazine's Best 50 Restaurants in the World 2005, Best Restaurant Good Housekeeping Food Award 2005, Condé Nast Traveller Best Food in Any UK Hotel 98% 2006, Condé Nast Traveller UK Gold List Best Hotel in World for Food 97.91% 2007, Condé Nast Traveller UK Best Food/Restaurant in the UK Hotel 97.5% 2008); *Recreations* scuba diving, water-skiing, karate; *Style—* Gary Jones, Esq; ✉ Le Manoir aux Quat'Saisons, Church Road, Great Milton, Oxfordshire OX44 7PD (☎ 01844 277205, fax 01844 278847, e-mail gary.jones@blanc.co.uk, website www.manoir.com)

JONES, George Quentin; s of John Clement Jones, CBE (d 2002), and Marjorie, *née* Gibson (d 1991); *b* 28 February 1945; *Educ* Highfield Sch Wolverhampton; *m* 1, April 1972 (m dis 1989), Diana, *née* Chittenden; 1 da (Jennifer Lucy b 2 Jan 1976), 1 s (Timothy Edward b 13 Jan 1979); m 2, 29 Dec 1990, Teresa Grace, da of John Lancelot Rolleston; *Career* trainee journalist Eastern Daily Press 1963–67, journalist South Wales Argus and Western Mail 1967–69, Reuters London 1969, Parly staff The Times 1969–73, Parly and political corr The Scotsman 1973–82; political corr: The Sunday Telegraph 1982–85, The Sunday Times 1985–86, The Daily Telegraph 1986–88; political ed The Daily Telegraph 1988–2007, multimedia political corr Press Assoc 2007–; regular broadcaster BBC and ind radio; chm Journalists Parly Lobby 1987–88, chm Parly Press Gallery 1996–97; *Style—* George Jones, Esq; ✉ The Press Association, 292 Vauxhall Bridge Road, London SW1V 1AE (☎ 0870 1203200, fax 0870 1203201)

JONES, Prof George William; OBE (1999); s of George William Jones (d 1973), of Wolverhampton, and Grace Annie, *née* Cowmeadow (d 1982); *b* 4 February 1938; *Educ* Wolverhampton GS, Jesus Coll Oxford (MA), Nuffield Coll Oxford (DPhil); *m* 14 Sept 1963, Diana Mary, da of Henry Charles Bedwell (d 1982), of Kidlington; 1 da (Rebecca b 1966), 1 s (Maxwell b 1969); *Career* lectr Univ of Leeds 1965–66 (asst lectr 1963–65); LSE: lectr 1966–71, sr lectr 1971–74, reader 1974–76, prof of govt 1976–2003 (emeritus prof 2003–), chm LSE Graduate Sch 1990–93, vice-chm Appts Ctee 1996–99, hon fell 2009–; Layfield Ctee on Local Govt Fin 1974–76, vice-chm Political Sci and Int Rels Ctee of SSRC 1978–81 (memb 1977–81); memb: Nat Consumer Cncl 1991–99, DOE Jt Working Pty on the Internal Mgmnt of Local Authorities in England 1992–93, DETR Beacon Cncls Advsy Panel 1999–2003, DETR Motorists Forum Consultation Working Gp 2000; hon fell Univ of Wolverhampton 1986; hon prof: Univ of Birmingham 2003–, Queen Mary Univ of London 2004–14; visiting research fell De Montfort Univ 2007–; hon memb: Soc of Local Authy Chief Execs (SOLACE) 2003–, Chartered Inst of Public Fin and Accountancy 2003–; assoc Centre for Public Service Partnerships 2010–12; FRHistS 1980, memb RIPA 1963 (memb Cncl 1984–90); *Books* Borough Politics (1969), Herbert Morrison (co-author, 1973 and 2001), Political Leadership in Local Authorities (jt ed, 1978), New Approaches to the Study of Central-Local Government Relationships (ed, 1980), The Case for Local Government (jt author, 1985), Between Centre and Locality (jt ed, 1985), West European Prime Ministers (ed, 1991), The Government of London (co-author, 1991), The Impact of Population Size on Local Authority Costs and Effectiveness (co-author, 1993), Local Government: The Management Agenda (1993), Joint Working Between Local Authorities (jt author, 1995), The Role of the Local Authority Chief Executive in Local Governance (jtly, 1996), The New Local Government Agenda (1997), At the Centre of Whitehall (jtly, 1998), Regulation Inside Government (jtly, 1999), The Future of Local Government: Has It One? (2008), Premiership (jtly, 2010), At Power's Elbow (jtly, 2013); *Recreations* cinema, eating, reading, dancing; *Clubs* National Film, Beefsteak; *Style—* Emeritus Prof G W Jones, OBE; ✉ Department of Government, London School of Economics and Political Science, Houghton Street, London WC2A 2AE (☎ 020 7955 7179, fax 020 7831 1707, e-mail g.w.jones@lse.ac.uk)

JONES, Geraint Martyn; s of Robert Kenneth Jones, of Luton, Beds, and Frances Elizabeth, *née* Mayo; *b* 15 July 1948, Luton; *Educ* St Albans Sch, Christ's Coll Cambridge (MA, LLM), Inns of Court Sch of Law; *m* 29 July 1978, Caroline Mary Jones (d 2012), da of Lt Peter Edwin Cecil Eyres, RNVR (d 1975); 1 s (Robert b 1980), 1 da (Louisa b 1982); *Career* called to the Bar Gray's Inn 1972; in practice (principally in commercial property, conveyancing, probate, trusts and charity law): London 1972–74, SE Circuit (mainly in Cambridge) 1974–; memb Chancery Bar Assoc, chm Rent Assessment Ctees 1985–2013, chm Leasehold Valuation Tribunals 1998–2013, chm Residential Property Tribunals 2007–13; judge First Tier Tribunal (Property Chamber) 2013–; mediator and dir Bellams Properties Ltd; Cambridge Bar Mess: chm 1999; memb SE Circuit Ctee 1991–94; asst cmmr Parly Boundary Cmmn 1992–95 and 2000–; chm Madingley Sch Tst 1988–91, chm of govrs Bourn Sch 1993–99; churchwarden Longstowe 2003–; memb: RYA, RNLI, Game Conservancy Tst, Nat Tst, BASC; Liveryman Worshipful Co of Glaziers 1992; *Recreations* sailing, shooting, jazz, carpentry, cooking; *Clubs* Grafham Water Sailing; *Style—* Geraint Jones, Esq; ✉ Fenners Chambers, 3 Madingley Road, Cambridge CB3 0EE (☎ 01223 368761, fax 01223 313007, e-mail geraint.jones@fennerschambers.co.uk or geraintmjones@hotmail.com)

JONES, Geraint Stanley; CBE (1993); s of Rev David Stanley Jones (d 1974); *b* 26 April 1936; *Educ* Pontypridd GS, UCNW Bangor (BA, DipEd); *m* 1961, Rhiannon, da of Emrys Williams (d 1971); 2 da (Sioned b 1965, Siwan b 1966); *Career* served RAEC, Sgt; BBC Wales: studio mangr 1960–62, TV prodn asst Current Affrs 1962–65, TV prodr Current Affrs 1965–69, prodr Features and Documentaries 1969–73, asst head of progs Wales 1973–74, head of progs Wales 1974–81, controller BBC Wales 1981–85, dir of public affrs 1986–87; md BBC Regnl Broadcasting 1987–89, chief exec S4C (Welsh Fourth Channel Authy) 1989–94; broadcasting conslt and prodr 1994–; visiting prof Int Acad of Broadcasting (IAB) Montreux; dir: WNO 1985–94, Wales Millennium Centre 1998–2005 (vice-pres 2008–); memb: Ct and Cncl UCW Aberystwyth 1990–96, Arts Cncl of Wales 1995–2000, BT Wales Forum 1995–2001, Ct Univ of Wales 1998–2000, Br Cncl Film and TV Advsy Ctee 1995–2002; chm: Ryan Davies Tst 1977–2008, Royal Welsh Coll of Music and Drama 1989–2000 (vice-pres 2000–), TV Prog Ctee Euro Broadcasting Union 1990–96, Nat Language Centre 1994–97, Sgrin Welsh Med Agency 1999–2004; pres Welsh Music Guild 2009–; vice-pres: Cardiff Business Club, Pendyrus Male Choir; memb UK Freedom from Hunger Ctee 1978–97; tstee: UNA Welsh Centre 1999–2005, Wales Video Gallery 2001–14, Pendyrus Tst 2001–08; Clwyd Theatr Cymru Devpt Tst 2004–; memb Bd Clwyd Theatr Cymru 2006–09; hon fell UCNW Bangor 1988, Hon LLD Univ of Wales 1998, Hon DLitt Univ of Glamorgan 1999; FRSA, FRTS, FRWCMD 2000; *Recreations* music and memories; *Clubs* Cardiff and County, Royal Over-Seas League; *Style—* Dr Geraint Stanley Jones, CBE

JONES, Gerald; MP; s of Colin Jones, and Patricia Irene, *née* Bevan, of New Tredegar, Caerphilly; *b* 21 August 1970, Caerphilly; *Educ* Bedwellty Comp Sch Monmouthshire, Ystrad Mynach Coll Caerphilly; *Partner* Tyrone Powell; *Career* worked in third sector and cncllr Caerphilly County BC 1995–2015, MP (Lab) Merthyr Tydfil & Rhymney 2015–; *Recreations* cinema, music, reading; *Style—* Gerald Jones, Esq, MP; ✉ House of Commons, London SW1A 0AA (e-mail gerald.jones.mp@parliament.uk, Twitter @GeraldJonesLab)

JONES, Rev Canon Glyndwr; s of Bertie Samuel Jones (d 1965), of Birchgrove, Swansea, and Elizabeth Ellen Jones (d 2001); *b* 25 November 1935; *Educ* Dynevor Sch Swansea, St Michael's Theol Coll Llandaff (DipTheol), Univ of Wales (MA); *m* 1, 13 Dec 1961, Cynthia Elaine Jenkins (d 1964); m 2, 23 July 1966, (Marion) Anita, da of David Morris (d 1969), of Plasmarl, Swansea; 1 da (Susan b 30 June 1968), 1 s (Robert b 11 Aug 1970); *Career* Nat Serv 1954–56, RAPC attached 19 Field Regt RA, served Korea, Hong Kong, demobbed Sgt AER; ordained Brecon Cathedral: deacon 1962, priest 1963; curate: Clydach 1962–64, Llangyfelach 1964–67, Sketty 1967–70; rector: Bryngwyn with Newchurch and Llanbedr, Painscastle with Llandewi Fach 1970–72; Missions to Seamen: port chaplain Swansea and Port Talbot 1972–76, sr chaplain Port of London 1976–81, sec gen The Missions to Seamen 1990–2000 (aux ministries sec 1981–85, asst gen sec 1985–90); memb Cncl: Marine Soc 1990–2000, Partnership for World Mission 1990–2000, Int Christian Maritime Assoc 1990–2000, Merchant Navy Welfare Bd 1990–99; hon chaplain Royal Alfred Seafarers Soc 1987–93, hon canon St Michael's Cathedral Kobe Japan 1988–; chaplain: Worshipful Co of Information Technologists 1989–2000, Worshipful Co of Innholders 1990–2002, Worshipful Co of Farriers 1990–2004, Worshipful Co of Carmen 1990–2004; chaplain to HM The Queen 1990–2005, chaplain to the Lay Sheriff of London 1993–94 and 1999–2000; commissary to bishop of Cyprus and the Gulf 1996–2000; tstee Eddie Baird Meml Tst 2002–08 (treas 2007–08); co-chm Orsett Churches Centre 2003–04, hon sec to the tstees Orsett Churches Centre 2004–07; memb: Batti Wallah's Soc (pres 2006–07), Thurrock Probus Club (pres 2005–06), Rotary Club of Grays Thurrock 2003 (vice-pres 2006–07, pres 2007–08, sec 2009–12); chaplain Little Ship Club London 1990–2000, govr Treetops Sch Thurrock 2008–12; Freeman City of London 1990, Hon Liveryman Worshipful Co of Carmen 1995, Hon Liveryman Worshipful Co of Farriers 1999; *Recreations* sport, music, reading, theatre, travel; *Clubs* Thurrock Rugby (chaplain), Grays Thurrock Rotary; *Style—* The Rev Canon Glyndwr Jones; ✉ 5 The Close, Grays, Essex RM16 2XU (☎ 01375 375053, e-mail glynita.tomdavey@blueyonder.co.uk)

JONES, (David) Graham; s of Mrs Dorothy Hartley, of Wakefield, W Yorks; *b* 16 June 1951; *Educ* Queen Elizabeth GS Wakefield, Keble Coll Oxford (MA), UCW Cardiff; *m* 1, 23 March 1977, Lynne Francis (d 1996); m 2, 5 March 2007, Virginia Frances Tooley; *Career* leader writer Glasgow Herald 1973–74; reporter: Sheffield Star 1973, The Sun 1974–79; Now! Magazine 1979–81 (reporter, dep foreign ed), Foreign Desk Daily Mail and Mail On Sunday 1981–83, Daily Telegraph 1983–89 (reporter, political staff, asst news ed, chief asst news ed, dep news ed), news ed Daily Star 1989–94, asst ed (news) Sunday Express 1994–96, ed News and Business CNNText 1996–98, sr ed CNNI Text 1998–2000, dep ed CNN.com Europe 2000–01, sr writer CNN.com International 2001–; *Books* Forked Tongues (1984), Own Goals (1985), The Forked Tongues Annual (1985), Plane Crazy (1986), I Don't Hate Men But.../I Don't Hate Women But... (1986), Boat Crazy (1987), The Official Candidate's Book of Political Insults (1987), I Love Sex/I Hate Sex (1989), The Book of Total Snobbery (1989); *Recreations* writing, current and international affairs, travel, gardening, photography, journalism training (seminars/workshops for Thomson Fndn and UNICEF in Ghana, Romania, Malaysia, Ukraine, Belarus, Russia, Pakistan, Mongolia and Papua New Guinea); *Style—* Graham Jones, Esq; ✉ 4 Dennis Road, East Molesey, Surrey KT8 9ED (☎ 020 8979 4198); CNN.com, CNN House, 16 Great Marlborough Street, London W1F 7HS (☎ 020 7693 1717)

JONES, Graham Peter; MP; *Children* 2 c; *Career* MP (Lab) Hyndburn 2010–; *Style—* Graham Jones, Esq, MP; ✉ 50 Abbey Street, Accrington, Lancashire BB5 1EE (☎ 01254 382283, fax 01254 398089, website http://hhgrahamjones.blogspot.com); House of Commons, London SW1A 0AA (e-mail graham.jones.mp@parliament.uk)

JONES, Gwyn; s of Edgar Jones (d 1994), and Laura, *née* Davies (d 1993); *b* 22 July 1960, Trawsfynydd; *Educ* Ysgol y Moelwyn Blaenau Ffestiniog, Liverpool Poly (BA), Coll of Law Chester; *m* 30 Aug 1986, Margaret, *née* MacMillan; 1 s (Mathew Gwyn b 21 Jan 1990), 1 da (Ruth Mererid b 17 Dec 1991); *Career* previously slr advocate specialising in gen crime; Leo Abse & Cohen Cardiff: articled clerk 1982–84, asst slr 1984–86, ptnr 1986–96; ptnr Gamlins Slrs Rhyl 1996–2013; dep dist judge 2001–13, dist judge (Crime and Family Jurisdiction) Magistrates Ct 2013–; chair Llamau Housing Soc Ltd 1989–92; chair Bod Alaw PTA 1999–2001; author of various articles on current legal issues; regular participant on BBC radio and TV progs; memb Law Soc; *Recreations* gardening, mountain biking, eating out; *Style—* Gwyn Jones, Esq; ✉ North Wales Magistrates Court, The Court House, Ffordd Conwy, Llandudno, Conwy LL30 1GA (☎ 01492 863854)

JONES, Dame Gwyneth; DBE (1986, CBE 1976); *b* 7 November 1936, Pontnewynydd, Wales; *Educ* Twmpath Secdy Modern Sch Pontypool, Royal Coll of Music, Accademia Chigiana Siena, Int Opera Centre Zürich; *Children* 1 da; *Career* principal dramatic soprano: ROH Covent Garden 1963–, Vienna Staatsoper 1966–, Bavarian State Opera 1966–, Deutsche Oper Berlin 1966–; guest artist: Met Opera NY, San Francisco, Chicago, LA, Paris, La Scala Milan, Rome, Florence, Hamburg, Stuttgart, Dresden, Barcelona, Madrid, Zürich, Oslo, Moscow, Geneva, Norway, Finland, Sweden, Buenos Aires, Tokyo, Hong Kong, Peking, Seoul; festivals: Bayreuth, Salzburg, Orange, Verona, Edinburgh; debut as dir Der Fliegender Holländer (new prodn, Deutsches Nat Theatre Weimar); hon memb Vienna State Opera 1990; pres Richard Wagner Soc London 1990;

J

Kammersängerin Bavaria 1977 and Austria 1978, Shakespeare Prize Hamburg 1988, Verdienstkreuz 1 Klasse FRG 1989, Premio Puccini Prize Torre del Lago 2003, Cymry for the World Honour Wales Millennium Centre 2004, Golden Medal of Honor Vienna 1991, Osterreichische Ehren Kreuz für Wissenschaft und Kunst (1 Klasse) 1998, Hon DMus: Univ of Wales 1978, Univ of Glamorgan 1995; Hon RAM 1980, fell Royal Welsh Coll of Music and Drama 1992, FRCM 1971 (ARCM); Commandeur de l'Ordre des Artes et des Lettres France 1992; *Roles* incl: Senta in Der Fliegende Holländer, Sieglinde, Guturne and Brünnhilde in Die Walküre, Siegfried, Götterdämmerung and Kundry in Parsifal, Isolde in Tristan und Isolde, Elisabeth and Venus in Tannhäuser, Ortud in Lohengrin, Annina, Octavian and Die Feldmarschallin in Der Rosenkavalier, Salome and Herodias, Ariadne in Ariadne auf Naxos, Farberin and Kaiserin in Die Frau ohne Schatten, Elektra and Klytaemnesta in Elektra, Helen of Egypt, Leonore in Fidelio, Erwartung, Esmeralda in Notre Dame, Lady Macbeth in Macbeth, Desdemona in Otello, Leonora in Il Trovatore, Elisabetta in Don Carlos, Aida in Aida, Tosca in Tosca, Madame Butterfly in Madame Butterfly, Turandot in Turandot, Minnie in La Fanciulla del West, Cherubini Medea in Medea, Bellini Norma in Norma, Monteverdi Poppea in L'Incoronazione di Poppea, La Voix Humaine, Janacek Kostelnicka in Jenufa, Kabanicha in Katia Kabanowa, Leokadia Begbick in Aufstieg und Fall Der Stadt Mahagonny, Queen of Hearts in Alice and Wonderland, Hanna Glawari in The Merry Widow, Ruth in Pirates of Penzance, Countess Pique-Dame; film, CD recordings and television roles incl: Isolde, Aida, Turandot, Elisabetta, Medea, Leonora, Desdemona, Poppea, Brünnhilde, Elisabeth/ Venus, Isolde, Octavian, Feldmarschallin, Fidelio Leonore, Elektra, Dyer's Wife, Erwartung, Hanna Glawari in The Merry Widow La Voix Humaine, Anne Langley Quartett; *Style*— Dame Gwyneth Jones, DBE; ✉ PO Box 2000, CH 8700 Küsnacht, Switzerland

JONES, Gwyneth Ann; da of Desmond James Jones, and Mary Rita, née Dugdale; *b* 14 February 1952; *Educ* Notre Dame Convent Sch Manchester, Univ of Sussex (BA); *m* 1976, Peter Wilson Gwilliam; 1 s (Gabriel Jimi Jones b 4 Sept 1987); *Career* author; memb: SE Arts Literature Panel 1988–94, Science Fiction Foundation 1986–; Richard Evans Meml Award for Science Fiction 2001, Pilgrim Award for Science Fiction Criticism 2008; *Children's Books* as Gwyneth Jones: Water In The Air (1977), The Influence of Ironwood (1978), The Exchange (1979), Dear Hill (1980), Seven Tales and a Fable (1995); as Ann Halam: Ally Ally Aster (1981), The Alder Tree (1982), King Death's Garden (1986), The Daymaker (1987), Transformations (1988), The Skybreaker (1990), Dinosaur Junction (1992), The Haunting Raven (1994), The Fear Man (1995, winner Children of the Night Award Dracular Soc 1995), Dr Franklin;s Island (2001), Siberia (2005, shortlisted Teenage Book Prize), Snakehead (2007); *Novels* Divine Endurance (1984), Escape Plans (1986), Kairos (1988), The Hidden Ones (1988), White Queen (1991, winner of James Tiptree Jr award), Flowerdust (1993), North Wind (1994, short listed Arthur C Clarke Award), Seven Tales And a Fable (two World Fantasy Awards, 1996), Phoenix Cafe (1997), Bold as Love (2001, Arthur C Clarke Award), Castles Made of Sand (2002), Midnight Lamp (2003, shortlisted Arthur C Clark Award), Life (2004, Philip K Dick Award), Band of Gypsys (2005), Rainbow Bridge (2006); *Recreations* walking, gardening, book reviewing; *Style*— Ms Gwyneth Jones; ✉ c/o David Higham Associates, 5–8 Lower John Street, Golden Square, London W1R 4HA (✆ 020 7437 7888, fax 020 7437 1072, e-mail gwyneth.jones@ntlworld.com, websites www.boldaslove.co.uk and http://homepage.ntlworld.com/gwynethann/)

JONES, Dr Hamlyn Gordon (Lyn); s of Douglass Gordon Jones (d 1978), and Mary Elsie, née Hoadley (d 1966); *b* 1947; *Educ* St Lawrence Coll Ramsgate, St John's Coll Cambridge (MA, Lister entrance scholarship, Wright Prize), Australian National Univ (PhD, ANU scholarship); *m* 1972, Amanda Jane, da of Sir James Perowne Ivo Myles Corry; 2 da (Katherine Myleta Gordon b June 1974, Julia Patricia Gordon b Nov 1976); *Career* res scientist Plant Breeding Inst Cambridge 1972–76, Title A res fellow St John's Coll Cambridge (Henry Humphreys Prize) 1973–76, lectr in botany Univ of Glasgow 1977–78, ldr Stress Physiology Gp East Malling Res Station 1978–88; Horticulture Research International: dir Crop Science Res 1988–95, dir Res Strategy 1995–97; prof of plant ecology Univ of Dundee 1997–2009 (emeritus prof 2009–); special prof Univ of Nottingham 1992–97, hon prof Univ of Birmingham 1995–98, emeritus prof Univ of Dundee 2009–, adjunct prof Univ of Western Australia 2013–; visiting prof: Univ of Toronto 1981, Univ of Basilicata 1989–90; memb: Cncl Soc of Experimental Biology 1986–90, Scientific Advsy Ctee Scottish Nat Heritage 2005–11; govr S Warks Coll of FE 1988–89, hon lectr Univ of Glasgow 1978–90, hon research prof Scot Crop Research Inst Invergowrie 1998–2010; author of over 230 scientific pubns; FIHort 1993; *Books* Plants and Microclimate (1983, last edn 2013), Remote Sensing of Vegetation (jtly, 2010) and joint ed of 4 books; *Recreations* tennis, mountains, lounging; *Style*— Dr Lyn Jones; ✉ Division of Plant Sciences, University of Dundee, James Hutton Institute, Invergowrie, Dundee DD2 5DA

JONES, Helen; MP; *b* 24 December 1954; *Educ* UCL, Univ of Liverpool, Manchester Metropolitan Univ (MEd); *m*; 1 s; *Career* former: teacher, devpt offr MIND, slr; MP (Lab) Warrington N 1997–; memb Chester City Cncl 1984–91; *Style*— Ms Helen Jones, MP; ✉ House of Commons, London SW1A 0AA (✆ 020 7219 4048); Constituency: Gilbert Wakefield House, 67 Bewsey Street, Warrington WA2 7JQ (✆ 01925 232480, fax 01925 232239)

JONES, Huw; s of Idris Jones (d 1993), and Olwen, née Edwards; *b* 5 May 1948; *Educ* Cardiff HS for Boys, Jesus Coll Oxford (MA); *m* 29 Aug 1972, Siân Marylka, da of Kazimierz Miarczynski; 2 c (Owain Elidir b 1973, Siwan Elenid b 1977); *Career* pop singer, recording artist and TV presenter 1968–76, dir/gen mangr Sain Recording Company 1969–81, chm Barcud Cyf (TV Facilities) 1981–93, md/prodr Teledu'r Tir Glas Cyf (ind prodn co) 1982–93, first chm Teledwyr Annibynnol Cymru (Welsh ind prodrs) 1984–86, chief exec S4C 1994–2005; dir: Sgrin Cyf 1996–2005, S4C Masnachol Cyf 1999–2005, SDN Ltd 1999–2005; dir Skillset Ltd 2001–05 (patron 2006–08), chm Skillset Cymru Cyf 2002–05; currently: chair Portmeirion Ltd, vice-chair Nant Gwrtheyrn Cyf; chair S4C Authy 2011–; former chm Broadcasting Avsy Ctee Welsh Assembly Govt 2008; memb: Welsh Language Bd 2007–12, RSPB Advsy Ctee for Wales 2007–12, RSPB Cncl 2008–13, Gorsedd of Bards, National Eisteddfod of Wales, Bd of Govrs Coleg Llandrillo Cymru 2009–12, Advsy Bd Investors in People 2010–12; vice-chair Wales Employment and Skills Bd 2008–12; tstee RTS 2013–; hon fell Univ of Wales Aberystwyth 1997, hon fell Bangor Univ 2013; FRTS 1999; *Recreations* reading, cycling, skiing; *Style*— Huw Jones, Esq; ✉ Y Bwlan, Llandwrog, Caernarfon, Gwynedd LL54 5SR

JONES, Hywel Ceri; CMG (2000); s of Gwilym Ceri Jones (d 1963), and Mary Symmons (d 1970); *b* 22 April 1937; *Educ* Pontardawe GS, Univ of Wales Aberystwyth (BA, DipEd, John and Elizabeth Williams scholar); *m* Morwenna, da of late Wilfred Carnsew Armstrong; 1 da (Hannah Ceri b 29 Aug 1967), 1 s (Gwilym Ceri b 5 May 1970); *Career* pres Students' Union Univ of Wales Aberystwyth 1961–62; Univ of Sussex: asst registrar 1962–65, dep dir Centre for Educnl Technol and Curriculum Devpt 1965–69, special asst to vice-chllr for planning and devpt 1969–73, visiting fell in educn and contemporary European studies 1973–80; EC: head Dept for Educn and Youth Policies 1973–79, dir Educn, Vocational Trg and Youth Policy 1979–88, dir Task Force for HR, Educn, Trg and Youth 1989–93, actg DG then dep DG Employment, Social Policy, Employment and Industrial Rels 1993–98; advsr to George Soros on the Open Soc's Network of Fndns 1998–99, European advsr to Welsh Office and chm Ctee on Wales and Europe 1998–99, chm Governing Bd of European Policy Centre Brussels 1999–2007; chm European Inst

for Educn and Social Policy Paris 2000–04, dir Network of European Fndns (NEF) 2003–07 (European policy advsr 2008–09); visiting prof Univ of Glamorgan 1999–2001; author of numerous articles on educn and trg and social policy in Europe; chm: prog ctees on educn and trg EU, Advsy Ctee for Vocational Trg EC, European Social Dialogue Ctee, European Social Fund Ctee, task force to prepare the social dimension to the enlargement of the EU; co-chair European Consortium of Fndn on Disability Rights 2008–, European advsr Freudenberg Fndn 2009–; vice-chm: European Centre for Vocational Trg (CEDEFOP), European Fndn for Living and Working Conditions Dublin; govr European Cultural Fndn 1999–2007; govr: NE Wales Inst of HE 2003–08, Bd ECORYS 2006–13 (dir ECORYS Tst 2006–13, memb Supervisory Bd 2007–13); tstee Federal Tst for Educn and Research 2006– (govr 2004–), tstee Equal Rights Tst 2011–; memb Bd Nat Playing Fields Assoc for Wales 2002–07, memb Bd Franco-Br Inst 2003–10; dir Tomorrow's Wales 2009–15, chm Bd Wales Governance Centre Univ of Cardiff 2012–15, tstee Bd Nat Museum of Wales 2014–, funding ambass Welsh Govt 2014–, chm St David's Day Ctee London 2014–15, vice-pres Int Eisteddfod Llangollen 2015–; Winston Churchill fell 1967, Eisenhower fell 1978; Hon DUniv: Sussex 1991, Leuven 1992, Open Univ 2000; Hon LLD Nat Cncl for Educnl Awards of Ireland 1992, Hon Dr Free Univ of Brussels 2002, hon doctorate Univ of Wales 2013; hon fell: Educn Inst of Scot 1988, Univ of Westminster 1990, Univ of Wales Aberystwyth 1990, Univ of Glyndwr 1993, Univ of Glamorgan 1994, Univ of Swansea 1995; fell Trinity St David's Univ Camarthen 2009, fell Inst for Welsh Affrs 2014; Gold Medal of the Republic of Italy 1987; *Recreations* travel, rugby, snooker, theatre; *Clubs* Reform, Fondation Universitaire (Brussels), Cardiff and County; *Style*— Hywel Ceri Jones, CMG; ✉ 38 Plymouth Road, Penarth CF64 3DH (✆ 02920 650119, e-mail hywelceri@hotmail.co.uk)

JONES, Hywel Vaughan; s of Cranoe Vaughan and Mari Elizabeth Jones; *b* 12 July 1971; *Educ* Ysgol Gyfun Rhymni Comp Sch Bargoed S Wales, S Glamorgan Inst of HE Cardiff; *m* Conny, née Degel; 2 s (Ieuan Vaughan Gunter b 22 March 2002, Johan Vaughan Gunther b 3 Dec 2005); *Career* chef; waiter Station Restaurant Newport 1987–88, asst chef: Farmer's Daughter Restaurant 1988, Roman Wine Bar & Restaurant Newport 1988–89; chef Le Cassoulet Cardiff 1989–90 (asst chef 1989), demi chef de partie Royal Garden Hotel 1992 (2 commis chef 1990, 1 commis chef 1991–92), chef Chez Nico and Nico at Ninety 1992–93, chef Harvey's and The Restaurant (owned by Marco Pierre White) 1993–94, sr chef de partie and jr sous chef Le Soufflé 1994–96, sous chef and sr sous chef Coast 1996–97, head chef Foliage at the Mandarin Oriental 1997–2002 (winner Michelin star 2002), chef and dir Lola's 2002, chef Pharmacy 2002–03, exec chef Luckham Park 2003– (winner Michelin star 2006); *Awards* nominated by Nico Ladenis, qv, for William Hepinstall Tst Scholarship 1992, bronze medallist Salon Culinaire Int 1992 (gold medallist 1996), semi finalist Nat Chef of the Year 1997, finalist Chef of the Year 2006, Hotel Chef of the Year Catey Award 2007; *Recreations* car racing, playing pool, cookery, music, mountain bike riding, reading, cycling, rugby (especially Welsh!); *Style*— Hywel Jones, Esq; ✉ 18 Burnfort Road, Newport, Gwent, South Wales NP20 3GU (✆ 01633 764708)

JONES, Prof Ian; *b* 13 June 1947; *Educ* Univ of Cambridge (MA), Univ of Birmingham (PhD); *Career* Univ of Birmingham: SRC res fell Dept of Physical Metallurgy 1972–74, res fell Dept of Metallurgy and Materials 1974–81, lectr Dept of Metallurgy and Materials 1981–86, sr lectr 1986–92, reader in the electron microscopy of materials 1992–96, prof of physical metallurgy 1996–; visiting prof Dept of Metallurgy and Materials Engrg Ohio State Univ Columbus 1992–1998, visiting prof Dept of Metallurgy and Mining Engrg Univ of Illinois Urbana-Champaign 1973 and 1984, visiting fell Theoretical Physics Div Atomic Energy Research Establishment 1973, distinguished foreign visitor fellowship Nagoya Inst of Technol Japan 1989; MIM CEng, FInstP; *Books* Chemical Microanalysis Using Electron Beams (1992), Materials Science for Electrical and Electronic Engineers (2000); also author of over 160 academic papers; *Style*— Prof Ian Jones; ✉ Department of Metallurgy & Materials, The University of Birmingham, Edgbaston, Birmingham B15 2TT (✆ 0121 414 5184, fax 0121 414 5232, e-mail i.p.jones@bham.ac.uk, website www.bham.ac.uk/metallurgy/staff/academic/ipjones.html)

JONES, Ian Geoffrey; s of Geoffrey Frederick Jones, and Ann Elizabeth, née Taylor; *b* 18 August 1965; *Educ* Bolton Sch, West Glamorgan Inst of Higher Educn (HND), Bournemouth Art Coll (PQE); *m* 21 Oct 1995, Elizabeth Caroline Hare; 1 s (Angus Ian b 28 March 1998), 1 da (Iona Elizabeth b 26 April 2000); *Career* chief photographer Skishoot 1987–91, freelance 1991–, Daily Telegraph photographer 1992–2008; projects incl maj home and world news assignments and Royal foreign tours; memb Old Boltonians' Assoc; highly commended Martini Royal Photographer Awards 1992, winner Canon News Photographer of the Year 1992 and Fuji News Photographer of the Year 1992, Martini Royal Photographer of the Year 1993 and 1994, Martini Royal Photographer of the Decade 1996, nominated Photographer of the Year Br Press Awards 2007; *Recreations* skiing, fishing; *Style*— Ian Jones, Esq; ✉ mobile 07850 329349, e-mail ianjonesphoto@ntlworld.com

JONES, Rt Rev Dr Idris; s of Edward Eric Jones (d 1983), and Alice Gertrude, née Burgess (d 1964); *b* 2 April 1943; *Educ* West Bromwich GS, UC of St David Lampeter (BA), New Coll Edinburgh (LTh), NY Seminary and Urban Theol Unit (DMin); *m* 27 Oct 1973, Alison Margaret, da of Ernest Abel Williams; 2 s (Adam Edward b 4 Oct 1977, Gareth Daniel b 27 July 1979); *Career* ordained: deacon 1967, priest 1968; curate St Mary Stafford 1967–70, precentor St Paul's Cathedral Dundee 1970–73, curate i/c St Hugh Gosforth 1973–80 (team vicar 1980), chaplain St Nicholas Hosp Newcastle 1975–80, rector Montrose with Inverbervie (Brechin) 1980–89, canon St Paul's Cathedral Dundee 1983, Anglican chaplain Univ of Dundee and priest i/c Invergowrie (Brechin) 1989–92, rector Ayr with Girvan and Maybole (Glasgow and Galloway) 1992–98, bishop of Glasgow and Galloway 1998–2009; pastoral dir Theol Inst 1995–98, Primus of Scottish Episcopal Church 2006–09, hon curate St Columba's Largs Dio (Glasgow and Galloway) 2010, nat spiritual dir Anglian Cursillo UK 2010–13, dir Scottish Episcopal Church Nominees 2014–; collector Trades House of Glasgow 2012–13; patron Hutcheson's Hosp, govr Hutcheson's GS 2002–09, dir Merchant's House Glasgow 2010; Master Incorporation of Skinners and Glovers of Glasgow, Freeman City of Glasgow, Deacon Convenor Incorporated Traders of Glasgow 2014–15; hon fell Univ of Wales Lampeter 2007; *Recreations* walking, playing piano, bird watching, golf, food and wine; *Clubs* Glasgow Western; *Style*— The Rt Rev Dr Idris Jones; ✉ 27 Donald Wynd, The Rise, Largs, North Ayrshire KA30 8TH (✆ 01475 674919, mobile 07702 589481, e-mail idrisjones43@ hotmail.co.uk)

JONES, Ieuan; s of David Edward Humphries Jones, of Mathrafal, Powys, and Beryl Elizabeth Mary, née Proudlove; *b* 24 January 1963; *Educ* Llanfair Caereinion Sch, Royal Coll of Music (Most Distinguished Student award, Tagore Gold medal, winner Royal Over-Seas League music competition, runner-up Israel Harp contest); *m* 18 June 1992, Penny Gore Browne, née Thomson; 1 step s (Edward), 1 step da (Alexandra); *Career* harpist; prof of harp RCM 1996–; appointed harpist to the House of Commons 1984–97; London debut Purcell Room 1985, Wigmore Hall debut 1987; recitals given and appearances with orchs in various countries incl: USA, Argentina, Uruguay, Mexico, Spain, Italy, Switzerland, Germany, Austria, France, Belgium, Netherlands, China, Philippines, Australia, Israel and Ireland; private appearance before HRH Queen Elizabeth The Queen Mother at the Royal Lodge Windsor 1986, guest appearance St James' Palace 1988 and Holyrood House 1989, world premiere Concerto for Harp and Marimba World Harp Festival 1994, cmmnd and premiered work by Jean-Michel Damase

Wigmore Hall 1994, Concertgebouw debut with Ginastera Concerto 1995, Hong Kong, Phillippines and Australia solo debut tour 1995, Far East tour (Bangkok, Hong Kong, Brunei, Australia, Philippines) 1997 and 1999; jury memb for int competitions incl Israel, Japan, Spain and London; recordings: The Uncommon Harp 1987, The Two Sides of Ieuan Jones 1988, ...In The French Style 1990, Mozart in Paris 1990, All Through the Night 1992, French Chamber Music 1994, William Alwyn 1994, Concerto D'Aranjuez/ Batiz 1995, The Liszt of the Harp 1999, Rodrigo – Concierto De Aranjuez 2003, Spohr – Flute and Harp 2008, Terzetti: The Debussy Ensemble 2012; ARCM 1981, DipRCM 1985; *Recreations* health and fitness, travel; *Clubs* Chelsea Arts; *Style*— Ieuan Jones, Esq; ✉ website www.ieuanjones.co.uk

JONES, Rt Rev James Stuart; s of Maj James Stuart Anthony Jones (d 1990), and Helen Deans Dick Telfer, *née* McIntyre (d 2002); *b* 18 August 1948; *Educ* Duke of York's RMS Dover, Univ of Exeter (BA), Alsager Coll (PGCE); *m* 19 April 1980, Sarah Caroline Rosalind, da of Rev Canon Peter Marrow; 3 da (Harriet Emma b 26 May 1982, Jemima Charlotte b 13 Aug 1984, Tabitha Rose b 14 Feb 1987); *Career* asst master Sevenoaks Sch 1971–75, prodr Scripture Union 1975–81, curate then assoc vicar Christ Church Clifton 1982–90, vicar Emmanuel Church Croydon 1990–94, bishop of Hull 1994–98, bishop of Liverpool 1998–2013; bishop to prisons 2007–13; memb House of Lords 2003–13; author and broadcaster; chair Hillsborough Ind Panel 2010–12, chair Ind Panel Future of Forestry 2011–12, advsr to home secretary on Hillsborough 2013, advsr to Waitrose on corp social responsibility, chair Gosport Ind Panel 2014–; ambass WWF 2006–13 (fell 2013–), vice-pres Town and Country Planning Assoc, patron UK Environmental Lawyers Assoc 2015; visitor St Peter's Coll Oxford 2007–13, fell John Moores Univ 2013; Freeman City of Liverpool 2016; Hon DD Univ of Hull 1998, Hon DLitt Univ of Lincolnshire and Humberside 2001; Hon DPhil: Liverpool Hope Univ 2009, Univ of Exeter 2013, Univ of Gloucestershire 2013; fell Soc of Environment 2013, fell Chartered Inst of Foresters 2014; *Books* incl: Following Jesus (1984), Finding God (1987), The Power and The Glory (1994), People of the Blessing (1998), The Moral Leader (2002), Jesus and the Earth (2003), Why do People Suffer? (2007), With my Whole Heart (2012); *Recreations* opera, walking; *Clubs* Athenaeum; *Style*— The Rt Rev James Jones; ✉ Mount Pleasant Cottage, Burythorpe, North Yorkshire YO17 9LJ (✆ 01653 658325)

JONES, Jenny; AM; da of Percy Jones, and Christine Heasman; *Educ* Westlain GS Brighton, Inst of Archaeology, UCL (BSc); *Career* archaeologist, formerly fin controller; memb Green Party (chm 1994–97); GLA: memb London Assembly (Green) London (list) 2000–, dep mayor 2003–04, previously Mayor's road safety ambass and Mayor's Green transport advsr; chair Planning and Housing Ctee; memb: Met Police Authy, Transport Ctee; chair London Food 2003–2008; cncllr S Camberwell ward Southwark Cncl 2006–10; *Recreations* cinema, reading; *Style*— Jenny Jones, AM; ✉ London Assembly, City Hall, Queens Walk, Southwark, London SE1 2AA (✆ 020 7983 4358, fax 020 7983 4398, e-mail jenny.jones@london.gov.uk)

JONES, Jenny; da of Peter Jones, and Helen Jones; *b* 3 July 1980, Bristol; *Educ* The Ridings HS, Filton Coll Bristol; *Career* snowboarder, coach and presenter; achievements incl: Gold medal Winter X Games 2009, Gold medal European Winter X Games 2010, Silver medal Winter X Games 2011, Bronze medal Winter Olympic Games 2014; ambass Snow-Camp Charity; *Recreations* snowboarding, surfing, cycling; *Clubs* British Ski and Snowboard; *Style*— Ms Jenny Jones; ✉ website www.jennyjonessnowboarder.com, Twitter @jennyjonessnow, Instagram @jennyjonessnow

JONES, John Elfed; CBE (1987), DL; s of Urien Maelgwyn Jones (d 1978); *b* 19 March 1933; *Educ* Blaenau Ffestiniog GS, Denbighshire Tech Coll, Heriot-Watt Coll; *m* 1957, Mary Sheila, da of David Thomas Rosser; 2 da (Bethan, Delyth); *Career* Flying Offr RAF; chartered electrical engr CEGB 1949–1969, dep md Anglesey Aluminium Metal Ltd 1969–79, under-sec (industry) Welsh Office 1979–82; chm: Welsh Water Authy 1982–89, Welsh Water plc 1989–93, HTV Wales/Cymru 1992–97, International Greetings plc 1996–2007; dep chm HTV (Group) plc 1992–97, chm Awen Cymru Ltd 2009–13; chm: Bwrdd Yr Iaith Gymraeg (Welsh Language Bd) 1988–93, Nat Assembly Advsy Gp (set up by sec of state for Wales) 1997–98, Exec Ctee Nat Eisteddfod of Wales 1998; pres: UCW Lampeter (St David's Univ) 1992–98, Campaign for the Protection of Rural Wales 1995–2001, Côr Bro Ogwr 1999–2008, The Miners Rest Porthcawl 2000–10, Princess of Wales Hosp Scanner Appeal 2000–, Cantorion Coety 2007–, Cwlwm Busnes Caerdydd 2009–; chm Menter Mantis Cyf 1999–2004; fell: Univ of Wales Aberystwyth 1991, NE Wales Inst 1996; Hon DUniv Glamorgan 1997, Hon LLD Univ of Wales 2000; CEng, CIMgt, FIET, FRSA; *Recreations* fishing (salmon and trout), attending Eisteddfodau, golf; *Clubs* Cardiff & County, Royal Porthcawl Golf; *Style*— John Elfed Jones, Esq, CBE, DL; ✉ Ty Mawr, Coety, Penybontarogwr, Morgannwg Ganol CF35 6BN (✆ 01656 653039, fax 01656 667204, e-mail john.jones2011@btinternet.com)

JONES, Prof Jonathan Dallas George; s of George Ronald Jones (d 1987), and Isabel Dallas Orr, *née* Pinkney; *b* 14 July 1954, London; *Educ* Hampton GS, Peterhouse Cambridge (BA), Univ of Cambridge (PhD); *m* 22 July 1991, Caroline Dean; 1 s (William George b 8 Feb 1992), 1 da (Philippa Susan b 23 April 1994), 1 other da (Gillian b 6 March 1983); *Career* postdoctoral research Harvard Univ 1981–82, Advanced Genetic Sciences Oakland CA 1983–88, Sainsbury Lab John Innes Centre Norwich 1988–; memb EMBO 1998; FRS 2003; *Recreations* sailing, music, children; *Clubs* Waverley and Oulton Broad Yacht; *Style*— Prof Jonathan Jones; ✉ The Sainsbury Laboratory, John Innes Centre, Colney Lane, Norwich NR4 7UH (✆ 01603 450327, fax 01603 450011, e-mail jonathan.jones@tsl.ac.uk)

JONES, Jonathan Guy; s of Leonard Martell Jones (d 1993), and Margaret Eleanor, *née* Jones (d 2006); *b* 21 May 1962; *Educ* Llandovery Coll, St Chad's Coll Durham (Horsfall scholar, organ scholar, BA), Inns of Court Sch of Law; *Career* called to the Bar: Middle Temple 1985 (bencher 2007), NI 2006; Legal Dept OFT 1989–93, Legal Advsr's Office Dept of Tport 1993–94, legal secretariat to the Law Officers Attorney-Gen's Chambers 1994–98, dep legal advsr HM Treasy 1998–2002, legal advsr DfES and dir Treasy Slr's Dept 2002–04, DG Attorney-Gen's Office 2004–09, dep treasy slr 2009–14, legal advsr Home Office and NI Office 2012–14, perm sec Govt Legal Dept (formerly Treasy Slr's Dept) 2014–; *Style*— Jonathan Jones, Esq

JONES, Karen Elisabeth Dind; CBE (2006); da of Eric Jones (d 1992), and Margaret, *née* Dind; *b* 29 July 1956; *Educ* UEA (BA), Wellesley Coll Mass; *m* Hamish Easton; 2 da (Rose b 16 June 1990, Molly b 3 Sept 1995), 1 s (Max b 2 Jan 1993); *Career* co-ed Straight Lines Magazine 1978–80, account planner Boase Massimi Pollitt 1980–81, operations dir Theme Holdings plc 1981–88; md and co-fndr: The Pelican Gp plc 1989–87, Punch Gp Ltd; chief exec Spirit Gp Ltd 1999–2006, co-fndr Food & Fuel Ltd 2006; non-exec dir: Gondola Holdings plc 2005–07, HBOS plc 2006–08, Virgin Active Gp Ltd 2008–11, ASOS plc 2009–15, Booker plc 2009–, Cofra Hldg ag 2008–, Firmenich 2011–, Corbin and King Ltd (formerly Rex Restaurants Ltd) 2012–; chm Hawksmoor 2013–; chllr UEA 2016; memb Bd Royal National Theatre Enterprises; memb Industrial Devpt Advsy Bd DTI 2004–10; finalist Veuve Clicquot Business Woman of the Year 1995; govr Ashridge Bus Sch 2005–15, memb Rebuilding Childhoods Bd NSPCC 2006–13; Hon DCL UEA 2013; FRSA; *Recreations* my children, food and wine, theatre, contemporary American and English literature; *Style*— Ms Karen Jones, CBE

JONES, Kelly; *Career* musician; vocalist and guitarist Stereophonics 1996–; also solo artist; *Albums* with Stereophonics incl: Word Gets Around 1997, Performance and Cocktails 1999, Just Enough Education to Perform 2001, You Gotta Go There To Come Back 2003, Language.Sex.Violence.Other? 2005, Live from Dakota 2006, Pull The Pin 2007, A Decade in the Sun – The Best of Stereophonics 2008, Keep Calm and Carry On 2009, Graffiti on the Train 2013, Keep the Village Alive 2015; solo album Only The Names Have Been Changed 2007; *Style*— Mr Kelly Jones; ✉ Natalie Seymour, c/o Nettwerk Management, Rear Building, 44 Chiswick Lane, London W4 2JQ (✆ 020 7456 9500, fax 020 7456 9501, e-mail natalie@nettwerk.com)

JONES, Kevan; MP; *b* 25 April 1964; *Educ* Portland Comp, Newcastle upon Tyne Poly, Univ of Southern Maine; *Career* memb Lab Pty 1982–; GMB Northern Region: political offr 1989–2001, regnl organiser 1992–99, sr organiser 1999–2001; memb Newcastle City Cncl 1990–2001 (chief whip, chair Public Health Ctee, cabinet memb for devpt and tport), MP (Lab) Durham N 2001–; memb: Co-op Pty, NE Tourism Advsy Bd; *Style*— Kevan Jones, Esq, MP; ✉ House of Commons, London SW1A 0AA

JONES, Laura Anne; da of John Dilwyn Jones, and Penelope Anne, *née* Haining; *b* 21 February 1979, Newport, Gwent; *Educ* Caerleon Comp Sch, Univ of Plymouth (BSc); *Career* memb Nat Assembly for Wales (Cons) S Wales E 2003–07; supporter: NSPCC, Cancer Research UK, Br Heart Fndn, Leukaemia Research, Red Cross; ambass Girl Guides; *Recreations* swimming, hockey, skiing, horse riding, cycling; *Clubs* Usk Conservative, Caerphilly Conservative; *Style*— Miss Laura Anne Jones; ✉ Llanusk Cottage, Llanbadoc, Monmouthshire NP15 1TA (✆ 07872 144938, e-mail lauraannejones@hotmail.co.uk)

JONES, Laurance Aubrey; s of Aubrey Joseph Goldsmid Jones (d 1990), of Godmanchester, Huntingdon, and Frances Laura, *née* Ward (d 1997); *b* 7 April 1936; *Educ* King's Sch Rochester; *m* 8 July 1961, Joan, da of Douglas Stanley Sargeant (d 1997), of Staplehurst, Kent; *Career* Nat Serv RAF 1954–56; Royal Insurance Group 1953–54 and 1956–57, National Employers Mutual General Insurance Association Ltd 1957–58, co sec Marchant & Tubb Ltd 1959–67, jt sec Tollemache & Cobbold Group Cambridge 1967–70, dep sec International Timber Corporation Ltd 1970–77, gp sec Land Securities plc 1977–98, memb and chm Land Securities Charities Ctee 1998–2007, tstee Land Securities Gp Pension Scheme 1999–2011; tstee Harold Samuel Educnl Tst 1998–; Freeman: Maidstone 1957, City of London 1981; Liveryman: Worshipful Co of Chartered Secretaries and Administrators 1981, Worshipful Co of Masons 1998; FCIS 1972 (ACIS 1968); *Recreations* golf, travel, bridge; *Clubs* City Livery, Broad Street Ward, United Wards' (City of London), Candlewick Ward; *Style*— Laurance Jones, Esq; ✉ 242 Cromwell Tower, Barbican, London EC2Y 8DD

JONES, Lucy Katharine; da of Anthony Tom Brett-Jones, CBE, and Ann, *née* Fox; *b* 21 February 1955; *Educ* Byam Shaw Sch of Art, Camberwell Sch of Art (BA), RCA (MA, Cubitt award for painting, Anstruther award for painting), Br Sch in Rome (Rome scholar in painting); *m* Peter Leach; *Career* self employed artist and painter; formerly visiting tutor at various art colls incl: Ruskin Sch of Art, Byam Shaw Sch of Art, West Surrey Coll of Art and Design, Winchester Sch of Art; currently pt/t tutor Chelsea Coll of Art and Slade Sch of Art; *Solo Exhibitions* Angela Flowers Gallery London 1986, 1987, and 1989, Spitalfields Health Centre in assoc with Whitechapel Art Gallery 1987, Drumcroon Art Educn Centre Wigan 1990, Flowers East London 1991, 1993, 1995, 1997, 1999 and 2000, Flowers Graphics London 1998 and 2001, Flowers West Santa Monica Calif 1999; *Group Exhibitions* incl: Royal Acad Summer Exhibition 1981, 1990, 2000, 2001 and 2002, The Pick of Graduate Art (Christies Inaugural) 1982, 10 Artisti della Accademia Britannica (Palazzo Barberini Rome) 1984, Canvas-New British Painters (John Hansard Gallery and Milton Keynes City Art Gallery) 1986, Artist of the Day (Angela Flowers Gallery) 1986, Young Masters (The Solomon Gallery London) 1986, Whitechapel Open 1987 and 1992, Passage West (Angela Flowers Ireland Co Cork) 1987, The Subjective City (The Small Mansion Arts Centre London) 1988, London Glasgow NY: New Acquisitions (Metropolitan Museum of Art NYC) 1988, Contemporary Portraits (Flowers East) 1988, Big Paintings (Flowers East) 1989, XXI International Festival of Painting Cagnes-sur-Mer-France 1989, Flowers at Moos (Gallery Moos NYC) 1990, The Subjective City (Cleveland Gallery Middlesbrough and tour) 1990, Rome 1980–90 (RCA) 1990, Rome scholars 1980–90 (RCA) 1990, Drumcroon The First Ten Years (Drumcroon Educn Art Centre) 1990, Anglo/Soviet Landscapes (Peterborough and Leningrad) 1991, Foregrounds and Distances (Galleria de Serpenti Rome) 1992, The Discerning Eye (Mall Galleries) 1992, But Big is Better (Flowers East) 1993, Overcoming Obstacles: Women Artists in NW Collections (Blackburn Museum and Art Gallery) 1993, featured artist Art 24 '93 (Basel) 1993, Two Women Artists (with Eileen Cooper, Collyer Bristow London) 1993, Inner Visions (Flowers East) 1994, Downeen Decade (Angela Flowers Gallery) 1994, Ireland Small is Beautiful Park XII: Night and Day (Flowers East) 1994, The Twenty Fifth Anniversary (Flowers East) 1995, John Moore's Exhbn (Walker Art Gallery) 1995, Small is Beautiful Part XIII: Food and Drink (Flowers East) 1995, In the Looking Glass: Contemporary Self Portraits by Women Artists (Usher Gallery Lincoln and touring) 1996, The Whitechapel Open (Whitechapel Art Gallery) 1998, The Hunting Art Prize Exhbn (RCA) 2001, Art-Tube 01 (42 artists on one Piccadilly Line tube train London Underground) 2001; *Work in Public Collections* Sheffield City Art Gallery, Univ of Reading, Arts Cncl, Security Pacific, Metropolitan Museum of Art, Rugby Museum, Drumcroon Education Art Centre Wigan, Unilever plc, Contemporary Art Soc, Arthur Andersen, Clifford Chance, Deutsche Bank AG London, Harris Museum and Art Gallery Preston, Procter & Gamble London, Univ of Hull, Univ of Southampton, Westminster and Chelsea Hosp; *Awards* Oppenheim-John Downes Meml Tst 1986, Daler-Rowney award (best work in oil) Royal Acad Exhibition 1989, John Moore's Exhbn prize winner Walker Art Gallery Liverpool 1995, Grand Award Young Print Royal Acad Summer Exhibition; *Recreations* swimming, music, opera, cooking, sailing; *Style*— Ms Lucy Jones; ✉ Angela Flowers Gallery plc, Flowers East, 82 Kingsland Road, London E2 8DP (✆ 020 8985 3333, e-mail gallery@flowerseast.com, website www.lucyjones.com)

JONES, Prof Malcolm Vince; s of Reginald Cross Jones (d 1986), and Winifred Ethel, *née* Vince (d 1992); *b* 7 January 1940; *Educ* Cotham GS Bristol, Univ of Nottingham (BA, PhD); *m* 27 July 1963, Jennifer Rosemary (d 2016), da of Frederick Walter Durrant (d 1987); 1 s (Alexander b 30 May 1967), 1 da (Helen b 5 Dec 1968); *Career* asst lectr in Russian Sch of Euro Studies Univ of Sussex 1965–67; Univ of Nottingham: lectr 1967–73, sr lectr 1973–80, prof Dept of Slavonic Studies 1980–97, dean Faculty of Arts 1982–85 (vice-dean 1976–79), pro-vice-chllr 1987–91, prof emeritus 1997–; memb Editorial Bd Birmingham Slavonic Monographs 1976–, gen ed Cambridge Studies In Russian Literature 1985–96; hon pres: Assoc of Teachers of Russian 1985–86, Br Universities Assoc of Slavists 1986–88 (hon sec 1974–76), Co-ordinating Cncl for Area Studies Assoc 1991–93 (hon vice-pres 1988–91), Univ of Nottingham Convocation 1992–97; hon vice-pres Br Assoc For Soviet, Slavonic and E European Studies 1988–90 (Hon life member 2005), memb Humanities Research Bd British Acad 1994–97; pres Int Dostoyevsky Soc 1995–98 (Hon life pres 2010); *Books* Dostoyevsky The Novel of Discord (1976), New Essays On Tolstoy (ed, 1978), New Essays On Dostoyevsky (jt ed, 1983), Dostoyevsky after Bakhtin (1990), Cambridge Companion to the Classic Russian Novel (jt ed, 1998), Dostoyevsky and the Dynamics of Religious Experience (2005), Slavianskii Mir, the story of Slavonic Studies at the University of Nottingham in the Twentieth Century (2009), The Vince Family 1848–1982 (2012); numerous articles in academic jls 1968–; *Recreations* painting; *Style*— Prof Malcolm Jones; ✉ University of Nottingham, Department of Russian and Slavonic Studies, University Park, Nottingham NG7 2RD (e-mail malcolmvjones@btinternet.com)

JONES, Marcus Charles; MP; *b* 5 April 1974; *Educ* St Thomas More Catholic Sch Nuneaton, King Edward VI Coll Nuneaton; *m* Suzanne; 1 s (Oliver), 1 da (Martha); *Career*

conveyancy mangr 1999–2010 Tustain Jones & Co Solicitors; cncllr Nuneaton and Bedworth Borough Cncl 2005–09 (ldr 2008–09), MP (Cons) Nuneaton 2010–; *Recreations* angling; *Style*— Marcus Jones, Esq, MP; ✉ House of Commons, London SW1A 0AA

JONES, Mark; s of David Jones, and Jean, *née* Wallet; *b* 10 May 1960; *Educ* John Cleveland Coll Hinckley, Trinity Coll Cambridge; *m* 1990, Annie, da of Bryson Ross; *Career* journalist; ed Londoner's Diary Evening Standard 1986–97, ed Campaign magazine 1989–90, exec features ed Evening Standard 1994–96, ed High Life magazine 1996–2003, editorial dir Cedar Communications 1997–; BSME Ed of the Year (Consumer Magazines) 1997, Travelex Travel Writer of the Year (Magazines) 1999; *Books* Invasion of the Rubbernecks (1990); *Recreations* football, cricket, Andalucia, gazing at rivers; *Clubs* Groucho, BSME, Racing Club de Blackheath; *Style*— Mark Jones, Esq

JONES, Sir Mark Ellis Powell; kt (2010); s of John Ernest Powell-Jones, of Cranleigh, Surrey, and Ann Elizabeth, *née* Murray; *b* 5 February 1951; *Educ* Eton, Univ of Oxford, Courtauld Inst of Art; *m* Dr Ann Camilla, da of Stephen Toulmin; 2 da (Sarah b 9 Oct 1974, Agnes b 7 Feb 1987), 2 s (Luke b 27 Aug 1985, William b 31 Dec 1988); *Career* keeper Dept of Coins and Medals British Museum 1990–92 (asst keeper 1974–90), dir National Museums of Scotland 1992–2001, dir V&A 2001–11; master St Cross Coll Oxford 2011–16; fndr dir SCRAN 1995; hon prof Univ of Edinburgh 1996; memb Advsy Ctee Royal Mint 1994–2004, sec British Art Medal Soc 1982–94 (pres 1998–2004), pres Fédération Internationale de la Médaille 1994–2000; ed The Medal 1983–95, memb Bd: Resource/MLA 2000–05, Crafts Cncl 2001–06, Ct RCA 2001–, Chllr's Forum Univ of Arts London 2002–06; tstee: Nat Tst 2005–, Pilgrim Tst 2006– (chm 2015–), Tullie House Museum, Compton Verney, Watts Gallery, Corning Museum; chm Nat Museum Dirs Conference 2006–09; memb Advsy Bd DCMS 2007–09; Liveryman Worshipful Co of Goldsmiths; Hon DLitt Royal Holloway Coll London 2001, Hon Dr of Art Univ of Abertay Dundee, Hon DLitt UEA, Hon LLD Univ of Dundee, hon fell Winchester Coll Oxford 2015, hon curator Ashmolean Museum; FRSE 1999; *Publications* The Art of the Medal (1977), Impressionist Paintings (1979), Catalogue of French Medals in the British Museum (Vol I 1982, Vol II 1988), Fake: The Art of Deception (ed, 1990), Why Fakes Matter (ed, 1992), Designs on Posterity (ed, 1994); *Clubs* Scottish Arts, Athenaeum; *Style*— Sir Mark Jones; ✉ 31 India Street, Edinburgh EH3 6HE (e-mail markellispowelljones@gmail.com)

JONES, Prof Martin Kenneth; s of John Francis Jones, and Margaret Olive, *née* Baldwin; *b* 29 June 1951; *Educ* Eltham Coll, Peterhouse Cambridge (Frank Smart prize); *m* 29 June 1985, Lucienne Mary, da of Clive Walker; 1 s (Alexander b 20 Dec 1987), 1 da (Leonie b 6 Aug 1990); *Career* environmental archaeologist Oxford Archaeological Unit 1973–78, res asst Botany Sch Univ of Oxford 1978–81, sr lectr Univ of Durham 1989–90 (lectr 1981–89), George Pitt-Rivers prof of archaeological science Univ of Cambridge 1990–, vice master Darwin Coll Cambridge 2012–; Hon DUniv Stirling 1999; FSA 1990, memb Academia Europaea (MAE) 2013; *Books* Environment of Man: The Iron Age to the Anglo Saxon Period (1981), Integrating the Substance Economy (1983), England before Domesday (1986), Archaeology and the Flora of the British Isles (1988), Molecular Information and Prehistory (1999), The Molecule Hunt (2001), Conflict (2006), Feast: Why Humans Share Food (2007), Archaeology Meets Science (2008); *Recreations* walking, sketching, cooking and eating; *Style*— Prof Martin Jones, FSA, MAE; ✉ Department of Archaeology, Downing Street, Cambridge CB2 3DZ (☎ 01223 333507, fax 01223 333503, e-mail mkj12@cam.ac.uk)

JONES, Martyn Eynon; s of Cledwyn Jones, and Megan Jones; *b* 22 July 1951; *Educ* Dynevor GS, Denbigh GS, Denbigh HS, UC Swansea (BSc); *m* 15 Sept 1973, Doreen Judith, da of late Russell, and Muriel Long, of Carlisle; 2 s (Alistair b 1979, Christopher b 1985); *Career* chartered accountant; Robson Rhodes and Deloitte Haskins & Sells 1972–77, Accountancy Tuition Centre 1977–81, under sec then sec Auditing Practices Ctee 1981–84, UK and Ireland advsr to Int Auditing Practices Ctee 1983–84; Deloitte & Touche LLP (formerly Touche Ross & Co): sr mangr 1984–87, nat audit tech ptnr 1987–2012; pro bono talks on employability skills at business schs and univs 2014–; memb: City Regulatory Panel CBI 1993–96, Corp Law Panel CBI 1996–2003, Companies Ctee CBI 2003–12; ICAEW: memb Cncl 2006–, memb Business Law Ctee 1993–2006, chm Special Reports of Accountants Sub-Ctee and Panel 1993–2000, and on Accountants Reports on Internal Controls over Financial Servs Orgns 1997–2013, memb Research Bd 1995–99, vice-chm Tech and Practical Auditing Ctee 1995–2006, advsr on Handbook 1995, chm Working Party on Guidance on Audit Ctees 2001, chm Centre for Business Performance 2002–06, chm Int Standards on Auditing Implementation Sub-Gp 2003–11, memb Corp Governance Ctee 2005–06, chm Ethics Standards Ctee 2006–11, vice-pres 2011–12, dep pres 2012–13, pres 2013–14, chm Bd 2013–14, chm Nominating Ctee 2013–14, chm Working Gp on Audit Insights on the Manufacturing Sector 2013, memb Tech Strategy Bd until 2011; chm: Task Force on future mission of audit and governing principles of auditing 1994, Working Party on reporting on prospective fin info 1996–2000, Ethics Standards Gp Consultative Ctee of the Accountancy Bodies 2006–11; memb: Audit Procedures Task Force Deloitte Touche Tohmatsu International 1990–97, Int Sub-Ctee Auditing Practices Bd 1991–2011, DTI Working Party on revision of company law on financial assistance for purchase of own shares 1993, Working Party on Statements on Investment Circular Reporting Standards 1997–99, Knowledge Task Force Deloitte Touche Tohmatsu 1998, Assurance and Advsy Services Deloitte Touche Tohmatsu 1998–99, Deloitte Touche Tohmatsu Global Service Innovation Bd 1999–2002, Audit Strategy Forum of the Consultative Ctee of Accountancy Bodies 1999–2003, Deloitte Touche Tohmatsu Technical Policy and Methodology Gp then Audit Task Force Leaders 1999–2009, Working Gp of Auditing Practices Bd ongoing concern issues during the current economic conditions 2008, Working Gp of Auditing Practices Bd on Clarified Int Standards on Auditing (UK and Ireland) 2009, Financial Reporting Cncl Advsy Gp on Guidance on Internal Control and Going Concern 2013, memb Takeover Panel 2013–14; patron Chartered Accountants Benevolent Assoc 2013–14; memb Advsy Bd Swansea Univ Sch of Business and Economics 2009–12, chair Advsy Bd Dept of Economics and Finance Brunel Univ 2014–; memb Worshipful Co of Chartered Accountants in England and Wales 2009–; FCA 1981, FRSA 1997; *Books* Safely past the perils – the new investment business accounting requirements (jtly, 1987), The Audit Committee and its Chairman (jtly, 1993), the Finance Director and the Audit Committee (jtly, 1993), Progress Reports and Updates on the Financial Aspects of Corporate Governance (jtly, 1993–), Corporate Governance Handbook (conslt ed, 1996–2003), Taking Fraud Seriously (jtly, 1996), Audit Committees – a framework for assessment (jtly, 1997), Avoiding Corporate Governance Overload (jtly, 1997), Implementing Turnbull (jtly, 1999), The Effective Audit Committe- a Challenging Role (2001); *Recreations* gardening, appreciating Georgian architecture, watching rugby, relaxing in Gower, South Wales and in Cumbria; *Style*— Martyn E Jones, Esq; ✉ Lorne Cottage, 23 Highland Road, Amersham, Bucks HP7 9AU (☎ 01494 722247, e-mail martyn.e.jones@btinternet.com)

JONES, Medwyn; s of Capt Ieuan Glyn Du Platt Jones (d 2008), and Margaret, *née* Owen; *b* 13 September 1955; *Educ* Scorton Sch, Chester GS, Univ of Sheffield (LLB), The Coll of Law; *m* 1990, Rita, da of Raymond Bailey (d 2003); 1 s (George Thomas b 1992), 1 da (Harriet Rhys b 1994); *Career* slr Theodore Goddard 1980–81 (articled clerk 1978–80); ptnr: Walker Martineau 1983–92 (slr 1981–83), Cameron Markby Hewitt 1992–94, Harbottle & Lewis LLP 1994–2014, Wiggin LLP 2014–; memb: Law Soc 1980, BAFTA 2001; Freeman City of London; *Recreations* skiing; *Style*— Medwyn Jones, Esq; ✉ Wiggin LLP, 10th Floor, Met Building, 22 Percy Street, London W1T 2BU

JONES, Prof (Richard) Merfyn; CBE (2011); s of John E Jones, of Llanfrothen, Gwynedd, and Elen Jones, *née* Roberts; *b* 16 January 1948, Tremadog, Gwynedd; *Educ* Ysgol Gynradd Llanfrothen, Ysgol Ardudwy, Univ of Sussex (BA), Univ of Warwick (MA, PhD); *m* 1; 2 c (Rhodri b 1978, Steffan b 1981); m 2, 30 Jan 2004, Nerys, *née* Thomas (d 2007); m 3, 25 July 2009, Catrin, *née* Richards; *Career* sr researcher Univ of Wales Swansea 1971–74; Univ of Liverpool: lectr 1975–80, memb Senate 1981–89, dir Dept of Continuing Educn 1982–85 (sr lectr 1980), actg dean Faculty of Educn 1985 and 1988–89, dir Centre for Community and Educnl Policy Studies 1986–89, memb Cncl 1988–89, fell Dept of Economic and Social History 1989–92, memb Ct 2002–; Univ of Wales Bangor: head Sch of History and Welsh History 1993–96, memb Senate and Cncl 1994–, prof of Welsh history 1995, dean Faculty of Arts and Social Sciences 1996–98, memb Bd of Celtic Studies 1998–, pro-vice-chllr 1998–2003, vice-chllr 2004–10 (actg vice-chllr 2003); visiting lectr: Univ of Paris VIII 1987–89, Univ of Tubingen 1997 (memb Advsy Bd Welsh Studies Centre 1996–); external examiner for numerous educnl insts; BBC: nat govr for Wales 2003–07, memb Bd of Govrs 2003–; memb: Advsy Bd N American Assoc for the Study of Welsh Culture and History 1995–, Mgmnt Bd Univ of Wales Press 2001–03, Hon Degree Ctee Univ of Wales 2003–; chair Broadcasting Cncl for Wales 2003–07, memb Broadcasting Standards Cmmn 2002–03, chair HE Wales, vice-pres Univs UK 2006–08 (memb Bd 2006–09), chair Review of HE in Wales 2008–09, chair Health Bd Betsi Cadwaladr Univ 2011–13, chair N Wales Inst of Welsh Affrs; tstee: Sr Clough Williams-Ellis Fndn, Royal Welsh Yacht Club; BAFTA Cymru Award 2000; memb Gorsedd of Bards Nat Eistedfodd of Wales 2004; FRHistS 1995; *Publications* North Wales Quarrymen 1874–1922 (1981), Hanes Cymru Yn Yr Ugeinfed Ganrif (History of Wales in the Twentieth Century, 1999), contrib to numerous articles; *Recreations* mountaineering, cooking; *Clubs* Athenaeum; *Style*— Prof Merfyn Jones, CBE; ✉ Cae Gwenllian, Pentrefelin, Gwynedd LL52 DRB

JONES, Dr Miah Gwynfor (Gwyn); s of Robert Jones (d 1979), of Porthmadog, Gwynedd, and Jane Irene, *née* Evans (d 1981); *b* 2 December 1948; *Educ* Ysgol Eifionydd Porthmadog, Univ of Manchester (BSc), Univ of Essex (PhD); *m* 10 Jan 1976, Maria Linda, da of Kenneth Johnson (d 1984), of Swansea; 2 da (Victoria Rachel Sian b 1980, Holly Alexandra Jane b 1982); *Career* British Steel 1975–77, ICL 1977–81, chm and chief exec Corporate Technology Group plc 1981–87, chm Welsh Devpt Agency 1988–93; non-exec dir: Tesco plc 1992–98, ACT Group plc 1989–95, Invesco English and Int Tst 1993–, Welsh Water Enterprises Ltd 1990–93; memb Cncl Univ of Wales 1990–95; nat govr for Wales BBC 1992–97, memb S4C Authy 1992–97, HBO & Co (UK) Ltd 1995–97; chm Corporate Technologies 1995–, dep chm Agenda Television Ltd 1997–2000, chm Agenda Online 1999–, exec chm Agenda Multimedia Ltd 2000–, dir Real Radio Ltd 2000–; hon fell Univ of Glamorgan (formerly Poly of Wales) 1991; FBCS; *Recreations* travel, boats, walking, opera; *Style*— Dr Gwyn Jones

JONES, Prof Michael Christopher Emlyn; s of late Reginald Luther Jones, and Megan Bevan Jones; *b* 5 December 1940; *Educ* Rugeley GS, Univ of Leicester, Trinity Coll Oxford (MA, DPhil, DLitt); *m* 1966, Elizabeth Marjorie, *née* Smith; 1 s; *Career* tutor in medieval history Univ of Exeter 1966–67; Univ of Nottingham: asst lectr 1967–69, lectr 1969–81, sr lectr 1981–84, reader in medieval history 1984–91, prof of medieval French history 1991–2002, emeritus prof 2002–; sr scholar Wolfson Fndn 1975, Euro fell Leverhulme Tst 1977, visiting fell All Souls Coll Oxford 1984–85; jt ed Renaissance and Modern Studies 1986–89, ed Nottingham Medieval Studies 1989–2008; jt literary dir Royal Hist Soc 1990–97; pres Lincoln Record Soc 2007–15; author of numerous papers and reviews in hist jls; FRHistS 1971, FSA 1977, Correspondant de l'Institut de France 2006, fell Historical Assoc 2012, membre correspondant Société d'Histoire et d'Archéologie de Bretagne 2015; *Books* Ducal Brittany 1364–1399 (1970, French edn 1998), Philippe de Commynes – Memoirs, the Reign of Louis XI (trans, 1972, internet edn 1999), Recueil des actes de Jean IV, duc de Bretagne (3 vols, ed, 1980–2001), Philippe Contamine – War in the Middle Ages (trans, 1984), John Le Patourel – Feudal Empires Norman and Plantagenet (ed, 1984), Gentry and Lesser Nobility in Later Medieval Europe (ed, 1986), The Family of Dinan in England in the Middle Ages (1987), The Creation of Brittany (collected papers, 1988), England and her Neighbours 1066–1453 – Essays in Honour of Pierre Chaplais (ed with Malcolm Vale, 1989), The Bretons (with Patrick Galliou, 1991, also French, Italian and Czech edns), Aimer les Châteaux de Bretagne (with Prof Gwyn Meirion-Jones, 1991, also English and German edns), Les Châteaux de Bretagne (with Prof Gwyn Meirion-Jones, 1992), Manorial Domestic Buildings in England and Northern France (ed with Prof Gwyn Meirion-Jones, 1993), Recueil des actes de Charles de Blois et Jeanne de Penthièvre, duc et duchesse de Bretagne (1341–1364) (1996), La Ville de Cluny et ses maisons XIe-XVe siècles (with Pierre Garrigou Grandchamp, Gwyn Meirion-Jones and Jean-Denis Salvèque, 1997), Catalogue sommaire des Archives du Fonds Lebreton, Abbaye Saint-Guénolé, Landévennec (1998), The Charters of Duchess Constance of Brittany and her Family, 1171–1221 (with Judith Everard, 1999), New Cambridge Medieval History, vol vi, c.1300-c.1415 (ed, 2000), Handbook of Dates for Students of British History (ed C R Cheney, 1945, revised edn 2000), The Seigneurial Residence in Western Europe AD c 800–1600 (ed with Prof Gwyn Meirion-Jones and Edward Impey, 2002), Between France and England: Politics, Power and Society in Late Medieval Brittany (collected papers, 2003), Letters, Orders and Musters of Bertrand du Guesclin, 1357–1380 (2004), Le Premier Inventaire du Trésor des Chartes des Ducs de Bretagne (1395): Hervé le Grant et les Origines du Chronicon Briocense (2007), Norwell Buildings (2009), Norwell Farms (2009), Willoughby by Norwell Deserted Village (with Elizabeth Jones, 2012), Norwell Church and Chapel (with Elizabeth Jones, 2013); *Recreations* browsing in book shops, gardening, philately, photography; *Clubs* MCC, Athenaeum; *Style*— Prof Michael Jones, FSA; ✉ Parr's Cottage, Main Street, Norwell, Nottinghamshire NG23 6JN (☎ 01636 636365, e-mail mcejones@btinternet.com)

JONES, Milton; s of Dr Colin Jones, and Isabel, *née* Wiesener; *b* 16 May 1964, London; *Educ* Latymer Upper Sch, Middx Poly; *m* 13 Sept 1986, Caroline, *née* Church; 5 c; *Career* stand up comic 1989–; involved with Christians in Comedy; Perrier Best Newcomer Edinburgh Fringe Festival 1996 (nominated 1997), Time Out Best Comedy Performer 2003; *Television* The Stand Up Show (BBC), The Comedy Store (five), The Strangerers (Sky); *Radio* The Very World of Milton Jones (BBC Radio 4) 1998, 1999 and 2001 (nomination Comedy Award 1999, Sony Bronze 2000), The House of Milton (BBC Radio 4) 2003, Another Case of Milton Jones 2005, 2007 and 2008; *Recreations* football; *Style*— Milton Jones, Esq; ✉ c/o Nick Ranceford Hadleigh, Noel Gay, 19 Denmark Street, London (☎ 020 7759 8353)

JONES, Morgan; *Career* qualified CA Touche Ross; fndr dir and jt chief exec Ashtenne1989–2005, currently jt chief exec Hansteen Hldgs plc; *Style*— Morgan Jones, Esq; ✉ Hansteen Holdings plc, 6th Floor, Clarendon House, 12 Clifford Street, London W1S 2LL

JONES, His Hon Judge Nicholas Graham; s of late Albert William Jones, and late Gwendolen Muriel Taylor-Jones, *née* Phillips; *b* 13 August 1948; *Educ* Latymer Upper Sch, St Catherine's Coll Oxford (MA); *m* 25 Sept 1976, Shelagh Ann, da of late Robert Maitland Farror; 1 s (Benjamin Nicholas Farror b 1986); *Career* film ed and prodr BBC 1969–73; called to the Bar Inner Temple 1975; recorder SE Circuit 1994–2001, circuit judge (SE Circuit) 2001–; *Recreations* sailing, walking, music; *Clubs* Royal London Yacht (rear cdre Yachting 2014–15), Royal Ocean Racing, Bar Yacht (cdre 2008–11); *Style*— His Hon Judge Nicholas Jones; ✉ Kingston Crown Court, 6–8 Penrhyn Road, Kingston upon Thames, Surrey KT1 2BB (☎ 020 8240 2500, fax 020 8240 2675)

JONES, Nicholas Keith Arthur (Nick); s of Keith Jones, and Anna, *née* Martin (d 2002); *b* 22 September 1963; *Educ* Shiplake Coll; *m* 1 (m dis); 1 da (Natasha b 2 June 1993), 1 s (Oliver b 8 April 1995); m 2, 30 Sept 1999, Kirsty Young, *qv*, da of John Young; 2 da (Freya b 15 Feb 2001, Iona b 5 April 2006); *Career* restaurateur; md: Cafe Boheme London 1992–, Soho House London 1995–, Babington House Somerset 1998–, Soho Kitchen Bar London 1999–, Electric Cinema and House London 2002–, Soho House NY 2003–, Cecconi's London 2005–, Cowshed Clarendon Cross London 2005–, High Road House and Brasserie Chiswick 2006–, Shoreditch House 2007–, Cowshed Carnaby 2007, Cecconi's West Hollywood 2009–, Pizza East Shoreditch 2009–, Dean Street Townhouse 2009–, Soho House W Hollywood 2010–, Soho House Berlin 2010–, Soho Beach House Miami 2010–, Cecconi's Miami 2010–, Pizza East Portobello 2011–, Pizza East Kentish Town 2012–, Dirty Burger Kentish Town 2012–, Chicken Shop Kentish Town 2012–, Soho House Toronto 2012–, Little House Mayfair 2012, Electric Diner London 2012–, Chicken Shop Tooting 2013–, Cowshed Primrose Hill 2013–, Dirty Burger Vauxhall 2013–, Chicken Shop and Dirty Burger Whitechapel 2014–, Barbour and Parlour Shoreditch 2014, Electric Cinema Shoreditch 2014, Soho House Chicago 2014–, Chicken Shop, Pizza East and Dirty Burger Chicago 2014–, Hubbard and Bell 2014–, Chicken Shop Holborn 2014–, Cheeky Holborn 2014–, Soho House Istanbul 2015–, Cecconi's Istanbul 2015–, Pizza East Istanbul 2015–, Chicken & Egg Shop Balham 2015, Soho Farmhouse Oxfordshire 2015–, Lotti's Amsterdam 2015, Soho House 76 Dean Street 2015–; patron PAC Project Frome, tstee The Roundhouse; *Books* Eat, Drink, Nap (2015); *Recreations* cooking, eating, drinking, napping; *Style—* Nick Jones, Esq; ✉ Soho House, 72–74 Dean Street, London W1D 3SG (☎ 020 7851 1171, 020 7851 1198, e-mail nickjones@sohohouse.com)

JONES, Nicholas Michael Houssemayne; s of Henry J E Jones, of Glos, and Patricia Rose, *née* Holland; *b* 27 October 1946; *Educ* Winchester, London Business Sch (MSc); *m* 1, 25 March 1971 (m dis 1999), Veronica Anne, da of Brig the Hon R G Hamilton-Russell, DSO, LVO, DL; 1 da (Rowena Rose b 5 Sept 1975), 1 s (Oliver Mark b 5 April 1977); m 2, 2 Feb 2002, Cherry Victoria Richardson, da of Sidney Smart; *Career* Peat Marwick Mitchell 1965–73, dir J Henry Schroder Wagg & Co 1975–87, md Lazard & Co 1987–2010 (vice-chm 1999–2008, sr advsr 2008–10); dir: Hilton Group plc 2002–06, Ladbrokes plc 2006–10 (dep chm 2009–10), Newbury Racecourse plc 2007–10, dir Candover Investments plc 2008–10; chm The National Stud 1991–2000, dir Br Horseracing Authy 2011–14; govr: James Allens Girls' Sch 1989–93, Birkbeck Coll London 1995–99; memb London Business Sch Advsy Cncl 1996–, memb Devpt Cncl Winchester Coll 2002–09, memb Patrons' Ctee, Royal Acad 2011–14; FCA 1969; *Recreations* racing, tennis, stalking, bridge, gardening; *Clubs* Turf, Jockey (steward and dir 2011–); *Style—* Nicholas Jones, Esq; ✉ The Manor, Coln St Dennis, Cheltenham, Gloucestershire GL54 3JU (e-mail colnvalleystud@hotmail.com)

JONES, Nigel Glanville Ollerton; s of David Jones, and Gill Jones; *b* 6 May 1958, Rustington, W Sussex; *Educ* St Edward's Sch Oxford; *m* 14 Aug 1982, Alyson, *née* Cuckney; 1 da (Katie b 25 Sept 1987), 1 s (Oliver b 13 Nov 1992); *Career* CA; Ernst & Young: joined as trainee, head of assurance UK 2003–, head of assurance Northern Europe, Middle East, India, Africa 2006–; *Recreations* rugby, tennis, sailing; *Style—* Nigel Jones, Esq; ✉ Ernst & Young, 1 More London, London SE1 2AF (☎ 020 7951 4203, e-mail njones@uk.ey.com)

JONES, Nigel Michael; s of Ralph Michael Jones, of Wolverhampton, and Patricia May, *née* Phelps; *b* 23 September 1960; *Educ* Wolverhampton GS, Keble Coll Oxford (exhibitioner, BA); *m* 27 June 1987, Gillian Hazel, da of Eric Keith Philpot; 2 s (Louis Frederick Bramley, Ethan Alexander Bramley), 1 da (Iona Nancy Bramley); *Career* grad trainee rising to head of account planning and bd dir BMP DDB 1984–98, fndr/managing ptnr Jones Mason Barton Antenen 1999–2000, chief exec Claydon Heeley Jones Mason 2000–05, chief exec DraftFCB Gp UK 2005–08, UK chm and chief exec Publicis 2008–; *Awards* US TV and Radio Commercials Festival Mobius award 1987, 1st prize IPA Advertising Effectiveness Awards 1988, 1st prize and grand prix IPA Advertising Effectiveness Awards 1990; *Recreations* music, playing guitar, chess, golf, Wolverhampton Wanderers; *Style—* Nigel Jones, Esq

JONES, Prof Norman; s of Edward Valentine Jones (d 2008), and Mary Alice, *née* Collins (d 2005); *b* 18 March 1938; *Educ* Evered HS, UMIST (BScTech, MScTech, PhD), Univ of Manchester (DSc); *m* 11 July 1964, Jenny, da of Fred Schofield (d 1946); 2 da (Alison Elizabeth b 29 Aug 1967, Catherine Ann b 8 March 1971); *Career* pt/t lectr Dept of Mech Engrg Manchester Coll of Sci and Technol 1961–63, James Clayton fell IMechE 1962–63, asst lectr Faculty of Technol Univ of Manchester 1963–65; asst prof: Dept of Mech Engrg Georgia Inst of Technol USA 1965–66, Dept of Engrg Brown Univ USA 1966–68; Dept of Ocean Engrg MIT USA: asst prof 1968–70, assoc prof 1970–77, prof 1977–79; Univ of Liverpool: prof of mechanical engrg (A A Griffith prof of mechanical engrg since 1993) 1979–2005 (emeritus prof 2005–), head Dept of Mech Engrg 1982–90, dir Impact Research Centre 1985–2005; hon ed-in-chief Int Jl of Impact Engineering 2008– (ed 1982–87, ed-in-chief 1988–2007), assoc ed Applied Mechanics Reviews 1995–2008; memb Editorial Bd: Jl of Ship Research 1972–80, Int Jl of Mechanical Sciences 1975–, Acta Mechanica Sinica 1991–, Dymat Jl 1992–96, Latin American Jl of Solids and Structures 2003–; memb: Ductile Collapse Ctee 3.1 Int Ship Structures Congress 1985–88, Safety in Mines Res Advsy Bd 1985–2005, Hull and Machinery Ctee Def Scientific Advsy Cncl 1989–95, Man-made Hazards Ctee Inter-Engrg Inst Hazards Forum 1990–99 (chm 1991–95), Solid Mechanics Conf Ctee Euro Mechanics Cncl 1990–2000 (chm 1995–2000), Euromech Cncl 1992–2000, UK Panel Int Union of Theoretical and Applied Mechanics 2000–07; sec Int Ship Structures Congress 1973–76; hon prof: Huazhong Univ of Sci and Technol Wuhan China 1987, Taiyuan Univ of Sci and Technol Shanxi China 1988; IMechE William Sweet Smith Prize 1989, Ludwig Mond Prize 1992, Eminent Scientist Award Wessex Inst of Technol 1998, Bronze Medal RINA 1998; memb ASME 1966 (fell 1990), PEng Massachusetts 1972, foreign fell Indian Nat Acad of Engrg 2005; FIMechE 1980, FRINA 1980, FREng 1998; *Books* Structural Crashworthiness (with T Wierzbicki, 1983), Structural Failure (with T Wierzbicki, 1989), Structural Impact (1989 and 1997, Chinese ed 1994, 2 edn 2012), Structural Crashworthiness and Failure (with T Wierzbicki, 1993), Structures Under Shock and Impact Vols IV to XI (with C A Brebbia, 1996–2010), Impact Loading of Lightweight Structures (with M Alves, 2005); *Recreations* walking, classical music; *Style—* Prof Norman Jones, FREng; ✉ Department of Engineering (Mechanical), The University of Liverpool, Harrison-Hughes Building, The Quadrangle, Liverpool L69 3GH (☎ 0151 794 4858, fax 0151 794 4848, e-mail norman.jones@liv.ac.uk)

JONES, His Hon Norman Henry; QC (1985); s of Warrant Offr Henry Robert Jones, DFM (d 1992), and Charlotte Isabel Scott, *née* Davis (d 2009); *b* 12 December 1941; *Educ* Bideford GS, N Devon Tech Coll, Univ of Leeds (LLB, LLM); *m* 28 March 1970, Trudy Helen, da of Frederick George Chamberlain (d 1974), of Werrington, Cambs; 2 s (Gareth b 22 Dec 1977, Nicholas b 14 April 1981), 1 da (Helena b 6 April 1983); *Career* called to the Bar Middle Temple 1968 (Harmsworth scholar); recorder 1987–92 (asst recorder 1984–87), circuit judge (NE Circuit) 1992–2001, sr circuit judge (NE Circuit) 2001–07, resident judge Bradford Combined Court 2000–01, resident judge Leeds Combined Court 2001–07, hon recorder Leeds 2001–07, asst surveillance cmmr 2007–; *Recreations* boats, walking; *Style—* His Hon Norman Jones, QC

JONES, Olwen Elizabeth; da of William Jones (d 1991), and Margaret Olwen Jones (d 1995); *b* 1 March 1945; *Educ* Harrow Sch of Art (NDD), Royal Acad Schs (silver medal in drawing, bronze medal in painting, David Murray travelling scholar); *m* 1970, Charles Bartlett, s of late Charles Henry Bartlett; *Career* artist; pt/t lectr: Putney Sch of Art 1966–71, Harrow Coll of Art 1970–86, City & Guilds of London Art Schs 1993–94; RE 1982, RWS 1992 (vice-pres 2004); *Exhibitions* solo exhbns incl: Zaydler Gallery London 1971, Oldham Art Gallery 1971, Dudley Museum and Art Gallery 1972, Halesworth Gallery 1973, travelling exhbn (Oldham Art Gallery, Wrexham Library and Art Centre, Lewes Art Centre) 1975, Craftsman Gallery Colchester 1977, Bohun Gallery Henley 1979, 1985, 1988 and 2002, travelling exhbn (Minories Colchester, Usher Gallery Lincoln, Univ of Durham, Oriel Theatre Clkwyd, Towner Art Gallery Eastbourne, Anthony Dawson Gallery London) 1984, Coach House Gallery Guernsey 1989, Printworks Colchester 1991 and 1993, Royal Exchange Theatre Manchester 1994, Hayletts Gallery Colchester 1994, Chappel Galleries Essex 1999, John Russell Gallery Ipswich 2002; gp exhbns incl: RA regularly 1996–, RE regularly 1968–, Barbican Centre London 1985 and 1987, Modern English Graphics Moscow; *Collections* work in numerous private and public collections incl: Dept of the Environment, Beecroft Art Gallery Southend, Bradford City Art Gallery, Graves Art Gallery Sheffield, Norwich Castle Museum, Nat Museum of Wales, Greenwich Library, Dudley Museums and Art Gallery, Reading Museums and Art Gallery, Usher Art Gallery Lincoln, art galleries of Huddersfield, Salford, Plymouth, Bolton, Keighley and Oldham; *Style—* Ms Olwen Jones

JONES, Paul Adrian; né Pond; s of Norman Henry Pond, of Worthing, W Sussex, and Amelia Josephine, *née* Hadfield; *b* 24 February 1942; *Educ* Portsmouth GS, Edinburgh Acad, Jesus Coll Oxford; *m* 1, 1963, Sheila MacLeod; 2 s (Matthew b 21 Oct 1963, Jacob b 10 Jan 1965); m 2, Fiona Jayne, da of Hugh Holbein Hendley; *Career* singer, musician, composer, actor, writer and presenter; memb: Br Actors' Equity, Musicians' Union, Br Acad of Songwriters, Composers and Authors; *Music* gp lead singer Manfred Mann 1962–66 (composer The One in the Middle, 5–4–3–2-1 for TV pop show Ready Steady Go! and others), solo singer 1966–; memb: The Blues Band 1979–, The Manfreds 1994–; songs recorded by numerous artists incl Helen Shapiro and Eric Clapton, has played harmonica for other recording artists, TV and TV advertisements, Royal Ballet Sinfonia featured soloist Street (world premiere) 1993; composer of theme music incl: BBC TV series The Wednesday Play and Fighting Back, films Privilege, The Committee and Intimate Reflections, BBC documentary The Last Vacation; *Theatre* incl: debut as Jack Argue in Muzeeka (Open Space Theatre) 1969, Conduct Unbecoming (Queen's Theatre 1969–70, Ethel Barrymore Theatre NY 1970–71), The Banana Box (Apollo Theatre) 1973, Pippin (Her Majesty's Theatre) 1973–74, Hamlet (Ludlow Festival) 1976, Drake's Dream (Shaftesbury and Westminster Theatres) 1977–78, Cats (New London Theatre) 1982, The Beggar's Opera/Guys and Dolls (Nat Theatre) 1982–83, The Pyjama Game (Leicester Haymarket and tour) 1985–86, Kiss Me Kate (RSC Stratford and tour, Old Vic) 1987, Julius Caesar (Ludlow Festival) 1989; *Films* Privilege 1966, The Committee 1968, Demons of the Mind 1971, The Blues Band 1980; *Television* incl: Top of the Pops, Ready Steady Go! (and other pop shows), A Bit of Discretion (Yorkshire TV) 1968, Square One (LWT) 1971, Z-Cars (BBC) 1972, The Protectors 1973, A Different Kind of Frost, Jackanory, The Sweeney, Space 1999, Great Big Groovy Horse, Twiggy Show (BBC), A Matter of Taste (BBC), The Songwriters (BBC) 1978, The Beggar's Opera (Channel 4) 1983, Weekend (Granada) 1983–84, A Plus 4 (Thames and Channel 4) 1984–85, Beat the Teacher 1985–86, John Lennon – A Journey in the Life 1985, A Royal Celebration 1985, Lyrics by Tim Rice 1985, Live from the Palladium 1988, Uncle Jack series 1990–95; author of play They Put You Where You Are (BBC) 1966; *Radio* Paul Jones on Music (Radio 4) 1983, Counterpoint (BBC World Serv) 1982–92, BBC Radio 2 1985–, GLR 1988–90, Jazz FM 1990–2004; *Recordings* incl: The Andrew Lloyd Webber Collection (Pickwick Records), The Blues Band: Few Short Lines (Repertoire Records), Groovin' With The Manfreds (EMI Records), Solo: Starting All Over Again (CBH Records); *Awards* UK Male Vocalist Br Blues Connection Awards 1990 and 1991, Scroll of Honour (Outstanding Contribution to the Blues) 1993, Gold Badge Award Br Acad of Songwriters, Composers and Authors 1996; Br Blues Awards: Harmonica Player of the Year 2010 and 2011, Broadcaster of the Year 2011, Lifetime Achievement 2011; Blues Fndn (USA) Keeping the Blues Alive 2011; *Recreations* music, books, walking, food, conversation, patron Cranleigh Arts Centre, Nat Jazz Archive; *Style—* Paul Jones, Esq; ✉ c/o Chatto and Linnit, 123a King's Road, London SW3 4PL (☎ 020 7352 7722, fax 020 7352 3450)

JONES, Peter David; CBE (2009); s of David Jones, and Eileen Jones; *b* 18 March 1966; *Career* entrepreneur; estab tennis acad at local club 1982, estab computer business 1984, head of Siemens PC business 1995, prop, chm and ceo Phones Int Gp 1998–, prop Peter Jones TV 2006–, chm and dir of numerous cos incl Red Letter Days, Wireless Logic and Expansys plc, owns capital investment business with portfolio of over 20 companies; TV appearances: Dragons' Den (BBC 2, 7 series) 2005– (investor in cos incl Concentrate, Wonderland Magazine, The Generating Co and Reggae Reggae Sauce), American Inventor 2006–07, Tycoon (ITV) 2007; Emerging Entrepreneur of the Year The Times/Ernst & Young 2001, 10th in Britain's Top Entrepreneurs under 40 Daily Telegraph 2006; *Style—* Peter Jones, Esq, CBE; ✉ website www.peterjones.tv

JONES, His Hon Judge Peter Henry Francis; s of Eric Roberts Jones, MBE, of Swansea (d 2004), and Betty Irene, *née* Longhurst (d 1981); *b* 25 February 1952; *Educ* Bishop Gore GS Swansea, Newport HS Gwent, Balliol Coll Oxford (MA); *m* 3 June 1978, Anne Elizabeth, da of David Jones, DFC (d 1995), of Cheadle; 2 da (Clare b 14 May 1980, Eleanor b 14 July 1982); *Career* admitted slr 1977; ptnr: Darlington & Parkinson Slrs London 1979–87, John Howell & Co Slrs Sheffield 1987–95; stipendiary magistrate then District Judge (Magistrates' Court) S Yorks 1995–2001, recorder 1997–2001, circuit judge 2001–; memb: Lord Chllr's Legal Aid Advsy Ctee 1983–92, Legal Aid Bd 1992–95, Sentencing Advsy Panel 1999–2005, Magistrates' Courts Rules Ctee 2001–04; *Recreations* tennis, watching rugby union, books; *Clubs* Dethreau Boat, Scorpions Cricket, Druidstone (Dyfed); *Style—* His Hon Judge Peter Jones; ✉ Sheffield Combined Court Centre, 50 West Bar, Sheffield S3 8PH

JONES, Prof Peter Howard; s of Thomas Leslie Jones (d 1963), of London, and Hilda Croesora, *née* Parkinson (d 1982); *b* 18 December 1935; *Educ* Highgate Sch, Queens' Coll Cambridge; *m* 1, 1960, (Elizabeth) Jean (d 2009), da of Robert James Roberton, JP (d 1972), of Morebattle, Roxburghshire; 2 da (Rachel (Mrs Michael Groves) b 1964, Laura b 1969); m 2, 2011, Lt Col Dr Diana M Henderson, da of Edna Smith; *Career* Br Cncl 1960–61, res scholar Univ of Cambridge 1961–63, asst lectr in philosophy Univ of Nottingham 1963–64, prof of philosophy Univ of Edinburgh 1984–98 (lectr then reader 1964–84, emeritus prof 1998–), dir Inst for Advanced Studies in the Humanities Edinburgh 1986–2000; assoc dean of arts 1975–78 (undergrad) and 1986–89 (grad); visiting prof of philosophy: Rochester Univ NY 1969–70, Dartmouth Coll NH 1973 and 1983, Carleton Coll MN 1974, Oklahoma Univ 1978, Baylor Univ TX 1978, Univ of Malta 1993, Belarusian State Univ 1997, Jagiellonian Univ Cracow 2001–2013; Mid-America distinguished visiting prof 1978; visiting fell: Humanities Res Centre ANU 1984 and 2002, Calgary Inst for the Humanities 1992; Lothian lectr 1993, Gifford lectr Univ of Aberdeen 1994–95, Loemker lectr Emory Univ GA 1995–96; lectr 1993–2013: Hungarian Acad of Science, Polish Acad of Arts and Sciences, St Petersburg Acad of Sciences, Swiss Acad of Humanities and Social Sciences, Yalta Malta Yalta 1995, The Windsor Meetings 1996–2001, RCDS 1999–2001; tstee: Nat Museums of Scotland 1987–99 (chm Client Ctee 1991–99), Univ of Edinburgh Devpt Tst 1990–98, Morrison's Acad 1984–98, AMAR Int Charitable Fndn 1994–99, Charlemagne Inst 1995–99, Fettes Tst 1995–2005, Fndn for Advanced Studies in Humanities 1997–2002, MBI Al Jaber Fndn, Policy Inst

J

1999–2008, Scots at War 1999–2014; memb: Ct Univ of Edinburgh 1987–90, CHOGM Planning Ctee Malta 1990, Cncl Royal Soc of Edinburgh 1992–95, UNESCO forum on tolerance Tblisi 1995, UNESCO dialogue on Europe and Islam 1997, Spoliation Advsy Panel 2000–; FRSE 1989, FRSA, FSA Scot; *Books* Philosophy and the Novel (1975), Hume's Sentiments (1982), A Hotbed of Genius (ed, 1986, 2 edn 1996), Philosophy and Science in The Scottish Enlightenment (ed, 1988), The Science of Man in the Scottish Enlightenment (ed, 1989), Revolutions in Science, 1789 – 1989 (1989), Adam Smith Reviewed (ed, 1992), Indigenous Peoples and Ethnic Minorities (1993), Family Values in the Mediterranean (1994), Educational Values (ed, 1994), Commonwealth Lectures (ed, 1997), James Hutton: Investigation of the Principles of Knowledge (ed, 1999), The Enlightenment World (ed, 2004, 2 edn 2006), Henry Home, Lord Kames: Elements of Criticism (ed, 2005), The Reception of David Hume in Europe (ed, 2005, 2 edn 2012), Ove Arup Masterbuilder of the Twentieth Century (2006, 2 edn 2008), Conversation: and the Reception of David Hume (2011), New Essays on Adam Smith's Moral Philosophy (jtly, 2012), The Reception of Edmund Burke in Europe (ed, 2016); over 150 articles on philosophical and cultural topics; *Recreations* 18th century music and culture, opera, clavichords conservation, gardening, boxing; *Clubs* Army and Navy; *Style—* Prof Peter Jones, FRSE; ✉ Hillside, Church Road, Wereham PE33 9AP

JONES, Peter Ivan; CBE (2008); s of Glyndwr Jones (d 1995), of Bridport, and Edith Evelyn, *née* Whittaker; *b* 14 December 1942; *Educ* Gravesend GS, LSE (BScEcon); *m* 1 (m dis 1969), Judith, *née* Watson; 1 da (Claire Amanda Markham b 1964), 1 s (Nicholas Francis Markham b 1968); m 2, 15 Aug 1970, Elizabeth, da of Raymond Gent; 1 da (Victoria Louise b 1975), 1 s (Matthew Alexander b 1978); *Career* dir Boase Massimi Pollitt Partnership 1968–75, chief exec Boase Massimi Pollitt plc 1989 (non-exec dir 1983–88), chm BBDO Ltd 1989–90, dir Omnicom Inc 1989–94, chief exec Omnicom UK plc 1989–94, pres Diversified Agency Services (DAS) 1994–97; pres Racehorse Owners' Assoc 1990–93, memb Br Horseracing Bd 1992–96, memb Horserace Betting Levy Bd 1993–95 and 1997–2007, chm Horserace Totalisator Bd 1997–2007 (memb 1995–2007); chm Dorset Police Authy 1997–2003 (memb 1995–2003), dir Goodwood Racecourse 2008–; 'The Scout' (columnist) Daily Express 2015–; govr LSE 2007–, tstee Animal Health Tst 2011–15, ; MIPA 1971; *Publications* Trainers Record (1973–87); *Recreations* watching all sport, computer programming; *Style—* Peter Jones, Esq, CBE; ✉ Melplash Farmhouse, Melplash, Bridport, Dorset DT6 3UH (☎ 01308 488383, e-mail pijones@hotmail.co.uk); 34 Rossetti Garden Mansions, Flood Street, London SW3 5QX (☎ 020 7352 8977)

JONES, Prof Philip; *Career* pro-vice-chllr Univ of Sheffield 1998–2004, dep vice-chllr and sub-warden Durham Univ 2004–07, vice-chllr Sheffield Hallam Univ 2007–; FRSA; *Style—* Prof Philip Jones; ✉ Sheffield Hallam University, City Campus, Howard Street, Sheffield S1 1WB

JONES, Sir Philip Andrew; KCB, ADC; *Career* joined RN 1978; CO HMS Beaver 1994, dir Navy Plans MOD 1997, CO HMS Coventry and capt 1st Frigate Sqdn 1999, military asst to the Chief of Defence Logistics 2002, dir Jt Maritime Operational Trg Staff 2003, asst COS to the C-in-C 2004, cdr Amphibious Task Gp 2006, Flag Offr Scotland, Northern England and NI 2008, Cdr UK Maritime Forces 2008, Asst Chief of the Naval Staff 2009, Dep C-in-C Fleet and COS Navy Command HQ 2011, Dep Fleet Cdr 2012, Fleet Cdr and Dep Chief of the Naval Staff 2012, First Sea Lord 2016–; *Style—* Sir Philip Jones, KCB, ADC

JONES, Prof Philip Douglas; s of Douglas Idris Jones, and Peggy Rita Yvonne, *née* Cleave; *b* 22 April 1952, Redhill, Surrey; *Educ* Glyn GS Ewell, Lancaster Univ (BA), Univ of Newcastle upon Tyne (MSc, PhD); *m* 4 Aug 1973, Ruth Anne; 1 da (Hannah Megan b 21 March 1977), 1 s (Matthew David b 14 Aug 1978); *Career* UEA: prof Sch of Environmental Sciences, dir Climatic Research Unit 1976–; memb Editorial Ctee Int Jl of Climatology until 1995, memb Editorial Bd Climatic Change; author of 200 scientific papers in peer-review jls; Hugh Robert Mill Medal Royal Meteorological Soc 1995 (jtly), Outstanding Scientific Paper Award Environmental Research Labs/NOAA 1997, Hans Oeschger Medal European Geophysical Soc 2002, Int Jl of Climatology Prize Royal Meteorological Soc 2002; hon degree Univ Rovira I Virgili Tarragona Spain 2012; memb: Academia Europaea 1998, American Meteorological Soc 2001; FRMetS 1992, fell American Geophysical Union 2009; *Books* Climate Since AD 1500 (co-ed, 1992), Climatic Variations and Forcing Mechanisms of the Last 2000 Years (co-ed, 1996), History and Climate: Memories of the Future (co-ed, 2001), Improved Understanding of Past Climatic Variability from Early European Instrumental Sources (co-ed, 2002); *Style—* Prof Philip Jones; ✉ Climatic Research Unit, School of Environmental Sciences, University of East Anglia, Norwich NR4 7TJ (☎ 01603 592090, e-mail p.jones@uea.ac.uk)

JONES, Philip Gwyn; s of Gwynfryn Jones, and Beatrice Evelyn Jones; *Educ* Bishop of Llandaff Sch, Univ of York; *m* ; 1 s, 1 da; *Career* rights asst Aladdin Books Ltd 1988–89; Collins Publishers (later Harper Collins Publishers): ed 1989–92, sr ed 1992–94, ed dir Fontana Press 1994–96, publishing dir Flamingo 1996–2004; publisher Granta Books and Portobello Books 2007–13 (fndr Portobello Books 2005); ed-at-large Scribe UK 2014–; tstee Royal Literary Fund 2012–, tstee English PEN 2014–, panellist Welsh Books Cncl; fell in creative writing Oxford Brookes Univ 2015–; *Publications* articles on the Bookseller website and Spectator blog; *Recreations* reading to my children, Italy, eating well; *Clubs* Electric House; *Style—* Philip Gwyn Jones, Esq

JONES, Philip Neville; s of James Neville Jones, of Hawarden, Flintshire, and Grace Linda, *née* Davies; *b* 8 June 1951, Hawarden, Flintshire; *Educ* Univ of Strathclyde, MSc, Inst of Mgmnt Servs (Dip); *m* 26 July 1975, Jacqueline, *née* Paterson; 3 s (Gareth b 18 Oct 1978, Matthew b 31 July 1981, Andrew b 21 July 1986); *Career* positions in prodn engrg, industrial engrg and mgmnt with Lucas/Girling, Firestone and Unilever; Dumfries and Galloway Cncl (formerly Dumfries and Galloway Regnl Cncl): asst regnl mgmnt servs offr Dept of Admin and Law 1980, asst dir of IT, corporate business mangr Office of the Chief Exec 1989, dep chief exec and head of corporate business 1995–98, interim chief exec 1998–99, chief exec 1999–2009; chm NHS Dumfries and Galloway 2014–; former hon sec SOLACE Scotland; chartered mangr CMI; *Recreations* playing golf, squash, watching football, walking, gardening, travelling; *Style—* Philip Jones, Esq

JONES, Rhiannon; QC (2015); *Educ* KCL (BMus, MA); *Career* called to the Bar (Inner Temple) 1993; memb: Personal Injury Bar Assoc, Professional Negligence Bar Assoc; AKC; *Style—* Ms Rhiannon Jones, QC

JONES, Rhidian Huw Brynmor; s of Rev Preb Ivor Brynmor Jones (d 1982), and Elizabeth Mary Jones (d 1996); *Educ* Queen Mary's GS Walsall, Keble Coll Oxford (MA); *m* 8 Aug 1970, Monica Marianne, da of Bror Eric Sjunne Sjöholm (d 1957), of Halmstad, Sweden; 1 da (Anna b 1978), 1 s (Gavin b 1982); *Career* trainee sec asst Selection Tst Ltd 1966–68, legal asst Total Oil GB Ltd 1968–69, co sec J E Lesser (Hldgs) Ltd 1969, asst sec Granada Group Ltd 1970–76, articled clerk and asst slr Herbert Smith 1976–80, sr asst slr Kenneth Brown Baker Baker (sic) 1980–81, ptnr Turner Kenneth Brown 1981–2002 (merged with Nabarro May 1995), head of corporate dept Nabarro 1999–2002, conslt Grundberg Mocatta Rakison LLP (merged with McGuireWoods 2009) 2003–12; non-exec dir: Mornington Building Society 1986–91, Serco Group Plc 1987–94 and 1996–2004, The Mortgage Agency plc 1988–93, Britannia Building Society 1993–2003 (dep chm 2000–2002), Ealing Hosp NHS Tst 2004–07, Unity Tst Bank plc 2004–13, Supervisory Bd Thompsons LLP 2012–16; vice-pres Ealing FC (RU), tstee and hon legal advsr Middx Co RFU Youth Tst 1994–2003; tstee: Middx Co RFU Memorial Fund 1996–2007, Middx Sports Fndn (chm 2008–), The Second World War Experience Centre 1998–2008 (chm 2007–08); former memb Cncl Anglo Swedish Soc, memb Swedish BV Soc 1997 (Viking 1998, Berserk 1999, Hirdman 2002); Freeman City of London Slrs' Co 1979, memb Ct of Assts Worshipful Co of Turners 2002 (Freeman 1992, Liveryman 1993, Master's Steward 2010, Renter Warden 2011, Upper Warden 2012, Master 2013, Dep Master 2014); FCIS 1976, memb Law Soc 1978, FCMI 1987, FInstD 1998 (MInstD 1987); *Recreations* rugby, military history, Celtic and Scandinavian studies; *Clubs* Rotary (London); *Style—* Rhidian Jones, Esq; ✉ Roseleigh, 80 Elers Road, Ealing, London W13 9QD (☎ 020 8579 9785, fax 020 8579 9892, mobile 07768 171475)

JONES, Richard; CBE (2015); *Career* director; *Theatre* incl: Too Clever by Half (Old Vic, Olivier Award), The Illusion (Old Vic, Evening Standard Award), A Flea in Her Ear (Old Vic), The Hairy Ape (Old Vic), Six Characters Looking for an Author (Young Vic), Hobson's Choice (Young Vic), The Good Soul of Szechuan (Young Vic), Annie Get Your Gun (Young Vic), The Government Inspector (Young Vic), Public Enemy (version of The Enemy of the People, Young Vic), The Trial (Young Vic), Into the Woods (Phoenix Theatre London, Olivier Award, Evening Standard Award), Tales from the Vienna Woods (NT), A Midsummer's Night Dream (RSC, Yale and Salamanca Festival), Holy Mothers (Ambassadors/Royal Court Theatre), Rumpelstiltskin – David Sawer (Birmingham Contemporary Music Gp, Spitalfields Festival London), La B?te (Eugene O'Neill Theater NY, Tony Nominated), Titantic (Lunt Fontaine Theater NY), Black Snow (American Rep Theatre NY), All's Well That Ends Well (Public Theatre NY); *Opera* incl: Der Ring des Nibelungen (ROH, Evening Standard Award), Anna Nicole (world premiere, ROH), Lady Macbeth of Mtsensk (ROH, Olivier Award), L'Heure Espagnol/Gianni Schicchi, The Gambler, Il Trittico (ROH), Gloriana, Boris Godunov (ROH), The Girl of the Golden West, Rodelinda, Cavalleria Rusticana, Pagliacci, The Trojans (ENO, Olivier Award), Lulu and Julietta (ENO), The Mastersingers of Nuremberg (ENO, 2 Olivier Awards), Wozzeck (WNO, Royal Philharmonic Soc Award), Hansel and Gretel (WNO, Olivier Award), Die Meistersinger von Nurnberg (WNO, South Bank Show Award), Der Rosenkavalier (Glyndebourne), Ariodante (Aix en Provence Festival), Lohengrin (Munich Opera), Billy Budd (Frankfurt Opera), Peter Grimes (La Scala, Milan), Un Ballo en Maschera (Bregenz Festival), L'Enfant et les Sortileges (Paris Opera), Der Zweig (Paris Opera), Julietta (Paris Opera), Der Fliegende Holländer (Amsterdam Opera), Jenufa (Amsterdam Opera), The Cunning Little Vixen (Amsterdam Opera), Billy Budd (Amsterdam Opera), Wozzeck (Komische Opera Berlin); *Style—* Richard Jones, Esq, CBE; ✉ c/o Judy Daish Associates Ltd; 2 St Charles Place, London W10 6EG (☎ 020 8964 8811, fax 020 8964 8966)

JONES, Richard Henry; QC (1996); s of Henry Ingham Jones (d 1993), and Betty Marian, *née* Allison (d 2010); *b* 6 April 1950; *Educ* Moseley GS Birmingham, St Peter's Coll Oxford (MA); *m* 1989, Sarah Jane, da of Peter Wildsmith; 1 s (Christopher b 12 March 1991), 1 da (Bryony Alice b 21 July 1994); *Career* called to the Bar Inner Temple 1972, in practice 1972–80 and 1986–, asst recorder 1999–2000, recorder 2000–; legal advsr: Crown Life Insurance Gp 1980–82, FT Gp 1982–86; chm Editorial Bd Counsel 2006–12, former chm Fin Reporting Cncl Disciplinary Tbnl; fell Soc of Advanced Legal Studies; *Publications* Investigations and Enforcement (2001); *Recreations* cricket and rugby (as spectator), walking, reading; *Clubs* MCC, RAC, London Scottish FC; *Style—* Richard Jones, Esq, QC; ✉ 5 Fountain Court, Steelhouse Lane, Birmingham B4 6DR (☎ 0121 606 0500)

JONES, Prof Robert Maynard; s of Sydney Jones (d 1956), of Cardiff, and Edith Jones (d 1981); *b* 20 May 1929; *Educ* Univs of Wales and Ireland (MA, PhD, DLitt); *m* 27 Dec 1952, Anne Elizabeth, da of John James (d 1979), of Clunderwen; 1 s (Rhodri Siôn), 1 da (Lowri Gwenllian); *Career* former head Dept of Welsh Language and Literature Univ of Wales Aberystwyth 1980 (lectr and sr lectr 1955–77, reader 1978, prof 1980, now emeritus prof); memb Editorial Bd Welsh Nat Dictionary; Welsh Arts Cncl Prizes 1956, 1959, 1971, 1987, 1990 and 1998; fell Yr Academi Gymreig 1965 (pres 2010); FBA 1993, FLSW 2011; *Books* Nid Yw D?r yn Plygu (1958), I'r Arch (1959), Cyflwyno'r Gymraeg (1964), Ci Wrth y Drws (1968), System in Child Language (1970), Traed Prydferth (1973), Tafod y Llenor (1974), Llên Cymru a Chrefydd (1977), Seiliau Beirniadaeth (1984–88), Selected Poems (1987), Casgliad o Gerddi (1988), Crio Chwerthin (1990), Dawn Gweddwon (1992), Cyfriniaeth Gymraeg (1994), Canu Arnaf (1995), Epistol Serch a Selsig (1997), Ysbryd y Cwlwm (1998), Ynghylch Tawelwch (1998), O'r Bedd i'r Crud (2000), Mawl a'i Gyfeillion (2000), Mawl a Gelynion ei Elynion (2002), Ôl Troed (2003), Dysgu Cyfansawdd (2003), Beirniadaeth Gyfansawdd (2003), Rhy Iach (2004), Y Fadarchen Hudol (2005), Meddwl y Gynghanedd (2005), Yr Amhortreadwy (2009), Bratiau Budron (2011), Y Cynllun Sy'n Canu (2011), Breuddwydion Maxine (2011), A Fydd y Cymry Cymraeg Mewn Pryd? (2011), Palu'r Ardd (2011), Right as Rain (2012), Storïau (2012), Hanes Beirniadaeth Gymraeg Ddiweddar (2012), Gobaith ac Anobaith Waldo ac RS (2012), Canolfan (2015), Problemau (2015), Ysgrifau Coffa (2016); *Style—* Prof Emeritus Robert Jones, FBA, FLSW; ✉ Tandderwen, Heol Llanbadarn, Aberystwyth, Dyfed SY23 1HB (☎ 01970 623603)

JONES, Robyn Anne; OBE (2011); da of David Lardge, and Patricia Mary, *née* Fenton Smith (d 1993); *b* 20 August 1961, Sutton Coldfield, W Midlands; *m* 30 Aug 1986 Timothy Jones, *qv*; 1 da (Tabitha b 5 Sept 1995), 1 s (Blake b 26 April 1999); *Career* grad trainee, asst cook then chef/mangr Grandmet (Compass) Catering 1981–83, catering mangr Gardner Merchant Ltd 1983–85, catering advsy offr Potato Mktg Bd London 1985–87, ops mangr High Table Ltd 1987–88, mangr then sr ops mangr Compass Services (UK) Ltd 1988–90, business devpt mangr Gazeway Catering 1990–91, ceo Charlton House Catering Services Ltd 1991–; tstee PM Tst; Booker Prize for Excellence 1993/94, Thames Valle Business Quality Award 1994, Thames Valley Business Enterprise Award 1996, Thames Valley Business Woman of the Year Award 1997, Virgin Atlantic Fast Tract 100 1997, Daily Telegraph/Energis Customer Service Award 2001, Daily Telegraph/Sage Growing Business Award 2002, Daily Telegraph/Sage Best Website Award 2002, Contract Caterer of the Year 2002, Deloitte & Touche Indy Winner 2003, Deloitte & Touche Indy 100 Winner 2004, Ernst & Young Southern Region Entrepreneur of the Year 2004, No 56 in CatererSearch 100 Listing of the Most Influential Figures in UK Hospitality 2005, Catey Award Food Service Caterer of the Year 2006; FIH, FHCIMA 1992 (MHCIMA 1985); *Recreations* swimming, cooking; *Style—* Mrs Robyn Jones, OBE; ✉ The Clock Tower, Wyfold Farm, Wyfold, Reading RG4 9HU

JONES, Roger; s of Bernard Jones, of Lampeter, Ceredigion, and Menna, *née* Evans; *b* 4 January 1961, Lampeter, Ceredigion; *Educ* Wycliffe Public Sch Stonehouse Glos; *m* 18 July 1992, Susan, *née* Raymond; 1 da (Rhiannon b 16 Oct 1993), 1 s (Richard b 23 March 1996); *Career* restaurateur; head chef Payne and Gunter, incl state banquets and Downing Street 1981–87, freelance chef 1987–98, prop and chef The Harrow at Little Bedwyn Wilts 1998–; fndr: Dine Australia 2006–, The Mamba Awards 2006–; conslt chef, wine conslt and judge Decanter World Wine Awards 2008–; journalism incl writing for The Caterer, Hotelkeeper Magazine (as wine conslt), Decanter Magazine (as panellist), Wiltshire Life; Master Chef of GB (fell 2011); *Awards* for The Harrow at Little Bedwyn: Michelin Star, Wine Spectator Best of Award of Excellence 2005, 2006 and 2007, AA Winelist of the Year 2006, Decanter Restaurant of the Year 2007, AA Restaurant of the Year; *Recreations* Welsh rugby; *Clubs* London Cornish RFC; *Style—* Roger Jones, Esq; ✉ The Harrow at Little Bedwyn, Marlborough, Wiltshire SN8 3JP (☎ 01672 870871, e-mail roger@harrowinn.co.uk, website www.theharrowatlittlebedwyn.com, www.rogerjonesconsultancy.com)

JONES, (James) Roger; s of Albert James Jones (d 1999), and Hilda Vera, *née* Evans (d 1989); *b* 30 May 1952; *Educ* Shrewsbury, St Catharine's Coll Cambridge (sr scholar, MA);

Career called to the Bar Middle Temple 1974 (Lloyd Jacob Meml exhibitioner, Astbury scholar), practised Oxford and Midland Circuit 1975–83, Office of the Parliamentary Counsel 1983–94, with Law Commission 1988–91, dep parliamentary counsel 1991–94; head Antique Dept Colefax & Fowler 1994–, dir Sibyl Colefax & John Fowler 1995–; *Recreations* walking the dog; *Style*— Roger Jones, Esq; ✉ Sibyl Colefax & John Fowler, 39 Brook Street, London W1K 4JE

JONES, Prof Ronald Mervyn; s of Cdr Glyn Owen Jones, MBE, OStJ (d 1987), and Doris, *née* Woodley (d 1983); *b* 24 April 1947; *Educ* Devonport HS Plymouth, Univ of Liverpool (MD); *m* 1, 1970 (m dis 1988), Angela Christine, *née* Parsonage; 1 da (Emily b 1976), 1 s (Alex b 1979); m 2, 1989, Caroline Ann, da of Dr Neill Wordsworth Marshall; 2 da (Catherine Elizabeth b 17 Feb 1992, Lucy Clare b 21 Jan 1995); *Career* memb Faculty: Karolinska Inst Stockholm 1978, Univ of Michigan 1979–80; conslt Nottingham Hosps 1981–82, sr lectr and conslt Guy's Hosp 1982–90, prof of anaesthetics Imperial Coll London and conslt anaesthetist St Mary's Hosp 1990–99; memb: Advsy Ctee on NHS Drugs Dept of Health 1990–99, Cncl Royal Coll of Anaesthetists 1997–2002 (dir of continuing educn and professional devpt); chm Assoc of Profs of Anaesthetics 1996–2001; civilian advsr to RN; academician Euro Acad of Anaesthesiology; hon life memb Aust Soc of Anaesthetists; FFARCS; *Books* Medicine for Anaesthetists (1989), Clinical Anaesthesia (1995); *Recreations* music, history, sailing; *Clubs* Royal Navy and Royal Marines Mountaineering; *Style*— Prof Ronald Jones

JONES, Prof Ronald Samuel; OBE (1998), JP; s of Samuel Jones (d 1974), of Oswestry, Shropshire, and Gladys Jane, *née* Philips (d 1953); *b* 29 October 1937; *Educ* Oswestry Boys' HS, Univ of Liverpool (BVSc); *m* 21 April 1962, Pamela, da of Wilfred Evans, of Pant Oswestry, Shropshire; 2 da (Rachel Mary Patricia b 1963, Alison Jane b 1966); *Career* Univ of Glasgow: house surgn 1960–61, univ asst 1961–62; Univ of Liverpool: lectr 1962–77, sr lectr 1977–86, reader 1986–89, prof 1990–, emeritus prof 2001; RCVS: memb Cncl 1986–98, treas 1993–95, pres 1996–97; chm Farriers' Registration Cncl 2010–12; John Henry Steele Medal RCVS 1989, Coll Medal RCA 1996; FRSM, FRCVS 1981 (MRCVS 1960), FSB 1988, Hon FRCA 2001, DVSc Pretoria 1992; *Recreations* gardening, horse racing, philately, fly fishing; *Clubs* Farmers, RSM; *Style*— Prof Ronald S Jones, OBE; ✉ 7 Birch Road, Oxton, Prenton, Merseyside CH43 5UF (☎ 0151 653 9008, fax 0151 653 7551)

JONES, Rupert Edward; *b* 26 September 1976; *Educ* Downside, Oxford Brookes Univ; *m* Sophie, *née* Breakwell; *Career* former head of real estate (Middle East) BNP Paribas 2005–8, fndr and chief exec Wulstan Capital 2009–; *Recreations* cricket, horse racing; *Style*— Rupert Jones, Esq; ✉ 11 Windlesham Grove, London SW19 6AW (☎ 020368 56861, e-mail rupertjones@live.com); Wulstan Capital, 80 Brook Street, Mayfair, London W1K 5DD (☎ 07584 160525, e-mail rupert.jones@wulstancapital.com)

JONES, Rupert James Livingston; s of Walter Herbert Jones (d 1982), and Dorothy Jocelyn, *née* Dignum (d 1989); *b* 2 September 1953; *Educ* KCS Wimbledon, Univ of Birmingham (LLB); *m* 24 June 1978, Sheila Carol, da of Andrew Kertesz (d 1993); 3 s (Oliver b 10 June 1984, Stephen b 13 Sept 1989, Michael b 20 Feb 1994), 1 da (Philippa b 31 Jan 1987); *Career* admitted slr 1978; ptnr: Allen and Overy 1985–97 (articled clerk 1976–78, asst slr 1978–85), Sonnenschein Nath & Rosenthal 1997–99, Buchanan Ingersoll 2000–02; counsel Weil, Gotshal & Manges 2002–; chm London Young Slrs Gp 1987–88 (Ctee 1984–89), memb Nat Ctee Young Slrs Gp 1986–89; chm: Whittington Ctee City of London Slrs Co 1992–94 (memb 1988–94), Planning and Environmental Law Ctee City of London Law Soc 2005–15 (memb 1997–); cncllr Dunsfold PC 2015–; Liveryman Worshipful Co of Slrs 1998 (memb 1985, asst 2011, Steward 2015); memb Law Soc 1976; *Recreations* gardening, cinema, motoring, computing; *Style*— Rupert Jones, Esq; ✉ Weil, Gotshal and Manges, 110 Fetter Lane, London EC4A 1AY (☎ 020 7903 1000, fax 020 7903 0990, e-mail rupert.jones@weil.com)

JONES, Russell Alan; *b* 26 May 1960; *Educ* Greenshaw HS Sutton, Univ of Kent at Canterbury (BA); *Career* orch personnel mangr Royal Liverpool Philharmonic Soc 1981–86, concerts mangr Scottish Chamber Orch 1986, chief exec and co sec Nat Fedn of Music Socs 1987–97, head of Business in the Arts ABSA 1997–99, dir of Prog Arts and Business 1999, dir of Operations Arts and Business 2000–01, dir of Policy and Public Affrs 2001–02; dir Assoc of Br Orchs 2002–07, vice-pres for mktg and membership devpt League of American Orchs NY 2007–12; NY Philharmonic: dir Friends Prog 2012–13, dir Individual and Planned Gifts 2013–14, dir Patron Prog 2014–15, sr devpt offr 2015–; admin Haydn Orch 1986–, jt fndr/admin/co sec Southwark Music Festival 1988–90; vice-pres Nat Fedn of Music Socs 1998, vice-pres Acad of Live and Recorded Arts 2000–04, chm Nat Music Cncl of GB 1995–2000 (memb Exec Ctee 1987–95), hon treas and sec Voluntary Arts Network 1991–97; memb: Cncl Amateur Music Assoc 1987–89, Cncl London Symphony Chorus 1987–89, 1991–94 and 1996–98, Steering Ctee Nat Music Day 1992–94, Musicians Benevolent Fund, Nat Campaign for the Arts, Nat Tst; pres American Friends of the Acad of St Martin in the Fields 2010–12; past master Billingsgate Ward Club; Freeman City of London 2003, Liveryman Worshipful Co of Musicians 2003; FRSA; Chevalier Order of Champagne; *Recreations* music, singing, piano, violin, current affairs, Br and American politics, cooking and entertaining, wine, badminton; *Style*— Russell Jones, Esq; ✉ 854 West 180th Street, Apartment 3C, New York, NY 10033, USA (☎ 001 202 390 1038)

JONES, Sarah; *b* 1 June 1968, Otley, W Yorks; *Educ* Univ of Leeds (MBA); *m*; 1 s, 1 da; *Career* BAE Systems: military project and contract mgmnt 1990–2000, COS 2001–02, dir RG Ammunition 2002–05; ceo learndirect Ltd 2005– (lead MBO 2011); non-exec dir Sheffield Children's Hosp Fndn Tst 2008–, non-exec dir Digital Outreach Ltd 2012–; former vol cnsllr prison service, sch govr; *Style*— Mrs Sarah Jones; ✉ learndirect Ltd, Dearing House, 1 Young Street, Sheffield S1 4UP

JONES, Simon Benedict; s of Harford Colin Jones, of High Peak, Derbys, and Josephine May, *née* Elliott (d 1969); *b* 2 May 1957, Chippenham, Wilts; *Educ* Manchester Grammar, Peterhouse Cambridge (scholar, BA); *m* 30 June 1984, Philippa Armorel, *née* Towler; 1 s (Timothy b 20 Jan 1991), 1 da (Christabel b 20 Sept 1993); *Career* dir of IT CAB International 1994–99, technol dir Dialog CD-ROM Div 1999–2001, head of technol UK Thomson Dialog 2001–04, chief info offr Dept for Int Devpt 2004–11, dir UN Int Computing Centre 2011–; govr Cholsey Primary Sch 1997–2011; *Publications* Modelling Under Uncertainty (jt ed, 1986); *Recreations* croquet, travel; *Clubs* Blewbury Croquet; *Style*— Simon Jones, Esq; ✉ International Computing Centre, Palais des Nations, 1211 Geneva 10, Switzerland (☎ 0041 22 929 1401, e-mail jones@unicc.org)

JONES, Stephen; s of Joseph Jones, of Manchester, and Constance, *née* Potter; *b* 15 November 1962, Ashton-under-Lyne, Lancs; *Educ* Manchester Grammar, Queen's Coll Cambridge (MA), Manchester Met Univ; *partner* Maria O'Malley; 3 s (Ocean b 16 Feb 1998, Macdara b 16 June 1999, Holden b 10 May 2004), 1 da (Pebbles b 17 April 2003); *Career* admitted slr 1986; Goldberg Blackburn & Howards (now Pannone LLP): trainee slr 1984–86, slr 1986–91; slr Russell Jones & Walker 1991–92, ptnr Pannone LLP 1992–2015, ptnr Leigh Day 2015–; slr to Royal Liverpool Children's Inquiry 2000, slr to Redfern Inquiry into tissue sampling in UK nuclear facilities 2007; memb: Clinical Negligence Panel Law Soc, Slrs' Referral Panel Action Against Medical Accidents (AvMA), MIND Legal Network; memb Law Soc 1984; *Recreations* following Manchester City FC home and away; *Style*— Stephen Jones, Esq; ✉ Leigh Day, Central Park Building C, Northampton Road, Manchester M40 5BP (☎ 0161 393 3530, e-mail sjones@leighday.co.uk)

JONES, Prof Stephen John Moffat; OBE (2010); s of Gordon Jones, of Marlow, Bucks, and Margaret, *née* Moffat; *b* 31 May 1957, W Kirby, Cheshire; *Educ* Liverpool Coll, St Martin's Sch of Art (BA); *Career* model millinery designer 1981–, estab diffusion range Miss Jones/Jones Boy 1989; first British milliner to work for French designer collections (clients have included Marc Jacobs, John Galliano, Comme des Garçons, Claude Montana and Christian Dior); designer of hats for film and music business; work in perm collections of: V&A London, Australian Nat Gallery Canberra, Met Museum of Art NY, Kyoto Costume Inst; references of work included in Status, Style, Glamour (Colin McDowell, Thames and Hudson, 1992); hon prof of millinery Univ of the Arts London 2008; Outstanding Contrib to Fashion Design British Fashion Award 2009; Royal Designer 2009; FRSA; *Publications* Hats, an Anthology by Stephen Jones, Stephen Jones & The Accent of Fashion; *Recreations* painting, sculpture; *Clubs* Arts; *Style*— Prof Stephen Jones, OBE; ✉ Stephen Jones Millinery Ltd, 36 Great Queen Street, Covent Garden, London (☎ 020 7242 0770, fax 020 7242 0796, website www.stephenjonesmillinery.com)

JONES, Stewart Elgan; QC (1994); s of Gwilym John Jones (d 1987), of Flecknoe, Warwickshire, and Elizabeth, *née* Davies; *b* 20 January 1945; *Educ* Cheltenham Coll, The Queen's Coll Oxford (MA); *m* 21 July 1979, Jennifer Anne, da of Maj James Ian Leonard Syddall (d 1963), of Riseley, Berks; 2 da (Eleanor b 1980, Clementine b 1981), 2 step c (Katherine b 1969, James b 1971); *Career* called to the Bar Gray's Inn 1972 (bencher 2002); memb Western Circuit, recorder of the Crown Court 1990–; *Recreations* home, hearth, the great outdoors, painting; *Style*— Stewart E Jones, Esq, QC; ✉ 3 Paper Buildings, Temple, London EC4Y 7EU (☎ 020 7583 8055, fax 020 7353 6271)

JONES, Susan Elan; MP; da of Richard James Jones, and Margaret Eirlys, *née* Thomas; *b* 1 June 1968, Wrexham, Wales; *Educ* Grango Comp Sch Wrexham, Ruabon Comp Sch, Univ of Bristol, Cardiff Univ; *Career* English teacher Tomakomai English Sch Japan 1990–91, English teacher Atsuma Bd of Educn Japan 1992–94, corp devpt fundraiser Muscular Dystrophy Gp 1995–96, fundraiser USPG 1997–2002, dir CARIS Haringey 2002–05, fundraising exec Housing Justice 2005–10; MP (Lab) Clwyd S 2010–, Lab whip 2011–15, shadow Wales Office min 2015–; *Publications* The Red Book of the Voluntary Sector (contrib, 2014); *Recreations* classical music; *Style*— Ms Susan Elan Jones, MP; ✉ House of Commons, London SW1A 0AA (e-mail susan.jones.mp@parliament.uk)

JONES, Terence Graham Parry (Terry); s of late Alick George Parry Jones, and Dilys Louise, *née* Newnes (d 1971); *b* 1 February 1942; *Educ* Royal GS Guildford, St Edmund Hall Oxford; *m* 20 June 1970, Alison, da of James Veitch Telfer; 1 da (Sally Louise Parry b 1974), 1 s (William George Parry b 1976); *Career* writer and performer; *Television* Monty Python's Flying Circus (BBC TV) 1969–74, Ripping Yarns (co-writer) 1978, More Ripping Yarns (dir and co-writer) 1980, Dr Fegg's Encyclopaedia (sic) of All World Knowledge (dir and co-writer) 1984, So This Is Progress (writer and presenter) 1991, Crusades (writer and presenter) 1994/95, Ancient Inventions (presenter, Discovery Channel) 1997, Longitude (screenplay writer) 1997, Gladiators – The Brutal Truth (presenter, BBC) 1999, Python Night anniversary (dir, BBC 2) 1999, narrator in Boy in Darkness (BBC Choice) 1999, The Hidden History of Ancient Egypt (Discovery/BBC) 2003, The Hidden History of Ancient Rome (Discovery/BBC) 2003, TheSurprising History of Sex and Love (Discovery/BBC) 2003, Terry Jones' Medieval Lives (presenter and writer, BBC) 2004, The Story of One (presenter and writer) 2005, Terry Jones' Barbarians (presenter and writer) 2006, Terry Jones' Great Map Mystery (BBC) 2007; *Film* Monty Python and the Holy Grail (dir, actor and co-writer) 1974, Monty Python's Life of Brian (dir, actor and co-writer) 1978, Monty Python's Meaning of Life (dir, actor and co-writer) 1981, Personal Services (dir) 1986, Erik the Viking (dir, writer and actor) 1989, The Wind in the Willows (dir, writer and actor) 1996, Asterix and Obelix (writer and dir, English version) 1999, BFI signature film for IMAX Theatre (writer and dir) 1999, BFG (sreenplay writer) 2003, Absolutely Anything (dir, co-writer and actor) 2015; *Theatre* Evil Machines (musical) 2008, The Doctor's Tale (opera) 2011; *Publications* Chaucer's Knight (1980), Fairy Tales (1981), The Saga of Erik the Viking (1983), Nicobobinus (1986), The Curse of the Vampire's Socks (1988), Attacks of Opinion (1988), Fantastic Stories (1992), Crusades (jtly, 1994), Lady Cottington's Book of Pressed Fairies (jtly, 1994), Fairy Tales and Fantastic Stories (1997), The Knight and the Squire (1997), The Starship Titanic (with Douglas Adams, 1997), The Lady and the Squire (2000), The Image of Chaucer's Knight (essay, 2000), Who Murdered Chaucer? (jtly, 2003), Terry Jones' Medieval Lives (jtly, 2004), Terry Jones' War on the War on Terror (2005), Terry Jones' Barbarians (jtly, 2006), Was Richard II a Tyrant? (in Fourteenth Century England Vol V, 2008), Trouble on the Heath (2011), Animal Tales (2011), Evil Machines (2011), Did John Gower Rededicate his Confession Amantis before Henry IV's Usurpation? (in Middle English Texts in Transition: A Festschrift dedicated to Toshiyuki Takamiya on his 70th birthday, ed Simon Horobin and Linne R Mooney, 2014); *Style*— Terry Jones, Esq; ✉ PO Box 63575, London N6 9BA

JONES, Thomas Henry (Tom); OBE (1996); s of Cadwaladr Jones (d 1986), and Olwen Ellyw, *née* Humphreys (d 1993); *b* 8 February 1950; *Educ* Tywyn Sch Merioneth, UCW Aberystwyth (BA); *m* 20 Sept 1980, Dr Margaret Elizabeth Jones, da of John Wyn Jones, of Welshpool, Powys; 2 s (Owain b 1 Sept 1985, Steffan b 24 Nov 1991), 1 da (Siwan b 12 Jan 1988); *Career* farmer; former vice-pres Farmers' Union of Wales, former pres Young Farmers' Clubs of Wales; former chm: Wales Ctee Nat Lottery Charities Bd, Berwyn Local Access Forum; chm Millennium Stadium Charitable Tst; memb: Richard's Cmmn on the Powers of the National Assembly for Wales, Legal Services Cmmn, European Economic and Social Ctee 2006–; non-executive dir Wales Office 2016–; formerly memb: S4C Authy, National Parks Review Panel, Agric Trg Bd; memb Countryside Cncl for Wales until 2002, govr Welsh Agricultural Colls, vice-pres Wales Cncl for Voluntary Action; tstee Community Fndn Wales; FRAgS; *Books* Brain Yn Y Brwyn (1976), Dyddiadur Ffarmwr (1985); *Style*— Tom Jones, Esq, OBE; ✉ Plas Coch, Dolanog, Welshpool, Powys (☎ 01938 810553)

JONES, Timothy Arthur; s of Canon Idwal Jones, and Jean Margaret Jones; *b* 20 April 1951; *Educ* Christ's Hosp (Almoners' nominee open scholar), Jesus Coll Cambridge, LSE, Coll of Law Chancery Lane; *Children* 1 da (Harriet b 1980); *Career* called to the Bar: Inner Temple 1975, King's Inn Dublin 1990, NI 1998; practising Midland Circuit (specialising in planning, local govt, and environment law); accredited mediator; memb: Planning and Environmental Bar Assoc, Admin Law Bar Assoc, CIARb Business Arbitration Scheme Panel of Arbitrators; neighbourhood planning examiner, village green inspr; Parly candidate (Lib later Lib Dem): Warwick and Leamington 1974, Mid Staffordshire 1983, 1987 and 1990; memb Lib Dem Federal Policy Ctee 1990–92, memb Brereton and Ravenhill Cncl (chm Planning Ctee 2003–), memb Rugeley Town Cncl 2011–15, sec Brereton Million; pres Cambridge Univ Liberal Club 1970, memb Standing Ctee Cambridge Union 1971; vice-chm League of Friends Rugeley Hosp 1985–89; govr Christ's Hosp; FCIArb (UK and int), FRGS, FRSA; *Publications* chapter on Town and Country Planning in Travellers and the Law (2007), chapter on The Impact of European Law on the UK in Criteria of Copenhagen; *Recreations* theatre, walking, ornithology, opera; *Style*— Timothy Jones, Esq; ✉ No 5 Chambers (Birmingham, London, Bristol & Leicester), Fountain Court, Steelhouse Lane, Birmingham B4 6DR (☎ 0845 210 5555, fax 0121 606 1501, e-mail planning@no5.com, website www.no5.com)

JONES, Timothy John; s of John Samuel Jones (d 2007), and Margaret, *née* Bull; *b* 17 November 1959, Newport, Gwent; *Educ* Croesyceiliog Sch Gwent, Univ of Bristol (BSc); *m* 30 Aug 1986, Robyn Jones, *qv*, *née* Lardge; 1 da (Tabitha b 5 Sep 1995), 1 s (Blake b 26 Apr 1999); *Career* grad trainee rising to audit asst mangr Price Waterhouse 1981–

J

86, fin controller Marvel Comics Ltd 1986–90, gp fin dir RWS Gp plc 1990–2000, fin dir Bybrook Ltd 1998–2000; co-fndr and chm CH&Co Catering 1991–; ACA 1984; *Recreations* golf, travel, music, wine; *Clubs* Oxfordshire Golf, Caversham Heath Golf, Huntercombe Golf; *Style*— Timothy Jones, Esq; ✉ Bryants Farm, Kiln Road, Dunsden, Reading RG4 9PB (☎ 0118 946 6300, fax 0118 946 6301, e-mail admin@chandco.net)

JONES, Sir Tom, né Thomas Jones Woodward; kt (2006), OBE (1999); *b* 7 June 1940; *m*; *Career* singer; formed first band Tommy Scott & The Senators 1963; released first solo single Chills and Fever 1964; hit singles incl: It's Not Unusual (1965, reached UK no 1), Thunderball (from film, 1966), Green Green Grass of Home (1966, UK no 1), Detroit City (1967, UK no 8), I'll Never Fall in Love Again (1967, UK no 2), I'm Coming Home (1967, UK no 2), Delilah (1968, UK no 2), 'Til (1971, UK no 2), A Boy From Nowhere (1987, UK no 2), Kiss (with Art of Noise, 1988, UK no 5); albums incl: Along Came Jones (1965, UK no 11), From The Heart (1966, UK no 23), Green Green Grass of Home (1967, UK no 3), Live At the Talk of the Town (1967, UK no 6), Delilah (1968, UK no 1), Help Yourself (1969, UK no 4), This Is Tom Jones (1969, UK no 2), Tom Jones Live In Las Vegas (1969, UK no 3), Tom (1970, UK no 4), She's A Lady (1971, UK no 9), 20 Greatest Hits (1975, UK no 1), I'm Coming Home (1978, UK no 12), Matador (musical soundtrack, 1987, UK no 26), Under Milk Wood (with George Martin, 1988), Carrying A Torch (with Van Morrison, 1991, UK no 44), The Lead and How to Swing It (1994), Reload (with 17 guest artists, UK no 1) 1999, Mr Jones 2002, Tom Jones & Jools Holland 2005; TV shows incl: Billy Cotton Band Show 1965, The Ed Sullivan Show 1965, Call In On Tom 1965, Sunday Night At The London Palladium, Spotlight 1967, This Is Tom Jones 1969, Comic Relief 1991, Tom Jones – The Right Time 1992, Amnesty International 40th Anniversary Special 2001, Pavarotti and Friends 2001, Prince's Trust Party in the Park 2001, King of the Teds 2012, coach The Voice 2012–; Mars Attacks (film) 1996; Nordhoff Robbins Silver Clef Award 2001, Brit Award for Outstanding Contribution to Music 2002; fell Welsh Coll of Music and Drama 1994; *Style*— Sir Tom Jones, OBE; ✉ website www.tomjones.com

JONES, Prof Trevor Mervyn; CBE (2003); s of Samuel James Jones (d 1992), of Finchampstead, Berks, and Hilda May, *née* Walley (d 1978); *b* 19 August 1942; *Educ* Wolverhampton Sch, King's Coll London (BPharm, PhD); *m* 9 April 1966, Verity Ann, da of Richard Bates (d 1963), of Emsworth, Hants; 1 da (Amanda Melissa (Mrs Lawrence Richard Kerr) b 1968), 1 s (Timothy Damian b 1971); *Career* formerly: lectr Univ of Nottingham, head of devpt The Boots Co Ltd, dir of R&D and med Wellcome plc, DG Assoc of the British Pharmaceutical Industry; BAC BV 2006–08, People in Health Ltd 2006–09, Kinetique Ltd; dir: Next Pharma Technologies Ltd 2005–11, SciClone Inc (USA) 2009–12, Tecnogen SpA 2010–12, ReNeuron Holdings Ltd 2000–12, Allergan Inc 2004–15, Synexus Ltd 2008–15; dir Verona Pharma plc 2006–15; currently dir: UK Stem Cell Fndn, Simbec-Orion Ltd, Arthurian Life Sciences Ltd, e-Therapeutics, Perceptive Bioscience Investment Ltd; memb: Advsy Bd MRC Social and Genetic Developmental Psychiatric Research Centre Inst of Psychiatry, WHO Cmmn on Intellectual Property Rights, Innovation and Public Health (CIPIH) 2004–06, Advsy Bd Aegate Ltd 2010–12, Bevan Cmmn, WGA 2014–; Fédération Internationale Pharmaceutique: pres Int Cmmn on Technol 1979–83, memb Bd of Pharmaceutical Scis 1980–84; pres Bd Maurice-Marie Janot Int Ctee, memb Bd of Hon Advsrs The Glynn Research Fndn, memb Bd Euro Fedn of Pharmaceutical Industry; chm Dept of Health Advsy Gp for Genetics Research 2003–07; non-exec memb Bd Merlin Ventures Ltd 1997–2012; former memb Bd: Medidesk Ltd, Datapharm Communications Ltd; sr advsr on clinical trials to S Korea Govt 2008–10; sometime visiting prof: KCL, Univ of Strathclyde, Univ of N Carolina; author of various pubns; memb Editorial Bd: Jl of Pharmacy and Pharmacology, Drug Development and Industrial Pharmacy, Int Jl of Pharmaceutics, Drugs and the Pharmaceutical Sciences; memb UK Medicines Cmmn 1982–94; former memb: Nuffield Cncl on Bioethics Expert Gp on the Use of Human Tissue, Cabinet Office Advsy Ctee on the Human Genome, Bd UK Sci Policy Support Gp, Cncl London Medicine, Advsy Bd MRC; tstee: Aviation Health Inst 1996–98, The Epilepsy Research Fndn 1996–2002, Northwich Park Inst for Med Research 1998–2004, Medicines for Malaria Venture 1999–2007, Br Urological Fndn 2005–07; dep chm Cncl KCL 2003–07; govr Croydon HS; Freeman: Worshipful Soc of Apothecaries 1988, City of London 1994; Hon PhD Univ of Athens 1993; Hon DSc: Univ of Strathclyde 1994, Univ of Nottingham 1998, Univ of Bath 2000, Univ of Bradford 2003; Harrison Meml Medal 1987, Gold Medal Comenius Univ 1992, Charter Gold Medal Royal Pharmaceutical Soc of GB 1996, SCRIP BTG Lifetime Achievement Award 2006; Hon FFPM (RCP) 1995, hon fell London Sch of Pharmacy 1998, FRPharmS, CChem, FRSC, FCPP, FRSM, FKC, hon fell Br Pharmacological Soc 2005, Hon FRCP 2005; *Books* Drug Delivery to the Respiratory Tract (1987), Advances in Pharmaceutical Sciences (1992); *Recreations* gardening, opera, golf, Welsh rugby; *Clubs* Athenaeum; *Style*— Prof Trevor Jones, CBE; ✉ Woodhyrst House, 18 Friths Drive, Reigate, Surrey RH2 0DS

JONES, Ven Dr Trevor Pryce; s of John Pryce Jones (d 1997), of Rhuddlan, N Wales, and Annie, *née* Jepson (d 1991); *b* 24 April 1948; *Educ* St Luke's Coll Exeter (CertEd), Univ of Southampton (BEd, BTh, ACP), Salisbury/Wells Theol Coll, Univ of Wales, Cardiff Law Sch (LLM), Durham Univ (DThM); *m* Susan Diane, da of Rev Peter John Pengelley; 1 da (Anna Catherine b 5 June 1982), 1 s (David Richard Pryce b 4 March 1985); *Career* asst teacher and lay chaplain Shaftesbury GS 1969–73; ordained: deacon 1976, priest 1977; asst curate Gloucester St George Lower Tuffley Glos 1976–79, warden Bishop Mascall Centre Ludlow 1979–84, memb Hereford Diocesan Educn Team 1979–84, diocesan communications offr Hereford 1981–86, team rector Hereford South Wye Team Miny 1984–87, officiating chaplain to the Forces 1985–97, prebendary of Hereford Cathedral 1993–97, archdeacon of Hertford 1997–2016 (archdeacon emeritus 2016–), hon canon Cathedral and Abbey Church of St Albans 1997–2016, chm St Albans and Oxford Miny Course 1998–2007; bishops' selector 2001–08, memb Gen Synod C of E 2000–05 and 2006–10, memb C of E Legal Advsy Cmmn 2006–11; chm St Albans Diocese Reach Out projects 1997–2009, chair Rural Strategy Advisory Gp (RUSTAG) 2001–16, chair Hockerill Educnl Fndn 2005–12, vice-chair Eastern Region Miny Course 2005–16, chair Reach Out Plus 1999–2012, memb Gen Synod Rule Ctee 2013–16; memb Ecclesiastical Law Soc 1997; *Recreations* country walks, vintage buses and trains, biography, holidaying in Sark; *Clubs* Royal Commonwealth, Royal Overseas League; *Style*— The Ven Dr Trevor Pryce Jones; ✉ 3 South Terrace, Longmeadow Road, Lympstone, Devon EX8 5LN (☎ 01395 268745, e-mail archdhert@stalbans.anglican.org)

JONES, Vincent Peter (Vinnie); s of Peter Jones, and Glenda, *née* Harris; *b* 5 January 1965; *Educ* Langleybury Sch, Bedmond Sch, Chancellors, Brookmans Park; *m* Tanya; 1 s (Aaron b 29 May 1991), 1 step da (Kaley b 15 April 1987); *Career* formerly amateur footballer Wealdstone; professional footballer: Wimbledon 1985–89 (debut v Nottingham Forest), Leeds United 1989–90 (joined for £650,000), Sheffield United 1990–91 (joined for £700,000), Chelsea 1991–92 (joined for £575,000), Wimbledon 1992–98 (rejoined for £700,000); player-coach QPR 1998, ret from football 1999; honours: 9 international caps for Wales (one as capt), FA Cup winners Wimbledon 1988, Div 2 Championship winners Leeds United 1990; currently actor; *Films* Lock, Stock and Two Smoking Barrels (Comedy Film of the Year 1998) 1998, Gone in Sixty Seconds 2000, Snatch 2000 (Best Actor Empire Film Awards 2001), Mean Machine 2002, A Night at the Golden Eagle 2002 (Best Supporting Actor New York Film Awards 2003), The Big Bounce 2004, Tooth 2004, Eurotrip 2004, Johnny Was 2005, She's the Man 2005, XMen 3: The Last Stand 2006, The Riddle 2007, The Condemned 2007, Strength and Honour 2007, 7–10 Split 2007, Tooth and Nail 2007, Hellride 2008, Loaded 2008, The Midnight Meat Train 2008, The Heavy 2009, Year One 2009, Legend of the Bog 2009, The Beeding 2010, Magic Boys 2010; *Television* Elementary 2013; presenter The 100 Greatest Sporting Moments (Channel 4) 2001; *Recreations* shooting, fishing, golf, charitable work; *Style*— Vinnie Jones, Esq

JONES OF BIRMINGHAM, Baron (Life Peer UK 2007), of Alvechurch and of Bromsgrove in the County of Worcestershire; Sir Digby Marritt Jones; kt (2005); s of late Derek Jones, of Bromsgrove, Worcs, and Bernice, *née* Marritt; *b* 28 October 1955; *Educ* Bromsgrove Sch (head boy 1974), UCL (LLB), Chester Coll of Law; *m* 1 November 1990, Patricia Mary; *Career* Edge & Ellison Slrs: articled clerk 1978–80, asst slr 1980–81, assoc ptnr 1981–84, ptnr 1984–, head of corp 1987–, dep sr ptnr 1990–, sr ptnr 1995–98; vice-chm corp fin KPMG 1998–99, DG CBI 2000–06, sr advsr Deloitte 2006–07; Govt's skills envoy 2006–07, min of state for trade and investment Dept for Business, Enterprise and Regulatory Reform 2007–08; currently: chm Triumph Motorcycles, chm Grove Industries, dep chm Unipart Expert Practices, non-exec dir Spicers Ltd, corp advsr JCB, sr global advsr Monitise plc, chm Neutrino Concepts Ltd, corp ambass to Jaguar Cars, sr advsr Harvey Nash plc, advsr Barburry Properties plc, chm Advsy Bd Argentex LLP, advsr SHP Ltd, corp ambass to Aon Risk Solutions, sr advsr Babcock Int Gp plc, non-exec chm Thatchers Cider Ltd, chm Cell Therapy Ltd, chm On-Logistics Ltd, corp ambass to Ravenscroft Securities of Guernsey, non-exec chm G-Labs Ltd; non-exec dir Leicester Tigers plc; vice-pres Birmingham Hospice, corp ambass Royal Br Legion; corp ambass: Cancer Research UK, Hospice of Hope Romania; chm of govrs Stratford-upon-Avon Coll; patron: Ladies Fighting Breast Cancer, Flying for Freedom, Avon River Tst, patron Birmingham Fndn; memb Law Soc 1980–; visiting prof Univ of Hull Business Sch; fell UCL, hon fell Cardiff Univ, hon fell Cardiff Met Univ; Hon DUniv: Univ of Central England, Univ of Birmingham, UMIST, Univ of Herts, Univ of Middx, Sheffield Hallam Univ, Aston Univ, Univ of Hull, Queen's Univ Belfast, Univ of Warwick, Univ of Bradford, Thames Valley Univ, Univ of Wolverhampton, Loughborough Univ, Univ of Nottingham; *Books* Fixing Britain: The business of re-shaping our Nation (2011); *Recreations* skiing, rugby, theatre, military history, recreational cycling; *Style*— The Lord Jones of Birmingham; ✉ c/o Lorraine Ellison, MBE (business manager, e-mail lorraine@digbylordjones.com, website www.digbylordjones.com, Twitter @digbylj)

JONES OF CHELTENHAM, Baron (Life Peer UK 2005), of Cheltenham in the County of Gloucestershire; Nigel David Jones; s of late A J Jones, and late Nora Jones; *b* 30 March 1948, Cheltenham, Glos; *Educ* Prince Henry's GS Evesham; *m* 21 May 1981, Katy, *née* Grinnell; 1 s, 2 da (twins); *Career* computer operator Westminster Bank Ltd 1965–67, computer programmer ICL Computers 1967–70, systems analyst Vehicle and General Insurance 1970–71, systems programmer Atkins Computing 1971, systems designer rising to project mangr ICL Computers 1971–92; cncllr (Cheltenham Park) Glos CC 1989–93; MP (Lib Dem) Cheltenham 1992–2005; exec memb: Cwlth Parly Assoc, Inter-Parly Union; chair Botswana Gp; Lib Dem spokesman on: England, Local Govt and Housing 1992, Sci and Technol 1993–, Consumer Affrs 1995–97, Sport 1997–99, Int Devpt 1999–; memb Select Ctee on: Standards and Privileges 1995–97, Sci and Technol 1997–99, Int Devpt 1999–2002, Public Accounts 2002–05, High Speed Rail (HS2) 2016; memb Lords Info Ctee 2005–; *Recreations* watching Cheltenham Town FC and Swindon Town FC, cricket, gardening; *Clubs* Reform, National Liberal; *Style*— The Rt Hon the Lord Jones of Cheltenham

JONES PARRY, Sir Emyr; GCMG (2007, KCMG 2002, CMG 1992); s of Hugh Jones Parry (d 1992), and Eirwen, *née* Davies (d 1985); *b* 21 September 1947, Carmarthen, Dyfed; *Educ* Gwendraeth GS, Cardiff Univ (BSc), Univ of Cambridge (PhD); *m* 30 July 1971, Lynn, *née* Noble; 2 s (Mark b 1977, Paul b 1979); *Career* various diplomatic serv postings 1973–97, dir EU FCO 1997–98, political dir FCO 1998–2001, ambass North Atlantic Cncl 2001–03, ambass and perm rep UN NY 2003–07; Aberystwyth Univ: pres 2008–, chllr 2014–; chair All Wales Convention 2008–09, chair Redress 2008–, chair Wales Millennium Centre 2010–; author of various scientific pubns 1973; various univ fellowships; Hon LLD Univ of Wales; FInstP, pres Learned Soc of Wales 2014–; *Recreations* sport, theatre, reading; *Style*— Sir Emyr Jones Parry, GCMG

JONES-DAVIES, Henry Ellis; s of late Dr Thomas Ellis Jones-Davies; *b* 30 March 1949, Caerfyrddin; *Educ* Rugby, St Peter's Coll Oxford (MA); *m* Frances Dorothy Roden; 3 s (Edward Owain Ellis b 1991, Tomos Llywelyn Ellis b 1993, Rhidian Glyndwr Ellis b 2000); *Career* dep leader archaeological expdn to Iran 1969 (memb 1968 expdn), dep leader expdn to N Afghanistan 1970, English teacher Hamburg 1974–75, worked PR co London 1975–78, exec asst to ceo of an industrial corp Jeddah Saudi Arabia 1978–80, fndr tourism business (expanded into PR, advtg and publishing) Turkey 1981–88, co-fndr (with Nigel Havers, *qv*) Pegasus Pictures London 1983–93, political risk analyst and relationship-builder BP Algiers 1993–96, fndr and ed Cambria – The Nat Magazine for Wales 1997–; Wales co-ordinator Anrhydedd Cymry'r Cyfanfyd (Worldwide Welsh Award), hon vice-pres Wales Heritage Campaign, dir Nat Welsh-American Fndn, memb Bd British-Irish Encounter 2004–07, pres Nat St David's Day Parade; frequent lectr in USA; FRGS; Hadhrami Medal of Honour; *Publications* I owe my life to... 125 Year of the International Red Cross (contrib), various articles and reviews; *Recreations* Welsh, European and political history, Celtic folk, classical, Christian and Islamic liturgical music, calligraphy, painting, running, mountaineering; *Style*— Henry Jones-Davies, Esq; ✉ Cambria Magazine, PO Box 22, Carmarthen SA32 7YH (☎ 01267 290188, e-mail editorial@cambriamagazine.com)

JONES-LEE, Prof Michael Whittaker; s of Lt-Col Walter Whittaker Jones-Lee (d 1977), of Leybourne, Kent, and Christina, *née* Hamilton (d 1985); *b* 3 April 1944; *Educ* Prince Rupert Sch Wilhelmshaven, Bishop Wordsworth's Sch Salisbury, Univ of Sheffield (BEng), Univ of York (DPhil); *m* 20 Dec 1969, Hazel, da of Arthur Stephen Knight (d 1999); 2 s (Rupert b 1974, Ben b 1976), 1 da (Sarah b 1979); *Career* sr lectr Dept of Political Econ Univ of St Andrews 1971–72; Univ of York: Esmée Fairbairn lectr in fin 1967–71, sr lectr Dept of Econs 1972–76, reader Dept of Econs 1976–77; Univ of Newcastle upon Tyne: prof Dept of Econs 1977–2009, head of dept 1984–95, dean Faculty of Social Science 1984–88, emeritus prof 2009–, strategic research advsr Business Sch 2013–; conslt: DfT, DEFRA, TRL, HSE, NICE, London Underground, Railtrack, New Zealand Land Tport Safety Authy, Rail Safety Standards Bd; specialist advsr to House of Lords Select Ctee on Economic Affrs Inquiry into Govt Policy on the Mgmnt of Risk 2005–06; adjunct prof of risk mgmnt Univ of Stavanger 2007–12; *Books* The Value of Life: An Economic Analysis (1976), The Value of Life and Safety (ed, 1982), The Economics of Safety and Physical Risk (1989), Economic Valuation with Stated Preference Techniques: A Manual (co-author, 2002); *Recreations* shopping and old sports cars; *Style*— Prof Michael Jones-Lee; ✉ Newcastle University Business School, 5 Barrack Road, Newcastle upon Tyne NE1 4SE (☎ 0191 208 1671, e-mail michael.jones-lee@ncl.ac.uk)

JONSSON, HE Benedikt; *b* 25 November 1954, Reykjavik, Iceland; *Educ* BA, MA; *m* Adalheidur Oskarsdottir; 4 c; *Career* Icelandic diplomat; first sec Miny of Foreign Affrs Reykjavik 1983–84, first sec Embassy of Iceland Moscow 1984–87, first sec Embassy of Iceland Paris and dep perm rep to OECD and UNESCO 1987–88, dep perm rep Cncl of Europe 1988, counsellor Embassy of Iceland Paris 1988–91, min-counsellor and head of dept Miny of Foreign Affrs Reykjavik 1991–95, ambass and dep perm sec of state Miny for Foreign Affrs Reykjavic 1995–97, ambass and perm rep to UN Office and other int orgns Geneva 1997–2001, ambass to Russian Fndn, Armenia, Azerbaijan, Belarus,

Georgia, Kazakhstan, Kyrgyzstan, Moldova, Tajikistan, Turkmenistan and Uzbekistan 2001–06, ambass and chief negotiator Directorate of External Trade Miny for Foreign Affrs Reykjavik 2006–08, perm sec of state Miny for Foreign Affrs Reykjavik 2008–09, ambass to the Ct of St James's 2009–14, ambass of Iceland to Denmark, Bulgaria, Romania and Turkey 2014–; *Style*— HE Mr Benedikt Jonsson; ✉ Embassy of Iceland, 2A Hans Street, London SW1X 0JE

JOPLING, Jay; s of Baron Jopling, PC, DL (Life Peer), *qv*, and Gail, *née* Dickinson; *Educ* Eton, Univ of Edinburgh; *m* 1997 (m dis 2008), Sam Taylor-Wood , *qv*; 1 da (Angelica b April 1997); *Career* opened White Cube 1993; *Style*— Jay Jopling, Esq; ✉ White Cube, 25–26 Masons Yard, London SW1Y 6BU (☎ 020 7766 3550, fax 020 7749 7480)

JOPLING, Baron (Life Peer UK 1997), of Ainderby Quernhow in the County of North Yorkshire; (Thomas) Michael Jopling; PC (1979); s of late Mark Bellerby Jopling; *b* 10 December 1930; *Educ* Cheltenham Coll, King's Coll Newcastle, Univ of Durham (BSc); *m* 1958, Gail, da of late Ernest Dickinson; 2 s; *Career* farmer; memb Nat Cncl NFU 1962–64; MP (Cons): Westmorland 1964–83, Westmorland and Lonsdale 1983–97 (Parly candidate (Cons) Wakefield 1959); PPS to Min of Agric 1970–71, asst Govt whip 1971–73, a Lord Cmmr of the Treasy (Govt whip) 1973–74, oppn whip 1974, oppn spokesman on Agric 1974–79, shadow min for agric 1975–76, Parly sec to Treasy and Govt chief whip 1979–83, min of agric, fisheries and food 1983–87; memb: Foreign Affrs Select Ctee 1987–97, Int Exec Cwlth Parly Assoc 1988–89 (memb UK Exec 1974–79 and 1987–97, vice-chm 1977–79), Select Ctee on Sittings of the House (Jopling Report, chm 1991–92); pres EEC Cncls of Agric and Fishery Ministers 1986; hon sec Br American Parly Gp 1987–2001; memb UK Delegation NATO Parly Assembly 1987–97 and 2001– (vice-pres 2014–), chm Ctee Civilian Aspects of Security 2011–14; ldr UK delegation OSCE Parly Assembly 1991–97; House of Lords: Select Ctee on EU Legislation 2000–03 and 2007–12 (Sub-Ctee D (Agriculture) 1997–99, Sub-Ctee C (Foreign Affrs and Defence) 2000–04 and 2010–15 (chm 2001–04), Sub-Ctee F (Home Office) 2006–10 (chm 2007–10)), Select Ctee on the Merits of Statutory Instruments 2004–07, Select Ctee on Int Relations 2016–; memb UK Exec Inter Parly Union 1997–; pres Auto Cycle Union 1988–2003; Hon DCL Univ of Newcastle 1992; DL: Cumbria 1991–97, N Yorks 1998–2005; *Style*— The Rt Hon Lord Jopling; ✉ Ainderby Hall, Thirsk, North Yorkshire YO7 4HZ; House of Lords, London SW1A 0PW

JORDAN, Andrew; s of Andrew Jordan (d 2003), of Belfast, and Bessie, *née* Gray (d 1977); *b* 12 March 1950; *Educ* Queen's Univ Belfast (BSc), Darwin Coll Cambridge (Dip Mathematical Statistics), Cranfield Sch of Mgmnt (MBA); *Career* statistician Unilever Research Ltd 1974–77, statistician Overseas Devpt Admin 1977–79, investment controller 3i 1980–84, ptnr PricewaterhouseCoopers (formerly Coopers & Lybrand before merger) 1985–2002; called to the Bar 2006; memn Hon Soc of the Inner Temple; chm of tstees The Migraine Tst 1996–; FRSS; *Recreations* skiing, waterskiing, opera, Cresta Run; *Clubs* St Moritz Tobogganing; *Style*— Andrew Jordan, Esq; ✉ 22 Northumberland Place, London W2 5BS (☎ 020 7229 0546, e-mail andrew@ajordan.net)

JORDAN, Prof Dame Carole; DBE (2006); da of Reginald Sidney Jordan, and Ethel May Jordan; *b* 19 July 1941; *Educ* Harrow Co GS for Girls, UCL (BSc, PhD); *Career* res assoc Jt Inst for Laboratory Astrophysics Univ of Colorado 1966, post doctoral appt UKAEA Culham Laboratory 1966–69; SRC's Astrophysics Res Unit Culham Laboratory: post doctoral res asst 1969–71, sr scientific offr 1971–73, princ scientific offr 1973–76; Univ of Oxford: former univ lectr Dept of Theoretical Physics, reader in physics 1994–96, prof of physics 1996–2008, emeritus prof 2008–; fell and tutor in physics Somerville Coll Oxford 1976–2008 (emeritus fell 2008–); RAS: sec 1981–90, vice-pres 1990–91 and 1996–97, pres (first female to hold position) 1994–96; memb SERC 1985–90, memb PPARC 1994–97; Gold Medal RAS 2005; FRAS 1966, memb IAU 1967, FRS 1990, Hon FInstP 2011 (FInstP 1973); *Recreations* gardening; *Style*— Prof Dame Carole Jordan, DBE, FRS; ✉ Department of Physics (Theoretical Physics), University of Oxford, 1 Keble Road, Oxford OX1 3NP (☎ 01865 273999, fax 01865 273947)

JORDAN, Caroline; *Educ* Univ of Oxford (MA), Univ of Manchester (PGCE); *Career* Wycombe Abbey Sch 1995–2005, headmistress St George's Sch Ascot 2005–11, headmistress Headington Sch 2011–; ISI inspector; GSA: memb Bd 2005, chm Educn Ctee, memb GSA/HMC Univ Ctee, pres 2016–; memb Bd ASCL 2005; *Style*— Ms Caroline Jordan; ✉ Headington School, Oxford OX3 7TD

JORDAN, Eddie; Hon OBE (2012); *b* 30 March 1948, Dublin; *m* Marie; 4 c (Zoe, Miki, Zak, Kyle); *Career* clerk Bank of Ireland 1967–70; racing driver: initially go-kart racing (winner Irish Kart Championship 1971), Formula Ford 1600 1974, Formula Atlantic 1977 (winner Irish Formula Atlantic Championship 1978), subsequently raced in Br Formula 3 series (as memb Team Ireland), world sport car champion (in a Porsche 908), then Formula 2 and test driver McLaren Formula 1 1979; fndr: Eddie Jordan Racing 1980 (raced in Britain (winner championship 1987, driver Johnny Herbert), European Formula 3 and Formula 3000 (champion 1989, driver Jean Alesi, gave first F3 drives for Ayrton Senna and Damon Hill)), Jordan Grand Prix 1990–2005 (entered Formula 1 1991, gave Michael Schumacher first F1 drive, one of only 5 teams to have won multiple Grands Prix in that time); currently BBC presenter covering F1; Irish Entrepreneur of the Year, James Joyce Award Univ Coll Dublin, Gold Medal TCD; hon doctorate Univ of Ulster, hon doctorate Dublin Inst of Technol; *Publications* An Independent Man (autobiography, 2007); *Recreations* football, horse racing, rock and roll music, playing drums in band V10; *Style*— Eddie Jordan, OBE

JORDAN, (Michael) Guy; s of Maj Michael Edward Jordan, of Plymouth, Devon, and Elizabeth Marcia Dermot, *née* Harris; *b* 10 June 1955; *Educ* Downside, Univ of Durham; *m* 12 July 1980, Helena Mary, *née* Moore; 2 s (Adam b 11 Oct 1986, Miles b 20 April 1991), 1 da (Lucy b 13 Dec 1988); *Career* admitted slr 1980; ptnr Masons 1986–2004, ptnr Forsters LLP 2004– (sr ptnr 2008–14); memb Law Soc 1980; *Recreations* painting, fishing, bee keeping; *Style*— Guy Jordan, Esq; ✉ Forsters LLP, 31 Hill Street, London W1J 5LS (☎ 020 7863 8333, e-mail guy.jordan@forsters.co.uk)

JORDAN, Dr Michael John; s of Dr John Jordan (d 1963), of Kidderminster, Worcs, and Margaret Tuer Jordan, MBE, *née* Harper (d 1992); *b* 26 May 1949; *Educ* Malvern Coll, Trinity Hall Cambridge, St Thomas' Hosp Med Sch; *m* 12 May 1984, (Gena) Rosamund, da of Alan Rigby Horler; 3 da (Camilla b 1986, Olivia b 1988, Isobel b 1991); *Career* Anaesthetics Dept St Thomas' Hosp: SHO 1976, registrar 1977, sr registrar 1979; visiting asst prof of anaesthesiology Univ of Texas Dallas 1981–82; conslt anaesthetist Bart's 1983–95, clinical dir of anaesthesia St Peter's Hosp Chertsey 1999–2003 (conslt anaesthetist 1995–2012); FFARCS 1978; memb: Anaesthetic Res Soc, Assoc of Anaesthetists, ret 2104; *Recreations* photography, music, cinema, theatre; *Clubs* Athenaeum, Sette of Odd Volumes; *Style*— Dr Michael Jordan; ✉ North Down, 2 Fort Road, Guildford, Surrey GU1 3TB (☎ 01483 567510, mobile 07787 409672, fax 01483 827489, e-mail mikejordan2011@sky.com)

JORDAN, Terence Frank; s of Frank William Jordan, of Papworth Everard, Cambridge, and Morfydd Enid Jordan; *b* 16 October 1941; *Educ* Leicester Coll of Art and Design (DipArch); *m* 1, 1963 (m dis 1976), Christine Ann; 1 s (Simon David b 23 April 1972), 1 da (Elizabeth Ann b 25 March 1964); m 2, 7 April 1978, Anita Lesley, da of Douglas Richard Reed, of Cambridge; 1 s (Daniel Thomas b 24 Nov 1981), 1 da (Sarah Louise b 7 Sept 1986); *Career* fndr ptnr Clark and Jordan 1973–76, md Covell Matthews Wheatley 1985–92 (fndr dir 1976), dir CMW Group plc 1990–92, fndr ptnr T Jordan Assoc 1993–96, md Corp Services Arlington Securities plc 1997–2006, dir T Jordan Assoc Ltd 2007–; former memb Mgmnt Ctee Cambridge Preservation Soc, former chm Fin and Property Ctee 1978–84; RIBA, FRSA; *Recreations* music, golf, gardening; *Style*— Terence Jordan, Esq; ✉ Grove Cottage, 40 Church Street, Haslingfield, Cambridge CB3 7JE (☎ 01223 872346, fax 01223 871432)

JORDAN, Baron (Life Peer UK 2000), of Bournville in the County of West Midlands; William Brian (Bill); CBE (1992); s of Walter Jordan (d 1974), and Alice, *née* Heath; *b* 28 January 1936; *Educ* Barford Rd Secdy Modern Birmingham; *m* 8 Nov 1958, Jean Ann, da of Ernest Livesey; 3 da (Pamela, Lisa, Dawn); *Career* former machine tool fitter GKN; pres AEEU 1986–95, gen sec Int Confedn of Free Trade Unions 1995–2001; formerly: memb NEDC, memb Gen Cncl and major ctees TUC, chair Euro-Strategy Ctee TUC, memb Exec Ctee and chair Engrg Ctee CSEU, pres Euro Metalworkers Fedn, memb Exec Cncl Int Metalworkers Fedn, memb Engrg Trg Authy, memb ACAS, memb UK Skills Cncl, memb Fndn for Mfrg and Industry, memb National Trg Task Force, NACETT, Duke of Edinburgh Conf Cncl, chm Engrg Cmmn; govr BBC 1988–98, memb Bd English Partnerships 1993–2003 (chm Homes and Communities Agency Pension Scheme 2003); currently: memb UN High Level Panel on Youth Employment, memb UN Global Compact Advsy Cncl, memb Cncl Industrial Soc, memb Cncl VSO, memb Br Overseas Trade Bd, memb Cncl Action Resource Centre, memb Invest in Br Campaign, vice-pres W Midland Productivity Assoc, govr LSE, Ashridge Mgmnt Coll, vice-pres Involvement and Participation Assoc (IPA), memb Advsy Bd Victim Support 1990–2007, memb Cncl Winston Churchill Tst, memb Steering Bd UK Nat Contact Point 2007–, pres RoSPA; memb RIIA; tstee: Party Tst, ReAction Tst; fell World Employment Forum; Hon Dr: Univ of Central England, Cranfield Univ; City and Guilds Insignia Award (hc); Hon FCGI; *Recreations* reading, most sports (particularly football, supporter Birmingham City FC); *Style*— The Rt Hon the Lord Jordan, CBE, RSA

JORDANOVA, Prof Ludmilla Jane; da of Ivan Nickolai Jordanov, and Phyllis Elisabeth, *née* Brown (d 2003); *b* 10 October 1949, Woking, Surrey; *Educ* Oxford HS for Girls, New Hall Cambridge (BA), Univ of Cambridge (PhD), Univ of Essex (MA); *m* 1970, Simon Thomas Emmerson (m dis 1974); 2 da with Karl Michael Figlio (Alix Green b 1977, Zara b 1985); *Career* res fell and dir of studies in history and philosophy of science New Hall Cambridge 1975–78, res offr Wellcome Unit for the History of Medicine Univ of Oxford 1978–79, res fell Wolfson Coll Oxford 1979; Univ of Essex: lectr in history 1980–88, sr lectr in history 1988–91, dean of students 1988–90, prof of history 1991–93, fndr and co-dir Interdisciplinary Centre for the Study of Children 1991–93; prof of cultural history Univ of York 1993–96, prof of visual arts UEA 1996–2003 (dean Schs of World Art Studies and Music 1999–2002), seconded as dir Centre for Res in the Arts, Social Scis and Humanities Univ of Cambridge 2003–05, fell Downing Coll Cambridge 2003–05 (dir of studies in history of art 2004–06), prof of modern history KCL 2006–; sr academic visitor Clare Coll Cambridge 1992, Wellcome research leave fell 1992–93, distinguished visiting prof Dept of English Univ of Alberta 1993, visitor Univ of Victoria 1994, Br Cncl sponsored lectr Australia 1995, visiting prof of science studies Univ of Calif San Diego 1996, visitor St John's Coll Cambridge 1999, Clark fell Clark Art Inst MA 2003, fell Inst for Advanced Studies in the Humanities Univ of Edinburgh 2003; memb Editorial Bd: Gender and History 1987–88, Science as Culture 1987–97, Social History of Medicine 1988–90, Art History 1988–92, British Jl for the History of Science 1989–, History of Human Sciences 1992–, Jl of the History of Sexuality 1993–96, Picturing History 1998–, The Historical Jl 2003–05 (memb Int Bd 2001–03 and 2006–); pres: Br Soc for the History of Sci 1998–2000 (memb Cncl 1980–82 and 1997–2001, vice-pres 1997–98 and 2000–01), History of Science Section BAAS 2006 (memb Section Ctee 2005–07, vice-pres 2007); vice-pres Royal Historical Soc 2001–04 (memb Cncl 1993–97, chair Gen Purposes Ctee 2002–); memb: Exec Ctee Soc for the Social History of Medicine 1977–79 and 1983–84, Panel 4 (History) Arts and Humanities Research Bd 1999–2002, Advsy Ctee St John's Coll Oxford Research Centre, Library Ctee Royal Soc 2003–06 and 2008–, Advsy Ctee CRESC Manchester and Open Univ until 2007, New Educn Hons Ctee until 2007; tstee Nat Portrait Gall 2001–09, external memb Appointments Ctee V&A 1989; govr St James Primary Sch Colchester 1990–93; memb: Soc for the Social History of Medicine, Scottish Assoc of Art Historians, Br Soc for the History of Sci, Historical Assoc; FRHistS 1989, FRSM 1999; *Books* Images of Earth: Essays in the History of the Environmental Sciences (co-ed and contrib, 1979, 2 edn 1997), Languages of Nature: Critical Essays on Science and Literature (ed and contrib, 1986), Sexual Visions: Images of Gender in Science and Medicine between the Eighteenth and Twentieth Centuries (1989), The Enlightenment and its Shadows (co-ed and contrib, 1990), Nature Displayed: Gender, Science and Medicine 1760–1820 (1999), History in Practice (2000, revised edn 2006), Defining Features: Scientific and Medical Portraits 1660–2000 (2000); author of articles in learned jls; *Recreations* friendship, listening to music, spending time in Edinburgh, travel, art museums; *Style*— Prof Ludmilla Jordanova; ✉ 23 Cavendish Place, Cambridge CB1 3BH (☎ 01223 243085); Department of History, King's College London, Strand WC2R 2LS (☎ 020 7848 1277, e-mail ludmilla.jordanova@kcl.ac.uk)

JOSEPH, Bernard Michael; s of Harry Toby Joseph (d 1989), of London, and Esther, *née* Markson (d 1999); *b* 27 September 1948; *Educ* Bede GS for Boys; *m* 12 Oct 1980, Ruth Lesley-Ann, *née* Trent (d 2011); 1 da (Danielle Natasha b 20 May 1983), 1 s (Darren Paul b 2 Sept 1985); *Career* CA; trainee Jennings Johnson 1971–75, Peat Marwick & Mitchell 1975–77, Nash Broad & Co 1977–79, sole practitioner 1979–88, ptnr Johnsons 1988–90, sr ptnr Joseph & Co 1990–; Freeman: City of London, Worshipful Co of CAs; FICA 1975; *Clubs* 41 (chm); *Style*— Bernard Joseph, Esq; ✉ 3 Hillersdon Avenue, Edgware, Middlesex HA8 7SG (☎ 020 8905 3721); Joseph & Co, PO Box 199, Edgware, Middlesex HA8 7FG (☎ 08707 104245, fax 0870 710 4245)

JOSEPH, David; CBE (2016); *Career* Universal Music UK: gen mangr Polydor 1998–2002, md then co-pres Polydor 2002–06, pres Unversal Music Operations 2006–08, chm and ceo 2008–; memb Cncl BPI 2005–, chm BRITs Ctee 2010–13, memb Cncl Arts Cncl England 2013–; *Style*— David Joseph, Esq, CBE; ✉ Universal Music UK, 364–366 Kensington High Street, London W14 8NS

JOSEPH, Derek Maurice; s of late Eugene Joseph, of London, and late Gertrude, *née* Enoch; *b* 10 December 1949; *Educ* Kilburn GS, Univ of Leeds (BCom); *m* 1980, Elizabeth, da of Charles Long; 1 da (Rosamond Amy b 6 June 1981), 1 s (Thomas Reuben b 24 April 1985); *Career* fin dir and sec Circle 33 Housing Tst 1975–79, md HACAS Group plc 1980–2003, dir Tribal Treasury Services 2003–10, dir Altair Consultancy & Advsy Services Ltd 2011–, md Financial Information Co 2008–12; non-exec chm Wadharma Investment plc 2001–07, non-exec chm A2Dominion Gp 2011–, non-exec dir Tilfen Land 2000–14, dep chm Basepoint plc 2001–, non-exec chm Tempus Wharf Freehold Ltd 2010–, non-exec dir General Industries plc 2014–15, finance dir General Industries plc 2015–; exec dir and sec London Housing Fndn 2008–, voluntary dir Theatre Royal Stratford East; FCIS 1985, AIS 2005; *Publications* various books and articles incl Private Finance Initiatives for Affordable Rental Housing (1997); *Recreations* theatre, travel, ardent supporter of Watford FC; *Clubs* House of St Barnabas; *Style*— Derek Joseph, Esq; ✉ Altair Consultancy, Unit 1, Tempus Wharf, 29a Bermondsey Wall West, London SE16 4SA

JOSEPH, Jane; da of Leonard Joseph (d 1989), and Hannah Joyce, *née* Stern (d 2011); *b* 7 June 1942; *Educ* Downe House, Camberwell Sch of Arts and Crafts (NDD, Leverhulme travelling award); *Career* painter and printmaker; Abbey Award in Painting British Sch at Rome 1991 and 1995; *Solo Exhibitions* Morley Gallery London 1973, 1997 and 2000, The Minories Colchester 1982, Angela Flowers Gallery 1987, Flowers East 1989 and 1992, Edinburgh Printmakers 1994, Scarborough Art Gallery 1999, Hebrew Union Coll

J

NY 2000, Italian Cultural Inst London 2000, Worcester City Art Gallery 2001, Victoria Art Gallery Bath 2002, Sch of Art Gallery Aberystwyth 2004, Etchings for Primo Levi (Mostyn Gallery Llandudno) 2012 and (London Jewish Cultural Centre) 2014, Common Grounds (Eagle Gallery London) 2013, Imprints (New Hall Murray Edwards Coll Cambridge) 2013, Seeing the Space (Southampton City Art Gallery) 2015; *Group Exhibitions* Artists Market, S Wales Gp 1971, Air Gallery 1981, Gardner Centre Univ of Sussex 1984, Imperial Coll London 1985, 100 Years – Artists and Morley (Morley Coll) 1990, Gardner Centre Univ of Sussex 1992, Cleveland Int Drawing Biennale, Int Print Biennale Bradford, London Gp, RA Summer Exhbns, Cheltenham Open Drawing Exhbns (Award winner 1998), Eagle Gallery London 2002, 2007, 2008 and 2009, Artspace Gallery London 2004, Biennal of Graphic Arts Ljubljana 2005, Drawing Breath (Wimbledon Coll of Art and tour) 2006, Artists and Morley 40 Years (Morley Coll) 2009, Ruth Borchard Self-Portrait Exhibition London 2013, Global Print (Alijo Portugal) 2013, 7th Int Printmaking Bienal Douro Portugal 2014, Garden (Campden Gallery Chipping Campden Glos) 2014, Contemporary and Modern British Drawings (The Art Stable Child Okeford Dorset) 2014, Editions (Eagle Gallery London) 2015, Intersecting Practice of Contemporary Printmaking in the UK (China Academy of Contemporary Art Hangzhou/ Impact 9, curated by Zhou Jian) 2015; *Work in Public Collections* Br Museum, Br Library, Castle Museum Norwich, Chelsea and Westminster Hosp, Govt Art Collection, Imperial Coll London, Univ of Northumbria at Newcastle, Unilever House, Brecknock Museum and Art Gallery Brecon, Paintings in Hosps, Ben Uri Gallery, New Hall Coll Cambridge, Fitzwilliam Museum Cambridge, Hebrew Union Coll NY, Worcester City Art Gallery, Lindley Library London, Nat Art Library, V&A, Yale Center for Br Art New Haven, Ashmolean Museum Oxford, Birmingham City Museum and Art Gallery, Sch of Art Gallery Aberystwyth, Whitworth Art Gallery, Univ of Manchester, Morley Coll London, Southampton City Art Gallery, Douro Bienal Printmaking Collection Portugal, Imperial Coll Healthcare Charity Art Collection London (public displays incl: Sea, Land and Journeying (Hammersmith Hosp) 2014–15, A View of London (Charing Cross Hosp) 2015–16); *Publications* A Little Flora of Common Plants (text by Mel Gooding), Kinderszenen (text by Anthony Rudolf), Seeds & Fruits (text by Mel Gooding); etchings accompanying If This is a Man and The Truce by Primo Levi; *Recreations* walking for observation, cinema, music; *Style—* Miss Jane Joseph; ✉ website www.janejoseph.co.uk; c/o Emma Hill, Eagle Gallery, 159 Farringdon Road, London EC1R 3AL (☎ 020 7833 2674, e-mail emmahilleagle@aol.com, website www.emmahilleagle.com)

JOSEPH, Jenny; da of Louis Joseph (d 1979), and Florence Ethel, *née* Cotton (d 1989); *b* 7 May 1932; *Educ* Badminton Sch, St Hilda's Coll Oxford (scholar, BA); *m* Charles Anthony Coles (decd); 1 s (Martin Louis b 1961), 2 da (Penelope Clare b 1963, Rebecca Ruth b 1965); *Career* poet, writer, broadcaster and lectr; newspaper reporter: Bedfordshire Times, Oxford Mail, Drum Publications (Johannesburg, South Africa); awarded travelling scholarship Soc of Authors 1995, FRSL; *Books* The Unlooked-for Season (1960, Gregory Award), Rose in the Afternoon and Other Poems (1974, Cholmondeley Award), The Thinking Heart (1978), Beyond Descartes (1983), Persephone: A Story in Prose and Verse (1986, James Tait Black Meml Award for Fiction), The Inland Sea (1989), Beached Boats (with photographs by Robert Mitchell, 1991), Selected Poems (1992), Ghosts and Other Company (1995), Extended Similes (1997), Warning (1997), All the Things I See (2000), Led by the Nose (2002), Extreme of Things (2006), Nothing Like Love (2009); for children (with Katherine Hoskyns): Boots (1966), Wheels (1966), Wind (1967), Water (1967), Tea (1968), Sunday (1968); *Style—* Miss Jenny Joseph; ✉ 17 Windmill Road, Minchinhampton, Gloucestershire GL6 9DX; c/o Johnson and Alcock Ltd, Clerkenwell House, 45–47 Clerkenwell Green, London EC1R 0HT

JOSEPH, Joe; *b* 20 May 1955; *m* Jane Louise, *née* Winterbotham; 2 s (Thomas Daniel b 20 Nov 1989, Charles Benjamin b 2 Dec 1992), 1 da (Eliza Rose b 6 March 1995); *Career* formerly with Reuters News Agency (London, NY), ldr writer, chief TV critic, feature writer and columnist The Times (formerly Tokyo corr); *Books* The Japanese: Strange but not Strangers (1993), Should I Flush My Goldfish Down the Loo? (2007); *Style—* Joe Joseph, Esq; ✉ The Times, 1 London Bridge Street, London SE1 9GF (☎ 020 7782 5000)

JOSEPH, Julian; *b* 1966; *Educ* Interchange's Weekend Arts Course Kentish Town, Berklee Sch of Music Boston (ILEA scholar, BA); *Career* pianist, composer; fndr: own quartet 1990, Julian Joseph Trio, Forum Project (8 piece), Electric Project; int tours of USA, Canada, Bermuda, India, Australia, Japan, S America, Europe and Caribbean as a soloist and with Branford Marsalis, Wynton Marsalis, Bobby McFerrin, Joe Williams, George Coleman, Chico Freemen, Arthur Blyth, Gary Bartz, Billy Cobham, Miroslav Vitous, Marta Sebestyen, Marcelo Bratke, Viktoria Mullova; festival appearances incl: Montreaux Jazz, North Sea, Nancy, Tourcoin, Brecon, Glasgow, Aldeburgh, City of London, Cheltenham, Bermuda, Audi Munich Piano Summer, House of Culture of the World (Berlin), St Lucia Jazz, Cork, Scarborough, Bath, Arundel; projects incl: The Two Sides of Julian Joseph Weekend Barbican 1994 (Classics meets Jazz with Royal Philharmonic Concert Orch, Total Jazz with Julian Joseph Big Band), Julian Joseph Jazz Series Wigmore Hall 1994 with Johnny Griffin, Eddie Daniels, Andy Sheppard and Jason Rebello, Ronnie Scott's Club, Jazz Café, Sweet Basils NY, BBC Proms Royal Albert Hall 1995 with Julian Joseph Big Band, Concertgebouw Amsterdam 1996, Queen Elizabeth Hall (premier performance of Electric Project) 1996, City of London Festival concert series with London Symphony (performing Gershwin's Rhapsody in Blue), concert series with Residence Orkest Hague 1996 (performance of Gershwin's Second Rhapsody), recital at Bridgwater Hall 1997, BBC Radio 3 London Jazz Festival cmmn (premiere), The Great Sage with BBC Concert Orch Strings and Julian Joseph Big Band 2002, The Great Exception with Halle Manchester (premiere) 2003, City of London Festival cmmn Rhapsody in Blue for Big Band (premiere) 2007, Bridgetown: A Fable of 1807 (jazz opera, premiere and tour) 2008, Shadowball (jazz opera, premiere) 2010 (commissioned by HMDT Music), Brown Bomber 2012 (Cultural Olympiad commission); presenter eight-part two-season television series Jazz with Julian Joseph (Meridian) 2000; writer and presenter Jazz Legends (BBC Radio 3) 2000–07, presenter Jazz Line-Up (BBC Radio 3) 2007–; patron: Band on the Wall Manchester, Firebird Tst, Pembroke Music Acad, Jazz Devpt Tst; Creative Industries Luminary for London 2004, Jazz Broadcaster of the Year Parly Jazz Awards 2006; Pro Cultura Hungarica 2004; *Recordings* The Language of Truth 1991, Reality 1993, Julian Joseph in Concert at the Wigmore Hall 1995, Universal Traveller 1996; *Style—* Julian Joseph, Esq; ✉ c/o James Joseph Music Management, 85 Cicada Road, Wandsworth, London SW18 2PA (☎ 020 8874 8647, fax 020 8877 1678, e-mail jj3@jamesjoseph.co.uk, website www.julianjoseph.com)

JOSEPH, Paterson; *b* 22 June 1964, London; *Educ* LAMDA; *Career* actor; jt patron www.offwestend.com 2006–09; memb Bd: Headlong Theatre 2008, LAMDA 2008; *Film* In the Name of the Father 1994, The Beach 1999, Aeon Flux 2005, The Other Man 2008, Stop the World (short) 2011, Between Lambs and Lions 2015; *Television* incl: Casualty 1997–98, Peep Show (Channel 4) 2003–15, Green Wing (Channel 4) 2004–06, That Mitchell and Webb Look 2006–, Jekyll (BBC 1) 2007, Survivors (BBC) 2008–10, The No 1 Ladies Detective Agency (BBC) 2009, Boy Meets Girl 2009, Case Histories 2011–13, The Hollow Crown 2012, Law and Order: UK 2013–14, The Leftovers 2014–15, Babylon 2014, Safe House 2015, You, Me, and the Apocalypse 2015; *Theatre* incl: Raping the Gold (Bush Theatre London) 1988 (Best Actor London Fringe Award 1988), Les Blancs (Royal Exchange Theatre Manchester) 2001 (Best Actor TMA Theatre Award 2001), The Royal Hunt of the Sun, The Emperor Jones (Olivier Theatre London), Sancho: An Age of Remembrance (Oxford Playhouse, Birmingham Rep and US tour), Julius Caesar (RSC), Saint Joan (NT); *Style—* Paterson Joseph, Esq; ✉ c/o Hamilton Hodell, 20 Golden Square, London W1F 9JL

JOSEPH, Richard Lewis; s of Alfred Joseph (d 1967), of London, and Rose Sarah, *née* Melzack (d 2000); *b* 24 July 1949; *Educ* Algernon Road Sch, Haberdashers' Aske's Sch; *m* March 1974, Linda Carol, da of Frank Hyams; 1 da (Danielle Frances b July 1978), 1 s (Mark Alan b Nov 1981); *Career* articled clerk: Lewis Bloom, Blick Rothenberg & Noble; qualified chartered accountant 1972, Stoy Hayward & Co 1972, Elliott Woolfe & Rose 1977–78, fin controller Unit Tst Gp 1978–82, private practice 1978–; fndr Micro Computer Gp of N London, chm Ctee N London Soc of CAs 1990–91 (joined 1986); London Soc of Chartered Accountants: chm 2000–01, chm Communications Ctee 1998–99, hon sec 2004–; chm LSCA Ed Bd 1992–96, memb Support Task Force ICAEW 1995–96, memb Ctee Edgware and Burnt Oak C of C; FCA (ACA 1972); *Recreations* golf, rock and country guitarist; *Clubs* Radlett Park Golf; *Style—* Richard Joseph, Esq; ✉ Richard Joseph & Co, 2nd Floor, 65 Station Road, Edgware, Middlesex HA8 7HX (☎ 020 8952 5407, e-mail rlj@richardjoseph.co.uk)

JOSEPH, Her Hon Judge Wendy Rose; QC 1998; da of Norman Joseph (d 1969), and Carole Esther, *née* Marks (d 2005); *b* 11 March 1952; *Educ* Cathays HS for Girls, Westridge Sch for Girls Pasadena CA, New Hall Cambridge; *Career* called to the Bar Gray's Inn 1975 (bencher 2004); asst recorder 1995, recorder 1998, circuit judge 2007–12, sr circuit judge 2012–; pres Mental Health Review Tbnl 2001–11; *Style—* Her Hon Judge Wendy Joseph, QC; ✉ Central Criminal Court, Old Bailey, London EC4M 7EH

JOSHI, Dr Hasmukh; MBE (2012); s of Prataprai Joshi (d 1992), of India, and Jasumati Joshi (d 2002); *b* 14 March 1946, India; *Educ* Gujarat Univ India (MB BS), Royal Coll of Physicians London (Dip); *m* 17 June 1978, Annie, *née* Leung ; 1 da (Dr Natasha Joshi b 7 June 1979), 1 s (Justin Joshi b 9 August 1985); *Career* GP Pontypool S Wales 1975–2011; former memb Bd and chair Assessment Ctee Postgraduate Medical Educn and Trg Bd; RCGP: examiner 1987–2013, memb Cncl 1995–2013, vice-chm 2007–10; FRCGP 1995 (MRCGP 1977); *Publications* Developing and Maintaining Assessment Systems (jt ed, 2006); *Recreations* cricket, rugby, golf; *Style—* Dr Hasmukh Joshi, MBE, FRCGP; ✉ 4 Uskvale Court, Usk Road, Pontypool NP4 8AS (☎ 01495 752453, e-mail hasmukhjoshi@btinternet.com); Ty Camlas, 4 Uskvale Court, Usk Road, Pontypool, Torfaen NP4 8AS (☎ 01495 753453)

JOSHI, Prof Heather Evelyn; CBE (2015, OBE 2002); *née* Spooner; da of Guy Malcolm Spooner, MBE (d 1989), and Molly Florence Spooner, MBE (d 1997); *b* 21 April 1946, Plymouth, Devon; *Educ* Tavistock Sch, St Hilda's Coll Oxford (MA), St Antony's Coll Oxford (MLitt); *m* 1, 26 June 1969 (m dis 1977), Vijay Ramchandra Joshi; *m* 2, 14 Oct 1982, Gregory Martin; 1 da (Julia Florence b 11 July 1982), 1 s (Benjamin William Malcolm b 8 Nov 1985 d 2009); *Career* asst res offr Inst of Economics and Statistics Univ of Oxford 1969–73, economic advsr Govt Economic Serv 1973–79, sr res fell Centre for Population Studies LSHTM 1979–87, sr research fell Dept of Economics Birkbeck Coll London 1987–89, sr lectr Centre for Population Studies LSHTM 1990–93, sr lectr then prof Social Statistical Research Unit City Univ 1993–98; Inst of Educn Univ of London: prof 1998–2011, dir Centre for Longitudinal Studies 2003–10 (dep dir 1998–2003), prof emerita 2011–; dir ESRC Millennium Cohort Study 2000–11; pres: Euro Soc for Population Economics 1996 (memb 1985–), Br Soc for Population Studies 2000 (memb 1976–); memb Royal Economic Soc 1970 (chair Ctee on Women in Economics 2001–04); AcSS 2000, FBA 2000; *Books* The Changing Population of Britain (ed, 1989), The Tale of Mrs Typical (jtly, 1996), Unequal Pay (jtly, 1998), Women's Incomes over the Lifetime (jtly, 2000), Children of the Twenty-First Century (jtly, 2005), Women and Employment (jtly, 2008), Children of the Twenty-first Century: Vol 2 (jtly, 2010); *Recreations* walking, listening to music; *Style—* Prof Heather Joshi, CBE; ✉ UCL Institute of Education, 20 Bedford Way, London WC1H 0AL (☎ 020 7612 6874, e-mail h.joshi@ucl.ac.uk)

JOSHI, Naresh; s of Narendra Joshi, and Sarala, *née* Shrestha; *b* 1 March 1962, Kathmandu, Nepal; *Educ* Guy's Hosp (MB BS), RCS (DO); *m* 6 April 1996, Frances Anne, *née* Mayhew; 1 da (Sarala Marie b 8 Oct 1997), 1 s (Naren Dominic b 16 Aug 1999); *Career* conslt opthalmic plastic surgn: Chelsea and Westminster Hosp 1996–, Royal Marsden 1996–, St John's Hosp 1996–; hon sr lectr Imperial Med Sch 1996–; memb: Br Ocuplastics Surgical Soc, Br Assoc of Aesthetic Plastic Surgns (BAAPS), Royal Coll of Opthamologists, RSM, BMA; FRCOphth 1990; *Recreations* golf, wines; *Clubs* Mosimanns, Hurlingham; *Style—* Mr Naresh Joshi; ✉ Cromwell Hospital, London SW5 0TU; Chelsea and Westminster Hospitals, London SW10 9NH (☎ 020 7460 5739)

JOSHI, Sanjay; s of R K Joshi and Kirin Joshi; *b* 2 May 1961; *Educ* Univ of Kent at Canterbury (BA(Econ), MA(Econ)); *m* Ranmali Deepika, *née* Ratnatunga; 1 s (Ravi), 1 da (Selina); *Career* research offr and lectr City Univ Business Sch 1984–86, sr economist CBI 1986–87, sr economist Baring Bros 1987–90, chief economist and head of bond research Daiwa Europe Ltd 1990–98, sr strategist SPP Investment Management 1998, currently head of fixed income London & Capital; regular pubns: Quarterly Fixed Income Strategy, Yen Weekly, Relative Value Perspective; regular portfolio selection The Economist 1990–; also contrib: CBI Economic Situation Report, Euromoney, IFR; memb: Nat Assoc for Business Economists, UK Soc for Business Economists (SBE), Harlequins RFC, memb Brentham CC; ECB level 1 coach; *Style—* Sanjay Joshi, Esq

JOSHUA, Rosemary; *Educ* Royal Coll of Music; *Career* soprano; *Performances* incl: Blonde in Die Entführung aus dem Serail (Buxton Festival), Zerlina in Don Giovanni (Scottish Opera), Adele in Die Fledermaus (ENO), Yum Yum in The Mikado (ENO), Norina in Don Pasquale (ENO), title role in Princess Ida (ENO), Pamina in The Magic Flute (Covent Garden Festival and Opera N Ireland, Brussels), Angelica in Orlando (Aix-en-Provence Festival), Sophie in Der Rosenkavalier (ENO, Deutsche Opera Berlin), Poussette in Manon (Royal Opera House), Poppea in Agrippa (Cologne Opera, Brussels and Paris), Susanna in Marriage of Figaro (Cologne Opera), Ilia in Idomeneo (Lisbon), Calisto title role in La Monnaie (Brussel), title role in Semele (BBC Proms1996, Aix-en-Provence, Innsbruck Festival, Flanders Opera and ENO), Gianetta in The Gondoliers (BBC Proms) 1997, Susanna in Le Nozze di Figaro, Susanna and Anne Trulove (Glyndebourne Festival), Cleopatra in Giulio Cesare (Florida), Juliet in Romeo and Juliet (San Diego), title role in The Cunning Little Vixen (Flanders Opera and the Theatre des Champs Elysées); future roles incl: Adele in Die Fledermaus (Metropolitan Opera New York), Euridice in Orfeo et Euridice, Micael in Saul, Sophie and Susanna (all at the Bavarian State Opera Munich) *Recordings* Orlando (with Les Arts Florissants and William Christie), Venus and Adonis (with René Jacobs), Sophie in Der Rosenkavalier, Sandman in Hansel und Gretel, Dido et Aeneas (with René Jacabs); *Awards* winner: Van Der Beugel Opera Prize, Royal Philharmonic Soc Debut Award 1992, Gold medal RCM; nominated for Laurence Olivier Award for Outstanding Achievement in Opera; *Style—* Ms Rosemary Joshua; ✉ c/o Askonas Holt, Lincoln House, 300 High Holborn, London WC1V 7JH

JOSIPOVICI, Prof Gabriel David; s of Jean Josipovici, and Sacha Elena, *née* Rabinovitch; *b* 8 October 1940; *Educ* Victoria Coll Cairo, Cheltenham Coll, St Edmund Hall Oxford; *Career* prof Univ of Sussex 1984– (formerly lectr and reader), Lord Northcliffe lectr Univ of London 1980–81, Lord Weidenfeld prof of comparative literature Univ of Oxford 1996–97; author; FRSL 1998, FBA 2001; *Plays* for the stage incl: Dreams of Mrs Fraser (Theatre Upstairs) 1972, Flow (Edinburgh Lyceum) 1973, Marathon (ICA) 1978; radio plays incl: Playback (1972), AG (1977), Vergil Dying (1980), Mr Vee (1989); *Books* The Inventory (1968), The World and The Book (1971), Mobius the Stripper (1975), Migrations (1977), Conversations in Another Room (1984), Contre-Jour (1986), In the Fertile Land (1987),

The Book of God: A Response to the Bible (1988), Steps: Selected Fiction and Drama (1990), The Big Glass (1991), Text and Voice: Essays 1981–91 (1992), In a Hotel Garden (1993), Moo Pak (1994), Touch (1996), Now (1998), On Trust (1999), A Life (2001), Goldberg: Variations (2002), The Singer on the Shore: Essays (2006), Everything Passes (2006), After (2009), Making Mistakes (2009), What Ever Happened to Modernism? (2010), Heart's Wings and Other Stories (2010), Only Joking (2010), Infinity (2012), Hotel Andromeda (2014), 'Hamlet' Fold on Fold (2016); *Style*— Prof Gabriel Josipovici; ✉ University of Sussex, Arts Building, Falmer, Brighton, East Sussex BN1 9SH (☎ 01273 606755)

JOSLIN, Paul; s of Edgar Alfred (d 1958), and Mary Elizabeth Elsie, *née* Buckeridge (d 2014); *b* 20 November 1950; *Educ* City of Portsmouth Tech HS, Royal Coll of Music (GRSM, LRAM, ARCM), Univ of Reading (MMus); *m* 2 August 1975, Gwenllian Elfyn, da of Rev Ifor Elfyn Ellis (d 2001), of St Asaph, N Wales; *Career* organist and choirmaster St Matthew's Fulham 1971–72, organist and dir of music St Paul's Onslow Sq London 1972–77; Holy Trinity Brompton London: associate dir of music 1977–79, organist and dir 1979–92; organist and dir: St Luke's Redcliffe Sq SW10 1992–97, St Jude Courtfield Gdns 1997–98; organist St Marylebone Crematorium London 2005–08 (actg organist 2004), actg organist St John the Baptist Holland Rd W14 2008–; asst conductor Brompton Choral Soc 1977–81, actg dir of music St Catherine Sch Twickenham 1993, organ conslt St Barnabas Ealing 2006–11, organ conslt Welsh Church of Central London 2016–; solo and organ accompanist; continuo work with London Bach Orch, Thames Chamber Orch and English Chorale, concerto soloist with and memb of English Chamber Orch, choral and orchestral conductor BBC Radio and TV (team organist and dir Daily Service 1989–94, organist Rome Pilgrimage Daily Service Tour 1992, Songs of Praise, Sunday Worship); dir of music (St Paul's Cathedral): Let's Celebrate 1993–96, London Bridges 1997, Feast of the Kingdom 1998, Partners in Mission 2000; recital Coventry Cathedral 2011; vice-pres London Organist Guild 1994–2008, visiting lectr Univ of Reading 1994–95; memb Cncl Br Inst of Organ Studies 1997–2001 (co-ordinator Historic Organ Scheme 2002–14), HOCS (Historic Organ Certificate Scheme) inspector for Central London and N Wales; recordings for Historic Organ Sound Archive Chelmsford and Birchanger 2006; *Recreations* architecture, swimming, 35mm photography, collection 78rpm classical records; *Style*— Paul Joslin, Esq; ✉ 109 Hanover Road, London NW10 3DN (☎ 020 8459 5547)

JOSS, Timothy Hans (Tim); *b* 27 June 1955; *Educ* Harrow, The Queen's Coll Oxford, Univ of Grenoble, RAM; *m* 1, 1983 (m dis 2008), Elizabeth Morag, *née* Wallace; 1 da (Hannah b 18 May 1987); m 2, 2012, Dr Vivienne Mary Hunt Parry, OBE; *Career* Live Music Now! 1980–82, music and dance offr NW Arts 1982–89, concerts dir Bournemouth Sinfonietta rising to sr mangr Bournemouth Orchs 1989–93, dir Bath Festivals Tst 1993–2004; chm: Cmmn for Community Music Int Soc for Music Educn 1992–94, Br Arts Festivals Assoc 1998–; dir Rayne Fndn 2005–14, fndr and chief exec AESOP (Arts Enterprise with a Social Purpose) 2014–, fndr Arts Impact Fund 2015; visiting sr fell cultural policy and mgmnt City Univ 2010–13; fndr and chair: Br Cncl for Sch Environments 2005–08, Public Engagement Fndn 2009–; chair Culture Forum 2010–11, fndr Nat Numeracy 2012, fndr and chair Arts Enterprises in Health and Social Care 2013–; memb Bd: London Sinfonietta 2003–12, Richard Feilden Fndn 2005–; FRSA, FRSPH; Chevalier dans l'Ordre des Arts et des Lettres 2007; *Books* Directory of Community Music (1993), New Flow – a better future for artists, citizens and the state (2008); *Style*— Tim Joss; ✉ AESOP, Lingermans, Burford Road, Brize Norton, Oxon OX18 3N2 (e-mail timjoss@ae-sop.org)

JOSSE, Dr (Silvain) Edouard; OBE (1983); s of Albert Josse (d 2001), of London, and Charlotte, *née* Karolicki (d 2000); *b* 8 May 1933; *Educ* Highgate Sch, Middx Hosp Med Sch, Univ of London (MB BS, MRCS, LRCP); *m* 1, 15 May 1960 (m dis 1983), Lea, da of Alter Majer Ber (d 1977); 2 s (David b 22 July 1961, Jeremy b 14 July 1968), 1 da (Anna b 19 Sept 1964); m 2, 27 Oct 1991, Yvonne, da of Harry Levine (d 1970); *Career* gen med practitioner 1962 (ret 1996), princ forensic med examiner Metropolitan Police 1965–2014, Tst Respiratory Physician North Middx Hosp, former regnl advsr in gen practice and assoc dean of postgrad med N (E) Thames Region Br Postgrad Med Fedn Univ of London 1974–95, former GP memb NE Thames RHA; former chm: Enfield and Haringey Local Med Ctee, Jt Ctee on Postgrad Training for Gen Practice; former memb: Standing Ctee on Postgrad Med and Dental Educn, Enfield and Haringey Family Practitioners' Ctee; sec gen UEMO 1982–86; memb Expert Witness Inst, former chm Soc of Expert Witnesses (memb Cncl); pres RSM Section for GP 2001–02; author of papers in Clinical Forensic Medicine and Education; clinical complaints advsr Medical Defence Union; Liveryman Worshipful Soc of Apothecaries; MA London 1989; memb RSM 1978 (Cncl 1997–2001); fell BMA 2002 (memb 1956–); FRCGP 1977, DMJ 1970, FACBS 2004, FFFLM 2005, FZS, AFP (pres 1998–2000), MLS, BAFS (memb Cncl 2003–05), MAE; *Recreations* skiing, gardening, history, good wine and malt whisky tasting; *Clubs* MCC, Middx CC, RAC; *Style*— Dr Edouard Josse, OBE; ✉ 2 Shirehall Gardens, London NW4 2QS (☎ 020 8202 7740, fax 020 8203 9891, mobile 07966 531334, e-mail eddiejosse@aol.com)

JOTISCHKY, Tim; s of late Laszlo Jotischky, and Helma, *née* Repczuk; *b* 16 May 1967, Twickenham, Gtr London; *Educ* St Paul's (sr scholarship), Exeter Coll Oxford (scholarship), City Univ Grad Sch of Journalism; *m* 1999, Jo, *née* Mitchell; 2 da (Millie b 2 Sept 2000, Eloise b 16 Aug 2003); *Career* reporter Eastern Daily Press 1989–91; Daily Mail: foreign ed 1994–98, exec news ed 1998–2000; ed Metro 2000–01, ed Scottish Daily Mail 2001–03, head of sport Daily Mail 2003–08, dep ed Sunday Telegraph 2008–13, head of business Telegraph Media Gp 2013–14; sr conslt PHA Media 2014–; *Recreations* running, reading, family, tennis, Chelsea FC; *Style*— Tim Jotischky, Esq; ✉ PHA Media, Hammer House, 117 Wardour Street, London W1F 0UN (☎ 020 7440 0361, e-mail timj@pha-media.com, website www.pha-media.com, Twitter @TimJotischky)

JOURDAN, Martin Henry; s of Henry George Jourdan (d 1990), of Dumfries, Scotland, and Jocelyn Louise, *née* Courtney (d 1962); *b* 7 October 1941; *Educ* Bishopshalt GS, Guy's Hosp Med Sch (MB BS, BSc, LRCP, PhD, MS); *m* 22 Oct 1966, May, da of John McElwain (d 1960), of Glasgow; 2 s (Iain Campbell b 1967, Adam Ramsay b 1985), 2 da (Anthea b 1969, Gabrielle b 1970); *Career* conslt surgn Guy's Hosp 1978–, external examiner in surgery to Univs of Bristol and W Indies 1978–87, reader in surgery Univ of London 1982, sub-dean Guy's Hosp Med Sch 1984–89, sr examiner in surgery Univ of London 1984–, memb Ct of Examiners RCS 1986–; Freeman City of London, Master Worshipful Soc of Apothecaries of London (memb Ct of Assts 2001–02); memb BMA, Surgical Res Soc Assoc of Surgns; FRSM, FRCS; *Recreations* tennis, reading, opera; *Clubs* Athenaeum; *Style*— Martin Jourdan, Esq; ✉ 55 Shirlock Road, Hampstead, London NW3 2HR (☎ 020 7267 1582); Department of Surgery, St Thomas' Hospital, London SE1 7EH (☎ 020 7928 9292 ext 1003, private room 020 7403 3817)

JOWELL, Prof Sir Jeffrey Lionel; KCMG, QC (1993); s of Jack and Emily Jowell, of Cape Town, SA; *b* 4 November 1938; *Educ* Univ of Cape Town (BA, LLB), Hertford Coll Oxford (MA, pres Oxford Union 1963), Harvard Law Sch (LLM, SJD); *m* 8 Dec 1963, Frances Barbara, da of Dr Moses Suzman, of Johannesburg, South Africa, and Helen Suzman, DBE; 1 da (Joanna b 2 Sept 1967), 1 s (Daniel b 11 June 1969); *Career* called to the Bar Middle Temple 1965 (hon bencher 1999, bencher 2013); res asst Harvard Law Sch 1966–68, fell Jt Centre Urban Studies Harvard and MIT 1967–68, assoc prof of law and admin studies York Univ Toronto 1968–71; LSE: Leverhulme fell in urban legal studies 1972–74, lectr in law 1974–75; UCL: prof of public law 1975–2006, dean Faculty of Law 1979–89 and 1998–2002 (head of dept 1982–89 and 1998–2002), vice-provost and head Grad Sch 1992–99, prof of law 2006–10, emeritus prof 2010–; dir Bingham Centre for the Rule of Law 2010–; Venice Cmmn (European Cmmn for Democracy Through Law): UK memb 2000–11, memb Governing Bd 2001–11, vice-pres 2003–06, chair Sub Cmmn on Democratic Instns 2009–11; memb Royal Cmmn on Environmental Pollution 2003–10, non-exec dir Office of Rail Regulation 2004–07, chair Br Waterways Ombudsman Ctee 2005–13; Lionel Cohen lectr in Hebrew Univ of Jerusalem 1986, JUSTICE Tom Sargant Memorial lectr 2006, Judicial Studies Bd of NI Ann lectr 2008, Eson Weinmann lectr Tulane Univ 2010, annual lectr Constitutional and Admin Bar Assoc 2010; visiting prof: Univ of Paris 1991, Univ of Aix-Marseilles 2002, Columbia Law Sch NY 2002; hon prof Univ of Cape Town 1999–2006 (Rabinowitz fell 2010); non-exec dir: UCL Press 1994–95, Camden and Islington Community Health Tst 1994–97; SSRC: chm Social Science and Law Ctee 1981–84, vice-chm Govt and Law Ctee 1982–84; memb: Nuffield Ctee Town and Country Planning 1983–86, Bd Inst of Cwlth Studies 1994–99, Cncl Justice 1997–, Bd Chancellor's Ctee to review Crown Office List 1999; chm Ctee of Heads Univ Law Schs 1984–86; Br delegate CSCE Conf Oslo 1991; chm Inst of Philanthropy 2000–04; tstee: John Foster Meml Tst 1986–, Int Centre for Public Law 1993–97, Prince of Wales's Inst of Architecture 1997–99, Prince of Wales's Fndn for Architecture and the Urban Environment 1998–99; chair Friends of the South African Constitutional Court Tst 2003–, Int Advsy Bd Freedom Under Law 2009–; memb editorial bds of various jls, convenor of numerous int workshops and confs on constitutional law and democratic principles, assisted with the drafting of various nat constitutions; hon fell UCL 1997; Hon DJur Univ of Athens 1987, Hon LLD Univ of Ritsumeikan 1988, Hon LLD Univ of Cape Town 2000, hon doctorate Univ of Paris 2 (2009); corresponding memb Acad of Athens 2009; *Books* Law and Bureaucracy (1975), Lord Denning: The Judge And The Law (jt ed, 1984), The Changing Constitution (jt ed, 1985, 1989, 1994, 2000, 2004, 2007 and 2011), Judicial Review (jt author, 1995, 2007 and 2013), Principles of Judicial Review (jt author, 1999), Understanding Human Rights Principles (jt ed, 2001), Delivering Rights (jt ed, 2003); numerous articles and reviews on public law, human rights and planning law; *Recreations* tennis, Exmoor and London; *Style*— Prof Sir Jeffrey Jowell, KCMG, QC; ✉ Blackstone Chambers, Middle Temple, London EC4Y 9BW (☎ 020 7583 1770)

JOWELL, Baroness (Life Peer UK 2015), of Brixton in the London Borough of Lambeth; Rt Hon Dame Tessa Jowell; DBE (2012), PC (1998); da of Dr Kenneth Palmer, and Rosemary Palmer; *b* 17 September 1947; *Educ* St Margaret's Sch Aberdeen, Univ of Aberdeen, Univ of Edinburgh, Goldsmiths Coll London; *m* 17 March 1979, David Mills; 1 s, 1 da, 3 step c; *Career* child care offr London Borough of Lambeth 1969–71, psychiatric social worker The Maudsley Hosp Camberwell 1972–74, asst dir MIND 1974–86, dir Community Care Special Action Project Birmingham 1987–90, dir Joseph Rowntree Fndn Community Care Programme 1990–92; Parly candidate Ilford N 1978 and 1979; MP (Lab): Dulwich 1992–97, Dulwich and West Norwood 1997–2015; min of state for public health Dept of Health and spokesperson for Women in the Commons 1997–1999, min of state for employment DfEE 1999–2001, sec of state for Culture, Media and Sport 2001–07, min for women 2005–06, min for the Olympics and London 2005–10, min with responsibility for humanitarian assistance, min for the Cabinet Office and Paymaster Gen 2009–10, shadow min for the Olympics and memb Olympic Bd 2010–12, shadow min for the Cabinet Office 2011; memb Expert Resource Gp Harvard Sch for Public Health Ministerial Health Leaders' Forum 2013, memb Advsy Bd Ministerial Leadership in Health Program Harvard Univ 2014; appointed expert by IOC Olympic Agenda Working Gp on Bidding Procedure 2014; cmmr for Mental Health Act 1985–90; cncllr London Borough of Camden 1971–86, vice-chm then chm Social Servs Ctee Assoc of Met Authorities 1978–86, govr Nat Inst for Social Work 1985–90; tstee Ditchley Fndn 2011– (memb Cncl of Mgmnt 2013–), chair City Safe Fndn 2012–, vice-pres RTS 2013–, tstee Tennis Fndn 2013; visiting fell Nuffield Coll Oxford 1993–2002, visiting sr fell Policy Studies Inst 1986–90, visiting sr fell King's Fund 1990–92, sr fell Inst of Govt 2011–, distinguished hon fell Faculty of Public Health 2014, Menschel fell in advanced leadership Harvard Sch for Public Health 2016; Hon LLD Univ of Aberdeen 2016; Freedom of the London Borough of Southwark 2012, Freedom of the City of London 2014; *Style*— The Rt Hon the Baroness Jowell, DBE; ✉ House of Lords, London SW1A 0PW

JOWITT, Prof Paul William; CBE (2011); s of late Stanley Jowitt, of Thurcroft, S Yorks, and late Joan Mary, *née* Goundry; *b* 3 August 1950; *Educ* Maltby GS, Imperial Coll London (BSc ((Eng)), PhD); *m* 11 Aug 1973, Jane Catriona, da of late Lt Ronald George Urquhart, of Romford, Essex; 1 s (Christopher b 17 Feb 1978), 1 da (Hannah b 29 June 1980); *Career* lectr in civil engrg Imperial Coll 1974–86 (warden Falmouth Hall 1980–86), chm Tynemarch Systems Engineering Ltd 1984–86 (dir 1984–91), ed Journal of Civil Engineering Systems 1985–; Heriot-Watt Univ: prof 1987–, head Dept of Civil Engrg 1988–91, head Dept of Civil and Offshore Engrg 1991–99; pres ICE 2009–10, dir Scottish Inst of Sustainable Technol, former bd memb Scotland Water, non-exec dir United Utilities Water 2009–11; author of various specialist tech pubns and jl articles; memb various nat and local assoc ctees ICE; CEng 1988, FICE 1994 (MICE 1988, pres), FRSA 1996, FRSE 2005, FCGI 2006, fell Instn of Professional Engrs NZ (FIPENZ) 2008, FREng 2012; *Recreations* painting, Morgan 3-wheelers, Jowett cars, restoring old houses, allotmenting, canal narrow boats; *Clubs* Chaps, Links, MTWC; *Style*— Prof Paul Jowitt, CBE; ✉ 14 Belford Mews, Edinburgh EH4 3BT; Heriot-Watt University, Edinburgh EH14 4AS (☎ 0131 451 3143, e-mail p.w.jowitt@hw.ac.uk)

JOY, His Hon Judge (Henry) Martin; s of Henry Joy, and Margaret Joy; *b* 18 April 1948; *Educ* Bradfield Coll, Univ of Southampton (LLB); *m* 1977, Hilary Ann Smyth; 1 s, 1 da; *Career* called to the Bar Lincoln's Inn 1971; in practice as barr 1971–2007, recorder 1993–2007, circuit judge (South Eastern Circuit) 2007–; *Style*— His Hon Judge Joy; ✉ c/o The South Eastern Circuit, 289–293 High Holborn, London WC1V 7HZ

JOYCE, Dr Bob; *b* 24 May 1958; *Educ* Univ of Leicester, Univ of Warwick (MBA); *m* m Amanda Joyce; *Career* exec dir product creation and delivery Jaguar Land Rover 2013–; FREng; *Style*— Dr Bob Joyce; ✉ Jaguar Land Rover, Abbey Road, Whitley, Coventry CV3 4LF

JOYCE, Prof Dominic; *b* 8 April 1968; *Educ* Queen Elizabeth's Hosp Bristol, Merton Coll Oxford (postmaster, sr scholar, Jr Mathematical Prize, Sr Mathematical Prize, Johnson Univ Prize, DPhil); *m* Jayne; 3 da (Matilda b 28 Aug 2000, Katharine b 2 July 2003, Margaret b 28 February 2008); *Career* jr research fell ChCh Oxford 1992–95, research memb Inst for Advanced Study Princeton 1993–94 (year abroad, also worked at Mathematical Sciences Research Inst (MSRI) Berkeley); Univ of Oxford: lectr in pure mathematics 1995–, prof of mathematics 2002–; tutorial fell in mathematics Lincoln Coll Oxford 1995–2006; EPSRC advanced research fell 2001–06; author of numerous conf proceedings, papers and articles in books and learned jls; second prize British Mathematical Olympiad 1986, Silver medal Int Mathematical Olympiad Warsaw 1986 (memb British team), Bronze medal Int Physics Olympiad London 1986 (memb British team); Jr Whitehead Prize London Mathematical Soc 1997, prize for young European mathematicians European Mathematical Soc 2000, Adams Prize 2004; FRS 2014; *Books* Compact Manifolds with Special Holonomy (2000), Calabi-Yau Manifolds and Related Geometries (jtly, 2003), Riemannian Holonomy Groups and Calibrated Geometry (2007); *Style*— Prof Dominic Joyce; ✉ Lincoln College, Oxford OX1 3DR; Mathematical Institute, 24–29 St Giles', Oxford OX1 3LB

JOYCE, Rosemary; *née* Jones; da of late J G M Jones, and V M Jones, *née* Fletcher; *b* 18 September 1963, Bromsgrove, Worcs; *Educ* Univ of Stirling (BA), Inst of Educn Univ of

J

London (MA, PGCE); *m* 1991; 2 da (Megan, Angharad (twins) b 5 Nov 2001); *Career* teacher: Millais Sch Horsham 1987–90, Aylesbury HS 1990–92, The Clarendon Sch Trowbridge 1993–2000; dep headteacher Nonsuch HS for Girls Cheam 2000–05, headteacher Tonbridge GS 2005–; NPQH; *Style*— Rosemary Joyce; ✉ Tonbridge Grammar School, Deakin Leas, Tonbridge, Kent TN9 2JR (☎ 01732 365125, fax 01732 359417, e-mail headteacher@tgs.kent.sch.uk)

JOYNES, Stephen Frederick (Steve); MBE (2006); s of Stephen Sidney Joynes (d 1988), and Doris Winifred, *née* Thurling (d 2008); *b* 24 February 1935, Walsall, W Midlands; *Educ* Blue Coat Secdy Modern and the academy of life; *m* 8 July 1978, Janet Lesley, *née* Cook; 1 s (Steven Earl b 8 Jan 1969); *Career* early career in building trade 1950–53; Nat Serv RAF 1953–56; fndr and prop: mobile fish and chip van 1956, Golden Grill Restaurant Wylde Green 1958, Midland Hotel Walsall 1961, County Hotel Walsall 1965, Chateau Impney Hotel Droitwich 1970, Barons Court Hotel Walsall Wood 1973, Hoar Cross Hall Spa Resort Hotel Hoar Cross 1989, Eden Hall Spa Newark 2002, Eden Day Spa Hoar Cross; memb of Midland Assoc of Restaurants, Caterers and Hoteliers; Salesman of the Year Autobar Vending Machines 1965, Most Excellent Spa Johansonns Award for Excellence, Best Health Spa Good Housekeeping, Lifetime Achievement Award and 3 Crystal Awards Thalgo, England's Leading Spa Resort World Travel Awards 2005, 2006, 2007, 2008, 2009, 2010 and 2011; *Books* Take Action, How To Make A Fortune By Being Nice To People; *Recreations* health, happiness, fitness, creating successful businesses and helping others to do the same; *Style*— Steve Joynes, Esq, MBE; ✉ Hoar Cross Hall Spa Resort, Hoar Cross, Staffordshire DE13 8QS (☎ 01283 575671, fax 01283 575224, e-mail marketing@hoarcross.co.uk, website www.hoarcross.co.uk)

JUBB, Brian Patrick; s of Charles Patrick Jubb (d 1992), and Patricia Elizabeth, *née* Parry (d 1968); *b* 25 August 1948; *Educ* The King's Sch Canterbury, Inns of Court Sch of Law; *m* 1, 16 Nov 1974 (m dis 1982), Susan Patricia Taylor; 1 da (Alexandra b 10 June 1978); m 2, 13 Sept 1985, Susan Elizabeth Lunn; 1 da (Lucy b 13 July 1988); *Career* called to the Bar Gray's Inn 1971, head of chambers 1994–; *Recreations* general aviation, scuba diving, reading; *Style*— Brian Jubb, Esq; ✉ Renaissance Chambers, Gray's Inn, London WC1R 5JA (☎ 020 7404 1111, fax 020 7430 1522 and 020 7430 1050)

JUBB, David; *Educ* Bedford Modern Sch, Bretton Hall Coll (BA), Univ of Bristol (MA), Central Sch of Speech and Drama (MA); *Career* theatre director; sch drama teacher 1992–95, lectr in performing arts Chippenham Coll 1995–96, project dir then venue dir Central Sch of Speech and Drama 1997–99, artistic dir Economical Truth Theatre 1997–2001, devpt prodr Battersea Arts Centre (BAC) 1999–2001 (assoc prodr 2001–04), fndr and dir Your Imagination 2001– (chair 2004–); BAC: artistic dir and chief exec 2004–08, jt artistic dir and chief exec 2008–12 (with David Micklem), artistic dir and chief exec 2012–; chair Bd of Tstees Kneehigh Theatre Cornwall 2008–13, chair London Theatre Consortium 2012–15; *Publications* https://issuu.com/jerwoodcf/docs/a11986_pl_the_producers_book; *Style*— David Jubb, Esq; ✉ Battersea Arts Centre, Lavender Hill, London SW11 5TN (☎ 020 7326 8224, e-mail davidj@bac.org.uk)

JUCKES, His Hon Judge Robert William Somerville; QC; s of Dr William Renwick Juckes, and Enid Osyth Juckes; *b* 1 August 1950; *Educ* Marlborough, Univ of Exeter; *m* 14 Sept 1974, Frances Anne, *née* MacDowell; 3 s (Timothy b 24 Aug 1979, Daniel b 22 May 1982, David b 30 Dec 1986); *Career* called to the Bar 1974; asst recorder 1992, recorder 1995; head of chambers 2000–03, circuit judge Midland Circuit 2007–; resident judge Worcester Crown Court 2011, hon recorder Worcester 2012; *Recreations* tennis, golf, cricket, Georgian history, historical novels particularly the works of Patrick O'Brien, culturing three sons and four grandchildren (thus far); *Style*— His Hon Judge Juckes, QC

JUDA, David; s of Paul Juda, and Annely Juda, CBE (d 2006); *Educ* Ibstock Place Froebel Sch, John Kelly Secdy Modern, Kilburn Poly; *m* March 1983, Yuko Shiraishi, *qv*, da of Masahiro Shinoda; *Career* dir Annely Juda Fine Art 1978 (joined 1967); memb Exec Ctee Fine Art 1971–2014; chm Soc of London Art Dealers 2014– (vice-chm 1986–90, 1995–2001 and 2014, memb 1970–); hon doctorate Norwich Univ Coll of the Arts (NUCA) 2012; *Recreations* skiing; *Clubs* Groucho; *Style*— David Juda, Esq; ✉ Annely Juda Fine Art, 23 Dering Street, London W1S 1AW (☎ 020 7629 7578, fax 020 7491 2139, e-mail ajfa@annelyjudafineart.co.uk)

JUDD, Baron (Life Peer UK 1991), of Portsea in the County of Hampshire; Frank Ashcroft Judd; s of Charles W Judd, CBE (d 1974), of Surrey, and Helen Osborn Judd, JP, *née* Ashcroft (d 1982); *b* 28 March 1935; *Educ* City of London Sch, LSE (BScEcon); *m* 1961, Christine Elizabeth Louise, da of Frederick Ward Willington (d 1966), of Kent; 2 da (Hon Elizabeth b 1967, Hon Philippa b 1969); *Career* F/O RAF 1957–59; sec gen Int Voluntary Serv 1960–66; MP (Lab): Portsmouth W 1966–74, Portsmouth N (following boundary change) 1974–79; memb Public Accounts Ctee 1966–69, chm PLP Overseas Aid and Devpt Gp 1967–70, PPS to Min for Housing and Local Govt 1967–70, jt sec All-Pty Parly Gp for UN 1967–72, memb Commons Select Ctee on Overseas Devpt 1969–74, jt PPS to Rt Hon Harold Wilson as Ldr of Oppn 1970–72, memb Br Parly Delgn to Cncl of Europe and WEU 1970–73 and 1997–2005, jr oppn def spokesman 1972–74, Parly under sec of state for def (RN) 1974–76, Parly sec Miny for overseas devpt 1976, min for Overseas Devpt 1976–77, min of state FCO 1977–79, rapporteur to Parly Assembly of the Cncl of Europe on the Conflict in Chechnya 1999–2004; assoc dir Int Defence & Aid Fund for Southern Africa 1979–80, dir VSO 1980–85, chm Centre for World Devpt Educn 1980–85, dir Oxfam 1985–91, chm Int Cncl of Voluntary Agencies 1985–90, memb House of Lords Oppn front bench foreign affrs team 1991–92; House of Lords princ front bench spokesman on: educn 1992–94, overseas devpt co-operation 1992–97; memb House of Lords oppn front bench defence team 1992–96; chm Geneva World Economic Forum Conf on future of Southern Africa 1990 and 1991, memb Governing Cncl Nat Housing and Tenant Resource Centre 1992–94; chm: Oxford Diocesan Bd for Social Responsibility 1992–95, Selly Oak Colls Birmingham 1994–97, European-Atlantic Gp 1997–99, Refugee Sub-Ctee of Ctee on Migration Refugees and Demography Parly Assembly of the Cncl of Europe 1998–2001; advsr on security matters, educn and community rels to The Forbes Tst 1992–2000, consIt World Humanity Action Tst 1993–96, advsr De Montfort Univ 1993–2012; memb: Int Cmmn on Global Governance 1992–2001, WHO Task Force on Health and Devpt 1994–98, Justice Goldstone's Int Working Gp on Human Duties and Responsibilities in the New Millennium 1997–99, Sub-Ctee on Environment, Agriculture, Public Health and Consumer Protection of Lords Ctee on European Communities 1997–2001, Procedure Ctee House of Lords 2001–04, Ecclesiastical Ctee House of Lords and House of Commons 2001–, Jt Ctee on Human Rights 2003–07, Lords Select Ctee on the EU Sub-Ctee F (Home Affairs, Educn and Health) 2010–15, Cmmn on Diplomacy LSE 2014–15, EU Justice Sub-Ctee House of Lords 2015–; pres ME Ctee Inter-Parly Union 2012–15; non-exec dir Portsmouth Harbour Renaissance Bd 1998–2006; memb: Labour Pty 1951–, Fabian Soc (former chm), Br Cncl, Unite, GMB, Governing Body Queen Elizabeth House Univ of Oxford 1989–94, NW Regnl Ctee Nat Tst 1996–2005, Oxfam Assoc 1997–2004, Royal Cwlth Soc, RIIA, Advsy Bd Centre for Human Rights LSE 2007–; pres: YMCA (England) 1996–2005, European Atlantic Gp 1999–2001, Friends of the Lake District 2005–12, W Cumbria Hospice at Home 2008–15; hon vice-pres: Campaign for Nat Parks 1998–, UN Assoc, Lakeland Housing Tst; govr: LSE 1982–2012 (emeritus govr 2012–), Westminster Coll Oxford 1992–98; convenor Social Responsibility Forum of Churches Together Cumbria 1999–2005; life memb Ct Univ of Newcastle, life memb Ct Lancaster Univ; tstee: International Alert 1994–2000 (chm 1997–2000), Ruskin Fndn 2002–11, Saferworld 2002–15; freedom of the City of Portsmouth 1995; hon pres Friends of the Royal Navy Museum 2002–12, hon fell Selly Oak Colls Birmingham; hon fell and Hon DLitt Univ of Portsmouth, Hon DLitt Univ of Bradford, Hon DLitt De Montfort Univ, Hon LLD Univ of Greenwich 1999, hon fell Lancaster Univ 2015; FRSA; *Books* Radical Future (jtly, 1967), Fabian International Essays (jtly, 1970), Purpose in Socialism (jtly, 1973), Imagining Tomorrow: Rethinking the Global Challenge (jtly, 2000); *Recreations* enjoying Cumbria, family holidays, listening to music, theatre; *Clubs* Cwlth Tst, Royal Overseas League; *Style*— The Lord Judd; ✉ House of Lords, London SW1A 0PW

JUDD, James; s of Eric Judd (d 1986), and Winifred Judd (d 1997); *b* 30 October 1949; *Educ* Hertford GS, Trinity Coll of Music; *m* 25 Sept 1993, Valerie; *Career* conductor; music dir Florida Philharmonic 1988–2001, music dir New Zealand Symphony Orch 1999–, Florida Grand Opera 1993–96; princ guest conductor Orchestre National de Lille; fndr memb Chamber Orch of Europe; has conducted numerous other major orchs incl: English Chamber Orch, Hallé Orch, Royal Philharmonic Orch, LSO, LPO, Royal Scottish National Orch, Vienna Symphony Orch, Prague Symphony Orch, Berlin Philharmonic, Orchestre National de France, Zurich Tonhalle, Orchestre de la Suisse Romande; also conducted numerous operas incl: Il Trovatore, La Traviata, The Barber of Seville, Rigoletto and The Marriage of Figaro (all with ENO), La Cenerentola (Glyndebourne Festival) 1985, Don Giovanni (US operatic debut, Miami) 1988; *Recordings* incl: Mahler Symphony No 1 (with Florida Philharmonic Orch), Elgar Symphony No 1 (with Hallé Orch) 1992, live recordings of Mahler Symphonies No 9 and 10, complete recordings of Meyerbeer and Donizetti operas on Opera Rara, various others with Euro Community Youth Orch, Gustav Mahler Youth Orch, English Chamber Orch, Hallé Orch and Chamber Orch of Europe; *Recreations* almost anything; *Style*— James Judd, Esq; ✉ Columbia Artists Management, New York (☎ 001 212 841 9560, website www.cami.com)

JUDD, Lionel Henry; s of John Basil Thomas Judd (d 1983), and Cynthia Margaret Georgina, *née* White-Smith; *b* 24 October 1945; *Educ* The Leys Sch Cambridge, Downing Coll Cambridge (MA); *m* 19 Sept 1970, Janet Elizabeth, da of Arthur Boyton Fraser (d 1966), of Stansted, Essex; 1 s (Edward b 1972), 1 da (Alexandra b 1975); *Career* admitted slr 1972; Cumberland Ellis Peirs (formerly Darley Cumberland): ptnr 1975–, managing ptnr 1997–2001, sr ptnr 2001–04, consIt 2005; memb Exec Ctee Abbeyfield Soc Bucks 1980–2013 (vice-chm 2005 and 2009, chm 2006–09); tstee: Downing Coll Boathouse Centenary Tst 1995–2008, Game Conservancy Ctee (Bucks branch) 1999–2012; pres Downing Coll Alumni Assoc 2015–16; tstee Aylesbury Cons Assoc 1999–, pres Wendover Cons Assoc 2005–; *Recreations* rowing, country pursuits, travel; *Clubs* Leander, Caledonian; *Style*— Lionel Judd, Esq; ✉ Little Coombe, Wendover, Buckinghamshire HP22 6EQ

JUDD, Very Rev Peter Somerset Margesson; DL (Essex 2009); s of William Frank Judd, of Monkton, Kent; *b* 20 February 1949, Calgary, Canada; *Educ* Charterhouse, Trinity Hall Cambridge (MA), Cuddeson Coll Oxford (CertTheol); *m* Judith Margaret; 1 s (Tom b 17 Dec 1981), 1 da (Alice b 29 Dec 1983); *Career* ordained: deacon 1974, priest 1975; curate St Philip with St Stephen Salford 1974–76; Clare Coll Cambridge: chaplain 1976–81, elected fell 1980, actg dean 1980–81; team vicar Hitcham and Dropmore Burnham Team Miny 1981–88, vicar of St Mary the Virgin Iffley 1988–97, rural dean of Cowley 1995–97, rector and provost of Chelmsford 1997–2000, dean of Chelmsford 2000–; *Recreations* architecture and art, listening to music, literature, drawing, fell walking, cooking; *Style*— The Very Rev the Dean of Chelmsford, DL; ✉ The Dean's House, 3 Harlings Grove, Waterloo Lane, Chelmsford CM1 1YQ; The Cathedral Office, Guy Harlings, New Street, Chelmsford CM1 1TY (☎ 01245 294492, fax 01245 294499, e-mail dean@chelmsfordcathedral.org.uk)

JUDGE, Lady; Barbara S Judge; CBE (2010); formerly Hon Barbara S Thomas; *née* Singer; d of Marcia Singer; *b* 28 December 1946; *Educ* Univ of Pennsylvania (BA), NY Univ Law Sch (ed NYU Law Review, John Norton Pomeroy Scholar, Jefferson Davis Prize in Public Law, seventeen other prizes in various subjects, JD); *m*; 1 s; *Career* assoc Paul Weiss Rifkind Wharton & Garrison (law firm) 1969–73, ptnr Kaye Scholer Fierman Hays & Handler 1978–80 (joined as assoc 1973), cmmr US Securities and Exchange Cmmn 1980–83 (fndr Int Ctee of Securities Regulators), regnl dir Hong Kong Samuel Montagu & Co Ltd 1984–86, sr vice-pres and head of Int Private Banking Gp Bankers Trust Co 1986–90, md mktg and int Cramer Rosenthal McGlynn Inc 1990–93, exec dir business and legal affrs News International plc 1993–94, chm Whitworths Group Ltd 1995–2000, exec chm Private Equity Investor plc 2000–04; dir LIXIL Corp Tokyo Japan 2015–; chm UK Atomic Energy Authy 2004–, chm Advsy Bd Int Energy Inst UCL 2011–, chm Nuclear Reform Ctee Tepco Tokyo 2013– (also chm Task Force on Nuclear Safety), currently memb Statoil Strategic Advsy Cncl; non-exec chm Axon Gp plc 1998–2003, non-exec dep chm Friends' Provident plc 1998–, dep chm Financial Reporting Cncl 2004–07, chm UK Pension Protection Fund 2010–, chm elect (first woman chm) IOD 2015–; non-exec dir: Capital Radio 1999–2005, Hardy Underwriting Gp 2004–08, Bekaert 2007–, Magna Int 2008–; memb: US-Hong Kong Econ Assistance Ctee, Cncl on Foreign Rels, Young Pres's Orgn (London, Hong Kong and Gotham NY chapters), Advsy Cncl Women's Economic Round Table, Forum UK, London and NY chapters Women's Forum; UK business ambass 2010–; memb Bd of Govrs Lauder Inst of Mgmnt and Int Studies Wharton Sch Univ of Pennsylvania 1985–, chm Governing Body SOAS 2004– memb Advsy Bd UAE 2009–, Steering Ctee Istanbul Int Energy and Climate Center Sabanci Univ 2011–; tstee: Royal Acad (memb Special Projects Advsy Ctee 1994–), Wallace Collection 2003–08; memb: Bd Int Salzburg Assoc (organisers of Salzburg Festival) 1987–92, Advsy Ctee LSO 1993–; dir Dementia UK 2014–; *Clubs* Reform, Economic (NY), River (NY), The Metropolitan (NY); *Style*— Lady Judge, CBE

JUDGE, Ian; s of John Judge, of Southport, Merseyside, and Marjorie Judge; *b* 21 July 1946; *Educ* King George V GS, Guildhall Sch of Music and Drama; *Career* stage director; *Theatre* joined RSC 1975; Stratford: Henry IV Parts 1 and 2, Henry V and Coriolanus (asst dir); assoc dir Poppy (Barbican, re-worked for the Aldephi), The Wizard of Oz (Stratford and Barbican) 1987 and 1988, The Comedy of Errors (UK and Asia/Aust tour) 1990, Love's Labour's Lost (UK and Japan) 1993, Twelfth Night (UK and world tour) 1994, The Relapse 1995, A Christmas Carol, Troilus and Cressida 1996, The Merry Wives of Windsor 1997; other directing credits incl: The Rivals and King Lear (Old Vic), The Orchestra (King's Head Theatre Club), Rookery Nook (Barbican Centre), Musical Chairs (Chichester Festival Theatre Studio), Friends of Dorothy and How Lucky Can You Get (Donmar Warehouse), Banana Ridge and Peter Pan (Shaw Festival Canada), Henry the Eighth and Love for Love (Chichester Festival Theatre), Macbeth (Sydney Theatre Co); *Musicals* incl: Oh Kay! (Chichester Festival Theatre, The Swan-Down Gloves (RSC)), Merrily We Roll Along (Guildhall Theatre Barbican, Arts Theatre Cambridge and Bloomsbury Theatre London), Bitter Sweet (New Sadler's Wells Opera), A Little Night Music (Chichester Festival Theatre and Piccadilly Theatre), Show Boat (RSC, Opera North and London Palladium), D'Oyly Carte in The Mikado (Savoy Theatre), West Side Story (Aust), The Roar of the Greasepaint – the Smell of the Crowd (London); *Opera* Ariodante (Buxton Festival), Faust (ENO and Opera North), The Merry Widow, Cavalleria Rusticana, Pagliacci, Don Quixote, La Belle Vivette, Mephistopheles, and Sir John in Love (all ENO), Macbeth, Tosca, Acis and Galatea, Boris Godunov and Attila (Opera North), Falstaff (Bremer Theatre Germany, Scottish Opera), Eugene Onegin (Grange Park Opera), Lohengrin (Wiesbaden Germany), The Tales of Hoffmann and Don Quixote (Victoria State Opera), Faust (Sydney Opera), Macbeth (Cologne Opera), The Flying Dutchman and Simon Boccanegra (ROH), The Tales of Hoffmann (Houston Grand Opera), Norma (Scottish Opera), Cosi Fan Tutte (Garsington Opera), Falstaff (Baden Baden Opera, Royal Albert Hall, Theatre du Chatelet Paris), Simon Boccanegra

(Washington Opera and Dallas Opera), Mefistofele (Teatro Colon Buenos Aires), La Boheme and Der Fliegende Holländer (Kirov Opera St Petersburg), Ernani (National Reisopera Holland), Salome (NYC Opera), Tosca, Madama Butterfly, Le Nozze di Figaro, Roméo et Juliette, Don Carlo, Tannhäuser (all Los Angeles Opera), Tannhäuser (Teatro Real Madrid) 2009, Simon Boccanegra (Canadian Opera Co Toronto) 2009, A Midsummer Night's Dream (Britten Theatre London) 2009, Die Gezeichneten (LA Opera); *Awards* Best Musical Revival Olivier Awards (for Show Boat), Green Room Theatre Best Dir Awards Victoria Aust (for Faust, The Tales of Hoffman, West Side Story); *Style—* Ian Judge, Esq; ✉ e-mail ijudge1@mac.com, website www.ianjudge.com

JUDGE, Sir Paul Rupert; kt (1996); s of Rupert Cyril Judge (d 1986), and Betty Rosa Muriel, *née* Daniels; *b* 25 April 1949; *Educ* Christchurch Sch Forest Hill, St Dunstan's Coll Catford, Trinity Coll Cambridge (MA), Wharton Business Sch Univ of Pennsylvania (MBA); *Family* 2 s (Christopher Paul, Michael James); *Career* Cadbury Schweppes plc: fin analyst then fin planning mangr Overseas Gp 1973–76, internal memb Gp Strategic Planning Project 1976–77, gp dep fin dir 1977–79, planning dir N American Region 1980, md Cadbury Schweppes Kenya Ltd 1980–82, md Cadbury Typhoo 1982–84, gp planning dir and memb Gp Exec Ctee 1984–85; Premier Brands Ltd: led MBO of food business of Cadbury Schweppes 1986, md 1986–87, chm 1987–89, co sold to Hillsdown Hldgs plc 1989; chm Food From Britain 1990–92, DG Cons Pty 1992–95, special advsr to Rt Hon Roger Freeman as Chllr of the Duchy of Lancaster 1995–96; non-exec dir: Grosvenor Development Capital plc 1989–93, Boddington Gp plc 1989–93, Strategy Ventures plc 1989–2002, WPP Gp plc 1991–97, Schroder Income Growth Fund plc 1995–2013 (chm 2005–13), Standard Bank Gp Ltd (Johannesburg) 2003–12, Tempur Sealy Int Inc (Kentucky) 2004–16, Eurasian Natural Resources Corporation plc 2007–13, Abraaj Capital Ltd Dubai 2009–15; pres: Assoc of MBAs 1997–, Chartered Mgmnt Inst 2004–05, Chartered Inst of Mktg 2008–14; memb: Cncl Food and Drink Fedn 1988–89, Milk Mktg Bd 1989–92, Cncl RASE 1991–96; chm: Advsy Bd Cambridge Univ Judge Business Sch 1991–2002, Br-N American Ctee 2001–14, Bd of Companions Inst of Mgmnt 2001–04; chm Br-Serbian Chamber of Commerce 2013–; tstee: Cambridge Fndn 1991–, Br Food Tst 1997–2007, Enterprise Education Tst 1998–2015 (chm 1999–2015), Royal Instn 1999–2005, American Mgmnt Assoc 2000–13 (dep chm 2005–13), Wharton EMEA Bd (chm 2000–10), Teachers' TV 2005–08 (chm); treas Imperial Soc of Knights Bachelor 1999–2006 (registrar 2006–13); dep chm Globe Theatre Devpt Cncl 2000–06; chm RSA 2003–06; govr: Bromsgrove Sch 1990–96, St Dunstan's Coll Catford 1997– (chm 2001–); listed in Business Magazine Top 40 under 40 1986, food industry personality of the year Food Processing Awards 1992; Freeman City of London 1970, Liveryman Worshipful Co of Marketors 1993 (Master 2005), alderman Tower Ward 2007–, Liveryman Worshipful Co of Clothworkers 2008–, Liveryman Worshipful Co of Educators 2013–, Sheriff of the City of London 2013–14, Foundation Master Guild of Entrepreneurs 2014–, Hon Liveryman Worshipful Co of Management Consultants 2015–; Hon LLD Univ of Cambridge 1995, Hon DLitt Univ of Westminster 2006, Hon DSc City Univ 2007; FRSA 1971, FInstD 1988, fell Mktg Soc 1991, CIMgt 1994; *Recreations* family, travel; *Clubs* Athenaeum, Mombasa (Kenya), Oriental; *Style—* Sir Paul Judge; ✉ 152 Grosvenor Road, London SW1V 3JL

JUKES, Graham Michael; OBE (2014); s of Thomas Jukes, and Edith Jukes; *b* 28 October 1952; *m* Barbara Jukes; 1 s (Henry Thomas); *Career* chief exec Chartered Inst of Environmental Health (CIEH) 2000–15 (dir CIEH Ltd 1999–2015, vice-pres 2016–), sr advsr Public Health England 2016–; dir: Specialist in Land Contamination Register (SiLC) Ltd 2010–15, Occupational Safety and Health Register (OSCHR) Ltd 2010–15, Inst of Food Safety Integrity and Protection (TiFSiP) Ltd 2014–15; company sec Int Fedn of Environmental Health 2000–15, tstee Assoc of London Environmental Health Practitioners (ALEHM) 2007–, vice-pres Environmental Protection UK 2016–; tstee and chm Reddiford Sch 2008–; FFPH 2004, chartered fell CIEH 2005 (memb 1970, fell 1990); *Style—* Graham Jukes, Esq, OBE, CFCIEH; ✉ e-mail grahamjukes@btinternet.com

JULIUS, Dr Anthony Robert; s of Morris and Myrna Julius; *b* 16 July 1956; *Educ* City of London Sch, Jesus Coll Cambridge (MA), Coll of Law, UCL (PhD); *m* 1, 1979 (m dis 1998), Judith, *née* Bernie; 2 s (Max Yoram b 8 December 1981, Theo Raphael b 6 September 1992), 2 da (Laura Yael b 12 July 1983, Chloe Anna b 10 February 1990); m 2, 1999, Dina, *née* Rabinovitch (d 2007); 1 s (Elon Lev b 12 Aug 2001); *Career* slr-advocate; ptnr Mishcon de Reya 1984–98 (head of litigation 1988–98, currently conslt); chm CentreCATH Univ of Leeds 2001–06, currently visiting prof English Dept Birkbeck Coll Univ of London; chair London Consortium; chair Law Panel Inst of Jewish Policy Research 1997–; co-fndr and tstee Diana, Princess of Wales Meml Fund 1997– (chm 1997–99, vice-pres 2002–), memb Advsy Bd Community Security Tst, memb Race and Faith Inquiry into MPS 2009; hon fell Soc for Advanced Legal Studies; Hon Dr Haifa Univ 2006; *Books* T S Eliot Anti-Semitism and Literary Form (1995, 2 edn 2003), Law & Literature (contrib, 1999), Idolising Pictures (2001), Transgressions: The Offences of Art (2002), Anti-Zionisms (pamphlet, 2004); *Recreations* cooking, writing; *Style—* Dr Anthony Julius; ✉ Mishcon de Reya, Summit House, 12 Red Lion Square, London WC1R 4QD (☎ 020 7440 7000, fax 020 7404 8171, e-mail anthony.julius@mishcon.co.uk)

JULIUS, Dame DeAnne; DCMG (2013), CBE (2002); da of Marvin G Julius, of Iowa, USA, and Maxine M, *née* Meeske; *b* 14 April 1949; *Educ* Iowa State Univ (BSc), Univ of Calif (MA, PhD); *m* 21 Nov 1976, Ian Alexander Harvey, *qv*, s of Dr Alexander Harvey (d 1987), of Cardiff; 1 da (Megan b 28 March 1979), 1 s (Ross b 9 Dec 1980); *Career* econ advsr World Bank 1975–82, md Logan Associates Inc 1982–86, dir of economics RIIA 1986–89; chief economist: Royal Dutch/Shell 1989–93, British Airways 1993–97, Monetary Policy Ctee Bank of England 1997–2001; non-exec dir: Ct of the Bank of England 2001–04, Lloyds TSB 2001–07, BP 2001–11, Serco 2001–07, Roche 2002–16, Deloitte 2011–14; sr advsr Fathom Financial Conslts 2008–11; chm: Banking Consumer Codes Review Gp 2000–01, RIIA 2003–12; chm UCL 2014–; *Books* Global Companies and Public Policy: The Growing Challenge of Foreign Direct Investment (1990), The Economics of Natural Gas (1990), The Monetary Implications of the 1992 Process (1990); *Recreations* skiing, hiking, Japanese gardens, bonsai; *Clubs* IOD; *Style—* Dame DeAnne Julius, DCMG, CBE; ✉ UCL Provost's Office, Gower Street, London WC1E 6BT (☎ 01372 451878, website www.deannejulius.com)

JUMAN, Curtis; *Career* md IT and Finance Gp UK Trade and Industry; *Style—* Curtis Juman, Esq; ✉ UK Trade and Investment, Kingsgate House, 66–74 Victoria Street, London SW1E 6SW

JUNG, Prof Roland Tadeusz; *Educ* Pembroke Coll Cambridge (exhibitioner, fndn scholar, MA, MB BChir, MD), St Thomas' Hosp London (LRCP (London), MRCS (England)); *Career* MRC clinical research scientific offr Dunn Nutrition Unit Cambridge 1977–79, sr registrar in endocrinology and diabetes Hammersmith Hosp and Royal Postgrad Med Sch London 1980–82, conslt physician/specialist in endocrinology and diabetes Ninewells Hosp Dundee 1982–2008; hon reader in med Ninewells Hosp and Med Sch Dundee 1991, clinical director of med Dundee Teaching Hosps NHS Tst 1991–94, dir for res devpt Tayside NHS Consortium 1997–2001, external examiner for medicine Univ of Oxford 2002–08, chair Prog Mgmnt Bd and memb Scientific Consultative Ctee Rowett Research Inst Univ of Aberdeen 2007–12, visiting prof Univ of Southampton 2009–; hon prof of medicine Univ of Dundee 1998–; chief scientist for Scottish Exec Health Dept 2001–07; Card Medal Western Gen Hosp Edinburgh 1987; biennial lecture named by Univ of Dundee Newton-Jung Diabetes Lecture 2012–, biennial lecture named by Tayside NHS Managed Clinical Network Jung-Newton Diabetes Lecture 2013–; memb Scottish Hosp Endowments Tst 1998–2001; chm Scottish Hosp Endowments Tst 2000–01; FRCPEd (chair UK Consensus Conf on Diabetes 2010), FRCP (London), MRCP (UK); *Books* Endocrine Problems in Cancer (jt ed, 1984), Colour Atlas of Obesity (1990); *Recreations* National Trust and Hampshire Cultural Trust volunteer; *Style—* Prof Roland Jung

JUNGELS, Dr Pierre Jean Marie Henri; Hon CBE (1989); s of Henri Jungels, and Jeanne Jungels; *b* 18 February 1944; *Educ* Univ of Liège (Ing Civ), Caltech (PhD); *m* 2, 1988, Caroline, da of Dr Z Benc, of Worcester; 2 step c and 2 c from previous m; *Career* gen mangr and chief exec Fina Petroleos (Angola) 1977–80, md and chief exec Fina plc (UK) 1980–89, exec dir Petrofina Gp 1989–95, md BG plc 1996, chief exec Enterprise Oil plc 1997–2001; chm Velocys plc (formerly Oxford Catalysts plc), chm Rockhopper Exploration plc, former chm OHM plc; non-exec dir: Woodside Petroleum Ltd until 2012, Baker Hughes Inc; pres Inst of Petroleum 1987–89 and 2002, co-chm Energy Inst 2002–03; *Style—* Dr Pierre Jungels, CBE

JUNIPER, Anthony Thomas (Tony); s of Austin Wilfred Juniper (d 1984), of Oxford, and Constance Margaret, *née* Eliston (d 2002); *b* 24 September 1960; *Educ* Oxford Sch, Oxford Coll of FE, Univ of Bristol (BSc), UCL (MSc); *m* Dec 1990, Susan Sparkes; 1 da (Madeleine b 1991), 2 s (Aneurin b 1994, Samuel b 1997); *Career* various posts: S Oxfordshire Countryside Educn Tst 1984, Nat Cmmn for Wildlife Conservation and Devpt Saudi Arabia 1988; freelance researcher 1988–89, contract worker UCL 1989, parrot conservation offr Int Cncl for Bird Preservation (now BirdLife Int) 1989–90; Friends of the Earth: sr campaigner (tropical rainforests) 1990–93, sr campaigner (biodiversity) 1993–95, dep campaigns dir 1995–97, campaigns dir 1997–98, policy and campaigns dir 1998–2003, vice-chair Friends of the Earth Int 2000–, exec dir Friends of the Earth England, Wales and NI 2003–08; special adsr Prince of Wales's Rainforest Project 2008–10, special advsr Prince's Charities Int Sustainability Unit 2010–, advsr Science Museum Climate Science Exhibit; co-fndr Robertsbridge Gp 2011–; sr assoc Cambridge Univ Prog for Industry 2008–13, fell Univ of Cambridge Prog for Sustainability Leadership 2013–; memb World Parrot Tst Scientific Ctee, founding bd memb Stop Climate Chaos 2005, founding memb Green New Deal Gp 2008–, tstee Beds, Northants and Cambs Wildlife Tst, patron Chartered Inst of Ecology and Environmental Mgmnt 2012–; Chromy Award Conscience Inst 2013; Hon DSc Univ of Brisol 2013, Hon DSc Univ of Plymouth 2013; hon fell Instn of Environmental Sciences 2009, hon fell Soc for the Environment 2013 (pres 2012–), FRSA; *Publications* Threatened Planet (1996), Parrots (with Parr, 1998, UK Library Assoc Reference Book of the Year 1999), Spix's Macaw – the race to save the world's rarest bird (2002), How Many Light Bulbs Does It Take to Change a Planet? (2007), Saving Planet Earth (2007), Harmony (with HRH The Prince of Wales and Ian Skelly, 2010), What Has Nature Ever Done For Us? (2013); also author of book chapters, scientific papers and magazine articles; contrib: BBC Wildlife magazine, The Ecologist, Bird Conservation International, Oryx, The Guardian, FT, The Independent, The Times, Resurgence Magazine, Sunday Times; ed Nat Geographic Green Magazine Supplement; *Recreations* family, natural history (especially ornithology), walking in wild places, all kinds of fishing, keeping fit, drawing and painting, gardening; *Style—* Tony Juniper, Esq; ✉ website www.tonyjuniper.com

J

JUNOR, Brian James Ross; s of Donald Junor, MBE (d 1986), of Dundee, and Ann Russell, *née* Mackie (d 1985); *b* 10 February 1946; *Educ* Dundee HS, Univ of St Andrews (MB ChB), Univ of Dundee (MD); *m* 1, 4 Feb 1972, Sheena MacLeod (d 1972), da of Sir Donald Douglas, of White House, Nevay Newtyle; m 2, 19 Jan 1979, Elizabeth Jane, da of John Fotheringham, OBE, of St Helen's, Fife; 1 s (Malcolm b 1980), 1 da (Katherine b 1982); *Career* sr registrar of medicine Aberdeen Royal Infirmary 1976–78, Aust Kidney Res Fndn fell Univ of Melbourne 1978–79, hon clinical lectr Univ of Glasgow 1979–, conslt nephrologist Gtr Glasgow Health Authy 1979–; currently sec Specialty Section in Nephrology Union of Euro Med Specialists; former memb Jt Ctee for Higher Med Training, former chm Specialist Advsy Ctee in Renal Diseases; memb BMA 1970, FRCPS 1982, FRCPE 1987; *Recreations* skiing, gardening, golf; *Style—* Brian Junor, Esq; ✉ The Barn, Ballagan, Strathblane, Glasgow (☎ 01360 770767); Renal Unit, Western Infirmary, Dunbarton Road, Glasgow (☎ 0141 211 2000, e-mail brian.junor@northglasgow.scot.nhs.uk)

JUNOR, Penelope Jane (Penny); da of Sir John Junor (d 1997), and Pamela Mary, *née* Welsh; *b* 6 October 1949; *Educ* Benenden, Univ of St Andrews; *m* 8 Sept 1970, James Stewart Leith; 3 s (Sam b 1 Jan 1974, Alexander b 23 July 1976, Jack b 17 Jan 1985), 1 da (Peta b 31 Dec 1987); *Career* trainee IPC Young Magazine Gp 1969–70, feature writer 19 Magazine 1970–71, writer Londoners' Diary Evening Standard 1971–73, freelance journalist 1974–, columnist Private Eye 1974–81, reporter Collecting Now (BBC) 1981, presenter 4 What It's Worth (Channel 4) 1982–89, co-presenter The Afternoon Show 1984–85, presenter The Travel Show (BBC) 1988–97, Paper Tigers (Radio Scotland) 2006, In the Footsteps of Fame (Radio Scotland) 2007; gen ed John Lewis Partnership 1994–99; patron Women's Health Concern 2002–, tstee beat (formerly Eating Disorders Assoc); *Books* Newspaper (1980), Babyware (1982), Diana, Princess of Wales (1982), Margaret Thatcher, Wife, Mother, Politician (1983), Burton – The Man Behind the Myth (1985), Charles (1987), Charles and Diana – Portrait of a Marriage (1991), Queen Elizabeth – Pictorial Celebration of Her Reign (1991), The Major Enigma (1993), Charles: Victim or Villain? (1998), Home Truths: Life Around My Father (2002), The Firm: The Troubled Life of the House of Windsor (2005), Wonderful Today: The Autobiography (with Pattie Boyd, 2007), My Life, My Way (with Cliff Richard, 2008), The Man Who Lives With Wolves (with Shaun Ellis, 2010), Prince William: Born To Be King (2012), Prince Harry: Brother, Soldier, Son (2014); *Recreations* Nordic walking; *Clubs* Groucho, Century; *Style—* Ms Penny Junor; ✉ c/o Jane Turnbull (☎ 01872 501317, e-mail jane.turnbull@btinternet.com); c/o Hilary Knight (☎ 01604 781818, e-mail hilary@hkmanagement.co.uk)

JUPP, Prof Jeffrey Addison; s of Leonard James Jupp (d 1988), and Elizabeth, *née* Addison (d 1984); *b* 31 December 1941; *Educ* Enfield GS, Queens' Coll Cambridge (MA); *m* 1965, Margaret Elizabeth, da of Ronald Peatchey; 1 da (Elizabeth Jane b 1971), 1 s (Richard James b 1974); *Career* Aerodynamics Dept Hawker Siddeley Aviation (subsequently British Aerospace) Hatfield: aerodynamicist 1964–73, head Fluid Motion Section 1973–80, type aerodynamicist Airbus and head Airbus Section 1980–84, asst chief aerodynamicist Devpts 1984; British Aerospace Airbus Ltd Filton: asst chief engr Airbus 1984–87, chief engr A330/A340 (BAe), chief engr Airbus 1988–92, dir Engrg 1993–98, dir Tech 1998–2001, ret; aerospace conslt 2000–; visiting prof: Mechanical Engrg Dept Univ of Bath 2000–, Shanghai Jiao Tong Univ 2009–12; non-exec dir Cranfield Aerospace Ltd 2002–16; chm: ARB Tech Ctee 1999–2004, Tech Bd SBAC 2000–2001, DTI Aerospace Innovation and Growth Team Environment, Safety and Security Working Gp 2003–06, External Advsy Panel Univ of Manchester Aerospace Research Inst 2007–13; former memb: Tech Dirs Ctee Airbus Industrie, Industry Advsy Ctee to Supervisory Bd of Euro (Cryogenic) Transonic Windtunnel Cologne; memb: ARB CAA 1995–2004, RAeS Medals and Awards Ctee 1998–2015, Greener by Design Exec 2005–14; chm Friends of Bath Abbey 2013–; author of numerous published lectures and papers; jt winner Esso Energy Award Royal Soc Gold Medal 1987, Br Bronze Medal Royal Aeronautical Soc 1992, Gold Medal Royal Aeronautical Soc 2002; FRAeS 1990, FREng 1996; *Recreations* croquet, listening to classical music, choral singing; *Style*— Prof Jeffrey Jupp, FREng, FRAeS; ✉ e-mail jeff.jupp@btinternet.com

JUPP, Miles Hugh Barrett; s of Peter Jupp, and Elizabeth, *née* Tebb; *b* 8 September 1979, Westminster; *Educ* Oakham Sch, Univ of Edinburgh (MA); *m* 28 June 2008, Rachel, *née* Boase; 4 s (Nye b 4 May 2009, Samuel, Atticus b 4 Aug 2012 (twins), Zebedee b 26 March 2015), 1 da (Eliza b 29 March 2011); *Career* actor, comedian and writer; performing stand-up comedy shows since 2000; *Television* incl: The Thick of It 2009 and 2012, Rev 2010–14, Have I Got News For You 2010–15, Mock the Week 2010–14, Would I Lie To You? 2012–14, Spy 2012; *Film* incl: Made In Dagenham 2010, The Monuments Men 2013, The Riot Club 2013, The Look of Love 2013, Tarzan 2016; *Theatre* People (NT) 2012–13, Neville's Island (Duke of York's) 2014, Rules for Living (NT) 2015; *Radio* The News Quiz 2015–; *Books* Fibber in the Heat (2012); *Recreations* cinema, cricket, music, travel, walking; *Style*— Miles Jupp, Esq; ✉ c/o Molly Wansell, 42 Management, 8 Fliteroff Street, London WC2H 8DL (☏ 020 7292 0554, e-mail mollywansell@42mp.com, website www.milesjupp.co.uk)

JURY CRAMP, Felicity; da of Cecil Walter Cramp (d 2007), of Horsham, W Sussex, and Hilary, *née* Napper (d 1971); *b* 9 July 1961; *Educ* Sir John Cass London (dip), Royal Coll of Art (MA); *Career* eyewear, watches and jewellery designer; early design experience with Alain Mikli Paris 1985–86, Optyl Vienna 1987, eyewear design/ prototype IDC Paris 1989–90, Betty Jackson 1990–91, conslt designer for eyewear, watches and jewellery Katharine Hamnett 1991–99, Patrick Cox 1997–2000, design dir for eyewear and watches Gucci 2000–15; fndr memb New RenaisCAnce (multi media co specialising in fashion and accessory design, display, styling and video prodn) 1991–97; exhbns incl: Fouts and Fowler Gallery London 1991, The World of The New RenaisCAnce (Royal Festival Hall and Parco Gallery Tokyo) 1992, Court Couture (Kensington Palace) 1992, Vision Gallery London 1992, Spectacles: A Recent History (Crafts Cncl) 1997; TV and video work incl title sequences for BBC1, Channel 4 and Carlton, window design for Liberty and Harvey Nichols London; *Style*— Ms Felicity Jury Cramp; ☏ 07775 782684, e-mail fjurycramp@me.com

K

KADO, Sven Alexander; s of Leonhardt Kado (d 1953), and Livia, *née* Kablitz; *b* 10 October 1944, Bad Mergentheim; *Educ* schooling in Germany, USA and France, Univ of Cologne, INSEAD Fontainebleau (MBA); *m* 9 Aug 1969, Suzanne Poensgen; 3 c (Carlos b 1980, Jeannette b 1982, Pascal b 1982); *Career* Orion Bank 1972–74; chief financial offr: Heimbach 1975–83, Nixdorf Computer 1984–90, Dyckerhoff 1991–97; sr advsr Principal Finance 1998–2000, chm MMC Germany 2000–; non-exec dir Compass Gp plc; memb Int Cncl INSEAD; *Recreations* field sports, skiing; *Clubs* Rotary; *Style—* Sven A Kado, Esq; ✉ Pienzenauerstrasse 31A, D-81679 Munich, Germany (☎ 00 49 89 9988 8875, fax 00 49 89 9988 8876); Marsh & McLennan Germany, Marstallstrasse 11, D-80539 Munich, Germany (☎ 00 49 89 2905 6641, fax 00 49 89 2905 6649, e-mail svenalexander.kado@mmc.com)

KAHN, Meyer; s of Ben Kahn (d 1966) and Sarah Kahn (d 1995); *b* 29 June 1939; *Educ* Univ of Pretoria (BA, MBA); *m* 1968, Lynette Sandra; 2 da (Deanne b 1969, Hayley b 1972); *Career* md Amrel 1972–77, exec chm OK Bazaars (1929) Ltd 1980–83 (md 1977–80); SAB Ltd/plc: gp md 1983–90, exec chm 1990–97; chief exec SA Police Service 1997–99; chm SAB Ltd/plc (now SABMiller plc) 1999–; pres SA Fndn 1995–96, prof extraordinaire Univ of Pretoria 1989, chm Miracle Drive 1990–2000; Top Five Businessmen SA 1983, Mktg Man of the Year SA 1987, Businessman of the Year SA 1990, Award for Business Excellence Univ of the Witwatersrand 1991, SA Police Star for Outstanding Service 2000; Hon Dr in Commerce Univ of Pretoria 1990; FInstM 1988; *Recreations* golf; *Clubs* Houghton Golf, The River, Wanderers Golf; *Style—* Meyer Kahn, Esq

KAHN, Paula; da of Cyril Maurice Kahn, and Stella, *née* Roscoe; *b* 15 November 1940; *Educ* Chiswick Co HS, Univ of Bristol (BA); *Partner* Annie Hedge (civil partnership 21 Dec 2005); *Career* teacher and admin 1962–66; Longman Group: ed then publisher, publishing dir, divnl md 1966–79, md ELT Div, Dictionaries Div and Trade and Reference Div 1980–85, md Int Sector 1986–88, chief exec of publishing 1988–89, chm and chief exec 1990–94; project dir World Learning Network 1995–96, md Phaidon Press 1996–97, chm Equality Works 1998–2008, chm NHS Islington (formerly Islington Primary Care Tst) 2002–13, chm NHS N Central London Cluster 2011–13, chm Cripplegate Fndn 2005–07 (govr 2000); chair: Camden Arts Centre 2007–13, Hidden Art 2007–12, Met Housing Tst 2013–; acting chair Bd Inst of Visual Arts 2008–09, tstee and treas Assoc of Charitable Foundations (ACF) 2013/2015–, tstee and treas Stuart Hall Fndn 2016–; CIMgt, FRSA; *Recreations* cinema, theatre, France, books; *Style—* Ms Paula Kahn; ✉ 4 Mica House, Barnsbury Square, London N1 1RN

KAHRMANN, Rainer Thomas Christian; s of Dr Johannes Wilhelm Karl Kahrmann, of Germany, and Therese, *née* Gillrath; *b* 28 May 1943; *Educ* Neusprachliches Gymnasium Erkelenz, Univ of Fribourg (LicRerPol, DrRerPol); *m* 8 Dec 1972, Christiane Jeanne Maria, *née* De Muller; 2 da (Louise b 27 Sept 1979, Alice b 19 Nov 1981); partner, Hilary Harrison-Morgan; 2 s (Frederic Johannes Christian, Maximilian Henry Thomas (twins) b 19 Oct 2001); *Career* apprenticeship Commerzbank AG Germany 1963–64, Dow Chemical Co (Dow Banking Corp) 1969–88, md EBC Amro Bank Ltd 1974–89, chm EBC Asset Mgmnt Ltd 1989–, sole md CBB Holding AG i L Cologne; *Recreations* work, family, antiquarian horology; *Style—* R C Kahrmann, Esq; ✉ c/o EBC Securities Services Limited, 9 Long Road, Canvey Island, Essex SS8 9JA (☎ 01268 514274, fax 01268 514027)

KAIN, Prof Roger James Peter; CBE (2005); s of Peter Albert Kain (d 1981), and Ivy, *née* Sharp (d 2005); *b* 12 November 1944; *Educ* Harrow Weald Middx Co GS, UCL (BA, PhD, DLit); *m* 1970, Annmaree, da of Sidney Frank Wallington; 2 s (Simon Peter Wallington b 1986, Matthew James Wallington b 1991); *Career* tutor Bedford Coll London 1971; Univ of Exeter: lectr 1972–91, prof of geography 1991–, head Sch of Geography and Archaeology 1999–2001, dep vice-chllr 2002–10; dean and chief exec Sch of Advanced Study Univ of London 2010–; Gill Meml Award RGS 1990, McColvin Medal Library Assoc 1996; Br Acad: treas 2001–, vice-pres (Research) 2014–; fell UCL 2002; FBA 1990, FSA 1992; *Books* The Tithe Surveys of England and Wales (1985), Atlas and Index of the Tithe Files (1986), Cadastral Maps in the Service of the State (1992), The Tithe Maps of England and Wales (1995), Historical Atlas of SW England (1999), English Maps: A History (1999), Tithe Surveys for Historians (2000), Historic Parishes of England and Wales (2001), Enclosure Maps of England and Wales (2004), England's Landscape: South-West England (2006); *Recreations* mountain walking, gardening, cycling; *Clubs* Athenaeum, Geographical; *Style—* Prof Roger Kain, CBE, FBA, FSA; ✉ University of London, Senate House, Malet Street, London WC1E 7HU (☎ 020 7862 8736, e-mail roger.kain@sas.ac.uk)

KAKKAD, Sunil Shantilal; s of Shantilal Kalyanji Kakkad (d 1996), of London, and Usha Shantilal, *née* Kanani; *b* 19 May 1959; *Educ* Alder Sch, Barnet Coll, Univ of Hull (LLB); *m* 23 Aug 1984, Darshna Sunil, da of Kantilal Vithaldas Hindocha, of Harrow, Middx; 1 s (Rajiv Sunil b 1990), 1 da (Radhika Sunil b 1996); *Career* admitted slr 1984; slr Hill Dickinson & Co 1984–89, ptnr Hill Taylor Dickinson 1989–2000, ptnr Lawrence Graham 2000–14, ptnr Wragge Lawrence Graham & Co 2014–; memb Law Soc; *Recreations* music, cinema, food; *Style—* Sunil Kakkad, Esq; ✉ Wragge Lawrence Graham & Co LLP, 4 More London Riverside, London SE1 2AU (☎ 020 7379 0000, fax 020 7379 6854, e-mail sunil.kakkad@wragge-law.com)

KAKKAR, Baron (Life Peer UK 2010), of Loxbeare in the County of Devon; Rt Hon Prof Ajay Kumar Kakkar; PC (2014); s of Prof Vijay Vir Kakkar, and Dr Savitri, *née* Karnani; *b* 28 April 1964, Dartford, Kent; *Educ* Alleyn's Sch Dulwich, KCL (BSc, MB BS), Imperial Coll London (PhD); *m* 30 Oct 1993, Nicola Susan, *née* Lear; 2 da (Hon India b 19 Jan 1995, Hon Tara b 17 Feb 1997); *Career* house physician and surgeon Kings Coll Hosp 1988–89, jr surgical trg 1989–92, clinical training fell MRC 1993–96, clinician scientist fell MRC 1996–99, sr lectr in surgery and hon conslt surgeon Hammersmith Hosp Imperial Coll London 1999–2004, prof of surgical sciences and hon conslt surgeon Barts and London Sch of Medicine and Dentistry Queen Mary Coll Univ of London and hon conslt surgeon Barts and the London NHS Tst 2004–11, prof of surgery UCL 2011–; conslt surgeon UC London NHS Fndn Tst 2007–; cmmr Royal Hosp Chelsea 2012–; chair Clin Qual UCL Partners Academic Health Science Systems 2009–, chm UCL Ptnrs Academic Health Science Network 2014–; dir Thrombosis Research Inst London 2008–; chm Governing Bd Alleyns Sch, tstee Dulwich Estate; hon fell Harris Manchester Coll Oxford 2010–; FRCS 1992, FRCP 2015; *Recreations* family; *Clubs* Athenaeum; *Style—* The Rt Hon Prof the Lord Kakkar; ✉ House of Lords, London SW1A 0AA (e-mail kakkara@parliament.uk)

KALETSKY, Anatole; s of Jacob Kaletsky (d 1989), and Esther, *née* Feinsilber; *b* 1 June 1952; *Educ* King's Coll Cambridge (hon sr scholarship, BA, DipEcon), Harvard Univ Graduate Sch (Kennedy memorial scholarship, MA); *m* 5 Dec 1985, Fiona Elizabeth, da of Christopher Murphy; 2 s (Michael b 10 Dec 1988, Jacob Alexander Christopher (Sasha) b 27 Feb 1992), 1 da (Katherine b 2 Nov 1986); *Career* fin writer The Economist 1976–79; The Financial Times: ldr and feature writer 1979–81, Washington corr 1981–84, int economics corr 1984–86, chief New York Bureau 1986–90, Moscow corr 1990, sr features writer April-Sept 1990; The Times: economics ed 1990–, assoc ed 1992–; Specialist Writer of the Year Br Press Awards 1980 and 1992, BBC Press Awards Commentator of the Year 1995; conslt: UN Devpt Ctee, UN Conf on Trade and Devpt, Twentieth Century Fund; memb Advsy Bd UK Govt Know-How Fund for Eastern Europe; numerous television and radio appearances; *Books* The Costs of Default (1985); *Style—* Anatole Kaletsky, Esq; ✉ The Times, 1 Pennington Street, London E1 9XN (☎ 020 7782 5000, fax 020 7782 5229)

KALKHOF, Peter Heinz; s of Heinz Emil Kalkhof (d 1945), and Kate Ottilie, *née* Binder (d 1976); *b* 20 December 1933; *Educ* Sch of Arts and Crafts Braunschweig, Acad of Fine Art Stuttgart, Slade Sch of Fine Art London, École des Beaux Arts Paris; *m* 1962, Jeanne The Soen Nio (d 1996); 1 s (Peter T L b 1964); *Career* artist; Slade Sch travel grant Br Isles 1961; lectr in painting Univ of Reading 1970–99 (pt/t lectr in lithography and etching 1964–70); artist in residence: Osnabruck Germany 1985, Künstlerhaus Schieder-Schwalenberg Germany 1995 (six months); memb Br Museum Soc; friend: Royal Acad, V&A, Tate Gallery; *Solo Exhibitions* Galerie in der Garage Stuttgart 1964, Oxford Gallery 1970, Annely Juda Fine Art London 1970, 1974, 1977, 1979, 1990, 1997 and 2002, Wellmann Galerie Düsseldorf 1973, Galerie HS Erkelenz 1974, Royal Shakespeare Theatre 1975, Oliver Dowling Gallery Dublin 1976, Kulturgeschichtliches Museum Osnabruck 1977, Hertfordshire Coll of Art and Design St Albans 1978, Kunstverein Marburg 1979, Goethe Inst London 1981, Juda Rowan Gallery London 1983, Galerie Altes Rathaus Worth am Rhein 1987, Landesmuseum Oldenburg 1988, Camden Arts Centre London 1989, Ostpreussisches Landesmuseum Luneburg 1989, Galerie Rösch Neubrunn 1993, Galerie Rösch Karlsruhe 1994, Rathaus Galerie Balingen Germany 1995, Prignitz Museum am Dom Havelberg Germany 1996, Stadt Museum Galerie Schieder-Schwalenberg Germany 1996, Galerie 'Planie' Reutlingen Germany 1998, St Hugh's Coll Oxford 1998, Gallery Rösch Houston TX 2000, t1+2 artspace London 2004, Annely Juda Fine Art London 2007, Merston Gallery 2011; *Group Exhibitions* incl: Spectrum 1971 (Alexandra Palace London) 1971, International Biennale of Drawing Middlesbrough 1973 and 1979, British Painting 74 (Hayward Gallery London) 1974, Celebrating 8 Artists (Kensington and Chelsea Arts Cncl Exhibition) 1977, Six Painters (Univ of Reading Art Gallery) 1984, Three Decades of Contemporary Art (Juda Rowan Gallery) 1985, From Prism to Paint Box (Welsh Arts Cncl touring exhbn) 1989–90, A Centenary Exhibition (Univ of Reading Art Gallery) 1992, Konstruktiv Tendens Gallery Stockholm 2002, Open Secret (Imperial War Museum) 2004, Summer Exhbn (Royal Acad) 2004 and 2007, Climate of Change (Union St London) 2007, Climate for Change (Finchley Road London) 2008; *Recreations* travelling, reading, listening to music, seeing films, visiting museums, exhibitions, art galleries etc; *Style—* Peter Kalkhof, Esq; ✉ c/o Annely Juda Fine Art, 23 Dering Street, London W1R 9AA (e-mail p.kalkhof@virgin.net)

KALKHOVEN, Ir Paul; *b* 25 May 1955; *Educ* Triniteits Lyceum Haarlem The Netherlands, Dept of Architecture and Town Planning Tech Univ Delft The Netherlands (Ingenieur); *Career* architect; MacCormac Jamieson & Prichard 1980–85, Foster & Partners 1986– (currently st ptnr); ARB 1984; *Style—* Ir Paul Kalkhoven; ✉ Foster and Partners, Riverside 3, 22 Hester Road, London SW11 4AN (☎ 020 7738 0455)

KALMS, Baron (Life Peer UK 2004), of Edgware in the London Borough of Brent; Sir Stanley Kalms; kt (1996); s of Charles Kalms (d 1978), and Cissie, *née* Schlagman (d 1990); *b* 21 November 1931; *Educ* Christ's Coll Finchley; *m* 28 Feb 1954, Pamela Audrey, da of Morris Jimack (d 1968), of London; 3 s (Hon Richard b 10 March 1955, Hon Stephen b 3 Dec 1956, Hon Paul b 6 March 1963); *Career* Dixons Group plc: joined 1948, chm 1971–2002, pres 2002–; non-exec dir British Gas plc (now BG plc) 1987–97; chm King's Healthcare NHS Tst 1993–96, memb Funding Agency for Schs 1994–97 (chm Fin Ctee 1994–97); non-exec dir Centre for Policy Studies 1991–2001; visiting prof Univ of N London Business Sch 1991; chm Strategy Ctee Henry Jackson Soc 2009–14; govr: Dixons Bradford City Technol Coll, NIESR 1995–2003; tstee: Industry in Education Ltd 1993–2002, The Economic Education Trust 1993–2002; dir and fndr Business for Sterling 1998–2001; pty treas Cons Pty 2001–03; Hon DLitt: CNAA/Univ of London 1991, Univ of Sheffield 2002; Hon Dr Univ of N London 1994, Hon DEcon Richmond 1996, Hon Degree Univ of Buckingham 2002; hon fell London Business Sch 1995; Hon FCGI 1988; *Publications* A Time for Change (1992); *Recreations* communal educnl activities, bridge, opera; *Clubs* Savile, Portland; *Style—* The Rt Hon the Lord Kalms; ✉ House of Lords, London SW1A 1PW (☎ 020 7629 1427, e-mail stanley.kalms@btinternet.com)

KALMUS, Prof George Ernest; CBE (2000); s of Hans Kalmus (d 1988), and Anna, *née* Rosenberg (d 1997); *b* 21 April 1935; *Educ* St Albans Co GS, UCL (BSc, PhD); *m* 15 June 1957, Ann Christine, da of Ernest Henry Harland (d 1984); 3 da (Susan Jane b 1960, Mary Elisabeth b 1962, Diana Christine b 1965); *Career* Lawrence Radiation Laboratory Univ of Calif Berkeley: res assoc 1962–63 and 1964–67, sr physicist 1967–71; UCL: res assoc 1959–62, lectr Physics Dept 1963–64, visiting prof 1984–; Rutherford Appleton Laboratory: gp ldr Bubble Chamber and Delphi Gps 1971–86, dir Particle Physics 1986–97, sr physicist 1998–2000, hon scientist 2000–; FRS 1988; *Recreations* skiing, reading; *Style—* Prof George Kalmus, CBE, FRS; ✉ 16 South Avenue, Abingdon, Oxfordshire OX14 1QH (☎ 01235 523340); Rutherford Appleton Laboratory, Chilton, Didcot, Oxfordshire OX11 0QX (☎ 01235 445443, fax 01235 446733, e-mail george.kalmus@stfc.ac.uk)

KAMANI, Mahmud; s of Abdullah Bhanji Khanji Kamani, and Roshan Abdullah Kamani, of Knutsford; *b* 12 December 1987, Mwanza, Tanzania; *Educ* Parrs Wood HS Manchester; *m* 12 Dec 1987, Aisha, *née* Jairath; 3 s (Umar b 21 March 1988, Adam b 5 June 1989, Samir b 1 Jan 1996); *Career* co-fndr and jt chief exec boohoo.com 2006–; *Style—* Mahmud Kamani, Esq; ✉ boohoo.com, 49/51 Dale Street, Manchester M1 2HF (e-mail mahmud.kamani@boohoo.com, website www.boohoo.com)

KAMARYC, Rosalynd; *Educ* Ballymena Acad, Queen's Univ Belfast (BA, MSc, PGCE); *Career* princ Queen's Gate Sch 2006–; *Style*— Mrs Rosalynd Kamaryc; ✉ Queen's Gate, 133 Queen's Gate, London SW7 5LE

KAMILL, Her Hon Judge Louise Naima Rachelle; da of Dr Mostapha Kamill, and Joan Mary, *née* Hirst; *b* 9 March 1951, London; *Educ* St Paul's Girls' Sch, UCL (LLB); *m* 1978, Max Lightwood; 2 da; *Career* called to the Bar Inner Temple 1974; recorder 1986–2008, circuit judge (South Eastern Circuit) 2008–; *Style*— Her Hon Judge Kamill; ✉ c/o The South Eastern Circuit, 289–293 High Holborn, London WC1V 7HZ

KAMPFNER, John; *b* 27 December 1962, Singapore; *Educ* Westminster Sch, Queen's Coll Oxford; *m* Lucy Ash; 2 da (Constance b 1993, Alex b 1997); *Career* journalist; foreign corr Daily Telegraph, chief political corr Financial Times, political commentator Today Programme (BBC Radio 4), ed New Statesman 2005–08 (previously political ed), chief exec Index on Censorship 2008–; chair Turner Contemporary 2008–; *Books* Inside Yeltsin's Russia: Corruption, Conflict, Capitalism (1994), Robin Cook (1998), Blair's Wars (2003), Freedom For Sale (2009); *Style*— John Kampfner, Esq

KANDER, Nadav; *b* 1961; *Career* photographer, established studio London working freelance on major advertising campaigns 1986– (incl Amnesty International, Dr Barnardos, Heals, Levis, Nike, Adidas and Stella Artois; *Exhibitions* Nat Portrait Gallery, V&A, Tate Liverpool, Royal Photographic Soc Bath, Photographers' Gallery London, Shine Gallery London, Leeds Met Univ Gallery, Acte II Gallery paris, Palais de Tokyo Paris, Shanghai Art Museum, Yancey Richardson Gallery NY, Fahey Klein Gallery LA, Peter Fetterman Gallery LA; *Awards* 2 Gold and 11 Silver Awards Assoc of Photographers, 7 Awards of Excellence Communication Arts, 2 Silver Awards D&AD, 2 Gold and 4 Silver Awards Art Director's Club of NY, Creative Review Annual, IPA Lucie Advtg Photographer of the Year; *Publications* Nadav Kander – Night (2001), Beauty's Nothing (2001); articles, reviews and editorial in various publications incl: Sunday Times Magazine, NY Times Magazine, Details, Dazed & Confused, Creative Review; *Style*— Nadav Kander; ✉ c/o Nadav Kander, Unit D, Imperial Works, Perren Street, London NW5 3ED (☎ 020 7485 6789, fax 020 7485 4321, e-mail mail@nadavkander.com)

KANE, Adam Vincent; QC (2015); s of Vincent Kane, OBE, and Mary, *née* Croad, of Cyprus; *b* 19 June 1969, Cardiff; *Educ* De La Salle Sch, Radyr Sch, UC Oxford (BA), Univ of Wolverhampton (CPE); *m* 8 July 2000, Emma, *née* Nott; 1 s (Charles b 29 June 2001), 2 da (Anna b 10 July 2003, Gisele b 4 Sept 2013); *Career* called to the Bar (Gray's Inn) 1993; memb: Criminal Bar Assoc, South Eastern Circuit; *Recreations* extreme gardening, vintage champagne; *Style*— Adam Kane, Esq, QC; ✉ Voronzoff Gate, Savernake Forest, Marlborough, Wiltshire; Chambers of Charles Bott, QC, Carmelite Street, London EC4Y 0DR (☎ 020 7936 6300)

KANE, Archie Gerard; s of Archie Kane (d 1990), and Rose Anne McGhee (d 1982); *b* 16 June 1952, Bellshill, Lanarkshire; *Educ* St Aloysius Coll Glasgow, Univ of Glasgow (BAcc), City Univ (MBA), Harvard Business Sch (AMP); *m* 26 Sept 1986, Diana Muirhead; 2 da (Rebecca b 3 Sept 1990, Brodie b 11 Nov 1992); *Career* asst mangr Price Waterhouse 1978–80, sr mgmnt auditor rising to finance dir General Telephone & Electronics Corporation 1980–85, finance dir British Telecom Yellow Pages Sales Ltd 1986, gp finance controller TSB Commercial Holdings Ltd 1986–89; TSB Bank plc: financial controller then dir of financial control Retail Banking Div 1989–91, dir of financial control then ops dir Retail Banking and Insurance 1991–94, gp strategic devpt dir 1994–96; Lloyds TSB Gp plc: project dir (post merger integration) 1996, retail financial servs dir 1996, dir of gp IT and ops 1997–99, gp exec dir IT & Ops 2000–03, gp exec dir Insurance and Investments 2003–, chief exec Scottish Widows plc 2003–, chm Lloyds TSB General Insurance Ltd 2003–, chm Scottish Widows Investment Partnership Gp Ltd 2003–; chm: Assoc of Payment Clearing Systems (APACS) 1991–93, ABI 2007– (memb Bd 1994–); memb: Takeover Panel, HM Treasy Retail Financial Servs Gp; MICAS, FCIBS 2005; *Recreations* golf, tennis, skiing; *Style*— Mr Archie Kane; ✉ Lloyds Banking Group plc, 25 Gresham Street, London EC2V 7HN (☎ 020 7356 1409, fax 020 7356 1195)

KANE, Carol; *b* 4 October 1966, Jarrow; *Educ* Berks Coll of Art (BA); *Career* design and buying dir Pinstripe Clothing 1993–2012, md Red Orange Clothing 2003–13, owner and jt ceo Boohoo.com 2006–; *Style*— Ms Carol Kane; ✉ boohoo.com, 49/51 Dale Street, Manchester M1 2HF

KANE, Martin Christopher; s of Bernard Kane, of Milngavie, Glasgow, and Rosina, *née* Maguire; *b* 3 June 1958; *Educ* St Andrew's HS Clydebank Glasgow, Edinburgh Coll of Art (BA); *m* 17 Oct 2002, Sharon, *née* Goodlet; 1 s (Christopher b 13 June 2003); *Career* artist; *Solo Exhibitions* Artist of the Day (Angela Flowers Gallery) 1988, Memory and Imagination (Jill George Gallery London) 1990, Reflections (Jill George Gallery London) 1992, Beyond the Wall (Jill George Gallery) 1993, New Paintings (Beaux Arts Gallery London) 1996, Both Sides of the Wall (Studio One Child Graddon Lewis London) 2002; *Group Exhibitions* incl: student annual exhibition (Royal Scottish Acad) 1986 and 1987, New Generation (Compass Gallery Glasgow) 1987, Obsessions (Raab Gallery London) 1987, Two Scottish Artists (Boundary Gallery) 1988, Int Art Fair (LA with Thumb Gallery) 1989, 1990, 1991 and 1992, Art 90, Art 91, Art 92, Art 93, Art 94, Art 95, Art 96, Art 99, Art 2000 and Art 2001 (Design Centre London), London to Atlanta (Thumb Gallery Atlanta) 1990, Lineart 95 (Gent) 1995, Small Paintings (Beaux Arts), 1st Int Art Fair New York 1998, Cabnet Paintings (Glasgow Print Studio) 2001, New Work 2003 (Seagull Gallery Gourock Scotland) 2003, Finding the Sacred in the 21st Century (Church of St John Edinburgh Festival) 2005, Glasgow Boys (Gatehouse Gallery Glasgow) 2006, Six Scottish Artists (Lyme Art Gallery Old Lyme CT) 2007, 100 Artists (Dovehill Studios Glasgow) 2016; *Public Collections* Glasgow District Cncl, Cleveland Museum Middlesbrough, CBS Collection, Scottish Devpt Agency Glasgow, Unilever plc Collection London, Gartmore Investments, Glasgow Museums Collection, Harry Taylor of Ashton; *Recreations* music, classic cars, reading; *Clubs* Glasgow Art, Mercedes-Benz; *Style*— Martin Kane, Esq; ✉ BeauxLondon, 48 Maddox Street, London W1S 1AY (website www.martinkane.net)

KANE, Russell; *b* 19 August 1980, Enfield, London; *Career* comedian; appearances at the Edinburgh Fringe Festival incl: The Theory of Pretension 2006, Gaping Flaws 2008, Fakespeare 2009 (also tour 2010), Human Dressage 2009 (also tour 2009–10), Smokescreens and Castles 2010 (Edinburgh Comedy Award 2010); television appearances incl: Big Brother's Big Mouth (E4) 2007 (presenter), Live at the Apollo (BBC1) 2008, I'm a Celebrity Get Me Out of Here Now (ITV2) 2009– (presenter), Freak Like Me (BBC3) 2010 (narrator and presenter), Let's Dance for Comic Relief (BBC1) 2010; *Style*— Mr Russell Kane; ✉ c/o Avalon UK, 4a Exmoor Street, London W10 6BD

KANIS, Prof John Anthony; s of Max Kanis (d 1957), of London, and Elizabeth Mary, *née* Mees (d 2003); *b* 2 September 1944, Wimbledon; *Educ* Univ of Edinburgh (MB ChB); *m* 1, 11 April 1966 (m dis 1984), Patricia Sheila, *née* Mclaren; 4 da (Lisa b 13 Dec 1967, Emma b 24 Sept 1969, Sarah b 4 July 1971, Rebecca b 2 Jan 1975); m 2, 19 June 1989, Monique Nicole Christiane, da of Georges Marie Benéton (d 1997); 1 step da (Natalie Beresford b 10 Dec 1978); *Career* Wellcome sr research fell Univ of Oxford 1976–79; conslt: Royal Hallamshire Hosp 1979–, Miny of Health France 1981–2000; prof of human metabolism Univ of Sheffield 1982–2003 (now emeritus); pres Euro Fndn for Osteoporosis and Bone Disease 1987–90, tstee Int Osteoporosis Fndn 1987–, advsr on osteoporosis WHO 1988–2002, dir WHO Collaborating Centre for Metabolic Bone Disease Sheffield 1988–2002; pres Int Osteoporosis Fndn 2008; ed Osteoporosis Int, author of 1000 scientific pubns on bone disease; MRCPath 1982, FRCP 1984, MD 1985, FRCPE 1986; *Books* Paget's Disease of the Bone, Osteoporosis; *Recreations* antiques restoration, genealogy; *Style*— Prof John Kanis; ✉ Centre for Metabolic Bone Diseases, University of Sheffield Medical School, Beech Hill Road, Sheffield S10 2RX (☎ 0114 285 1109, fax 0114 285 1813, e-mail w.j.pontefract@sheffield.ac.uk)

KANTOROWICZ-TORO, Donald; s of Rodolph Kantorowicz, and Blanca Livia, *née* Toro; *b* 4 August 1948, Cali, Colombia; *Educ* Jesuit Sch Cali Colombia, Hochschule für Welthandel Vienna (MBA), Faculté de Droit et Sciences Economiques Paris (DEconSc); *m* 1, 12 Sept 1973 (m dis 1986); 2 da (Melanie Tatiana (Mrs Elwes) b 1976, Johanna Joy b 1978); m 2, 16 July 1999 (m dis 2006), Laura Puyana-Bickenbach; m 3, 6 Oct 2012, Anna Borysevych Korinko; 2 da (Bianca Livia, Angelika Sophia (twins) b 8 Jan 2016); *Career* Banque de L'Union Européenne Paris 1969–71, vice-pres and mangr Bank of America Paris and Madrid 1972–79, md and chief exec Consolidado UK/Vestcor Partners Ltd 1980–94, md Merrill Lynch 1995–2013, exec dir Julius Baer 2013; memb French Fin Assoc Paris; *Recreations* skiing, sailing, classical music, history; *Clubs* Overseas Bankers, Cercle Interallie Paris, Club de los Andes (fndr and pres); *Style*— Donald Kantorowicz-Toro, Esq; ✉ 11 South Terrace, London SW7 2BT (☎ 020 7584 8185, mobile 07770 832941, e-mail d@kantorowicz.net); Houston Palace, 7 Avenue Princesse Grace 98000, Monaco (mobile 00336 0793 4561, e-mail donald.kantorowicz@juliusbaer.com); 45-B Prospekt Lenina Apto. 90, 61000 Kharkiv, Ukraine (mobile 00380 5777 30770)

KAPADIA, Asif; *b* 1973, Hackney, London; *Educ* RCA; *Career* film dir; work incl commercials for AMV BBDO and 180 Amsterdam; *Film* dir: The Waiting Room (screened at British and Munich short film festivals) 1996, The Sheep Thief (graduation film, screened Channel 4, and London, Clermont-Ferrand, NY, Texas and Cork Film Festivals) 1997, Hot Dog (short film for Channel 4/Ideal World's Spotlight Series) 1998, The Warrior 2001 (also co-writer), Cinema16 2003, The Return 2006; *Awards* for The Waiting Room: RTS Student Award; for The Sheep Thief: Grand Jury Prize Cannes Int Film Festival 1998, Grand Prix European Short Film Festival Brest, Direction Prize Poitiers Film Festival; for The Warrior: BAFTA Alexander Korda Award (for Outstanding Br Film of the Year) 2003; BAFTA Carl Foreman Award (for special achievement by a dir, screenwriter or prodr in their first feature film) 2003; *Style*— Asif Kapadia, Esq; ✉ c/o Paul Weiland Film Company, 14 Newburgh Street, London W1F 7RT (☎ 020 7287 6900, fax 020 7434 0146)

KAPOOR, Sir Anish; kt (2013), CBE (2003); *b* 1954, Bombay, India; *Educ* Hornsey Coll of Art London, Chelsea Sch of Art; *Career* artist, sculptor; teacher Wolverhampton Poly 1979, artist in residence Walker Art Gallery Liverpool 1982; subject of numerous books, articles and reviews; memb Arts Cncl of England 1998–; hon dr London Inst 1997, Hon FRIBA 2001; *Solo Exhibitions* incl: Patrice Alexandre Paris 1980, Lisson Gallery 1983, 1985, 1988, 1989–90 and 1993, Walker Art Gallery Liverpool 1982 and 1983, Barbara Gladstone Gallery NY 1984, 1986, 1989–90 and 1993, Stedelijk Van Abbemuseum Erndhoven 1986, Anish Kapoor: Recent Sculpture and Drawings (Univ Gallery Massachusetts) 1986, Anish Kapoor: Works On Paper 1975–87 (Ray Hughes Gallery) 1987, Kohji Ogura Gallery Japan 1989, Br Pavilion Venice 1990, Anish Kapoor Drawings (Tate Gallery) 1990–91, Centre National d'Art Contemporain Grenoble 1990–91, Palacio de Velazquez Madrid 1991, Kunstverein Hannover 1991, Feuerle Köln 1991, The Sixth Japan Ushimado Int Art Festival Japan 1991, Galeria Soledad Lorenzo Madrid 1992, San Diego Museum of Contemporary Art 1992–93, Designs for a Dance (South Bank Centre London) 1993, Tel Aviv Museum of Art 1993, Mala Galerija Moderna Galerija Ljubljana 1994, Echo (Kohji Ogura Gallery) 1994, Anish Kapoor (Tillburg Nishimura Gallery Tokyo) 1995, Prada Milanoarte Milan and also Lisson Gallery London 1995–96, Anish Kapoor. Sculptures (Aboa Vetus & Ars Nova Finland) 1996, Anish Kapoor: Two Sculptures (Kettle's Yard Cambridge) 1996, Galleria Massimo Minini Brescia 1996, Gourd Project 1993–95 (Freddie Fong Contemporary Art San Francisco) 1996, Kunst-Station Sankt Peter Cologne 1996, Hayward Gallery London 1998, Lisson Gallery London 1998, Barbara Gladstone Gallery NY 1998, CAPC Bordeaux 1998, Baltic Centre for Contemporary Art Gateshead 1999, Scai The Bathhouse Tokyo 1999, Museé d'Art Contemporain de Bordeaux 1999, Blood (Lisson Gallery London) 2000, The Edge of the World (installation, Axel Vervoordt Kanal Wijnegem Belgium) 2000, Blood Solid (fig-1 London) 2000, Taratantara (installation, Baltic Centre Gateshead and Piazza del Plebiscito Naples) 2000, Taidehalli Helsinki 2001, Barbara Gladstone NY 2001, Marsyas (installation, Tate Modern) 2002, Painting (Lisson Gallery London) 2003, Kukje Gallery Seoul 2003, Galleria Continua San Gimignano Italy 2003, Idomeneo (set design, Glyndebourne) 2003, My Red Homeland (Kunsthaus Bregenz) 2003, Nat Archaeological Museum Naples 2003, Whiteout (Barbara Gladstone Gallery NY) 2004, Cloud Gate (Chicago Millennium Park) 2004, Massimo Minini Gallery Brescia 2004, Melancholia (MAC Grand-Hornu Belgium) 2004, Japanese Mirrors (SCAI Tokyo) 2005, My Red Homeland (CAC Malaga) 2006, Regen Projects LA 2006, Ascension (BBCC Rio de Janeiro and Brasilia) 2006 and (Sao Paulo) 2007, Sky Mirror (Rockefeller Center NY) 2006, Lisson Gallery London 2006, Works on Paper (Gladstone Gallery NY) 2007, Anish Kapoor: Past, Present, Future (ICA Boston) 2008; *Group Exhibitions* incl: Art Into Landscape 1 (Serpentine Gallery London) 1974, Young Contemporaries (Royal Academy London) 1975, London/New York 1982 (Lisson Gallery London) 1982, Paris Biennale (Paris) 1982, India: Myth and Reality (MOMA Oxford) 1982, Finland Biennale (Helsinki) 1983, Sculpture 1983 (Van Krimpen Gallery Amsterdam) 1983, New Art (Tate Gallery) 1983, An International Survey of Recent Painting and Sculpture (MOMA NY) 1984, Nouvelle Biennale de Paris (Paris) 1985, Europa oggi/Europe now (Museo d'Arte Contemporánea Italy) 1988, Starlit Waters, British Sculpture: An International Art 1968–88 (Tate Gallery Liverpool) 1988, Heroes of Contemporary Art (Galerie Saqqarah Switzerland) 1990–91, British Art Now (touring) 1990–91, Gallery Shirakawa Kyoto 1991, Feuerle Gallery 1991, Anish Kapoor and Abstract Art in Asia (Fukuoka Art Museum Japan) 1991–92, Whitechapel Open 1992, British Sculpture from the Arts Cncl Collection (Derby Museum and Art Gallery) 1993, Punti Dell'Arti (Italian Pavilion Venice Biennale) 1993, Art Against Aids (Venice Biennale) 1993, Sculpture (Leo Castelli Gallery NY) 1993, Sculptors' Drawings (Tate Gallery) 1994, Re Rebaudengo Sandretto Collection Turin 1994, Ars 95 Helsinki (Museum of Contemporary Art Helsinki) 1995, Ideal Standard Summertime (Lisson Gallery London) 1995, British Abstract Art Part II: Sculpture (Flowers East Gallery London) 1995, Fémininmasculin. Le sexe de l'art (Centre Georges Pompidou Paris) 1996, New Art on Paper 2 (Philadelphia Museum of Art) 1996, Un siècle de sculpture anglaise (Jeu de Paume Paris) 1996, Anish Kapoor, Barry X Ball (Angles Gallery Santa Monica USA) 1996, 23rd Int Biennial of Sao Paolo 1996, Modern Galerija Ljubljana (MOMA Sarajevo Ljubljana Slovenia) 1996, Betong (Malmö Konsthall) 1996, entgegen (Mausoleum am Dom Graz) 1997, Arte Continua (Chiesa di San Guisto and Pinacoteca Civica Volterra Italy) 1997, Belladonna (ICA London) 1997, Changing Spaces (Detroit Inst of Arts) 1997/98, Wounds: Between Democracy and Redemption in Contemporary Art (Moderna Museet Stockholm) 1998, Then and Now (Lisson Gallery London) 1998, Prime (Dundee Contemporary Art Dundee) 1999, Shape of the Century (Salisbury Festival) 1999, Den Haag Sculptuur (The Hague) 1999, Art Worlds in Dialogue (Museum Ludwig Cologne) 1999, Together: Artists in Support for the Homeless (The Passage House London) 1999, Beauty – 25th Anniversary (Hirschhorn Museum and Sculpture Garden Washington DC) 1999, Retrace Your Steps: Remember Tomorrow (Soane Museum London, curated by Hans Ulrich Obrist) 1999, Blue (New Walsall Museum Walsall) 2000, Groenningen Exhibition 2000 (Charlottenborg Copenhagen) 2000, Sinn und Sinnlichkeit (Neues Museum Weserburg Bremen) 2000, La Beauté (Papal Palace

Avignon) 2000, Lyon Biennale (Lyon) 2000, 1951–2001 Made in Italy (triennale, Palazzo dell'Arte Milan) 2001, BO01 (Conceptthaus Malmo) 2001, Drawings (Regen Projects LA) 2001, Field Day: Sculpture form Britain (Tapei Fine Art Museum Japan) 2001, Homage to Rudolf Schwarzkogler (Galerie Krinzinger Vienna) 2002, Kaash (touring collaborative dance prodn) 2002, this ain't no tupperware (Kunststof, Kortrijk and Herford Belgium) 2002, Colour White (De La Warr Pavilion) 2002, No Object, No Subject, No Matter... (Irish MOMA) 2002, Remarks on Colour (Sean Kelly Gallery NY) 2002, Blast to Freeze (Kunstmuseum Wolfsburg) 2002–03, Retrospectacle: 25 Years of Collecting Modern and Contemporary Art (Denver Art Museum) 2002–03, Mind Space Ho-Am Art Gallery Seoul 2003, Beaufort 2003 (Ostend) 2003, Himmelschwer Graz 2003, Ineffable Beauty (Kunsthalle Erfurt) 2003, In Good Form (Longside Gallery Yorks Sculpture Park) 2003, Longside Gallery Yorks Sculpture Park 2003, Saved! (Hayward Gallery) 2003–04, Pain: passion Companssion Sensibility (Science Museum London) 2004, Lustwarande 04 (Tilburg) 2004, Gwangju Biennale Korea 2004, Arts and Architecture 1900–2000 (Genova Palazzo Ducale) 2004, Kanazawa Museum 2004, Universal Experience (MCA Chicago) 2005, Colour after Klein (Barbican) 2005, British Sculpture Show (Kunsthalle Würth) 2005, God is Great (Venice) 2005, Museo Madre Naples 2005, Arte all'Arte (San Gimignano) 2005, Sixty Years of Sculpture (Arts Cncl Collection) 2006, The Sublime is Now (Museum Franz Gertsch Switzerland) 2006, Sculpture (Thaddaeus Ropac Salzburg) 2006, The Expanded Eye (Kunsthaus Zurich) 2006, Surprise, Surprise (ICA London) 2006, How to Improve the World (Hayward Gallery London) 2006, Super Vision (ICA Boston) 2006, Asia Pacific Triennial of Contemporary Art (Queensland Art Gallery) 2006–07, One Colour (Galleria Continua Beijing) 2007, Timer (Milan) 2007, Contrepoint III (Louvre Paris) 2007, Blake's Shadow (Whitworth Art Gallery Manchester) 2008, Blood on Paper – the Art of the Book (V&A) 2008, Traces du Sacré (Centre Georges Pompidou Paris) 2008, Ambition of Art (Intitut d'art contemporian Lyon) 2008; *Works in Collections* incl: Tate Gallery London, Hirshhorn Museum and Sculpture Park Washington DC, MOMA NY, Art Gallery of New South Wales Sydney, Rijksmuseum Kroller-Muller Otterlo, Moderna Museet Stockholm, Tel Aviv Museum of Art Israel, Vancouver Art Gallery and San Diego Museum of Contemporary Art; *Awards* Premio Duemila Venice Biennale 1990, Turner Prize 1991; *Style—* Sir Anish Kapoor, CBE

KAPOSI, Dr Agnes Aranka; da of Imre Kristof (d 1962), and Magda Csengeri; *b* 20 October 1932; *Educ* Kossuth Zsuzsa Girls' Sch Budapest, Tech Univ of Budapest (Dipl Ing), PhD (UK); *m* 1952, Janos Ferenc Kaposi, s of Ernö Kaposi; 2 da (Esther Julia b 1959, Anna Jane b 1963); *Career* sr res engr and head of Digital Systems Gp Ericsson Telephones Beeston 1957–60, princ res engr and head of Storage Electronics ICL Research Laboratories Stevenage 1960–64, lectr Cambridgeshire Coll of Arts and Technol 1964–67, princ lectr and dir of res and postgrad studies Kingston Poly (now Univ of Kingston upon Thames) 1967–77, head Dept of Electrical and Electronic Engrg South Bank Poly (now South Bank Univ) 1977–88; formerly: ptnr Polytechnic Consultants, dir ARC Consultants Ltd; ptnr Kaposi Associates 1986–; visiting prof Engrg Design Centre City Univ 1990–95, academic govr Richmond The American Int Univ in London 1992–, memb Nat Bd Academic Accreditation of the Hungarian Govt 1994–97; former memb WSET Ctee Office of Sci and Technol; Instn of Electrical Engrs: memb Cncl, memb Int Bd, memb Accreditation Ctee, memb Pool of Accreditors, former memb Public Affrs Bd, chair London Branch 1994–95; memb Nominations Ctee Engrg Cncl 1986–96; EPSRC (formerly SERC): memb, memb Electromechanical Engrg Ctee, memb Info Technol Liaison Ctee 1989–93; memb Cncl Women's Engrg Soc 1990–94; FIEE 1977 (MIEE 1958), FREng 1992; *Books* Systems, Models and Measures, Systems for computer systems professionals, A first systems book (with M Myers, 1994); *Recreations* reading, music, walking, debating, bridge; *Style—* Dr Agnes Kaposi, FREng; ✉ Kaposi Associates, 3 St Edwards Close, London NW11 (☎ 020 8458 3626, fax 020 8458 0899)

KAPP, Carlo David; s of Robert Scope Kapp (d 1975), and Paola Luisa, *née* Putoto (d 2009); *b* 31 July 1947; *Educ* Ladybarn Sch Manchester; *m* 1, 28 March 1970 (m dis 1978), Jean Gillian, da of Aubrey Charles Overington (d 1980), of Richmond, Surrey; 1 da (Kelli Anne b 4 July 1977); m 2, 30 Oct 1979 (m dis 2007), Basia Evelyn, da of Dr Abraham Seinwel Bardach (d 1988), of London; 1 s (Daniel Joseph Scope b 5 Oct 1980), 1 da (Pippa Luisa b 25 Feb 1983); m 3, 9 June 2011, Ann Charlotte, da of Prof Axel Montenbruck, of Berlin, Germany; *Career* creative servs mangr Estée Lauder Group (UK) 1974–81; chm and md: Dawson Kapp Overseas 1981–88, The DKO Group plc 1988–2001; chm: The Best Group Ltd 1988–2001, Euro Shopfittings Ltd 1998–; ceo 360 Squared; chm Coral Fndn; FRGS; *Recreations* shooting, travel, exploring, eco projects, philanthropy, Africa; *Clubs* Anabels, Soho House; *Style—* Carlo Kapp, Esq; ✉ 2/3 Ledbury Mews North, Notting Hill, London W11 2AF (☎ 07802 201666, e-mail carlo@kapps.eu)

KAPPES, Anthony Edward; MBE (2009); *b* 1 March 1973, Stockport, Cheshire; *Career* Paralympic cyclist; achievements incl: 2 Gold medals (kilo and sprint) World Disability Championships 2006, 2 Gold medals (kilo and sprint) World Disability Championships 2007, 2 Gold medals (kilo and sprint) Paralympics Beijing 2008, 2 Gold medals (kilo and sprint) World Disability Championships 2012, Gold medal (individual sprint) Paralympic Games 2012; *Style—* Anthony Kappes, Esq, MBE; ✉ c/o British Cycling, Stuart Street, Manchester M11 4DQ

KAPPLER, David; s of Alec Kappler (d 1995), and Hilary, *née* Coleman; *b* 24 March 1947; *Educ* Lincoln Sch; *m* 1970, Maxine; 3 da (Suzanne b 1973, Isabel b 1975, Sally b 1981); *Career* fin dir: Jeyes Gp 1977–84, Trebor Gp 1984–89; Cadbury Schweppes plc: fin dir (Cadbury Ltd) 1990–91, fin dir confectionery 1991–93, corp fin dir 1994–95, chief fin offr 1995–2004; non-exec chm Premier Foods plc 2004–10, chm ADS2Brands Ltd 2011–15; non-exec dir: Camelot plc 1997–2004, HMV Gp plc 2002–06 (chm 2005), Shire plc 2004–16 (also dep chm), Flybe plc 2015–, InterContinental Hotels Gp plc 2004–14; Leverhulme Prize (CIMA) 1968; FCMA 1970; *Recreations* watching sports, playing golf, wine; *Clubs* Harewood Downs Golf, RAC; *Style—* David Kappler, Esq

KARAT, David Spencer; s of Lt Rene Karat, and Frances, *née* Levy; *b* 1 August 1951; *Educ* Merchant Taylors, Univ of Leicester (LLB); *m* 1, 1 Sept 1976 (m dis 2003), Shirley Lessels; 2 da (Florence Louisa b 22 Sept 1980, Emma Rachel b 21 May 1985); m 2, 19 July 2005, Aurore L'Heritier; 2 s (Joshua b 30 Sept 2006, Noah b 8 Feb 2009); *Career* slr Slaughter & May 1976, gp counsel Royal Bank of Canada 1980; Merrill Lynch: assoc dir 1984, exec dir 1986, md 1989, head Fin Instns Gp; md and head of capital mkts Salomon Brothers International Limited 1990–96, md and co-head Fin Instns BZW 1996–97, md Fin Instns Barclays Capital 1997, ptnr Deloitte & Touche 1998–2003, founding ptnr Clarat Ptnrs 2003–12, md Intermezzo Capital Ltd 2007–14, ptnr Vestra Wealth LLP 2009, founding ptnr Clearhaven Capital Partners 2012–14; memb: Bd Movement Reform Judaism 2012–, Faculty Cambridge Co-exist Leadership Prog 2013; vice-chm Inst for Jewish Policy Research 2014–, chm Religious Literacy Partnership 2016–; *Recreations* classic cars, motorbikes, theatre, jazz and classical music, small-holder farming; *Clubs* RAC; *Style—* David S Karat, Esq; ✉ c/o 64 New Cavendish Street, London W1G 8TB (e-mail david@davidkarat.com)

KARIM, Sajjad Haider; MEP; s of Fazal Karim, and Shamshad Karim; *b* 11 July 1970; *Educ* Mansfield HS, Nelson and Colne Coll, London Guildhall Univ, Coll of Law Chester; *m* 17 Aug 1997, Zahida; 2 c (Bilal Haider b 24 Jan 2000, Rabia Iman b 27 Sept 2002); *Career* ptnr: SFN Slrs 1995–2001, Marsdens Slrs 2001–; MEP (Lib Dem) NW England 2003–07, MEP (Cons) NW England 2007–; cnclr Pendle BC 1994–2002; memb Law Soc 1997; *Style—* Sajjad Karim, Esq, MEP; ✉ Marsdens Solicitors, 20A-22A Manchester Road, Nelson, Lancashire BB9 7EG (☎ 01282 611899, fax 01282 611988, e-mail sajjad.karim@marsdens.uk.com)

KARMEL, Annabel Jane Elizabeth; MBE (2006); da of late Gordon Karmel, and Evelyn Stoutzkerr; *b* 10 May 1959; *Educ* St Paul's Girls' Sch London, RCM, Royal Conservatoire The Hague; *m* 19 Aug 1984 (m dis); 3 da (Natasha d 1987, Lara b 4 Nov 1989, Scarlett b 24 Feb 1992), 1 s (Nicholas b 6 Aug 1988); *Career* early career as musician (harpist); currently parenting author on feeding babies and children; regular contrib: Mother and Baby, Tesco Baby and Toddler Club, Maternity and Infant; TV appearences incl: Annabel's Kitchen (CITV), Daybreak (ITV), Saturday Kitchen (BBC 1); food ranges incl: Annabel Karmel's chilled ready meals for toddlers 2007, pasta sauce and pasta shapes 2008, range of meals (Food Service, served in select leisure parks and resorts, restaurant and hotel chains), co-branded Disney snacks for toddlers 2009, AK by NUK Equipment 2011, organic baby purees 2012, Australian frozen food range of ready meals and purées for babies and toddlers 2015; apps incl: Essential Guide to Feeding Your Baby and Toddler App 2013, Annabel's Family Cooking App 2015; memb: Equity, Soc of Authors; *Publications* New Complete Baby and Toddler Meal Planner (1991), Small Helpings (1994), New Baby and Toddler Cookbook (1995), Quick Children's Meals (1997), Annabel Karmel's Feeding Your Baby and Toddler (1999), Favourite Family Recipes (1999), Eat Up Charity Cookbook for NSPCC (1999), Complete Party Planner (2000), Superfoods For Babies and Children (2001), Annabel Karmel's Complete First Year Planner (2003), Lunchboxes and Snacks (2003), Top 100 Baby Purees (2005), Children's First Cookbook (2005), Annabel Karmel's After School Meal Planner (2006), The Fussy Eaters' Recipe Book (2007), Mummy and Me Cookbook (2008), Baby's First Year (2008), Baby and Toddler Food Diary (2008), Top 100 Finger Foods (2009), Cook It Together (2009), I Can Eat A Rainbow (2009), Your Feeding Questions Answered (2009), Top 100 Pasta Dishes (2010), Top 100 Meals in Minutes (2011), Annabel's Kitchen: My First Cookbook (2011), 100 Family Meals (2011), Easting for Two (2012), Quick and Easy Toddler Recipes (2013), Quick and Easy Weaning (2014), Annabel's Family Cookbook (2014), Busy Mum's Cookbook (2015), New Complete Baby and Toddler Meal Planner 25th Anniversary Edition (2016); *Recreations* skiing, bridge, films, cooking, spending time with my children, travel, walking my dogs Bono, Hamilton and Sabre; *Clubs* Arts, 5 Hertford Street; *Style—* Ms Annabel Karmel, MBE; ✉ Karmel Foods Limited, 18A Pindock Mews, London, W9 2PY (☎ 020 7289 3808, e-mail sarah@annabelkarmel.com, website www.annabelkarmel.com, Facebook @annabelkarmeluk, Twitter @annabelkarmel, Instagram @annabelkarmel)

KARMILOFF-SMITH, Prof Annette Dionne; CBE (2004); da of late Jack Smith, and Doris Ellen Ruth, *née* Findlay; *b* 18 July 1938; *Educ* Edmonton Co GS, Inst Français de Londres, Univ of Lille (Certificat d'Etudes Bilingues), Holborn Coll of Law and Languages (Dip Int Conf Interpreting), Univ of Geneva (Diplôme Général de Psychologie de l'Enfant, Licence en Psychologie, Diplôme de Spécialisation en Psychologie Génétique, Doctorat en Psychologie Génétique et Expérimentale); *m* 1, 1966 (m dis 1991), Igor Alexander Karmiloff; 2 da; m 2, 2001, Mark Henry Johnson; *Career* int conf interpreter UN 1966–70, research conslt UNWRA/UNESCO Inst of Educn Beirut 1970–72, research collaborator Int Centre for Genetic Epistemology Geneva 1972–76, chargé du cours Faculty of Med Univ of Berne 1977–79, dir of studies Univ of Geneva 1979, visiting research assoc Max-Planck Inst Nijmegen 1978–82, special appointment career scientist Cognitive Devpt Unit MRC 1988–98 (sr scientist 1982–88), hon prof of psychology UCL 1982–98, head Neurocognitive Devpt Unit Inst of Child Health 1998–2006, professorial research fell Birkbeck Univ London 2007–; visiting lectr: Free Univ of Brussels 1985, Max-Planck Inst Munich 1986, Univ of Chicago 1987, Univ of Barcelona 1988, Carnegie Mellon Univ Pittsburgh 1991–92, Univ of Aix-Marseilles 1995, Univ of Madrid 1995; Sloan fell: Yale Univ 1978, Univ of Calif Berkeley 1981; hon professorial fell in cognitive science Univ of Sussex 1979–81; memb and former memb editorial bds on numerous learned jls 1982–, author of numerous book chapters and of articles in learned journals; memb: Soc for the Study of Behavioural Phenotypes, Br Psychological Soc (memb Cncl 1988–91), US Soc for Philosophy and Psychology; distinguished fell US Cognitive Science Soc 2008; memb Academia Europaea 1991, FBA 1993, FRSA 1996, FMedSci 1999; *Books* A Functional Approach to Child Language (1979, 2 edn 1981), Child Language Research in ESF Countries (jtly, 1991), Beyond Modularity: A Developmental Perspective on Cognitive Science (1992, British Psychological Society Book Award 1995), Baby It's You: A unique insight into the first three years of the developing baby (1994), Rethinking Nativism: Connectionism in a Developmental Framework (jtly, 1996), Everything Your Baby Would Ask (jtly, 1999); *Recreations* antique collecting, working out, going on multiple diets, writing/reading poetry; *Style—* Prof Annette Karmiloff-Smith, CBE, FBA, FMedSci

K

KARNEY, (Eur Ing) Andrew Lumsdaine; s of Rev Gilbert Henry Peter Karney (d 1996), and Celia Finch Wigham, *née* Richardson (d 1994); gf Rt Rev Arthur B L Karney, First Bishop of Johannesburg; *b* 24 May 1942; *Educ* Rugby, Trinity Coll Cambridge; *m* 1969, Beryl Fleur Goldwyn, MRAD, prima ballerina of Ballet Rambert 1950–60, da of late Louis Goldwyn, of Australia; 1 s (Peter John b 1972); *Career* teacher UN Relief and Works Agency Beirut and Gaza 1963–64, devpt engr STC London and Paris 1965–68, sr scientist Gen Electric Co 1968–71, planning engr communications Gas Cncl (now BG Gp) 1972–73; Logica plc 1973–94: chm Logica Space and Communications Ltd 1984–94, fndr dir Logica General Systems Spa (Italy) 1984–94, fndr dir Logica Ltd (Hong Kong) 1986–94, corp devpt dir Logica plc 1986–94, dir Logica Data Architects Inc (USA) 1988–90, dir Logica Aerospace and Defence Ltd 1989–91, fndr dir Speedwing Logica Ltd (joint venture between British Airways and Logica) 1990–94; fndr dir Cable London plc 1984–86; non-exec chm Language Line Ltd 1996–99 and 2003–06, non-exec chm Conclusive Logic Ltd 2000–02, non-exec dep chm Communicandum Ltd 1999–2003; non-exec dir: Integrated Micro Products plc 1995–96, Guardian Media Gp plc 1997–2006, ViewGate Networks Ltd 1997–2001, Telematix Ltd 2000–01, Netcentric Systems Ltd 2000–01, Guardian Newspapers Ltd 2001–06, Baronsmead VCT3 plc 2001–16 (sr ind dir); ind conslt to various UK and int companies; memb Ctee Nat Electronics Cncl 1989–99, chm and tstee Integrity Action (int NGO London, Jerusalem, Ramallah, Jakarta, Nairobi and Bishkek) 2005–13, tstee Medical Aid for Palestinians 2009–; Freeman City of London, Liveryman Worshipful Co of Info Technologists; memb Chatham House; CEng, Eur Ing, FIET, FInstD, FRSA; *Recreations* travel, photography, scuba diving; *Style—* Mr Andrew Karney; ✉ The Old Rectory, Credenhill, Herefordshire HR4 7DJ (☎ 01432 761655, mobile 07956 366086, e-mail andrew@karney.com, website www.karney.com)

KARP, Her Hon Judge Rachel Vivienne; *Career* admitted slr 1986; dep district judge then district judge 2004, circuit judge (South Eastern Circuit) 2013–; *Style—* Her Hon Judge Karp; ✉ Willesden County Court, 9 Acton Lane, Harlesden, London NW10 8SB

KARSTEN, His Hon Ian George Francis; QC (1990); s of late Dr Frederick Karsten, and late Edith Karsten; *b* 27 July 1944; *Educ* William Ellis Sch Highgate, Magdalen Coll Oxford (MA, BCL); *m* 25 May 1984 (m dis 2002), Moira Elizabeth Ann, da of Wing Cdr Laurence O'Hara; 2 da (Lucy Caroline Jane b 9 Oct 1985, Emma Catherine Louise b 17 June 1988), 1 s (Charles Frederick Laurence b 9 Feb 1993); *Career* called to the Bar Gray's Inn 1967, in practice Midland & Oxford Circuit 1970–, recorder of the Crown Court 1994–, head of chambers, circuit judge (SE Circuit) 1999–2014; lectr in law: Univ of Southampton 1966–70, LSE 1970–88; delegate to Hague Conf on Private Int Law 1973–77 (Convention on the Law Applicable to Agency, appointed rapporteur), ldr UK Delegation to Unidroit Conf (Convention on Agency in the Int Sale of Goods) Bucharest 1979 and Geneva 1983;

diplomé Hague Acad of Int Law; *Books* Conflict of Laws – Halsbury's Laws of England (co-author 4 edn, 1974); *Recreations* opera, travel, chess; *Style*— His Hon Ian Karsten, QC; ✉ Crown Court at Blackfriars, 1–15 Pocock Street, London SE1 0BJ

KARU, Her Hon Judge Usha; *b* 18 December 1958, New Delhi, India; *m* 1987, Lee Karu, QC; 2 s; *Career* called to the Bar Middle Temple 1984 (bencher 2012); in practice as criminal barr 1984–2005, asst recorder 1998–2000, recorder 2000–05, circuit judge (South Eastern Circuit) 2005–; tbnl judge Mental Health Review Tbnl 2011–, circuit judge cmmr Judicial Appointments Cmmn 2014–; *Recreations* gardening, theatre, travel; *Style*— Her Hon Judge Karu; ✉ c/o Judicial Secretariat, City of London Magistrates Court, 3rd Floor, 1 Queen Victoria Street, London EC4N 4XY

KASKI, Prof Juan Carlos; s of Moises Kaski, and Ofelia, *née* Fullone; *b* 3 May 1950, Mar del Plata, Argentina; *Educ* Universidad del Salvador Buenos Aires (Gold Medal, MD, DM), Univ of London (DSc); *m* 19 Sept 1975, Dr Marta Carpani; 2 s (Juan-Pablo b 3 June 1977, Diego b 3 Oct 1979), 1 da (Maria-Cecilia b 16 Feb 1984); *Career* med intern Universidad del Salvador Buenos Aires 1974–75, resident (internal med) Rawson Hosp Buenos Aires 1975–78; Ramos Mejia Hosp Buenos Aires: chief resident 1978–79, cardiology fell and registrar 1979–82, head of coronary disease research 1986–88; sr registrar and lectr in cardiology Hammersmith Hosp London 1988–91 (research fell 1982–86; St George's Hosp London: lectr in cardiology 1991–95, sr lectr and hon conslt cardiologist 1995–97, Br Heart Fndn Sugden sr lectr 1996–98, Br Heart Fndn Sugden reader in cardiology 1998–99, prof of cardiovascular science and hon conslt 1999–, head Cardiological Sciences, dir Coronary Artery Disease Research Unit, chm Cardiovascular Research Gp 2007, head of dept Cardiovascular Sciences Research Centre 2009–; head Cardiovascular Biology Res Centre SEUL London 2003, dep head Div of Cardiac and Vascular Sciences SGUL London 2004, dir Heart and Brain Research Inst SGUL Univ of London 2013; scientfic advsr Miny for Health São Paulo 1992–, advsr St Pau Hosp Directorate Univ of Barcelona 1999–, external advsr Argentine Fund for Promotion of Science and Technol (FONCYT) 2000–; chm Working Gp on Microcirculation European Soc of Cardiology 1994–96 (vice-chm 1992–94); memb: Steering Ctee Cardiovascular Research Gp R&D Ctee St George's Hosp Med Sch 1997–, Educn and Trg Prog Ctee European Soc of Cardiology 1997–, Project Grants Ctee 1 Br Heart Fndn 2002–; pres Int Soc of Cardiovascular Pharmacotherapy (ISCP) 2010 (UK govr 2005, vice-pres 2008–); chm CEM Ctee Int Soc of Cardiovascular Pharmacotherapy 2006; assoc ed Cardiovascular Drugs and Therapy 2006; memb: Br Cardiac Soc, Argentine Soc of Cardiology, Atherosclerosis and Coronary Circulation Cncl, American Heart Assoc; ed-in-chief ISCP Parmacotherapy book series 2012; Distinguished Cardiologist Award Fukushima Univ 2002, Gold Medal Spanish Soc of Cardiology 2003, Raices Award Argentine Miny of Health and Innovation 2011; hon prof Univ of São Paulo 1998, prof (hc) Universidad del Salvador Buenos Aires 1998, scientiae magistri Univ of Rome 1998, hon prof Catholic Univ Rome 2007; fell NY Acad of Sciences 1993, fell Societa Medico-Chirurgica Univ of Bologna 1994; FACC 1990, FESC 1991, FRCP 1999, fell Royal Soc of Med Catalonia 2007, fell American Heart Assoc 2011; *Publications* author of five books, over 150 book chapters, 600 abstracts and 500 papers in peer-reviewed jls; *Recreations* collecting illuminated manuscripts, photography, tennis; *Style*— Prof Juan Carlos Kaski; ✉ St George's Hospital Medical School, Cranmer Terrace, London SW17 0RE (☎ 020 8725 2628, fax 020 8725 3416, e-mail jkaski@sgul.ac.uk)

KASSIMATIS, Philippos; s of George Kassimatis, and Anastasia, *née* Dimitropoulos (d 2007); *b* 20 June 1974, Athens, Greece; *Educ* BNC Oxford (MEng, Edward Shepee Univ Prize), Yale Univ (MA, MBA); *m* Ritika Dhamija; *Career* sr assoc Investment Banking Merrill Lynch NY 1999–2002, vice-pres Global Foreign Exchange Merrill Lynch London 2003–05, md and global head of FX structuring Barclays Capital 2005–, founding ptnr Panthir Capital 2008–, founding ptnr Maven Global 2014–; *Style*— Philippos Kassimatis, Esq; ✉ 26 Upper Brook Street, London W1K 7QE (☎ 020 7491 4864, e-mail pkassimatis@hotmail.com)

KASYMOV, HE Erkin; *b* 19 May 1951, Dushanbe, Tajikistan; *m* Eleonora Kasymova; *Career* Tajakistani diplomat; ambass to the Ct of St James's 2008–; *Style*— HE Mr Erkin Kasymov; ✉ Embassy of Tajikistan, 26–28 Hammersmith Grove, London W6 7BA

KATIN, Dr Peter Roy; s of Jerrold Katin (d 1991), and Gertrude Kate May (d 1976); *b* 14 November 1930; *Educ* Royal Acad of Music; *Career* pianist; musical talent evident at age of four, admitted to Royal Acad of Music at age of twelve; debut: Wigmore Hall 1948, Henry Wood Promenade Concert (with Tchaikovsky's second Concerto) 1952; first postwar Br artist to make a solo tour of the USSR 1958; early influences incl: Clifford Curzon, Claudio Arrau, Myra Hess; recordings incl: complete Mozart Sonatas, Chopin Nocturnes and Impromptus, complete Chopin Waltzes and Polonaises, complete Grieg Lyric Pieces, Clementi, Schubert and Chopin (on square pianos), works by Schubert, Liszt, Tchaikovsky, Schumann, Rachmaninov, Brahms, Scarlatti and Mendelssohn; composer of various piano pieces and songs, the song cycle Sequence (words by Charlotte Morrow) and various cadenzas to Beethoven and Mozart Concertos; series of subscription recitals and master classes for young artists 1968–78, prof Royal Acad of Music 1956–60, visiting prof Univ of W Ontario 1978–84, prof Royal Coll of Music 1992–2001; writer of articles on various aspects of music-making and composing, currently writing autobiography; Eric Brough Meml Prize 1944, Chopin Arts Award 1977; Hon DMus 1994; ARCM 1952, FRAM 1960; *Recreations* theatre, literature, writing, photography, record collections; *Style*— Dr Peter Katin; ✉ 41 First Avenue, Bexhill-on-Sea, East Sussex TN40 2PL (e-mail peter.katin@btinternet.com, website www.peterkatin.com)

KATWALA, Sunder; *m* Stacy; 4 c (Zarina, Jay, Sonny, Indira); *Career* currently dir British Future; previously: writer and internet ed The Observer, research dir Foreign Policy Centre, cmmng ed for politics and economics Macmillan; gen sec Fabian Soc 2003–11; *Style*— Sunder Katwala, Esq; ✉ British Future, Kean House, 6 Kean Street, London WC2B 4AS

KATZ, Alan Jacob; s of Berl Katz, and Edith Lena, *née* Seidel; *b* 29 September 1945; *Educ* Salford GS, LSE (BSc); *m* Susan Ernesta, *née* Rees; 2 da (Nicola b 6 March 1977, Joanna b 8 Dec 1979); *Career* chartered accountant; Arthur Andersen: articled clerk 1966–69, mangr 1972–78, ptnr 1978–98, conslt 1998–; conslt: Ernst and Young 2000–05, LECG 2003–; sr moderator JIEB Examination 2004–; res fell ICRA Lancaster Univ 1999–; memb ICA 1969, MIPA 1989, MSPI 1991, MABRP 2000; *Recreations* walking, swimming, theatre; *Clubs* St James (Manchester), Rotary (Ambleside Kirkstone); *Style*— Alan Katz, Esq; ✉ International Centre for Research in Accounting, Lancaster University, Lancaster LA1 4YX (☎ 01524 565201, fax 01524 594334)

KATZ, Andrew James Stewart; s of Stewart Katz, and Janet, *née* McDonnell (d 2004); *b* 13 April 1966, Melton Mowbray, Leics; *Educ* Uppingham (entrance scholar), Churchill Coll Cambridge (entrance scholar, MA), Inns of Court Sch of Law; *m* 1 April 1996, Lucy, *née* Pollard; 1 s (Oscar Guy b 17 Oct 1999), 1 da (Isabelle Lucy b 21 May 2002); *Career* called to the Bar Inner Temple 1990, admitted slr 1993; barr Winward Fearon & Co 1991–93; slr: Brethertons 1993–99 (ptnr 1996), Moorcrofts LLP 2000– (ptnr 2001); memb: Bd Telecommunications Industry Assoc 2001–03, Ctee Open Source Specialist Gp BCS; supporter Open Rights Gp, UK Licence contrib Creative Commons; ed Int Free and Open Source Software Law Review; fell Free Software Fndn Europe; memb Law Soc 2003; *Books* A Manager's Guide to IT Law (contrib, 2004); *Recreations* reading, wine, food, web 2.0, music; *Style*— Andrew Katz, Esq; ✉ Moorcrofts LLP, James House, Dedmere Road, Marlow, Buckinghamshire SL7 1FJ (☎ 01628 470003, fax 01628 470001, e-mail andrewk1@moorcrofts.com, website www.moorcrofts.com)

KATZ, Ian; *b* S Africa; *Educ* New Coll Oxford; *m* Justine Roberts; *Career* grad trainee Sunday Correspondent 1989–90; The Guardian 1990–2013 (latterly dep ed), ed Newsnight BBC 2013–; *Style*— Ian Katz, Esq; ✉ BBC Newsnight, Zone D, 3rd Floor, BBC Broadcasting House, Portland Place, London W1A 1AA

KAUFMAN, Rt Hon Sir Gerald Bernard; kt (2004), PC (1978), MP; s of Louis Kaufman, and Jane Kaufman; *b* 21 June 1930; *Educ* Leeds GS, The Queen's Coll Oxford; *Career* political staff Daily Mirror 1955–64, political corr New Statesman 1964–65, Lab Pty press liaison offr 1965–70; MP (Lab): Manchester Ardwick 1970–83, Manchester Gorton 1983–; Parly under sec Environment 1974–75, Parly under sec Industry 1975, min of state Dept of Industry 1975–79; oppn front bench spokesman and memb Shadow Cabinet: Environment 1980–83, Home Affrs 1983–87, Foreign and Cwlth Affairs 1987–92; memb Labour Party NEC 1991–92; chm House of Commons: Nat Heritage Ctee 1992–97, Culture, Media and Sport Ctee 1997–2005, All-Pty Dance Gp 2006–, All-Pty Opera Gp 2010–; memb Royal Cmmn into reform of House of Lords 1999; chm Booker Prize judges 1999; *Style*— The Rt Hon Sir Gerald Kaufman, MP; ✉ 87 Charlbert Court, Eamont Street, London NW8 7DA (☎ 020 7219 3000)

KAUFMANN, Julia Ruth; OBE (1997); da of Felix Kaufmann, of Fort Lauderdale, FL, and Ruth Armley, *née* Arnold; *b* 1941, London; *Educ* Ursuline Convent Wimbledon, Univ of London (BEd), Brunel Univ (Dip Social Policy); *m* (m dis); 2 s (Luke Kelly b 1962, Oisin Kelly b 1965), 1 da (Tara Kaufmann b 1964); *Career* co-dir Social Educn Unit Centre for Human Rights and Responsibilities 1976–78, chief exec Gingerbread (assoc for one parent families) 1979–87, dir BBC Children in Need Appeal 1987–2000, voluntary sector conslt 2001–; memb Nat Lotteries Charities Bd 1994–99, pt/t cmmr Postcomm 2000–06, memb Employment Rels Advsy Panel on Public Appts 2001–05, memb Bd Capacity Builders 2006–09; chair: Nat Assoc of Toy Libraries 2000–, Whizz-Kidz 2006–08, Eaves Housing for Women 2011–12; princ advsr John Lyon's Charity 2001–; sr assoc Inst for Voluntary Action Research 2010–; *Style*— Ms Julia Kaufmann, OBE; ✉ 2 Carberry Road, Upper Norwood, London SE19 3RU (☎ 020 8653 3877, e-mail julia.kaufmann@btinternet.com)

KAUR, Pervinder; da of Sarwan Singh (d 1988), and Surjit Kaur; *b* 28 November 1971, Nottingham; *Educ* Fernwood Comp Sch Nottingham, Bilborough Sixth Form Coll, Univ of Sheffield (LLB), Coll of Law Chester (Dip); *Career* admitted slr 1996; Addleshaw Goddard: trainee slr 1994–96, slr 1996–2004, legal dir 2004–, ptnr 2008–; memb: Charity Law Assoc, Law Soc 1996; *Recreations* photography, tennis, fashion, travel; *Style*— Miss Pervinder Kaur; ✉ Addleshaw Goddard, Sovereign House, Sovereign Street, Leeds LS1 1HQ (☎ 0113 2092381, fax 0113 2092060, e-mail pervinder.kaur@addleshawgoddard.com)

KAVANAGH, Prof Dennis Anthony; s of Patrick Joseph Kavanagh, and Agnes, *née* Campbell; *b* 27 March 1941; *Educ* St Anselm's Coll, Univ of Manchester (BA, MA); *m* 13 Aug 1966, Monica Anne, *née* Taylor; 3 da (Jane b 24 July 1968, Catherine b 4 Nov 1972, Helen b 3 Jan 1981), 1 s (David b 20 Nov 1970); *Career* prof of politics Dept of Politics Univ of Nottingham 1982–95, prof of politics Dept of Politics Univ of Liverpool 1996–2006 (now emeritus prof); visiting prof: European Univ Inst Florence 1977, Univ of Calif San Diego 1979, Stanford Univ 1985; memb ESRC Cncl, Liverpool Democracy Cmmn; Ford Fndn Fell Stanford Univ Calif 1969–70; *Books* Constituency Electioneering, The British General Election of February 1974 (with Dr David Butler, *qv*), The British General Election of 1979 (with David Butler), British Politics Today (with W Jones), New Trends in British Politics (ed, with Prof Richard Rose, FBA, *qv*), The Politics of the Labour Party (ed), Political Science and Political Behaviour, The British General Election 1983 (with David Butler), Thatcherism and British Politics, The British General Election of 1987 (with David Butler), Consensus Politics from Attlee to Thatcher (with Peter Morris), The Thatcher Effect (ed, with Anthony Seldon), Comparative Government and Politics, Personalities and Politics, The British General Election of 1992 (with David Butler), The Major Effect (with Anthony Seldon), Electoral Politics, The New Marketing of Politics, The British General Election of 1997 (with David Butler), The Reordering of British Politics, Oxford Dictionary of Political Biography, The Powers Behind the Prime Minister (with Anthony Seldon), British Politics: Continuities and Change, The British General Election of 2001 (with David Butler), The British General Election of 2005 (with David Butler), The Blair Effect 2001–05 (with Anthony Seldon), The British General Election of 2010 (with Philip Cowley), Philip Gould An Unfinished Life (ed), The British General Election of 2015 (with Philip Cowley); *Recreations* running, tennis, music, obituaries; *Clubs* RSA, Bowdon Lawn Tennis, Hale Lawn Tennis; *Style*— Prof Dennis Kavanagh; ✉ Lynton, Belgrave Road, Bowdon, Cheshire WA14 2NZ (e-mail dennis.kavanagh@talktalk.net)

KAVANAGH, Giles; s of Joseph Kavanagh, of Belfast, and Bernadette, *née* Kelly; *b* 2 May 1959, Belfast; *Educ* St Malachy's Coll Belfast (Mellon Fndn scholar), St John's Coll Cambridge (pres Cambridge Union); *m* 1996 (m dis); 2 da (Tierney Rose b 7 April 1998, Erin Aoife Bernadette b 9 July 2001), 1 s (Conall Joseph b 22 March 2000); *Career* called to the Bar Middle Temple 1984 (scholar); barr 1984–98, ptnr Barlow Lyde & Gilbert 1998–2012 (head of aerospace 2004–12), ptnr Holman Fenwick Willan 2012–; past chm Air Law Gp Ctee RAeS; *Recreations* golf, swimming, tennis; *Clubs* RAC; *Style*— Giles Kavanagh, Esq; ✉ until March 2012: Barlow Lyde & Gilbert, Beaufort House, 15 St Botolph Street, London EC3A 7NJ (☎ 020 7643 8008, e-mail gkavanagh@blg.co.uk); after March 2012: Holman Fenwick Willan, Friary Court, 65 Crutched Friars, London EC3N 2AE

KAVANAGH, Peter Richard Michael; s of Patrick Bernard Kavanagh, CBE, QPM, (d 2013), and Beryl Annie, *née* Williams (d 1984); *b* 20 February 1959; *Educ* Wimbledon Coll, Gonville& Caius Coll Cambridge (MA); *m* 16 Nov 1985, Vivien Mary, da of Gordon Samuel Hart, of Bromham, Beds; 1 da (Emma b 1988); *Career* admitted slr 1984; ptnr Theodore Goddard 1989–2002, ptnr Hunton & Williams 2002–07, business affrs dir Ambassador Theatre Gp Ltd 2007–; memb Law Soc; *Style*— Peter Kavanagh, Esq; ✉ The Ambassador Theatre Group Limited, 39–41 Charing Cross Road, London WC2H 0AR (☎ 020 7534 6100, e-mail peterkavanagh@theambassadors.com)

KAVANAGH, Trevor Michael Thomas; s of Bernard George Kavanagh (d 1978), and Alice Rose, *née* Thompson; *b* 19 January 1943; *Educ* Reigate GS; *m* 1967, Jacqueline Gai, da of John Swindells; 2 s (Benjamin b 14 June 1969, Simon John b 20 March 1971); *Career* journalist The Sun (political ed until 2006); chm The Lobby House of Commons Westminster 1990–91, chm Parly Press Gall 2000–01; Journalist of the Year and Specialist Reporter of the Year British Press Awards 1997; *Recreations* golf, swimming; *Clubs* RAC, Pall Mall; *Style*— Trevor Kavanagh, Esq

KAWCZYNSKI, Daniel; MP; *b* 1972; *Educ* Univ of Stirling; *Career* MP (Cons) Shrewsbury and Atcham 2005– (Parly candidate (Cons) Ealing Southall 2001); *Style*— Daniel Kawczynski, Esq, MP; ✉ House of Commons, London SW1A 0AA

KAY, Prof (Anthony) Barrington (Barry); s of Anthony Chambers, and Eva Gertrude, *née* Pearcey (later Mrs Kay, now Mrs Reuben); *b* 23 June 1939; *Educ* King's Sch Peterborough, Univ of Edinburgh (MB ChB, DSc), Jesus Coll Cambridge (MA, PhD), Harvard Med Sch; *m* 1966, Rosemary Margaret, da of Hugh Johnstone; 3 da (Emma Rosalind b 21 Sept 1968, Rebecca b 13 May 1975, Eleanor Elizabeth b 19 Nov 1976); *Career* various posts as house physician and surgn City and Eastern Gen Hosps Edinburgh 1963; student Univ of Cambridge 1964–65; house physician City Hosp Edinburgh 1965–66; post grad student Dept of Pathology Univ of Cambridge and hon registrar Addenbrooke's Hosp Cambridge 1966–69; research fell Harvard Med Sch at Robert B Brigham Hosp Boston

1969–71; Univ of Edinburgh: lectr in respiratory diseases 1971–74, pt/t sr lectr 1974–76, sr lectr in experimental pathology 1977–79, reader Dept of Pathology 1979–80; dep dir and conslt Immunology Div SE Scot Regnl Blood Transfusion Serv Royal Infirmary Edinburgh 1974–76; prof of clinical immunology and dir Dept of Allergy and Clinical Immunology Nat Heart and Lung Inst London 1980–2004, prof emeritus of allergy and clinical immunology and sr research investigator NHLI Div Imperial Coll 2004–; hon conslt physician Royal Brompton and Nat Heart and Lung Hosp 1980–, conslt physician (allergy) The London Clinic 2005–, scientific advsr House of Lords Select Ctee on Allergy 2006–07; co-fndr and dir Circassa Ltd; pres: European Acad of Allergology and Clinical Immunology 1989–92, Br Soc of Allergy and Clinical Immunology 1993–; T K Stubbins research fell RCP 1969–71; scientific achievement award Int Assoc of Allergology and Clinical Immunology 1991, Citation Superstar of the UK ISI Web of Science 1999, seventh most-cited UK biomedical researcher of decade Science Watch 2000, ISI Highly Cited researcher 2000, Paul Ehrlich Medal European Acad of Allergology and Clinical Immunology 2005; hon fell: American College of Allergy 1986, American Acad of Asthma, Allergy and Immunology 2004; hon memb: American Assoc of Physicians 1988, Hungarian Soc of Allergology and Clinical Immunology 1990, Swiss Soc of Allergology and Clinical Immunology 1991, Br Soc of Allergy and Clinical Immunology 2008; Hon DUniv (laurea honris causa) Univ of Ferrara Italy 2000; FRCPE 1975, FRCP 1980, FRCPath 1989, FRSE 1993, FMedSci 1999; *Books* Clinical and Experimental Allergy (co-ed, since 1984), Asthma: Clinical Pharmacology and Therapeutic Progress (ed, 1986), Allergy and Inflammation (ed, 1987), Allergic Basis of Asthma (ed, 1988), Allergy and Asthma: New Trends and Approaches to Therapy (ed, 1989), Eosinophils, Allergy and Asthma (ed, 1990), Eosinophils in Allergy and Inflammation (ed, 1993), Allergy and Allergic Diseases (ed, 1997); also numerous scientific articles on asthma and allergy; *Recreations* Baroque and modern bassoon, tennis, country walks; *Clubs* Hurlingham, Chelsea Arts; *Style—* Prof Barry Kay, FRSE; ✉ Sir Alexander Fleming Building, Leukocyte Biology Section, Imperial College, NHLI Division, South Kensington Campus, London SW7 2AZ (☎ 020 7594 3174, fax 020 7594 1475)

KAY, Brian Christopher; s of Noel Bancroft Kay (d 1980), of York, and Gwendoline, *née* Sutton (d 2004); *b* 12 May 1944; *Educ* Rydal Sch, King's Coll Cambridge (choral scholar), New Coll Oxford; *m* 1, 1970, Sally, *née* Lyne; 1 s (Jonathan b 22 June 1973), 1 da (Charlotte Joanna b 24 Feb 1975); m 2, 1983, Gillian Elizabeth Fisher, *qv*; *Career* conductor, singer, radio and TV presenter; fndr memb and bass The King's Singers 1968–82, chorus master Huddersfield Choral Soc 1984–93, freelance singer various vocal gps incl John Alldis Choir, London Voices and BBC Singers; conductor: Cecilian Singers of Leicester 1987–91, Cheltenham Bach Choir 1989–97, Mary Wakefield Westmorland Festival 1996–2003, Leith Hill Musical Festival 1996–2016, Bradford Festival Choral Soc 1998–2002, Burford Singers 2002–, The Really Big Chorus 2005–; presenter various BBC progs incl: Cardiff Singer of the World (BBC TV), Choir of the Year (BBC TV), Mainly for Pleasure (Radio 3) 1983–91, Music in Mind (weekly prog Radio 4) 1989–96, arts prog Radio 2, Record Review (World Serv), Brian Kay's Sunday Morning (Radio 3) 1992–2001, Classics with Kay (weekly prog World Serv) 1996–98, Comparing Notes (Radio 4) 1996–98, Friday Night is Music Night (Radio 2) 1998–2007, Choirworks (Radio 3) 1998–99, Brian Kay's Light Programme (Radio 3) 2002–07, Melodies for You (Radio 2) 2003–04; Music Presenter of the Year Award Sony Radio Awards 1996; appeared in feature film Amadeus as voice of Schickenaeder; lay vicar Westminster Abbey 1968–71; pres: Harrogate Choral Soc, Market Harborough Singers, Nottingham Choral Tst, Derbyshire Singers, Bristol Bach Choir, English Arts Chorale, Joyful Co of Singers; vice-pres: Assoc of Br Choral Dirs, Royal Sch of Church Music; *Recreations* reading, gardening, the local pub; *Style—* Brian Kay, Esq

KAY, (Robert) Jervis; QC (1996); s of late Philip Jervis Kay, VRD, of Suffolk, and late Pamela, *née* Carter; *Educ* Wellington Coll, Univ of Nottingham (LLB); *m* 1, 1975 (m dis 1986), Rosemary, da of late Dr Arthur Pollard; m 2, 1988, Henrietta Kathleen (d 2011), da of late Maj Guy Ward, RA, and Elizabeth Ward; 3 da (Pamela Felicity Iona b 1988, Katherine Elizabeth Skye b 1993, Lucinda Valentine Ailsa b 1995), 1 s (Philip-Alexander Guy Jervis b 1990); *Career* called to the Bar Lincoln's Inn 1972 (bencher 2005), called to the Bar of NSW 1984, called to the Bar of Antigua and Barbuda 1998, Admiralty Registrar and Master of the Queen's Bench 2009–; *Books* Atkins Court Forms (ed Vol 3, Admiralty, 1979, 1990, 1994, 2000, 2004 and 2008); *Recreations* sailing, golf, cricket, reading; *Clubs* Turf, MCC, Royal Ocean Racing, Bar Yacht; *Style—* Master Kay, QC; ✉ Royal Courts of Justice, Strand, London WC2A 2LL

KAY, Prof John Anderson; CBE (2014); s of James Scobie Kay (d 1983), and Allison, *née* Anderson (d 2006); *b* 3 August 1948; *Educ* Royal HS Edinburgh, Univ of Edinburgh (MA), Nuffield Coll Oxford (MA); *m* 1, 1986 (m dis 1995), Deborah, da of Raymond Freeman; m 2, 2009, Mika Oldham; *Career* Univ of Oxford: fell St John's Coll Oxford 1970–, univ lectr in economics 1971–79; Inst for Fiscal Studies: research dir 1979–82, dir 1982–86; London Business Sch: prof of economics 1986–96, dir Centre for Business Strategy 1986–91; dir Saïd Business Sch Univ of Oxford 1997–99; chm Clear Capital Ltd 2004–08; dir: Govett Strategic Investment Trust plc 1982–95, London Economics 1986–2000 (chm 1986–96), Investors' Compensation Scheme 1988–95, Halifax Building Society (now Halifax plc) 1991–2000, Foreign & Colonial Special Utilities Investment Trust plc 1993–2003, Undervalued Assets Trust plc 1994–2005, Value and Income Trust plc 1994–, Law Debenture Corporation 2004–14, Scottish Mortgage Investment Tst plc 2008–, Buddi 2012, Norges Bank Investment Mgmnt (NBIM) 2013; chm Kay Review on Short-Termism Dept of Business, Innovation and Skills 2011–12; memb Bd Social Market Fndn 1992–94, memb Scottish Govt Cncl of Economic Advisors 2007–10; Hon DLitt Heriot Watt Univ 2008; FBA 1997, FRSE 2007; *Books* Concentration in Modern Industry (with L Hannah, 1977), The Reform of Social Security (with A W Dilnot and C N Morris, 1984), The Economic Analysis of Accounting Profitability (with J Edwards and C Mayer, 1987), The British Tax System (with M A King, 1989), Foundations of Corporate Success (1993), The Business of Economics (1996), The Truth about Markets (2003), Culture and Prosperity (2004), Everlasting Light Bulbs (2004), The Hare and the Tortoise (2006), The Long and the Short of It (2009), Obliquity (2010), Other People's Money (2015); *Recreations* travelling, walking; *Style—* Prof John Kay, CBE, FBA, FRSE; ✉ The Erasmus Press, PO Box 4026, London W1A 6NZ (☎ 020 7224 8797, e-mail johnkay@johnkay.com, website www.johnkay.com)

KAY, Nicholas Peter; KCMG (2016, CMG 2007); s of Ralph Peter Kay, of Toddington, Glos, and Josephine Alice, *née* Poyner; *b* 8 March 1958, Louth, Lincs; *Educ* Abingdon Sch, St Edmund Hall Oxford (BA), Univ of Reading (MA); *m* 1986, Susan, *née* Wallace; 1 s (Joseph b 20 July 1987), 2 da (Hannah b 22 Dec 1988, Matilda b 15 Oct 1991); *Career* English language teacher Spain, Peru, Brazil, Saudi Arabia, Cyprus and UK 1980–94; FCO: joined 1994, head Pakistan and Afghanistan Section 1994–96, dep head of mission Havana 1997–2000, dep head Policy Planning Staff 2000–02, cnsllr and dep head of mission Madrid 2002–06, UK regnl coordinator Southern Afghanistan and head Helmand PRT 2006–07, ambass to Democratic Repub of Congo (concurrently non-resident ambass to Repub of Congo) 2007–10, ambass to Sudan 2010–12, dir (Africa) FCO 2012–13, special rep of the Sec-Gen to Somalia and head UN Assistance Mission in Somalia (UNSOM) 2013–16; *Publications* Letterwriter (software, 1988); *Recreations* water sports, travel, vegetarian food; *Style—* Sir Nicholas Kay, KCMG; ✉ c/o Foreign and Commonwealth Office, King Charles Street, London SW1A 2AH (e-mail nicholas.kay@gmail.com, Twitter @NicholasK111)

KAY, Richard; *m* 1998, Emma, *née* Wilkins; 2 da, 1 s; *Career* Daily Mail: reporter 1980–82, Belfast correspondent 1982–85, royal correspondent and feature writer 1986–2003, diary ed and columnist 2003–14, ed-at-large 2014–; Royal Reporter of the Year What the Papers Say Awards 1997; *Books* Desert Warrior (1993); *Style—* Richard Kay, Esq; ✉ Daily Mail, Northcliffe House, 2 Derry Street, Kensington, London W8 5TT (☎ 020 3615 1155)

KAY, Steven Walton; QC (1997); s of Maj John Kay, of Epsom, Surrey, and Eunice May; *b* 4 August 1954; *Educ* Epsom Coll, Univ of Leeds (LLB); *m* 1, (m dis); 1 s (Alexander b 1991); m 2, 14 Feb 2000, Valerie, *née* Logan; 1 da (Madeleine Lily b 2000); *Career* called to the Bar Inner Temple 1977 (bencher 2009); recorder of the Crown Court 1997–, specialist in criminal law, war crimes (def counsel before UN War Crimes Tribunal for former Yugoslavia and Rwanda), assigned defence counsel in trial of ex-Pres Slobodan Milosevic at ICTY The Hague 2001, counsel at ICC to Pres Uhuru Kenyatta of Kenya 2011–; estab Int Criminal Law Bureau 2008; memb Working Party on Efficient Disposal of Business in the Crown Court 1992, sec Criminal Bar Assoc 1993–95 and 1995–96; memb: Bail Issues Steering Gp 1993, Legal Servs Ctee Bar Cncl 1993, Nat Steering Gp for Recommendation 92 1993, Bar Standards Review Body 1994; co-chair IBA War Crimes Ctee 2013–; organiser of numerous confs and deliverer of various lectures on criminal law; frequent commentator on radio, TV and in press on criminal judicial system; memb South Eastern Circuit; dir: Melbury House Music Ltd 2012, Laughing Budgie Records Ltd 2013; *Recreations* golf, counting crows, works of pg, gardening, music, opera; *Clubs* Hurtwood Park Polo, Drift Golf, Old Epsomian, International Gentlemen's Sailing; *Style—* Steven Kay, QC; ✉ 9 Bedford Row, London WC1R 4AZ (☎ 020 7489 2727, fax 020 7489 2828, e-mail goodnightvienna@gmail.com, website www.internatinallawbureau.com and www.9bri.co.uk)

KAY, Susan Elaine; da of Donald Jackson Hodgson, of Manchester, and Joyce, *née* Martyn; *b* 24 June 1952; *Educ* Brookway HS Manchester, Mather Coll of Educn (Cert in Teaching), Univ of Manchester (BEd); *m* 1974, Norman Kay, s of Norman Kay (d 1975); 1 s (Tristan Andrew b 18 Feb 1979), 1 da (Sarah Elizabeth b 23 April 1982); *Career* author; infant sch teacher until 1979; *Books* Legacy (1985, Historical Novel prize in memory of Georgette Heyer 1985, Betty Trask Award for a first novel 1985), Phantom (1990, winner Romantic Novel of the Year Award 1991, ALA Best Book for Young Adults Award 1991); *Recreations* theatre, craft work, writing; *Style—* Mrs Susan Kay; ✉ c/o Heather Jeeves Literary Agency, 9 Kingsfield Crescent, Witney, Oxfordshire OX8 6JB (☎ 01993 700253)

KAY, Vernon; s of Norman Kay, of Bolton, and Gladys Kay; *b* 28 April 1974, Bolton; *Educ* St Joseph's RC Sch Horwich, St John Rigby Coll Orrell, Manchester Met Univ; *m* 12 Sept 2003, Tess Daly, *qv*; 2 da (Phoebe Elizabeth b 2004, Amber Isabella b 2009); *Career* TV and radio presenter; former model; supporter NCH, ambass Prince's Tst; pres Bolton FC Jr Whites, memb Br Model Flying Assoc; hon doctorate Univ of Bolton 2009; *Television* as presenter incl: T4 (Channel 4), Celebrities Under Pressure (ITV) 2003, Boys and Girls (Channel 4) 2003, Head Jam (BBC2 and BBC3) 2004, Wife for William (E4) 2004, Hit Me Baby One More Time (ITV and NBC) 2005, Family Fortunes (now All Star Family Fortunes) 2006–, Just the Two of Us (BBC1) 2006–07, The World's Greatest Elvis (BBC1) 2007, Gameshow Marathon (ITV1) 2007, Beat the Star (ITV1) 2008, The Whole 19 Yards (ITV1) 2010, Skating with the Stars (ABC) 2010, Million Dollar Mind Game 2011, Homes for the Holidays (Channel 4) 2011; *Radio* sometime presenter Xfm, presenter BBC Radio 1 2006–12; *Clubs* Fifty, Soho House; *Style—* Vernon Kay, Esq; ✉ c/o George Ashton, James Grant Media Ltd, 94 Strand on the Green, Chiswick, London W4 3NN (☎ 020 8742 4950, fax 020 8742 8951, e-mail enquiries@jamesgrant.co.uk)

K

KAY-PRICE, Rosalind Jane (Rosie); da of Stefan G Kay, of Edinburgh, and Helen E, *née* Irving; *b* 27 March 1976, Berwick upon Tweed, Northumberland; *Educ* Royal HS Edinburgh, London Contemporary Dance Sch (BA), Merce Cunningham Sch NY; *m* Louis A Price; *Career* dancer and choreographer; soloist and teacher Ballet Poznanski (Poland) 1998–2000, artistic dir Rosie Kay Dance Co 1999– (nominated Critics Circle and UK Best Ind Co Nat Dance Awards, winner Best Ind Dance Co Nat Dance Awards), memb Green Candle Dance Co 2000–01, memb Der Blaue Vogel Theatre Co (Berlin) 2001–02, dance artist-in-residence DanceXchange Birmingham Hippodrome 2003, dance artist Oakview 2004–05, guest choreographer / artist-in-residence Univ of Wolverhampton, assoc lectr Manchester Met Univ 2004–05, assoc artist Dance Xchange Birmingham Hippodrome 2008–, subject ldr contemporary strand Centre for Advanced Trg W Midlands 2009–12, Leverhulme artist in residence Sch of Anthropology and Museum Ethnography Univ of Oxford; Young Achiever of Scotland 1999; fell Rayne Fndn 2007–10 (incl attachment to 4 Rifles Battalion (choreographic research) 2008); *Productions* Patisserrie (Edinburgh Festival, Poland, Germany and UK tour) 1999 (Choreography Prize Int Solo Dance Theatre Festival 2000, first prize Sardinian Int Dance Festival 2008), Say it Quietly (Edinburgh Festival) 2000, Don't Play Me Play Games (Edinburgh Festival and The Place London) 2001, Honey You're a Pig (UK tour) 2002 (Bonnie Bird New UK Choreography Award Laban Centre 2003), Asylum (UK tour) 2004–05 (Creative Class of 2005 Channel 4), The Wild Party (film) 2005, 22 (film), Mars (Birmingham Royal Ballet) 2005, Trapped (Ludus Dance Co) 2006, The Class Club (Barbican) 2006–07, Ballet on the Buses (Birmingham Royal Ballet) 2007, The Wild Party (UK tour incl Edinburgh, Belfast and Lichfield Festivals, London, Birmingham and Warwick) 2006–08 (Sunday Herald Cultural Highlight of the Year 2006), Double Points: K (Int Dance Festival Birmingham, Edinburgh Festival and UK tour) 2008, Supernova (UK tour 2008–09) Double Points: 3X (commissioned by watching Dance Project Univ of Manchester) 2009, 5 SOLDIERS – The Body Is The Frontline (co-commission Int Dance Festival Birmingham and Warwick Arts Centre, Br Dance Edn and UK tour incl Rifles Club, int tour Germany and Spain) 2010–11 and (UK tour to theatres and military bases) 2015 (Time Out Critics Choice Award, Radio 4 Today Prog and The Times Eds Choice Award, nominated Best Choreography (Modern) Critics Circle, Special Commendation Award Royal Soc for Public Health), The Great Train Dance 2011 (cultural Olympiad outdoor work Severn Valley Railway), There is Hope (nat tour) 2012–13, Sluts of Possession (Edinburgh Fringe collaboration with Pitt Rivers Museum Univ of Oxford) 2013, 5 Soldiers (film and exhibition, Special Mention Imperial War Museum Short Film Festival), Caught in the Crossfire – Artists' responses to conflict peace and reconciliation (Herbert Gallery Coventry, Dresden Stadt Museum), Haining Dreaming (outdoor work Selkirk) 2013, choreography for feature film Sunshine on Leith 2013 and BBC film Brummoves 2014, Orango (choreographer and dancer, BBC Proms) 2015, The Machine Show (asst dir and choreographer, Birmingham Int Dance Festival) 2016; *Publications* Choreographies of 21st Century War (contrib), The Body is The Frontline, Choreographing lived experience: dance, feelings and the storytelling body (with Karin Eli, in Medical Humanities Jl), Spectators aesthetic experience of sound and movement in dance performance: a transdisciplinary investigation (jtly, in Psychology of Aesthetics, Creativity, and the Arts, Vol 10, 2016); *Recreations* reading, writing, theatre, music, art, walking, food and wine; *Clubs* Royal High Sch London, RSA; *Style—* Ms R J Kay-Price; ✉ website http://www.rosiekay.co.uk

KAYE; *see also:* Lister-Kaye

KAYE, Dr Georges Sabry; s of Dr Georges Kaye, of Beirut, The Lebanon, and Claire, *née* De Las Cases; *b* 21 May 1949; *Educ* Villa St Jean, Fribourg, Ratcliffe, KCL (BSc), Westminster Hosp Med Sch (MB BS); *m* Pamela Jean Harrison-Kaye; 3 c from previous m (Charles, Alice, Olivia); *Career* physician i/c Occupational Health Dept Cromwell Hosp 1982–2004; European med dir to General Electric Co 1982–2005; also former med dir to:

Salomon Bros Int Ltd, Citigroup, Pendragon Capital Mgmnt Ltd, Air France, Hill Samuel Financial Services; currently physician to: ABF, Fortnum & Mason, Primark; memb International Commission on Occupational Health; memb BMA and RSM; AFOM 1986; *Books* La Soif (The Thirst) (1976), Musings upon a Busy Doctor's Life (2000), The Tortured Wounded Healer that is Today's Patient (2000); *Recreations* French literature, lute playing; *Clubs* The Reform; *Style*— Dr Georges Kaye; ✉ 4 Manson Mews, South Kensington, London SW7 5AF (☎ 020 7370 0920, e-mail GSK@georgeskaye.com); Le Couvent de Bajou, 09130, Artigat, France (☎ 0033 5 3401 4233)

KAYE, Jeremy Robin; s of Kenneth Brown Kaye (d 1985), of Doncaster, and Hannah Eleanor Christabel, *née* Scott (d 1991); *b* 25 September 1937; *Educ* Eastbourne Coll, Worcester Coll Oxford (MA); *Career* Nat Serv Bombardier RA 1956–58; called to the Bar Inner Temple 1962; asst sec Limmer and Trinidad Lake Asphalt Co Ltd 1962–67, chief legal offr and asst sec Limmer Holdings Ltd 1967–72; sec: Arbuthnot Latham Holdings Ltd 1975–81, Dow Scandia Holdings Ltd 1982–86, Arbuthnot (formerly Secure Trust) Banking Gp plc 1987–, Arbuthnot Fund Mangrs Ltd 1987–, Secure Trust Bank plc 1992–2014; dir: Arbuthnot Latham Bank Ltd 1984–91 (sec 1973–91); lay chm East Grinstead Deanery 1977–87 (sec 1967–77, treas 1993–2011); Diocese of Chichester: memb Synod 1970–73 and 1988–, memb Bd of Fin 1992–2013, treas 2002–11, dep chm 2010, chm 2011–13; FCIS; *Recreations* gardening, cricket, golf; *Clubs* MCC, Holtye Golf; *Style*— Jeremy Kaye, Esq; ✉ Mallards, 52 Moat Road, East Grinstead, West Sussex RH19 3LH (☎ 01342 321 294); Arbuthnot House, 7 Wilson Street, London EC2M 2SN (☎ 020 7012 2430, fax 020 7012 2401)

KAYE, Laurence Martin; s of Moss Kaye, and Beatrice, *née* Herman; *b* 1 September 1949; *Educ* Haberdashers' Aske's, Sidney Sussex Coll Cambridge (Whittaker scholar, MA); *m* 1 July 1976, Lauren Merrill, *née* Shaymow; 1 s (David Benjamin b 22 Sept 1978), 1 da (Debra Ann b 16 Oct 1981); *Career* admitted slr 1975; ptnr: Brecher & Co 1977 (articled clerk 1972–75), Saunders Sobell Leigh & Dobin 1980–94, The Simkins Partnership (head of publishing and new media) 1994–98, Paisner & Co (head of e-commerce) 1998–2000, Andersen Legal (head of technology and e-business) 2000–02; slr in private practice (Laurence Kaye Slrs, specialists in digital media and internet law) 2002–13, conslt Shoosmiths LLP 2013–, fndr Laurence Kaye Consulting 2016–; legal advsr to Euro Publishers' Cncl; former chm: Mount Vernon Cleft Lip and Palate Assoc Ltd, Meher Baba Assoc Ltd; fndr chm UK Friends of The Abraham Fund Initiatives; Liveryman Stationers' Co; memb: Law Soc, Int Bar Assoc; *Recreations* tennis, golf, theatre, music, yoga; *Clubs* Radlett Lawn Tennis; *Style*— Laurence Kaye, Esq; ✉ e-mail laurie@laurencekaye.com

KAYE, His Hon Roger Godfrey; TD (1980, 1985), QC (1989); s of Anthony Harmsworth Kaye (d 1971), and Heidi Alice, *née* Jordy (d 1984); *b* 21 September 1946, London; *Educ* King's Sch Canterbury, Univ of Birmingham (LLB); *m* 15 April 1974, Melloney Rose, da of Rev H Martin Westall (d 1994); *Career* called to the Bar Lincoln's Inn 1970 (bencher 1997); jr Treasy counsel in Insolvency Matters 1978–89, dep High Court bankruptcy registrar 1984–2001, dep High Court judge 1990–, recorder 1995–2005, specialist chancery and mercantile circuit judge (NE Circuit) 2005–16; chm: Bar Cncl Fees Collection Ctee 1990–93, Bristol and Cardiff Chancery Bar Assoc 1990–95; memb Bar Cncl Professional Conduct Ctee 1995–97; dep chllr: Dio of St Albans 1995–2002, Dio of Southwark 1995–99, Dio of Hereford 1997–2000; chllr: Dio of Hertford 2000–, Diocese of St Albans 2002–; Hon Col 3 & 5 (V) MI Bn 1998–2011; Freeman City of London 1997; FRSA 1995, FCIArb 2001; *Recreations* going home; *Clubs* Athenaeum, RAC, Army and Navy, Special Forces, Northern Counties; *Style*— His Hon Roger Kaye, TD, QC

KAYE, Simon; s of Isaac Kaye (d 1964), of London, and Dora, *née* Libovitch (d 1964); *b* 22 July 1935; *Educ* Wycombe Sch; *m* 8 Sept 1957, Sylvia Adrienne, da of Michael Kagan (d 1982); 2 s (Jeremy b 22 Oct 1959, Trevor b 6 May 1966), 1 da (Elaine b 24 Sept 1962); *Career* film sound recordist; entered film industry 1953, sound mixer 1962, dir Siren Sound 1967–89, recorded over 100 Br and American films; winner of Oscars (for Platoon and Last of the Mohicans), 2 other Oscar nominations (for Reds and Gandhi), 3 BAFTA Awards (for Oh! What a Lovely War, A Bridge Too Far and Cry Freedom), 10 Br Acad Award nominations (for The Charge of the Light Brigade, The Lion in Winter, Oh! What a Lovely War, Sunday Bloody Sunday, A Bridge Too Far, Reds, Gandhi, Indiana Jones and the Temple of Doom, Cry Freedom and Last of the Mohicans), Cinema Audio Soc Best Sound Award 2004 (for The Life and Death of Peter Sellers); other credits incl: Shadowlands, Lost in Space, The Bone Collector, Under Suspicion, Spy Game, Tomb Raider II, Life and Death of Peter Sellers, Being Julia, Fateless, The Door; memb: BAFTA, Acad Motion Pictures Arts and Sciences, Cinema Audio Soc, Assoc Motion Picture Sound; *Style*— Simon Kaye, Esq; ✉ 39 Bellfield Avenue, Harrow Weald, Middlesex HA3 6ST (☎ 020 8428 4823)

KAYE, Prof Stanley Bernard; *b* 5 September 1948; *Educ* Roundhay Sch Leeds, Charing Cross Hosp Med Sch London (BSc, MB BS, MD); *Career* jr hosp posts in med oncology and gen med 1972–79, acting staff specialist in med oncology Ludwig Institute for Cancer Research Sydney 1980–81, prof of med oncology Univ of Glasgow 1985–2000 (sr lectr 1981–85), prof of med oncology and former head Drug Devpt Unit Inst of Cancer Research and Royal Marsden Hosp 2000–; research dir London Cancer Alliance 2014–; Cancer Research UK: memb Scientific Exec Bd 2002–07, chm Clinical and Translational Research Ctee 2004–07; non-exec dir North Glasgow Univ Hosp NHS Trust 1999–2000; memb MRC Cancer Therapy Ctee 1986–93, memb Gynaecological Cancer Working Pty 1990, memb Working Parties on Lung and Gynaecological Cancer 1986–90; memb: Scottish Cancer Coordinating and Advsy Ctee 1992, Scottish Cancer Therapy Network 1993; clinical ed British Jl of Cancer 1993; memb editorial bds of various cancer-related jls; author of various med pubns; FRCP 1989, FRCPGlas 1992, FRCR 1993, FRSE 2001, FMedSci 2004; *Recreations* playing several sports badly; *Style*— Prof Stanley Kaye; ✉ Royal Marsden Hospital, Sutton, Surrey SM2 5PT (e-mail stan.kaye@rmh.nhs.uk)

KEABLE, Nicholas Simon Phillip-James (Nick); s of John Todhunter Keable (d 1996), and Norma Sybil, *née* Norton (d 2006), of Sanderstead, Surrey; *b* 6 June 1966; *Educ* Ratcliffe Coll, RMA Sandhurst, Harvard Business Sch; *m* 1998, Tanya Towhidi; 2 da (Shakila b 1998, Layla b 1999); *Career* cmmnd Grenadier Gds 1986–94, latterly Capt (ops offr); Euro Parl 1994–96, with PPS Gp 1997–2005 (latterly md), vice-pres Saint Consulting Gp 2005–11, ceo Development Intelligence 2011–; cncllr (Cons) London Borough of Croydon 1998–2002; MInstD; *Style*— Nick Keable, Esq; ✉ Development Intelligence, 85 Buckingham Gate, London SW1E 6PD

KEAL, Anthony Charles (Tony); s of Maj Kitchener Keal, of Thornton Dale, N Yorks, and Joan Marjorie, *née* Ayling; *b* 12 July 1951; *Educ* Stowe, New Coll Oxford (BA); *m* 24 Nov 1979, (Janet) Michele, da of late John Charles King, of Javea, Spain; 4 s (Julian Charles b 1982, Jonathan David b 1986, Christopher James b 1987, Alexander Anthony b 1989); *Career* slr Allen & Overy 1976, slr and co sec Libra Bank plc 1976–78, ptnr Allen & Overy 1982–2005 (slr 1978–82), ptnr Simpson Thacher & Bartlett LLP 2005–; memb Law Soc; *Recreations* sailing, travel, skiing, family, opera; *Style*— Tony Keal, Esq; ✉ Simpson Thacher & Bartlett LLP, Citypoint, One Ropemaker Street, London EC2Y 9HU

KEALEY, Gavin Sean James; QC (1994); s of Paul E Kealey, and Evelyn, *née* Fegali; *b* 2 September 1953; *Educ* Charterhouse, UC Oxford (Fletcher scholar, BA); *m* 28 Feb 1981, Karen Elizabeth, da of Robert Nowak; 3 da (Alexandra Louise b 22 March 1983, Eleanor Victoria b 26 March 1986, Rowena Charlotte Ambrosiana b 19 Feb 1992); *Career* lectr in laws KCL; called to the Bar Inner Temple 1977; recorder 2000–10, head of chambers

2001–, dep judge of the High Court (Queen's Bench Div Commercial Court) 2002–; *Style*— Gavin Kealey, Esq, QC; ✉ 7 King's Bench Walk, Temple, London EC4Y 7DS (☎ 020 7910 8300, fax 020 7910 8400)

KEANE, Fergal Patrick; OBE (1997); s of Eamon Brendan Keane (d 1990) and Mary, *née* Hasset; *b* 6 January 1961; *Educ* Terenure Coll Dublin, Presentation Coll Cork; *m* 11 July 1986, Anne Frances, da of Frank Coleman Flaherty; *Career* trainee reporter Limerick Leader 1979–82; reporter: Irish Press Group Dublin 1982–84, Radio Telefis Éireann Belfast 1986–89 (Dublin 1984–86); BBC Radio: Northern Ireland corr 1989–91, Southern Africa corr 1991–94, Asia corr 1994–; BBC special correspondent 1997–; presenter Fergal Keane's Forgotten Britain (BBC TV) 2000; Hon DLitt Univ of Strathclyde 2001 *Awards* Reporter of the Year Sony Silver Award 1992 and Sony Gold Award 1993, Amnesty International Press Awards Int Reporter of the Year 1993, RTS Journalist of the Year 1994, BAFTA 1998, James Cameron Prize 1998, Sony Gold Award 2008; *Books* Irish Politics Now (1987), The Bondage of Fear (1994), Season of Blood: A Rwandan Journey (1995), Letter to Daniel: Despatches from the Heart (1996), Letters Home (1999), A Strangers Eye (2000), All of these People (2005), Road of Bones: The Siege of Kohima (2010); *Recreations* fishing, golf, poetry; *Style*— Fergal Keane, Esq, OBE; ✉ c/o BBC News and Current Affairs, Radio, Broadcasting House, London W1A 1AA

KEANE, Prof John Charlick; s of Ronald Melville Keane (d 1974), of Adelaide, and Mavis Matilda, *née* Charlick (d 1978); *b* 3 February 1949; *Educ* King's Coll Adelaide, Univ of Adelaide (Tinline scholar, BA, Archibald Grenfell Price prize, Charles Fenner prize), Univ of Toronto (Canadian Cwlth scholar and fell, MA, PhD); *m* Kathleen Margaret, *née* O'Neil; 4 c (Rebecca Allison b 1974, Leo Lawson-O'Neil b 1980, George b 1991, Alice b 1992); *Career* prof of politics Univ of Westminster 1988– (dir Centre for the Study of Democracy 1989–); Nuffield fell King's Coll Cambridge 1979–80, visiting lectr Inter-Univ Centre of Dubrovnik Yugoslavia 1982, 1983 and 1985, Social Scis Research Cncl fell Freie Universität Berlin FRG 1983, DAAD research fell Universität Bielefeld FRG 1984, overseas teaching and research fell Griffith Univ Aust 1984, research fell Zentrum für Interdisziplinäre Forschung Universität Bielefeld FRG 1987, visiting sr fell Dept of Politics and Soc Scis Euro Univ Inst Florence 1990, visiting prof Depts of Political Sci and Communications Univ of Calif San Diego 1990 and 1994, visiting prof Central Euro Univ Prague 1990, Andrew Mellon sr fell American Philosophical Soc Philadelphia 1991–92, Karl Deutsch prof Wissenschftszentrum Berlin 2001, sr fell IPPR London 2002–03; Anglo-German Br Cncl Research Award Universität Bremen and Freie Universität Berlin FRG 1991, PCFC Award Europe in the Twenty-First Century 1992–93, Univ of Westminster Euro Awareness Fund 1992, Br Cncl travel grant 1993, DEVR/QR Research Assessment Exercise Award CSD 1993–, Deutsch-Englische Gesellschaft fell 1994; memb: Governing Bd Institutum Studium Humanitatis Ljubljana Slovenia 1992–, Assoc Thomas Paine (Paris) 1990–, Editorial Bd The Political Quarterly 1989–, Jan Hus Educnl Fndn (with frequent contribs to parallel university lectrs and seminars in Brno and Prague) 1984–89; Superdon Award The Times (London) 1994; FRSA 1992, FBA 1998–99; *Books* Public Life and Late Capitalism: Towards a Socialist Theory of Democracy (1984), Contradictions of the Welfare State (ed and translator, 1984), The Power of the Powerless: Citizens Against the State in Central-Eastern Europe (ed, 1985), Disorganized Capitalism (ed and co-translator, 1985), After Full Employment (co-author with John Owens, 1986), Nomads of the Present: Social Movements and Individual Needs in Contemporary Societies (co-ed with Paul Mier, 1988), Civil Society and the State: New European Perspectives (ed and translator, 1988), Democracy and Civil Society (1988), The Media and Democracy (1991), Tom Paine: A Political Life (1995), Reflections on Violence (1996), Civil Society: Old Images, New Visions (1998), Václav Havel: A Political Tragedy in Six Acts (1999), On Communicative Abundance (2000), Whatever Happened to Democracy? (2002), Global Civil Society (2003); *Recreations* walking, running, gardening, journalism, film, theatre, cooking; *Style*— Prof John Keane; ✉ Centre for the Study of Democracy, 100 Park Village East, London NW1 3SR (☎ 020 7911 5138, fax 020 7911 5164, e-mail csd@westminster.ac.uk)

KEANE, John Granville Colpoys; s of Granville Keane (d 1990), and Elaine Violet Meredith Doubble (d 2004); *b* 12 September 1954; *Educ* Wellington, Camberwell Sch of Art (BA); *m* June 1996, Rosemary Anne McGowan (television prodr); 1 da (Calypso McGowan b 7 April 1997), 1 s (Theodore Granville Peter b 28 June 2002); *Career* artist; official Br war artist Gulf Crisis 1991; work in several public collections incl: Imperial War Museum, Ulster Museum, Nat Army Museum, Nat Portrait Gallery, Wolverhampton Museum, The Lowry Salford, UN; commissioned portraits incl Mo Mowlam, Jo Snow, Greg Dyke, David Puttnam and Kofi Annan; artist in residence Whitefield Sch London 1985–86, visiting prof Univ of the Arts London, res fell Camberwell Coll of Arts, artist in residence Independent on Sunday 2000–01, artist in residence Sch of Int Relations Univ of St Andrew's 2014–17; FRSA 2005; *Solo Exhibitions* incl Peking, Moscow, Milton Keynes (Minsky's Gallery London) 1980, Some of it Works on Paper (Centre 181 London) 1982, War Efforts (Pentonville Gallery London) 1984, Conspiracy Theories (Angela Flowers Gallery London) 1985, Perspective '85 (Basel Art Fair Switzerland) 1985, Work Ethics (Angela Flowers Gallery London) 1986, Bee Keeping in the War Zone (Angela Flowers Gallery) 1988, Against the Wall (Turnpike Gallery Leigh Gtr Manchester) 1988, The Accident (cmmnd painting and screenprint for Greenpeace, Flowers East London) 1988, Divided States (Terry Dintenfass Gallery NY) 1989, Forum (Hamburg Germany) 1989, The Other Cheek? (Flowers East London) 1990, Cloth Caps and Hang-Gliding (cmmnd exhibition about Ollerton Mining Community, Angel Row Gallery Nottingham) 1991, Before the War (Kelvingrove Art Gallery Glasgow) 1991, Gulf (Imperial War Museum London) 1992, Fairytales of London (Lannon Cole Gallery Chicago) 1992, Burden of Paradise, Paintings of Guatemala (Flowers East) 1992, The Struggle for the Control of the Television Station (Terry Dintenfass Gallery, Flowers East) 1993, Gulf (Norton Gallery of Art Florida) 1993, Graham Greene and the Jungle of Human Dilemma (Flowers East) 1995, Truth, Lies and Super-8 (Flowers East) 1997, Conflicts of Interest Touring Retrospective (Wolverhampton City Art Gallery, Ulster Museum, Belfast & Laing Gallery, Newcastle upon Tyne) 1998, Trading Flaws and Sporting Mistakes, Flowers West (Los Angeles), Making a Killing (Flowers East) 2000, Exchange Rates (Gwenda Jay Addington, Chicago) 2000, Saving the Bloody Planet (in assoc with Greenpeace), Flowers East 2001, Recent Events (Flowers Central) 2002, The Inconvenience of History (The London Inst Gallery, in assoc with Christian Aid) 2004, Back to Fundamentals (Flowers East, Ferens Art Gallery Hull) 2004, Fifty Seven Hours in the House of Culture (Flowers East, Sakharov Museum Moscow) 2006, Guantanamerica (Flowers NY) 2006, Children in Conflict (with Christian Aid, Wolverhampton Art Gallery and Aberdeen Art Gallery) 2008, Intelligent Design (Flowers East) 2009, Scratching the Surface, Joining the Dots (Flowers Gallery) 2012, Fear (Flowers Gallery) 2013, Speaking Power to Truth (Flowers Gallery) 2015, The Wisdom of Hindsight (Flowers Gallery) 2015; *Books* Conflicts of Interest (by Mark Lawson, 1995), Troubles My Sight (with Mark Lawson, 2015); *Recreations* tennis, snooker, unpopular music; *Clubs* Groucho, Chelsea Arts, Thorpeness Country; *Style*— John Keane, Esq; ✉ Flowers Gallery, 82 Kingsland Road, London E2 8DP (☎ 020 920 7777, fax 020 920 7770); website www.johnkeaneart.com

KEANE, Philip Vincent; s of Bernard Vincent Keane (d 1983), of London, and Brenda Ellen Margaret, *née* Ford; *b* 11 August 1940; *Educ* Wimbledon Coll GS, LSE (BSc); *m* 18 Sept 1965, (Kathleen) Winifred, da of William Aloysius Thomson (d 1987), of London; 2 da (Angelina Teresa b 14 Sept 1968, Noelle Francesca b 16 Dec 1969); *Career* sr investment analyst Esso Pension Tst 1967–71, head of investment res Mercantile & General

Reinsurance 1971–75, equity fund mangr Prudential Pensions 1976–77, investment mangr Rea Bros Ltd 1977–81; dir: Wardley Investment Mgmnt Ltd, HK Unit Tst Managers Ltd 1981–82, Rea Bros (Investment Mgmnt) Ltd 1982–89, CS Investment Mgmnt Ltd 1989–91; assoc dir IBJ Asset Management International Ltd (subsid of the Industrial Bank of Japan, and formerly IBJ International plc) 1991–; AIIMR; *Recreations* travel, photography, skiing, literature; *Style—* Philip Keane, Esq; ✉ 70 Pine Grove, off Lake Road, Wimbledon, London SW19 7HE

KEARNS, Hon Mr Justice Nicholas J; s of William Kearns (d 1995), and Joan, *née* Welland; *b* 13 April 1946, Dublin; *Educ* St Mary's Coll Rathmines, UCD, King's Inns Dublin; *m* 18 Sept 1971, Eleanor; 4 s (Stephen, Daniel, Simon, Nicholas); *Career* called to the Bar: King's Inns Dublin 1968, England and Wales 1980; sr counsel 1982–98, judge of the High Court of Ireland 1998–2004 (pres 2009–), judge of the Supreme Court of Ireland 2004–; subst/alternate judge European Court of Human Rights 2001, 2007 and 2008, judge Permanent Court of Arbitration The Hague 2005; bencher Middle Temple 2006–; chair Referendum Cmmn (on citizenship) 2004, chair Family Law Reporting Ctee (tasked with overseeing Family Law Reporting Project) 2008–09; co-fndr Assoc of European Competition Law Judges (vice-pres 2008–); *Recreations* reading, writing, walking, golf; *Style—* The Hon Mr Justice Nicholas Kearns; ✉ President of the High Court, Four Courts, Inns Quay, Dublin 7, Ireland

KEATES, Chris; *Educ* Univ of Leicester (BA); *Career* gen sec NASUWT 2004–; *Style—* Ms Chris Keates; ✉ NASUWT, 6th Floor, Orion House, 5 Upper St Martin's Lane, London WC2H 9EA (☎ 020 7420 9670, e-mail chris.keates@mail.nasuwt.org.uk, website www.nasuwt.org.uk)

KEATES, Jonathan Basil; s of Richard Herbert Basil Keates (d 1949), and Sonia Evangeline, *née* Wilcox; *b* 7 November 1946, Paris; *Educ* Bryanston (scholar), Magdalen Coll Oxford (MA), Univ of Exeter (PGCE); *Career* author; asst English master City of London Sch 1974–2013, chm Venice In Peril Fund 2013–; regular contrib to: The Spectator, The Literary Review, TLS; Hawthornden Prize 1984, James Tait Black Prize 1984; judge Booker Prize 1991; FRSL 1993 (memb Cncl 2014–), FSA 2009; *Books* The Companion Guide to Shakespeare Country (1979), Allegro Postillions (1983), Handel: the man and his music (1985), The Stranger's Gallery (1986), Tuscany (1988), Umbria (1991), Italian Journeys (1991), Stendhal (1994), Purcell (1995), Soon To Be A Major Motion Picture (1997), Smile Please (2000), The Siege of Venice (2005), Handel (2008), The Portable Paradise (2011), Robert Browning (2012), William III and Mary II (2015); *Recreations* music, travel, libraries, friendship; *Clubs* Athenaeum; *Style—* Jonathan Keates, Esq, FRSL; ✉ 5 Houblon Road, Richmond, Surrey TW10 6DB (☎ 020 8940 9679, e-mail jonnokeates@blueyonder.co.uk); c/o Peter Staus, Roger, Coleridge & White Ltd, 20 Powis Mews, London W11 1JN (☎ 020 7221 3717)

KEATING, John David; s of Peter Steven Keating (d 1944, war casualty), of York, and Muriel Emily Alice Lamport; *b* 18 June 1943; *Educ* King Edward VI Chelmsford, Highbury Coll Portsmouth; *m* 28 Aug 1970, Linda Margaret, da of Sidney Reginald Hall, of London; 1 s (Matthew b 1971), 1 da (Sarah b 1973); *Career* seagoing purser with P&O 1960–70, Lt Reserve Serv RN 2 Submarine Div 1970–71; asst to md CWS 1972–74, UK divnl accountant Borden Chemical Corp 1975–81, fndr dir and proprietor WRA Ltd 1982–; dir: WRA Holdings Ltd 1984–, WRA (Offshore) Ltd (Sub-Sea Devpt) 1985–, Russell Square Management Co Ltd 1991–, Martel-Wessex Composites Ltd 1991–; md Wessex Resins & Adhesives Ltd; elected memb for Ringwood South Ward of New Forest DC 1987–; FCCA 1977 (ACCA), MHCIMA; *Recreations* sailing, skiing; *Clubs* Naval, Royal Naval Sailing Assoc, Royal Lymington Yacht, Ski Club of GB; *Style—* John Keating, Esq; ✉ Okefield Lodge, Beaulieu Road, Lyndhurst, Hampshire SO43 7DA (☎ 02380 283672)

KEATING, Prof Michael James; s of Michael Joseph Keating (d 1974), and Margaret Watson, *née* Lamb (d 2001); *b* 2 February 1950, Hartlepool, Co Durham; *Educ* Univ of Oxford (BA, MA), CNAA (PhD); *m* 22 Feb 1975, Patricia Ann, *née* McCusker; 1 s (Patrick David b 24 Feb 1979); *Career* pt/t lectr Glasgow Coll of Technol 1972–75, sr res offr in govt Univ of Essex 1975–76, lectr in politics North Staffordshire Poly 1976–79, lectr and sr lectr Univ of Strathclyde 1979–88, prof of political science Univ of Western Ontario 1988–99, prof of politics Univ of Aberdeen 1999, prof of political science European Univ Inst Italy 2000–; FRSE, AcSS, FBA, MAE; *Books* Labour and Scottish Nationalism (jtly, 1979), Regional Government in England (jt ed, 1982), The Government of Scotland (jtly, 1983), Labour and the British State (jtly, 1985), Regions in the European Community (jt ed, 1985), Decentralisation and Change in Contemporary France (jtly, 1986), Remaking Urban Scotland: Strategies for Local Economic Development (jtly, 1986), The City that Refused to Die: Glasgow – The Politics of Urban Regeneration (1988), State and Regional Nationalism: Territorial Politics and the European State (1988), Politics and Public Policy in Scotland (jtly, 1991), Comparative Urban Politics: Power and the City in the United States, Canada, Britain and France (1991), The Politics of Modern Europe: The State and Political Authority in the Major Democracies (1993, 2 edn 1999), The European Union and the Regions (jt ed, 1995), Nations against the State: The New Politics of Nationalism in Quebec, Catalonia and Scotland (1996, 2 edn 2001), The Political Economy of Regionalism (jt ed, 1997), The New Regionalism in Western Europe: Territorial Restructuring and Political Change (1998), Remaking the Union: Devolution and British Politics in the 1990s (jt ed, 1998), Paradiplomacy in Action: The External Activities of Subnational Governments (jt ed, 1999), Plurinational Democracy: Stateless Nations in a Post-Sovereignty Era (2001), Minority Nationalism and the Changing International Order (jt ed, 2001), The Dynamics of Decentralization: Canadian Federalism and British Devolution (jt ed, 2001), Culture, Institutions and Economic Development: A Study of Eight European Regions (jtly, 2003), The Regional Challenge in Central and Eastern Europe: Territorial Restructuring and European Integration (jt ed, 2003), The Government of Scotland: Public Policy Making after Devolution (2005), European Integration and the Nationalities Question (jt ed, 2006), Devolution and Public Policy: A Comparative Perspective (jt ed, 2006), Scottish Social Democracy (ed, 2007), The Independence of Scotland (2009), The Crisis of European Social Democracy (jt ed, 2013), Rescaling the European State (2013); *Recreations* traditional music, sailing, hiking, cooking; *Style—* Prof Michael Keating; ✉ University of Aberdeen, Aberdeen AB24 3QY

KEATING, Roland Francis Kester (Roly); *b* 5 August 1961; *Educ* Balliol Coll Oxford; *m*; 1 s, 2 da; *Career* BBC gen trainee incl attachments to Radio Ulster, Kaleidoscope, Everyman and Newsnight 1983, prodr and dir Bookmark, Omnibus, Arena and numerous music and arts programmes incl Made in Ealing and Philip Roth – My True Story 1985, fndr prodr The Late Show 1988, ed The Late Show 1990 (winner BP Arts Journalism Award), ed Bookmark 1992 (winner BAFTA Best Documentary award and Int Emmy nomination), exec prodr series incl A History of British Art, The House Detectives and How Buildings Learn 1993, devised and launched heritage magazine One Foot in the Past for BBC2, head of devpt music and arts with special responsibility for New Services BBC 1995, seconded to BBC Broadcast to develop factual channel propositions for BBC Worldwide/Flextech joint venture, head of programming UKTV 1997, overseer all new services incl BBC Choice and BBC Knowledge, controller Digital Channels BBC 1999, controller arts commissioning for all BBC TV channels 2000, controller BBC4 2001–04 (Channel of the Year MediaGuardian Edinburgh Int TV Festival), controller BBC2 2004–08, dir of archive content BBC 2008–12, chief exec Br Library 2012–; chair: Knowledge Quarter 2014–, Conference of European Nat Libraries 2015–; memb Bd Barbican Centre 2009–, tstee Turner Contemporary 2009–; hon PhD (univ of Lincoln 2013, univ of York (2014), univ of Warwick (2015); *Clubs* Soho House; *Style—* Roly Keating; ✉ British Library, 96 Euston Road, London NW1 2DB

KEATLEY, John Rankin Macdonald; s of James Walter Stanley Keatley (d 1978), of Royston, and Helen Rankin Thompson; *b* 20 August 1933; *Educ* Aldenham, RAC Cirencester; *m* 1964 (m dis 1980), Carolyn Margaret, da of Rodney Telford Morell, of Melbourne, Aust; 1 s (James b 1965), 1 da (Arabella (Mrs White) b 1967); *Career* 2 Lt Duke of Wellington's Regt, Korea 1952–53, Capt Hertfordshire Regt TA 1953–60, GS03 162 Brigade 1958; Parly candidate (Cons) Hemsworth 1964; leader Cambridge CC 1967–69; dir REA Holdings plc 1978–2015; chm: The Keatley Tst 1968–, Lansdowne Club 1979–97; fndr tstee Cambridge Museum of Technol 1970–2009, patron Decorative Arts Soc 1990–; pres: SW Cambridgeshire Cons Assoc 1987, S Cambridgeshire Cons Assoc 1999–2002, Arts Cncl of North Hertfordshire 1991–2000, Guild of Glass Engravers 2001–10 (patron 2010–); chm S Cambridgeshire Cons Fedn 2001–03; memb: Ctee Contemporary Art Soc 1989–95 (buyer 1990), Syndicate Fitzwilliam Museum Cambridge 1990–, Crafts Advsy Ctee Br Library Oral History Project 2004–; fndr patron Herts Heritage Fund 1988–; advsr to the Silver Tst (10 Downing St collection) 2015–; hon fell Guild of Designer Bookbinders 1989, assoc memb Worshipful Co of Goldsmiths 2014; Commonplace Reflections (2002), A Keatleian Miscellany (2006); *Recreations* art, music, gardening; *Style—* J R M Keatley, Esq; ✉ White Lodge, Melbourn, Royston, Hertfordshire SG8 6AF (☎ 01763 260680)

KEBEDE, HE Berhanu; *b* 11 April 1956, Addis Ababa; *Educ* Haile Selassie I Secdy Sch, Addis Ababa Univ, Free Univ of Brussels (MA); *m*; 3 c; *Career* Ethiopian diplomat; joined Miny of Foreign Affrs as Ethiopian-EEC rels desk offr 1978, economist Ethiopian Mission Brussels 1983, head Western European Div Miny of Foreign Affrs 1992–93, DG Int Orgn and Economic Cooperation Miny of Foreign Affrs 1992–2000, charge d'affaires Ethiopian embassy Russian Fedn 2000–02, ambass to Sweden, Norway, Denmark, Finland and Iceland 2002–06, ambass to Ct of St James's 2006–; *Style—* HE Mr Berhanu Kebede; ✉ Ethiopian Embassy, 17 Princes Gate, London SW7 1PZ (☎ 020 7838 3888)

KECK, Colleen; *b* 23 October 1958; *Educ* Univ of Saskatchewan (BA, LLB), Univ of London (LLM); *Career* corp lawyer specialising in IT, intellectual property (commercial) and pharmaceutical law; admitted slr and called to the Bar Alberta Canada 1983, admitted slr England and Wales 1988; articled student Bennett Jones Barristers and Solicitors Canada 1982–83, barr and slr Home Oil Co Ltd 1983–88, ptnr Allen & Overy 1992– (asst 1988–92); dep chm Copyright Tbnl 2011–; publisher/lectr on pharmaceutical, intellectual property, IT and media topics; memb: Law Soc of England and Wales, Law Soc of Alberta, Canadian Bar Assoc; *Style—* Ms Colleen Keck

KEEBLE, Giles; JP (2008); s of Thomas Whitfield Keeble (d 1994), and Ursula, *née* Scott-Morris; *b* 12 November 1949; *Educ* The King's Sch Canterbury, St John's Coll Cambridge (MA); *m* 1, 1981 (m dis 1988), Gillian, *née* Perry; 2 s (Nicholas, Sam); m 2, 1992, Caroline, *née* de Méric; 1 da (Fizzy), 2 step da (Polly, Chlöe); *Career* account handler JWT 1971–73, account mangr BMP 1973–75, sr account mangr and account planner FGA 1975–76; copywriter: FGA 1976–77, Abbott Mead Vickers 1978–81, WCRS 1981–88 (dir 1984); creative ptnr Leo Burnett 1994–95 (exec creative dir 1988–94), exec creative dir The Open Agency (Abbott Mead Vickers advertising and design subsid) 1996–99, gp creative dir Publicis Ltd 1999–2001, regnl creative dir Lowes Asia Pacific 2001–02, strategic and creative brand consultancy 2002–; winner various advertising industry awards; *Recreations* sport, music, reading, friends; *Clubs* Hawks' (Cambridge); *Style—* Giles Keeble, Esq, JP; ✉ e-mail giles.keeble@btinternet.com

K

KEEFE, Denis Edward Peter Paul; CMG (2016); s of John Victor Keefe (d 2005), and Oonagh Rose, *née* McAleer (d 2008); *b* 29 June 1958, Bury St Edmunds, Suffolk; *Educ* Campion Sch Hornchurch, Churchill Coll Cambridge (MA), Hertford Coll Oxford, Malmö Univ Sweden (distance); *m* 7 May 1983, Catherine Ann Mary, *née* Wooding; 3 s, 3 da; *Career* diplomat; Southern European Dept FCO 1982–83, 2 sec Prague 1984–88; FCO: 1 sec European Community Dept 1988–90, Germany desk offr Western European Dept 1990–91, European corr Common Foreign and Security Policy Dept 1991–92; head Political Section Nairobi 1992–95, dep head South Asia Dept FCO 1996–97, cnsllr and head Asia-Europe Meeting Unit FCO 1997–98, dep head of mission Prague 1998–2002, CONTEST team ldr Cabinet Office 2002–03, head China Hong Kong Dept FCO 2003–04, head Far East Gp 2004–06, ambass to Georgia 2007–10, dep head of mission Br Embassy Moscow 2010–14, ambass to Serbia 2014–; *Style—* HE Mr Denis Keefe, CMG; ✉ c/o FCO, King Charles Street, London SW1A 2AH

KEEFFE, Barrie Colin; s of late Edward Thomas Keeffe, and late Constance Beatrice, *née* Marsh; *b* 31 October 1945; *Educ* East Ham GS; *m* 1, 1969 (m dis 1979), Dee Sarah Truman; m 2, 1981, Verity Eileen Proud, *née* Bargate (d 1981); 2 step s; m 3, 1983 (m dis 1993), Julia Lindsay; m 4, 2012, Jacky Stoller; *Career* actor Nat Youth Theatre, journalist, writer in residence Shaw Theatre, resident playwright Royal Shakespeare Co 1978, assoc writer Theatre Royal Stratford East 1986–91; also theatre and radio plays dir; memb Bd of Dirs: Soho Theatre Co 1978–89, Theatre Royal Stratford 1989–91; tutor City Univ 2002–05; Judith E Wilson fell Christ's Coll Cambridge 2003–04, visiting tutor/patron in writing for performance Rusking Coll Oxford 2010–, writer in residence Univ of Kingston 2010–; UN ambass 1995; Hon DLitt Univ of Warwick 2010; *Theatre* Only a Game 1973, A Sight of Glory 1975, Scribes 1975, Here Comes the Sun 1976, Gimme Shelter 1977, A Mad World My Masters 1977, Barbarians 1977, Gotcha 1977, Frozen Assets 1978, Sus 1979, Bastard Angel 1980, She's So Modern 1980, Black Lear 1980, Chorus Girls 1981, Better Times 1985, King of England 1988, My Girl 1989, Not Fade Away 1990, Wild Justice 1990, I Only Want to be With You 1995, The Long Good Friday 1996, Shadows on The Sun 2001, Still Killing Time 2007, My Girl 2 2015; *Television* plays: The Substitute 1972, Gotcha 1977, Not Quite Cricket 1977, Nipper 1977, Champions 1978, Hanging Around 1978, Waterloo Sunset 1979, King 1984; TV series No Excuses 1983, Paradise 1991; *Films* The Long Good Friday 1981, SUS 2010; *Awards* French Critics Prix Revelation 1978, Giles Cooper Best Radio Plays 1980, Mystery Writers of America Edgar Allan Poe Award 1982; *Novels* Gadabout (1969), No Excuses (1983); *Recreations* origami; *Style—* Barrie Keeffe, Esq; ✉ 33 Brookfield, Highgate West Hill, London N6 6AT (e-mail barrie.okeeffe@gmail.com)

KEEGAN, Sir Donal Arthur John; KCVO (2012), OBE (1999); s of Daniel McManus Keegan, of Balliniska, Co Londonderry, and Geraldine, *née* Halpin (d 1979); *b* 8 October 1938; *Educ* St Columb's Coll Londonderry, Queen's Univ Belfast (BSc, MB BCh, BAO); *m* 5 March 1973, Elizabeth, *née* Nelson; 1 da (Rosemary Elizabeth Catriona b 6 Nov 1974); *Career* conslt physician Altnagelvin Hosp Londonderry 1975–2003 (now emeritus); visiting prof Faculty of Life and Health Scis Univ of Ulster 2008–13; chm: Regnl Advsy Ctee on Cancer 1997–2006, Central Med Advsy Ctee 1999–2003, NI Cncl for Postgrad Med and Dental Educn 1999–2004; med dir Med Distinction and Meritorious Serv Awards Ctee 2002–04; fndr memb Scottish Rehabilitation Gp 1971–75, memb Br Soc for Rheumatology 1970, memb BMA 1975; WHO Fellowship 1975; Hon Col 204 (N Irish) Field Hosp (V) 2005–11; pres RFCA NI 2009–13; HM Lord-Lt Londonderry 2002–13; Freeman City of London 2013; FRCPI 1973, FRCP 1989, FRCPEd 1990; *Publications* various papers on internal med and rheumatology; *Recreations* fishing, shooting; *Clubs* RSM; *Style—* Sir Donal Keegan, KCVO, OBE, FRCP; ✉ Auskaird, 5 Greenwood, Culmore, Londonderry BT48 8NP (☎ 028 7135 1292); Altnagelvin Hospital, Londonderry BT47 6SB (☎ 028 7134 5171)

KEEGAN, Sir John Desmond Patrick; kt (2000), OBE (1991); s of Francis Joseph Keegan (d 1975), of London, and Eileen Mary, *née* Bridgman (d 2001); *b* 15 May 1934; *Educ* King's

Coll Taunton, Wimbledon Coll, Balliol Coll Oxford (MA); *m* 10 Dec 1960, Susanne Ingeborg, da of Dr Thomas Everett, of Horsington, Somerset (d 1974); 2 da (Lucy Newmark b 1961, Rose Keegan b 1965), 2 s (Thomas b 1963, Matthew b 1965); *Career* sr lectr in war studies RMA Sandhurst 1960–86, defence ed Daily Telegraph 1986–; Lees Knowles lectr in mil history Cambridge 1986–87; cmmr Cwlth War Graves Cmmn 2001–; visitor Sexey's Hosp Bruton Somerset, tstee Nat Heritage Meml Fund 1999–2000; fell Princeton Univ 1984, Delmas distinguished prof of history Vassar Coll 1997; Reith lectr 1998; hon fell Balliol Coll Oxford 1999, Hon LLD Univ of New Brunswick 1997, Hon DLit Queen's Univ Belfast 2000, Hon DLitt Univ of Bath 2002, FRHistS, FRSL; *Books* The Face of Battle (1976), World Armies (1978), Six Armies in Normandy (1982), The Mask of Command (1987), The Price of Admiralty (1988), The Second World War (1989), A History of Warfare (1993, Duff Cooper prize 1993), Warpaths (1995), The Battle for History (1995), War and Our World, the Reith Lectures (1998), The First World War (1998, Westminster Medal), Intelligence in War (2003), The Iraq War (2004); *Clubs* Garrick, Beefsteak, Pratt's, The Brook (NY); *Style*— Sir John Keegan, OBE, FRSL; ✉ The Manor House, Kilmington, Warminster, Wiltshire BA12 6RD (☎ 01985 844856); The Daily Telegraph, 1 Canada Square, Canary Wharf, London E14 5DT (☎ 020 7538 5000)

KEEGAN, Nicholas Francis; s of J P Keegan (d 1977), of IOM, and C H Keegan, *née* Glynn (d 1993); *b* 16 September 1955, Solihull; *Educ* Douai Sch Woolhampton, CCC Oxford (MA); *m* 10 Oct 1992, Sally Anne, *née* Woodburn; 2 da (Louise Harriet b 2 Aug 1993, Caroline Vivien b 18 Apr 1995); *Career* Price Waterhouse London 1978–82, Hill Samuel & Co Ltd 1982–87, Barclays de Zoete Wedd Ltd 1987–92 (dir corp fin 1990–92); gp fin dir: Newman Tonks Gp plc 1992–97, Frederick Cooper plc 1997–2001, Evenser Gp Ltd 2001–04; chief fin offr CompAir Holdings Ltd 2005–09, fin dir Egbert Taylor Gp Ltd 2013–14; non-exec dir: Interserve plc 2003–09, Staffline Recruitment Gp plc 2004–14; hon treas SENSE Nat Deafblind and Rubella Assoc 2011–; FCA 1991; *Recreations* opera, swimming, tennis; *Clubs* Oxford and Cambridge; *Style*— Nicholas Keegan, Esq; ✉ Alderminster Lodge, Stratford-upon-Avon, Warwickshire CV37 8NY (☎ 01789 450493, fax 01789 450148, e-mail nick.keegan@btinternet.com)

KEEGAN, William James Gregory; CBE (2009); s of William Patrick Keegan (d 1995), of Durham, and Julia Sheila, *née* Buckley (d 1976); *b* 3 July 1938; *Educ* Wimbledon Coll, Trinity Coll Cambridge (MA); *m* 1, 7 Feb 1967 (m dis 1982), Tessa, *née* Young (wid of John Ashton); 2 s, 2 da; m 2, 24 Oct 1992, Hilary Stonefrost , *qv*, da of Maurice Stonefrost, CBE, DL, and Audrey Stonefrost; 2 da (Caitlin Clare b 5 Sept 1994, Lucinda Grace Julia b 18 Dec 1997), 1 s (James Patrick William (twin) b 18 Dec 1997); *Career* Nat Serv 5 Royal Tank Regt RASC (cmmnd 1958) 1957–59; journalist: Financial Times 1963–64, Daily Mail and News Chronicle 1964–67; economics corr Financial Times 1967–76, worked Econ Intelligence Dept Bank of England 1976–77, economics ed The Observer 1977–2003 (assoc ed 1982–2003, sr economics commentator 2003–); memb: BBC Advsy Ctee on Business and Industrial Affrs 1981–88, Cncl Employment Inst 1987–92, Advsy Bd Dept of Applied Economics Univ of Cambridge 1988–92, Nat Cncl The Catalyst Forum, Advsy Bd Mile End Gp Queen Mary Univ of London 2011–; chm Bd Contributing Edn OMFIF (Official Monetary and Financial Instns Forum) 2010–; visiting prof of journalism Univ of Sheffield 1989– (hon res fell 1990–), visiting prof of economics Queen Mary Univ of London 2012–14, visiting prof KCL 2015–; govr NIESR 1998–; Hon DLitt: Univ of Sheffield 1995, City Univ 1998; *Books* fiction: Consulting Father Wintergreen (1974), A Real Killing (1976); non-fiction: Who Runs The Economy (jtly, 1978), Mrs Thatcher's Economic Experiment (1984), Britain Without Oil (1985), Mr Lawson's Gamble (1989), The Spectre of Capitalism (1992), 2066 And All That (2000), The Prudence of Mr Gordon Brown (2003), Saving the World? Gordon Brown Reconsidered (2012), Mr Osborne's Economic Experiment (2015); *Clubs* Garrick, MCC; *Style*— William Keegan, Esq, CBE; ✉ 76 Lofting Road, Islington, London N1 1JB (☎ 020 7607 3590); The Observer, King's Place, 90 York Way, London N1 9GU (☎ 07775 620410)

KEEHAN, Hon Mr Justice; Sir Michael Joseph Keehan; kt (2013), QC (2001); *Educ* Univ of Birmingham (LLB); *m* 16 July 1988, Sarah, *née* Monk; 2 da (Bethany b 3 April 1990, Eleanor b 13 Aug 1990); *Career* called to the Bar Middle Temple 1982; recorder 2000, judge of the High Court of Justice (Family Div) 2013–; *Recreations* gardening, music, reading, travel, walking; *Style*— The Hon Mr Justice Keehan; ✉ Royal Courts of Justice, Strand, London WC2A 2LL

KEELEY, Barbara; MP; da of Edward Keeley (d 2003), of Leeds, and Joan Keeley (d 1995); *Educ* Mount St Mary's Coll Leeds, Univ of Salford (BA); *m* Colin Huggett; *Career* systems engr IBM until 1989 (latterly field systems engrg mangr), ind conslt in community regeneration and orgn devpt 1990–94 and 1995–2001, area mangr Business in the Community 1994–95, conslt and advsr to Princess Royal Tst for Carers 2001–05; MP (Lab): Worsley 2005–10, Worsley and Eccles S 2010–; PPS to Rt Hon Harret Harman QC, MP (as Min for Women) 2007–08, memb Finance and Servs Ctee 2006–, chair Women's PLP Ctee 2007–08, govt asst whip HM Treasy 2008–09, dep ldr of the House of Commons 2009–10, shadow financial sec to the Treasy 2015, shadow min for older people, socail care and carers 2016–; cncllr Trafford MBC 1995–2004; dir Pathfinder Children's Tst Trafford 2002–04; memb: GMB, Fabian Soc, Amnesty Int; *Recreations* jogging, swimming, listening to live music; *Style*— Ms Barbara Keeley, MP; ✉ House of Commons, London SW1A 0AA (☎ 020 7219 8025, website www.barbarakeeley.co.uk); Constituency Office ☎ 0161 799 4159

KEELING, Christopher Anthony Gedge; s of Sir Edward Keeling, MC, MP, DL (d 1954), of London, and Martha Ann, *née* Darling (d 1988); *b* 15 June 1930; *Educ* Eton, RMA Sandhurst; *m* 1, 20 Sept 1955 (m dis 1972), Veronica, da of Alec Waugh, writer (d 1980), of Edrington, Berks; 2 s (Simon Alexander Edward d 1982, Julian James), 1 da (Nicola Sara); m 2, 1974, Rachael Macdonald; *Career* Capt Grenadier Gds 1948–56; dir and chm various Lloyd's Agency Cos; Freeman City of London, Liveryman Worshipful Co of Fishmongers 1955; ACII; *Recreations* shooting, reading, watching cricket; *Clubs* White's, MCC, Beefsteak, City of London; *Style*— Christopher Keeling, Esq; ✉ Leyden House, Thames Bank, London SW14 7QR (☎ 020 8876 7375); Hampden Agencies Limited, 85 Gracechurch Street, London EC3V 0AA (☎ 020 7863 6542, fax 020 7863 6728, e-mail christopher.keeling@hampden.co.uk)

KEELING, Dr John David; s of David Keeling, of Worthing, W Sussex, and Helen, *née* Weir; *b* 31 October 1958, Aberdeen; *Educ* Trinity Sch Croydon, Guy's Hosp Med Sch, KCH Med Sch (MB BS), Keele Univ (MBA); *m* 2 Aug 1980, Catherine, *née* Tanguy; 1 da (Elizabeth Helen Moncur b 31 Dec 1983), 1 s (James Edward David b 3 April 1985); *Career* RMO 9/12L 1985–87, RMO 8 Regt RCT 1987–88, RMO 14/20KH 1990, RMO 6GR 1990–92, SMO Celle 1992–93, SMO ATR Pirbright 1993–97, CO 22 Field Hosp 1997–99, SO1 Med NATO Surgn Gens Dept 1999–2000, SMO ATR Pirbright 2000–01, clinical servs dir Army Primary Healthcare Serv 2003–07, DACOS Med HQ LAND 2007–08, D Healthcare 2008–11, dir APHCS 2011–13; memb Cncl BMA 2000–08, chm BMA Pension Tstees Ltd 2003– (dir 2002–); DRCOG 1990, FRCGP 2004 (MRCGP 1988); *Recreations* reading, wine, music, visual arts, fly fishing; *Style*— Dr John Keeling; ✉ BMA Pension Trustees Ltd, BMA House, Tavistock Square, London WC1H 9JP

KEEN, Nigel John; s of Peter John Keen (d 1985), and Margaret Alice, *née* Peach (d 2010); *b* 21 January 1947; *Educ* Charterhouse, Peterhouse Cambridge (MA); *m* 2 Sept 1972, Caroline Jane, *née* Cumming; 2 s (Dominic John b 22 March 1977, Thomas Christopher b 30 Jan 1990); *Career* auditor Touche Ross & Co 1968–74, dir European Banking Co Ltd 1974–83; chm: Cygnus Gp of Cos 1983–2001, Oxford Instruments plc 1999–2016, Axis-Shield plc 1999–2010, Deltex Medical Gp plc 2000–, Laird plc 2000–14, Bioquell plc 2009–16, Syncona Ptnrs LLP 2013–, Oxford University Innovation Ltd 2014–, Oxford Academic Health Sci Network 2013–; dir Channel Islands Development Corp Ltd 1998–2007; tstee David Shepherd Wildlife Fndn 1999–; FCA 1979, FIET 2011; *Recreations* opera, golf; *Clubs* HAC; *Style*— Nigel Keen, Esq; ✉ Syncona Partners, 215 Euston Road, London NW1 2BE (☎ 020 7611 2031, e-mail n.keen@synconapartners.com)

KEEN, Baron (Life Peer UK 2015) of Elie in Fife; Richard Sanderson Keen; QC (Scot 1993); s of Derek Michael Keen, of Wester Balgedie, Kinross-Shire, and Jean, *née* Sanderson; *b* 29 March 1954; *Educ* King's Sch Rochester, Univ of Edinburgh (Beckman scholar, LLB); *m* 7 April 1980, Jane Carolyn, da of Dr William Marr Anderson; 1 s (Jamie Marr Sanderson b 29 Sept 1983), 1 da (Sophie Jane b 29 Sept 1985); *Career* called to the Bar Middle Temple 2010 (bencher); admitted Faculty of Advocates 1980, standing jr counsel DTI Scotland 1986–93; treas Faculty of Advocates 2006–07 (dean of faculty 2007–14); chm Scottish Cons and Unionist Pty 2014–15; tstee Nat Library of Scotland; Advocate Gen for Scotland 2015–; *Recreations* opera, golf, shooting, skiing; *Clubs* New (Edinburgh), Golf House (Elie), Hon Co of Edinburgh Golfers (Muirfield), Royal and Ancient Golf Club of St Andrews; *Style*— The Lord Keen of Elie, QC; ✉ Private Office of the Advocate General, Dover House, Whitehall, London SW1A 2AU; 27 Ann Street, Edinburgh EH4 1PL; The Castle, Elie, Fife KY9 1DN (e-mail rsk@rskeenqc.com)

KEENE, Rt Hon Sir David Wolfe; kt (1994), PC (2000); s of Edward Henry Wolfe Keene (d 1987), and Lilian Marjorie, *née* Conway; *b* 15 April 1941; *Educ* Hampton GS, Balliol Coll Oxford (Eldon scholar, BA, BCL, Winter Williams prize), Inner Temple (Public Int Law prize); *m* 1965, Gillian Margaret, da of Geoffrey Lawrance; 1 da (Harriet Margaret b 1968), 1 s (Edward Geoffrey Wolfe b 1970); *Career* called to the Bar Inner Temple 1964 (bencher 1987, treas 2006); QC 1980–94, recorder of the Crown Court 1989–94, judge of the High Court of Justice (Queen's Bench Div) 1994–2000 (dep High Ct judge 1993), Lord Justice of Appeal 2000–09; judge Employment Appeal Tbnl 1994–2000, dep pres QFC Civil and Commercial Court Qatar 2011–13, chm QFC Regulatory Tbnl Qatar 2013–; arbitrator Kuala Lumpur Regnl Centre for Arbitration 2014–; chm Argentum Capital Ltd 2012–14; visitor Brunel Univ 1995–2000; chm Examination-in-Public Cumbria Structure Plan 1980, inspector County Hall (London) Public Inquiry 1987, chm Planning Bar Assoc 1994, sometime memb Final Selection Bd Planning Inspectorate DOE, memb QC Selection Panel 2010–12, memb Arbitrators Panel Sport Resolutions 2011–; chm Judicial Studies Bd 2003–07 (memb 1998–, chm Equal Treatment Advsy Ctee 1998–2003), memb Bowman Ctee on the Crown Office 1999–2000, memb Bd Sch of Advanced Studies London Univ 2007–10; memb Exec Ctee Amnesty International (Br section) 1965–68; tstee: Oxford Philomusica 2009–, Slynn Fndn 2010–; Hon LLD Brunel Univ 2000, hon fell: Soc for Advanced Legal Studies 1998– (chm Planning Law Reform Gp), Balliol Coll Oxford 2004; ACIArb 2010; *Books* The Adult Criminal (co-author 1967); *Clubs* Athenaeum, Garrick; *Style*— The Rt Hon Sir David Keene; ✉ 39 Essex Chambers, 81 Chancery Lane, London WC2A 1DD

KEENE, Gareth John; s of Victor Horace Keene (d 1993), and Muriel Olive, *née* Whitehead (d 2002); *b* 31 March 1944; *Educ* Tonbridge, St John's Coll Cambridge (Choral scholar, MA, LLM); *m* 1, 1969 (m dis 1983), Georgina Garrett Thomas; 3 s (Timothy b 1973, David b 1975, Jonathan b 1979); m 2, 1983, Charlotte Louise, da of Peter Frank Lester (d 1985), of Devon; *Career* called to the Bar Gray's Inn 1966; sec Allen & Hanburys Ltd 1968–73, admin Dartington Coll of Arts 1973–78 (govr 1989–2008, vice-chm 2001–08), sec The Dartington Hall Tst 1978–83; dir: TSW Television South West Holdings plc 1980–92, Gamida for Life BV Netherlands 1989–2009; chm: Gamidor Technical Services Ltd 1994–2015, Evans Estates (1956) Ltd 2007–2014; chm: EU Chamber Orchestra Tst 1995–, Beaford Arts Centre 1987–2002 (tstee 1980–2002), Dartington N Devon Fndn 2002– (tstee 1991–), SW Film and Television Archive 2006–08 (tstee 1992–2008); govr Judd Sch 2007–15; tstee: IMS Prussia Cove 1983–90, Dartington Int Summer Sch Fndn 2008–; FRSM; *Books* Sacred and Secular (with Adam Fox, 1975); *Recreations* singing, small holding, travel; *Style*— Gareth Keene, Esq; ✉ Buttermead, Manaton, Newton Abbot, Devon TQ13 9XG (☎ and fax 01647 221208, e-mail gareth@gckeene.com); Windy Edge, Concordia, Tobago, West Indies (☎ and fax 001 868 639 5596)

KEENE, Martin Elliott; MVO (2007); s of John Keene, and Pamela, *née* Richards; *b* 8 September 1957; *Educ* Felsted, Sidney Sussex Coll Cambridge (BA); *Career* photographer: Torquay Herald Express 1978–82, Torbay News Agency 1982–87; The Press Association: joined as staff photographer 1987, special responsibility for royal coverage 1990, chief photographer 1992–95, picture ed 1995, currently head of pictures; *Books* Practical Photojournalism – a professional guide (1993); *Style*— Martin Keene, Esq, MVO; ✉ The Press Association, 292 Vauxhall Bridge Road, London SW1V 1AE

KEENE, Raymond Dennis; OBE (1985); s of Dennis Arthur Keene (d 1992), of Worthing, W Sussex, and Doris Anita, *née* Leat (d 1969); Grant of Arms College of Arms 2007; *b* 29 January 1948; *Educ* Dulwich Coll, Trinity Coll Cambridge (MA); *m* 1974, Annette Sara, da of Dr Walter Goodman; 1 s (Alexander Philip Simon b 21 March 1991); *Career* chess corr: The Spectator 1977–, The Times 1985–, Thames Television 1986–90, Channel 4 TV 1993–, Classic FM Radio 1993–, Sunday Times 1996– International Herald Tribune 2001–2008; columnist: daily The Times 1997–, weekly IQ 1997–, The Australian, The Daily Yomiuri, The Gulf News; chess contrib to Encyclopaedia Britannica; memb Eng Olympic chess team 1966, 1968, 1970, 1972, 1974, 1976, 1978 and 1980, Br Chess Champion 1971, Olympic Bronze medal 1976, Bronze medal Euro Team Championship Skara Sweden 1980, Gold Medal EEC Team Championship Berlin 1980, Bronze medal Cwlth Chess Championship Melbourne 1983; dep chm Braingames Asia 2002–, dir Hardinge/Simpole Publishing 2002–; winner various int chess tournaments: Johannesburg 1973, Camagüey (Cuba) 1974, Alicante 1977, Sydney 1979, Dortmund 1980, London (Lloyds Masters) 1981, Adelaide 1983, Valletta 1985; chess grandmaster 1976 (life title); chief organiser: World Chess Championship between Kasparov and Karpov London 1986, World Memory Championship London 1991, World Draughts Championship London 1992, second World Memory Championship London 1993, World Chess Championship between Kasparov and Short London 1993, World Draughts Championship Human v Computer Boston 1994, third World Memory Championship London 1994, World Chess Championship between Kasparov and Kramnik London 2000; organiser: First Mind Sports Olympiad Royal Festival Hall 1997, Second Mind Sports Olympiad London 1998, Third Mind Sports Olympiad London 1999, seven Brighton Int Chess Tournaments (with Julian Simpole), World Memory Championships Kingdom of Bahrain (with Tony Buzan) 1991–2008, 19th and 20th World Memory Championships Guangzhou 2010–11, 21st and 22nd World Memory Championship London, 23rd World Memory Championship Hainan, 24th World Memory Championship Chengdu; Int Arbiter Mental World Records, World Chess Federation-Fide-Official Organiser, World Chess Federation Int Arbiter, organiser Brain of the Year Award 2013 and 2014, organiser 23rd World Memory Championship Hainan China 2014; ceo Mind Sports Olympiad 1998, fndr IMPALA London Ltd (Int Media Prodn and Literary Activities) 2005, fndr and sole prop Impala Films 2006; dir: Festival of the Mind Int Brain Trust Charity, Outside Inside Pathways 2013–, World Peace and Prosperity Fndn 2013–, chm Howard Staunton Soc 2003–; Freeman City of London 2001, Officer of the Companionate of the White Swan 2014, Officer of the Order des Coteaux de Champagne, Commander's Cross Companionate of the White Swan 2015, Archivist and Grand Cross of Justice of the Autonomous Grand Priory of the Military and Hospitaller Order of St Lazarus of Jerusalem, ennoblement to the rank of Count of Torres Vedras by the House of Saxe-Coburgo-Braganca 2015; *Books* author of 199 books on chess (world record), art criticism, thinking and genius incl:

Duels of the Mind, Kingfisher Pocket Book of Chess, Batsford Chess Openings (with Garry Kasparov), Buzan's Book of Genius (co-author); Official Biography of Tony Buzan (2013), Lorraine Gill The 10th Muse (2014); *Recreations* attending ballet, theatre, opera, collecting modern British art; *Clubs* RAC, Garrick; *Style*— Raymond Keene, Esq, OBE; ✉ 86 Clapham Common North Side, London SW4 9SE (✆ 020 7228 7009, fax 020 7924 6472); The Times, The News Building, 1 London Bridge Street, London SE1 9SF (e-mail rdkobe@aol.com)

KEENS, David Wilson; s of Wilson Leonard Keens (d 1959), and Olive Ivy, *née* Collins; *b* 16 August 1953; *m* (m dis 2009), Shirley Ann, da of Cyril Charles Cardnell; 1 s (Benjamin David b 17 Nov 1983), 1 da (Emma Louise b 15 Oct 1985); *Career* Gale Brown & Co Essex: articled clerk 1970–75, chartered accountant 1975–77; successively chief fin offr (Tunis), fin controller (Liverpool), fin dir (Lancs) and planning dir and treas (Berks) RJR Nabisco Inc 1977–86, dir of treasy then gp fin dir Next plc 1986–2015; non-exec dir and audit chair J Sainsbury 2015–, non-exec dir, sr ind dir and audit chair Auto Trader plc 2015–; FCCA, MCT; *Style*— David Keens, Esq; ✉ e-mail davidwkeens@gmail.com

KEEYS, Geoffrey Foster; s of Richard Kipling Foster Keeys, and Joan, *née* Anderson; *b* 29 October 1944; *Educ* Abingdon Sch, Univ of Manchester (LLB); *m* 4 April 1970, Christine Mary (Donna), da of Henry Albert Lavers, of Newbury, Berks; 1 da (Georgia Ellen b 22 May 1974), 1 s (Henry Foster b 16 April 1976); *Career* graduate trainee Mobil Oil 1966–68, various personnel positions to dir of personnel and industrial relations (Europe and rest of world) Massey Ferguson 1968–82, dir Gp Personnel Chubb & Son plc 1982–84, dir Personnel and Business Servs Prudential Corporation plc 1984–95, vice-chm Strategic Thinking Gp 1995–, dir Incite Solutions Ltd 2007–; angel investor 2004–; non-exec dir HM Prison Service until 1993–95; memb Advsy Bd Fredericks Fndn Glos 2014–, tstee Water City Music 2016–; memb IOD, FIPM; *Recreations* national hunt horse racing, golf, cricket; *Style*— Geoffrey Keeys; ✉ Strategic Thinking Group, 180 Piccadilly, London W1J 9HF (✆ 020 7917 2867)

KEHOE, Catherine; da of Wayne Rathwell (d 2012), and Ann, *née* McKenzie; *b* 21 November 1968, Croydon, Surrey; *Educ* Univ of London (BA); *m* 1, 1994, Jeffrey Kehoe; 2 s (Dominic b 15 Oct 1994, Laurence b 9 Sept 1996); m 2, 12 Oct 2008, Jason Smith; 1 s (James b 15 Jan 2009); *Career* head of brand communications Royal and Sun Alliance 1991–2000, head of strategy and mktg and head of mktg communications BT 2000–05, mktg dir Yell Ltd 2005–07; Lloyds Banking Gp: brand and mktg dir Lloyds TSB and Bank of Scotland 2007–11, gp brands and mktg dir 2011–13, md brand and mktg 2013–; memb: Financial Services Forum 2008, Mktg Soc 2008, ISBA 2011, Mktg Gp of GB; *Style*— Ms Catherine Kehoe; ✉ Lloyds Banking Group, 7th Floor, Bishopsgate Exchange, 155 Bishopsgate, London EC2M 3YB (✆ 07730 426246, e-mail catherine.kehoe@lloydsbanking.com)

KEIGHLEY, Prof Michael Robert Burch; s of Rev Dr R A S Keighley, TD (d 1988), and Dr J V Keighley, *née* Burch (d 2000); *b* 12 October 1943; *Educ* Monkton Combe Sch, Bart's Med Coll London (MB BS, MS), Univ of Durham (MA); *m* 27 Sept 1969, Dr D Margaret Keighley, MBE, da of J H Shepley (d 1985); 1 da (Helen Louise b 28 Oct 1971), 1 s (Nicholas John Alexander b 23 Jan 1974); *Career* Univ of Birmingham: prof of gastrointestinal surgery 1985–88, Barling prof and head Dept of Surgery 1988–2004, emeritus prof (also prof CMC Vellore S India); Hunterarian prof RCS 1976, Jacksonian prize RCS 1980, Boerhaave prof of surgery Univ of Leiden 1985, Eybers visiting prof Univ of Bloemfontein 1988, visiting prof Harvard Univ 1990, Penman visiting prof Univ of Cape Town 1991, Alan Parks visiting prof St Marks' London 1995, Turnbull visiting prof Univ of Washington 1997, Henry Bacon prof Indian Surgical Assoc 1997, visiting prof Hong Kong and China 1999, visiting prof Karolinska Inst Stockholm 2001; chm: Public Affairs Ctee United European Gastroenterology Fedn (UEGF) 2001–05, PR and Ethics Ctee Assoc of Coloproctology of GB & I (ACPGBI) 2002–05; treas and memb Cncl Br Jl of Surgery 1995–2001; chm and pres Bowel Disease Research Fndn 2003–08 (currently tstee); memb: American Soc of Colorectal Surgns (Int Community Impact Award 2008), Br Soc of Gastroenterology (formerly memb Cncl), Coloproctology Section RSM (formerly pres and memb Cncl), Cncl Surgical Res Soc, Assoc of Surgns of GB & I; hon fell Brazilian Coll of Surgns, hon fell Royal Australasian Coll of Surgns, hon memb Portuguese Soc of Surgery; pres MASIC Fndn 2016; reader C of E; FRSC (Edinburgh) 1970, FRCS 1971; *Books* Antimicrobial Prophylaxis in Surgery (1980), Inflammatory Bowel Diseases (1983, 1990 and 1997), Gastrointestinal Haemorrhage (1985), Textbook of Gastroenterology (1986 and 1993), Surgery of the Anus, Rectum & Colon (1993, 1999, 2008 and 2016), Atlas of Colorectal Surgery (1996), Flesh and Bones: Surgery; *Recreations* painting, music, writing, travel, botany, walking, sailing; *Clubs* RSM, Athenaeum; *Style*— Prof Michael Keighley; ✉ Whalebone Cottage, Vicarage Hill, Tanworth in Arden, Warwickshire B94 5AN (✆ 01564 741865, e-mail keighleycolo@btinternet.com)

KEIL, Charles George; *b* 7 March 1933; *Educ* St Bartholomew's GS Newbury, QMC London (BSc(Eng)); *m* 23 April 1960, Janette Catherine; 1 da (Fiona b 1962), 2 s (Duncan b 1963, Ewan b 1964); *Career* fighter pilot RAF 1951–55, Flt Lt; served Canada, Germany, France, Cyprus; ed of monthly aviation jl Aircraft Engineering 1959–65, assoc ed (London) Indian Aviation 1963–66, gp ed Thomas Reed Pubns Ltd 1965–66, dir John Fowler & Ptnrs Ltd (PR conslts) 1966–73, md Harrison Cowley PR Birmingham Ltd 1974–94, chm Harrison Cowley Ltd 1988–2001, chm Brumhalata Storytelling Co 1995–99, chm Tindal Street Press 2000–02; dir Nat Acad of Writing 1998–2003; chm Birmingham Readers' and Writers' Festival 1992–96, mktg dir Birmingham Centre for Drama 1994–95, dir Birmingham Rep Theatre 2001–07; mktg advsr Business in the Arts 1992–2002, session ldr Understanding Industry 1992–2000, memb Servs Ctee Birmingham City 2000 1995–98, memb New Partners Ctee Arts and Business 2001–05, memb Friends Ctee Barber Inst of Fine Arts 2010–15; judge RTS Midlands Centre Awards 1996–2004; govr St George's Sch Edgbaston 2006–08; MRAeS, CEng; *Books* Aerodynamics (jt ed and trans with Janette C Loder, textbook), Sabre – from the Cockpit; *Recreations* reading, golf, theatre-going, music, aviation; *Clubs* RAF; *Style*— Charles Keil, Esq; ✉ Illyria, 536 Streetsbrook Road, West Midlands B91 1RD (✆ 0121 705 0773, e-mail charlesgkeil@aol.com)

KEIR, Colin; s of John Keir, and Catherine, *née* Bonnar; *b* 9 December 1959, Edinburgh; *Educ* Craigmount HS Edinburgh; *Career* memb City of Edinburgh Cncl 2007– (convener Regulatory Ctee 2007–11), MSP (SNP) Edinburgh Western 2011–16; co-convener Cross Pty Gp on Taiwan 2011–16, convener Cross Pty Gp on Aviation 2012–16; ordinary memb Cross Pty Gp on: China 2011–16, Germany 2011–16; non-exec dir EDI Gp 2009–11, dir East Craigs Office Supplies; convener Mgmnt Ctee Pentland Hills Regnl Park 2007–11; Scottish Schs 500m champion 1977; *Recreations* golf, football, rugby, fly fishing; *Clubs* RHC Cougars Rugby; *Style*— Colin Keir, Esq; ✉ Ankerdoon, 16 Alvah Terrace, Banff, Aberdeenshire, Scotland AB45 1BG

KEIRLE, David Alan; s of Alan George Keirle, of St Albans, Hertfordshire, and Frances, *née* Windsor (d 1966); *b* 19 October 1955; *Educ* Borehamwood GS, Poly of the South Bank (BA), RIBA (postgrad Dip Arch); *m* 1982, Lesley Anne, da of Charles Edwards; 3 s (Matthew Alan b 1986, Simon Alexander b 1988, Nicholas Andrew b 1991); *Career* Newan Levinson Ltd: joined 1977, chartered architect 1983, ptnr 1986, dir 1987; formed Keirle Salter Simons Architects 1991, fndr and chm KSS Design Gp; projects incl Basketball Arena Building for London 2012 Olympics; ARIBA 1983; *Recreations* family, flying, skiing; *Style*— David Keirle, Esq; ✉ KSS Design Group, 1 James Street, London W1U 1DR

KEITH, Dame Penelope Anne Constance; DBE (2014, CBE 2007, OBE 1989), DL; da of Frederick Arthur William Hatfield, and Constance Mary, *née* Nutting; *b* 2 April 1940; *Educ* Webber Douglas Acad; *m* 1978, Rodney Timson; *Career* actress; worked in repertory Chesterfield, Lincoln, Manchester and Salisbury, seasons with RSC; pres Actors' Benevolent Fund 1989; pro-chllr Univ of Surrey; govr Queen Elizabeth's Fndn for the Disabled People 1990, patron Guildford Sch of Acting; tstee Yvonne Arnaud Theatre Guildford; memb HFEA 1990; High Sheriff Surrey 2002–03; *Theatre* roles incl: Maggie Howard in Suddenly at Home (Fortune) 1971, Sarah in The Norman Conquests (Greenwich and Globe) 1974, Lady Driver in Donkey's Years 1976, Orinthia in The Apple Cart (Chichester and Phoenix) 1977, Epifania in the Millionairess (Haymarket) 1982, Sarah in Moving (Queen's) 1981, Maggie in Hobson's Choice (Haymarket) 1982, Lady Cicely Waynflete in Captain Brassbound's Conversion (Haymarket) 1982, Judith Bliss in Hayfever (Queen's) 1983, The Dragon's Tail (Apollo) 1985, Miranda (Chichester) 1987, The Deep Blue Sea (Haymarket) 1988, Dear Charles (Yvonne Arnaud Theatre) 1990, The Merry Wives of Windsor (Chichester) 1990, The Importance of Being Earnest 1992, On Approval, Glyn and It (all Yvonne Arnaud Theatre) 1994, Good Grief (Theatre Royal Bath) 1998, Monsieur Amilcar (Chichester), Star Quality (Apollo) 2001–02, Time and the Conways (Theatre Royal Bath) 2003–04, Blithe Spirit (Savoy) 2004–05, Importance of Being Ernest (Vaudeville) 2008, The Rivals (Haymarket) 2011, The Way of the World (Chichester) 2012; dir: Relatively Speaking 1992, How the Other Half Loves 1994, Mrs Warren's Profession (Yvonne Arnaud Theatre) 1997; *Television* Six Shades of Black, Kate, The Pallisters, Jackanory, Saving it for Albie, The Morecambe and Wise Christmas Show, Tickle on the Tum, Woof, The Good Life, To the Manor Born, Law and Disorder, Sweet Sixteen, Executive Stress, No Job for a Lady, Next of Kin, Coming Home, Private Lives, Waters of the Moon, On Approval, Death Comes to Pemberley; former presenter: What's My Line, Capability Brown, Growing Places, Behind the Scenes; *Film* The Priest of Love; *Awards* BAFTA 1976 and 1977, SWET 1976, Variety Club of GB 1976 and 1979, Pye Female Comedy Star 1977, Radio Industries 1978 and 1979, Daily Express 1979/80/81/82, BBC TV Swap Shop 1977–78 and 1979–80, TV Times 1976, 1977–78, 1979–80, 1983 and 1988, United States TV and Radio Mobius 1988; *Style*— Dame Penelope Keith, DBE, DL; ✉ c/o Actors' Benevolent Fund, 6 Adam Street, London WC2N 6AD (✆ 020 7836 6378, fax 020 7836 8978)

KEITH-LUCAS, Peter; s of Prof Bryan Keith-Lucas, and Mary Keith-Lucas; *Educ* Bradfield Coll, The Queen's Coll Oxford (MA); *Career* admitted slr 1976; chief exec Medina BC 1988–89, dir of central servs Swansea CC 1989–96, dir of legal and admin servs City and Co of Swansea 1996–97, ptnr (local govt) Wragge & Co 1997–; lectr on local govt law, constitutions and probity; Society of Town Clerks Prize for Local Govt Law 1976; pres Assoc of Cncl Secs and Slrs 1996–97; *Books* The Monitoring Officer, Facilitating Executive Government (2002); *Recreations* tennis, sailing; *Clubs* Swansea Lawn Tennis and Squash Racquets, Priory (Edgbaston); *Style*— Peter Keith-Lucas, Esq; ✉ 50 Greenfield Road, Harborne, Birmingham B17 0EG (✆ 0121 244 3472); Wragge & Co, 55 Colmore Row, Birmingham B3 2AS (✆ 0121 214 1084, fax 0121 214 1099, mobile 07767 256566)

K

KELJIK, Christopher Avedis; OBE (2006); s of Garbis Keljik (d 1984), and Suzanne Keljik (d 2007); *b* 1948; *Educ* Merchant Taylors', Univ of Kent (BA), Stanford Univ (Sr Exec Prog); *m* 1978, Doreen; 2 s (James, Edward); *Career* CA; Ball Baker Deed, Deloitte Haskins and Sells, Standard Chartered; sr ind dir: Foreign & Colonial Investment Trust 2005–, Millennium & Copthorne Hotels plc 2006–12, Asian Total Return Investment Co plc 2007–; non-exec dir: Jardine Lloyd Thompson plc 2005–10, Sanditon Investment Tst plc 2014–, Waverton Investment Mgmnt 2014–; FCA 1979; *Recreations* music, travel; *Clubs* Travellers; *Style*— Christopher Keljik, Esq, OBE

KELLEHER, Patricia Mary (Tricia); *b* 17 March 1962; *Educ* Grays Convent RC Comp Sch, Palmer's Sixth Form Coll Grays, Lady Margaret Hall Oxford (MA), Univ of Nottingham (PGCE), Univ of Sussex (MA); *Career* history teacher Haberdashers' Aske's Sch for Girls Elstree 1985–88; Brighton & Hove GDST: asst history teacher 1988–92, head of year 7 1990–97, head of history 1992–97; dep headmistress Brentwood Sch 1997–2001, princ Stephen Perse Fndn 2001–; *Recreations* theatre, cinema, music, travel, walking; *Style*— Miss Tricia Kelleher; ✉ The Stephen Perse Foundation, Union Road, Cambridge CB2 1HF

KELLEY, John Victor; s of William Kelley (d 1988), and Beatrice, *née* Armitage (d 1984); *b* 20 February 1947; *Educ* Harold Hill GS; *m* 1974 (sep), Anne; 1 s (John William b 28 Feb 1980), 1 da (Rosemary Anne b 26 June 1982); *Career* jr art dir Brunning Advertising 1963–66; copywriter: Foote Cone & Belding 1966–69, PKL (later BBDO) 1969–75, Collett Dickensen Pearce 1976–81 (rising to gp head); fndr ptnr Lowe Howard Spink 1981–82, copywriter/bd dir Abbott Mead Vickers 1982–83, creative dir Geers Gross 1983–85, vice-chm and exec creative dir Abbott Mead Vickers 1985–93, creative dir Publicis 1993–95, vice-chm and sr creative TBWA 1996–97, jt creative dir TBWA Simons Palmer 1997–98, exec creative dir (Ford Europe) Ogilvy & Mather 1998–; D&AD Silver Awards for: best 15 sec TV commercial (Great Northern Bitter) 1973, most outstanding direction of TV campaign (Daily Express) 1977, most outstanding 45 sec TV commercial (Heineken) 1981, most outstanding typography in an advertisement (Long John Whisky) 1981, most outstanding direction of cinema commercial (Benson & Hedges) 1982; other awards incl: Br TV ITV Award for best commercial (EMI Records) 1978, Film & TV Festival of NY Gold Award (Bass Charrington) 1984, Br Cinema Advtg Awards Gold Award (Britvic Corona) 1988, NY One Show Merit Awards (Cow & Gate) 1990 and 1991, Gold Award APG (Hula Hoops) 1996, Gold Award APG (Ford Transit) 1999; former memb Exec Ctee D&AD; *Style*— John Kelley, Esq; ✉ Ogilvy & Mather, 10 Cabot Square, Canary Wharf, London E14 4QB (✆ 020 7345 3000)

KELLIE, Ian; s of Lionel Kellie (d 1996), and Doris, *née* Stead; *b* 7 July 1950, Surrey; *Educ* Queen Elizabeth GS Hexham, Univ of Durham (BSc), St John's Coll York (PGCE), Univ of Bristol (MEd); *m* 1979 (m dis 2002); 2 s (Simon b 8 Jan 1982, Peter b 2 Jan 1984); *Career* chemistry master St Bees Sch Cumbria 1972–75, second in chemistry dept Cotham GS Bristol 1975–82, head of science Ashton Park Sch Bristol 1982–88; Sir Thomas Rich's Gloucester: dep headmaster 1988–94, headmaster 1994–2013, ret; *Recreations* walking, cycling, table tennis; *Style*— Ian Kellie, Esq

KELLNER, Peter Jon; s of Michael Kellner (d 1991), and Lily, *née* McVail (d 2004); *b* 2 October 1946, Lewes, Sussex; *Educ* Minchenden GS London, Royal GS Newcastle upon Tyne, King's Coll Cambridge (BA); *m* 1, 1972, Sally, *née* Collard; 2 da (Tara b 1977, Katherine b 1979), 1 s (Michael b 1981); m 2, 1988, Catherine Margaret Ashton (Rt Hon Baroness Ashton of Upholland), *qv*; 1 s (Hon Robert b 1989), 1 da (Hon Rebecca b 1992); *Career* journalist Sunday Times 1969–80, political ed New Statesman 1980–87; political columnist: The Independent 1986–92, Sunday Times 1992–96, The Observer 1996–97, London Evening Standard 1997–2003; political analyst BBC2 Newsnight 1990–97; YouGov plc: chm 2001–07, pres 2007–16; memb Cncl NIESR 2013–; tstee: Action on Smoking and Health 2009–, Hansard Soc 2012–15; visiting prof Univ of Hertfordshire 2006; Journalist of the Year British Press Awards 1978, Chm of the Year Quoted Companies Alliance 2006, Special Recognition Award Political Studies Assoc 2011; Hon DLitt Univ of Hertfordshire 1998; Callaghan: The Road to Number 10 (co-author, 1976), The Civil Servants: An Inquiry into Britain's Ruling Class (co-author, 1980), The New Mutualism (co-author, 1998), Democracy (2009); *Style*— Peter Kellner, Esq

KELLY, Bernard Noel; s of Sir David Kelly, GCMG, MC (d 1959), of Co Wexford, and Comtesse Renée Marie Noële Ghislaine de Vaux (d 1995); *b* 23 April 1930; *Educ*

Downside; *m* 11 July 1952, Lady Mirabel Magdalene Fitzalan Howard (d 2008); 7 s, 1 da; *Career* Capt 8 Queen's Royal Irish Hussars incl reserves 1948–60; admitted slr 1956; ptnr Simmons and Simmons 1958–62; banker; md Compagnie Monegasque de Banque SAM 1976–80; dir: S G Warburg & Co 1963–76, Barnes Gp Inc USA 1975–91, Insilco USA 1978–89, Lazard Bros and Co Ltd 1980–90 (vice-chm and md 1981–85), PXRE USA 1988–2002, American Phoenix Investment Ltd 1990–99, Société Générale Investissement (LUX) 1990–2010, Campbell Lutyens & Co Ltd (chm 1990–92); chm: Langbourne Income Growth & Property Unit Trust 1984–2010, International Select Fund Ltd 1989–96, LET Ventures plc 1990–95, Nexus Gp Ltd 1993–, Discovery Gp of Funds 1997–2003, First Equity Ltd 2000–14; dir: Gen Med Clinic 1998–2012, PXP International Ltd 2000–03; *Clubs* Athenaeum, Brooks's, Kildare Street and Univ (Dublin); *Style*— Bernard Kelly, Esq; ✉ 45 Fernshaw Road, London SW10 0TN (☎ 020 7352 8272)

KELLY, Prof Catriona Helen Moncrieff; da of Alexander Kelly (d 1996), and Margaret Moncrieff Kelly (d 2008); *b* 6 October 1959; *Educ* Godolphin & Latymer Sch, St Hilda's Coll Oxford (BA), Univ of Oxford (DPhil); *m* 1993, Prof Ian Thompson; *Career* ChCh Oxford: sr scholar 1983–87, jr research fell 1987–90, Br Acad fell 1990–93; lectr in Russian language and literature SSEES Univ of London 1993–96; Univ of Oxford: lectr 1996–97, reader 1997–2002, prof of Russian 2002–, tutorial fell New Coll; FBA 2007; *Publications* Petrushka, the Russian Carnival Puppet Theatre (1990), An Anthology of Russian Women's Writing 1777–1992 (ed, 1994), A History of Russian Women's Writing, 1820–1992 (1994), Constructing Russian Culture in the Age of Revolution (co-ed, 1998), Russian Cultural Studies: An Introduction (co-ed, 1998), Utopias: Russian Modernist Texts 1905–1940 (ed, 1999), Russian Literature, Modernism, and the Visual Arts (co-ed, 2000), Refining Russia: Advice Literature, Polite Culture, and Gender from Catherine to Yeltsin (2001), Russian Literature: A Very Short Introduction (2001), Comrade Pavlik: The Rise and Fall of a Soviet Boy Hero (2005), Children's World: Growing Up in Russia 1890–1991 (2007), Gorodok v Tabakerke: Detstvo v Rossii ot Nikolaya II do Borisa Yel'tsina (jt ed, 2008), Soviet and Post-Soviet Identities (co-ed, 2012), Russian Cultural Anthology After the Collapse of Communism (co-ed, 2012), St Petersburg: Shadows of the Past (2014), Socialist Churches: Radical Secularization and the Preservation of the Past in Petrograd and Leningrad, 1918–1988 (2016); also author of book chapters, chapters in specialised volumes and articles in professional jls; reviews published in jls incl: The Guardian, TLS, Evening Standard, The Independent, FT, Jl of Modern History, American Historical Review; *Recreations* visual arts, travel, slash and burn gardening; *Style*— Prof Catriona Kelly, FBA; ✉ e-mail catriona.kelly@new.ox.ac.uk

KELLY, Christopher (Chris); *b* 1978, Wolverhampton, W Midlands; *Educ* Wolverhampton GS, Oxford Brookes Univ, Imperial Coll London (MBA); *Career* dir Keltruck Ltd; MP (Cons) Dudley S 2010–15; *Recreations* swimming, squash, tennis, golf, running; *Style*— Chris Kelly, Esq; ✉ House of Commons, London SW1A 0AA

KELLY, Sir Christopher William; KCB (2001); s of Dr Reginald Edward Kelly (d 1990), and Peggy Kathleen, *née* Stone (d 2008); *b* 18 August 1946; *Educ* Beaumont Coll, Trinity Coll Cambridge (MA), Univ of Manchester (MA Econ); *m* 1970, Alison Mary Collens, da of Dr Henry Durant (d 1982), and Peggy Durant (d 2010); 2 s (Jake b 1974, Toby b 1976), 1 da (Rachel b 1980); *Career* HM Treasy: asst princ 1970, private sec to Fin Sec 1971–73, sec to Wilson Ctee of Inquiry into Fin Instns 1978–80, asst sec 1981, under sec Pay and Industrial Relations Gp 1987–90, under sec Social Servs and Territorial Gp 1990–92, under sec Gen Expenditure Policy Gp 1992–94, dir of fiscal and monetary policy 1994–95, dir of budget and public fins 1995; head Policy Gp Dept of Social Security 1995–97, perm sec Dept of Health 1997–2000; chm Ctee on Standards in Public Life 2001–13; memb Bd Nat Consumer Cncl 2001–08; chm: NSPCC 2002–10, Financial Ombudsman Serv 2005–12 (non-exec dir 2002–12), King's Fund 2010–, TPO Fndn 2012–, Responsible Gambling Strategy Bd 2013–, snr ind dir Co-operative grp 2014–; *Recreations* walking; *Style*— Sir Christopher Kelly, KCB

KELLY, Crispin Noel; s of Bernard Kelly, *qv*, of London, and Lady Mirabel, *née* Fitzalan Howard; *b* 21 October 1956; *Educ* Magdalen Coll Oxford (MA), AA Sch of Architecture (Dip); *m* 9 July 1982, Frances, da of Charles Pickthorn; 4 c (Alex b 9 Aug 1984, Christian b 18 Jan 1987 d 1987, Jessica b 12 July 1988, Rowan b 28 Aug 1998); *Career* architect; fndr and md Baylight Properties plc 1982; pres AA 2001–03; RIBA 1994; *Books* Building More Homes (with R Ehrman, 2003); *Style*— Crispin Kelly

KELLY, Prof Deirdre; CBE (2016), DL (W Midlands 2008); da of Frank Kelly, and Kathy, *née* Scannell; *b* 1 February 1950, Calcutta; *Educ* Convent of Holy Child Killiney Dublin, TCD (MB BCh, BAO, MD); *m* 1, 1973, Miles Parker; 2 s (Eoin Parker b 1978, Lochlinn Parker b 1980); m 2, 1997, Sir Ian Byatt, *qv*; *Career* lectr in medicine TCD 1980–82, Wellcome research fell Royal Free Hosp 1982–84, lectr in child health St Bartholomew's Hosp 1987, asst prof in pediatrics Univ of Nebraska 1987–89, founding dir Liver Unit Birmingham Children's Hosp 1989– (med dir 2000–07), hon prof of paediatric hepatology Birmingham Children's Hosp 2001–; assoc non-exec dir Royal Wolverhampton NHS Tst 2013–15, non-exec dir Health Research Authy 2015–; chm Nat Advsy Cmmn (formerly Panel) Enquiry into Child Health 2004–09, chm Coll Speciality Advsy Ctee RCPCH 2004–07, memb Bd Healthcare Cmmn 2007–09, memb Bd Care Quality Cmmn 2008–13; memb: Advsy Ctee on Safety of Blood, Tissues and Organs 2008–12, Advsy Gp on Hepatitis 2010–15, Prog Devpt Gp NICE 2011–12, GMC 2013–; pres: Int Pediatric Transplant Assoc 2002–05, Br Soc of Paediatric Gastroenterology, Hepatology and Nutrition 2004–07, European Soc of Paediatric Gastroenterology, Hepatology and Nutrition 2007–10; chm Lunar Soc 2007–09; govr: St Martin's Sch Solihull 2004–05, Health Fndn 2008–16; Hospital Doctor of the Year 1991, Midlands Woman of Achievement 1996, Alumni Award TCD 2011, Lunar Society Medal 2012; FRCPI 1990, FRCP 1995, FRCPH 1997; *Publications* incl: Pediatric Gastroenterology and Hepatology (1996), Diseases of the Liver and Biliary System in Children (1999, 3 edn 2008), Paediatric Solid Organ Transplantation (2000, 2 edn 2007), Practical Approach to Paediatric Gastroenterology, Hepatology and Nutrition (2014), contrib on clinical and basic science related to paediatric liver disease; *Recreations* gardening, opera, travel, walking; *Clubs* Royal Over-Seas League; *Style*— Professor Deirdre Kelly, CBE, DL; ✉ Liver Unit, Birmingham Children's Hospital, Steelhouse Lane, Birmingham B4 6NH (☎ 0121 333 8235, e-mail deirdre.kelly@bch.nhs.uk, website www.bch.nhs.uk, Twitter @KellyDA60)

KELLY, Desmond Hugh; OBE (2005); s of Fredrick Henry Kelly (d 1973), of Salisbury, Southern Rhodesia, and Mary Josephine, *née* Bracken; *b* 13 January 1942; *Educ* Christian Brothers Coll Bulawayo, Elaine Archibald Ballet Sch Bulawayo, Ruth French Dance Acad London; *m* 4 Jan 1964, Denise Jeanette, da of Henri Charles le Comte; 1 da (Emma Louise b 30 Dec 1970), 1 s (Joel Henry b 1 June 1973); *Career* dancer; princ London Festival Ballet 1964 (joined 1959), Zurich Ballet 1966–67, ballet master teacher and princ dancer New Zealand Ballet 1967–68, Nat Ballet of Washington 1968–70 (most notable role James in La Sylphide with Margot Fonteyn), The Royal Ballet 1970–76 (ballets incl Swan Lake, Giselle and Romeo and Juliet); Sadler's Wells Royal Ballet: princ dancer 1976–78, ballet master 1978–, asst to dir 1988, asst dir 1990–2008, int guest teacher; currently artistic dir Elmhurst Sch for Dance; roles incl: Thomas in La Fille Mal Gardée, Dr Coppélius in Coppélia, Dago in Façade, Mr Hobson in David Bintley's Hobson's Choice; various TV appearances; Critics Circle Special Dance Award 2007, Royal Ballet Govrs' Gold Medal 2008; DLitt: Univ of Birmingham 2007, Univ of Leicester 2007; *Recreations* theatre, gardening, cooking, reading; *Style*— Desmond Kelly, Esq, OBE; ✉ Elmhurst School for Dance, 249 Bristol Road, Edgbaston, Birmingham B5 7UH (☎ 0121 472 6655, fax 0121 472 6654, e-mail enquiries@elmhurstdance.co.uk)

KELLY, (Reay) Diarmaid Anthony; s of Capt Edward Raymond Anthony Kelly (d 1991), of Belgrave Mews North, London, and Bridget Ramsay, *née* Hornby; *b* 8 July 1959; *Educ* Ampleforth; *m* 18 April 1991, Candida, eld da of Peter Meinertzhagen; 2 s (Barnaby b 15 Jan 1993, Augustus b 15 June 1995); *Career* sales exec Henderson Crosthwaite & Co 1981–84, dir Baring Securities Ltd (later ING Baring Securities Ltd) 1984–96, fndr dir CrossBorder Capital 1996–; *Recreations* racing; *Clubs* Boodle's, Pratt's, Turf; *Style*— Diarmaid Kelly, Esq

KELLY, Prof Francis Patrick (Frank); CBE (2013); s of Francis Kelly, and Margaret, *née* McFadden; *b* 28 December 1950; *Educ* Van Mildert Coll Durham (BSc), Emmanuel Coll Cambridge (PhD); *m* 1972, Jacqueline Pullin; 2 s; *Career* operational res analyst Scicon Ltd 1971–73; Univ of Cambridge: asst lectr in engrg 1976–78, lectr Statistical Laboratory 1978–86, Nuffield Fndn sci res fell 1986–87, reader in mathematics of systems 1986–90, prof of the mathematics of systems 1990–, dir Statistical Laboratory 1991–93, Royal Soc Leverhulme Tst sr research fell 1994–95; chief scientific advsr Dept for Transport 2003–06, master Christ's Coll Cambridge 2006–16 (fell 1976–); Rollo Davidson Prize 1979, Guy Medal in silver RSS 1989, Lanchester Prize Operation Res Soc of America 1992, Clifford Paterson lectr Royal Soc 1995, Blackett lectr Operational Res Soc 1996, Naylor Prize London Mathematical Soc 1997, IEEE Koji Kobayashi Award 2005, INFORMS John von Neumann Theory Prize 2008, Sigmetrics Achievement Award 2009, Gold Medal Assoc of European Operational Research Societies 2009, Beale Medal Operational Research Soc 2011, foreign memb Nat Acad of Engrg 2012,Saul Gass Expository Writing Award Inst for Operations Research and the Management Sciences (INFORMS), Alexander Graham Bell Medal IEEE 2015, David Crighton Medal London Mathematical Soc and IMA 2015; dir Autonomy 2010–11; chair Cncl for the Mathematical Sciences 2010–13; assoc ed: Stochastic Models 1983–86, Annals of Probability 1984–90, Jl of the Royal Statistical Soc 1986–90, Probability in the Engineering and Informational Scis 1986–96, Combinatorics, Probability and Computing 1991–95, Queueing Systems 1995–2011, Mathematics of Operations Research 2003–05; Hon DSc Heriot-Watt Univ 2001, Hon DSc Eindhoven Univ of Technol 2011, Hon DSc Imperial Coll London 2015; FRS 1989; *Books* Reversibility and Stochastic Networks (1979), Stochastic Networks (with E Yudovina, 2014); numerous articles in mathematical & statistical jls; *Recreations* skiing, golf; *Clubs* Royal Society, Oxford and Cambridge; *Style*— Prof Frank Kelly, CBE, FRS; ✉ Statistical Laboratory, Centre for Mathematical Sciences, Wilberforce Road, Cambridge CB3 0WB (☎ 01223 337963, fax 01223 337956)

KELLY, Iain Charles MacDonald; *b* 5 March 1949, Cardiff; *Educ* Univ of Wales Aberystwyth (BSc), Univ of London (Dip); *m* Linda; 2 s; *Career* diplomat; desk offr Caribbean Dept FCO 1974–75, Russian language trg 1975–76, 3 sec Moscow 1976–79, 3 sec Kuala Lumpur 1979–82, desk offr East European and Soviet Dept FCO 1982–85, Turkish language trg 1985–86, consul Istanbul 1986–88, desk offr North and South Korea FCO 1988–90, consul LA 1990–92, head Commercial Dept Moscow 1992–95, consulate-gen Amsterdam 1996–98, sr memb Jesus Coll Oxford 1998–99, ambass to Belarus 1999–2003, dep head Whitehall Liaison Dept FCO 2003–07, sr memb St Antony's Coll Oxford 2007, ambass to Uzbekistan 2007–09; FRGS; *Style*— Mr Iain Kelly; ✉ c/o FCO, King Charles Street, London SW1A 2AH

KELLY, James; MSP; s of Frank Kelly, and Lilian, *née* Reid; *b* 23 October 1963, Glasgow; *Educ* Glasgow Coll of Technol (BSc); *m* 12 June 1992, Alexandra, *née* Mullan; 2 da (Carys b 9 Jan 1998, Erin b 18 July 2000); *Career* analyst programmer Argyll and Clyde Health Bd 1985–88, computer auditor and fin officer Scottish Power 1988–99, sr analyst Scottish Electricity Settlements 1999–2004, business analyst SAIC 2004–07; MSP (Scot Lab) Glasgow Rutherglen 2007–; CIMA 1994; *Recreations* half marathons, five-a-side football, golf; *Style*— James Kelly, Esq, MSP; ✉ The Scottish Parliament, Edinburgh EH99 1SP

KELLY, John Anthony Brian; RD (1974); s of Lt Cdr Brian John Parmenter Kelly, DSC (d 1994), of Bangor, Co Down, and Ethne Mary, *née* Ryan (d 1977); *b* 21 August 1941; *Educ* Bangor GS, Fort Augustus Abbey Sch, Queen's Univ Belfast (LLB); *m* 27 March 1971, Denise Anne, da of Ronald James Circuit, of St Albans; 2 da (Katrina b 1973, Joanna b 1975), 2 s (Christopher b 1977, Nicholas b 1982); *Career* Lt Cdr RNR 1959–84; Price Waterhouse and Co 1963–68 (qualified 1967), exec Old Broad St Securities 1968–70, exec and assoc Laurie Milbank and Co 1971–78, dir Brown Shipley and Co Ltd 1982–92 (mangr 1978); dir: Close Brothers Ltd 1992–96, Close Securities Ltd 1997–2012; non-exec dir: Cosalt plc 1986–2010 (chm 2005–08), SEP Industrial Holdings plc 1996–2001, Clugston Group Ltd 1997–, iRevolution Gp plc 2001–02, GSH Gp plc 2007–2008 (chm 2008); Liveryman Worshipful Co of Founders (Master 2007–08); FCA; *Recreations* walking, reading, poetry, golf; *Clubs* The Naval, Royal Ulster Yacht, Beaconsfield Golf; *Style*— John Kelly, Esq, RD; ✉ Cherrytrees, Penn Road, Beaconsfield, Buckinghamshire HP9 2LW (e-mail kellycherrytrees@hotmail.com)

KELLY, Prof John Stephen; s of Michael Kelly (d 1982), and Joan, *née* Trebble; *b* 4 February 1942; *Educ* Trinity Coll Dublin (fndn scholar, univ prize in Old and Middle English, Henry Hutchinson Stewart literary scholarship, vice-chllr's prize for English prose, BA, univ research exhbn), St Catharine's Coll Cambridge (Gardiner meml scholar, PhD); *m* 1966, Christine Juliet, eld da of Capt Michael Rahilly, RN; 1 da (Katharine Sophia b 1971), 2 s (Tom Michael b 1974, Ned b 1978); *Career* lectr in English Univ of Kent at Canterbury 1968–76; St John's Coll Oxford: fell and tutor in English 1976, sr English fell 1980, tutor for admission 1982–85, vice-pres 1991, prof of English 1997–; Lamont visiting prof Union Coll Schenectady NY 1990, Donnelly visiting prof of Irish studies Notre Dame Univ 1999; dir Yeats Summer Sch 1971–76; founding memb Int Assoc for the Study of Anglo-Irish Literature (IASAIL) 1969 (treas 1969–71); Leverhulme Fellowship 1972–73, sr research fell Univ of Leicester 1973–74, Br Acad Readership 1988–90; O'Donnell lectr Univ of Oxford 1991, Churchill lectr Univ of Bristol 1992; curator Oxford Playhouse (univ theatre) 1978–83, sr memb Experimental Theatre Club Univ of Oxford 1978–87; hon fell Trinity Coll Dublin 1998; *Books* The Collected Letters of W B Yeats (ed, vol I 1986, vol II 1997, vol III 1994, vol IV 2005), The Spirit of the Nation (ed, 1999), Poems and Ballads of Young Ireland (ed, 2000); ed of editions: James Joyce, John Mitchel, James Fintan Lalor, James Clarence Mangan, Gerald Griffin, John Banim, Thomas Davis, William Allingham, Samuel Ferguson, Charles Kickham; *Recreations* theatre, cinema, running; *Style*— Prof John Kelly; ✉ St John's College, Oxford OX1 3JP (☎ 01865 277300, fax 01865 277435, e-mail john.kelly@sjc.ox.ac.uk)

KELLY, Judith Pamela (Jude); CBE (2015, OBE 1997); da of John Kelly, of Wimbledon, London, and Ida Kelly; *b* 24 March 1954; *Educ* Calder HS Liverpool, Univ of Birmingham; *m* Michael Bird (professionally known as Michael Birch); 1 da (Caroline b 21 Oct 1986), 1 s (Robbie b 4 Sept 1989); *Career* director; began career as freelance folk and jazz singer 1970–75, actress with Michael Bogdanov's Co (Leicester Phoenix Theatre) 1975–76, fndr dir Solent People's Theatre Hampshire (over 42 community shows) 1976–80, artistic dir BAC 1980–85 (also co-fndr BAC based General Theatre Co 1983), freelance dir Nat Theatre of Brent 1982–85, artistic dir York Festival and Mystery Plays 1988 (joined pt/t 1985–88), chief exec West Yorkshire Playhouse 1993–2002 (artistic dir 1988–2002), fndr artistic dir Metal (artists' lab) 2002–05 (chair 2005–), artistic dir South Bank Centre 2005–; BAC prodns incl: rodns incl: Fascinating Aida 1983, Second from Last in the Sack Race (also tour) 1983, The Devil Rides Out – A Bit (also Lyric Hammersmith and tour) 1984; Nat Theatre of Brent prodns incl Harvey and the Wallbangers (3 nat tours, 2 TV shows); other prodns incl: The Pink Briefcase (Lyric Hammersmith and tour) 1985, Lynchville (RSC festival, joined as asst dir) 1986, Sarcophagus 1987 (The Pit, transferring to Mermaid (two nominations Olivier Awards)), Affairs in a Tent 1988, A Garden Fête 1988 (both Bristol Old Vic); West Yorkshire Playhouse prodns incl: Wild Oats, Safe in our Hands, Getting Attention, The Pope and the Witch, Second from last in the Sack Race, Pratt of the Argus, The Revenger's Tragedy, Wicked Old Man, Happy Days, The Taming of the Shrew, Comedians, Gypsy, The Merchant of Venice, Mail Order Bride, Call in the Night, King Lear, Beatification of Area Boy, World Goes 'Round, A Perfect Ganesh, Odysseus Thump, Queen, Blast from the Past, Macbeth, Singin' in the Rain (transferred to RNT, Olivier Award for Outstanding Musical Production 2001), Half a Sixpence; freelance prodns incl: When We Are Married, Othello (for Shakespeare Theatre Washington DC), The Elixir of Love (for ENO), Saturday Sunday and Monday; formed resident ensemble company at West Yorkshire Playhouse led by Sir Ian McKellen (prodns incl: The Seagull, The Tempest); fndr memb Noroc 1992 (cultural exchange initiative between Br and Romania); visiting prof: Univ of Leeds 2002–, Kingston Univ 2002–; chair: Common Purpose Charitable Tst 1997–, Qualifications and Curriculum Authy Advsy Gp on the Arts 2001, Arts, Educn and Culture Ctee London 2012 Olympic Games Bid 2004–05, Culture, Ceremonies and Educn London Organising Ctee of the Olympic Games 2005–; dep chair NACCCE (National Advsy Ctee on Creative and Cultural Educn) 1998–2000, represents UK for UNESCO on cultural matters 1998–2000; memb: Leeds Initiative, Cncl and Ct Univ of Leeds, Arts Cncl Drama Panel 1995–97, Cncl RSA 1998–99, Bd RJC Reggae, Jazz, Contemporary Dance Co 2001–; awarded Br Jr C of C Outstanding Young Person's Cultural Achievement 1993; Hon Dr: Leeds Met Univ 1995, Univ of Bradford 1996, Univ of Leeds 2000, Univ of York 2001, Open Univ 2001; *Recreations* windsurfing; *Style*— Ms Jude Kelly, CBE; ✉ Metal, 198A Broadhurst Gardens, London NW6 3AY (e-mail jude@metalculture.com)

KELLY, Laurence Charles Kevin; s of Sir David Kelly, GCMG, MC (d 1959), and Comtesse Renée Marie Noële Ghislaine de Vaux (d 1995); *b* 11 April 1933, Brussels; *Educ* Downside, New Coll Oxford (MA); *m* 1963, Linda Kelly, *qv*, da of Maj R G McNair Scott (d 1995), and Hon Mrs Scott (d 1996), of Old Basing, Hants; 1 s, 2 da; *Career* Lt Life Gds 1949–52; served FO (Northern Dept) 1955–56, Guest Keen and Nettlefolds 1956–72; Helical Bar plc: non-exec dir 1972–93, dep chm 1981–84, chm 1984–88, vice-chm 1988–93; dir: GKN Int Trading 1972, Morganite Int Ltd 1984–92, KAE Mintel Int Ltd 1985–2003; chm Queenborough Steel Co 1980–89; vice-chm British Steel Consumers' Cncl 1974 (res 1985); memb: Bd NI Devpt Agency 1972–78, Monopolies and Mergers Cmmn 1982–88; chm Carmelite Church Choir Tst 1997–, sr tstee Apollo Fndn Charity 1984–2013; sr assoc memb St Antony's Coll Oxford 1985–92; FRGS 1972, FRSL 2003; *Books* Lermontov – Tragedy in the Caucasus (1978), Travellers' Companion to St Petersburg (1981), Travellers' Companion to Moscow (1983), Travellers' Companion to Istanbul (1987), Proposals (with Linda Kelly, 1989), Diplomacy and Murder in Tehran: Alexander Griboyedov and Imperial Russia's Mission to the Shah of Persia (2001); *Recreations* swimming, opera; *Clubs* Brooks's, Turf, Beefsteak, Univ (Dublin); *Style*— Laurence Kelly, Esq; ✉ 44 Ladbroke Grove, London W11 2PA (☎ 020 7727 4663)

KELLY, Linda; da of Ronald McNair Scott (d 1995), and Hon Mary McNair Scott *née* Berry (d 1996); *b* 1 October 1936; *Educ* Southover Manor, Byam Shaw Sch of Art; *m* 20 April 1963, Laurence Kelly, *qv*, s of Sir David Kelly, GCMG, MC; 2 da (Rosanna b 21 May 1964, Rachel b 19 Sept 1965), 1 s (Nicholas b 24 Nov 1967); *Career* copywriter Condé Nast Pubns 1956–60, travel ed Vogue 1960–63; conslt Capuchin Classics 2009; tstee: London Library 2001–04, Wordsworth Tst 2001–07 (currently fell); FRSL; *Books* The Marvellous Boy (1971), The Young Romantics (1976), The Kemble Era (1980), Women of The French Revolution (1987), Juniper Hall (1991), Richard Brinsley Sheridan (1997), Susanna, the Captain and the Castrato (2004), Ireland's Minstrel (2006), Alyson: A Painter's Journey (2008), Holland House: A History of London's Most Celebrated Salon (2013); anthologies: Feasts (with Christopher Bland, 1986), Proposals (with Laurence Kelly, 1989), Happiness (with John Train, 2008), Animals and Us (with John Train, 2011), Garden Magic (with John Train) 2013, Joy of the Seasons (with John Train) 2014; *Recreations* reading, opera-going, family life; *Clubs* Grillions; *Style*— Ms Linda Kelly; ✉ 44 Ladbroke Grove, London W11 2PA (☎ 020 7727 4663)

KELLY, Linda Mary; da of late John Nicholl Millar, and Vicenta Amy Gibson, *née* Smith; *b* 2 January 1955; *m* 24 April 1987, Brian James Kelly; 2 da (Natasha Vicenta b 4 Dec 1987, Kirsty Marion b 6 Aug 1998); *Career* hosp pharmacist Royal Free Hosp and Oldchurch Hosp 1977–78, various mktg and product devpt posts Merck Sharp and Dohme Pharmaceuticals 1978–87, new product planning mangr rising to mktg dir Smith Kline Beecham 1988–91, sales and mktg dir then md (UK and Ireland) Bristol Myers Squibb Pharmaceuticals 1991–95, pres (UK) Astra Pharmaceuticals Ltd (now Astra Zeneca) 1995–99 (also chm Pension Fund and tstee Astra Fndn), full time study at Christies Educn 1999–2000, chief exec Parkinson's Disease Soc 2001–05, chief exec Lloyds TSB Fndn 2006–12; full time study SOAS 2013–; MRPharmS, FRSA; *Recreations* walking, the arts; *Style*— Mrs Linda Kelly

KELLY, Lorraine; OBE (2012); *b* 30 November 1959, Glasgow; *Educ* Claremont HS East Kilbride; *m* 5 Sept 1992, Steve Smith; 1 da (Rosie b June 1994); *Career* television presenter; researcher BBC Scotland 1983–84; TV-am: joined as reporter 1984, presenter Good Morning Britain 1990; presenter: GMTV 1993–2010, Lorraine (ITV) 2010–, Daybreak (ITV) 2012–; rector Univ of Dundee 2004–07, patron Help for Heroes; Hon Col Black Watch Cadets 2009; Hon LLD Univ of Dundee 2008; *Books* Between You and Me (autobiography, 2008), Lorraine On Looking Good (2009), Lorraine Kelly's Scotland (2014); *Style*— Ms Lorraine Kelly, OBE; ✉ c/o Roar Global Ltd, Roar House, 46 Charlotte Street, London W1T2GS (e-mail info@roarglobal.com, website www.lorrainekelly.tv, Twitter @reallorraine)

KELLY, (Richard) Martin; s of Norman Keith Kelly, of Bishop Burton, and Gwendoline, *née* Fisher; *b* 25 April 1954; *Educ* Beverley GS, Leeds Poly (Dip Landscape Architecture), Oxford Poly (Dip Urban Design, MA); *m* 10 May 1986 (m dis), Anna Acton-Stow; 1 da (Victoria Grace b 1987); *Career* asst planning offr Landscape and Reclamation Section Sheffield Met Dist Cncl until 1979; currently md Derek Lovejoy Partnership London (joined 1979, ptnr 1986); landscape infrastructure work undertaken for public and private sector clients; expert witness at public enquiries; dir Derek Lovejoy Touchstone Ltd; memb SE Chapter Landscape Ctee; author various articles and book reviews for tech press; FLI 1990, FIHT 1990; *Style*— Martin Kelly, Esq

KELLY, Matthew; né David Alan Kelly; s of Ronald Nugent Kelly, and Olive Hilda, *née* Rixon; *b* 9 May 1950; *Educ* Urmston GS, Manchester Poly (DipEd), Open Univ (BA); *m* 1970, Sarah Elizabeth, *née* Gray; 1 s (Matthew David (stage name Matthew Rixon) b 1970), 1 da (Ruth Emma b 1972); *Career* actor and television presenter; theatre 1967–, TV 1977–; credits incl: Game for a Laugh (LWT) 1981–83, You Bet! (LWT) 1990–95, Stars in their Eyes (Granada) 1990–2004, City Hospital (BBC) 2002–04, Bleak House (BBC) 2005, Egypt: The Pharoah and The Showman and The Temple of Sands (BBC) 2005, Cold Blood (Granada) 2005 and 2006 (RTS Award for Best Performer in a Drama, Silver Medal NY Int Programming Awards), Where the Heart Is 2006, Marple 2006, Forensic Casebook (ITV), My Family At War (BBC) 2009, Moving On (BBC), Benidorm (ITV), MI High (BBC); recent theatre performances incl: Lenny in Of Mice and Men (Birmingham Rep and West End, Olivier Award Best Actor 2004), Mirandolina (Manchester Royal Exchange Theatre) 2006, Amadeus (Wilton's Music Hall) 2006, Forgotten Voices (Riverside Studios) 2007, Endgame (Liverpool Everyman) 2008, Victory (Arcola Theatre), Who's Afraid of Virginia Woolf? (Trafalgar Studios), Troilus and Cressida (Shakespeare's Globe) 2009, Comedians (Lyric Hammersmith) 2009, Waiting For Godot (Theatre Royal Haymarket and tour of Australia, NZ and S Africa) 2010, Sign of the Times (West End) 2011, Lend Me a Tenor, The Musical (West End) 2011, Spamalot (UK tour) 2010–11, Buried Child (Curve Leicester) 2011–12, Legally Blonde (UK tour) 2011–12, Educating Rita (Menier Chocolate Factory and Edinburgh Festival) 2012, The Seagull (Southwark Playhouse) 2012, God of Carnage (Nuffield Southampton) 2013, The History Boys (Sheffield Crucible) 2013, To Sir With Love (Royal and Derngate and UK tour) 2013, Twelfth Night (Liverpool Everyman) 2014, Kafka's Dick (Theatre Royal Bath) 2014; film credits incl: Showreel 2009, Tribute, Two Stops to Bank, Tortoise; pres Neuromuscular Centre Cheshire 1990–; hon memb Stretford and Urmston Rotary; Paul Harris fell 2003; Hon DLitt Univ of Chester 2010, hon fell Liverpool John Moore's Univ 2011; *Style*— Matthew Kelly, Esq

KELLY, Matthias John; QC (1999), SC (2005); s of Ambrose Kelly (d 2001), and Anne Kelly (d 1973); *b* 21 April 1954; *Educ* St Patrick's Secdy Sch Dungannon, St Patrick's Acad Dungannon, Trinity Coll Dublin (BA, LLB), Cncl of Legal Educn London; *m* 5 May 1979, Helen Ann, da of Peter Joseph Holmes (d 1974), and Eileen Holmes (d 2010), of Longford, Ireland; 1 s (Peter b 1986), 1 da (Anne b 1987); *Career* called to the Bar: Gray's Inn 1979 (bencher 2002), NI 1983, Repub of Ireland 1983; admitted attorney: NY 1986, USA Federal Bar 1987; recorder of the Crown Court 2002–, SC Repub of Ireland 2005; conslt EU Cmmn Health and Safety UK 1994–96; chm: Bar Conference Eng and Wales 2001, Personal Injuries Bar Assoc 2001–02 (sec 1994–2000, vice-chm 1999–2001), Bar Cncl of Eng and Wales 2003 (memb 1997–2004, chm Policy Ctee 1999–2000, chm Public Affrs Gp 2001–, vice-chm 2001–02); memb: Mgmnt Ctee Gray's Inn 1993–95, Ogden Working Pty 1997–2003, Blackwell Ctee on non-legally qualified claims handlers 1999–2000; vice-chm Appeals Panel Inst of Actuaries 2002–; chm: EVA Campaign 1989–93, Children Act Housing Action Gp 1990–94, Mgmnt Ctee Alcohol Recovery Project 1993–96; dir Allied Irish Bank (GB) Gp 2004–12; hon life memb Br Soc of Criminology 1986; formerly FRSA and FRSM; *Publications* Child Abuse, uncovering the facts (New Law Jl, 1994), Achieving Full Compensation (New Law Jl, 1994), author of chapter on multipliers Manual of Personal Injuries (1997, 2 edn 2000, 3 edn 2007, jt ed 1 and 2 edns), Legal Aid (The Lawyer, 1999), Multipliers (article for newsletter of ICA 1999), Review of the Leading PI cases in 1999/2000 (The Lawyer, 2000), Review of law on dependency claims in fatal accident claims (Jl of Personal Injury Law, 2000), Independence Day for the Bar (Human Rights, The Times, 2001), Are brokers' fees recoverable? (2002), Munkman on Employers' Liability (jt ed and contrib, 13 edn 2002), Funding awards: all change? (Solicitors' Jl, 2002), A comparison of Securities litigation in the US and the EU (with Arthur A Eubank, Jr, PhD, Int Atlantic Economic Conference, 2008), chapter on UK damages in Contemporary Studies in Economic and Financial Analysis Vol 91, Personal Injury and Wrongful Death Damages Calculations, a Transatlantic Dialogue (2009); also on ed panel for Specialist Research papers on Personal Injury (1996–2000); *Recreations* walking, cycling, reading; *Style*— Matthias Kelly, Esq, QC; ✉ 39 Essex Chambers, 81 Chancery Lane, London WC2A 1DD (☎ 020 7832 1111, fax 020 7353 3978, DX 298 Chancery Lane)

KELLY, Dr Michael; CBE (1983), JP (Glasgow 1973), DL (1983); s of David Kelly (d 1972); *b* 1 November 1940; *Educ* Univ of Strathclyde (BSc, PhD); *m* 1965, Zita, da of Hugh Harkins; 3 c; *Career* economics lectr Univ of Aberdeen and Univ of Strathclyde 1967–84, md Michael Kelly Associates 1983–; columnist The Scotsman 2000–; chm RSSPCC 1987–96, pres Strathclyde Branch Inst of Mktg 1986–89, dir Celtic FC 1990–94; chm Glasgow Central CLP 2004–; memb: Scottish ABSA 1986–90, Scottish Ctee Nat Art Collections Fund 1990–94, External Relations Advsy Gp ESRC 2001–05; Lord Provost of Glasgow (and ex officio Lord-Lt) 1980–84, Lord Rector Univ of Glasgow 1984–87; Hon LLB Univ of Glasgow 1983; FIM 1989; OStJ 1984, Knight's Cross Order of Merit (Poland) 1998; *Books* Paradise Lost, The Struggle for Celtic's Soul (1994), London Lines: The Capital by Underground (1996); *Recreations* golf, photography, philately, sking; *Style*— Dr Michael Kelly, CBE, DL; ✉ 50 Aytoun Road, Glasgow G41 5HE (e-mail kellymkelly1@aol.com)

KELLY, Prof Michael Howard; OBE (2014); s of Kenneth Howard Kelly (d 2004), of Hull, and Kathleen Mary, *née* Lucas (d 1994); *b* 19 November 1946; *Educ* Hull GS, Univ of Warwick (BA, PhD), Univ of Southampton Mgmnt Sch (MBA); *m* 3 Jan 1975, Josephine Ann, da of Patrick Joseph Doyle, of Dublin; 2 s (Thomas Doyle b 1980, Paul Doyle b 1983); *Career* lectr in French UC Dublin 1972–86, prof of French Univ of Southampton 1986–; sec Euro Language Cncl; memb: Advsy Bd Language and Intercultural Communication, Editorial Bd Arts and Humanities in HE, Advsy Bd Modern and Contemporary France; assoc ed French Cultural Studies, ed Synergies Royaume-Uni et Irlande, ed European Jl of Language Policy; dir Routes into Languages prog; formerly: pres Assoc of Univ Profs of French, chm Irish Cncl for Civil Liberties, chair Univ Cncl of Modern Languages, memb Nuffield Languages Inquiry; dir HE Acad Subject Centre for Languages, Linguistics and Area Studies, dir Links into Languages Prog; FRSA, Hon FCIOL; Officier des Palmes Académiques, Chevalier des Arts et des Lettres; *Books* Pioneer of the Catholic Revival: Emmanuel Mounier (1979), Modern French Marxism (1982), Hegel in France (1992), French Cultural Studies: An Introduction (1995), Pierre Bourdieu: Language, Culture and Education (1999), French Culture and Society (2001), Third Level, Third Space (2001), A New Landscape for Languages (2003), The European Language Teacher (2003), Cultural and Intellectual Rebuilding of France (2004), Languages at War (2012), Languages and the Military (2012), Interpreting the Peace (2013); *Recreations* tennis, choir, cinema, golf; *Style*— Prof Michael Kelly, OBE; ✉ School of Humanities, University of Southampton, Highfield, Southampton SO17 1BF (☎ 023 8059 2191, fax 023 8059 3868, e-mail m.h.kelly@soton.ac.uk)

KELLY, Prof Michael Joseph; s of Steve Kelly (d 1988), and Mary Constance, *née* Powell (d 1987); *b* 14 May 1949, New Plymouth, NZ; *Educ* Francis Douglas Meml Coll NZ, Victoria Univ of Wellington (scholar, MSc, DSc), Univ of Cambridge (MA, PhD, ScD); *m* 1 June 1991, Ann Elizabeth, da of Dr Daniel Brumhall Cochrane Taylor (d 2003); 1 da (Constance Frances b 12 Feb 1993); *Career* res fell Trinity Hall Cambridge 1974–77, IBM res fell Univ of Calif 1975–76, SRC advanced fell Cavendish Laboratory and staff fell Trinity Hall Cambridge 1977–81 and 2002–16 (emeritus fell 2016–), res asst GEC 1981–92; Univ of Surrey: prof of physics and electronics 1992–96, head Electronic and Electrical Engrg Dept 1996–97, head Sch of Electronics, Computing and Mathematics 1997–2001, visiting prof 2002–; Prince Philip prof of technol Univ of Cambridge 2002–16 (emeritus prof 2016–), dep head Dept of Engrg Univ of Cambridge 2002–04, exec dir Cambridge-MIT Inst 2003–05, chief scientific advsr to the Dept for Communities and Local Govt 2006–09; visiting prof MIT 2004–06, visiting prof MacDiarmid Inst Wellington NZ 2012–13, memb Skoltech Int Advsy Panel 2014–; dir: Centre for Solid State Electronics, Advanced Technol Inst Sch of Electronics, Computing and Mathematics 2001–02; conslt GEC Marconi 1992–93, visiting researcher Cavendish Laboratory 1988–92, non-exec dir Laird plc 2006–15; Rutherford Meml lectr Royal Soc 2000; Paterson Medal and Prize Inst of Physics 1989, Nelson Gold Medal GEC 1991, Royal Acad of Engrg Silver Medal 1999, Hughes Medal of the Royal Soc 2006; holder of 13 patents on semiconductor devices, author of 270 papers, review articles and book chapters in refereed jls; memb: American Inst of Physics, Cncl of Univ of Surrey 1996–2001, Cncl Royal Soc 2001–02; fell Trinity Hall 1989–92 and 2002–16 (emeritus fell 2016–), Erskine fell Univ of Canterbury NZ 1999; Hon DSc Victoria Univ of Wellington 2002; CPhys, FInstP 1988 (memb Cncl 1997–2001, vice-pres 2001–05), FIET 1989, FRS 1993, FREng 1998, Hon FRSNZ 1999, SMIEEE 2003 (MIEEE 1998), memb Academia Europaea 2009, fell ERA Fndn 2014; *Books* The Physics and Fabrication of Microstructures and Microdevices (ed, 1986), Low Dimensional Semiconductors: Physics, Materials, Technology, Devices (1995); *Recreations* music, literature; *Style*— Prof Michael Kelly, FRS, FREng; ✉ Electrical Engineering Division, Centre for Advanced Photonics and Electronics, 9 JJ Thomson Avenue, Cambridge CB3 0FA (☎ 01223 748303, fax 01223 748348, e-mail mjk1@cam.ac.uk)

KELLY, Neil; WS; s of Neil Kelly, and Bridget, *née* Morgan; *b* 28 June 1961, Bellshill, Lanarkshire; *Educ* St Patrick's HS Coatbridge, Univ of Aberdeen (LLB, DipLP); *m* 3 Sept 1994, Alison, *née* Whyte; 2 s (Nicholas, Christopher), 1 da (Elizabeth); *Career* ptnr MacRoberts slrs 1991– (joined as trainee 1983); NP; convener Scottish region Adjudication Soc; memb Law Soc of Scotland; Hon RICS, Hon FRIAS; MacRoberts on Scottish Building Contracts (contrib, 1999, 3 edn 2014); *Recreations* travel, opera, classical music; *Style*— Neil Kelly, Esq, WS; ✉ 64 Pentland Terrace, Edinburgh EH10 6HE (☎ 0131 445 1148, e-mail njkopera@blueyonder.co.uk); MacRoberts, 30 Semple Street, Edinburgh EH3 8BL (☎ 0131 229 5046, fax 0131 229 0849, e-mail neil.kelly@macroberts.com)

KELLY, Owen Dennis; OBE (2014); *Educ* Univ of Edinburgh; *Career* govt official 1988–2008, chief exec Scottish Financial Enterprise 2008–; *Style*— Owen Kelly, Esq, OBE; ✉ Scottish Financial Enterprise, 24 Melville Street, Edinburgh EH3 7NS

KELLY, Peter; *b* 1931; *Educ* Loxford Central Sch Ilford, West Ham Sch of Art and Technol, Central Sch of Art and Design; *Career* artist; Nat Serv Royal Signals 1950–52; graphic designer 1952–57, painter and illustrator 1957–; cmmns from numerous British and foreign companies and galleries; RBA 1982 (ARBA 1980); *Solo Exhibitions* Hallam Gallery London, John Adams Fine Art London; *Two-Man Exhibitions* Llewelyn Alexander Gallery London, John Adams Fine Art London, Adam Gallery Bath; *Group Exhibitions* incl: Waterman Fine Art, Mall Gallery, Westminster Central Hall, Roy Miles Gallery, RA Summer Exhbn, Royal Soc of Portrait Painters; *Awards* Laing Competition (5 times), Berol Drawing Prize, painting prize Beecroft Gallery Essex, Pro Arte Brush Award, RBA Daler Rowney Award, Higgs & Hill Bursary, Artist Magazine Drawing Prize, De Lazlo Medal 1997, Jeffrey Archer Prize; *Clubs* NEAC; *Style*— Peter Kelly, Esq; ✉ c/o John Adams Fine Art, 200 Ebury Street, London SW1W 8UN (website www.johnadamsfineart.com)

KELLY, Dr William Francis; s of William Francis Kelly (d 1951), of Wolverhampton, and Lilian Rose, *née* Foister (d 1986); *b* 16 June 1942; *Educ* Royal Wolverhampton Sch, Univ of London (BSc), St Mary's Med Sch London (MB BS, MD), Open Univ (BA); *m* 21 Aug 1971, Miranda Jane, da of Leonard Oscar Goddard, of Wonersh, Surrey; 1 s (Adam John William b 1974), 1 da (Juliet Miranda b 1977 d 1995); *Career* qualified CA 1964 (resigned 1972); conslt physician S Tees Acute Hosps 1983–2006 (chm Sr Med Staff Ctee 1990–93), ret from practice 2006; clinical lectr Univ of Newcastle 1988 (hon sr lectr 1998–2006), hon lectr Univ of Durham 2006; author of articles in endocrine and diabetic jls, editorial asst Clinical Endocrinology 1986–93, memb Editorial Bd Cinical Endocrinology 1994–97; chm Northern Region Advsy Gp for Diabetes 1993–96; examiner RCP 1998; memb: Br Diabetic Assoc 1976 (pres S Tees Branch), Endocrine Section RSM 1978–98, FRCP 1989 (MRCP 1975), FRCP(Ed) 1996; *Recreations* walking, literature, photography; *Style*— Dr William Kelly; ☎ 01287 624192

KELMAN, Alistair Bruce; s of James Bruce Edward Kelman (d 1983), of London, and Florence Gwendoline, *née* Cutts (d 1987); *b* 11 August 1952; *Educ* Haberdashers' Aske's, Univ of Birmingham (BSc); *m* 2 Sept 1978, Diana Elizabeth, da of Prof Joseph Tinsley, of Aberdeen; *Career* called to the Bar Middle Temple 1977; specialist in computer law 1979–2000; litigation: R v Bedworth (computer addiction defence) 1993, McConville v Barclays and others (group action against UK banks over phantom withdrawals from automatic teller machines) 1993, IBCOS v Poole and Barclays (software copyright in the UK) 1994; currently ceo: Cachebox TV Ltd, Playback Hldgs Ltd; forensic computing expert witness and advsr on computer related problems, disclosure, reliability of digital evidence, electronic commerce and network security; inventor: technols for protecting privacy in digital TV (awarded patents 2011, 2013 and 2016), technols for protecting TV watershed (awarded UK patent 2013 and US patent 2016), cryptographic system for use in domestic medical care (awarded patent 2014); visiting fell LSE Computer Security Research Centre 1994–; head of legal content to Epoq Software Ltd 2002–08; reviewer ESPRIT multimedia projects for EC 1989–96; fndr memb Parly Info Technol Ctee House of Commons; AMBCS 1982, ACIArb 1986; *Books* The Computer in Court (with R Sizer, 1982), Computer Fraud in Small Businesses (1985), E-Commerce: Law and Practice (with M Chissick, 1999, 3 edn 2001); *Recreations* writing, cycling on Brompton folding bicycle; *Style*— Alistair Kelman; ✉ 37 Station Road, Hendon, London NW4 4PN (☎ 07709 191491, e-mail ali.kelman@gmail.com, website www.alikelman.com)

KELNAR, Prof Christopher John Harvey; s of Dr John Kelnar (d 1979), of London, and Rose, *née* Stoller (d 1992); *b* 22 December 1947; *Educ* Highgate Sch, Trinity Coll Cambridge (MA, MB BChir, MD), Bart's Med Coll London (DCH); *m* Alison Frances, da of Dr Ernst Adolf Schott (d 1984); 2 da (Clare Deborah Rosemary b 5 April 1976, Rachel Catherine Ruth b 9 May 1978), 1 s (David John Samuel b 12 June 1981); *Career* successively registrar in paediatrics rising to research fell in paediatric endocrinology Middx Hosp London, sr paediatric registrar Hosp for Sick Children Great Ormond St, clinical tutor Inst of Child Health London 1976–83, conslt paediatrician, endocrinologist and diabetologist Royal Hosp for Sick Children Edinburgh until 2011 (ret), prof Dept of Child Life and Health Univ of Edinburgh 1983–2011 (ret, hon prof 2011–); vice-chm Scottish Intercollegiate Guideline Network (SIGN) 2002–09, chm Clinical Fellowship Programme Euro Soc for Paediatric Endocrinology 2002–11; post doctoral fell in Edocinology: Human Reproductive Sciences Unit Edinburgh, Oregon Health Sciences Univ USA 1999–2000; memb: Cncl RCPEd, Exec Ctee Surveillance Unit Royal Coll of Paediatrics and Child Health; pres European Soc for Paediatric Endocrinology 2010–11; Sydney Watson Smith and Charles McNeil lectr RCPEd, European Soc for Paediatric Endocrinology Outstanding Clinician Award 2012; memb Cncl European Soc for Paediatric Endocrinology (also memb Scientific Ctee 1995, chair Corporate Liaison Bd 2006–12, pres 2010–11); memb: Br Soc for Paediatric Endocrinology and Diabetes; FRCPEd 1985, FRCP, FRCPCH; *Books* The Sick Newborn Baby (with D R Harvey, 1981, 4 edn 2005), Childhood and Adolescent Diabetes (ed, 1995), Growth Disorders – Pathophysiology and Treatment (2 edn 2007), ESPE Classification of Paediatric Endocrine Diagnoses (2007), The Endocrine Consquences of Curing Childhood Cancer (2009); contrib chapters to other med books and author of over 200 reviews and original scientific papers; *Recreations* music, gardening; *Style*— Prof Christopher Kelnar; ✉ e-mail christopher.kelnar@gmail.com

KELNER, Simon; *b* 9 December 1957; *Educ* Bury GS, Preston Poly; *Career* trainee reporter Neath Guardian 1976–79, sports reporter Extel 1979–80, sports ed Kent Evening Post 1980–83, asst sports ed The Observer 1983–86, dep sports ed The Independent 1986–89; sports ed: Sunday Correspondent 1989–90, The Observer 1990–91; ed Observer Magazine 1991–93 (Magazine of the Year 1992), sports ed Independent on Sunday 1993–95 (launched first national sports section); The Independent: night ed 1995, features ed 1995–96; ed Night & Day magazine Mail on Sunday 1996–98, ed-in-chief The Independent 1998–2011 (md 2008–10), ed-in-chief i 2010–11, chief exec Seven Dials PR 2013–; hon fell Univ of Central Lancashire, visiting fellowship Univ of Glos; Hon Dr Univ of Bolton; *Awards* Editor of the Year What the Papers Say Awards 1999 and 2003, The Edgar Wallace Award 2000, Newspaper of the Year Br Press Awards 2004, Newspaper of the Year What the Papers Say Awards 2004, GQ Editor of the Year GQ Awards 2004 and 2010, Media Achiever of the Year Campaign Media Awards 2004, Marketeer of the Year Marketing Week Effectiveness Awards 2004. Newspaper of the Year London Press Club 2004, Editorial Intelligence Comment Award 2010; Hon DLitt Univ of Ulster 2013; *Publications* To Jerusalem and Back (1996); *Style*— Simon Kelner, Esq; ✉ Seven Dials, 56a Poland Street, London W1F 7NN

KELSALL, Prof Malcolm Miles; s of Alec James Kelsall, and Hetty May, *née* Miles; *b* 27 February 1938; *Educ* William Hulme's GS Manchester, Brasenose Coll Oxford (state scholar, MA, Sr Hulme scholar, BLitt); *m* 5 Aug 1961, Mary Emily, da of George Hurley Ives (d 1978); *Career* staff reporter The Guardian 1961, asst lectr Univ of Exeter 1963–64, lectr Univ of Reading 1964–75, prof and head English Dept UC Cardiff 1975–88, prof Univ of Wales Cardiff 1988–2003 (emeritus prof 2003–); visiting prof: Univ of Paris 1978, Univ of Hiroshima 1979, Univ of Wisconsin 1996; visiting scholar in residence Int Center for Jefferson Studies 1997; advsy ed: The Byron Journal, Litteraria Pragensia; memb: Mgmnt Ctee Welsh Nat Drama Co 1976–77, Int Advsy Bd Messolonghi Byron Soc; *Books* Sarah Fielding's David Simple (ed, 1969), Thomas Otway's Venice Preserved (ed, 1969), William Congreve's Love for Love (ed, 1969), Joseph Trapp's Lectures on Poetry (ed, 1973), JM Synge's The Playboy of the Western World (ed 1975), Christopher Marlowe (1981), Congreve: The Way of the World (1981), Joseph Trapp's The Preface to the Aeneis (ed 1982), Studying Drama (1985), Byron's Politics (1987, awarded Elma Dangerfield prize, 1991), Encyclopedia of Literature and Criticism (ed, 1990), The Great Good Place: The Country House and English Literature (1992), British Academy Warton Lecture (1992), Jefferson and the Iconography of Romanticism (1999), Literary Representations of the Irish Country House (2003), The Cambridge Companion to Byron (contrib, 2004), Marchand Lecture (2005), The Cambridge Companion to Pope (contrib, 2007), The Oxford History of Classical Reception in English Literature 1660–1790 (contrib, 2012); *Recreations* theatre, long distance walking; *Style*— Prof Emeritus Malcolm Kelsall; ✉ 17 Withyholt Park, Charlton Kings, Gloucestershire GL53 9BP (☎ 01242 530335, e-mail malcolm.kelsall@btinternet.com)

KELSEY, Alan Howard Mitchell; s of Emanuel Kelsey (d 1985), of London, and Dorothy Mitchell, *née* Smith; *b* 10 April 1949; *Educ* KCS Wimbledon, Oriel Coll Oxford (MA); *m* 1, 12 March 1977 (m dis 2011), Sarah D'Oyly, da of Robin Carlyle Sayer, of Little Walsingham, Norfolk; 1 da (Keziah b 19 Jan 1978), 2 s (Guy b 22 Feb 1980, William b 27 July 1981); *m* 2, Catherine, da of Sir Conrad Swan, of Boxford Hall, Suffolk; *Career* Kitcat & Aitken: tport investment analyst 1975–88, head of res 1987–89, head of corp fin 1989–90; dir: RBC Dominion Securities International 1988–91, RBC Dominion Securities Inc 1989–91, Merrill Lynch International (formerly Smith New Court) 1992–96; gp dir of corporate devpt National Express Group plc 1996–98; md and global head of Tport Industry Gp WestLB Panmure 1999–2002, co-head corp broking WestLB Panmure 2001–02; chm Nord Anglia Educn plc (now Nord Anglia Educn) 2005– (non-exec dir 2003–05); sr ind dir: PD Ports 2004–06, Stobart Gp 2011–13; chm Explore Learning 2013–; tstee Prince's Teaching Inst 2007–; FCILT; *Recreations* fishing; *Clubs* Brooks's; *Style*— Alan Kelsey, Esq; ✉ The Old Rectory, Wetherden, Suffolk IP14 3LP (☎ 07768 173388)

KELSEY, Linda; da of Samuel Cohen, and Rhona, *née* Fox, of London; *b* 15 April 1952; *Educ* Woodhouse GS, Univ of Warwick; *m* 1972 (m dis 1980); partner Christian Testorf; 1 s (Thomas Testorf b 1988); *Career* trainee sub ed Good Housekeeping 1970–72, sub ed, asst features ed then features ed Cosmopolitan 1972–78; dep ed Company Magazine 1978–81, dep ed Options Magazine 1981–82, ed Cosmopolitan 1985–89 (dep ed 1982–85), ed SHE Magazine 1989–95, ed-at-large Nat Magazine Co 1996–; chair Br Soc of Magazine Editors 1987 (memb), memb Women's Financial Forum 1993; Editor of the Year award for Cosmopolitan Periodical Publishers Assoc 1989, Women's Magazine Editor of the Year award for SHE Br Soc of Magazine Editors 1990; *Recreations* family, reading, trekking, walking; *Clubs* Groucho, RAC; *Style*— Ms Linda Kelsey; ✉ c/o National Magazine Co, 72 Broadwick House, London W1F 9EP

KELSEY, Timothy Claude; s of Michael Kelsey (d 2010), and Anthea, *née* McFarlane; *b* 7 May 1965, Welwyn Garden City, Herts; *Educ* Wellington Coll Berks, Magdalene Coll Cambridge (late exhibitioner, MA); *m* (m dis), Alison Kelsey; 4 s; 2 s with Hilary Rowell; *Career* foreign stringer (Turkey) The Independent 1988–90, reporter Independent on Sunday 1990–95; Sunday Times: Insight Team 1995–97, focus ed 1997–98, news ed 1998–2000; ceo Dr Foster 2000–06, prog dir NHS Choices 2007–08, exec char Dr Foster Intelligence 2006–10, McKinsey & Co 2010–11, exec dir transparency and open data Cabinet Office HM Govt 2012, nat dir for patients and information NHS England 2012–; UK Govt advsr on transparency and open data 2011–; memb Nat Quality Bd 2009–12, tstee Nuffield Tst; Ind Healthcare Award for Innovation 2007, Health Investor Award for Outstanding Individual 2008; *Publications* Dervish: Invention of Modern Turkey (1996); *Recreations* my family, music, sailing, writing; *Clubs* Royal Dart Yacht, Naval and Military; *Style*— Timothy Kelsey, Esq; ✉ NHS England, Quarry House, Leeds LS2 7UE (e-mail tim.kelsey@nhs.net, Twitter @tkelsey1)

KELSEY-FRY, John; QC (2000); s of Dr Ian Kelsey-Fry, and Mary Josephine, *née* Fitzpatrick-Casey; *m* 29 July 2000, Sally Halkerston, da of Rod Muddle; *Career* called to the Bar Gray's Inn 1978; sr treasury counsel Central Criminal Court 1997–2000 (jr 1992–97); *Recreations* horseracing, golf; *Style*— John Kelsey-Fry, Esq, QC; ✉ Cloth Fair Chambers, 39–40 Cloth Fair, London EC1A 7NR (☎ 07875 012444)

KEMBALL, Christopher Ross Maguire; MBE (Mil 1973); s of John Patrick Gerard Kemball (d 2003), of Vila Praia De Ancora, Portugal, and Rachel Lucy, *née* Vernon; *b* 29 December 1946; *Educ* Ampleforth, Pembroke Coll Cambridge (BA); *m* 3 Feb 1979, Frances Maria, da of Flt Lt Richard Peter Monico, RAF (d 1945); 1 s (Charles b 1983); *Career* Regular Army Capt (actg Maj) Royal Green Jackets 1968–75, Sultan's Armed Forces, Maj Northern Frontier Regt 1972–73; dir Kleinwort Benson Ltd 1975–86, vice-chm Kleinwort Benson Hldgs Inc 1984–86, md Dillon Read & Co Inc 1986–91, exec md and co-head Dillon Read Ltd 1987–91, head of corp fin (emerging markets) and dir Baring Brothers & Co Ltd (now ING Barings) 1992–98, md corp fin ING Barings 1999–2000, vice-chm Hawkpoint Partners Ltd 2000–; chm: Berendsen Service Gp plc 2005– (non-exec dir 1998–), Frontier Medex Ltd 2010–; chm Progressive Supranuclear Palsy Assoc 2010–; *Recreations* opera, swimming, skiing, shooting, sailing, beekeeping; *Clubs* Royal Green Jackets, Brooks's; *Style*— Christopher Kemball, Esq, MBE; ✉ Hawkpoint Partners Ltd, 41 Lothbury, London EC2R 7AE (☎ 020 7665 4500)

KEMBALL, Air Marshal Sir John; KCB (1990), CBE (1981), DL (Suffolk 1999); s of Richard Charles Kemball (d 1983), of Suffolk, and Margaret James, *née* Robson (d 1987); *b* 31 January 1939, Bury St Edmunds, Suffolk; *Educ* Uppingham, Open Univ (BA, 1990); *m* 1962, Valerie Geraldine, da of Maj Albert John Webster, RA (d 1998); 2 da (Katherine b 1964, Samantha b 1966); *Career* cmmnd RAF 1957, served UK, France, Middle East, USA, cmd No 54 Sqdn 1976–78, RAF Laarbruch 1978–81, Cmdt RAF Central Flying Sch 1983–85, Cdr Br Forces Falkland Islands 1985–86, Chief of Staff and dep C-in-C Strike Cmd 1989–93, ADC to HM The Queen 1984–85, co-ordinator Br-American Community Rels MOD 1994–2004; chief exec Racing Welfare 1995–2004, pres Corp of Commissionaires 2002–08; memb ICL Def Advsy Bd 1996–2000; chm Essex Rivers NHS Healthcare Tst 1993–96; pres RAF Assoc 1995–98 (life vice-pres); Hon Col 77 Regt RE (V) 1993–96; High Sheriff Suffolk 2007–08; Freeman City of London 1995; FRAeS 2003 (pres Southend branch 2001–09); *Recreations* riding, gardening; *Clubs* RAF; *Style*— Air Marshal Sir John Kemball, KCB, CBE, DL, FRAeS

KEMBERY, John Philip; s of Alec George Kembery, of Keynsham, Somerset; *b* 6 October 1939; *Educ* Queen Elizabeth's Hosp Bristol, Univ of Surrey; *m* 1964, Marjorie Carolyn, da of Gilbert James Bowler, of Much Cowarne, Herefords; 2 s (Jonathan Alexander b

1967, Nicholas Philip b 1969); *Career* md: Alcan Extrusions 1975–80, Alcan Metal Centres 1980–81; chm: McKechnie Metals non-ferrous metal mfrs (md 1981–87), PSM Int plc, EADIE IND Ltd 2001–; dir and chm Metals and Engrg Divs McKechnie plc 1986–92, business conslt and chm MW Technologies 1992–95; exec chm Belgravium Technologies plc (formerly Eadie Holdings plc) 1997– (dir 1996–); non-exec chm: Wheelpower International 1993–94, Black and Luff Holdings Ltd 1994–98, Sunleigh plc 1995–98; non-exec dir: Trigon Cambridge Ltd 1993–95, Europower plc (formerly Brasway plc) 1994–2000, Crosrol Ltd 1995–, Trigon Packaging Systems (Europe) Ltd, Trigon Packaging Systems (UK) Ltd; pres Br Non-Ferrous Metals Fedn 1988–90; CEng, FIM, FInstD; *Recreations* golf, shooting, good food; *Style*— John Kembery, Esq; ✉ 12 Parkfields, Arden Drive, Dorridge, West Midlands B93 8LL (☎ 01564 730168, fax 01564 778057, mobile 07770 731021, e-mail john@kembery.net)

KEMBLE, Tom; s of Brian Kemble, MBE, of Wiltshire, and Sarah Hemus, of Somerset; *b* 20 May 1983, London; *Educ* Stowe, Univ of Nottingham (BA); *Career* sous chef Hedone London 2011–12, chef Faviken Sweden 2013, head chef Bonhams Restaurant London 2014– (1 Michelin Star 2016–); *Style*— Tom Kemble, Esq; ✉ Bonhams Restaurant, 7 Haunch of Venison Yard, London W1K 5EU (☎ 020 7468 5867, e-mail tom.kemble@bonhams.com, Twitter @DineatBonhams)

KEMP, Prof Bruce Ernest; s of Norman Beck Kemp (d 1956), and Mary Frances, *née* Officer (d 2015); *b* 15 December 1946, Sydney, Aust; *Educ* Univ of Adelaide (BAgrSc), Flinders Univ (PhD); *m* 23 Jan 1970, Alison Virginia; 3 s (Robert E S b 18 May 1977, William E B b 12 March 1980, Charles E F b 9 March 1983); *Career* postdoctoral fell Sch of Med Univ of Calif Davis 1974–76, Nat Heart Fndn fell Flinders Med Centre 1977–78; Univ of Melbourne: Queen Elizabeth II fell Howard Florey Inst 1979, sr research fell Howard Florey Inst 1980–84, sr research fell Repatriation Gen Hosp Heidelberg Victoria 1984–88, CSIRO Molecular and Health Technologies 2004–08, Pehr Edman fell St Vincent's Inst of Med Research 1989–2003 and 2009–, currently professorial assoc St Vincent's Hosp Victoria; research collaboration with Agen Biomedical 1987–99, memb Scientific Advsy Bd Besagen (formerly Bresatec Pty Ltd) 1993–2003, co-fndr and memb Scientific Advsy Bd Mercury Therapeutics Inc 1999–; memb Bd Genomic Disorders Research Centre (GDRC, formerly Mutation Research Centre) 1996–2003, memb Scientific Advsy Bd and Mgmnt Ctee Nat Serology Reference Lab (NSRL) 1997–2006; memb Editorial Bd: Cellular Signalling 1988–2003, Biochim Biophys Acta 1992–97, Biochemistry Jl 1994–96, Jl of Biological Chemistry 1998–; memb: Aust Soc for Biochemistry and Molecular Biology, Aust Soc for Med Research, Aust Soc for Microbiology, AAAS; Selwyn Smith Prize for Med Research 1988, Newman Award for Excellence in AIDS Research (jtly) 1989, AIDS Tst of Aust Award 1989, Wellcome Aust Medal for Med Research and Technol Devpt 1990, Wellcome Rapid Diagnostics Award 1991, Lemberg Medal Aust Soc for Biochemistry and Molecular Biology 1996, Royal Soc of Victoria Research Medal 1996, Max Planck Award 2000, Centenary Medal 2003, Leach Medal 2016; FAAS 2000, FRS 2002, Fedn fell 2003, FAAAS 2007; *Publications* Peptides and Protein Phosphorylation (ed, 1990); author of over 360 articles in jls and contribs and chapters to books; *Recreations* tennis; *Clubs* North Kew Tennis, Univ House (Melbourne); *Style*— Prof Bruce Kemp, FRS; ✉ St Vincent's Institute of Medical Research, 41 Victoria Parade, Fitzroy, Victoria 3065, Australia (☎ 00 61 3 9288 2480, fax 00 61 3 9416 5676, e-mail bkemp@svi.edu.au)

KEMP, His Hon Judge Charles James Bowring; s of Capt Michael John Barnett Kemp, ERD (d 1982), of Winchcombe, Glos, and Brigid Ann Vernon-Smith, *née* Bowring; *b* 27 April 1951; *Educ* Shrewsbury, UCL (LLB); *m* 21 Dec 1974, Fenella Anne, da of Harry Herring (d 1995), of Cropwell Butler, Notts; 1 da (Sophie b 11 Feb 1977), 1 s (Marcus b 28 Feb 1979); *Career* called to the Bar Gray's Inn 1973; recorder 1991–98, circuit judge 1998–; memb: Sussex Probation Bd 2001–07, Sussex Courts Bd 2004–07, Surrey and Sussex Courts Bd 2007–10; vice-pres E Sussex Magistrates Assoc 2013–; *Recreations* tennis, swimming, cricket, golf, country pursuits, music; *Clubs* Piltdown Golf, Harbour Club Portscatho; *Style*— His Hon Judge Kemp; ✉ Lewes Combined Court Centre, 182 High Street, Lewes, East Sussex BN7 1YB (☎ 01273 480400, e-mail c.kemp2@me.com)

KEMP, Gene; da of Albert Rushton, of Tamworth, Staffs, and Alice Anne, *née* Sutton; *Educ* Wigginton C of E Sch, Tamworth Girls' HS, Univ of Exeter (BA); *m* 1 (m dis), Norman Charles Pattison, s of Charles Pattison; m 2, Allan William Kemp, s of late William Kemp; 1 s (Richard William), 2 da (Judith Eve, Chantal Jennifer); *Career* author; teacher: Wychbury HS Hagley, Drewsteignton CP Sch, St Sidwell's Combined Sch Exeter, Rolle Coll; govr: Central and Middle Schs Exeter 1975–85, Montgomery Sch Exeter 1994–96, St Sidwell's Sch Exeter 2001–04; memb: Lab Pty, Soc of Authors; Hon MA Univ of Exeter 1984; *Awards* The Other Award 1977, Carnegie Medal 1978; shortlisted: Whitbread Award 1985, Smarties Award 1986 and 1990; *Books* incl: Tamworth Pig Stories, Cricklepit Combined School Stories (incl The Turbulent Term of Tyke Tiler, Gowie Corby Plays Chicken and Just Ferret), The Well, Dog Days and Cat Naps (short stories), Mr Magus is Waiting for You (TV drama), Ducks and Dragons (poetry, ed), The Mink War (narrative poem), Roundabout, Puffin Book of Ghosts and Ghouls, The Wacky World of Wesley Baker, Zowey Corby's Story (fiction), Goosey Farm, Rebel, Rebel (anthology), Goosey Farm: The Wishing Tower, Bluebeard's Castle, Snaggletooth's Mystery, Seriously Weird, Haunted Piccolo, Nothing Scares Me; *Recreations* gardening, politics, reading, grandchildren; *Style*— Mrs Gene Kemp; ✉ c/o Philippa Milnes-Smith, Lucas Alexander Whitley Ltd, 14 Vernon Street, London W14 0RJ (☎ 020 7471 7900); c/o Faber & Faber Ltd, 3 Queen Square, London WC1N 3AU (☎ 020 7465 0045, fax 020 7465 0034); c/o Puffin, 27 Wrights Lane, London W8 5TZ (☎ 020 7416 3000, fax 020 7416 3099); c/o Orchard Books, 96 Leonard Street, London EC2A 4XD (☎ 020 7739 2929); e-mail genekemp6@aol.com

KEMP, Kit; MBE (2012); da of William Henry Thomas (d 1982), and Stella Gould (d 1999); *b* 29 November 1956, Southampton; *m* 6 July 1983, Timothy J R Kemp, MBE; 3 da (Tiffany b 28 Feb 1986, Willow b 19 Oct 1987, Araminta b 26 July 1990); *Career* interior designer; early career working in architectural practice, then started own design co; opened (with Tim Kemp) Dorset Square Hotel London 1985, co-fndr (with Tim Kemp) Firmdale Hotels 1986–; hotels incl: The Soho Hotel, Charlotte Street Hotel, Covent Garden Hotel, The Pelham Hotel, Knightsbridge Hotel, Number Sixteen, Haymarket Hotel; numerous design and hotel awards, Queen's Award 2000 and 2006, Crown Estate Urban Business Award 2007; *Recreations* riding, horses; *Style*— Mrs Kit Kemp, MBE; ✉ Firmdale Hotels, 18 Thurloe Place, London SW7 2SP (☎ 020 7581 4045, e-mail kitk@firmdale.com)

KEMP, Prof Martin John; s of Frederick Maurice Kemp (d 1990), of Watton, Norfolk, and Violet Anne, *née* Tull (d 2000); *b* 5 March 1942; *Educ* Windsor GS, Downing Coll Cambridge (MA), Courtauld Inst of Art London; *m* 27 Aug 1966 (m dis 2005), Jill, da of Dennis William Lightfoot, of Bisham, Bucks; 1 da (Joanna b 1972), 1 s (Jonathan b 1976); *Career* lectr in history of western art Dalhousie Univ Nova Scotia 1965, lectr in fine arts Univ of Glasgow 1966–81; Univ of St Andrews: prof of fine arts 1981–90, memb Ct 1988–91, prof of the history and theory of art 1991–95, provost St Leonard's Coll 1991–94; prof of history of art Univ of Oxford 1995–2008 (currently emeritus prof); memb Inst for Advanced Study Princeton 1984–85, Slade prof Univ of Cambridge 1987–88, Benjamin Sonenberg visiting prof Inst of Fine Arts NYU, Wiley prof Univ of N Carolina Chapel Hill 1993, Br Acad Wolfson research prof 1993–98, visiting scholar Getty Research Inst LA 2002–, Mellon research fell Canadian Centre for Architecture Montreal 2004, sr fell I Tatti Harvard 2010, Page-Barbour lectr Univ of Virginia 2012, Robert Janson La Palme lectr Princeton Univ 2013; tstee: Nat Galleries of Scotland 1982–87, V&A 1986–89, Br Museum 1995; hon prof of history Royal Scottish Acad 1985–, pres Leonardo da Vinci Soc 1987–96, chm Assoc of Art Historians 1989–92, memb Exec Scottish Museums Cncl 1990–96, dir and chm Graeme Murray Gallery 1990–92; dir: Interalia Bristol 1992–99, Museums Training Inst 1993–99, Wallace Kemp/Artakt 2001–03; memb Cncl Br Soc for the History of Science 1994–97; fell Downing Coll Cambridge 1999; Hon DLitt Heriot-Watt Univ 1995, hon doctorate Appsala Univ 2009; hon memb American Acad of Arts and Sciences 1996, hon fell Glyndwr Univ 2009, hon fell Trinity Coll Oxford; FRSA 1983–98, HRSA 1985, FRIAS 1988, FBA 1991, FRSE 1992; *Books* incl: The Science of Art – Optical Themes in Western Art from Brunelleschi to Seurat, Behind The Picture – Art and Evidence in the Italian Renaissance, The Oxford History of Western Art, Visualizations, The 'Nature' Book of Art and Science, Spectacular Bodies (with Marina Wallace), Leonardo, The Human Animal, La Bella Principessa, Christ to Coke: How Image becomes Icon, The Chapel of Trinity College Oxford (2013) Art in History: 600BC-2000AD (2015); *Recreations* sport (especially hockey), early and modern music, modern dance; *Style*— Prof Martin Kemp, FBA, FRSE; ✉ Trinity College, Oxford OX1 3BH; c/o agent Caroline Dawnay (e-mail cdawnay@unitedagents.co.uk)

KEMP, (Bernard) Peter; s of William Gordon Kemp, of Chorley, Lancs, and Teresa, *née* Howarth; *b* 16 October 1942; *Educ* Thornleigh Coll Bolton, King's Coll London (BA, MPhil); *Career* lectr in English Middx Poly 1968–88; regular book reviewer: The Listener 1978–91, TLS 1980– (weekly TV and radio column 1982–86); chief fiction reviewer Sunday Times 1995– (regular fiction reviewer 1987–95, fiction ed 1995–2010); theatre reviewer The Independent 1986–90; regular broadcaster on: Front Row, Saturday Review, Night Waves, Open Book; FRSL 2015; *Books* Muriel Spark (1974), H G Wells and The Culminating Ape (1982, 2 edn 1996), The Oxford Dictionary of Literary Quotations (ed, 1997, 2 edn 2003); *Recreations* travel, art galleries, music, gardening; *Style*— Peter Kemp, Esq; ✉ The Sunday Times, 1 Pennington Street, London E1 9XW

KEMP, Richard Harry; s of Thomas Kemp (d 2007), and Audrey, *née* Withers (d 1965); *b* 8 July 1956, Romford, Essex; *Educ* Oakham Sch, St Catharine's Coll Cambridge (MA), Université Libre de Bruxelles; *m* 20 June 1987, Margaret, *née* Wade; 2 s (Christopher b 26 Feb 1988, Nicholas b 6 May 1990); *Career* admitted slr 1980; with Clifford-Turner 1978–84, with Hopkins & Wood 1984–91 (ptnr 1985), ptnr and co-fndr London office Hammond Suddards 1992–95, ptnr Garretts 1995–97 (first head European intellectual property/IT practice 1996), fndr and managing ptnr Kemp & Co 1997–2001 (ldr Legal Business Technol Team of the Year 2002), fndr and sr ptnr Kemp Little LLP 2001–14, fndr Kemp IT Law 2014 (UK IT Law Firm of the Year Finance Monthly 2015); memb Bd Computer Law Assoc 2002–06; memb Law Soc; *Clubs* Hurlingham; *Style*— Richard Kemp, Esq; ✉ Kemp IT Law, 21 Napier Avenue, London SW6 3PS (☎ 020 3011 1670, e-mail richard.kemp@kempitlaw.com)

KEMP, Prof Roger John; s of late Ivor Kemp, and Audrey, *née* Hobbs; *b* 18 December 1945; *Educ* Hitchin GS, Univ of Sussex (BSc); *m* 3 Aug 1968, Joan Caroline, da of Kenneth and Winifred Walker (both decd); 1 da (Deborah Rachael b 29 Oct 1971), 1 s (Nicholas Ian b 15 Dec 1972); *Career* electrical and mechanical engr; science teacher Malaysia VSO 1964–65, various engrg appts 1969–85, engrg dir GEC Transportation Projects Ltd Manchester 1985–89, directeur des Études d'Ensemble GEC Alsthom SA Paris 1989–91, project dir Eurostar Paris 1991–93, safety dir ALSTOM Transport 2000–03, prof of engrg Lancaster Univ 2003– (visiting prof 1998–2003); memb various professional ctees and author of numerous papers in various professional jls; CEng, FIEE, FIMechE, FREng 1995; *Recreations* playing double bass, music, theatre; *Style*— Prof Roger Kemp, FREng; ✉ Engineering Department, Lancaster University, Lancaster LA1 4YW (e-mail r.kemp@lancaster.ac.uk)

KEMP, Ross; s of John Kemp, of Norfolk, and Jean Kemp; *b* 21 July 1964, Essex; *Educ* Webber Douglas Theatre Sch; *Career* actor and presenter; estab prodn co Mongoose TV; *Theatre* early career at Westcliffe-on-Sea Rep Theatre; roles incl Petruchio in Taming of the Shrew; *Television* incl: Emmerdale Farm 1986–87, Birds of a Feather 1989, EastEnders (as Grant Mitchell) 1990–99 and 2005 (Best Actor Br Soap Awards 1999 and 2001), City Central 1998, Hero of the Hour 2000, Without Motive 2000, In Defence 2000, A Christmas Carol 2000, Ultimate Force I, II and III 2002 and 2005, The Crooked Man 2003, A Line in the Sand 2004, Spartacus 2004, Lethal Attraction 2004, Ross Kemp on Gangs 2006 (Best Factual Series BAFTA Awards 2006), Ross Kemp on Afghanistan 2007, Ross Kemp: A Kenya Special 2008, Ross Kemp Meets the Glue Kids of Kenya 2008, Ross Kemp in Search of Pirates 2009, Extreme Worlds 2011; *Publications* Gangs (2007), Gangs 2 (2008), Ross Kemp on Afghanistan (2009), Warriors (2010), Devil to Pay (2011); *Clubs* Chelsea Arts, Groucho, Home House; *Style*— Ross Kemp, Esq; ✉ c/o Waheed Alli, 4th Floor, Aldwych House, 81 Aldwych, London WC2B 4HN (☎ 020 7061 3885)

KEMP, Prof Terence James; s of Thomas Brynmor Kemp (d 1978), and Emily Maud, *née* Spriggs (d 1982); *b* 26 June 1938; *Educ* Cardiff HS, Watford GS, Jesus Coll Oxford (MA, DPhil, DSc); *m* 8 April 1961, Sheila Therese, da of Henry Francis Turner (d 1972); 1 s (Jeremy b 1964), 2 da (Celia b 1966, Penelope b 1969); *Career* Univ of Warwick: asst lectr 1965, lectr 1966, sr lectr 1970, reader 1974, prof 1980– (emeritus 2006–), pro-vice-chllr 1983–89, seconded pt/t to Quality Assurance Agency 1995–2009; specialist subject assessor HEQC 1993–95; sr ed Progress in Reaction Kinetics and Mechanism, assoc ed Science Progress; memb Evaluation Ctee: Univ of Malta 1990, Univ of Namibia 1993, Univ of Qatar 2001; CChem, FRSC 1969, FRSA 1986; Order of Merit Polish Repub 1985; *Books* Introductory Photochemistry (1971), Dictionary of Physical Chemistry (1992); *Recreations* philately, cinema, walking; *Style*— Prof Terence Kemp; ✉ 7 Barford Road, Kenilworth CV8 2AY (☎ 01926 730746, e-mail terry-sheila@ntlworld.com)

KEMSLEY, Arthur Joseph; s of Joseph Alfred Kemsley (d 1966), of Stepney, London, and Ivy Elizabeth Everet; *b* 21 May 1936; *Educ* Nicholas Gibson Secdy Sch; *m* 1967, Maureen (d 1989); 1 da (Gemma Louise b 29 Sept 1983); *Career* SAC RAF 1953–58; photographer; copy boy Advertising Dept Kemsley Newspapers 1951–52, gen asst Pathe Pictorial 1952–53; BAA (formerly Heathrow Airport Ltd): joined 1958, chief photographer 1965–89, TV prodr/dir 1989–; R&D on video-visual imaging system for recording condition and quality of runway approach lights at airports (first of its kind) 1993–95, currently working on range of aviation safety progs covering all aspects of airport ops incl digital imaging and computer based interactive trg for airport staff; dir Airside Training Co 2001; developing immersive learning for aviation airside ops using DVD interactive technol; aviation trg with Aircraft Service Int Gp 2002; trg conslt Air France Services Ltd 2005– (now Cobalt Ground Solutions Ltd after 2009 merger with KLM Ground Services); development of interactive CBT trg courses for aircraft ground handling learning 2013–14; 2 Gold and 3 Silver Medals World Airports Photographers competition 1988, Bronze Medallion USAF (for photographing the space shuttle Discovery); *Recreations* research and development for future aviation trg; *Style*— Arthur Kemsley, Esq; ✉ Cobalt Ground Solutions Limited, Room 2535, Terminal 4, Heathrow Airport, Middlesex TW6 1RR

KENCH, Eric Arthur; s of Joseph Peter Kench (d 2005), of Oxon, and Ethel Catherine, *née* Younger; *b* 30 September 1952, Henley on Thames, Oxon; *Educ* Henley GS; *m* 20 July 1974, Kathleen Jennifer, da of Philip Hague (d 1980); 1 s (David b 1979), 2 da (Caroline b 1981, Sarah b 1982); *Career* chartered accountant; fndr E A Kench & Co (now Kench & Co Ltd) 1982–; former chm Thames Valley Young Chartered Accountants Gp; ICAEW: memb Smaller Practitioners' Ctee 1984–90, memb Gen Practitioner Bd 1990–2000 (vice-

K

chm 1998–2000), vice-chm Gen Practitioner Panel 2000–03, chm Practice Soc 2004–07; memb: Cncl 2004–08, Practice Advsy Bd 2007–11, Practice Ctee 2011–13, Ethical Standards Ctee 2013–15, Learning and Professional Devpt Bd 2015–; pres Thames Valley Soc of Chartered Accountants 1987–88; Liveryman Worshipful Co of Chartered Accountants in England and Wales; FCA; *Recreations* squash, flying (private pilot), reading, working; *Style—* Eric Kench, Esq; ✉ Kench & Co Ltd, 10 Station Road, Henley-on-Thames, Oxfordshire RG9 1AY (☎ 01491 578207, e-mail erickench@kench.co.uk)

KENDAL, Felicity Anne; CBE (1995); da of Geoffrey Kendal (d 1998), of Chelsea, London, and Laura May, *née* Liddell (d 1992); *Educ* convents in India; *m* 1, 1969 (m dis 1976), Drewe Henley; 1 s (Charles b 23 Jan 1973); m 2, 1983 (m dis 1991), Michael Edward Rudman, s of Duke Rudman, of Dallas, Texas; 1 s (Jacob Henry b 1 Oct 1987); *Career* grew up touring and acting with parents' theatre co in India and Far East, London debut in Minor Murder (Savoy) 1967; *Theatre* Henry V and The Promise (Leicester) 1968, Back to Methuselah (NT) 1969, A Midsummer Night's Dream and Much Ado About Nothing (Regents Park) 1970, Kean (Oxford 1970 and London 1971), Romeo and Juliet,' Tis Pity She's a Whore 1972, The Three Arrows 1972, The Norman Conquests (Globe) 1974, Once Upon a Time (Bristol) 1976, Arms and the Man (Greenwich) 1978, Clouds (Duke of York's) 1978, Amadeus (NT) 1979, Othello (NT) 1980, On the Razzle (NT) 1981, The Second Mrs Tanqueray (NT) 1981, The Real Thing (Strand) 1982, Jumpers (Aldwych) 1985, Made in Bangkok (Aldwych) 1986, Hapgood (Aldwych) 1988, Much Ado About Nothing and Ivanov (Strand) 1989, Hidden Laughter (Vaudeville) 1990, Tartuffe (Playhouse) 1991, Heartbreak House (Yvonne Arnaud Guildford and Haymarket) 1992, Arcadia (RNT) 1993, An Absolute Turkey (Globe) 1994, Indian Ink (Aldwych) 1995, Mind Millie for Me (Haymarket) 1996, Waste (Old Vic) 1997, The Seagull (Old Vic) 1997, Alarms and Excursions (Gielgud Theatre) 1998, Fallen Angels (Apollo) 2000, Humble Boy (Gielgud Theatre) 2002, Happy Days (Arts Theatre) 2004, Amy's View (Garrick Theatre) 2006, The Vortex (Apollo Theatre) 2008, The Last Cigarette (Trafalgar Studios) 2009, Mrs Warren's Profession (Comedy Theatre) 2010, Relatively Speaking (Wyndham Theatre) 2013, Chin Chin (UK Tour) 2013, Hay Fever (UK Tour/Australia Tour) 2014, Hay Fever (Duke of York's Theatre) 2015; *Television* Barbara in The Good Life 1975–77, Twelfth Night 1979, Solo 1980 and 1982, The Mistress 1985, The Camomile Lawn 1992, Honey for Tea 1994, How Proust Can Save Your Life 1999, Rosemary and Thyme 2003–05, Doctor Who 2008, Strictly Come Dancing 2010, Indian Shakespeare Quest 2012, Piers Morgan Life Stories 2012, Secrets of the Workhouse 2013; *Films* Shakespeare Wallah 1965, Valentino 1976, Parting Shots 1998; *Awards* Variety Club Most Promising Newcomer 1974, Best Actress 1979, Clarence Derwent Award 1980, Variety Club Best Actress Award 1984, Evening Standard Best Actress Award 1989, Actress of the Year Sony Radio Awards 1992, Variety Club Best Actress Award 2000; *Books* White Cargo (autobiography, 1998); *Style—* Miss Felicity Kendal, CBE; ✉ c/o United Agents, 12–26 Lexington Street, London W1F 0LE (☎ 020 3214 0800)

KENDALL, Bridget; MBE (1994); da of David George Kendall, and Diana Louise, *née* Fletcher; *b* 27 April 1956; *Educ* Perse Sch for Girls Cambridge, Lady Margaret Hall Oxford (BA), Harvard Univ (Harkness fell), St Antony's Coll Oxford, Voronezh Univ (Br Cncl scholar), Moscow State Univ (Br Cncl postgrad scholar); *Partner* Amanda Farnsworth (civil partnership); *Career* BBC: prodr and reporter BBC World Service, BBC Radio 4 and Newsnight 1983–89, Moscow corr 1989–93, made series of special reports on Russia for Newsnight and Panorama 1993–94, Washington corr 1994–98, diplomatic corr 1998–2016, host The Forum (flagship radio prog) 2008–; Master Peterhouse Univ of Cambridge 2016–; tstee Asia House 2011–14, memb Advsy Cncl Wilton Park 2013–; visiting prof Univ of Lincoln 2005–; James Cameron Meml Award for Journalism 1992, Voice of the Listener and Viewer Award for Excellence in Broadcasting 1993, Int Reporter Award Political Studies Assoc 2015; hon fell St Antony's Coll Oxford, hon fell LMH Oxford 2015; Hon DUniv Univ of Central England in Birmingham 1997, Hon LLD Univ of St Andrews 2001, Hon LLD Univ of Exeter 2002; *Books* The Day That Shook the World (contrib, 2001), The Battle for Iraq (contrib, 2003), Int News Reporting: Frontlines and Deadlines (contrib, 2009), The Two Princesses (foreword, 2010), The Secret City (foreword, 2012), 1009: Russians Remember a Turning Point (foreword, 2013); *Recreations* literature, music, theatre and film; *Style—* Ms Bridget Kendall, MBE; ✉ Peterhouse, Trumpington Street, Cambridge CB2 1RD

KENDALL, David Richard; s of Frederick Richard Kendall, of Lutterworth, Leics, and Gwendoline Florence, *née* Blackwell; *b* 17 September 1955; *Educ* Lutterworth GS, Univ of Birmingham (LLB), City of London Poly (MA), Sprachen und Dolmetsch Institut Munich (Dip); *m* 28 June 1980, Marsha Alexa, da of Allan Rothenberg; 1 da (Sarah Louise b 13 Feb 1982), 2 s (Ralph Alexander b 14 Sept 1984, Ian William b 1 April 1986); *Career* Messrs Hedleys: articled clerk 1979–81, asst slr 1981–85, ptnr 1985–88; ptnr D J Freeman 1988–2003 (head Insurance Dept 1991–2003), sr ptnr Kendall Freeman 2003–07; ptnr: Edwards Angell Palmer & Dodge 2008–11, Edwards Wildman Palmer 2011–15, Cooley 2015–; panel arbitrator Lloyd's 1993–; chm Br Insurance Law Assoc 2012–14; memb: Law Soc 1977, Fedn of Defence and Corp Counsel 1993, Cncl Br Insurance Law Assoc; ARIAS; *Recreations* tennis, woodwork; *Style—* David Kendall, Esq; ✉ Cooley (UK) LLP, Dashwood, 69 Old Broad Street, London EC2M 1QS (☎ 020 7583 4055, e-mail dkendall@cooley.com)

KENDALL, (Gilbert) John; s of Arthur Charles Kendall (d 1983), of Crickhowell, Powys, and Hilda Mary, *née* Morgan (d 2001); *b* 31 May 1950, Oxford; *Educ* Rugby (scholar), New Coll Oxford (exhibitioner, MA), KCL; *m* 4 Oct 1986, Jennifer Lynne, da of Peter Owen Watton; *Career* slr; articled clerk Stephenson Harwood 1973; Allen & Overy: slr 1977–, ptnr 1985–98, specialist in litigation, arbitration and construction law, managing ptnr Litigation Dept 1994–97; ind mediator 1998–2012; mayor Presteigne and Norton Town Cncl 2011–12; Freeman City of London; *Publications* Expert Determination (4 edn, 2008, with Clive Freedman and James Farrell (5 edn renamed Kendall on Expert Determination by Freedman and Farrell only, 2015)), author of numerous articles; *Recreations* opera; *Style—* John Kendall, Esq; ✉ The Manor House, St David's Street, Presteigne, Powys LD8 2BP (☎ 01544 260019, e-mail johnkendall475@gmail.com)

KENDALL, Prof Kevin; Cyril Kendall (d 1960), of Accrington, Lancs, and Margaret, *née* Swarbrick (d 1950); *b* 2 December 1943; *Educ* St Marys Coll Blackburn, Univ of London (BSc), Cavendish Lab Cambridge (PhD), Monash Univ; *m* 1969, Patricia Jennifer, da of Jim Heyes; 1 da (Michaela b 21 Aug 1970), 1 s (Alexander b 8 Nov 1971); *Career* researcher Joseph Lucas 1961–66, scientist BR 1969–71, fell Monash Univ 1972–74, fell Univ of Akron 1974, scientist ICI Runcorn 1974–93, prof of materials science Keele Univ 1993–2000, prof of formulation engrg Univ of Birmingham 2000–11; fndr dir Adelan Ltd 1996–; FRS 1993; *Publications* Molecular Adhesion and its Applications (2001), High Temperature Solid Oxide Fuel Cells (2003), Adhesion of Cells, Viruses and Nanoparticles (2010); numerous papers in learned journals 1971–20135; *Recreations* walking, cycling; *Style—* Prof Kevin Kendall, FRS; ✉ Metallurgy and Materials, University of Birmingham, Edgbaston, Birmingham B15 2TT (☎ 0121 414 2739); Wycherley, Tower Road, Ashley Heath, Market Drayton, Shropshire TF9 4PY (☎ 01630 672665, e-mail k.kendall@bham.ac.uk)

KENDALL, Nicholas John (Nick); s of Leonard and Barbara Kendall; *b* 29 September 1959; *Educ* Manchester Grammar, ChCh Oxford (BA); *m* 23 Sept 1989, Patrice Rosanna, da of Roy Charlton Chasteau; *Career* account exec Sharps Advertising 1981–82, account planner Burkitt Weinreich Clients & Co 1982–87; Bartle Bogle Hegarty: account planner 1987–93, bd dir 1989–, head of planning 1993–99, global planning dir 1999–2003; Keeper of the Quaich 2009; Gold IPA Effectiveness Awards 1992; memb Effectiveness Ctee IPA 1993, convenor of judges IPA Effectiveness Awards 1998, designer and chief examiner IPA Dip professional qualification 2006 and 2007; memb MRS; *Recreations* my wife, pottery; *Style—* Nick Kendall, Esq; ✉ Bartle Bogle Hegarty, 60 Kingly Street, London W1R 6DS (☎ 020 7734 1677, fax 020 7437 3666)

KENEALLY, Thomas Michael (Tom); AO (1983); *m*, Judith; 2 da (Margaret, Jane); *Career* author and playwright; contrib to numerous magazines and newspapers incl: New York Times Book Review, Boston Globe, Washington Post, The Times, The Guardian, The Independent, Observer Colour Magazine, Time, Newsweek, The Australian, Sydney Morning Herald, Medical Journal of Australia; work translated into over 15 languages incl: French, German, Spanish, Hebrew, Czechoslovakian, Flemish, Japanese; distinguished prof Dept of English Creative Writing Sch Univ of Calif Irvine 1991–95 (prof 1985–), visiting prof and Berg prof Dept of English Creative Writing Sch New York Univ 1988; inaugural memb Australia-China Cncl 1978–83; pres: Aust Nat Book Cncl 1985–89, Aust Soc of Authors 1990 (cncl memb 1981–, chm 1987–90); dir Australian Republican Movement Movement 1993– (inaugural chairperson 1991–93); memb: Lit Bd Aust Cncl 1985–, Advsy Panel Aust Constitutional Cmmn 1985–88, Aust Writers' Guild, US Screenwriters' Guild; Hon DLit: Queensland Univ 1993, Nat Univ of Ireland 1994, Fairleigh Dickenson Univ USA 1994, Rollins Coll USA 1995; Dr (hc) Univ of W Sydney 1997; Univ Medal Univ of Calif Irvine 1995; FRSL, FAAAS 1993; *Books* incl: Bring Larks and Heroes (1967, Miles Franklin Award), Three Cheers for the Paraclete (Miles Franklin Award 1968), The Survivor (1969, Captain Cook Bi-Centenary Prize 1970), The Chant of Jimmie Blacksmith (1972, Booker McConnell shortlisted, RSL Prize 1973, later filmed), Gossip from the Forest (1975, The Age Fiction Prize, Booker McConnell shortlisted 1977, filmed 1979), Ned Kelly and the City of Bees (for children, 1978), Confederates (1979, Booker McConnell shortlisted), Schindler's Ark (1982, Booker McConnell Prize, Los Angeles Times Prize for Fiction 1983, titled Schindler's List in US), A Family Madness (1985), The Playmaker (1987), Towards Asmara (1989), Flying Hero Class (1991), Now And In Time To Be (1991), Place where Souls are Born (1992), Woman of the Inner Sea (1992), Jacko (1993), A River Town (1995), Bettany's Book (2000), The Office of Innocence (2002), The Tyrant's Novel (2004), The Widow and Her Hero (2007), The People's Train (2009), Australians: Eureka to the Diggers (2011), Daughters of Mars (2012), Shame and the Captives (2013), Napoleon's Last Island (2015 (Australia) and 2016 (UK)); *Non-Fiction* The Utility Player (1993), Our Republic (1993), Homebush Boy – A Memoir (1995), The Great Shame (1999), American Scoundrel (2002), Lincoln (2004), The Commonwealth of Thieves: The Story of the Founding of Australia (2006), Australians: Origins To Eureka (2009), Three Famines (2011), Australians: Eureka to the Diggers (2011), Australians: Flappers to Vietnam (2013); *Plays* incl: Childermas (1968), An Awful Rose (1972), Gossip from the Forest (1983), The Playmaker (adapted from novel, 1988); *Film and Television scripts* incl: Too Many People are Disappearing, Silver City (Critics' Circle award for Best Screenplay 1985), Libido, Catalpa – The Australian Break, Corroboree; *Style—* Tom Keneally, Esq, AO, FRSL

KENILWORTH, 4 Baron (UK 1937); (John) Randle Siddeley; only s of 3 Baron Kenilworth (d 1981); *b* 16 June 1954; *Educ* Northease Manor, London Coll of Furniture; *m* 1, 1983 (m dis 1990), Kim, only da of Danie Serfontein, of Newcastle upon Tyne; m 2, 15 Aug 1991, Mrs Kiki McDonough, *née* Axford; 2 s (Hon William Randle b 24 Jan 1992, Hon Edward Oscar b 4 Feb 1994); *Heir* s, Hon William Siddeley; *Career* dir: Siddeley Landscape Designs, Randle Siddeley Assocs; *Style—* The Rt Hon the Lord Kenilworth; ✉ e-mail randle@randlesiddeley.co.uk

KENNA, Michael; s of Walter Kenna (d 2006), and Eva, *née* Sherrington (d 1968); *b* 20 November 1953, Widnes, Cheshire; *Educ* St Joseph's Coll Upholland, Banbury Sch of Art, London Coll of Printing (HND Photography); *m* 1, 1981 (m dis 1990), Kathryn Grady Crawley; 1 da (Olivia Morgan b 1985); m 2, 1991 (m dis 2007), Camille Solyagua; m 3, 2011, Mamta Mani; *Career* fine art photographer/master printer since 1978 (specialising in the interaction between the natural landscape and urban structures); advertising clients 1990– incl: Adidas, Audi, Bank of America, BMW, British Rail, British Airways, Isuzu, Jeep Chrysler, Landrover, Mazda, Mazerati, Moët et Chandon, RAF, Rolls Royce, Saab, Spanish Tourist Bd, Toshiba, Volvo; Hon MA Brooks Inst Santa Barbara CA; Chevalier de l'Ordre des Artes et des Lettres 2000; *Solo Exhibitions* recent exhibitions incl: Michael Kenna-Saturo Hoshino (Staniar Gallery Washington and Lee Univ USA and Zeit Gallery Tokyo) 2009, Michael Kenna – Retrospective (Centro Andaluz de al Fotografia Almeria Spain) 2009, Charles A Hartman Fine Art Portland USA 2009, Michael Kenna – Landscape and Memories (Kushiro Art Museum Japan and Galerie Box Brussels) 2009, Michael Kenna – Retrospective (Bibliotheque Nationale de France and Galerie Obscura Paris) 2009, Plum Blossoms Gallery Hong Kong 2010, A Gallery for Fine Photography New Orleans 2010, Galerie Wouter van Leeuwen Amsterdam 2010, BLD Gallery Tokyo 2010, Craig Krull Gallery LA 2010, Shanghai Int Art Exhbn 2010, Stephen Wirtz Gallery San Francisco 2010, Michael Kenna – Immagini dei Settimo Giorno (Palazzo Magnani Museum Italy) 2010, Catherine Edelman Gallery Chicago 2010, Bernheimer Gallery Munich 2010 and 2011, G Gibson Gallery Seattle 2010 and 2011, Michael Kenna – Landscapes and Memory (Miyanomori Art Museum Sapporo Japan) 2010, Robert Mann Gallery NY 2010, Timeless Gallery Beijing 2011, Elipsis Gallery Istanbul 2011, Rebekah Jacob Gallery Charleston S Carolina 2011, Plum Blossoms Gallery Hong Kong 2011, Taiwan Photo Art Fair 2011, Birgit Filzmaier Fine Art Zurich 2011, Venezia (Jardin Raymond VI du Musees des Abbatoirs Toulouse and Columbia Museum of Art) 2011, Le Souffle des Arts Bargeme France 2011, Galerie de la Rue Saint-Victoire Brittany France 2011, Impossible to Forget (Casa Samano Museum Bogota) 2011, Casalgrande Padana Italy 2011, Michael Kenna – Retrospective (Moscow Museum of Modern Art) 2011, Galerie Troncin-Denis Nancy France 2011, Galerie Camera Obscura Paris 2011, Weston Gallery Carmel CA 2011, Gallery KONG Seoul 2011, Asia View (1839 Gallery Taipei) 2012, In France (BLD Gallery Tokyo) 2012, Galeria PH Neutro Verona 2012, Galeria Galaverni Italy 2012, Hokkaido to Huangshan (M97 Gallery Shanghai) 2012, Huangshan (Albrecht Gallery Berlin) 2012, Tranquil Morning (Galerie KONG Seoul) 2012; *Group Exhibitions* recent exhibitions incl: Paris – zwischen Traum und Nostalgie (Birgit Filzmaier Fine Art Zurich) 2009, L'Art del Mar (Fundacio Forum Tarragona Spain) 2009, Les Nuages...la-bas...les merveilleux nuages (Musee Malraux Le Havre France) 2009, Right through the very heart of it (Robert Mann Gallery NY) 2009, Voyages Pittoresques en Normandie (Musee de Beaux Caen France) 2009, Picturing Eden (Ringling Museum of Art Sarasota FL) 2009, High Modernism: Alfred Steigliz and His Legacy (Amon Carter Museum TX) 2009, 8th NW Biennial (Tacoma Art Museum Washington USA) 2009, Le Stanze della Fotografia (Palazzo della Ragione Milan 2010, Proof (Catherine Edelman Gallery Chicago) 2010, Epilogues 2 (Robert Mann Gallery NY) 2010, Blow Up (G Gibson Gallery Seattle) 2010, Versaille Photographie 1859–2009 (Chateau de Versailles France) 2010, On Site/In Site: Selections from the Permanent Collection (De Saisset Museum Santa Clara Univ CA) 2010, 10 Ans 1999–2009 Parcour d'Une Collection (Theatre de la Photographie et de l'Image Nice) 2010, Ulsan Int Photography Festival S Korea 2011, Regards Croiss sur 60 ans de Photographie (Le Royal Monceau Raffles Paris) 2011, Collecting for the Future: The Safeco Gift and New Acquisitions (Tacoma Art Museum Washington USA) 2011, Twentieth Anniversary Exhbn (G Gibson Gallery Seattle) 2011, The Industrial Modern (Madison Museum of Contemporary Art Wisconsin) 2011, L'Arbre et le Photographe (Ecole Nationale Superieure des Beaux-Arts Paris) 2012; *Selected*

Collections work included in the permanent collections of numerous museums incl: Australian Nat Gallery Canberra, Bibliothèque Nationale de France, Fine Los Angeles County Museum of Art CA, Maison Européenne de la Photographie Paris, Musee National d'Art Moderne Paris, Museum of Fine Arts Boston, Museum of Fine Arts Houston, National Gallery of Art Washington DC, Rijksmuseum Amsterdam, San Francisco MOMA, Shanghai Art Museum, Smithsonian American Art Museum Washington DC, Tokyo Met Museum of Photography, Umleckoprmyslové Museum v Praze Prague, V&A London; *Awards* Imogen Cunningham Award (San Francisco) 1981, Art in Public Buildings Award (California Arts Cmmn Sacramento) 1987, The Inst for Aesthetic Devpt Award (Pasadena) 1989, Golden Saffron Award (Consuegra Spain) 1996; *Selected Books and Catalogues* The Hound of the Baskervilles (photographic illustrations, 1985), Michael Kenna 1977–1987 (1987), Night Walk (1988), Le Desert de Retz (1990), Michael Kenna (1990), The Elkhorn Slough and Moss Landing (photographic illustrations, 1991), Michael Kenna – A Twenty Year Retrospective (1994), The Rouge (1995), Les Notre's Gardens (1997), Monique's Kindergarten (1997), Night Work (2000), L'Impossible Oubli (2001), Easter Island (2002), Et la Dentelle (2003), Ratcliffe Power Station (2004), Retrospective Two (2004), Michael Kenna – A Retrospective (2009), Immagini del Settimo Giorno (2010), China (2014), France (2014), Forms of Japan (2015); *Recreations* marathon running, guitar playing, singing, reading, travelling; *Clubs* Chelsea Arts; *Style*— Michael Kenna, Esq; ✉ website www.michaelkenna.com

KENNAIR, William Brignall; s of late Joseph Terry Kennair, and late Nancy, *née* Neasham; *b* 6 June 1956; *Educ* Royal GS Newcastle upon Tyne, UCL (LLB); *m* 2 Aug 1980, Karen Elizabeth, da of late Keith John Williams, of Cardiff; *Career* sr ptnr John Venn & Sons London 1999– (ptnr 1986–), Scrivener Notary (John Venn & Sons, Scrivener Notaries and Translators); assoc memb American Bar Assoc 1994–; dir Soc of Scrivener Notaries London (representative to the Union Internationale du Notariat (UINL)), memb Gen Cncl UINL, former Chargé d'Affaires for UINL to UN Cmmn for Int Trade Law (UNCITRAL), treas UINL Cmmn Consultative; memb European Notarial Acad 2010–; games maker Protocol Language Team London 2012 Olympic Games; Freeman City of London 1983–; Liveryman Worshipful Co of Scriveners 1983– (memb Ct of Assts 2000–, Master 2008–09 and 2012), Liveryman Worshipful Co of Information Technologists 2009– (Freeman 1993–2009, Court Liveryman 2013–15, dir 2015–); *Books* contrib section on Notaries in Halsbury's Laws of England 4 edn vol 33, General Usage of International Digitally Ensured Commerce (GUIDEC) for ICC (2 edn, 2001), Halsbury's Laws of England (conslt ed Notaries section, 5 edn, 2008); *Recreations* cuisine, wine, travel; *Style*— William Kennair, Esq; ✉ John Venn & Sons, 95 Aldwych, London WC2B 4JF (☎ 020 7395 4300, fax 020 7395 4310, e-mail kennair@johnvenn.co.uk, website www.johnvenn.co.uk)

KENNARD, Peter; *b* 1949, London; *Educ* Byam Shaw Sch of Art, Slade Sch of Art, RCA; *Career* artist/photographer; pt/t lectr Byam Shaw Sch of Art, pt/t lectr NE Londom Poly 1980–82, lectr West Surrey Coll of Art and Design 1989–94, sr lectr RCA 1994–; photomontages used for varied film and video work incl: Lab Pty election broadcast 1983, State of Emergency – South Africa (Bandung File Channel 4) 1986, Heartfield – The Father of Photomontage (Granada TV) 1991; work published in newspapers and jls incl: The Guardian (regular contrib), The Listener, Time Magazine, Washington Post, New Scientist, Sunday Times; book covers cmmnd by: Penguin, Pluto Press, Paladin, Verso; work in the collections of: Magdalen and St Catherine's Colls Oxford, V&A, Imperial War Museum, Arts Cncl of GB, Saatchi Collection London; *Exhibitions* one man incl: St Catherine's Coll Oxford 1968, Gardner Arts Centre Univ of Sussex (artist in residence) 1971, Photographers Gallery Univ of Southampton 1973, A Document of Chile (Half Moon Gallery London and touring) 1978, Images for Disarmament (ICA London and Arnolfini Gallery Bristol) 1981, Despatches from an Unofficial War Artist (opening GLC Peace Year County Hall London and touring) 1982–83, Images Against War 1965–85 (Barbican Centre London) 1985, Photomontages for Peace (UN Palais des Nations Geneva) 1989, Images for the End of the Century (Gimpel Fils Gallery London and Imperial War Museum London) 1990, Reading Room (Gimpel Fils Gallery) 1996, Zelda Cheatle London 1997, Dazed and Confused Gallery London 1997; group incl: Photographer as Printmaker (Arts Cncl touring) 1981, Art of the Comic Strip (Gimpel Fils Gallery London) 1984, Whitechapel Open 1985–88, Invention D'un Art (Pompidou Centre Paris) 1989, Shocks to the System (Festival Hall London and touring) 1991, Photomontage Now (Manchester City Art Gallery) 1991, The Cutting Edge (Barbican Art Gallery London) 1992, Do You Speak English? (Int Artists' Centre Poznan Poland), Where is Home? (Kent Gallery New York) 1994, No More Hiroshimas (Phoenix Gallery Brighton) 1995, Gimpel Fils Gallery London 1996, The Power of the Poster (V&A Museum London) 1998, Art in Exile (Brixton Art Gallery London) 1999, Housing and Homelessness (Candid Gallery London) 1999; curator Look Out (Wolverhampton City Art Gallery and touring) 2000; work in public collections incl: Antwerp Art Gallery, Arts Council of Britain, Gallery of Modern Art Glasgow, Imperial War Museum London, Oxford National Museum of Photography, Film and Television Bradford, Science Museum London, University College London, V&A Museum London; *Books* No Nuclear Weapons (jtly, 1981), Jobs for a Change (1983), Keep London out of the Killing Ground (jtly, 1983), Target London (1985), About Turn (jtly, 1986), Images for the End of the Century (1990); *Style*— Peter Kennard, Esq

KENNAUGH, Peter; MBE (2013); *b* 15 June 1989, Douglas, Isle of Man; *Career* cyclist; achievements in team pursuit incl: Gold medal European Elite Championships 2011, Bronze medal World Championships 2011, Gold medal World Championships 2012, Gold medal Olympic Games 2012; *Style*— Mr Peter Kennaugh, MBE

KENNEDY, Dr Alexander; s of late Alexander Kennedy, and late Florence Edith, *née* Callin; *b* 20 April 1933, Chorlton-cum-Hardy, Lancs; *Educ* Merchant Taylors', Univ of Liverpool (MB ChB, MD); *m* 6 Aug 1960, Marlene Joan Campbell, da of Alfred Beveridge (d 1939), of Edinburgh; 1 da (Fiona b 1963), 1 s (Alistair b 1969); *Career* RAF Med Branch, Flt Lt pathologist RAF Hosp Wroughton 1958–61; lectr in pathology Univ of Liverpool 1961–67, visiting asst prof Dept of Pathology Univ of Chicago 1968, sr lectr Dept of Pathology Univ of Sheffield 1968–77, hon conslt pathologist Sheffield Area HA 1969–77, formerly conslt histopathologist Northern Gen Hosp NHS Tst Sheffield, hon clinical lectr Univ of Sheffield 1977–1997; pres Sheffield Medico-Chirurgical Soc 1997–98; memb: Pathological Soc of GB and Ireland, Int Acad of Pathology, British Thoracic Soc; Tport Campaign, Peak District and S Yorks Branch CPRE 1999–; formerly churchwarden St Andrew's Sharrow; FRCPath 1985 (MRCPath 1966); *Books* Essentials of Surgical Pathology – A Programmed Instruction Text (with A C Daniels and F Strauss, 1974), Basic Techniques in Diagnostic Histopathology (1977); articles on heart disease and medical aspects of cycling; *Recreations* cycling, walking, music, gardening, genealogy, earth sciences; *Style*— Dr Alexander Kennedy; ✉ 16 Brincliffe Gardens, Sheffield S11 9BG (e-mail sandy.kennedy@care4free.net)

KENNEDY, Alison Louise; da of Prof R Alan Kennedy, and Edwardine Mildred, *née* Price; *b* 22 October 1965; *Educ* HS of Dundee, Univ of Warwick (BA); *Career* writer; co-ordinator of creative writing for Project Ability 1989–94, writer in residence SAC/Strathclyde Regnl Social Work Dept 1990–92; judge on Booker Prize 1996, memb Granta Best Young British Novelists list 2003; Hon DLitt Univ of Glasgow; FRSL, FRSA; *Awards* Social Work Today Special Award 1990, Scottish Arts Cncl Book Award 1991, 1994, 1995, 1997 and 1999, Saltire First Book Award 1991, Mail on Sunday/John Llewelyn Rhys Prize 1991, Best of British Young Novelist list Granta 1993, Edinburgh Festival Fringe First 1993, Somerset Maugham Award 1994, Saltire Best Book Award 1995 and 2007, Encore Award 1996, Premio Napoli 2007, Austrian State Prize for Int Literature 2008, Eifel Int Literature Prize 2008, Costa Book of the Year Award 2008 (for Day); *Film* Stella Does Tricks 1997; *Books* Night Geometry and the Garscadden Trains (1991), Looking for the Possible Dance (1993), Now That You're Back (1994), So I am Glad (1995), Original Bliss (1997), The Life And Death of Colonel Blimp (1997), Everything You Need (1999), Indelible Acts (2002), Paradise (2004), Day (2007), What Becomes (2009), The Blue Book (2011), All The Rage (2014), Dr Who and The Drosten's Curse (2015), Serious Sweet (2016); *Recreations* cinema, banjo, sleep; *Style*— Miss A L Kennedy; ✉ c/o Antony Harwood, Antony Harwood Ltd, 103 Walton Street, Oxford OX2 6EB (☎ 01865 559615, fax 01865 310660, e-mail info@a-l-kennedy.co.uk)

KENNEDY, Dr Cameron Thomas Campbell; s of Thomas Kennedy (d 1981), and Dorian, *née* Talbot; *b* 30 January 1947; *Educ* Forest Sch, Queens' Coll Cambridge and UCH (MA, MB BChir); *m* 19 May 1973, Dr Rosalind Penelope, da of Raymond Whittier Baldwin, of Alderley Edge, Cheshire; 3 s (Nicholas b 5 June 1979, Thomas b 3 March 1981, Stephen b 29 Jan 1984); *Career* registrar in dermatology London Hosp 1973–75, sr registrar St George's Hosp 1975–80; Bristol Royal Infirmary: conslt dermatologist 1981–, postgrad clinical tutor 1985–89; conslt dermatologist: Southmead Hosp Bristol 1981–2015, Bristol Children's Hosp 1981–; memb Bd Br Jl of Dermatology 2005–; hon chm Br Soc of Paediatric Dermatology 1994–97 (hon treas/sec 1991–94), pres Section of Dermatology RSM 2001–02 (appointed hon memb 2007); memb Br Assoc of Dermatologists, non-resident fell American Acad of Dermatology; FRCP 1986, FRSM; *Publications* Your Questions Answered: Common Skn Disorders, Rook's Textbook of Dermatology (contrib), Textbook of Paediatric Dermatology (contrib); *Recreations* gardening, reading, badminton; *Clubs* Bristol Savages; *Style*— Dr Cameron Kennedy; ✉ 16 Sion Hill, Clifton, Bristol BS8 4AZ (☎ 0117 974 1935, e-mail camken49@gmail.com); Bristol Royal Infirmary, Department of Dermatology, Marlborough Street, Bristol BS2 8HW (☎ 0117 342 2520, e-mail cameron.kennedy@uhbristol.nhs.uk)

KENNEDY, Prof Clive Russell; s of Thomas Kennedy (ka 1941), of Paisley, Renfrewshire, and Victoria Alice, *née* Russell; *b* 17 June 1941, Liverpool; *Educ* Liverpool Coll, Univ of Liverpool (BSc, PhD, DSc); *m* 1, 23 Feb 1963, Beryl Pamela (d 1978), da of David Redvers Jones (d 1979), of Nantgaredig, Carmarthen; 1 s (Aidan b 1970), 1 da (Kate b 1971); m 2, 5 May 1979 (m dis 1998), Margaret Hilary, da of Bernard Wise (d 1973), of Oxford; m 3, 4 Sept 1999, Patricia Frances, da of Huw Jones, of Reading; *Career* parasitologist and teacher; asst in zoology UC Dublin 1963–64, asst lectr in zoology Univ of Birmingham 1964–65; Univ of Exeter: lectr in biological sci 1965–76, reader in zoology 1976–86, prof of parasitology 1986–2001, dean of sci 1990–93, head Sch of Biological Sci 1996–2000, emeritus prof 2001–; visiting research fell: Univ of Tromsø 1977, Univ of Queensland 1993–94; visiting prof: King's Coll London 1986–90, Univ Roma Tor Vergata 1996–2001; Royal Soc sponsored exchanges to: Acad of Scis USSR Leningrad 1984, Academia Sinica Wuhan 1988, Acad of Scis Argentina 1993; Br Cncl CINVESTAV Mexico 1988 and 1990; memb Exec Ctee Field Studies Cncl 1982–86; memb: Regnl Fisheries Advsy Ctee Nat Rivers Authy, Fisheries Soc of the Br Isles 1969 (meeting sec 1969–74, hon sec 74–77), Ctee NERC 1984–88; Pavlovsky Meml Medal Zoological Inst ANSSSR 1984; hon memb: Br Soc of Parasitology (memb 1968, vice-pres 1992–94, pres 1994–96), Russian Parasitology Soc, Scandinavian Soc for Parasitology; *Books* Ecological Animal Parasitology (1975), Ecological Aspects of Parasitology (1976), Ecology of the Acanthocephala (2006), numerous papers in sci jls; *Recreations* walking, churches, glass, rugby; *Style*— Prof Clive Kennedy; ✉ School of Biological Sciences, The University, Exeter EX4 4PS (☎ 01392 263757, fax 01392 263700, e-mail c.r.kennedy@exeter.ac.uk)

KENNEDY, Danny; MLA; s of John Trevor Kennedy, and Mary Ida, *née* Black; *b* 6 July 1959, Newry, NI; *Educ* Newry HS; *m* 26 March 1988, Karen Susan, da of Robert McCrum; 2 s (Stephen Daniel b 17 March 1990, Philip Robert b 7 Oct 1992), 1 da (Hannah Ruth b 30 Nov 1997); *Career* BT NI 1978–98; cncllr Newry and Mourne DC 1985–2010 (chair 1994–95); memb UUP 1974–; MLA (UUP) Newry and Armagh 1998–, chm Educn Ctee 2001–03, min for employment and learning 2010–11, min for regnl devpt 2011–; memb NI Tourist Board 1996–98; govr: Bessbrook Primary Sch, Newry HS; *Recreations* family, church activities, sports (as a spectator), reading; *Style*— Danny Kennedy, Esq, MLA; ✉ Northern Ireland Assembly, Parliament Buildings, Stormont Estate, Belfast BT4 3XX (☎ 028 9052 1336, fax 028 9052 1757, e-mail danny.kennedy@mla.niassembly.gov.uk); Advice Centre, 47 Main Street, Markethill, Co Armagh BT60 1PH (☎ 028 3755 2831)

KENNEDY, Jane; *b* 28 February 1953; *Educ* Sch of Architecture Univ of Manchester, Sch of Architecture Manchester Poly (DipArch); *m* John Maddison, artist and writer; 2 s; *Career* asst in Historic Buildings Gp Planning Dept Gtr Manchester Cncl 1974–75, Manchester Poly 1975–78, architect with Br Waterways Bd Rugby 1978–80, asst to David Jeffcoate Architect London 1980–81, pt/t work (due to family) 1981–86, historic buildings architect Planning Dept Norwich City Cncl 1986–88; Purcell Miller Tritton and Partners: joined Norwich Office as asst 1988, assoc 1989, ptnr Ely Office 1992– (chm 2000–13); cmmr English Heritage 2006–14 (conslt inspecting architect 1994–2001); surveyor to the Fabric of Ely Cathedral 1994– (asst surveyor 1990), memb Cncl for the Care of Churches 1996–2003, architect to the fndn ChCh Oxford 2008–, memb Heritage Advsy Panel Canal and River Tst 2012–, tstee Historic Royal Palaces 2015–; occasional lectr at Univs of York, Cambridge and Edinburgh; tstee and chm Church and Community Tst 1992–2003 (chm 1999–2003), sec Cathedral Architects Assoc 1999–2006, architect to St Nicholas Cathedral Newcastle upon Tyne 2006–; memb: The Victorian Soc (ctee memb Manchester and E Anglia), Soc for the Protection of Ancient Buildings, National Tst, Heritage Advsy Ctee Canal and River Tst 2012–; RIBA 1979; memb: ARCUK 1979, IHBC 1997; FRSA 1994; *Recreations* walking and family life; *Style*— Ms Jane Kennedy

KENNEDY, Dr Joanna Alicia Gore; OBE (1995); *née* Ormsby; da of Capt Gerald Anthony Gore Ormsby, DSO, DSC, RN (d 1992), and Nancy Mary (Susan), *née* Williams (d 1974); *b* 22 July 1950; *Educ* Queen Anne's Sch Caversham, Lady Margaret Hall Oxford (MA); *m* 21 July 1979, Richard Paul Kennedy, *qv*; 2 s (Peter b 1985, David b 1988); *Career* Ove Arup & Ptnrs consltg engrs: design engr 1972, sr engr 1979, assoc 1992, assoc dir 1994, dir 1996–2013; ldr Arup Project Mgmnt Europe 2006–10, ldr Arup Global Prog and Project Mgmnt 2010–13; dir Engrg and Technol Bd 2002–05; memb: Engrg Cncl 1984–86 and 1987–90, Cncl ICE 1984–87, Advsy Cncl RNEC Manadon 1988–94, Engrg Bd SERC 1990–93, Engrg and Technol Bd SERC 1993–94, EPSRC 2002–06 (memb Tech Opportunities Panel 1994–97); dir Port of London Properties Ltd 2001–05, dir Native Land Ltd 2016–; cmmr Royal Cmmn for the Exhbn of 1851 2003–12; memb: Cncl Univ of Southampton 1996–99, Bd Port of London Authy 2000–09 (vice-chm 2008–09), Cncl RCA 2001–16; tstee: Science Museum 1992–2002, Arup 1998–2005, Cumberland Lodge 2002–11 and 2013–, Nat Portrait Gallery 2015–; patron Women into Science, and Egrg (WISE) 2008–, tstee Ove Arup Fndn 2010–, memb Bd ERA Fndn 2014–; Woman of the Year Inspire Award for the Built Environment 2007, Woman of Outstanding Achievement Award 2008, CBI/Real Business First Women Award for Engrg 2013; Hon DSc Univ of Salford 1994; FICE 1992, FRSA, FREng 1997, Smeatonian Soc of Civil Engrs 2005; *Recreations* sailing; *Style*— Dr Joanna Kennedy, OBE, FREng, FICE; ✉ 9 Luscombe Road, Poole, Dorset BH14 8ST (e-mail jo.kennedy@gmail.com)

KENNEDY, Louise; da of James Kennedy (d 2007), and Margaret, *née* McCormack (d 1984); *b* 28 June 1960, Ireland; *Educ* St Annes Mount Merrion Ave Dublin, Grafton Acad of Fashion Design Dublin; *Career* fashion designer (under own label) 1984–; designer of inauguration outfit for Mary Robinson (first female pres of Ireland) 1984, selected to join Br Designer Gp and exhibit at London Designer Show 1990, elected Tipperary Person

K

of the Year (for outstanding achievements in Irish fashion 1992), opened flagship retail outlets in Dublin and London, designed uniforms for Aer Lingus 1997, launched Crystal Collection in conjunction with Tipperary Crystal 1999, first female style envoy for Mercedes Benz Ireland 2009 (remains ambass), launched bespoke bridal collection 2011; ambass Great Britain Campaign 2014; other awards incl: Best Irish Coat Collection 1985, Irish Designer of the Year 1989 and 1990, Best Suit and Best Coat Award 1991, Best Irish Designer Collection (Fashion Oscar Award) 1992, Best Coat and Suit Collection Designer of the Year Awards 1993, first female designer to receive award for Outstanding Achievements in Fashion from Irish Clothing Industry 1994, Veuve Clicquot Irish Business Woman of the Year 2003, Veuve Clicquot Irish Business Woman of the Year 2004, Company of the Year Irish Post Awards 2014; hon doctorate Dublin Inst of Technol 2014; *Style*— Ms Louise Kennedy; ✉ c/o Sarah-Kate Caughey, Dublin Flagship Store, 56 Merrion Square, Dublin 2, Ireland (☎ 00353 1 662 0056); London Flagship Store, 9 West Halkin Street, London SW1X 8JL (☎ 020 7235 0911); website www.louisekennedy.com

KENNEDY, Lulu; MBE (2012); da of John Paul Kennedy, and Dr Ruth Kennedy, *née* Knopfler; *b* 28 December 1969, Newcastle; *Educ* Middlesex Univ (BA); *Career* dir: Fashion East 2000–, MAN 2005–; md Lulu & Co 2010–; ed-at-large LOVE 2012; FRSA 2006; *Style*— Ms Lulu Kennedy, MBE; ✉ Fashion East, The Old Truman Brewery, 91 Brick Lane, London E1 6QL (☎ 020 7770 6150, e-mail katie@fashioneast.co.uk, website www.fashioneast.co.uk)

KENNEDY, Dr Malcolm William; CBE (2000); s of William Kennedy (d 1970), of Gosforth; *b* 13 March 1935; *Educ* Univ of Durham (BSc), Univ of Newcastle upon Tyne (PhD); *m* June 1962, Patricia Ann, da of George Arthur Forster; 1 da (Clare Rachel b 10 Oct 1967 d 2004); *Career* apprentice to C A Parsons & Co Ltd; Merz and McLellan: joined 1964, ptnr 1981, sr ptnr 1988–91, first chm and md (following incorporation) 1991–94, chm 1995–; non-exec dir Port of Tyne Authy 1994–2001, chm PB Power Ltd 1999–2002, chm NEA 2001–07, dir New and Renewables Energy Centre 2003–12, dir Renewable Energy Generation 2007–, chm Applied Superconductor Ltd 2011–; advsr Dept of Energy on privatisation of electricity indust 1987–90; memb: Electricity Panel MMC 1992–98; IEE: vice-pres 1989–92 and 1994–97, dep pres 1997–99, pres 1999–2000; CEng 1967, FIEE 1974, FREng 1986, FRSE 2002; *Recreations* Methodist local preacher, cricket, railways; *Clubs* National; *Style*— Dr Malcolm Kennedy, CBE, FREng, FRSE

KENNEDY, Michael Gerard (Mike); CBE (2008); s of Peter Thomas Kennedy, of Coventry, and Eileen Mary, *née* Mulligan; *b* 19 June 1954, Doncaster, S Yorks; *Educ* Ullathorne Sch Coventry, Univ of Leeds (LLB), KCL (Dip); *m* 19 May 1979, Valerie Anne, *née* Buck; 3 da (Joanna Mary b 31 Dec 1980, Helen Elizabeth b 23 April 1983, Katharine Lydia b 19 March 1987); *Career* admitted slr 1980; various posts CPS HQ 1987–96, asst chief crown prosecutor 1996–99, chief crown prosecutor Sussex 1999–2001, pres Eurojust 2001–07, chief operating offr CPS 2007–13; conslt national and international criminal justice 2013–; *Recreations* sailing, rugby, reading; *Style*— Mike Kennedy, Esq, CBE; ☎ 07808 511293, e-mail mgkennedy12@gmail.com

KENNEDY, Nigel Alan; s of Alan Ridsdale Kennedy (d 1980), and Joan, *née* Mellows (d 2012); *b* 2 February 1956; *Educ* Ardingly, Trinity Coll Oxford (MA); *m* 11 Sept 1982, Nicola Helen, da of Christopher Maurice Spencer (d 2013); 2 da (Rachel b 21 Dec 1985, Rosalind b 16 Feb 1988), 2 s (Michael b 4 June 1990, Rory b 16 June 1997); *Career* Mobil Oil Co Ltd London 1979–81, Total Oil Great Britain Ltd London 1981–84, Total Compagnie Française des Pétroles Paris 1984–86, The Communication Group plc 1986–93, gp chief exec Grayling 1993–2009, communications conslt 2010–; chm Commucan 2010–, dir Frugalpac 2015–; tstee Young Epilepsy 2012–; *Recreations* soccer, cricket, tennis, squash, travel; *Clubs* Le Beaujolais, Oxford and Cambridge; *Style*— Nigel Kennedy; ✉ Commucan Ltd, Somerset House, Strand, London WC2R 1LA (☎ 020 7257 9562, e-mail nigel.kennedy@commucan.com or nigel.a.kennedy@gmail.com, website www.commucan.com)

KENNEDY, Nigel Paul; s of John Kennedy, and Scylla, *née* Stoner; *b* 28 December 1956; *Educ* Yehudi Menuhin Sch, Juilliard Sch of Performing Arts; *Career* solo violinist; debut at Festival Hall with Philharmonia Orch 1977, Berlin debut with Berlin Philharmonia 1980, Henry Wood Promenade debut 1981, New York debut with BBC Symphony Orch 1987, tour of Hong Kong and Aust with Hallé Orch 1981, extensive tours USA and Europe; recordings incl: Tchaikovsky, Sibelius, Vivaldi (Double Platinum Disc), Elgar Violin Concerto (Record of the Year 1985, Gold Disc), Bruch and Mendelssohn (Gold Disc), Walton Violin and Viola, Let Loose, Kafka, Classic Kennedy, The Kennedy Experience; *Style*— Nigel Kennedy, Esq

KENNEDY, Rt Hon Sir Paul Joseph Morrow; kt (1983), PC (1992); s of late Dr Joseph Morrow Kennedy, of Sheffield, and late Bridget Teresa Kennedy; *b* 12 June 1935; *Educ* Ampleforth, Gonville & Caius Coll Cambridge; *m* 1965, Hon Virginia, da of late Baron Devlin; 2 s, 2 da; *Career* called to the Bar Gray's Inn 1960 (bencher 1982, vice-treas 2001, treas 2002); recorder of the Crown Court 1972, QC 1973, judge of the High Court of Justice (Queen's Bench Div) 1983–92, presiding judge NE Circuit 1985–89, a Lord Justice of Appeal 1992–2005, vice-pres Queen's Bench Div of the High Court 1997–2002; interception of communications cmmr 2006–12; main bd memb Judicial Studies Bd 1993–96 (chm Criminal Ctee 1993–96), chm Advocacy Studies Bd 1996–99, memb Ct of Appeal of Gibraltar 2006–15 (pres 2011–15); hon fell Gonville & Caius Coll Cambridge 1998; Hon LLD Univ of Sheffield 2000; *Style*— The Rt Hon Sir Paul Kennedy

KENNEDY, Prof Paul M; CBE (2000); *b* 1945; *Educ* Univ of Newcastle upon Tyne (BA), Univ of Oxford (DPhil); *m* 1, Catherine (d 1998); 3 s; m 2, Cynthia Farrar, 2001; *Career* UEA: lectr 1970–75, reader 1975–82, prof 1982–83; J Richardson Dilworth prof of history Yale Univ 1983– (dir of int security studies); co-dir of the Secretariat to the Int Advsy Gp Report – The UN in its Second Half Century; res awards from British Acad, Leverhulme Fndn, Alexander von Humboldt Fndn, Beit Fund Oxford, Social Science Res Cncl, German Academic Exchange Serv; Hon MA Yale Univ, Hon DLitt Univ of Newcastle, Hon DHL Long Island Univ, Hon DHL Univ of New Haven, Hon LLD Ohio Univ, Hon DLitt UEA, Hon Doctorate Univ of Leuven and 6 other hon degrees; supernumary fell St Antony's Coll Oxford; fell: Inst for Advanced Study Princeton 1978–79, American Philosophical Soc, Soc of American Historians, Alexander von Humboldt Fndn; FRHS, FAAAS, FBA; *Books* Pacific Onslaught 1941–43 (1972), Conquest: The Pacific War 1943–45 (1973), The Samoan Tangle: A Study in Anglo-German-American Relations 1878–1900 (1974), The Rise and Fall of British Naval Mastery (1976), The Rise of the Anglo-German Antagonism 1860–1914 (1980), The Realities Behind Diplomacy: Background Influences on British External Policy 1865–1980 (1981), Strategy and Diplomacy, 1870–1945: Eight Essays (1983), The Rise and Fall of the Great Powers: Economic Change and Military Conflict from 1500–2000 (1988), Preparing for the Twenty-First Century (1993), The Parliament of Man: The Past, Present and Future of the United Nations (2006), Engineers of Victory (2013); reg contrib to numerous jls and publications incl The New York Times, The Los Angeles Times, The Atlantic and others; *Recreations* hawk watching, old churches, helping to run local soup kitchen; *Style*— Prof Paul Kennedy, CBE, FBA; ✉ Department of History, Yale University, New Haven, Connecticut, USA (☎ 00 1 203 432 6246, fax 00 1 203 432 6250)

KENNEDY, Prof Peter Graham Edward; CBE (2010); s of Philip Kennedy, of London, and Trudie Sylvia, *née* Summer; *b* 28 March 1951; *Educ* UCS London, UCL and UCH (MB BS, MD, PhD, DSc), Univ of Glasgow (MPhil, MLitt); *m* 6 July 1983, Catherine Ann, da of Christopher King; 1 s (Luke b 1988), 1 da (Vanessa b 1991); *Career* hon res asst MRC Neuroimmunology Project UCL 1978–80, sr registrar (formerly registrar) in neurology Nat Hosp London 1981–84, asst prof of neurology Johns Hopkins Univ Sch of Med 1985, Burton prof and head Dept of Neurology Univ of Glasgow 1987– (sr lectr in neurology and virology 1986–87), conslt neurologist Inst of Neurological Sciences Glasgow 1986–; visiting fell in med Jesus Coll Cambridge 1992, Fogarty int scholar-in-residence Nat Insts of Health USA 1993–94 (awarded Fogarty medal); memb Med Res Advsy Ctee Multiple Sclerosis Soc 1987–98, chm Med Res Advsy Ctee Scot Motor Neurone Disease Assoc 1987–97, chm Scientist Panel on Infections incl AIDS of the Euro Fedn of Neurological Societies 2000–06; sr assoc ed Jl of Neurovirology; memb Editorial Bds: Neuropathology and Applied Neurobiology 1986–92, Brain 1997–2004, Jl of Neuroimmunology, Jl of the Neurological Sciences 1997–2013, Scottish Medical Jl, Jl of Neuroparasitology; BUPA Med Fndn Doctor of the Year Res Award 1990; Fleming Lecture RCPSGlas 1990, Linacre Medal and Lecture RCP 1991, T S Srinivasan Endowment Lecture and Gold Medal 1993, J W Stephens Lecture Denver Colorado 1994, Brain Bursary Lecture King's College Hosp 1999, Livingstone Lecture RCPSGlas 2004, Int Soc for Neurovirology Distinguished Service Award 2010, Sir James Black Medal Royal Soc of Edinburgh 2014; pres Int Soc for Neurovirology 2004–10 (pres elect 2003–04), sec Int Soc for Neurovirology 2000–03; memb: Assoc of Br Neurologists, American Neurological Assoc, Soc for Gen Microbiology, Assoc of Clinical Profs of Med, Scottish Assoc of Neurological Sciences, Scottish Soc of Physicians, Royal Medico-Chirurgical Soc Glasgow, Assoc of Physicians of GB and I; fell Br Astronomical Assoc; FRCP 1988, FRCPG 1989, FRSE 1992, FRCPath 1997 (MRCPath 1988), FMedSci (fndr) 1998, FRAS 2004, FRSM; *Books* Infections of the Nervous System (ed with R T Johnson, 1987), Infectious Diseases of the Nervous System (ed with L E Davis, 2000), The Fatal Sleep (2007), Reversal of David (novel, 2014), Brothers in Retribution (novel, 2015); author of numerous papers on neurology, neurovirology and sleeping sickness; *Recreations* astronomy, philosophy, walking in country, tennis, reading, music, cycling; *Style*— Prof Peter Kennedy, CBE, FRSE; ✉ 23 Hamilton Avenue, Pollokshields, Glasgow G41 4JG (☎ 0141 427 4754); Glasgow University Department of Neurology, Institute of Neurological Sciences, Southern General Hospital, Glasgow G51 4TF (☎ 0141 201 2500, fax 0141 201 2993, e-mail peter.kennedy@glasgow.ac.uk)

KENNEDY, Seema; MP; *Career* MP (Cons) S Ribble 2015–; *Style*— Mrs Seema Kennedy, MP; ✉ House of Commons, London SW1A 0AA

KENNEDY, Tessa Georgina; da of late Geoffrey Farrer Kennedy, and Daska McLean, *née* Ivanovic; *b* 6 December 1938; *Educ* Oak Hall Haslemere, Ecole des Beaux Arts Paris; *m* 1, 27 Jan 1958 (m dis 1969), Dominick Evelyn Bede Elwes, s of Simon Elwes (d 1975); 3 s (Cassian b 1959, Damian b 1960, Cary b 1962); m 2, 26 June 1971, Elliott Kastner; 1 s (Dillon b 1970), 1 da (Milica b 1972); *Career* interior designer; former clients incl: John Barry, Sam Spiegel, Richard Burton, De Beers, BUPA Hosps, HM King Hussein of Jordan, Michael Winner, Candice Bergen, Rudolf Nureyev, George Harrison, Pierce Brosnan, Claridges, Berkeley Hotels, Port Lympne Zoo, Aspinalls Casino, Ritz Bar, Ritz Casino; current clients incl Bibi's Restaurant and private residences in Moscow; D&D Designer of the Year 2003, D&D Best Traditional Commerical Design 2003; fell Int Interior Design Assoc (IIDA), memb Br Int Design Assoc (BIDA); *Recreations* tennis, movies, watching American football; *Clubs* Vanderbilt, Harbour; *Style*— Miss Tessa Kennedy; ✉ Tessa Kennedy Design Ltd, Studio 5, 2 Olaf Street, London W11 4BE (☎ 020 7221 4546, fax 020 7229 2899, e-mail info@tessakennedydesign.com)

KENNEDY OF SOUTHWARK, Baron (Life Peer UK), of Newington in the London Borough of Southwark; Roy Francis Kennedy; s of John Kennedy, and Frances, *née* Hoban; *b* 9 November 1962, Lambeth, London; *Educ* St Thomas the Apostle Sch London; *m* 31 Jan 2004, Alicia Kennedy; *Career* Labour Party: official for over 20 years, regnl dir E Midlands 1997–2005, dir of finance and compliance 2005–10; electoral cmmr 2010–14; cncllr London Borough of Lewisham 2014–; memb Co-operative Pty; vice-pres Southwark Chamber of Commerce; govr Morley Coll London; *Recreations* reading, films, walking, travel; *Style*— The Lord Kennedy of Southwark; ✉ House of Lords, London SW1A 0PW (☎ 020 7219 5353, e-mail kennedyro@parliament.uk)

KENNEDY OF THE SHAWS, Baroness (Life Peer UK 1997), of Cathcart in the City of Glasgow; Helena Ann Kennedy; QC (1991); da of late Joshua Patrick Kennedy, of Glasgow, and Mary Veronica, *née* Jones; *b* 12 May 1950; *Educ* Holyrood Secdy Sch Glasgow, Cncl of Legal Educn; *m* 1986, Dr Iain Louis Hutchison; 1 s (Hon Roland), 1 da (Hon Clio); 1 s (Keir) from previous partner Roger Ian Mitchell; *Career* called to the Bar Gray's Inn 1972 (bencher 1999–); in practice: Garden Court 1974–84, Tooks Court 1984–90, Doughty Street Chambers 1990–; specialises in criminal law (acted in Brighton Bombing Trial and Guildford Four Appeal); broadcaster and journalist on law and women's rights; chair: London Int Festival of Theatre 1993–2002, Br Cncl, Human Genetics Cmmn 1999–2007; memb Advsy Cncl of the World Bank Inst; chllr Oxford Brookes Univ 1994–2001; contrib to: The Bar on Trial (1982), Child Sexual Abuse Within the Family (1985), Balancing Acts (1989); created Blind Justice (BBC, 1987); presenter: Heart of the Matter (BBC, 1987), Raw Deal (1989), The Trial of Lady Chatterley's Lover (1990), Time Gentleman, Please (BBC Scotland, awarded TV Prog Award Industrial Journalism Awards 1994), Hypotheticals; vice-pres Haldane Soc; chair: Standing Ctee for Youth Justice, Charter 88 until 1997, Br Cncl 1998–, London Int Festival Theatre 1993–2002; patron Liberty; memb Cncl Howard League for Penal Reform; pres National Children's Bureau 1998–; vice-pres Nat Assembly of Women; cmmr Nat Cmmn on Educn; pres: North of England Educn Conf 1994;18 Hon LLD from Br Univs; hon memb Academie Universelle des Cultures Paris; hon fell: Inst of Advanced Legal Studies, Univ of London; fell City and Guilds London Inst; FRSA; *Awards* Women's Network Award 1992, UK Woman of Europe Award 1995, Campaigning and Influencing Award Nat Fedn of Women's Institutes 1996, The Times Newspaper Lifetime Achievement Award in the Law 1997; *Publications* incl: Eve Was Framed (1992), Learning Works (report for the Further Educn Funding Cncl, 1997), Just Law: The Changing Face of Justice (2004); *Style*— Helena Kennedy, QC; ✉ c/o Hilary Hard, 12 Athelstan Close, Harold Wood, Essex RM3 0QJ (☎ and fax 01708 379482, e-mail hilary.hard@btinternet.com)

KENNEDY-SANIGAR, Patrick; s of William Adrian George Sanigar, of Ely, Cambs, and Patricia Anne, *née* Kay; *b* 27 September 1957; *Educ* Soham GS, Soham Village Coll, Gordonstoun, Canterbury Coll of Art Sch of Architecture (BA, DipArch); *m* 12 Oct 1989, Melena Kay, da of Alan Mark Kennedy; 3 da (Courtney Oneka b 24 July 1991, Ottilie Fabien b 6 April 1993, Sydney Camille b 27 Aug 1995); *Career* head of design Townscape Homes Ltd 1981 (site agent 1979); fndr: Townscape Designs Ltd (dir and head of design) 1982, Townscape Interiors Ltd 1984, Harbour Studios 1986 (having resigned all directorships of the Townscape Group); head of design 691 Promotions Ltd 1991–95, head of design servs Faithdean Interiors Ltd Chatham 1995–97 (design conslt 1991–95); dir: Domus Estates Ltd 1992–99, Honeywood Forestry Ltd 1993, Space Shuffle Ltd 2001; projects incl: The Tube shoe retail chain 1985 (featured Designers Journal 1986), restoration in assoc with Lionel March The How House (LA) 1986, The Cocoon concert bldg 1991, Swedish Knotty Timber project 1991–92 and 1994–95, The Penguin Café Canterbury, The Kent Bio-power Renewable Energy Project 1993–95, The Millennium Underground Dwelling Project 2000, Earth Studio Three Project 2006, Ruffynes Oast 2009 (award winner), Potter's Farm Barn (The Barn that Flew); memb Visiting Bd Panel RIBA 1987–89, judge Property Awards 2013; FCSD 1988 (co chm of Interiors Gp and memb Cncl 1990), fell Br Inst of Interior Design 1988; *Recreations* qualified gymnasium instructor, swimming, earth sheltered housing; *Style*— Patrick

Kennedy-Sanigar, Esq; ✉ Space Shuffle, The Apple Barn, Brogdale Farm, Brogdale Road, Faversham, Kent ME13 8XZ (☎ 01795 597969, e-mail patrick@spaceshuffle.com, designers@spaceshuffle.com or missioncontrol@spaceshuffle.com, website www.spaceshuffle.com)

KENNELLY, Brendan; *b* 1936; *Educ* St Ita's Coll Co Kerry, TCD (BA, MA, PhD), Univ of Leeds; *Career* poet, dramatist and lectr; lectr TCD 1963–71, Guidersleeve prof Barnard Coll NYC 1971, Cornell prof of literature Swarthmore Coll Penn 1971–72, prof of modern literature TCD 1973–2004; hon doctorate Trinity Coll Conn 1992; *Publications* The Real Ireland (text, photos by Liam Blake, 1984), Ireland Past and Present (ed, 1985), Landmarks of Irish Drama (1988); *Poetry* My Dark Fathers (1964), Collection One – Getting Up Early (1966), Good Souls to Survive (1967), Dream of a Black Fox (1968), A Drinking Cup (1970), Selected Poems (1969), The Penguin Book of Irish Verse (ed, 1970, 2 edn 1981), Selected Poems (1971), Love Cry (1972), The Voices (1973), Shelley in Dublin (1974), A Kind of Trust (1975), New and Selected Poems (1976), Islandman (1977), A Small Light (1979), The Boats Are Home (1980), The House That Jack Didn't Build (1982), Moloney Up and At It, Cromwell (1983 Eire, 1987 UK), Selected Poems (1985), Mary (1987), Love of Ireland – Poems from the Irish (trans, 1989), A Time for Voices – Selected Poems 1960–90 (1990), The Book of Judas (1991, Sunday Independent/Irish Life Award for Poetry), Joycechoyce: The poems in verse and prose of James Joyce (ed jtly with A N Jeffares, 1992), Breathing Spaces (1992), Poetry My Arse (1995), The Man Made of Rain (1998), Begin (1999), Glimpses (2001), The Little Book of Judas (2002), Martial Art (2003), Familiar Strangers: New and Selected Poems 1960–2004 (2004), Now (2006); Reservoir Voices (2009); *Novels* The Crooked Cross (1963), The Florentines (1967); *Plays* Antigone (1983, Peacock Theatre Dublin), Medea (1988, Dublin Theatre Festival), Cromwell (1986, Damer Hall Dublin), Trojan Women (1993, Peacock Theatre Dublin), Blood Wedding (1996, Newcastle Playhouse); *Style—* Brendan Kennelly, Esq; ✉ Department of English, Trinity College, Dublin 2, Ireland (☎ 00 353 1 896 2301 or 00 353 1 896 1111, fax 00 353 1 677 2694)

KENNERLEY, Peter Dilworth; TD (1989); s of John Dilworth Kennerley (d 2006), and Margery, *née* Dugard (d 1977); *b* 9 June 1956; *Educ* Collyers Sch, Sidney Sussex Coll Cambridge (MA); *m* 1989, Hon (Anne Marie) Ghislaine du Roy, da of late Hon Sir Thomas Galbraith, KBE, MP; 2 da (Sarah Marie Louise b 30 Jan 1991, Julia Anne Delphine b 13 Feb 2002), 1 s (Samuel John Maximilian b 21 July 1992); *Career* TA Maj Royal Yeo 1986; Simmons & Simmons: joined 1979, admitted slr 1981, ptnr 1986–99; co sec and gen counsel Scottish & Newcastle plc 1999–2008, group legal advisor and co sec Aggreko plc 2008–; sec Panel on Takeovers and Mergers 1986–88; cncllr London Borough of Wandsworth 1994–98; Parly candidate (Cons) Doncaster N 1997, Scottish Parly candidate (Cons) Carrick, Cumnock and Doon Valley 2011; memb Law Soc; *Clubs* Cavalry and Guards'; *Style—* Peter Kennerley, Esq

KENNEY, Edward John; s of George Kenney, and Emmie Carlina Elfrida, *née* Schwenke; *b* 29 February 1924; *Educ* Christ's Hosp, Trinity Coll Cambridge (Craven scholar, Craven student, Chancellor's medallist, MA); *m* 18 June 1955, (Gwyneth) Anne, da of late Henry Albert Harris; *Career* served WWII: Royal Signals UK and India 1943–46, cmmnd 1944, Lt 1945; asst lectr Univ of Leeds 1951–52; Univ of Cambridge: res fell Trinity Coll 1952–53, asst lectr 1955–60, lectr 1966–70, reader in Latin lit and textual criticism 1970–74, Kennedy prof of Latin 1974–82; Peterhouse Cambridge: fell 1953–91, dir of studies in classics 1953–74, librarian 1953–82, tutor 1956–62, sr tutor 1962–65, Perne librarian 1987–91, domestic bursar 1987–88; jt ed: Classical Quarterly 1959–65, Cambridge Greek and Latin Classics 1970–; Sather prof of classical lit Berkeley 1968, Carl Newell Jackson lectr Harvard Univ 1980 (James C Loeb fell in classical philology 1967–68); author of articles and reviews in classical jls; pres: Jt Assoc of Classical Teachers 1977–79, Classical Assoc 1982–83, Horatian Soc 2002–07; treas and chm Cncl of Almoners Christ's Hospital 1984–86; FBA 1968, foreign memb Royal Netherlands Acad of Arts and Scis 1976; *Books* P Ouidi Nasonis Amores etc (ed, 1961, 2 edn 1995), Ovidiana Graeca (ed with Mrs P E Easterling, 1965), Appendix Vergiliana (ed with W V Clausen, F R D Goodyear, J A Richmond, 1966), Lucretius De Rerum Natura III (ed, 1971, 2 edn 2014), The Classical Text (1974, Italian trans 1995), Cambridge History of Classical Literature II (ed and contrib, 1982), The Ploughman's Lunch (1984), Ovid, Metamorphoses (introduction and notes, 1985), Ovid, The Love Poems (introduction and notes, 1990), Apuleius, Cupid & Psyche (ed, 1990), Ovid, Sorrows of an Exile (introduction and notes, 1992), Ovid, Heroides XVI-XXI (ed, 1996), Apuleius, The Golden Ass (trans, introduction and notes, 1998, Folio Soc edn 2016), Ovidio Metamorfosi Vol IV Libri VII-IX (2011); *Recreations* discursive reading, listening to the wireless; *Style—* Prof E J Kenney, FBA; ✉ 4 Belvoir Terrace, Trumpington Road, Cambridge CB2 7AA

KENNICUTT, Prof Robert Charles; s of Robert Charles Kennicutt (d 1996), and Joyce Ann, *née* Laird (d 2009); *b* 4 September 1951, Baltimore, MD; *Educ* Rensselaer Poly Inst NY (BS), Univ of Washington (MS, PhD); *Family* 1 da (Laura b 18 Sept 1982); *Career* adjunct research fell California Inst of Technol and Carnegie postdoctoral fell Hale Observatories 1978–80, asst prof then assoc prof Dept of Astronomy Univ of Minnesota 1980–88; Univ of Arizona: astronomer Steward Observatory 1988–2005 (memb Cncl 1989–2005), assoc prof 1988–92, dep head Dept of Astronomy 1991–98 (academic dir 1990–98), prof 1992–2005; Univ of Cambridge: Plumian prof of astronomy and experimental philosophy 2005–, professorial fell Churchill Coll 2006–, dir Inst of Astronomy 2008–11, head Sch of Physical Sciences 2012–15; visiting positions and lectureships incl: visiting fell Leiden Observatory 1982, Beatrice M Tinsley centennial visiting prof Univ of Texas 1994, Adriaan Blaauw visiting prof Univ of Groningen 2001, Whitford lectr Univ of Wisconsin 2002, Caroline Hershel distinguished visitor Space Telescope Science Inst Baltimore 2006–07, Lyman Spitzer lectr Princeton Univ 2007, Bruno Rossi lectr Arcetri Observatory Florence 2008, Vaucouleurs lectr Univ of Texas 2015, Hintze lectr Univ of Oxford 2016; memb Fachbeirat Max Planck Inst Extraterrestrial Physics 2013–; ed-in-chief The Astrophysical Jl 1999–2006, memb Int Advsy Ctee Chinese Jl of Astronomy and Astrophysics 2002–08, memb Editorial Bd Cambridge Univ Press Astrophysics Series 2007–; memb of numerous professional ctees incl: Nat Acad of Sciences/Nat Research Cncl Ctee on Astronomy and Astrophysics 1998–2001, Hubble Space Telescope Science Inst Cncl 2000–04, Advsy Ctee Nat Science Fndn Nat Virtual Observatory 2002–06, NASA Science Mission Directorate Evaluation Team 2004–05, Astrophysics Sub-Ctee NASA Advsy Cncl 2006–09, Scientific Advsy Ctee European Virtual Observatory Project 2006–09, Wissenschaftlicher Beirat Astrophysikalishe Inst Potsdam 2006–11, Int Advsy Bd Netherlands Research Sch for Astronomy 2008–, STFC Programmatic Review Panel 2008; Alfred P Sloan fell 1983–87; Dannie Heineman Prize American Inst of Physics/American Astronomical Soc 2007, Gruber Cosmology Prize 2009; memb: Nat Acad of Sciences (USA) 2006, IAU, American Astronomical Soc (vice-pres 1998–2001, memb Exec Ctee 1999–2001), Astronomical Soc of the Pacific; FRAS, fell American Acad of Arts and Sciences 2001, FRS 2011; *Recreations* rock collecting; *Style—* Prof Robert C Kennicutt; ✉ Institute of Astronomy, Madingley Road, Cambridge CB3 0HA (e-mail robk@ast.cam.ac.uk)

KENNY, Julie Ann; CBE (2002), DL (S Yorks 2005); *née* Bower; da of Cyril Bower (d 1992), and H J Johanna, *née* Klement (d 2010); *b* 19 August 1957, Sheffield; *m* (m dis); 2 s (Oliver James Paul b 19 Jan 1989, Laurence Jason Peter b 6 Jan 1992), 1 da (Charlotte Louise b 20 Nov 1993); *Career* litigation lawyer in private practice and with local authorities until 1989, md Pyronix Ltd and chief exec Secure Holdings Ltd 1989–; chm and chief exec Pyronix Ltd and Secure Hldgs Ltd 2011–; chm: Regnl Industrial Devpt Bd 1996–2002, Rotherham New Deal Employers' Coalition 2000–02, S Yorks Steel Task Force 2000–02, Business Link S Yorks 2001–05, S Yorks New Deal Employers' Coalition 2002–05, Rotherham Partnership 2002–05, Small Business Cncl 2005–07, Yorks Forward 2010–12 (memb Bd 2003–12); memb Bd: Br Security Industry Assoc 1992–2013 (chm Security Equipment Manufacturers' Section 1998–2000 and 2002–04, chm 2010–12), S Yorks Investment Fund 2000–05, S Yorks Learning and Skills Cncl 2001–02, S Yorks Partnership 2004–07, Creative Sheffield 2005–, Panel for Regulatory Accountability 2005–07, Socio-Economic Gp Skills Alliance 2005–07, Small Business Service Strategy Bd 2006–07, Univ of Sheffield Mgmnt Sch Advsy Bd 2006–08, Administrative Burdens Advsy Bd 2006–07, Small Business Forum 2007–10, UK Cmmn for Employment and Skills 2007–, Better Regulation Stakeholder Gp 2007–10, Barnsley and Rotherham C of C 2008–09; intervention cmmr Doncaster Metropolitan BC 2010–14; memb Regnl Cncl Engrg Employers Fedn 2009–10; hon dir Rotherham C of C 2004–10 (memb Bd and pres 2000–04); tstee Rudston Prep Sch 2002–05, govr Mount St Mary's Coll 2008–12, ambass Whirlow Hall Farm Tst 2008–, govr Maltby Acad 2010– (chm of govrs 2010–), tstee Rotherham Hospice 2010–, pres NSPCC Sheffield and Hallamshire Branch 2012–14, S Yorks Community Fndn 2013–, Sheffield City Region Local Enterprise Partnership 2013–, chair Maltby Learning Tst 2014–, dir and tstee Nat Coal Mining Museum 2014–, dir and tstee Gallery Town Ltd (Rotherham) 2014–, chair Wentworth Woodhouse Preservation Tst 2014–, intervention cmmr Rotherham Metropolitan BC 2015–; patron: Inspiring Women (Women In Business), In2Change, St Luke's Hospice, Gallery Town Ltd (Rotheram); High Sheriff S Yorks 2012–13; Hon Doctorate Sheffield Hallam Univ 2006; fell Inst of Legal Execs 1983–2010, FRSA 2002, assoc memb RSM 2008–11; *Style—* Mrs Julie Kenny, CBE, DL; ✉ Pyronix Ltd, Secure House, Braithwell Way, Hellaby, Rotherham, South Yorkshire S66 8QY (☎ 01709 535218, fax 01709 700101, e-mail juliek@pyronix.com)

KENNY, Prof Phillip Herbert; s of Robert Kenny, of King's Lynn, and Moira, *née* Davies; *b* 9 August 1948; *Educ* Univ of Bristol (LLB), Univ of Cambridge (Dip Criminology), Columbia Univ (LLM); *m* 7 Aug 1970, Ann Mary, da of Harold Langley (d 1970), of Winchester; 1 s (Stephen b 1982), 3 da (Julia b 1975, Angharad b 1977, Helen b 1979); *Career* slr; head of Law Dept Univ of Northumbria at Newcastle (formerly Newcastle Poly) 1980–, former univ and poly lectr, legal dir Educn Assets Bd; conslt Messrs Dickinson Dees Slrs Newcastle upon Tyne; *Publications* Conveyancing Law, Study of Law, Conveyancing Law and Practice, Licensed Conveyancers the New Law, Sweet and Maxwell's Law Files, Mines and Minerals in Conveyancing, Property Law Statutes, Leasehold Reform Housing and Urban Development Act 1994, Covenants for Title, Trusts of Land and Appointment of Trustees, Mobile Homes an Occupiers Guide (Shelter); *Recreations* shooting, walking, sailing, golf; *Clubs* Keswick Golf; *Style—* Prof Phillip Kenny; ✉ 105 Kenton Road, Gosforth NE3 4NL; University of Northumbria at Newcastle, Ellison Building, Ellison Place, Newcastle upon Tyne NE1 8ST (☎ 0191 232 6002, fax 0191 235 8017)

K

KENRICK, Martin John; s of William Edmund Kenrick (d 1981), of Birmingham, and Elizabeth Dorothy Magdalen, *née* Loveday (d 1999); family non-conformists who settled with others in Midlands; *b* 5 February 1940; *Educ* Newlands, Rugby, TCD (MA, BComm), Cranfield Univ (MBA); *m* 21 Feb 1970, Christine Mary, da of Charles Ronald Wingham (d 1972), of St Albans, Herts; 2 da (Tanya b 1972, Helen b 1973), 1 s (Hilgrove b 1977); *Career* guardian Birmingham Assay Office 1971–2007, cmmr of taxes 1972–2009, chm Archibald Kenrick & Sons Ltd 1978–91 (md 1973–78); dir: Birmingham R&D Ltd 1985–2003 (chm 1985–87), Rote Public Relations 1991–92, Jones & Barclay Ltd 1991–93, Martin Kenrick Associates 1991–2004, Turnock Ltd 2001–02, Swan Laundry Ltd 2001–02, Cape Instruments Ltd 2001–04; managing conslt Directormatch 1993–2004; Univ of Birmingham: hon life memb Ct of Govrs 1978–2012, memb Cncl 1981–96, memb Fin and Gen Purpose Ctee 1987–88; memb Mgmnt Ctee W Midlands Regnl Mgmnt Centre 1978–82; Birmingham C of C and Industry: memb Cncl 1981–98, memb Gen Purposes Ctee 1982–93, chm Educn Ctee 1985–89, memb Working Pty for Industry Year 1985–86, vice-pres 1988–90, pres 1990–91; dir: Birmingham Chamber Training Ltd 1986–87, Black Country Museum Tst 1987–2003; chm: Policy Gp Birmingham Local Employer Network 1987–89, W Midlands Region Industry Matters 1987–90, Birmingham Educn Business Partnership 1989–93, Police Advsy Ctee Birmingham City Centre 1995–2000; govr Fndn for Schs of King Edward VI Birmingham 1990–93; *Recreations* ornithology, skiing, tennis, gardening; *Clubs* W Midland Bird (chm 2007–13), Edgbaston Priory Tennis, Cutnall Green Tennis, Belbroughton and District Probus, Worcestershire Wildlife Trust; *Style—* Martin J Kenrick, Esq; ✉ September House, Woodrow, Chaddesley Corbett, Worcestershire DY10 4QE (☎ 01562 777415, e-mail martin@kenrick.co.uk, website www.kenrick.co.uk)

KENSINGTON, Bishop of 2015–; Rt Rev Dr Graham Tomlin; *m* 1982, Janet, *née* Wynn Owen; 1 s (Sam b 1986), 1 da (Sian b 1988); *Career* ordained: deacon 1986, priest 1987; curate Exeter, chaplain Jesus Coll and tutor Wycliffe Hall Oxford (also vice-princ Wycliffe Hall), princ St Mellitus Coll, princ St Paul's Theological Centre; Silver Rose of St Nicholas 2016; *Recreations* cricket, golf, music, reading, travel, football; *Clubs* MCC; *Style—* The Rt Rev the Bishop of Kensington

KENSINGTON, 8 Baron (I 1776 and UK 1886); Hugh Ivor Edwardes; s of Capt Hon Owen Edwardes (d 1937, 2 s of 6 Baron Kensington, CMG, DSO, TD, JP, DL); suc unc, 7 Baron, 1981; *b* 24 November 1933; *Educ* Eton; *m* 1961, Juliet Elizabeth Massy, da of Capt Alexander Massy Anderson (d 1943); 1 da (Hon Amanda b 1962), 2 s (Hon Owen b 1964, Hon Rupert b 1967); *Heir* s, Hon Owen Edwardes; *Career* farmer and thoroughbred breeder; *Recreations* horse breeding, shooting; *Clubs* Boodle's, Victoria Country (Pietermaritzburg); *Style—* The Rt Hon the Lord Kensington; ✉ Friar Tuck, PO Box 549, Mooi River, 3300 Natal, South Africa (☎ 00 27 08 2584 4801)

KENT, Alastair; OBE (2011); *Career* dir Genetic Alliance UK; FRSM; *Style—* Alastair Kent, Esq, OBE; ✉ Genetic Alliance UK, Unit 4D, Leroy House, 436 Essex Road, London N1 3QP

KENT, HE Mark Andrew Geoffrey; *m* Martine Delogne; 1 s, 1 da; *Career* Near East and North Africa Dept FCO 1987–89, 3 then 2 sec Brasilia 1989–93, 1 sec external rels UK Perm Representation to EU Brussels 1993–98, News Dept FCO 1998–2000, 1 sec then consul gen and commercial cnsllr Mexico City 2000–04, int affrs advsr to Supreme Allied Cdr Europe SHAPE Belgium 2004–05 (secondment), head Migration Gp FCO 2005–07, ambass to Vietnam 2007–10, Thai language and other trg 2010–12, ambass to Thailand 2012–16, ambass to Argentina 2016–; *Style—* HE Mr Mark Kent; ✉ c/o FCO (Buenos Aires), King Charles Street, London SW1A 2AH

KENT, Michael Harcourt; QC (1996); s of late Capt Barrie Harcourt Kent, RN, of Petersfield, Hants, and Margaret, *née* Wightman; *b* 5 March 1952; *Educ* The Nautical Coll Pangbourne, Univ of Sussex (BA); *m* 1977, Sarah Ann, da of Alan John Ling; 2 s (Rupert Haworth Harcourt b 2 April 1982, Leo Jonathan Harcourt b 2 Feb 1985); *Career* called to the Bar Middle Temple 1975; memb Supplementary Panel of Jr Counsel to the Crown (Common Law) 1988–96, recorder 2000– (asst recorder 1999–2000); asst boundary cmmr 2001–08, dep judge High Ct 2010–; chm London Common Law and Commercial Bar Assoc 2011–13; *Recreations* sailing; *Style—* Michael Kent, Esq, QC; ✉ Crown Office Chambers, 2 Crown Office Row, Temple, London EC4Y 7HJ (☎ 020 7797 8100, fax 020 7797 8101, e-mail kent@crownofficechambers.com)

KENT, Pauline; da of Roy Kent, of Felmingham, Norfolk, and Irene, *née* Rimes; *b* 30 June 1961; *Educ* Orme Girls' Sch Newcastle-under-Lyme, Univ of Birmingham (BA); *m* 1992,

Jeremy Budden, s of Michael Budden; 1 da (Olivia Clementine b 4 Oct 1994), 1 s (Matthew b 10 Sept 1996); *Career* copywriter/account exec Lynne Franks PR 1982–84, account mangr Grant Spreckley Williams 1984–87, account mangr then account dir VandenBurg PR 1987–90, dir VandenBurg Kent 1990–93, creative dir Countrywide Porter Novelli 1993–; PRCA awards for: Reed Employment 1989, launch of first UK Disney Store 1990, Nivea/Fashion Targets Breast Cancer Campaign 1996; author of various articles in the trade and nat press; memb Business in the Community Task Force; *Recreations* walks by the sea, writing children's stories (for own children), cycling, relaxing with friends and family; *Style—* Ms Pauline Kent

KENT, Dr Peter; s of Harold Kent, and Lilian, *née* Melling; *b* 19 April 1961, Liverpool; *Educ* Univ of Sheffield (BA), St Katharine's Liverpool (PGCE), Univ of Salford (MA), Univ of Leicester (MBA, DEd); *m* 9 July 1988, Sian, *née* White; 1 da (Hannah b 2 July 1991), 2 s (Andrew b 6 Jan 1994, Matthew b 27 May 1997); *Career* Queen Elizabeth's GS Blackburn 1983–93, head of English Liverpool Coll, dep head Lawrence Sheriff Sch Rugby 1997–99, head Lawrence Sheriff Sch 1999–, exec headteacher Blue Coat Sch Coventry 2008–09; pres ASCL 2014–15; lay reader Church of England; *Publications* The Cultural Jigsaw, Educational Management and Administration Vol 38; *Recreations* cricket, music, reading, walking, football; *Style—* Dr Peter Kent; ✉ Lawrence Sheriff School, Clifton Road, Rugby CV21 3AG (☎ 01788 843727, e-mail peter.kent@lawrencesheriffschool.com, website www.lawrencesheriffschool.net)

KENT, Roderick David; s of Dr Basil Stanley Kent (d 1991), of Ramsdell, Hants, and Vivien Margaret, *née* Baker (d 2006); *b* 14 August 1947; *Educ* King's Sch Canterbury, CCC Oxford (MA), INSEAD (MBA); *m* 12 Aug 1972, Belinda Jane, da of W H Mitchell (d 1983), of Grouville, Jersey; 3 da (Sophie b 1974, Nicola b 1976, Tiffany b 1978); *Career* with J Henry Schroder Wagg & Co Ltd 1969–71, Banque Blyth (Paris) 1971, Triumph Investment Tst 1972–74; Close Brothers Gp: dir Close Brothers 1974–84, md Close Brothers 1975–84, md Close Brothers Gp plc 1984–2002, non-exec dir 2002–, non-exec chm 2006–08; chm: Bradford & Bingley 2002–08, BT Pension Scheme 2008–; non-exec dir: Wessex Water plc 1989–98, English and Scottish Investors plc 1989–98, M & G Group plc 1995–99 (chm), Whitbread plc 2002–08; chm Grosvenor Ltd 2000–, non-exec dir Grosvenor Gp Ltd 2000–; govr Wellcome Tst 2008–; Liveryman of Worshipful Co of Pewterers; *Recreations* sport; *Style—* Roderick Kent, Esq

KENT, Sarah Ann; da of Hugh Kent (d 1989), of Cornwall, and Joan Eileen, *née* Mather (d 1972); *b* 19 November 1941; *Educ* Haberdashers' Aske's Sch for Girls, Slade Sch of Fine Art (Dip Fine Art, Painting and Printmaking), UCL (MA), Univ of London Inst of Educn (Advanced Dip Art Educn); *m* 1961 (m dis 1965), John Howard Drane; 1 s (Matthew Pendarell); *Career* artist, exhibition curator, lectr, broadcaster, writer and magazine ed; pt/t lectr various art schs 1965–77 (incl Hornsey, London Coll of Printing, Harrow and Byam Shaw); lectr in art history and criticism: City Literary Inst London 1965–76, Extra-mural Dept Univ of London 1967–75; visiting lectr: Tate Gallery, Hayward Gallery, Courtauld Inst, Serpentine Gallery, Nat Portrait Gallery, Whitechapel, RCA, South London Gallery; visual arts ed: Time Out magazine 1976–2006, 20/20 magazine 1989–90; dir of exhibitions ICA London 1977–79; *Exhibitions as curator* since 1979: Br section of Lichtbildnisse (historical survey of portrait photography Bonn) 1982, Problems of Picturing (Serpentine Gallery) 1984, Retrospective of Elisabeth Frink's Sculpture, Drawings and Prints (Royal Acad) 1985, Br section of Sydney Biennale (Art Gallery of NSW) 1986, Peripheral States (Benjamin Rhodes London), Photo 94 (Photographers' Gallery), Artist of the Day (Flowers East Gallery) 1995, Whistling Women (Royal Festival Hall) 1995, Critic's Choice (FACT Gallery) 2005, Fresh Faced and Wild Eyed (Photographers' Gallery) 2008, A View From A Window: Shelagh Wakely (Camden Arts Centre) 2014; *Exhibitions as artist* solo: Redmark Gallery London 1968, Design Progression London 1970; mixed: Young Contemporaries 1965, Arts Cncl Touring 1965, Slade/Royal Coll Show 1966, Free Painters and Sculptors 1966, Ben Uri Gallery 1966, Reeves Bicentennial Exhibition 1966, Survey '67 (Camden Arts Centre) 1967, Lancaster Arts Festival 1967, Arts Cncl Touring Exhibition 1969–71, Cleveland Int Drawing Biennale 1973 (prizewinner), Cleveland Int Drawing Biennale Touring Exhibition 1979–80, Aspects of Drawing (House Gallery London) 1981, Fully Exposed – The Male Nude in Photography (Photographers' Gallery London) 1990, Artists in the Arts (John Jones Gallery London) 1992; work in collections incl: Arts Cncl of GB, Camden Arts Cncl, Cleveland BC, numerous private collections; *as writer and broadcaster* numerous contribs to TV and radio incl: Art and Technology, Arena, The South Bank Show, The Late Show, J'Accuse, Private View, Critics' Forum, Third Ear, Third Opinion, After Eight, Kaleidoscope, Meridian, Nightwaves, Woman's Hour, The World At One, Today, Last Word; numerous contribs to art jls and magazines incl: Studio International, Art Monthly, Flash Art, Artscribe, Arte, Tema Celeste, Art in America, Time Out, Dance Now, Art World, Phillips de Pury Magazine, Art & Auction, Brooklyn Rail, The Arts Desk, London Dance; memb Jury: Turner Prize Tate Gallery 1992, Gulbenkian New Horizons Award 1992, Barclay Young Artists Awards 1993, SE Arts Purchasing Award 1993, British Tport Painting Competition 1993, Arts Fndn Fellowship 1995, Northern Graduates Fine Arts Prizes 1996, John Kobal Photographic Portrait Award Nat Portrait Gallery 1998, Bloomberg New Contemporaries 2000, Schweppes Photographic Portrait Award (Nat Portrait Gallery) 2004, Emerging Artist Award British Oxygen Co 2004 and 2005, Pirye Prize (Ruskin Sch of Art/ Oxford Univ Press) 2007, London Int Creative Competition 2008–10, Harper's Bazaar Art Power 20 2010, GAM Award for MA grads (City & Guilds Art Sch) 2013, Arts Fndn Arts Journalism Fellowship 2013, Sculpture Shock (Royal Br Soc of Sculptors) 2013, Olivier Dance Awards 2014–15; external examiner: Chelsea Sch of Art (Sculpture MA) 1986–90, Trent Poly (MA Fine Art) 1982–86, Staffs Poly (Sculpture BA) 1990–93, Univ of Nottingham (Contemporary Art Practice BA) 1993–95, Glasgow Sch of Art (Fine Art MA) 1993–97; *Publications* Berlin a Critical View: Ugly Realism 20's-70's (with Eckhart Gillen, 1978), Elisabeth Frink: Sculpture (1985), Women's Images of Men (with Jacqueline Morreau, 1985 and 1990), Shark Infested Waters (1994), Composition (1995), Stephen Balkenhol (1996); contrib to: Fotografie als Kunst: Kunst als Fotografie (by Floris M Neususs, 1979), Lichtbildnisse (by Klaus Honeff, 1982), Drawings and Graphics (by Jacqueline Morreau, 1986), Nudes in Budapest (by James Cotier, 1992), Paula Rego: Dancing Ostriches (1996), The Saatchi Decade (1999), London from Punk to Blair (2003), Flowers: Jo Self (2003), Border Crossings: Pedro Cabrita Reis (2005), Close Encounters (365 days): Roelof Bakker (2007), Demons, Yarns and Tales: Tapestries by Contemporary Artists (2008), London After Dark (365 nights): Roelof Bakker 2010, Blowing Hot and Cold: Rose Finn-Kelcey (2013), Thinking Aloud: Shelagh Wakely (2013); photographs published in: The Naked and the Nude (by Jorge Lewinski, 1987), Fully Exposed: the Male Nude in Photography (by Emmanuel Cooper, 1990), Running Scared (by Peter Lehman, 1993), The Boy (by Germaine Greer, 2003); *Recreations* dancing, performing, walking, singing; *Style—* Ms Sarah Kent; ✉ e-mail skent235@btinternet.com

KENT, Trevor Lincoln; s of Ernest George Kent (d 1987), and Evelyn Gertrude Mary Kent (d 1999), of Gerrards Cross, Bucks; *Educ* Thorpe House Sch, Denstone Coll, London Coll of Commerce; *m* 1979, Angela Christine (d 1996), da of Gp Capt John Thornhill Shaw, DSO, DFC, AFC (d 1975), and Doreen Lilian Shaw (d 2004), of Berwick upon Tweed; 4 s (Toby d 1980, Lincoln b 1982, Warwick b 1983, Leicester b 1987); *Career* princ Trevor Kent & Co estate agents and auctioneers 1971–; freelance writer and broadcaster specialising in residential property and related finance; co-presenter: Moving and Improving, Housebuying Explained, Hot Property, Only Follies and Houses, The French Collection (Channel 4); specialist commentator: BBC, ITN, Sky News, IRN, Steve Wright and Jeremy Vine Shows BBC Radio 2, BBC Radio Five Live, BBC Radio London; past columnist: International Property, Estate Agency News, English Homes, The Negotiator, EstateAgentToday.co.uk; current columnist PropertyIndustryEye.co.uk; former media spokesman Nat Assoc of Estate Agents (pres 1989–90); memb Govt's Inter-Professional Working Pty on the Transfer of Residential Property 1989–90; dist cncllr South Bucks DC 1978–82; licensed asst C of E; hon memb Du Page Assoc of Realtors Chicago USA; *Recreations* cricket, watching the garden grow, auctioneering for charities, not dieting; *Clubs* Middlesex and Bucks County Cricket; *Style—* Trevor Kent, Esq; ✉ Kent House, Oxford Road, Gerrards Cross, Buckinghamshire SL9 7DP (☎ 01753 885522, fax 01753 887777, website www.trevorkent.com)

KENTFIELD, Graham Edward Alfred; s of Edward Leonard Harvey Kentfield (d 1984), and Frances Elfrida May, *née* Tucker (d 2000); *b* 3 September 1940; *Educ* Bancroft's Sch, St Edmund Hall Oxford (BA); *m* 29 April 1965, Ann Dwelley, da of James Préaud Hewetson; 2 da; *Career* Bank of England: joined 1963, Economic Intelligence Dept 1964–66, seconded to Dept of Applied Economics Univ of Cambridge 1966–67, Foreign Exchange Operations 1967–69, Overseas Dept 1969–74 (a mangr 1972–74), mangr Monetary Policy Forecasting 1974–76, Govrs speechwriter 1976–77, ed Bank of England Quarterly Bulletin 1977–80, sr mangr Financial Statistics Div 1980–84, advsr Banking Dept 1984–85, dep chief Banking Dept 1985–91, chief Banking Dept and chief cashier 1991–94, dep dir and chief cashier 1994–98; chm: Insolvency Practices Cncl 2000–04, Building Societies Tst Ltd 2002–; memb: Building Societies Investor Protection Bd 1991–2001, Financial Law Panel 1994–98, Cncl London Univ 2000–08; tstee Chartered Inst of Bankers Pension Fund 1994–2006 (chm 2000–06); tstee Overseas Bishoprics Fund 1999– (chm 2005–12); hon treas Soc for the Promotion of Roman Studies 1991–2010; FCIB; *Recreations* Roman history, genealogy, philately; *Style—* Graham Kentfield, Esq; ✉ 27 Elgood Avenue, Northwood, Middlesex HA6 3QL (☎ 01923 825401)

KENTON, Jeremy Martin; s of Dr Ralph J Kenton (d 1988), of Westcliff-on-Sea, Essex, and Veronica Maisie, *née* Field (d 1994); *b* 11 December 1955; *Educ* Chigwell Sch, Br Coll of Naturopathy and Osteopathy (Dip Osteopathy, Dip Naturopathy); *m* 21 July 1990, Sharon Anna, da of Reginald Eric Calder; 1 da (Claudia Elizabeth b 7 Oct 1992), 1 step da (Katrina Anna b 12 July 1986); *Career* osteopath; lectr Br Coll of Naturopathy and Osteopathy London 1979–, private osteopath London and Javea 1979–; sr clinician Br Coll of Naturopathy and Osteopathy Teaching Clinic 1981–92, Br delegate to Euro Osteopathic Liaison Ctee Brussels 1983–87, fndr Ctee Cncl for Complementary and Alternative Med 1984; pres Br Naturopathic and Osteopathic Assoc 1988–90 (memb 1979–); memb: Gen Cncl and Register of Osteopaths 1987– (memb Cncl 1989–92, pres 1990), memb Gen Osteopathic Cncl 1998–; regular broadcaster on nat and local radio and TV 1980–, author of numerous articles in newspapers and magazines, host The Health Appointment (weekly radio broadcast, Overseasfm); advsr on osteopathy to All-Pty Gp House of Commons; expert medical witness; DO 1979, ND 1979; *Publications* Competence in Osteopathic Practice (1994), regular contrib to numerous jls and periodicals on health, medical health correspondent and broadcaster; *Recreations* family, patients, horse riding, motor racing, music, theatre, sailing, powerboating; *Clubs* East India, New Cavendish; *Style—* Jeremy M Kenton, Esq; ✉ e-mail jeremymkenton@aol.com, www.osteopath-kenton.co.uk

KENWAY, Prof Richard Donovan; OBE (2008); s of Alfred Bertram Kenway (d 2008), and Sheila Ethel Donovan (d 1994); *b* 8 May 1954; *Educ* Univ of Exeter (BSc), Jesus Coll Oxford (grad scholar, DPhil); *m* 11 Feb 1981, Anna Cass; 3 c (Owain Alfred b 11 March 1982, Angharad Sonia b 9 April 1985, Carys Sheila b 23 Oct 1986); *Career* research assoc Brown Univ USA 1978–80, postdoctoral fell Los Alamos Nat Lab USA 1980–82; Univ of Edinburgh: SERC postdoctoral fell 1982–83, lectr in physics 1983–90, reader 1990–94, chm Edinburgh Parallel Computing Centre 1997– (dir 1993–97), Tait prof of mathematical physics 1994–, head Dept of Physics and Astronomy 1997–2000, asst princ 2002–05, vice-princ 2005–, head Sch of Physics and Astronomy 2008–11; chm UK Nat e-Science Centre 2001–11; chm Particle Physics Theory Ctee PPARC 1997–2000, sr res fell PPARC 2001–04, chm Scientific Steering Ctee of Partnership for Advanced Computing in Europe (PRACE) 2010–12; memb American Physical Soc 1976; FInstP 2001 (MInstP 1982), FRSE 1997, FLSW 2015; *Publications* author of 140 publications in Elementary Particle Physics, High Performance Computing, and Condensed Matter Physics; *Recreations* munroing, running; *Style—* Prof Richard Kenway, OBE, FRSE, FInstP; ✉ School of Physics and Astronomy, University of Edinburgh, James Clerk Maxwell Building, Peter Guthrie Tait Road, Edinburgh EH9 3FD (☎ 0131 650 5245, fax 0131 650 5902, e-mail r.d.kenway@ed.ac.uk)

KENWRIGHT, Bill; CBE (2001); s of Albert Kenwright, of Liverpool, and Hope, *née* Jones; *b* 4 September 1945; *Educ* Liverpool Inst HS for Boys; *m* (m dis) Anouska Hempel (Lady Weinberg); *Career* stage and film producer; actor 1964–70, theatre prodr 1970–; exec prodr Theatre Royal Windsor chm and prodr Olivier Awards Soc of London Theatres; chm Everton FC 2004– (dep chm 1999–2004); hon prof Thames Valley Univ; Hon Dr: John Moores Univ Liverpool, Nottingham Trent Univ, Univ of West London; *Theatre* West End productions: Let the Right One In (Apollo), Twelve Angry Men (Garrick), Cabaret (Savoy), Blood Brothers (Phoenix), Dreamboats and Petticoats (Wyndhams), Soul Sister (Savoy), Volcano (Vaudeville), Written on the Heart (RSC Duchess), Three Days in May (Trafalgar), The Pitmen Painters (Duchess), The Wizard of Oz (Palladium), The Country Girl (Apollo), Bedroom Farce (Duke of York's), A Daughter's a Daughter (Trafalgar), One the Waterfront (Haymarket), Woman in Mind (Haymarket), Plague Over England (Duchess), Sunset Boulevard (Comedy), The Vortex (Apollo), Absurd Person Singular (Garrick), Joseph and the Amazing Technicolor Dreamcoat (Adelphi), The Lette (Wyndhams), Treats (Garrick), The Glass Menagerie (Apollo), Cabaret (Lyric), The Canterbury Tales (RSC Gielgud), The Crucible (RSC Gielgud), Whistle Down the Wind (Palace), A Man for All Seasons (Theatre Royal Haymarket), The Night of the Iguana (Lyric), Scrooge (London Palladium), A Few Good Men (Haymarket), The Big Life (Apollo), Elmina's Kitchen (Garrick), Festen (Lyric), All's Well that Ends Well (RSC Gielgud), Hay Fever (Haymarket), Filumena (Piccadilly), The Gift of the Gorgon (Wyndhams), The Taming of the Shrew and The Tamer Tamed (RSC Queen's), The Secret Rapture (Lyric), the RSC Jacobean season (Gielgud), Via Dolorosa (Duchess), Sleuth (Apollo), The Constant Wife (Lyric), Cat on a Hot Tin Roof (Lyric), Ghosts (Comedy), Fallen Angels (Apollo), Long Day's Journey into Night (Lyric), Brief Encounter (Lyric), Miss Julie (Haymarket), Stepping Out (Albery), Hurlyburly (Queen's), Lady Windemere's Fan ((Haymarket), Passion (Queen's), Company (Albery), The Miracle Worker (Wyndhams), No Man's Land and Moonlight (Comedy), Mind Millie for Me, The Master, A Streetcar Named Desire (all Haymarket and directed by Peter Hall), The School of Wives (Piccadilly), Hamlet, An Absolute Turkey (both Gielgud), Lysistrata (Old Vic, Athens), Separate Tables (Albery), She Stoops to Conquer (Queen's), Waiting for Godot, The Misanthrope, Major Barbara, Kafka's Dick (all Piccadilly), The Go Between (Apollo), How the Other Half Loves (Haymarket), The War of the Worlds (Dominion), Evita (Dominion); Broadway productions: Blood Brothers (Music Box Theatre) 1993–95, A Doll's House (Belasco Theatre) 1997, The Chairs (Theatre de Complicite, Golden Theatre) 2000; prodr Peter Hall Co season (Picadilly): Waiting for Godot, The Misanthrope, Major Barbara, Filumena, Kafka's Dick; prodr (dir by Sir Peter Hall, *qv*): Mind Millie for Me (Theatre Royal Haymarket), The Master Builder (Theatre Royal Haymarket and Toronto), Hamlet (Gielgud), An Absolute Turkey (Globe), The Gift of the Gorgon

(Wyndham's), Lysistrata (Old Vic, Athens and Wyndham's), Separate Tables (Albery), She Stoops To Conquer (Queen's); as dir incl: Whistle Down the Wind, Joseph, Jesus Christ Superstar, Evita, Blood Brothers; *Films* Stepping Out 1991, The Day After the Fair, Zoe, Cheri, Broken (Best Br Ind Film 2013); *Awards* winner numerous awards incl: Tony Awards, Olivier Awards, Evening Standard Awards, Scouser of the Year 1991 and 1992, gold badge BASCA, Bernard Delfont Award Variety Club 2002, Lifetime Achievement Award Theatrical Management Assoc 2008; nominated London Theatre Critics' Award (for West Side Story) and Tony Award (for Blood Brothers); *Recreations* football; *Style*— Bill Kenwright, Esq, CBE; ✉ Bill Kenwright Ltd, BKL House, 1 Venice Walk, London W2 1RR (☎ 020 7446 6200, fax 020 7446 6222)

KENYON, Guy Stuart; s of Horace Stuart Kenyon (d 1997), of Hunstanton, Norfolk, and Katherine Mary, *née* Chapman; *b* 6 January 1948; *Educ* Perse Sch Cambridge, Univ of Edinburgh (BSc, MB ChB, MD), Univ of Surrey (MBA); *m* 30 Sept 1989, Judith Elizabeth, da of Edward Meirion Morgan, of Kettering, Northants; 2 s (James Edward Stuart b 1 Feb 1991, Benjamin Raymond Guy b 20 Dec 1993); *Career* RNR 1979–88, Surgn Lt Cdr; training in gen surgery United Bristol and Royal Northern Hosps 1977–80, registrar and sr registrar in otolaryngology London Hosp, Royal Free Hosp and Royal Surrey County Hosp Guildford 1981–87; conslt surgn in otolaryngology: London Hosp 1987–, Hosps for Sick Children London 1987–92, conslt surgn St Luke's Hosp for the Clergy 1987–; contrib papers on neuro-otology and head and neck cancer; memb: Med Soc of London, The Otorhinolaryngological Res Soc 1983, The Joseph Soc 1987; FRCSEd 1980, FRCS 1982; *Books* Hutchinson's Clinical Examination (1984 and 1994), Textbook of Otolaryngology (contrib, 1988), many articles in medical journals; *Recreations* skiing, swimming, music, reading; *Clubs* RSM, Royal Naval Medical, Blizzard; *Style*— Guy Kenyon, Esq; ✉ Pentlands, East Common, Harpenden, Hertfordshire AL5 1DG (☎ 01582 767593, fax 01582 767751)

KENYON, Ian Peter; s of Peter Kenyon (d 1986), and Barbara, *née* Thirlby; *b* 23 September 1961, Wimbledon; *Educ* Bradfield Coll, Univ of Nottingham (BSc); *m* 1989, Louise, *née* Tucker; 2 da (Alice b 23 Oct 1994, Fiona b 5 Sept 1996) 1 s (Richard b 26 Feb 2001); *Career* Price Waterhouse 1983–89, St Ives plc 1989–94, Kingfisher plc 1994–2002, dir financial reporting Sainsburys 2002–05, gp finance dir Carpetright plc 2005–08, chief finance offr Carphone Warehouse Retail 2008–12, gp finance dir HMV plc 2012–13, chief financial offr Cancer Research UK 2013–; treas Guildford Cathedral; Liveryman Worshipful Co of Glovers; ACA 1986; *Recreations* church, tennis; *Style*— Ian Kenyon, Esq

KENYON, Dr Julian N; s of Dr Joseph Bernard Kenyon, of Worsthorne, Lancs, and Marie Therese, *née* Rudant; *b* 8 March 1947; *Educ* Lancaster Royal GS, Univ of Liverpool Med Sch (scholar, MB ChB, MD); *m* 1, 1970 (m dis 1985), Margaret Angela, *née* O'Connor; 2 da (Rachel b 31 March 1973, Abigail b 28 Feb 1984), 2 s (Benjamin b 21 Nov 1974, Rupert b 18 Jan 1978); m 2, 1987, Rachel Staveley Jessel (m dis 1999), da of Dr Thomas Bonsor Staveley Dick; 1 da (Meri Barbara b 9 June 1989), 1 s (Micha Tom b 26 Sept 1993); m 3, 2000, Tanya Cartwright, da of Norman Armitage, and Lois Armitage; *Career* house surgn Broadgreen Hosp Liverpool 1971 (house physician 1970–71), demonstrator Dept of Anatomy Univ of Liverpool Med Sch 1971–72, lectr in child health Univ of Liverpool 1972–74, princ in gen practice Crosby Liverpool 1974–76, full-time private practice in med alternatives 1976–82; fndr Cancer ImmunotherapyUK Ltd; currently dir: The Dove Healing Tst, The Dove Clinic for Integrated Med; former co-dir The Centre for the Study of Complementary Med Southampton; hon specialist Pain Relief Fndn Clinic Walton Hosp Liverpool 1980–82, visiting prof Calif Inst for Human Sci; pres Int Assoc of Auricular Therapy; memb: Ctee Br Holistic Med Assoc, Bd of Advsrs Findhorn Holistic Health Centre Forres Scotland, Br Soc for Clinical Ecology, Br Med Acupuncture Soc (fndr chm 1980); pres Int Auricular Med Soc, fndr chm Br Soc of Integrated Med 2002; FRCSEd 1972; contrib, author or ed of numerous books and booklets on acupuncture and several pubns in the cancer field; *Recreations* playing violin, gardening; *Style*— Dr Julian N Kenyon; ✉ The Dove Clinic for Integrated Medicine, Hockley Mill Stables, Church Lane, Twyford, Winchester, Hampshire SO21 1NT (☎ 01962 718000, fax 01962 718011; 19 Wimpole Street, London W1G 8GE (☎ 020 7580 8886, fax 020 7580 8884); The Old Brewery, High Street, Twyford, Winchester, Hampshire SO21 1RG (☎ 01962 712226, fax 01962 717060); websites www.doveclinic.com, www.eecp.co.uk, www.spdt.org.uk and www.propanc.com

KENYON, Sir Nicholas; kt (2008), CBE (2001); *b* 1951; *Educ* Balliol Coll Oxford (BA); *m*; 4 c; *Career* English Bach Festival 1973–76, Music Div BBC 1976–79; music critic: The New Yorker 1979–82, The Times 1982–85; music ed The Listener 1982–87, ed Early Music 1983–92; music critic The Observer 1985–92; BBC Radio: controller Radio 3 1992–98, BBC Proms 1996–2007, controller millennium progs 1998–2000, controller BBC Proms, live events and TV classical music 2000–07; md Barbican Centre 2007–; *Publications* The BBC Symphony Orchestra – The First 50 Years, Simon Rattle: From Birmingham to Berlin, Authenticity and Early Music (ed), BBC Proms Pocket Guide to Great Symphonies, BBC Proms Guide to Great Concertos (ed), BBC Proms Guide to Choral Works (ed), BBC Proms Guide to Great Orchestral Works (ed), The Faber Pocket Guide to Mozart (2005), The Faber Pocket Guide to Bach (2011), The City of London: A Companion Guide (2012); *Style*— Sir Nicholas Kenyon; ✉ Barbican Centre, Silk Street, London EC2Y 8DS

KENYON, Ronald James; s of Fletcher Kenyon (d 1981), of Penrith, Cumbria, and Isabella, *née* Winter; *Educ* Queen Elizabeth's GS Penrith, Trent Poly; *m* 27 April 1985, Anne Christine, da of William Eckersall; 1 s (Michael Fletcher b 14 Oct 1990), 1 da (Catherine Sarah b 31 Oct 1993); *Career* chartered accountant; articled clerk F T Kenyon and Son (founded by gf), ptnr Saint and Co (formerly F T Kenyon and Son then Kyle Saint and Co) 1980–2011, ret; dir Penrith Building Soc 1993–2003; pres Penrith Chamber of Trade 2006–08; chm: Cumberland Dist Soc of CAs 1991, Penrith Civic Soc 1989–91, Eden Climbing Wall 1992–, Eden Sports Cncl 1996–2006, Penrith Partnership 1999, Penrith Running Track Gp 2004–06, Penrith Castle Park Devpt Gp 2013–; treas: Penrith Amateur Savoyards 1981–84, Eden Valley Visitors Assoc 1983–2000, Penrith Agric Soc 1986–2010 (also now hon life memb), Penrith Lions 1988–90, Greenpeace Eden Valley Support Gp 1991–93, Juniper Tst 1996–2002 and 2011–, Penrith Partnership 1998–, Friends of Penrith Cinema 2012; dir: Keswick Museum and Art Gallery 2011–15, NCL (Eden) 2011–, NCL (Trading) 2012–, Eden Housing Assoc 2012–14; memb: Penrith Mountain Rescue Team 1967–92 (pres 1992–2013), Tibet Support Gp; tstee Mountain Heritage Tst 2003–13; gamesmaker Paralympic Games London 2012; cncllr Penrith Town Cncl 2015–; winner Penrith Sports Superstar 1976; FCA (ACA 1975); *Books* Rock Climbers' Guide – North of England (1978), Rock Climbers' Guide – Borrowdale (1986, 1990 and 2016), Recent Developments of Rock Climbs in the Lake District (1984, 1986, 1988, 1990 and 1996), Eden Valley and South Lakes Limestone (2012), Scafell and Wasdale (2014); *Recreations* rock climbing, fell running, ski touring; *Clubs* Eden Valley Mountaineering, Fell and Rock Climbing (vice-pres 1992–94, sec Guidebook Ctee 1998–, hon memb 2011, pres 2014–16), Borderliners Orienteering, Eden Runners (jrs treas and coach 2003–), Climbers, Alpine, Scottish Mountaineering; *Style*— Ronald Kenyon, Esq; ✉ 30 Wordsworth Street, Penrith, Cumbria CA11 7QY (☎ 01768 864728, mobile 07775 768569, e-mail ron@jaggedlakes.plus.com)

KEOGH, Prof Sir Bruce E; KBE (2003); s of Gerald Keogh, and Marjorie Beatrice, *née* Craig; *b* 24 November 1954, Harare, Zimbabwe; *Educ* St George's Coll Harare, Charing Cross Hosp Medical Sch (MB, BS), Univ of London (MD); *m* 1979, Ann Katherine, *née* Westmore; 4 s (Robert, Christopher, William, Michael); *Career* Br Heart Fndn sr lectr in cardiac surgery Royal Postgrad Medical Sch Hammersmith Hosp 1991–95 (memb Research Ethics Ctee 1993–95), conslt in cardiothoracic surgery Univ Hosp Birmingham NHS Tst 1995–2004 (assoc medical dir 1998–2003), prof of cardiac surgery UC London and Royal Free Medical and dir of surgery Heart Hosp London 2004–07, medical dir NHS 2007–13, DG Medical Directorate Dept of Health 2007–13, nat medical dir NHS England 2013–; cmmr Cmmn for Health Improvement 2002–04 (also chm Jt Cmmn for Health Improvement and Audit Cmmn Nat Service Framework Prog Bd), cmmr Healthcare Cmmn 2004–07 (also chair Clinical Advsy Gp); memb: NHS Nat Taskforce for Coronary Heath Disease 2000–07, NHS Standing Medical Advsy Ctee 2002–04, Dept of Health Prog Bd for Coronary Heart Disease 2003–07, Cncl Br Heart Fndn 2007–15; Soc for Cardiothoracic Surgeons of GB and Ireland: Ronald Edwards Medal 1991, fndr and co-ordinator Nat Adult Cardiac Surgical Database 1995–2004, hon sec 1999–2003, pres 2006–08; Cardiothoracic Section RSM: memb Cncl 1992–99, hon sec 1993–99, pres 2005–07; US Soc of Thoracic Surgeons: int memb 1995–, memb US Adult Cardiac Surgery Database Ctee 1997–2009, memb Technol Ctee 1997–2000, memb Bd of Dirs 2005–11, int dir 2005–11, Ferguson lecture 2009; European Assoc for Cardio-Thoracic Surgery: chm Database Ctee 2000–07, sec-gen 2004–07, dir European Acad of Thoracic and Cardiovascular Surgery; RCS: memb Clinical Effectiveness Ctee 1998–2004, memb Intercollegiate Specialist Advsy Ctee on Higher Surgical Training in Cardiothoracic Surgery 1999–2003, memb Intercollegiate Examination Bd in Cardiothoracic Surgery 1999–2003, memb Steering Gp Nat Confidential Enquiry into Perioperative Outcome and Death 2000–07, memb Cncl Royal Coll of Surgeons of England 1999–2002 and 2006–08, Tudor Edwards Medal 2007, Hunterian Orator and Medal 2013; memb American Assoc for Thoracic Surgery 2007, hon memb Br Soc of Interventional Radiology 2010; visiting prof: Univ of Colorado, Chinese Univ of Hong Kong 2007, Clinical Excellence Cmmn Australia 2014; memb Editorial Bd: Jl RSM 1994–99, CTSNet 1999–2007; Heart 2000–04; author of numerous pubns on cardiac surgical outcomes, public disclosure and surgery for heart failure; Robert Gross lecture Boston Children's Hosp and Harvard Medical Sch 2010, inaugural John Snow orator Royal Coll of Anaesthetists 2014; vice-patron Royal Br Legion Poppy Factory 2011–, tstee Scar Free Fndn (formerly The Healing Fndn) 2014–, pres Ex Fide Feducia Tst 2016–; Hon MD Univ of Sheffield 2009, Hon MD Univ of Birmingham 2009, Hon DSc Univ of Toledo 2009, Hon DSc Univ of Coventry 2010; FRCSEd 1985 (King James IV Professorship 2005, McKeown lecture and Medal 2012), FESC 1992 (memb Scientific Ctee 1999–2001), fell European Bd of Thoracic and Cardiovascular Surgns (FETCS) 1999, hon FRCP 2007, hon FRCGP 2009, hon fell American Coll of Surgeons 2009, hon fell Royal Coll of Surgeons in Ireland 2010, hon FRCA 2011, hon fell American Surgical Assoc 2016; *Publications* Normal Surface Anatomy (1984), The Evidence Base for Cardiothoracic Surgery (jt ed, 2004); *Recreations* diving, photography; *Clubs* Lunar Soc; *Style*— Prof Sir Bruce Keogh, KBE; ✉ NHS England, Skipton House, 80 London Road, London SE1 6LH (e-mail bruce.keogh@nhs.net)

K

KEOGH, Colin Denis; s of John Denis Keogh, and Hillary Joan, *née* Campbell; *b* 27 July 1953; *Educ* St John's Coll, Eton, UC Oxford (MA), INSEAD (MBA); *m* 26 Aug 1978, Joanna Mary Martyn, da of John Frederick Leapman; 2 s (Thomas b 27 March 1983, William b 6 May 1987), 2 da (Kate b 6 Nov 1984, Georgina b 10 Aug 1990); *Career* Arthur Andersen & Co 1978–82, INSEAD 1982–83, Saudi Int Bank 1983–85; Close Brothers Gp plc: joined 1985, dir Close Brothers Ltd 1986–95, gp dir 1995, chm Close Brothers Corporate Finance Ltd 1995–98, gp chief exec 2002–09; *Recreations* sport, theatre; *Style*— Colin Keogh, Esq

KER, David Peter James; s of Capt David John Richard Ker, MC, DL, JP (d 1997), of Aldworth, Reading, Berks, and Virginia Mary Eloise, *née* Howard, of Suffolk and Berks; *b* 23 July 1951; *Educ* Eton; *m* 27 June 1974, Alexandra Mary, da of Vice Adm Sir Dymock Watson, KCB, CBE, DL (d 1987), of Trebinshwyn, Powys; 1 da (Clare Rose (m Donald Rice, s of Sir Tim Rice, *qv*) b 23 Nov 1977), 2 s (David Edward Richard b 18 Dec 1979 d 1980, David Humphrey Rivers b 11 Oct 1982); *Career* fndr and sole proprietor David Ker Fine Art 1980–; dir: Parc St Roman SA 1977–79, Oceanic Development Co (Bahamas) Ltd 1979–80, Ker Management Ltd 1980–, Belgrave Frames Ltd 1986–92, John Paravicini Ltd 1988–92, James Roundell Ltd 1995–, Dickinson Roundell Inc USA 1998–, Humphrey Butler Ltd 2001–08; md Simon C Dickinson Ltd; memb Soc of London Art Dealers 1986 (memb Ctee 2001–); *Recreations* shooting, fishing, collecting fine art, racing; *Clubs* White's, Beefsteak, Pratt's, The Brook (NY); *Style*— David Ker, Esq; ✉ 58 Jermyn Street, London SW1Y 6LX (☎ 020 7493 0340, fax 020 7493 0796, mobile 07899 668972, e-mail ker@simondickinson.com)

KERR, Alan Grainger; OBE (2000); s of Joseph William Kerr (d 1974), and Eileen, *née* Allen (d 1989); *b* 15 April 1935; *Educ* Methodist Coll Belfast, Queen's Univ Belfast (MB BCh, BAO, DRCOG); *m* 1, 14 April 1962, Patricia Margaret (d 1999), da of Edward Stewart McNeill; 2 s (Jonathan Richard b 5 June 1963, Anthony Michael b 16 Oct 1965), 1 da (Rosalind Patricia b 18 Dec 1966); m 2, 21 April 2015, Victoria, *née* Shannon; *Career* basic med trg Belfast Hosps, otolaryngology trg Belfast Hosps and Harvard Med Sch, conslt otolaryngologist Royal Victoria Hosp and Belfast City Hosp 1968–2003; prof of otorhinolaryngology Queen's Univ Belfast 1979–81; Harrison prize RSM, Jobson Horne prize BMA, Howells prize Univ of London 1988 and 1998; past pres: Section of Otology RSM, Otorhinolaryngological Res Soc, Int Otopathology Soc, Br Assoc of Otorhinolaryngologists, Irish Otolaryngological Soc, Int Soc for Otologic Surgery; FRCS 1964, FRCSEd 1987; *Books* Scott-Brown's Otolaryngology (ed, 5 edn 1987, 6 edn 1996); *Recreations* tennis, skiing, bowling; *Clubs* RSM; *Style*— Alan Kerr, Esq, OBE; ✉ 6 Cranmore Gardens, Belfast BT9 6JL (☎ 028 9066 9181, fax 028 9066 3731)

KERR, Caroline; da of John Joseph Kerr, and Maureen, *née* McNulty; *b* 27 May 1962; *Educ* St Catherine's Sr Sch Strawberry Hill, Newnham Coll Cambridge (BA); *Career* ITN: trainee 1984–86, prodr 1986–89, reporter Channel 4 Daily 1989–92 (assignments incl fall of Berlin Wall and subseq end of communist rule in Eastern Europe, Gulf War from Jordan, Israel and liberated Kuwait), gen reporter ITN 1992–94 (assignments incl Bangkok riots 1992, Bombay bombings 1993), Asia corr 1994–96, sr reporter 1996–98, business and economics ed 1998–2004; co-fndr Millbank Media 2006–; ind editorial advsr BBC Tst 2007–; hon assoc Newnham Coll; *Style*— Ms Caroline Kerr; ✉ Millbank Media, 4 Millbank, London SW1 3JA (website www.millbankmedia.com)

KERR, Prof David James; CBE (2002); s of Robert James Andrew Kerr (d 1986), and Sarah Pettigrew, *née* Hogg (d 1976); *b* 14 June 1956; *Educ* Univ of Glasgow (BSc, MB ChB, MD, MSc, PhD, DSc, Bellahouston Prize); *m* 11 July 1980 (m dis 2013), Annie, *née* Young; 1 s (Stewart), 2 da (Sarah, Fiona); m 2, 13 Aug 2013, Rachel, *née* Midgley; 1 da (Solace b 14 July 2010), 1 s (James Robert, b 31 Dec 2012); *Career* hon sr registrar Beatson Inst for Cancer Research Glasgow 1986–88; Cancer Research Campaign (CRC) Dept of Med Oncology Univ of Glasgow: CRC sr research fell and hon sr registrar 1988–89 (CRC research fell and hon registrar 1984–86), CRC sr fell, sr lectr in med oncology, hon conslt physician and ldr Pharmacology Gp 1989–92; prof of clinical oncology and clinical dir CRC Inst for Cancer Studies Univ of Birmingham 1992–2001, hon conslt physician Birmingham Oncology Centre Queen Elizabeth Hosp and City Hosp Birmingham 1992–2001, Rhodes prof of cancer therapeutics and clinical pharmacology and head Dept of Clinical Pharmacology Univ of Oxford 2001–, hon conslt in med oncology Radcliffe Hosps Tst Oxford 2001–, prof of Cancer Medicine Univ of Oxford 2011–; adjunct prof of medicine Weill-Cornell College of Medicine NY 2009–; chief research advsr and memb

Supreme Health Cncl Qatar 2009–11; fell CCC Oxford 2001–, hon fell Harris Manchester Coll Oxford; MA (by incorporation) Univ of Oxford 2002; FRCPGlas 1995, FRCP 1996, FMedSci 2000, FRCPEd 2008, Hon FRCGP 2009; *Publications* incl: Oxford Textbook of Oncology (3 edn, 2014); also author of numerous papers in learned jls; *Recreations* playing drums in a rock 'n' roll band; *Clubs* Reform, Partick Thistle Supporters; *Style*— Prof David Kerr, CBE

KERR, Rev Fergus Gordon Thomson; OP (1956); s of George Gordon Kerr (d 1967), of Banff, and Jean, *née* Smith (d 2000); *b* 16 July 1931, Banff; *Educ* Banff Acad, Univ of Aberdeen (MA), Le Saulchoir Paris (STL); *Career* Flying Offr RAF 1953–55; prior: Blackfriars Oxford 1969–78, Blackfriars Edinburgh 1988–94; regent Blackfriars Oxford 1998–2004; ed New Blackfriars 1992–; Hon DD Univ of Aberdeen 1995; FRSE 2003; *Books* Theology after Wittgenstein (1986), Immortal Longings (2001), After Aquinas (2003), Twentieth Century Catholic Theologians (2007); *Recreations* walking, reading fiction; *Style*— The Rev Fergus Kerr, OP; ✉ 24 George Square, Edinburgh EH8 9LD (☎ 0131 650 0901, e-mail fergus.kerr@english.op.org)

KERR, Glynn; s of Geoffrey Douglas Kerr, amd Myra Maureen, *née* Platt; *b* 17 February 1958, Skegby, Notts; *Educ* Coventry Univ; *m* 1, 1979 (m dis 2006), Janice May, *née* Edmonds; 1 da (Heather Jayne b 21 Dec 1984) and 1 s (Douglas Alistair b 25 Aug 1986); m 2, 28 Oct 2007, Diane Marie, *née* Sgro; *Career* motorcycle designer and conslt; former bodywork designer TVR; BMW Munich: exterior designer 1982–84, sr designer motorcycle division 1984–87; chief designer Global Design Amsterdam (now GK Design Europe) 1987–90, ind conslt 1990– (clients incl: Ducati, Triumph, Aprilia, Honda, Bajaj, Kymco, Kawasaki, Yamaha), creative dir Motovisions California 2006–15; co-fndr and pres Motorcycle Design Assoc 2001–; former lectr Art Center Coll of Design Europe, reg speaker on bike design and rendering techniques, regular columnist: Motorcycle Consumer News (USA), Two Wheels (Australia), Bike (India), Solo Moto Trienta (Spain); *Style*— Glynn Kerr, Esq; ✉ e-mail glynnkerr@yahoo.com, website www.coroflot.com/glynnkerr

KERR, John Neilson; WS (1980); s of John Kerr (d 2000), of Edinburgh, and Helen, *née* Clark (d 2000); *b* 23 September 1956, Edinburgh; *Educ* John Watson's Sch Edinburgh, Univ of Edinburgh (LLB); *m* 12 Oct 1991, Adrienne, *née* Thompson; 2 s (Struan b 17 Feb 1994, Moray b 7 April 1996); *Career* slr; NP 1980; ptnr Anderson Strathern (formerly Strathern & Blair WS) 1984– (apprentice 1978–80); *Clubs* Stewart's Melville Rugby; *Style*— John N Kerr; ✉ Anderson Strathern, 1 Rutland Court, Edinburgh EH3 8EY (☎ 0131 625 7240, fax 0131 270 7704, e-mail john.kerr@andersonstrathern.co.uk)

KERR, Rear Adm Mark William Graham; DL (County of Powys 2013); s of Capt M W B Kerr, DSC, RN (d 1986), and Coralie Erskine (Pat), *née* Clark; *b* 18 February 1949, Malta; *Educ* Marlborough, New College Oxford (BA); *m* 16 Sept 1978, Mary Louisa; 1 da (Eleanor b 3 Feb 1980), 2 s (Harry b 21 Oct 1981, Robert b 29 Sept 1983); *Career* cmd HMS Alert 1976, RN staff course 1981–82, cmd HMS Beachampton 1982–84, RN Schs Presentation Team 1984–85, exec offr HMS Ariadne 1985–88, cmd HMS Broadsword 1988–90, MOD 1990–94, cmd HMS Cumberland 1994–95, RN Presentation Team 1996, Dep Flag Offr Sea Trg 1997–99, Cdre Britannia RNC Dartmouth 1999–2002, Naval Sec and DG HR (Navy) 2002–04, chief exec Powys CC 2004–09, interim dir Nat Botanical Garden of Wales 2009–10; memb: Naval Review 1977, Assoc of Local Authy Chief Execs (ALACE), Soc of Local Authy Chief Execs (SOLACE) 2004–09 (vice-chair Wales 2008–09), Royal Navy Club of 1765 and 1785 1988; pres Friends of Gwent and Powys Army Cadet Force 2013–14 (vice-pres 2011–13); tstee Nat Botanic Garden of Wales 2011–15 (chm Regency Restoration Steering Ctee 2014–15), tstee Brecon Univ Scholarship Fund 2014–, memb Cncl RNLI 2012–, pres Powys branch SSAFA 2012–; Hon Col Powys Army Cadet Force 2006–11; FCIPD 2002–09; *Recreations* skiing, gardening, reading, hill walking, photography; *Clubs* Royal Navy Winter Sports Assoc; *Style*— Rear Adm Mark Kerr, DL; ✉ Ty Llyn, Llangors, Powys LD3 7UD (☎ 01874 658276, e-mail mark.kerr4@btopenworld.com)

KERR, Lord Ralph William Francis Joseph; DL (Derbyshire 2005); s of 12 Marquess of Lothian, KCVO; *b* 7 November 1957; *Educ* Ampleforth; *m* 1, 1980 (m dis 1987), Lady Virginia Mary Elizabeth, da of 11 Duke of Grafton, KG; m 2, 5 March 1988, Marie-Claire, yr da of (Michael) Donald Gordon Black, MC, of Cupar, Fife; 4 s (John Walter Donald Peter b 8 Aug 1988, Frederic James Michael Ralph b 23 Oct 1989, Francis Andrew William George b 5 Sept 1991, Hugh Alexander Thomas Joseph b 15 Aug 1999), 2 da (Amabel Mary Antonella b 5 Jan 1995, Minna Alice Priscilla Elizabeth b 31 March 1998); *Heir* s, Marquis of Lothian; *Career* political researcher, currently estate mangr, songwriter, Sotheby's rep; dir Grange Estates (Newbattle) Ltd until 2013, pres of tstees Treetops Hospice 1988–, county pres St John Ambulance 1994–2000 (vice-pres Derbys 2000–), pres Melbourne Male Voice Choir, patron Castle Donington Museum Tst, vice-pres Br Assoc Order of Malta 2013–; memb Queen's Body Guard for Scotland (Royal Co of Archers); High Sheriff Derbys 2008–09; Knight of Honour and Devotion SMOM; *Recreations* playing the piano, reading, walking; *Clubs* Boodle's, Brooks's, Turf, White's; *Style*— The Lord Ralph Kerr, DL; ✉ Melbourne Hall, Melbourne, Derby DE73 8EN (☎ 01332 862163, e-mail melbhall@globalnet.co.uk); 20 Upper Cheyne Row, London SW3 5JN (☎ 020 7352 7017)

KERR, Sir Ronald James (Ron); kt (2011), CBE; *Career* formerly: dir of ops NHS Exec, regnl dir North Thames Regnl Office, chief exec SE London Commissioning Agency, chief exec Nat Care Standards Cmmn, chief exec United Bristol Healthcare NHS Tst, chief exec Guy's and St Thomas's NHS Fndn Tst 2007–; chm Assoc of UK Univ Hosps; *Style*— Sir Ron Kerr, CBE; ✉ Guy's and St Thomas's NHS Foundation Trust, Gassiot House, St Thomas's Hospital, London SE1 7EH

KERR, Rose; da of William Antony Kerr, of Almeley, Herefordshire, and Elizabeth, *née* Rendell; *b* 23 February 1953; *Educ* Convent of Sacred Heart Hammersmith, Belmont Abbey Hereford, SOAS Univ of London (BA), Languages Inst of Beijing; *m* Stephen Charles Lord; *Career* fell Percival David Fndn of Chinese Art 1976–78; V&A Far Eastern Dept: res asst 1978, asst keeper 1979, keeper 1987; dep keeper V&A Asian Dept, ret 2003; memb: Exec Cncl GB-China Assoc 1989, Cncl Oriental Ceramic Soc (pres), Br Assoc for Chinese Studies, GB-China Educational Tst 1995 (chm); tstee Worcester Porcelain Museum 2008; keeper emeritus Far Eastern Dept V&A 2005; hon assoc Needham Research Inst Cambridge 2003, hon fell Univ of Glasgow 2004; *Books* Kiln Sherds of Ancient China (with P Hughes-Stanton, 1980), Guanyin – A Masterpiece Revealed (with John Larson, 1985), Chinese Ceramics – Porcelain of the Qing Dynasty (1986), Later Chinese Bronzes (1990), Chinese Art and Design (The T T Tsui Gallery of Chinese Art) (ed and contrib, 1991), Ceramic Evolution in the Middle Ming Period (with Rosemary E Scott, 1994), Chinese Qing Dynasty Ceramics in the Collection of England's Victoria & Albert Museum (1996), Blanc de Chine: Porcelain from Dehua (jtly, 2001), Ceramics of the Song Dynasty (2004), Science and Civilisation in China vol 13 no 5: Ceramic Technology (jtly, 2004), Song China Through 21st Century Eyes (2009); *Recreations* walking, reading, gardening; *Style*— Ms Rose Kerr

KERR, Hon Mr Justice; Sir Timothy Julian (Tim) Kerr; QC (2001); s of Sir Michael Kerr (d 2002), and Julia, *née* Braddock; *b* 15 February 1958, London; *Educ* Westminster (Doncaster scholarship), Magdalen Coll Oxford (BA); *m* 4 Aug 1990, Nicola, da of late Dominic Croucher; 3 s (Gavin Michael b 22 June 1989, George Alfred b 27 Oct 1998, Marcel Robert Shyam b 26 Jan 2001); *Career* called to the Bar Gray's Inn 1983 (Holt scholar, Birkenhead scholar); pt/t chm Employment Tbnls 2001–06, Chancery recorder NE Circuit 2009–15, dep judge of the High Ct (Chancery Div) 2013–15, judge of the High Court of Justice (Queen's Bench Div) 2015–; memb Panel of Arbitrators FA Premier League 2008–15, memb Panels of Arbitrators (chm) Sport Resolutions UK 2009–15, chm Int Cricket Cncl Anti-Doping Tbnl 2011–15; *Books* Sports Law (jtly, 1999, 2 edn 2012); various articles in learned jls; *Recreations* physical exercise, travel, music, theatre, languages (French, German and Spanish), Chelsea FC; *Style*— The Hon Mr Justice Kerr, QC; ✉ Royal Courts of Justice, Strand, London WC2A 2LL (☎ 020 7632 8500, fax 020 7583 9123, e-mail kerr@11kbw.com)

KERR OF KINLOCHARD, Baron (Life Peer UK 2004), of Kinlochard in Perth and Kinross; Sir John Olav Kerr; GCMG (2001, KCMG 1991, CMG 1987); s of Dr and Mrs J D O Kerr; *b* 22 February 1942; *Educ* Glasgow Acad, Pembroke Coll Oxford; *m* 1965, Elizabeth Mary, da of Wilfrid George Kalaugher, of Marlborough, Wilts; 2 s, 3 da; *Career* HM Dip Serv: joined 1966, served FO, Moscow, Rawalpindi, FCO and HM Treasy, princ private sec to Chancellor of the Exchequer 1981–84, head of Chancery Washington 1984–87, asst under sec of state FCO 1987–90, ambass and UK perm rep to EC 1990–95, ambass Washington 1995–1997, perm under-sec of state FCO and head of the Diplomatic Serv 1997–2002; sec-gen European Convention 2002–03; dep chm Royal Dutch Shell plc 2005–12, dep chm Scottish Power 2012– (dir 2009–); dir: Shell Transport and Trading Co 2002–05, Scottish American Investment Co 2002–, Rio Tinto plc 2003–15; chm: Imperial Coll London 2005–11, Centre for European Reform 2008–; memb House of Lords EU Select Ctee 2006–10 and 2014–15, memb House of Lords Economic Affrs Select Ctee 2015–; tstee: Rhodes Tst 1997–2010, Nat Gallery 2002–10, Fulbright Cmmn 2004–09, Carnegie Tst 2005–, Refugee Cncl 2016–; hon pres St Andrew's Clinics for Children; *Style*— The Rt Hon the Lord Kerr of Kinlochard, GCMG

KERR OF TONAGHMORE, The Rt Hon Lord (Law Lord, 2009), of Tonaghmore in the County of Down; Rt Hon Sir Brian Francis Kerr; kt (1993), PC (2004); s of James William Kerr (d 1959), of Lurgan, Co Armagh, and Kathleen Rose, *née* Murray (d 1996); *b* 22 February 1948; *Educ* St Colman's Coll Newry, Queen's Univ Belfast (LLB); *m* 31 Oct 1970, Rosemary Gillian Owen, da of John Owen Widdowson; 2 s (John James b 6 May 1977, Patrick Brian b 11 Jan 1980); *Career* called to the Bar NI 1970 (England and Wales 1974), QC (NI) 1983, sr crown counsel NI 1988–93 (jr crown counsel 1978–83), bencher Inn of Court NI 1990–, judge of the Supreme Court of NI 1993–2004, Lord Chief Justice of NI 2004–09, a Lord of Appeal in Ordinary 2009, a Justice of the Supreme Court 2009–; chm: Mental Health Cmmn NI 1988, Distinction and Meritorious Servs Awards Ctee 1997–2001; memb: Br-Franco Judicial Cooperation Ctee 1995–2001, Judical Studies Bd for NI 1995–2004; Eisenhower fell for NI 1999; hon bencher: Gray's Inn 1997, King's Inn Dublin 2004; *Style*— The Rt Hon the Lord Kerr of Tonaghmore; ✉ Supreme Court, Parliament Square, London SW1P 3BD

KERR-DINEEN, Michael Norman Colin; s of Frederick George Kerr-Dineen (d 1988), and Hermione Iris, *née* Macdonald; *b* 14 July 1952; *Educ* Marlborough, Univ of Edinburgh (MA); *m* 1, 1976 (m dis 1981), Catharine, da of Alexander McCrindle; 1 s (Robert Crockford b 4 Oct 1979); m 2, 1988 (m dis 1995), Sally, da of Raymond Leonard; 1 s (Luke Giles b 26 Feb 1989), 1 da (Iris Sophie b 20 May 1992); m 3, 1997, Jacqui, da of Donald Graham; 2 s (Edward Graham b 22 Feb 1997, Thomas Michael b 14 July 1998), 1 da (Natasha Marie b 18 Oct 2000); *Career* Economic Intelligence Dept Bank of England 1975–79, PA to chm and chief exec British National Oil Corporation 1979–81, exec Alastair Morton & Co 1981–82; md: Guinness Peat Group 1982–88, Cambridge International Partners NY 1988–89; chief exec: UBS Laing & Cruickshank Investment Management (formerly Laing & Cruickshank Investment Management) 1989–2006, Cheviot Asset Mgmnt Ltd 2006–13, sr advsr Quilter Cheviot 2013–; dir Old Oak Hldgs 2007–; *Recreations* horse racing, golf, skiing, opera; *Clubs* Athenaeum, Derby, Turf, MCC, Swinley Forrest; *Style*— Michael Kerr-Dineen, Esq; ✉ Cheviot Asset Management Limited, One Kingsway, London WC2B 6AN (☎ 07920 279560, website www.quiltercheviot.com)

KERR-DINEEN, Sarah; *Educ* Trinity Coll Cambridge, ChCh Oxford; *Career* boarding housemistress and director of studies St Edward's Oxford, warden Forest Sch 2009–15, head Oundle Sch 2015–; *Style*— Mrs Sarah Kerr-Dineen

KERR-MUIR, James; *Educ* Univ of Oxford (BA), Harvard Business Sch (MBA); *Career* formerly vice-pres fin Redpath Industries Toronto, md UK Div Tate & Lyle 1987–91 (gp fin dir 1984–88), fin dir Kingfisher plc 1992–95; chm: The Outdoor Gp Ltd 1996–99, Freeport plc 1996–2001, Ehrmanns Holdings Ltd 2000–03, Davenham Gp plc 2000–, Senior plc 2001– (non-exec dir 1996–, dep chm 2000–01), Hardys Hansons plc 2004–, Acertec plc 2006–; dep chm Birmingham Midshires 1997–2001; dir Wilson Connolly Holdings plc 2003; non-exec dir: Graseby plc 1992–97, The Boddington Gp plc 1993–95, Gartmore Fledgling Tst plc 1994–, Yates Gp plc 1998–2004; *Style*— James Kerr-Muir, Esq

KERRIDGE, Tom; s of Michael John Kerridge (d 1991), and Jackie, *née* Cook; *b* 27 July 1973, Salisbury, Wilts; *Educ* Saintbridge Sch Gloucester; *m* 14 Oct 2000, Beth, *née* Cullen; 1 s (Acey b 21 Dec 2015); *Career* restaurateur; commis chef Calcot Manor Tetbury 1991–92, commis/chef de partie The Painswick Hotel Gloucester 1992–94, chef de partie The Country Elephant Gloucester 1994–96, chef de partie Capital Hotel London 1996, sous chef Stephen Bull St Martins Lane London 1996–99, sous chef Rhodes in the Square London 1999, sous chef Odettes Restaurant London 1999–2001, head chef Bellamys Dining Room London 2001, head chef Great Fosters Hotel Surrey 2001, sr sous chef Monsieur Max Restaurant Hampton 2001–03, head chef Adlards Norwich 2003–05, chef proprietor The Hand and Flowers Marlow 2005– (Michelin Star 2006– (second Michelin star 2012–), 3 AA Rosettes 2007 and 2008), chef/owner The Coach Marlow 2014–; memb HMICA 2007; *Style*— Tom Kerridge, Esq; ✉ The Hand and Flowers, 126 West Street, Marlow, Buckinghamshire SL7 2BP (☎ 01628 482277, e-mail contact@thehandandflowers.co.uk, website www.thehandandflowers.co.uk)

KERRIGAN, Greer Sandra; CB (2006); da of Wilfred McDonald Robinson (d 1998), of Trinidad, and Rosina, *née* Ali (d 1964); *b* 7 August 1948; *Educ* Bishop Anstey HS Trinidad, Coll of Law Cncl of Legal Education; *m* 11 May 1974, Donal Brian Matthew Kerrigan, s of Daniel Patrick Kerrigan, QC; 1 s (Dylan Brian Rum b 25 April 1976), 1 da (Lanra Lee Gin b 24 Jan 1979); *Career* legal advsr to Public Utilities Cmmn Trinidad 1972–74, various positions DSS 1974–96, formerly legal dir Dept of Health, latterly legal dir Law, Governance and Special Policy Gp Dept for Work and Pensions; *Recreations* bridge, reading, travelling; *Style*— Mrs Greer Kerrigan, CB

KERRIGAN, Prof Herbert Aird; QC (1992); s of Herbert Kerrigan (d 1975), and Mary Agnes Wallace Hamilton or Kerrigan (d 1982); *b* 2 August 1945, Glasgow; *Children* 1 s (Darrin John Gilfillan b 8 Oct 1969); *Career* lectr in criminal law, criminology and Scots law 1969–74; called to the Bar (Scotland) 1970; memb: Faculty of Advocates 1970, Hon Soc of Middle Temple 1990; reader Church of Scotland 1969–, pres Edinburgh Royal Infirmary Samaritan Soc 1979–; *Clubs* New (Edinburgh); *Style*— Prof H A Kerrigan, QC; ✉ Airdene, 20 Edinburgh Road, Dalkeith EH22 1JY (☎ 07725 953772, e-mail kerrigan@kerriganqc.com); Parliament House, Edinburgh EH1 1RF (☎ 0131 660 3007); 9–12 Bell Yard, London WC2A 2JR

KERRIGAN, Prof John Francis; s of late Stephen Francis Kerrigan, and Patricia, *née* Baker; *b* 16 June 1956; *Educ* St Edward's Coll Liverpool, Keble Coll Oxford (BA); *Children* 1 da; *Career* jr research fell Merton Coll Oxford 1979–82 (Domus sr scholar 1977–79); Univ of Cambridge: lectr in English 1986–98 (asst lectr 1982–86), reader in English lit 1998–2001, prof of English 2001–, chair Bd English Faculty 2003–06; fell St John's Coll Cambridge 1982– (dir of studies in English 1987–97); visiting prof Meiji Univ Tokyo 1986, visiting fell Jadavpur Univ Calcutta and Univ of Delhi 2008, visiting prof UCLA 2009, Alice Griffin Shakespeare fell Univ of Auckland 2011; Br Acad research readership 1998–2000, Leverhulme Tst Research Fellowship 2012–13; Chatterton lectr Br Acad 1988, J A W Bennett meml lectr Perugia 1998, Acad for Irish Cultural Heritage lectr Derry 2003, F W Bateson lectr Oxford 2004, Nicholson lectr and Poetics lectr Univ of Chicago 2007, Shakespeare lectr Br Acad 2009, Andrew Lang lectr Univ of St Andrews 2009, Wells Shakespeare Lectures Univ of Oxford 2016; Charles Oldham Shakespeare Prize 1976, Matthew Arnold Meml Prize Univ of Oxford 1981, Truman Capote Award for Literary Criticism 1998; tstee Dove Cottage Wordsworth Tst 1984–2001, fell Wordsworth Tst 2001; fndn fell English Assoc 1999, FBA 2013; *Publications* Shakespeare: Love's Labour's Lost (ed, 1982), Shakespeare's Sonnets and A Lover's Complaint (ed, 1986, 2 edn 1995), Hugh Sykes Davies: Wordsworth and the Worth of Words (ed with J Wordsworth, 1987), Motives of Woe: Shakespeare and Female Complaint (1991), English Comedy (jt ed, 1994), Revenge Tragedy: Aeschylus to Armageddon (1996), The Thing About Roy Fisher: critical studies (ed with P Robinson, 2000), On Shakespeare and Early Modern Literature: essays (2001), Archipelagic English (2008), Shakespeare's Binding Language (2016); reviewer: London Review of Books, TLS; *Recreations* music; *Style*— Prof John Kerrigan; ✉ St John's College, Cambridge CB2 1TP (☎ 01223 338620, e-mail jk10023@cam.ac.uk)

KERSHAW, David Andrew; s of Lawrence Morris Kershaw (d 1991), of Malaga, Spain, and Rona, *née* Levy; *b* 26 February 1954; *Educ* Bedales, Univ of Durham (BA), London Business Sch (MBA); *m* 1993, Clare Elizabeth, *née* Whitley; 1s (Tom b 1997), 1 da (Emma b 1998); *Career* advtg exec; account exec Wasey Campbell Ewald 1977–80, London Business Sch 1980–82; Saatchi & Saatchi Advertising: account dir 1982–86, gp account dir 1986–90, md 1990–94, chm and ceo 1994–95, resigned; ptnr M&C Saatchi 1995–; memb Mktg Soc, FIPA; *Recreations* Arsenal, music (playing clarinet), opera, golf, tennis; *Clubs* RAC, Groucho; *Style*— David Kershaw, Esq; ✉ M&C Saatchi Ltd, 34–36 Golden Square, London W1F 9EE (☎ 020 7543 4510, fax 020 7543 4502, e-mail davidk@mcsaatchi.com)

KERSHAW, David Robert; s of late Noel Ernest Kershaw, TD, and Dorothy Anne, *née* Cheyne, b 1953; *b* Dunedin, NZ; *Educ* Urmston GS Manchester, Trinity Coll Cambridge (MA), Univ of London (MA); *m* 1978, Christine Anne, da of John Spear Sexton (d 1986); 3 s (Oliver James b 1979, Toby Thomas b 1984, Charles Henry Alexander b 1986), 1 da (Isabelle Alice Katharine b 1989); *Career* admitted slr 1978; specialist in corporate fin, mergers and acquisitions, equity capital markets and restructuring; ptnr Ashurst 1986–2010; memb City of London Law Soc; memb Trinity Law Assoc, past chair Trinity Coll Alumni Advsy Bd; chm of tstees Royal Cwlth Soc for the Blind Pension Fund, tstee The Mayor's Music Fund (for young Londoners); memb Br Humanist Assoc; Freeman City of London Slrs' Co; *Publications* Joint Ventures in English and German Law, Property Joint Ventures; *Recreations* classical guitar, violin, sailing, tennis, literature; *Clubs* ELLSO Performance Ensemble, London Baroque Strings, Tunbridge Wells LTC, Tonbridge Sch Parents' Arts Soc; *Style*— David R Kershaw, Esq; ✉ e-mail drkershaw@googlemail.com

KERSHAW, Elizabeth Ann (Liz); da of Lawrence Colin Ward Kershaw, and Grace Elizabeth, *née* Milburn; *b* Sheffield; *Educ* Cheltenham Ladies' Coll, King Edward VII Sch Sheffield, Univ of Sheffield (BA); *Children* 1 s (Oliver Patrick Lawrence b 27 Oct 2001); *Career* National Magazine Co: publisher Harpers & Queen 1990–93, publishing dir Good Housekeeping 1993–98, memb Bd 1993–, publishing dir Cosmopolitan Gp 1998–2000, exec gp publishing dir Harpers & Queen, Esquire, Country Living and Focus 2000–02, exec gp publishing dir Women's Interest Gp (Good Housekeeping, Country Living, House Beautiful and Coast) 2002–; emeritus dir Cosmetic Executive Women (CEW), memb Advsy Bd Fragrance Fndn; memb: IOD, Marketing Soc, Womens' Advtg Club of London; PPA Publisher of Year 1995; Freeman City of London, Liveryman Worshipful Co of Gunmakers; *Style*— Ms Liz Kershaw

KERSHAW, Prof Sir Ian; kt (2002); s of Joseph Kershaw (d 1969), and Alice, *née* Robinson; *b* 29 April 1943, Oldham, Lancs; *Educ* Univ of Liverpool (BA), Merton Coll Oxford (DPhil); *m* 29 Oct 1966, Betty, *née* Gammie; 2 s (David b 7 Oct 1970, Stephen b 22 Jan 1973); *Career* Univ of Manchester: lectr in medieval history 1971–74 (asst lectr 1968–71), lectr then sr lectr in modern history 1974–87 (reader-elect 1987); prof of modern history Univ of Nottingham 1987–89, prof of modern history Univ of Sheffield 1989–2008; actg prof of contemporary European history Ruhr-Univ Bochum 1983–84; Deutscher Akademischer Austauschdienst (DAAD) Scholarship 1974, Alexander von Humboldt-Stiftung Fellowship 1976–77 (continuation 1985, 1997 and 1999), Br Acad-Akademie der Wissenschaften der DDR Exchange Scholarship 1981, Leverhulme Fellowship 1982, Br Acad-Polish Acad of Sciences Exchange Scholarship 1989, Wissenschaftskolleg zu Berlin Fellowship 1989, Leverhulme Tst Research Award 1991, Br Acad-Leverhulme Fndn Sr Scholarship 1994–95, Leverhulme Major Research Fellowship 2002–; keynote lectures incl: Commemoration of Reichskristallnacht Paulskirche Frankfurt 2000, Remembering the Future: Oxford Int Conf 2000, 1st Glasgow Holocaust Meml Lecture 2001, 1st London Holocaust Meml Lecture 2002, Trevelyan Lecture Cambridge 2002, Sir Frank Stenton Meml Lecture 2002, 1st BBC-Open Univ Televised History Lecture 2005, Ramsay Murray Lecture Cambridge 2005, Ashby Lecture Cambridge 2010; conslt for BBC documentaries: The Nazis. A Warning from History (series) 1994–97, Hitler's War in the East (series) 1997–99, Timewatch: Operation Sealion 1998, Timewatch: Himmler 2001, Timewatch: The Making of Adolf Hitler 2002, Auschwitz – The Nazis and the Final Solution (series) 2003–05, The Dark Charisma of Adolf Hitler 2012; conslt and academic advsr to ZDF (Zweites Deutsches Fernsehen); newspaper contrib, various TV and radio broadcasts; Hon Dr: Univ of Manchester 2004, Univ of Stirling 2004, Queen's Univ Belfast 2007, Univ of Sheffield 2009, Univ of Oxford 2010, Univ of Leeds 2012, Univ of Huddersfield 2013; hon fell Merton Coll Oxford 2005; FRHistS 1991 (also 1972–74), FBA 1991; Bundesverdienstkreuz (Germany) 1994; *Publications* Bolton Priory Rentals and Ministers' Accounts, 1473–1539 (ed, 1969), Bolton Priory: The Economy of a Northern Monastery (1973), Der Hitler-Mythos: Volksmeinung und Propaganda im Dritten Reich (1980, revised edn 1999), Popular Opinion and Political Dissent in the Third Reich: Bavaria, 1933–1945 (1983, revised edn 2002), The Nazi Dictatorship: Problems and Perspectives of Interpretation (1985, 4 edn 2000), The 'Hitler Myth': Image and Reality in the Third Reich (1987), Weimar: Why did German Democracy Fail? (ed, 1990), Hitler: A Profile in Power (1991, 2 edn 2001), Stalinism and Nazism: Dictatorships in Comparison (ed with Moshe Lewin, 1997), Hitler, 1889–1936: Hubris (1998, revised edn 2001), Hitler, 1936–1945: Nemesis (2000, revised edn 2001), The Bolton Priory Compotus 1286–1325 (ed with David M Smith, 2001), Making Friends With Hitler: Lord Londonderry, the Nazis and the Road to War (2004), Fateful Choices: Ten Decisions That Changed the World (2007), Luck of the Devil: The Story of Operation Valkyrie (2009), The End: Hitler's Germany 1944–45 (2011), To Hell and Back: Europe 1914–49 (2015); regular reviewer and author of 100 articles in learned jls; *Awards* Bruno-Kreisky Prize (Austria) for Political Book of the Year 2000, Wolfson Literary Award for History 2000, Damals Book of the Year 2000, Br Acad Book Prize 2001, Norton Medlicott Medal Historical Assoc 2004, Elizabeth Longford Prize for Historical Biography 2005, Leipzig Book Prize for European Understanding 2012, Meyer-Struckmann Prize (Germany) 2013; shortlisted: Samuel Johnson Prize 1999, Whitbread Biography Prize 1999 and 2002, Los Angeles Times Book Prize 2000, WH Smith Prize 2001, James Tait Black Meml Prize 2002, Military History Book of the Year 2008; *Recreations* rugby league, cricket, football, classical music, opera, jazz, wine, real ale; *Style*— Prof Sir Ian Kershaw

KERSHAW, Nicholas John; s of Henry Kershaw (d 1995), and Daphne Kershaw; *b* 16 November 1963; *Educ* Bolton Sch, KCL (LLB), Inns of Court Sch of Law; *m* 1994, Karen; 2 da (Lucy b 21 June 1997, Natalya b 3 April 2004); *Career* called to the Bar Eng and Wales 1988, advocate Jersey 1996; sr offr UBS 1987–89, lawyer Clifford Chance 1990–93, ptnr Ogier 1997– (joined 1993, currently gp ceo); *Recreations* golf, skiing, running, tennis; *Style*— Nicholas Kershaw, Esq; ✉ Ogier, Whiteley Chambers, Don Street, St Helier, Jersey JE4 9WG (☎ 01534 504263, fax 01534 504444, e-mail nick.kershaw@ogier.com)

KERSHAW, Nigel; OBE (2010); *b* 1951, London; *Career* chm Exec Gp Big Issue Gp, chief exec Big Issue Invest; *Style*— Nigel Kershaw, Esq, OBE; ✉ Big Issue Invest, 1–5 Wandsworth Road, Vauxhall, London SW8 2LN

KERSHAW, Stephen (Steve); s of John Bertram Kershaw, of Ashington, Egley Road, Mayford, Woking, Surrey, and Joyce Mary, *née* Robson; *b* 24 April 1955; *Educ* Dr Challoner's GS Amersham Bucks; *m* 1978, Alison Deborah, da of Thomas Charles Garrett, of 10 Brushwood Drive, Chorleywood; 1 da (Deborah Stephanie b 12 Dec 1982), 1 s (Carl Thomas b 15 Sept 1985); *Career* salesman Cavenham Foods 1973–75; Wilkinson Sword Ltd: salesman 1975–76, mktg asst 1977–78, product mangr 1978; Cadbury Ltd: product mangr 1978–79, sr product mangr 1980–82, product gp mangr 1983–84; head of mktg Britvic Ltd 1984–86; Bartle Bogle Hegarty advtg: successively account dir, business devpt dir/mgmnt rep, then bd dir/team ldr 1986–98, md 1998–; memb Mktg Soc; *Style*— Steve Kershaw; ✉ Bartle Bogle Hegarty, 60 Kingly Street, London W1B 5DS (☎ 020 7734 1677, fax 020 7437 3666)

KERSHAW, Walter; s of Walter Kershaw (Flt Sgt RAF 19 Sqdn Duxford Battle of Britain, d 1998), and Florence, *née* Ward (d 2010); *b* 7 December 1940, Rochdale, Greater Manchester; *Educ* De La Salle Coll Salford, Durham Univ (BA); *m* Gillian Halliwell; 1 s (Paul b 15 Feb 2002 (twin)), 1 da (Isabelle b 15 Feb 2002 (twin)); *Career* war artist King's Regt NI 1976; artist and pioneer of large external mural painting; UK work: Manchester Trafford Park 1993, Science Museum, Manchester United FC, CEGB, Univ of Salford 1979–89, Br Aerospace and Granada TV 1984–88, Wensum Lodge Norwich 1985, Italian Consulate Manchester 1991, P&O Manchester Arndale 1996, Dulwich Outdoor Gallery 2014, Avro Heritage Museum 2015; work abroad: Brazil, São Paulo and Recife 1983–95, Sarajevo Int Arts Festival 1996, Briggs of Burton 1999, Airtours 1999, Leonard Cheshire Homes 2002, Yuri Gagarin Mural Manchester 2011; works exhibited: V&A, Tate Gallery, Nat Portrait Gallery, Gulbenkian Fndn, Arts Cncl and Br Cncl Berlin, Brazil and Edinburgh; in conversation BBC Radio Four with Sue MacGregor 1984, guest The One Show (BBC 1) 2012; Gulbenkian Fndn Award for External Murals 1977–79; *Recreations* travel, photography, cricket, opera, tennis, walking, cycling; *Style*— Walter Kershaw, Esq; ✉ Studio 193, Todmorden Road, Littleborough, Lancashire OL15 9EG (☎ 01706 379 653, website www.walterkershaw.co.uk)

KERSLAKE, Baron (Life Peer 2015), of Endcliffe in the City of Sheffield; Sir Robert (Bob) Kerslake; kt (2005); *Educ* Univ of Warwick; *Career* chief exec: London Borough of Hounslow until 1997, Sheffield City Cncl 1997–2008, Homes and Communities Agency 2008–10; perm sec Dept for Communities and Local Govt 2010–, head of the Civil Serv 2012–14; chair KCH NHS Fndn Tst; *Style*— The Lord Kerslake; ✉ Department for Communities and Local Government, Eland House, Bressenden Place, London SW1E 5DU

K

KERVIN, Alison; *Career* chief sports feature writer The Times, chief sports interviewer Daily Telegraph, currently sports ed Mail on Sunday; contrib: The Spectator, New Statesman, Company, Woman's Own, Vogue, New York Times, Sydney Morning Herald, Tatler; *Books Fiction* incl: The WAG's Diary (2007), A WAG Abroad (2008), Celebrity Bride (2009), WAGs at the World Cup (2010), Mother and Son (2014); *Non-Fiction* incl: A Guide to Sports Writing (1997), Guide to the 1999 World Cup (1999), Denise Lewis: Personal Best (2001), Jason Leonard: Full Time (2004), Clive Woodward: The Biography (2004), Thirty Bullies: A History of the World Cup (2007), Phil Vickery: Raging Bull (2010); *Style*— Ms Alison Kervin; ✉ The Mail on Sunday, Northcliffe House, 2 Derry Street, Kensington, London W8 5TS

KERWIN, Prof David George; s of late William George Kerwin, and Margaret Winifred, *née* Bolger; *b* 26 May 1948, Liverpool; *Educ* Sir John Deane's GS Northwich, Keele Univ (CertEd, BEd), Univ of Leeds (MA), Loughborough Univ (PhD); *m* 15 Aug 1972, Linda Anne; 2 s (Thomas David b 1977, Samuel John William b 1980); *Career* school teacher Cheshire LEA 1970–72, lectr Stockport Coll 1972–75, sr lectr Bedford Coll of HE 1976–81; Loughborough Univ: lectr 1982–90, sr lectr 1990–99, head of sports science 1996–99; prof and head of sport and exercise science Univ of Bath 1999–, prof of biomechanics Cardiff Sch of Sport Cardiff Met Univ Wales 2005–11 (prof emeritus of biomechanics 2011–); memb: Scientific Cmmn Fedn Internationale Gymnastique (FIG) until 2012, Scientific Advsy Bd NZ Sports Cmmn until 2006, Scientific Advsy Bd British Gymnastics Med Cmmn until 2006, Engrg and Physical Sciences Research Cncl Peer Review Coll 2006–14 (princ investigator EPSRC SESAME research project 2006–10); biomechanics ed Jl of Sports Sciences until 2002, memb Editorial Bd Jl of Sports Engrg and Technol 2008–12, author of numerous articles and papers in learned jls; European Athletics Technol Innovation Award 2010, Geoffrey Dyson Award Int Soc of Biomechanics in Sports Taipei Taiwan 2013, Dyson Award Int Soc of Biomechanics in Sports (ISBS) 2013; hon fell Cardiff Met Univ 2013; fell British Assoc of Sport and Exercise Sciences (BASES) 1999 (memb 1976), FRSM 2006, fell Int Soc of Biomechanics in Sports (ISBS) 2010; *Publications* numerous articles in books and jls on sports biomechanics, sports technology and coaching; *Recreations* golf, sport, theatre, television; *Clubs* Cumberwell Park Golf, Falmouth Golf, Falmouth Decorative and Fine Arts Soc, Nat Tst, Merlin Cinema; *Style*— Prof David Kerwin; ✉ e-mail dkerwin@cardiffmet.ac.uk and davidkerwin@icloud.com, website http://www3.uwic.ac.uk/english/sport/about/staff/academic/bio/pages/david-kerwin.aspx

KESSLER, George Bernard; CBE (2001); s of William Kessler, of London, and Joanna, *née* Rubner; *b* 17 August 1953; *Educ* City of London Sch, Univ of Nottingham (BSc); *m* 25 Oct 1986, Deborah Susan, da of Beni Baltfried Jaffe, of London; 2 da (Madeleine b 1987, Flora b 1988); *Career* conslt Logica 1974–77, various positions Kesslers Int 1977–90, dir Kesslers Int Ltd 1988–, ops dir Kesslers Gp 1990–, md Kesslers Manufacturing 1990–, md Kesslers Int Ltd 2000–; dir: Bridgewater Distribution & Mgmnt Ltd 1989–, Newham Schools & Industry Liaison Ctee 1989–91, Kesslers Investment Ltd 1989–, Newham Educn Employer Partnership 1991, Kesslers Int Holding Co Ltd 1991–, Carpenters Road Properties Ltd 1991–, Brand Technology Ltd 1991–, Tower Hamlets Educn Business Partnership 1993–95, Roegate Ltd 1994–2002, Point Topic Ltd 1998, London First 1999– (memb Educn Advsy Gp 1995–96), Business Educators 2001–04, Loopweave Ltd 2003–, Kesslers Properties North Ltd 2005–, Kesslers Properties South Ltd 2005–, Kesslers Int Gp Ltd 2005–, Carpenters Road Hldgs Ltd 2005–; chm: Newham Compact 1988–95 (fndr), Newham Community Coll 1992–93 (chm of govrs 1994–95), London Regnl Competitiveness Gp 1995–98, Educn & Employability Gp 1996–97, LDP Business Support Task Force 1998–2000, London TEC Cncl 1999–2001 (memb 1996–1999), London Devpt Agency Prodn Industry Cmmn 2002–, 3H 2005–; dep chm London E TEC 1994–2001 (fndr memb 1990, chm Educn Advsy Gp 1991–96, memb Ethnic Minorities Focus Gp 1996–98), London Innovation and Knowledge Transfer Strategy 2001–08, vice-chm London Section Britain in Europe 2002–05, dep chm London Devpt Agency Business Competitiveness Agency 2001–04; fndr memb Campaign for Learning 1995–97 (memb Steering Ctee 1994–97); memb: Royal Inst 1978–2006, Bd E London Strategic Forum

1992–96, RSA Learning Soc Exchange 1993–95, London Regnl Ctee FE Funding Cncl 1993–99, RSA Learning Advsy Gp 1994–98, Industry Forum 1994–, Bd Futures 1995–96, Fndn for Sci and Technol 1995–2000, CBI Educn and Trg Advsy Gp 1996–98, Bd Business Link London 1996–2001, Bd London Mfrg Gp 1996–, Ind Review Panel Cncl Membs' Allowances 1997–98, Steering Ctee EU Presidency Life Long Learning Conf 1997–98, Newham & Tower Hamlets Steering Ctee on Welfare to Work 1997–98, Task Force to Advise on Mfrg in London 1998–99, Bd London Devpt Partnership (LDP) 1998–2000, LDP Skills Strategy Task Force 1998–2000, TEC Nat Cncl 1998–2001 (memb Trg and Educn Ctee 1997–98), London Mfrg Task Force 2000–01, Bd London European Prog Ctee 2000–01, Bd London and SE Regnl Industrial Devpt Bd 2001–02, Bd N London LSC 2001–03, Bd Cultural Strategy Gp 2001–03, Bd London Int Festival of Theatre 2001–04, London Devpt Agency People's Educn and Trg Ctee 2001–04, Made in London SRB Steering Gp 2000–, Bd London Devpt Agency 2000–08, Gordon Brown's Task Force to review Modern Apprenticeships 2003–, Advsy Bd Britain in Europe, London Devpt Agency Corp Affrs Ctee 2004–08, London Devpt Agency Regeneration and Devpt Ctee 2004–08, London Regional Ctee Prince's Tst 2005–12, judging panel RCA design competition 2005–, EEF Economics Affrs Ctee 2008–, London Economic Policy Ctee 2010–, Bd LIFT 2012–, Economic Plan for London 2014–; memb Advsy Cncl: New Voice for London 1999–2000, E London Business Alliance 1999–2001, Employment Cmmn for London 1999–2002, London Borough Grants Reference Gp 2000–02; princ sponsor NIACE Learning Works Award 1999–2003; chair Steering Gp to select Regnl Centre for Mfrg Excellence 2001–02; memb judging panel: London Smart Awards 1999–2000, DTI Design & Mfrg Task Force 1999–2000; govr Stratford Sch 1996–97; Hon Dr Univ of East London 2005–; MRI 1975, FRSA 1994, CIMechE 2001 (memb Ctees 2010–); *Recreations* contemporary art, reading, theatre; *Clubs* Savile; *Style*— George Kessler, Esq, CBE; ✉ 22 Tanza Road, London NW3 2UB; Kesslers International Ltd, No 1 International Business Park, Rick Roberts Way, Stratford, London E15 2NF (☎ 020 8522 3000, fax 020 8522 3129, e-mail kesslerg@kesslers.com)

KESTENBAUM, Baron (Life Peer UK 2011), of Foxcote in the County of Somerset; Jonathan Andrew Kestenbaum; s of Ralph Kestenbaum, of Switzerland, and Gaby, *née* Schwalbe; *b* 5 August 1959, Tokyo, Japan; *Educ* Hasmonean GS, LSE (BA), Univ of Cambridge (post grad research, Soccer half blue), Hebrew Univ Jerusalem (MA), Cass Business Sch (MBA); *m* 9 Dec 1984, Deborah Jane; 4 c; *Career* chief exec Office of Chief Rabbi 1991–96, chief exec UJIA, COS to Sir Ronald Cohen, *qv* (chm Apax Partners Ltd) and chief exec Portland Tst until 2005, chief exec NESTA 2005–10, chief operating offr RIT Capital Ptnrs plc, chm Five Arrows Ltd 2010–13, chm Capital Hldgs Fund plc 2014–; dir: Bd TSB, J Rothschild Capital Mgmnt Ltd 2011–, Pershing Square Hldgs 2014–; tstee: Rowley Lane Recreational Tst, RSC; non-exec bd memb Profero 2008–14; chllr Plymouth Univ 2013–; *Recreations* soccer, tennis; *Style*— The Lord Kestenbaum; ✉ RIT Capital Partners plc, Spencer House, 27 St James's Place, London SW1A 1NR

KESWICK, Hon Lady (Annabel Thérèse (Tessa)); *née* Fraser; yr da of 15 Lord Lovat, DSO, MC, TD (d 1995); *b* 15 October 1942; *Educ* Woldingham, French Baccalaureat Course (Paris); *m* 1, 1964 (m dis 1978), 14 Lord Reay; 2 s, 1 da; m 2, 1985, Sir Henry Neville Lindley Keswick, *qv*, eld s of Sir William Johnston Keswick (d 1990); *Career* special advsr to Rt Hon Kenneth Clarke QC, MP (as Sec of State for Health then Educn and Sci, Home Sec and Chllr of the Exchequer) 1989–95, exec dir Centre for Policy Studies 1995–2004, dep chm Centre for Policy Studies 2004–; non-exec dir Daily Mail and General Tst plc 2013–; Parly candidate (Cons and Unionist) Inverness, Nairn and Lochaber 1987; pres Devizes Cons Assoc 2002–; chllr Univ of Buckingham 2013–; FKC 2007; *Publications* incl: A Conservative Agenda (co-author, 1996), Conservative Women (1999), Second Amongst Equals (2000); over 100 public policy pamphlets on the EU, the Constitution, law and order, education, health, tax and regulatory affairs, and women's issues; *Recreations* reading, travel; *Style*— The Hon Lady Keswick; ✉ 6 Smith Square, London SW1P 3HT; The Centre for Policy Studies, 57 Tufton Street, London SW1P 3QL (☎ 020 7222 4488)

KESWICK, Sir (John) Chippendale Lindley (Chips); kt (1993); s of Sir William Johnston Keswick (d 1990), and Mary, *née* Lindley (d 2009); bro of Sir Henry Keswick *qv*, and Simon Lindley Keswick *qv*; *b* 2 February 1940; *Educ* Eton, Univ of Aix Marseilles; *m* 1966, Lady Sarah Ramsay, da of 16 Earl of Dalhousie, KT, GCVO, GBE, MC (d 1999); 3 s (David b 1967, Tobias b 1968, Adam b 1973); *Career* Hambros Bank Ltd: chief exec 1985–95, chm and chief exec 1986–95, non-exec chm 1995–98; chief exec Hambros 1995–98 (jt dep chm 1990–95, chm 1997–98); non-exec dir: Persimmon plc 1984–2006, The Edinburgh Investment Trust plc 1992–2001, De Beers Consolidated Mines Ltd 1993–2006, Bank of England 1993–2001, IMI plc 1994–2003, Anglo American plc 1999–2001, Investec Bank (UK) 2000–10, Arsenal Hldgs plc 2005–, Arsenal FC plc 2005–; memb Queen's Body Guard for Scotland (Royal Co of Archers); *Recreations* bridge, country pursuits; *Clubs* White's, Portland; *Style*— Sir Chips Keswick; ✉ 1 Charterhouse Street, London EC1N 6SA (☎ 020 7421 9823, fax 020 7242 6277)

KESWICK, Sir Henry Neville Lindley; kt (2009); s of Sir William Johnston Keswick (d 1990), and Mary, *née* Lindley (d 2009); bro of Sir (John) Chippendale Lindley (Chips) Keswick, *qv* and Simon Lindley Keswick *qv*; *b* 29 September 1938; *Educ* Eton, Trinity Coll Cambridge (MA); *m* 1985, Annabel Thérèse (Tessa), *qv*, da of 15 Lord Lovat; *Career* Nat Serv cmmnd Scots Guards 1956–58; prop The Spectator 1975–80; dir: Jardine Matheson & Co Ltd 1967 (chm 1972–75), Sun Alliance & London Insurance 1975–96, Royal & Sun Alliance Insurance Group plc 1989–2001 (dep chm 1993–96), Robert Fleming Holdings 1975–2000, Mandarin Oriental Ltd, Dairy Farm Int Ltd, The Telegraph Gp Ltd 1990–2004, Rothschilds Continuation Holdings AG 2006–11; dir Matheson & Co Ltd 1975– (chm 1975–2016), chm Jardine Matheson Holdings Ltd, chm Jardine Strategic Holdings Ltd; chm National Portrait Gallery 1994–2001, jt vice-chm Hong Kong Assoc (chm 1988–2001), tstee Royal Botanic Gardens Kew 2008–, memb Cncl Nat Tst 2009–10; *Recreations* country pursuits; *Clubs* White's, Turf, Portland, Third Guards'; *Style*— Sir Henry Keswick; ✉ Matheson & Co Ltd, 3 Lombard Street, London EC3V 9AQ (☎ 020 7816 8100, fax 020 7623 5024)

KESWICK, Simon Lindley; s of Sir William Johnston Keswick (d 1990), and Mary, *née* Lindley (d 2009); bro of Sir (John) Chippendale Lindley (Chips) Keswick, *qv* and Sir Henry Neville Lindley Keswick *qv*; the firm of Jardine Matheson was founded in 1832 by William Jardine and James Matheson; the Keswicks of Dumfries married into the Jardine family in the mid-nineteenth century; *b* 20 May 1942; *Educ* Eton, Trinity Coll Cambridge; *Career* dir: Jardine Matheson Holdings Ltd 1972– (chm 1983–89), Matheson & Co 1982–, Jardine Strategic Hldgs Ltd 1987– (chm 1987–89), Jardine Lloyd Thompson Group plc 2001–; chm Trafalgar House plc 1993–96, Kwik Save Group plc 1990–98; dir: HSBC 1983–88, Fleming Mercantile Investment Tst 1988–2007 (chm 1990–2003), Hanson plc 1991–2005, Wellcome plc 1995–96, Hong Kong Land Hldgs Ltd 2013– (chm 1983–2013), Mandarin Oriental Int Ltd 2013– (chm 1984–2013), Dairy Farm Int Hldgs Ltd 2013– (chm 1984–2013); tstee: Br Museum 1989–99, Henry Moore Fndn 2003–13; *Style*— Simon Keswick, Esq; ✉ Matheson & Co, 3 Lombard Street, London EC3V 9AA

KETTLE, Martin James; s of Arnold Kettle, and Margot Kettle; *b* 7 September 1949, Leeds; *Educ* Leeds Modern Sch, Balliol Coll Oxford; *m* Alison Hannah; 2 s; *Career* journalist and writer; formerly: political corr Sunday Times, Washington corr The Guardian; currently asst ed and chief leader writer The Guardian; govr Trinity-Laban Conservatoire of Music and Dance; *Books* Policing the Police (with Peter Hain 1980), Uprising (with Lucy Hodges 1982), Guardian Guide to the New Europe (ed, 1993), The Single Currency: Should Britain Join? (1997), The Bedside Guardian (ed, 2008); *Recreations* music, walking, watching cricket, friends; *Clubs* Yorks CCC; *Style*— Martin Kettle, Esq; ✉ The Guardian, 90 York Way, London N1 9GU (☎ 020 3353 3521, e-mail martin.kettle@guardian.co.uk)

KETTLEY, John Graham; s of Harold Kettley (d 2005), of Littleborough, Lancs, and Marian, *née* Greenwood (d 2013); *b* 11 July 1952, Halifax, W Yorks; *Educ* Todmorden GS, Lanchester Poly Coventry (BSc); *m* 12 Sept 1990, Lynn Nicola; 2 s (Charles William b 19 Sept 1992, George Kit b 26 Sept 1994); *Career* Meteorological Office 1970–2000 (Meteorological Res Flight Farnborough then Fluid Dynamics Dept Bracknell 1970–79), television weatherman for BBC and ITV Nottingham Weather Centre 1980–85, forecaster BBC Television and Radio 1985–2000, resident weather expert The Travel Show BBC 2 1987–89, weather and sports features presenter BBC Radio 5Live 2001–08, interviews for Channel 5 News 2012–, regular radio broadcasts for TalkSport, TalkRadio and LBC; currently freelance presenter and weather conslt John Kettley Enterprises; weekly weather article Mail On Sunday 2005–, John Kettley Weather Show airing monthly on Siren FM Univ of Lincoln; ptnr British Weather Services; RGS presentations 2013; guest appearances on Blankety Blank (BBC), Telly Addicts (BBC), Through the Keyhole (BBC and ITV), Style Challenge (BBC) 1997, Call My Bluff (BBC), Watchdog (BBC), Test the Nation (BBC), Ant and Dec's Saturday Night Takeaway (ITV) 2007, Weakest Link (BBC) 2008, Loose Women (ITV) 2009, Great British Weather (BBC) 2011, Sarah Millican Show (BBC) 2012, Eggheads (BBC 2) 2013; subject of song John Kettley is a Weatherman (Tribe of Toffs) 1988; ambass Cricket World Cup England 1999, presenter and host Triangular NatWest One-Day Int cricket: England, Australia and Pakistan 2001, England, India and Sri Lanka 2002; conslt to Dick Francis for novel Second Wind (1999); corporate video presenter for cos incl: Boots, Crown Paints, North Herts Dist Cncl; endorsements for Crystal Canopies and Homesun 2011; endorsements and corporate video prodns for: Camping and Caravanning Club 2012, Canary Islands Tourist Website 2014; The Pennine Way 50th Anniversary 2015; FRMetS; *Books* Weatherman (autobiography, 2009); *Recreations* cricket, horse racing, photography, fell walking, gardening, cycling; *Clubs* Lord's Taverners; *Style*— John Kettley, Esq; ✉ Ambition Management, Carina Marina, Nottingham (☎ 0115 950 2010, websites www.johnkettley.co.uk and (book publisher) www.gnbooks.co.uk); Personal Appearances Agency, 20 North Mount, 1147–1161 High Road, Whetstone, London N20 0PH (☎ 020 8343 7748); The Speakers Agency (☎ 01522 522620, website www.speakersagency.com)

KEY, Geoffrey George Bamford; s of George Key (Sgt RA, d 1967), and Marion, *née* Bamford (d 2004); *b* 13 May 1941; *Educ* Manchester High Sch of Art, Manchester Regnl Coll of Art (NDD, Dip of Associateship of Manchester, Postgrad in Sculpture); *Partner* Judith M O'Leary; *Career* painter and sculptor; major exhibitions: Salford Art Gallery 1966, Univ of Manchester 1969, Erica Bourne Gallery London 1974, Salon d'Automne Clermont Ferrand France 1974, Nancy France 1974, Gallery Tendenz Germany 1977, Lausanne Switzerland 1980, Madison Avenue NY 1980, Solomon Gallery Dublin 1983, Solomon Gallery London 1985, Damme Belgium 1990, Moret-sur-Loing France 1991, Hong Kong 1992, 1993 and 1994, Art 95 London, Arley Hall Cheshire 1995–97, Joshua Fine Art Kuala Lumpur Malaysia 1997, Harrods Knightsbridge 1999, Rotunda Hong Kong 2000, Oriel Gallery Dublin 2001, 2003 and 2006, The Biscuit Factory Newcastle upon Tyne 2007, ClarkArt Cheshire 2008, CollectArt Cheshire 2010–11, Messum's Cork St London 2013 and 2014, Art Decor Gallery Lancs 2015; work in public and corp collections incl: Salford Art Gallery, Astley Cheetham Art Gallery, Manchester City Art Gallery, Rutherston Loan Collection, Bolton Art Gallery, NW Arts Bd, Univ of Manchester, Wigan Met Borough, Granada TV, New Salford Players Theatre (mural), Wilsons Brewery, Manchester Museum of Science and Industry, Mather & Platt, Peak Translations, Nat West Bank, Tameside Museum Serv, Llewellyn Ryland, Nat Art Library V&A, Chateau de St Ouen France, Jockey Club Hong Kong, Mandarin Hotel Hong Kong, Perrier, Chateaux Relais, Society Relais; memb Friends of Salford Art Gallery, patron Salford Art Club; *Books* G Key A Book of Drawings and Interview (1975), Daydreams (1981), Clowns (2001), Geoffrey Key Twentieth Century Drawings (2002), Images (2004), Geoffrey Key Paintings (2008), Birds (2010), Signature Book (2011), Infinite Jest (2015); *Recreations* collecting apothecary ceramics; *Style*— Geoffrey Key, Esq; ☎ 0161 736 6014, website www.geoffreykey.com

KEYES, Marian; da of Ted Keyes, and Mary, *née* Cotter; *Educ* UC Dublin (BCL); *m* 29 December 1995, Tony Baines; *Career* writer; books translated into 30 languages; Irish Tatler Literary Award 2001, Irish World Literary Award 2002, Popular Fiction Book of the Year Br Book Awards 2007 and 2009; *Books* Watermelon (1995), Lucy Sullivan is Getting Married (1996), Rachel's Holiday (1998), Last Chance Saloon (1999), Sushi for Beginners (2000), Under the Duvet (2001), Angels (2002), The Other Side of the Story (2004), Further Under the Duvet (2005), Anybody Out There? (2006), This Charming Man (2008), The Brightest Star in the Sky (2009), Saved by Cake (2012), The Mystery of Mercy Close (2012), The Woman Who Stole My Life (2014), Making It Up As I Go Along (2016); *Style*— Ms Marian Keyes; ✉ c/o J Lloyd, Curtis Brown, 28–29 Haymarket, London SW1Y 4SP (☎ 020 7396 6600); website www.mariankeyes.com

KEYES, Timothy Harold (Tim); s of Edward Keyes (d 1999), and Mary, *née* Mylchreest; *b* 15 December 1954; *Educ* Christ's Hosp, Wadham Coll Oxford, Univ of Exeter (PGCE); *m* 1979, Mary Anne, da of Robert Lucas; 2 s (Samuel b 6 Sept 1986, William b 26 April 1989); *Career* teacher Tiffin GS Kingston upon Thames 1979–83, teacher Whitgift Sch Croydon 1983–88, head of classics Perse Sch Cambridge 1988–93, dep head Royal GS Guildford 1993–98, headmaster King's Sch Worcester 1998–; *Recreations* church bellringing, choral singing, Yorkshire cricket; *Clubs* East India; *Style*— Tim Keyes, Esq; ✉ The King's School, 5 College Green, Worcester WR1 2LH (☎ 01905 721700, fax 01905 721710, mobile 07753 681211, e-mail headmaster@ksw.org)

KEYNES, Prof Simon Douglas; s of Prof Richard Darwin Keynes, CBE, ScD, FRS, and Hon Anne Pinsent Keynes, da of 1 Baron Adrian, OM, FRS; *b* 23 September 1952; *Educ* King's Coll Choir Sch Cambridge, Leys Sch Cambridge, Trinity Coll Cambridge (BA, PhD, LittD); *Career* res fell Trinity Coll Cambridge 1976–79; Univ of Cambridge: asst lectr Dept of Anglo-Saxon, Norse, and Celtic 1978–82, lectr 1982–92, reader in Anglo-Saxon history 1992–99, Elrington and Bosworth prof of Anglo-Saxon 1999–, head of dept 1999–2006; Liveryman Worshipful Co of Goldsmiths; FRHistS 1982, FSA 1985, FBA 2000; *Books* incl: The Diplomas of King Aethelred the Unready 978–1016 (1980), Alfred the Great (1983), Facsimiles of Anglo-Saxon Charters (1991), The Liber Vitae of the New Minster Winchester (1996); *Clubs* Roxburghe; *Style*— Prof Simon Keynes; ✉ Trinity College, Cambridge CB2 1TQ (☎ 01223 338421, e-mail sdk13@cam.ac.uk)

KEYS, Richard John; s of Henry John Keys (d 2007), of Rustington, W Sussex, and Bessie, *née* Taylor (d 1995); *b* 10 April 1951; *Educ* Lewes Co GS for Boys; *m* 5 Oct 1974, Helen Kathryn, da of Alan Herbert Jackson; 2 da (Emily Sarah b 19 Feb 1986, Letitia Mary b 2 March 1990); *Career* articled clerk Singleton Fabian Derbyshire 1969–73; PricewaterhouseCoopers (formerly Coopers & Lybrand before merger): joined Cooper Bros & Co 1973, ptnr 1984–2010, seconded to Dept of Environment (water finance) 1983–84, memb Energy Water and Tport Market Bd 1989–98 (chm 1989–96), memb Audit Bd 1993–96; professional standards and risk mgmnt leader UK Assurance 2004–07, global ldr/global chief accountant Accounting Consltg Servs 2007–10, memb Global Assurance Leadership Team 2007–10; memb: Tech Ctee ICAEW 1988–90, Advsy Cncl Int Financial Reporting Standards 2009–10, Audit and Risk Ctee RBG Kew 2011–15; dir: Sainsbury's Bank plc 2011– (chair Audit Ctee), Glaziers Hall Ltd 2012– (chm 2016–), NATS Holdings

Ltd 2013– (chair Audit Ctee), Wessex Water Services Ltd 2016–; non-exec dir Dept for Int Devpt 2013– (chair Audit Ctee); lay memb Cncl Univ of Birmingham 2010–15 (chair Audit Ctee); Liveryman and Ct Asst Worshipful Co of Glaziers & Painters of Glass 2010 (Freeman 2003); FCA (ACA 1973); *Recreations* shooting, opera, fly fishing; *Clubs* Reform, Lansdowne; *Style*— Richard Keys, Esq; ✉ e-mail rjkeys@btopenworld.com

KEYSER, His Hon Judge Andrew John; QC (2006); *b* 19 December 1963; *Educ* Cardiff HS, Balliol Coll Oxford; *Career* called to the Bar 1986; recorder 2002, dep High Court judge 2008, circuit judge (North Eastern Circuit) 2011–12, specialist mercantile circuit judge (Wales Circuit) 2012–; *Style*— His Hon Judge Keyser, QC; ✉ Cardiff Civil Justice Centre, 2 Park Street, Cardiff CF10 1ET

KEYTE, Malcolm William; s of William Keyte (d 1977), of Sandsgate, Devon, and Grace Mary, *née* Bocking (d 1983); *b* 23 February 1944; *Educ* Tonbridge (athletics and 1st VIII cross country); *m* May 1983, Nicola Anne, da of Arthur Leonard Spiller; 3 da (Sophie Victoria b 30 March 1985, Charlotte Mary b 10 Jan 1987, Alice Joanna b 18 Dec 1990), 1 s (Thomas William b 25 March 1993); *Career* princ Keyte & Co Chartered Accountants 1973–2013 (articled clerk 1961–67); Croydon and Dist Soc of Chartered Accountants: memb 1968–, pres 1991–92, chm Gen Practitioner Bd 1994–2001; memb: Gen Practitioner Bd/Panel ICAEW 1994–2002, Cncl Small Firms Lead Body 1995–98; chm S London HMRC Working Together Ctee 2000–14; treas Tonbridge Sch Parents Arts Soc 2007–10; memb Warlingham RFC 1st XV and 1st VII 1965–69, capt Purley Squash Club 1981–84; fell WWF 1985–; FCA 1979 (ACA 1968); *Recreations* gardening, tennis, walking; *Style*— Malcolm W Keyte, Esq; ✉ Keyte & Co, Coombe Avenue, Croydon CR0 5SD (☎ 020 8688 6551)

KHALILI, Prof Nasser David; *b* 18 December 1945, Iran; *Educ* schooling in Tehran, Queens Coll NY (BA), SOAS Univ of London (PhD); *m* 1978, Marion Easton; 3 s (Daniel b 5 Aug 1981, Benjamin, Raphael (twins) b 2 May 1984); *Career* scholar, art collector and philanthropist; army medic Iranian military 1967–67; fndr Khalili Family Tst 1970, 8 collections totalling approx 25,000 objects: The Arts of the Islamic World 1970, Hajj and the Arts of Pilgrimage 1970, Aramaic Documents 1975 Japanese Art of the Meji Period 1978, Spanish Damscened Metalwork 1979, Swedish Textile Art 1980, Enamels of the World 1981, Japanese Kimonos 1988; estab Khalili Chair of Islamic Art at SOAS Univ of London 1989, estab Khalili Research Centre for Art and Material Culture of the Middle East Univ of Oxford 2005; memb Int Bd of Overseers Tufts Univ USA 1997, tstee Boston Univ 2003, assoc res prof SOAS Univ of London 2003; estab Nasser David Khalili Charitable Settlement 1992, fndr and chm Maimonides Fndn 1995–; memb Elias Ashmole Gp Ashmolean Museum Oxford 2000, memb Chancellor's Ct of Benefactors Oxford 2006; patron of arts Vatican Museums 2002; goodwill ambass UNESCO 2012; High Sheriff of London Award 2007, Queen's Coll President's Award 2010, Queen's Coll President's Medal in recognition of outstanding service to humanity 2013, Laureate of the Dialogue of Cultures Award French National Assembly 2014; hon fell: Univ of London 1991, Wolfson Coll Oxford 2005; Hon Dr: Boston Univ 1997 and 2003, Univ of the Arts London 2005; tstee City of Jerusalem 1996; Knight Cdr Royal Order of Francis I 2003, Knight Cdr Pontifical Equestrian Order of Pope St Sylvester 2009 (Knight 2004); *Style*— Professor Nasser D Khalili

KHALIQ, Imtaz; MBE (2010); da of Abdul Khaliq, and Gultaz Khaliq; *b* 28 July 1964, Yorks; *Educ* Buttershaw Upper Sch Bradford, Leeds Coll of Art (Dip), Univ of Arts London (HND), Univ of Westminster (BA); *m* Oct 2007, Dr Karl Rattray; 2 c; *Career* bespoke tailor; Imtazia Tailor 1983–87, fashion conslt Harrods 1987–88, fashion conslt Harvey Nichols 1989–90, head of design and manufacturing Couturier Guy Faustaire 1989–91, founded own business Wilton Square N1 1991–, New Bond St W1 1996–2003, Independent Place E8 2004–08; clients incl: Michelle Pheiffer, The Baroness Dean of Thornton-le-Fylde, PC, Kay Burley, Dawn Airey, Dina Carroll, Dawn Butler, MP, *qqv*, Sian Lloyd; visiting lectr Univ of Westminster 1997–2000, teacher Univ of the Arts London 2000–03, advsr to gender studies MPhil Kings Coll Cambridge; Best Creative Business Precious Award 2008, Best Women's Business Mayor of Hackney Award 2009; FRSA 2010; *Recreations* reading, walking and exciting adventures; *Style*— Ms Imtaz Khaliq, MBE; ✉ 39 Wilton Square, London N1 3DW (☎ 020 7683 7022, mobile 07958 550816, e-mail info@imtaz.com, website www.imtaz.com)

KHALIQUE, Nageena; QC (2015); *b* 10 December 1961, Nottingham; *Educ* Nottingham HS for Girls, UCL, City Univ, Inns of Ct Law Sch; *m* 29 Aug 1992, Andrew Mark Sean Brown; 1 s (Joseph Louis Khalique-Brown b 7 July 1997), 1 da (Hannah Rose Khalique-Brown b 2 April 1999); *Career* trained as dentist specialising in oral and maxillofacial surgery, registrar in maxillofacial surgery 1992; called to the Bar 1994; dep head, head Public Law, Court of Protection Gp and head Inquests and Public Inquiries Team No. 5 Chambers; memb ALBA (Constitutional and Administrative Law Bar Assoc), memb PNBA (Professional Negligence Bar Assoc); *Recreations* music, skiing; *Style*— Miss Nageena Khalique, QC; ✉ No. 5 Chambers, Fountain Court, Steelhouse Lane, Birmingham B4 6DR

KHAN, Akram Hossain; MBE (2005); *b* 29 July 1974; *Educ* Rutlish HS Merton Park, Prayag Sangeet Samati (Dance Bd of India, Sr Dip), De Montfort Univ (BA), Northern Sch of Contemporary Dance Leeds (BPA); *m* Shanell Winlock; *Career* choreographer and dancer; teacher: Bangladesh Centre London 1986, Leicester Cncl 1994–95, Merton Adult Inst London 1992–, Acad of Indian Dance London 1994–96, Wakefield Arts Centre 1996; Jonathan Burrows Co: Freiburg Residency 1998, Kevin Volans Evening 1999; choreographer in residence Royal Festival Hall 2001–03, assoc artist Royal Festival Hall 2003–, assoc artist Sadler's Wells Theatre 2005–; Hon Dr Arts De Montfort University 2004; *Performances* nat performances incl: Bangladesh Festival (Cwlth Inst) 1983–86, Bangladesh Festival of Freedom London 1984–86, Ora Kadam Ali (Cwlth Inst) 1985, Makhon Churi-Krishna (Trevini Co) 1985, Jungle Book (Br Arts Cncl, touring) 1984–85, Treveni Co 1986, Round House 1986, Mahabharata (RSC, world tour) 1988, solo performance tour 1992, solo performance (Cwlth Inst and Bhavan) 1992, Treveni (tour) 1992, Merton Festival 1993–95, vision prodn (The Place Theatre) 1995, Indian Dance Festival (Phoenix Theatre) 1995, Homage to the Four Tops (Glasgow Festival) 1996, Dance Umbrella Festival (Cochrane Theatre) 1996, X-10-DED (Woking Dance Umbrella) 1996, Ross-on-Wye Int Festival 1997, Purush (Birmingham) 1997, Watermans Arts Centre 1998, Interface (Interface Festival) 1998, Choreolab 1999, Per4mance (short film) 1999, Saint (CADMAD Cardiff) 1999, Desert Steps (QEH London) 1999, Saint (Greenwich and Docklands Int Festival) 1999, No Male Egos (Purcell Room London) 1999, Loose in Flight 2000, Fix 2000, Rush 2000 (added to A-level syllabus 2004), Related Rocks 2001, kaash 2002, ma 2004, zero degrees (Sadler's Wells) 2005 (nominated Best New Dance Prodn Laurence Olivier Awards 2006), sacred monsters 2006, variations for vibes, strings & pianos 2006; int performances incl: Mahabharata (int tour) 1987–89, solo performance (India and Bangladesh) 1990, Lucknow and TV interview (Bombay) 1993, solo performance (Divya Drishti Indian TV), vision prodn Bangladesh 1995, X-10-DED (Oriental Festival Germany) 1997; *Awards* Jerwood Choreography Award 1999, Outstanding Newcomer to Dance Dance Critics Circle 2000, Outstanding Newcomer Time Out Live Award 2001, Best Choreography (modern section) Critics' Circle National Dance Awards 2003, Most Promising Newcomer in Dance International Movimentos Tanzpreis Berlin 2004, Outstanding Male or Female Artist (modern) Critics' Circle National Dance Awards 2005, South Bank Show Dance Award 2005 (nominated 2000); *Recreations* singing, playing the guitar; *Style*— Akram Khan, Esq, MBE; ✉ website www.akramkhancompany.net

KHAN, Asif; *b* 1979, London; *Educ* Bartlett Sch UCL (Donaldson medal), Architectural Assoc (DipArch, Baylight Scholarship); *m* 2004, Sakiko Kohashi; *Career* architect; visiting prof (Architecture MA) RCA; works incl: West Beach Café Littlehampton 2008, Milan Salone Satellite 2009, Coca-Cola Beatbox (London Olympics) 2012, Parhelia (for Swarovski, Design Miami) 2012, MegaFaces Pavilion (Winter Olympics Sochi) 2014 (Innovation Grand Prix Cannes Lions 2014, Red Dot Design Award, D&AD Award 2015, ADC Global Award), British Pavilion Milan Expo 2015 (finalist), Guggenheim Museum Helsinki 2015 (finalist), Serpentine Summer House 2016, Museum of London (finalist); Design Museum: designer in residence 2010, memb Bd of Tstees 2015; honourable mention MAXXI MoMA/PS1 Young Architects Program 2010, Designers to Watch New York Times 2010, Designer of the Future Design Miami 2011, Telegraph Amazing 15 2012; *Style*— Asif Khan, Esq; ✉ Asif Khan Ltd, 1–5 Vyner Street, London E2 9DG (☎ 020 8980 3685, website www.asif-khan.com, Twitter @asif_can)

KHAN, Prof Geoffrey Allan; s of Clive Khan, and Diana Margaret Hodson; *b* 1 February 1958; *Educ* SOAS Univ of London (BA, PhD); *m* 21 Jan 1984, Colette Winefride Mary, da of Alfred A Alcock; 1 da (Hannah Maryam b 26 Feb 1987), 1 s (Jonathan Anthony b 24 Oct 1989); *Career* research assoc Taylor-Schechter Genizah Research Unit 1987–93 (research asst 1983–87); Univ of Cambridge: lectr in Hebrew and Aramaic (Semitic languages) 1993–99, prof of Semitic philology 2002– (reader 1999–2002), regius prof of Hebrew 2012–; Lidzbarski Gold Medal for Semitic Philology 2004; fell Inst for Advanced Studies Jerusalem 1990–91, hon fell Acad of the Hebrew Language 2011, visiting memb Inst for Advanced Study Princeton 2015, Lady Davis visiting prof Hebrew Univ Jerusalem 2015, Sackler fell Univ of Tel Aviv 2015, hon extraordinary prof Univ of Stellenbosch 2016; FBA 1998, hon fell Acad of the Hebrew Language 2011, fell Academia Europea 2014, hon memb American Oriental Soc 2015; *Books* Studies in Semitic Syntax (1988), Karaite Bible Manuscripts from the Cairo Genizah (1990), Arabic Papyri: Selected material from the Khalili Collection (1992), Arabic Legal and Administrative Documents in the Cambridge Genizah Collections (1993), Bills, Letters and Deeds. Arabic Papyri of the Seventh-Eleventh Centuries (1993), A Grammar of Neo-Aramaic (1999), The Early Karaite Tradition of Hebrew Grammatical Thought (2000), Early Karaite Grammatical Texts (2001), Exegesis and Grammar in Medieval Karaite Texts (2002), The Neo-Aramaic Dialect of Qaraqosh (2002), The Karaite Tradition of Hebrew Grammatical Thought in its Classical Form (2003), The Jewish Neo-Aramaic Dialect of Sulemaniyya and Halabja (2004), Arabic Documents from Early Islamic Khurasan (2007), Neo-Aramaic Dialect Studies (2008), The Neo-Aramaic Dialect of Barwar, 3 Vols (2008), The Jewish Neo-Aramaic Dialect of Urmi (2009), The Jewish Neo-Aramaic Dialect of Sanandaj (2010), Semitic Languages: An International Handbook (jt ed, 2011), Studies on the Text and Versions of the Hebrew Bible in Honour of Robert Gordon (jt ed, 2011), A Short Introduction to the Masoretic Hebrew Bible and its Reading Tradition (2012), The Encyclopedia of Hebrew Language and Linguistics (ed-in-chief, 4 vols, 2013), Neo-Amaric and its Linguistic Context (ed, with L Napiorkowska as co-ed, 2015), The Neo-Aramaic Dialect of the Assyrian Christians of Urmi (4 vols: Vol 1, Grammar: Phonology and Morphology, Vol 2, Grammar: Syntax, Vol 3, Lexical Studies and Dictionary, Vol 4, Texts, 2016); also author of numerous articles and reviews in learned jls; *Recreations* mountain walking; *Style*— Prof Geoffrey Khan, FBA; ✉ Faculty of Asian and Middle Eastern Studies, Sidgwick Avenue, Cambridge CB3 9DA (☎ 01223 335114, fax 01223 335110, e-mail gk101@cam.ac.uk)

KHAN, (Mohammed) Ilyas; s of Mohammed Yasin Khan (d 1970), of Gillingham, Kent, and Hafiza Begum; *b* 14 October 1945; *Educ* Duke of Gloucester Sch Nairobi Kenya; *m* 14 April 1972, Amtul Naseer, da of Abdul Rehman Qureshi (d 1965); 1 da (Maham Hina b 1988), 1 s (Shamail Ahmed Nadeem b 1992); *Career* Cncl of Legal Educn 1965–68, called to the Bar Lincoln's Inn 1969, res magistrate Kenya 1977–80, immigration adjudicator 1992– (pt/t 1983–92), special asylum adjudicator 1993–, dep regnl adjudicator 2003–05, designated immigration judge 2005–; recorder of the Crown Ct 1996– (asst recorder 1991); *Recreations* cricket, squash; *Style*— Ilyas Khan, Esq; ✉ 12 Halfway Close, Great Barr, Birmingham B44 8JL

KHAN, Irene Zubaida; *b* 24 December 1956, Dhaka, Bangladesh; *Educ* Univ of Manchester, Harvard Law Sch; *Career* fndr memb Concern Universal 1977, human rights activist Int Cmmn of Jurists 1979; UNHCR: joined 1980, various positions at HQ and in field ops, sr exec offr to UN High Cmmr 1991–95, chief of mission India 1995–98, dep dir of int protection 1999–2001; sec gen Amnesty Int 2001–; hon dr: Ferris Univ Japan, Ghent Univ, Staffordshire Univ, Univ of London; Ford Fndn fell; Pilkington Woman of the Year Award 2002, City of Sydney Peace Prize 2006, John Owens Distinguished Alumni Award Univ of Manchester; *Books* The Unheard Truth: Poverty and Human Rights (2009); *Style*— Dr Irene Khan

KHAN, Rosemarie; OBE (1999); *b* 29 July 1947; *Educ* GDC (Dip Dental Hygiene), Univ of Manchester (BEd, MEd); *m* Mohammad Aslam; 1 s (Alexander b 24 Nov 1965), 1 da (Sophia b 5 June 1973); *Career* formerly dental hygienist Dental Dept St Mary's Hosp Whitworth Park Manchester, dental hygienist in gen dental practice 1971–2000, tutor dental hygienist Univ of Manchester Dental Hosp 1971–98, oral health promotion mangr Sheffield Primary Dental Care Serv 1998–2004, tutor dental hygienist Gtr Manchester Sch for Dental Care Professionals 2004–; nat pres Br Dental Hygienists Assoc (BDHA) 1984–86 (memb Cncl 1981–84), UK dir Int Dental Hygienists Fedn 1986–89; memb: Central Examining Bd for Dental Hygienists 1976–98, Panel of Examiners Central Examining Bd for Dental Hygienists 1982–99, Registration Assessment Panel Dental Care Professionals 2009–; elected memb GDC 1991–2009 (memb Dental Auxiliaries Ctee 1985–98, memb Inspection Panel 2009–); BDHA Leatherman 1995, BDA Roll of Distinction 1999; *Recreations* family, reading, travel; *Style*— Mrs Rosemarie Khan, OBE; ✉ Greater Manchester DCP School, 4th Floor, St James's House, Pendleton Way, Salford M6 5FW

KHAN, Rt Hon Sadiq; MP, PC (2009); s of Amanullah Ahmed Khan (d 2003), and Sehrun Nisa Khan; *b* 8 October 1970, Tooting, London; *Educ* Ernest Bevin Secdy Comp Tooting, Univ of N London (LLB), Coll of Law Guildford (Sweet & Maxwell Law Prize, Windsor fell, Esso Law Award); *m* 1994, Saadiya Ahmad; 2 da; *Career* solicitor; ptnr: Christian Fisher Slrs 1998–2000 (trainee slr 1993–95, slr 1995–98), Christian Fisher Khan Slrs 2000–02, Christian Khan Slrs 2002–04 (also co-fndr); MP (Lab) Tooting 2005–16; cncllr (Lab) Wandsworth BC 1994–2006 (dep ldr Lab gp 1996–2001); min of state for transport 2009–10, shadow lord chllr and justice sec (political and constitutional reform) 2010–15, shadow min for London 2013–15, Mayor of London (Lab) 2016–; chair: Liberty 2001–04, Legal Affrs Ctee Muslim Cncl of Britain (MCB) 2004–05; vice-chair Legal Action Gp (LAG) 1999–2004; fndr Human Rights Lawyers Assoc; memb: Unison, Co-op, GMB, CWU, Fabian Soc, Friends of the Earth, Law Soc 1993–; govr Fircroft Primary Sch 1993–, chair of govrs Gatton Primary Sch 2004–; Newcomer of the Year Spectator Parly Awards 2005, Achievement and Inspiration Award Fedn of Student Islamic Societies 2012, Patchwork Lab MP of the Year and Overall MP of the Year 2013; *Publications* Challenging Racism (2003), Police Misconduct (2005); author of articles in various pubns on variety of matters; *Recreations* playing and watching sports, cinema, family, friends, local community, lifelong supporter of Liverpool FC; *Style*— The Rt Hon Sadiq Khan, Esq, MP; ✉ House of Commons, London SW1A 0AA (☎ 020 7219 6967, fax 020 7219 6477, e-mail sadiqkhanmp@parliament.uk); Tooting Labour Party, 58 Trinity Road, London SW17 7RH (☎ 020 8767 9660, fax 020 8772 4593, e-mail tooting@email.org.uk, website www.sadiqkhan.org.uk)

KHAN, Sara; *Career* author, dir and co-fndr Inspire 2009–; contrib: Guardian, Independent, Telegraph, New Statesman, Huffington Post; Top 10 Influencer BBC Woman's Hour Power List 2015; Kraemer ME distinguished scholar in residence William and Mary Sch of Law Williamsburg Virginia USA 2015; *Publications* Retrieving the Equilibirum and Restoring Justice: Using Islam's Egalitarian Teachings to Reclaim Women's Right (in Sensible Religion, 2014), The Battle for British Islam: Reclaiming Muslim Identity from Extremism (2016); *Style—* Ms Sara Khan; ✉ Twitter @WeWillInspire

KHANDEKAR, Ashutosh; *b* 6 April 1965, Mumbai, India; *Educ* Univ of Oxford (MA); *Career* ed-in-chief Opera Now magazine 1997–; tstee: Iford Opera Wilts, Frome Festival Somerset; *Recreations* cinema, gardening, music, opera, travel; *Style—* Ashutosh Khandekar, Esq; ✉ Opera Now, Rhinegold Publishing, Rhinegold House, 20 Rugby Street, London WC1N 3QZ (e-mail opera.now@rhinegold.co.uk, website www.operanow.co.uk)

KHANNA, Karunesh; *Educ* Inst of Hotel Mgmnt Calcutta; *Career* sous chef Taj Palace Hotel 1995–99, exec chef Taj Chandela India 1999–2001, exec sous chef Taj Exotica 2001–03, exec chef Taj Holiday Village Goa 2003–04, head chef Amaya London 2004– (Michelin star 2006–); Craft Guild of Chefs Ethnic Chef Award 2011; *Style—* Karunesh Khanna, Esq; ✉ Amaya, Halkin Arcade, Motcomb Street, London SW1X 8JT

KHAW, Prof Kay-Tee; CBE (2003); da of Kai-Boh Khaw (d 1972), of Kuala Lumpur, and Chweegeok, *née* Tan; *b* 14 October 1950; *Educ* Victoria Inst Kuala Lumpur, Univ of Cambridge (MA, MB BChir), LSHTM (MSc); *m* 1980, Dr James William Fawcett; 1 da (Nicola b 21 Dec 1981), 1 s (Andrew b 14 Feb 1984); *Career* house physician and surgn St Mary's Hosp 1975–76, SHO Whittington Hosp 1977–78, registrar KCH 1978–79; Wellcome Tst res fell: St Mary's Hosp and LSHTM 1980–82, Univ of Calif 1982–84; asst prof Univ of Calif 1985–89; Univ of Cambridge: sr registrar (community med) 1986–89, prof of clinical gerontology 1989–; fell Gonville & Caius Coll Cambridge 1992–; FRCP, FFPHM, FMedSci; *Style—* Prof Kay-Tee Khaw, CBE; ✉ Clinical Gerontology Unit, University of Cambridge, Addenbrooke's Hospital, Cambridge CB2 2QQ (☎ 01223 217292, fax 01223 336928)

KHEMKA, Dame Asha; DBE (2014, OBE 2009); *née* Agarwal; da of Mr R C Agarwal (d 2004), and Mrs M Agarwal (d 1964), *née* Devi; *b* 21 October 1951, Sitamarhi, India; *Educ* Cardiff Univ (BEd, Cert Ed); *m* 19 Feb 1967, Shankar Lal Khemka; 1 da (Shalini Khemka b 7 Sept 1972), 2 s (Sheel Kemkha b 14 April 1974, Dr Sneh Khemka b 18 Sept 1975); *Career* lectr Oswestry Coll 1987–1995, dir of quality and dep head of faculty Tamworth Coll 1995–2001, assoc inspector Ofsted 1996–2005, asst princ Stafford Coll 2001–04, dep princ New Coll Nottingham 2004–06, princ and chief exec W Notts Coll Gp 2006–; memb Bd: Assoc of Coll (AoC), Educn and Training Fndn (ETF), Univ of Nottingham; chair: AoC India, AoC Quality and Policy Gp; memb Educn Hons Ctee 2015–, Vision Studio Sch Bd; tstee and fndr Inspire and Achieve Fndn; memb Bd Notts and Derbyshire Local Enterprise Partnership, memb Bd Indo Br Trade Cncl; National Jewel Award for Excellence in Healthcare and Educn 2007, Asian Woman of the Year (outstanding contrib to educn) 2008, Midlands Businesswoman of the Year 2009, NRI Welfare Soc of India Gold Medal (for work in educn as a non-resident Indian) 2010, Inspirational Woman of the Year Derbyshire and Notts Chamber of Commerce 2011; Woman of the Year 2014 GG2 Awards; Inaugural Winner Dadabhai Naoroji Award for Educn 2014; *Recreations* cinema, music, travel, entertaining; *Style—* Dame Asha Khemka, DBE; ✉ West Nottinghamshire College, Derby Road, Mansfield NG18 5BH (☎ 01623 413606, e-mail asha.khemka@wnc.ac.uk, website www.wnc.ac.uk, Twitter @DameAsha)

KHERAJ, Naguib; *b* London, 1964; *Educ* Dulwich Coll, Robinson Coll Cambridge; *m* Nazira Jiwan Hirji; 1 s (Ali Hirji b 2002); *Career* Salomon Bros 1986–96 (joined Investment Banking Div, appointed chief financial offr 1993), co-head of global capital markets and memb Exec Ctee Robert Fleming 1996–97, joined Barclays 1997, successively chief operating offr then global head of investment banking Barclays Capital and dep chm Barclays Global Investors, chief exec Barclays Private Clients 2003–04, gp finance dir Barclays plc 2004–07, memb Barclays Gp Exec Ctee, Bd Barclays plc and Bd Barclays Bank plc 2004–07; chief exec JPMorgan Cazenove 2008–10; vice-chm Barclays Bank 2011–12; non-exec dir Standard Chartered 2014–, non-exec dir Rothesay Life 2014–; chm Aga Khan Fndn (UK); memb: Bd of Govrs Inst of Ismaili Studies, Investment Ctee Wellcome Tst, US-UK Fulbright Cmmn, Bd of Tstees Aga Khan Univ; *Style—* Naguib Kheraj, Esq

KHMELNITSKII, Prof David; s of Ephraim A Khmelnitskii (d 1984), and Ida S, *née* Borodyanskaya (d 1998); *b* 5 December 1944; *Educ* Landau Inst for Theoretical Physics Moscow (PhD, DSc); *m* 20 Jan 1981, Ellen, da of Pietr Kaminskii; 2 da (Anna b 22 Aug 1981, Eugenia b 28 Nov 1984); *Career* grad student and researcher L D Landau Inst Moscow 1969–84 (gp leader 1989), gp leader Inst for Solid State Physics 1985–89, sr research fell Trinity Coll Cambridge 1991–2011 (emeritus fell 2011–); hon prof Univ of Cambridge 2002–13 (prof emeritus 2013–); Hewlett-Packard Europhysics Prize 1993, Landau-Weizmann Award 1995; *Style—* Prof David Khmelnitskii; ✉ Cavendish Laboratory, University of Cambridge, Cambridge CB3 0HE (☎ 01223 337289, fax 01223 337356, e-mail dek12@cam.ac.uk)

KHOO, Francis Kah Siang; s of late Teng Eng, and late Swee Neo, *née* Chew; *b* 23 October 1947; *Educ* Univ of Singapore (LLB), Univ of London (MA); *m* 29 Jan 1977, Dr Swee Chai Ang, da of late Peng Liat Ang; *Career* advocate and slr Singapore 1971–77, business, political journalist and cartoonist London 1980–87, gen sec War on Want London (Br Devpt Aid Agency) 1988–89, slr Law Soc of England and Wales 1998–; vice-chm and fndr memb Medical Aid for Palestinians 1984–; chm, tstee and sec Radicle 2000–; memb: NUJ 1979–, Singapore Law Soc 1971–; *Books* Bungaraya Blooms All Day (1978), The Rebel and the Revolutionary (1994), Our Thoughts are Free (2009); *Recreations* song-writing, swimming, camera designing; *Style—* Francis Khoo, Esq; ✉ 285 Cambridge Heath Road, Bethnal Green, London E2 0EL (☎ 020 7729 3994, e-mail fkhoo@btinternet.com)

KHOURY, Dr Ghassan George; s of George Sammaan Khoury, of Amman, Jordan, and Margaret, *née* Rizik; *b* 14 July 1954; *Educ* Bryanston, UCL, UCH; *m* 7 Aug 1984, Sonia, da of Jubran Khoury, of Jifna, Ramallah, Palestine; 2 s (George Ghassan b 1986, Timothy b 1993), 2 da (Genevieve b 1996, Emma b 1997); *Career* lectr in radiotherapy and oncology Univ of Leeds 1986–89, conslt and head Radiotherapy and Oncology Dept Portsmouth 1989–; memb: BMA 1978, British Gynaecological Cancer Soc 1991, Faculty of Clinical Oncology RCR 1998, Br Uro-oncologyGp 2004, Med Advsy Ctee Spire Hosp Portsmouth 2004; chair Whitburn Charitable Tst 1989–; MRCP 1981, FRCR 1985 (elected memb Cncl 2010–13), FRCP 1998; *Recreations* swimming, skiing, reading, opera, theatre; *Style—* Dr Ghassan Khoury; ✉ Portsmouth Oncology Centre, Queen Alexandra Hospital, Cosham, Portsmouth PO6 3LY (☎ 02392 286000, e-mail ggkhoury@hotmail.com)

KIBAZO, Joel Serunkuma; s of Godfrey Serunkuma Lule, and Margaret Mary, *née* Namusisi; *b* 24 June 1961; *Educ* HS for Boys Swindon, Kingsbury HS London, Sunderland Poly (BA), Univ of Reading (MA), Univ of Bradford (MBA); *Family* 2 da (Jennifer b 27 March 1998, Jade b 2 Dec 2001); *Career* trainee reporter New Life 1986–87, political corr The Voice 1987–88, Financial Times 1988–2000, dir of communications and public affairs The Commonwealth Secretariat 2000–06, ptnr JK Associates 2007–; memb Policy Ctee Centre for the Study of African Economies Univ of Oxford; fell of Africa Research Gp Univ of Bradford; assoc fell Chatham House; *Recreations* swimming, African history, Third World development issues; *Style—* Joel Kibazo, Esq; ✉ JK Associates, Devlin House, 36 St George Street, Mayfair, London W1S 2FW (☎ 020 7529 1402, mobile 07887 788566, e-mail joel@joelkibazo.com)

KIBBLE, Richard David; s of David John Kibble, of Lewes, E Sussex, and Maureen Carol, *née* Scott; *b* 14 February 1968, Cuckfield, Sussex; *Educ* New Coll Oxford (BA); *m* 20 March 1993, Alison Caroline, *née* Mitchell; 1 s (Zachary David b 31 July 2003); *Career* Marakon Assocs: joined 1990, ptnr 1999–2008, managing ptnr 2005–08; ptnr PricewaterhouseCoopers 2008–; memb Regeneration Ctee Business in the Community; *Recreations* squash, tennis, cycling, bridge, chess; *Clubs* RAC; *Style—* Richard Kibble, Esq

KIDBY, Robert James; s of late James Clarence Kidby, and Myrtle Eileen, *née* Wright; *b* 27 February 1951; *Educ* Steyning GS, Univ of London (LLB); *m* 3 Dec 1977, Stephanie Elizabeth Mary, da of Morris Shipley (decd); 1 s (Samuel Robert b 4 Aug 1985), 1 da (Harriet Elizabeth Cynthia b 6 Nov 1988); *Career* admitted slr 1977; ptnr: Durrant Piesse 1985–88, Lovells (previously Lovell White Durrant) 1988–2010; dir Welbeck Land Ltd 2010–13, dir Stupid Music Ltd 2014–; memb: Bd Alexandra Park and Palace Tst; appeal steward Br Boxing Bd of Control; tstee Caudwell Children 2016–; Freeman Worshipful Co of Slrs 1984; *Recreations* electric guitar, Antarctic memorabilia; *Clubs* Flyfishers, MCC, Ivy; *Style—* Robert Kidby, Esq; ✉ 29 Sotheby Road, London N5 2UP (☎ 07850 236191, e-mail bob@bobkidby.co.uk)

KIDD, Andrew Nicholson; s of Albert Kidd, of Santa Fe, NM, and Elizabeth, *née* White; *b* 18 September 1968, Houston, TX; *Educ* American Sch London, Brown Univ Providence (AB); *m* 9 July 1993, Solange, *née* Weinberger; 2 s (Nicolas b 13 June 1997, Oliver b 12 Feb 2001); *Career* editorial dir Penguin 1994–2002, publisher Picador and Pan Macmillan 2002–08, md Aitken Alexander Assocs 2008–14, co-fndr Alexi Books Ltd 2014–; *Recreations* laundry; *Style—* Andrew Kidd, Esq; ✉ Alexi Books Ltd, 77 Barnsbury Street, London N1 1EJ (e-mail andrew@alexibooks.com, website www.alexibooks.com)

KIDD, Jodie; da of John Edward Aitken Kidd, and Wendy Madeleine, *née* Hodge; *b* 25 September 1978, Guildford, Surrey; *m* 1 (m dis); *m* 2, David Blakeley; 1 s from a previous relationship (Indio Vianni b 5 Sep 2011); *Career* fashion model; campaigns incl: Chloé Innocence, Yves Saint Laurent, Green Lamb Golf Clothing 2014–16; magazine covers incl: Elle (USA, Portugal, Italy, Singapore and Sweden), British Vogue, The Face; collaboration on range of leather travel wallets with Debrett's 2014; *Television* incl: Fashion Avenue, Jack Osborne's Adrenaline Junkie (ITV2) 2008, Who Do You Think You Are (BBC1) 2008, Strictly Come Dancing (BBC1) 2008, Britain's Next Top Model 2009, I Believe In Miracle Healing (BBC3) 2010, Countrytracks (BBC1), Ration Book Britain (BBC1), Objects of Desire (Sky Arts), Celebrity Antiques Road Trip (BBC 1) 2013, Countdown (Channel 4) 2013, Celebrity Masterchef (runner up, BBC1) 2014, The Equestrian Season (presenter, CNN) 2014, The Classic Car Show (co-presenter) 2014; fndr Jodie Kidd Fndn; *Style—* Ms Jodie Kidd; ✉ c/o Claire Morgan, M&C Saatchi Merlin, 36 Golden Square, London W1F 9EE (e-mail claire.morgan@mcsaatchimerlin.com, Twitter @RealJodieKidd)

KIDD, William (Bill); MSP; *b* 24 July 1956, Glasgow; *Career* cncllr Glasgow City Cncl 2007–09; MSP (SNP): Glasgow 2007–11, Glasgow Anniesland 2011–; chief whip Scottish Govt 2012–; co-pres Parliamentarians for Nuclear Non-Proliferation and Disarmament, memb Global Cncl Abolition 2000; *Recreations* reading, travel; *Style—* Bill Kidd, Esq, MSP; ✉ Room 1.16, Glasgow Clyde College, Glasgow G12 0YE; Room 5.08, The Scottish Parliament, Edinburgh EH99 1SP

KIDGELL, John Earle; CB (2003); s of Maj Gilbert James Kidgell, TD, RA and TA (d 1989), and Cicely Alice Whitfield, *née* Earle (d 1982); *b* 18 November 1943; *Educ* Eton House Sch Southend, Univ of St Andrews (MA), LSE (MSc); *m* 30 March 1968, Penelope Jane, da of Kenneth Tarry (d 1970); 2 da (Clare Louise b 1972, Alexandra Frances b 1981), 1 s (James Kenneth b 1974); *Career* NIESR 1967–70, Gallup Poll 1970–72, statistician Central Statistical Office and Treasury 1972–79, chief statistician DOE and PSA 1979–88, under sec (grade 3) Office for National Statistics (formerly Central Statistical Office) 1988– (dir Macro-Economic Statistics and Analysis Gp 1994–99, dir Economic Statistics 1999–2002); *Recreations* tennis, hill walking, golf, reading; *Style—* John Kidgell, Esq, CB

KIDRON, Baroness (Life Peer UK 2012), of Angel in the London Borough of Islington; Beeban Tania Kidron; OBE (2012); da of Michael Kidron, and Nina Kidron; *b* 2 May 1961, London; *Educ* Nat Film Sch; *m* Lee Hall; 2 c (Noah, Blaze); *Career* film dir, dir Cross Street Films; co-fndr FILMCLUB 2006; memb Cncl Inst of Contemporary Art; govr Paul Hamlyn Fndn; patron Artangel, tstee Into Film, pres Voluntary Arts; hon doctorate Kingston Univ 2010; memb: AMPAS, Directors' Guild of America, Directors UK; *Television* incl: Carry Greenham Home 1983 (Golden Hugo Chicago Int Film Award), Oranges Are Not The Only Fruit 1989 (Best Drama BAFTA, Best Feature San Francisco Int Lesbian and Gay Film Festival, Outstanding TV Movie GLAAD, FIPA D'argent Cannes Film Festival, Special Prize for Ficiton Prix Italia), Great Moments in Aviation 1993, Hookers Hustlers Pimps and Their Johns 1993 (Most Erotic Br TV Show Erotic Award), Eve Arnold: A Portrait 1996, Texarkana 1998, Cinderella 2000, Murder 2002, Antony Gormley: Making Space 2007, Storyville: Sex, Death and the Gods 2011; *Film* incl: Vroom 1990, Used People 1992, Amy Foster 1997, Bridget Jones: The Edge of Reason 2004 (Evening Standard Readers' Film of 2004), InRealLife 2013; *Radio* Democracy and Language 2001, Wild Things 2002; *Recreations* visual arts, theatre, film, food, old buildings, shouting at the Today Programme (Radio 4); *Style—* The Baroness Kidron, OBE; ✉ House of Lords, London SW1A 0PW

KIDSTON, Cath; MBE (2010); da of Archibald Kidston (d 1978), and Susan, *née* Pease (d 1991); *b* 6 November 1958, London; *Educ* West Heath Girls Sch Sevenoaks, Southover Sch Lewes; *m* Hugh Padgham, *qv*; *Career* interior designer; asst to Nicky Haslam 1984–87, jt prop Curtainalia & Interior Design store 1987–92, fndr and creative dir Cath Kidston Ltd (68 UK and 105 Asia stores) 1992–2014; memb RSA 2002; *Publications* Vintage Style (1999), Tips for Vintage Style (2004), Cath Kidston In Print (2005), Make! (2008), Sew! (2009), Stitch! (2010), Patch! (2011), Coming Up Roses (2013); *Recreations* family, car boot sales, art exhibitions, travel; *Style—* Miss Cath Kidston, MBE; ✉ c/o The Communications Store, 2 Kensington Square, London W8 5EP (e-mail contactcathk@gmail.com)

KIELY, John Andrew; s of Nicholas Joseph Kiely (d 1989), and Maureen, *née* O'Neill; *b* 12 December 1961; *Educ* Stonyhurst, UCL (BA); *m* 1 June 1991, Sarah, da of Maj Peter Challen; 1 s (Alexander Fergus), 2 da (Georgia Francesca, Eloise India); *Career* Broad Street Associates PR 1986–88, fndr dir Square Mile Communications 1988–95, dir Bell Pottinger Financial (formerly Lowe Bell Financial) 1995–98, md Smithfield Consultants 1998–; *Recreations* most sports; *Clubs* Queen's, Rye Golf, Royal Worlington and Newmarket Golf, Worplesdon Golf, Royal St George's Golf; *Style—* John Kiely, Esq; ✉ Smithfield, 10 Aldersgate Street, London EC1A 4HJ

KIERNAN, Peter Anthony; s of Joseph Patrick Kiernan (d 1980), and Mary (Molly) Kiernan (d 1989); *b* 11 September 1960, Watford, Herts; *Educ* St Michael's Sch Garston, Downing Coll Cambridge (MA); *m* 20 April 1991, Felicity Ann, *née* Pearce; 1 da (Mary Grace Elizabeth b 9 Nov 1996); *Career* Peat Marwick Mitchell & Co 1982–86, dir S G Warburg & Co Ltd (and md of successor orgns) 1986–2000, md Investment Banking Div Goldman Sachs Int 2000–03, md Lazard 2004–11 (head UK Banking 2004–06), chm European Investment Banking Canaccord Genuity 2013– (vice-chm 2012–13), sr advsr Canaccord Genuity 2015–; non-exec dir: Tungsten Corporation plc 2012–, Listrac Hldgs Ltd 2016–, London First 2016–; sr advsr: Bell Pottinger 2012–, UK Bd Practice Heidrick & Struggles

2015; FCA; *Recreations* family and friends, skiing, watching sports; *Style*— Peter Kiernan, Esq; ✉ Canaccord Genuity, 88 Wood Street, London EC2V 7QR

KIFF, Rhys David; *b* 25 February 1970, Cardiff; *Educ* Cardiff HS, Jesus Coll Oxford (BA); *m* 27 Feb 1993, Helena, *née* Miller; 1 s (Geraint b Sept 1993); *Career* Citibank NA 1991–94, Swiss Bank Corp 1994–98, Credit Suisse First Boston 1998–2004, md Barclays Capital 2004–; *Recreations* classical music, theatre, wine; *Style*— Rhys Kiff, Esq; ✉ Barclays Capital, 5 The North Colonnade, Canary Wharf, London E14 4BB (☎ 020 7773 5007, e-mail rhys.kiff@barcap.com)

KILBURN, Alan Edward; OBE (1990); s of Edward Kilburn (d 1979), and Ethel, *née* Doidge (d 1997); *b* 15 April 1936; *Educ* Wellfield A J Dawson GS Wingate; *m* 27 July 1963, Doreen, da of Richard Edward Gratton; 1 s (Matthew Charles b 24 Nov 1970), 1 da (Jessica b 9 Jan 1974); *Career* Peterlee Devpt Corp 1952–63; housing mangr: Ashington UDC 1963–65, Knottingley UDC 1965–66, Felling UDC 1966–69; asst dir of housing Newcastle upon Tyne City Cncl 1969–73, regnl dir N Br Housing Assoc Ltd 1973–74, dep dir of housing Nottingham City Cncl 1974–76, chief exec Home Housing Assoc 1976–98; int housing advsr 1998–; chm Affinity Sutton Gp 2006–10; non-exec dir Barratt Developments plc 1998–2006; dir: Azure Charitable Enterprises, Managed Business Space Ltd; memb Inquiry into Br Housing 1985 and 1991; fell Inst of Housing 1972 (pres 1982–83); *Recreations* sport: assoc football, rugby football, cricket, golf; theatre and music; *Style*— Alan Kilburn, Esq, OBE

KILCLOONEY, Baron (Life Peer UK 2001), of Armagh in the County of Armagh; John David Taylor; PC (NI 1970); s of George David Taylor (d 1979), of Armagh, and Georgina, *née* Baird (d 1986); *b* 24 December 1937; *Educ* Royal Sch Armagh, Queen's Univ Belfast (BSc); *m* 1970, Mary Frances, da of Ernest Leslie Todd (d 1985); 1 s (Jonathan), 5 da (Jane, Rachel, Rowena, Alex, Hannah); *Career* memb (UUP): NI Parliament Stormont (memb for S Tyrone) 1965–72 (min of Home Affrs 1970–72), NI Assembly (memb for Fermanagh and S Tyrone) 1973–74, NI Constitutional Convention (memb for N Down) 1975–76, NI Assembly (memb for N Down) 1983–86, New NI Assembly 1997–2007; MEP NI 1979–89; MP (UUP) Strangford 1983–2001; memb Parly Assembly WEU 1996–2001; ind crossbencher House of Lords 2001–; chartered engr; dir: West Ulster Estates Ltd 1968–, Bramley Apple Restaurant Ltd 1974–, Ulster Gazette (Armagh) Ltd 1983–, Gosford Housing Assoc (Armagh) Ltd 1978–, Carrickfergus Advertiser Ltd 1992–, Cerdac Print (Belfast) Ltd, Tyrone Printing Ltd, Tyrone Courier Ltd, Tyrone Constitutions Ltd, Sovereign Properties (NI) Ltd, Tontine Rooms Holding Co Ltd, Ulsternet (NI) Ltd, Outlook Press Ltd, Coleraine Chronicle Ltd, Northern Constitution Ltd, Northern Newspapers Ltd, Midland Tribune Ltd 2004–, Alpha Publications Ltd 2004–, Tuam Herald Ltd 2004–, East Antrim Newspapers Ltd, BOL Properties (Repub of Ireland) Ltd, Elder Presbyterian Church in Ireland; memb Bd: Charles Sheils Houses, Gosford Voluntary Housing Assoc, Royal Sch Armagh; memb: RHS, Inst of Civil Engrs of Ireland, Inst of Highway Engrs; Hon PhD Eastern Mediterranean Univ 1998; *Publications* Ulster: The Economic Facts (1971); *Recreations* gardening, foreign travel; *Clubs* Armagh County (Armagh City), Farmers'; *Style*— The Rt Hon the Lord Kilclooney, PC; ✉ Mullinure, Armagh BT61 9EL (☎ and fax 028 3752 2409); House of Lords, London SW1A 0PW (☎ 020 7931 7211, fax 020 7931 7211)

KILGALLON, William (Bill); OBE (1992); s of William Kilgallon (d 1984), of Co Mayo and Leeds, and Bridget Agnes, *née* Earley; *b* 29 August 1946, Manulla, Co Mayo, Ireland; *Educ* St Michael's Coll Leeds, Ushaw Coll Durham, Gregorian Univ Rome (STL), London Sch of Economics (DSA), Univ of Warwick (MA), Lancaster Univ (MSc); *m* 20 Jan 1978, Stephanie, da of Benjamin Martin; 3 s (Stephen b 1979, Michael b 1980, Christy b 1996, adopted 2010); *Career* RC priest Dio of Leeds 1970–77: asst priest St Anne's Cathedral 1970–74, fndr chm St Anne's Shelter and Housing Action 1971–74, social work trg 1974–76, social worker Leeds Catholic Children's Soc 1976–77; returned to lay state 1977, mangr St Anne's Day Centre 1977–78, chief exec St Anne's Shelter and Housing Action 1978–2002, chief exec Social Care Inst for Excellence 2003–07, chief exec St Gemma's Hospice Leeds 2007–10; dir Nat Office for Professional Standards Catholic Church in NZ 2013–; memb (Lab) Leeds City Cncl 1979–92: chm Housing Ctee 1984–88, chm Social Serv Ctee 1988–90, Lord Mayor of Leeds 1990–91, chm Environment Ctee 1991–92; NHS: memb Leeds Family Practitioner Ctee 1978–80, memb Leeds AHA 1980–82, memb Leeds Eastern District HA 1982–86, non-exec dir and vice-chm Yorkshire RHA 1990–92 (memb 1986–90), chm Leeds Community and Mental Health Servs Teaching NHS Tst 1992–98, chm Leeds Teaching Hosps NHS Tst 1998–2002; ldr of inquiry into: abuse in children's home Northumberland 1994–95, community health care North Durham NHS Tst 1997–98; memb: Cncl NHS Confedn 1997–2002 (vice-chm 1998–2000), Independent Reference Gp on Mental Health Dept of Health 1997–99, Reference Gp on Nat Health Serv Framework for Mental Health 1998–99, CCETSW 1998–2001, Nat Task Force on Learning Disability 2001–04; non-exec dir Places for People Gp 2004–05, ind memb W Yorks Police Authy 2007–09, chair Nat Catholic Safeguarding Cmmn 2008–10, memb Pontifical cmmn for the Protection of Minors 2014–; Hon LLD Univ of Leeds 1997, Hon DUniv Leeds Met Univ 2000; FRSA 1992; *Recreations* reading, walking, travel, sport – Rugby League and cricket; *Style*— Bill Kilgallon, OBE; ✉ National Office for Professional Standards, PO Box 301398, Albany, Auckland 0752, New Zealand (e-mail prof.standards@nzcbc.org.nz)

KILLANIN, 4 Baron (UK 1900); (George) Redmond Fitzpatrick Morris; s of 3 Baron Killanin, MBE, TD (d 1999); *b* 26 January 1947; *Educ* Gonzaga Coll Dublin, Ampleforth, TCD; *m* 1972 (m dis 1999), Pauline, da of Geoffrey Horton, of Cabinteely, Co Dublin; 1 s (Hon Luke), 1 da (Hon Olivia); m 2, 2000, Sheila Elizabeth, da of Patrick and Mary Lynch, of Dublin; 1 da (Hon Hannah), 1 s (Hon George); *Heir* s, Hon Luke Morris; *Career* film prodr; *Films* incl: The Wind That Shakes The Barley 2006, Notes on a Scandal 2006, The Reader 2008 (nominated Best Picture Acad Award 2009); *Recreations* film, music; *Clubs* Groucho; *Style*— The Rt Hon the Lord Killanin

KILLEARN, 3 Baron (UK 1943); Sir Victor Miles George Aldous Lampson; 4 Bt (UK 1866); s of 1 Baron Killearn, GCMG, CB, MVO, PC (d 1964), by his 2 w Jacqueline Aldine Leslie, da of late Marchese Senator Sir Aldo Castellani, KCMG; suc half-bro, 2 Baron Killearn (d 1996); *b* 9 September 1941, Cairo, Egypt; *Educ* Eton; *m* 1971, Melita Amaryllis Pamela Astrid (d 2014), da of Rear Adm Sir Morgan Charles Morgan-Giles, DSO, OBE, GM, DL, (MP Winchester 1964–79); 2 da (Hon Pamela Camilla Roxana b 1973, Hon Miranda Penelope Amber b 1975), 2 s (Hon Miles Henry Morgan b 1977, Hon Alexander Victor William b 1984); *Heir* s, Hon Miles Lampson; *Career* late Capt Scots Gds; ptnr Cazenove & Co 1979–2002; non-exec chm: Henderson Global Investors Hldgs Ltd 2001–05, Vietnam Dragon Fund 2005–11; non-exec dir: AMP Ltd 1999–2003, Maxis Communications Berhad 2002–06, Shanghai Real Estate Ltd 2003–07, Ton Poh Emerging Thailand Fund 2005; *Clubs* White's, Hong Kong; *Style*— The Lord Killearn

KILLEN, Fiona Mary; da of Thomas Killen, of Scotland, and Anne, *née* Thomas, of Wales; *b* 24 February 1969, Hamilton; *Educ* Univ of Leeds (BA), Univ of Edinburgh (LLB, LLM, DipLP); *m* 7 June 2003, Lloyd Quinan; 1 da; *Career* slr and NP; political researcher UK Parl and US Senate 1990–92, asst dir RICS Scotland 1994–96; Univ of Edinburgh: co-ordinator Scottish Univs Research Consortium 1996–98, tutor in public law 1999–2003; legal researcher Scottish Law Cmmn 1998–99, sr legal research specialist Scot Parl 1999–2001; Anderson Strathern: joined 2002–, head of parly and public law 2005–, ptnr 2006–; memb: Br Assoc for Sport and the Law (BASL), Erin Tst; former memb Bd: Scottish Human Rights Centre, Scot Civic Forum; memb: Law Soc of Scot 2003, Assoc of Regulatory and Disciplinary Lawyers 2005; jt winner Specialist Client Team of the Year Scottish Legal Award 2006; University Research in Scotland: Developing a Policy Framework (co-author, 1997), Inter-disciplinary Research: Process, Structures and Outcome (co-author, 1998), Annotated Transport and Works (Scotland) Act 2008; *Recreations* running, football, travel, music, reading; *Style*— Ms Fiona Killen; ✉ Anderson Strathern, 1 Rutland Court, Edinburgh EH3 8EY (☎ 0131 270 7700)

KILLEN, Prof John Tyrrell; s of John Killen (d 1975), and Muriel Caroline Elliott, *née* Bolton (d 1975); *b* 19 July 1937; *Educ* The High Sch Dublin, Trinity Coll Dublin (fndn scholar, vice-chllr's Latin medallist, BA), St John's Coll Cambridge (Robert Gardiner meml scholar, PhD); *m* 1964, Elizabeth Ann, da of J W Ross; 1 s (Richard James b 3 April 1966), 2 da (Sheelagh Margaret b 22 Feb 1968, Nicola Jane b 25 Feb 1971); *Career* Univ of Cambridge: asst lectr in classics 1967–70, lectr 1970–90, chm Faculty Bd of Classics 1984–86, reader in Mycenaean Greek 1990–97, prof of Mycenaean Greek 1997–99, emeritus prof 1999–; Churchill Coll Cambridge: Gulbenkian research fell 1961–62, fell and librarian 1962–69; Jesus Coll Cambridge: lectr 1965–97, fell 1969–, actg bursar 1973, sr bursar 1979–89, dir Quincentenary Devpt Appeal 1987–90; FBA 1995; *Publications* Corpus of Mycenaean Inscriptions from Knossos (with J Chadwick et al, 1986–98), The Knossos Tablets (with J-P Olivier, 5 edn 1989), Economy and Administration in Mycenaean Greece: Collected Papers on Linear B (ed M Del Freo, 3 vols, 2015); also author of numerous articles in learned jls; *Recreations* golf, watching sport on TV, reading the FT, music; *Style*— Prof John Killen, FBA; ✉ Jesus College, Cambridge CB5 8BL (☎ 01223 339339, fax 01223 332 4910)

KILMISTER, (Claude Alaric) Anthony; OBE (2005); s of Dr Claude Emile Kilmister (d 1951), and Margaret E Gee (d 1999); *b* 22 July 1931, Swansea, Wales; *Educ* Shrewsbury; *m* 1, 24 May 1958, Sheila, *née* Harwood (d 2006); m 2, 3 Feb 2016, Christine Margaret, da of late Herbert Batho; *Career* Nat Serv 1950–52, cmmnd Army; with NCB 1952–54, Cons Pty Orgn 1954–60; gen sec Cinema and TV Benevolent Fund 1962–72 (asst sec 1960–61), exec dir Parkinson's Disease Soc 1972–91, memb Ctee Action for Neurological Diseases 1987–91, pres Prostate Action (formerly Prostate Research Campaign UK) 2004–12 (fndr 1994–), vice-pres Prostate Cancer UK 2012–; pres Anglican Assoc 2007– (memb Exec Ctee 1976–); memb: Int Cncl for the Apostolic Faith 1987–93, Ctee Assoc for the Apostolic Ministry 1989–96; Prayer Book Soc: fndr memb and dep chm incl BCP Action Gp (its forerunner) 1972–89, chm 1989–2001, vice-pres 2001–, pres St Alban's Branch 2006–; Freeman City of London 2003–; MA (Lambeth) 2002; *Books* The Good Church Guide (1982), When Will Ye be Wise? (1983), My Favourite Betjeman (1985), The Prayer Book and Ordination: A Prayer Book View of Women Bishops (2006); *Recreations* reading, writing, walking, cinema, music, travel; *Style*— Anthony Kilmister, Esq, OBE; ✉ 11 Homewood Court, Cedars Village, Chorleywood, Hertfordshire WD3 5GB (☎ 01923 447367)

KILMORE, Bishop of (RC) 1998–; Most Rev Philip Leo O'Reilly; s of Terence O'Reilly (d 1973), of Cootehill, Co Cavan, and Maureen, *née* Smith (d 1951); *b* 10 April 1944; *Educ* St Patrick's Coll Cavan, St Patrick's Coll Maynooth, Gregorian Univ Rome (BSc, BD, Higher DipEd, STD); *Career* St Patrick's Coll Cavan 1969–76, Irish Coll Rome 1976–81, Bailieborough Community Sch 1981–88, Dio of Minna Nigeria 1988–90, St Paul's Missionary Seminary Abuja Nigeria 1990–95, Parish of Castletara Kilmore 1995–97, coadjutor bishop of Kilmore 1997–98; *Books* Word and Sign in the Acts of the Apostles. A Study in Lucan Theology (1986); *Recreations* reading, walking, golf; *Style*— The Most Rev the Bishop of Kilmore; ✉ Bishop's House, Cullies, Cavan, Republic of Ireland (☎ 00 353 49 4331496, e-mail bishop@kilmorediocese.ie)

K

KILMOREY, 6 Earl (I 1822); Sir Richard Francis Needham; kt (1997), PC (1994); also Hereditary Abbot of the Exempt Jurisdiction of Newry and Mourne, Viscount Kilmorey (I 1625) and Viscount Newry and Morne (I 1822); s of 5 Earl of Kilmorey (d 1977), and Helen, da of Sir Lionel Faudel-Phillips, 3 and last Bt; *b* 29 January 1942; *Educ* Eton; *m* 1965, Sigrid Juliane, da of late Ernst Thiessen, and Mrs John Gairdner; 2 s (Robert, Viscount Newry and Morne b 1966, Hon Andrew b 1969), 1 da (Lady Christina b 1977); *Heir* s, Viscount Newry and Morne, *qv*; *Career* PA to Rt Hon James Prior MP (oppn spokesman on employment) 1974–79; MP (Cons): Chippenham 1979–83, Wilts N 1983–97; memb Public Accounts Ctee 1982–83; PPS to: Rt Hon James Prior as sec of state for NI 1983–84, Rt Hon Patrick Jenkin as sec of state for environment 1984–85; min of health for NI 1985–89, min of environment for NI 1985–92, min for the economy for NI 1989–92, min of trade DTI 1992–95; chm: Gleneagles Hospital UK Ltd 1995–2001, Biocompatibles Int plc 2000–06, Avon Rubber plc 2007–12, Tetra Strategy 2009–, Rose plc 2009–15; dir: Dyson Ltd 1995–2011, NEC Europe Ltd 1997–, Smarta.com 2009–, Lonrho plc 2011–12, Rank plc 2012–; exec dir GEC plc 1995–97, non-exec dir Meggitt plc 1997–2002, non-exec dir Halsbury Homes Ltd 2015–; pres Br Exporters Assoc 1997–; govr Br Inst of Florence 1983–85; fndr memb: Anglo-Japanese 2000 Gp, Anglo-Korean Forum for the Future; formerly cncllr (Cons) Somerset CC; Hon LLD Univ of Ulster 2010; Order of the Rising Sun (Gold and Silver Star) Japan; *Publications* The Honourable Member (1983), Battling for Peace (1998); *Clubs* Pratt's, Brooks's; *Style*— The Rt Hon the Earl of Kilmorey, PC

KILPATRICK, Helen Marjorie; CB (2010); da of Henry Ball, and Nan Dixon Ball; *b* 9 October 1958; *Educ* King's Coll Cambridge (BA); *Career* controller of financial servs London Borough of Greenwich 1989–95, dir for resources, co treas and dep chief exec W Sussex CC 1995–2005, treas Sussex Police Authy 1995–2005, DG financial and commercial Home Office 2005–13, govr Cayman Islands 2013–; *Style*— Ms Helen Kilpatrick, CB; ✉ c/o FCO (George Town), King Charles Street, London SW1A 2AH

KILROY, Thomas; s of Thomas Kilroy, of Callan, Co Kilkenny, Ireland, and Mary, *née* Devine; *b* 23 September 1934; *Educ* St Kieran's Coll Kilkenny, Univ Coll Dublin; *m* 1, 1963 (m dis 1980), Patricia, *née* Cobey; 3 s; m 2, 1981, Julia Lowell, *née* Carlson; 1 da; *Career* writer; lectr in Eng Univ Coll Dublin 1965–73, prof of modern Eng Univ Coll Galway 1979–89 (now emeritus); Guardian Fiction Prize 1971, short listed for Booker Prize 1971, Heinemann Award for Literature 1972, AIB Literary Prize 1972, American-Irish Fndn Award 1975, Irish Times Special Tribute Award 2004, Pen Ireland Cross Award 2008; memb: Irish Acad of Letters, Aosdána; hon fell TCD; FRSL; *Novels* The Big Chapel 1971; *Plays* The Death and Resurrection of Mr Roche 1968, The O'Neill 1969, Tea and Sex and Shakespeare 1976, Talbot's Box 1977, Double Cross 1986, The Madame MacAdam Travelling Theatre 1991, Gold in the Streets 1993, The Secret Fall of Constance Wilde 1997, The Shape of Metal 2003, My Scandalous Life 2004, Christ Deliver Us! 2010, Blake 2013; *Adaptations* The Seagull 1981, Ghosts 1989, Six Characters in Search of An Author 1996, Previous Relations 2001, Henry IV 2005; *Style*— Thomas Kilroy, Esq, FRSL; ✉ Kilmaine, County Mayo, Ireland (☎ 00 353 93 33361); c/o Alan Brodie Representation, Paddock Suite, The Courtyard, 55 Charterhouse Street, London EC1M 6HA (☎ 020 7253 6226, fax 020 7183 7999, website www.alanbrodie.com)

KILSHAW, David Andrew George; OBE (1999); s of George Arthur Kilshaw (d 1963), and Margaret Annie, *née* Bridgwater (d 1991); *b* 18 March 1953; *Educ* Keil Sch Dumbarton; *m* 17 June 1976, Judith Margaret, da of John Sydney Milner; 3 s (Ross David b 26 May 1980, Craig John b 18 Feb 1982, Iain George b 21 Oct 1985); *Career* qualified asst Messrs Brunton Miller, Alexander & Martin Slrs Glasgow 1979–80 (legal apprenticeship 1974–79), slr Borders Regnl Cncl 1980–82, NP 1982, ptnr Messrs Cullen Kilshaw Slrs Galashiels, Melrose and Peebles 1982–; chm Borders Health Bd 1993–2001 (non-exec memb 1991–93); memb Law Soc of Scotland 1979; *Recreations* golf, fishing, listening to music; *Style*— David Kilshaw, Esq, OBE; ✉ Cullen Kilshaw, Solicitors and Estate Agents, 27 Market Street, Galashiels TD1 3AF (☎ 01896 758311, fax 01896 758112)

KIMBERLEY, 5 Earl of (UK 1866); Sir John Armine Wodehouse; 12 Bt (estab 1611); also 7 Baron Wodehouse (GB 1797); s of 4 Earl of Kimberley (d 2002), and Carmel June, *née* Maguire (d 1992); *b* 15 January 1951, London; *Educ* Eton, UEA (BSc, MSc); *m* 1973, Hon Carol Lylie, 2 da of 3 Baron Palmer (d 1990); 1 da (Lady Katherine b 1976), 1 s (David Simon John, Lord Wodehouse b 1978); *Heir* s, Lord Wodehouse; *Career* systems programmer with Glaxo 1979–95 (joined as res chemist 1974), advanced technology and informatics specialist GlaxoSmithKline (formerly Glaxo Wellcome) 1996–2000, sr internet analyst GlaxoSmithKline 2001–12, ret; chm: UK Info Users Gp 1981–83, UIS Users Gp 1991–93; reader C of E 2008–; fell Br Interplanetary Soc 1984 (assoc fell 1981–83); FRSA, MBCS CITP 1988, CEng 1993; *Recreations* photography, computing, spaceflight; *Style*— The Rt Hon the Earl of Kimberley; ✉ Fieldfares, Ferry Lane, Medmenham, Marlow, Buckinghamshire SL7 2EZ (e-mail lordkimberley@gmail.com)

KIMMINS, Malcolm Brian Johnston; CVO (2002), DL (2008); s of Lt-Gen Sir Brian Charles Hannam Kimmins, KBE, CB, DL (d 1979), and Marjory, *née* Johnston (d 1992); *b* 12 February 1937; *Educ* Harrow, Grenoble Univ; *m* 1968, Jane, da of Thomas Douglas Pilkington; 2 da (Katie b 1969, Mary-Anne b 1974), 1 s (Charles b 1971); *Career* 15/19 King's Royal Hussars 1955–57; chm and md William Sanderson & Son Ltd, chm Corney & Barrow Gp Ltd; dir: Shepherd Neame Ltd, Newbury Racecourse plc, Laurent Perrier UK; tstee Ascot Authy 1989–2002; High Sheriff Royal Co of Berkshire 2003–04; *Recreations* horse racing, golf, shooting; *Clubs* White's, Jockey, Swinley Golf, Royal St George's Golf; *Style*— Malcolm Kimmins, Esq, CVO, DL; ✉ Wick Lodge, Hoe Benham, Newbury, Berkshire RG20 8EX (☎ 01488 608368, mobile 07785 557877, e-mail mbj.kimmins@btinternet.com)

KINAHAN, Col Daniel de Burgh (Danny); MP, DL; s of Sir Robin Caldwell Kinahan, ERD, JP (d 1997), and Coralie Isabel, *née* de Burgh; *b* 14 April 1958, Belfast; *Educ* Stowe, Univ of Edinburgh (BCom), RMA Sandhurst; *m* 8 June 1991, Anna Marguerite, *née* Bence-Trower; 3 da (Eliza b 1993, Tara b 1994, Mia b 1998), 1 s (Hugo b 1996); *Career* Capt Blues and Royals 1976–1984, Sqdn Ldr North Irish Horse (Hon Col 2014); mangr Short Bros 1985–88, Christie's rep Ireland/ NI 1988–2003; cncllr Antrim BC 2005–09, MLA (UU) South Antrim 2009–15, MP (UU) South Antrim 2015–; chair Stormont All-Pty Gps: Ethnic, Country Sport, Environment, Social Economy; All-Pty Parly Gps: chair Educn, sec Union, co-chair Developing Democracy, vice-chair Cancer, memb Military Covenant; NI chair Historic Houses Assoc; *Recreations* cinema, golf, music, reading, shooting, skiing, tennis, travel, walking; *Clubs* Army & Navy, Ulster Reform, Down Hunt; *Style*— Col Danny Kinahan, MP, DL; ✉ Castle Upton, Templepatrick, Co Antrim (☎ 028 9443 3480); House of Commons, London SW1A 0AA

KINCH, His Hon Judge Christopher Anthony; QC (1999); s of Anthony Kinch, CBE (d 1999), and Barbara, *née* Paton Walsh (d 1992); *b* 27 May 1953; *Educ* Bishop Challoner Sch Bromley, ChCh Oxford (MA); *m* Carol Lesley, *née* Atkinson; 1 s (Samuel George b 1998), 2 da (Eleanor Kathleen b 2001, Martha Rose b 2004); *Career* called to the Bar Lincoln's Inn 1976 (bencher 2007), in practice 1977–2012, recorder of the Crown Court 1998, head of chambers 23 Essex Street 2005–09, circuit judge South Eastern Circuit 2012–, sr circuit judge and resident judge Woolwich Crown Court 2013–; hon recorder Royal Borough of Greenwich 2014–; chm Kent Bar Mess 2001–04; stagiaire EC Cmmn 1976–77; dir of educn Criminal Bar Assoc 2005–08 (vice-chair 2009–10, chm 2010–11), chair Bar Nat Mock Trial for Schs Competition Working Pty 1999–2009; tstee Citizenship Fndn 2006–15; *Style*— His Hon Judge Kinch, QC

KINCLAVEN, Hon Lord; Alexander Featherstonhaugh Wylie; s of Ian Hamilton Wylie (d 1991), and Helen Jane, *née* Mearns (d 1993); *b* 2 June 1951; *Educ* Univ of Edinburgh (LLB); *m* 12 July 1975, Gail Elizabeth Watson, da of Winifred and William Duncan; 2 da (Claire Elizabeth b 4 Aug 1981, Nicola Jane b 1 April 1985); *Career* admitted slr Scotland 1976, admitted Faculty of Advocates 1978, in practice 1978–2005, standing jr counsel to Accountant of Ct 1986–89, advocate depute 1989–92, QC (Scot) 1991, senator Coll of Justice 2005–; called to the English Bar Lincoln's Inn 1990; jt chm Discipline Ctee ICAS 1994–2005, memb Scottish Cncl of Law Reporting 2001–05, pt/t chm Police Appeals Tribunal 2001–05, pt/t memb Scottish Legal Aid Bd 1994–2002, memb Scottish Cases Review Cmmn 2004–05; pt/t sheriff 2000–05; FCIArb 1991 (ACIArb 1977); *Style*— The Hon Lord Kinclaven; ✉ Supreme Courts, Parliament House, 11 Parliament Square, Edinburgh EH1 1RQ

KINDER, John Russell; s of Herbert Kinder, of Leicester, and Kathleen Margaret, *née* Sarson; *b* 10 November 1937; *Educ* Wyggeston GS Leicester, CCC Oxford (MA); *m* 1964, Diana Christine, da of Frederick Gordan Evans (d 1984); 4 s (Mark Russell b 1966, Andrew John b 1967, Stephen James b 1970, Jonathan Charles b 1974); *Career* RAF 1956–58; dir William Brandts Sons & Co Ltd 1975–77, jt md Warwick Engineering Investment Ltd 1978–80, md and dir CH Industrials plc 1980–90, chief exec Kinder Consultants mgmnt conslts 1992–, financial dir Reflec plc 2005–; dir Serious Banking Complaints Bureau (SBCB) Ltd 2014–; chief exec Westminster Fndn for Democracy 2002–03; dir: Aston Martin Lagonda 1980–83, Aston Martin Tickford 1981–90; chm of tstees Priors Court Sch 2002–10; FCA; *Recreations* tennis, sailing, christian youth work; *Clubs* National, Hurlingham, Oxford Kilburn (pres 2001–), Brentham (chm 2010–16), Swanage Sailing; *Style*— John Kinder, Esq; ✉ Kinder Consultants, 23 Woodville Gardens, Ealing, London W5 2LL (☎ 07860 848747, e-mail john@jkinder.co.uk)

KINDRED, Nyree; MBE (2009); *née* Lewis; *b* 21 September 1980, Rhonda Valley, Wales; *m* Sascha Kindred, OBE, *qv*; 1 da (Ella b 2011); *Career* Paralympic swimmer; achivements incl: Silver medal 100m backstroke Paralympics Sydney 2000, 2 Bronze medals (100m breaststroke and 4x50m ind medley) Paralympics Sydney 2000, 2 Gold medals (100m backstroke and 4x50m ind medley relay), 2 Silver medals (100m breaststroke and 200m ind medley) and 1 Bronze medal 400m freestyle Paralympics Athens 2004, Silver medal 100m backstroke Paralympics Beijing 2008, Silver medal 100m backstroke Paralympics London 2012; *Style*— Mrs Nyree Kindred, MBE; ✉ c/o British Paralympic Association, 40 Bernard Street, London WC1N 1ST

KINDRED, Sascha; OBE (2009); *b* 13 December 1977, Münster, Germany; *m* Nyree Kindred, MBE, *qv*; 1 da (Ella b 2011); *Career* Paralympic swimmer; achivements incl: Silver medal 100m breaststroke Paralympics Atlanta 1996, 2 Gold medals (200m medley and 100m breaststroke) Paralympics Sydney 2000, Silver medal 4x100m medley Paralympics Sydney 2000, Bronze medal 4x50m freestyle relay Paralympics Sydney 2000, 2 Gold medals (200m individual medley and 100m breaststroke) Paralympics Athens 2004, Bronze medal 4x50m freestyle Paralympics Athens 2004, Gold medal Paralympic World Cup Manchester 2006, 2 Gold medals (200m individual medley and 100m breaststroke) Paralympics Beijing 2008, Bronze medal 50m butterfly Paralympics Beijing 2008, Silver medal 200m individual medley Paralympics London 2012; *Style*— Sascha Kindred, Esq, OBE; ✉ c/o British Paralympic Association, 40 Bernard Street, London WC1N 1ST

KING, Alastair John; s of Bernard Frank Beaumont King, and Jean, *née* Ferguson; *b* 22 December 1967; *Educ* Bath Coll of HE (BA), Univ of Birmingham (MA), Univ of Kansas (MMus); *m* 12 Oct 2002, Claire, *née* Holyoake; 1 s (Harry Francis b 30 Jan 2004), 1 da (Ella Sophia b 17 Sept 2006); *Career* composer; orchestrator and conductor on films incl: King Arthur 2004, Kingdom of Heaven 2005, The Island 2005, Wallace and Gromit: The Curse of the Were-Rabbit 2005, Curious George 2006, Pirates of the Caribbean: Dead Man's Chest 2006, Over the Hedge 2006, Harry Potter and the Order of the Phoenix 2007, Bee Movie 2007, St Trinians 2007, Made of Honor 2008, You Don't Mess with the Zohan 2008, Bedtime Stories 2008, The Maiden Heist 2009, Dorian Gray 2009, Harry Potter and the Half-Blood Prince 2009, St Trinians II 2009, Grown Ups 2010, Prince of Persia 2010, Just Go With It 2011, African Cats 2011, The Zookeeper 2011, Jack and Jill 2011, Chimpanzee 2012, That's My Boy 2012, Unfinished Song 2012, Chimpanzee 2012, Total Recall 2012, Grown Ups 2 2013, Winter's Tale 2014, Exodus: Gods and Kings 2014, Mordecai 2015, The Martian 2015, Dad's Army 2016; film composition 113 Degrees 2012; orchestrator and conductor on TV incl: Downton Abbey 2010–15, Mr Selfridge 2013–16, Grantchester 2015–16, Doctor Who 2015, A Midsummer Night's Dream 2016; TV compositions incl: The Last Detective 2003 and 2007, The Br Book Awards 2004–11, Dan Cruickshank's Adventures in Architecture 2008, The Crime Thriller Awards 2008–13, North America 2013; memb Performing Right Soc 1991, memb Br Acad of Composers and Songwriters 1999; *Compositions* concert works incl: In Just 1997, Irpy 1998, Straight on Til Morning 1999, Hit the Ground (Running, Running, Running) 2000 (finalist Masterprize 2001), Time Let Me Play 2001, Dance Marathon ($1000 Stake) 2001, Three Dance Miniatures 2002, The Games We Play (written for Evelyn Glennie, *qv*) 2003, Hints of Immortality 2004, Concerto for Youth Orchestra 2004, Volante 2005, Arrow 2010, Concertinfouro 2012; *Recreations* football, badminton; *Style*— Alastair King, Esq; ✉ Chester Music, 14–15 Berners Street, London W1T 3LJ (☎ 020 7612 7400, e-mail alastairj.king@mac.com, website http://web.me.com/alastairj.king/alastair_king/home.html)

KING, Prof Andrew John; s of Neville Douglas King (d 1999), and Audrey Kathleen, *née* Manix (d 2001); *b* 8 April 1959, Greenford, Middx; *Educ* Eliots Green GS, KCL (BSc), Nat Inst for Med Research and KCL (PhD); *m* Dr Scott Thomas Bryan; *Career* Univ of Oxford: Douglas McAlpine jr research fell in neurology Green Coll 1983–86, SERC postdoctoral fell 1984–86, E P Abraham Cephalosporin jr research fell in med scis Lincoln Coll 1986–89, research fell Lister Inst 1986–91, Wellcome Tst sr research fell 1991–2006, univ research lectr 1996–2000, reader in auditory physiology 2000–04, sr research fell in med scis Merton Coll 2002–07, prof of neurophysiology 2004–, Wellcome Tst princ research fell 2006–, supernumerary fell Merton Coll 2007–; visiting scientist Eye Research Inst of Retina Fndn Boston USA 1988; chief scientific advsr Deafness Research UK 2011–13; sr ed eLife; Layton Science research award KCL 1980, Wellcome Prize medal and lecture in physiology 1990; FMedSci 2011; *Publications* Auditory Neuroscience: Making Sense of Sound (jtly, 2011); over 180 scientific articles; *Recreations* gardening, cooking, Renaissance and Baroque music; *Style*— Prof Andrew King; ✉ Department of Physiology, Anatomy and Genetics, Sherrington Building, University of Oxford, Parks Road, Oxford OX1 3PT (e-mail andrew.king@dpag.ox.ac.uk, website www.dpag.ox.ac.uk/team/group-leaders/andrew-king)

KING, Prof Anthony Stephen; s of Harold Stark King (d 1949), and Marjorie Mary, *née* James (d 1982); *b* 17 November 1934; *Educ* Queen's Univ Kingston Ontario (BA), Univ of Oxford (BA, DPhil); *m* 1, Vera Korte (d 1972); *m* 2, Janet Frances Mary, da of Adm of the Fleet Sir Michael Pollock, KGCB, DSO, of Churchstoke, Powys; *Career* fell Magdalen Coll Oxford 1961–65; Univ of Essex: sr lectr in govt 1966–67, reader 1967–69, prof 1969–, academic pro-vice-chllr 1986–89; fell Center for Advanced Study in the Behavioral Scis Stanford Calif 1977–78, visiting prof of public int affrs Princeton Univ 1984, hon foreign memb American Acad of Arts and Sciences 1993–; memb: Ctee on Standards in Public Life 1994–98, Royal Cmmn on Reform of House of Lords 1999; hon life fell RSA 2006; FBA 2010; *Books* Westminster and Beyond (with Anne Sloman, 1973), British Members of Parliament (1974), Why is Britain Becoming Harder to Govern? (ed, 1976), Britain Says Yes: The 1975 Referendum on the Common Market (1977), The British Prime Minister (ed, 2 edn 1985), The New American Political System (ed, 2 edn 1990), Britain at the Polls (ed, 1992), SDP: The Birth, Life and Death of the Social Democratic Party (with Ivor Crewe, 1995), Running Scared: Why America's Politicians Campaign Too Much and Govern Too Little (1997), New Labour Triumphs (ed, 1997), British Political Opinion 1937–2000: The Gallup Polls (ed, 2001), Does the United Kingdom Still Have a Constitution? (2001), Britain at the Polls 2001 (ed, 2001), Leaders' Personalities and the Outcomes of Democratic Elections (ed, 2002), Britain at the Polls, 2005 (ed, 2005), The British Constitution (2007), The Founding Fathers v the People: Paradoxes of American Democracy (2012), The Blunders of Our Governments (with Ivor Crewe, 2013), Who Governs Britain? (2015); *Recreations* music, holidays, friendship; *Style*— Prof Anthony King; ✉ Department of Government, University of Essex, Wivenhoe Park, Colchester, Essex CO4 3SQ (☎ 01206 873393, e-mail kinga@essex.ac.uk)

KING, Prof Bernard; CBE (2004); *b* 4 May 1946; *Educ* Synge St Christian Brothers Sch Dublin, Coll of Technol Dublin, Aston Univ (MSc, PhD); *m* 29 July 1970, Maura Antoinette, da of Mathew Collinge; 2 da (Madge b 5 Feb 1973, Sinead b 26 June 1977); *Career* pt/t lectr in microbiology Birmingham Poly 1970–72, research fell Aston Univ 1971–76; Dundee Coll of Technol: lectr in microbiology 1976–79, sr lectr 1979–83, head Dept of Molecular and Life Scis 1983–91, prof 1985–91, dean Faculty of Sci 1987–89; asst princ Robert Gordon Inst of Technol 1991–92, princ Dundee Inst of Technol 1992–94, princ and vice-chllr Univ of Abertay Dundee 1994–; memb: Universities UK (formerly CVCP), Ctee of Euro Rectors, Bd Cncl for Industry and Higher Educn, Higher Educn Acad; govr Unicorn Preservation Soc; FIWSc 1975, CBiol, FIBiol 1987, CCMI (CIMgt 1999); *Recreations* sailing, late medieval music, opera, reading; *Style*— Prof Bernard King, CBE; ✉ University of Abertay Dundee, Kydd Building, Bell Street, Dundee DD1 1HG (☎ 01382 308012, fax 01382 308011, e-mail b.king@abertay.ac.uk)

KING, Prof Christine Elizabeth; CBE (2007), DL (Staffs); da of late William Edwin King, and late Elizabeth, *née* Coates; *Educ* Univ of Birmingham (BA, MA), Cncl for National Academic Awards (PhD); *Career* teacher Southampton Sixth Form Coll 1967–70, lectr Preston Poly 1970–74, staff tutor Open Univ 1974–75; Univ of Central Lancs (formerly Lancs Poly): research asst 1975–78, successively lectr, sr lectr, princ lectr then head of history 1978–85, head Sch of Historical and Critical Studies 1985–87, dean Faculty of Arts 1987–90; Staffordshire Univ (formerly Staffordshire Poly): asst dir and dean Faculty of Business Humanities and Social Sciences 1990–92, pro-vice-chllr 1992–95, vice-chllr 1995–; Hon DLitt: Univ of Birmingham 1998, Univ of Portsmouth 2001; Hon DUniv: Derby 2001, Portsmouth 2001; Hon Dr (hc) Univ of Edinburgh 2005, Mensión de Honor Consejo Superior Europeo de Doctores ESERP Barcelona-Madrid 2007; hon fell Univ of Central Lancs 2001; CIMgt, FRSA, FRHistS; *Publications* author of numerous articles and chapters in books and learned jls incl: Resistance in Nazi Germany (Bulletin of John Rylands Library, Vol 70, No3, 1988), The Jehovah's Witnesses (chapter in A Mosaic of Victims: Non-Jews persecuted and murdered by the Nazis, 1990), His Truth Goes Marching On (chapter in Popular Culture and Pilgrimage, 1992), Through the Glass Ceiling: Effective Management Development for Women (ed 1993), The Student Experience (chapter in The Changing University, 1995), Making Things Happen (chapter in Managing Innovation and Change in Universities and Colleges, 1995), The Death of a King (chapter in The Changing Face of Death, 1997), Networking and Mentoring (chapter in Women as Leaders in Higher Education, 1997); *Style*— Prof Christine E King, CBE, DL; ✉ Staffordshire University, Beaconside, Stafford ST18 0AD (☎ 01785 353200, fax 01785 353230, e-mail c.e.king@staffs.ac.uk)

KING, Christopher John; s of Kavan John King, of New Malden, Surrey and Gwendoline June, *née* Kent (d 1985); *b* 15 October 1959; *Educ* KCS Wimbledon, Univ of Edinburgh; *m* 1989, Gayle Shiona, da of John Thomson, of Dollar, Clackmannanshire; 2 s (James Alexander b 4 Oct 1990, Thomas William b 20 July 1997), 1 da (Georgie Louisa b 10 Feb 1992); *Career* cmmnd Royal Regt of Fus 1978–; brand mangr Procter & Gamble Ltd 1982–84, account supervisor Ted Bates Advertising 984, account dir Grey

Advertising Ltd 1985–87, bd dir Jenner Keating Becker Reay 1989–91 (account dir 1987–88), Reay Keating Hamer 1991–94; Grey Advertising (formerly Mellors Reay and Ptnrs): joined as bd dir 1994, subsequently vice-chm, gp md 1998–; MIPA; *Style*— Christopher King, Esq; ✉ Grey Advertising, The Johnson Building, 77 Hatton Garden, London EC1N 8JS

KING, Danielle (Dani); MBE (2013); *b* 21 November 1990, Southampton, Hants; *Career* track and road cyclist; achievements incl: Gold medal (team pursuit) European Elite Championships 2011, Bronze medal (scratch) and Gold medal (team pursuit) World Championships 2011, Gold medal (team pursuit) World Championships 2012, Gold medal (team pursuit) Olympic Games 2012, Gold medal (team pursuit) World Championships 2013, Gold medal (team pursuit), Silver medal (points race) European Championships 2013; *Style*— Ms Dani King, MBE; ✉ c/o Steve Fry, M2 Sports Management, 4 Farriers Gate, Bassaleg, Newport NP10 8FX (e-mail steve@m2sportsmanagement.com)

KING, Prof Sir David Anthony; kt (2003); s of Arnold Tom Wallis King, of Johannesburg, South Africa, and Patricia Mary Bede, *née* Vardy; *b* 12 August 1939; *Educ* St John's Coll Johannesburg, Univ of the Witwatersrand (BSc, PhD), UEA (ScD), Univ of Cambridge (ScD); *m* 5 Nov 1983, Jane Margaret Lichtenstein (uses maiden name), da of Hans Lichtenstein, of Llandrindod Wells, Wales; 3 s (Benjamin Tom b 11 Nov 1973, Tobias Alexander b 15 Sept 1975, Zachary Adam b 17 Sept 1986), 1 da (Emily Sarah b 20 Feb 1984); *Career* Shell scholar Imperial Coll London 1963–66, lectr in chemical physics UEA 1966–74, Brunner prof of physical chemistry Univ of Liverpool 1974–88; Univ of Cambridge: 1920 prof of physical chemistry 1988–2005, head Dept of Chemistry 1993–2000, dir of research 2005–; fell St John's Coll Cambridge 1988–95, master Downing Coll Cambridge 1995–2000, fell Queens' Coll Cambridge 2001–08, chief scientific advsr to UK Govt and head Office of Sci and Innovation 2000–07, dir Smith Sch of Enterprise and the Environment Univ of Oxford and fell Univ Coll Oxford 2008–12, sr science advsr UBS 2008–13, chief scientific advsr to President Kagame of Rwanda 2009–13, Bd pres Collegio Carlo Alberto Turin 2009–12, chllr Univ of Liverpool 2010–13, UK foreign sec's special rep for Climate Change 2013–; pres AUT 1976–77; chm Leverhulme Tst Res Awards Advsy Ctee 1995–2000, memb Direction Ctee Fritz Haber Inst Berlin 1981–93; ed Chemical Physics Letters 1989–2001, chm Kettle's Yard (House and Art Gallery) Cambridge 1989–2000; pres Br Science Assoc 2008–09 (hon fell 2009), chair Bd Future Cities Catapult 2013–, dir Cambridge Kaspakas 2013–; Br Vac Cncl medal and award for research 1991, Greenpeace Business Lectr 2004, World Wildlife Fund Awareness Award 2004, Arthur W Adamson Award American Chemical Soc 2009; FInstP 1977 (MInstP 1967), FRSC 1974 (medal and award for surface chem 1978, Tilden lectr 1988–89, Liversidge lecture and medal 1997), FRS 1991 (Rumford medal and prize 2002), foreign fell American Acad of Arts and Sciences 2002; Officier dans l'ordre Legion d'Honeur 2009; *Publications* The Hot Topic (with Gabrielle Walker, 2008); numerous scientific pubns on the chemical physics of solid surfaces and gas/surface interactions and on science policy; *Recreations* art, photography; *Clubs* Athenaeum; *Style*— Prof Sir David King, FRS; ✉ 20 Glisson Road, Cambridge CB1 2HD

KING, Ian Ayliffe; s of Jack Edward King (d 1990), of Henley-on-Thames, Oxon, and Hilda Bessie King (d 2002); *b* 25 April 1939; *Educ* Bromsgrove Sch; *m* 1, 1963 (m dis 2004), Rosemary, *née* Wolstenholme; 4 c (Joanna b 1965 d 2010, Giles b 1966, Oliver b 1972, Philippa b 1977); m 2, 2004, Jane Margaret FitzGibbon, *née* Liddington; *Career* chartered accountant; ptnr Baker Tilly (formerly Chalmers Impey) 1968–2004 (nat chm HLB Kidsons 1992–2002); dir: E Walters (Ludlow) Ltd 1968–85, Baker & Sons (Margate) Ltd 1975–2010, Beoley Hall (1992) Ltd 2004–, V-Viz Ltd 2005–13, The All England Lawn Tennis Ground Ltd 1991–96, LTA Tst Ltd 1991–94, The Queen's Club Ltd 1993–2007, The South Birmingham Mental Health NHS Tst Ltd 1994–97, The Int Tennis Hall of Fame 1995–2005, ITF Ltd 1995–2005 (memb Fin Ctee, chm Women's Circuit Ctee, chm Constitutional Ctee, hon life cnsllr 2006–); tstee: Sir Barry Jackson Tst, The Jack Kendall Tennis Tst; govr Whitford Hall Sch 1973–90; LTA: memb Cncl 1981–, memb Bd of Mgmnt 1984–2004 (chm 1991–93), dep pres 1988–90, pres and chm Cncl 1991–93, int rep 1995–2004, dir Int and Professional Tennis Div Bd, chm Anti-Doping Ctee; memb Ctee of Mgmnt of the Championships Wimbledon 1987–2005; pres Herefordshire and Worcestershire LTA 2002– (memb Ctee 1969–, chm 1980–2002); Liveryman Worshipful Co of Chartered Accountants in England and Wales 1991; FCA 1962; *Recreations* tennis, cricket, theatre, travel; *Clubs* All England Lawn Tennis, Queen's, Barnt Green Tennis, Edgbaston Priory Tennis, The International Lawn Tennis Clubs of GB and Aust, Bromsgrove Tennis, Worcs CCC; *Style*— Ian King, Esq; ✉ 2 Beoley Hall, Beoley, Redditch, Worcestershire B98 9AL (☏ 01527 591548, fax 01527 597823, e-mail ian_a_king@hotmail.com)

KING, Ian Charles; *b* 28 December 1934; *Educ* UCS Hampstead, Bartlett Sch of Achitecture Univ of London (Dip Arch); *m* 1 (m dis); m 2, 5 Feb 1980, Nathalie Wareham, *née* Singh; *Career* architect in private practice 1964–, Ian C King Associates Architects; Freeman City of London 1981; Liveryman: Worshipful Co of Glass Sellers 1982, Worshipful Co of Chartered Architects 1988; RIBA 1960; *Recreations* lawn tennis, theatre, veteran cars; *Clubs* All England Lawn Tennis and Croquet, Hurlingham (past chm); *Style*— Ian C King, Esq; ✉ Flat 28, Sherwood Court, Riverside Plaza, Chatfield Road, London SW11 3UY; 5 St George's Court, 131 Putney Bridge Road, London SW15 2PA (☏ 020 8871 2022, fax 020 8871 2989, e-mail ian@iancking.co.uk)

KING, Jeremy Richard Bruce; OBE (2014); s of Charles Henry King (d 2003), and Molly, *née* Chinn; *b* 21 June 1954, Taunton, Somerset; *Educ* Christ's Hosp; *m* 9 Jan 1982, Debra Hauer; 2 da (Hannah b 16 April 1991, Margot b 1 June 1993), 1 s (Jonah b 30 May 1995); *Career* restaurateur; dir and prop (with Chris Corbin, OBE, *qv*) Caprice Holdings Ltd 1981–2003; restaurants opened incl: Le Caprice 1981, The Ivy 1990, J Sheekey 1998; dir and prop (with Chris Corbin): The Wolseley 2003–, St Alban 2007, The Delaunay 2011–; Caterer and Hotelkeeper Restaurateur of the Year 1993 (jtly); chm Tate Catering, memb Cncl Tate Modern, dir Tate Enterprises Ltd 2006–; *Clubs* Garrick, RAC; *Style*— Jeremy King, Esq, OBE; ✉ Rex Restaurant Associates, 170 Piccadilly, London W1J 9EJ (☏ 020 7647 1810, fax 020 7439 0420, e-mail jeremy.king@rexra.com)

KING, Prof John B; *Educ* MB BS, LRCP; *Career* hon sr lectr and hon conslt in orthopaedic and trauma surgery Sch of Med and Dentistry St Bartholomews, Royal London Hosp, Queen Mary Coll London, former dir Academic Dept of Sports Med The London Hosp Med Coll, hon conslt Sports Clinic The London Hosp; former chm Br Assoc of Sports Med, former sr examiner in sports med Worshipful Soc of Apothecaries, former external advsr to Bath Distance Learning Course for Doctors in Sports Med, former orthopaedic conslt to Nat Sports Centre Crystal Palace London; academic assoc The Univ of London Interdisciplinary Research Centre in Biomedical Materials, former memb Editorial Bd Int Jl of Orthopaedic Trauma; Robert Milne prize in orthopaedic and related subjects 1977, Br Orthopaedic Assoc Euro travelling fell 1977, Sir Roger Bannister Medal for Lifetime Services to Sport and Exercise Medicine; pres European Coll of Sport and Exercise Medicine (ECOSEP); hon fell Faculty of Sport and Exercise Medicine Royal Colls of Surgery Ireland; memb: Br Assoc for Surgery of the Knee (fndr memb), BMA, RSM, Br Orthopaedic Assoc, Int Soc of Arthroscopy, Knee Surgery and Orthopaedic Sports Medicine (ISAKOS), Euro Soc of Sports Traumatology, Knee Surgery and Arthroscopy; hon life memb Br Assoc of Sport and Exercise Medicine (BASEM); hon fell: Queen Mary Univ of London, Faculty of Sports Med Royal Coll of Medicine Ireland and RCSI, FSEM; FRCS, fell Inst of Sport and Exercise Medicine; *Publications* author of more than 100 pubns in learned jls and books; *Clubs* Athenaeum; *Style*— Prof John B King; ✉ The London Independent Hospital, Beaumont Square, London E1 4NL (☏ 020 7790 4405)

KING, Julian; CMG (2006); *b* 22 August 1964; *m* 1992, Lotte Knudsen; *Career* diplomat; joined FCO 1985, 3 then 2 sec Paris 1987, Luxembourg and The Hague 1991, 2 then 1 sec FCO 1992, private sec to Perm Under-Sec of State 1995, 1 sec then counsellor UK Rep Brussels 1998, counsellor and head of chancery UK Mission NY 2003, UK rep Political and Security Ctee Brussels 2004, head Cabinet to European Cmmr for Trade 2008, ambass to Ireland 2009–12; *Style*— Mr Julian King, CMG

KING, Justin Matthew; CBE (2011); s of Alan Sydney King, of Alton, Hants, and Elaine, *née* Adams; *b* 17 May 1961; *Educ* Tudor Grange Sch Solihull, Solihull Sixth Form Coll, Univ of Bath (BSc); *Children* 1 da, 1 s; *Career* univ sponsorship to Lucas Electrical Birmingham 1979–83; various positions Mars Confectionery incl: mfrg mangr 1983–84, servs buyer 1984–85, nat account mangr 1986–89; various positions Pepsi Cola International incl: sales devpt mangr Cyprus 1989–90, sales and mktg dir Egypt 1990; md Haagen-Dazs UK Ltd 1990–93, mktg dir Allied Maples (Div of Asda plc) 1993–94, product devpt dir Asda 1997–98 (dir of drinks and kiosks 1994–97), dep trading dir Asda plc 1998–2000, head of foods M&S 2000–03, chief exec J Sainsbury plc 2004–2014; vice-chm Terra Firma 2015; *Recreations* sailing; *Clubs* Hayling Island Sailing; *Style*— Justin King, Esq, CBE

KING, Laurence Richard; s of (Cecil) Francis Harmsworth King, of London, and Jenifer Mary, *née* Beckett; *b* 28 July 1955, Accra; *Educ* Winchester, Jesus Coll Cambridge (BA); *m* (m dis 2006), Caroline Monica Elizabeth Ann, *née* Schofield; 1 da (Elizabeth Margaret b 1998); *Career* Calmann & King Ltd (formerly John Calmann & Cooper Ltd until 1983): asst ed 1976–80, sales dir 1980, md 1983–2001; fndr Laurence King Publishing Ltd 1991; *Style*— Mr Laurence King; ✉ Laurence King Publishing, 361–373 City Road, London EC1V 1LR (☏ 020 7841 6900, fax 020 7841 6910, e-mail enquiries@laurenceking.com)

KING, Lindy; *Career* dir Peters Fraser & Dunlop until 2007, co-chair United Agents 2007–; clients incl Tara FitzGerald, Miriam Margolyes, OBE, Dougray Scott, Keira Knightley, Tom Hardy and Ewan McGregor, *qqv*; *Style*— Ms Lindy King; ✉ United Agents Ltd, 12–26 Lexington Street, London W1F 0LE

KING, Malcolm James Geoffrey; s of late Douglas James Edward King, of Hadley Wood, Herts, and late Betty Alice, *née* Martin; *b* 10 April 1945; *Educ* Harrow, Coll of Estate Mgmnt, Univ of Western Ontario (MBA); *m* 1, 6 June 1970 (m dis 2001), Jennifer Kate, da of Arthur Charles Rose; 1 da (Annabel Kate b 11 Jan 1973), 1 s (Oliver James b 25 March 1975); m 2, 2 May 2003, Dr Josephine Angela Emery, da of Jack Thomas; *Career* chartered surveyor Gerald Eve 1963–68; King & Co: joined 1968, head Investment Dept 1970, assoc 1972–75, ptnr 1975–88, jt sr ptnr 1988–94, sr ptnr 1994–2005, int chm 1994–2006; non-exec dir: Redrow plc 2004–10, Yatra Capital plc, C Le Masurier Ltd; Freeman City of London; Liveryman: Worshipful Co of Wheelwrights, Worshipful Co of Chartered Surveyors; FRICS; *Recreations* fly fishing, golf, shooting, stalking, flying, gardening; *Clubs* The Machrie, Essendon Country; *Style*— Malcolm King, Esq; ✉ Eversleigh Ltd, Marquis House, 68 Gt North Road, Hatfield, Hertfordshire AL9 5ER

K

KING, Martina; *née* Doyle; *b* 7 March 1961; *Educ* Bonus Pastor RC Sch Bromley Kent; *m* 1995, Simon King; *Career* personnel exec GLC 1980–82, telephone sales canvasser The Observer 1982–84; The Guardian 1984–93: classified sales exec 1984–86, display sales exec 1986–88, gp head (Display Sales) 1988–89, display sales mangr 1989–93; Capital Radio 1993–99: client sales dir Jan-Aug 1993, sales dir Aug 1993–94, station dir 1994–97, md 1997–99; md TSMS Gp Ltd 1999, md Yahoo! UK & Ireland 1999–2003, md country ops Yahoo! Europe 2003–04, ceo Featurespace 2012–; non-exec dir: Johnston Press plc 2003–, Capita Gp plc 2005–, IMD plc 2005–, Debenhams plc, Cineworld plc; chm Radio Advertising Bureau 2007–; memb Mayor's Cmmn on the Creative Industries London Devpt Agency; tstee: Help a London Child, Ahoy Centre; govr Woodbridge Sch 2007–; *Recreations* sport, music, family life and friends; *Style*— Mrs Martina King

KING, Mary Elizabeth; MBE (2013), DL (Devon 2016); da of late Lt Cdr Michael Dillon Harding Thomson, RN, and Patricia Gillian, *née* Hole; *b* 8 June 1961; *Educ* King's GS Ottery St Mary, Evendine Court Malvern (cordon bleu coll); *m* 1995, (Alan) David Henry King; 1 da (Emily Maria b Jan 1996), 1 s (Fredrick Arthur b Nov 1998); *Career* three day eventer; began with Axe Vale Pony Club, trained with Sheila Willcox 1977–80, fndr own yard 1981; achievements incl: winner Windsor Horse Trials 1988, 1989 and 1992, Br Open champion 1990, 1991, 1996 and 2007, team Gold medal European Championships 1991, winner Badminton Horse Trials 1992 and 2000 (runner-up 1989 and 1997), winner Althorp Maverick Championships 1993, team Gold medal and individual fourth place World Equestrian Games 1994, winner Punchestown and Compiègne Int Events 1995, team Gold medal and individual Bronze medal European Championships 1995, winner Burghley Horse Trials 1996, team Gold medal European Open Championships 1997, team Silver medal Olympic Games Athens 2004, team Silver medal World Equestrian Games 2006, team Gold and individual Silver European Championships 2007, team Bronze medal Olympic Games Beijing 2008, team Gold medal and individual Silver medal European Championships 2009, team Gold medal World Equestrian Games 2010, first and second Rolex Kentucky CCI**** 2011, winner HSBC FEI Classics 2011, team Silver medal Olympic Games London 2012; GB rep Olympic Games: Barcelona 1992, Atlanta 1996, Sydney 2000, Athens 2004, Beijing 2008, London 2012; ranked no 1 British event rider 1993, 1994 and 1997, ranked no 1 World event rider 2011, holds world record for consecutive three day event wins (5 in 1991–92); Sun Systems Outstanding Rider of the Year 1990, Animal Health Tsts Equestrian Personality of the Year 1991, The Times/Minet Supreme Award 1992; watch leader on the Sir Winston Churchill tall ship 1980, chalet girl Zermatt 1980–81; *Books* Mary Thomson's Eventing Year (1993), All the King's Horses (1997), William and Mary (1998), Mary King – My Way (2014); *Video* Mary Thomson – Rider of the World (1995), Mary King: The Autobiography (2011); *Recreations* tennis, snow and water skiing, deep sea diving; *Style*— Mrs David King, MBE, DL; ✉ Thorn House, Salcombe Regis, Sidmouth, Devon EX10 0JH

KING, Prof Michael Bruce; s of Bruce Eugene King, of Napier, NZ, and Patricia Alfredith, *née* Maxwell; *b* 10 February 1950; *Educ* Univ of Canterbury Christchurch (sr scholar in zoology, BSc), Sch of Med Univ of Auckland (sr scholar in med, Sims travelling Cwlth scholar, BSc, MB ChB, MD, sr prize for med), Univ of Aberdeen (Dip Health Economics), Univ of London (PhD); *Career* pre-registration/physicians trg Auckland 1976–77, GP trg Hammersmith Hosp 1978–81, trg in psychiatry Royal Bethlem and Maudsley Hosps 1981–84; Inst of Psychiatry: res worker/hon sr registrar 1984–86, clinical lectr/hon sr registrar 1986–88, sr lectr/hon conslt 1988–89, hon sr lectr 1989–; Dept of Psychiatry Behavioural Sciences Royal Free and UC Med Sch: sr lectr and hon conslt 1989–94, reader, hon conslt and head of dept 1994–96, prof and head of dept 1996–2004, head of Royal Free Campus mental health sciences 2004–09, dir mental health services 2009–; memb: Dept of Health's Expert Advsy Gp on AIDS 1992–98, AIDS Working Pty RCGP 1994–98, Cncl Section of Psychiatry RSM (past pres); memb: Educn Ctee RCPysch 1992–95, Steering Gp for the Mental Health Fndn/Dept of Health Sr Educnl Fellowship in Mental Health and Gen Practice 1993–97, Public Health and Health Services Research Bd MRC 1998–2002, Standing Ctee Assoc of Univ Teachers of Psychiatry, Primary Care Working Pty Mental Health Fndn, Nat Panel of Referees for the Nat Mental Health R&D Prog (NHS Mgmnt Exec), NIHR Clinical Evaluation and Trials Bd 2007–10; asst ed Jl of Psychosomatic Research 1990–93; memb Editorial Bd: Br Jl of General Practice 1993–99, Br Jl of Psychiatry; memb Int Editorial Bd AIDS Care; author of numerous original papers in learned jls; Dennis Hill Prize Maudsley Hosp/Inst of Psychiatry 1983; FRCGP 1991 (MRCGP), FRCP 1996 (MRCP), FRCPsych 2000 (MRCPsych); *Books* Male Victims of Sexual Assault (ed and jt author, 1992, 2 edn 2000), AIDS, HIV and Mental Health (1993); contrib: Eating Disorders and Disordered Eating (1988), The Scope of Epidemiological Psychiatry (1989), Epidemiology and the Prevention of Psychiatric Disorder (1989), The Public Health Impact of Mental Disorder (1990), Principles of Social Psychiatry (1993), Recent Advances in Clinical Psychiatry (1993), The Medical Annual 1993/94 (1993), Psychiatry and General Practice (1994), Research Foundations for Psychotherapy Research (1995), Assessment of Parenting (1995), Evidence Based Counselling and Psychological Therapies (2000), The Trauma of Sexual Assault: Treatment, Prevention and Policy (2002), Identity and Health (2004), Textbook of Men's Mental Health (2007), Handbook of Liaison Psychiatry (2007); *Recreations* swimming, running, languages; *Style*— Prof Michael King; ✉ Division of Psychiatry, Faculty of Brain Sciences, University College London Medical School, First Floor, Charles Bell House, 67–73 Riding House Street, London W1W 7EH (☎ 020 7679 9024, e-mail michael.king@ucl.ac.uk)

KING, (Austin) Michael Henry; s of Gerald King (d 1970), of Bath, and Pauline King, MBE, *née* Gillow; *b* 9 February 1949, Bath; *Educ* Stonyhurst Coll; *m* 18 Oct 1975, Frances-Anne, *née* Sutherland; 3 s (Edward John b 16 July 1978, Dominic Henry b 27 March 1982, Piers Michael Hugo b 27 Nov 1987); *Career* articled clerk Stone King & Wardle and Charles Russell & Co 1969–74, admitted slr 1974; Stone King (Bath and London): ptnr 1975–2014, opened London office 1990, head Charity Unit 1993–2010, sr ptnr and chm 1996–2014, conslt 2014–; 5 appts by Charity Cmmn as interim mangr of charities under investigation; memb Exec Ctee Charity Law Assoc 1993–2006 (chm 1997–2000), pres Bath Law Soc 2001–02; chm Catholic Charity Conf 1990–2015; several appts as tstee of charitable orgns and govr of schs incl tstee and hon sec Bath Royal Literary and Scientific Inst, chm Kilmersdon Rural Housing Assoc, govr Royal HS Bath, current positions incl chm British Hospitalité Tst, chm Prior Park Educnl Tst Bath, tstee Holburne Museum of Art, tstee Stone King Fndn; *Publications* The Charities Act Explained (2000), Charities Act 2006: A Guide to the New Law (2006); *Recreations* sailing, shooting, tennis, watching rugby; *Clubs* Lansdowne; *Style*— Michael King, Esq; ✉ Stone King LLP, Boundary House, 91 Charterhouse Street, London EC1M 6HR

KING, Eur Ing Prof Michael Stuart; s of Edward Roy King (d 1963), of Thornham, Norfolk, and Jessie Margaret, *née* Davis (d 1994); *b* 2 June 1931; *Educ* St Edward's Sch Oxford, Univ of Glasgow (BSc), Univ of Calif (MS, PhD); *m* 1, 9 June 1962 (m dis 1983), Margaret Helen Hoeschen, da of Theodore de Vassily Bujila (d 1979), of Montreal, Canada; 1 da (Sarah Bernadine Margaret b 1966), 2 s (Bernard John Edward b 1967, David Matthew Stuart b 1971); *m* 2, 21 Oct 1989, (Shirley) Georgina King, OBE, da of Dr the Hon Walter Symington Maclay (d 1963), of Newbury, Berks; *Career* prof of geological engrg Univ of Saskatchewan 1966–81, prof of mechanical engrg Univ of Calif Berkeley 1981–86, Phoebe Apperson Hearst distinguished prof 1986, oil industry prof of petroleum engrg Imperial Coll London 1986–96 (prof emeritus 1996, sr research fell 2001); FIMechE 1985, FGS 1985, Eur Ing 1991; *Recreations* field sports, music; *Style*— Eur Ing Prof Michael King; ✉ Cedar House, Hellidon, Daventry, Northamptonshire NN11 6GD (☎ 01327 261919, e-mail kinghellidon@gmail.com); Department of Earth Science and Engineering, Imperial College London, London SW7 2AZ (e-mail m.s.king@imperial.ac.uk)

KING, Mike; *b* 22 September 1962; *Educ* St Benedict's Ealing; *Career* photographer; progressively: jr in small sports photographic agency, with Allsport agency, chief sports photographer The Observer; currently with The Daily Telegraph; chair SJA Sports Photographer of the Year 2011 and 2012; official photographer to the commemorative London 2012 Olympic and Paralympic book, official photographer to the North Pole, Antarctic ice marathon and Tough Guy endurance event; Sports Cncl Black and White Photographer of the Year 1989, Nikon Sports Photographer of the Year 1989 and 1990, IAF Athletics Photographer of the Year, Sport England Sports Photographer of the Year 1999, Sport England Sports Picture of the Year 2001; *Recreations* cycling; *Style*— Mike King, Esq; ✉ 28 Beauval Road, London SE22 8UQ (☎ 020 8299 0484)

KING, Neil Gerald Alexander; QC (2000); s of Joseph King (d 2005), and Leila, *née* Saxton; *b* 14 November 1956, London; *Educ* Harrow, New Coll Oxford (MA); *m* 15 July 1978, Matilda, *née* Oppenheimer; 4 da (Dorothy b 2 April 1987, Hannah b 2 Dec 1988, Elsa b 17 April 1990, Lily b 2 Aug 1993); *Career* called to the Bar 1980; practising barr, currently head of chambers Landmark Chambers; memb Planning and Environment Bar Assoc; dir: Garsington Opera Ltd, Harrison Housing Ltd, Scarista House Ltd, White Lodge Properties Ltd; *Recreations* golf, walking, opera (especially Verdi), pianism; *Clubs* Isle of Harris Golf, Royal Jersey Golf, Huntercombe Golf, RAC, Army and Navy, Royal St George's; *Style*— Neil King, Esq, QC; ✉ The White House, Whitchurch-on-Thames, Reading RG8 7HA (☎ 0118 984 2800, fax 0118 984 1264, e-mail neil_ga_king@msn.com); Landmark Chambers, 180 Fleet Street, London EC4A 2HG (☎ 020 7421 1330, e-mail nking@landmarkchambers.co.uk)

KING, Robert John Stephen; s of Stephen King, of Wolverhampton, and Margaret Digby; *b* 27 June 1960; *Educ* Radley, St John's Coll Cambridge (MA); *m* Viola Scheffel; 1 s, 1 da; *Career* conductor and harpsichordist; dir The King's Consort (Baroque orch) 1980–; conductor and dir on over 100 records on Hyperion and Vivat; artistic dir ION Festival Nürnberg 2003–07; guest dir: New World, Seattle, Houston, Oregon, Detroit, Atlanta, National, Minnesota and Pacific Symphony Orchestras, Calgary Philharmonic, Manitoba Chamber Orchestra, Bergen Philharmonic, Danish Nat Radio, Stavanger, Malmo, Trondheim, Sondjelands, Norrkoping, Aarhus, Aalborg and Iceland Symphony Orchestras, RAI Nat Symphony Orchestra, Orchestra Verdi Milan, NDR, WDR, Hamburg and Muchich Radio Orchestras, Zurich Chamber Orchestra and RTSI Symphony, Monte Carlo Philharmonic, Nederlands Kamerorkest, Orquesta Cuidad de Barcelona, Orquesta de Navarra, Orquesta e Coro Ciudad de Madrid, Real Filharmonia de Galicia, Real Orquesta Sinfonica de Sevilla, Hong Kong Sinfonietta, Nederlands Kamerkoor, Orfen Donostiarra, Swiss Radio Choir, Collegium Vocale Ghent, BBC Singers; operatic work incl: Handel Ottone (Japan and UK), Handel Ezio (Paris), Purcell The Indian Queen (UK and Germany), Purcell The Fairy Queen (Spain and UK), Gluck Armide (Buxton Festival); concert tours: France, Holland, Belgium, Spain, Finland, Italy, Japan, Hong Kong, Mexico, Taiwan, Turkey, S America, USA; TV and radio appearances throughout Europe and the UK; film soundtracks incl: The Da Vinci Code, Pirates of the Caribbean, The Chronicles of Narnia, Kingdom of Heaven, Shrek 2; *Publications* Henry Purcell (1994), English Church Music Vol 1 (2010) and Vol 2 (2011); ed of much 1600–1750 music; *Recreations* skiing, lupin growing, Hebridean sheep farming; *Style*— Robert King, Esq; ✉ c/o The King's Consort, The Old Rectory, Alpheton, Suffolk CO10 9BT (e-mail info@tkcworld.org)

KING, Prof Roger Patrick; *b* 31 May 1945; *Educ* St Anselm's GS Birkenhead, St George's GS Hong Kong and Singapore, Wimbledon Coll, Univ of London (external BSc), Univ of Birmingham (MSc); *m*; *Career* exec offr Miny of Housing & Local Govt London 1963–64, sales mangr United Glass Ltd 1964–65, sales mangr Marley Tiles Ltd 1965–66; lectr then sr lectr in social science Manchester Poly 1970–75; princ lectr Dept of Behavioural Sciences Huddersfield Poly 1976–82 (head of dept 1982–85); Univ of Lincs and Humberside (Humberside Poly until 1992): dep dir (resources) 1985–89, dir and chief exec 1989–92, vice-chllr 1992–2000, personal professorship 1992–; visiting research prof Open Univ 2003–11, visiting research fell Assoc of Cwlth Univs 2003–, research assoc LSE 2007–, visiting prof Univ of Bath 2011–; chm Inst for Learning and Teaching 1997–2001;

Br Cncl: memb Ctee for Asia and the Oceans 1991–95, memb Ctee for Int Co-operation in Higher Educn 1991–; memb Funding Gp PCFC 1988–89, memb Libraries and Learning Resources Review Gp and chm Managing Libraries Sub-Gp HEFCE 1993–94, memb HEFCE Ctee on Learning and Teaching 1998–; Ctee of Dirs of Polys: memb Funding of Teaching Gp 1991–, memb Student Issues Gp 1992–; CVCP: memb Fin Ctee 1992–, memb European Ctee 1992–, memb Student Affairs Ctee 1992–; memb Exec Bd Poly and Colls Employers Forum 1992–, memb Cncl Humberside TEC 1991–; chm Int Centre for Mgmnt Educn Singapore 1992–; CNAA: memb Combined Studies (Social Sciences) Sub-Ctee 1985–88, memb Sociological Studies Bd 1984–88; memb: Political Studies Assoc, Soc for Research into HE, HE Cmmn 2013–; chair Bd of Govrs UK Coll of Business and Computing 2015–; author of numerous res papers and pubns; *Publications* Governing Universities Globally (2009), Handbook on Globalization of Higher Education (2013), Regulating Higher Education (2013); *Style*— Prof Roger King; ✉ Griffins, Hanging Birch Lane, Horam, Heathfield, East Sussex TN21 0BH (☎ and fax 01435 813443)

KING, Ronald Gordon; s of Basil Frederick Gordon King (d 1991), and Jacqueline Marie Catherine, *née* Timmermans (d 1994); *b* 31 December 1946; *Educ* Jesuit Coll Antwerp; *Career* ed: Viewpoint 1965–, The Keys of Peter 1969–, Warfare 1972–; librarian: The Times 1969–86, Today 1986–92, CSO Research 1992–; dir Christian Social Order; sec: Christian Centre Pty, Napoleon Soc, Pugin Gild; librarian Army and Navy Club 1969–99; *Books* Catholicism and European Unity (1980), Zionism and the Vatican (1981), Napoleon and Freemasonry (1985), NATO's First War (1999), Beria Was on Our Side (2001); *Style*— Ronald King, Esq; ✉ 157 Vicarage Road, London E10 5DU (☎ and fax 020 8539 3876, e-mail keys@fsmail.net)

KING, (Derek) Ross; s of David Johnston King, of Glasgow, and Isabel Moore McLeod, *née* Ross; *b* 21 February 1964; *Educ* Victoria Drive Secdy Sch Glasgow; *m* 30 May 1999, Helen Way; *Career* actor, radio and TV presenter; *Theatre* Franknfurter in The Rocky Horror Show, Wallace Spencer in Summer Holiday, Toby McWiry in Dick Whittington (Sadlers Wells), Fancourt Babberly in Charleys Aunt; others incl: She Stoops to Conquer, Guys and Dolls, Joseph, Butterfly Children, Life and Limb (LA, dir); pantomimes incl: Cinderella, Dick Whittington, Snow White, Jack and the Beanstalk, Mother Goose, Babes in the Wood; *Film* She Said I Love You, Do it for Uncle Manny, Comfort and Joy, The Girl in the Picture, Half Past Dead, The Day After Tomorrow; *Television* for BBC: Pebble Mill, The Ross King Show, The 8.15 from Manchester, Holiday, King of the Road, Summer in the City, Hot Chefs, Newshound, Pop Goes Summer, The Wetter the Better, CTV1; for ITV: Run the Gauntlet, My Secret Desire, Young Krypton, Quiz Night, Pick of the Week, Auto TX, Who's Into, Living It Up, The Calendar Fashion Show, Mini Champions; American Juniors (Fox TV); Living TV: Charmed: Behind the Magic, Will & Grace: Access All Areas, According to Jim: Access All Areas; *Radio* Ross King Show (Capital Radio), Ross King Show (Radio Clyde), Sportsbeat and various others incl Olympics (Radio 5), The Eurochart (ILR Network), Ok to Talk (Talk Radio), Ross King's Sportstars (Talk Radio), The King in LA; *Awards* Local Radio DJ of the Year Sony Radio Awards and Smash Hits, Sony Radio Award for outstanding sports presentation of Barcelona Olympics; *Recreations* sport, theatre, cinema; *Clubs* Ham Polo; *Style*— Ross King, Esq

KING, Prof Roy D; s of Leonard Stanley King (d 1991), of Potters Bar, Herts, and Helena, *née* Loe (d 1978); *b* 1 January 1940, Potters Bar; *Educ* Stationers' Co's Sch, Univ of Leicester (BA), Univ of Cambridge (DipCrim), LSE (PhD); *m* 20 Feb 1965, Janet MacDonald, *née* Price; 2 s (Simon Henry b 1970, Matthew David b 1974); *Career* res offr Inst of Social Psychiatry 1963–64, res offr Inst of Educn London 1964–67, lectr Univ of Southampton 1967–72, visiting fell Yale Law Sch 1972–73, sr lectr Univ of Southampton 1974–79, prof of social theory and instns Univ of Wales Bangor 1979–83, visiting prof Univ of Wisconsin 1983–84, prof of criminology and criminal justice Univ of Wales Bangor 1984–2004, sr res fell Inst of Criminology Cambridge 2004–; memb Parole Bd for Eng and Wales 1968–72 and 2001–07; conslt: Amnesty Int, Netherlands Helsinki Ctee, Cncl of Europe; memb: Br Soc of Criminology, American Soc of Criminology; *Books* Patterns of Residential Care (1970), A Taste of Prison (1975), Albany: Birth of a Prison – End of an Era (1977), Future of the Prison System (1981), Prisons in Context (1994), The State of Our Prisons (1995), Doing Research on Crime and Justice (2007); *Recreations* family, walking, running, cycling, piano, opera; *Style*— Prof Roy King

KING, Stephen Daryl; s of Harold King, and Joan, *née* Squire; *b* 19 November 1963; *Educ* Vyners GS Ickenham, New Coll Oxford (BA), DipABRSM; *m* 1991, Yvonne Miriam, da of Maurice Nathan; 3 da (Helena Rachel b 1993, Olivia Esther b 1995, Sophie Leah b 1997); *Career* economist HM Treasy 1985–88; James Capel: Euro economist 1988–89, Japanese economist 1989–92, dep chief economist 1992–96, chief Euro economist 1996–98; group chief economist HSBC plc 1998–; memb Shadow Cncl European Central Bank 2007–10; columnist The Independent 2001–12, columnist The Times 2012–; memb Financial Times A List 2012–14, memb Financial Times Exchange 2014–; *Books* EMU: Four Endings and a Funeral (1996), Strainspotting: Moving to a Single European Interest Rate (1997), Bubble Trouble: The US Bubble and How It Will Burst (1999), Decline and Fall: Bubbles, Busts and Deflation (2002), The Consumer Takes it All (2002), Thinking the Unthinkable (2003), The Lucky and the Losers (2004), China, the Renminbi and the World Financial Order (2005), Global Imbalances: Economic Myth and Political Reality (2006), Money Makes the World Go Round (2007), Losing Control: The Emerging Threats to Western Prosperity (2010), The Southern Silk Road (2011), When the Money Runs Out: The End of Western Affluence (2013); *Recreations* music, playing piano, cooking, travelling, Chelsea FC; *Clubs* Groucho; *Style*— Stephen King, Esq; ✉ HSBC Bank plc, Level 40, 8 Canada Square, London E14 5HQ (☎ 020 7991 6700, fax 020 7992 4864, e-mail stephen.king@hsbcib.com)

KING, Stephen James (Steve); s of Joseph Henry King, of Leicester, and Jean, *née* Bond; *b* 11 September 1956; *Educ* Bosworth Upper Sch, Charles Keene Coll Leicester (OND); *m* 14 July 1984, Philippa Jane, da of George Walter Lay; 1 s (James b 21 May 1992); *Career* presenter and prodr: Loughborough Hosp Broadcasting 1978–81, University Radio Loughborough 1978–81, Centre Radio Leicester 1981–83; Viking Radio Hull: joined as presenter 1984, head of music Viking Radio 1985–88, presentation controller 1988–89, prog controller 1989–91, also gen mangr Viking FM 1990–91; prog controller Hallam FM Sheffield, Yorks regnl prog controller Metro Radio Group plc (parent co of Viking Radio and Radio Hallam, and others) 1993–, prog dir Radio Hallam Ltd 1993–96, md Radio Aire Ltd (parent co of 96.3 Aire FM and magic 828, pt of Emap Radio Ltd) 1996–; dir GE Digital Ltd 1998–; *Recreations* national economics, football, cycling; *Style*— Steve King, Esq; ✉ Radio Aire Ltd, 51 Burley Road, Leeds LS3 1LR (☎ 0113 245 2299, fax 0113 244 0445)

KING, Thomas George (Tom); s of Thomas Herbert King (d 1974), of Cambridge, and Cecilia Edith, *née* Tromp (d 1986); *b* 21 May 1938; *Educ* Perse Sch Cambridge, Royal Sch of Mines Imperial Coll London (BSc, ARSM, Inst of Petroleum Prize 1958); *m* Jan 1960, Judith Mary Clarke; 2 s (Aivars Thomas b Feb 1961, Warwick Ralph b July 1962), 1 da (Tania Ann b Nov 1963); *Career* Shell Group of Cos 1960–66; Gulf Oil Corp 1966–82: Kuwait Oil Co 1966–74, gen mangr Zaïre Gulf Oil 1974–78, mangr planning 1978–79, vice-pres and gen mangr Cabinda Gulf Oil 1979–82; dir of ops Burmah Oil 1984–86 (gen mangr UK 1982–84), pres and chief exec Trafalgar House Oil and Gas Inc 1986–87; LASMO plc: dir Prodn 1988–89, dir Exploration and Prodn 1990–93, dir New Business 1993–97, non-exec dir 1997–99; non-exec chm: Pipeline Engineering plc 1997–2004, Metoc plc 1997–2010 (conslt 2010–); memb Soc of Petroleum

Engrs (SPE), FGS, FInstPet, FInstD; Chevalier de l'Ordre National du Zaïre; *Recreations* rugby, cricket, boating; *Clubs* Royal Lymington Yacht, Lentune Probus (chm); *Style—* Tom King, Esq; ✉ mobile 07753 608942, e-mail thomasgking@btinternet.com or thomas.king@quarrmeadow.co.uk

KING, Hon Mr Justice; Sir Timothy Roger Alan King; kt (2007); s of Harold Bonsal King (d 1992), of Liverpool, and Dorothy, *née* Watts; *b* 5 April 1949; *Educ* Liverpool Inst (Margaret Bryce scholar), Lincoln Coll Oxford (MA, BCL); *m* 7 June 1986, Bernadette Tracy, *née* Goodman; *Career* called to the Bar Lincoln's Inn 1973 (bencher 2000), practising barr Northern Circuit 1973–2007, QC 1991, recorder 1991–2007, judge of the High Court of Justice (Queen's Bench Div) 2007–; *Recreations* travel; *Clubs* Liverpool Athenaeum; *Style—* The Hon Mr Justice King; ✉ Royal Courts of Justice, Strand, London WC2A 2LL

KING, His Hon Timothy Russell; s of Charles Albert King (d 1988), and Elizabeth Lily, *née* Alexander (d 1996); *b* 4 June 1946; *Educ* St Mary's Coll Southampton, Inns of Court Sch of Law; *m* 1, 1973 (m dis 1979); 2 s (Anthony Laurence b 25 Nov 1973, Gregory James b 14 Oct 1974); m 2, 1989, Rotraud (Jane) Webster-King, da of Wilhelm Karl Oppermann (d 1994), of Hannover, Germany; *Career* HM Dip Service (Colonial Office) 1966–67; called to the Bar Gray's Inn 1970; in practice 1971–86, dep judge advocate 1986–90, asst judge advocate-gen 1990–95, asst recorder 1989–93, recorder of the Crown Court 1993–95, circuit judge (South Eastern Circuit) 1995–2012; legal memb Mental Health Review Tbnl 2002–; chm Advsy Ctee on Conscientious Objectors 2008–, memb Public Chairs Forum 2010– (memb Mgmnt Ctee 2011–); pres St Leonard's Soc 1998–2006; *Recreations* skiing, classical music, reading, walking, cooking and (occasional) golf; *Clubs* Royal London Yacht (Cowes), Osborne Golf; *Style—* His Hon Timothy King

KING OF BOW, Baroness (Life Peer UK 2011), of Bow in the London Borough of Tower Hamlets; Oona Tamsyn King; da of Prof Preston King, *qv*, and Hazel King; *b* 22 October 1967; *Educ* Haverstock Comp, Univ of York (BA), Univ of Calif Berkeley (scholar); *m* 15 July 1994, Tiberio Santomarco, s of Tulio Santomarco; 2 s (Elia b 25 June 2005, Tullio Jahan b 10 Oct 2013), 2 da (Kaia b 31 Aug 2007, Ariel b 27 Aug 2011); *Career* researcher (Socialist Gp) Euro Parliament 1990–91, political asst to Glyn Ford, MEP 1991–93, memb John Smith's Campaign team 1992, freelance speech writer 1993–94, political asst to Glenys Kinnock, MEP 1994–95, TU organiser GMB 1995–97, MP (Lab) Bethnal Green and Bow 1997–2005; PPS to Stephen Timms, MP 2003–05; PPS to Patricia Hewitt 2003–05; memb Select Ctee on Int Devpt 1997–2001, memb Select Ctee DTLR 2001–05 (memb Urban Affrs Sub-Ctee); chair All-Pty Parly Gp on Rwanda, the Great Lakes and the Prevention of Genocide, vice-chair All-Pty Gp on Bangladesh 1997–2005; chair Lab Campaign for Electoral Reform, vice-chair London Lab Gp of MPs; sr advsr to the PM 10 Downing St 2007–09, diversity exec Channel 4 2009–; House of Lords: shadow educn min 2014–, whip's office 2014–, shadow equalities spokesperson 2014–; chair Rich Mix Cultural Fndn 2000–10; vice-chair Br Cncl 2000–02; treas All-Pty Parly Gp of the Friends of Islam House of Commons; patron Progress; memb: Amnesty International, Jewish Cncl for Racial Democracy, One World, 1990 Trust, Fabian Soc, Campaign for Electoral Reform, Britain in Europe; tstee Tower Hamlets Youth Sports Fndn 2013–; hon degree Univ of Sussex 2013; *Books* House Music – the Oona King Diaries (2007, e-book 2013); *Recreations* cinema, music, travel, ice skating; *Style—* The Baroness King of Bow; ✉ House of Lords, London SW1A 0PW

KING OF BRIDGWATER, Baron (Life Peer UK 2001), of Bridgwater in the County of Somerset; Thomas Jeremy (Tom) King; CH (1992), PC (1979); s of John H King, JP, of Langford, Somerset; *b* 13 June 1933; *Educ* Rugby, Emmanuel Coll Cambridge; *m* 1960, (Elizabeth) Jane, 3 and yst da of late Brig Robert Tilney, CBE, DSO, TD, DL, Lord of the Manor of Sutton Bonington (maternal gs of Sir Ernest Paget, 1 Bt); 1 s, 1 da; *Career* Nat Serv Somerset LI and King's African Rifles (Tanganyika and Kenya), formerly with E S & A Robinson Ltd Bristol (rising to div gen mangr), chm Sale Tilney & Co 1971–79 (dir 1965–79); MP (Cons) Bridgwater 1970–2001; PPS: to Min of Posts and Telecommunications 1970–72, to Min for Industrial Devpt 1972–74; vice-chm Cons Parly Industry Ctee 1974; oppn front bench spokesman on: industry 1975–76, energy 1976–79; min of state for local govt and environmental servs DOE 1979–83; sec of state for: environment Jan-June 1983, transport June-Oct 1983, employment Oct 1983–85, Northern Ireland 1985–1989, defence 1989–1992; chm Intelligence and Security Ctee 1994–2001, memb House of Lords Select Ctee on Communications, memb House of Lords Select Ctee on the Inquiries Act 2005; memb Ctee on Standards in Public Life 1994–97; dir London Int Exhbn Centre (ExCel); *Style—* The Rt Hon the Lord King of Bridgwater, CH, PC

KING OF LOTHBURY, Baron (Life Peer UK 2013), of Lothbury in the City of London; Prof Mervyn Allister King; KG (2014), GBE (2011); s of Eric Frank King, and Kathleen Alice, *née* Passingham; *b* 30 March 1948; *Educ* Wolverhampton GS, King's Coll Cambridge (MA); *Career* jr res offr Dept of Applied Economics (memb Cambridge Growth Project) 1969–73, Kennedy scholarship Harvard Univ 1971–72; Univ of Cambridge: res offr Dept of Applied Economics 1972–76, fell and dir studies St John's Coll 1972–77, lectr Faculty of Economics 1976–77; Esmée Fairbairn prof of investment Univ of Birmingham 1977–84, prof of economics LSE 1984–95; Bank of England: chief economist 1991–98, exec dir 1991–98, dep govr 1998–2003, govr 2003–13; prof of economics and law NYU 2014–, school prof of economics LSE 2015–; visiting prof of economics: Harvard Univ 1982–83 and 1990, MIT 1983–84; visiting fell Nuffield Coll Oxford 2002–; pres Euro Economic Assoc 1993, pres IFS 1999–2003; chm Interim Financial Policy Ctee 2011–13, vice-chair Systemic Risk Bd 2011–; memb: Prog Ctee Econometric Soc Congress 1974, 1979, 1985, Meade Ctee on Taxation (sec) 1975–78, CLARE Gp 1976–85, Editorial Bd Jl of Industrial Economics 1977–83, Economics Ctee ESRC 1980–82, Cncl and Exec Ctee Royal Economic Soc 1981–86, Res Ctee ENSAE Paris 1985–88, Economic Policy Panel 1985–86 and 1990–91, Bd The Securities Assoc 1987–89, City Capital Markets Ctee 1989–91; res assoc NBER 1978–, co-dir ESRC Res Prog on Taxation Incentives and Distribution of Income LSE 1979–89, research fell Centre for Economic Policy Res 1984–, co-dir (with C Goodhart) Financial Markets Gp LSE 1987–91; asst ed Economic Jl 1974–75, managing ed Review of Economic Studies 1978–83, assoc ed Jl of Public Economics 1982–98, memb Editorial Bd American Economic Review 1985–88, chm Soc of Econ Analysis 1984–86; Walras-Bowley lectr Econ Soc 1987, Review of Economics lectr Cambridge 1986, assoc memb Inst of Fiscal and Monetary Policy Miny of Fin Japan 1986–91; conslt: NZ treasy 1979, OECD 1982, Royal Cmmn on Distribution of Income and Wealth 1975; tstee Kennedy Meml Tst 1990–2000; res fell INSEE Paris 1977, hon res fell UCL 1977–79; Helsinki Univ medal 1982; hon degrees: London Guildhall Univ 2001, City Univ 2002, Univ of Birmingham 2002, LSE 2003, Univ of Wolverhampton 2003, Univ of Edinburgh 2005, Univ of Helsinki 2006, Univ of Cambridge 2006, Univ of Worcester 2008, Univ of Abertay Dundee 2013; FBA 1992; *Books* Indexing for Inflation (ed with T Liesner, 1975), Public Policy and the Corporation (1977), The British Tax System (with J A Kay, 1978, 5 edn 1990), The Taxation of Income from Capital: A Comparative Study of the US, UK, Sweden and West Germany (with D Fullerton et al, 1984), The End of Alchemy (2016), author of numerous articles; *Clubs* Brooks's, Garrick, Athenaeum, All England Lawn Tennis and Croquet; *Style—* The Lord King of Lothbury, KG, GBE; ✉ House of Lords, London SW1A 0PW (e-mail office@mervynking.com)

KING OF WEST BROMWICH, Baron (Life Peer UK 1999), of West Bromwich in the County of West Midlands; Tarsem King; JP (West Bromwich 1987); s of Ujagar Singh, of Kultham, Punjab, India, and Dalip Kaur; *b* 24 April 1937; *Educ* Khalsa HS Dosanjh Kalan, Univ of India (BA), Nat Foundry Coll (Dip Foundry Technol and Mgmnt), Aston Univ (Postgrad Dip Mgmnt Studies), Teacher Trg Coll Wolverhampton (Teacher's Cert), Univ of Essex (MSc); *m* 1957, Mohinder Kaur, da of Gurdev Singh, and Satwant Kaur; 1 s (Hon Rajinder Singh b 1972); *Career* lab asst 1960–62, foundry trainee 1964–65, teacher 1968–74 (dep head of mathematics 1974–90), md Sandwell Polybags Ltd 1990–2007; sits as Labour Peer in House of Lords; dep ldr Sandwell Cncl 1992, ldr Sandwell MBC 1997–2000, mayor of Sandwell 2001 (dep mayor 1982); chm West Bromwich Town Ctee 2002–07; tstee S Staffs Water Disconnections Charitable Tst, vice-pres West Bromwich and District YMCA; Hon Alderman Met Borough of Sandwell, Hon Freeman Met Borough of Sandwell; Hon PhD Univ of Wolverhampton; *Recreations* reading, music; *Style—* The Rt Hon the Lord King of West Bromwich; ✉ House of Lords, London SW1A 0PW (☎ and fax 0121 532 5688)

KING-FARLOW, Charles Roderick; s of Roderick Sydney King-Farlow (d 1988), and Alice Frances Joan, *née* Ashley (d 1988); *b* 16 February 1940; *Educ* Eton, Trinity Coll Oxford (MA); *m* 1965, Tessa King-Farlow, *qv*, da of Robert Lawrence Raikes (d 1989); 1 da (Alice Caroline 1968), 1 s (Joshua Michael b 1971); *Career* admitted slr 1965; ptnr Pinsent Curtis (formerly Pinsent & Co) 1969–2001; dir ISS UK Ltd 1969–2001; conslt Martineau Johnson 2002–08, conslt Pemberton Greenish 2009–11; pres Birmingham Law Soc 1991–92; vice-pres Fedn of European Bars 1992–93; Law Soc: hon auditor 1995–97, memb Audit Ctee 1997–99; chm Midlands Arts Centre 1985–89, chm Clent Hills Ctee of the Nat Tst 2000–09, chm John Feeney Charitable Tst 2013–16; memb: CBSO Cncl of Mgmnt 1972–80, Taxation Ctee of Historic Houses Assoc 1980–2011, Friends of Birmingham Museums and Art Gallery Ctee 1972–78 and 1983–88, Bd Birmingham Opera Co 1987–92 and 1999–2010, Public Art Cmmns Agency 1990–2000; tstee The Wye and Usk Fndn 1997–2012; *Recreations* bridge, fishing, skiing; *Clubs* Athenaeum, Midland Flyfishers; *Style—* Charles King-Farlow, Esq

KING-FARLOW, Tessa; da of Robert Lawrence Raikes (d 1989), and Cilla, *née* Brierley (d 2004); *b* 2 February 1941, Aldershot, Hants; *Educ* Downe House, Univ of Birmingham (BA); *m* 1965, Charles Roderick King-Farlow, *qv*; 1 da (Alice Caroline b 1968), 1 s (Joshua Michael b 1971); *Career* garden designer; chair Birmingham Royal Ballet 2004–09 (memb Bd 1991–2003); govr: Royal Ballet Sch 1997–2002, Elmhurst Sch for Dance 2002–04; memb: Advsy Ctee Birmingham Botanical Gardens 1982–2000, Bd City of Birmingham Touring Opera 1990–2001, Bd Ikon Gallery 1992–2001, Bd Kings Norton Community Devpt Tst 2002–04; chair Cncl of Birmingham Cathedral 2003–04; tstee Music in May St Ives 2008–11, tstee Sacconi Tst 2011–, tstee ROH Benevolent Fund 2011– (chm 2013–); JP Birmingham Bench 1981–2001, High Sheriff W Midlands 2001–02; Hon DMus Univ of Birmingham 2009; *Recreations* gardening, travel, performing arts, visual arts; *Style—* Mrs Tessa King-Farlow; ✉ e-mail tessa@king-farlow.com

KINGARTH, Rt Hon Lord; Hon Derek Robert Alexander Emslie; PC (2006); 2 s of Baron Emslie, MBE, PC (Life Peer) (d 2002); bro of Hon Nigel Hannington Emslie (Hon Lord Emslie) and Dr the Hon Richard Emslie, *qqv*; *b* 21 June 1949; *Educ* Edinburgh Acad, Trinity Coll Glenalmond, Gonville & Caius Coll Cambridge (BA, history scholar), Univ of Edinburgh (LLB); *m* 1974, Elizabeth Jane Cameron, da of Andrew Maclaren Carstairs; 3 c; *Career* advocate, QC (Scot 1987); standing jr counsel DHSS 1979–87, standing jr counsel MDDUS 1980–87, advocate depute 1985–88, pt/t chm Pension Appeal Tbnl 1988–95, pt/t chm Medical Appeal Tbnl 1990–95; vice-dean Faculty of Advocates 1995–97, senator of the Coll of Justice 1997–; *Style—* The Rt Hon Lord Kingarth; ✉ Supreme Courts, Edinburgh EH1 1RQ

K

KINGDOM, David; s of Eric Kingdom, of Scarborough, N Yorks, and Patricia Anne Kingdom; *b* 26 May 1955, Hull; *Educ* Riley HS Hull, Hull Sch of Architecture (DipArch), Leeds Met Univ (Dip Arbitration and Construction Law); *m* 1987 (m dis); 1 s (Louis Michael Alexander b 25 March 1990); *Career* architect: Br Rail Chief Architect's Dept York 1974–84, Deutsche Bundesbahn Architekten Frankfurt 1984–85, Fitzroy Robinson Partnership 1985–87, Abbey Hanson Rowe Huddersfield 1987–99; ptnr Abbey Holford Rowe Manchester 1999–2002, dir Aedas Architects Manchester and London 2002–12 (ptnr 1994–2012, conslt dir 2012–), chm Kingdom Architects + Planners Ltd Guernsey, currently dir InstaSnitch Ltd (smartphone customer service app provider); dir Bd Br Aviation Gp 2008–14; pres Guernsey Soc of Architects 2015–; memb Interact Construction Club (past chm); RIBA 1982, MAPM 1994, ACIArb 1999, MCMI; *Recreations* fell walking, horse riding, airport planning and design; *Clubs* Manchester Interact Soc, Br Aviation Gp, East India, Guernsey Soc of Architects; *Style—* David Kingdom, RIBA; ✉ Kingdom Architects + Planners Ltd, Somerville House, 31 Mount Row, St Peter Port, Guernsey GY1 1NU (☎ 01481 713440, mobile 07831 217775, e-mail kingdom@kingdomarchitecture.com, websites www.kingdomarchitecture.com and www.instasnitch.com)

KINGHAM, Richard; s of James Richard Kingham (d 1977), and Loretta Catherine Kingham; *b* 2 August 1946, Lafayette, IN, USA; *Educ* Woodward Sch Washington DC, George Washington Univ (BA, tstee scholar), Univ of Virginia Sch of Law (JD, Order of the Coif); *m* 6 July 1968, Justine, *née* McClung; 1 s (Richard Patterson b 4 Nov 1987); *Career* memb DC Bar 1973, registered foreign lawyer England & Wales 1993; editorial asst Washington Star 1964–68 and 1969–70; US Army 1968–69; Virginia Govr's Cncl on the Environment 1971; Covington & Burling: assoc Washington 1973–81, ptnr 1981–, coordinator Food and Drug Practice Gp Washington 1981–84, managing ptnr London office 1996–2000, memb Mgmnt Ctee 2000–04, coordinator Life Sciences Industry Gp 2001–, coordinator Industry, Regulatory and Legislative Umbrella Gp 2005–15; lectr Univ of Virginia Sch of Law 1977–90, lectr in grad prog of pharmaceutical med Cardiff Univ 1998–2016, adjunct prof Georgetown Univ Law Centre 2003–; memb Ctee: Inst of Med Nat Acad of Sciences USA, Nat Advsy Allergy and Infectious Diseases Cncl Nat Insts of Health USA, Dean's Cncl and Business Advsy Cncl Univ of Virginia Sch of Law; memb Clinical Trials and Regulatory Pathways for Neglected Diseases Working Party Center for Global Development 2010–11; rapporteur China Drug Administration Law Initiative Pharmaceutical Law Institute Tsinghua Univ Law Sch Beijing, advsr Health Policy Initiative on Drug Regulatory Reforms Indian Cncl for Research on Int Economic Relations New Delhi 2013–; author of numerous articles in professional jls; Distinguished Service and Leadership Award US Food and Drug Law Inst 2013; *Books* Global Pharmacovigilance Laws and Regulations (US chapter, 2009), Practical Guide to Food and Drug Law and Regulation (international chapter, 4 edn 2012), Life Sciences Law Review (gen ed and US chapter, 2013); *Recreations* vertebrate palaeontology; *Clubs* Reform; *Style—* Richard Kingham, Esq; ✉ Covington & Burling LLP, 265 Strand, London WC2R 1BH (☎ 020 7067 2000, e-mail rkingham@cov.com)

KINGHAN, Neil; CB (2005); s of Derek Kinghan (d 1991), and Esmé, *née* Webb (d 2014); *b* 20 August 1951; *Educ* Brentwood Sch, Hertford Coll Oxford (MA, MPhil), UCL (MA); *m* 1994, Dr Lilian Pusavat; *Career* DOE: private sec to Parly Under Sec 1978–80, princ 1980–87, private sec to Mins of Housing Ian Gow, John Patten and Michael Howard 1984–87, head Sport and Recreation Div 1987–90, head Homelessness Policy Div 1990–92, dir Housing Policy and Private Sector 1992–94, dir Departmental Task Force 1994–96, dir Local Govt Fin Policy 1996–97; Local Govt Assoc: dir of local govt fin 1997–2001, dir Econ and Environmental Policy Div 2002–03; DG Local and Regnl Governance Gp then Fire and Resilience Gp Dept for Communities and Local Govt (formerly ODPM) 2003–07; conslt: Essex CC 2007–08, Salops CC 2008–09; chm Fire Service Coll 2008–09, DG Equality and Human Rights Cmmn 2009–10; advsr Assoc of Chief Execs of Voluntary Orgns 2011–13, conslt Executive Action until 2013, ind reviewer of the Riot (Damages) Act 1886 for the Home Office until 2013; review of riot in Clapham Junction for Wandsworth Cncl 2011; currently PhD student of US history UCL; FRSA 2007–15; *Recreations* cricket, skiing, buying books; *Clubs* Surrey CC, Athenaeum; *Style—* Neil Kinghan, Esq, CB

KINGHORN, Prof George Robert; OBE (2012); s of Alan Douglas Kinghorn, of Allendale, Northumberland, and Lilian Isobel, *née* Henderson; *b* 17 August 1949, South Shields, Co Durham; *Educ* Royal GS Newcastle upon Tyne, Univ of Sheffield (MB ChB, MD); *m* 14 July 1973, Sheila Anne, da of Haydn Wilkinson Littlewood, of Sheffield; 1 s (Robert b 1978), 1 da (Joanne b 1982); *Career* trg in gen med Royal Hosp and Royal Infirmary Sheffield 1972–76, sr registrar in genito-urinary med Royal Infirmary Sheffield 1976–78, conslt in genito-urinary med General Infirmary Leeds 1979–; dir S Yorks Comprehensive Local Research Network 2011–, dir NIHR S Yorks Clinical Research Network 2011–14; Univ of Sheffield: sr clinical lectr i/c Sub-Dept of Genito-Urinary Med 1979–2005, hon prof of genito-urinary med 2005–; Sheffield Teaching Hosps NHS Fndn Tst: conslt physician in genito-urinary med 1979–2013, clinical dir of communicable diseases 1991–2010, conslt advsr on clinical research 2014–; WHO conslt: Sri Lanka 1985, Tunisia 1987; EEC conslt Kenya 1988; chm Advsy Sub-Ctee on Genito-Urinary Med Trent Region 1989–93 (memb 1978–, vice-chm 1985–89), memb Trent Regnl Med Ctee 1989–93; chm: Special Advsy Ctee in Genito-Urinary Med 1986–87 (memb 1981–84, sec 1984–86), Regnl Educn Ctee Genito-Urinary Med 1993–97, Ctee on Genito-Urinary Med RCP 1991–95 (memb 1983–86, hon sec 1986–90), Herpes Simplex Panel 2003–08; hon sec Br Co-operative Clinical Gp 1983–93 (chm 1996–99); memb: Clinical Medicine Bd RCP 1994–95, PHLS STI/HIV Ctee 1996–2002, Nat Ctee Providers of AIDS Care and Treatment (PACT) 1996–, MRC Ctee on Epidemiological Studies in AIDS (CESA) 1998–2002, Exec Ctee Br HIV Assoc 1999–2001, Jt Liaison Ctee on GU Med RCP 1999–2001, Nat Sexual Health and HIV Strategy Working Gps 1999–2001, MRC Sexual Health and HIV Research Ctee 2003–, Ind Advsy Gp in Sexual Health and HIV 2003–10, Coll of Experts 2006–; tstee: Med Fndn for AIDS and Sexual Health (MedFASH) 2002–, Br Assoc for Sexual Health and HIV (BASHH) 2003–; memb Editorial Bd: Int Jl of STD and AIDS 1990–, Sexually Transmitted Infections 1990–2012; Freeman City of London 2011; memb: Med Soc for Study of Venereal Diseases 1976– (pres 1999–2001, tstee 1999–2003), E Midlands Soc of Physicians 1979–, Assoc of Genito-Urinary Medicine; MRCP 1986, FRCP 1988; *Publications* author of 3 books, 48 book chapters and over 250 peer reviewed publications; *Recreations* travel, gardening, home computers, sport; *Clubs* Royal Soc of Med, Soc of Apothecaries; *Style—* Prof George Kinghorn, OBE; ✉ e-mail g.r.kinghorn@virgin.net, g.r.kinghorn@sheffield.ac.uk, george.kinghorn@sth.nhs.uk

KINGSHOTT, (Albert) Leonard; s of Albert Leonard Kingshott, of Ingatestone, Essex, and Katherine Bridget, *née* Connelley; *b* 16 September 1930; *Educ* LSE (BSc); *m* 10 Aug 1957, Valerie, da of Ronald Simpson (d 1964); 1 da (Nicola b 1958), 2 s (Adrian b 1960, Brendan b 1962); *Career* RAF (FO) 1952–55; fin analyst BP Corp 1955–59, economist British Nylon Spinners 1960–62, fin mangr Iraq Petroleum Co 1963–65; treas 1965–70: Ford of Europe, Ford Motor Co, Ford of Britain; fin dir Whitbread Group 1970–72, md (fin) British Steel Corp 1972–77; Lloyds Bank plc: dir Merchant Banking Div 1977, dir Int Banking Div 1977–89, exec dir Europe 1980, exec dir Marketing & Planning 1983, dep chief exec Marketing & Planning 1985 and dir several assoc cos; exec dir (banking) The Private Bank and Tst Co Ltd 1989–91, exec dir Rosehaugh plc 1991 (chm 1992–93); appointed Crown Agent 1989–91, memb Monopolies and Mergers Cmmn 1990–96; dir Mutual Management Services 1993–96, md MicroTrace Ltd 1996–; chm Delamas Properties Ltd 1997–; md Trace Tag Ltd 2001–; non-exec dir: Shandwick IPR (formerly Shandwick International plc) 1993–99, New Markets Foods Ltd 1994–97; chm Oakbridge Counselling Gp 1990–96; govr and assoc memb Faculty Ashbridge Mgmnt Coll; FCIS; *Books* Investment Appraisal (1967); *Recreations* reading, chess, golf; *Style—* Leonard Kingshott, Esq; ✉ 4 Delamas, Beggar Hill, Fryerning, Ingatestone, Essex

KINGSLAND, Prof Charles Richard; s of Richard Alan Kingsland, of Nottingham, and Noreen Monica, *née* Hayes; *b* 29 October 1957, Nottingham; *Educ* Mundella GS Nottingham, Univ of Liverpool (MB ChB, MD, DRCOG); *m* (m dis), Catharine Anne, da of Peter O'Neill; 1 s (Joseph Edward), 2 da (Charlotte Alexandra, Lucy Elizabeth); *Career* house offr Royal Liverpool Hosp 1982–83, registrar Liverpool Hosps 1983–87, res fell Middx Hosp 1987–89, sr lectr in obstetrics and gynaecology Univ of Liverpool 1992–93 (lectr 1989–92), conslt 1993–; fellows rep Cncl RCOG 2010–; memb Br Fertility Soc (memb Ctee 1992–); FRCOG 1998 (MRCOG 1987); *Recreations* soccer, hiking, skiing; *Clubs* Liverpool Artists; *Style—* Prof Charles Kingsland; ✉ The Women's Hospital, Crown Street, Liverpool L8 7SS (☎ 0151 708 9988, fax 0151 702 4137, e-mail ckingsland@yahoo.com)

KINGSLEY, Sir Ben; kt (2002); s of Rahimtulla Harji Bhanji, and Anna Lyna Mary, *née* Goodman; *b* 31 December 1943, Yorks; *Educ* Manchester Grammar; *Career* actor; associate artist RSC; patron and affiliated memb of many charitable organisations; Hon MA Univ of Salford 1984: Hon DLitt: Univ of Sussex, Univ of Hull; memb: BAFTA 1983, AMPAS; Padma Sri (India) 1986; *Theatre* incl: RSC 1967–86 (title roles incl Hamlet and Othello), Nat Theatre 1977–78 (leading roles incl Mosca in Volpone), Waiting for Godot (Old Vic) 1997; *Film* incl: Gandhi, Betrayal, Turtle Diary, Harem, Silas Marner, Maurice, Slipstream, Testimony, Pascali's Island, Without a Clue, Murderers Amongst Us, Fifth Monkey, The Children, Bugsy, Sneakers, Searching for Bobby Fischer, Dave, Schindler's List, Death and the Maiden, Species, Twelfth Night, The Assignment, Photographing Fairies, Sweeney Todd, Weapons of Mass Distraction, The Confession: Crime & Punishment, Alice in Wonderland, Spookey House, Sexy Beast, Rules of Engagement, What Planet are you From, The Triumph of Love, Anne Frank: The Whole Story, Artifical Intelligence: AI, Suspect Zero, Sound of Thunder, House of Sand and Fog, Thunderbirds, Oliver Twist, Last Legion, You Kill Me, Elegy, The Wackness, Transsiberian, War Inc, Love Guru, 50 Dead Men Walking, Shutter Island, Prince of Persia, Hugo, The Dictator 2012, Iron Man 3 2013, Ender's Game 2013, Marvel One-Shot: All Hail the King (short) 2014; *Awards* incl: Oscar, BAFTA (twice), Golden Globe (twice), NY Critics', LA Critics', Grammy, Simon Wiesenthal Humanitarian, Berlin Golden Camera, Evening Standard Best Actor Award (for Schindler's List) 1995, European Film Acad Best Actor Award 2001, Br Ind Film Award for Best Actor 2001, Screen Actor's Guild Best Actor Award 2002, Broadcast Critics' Award for Best Actor 2002, Star on Hollywood Walk of Fame 2010, Albert R Broccoli Award for Worldwide Contribution to Entertainment BAFTA LA Britannia Awards 2013, National Leadership Award US Holocaust Meml Museum 2014; *Style—* Sir Ben Kingsley; ✉ c/o Independent Talent Group, 40 Whitfield Street London W1T 2RH (☎ 020 7636 6565, fax 020 7323 0101)

KINGSLEY, David John; OBE (2006); s of Walter John Kingsley, and Margery, *née* Walden; *b* 10 July 1929; *Educ* Southend HS for Boys, LSE (BSc(Econ)); *m* 1, July 1955 (m dis), Enid Sophia, da of Thomas Jones, MBE (d 1985), of Llandeilo; 2 da (Nichola Sophia b 1962, Nadia b 1964); *m* 2, May 1968 (m dis), Gillian (d 2000), da of George Leech (d 1978); 2 s (Andrew John b 1966, Paul David b 1967); *m* 3, 25 Oct 1988, Gisela Irene, *née* Reichardt; *Career* dir Benton and Bowles Advertising Agency 1961–64, fndr and ptnr Kingsley Manton & Palmer Advertising Agency 1964–78, dir and chm Kimpher Group Communications Group 1969–78, ptnr and chm Kingsley & Kingsley Business Consultancy 1974–, dir Francis Kyle Gallery 1978–, chair Worldaware – the centre for world devpt educn, chm Cartoon Arts Tst 1994–2001, chair Discover 1997–2006; dir: Mediawise 2003–06, Fun Radio UK 2004–; advsr Institute of Global Ethics 2002–; memb Devpt Ctee RCM; tstee: The Ireland Fund (UK) 1986–2002, @Bristol 1995–2003, Royal Philharmonic Orch; Lab Parly candidate East Grinstead 1952–54; advsr to: Lab Pty and Govt on Communications 1962–70, Govt of Zambia 1974–82, Govt of Mauritius 1977–81, SDP 1981–87; organiser and creator: The Greatest Children's Party in the World for the Int Year of the Child 1980, HM The Queen's 60th Birthday Celebration, the Creative Summit 1999; hon doctorate Soka Univ Tokyo; LSE: govr LSE (memb Cncl) 1966–2006 (now emeritus govr), hon fell, chair LSE Alumni Assoc; hon memb RCM; FRSA, FIPA, MCSD; *Books* Albion in China (1979), How World War II was Won on the Playing Fields of LSE; *Recreations* music, books, creating happy public events, travel, art; *Clubs* Reform; *Style—* David J Kingsley, Esq, OBE; ✉ Kingsley & Kingsley, 81 Mortimer Road, London N1 5AR (☎ 020 7275 8889, e-mail kingsleydavid@btconnect.com)

KINGSLEY, Nicholas William; s of Philip Francis Kingsley (d 2004), and Joan Rosamond, *née* Holliday (d 2004); *b* 14 September 1957, London; *Educ* St Paul's, Keble Coll Oxford (MA); *m* 14 June 1980, Susan Mary, *née* Summerhayes; *Career* archive trainee Bodleian Library Oxford 1978–79, modern records archivist Glos Record Office 1982–89 (asst archivist 1979–82), city archivist Birmingham CC 1989–96, mangr Birmingham Central Library 1996–2000, county and diocesan archivist Glos Record Office 2000–05, head Archives Sector Devpt and sec Historical Manuscripts Cmmn Nat Archives 2005–15, ret; Nat Cncl of Archives: memb 1991–2010, sec 1993–99, vice-chm 2000–01, chm 2001–05; memb Bd Museums Libraries and Archives Cncl 2004–06; author of articles for Country Life and professional jls; chm: Victoria County History Nat Ctee 2005–11, DLM Forum EU 2006, Victoria History Tst Advsy Ctee 2011–13; dir and tstee Glos County History Tst 2010–, dir and tstee Victoria County History Tst 2013–; Hon DLitt Univ of Birmingham 2006; memb then registered memb Soc of Archivists (now Archives and Records Assoc) 1979–; FSA 2003; *Books* The Country Houses of Gloucestershire: 1500–1660 (1989, 2 edn 2001), The Country Houses of Gloucestershire: 1660–1830 (1992), The Country Houses of Gloucestershire: 1830–2000 (jtly, 2001); Handlist of the Contents of the Gloucestershire Record Office (1988, 4 edn 2002), Archives Online (1998), Changing the Future of the Past (2003); Landed Families of Britain and Ireland (2013–); *Recreations* visiting historic buildings, historical research, photography, food, genealogy; *Style—* Nicholas Kingsley, Esq; ✉ 38 Dial Hill Road, Clevedon, North Somerset BS21 7HN (☎ 01275 542263, e-mail nick.kingsley@blueyonder.co.uk, website website www.landedfamilies.blogspot.co.uk)

KINGSLEY, Stephen Michael; s of Ernest Robert Kingsley, of Cheadle, Cheshire, and Ursula Renate, *née* Bochenek (d 1972); *b* 1 June 1952; *Educ* Cheadle Hulme Sch, Univ of Bristol (BSc); *m* 18 March 1982, Michelle, da of Oscar Solovici (d 1983), of Paris; 1 da (Natalie b 1984); *Career* Arthur Andersen: joined 1973, mangr 1979–86, ptnr 1986–2002, head London Capital Markets Gp 1987–92, dir Euro regnl capital mkts 1988–93, dir Euro regnl banking and capital mkts 1993–2002, dir Euro Financial Risk Mgmnt Practice 1995–2002; managing pntr Global Financial Services Industry 2001–02, ptnr DiamondCluster International 2002–04, ceo sales and business devpt Aon Europe 2004–06, head of UK financial servs practice BearingPoint Inc 2006–07, dir LECG London 2007–09, sr md FII Consulting 2009–; non-exec dir: Britannia Building Soc 2008–09, Cooperative Financial Services Gp 2009–; memb Tech Panel Securities and Investments Bd 1985–87; visiting lectr Coll of Petroleum Studies Oxford; memb Worshipful Co of Int Bankers; FCA; *Books* Managing A Foreign Exchange Department (contrib, 1985), Currency Options (contrib, 1985), European Banking and Capital Markets – a strategic survey; *Recreations* travel, ballet, classical music, current affairs; *Style—* Stephen Kingsley, Esq; ✉ 23 Gloucester Walk, London W8 4HZ (☎ 020 7937 4525); FII Consulting, 322 High Holborn, London WC1 7PB (e-mail stephen.kingsley@fiiconsulting.com)

KINGSNORTH, Prof Andrew Norman; s of John Norman Kingsnorth, of Eynsford, Kent, and Kathleen Dorothy, *née* Bassett; *b* 20 November 1948, Dartford, Kent; *Educ* Sevenoaks Sch, Royal Free Hosp Sch of Med (BSc, MB BS, MS); *m* 1 June 1974, Jane Mary, da of Mervyn Bryant Poulter; 2 s (Edward Anthony b 1 July 1977, Peter John b 27 March 1982), 1 da (Bryony Jane b 30 June 1980); *Career* house surgn Addenbrooke's Hosp Cambridge 1974–75, sr house offr Norwich Hosps 1976–77, registrar John Radcliffe Hosp Oxford 1977–80, res fell Harvard Univ Boston 1980–81, lectr in surgery Univ of Edinburgh 1982–86, jr conslt Groote Schuur Hosp Cape Town SA 1986–87, sr lectr and reader in surgery Univ of Liverpool 1987–96, prof of surgery Plymouth Postgrad Med Sch 1996–2002, conslt surgeon Derriford Hosp Plymouth 2002–13, hon prof Peninsula Medical Sch 2003–17, clinical dir of surgery; RCS: Arris and Gale lectr 1984, memb Ct of Examiners 1994–2000, tutor in Telemedicine 1999–2002, Hunterian Prof 2008; pres Section of Surgery RSM 2010–11; exec-dir Hernia Int; Rodney Smith prize Pancreatic Soc 1993; magistrate Plymouth Bench 2007–15; FACS, FRCS; *Books* Fundamentals of Surgical Practice (jtly, 1998, 3 edn 2011) Incisional Hernia (jtly, 2000), Principles of Surgical Practice (jtly, 2001), Advanced Surgical Practice (jtly, 2002), Management of Abdominal Hernias (jtly, 2013); also author of over 200 articles in scientific jls; *Recreations* duplicate bridge, rambling, gardening; *Clubs* Bigbury Golf, Newton & Noss Bridge; *Style—* Prof Andrew Kingsnorth; ✉ Rowden House, Stoke Road, Noss Mayo, Plymouth PL8 1JG (e-mail kingsnortha@hotmail.com)

KINGSTON, Jeremy Henry Spencer; s of William Henry Kingston (d 1989), of Brighton, E Sussex, and Elsie, *née* Cooper (d 1980); *b* 5 August 1931; *Educ* Reigate GS; *m* 1967 (m dis 1996), Meg, da of James Ritchie, of Dumbarton; 2 s (Benjamin James b 1968, Rufus William b 1970); *Career* Nat Serv 2 Lt Royal Signals; casually employed Chelsea 1951–55 (coffee houses, sculpture model, barr's clerk's clerk), sec to John Lehmann 1955–57; playwright: No Concern of Mine (Westminster) 1958, Signs of the Times (Vaudeville) 1973, Oedipus at the Crossroads (King's Head) 1977, Making Dickie Happy (Rosemary Branch) 2004, Oedipus the King (Tristan Bates) 2014; theatre critic: Punch 1964–75, The Times 1985–; winner Ware Open Poetry Competition 2008; *Books* Love Among The Unicorns (1968), On the Lookout (poems, 2008), Who is He, Who Am I, Who Are They? (poems, 2013), Sherlock Holmes and a Scandal in Batavia (2015), and three children's books; *Recreations* long conversations over meals; *Style—* Jeremy Kingston, Esq; ✉ 65 Romulus Court, Brentford Dock, Middlesex TW8 8QL (☎ 020 8568 4714, e-mail jhskingston@aol.com); The Times, 3 Thomas More Square, London E98 1XY

KINGSTON, (William) Martin; QC (1992); s of William Robin Kingston, of Bishops Frome, Worcs, and Iris Edith, *née* Grocott; *b* 9 July 1949; *Educ* Middlewich Secdy Modern Sch, Hartford Coll of Further Educn, Univ of Liverpool (LLB); *m* 9 Sept 1972, Jill Mary, da of Robert Philip Sidney Bache; 2 da (Joanna Jessie b 3 Feb 1976, Emma Rachel b 9 Dec 1980), 1 s (Thomas Henry Robin b 22 June 1978); *Career* called to the Bar Middle Temple 1972, recorder 1991–99 (asst recorder 1987–91); dep chm Agricultural Lands Tbnl 1985–, asst cmmr Parly Boundary Cmmn for England 1992–; *Recreations* fly fishing, skiing, reading, holidays; *Style—* Martin Kingston, Esq, QC; ✉ No 5 Chambers, Greenwood House, 4–7 Salisbury Court, London EC4Y 8AA (☎ 0845 210 5555)

KINGSTON, Bishop of 2002–; Rt Rev Dr Richard Ian Cheetham; s of John Brian Margrave Cheetham, and Mollie Louise, *née* Cannell; *b* 18 August 1955; *Educ* Kingston GS, CCC Oxford (MA, PGCE), Ripon Coll Cuddesdon (CertTheol), KCL (PhD); *m* 1977, Felicity Mary; 1 s (Michael b 1979), 1 da (Sarah b 1981); *Career* sci teacher Richmond Sch Yorks 1978–80, physics teacher Eton Coll 1980–83, investment analyst Legal & Gen London 1983–85; ordinand 1985–87, asst curate Holy Cross Newcastle upon Tyne 1987–90, vicar St Augustine Luton 1990–99, rural dean of Luton 1995–98, archdeacon of St Albans 1999–2002; Anglican pres Christian Muslim Forum 2012–15 (co-chair 2008–12); chair Southwark Diocesan Bd of Educn 2002–15, pres London SW YMCA 2002–; memb Cncl Roehampton Univ 2006–12, chair Br Regnl Ctee St George's Coll Jerusalem

2013–; patron Fircroft Tst; pres Old Kingstonian Hockey Club 2009–15; hon research fell KCL 2011–, Whitelands professorial fell in Christian theology and contemporary issues Univ of Roehampton 2014–; *Publications* Collective Worship: Issues and Opportunities (2004); *Recreations* hockey, squash, tennis, walking, cinema, theatre; *Style—* The Rt Rev the Bishop of Kingston; ✉ Kingston Episcopal Area Office, 620 Kingston Road, Raynes Park, London SW18 8DN (☎ 020 8545 2443, e-mail bishop.richard@southwark.anglican.org, website www.southwark.anglican.org and www.bishoprichardcheetham.com)

KINGSTON, (John) Simon; s of Leonard James Kingston (d 1981), and Elisabeth Archer (d 2000); *b* 29 May 1949, London; *Educ* Highgate Sch, Oxford Poly; *m* 19 Dec 1970, Anna Mary, *née* Latham; 2 s ((John Louis) James b 1973, Charles Edward b 1974); *Career* ed: Faber and Faber 1969–70, Routledge 1971–72, Blandford Press 1973–74, G Bell and Sons 1974–79; variously ed, head of London office and head of editorial, mktg and admin Gordon Fraser 1980–89, gen mangr Marshall Cavendish Books 1989–93; SPCK: dir of publishing 1993, sr exec offr 2006, ceo and gen sec SPCK 2007–14; presenter The Book Show Premier Radio 2015–; dir Read For Your Life, dir World Mission Assoc, chair Religious Publishers Gp Publishing Assoc 2001–07; memb: British Soc for Eighteenth-Century Studies, Int Laurence Sterne Fndn; tstee Overseas Bishoprics' Fund 2008–13, memb NCVO Members Assembly 2009–11; Freeman City of London, Liveryman Worshipful Co of Vintners; MInstD 2004; *Recreations* photography, the eighteenth century; *Style—* Simon Kingston, Esq; ✉ 2 The Glebe, Wheatley, Oxford OX33 1YN (☎ 01865 429613, e-mail simon.kingston@oxfordbrookes.net)

KININMONTH, James Wyatt; s of late Peter Wyatt Kininmonth, of Ashmore, Dorset, and Priscilla Margaret, *née* Sturge; *b* 26 September 1952; *Educ* Harrow, RMA Sandhurst; *m* 19 March 1977, Susie, da of late Richard William Griffin, of Albermarle, USA; 2 da (Annabel b 1980, Harriet b 1983), 1 s (Charles b 1985); *Career* 5 Royal Inniskilling Dragoon Gds 1973, Capt 1977, trans to Reserve 1978; dir Kininmonth Holdings 1982–85; md Kininmonth Lambert North America 1987–91 (dir 1985–); dir: Lowndes Lambert North America Ltd 1990–92, Cooper Gay & Co Ltd 1992–2014, J W Kininmonth & Co Ltd 2014–; non-exec dir James Hampden Int Insurance Brokers 2016–; memb Lloyd's 1983–, dir Assoc of Lloyd's Members 2009–, chm of tstees Lloyd's Patriotic Fund 2015–; dir Nat Migraine Centre 2011–; Freeman City of London; Assistant Worshipful Co of Haberdashers 1982; *Recreations* shooting, skiing, golf; *Clubs* City of London, Royal & Ancient, George; *Style—* J W Kininmonth, Esq; ✉ Old Mill Barn, Isfield, East Sussex TN22 5XJ (☎ 01825 750732, e-mail james@kininmonth.com)

KINLOCH, Prof Anthony James; *b* 7 October 1946; *Educ* Queen Mary Coll London (PhD), Univ of London (DSc); *m* 1969, Gillian Patricia; 2 s (Ian Anthony b 1975, David Michael Robert b 1981), 1 da (Elizabeth Sarah b 1978); *Career* Royal Armaments R&D Establishment MOD 1972–84; Imperial Coll London: sr lectr 1984–85, reader in engrg adhesives 1985–90, prof of adhesion 1990–, head Mechanical Engrg Dept 2007; visiting appts: Nat Bureau of Standards Washington DC 1982, Ecole Polytechnique Fédérale de Lausanne 1986, Univ of Utah 1988; UK ed Jl of Adhesion 1985–; US Adhesion Soc Award 1992, Griffith Medal and Prize Inst of Materials 1996; Thomas Hawksley Meml Lectr (Adhesives in Engrg) IMechE 1996, Thomas Hawksley Gold Medal IMechE 1998, Wake Meml Medal Inst of Materials 2002; chair Soc Adhesives Inst of Materials 2000–02; memb: Cncl Inst of Materials 1997–02, EPSRC Coll for Structural Materials 1994–; fell US Adhesion Soc 1995 (pres 2002–04), CChem 1982, FRSC 1982, FIM 1982, CEng 1988, FREng 1997, FCGI 2001, FRS 2007; *Publications* author of two books and more than 200 scientific papers in the field of composite materials, adhesion and adhesives; *Recreations* opera, tennis, walking; *Style—* Prof Anthony J Kinloch, FREng, FRS; ✉ Department of Mechanical Engineering, Imperial College London, Exhibition Road, London SW7 2BX (☎ 020 7594 7081, fax 020 7594 7238)

KINLOCH, Sir David Oliphant; 5 Bt (UK 1873), of Kinloch, Co Perth; s of Sir John Kinloch, 4 Bt (d 1992), and Doris Ellaline, *née* Head (d 1997); *b* 15 January 1942; *Educ* Charterhouse; *m* 1, 1968 (m dis 1979), Susan Minette, da of Maj-Gen Robert Elliott Urquhart, CB, DSO; 3 da (Katherine Cecilia b 1972, Emily Nicole b 1974, Nicola Marjorie b 1976); m 2, 1983, Sabine, da of Philippe de Loës, of Geneva, Switzerland; 1 s (Alexander Peter b 1986), 1 da (Sophie b 1994); *Heir* s, Alexander Kinloch; *Career* chartered accountant; dep chief exec Caledonia Investments plc; dir: British Empire Securities and General Trust plc, Sterling Industries plc, Amerindo Internet Fund plc; chm: ISIS Asset Management plc, JPMorgan Fleming Chinese Investment Trust plc, Radio Investments Ltd, Wallem Group Ltd; *Style—* Sir David Kinloch, Bt; ✉ House of Aldie, Fossoway, Kinross-shire KY13 0QH; 29 Walpole Street, London SW3 4QS

KINLOCH ANDERSON; *see:* Anderson

KINMONTH, Prof Ann Louise; CBE (2002); da of Maurice Henry Kinmonth, of East Langton, Leics, and Gwendolyn Stella, *née* Phillipps; *b* 8 January 1951; *Educ* Market Harborough GS, New Hall Cambridge (exhibitioner, MB BChir, MA, MD), LSHTM (MSc), St Thomas' Hosp London (exhibitioner); *Career* res fell Univ Dept of Paediatrics Oxford 1978–81, vocational trg for gen practice Berinsfield Oxon 1981–82, princ in gen practice Aldermoor Health Centre Southampton 1983–96, prof of primary med care Univ of Southampton 1992–96 (reader 1990–92); Univ of Cambridge: prof of gen practice 1997–2011, clinical dir of studies St John's Coll 2001– (fell 1997–), hon dir of research and emeritus prof 2011–; sr investigator NIHR 2009–14; James Mackenzie Prize for contribs to research and practice RCGP, William Pickles lectr 2001, Maurice Wood Award N American Primary Care Research Gp 2006; author of pubns on the orgn and delivery of diabetes care in childhood and adult life, on preventive med and gen practice; memb: British Diabetic Assoc, Norfolk Naturalists Tst; patron ZSL; overseas memb Inst of Medicine USA 2007, foreign Assoc Inst of Medicine 2007–; FZS, FRCP, FRCGP, FMedSci; *Recreations* walking, sailing wooden boats, conservation and sustainability; *Style—* Prof Ann Louise Kinmonth, CBE; ✉ Primary Care Unit, Institute of Public Health, University Forvie Site, Robinson Way, Cambridge CB2 0SR (☎ 01223 763830, fax 01223 762515, e-mail alk25@medschl.cam.ac.uk)

KINNAIRD, Nicky; MBE (2009); *Educ* Victoria Coll Belfast, Univ of Reading (BSc); *Career* chartered surveyor 1987–92; fndr Space NK Ltd lifestyle concept store Covent Garden 1993, fndr Space NK Apothecary luxury skincare and make-up boutiques (now trading at 54 UK locations) 1996, opened SPAce NK day spa Notting Hill 2000; Space NK signature products launched internationally 2001, launched Space NK online store 2004, opened first Space NK Apothecary store in US 2007, launched Space NK US online store 2007; Cosmetic Exec Women (UK) Achievers Award 2003, Save the Children Woman of Achievement Award 2005, Invest Northern Ireland Female Entrepreneur of the Year Award 2006, Irish Tatler Woman of the Year Award 2006, WWD Beauty Biz Award for the Most Innovative Marketer of the Year (Prestige Person category) 2008; hon doctorate Queens Univ Belfast 2006; *Books* Awaken Your Senses, Change Your Life (2002); *Recreations* running, yoga, pilates, tennis, cinema, art, books; *Style—* Ms Nicky Kinnaird, MBE; ✉ Space NK Ltd, 5th Floor, Shropshire House, 11–20 Capper Street, London WC1E 6JA (☎ 020 7299 4999, fax 020 7299 4998, e-mail nk@spacenk.com)

KINNEAR, Rory; s of Roy Kinnear (d 1988), and Carmel Cryan; *b* 17 February 1978, London; *Educ* St Paul's, Balliol Coll Oxford, LAMDA; *Career* actor; *Theatre* incl: The Seagull (Theatre Royal Northampton) 2002, The Tempest (Theatre Royal Plymouth) 2002, The Taming of the Shrew (RSC) 2003, The Tamer Tamed (RSC) 2003, Hamlet (Old Vic) 2004, Festen (Almeida Theatre) 2004, Mary Stuart (Donmar Warehouse) 2005, Southwark Fair (NT) 2006, The Man of Mode (NT) 2007 (Best Performance in a Supporting Role Laurence Olivier Award 2008), Philistines (NT) 2007, Othello (NT) 2013 (Best Actor Evening Standard Theatre Award 2013 (jtly with Adrian Lester, OBE, *qv*), Best Actor Olivier Award 2014); *Television* incl: Mansfield Park 2007, Messiah: The Rapture 2008, The Curse of Steptoe 2008, Margaret Thatcher: The Long Walk to Finchley 2008, Cranford 2009, Vexed 2010, Women in Love 2011, The Mystery of Edwin Drood 2012, The Hollow Crown 2012, Count Arthur Strong 2013, Southcliffe 2013, Lucan 2013, Penny Dreadful 2014; *Film* incl: Quantum of Solace 2008, Wild Target 2009, Skyfall 2012, Cuban Fury 2014, The Imitation Game 2014; *Style—* Mr Rory Kinnear; ✉ c/o Markham, Froggatt and Irwin Ltd, 4 Windmill Street, London W1T 2HZ

KINNOCK, Baron (Life Peer UK 2005), of Bedwellty in the County of Gwent; Neil Gordon Kinnock; PC (1983); s of late Gordon H Kinnock, steelworker and former coalminer, and Mary, *née* Howells, nurse; *b* 28 March 1942; *Educ* Lewis Sch Pengam, UC Cardiff (BA, DipEd); *m* 25 March 1967, Glenys Elizabeth (Baroness Kinnock of Holyhead, *qv*), da of Cyril Parry; 1 s (Hon Stephen Nathan), 1 da (Hon Rachel Nerys Helen); *Career* UC Cardiff: pres Socialist Soc 1963–66, pres Union 1965–66, hon fell 1982; tutor organiser WEA 1966–70, memb Welsh Hosp Bd 1969–71, former memb BBC Gen Advsy Cncl; MP (Lab): Bedwellty 1970–83, Islwyn 1983–95; PPS to Sec of State for Employment 1974–75, memb Nat Exec Lab Party 1978–94, princ oppn front bench spokesman on educn 1979–83 (memb Shadow Cabinet 1980–92), leader Lab Pty and HM Oppn 1983–92, chm Lab Party 1987–88; EC: tport cmmr 1995–99, vice-pres for reform and cmmr for Audit, Personnel and Admin, Languages and Logistics 1999–2004; chair Br Cncl 2004–09; pres Univ of Cardiff 1998–2009; memb TGWU; Alexis de Tocqueville Prize European Inst of Public Admin 2003, Danish Shipowners' Cncl Prize 2004, Oliver Tambo Medal Repub of S Africa 2014; Hon LLD: Univ of Wales 1992, Univ of Glamorgan 1996; *Publications* Wales and the Common Market (1971), Making Our Way – Investing in Britain's Future (1986), Thorns and Roses (1992); *Recreations* music (esp male voice choral work and opera), the theatre, rugby and association football, cricket, being with family; *Style—* The Rt Hon the Lord Kinnock; ✉ House of Lords, London SW1A 0PW

KINNOCK, Hon Stephen; MP; s of The Rt Hon the Lord Kinnock, *qv*, and Baroness Kinnock of Holyhead, *qv*; *Career* MP (Lab) Aberavon 2015–; *Style—* Hon Stephen Kinnock, Esq, MP; ✉ House of Commons, London SW1A 0AA

KINNOCK OF HOLYHEAD, Baroness (UK Life Peer 2009), of Holyhead in the Co of Ynys Môn; Glenys Elizabeth; *b* 7 July 1944, Roade, Northampton; *Educ* Holyhead Comprehensive Sch, Univ Coll Cardiff (BA, DipEd); *m* 25 March 1967, Baron Kinnock (Life Peer), *qv*; 1 s (Hon Stephen Nathan), 1 da (Hon Rachel Nerys Helen); *Career* sec Socialist Soc UC Cardiff 1964–66, chm NUS Cardiff 1965–66, sch teacher 1966–93; MEP (Lab): South Wales East 1994–99, Wales 1999–2009; co-pres ACP/EU Jt Parly Assembly 2002–; memb: Devpt and Cooperation Ctee European Parl, Foreign Affairs Ctee; European Parl Lab Pty spokesperson on Int Devpt; min of state for Europe 2009–10; pres: One World Action, Wales Cncl for Voluntary Action, Coleg Harlech; vice-pres Parliamentarians for Global Action, SE Wales Racial Equality Cncl, St David's Fndn, Special Needs Advsy Project (SNAP) Cymru, UK Nat Breast Cancer Coalition Wales, Community Enterprise Wales, Charter Housing, UK Women of the Year Lunch and Assembly; patron: Saferworld, Drop the Debt Campaign, Welsh Woman of the Year, Burma Campaign UK, Crusaid, Elizabeth Hardie Ferguson Tst, Med Fndn for Victims of Torture, Nat Deaf Children's Soc; memb Cncl: VSO, Br in Europe; memb Bd World Parliamentarian Magazine; memb Advsy Bd Int Research Network on Children and Armed Conflict; hon fell: Univ of Wales Coll Newport, Univ of Wales Coll Bangor Hon Dr: Thames Valley Univ, Brunel Univ, Kingston Univ; FRSA; *Publications* Voices for One World (1997), Eritrea – Images of War and Peace (1989), Namibia – Birth of a Nation (1991), Could Do Better – where is Britain in the European league tables?, By Faith & Daring (1993), Zimbabwe: On the Brink (2003); *Recreations* theatre, cooking, grandchildren, reading; *Style—* The Baroness Kinnock of Holyhead

KINNOULL, 16 Earl of (S 1633); Charles William Harley Hay; also Viscount Dupplin, Lord Hay of Kinfauns and Lord Hay of Pedwarden; s and h of 15 Earl of Kinnoull, Arthur William George Patrick Hay (d 2013), and Countess of Kinnoull, Gay Ann Hay, *née* Lowson; *b* 20 December 1962; *Educ* Eton, ChCh Oxford (MA), City Univ, Inns of Court Sch of Law; *m* 15 June 2002, Catherine Clare Crawford, da of His Hon William Crawford, of Dalgonar, Dumfriesshire; 3 da (Lady Alice, Lady Catriona (twins) b 25 Sept 2003, Lady Auriol b 15 March 2007), 1 s (William Thomas Charles (Viscount Dupplin) b 24 June 2011); *Heir* s, Viscount Dupplin; *Career* called to the Bar Middle Temple 1990; investment banker with Credit Suisse First Boston Ltd 1985–88, underwriter with Hiscox Group at Lloyd's 1990; dir: Hiscox Underwriting Ltd 1995–97, Construction and General Guarantee Insurance Company Ltd 2001–15, Heritage Group Ltd 2001–05; md Europe Hiscox Insurance Co Ltd 1995–2001, dir Amorphous Sugar Ltd 2001–15, dir HIM Capital Ltd 2007–09; chief exec Hiscox Insurance Co (Bermuda) Ltd 2009–12; dir M&A Hiscox plc 2000– (memb Exec Mgmnt Ctee 2004–14), co sec Hiscox Ltd 2009–12; dir: Assoc of Bermuda Insurers and Reinsurers 2009–12, Reinsurance Assoc of America 2009–12, Assoc of Bermuda Int Companies 2011–12; dir and memb Bd Horsecross Arts Ltd 2014–; sits in House of Lords as crossbench peer 2015–; memb House of Lords Select Ctees: on Social Mobility 2015–, on Trade Union Bill 2016–; tstee Royal Caledonian Charities Tst 1992– (chm 1996–2009, pres 2013–), chm Red Squirrel Survival Tst 2013–; memb Devpt Ctee ChCh Oxford 2003–09, memb Perth City Devpt Bd 2014–, chm Culture Perth & Kinross 2016–; Lt Atholl Highlanders 1992– (Capt 2008–), memb Queen's Body Guard for Scotland (Royal Co of Archers) 2000–; pres (London membs) Nat Tst for Scotland 2007–12; Freeman City of London 2008; FRPSL 2006 (MRPSL 1999); *Recreations* skiing, real tennis, philately, motor cars, racing; *Clubs* White's, Turf, Pratts, Royal Perth, MCC, Jockey (Vienna); *Style—* The Earl of Kinnoull; ✉ 17 Cumberland Street, London SW1V 4LS (☎ 020 7976 6973); Pitkindie, Abernyte, Perthshire (☎ 01828 686342, e-mail dupplinc@yahoo.co.uk)

KINSELLA, Sophie; *b* 12 December 1969, London; *Educ* Putney HS, Sherborne, New Coll Oxford; *m* Henry Wickham; 4 s (Freddy b 1997, Hugo b 1999, Oscar b 2006, Rex William b 2010), 1 da Sybella (b 2011); *Career* author; early career as financial journalist; *Books* The Shopaholic series: The Secret Dreamworld of a Shopaholic (2000), Shopaholic Abroad (2001), Shopaholic Ties The Knot (2001), Shopaholic & Sister (2004), Shopaholic & Baby (2007), Mini Shopaholic (2010), Shopaholic to the Stars (2014); others incl: Can You Keep a Secret? (2005), The Undomestic Goddess (2006), Remember Me? (2008), Twenties Girl (2009), I've Got Your Number (2012), Wedding Night (2013), Finding Audrey (2015); *Style—* Ms Sophie Kinsella

KINSELLA-BEVAN, Col Richard Dennis; s of late Lt Col Richard Bevan, of Bowelk House, Co Monaghan, and Margot, *née* Kinsella; *b* 5 January 1943; *Educ* Brighton Coll, King's Coll Cambridge (MA); *m* 1971, Kitty, da of late Capt A B B J Goor, KRRC, and Judith Bloomfield; 1 s (Desmond b 1 Oct 1975), 2 da (Emma-Louise b 16 March 1977, Edwena b 6 Sept 1979); *Career* cmmnd 5th Royal Inniskilling Dragoon Gds 1965; served: N Africa, Cyprus, Oman, Dhofar War (Sultan's Commendation), BAOR, Iraq; psc, Cmd Sultan's Armoured Regt 1984–87 (Sultan's Commendation Medal and Order of the Special Emblem); Head Secretariat National Employers' Liaison Ctee for the Reserve Forces 1992–95; Sr Br Loan Serv Offr (Army) Sultanate of Oman 1996–99 (DSM); chm SSAFA Forces Help Repub of Ireland 1999– (pres 2016–); registrar Med Soc of London 1999–2009, exec sec Harveian Soc 1999–2009; dir St George's Court Pimlico; tstee Seaton Tst 1999, chm of tstees Royal Drummond Instn 2010–; author of articles in mil jls; Freeman City of London, Liveryman Worshipful Co of Farriers (memb Ct of Assts 2003–, Master

K

2007), memb Farriers' Registration Cncl 2004–07; FRGS 1985 (Baram-Rejang Expdn 1961, Kinabalu 1962); *Recreations* field sports (MH Shrivenham Beagles 1987–88); *Clubs* Cavalry and Guards', Kildare Street and University (Dublin); *Style*— Col Richard Kinsella-Bevan; ✉ Knockbrack Grange, Oldcastle, County Meath, Ireland

KINSEY, Julian; s of Tom Kinsey, of Solihull, and Ruth, *née* Owen-Jones; *b* 8 October 1959, Birmingham; *Educ* Solihull Sch, Univ of Sheffield (LLB), Chester Coll of Law; *m* 1 July 1989, Amanda *née* Cundy; 1 s (George b 1 Oct 1992); *Career* admitted slr 1984; trainee Rigby Loose & Mills 1982–84, Linklaters 1984–86, Harbottle & Lewis 1986–88, Bond Pearce 1988– (ptnr 1993–, currently head of banking); *Recreations* family, cricket, music; *Clubs* Tideford Cricket (tstee); *Style*— Julian Kinsey, Esq; ✉ Bond Pearce LLP, 3 Temple Quay, Temple Back East, Bristol BS1 6DZ (☎ 0845 415 0000, e-mail julian.kinsey@bondpearce.com)

KINSMAN, Prof Rodney; s of John Thomas Kinsman, and Lilian, *néa* Bradshaw; *b* 9 April 1943; *Educ* Mellow Lane GS, Central Sch of Art (NDD); *m* Lisa Sau-Yuk, *née* Ngai; 1 s (Brandon Lee b 19 June 1968), 2 da (Charlie Sam b 24 Nov 1973, Chloe Jessica b 4 Jan 1975); *Career* furniture designer; chm and md OMK Design Ltd (fndr 1966), Kinsman Assoc 1981; work in exhibitions incl: The Way We Live Now (V&A Museum) 1979, Sit (RIBA) 1980, The Modern Chair (ICA) 1989, The Review (Design Museum London) 1989, Evolution of the Modern Chair (Business Design Centre London) 1989, BBC Design Awards (Design Centre London) 1990, In Focus OMK The Designs of Rodney Kinsman (Design Museum) 1992; also chosen to represent Britain in numerous foreign exhibitions; designs featured in: various Museum permanent collection UK and abroad incl V&A, numerous publications, TV and radio broadcasts; awards incl: Observer Design award UK 1969, Design Council award 1984, Resources Cncl Inc 1987, Product Design award USA 1987, Industrial Design Designers Choice USA 1988, D&AD Silver award for most outstanding Br product design for the home UK 1989, The British Design award 1991, Design Cncl Millennium Product 1998; prof: The London Inst 1996, Univ of the Arts London 2005; visiting prof: RCA 1985–86 (external examiner 1987–89), St Martin's and Central Sch of Art; memb BA Advsy Cncl St Martin's and Central Sch of Art 1989–90; govr Univ of the Arts 1998–2010; Hon FRCA 1988; FCSD 1983, FRSA 1991, RDI 1990; *Publications* Rodney Kinsman – The Logical Art of Furniture (monograph, 1992); *Recreations* polo, skiing; *Clubs* Reform, Chelsea Arts, Groucho; *Style*— Prof Rodney Kinsman, RDI; ✉ OMK Design Ltd, Stephen Building, 30 Stephen Street, London W1P 1QR (☎ 020 7631 1335, fax 020 7631 3227, e-mail enquiries@omkdesign.com, website www.omkdesign.com)

KIRBY, (Bernard William) Alexander (Alex); s of Frederic William Kirby (d 1953), and Vera Beryl, *née* Crawshaw (d 1989); *b* 11 July 1939, Liverpool; *Educ* King's Coll Taunton, Keble Coll Oxford; *m* 8 April 1972, Belinda Anne, da of Hugh Alfred Andrews (d 1991), and Anne Andrews (d 2009); 2 s (Edmund b 29 Dec 1978, Thomas b 14 April 1982); *Career* asst curate Isle of Dogs 1965–66, community relations offr London Borough of Newham 1967–70, ed Race Today magazine 1970–73, co-ordinator Br Volunteer Prog Burkina Faso and Niger 1974–75, researcher Prog to Combat Racism World Cncl of Churches 1976–78; BBC: journalist World Service News 1978–83, stringer N Africa 1983–84, actg bureau chief and Cairo corr 1986, reporter BBC Radio News 1986–87, agric and environment corr 1987–96, religious affairs corr 1996–98, presenter Costing the Earth (BBC Radio 4) 1998–2005; environment corr BBC News Online 1998–2005; jt fndr/ed Climate News Network 2013; advsr UN Environment Prog 2004–, conslt UN Sec-Gen's High-Level Global Sustainability Panel 2011–12; chm World Water Forum of Journalists 2006–, assoc Conservation Fndn, advsr Islam in Peace campaign, fndr memb Science and Faith Unite on Biodiversity, memb Advsy Ctee China Climate Change Communication Project Renmin Univ Beijing 2012–, memb Bd Zoi Environment Network Geneva 2012–; memb Royal Inst; *Recreations* walking, drinking beer; *Style*— Alex Kirby; ✉ 28 Prince Edward's Road, Lewes, East Sussex BN7 1BE (☎ 01273 474935, e-mail alexkirby_uk@yahoo.co.uk)

KIRBY, Jill; *Educ* Univ of Bristol (LLB); *m* Richard C Kirby, *qv*; *Career* admitted slr 1981; conslt Renewing One Nation 2001–03, Tax Reform Cmmn 2005–06, dir Centre for Policy Studies 2007–11; Choosing to be Different: women, work and the family (2003), The Price of Parenthood (2005), The Nationalisation of Childhood (2006), Who Do They Think We Are (2008); *Style*— Mrs Jill Kirby

KIRBY, John Patrick; s of Robert Kirby, of Liverpool, and Matilda, *née* Carroll (d 1976); *b* 2 February 1949; *Educ* Cardinal Godfrey Tech Sch Liverpool, St Martin's Sch of Art (BA), Royal Coll of Art (MA); *Career* artist; shipping clerk American Express Company Liverpool 1965–67, book salesman Burns & Oates 1967–69, voluntary social worker Boy's Town of Calcutta India 1969–71, asst warden Sydney House Hostel 1971–72, probation offr London and Plymouth 1972–77, asst stage doorman Royal Opera House 1977–78, market stall holder Kensington High St 1978–79, probation offr Brixton 1979–82, mothers' help London 1985, hosp porter London 1986; *Solo Exhibitions* incl: Other People's Lives (Angela Flowers Gallery Ireland) 1988, Still Lives (Flowers East London) 1989, New York and Related Works (Flowers East) 1991, Homeland (Lannon Cole Gallery Chicago) 1991 and (Flowers East) 1992, The Sign of the Cross (Angela Flowers Gallery London) 1993, The Company of Strangers (Flowers East) 1994, The Company of Strangers (Ferens Art Gallery Hull) 1995, Art Basle 27 Switzerland 1996, John Kirby (Il Polittico Rome) 1997, In the Dark (Flowers East) 1997, Lost Children (Flowers West Santa Monica CA) 1998, Lost Children (Flowers East) 1999, Il Polittico Rome 2000, New Prints and Monoprints (Flowers Graphics) 2000; work displayed in numerous group exhibitions and public collections; *Recreations* watching TV, contemplating suicide; *Clubs* Copacabana; *Style*— John Kirby, Esq; ✉ c/o Flowers East, 82 Kingsland Road, London E2 8DP (☎ 020 8985 3333, fax 020 8985 0067)

KIRBY, Maj-Gen Norman George; OBE; s of George William Kirby (d 1978), and Laura Kirby (d 1980); *Educ* King Henry VIII Sch Coventry, Univ of Birmingham (MB ChB); *m* 1 Oct 1949, Cynthia Maire, da of Thomas Ian Bradley (d 1954); 1 s (Robert b 22 June 1954), 1 da (Jill b 11 Nov 1958); *Career* regtl MO 10 Parachute Regt TA 1950–51, offr i/c 5 Parachute Surgical Team 1956–59 (served Suez landing 1956), offr i/c Surgical Div BMH Rinteln 1959–60, OC and surgical specialist BMH Tripoli 1960–62, OC and conslt surgn BMH Dhekelia 1967–70, chief conslt surgn Cambridge Mil Hosp 1970–72, conslt surgn HQ BAOR 1973–78; 1978–82: dir of Army surgery, conslt surgn to the Army, hon surgn to the Queen; Hon Col: 308 Gen Hosp RAMC TA 1982–87, 144 Para Field Sqdn RAMC TA 1985–96; Col Cmdt RAMC 1987–92; surgical registrar: Plastic Surgery Unit Stoke Mandeville Hosp 1950–51, Birmingham Accident Hosp 1953–55, Postgrad Med Sch Hammersmith 1964; hon conslt surgn Westminster Hosp 1979–; Guy's Hosp: conslt A&E surgn 1982–93, dir Clinical Servs, Accidents, Emergencies and Admissions 1985–93, conslt A&E surgn Nuffield House Guy's Hosp 1993–2005; chm: A&E Ctee SE Thames RHA 1983–88, Army Med Dept Working Pty Surgical Support for BAOR 1978–80; memb Med Ctee Defence Scientific Advsy Cncl 1979–82, examiner in anatomy RCS Edinburgh 1982–90, memb Ct of Examiners RCS 1988–94; pres: Br Assoc for A&E Med 1990–93, Mil Surgical Assoc 1991–92; vice-pres: Br Assoc of Trauma in Sport 1982–88, Faculty of A&E Med 1993–94; hon librarian RSM 1993–98; memb Cncl: ICS 1980, Royal Coll of Surgns 1989–94; McCombe lectr RCS Edinburgh 1979, Mitchener medal RCS 1982, memb Editorial Bd Br Jl of Surgery and Injury 1979–82, librarian Med Soc of London 1988–92 (pres 1992–93); ed Transactions 2003–11; Freeman City of London 1980, Liveryman Worshipful Soc of Apothecaries of London; OStJ; Hon FACEP, FRCS, FICS, FRCSEd, FRCEM (FFAEM), DMCC, fndr memb Inst of Expert Witnesses; *Books* Field Surgery Pocket Book (1981), Baillieres First Aid (1985), Accidents and Emergencies (pocket reference, 1991), Medical Care of Catastrophies (handbook, co-ed, 1996); *Recreations* travel, reading, archaeology; *Clubs* Probus; *Style*— Maj-Gen Norman Kirby, OBE; ✉ 14 Hillview Crescent, Baldwins Gate, Newcastle under Lyme ST5 5DE

KIRBY, Richard Charles; s of Charles Neil Vernon Kirby (d 1970), and Nora Helena, *née* Corner (d 1997); *b* 18 September 1946; *Educ* Sevenoaks Sch, Jesus Coll Oxford (MA); *m* 18 May 1985, Jill Kirby, *qv*, da of Kenneth Fernie, of Rugby, Warwicks; 3 s (Thomas Charles b 1986, James Edward b 1988, Robert Alexander b 1992 d 2004); *Career* admitted slr 1971; ptnr Speechly Bircham 1973–2012 (managing ptnr 1989–91), conslt Charles Russell Speechlys 2012–; memb Ctee London Young Slrs 1973–74; cncllr Tonbridge and Malling Borough 1971–84 (ldr 1979–82); memb: Exec Tonbridge and Malling Cons Assoc 1978–84 (vice-chm and treas 1979–84), Exec SE region Nat Housing and Town Planning Cncl 1980–83, Cncl Together Working for Wellbeing (formerly Mental After Care Assoc) 1982–2008 (hon treas 1987–2007); dir Hortons' Estate Ltd 1996–2015 (dep chm 2002–07); tstee and treas Friends of Long Compton Church 2011–; slr Worshipful Co of Pewterers 1981–2014 (Hon Freeman 1991, Liveryman 2000); Freeman City of London 1992; *Recreations* reading, theatre, walking, gardening; *Clubs* Carlton; *Style*— Richard C Kirby, Esq; ✉ Yerdley House, Long Compton, Warwickshire CV36 5LH (☎ 01608 684923); Charles Russell Speechlys, 5 Fleet Place, London EC4M 7RD (☎ 020 7427 6498, fax 020 7203 0200, e-mail richard.kirby@crsblaw.com)

KIRBY, Simon Gerard; MP; *b* 22 December 1964, Hastings, E Sussex; *Educ* Hastings GS, Open Univ (BSc); *m* Elizabeth Anne; 2 da, 4 s; *Career* md C-Side Ltd 1989–2001; MP (Cons) Brighton Kemptown 2010–; *Style*— Simon Kirby, Esq, MP; ✉ House of Commons, London SW1A 0AA

KIRDAR, Nemir Amin; s of Amin Jamil Kirdar (d 1958), and Nuzhet Mohammed Ali Kirdar (d 1982); *b* 28 October 1936; *Educ* Coll of the Pacific Calif (BA), Fordham Univ (MBA), Harvard Univ; *m* 1 Feb 1967, Nada, da of Dr Adnan Shakir; 2 da (Rena b 1968, Serra b 1975); *Career* Allied Bank International NY 1969–73, Nat Bank of N America NY 1973–74, Chase Manhattan Bank NY 1974–81, fndr, exec chm and ceo Investcorp 1982–; fndr memb Int Business Cncl World Econ Forum; chm Advsy Bd MEC St Anthony's Coll Oxford 2015; memb: Advsy Bd Sch of Int and Public Affairs Columbia Univ NYC, Bd of Tstees Brookings Instn Washington DC, Bd of Tstees Eisenhower Exchange Fellowship Philadelphia, UN Investments Ctee (overseeing UN Pension Fund) NYC, Int Cncl Belfer Center for Science and Int Affairs John F Kennedy Sch of Govt Harvard Univ, Panel of Sr Advsrs Chatham House London, Cncl for Arab and Int Relations Kuwait, Bd of Tstees Silatech Doha; hon fell St Antony's Coll Oxford 2009; *Publications* Saving Iraq: Rebuilding a Broken Nation (2009), In Pursuit of Fulfilment (2012), Need Respect Trust (2013); *Recreations* reading, skiing, tennis, golf, architecture, antiques; *Clubs* Metropolitan (Washington DC), Knickerbocker (NY), Brook (NY); *Style*— Nemir Kirdar, Esq; ✉ Investcorp International, 48 Grosvenor Street, London W1K 3HW (☎ 020 7629 6600, fax 020 7887 3333, e-mail nkirdar@investcorp.com)

KIRK, Matthew J L; s of Sir Peter Kirk (d 1977), and Elizabeth, *née* Graham; *b* 10 October 1960; *Educ* Felsted, St John's Coll Oxford (MA), Ecole Nationale d'Adminstration Paris (Diplome International d'Administration Publique); *m* 20 May 1989, Anna Thérèse, *née* Macey; 2 da (Georgina b 1995, Alexandra b 1998); *Career* joined HM Dip Serv 1982; served: UK mission to UN NY 1982, FCO 1983–84, Br Embassy Belgrade 1984–87, Office of the Gov of Gibraltar 1988, FCO 1988–92, Br Embassy Paris 1992–97, FCO 1997–98, Cabinet Secretariat 1998–99, FCO 1999–2002; ambass to Finland 2002–06; dir of external relationships Vodafone Gp plc 2006–; FRGS 1988; *Recreations* music, reading, walking, tennis; *Clubs* Brooks's, Beefsteak; *Style*— Matthew Kirk, Esq

KIRK, Prof Raymond Maurice; *b* 31 October 1923; *Educ* County Secdy Sch W Bridgford Nottingham, Univ of London (MB BS, MS); *m* 2 Dec 1952, Margaret; 1 s (Jeremy), 2 da (Valentine, Louise); *Career* Lt RN 1942–46; hon consulting surgn Royal Free Hosp (conslt surgn 1964–89), hon prof of surgery Royal Free and UCL Sch of Med Scis 2004–; RCS: memb Ct of Examiners 1975–81, memb Cncl 1983–91, ed Annals 1985–92, former dir Overseas Doctors Trg Scheme; examiner: Univ of London, Univ of Kuwait, Univ of Liverpool, Univ of Bristol, Univ of Khartoum, Univ of Malta, Univ of Colombo, RCPSG; former pres Surgical Section RSM; past pres: Med Soc London, Hunterian Soc; memb: Soc of Academic and Res Surgery, British Soc of Gastroenterology, Assoc of Surgns of GB and Ireland, Soc of Authors (memb Cncl Med Section 1996–2000); hon fell: Assoc of Surgeons of Poland, Coll of Surgeons of Sri Lanka; FRCS, FRSM; *Books* A Manual of Abdominal Operations (1967), Surgery (jtly, 1973), Basic Surgical Techniques (1973, 6 edn 2010), Kirk's General Surgical Operations (1978, 6 edn 2012), Complications of Surgery of the Upper Gastrointestinal Tract (jtly, 1986), A Career in Medicine (1998), Clinical Surgery in General (jt ed, 1993, 4 edn 2004), Essential General Surgical Operations (jt ed, 2001, 2 edn 2007); *Recreations* opera, travel; *Style*— Prof Raymond Kirk; ✉ 10 Southwood Lane, Highgate Village, London N6 5EE (☎ 020 8340 8575)

KIRKBY, Prof Michael John (Mike); s of John Lawrence Kirkby (d 1989), of London, and Hilda Margaret, *née* Potts (d 1974); *b* 6 May 1937; *Educ* Radley, Univ of Cambridge (BA, PhD); *m* 1, 24 July 1963 (m dis 1975), Anne Veronica Tennant, da of Philip Whyte (d 1983), of Bedford; 1 s (David b 1967), 1 da (Clare b 1970); m 2, 15 May 1976, Fiona Elizabeth, da of Donald Weston Burley (d 1995); 2 s (John b 1978, Nicholas b 1982); *Career* Nat Serv 2 Lt REME 1955–57; lectr in geography Univ of Bristol 1967–72, prof of physical geography Univ of Leeds 1973–2002, emeritus prof 2002–; author of numerous scientific pubns; memb BGRG/BSG 1966; chartered geographer 2003; RGS Founders' Medal 1999, EGU John Dalton Medal 2008; FRGS 1963, fell AGU 2004, pres BSG 2014–;; *Books* Hillslope Form and Process (with M A Carson, 1972), Hillslope Hydrology (ed, 1978), Soil Erosion (ed with R P C Morgan, 1980), Computer Simulation in Physical Geography (jtly, 1987 and 1993), Channel Network Hydrology (ed with K J Beven, 1993), Process models & theoretical geomorphology (ed, 1994), Dryland Rivers (ed with L J Bull, 2002), Critical Concepts in Geography: Hillslope Geomorphology (ed, 2004), Hydro-geomorphology, Erosion and Sedimentation (ed, 2011); managing ed Earth Surface Processes and Landforms 1976–2007; *Recreations* hill walking, photography; *Style*— Prof Mike Kirkby; ✉ School of Geography, University of Leeds, Leeds LS2 9JT (☎ 0113 343 3310, fax 0113 343 6758, e-mail m.j.kirkby@leeds.ac.uk)

KIRKHAM, Donald Herbert; CBE (1996); s of Herbert Kirkham (d 1987), and Hettie, *née* Trueblood (d 1999); *m* 17 Sept 1960, Kathleen Mary, da of Christopher Lond (d 1999); 1 s (Richard b 1963), 1 da (Sarah b 1966); *Career* Nat Serv Army 1954–56; The Woolwich Building Society: joined Lincoln Branch 1959, branch mangr Worcester 1963, gen mangr's asst 1967, business prodn mangr 1970, asst gen mangr of ops 1972, gen mangr 1976, appointed to Local Bd for Scotland and NI 1979–84, dep chief gen mangr 1981, memb Main Bd 1982, chief exec 1986–95, non-exec dir 1996–97; vice-pres Chartered Building Societies Inst 1986 (pres 1981–82), pres Cncl ICSA 1991; chm: Met Assoc of Building Societies 1988–89, Building Societies Assoc 1994–95 (dep chm 1993–94), Banque Woolwich SA 1995–2001, Banca Woolwich SpA 1995–2002, Woolwich Insurance Services Ltd 1995–96; memb Bd: Horniman Museum 1989–2004 (chm 1996–2004), Gresham Insurance Co Ltd 1995–96, Building Societies Investor Protection Bd 1995–97, Bexley and Greenwich HA 1996–98, and 1999–2001, Ranyard Meml Charitable Trust 2001–10, Oxleas NHS Fndn Tst 2006–09; Freeman City of London, Liveryman Worshipful Co of Chartered Secretaries and Administrators (memb Ct of Assts, Master 2003–04); Hon DBA 1991; FCIS 1973, FCIB 1993; *Recreations* boating; *Clubs* Christchurch

Sailing; *Style*— Donald Kirkham, Esq, CBE; ✉ 2 Chaundrye Close, The Court Yard, Eltham, London SE9 5QB (☎ 020 8859 4295, e-mail donaldhk@aol.com)

KIRKHAM, Her Hon Frances Margaret; CBE (2011); da of Brian Llewellyn Morgan Davies, and Natalie May Davies; *b* 29 October 1947; *Educ* KCL (BA, AKC, Merchant Taylor's Prize and Edward Jones medal and exhbn); *m* 27 March 1971, Barry Charles Kirkham, s of Stanley Edward Kirkham; *Career* Bank of England 1969–73, Lloyds Bank Int 1973–74; admitted slr 1978; Pinsent & Co 1976–84, Bettinsons 1984–87, Edge & Ellison 1987–95, Dibb Lupton Alsop 1995–2000, circuit judge (Midland Circuit) 2000–11, designated judge Technol and Construction Court 2000–11, judge Qatar Int Court 2013–; cmmr Parly Boundary Cmmn 2000; memb: Working Pty on Civil Justice Reform 1992–93, Law Soc Civil Litigation Ctee 1988–92, Birmingham Law Soc Civil Litigation Ctee 1992–93, Cncl CIArB 1992–97 and 2000, W Midlands Branch CIArb (chm 1994–97), Advsy Bd for Centre for Advanced Litigation Nottingham Law Sch 1992–97, Judicial Appointments Cmmn 2006–; fndr chm W Midlands Assoc of Women Slrs 1983, sec UK Assoc of Women Judges 2003–06; non-exec dir Royal Orthopaedic Hosp NHS Fndn Tst 2011–; hon memb: Technol and Construction Slrs Assoc (TeCSA) 2005, Arbrix; hon lifetime memb Soc of Construction Law 2015; chm of govrs Heathfield Sch Pinner 1984–91 (govr 1981–91); memb Law Soc; FCIArb, chartered arbitrator; hon bencher Inner Temple 2011; *Recreations* time with friends, sailing, skiing, walking, music, theatre; *Clubs* Bank of England Sailing, Univ Women's; *Style*— Her Hon Frances Kirkham, CBE; ✉ Atkin Chambers, 1 Atkin Building, Gray's Inn, London WC1R 5AT

KIRKHAM, Baron (Life Peer UK 1999), of Old Cantley in the County of South Yorkshire; Sir Graham Kirkham; kt (1996), CVO (2001); *b* 14 December 1944, Doncaster; *Educ* Maltby GS; *m* ; 1 s, 1 da; *Career* fndr DFS Furniture Co Ltd 1969–2010, ptnr Black Diamond Investments 2010–; dir Iceland Frozen Foods 2012–; sr party treas Cons Pty 1997–98; chm Duke of Edinburgh's Award, dep patron Outward Bound Tst, dep pres Animal Health Tst; *Style*— The Lord Kirkham, CVO; ✉ House of Lords, London SW1A 0PW; Black Diamond Investments LP, 8 Ebor Court, Redhouse Interchange, Adwick-le-Street, Doncaster DN6 7FE

KIRKHILL, Baron (Life Peer UK 1975), in District of City of Aberdeen; John Farquharson Smith; s of Alexander Findlay Smith; *b* 7 May 1930; *Educ* Robert Gordon's Colls Aberdeen; *m* 1965, Frances Mary Walker Reid; 1 step da; *Career* Lord Provost of the City and Royal Burgh of Aberdeen 1971–75, min of state Scottish Office 1975–78, chm North of Scotland Hydro-Electric Bd 1979–82; delg to Parly Assembly Cncl of Europe and WEU 1987–01, chm Ctee on Legal Affrs and Human Rights 1991–95; Hon LLD Univ of Aberdeen 1974; *Style*— The Rt Hon the Lord Kirkhill; ✉ 3 Rubislaw Den North, Aberdeen AB15 4AL (☎ 01224 314167)

KIRKHOPE, Timothy John Robert; MEP; s of John Thomas Kirkhope (d 1991), of Newcastle upon Tyne, and Dorothy Buemann Kirkhope, *née* Bolt (d 1973); *b* 29 April 1945, Newcastle-Upon-Tyne; *Educ* Royal GS Newcastle upon Tyne, Coll of Law Guildford; *m* 1969, Caroline, da of Christopher Thompson Maling (d 1975), of Newcastle upon Tyne; 4 s (Justin b 1970, Rupert b 1972, Dominic b 1976, Alexander 1979); *Career* slr; ptnr with Wilkinson Maughan Newcastle upon Tyne (now Eversheds) 1977–87, constlt 1987–90; MP (Cons) Leeds NE 1987–97; House of Commons: PPS to David (now Sir David) Trippier as Min of State for the Environment and Countryside 1989–90, asst Govt whip 1990–92, Lord Cmmr to the Treasy (Govt whip) 1993–95, vice-chamberlain HM's Household 1995, under sec of state Home Office 1995–97; slr and business conslt 1997–; dir Bournemouth and West Hampshire Water Co 1999–2011; MEP (Cons) Yorkshire & the Humber 1999–; European Parl: Cons chief whip 1999–2001, Cons spokesman on Justice and Home Affairs 1999–2007 and 2009–, Cons spokesman on Transport and Tourism 2007–09, ldr Cons in European Parl 2004–07 and 2008–10, chm European Parl Perm Delgn to Aust and NZ 2008–09, fndr and first chm European Conservatives and Reformists Gp European Parl 2009–11, memb European Parl Delgn to the USA 2009–, memb and vice-chm Special Ctee on Organised Crime, Corruption and Money Laudering (CRIM) 2012–14; memb: Bd Cons Party 2005–10, Northern Bd Cons Party 2007–; memb 'Future of Europe' Constitutional Convention 2002–03; chm: Kirkhope Cmmn on Asylum 2003, Kirkhope Cmmn on Immigration 2004; vice-chm Constitutional Affairs Ctee 2007–09; memb: Newcastle Airport Controlling Bd 1981–85, Northern Region HA 1982–86, Mental Health Act Cmmn 1983–86; cncllr Northumberland CC 1981–85; tstee BRASS (Biwater Retirement and Security Scheme) Pension Fund 2011–; govr Newcastle upon Tyne Royal GS 1986–99, dep chm Governing Bodies Assoc for Ind Schs 1990–98; *Publications* A Simplifying Treaty for Europe (2004); *Recreations* swimming, tennis, golf, flying (holds private pilot's licence); *Clubs* Northern Counties (Newcastle upon Tyne), Dunstanburgh Castle Golf (Northumberland), IOD; *Style*— Timothy Kirkhope, Esq, MEP; ✉ ASP 9G305, European Parliament, Rue Wiertz, B-1047 Brussels, Belgium (☎ 0032 2284 7321, fax 0032 2284 9321, e-mail timothy.kirkhope@europarl.europa.eu or timothy@kirkhope.org.uk)

KIRKLAND, Prof Angus Ian; s of Hugh Thomson Kilpatrick Kirkland, of Rayleigh, Essex, and Kathleen Theresa, *née* Doherty; *b* 29 August 1965, Rochford, Essex; *Educ* Univ of Cambridge (MA, PhD), Univ of Oxford (MA, DPhil); *m* 19 July 2008, Keiren Elizabeth; 1 da (Sophie Elizabeth b 27 July 1990); *Career* Univ of Cambridge: Br Ramsay fell 1991–93, sr res fell 1993–2003; Univ of Oxford: Leverhulme sr res lectr 2003–05, prof of materials 2005–; fell: Fitzwilliam Coll Cambridge 1992–2003, Linacre Coll Oxford 2003–; FRSC 2000 (MRSC 1989), CChem 2000, fell Royal Microscopical Soc (FRMS), FInstP 2014; over 300 papers in scientific jls; *Recreations* horse racing; *Clubs* Hawkes, Royal Ascot Racing; *Style*— Prof Angus Kirkland; ✉ University of Oxford, Dept of Materials, Parks Road, Oxford OX1 3PH

KIRKPATRICK, Prof Janice Mary; OBE (2013); da of James Burns Kirkpatrick, and Jane Henry Copeland Borthwick Kirkpatrick; *b* 16 April 1962; *Educ* Dumfries Acad, Glasgow Sch of Art (BA, MA), Univ of Glasgow (DLitt); *m* 2008, Ross Buchanan Hunter, *qv*; *Career* designer; creative dir and fndr Graven Images Ltd 1985–; visiting lectr Glasgow Sch of Art 1993–96, visiting prof Univ of Glasgow 1999–; dir and chair: The Lighthouse Tst 1998–2007, Glasgow Sch of Art 1999–; memb D&AD; FSCD, FRSA; *Awards* RSA 1983, Scottish Film Cncl 1983, Newberry Medal 1984, commended finalist Prince Philip Designer of the Year Award 1994, Conran Fndn Archive Collector 1996; *Publications* New Packaging Design (2009); contrib magazines incl: Creative Review, Design Review, Architectural Journal, Scottish Homes and Interiors; delivered numerous papers on design issues; *Recreations* Clydesdale horses, horsemanship, beekeeping, British Saddleback pigs; *Style*— Prof Janice Kirkpatrick, OBE; ✉ Graven Images Ltd, 175 Albion Street, Glasgow G1 1RU (☎ 0141 552 6626, fax 0141 552 0433, e-mail janice@graven.co.uk)

KIRKPATRICK, (William) Niall Alexander; s of William Arthur Kirkpatrick, of Chard, Som, and Marlise Meta Erna, *née* Filippa; *b* 29 December 1959, Aldershot, Hants; *Educ* Wellington Coll, Guy's Hosp (BDS, MB, BS); *Career* conslt craniofacial plastic surgn 2003, head Craniofacial Unit Chelsea and Westminster Hosp 2003–; conslt plastic surgn Head and Neck Unit Charing Cross Hosp 2003–09 (currently hon conslt plastic surgeon), conslt plastic surgeon Royal Marsden Hosp London 2009–13; private conslt; chm, med dir and tstee Facing the World Charity; conslt plastic surgn www.essentiallymedical.co.uk; lectr Dept of Anatomy Guy's and St Thomas' Hosp London 1992–93, clinical tutor Imperial Coll London, hon clinical sr lectr Imperial Coll London; author of numerous articles in professional jls; memb: W London Cancer Network Head and Neck Cancer Multi-Disciplinary Team, W London Skin Cancer TWG Multidisciplinary Team; JPRAS Prize 2006; memb: Chelsea Clinical Soc, Br Assoc of Plastic, Reconstructive and Aesthetic Surgns (BAPRAS), Br Assoc of Aesthetic Plastic Surgns (BAAPS), Int Soc Aesthetic Plastic Surgery (ISAPS), European Soc of Craniofacial Surgery (ESCFS), Br Assoc of Head and Neck Oncologists (BAHNO), Br Assoc of Oral Maxillofacial Surgns (BAOMS), BMA, RSM (hon sec 2005–06, pres 2007–08); FRCS 1996 (plast 2001); *Style*— Mr Niall Kirkpatrick; ✉ The Consulting Suite, 212–214 Great Portland Street, London W1W 5QN (☎ 020 7927 6512, fax 020 7297 6511, niallkirkpatrick@theconsultingsuite.co.uk); The Cadogan Clinic, 120 Sloane Street, London SW1X 9BW (☎ 020 7901 8500, e-mail info@cadoganclinic.com); Chelsea and Westminster Hospital, 369 Fulham Road, London SW10 9NH (☎ 020 8746 8358, fax 020 8746 8689, e-mail niall.kirkpatrick@chelwest.nhs.uk)

KIRKWOOD, Bryan; *b* Bellshill, Lanarkshire; *Career* story ed Coronation Street (ITV) 2004–05, prodr Hollyoaks (Channel 4) 2006–09, exec prodr EastEnders (BBC 1) 2010–12, Lime Pictures 2012–; *Style*— Bryan Kirkwood, Esq

KIRKWOOD, Colin Bennie; s of Matthew Chrystal Kirkwood (d 1991), of Killearn, Stirlingshire, and Charlotte Margaret, *née* Bennie (d 1993); *b* 6 December 1951; *Educ* Glasgow Acad, Napier Coll of Science and Technol Edinburgh (Dip Book and Periodical Publishing); *m* 4 April 1987, Isabel Mary, da of David Gordon Johnstone (d 1976); 1 s (Matthew David b 1989), 1 da (Rosanna Mary b 1991); *Career* The Aberdeen University Press Ltd 1990–92, publishing conslt 1992–93, publishing dir Times Books/Bartholomew Div HarperCollins Publishers Ltd 1993–94, publishing and mktg conslt 1994–95, mktg dir Colin Baxter Photography Ltd 1995–2006, mktg conslt 2006–07; CairnGorm Mountain Ltd: mktg exec 2007–11, mktg, PR and sales mangr 2011–14; md Piccolo Press 2015–; chm Scot Young Publishers Soc 1979, chm Scot Publishers Assoc 1984–86, dir Tuckwell Press 1994–95, memb Bd Edinburgh Book Festival 1984–89, ed Charles Rennie Mackintosh Soc Newsletter 1976–84; *Books* The National Book League (1972); *Recreations* skiing, tennis, walking, cooking, architecture; *Style*— Colin B Kirkwood, Esq; ✉ Easter Coulnakyle, Nethy Bridge, Inverness-shire PH25 3EA (☎ 01479 821393)

KIRKWOOD, Nicholas; s of John Kirkwood, and Wendy, *née* Schneidau; *b* 10 July 1980, UK; *Educ* Central St Martins, Cordwainers Coll; *Career* shoe designer; launched first collection 2005, consultant dir Pollini 2008–, fndr and creative dir Nicholas Kirkwood Ltd; Italian Vogue/Alta Roma Accessories Designer of the Year 2007, Emerging Talent for Accessories Br Fashion Award 2008, Conde Nast Footwear News Designer of the Year 2008, Accessory Designer of the Year Elle Style Award 2013; *Recreations* cinema, fashion, horse racing, music, opera, travel; *Clubs* Soho House; *Style*— Nicholas Kirkwood, Esq; ✉ 5b Mount Street, London W1K 3NE (e-mail studio@nicholaskirkwood.com)

KIRKWOOD OF KIRKHOPE, Baron (Life Peer UK 2005), of Kirkhope in Scottish Borders; Sir Archibald Johnstone (Archy) Kirkwood; kt (2002); s of David Kirkwood, of Glasgow, and Jessie Barclay (d 1980); *b* 22 April 1946; *Educ* Heriot-Watt Univ (BSc); *m* 1972, Rosemary Jane, da of Edward John Chester; 1 s, 1 da; *Career* slr; MP (Lib until 1988, now Lib Dem) Roxburgh and Berwickshire 1983–2005; House of Commons: Lib spokesman on health and social security 1985–87, Alliance spokesman on overseas devpt 1987, Lib spokesman on Scotland 1987–88, SLD spokesman on welfare, health and educn 1988–89, Lib Dem convenor and spokesman on welfare and social security 1989–94, Lib Dem chief whip 1992–97 (dep 1989–92), Lib Dem spokesman on community care 1994–97, spokesman House of Commons Cmmn 1997–2005, chm Social Security Select Ctee 1997–2001, chm Work and Pensions Select Ctee 2001–05, sponsored Private Member's Bills leading to Access to Personal Files Act 1987 and Access to Medical Reports Act 1988; chm Lib Dem Campaigns Ctee 1989–92; chm Rowntree Reform Tst 1985–2007; former memb Bd of Govrs Westminster Fndn for Democracy; *Recreations* music; *Style*— The Lord Kirkwood of Kirkhope

KIRSCHEL, Laurence Grant; s of Eric Kirschel, and Ruth, *née* Novak; *b* 17 December 1962, Middlesex; *Educ* Franklin House London, Carmel Coll Wallingford; *Children* 1 s (Davar Ethan b 3 Aug 2000); *Career* property developer; estab main company 1983; tstee Kirschel Fndn; FRICS; *Style*— Laurence Kirschel, Esq; ✉ 26 Soho Square, London W1D 4NU (☎ 020 7437 4372, fax 020 7437 3800, e-mail laurence@26sohosq.com)

KIRSTEIN, Prof Peter Thomas; CBE (2003); s of Walter Kirstein (d 1983), of London; *b* 20 June 1933; *Educ* Highgate Sch, UCLA, Gonville & Caius Coll Cambridge (BA), Stanford Univ (MSc, PhD), Univ of London (DSc); *m* 5 July 1958, Gwen Margaret Oldham; 2 da (Sarah Lynn b 1964, Claire Fiona b 1971); *Career* res assoc and lectr W W Hansen Laboratory of Physics Stanford Univ 1957–58, accelerator physicist Centre of European Nuclear Research Geneva 1959–63, scientific rep Europe General Electric Company of USA 1963–67, prof of computer systems Univ of London 1970–73 (reader in information processing 1967–70); UCL: prof 1973–, head Dept of Computer Science 1980–95, dir of research 1995–2006, hon fell 2006; pioneer Internet Hall of Fame 2012; Sr Award IEE 1999, ComSoc Award IEEE 1999, Postel Award 2003, Lifetime Achievement Award RAE 2006, Marconi Award 2015; foreign hon memb AAAS 2002, foreign assoc Nat Acad of Engrg (USA) 2009; FIEE 1965, FInstP 1965, SMIEEE 1975, FREng 1985, distinguished FBCS 2003 (FBCS 1964); *Books* Space Charge Flow (1967); *Recreations* skiing, tennis, bridge; *Clubs* Alpine Ski; *Style*— Prof Peter Kirstein, CBE, FREng; ✉ 31 Bancroft Avenue, London N2 0AR (☎ 020 8340 3154); Department of Computer Science, University College London, Gower Street, London WC1E 6BT (☎ 020 7679 7286, fax 020 7387 1397, e-mail kirstein@cs.ucl.ac.uk)

KIRWAN, Prof Laurence Anthony; s of Maurice Kirwan (d 2003), and Bertha, *née* Endbinder (d 1999); *b* 31 March 1952, Liverpool; *Educ* Victoria Univ of Manchester (MB, ChB); *Career* plastic surgn in private practice; attending surgeon Section of Plastic Surgery Greenwich Hosp Assoc CT 1987–, sr attending surgeon Section of Plastic Surgery Norwalk Hosp CT 1987–, attending staff Section of Plastic Surgery NY Eye and Ear Infirmary 1996–, attending surgeon Centre for Specialty Surgery NY; conslt plastic surgeon: London Welbeck Hosp, Hosp of St John & St Elizabeth London 2000–, Princess Grace Hosp 2011; prof Int Sch of Aesthetic Plastic Surgery Univ of Belgrade 1996; founding dir Doctors For All People AmeriCares Fndn 1989, jt dir AmeriCares Mission Armenia 1989; memb: Connecticut Med Soc 1987, American Soc of Plastic and Reconstructive Surgeons 1987, Fairfield County Medical Assoc 1987, NY Regnl Soc of Plastic and Reconstructive Surgery 1995, American Soc for Aesthetic Plastic Surgery 1997; diplomate American Bd of Plastic Surgery 1989; FRCS 1979, FACS 1993; *Publications* incl: Three-Dimensional Liposculpture of the Iliac Crest and Lateral Thigh (Aesthetic Surgery Jl, 17, 1997), Simultaneous Areolar Mastopexy / Breast Augmentation – The SAMBA Procedure (Aesthetic Surgery Jl, 19, 1999), A Classification and Algorithm for Treatment of Breast Ptosis (Aesthetic Surgery Jl, 22, 2002), My Mole Book: A Children's Information Book (2003), Cutting Edge (2004), Breast Auto-Augmentation (Canadian Jl of Plastic Surgery, 15(2), 2007), Ophelia Blue Eyes (2009), Breast Auto-Augmentation: A Versatile Method of Breast Rehabilitation. A Retrospective Series of 107 Procedures (Archives of Plastic Surgery, 2015); numerous articles in professional jls; *Recreations* writing, spending time with family, acting; *Clubs* Home House; *Style*— Prof Laurence Kirwan; ✉ Ground Floor Suite, 56 Harley Street, London W1G 9QA (☎ 020 7637 4455, e-fax 020 7657 4475, e-mail drkirwan@drkirwan.com, website www.cosmeticplasticsurgery.uk.com, Twitter @drkirwan)

KISSACK, Nigel Euan Jackson; s of Maj Henry Jackson Kissack, RE (ret), of Sydney, Aust, and formerly Isle of Man, and Valerie Kissack; *b* 8 April 1955; *Educ* King William's Coll IOM, Univ of Sheffield (LLB), Chester Coll of Law; *m* 11 Oct 1980, Kathryn Margaret, da of Thomas Lloyd-Jones, of Hale, Cheshire; 1 da (Annabel Laura Jayne b 4 Aug 1982), 1 s (Richard Lloyd b 2 Aug 1984); *Career* admitted slr 1979; ptnr DLA 1980–97, ptnr Pinsent Masons 1997–13 (head of litigation 1997–2012); *Recreations* rugby, cricket, cycling, reading, golf, skiing; *Style*— Nigel Kissack, Esq

KISSMANN, Edna; da of Karl Kissmann (d 1983), of Jerusalem, and Frieda Mosser Kissmann, of Tel Aviv; *b* 20 December 1949; *Educ* Hebrew Univ HS, Hebrew Univ (BA), Univ of Boston Sch of Public Communications (MSc); *Career* asst press sec PM's Office Govt of Israel 1975, md Ruder and Finn PR Ltd Israel 1976–77 (assoc dir 1973–75); Burson-Marsteller Inc NY: account exec 1978–79, account supervisor 1979–80, client servs mangr 1980–82, gp mangr 1982–85, vice-pres then sr vice-pres, exec vice-pres and unit mangr i/c healthcare communications practice 1985–88; Burson-Marsteller London: EUP/unit mangr of healthcare and mktg 1988–89, jt md 1989–92; chief Burson-Marsteller Germany 1992–93; Burson-Marsteller London: global head of healthcare practice 1994–97, chief knowledge offr worldwide 1997–99; winner of several internal Burson-Marsteller awards; vice-chm Europe 1993; memb Bd: Business in the Community, London First Centre; fndr memb Israel PR Assoc 1974 (memb London 1990); *Recreations* music, theatre, travel, people, good food and wine; *Clubs* The Reform; *Style*— Miss Edna Kissmann

KISZELY, Lt-Gen Sir John Panton; KCB (2004), MC (1982), DL (Glos 2010); s of Dr John Kiszely (d 1995), and Maude, *née* Panton (d 2010); *b* 2 April 1948; *Educ* Marlborough, RMAS; *m* 28 July 1984, Hon Arabella Jane, da of 3 Baron Herschell, *qv*; 3 s (Alastair b 17 Feb 1986, Matthew b 27 Nov 1987, Andrew b 28 April 1990); *Career* CO 1 Bn Scots Guards 1986–88 (mentioned in despatches 1988), Cdr 22 Armd Bde 1991–93, Cdr 7 Armd Bde 1993, Dep Cmdt Staff Coll Camberley 1993–96, GOC 1 (UK) Armd Div 1996–98, ACDS (Resources and Plans) MOD 1998–2001, Dep Cdr NATO Force Bosnia 2001–02, Cdr Regnl Forces 2002–04, Dep Cdr Multinational Force Iraq 2004–05, DG Defence Acad 2005–08; Regtl Lt Col Scots Gds 1995–2001, Col Comdt The Intelligence Corps 2000–08, Hon Col Univ of London Offr Trg Corps 2003–09; visiting prof in war studies KCL 2008–13; nat pres Royal Br Legion 2009–12, tstee Imperial War Museum 2008–, memb Advsy Bd Baltic Defence Coll 2011–, vice patron Disabled Sailors Assoc 2010–; Queen's Commendation for Valuable Service 1996; memb Hon Co of Glos; Liveryman Worshipful Co of Painter-Stainers; CRAeS 2006; Offr Legion of Merit (USA) 2005; *Publications* contrib: The Science of War: Back to First Principles (1983), Military Power: Land Warfare in Theory and Practice (1997), The Falklands Conflict Twenty Years On (2004), The Past as Prologue: History and the Military Profession (2006), The Impenetrable Fog of War (2008), Coalition Command in Contemporary Operations (2008), British Generals in Blair's Wars (2013); author of numerous articles in military jls; *Recreations* sailing, fishing, music; *Clubs* Royal Solent Yacht, Cavalry and Guards'; *Style*— Lt-Gen Sir John Kiszely, KCB, MC, DL; ✉ c/o HQ Scots Guards, Wellington Barracks, Birdcage Walk, London SW1E 6HQ (☎ 020 7930 4466)

KITCHEN, Michael; s of Arthur Kitchen, and Betty, *née* Allen; *b* 31 October 1948; *Educ* City of Leicester Boys GS, RADA; *Children* 2 s (Jack b 7 Oct 1988, Jamie b 25 Nov 1995); *Career* actor; writer of two screenplays and short stories; *Theatre* work incl: Nat Theatre 1974–84, RSC 1987 (roles incl Hogarth, Mercutio, Bolingbroke), Lenny in The Homecoming (West End); *Television* numerous appearances incl: Caught on a Train, Brimstone and Treacle, Home Run, Benefactors, The Brontës, Freud, No Man's Land, Savages, Chancer, The Justice Game, Bedroom Farce, King Lear, A Comedy of Errors, School Play, Love Song, Ball Trap at the C?te Sauvage, To Play the King, Dandelion Dead, Buccaneers, The Hanging Gale, Reckless, Wilderness, Oliver Twist, The Secret World of Michael Fry, Foyle's War, Alibi, Falling, Mobile, Hacks, Brian Pern – Life of Rock; *Film* incl: Out of Africa, The Russia House, Fools of Fortune, The Dive, Pied Piper, Unman Wittering and Zigo, The Bunker, The Enchanted April, Hostage, The Guilty, The Trial, Mrs Dalloway, Goldeneye, The Last Contract, The World is Not Enough, Proof of Life, My Week With Marilyn; *Recreations* music, guitar, piano, composition, pilot's licence, sailing, tennis, skiing, swimming; *Style*— Michael Kitchen, Esq; ✉ c/o Independent Talent Group, 40 Whitfield Street, London W1T 2RH (☎ 020 7636 6565)

KITCHENER, Prof Henry Charles; *b* 1 July 1951; *Educ* Eastwood HS, Univ of Glasgow (MB ChB, MD); *m* 12 June 1977, Valerie Anne, 1 da (Sophie); *Career* Florence and William Blair-Bell res fell 1980–82, lectr in obstetrics and gynaecology Univ of Singapore 1983–84, William Blair-Bell meml lectr RCOG 1985, conslt obstetrician and gynaecologist specialising in gynaecological oncology Aberdeen Royal NHS Tst 1988–96, prof of gynaecological oncology Univ of Manchester 1996–; pres Br Soc for Colposcopy and Cervical Pathology (BSCCP) 2000–03 (vice-pres 1997–99), memb Gynaecological Visiting Soc of GB and I; FRCSGlas 1989, FRCOG 1994 (MRCOG 1980); *Recreations* golf, hill walking; *Clubs* Prestbury Golf, Royal Dornoch Golf; *Style*— Prof Henry Kitchener; ✉ Southlands, Bridge End Drive, Prestbury, Cheshire SK10 4DL (e-mail hckitchener@aol.com); Department of Obstetrics and Gynaecology, St Mary's Hospital, Oxford Road, Manchester M13 0JH (☎ 0161 276 6461, fax 0161 273 6134)

KITCHENER-FELLOWES; *see:* Fellowes

KITCHIN, Alan William Norman; s of Norman Tyson Kitchin (d 1995), and Shirley Boyd, *née* Simpson; *Educ* Oundle, Univ of Cambridge (Squire univ scholar, BA, Tapp postgrad scholar, MA); *Career* admitted slr 1978; Ashurst Morris Crisp (now Ashurst): ptnr 1986–, ptnr in charge Tokyo office 1991–2003, managing ptnr Asia 1998–2003, head worldwide Japanese practice 2003–; chm Infrastructure and Privatisation Ctee Law Asia; *Books* International Trade for the Nonspecialist (co-author); *Recreations* golf, tennis; *Clubs* Walton Heath Golf, Luffenham Heath Golf, Reform, Kasumigaseki Golf Tokyo; *Style*— Alan Kitchin, Esq; ✉ Ashurst, Broadwalk House, 5 Appold Street, London EC2A 2HA (☎ 020 7638 1111, fax 020 7972 7990, e-mail alan.kitchin@ashursts.com)

KITCHIN, Rt Hon Lord Justice; Sir David James Tyson; kt (2005), PC (2011), QC (1994); s of Norman Tyson Kitchin (d 1995), and Shirley Boyd, *née* Simpson (d 2002); *b* 30 April 1955; *Educ* Oundle, Fitzwilliam Coll Cambridge (MA); *m* 28 Oct 1989, Charlotte, da of Cdr David Jones; 1 da (Lara b 16 June 1991), 1 s (James b 2 July 1993); *Career* called to the Bar Gray's Inn 1977 (bencher 2003), judge of the High Court of Justice (Chancery Div) 2005–11, Chancery supervising judge Midland, Wales and Western Circuits 2009–11, Lord Justice of the Court of Appeal 2011–; chm Vet Code of Practice Ctee Nat Office of Animal Health 1995–2001, memb Enlarged Bd of Appeal European Patent Office 2009–11; chm Intellectual Property Bar Assoc 2004–05, memb Bar Cncl 2004–05; memb Cncl Queen Mary London 2006–11, hon fell Fitzwilliam Coll Cambridge 2012, chm Advsy Cncl Centre for Commercial Law Studies Queen Mary Univ of London 2015–; Hon LLD Queen Mary Univ London 2015; *Recreations* golf, tennis, theatre; *Clubs* Walton Heath, Leander, Hawks' (Cambridge); *Style*— The Rt Hon Lord Justice Kitchin; ✉ Royal Courts of Justice, Strand, London WC2A 2LL

KITCHING, Alan; *b* 29 December 1940; *m* 1, 1962, Rita, *née* Haylett (d 1984); 2 s; m 2, 2007, Celia, *née* Stothard (d 2010); *Career* compositor to J W Brown & Son Darlington 1956–61, fndr (with Anthony Froshaug) Experimental Printing Workshop Sch of Art Watford Coll of Technol 1964 (first year work exhibited ICA 1965), freelance design practice working in magazine and book design 1971–78, fndr (with Derek Birdsall) Omnific Studios Partnership Covent Garden 1978–86, subsequently estab letterpress studio Islington 1986, fndr/designer The Typography Workshop Clerkenwell 1989–; pt/t teacher of typography Central Sch of Art & Design London 1968–72, visiting lectr in typography RCA 1988–2006, visiting prof London Inst 2001, visiting prof Univ of the Arts London 2001; estab letterpress workshops RCA 1992, subsequent workshops at Univs of Brighton and Middx and Glasgow, Hereford, Falmouth and Exeter Schs of Art, workshop/lecture tour Norway 1997, Germany 1999, Denmark and Holland 2000, Barcelona Forum LAUS 2004, SUPSI-LCV Lugano 2007 and 2009, lectures incl ATypI Lyon 1998, Univ of NSW Sydney and AGI Ideas Melbourne 2002, Typo3 Johannesburg 2003 and Biblioteket Stockholm 2007; designer millennium stamp for Royal Mail 1999; memb AGI 1994, RDI 1994; FRCA 1998 (hon FRCA 2006); *Exhibitions* Pentagram Gall London (first exhbn of letterpress work) 1992, RCA (retrospective exhbn of typography and printing) 1993, Type Art '98 (Coningsby Gallery) 1998, Pentagram Gall London (solo) 2002, Typography: Alan Kitching (St Bride Library) (solo show and retrospective with lectures) 2007, retrospective at Somerset House 2016, The Lettering Arts Centre Snape Suffolk 2016; contrib to/participant in: Communicate: Independent British Graphic Design since the Sixties (Barbican Art Gallery) 2004, 26 Letters: Illuminating the Alphabet (Br Library) 2004–05, Advanced Graphics London 2010, RA Summer Show 2011 and 2012; *Books and Publications* Typography Manual (Watford Sch of Art, 1970), Broadside (occasional pubn devoted to the typographic arts, 1 edn 1988), A-Z of Letterpress (2015), Alan Kitching a Life in Letterpress (2016); *Clubs* Chelsea Arts, London Sketch; *Style*— Alan Kitching, RDI, AGI, Hon FRCA; ✉ The Typography Workshop, 19 Cleaver Street, London SE11 4DP

KITCHING, John; s of Douglas Eric Kitching, of Barwell, Leics (d 1992), and Dorothy Violet, *née* Mellors (d 2005); *b* 7 July 1950, Surrey; *Educ* Davidson HS Croydon; *m* 1, 16 March 1973; 1 da (Sarah Elaine b 16 May 1975); m 2, 15 May 1982, Elaine, *née* Flint; 1 da (Elizabeth Elzine b 24 March 1983); *Career* early career as building services design engr then various sr mgmnt roles Harris Queensway; Carpetright plc: joined 1988, sales dir 1992, md 1996, chief exec Europe 2005, chief exec Storey Carpets 2007–; MInstD; *Recreations* authy on the life and times of Queen Victoria, classic 20th century Br motor cars; *Style*— John Kitching, Esq; ✉ Carpetright plc, Harris House, Purfleet By-Pass, Purfleet, Essex RM19 1TT (☎ 01708 802000, fax 01708 805423)

KITCHING, Paul; s of William Kitching (d 1968), and Angela Ainslie (d 2002); *b* 23 March 1961; *Educ* Dryden Rd HS Gateshead, Newcastle Coll of Art & Technol; *Career* commis chef: Viking Hotel 1981–83, Middlethorpe Hall York 1983–84; sous chef: Restaurant 74 Canterbury (joined as commis chef) 1984–87, Gidleigh Park 1987–90 (joined as 3 chef); head chef Nunsmere Hall Hotel 1990–96, head chef and owner Juniper 1996–2008, head chef and owner 21212 Edinburgh 2009–; *Awards* for Nunsmere Hall Hotel: 3 stars Good Food Guide and Co Restaurant of the Year 1993 and 1995, 3 AA rosettes 1993–96, 3 AA red stars (for hotel), Egon Ronay 77% (for hotel); for Juniper: Cheshire Life Newcomer of the Year, City Life Best Restaurant, Manchester Evening News Best Dinner, 3 stars Good Food Guide and Co Restaurant of the Year 1997, Cheshire Life Restaurant of the Year 1998, 7 out of 10 Good Food Guide (annually) 1998–2007, Michelin rosette (annually) 1998–2007, Highest Rated Restaurant in Manchester, Gtr Manchester, Lancashire, and Cheshire 1996–99, Highest Rated Restaurant in the North West, placed 17th in top 50 Restaurants 2000–2001, 4 AA rosettes (annually) 2002–07, Good Food Guide Restaurant of the Year 2003, Guardian Weekend 18.5/20 and Restaurant of the Year 2003, Metro News Restaurant of the Year 2003, Life Magazine Northwest Chef of the Year 2003, Life Magazine Restaurant of the Year (Cheshire) 2007; for 21212: Best New Restaurant in the UK Nat Restaurant Award 2009, Eat Scotland Gold Award, Most Sylish Hotel Style Award 2009, Michelin star 2010–, AA 5 star Restaurant with Rooms, Best Newcomer CIS Award 2010, Chef of the Year CIS Award 2011, Restaurant of the Year CIS Award 2012, Prince Philip Medal 2012, 4 AA rosettes, listed in AA Guide 2013–; Restaurant Chef Award Craft Guild of Chefs Awards 2014; *Recreations* history of the American Civil War 1861–65; *Style*— Paul Kitching, Esq; ✉ 21212, 3 Royal Terrace, Edinburgh EH7 5AB

KITNEY, Prof Richard Ian; OBE (2001); s of Leonard Walter Richard Kitney, and Gladys Simpson, *née* Byrne; *b* 13 February 1945; *Educ* Enfield GS, Univ of Surrey (DipEE, MSc), Imperial Coll London (PhD, DIC) Univ of London (DSc); *m* 7 May 1977, Vera Theresa; 2 s (Andrew John b 18 March 1978, Paul David b 30 July 1980); *Career* electronics engr Thorn EMI 1963–72, lectr in biophysics Chelsea Coll London 1972–78; Imperial Coll London: lectr 1978–85, reader 1985–89, prof 1989–, dir Centre of Biological and Med Systems 1991–97, head of dept 1997–2001, dean Faculty of Engrg 2003–07; visiting prof: Georgia Inst of Technol 1981–90, MIT 1991–; govr Imperial Coll London 1995–98, govr Royal Post Grad Med Sch 1995–98; tech dir Intravascular Research Ltd 1987–94, dir St Mary's Imaging plc 1991–96, chm Visbion Ltd 2007–; tstee Smith and Nephew Fndn 1996; regular contrib to BBC radio progs, also occasional film and TV work; Freeman City of London 1996, Liveryman Worshipful Co of Engrs 1995; FIEE 1993, FRSM 1994, FRCPEd 1996, FREng 1999, fell World Technology Network 2000, FRSA 2001, FRSE 2016; *Publications* 175 full research papers, 152 refereed conference papers, 3 inquiry reports and 3 books (full details at http://www.imperial.ac.uk/people/r.kitney); *Recreations* history, cooking, France; *Clubs* Athenaeum; *Style*— Prof Richard Kitney, OBE; ✉ Department of Bioengineering, Imperial College, London SW7 2AZ (☎ 020 7594 6226, fax 020 7584 4297, mobile 07785 341922, e-mail r.kitney@imperial.ac.uk)

KITTEL, Gerald Anthony (Gerry); s of Francis William Berthold Kittel (d 2000), of Pinner Hill, Middx, and Eileen Winifred, *née* Maybanks (d 1973); *b* 24 February 1947; *Educ* Merchant Taylors', Univ of Poitiers (Dip), Ealing Poly; *m* 26 April 1975, Jean Samantha, *née* Beveridge; 2 s (Christian b 1969, Ashley b 1976), 1 da (Natalie b 1979); *Career* currently chm City Road Communications Ltd, dir KML Ltd; chief exec The Invention Shop Ltd, chm Open Internet Solutions Ltd (Mabel Maybanks cosmetics range, Bar-Star promotional bar products for the drinks and retail trades and specialist in social networking platforms and online marketing), chief exec Osmatic Systems (manufacturers of on-license beer dispense and control systems and CO2 recyclers), chm Osmatic Systems LLC (US agents); MInstM, MIPA, MCIM, MInstD; *Recreations* riding, carting, farming; *Clubs* Old Merchant Taylors' Soc; *Style*— Gerry A Kittel, Esq; ✉ Oakhurst, Meres Lane, Five Ashes, Mayfield, East Sussex TN20 6JT (☎ 01435 873008, e-mail gerry.kittel@openinternetsolutions.com)

KITTMER, HE John; s of Roy Kittmer, of Brandesburton, Yorks, and Jean, *née* Southern; *b* 6 July 1967, Cuckfield, W Sussex; *Educ* Christ's Coll Cambridge (BA), KCL (MA); *Partner* David Bates (civil partnership 30 March 2007); *Career* diplomat and civil servant; DfEE: private sec to Parly Under Sec of State 1995–97, team ldr social policy EU Div 1997–98; first sec employment and social policy UK Perm Rep to EU 1998–2002; FCO: section head EU Accession Treaty and Bill EU Directorate 2003, section head peacekeeping and international policing Conflict Group 2003–04; dep dir EU & International Better Reg Exec Cabinet Office 2006–07; DEFRA: team ldr Animal Welfare Bill 2004–06, dep dir exotic animal diseases 2008, princ private sec to Sec of State 2008–10, dep dir inland waterways & EU strategy support 2011–12; ambass to Greece 2013–; *Style*— HE Mr John Kittmer; ✉ c/o Foreign & Commonwealth Office (Athens), King Charles Street, London SW1A 2AH; British Embassy Athens, 1 Ploutarchou Street, 106 75 Athens, Greece (☎ 0030 210 727 2602, fax 0030 210 727 2723)

KITZINGER, Uwe; CBE (1980); *b* 12 April 1928; *Educ* Watford GS, Balliol Coll and New Coll Oxford (MA, MLitt, pres Oxford Union 1950); *m* 1952, Sheila Helena Elizabeth, *née* Webster, MBE (d 2015); 5 da; *Career* Cncl of Europe 1951–56, fell Nuffield Coll 1956–76 (emeritus fell 1976–), fndr ed Journal of Common Market Studies 1961–; visiting prof: Univ of the West Indies 1964–65, Harvard Univ 1969–70, Paris Univ 1970–73; advsr to vice-pres of EC Cmmn i/c external rels Brussels 1973–75, dean Euro Inst of Business

Admin INSEAD Fontainebleau 1976–80 (hon alumnus 1980–), dir Oxford Centre for Mgmnt Studies 1980–84, fndr pres Templeton Coll Oxford 1984–91 (hon fell 2001–), visiting scholar Harvard Univ 1993–2003 (affiliate 2003–), sr res fell Atlantic Cncl 1993–; fndr chm: Ctee on Atlantic Studies 1967–70, Major Projects Assoc 1981–86; fndr pres Int Assoc of Macro-Engr Socs 1987–92 and 1996–2001; chm Oxfordshire Radio Ltd 1988, co-fndr Lentils for Dubrovnik 1991–93; pres Fedération Britannique des Alliances Francaises 1999–2004, chair GARIWO Campaign for Civil Courage Sarajevo 2001–12; patron Asylum Welcome 2004–; memb Br Univs Ctee of the Encyclopedia Brittanica 1967–98; memb Int Bds: Conflict Mgmnt Gp Cambridge MA 1997–2003, Inst for Transition to Democracy Zagreb 1997–2016; memb Cncl: RIIA 1973–85, European Movement 1974–76, Oxfam 1981–85, Fondation Jean Monnet 1990–, Tufts Inst for Global Leadership 2006–16; Global Citizenship Award Tufts Univ 2016; hon fell Green Templeton Coll Oxford 2008–; Hon LLD 1986; Order of the Morning Star (Croatia) 1997; *Books* German Electoral Politics (1960), The Challenge of the Common Market (1961), The Politics and Economics of European Integration (1963), Britain, Europe and Beyond (1964), The European Common Market and Community (1967), The Second Try (1968), Commitment and Identity (1968), Diplomacy and Persuasion (1973), Europe's Wider Horizons (1975), The 1975 Referendum (with D Butler, 1976, republished 1996), Macro-Engineering and the Earth (with E Frankel, 1998); documents, books articles and press cuttings on Britain's relations with the emergent EU from 1945 to 1976 deposited in the Historical Archives of the EU European Univ Inst Florence 2012 (http://www.eui.eu/HAEU/pdfinv/inv-uwkns.pdf); *Recreations* sailing (ketch 'Anne of Cleves'); *Clubs* Royal Thames Yacht; *Style—* Uwe Kitzinger, Esq, CBE; ✉ Standlake Manor, Witney, Oxfordshire (☎ 01865 300266, e-mail uwe_kitzinger@yahoo.com); La Rivière, 11100 Bages, France (☎ 0033 468 417013)

KLASS, Myleene; *b* 6 April 1978, Norfolk; *m* 2011 (m dis 2013), Graham Quinn; 2 da (Ava Bailey b 2007, Hero Harper b 2011); *Career* TV presenter and former singer; memb Hear'Say 2001–02, subsequently solo artist; albums with Hear'Say: Popstars 2001, Everybody 2001; solo albums: Moving On 2003, Myleene's Music For Romance 2007, Mylene's Music for Mothers 2008; singles with Hear'Say: Pure and Simple 2001 (UK no 1), The Way To Your Love 2001 (UK no 1), Everybody 2001, Lovin' Is Easy 2002; presenter: CD:UK (ITV) 2005–06, The One Show (BBC) 2007, Last Choir Standing (BBC) 2008, 10 Years Younger (Channel 4) 2008–09, I'm A Celebrity...Get Me Out Of Here! (US version) 2009, Popstar to Operastar (ITV) 2010–; *Style—* Ms Myleene Klass; ✉ c/o Roar Global Ltd, ROAR House, 46 Charlotte Street, London W1T 2GS

KLASSNIK, Robin; OBE (2014); s of Dr Benjamin Klassnik, and Leila Fabian, *née* Hammerschalg; *b* 28 January 1947; *Educ* Haverstock Comprehensive Sch, Hornsey Coll of Art, Leicester Coll of Art (BA); *m* 1 Dec 1979, Kathryn, da of Henry Halton; 1 s (Tomas b 2 Jan 1981), 1 da (Zoë b 9 Oct 1983); *Career* artist, lectr, gallery owner; fndr, owner and dir Matts Gallery 1979–; gp ldr Fndn Course London Coll of Printing 1979–82, head Complementary Studies Byam Shaw Sch of Art 1982– (visiting lectr 1977–82), res asst (sculpture theory) Statens Kunstakademie Oslo Norway 1990–91; guest lectr: Poznan Acad of Fine Art, Maidstone Sch of Art, Camberwell Sch of Art, Brighton Poly, Slade Sch of Fine Art, Statens Kunstakademie Oslo, Goldsmiths Coll London, RCA London, Valands Konsthogskola Göteborg Sweden, Bath Coll of HE, Chelsea Coll of Art & Design (external examiner sculpture MA); dir New Contemporaries; publisher of artists books and bookworks; *Solo Exhibitions* incl: Walk Through Painting (Pavilions in the Park Croydon) 1969, Nine Till Four (Acland Burghley Sch) 1969, Postal Sculpture (Boyd Inst and James Carters Bookshop) 1970, 34'3' x 57' x 11'6' (New Gallery) 1970, Galeria Dois Porto Portugal 1974, Open Studio Martello St 1974, Galeria Akumulatory 2 Poznan Poland 1975, Space Open Studios 1976, Nearly a Sculpture (Galeria Akumulatory 2, Galeria Pawilon Kraków, Whitechapel Art Gallery) 1978–79, Five Pheromones The Incomplete Documentation (Matts Gallery) 1980, Three Works (Spectro Art Gallery Newcastle upon Tyne) 1981, To Be Or Not To Be Original That is The Question (Galeria Akumulatory 2, Piwna 20/26 Warsaw Poland) 1983; *Recreations* cricket; *Clubs* Burger King; *Style—* Robin Klassnik, Esq, OBE; ✉ Matt's Gallery, 42–44 Copperfield Road, London E3 4RR

KLEEMAN, David George; s of Jack Kleeman (d 1984), and Ruth, *née* Stephany (d 1981); *b* 20 August 1942; *Educ* St Paul's, Trinity Hall Cambridge (MA); *m* 1968, Manuela Rachel, da of Edouard Cori, of Paris; 4 da (Susanna b 1970, Nicole b 1973, Julie b 1974, Jenny b 1978); *Career* md Daman Financial Services Ltd; former chm: Computerlinks AG, Transense Technologies plc, Fayrewood plc; memb Bd Genesis Housing Gp 2006–12; dir of other public and private cos; sr ptnr Pickering Kenyon Slrs 1971–84; chm Enfield & Haringey HA 1991–95, dep chm NHS Logistics Authy 1995–2001; non-exec dir Housing Corp (responsible for Merseyside and the NW) 1990–98; chm Springboard Housing Assoc 2000–07; *Recreations* fly fishing, reading, opera; *Clubs* MCC, Fly Fishers, Piscatorial Soc; *Style—* David Kleeman, Esq; ✉ 15 St Stephens Close, London NW8 6DB (☎ 020 7449 9371, e-mail david@damanfinancial.co.uk)

KLEIN, Dr Gillian; *née* Falkow; da of Harry Falkow (d 1980), of Johannesburg, South Africa, and Enid, *née* Ash (d 1985); *Educ* Univ of the Witwatersrand (BA, Dip Library and Info Sci), Univ of Central England Birmingham (PhD); *Children* 1 s (Graeme b 31 Dec 1961), 1 da (Leanne b 20 March 1964); *Career* info offr private indust 1960–61, sch librarian 1967–74, librarian ILEA Centre for Urban Educnl Studies 1974–81, teacher fell Inst of Educn Univ of London 1981–82, resources advsr ILEA 1982–90; visiting lectr: Brighton Poly 1986–89, Poly of N London 1987–90, Univ of Warwick 1989–95, SOAS Univ of London 1996–2000; fndr and ed Race Equality Teaching Jl 1982–, editorial dir Trentham Books Ltd 1984–2012, publisher Trentham Books (IOE Press) 2013–; rapporteur Cncl of Europe Multicultural Studies in Higher Educn 1983–86; conslt: Children's Book Project of Thailand 1991–, ANC Centre for Educnl Policy; chair Anne Frank Tst 2003–06 (tstee 1993–2007); hon DUniv Birmingham City Univ 2009; FRSA 1993–2009; *Publications* incl: Fancy Dress Party (1981), Resources for Multicultural Education (1982), Scrapbooks (1983), School Libraries for Cultural Awareness (1985), Reading into Racism (1985), Agenda for Multicultural Teaching (jtly, 1986), Education towards Race Equality (1993), A Vision for Today – John Eggleston's Writings on Education (jtly, 2003), Equal Measures (jtly, 2004); *Recreations* family and friends, travel, theatre, art and architecture, swimming, reading, food; *Style—* Dr Gillian Klein; ✉ Trentham Books, IOE Press, Inst of Education, Univ of London, 20 Bedford Way, London WC1H 0AL

KLEIN, Roland; s of Fernand Klein (d 1982), and Marguerite, *née* Meyer (d 1987); *b* 3 July 1938; *Educ* CEC, BEPC and Beaux Arts Rouen France, Ecole de la Chambre Syndicale de la Haute Couture Parisienne and CAP Paris France; *Career* designer; Nat Serv France 1959–60; asst tailor Jean Patou Paris 1958–59, asst designer Christian Dior Paris 1960–61, asst designer Jean Patou and Karl Lagerfeld 1961–63, designer Nettie Vogue London 1963–66, design dir Marcel Fenez London 1970–88 (designer 1966–70), designer Roland Klein Ltd London and Tokyo 1988–, interior designer 2001–; major projects incl: conslt designer British Airways corporate image clothing 1986, Max Mara and Marina Rinaldi Italy 1988–, British Telecom corporate image clothing 1991, Halifax Building Society 1992, Midland Bank plc 1993, Russell & Bromley 1993; memb Br Interior Designer Assoc 2007–; Fil D'or 1987; *Style—* Roland Klein, Esq; ✉ Roland Klein Ltd, 16 Bolton Gardens, London SW5 0AJ (☎ 07960 824802, e-mail rmklondon@aol.com)

KLEINMAN, Daniel; s of Emmanuel (Ted) Kleinman (d 1987), and Mary, *née* Cockburn (d 2001); *b* 23 December 1955, London; *Educ* St Mary's Jr Sch Hendon, Orange Hill GS Burnt Oak, Hornsey Sch of Art (BA); *m* 5 August 1994, Judy, *née* Banks; *Career* played in various bands incl Bazooka Joe and Adam and the Ants; illustrator through Ian Femming Assocs until 1983, dir Limelight Films 1983–97, dir Spectre 1997–2003, dir Kleinman films 2003–05, dir Rattling Stick 2005–; dir of James Bond title sequences: Goldeneye 1995, Tomorrow Never Dies 1997, The World is Not Enough 1999, Die Another Day 2002, Casino Royale 2006, Skyfall 2012; *Awards* Lion d'Or Cannes 1992, 2001, 2002, 2003 (for Johnnie Walker 'Fish'), 2004 (for John Smiths 'Diving Mum and Ball Skills'), 2005 (for NSPCC 'Ventriloquist'), 2006 (for Sony Playstation 'Golfers, Traders, Athletes'), 2008 (for Monster.com 'Stork' and Smirnoff 'Sea'), 2009 (for Monster.com 'Double Take') and 2010 (for Plane Stupid 'Polar Bear'), Grand Prix Cannes 2006, Gold Award BTAA 1996, 1997, 1998, 1999, 2000, 2001, 2002, 2003, 2004, 2005, 2006, 2007, 2010 and 2011, Pencils D&AD 2001, 2002, 2003, 2004, 2005, 2006 and 2010, Gold Award Creative Circle 1996, 1997, 1998, 1999, 2000, 2001, 2002, 2003, 2004, 2005, 2006 and 2010, President's Award Creative Circle 2005, Gold NY Film Festival 2001, Chm's Award BTAA 2005, Gold One Show NYC 2006, Ad Week Dir of the Decade 2010; *Recreations* painting, growing vegetables and sweet peas, whistling out of tune; *Clubs* Century; *Style—* Daniel Kleinman, Esq; ✉ Rattling Stick, 1 Portland Mews, London W1F 8JE (☎ 020 7851 2000, e-mail info@rattlingstick.com, website www.rattlingstick.com)

KLEINWORT, Sir Richard Drake; 4 Bt (UK 1909), of Bolnore, Cuckfield, Sussex; DL (West Sussex 2005); s of Sir Kenneth Drake Kleinwort, 3 Bt (d 1994), and his 1 w, Lady Davina Rose Pepys (d 1973), da of 7 Earl of Cottenham; *b* 4 November 1960; *Educ* Stowe, Univ of Exeter (BA); *m* 29 Nov 1989, Lucinda, da of William Shand Kydd, of Bucks; 3 s (Rufus Drake b 16 Aug 1994, Tristan William b 10 July 1997, Ivo John b 24 June 1999), 1 da (Heloise b 28 Feb 1996); *Heir* s, Rufus Kleinwort; *Career* Kleinwort Benson Geneva 1979, Banco General de Negocios Buenos Aires 1983, banker corp fin Deutschebank AG Hamburg and Frankfurt 1985–88, Biss Lancaster plc 1988–89, Grandfield Rork Collins Financial 1989–91, dir Cardew & Co 1994–2000 (ptnr 1991–94), head of financial PR Ogilvy 2000–01, chm The Richard Kleinwort Consultancy Gp 2001–; non-exec dir RDF Gp plc 2008–10, non-exec chm Hungry Hamsters Ltd 2009–11, vice-chm Cubitt Consulting 2010–; memb Advsy Bd Kleinwort Benson 2011–; patron The Cuckfield Soc, vice-patron Sussex Young Cricketers Educn Tst (SYCET) 2008–; pres The Little Black Bag Housing Assoc; fell World Scout Fndn Geneva; chm Knepp Castle Polo Club 1997–2006; govr Stowe Sch 1999–2004, chm The Stowe Sch Fndn, chm The Campaign for Stowe until 2004; dir Steppes East Ltd; vice-pres Chichester Cathedral Millennium Endowment Appeal; memb: The Sussex Club, Royal Horticultural Soc, S of England Agric Soc, The Countryside Alliance, Inst King Edward VII Hosp Midhurst, Compagnie Internationale de la Chasse (CIC), Cncl of Ambassadors WWF UK; ambassador Study Support Prog Prince's Tst; tstee: The Ackroyd Tst, The Ernest Kleinwort Charitable Tst; High Sheriff W Sussex 2008–09; *Recreations* my family, laughter, travel, sports (in general), watching England win; *Clubs* MCC, Turf, WWF (1001), White's, The Benedicts, Arts; *Style—* Sir Richard Kleinwort, Bt, DL; ✉ Kleinwort Benson, 14 St George Street, London W1S 1FE

K

KLEMPERER, Prof Paul David; s of late Hugh G Klemperer, and late Ruth, *née* Jordan; *b* 15 August 1956; *Educ* King Edward's Sch Birmingham, Peterhouse Cambridge (BA), Stanford Univ (top student award, MBA, PhD); *m* 1989, Margaret, *née* Meyer; 2 s (David b 1995, William b 1997), 1 da (Katherine b 1997); *Career* conslt Andersen Consulting (now Accenture) 1978–80, Harkness fell of the Cwlth Fund 1980–82; Univ of Oxford: lectr in operations research and mathematical economics 1985–90, reader in economics 1990–95, Edgeworth prof of economics 1995–, John Thomson fell and tutor St Catherine's Coll 1985–95, fell Nuffield Coll 1995–; memb Competition Cmmn 2001–05; visiting positions: MIT 1987, Univ of Calif Berkeley 1991 and 1993, Stanford Univ 1991 and 1993, Yale Univ 1994, Princeton Univ 1998; princ auction theorist UK 3G auction UK Radiocommunications Agency 2000; conslt: US Federal Trade Cmmn 1999–2001, Bank of England 2007–, US Treasy 2008–09, Bank of Canada 2009; advsr to EU, US, UK and other govts and private firms; ed RAND Jl of Economics 1993–99; assoc ed or memb Editorial Bd: Oxford Economic Papers 1986–2000, Review of Economic Studies 1989–97, Jl of Industrial Economics 1989–96, International Jl of Industrial Organization 1993–, European Economic Review 1997–, Review of Economic Design 1997–2000, Economic Policy 1998–99, Economic Jl 2000–04, Frontiers in Economics 2000–, BE Jl of Economic Analysis and Policy 2001–, Jl of Competition Law and Economics 2004–; memb Cncl: Econometric Soc 2001–06, Royal Economic Soc 2001–05 (also memb Exec Ctee), European Economic Soc 2002–07; hon fell ESRC Centre for Economic Learning and Social Evolution (ELSE) 2001, fell European Econ Assoc 2004, foreign hon memb American Acad of Arts and Sciences 2005, hon memb Argentine Econ Assoc 2006; fell Econometric Soc 1994; FBA 1999; *Publications* The Economic Theory of Auctions (2000), Auctions: Theory and Practice (2004); author of articles in economics jls on industrial organization, auction theory, and other economic theory and policy; *Style—* Prof Paul Klemperer, FBA; ✉ Nuffield College, Oxford OX1 1NF (☎ 01865 278588, e-mail paul.klemperer@economics.ox.ac.uk, website www.paulklemperer.org)

KLIMENTOVA, Daria; da of Zdenek Kliment, of Prague, and Ludmila Klimentova; *b* 23 June 1971; *Educ* Sch of Music and Dance Prague State Conservatory; *m* Ian Comer; 1 da (Sabina b 6 Nov 2000); *Career* ballet dancer; studied with Prof Dr Olga Paskova and Prof Jaroslav Slavicky; soloist Nat Theatre Ballet Prague 1989–92, princ Capab/Kruik Ballet Cape Town 1992–93, princ Scottish Ballet 1993–96, princ English Nat Ballet 1996–; appeared with: Prague Festival Ballet Portugal and USA, Nat Theatre Ballet of Brno Germany tour; guested in ballet galas all over the world; subject of profile on Czech TV 1998; dir of int ballet classes Prague 2002–; *Roles* with Nat Theatre Ballet of Prague incl: Aurora in Sleeping Beauty, Margarita in Lady with Camellias, Kitri in Don Quixote, title role in Sylvia, solo in Paguita, solo in Return to a Strange Land, Princess in From Tale to Tale, Diverttimento m 15, Double Concerto, Concerto, A Million Kisses to my Skin; with Capab/Kruik Ballet incl: solo in Walpurgisnacht, solo in Four Last Songs, Titania in A Midsummer Night's Dream, Sugar Plum Fairy/Snow Queen in The Nutcracker, title role in Raymonda, Ophelia in Hamlet; with The Scottish Ballet incl: Swanilda in Coppélia, Solo Navy in Bruch Violin Concerto No 1, Wendy in Peter Pan, title role in Anna Karenina, Odette/Odile in Swan Lake, title role in La Sylphide, A Fond Kiss, Haydn Pieces, The Scotch Symphony; with English Nat Ballet incl: title role in Giselle, title role in Paguita, Mazurka in Les Sylphides, Ballerina in Eludes, Dream Alice in Alice in Wonderland, Ben Stevenson's 3 Preludes, Cut to the Chase, Nikya in La Bayadere, Sphinx Voluntaries, Tchaikovsky pas de deux, title role in Manon; *Film* Lady with Camellias (Czech Republic) 1992, A Midsummer Night's Dream (South Africa) 1993, Daria Klimentova (documentary), Daria Klimentova Masterclasses (Czech Republic) 2003, Terra Musica – Daria's Masterclasses 2006, Daria Klimentova – Portrait 2006, Terra Musica – Snow Queen in London (documentary) 2007, Daria Klimentova – Around the world with point shoes (documentary, Prague) 2008, Agony & Ecstasy (documentary), Giselle (Czech Republic); *Awards* second prize nat ballet competition Brno Czech Republic 1987, Prize of Paris Dance Fndn 1989, Prix de Lausanne Tokyo 1989, winner int ballet competition Pretoria 1991, Life Achievement from Beryl Grey 2011, Best Female Dancer 2012; *Publications* ballet calenders 2003–07, incl: Ballet Calendar 2003, English Nat Ballet Calendar 2004; Agony & Ecstasy: My Life in Dance (autobiography); *Recreations* photography, nature and animals, art, computers; *Style—* Miss Daria Klimentova; ✉ English National Ballet, Markova House, 39 Jay Mews, London SW7 2ES (☎ 020 7581 1245, fax 020

7225 0827, e-mail daria@ntlworld.com, website www.balletmasterclass.com and www.dariaklimentova.co.uk)

KLINOWSKI, Prof Jacek Maria; s of Dr Czeslaw Klinowski (d 1984), of Krakow, Poland, and Dr Julia Klinowska, *née* Penkala (d 2008); *b* 11 October 1943, Krakow, Poland; *Educ* Jagiellonian Univ Krakow (MSc, Dr rer nat), Univ of London (DIC, PhD), Univ of Cambridge (MA, ScD); *m* 11 May 1967, Dr Margaret Klinowska, *née* Townsend; 1 da (Dr Teresa Klinowska b 30 July 1969); *Career* lectr in chemistry Jagiellonian Univ 1965–68, res fell Univ of Aberdeen 1968–69, res fell Imperial Coll London 1969–79; Univ of Cambridge: sr res assoc 1980–85, asst dir of res 1985–98, reader in chemical physics 1998–2000, prof of chemical physics 2000–11, professorial fell Peterhouse; hon prof Jagiellonian Univ Kraków; visiting prof: Univ of Poznan, Univ of Aveiro, Univ of Cagliari; ed-in-chief Solid State Nuclear Magnetic Resonance 1992–2000; author of over 500 scientific pubns; Marie Curie Medal Polish Chemical Soc; hon memb Polish Chemical Soc 1994, foreign memb Polish Acad of Arts and Sciences 1993, presidential prof Repub of Poland 1988; *Books* incl: Cinema, the Magic Vehicle: A Guide to Its Achievement: The Cinema Through 1949 Journey 1 (with Adam Garbicz, 1980), Cinema, the Magic Vehicle: A Guide to Its Achievement: The Cinema in the Fifties Journey 2 (with Adam Garbicz, 1980), Fundamentals of Nuclear Magnetic Resonance (with Jacek W Hennel, 1993), A Primer of Magnetic Resonance Imaging (with Jacek W Hennel and Teresa Kryst-Widzgowska, 1997), New Techniques in Solid-State NMR (ed, 2004); *Recreations* cinema (sometime film critic), music; *Style—* Prof Jacek Klinowski; ✉ e-mail jk18@cam.ac.uk

KLUG, Sir Aaron; OM (1995), kt (1988); s of Lazar Klug (d 1971), of Durban, South Africa, and Bella, *née* Silin (d 1932); *b* 11 August 1926; *Educ* Durban HS, Univ of the Witwatersrand (BSc), Univ of Cape Town (MSc), Univ of Cambridge (PhD, ScD); *m* 8 July 1948, Liebe, da of Alexander Bobrow (d 1983), and Annie Bobrow, of Cape Town; 2 s (Adam Brian Joseph b 1954 d 2000, David Rupert b 1963); *Career* Nuffield research fell Birkbeck Coll London 1954–57, ldr virus research project 1958–61; Univ of Cambridge: fell Peterhouse 1962–93, dir of natural sci studies Peterhouse 1962–85, memb staff MRC Laboratory of Molecular Biology 1962–, jt head structural studies 1978–86, dir of laboratory 1986–96, hon prof 1989–96; awards: Heineken prize Royal Netherlands Acad 1979, Louisa Gross Horwitz prize Columbia Univ 1981, Nobel prize for chemistry 1982; Hon DSc: Chicago 1978, Witwatersrand 1984, Hull 1985, St Andrews 1987, Western Ontario 1991, Warwick 1994, Cape Town 1997, London 2000, Oxford 2001; Hon Dr Columbia 1978, Dr (hc) Strasbourg 1978, Hon Dr Stockholm 1980, Hon PhD Jerusalem 1984, Hon DLitt Cambridge 1998, Hon DUniv Stirling 1998; hon fell: Trinity Coll Cambridge 1983, Peterhouse Cambridge 1993; hon memb: Worshipful Co of Salters 1995, Biochem Soc (Harden medal 1985); foreign assoc: American Acad of Arts and Sciences 1969, Nat Acad of Sciences of USA 1984, Max-Planck-Gesellschaft FRG, Académie des Sciences Paris 1989, American Philosophical Soc 1998, Japan Acad 2001; Hon FRCP 1986 (Baly medal 1987), Hon FRCPath 1991, FRS 1969 (Copley medal 1985, pres 1995–2000); Order of Mapungubwe Gold (South Africa) 2006; *Recreations* reading, ancient history; *Style—* Sir Aaron Klug, OM, PPRS; ✉ MRC Laboratory of Molecular Biology, Hills Road, Cambridge CB2 2QH (☎ 01223 248011, fax 01223 412231)

KNAGG, John Worsley; OBE (1996); s of Albert Knagg, and Ivy, *née* Worsley; *b* 22 September 1953, Manchester; *Educ* Bury GS, Worcester Coll Oxford (MA), UCNW Bangor (PGCE), Univ of Edinburgh (MSc), Henley Mgmnt Coll; *Children* 2 s (Alex b 9 July 1995, Martin b 14 Aug 1996), 1 da (Emily b 29 June 1998); *Career* British Cncl: dir Porto 1987–90, dep dir Singapore 1993–98, dir Ecuador 1998–2001, dir Chile 2001, currently head of research and consultancy for English; chair Educn Ctee British Sch Quito 1999–2001; *Style—* John Knagg, Esq, OBE

KNEALE, Prof (Robert) Bryan Charles; s of William Thomas Kneale (d 1963), of Douglas, IOM, and late Lilian, *née* Kewley; *b* 19 June 1930; *Educ* Douglas HS IOM, Douglas Sch of Art IOM, Royal Acad Schs (Rome scholar); *m* 1956, Doreen, da of Clifford Lister; 1 da (Katherine b 1957), 1 s (Simon Benedict b 1960, d 1996); *Career* painter until 1959; first exhibition of paintings Redfern Gallery 1954, recipient Daily Express Young Painters prize 1955; sculptor (mainly in bronze) 1960–, regular exhibitor Redfern Gallery until 1986; head of sculpture Hornsey Coll of Art and Design 1968, prof of sculpture Royal Acad 1980–87; RCA: tutor 1963–80, sr tutor 1980–85, head of sculpture 1985–90, prof of drawing 1990–95; Leverhulme prize 1952, Arts Cncl purchase award 1969; RA 1974 (ARA 1971, tstee Royal Acad), sr fell RCA; *Exhibitions* incl: John Moores 1961, Sixth Congress of Architects Union (Southbank) 1961, Art d'Aujourd'hui Paris 1963, Battersea Park Sculpture Int 1963–66, Profil 2 Bochom 1964, Retrospective (Whitechapel Gallery) 1966, English Eye 1965, British Sculpture of the 60's (Tate Gallery) 1966, City of London Open Air Sculpture 1968, British Sculptors Winter Exhibition (Royal Acad) 1972 (also curator), Holland Park 1973, New Art (Hayward Gallery) 1975, Silver Jubilee Exhibition of British Sculpture (Battersea Park) 1977 (also curator), Monumental Sculpture (Manx Millenium) 1979, Serpentine Gallery 1979, Royal Acad 1985, Retrospective (Henry Moore Gallery) 1986, Fitzwilliam Museum 1987, Sal Uno Rome 1988, Drawing Retrospective (Natural History Museum) 1991, Sculpture and Drawing (bone drawings and sculpture retrospective Manx Museum and National Tst) 1992, Chelsea Harbour sculpture 1993, Retrospective (Royal West of England Acad) 1995, Discerning Eye 1995–96, Goodwood Sculpture Park 1996–99, Sculpture for Manx Government Building 1996, Lewes Festival 1997, Bronze Doors for Portsmouth Cathedral 1997, sculpture for Westminster Cathedral 1998 and 1999, Angela Flowers East Figurative Arts 1998, Holland Park Sculpture Exhbn Bronze 2000, New Arts Centre Roche Court 2000, Eye of the Storm Mandria Park Turin 2000, Hart Gallery 2002 and 2004, Cass Sculpture Fndn Gallery 2005, sculpture for Nobles Hosp IOM 2005, sculpture for Castletown Hosp IOM 2005, sculpture for Malew Church IOM 2006, sculpture for Tower Bridge House London 2007, sculpture for RTZ Building Paddington 2007; *Clubs* Chelsea Arts, Arts; *Style—* Prof Bryan Kneale, RA; ✉ Hart Gallery, 113 Upper Street, London N1 1QN (☎ 020 7704 1131, fax 020 7288 2922); Beaux Arts Gallery, 22 Cork Street, London W1 3NA (☎ 020 7437 5799)

KNEALE, David Arthur; *b* 20 August 1954; *Educ* Douglas HS IOM, Univ of Nottingham (BA); *m* 13 May 1996, Jacqueline Sylvia, da of Sylvia Agnes Paterson; *Career* treas Student Union Univ of Nottingham 1975–76; The Boots Company 1976–99: asst expense controller 1976–77, pet food buyer 1978–80, leisure gp mangr 1980–82, cosmetics gp mangr 1982–83, asst merchandise controller (med merchandise) 1983–85, asst mktg controller (food and own brand meds) 1985–86, buying controller (personal care business centre) 1986–89, gen mangr (personal care) 1989–92, gen mangr (beauty and personal care) 1992–95, dir of merchandise and mktg 1995–97, md int retail devpt 1997–99; md Waterstone's Booksellers Ltd 1999–2001; dir of trading Boots UK and Ireland 2002–05, ceo Clicks Gp S Africa 2006–; *Recreations* reading, cinema, travel; *Style—* David Kneale, Esq; ☎ 0027 21 460 1849

KNEALE, Matthew Nicholas Kerr; s of Nigel Kneale, of London, and Judith Kerr; *b* 24 November 1960; *Educ* Latymer Upper Sch, Magdalen Coll Oxford (BA); *m* 2000, Shannon Lee, da of Gary Russell; 1 s (Alexander b 2001), 1 da (Tatiana b 2004); *Career* writer; former English teacher Japan; *Books* Mr Foreigner (1988, Betty Trask Award 1987, Somerset Maugham Award 1988), Inside Rose's Kingdom (1989), Sweet Thames (1992, John Llewellyn Rhys Award 1993), English Passengers (2000, shortlisted Booker Prize 2000, Whitbread Book of the Year Award 2000, shortlisted Miles Franklin Award (Australia) 2001, Relay Prix d'Evasion (France) 2002), Small Crimes in an Age of Abundance (2005), When We Were Romans (2007); *Recreations* mountain walking, cycling, photography, travel (85 countries and 7 continents); *Style—* Matthew Kneale, Esq; ✉ c/o Rogers, Coleridge & White, 20 Powys Mews, London W11 1JN (☎ 020 7221 3717, e-mail matthew.kneale@attglobal.net)

KNECHT, Prof Robert Jean; s of Jean Joseph Camille Knecht (d 1970), and Odette Jeanne Eugenie Juliette, *née* Mioux (d 1983); *b* 20 September 1926; *Educ* Lycée Français London, Salesian Coll Farnborough, KCL (BA, MA), Univ of Birmingham (DLitt); *m* 1, 8 Aug 1956, Sonia Mary Fitzpatrick (d 1984), da of Dr Hubert Hodge; m 2, 28 Aug 1986, Maureen Joan, *née* White; *Career* Univ of Birmingham: asst lectr in modern history 1956–59, lectr 1959–68, sr lectr 1968–78, reader 1978–85, prof of French history 1985–92, emeritus prof and hon sr res fell in modern history 1992–97, fell Inst for Advanced Research in Arts and Social Scis 1998–; chm: Soc for Renaissance Studies 1989–92, Bd of Govrs Wroxall Abbey Sch Warwick 1989–92; co fndr Soc for Study of French History (chm 1995–98); memb Société de l'Histoire de France; Enid McLeod Literary Prize 2008; FRHistS; Officier dans l'Ordre des Palmes Académiques 2010 (Chevalier 2001); *Books* The Voyage of Sir Nicholas Carewe (1959), Francis I (1982), French Renaissance Monarchy (1984), The French Wars of Religion (1989), Richelieu (1990), Renaissance Warrior and Patron (1994), The Rise and Fall of Renaissance France (1996), Catherine de' Medici (1998), Un Prince de la Renaissance: François 1er et son royaume (1998), The French Civil Wars (2000), The French Religious Wars (2002), The Valois (2004), The French Renaissance Court (2008), Hero or Tyrant: Henry III, King of France (2014), Francis I and Sixteenth-Century France (2015); *Recreations* travel, art, music, photography; *Style—* Prof Robert Knecht; ✉ 79 Reddings Road, Moseley, Birmingham B13 8LP (☎ and fax 0121 449 1916, e-mail r.j.knecht@btinternet.com)

KNIBB, Prof Michael Anthony; s of Leslie Charles Knibb (d 1987), and Christian Vera, *née* Hoggar (d 1978); *b* 14 December 1938; *Educ* Wyggeston Sch Leicester, KCL (BD, PhD), Union Theol Seminary NY (STM), CCC Oxford; *m* 30 Dec 1972, Christine Mary, da of John Henry Thomas and Patricia Mary Burrell, of Leicester; *Career* Old Testament studies KCL: lectr 1964–82, reader 1982–86, prof 1986–97, Samuel Davidson prof 1997–2001; head Theology and Religious Studies Dept KCL 1989–93 and 1998–2000; Sch of Humanities KCL: dep head 1992–97, head 2000–01, prof emeritus 2001–; Schweich lectr British Acad 1995; memb SOTS 1965–, ed SOTS Book List 1980–86; hon sec Palestine Exploration Fund 1969–76; memb: Studiorum Novi Testamenti Societas 1980– (jt convener of seminar on early Jewish writings and the New Testament 1986–91), Cncl British Acad 1992–95, Humanities Research Bd 1995–98 (chm Postgraduate Ctee 1996–98); memb Governing Body: Watford GS for Girls 1993–2002, SOAS Univ of London 2000–10 (vice-chair 2006–10); FBA 1989, FKC 1991, FRAS 1993; *Books* The Ethiopic Book of Enoch (1978), Commentary on 2 Esdras (1979), Het Boek Henoch (1983), The Qumran Community (1987), Translating the Bible: The Ethiopic Version of The Old Testament (1999), Essays on the Book of Enoch and Other Early Jewish Texts and Traditions (2009), The Ethipic Text of the Book of Ezekiel: A Critical Edition (2015); *Recreations* hill walking; *Clubs* Athenaeum; *Style—* Prof Michael A Knibb, FBA; ✉ 6 Shootersway Park, Berkhamsted, Hertfordshire HP4 3NX (☎ 01442 871459)

KNIGHT, Prof Alan Sydney; s of William Henry Knight (d 1998), and Eva Maud, *née* Crandon (d 1979); *b* 6 November 1946; *Educ* Christ's Hosp, Balliol Coll Oxford (BA), Nuffield Coll Oxford (DPhil); *m* 1, 1969 (m dis), Carole, da of Gordon Jones; 1 da (Katharine b 1974); m 2, 1985, Lidia, da of Juan Lozano Martin; 2 s (Alexander b 1980, Henry b 1982); *Career* res fell Nuffield Coll and lectr in politics Balliol Coll Oxford 1971–73, lectr in modern history Univ of Essex 1973–85, visiting prof Centre for US-Mexican Studies Univ of Calif San Diego 1986; Univ of Texas: Worsham Centennial prof of history 1986–90, C B Smith sr prof of history 1990–92; Univ of Oxford: prof of Latin America history and dir Latin American Centre 1992–, fell St Antony's Coll 1992–; memb: Soc for Latin American Studies 1982–, Latin American Studies Assoc 1986–; Bolton prize Conf on Latin American History 1987, Beveridge prize American Historical Soc 1987, Guggenheim fell 1990–91; FBA 1998; *Books* The Mexican Revolution (1986), US-Mexican Relations 1910–40: An Overview (1987), The Mexican Petroleum Industry in the Twentieth Century (ed, 1992); *Recreations* kayaking; *Style—* Prof Alan Knight, FBA; ✉ St Antony's College, Oxford OX2 6JF (☎ 01865 274490, fax 01865 274489)

KNIGHT, Very Rev Alexander Francis; OBE (2006); s of Benjamin Edward Knight (d 1998), of Bridport, and Dorothy Mary, *née* Sherwood (d 2015); *b* 24 July 1939; *Educ* Taunton Sh, St Catharine's Coll Cambridge (MA), Wells Theol Coll; *m* 23 June 1962, Sheelagh Elizabeth, *née* Desmond Faris; 3 da (Catharine Mary b 2 April 1964, Susannah Elizabeth b 8 June 1966, Helen Clare b 31 Dec 1968), 1 s (William Benjamin James b 22 Jan 1971); *Career* asst curate Hemel Hempstead 1963–68, chaplain Taunton Sch 1968–74, dir The Bloxham Project 1975–81, dir of studies Aston Trg Scheme 1981–83, priest-in-charge Easton and Martyr Worthy 1983–91, archdeacon of Basingstoke 1990–98, canon residentiary of Winchester Cathedral 1991–98, dean of Lincoln 1998–2006 (now emeritus), dean Priory of England and the Islands of the Ven Order of the Hosp of St John of Jerusalem 2007–13; Hon DLitt Univ of Lincoln; KStJ; *Recreations* gardening, theatre, walking; *Style—* The Very Rev Dr Alec Knight, OBE; ✉ Shalom, Clay Street, Whiteparish, Salisbury, Wiltshire SP5 2ST (☎ 01794 884402)

KNIGHT, Andrew Stephen Bower; s of M W B Knight, and S E F Knight; *b* 1 November 1939; *m* 1, 1966 (m dis), Victoria Catherine Brittain; 1 s (Casimir); m 2, 1975 (m dis 1991), Sabiha Rumani Malik; 2 da (Amaryllis, Afsaneh); m 3, 2006, Marita Georgina Phillips Crawley; *Career* ed The Economist 1974–86; Daily Telegraph plc: chief exec 1986–89, ed-in-chief 1987–89; exec chm News International plc 1990–94 (non-exec chm 1994–95), dir News Corporation 1991–2012; dep chm Home Counties Newspapers Holdings plc 1996–98; non-exec dir: RIT Capital Partners 1996–2008, Templeton Emerging Markets Investment Tst plc; chm J Rothschild Capital Mgmnt 2008–12; Stanford Univ: memb Advsy Bd Centre for Econ Policy Res 1981–, memb Advsy Cncl Inst of Int Studies; govr Ditchley Fndn 1981– (memb Mgmnt Cncl 1982–2013), dir Anglo Russian Opera & Ballet Tst; *Clubs* Brooks's, Beefsteak, RAC, Tadmarton Heath; *Style—* Andrew Knight, Esq; ✉ Compton Scorpion Manor, Shipston-on-Stour, Warwickshire CV36 4PJ

KNIGHT, Angela; CBE (2007); da of late Andrew McTurk Cook, and late Barbara Cook; *b* 31 October 1950; *Educ* Sheffield Girls HS, Univ of Bristol (BSc); *m* 7 Feb 1981 (m dis), David George Knight; 2 s; *Career* devpt engr Air Products Ltd 1972–77, fndr and md engrg co specialising in heat treatment of metals 1977–92; cncllr Sheffield City Cncl 1987–92 (spokesman on educn, planning and industry), MP (Cons) Erewash 1992–97; memb Educn Select Ctee 1992–93, sec Backbench Environment Ctee 1992–93, PPS DTI 1993–94, PPS to Chllr of the Exchequer 1994–95, economic sec to the Treasy 1995–97; chief exec Assoc of Private Client Investment Managers and Stockbrokers (APCIMS) 1997–2006, chief exec British Bankers Assoc (BBA) 2007–; non-exec dir: Scottish Widows 1997–2006, South East Water 1998–2004, LogicaCMG plc 1999–2008, Port of London Authy 2002–08, Lloyds TSB 2003–06, Int Fin Servs London 2003–10, Brewin Dolphin plc 2007, Fin Servs Skills Cncl 2008–; *Clubs* London Capital; *Style—* Ms Angela Knight, CBE

KNIGHT, Prof Bernard Henry; CBE (1993), GSM (Malaya) 1956; s of Harold Ivor Knight (d 1984), of Cardiff, and Doris, *née* Lawes (d 1995); *b* 3 May 1931; *Educ* St Illtyd's Coll Cardiff, Welsh Nat Sch of Med (MD BCh), DMJ (Path); *m* 11 June 1955, Jean Gwenllian, da of Charles Ogborne (d 1947), of Swansea; 1 s (Huw David Charles b 1964); *Career* Short Serv Cmmn Capt RAMC specialist in pathology Malaya 1956–59; called to the Bar Gray's Inn; lectr in forensic med Univ of London 1959–62, sr lectr Univ of Newcastle 1965–68, prof of forensic pathology Univ of Wales 1980–96 (sr lectr 1968–76, reader

1976–80, now emeritus prof), Home Office pathologist 1965–96, conslt pathologist Cardiff Royal Infirmary, dir Wales Inst of Forensic Med 1989–96, pathology ed Forensic Sci Int; memb GMC 1979–94, vice-pres Int Acad of Legal Med 1982–86, pres Forensic Sci Soc 1987–89, memb Cncl RCPath, memb Home Office Policy Advsy Bd on forensic pathology, pres Br Assoc of Forensic Med 1991–93 (former sec), hon memb Finnish, Hungarian and German Socs of Forensic Med; Hon DSc Univ of Glamorgan 1996, Hon LLD Univ of Wales 1998, Hon DM Univ of Turkh Finland, Hon PhD Univ of Tokyo, Hon PhD Univ of Coimbra Portugal; hon fell Metropol Univ Swansea, fell Faculty for Medicine Royal Coll of Physicians; Hon FRSM; MRCP, FRCPath; *Books* crime novels: The Lately Deceased (1963), The Thread of Evidence (1965), Russian Roulette (1968), Policeman's Progress (1969), Tiger at Bay (1970), Deg Y Dragwyddoldeb (1972), The Expert (1976); historical novels: Lion Rampant (1974), Madoc Prince of America (1977), The Sanctuary Seeker (1998), The Poisoned Chalice (1998), Crowner's Quest (1999), The Awful Secret (2000), The Tinner's Corpse (2001), The Grim Reaper (2002), Fear in the Forest (2003), Brennan (2003), The Witch Hunter (2004), Figure of Hate (2005), The Tainted Relic (2005), The Elixir of Death (2006), The Sword of Shame (2006), The Noble Outlaw (2007), The Manor of Death (2008), Crowner Royal (2009), A Plague of Heretics (2010), Where Death Delight (2010), The Sacred Stone (2010), According to the Evidence (2010), Grounds for Appeal (2011), Hill of Bones (2011), Dead in the Dog (2012), The First Murder (2012), Crowner's Crusade (2012), The False Virgin (2013); Autopsy: The Memoirs of Milton Helpern (biography, 1977); popular non-fiction: Murder Suicide or Accident (1971), Discovering the Human Body (1980); textbooks: Legal Aspects of Medicine (5 edn, 1992), Sudden Death In Infancy (1982), Coroner's Autopsy (1983), Lawyer's Guide to Forensic Medicine (1983, 2 edn 1998), Essentials of Forensic Medicine (with Polson and Gee, 1985), Forensic Medicine (1986), Forensic Pathology (1991, 3 edn 2004), Simpson's Forensic Medicine (11 edn, 1996), Estimation of Time Since Death (2 edn, 2002); *Recreations* writing: crime and history novels, biography, radio and TV drama; *Style—* Prof Bernard Knight, CBE; ✉ 26 Millwood, Lisvane, Cardiff CF14 0TL (e-mail knight.j4@sky.com)

KNIGHT, Beverley; MBE (2006); *b* 22 March 1973, Wolverhampton, Staffs; *Career* singer, songwriter and record producer; top 20 singles incl: Made it Back 99 1999, Greatest Day 1999, Get Up 2001, Shoulda Woulda Coulda 2002, Come As You Are 2004, Keep This Fire Burning 2005, Piece of My Heart 2006; albums: The B-Funk 1995, Prodigal Sista 1998, Who I Am 2002, Affirmation 2004, Voice – The Best of Beverley Knight 2006 (platinum), Music City Soul 2007, 100% 2009; collaborations incl: Hard Times (Courtney Pine) 2000, Main Vein, A Foolsophy (Jamiroquai) 2001, Do They Know It's Christmas (Band Aid 20) 2004, Where in the World (Jools Holland) 2005; resident singer Just the Two of Us (BBC1 series) 2006, host Beverley's Gospel Nights BBC Radio 2; ambass: Christian Aid, Stop AIDS Campaign, Terrence Higgins Tst, Rainbow Tst, Elton John Aids Fndn; Best R&B Artist and Best Producer Black Music Awards 1996, Best R&B Act MOBO Awards 1998 and 1999, Best Album MOBO Awards 1999, Best Br Music Act EMMA Awards 1999, Trailblazing Artist BBM/BMC Awards 2003, Lifetime Acheivement Urban Music Awards 2004; *Style—* Ms Beverley Knight, MBE; ✉ c/o The Outside Organisation Limited, Butler House, 177–178 Tottenham Court Road, London W1T 7NY (☎ 020 7436 3633, fax 020 7436 3632); DWL Limited, 53 Goodge Street, London W1T 1TG (☎ 020 7436 5529, fax 020 7637 8776)

KNIGHT, Brien Walter; s of Edward Alfred Knight (d 1993), of Sussex, and Winifred, *née* Stolworthy (d 1976); *b* 27 June 1929; *Educ* Woodhouse GS, Sir John Cass Business Sch City of London; *m* 1, 1955, Annette (d 2013), da of Alfred Scotten (d 1964), of Barnet; 4 da (Carolyn b 1961, Judith b 1964, Emma b 1966, Sophie b 1968), 1 s (Darrell b 1963); m 2, 1987, Maria Antoinette (Rita), da of Abraham Van Der Meer (d 1958), of Holland; *Career* dir: Knight Strip Metals Ltd 1951 (chm 1970–), Sterling Springs Ltd 1952–, Knight Precision Wire Ltd 1979– (chm 1979–); Precision Metals EU (Belgium) 1973–, Knight Precision Metals Ltd 2011 (chm), Knight Gp (UK and Europe) 2012; chm: Knuway Investment Ltd 1973–; gp chm Saltley Business Park 2000; FInstD; *Recreations* DIY; *Style—* Brien Knight, Esq; ✉ Sherborne, Nightingales Lane, Chalfont St Giles, Buckinghamshire HP8 4SR; Linkside, Summit Road, Cranborne Road, Potters Bar, Hertfordshire EN6 3JL (e-mail brien.knight@knight-group.co.uk)

KNIGHT, Charles Henry; s of Robert W S Knight, DL (d 2004), and Susan M, *née* Ball; *b* 30 March 1966, Southerndown, Glamorgan; *Educ* Radley Coll, London South Bank Univ (BSc); *m* 1993, Lalley, *née* Usher-Smith; 2 da (Ophelia b 1997, Anastasia b 1999), 1 s (Henry b 2007); *Career* investment surveyor Grimley J R Eve 1989, assoc ptnr GVA Grimley 1993, fndr shareholder and dir Mansford Wales Ltd 1997, main bd dir Mansford Hldgs plc 2001–, managing ptnr Mansford Real Estate LLP 2008–; memb Investment Property Forum; Commercial Devpt of the Year (Old Brewery Quarter Cardiff) Western Mail Welsh Property Awards 2005; memb CLA; High Sheriff Mid Glamorgan 2007–08; MRICS 1991; *Recreations* golf, shooting, boating, tennis; *Clubs* Royal Porthcawl Golf, Seaview Yacht; *Style—* Charles Knight, Esq; ✉ Tythegston Court, Mid Glamorgan CF32 0NE (☎ 01656 773366); Mansford LLP, St Albans House, 57–59 Haymarket, London SW1Y 4QX (☎ 020 7838 0111, e-mail cknight@mansford.com)

KNIGHT, Prof Charles James; s of Alfred Charles James Knight, and Janet Elizabeth Knight; *Educ* Canford Sch, Magadalene Coll Cambridge (MA, MD), Merton Coll Oxford (BM BCh); *Career* hon sr registrar and Br Heart Fndn research fell Royal Brompton Hosp 1994–96, sr registrar St George's Hosp 1996–99, conslt cardiologist Barts Health, exec dir Barts Heart Centre 2014–, md St Bart's Hosp 2015–; hon sec Br Cardiovascular Soc 2008–11; hon prof Queen Mary London 2014–; FRGS, FRCP 2003 (MRCP 1992), FACC, FESC; *Recreations* bridge, gardening; *Style—* Prof Charles Knight; ✉ Bart's Heart Centre, St Bartholomew's Hospital, West Smithfield, London EC1A 7BE

KNIGHT, Rt Hon Gregory (Greg); kt (2013), PC (1995), MP; s of late Albert George Knight, of Leicester, and late Isabella, *née* Bell; *b* 4 April 1949; *Educ* Alderman Newton's GS Leicester, Coll of Law Guildford; *Career* admitted slr 1973, practising until 1983 and 2000–06; Leicester City cncllr 1976–79, Leicestershire co cncllr 1977–83; former chm Public Protection Ctee; MP (Cons): Derby N 1983–97, Yorkshire E 2001–; PPS to Rt Hon David Mellor, QC, *qv*, 1987–89, asst Govt whip 1989, a Lord Cmmr of the Treasury (Govt whip) 1990–93, Treasurer HM Household (dep chief whip) 1993–96, min of state DTI 1996–97, oppn spokesman for Shadow Ldr of the House 2001–02; shadow min for: Culture 2002–03, Railways and Aviation 2003–05, Roads 2005–06; chair All Party Parly Historic Vehicles Gp 2001–, chm House of Commons Select Ctee on Procedure 2006–12, vice chamberlain Royal Household (sr whip) 2012–13; business exec 1997–2001; former dir Leicester Theatre Tst Ltd (former chm Fin Ctee); memb Law Soc 1973; *Books* Westminster Words (1988), Honourable Insults (1990), Parliamentary Sauce (1993), Right Honourable Insults (1998), Naughty Grafitti (2005), Dishonourable Insults (2011); *Recreations* arts (especially music), classic cars; *Style—* The Rt Hon Sir Greg Knight, MP; ✉ House of Commons, London SW1A 0AA (e-mail secretary@gregknight.com)

KNIGHT, Ian; *Career* non-exec chm: QDS Environmental Ltd 2001–, DeltaSimons Environmental Conslts Ltd 2001–; non-exec dir: Mouchel Parkman plc 2001–, Morson Gp plc 2006–, Elco Motors Ltd 2007–; *Style—* Ian Knight, Esq

KNIGHT, (William) Jeremy Jonathan; s of Richard Beatty MacBean Knight, of Brighton, and Yvonne Stephanie, *née* Searles; *b* 27 May 1951; *Educ* Brighton Coll; *m* 15 March 1975, Marian Margaret, da of Albert Edward Hoare; 2 s (Richard Andrew b 6 Feb 1978, Simon Peter Edward b 7 July 1979); *Career* CA/insolvency practitioner; articled clerk Graves Goddard & Horton-Stephens 1969–73, National Trading Co Johannesburg 1973–74, Peat Marwick Mitchell 1974–76; ptnr: Chater Spain Brothers 1978–88 (joined 1976), Moores Rowland (following merger) 1988–89; sole practitioner specialising in insolvency Jeremy Knight & Co Brighton and Croydon 1989–; pres SE Soc of CAs 1991–92, memb Cncl ICAEW 1995–2005; FCA 1975, MIPA 1987; *Recreations* flying, motor racing; *Style—* W J J Knight, Esq; ✉ 48 Welbeck Avenue, Hove, East Sussex BN3 4JN (☎ 01273 558045); Jeremy Knight & Co, 68 Ship Street, Brighton, East Sussex BN1 1AE (☎ 01273 203654 or 020 8680 4274, fax 01273 206056, mobile 07766 303997, e-mail jknight@jeremyknight.co.uk)

KNIGHT, Julian; MP; *b* 5 January 1972, Chester; *Educ* Univ of Hull (BA); *m* Philippa, *née* Harrison; *Career* personal finance and consumer affrs reporter BBC 2002–07, money and property ed Independent on Sunday; Pensions Journalist of the Year 2006; MP (Cons) Solihull 2015–; *Books* Wills, Probate and Inheritance Tax for Dummies (2005), Cricket for Dummies (2006), Politics for Dummies (2010); *Recreations* cinema, cricket, reading, tennis, walking, cycling; *Style—* Julian Knight, Esq, MP; ✉ House of Commons, London SW1A 0AA (☎ 020 7219 3577, e-mail julian.knight.mp@parliament.uk, website www.julianknight.org.uk, Twitter @JulianKnight15)

KNIGHT, Dr Lorna A; da of Gerald A Knight (d 1991), and Sybil E, *née* Cole (d 1999); *b* 12 February 1949, Taunton, Somerset; *Educ* Bedford Coll Univ of London (BA, PhD); *m* 1, 15 Sept 1973, Ian M Sinclair; 2 s (Simon J b 11 July 1977, Christopher M b 17 Feb 1981); m 2, 28 Aug 2004, Ian S McTier; *Career* lectr in French Univ of Strathclyde 1973–77; Dictionaries Div HarperCollins Publishers: lexicographer 1979–85, managing ed 1985–89, publishing mangr 1989–95, publishing dir 1995–2002, md Collins Dictionaries 2002–; princ flautist Glasgow Orchestral Soc 1973–; main contrib to numerous Collins Dictionaries 1975–, Collins-Robert French-English Dictionary (co-author, 1978), Collins German-English Dictionary (co-author, 1980); *Recreations* classical music, dance, keeping fit; *Style—* Dr Lorna Knight; ✉ HarperCollins Publisher, Dictionaries Division, Westerhill Road, Glasgow G64 2QT (☎ 0141 306 3679)

KNIGHT, Matthew; s of Nicholas Knight, and Patricia Knight; *Educ* Eltham Coll, Univ of Newcastle upon Tyne, Coll of Law Guildford; *Career* articled clerk Farrer & Co 1981–83, asst slr Sinclair Roche & Temperley 1983–85, ptnr Cripps Harries Hall 1986–94 (asst slr 1985–86), sr ptnr Knights Slrs 1994–; memb Law Soc 1981–; Liveryman Worshipful Co of Broderers; *Recreations* hunting, shooting, skiing, sailing, running, reading, riding; *Style—* Matthew Knight, Esq; ✉ Knights, Regency House, 25 High Street, Tunbridge Wells, Kent TN1 1UT (☎ 01892 537311, fax 01892 526141, e-mail matthew.knight@knights-solicitors.co.uk)

KNIGHT, Michael James; s of Charles Knight (d 1988), of London, and Ellen, *née* Murphy (d 1997); *b* 29 August 1939; *Educ* St Bonaventures Sch London, KCL, St George's Hosp London (MB BS, MS); *m* 1981, Phyllis Mary, da of William Ansel Purcell; 1 s (William Robert Charles b 1981), 1 da (Ellen Harrison b 1983); *Career* surgical registrar: Royal Hampshire County Hosp Winchester 1965–69, St George's Hosp 1969–71 (surgical res fell 1971–72); surgical res fell Washington Univ St Louis MO 1972–73, sr surgical registrar St George's Hosp London 1973–78, Hunterian prof RCS 1975, hon sr lectr St George's Hosp Med Sch; conslt surgn: St James's Hosp London 1978–88, St George's Hosp London 1978–, Royal Masonic Hosp London 1979–97; ind advsr to the Health Servs Cmmr for England 1998–2006; memb: Pancreatic Soc of GB and I (pres 1987), RSM, Euro Soc of Surgical Res, Ct of Examiners RCS 1988–98; examiner in surgery Univ of London, external examiner RCS in I, Edinburgh and Univ of Colombo; author of numerous pubns on gastroenterology, hepatic, pancreatic and biliary tract diseases; FRCS 1967 (MRCS 1963), LRCP; *Recreations* music; *Style—* Michael Knight, Esq; ✉ 33 Sherwood Court, Chatfield Road, London SW11 3UY

KNIGHT, Nicholas David Gordon (Nick); OBE (2010); s of Michael Anthony Gordon Knight, and Beryl Rose Knight; *b* 24 November 1958; *Educ* Hinchingbrooke Sch Huntingdon, Huntingdon Tech Coll, Chelsea Coll London, Bournemouth and Poole Coll of Art (PQE DipAD); *m* 1995, Charlotte Esme, *née* Wheeler; 2 da (Emily Ruby b 1993, Ella May b 1994), 1 s (Calum Kingsley b 1997); *Career* photographer; commissioning picture ed i-D Magazine 1990, contracted photographer for Vogue 1995–; dir SHOWStudio Ltd; dir NK Image Ltd; lectr: V&A, RCA, Manchester Coll of Art; prof Univ of the Arts London 2007–; fashion and advtg campaigns incl: Yves Saint Laurent, Lancôme, Guerlain, Christian Dior, Levis, Yohji Yamamoto, Jil Sander, Alexander McQueen, Mercedes, Royal Mail, Royal Ballet; record covers for: David Bowie, George Michael, Rolling Stones, Bjork, Massive Attack; *Exhibitions* Photographers Gallery 1982, 20 For Today (Nat Portrait Gallery) 1986, 14–21 Youth Culture Exhbn (V&A) 1986, Out of Fashion (Photographers Gallery) 1989, Ils Annoncent la Colour (Les Rencontres d'Arles) 1989, Vanités (Paris) 1993, Plant Power (permanent exhbn cmmnd by Nat History Museum) 1993, Biennale di Firenze – Art/Fashion (with Alexander McQueen) 1996, JAM (Barbican Art Gallery) 1997, Contemporary Fashion Photography (V&A) 1997, Look at Me – Fashion Photography 1965 to Present (travelling) 1998, Shoreditch Biennale 1998, Addressing the Century: 100 Years of Art & Fashion (Hayward Gallery) 1998, Silver & Syrup (V&A) 1999, Century City Tate Modern 2001; *Awards* Kodak 1985 and 1987, D&AD Award 1985, Magazine Publishing Award 1986, Club des Directors Artistique Award 1988, Expansion Magazine Awards 1988, Halina Award 1989, Gold Award USA 1989, Int Festival de la Photo de Mode 1991 and 1992, voted by GQ magazine as one of Britain's best dressed men 1992, 2002 and 2006, Int Festival de la Photo de Mode Award 1994, voted most influential fashion photographer in the world Face Magazine 1995, Royal Mail Innovation Award 1996, D&AD Silver Award 1997, The Power of Photography Award 1998, Total Publishing 'Best Front Cover of the Year' for Dazed & Confused Magazine 1999, D&AD Silver Award for Best Music Poster for Massive Attack album 'Mezzanine' 1999, Design Distinction Award from Int Design Magazine for front cover of Visionaire Magazine, Fashion Tribute Moet & Chandon 2006; Hon MA Anglia Polytechnic Univ 2000, Hon Dr Univ of the Arts London 2014; hon fell Bournemouth and Poole Coll of Art and Design 1998; *Books* Skinheads (1982), NICKNIGHT (retrospective by Schirmer Mosel, 1994), Flora (Herbarium samples from the Nat History Museum, 1997), Nick Knight: Retrospective 1994–2009 (2009); *Recreations* architecture, natural history; *Style—* Nick Knight, Esq, OBE; ☎ 020 8940 1086, fax 020 8948 8761, e-mail info@nkimage.com, websites www.nickknight.com and www.showstudio.com

KNIGHT, Peter John; s of William Knight (d 1974), of Ware, Herts; *b* 16 April 1950; *Educ* Trinity Hall Cambridge (MA); *m* Aug 1975, Jennifer Joan, da of late Wilfred Walter Townsend; 4 s (Jonathan William b May 1979, Robert Peter b Dec 1980, Oliver James b July 1984, Christopher Richard b Feb 1987); *Career* admitted slr England and Wales, Hong Kong and NSW Aust; Baker & McKenzie: slr London 1975–76 and 1979–82, slr Sydney 1976–79, managing ptnr Singapore 1987–90 (ptnr 1983–87), ptnr London 1990–; chm Br Assoc of Singapore 1989–90; memb Ctee: Asia Pacific Advsy Gp (DTI) 1992–98, London C of C 1993–; memb Bd of Advsrs Japanese and SE Asian Studies, chm Cambridge in the Capital 1995–98; govr Tanglin Tst Schs 1987–90; memb: Law Soc of England and Wales, Law Soc of Singapore; *Recreations* tennis, sailing, golf, early music, opera, theatre; *Style—* Peter J Knight, Esq; ✉ Baker & McKenzie LLP, 100 New Bridge Street, London EC4V 6JA (☎ 020 7919 1000, fax 020 7919 1999)

KNIGHT, Prof Sir Peter Leonard; kt (2005); s of late Joseph Knight, and late Eva Lillian Knight; *b* 12 August 1947; *Educ* Bedford Modern Sch, Univ of Sussex (BSc, DPhil); *m* 1965, Christine Mary, *née* Huckle; 2 s (David b 1965, Phillip b 1967), 1 da (Victoria b 1971); *Career* res assoc Univ of Rochester NY 1972–74, SRC res fell Univ of Sussex 1974–76, Jubilee res fell Royal Holloway Coll London 1976–78; Imperial Coll London: SERC advanced fell 1978–83, lectr 1983–87, 1987–88, prof 1988–, head of laser optics

K

and spectroscopy 1991–2000, head of quantum optics and laser science 2001–02, head Physics Dept 2002–05, sr princ Faculty of Natural Sciences 2008– (actg princ 2004–05, princ 2005–08, dep rector (research) 2009–10); sr research investigator and sr fell in residence Kavli Royal Soc Int Centre Chicheley Hall 2010–; chief scientific advsr Nat Physical Lab 2002–05, chair Defence Scientific Advsy Cncl MOD 2007–10, memb Cncl Science Technol Facilities Cncl 2009–12; co-ordinator SERC Initiative in Non-Linear Optics 1988–92 (chm 1992–93), chm Quantum Electronics Div Euro Physical Soc 1988–92, pres Physics Section of BAAS 1994–95, dir Optical Soc of America 1999–2005; ed: Jl of Modern Optics 1987–2006, Jl of Contemporary Physics 1993–; Alexander von Humbolt Res Award 1993, European Physical Soc lectr 1998–99, Einstein Medal and Prize for Laser Sci Soc of Optical and Quantum Electronics 1996, Parsons Medal Inst of Physics and Royal Soc 1997, Thomas Young Medal and Prize Inst of Physics 1999, Ives Medal Optical Soc of America 2008, Glazebrook Medal Ist of Physics 2009, Royal Medal of the Royal Soc 2010; memb: Mexican Acad of Scis 2000, Academia Europaea 2001, German Nat Acad of Sci 'Leopoldina'; Dr (hc): INAOE Mexico 1998, Slovak Acad of Sciences 2000; memb of cncl Sussex Univ 2013–; DSc (hc): Univ of Sussex 2010, Heriot-Watt Univ 2010, Royal Holloway Univ of London 2013, Macquarie Univ 2014; fell Optical Soc of America (vice-pres 2002, pres 2004); FInstP (pres 2011–), FRS 1999; Principles of Quantum Optics (1983), Introductory Quantum Optics; also author of over 400 articles in scientific literature; *Recreations* traditional music; *Clubs* Athenaeum; *Style*— Prof Sir Peter Knight, FRS; ✉ Blackett Laboratory, Imperial College, London SW7 2AZ (☎ 020 7594 7727, fax 020 7594 8802, e-mail p.knight@imperial.ac.uk)

KNIGHT, Dr Roger John Beckett; s of Lt Cdr John Beckett Knight (d 1983), of Bromley, Kent, and Alyson Yvonne Saunders, *née* Nunn; *b* 11 April 1944; *Educ* Tonbridge, Trinity Coll Dublin (MA), Univ of Sussex (PGCE), UCL (PhD); *m* 1, 3 Aug 1968 (m dis 1980), Helen Elizabeth, da of Dr William Magowan (d 1980), of Hawkhurst, Kent; 2 s (William b 1973, Richard b 1976); m 2, 31 Jan 1998, Jane Hamilton-Eddy, *née* Coffey; *Career* National Maritime Museum: custodian Manuscripts 1977–81 (dep 1974–77), dep head Books and Manuscripts 1981–84, head Info Project Gp 1984–86, head Documentation Div 1986–88, head Collections Div and chief curator 1988–93, dep dir and head Display Div 1993–95, dep dir and head Information Div 1995–97, dep dir 1997–2000; prof of naval history Univ of Greenwich 2006–09 (visiting prof 2000–06 and 2009–14), sr research fell IHR Univ of London; memb: Ctee Greenwich Soc 1988–90, Cncl Soc for Nautical Res 1975–79 (vice-pres 1992–2006), Cncl Navy Records Soc 1975–2008 and 2014–; tstee National Maritime Museum Cornwall 1998–2002; Caird Medal, Nat Maritime Museum 2014; FRHistS; *Books* Guide to the Manuscripts in the National Maritime Museum (1977, 1980), The Journal of Daniel Paine, 1794–1797 (with Alan Frost, 1983), Portsmouth Dockyard in the American War of Independence, 1774–1783 (1986), British Naval Documents 1204–1960 (jt ed, 1993), The Pursuit of Victory: The Life and Achievement of Horatio Nelson (2005, Mountbatten Maritime Prize Br Maritime Charitable Fndn 2005, Duke of Westminster's Medal RUSI 2006), Sustaining the Fleet 1793–1815: War, the British Navy and the Contractor State (with Martin Wilcox, 2010), Britain Against Napoleon: the Organization of Victory, 1793–1815 (2013), William IV Penguin Monarch Series (2014); *Recreations* music, walking the Sussex Downs; *Clubs* Athenaeum; *Style*— Dr Roger Knight; ✉ Institute of Historical Research, University of London, Senate House, Malet Street, London WC1E 7HU (☎ 020 7862 8740

KNIGHT, Stephen; AM; s of Dr David JE Knight, and Ruth M *neé* Fry; *b* 15 May 1970, Roehampton; *Educ* Univ of Southampton; *Partner* Jennifer Churchill; 2 da; *Career* cncllr London Borough of Richmond upon Thames (dep ldr 2006–10), memb London Assembly (Lib Dem) 2012–; *Recreations* sailing; *Clubs* RSA; *Style*— Cllr Stephen Knight, AM; ✉ London Assembly, City Hall, The Queen's Walk, London SE1 2AA

KNIGHT, Stephen Charles; s of Reginald Frank Knight (decd), of Street, Somerset, and Sheila Ethel Clarice, *née* Jones (decd); *b* 25 November 1954; *Educ* Colfe's Sch, Bromley Coll; *m* 30 July 1977, Lesley Joan, da of Harold Leonard Davison, of Petts Wood, Kent; 2 s (Timothy David Stephen b 1988, Joshua James Stephen b 1990); *Career* gen mangr mktg and devpt Newcross Building Society 1983–84, vice-pres Citibank 1984–87, chm Private Label Mortgage Services Ltd 1987–2000; chm GMAC RFC Ltd 2000–08, ceo Portillion Ltd 2008–; FCIB 1977; *Publications* The Art of Marketing Mortgages (1997), Creator and Trader: A Vision for Growth in the UK Mortgage Market (2006), Life with Granny Glasses (2013); *Recreations* sport, writing; *Clubs* IOD; *Style*— Stephen Knight, Esq

KNIGHT, Tina Patricia; da of Jack Leonard King (d 1983), of London, and Nellie Irene, *née* Baxter (d 1999); *Educ* Walthamstow Co HS for Girls, SW Essex Tech Coll; *Career* mgmnt conslt and trouble-shooter until 1978, md GSC (UK) Ltd 1978–84, mgmnt conslt Scientific Staff Consultants 1984–85, prop Nighthawk Enterprises 1985– (prop and md Nighthawk Electronics Ltd 1985–2002, md Nighthawk Traders Ltd 1986–2002); non-exec dir Essex TEC 1990–2000, chm Millbrook Bakeries Ltd 2002–03, dep chm EWP 2002–, chief exec Entrepreneurial Exchange 2002–, chm CHA 2003–, dir PSA 2004–08, dir Northern Cyprus Property Centre Ltd 2005–10, dist cncllr Uttlesford 2005–; numerous TV and radio appearances incl: Election Special (Channel 4), Question Time (BBC 1) and various regnl broadcasting appearances; also professional after-dinner and conf speaker incl: Nat Conf Small Business Bureau, Women in Business Int Conf; memb: Bd Prince's Youth Business Tst 1990, Ctee China-Britain Trade Gp 1990, Ctee Advsy Unit Small Business Bureau 1991, Bd TAVRA 1992, Bd East of England Industry Devpt Bd (EEIDB) 1999–2002; chm Women Into Business 1995 (dep chm 1992–95), vice-chm London Businessmen's Network 1994, vice-pres Small Business Bureau; runner-up TSB/Options Magazine Women Mean Business 1988, TOBIE Award 1989, runner-up Veuve Clicquot Business Woman of the Year 1989, Starr Award Top Entrepreneur of the World 1998, Global Summit of Women Award UK BusinessPioneer 1998, Br Assoc of Women Entrepreneurs (BAWE) Award for Br Entrepreneur of the Year 1999, BAWE Joyce Award 2006; chm Addenbrooke's Hosp Food Chain Appeal, tstee Galapagos Conservation Tst 2005–08, hon pres Tang Ting Twinning Assoc; FInstD 1987, FRSA 1992, fell PSA 1999; *Recreations* bridge, theatre, opera, bookbinding, fishing, art galleries, needlepoint; *Clubs* Mosimann's, Univ Women's, English Speaking Union; *Style*— Tina Knight; ✉ Nighthawk Enterprises, PO Box 44, Saffron Walden, Essex CB11 3ND (☎ 01799 540881, fax 01799 541713, e-mail tpk@nighthawk.co.uk)

KNIGHT, (Christopher) William; s of Claude Knight (d 1993), and Hon Priscilla (d 1995), da of 2 Baron Monk Bretton, CB; *b* 10 April 1943, Lewes, E Sussex; *Educ* Eton; *m* 6 Sept 1969, Jonkvrouw Sylvia Caroline, da of Jonkheer Emile van Lennep (d 1996); 2 da (Alexa Isobel (Mrs Mark Ridley) b 9 Nov 1971, Louisa Jane (Viscountess Hereford) b 15 Oct 1977), 1 s (Christopher Thorburn b 20 Oct 1973); *Career* princ mangr Portugal The Bank of London and S America 1982–84; dir: Lloyds Merchant Bank 1985–91, Lloyds Investment Mangrs 1987–91; md Lloyds Bank Fund Mgmnt 1988–91, fndr William Knight and Associates 1991; chm: J P Morgan Chinese Investment Tst, Myanmar Investments Int Ltd, Henry Cotton's Greater China Ltd, Homestrings Ltd; dir: L China, Axis Fiduciary Ltd, Guardian Ceylon Investment Co plc, Homestring LLC, Smith-Tan Phoenix Asia Fund Ltd, LGNet Gp plc; *Recreations* cricket, opera, travel writing, wine, contemporary global politics; *Clubs* Boodle's, Shek-O, Hurlingham; *Style*— William Knight, Esq; ✉ 82 Lansdowne Road, London W11 2LS (☎ 020 7221 3911, fax 020 7221 2178, e-mail william.wknight@gmail.com)

KNIGHT, William John Langford (Bill); OBE (2012); s of William Knight, and Gertrude Alice, *née* Wallage; *b* 11 September 1945; *Educ* Sir Roger Manwood's Sch Sandwich, Univ of Bristol (LLB); *m* 21 April 1973, Stephanie Irina, da of Lt-Col Edward Jeffery Williams; 1 da (Sarah b 1977), 1 s (Sam b 1980); *Career* admitted slr 1969; Simmons & Simmons Slrs: joined 1967, ptnr 1973–2001, i/c Hong Kong office 1979–82, head Corp Dept 1994–96, sr ptnr 1996–2001; dep chm Cncl of Lloyd's 2003–08 (memb 2000–08); former chm Standing Ctee on Co Law for Law Soc; chm: London Weighting Advsy Panel for GLA 2001–02, Enforcement Ctee Gen Insurance Standards Cncl 2002–04, Financial Reporting Review Panel 2004–12; dir Financial Reporting Cncl 2008–12 (memb 2004–07); memb Gaming Bd for GB 2004–05, gambling cmmr 2005–12; specialist advsr Treasy Select Ctee for FSA Report into RBS 2011–12; currently professional photographer specialising in portraits, theatre and opera (exhibn The Refugee's Gift at St Martin's in the Fields 2014, portrait of Elsbeth Juda accepted by National Portrait Gallery 2014); tstee: City of London Acad Islington 2008–12, Nat Life Stories 2011–; chm of govrs Argyle Primary Sch Camden 2010–12; Liveryman City of London Slrs' Co (memb Ct of Assts 2002–, Master 2007); FRSA; *Books* The Acquisition of Private Companies and Business Assets (1975, 7 edn 1997); *Recreations* Arsenal, tennis; *Clubs* Travellers, Hong Kong, City Law; *Style*— Bill Knight, Esq, OBE; ✉ website www.knightsight.co.uk

KNIGHT OF COLLINGTREE, Baroness (Life Peer UK 1997), of Collingtree in the County of Northamptonshire; Dame (Joan Christabel) Jill Knight; DBE (1985, MBE 1964); da of A E Christie (d 1933); *b* July 1923; *Educ* Fairfield Sch, King Edward GS for Girls Birmingham; *m* 1947, Montague Knight (decd), s of Leslie Knight of Harpole Hall, Northampton; 2 s; *Career* MP (Cons) Birmingham Edgbaston 1966–97 (Parly candidate (Cons) Northampton 1959 and 1964); memb: Race Relations and Immigration Select Ctee 1969–72, Home Affrs Select Ctee 1980–84 and 1992–97, Privileges and Standards Select Ctee 1993–97; chm Cons Backbench Ctee Health and Social Services 1981–97, memb Cncl Europe 1977–88 and 1999–2010, chm Lords and Commons All Pty Child Protection Gp 1983–97, pres W Midlands Cons Political Centre 1980–83, vice-chm 1922 Ctee 1992–97, chm Inter-Parliamentary Union 1994–97 (memb Exec Ctee 1992–97), vice-chm Assoc of Cons Peers 2002–06, chm All Pty Parly Gp for Northern Cyprus 2004–12; dir Computeach International Ltd 1990–2002, dir Heckett Multiserv 1999–2002; memb Northampton Borough Cncl 1956–66; lectr and broadcaster; vice-pres Br Fluoridation Soc 1994–; chm Bd Sulgrave Manor (ancestral home of George Washington) 2007–12 (pres 2012–); Hon DSc Aston Univ 1998; *Publications* About the House (1997); *Style*— The Baroness Knight of Collingtree, DBE; ✉ House of Lords, London SW1A 0PW

KNIGHT OF WEYMOUTH, Baron (Life Peer UK 2010), of Weymouth in the County of Dorset; Rt Hon James Philip (Jim) Knight; PC (2008); s of late Philip John Knight, and Hillier, *née* Howlett; *b* 6 March 1965; *Educ* Eltham Coll, Fitzwilliam Coll Cambridge; *m* 1989, Anna, *née* Wheatley; 1 da (Ruth Bridget b 31 Aug 1988), 1 s (Fergus James b 26 Sept 1990); *Career* actor and theatre mangr 1987–91, publisher of telephone directories Dentons Directories Ltd 1991–2001 (co dir 1998–2001); MP (Lab) S Dorset 2001–10 (Parly candidate (Lab) S Dorset 1997, European Parly candidate (Lab) SW England 1999), memb House of Commons Defence Ctee 2001–03, Parly sec DEFRA 2005–06, min of state DfES 2006–07, min of state Dept for Children, Schs and Families 2007–09, min of state for employment and welfare reform Dept for Work and Pensions 2009–10; memb Frome Town Cncl 1995–2001 (mayor 1998–99), memb Medip DC 1997–2001 (dep ldr 1999–2001); *Style*— The Lord Knight of Weymouth, PC

KNIGHTLEY, Keira; da of Will Knightley, and Sharman MacDonald; *b* 1985; *m* 2013, James Righton; *Career* actress; *Films* incl: Star Wars: Episode I – The Phantom Menace 1999, The Hole 2001, Bend It Like Beckham 2002, Pirates of the Caribbean: The Curse of the Black Pearl 2003, Love Actually 2003, King Arthur 2004, The Jacket 2005, Pride & Prejudice 2005, Domino 2005, Pirates of the Caribbean: Dead Man's Chest 2006, Pirates of the Caribbean: At World's End 2007, Atonement 2007, Silk 2007, The Edge of Love 2008, The Duchess 2008, Never Let Me Go 2010, Last Night 2010, London Boulevard 2010, A Dangerous Method 2011, Seeking a Friend for the End of the World 2012, Anna Karenina 2012, Can a Song Save Your Life? 2013; *Theatre* The Misanthrope (Comedy Theatre) 2009–10, The Children's Hour (West End) 2011; *Awards* London Critics Circle Award for Best Newcomer 2003, Best Int Actress Irish Film and TV Festival 2004, Breakthrough Award Hollywood Film Festival 2004, nomination Golden Globe Awards and Oscars (for Pride & Prejudice) 2006; *Style*— Ms Keira Knightley; ✉ c/o United Agents Limited, 12–26 Lexington Street, London W1F 0LE (☎ 020 3214 0800, fax 020 3214 0801, website www.unitedagents.co.uk)

KNIVETON, Prof Patrick; s of Edward George Kniveton (d 1985), and Winifred Mary, *née* Hopwood (d 2008); *Educ* BSc, MBA; *m* 22 Oct 1988, Melanie, *née* Lucas; 1 s (Thomas Edward b 22 Oct 1990), 2 da (Catherine Elizabeth b 21 March 1994, Ruth Frances b 8 Dec 1997); *Career* head of business mgmnt Gas Turbine Operations Engrg 1999–2007, head of infrastructure Rolls-Royce Marine Power 2007–09, head of engrg improvement Rolls-Royce Submarines 2009–14, head of engrg skills Rolls-Royce Submarines 2014–; pres Instn of Mechanical Engrs 2013–14 (vice-pres 2004–07, dep pres 2011–13); visiting prof Univ of Derby 2014–; CEng, FIMechE, CCMI; *Recreations* skiing, walking, theatre, badminton, cycling; *Style*— Prof Patrick Kniveton; ✉ Rolls-Royce, WW-G, PO Box 2000, Raynesway, Derby DE21 7XX

KNOBEL, Lance; s of Lawrence Roy Knobel (d 1990), and Gladys, *née* Smith (d 1994); *b* 6 November 1956; *Educ* New Trier East HS Winnetka Illinois, Princeton Univ (BA), Worcester Coll Oxford (MA); *Career* asst ed The Architectural Review 1980–82; ed: Designer's Journal 1983–87, Management Today 1987–89; md New International Media Milan Italy 1989–90, editorial dir Haymarket Marketing Publications 1990 (publishing devpt dir 1991–92), md and ed-in-chief World Link Publishing 1992–2000, head of prog World Economic Forum's Annual Meeting Davos 2000, advsr PM's Strategy Unit 2001–02, currently co-fndr and ed-in-chief Q Network Inc; *Books* Faber Guide to Twentieth Century Architecture (1985), Office Furniture (1987), International Interiors (1989); *Recreations* scuba diving, trumpet playing, tennis, skiing; *Style*— Lance Knobel, Esq; ✉ website www.davosnewbies.com

KNOPF, His Hon Elliot Michael; s of Harry Knopf (d 1976), and Clara Renée, *née* Weingard (d 2009); *b* 23 December 1950; *Educ* Bury GS, UCL (LLB); *m* 8 Feb 1976, Elizabeth Carol, da of Eugene Lieberman; 1 s (Anthony Martin b 17 Dec 1979), 1 da (Marcelle Rebecca b 4 Feb 1983); *Career* articled clerk Conn Goldberg Slrs Manchester 1974–76; Pannone March Pearson Slrs Manchester: admitted slr 1976, asst slr 1976–79, equity ptnr 1979–91; dep district registrar of the High Court and dep registrar of Co Court (Northern Circuit) 1987–91, district judge of the High Court and Co Court 1991–2002, asst recorder of Crown Court (Northern Circuit) 1996–2000, recorder of Crown Court (Northern Circuit) 2000–02, circuit judge (Northern Circuit) 2002–15, dep High Court judge 2008–15; memb Law Soc 1976–; *Recreations* reading, swimming, walking, theatre, foreign travel, the family; *Style*— His Hon Elliot Knopf; ✉ Bolton Combined Courts, Blackhorse Street, Bolton BL1 1SU (☎ 01204 392881)

KNOPFLER, Mark; s of Erwin Knopfler (d 1993), and Louisa Knopfler; *b* 12 August 1949; *Career* musician; former journalist Yorkshire Evening Post and teacher; fndr Dire Straits 1977; has produced: Bob Dylan, Randy Newman and others; albums with Dire Straits: Dire Straits (1978, reached UK no 5), Communique (1979, UK no 5), Making Movies (1980, UK no 4), Love Over Gold (1982, UK no 1), Alchemy – Dire Straits Live (live, 1984, UK no 3), Brothers In Arms (1985, UK no 1, formerly best ever selling UK album), Money For Nothing (compilation, 1988, UK no 1), On Every Street (1991, UK no 1), On the Night (1993), Live at the BBC (1995), Sultans of Swing: The Very Best of Dire Straits (compilation, 1998), Private Investigations: The Best of Dire Straits and Mark Knopfler

(2005); solo soundtrack albums: Local Hero (1982, UK no 14), Cal (1984, UK no 65), Comfort and Joy (1984), The Princess Bride (1987), Last Exit to Brooklyn (1989), Wag the Dog (1998), Metroland (1999), Shot at Glory (2002); other albums: Stay Tuned (with Chet Atkins, 1986), Missing...Presumed Having A Good Time (as Notting Hillbillies, 1990, UK no 2), Neck And Neck (with Chet Atkins, 1990, UK no 41), Golden Heart (1996), Sailing to Philadelphia (2000), The Ragpicker's Dream (2002), Shangri-La (2004), All the Roadrunning (with Emmylou Harris, 2006); has won Ivor Novello (incl Lifetime Achievement 2012), BRIT, MTV and Grammy awards; *Style*— Mark Knopfler, Esq

KNOPS, Prof Robin John; s of Joseph Nicholas Jean Toussaint Knops (d 1978), of Weymouth, Dorset, and Rita Josephine, *née* Colombo (d 1997); *b* 30 December 1932; *Educ* Thames Valley GS Twickenham, Univ of Nottingham (BSc, PhD); *m* 2 Sept 1965, Margaret Mary, da of Michael McDonald (d 1977), of Newcastle upon Tyne; 4 s (Andrew b 10 June 1966, Peter b 4 May 1968, Joseph b 12 April 1970, Robert b 22 Oct 1971), 2 da (Geraldine b 9 Aug 1974, Catherine b 9 Jan 1980); *Career* lectr in mathematics Univ of Nottingham 1959–62 (asst lectr 1956–59), reader in continuum mechanics Univ of Newcastle upon Tyne 1968–71 (lectr in applied mathematics 1962–68); Heriot-Watt Univ: prof of mathematics 1971–98, head of dept 1971–83, dean of science 1984–87, vice-princ 1988–95, special advsr to princ 1995–97, sr research fell 1997–98, prof emeritus 1998–; memb Bd of Govrs Scottish Coll of Textiles 1992–98; pres: Edinburgh Mathematical Soc 1974–75, Int Soc for the Interaction of Mechanics and Mathematics 1991–95 (vice-pres 1995–99); Leverhulme emeritus fell 2000–02, Hon DSc Heriot-Watt Univ 1999; FRSE 1975 (memb Exec Ctee 1982–92, memb Cncl 1982–87, meeting sec 1982–87, curator 1987–92), FRSA 1989–2000; *Books* Uniqueness Theorems in Linear Elasticity (with L E Payne, 1971); *Recreations* walking, reading; *Style*— Prof R J Knops, FRSE; ✉ Heriot-Watt University, Edinburgh EH14 4AS (✆ 0131 451 3363, e-mail r.j.knops@hw.ac.uk)

KNOTT, Herbert Espenett (Herbie); s of Lt-Col Roger Birbeck Knott, OBE, MC (d 1960), and Eva, *née* Conroy (d 1995); *b* 11 March 1949; *Educ* Rugby, UC Oxford (MA); *Career* mgmnt trainee Atlas Express Ltd 1972–73; photojournalist: London Evening Standard 1977–80, NOW! magazine 1980–81, Sunday Times 1981–86, The Independent 1986–96, freelance 1996–; visiting lectr London Sch of Photojournalism 1998–2000; contrib exhibitions: Br Press Photographers Assoc Exhibitions 1986–89, World Press Photo 1987, 1989 and 1998, Telegraph Magazine 25th Anniversary, Witness (NT) 1990, Politicians (Impressions Gallery York) 1992 (Stills Gallery Edinburgh) 1993 and (Battersea Arts Centre London) 1994, Fashion Exposures (London) 1993–2002, London Exhibition (Zwemmer Gallery London) 1994, The Oblique View – 10 Years of The Independent (Visa pour l'Image Perpignan) 1997, Ilford Printers (RPS Bath) 1998, Eden Project (Royal Acad) 2001 (with Nicholas Grimshaw), Redesign – Sustainability in New British Design (Br Cncl Norway, China and Kenya) 2001, Skin – Surface, Substance and Design (Cooper-Hewitt Nat Design Museum NY) 2002, The Lost Gardens of Heligan 25th Anniv Exhibition (Heligan Gardens, Cornwall) 2015, Changing Britain (Hayward Gallery, London) 2015; *Awards* Nikon Photographer of the Month June 1983 and Dec 1990, Nikon Photographer of the Election 1987; *Books* How They Made Piece of Cake (with Robert Eagle, 1988), Black and White (1990), Glasmoth – Moscow and Back by Tiger Moth (with Jonathan Elwes, 1990); *Recreations* gardening, supporting AFC Wimbledon, Cycling; *Style*— Herbie Knott, Esq; ✉ c/o Rex Features Ltd, Vine Hill, London EC1R 5DZ (✆ 020 7278 7294, mobile 07905 105009)

KNOTT, Prof John Frederick; OBE (2004); s of Fred Knott, of Bristol, and Margaret, *née* Chesney; *b* 9 December 1938; *Educ* Univ of Sheffield (BMet), Univ of Cambridge (PhD, ScD); *m* 1, 16 April 1963 (m dis 1986), Christine Mary, da of William Roberts; 2 s (William Frederick b 28 April 1965, Andrew John b 10 May 1966); *m* 2, 15 Sept 1990, Susan Marilyn (formerly Mrs Cooke), da of William Jones; 2 step s (Paul Antony b 6 Dec 1966, James Daniel b 21 April 1981); *Career* res offr Central Electricity Res Laboratories Leatherhead 1962–66; Univ of Cambridge: lectr Dept of Materials Sci and Metallurgy 1967–81, univ reader in mechanical metallurgy 1981–90; Churchill Coll Cambridge: Goldsmiths' fell 1967–91, vice-master 1988–90, extra-ordinary fell 1991–2006; Univ of Birmingham: prof and head of Sch of Metallurgy and Materials 1990–96, Feeney prof 1994–2007, dean of engrg 1995–98; hon prof Beijing Univ of Aeronautics and Astronautics 1992–, hon prof Xian Jiaotong Univ 1995–; pres Int Congress on Fracture 1993–97 (hon fell 1984); chm Materials, Manufacturing and Structures Advsy Bd (formerly Materials and Processing Advsy Bd) Rolls-Royce 2000–11 (memb 1987–); memb: Tech Assessment Gp on Structural Integrity 1988– (chair 2010–), Research Bd of the Welding Inst 1989–, EPSRC/DTI LINK Ctee (EEM) 1992–99, Nuclear Safety Advsy Ctee 1992–2005 (actg chm 2003–04, chm Sub Ctee on Research 2000–05), EPSRC Prog Mgmnt Ctee for Structural Integrity 1998–2001, MOD Research Prog Gp 2003–, Graphite Tech Advsy Gp 2004–, Defence Nuclear Safety Ctee 2006–; ed Materials Science and Technology Jl 2003–14; foreign memb Acad of Sciences of the Ukraine 1992; foreign assoc US Nat Acad of Engrg 2003; visiting fell Japan Soc for the Promotion of Sci 1980; gave Royal Soc/Royal Acad of Engrg lecture at the Royal Soc 1999; Sheffield Soc of Engrs and Metallurgists prize 1958, Mappin medal 1959, Nesthill medal 1959, L B Pfeil prize for Physical Metallurgy 1973, Rosenhain medal for Physical Metallurgy 1978, Leslie Holliday prize (Materials Sci Club) 1978, Inst of Materials Griffith Medal 1999, Robert Franklin Mehl award Minerals, Metals & Materials Society 2005, Leverhulme Medal Royal Soc 2005, Hatfield lectr IMMM 2006, Brooker Medal Welding Inst 2007, Platinum Medal IMMM 2009, Cottrell Gold Medal Int Congress on Fracture 2013; Hon DEng Univ of Glasgow 2004, Hon DEng Univ of Sheffield 2010; hon memb Inst of Metals Japan 2005, foreign fell Indian Nat Acad of Engrg 2006; FIM 1974 (AIM 1963), CEng 1978, FWeldI 1985, FRSA 1985, FREng 1988, FRS 1990, FIMechE 1994; *Books* Fundamentals of Fracture Mechanics (1973), Worked Examples in Fracture Mechanics (with Dr David Elliott, 1979), Fracture Mechanics – Worked Examples (with Dr Paul Withey, 1993); *Publications* author of more than 325 publications in jls and conference proceedings; *Recreations* bridge, cryptic crosswords, listening to traditional jazz (preferably in live performance), playing the tenor recorder with enthusiasm rather than skill; *Style*— Prof John Knott, OBE, FRS, FREng; ✉ 43 West Street, Stratford upon Avon CV37 6DN (✆ 01789 261977); The University of Birmingham, School of Metallurgy and Materials, Edgbaston, Birmingham B15 2TT (✆ 0121 414 6729, e-mail j.f.knott@bham.ac.uk)

KNOTT, HE (Graeme) Jonathan; *m* Angela Susan; 1 da, 2 s; *Career* diplomat; desk offr Anti Drugs Cooperation Dept FCO 1988–90, desk offr Sanctions Enforcement Gulf War Emergency Unit FCO 1990–91, third later second sec (political) Havana 1991–95, dep European corr EU Directorate FCO 1995–96, first sec Mexico 1996–2000, first sec UK Delgn Paris 2000–05, dir FCO Services Change Prog 2005–06, head Financial Planning and Performance Dept FCO 2006–08, dep head of mission and dir UKTI Seoul 2008–11, ambass to Hungary 2012–; *Style*— HE Mr Jonathan Knott; ✉ FCO (Budapest), King Charles Street, London SW1A 2AH

KNOWLES, Sir Charles Francis; 7 Bt (GB 1765), of Lovell Hill, Berkshire; s of Sir Francis Gerald William Knowles, 6 Bt, FRS (d 1974), and Ruth, *née* Brooke-Smith; *b* 20 December 1951; *Educ* Marlborough, Oxford Sch of Architecture (DipArch); *m* 1979, Amanda Louise Margaret, da of Lance Lee Bromley, Esq, MChir, FRCS, of London; 2 s ((Charles) William Frederick Lance b 1985, Edward Francis Annandale Bromley b 7 April 1989); *Heir* s, William Knowles; *Career* dir: Charles Knowles Design Ltd (architects), Richmond Knowles Architects; works incl: new Battersea Dogs Home London and Old Windsor, refurbishment of Bank of England, historic country houses and listed London properties;

RIBA 1978, FRSA 1984; *Recreations* flying, shooting, architecture, countryside; *Style*— Sir Charles Knowles, Bt; ✉ Wyndham Croft, Turners Hill, West Sussex RH10 4PS

KNOWLES, Rev Graeme Paul; CVO (2011); s of Stanley Knowles, and Grace Edith Ellen, *née* Pratt; *b* 25 September 1951; *Educ* KCL (AKC), St Augustine's Coll Canterbury (Bishop Hanson prize); *m* 1973, Susan Gail, *née* Marsden; *Career* ordained: deacon 1974, priest 1975; curate St Peter in Thanet 1974–79, sr curate and precentor Leeds Parish Church 1979–81, chaplain precentor Portsmouth Cathedral 1981–87, vicar of Leigh Park 1987–93, rural dean of Havant 1990–93, archdeacon of Portsmouth 1993–98, dean of Carlisle 1998–2003, bishop of Sodor and Man 2003–07, dean of St Paul's 2007–11; chm Cncl for the Care of Churches 2003–09; registrar Sons and Friends of the Clergy 2012–; memb Legislative Cncl Tynwald Ct 2003–07; hon chaplain RNR; FKC 2011; *Recreations* music (Victorian and Edwardian ballads), novels of E F Benson; *Clubs* Garrick; *Style*— The Rev Graeme Knowles

KNOWLES, His Hon Judge Graham Roy; QC (2009); *b* 20 February 1968, Manchester; *Educ* Queen Elizabeth II HS Peel, King's Coll Cambridge (MA); *Career* called to the Bar 1990 (Astbury law scholar); junior of the Northern Circuit 1994, recorder 2005, circuit judge (Northern Circuit) 2010–; *Style*— His Hon Judge Knowles, QC; ✉ The Law Courts, Openshaw Place, Ring Way, Preston PR1 2LL (✆ 01772 844700)

KNOWLES, Hon Mr Justice Robin Knowles; CBE (2006), QC (1999); s of Norman Richard Knowles, of Alkham, Kent, and Margaret Mary, *née* Robinson; *b* 7 April 1960; *Educ* Sir Roger Manwood's GS, Trinity Coll Cambridge; *m* 1987, Gill, *née* Adams; 1 da (Emma Kathleen b 26 April 1991); *Career* called to the Bar 1982, asst recorder 1998, recorder 2000, judge of the High Court of Justice (Queen's Bench Div) 2014–; tstee and memb Mgmnt Ctee Bar Pro Bono Unit 1996–, tstee RCJ Advice Bureau 1999–, chm N American Ctee of the Commercial Bar Assoc 2000–, tstee Bar in the Community 2001–, tstee Slrs Pro Bono Gp 2001–; memb Exec of the Commercial Bar Assoc 1999–, memb various Bar Cncl, Commercial Bar Assoc and Inn ctees and working parties; memb: Middle Temple, Gray's Inn, Commercial Bar Assoc, Chancery Bar Assoc, S E Circuit; *Recreations* the East End of London; being with family and friends; *Style*— Hon Mr Justice Knowles, CBE, QC; ✉ The Royal Courts of Justice, Strand, London WC2A 2LL

KNOWLES-CUTLER, Angus; s of Charles Knowles, and Joyce, *née* Bradbury, of Bradford on Avon; *b* 1 September 1962, Bradford; *Educ* Bedford Modern Sch, CCC Cambridge; *m* 13 March 1993, Laura, *née* Culbert; 2 da (Charlotte Culbert Knowles-Cutler b 10 Oct 1997, Elise Avery Knowles-Cutler b 19 Nov 1999); *Career* vice-pres Cap Gemini Ernst & Young 1997–2001; Deloitte LLP: ptnr and head of post-merger integration EMEA 2001–, sr ptnr London 2013–, UK head of transaction servs 2013–15, vice-chm 2015–, chm UK-China Practice 2016–; Freeman City of London 2013, Liveryman Worshipful Co of Gardeners 2016; FRSA 2015; *Books* Golbaltown (2013), Agiletown (2014), From Brawn to Brains (2015); *Recreations* family, gardening, music, shooting, travel; *Clubs* RAC, RSA; *Style*— Angus Knowles-Cutler, Esq; ✉ Worples Field, Farley Common, Westerham, Kent TN16 1UB (✆ 07968 025680, Twitter @AngusCutler); Deloitte LLP, Athene Place, 66 Shoe Lane, London EC4A 3BQ (✆ 020 7007 2946, e-mail aknowlescutler@deloitte.co.uk)

KNOWLSON, Prof James Rex; OBE (2014); s of Francis Frederick Knowlson (d 1972), of Ripley, Derbys, and Elizabeth Mary, *née* Platt (d 2004); *b* 6 August 1933; *Educ* Swanwick Hall GS, Univ of Reading (BA, DipEd, PhD); *m* Elizabeth Selby, da of Thomas Albert Coxon (d 1985); 2 s (Gregory Michael b 1960, Richard Paul b 1963), 1 da (Laura Elizabeth b 1968); *Career* asst master Ashville Coll Harrogate 1959–60, lectr in French Univ of Glasgow 1963–69 (asst lectr 1960–63); Univ of Reading: lectr 1969–75, Leverhulme research fell 1975–76, sr lectr 1975–78, reader 1978–81, prof of French 1981–98, emeritus prof 1998–; fell Nat Humanities Center USA 2002–03, Leverhulme emeritus fell 2003–04; memb Soc of Authors 1987; Hon DLitt Univ of Reading; Officier dans l'Ordre des Palmes Académiques 2011; *Books* Samuel Beckett: An Exhibition (1971), Light and Darkness in the Theatre of Samuel Beckett (1972), Universal Language Schemes in England and France 1600–1800 (1975), Happy Days/Oh les beaux jours (ed, 1978), Frescoes of the Skull: The Later Prose and Drama of Samuel Beckett (with John Pilling, 1979), Samuel Beckett's Krapp's Last Tape (ed, 1980), Happy Days (ed, 1985), The Theatrical Notebooks of Samuel Beckett Vol III – Krapp's Last Tape (ed, 1992), Waiting for Godot Vol I (ed, 1993), Damned to Fame: The Life of Samuel Beckett (1996), Images of Beckett (with John Haynes, 2003), Beckett Remembering, Remembering Beckett (with Elizabeth Knowlson, 2006); *Recreations* badminton, cricket, theatre; *Style*— Prof James Knowlson, OBE; ✉ 259 Shinfield Road, Reading, Berkshire RG2 8HF (✆ 0118 962 1587); Department of French, The Faculty of Letters and Social Sciences, The University of Reading, Whiteknights, Reading, Berkshire RG6 6AE (✆ 0118 931 8776, e-mail j.r.knowlson@reading.ac.uk)

KNOX, Ian Campbell; s of Eric Campbell Knox, and Mary Fyfe, *née* Beattie; *b* 18 January 1954; *Educ* Royal HS Edinburgh, Waid Acad Anstruther, Edinburgh Coll of Art, Br Cncl scholarship to Budapest, Nat Film Sch; *m* Sarah Cartwright; 2 da (Kita b 7 Aug 2008, Anna-May b 23 June 2010); *Career* freelance writer and director 1980–; many British film and TV drama credits, currently working on feature film La Americana; film credits incl: The Stronger, The Privilege, Shoot for The Sun, Down Where The Buffalo Go, The Police, Martino Unstrung; *Awards* BAFTA Award for Best Short film (for The Privilege), Bilbao Film Festival Award for Best Short Fiction (The Privilege), Scottish Radio and TV Awards for Best Play (for Workhorses); *Recreations* music, design, motor cycles; *Clubs* Soho House; *Style*— Ian Knox, Esq; ✉ 22 Ruston Mews, London W11 1RB (✆ 020 7792 0101, e-mail knoxyfilm@gmail.com)

KNOX, Lesley Mary; *née* Samuel; da of Prof Eric Samuel, CBE, of SA, and Vera Eileen; *b* 19 September 1953; *Educ* Cheltenham Ladies' Coll, Univ of Cambridge (MA); *m* 1, 1983 (m dis); *m* 2, 1991, Brian Knox; 1 da (Fenella Megan b 27 June 1994); *Career* slr Slaughter & May 1979, attorney Shearman & Sterling USA 1980; Kleinwort Benson: joined 1981, dir 1986, head of institutional asset mgmnt 1991; non-exec directorships incl: Alliance Tst plc 2001–11 (chm 2004–11), Hays plc 2002–11, SABMiller plc 2011–, Remco, Thomas Cook Gp plc 2016–, Legal and General Gp plc 2016–; chm: Grosvenor Gp 2010–, Centrica plc 2012–, Remco; chair V&A at Dundee 2010; *Recreations* textile design, family, collector of contemporary art; *Clubs* Athenaeum, New (Edinburgh); *Style*— Mrs Lesley Knox

KNOX-JOHNSTON, Sir William Robert Patrick (Robin); kt (1995), CBE (1969), RD (1978, and Bar); s of David Robert Knox-Johnston (d 1970), and Elizabeth Mary, *née* Cree (d 2004); *b* 17 March 1939; *Educ* Berkhamsted Sch; *m* 1962, Suzanne (d 2003), da of Denis Ronald Singer; 1 da (Sara b 1963); *Career* yachtsman; first person to circumnavigate the world non-stop and single handed 14 June 1968–22 April 1969, Br Sailing Trans Atlantic Record (10 days 14 hours 9 mins) 1986, World Champion Class II multihulls 1985, co-skipper Enza NZ (world's fastest circumnavigation under sail, 74 days 22 hours 17 mins 22 secs) 1994, fourth Velux 5 Oceans solo around the world race 2007; fndr and chm Clipper Ventures 1995–; pres Sail Trg Assoc 1993–2002, hon pres Cruising Assoc; tstee: Greenwich Maritime Museum 1992–2002, National Maritime Museum Cornwall 1997–2006, Cutty Sark Tst until 2015; memb: Lottery Panel Sports Cncl 1995–2000, Cncl Sport England 2000–02; UK Yachtsman of the Year 1969, 1995, 2007 and 2015, RIN Gold medal 1992, Int Sailor of the Year 1995, Hall of Fame Int Sailing Fedn 2010, Hon Capt RNR 2015; Hon Keeper of the Quaich 2009; Younger Bro Trinity House 1973–; Freeman: City of London, London Borough of Bromley; Hon DSc Maine Maritime Acad, Hon DTech Southampton Inst of Technol 1993, hon doctorate Univ of Exeter 2008, hon doctorate Univ of Hull, hon doctorate Univ of Roehampton; fell Liverpool John Moore Univ 2006; FRIN 1994; *Books* World of my Own (1969), Sailing (1975), Twilight of Sail

(1978), Last but not Least (1978), Bunkside Companion (1982), Seamanship (1986), The BOC Challenge (1986–87), The Cape of Good Hope (1989), The History of Yachting (1990), The Columbus Venture (1991, Book of the Sea Award), Sea, Ice and Rock (with Sir Christian Bonington, CBE, *qv*, 1992), Cape Horn (1994), Beyond Jules Verne (1995), Force of Nature (2007), Knox-Johnston of Sailing (2010); *Recreations* sailing; *Clubs* Royal Yacht Sqdn (hon), RNSA (Hon Rear Cdre); hon memb Yacht Clubs: Royal Irish, Royal NI, Royal Harwich, Royal Southampton, Royal Western, National (Dublin), Royal Bombay (India), Fremantle Sailing (Aust), Benfleet, Howth (Ireland), Liverpool, Royal Southern, Cruising Assoc, Island Sailing, Royal Western, Erith, Royal Ocean Racing; *Style*— Sir Robin Knox-Johnston, CBE, RD*; ✉ 1 Tower Street, Old Portsmouth PO1 2JR (e-mail rknoxjohnston@clipper-ventures.com)

KNOX-PEEBLES, Brian Philip; s of Lt-Col George Edward Knox-Peebles, RTR, DSO (d 1969), and Patricia, *née* Curtis-Raleigh (d 2002); *b* 19 June 1936, Canterbury, Kent; *Educ* Wellington (head of coll, Queen's Medal), Göttingen Univ W Germany, BNC Oxford (MA, William Hulme exhibitioner); *m* 20 Aug 1960, Rose Mary, da of Capt Cyril Telford Latch; 3 da (Nina b 16 Nov 1962, Fleur b 3 Feb 1964, Bryonie b 16 Nov 1967), 1 s (Brendan b 21 Sept 1965); *Career* Daily Mail 1963–64, Evening Standard 1964–65, The Times 1965–67, United Newspapers plc 1967–89; dir: Punch Publications 1969–86 (publisher 1984–86) Bradbury Agnew Ltd 1979–82, United Provincial Newspapers 1981–89, Webster & Horsfall 1987–2009; gp mktg dir United Newspapers plc 1974–89; fndr and chm Consultants in Media; fndr memb and first pres Int Newspaper Mktg Assoc (Europe), memb Mktg Ctee Int Fedn of Newspaper Publishers; former Euro dir Int Circulation Managers' Assoc; memb IOD 1982–89; *Books* The Fleet Street Revolution; *Recreations* cinema, music, walking, swimming, reading, writing; *Clubs* Hurlingham; *Style*— Brian Knox-Peebles, Esq; ✉ 7 Bulmer Mews, London W11 3NZ (☎ 020 7727 9595, e-mail brian@knox-peebles.co.uk)

KOBBORG, Johan; s of Martinus Vedel Kobborg, and Käthe Kobborg; *Career* dancer; joined Royal Danish Ballet 1988 (princ dancer 1994), princ dancer Royal Ballet 1999–2013, currently freelance dancer and choreographer; performances incl: Swan Lake, Giselle, La Bayadere, Don Quixote, Coppélia, La Sylphide, Hamlet, Romeo and Juliet, Nutcracker, La Fille Mal Gardee, Onegin, Paquita, Napoli, The Dream, Le Corsaire, Agon, Etudes, Flowerfestival in Genzano, In the Middle Somewhat Elevated, Vestris, Songs of the Earth, Rendezvous, The Concert; TV and video performances incl: Hamlet, Don Quixote, Bournonville Ballet Technique, Sleeping Beauty, Mime Matters; galas incl: Stars of the 21st Century (Paris, NY, Canada), Nijinsky Gala (Germany), John Cranka Gala (Stuttgart), Stars of American Ballet (Italy); guest appearances with companies incl: Bolshoi Ballet, La Scala, Nat Ballet of Canada, Teatro San Carlo, Stuttgart Ballet, Hamburg Ballet, Finnish Nat Ballet, Scottish Ballet, Nat Ballet of Japan, Hanover Ballet; prodr: The Bournonville Gp Italy 1999, Johan Kobburg and Friends Copenhagen 2001; Gold Medal Erik Bruhn Competition 1993, Grand Prix and Gold Medal Nureyev Int Ballet Competition 1994, Grand Prix and Gold Medal Jackson Int Ballet Competition 1994, Best Male Dancer Critics Circle Award 2001; *Style*— Johan Kobborg, Esq

KOCHHAR, Prof Ashok Kumar; s of Sansar Chand Kochhar (d 1997), and Satya, *née* Vohra; *b* 31 January 1949; *Educ* MLM Senior Secdy Sch Firozpur India, RSD Coll Firozpur India, Government Coll Ludhiana India, Univ of London (BSc Engrg), Univ of Bradford (PhD); *m* 1987, Dr Rupa Mehta; *Career* graduate engr Rolls Royce 1970–71 (engrg apprentice 1966–70); Univ of Bradford: researcher 1971–74, postdoctoral research fell 1974–76, lectr 1976–83, reader 1983–86, prof of mfrg systems engrg 1986–92; UMIST: Lucas prof of mfrg systems engrg and head Mfrg Div 1992–98, head Dept of Mechanical Engrg 1997–98; inaugural head/exec dean Sch of Engrg and Applied Science Aston Univ 1999–; visiting prof Indian Inst of Technol Delhi 2009, visiting professorial fell Univ of NSW 2009, visiting researcher John Hopkins Univ Carey Business Sch 2009; academic advsr: Hong Kong Poly Univ 2004–14, Universiti Putra Malaysia, Universiti Technology Mara; dir Birmingham Technol Ltd 2001–; memb Editorial Bd: Jl of Engrg Manufacture, Int Jl of Advanced Mfrg Technol, Integrated Mfrg Systems, Int Jl of Mfrg Systems Design; memb: Int Fedn of Info Processing Gp on Computer-Aided Prodn Mgmnt, DTI/Br Cncl sponsored missions to Japan, Korea, China, Hong Kong and India, Design and Integrated Prodn Coll EPSRC; memb Global Research Awards Panel Royal Acad of Engrg 2001–, memb UK Research Assessment Exercise Panels 2001 and 2008; conslt to several mfrg companies; author of over 150 papers in jls and conf proceedings; memb Ct Cranfield Univ 1997–98; FIET 1989 (memb Cncl 2000–), FIMechE 1992, FREng 1997; *Awards* Donald Julius Groen Prize IMechE 1988, Joseph Whitworth Prize IMechE 1988 and 1998, Nat Mfrg Intelligence Award DTI, A M Strickland Prize IMechE 1999; *Books* Development of Computer-Based Production Systems (1979), Micro-Processors and Their Manufacturing Applications (with N D Burns, 1983), Integrating Micro-Processors into Product Design (with N D Burns, 1983), Proceedings of the 30th International MATADOR Conference (ed, 1993), Proceedings of the 31st International MATADOR Conference (ed, 1995), Proceedings of the 32nd International MATADOR Conference (ed, 1997), Managing By Projects For Business Success (with John Parnaby and Stephen Wearne, 2003); *Recreations* reading, current affairs, music, internet, swimming; *Style*— Prof Ashok Kochhar, FREng; ✉ School of Engineering and Applied Science, Aston University, Aston Triangle, Birmingham B4 7ET (☎ 0121 204 3672, fax 0121 204 3678, e-mail a.k.kochhar@aston.ac.uk)

KOCHHAR, Atul; *b* 31 March 1969, Jamshedpur, India; *Career* head chef Tamarind London 1994–2002 (Michelin star); chef patron: Benares London 2003– (Michelin star 2007–), Ananda Dublin 2008–, Vatika Hants 2009–, Rang Mahal Dubai 2012–, Indian Essence Kent 2012–, Sindhu Marlow 2014–, Benares Madrid 2015–, NRI Mumbai 2015–, LIMA Mumbai 2016–; exec chef Colony London 2010–; ambass Br Asian Tst; Triangle Media Gp Cordon Bleu Award 2010; hon doctorate Southampton Solent Univ 2010; *Books* Indian Essence (2004), Fish, Indian Style (2008), Indian Essence (2008), Curries of the World (2012), Benares Cookbook (2015); *Style*— Atul Kochhar, Esq; ✉ Benares Restaurant & Bar, 12a Berkeley Square House, Berkeley Square, London W1J 6BS (☎ 020 7629 8886, e-mail marketing@benaresrestaurant.co.uk or reservations@benaresrestaurant.co.uk, website www.benaresrestaurant.co.uk, Twitter @atulkochhar, Instagram @atulkochhar)

KOEFOED-NIELSEN, Kester Carl (Kes); *see:* Kes Nielsen

KOERNER, Prof Joseph Leo; s of Henry Koerner, the artist (d 1991), and Joan Frasher Koerner; *b* 1958, Pittsburgh, PA; *Educ* Yale Univ (BA), Univ of Cambridge (MA), Univ of Heidelberg, Univ of Calif Berkeley (MA, PhD); *Family* 1 s (Benjamin Henry Anders b 2 Oct 1991), 1 da (Sigrid Anna Gunhild b 6 May 1995); m, 28 June 2003, Margaret Koster; 1 s (Leo Anselm b 3 June 2004), 1 da (Lucy Willa b 16 Jan 2006); *Career* Soc of Fellows Harvard Univ 1986–89, prof of history of art and architecture Harvard Univ 1989–99, prof of modern art history Univ of Frankfurt 1999–2000, prof UCL 2000–04, prof Courtauld Inst of Art London 2004–06, Victor S Thomas prof of history of art Harvard Univ 2006–; curator Henry Koerner retrospective Austrian Nat Gallery 1997; writer-presenter Northern Renaissance (BBC TV) 2006, writer-presenter Vienna: City of Dreams (BBC TV) 2007; Jan Mitchell Prize for the History of Art 1992, Andrew W Mellon Distinguished Achievement Award 2009; Phi Beta Kappa 1979; memb American Acad of Arts and Sciences 1995, memb American Philosophical Soc 2008, sr fell Harvard Soc of Fells 2008–; *Books* Die Suche nach dem Labyrinth (1983), Paul Klee: Legends of the Sign (with Rainer Crone, 1991), Caspar David Friedrich and the Subject of Landscape (1990), The Moment of Self-Portraiture in German Renaissance Art (1993), The Reformation of the Image (2004); *Recreations* mountaineering, cycling, piano; *Clubs* Savile, Cambridge Scientific; *Style*— Prof Joseph Leo Koerner; ✉ Department of History of Art and Architecture, Harvard University, Cambridge, MA 02138, USA

KOHLI, Jitinder; s of Inder Pal Kohli, and Swarn Kohli; *b* 2 February 1973; *Educ* Univ of Oxford (BA), Univ of Southampton (MSc); *Career* civil servant; head Productivity and Structural Reform Team HM Treasy 2003–04, dir of active communities Home Office 2004–05, chief exec (DG) Better Regulation Executive Dept for Business, Enterprise and Regulatory Reform 2005–09, DG strategy and communications Dep for Business, Innovation and Skills 2009, sr fell Center for American Progress Washington DC 2009–; dir Deloitte Consulting Washington DC; memb Bd Circle Anglia Housing Gp; chair EPIC Tst, fell Young Fndn 2009–; *Publications* reports for Centre for American Progress and Young Fndn; *Style*— Jitinder Kohli, Esq

KOHNER, Prof Eva Maria; OBE (1994); da of Baron George Nicholas Kohner, of Szaszberek (d 1945), of Hungary, and Andrea Kathleen, *née* Boszormenyi (d 1985); *b* 23 February 1929; *Educ* Baar-Madas Presbyterian Boarding Sch for Girls, Royal Free Hosp Sch of Med Univ of London (BSc, MB BS, MD); *m* 26 April 1961 (m dis 1979), Steven Ivan Warman; *Career* med registrar med ophthalmogy Lambeth Hosp 1963–64, res fell Royal Postgraduate Med Sch Hammersmith Hosp London 1965–68, MRC Alexander Wernher Piggott Meml fell NY 1968–69; Moorfields Eye Hosp and Hammersmith Hosp: sr registrar and lectr 1970–77, conslt med ophthalmologist 1977–88, prof med ophthalmology (first full-time prof in Britain) 1988–; worked in field of treatment of diabetic eye disease by laser (in part instrumental in this treatment now being available to all patients in the UK and Europe) and pathogenic mechanisms in diabetic eye disease, instigated (with colleagues) yearly screening for eye disease in diabetic patients; FRCP 1977 (MRCP 1963), FRCOphth 1991; *Books* over three hundred publications in field of retinal vascular disease; *Recreations* art, travel; *Clubs* Athenaeum (first female intake in 2002); *Style*— Prof Eva Kohner, OBE; ✉ 32 Monckton Court, Strangways Terrace, London W14 8NF

KOK, Nicholas Willem; s of Felix Kok, and Ann, *née* Steel; *b* 30 December 1962; *Educ* King's Sch Worcester, New Coll Oxford (organ scholar, BA, ARCO, FRCO), RCM (Lofthouse Memorial Prize, Countess of Munster Award); *m* 19 Sept 1992, Sarah, *née* Hickson; *Career* conductor; music dir Janet Smith and Dancers 1985–87, asst conductor/repetiteur ENO and music advsr Contemporary Opera Studio 1989–93, princ conductor and artistic dir ViVA: the orchestra of the east midlands 1996–; involved in setting up Almeida Opera; conductor: ENO, Opera North, Stuttgart Opera, Köln Opera, English Touring Opera, Opera Rara, Opera Factory, Dublin Grand Opera, The Opera Co, The Philharmonia, London Philharmonic, Royal Scottish Nat Orch, London Sinfonietta, Scottish Chamber Orch, Ulster Orchestra, Halle, CBSO, Bournemouth Sinfonietta, Endymion Ensemble, Premiere Ensemble, Trinity Coll of Music Sinfonia, London Pro Arte Orch, Philippines Philharmonic, Alvin Ailey Dance Theater London Coliseum, Orch of St John's, Nash Ensemble; television and radio incl: The Return of Ulysses, The Fairy Queen, Arion and the Dolphin, The Soldier's Tale, The Carnival of the Animals, Reginald Smith Brindle's Journey Towards Infinity, Erollyn Wallen's Mondrial, A Man For All Seasons and other broadcasts of several operas; interviewer/commentator: Cardiff Singer of the World, Sainsbury's Choir of the Year, BBC Proms; *Style*— Nicholas Kok, Esq; ✉ c/o Rayfield Allied, Southbank House, Black Prince Road, London SE1 7SJ

KOKOSALAKI, Sophia; da of Vasilios Kokosalakis, and Stella, *née* Leonidaki; *b* 3 November 1972, Athens, Greece; *Educ* Univ of Athens (BA), Central St Martins Sch of Art (MA); *Career* fashion designer; first catwalk show autumn/winter 1999–2000 London Fashion Week, catwalk show for Ruffo Research spring/summer 2001 and autumn/winter 2001–02, debut catwalk presentation thirteenth collection (spring/summer 2005) Paris Fashion Week; chief designer Olympic Games 2002–04 (design for opening ceremony and officials uniforms Athens 2004); guest designer Fendi 2002; creative dir for relaunch of Vionnet 2006–07; Sophia Kokosalaki Ltd (jt venture with Staff Int Spa) 2007; Best New Designer Elle Style Awards 2001, Arts Fndn Award 2002, Best New Designer Lycra Awards 2003; voted one of Britain's 'cool brand leaders' 2004; *Style*— Miss Sophia Kokosalaki; ✉ Unit 7, 47–49 Tudor Road, London E9 7SN (☎ 020 8986 6001, e-mail sophia@sophiakokosalaki.com)

KOLBERT, His Hon Dr Colin Francis; s of Arthur Richard Alexander Kolbert (d 1992), of Barnet and Barnstaple, and Dorothy Elizabeth, *née* Fletcher (d 1996); *b* 3 June 1936; *Educ* Queen Elizabeth's Barnet, St Catharine's Coll Cambridge (MA, PhD), St Peter's Coll Oxford (MA, DPhil); *m* 12 Sept 1959, Jean Fairgrieve, da of Stanley Hutton Abson (d 1964), of Friern Barnet; 2 da (Julia Catharine b 1963, Jennifer Sally b 1965); *Career* RA 1954–56, Cambridge Univ OTC (TAVR) 1969–74; called to the Bar Lincoln's Inn 1961 (bencher 2005); fell and tutor in jurisprudence St Peter's Coll Oxford 1964–68, fell Magdalene Coll Cambridge 1968– (tutor 1969–88), lectr in law Dept of Land Economy Cambridge 1968–88; recorder SE Circuit 1985–88; circuit judge: SE Circuit 1988–90, NE Circuit 1990–95; ind bd memb and tbnl chm SFA 1995–2001, dep chm Regulatory Decisions Ctee FSA 2001–06; asst surveillance cmmr 2001–13; Freeman City of London 1997, Liveryman Wax Chandlers' Company 1999 (Master 2009); FCIArb 1997; *Clubs* Hawks' (Cambridge), MCC, Farmers, Cambridge Univ Rugby (tstee 1988–2011); *Style*— His Hon Dr Colin Kolbert; ✉ Magdalene College, Cambridge CB3 0AG; Outer Temple Chambers, 222 Strand, Temple, London WC2R 1BA

KOLTAI, Ralph; CBE (1983); s of Dr Alfred Koltai (d 1970), and Charlotte, *née* Weinstein (d 1987); *b* 31 July 1924; *Educ* Berlin, Central Sch of Arts and Crafts London (DipAD); *m* 29 Dec 1954 (m dis 1976), Mary Annena, da of late George Stubbs, of Liverpool; *Career* stage designer and director; RASC attached Intelligence Corps, served Nuremberg War Crimes Trial and War Crimes Interrogation Unit 1944–47; assoc designer RSC 1963–66 and 1976–; first prodn Angelique for London Opera Club 1950; Retrospective Exhibition (London) 1997; designs for: Royal Opera House, Sadler's Wells, Scottish Opera, Nat Welsh Opera, Ballet Rambert; RDI 1984; hon fell The London Inst 1996; fell: Acad of Performing Arts Hong Kong 1994, Rose Bruford Coll; FRSA; *Theatre* RSC prodns incl: The Caucasian Chalk Circle 1962, The Representative 1963, The Birthday Party 1964, The Jew of Malta 1964, Timon of Athens 1965, Little Murders (Drama Critics Award) 1967, Major Barbara 1970, Old World 1976, Wild Oats 1977, The Tempest 1978, Hamlet 1980, The Love Girl and The Innocent (Drama Critics Award) 1981, Molière 1982, Much Ado About Nothing 1982, Cyrano de Bergerac (SWET Award) 1984, Troilus and Cressida 1985, Othello 1986; NT prodns incl: As You Like It (Drama Critics Award) 1967, Back To Methuselah 1969, State of Revolution 1977, Brand (SWET Award) 1978, Richard III 1979, Man and Superman 1981; other prodns incl: Wagner's complete Ring Circle (ENO) 1973, Tannhauser (Sydney) 1973 and Geneva 1986, Fidelio (Munich) 1974, Bugsy Malone 1983, Pack of Lies 1983, Metropolis 1989, dir and designer of The Flying Dutchman 1987 and La Traviata (Hong Kong Arts Festival) 1990, The Planets (Royal Ballet) 1990, The Makropulos Affair (Norwegian Opera) 1992, Hair (Old Vic) 1993, La Traviata (Swedish Opera) 1993, Otello (Essen Opera) 1994, Madam Butterfly (Tokyo) 1995, Twelfth Night (Copenhagen) 1996, Carmen (Royal Albert Hall) 1997, Simon Boccanegra (WNO) 1997, Dalibor (Edinburgh Festival) 1998, A Midsummer Night's Dream (Copenhagen) 1998, Don Giovanni (Kirov Opera) 1999, Genoveva (Edinburgh Festival, Prague and Venice) 2000–01; has worked throughout Europe and in Argentina, USA, Canada, Aust and Japan; retrospective exhibitions in London 1997, Beijing 1998, Hong Kong, Taipei and Prague 1999; *Awards* incl: co-winner Individual Gold Medal Prague Quadriennal 1975, Golden Triga 1979 and 1991, Individual Silver Medal 1987;

Publications Ralph Koltai – Designer for the Stage (1997); *Recreations* wildlife photography; *Style*— Ralph Koltai, Esq, CBE

KONDRACKI, Henry Andrew; s of Pawel Kondracki (d 1986), of 12 Union St, Edinburgh, and Boyce Matilda, *née* Hills (d 1988); *b* 13 February 1953; *Educ* Bellevue Secdy Sch Edinburgh, Byam Shaw Sch of Art London, Slade Sch of Fine Art (BA, Sir William Coldstream prize for best figurative work, Slade prize for Fine Art 1985 and 1986); *m* 2 Oct 1985, Sara, da of Dr Mohamed Gawad Elsarrag; 3 s (Patrick, Miles, Edward); *Career* artist; *Solo Exhibitions* Traverse Theatre Club Edinburgh 1979, The Artist's Collective Gallery Edinburgh 1984 and 1992, Vanessa Devereux Gallery London 1987 and 1989, Michael Wardell Gallery Melbourne Aust 1988, William Jackson Gallery London 1991 and 1994, Flowers East Gallery London 1995, 1996, 1998 and 2001, Bellevue Gallery Edinburgh 1997, Flowers West Gallery Los Angeles 2000; *Group Exhibitions* Royal Scottish Acad Edinburgh 1984 and 1988, The Peter Moores Exhibition (Walker Gallery Liverpool) 1986, Royal Acad Summer Show 1989, 1990 and 2000 (invited artist 1993 and 1994), Polish Roots British Soil (Edinburgh City Art Centre touring show) 1993, John Moores Liverpool Exhibition 19 1995 (prizewinner), Contemporary Painting Scotland (The Rotunda Hong Kong) 1996, Flowers West Gallery Los Angeles 1998; *Work in Public Collections* Granada Fndn Manchester, Br Arts Cncl, Br Cncl, UCL, Manchester City Art Gallery, Guildhall London, Glasgow Art Galleries and Museums, City Art Centre Edinburgh; *Prizes and Awards* incl: South Bank Bd Prize 1987, Spectator Art Prize 1991, John Moores Exhibition 2nd Prize 1995, Noble Grossard Scotland on Sunday 3rd Prize 1997, Cheltenham Drawing Competition Prize 1999, Hunting Group Regnl Prize 2000, Hunting Gp Prize 2004; *Style*— Henry Kondracki, Esq

KOOPS, Eric Jan Leendert; LVO (1997); s of Leendert Koops (d 1990), of Hellingly, E Sussex, and Daphne Vera, *née* Myhill (d 1998); *b* 16 March 1945; *Educ* Eastbourne Coll, Lancaster Univ (BA); *m* 1, 1968 (m dis 1985); 1 da (Amanda Charlotte b 25 Sept 1972), 1 s (Mark Alexander b 20 Feb 1975); m 2, 1987, Hon Mrs Justice Hogg, DBE, *qv*, da of Baron Hailsham of St Marylebone, KG, CH (d 2001); 1 da (Katharine Mary b 17 March 1989), 1 s (William Quintin Eric b 21 Dec 1991); *Career* TA 2 Lt 4/5 KORR 1964–67; corporate advsr and co dir; Parly candidate (Cons) Wakefield 1974; fdnr and chm Friends of Africa Fndn 2000–, chm Friends of Kenya Ltd 2003–; vice-pres Political Ctee Carlton Club 1988– (chm 1984–88); hon chm: The Duke of Edinburgh's Award, World Fellowship 1987–97; tstee: The Duke of Edinburgh's Award Int Fndn 1994–97, Inst for Policy Research; FCA 1971; *Publications* Money for our Masters (1970), Airports for the Eighties (1980); *Recreations* travel, cricket, biographies; *Clubs* Carlton, MCC, Muthaiga Country; *Style*— Eric Koops, Esq, LVO; ✉ Forest Lodge, Wych Cross, Forest Row, East Sussex RH18 5JP (☎ 01342 824096)

KOPELMAN, Prof Peter Graham; s of Dr Harry Kopelman (d 2009), and Joan, *née* Knowlman (d 1995); *b* 23 June 1951; *Educ* Felsted, St George's Hosp Med Sch London (MB BS, MD, Prize for Pathology); *m* 1981, Susan Mary, *née* Lewis; 2 da (Sarah b 22 Oct 1981, Claire b 3 May 1983), 1 s (Thomas b 25 Sept 1989); *Career* St George's Hosp London: hon registrar in gen med 1978, research registrar Dept of Med 1978–79, registrar in gen med 1979–80; conslt physician Newham Healthcare NHS Tst London 1986–95, sr lectr in med The London Hosp 1986–96 (lectr in gen med, metabolism, diabetes and endocrinology 1980–86); Bart's and The London Queen Mary's Sch of Med and Dentistry Univ of London: sr clinical tutor 1990–97, reader in med 1996–98, prof of clinical med 1998–2006, dep warden 2001–06, vice-princ 2003–06; chm Med Studies, memb Cncl Univ of London 2001–06, assoc non-exec dir NE London SHA 2004–06, non-exec dir St George's Healthcare NHS Tst 2010–15; dean Faculty of Health UEA 2006–08, princ St George's Univ of London 2008–15; chair London Medicine Gp 2009–15, censor RCP; memb: Scientific Advsy Ctee on Nutrition 2001–11, Governance Bd Centre for Workforce Intelligence 2010–13; RCP: chm Clinical Nutrition Ctee 1998–2004, chm Working Pty on Management of Obesity and med Aspects of Nutrition, pres Euro Assoc for the Study of Obesity 2003–06, scientific advsr GOS Foresight Obesity Project 2005–10, memb HEFCE Research & Innovations Ctee 2007–13, chm NIHR Clinical Academic Careers Panel 2008, Med Educn England Bd 2009–12, dep chair London Higher 2010–15, chair UCEA Cinical Academic Staff Advsy Gp 2010–15, vice-chair UUK Health Educn and Research Policy Network 2011–15, chair Faculty Bd Royal Pharmaceutical Soc 2013–; adjunct prof Thomas Jefferson Univ Philadelphia 2016; memb Bd of Tstees Univ of London 2011–14; memb: GMC, Med Def Union, RCP, Diabetes UK, MRS, Assoc for the Study of Med Educn, Assoc of Physicians; tstee Int Assoc for the Study of Obesity 2002–06; govr Bancroft's Sch Woodford Green 2015–; DSc (hc) Univ of London 2016, DSc (hc) Univ of Nicosia Cyprus 2016; FRCP 1992, FFPH by distinction 2005, FAcadMed 2015; *Publications* author of numerous scientific papers and book chapters on metabolism, obesity and medical education; *Recreations* all sports (with enthusiastic son), music (with daughters), painting and drawing, reading modern literature, political biographies; *Clubs* Athenaeum; *Style*— Prof Peter Kopelman; ✉ St George's, University of London, Cranmer Terrace, London SW17 0RE (☎ 020 8725 5008, fax 020 8672 6940, e-mail pkopelman@sgul.ac.uk)

KOPPEL, Jessica Esther (Jess); da of Heinz Koppel (d 1980), and Renate Koppel; *b* London; *Educ* Penglais Aberystwyth, Cardiff Coll of Art (Higher Nat Dip Photography); *Career* photographer; asst to Bryce Attwell 1984–85, freelance photographer 1985– (specialising in food and still life); numerous exhibitions incl: Stages Photographers Gallery 1988, Assoc of Photographers Gallery, F45 Womens Exhibition every year; winner: Silver award Assoc of Photographers, Clio Gold award Int Food Packaging 1988, award of Excellence Mead Show 1989; *Books* incl: Sophie Grigson's Ingredients Book, 10 Minute Cuisine, Henrietta Green's Country Kitchen, Sophie Grigson's Eat Your Greens, Sophie Grigson's Meat Course, Sophie Grigson's Taste of the Times; *Style*— Ms Jess Koppel; ✉ Jess Koppel Studio (*website* www.jesskoppel.com)

KOPS, Bernard; s of Joel Kops, and Jenny Zetter; *b* 28 November 1926, Stepney, London; *Educ* Stepney Jewish Sch; *m* 1956, Erica, *née* Gordon; 4 c; *Career* writer, poet and broadcaster; lectr in drama The Spiro Inst 1985–86; writer in residence at various instns incl: ILEA, Surrey Educn Authy, Feltham Young Offenders Inst, The Paines Plough Co, City Literary Inst; Arts Cncl bursary 1957–2004, C S Lewis fellowship, awarded Civil List pension for services to literature 2009; *Novels* incl: Awake for Mourning (1958), The Dissent of Dominick Shapiro (1966), The Passionate Past of Gloria Gaye (1972), Partners (1975), On Margate Sands (1978), The Odyssey of Samuel Glass (2012); *Non-Fiction* Neither Your Honey Nor Your Sting – An Offbeat History of the Jews (1985), The World is a Wedding (autobiography, 1963, 1975), Collected Plays: Vol 1 (1998) Vol 2 (2000), Vol 3 (2002), Shalom Bomb (autobiography, 2000), Bernard Kops East End, The World is a Wedding (2007); subject of Bernard Kops: Fantasist, London Jew, Apocalyptic Humorist by William Baker and Jeanette Roberts Shumaker 2014 (2014); *Poetry* Poems (1955), Poems and Songs (1958), Anemone for Antigone (1959), Erica, I Want You to Read Something (1967), For the Record (1971), Barricades in West Hampstead (1988), Grandchildren and Other Poems (2000), This Room in the Sunlight (2009), Selected Poetry: Whitechapel Dreams (2009); *Stage Plays* incl: The Hamlet of Stepney Green (1956), The Dream of Peter Mann (1959), Enter Solly Gold (1961, televised 1968), Stray Cats and Empty Bottles (1967, televised 1967), Ezra (1981, on radio 1980), Simon at Midnight (1985, on radio 1982), More Out Than In (1980, on radio 1985), Kafe Kropotkin (1988, also on radio), Sophie! the Last of the Red Hot Mamas (1990), Moss (1991, on radio 1983, televised 1976), Playing Sinatra (1992), Dreams of Anne Frank (1992, winner London Fringe Awards 1993), Who Shall I Be Tomorrow (1992), Call in the Night (1995), Golem (1996), Jacob and the Green Rabbi (1997), Houdini (1999), Cafe Zeitgeist (1999), Riverchange (2000), The Opening (2001), I am Isaac Babel (2002), Returning we hear the Larks (2004), Knocking on Heaven's Door (2005), Rogues and Vagabonds (2008); *Radio Plays* incl: Return to Stepney Green (1957), Home Sweet Honeycomb (1962), Israel Pt 1 (1963), Israel Pt 2 (1964), I Grow Old, I Grow Old (1979), Over the Rainbow (1981), Trotsky was My Father (1984), Congress in Manchester (1990), Soho Nights (serial, 1993), Sailing With Homer (1994, Writer's Guild Award 1994/95), The Jericho Players (1996), Rogues and Vagabonds (1998), Monster Man (1999), Falling in Love Again (2000), The Lost Love of Phoebe Myers (2006), Whitechapel Dreams (2009), Harry and the Angels (2010); *Television Drama/Documentary* incl: I Want to Go Home (1963), The Lost Years of Brian Hooper (1965), It's A Lovely Day Tomorrow (1975), The Geese that Shrieked and The Boy Philosopher (adaptions from Isaac Bashevis Singer 1975), Rocky Marciano is Dead (1977), Nightkids (1983); *Recreations* walking, cooking, surviving; *Style*— Bernard Kops; ✉ 41b Canfield Gardens, London NW6 3JL (e-mail bernardkops@blueyonder.co.uk); c/o Emily Hayward (agent) (☎ 020 7300 7266, e-mail emily@knighthallagency.com)

KORLIPARA, Dr Krishna Rao; s of Laxminarayana Korlipara, of Denduluru, India, and Krishnaveni, *née* Kodali; *b* 14 September 1938, Denduluru, India; *Educ* Kasturba Med Coll Karnatak Univ Mangalore S India (MB BS); *m* 3 May 1963, Uma Devi Korlipara, da of Rajendra Vara Prasad Veeramachaneni; 3 da (b 1964, 1965 and 1968), 1 s (b 1970); *Career* sr house offr in gen med: Manor Park Hosp Bristol 1965–66, Huddersfield 1967, Mansfield Hosp Notts 1967–68; registrar in gen med Bolton Gen Hosp 1969–72, princ in gen practice Horwich 1972–2008, pt/t clinical asst in cardiology Wythenshawe Hosp Regional Cardiac Centre Univ of S Manchester 1977–99, trainer in gen practice 1984–94, pt/t sessional GP 2008–09; fndr chm: Bolton Dist Med Services Ltd (first GP co-operative in UK) 1977–2002 (pres 2002–05), Nat Assoc of GP Co-Operatives 1981–97 (pres 1997–2003); chief exec and pres CMEDS (Bolton) Ltd 2005–07; chm: Rivington View Ltd 1986–, Bharatiya Vidya Bhavan (Manchester) Ltd (Indian Inst of Culture in Britain) 1996–99; GMC: memb 1984–2008, former med screener for professional conduct and performance, memb Registration Ctee, former memb Ctee on Professional Performance, former chm GP Consultative Gp on Revalidation, former memb Revalidation Steering Gp, former memb Professional Conduct Ctee, Overseas Ctee and Health Ctee; chm: NW Regnl Steering Gp NHS Direct 1999–2001, GP Collaborative Consortium 2011–12; memb: Bolton Local Med Ctee 1993–, Exec Ctee PCD-UK (Primary Care Diabetes in UK, a section of Br Diabetic Assoc) 1997–99; gen sec Overseas Doctors Assoc UK 1979–84; memb Salford Univ Assembly 2009–12; Fellowship Award for Outstanding Services to the Profession BMA 2012; memb: Med Protection Soc 1965–, Bolton Med Soc 1972 (pres 1992–93), BMA 1978–; FInstD 1994, MRCGP 2001; contrib numerous articles in learned jls incl: Int Jl of Clinical Practice, Cardiology News, Br Jl of Cardiology, Br Jl of Gen Practice; *Recreations* reading, meditating; *Style*— Dr Krishna Korlipara; ✉ mobile 07867 503559, e-mail kkorlipara@gmail.com; Rivington View Nursing Home, Albert Street, Horwich, Bolton BL6 7AW (☎ 01204 694325, website www.rivingtonview.com)

K

KORNBERG, Prof Sir Hans Leo; s of Max Kornberg; *b* 14 January 1928; *Educ* Queen Elizabeth GS Wakefield, Univ of Sheffield; *m* 1, 1956, Monica King (d 1989); 2 s (Jonathan, Simon (twins)), 2 da (Julia, Rachel); m 2, 28 July 1991, Donna, da of William B Haber, of Los Angeles; *Career* prof of biochemistry Univ of Leicester 1960–75, Sir William Dunn prof of biochemistry Univ of Cambridge 1975–95, fell Christ's Coll Cambridge 1975– (master 1982–95), univ prof and prof of biology Boston Univ 1995–, dir The Univ Profs 2002–05 and 2007–11; a managing tstee Nuffield Fndn 1973–93, chm Royal Cmmn on Environmental Pollution 1976–81, chm Sci Advsy Ctee and chm Kuratorium Max-Planck Inst Dortmund 1979–89, memb AFRC 1981–85, memb Advsy Cncl for Applied Res & Devpt 1982–85, chm Advsy Ctee for Genetic Modification 1986–95, memb Priorities Bd for Res in Agric and Food 1985–90, dir UK Nirex 1987–95, memb Advsy Ctee Harkness Fellowships 1989–94, govr Wellcome Tst 1990–95; pres: Br Assoc 1984–85, Biochemical Soc 1990–95, Int Union of Biochemistry and Molecular Biology 1991–94, Assoc Sci Educn 1991–92; memb various int acads; Hon DSc: Cincinnati, Warwick, Leicester, Sheffield, Bath, Strathclyde, South Bank, Leeds, La Trobe Univ Melbourne; Hon DUniv Essex, Hon MD Leipzig, Hon LLD Univ of Dundee; hon fell: Brasenose Coll Oxford, Worcester Coll Oxford, Wolfson Coll Cambridge; FIBiol, FRSA, Hon FRCP 1989, FRS 1965, Hon FRSB; *Publications* Energy Transformations in Living Matter (jtly, 1957); numerous publications in scientific journals; *Clubs* Oxford and Cambridge; *Style*— Prof Sir Hans Kornberg, FRS; ✉ Biology Department, Boston University, 5 Cummington Mall, Boston, MA 02215, USA (☎ 00 1 617 353 2440, fax 00 1 617 353 6340, e-mail hlk@bu.edu)

KORNER, Her Hon Judge Joanna Christian Mary; CMG (2004), QC (1993); da of John Hugh George Korner, of House of Elrig, Portwilliam, and Martha Maria Emma, *née* Tupay von Isertingen; *b* 1 July 1951; *Educ* Queensgate Sch London, Inns of Court Sch of Law; *Career* called to the Bar Inner Temple 1974 (bencher 1996); tenant in chambers 1975, recorder of the Crown Court 1995–2012 (asst recorder 1992–95), circuit judge (South Eastern Circuit) 2012–; int course dir Judicial Coll 2014–; sr prosecuting counsel Int Criminal Tbnl for the Former Yugoslavia The Hague 1999–2004 and 2009–12, conslt to chief prosecutor Bosnia and Herzegovina 2004–05; chair Advocacy Trg Cncl Int Ctee 2004–11, chair Advsy Ctee on Conscientious Objectors 2013–; memb: SE Circuit, Crown Court Rules Ctee 1994–2000; *Recreations* collecting books and porcelain, tennis, cinema; *Clubs* Reform; *Style*— Her Hon Judge Korner, CMG, QC

KORNICKI, Prof Peter Francis; s of Sqdn Ldr F Kornicki, of Worthing, W Sussex, and P C Kornicki; *b* 1 May 1950; *Educ* St George's Coll Weybridge, Lincoln Coll Oxford (BA, MSc), St Antony's Coll Oxford (DPhil); *m* 1, 1975, C O Mikolaski (d 1995); 1 s (Martin b 15 July 1985), 1 da (Alice b 24 Sept 1990); m 2, 1998, Prof F Orsini; *Career* lectr in Japanese Univ of Tasmania 1978–82, assoc prof Univ of Kyoto 1982–84; Univ of Cambridge: lectr 1985–95, chm Faculty of Oriental Studies 1993–95, reader 1995–2001, prof 2001–14, emeritus prof 2014–, Sandars reader in bibliography 2007–08, dep warden Robinson Coll 2008–16; author of numerous articles and reviews; pres European Assoc for Japanese Studies 1997–2000, chm African and Oriental Studies Section Br Acad 2006–; Special Prize Japan Fndn 1992, Yamagata Banto Prize Japan 2013; tstee Corbridge Tst, tstee Bell Tst; DLitt Univ of Oxford 2011; memb: Accademia Ambrosiana Milan 2011, Academia Europaea 2012; FBA 2000; *Books* Early Japanese Books in Cambridge University Library (1991), The Book in Japan: A Cultural History (1998), Catalogue of the early Japanese books in the Russian State Library Vol 2 (2004), Having Difficulty with Chinese? The rise of the vernacular book in Japan, Korea and Vietnam (2008), The Female as Subject: Women and the Book in Japan (2010), F V Dickins's Letters to Ernest M Satow, Kumagusu Minakata and others (transcribed, edited and annotated with Haruko Iwakami, 2011), The History of the Book in East Asia (ed with Cynthia Brokaw, 2011); catalogues for the British Library and British Museum; *Recreations* languages, cooking, hiking; *Style*— Prof Peter Kornicki; ✉ Robinson College, Cambridge CB3 9AN (☎ 01223 339156, e-mail pk104@cam.ac.uk)

KOSCIUSZKO, Stefan Henry; s of Konstanty Kosciuszko (d 1985), and Elizabeth, *née* Havelock; *b* 2 June 1959, NYC; *Educ* Gordonstoun, Divine Mercy Coll, Univ of Keele (BA, Josiah Wedgwood Meml Prize Award); *m* 15 Jan 1985, Takako, *née* Yamaguchi; 2 da (Krystyna Midori Havelock b 18 May 1989, Rachel Sayaka Havelock b 7 Aug 1991); *Career* National Westminster Bank 1980–82, Sumitomo Bank London and Tokyo 1982–85, Chemical Bank London and Tokyo 1985–88; Schroders: gen mangr Tokyo 1988–91, London 1992–95, dir 1995–98, head of Asia Pacific equity capital markets 1995–97, head of corp fin Indonesia 1997–98; md Gavin Anderson 1999–2000, dir Credit Suisse First Boston 2000–02, chief exec Asia House 2002–07, COS Hinduja Gp and ceo AMAS-IPS 2007–, md and head Asia-Pacific Distribution CQS 2013–14, vice-chm Asia Pacific CQS 2014–16; exec dir Pakistan Britain Trade & Investment Forum 2003–07, sec Indo British Partnership Network 2005–07, exec dir UK-Korea Forum for the Future 2007–; memb: Chm's Ctee China Now 2006–08, Bd Ishi Project Univ of Cambridge 2009–; govr Gainsborough House Museum 2002–06, sec Sudbury Soc 2002–06; tstee Digital Himalaya Tst 2008–; FRSA 2006; *Recreations* sports, chess, fine wine, antiques, English medieval history, Asian culture and history; *Clubs* Naval and Military; *Style—* Stefan Kosciuszko, Esq; ✉ Swarthgill House, Garsdale, Sedbergh, Cumbria LA10 5PD (e-mail stefan@kosciuszko.com)

KOUVARITAKIS, Prof Basil; s of Alexander Kouvaritakis (d 1984), and Xanthippi, *née* Vasileiou (d 1988); *b* 19 December 1948; *Educ* Varvakeios Model Sch Athens, Atlantic Coll S Wales (Schilizzi Fndn scholar), UMIST (BSc, IEE Prize, MSc, PhD); *m* 14 Sept 1974, Sheila, *née* Kennedy; 2 s (Philip, Nicholas); *Career* demonstrator UMIST 1972–74, asst researcher Univ of Cambridge 1974–78, lectr Univ of Bradford 1978–80, fell St Edmund Hall Oxford 1981–, prof of engrg sci Univ of Oxford 1998– (lectr 1981–96, reader 1996–98); MIEE 1980; *Books* Nonlinear Predictive Control: Theory and Practice (jt ed, 2001), Predictive Control: Classical, Robust and Stochastic (with Mark Cannon, 2015); author of over 200 articles in scientific jls;; *Recreations* memb various orchestras, chamber music and duet performances, cycling, walking; *Style—* Prof Basil Kouvaritakis; ✉ Huggins Cottage, Old Road, Headington, Oxford OX3 8SZ; Department of Engineering Science, University of Oxford, Parks Road, Oxford OX1 3PJ (☎ 01865 765876, e-mail basil.kouvaritakis@eng.ox.ac.uk)

KOVAR, Dr Ilya Zdenek; TD; s of Victor Kovar (d 1971), and Nina Kovar (d 2009); *b* 17 March 1947, Prague; *Educ* Sydney Boys' HS Aust, Univ of Sydney (MB BS); *m* 29 Dec 1974 (m dis), Cynthia Rose, da of Norbert Sencier; 3 s (Simon b 10 Oct 1976, Benjamin b 23 March 1979, David b 31 May 1984), 1 da (Sarah b 5 Aug 1981); *Partner* since 2003, Mary; *Career* sr lectr in child health at Charing Cross and Westminster Med Schs and conslt paediatrician Charing Cross Hosp London 1984– (pt/t since 2011), currently conslt in paediatrics and perinatal med Chelsea and Westminster Hosp London; hon sr lectr Imperial Coll, visiting prof in UK and int medical-legal practice; vice-pres Partnerships World Assoc of Disaster and Emergency Med; advsr UK and int govts; author of med, scientific, clinical articles and med texts; Lt Col RAMC(V) (ret); FRCPCH, FRCP, FRCP(C), FAAP, DRCOG; *Books* Textbook for DCH (1984, 1991), Make it Better (1982); *Recreations* riding, reading, music, family, travel; *Clubs* Naval and Military; *Style—* Dr Ilya Kovar, TD; ✉ Neonatal Unit, Chelsea and Westminster Hospital, London SW10 9NH (☎ 020 3315 7195, e-mail ilyakovar@icloud.com)

KRAEMER, Nicholas Thomas Wilhelm; s of Dr William Paul Kraemer (d 1982), of London, and Helen, *née* Bartrum; *b* 7 March 1945; *Educ* Lancing, Dartington Coll of Arts, Univ of Nottingham (BMus, ARCM), Guildhall Sch of Music; *m* 22 April 1984, Elizabeth Mary, da of John Anderson; 2 da (Emma b 1986, Chlöe b 1993), 3 s (Dominic b 1988, Matthew b and d 1990, Daniel b 1991); *Career* conductor and harpsichordist: Monteverdi Orchestra and English Baroque Soloists 1970–80, Acad of St Martin in the Fields 1972–80; musical dir: Unicorn Opera Abingdon 1971–75, West Eleven Children's Opera 1971–88; fndr and dir Raglan Baroque Players 1978–2003, musical dir Opera 80 1980–83, princ conductor Divertimenti 1980–95, assoc conductor BBC Scottish Symphony Orchestra 1983–85, artistic dir London Bach Orchestra 1985–93, artistic dir Irish Chamber Orch 1985–90, princ conductor Manchester Camerata 1992–95 (perm guest conductor 1995–); guest conductor: Music of the Baroque Chicago (princ guest conductor 2003–), Manchester Camerata, Collegium Musicum Winterthur, Halle Orchestra, Scottish Chamber Orchestra, St Paul Chamber Orchestra, Berlin Philharmonic, ENO, Northern Sinfonia, Bergen Philharmonic, BBC NOW, Chicago Symphony Orch, Detroit Symphony Orch, Toronto Symphony Orch, BBC Philharmonic, Minnesota Orch, Orch Ensemble Kanazara (Japan), Philharmonia Baroque (USA), Irish Chamber, Lapland Chamber Orchestras, Grange Park Opera, Buxton Festival Opera, Aalborg Symphony Orchestra, Trinity Laban Conservatiore Greenwich; princ guest conductor Kristiansand Symphony; prog dir Bath Festival 1994; memb Royal Soc of Musicians; *Recreations* watching sport, keeping fit; *Style—* Nicholas Kraemer; ✉ c/o Caroline Phillips Management, 11 Pound Pill, Corsham, Wiltshire SN13 9HZ (☎ 01249 716716)

KRAMER, Prof Matthew Henry; s of Alton Kramer (d 2007), and Eunice Bixon Kramer (d 1993); *b* 9 June 1959, Boston, MA; *Educ* Cornell Univ (BA), Harvard Univ (JD), Univ of Cambridge (PhD, LLD); *Career* fell and dir of studies in law Churchill Coll Cambridge 1994–, prof of legal and political philosophy Univ of Cambridge 2002–; dir Cambridge Forum for Legal and Political Philosophy 2001–; subject ed Routledge Encyclopedia of Philosophy 2000–; vice-pres UK Assoc for Legal and Social Philosophy 1998–99; Br Acad Research Leave Award 1998, Guggenheim Fndn Fellowship 2001–02, Leverhulme Tst Major Research Fellowship 2005–07; FBA; *Books* John Locke and tthe Origins of Private Property (1997), Hobbes and the Paradoxes of Political Origins (1997), A Debate over Rights (1998), In the Realm of Legal and Moral Philosophy (1999), In Defense of Legal Positivism (1999), Rights, Wrongs, and Responsibilities (2001), The Quality of Freedom (2003), Where Law and Morality Meet (2004), Objectivity and the Rule of Law (2007), Moral Realism as a Moral Doctrine (2009), The Ethics of Capital Punishment (2011), Torture and Moral Integrity (2014), Liberalism with Excellence (2017); *Recreations* Shakespearean drama, Bible commentary, long-distance running; *Style—* Prof Matthew Kramer; ✉ Churchill College, Cambridge CB3 0DS (☎ 01223 336231, fax 01223 336180, e-mail mhk11@cam.ac.uk, website www.law.cam.ac.uk/people/academic/mh-kramer/51)

KRAMER, His Hon Judge Stephen Ernest; QC (1995); s of Frederic Kramer, of Peterborough, and Lotte Karoline, *née* Wertheimer; *b* 12 September 1947; *Educ* Hampton GS, Keble Coll Oxford (Open exhibitioner, MA), Coll of Law, Université de Nancy; *m* 12 March 1978, Miriam, da of Siegfried Leopold (d 1992), and Charlotte Leopold (d 1997); 1 da (Joanna Louise b 13 Sept 1981), 1 s (Robert Paul b 13 Oct 1982); *Career* called to the Bar Gray's Inn 1970 (bencher 2001); standing counsel (Crime) Customs and Excise SE Circuit 1989–95, recorder of the Crown Court 1991–2003 (asst recorder 1987–91), circuit judge (SE Circuit) 2003–05, sr circuit judge (sitting at Central Criminal Court) 2005–; chm Liaison Ctee Bar Cncl/Inst of Barristers Clerks 1996–99; memb: Bar Cncl 1993–95, Ctee Criminal Bar Assoc 1993–98 (actg vice-chm 1998–99, vice-chm 1999–2000, chm 2000–01), Ctee SE Circuit 1997–2000; Parly candidate (Lib) Twickenham 1974 (both elections); govr Hampton Sch 2005–15; *Recreations* theatre, music, swimming, recreational cycling, watching rugby union; *Style—* His Hon Judge Stephen Kramer, QC

KRAMER, Baroness (Life Peer UK 2010), of Richmond Park in the London Borough of Richmond upon Thames; Susan Veronica Kramer; *Educ* St Paul's Girls' Sch, St Hilda's Coll Oxford, Univ of Illinois (MBA); *Career* former vice-pres Citibank, MP (Lib Dem) Richmond Park 2005–10; memb: Women Lib Dems Exec 1997–2000, London Regnl Exec 1997–2003, Lib Dem Fed Exec 2001–04; fndr Future Water Int, memb Bd Tport for London 2000–05; *Style—* The Baroness Kramer; ✉ House of Lords, London SW1A 0PW

KREBS, Baron (Life Peer UK 2007), of Wytham in the County of Oxfordshire; Prof Sir John Richard Krebs; kt (1999); s of Sir Hans Krebs (d 1981), of Oxford, and Margaret Cicely, *née* Fieldhouse (d 1993); *b* 11 April 1945, Sheffield, S Yorks; *Educ* City of Oxford HS, Pembroke Coll Oxford (MA, DPhil); *m* 1, 3 Aug 1968 (m dis 2012), Katharine Anne, da of John Fullerton (d 1973); 2 da (Emma Helen b 1977, Georgina Clare b 1980); m 2, 22 June 2013, Sarah Margaret, da of Prof David Harris (d 2013), of Rickmansworth, Herts; *Career* asst prof Inst of Animal Resource Ecology Univ of British Columbia 1970–73, lectr in zoology UCNW Bangor 1973–75, fell Wolfson Coll Oxford 1975–81, lectr in zoology Edward Grey Inst Oxford 1975–88 (demonstrator in ornithology 1970), Royal Soc research prof and fell Pembroke Coll 1988– (EP Abraham fell 1981–88), chief exec Natural Environment Research Cncl 1994–99, chm UK Food Standards Agency 2000–05, princ Jesus Coll Oxford 2005–15; sr scientific conslt AFRC 1991–94; chair House of Lords Sci and Technol Ctee 2010–14; tstee Nuffield Fndn 2007–; Zoological Soc of London: Scientific Medal 1981, Frink Medal 1996; Linnean Soc Bicentenary Medal 1983; American Ornithologists Union: Elliot Coues Award 1999, Assoc Study Animal Behaviour Medal 2000; Royal Soc of the Promotion of Health Benjamin Ward Richardson Gold Medal 2002, Woodridge Medal British Veterinary Assoc 2003, Croonian Lecture Royal Soc 2004, Harben Gold Medal RIPH 2006; pres Br Science Assoc 2012–13; memb: Max Planck Soc 1985–, AFRC 1988–94, Cncl Zoological Soc of London 1991–92, Academia Europaea 1995; hon memb: Br Ecological Soc 1999, UK Nat Heart Forum 2008; foreign memb American Philosophical Soc 2000; fell American Acad of Arts and Sciences 2000, foreign memb US Nat Acad of Sci 2004, memb German Nat Acad of Sciences (Leopoldina) 2013; Hon DSc: Univ of Sheffield 1993, Univ of Wales 1997, Univ of Birmingham 1997, Univ of Exeter 1998, Univ of Stirling 2000, Univ of Warwick 2000, Cranfield Univ 2001, Univ of Kent 2001, Univ of Plymouth 2001, Queen's Univ Belfast 2002, Heriot-Watt Univ 2002, South Bank Univ 2003, Lancaster Univ 2005, Univ of Guelph 2006, Univ of Aberdeen 2010, Newcastle Univ 2012, Univ of Western Ontario 2015; hon fell Univ of Cardiff 1999, hon fell German Ornithologists' Soc 2003; hon fell Univ of Wales Inst Cardiff 2006; Hon Freeman City of London, hon memb Salters' Co 2007; FRS 1984, FMedSci 2004, hon FZS 2006; *Books* Behavioural Ecology (with N B Davies, 1978, 1984, 1991 and 1997), Introduction to Behavioural Ecology (with N B Davies, 1981, 1987 and 1993 and with N B Davies and S West, 2012), Foraging Theory (with D W Stephens, 1986), A Very Short Introduction to Food (2013); *Recreations* running, gardening, travel, walking, cooking; *Style—* The Rt Hon the Lord Krebs, FRS; ✉ e-mail john.krebs@zoo.ox.ac.uk

KREINCZES, Gerald Michael; s of Maurice Kreinczes (d 1985), of London, and Alice, *née* Baker; *b* 28 October 1951; *Educ* Kingston GS, Lancaster Univ (BA); *m* 1976, Catherine, da of Francis J Cronin (d 1993); 1 da (Nicola Catherine b 17 Aug 1985), 1 s (Christopher Gerald b 22 April 1988); *Career* graduate trainee AGB Market Research 1974–75, Findus Ltd 1975–79, dir/head of mktg Allen Brady & Marsh Ltd 1979–84, dir Mgmnt and Mktg Servs Publicis Ltd 1984–86, planning dir Dorlands 1986–89, exec planning dir Allen Brady & Marsh 1989–90, ptnr The Kreinczes Partnership 1990–92, exec planning dir Kevin Morley Marketing 1992–96, planning dir Lintas i 1996, vice-chm Ammirati Puris Lintas 1996–99, chm Occam Insight 2000–; memb: Mktg Soc, IOD; MCIM; *Recreations* sailing, music, reading; *Style—* Gerald Kreinczes, Esq; ✉ Occam Insight, 14 Nunhead Grove, London, SE15 3LY (☎ 020 7928 8199)

KRIEGER, Ian Stephen; s of Sid Krieger, and Raie, *née* Dight; *b* 2 February 1952; *Educ* Christ's Coll Finchley, Univ of Kent (BA); *m* Caron Meryl, *née* Gluckstein; 3 s (James Michael b 1990, Elliott Charles b 1992, Ben Scott b 1995); *Career* Arthur Andersen: articled clerk 1973–76, CA 1976, ptnr 1985–2002; vice-chm Deloitte LLP 2002–12; non-exec dir: Premier Foods plc, Safestore Holdings plc, Capital & Regnl plc, Anthony Nolan (also vice-chair), Nuffield Tst; FCA 1981; *Books* Management Buy-Outs (1990); *Style—* Ian Krieger, Esq; ✉ 37 Norrice Lea, London N2 0RD (☎ 07836 659327)

KRUT, Ansel Jonathan; s of Dr Louis Harold Krut, and Rhoda, *née* Robinson; *b* 19 March 1959; *Educ* Univ of the Witwatersrand (BA), RCA (MA); *Career* artist; Cité International des Arts Paris 1982–83, Rome prize Br Sch Rome 1986–87, subsequently lived and worked in Rome 1987–90, returned London 1990; *Exhibitions* Fischer Fine Art London (one man) 1989 and 1990, Gillian Jason Gallery London (one man) 1994, Royal Acad Summer Show 1985, John Moores 14 Liverpool 1985, 12 British Artists (Künstlerhaus Vienna) 1986, The Human Touch (Fischer Fine Art London) 1986, Artists at the Br Sch at Rome (Rome) 1987, The Self Portrait (Bath and touring) 1988, 3 Ways (Budapest and touring Eastern Europe) 1989, 10 Years of the Br Sch at Rome (RCA London) 1990, The Discerning Eye (Mall Galleries London) 1991, A View of the New (Royal Over-Seas League London) 1991, 20th Century British Art Fair (London) 1992, Contemporary Portraits, Real and Imagined (Gillian Jason Gallery) 1993, Jason and Rhodes Gallery (one man) 1996 and 1998, George Adams Gallery (One Man) 2000; work in public collections: Arts Cncl of GB, Br Cncl London, Contemporary Art Soc London, Johannesburg Art Gallery, Govt Art Collection London, The Harris Museum and Art Gallery Preston Lancs, Mercer Art Gallery Harrogate; *Style—* Ansel Krut, Esq

KUENSSBERG, HE Joanna Kate; da of Nicholas Christopher Kuenssberg, and Sally Carolyn Glen Kuenssberg; *Educ* New Coll Oxford (BA); *m* 1997; 3 s; *Career* diplomat; desk offr Dept of Environment 1995–96, project mangr European Cmmn 1996–97, dep head Enlargement Section EU Dept FCO 1997–99, seconded to Hungarian Miny of Foreign Affrs 1999–2000, seconded to Quai d'Orsay EU Directorate 2000–01, first sec (EU/economic) Paris 2001–04, business team ldr Global Business/Sustainable Devpt and Business Gp FCO 2004–07, project mangr Consular Strategy Prog FCO 2008–09, Russian language trg 2009–10, Policy Unit FCO 2010, Portuguese language trg 2010, chargé d'affaires Lisbon 2011, dep head of mission Lisbon 2010–14, high cmmr to Mozambique 2014–; *Style—* HE Ms Joanna Kuenssberg; ✉ c/o FCO (Maputo), King Charles Street, London SW1A 2AH

KUENSSBERG, Laura; *Career* chief political corr BBC News 2009–11, business ed ITV News 2011–13, chief corr and presenter Newsnight (BBC 2) 2014–15, political ed BBC News 2015–; *Style—* Ms Laura Kuenssberg

KUENSSBERG, Nicholas Christopher (Nick); OBE (2004); s of Dr Ekkehard von Kuenssberg, CBE (d 2000), and Constance, *née* Hardy (d 2004); *b* 28 October 1942, Edinburgh; *Educ* Edinburgh Acad, Wadham Coll Oxford (BA), Manchester Business Sch; *m* 27 Nov 1965, Sally Kuenssberg, CBE, da of Hon Lord Robertson (Lord of Session); 1 s (David b 1971), 2 da (Joanna b 1973, Laura b 1976); *Career* worked for Coats Patons in Europe and Latin America 1965–78; chm: Dynacast International Ltd 1978–91, David A Hall Ltd 1996–98, GAP Gp Ltd 1996–2005, Stoddard International plc 1998–2000, Canmore Partnership Ltd 1999–, iomart gp plc 2000–08, Keronite Ltd 2005–07, eTourism Ltd 2007–08, Scott & Fyfe Ltd 2009–, mLED Ltd 2010–, Social Investment Scotland 2013–, K2L Ltd 2013–, Health Matters Gp Ltd 2015–; md Dawson International plc 1994–95 (dir 1991–95); dir: J & P Coats Ltd 1978–91, West of Scotland Bd Bank of Scotland 1984–88, Scottish Power plc (formerly South of Scotland Electricity Bd) 1984–97, Coats Patons plc 1985–91, Coats Viyella plc 1986–91, Standard Life Assurance Co 1988–99, Baxi Partnership Ltd 1996–99, Chamberlin & Hill plc 1999–2006, RingProp plc 2002–06, Amino Technologies plc 2004–07, Quality Assurance Agency for Higher Educn UK 2007–10; chm: Assoc of Mgmnt Educn & Trg in Scotland 1996–98, IoD Scotland 1997–99, Scottish Networks International 2001–08, ScotlandIS 2001–03, Scotland the Brand 2002–05, Social Investment Scotland 2013–; memb: Scottish Legal Aid Bd 1996–2004, Advsy Gp to Sec of State on Sustainable Devpt 1996–99, Scottish Environment Protection Agency 1999–2007 (dep chm 2003–07), Scottish Ctee Br Cncl 1999–2008, Quality Assurance Agency Scotland 2004–10 (chm 2007–10); public interest memb Cncl Inst of Chartered Accountants Scotland 2008–12; tstee David Hume Inst 1994–2008, tstee Pitlochry Festival Theatre 2011–; visiting prof Strathclyde Business Sch 1988–91 (visiting fell 1986–87), govr Queen's Coll Glasgow 1989–91; chm: The Glasgow Sch of Art 2003–10 (dir 2001–); hon prof Univ of Glasgow 2008–; dir Citizens Theatre Glasgow 2000–03, dir Pitlochry

Festival Theatre 2010–16; Hon DUniv Glasgow 2011; FCIS 1977, CCIMgt 1989, FRSA 1993, FInstD 1996; *Publications* The David Hume Institute: The first decade (ed, 1995), Argument Amongst Friends: Twenty-five Years of Sceptical Enquiry (ed, 2010), various articles in professional jls; *Recreations* travel, languages, opera, sport, Pitlochry Festival Theatre; *Style*— Nick Kuenssberg, OBE, DUniv; ✉ e-mail horizon@sol.co.uk

KUHN, Prof Annette; *Educ* Univ of Sheffield, Univ of London (PhD); *Career* various posts incl writer, ed, lectr and TV prodr; reader in film and TV studies Univ of Glasgow 1991–98 (lectr 1989–91), reader in cultural research Lancaster Univ 1998–2000, prof of film studies Lancaster Univ 2000–06, prof of film studies Queen Mary Univ of London 2006– (emeritus prof 2014–); Fulbright sr research scholar Mount Holyoke Coll; visiting appts: Humanities Research Centre ANU, Stockholm Univ; co-ed Screen until 2014; memb Editorial Bd: Jl of British Cinema and TV, Memory Studies, Transformations – the Jl of Inclusive Scholarship and Pedagogy, Aura: Filmvetenskaplig Tidskrift, Culture Unbound – Jl of Current Cultural Research, Film Jl, Image and Text, Legenda (moving image book series), Feminist Media Histories: An International Journal; former memb Editorial Bd: Visual Studies, Secuencias – revista de historia del cine; FBA 2004; Feminism and Materialism (jt ed, 1978), Ideology and Cultural Production (jt ed, 1979), Women's Pictures: Feminism and Cinema (1982, 2 edn 1994), The Power of the Image: Essays on Representation and Sexuality (1985), Cinema, Censorship and Sexuality (1988), The Women's Companion to International Film (ed, 1990), Alien Zone: Cultural Theory and Contemporary Science Fiction Cinema (ed, 1990), Family Secrets: Acts of Memory and Imagination (1995, revised edn 2002), Queen of the Bs: Ida Lupino Behind the Camera (ed, 1995), Screen Histories: A Screen Reader (jt ed, 1998), Alien Zone II: The Spaces of Science Fiction Cinema (ed, 1999), An Everyday Magic: Cinema and Cultural Memory (2002), Screening World Cinema (jt ed, 2006), Locating Memory: Photographic Acts (jt ed, 2006), Ratcatcher (2008), Screen Theorizing Today: A Celebration of Screen's Fiftieth Anniversary (ed, 2009), Oxford Dictionary of Film Studies (jtly, 2012), Little Madnesses: Winnicott, Transitional Phenomena and Cultural Experience (2013); also author of book contribs, academic articles and reviews; *Style*— Prof Annette Kuhn; ✉ School of Languages, Linguistics and Film, Queen Mary, University of London, Mile End Road, London E1 4NS

KUKADIA, Nish; s of Pravin Kukadia, and Aruna, *née* Vara; *b* 17 March 1982, London; *m* 18 July 2007, Shreya, *née* Shah; 2 s (Rian, Arin b 3 Dec 2015 (twins)); *Career* planning Mediaedge:cia (now MEC) 2004–06, dir London Express bvba 2006–07; SECRETSALES.com: co-fndr (with bro Sach Kukadia, *qv*) and dir 2006–10, ceo 2010–; advsr: Silkfred.com, Oppermann-London.com, cornerstone.co.uk; *Awards* Future Fifty Co Tech City UK 2013, Times Tech Track The Sunday Times 2014, Entrepreneurs of the Year Lloyds English Asian Business Awards 2014, Department Store of the Year Online Retail Awards 2014, Mid-Sized Retailer of the Year Online Retail Awards 2014, Fashion Entrepreneur of the Year Great British Entrepreneur Awards 2014, RetailWeek Top 50 Etail Power List 2015, Top 100 People in UK Fashion Drapers 2015, Entrepreneur of the Year Asian Achievers Awards 2015, Etailer of the Year <£50M Drapers 2016; *Books* Haberdashers' Aske's, Univ of Manchester (BSc), London Business Sch; *Recreations* cinema, fashion, motorsport, music, reading, skiing, travel, walking; *Style*— Nish Kukadia, Esq; ✉ SECRETSALES.com, Newcombe House, 45 Notting Hill Gate, London W11 3LQ

KUKADIA, Sach; *b* 9 November 1988; *Educ* UMIST, Manchester Business Sch; *Career* dir London Express UK Ltd 1999–2007, founding ptnr Naughtiness Promotions 2001–04, founding ptnr (with bro Nish Kukadia, *qv*) and buying dir SECRETSALES.com 2007–; *Awards* Best Family Business Lloyd's EA Business Awards 2014, Department Store of the Year Online Retail Awards 2014, Mid-sized E-tailer of the Year Online Retail Awards 2014, Fashion Entrepreneur of the Year Great British Entrepreneur Awards 2014, Entrepreneur of the Year Asian Achievers Awards 2015, Best Purely Retailer ~£50m Drapers Digital Awards 2016, Top 100 Most Influential People in Fashion Drapers Fashion Magazine 2016; *Recreations* cinema, cricket, fashion, golf, motorsport, music, reading, skiing, tennis, travel; *Style*— Sach Kukadia, Esq; ✉ SECRETSALES.com, Newcombe House, 45 Notting Hill Gate, London W11 3LQ (Twitter @SachKukadia)

KULUKUNDIS, Sir Eddie; kt (1993), OBE (1988); s of George Elias Kulukundis (d 1978), and Eugenia, *née* Diacakis (d 1993); 5th generation shipping family; *b* 20 April 1932, London; *Educ* Collegiate Sch NYC, Salisbury Sch Connecticut, Yale Univ; *m* 4 April 1981, Susan Hampshire, OBE, *qv*, da of George Kenneth Hampshire (d 1964); *Career* theatrical producer and co-producer of over 80 shows in the West End and NY 1969–1996; chm: Knightsbridge Theatrical Productions Ltd 1970–2006, London Coaching Fndn 1990–2006, Sport Aid Fndn 1988–93 (govr 1977–2006, tstee Sports Aid Fndn Tst 1987–2006), Ambassadors Theatre Gp 1992–2010 (life pres 2010–), Br Athletic Charitable Tst (previously Br Athletics Field Events Charitable Tst) 1996–2009; vice-pres: Traverse Theatre Club 1988–, UK Athletics 1998–2003; tstee: Salisbury Sch Connecticut 1983–, Theatre Trust 1976–95; govr: Royal Shakespeare Theatre 1976–2003 (vice-chm Royal Shakespeare Theatre Tst 1984–88 (dir 1968)), The Raymond Mander & Joe Mitchenson Theatre Collection Ltd 1981–2001; dir: Rethymnis & Kulukundis Ltd 1964–, Rethymnis & Kulukundis (Chartering) Ltd 1969–, London & Overseas Freighters plc 1980–85 and 1989–97, Soc of London Theatre 1973–2003, Hampstead Theatre Ltd 1969–2004, Hampstead Theatre Trust 1980–2003; memb: Baltic Exchange 1959–2001, Lloyd's 1964–95 (memb Cncl 1983–89), Richmond Theatre Tst 2001–; hon vice-pres SOLT 2003 (memb Bd 1973–2003); *Productions* London prodns incl (some jtly): Enemy 1969, The Happy Apple 1970, Poor Horace 1970, The Friends 1970, How the Other Half Loves 1970, Tea Party and the Basement (double bill) 1970, The Wild Duck 1970, After Haggerty 1971, Hamlet 1971, Charley's Aunt 1971, Straight Up 1971, London Assurance 1972, Journey's End 1972, Small Craft Warnings 1973, A Private Matter 1973, Dandy Dick 1973, The Waltz of the Toreadors 1974, Life Class 1974, Pygmalion 1974, Play Mas 1974, The Gentle Hook 1974, A Little Night Music 1975, Entertaining Mr Sloane 1975, The Gay Lord Quex 1975, What the Butler Saw 1975, Travesties 1975, Lies 1975, The Seagull 1975, A Month in the Country 1975, A Room with a View 1975, Too True to be Good 1975, The Bed Before Yesterday 1975, Dimetos 1976, Banana Ridge 1976, Wild Oats 1976, Candida 1977, Man and Superman 1977, Once a Catholic 1977, Privates on Parade 1978, Gloo Joo 1978, Bent 1979, Outside Edge 1979, Last of the Red Hot Lovers 1979, Beecham 1980, Born in the Gardens 1980, Tonight at 8.30 1981, Steaming 1981, Arms and the Man 1981, Steafel's Variations 1982, Messiah 1983, Pack of Lies 1983, Of Mice and Men 1984, The Secret Diary of Adrian Mole Aged 13–3/4 1984, Camille 1985, The Cocktail Party 1986, Curtains 1987, Separation 1989, South Pacific 1989, Married Love 1989, Over My Dead Body 1989, Never the Sinner 1990, King and I 1991, Carmen Jones 1991, Noel & Gertie 1992, Slip of the Tongue 1992, Shades 1992, Annie Get Your Gun 1992, Making it Better 1992, The Prime of Miss Jean Brodie 1994, The Killing of Sister George 1995; NY prodns (jtly): How the Other Half Loves, Sherlock Holmes, London Assurance, Travesties, The Merchant, Players, Once a Catholic; *Recreations* theatre, athletics; *Clubs* Garrick; *Style*— Sir Eddie Kulukundis, OBE; ✉ c/o The Ambassador Theatre Group, 39–41 Charing Cross Road, London WC2H 0AR (☎ 020 7854 7000)

KUMAR, Sir Harpal Singh; kt (2016); s of Mohinder Singh Kumar, and Prem Kaur Kumar; *b* 13 January 1965, London; *Educ* St John's Coll Cambridge (MEng, MA, Mobil Prize, Met Box Prize, Hughes Prize), Harvard Business Sch (MBA, Ford Prize, Wolfe Prize); *m* 27 July 1998, Benita, *née* Sokhey; 1 s (Jamanvir b 8 April 2002), 1 da (Jyotika b 29 March 2004); *Career* assoc McKinsey and Co Inc 1987–89 and 1991–93; chief exec: Papworth Tst 1993–97, Nexan Gp plc 1997–2002, Cancer Research Technol 2002–07, Cancer Research UK 2007– (chief operating offr 2004–07); memb: Nat Cancer Res Inst, UK Clinical Res Collaboration, Inst of Cancer Res, American Assoc for Cancer Res, American Soc of Clinical Oncology; *Recreations* theatre, opera, football; *Style*— Sir Harpal Kumar; ✉ Cancer Research UK, Angel Building, 407 St John Street, London EC1V 4AD (☎ 020 3469 8469, e-mail harpal.kumar@cancer.org.uk, website www.cancerresearchuk.org)

KUMAR, Prof Parveen June; CBE (2001); da of Cyril Proshuno Fazal Kumar (d 1982), and Grace Nazira, *née* Faiz (d 2001); *b* 1 June 1942; *Educ* Lawrence Sch Sanawar N India, Maida Vale HS, Bart's Med Coll, Univ of London (BSc, MB BS, MD); *m* Dr David G Leaver (d 2003), s of Frances Joseph Leaver; 2 da (Rachel Nira b 28 March 1972, Susannah Kiran b 22 July 1974); *Career* house physician Bart's 1966–67, house surgn Royal Berks Hosp Reading 1968, research registrar in bacteriology Bart's 1968–69, house physician Royal Postgrad Med Sch 1969–70, registrar, sr registrar then lectr Bart's 1970–85, conslt physician St Leonard's and Hackney Hosps 1983, sr lectr in gastroenterology and hon conslt physician Bart's and Homerton Hosps (City and Hackney HA) 1985–94, reader in gastroenterology 1994–2007, currently prof of med and educn and hon conslt physician and gastroenterologist Bart's and The London Sch of Medicine and Dentistry Queen Mary Univ of London and BartsHealthcare NHS Tst, hon conslt physician Homerton Hosp; coll tutor RCP 1988–93, clinical tutor BPMF 1988–96, dir of postgraduate med educn Royal Hosps Tst 1993–96, undergraduate sub-dean Bart's & London Sch of Med and Dentistry 1996–98; RCP: procensor then censor 1996–98, dir Continuing Medical Educn 1998–2002, vice-pres (academic) 2003–05, currently sr examiner; non-exec dir: Nat Inst for Clinical Excellence 1999–2002, Barts and the London NHS Tst 1999–2003; chm Medicines Cmmn UK 2002–05; pres BMA 2006–07; tstee: Med Coll of St Bartholomews 2001–10, Cancer Backup 2003–07; govr: BUPA Fndn until 2013, Tropical Health and Educn Tst until 2014, Br Soc of Gastroenterology; pres Royal Medical Benevolent Fund 2013–, pres Medical Women's Fedn 2016–18; memb Int Advsy Bd S African Consortium for Research Excellence (SACORE) 2010–16, memb Access Review Ctee and Publications Ctee Genomics England 2016–, chair Devpt Bd and Equality and Diversity Ctee Royal Coll of Physicians 2016–, chair Bd of Science BMA 2016–; examiner of univ degrees UK and abroad; co-fndr and co-ed Kumar and Clark's Clinical Medicine Textbook, author of published papers and lectr at home and abroad; tstee Br Youth Opera; Asian Woman of the Year 1999, Gold Medal BMA 2007; memb: Br Soc of Gastroenterology (elected memb Cncl 2001–04), Royal Soc of Med (co-opt memb Cncl 2008–, pres 2010–12); Hon DM: Univ of Nottingham, Univ of Brighton, Univ of Sussex, Univ of Plymouth; Hon DEd TCD, Hon DSc Univ of Hull and York, hon fell Manfield Coll Oxford, Hon DSc Univ of Glasgow; Hon FRCPath, hon fell RSM 2014, FRCP, FRCPE, FICG, FAIP, FIMA; *Books* Gastrointestinal Radiology (jtly, 1981), Kumar and Clark's Clinical Medicine (jtly 1987, 9 edn 2016), Kumar and Clark's Acute Clinical Medicine (co-ed, 2 edn 2006), Kumar and Clark's Medical Management and Therapeutics (2011), Clinical Cases (2013); series co-ed of several other books; *Recreations* opera, skiing, walking; *Clubs* RAC, Int Women's Fedn (IWF); *Style*— Prof Parveen Kumar, CBE; ✉ c/o N J Kingston, Blizzard Institute, Barts and the London School of Medicine and Dentistry, Queen Mary University of London, Newark Street, London E2 2AT (e-mail n.j.kingston@qmul.ac.uk)

K

KUNKLER, Prof Ian Hubert; s of Dr Peter Bertrand Kunkler, of Las Fuentes, Spain, and Pamela, *née* Hailey (d 1988); *b* 22 July 1951; *Educ* Clifton, Univ of Cambridge (MA, MB BChir), St Bartholomew's Hosp London; *m* 18 July 1981, Dr (Alison) Jane Kunkler, da of late Ronald George Pearson, of Kenya; *Career* house offr Univ of Leicester Med Sch 1978–79, sr house offr in gen med Nottingham City Hosp 1979–81, sr registrar Western Gen Hosp Edinburgh 1984–88 (registrar 1981–83), EEC and French Govt clinical res fell Inst Gustave Roussy Paris 1986–87; conslt in radiotherapy and oncology: Sheffield 1988–92, Edinburgh 1992–; hon prof of clinical oncology Univ of Edinburgh 2007–; author of papers on bone scanning in breast cancer, radiotherapy in breast and laryngeal cancer and the value of clinic follow-up in cervical cancer; pres London Med Gp 1977, convener annual conference Pain – A Necessity? Charing Cross Med Sch; pres British Oncological Assoc 2000–02; memb BMA 1978, DMRT Edinburgh 1983, FRCR 1985, FRSM 1989, FRCPE 1994, FRSA 1996; *Books* Cambridge University Medical Journal (ed, 1974), Walter and Miller's Textbook of Radiotherapy (jt author, 6 edn, 2002); *Recreations* fly fishing; *Style*— Prof Ian Kunkler

KUPER, Prof Adam Jonathan; s of Simon Meyer (d 1963), of Johannesburg, and Gertrude, *née* Hesselson (d 1987); *b* 29 December 1941; *Educ* Parktown Boys HS Johannesburg, Univ of the Witwatersrand Johannesburg (BA), King's Coll Cambridge (PhD); *m* 16 Dec 1966, Jessica Sue (d 2012), da of Sidney Cohen (d 1986), of Johannesburg; 2 s (Simon b 1969, Jeremy b 1971), 1 da (Hannah b 1974); *Career* lectr in social anthropology Makerere Univ of Kampala 1967–70, lectr in anthropology UCL 1970–76, prof of African anthropology and sociology Univ of Leiden 1976–85, prof of social anthropology Brunel Univ 1985–2007, Centennial prof LSE 2013–; visiting appts: asst prof Univ of Calif 1969, planner Nat Planning Agency Office of PM Jamaica 1972, prof Univ of Gothenburg 1975, prof Yale Univ 2009; fell Centre for Advanced Study in the Behavioural Sci Calif 1980–81, memb Inst for Advanced Study Princeton 1994–95; chm Euro Assoc of Social Anthropologists 1989–90; Hon Dr Univ of Gothenburg 1978; memb Academia Europaea, FBA 2000; *Books* Kalahari Village Politics (1970), Councils in Action (ed, 1971), The Social Anthropology of Radcliffe-Brown (ed, 1977), Wives for Cattle: Bridewealth and Marriage in Southern Africa (1982), Anthropology and Anthropologists: The Modern British School (1983), The Social Science Encyclopaedia (ed, 1985), South Africa and the Anthropologist (1987), The Invention of Primitive Society: Transformations of an Illusion (1988), Conceptualizing Society (ed, 1992), The Chosen Primate (1994), Culture: The Anthropologists' Account (1999), Among the Anthropologists (1999), The Reinvention of Primitive Society (2005), Incest and Influence: The private life of the English bourgeoisie (2009); *Recreations* golf; *Clubs* Hampstead Golf, Cambridge; *Style*— Prof Adam Kuper; ✉ 16 Muswell Road, Muswell Hill, London N10 2BG (☎ 020 8883 0400)

KUPFERMANN, Jeannette Anne; da of Nathan Weitz (d 1987), and Eva Tarnofsky (d 2000); *b* 28 March 1941; *Educ* Hendon Co GS, LSE (BA), UCL (MPhil); *m* 25 June 1964, Jacques H Kupfermann (d 1987), s of Elias Kupfermann (k ca 1940); 1 s (Elias Jonathan b 16 April 1965), 1 da (Mina Alexandra b 10 May 1967); *Career* res librarian Wenner-Gren Fndn Anthropological Res NY 1963–65, actress Woodstock Playhouse NY 1964–67, ante-natal teacher Nat Childbirth Tst 1972–85, res asst Univ of London 1976–77; broadcasting 1972–; writer: Man and Myth (Radio 3, award for best radio documentary series 1976), An Introduction to Social Anthropology (1980); presenter and contrib LWT and Thames TV 1970–, panelist on Tomorrow's Child; writer of documentaries Channel 4 and five; tech advsr to film dirs: Fred Zinnemann (The Dybbuk) 1972, Barbra Streisand (Yentl) 1982; journalist: Woodstock Times 1965–67, Sunday Times 1984–88, Daily Telegraph 1987; TV critic and feature writer: Daily Mail 1984–, Sunday Times Magazine, You, She, New Woman, The Mail on Sunday, Aspire magazine; guest lectr and motivational speaker 2007–; tstee Frimley Hosp Tst; memb Br Broadcasting Press Guild 1988; *Books* The Mistaken Body (1978), When The Crying's Done – A Journey Through Widowhood (1992), The American Madonna (2002), Loneliness and How to Overcome It (2008), The Chartres Street Cats (children's book, 2014), Living with the Leopard (2015); *Recreations* dancing, choreography, gardening, walking, painting (water colours), cooking, 17th century embroidery, growing old-fashioned roses; *Style*— Ms Jeannette Kupfermann;

✉ Features Department, Daily Mail, Northcliffe House, 2 Derry Street, London W8 5EE (✆ 020 7583 8000)

KURBAAN, Dr Arvinder Singh; s of Meherban Singh Kurbaan, and Satinder Pal Kurbaan; *b* 17 January 1966; *Educ* UMDS London (BSc, MB BS), Nat Heart and Lung Inst and Imperial Coll Sch of Med London, Univ of London (MD); *Career* trg posts: Guy's and associated hosps London 1990–93, Bart's 1993–94, Harefield Hosp Middx 1994–95, Imperial Coll London 1995–96, Royal Brompton Hosp 1995–98, Chelsea & Westminster Hosp 1996–98, St Mary's Hosp London 1998–2000; conslt cardiologist London Chest Hosp and Homerton Hosp 2000–; memb: RSM, BMA, Br Cardiac Soc, Br Cardiovascular Intervention Soc, Br Pacing and Electrophysiology Gp; memb Amnesty Int; FRCP 2003 (MRCP 1993); *Publications* author of numerous papers, book chapters, abstracts and presentations; *Recreations* tennis, cricket, skiing, watching films; *Style*— Dr Arvinder Kurbaan; ✉ London Heart Centre, 22 Upper Wimpole Street, London W1G 6NB

KUREISHI, Hanif; CBE (2008); *b* 5 December 1954, Kent; *Educ* KCL; *Career* novelist and scriptwriter; writer in residence Royal Court Theatre 1982; Chevalier de l'Ordre des Arts et des Lettres (France); *Plays* Outskirts (George Devine Award 1981), Sleep With Me (1999), When Night Begins (2004); *Fiction* The Buddha of Suburbia (1990, Whitbread First Novel Award, also televised), The Black Album (1995), Love in a Blue Time (short stories, 1997), Intimacy (1998), Midnight All Day (short stories, 1999), Gabriel's Gift (2001), The Body (2002); *Non-Fiction* Dreaming and Scheming (essays, 2002), My Ear at His Heart (2004); *Screenplays* My Beautiful Laundrette (1984, Oscar nomination), Sammy and Rosie Get Laid (1988), London Kills Me (1991, also dir), My Son the Fanatic (1998), The Mother (2003), Venus (2006); *Style*— Hanif Kureishi, Esq, CBE; ✉ c/o Peter Straus, Rogers, Coleridge & White Ltd, 20 Powis Mews, London W11 1JN (✆ 020 7221 3717, fax 020 7229 9084, e-mail matthew@rcwlitagency.co.uk)

KURTZ, Prof Donna Carol; *b* Cincinnati, OH, USA; *Educ* Univ of Cincinnati (BA), Yale Univ (MA), Univ of Oxford (DPhil); *Career* Univ of Oxford: Beazley archivist and prof of classical art Faculty of Classics (1979–2011), emeritus fell Wolfson Coll, sr research fell Oxford e-Research Centre, research affiliate Oxford Internet Inst, hon life memb Hellenic Soc, dir: of The Cultural Heritage Programme, CLAROS, THe World of Art on the Semantic Web, Digital Cultural Heritage India and China; *Books* incl: The Iconography of the Athenian White-Ground Lekythos (1968), Greek Burial Customs (with John Boardman, 1971), Athenian White Lekythoi: Patterns and Painters (1975), The Man-Eating Horses of Diomedes in Poetry and Painting (1975), The Eye of Greece: Studies in the Art of Athens (ed with Brian Sparkes, 1982), Mr Hattatt's Painter (1982), The Berlin Painter (1983), Gorgo's Cup: An Essay on Connoisseurship (1983), Vases for the Dead: An Attic Selection 750–400 BC (1984), The Achilles Painter's Early White Lekythoi (1990), Studies in Greek Vases and their Paintings: An Introduction to Classical Archaeology (1992), The Reception of Classical Art in Britain: An Oxfird Story of Plaster Casts from the Antique (2000), Reception of Classical Art: An Introduction (ed, 2004); *Publications* Articles on digital technologies for cultural heritage; *Recreations* Digital technologies for Global Cultural Heritage; *Style*— Prof Donna C Kurtz; ✉ OeRC, 6 Keble Road, Oxford OX1 3QG

KUSHNER, Her Hon Judge Lindsey Joy; QC (1992); da of Harry Kushner, of Manchester, and Rita, *née* Alexander; *b* 16 April 1952; *Educ* Manchester HS for Girls, Univ of Liverpool (LLB); *m* 15 Aug 1976, David Norman Kaye; 1 s (Alexander Lewis b 8 Sept 1979), 1 da (Tamara Ruth b 21 July 1981); *Career* called to the Bar 1974, pupilled to His Hon Judge Charles Bloom, QC, *qv*, recorder 1993–2000 (asst recorder 1989–93), circuit judge (Northern Circuit) 2000–; legal chm: Medical Appeal Tbnl 1989–2000, Disablement Appeal Tbnl 1992–99; former memb Ethnic Minorities Advsy Ctee Judicial Studies Bd; *Recreations* cooking, cinema; *Style*— Her Hon Judge Kushner, QC; ✉ Courts of Justice, Crown Square, Manchester M3 3PL

KUTAPAN, Nicola Annette; da of Peter Kutapan (d 1965), and Molly Grace, *née* Hawkins; *b* 21 April 1958; *Educ* Greycoat Hosp Sch; *Children* 1 s (b 1995); *Career* dir Seven Dials Monument Co 1986–; 300 Group (all-pty campaign for more women in Parliament and public life): chair 1992–94, treas 1994–95; head of admin CPSA 1992–95, chair Opportunity 2000 Women's Advsy Panel 1993; Lab Pty: Parly candidate Solihull 1992, vice-chair Holborn and St Pancras CLP, sec London Central Euroconstituency; London Borough of Camden: cncllr 1986–90, vice-chair Planning Ctee and chair Planning Sub-Ctee, vice-chair Employment Ctee, chair Public Control Sub-Ctee; dir Fitzrovia Trust 1989–92, govr St Joseph's Sch 1989–91; *Style*— Miss Nicola Kutapan; ✉ 11 Hunter House, King James Street, London SE1 0AG (✆ 020 7928 6403)

KVERNDAL, Simon Richard; QC (2002); s of Ole Sigvard Kverndal (d 2003), of Colgates, Halstead, Kent, and Brenda, *née* Skinner; *b* 22 April 1958; *Educ* Haileybury, Sidney Sussex Coll Cambridge (MA); *m* 1997, Sophie Rowsell; *Career* called to the Bar Middle Temple 1982, practising barr in commercial and maritime law 1983–; Lloyd's (LOF) salvage arbitrator 2006–; Liveryman Worshipful Co of Shipwrights 1983 (memb Ct of Assts 1999); *Recreations* real tennis, rackets, wine tasting, opera, the Church of England; *Clubs* Hawks' (Cambridge), Queen's, MCC, Garrick, Mjolnirs Rackets; *Style*— Simon Kverndal, Esq, QC; ✉ 17 Heathfield Terrace, London W4 4JE; Quadrant Chambers, 10 Fleet Street, London EC4Y 1AU (✆ 020 7583 4444, fax 020 7583 5544, e-mail simon.kverndal@quadrantchambers.com)

KWARTENG, Dr Kwasi Alfred Addo; MP; *b* 26 May 1975, London; *Educ* Eton (King's scholar, Newcastle scholar), Trinity Coll Cambridge (MA, PhD), Harvard Univ (Kennedy scholar); *Career* MP (Cons) Spelthorne 2010–; *Style*— Dr Kwasi Kwarteng, MP; ✉ The Spelthorne Conservative Association, 55 Cherry Orchard, Staines, Middlesex TW18 2SQ; House of Commons, London SW1A 0AA

KWEI-ARMAH, Kwame (né Ian Roberts); OBE (2012); *b* 1967, Tottenham, London; *Educ* London Coll of Printing; *m* (m dis); 3 c; *Career* actor, playwright and singer; writer in residence Bristol Old Vic 1999–2001; *Theatre* as writer incl: Blues Brother, Soul Sister (also actor, Bristol Old Vic) 1999, Big Nose (also actor, Belgrade Coventry) 1999, A Bitter Herb (Bristol Old Vic) 2001 (Peggy Ramsay Award), Elmina's Kitchen (also actor, NT and Garrick Theatre) 2003 (Evening Standard Most Promising Playwright Award 2003, nominated Best New Play Laurence Olivier Awards 2003, nominated Best New Writer for screen adaptation BAFTA Awards), Fix Up (NT) 2004; *Television* incl: The Latchkey Children 1980, Casualty 1999–2004 (Favourite TV Actor Screen Nat Film and TV Awards 2003), Comic Relief Does Fame Academy (winner) 2003, Pride 2004; *Films* incl: Cutthroat Island 1995, My West 1998, The 3 Kings 2000; *Albums* Kwame 2003; *Style*— Kwame Kwei-Armah, Esq, OBE; ✉ c/o Lou Coulson Associates, 1st Floor, 37 Berwick Street, London W1F 8RS (✆ 020 7734 9633, fax 020 7439 7569)

KYLE, Dr Peter McLeod; s of late Andrew Brown Kyle, of Ravens Court, Thorntonhall, and late Janet, *née* McLeod; *b* 19 August 1951; *Educ* Glasgow HS, Univ of Glasgow (MB ChB); *m* 25 March 1982, Valerie Anne, da of late James Steele, of Mairi Lodge, Hamilton; 1 s (Alasdair McLeod b 23 Jan 1983), 2 da (Catriona Jane b 20 Dec 1984, Gillian Fiona b 16 Feb 1989); *Career* clinical dir of ophthalmology Southern Gen Hosp Glasgow 1993–98 (conslt 1982–2010), memb Med Appeal Tbnl 1985–, memb Criminal Injuries Compensation Tbnl 2010–; hon clinical sr lectr Univ of Glasgow 1985 (lectr in ophthalmology 1980–84), ophthalmology convenor RCPSGlas; memb Gen Optical Cncl, GMC Fitness to Practice panellist 2010–; memb Trades Houses of Glasgow 1997–, Deacon Incorporation of Barbers of Glasgow 1998–99, Liveryman Worshipful Co of Spectacle Makers 2004; FRCS (Glasgow and Edinburgh), FRCOphth; *Books* Current Ophthalmic Surgery (1990); *Clubs* Glasgow Art, Golf House (Elie); *Style*— Dr Peter Kyle; ✉ The Stables, Chapel Green, Earlsferry, Fife KY9 1AD

L

LA TROBE-BATEMAN, Richard George Saumarez; s of John Saumarez La Trobe-Bateman (d 1996), of Sark, CI, and Margaret Jane, *née* Schmid; *b* 17 October 1938; *Educ* Westminster, St Martin's Sch of Art, RCA (MDesRCA); *m* 26 April 1969, Mary Elizabeth, OBE (2001), da of Arthur Jolly, JP (d 1984), of Hove, E Sussex; 2 da (Emily b 1971, Alice b 1976), 1 s (Will b 1973); *Career* studied sculpture under Anthony Caro at St Martin's Sch of Art 1958–61, studied furniture under David Pye at RCA 1965–68; exhbns at UK Design Centre, Crafts Cncl, V&A, Br Craft Centre and Contemporary Applied Art and in Belgium, Holland, Denmark, Austria, France, USA and Japan; works in public collections incl: V&A, Crafts Cncl, Leeds City Art Collection, Tyne & Wear Art Collection (Shipley Art Gallery), Portsmouth Museum and Art Gallery, Craft Study Centre Bath, Contemporary Arts Soc, Cheltenham Art Gallery; public footbridges in Britain (Cumbria, Essex and Kent) incl bridge at Nat Pinetum Kent, Swing-Lift Bridge Quenington Glos 2002 (winner Wood Awards 2003), Parrett Bridge Somerset 2005–06, footbridges at Tassajara and Napa CA USA 2005 and 2011, rolling bridge Buscot Oxon 2010; memb Crafts Cncl 1982–86 (work presented to HRH Prince of Wales by Craft Cncl 1984); prof of furniture San Diego State Univ 1986–87; *Books* Making Triangles (2012); *Clubs* Contemporary Applied Arts; *Style—* Richard La Trobe-Bateman, Esq; ✉ Elm House, Batcombe, Shepton Mallet, Somerset BA4 6AB (☎ 01749 850442)

LACE, Garry Marc; s of John Cresswell Lace (d 1989), and Carole Anne, *née* Harrison; *b* 8 May 1967; *Educ* Thomas Rotherham Sixth Form Coll, Univ of Manchester (BA); *m* 12 July 1997, Katherine; 1 s (Thomas Cresswell b 27 May 1998), 1 da (Eleanor Daisy b 27 April 2003); *Career* grad trainee Saatchi & Saatchi 1990, bd dir Euro RSCG 1995, TBWA: jt md 1999, ceo 2001; ceo Grey London 2002–04, ceo Lowe London 2005–; memb Cncl IPA 1999–; patron: Sparks, NCH; MInstD, FIPA 2002 (MIPA 1999); *Recreations* tennis, skiing, opera; *Clubs* Solus; *Style—* Garry Lace, Esq

LACEY, Prof (John) Hubert; s of Percy Hubert Lacey (d 2013), and Sheila Margaret, *née* Neal; *b* 4 November 1944; *Educ* Loughborough GS, Univ of St Andrews (MB ChB), Univ of London (MPhil), Univ of Dundee (MD), RCOG (DipObst); *m* 7 Feb 1976, Susan Millicent, da of late Richard England Liddiard, CBE, of Wimbledon; 1 da (Emma Louise Susan b 1978), 2 s (Ben William Hubert b 1979, Jonathan Rupert Neal b 1982); *Career* jr hosp appts Dundee, St Thomas' and St George's Hosps London 1969–78; Univ of London: sr lectr 1978–86, reader 1987–91, prof 1991–2011, emeritus prof 2011–; hon conslt psychiatrist: Middx Hosp 1978–80, St George's Hosp London 1980–; dir and consl i/c Eating Disorders Service 1980–, head of psychiatry St George's Hosp Med Sch London 1987–2003 (chm Dept of Psychiatry 1991–2003); clinical dir: Pathfinder Hosp Tst 1993–2000, SW London St Georges NHS Tst 2000–10; dir: Yorks Centre for Eating Disorders Leeds NHS Tst 2004–07, Peninsular Eating Disorders Unit Exeter and Devon NHS Tst 2005–08; medical dir Newbridge Healthcare Systems 2007–; consl and dir Nightingale Hosp London 2007–, consl and med advsr Priory Hospital Gp; non-exec dir Merton Sutton and Wandsworth HA 1994–96; pres Euro Cncl on Eating Disorders; past pres Int Coll of Psychosomatic Med, elector Ct of Electors RCPsych 2001–08 (memb Cncl, former chm gen psychiatry); tstee Bd Beat (Eating Disorders charity) 2013–, chm cncl Beat 2015–; NHS Modernisation Award 2003; charity warden 2012–; Freeman: City of London 1986, Worshipful Co of Plaisterers 1986 (Master 2010–11); FRCPsych 1985 (MRCPsych 1974); *Books* Psychological Management of the Physically Ill (1989), Overcoming Anorexia (2007), Bulimia, Binge-eating and their Treatment (2010), Managing Severe and Enduring Anorexia Nervosa: A Clinician's Guide (2016); Over 170 peer-reviewed papers in scientific journals; *Recreations* music, travel, interior decoration, hill walking; *Clubs* Athenaeum; *Style—* Prof J Hubert Lacey; ✉ 5 Atherton Drive, Wimbledon, London SW19 5LB (☎ 020 8947 5976, e-mail jhubertlacey@hotmail.com); Newbridge House, 147 Chester Rd, Streetly, Sutton Coldfield, Birmingham B74 3NE (☎ 01215 808362)

LACEY, Nicholas Stephen; s of John Stephen Lacey (d 2005), of Highgate, London, and Norma, *née* Hayward (d 1995); *b* 20 December 1943; *Educ* Univ Coll Sch, Emmanuel Coll Cambridge (MA), Architectural Assoc London (AADip); *m* 1, 1965 (m dis 1976), Nicola, da of Dr F A Mann (d 1991); 2 s (Joshua b 1968, William b 1973), 1 da (Olivia b 1970); m 2, 1981 (m dis 2009), Juliet, da of Dr Wallace Aykroyd, CBE (d 1979); 2 da (Laetitia b 1978, Theodora b 1980); *Career* ptnr: Nicholas Lacey & Assoc Architects 1971–83, Nicholas Lacey & Ptnrs Architects 1983–; dir ContainerSpace Ltd 2003; winner: Wallingford Competition 1972, Crown Reach 1977; jt winner Arunbridge 1977, prize winner Paris Opera House Competition 1983; *Recreations* music, theatre, sailing; *Clubs* Athenaeum; *Style—* Nicholas Lacey, Esq; ✉ Nicholas Lacey & Partners, Reeds Wharf, Mill Street, London SE1 2AX (☎ 020 7231 5154, fax 020 7231 5633)

LACEY, Prof Nicola Mary; da of John McAndrew (d 1995), and Gillian, *née* Wroth; *b* 3 February 1958, Liverpool; *Educ* Malvern Girls' Coll, UCL (LLB, Hurst prize, Maxwell law prize, Maxwell medal), UC Oxford (BCL); *m* 1991, David Soskice; *Career* lectr Faculty of Laws UCL 1981–84, fell and tutor in law New Coll Oxford 1984–95 (tutor for admissions 1988–91), CUF lectr Univ of Oxford 1984–95, prof of law Birkbeck Coll London 1995–97 (head Dept of Law 1996–97), prof of criminal law LSE 1998–2010 (dir doctoral prog Law Dept 2000–02), currently sch prof of law, gender and social policy LSE; visiting scholar Stanford Law Sch 1992, guest prof Law Faculty Humboldt Univ Berlin 1996, fell Wissenschaftskolleg zu Berlin 1999–2000, visitor Global Law Sch NY Univ 2001 and 2003, prof Programme in Ethics, Politics & Economics Yale Univ 2004, visiting scholar Harvard Univ Center for European Studies 2007, visiting prof Harvard Law Sch 2013, distinguished visiting prof Global Law Sch NYU 2014; ANU: visiting prof Law Sch 1992, visiting fell Dir's Section Res Sch of Social Sciences 1995–96, adjunct prof Law Prog Res Sch of Social Sciences 1999–2001, adjunct prof Social and Political Theory Prog Res Sch of Social Sciences 2002–07; Univ of Oxford: memb Working Pty on Sexual Harrassment 1988, memb Rules Ctee Panel Disciplinary Ct 1988–91, memb Gen Purposes Ctee Law Bd 1989–91, memb Proctors' Advsy Panel on Sexual Harrassment 1991–94, memb Grad Studies Ctee in Law 1993–95, sr research fellow All Souls Coll and prof of law 2010–13; co-dir Cmmn on Gender, Inequality and Power LSE Gender Inst 2014–15; articles co-ed Modern Law Review 2001–04; assoc ed: Int Jl of the Sociology of Law 1988–91, Social and Legal Studies 1991–2000; Hamlyn lectr 2007, Clarendon law lectr 2007; memb Editorial Bd: Law and Philosophy series of monographs 1988–, New Community 1993–94, Clarendon Studies in Criminology 1994–95, Oxford Jl of Legal Studies 1994–95, Current Legal Problems 1994–2009, Policy Studies 1995–, Cambridge Studies in Law and Society 1996–, Economy and Society 1997–2001, Modern Law Review 1998–; memb: Advsy Gp on draft bill of rights for Inst of Public Policy Res (published 1991), Advsy Bd Law in Context series 1995–, Int Editorial Advsy Bd Buffalo Criminal Law Review 1996–; memb Criminal Justice Ctee Justice 1993–95, memb Ctee on Women's Imprisonment Prison Reform Tst 1998–2000; memb Planning Ctee 14th World Congress of the Int Assoc for Philosophy of Law and Social Philosophy Edinburgh 1988–89; tstee and memb Cncl Charter 88 1989–91; hon fell New Coll Oxford 2007; Hans Sigust Prize 2011; FBA 2001 (chair Law Section 2010–13, memb Policy Gp on Imprisonment 2012–14); *Publications* State Punishment: Political Principles and Community Values (1988), Reconstructing Criminal Law: Critical Perspectives on Crime and the Criminal Process (jtly, 1990, 3 edn 2003), The Politics of Community: A Feminist Analysis of the Liberal-Communitarian Debate (jtly, 1993), Criminal Justice: A Reader (ed, 1994), Unspeakable Subjects: Feminist Essays in Legal and Social Theory (1998), A Life of H L A Hart: The Nightmare and the Noble Dream (2004, RSA Swiney Prize 2004), The Prisoners' Dilemma: Political Economy and Punishment in Contemporary Democracies (2008), Women, Crime and Character: From Moll Flanders to Tess of the D'Urbervilles (2008), In Search of Criminal Responsibility: Ideas, Interests and Institutions (2016); author of numerous articles in learned jls and contributions to books; *Style—* Prof Nicola Lacey, FBA

LACEY, Peter; s of Ernest Lacey, of Ipswich, Suffolk, and Elsie, *née* Bolt; *b* 11 August 1946; *Educ* St Joseph's Coll Ipswich, Balliol Coll Oxford (MA, DipEd); *m* 1969, Naomi Ruth; 3 s (Jonathan b 25 June 1975, Timothy b 10 Nov 1977, Jeremy b 9 Dec 1981); *Career* teacher The Leys Sch Cambridge 1972–92, headmaster The King's Sch Gloucester 1992–; memb HMC 1994; memb Area Child Protection Ctee; FRCA; *Recreations* sport, golf, wine writing; *Clubs* MCC; *Style—* Peter Lacey, Esq; ✉ King's School House, College Green, Gloucester GL1 2BG (☎ 01452 524260); The King's School, Gloucester GL1 2BG (☎ 01452 337337, fax 01452 337319, e-mail headmaster@thekingsschool.co.uk)

LACEY, Air Vice-Marshal Richard Howard; CBE (2004); s of Henry Howard Lacey (d 1996), of Croydon, Surrey, and Mary Elliott Lacey; *b* 11 December 1953; *Educ* Peterhouse Cambridge (MA), RAF Coll Cranwell, RCDS; *m* 30 May 1980, Cate; 1 da (Alexandra b 23 June 1981), 1 s (Gregory b 7 May 1984); *Career* advanced flying trg RAF Shawbury 1978 (qualified helicopter pilot), ops 72 and 28 Sqdns UK, NI and Hong Kong 1978–83, trg as helicopter flying instr 1984–85, Flight Cdr 72 Sqdn NI 1985–87, RAF Staff Coll 1989, Personal Staff Offr to COS RAF Strike Command then C-in-C Gulf War 1989–91, promoted Wing Cdr 1991, cmd 33 Sqdn RAF Odiham 1992–94, served Air Plans and Progs MOD 1994–97, promoted Gp Capt, asst dir Jt Warfare Commitments Area MOD, cmd RAF Benson 1997–99, RCDS 2000, promoted Air Cdre, dir NATO Policy MOD 2000–03, Cdr Br Forces Falkland Islands 2003–05, UK Nat Mil Rep SHAPE Belgium 2005–06, Cdr Br Forces Cyprus 2006–08, ret 2009; dir of strategy Sodexo Defence Ltd 2009–14, ret; Gentleman Usher to HM The Queen 2010–; *Recreations* industrial archaeology, photography, model engineering; *Clubs* RAF; *Style—* Air Vice-Marshal Richard Lacey, CBE; ✉ e-mail cateandrichlacey@gmail.com

LACEY, Robert; *b* 3 January 1944; *Educ* Bristol GS, Selwyn Coll Cambridge; *m* 2012, Lady Jane Rayne, *née* Stewart; *Career* historian and biographer; early career as journalist for Illustrated London News and later Sunday Times; Royal commentator Good Morning America (ABC); *Books* Robert, Earl of Essex (1971), Henry VIII (1972), The Queens of the North Atlantic (1973), Sir Walter Raleigh (1973), Majesty (1977), The Kingdom (1981), Princess (1982), Aristocrats (1983), Ford (1986), Little Man: Meyer Lansky and the Gangster Life (1991), Grace (1994), Sotheby's: Bidding for Class (1998), The Year 1000: What Life Was Like at the Turn of the First Millennium (with Danny Danziger, 1999), The Queen Mother's Century (with Michael Rand, 1999), Royal (2002), Monarch, Life and Reign of Elizabeth II (2002), Great Tales from British History, Volume 1 (2003), Great Tales from British History, Volume 2 (2005), Great Tales from British History, Volume 3 (2006), Inside the Kingdom (2009), The Queen: a Life in Brief (2012), Model Woman, Eileen Ford and the Business of Beauty (2015); *Recreations* opera, reading, swimming, water skiing; *Clubs* Chelsea Arts, Savile, Denham Waterski; *Style—* Robert Lacey, Esq; ✉ c/o Jonathan Pegg Literary Agency, 32 Batoum Gardens, London W6 7QD

LACHMANN, Prof Sir Peter Julius; kt (2002); s of Heinz Ulrich Lachmann (d 1971), of London, and Thea Emilie, *née* Heller (d 1978); *b* 23 December 1931; *Educ* Christ's Coll Finchley (state scholar, HSC), Trinity Coll Cambridge (scholar), UCH (Goldsmid scholar, MA, MB BChir, PhD, ScD (Cantab), Fellowes Silver medal, Tuke Silver medal, Liston Gold medal); *m* 7 July 1962, Sylvia Mary, da of Alan Stephenson; 2 s (Robin b 20 June 1965, Michael b 20 Aug 1970), 1 da (Helen b 16 Sept 1967); *Career* house surgn Newmarket General Hosp 1956–57, house physician Med Unit UCH and Rheumatism Unit Canadian Red Cross Meml Hosp 1957–58, John Lucas Walker student, res scholar and BMA science res scholar Trinity Coll Cambridge 1958–60, visiting investigator and asst physician Rockefeller Univ 1960–61; Dept of Pathology Univ of Cambridge: Arthritis and Rheumatism Cncl fell 1962–64, asst dir of res Immunology Div 1964–71; dir of med studies Christ's Coll Cambridge 1969–70 (fell 1962–71), prof of immunology RPMS Univ of London 1971–75; Univ of Cambridge: fell Christ's Coll 1976–, Sheila Joan Smith prof of immunology 1977–99, emeritus prof 1999–, hon dir MRC Molecular Immunopathology Unit 1980–97; consl WHO 1968, hon consl pathologist Hammersmith Hosp 1971–75, hon consl clinical immunologist Cambridge HA 1976–99; visiting investigator: Basel Inst for Immunology 1971, Scripps Clinic and Res Fndn 1975, 1980, 1986 and 1989; SmithKline and French visiting prof Aust 1984, Mayerhoff visiting prof Dept of Chemical Immunology Weitzmann Inst 1989; visiting prof: Dept of Med RPMS 1986–90, College de France 1993; memb: Medical Advsy Ctee British Council 1983–97, Gene Therapy Advsy Ctee Dept of Health 1993–96, Int Bioethics Ctee UNESCO 1993–98, Scientific Advsy Bd SmithKline Beecham 1995–2000, Exec Ctee Inter-Acad Med Panel 2000–06; chm: Int Archive Advsy Gp DEFRA 2002–08, Research Advsy Ctee CORE 2003–09; non-exec dir Adprotech plc 1997–2000 (chm Scientific Advsy Bd 1997–2004); fndr and chm Scientific Advsy Bd Gyroscope Therapeutics 2016; RCPath: memb Cncl 1982–85 and 1989–93, pres 1990–93; biological sec and vice-pres Royal Soc 1993–98; pres: Fedn of European Academies of Med 2004–05 (vice-pres 2002–03), Henry Kunkel Soc 2003–05; nat patron Lupus (UK) 1996–; tstee: Darwin Tst 1991–2001, Arthritis Research Campaign 2000–06, Academia Europaea 2007–10; assoc ed Clinical and Experimental Immunology 1990–2001, pres Cncl and memb Bd of Dirs Int Jl of Experimental Pathology 1991–2014; memb: Br Soc for Immunology 1959 (memb Ctee 1966–69), Gold medallist European

Complement Network 1997, Med and Europe Sr Prize Inst des Sciences de la Santé 2003; fell Royal Postgrad Med Sch 1995, foreign fell Indian Nat Sci Acad 1996, fndr fell UCL Hosp 1999, fell Imperial Coll London 2001, hon fell Trinity Coll Cambridge 2007, hon memb Czech Acad of Medicine 2012; Hon DSc Univ of Leicester 2005; American Assoc of Immunologists 1966, Norwegian Acad of Science and Letters 1991, Academia Europaea 1992; hon memb: Societé Française d'Immunologie 1986, Assoc of Physicians 1999; hon fell Faculty of Pathology RCPI 1993; FRSM, FRS 1982, fndr fell and pres Acad of Med Sci 1998–2002; FRCP 1973, FRCPath 1981, FRS 1982, FMed Sci 1998; *Publications* Clinical Aspects of Immunology (co-ed, 5 edn 1993), First Steps – a personal account of the formation of the Academy of Medical Sciences 2010; author of numerous papers in professional jls on complement and immunopathology, and on evolution, ethics and religion; *Recreations* mountain walking, keeping bees; *Clubs* Athenaeum; *Style*— Prof Sir Peter Lachmann, FRS, FMedSci; ✉ Conduit Tail, 38 Conduit Head Road, Cambridge CB3 0EY (✆ 01223 357842, fax 01233 300169); Department of Veterinary Medicine, Madingley Road, Cambridge CB3 0ES (✆ 01223 766242, fax 01223 766244, e-mail pjl1000@cam.ac.uk)

LADER, Philip; *Educ* Duke Univ Durham N Carolina (Phi Beta Kappa), Univ of Michigan (MA), Pembroke Coll Oxford, Harvard Law Sch (JD); *m* Linda LeSourd Lader; 2 da (Mary-Catherine, Whitaker); *Career* businessman and educator, diplomat of the USA; formerly: pres Sea Pines Company (developer/operator award-winning large-scale recreation communities), exec vice-pres US holding co of late Sir James Goldsmith, pres univs in S Carolina and Aust; one-time chm South Carolina Cncl on Small and Minority Business and fndr dir South Carolina Jobs-Economic Devpt Authy, candidate govr S Carolina 1986, subsequently joined Govt Serv, becoming White House dep chief of staff/asst to Pres Clinton and dep dir for mgmnt Office of Mgmnt and Budget, then administrator US Small Business Admin and memb Pres Clinton's Cabinet; American ambass to the Ct of St James's 1997–2001; non-exec chm WPP Gp plc 2001–, sr advsr Morgan Stanley Int 2001–; non-exec dir: WPP Gp, AES Corp, Marathon Oil Corp, RAND Corp, RUSAL Corp; memb: Cncl on Foreign Rels, Chief Execs Orgn, American Assoc of Royal Acad of Arts Tst; former memb Lloyd's Cncl; tstee: Smithsonian Museum of American History, Salzburg Seminar; former tstee: Br Museum, Windsor Leadership Tst, St Paul's Cathedral Fndn; memb: Advsy Bd Br-American Business Cncl, The Prince's Tst; memb: Int Advsy Bd Columbia Univ, Bd of Visitors Harvard Law Sch, Bd of Visitors Yale Divinity Sch; formerly: pres Business Execs for Nat Security, memb Bds American Red Cross and Duke Univ's Public Policy Inst; fndr Renaissance Weekends (family retreats for innovative ldrs) 1981; hon fell: Pembroke Coll Oxford, London Business Sch, John Moore's Univ; recipient hon doctorates from 14 univs; *Style*— The Hon Philip Lader

LADHA, Hash; *Educ* Univ of Wales; *Career* mktg dir New Look 2004–07, mktg and operations dir ASOS.com 2007–10; Aurora: gp multichannel dir 2010–12, dep md Oasis 2012–13, chief operating offr Oasis 2013–; *Style*— Mr Hash Ladha; ✉ Oasis, 1st floor, 69–77 Paul Street, London EC2A 4PN

LAFFERTY, Henry; *Educ* London Business Sch (Sloan fell, MSc); *Career* formerly: various sr positions Nat Freight Corp, gp fin dir Jarvis plc, chief exec PatientFirst Partnerships; chm City of London Gp (memb Bd 2006–), pt/t exec dir InvestSelect plc; fell CIMA; *Style*— Henry Lafferty, Esq; ✉ City of London Group plc, 30 Cannon Street, London EC4M 6WH (✆ 020 7634 9800)

LAIDLAW, Charles David Gray; s of George Gray Laidlaw, and Margaret Orr, *née* Crombie; *b* 23 January 1954; *Educ* Strathallan Sch, Univ of Edinburgh (LLB); *m* 27 June 1986, Lucy Elizabeth, *née* Brooks; 2 s (Robert Gray b 27 June 1989, Douglas John b 8 May 1991); *Career* political writer D C Thompson Group 1977–79 (reporter 1975–77), reporter Sunday Express 1980, def intelligence analyst MOD 1980–83, exec Good Relations 1983–85, mangr PA Consulting Group 1985–87, gp mangr Reginald Watts Associates 1987–88; dir: Burson-Marsteller and Burson-Marsteller Financial 1988–90, TMA Group 1990, Citigate Scotland 1991–96; chief exec Scottish and Westminster Communications 1992–96, head of media and public relations Scottish Rugby Union 1996–98, sec Club Scotland 1998–2001, md David Gray PR 2002; Freeman City of Glasgow (hereditary); memb Grand Antiquary Soc; MIPR 1986; *Recreations* rugby, running, writing; *Clubs* London Scottish, N Berwick RFC; *Style*— Charles Laidlaw, Esq; ✉ Gullane Business Centre, 12A Lammermuir Terrace, Gullane, East Lothian EH31 2HB (e-mail info@davidgraypr.com)

LAIDLAW, Baron (Life Peer UK 2004), of Rothiemay in Banffshire; Irvine Alan Stewart Laidlaw; s of late Roy Alan Laidlaw, of Keith, Scotland; *Educ* Merchiston Castle Sch Edinburgh, Univ of Leeds (BA), Columbia Univ (MBA); *m* 1, 1965 (m dis 1985), Anne Marie, da of late Knut Bakkevig; *m* 2, 1987, Christine, da of late Francis O'Day; *Career* fndr and chm Inst for Int Research Ltd 1974–2005, chm Abbey Business Centres 1997–, memb Global Advsy Bd Wall St 2000–; fndr Laidlaw Youth Tst 2003; memb House of Lords 2004–10; Hon DL St Andrew's Univ 2002, Hon DHC Univ of Aberdeen 2007; *Clubs* Royal Thames Yacht, NY Yacht; *Style*— The Lord Laidlaw

LAIDLAW, Jonathan James; QC (2008); *b* 28 February 1960; *Educ* Univ of Hull (LLB); *Career* called to the Bar Inner Temple 1982; Treasy counsel Central Criminal Court 1995–2001, recorder 1998–, sr Treasy counsel 2001–08, first sr Treasy counsel 2008–10; *Style*— Jonathan Laidlaw, Esq, QC; ✉ 2 Hare Court, Temple, London EC4Y 7BH (✆ 020 7353 5324)

LAIDLAW, (William) Samuel Hugh (Sam); s of Sir Christophor Laidlaw, qv, of Chelsea, London, and Nina Mary, *née* Prichard; *b* 3 January 1956, London; *Educ* Eton, Gonville & Caius Coll Cambridge (MA), INSEAD Fontainebleau (MBA); *m* 15 April 1989, Deborah Margaret, *née* Morris-Adams; 3 s (Arthur Charles Hugh b 12 May 1990, Humphrey Thomas Christopher b 27 Aug 1992, Fergus Richard Playfair b 1 Dec 1995), 1 da (Clementine Selina b 29 Sept 1998); *Career* admitted slr 1980; formerly: exec vice-pres Chevron Corporation, ceo Enterprise Oil, pres and chief operating offr Amerada Hess; ceo Centrica plc 2006–; non-exec dir Hanson plc 2003–07, non-exec dir HSBC Hldgs plc 2008–; lead non-exec dir Dept for Tport 2010–, memb PM's Business Advsy Gp 2010–12; chm CBI HE Task Force; dir Business Cncl for Int Understanding; tstee RAFT; FRSA; *Recreations* sailing; *Clubs* Royal Yacht Squadron, Royal Thames Yacht, Bucks; *Style*— Sam Laidlaw, Esq; ✉ Centrica plc, Millstream, Maidenhead Road, Windsor, Berkshire SL4 5GD (✆ 01753 494000, fax 01753 494616)

LAINE, Dame Clementine Dinah (Cleo); (Lady Dankworth); DBE (1997, OBE 1979); da of Alexander Campbell, and Minnie, *née* Bullock; *b* 28 October 1927; *m* 1, 1947 (m dis 1958), George Langridge; 1 s; *m* 2, 1958, Sir John Philip William Dankworth, CBE (d 2010); 1 s, 1 da; *Career* vocalist; with The Dankworth Orchestra 1953–58; has appeared on television numerous times and made guest appearances with symphony orchestras in England and abroad; fndr Wavendon Stables Performing Arts Centre (with John Dankworth) 1970; jt 70 birthday tribute (with John Dankworth) BBC Proms 1997; Hon MA Open Univ 1975; Hon DMus: Berklee Coll of Music, Univ of York, Univ of Cambridge, Univ of Bedfordshire, Brunel Univ; Freeman Worshipful Co of Musicians 2002; *Theatre* incl: lead in Seven Deadly Sins (Edinburgh Festival and Sadler's Wells) 1961, A Time to Laugh, Hedda Gabler 1966, The Women of Troy 1967 (both Edinburgh Festival), lead in Showboat 1972, Colette 1980, The Mystery of Edwin Drood 1986 (winner of Theatre World Award, nominated for a Tony Award and Drama Desk Award), Into The Woods (US tour) 1989; *Film* Last of the Blonde Bombshells 2000; *Recordings* albums incl: Cleo Laine Jazz 1991, Nothing Without You 1992, Blue and Sentimental 1994, Solitude 1995, The Very Best of Cleo Laine 1997; Gold records incl: Feel the Warm, I'm a Song, Live at Melbourne; Platinum records incl: Best Friends,

Sometimes When We Touch; *Awards* incl: Golden Feather Award LA Times 1973, Edison Award 1974, Variety Club 1977, Singer of the Year (TV Times) 1978, Grammy Award (best female jazz vocalist) 1985, Theatre World Award 1986, Presidential Lifetime Achievement Award (Nat Assoc of Recording Merchandisers (NARM)) 1990, Vocalist of the Year (British Jazz Awards) 1990, Lifetime Achievement Award (USA) 1991, Distinguished Artists award (Int Soc for the Performing Arts Fndn (ISPA)) 1999, Back Stage Bob Harrington Lifetime Achievement Award (with John Dankworth) 2001, BBC British Jazz Awards Lifetime Achievement Award (with John Dankworth) 2002; *Books* Cleo (autobiography, 1994), You Can Sing if You Want To (1997); *Style*— Dame Cleo Laine, DBE; ✉ The Old Rectory, Wavendon, Milton Keynes, Buckinghamshire MK17 8LU (✆ 01908 583151, fax 01908 584414)

LAING, Christopher Maurice; OBE (2000), DL (Herts 2000); s of Sir Kirby Laing, JP, DL, FREng (d 2009), and Joan Dorothy, *née* Bratt (d 1981); *b* 1 May 1948; *Educ* St Lawrence Coll Ramsgate, Herts Coll of Building St Albans; *m* 15 May 1971, Diana Christina, *née* Bartlett; 2 s, 2 da; *Career* with John Laing Services Ltd 1971–2002, dir John Laing Construction Ltd 1986–2001, md Grosvenor Laing Urban Enterprise Ltd 1987–97; dir: Crofton Country Centre Ltd 1989–98, Crofton Trust Ltd 1989–98, Br Sch of Osteopathy 1992–98, Tyringham Foundation Ltd 1993–2008, Chartered Inst of Building Benevolent Fund Ltd 1994–2002, Construction Industry Relief and Assistance for the Single Homeless Ltd 1996–2004, Laing Construction plc 1998–2001; non-exec dir: NPFA Services Ltd 1987–2000, Eskmuir Properties plc 1990–98 and 2000– (chm 2005–), Englemere Ltd 1992–2012; pres Chartered Inst of Building 1992–93 (vice-pres 1989–92); chm: Nat Playing Fields Assoc 1993–2000 (memb Cncl 1985–2000), Herts Groundwork Tst 1998–2006, N London Leadership Team 1993–95, Upper Lee Valley Partnership SRB Gp 1995–97; memb Cncl: Tidy Britain Gp 1993–2002, Euro Cncl for Building Professionals 1993–2002; tstee: Global Action Plan 2001–04, Groundwork UK 2003–04, Herts In Trust 2003–08, Herts Community Fndn 2003–08; pres Cncl St Lawrence Coll 2010–; High Sheriff Herts 2001–02; Lord's Taverners: pres St Albans Chapter 2000–10, treas 2004–05, tstee 2005–11, chm of fndn 2006–11; Master Worshipful Co of Paviors 2008–09 (Liveryman 1971, memb Ct of Assts 1993–); *Recreations* golf, shooting, tennis, swimming; *Clubs* RAC, Temple Golf, Royal Cinque Ports Golf, NRA, North London Rifle; *Style*— Christopher Laing, Esq, OBE, DL; ✉ Brookend, Lashbrook Road, Lower Shiplake, Oxfordshire RG9 3NX

LAING, Eleanor; MP; da of Matthew Pritchard (d 1995), and Betsy, *née* McFarlane (d 1999); *Educ* Univ of Edinburgh (BA, LLB, first woman pres of union); *m* 1983 (m dis 2003), Alan Laing, s of Alan and Margaret Laing; 1 s (b 14 June 2001); *Career* lawyer Edinburgh, City of London and industry 1983–89; special advsr to Rt Hon John MacGregor, MP as: sec of state for educn 1989–90, Ldr of the House of Commons 1990–92, sec of state for Tport 1992–94; MP (Cons) Epping Forest 1997– (Parly candidate Paisley N 1987); oppn whip 1999, oppn front bench spokesman on constitutional affrs 2000–01, oppn frontbench spokesman on educn and skills 2001–04, shadow min for women and equality 2004–07, shadow sec of state for Scotland 2005, shadow min for justice 2007–10, memb Political and Constitutional Reform Select Ctee, first dep chm Ways and Means 2013–, dep speaker House of Commons 2013–; memb Scottish Affairs Select Ctee, chm All Pty Parly Gp on Magna Carta 800th Anniversary; chm Soc of Cons Lawyers 2010–13; *Recreations* music, theatre, golf; *Style*— Mrs Eleanor Laing, MP; ✉ House of Commons, London SW1A 0AA (✆ 020 7219 3000)

LAING, Gerald; *see:* Ogilvie-Laing, Gerald

LAING, Jennifer Charlina Ellsworth; da of James Ellsworth Laing, FRCS (d 1983), and Mary McKane, *née* Taylor (d 2007); *Educ* Godolphin, North Western Poly; *m* (m dis); *Career* bd dir: Saatchi & Saatchi Garland Compton 1977, Leo Burnett 1978; Saatchi & Saatchi Advertising: dep chm 1983–87, jt chm 1987–88, chm and chief exec Aspect Hill Holliday 1988, mgmnt buyout to form Laing Henry Limited 1991–95 (sold to Saatchi & Saatchi Advertising 1995), chairman Saatchi & Saatchi Advertising (London) 1995–97, memb Exec Bd Saatchi & Saatchi Advertising Worldwide 1996–2000, chief exec N American ops Saatchi & Saatchi (New York) 1997–2001; assoc dean of external rels London Business Sch 2002–07; non-exec dir: Remploy Ltd, Great Ormond Street Hosp for Children NHS Trust, Hudson Highland Gp Inc 2003–, InterContinental Hotels Gp plc 2005–; fell Mktg Soc, FIPA; *Recreations* racing, gardening, opera; *Style*— Miss Jennifer Laing

LAING, (John) Stuart; s of late Dr Denys Laing, and Dr Judy Laing, *née* Dods; *b* 22 July 1948; *Educ* Rugby, CCC Cambridge (MA, MPhil); *m* 12 Aug 1972, Sibella, da of Sir Maurice Dorman, GCMG, GCVO, of West Overton, Wiltshire; 1 s (James b 1974), 2 da (Catriona b 1979, Hannah b 1985); *Career* diplomat then academic; entered HM Dip Serv 1971, FCO 1971–72, MECAS Lebanon 1972–73, Jeddah 1973–75, UK Perm Representation to EC 1975–78, FCO 1978–83, Cairo 1983–87, FCO 1987–89, Prague 1989–92, Riyadh 1992–95, head Know How Fund for Central Europe (FCO and later DFID) 1995–98, high cmmr to Brunei 1998–2002, ambass to Oman 2002–05, ambass to Kuwait 2005–08; Master Corpus Christi Coll Cambridge 2008–; tstee Educn Devpt Tst; *Books* Unshook till the End of Time: a History of Britain and Oman (jtly, 2012); *Recreations* playing music, hill walking; *Clubs* Oxford and Cambridge; *Style*— Stuart Laing, Esq; ✉ Corpus Christi College, Cambridge CB2 1RH

LAING, Susan Anne (Sue); da of Angus Murray Laing (d 1984), and Anne Catherine, *née* Wilson-Walker (d 2012); *Educ* Wycombe Abbey, St Hugh's Coll Oxford; *m* 17 March 1984, Wolfgang Bauer; 2 s (Georg b 11 Sept 1985, Angus b 31 Oct 1987), 1 da (Ruth b 7 Dec 1990); *Career* admitted slr 1978; Boodle Hatfield: asst slr 1978–81, ptnr 1981–, head Tax and Fin Planning Dept 2001–11; memb: Law Soc, Soc of Tst & Estate Practitioners, Gen Anti Abuse Rule (GAAR) Advsy Panel, Professional Advsrs to Int Art Market (PAIAM), CLA Tax Ctee; *Recreations* playing piano, sailing, walking; *Style*— Miss Sue Laing

LAIRD, Baron (Life Peer UK 1999), of Artigarvan in the County of Tyrone John Dunn; s of Dr Norman Davidson Laird, OBE, JP, MP (d 1970), of Belfast, and Margaret, *née* Dunn (d 1983); *b* 23 April 1944; *Educ* Royal Belfast Academical Instn; *m* 24 April 1971, Caroline Ethel, da of William John Ferguson, of Dromore, Derrygonnelly, Co Fermanagh; 1 da (Alison Jane b 24 March 1976), 1 s (John) David b 18 Oct 1977; *Career* Belfast Saving Bank: bank official 1963–67, bank inspr 1967–68, computer programmer 1968–73; memb (UUP): St Anne's Div Belfast NI House of Commons 1970–73, W Belfast NI Assembly 1973–75, NI Convention 1975–76; hon treas UUP 1974–76; chm John Laird Public Relations 1976–2001; chm NI Branch Inst of PR 1989–92, visiting prof of PR Univ of Ulster 1993–; chm Ulster Scots Agency 1999–2004; Freeman City of London 2012; FCIPR 1991 (Lifetime Achievement Award 2011); *Books* A Struggle to be Heard – by a True Ulster Liberal (2010); *Videos* Trolleybus Days in Belfast (1992), Swansong of Steam in Ulster (1993), Waterloo Sunset (1994), Rails on the Isle of Wight (1994), The Twilight of Steam in Ulster (1994); *Recreations* transport, travel, cricket, history; *Style*— The Rt Hon Lord Laird; ✉ House of Lords, London SW1A 0PW

LAIRD, Robert Edward; s of Robert Laird (d 1975), of Seaford, E Sussex, and Esther Margaret, *née* Stoney (d 1976); *b* 25 December 1940; *Educ* Aldenham, Harvard Univ; *m* 8 Aug 1964, Mary Theresa, da of Martin Cooke (d 1969), of Galway, Ireland; 2 s (Robert Richard Martin b 1964, Julian Alexander b 1968), 1 da (Caroline b 1971); *Career* various appts Unilever Ltd 1959–76, dir Carnation Foods 1977–80, md Vandemoortele 1980–86, chm Polar Entertainment Gp 1986–88, dir Keith Butters Ltd 1988–89, head of mktg Tate & Lyle Sugars 1989–96; behavioural conslt 1996–; memb Sugar Bureau Ctee 1991–96;

Advtg Assoc: memb Int Working Pty 1992–95, chm Food Advtg Ctee 1992–96 (memb 1991), chm Public Affrs Prog Gp 1993–95, memb Exec Ctee 1995–96; memb Cncl Coronary Prevention Gp; Co Donegal Historical Soc 2003–; memb: Int Soc of Genetic Genealogy 2007–, Irish Family Research 2007–, Scottish Genealogy Soc 2007–; Freeman: City of London 1984, Worshipful Co of Upholders 1984; MInstM 1978, FIMgt 1980, MInstD 1982; *Recreations* golf, reading, genealogy, horse racing; *Clubs* Carlton, Old Aldenhamians, Harvard Business Sch Club of London, The Sportsman; *Style*— R E Laird, Esq; ✉ Suite 262, 22 Notting Hill Gate, London W11 3JE (☎ 07973 262012, e-mail lboblaird@aol.com)

LAITY, Mark Franklyn; s of Frank Laity, of Cornwall, and Pamela, *née* Dunn; *b* 18 December 1955; *Educ* Redruth County GS, Univ of York (MA); *m* 6 Oct 1990 (m dis 2010), Sarah Lisa, da of Edward Thomas Parker-Gomm; *Career* trainee and reporter Western Mail 1978–81, news prodr BBC Radio Wales 1981–83; prodr BBC Radio 4: Today 1983–86, Analysis 1986–88; dep ed The World This Weekend Radio 4 1988–89, defence corr BBC 1989–2000; NATO: dep spokesman and special advsr to Sec Gen 2000–03, special advsr on strategic communications to Supreme Allied Cdr Europe (SACEUR) 2004–05, chief of public information Supreme HQ Allied Powers Europe (SHAPE) 2005–06, NATO spokesman Kabul 2006–07 and 2008, chief of strategic communications SHAPE 2007–; NATO Meritorious Service Medal; *Publications* Preventing War in Macedonia: Pre-Emptive Diplomacy for the 21st Century (2008), Strategy in NATO: Preparing for an Imperfect World (contrib, 2014); *Recreations* sailing, reading military and maritime history literature; *Clubs* RAF, Thames Sailing; *Style*— Mark Laity, Esq; ✉ SHAPE, B-7010, Belgium (☎ 00 32 475 777739, e-mail markflaity@hotmail.com or mark.laity@shape.nato.int)

LAKE, (Charles) Michael; CBE (1996); s of Stanley Giddy, and late Beryl, *née* Heath; step s of late Percival Redvers Lake; *b* 17 May 1946; *Educ* Humphry Davy GS Penzance, RMA Sandhurst; *m* 1970, Christine, *née* Warner; 3 da (Catherine b 26 Jan 1972, Anna b 25 Feb 1974, Victoria b 25 Oct 1978); *Career* cmmnd RCT 1965, various regtl appts in Germany, Hong Kong, NI and Oman 1965–77, attached Cmdt-Gen RM 1977–78, directing staff Staff Coll 1982–83, Cmd 1st Div Tport Regt 1983–86, Cdr Tport HQ British Forces Riyadh Gulf War 1990–91, Regtl Col Royal Logistic Corps 1992–96, ret 1997; DG Help the Aged 1996–; memb: Bd HelpAge Int 1996–2004, Cncl Occupational Pensions Advsy Serv 1997–2001, Benevolent and Strategy Ctee Royal Br Legion 1997–2005, Bd Network Housing Assoc 1999–2001, Cncl Disasters Emergency Ctee 1999–, Cncl Oxford Inst of Ageing 2000, Advsy Bd Oxford Centre for Population Ageing Univ of Oxford 2000–; lay memb Lord Chllr's Advsy Ctee on Conscientious Objectors 2002; vice-chair Air Ambulance Fndn (AAF) 2003–04, chm Br Gas Energy Tst 2004–; tstee: Disasters Emergency Ctee 1999–, Pensions Policy Inst 2001–; Chelsea Arts Club: dir and memb Bd 1997, currently chm Mgmnt Bd; Freeman City of London 1995, Liveryman Worshipful Co of Carmen 1995; FILog 1995; *Recreations* all sports, avid golfer, declining cricketer, rugby, post impressionist art; *Clubs* Sloane, Chelsea Arts, Fadeaways, Penguin Int Rugby, West Cornwall Golf, North Hants Golf, MCC; *Style*— Michael Lake, Esq, CBE; ✉ Help The Aged, 207–221 Pentonville Road, London N1 9UZ (☎ 020 7278 1114, fax 020 7239 1809)

LAKER, Dr Michael Francis (Mike); s of Sqdn Ldr Walter John Laker (d 2001), of Ledbury, and Joyce, *née* Ashill (d 2001); *b* 9 June 1945, Newport, Gwent; *Educ* Newport HS, Univ of London (MD, BS, Dip BioChemistry); *m* 13 Dec 1969, Alison Jean, da of Thomas Borland (d 1986), of Tunbridge Wells; 2 da (Hannah b 1974, Bethan b 1977), 2 s (Christopher b 1981, Jonathan b 1983); *Career* lectr in chemical pathology and metabolic disorders St Thomas' Hosp Med Sch 1973–80, res fell Dept of Med Univ of Calif San Diego 1979–80, sr lectr in clinical biochemistry and metabolic med Univ of Newcastle upon Tyne and conslt chemical pathologist Newcastle HA 1980–89, reader in clinical biochemistry and metabolic med Univ of Newcastle upon Tyne 1989–2006 (sub dean for admissions Med Sch 1990–98, lay memb Audit Ctee 2011–, memb Ct 2014–), conslt in clinical biochemistry Royal Victoria Infirmary and Associated Hosps NHS Tst 1989–2006, med dir Newcastle upon Tyne Hosps NHS Trust 1998–2006, med advsr N E Stretegic Health Authy 2006–10, non-exec dir City Hosps Sunderland 2014–; memb Ctee Br Hyperlipidaemia Assoc; FRCPath 1988; *Books* Short Cases in Clinical Biochemistry (1984), Cholesterol Lowering Trials – Advice for the British Physicians (1993), Clinical Biochemistry for Medical Students (1995), Multiple Choice Questions in Clinical Pathology (1995), Understanding Cholesterol (2003); *Recreations* music, gardening, golf; *Style*— Dr Mike Laker; ✉ 9 Campus Martius, Heddon-on-the-Wall, Northumberland NE15 0BP (e-mail mikelaker@btinternet.com)

LAKHANI, Prof Mayur Keshavji; CBE (2007); s of Keshavji V Lakhani (d 1989), and Shantaben K, *née* Moijaria (d 2002); *b* 20 April 1960, Uganda; *Educ* Univ of Dundee (MB ChB); *m* 3 July 1988, Mayuri M, *née* Jobanputra; 2 da (Sonam b 15 Feb 1991, Priyanka b 19 June 1992), 1 s (Rahul b 13 Feb 1995); *Career* princ in gen practice Highgate Medical Centre Loughborough 1991; visiting prof Dept of Health Sciences Univ of Leicester Medical Sch 2006; chm Nat Cncl for Palliative Care 2008–; co-clinical lead NHS East Midlands Next Stage Review 2007–08; chm: Editorial Steering Gp NHS Clinical Knowledge Summaries Service 2007, Dept of Health Inquiry into Access to Primary Care for Black and Minority Ethnic People 2007–08 (report published No Patient Left Behind 2008), Primary and Community Care External Working Gp CLIC-Sargeant 2008, Early Diagnosis of Cancer Sub-Ctee Nat Patient Safety Agency 2008; NHS GP appraiser; DFFP; FRCGP (MRCGP 1991, chm Cncl 2004–07, nationally elected memb Cncl 2008), FRCPEd, FRCP; *Publications* incl: A Celebration of General Practice (ed, 2003), Recent Advances in General Practice (jt ed, 2005), BMJ (contrib, 2006), Roadmap for General Practice (2007); articles on quality of care, health policy and on early diagnosis of cancer; *Recreations* tennis; *Style*— Prof Mayur Lakhani, CBE; ✉ Highgate Medical Centre, 5 Storer Close, Sileby, Loughborough LE12 7UD (☎ 01509 816364, fax 01509 815528, e-mail mklakhani@aol.com)

LAKIN, His Hon Peter Maurice; s of Ronald Maurice Lakin (d 1985), of Coventry, and Dorothy Kathleen, *née* Cowlishaw (d 2009); *b* 21 October 1949; *Educ* King Henry VIII GS Coventry, Univ of Manchester (LLB); *m* 11 Dec 1971, Jacqueline, da of John Alexander Jubb; 1 s (Michael John b 25 May 1975), 1 da (Emma Jane b 14 May 1977); *Career* asst slr Conn Goldberg Solicitors 1974–76 (articled clerk 1971–74), ptnr (i/c Forensic and Criminal Litigation) Pannone and Partners Solicitors 1976–95; recorder of the Crown Court 1993–95, circuit judge (Northern Circuit) 1995–2014, resident judge Minshull St Crown Court Manchester 2006–14; memb Law Soc 1974; *Recreations* fell walking, gardening, opera, grandchildren; *Style*— His Hon Peter Lakin; ✉ e-mail pmlakin@googlemail.com

LAL, Prof Deepak Kumar; s of Nand Lal (d 1984), of New Delhi, India, and Shanti, *née* Devi; *b* 3 January 1940; *Educ* Doon Sch Dehra Dun, Stephen's Coll Delhi (BA), Jesus Coll Oxford (MA, BPhil); *m* 11 Dec 1971, Barbara, da of Jack Ballis (d 1987), of New York, USA; 1 da (Deepika b 17 March 1980), 1 s (Akshay b 18 Aug 1981); *Career* Indian Foreign Serv 1963–65, lectr ChCh Oxford 1966–68, res fell Nuffield Coll Oxford 1968–70, reader political econ UCL 1979–84 (lectr 1970–79), prof of political econ Univ of London 1984–93 (emeritus 1993), James S Coleman prof of devpt studies UCLA 1990–2009 (emeritus prof 2010); conslt Indian Planning Cmmn 1973–74, res admin World Bank Washington DC 1983–87; conslt since 1970: ILO, UNCTAD, OECD, UNIDO, World Bank, Miny of Planning South Korea and Sri Lanka; co-dir: Trade Policy Unit Centre for Policy Studies London 1993–96, Trade and Devpt Unit Inst of Econ Affrs 1997–2002; hon prof Universidad Peruana de Ciencias Aplicades 2010, hon prof UPC Peru 2010, sr fell Cato Inst 2010–, distinguished fell Bharti Inst of Public Policy Indian Sch of Business 2015–; Wincott Meml Lecture 1989, Ohlin Meml Lecture 1995, Shenoy Meml Lecture 1996, Peking Univ Centennial Lecture 1998, Hal Clough Lecture 1998, Julian Simon Meml Lecture 2000, Sven Rydenfeldt Meml Lecture 2001, The Wendt Lecture 2002, The Snape Meml Lecture 2006, Fulvio Guerrine Lecture Turin 2010, Telders Lecture Utrecht 2010; pres Mont Pelerin Soc 2008–10; Int Freedom Award for Economics 2007; Dr (hc) Université Paul Cezanne Aix Marseille III 2009; *Books* Wells and Welfare (1972), Methods of Project Analysis (1974), Appraising Foreign Investment in Developing Countries (1975), Unemployment and Wage Inflation in Industrial Economies (1977), Men or Machines (1978), Prices for Planning (1980), The Poverty of Development Economics (1983, 3 edn 2002), Labour and Poverty in Kenya (with P Collier, 1986), Stagflation, Savings and the State (ed with M Wolf, 1986), The Hindu Equilibrium (1988 and 1989, revised and abridged edn 2005), Public Policy and Economic Development (ed with M Scott, 1990), Development Economics, 4 vols (ed 1992), The Repressed Economy (1993), Against Dirigisme (1994), The Political Economy of Poverty, Equity and Growth (with H Myint, 1996), Unintended Consequences (1998), Unfinished Business (1999), Trade, Development and Political Economy (ed with R Snape, 2001), In Praise of Empires (2004), Reviving the Invisible Hand (2006), Lost Causes (2012), Poverty and Progress (2013); *Recreations* opera, theatre, golf; *Clubs* Reform; *Style*— Prof Deepak Lal; ✉ 2 Erskine Hill, London NW11 6HB (☎ 020 8458 0333, mobile 07981 961815, website www.econ.ucla.edu/lal); A 30 Nizamuddin West, New Delhi 110013, India (☎ 00 9111 4607 5900); 8283 Bunche Hall, UCLA, 405 Hilgard Avenue, Los Angeles, CA 90095, USA (☎ 00 1 310 825 1011, fax 00 1 310 825 9528, e-mail dlal@ucla.edu)

LALLA-MAHARAJH, Julia; OBE (2016); *b* 25 February 1970, London; *Educ* James Allen's Girls' Sch, Thames Valley Univ; *Career* London First 1995–99 (dir of transport) 2001–06; Bass plc 1999–2001, volunteer VSO Cambodia 2007 and Ethiopia 2008, fndr and ceo Orchid Project; winner Davos Debates 2010; winner Social Change Awards, Influencer of the Year 2011, listed in Directory of Social Change, honoured by HM The Queen as Woman Agent of Change 2011, listed in Evening Standard Power 1000 (London's most influential people) 2013, 2014 and 2015; *Style*— Ms Julia Lalla-Maharajh, OBE; ✉ Orchid Project, The Foundry, 17–19 Oval Way London SE11 5RR (website www.orchidproject.org, Twitter @OrchidProject)

LAMB, Dr Andrew Martin; s of late Harry Lamb, and late Winifred, *née* Emmott; *b* 23 September 1942; *Educ* Werneth Sch Oldham, Manchester Grammar, CCC Oxford (MA, DLitt); *m* 1 April 1970, Wendy Ann, da of Frank Edward Davies (decd); 1 s (Richard Andrew b 1976), 2 da (Helen Margaret b 1972, Susan Elizabeth b 1973); *Career* investment mangr then asst gen mangr MGM Assurance 1976–88, chief investment mangr Friends Provident Life Office 1988–98, dir (operational projects) Friends Ivory & Sime plc 1998–2000; music historian; FIA 1972; *Books* Jerome Kern in Edwardian London (1985), Gänzl's Book of the Musical Theatre (with Kurt Gänzl, 1988), Light Music from Austria (1992), Skaters' Waltz: The Story of the Waldteufels (1995), An Offenbach Family Album (1997), Shirley House to Trinity School (1999), 150 Years of Popular Musical Theatre (2000), Leslie Stuart – Composer of Florodora (2002), Leslie Stuart's My Bohemian Life (ed, 2003), Fragson: The Triumphs and the Tragedy (with Julian Myerscough, 2004), The Merry Widow at 100 (2005), A Life on the Ocean Wave: The Story of Henry Russell (2007), William Vincent Wallace: Composer, Virtuoso and Adventurer (2012); contrib to: Gramophone, Opera, The New Grove Dictionary of Music & Musicians, The Oxford Dictionary of National Biography; *Recreations* cricket, music, family; *Clubs* Lancashire CCC; *Style*— Dr Andrew Lamb; ✉ 1 Squirrel Wood, West Byfleet, Surrey KT14 6PE (☎ 01932 342566, e-mail fullerswood@gmail.com)

LAMB, Dave; s of Jim Lamb (d 2009), and Shirley, *née* Hopson; *b* 17 January 1969, London; *Educ* Univ of Warwick (BA); *m* July 2004, Nicola Frances, *née* Dowbiggin; 1 da (Betty Rose b June 2008); *Career* comic actor, writer and voice over artist; founding dr Top Dog Prodns; *Film* Hunting the Beast 2005, Send in the Clowns 2006; writer: Hung, Drawn and Slaughtered 2013, Spanish Rock 2013; *Theatre* Caught in the Net (Vaudeville Theatre) 2002, Finding Bin Laden (Gilded Balloon) 2003; *Television* Goodness Gracious Me 1997–2001, Armstrong & Miller 1997–2001, People Like Us 1997, Barking 1998, How Do You Want Me? 1998–99, Hippies 1999, Dark Ages 1999, Rhona 2000, 2DTV 2001–05, Dr Terrible's House of Horrible 2001, Fun At The Funeral Parlour 2001, We Know Where You Live 2001, My Parents Are Aliens 2003 and 2005, French and Saunders 2004, Eastenders 2004, Doc Martin 2004, Comedy Connections 2005, Bromwell High 2005, The Smoking Room 2005, Broken News 2005, The Late Edition 2006, City Lights 2007, Grownups 2007, The Life and Times of Vivienne Vyle 2007, Catwalk Dogs 2007, Moving Wallpaper 2008–09, Miranda 2009, Coming of Age 2009, The Zoo Factor 2010–, Reggie Perrin 2010, Sports Mash 2010, Rock and Chips 2010–11, Alexander Armstrong's Big Ask 2011, Horrible Histories Gory Games 2011–, Bleak Old Shop of Stuff 2012; writer: Spitting Image 1996, The Russ Abbot Show 1996, Oddballs 1996, Saturday Live 1996, The Cheese Shop 1996–97, The End of the Year Show 1997, The Jack Docherty Show 1997–98, Barking 1998, The Outlaw 1998, Terry and John 1999, 2DTV 2001–05, Live with Christian O'Connell 2003; voice overs: Come Dine With Me 2004–, Those TV Times 2009, Big Barn Farm 2010–; *Radio* Weekending 1994–97, The Game's Up 1995–96, You Cannot Be Serious 1995–97, The Cheeseshop 1997–2000, The Alan Davies Show 1997–98, Rent 1997–98, The Way It Is 1997–2002, Another Case of Milton Jones 1998–99, The Dominic Holland Show 2000, The Bigger Issues 2000–03, At Home with the Snails 2001–02, Whole Nother Story 2001–03, The Hudson & Pepperdine Show 2001–05, All The Young Dudes 2002, Artists 2003, Double Income No Kids Yet 2003, Wild Things 2003, Baggy Trousers 2003, London Europe 2003–04, The Rapid Eye Movement 2004, Fifteen Minute Musical 2004–, The Very World of Milton Jones 2005–, Be Prepared 2005, Bearded Ladies 2005, Life In London 2006–, Vent 2006–, Look Away Now 2007–, Elvenquest 2009–, The Music Teacher 2010–, Revenge of the First King of Mars 2010, Dave Against the Machine 2011, Stormchasers 2012; writer: Weekending 1994–97, News Huddlines 1994–98, The Game's Up 1995–96, You Cannot Be Serious 1995–97 (Radio Light Entertainment Peter Titheridge Award 1996–97), The Cheeseshop 1997–2000, The Way It Is 1997–2002, The Bigger Issues 2000–03, London Europe 2003–04, Look Away Now 2007–11, Dave Against the Machine 2011, Hobby Bobbies 2013–; prodr/dir Mission Improbable 2012–; *Clubs* Groucho, Century; *Style*— Dave Lamb, Esq; ✉ c/o Joe Hutton, BWH, Fifth Floor, 35 Soho Square, London W1D 3QX (☎ 020 7734 0657)

LAMB, Elspeth; da of John Cunningham Lamb (d 1961), and Margaret Paterson Lyon (d 1988); *b* 28 March 1951; *Educ* Glasgow Sch of Art, Manchester Poly (post grad in printmaking), Ruskin Sch of Drawing Oxford; *Partner* Malcolm Gray; *Career* lectr in etching Glasgow Sch of Art 1975–76, lectr Printmaking, Drawing and Painting Dept Edinburgh Coll of Art 1978– (actg head of dept 1995–99); visiting lectr: Glasgow Sch of Art 1988, 1991, 1993, 1994 and 1995, Univ of Ulster 1991, 1993, 1994 and 1996, Grays Sch of Art Aberdeen 1991, Univ of Newcastle 1991 and 1992, Queens Univ Kingston Ontario 1992, Canberra Sch of Art Aust 1993, Monash Univ Gippsland Aust 1993, Ballarat Univ Art Sch Victoria Aust 1993, Slade Sch of Art UCL 1994, The Joan Miro Fndn Spain 1994, 1996 and 1997, Hornsea Sch of Art Middx Univ 1995 and 1996; artist in res: Grafikan Paja Jyvaskyla Finland 1991, Open Studio Toronto 1992, Canberra Sch of Art 1993, Malasplna Printmakers Vancouver 1995; fndr Bon a Tirer Editions (first ind lithography workshop in Scotland) 1986; appeared various arts progs television and radio, subject of various jl and newspaper articles; memb Visual Arts Awards Panel

Scottish Arts Cncl 1994–; ARSA 1991, RGI 1992; *Solo Exhibitions* Glasgow Sch of Art 1974, Univ of Glasgow 1975, Glasgow Print Studio Gallery 1986, Taller Galeria Fort (Spain) 1986, Int Festival Exhbn Scottish Gallery (Edinburgh) 1987, Mercury Gallery (London) 1988 and 1990, Touchstones (City of Culture exhbn Glasgow Print Studio) 1990, Edinburgh Printmakers Gallery 1990, Cornerstones (Mayfest exhbn Compass Gallery Glasgow) 1992, Edinburgh Coll of Art Int Festival 1992, Electra Fine Art Gallery (Toronto) 1992 and 1995, Foyer Gallery (Canberra Sch of Art) 1993, Malaspina Gallery (Vancouver) 1995; *Group Exhibitions* incl: Glasgow Print Studio Gallery 1981, Corners Gallery (Glasgow) 1983, Grease and Water (Arts Cncl tour) 1983, Etching (Ats Cncl tour) 1983, New Scottish Prints (NY and tour of N America) 1983, Wenniger Gallery (Boston) 1984, Print Exhibition (Cadaques Spain) 1984, Printmakers Drawings (Mercury Gallery Edinburgh) 1987, Ravensdale Gallery (London) 1987, New Scottish Art (Turberville-Smith London) 1987, Culture City Prints (Amsterdam) 1987, The Lillie Art Gallery (Glasgow) 1987, With an Eye to the East (Scottish Arts Cncl travelling gallery) 1989, Critic's Choice (Bohun Gallery London) 1989, Grafika Creativa (Aalto Museum Jyvaskyla Finland) 1990, Union of Artists Gallery (Red Square Moscow) 1991, Henry Moore Gallery (RCA) 1991, Xian Acad of Fine Arts (China) 1994, Celtic Connections (Glasgow) 1995, Exhibition Costillo de Soutomaior (Pontevedra Spain) 1995, Brought to Book (Collins Gallery Glasgow) 1995, Scottish Art Gallery Shek-O (Hong Kong) 1996, Otra Vez Gallery (LA) 1996; Int Print Biennales: Ljubljana 1985, Bradford 1985 and 1990, Berlin 1987, Varna Bulgaria 1989, Kochi-Chi Japan 1990, Kanagawa Japan 1990, Cracow 1991 and 1994, La Louviere Belgium 1992, Katowice Poland 1992 and 1994, Beograd 1997, Portland USA 1997; various art fairs 1981–; *Work in Public Collections* Br Cncl London, Japanese Consular Collection London, Scottish Arts Cncl, BBC, Glasgow Museums and Art Galleries Kelvingrove, Leeds Art Galleries, Inverness Art Galleries, The Arts in Fife, City Arts Centre Edinburgh, Perth Art Galleries and Museums; *Awards* RSA Meyer Oppenheim Award 1973, Scottish Young Contemporaries Prize 1973, Scottish Arts Cncl Award 1975 and 1979, SSA Educational Inst of Scotland Award 1983, Mini-print Int Prize Spain 1983, Edinburgh Coll of Art res bursary (to study at Tamarind Inst of Lithography Univ of New Mexico) 1985, Scottish Print Open IV Rives Arches Mill Award 1987, RSA W&J Burness Award 1989, Hope Scott Tst Award 1989, 1992 and 1995, Lady Artists Club Tst Award 1989, Scottish Arts Cncl bursary (for USA project) 1989, Int Print Biennale Gerhardt & Leimar Award Bradford 1990, RGI Bank of Scotland Award 1990, Scotland on Sunday Paper Boat Award (for Cornerstones exhbn Glasgow Mayfest) 1992, RSA Satire Soc Award 1993, RSA Gillies Award (to study in New Mexico) 1995, Portland Museum Oregon Int Print Exhbn Purchase Award 1997; The Best of British Women (1995), Best of Printmaking (1997); various edns of lithographs; *Recreations* travel, hill walking, swimming, badminton, aerobics; *Clubs* Western Baths (Glasgow); *Style*— Ms Elspeth Lamb; ✉ Bon a Tirer Editions, 15 East Campbell Street, Glasgow G1 1DG (☎ 0141 552 7250)

LAMB, Harriet; CBE (2006); da of late Gilbert Lamb, and Sarah, *née* Tennyson d'Eyncourt; *Educ* Trinity Hall Cambridge (BA), Inst of Devpt Studies Univ of Sussex (MPhil); *Partner* Steve Percy; 1 da (Neena b 28 Feb 1992), 1 s (Oscar b 26 July 1996); *Career* Northern Region Low Pay Unit 1987–90, NE Refuge Service 1990–92, World Devpt Movement 1993–99, Fairtrade Labelling Orgns Int 1999–2001, exec dir Fairtrade Fndn 2001–12, ceo Fairtrade Int 2012–; Cosmopolitan Magazine Ultimate Eco-Queen 2007, Outstanding Woman in Business Nat Business Award 2008; *Books* Fighting The Banana Wars and other Fairtrade Battles (2008); *Recreations* cycling, gardening; *Style*— Ms Harriet Lamb, CBE; ✉ The Fairtrade Foundation, 3rd Floor, Ibex House, 42–47 Minories, London EC3N 1DY

LAMB, John Tregea; s of late Roger Craven Lamb, of Scaynes Hill, W Sussex, and Katherine Honor Lamb; *b* 1 August 1952; *Educ* Felsted, Poly of N London (BA); *Children* 2 da (Mary Jane b 14 March 1973, Naomi b 26 Oct 1987), 2 s (Jamie b 25 Nov 1974, Max b 4 April 1984); *Career* trainee exec Richmond Towers PR 1970–71, trainee reporter Camberley News Surrey 1971–73, sub ed National Newsagent 1976–77, reporter Computing magazine 1977–78, news ed Computer Talk 1978–80, freelance journalist covering computer and electronics field 1980–88, ed Computer Weekly 1988–96, ed Computer Age supplement Sunday Business 1996, ed-in-chief Information Week 1998–99, ed Butler Gp Review 2002–04, ed IT Strategy, ed Information Economics Jl 2003–04, publisher Ability magazine 2004; dir IT Media Conferences 1999; Liveryman Worshipful Co of Info Technologists; MBCS; *Recreations* gardening, sailing; *Style*— John Lamb, Esq; ✉ Pellingbrook, Lewes Road, Scaynes Hill, Haywards Heath, West Sussex RH17 7NG

LAMB, Martin James; s of Dr Trevor A J Lamb, of Knowle, W Midlands, and Shirley, *née* Hubbard; *b* 7 January 1960, Leeds; *Educ* Bradford GS, Solihull Sixth Form Coll, Imperial Coll London (BSc), Cranfield Business Sch (MBA); *m* 13 Aug 1983, Jayne Louise, *née* Bodenham; 4 da (Charlotte b 13 Dec 1989, Rebecca b 15 Aug 1991, Georgia b 23 Feb 1994, Victoria b 29 April 1996); *Career* grad trainee IMI Cornelius Inc USA 1982–83, project engr IMI Air Conditioning UK 1983–85, R&D mangr Coldflow Ltd 1985–87, md IMI Cornelius (UK) Ltd 1991–96 (mktg dir 1987–91), chief exec IMI plc 2001– (exec dir 1996–2000); non-exec dir: Spectris plc 1999–2006, Severn Trent plc 2008–, Mercia Technols plc 2015–; chm: Evoque Water Technologies LLC 2014–, Rotork plc 2015– (non-exec dir 2014); tstee City Technol Coll Birmingham 1997–2008; Hon Dr Univ of Central Eng 2006; CCMI 2002; *Recreations* family, tennis, golf; *Style*— Martin Lamb, Esq; ☎ 07714 836094, e-mail martin@mjlamb.org

LAMB, Prof Michael Ernest de Lestang; s of Francis B W Lamb (d 1979), and M M Michelle, *née* Nageon de Lestang; *b* 22 October 1953, Lusaka, Zambia; *Educ* Univ of Natal Durban (BA), Johns Hopkins Univ (MA), Yale Univ (MPhil, MS, PhD); *m* 22 Oct 2005, Hilary S Clark; 3 s (Damon b 8 April 1982, Darryn b 21 Aug 1986, Philip b 12 Aug 1996), 1 da (Jeanette b 13 May 1992), 4 step da (Aya b 10 Oct 1982, Amy b 21 May 1990, Kate b 9 Nov 1992, Lily b 23 Sept 1995); *Career* Univ of Wisconsin 1976–78, Univ of Michigan 1978–80, Univ of Utah 1980–87, Nat Inst of Child Health and Human Devpt 1987–2004, Univ of Cambridge 2004– (dir of studies in psychology Sydney Sussex Coll 2012–); memb ESRC 2006–11 (chair Int Advsy Ctee 2007–11, memb Audit Ctee 2006–11), memb Sub-Panel 4 (Psychology, Psychiatry and Neuroscience) Research Excellence Framework 2014 HEFCE 2011–14, pres Div 7 (Developmental Psychology) American Psychological Assoc (APA) 2017–18; memb Panel Scottish Child Abuse Inquiry 2015–19; tstee Fatherhood Inst 2005–09; Young Psychologist Award American Psychological Assoc 1976, Boyd McCandless Young Scientist Award 1978, Univ of Utah Superior Res Award 1985, Univ of Utah Distinguished Res Award 1986, Hammer Award US Govt 1998, Cattell Award for Lifetime Achievement and Contributions American Psychological Soc/Assoc for Psychological Science 2003–04, Distinguished Scientific Contributions Award American Psychology-Law Soc 2013, G Stanley Hall Award for Lifetime Contribution to Developmental Psychology APA 2014, Distinguished Scientific Award for Lifetime Contributions to Psychology in the Public Interest APA 2015, Distinguished Scientific Award for Lifetime Contributions to the Application of Psychology APA 2015; PhD (hc) Univ of Goteburg Sweden 1995, DCL (hc) UEA 2006, PhD (hc) Univ of Abertay 2015; fell Assoc for Psychological Science, memb Soc for Res in Child Devpt; fell Sidney Sussex Coll Cambridge 2008; FAcSS 2014; *Books* The Role of the Father in Child Development (ed, 1976, 5 edn 2010), Social and Personality Development (ed, 1978), Social Interaction Analysis: Methodological Issues (co-ed, 1979), Advances in Developmental Psychology, (co-ed, Vol 1 1981, Vol 2 1982, Vol 3 1983, Vol 4 1986), Infant Social Cognition: Empirical and Theoretical Considerations (co-ed, 1981), Child Psychology Today (jtly, 1982, 2 edn 1986), Development in Infancy: An Introduction (jtly, 1982, 4 edn 2002), Socialization and Personality Development (jtly, 1982), Non-Traditional Families (ed, 1982), Sibling Relationships: Their Development and Significance Across the Lifespan (co-ed, 1982), Fatherhood and Family Policy (co-ed, 1983), Developmental Psychology: An Advanced Textbook (co-ed, 1984, 7 edn 2015), Infant-Mother Attachment (jtly, 1985), Adolescent Fatherhood (co-ed, 1986), The Father's Role: Applied Perspectives (ed, 1986), The Father's Role: Cross-Cultural Perspectives (ed, 1987), Infant Development: Perspectives from German-Speaking Countries (co-ed, 1991), Child-Care in Context: Cross-Cultural Perspectives (co-ed, 1992), Adolescent Problem Behavior: Issues and Research (co-ed, 1994), Images of Childhood (co-ed, 1996), Investigative Interviews with Children: A Guide for Helping Professionals (jtly, 1998), Parenting and Child Development in 'Nontraditional' Families (ed, 1999), Conceptualizing and Measuring Father Involvement (co-ed, 2004), Hunter-Gatherer Childhoods: Evolutionary Developmental and Cultural Perspectives (co-ed, 2005), Child Sexual Abuse: Disclosure, Delay and Denial (co-ed, 2007), Tell me what happened: Structured investigative interviews of child victims and witnesses (jtly, 2008), Handbook of Lifespan Development: social and personality development (co-ed, 2010), The Role of the Father in Child Development (ed, 2010), Children's Testimony (co-ed, 2011), Children and Cross-Examination: Time to Change the Rules? (co-ed, 2012), Development in Infancy (jtly, 2013), Fathers in Cultural Context (jtly, 2013); Handbook of child psychology and developmental science (co-ed, 2015); also author of several hundred articles in learned jls; jl ed Psychology, Public Policy and Law 2013–18; *Style*— Prof Michael Lamb; ✉ Department of Psychology, University of Cambridge, Free School Lane, Cambridge CB2 3RQ (☎ 01223 334523, fax 01223 334550, e-mail mel37@cam.ac.uk)

LAMB, Rt Hon Norman Peter; MP; s of Hubert Horace Lamb (d 1997), of Holt, Norfolk, and Beatrice Moira, *née* Milligan; *b* 16 September 1957; *Educ* Univ of Leicester (LLB); *m* 14 July 1984, Mary Elizabeth Lamb; 2 s (Archie b 9 Feb 1988, Edward b 30 May 1991); *Career* trainee slr then sr asst slr Norwich CC 1982–86, slr then ptnr Steele & Co Slrs 1986–2001; cncllr Norwich CC 1987–91; MP (Lib Dem) Norfolk N 2001–; dep spokesman for int devpt 2001–03, memb Treasy Select Ctee 2003–05, Lib Dem shadow spokesman for Trade and Industry 2005–06, chief of staff to Sir Menzies Campbell 2006, Lib Dem shadow sec of state for Health 2006–10, asst whip 2010–12, chief Parly and political advsr to Dep PM 2010–12, Parly under sec for employment relations, consumer and postal affrs Dept for Business, Innovation and Skills 2012, min for care and support Dept of Health 2012–15; visiting fell Nuffield Coll Oxford 2014–; *Publications* Remedies in the Employment Tribunal (1998); *Recreations* art, cycling, Norwich City FC; *Style*— The Rt Hon Norman Lamb, MP; ✉ House of Commons, London SW1A 0AA (☎ 020 7219 0542, e-mail norman.lamb.mp@parliament.uk)

LAMB, Hon Timothy Michael (Tim); 2 s of 2 Baron Rochester, and late Mary *née* Wheeler; *b* 24 March 1953, Hartford, Cheshire; *Educ* Shrewsbury, The Queen's Coll Oxford (MA); *m* 23 Sept 1978, Denise Ann, da of John Buckley, of Frinton-on-Sea, Essex; 1 da (Sophie b 15 Sept 1983), 1 s (Nicholas b 9 Nov 1985); *Career* professional cricketer with: Middlesex CCC 1974–77, Northants County Cricket Club 1978–83; sec/gen mangr Middlesex CCC 1984–88; ECB (formerly TCCB): cricket sec 1988–96, chief exec 1996–2004; chief exec Sport and Recreation Alliance (formerly CCPR) 2005–14, dir TML Sports Connections Ltd 2014–; memb Sport Honours Ctee Cabinet Office 2011–; *Recreations* golf, travel, watching sport, walking; *Clubs* hon life memb: MCC, Middx CCC, Northants CCC, Durham CCC; *Style*— The Hon Tim Lamb

LAMB, His Hon Judge Timothy Robert; QC (1995); s of Stephen Falcon Lamb (d 1992), and Pamela Elizabeth, *née* Coombes (d 2010); *b* 27 November 1951, Brentwood, Essex; *Educ* Brentwood Sch, Lincoln Coll Oxford (MA); *m* 1978, Judith Anne, da of Francis Ryan; 1 s (Jonathan Francis b 31 Aug 1981), 1 da (Victoria Josephine b 8 Aug 1983); *Career* called to the Bar Gray's Inn 1974 (bencher 2003); recorder 2000–08, jt head of chambers 3 Paper Bldgs Temple 2004–08, circuit judge 2008–; memb Law Reform Ctee Bar Cncl 2005–08, memb Lord Chancellor's North and East London Magistrates' Advsy Ctee 2012–; memb: LCLCBA, TECBAR, PIBA; *Recreations* family, travel, watersports; *Style*— His Hon Judge Timothy Lamb, QC; ✉ Kingston Crown Court, 6–8 Penrhyn Rd, Kingston-upon-Thames, Surrey KT1 2BB; County Court at Central London, Royal Courts of Justice, Thomas More Building, Strand, London WC2A 2LL

LAMB, Dr Trevor Arthur John; s of Arthur Bradshaw Lamb, and Ruth Ellen, *née* Eales; *b* 7 December 1929; *Educ* Wanstead GS, QMC London (BSc, PhD); *m* 1952, Shirley Isabel, da of Sidney Charles Hubbard (d 1971); 2 s (John b 1957, Martin b 1960), 2 da (Susan b 1960, Karen b 1964); *Career* pt/t lectr Univ of London 1950–52, section ldr Bristol Aeroplane Co Engine Div 1952–56, section head (engrg res) Imperial Chemical Industries 1956–58, factory mangr then gen mangr Leeds Plant Marston Excelsior Ltd (subsid of ICI Metals Div, became Imperial Metal Industries Ltd, styled IMI Ltd) 1958–62, md then exec chm Radiator Gp IMI Ltd 1962–74; IMI plc: main bd dir of overseas and mktg 1974–87, exec chm Australasian, Refinery and Fabrication Gps 1974–77, exec chm Valve Gp 1977–89, exec chm Fluid Power Gp 1981–91, conslt 1992–94; non-exec dir: W Canning plc 1980–96, Richard Burbidge Ltd 1992–96; business conslt 1992–; govr The City Technol Coll Kingshurst 1989–93; Eur Ing, CEng, FIMechE; *Recreations* music, golf, tennis, swimming; *Style*— Dr Trevor Lamb; ✉ Heronbrook House, 75 Bakers Lane, Knowle, Warwickshire B93 8PW (☎ 01564 773877, fax 01564 779428, e-mail drtrevorlamb@aol.com)

LAMBERT, Air Cdre Andrew; s of Maj N L Lambert; *b* 12 October 1948, Salisbury, Wilts; *Educ* Wellington, RAF Coll Cranwell, Univ of Cambridge (MPhil); *m* 8 March 1975, Prudence Tonkin; 1 s, 1 da; *Career* flying trg as navigator, completed tours 54(F), 31 and 23(F) Sqdns, memb Weapons Instr Staff Phantom Operational Conversion Unit 1979, promoted Sqdn Ldr 1981, Weapons Ldr 23 Sqdn 1981, Flight Cdr 23 Sqdn Falkland Islands 1983, cmd Phantom Weapons Instr Sch 1983–85, RAF Staff Coll 1986, promoted Wing Cdr 1988, posted Plans Branch HQ Strike Command 1988, Sqdn Cdr 23 Sqdn 1991–93 (cmd Operation Deny Flight Bosnia), Dir of Defence Studies RAF 1995–97, Air Cdr and COS Br Forces Falkland Islands 1997–98, Cdr Br Forces Op Warden 1999, Dep Cdr CAOC3 Reitan 2000–01, Asst Cmdt (Air) Jt Services Command and Staff Coll 2001–03; lectr and advsr on coercive techniques, published several monographs, guest lectr in cruise ships; RAF advsr and dir UKNDA; Nicolson Trophy for Best Qualified Weapons Instr 1978, Wilkinson Battle of Britain Meml Sword, QCVSA; fell commoner Downing Coll Cambridge; MRIN, MRUSI; *Recreations* sailing, sub aqua diving, ancient history; *Style*— Air Commodore Andrew Lambert; ✉ c/o RAF Club, 128 Piccadilly, London W1J 7PY; ☎ and fax 01363 83150, e-mail andrewlambert99@hotmail.com

LAMBERT, Prof Andrew David; s of David George Lambert, of Beetley, Norfolk, and Nola, *née* Burton; *b* 31 December 1956; *Educ* Hamond's Sch Swaffham, City of London Poly (BA), King's Coll London (MA, PhD); *m* 27 Nov 1987, Zohra, da of Mokhtar Bouznat, of Casablanca, Morocco; 1 da (Tama-Sophie b 29 May 1990); *Career* lectr modern int history Bristol Poly 1983–87, conslt Dept of History and Int Affrs RNC Greenwich 1987–89, sr lectr in war studies RMA Sandhurst 1989–91; KCL: lectr 1991–96, sr lectr in war studies 1996–99, prof of naval history 1999–2001, Laughton Prof of naval history 2001–; hon sec Soc Navy Records 1996–2005; writer and presenter War at Sea (BBC 2) 2004; FRHistS 1990; *Books* Battleships in Transition: The Creation of the Steam Battlefleet 1815–1860 (1984), The Crimean War: British Grand Strategy Against Russia 1853–56 (1990), The Last Sailing Battlefleet: Maintaining Naval Mastery 1815–1850 (1991), The Foundations of Naval History (1998), War at Sea in the Age of Sail (2000), Nelson: Britannia's God of War (2004), Admirals (2008), Franklin: Tragic Hero of Polar Navigation (2009), The Challenge: Britain Against America in the Naval War of 1812 (2012); *Recreations* running; *Style*— Prof Andrew Lambert; ✉ Department of War Studies, King's College London, Strand, London WC2R 2LS (☎ 020 7848 2179, fax 020 7848 2026, e-mail andrew.lambert@kcl.ac.uk)

LAMBERT, Eva Margaret; MBE (2016); da of Frank Holroyd (d 1978), and Elsie Irene, *née* Fearnley (d 2010); *b* 17 September 1946; *Educ* Elland GS; *m* 1; 1 s (Terry Graham b 16 Dec 1966), 1 da (Justine Louise b 30 July 1968); m 2, 17 April 1982, Robert Stephen Lambert, s of Robert Lambert; 1 da (Jemma Louise b 13 April 1983); *Career* NHS: health service administrator 1973–83, fin accountant 1983–85, mgmnt accountant 1985–86, dep fin mangr 1986–90, dep unit gen mangr 1990–91, divnl gen mangr 1991–92, chief exec Huddersfield NHS Tst 1992–97, ret; ind conslt Freshstart Consulting 1997–, chief exec Pennell Initiative for Women's Health 1999–2004; co sec R Lambert Transport Ltd; vice-chair Huddersfield Mencap 2007–08 (chair 2005–07), tstee Kirklees Active Leisure Tst 2002–07, govr Greenhead Coll Huddersfield (vice chair of govrs 2008–10, chair of govrs 2010–15); FIMgt, AAT 1982, FCCA 1993 (ACCA 1987), FRSA 2002; *Recreations* tennis, golf, handicrafts; *Clubs* Huddersfield Lawn Tennis and Squash; *Style*— Mrs Eva Lambert, MBE; ✉ 206a Laund Road, Salendine Nook, Huddersfield, West Yorkshire HD3 3UD (☎ 01484 340049, mobile 07920 841147, e-mail eva17lambert@hotmail.co.uk)

LAMBERT, Jean; MEP; da of Frederick Archer, and Margaret, *née* McDougall; *b* 1 June 1950; *Educ* Palmer's Girls GS, St Paul's Coll Cheltenham, Univ Coll Cardiff (BA), (PGCE, ADB Ed); *m* 1977, Stephen Lambert; 1 s, 1 da; *Career* secdy sch teacher 1972–89, pt/t teacher 1992–99; Green Pty: memb 1977–, princ speaker 1984 and 1998–99, political liaison with Green Gp in Euro Parl 1989–92, chair Pty Exec 1994; MEP (Green) London 1999–, vice-pres Green/EFA Gp 2001–06, memb European Parl Ctee on Employment and Social Affrs, memb EP Delgn to India and SAARC; memb: Charter 88, Waltham Forest Race Equality Cncl, Cncl Liberty, Mgmnt Ctee Make Votes Count; patron East London Out Project; *Publications* No Change? No Chance! Green Politics Explained (1997), Research into Women and Decision-Making in EP Green Parties (1995); *Recreations* dancing, detective fiction; *Style*— Mrs Jean Lambert, MEP; ✉ Green MEP Office, Suite 58, The Hop Exchange, 24 Southwark Street, London SE1 1TY (☎ 020 7407 6269, fax 020 7234 0183, e-mail jeanlambert@greenmeps.org.uk)

LAMBERT, Nigel Robert Woolf; QC (1999); s of Dr E Vivian Lambert, MB, BS, MRCS, LRCP (d 1970), and Sadie, *née* Woolf (d 1966); *b* 5 August 1949; *Educ* Cokethorpe Sch Oxford, Coll of Law; *m* 1975, Roamie Elisabeth, da of late Philip Sado, and Mrs Renée Sado; 1 s (David Vivian Robin b 11 Dec 1978), 1 da (Talia Susanna b 15 April 1981); *Career* called to the Bar Grays Inn 1974 (bencher 2003), add eundem memb Inner Temple 1986; recorder 1996– (asst recorder 1993–96), dep head of chambers 2004–09, head of chambers 2009–14; memb: Bar Cncl 1993–2000, Professional Standards Ctee 1993–95 and 1997–99, Public Affairs Ctee 1994, Fin Ctee 1994, Legal Aid and Fees Ctee 1996, South Eastern Circuit Ctee 1992–, Criminal Bar Assoc Ctee 1993–2000, Criminal Bar Assoc, Justice, South Eastern Circuit Exec Ctee 2001–07, Inner Temple Bar Liaison Ctee 2002–03, Inner Temple Circuit Ctee 2002–03; chm: North London Bar Mess 2001–07 (jr 1992–99), South Eastern Circuit/Inst of Barristers' Clerks Ctee 2001–07; govr Cokethorpe Sch 1971–78, life vice-pres Cokethorpe Old Boys' Assoc; *Recreations* supervising, organising, gossiping; *Clubs* Garrick, MCC; *Style*— Nigel Lambert, Esq, QC; ✉ Carmelite Chambers, 9 Carmelite Street, London EC4Y 0DR (☎ 020 7936 6300, e-mail nlambertqc@carmelitechambers.co.uk)

LAMBERT, Stephen; s of Roger Lambert, of London, and Monika, *née* Wagner; *b* 22 March 1959; *Educ* Thames Valley GS, UEA, Univ of Oxford; *m* 8 April 1988, Jenni, da of Martin Russell, of South Africa; 1 da (Jessica b 1988), 1 s (Harry b 1992); *Career* BBC TV: joined 1983, Documentary Dept prodr/dir 40 Minutes 1987–90 and Inside Story 1991–92, series prodr/dir True Brits 1994, exec prodr BBC1 and BBC2 series 1996–99, series ed Modern Times (BBC2) 1994–98; RDF Media: dir of progs 1998–2005, chief creative offr 2005–07; chief exec Studio Lambert 2008–; ed Real Life (ITV) 1999–2001; Commissioning Ed of the Year Broadcast Prodn Awards 1997; memb BAFTA; FRSA; *Books* Channel Four (1982); *Recreations* sailing, skiing; *Style*— Stephen Lambert, Esq; ✉ e-mail stephen.lambert@studiolambert.com

LAMBERTS, Prof Koen; *Career* lectr Univ of Birmingham 1992; Univ of Warwick 2000–13: faculty chair for science, pro-vice-chllr for research (Science and Medicine), dep vice-chllr, provost; vice-chllr Univ of York 2014–; *Style*— Prof Koen Lamberts; ✉ University of York, York YO10 5DD

LAMBERTY, Mark Julian Harker; s of Dr G B Lamberty (d 1982), of Rossendale, Lancs, and Dr D S Lamberty; *b* 17 August 1947; *Educ* Rugby, Keble Coll Oxford (MA), Univ of Oxford (postgrad BCL); *m* 17 Aug 1991, Pamela Jean Wilson; *Career* called to the Bar Gray's Inn 1970; practising barr specialising in serious crime; former head of chambers; *Recreations* cricket; *Clubs* Norden Cricket (tstee); *Style*— Mark Lamberty, Esq; ✉ St Johns Buildings, 24a-28 St John Street, Manchester M3 4DJ

LAMBIE, James (Jim); s of Robert Lambie, and Cecilia, *née* Blair; *b* 28 April 1964, Bellshill, N Lanarkshire; *Educ* Glasgow Sch of Art (BA); *Family* 1 c (Van); *Career* installation artist; Paul Hamlyn Award 2000, nominated Turner Prize 2005; *Solo Exhibitions* Ultralow (Carnival Soho) 1998, ZOBOP (The Showroom Gallery London) 1999, Voidoid (Transmission Gallery Glasgow) 1999, Weird Glow (Sadie Coles HQ London) 1999, Sonia Rosso (Pordenone Italy) 2000, Triangle Paris 2000, Konrad Fisher Dusseldorf 2000 and 2004, Blank Generation (Jack Hanley San Francisco) 2001, The Modern Institute Glasgow 2001, Sadie Coles HQ London 2001, Boy Hairdresser (Anton Kern NY) 2001, Salon Unisex (Sadie Coles HQ London) 2002, The Breeder projects (Athens) 2002, Acid Trails (Basel/Miami Beach Art Fair and The Modern Institute) 2002, Kebabylon (Inverleith House Edinburgh) 2003, Male Stripper (Museum of Modern Art Oxford) 2003, Mars Hotel (Franco Noero and Sonia Rosso Turin) 2004, Grand Funk (OPA Mexico) 2004, Mental Oyster (Anton Kern NY) 2004, My Boyfriend's Back (Konrad Fischer Galerie Dusseldorf) 2004, Concentrations 47: Jim Lambie (Dallas Museum of Art) 2005, Shoulder Pad (Sadie Coles HQ London) 2005, The Byrds (The Modern Institute Glasgow) 2005, P.I.L. (Mizuma Art Gallery Tokyo) 2006, Directions – Jim Lambie (Hirshhorn Museum & Sculpture Garden Washington DC) 2006; *Style*— Jim Lambie, Esq; ✉ c/o The Modern Institute, Suite 6, 73 Robertson Street, Glasgow G2 8QD (☎ 0141 248 3711, e-mail mail@themoderinstitute.com)

LAMBIE-NAIRN, Martin John; s of Joan Louise Lambie, and Stephen John Lambie-Nairn; *b* 5 August 1945, Purley, Surrey; *Educ* King Ethelbert's Secdy Sch, Canterbury Coll of Art; *m* 19 Dec 1970, Cordelia Margot, *née* Summers; 1 s (Van), 2 da (Fenn, Flavia); *Career* asst graphic designer BBC 1965, graphic designer Rediffusion 1966, freelance graphic designer 1967, art dir Conran Associates 1968, dep sr designer ITN 1968, graphic designer LWT 1970–76, chm and creative dir Lambie-Nairn & Company (brand identity for TV and commercials prodns) 1990–97, creative dir Lambie-Nairn (The Brand Union Ltd) 1997–2008, ptnr MLN Partnership 2008–09, creative dir Heavenly Gp Ltd 2008–11, conslt creative dir TNS 2011–14, fndr MLN Creative Consultancy 2014; chm Red + White Studio 2015–; work incl: Channel 4 TV corp identity 1982, Anglia TV corp identity 1988, review of on-screen presentation for BBC1 and BBC2 1989, TFI corp identity 1989, BBC1 and BBC2 channel identities 1991, RTSI corp identity 1992, Carlton TV corp identity 1992–97, ARTE (France & Germany) 1995, ITN corp identity 1995, BBC corp identity 1997, Millennium Experience corp identity 1998, O2 corp identity 2002; prof Faculty of Design, Architecture and Fine Art Lincoln Univ 2005; devisor of Spitting Image (ITV); chm Graphics Jury BBC Design Awards 1987; pres D&AD 1990 (memb Exec Ctee 1985, chm Corporate Identity Jury 2000); memb: BAFTA, RTS; hon fell Kent Inst of Art and Design 1994; Hon DA Lincoln Univ 2004; FCSD 1982, RDI 1987, FRTS 2004; *Awards* winner (with Daniel Barber) BAFTA Award for BBC2 identity 1992, recipient RTS Judges' Award for 30 years of creativity 1995, Lambie-Nairn & Co recipient of Queen's Award for Export Achievement 1995, President's Award D&AD 1997, Prince Philip Designers Prize 1998; Hon DA; *Books* Brand Identity for Television with Knobs On (1997); *Recreations* opera; *Style*— Martin Lambie-Nairn, Esq

LAMBIRTH, Andrew Gordon; s of Gordon Frank Trevallion Lambirth, of Ottery St Mary, Devon, and Adelaide Harriet, *née* Betteridge; *b* 2 January 1959; *Educ* St John's Sch Leatherhead, Univ of Nottingham (BA); *Career* porter Sotheby's London 1981–82, freelance researcher and writer 1983–, ed and collaborator on Eileen Agar's autobiography A Look At My Life (1988) 1985–88, cataloguer and conslt on papers of Malcolm Muggeridge 1987–88, contrib ed Royal Academy Magazine 1990–2002; art critic The Spectator 2002–14; *Monographs* incl: Allen Jones (1997 and 2005), Josef Herman (1998), Aubrey Beardsley (1998), Kitty North (1998), William Shakespeare (1999), W B Yeats (1999), Ken Kiff (2001), Ron King (2002), Craigie Aitchison (2003), R B Kitaj (2004), Maggi Hambling (2006), Roger Hilton (2007), Nigel Hall (2008), Stephen Chambers (2008), Rose Hilton (2009), John Hoyland (2009), Trevor Felcey (2009), John Armstrong (2009), Margaret Mellis (2010), David Inshaw (2010), Brian Horton (2012), A is a Critic: Writings from The Spectator (2013), Sarah Adams (2013), Francis Davison (2013), Craigie Aitchison Prints (2013), Patrick George (2014), David Tress (2015); *Recreations* reading, walking and looking; *Style*— Andrew Lambirth, Esq; ✉ Stebbings, Back Lane, Washbrook, Suffolk IP8 3JA

LAMBTON, (Lady) Lucinda; eld da of Antony Lambton (6 Earl of Durham who disclaimed peerage 1970); does not use courtesy title of Lady; *b* 10 May 1943; *m* 1, 16 Jan 1965, Henry Mark Harrod, s of Sir (Henry) Roy Forbes Harrod; 2 s (Barnaby, Huckleberry); m 2, 11 Jan 1986 (m dis), Sir Edmund Fairfax-Lucy, 6 Bt, of Charlecote Park, Warwick; m 3, 11 May 1991, as his 2 w, Sir Peregrine Gerard Worsthorne; *Career* photographer, writer and broadcaster; broadcaster many progs for BBC Radio 4; hon FRIBA; *Television* 55 progs for BBC, 25 progs for ITV; incl: On The Throne, Animal Crackers, Cabinet of Curiosities, The Great North Road, Desirable Dwellings, Hurray for Today (on modern architecture, six part series), Hurray for Today USA (six part series), The Alphabet of Britain (24 part series), One Foot in the Past (thirteen contribs), The Other House of Windsor, Travels with Pevsner, Old New World (3 part series), Sublime Suburbia (24 part series), Treasures of Jamaica; *Books* Vanishing Victoriana, Temples of Convenience (1978, 1995 and 2007), Chambers of Delight, Beastly Buildings (1985), Album of Curious Houses (1988), Magnificent Menagerie (1992), Lucinda Lambton's A-Z of Britain (1996), Old New World (2000), The House of Tekelden (jtly, 2005), The Queen's Dolls' House (2010), Palaces for Pigs, Animal Architecture and Other Beastly Buildings (2011); *Clubs* Chelsea Arts; *Style*— Lucinda Lambton; ✉ The Old Rectory, Hedgerley, Buckinghamshire SL2 3UY (☎ 01753 646167, fax 01753 646914, e-mail lucinda.lambton@virgin.net)

LAMING, Baron (Life Peer UK 1998), of Tewin in the County of Hertfordshire; Rt Hon Sir (William) Herbert Laming; kt (1996), CBE (1985), PC (2014), DL (Herts 1999); s of William Angus Laming, and Lillian, *née* Robson; *b* 19 July 1936; *Educ* Univ of Durham (DSocSci); *m* 1962, Aileen Margaret, *née* Pollard (d 2010); *Career* probation offr then sr probation offr Nottingham Probation Serv 1961–68, asst chief probation offr Nottingham City and Co Probation Serv 1968–71, deputy dir then dir Hertfordshire CC Social Servs 1971–91, chief inspr Social Servs Inspectorate DHSS 1991–98; chair: Ind Inquiry into Care and Treatment of Miss Justice Cummins 2000, Review of the Mgmnt of Prison Serv 2000, Victoria Climbié Inquiry 2001–03, The Protection of Children in England 2009–; convenor Crossbench Gp House of Lords 2011–15, chm Ctees House of Lords 2015–; pres Assoc of Dirs of Social Servs 1982–83; *Style*— The Rt Hon Lord Laming, CBE, DL; ✉ House of Lords, London SW1A 0PW

LAMMER, Dr Peter; s of Alfred Ritter von Lammer (d 2000), and Benedicta, *née* Gräfin Wengersky; *b* 18 December 1958; *Educ* Alleyn's Sch Dulwich, Univ of Warwick (BSc), St John's Coll Oxford (DPhil); *Children* 1 da (b 2008); *Career* co-fndr and jt ceo (with Dr Jan Hruska, *qv*) Sophos plc 1985–2005 (non-exec dir 2006–15); KM; *Recreations* forestry, stalking, bridge, skiing, old sports cars; *Clubs* Travellers; *Style*— Dr Peter Lammer; ✉ Sophos plc, The Pentagon, Abingdon Science Park, Abingdon OX14 3YP (☎ 01235 559933, fax 01235 544181)

LAMMY, Rt Hon David; PC (2008), MP; s of Rosalind Lammy; *b* 19 July 1972; *Educ* King's Sch Peterborough, Univ of London (LLB), Inns of Court Sch of Law, Harvard Law Sch (LLM); *m* Nicola Green; 2 s; *Career* barr 3 Serjeant's Inn 1994–98, attorney Howard Rice USA 1997–98, barr DJ Freeman 1998–2000, GLA (Lab) 2000, MP (Lab) Tottenham 2000– (by-election); PPS to Rt Hon Estelle Morris, MP 2001–02; Parly under sec of state: Dept of Health 2002–03, DCA 2003–06, DCMS 2006–07, Dept of Innovation, Univs and Skills 2007–08; min of state Dept of Business, Innovation and Skills (formerly Dept of Innovation, Univs and Skills) 2008–10; memb Select Ctee: Public Admin 2000–01, Procedure 2000–01; memb All-Pty Gp: Rwanda and the Prevention of Genocide, Br-Caribbean, Aids; memb Parly Cwlth Assoc; author of numerous articles for nat newspapers, incl The Guardian, The Independent, New Statesman and The Spectator; memb: Soc of Lab Lawyers, Christian Socialist Movement; tstee Action Aid 2001–06 (hon ambass 2006–); *Books* Out of the Ashes: Britain after the Riots; *Recreations* film, live music, Spurs FC; *Style*— The Rt Hon David Lammy, MP; ✉ House of Commons, London SW1A 0AA (☎ 020 7219 0767, fax 020 7219 0357)

LAMONT, (Archibald) Colin (Neil); s of Archie and Christabel, of Argyll; *b* 20 June 1956, Greenock, Renfrewshire; *Educ* Greenock Acad, Univ of Glasgow (BA), Royal Scottish Acad of Music & Drama (Dip Speech & Drama, winner Duncan Macrae Meml Competition), Jordanhill Coll of Educn Glasgow (PGCE); *Career* media conslt, actor, writer and broadcaster; secdy teacher, mgmnt trainee Clydesdale Bank Ltd 1973–77; Scottish Opera Theatre Royal Glasgow: touring mangr and presenter 1980, dir educn prog 1981–84, mktg offr 1983; asst mangr Pitlochry Festival Theatre 1981; announcer/newscaster: Grampian Television Aberdeen 1984–85, Scottish Television Glasgow 1985–88, Border Television Carlisle 1985–89, gen mangr and controller of programmes CentreSound Radio (now Central FM) Stirling 1989–90, mgmnt conslt 1990–91; sr prodr/presenter: Red Rose Radio Preston 1992–94, Central Scotland Radio Edinburgh, Scot FM Leith 1994–97, EMAP Radio, Hallam FM Sheffield, TFM Middlesbrough, Magic AM Liverpool, Leeds and Hull 1997–98, BRH Carlisle, Century Radio Manchester, Nottingham and Newcastle 1998–2000, The Wireless Gp 96.3 QFM Glasgow and AM NW Yorks and the Midlands 2000–02, EMAP Radio, Sheffield, Leeds and Hull and Magic AM Yorks, Lincs and the Midlands 2002–04, SRH (Scottish Radio Holdings) Radio Forth Edinburgh 2003–05, SRH Radio Clyde Glasgow 2004–05; UTV Radio: Q96 Glasgow 2006, Talk 107 Edinburgh 2006–08; dir of radio Lanarkshire's L107 Hamilton 2008–11, STV Glasgow 2011, internet pioneer Public Access Radio 2012–, prodr presenter The World's Top Talk Show (www.scottie-mcclue.com); guest appearances: BBC Radio 4, BBC World Serv, BBC Radio Scotland, Talk Radio London, Cwlth Broadcasting Assoc (London and around the world), Your Radio Glasgow 2014–15, GO Radio Glasgow 2015–; conductor Hallé orch Manchester Arena, The Chieftain Bearsden and Milngavie Highland Games 2007; columnist: Daily Record, The Sun; contrib to many pubns and newspapers; writer Going Live (sitcom) 2010; visiting lectr: Stevenson Coll Edinburgh, Univ of Salford; teacher

L

2012–, various appts incl St Columba's HS Gourock, Eastwood HS East Renfrewshire, Notre Dame HS Glasgow, Isobel Mair Sch, Mearns Castle HS E Renfrewshire, on staff of Gordonstoun Int Summer Sch 2014– (teacher of English as an additional language and English Lit, asst housemaster Windmill Lodge 2016), int tutor 2015–; memb: Equity, Exec Ctee Sea Cadet Corps 1975–80, Soc of Friends and Descendants of the Knights of the Garter St George's Chapel Windsor 1977–; *Publications* An Audience With Scottie McClue (video, 1996), The Best of Scottie McClue (CD, 1999); *Recreations* music, conversation, working field-trials labradors, classic motoring (owner/driver), classic coastal cruising (owner/master/skipper); *Clubs* Royal Over-Seas League; *Style—* Colin Lamont, Esq; ✉ e-mail bigtalkman@btinternet.com, scottie@scottie-mcclue.com or bookings@scottie-mcclue.com, website www.scottie-mcclue.com

LAMONT, Graham William; s of Gordon Lamont (d 1999), of Workington, and Marjorie, *née* Tinnion; *b* 7 May 1952, Workington, Cumbria; *Educ* Workington Tech Coll, W Cumbria Coll (HNC); *m* 1, 2 Nov 1974, Carol Joan, *née* Wigham (d 1984); 1 s (Christopher Ian b 2 Jan 1981); m 2, 22 March 1986, Maggie, *née* Rudd; *Career* chartered sec 1973, CA 1978; internal auditor Nat Bus 1968–71, trainee CA John Armstrong Co 1971–79, ptnr Lamont Pridmore Chartered Accountants 1979–; chm Coll Collaboration Task Force 2004–06; vice-chm: Cumbria Sub Regnl Assembly 1999–2002 (memb 2002–07), West Cumbria Strategic Partnership 2007–10; founding pres Cumbria C of C 1998–2006, non-exec dir Activ8 Business Link Cumbria 2001–05; memb: Cumberland Soc of CAs 1987–94 (courses chm 1990–93, chm 1992–93), Northern Soc of CAs 1991–93 (memb Tech Advsy Ctee 1993–94), Cumbria Panel Rural Devpt Cmmn 1995–97, Fin Servs Authorisation Ctee Inst of CAs 1997–98, Cumbria Foot and Mouth Taskforce 2001, Northwest Bd Learning and Skills Cncl 2006–11, Practice Ctee ICAEW 2015–; private sector memb Cumbria Local Enterprise Partnership 2013–15; non-exec dir West Cumbria Health Care Tst 1993–2001; non-exec memb: Enterprise Cumbria 1998–2001, Govt Task to merge Business Link Cumbria 1996–97, Selection Panel Ind Membs of Cumbria Police Authy 1998–2004, Cumbria Learning and Skills Cncl 2001–08 (chm 2006–08); ind memb Cumbria Vision 2004–05; judge Nat Business Awards 2007–; govr: St Bees Sch 1997–2002, Lakes Coll West Cumbria 2001–04, Carlisle Coll 2002–04; author and lectr for ICAEW (incl ed Adding Value newsletter 2000–05); jt chm Theatre by the Lake Keswick 1984–, conference chm Lakes Residential Weekend 1990–2004; High Sheriff Cumbria 2008–09; FCA, FCCA (ACCA 1985), ACIS, MCMI 1990, AIMC 2002, FRSA 2007; *Recreations* theatre, art, reading, golf, jogging; *Style—* Graham Lamont, Esq; ✉ Lamont Pridmore, Milburn House, 3 Oxford Street, Workington, Cumbria CA14 2AL (☎ 01900 65955, fax 01900 65999, e-mail graham@lamontpridmore.co.uk, website www.lamontpridmore.co.uk)

LAMONT, John Robert; MSP; s of Robert Lamont, and Elizabeth, *née* Wilson; *b* 15 April 1976, Irvine, Ayrshire; *Educ* Kilwinning Acad, Univ of Glasgow (LLB), Coll of Law Chester; *Career* trainee slr then assoc Freshfields 2000–04, assoc Bristows 2004–05, sr slr Brodies 2005–07; MSP (Cons): Roxburgh and Berwickshire 2007–11, Ettrick, Roxburgh & Berwickshire 2011–; memb Law Soc of Eng and Wales 2002; *Recreations* swimming, running, cycling; *Style—* John Lamont, Esq, MSP; ✉ Scottish Parliament, Edinburgh EH99 1SP (☎ 0131 348 6533)

LAMONT OF LERWICK, Baron (Life Peer UK 1998), of Lerwick in the Shetland Islands; Rt Hon Norman Stewart Hughson Lamont; PC (1986); s of Daniel Lamont and Irene Lamont; *b* 8 May 1942; *Educ* Loretto (scholar), Fitzwilliam Coll Cambridge (pres Cambridge Union); *m* 1971 (m dis 2000), Alice Rosemary, da of Lt-Col Peter White; 1 s, 1 da; *Career* PA to Duncan Sandys 1965, Cons Res Dept 1966–68, investment banker N M Rothschild & Sons 1968–79 (dir Rothschild Asset Management); Parly candidate (Cons) Hull E 1970, MP (Cons) Kingston upon Thames 1972–97, Parly candidate (Cons) Harrogate and Knaresborough 1997; chm: Coningsby Club 1970–71, Bow Gp 1971–72; PPS to Arts Min 1974; oppn spokesman: on consumer affairs 1975–76, on industry 1976–79; under-sec of state Dept of Energy 1979–81; Min of State: DTI 1981–85, for Defence Procurement 1985–86; Financial Sec to Treasy May 1986-July 1989, Chief Sec to the Treasy July 1989-Nov 1990, Chancellor of the Exchequer 1990–93, chm G7 Finance Min 1992, chm EU Finance Mins 1993, memb House of Lords Select Ctee on Euro Union Affairs 1999–2003; non-exec dir N M Rothschild & Sons Ltd 1993–95, chm and dir of various investment tsts 1995–, adsvr to Monsanto Co 1995–2000; dir: Balli plc 1995–, Compagnie Internationale de Participations Bancaires et Financieres 1999–, RAB Capital 2004–; chm Jupiter Adria 2006–; advsr to the Romanian Govt 1997–98, advsr to the Western Union Co 2005–07, pres Br-Romanian C of C 2002–, chm Br Iranian C of C 2004–, chm Clan Lamont Soc 2007–09; vice pres Bruges Gp 2006–; awarded Star of Merit (Chile) 2000, Cdr Order of Faithful Service (Romania) 2010; *Books* In Office (1999), Sovereign Britain (1994); *Style—* The Rt Hon the Lord Lamont of Lerwick, PC; ✉ c/o Balli plc, 5 Stanhope Gate, London W1Y 5LA

LAMPARD, Clive; s of Roy Lampard (d 1978), of Maidstone, and Renee Lampard; *b* 25 May 1959; *Educ* Oakwood Park GS Maidstone, Westfield Coll London (BA, MA); *m* 1984, Julia Catherine, da of James Bernard Carr; 1 da (Sarah b 13 Jan 1987), 2 s (Daniel b 22 March 1989, Luke b 12 June 1992); *Career* articled clerk Slaughter and May 1983–85; ptnr Macfarlanes 1991– (joined 1989, currently head Corporate Real Estate Practice); author of various articles; govr The Hall Sch Hampstead; memb Law Soc; *Recreations* family, wine, sport, church; *Style—* Clive Lampard, Esq; ✉ Macfarlanes, 20 Cursitor Street, London EC4A 1LT (☎ 020 7831 9222, fax 020 7831 9607, e-mail clive.lampard@macfarlanes.com)

LAMPARD, Frank James; OBE (2015); s of Frank Lampard, the West Ham and England footballer; *b* 21 June 1978, Romford, Essex; *Children* 2 da (Luna Patricia b 2005, Isla b 2007); *Career* professional footballer; clubs: West Ham United FC 1995–2001, Swansea City (on loan) 1995–96, Chelsea FC 2001– (winners: FA Premiership 2005 and 2006 (runners-up 2004 and 2007), League Cup 2005 and 2007, FA Cup 2007 and 2009 (finalists 2002), FA Charity/Community Shield 2005 and 2009, Europa League 2013; finalists UEFA Champions League 2008); England: 100 caps, 29 goals, debut v Belgium 1999, memb squad European Championships 2004 and World Cup 2006, 2010 and 2014; runner-up PFA Player of the Year 2004 and 2005, England Footballer of the Year 2004 and 2005, Football Writers Footballer of the Year 2005 (runner-up 2004), runner-up European Footballer of the Year and World Player of the Year 2005; *Style—* Mr Frank Lampard, OBE; ✉ c/o Chelsea Football Club, Fulham Road, London SW6 1HS

LAMPORT, Sir Stephen Mark Jeffrey; KCVO (2002, CVO 1999), DL (Surrey 2006); s of Eric George Lamport, of Horsted Keynes, W Sussex, and Jeanne Helen, *née* Jeffries (d 2013); *b* 27 November 1951; *Educ* Dorking Co GS, CCC Cambridge (MA), Univ of Sussex (MA); *m* 1979, Angela Vivien Paula, da of Peter De La Motte Hervey; 2 s (Edward b 1983, William b 1985), 1 da (Alexandra b 1990); *Career* HM Dip Serv: joined 1974, third later second sec Br Embassy Tehran 1975–79, private sec to Douglas Hurd as minister of state 1981–83, private sec to Malcolm Rifkind as min of state 1983–84, first sec Br Embassy Rome 1984–88, FCO 1988–93 (appointed counsellor 1990), private sec and treas to HRH The Prince of Wales 1996–2002 (dep private sec 1993–96); gp dir for public policy and govt affrs Royal Bank of Scotland 2002–07, Receiver Gen Westminster Abbey 2008–; non-exec dir Brewin Dolphin Holdings plc 2007–16; memb Bd RAC 2012–; tstee: Queen Mother Meml Fund 2003–06, Surrey Community Fndn 2006–10 (vice-pres 2010–); memb: Cncl Arvon Fndn 2004–08, Cncl Guildford Cathedral 2006–10, Scottish Nat Ballet Tramway Appeal 2007–09; chm Advsy Panel for Nat Floods Appeal Br Red Cross 2007–08, memb Advsy Cncl Inst of Business Ethics 2016–; ind person Westminster City Cncl 2015–; memb Ct Royal Fndn of St Katharine 2004–; *Books* The Palace of Enchantments (with Douglas Hurd, *qv*, 1985); *Clubs* RAC, Grillions; *Style—* Sir Stephen Lamport, KCVO, DL; ✉ Westminster Abbey, London SW1P 3PA

LAN, Dr David; CBE (2014); *b* 1 June 1952, Cape Town; *Educ* Univ of Cape Town (BA), LSE (BSc, PhD); *Career* playwright, translator, social anthropologist, theatre dir; writer in residence Royal Court Theatre 1995–97, artistic dir Young Vic Theatre 2000–, consulting artistic dir Performance Arts Center World Trade Center 2013–15; *Theatre* prodns at Young Vic incl: 'Tis Pity She's a Whore 1999, Julius Caesar 2000, A Raisin in the Sun 2001 and 2005, Doctor Faustus 2002, The Daughter in Law 2002, The Skin of our Teeth 2004, Joe Turner's Come and Gone 2010; other prodns incl: The Glass Menagerie (Watford) 1998, As You Like It (Wyndhams) 2005, Blackta 2012; *Film* for BBC: The Sunday Judge 1985, Welcome Home Comrades 1986, Dark City (writer) 1996, Artist Unknown 1996, Royal Court Diaries (dir) 1997; *Plays* incl: Painting a Wall (Almost Free) 1974, Bird Child (Royal Court) 1974, The Winter Dancers (Royal Court) 1977, Sergeant Ola (Royal Court) 1979, Flight (RSC) 1986, Desire (Almeida) 1990, The Ends of the Earth (NT) 1996; *Translations* Ghetto 1989 (NT), Hippolytos (Almeida) 1991, Ion (RSC) 1994, Uncle Vanya (RSC/Young Vic) 1998, La Lupa (RSC) 1999, The Cherry Orchard (NT) 2000, The Magic Flute 2008; *Libretti* Tobias and the Angel (music J Dove) 1999, Ion (music Param Vir) 2000 and 2003; *Books* Guns and Rain: Guerrillas and Spirit Mediums in Zimbabwe (1985); *Style—* Dr David Lan; ✉ c/o Young Vic Theatre, 66 The Cut, London SE1 8LZ

LANCASTER, His Hon Judge Anthony Trevor; s of Thomas William Lancaster (decd), and Jean Margaret, *née* Grainger; *b* 26 June 1948; *Educ* Austin Friars Sch Carlisle, Univ of Leeds (LLB); *Family* 3 s (Philip James b 23 Dec 1974, John Andrew b 7 May 1977, David Francis b 29 March 1981), 1 da (Helen Alice b 4 Aug 1991); m 1, 11 May 1997 (m dis 2011), Beverley Anne, *née* Conlon; 1 s (Matthew Charles b 31 Oct 1998), 1 da (Rebecca Niamh b 10 Nov 2000); m 2, 2 March 2012, Louise, *née* Askins; *Career* admitted slr 1973; registrar County Court 1988–91, district judge 1991–2001, recorder of the Crown Court 1999–2001 (asst recorder 1995–99), circuit judge (NE Circuit) 2001–; pres Assoc District Judges 2000–01, pt/t chm Social Security Appeals Tbnl 1985–88; memb Law Soc 1973; *Style—* His Hon Judge Lancaster; ✉ c/o Law Courts, Quayside, Newcastle upon Tyne NE1 1EE (☎ 0191 201 2000, fax 0191 201 2001)

LANCASTER, (John) Mark; TD (2002), MP; s of Rev Ron Lancaster, MBE; *b* 12 May 1970, Cambridge; *Educ* Univ of Buckingham (BSc, PhD), Univ of Exeter (MBA); *m* (m dis); m 2, 14 Feb 2014, Caroline Dinenage, MP, *qv*; *Career* Gap Year Cmmn, offr Queens Gurkha Engineers (served Hong Kong), Lt Col TA (served Kosovo and Bosnia as part of UN peacekeeping force), served Afghanistan 2006; md Kimbolton Fireworks; Parly candidate (Cons) Nuneaton 2001; MP (Cons): Milton Keynes NE 2005–10, Milton Keynes N 2010–; PPS to Sec of State for Int Devpt 2010–12, Lord Cmmr to HM Treasy 2012–15, min for defence personnel 2015–; *Recreations* collecting and restoring classic British motorcycles; *Clubs* Army and Navy; *Style—* Mark Lancaster, TD, MP; ✉ House of Commons, London SW1A 0AA (☎ 020 7219 8414, fax 020 7219 6685, e-mail lancasterm@parliament.uk); Constituency Office, Suite 102, Milton Keynes Business Centre, Foxhunter Drive, Milton Keynes MK14 6ED (☎ 01908 686830, website www.lancaster4mk.com, Twitter @MarkLancasterMP)

LANCASTER, Bishop of (RC) 2001–; Rt Rev Patrick Augustine O'Donoghue; s of Daniel O'Donoghue (d 1970), of Mallow, Co Cork, and Sheila, *née* Twomey (d 1985); *Educ* Patrician Acad Mallow, Campion House Coll Osterley, St Edmund's Coll Ware; *Career* ordained RC priest 1967; Dio of Westminster: memb Diocesan Mission Team 1970–73, rector Allen Hall Diocesan Seminary Chelsea 1985–90, admin Westminster Cathedral 1990–93, aux bishop of Westminster with responsibility for the West Area 1993–2001; involvement with other orgns incl: The Passage Day Centre for the Poor, Cardinal Hume Centre for Young Homeless, The Lillie Road Centre for Children in Care, Acton Homeless Concern, Christian Arts Tst; *Recreations* walking (in countryside), travel, theatre, football (spectator); *Style—* The Rt Rev the Bishop of Lancaster; ✉ Bishop's Apartment, Cathedral House, Balmoral Road, Lancaster LA1 3BT (☎ 01524 596050, fax 01524 596053, e-mail bishop@lancasterrcdiocese.org.uk)

LANCASTER, Roger; *b* 4 February 1951; *Educ* Univ of Leicester (LLB); *m* Margaret; 2 s, 1 da; *Career* admitted slr 1975; former sr ptnr and head of planning and environmental law Halliwell Landau; called to the Bar, practising fom King's Chambers Manchester; *Recreations* cricket, squash; *Style—* Roger Lancaster, Esq

LANCASTER, Stuart; *b* 9 October 1969, Penrith, Cumbria; *m* Nina; 1 da (Sophie), 1 s (Dan); *Career* rugby coach and former player; player (flanker) Leeds RFC 1992–2000, head Leeds RFU Acad 2001–05, dir of rugby Leeds Carnegie 2006–07, head of elite player devpt RFU and head coach England Saxons 2007–11, head coach England 2012– (caretaker coach 2011–12); *Style—* Mr Stuart Lancaster; ✉ c/o Rugby Football Union, Rugby House, Twickenham Stadium, 200 Whitton Road, Twickenham TW2 7BA

LANCE, Prof (Edward) Christopher; s of F Nevill Lance (d 1987), and Elizabeth, *née* Bagnall (d 1989); *b* 17 January 1941; *Educ* Dulwich Coll, Trinity Coll Cambridge (MA, PhD); *m* 9 April 1966, Mary Margaret, *née* Hall; 1 s (Stephen b 1969), 1 da (Elizabeth b 1971); *Career* lectr in pure maths Univ of Newcastle 1965–73, reader Univ of Manchester 1973–78, prof of mathematics Univ of Leeds 1980–; visiting prof Univ of Pennsylvania USA 1971–72, 1978–80 and 1992–93; vice-pres London Mathematical Soc 1988–90, sec Euro Mathematical Soc 1990–94; *Recreations* hill walking, music; *Style—* Prof Christopher Lance

LANCELEY, Ian Kenneth; s of Thomas Peter Kenneth Lanceley (d 2011), and Barbara Doreen, *née* Allen (d 2015); *b* 12 February 1946; *Educ* Blundell's, Coll of Law; *m* 12 Dec 1980, Valerie, da of Frederick William Kay (d 1987), of Richmond, North Yorks; 2 s (Adam b 1981, Charles b 1983); *Career* admitted slr (with hons)1971; ptnr Freeborough Slack & Co 1977–85, sr ptnr Freeboroughs 1985–98, ptnr WH Matthews and Co (incorporating Freeboroughs) 1998–2010; dep magistrate Metropolitan Stipendiary 1985–90; memb Law Soc; *Recreations* family, golf, wine drinking; *Clubs* Roehampton, Royal Wimbledon Golf; *Style—* Ian K Lanceley, Esq; ✉ 19 Penrhyn Road, Kingston upon Thames KT1 2BZ (☎ 020 8549 0264, e-mail ikl@whmatthews.com)

LANCELOT, Canon Dr James Bennett; s of Rev Roland Lancelot (d 1983), and Margaret, *née* Tye (d 1998); *b* 2 December 1952; *Educ* St Paul's Cathedral Choir Sch, Ardingly, RCM, King's Coll Cambridge (Organ scholar, MA, MusB); *m* 31 July 1982, Sylvia Jane, da of Raymond Hoare, of Cheltenham; 2 da (Rebecca b 1987, Eleanor b 1989); *Career* asst organist Hampstead Parish Church and St Clement Danes Church 1974–75, sub-organist Winchester Cathedral 1975–85, master of the choristers and organist Durham Cathedral 1985–, conductor Univ of Durham Choral Soc 1987–2013, organist Univ of Durham 2002–, fell St Chad's Coll Durham 2006–; numerous recordings; lay canon Durham Cathedral 2002–; pres Cathedral Organists' Assoc 2001–03, pres Darlington and District Organists' and Choirmasters' Assoc 2004–05, pres Incorporated Assoc of Organists 2013–; hon fell Guild of Church Musicians 2002, hon fell Royal Sch of Church Music 2008; hon DMus Durham Univ 2014; FRCO (chm 1969), ARCM 1970; *Books* Durham Cathedral Organs (co-author with Richard Hird, 1991), The Sense of the Sacramental (contrib, 1995); *Recreations* railways; *Style—* Canon Dr James Lancelot; ✉ 6 The College, Durham DH1 3EQ (☎ 0191 386 4766)

LAND, (John) Anthony; *b* 21 September 1939; *Educ* Westminster (Queen's scholar), Trinity Coll Cambridge (minor scholar, BA); *m* Deborah Lucy Irene; 2 c; *Career* asst mangr (special pubns) The Times 1962–65; Readers' Digest London: asst then dep ed (magazines) 1965–71, managing ed (magazines) 1971–74, exec dir (books) 1974–77; Consumers' Assoc: head of publishing 1977–91, asst dir 1987–91; freelance conslt (Thames and Hudson, Joseph Rowntree Fndn, The Planning Exchange, Asia Inc) 1991–93; Design Cncl: dir of publishing 1991–94, resources dir and sec to the Cncl 1994–2000; mgmnt and editorial conslt 2001– (Equal Opportunities Cmmn, Gen Social Care Cncl, Social Care Inst for Excellence, Royal Soc, Kensington and Chelsea PCT); non-exec dir: Book Tst London 1989–96, Health and Social Care Information Centre Leeds 2005–, Dr Foster Intelligence 2006–10; chm Campden Hill Residents' Assoc 1994–2001; memb Parly and Legal Ctee PPA 1989–94; Hon DLitt Univ of Brighton; ACCA (Charterd Dip Accounting and Fin); *Recreations* swimming, walking, opera, travel, history; *Style—* Anthony Land, Esq

LAND, (Harold) Brook; s of David Land (d 1995), of London, and Zara, *née* Levinson; *b* 12 March 1949; *Educ* St Paul's; *m* 7 Dec 1975, Anita Penny, da of Leslie Grade; 1 da (Lesley Olivia b 19 Jan 1981), 1 s (Daniel Edward b 30 April 1983); *Career* Nabarro Nathanson Solicitors: articled clerk 1967–72, asst slr 1972–74, ptnr 1974–96, conslt 1996–; memb Law Soc 1972; non-exec chm: RPS Gp plc 1997–, Medal Entertainment and Media plc 2001–; non-exec dir: JLI Gp plc 1989–98, Signet Gp plc 1995–2008, Brown Lloyd James Ltd 1997–2006, Crown Personnel plc 1998–2005; chm Theatre Royal Brighton Ltd 1996–99; *Recreations* reading, family, Arsenal; *Style—* Brook Land, Esq; ✉ 10 Wyndham Place, London W1H 2PU (☎ 020 7723 2456, fax 020 7723 7567, e-mail brook@brookl.co.uk)

LAND, Dr John Melville; s of Ernest G E Land (d 1979), and Joyce Land (d 2012); *b* 19 February 1950; *Educ* Hymers Coll Hull, Univ of London (BSc, PhD), London Business Sch (MBA), Merton Coll Oxford (BM BCh); *Career* jr med positions 1980–81, Hammersmith Hosp London 1981, Brompton Hosp London 1982, John Radcliffe Hosps Oxford 1982–92, conslt Neurometabolic Unit National Hosp London 1992–, clinical head of service Biochemical Med UCLH Tst 2002–; Salters fell Univ of Pennsylvania 1974–75, Brian Johnson Prize in pathology Univ of Oxford 1979, NHS Exec Bursary 1994–97; corresponding memb American Soc of Neurochemistry 2003; FRSM 1985, MRCPath 1999, FRCP 2007; *Publications* author of many pubns in med and biochemical jls; *Recreations* cricket, walking, cooking; *Clubs* Savile; *Style—* Dr John Land; ✉ Neurometabolic Unit, National Hospital, Queen Square, London WC1N 3BG (☎ 020 7829 8768, e-mail john.land@uclh.org)

LAND, Prof Michael Francis; s of Prof Frank William Land (d 1990), and Nora Beatrice, *née* Channon (d 1985); *b* 12 April 1942; *Educ* Birkenhead Sch, Jesus Coll Cambridge (BA, Frank Smart Prize in zoology), UCL (PhD); *m* 1 (m dis 1980), Judith Drinkwater; 1 s (Adam Michael b 1969); m 2, 10 Dec 1980, Rosemary, da of James Clarke; 2 da (Katharine Rosemary b 1981, Penelope Frances b 1983); *Career* asst prof Univ of Calif Berkeley 1969–71 (Miller fell 1967–69); Sch of Biological Sciences Univ of Sussex: lectr 1972–78, reader 1978–84, prof 1984–; sr visiting fell Aust Nat Univ Canberra 1982–84; memb Editorial Bd Jl of Comparative Physiology; Frink Medal Zoological Soc of London 1994; FRS 1982; *Publications* Animal Eyes (2002, 2 edn 2012), Looking and Acting (2009), The Eye: a Very Short Introduction (2014); author of 180 publications on aspects of animal and human vision in learned jls and popular sci jls; *Recreations* gardening, music; *Style—* Prof Michael Land, FRS; ✉ Dart Cottage, The Elms, Ringmer, East Sussex, BN8 5EZ; School of Life Sciences, University of Sussex, Brighton BN1 9QG (☎ 01273 813911)

LAND, Ralph Richard; CBE (1996, OBE 1985); s of Louis Landsberger (d 1976), of London, and Sofia, *née* Weinberger (d 1999); *b* 24 October 1928, Berlin; *Educ* Willesden Co GS, LSE (BSc (Econ)); *m* 3 April 1954, Jacqueline-Marie (d 2009), da of Gustave Bourdin; 2 s (Bryan Christopher b 23 July 1959, Anthony Michael b 6 July 1960); *Career* mgmnt accountant J Lyons & Co Ltd 1952–59, Leo Computers, English Electric Computers and ICL 1959–76 (gen mangr Eastern Europe Div ICL 1964–72, mktg dir Western European Div ICL 1972–74, md ICL Deutschland GMBH 1974–76), gen mangr Eastern Export Ops Rank Xerox Ltd 1976–91, dir of Eastern European affrs Rolls-Royce plc 1991–94 (advsr to the Bd 1994–96), chm Cyberaction Ltd 1997–2000, dir Financial Information Technology Ltd 1999–, chm PCG Worldwide Ltd 2002–05, dir Penatrada Ltd; non-exec dir Int Advsy Bd ICL plc 1991–2001, memb Int Advsy Bd American Phoenix Life and Reassurance Co 1998–2001; chm Russo-British C of C 1995–2004; UNICE Working Gp on Eastern and Central Europe and Taskforce on Enlargement 1995–2000, E European Trade Cncl (EETC)/DTI; co-chm British Romanian C of C 1998–2007, dep chm Westminster Fndn for Democracy 1993–97; memb: Advsy Bd British Know How Fund 1991–99, Advsy Bd Iman Fndn 2014–; frequent lectr at confs and seminars on Eastern Europe, TV and radio commentator on Eastern European business matters; chm Br Consultancy Charitable Tst 2006–, tstee Healthprom; former tstee: Hamlet Tst, BBC World Serv Tst, BESO; memb: Lab Pty, Br Computer Soc, Ad Hoc Soc 2006–, Ctee LEO Soc 2009–, VAP Ctee TWINSUK Research Project St Thomas's Hosp 2015; dir Mid-Atlantic Club 2011–; memb RIIA; FRSA 1992; *Publications* Leo: The Incredible Story of the World's First Business Computer (contrib, 1997); author of numerous articles; *Recreations* travel, opera and music, photography, food and drink; *Clubs* Reform, Rotary Club of London (pres 2009–10); *Style—* Ralph Land, Esq, CBE; ✉ 27 Alder Lodge, 73 Stevenage Road, London SW6 6NP (☎ 020 7385 3054, fax 020 7610 1116, mobile 07785 257388, e-mail r.land@btinternet.com)

LAND, Sonia; da of Tan Peng Liat (d 1965), and Md Lioh Ta Fan; *b* 29 January 1948, Singapore; *Educ* Singapore Chinese Girls' Sch, Raffles Inst, Univ of Singapore (BAcc); *m* 27 Sept 1975, Nicholas Charles Edward Land; 1 s (Christopher Mark Nicholas b 30 Dec 1983); *Career* Ernst & Young 1971–75, mgmnt accountant Trust Houses Forte 1975–76, financial and mgmnt accountant BB Mason Ltd 1976–77, financial dir Granada Publishing Ltd 1977–83, gp finance dir William Collins Plc 1983–88, exec dir Newmarket Venture Capital Plc 1988, dir of planning News International plc 1988–90, ceo HarperCollins Publishing Gp UK and Europe 1989–90, ceo Sheil Land Assocs Ltd 1990–; non-exec dir: Mirror Gp 1993–98, Waterford Wedgewood Gp 1994–98; fell Certified and Corporate Accountants 1974; *Recreations* tennis, gardening, travel, cooking; *Style—* Mrs Sonia Land; ✉ Sheil Land Associates Ltd, 52 Doughty Street, London WC1N 2LS (☎ 020 7405 9351, fax 020 7831 2127, e-mail sland@sheilland.co.uk)

LANDALE, Sir David William Neil; KCVO (1993), DL (Nithsdale and Annandale (Dumfriesshire) 1984); s of David Fortune Landale (d 1970), and Louisa Mary Dorothy Charlotte, *née* Forbes, (d 1956), yst da of Charles Forbes of Falkirk; *b* 27 May 1934; *Educ* Eton, Balliol Coll Oxford (MA); *m* 1961, Melanie, da of Sir Harold Roper, CBE, MC, MP (Cons) for N Cornwall 1949–59 (d 1971); 3 s (Peter b 1963, William b 1965, Jamie b 1969); *Career* Black Watch Royal Highland Regt 1952–54; Jardine Matheson & Co Ltd: joined 1958, dir 1967–75, worked in Hong Kong, Thailand, Taiwan and Japan; dir: Matheson & Co Ltd 1975–98, Pinneys Holdings Ltd 1982–87; chm: T C Farries & Co Ltd 1982–96, Timber Growers UK Ltd 1985–87; appointed sec and keeper of records of The Duchy of Cornwall 1987–93, dir Dumfries & Galloway Enterprise Co 1993–95; pres Royal Highland Agric Soc of Scotland 1994–95; chm: Royal Highland Agric Soc Ingliston Devpt Tst 1995–97, Royal Scottish Forestry Soc Tst Co (Cashel) 1996–, Malcolm Sargent Cancer Care for Children for Scotland 1996–99 (also tstee), Maggie Keswick Jenks Cancer Caring Centre Tst 1996–2006; convenor Crichton Fndn 1998–2001 (chm 1998–2000); hon doctorate: Univ of Paisley 2001, Univ of Glasgow 2002; *Recreations* all countryside pursuits, theatre, reading (history); *Clubs* Boodle's, Pratt's, New (Edinburgh); *Style—* Sir David W N Landale, KCVO, DL; ✉ Bankhead, Dalswinton, Dumfries DG2 0XY (☎ 01387 740208, e-mail sirdavid.landale@btinternet.com)

LANDAU, Dr David; Hon CBE (2007); s of Aharon Landau, of Jerusalem, and Evelyne, *née* Conti, of Italy; *b* 22 April 1950, Tel Aviv, Israel; *Educ* Liceo Berchet Milan (Maturità Classica), Pavia Univ (MD), Wolfson Coll Oxfd or(MA); *m* 2001, Marie-Rose *née* Kahane; 1 s (Max b 2004), 1 da (Mia b 2004 (twin)); *Career* curator Mantegna exhbn Oxford 1979, print curator The Genius of Venice 1500–1600 exhbn Royal Acad 1983, chm Steering Ctee Andrea Mantegna exhbn Royal Acad and Met Museum NYC 1992; co-fndr Italian ice cream business 1983–86; Loot (classified listings paper): fndr and jt md 1985–95, chm 1995–2000; fndr of other jls: Print Quarterly 1984 (ed 1984–2010, tstee 2010–), Via Via (Holland) 1986, Modern Painters 1988; chm Saffron Hill Investors (Guernsey) 2000–; fndr treas and chm Free Ad Paper Int Assoc 1986–91 (ctee offr 1991–93), jt fndr and treas Young British Friends of the Art Museums of Israel charity 1988–95 (tstee 1995–2008), tstee Nat Gallery 1996–2003, tstee Nat Gallery Tst 1995–, dir Nat Gallery Co 1995–2003 (chm 1998–2003), memb Ctee Nat Art Collections Fund 1996–2010, treas Venice in Peril Fund 1997–2010 (tstee 1996–2012); dir Getty Images 2003–06, dir Yad Hanadiv (a Rothschild Fndn) 2012–, dir Yad Hanadiv Israel 2012–; tstee: NGT Fndn 1997–, Rothschild Fndn (Hanadiv) Europe 2001–, Warburg Charitable Tst 2001–09, Borletti Buitoni Charitable Tst 2002–, Courtauld Inst 2002–12, Fondazione dei Musei Civici di Venezia 2010; fell Worcester Coll Oxford 1980–2009; Commendatore dell'Ordine al Merito della Repubblica Italiana 2007; *Books* Il Catalogo Completo dell'Opera Grafica di Georg Pencz (catalogue of the prints of Georg Pencz, 1978), Federica Galli – Catalogo Completo delle Acqueforti (1982), The Renaissance Print (with Prof Peter Parshall, 1994); numerous articles in jls incl: The Burlington Magazine, Master Drawings, Print Collector, Print Quarterly, Art International, Oxford Art Jl; *Recreations* looking at and collecting art, opera; *Style—* Dr David Landau, CBE; ✉ Chesa Carla, CH-7505 Celerina, Switzerland (☎ 0041 81 832 1550, fax 0041 81 833 3620, e-mail dlandau@saffronhill.com)

LANDAU, Toby Thomas; QC (2008); s of Dr Thomas L Landau (d 1991), and Marianne, *née* Samson; *b* 9 October 1967, London; *Educ* Univ Coll Sch London, Merton Coll Oxford (MA, BCL, Eldon law scholar, Slaughter & May Prize, coll exhibitioner, Fowler Prize), Inns of Ct Sch of Law, Harvard Law Sch USA (Kennedy scholar, LLM); *m* Sept 1998, Nudrat B Majeed; 1 da (Zakiya Marianne b 4 Sept 2002); *Career* called to the Bar: Eng and Wales 1993, NI 2000, Br Virgin Islands 2011; admitted attorney and cnsllr-at-law NY 1994; lawyer Civil Appeals Office Court of Appeal 1991, law tutor Univ of London 1991–92, memb Essex Ct Chambers 1993–, practising barr specialising in int and commercial law and arbitration; dir of studies, lectr and legal conslt Miny of Justice Thailand 1993–94; visiting prof in arbitration law KCL; visiting lectr: Chulalongkoun Univ and Judge's Inst 1993, Asser Inst The Hague 1995–2004, Int Devpt Law Orgn Rome 2003 and 2004, Pakistan Coll of Law Lahore 2005; memb Govt's Standing Ctee on Private Int Law 1997–, memb Attorney-Gen of Singapore's Panel of Counsel 2012; memb: Bd London Ct of Int Arbitration, Int Arbitration Inst, Swiss Arbitration Assoc, American Soc of Int Law, Commercial Bar Assoc, Int Law Assoc; FCIArb; incl: The English Arbitration Act 1996: Texts and Notes (jtly, 1998), The English Arbitration Act 1996: An Approach to Harmonisation (1999), Commentary on WIPO Arbitration Rules (2000), The Written Form Requirement for Arbitration Agreements: When 'Written' Means 'Oral' (2002); *Style—* Toby Landau, Esq, QC; ✉ Essex Court Chambers, 24 Lincoln's Inn Fields, London WC2A 3EG

LANDER, Geoffrey Ian; s of Victor Lander; *b* 11 January 1951; *m* Lynn; *Career* Nabarro Nathanson: joined as trainee slr 1973, ptnr 1980–2002, head Property Dept 1995–2002; princ Tricore Equity Ptnrs LLP 2002–; non-exec dir: Dolphin Square Tst Ltd 1999–, Plato Enterprises 2005–, TTA Gp 2006–; featured in Euromoney Guide to World's Leading Real Estate Lawyers; past chm CoreNet Global UK (formerly NACORE, also past chm European Advsy Bd), pres Br Cncl for Offices 1998–99; memb Exec Ctee and Bd UK Branch American C of C; memb Law Soc 1976; *Recreations* watching Manchester Utd, bridge, golf; *Style—* Geoffrey Lander, Esq

LANDER, Nicholas Laurence (Nick); s of Israel Lennard Lander (d 1991), and Pauline, *née* Shalyt; *b* 8 April 1952, Manchester; *Educ* Manchester Grammar, Jesus Coll Cambridge, Manchester Business Sch; *m* 22 Oct 1981, Jancis Robinson, OBE, *qv*; 2 da (Julia Margaux b 10 July 1982, Rose Ellen b 6 March 1991), 1 s (William Isaac b 5 Sept 1984); *Career* restaurant corr FT 1989–; hospitality conslt: Southbank Centre, Somerset House, ROH, The Ashmolean; *Publications* The Art of The Restaurateur (2012); *Recreations* cooking for friends, reading, restaurants; *Clubs* Manchester United; *Style—* Nick Lander, Esq; ✉ Financial Times, 1 Southwark Bridge, London SE1 9HL

LANDER, Sir Stephen James; KCB (2000, CB 1995); *b* 1947; *Educ* Bishop's Stortford Coll, Queens' Coll Cambridge (open exhibitioner, MA, PhD); *m* Felicity Mary, *née* Brayley; 1 s (decd), 1 da; *Career* Inst of Historical Research 1972–75, DG Security Service (MI5) 1996–2002 (joined 1975); non-exec dir: HM Customs and Excise 2002–05, Northgate Information Solutions 2004–08, Steamshield Networks Ltd 2004–07; ind cmmr to Law Soc 2002–05, chair Serious Organised Crime Agency 2004–09, memb Slr's Regulation Authy 2006–09, panel chair Judicial Appointments Cmmn 2008–12, lay memb Special Immigration Appeals Cmmn 2011–; tstee Dawes Tst 2012–; Hon LLD Hertfordshire Univ 2005, Hon DSc Cranfield Univ 2007; *Style—* Sir Stephen Lander, KCB

LANDERS, Dr John Maxwell; s of William Maxwell Landers (d 2003), and Muriel, *née* Wilkinson (d 2007); *b* 25 January 1952; *Educ* Southgate Tech Coll, Hertford Coll Oxford (MA), Churchill Coll Cambridge (PhD), Univ of Oxford (LittD); *m* 1991, Diana Parker; *Career* oil demand analyst Shell UK Oil 1979–80, lectr in biological anthropology UCL 1980–90 (tutor Human Scis Interdisciplinary Prog 1984–87, departmental tutor Anthropology Dept 1987–90); Univ of Oxford: fell All Souls Coll and univ lectr in historical demography 1991–2005, princ Hertford Coll 2005–11 (sr research fell 2011–), univ assessor 1994–95, academic sec All Souls Coll 1994–98, memb Jt Ctee Hon Sch of Human Sci 1996–2000, memb Hebdominal Cncl and Gen Bd of the Faculties 1997–2000, chm of curators Examination Schs 1998–2000, memb Communications and IT Ctee 1998–2000, convenor of MSt grad degree and memb Grad Studies Ctee Modern History Faculty 2002–05, chm Mgmnt Ctee Wellcome Unit for the History of Medicine 2003–05; chm Gen Bd Review Ctee Dept of Statistics 1998; memb: Ctee Soc for the Study of Human Biology 1988–92, Advsy Ctee Centre for Metropolitan History Inst of Historical Research Univ of London 1988–95, Review Panel ESRC Cambridge Gp for the History of Population and Social Structure 1993, Visitors Ctee Pitt-Rivers Museum 1996–2014 (chm 1999–2014), History of Medicine Ctee Wellcome Tst 1995–2001 (vice-chm 2000–01); hon sec Br Soc for Population Studies 1990–94, sr treas Oxford Union Soc 1996–98, chair Animals in Science Ctee 2013–, external chair Audit Ctee All Souls Coll Oxford 2015–; memb Int Union for the Scientific Study of Population 1987–; FRHistS 2002; *Publications* Death and the Metropolis (1993), The Field and the Forge (2003); author of numerous articles in learned jls and chapters in books incl Jl of Historical Geography, Population Studies, Fertility and Resources, Social History of Medicine, Medical History, Darwinism and Historical Demography, Historical Epidemiology and the Health Transition; *Recreations* cinema, reading, theatre, running; *Clubs* Athenaeum, Oxford and Cambridge; *Style—* Dr John Landers; ✉ Hertford College, Catte Street, Oxford OX1 3BW

LANDON, Prof John; s of Charles Landon, and Ellen, *née* Hutton; *b* 2 December 1931; *Educ* King William's Coll Isle of Man, St Mary's Hosp Med Sch (MD); *m* Mary Ursula; 2 s (Ewan, Mark), 1 da (Bridget); *Career* prof of chemical pathology Bart's Med Coll 1968–95, chm and research dir MicroPharm Ltd 1998–; FRCP; *Style—* Prof John Landon; ✉ MicroPharm Limited, Station Road Industrial Estate, Newcastle Emlyn, Carmarthenshire SA38 9BX (☎ 01239 710529)

L

LANDSMAN, Dr David Maurice; OBE (2001); s of Sidney Landsman (d 1998), and Miriam, *née* Cober; *b* 23 August 1963; *Educ* Chigwell Sch, Oriel Coll Oxford (MA), Clare Coll Cambridge (MPhil, PhD); *m* 1990, Catherine Louise, da of Geoffrey Holden; 1 s (Henry Francis Hugh b 1992); *Career* Univ of Cambridge Local Examinations Syndicate 1988–89; joined FCO 1989, second sec Athens 1991–94, dep head of mission Belgrade 1997–99, head Br Embassy Office Banja Luka and concurrently first sec Budapest 1999–2000, head Br Interests Section Belgrade then charge d'affaires 2000–01, ambass Tirana 2001–03, head Counter Proliferation Dept 2003–06, seconded as int affrs advsr De La Rue Identity Systems 2006–08, Balkans dir FCO 2008, ambass to Greece 2009–13; exec dir Tata Ltd 2013–; dir UK-India Business Cncl 2013–; memb IoD; *Publications* author of articles on Greek and Balkan languages; *Recreations* travel, languages, music, food, wildlife; *Clubs* Athenaeum; *Style*— Dr David Landsman, OBE; ✉ Tata Limited, 18 Grosvenor Place, London SW1X 7HS (e-mail tata@tata.co.uk)

LANDY, Michael; *Career* artist; works incl: Breakdown 2001, Nourishment 2002, Art Bin 2010; RA 2008; *Style*— Michael Landy, Esq

LANE, Abigail; *b* 1967, Penzance, Cornwall; *Educ* Bristol Poly, Goldsmiths Coll London (BA); *Career* artist; co-fndr Showroom Dummies 2003–; *Solo Exhibitions* Abigail Lane: Making History (Karsten Schubert Gallery London, collaboration with Interim Art) 1992, Emi Fontana Milan 1994, Skin of the Teeth (ICA London) 1995, 25 Watt Moon (Ridinghouse Editions London) 1996, Bonnefanten Museum Maastricht 1996–97, Another Time, Another Place (Galerie Chantal Crousel Paris) 1997, Andréhn-Schiptjenko Stockholm 1997, Never, never mind (Victoria Milo Gallery London) 1998, Whether the roast burns, the train leaves or the heavens fall (Museum of Contemporary Art Chicago) 1998, Inspirator (Andréhn-Schiptjenko Gallery Stockholm) 2001, Tomorrow's World, Yesterday's Fever (Mental Guests Incorporated) (Milton Keynes Gallery and Victoria Miro Gallery London) 2001; *Group Exhibitions* Freeze (Surrey Docks London) 1988, The New Contemporaries (ICA London) 1989, Home Truths (Castello di Rivara Turin) 1989, Modern Medicine (Building One London) 1990, Show Hide Show (Anderson O'Day Gallery London) 1991, Group Show (Emi Fontana Milan) 1992, Etats Spécifiques (Musée des Beaux-Arts Le Havre) 1992, Group Show (Kunsthalle Luzern) 1992, 20 Pièces Fragiles (Galerie Barbara et Luigi Polla Geneva) 1992, Group Show (Barbara Gladstone Gallery and Stein Gladstone Gallery NY) 1992, Group Show (Galerie Tanja Grunert Cologne) 1992, Privacy (Documentario Milan) 1992, Visione Britannica (Valentina Moncada & Pino Casagrande Rome) 1993, Displace (Cohen Gallery NY) 1993, Ha – Ha (Killerton House Gardens and Spacex Gallery Exeter) 1993, Peccato di Novita (Emi Fontana Milan) 1993, Recent British Sculpture from the Arts Council Collection (nat touring exhbn) 1993–94, photo 94 (The Photographers' Gallery London) 1994, Punishment + Decoration (Hohenthal und Bergen Cologne) 1994, Cyberintimismo (Erotica Bologna) 1994, Domestic Violence (Gio Marconi Milan) 1994, Not Self-Portrait (Karsten Schubert Gallery London) 1994, Some Went Mad, Some Ran Away... (Serpentine Gallery London) 1994, Ars Lux (billboard project, various sites Bologna) 1994, Fiction/Non-Fiction (Galleria Bonomo Rome) 1994, Some Went Mad, Some Ran Away... (Nordic Arts Centre Helsinki, Kunstverein Hannover, MCA Chicago and Portalen Copenhagen) 1995, Corpus Delicti (Kunstforeningen Copenhagen) 1995, Here and Now (Serpentine Gallery London) 1995, Karaoke: 4 for 4 and 2 to 2 Too (South London Gallery) 1995, Group Show of Young British Artists (Shoshana Wayne Gallery Santa Monica) 1995, Brill: works on paper by 'Brilliant!' artists (Montgomery Glasoe Fine Art Minneapolis) 1995, 4th International Istanbul Biennial 1995, Images of Masculinity (Victoria Miro Gallery London) 1995–96, Brilliant! New Art from London (Walker Art Center Minneapolis) 1995–96, Brilliant! New Art From London (Contemporary Arts Museum of Houston) 1996, #10 (Rhona Hoffman Gallery and Gallery 312 Chicago) 1996, Chaos, Madness. Permutations of Contemporary Art (Kunst Halle Krems) 1996, An exhibition of young British artists (Roslyn Oxley Gallery Sydney and RMIT Gallery Melbourne) 1996, From Figure to Object (Karsten Schubert Gallery and Frith Street Gallery London) 1996, Painting – The Extended Field (Magasin 3 Stockholm Konsthall) 1996–97, Intérieurs – Fischli & Weiss – Clay Ketter – Abigail Lane (Galerie Chantal Crousel Paris) 1996–97, Full House (Kunstmuseum Wolfsburg) 1996–97, Painting – The Extended Field (Rooseum Center for Contemporary Art Mälmo) 1997, L'Empreinte (Centre Pompidou Paris) 1997, Material Culture: The Object in British Art of the 1980's and 1990's (Hayward Gallery London) 1997, Gothic (ICA Boston touring to Portland Art Museum) 1998, Apocalyptic Wallpaper (Wexner Center for the Arts Columbus) 1997, L'Autre (4e Biennale de Lyon Halle Tony Garnier Lyon) 1997, Sensation. Young British Artists from the Saatchi Collection (Royal Acad of Arts London) 1997, Minor Sensation (Victoria Miro Gallery London) 1997, Art from the UK: Abigail Lane, Mona Hatoun, Rachel Whiteread, Douglas Gordon (Sammlung Goetz Munich) 1997–98, Exterminating Angel (Galerie Ghislaine Hussenot Paris) 1998, Close Echoes. Public Body & Artificial Space (City Gallery Prague and Kunst Halle Krems) 1998, London Calling (Br Sch at Rome) 1998, Fotografie als Handlung 4. Internationale Foto-Triennale Esslingen (Galerien der Stadt Esslingen Esslingen am Neckar) 1998, Trance (Philadelphia Museum of Art) 1998–99, Emotion – Junge britische und amerikanische Kunst in der Sammlung Goetz (Deichtorhallen Hamburg) 1998–99, Sensation. Yonug British Artists from the Saatchi Collection (Hamburger Bahnhof Berlin) 1998–99, Moving Images without Tears (Galerie Vera Munro Hamburg) 1998–99, Graphic! British Prints Now! (Yale Center for British Art New Haven) 1999, Mayday (Centre d'Art Neuchâtel) 1999–2000, De Schreeuw/The Scream (Galerij 't Leerhuys Bruges) 1999–2000, Raw (Victoria Miro Gallery London) 2000, Close Up (Kunstverein Freiburg im Marienbad, Kunsthuas Basselland and Kunstverein Hannover) 2000–01, Uncovered (The Gallery Univ of Essex) 2001, Summer Exhibition (Royal Acad of Arts London) 2001, Works on paper: from Acconci to Zittel (Victoria Miro Gallery London) 2001; *Style*— Ms Abigail Lane

LANE, Prof Christel; da of Erich Noritzsch (d 1985), of Flensburg, Germany, and Paula, *née* Lessman (d 1995); *b* 10 December 1940, Flensburg, Germany; *Educ* Univ of Essex (BSocSci), LSE (PhD); *m* 1962, David Lane, 1 s (Christopher b 1964), 1 da (Julie b 1973); *Career* post-doctoral research fell Univ of Cambridge 1976–79, lectr Univ of Aston 1981–90, lectr, reader and prof Univ of Cambridge 1990–, fell St John's Coll Cambridge 1990–; pres Soc for Advancement of Socio-Economics 2006; *Books* Christian Religion in the Soviet Union (1976), Rites of Rulers (1981), Management and Labour in Europe (1989), Industry and Society in Europe (1995), Trust Within and Between Organisations (1998), National Capitalisms, Global Production Networks (2009), Capitalist Diversity and Diversity within Capitalism (jt ed, 2012), The Cultivation of Taste, Chefs and the Organization of Fine Dining (2014); *Recreations* walking, contemporary novels, travel; *Style*— Prof Christel Lane; ✉ 3 Barrow Road, Cambridge CB2 8AP (☎ 01223 359113); Department of Sociology, Free School Lane, Cambridge CB2 3RQ (☎ 01223 330521, fax 01223 334550, e-mail col21@cam.ac.uk)

LANE, David Ian; *see:* David Ian

LANE, Prof Sir David Philip; kt (2000); *b* 1 July 1952; *Educ* John Fisher Sch, UCL (BSc, PhD); *Career* post doctoral res fell 1976–77, lectr Zoology Dept Imperial Coll of Science and Technol London 1977–81, Robertson res fell and CRI fell Cold Spring Harbor Laboratories USA 1978–80, lectr Biochemistry Dept Imperial Coll London 1981–85, princ scientist ICRF 1988–90 (sr head scientist 1985–88), dir Cell Transformation Res Gp Cancer Research Campaign 1990–; Gibb fell CRC 1990; fndr dir and chief scientific offr Cyclacel 1997–; memb: EMBO 1990, CRC Scientific Ctee 1995– (former memb Grants Ctee), Cncl Royal Soc of Edinburgh 1995–; author of over 160 papers; Charles Rodolphe Brupbacher Fndn Prize 1993, Howard Hughes Int Scholar Award 1993–98, Joseph Steiner Prize 1993, Jan Waldenstrom Lecture 1994, Yvette Mayent Prize 1995, Lennox Black Prize 1995, Mayenberg Prize 1995, Paul Erlich Prize 1998; FRSE 1992, FRS 1996; *Style*— Prof Sir David Lane, FRS, FRSE; ✉ Cancer Research Campaign, Laboratories, Department of Surgery and Molecular Oncology, Dundee University Medical School, Dundee DD1 9SY

LANE, David Stuart; s of Reginald Lane, and Mary Lane; *b* Fleur de Lys, Monmouthshire; *Educ* King Edward's Camp Hill GS Birmingham, Univ of Birmingham (BSocSc), Nuffield Coll Oxford (DPhil), Univ of Cambridge (PhD, by incorporation); *m* Christel, *née* Noritzsch; 1 s (Christopher), 1 da (Julie); *Career* Univ of Birmingham: lectr Faculty of Commerce and Social Sci 1962–64, lectr Centre for Russian and E Euro Studies 1964–67, prof of sociology 1981–90; Univ of Essex: lectr 1967–71, reader 1971–73, chm Sociology Dept 1972–73; Emmanuel Coll Cambridge: univ lectr 1974–80 and 1990–92, reader 1992–2000, fell 1974–80 and 1990–2000, emeritus fell 2000–; sr research assoc: Univ of Cambridge (emeritus reader 2000–), Leverhulme project on transformation of Russia and Ukraine 2004–07; Br Acad research award to study effects of unemployment in Ukraine and China, research supported by ESRC on new economic and political elites in Russia and political economy of Russian oil and financial system; memb New Modes of Governance within the European Union inter-univs consortium EU; visiting scholar Woodrow Wilson Centre Washington DC 1982, 1986 and 1995; visiting prof: Cornell Univ USA 1987, Univ of Graz Austria 1991 and 1996, Harvard Univ 1993 and 2001, Sabanci Univ Istanbul 2000–02; participant Valdai Conf Russia 2012–; chm W Midlands Branch Campaign for Mentally Handicapped People 1982–83, sec W Midlands Cncl for Disabled People 1983–86, exec ed Disability, Handicap and Society jl 1985–89, vice-chm Birmingham Elfrida Rathbone Assoc 1986–90, memb Exec Br Sociological Assoc 1987–92, jt chm and fndr first Euro Sociological Conf 1992, fndr memb and vice-pres Euro Sociological Assoc (memb Exec Ctee 1999–2001), memb Exec Ctee European Sci Fndn Network on Transition 1994–98, vice-pres Soc for Cooperation in Russian and Soviet Studies 2013; memb Editorial Bd Mir Rossii (Moscow); holder Br Acad Network Award supporting Network for Studies of Strategic Elites and European Enlargement 2004–09; FAcSS 2015; *Books* incl: The Roots of Russian Communism (1969), Politics and Society in the USSR (1970), The Socialist Industrial State – Towards a Political Sociology of State Socialism (1976), Current Approaches to Down's Syndrome (jt ed, 1985), Soviet Economy and Society (1985), Soviet Labour and the Ethic of Communism – Employment and the Labour Process in the USSR (1987), Soviet Society under Perestroika (1991), Russia in Flux (ed, 1992), Russia in Transition (ed, 1995), The Rise and Fall of State Socialism (1996), The Transition from Communism to Capitalism: Ruling Elites from Gorbachev to Yeltsin (jtly, 1998), The Political Economy of Russian Oil (ed and contrib, 1999), The Legacy of State Socialism and the Future of Transformation (ed and contrib, 2002), Russian Banking: Evolution, Problems and Prospects (ed and contrib, 2002), Pod"em i upadok gosudarstvennogo sotsialisma (2006), Varieties of Capitalism in Post-Communist Countries (jt ed and contrib, 2006), The Transformation of State Socialism: System Change, Capitalism or Something Else? (ed and contrib, 2007), Revolution in the Modern World: Social Identities, Globalisation and Modernity (ed and contrib, 2007), European Union and World Politics (jt ed and contrib, 2009), Migration and Mobility in Europe (jt ed 2009), Rethinking the Coloured Revolutions (jt ed and contrib 2010), Elites and Classes in the Transformation of State Socialism (2011), Elites and Identities in Post-Soviet Space (ed and contrib, 2012), The Capitalist Transformation of State Socialism (2013), The Eurasian Project and Europe (with Vsevolod Samokhvalov, 2015); author of articles in pubns incl: European Societies, Jl of Post-Communist and Transition Studies, New Political Economy, Political Studies, Polis, Br Jl Politics and Int Relations, Sociology, Competition and Change, Mir Rossii, POLIS (Moscow), Historical Social Research, Perspectives on European Politics and Society, Studies in Comparative International Development; *Recreations* playing squash, cinema, theatre, supporting Arsenal FC; *Style*— David Lane; ✉ Emmanuel College, Cambridge CB2 3AP (☎ 01223 359113, fax 01223 334550, e-mail dsl10@cam.ac.uk)

LANE, (Sara) Elizabeth; da of Rt Hon Sir Lionel Heald, QC, MP (d 1981), and Daphne Constance Heald, CBE; *b* 30 April 1938; *Educ* Heathfield Sch Ascot, Paris; *m* 15 May 1963, George Henry Lane, MC (d 2010), s of Ernest Lanyi, of Budapest, Hungary; *Career* dir Seek & Find Ltd 1963–68, advsr on works of art and assoc Baron Martin von Koblitz 1968–78, dir Christie Manson & Woods Ltd 1978–; *Recreations* country pursuits; *Style*— Mrs George Lane; ✉ 12 Petersham Place, London SW7 5PX; Christie Mansion & Woods Ltd, 8 King Street, St James's, London SW1Y 6QT (☎ 020 7839 9060, e-mail elane@christies.com)

LANE, Mark Alastair; *b* 18 March 1950; *Educ* Cranleigh Sch Surrey, Trinity Coll Cambridge (Keasby award), Coll of Law Guildford; *m* Judy West; 1 s (Benjamin), 1 da (Sarah); *Career* admitted slr: England and Wales 1975, Hong Kong 1984; trainee slr Stephenson Harwood 1973–75; slr Macfarlanes 1975–76, lectr Coll of Law London 1976–79; slr: A G Qarooni Iliffe & Edwards (Bahrain) 1979–81, Cameron McKenna 1982–85; Pinsent Masons LLP (formerly Masons): slr 1986–88, ptnr 1988–, head Water Sector Gp 1995–, ed-in-chief Pinsent Masons Water Yearbook; former chair Water Ctee Int Bar Assoc, co-vice-chair Int Construction Projects Ctee Int Bar Assoc; memb Exec Ctee European Construction Inst; memb City of London Slrs Co; memb Worshipful Co of Water Conservators; FRSA; *Recreations* tennis, running, gardening, sculpting, collecting antiques; *Style*— Mark Lane, Esq; ✉ Pinsent Masons LLP, 30 Aylesbury Street, London EC1R 0ER (e-mail mark.lane@pinsentmasons.com)

LANE, Dr Nancy Jane; OBE (1994); da of Temple Haviland Lane (d 1994), of Nova Scotia, and Frances de Forest, *née* Gilbert (d 1967); *Educ* Dalhousie Univ Canada (Allan Pollock scholar, Khaki Univ scholar, Ross Stewart Smith scholar, B'nai B'rith prize, Eugene Harris prize in zoology, BSc, Univ Gold medal, MSc), LMH Oxford (DPhil), Univ of Cambridge (PhD, DSc); *m* 22 Dec 1969, Prof R N Perham, FRS, FMedSci (d 2015); 1 da (Temple Helen Gilbert b 8 Oct 1970), 1 s (Quentin Richard Haviland b 14 Oct 1973); *Career* res asst prof Dept of Pathology Albert Einstein Coll of Med NY 1964–65, res staff biologist Dept of Biology Yale Univ 1965–68; Univ of Cambridge: research fell Girton Coll 1968–70, official fell and lectr in cell biology Girton Coll 1970–04 (subsequently life fell), tutor Girton Coll 1975–98, sr princ scientific offr ARC Unit of Invertebrate Chemistry and Physiology (later AFRC Unit) Zoology Dept 1982–90 (sr scientific offr 1968–73, princ scientific offr 1973–82), sr res assoc Zoology Dept 1990–, project dir Women in Sci, Engrg and Technol Initiative (WiSETI) 1999–2007; visiting prof: Siena Univ 1990–93, Padua Univ 1991–94; memb: PM's Advsy Panel for the Citizen's Charter 1991–93; chair: BTEC's Advsy Bd for Science and Caring 1991–94, Working Pty for Women in Science and Engrg (OST) Cabinet Office 1993–94, Athena Project 1998–2007 (vice-chair 1998–2003, chair 2004–07); dir WOYLA 1997–2004 (memb Cncl 2005–), ptnr Women Resource Centre DTI 2004–07; ed-in-chief Cell Biology International 1995–98, chair Editorial Ctee Science and Public Affairs (SPA) (now People and Science) 2001–13, co-author Set Fair Greenfield Report 2002, assoc ed 5 learned jls; non-exec dir: Smith and Nephew plc 1991–2000, Peptide Therapeutics plc 1995–98; memb: science GNVQ Advsy Ctee NCVQ 1993, Forum UK 1994–2008, Cmmn on Univ Career Opportunities CVCP 1996–2000, Exec Cncl Bioscience Fedn 2002–06, Scientific, Engrg and Environment Advsy Ctee Br Cncl (SEEAC) 2003–07, memb UNESCO Ctee for Natural Sci 2005–10, Scientific Ctee for Women in Sci and Technol UNESCO, Selection Bd Vanier/Banting Canada Graduate Scholarships Prog 2009–11; chair UK

Experts Database 2005; ptnr UK Resource Centre for Women in Sci 2005–07, gender equality champion Zoological Dept Univ of Cambridge 2013–; elected to Nova Scotia Hall of Fame for Science (Canada) 2006; Hon LLD Dalhousie Univ 1985, Hon DSc Univ of Salford 1994; Hon ScD: Sheffield Hallam Univ 2002, Oxford Brookes Univ 2003, Univ of Surrey 2005, Heriot-Watt Univ Edinburgh 2015; pres Inst of Biology 2002–04 (pres elect 2001–02); memb: Soc for Experimental Biology 1962, American Soc for Cell Biology 1965, Histochemical Soc 1965, American Assoc for the Advancement of Science 1965, Br Soc for Cell Biology 1980 (sec 1982–90), Br Soc for Developmental Biology 1980; fell Royal Microscopical Soc 1965; MRI 1987, MInstD 1991, FZS 1986 (memb Cncl 1998–2001, vice-pres 1999–2001), FSB 1991, FRSA 1992, Hon Fell BAAS 2005, CBiol, FIBiol; *Publications* author of over 190 scientific papers; *Recreations* theatre, dance and opera, 20th Century art, travelling; *Clubs* IOD, RSA; *Style—* Dr Nancy J Lane, OBE; ✉ 107 Barton Road, Cambridge CB3 9LL (☏ 01223 363710); Department of Zoology, Downing Street, Cambridge CB2 3EJ (e-mail njl1@cam.ac.uk)

LANE, (Alan) Piers; AO; s of Peter Alan Lane (d 2002), and Enid Muriel, *née* Hitchcock (d 2005); *b* 8 January 1958, London; *Educ* Kelvin Grove HS Brisbane, Queensland Conservatorium of Music, RCM London; *Career* concert pianist; prof Royal Acad of Music 1989–2007, writer and presenter BBC Radio 3 (54 programmes The Piano 1998–99), presenter of Legends series (BBC) 2000–03; artistic dir: Australian Festival of Chamber Music 2007–, Myra Hess Memorial Day Nat Gallery 2007–13, Sydney Int Piano Competition of Australia 2015; critic CD Review; appeared with orchs incl: Royal Philharmonic, London Philharmonic, the Philharmonia, Hallé Orch, BBC Welsh, BBC Scottish, BBC Concert, BBC Symphony, BBC Philharmonic, Scottish Chamber Orch, Australian Chamber Orch, New Zealand Symphony Orch, Bombay Chamber Orch, Adelaide Symphony Orch, American Symphony, Ensemble Kanazawa, Cape Town Symphony, Transvaal Philharmonic, Natal Philharmonic, Royal Liverpool Philharmonic, RTE Orch, Queensland Symphony, W Aust Symphony, Tasmanian Symphony, Melbourne Symphony, Czech Philharmonic, Queensland Philharmonic, Auckland Philarmonic, Christchurch Symphony, Montpellier Philharmonic Orch, Royal Oman Symphony, Brabants Orkester, Noorhollands Philharmonisch Orkest, Gothenburg Philharmonic, Aarhus Philharmonic, Romanian Radio Orch, CBSO, Orchestre National de France, Bournemouth Symphony, Australian Chamber Orchestra, Prague Chamber Orchestra, Janacek Philharmonic, Warsaw Philharmonic, Polish Radio Symphony, Helsingborg Symphony; toured extensively in UK, Ireland, Aust, NZ, S America, Western and Eastern Europe, USA, Africa, Japan, India, Sweden, Denmark, Norway, Canada, Korea, Thailand; special prize Bartók-Liszt Int Competition Budapest 1976, best Australian pianist Sydney Int Piano Competition 1977, winner Royal Over-Seas League Competition 1982; dir and tstee The Hattori Fndn; pres European Piano Teachers' Assoc 2014–; patron: Queensland Music Teachers' Assoc, Accompanists' Guild Queensland; memb jury Int Piano Competition in Tbilisi 2001 and Sydney 2004; memb: Liszt Soc, Delius Soc; vice-pres: Putney Music Club, Delius Soc, Int Ernest Bloch Soc; patron The Old Granary Studio, patron Youth Music Fndn Aust, patron Tait Meml Tst; Churchill fell 1979; Hon DUniv Griffith Univ 2007, Hon Doctorate James Cook Univ 2015; Hon RAM 1994; *Recordings* Moszowski and Paderewski Concertos (with BBC Scottish Symphony Orch and Jerzy Maxymiuk, 1991), Complete Études of Scriabin 1992, works by Mussorgsky, Balakirev and Stravinsky 1992, Piano Quintet by Brahms (New Budapest Quartet) 1992, Violin Virtuoso (with Tasmin Little) 1992, Sonatas by Shostakovich, Prokofiev, Schnittke and Rachmaninoff (with cellist Alexander Baillie), Franz Waxman Rhapsody (with Queensland Symphony Orch and Richard Mills), d'Albert Concertos (with BBC Scottish Orch and Alun Francis) 1994, Busch Concerto (with Royal Philharmonic and Vernon Handley) 1994, Vaughan-Williams and Delius Concertos plus Finzi Eclogue (with RLPO and Vernon Handley) 1994, Piano pieces by Alan Bush 1994, Elgar Piano Quintet (with Vellinger String Quartet) 1994, Virtuoso Strauss Transcriptions 1995, Concertos by Parry and Stanford 1995, French Violin Sonatas by Ravel, Debussy and Poulenc (with Tasmin Little) 1995, Delius Violin Sonatas (with Tasmin Little) 1997, d'Albert Solo Piano Works 1997, Saint-Saëns Complete Etudes 1998, Kullak & Dreyschock Concertos (with BBCSO and Niklas Willen) 1999, Complete Scriabin Preludes 2000, Carnival of the Animals (with Kathryn Stott, BBCCO and Barry Wordsworth) 1999, Grainger Piano Transcriptions 2001, Bach Transcriptions by Grainger, Friedman and Murdoch 2002, Finzi Eclogue (with Eng Chamber Orchestra and Nicholas Daniel) 2002, Moscheles Concert Etudes 2003, Henselt Concert Etudes 2004, Stanford Piano Quintet (with Vanburgh String Quartet) 2004, Alnaes and Sinding Concertos (with Bergen Philharmonic and Andrew Litton) 2006, Delius Songs (with Yvonne Kenny) 2006, Bloch Piano Quintets (with Goldner String Quartet) 2007, Bach/d'Albert Transcriptions 2009, Bridge Piano Quintet (with Goldner String Quartet) 2008, Dvorak Piano Quintets (with Goldner String Quartet) 2009, Mozart Concertos 482 and 491 (with Queensland Orch and Johannes Fritsch) 2009, Elgar Piano Quintet (with Goldner String Quartet) 2010, Virtuoso Clarinet with Michael Collins 2010, Harty Piano Quintet (with Goldner String Quartet) 2011, Berlioz, Liszt and Roger (with Philip Dukes) 2012, Strauss and Respighi Violin Sonatas (with Tamsin Little) 2012, Piers Lane Goes to Town 2013, British Violin Sonatas Vol I (with Tamsin Little) 2013, Arensky and Taneyev Piano Quintets (with Goldner String Quartet) 2013, Pierné Piano Quintet (with Goldner String Quartet) 2014, The Hour of Dreaming (with Lorna McGhee) 2014, Bruch Piano Quintet and Swedish Dances (with Goldner String Quartet) 2014, The Hour of Dreaming (with Lorna McGhee) 2014, Bruch Piano Quintet and Swedish Dances (with Golden String Quartet) 2015, Schubert Complete Works for Violin and Piano (with Tamsin Little and Timothy Hugh) 2015; *Style—* Piers Lane, Esq, AO; ✉ c/o Dr Sibylle Jackson at Hazard Chase, 25 City Road, Cambridge CB1 1DP (☏ 01223 312400, fax 01223 460827, e-mail sibylle.jackson@hazardchase.co.uk, websites www.pierslane.com and www.facebook.com/pierslane)

LANE, Robert Charles; CBE (2001); s of Sidney Arthur Lane (d 2011), and Eileen Ethel Anna, *née* Cleave (d 1991); *b* 29 August 1958, London; *Educ* Buckhurst Hill HS, UCL (LLB), Coll of Law; *m* 26 April 1986, Margaret Enid, da of Rev Stanley Peter Handley Stubbs, of London; 2 s (Edward b 2 Aug 1988, William b 20 May 1990), 1 da (Alice b 28 Aug 1991); *Career* articled clerk then slr Slaughter and May 1980–88; Cameron McKenna LLP (formerly McKenna & Co): slr 1988–90, ptnr 1990–, currently head Regulated Industries Gp; former chm Power Sector Advsy Gp UK Trade & Investment (BIS and FCO), exec memb Parly Gp for Energy Studies, exec memb Br Energy Assoc, former chm Utilities Ctee Int Bar Assoc; memb Kensington Soc; tstee and chm Orchid Cancer Charity; Freeman City of London 1987, Liveryman Worshipful Co of City of London Slrs 1988, Liveryman Worshipful Co of Wax Chandlers 2016; memb Law Soc 1982; *Recreations* opera, cricket, family, rugby, Joseph Crabtree Scholar; *Clubs* City of London, RAC, Garrick; *Style—* Robert Lane, Esq, CBE; ✉ CMS Cameron McKenna LLP, Cannon Place, 78 Cannon Street, London EC4N 6HL (☏ 020 7367 3000, fax 020 7367 2000, e-mail robert.lane@cms-cmck.com)

LANE, Prof Stuart N; *Educ* Fitzwilliam Coll Cambridge, City Univ London; *Career* fell, tutor and dir of studies in geography Fitzwilliam Coll Cambridge 1994–2000, asst univ lectr then univ lectr in geography Univ of Cambridge 1994–2000, prof of physical geography Univ of Leeds 2000–04, prof of physical geography and dir Inst of Hazard and Risk Research Univ of Durham 2004–11, prof of geomorphology Univ of Lausanne 2011–; adjunct prof INRS-Georesources Quebec 2001–; visiting scientist: Nat Inst for Water and Atmospheric Research NZ 1998, Dept of Geography Univ of Montreal 1998; memb: Photogrammetric Soc 1993–, European Geophysical Soc 1995–, American Geophysical Union 1995–, Int Assoc of Hydraulics Research 1997–; refereeing ed and memb Int Editorial Bd Photogrammetric Record 2002–, memb Editorial Advsy Bd Jl of River Basin Mgmnt 2003–; memb Editorial Bd: Transactions of the Inst of British Geographers 2003–, Earth Surface Processes and Landforms 2004–; tstee Yorkshire Dales Rivers Tst; Jan de Ploey Award Int Assoc of Geomorphologists 1997, Harold J Schoemaker Award Int Assoc of Hydraulics Research 2001 (jtly), President's Prize Remote Sensing and Photogrammetry Soc 2001, Philip Leverhulme Prize Leverhulme Tst 2002, R A Bagnold Medal European Goescience Union 2011, Victoria Medal RGS 2012; FRGS 1991; *Style—* Prof Stuart N Lane; ✉ Institute of Earth Surface Dynamics, Quartier Mouline, University of Lausanne, CH1015 Lausanne, Switzerland

LANE FOX, Robin James; s of James Henry Lane Fox, of Middleton Cheney, Oxon, and Anne, *née* Loyd; *b* 5 October 1946; *Educ* Eton, Magdalen Coll Oxford (MA); *m* 26 June 1970 (m dis 1993), Louisa Caroline Mary, da of Maj Charles Farrell, MC, of Watlington, Oxon; 1 da (Martha b 10 Feb 1973), 1 s (Henry b 19 Oct 1974); *Career* fell Magdalen Coll Oxford 1970–73, lectr in classics Worcester Coll Oxford 1974–76, res fell classical and Islamic history Worcester Coll Oxford 1976–77, fell and tutor New Coll Oxford 1977–, univ reader in ancient history Univ of Oxford 1990–; gardening columnist Financial Times 1970–, writer-presenter Travelling Heroes (BBC 4) 2010; Br Press Award Leisure Journalist of Year 1988; garden master New Coll Oxford 1979–; FRSL 1974; *Books* Alexander The Great (1973), Variations On A Garden (1974), Search for Alexander (1980), Better Gardening (1982), Pagan and Christians (1986), The Unauthorised Version (1991), The Long March (2004), The Making of Alexander (2004), The Classical World: From Homer to Hadrian (2005), Travelling Heroes (2008), Brill's Companion to Ancient Macedon (2011); *Recreations* gardening, travelling, remembering foxhunting; *Clubs* Beefsteak; *Style—* Robin Lane Fox, Esq, FRSL; ✉ c/o New College, Oxford OX1 3BN (☏ 01865 279 555)

LANE-SMITH, Roger; s of Harry Lane-Smith (d 1979), of Cheshire, and Dorothy, *née* Shuttleworth; *b* 19 October 1945; *Educ* Stockport GS, Guildford Coll of Law (Robert Ellis Memorial prizeman); *m* 1969, Pamela Mary, da of Leonard Leigh; 1 s (Jonathan Roger b 10 Nov 1973), 1 da (Zoe Victoria b 21 June 1971); *Career* admitted slr 1969; ptnr David Blank & Co Manchester 1973–77; Alsop Wilkinson: managing ptnr Manchester Office 1977–88, managing ptnr London Office 1988–92, chm 1992–96; DLA Piper Rudnick Gray Cary (formerly Dibb Lupton Alsop): dep sr ptnr 1996–98, sr ptnr and chm 1998–2005, conslt 2005–; non-exec chm JJB Sports plc 2005– (non-exec dir 1998–); non-exec dir: MS Int plc, Timpsons plc, Civica plc 2007–; memb Cncl CBI; winner Robert Ellis Meml prize; memb Law Soc; *Recreations* golf, tennis, shooting, deep-sea fishing; *Clubs* Mark's, St James'; *Style—* Roger Lane-Smith, Esq; ✉ JJB Sports plc, Martland Park, Challenge Way, Wigan, Lancashire WN6 0LD

LANG, Belinda Lucy; da of Jeremy Hawk, of London, and Joan, *née* Heal; *b* 23 December 1955; *Educ* Lycee Français de Londres, Central Sch of Speech and Drama; *m* 15 Oct 1988, Hugh Munro, s of John Hugh Munro Fraser (d 1987); 1 da (Lily Irene b 1990); *Career* actress and dir; co-fndr Haig-Lang Productions 2004; *Theatre* incl: Present Laughter (Vaudeville) 1981, Hobsons Choice (Haymarket) 1982, Antigone and Tales from Hollywood (NT) 1983–84, Clandestine Marriage (Albery) 1984, Mrs Klein (Apollo) 1989, Thark (Lyric Hammersmith) 1989, Dark River (Orange Tree) 1992 (nominated London Fringe Award), On Approval (Peter Hall Co) 1994, Dead Funny (Savoy and tour) 1996, Blythe Spirit (Chichester Festival) 1997, My Boy Jack (Hampstead Theatre) 1997, Things We Do for Love (Duchess Theatre) 1999, Life x Three (Savoy Theatre) 2002, Three Sisters Two (Orange Tree) 2002, The Secret Rapture (Lyric Theatre) 2003, My Boy Jack (tour, Haig-Lang Prodns) 2004, What the Butler Saw (Hamspstead Theatre and Criterion Theatre) 2005, Hay Fever (Haymarket Theatre) 2006 and (Royal Exchange) 2008 (nominated Best Actress MEN Award), Private Lives (Bath and Haig-Lang) 2006, Ring Around The Moon (Playhouse) 2008; dir: Present Laughter (nat tour) 2010, The Reluctant Debutante (nat tour) 2011; *Television* incl: To Serve Them All My Days (BBC) 1980, Dear John (BBC) 1985, The Bretts (Central) 1986, Bust (LWT) 1988, Alleyn Mysteries (BBC) 1990 and 1993–94, Second Thoughts (LWT) 1991–94, 2 Point 4 Children (BBC) 1991–99, Justice in Wonderland (BBC) 2000; *Recreations* walking, reading; *Style—* Miss Belinda Lang

LANG, Hon Mrs Justice; Dame Beverley Ann Macnaughton Lang; DBE (2011), QC (2000); *Career* called to the Bar Inner Temple 1978; recorder 2006, judge of the High Court of Justice (Queen's Bench Div) 2011–; hon fell Lady Margaret Hall Oxford 2012; *Style—* The Hon Mrs Justice Lang, DBE; ✉ Royal Courts of Justice, Strand, London WC2A 2CL

LANG, Dr Brian Andrew; CBE (2016); s of Andrew Ballantyne Lang, and Mary Bain, née Smith; *b* 2 December 1945; *Educ* Royal High Sch Edinburgh, Univ of Edinburgh (MA, PhD); *m* 1, 1975 (m dis 1982); 1 s; m 2, 1983 (m dis 2000); 1 s, 1 da; m 3, 2002, Tari Hibbitt, *qv*, da of late Suwondo Budiardjo, and Carmel Budiardjo; *Career* social anthropological field res Kenya 1969–70, lectr in social anthropology Aarhus Univ Denmark 1971–75, scientific staff SSRC 1976–79, sec Historic Bldgs Cncl for Scotland (Scottish Office) 1979–80, sec Nat Heritage Meml Fund 1980–87, dir of public affairs National Trust 1987–91, chief exec and dep chm The British Library 1991–2000; chm Euro Nat Libraries Forum 1993–2000, chair Heritage Image Partnership 2000–02, memb Cncl National Trust Scotland 2001–04, tstee Hopetoun House Preservation Trust 2001–05, chm Newbattle Abbey Coll Tst 2004–08, chm Edinburgh World Heritage 2015–; princ and vice-chllr Univ of St Andrews 2001–08; bd memb Scottish Enterprise Fife 2003–08, memb Scottish Exec Cultural Cmmn 2004–05; Pforzheimer lectr Univ of Texas 1998, visiting prof Napier Univ Edinburgh 1999–, visiting scholar Getty Inst LA 2000; memb: Library and Information Services Cncl (England) 1991–94, Library and Information Cmmn 1995–2000, Cncl St Leonards Sch St Andrews 2001–08; tstee: 21st Century Learning Initiative 1995–99, Nat Heritage Meml Fund 2004–11, Nat Museums of Scotland 2014–; chair Ctee for Scotland Heritage Lottery Fund 2005–11, chm Royal Scottish Nat Orchestra 2008–15; pres Inst of Info Scientists 1993–94 (hon fell 1994); Dr (hc) Univ of Edinburgh 2008, Hon LLD Univ of St Andrews 2008; Hon FLA 1997, FRSE 2006; *Publications* numerous articles, contribs to professional jls; *Recreations* music, museums and galleries, pottering; *Clubs* New (Edinburgh); *Style—* Dr Brian Lang, CBE, FRSE; ✉ 4 Manor Place, Edinburgh EH3 7DD

LANG, Rt Rev Declan; *see:* Clifton, Bishop of (RC)

LANG, Tari; da of Suwondo Budiardjo (d 1996), and Carmel, *née* Brickman; *b* 18 June 1951; *m* 1, 1971 (m dis 1996), Roger Hibbitt, s of John A Hibbitt; 1 da (Claire b 28 June 1976), 1 s (Laurence b 9 June 1978); m 2, 2002, Dr Brian Andrew Lang, *qv*, s of Andrew Ballantyne Lang; *Career* fndr dir Clasma Software Ltd 1980–86, md UK The Rowland Co 1988–95, chief exec UK Edelman Public Relations Worldwide 1995–2002 (dep md UK and md European Business and Technol 1995–98), founding ptnr ReputationInc 2002–09, ptnr Lang Consultancy 2009–; memb Bd: Nat Theatre of Scotland, Edinburgh Int Festival, Nat Galleries of Scotland; memb Bd of Govrs Royal Conservatoire Scotland; *Recreations* theatre, cinema, opera; *Style—* Ms Tari Lang; ✉ 4 Manor Place, Edinburgh EH3 7DD (e-mail tari@lang-uk.com, website www.lang-uk.com)

LANG, Prof Tim; s of Robert Anthony Lang (d 1996), and Katharine Margaret, *née* Alcock (d 2004); *b* 7 January 1948, Lincoln; *Educ* Uppingham, Univ of Leeds (BA, PhD); *m* 2 April 2004, Valerie Elizabeth Castledine, *née* Boon; *Career* dir: London Food Cmmn 1984–90, Parents for Safe Food 1990–94; prof of food policy: Thames Valley Univ 1994–2002, City Univ 2002–; conslt WHO 1996–2003, advsr House of Commons Health and Agric

L

Ctees (inquiries incl: Food Standards Agency Bill 1998–99, Food Standards Agency 2000, Globalisation 2000, Obesity 2003–04), tech advsr to French Presidency of the European Cmmn Food and Nutrition Initiative 1999–2000, chair Sustain 1999–2005, cmmr for land use and natural resources Sustainable Devpt Cmmn 2006–11; memb Cncl of Food Policy Advsrs 2008–10; tstee: Food Cmmn (UK) 1990–2010, Friends of the Earth 1994–2001; memb Bd The Rodale Inst USA 1997–2007; vice-pres Chartered Inst of Environmental Health 1999–, pres Garden Organic 2008; tstee Borough Market 2008; Caroline Walker Award 2002, BBC Radio 4 Food & Farming Derek Cooper Award 2003; FRSA 1998, FFPH 2001, Hon fell Cardiff Metropolitan Univ 2007, Hon DSc Univ of Lincoln 2009, fell Faculty of Public Health RCP, Hon FRSL 2014; *Publications* More than we can Chew (jtly, 1982), Food Irradiation: the Myth and the Reality (jtly, 1990), P is for Pesticides (jtly, 1991), The New Protectionism (jtly, 1993), The Unmanageable Consumer: Contemporary Consumption and its Fragmentation (jtly, 1995), The Atlas of Food (jtly, 2003, André Simon Food Book of the Year Award 2003), Food Wars: The Battle for Mouths, Minds and Markets (jtly, 2004), Food Policy (jtly, 2009), Ecological Public Health (jtly, 2012); *Recreations* reading the papers; *Style—* Prof Tim Lang; ✉ City University London, Northampton Square, London EC1V 0HB (☎ 020 7040 8798, e-mail t.lang@city.ac.uk)

LANG OF MONKTON, Baron (Life Peer 1997), of Merrick and the Rhinns of Kells in Dumfries and Galloway; Rt Hon Ian Bruce Lang; PC (1990), DL (Ayrshire & Arran 1998); s of late James Fulton Lang, DSC; *b* 27 June 1940; *Educ* Lathallan Sch, Rugby, Sidney Sussex Coll Cambridge (BA); *m* 1971, Sandra Caroline, da of John Alastair Montgomerie, DSC; 2 da; *Career* MP (Cons): Galloway 1979–83, Galloway and Upper Nithsdale 1983–97 (Parly candidate (Cons): Central Ayrshire 1970, Glasgow Pollok 1974); asst govt whip 1981–83, a Lord Cmmr of the Treasy 1983–86; Parly under-sec of state: Dept of Employment 1986, Scottish Office 1986–87; min of state Scottish Office 1987–90, sec of state for Scotland 1990–95, pres Bd of Trade (sec of state for Trade and Industry) 1995–97; memb House of Lords Constitution Ctee 2001–05 and 2013– (chm 2014–), memb Select Ctee on the Barnett Formula 2009, chm PM's Advsy Ctee on Business Appts 2009–14; chm Marsh & McLennan Companies Inc 2011–16 (dir 1997–2011), dir Charlemagne Capital Ltd 2006–; chm Patrons of Nat Galleries of Scotland 1999–2007; govr Rugby Sch 1999–2007; memb Queen's Body Guard for Scotland (Royal Co of Archers) 1974; OStJ 1974; *Publications* Blue Remembered Years (2002); *Clubs* Prestwick Golf, Pratt's; *Style—* The Rt Hon Lord Lang of Monkton, PC, DL; ✉ House of Lords, London SW1A 0PW

LANGDON, (Richard) Benedict (Ben); s of David Langdon, OBE, of Prestwood, Bucks, and April Yvonne Margaret, *née* Sadler-Phillips; *b* 28 August 1963; *Educ* Royal GS High Wycombe, Jesus Coll Oxford (BA); *m* 21 Oct 1989, Vicky, da of George Henderson; 1 s (Max David b 25 Sept 1992), 1 da (Ruby Louise b 25 April 1994); *Career* account mangr: Allen Brady & Marsh advtg agency 1985–87, Lowe Howard Spink 1987–88; Still Price Court Twivy D'Souza Lintas: account dir 1989–90, bd/gp account dir 1990, new business dir 1991–93; md Addition Marketing Jan-June 1993, client servs dir McCann-Erickson Advertising 1993, chief-exec Collett Dickenson Pearce 1995–96 (md 1993–95), chief-exec and md McCann-Erickson Advertising 1996–1999, ceo and chm McCann-Erickson UK & Ireland 1999–2003, regional dir McCann-Erickson EMEA 2000–03, co-fndr Ben Mark Orlando Jan-Mar 2004, chm Euro RSCG Worldwide UK and Euro RSCG London 2004–05, ceo Digital Marketing Group plc 2006–11, owner Tradigital Ltd 2011–; non-exec dir Hay & Robertson plc 1999–2001; *Recreations* golf, soccer; *Clubs* Harewood Downs Golf (Little Chalfont); *Style—* Ben Langdon, Esq

LANGDON, Prof John Dudley; s of Jack Langdon (d 1984), of London, and Daphne Irene Heloise, *née* Liebsch (d 1988); *b* 24 March 1942, London; *Educ* Highgate Sch, London Hosp Med Coll (BDS, MB BS, MDS, Med, Surgery and Pathology prize, London prize, Annual Award of Merit American Soc of Dentistry for Children, Harold Fink prize, Charrington prize, James Anderson prize), RCS (LDS); *Career* house surgn Royal London Hosp 1965, sr house surgn Dept of Oral Surgery Royal Dental and St George's Hosp 1965–66, SHO Dept of Oral Surgery Eastman Hosp 1966; registrar: Dept of Oral Surgery Royal London Hosp 1967 (Oral Surgery and Conservative Dentistry 1966–67), Oral Surgery and Maxillofacial Unit Honey Lane Hosp 1967–68; pt/t demonstrator Dept of Dental Anatomy London Hosp Med Coll 1968–69, locum registrar Dept of Oral Surgery St Thomas' Hosp 1969, pt/t lectr London Hosp Med Coll 1970–73, house physician Harold Wood Hosp 1974 (house surgn 1973), locum conslt oral surgn Oldchurch Hosp 1974; sr registrar Dept of Oral and Maxillofacial Surgery: Royal London Hosp 1974–76, KCH 1976–77; tutor RCS 1977, conslt oral and maxillofacial surgn Queen Mary's Hosp 1977–83 (hon conslt 1983–90), sr lectr/conslt Dept of Oral and Maxillofacial Surgery King's Coll Sch of Med and Dentistry 1983–92, special lectr in oral surgery Dental Sch Univ of Bristol 1987–93, prof of oral and maxillofacial surgery King's Coll Sch of Med and Dentistry 1992–2004 (vice-dean Faculty of Clinical Dentistry 1987–90), exec dir of patient servs King's Dental Inst 1994–, dir of modernisation and health services delivery Guy's, King's & St Thomas' Dental Inst 2002–04; hon conslt: St George's Healthcare NHS Tst 1984–2000, Royal Surrey and St Luke's NHS Tst 1993–2000, Epsom Healthcare NHS Tst 1994–2003; chm Intercollegiate Bd in Oral & Maxillofacial Surgery 1998–2001; pres: Section of Odontology RSM 1998–99, Br Assoc of Head and Neck Oncologists 1998–2001, Inst of Maxillofacial Prosthetists & Technologists 1999–2001, Br Assoc of Oral and Maxillofacial Surgns 2003; memb: Cncl Assoc of Head and Neck Oncologists of Great Br 1981–84, Academic Advsy Ctee Oral and Maxillofacial Surgery 1989–97, SAC in oral surgery and oral med 1989–94, Speciality Advsy Bd in oral and maxillofacial surgery RCS (Ed) 1990–98 (chm), Bd Faculty of Dental Surgery RCSE 1994–, BDA, BMA, Br Soc of Dental Res, Craniofacial Soc of Great Britain, Euro Assoc for Cranio-Maxillo-Facial Surgery; hon treas Br Assoc of Oral and Maxillofacial Surgns 1992–2004; fndr memb Maxillofacial Study Gp, hon sec (Odontology) RSM 1993–95; fndn fell Asian Assoc of Oral and Maxillofacial Surgns; ed (Oncology Section) Int Jl of Oral and Maxillofacial Surgery 1988–, conslt ed (Oral Oncology) Euro Jl of Cancer 1991–; fell: Br Assoc of Oral and Maxillofacial Surgns, Int Assoc of Oral and Maxillofacial Surgns, Acad of Med Science (fndr fell), Int Acad of Oral Oncology (fndr fell and exec dir), KCL, Acad of Med Sciences; FKC 2002, FDS 1972, FRCS 1985; *Books* Malignant Tumours of the Oral Cavity (with J M Henk, 1985), Cancer of the Mouth, Jaws and Salivary Glands (with J M Henk, 1994), Surgical Pathology of the Mouth and Jaws (with R A Cawson and J Eveson, 1995), Surgical Anatomy of the Infratemporal Fossa (with B K B Berkovitz and B J Moxham, 2003), Operative Oral and Maxillofacial Surgery (with M F Patel, R A Ord and P Brennan, 2010); *Recreations* gardening, opera, antiques, cooking, church bell ringing; *Style—* Prof John Langdon; ✉ The Old Rectory, Limington, Somerset BA22 8EQ (☎ 01935 840127)

LANGHAM, Lorraine; da of Leslie Goodge, of Cooden, E Sussex, and Josephine, *née* Cole (d 2006); *b* 29 March 1964, Dunstable, Beds; *m* 2006, Leon Panitzke; *Career* LGTB 1980–85, London Borough of Hounslow 1985–89, London Borough of Hammersmith and Fulham 1989, London Borough of Harrow 1989–93, London Borough of Camden 1993–96, London Borough of Hackney 1996–2000, Renaissance – Partners in Communication 2000–05, md Verve Communications 2005–07; Ofsted: dir corporate services 2007–09, dir organisational devpt 2009–12, chief operating offr 2012–, chief operating offr Brent Cncl 2015–; FCIPR 2000, Dir FInstD 2012; *Style—* Mrs Lorraine Langham; ✉ Brent Council, Civic Centre, Engineer's Way, Wembley, HA9 0FJ

LANGHAM, Tony; s of Trevor Langham, and Margaret, *née* Harris; *b* 4 June 1961; *Educ* Holgate Comp, Univ of Birmingham (BA); *m* 1993, Clare, da of Anthony Parsons (d 1964); 2 s ((Charles) Alexander b 10 Jan 1994, Theodore Maximilian b 14 Oct 1996); *Career* sr researcher MORI 1982–84, jt head of retail fin PR Dewe Rogerson 1984–89; Lansons: co-fndr (with Clare Parsons) 1989–, chief exec 2001–; non-exec chm unbiased.co.uk 2011–, chm PRCA PR Cncl 2014–15; chm Great British Racing 2016–; memb MRS 1986, MIPR 1989, FCIPR 2007; *Recreations* performing arts, travel, history, sport; *Style—* Tony Langham, Esq; ✉ Lansons, 24a St John Street, London EC1M 4AY (☎ 020 7490 8828, fax 020 7490 5460, e-mail tonyl@lansons.com, Twitter @TonyLangham)

LANGHORNE, Richard Tristan Bailey; s of Eadward John Bailey Langhorne, MBE (d 1995), of Chichester, and Rosemary, *née* Scott-Foster; *b* 6 May 1940; *Educ* St Edward's Sch Oxford, St John's Coll Cambridge (MA); *m* 18 Sept 1971, Helen Logue (d 2005), da of William Donaldson, CB (d 1988); 1 s (Daniel b 22 Nov 1972), 1 da (Isabella b 29 Aug 1975); *Career* lectr in history Univ of Kent 1966–75 (master Rutherford Coll 1971–74), fell St John's Coll Cambridge 1975– (steward 1975–79, bursar 1975–87), dir Centre of Int Studies Univ of Cambridge 1987–93, dir and chief exec Wilton Park FCO 1993–96, prof of political science and dir Grad Div of Global Affrs Rutgers Univ 1996–; visiting prof: Sch of Int Rels Univ of Southern Calif 1986, Canterbury Christchurch Univ 2005; hon prof of int rels Univ of Kent at Canterbury 1994, hon prof of global affrs Univ of Buckingham 2006– (also prog co-dir MA in global affrs); chm Br Int History Assoc 1988–93; FRHistS 1985; *Books* The Collapse of the Concert of Europe 1890–1914 (1982), Diplomacy and Intelligence during the Second World War (ed, 1985), The Practice of Diplomacy (with K A Hamilton, 1994), The Coming of Globalization (2000), Guide to International Relations and Diplomacy (ed, 2002), Diplomacy (ed, 3 vols, 2004), Diplomacy and Governance (2004), The Essentials of Global Politics (2006); *Recreations* cooking, music, railways; *Clubs* Athenaeum; *Style—* Richard Langhorne, Esq; ✉ Carleton House, King Street, Fordwich, Canterbury, Kent CT2 0DA (☎ 01227 712454); 123 Washington Street, #510, Newark, NJ 07102, USA

LANGLANDS, Sir (Robert) Alan; kt; *b* 29 May 1952; *Educ* Allan Glen's Sch Glasgow, Univ of Glasgow (BSc), Inst of Health Service Mgmnt; *m* 1977, Elizabeth McDonald; 1s, 1 da; *Career* with Argyll and Clyde Health Bd 1976–78, with dist maternity services S Lothian 1978–82, unit admin Middx Hosp 1981–82, with Middx Hosp, UCH and Soho Hosp for Women 1982–85, dist gen mangr Harrow HA 1985–89, healthcare mgmnt conslt in private practice 1989–90, regnl gen mangr NW Thames RHA 1990–93; Dept of Health NHS Exec: dep chief exec 1993–94, chief exec 1994–2000; princ and vice-chllr Univ of Dundee 2000–09, chief exec HE Funding Cncl for England 2009–13, vice-chllr Univ of Leeds 2013–; chair: Cmmn on Good Governance in the Public Servs 2004–05, Gateways to the Professions 2004–05, UK Biobank Ltd 2004–12, FBbk 2015, The Health Fndn; memb Advsy Bd: INSEAD 1999–2003, Johns Hopkins Univ Bioethics Inst 2000–04; hon prof Warwick Business Sch; Hon DUniv Glasgow 2001; Hon FFPH (Hon FFPHM 1994), FIA 1999, FCGI 2000, CCMI (CIMgt 2000), Hon FRCP 2001, Hon FRCGP 2001, Hon FRCSE 2001, Hon FRCPSGlas 2002, Hon FMedSci, HON FRCP (Edin) 2014, Hon LLD Dundee 2010, Hon D Univ Edin 2010, Royal Northern Coll of Music bd memb 2014, FRSE; *Recreations* living and walking in Scotland and Yorkshire; *Style—* Sir Alan Langlands, FRSE

LANGLEY, Anthony John (Tony); s of John James Langley, of Nottingham, and Kathlene Grace, *née* Hunt; *b* 2 December 1954, Nottingham; *Educ* Gedling Secdy Modern, Arnold & Carlton Coll of FE Nottingham; *m* 12 May 1994, Amanda Jane, *née* Drakes; 1 da (Charlotte Audrey b 31 Oct 1991), 2 s (Bernard James b 31 March 1993, William Anthony b 24 March 1995); *Career* F S Hunt & Co Ltd (family business) 1974–75, chm and ceo Langley Hldgs plc 1975–; *Recreations* sailing, skiing, tennis, flying (helicopters and aeroplanes); *Clubs* Royal London Yacht, Royal Thames Yacht, Yacht Club Costa Smerelda; *Style—* Tony Langley, Esq; ✉ Langley Holdings plc, Thrumpton Lane, Retford, Nottinghamshire DN22 7AN (☎ 07785 265829, website www.langleyholdings.com)

LANGLEY, Sir (Julian Hugh) Gordon Langley; kt (1995); s of Gordon Thompson Langley (d 1943), and Marjorie, *née* Burgoyne (d 2000); *b* 11 May 1943; *Educ* Westminster, Balliol Coll Oxford (MA, BCL); *m* 20 Sept 1968, Beatrice Jayanthi, da of Simon Tennakoon (d 1986), of Colombo, Sri Lanka; 2 da (Ramani Elizabeth b 1969, Sharmani Louise b 1972); *Career* called to the Bar Inner Temple 1966 (bencher 1996); QC 1983–95, recorder 1986–95, judge of the High Court of Justice (Queen's Bench Div) 1995–2007, chm Takeover Panel 2010–; *Recreations* music, sport; *Style—* Sir Gordon Langley; ✉ Fountain Court Chambers, Temple, London EC4Y 9DH

LANGMEAD, Jeremy John; s of John Sambrook, and Juliet Langmead, *née* Popplewell; *b* 3 November 1965; *Educ* St Joseph's Coll Ipswich, Central St Martin's Sch of Art London (BA); *m* 1992 (sep), India Knight, da of Michel Aertsens; 2 s (Oscar Augustus b 8 Dec 1992, Archie Jack b 8 Nov 1995); *Career* journalist; previous appts with Tatler, Elle Decoration and Mirabella magazines and freelance contrib to various newspapers incl Sunday Times, Evening Standard and The Guardian; Style ed The Sunday Times 1995–2000 (dep Style ed 1994–95), ed Nova 2000–01, Life and Style ed Evening Standard 2001–02, ed-in-chief Wallpaper* 2002–07, ed Esquire 2007–10, ed-in-chief Mr Porter 2010–; *Recreations* travelling, cycling and socialising; *Style—* Jeremy Langmead, Esq

LANGRIDGE, Matthew; *b* 20 May 1983, Crewe; *Career* rower; GB nat sr rowing debut 2003; achievements incl: Bronze medal (coxless pair) World Championships 2007, Silver medal (eights) Olympic Games Beijing 2008, Gold medal (coxless four) World Championships 2009, Gold medal (coxless four) World Championships 2011, Bronze medal (eights) Olympic Games 2012; *Clubs* Leander; *Style—* Matthew Langridge, Esq

LANGSLOW, Dr Derek Robert; CBE (2000); s of Alex Langslow (d 1993), and Beatrice, *née* Wright (d 1992); *b* 7 February 1945; *Educ* Ashville Coll Harrogate, Queens' Coll Cambridge (MA, PhD); *m* 1969, Helen Katherine Addison; 1 s (Ian b 1975), 1 da (Sarah b 1980); *Career* res fell Univ of Cambridge 1969–72, lectr in biochemistry Univ of Edinburgh 1972–78; Nature Conservancy Cncl: sr ornithologist 1978–84, asst chief scientist 1984–87, dir policy planning and servs 1987–90; chief exec English Nature 1990–2000, memb Agric and Environment Biotechnol Cmmn 2000–05; dir Br Waterways 2000–06, dep chm Harwich Haven Authy 2001–09; chm E of Eng Tourist Bd 2006–10; chm: Rail Passengers Eastern Eng 2000–05, Rail Passengers Cncl 2005–11; dir Marine Mgmnt Orgn 2010–; tstee: Heritage Lottery Fund 2002–08, Natural History Museum London 2008–; author of more than 50 scientific pubns; *Style—* Dr Derek Langslow, CBE; ✉ 4 Engaine, Orton Longueville, Peterborough PE2 7QA (☎ 01733 232153, e-mail derek.langslow@btinternet.com)

LANGSTAFF, Hon Mr Justice; Sir Brian Frederick James Langstaff; kt (2005); s of Frederick Sydney Langstaff, of Boxted, Essex, and Muriel Amy Maude, *née* Griffin; *b* 30 April 1948, Perth, Scotland; *Educ* George Heriot's Sch Edinburgh, St Catharine's Coll Cambridge (BA); *m* 19 July 1975, Deborah Elizabeth, da of Samuel James Weatherup (d 1953), of NI; 1 da (Kerry b 1978), 1 s (Nicholas b 1980); *Career* called to the Bar Middle Temple 1971 (bencher 2002), called to the Bar of NI 1999; sr lectr in law Chelmer Coll 1971–75 (formerly lectr), Harmsworth scholar 1975, in practice 1975–2005, QC 1994, recorder 1995–2005 (asst recorder 1991–95), judge Employment Appeal Tbnl 2000–03, head of chambers 2002–05, judge of the High Court of Justice (Queen's Bench Div) 2005–; pres Employment Appeal Tbnl 2012–15; leading counsel Bristol Royal Infirmary Inquiry 1998–2001; memb Exec Ctee: Personal Injury Bar Assoc 1995–2002 (chm 1999–2001),

Industrial Law Soc 1997–2005 (hon vice pres 2005–), Bd of Govrs local primary sch; chm: Law Reform Ctee of Bar Cncl 2001–02 (vice-chm 1999–2001), working pty on structured settlements for Master of Rolls 2001–02, Serious Personal Injury and Clinical Negligence Ctee Civil Justice Cncl 2003–05, Tbnls Procedure Ctee 2012–16; advsy ed OHS&E 1997–2000; *Books* Concise College Casenotes Series: Equity & Trusts (1975); contrib Health and Safety at Work (Halsbury's Laws, 4 edn), Bullen & Leake's Precedents of Pleading (conslt ed, 1999, 15 edn 2003, 18 edn 2015), Munkman on Employers' Liability (contrib, 2000, 2006, 2009 and 2013), Personal Injury Handbook (ed and contrib, 2001 and 2006), Personal Injury Schedules (2002, 2005 and 2009); *Recreations* sport, tennis, swimming, walking, travel, watching TV, mowing the lawn; *Style—* The Hon Mr Justice Langstaff; ✉ Royal Courts of Justice, Strand, London WC2A 2LL

LANGSTAFF, Rt Rev James Henry; *see:* Rochester, Bishop of

LANGTON, Simon Guy Charles; s of David Langton (d 1994), of Stratford-upon-Avon, Warks, and Mona Rosemary, *née* Copeman (d 1972); *b* 5 November 1941; *Educ* Bloxham Sch; *m* 1, 1971 (m dis 1973), Victoria Master; *Career* director; asst stage mangr Folkestone Repertory Theatre 1959, stage mangr Theatre Royal Windsor 1960–62, BBC TV 1963–71, freelance dir 1971–; memb: Dirs' Guild of GB 1980, Dirs' Guild of America 1983; *Television and Film* credits incl: Microbes & Men (BBC) 1972, Love For Lydia (LWT) 1973, Upstairs Downstairs (LWT) 1974, Duchess of Duke Street (BBC) 1976, Gate of Eden (YTV) 1977, Danger UXB (Euston Films) 1978, Rebecca (BBC) 1979, Therese Raquin (BBC) 1980, Nelson (ATV) 1980, Smiley's People (BBC) 1981, Lost Honour of Katherine Beck (CBS) 1982, Casanova (ABC) 1984, Anna Karenina (CBS) 1985, Laguna Heat (HBO) 1986, Dos Destinos (corporate film for BA) 1986, Whistle Blower (feature) 1987, Out of Darkness (ABC/Robert Halmi) 1987, Mother Love (BBC) 1988, Jeeves & Wooster II (Carnival Films) 1990, Headhunters (BBC) 1992, The Cinder Path (YTV) 1993, Pride and Prejudice (BBC) 1994, Stanley's Search for Dr Livingstone (Hallmark Films) 1997, Nancherrow (Portman Prodns/Telemunchen) 1998, Scarlet Pimpernel (BBC) 2000, Murder Rooms (BBC) 2001, Agatha Christie's The Hollow (LWT) 2003, Rosemary and Thyme 2004 and 2005, Midsomer Murders 2009; *Theatre* co-prodr The Old Masters (West End) 2004; *Awards* Peabody Award (for Smiley's People), Tric Award (for Mother Love), Best Drama RTS Award (for Scarlet Pimpernel) 2002; for Pride and Prejudice 1996: Tric Award for Best Drama, Broadcasting Press Guild Award for Best Drama Serial, Banff Television Festival Award for Best Mini Series and Grand Prize for Best Programme; nominations incl: BAFTA 1972 (for Microbes & Men), BAFTA 1979 (for Therese Raquin), BAFTA (Mother Love), BAFTA for Best Serial 1996 (for Pride and Prejudice); nominations for Smiley's People: BAFTA, Emmy, Peoples Award; *Recreations* natural history; *Clubs* Garrick; *Style—* Simon Langton, Esq; ✉ c/o Charles Collier, Tavistock Wood, 45 Conduit Street, London W1S 2YN (☎ 020 7494 4767)

LANKESTER, Sir Timothy Patrick (Tim); KCB (1994); s of Robin Prior Archibald Lankester, and Jean Dorothy, *née* Gilliat; *Educ* Monkton Combe Sch, St John's Coll Cambridge (BA), Jonathan Edwards Coll Yale Univ (Henry fell, MA), St John's Coll Oxford (Fereday fell); *m* 1968, Patricia, *née* Cockcroft; 3 da (Alexandra Kim b 30 April 1970, Olivia Mary b 28 Sept 1971, Laura Camilla b 9 Oct 1981); *Career* economist World Bank 1966–73 (Washington until 1969 and New Delhi until 1973); HM Treasy: princ 1973–77, asst sec 1977, private sec to Rt Hon James Callaghan 1978–79, private sec to Rt Hon Margaret Thatcher 1979–81, seconded to S G Warburg and Co Ltd 1981–83, under sec 1983–85, econ minister Washington (and exec dir World Bank and IMF) 1985–88, dep sec (and dir European Investment Bank) 1988–89; perm sec: ODA 1989–94, Dept for Educn 1994–95; dir SOAS Univ of London 1996–2000, pres Corpus Christi Coll Oxford 2001–10; dep chm British Cncl 1998–2003; chm Cncl London Sch of Hygiene and Tropical Medicine 2007–15, chm of govrs Contemporary Dance Tst 2007–13; hon fell: SOAS, St John's Coll Cambridge, CCC Oxford; *Style—* Sir Tim Lankester, KCB; ✉ e-mail tim.lankester@ccc.ox.ac.uk

LANNON, Dr Dame Dr Frances; DBE (2016); da of Martin Lannon, and Margaret, *née* O'Hare; *b* 22 December 1945, Newcastle upon Tyne; *Educ* Sacred Heart GS Newcastle upon Tyne, Lady Margaret Hall Oxford (MA), St Antony's Coll Oxford (DPhil); *Career* lectr in history Queen Mary Coll London 1975–77; Lady Margaret Hall Oxford: fell and tutor in modern history 1977–2002, princ 2002–; visiting prof Univ of South Carolina 1986, fell Woodrow Wilson Center Washington DC 1992; FRHistS 1986; Privilege, Persecution and Prophecy: The Catholic Church in Spain 1875–1975 (1987), Elites and Power in Twentieth-Century Spain: Essays in Honour of Sir Raymond Carr (ed with Paul Preston,1990), The Spanish Civil War (2002), Lady Margaret Hall, Oxford: The First 125 Years 1879–2004 (2004); *Clubs* Reform; *Style—* Dr Dame Frances Lannon, DBE; ✉ Lady Margaret Hall, Oxford OX2 6QA (☎ 01865 274302, fax 01865 274294, e-mail frances.lannon@lmh.ox.ac.uk)

LANSDOWNE, 9 Marquess of (GB 1784) Charles Maurice Petty-Fitzmaurice; LVO (2002), DL (Wilts 2015); also Baron Kerry and Lixnaw (I 1295), Earl of Kerry, Viscount Clanmaurice (both I 1723), Viscount FitzMaurice, Baron Dunkeron (both I 1751), Earl of Shelburne (I 1753), Lord Wycombe, Baron of Chipping Wycombe (GB 1760), Earl Wycombe, and Viscount Calne and Calstone (both GB 1784); assumption of additional surnames of Petty-Fitzmaurice recognised by decree of Lord Lyon 1947; s (by 1 m) of 8 Marquess (d 1999), and Barbara Stuart Chase (d 1965); *b* 21 February 1941; *Educ* Eton; *m* 1, 1965 (m dis 1987), Lady Frances Eliot (d 2003), da of 9 Earl of St Germans; 2 da (Lady Arabella Helen Mary (Lady Arabella Unwin) b 1966, Lady Rachel Barbara Violet (Lady Rachel Spickernell) b 1968), 2 s (Simon Henry George, Earl of Kerry b 1970, Lord William Nicholas Charles b 1973); m 2, 1987, Fiona Mary, da of Donald Merritt; *Heir* s, Earl of Kerry; *Career* page of honour to HM The Queen 1956–57; served: Kenya Regt 1960–61, Wiltshire Yeomanry (TA), amalgamated with Royal Yeomanry Regt 1963–73; cncllr: Calne and Chippenham RDC 1964–73, Wilts CC 1970–85, N Wilts DC (chm 1973–76); memb: SW Econ Planning Cncl 1972–77 (chm Working Ctee on Population and Settlement Pattern), Historic Bldgs and Monuments Cmmn 1983–89, Cncl Duchy of Cornwall 1990–2002; pres: Wilts Playing Fields Assoc 1965–75, Wilts Assoc of Boys' Clubs and Youth Clubs 1976–2003, NW Wilts Dist Scout Cncl 1977–88, HHA 1988–93 (dep pres 1986–88), South West Tourism 1989–2006, Wiltshire Historic Buildings Tst 1994–, The Wilts and Berks Canal Partnership 2001–; Parly candidate (Cons) Coventry NE 1979; HM Vice Lord-Lt Wilts 2012–15; Liveryman Worshipful Co of Fishmongers; *Clubs* Turf, Brooks's; *Style—* The Most Hon the Marquess of Lansdowne, LVO, DL; ✉ Bowood House, Calne, Wiltshire SN11 0LZ (☎ 01249 812102)

LANSLEY, Baron (Life Peer UK 2015), of Orwell in the County of Cambridgeshire; Rt Hon Andrew David Lansley; CBE (1996), PC (2010), DL (2016); s of Thomas Stewart Lansley, OBE, of Hornchurch, Essex, and Irene, *née* Sharp; *b* 11 December 1956; *Educ* Brentwood Sch, Univ of Exeter (BA, pres Guild of Students); *m* 1, 1985 (m dis); 3 da (Katherine Elizabeth Jane b 1987, Sarah Isabel Anne b 1989, Eleanor Rose Amy b 1993); m 2, 2001, Sally Anne, da of Donald Low, of Cheshire; 1 da (Martha Rose Low b 2003), 1 s (Charles Frederick Low b 2004); *Career* private sec to Sec of State for Trade and Industry 1984–85 (joined DOI 1979), princ private sec to Chancellor of the Duchy of Lancaster Cabinet Office 1985–87, dep DG Assoc of British Chambers of Commerce 1989–90 (dir policy and progs 1987–89), dir Conservative Research Dept 1990–95, dir Public Policy Unit 1995–97; MP (Cons) S Cambridgeshire 1997–2015; a vice-chm Cons Pty 1998–99; shadow min for the Cabinet Office 1999–2001, shadow chllr of the Duchy of Lancaster 1999–2001, shadow sec of state for health 2003–10, sec of state for health 2010–12, ldr House of Commons and Lord Privy Seal 2012–14; memb House of Lords 2015–; memb: Health Select Ctee 1997–98, Trade and Industry Select Ctee 2001–03; memb Exec Ctee Nat Union of Cons and Unionist Assocs 1990–95; *Publications* A Private Route (1988), Conservatives and the Constitution (with R Wilson, 1997), Extending the Reach (2003); *Recreations* history, political biographies, travel, cricket; *Style—* The Rt Hon the Lord Lansley, CBE, DL; ✉ House of Lords, London SW1A 0PW (☎ 020 7219 3000, e-mail lansleya@parliament.uk)

LANTOS, Prof Peter Laszlo; s of Sandor Leipniker (d 1945), and Ilona, *née* Somlo (d 1968); *b* 22 October 1939; *Educ* Med Sch Szeged Univ Hungary (MD), Univ of London (PhD, DSc); *Career* Wellcome research fell 1968–69, sr lectr and hon conslt in neuropathology Middx Sch of Med 1976–79 (research asst 1969–73, lectr in neuropathology 1974–75), prof of neuropathology Inst of Psychiatry 1979–2001 (prof emeritus 2001–); hon conslt in neuropathology: Bethlem Royal and Maudsley Hosps 1979–2002, KCH 1985–2002, St Thomas' Hosp 1992–2002; dir Neuropathology Serv King's Neuroscience Centre 1995–2002; chm: Scientific Advsy Panel Brain Research Tst 1985–91, Neuropathology Sub-Ctee RCPath 1986–89 (chm Panel of Examiners in Neuropathology 1983–89), Academic Bd Inst of Psychiatry 1988–91; cncllr Int Soc of Neuropathology 1995–, advsr German Federal Miny for Educn and Research 2000–02; tstee: Psychiatry Research Tst 1996–, Alzheimer's Research UK 2001–14; memb: Pathologic Soc of GB and I 1971, Br Neuropathological Soc 1972 (pres 1995–97), Samantha Dickson Research Tst 2003–, Med Advsy Ctee Multiple Sclerosis Soc; FRCPath 1987 (MRCPath 1975), FMedSci 2001; *Books* Greenfield's Neuropathology (ed, 1997 and 2002); contrib: Brain Tumours: Scientific Basis, Clinical Investigation and Current Therapy (1980), Histochemistry in Pathology (1983), Scientific Basis of Clinical Neurology (1985), Schizophrenia: The Major Issues (1988), Systemic Pathology (3 edn, 1990), Oxford Textbook of Pathology (1992), WHO Tumours of the Nervous System (2000), Dementia (2000), Early-onset Dementia (2001), Neurodegeneration (2003); Parallel Lines (autobiography, 2006), Closed Horizon (fiction, 2012); *Plays* The Visitor (workshop reading Soho Theatre) 2013 and (Park Theatre) 2014, Distorting Mirrors (rehearsed reading Tristan Bates Theatre, Actors Centre and The Theatre Room) 2015; *Recreations* travel, theatre, fine arts; *Clubs* Athenaeum; *Style—* Prof Peter Lantos

LAPOTAIRE, Jane Elizabeth Marie; da of Louise Elise Burgess Lapotaire; *b* 26 December 1944; *Educ* Northgate GS Ipswich, Bristol Old Vic Theatre Sch; *m* 1, 1965 (m dis 1967), Oliver Wood; m 2, 1974 (m dis 1982), Roland Joffé, *qv*; 1 s (Rowan b 1973); *Career* actress; pres Bristol Old Vic Theatre Club 1985–2009, memb Marie Curie Meml Fndn Appeals Ctee 1986–88, hon pres Shakespeare's Globe Friends 1986–2003, hon assoc artist RSC 1993–, visiting fell Univ of Sussex 1986–2001, visiting artist in residence Univ of Washington St Louis 1999; Hon DLitt: Univ of Bristol 1997, UEA 1998, Univ of Warwick 2000, Univ of Exeter 2004; hon fell Univ of Exeter 2006; *Theatre* RSC various periods 1974–94 incl: Viola in Twelfth Night, Sonya in Uncle Vanya, Rosaline in Love's Labour's Lost 1978–79, Misalliance 1986, Archbishop's Ceiling 1986, Gertrude in Kenneth Branagh's Hamlet 1993, Mrs Alving in Ghosts 1993 & 1994, Katherine of Aragon in Henry VIII 1996–98, Duchess of Gloucester in Richard II 2013–14; NT various periods 1967–84 incl: Measure for Measure, Flea in Her Ear, Dance of Death, Way of the World, Merchant of Venice, Oedipus, The Taming of the Shrew, Eileen in Kick for Touch 1983, Belvidera in Venice Preserv'd, Antigone 1984; other credits incl: Bristol Old Vic Co 1965–67, Vera in A Month in the Country, Lucy Honeychurch in A Room with a View (both Prospect Theatre Co West End) 1975–76, Rosalind in As You Like It (Edinburgh Festival) 1977, title role in Piaf (The Other Place, RSC, Aldwych, Wyndhams and Broadway) 1978–81, title role in St Joan (Compass Co) 1985, Double Double (Fortune) 1986, Greenland (Royal Court) 1988, Joy Davidman in Shadowlands (Queen's) 1990; *Television* freelance 1971–74 and 1976–78; credits incl: Marie Curie (Emmy and BAFTA nomination) 1977, Antony and Cleopatra 1981, Macbeth 1983, Seal Morning 1985, Napoleon and Josephine 1987, Blind Justice (BAFTA nomination) 1988, The Dark Angel 1989, Love Hurts (series 1 and II, BBC) 1991–92, Big Battalions 1992, Trial and Retribution 2008; *Films* Eureka 1983, Lady Jane 1986, Surviving Picasso (Merchant Ivory) 1996; *Awards* incl: Emmy and BAFTA nominations 1976 for Marie Curie, Helen Hayes Award USA for Katharine of Aragon 1999; awards for performance in Piaf: SWET Award 1979, London Critics' Award 1980, Variety Club Award 1980, Broadway Tony Award 1981; for Blind Justice: Br Press Guild Best Actress Award 1988, Variety Club Award 1989 for Shadowlands; *Books* Grace and Favour (autobiography, 1989), Out of Order (1999), Time Out Of Mind (2003), Everybody's Daughter Nobody's Child (2007); *Recreations* walking, cooking; *Style—* Ms Jane Lapotaire; ✉ c/o Andy Herrity, Gardner Herrity, 24 Conway Street, London W1T 6BT (☎ 020 7388 0088)

LAPPING, Anne Shirley Lucas; CBE (2005); da of Frederick Stone, and Dr Freda Lucas Stone; *b* 10 June 1941; *Educ* City of London Sch for Girls, LSE; *m* 1963, Brian Michael Lapping, *qv*; 3 da (Harriet, Claudia, Melissa); *Career* journalist: New Society 1964–68, London Weekend Television 1970–73, The Economist 1974–82; md: Brook Lapping Productions 1982–2013, Scott Tst 1995–; non-exec dir: Channel 4 TV 1989–95, NW London Mental Health Tst 1993–98; vice-chair Central and NW London Mental Health Tst 2000–04; govr LSE 1995–2016 (vice-chair of govrs 2007–14, emeritus govr 2016–); memb: Nat Gas Consumers Cncl 1978–79, Social Science Research Cncl 1978–82; tstee Open Democracy 2014–; *Recreations* literature, cooking; *Style—* Anne Lapping, CBE; ✉ 61 Eton Avenue, London NW3 3ET (☎ 020 7586 1047)

LAPPING, Brian Michael; CBE (2005); s of Max Lapping, and Doris Lapping; *b* 13 September 1937, London; *Educ* City of London Sch, Pembroke Coll Cambridge (open scholar, BA); *m* 1963, Anne Shirley Lucas Lapping, *qv*; 3 da (Harriet, Claudia, Melissa); *Career* early career as journalist on Daily Mirror, Guardian, Financial Times and New Society until 1970; Granada Television 1970–88: exec prodr World in Action 1976–79, End of Empire 1985, creator Hypotheticals current affrs format (30 progs produced for Granada); fndr Brian Lapping Associates (independent prodn co) 1988–, merged with Brook Assocs to form Brook Lapping Prodns 1997; Brian Lapping Associates progs incl: further Hypotheticals series (annually on BBC 2), Countdown to War (ITV) 1989, The Second Russian Revolution (BBC2, Discovery US, NHK Japan) 1991 (RTS and Broadcasting Press Guild Best Documentary Series Awards, Silver Medal Int Film and TV Festival NY 1992), Question Time (BBC1) 1991–94, The Washington Version (BBC2 and Discovery US) 1992, Woolly Al Walks the Kitty Back (BBC2 and Discovery US) 1992, Off the Back of a Lorry (BBC1) 1993, Watergate (BBC2 and Discovery US) 1994, Fall of the Wall (BBC2, Spiegel TV and Discovery US) 1994, The Death of Yugoslavia (BBC2, ORF Austria, Discovery US, Canal Plus France) 1995 (RTS Judges' Award 1996, Best Ind Prodn and Best News and Current Affrs Prodn Indie Awards 1996, Broadcasting Press Guild Best Documentary Series 1996, George Foster Peabody Award Univ of Georgia 1996, BAFTA Best Documentary 1996, duPont Gold Baton Columbia Univ 1996), The 50 Years War: Israel and the Arabs (BBC 2, PBS) 1998, The Money Changers (a history of European Monetary Union) 1998, Hostage (C4, PBS, Canal Plus) 1999, Playing the China Card (C4, PBS) 1999 (George Foster Peabody Award Univ of Georgia 2000), Endgame in Ireland (BBC2, PBS) 2000, Avenging Terror (C4, PBS, France 2, ZDF, NHK) 2002, The Fall of Milosevic (BBC2, Discovery) 2003, Israel and the Arabs: Elusive Peace (BBC2, Arte, PBS) 2005 (RTS Journalism Programme of the Year 2004–05, duPont Gold Baton Columbia Univ 2007), Iran & the West (BBC 2, Nat Geographic US and others) 2009 (Grierson and many other awards), Putin, Russia and the West (BBC 2, Nat Georgraphic US and others) 2012, The Iraq War (BBC 2, Nat Geographic US, Canal+, NHK, ABC, SVT, NRK, RDI/Radio Canada, VPRO, DRTV, TVP, etc) 2013;

L

chm Teachers' TV Dept of Educn 2003–11; *Awards* incl: various for World in Action, RTS Best Documentary Series for The State of the Nation 1979, Silver Medal Int Film and TV Festival NY for Hypotheticals prog Kidnapped 1984, Broadcasting Press Guild Best Documentary Series for Apartheid 1984, Gold Medal Int Film and TV Festival NY for Breakthrough at Reykjavik 1988 (also finalist Prix Italia) and for Countdown to War 1989; News World First Documentary Award 2003, BAFTA Personal Award for Creative Contribution to Television 2003, Broadcasting Press Guild Award for Outstanding Contribution to Broadcasting 2003, numerous awards (incl Grierson, Peabody, etc) for Iran & the West 2010; *Books* More Power to the People (jtly, 1964), The Labour Government 1964–70 (1970), End of Empire (1985), Apartheid: A History (1986); *Recreations* tending vines; *Style*— Brian Lapping, Esq, CBE; ✉ Brook Lapping Productions Ltd, Portland House, Bressenden Place, Victoria, London SW1E 5RS (☎ 020 7428 3100, fax 020 7284 0626)

LAPTHORNE, Sir Richard Douglas; kt (2010), CBE (1997); *b* 25 April 1943; *Educ* Calday Grange GS, Univ of Liverpool (BCom); *m* 1967, Valerie, *née* Waring; 2 s, 2 da; *Career* trainee Unilever Audit UCMDS 1965–67, fin accountant Lever Brothers (Zambia) Ltd 1967–69, accountant Unilever Pensions 1969–71, chief accountant Food Industries Ltd 1971–74, commercial offr Urachem Div Unilever Holland 1974–75; commercial dir: Synthetic Resins Ltd 1975–77, Sheby SA Paris 1977–80, Urachem Div 1980–81, Crosfields Chemicals Ltd 1981–83; Courtaulds plc: gp fin controller 1983–86, gp fin dir 1986–92, pres Courtaulds United States Inc 1986–92; British Aerospace plc: fin dir 1992–98, vice-chm 1998–99; non-exec chm: Amersham International plc 1996–97 (non-exec dir 1988–2003), Nycomed Amersham (following merger, now Amersham plc) 1999–2003 (dep chm 1997–99), Morse Group Ltd 1998–2008, Avecia 1999–2005, TI Automotive 2001–03, Cable and Wireless plc 2003–, New Look 2005–, McLaren Gp 2009–; non-exec dir: Orange plc 1996–99, Robert Fleming Holdings Ltd 1998–2002, Oasis International Leasing Ltd (Abu Dhabi) 1997–2006, McLaren Automotive 2009–; tstee: Royal Botanic Gardens Kew 1998– (HM The Queen's rep 2004–), Calibre (books for the blind) 1999–2008, Tommys Campaign 2002–; memb: Industry Devpt Advsy Bd 1996–2000, Advsy Bd Cancer Research Campaign 1998–2001; FCCA, FCMA, FCTA, CIMgt; *Recreations* gardening, opera, travel; *Style*— Sir Richard Lapthorne, CBE

LARCOMBE, Brian; *Career* 3i Group plc: joined 1974, local dir 1982, regnl dir 1988, fin dir 1992–97, chief exec 1997–2004; chm Bramdean Alternatives Ltd 2007–; non-exec dir: Smith & Nephew plc 2002–, Party Gaming plc 2005–06, Gallaher Gp plc 2005–06, F&C Asset Mgmnt plc 2005–, Gategroup Hldg AG 2008–, Incisive Media Hldgs 2010–; chm Br Venture Capital Assoc 1994–95; *Style*— Brian Larcombe, Esq

LARCOMBE, Richard; s of James Larcombe, and Anna, *née* Knight; *b* Oxford; *Educ* Stowe, Univ of Leeds, Int Inst for Mgmnt Devpt (IMD); *m* Jemma, *née* Harris; 2 s (Oscar James Joby b 7 June 2013, Theo Edward Beau b 26 Jan 2015); *Career* account exec Grey London 1996–98, account dir AMV BBDO 1998–2004, head of mktg News UK 2004–10; Virgin Media: dir of advtg and sponsorship 2010–13, dir of brand and mktg 2013–16; dir of brand and mktg Tesco 2016–; memb Exec Ctee ISBA 2013–, mentor Mktg Acad 2014–; *Clubs* Soho House, House of St Barnabas, Putney Lawn Tennis, Spencer Hockey; *Style*— Richard Larcombe, Esq; ✉ Virgin Media, Media House, Bartley Wood Business Park, Hook, Hampshire RG27 9UP

LAREDO, Jaime; *b* 1940; *Career* violinist; pupil of: Antonio de Grassi, Frank Houser, Josef Gingold, Ivan Galamian; debut recital 1948, orchestral debut 1951, youngest winner ever (age 17) Queen Elizabeth competition Brussels 1959; festival appearances with major orchestras worldwide incl: Spoleto, Tanglewood, Hollywood Bowl, Mostly Mozart, Ravinia, Blossom, Marlboro, Edinburgh, Harrogate, The Proms; guest soloist and/or conductor with orchestras incl: Chicago Symphony, Boston Symphony, Philadelphia Orch, NY Philharmonic, London Symphony, Scottish Chamber Orch, NY String Orch; dir Chamber Music at the 92nd Street Y series NY, memb Kalichstein/Laredo/Robinson Trio (Musical America's Ensemble of the Year 2002), memb Ax, Stern, Laredo Ma Quartet (Grammy Award for piano quartets), teacher Artist Faculty Curtis Inst, chamber musician, dir and soloist with int chamber orchestras incl: Scottish Chamber, English Chamber Orchestra, Orchestra of St Luke's; holds post as Distinguished Artist with St Paul Chamber Orchestra; numerous tours worldwide, numerous recordings incl The Complete Cycle of Beethoven Trios with Kalichstein/Laredo/Robinson Trio; awarded Handel medallion NY; *Style*— Jaime Laredo; ✉ c/o Askonas Holt, Lincoln House, 300 High Holborn, London WC1V 7JH (☎ 020 7400 1751, e-mail info@askonasholt.co.uk)

LARKEN, Rear Adm (Edmund Shackleton) Jeremy; DSO (1982); s of Rear Adm Edmund Thomas Larken, CB, OBE (d 1965), and Eileen Margaret, *née* Shackleton (d 2009); *b* 14 January 1939; *Educ* Bryanston, BRNC Dartmouth; *m* 1, 1963 (m dis 1987), Wendy Nigella, *née* Hallett; 2 da (Juliet b 1963, Henrietta b 1968); m 2, 1987 (m dis 1997), Anthea Larken, CBE, *qv*; m 3, 1997, Helen Denise, da of Bernard Barry Shannon (d 1977), of Mold; 1 s (Thomas b 1996), 1 da (Isobel b 1999); *Career* joined RN 1957, specialised in submarines 1961, navigation 1964, exchange with USN Submarine Force 1971–73; cmd: HMS Osiris 1969–70, Glamorgan 1975, Valiant 1976–77, Third Submarine Sqdn 1979–81, HMS Fearless 1981–83 (incl Falklands Campaign); Naval Plans 1983–84, Dir Naval Staff Duties 1985, Cdre Amphibious Warfare and Cmd UK/NL Amphib Force 1985–87; Rear Adm 1988, ACDS (Overseas) 1988–90; md Operational Command Training Organisation Ltd (OCTO) 1991–; govr Bryanston Sch 1988–99; FInstD; *Books* The Defence Case – Sense in Defence (with Cdre Michael Clapp, Alexander Clarke and Maj Gen Julian Thompson); *Recreations* crisis management, leadership, maritime and aviation interests, history and strategy, sailing, theatre, reading, home, family and friends; *Clubs* Reform; *Style*— Rear Admiral Jeremy Larken, DSO; ✉ OCTO, Caerlleon House, 142 Boughton, Chester CH3 5BP (e-mail jeremy.larken@octo.uk.com)

LARKIN, Judith Mary; da of Patrick John Larkin, and Sylvia May, *née* Silverthorne; *b* 22 May 1952; *Educ* The North London Coll Sch, City of London Poly; *Career* trainee Unilever plc 1971, corporate PR specialist in IT, telecommunications and electronics industries, head of corporate PR Logica plc 1979–84; dir: Traverse-Healy & Regester 1984–87, Charles Barker 1987; md Fleishman-Hillard UK Ltd 1990–94, fndr ptnr Regester Larkin Ltd 1994, fndr ptnr Risk Principals Ltd 2006; chm Br Gp Int PR Assoc; memb Bd Issue Mgmnt Cncl 1997; FIPR 1997 (MIPR 1985); *Books* Risk Issues and Crisis Management (with Michael Regester, 1997); *Style*— Ms Judith Larkin

LARRECHE, Prof Jean-Claude; s of Pierre Albert Alexis Larreche, of Pau, France, and Odette Jeanne Madeleine, *née* Hau-Sans; *b* 3 July 1947; *Educ* Lyon (INSA), Univ of London (MSc), INSEAD (MBA), Stanford Univ (PhD); *m* 10 Sept 1971, Denyse Michèle Joséphine, da of Michel Francis Henri Gros, of Besancon, France; 1 da (Sylvie b 1975), 1 s (Philippe b 1978); *Career* INSEAD: prof of mktg 1974–, dir Euro Strategic Mktg Inst 1985–89, Alfred H Heineken chair 1993–, dir Competitive Fitness of Global Firms Initiative 2000–02; non-exec dir: Reckitt and Colman plc (London) 1983–99, Reckitt Benckiser (London) 1999–2001; chm StratX Paris France 1985–, memb Bd The Mac Group Boston 1986–89; memb: America Mktg Assoc 1973, Inst of Mgmnt Sci 1975; FInstD; *Publications* The Momentum Effect: How to Ignite Exceptional Growth (2008), Markstrat: A Strategic Marketing Simulation (jtly); more than 100 books and articles on the subject of marketing and strategy; *Recreations* golf, marathon running, sailing; *Style*— Prof Jean-Claude Larreche; ✉ 85 Rue Murger, 77780, Bourron Marlotte, France (☎ 00 33 1 64 45 62 00, fax 00 33 1 64 45 98 76); INSEAD, 77305, Fontainebleau, France (☎ 00 33 1 60 72 41 51, fax 00 33 1 60 74 55 00, e-mail jean-claude.larreche@insead.edu)

LARVIN, Prof Michael; s of late John Larvin, of Marske by the Sea, Redcar, and Mary, *née* Cairns; *b* 13 September 1956, Gateshead, Co Durham; *Educ* Sir William Turner's Sch Coatham, Guy's Hosp Med Sch Univ of London (BSc, MB BS), Univ of Leeds (MD), Inst of Educn Univ of London (MA); *m* 25 July 1981, Keyna, *née* O'Donnell; 3 da (Elizabeth b 31 August 1982, Catherine b 18 March 1984, Abigail b 24 Feb 1996), 2 s (Christopher b 19 Dec 1985, David b 12 Nov 1990); *Career* jr surgical trg Guy's Hosp and Northwick Park Hosp 1981–85, research fell Univ of Leeds 1985–88, registrar Guy's Hosp 1989, lectr St James's Univ Hosp Leeds 1990–93, conslt surgn Univ Hosp Lewisham 1993–96, conslt surgn and sr clinical lectr Leeds 1996–2002, prof of surgery Univ of Nottingham 2002–12, prof and head Medical Sch Univ of Limerick Ireland 2012–; dir of educn Royal Coll of Surgeons of England 2008–12; American gastroenterology int fell 1988, Pancreatic Soc travelling fell 1988, Hunterian prof of surgery RCS 1996–97, Rovsing medal Denmark 1998; patron Pancreatitis Supporters' Network 1997–, supporter Chernobyl Children's Tst 1998–; pres Pancreatic Soc of GB & I 2002, tutor RCS 2000–08, dir NHS Specialist Library for Surgery 2007–10, dir of educn RCS 2008–; memb: BMA 1981, Pancreatic Soc 1985, Pancreas Club USA 1987, Br Soc of Gastroenterology 1989, Soc for Surgery of the Alimentary Tract USA 1997, Int Assoc of Pancreatology 1997, American Pancreatic Assoc 2004; FRCSGlas 1986, FRCS 2001; *Books* over 100 scientific publications; books incl: STEP Foundation (ed, 4 vols and eSTEP, 2006), STEP Core (ed, 4 vols and eSTEP, 2006), Making Sense of Your Surgical Attachement (jt ed, 2007), EMQs and MCQs for Surgical Finals (jtly, 2011); *Recreations* swimming, cricket, baseball, socer, rugby, reading, electronics and computing; *Style*— Prof Michael Larvin; ✉ Medical School, University of Limerick, Ireland (☎ 00 353 61 202595, e-mail michael.larvin@ul.ie)

LASCELLES, Angela Marion; da of James Anthony Greig (d 1967), of Mersham, Kent, and Juliet Felicia, *née* Colvile; *Educ* Ashford Sch, Univ of London (BA); *m* 1974, Richard Lascelles, s of Dr William Lascelles; 2 s (Edward b 1975, Simon b 1978), 1 da (Rosalind b 1981); *Career* private clients Phillips & Drew Stockbrokers 1968–70, investment analyst Spencer Thornton Stockbrokers 1970–72, investment mangr Dawnay Day (Merchant Bank) 1972–74, Associated British Foods Pension Fund 1975–79, Courtaulds Pension Fund 1979–86, exec dir OLIM Ltd 1986–; jt investment dir Value & Income Trust plc 1986–; govr: The London Inst 1989–92, West Heath Sch 1996–97; vice-pres Epilepsy Soc; AIIMR; *Recreations* tennis, music; *Style*— Mrs Angela Lascelles; ✉ OLIM Ltd, 15 Berkeley Street, London W1J 8DY (☎ 020 7408 7290)

LASCELLES-HADWEN, Francis Edward; s of Edward Hubert Lascelles Hadwen, diplomat (d 1947), and Margaret, *née* Turnbull Fernie; *b* 13 December 1926; *Educ* The Hall, St Paul's, Magdalen Coll Oxford (MA), Aston Univ (DPM); *m* 1 (m dis), Lady Julia Blunt-Mackenzie, da of 4 Earl of Cromartie, MC, TD, JP (d 1989); 1 s, 1 da; m 2 (m dis), Clare, da of H G Liversidge, of Nairobi; 2 s; *Career* Nat Serv RN 1945–47, sec to Capt HMS Woodbridge Haven, asst to Cdre HMS Pembroke; Army SSC 1963–66, instr Sandhurst candidates ASE Beaconsfield; educn and trg offr: Tournai and Oudenarde Barracks, Aldershot, attached Welch Regt, Sch of Infantry Warminster; various commercial positions City of London; visiting lectr in econs Brighton Tech Coll and Poly 1967–70; exec dir Partington's advertising and PR; broker Lloyd's of London, Stock Exchange with Coates Son & Co; dir Finchcastle Ltd fin conslts; memb: LCC for Clapham Div of Wandsworth 1955–58, Housing, Town Planning and Rivers Ctees, TA Forces Assoc Co of London; govr Larkhall and Heathbrook Schs London, hon sec personal staff Rt Hon Sir W Churchill KG prior to second admin; memb: Ladywood Police Consultative Ctee 1987–89, Harborne and Quinton Police Liaison Ctee 1987, Birmingham City Centre Crime Prevention Panel 1987– (chm 1989–90, vice chm 1991–92), Birmingham and Sutton Coldfield Crime Prevention Panel 1987–90, Quinborne Community Assoc Cncl 1987–89; convenor local Neighbourhood Watch Scheme; govr: Duddeston Manor Saltley (vice chm 1990–91)St Georges C of E Jl (vice-chm 1989); chm Fin Ctee (support) SSAFA and FHS W Mids Central 1989–90; del: Ladworth project Inter-Agency Conference 1988, Birmingham Heartlands Inter-Agency Conference 1988–89; police lay visitor 1988–93; memb Harborne and Quinton Police Consultative Ctee 1989; invited to give evidence to Ctee on Press Privacy and Related Matters 1989, memb sub ctee to report on police leadership and composition to the PM and Home Sec 1990; del for: Birmingham Crime Concern Tst Conf Westminster 1989, Lay Visitors Conf Univ of London 1990; memb Rann Project Steering Ctee 1989–90, memb Nat Art Collection Fund; Friend of the Bodleian Oxford involved in discussions on new building plans completion 2014; FRSA; *Recreations* the South of France, Monte Carlo, 18 Century Dukes, owning Pekingese dogs, the second chamber and the constitution; *Clubs* Oxford Union; *Style*— Francis Lascelles-Hadwen, Esq; ✉ 19 Weather Oaks, Birmingham B17 9DD

LASK, Prof Bryan; s of Dr Aaron Lask, and Rita, *née* Flax (d 1989); *b* 18 February 1941; *Educ* St Paul's, St Bartholomew's Hosp London, Inst of Psychiatry; *children* 2 s (Gideon, Adam); *Career* medical dir mental health Care UK; hon conslt Gt Ormond St Hosp London; emeritus prof Univ of London, visiting prof Univ of Oslo; past pres Eating Disorders Research Soc; former ed Jl of Family Therapy, former ed Clinical Child Psychology and Psychiatry, ed Advances in Eating Disorders – Theory, Research and Practice (jl); Lifetime Achievement Award Acad for Eating Disorders; fell Int Coll of Psychosomatic Medicine, FRCPsych, FRCPCH; *Books* Child Psychiatry & Social Work (1981), Children's Problems (1985, 2 edn 1994), Childhood Illness – The Psychosomatic Approach (1989), Eating Disorders in Childhood and Adolescence (1993, 4 edn 2013), Eating Disorders in Childhood and Adolescence – A Parent's Guide (1999, 3 edn 2013), Psychosocial Aspects of Cystic Fibrosis (2000), Practical Child Psychiatry (2003), Who's Who of the Brain (2008), Eating Disorders and the Brain (2011), Can I Tell You About Eating Disorders? (2014); *Recreations* sports, theatre, music; *Style*— Prof Bryan Lask; ✉ Child and Family Practice, 8 Ridgmount Street, London WC1 E7AA

LASKEY, Prof Ronald Alfred; CBE (2011); *b* 26 January 1945; *Educ* The Queen's Coll Oxford (open major scholar, MA, DPhil); *Career* scientific staff: Dept of Molecular Virology ICRF 1970–73, MRC Lab of Molecular Biology Cambridge 1973–83; professorial fell Darwin Coll Cambridge 1982–, Charles Darwin prof of embryology Univ of Cambridge 1983–2011, Cancer Research Campaign (CRC) dir Wellcome/CRC Inst Univ of Cambridge 1991–2001, dir MRC Cancer Cell Unit 2000–10, co-dir Hutchison/MRC Research Centre 2000–10; vice-chm MRC Cell Bd 1989–1992, convenor Cell and Devpt Biology Academia Europaea 1991–96, tstee Strangeways Research Lab Cambridge 1993–2010; pres Br Soc for Cell Biology 1995–99, vice-pres Acad of Med Sci 2007–12; ed Current Opinion in Genetics and Devpt 1990–99 (memb Editorial Bd 1999–2010), assoc ed: Cell 1982–2009, Current Biology 1991–99, Molecular Cell 1997–2014; memb: Cncl Royal Soc 1988–90, Scientific Ctee Cancer Research Campaign 1993–2001, Scientific Ctee EMBL Heidelberg 1999–2004, Scientific Ctee Max Planck Inst for Biochemistry 2000–10 (chair 2002–10), Cncl ICRF 2000–02, Scientific Advsy Bd Cytosystems 2006–12, UK Panel for Research Integrity 2006–, Bd UK Panel for Research Integrity 2007–11, Cancer Research UK London Research Inst 2005–12, Louis Jeantet Fndn 2008– (vice-pres 2010–); pres Biochemical Soc 2012–14 (hon memb 2011), tstee Inst of Cancer Research 2007–13; memb: EMBO 1982, Academia Europaea 1988; hon foreign memb Japanese Biochemical Soc, hon memb Dept of Biochemistry Univ of Oxford 1997–, hon fell Queens' Coll Oxford 2011; Hon LLD Univ of Dundee 2014; FRS 1984, FMedSci 1998, FLSW 2013; *Awards*: Colworth Medal Biochemical Soc 1979, Alkis Seraphim meml lectr 1984, L'Institut Jacques Monod Medal 1986, Runnström lectr, Medal and Prize Univ of Stockholm 1991, Earl King meml lectr Royal Postgrad Med Sch 1991, Frank Rose meml lectr Br Assoc Cancer Research 1997, Biochemical Soc CIBA Medal 1997, Bidder lectr Soc of

Experimental Biology 1998, Feldberg Prize for Med Research Germany 1998, Louis-Jeantet Prize for Med Switzerland 1998, Univ Medal Charles Univ Prague 1999, BBC Tomorrow's World Health Innovation Award 2000, Croonian lectr Royal Soc 2001, Wenner Gren lectr Univ of Stockholm 2001, Kettle lectr RCPath 2003, Mühlbock lectr European Assoc of Cancer Research 2006, Medical Futures Cancer Innovation Award 2007, Royal Medal Royal Soc 2009, Werner Heisenberg lectr Bavarian Acad 2010, Lifetime Achievement in Cancer Research Prize Cancer Research UK 2014; DSc (hc) Univ of London 2014; *Style*— Prof Ronald A Laskey, CBE, FRS, FMedSci, FLSW; ✉ Department of Zoology, University of Cambridge, Downing Street, Cambridge CB2 3EJ (☎ 01223 334106/7, e-mail ral19@cam.ac.uk)

LASOK, Dr (Karol) Paul Edward; QC (1994); s of Prof Dominik Lasok, QC (d 2000), and Sheila May, *née* Corrigan; *b* 16 July 1953; *Educ* Jesus Coll Cambridge (MA), Univ of Exeter (LLM, PhD); *m* 23 Feb 1991, Karen Bridget Morgan, da of Rev Dr Hugh Griffith, HCF (d 1991); 2 da (Frances Katharine Marina b 10 June 1993, Anna Zofia Christina b 18 June 1997); *Career* called to the Bar Middle Temple 1977 (bencher 2002); legal sec Court of Justice of European Communities 1980–84 (locum tenens March-May 1985); private practice: Brussels 1985–87, London 1987–; chm Bar European Gp 2007–09, chm VAT Practitioners' Gp 2009–11; memb Editorial Bd: European Competition Law Review, Law and Justice; Tax Lawyer of the Year 2005; *Books* The European Court of Justice Practice and Procedure (2 edn, 1994), Law & Institutions of the European Union (7 edn, 2001); contrib: Halsbury's Laws of England 4 edn vols 51 and 52 (1986), Stair Memorial Encyclopaedia of the Laws of Scotland, Weinberg & Blank on Take-overs and Mergers (1989), Judicial Control in the EU (2004), Atkin's Court Forms Vol 10 (2009), Value Added Tax: Commentary and Analysis (2009), Atkin's Court Forms Vol 16 (2011); *Recreations* walking, music, amusing daughters; *Clubs* Athenaeum; *Style*— Dr Paul Lasok, QC; ✉ 57 Ellington Street, London N7 8PN (☎ 020 7607 5874); Monckton Chambers, 1 & 2 Raymond Buildings, Gray's Inn, London WC1R 5NR (☎ 020 7405 7211, fax 020 7405 2084)

LAST, Andrew John; s of Prof John William Last, CBE, of Llannerch Hall, Clwyd, and Susan Josephine, *née* Farmer; *b* 2 January 1969; *Educ* Birkenhead Sch, Trinity Coll Oxford (MA); *m* 14 June 1997, Sarah Jane, da of Giles Bartleet; 2 s (Henry Jack b 16 July 1998, Jordan Michael Benedict b 12 Jan 2001); *Career* account exec Pettifor Morrow & Associates Ltd 1990–92, account mangr Nexus Public Relations 1992–96, conslt Bell Pottinger Consultants 1996–99, founding dir salt 2000–; Freeman City of London 1997; assoc memb IPR 1998; *Recreations* football, golf, cricket, antique maps; *Clubs* RAC, Rodmell Cricket; *Style*— Andrew Last, Esq; ✉ salt, Cranmer House, 39 Brixton Road, London SW9 6DZ (☎ 020 8870 6777, email andy.last@saltlondon.com, Twitter @saltylast)

LASZLO; *see:* de Laszlo

LATCHMAN, Prof David Seymour; CBE (2010); *b* 22 January 1956; *Educ* Haberdashers' Aske's, Queens' Coll Cambridge (entrance scholar, fndn scholar, BA, coll prizes), Univ of Cambridge (bachelor scholar, MA, PhD), Univ of London (DSc); *Career* postdoctoral research fell Eukaryotic Molecular Genetics Gp Cancer Research Campaign Dept of Biochemistry Imperial Coll London 1981–84, lectr in molecular genetics Dept of Biology (formerly Zoology) UCL 1984–88, dir Medical Biology Unit Dept of Biochemistry and Molecular Biology UCL and Middx Sch of Med 1988–91 (reader 1990); UCL: prof of molecular pathology (established chair) and head Dept of Molecular Pathology 1991–99, chm Div of Pathology 1995–99, dir Windeyer Inst of Med Scis 1996–99, dep head UCL Grad Sch 1998–99, dean and prof of human genetics Inst of Child Health Gt Ormond Street Hosp UCL 1999–2002 (non-exec dir Gt Ormond Street Hosp for Children NHS Tst 2001–02), master Birkbeck Coll London and prof of genetics Birkbeck Coll and UCL 2003–; chm Science Expert Advsy Ctee Univ of London; memb Univ of London: Central Equipment and Scholarships Fund, Examinations and Assessment Cncl Advsy Bd, Examinations Bd and Biological Subjects Advsy Panel; chair London Ideas Genetics Knowledge Park 2002–08, chm London Higher, bd observer London Devpt Agency; chm Scientific Advsy Bd Nat Inst for Biological Standards, vice-chm Med Advsy Panel Parkinson's Disease Soc; memb: Br Heart Fndn Project Grants Ctee, Advsy Bd MRC, Biological Standards Bd Nat Inst for Biological Standards, Examining Panel in Genetics RCP, Health Protection Agency, Genetics and Insurance Ctee, HEFCE Research Strategy Ctee, UUK Research Strategy Ctee, Cncl Lifelong Learning UK, Bd London First, London Cncl CBI; patron Women and Children First; memb: Biochemical Soc, Soc for General Microbiology, AAAS, American Soc for Microbiology, NY Acad of Scis; pres The Maccabeeans; FRCPath; *Books* Gene Regulation – a eukaryotic perspective (1990, 5 edn 2005), Eukaryotic Transcription Factors (1991, 5 edn 2008), Transcription Factors: a practical approach (ed, 1993, 2 edn, 1999), From Genetics to Gene Therapy (ed, 1994), PCR Applications in Pathology (ed, 1994), Genetic Manipulation of the Nervous System (ed, 1996), Landmarks in Gene Regulation (ed, 1997), Basic Molecular and Cell Biology (ed, 1997), Stress Proteins (ed, 1999), Viral Vectors for Treating Diseases of the Nervous System (ed, 2003); *Recreations* book collecting, opera; *Clubs* Athenaeum; *Style*— Prof David Latchman, CBE; ✉ Birkbeck College, Malet Street, London WC1E 7HX (☎ 020 7631 6274, fax 020 7631 6259, e-mail master@bbk.ac.uk)

LATCHMORE, Andrew Windsor; s of Arthur John Craig Latchmore, MBE, FRCS (d 1998), and Joyce Mary Latchmore, JP, *née* Raper (d 1993); *b* 9 February 1950; *Educ* Oundle, Univ of Leeds (LLB); *m* 1 (m dis 1989), Jillian Amanda, da of Victor Hugo Watson (d 2015); 1 da (Lucy Emma 1979), 1 s (Jolyon Guy 1981); m 2, Clarissa Mary, da of Maj Peter J Orde (d 2001); 1 da (Chloe Roseanna b 1991), 1 s (Max Andrew b 1993); *Career* admitted slr 1975; Eversheds: (formerly Hepworth and Chadwick): ptnr 1978–2004, chm of commercial property 1991–98, nat managing ptnr Client Servs 1998–2000; ptnr Shulmans LLP (formerly Shulmans) 2004–; chm Leeds Property Forum 2011–, dep chm Leeds Business Improvement District 2015–; memb Exec Bd Br Cncl for Offices 2001–05 (chm Northern Chapter 1999–2005); govr Gateways Sch 1992–94 (sec to govrs 1977–92), chair of govrs of Queen Mary's Sch Baldersly 2004–07; hon sec Leeds Law Soc 1986–90; memb Law Soc; *Recreations* music, opera, golf, tennis, skiing, walking, travel; *Clubs* Alwoodley Golf; *Style*— Andrew Latchmore, Esq; ✉ Shulmans LLP, 10 Wellington Place, Leeds LS1 4AP (☎ 0113 245 2833, fax 0113 246 7326, e-mail alatchmore@shulmans.co.uk)

LATHAM, Rt Hon Sir David Nicholas Ramsay; kt (1992), PC (2000); s of Robert Clifford Latham, CBE (d 1995), of Cambridge, and Eileen Frances, *née* Ramsay (d 1969); *b* 18 September 1942; *Educ* Bryanston, Queens' Coll Cambridge (MA); *m* 6 May 1967, Margaret Elizabeth, *née* Forrest; 3 da (Clare Frances (Mrs Jonathan Speight) b 2 Aug 1969, Angela Josephine (Mrs Ian Taylor) b 23 Jan 1972, (Rosemary) Harriet (Mrs Charles Waggett) b 10 Dec 1974); *Career* called to the Bar Middle Temple 1964 (bencher 1989); jr counsel to the Crown Common Law 1979–85, jr counsel to Dept of Trade in export credit guarantee matters 1982–85, QC 1985, recorder of the Crown Court 1983–92, judge of the High Court of Justice (Queen's Bench Div) 1992–2000, presiding judge Midland & Oxford Circuit 1995–99, Lord Justice of Appeal 2000–09; vice-pres Court of Appeal Criminal Div 2006–09, chm Parole Bd 2009–12; memb: Gen Cncl of the Bar 1986–92, Judicial Studies Bd 1988–91, Cncl Legal Education 1988–96, Sentencing Guidelines Cncl 2006–09; vice-chm Cncl of Legal Educn 1992–96; tstee Slynn Fndn 2013–; *Recreations* reading, music, food, drink; *Clubs* Travellers, Beefsteak, Leander; *Style*— The Rt Hon Sir David Latham; ✉ 3 Manor Farm Close, Pimperne, Dorset DT11 8XL

LATHAM, Derek James; s of James Horace Latham, DFC (d 1996), of Newark-on-Trent, and Mary Pauline, *née* Turner (d 1974); *b* 12 July 1946; *Educ* King Edward VI GS Retford, Leicester Sch of Architecture, Trent Poly Nottingham (DipArch, DipTP, DipLD); *m* 14 Sept 1968, Pauline Elizabeth, OBE, da of Philip George Tuxworth, of Lincs; 1 da (Sarah Jane b 1972), 2 s (Benjamin James b 1974, Oliver James b 1981); *Career* Clifford Wearden & Assocs (architects and planners) London 1968–70, housing architect and planner Derby CC 1970–73, design and conservation offr Derbyshire CC 1974–78, tech advsr Derbyshire Historic Bldgs Tst 1978–, princ Derek Latham and Assocs 1980–89, chm Derek Latham and Company 1989–; md Michael Saint Developments Ltd 1984–96; dir: Acanthus Associated Architectural Practices Ltd 1984–98 (chm 1987–89), Omega Two Ltd (artworks advsrs) 1990–, Acanthus Europe 1993–98, Church Converts Ltd 1996–; chm Opun (Architecture and Built Environment Centre for the East Midlands) 2002–05 (memb Ctee 2010–), chm Regeneration E Midlands 2005–10; chair Technical Panel Derbyshire Historic Buildings Tst 1974–78 (technical advsr 1978–), memb Exec Ctee Cncl for Care of Churches 1985–91, architectural advsr Peak Park Tst 1986–, concept co-ordinator Sheffield Devpt Corp 1987–89; master planner Derby City Challenge 1992–94; memb Regnl Ctee HLF 2001–06; memb: Soc for the Protection of Ancient Buildings 1974 (memb Ctee 1993–2001), Ancient Monument Soc 1975, Assoc of Heritage Interpretation 1976–2010, RSA 1989 (chm RSA Dean Clough 1995–98), EASA 1991–2015, Urban Design Gp 1991–2015, Inst of Historic Bldg Conservation 1997–2015, Inst of Environmental Mgmnt and Assessment 1998–2008, EH/Cabe Urban Panel 2010–; regnl ambass CABE 2001–11 (educn enabler 2002–11), client deisgn advsr RIBA 2005–; visiting prof Univ of Derby 2013–; external examiner: Leicester Sch of Architectural Conservation Studies 1983–86, Leicester Sch of Architecture 1988–92, Sch of Architecture Univ of Nottingham 1996–99; govr Nottingham Sch of Interior Design 1986–90, memb Ct Univ of Derby 1995–; memb Register of Architects Accredited in Building Conservation 2001–15; tstee Little Eaton Sr Citizens' Welfare Club 2010–, tstee and dir Derwent Valley Heritage Tst and chair Derwent Valley Cycleway Gp 2015–; Hon Dr Univ of Derby 2008; RIBA 1971, MRTPI 1974, ALI 1978, Academician Acad of Urbanism 2006 (chm Place Partnering Ctee); *Publications* Creative Re-use of Buildings: Donhead 2000; *Recreations* squash, sailing, rambling, cycling, swimming, riding; *Clubs* Duffield Squash and Lawn Tennis, Little Eaton Lawn Tennis (pres 1991–2003); *Style*— Derek J Latham, Esq; ✉ Hieron's Wood, Vicarage Lane, Little Eaton, Derby DE21 5EA (☎ 01332 832371); Latham Architects, St Michaels, Derby DE1 3SU (☎ 01332 365777, fax 01332 290314, e-mail derek@lathamarchitects.co.uk)

LATHAM, John Charles; *Career* formerly vice-pres Int Business Devpt Laureate Educn Inc, currently pres and ceo Univ of Law; former memb Bd QAA; founding tstee N Liverpool City Acad; *Style*— John Latham, Esq; ✉ The University of Law, Braboeuf Manor, Portsmouth Road, Guildford, Surrey GU3 1HA

LATHAM, Sir Michael Anthony; kt (1993), DL (Leics 1994); s of Wing Cdr S H Latham (d 1993); *b* 20 November 1942; *Educ* Marlborough, King's Coll Cambridge, Dept of Educn Univ of Oxford; *m* 1969, Caroline Susan (d 2006), da of Maj T A Terry, RE (d 1971); 2 s; *Career* housing and local govt offr CRD 1965–67, co-opted memb GLC Housing Ctee 1967–73, memb Westminster City Cncl 1968–71, dir and chief exec House Builders Fedn 1971–73; MP (Cons): Melton 1974–83, Rutland and Melton 1983–92; memb: Select Ctee on Energy 1979–82, Public Accounts Ctee 1983–92; pres: Br Flat Roofing Cncl 1995–99, Flat Roofing Alliance 2000–09, European Construction Inst 2002–08; chm: Construction Industry Bd 1995–96, Jt Major Contractors' Gp 1996–, Jt Industry Bd for the Electrical Contracting Industry 1998–, Willmott Dixon Ltd 1999–2002 (non-exec dir 1996–99, dep chm 2002–09, partnering advsr 2010–), Partnership Sourcing Ltd 2000–05, Construction Skills (formerly Construction Industry Trg Bd) 2002–10, Roofing Industry Alliance 2003– (dep chm 1997–2003), Collaborative Working Centre Ltd 2003–, E C Harris Public Sector Exec 2004–07; patron Nat Fedn of Roofing Contractors 2010–; dep chm BIW Technologies Ltd 2000–05; non-exec dir James R Knowles construction conslts 1997–2003; dep chm Inspace plc 2008–09 (conslt on partnering 2005–08); visiting prof: Univ of Northumbria 1995–2000, Bartlett Sch of Architecture UCL 1997–2000, Univ of Central Eng 2001–08, Univ of Leeds 2008–; reviewer Jt Govt/Indust Review on Procurement/Contractual Problems in the Construction Indust 1993–94; hon vice-pres Anglo-Israel Assoc 1994– (pres 1990–94), vice-pres Cncl of Christians and Jews 2000– (jt hon treas 1996–2000); tstee Oakham Sch 1987–2001; Anglican lay reader 1988–; hon fell: Chartered Inst of Building Services Engineers 2002, Chartered Inst of Purchasing and Supply 1994, ICE 1995, CIOB 1995, Landscape Inst 1997, Royal Acad of Engrg 1997, Royal Incorporation of Architects in Scotland 1998, RIBA 2000; hon memb RICS 1996; Hon LLD Nottingham Trent Univ 1995, Hon DEng Univ of Birmingham 1998, Hon DCL Univ of Northumbria 1999, Hon DTech Loughborough Univ 2004; FRSA 1992; *Recreations* cricket, fencing, gardening, listening to classical music; *Clubs* Carlton; *Style*— Sir Michael Latham, DL; ✉ 508 Hood House, Dolphin Square, London SW1V 3NH

LATHAM, (Edward) Michael Locks; DL (Cornwall 1995); s of Edward Bryan Latham, CBE (d 1980); *b* 7 January 1930; *Educ* Stowe, Clare Coll Cambridge (MA); *m* 1955, Joan Doris, da of Charles Ellis Merriam Coubrough (d 1967); 1 s (Richard b 28 June 1957), 2 da (Mrs Philippa French b 24 June 1960, Mrs Sarah Phillips b 14 Sept 1963); *Career* chm James Latham plc 1973–87 (dir 1957–91); sr delegate EC of G8 and to trade bodies concerned with Forest Products in EEC memb states 1972–2005, pres UCBT (Union for Tropical Timber Trade) 1985–86, convenor of successive int conferences in Washington DC, Hong Kong and Rio de Janeiro, princ guest speaker German Timber Trade AGM Munich 1988; vice-pres Royal Cornwall Agric Assoc 1993– (pres 1992–93); Co Cdr St John Ambulance Cornwall 1992–98; High Sheriff Cornwall 1992; *Recreations* motoring, exploring countryside; *Clubs* STD Register, Club Talbot; *Style*— E Michael Latham, Esq, DL

LATHAM, Pauline Elizabeth; OBE (1992), MP; da of Philip Tuxworth, and Anne Frances Warrener, *née* Millhouse; *b* 4 February 1948, Sleaford, Lincs; *Educ* Bramcote Hills Technical GS; *m* 14 Sept 1968, Derek James Latham; 1 da (Sarah Jane (Mrs Salter) b 15 March 1972), 2 s (Benjamin James b 28 Feb 1974, Oliver James b 25 June 1981); *Career* Mayor of Derby 2007–08, MP (Cons) Mid Derbys 2010–; chm and fndr memb Grantmaintained Schs Advsy Ctee; govr and chm Ecclesbourne Sch; *Style*— Mrs Pauline Latham, OBE, MP; ✉ House of Commons, London SW1A 0AA

LATYMER, 9 Baron (E 1431–32); Crispin James Alan Nevill Money-Coutts; eldest s of 8 Baron (d 2003); *b* 8 March 1955; *Educ* Eton, Keble Coll Oxford; *m* 1, 1978 (m dis 1995), Hon Lucy Rose Deedes, yst da of Baron Deedes (Life Peer); 2 da (Hon Sophia Patience b 1985, Hon Evelyn Rose b 1988), 1 s (Hon Drummond William Thomas b 11 May 1986); m 2, 1995, Shaunagh Anne Henrietta, former w of Thomas Peter William Heneage, and da of (George Silver) Oliver Annesley Colthurst; *Heir* s, Hon Drummond Money-Coutts; *Career* E F Hutton, Bankers Trust International, European Banking Co, Coutts & Co, Cazenove & Co; non-exec dir: Manek Investment Mgmnt, Throgmorton Tst plc 2007– (chm 2012–); chm UCLH Charity 2007–15; tstee Astor Fndn 1992–; *Books* Where the Ocean Meets the Sky (2009); *Clubs* House of Lords Yacht, Ocean Cruising, Velo Club Rocacorba; *Style*— The Rt Hon the Lord Latymer

LAUDERDALE, 18 Earl of (S 1624); Sir Ian Maitland; 14 Bt (NS 1680); s of 17 Earl of Lauderdale (d 2008); *b* 4 November 1937; *Educ* Radley, BNC Oxford (MA); *m* 27 April 1963, Ann Paule, da of Geoffrey B Clark, of London; 1 s, 1 da; *Heir* s, Master of Lauderdale, Viscount Maitland; *Career* Lt RNR 1963–73; has held various appts in mfrg industry; National Westminster Bank plc: joined 1974, asst regnl mangr N Africa 1985, regnl mangr N Africa 1986, regnl mangr Middle East 1989, sr regnl mangr Africa and ME 1991–95; dir Maitland Consultancy Services Ltd 1995–2007; marketing advsr LSE 1995–2001; lectr: British Cncl Anglo-Egyptian Banking Seminar Alexandria 1994,

L

Euromoney Pubns and NY Inst of Finance Central Europe, Africa, Asia and ME 1996–2006, LSE British Chevening Gurukul Scholarship Prog 1999; dir Tachbrook St Residents' Assoc, dir Pimlico Fedn of Residents' Assocs until 2013; memb Queen's Body Guard for Scotland (Royal Co of Archers); Liveryman Worshipful Co of Fan Makers; *Recreations* sailing, photography; *Clubs* Royal Ocean Racing, New (Edinburgh), Puffins; *Style*— The Earl of Lauderdale; ✉ 150 Tachbrook Street, London SW1V 2NE (website www.clanmaitland.org.uk); Newlands Barn, by Thornhill, Dumfriesshire

LAUE, Prof Ernest Douglas; *b* 18 August 1955; *Educ* RSC, CNAA (PhD); *Career* Univ of Cambridge: demonstrator then lectr Dept of Biochemistry 1985–99, fell St John's Coll 1987– (coll lectr in biochemistry 1987–2000), reader in structural biology 1999–2000, prof of structural biology 2000–; memb: Biochemistry and Biophysics Sub-Ctee SERC 1987–91, Advsy Ctee on NMR MRC 1994–98, Review of Structural Biology BBSRC 1996, BMS Ctee Network Gp BBSRC 1997–2004, Infrastructure Panel Wellcome Tst 1997–99, Advsy Bd MRC 2002–, Tools and Resources Strategy Panel BBSRC 2004–; author of numerous research papers and articles in learned jls particularly on the structure and function of macromolecules; conslt: Dupont Pharmaceutical Co 1991–2001, Mitotix Inc 1996–2000; memb EMBO 2010–; *Style*— Prof Ernest Laue; ✉ University of Cambridge, Department of Biochemistry, 80 Tennis Court Road, Old Addenbrooke's Site, Cambridge CB2 1GA (☎ 01223 333677, fax 01223 766002)

LAUGHTON, Prof Michael Arthur; s of William Arthur Laughton (d 1986), of Barrie, Ontario, Canada, and Laura, *née* Heap (d 1987); *b* 18 December 1934, Madras, India; *Educ* King Edward Five Ways Birmingham, Etobicoke Collegiate Inst Toronto, Univ of Toronto (BASc), Univ of London (PhD, DSc(Eng)); *m* 1960 (m dis 1994), Margaret Mary, yr da of Brig George Vincent Leigh Coleman, OBE (QVOCG Indian Army, d 1970); 2 da (Joanna Margaret (Mrs Brogan-Higgins) b 28 June 1963, Katherine Alice (Dr Gardner) b 22 Nov 1965), 2 s (Mark Michael b 30 July 1968, Thomas George b 16 May 1971); *Career* graduate apprentice GEC Witton Birmingham 1957–59, project engr GEC Engineering Computer Services 1959–61; QMC London (later Queen Mary & Westfield Coll London, now Queen Mary Univ of London): DSIR res student 1961–64, lectr Dept of Electrical Engrg 1964–72, reader in electrical engrg 1972–77, prof 1977–2000, emeritus prof 2000–, dean Faculty of Engrg 1983–85, pro-princ 1985–89; dean Faculty of Engrg Univ of London 1990–94; visiting prof: Univ of Purdue USA 1966, Univ of Tokyo Japan 1977, Imperial Coll 2002–; external examiner numerous univs UK and abroad 1970–; co-ed and fndr Int Journal of Electrical Power and Energy Systems 1978–; chm: Tower Shakespeare Company Ltd 1985–93, Queen Mary College Industrial Research Ltd 1988–91 (dir 1979, chm 1990–91); organising sec Power Systems Computation Confs 1963–81 (chm Exec Ctee 1981–2014, pres Cncl 2014–); chm Working Gp on Renewable Energy 1986–90 (Watt Ctee on Energy 1986–94); memb: Info Ctee Royal Society 1988–92, British Scholars Selection Ctee Fulbright Cmmn 1991–, House of Lords Select Ctee on the Euro Communities (specialist advsr to Sub Ctee B (Energy, Tport and Technol) on Inquiries into Renewable Resources 1988 and Efficiency of Electricity Use 1989), Cncl IEE 1990–94, House of Commons Welsh Ctee (specialist advsr on Inquiry on Wind Energy) 1994, Energy Policy Advsy Gp Royal Soc 2001–, Int Ctee Royal Acad of Engrg 2002–06; memb Ct Cranfield Inst of Technol 1991–96; IEE Career Achievement Medal 2002; Freeman City of London 1990; Liveryman: Worshipful Co of Barbers 1995, Engrs Co 2009; CEng 1965, MRI 1973–91, FIEE 1977 (MIEE 1968), FREng 1989, FIEEE 2010; *Publications* Electrical Engineers Reference Book (with: M G Say 1985, G R Jones 1993, D G Warne 2002), Expert System Applications in Power Systems (ed with T S Dillon, 1990), Renewable Energy Sources (ed 1990); author of numerous papers on electrical power and energy systems, control and computation; *Recreations* music, following rugby and cricket; *Clubs* Athenaeum; *Style*— Prof M A Laughton, FREng; ✉ 28 Langford Green, Champion Hill, London SE5 8BX (☎ 020 7326 0081, e-mail michael.laughton1@btinternet.com)

LAUNDER, Prof Brian Edward; s of Harry Edward Launder (d 1997), of Manchester, and Elizabeth Ann, *née* Ayers (d 2003); *b* 20 July 1939; *Educ* Enfield GS, Imperial Coll London (BSc(Eng), Bramwell Medal, Unwin Premium, ACGI), MIT (SM, ScD), Univ of London (DSc(Eng)), Victoria Univ of Manchester (DSc), UMIST (DEng); *m* 20 Sept 1968, Dagny, da of Svend Simonsen; 1 da (Katya Jane b 18 July 1970), 1 s (Jesper David b 12 May 1973); *Career* res asst MIT 1961–64, reader in fluid mechanics Imperial Coll London 1972–76 (lectr in mech engrg 1964–72), prof of mech engrg Univ of Calif Davis 1976–80; UMIST (now Univ of Manchester): prof of mech engrg 1980–98, head of Thermodynamics & Fluid Mechanics Div 1980–90, head of Mech Engrg Dept 1983–85 and 1993–95, res prof 1998–, chm Environmental Strategy Gp 1998–2004; adjunct prof Pennsylvania State Univ 1984–88; assoc ed ASME Fluids Engrg Jl 1978–81, ed-in-chief Int Jl of Heat & Fluid Flow 1987–2012; regnl dir Tyndall Centre for Climate Change Res 2000–06; hon prof Nanjing Univ of Aeronautics and Astronautics PRC 1993; Hon DUniv INP Toulouse 1999, DSc (hc) Aristotle Univ of Thessaloniki 2005, Paul Cézanne Aix-en-Provence 2008, hon dip Russian Acad of Science Novosibirsk 2013; FIMechE 1981, FASME 1983, FRS, FREng 1994, FRAeS 1996, FCGI 2003; *Books* Mathematical Models of Turbulence (with D B Spalding, 1972), Turbulence Models and their Application (with W C Reynolds and W Rodi, 1985), Closure Strategies for Turbulent and Transitional Flows (with N Sandham, 2002), Geo-Engineering Climate Change: Environmental Necessity or Pandora's Box? (ed, with JMT Thompson, 2010), Turbulence Modelling for Engineering and the Environment (with K Hanjalic, 2011); also author of over 200 scientific articles on turbulence and turbulent flow; *Recreations* photography, country walking, French life, literature, culture, food and wine; *Style*— Prof Brian Launder, FRS, FREng; ✉ School of Mechanical, Aerospace and Civil Engineering, University of Manchester, George Begg Building, Sackville Street, Manchester M13 8LP (☎ 0161 360 3801, e-mail brian.launder@manchester.ac.uk)

LAUNER, Dr Michael Andrew (Mike); s of Ellis Launer (d 1978), of Manchester, and Sylvia Launer, *née* Cohen (d 1985); *b* 29 May 1947, Manchester; *Educ* Manchester Grammar, Univ of Leeds (DPM), Open Univ (BA), Liverpool John Moores Univ (MA), Open Univ (Dip); *m* Nov 1972, Hilary Elizabeth, da of Herbert Frederick Coates (d 1955), of Milford Haven, Wales; 1 s (Jack Simon b 1974); *Career* conslt psychiatrist Burnley Healthcare Tst 1977–2004, fndr Unit for the Treatment of Eating Disorders Burnley 1984, medical dir (North West) Partnership in Care 2004–11, conslt psychiatrist in eating disorders Priory Hospital Preston 2014–15, DCL Open Univ 2009; clinical advsr Care Quality Cmmn 2011; pioneer in use of Clozapine for schizophrenia; freelance contrib: Hospital Doctor, local radio, TV and newspapers; hon lectr Univ of Manchester 2011; Law Society approved expert witness; professional memb Mental Health Cmmn Isle of Man 2012–15; opinion ldr on schizophrenia; medio-legal work 1979–; Unsung Hero of the NHS Daily Mail 2001, winner Medical Section Laing & Buisson Award 2010, runner-up BMA News Writing Competition 2010; LRCP, MRCS 1970, MRCPsych 1975, memb BMA; FRSA 1996; *Books* The Pleasure Man (2004), Dead in El Paso (2006), Spy Doctors and the Arab Spring (2013); *Recreations* writing, sport as a spectator, novelist and communicator; *Style*— Dr Mike Launer; ✉ e-mail mikelauner@yahoo.co.uk

LAURENCE, George Frederick; QC (1991); s of Dr George Bester Laurence (d 1993), of SA, and Anna Margaretha, *née* Niemeyer; *b* 15 January 1947; *Educ* Pretoria Boys HS, Univ of Cape Town (Smuts Meml scholar, BA), UC Oxford (Rhodes scholar, MA); *m* 1, 27 Aug 1976, (Ann) Jessica (d 1999), da of John Gordon Chenevix Trench; 1 da (Catherine Ann b 28 Aug 1978), 1 s (Benjamin George b 24 Oct 1981), 1 step s (Thomas James Yardley b 14 Sept 1974); m 2, 25 July 2000 (Anne) Jacqueline, da of Dr Hugh Baker; 1 da (Claire Elizabeth b 29 Oct 2001), 1 s (Edward Stephen b 3 March 2003); *Career* called to the Bar Middle Temple 1972 (Harmsworth scholar, bencher 1999); memb: Administrative Law Bar Assoc, Parly Bar Mess, Planning and Environmental Bar Assoc, Chancery Bar Assoc, Justice, Amnesty International; fell Soc of Advanced Legal Studies 1999–; *Recreations* cricket, tennis, theatre; *Clubs* Grannies Cricket; *Style*— George Laurence, Esq, QC; ✉ 12 New Square, Lincoln's Inn, London WC2A 3SW (☎ 020 7419 8000, fax 020 7419 8050, e-mail clerks@newsquarechambers.co.uk)

LAURENCE, Vice Adm Sir Timothy James Hamilton (Tim); KCVO (2011, MVO 1989), CB (2007); yr s of Cdr Guy Stewart Laurence, RN (d 1982), and Barbara Alison, *née* Symons; *b* 1 March 1955; *Educ* Sevenoaks, RNC Dartmouth, UC Durham; *m* 12 Dec 1992, HRH The Princess Royal (*see* Royal Family section); *Career* cmmnd RN 1979, Cdr 1988, Capt 1995, Cdre 1998, Rear Adm 2004, Vice Adm 2007; asst navigating offr HM Yacht Britannia 1979, cmd HMS Cygnet 1981–82 (despatches), equerry to HM The Queen 1986–89, cmd HMS Boxer 1990–91, MOD 1992–95, cmd HMS Cumberland 1995–96, cmd HMS Montrose and Capt Sixth Frigate Sqdn 1996–97, MOD 1997–98, JSCSC (Asst Cmdt (Maritime)) 1999–2001, MOD (dir Navy Resources and Plans (DNRP)) 2001–04, ACDS (Resources and Plans) 2004–07, chief exec Defence Estates 2007–10; ADC 2004 (personal ADC to HM The Queen 2005); ret from RN 2010; now pursues a portfolio of non-exec and charitable interests with particular emphasis on property and regeneration; memb Bd Capita Symonds 2011–15, non-exec chm Dorchester Regeneration, chm Major Projects Assoc, sr military advsr PA Consulting 2011–16, chm Purfleet Centre Regeration Ltd; chm English Heritage 2016–, vice chm Cwlth War Graves Cmmn 2016–; tstee RNLI, memb Bd HMS Victory Preservation Co; Hudson fell St Antony's Coll Oxford 1998–99; memb: RUSI, IISS, RICS; Master Worshipful Co of Coachmakers & Coach Harness Makers 2010; FRGS, AMNI; *Style*— Vice Adm Sir Tim Laurence, KCVO, CB, ADC; ✉ c/o Buckingham Palace, London SW1A 1AA

LAURENS, Simon; *b* 1967, Jersey; *Career* Paralympic equestrian; achievements incl: 2 Gold medals FEI World Para Dressage Championships 2007, Gold medal team event Paralympics Beijing 2008, Silver medal freestyle test Paralympics Beijing 2008, Gold medal team event European Championships Norway 2009, two Bronze medals (individual event and freestyle) European Championships Norway 2009; *Style*— Simon Laurens, Esq

LAUTERPACHT, Prof Sir Elihu; kt (1998), CBE (1989), QC (1970); s of Sir Hersch Lauterpacht, QC (d 1960), and Rachel, *née* Steinberg (d 1989); *b* 13 July 1928; *Educ* Harrow, Trinity Coll Cambridge (MA, LLM, LLD); *m* 1, 1955, Judith Maria (d 1970), er da of Harold Hettinger; 1 s (Michael), 2 da (Deborah, Gabriel); m 2, 1973, Catherine Josephine, da of Francis Daly (d 1960); 1 s (Conan); *Career* international lawyer; called to the Bar Gray's Inn 1950 (bencher 1983); Univ of Cambridge: dir Lauterpacht Centre for Int Law 1983–95, hon prof of int law 1994–; judge (ad hoc) Int Court of Justice 1993–; pres: Eastern Regn UN Assoc 1991–2001, World Bank Admin Tbnl 1979–98; chm: Asian Devpt Bank Admin Tbnl 1993–95, Dispute Settlement Panel N American Free Trade Agreement 1996, World Bank Center for the Settlement of Investment Disputes Arbitration Panels 1997–, UN Compensation Cmmn 1998–99, Eritrea-Ethiopia Boundary Cmmn 2001–; memb Perm Court of Arbitration; govr Westminster Sch 1990–2001; hon memb American Soc of Int Law; Hague Prize for Int Law 2013; *Clubs* Garrick; *Style*— Prof Sir Elihu Lauterpacht, CBE, QC; ✉ 20 Essex Street, London WC2R 3AL (☎ 020 7583 9294, fax 020 7583 1341)

LAVENDER, Justin; s of late Alexander Desmond Lavender, of Christchurch, Dorset, and Hilary May, *née* Coleman; *b* 4 June 1951, Bedford; *Educ* Bedford Modern Sch, QMC London, Guildhall Sch of Music and Drama; *m* 1; 1 s (William b 4 May 1982), 1 da (Catherine b 21 Jan 1984); m 2, Louise, da of Derek William Crane; *Career* tenor; has performed with all major Br orchs; prof of vocal studies RCM 2007–, vocal conslt King's Coll Cambridge, visiting tutor Birmingham Conservatoire, hon prof Confucius Inst NC USA, vocal conslt to the choir of Canterbury Cathedral; *Performances* professional debut as Nadir in The Pearl Fishers (Sydney Opera House) 1980; other debuts incl: Arnold in Rossini's Guillaume Tell (Royal Opera House) 1990, Tamino in Die Zauberflöte (Vienna State Opera) 1990, title role in Rossini's Le Comte d'Ory (La Scala Milan) 1991, Demodokos in Dallapiccola's Ulisse (Salzburg Festival) 1993; concert performances incl: Schubert's Mass in E Flat (Giulini and Berlin Philharmonic) 1988, Bartók's Cantata Profana (Solti and London Philharmonic) 1988, Schnittke's Faust Cantata (Abbado and Vienna Symphony) 1991 (Slatkin and BBC) 2001, Gerontius (Slatkin and Philharmonia) 1996, title role in Gounod's Faust (Royal Opera House) 2004; appeared in The Life of David Gale (film) 2002; *Recordings* incl: videos of Oedipus Rex 1983 and Mitridate 1993, audio of La Noche Triste 1989, La Favorite 1991, Messiah 1993, I Puritani 1993, The Wreckers 1994, Rossini and Donizetti arias 1994, Britten Song Cycles 1996, Bomtempo Mattutina dei Morti 1996, Mozart Arias 1997, Alceste 1998, War and Peace 1999, Schnittke Faust Cantata 2004, Elgar Dream of Gerontius 2006, Jana?ek Ot?enas 2008; *Publications* numerous contribs to professional jls, feature articles in Irish Examiner and China World News Jl; *Recreations* rowing, sailing, railway modelling, Mandarin Chinese; *Style*— Justin Lavender, Esq; ✉ e-mail justinlavender@ntlworld.com, website www.justinlavender.co.uk

LAVENDER, Nicholas; QC (2008); *m* 2002, Anuja Dhir (Her Hon Judge Dhir, QC, *qv*); 1 d (Nikita b 2003), 2 s (Sachin b 2004, Arjun b 2006); *Career* called to the Bar 1989; recorder 2011–, dep judge of the High Court of Justice 2013–; memb Serle Court; memb Bar Cncl 1994– (chm 2014); FCIArb; *Style*— Nicholas Lavender, Esq, QC; ✉ Serle Court, 6 New Square, Lincoln's Inn, London WC2A 3QS

LAVER, Prof John David Michael Henry; CBE (1999); s of Harry Frank Laver (d 1985), and Mary, *née* Brearley (d 1994); *b* 20 January 1938, Nowshera, India; *Educ* Churcher's Coll Petersfield, Univ of Edinburgh (MA, DipPhon, PhD, DLitt); *m* 1, 29 July 1962 (m dis 1974), Avril Morna Anel Macqueen, *née* Gibson; 2 s (Nicholas b 1963, Michael b 1965), 1 da (Claire b 1968); m 2, 1 Aug 1974, Sandra, da of Alexander Traill, of Bonnyrigg, Midlothian; 1 s (Matthew b 1972); *Career* lectr in phonetics Univ of Ibadan 1964–66 (asst lectr 1963–64); Univ of Edinburgh: lectr in phonetics 1966–76, sr lectr 1976–80, reader 1980–85, personal chair in phonetics 1985–2000, chm Centre for Speech Technol Res 1989–94 (dir 1984–89), research prof in the Faculty of Arts 1994–2000, vice-princ 1994–97; res chair in speech sciences Queen Margaret Univ Edinburgh 2001–04 (vice-princ 2002–03, dep princ 2003–04), prof emeritus 2004–; pres Int Phonetic Assoc 1991–95 (memb Cncl), memb Bd Euro Speech Communication Assoc 1988–93, chm Bd of Governance Trinity Coll Dublin Long Room Hub 2007–09; Hon DLitt: De Montfort Univ 1999, Univ of Sheffield 1999, Queen Margaret Univ 2006; Hon LittD TCD 2013; FIOA 1988–2001, FBA 1990 (chm Humanities Research Bd 1994–98, memb Cncl 1998–2001), FRSE 1994 (vice-pres 1996–99, fellowship sec 1999–2002, Bicentenary medal 2004, Royal Medal 2007), hon fell Royal Coll of Speech and Language Therapists (Hon FRCSLT) 2003; *Books* Voice Quality: A Classified Research Bibliography (1979), The Phonetic Description of Voice Quality (1980), The Gift of Speech (1991), Principles of Phonetics (1994); *Recreations* lexicography, bird watching; *Style*— Prof John Laver, CBE, FBA, FRSE; ✉ Easter Bleaton House, By Bridge of Cally, Blairgowrie, Perthshire PH10 7LJ

LAVERICK, David John; s of Wilfred Henry Laverick (d 1992), of Redcar, Cleveland, and (Ivy Mabel) Doreen, *née* Lockhart; *b* 3 August 1945, Stockton, Co Durham; *Educ* Sir William Turner's Sch Redcar, KCL (Halliday Prize), Coll of Law Lancaster Gate; *m* 5 Oct 1968, Margaret Elizabeth, da of Gerald Myatt; 3 s (John Lockhart b 23 Feb 1971, Andrew Duncan b 16 Oct 1972, Benjamin Ian b 9 Aug 1975); *Career* asst slr: Beds CC 1970–72, Lincs (Lindsey) CC 1972–74; dir of admin and slr E Lindsey DC 1973–75, dir

Cmmn for Local Admin in England 1975–95 (local govt ombudsman), chief exec Family Health Serv Appeal Authy 1995–2001, pensions ombudsman 2001–07; pres Adjudication Panel for England 2001–10, princ judge First-tier Tbnl (Gen Regulatory Chamber) 2010–; formerly: legal memb Mental Health Review Tbnl, regnl chm Anchor Housing Assoc, hon sec Tuke Housing Assoc; memb Law Soc 1970 (Beds Law Soc prizewinner); *Recreations* Scottish country dancing, digital photography; *Style*— David Laverick, Esq; ✉ e-mail davidjl39@gmail.com

LAVERICK, Peter Michael; s of Lt Peter Laverick, and Joyce Margaret Carpenter; *b* 7 June 1942; *Educ* Canford Sch, Sch of Law; *m* 25 Feb 1972, Elaine Ruth, da of Leopold Steckler; 2 da (Helen Tanya b 1973, Elise Laverick, *qv*, b 1975); *Career* Capt GS (attached Coldstream Guards) 1968–71; slr 1966, Notary Public 1985, sr ptnr Bennett Griffin Worthing, pres Worthing Law Soc 1995; memb Co of Watermen and Lightermen of the River Thames; *Recreations* playing the tuba, sailing and skiing, rowing, punting and skiffing; *Clubs* Leander, Thames Rowing, Thames Punting, Thames Valley Skiff; *Style*— Peter M Laverick, Esq; ✉ North Barn, Poling, West Sussex (☎ 01903 883205); Bennett Griffin, 23 Warwick Street, Worthing, West Sussex (☎ 01903 229910, fax 01903 229160, e-mail peter@laverick.net)

LAVERNE, Lauren; da of Dr Leslie Ross Gofton, and Cecilia, *née* Watson; *b* 28 April 1978, Sunderland; *Educ* City of Sunderland Coll; *m* Graeme Fisher; 2 s (Fergus, Mackenzie); *Career* television and radio presenter; former singer and guitarist Kenickie; columnist for Red, Grazia and Observer magazine; *Albums* At the Club 1997, Get In 1998; *Television* incl: CD:UK (ITV) 2005–06, The Culture Show (BBC) 2006–10, 10 O'Clock Live (Channel 4) 2011–; other appearances incl: Never Mind the Buzzcocks, Mock the Week, Have I Got News For You, Would I Lie To You?; *Radio* Xfm: Saturday morning show 2002–04, drivetime slot 2004–05 (Best Newcomer Commercial Radio Awards 2004), breakfast show 2005–07; currently BBC Radio 6 Music (Music Radio Personality of the Year Sony Radio Acad Silver Award 2012); *Books* Candy Pop – Candy and the Broken Biscuits (2011); *Style*— Ms Lauren Laverne; ✉ c/o Presenters Department, Independent Talent Group, Oxford House, 76 Oxford Street, London W1D 1BS; Twitter @laurenlaverne

LAVERTY, Paul; *Career* screenwriter; *Films* Carla's Song 1996 (Golden Medal Venice Film Festival 1996), My Name Is Joe 1998 (People's Choice Award Locarno Film Festival, Best Non-American Foreign Film Danish Film Academy), Bread and Roses 1999 (nominated Palme D'Or Cannes Film Festival), Sweet Sixteen 2002 (Best Screenplay Cannes Film Festival, Best Br Ind Film of the Year Br Ind Film Awards, FIPRESCI Award for Best Film European Film Awards, Golden Spike Valladolid Film Festival), Ae Fond Kiss 2004 (German Cinema Owners Prize and Ecumenical Prize Berlin Film Festival, Best Film Motovun Film Festival), Tickets 2005 (co-writer), Cargo 2006, The Wind That Shakes The Barley 2006 (Palme d'Or Cannes Film Festival 2006), It's A Free World 2007, In The Name of Christ 2007, Looking for Eric 2009, Route Irish 2009; *Style*— Paul Laverty Esq; ✉ c/o Sixteen Films Ltd, 187 Wardour Street, London W1F 8ZB

LAVERY, Bryony Mary; da of Harold Shepherd (d 1997), of Scarborough, N Yorks, and Kathleen Betty Shepherd (d 1996); *b* 21 December 1947, Wakefield, W Yorks; *Educ* Wheelwright GS for Girls, Univ of London (BA); *m* 13 Sept 1969, Paul Lavery (d 1991); *Career* playwright; dir Performing Arts Labs, former artistic dir Gay Sweatshop and Les Oeufs Malades, former writer in residence Unicorn Theatre for Children, former tutor Univ of Birmingham; Hon Dr Arts De Montfort Univ; FRSL 2002; *Stage Plays* incl: Missing 1979, Calamity 1983, The Origin of the Species 1984, Wicked 1990, Her Aching Heart 1991 (Pink Paper Play of the Year 1991), Nothing Compares to You 1995, Ophelia 1996, More Light 1997, Goliath 1997, Frozen 1998 (Best New Play TMA 1998, Eileen Anderson Best New Play Award 1998), A Wedding Story 2000, Behind The Scenes at The Museum 2000, Illyria 2000, Magic Toyshop 2001, Precious Bane 2003, Thyestes 2003, A Doll's House 2004, Last Easter 2004, Dracula 2005, Smoke 2006, Yikes 2006, Uncle Vanya 2007, Last Easter 2007, Stockholm 2007; *Radio Plays* incl: No Joan of Arc (nominated Sony Award), Velma and Therese, The Smell of Him, Requiem, Wuthering Heights (adaptation), Lady Audley's Secret (adaptation), Wise Children (adaptation); *Style*— Ms Bryony Lavery; ✉ c/o United Agents, 12–26 Lexington Street, London W1F 0LE (☎ 020 3214 0800, fax 020 3214 0801, website www.unitedagents.co.uk)

LAVERY, Ian; MP; *m* Hilary; 2 s (Ian, Liam); *Career* MP (Lab) Wansbeck 2010–; *Style*— Ian Lavery, Esq, MP; ✉ House of Commons, London SW1A 0AA

LAVINGTON, Prof Simon Hugh; s of Edgar Lavington (d 1982), of Wembley Park, London, and Jane, *née* Nicklen (d 2004); *b* 1 December 1939; *Educ* Haileybury and ISC, Univ of Manchester (MSc, PhD); *m* 6 Aug 1966, Rosalind Margaret, da of Rev George Charles William Twyman, ISO (d 1991), of Herstmonceux, E Sussex; 2 s (Damian b 25 Aug 1968, Dominic b 9 April 1970), 2 da (Hannah b 7 Sept 1971, Tamsin b 19 May 1973); *Career* sr lectr Univ of Manchester 1974–86 (lectr 1965–74); prof Univ of Ife Nigeria 1976–77, prof Univ of Essex 1986–2002 (emeritus prof 2002–); memb various BCS ctees; UN tech expert 1975; CEng, FBCS 1978, FIEE 1985, FRSA 1988; *Books* Logical Design of Computers (1969), History of Manchester Computers (1975), Processor Architecture (1976), Early British Computers (1980), Information Processing 80 (1980), Emerging Trends in Database and Knowledge – Base Machines (1995), Mining Very Large Databases with Parallel Processing (1998), The Pegasus Story: a history of a vintage British computer (2000), Moving Targets: Elliott-Automation and the dawn of the computer age in Britain 1947–67 (2011), Alan Turing and his Contemporaries: Building the World's First Computers (2012); *Recreations* sailing, walking; *Style*— Prof Simon Lavington; ✉ Lemon Tree Cottage, High Street, Sproughton, Suffolk IP8 3AH (☎ 01473 748478, e-mail lavis@essex.ac.uk)

LAW, Andrew Jonathan Parker (Andy); s of Peter Leslie Law, and Audrey Iris, *née* Potter; *b* 25 May 1956; *Educ* Portsmouth GS, Univ of Bristol (BA); *m* 12 April 1986, Amanda Mary, da of Ronald Ernest Southey; 1 s (Thomas Andrew Peter (Tom) b 27 Dec 1988), 2 da (Olivia Rosie Jean b 31 Jan 1993, Venetia Elizabeth b 25 Sept 1997); *Career* account supervisor Wasey Campbell-Ewald advtg 1980 (trainee 1978, asst account exec 1979), account dir Foote Cone & Belding 1981–83 (account supervisor 1980), account dir Collett Dickenson Pearce & Partners 1983–90 (London bd dir 1985, int bd dir 1988); Chiat/Day: business devpt dir 1990–92, client servs dir 1992–93, md London 1993–95, managing ptnr Chiat/Day Inc 1994–95; fndr, chm and ceo St Luke's Holdings Ltd (after MBO of Chiat/Day London) 1995–; worldwide chm and fndr The Law Firm Global Advertising Network 2005; Entrepreneur of the Year 2002; FRSA 2003; *Publications* Open Minds: 21st Century Business Lessons and Innovations from St Luke's, Experiment at Work; *Recreations* family, reading and translating the classics; *Style*— Andy Law, Esq

LAW, Chris M A; MP; s of John Law (d 1993), and Jean Grubb (d 2000); *b* 21 October 1969, Edinburgh; *Educ* St Andrew's Univ (MA), PGDip, CeMAP (professional mortgage adviser); *Career* owner Freewheeling Travels (Himalayan motorcycle expedition leader) 1996–2003, dir and prop CMAC Ltd 2004–; MP (SNP) Dundee West 2015–; fndr Spirit of Independence (political orgn) 2014–; *Recreations* cinema, reading, travel, walking, motorcycling; *Style*— Chris Law, Esq, MP; ✉ 2 Marshall Street, Lochee, Dundee DD2 3BR (☎ 01382 848906, website www.chrislaw.scot, Twitter @ChrisLawSNP); House of Commons, London SW1A 0AA

LAW, (David) Jude; s of Peter Law, and Maggie Law; *b* 29 December 1972, Lewisham, London; *Career* actor; *Theatre* incl: Les Parent Terribles (RNT and Broadway) 1994–95, Death of a Salesman (West Yorkshire Playhouse) 1994, 'Tis Pity She's a Whore (Young Vic) 1999, Dr Faustus (Young Vic) 2002, Hamlet (Wyndham's Theatre) 2009 (Best Shakespearean Performance Critics' Circle Theatre Award 2010), Anna Christie (Donmar Warehouse) 2011, Henry V (Noel Coward Theatre) 2013–14; *Film* incl: Wilde 1997, Gattaca 1997, Midnight in the Garden of Good and Evil 1997, The Wisdom of Crocodiles 1998, The Talented Mr Ripley 1999, Existenz 1999, Love, Honour and Obey 2000, Enemy at the Gates 2001, A.I. 2001, The Road to Perdition 2002, Cold Mountain 2003, I Heart Huckabee's 2004, Closer 2004, Alfie 2004, The Aviator 2004, Sky Captain and the World of Tomorrow 2004, All the King's Men 2006, The Holiday 2006, My Blueberry Nights 2007, The Imaginarium of Doctor Parnassus 2009, Sherlock Holmes 2009, Repo Men 2010, Contagion 2011, Hugo 2011, Sherlock Holmes: A Game of Shadows 2011, Anna Karenina 2012; *Style*— Jude Law, Esq

LAW, Richard Alastair; *b* 29 April 1953; *Educ* Rendcomb Coll, Exeter Coll Oxford (MA); *Career* CA; former ptnr Ernst & Young LLP; memb Tax and Child Support Tbnls; FCA, CTA; *Recreations* rugby union, National Hunt racing, cricket; *Style*— Richard A Law, Esq

LAW, Roger; s of George Law, and Winifred Law; *b* 6 September 1941; *Educ* Littleport Secdy Modern Sch, Cambridge Sch of Art; *m* 2 March 1960, Deirdre Amsden; 2 c (Shem b 26 July 1962, Sophie b 15 Sept 1965); *Career* cartoonist and illustrator; The Observer 1962–65, Sunday Times 1965–67, artist in residence Reed Coll Oregon USA 1967, first puppet film The Milkman 1967, freelance illustrator Pushpin Studios NY 1968–69, caricaturist and features ed Sunday Times 1971–75; Luck and Flaw: formed with Peter Fluck 1976, BBC Arena Art Documentary Luck and Flaw Show 1979; Spitting Image: co-fndr 1982, creative dir Spitting Image Productions 1983–97, first series televised 1984, first American show (NBC TV) 1986, final (18) series 1996, presenter Spitting Images (BBC Radio 4) 2008; The Win'gin Pom (TV puppet series) 1991, Whatever Happened to Spitting Image? (documentary, BBC 4) 2014; Potshots Film (Ceramic Millennium Amsterdam) 1999; presenter: Art Made in China (series of 5 progs) 2008, Whatever Happened to the Teapots? (BBC Radio 4) 2009, Spitting in Russian (BBC Radio 4) 2010, The Secrets of the Art and the Artist Caravaggio (BBC Radio 4) 2010, Archive on 4 – Satire the Great British Tradition (BBC Radio 4) 2010, I'm a Celebrity Get Me Into Here (BBC Radio 4) 2010, The New Silk Road (BBC Radio 4) 2011, Roger's Rabbits (BBC Radio 4) 2011, Roger Law's Chinese Curiosities (BBC Radio 4) 2012, South Africa Spits Back (BBC Radio 4) 2013, Wow! How Did They Do That? (BBC Radio 4) 2013, Roger Law's Chinese Curiosities II (BBC Radio 4) 2014, Roger Law: Art and Seoul (BBC Radio 4) 2015; film A Law Unto Himself by Catherine Hunter (Australian Broadcasting Corporation) 2012; elected memb Alliance Graphic Int (AGI) 1993; memb: RDI, Royal Soc for the Encouragement of Arts Manufacturing and Commerce 1999; Hon DLitt Loughborough Univ 1999; fell of Int Specialised Skills Australia 1997, hon FRCA 2004; *Exhibitions* Cutting Edge Major Installation (Barbican Art Gallery) 1992, Seven Deadly Sins (with Janice Tchalenko, V&A) 1993, Teapot Mania (with Janice Tchalenko, Norwich Castle Museum) 1995, Modern Antiques (with Janice Tchalenko, Richard Dennis Gallery) 1996, Puppet Installation (Royal Acad of Art) 1997, Aussie Stuff (Rebecca Hossack Gallery) 2000, Risk Takers and Pioneers (Ceramic Exhibition Centenary Gallery) 2001, The Land of Oz (The Fine Art Soc) 2005, Still Spitting at Sixty (Newsroom Archive and Visitor Centre) 2005, Rude Britannia: British Comic Art (Tate Britain) 2010, Porcelain City – Jingdezhen (V&A) 2011, Her Maj – 60 Years of Unofficial Portraits of the Queen (Cartoon Museum) 2012, Travelling Light (Sydney) 2012, Spitting Image from Start to Finish (Cartoon Museum) 2014, Collect 2014, Sladmore Contemporary (Saatchi Gallery) 2014, Roger Law – Porcelain (Sladmore Contemporary Gallery) 2014, Collect 2015, Sladmore Contemporary (Saatchi Gallery) 2015, Transported: Roger Law & Stephen Bird (The Scottish Gallery Edinburgh) 2016; *Collections* V&A Museum Ceramic Collection, British Cncl, Print Collection of the Nat Gallery of Australia; *Awards* D&DA award Magazine Illustration 1967 (Roger Law); for Luck and Flaw: Assoc of Illustrators awards Consistent Excellence 1984, D&DA award 1984; for Spitting Image: BPG TV award Best Light Entertainment Prog 1984, Emmy award 1984 and 1986, Grammy award 1987, Int Film and TV award NY 1989, BAFTA award 1989; Gold award NY Film and TV Festival 1991, Emmy award 1994 (Peter and the Wolf Puppets), Lifetime Achievement award Cartoon Art Tst 1998, Political Satire award Political Studies Gp 2000; *Publications* Synthetic Fun (with Jeremy Sandford, 1965), A Christmas Carol (with Peter Fluck, 1979), The Appallingly Disrespectful Spitting Image Book (1985), Treasure Island (with Peter Fluck, 1986), Spitting Images (1987), The Spitting Image Giant Komic Book (1988), Goodbye Magazine (1992), A Nasty Piece of Work (with Lewis Chester, 1992), Thatcha The Real Maggie Memoirs (1993), Aussie Stuff (exhibition catalogue, 2000), The Land of Oz (exhibition catalogue, 2005), Still Spitting at Sixty (autobiography, 2005), Porcelain City – Jingdezhen (exhibition catalogue, 2011), Roger Law (exhibition catalogue, 2014_; *Recreations* making mischief; *Clubs* The Academy (Lexington Street London); *Style*— Roger Law; ✉ e-mail roger_law@spittingimage.uk.com

LAWDEN, James Anthony Henry; s of Maj Henry Tipping Lawden, MC (d 1981), of Roehampton, and Claire Phyllis, *née* Berthoud (d 1962); *b* 10 August 1955; *Educ* Winchester, New Coll Oxford (MA); *m* 6 June 2012, Hikari, da of Takashi and Keiko Haraguchi, of Seijo, Tokyo; *Career* admitted slr 1981; Freshfields Bruckhaus Deringer (formerly Freshfields) 1979–2015: seconded with Aoki, Christensen & Nomoto Tokyo 1984–85, ptnr 1988, resident ptnr Tokyo Office 1992–95, resident ptnr Bangkok Office 1995–2001 (managing ptnr 1998–2001), resident ptnr Tokyo Office 2001–15, (managing ptnr 2005–09 and 2011–15); sr counsel Weerawong, Chinnavat & Peangpanor Ltd Bangkok 2015–; co-chm Foreign Lawyers Assoc of Japan 2010–15; memb Law Soc; *Recreations* tennis, golf, squash, travelling; *Clubs* Naval and Military, Roehampton, Tokyo American, Tokyo Lawn Tennis, Bangkok, Bankok British, Royal Bangkok Sports; *Style*— James Lawden, Esq; ✉ e-mail jahlawden@gmail.com; Weerawong, Chinnavat & Peangpanor Ltd, 22nd Floor, Mercury Tower, 540 Ploenchit Rad, Lumpini, Pathumwan, Bangkok 10330 (☎ 00 66 2 264 8016, mobile 00 66 98 282 1384, e-mail james.l@weerawongcp.com)

LAWES, William; *Educ* Victoria Univ of Wellington NZ, Gonville & Caius Coll Cambridge; *Career* Freshfields Bruckhaus Deringer: joined 1986, ptnr 1994–2011, sr ptnr (chm) 2011–; visiting fellow Centre for Corporate Reputation Oxford; *Style*— William Lawes, Esq; ✉ Freshfields Bruckhaus Deringer, 65 Fleet Street, London EC4Y 1HS

LAWLER, Geoffrey John; s of Maj Ernest Lawler (d 2004), and Enid Florence Lawler (d 1998), of Richmond, N Yorks; *b* 30 October 1954; *Educ* Colchester Royal GS, Richmond Sch, Univ of Hull (BSc); *m* 1989 (m dis 1998), Christine Roth, da of C Roth, of Wyoming, USA; *Career* Cons Res Dept 1980–82, PR exec 1982–83, md The Public Affairs Company (GB) Ltd 1987–, dir Democracy International Ltd 1995–2006, vice-pres International Access Inc 1987–95, sr advsr Keene Public Affrs Ltd 2010–13; FCO observer Russian elections 1993, 1995 and 1996, UN observer South African elections 1994, EC observer Liberia 1997, OSCE observer Ukraine 2014; MP (Cons) Bradford N 1983–87; vice-pres Bradford N Cons Assoc 1987–2001; pres: Univ of Hull Students' Union 1976–77, Br Youth Cncl 1984–87, W Yorks Youth Assoc 1995–2004 (vice-pres 1986–95); chm Aromatherapy Regulation Gp 2001; exec memb Assoc of Former MPs 2012–15; memb Cncl UKIAS 1987–93; Freeman City of London; *Recreations* cricket, travel; *Style*— Geoffrey Lawler, Esq; ✉ The Public Affairs Company, Castlehill House, Otley Road, Leeds LS6 3AA (☎ 0113 278 0211)

LAWLER, His Hon Judge Simon William; QC (1993); s of Maurice Rupert Lawler, of W Yorks, and Daphne Lawler; *b* 26 March 1949; *Educ* Winchester Secdy Modern, Peter Symonds' Sch Winchester, Univ of Hull (LLB); *m* 7 Jan 1985, Josephine Sallie, da of Norman Hanson Day; 2 s (Rupert Hanson b 28 June 1986, Toby William b 3 June 1988);

L

Career called to the Bar Inner Temple 1971, memb chambers 6 Park Square Leeds 1971–2002, recorder 1989–2002 (asst recorder 1983–89), circuit judge (NE Circuit) 2002–; *Recreations* opera, gardening, cricket; *Style*— His Hon Judge Lawler, QC; ✉ Sheffield Crown Court, 50 West Bar, Sheffield, South Yorkshire S3 8PH (☎ 0114 281 2400)

LAWLEY, Susan (Sue); OBE (2001); da of Thomas Clifford Lawley (d 1972), and Margaret Jane Lawley (d 2011); *b* 14 July 1946; *Educ* Dudley Girls' HS, Univ of Bristol (BA); *m* 1, David Arnold Ashby; 1 s (Thomas David Harvey b 1976), 1 da (Harriet Jane b 1980); m 2, Roger Hugh Williams; *Career* trainee reporter and sub ed Western Mail and South Wales Echo 1967–70, BBC Plymouth 1970–72 (freelance reporter, sub ed, TV presenter); govr Nat Film & TV Sch 1990–95; Hon LLD: Univ of Bristol 1989, Univ of Wolverhampton 1995; Hon MA Univ of Birmingham 1989; *Television* presenter BBC: Nationwide 1972–75 and 1977–81, Tonight 1976, Budget and general election progs Nine O'Clock News 1981–82, Six O'Clock News 1982–86, chat shows and other special series incl: News '45, Hospital Watch, Here and Now, general election progs; *Radio* presenter Desert Island Discs (BBC Radio Four) 1988–2006, chair Reith Lectures 2001–; *Recreations* eating, biographies, bridge, golf; *Clubs* NZ Golf; *Style*— Ms Sue Lawley

LAWRENCE, Andrew; *b* 23 April 1954; *Educ* Univ of Edinburgh (BSc), Univ of Leicester (PhD); *Partner* Debbie Capel; 4 c (Zoë, Kit, Dylan, Jake); *Career* exchange scientist Centre for Space Research MIT 1980–81, sr research fell Royal Greenwich Observatory 1981–84; Queen Mary & Westfield Coll London: SERC postdoctoral research asst Sch of Mathematical Scis 1984–87, SERC advanced fell Sch of Mathematical Scis 1987–89, lectr Dept of Physics 1989–94; Univ of Edinburgh: regius prof 1994–, head Sch of Physics 2004–08; assoc scientist SLAC 2008–; chair Astronomy Grants Panel Science and Technol Facilities Cncl 2010–13; former memb: Cncl PPARC, ESO Survey Working Gp, Astronomy Ctee PPARC; former chm Space Sci Advsy Ctee BNSC/PPARC; FRSE, FRAS; *Publications* author of over 200 articles, reports etc in scientific jls; *Recreations* drama, literature, art and music; *Style*— Prof Andrew Lawrence, FRSE; ✉ Institute for Astronomy, Royal Observatory, University of Edinburgh, Blackford Hill, Edinburgh EH9 3HJ (☎ 0131 668 8356, fax 0131 668 8416, e-mail al@roe.ac.uk)

LAWRENCE, Christopher; s of Sir Henry Lawrence, of Bristol, and Penelope Rowland-Lawrence; *b* 10 December 1979, London; *Educ* UCL (BEng); *m* Lorna Paterson; *Career* visual effects supervisor; films incl: Troy 2004, Harry Potter and the Goblet of Fire 2005, Superman Returns 2006, WALL-E 2008, Nanny McPhee and the Big Bang 2010, Prince of Persia: The Sands of Time 2010, Gravity 2013 (Best Special Visual Effects BAFTA 2014, Best Visual Effects Acad Award 2014); *Style*— Christopher Lawrence, Esq; ✉ Framestore, 9 Noel Street, London W1F 8GH

LAWRENCE, HE Claire; *Educ* Univ of Cambridge (MA); *m* 1 July 2006, Mark Gee; 1 s (Theodor Gee b 12 Nov 2014); *Career* diplomat; desk offr EU Directorate 2000–01, Afghan Crisis Unit FCO 2001–02, Mandarin language training 2002–03, consul Guangzhou 2003–06, sr mgmnt offr Freetown 2006–08, first sec UK Permanent Representation to the EU Brussels 2008–11, dep Western Balkans dir and dep head Western Balkans and Enlargement Dept 2011–14, ambass to Lithuania 2015–; *Recreations* literature, art, ballet, classical music; *Style*— HE Ms Claire Lawrence; ✉ c/o FCO (Vilnius), King Charles Street, London SW1A 2AH

LAWRENCE, Dr Clifford Maitland; s of Ronald Douglas Lawrence, and Irene Rose Emma, *née* Abell; *b* 29 November 1950; *Educ* East Ham GS, Univ of Sheffield Med Sch (MB ChB, MD); *m* 2 April 1977, (Patricia) Anne; 3 s (Thomas b 12 Sept 1981, Christopher b 22 June 1986, James b 29 Jan 1991), 1 da (Joanna b 23 Feb 1984); *Career* dermatologist N Staffs Hosp Centre and Royal Victoria Infirmary Newcastle; chm British Soc for Dermatological Surgery; author of papers on: skin surgery, psoriasis, dithranol inflammation; FRCP 1993 (MRCP 1978), MD 1988; *Books* Physical Signs in Dermatology – A Color Atlas and Text (with N H Cox, 1993, 2 edn 2002), Diagnostic Picture Tests in Dermatology (with N H Cox, 1995), An Introduction to Dermatological Surgery (1996, 2 edn 2002), Diagnostic Problems in Dermatology (with N H Cox, 1998); *Recreations* gardening; *Style*— Dr Clifford Lawrence; ✉ Department of Dermatology, Royal Victoria Infirmary, Newcastle upon Tyne NE1 4LP (☎ 0191 282 4548)

LAWRENCE, David Charles; s of Charles Alfred Lawrence, of Bradford on Avon, Wiltshire, and Muriel Betty, *née* Fife; *b* 11 October 1961; *Educ* Reading Sch, Univ of Newcastle upon Tyne (BA, BArch); *m* 22 Aug 1987, Ingrid, da of Malcolm Bell; 2 da (Harriet Kristina b 17 July 1993, Flora Anna b 28 Dec 1996); *Career* architect; assoc dir Fitzroy Robinson London 1986–96, sr assoc Abbey Hanson Rowe London 1996–97, dir Hamiltons Architects 1997–2010, md Bogle Flanagan Lawrence Silver Ltd 2010–13, md Flanagan Lawrence Ltd 2013–; ARB 1986, RIBA 1986; *Recreations* running, music, art, cycling, swimming; *Style*— David Lawrence, Esq; ✉ Flanagan Lawrence Ltd, 66 Porchester Road, London W2 6ET (☎ 020 7706 6220, e-mail d.lawrence@flanaganlawrence.com)

LAWRENCE, Felicity Jane Patricia; da of Prof Clifford Hugh Lawrence, and Helen Maud, *née* Curran; *b* 15 August 1958; *Educ* Ursuline Convent Wimbledon, St Anne's Coll Oxford (BA); *Career* ed New Health Magazine 1984–86; Daily Telegraph plc: ed Sunday Magazine 1986–88, former ed Weekend Magazine and head of devpt magazines; The Guardian 1995– (currently special corr); aid work in Pakistan's NW Frontier Province 1989–91; *Publications* Additives: Your Complete Survival Guide (ed), Not On The Label (2004), Eat Your Heart Out (2008); *Style*— Ms Felicity Lawrence; ✉ The Guardian, King's Place, London N1 9GU

LAWRENCE, Francine; *Educ* Twickenham Art Sch; *m* Jan 1998, Malcolm Macalister Hall; *Career* won Thames TV Design bursary and travelled Caribbean, exhibition of photographs on return, asst art dir Fontana and freelance work for Virago Books, art ed Woman's Journal, art dir and assoc ed Living, ed Country Living 1989–95 (art dir 1985), freelance journalist and photographer 1995–, conslt ed Heritage Today magazine English Heritage 2003–08, editorial dir Simon & Schuster Illustrated 2009–12; lectr in magazine journalism City Univ London 2003–; contrib to various magazine titles; UK co-ordinator FOSCO (charity for street children in Colombia); Designer of The Year Award Periodical Pubns Assoc 1988, Marc Boxer Award for Art Editors 1989; chair Br Soc of Magazine Eds 1991; *Recreations* photography, gardening, travel; *Style*— Ms Francine Lawrence; ✉ e-mail francine.lawrence@btinternet.com, website www.rhodeslawrence.co.uk

LAWRENCE, Sir Ivan John; kt (1992), QC (1981); s of Leslie Lawrence (d 1989), and Sadie Lawrence (d 1992); *b* 24 December 1936; *Educ* Brighton Hove and Sussex GS, ChCh Oxford (MA); *m* 1966, Gloria Helene, *née* Crankshaw; 1 da (Rachel Camilla b 22 June 1968 d 2013); *Career* Nat Serv RAF 1955–57; called to the Bar Inner Temple 1962 (Yarborough-Anderson scholar, master of the bench 1990), in practice SE Circuit, recorder of the Crown Court 1985–2002 (asst recorder 1983–85), head of chambers 1997–2000, visiting prof of law Univ of Buckingham 2004–, elected memb Gen Cncl of the Bar 2005–11; MP (Cons) Burton 1974–97; memb: Expenditure Select Ctee 1974–79, Foreign Affrs Select Ctee 1983–92; chm: Cons Parly Legal Ctee 1987–97, All-Pty Jt Parly Barristers Gp 1987–97, Cons Parly Home Affrs Ctee 1988–97, Home Affrs Select Ctee 1992–97, Exec Ctee UK Branch Cwlth Parly Assoc 1994–97; promoted Nat Lottery as private members bill (1990) leading to introduction of Nat Lottery following Govt bill (1992); chm and vice-chm Cons Friends of Israel 1994–97; memb: Board of Deputies of British Jews 1979–, Exec 1922 Ctee 1988–89 and 1992–97, Cncl of Justice 1989–95, Exec Ctee Soc of Cons Lawyers 1989–95 and 1998– (chm Criminal Justice Ctee 1997–, vice pres 2015–); chm Burton Breweries Charitable Tst 1979–97, pres Brighton Hove and Sussex GS Old Boys Assoc 1999–; contrib to newspapers and magazines on political and legal subjects, also broadcaster, lectr and after dinner speaker; visiting prof of law BPP Univ 2014–; Hon LLD Univ of Buckingham 2013; Freeman of City of London 1993; fell Soc of Advanced Legal Studies; *Books* My Life of Crime (memoir, 2010); *Recreations* piano, squash, travel, friends; *Style*— Sir Ivan Lawrence, QC; ✉ 5 Pump Court Chambers, 5 Pump Court, Temple, London EC4Y 7AP (☎ 020 7353 2532, fax 020 7353 5321)

LAWRENCE, Jill; *b* 17 April 1947; *Educ* Loughborough Univ (BA); *m*; *Career* designer and conslt; industrial design and devpt conslt to global int corporations; BA and MA course conslt and examiner; FRSA 1982; *Style*— Ms Jill Lawrence

LAWRENCE, John Wilfred; s of Wilfred James Lawrence, and Audrey Constance, *née* Thomas; *b* 15 September 1933, Hastings, E Sussex; *Educ* Salesian Coll Cowley Oxford, Hastings Sch of Art, The Central Sch of Art and Design; *m* 14 Dec 1957, Myra Gillian, da of Dr George Douglas Hutton Bell, CBE, FRS; 2 da (Emma b 26 July 1958, Kate b 6 Feb 1960); *Career* book illustrator; lectr in illustration: Brighton Poly 1960–68, Camberwell Sch of Art 1960–92; visiting prof in illustration: London Inst, Anglia Ruskin Univ Cambridge Sch of Art 2001–15; external assessor of illustration: Bristol Poly 1978–82, Brighton Poly 1982–85, Exeter Coll of Art 1986–89, Duncan of Jordanstone Coll of Art 1986–89, Kingston Poly 1990–93, Edinburgh Coll of Art 1991–94; work represented in: Ashmolean Museum, V&A, Nat Museum of Wales, Manchester Metropolitan Univ, collections abroad; memb: Art Workers' Guild 1972 (Master 1990), RE 1987, Soc of Wood Engravers, Wynkyn de Worde; *Books* The Giant of Grabbist (1968), Pope Leo's Elephant (1969), Rabbit and Pork Rhyming Talk (1975), Tongue Twisters (1976), George His Elephant and Castle (1983), Good Babies Bad Babies (1987), This Little Chick (2002, New York Times Certificate of Excellence), Tiny's Big Adventure (by Martin Waddell, *qv*, 2004), Lyra's Oxford (by Philip Pullman, *qv*, 2003), Secret Seahorse (by Chris Butterworth, 2006), Once Upon a Time in the North (by Philip Pullman, 2008), Treasure Island (by Robert Louis Stevenson, 2009), The Arthur Trilogy (by Kevin Crossley-Holland, *qv*, 2010), Wayland the Smith (by Tony Mitton, 2012); illustrator of more than 300 books; *Clubs* Double Crown; *Style*— John Lawrence, Esq; ✉ 6 Worts Causeway, Cambridge CB1 8RL (☎ 01223 247449, e-mail johnlawrence326@btinternet.com)

LAWRENCE, Michael John; s of Geoffrey Frederick Lawrence, of London, and Kathleen, *née* Bridge (d 1981); *b* 25 October 1943; *Educ* Wembley County GS, Univ of Exeter (BSc), Univ of Bristol (PhD); *m* 1967, Maureen, da of Terence Henry Blennerhassett; 3 c; *Career* postgrad research in solid state physics Univ of Nottingham 1965–66, research fell Univ of Bristol 1966–69; Price Waterhouse: joined 1969, qualified CA 1972, ptnr 1978–88; gp fin dir Prudential Corporation plc 1988–93, chief exec London Stock Exchange 1994–96; non-exec dir: Port of London Authy 1983–89, London Transport Bd 1994, Yattendon Investment Tst 1998–; external memb Cncl Defence Research Agency 1990, chm Hundred Gp of Fin Dirs 1992–93; memb Bow Gp 1970–74, cncllr London Borough of Hillingdon 1974–79 (chm Fin Ctee 1978–79); Freeman City of London 1974, memb Ct of Assts Worshipful Co of Tin Plate Workers; FCA; *Recreations* flying, sailing, bridge, tennis; *Style*— Michael Lawrence, Esq

LAWRENCE, Dr Peter Anthony; s of Instr Lt Ivor Douglas Lawrence (d 1990), of Swanage, Dorset, and Joy Frances, *née* Liebert (d 1999); *b* 23 June 1941; *Educ* Wennington Sch Wetherby, Univ of Cambridge (MA, PhD); *m* 9 July 1971, (Ruth) Birgitta, da of Prof Ake Haraldson (d 1985), of Uppsala, Sweden; *Career* Cwlth (Harkness) fell 1965–67, Genetics Dept Univ of Cambridge 1967–69, MRC Lab of Molecular Biology Cambridge 1969–, Zoology Dept Univ of Cambridge 2006–; Prince of Asturias Award for Technical and Scientific Research 2007 (with Gines Morata); FRS 1983; *Books* Insect Development (ed, 1976), The Making of a Fly (1992), Principles of Development (jtly, 1998, 5 edn 2015), Generation and Interpretation of Morphogen Gradients (ed); *Recreations* Ascalaphidae, fungi, gardening, golf, theatre, trees; *Style*— Dr Peter Lawrence, FRS; ✉ 9 Temple End, Great Wilbraham, Cambridge CB21 5JF (☎ 01223 880505); Department of Zoology, University of Cambridge, Downing Street, Cambridge CB2 3EJ (☎ 01223 769015, e-mail pal38@cam.ac.uk)

LAWRENCE, Sandra Elizabeth; da of Brig Roderick Gwynne Lawrence, OBE (d 1976), and Gillian Winifred, *née* Bishop (d 1994); *Educ* St Mary's Sch Wantage, St Martin's Sch of Art London, Byam Shaw Sch of Art London, Simi's Acad Florence; *Career* painter (chiefly wild life, still life and portraits); exhibited Royal Acad, Royal Soc of Portrait Painters, Royal Inst of Painters in Watercolour, Francis Kyle, Fischer Fine Art, Pastel Soc, Grosvenor Gallery, Royal Inst of Oil Painters, Inst of Fine Arts Glasgow, Tryon and Swann Gallery, New York, Caracas, Palm Beach, Singer & Friedlander Sunday Times Watercolour Competition 1997–98, Hunting Art Prizes 1997–2002; designed: Overlord Embroidery D-Day Museum Portsmouth 1968–72, 275ft of cartoons which hang in the Pentagon Washington DC (awarded Cert of Appreciation by the Pentagon 2009); ROI 1980; *Recreations* travel, music, reading; *Clubs* Chelsea Arts; *Style*— Sandra Lawrence; ✉ 12 Paultons House, Paultons Square, London SW3 5DU (☎ 020 7352 0558, website www.sandralawrence.co.uk)

LAWRENCE, Susanne; da of Julian Lawrence (d 2008), and Irene Leah Esme, *née* Conn (d 1980); *b* 15 December 1944, London; *Educ* Brondesbury & Kilburn HS for Girls, City of London Coll (Dip), Inst of Public Relations City of London Coll (Cert), Coll for the Distributive Trades; *Career* PR consultancy with Wilcox Press & PR, International News Service and Good Relations 1963–68, editorial asst, asst ed then dep ed Personnel Management 1968–74, ed Personnel Management monthly jl of IPM 1974–94, co-fndr, editorial dir and dep md Personnel Publications Ltd 1981–93, dep chm Personnel Publications Ltd 1993–2008, chief exec Indigo Publishing Ltd 1996–2010; launched: Transition magazine for Br Assoc for Commercial & Industrial Educn 1985, Personnel Management Plus mid-monthly magazine for IPM 1990, Human Resource Management Journal as jt publisher 1990–2005, Newsline for Nat Fedn of Retail Newsagents 1994, People Management for Inst of Personnel and Devpt 1995, Supply Management for Chartered Inst of Purchasing and Supply 1996, newsletters for Employers Forum on Age and Employers Forum on Disability 1996; published Charity magazine for Charities Aid Fndn 1996–98, relaunched and ed Worldlink and website for World Fedn of Personnel Management Assocs 1998–2008, relaunched and ed NNA News 2006–; memb Editorial Bd Vision (magazine of Br WIZO) 1997–2003; awards incl: Specialist Journalist of the Year Blue Circle Awards for Industrial Journalism 1980, Best Specialist Columnist Magazine Publishing Awards 1983, highly commended Ed of the Year Award PPA 1993; fndr and hon sec: Equal Pay and Opportunity Campaign 1974–87, David Wainwright Equal Opportunity Devpt Tst 1987– (chair of tstees); has served as judge in advtg awards, WIZO Short Story Competition, Personnel Mangr of Year Awards, Parents at Work Employer Awards and in trade union jl awards; life memb Nat Union of Journalists; chartered fell Chartered Inst of Personnel and Devpt; MIPR 1968, FCIPD 1992, FRSA 1998; *Recreations* food, cinema, theatre, travel, art and art history, architecture and design; *Style*— Ms Susanne Lawrence; ✉ Waltham Lodge, 47B Netherhall Gardens, London NW3 5RJ (☎ 020 7435 4140, e-mail susannelawrence@gmail.com)

LAWRENCE, Dr Vanessa Vivienne; CB (2008); da of Leonard Walter Sydney Lawrence (d 1972), and Margaret Elizabeth, *née* Summers; *b* 14 July 1962, Beaconsfield, Bucks; *Educ* St Helen's Sch Northwood, Univ of Sheffield (BA), Univ of Dundee (MSc); *Career* Longman Gp UK Ltd: publisher 1985–89, sr publisher 1989–91, publishing mangr 1991–93; dir GeoInformation Int Pearson Gp Ltd 1993–96; Autodesk Inc: regnl business devpt mangr EMEA West Region 1996–2000, global mangr strategic mktg and communications GIS Solutions Div 2000; DG and ceo Ordnance Survey 2000–14, sec gen

Ordnance Survey Int 2014; chair UK ACE Assoc (formerly Agency Chief Executives' Assoc) 2003–08, non-exec dir ODPM 2002–06, chair UN Ctee of Experts on Global Geospatial Information Mgmnt 2011–; non-exec dir Satellite Applications Catapult Ltd 2015–; memb: Cncl Remote Sensing Soc 1991–94, Cncl Inst of Br Geographers 1994–95, Research Resources Bd ESRC 1995–99, Cncl Assoc for Geographical Info 1996–2001 (chair 1999–2000), Cncl RGS 2002–, Bd Open Geospatial Consortium 2005–; visiting prof: Univ of Southampton 2000–, Kingston Univ 2003–; Univ of Southampton: memb Ct 2001–11, memb Cncl 2002–09, memb Bd of Advsrs Sch of Mgmnt 2005–11; memb Cncl Univ of Cambridge 2009–12; hon vice-pres Geographical Assoc 2006–; patron: Coastin' 2002–06, MapAction 2006–, Cure Parkinson's Tst 2007–; Hon Col 135 Ind Geographic Sqdn Royal Engrs (Volunteers) 2008–; SE Dir of the Year Inst of Dirs 2008; Hon DSc: Univ of Sheffield 2001, Nottingham Trent Univ (on behalf of Southampton Inst) 2002, Kingston Univ 2002, Univ of Glasgow 2005, Univ of Southampton 2014, Royal Holloway Univ of London 2014; Hon DUniv Oxford Brookes 2001, Hon LLD Univ of Dundee 2003; hon fell UCL 2003; FRGS 1987, CGeog 2002, CCMI 2003, assoc fell Remote Sensing and Photogrammetry Soc 2001, Hon FInstCES 2001, FRICS 2003, Hon FREng 2008, FRSGS 2014; *Recreations* scuba diving, sailing, walking, collecting antique maps, tennis; *Clubs* Rickmansworth Sailing, Horsley Sports; *Style—* Dr Vanessa Lawrence, CB; ☎ 07733 001645, e-mail vanessa_lawrence@yahoo.co.uk

LAWRENCE, Sir William Fettiplace; 5 Bt (UK 1867), of Ealing Park, Middx; OBE (2003); s of Maj Sir William Lawrence, 4 Bt (d 1986), and Pamela Mary, *née* Gordon; *b* 23 August 1954, Walcote, Leics; *Educ* King Edward VI Sch Stratford-upon-Avon; *m* 2005, Tamar Bubashvili, da of Revaz Bubashvili, and Mariam, *née* Khizanishvili, of Tbilisi, Georgia; *Heir* cous, Aubrey Lawrence; *Career* asst fin accountant: W B Bumpers Ltd, Rockwell International 1980–81; gen mangr Newdawn & Sun Ltd 1981–98; proprietor William Lawrence Wines; dir: Unicorn Tourism Ltd 1994–98, South Warwickshire Business Partnership 1995–, Stratford-upon-Avon & District Marketing Ltd 1995–97, Stratford-upon-Avon Crossroads Care Attendant Scheme Ltd 1996–99, Midland Music Festivals 1996–98; cncllr Stratford-on-Avon DC 1982 (chm 1990–91, vice-chm 2009–10); memb S Warks Health Authy 1984–92, non-exec/assoc dir S Warks General Hospitals NHS Tst 1993–2003; past non-exec dir Orchestra of the Swan; memb W Midlands Arts 1984–91, chm Heart of England Tourist Bd 1991– (non-exec dir 1989–); chm Tourism for All 2002–; exec memb Stratford District Cncl for Voluntary Serv 1986–91; pres: Stratford and Dist MENCAP, Stratford-upon-Avon Chamber Music Soc, Birmingham Symphonic Wind, Br Toilet Assoc; tstee Holiday Care Serv 2001–; memb: Warks Branch Rural Devpt Cmmn 1995–98, W Midlands Life 1999–, W Midlands Business Cncl 2002–, W Midlands Regnl Assembly 2003–, Local Govt Assoc Tourism Exec Culture and Sport, Ministerial Advsy Gp 2012 Games, BBFC, Assoc of Train Operating Companies Disability Reference Panel 2009–; conslt to: The Insite Consultancy on Disability Awareness Training 1995–2000, Heritage House Gp, Healthmatic Ltd; membCt Univ of Birmingham 1990–; former govr Royal Shakespeare Theatre; formerly: pres Action Unlimited Tst, dir Cncl for the Advancement of the Arts Recreation and Education, memb Corporation Stratford-upon-Avon Coll, govr King Edward VI Sch Stratford-upon-Avon, govr Stratford-upon-Avon GS for Girls, tstee Live Music Now 2006; Hon MA Univ of Worcester 2006; fell Tourism Soc 2003, FRSA 2005; *Recreations* wine, gardening, travel; *Style—* Sir William Lawrence, Bt, OBE; ✉ The Knoll, Walcote, Alcester, Warwickshire B49 6LZ (☎ 01789 488303, mobile 07973 202113, e-mail sirwlawrence@cix.co.uk or sirwlawrence@orange.net)

LAWRENCE OF CLARENDON, Baroness (Life Peer UK 2013), of Clarendon in the Commonwealth Realm of Jamaica; Doreen Delceita Lawrence; OBE; *b* 24 October 1952; *Career* campaigner; fndr Stephen Lawrence Charitable Tst; chllr De Montfort Univ 2016–; *Style—* The Baroness Lawrence of Clarendon, OBE; ✉ House of Lords, London SW1A 0PW

LAWRENSON, Prof Peter John; s of John Lawrenson (d 1949), of Prescot, and Emily, *née* Houghton (d 1979); *b* 12 March 1933, Prescot, Merseyside; *Educ* Prescot GS, Univ of Manchester (BSc, MSc, DSc); *m* 5 April 1958, Shirley Hannah, da of Albert Edward Foster, of Macclesfield; 1 s (Mark b 1958), 3 da (Ruth b 1960, Rachel b 1963, Isobel b 1965); *Career* res engr GEC 1956–61; Univ of Leeds: lectr 1961, reader 1965, prof 1966–91, head Dept of Electrical and Electronic Engrg 1974–84, chm Faculty of Sci and Applied Sci 1978–80, chm Faculty of Engrg 1980–81; Switched Reluctance Drives Ltd: chm 1980–97, non-exec dir 1997–2002; consit Rolls-Royce plc 2000–02; author of over 120 papers for various sci jls; awards: Inst Premium IEE 1981, Alfred Ewing Gold Medal Royal Soc and Inst of Civil Engrs 1983, Esso Energy Gold Medal Royal Soc 1985, Faraday Medal IEE 1990, Edison Medal 2005, Sir Frank Whittle Medal 2005; pres IEE 1992–93; memb Cncl Univ of Buckingham 1987–93; services to Collinghurst and Linton Parish Cncl 2003–10; FIEE 1974, FIEEE 1975, FREng 1980, FRS 1982; *Books* Analysis and Computation of Electric & Magnetic Fields (with K J Binns, 1963 and 1973), Per Unit Systems (with M R Harris & J M Stephenson, 1970), The Analytical and Numerical Solution of Electric and Magnetic Fields (with K J Binns and C W Trowbridge) 1992; *Recreations* chess, bridge, tennis, gardening, walking; *Style—* Prof Peter Lawrenson, FREng, FRS; ✉ Nidec Motor UK Technology Centre, East Park Road, Harrogate HG3 1PR (☎ 01483 845200)

LAWRIE, His Hon Judge Ian; QC (2011); *Educ* Univ of Warwick (LLB); *Career* called to the Bar 1985; head of chambers 3 Paper Buildings until 2015, circuit judge (Western Circuit) 2015–; *Style—* His Hon Judge Lawrie, QC; ✉ The Law Courts, Armada Way, Plymouth PL1 2ER

LAWRIE, Paul; OBE (2013, MBE 2000); *b* 1 January 1969; *m* 1991, Marian; 2 s (Craig, Michael); *Career* professional golfer; turned professional 1986; tournament victories: Catalonian Open Spain 1996, Qatar Masters 1999, Open Championship at Carnoustie 1999, Dunhill Links Championship 2001, Wales Open 2002, Open de Andalucia de Golf 2011; memb European Ryder Cup Team 1999; *Style—* Paul Lawrie, Esq, OBE; ✉ c/o IMG, McCormack House, Chiswick, London W4 2TH (☎ 020 8233 5300, fax 020 8233 5301)

LAWS, Rt Hon David Anthony; PC (2010); s of D A Laws, and Mrs M T Savidge; *b* 30 November 1965; *Educ* St George's Coll Weybridge, King's Coll Cambridge (scholar, BA); *Career* vice-pres JP Morgan & Co 1987–94, md Barclays de Zoete Wedd 1992–94; Lib Dems: econ advsr 1994–97, dir of policy and research 1997–99; MP (Lib Dem) Yeovil 2001–15, memb Treasy Select Ctee 2001–03; spokesman for defence 2001–02, Lib Dem shadow chief sec 2002–05, Lib Dem spokesman on work and pensions 2005–10, chief exec to the Treasy 2010; Observer Mace Nat Debating Champion 1984; *Style—* The Rt Hon David Laws; ✉ House of Commons, London SW1A 0AA (☎ 020 7219 8413); Constituency Office: 5 Church Street, Yeovil, Somerset BA20 1HB (☎ 01935 423284)

LAWS, Rt Hon Lord Justice; Hon Sir John Grant McKenzie; kt (1992), PC (1999); s of Dr Frederic Laws (d 1961), and Dr Margaret Ross Laws, *née* McKenzie; *b* 10 May 1945; *Educ* Durham Sch (King's scholar), Exeter Coll Oxford (Sr open classical scholar, BA, MA); *m* 1973, Sophie Susan Sydenham Cole, *née* Marshall; 1 da (Margaret Grace McKenzie b 1980); *Career* called to the Bar Inner Temple 1970 (Marshall Hall scholar), recorder 1985–92 (asst recorder 1983–85), first jr counsel to the Treasy in Common Law 1984–92, bencher Inner Temple 1985, judge of the High Court of Justice (Queen's Bench Div) 1992–97, Lord Justice of Appeal 1999–; called to the Bar: New South Wales 1987, Gibraltar 1988; pres Bar Euro Gp 1994–; hon fell: Robinson Coll Cambridge, Exeter Coll Oxford; judicial visitor UCL 1997–; *Recreations* Greece, living in London, philosophy; *Clubs* Garrick; *Style—* The Rt Hon Lord Justice Laws; ✉ c/o Royal Courts of Justice, Strand, London WC2A 2LL

LAWS, Sir Stephen Charles; KCB (2011, CB 1996), QC; s of late Dennis Arthur Laws, MC, and late Beryl Elizabeth, *née* Roe; *b* 28 January 1950; *Educ* St Dunstan's Coll Catford, Univ of Bristol (LLB); *m* 1, Angela Mary (d 1998), da of John William Deardon; 3 da (Clare Theresa b 10 Aug 1976, Mary Veronica b 20 May 1980, Philippa Jane b 24 Nov 1982), 2 s (Michael Benedict b 11 Feb 1978, Patrick Joseph b 30 July 1985); m 2, Elizabeth Ann Owen, da of Robert Williams; 1 step s (Matthew Thomas David Owen b 16 Jan 1978), 1 step da (Katherine Louise Owen b 26 Nov 1979); *Career* asst lectr Univ of Bristol 1972–73; called to the Bar Middle Temple 1973 (bencher 2008); pupil of Michael Hutchison then Andrew Longmore 1973–74, legal asst Home Office 1975–76; Parly Counsel: asst 1976–82, seconded to Law Cmmn 1980–82 and 1989–91, sr asst 1982–85, dep parly counsel 1985–91, parly counsel 1991–2006, first parly counsel 2006–12; chm Advsy Bd Big Data for Law research project 2014–15; chm Civil Service Benevolent Fund (now Charity for Civil Servants) 2009–12, memb McKay Cmmn 2012–13, memb Expert Panel Strathclyde Review of Secondary Legislation and the Primacy of the House of Commons 2015; sr assoc research fell Inst of Advanced Legal Studies 2012–, hon sr research assoc UCL 2013–, memb Advsy Bd Law Sch Univ of Bristol 2013–, hon fell Univ of Kent Law Sch 2015–; Hon LLD Univ of Bristol 2012, Hon LLD Univ of London 2014; *Publications* Halsbury's Laws: Statutes Title (1983), Drafting Legislation: A Modern Approach (contrib, 2008), Plus ça Change? Continuity and Change in UK Legislative Drafting Practice (in European Jl of Law Reform 2009), Giving Effect to Policy in Legislation: How to Avoid Missing the Point (in Statute Law Review, 2011), Law in Politics, Politics in Law (contrib, ed Feldman, 2013), Parliament: Legislation and Accountability (contrib, eds Horne and Le Sueur, 2016); *Recreations* Italy, medieval and constitutional history, gadgets, cricket watching, golf; *Clubs* St Thomas More Soc, Statute Law Soc, Soc of Legal Scholars, Study of Parliament Group, Canterbury Golf; *Style—* Sir Stephen Laws, KCB, QC; ✉ e-mail sc.laws@me.com, Twitter @sc_laws

LAWSON, Hon Mrs (Rosamond Mary); only da of 2 Viscount Monckton of Brenchley, CB, OBE, MC, DL, FSA (d 2006); *b* 26 October 1953; *Educ* Ursuline Convent Tildonk Belgium; *m* 30 Dec 1991, as his 2 w, Dominic Ralph Campden Lawson, *qv*, s of Baron Lawson of Blaby, PC (Life Peer), *qv*; 2 da; *Career* asst md Cartier London 1979, sales and exhibition mangr Tabbah Jewellers (Monte Carlo) 1980, promotions mangr Asprey 1982–85, md Tiffany London 1986–97 (pres 1997–2000), non-exec chm Asprey & Garrard 2002–04 (chief exec 2000–02); pres KIDS 2003– (chm 1999–2003); patron: Acorn Hospice, Downside Up, Downs Ed; tstee Gilbert Collection 2003–; Liveryman Worshipful Co of Goldsmiths 2000 (Freeman 1982); *Recreations* books, dogs, voyages; *Style—* The Hon Mrs Lawson

LAWSON, Celia; s of Bernard Macnamara, and Winifred Anne, *née* Conlon; *b* 22 July 1955, Edinburgh; *Educ* St Margaret's Convent Edinburgh; *m* 21 July 1979, Iain McDonald Lawson; 2 da (Laura Anne b 21 April 1981, Rachel Louise b 3 Feb 1983); *Career* previously memb former Ind Broadcasting Authy; cncllr: Renfrew DC 1992–, Renfrewshire Cncl (Paisley East and Ralston Ward, provost 2007–); involvement with: Accord Hospice, St Vincent's Hospice, Paisley Crime Prevention Panel, Barlinnie Visiting Ctee; tstee: Miss Elizabeth Kibble Tst, Peter Brough Tst; past memb St Vincent de Paul; *Recreations* reading, travel; *Style—* Mrs Celia Lawson; ✉ 27 Ben Lui Drive, Hawkhead, Paisley, Renfrewshire PA2 7LU (☎ 0141 562 6675, e-mail c.lawson27@hotmail.co.uk)

L

LAWSON, Prof Colin James; CBE (2016); s of Eric William Lawson (d 1998) and Edith Mary, *née* Pounder (d 1998); *b* 24 July 1949, Saltburn-by-the-Sea, Cleveland; *Educ* Keble Coll Oxford (MA), Univ of Birmingham (MA), Univ of Aberdeen (PhD), Univ of London (DMus); *m* 16 April 1982, (Aileen) Hilary, *née* Birch; 1 s (Oliver James b 10 Jan 1985); *Career* lectr in music Univ of Aberdeen 1973–77, successively lectr, sr lectr and reader in music Univ of Sheffield 1978–97, prof of performance studies Goldsmiths Coll 1998–2001, pro-vice-chllr Thames Valley Univ 2001–05, dir Royal Coll of Music 2005–; princ clarinet: English Concert, London Classical Players, King's Consort; solo appearances worldwide incl Carnegie Hall and Lincoln Center NY; tstee London Music Masters; FLCM 2005, FRCM 2005, FRNCM 2009, Hon FRAM 2015; Cambridge Companion to the Clarinet (ed, 1995), Mozart Clarinet Concerto (1996), Brahms Clarinet Quintet (1998), Historical Performance of Music (1999), The Early Clarinet (2000), Cambridge Companion to the Orchestra (ed, 2003), Cambridge History of Musical Performance (co-ed, 2012); *Recreations* travel, acquisition of early clarinets; *Clubs* Athenaeum; *Style—* Prof Colin Lawson, CBE; ✉ Royal College of Music, Prince Consort Road, London SW7 2BS (☎ 020 7591 4363, e-mail clawson@rcm.ac.uk)

LAWSON, Prof David Hamilton; CBE (1993); s of David Lawson (d 1956), of East Kilbride, and Margaret Harvey, *née* White (d 1982); *b* 27 May 1939, Glasgow; *Educ* HS of Glasgow, Univ of Glasgow (MB ChB, MD); *m* 1, 7 Sept 1963, Alison (d 1996), da of William Diamond (d 1974); 3 s (Derek b 1965, Iain b 1967, Keith b 1970); m 2, Sept 2010, Avril Eleanor Yarrow Scott; *Career* visiting conslt Univ Med Center Boston Mass 1972–90; conslt physician: Royal Infirmary Glasgow 1973–2003, Dental Hosp Glasgow 1984–2003; visiting prof Sch of Pharmacy Univ of Strathclyde 1976–2006, hon prof of med Univ of Glasgow 1993–; chm Scottish Medicines Consortium 2001–04; hon conslt physician Glasgow Royal Infirmary 2003–; advsr on adverse drug reactions WHO Geneva 1984–89, external assessor Scientific Branch Civil Serv Cmmn 1986–99; Dept of Health London: chm Ctee on Review of Med 1987–91 (memb 1979–91), memb Ctee on Safety of Med 1987–93, chm Medicines Cmmn 1994–2001, tstee RCPE 2006– (vice-pres 1998–99); pres Antonine Probus Club 2008–09, chm Bd of Tstees Drug Safety Research Unit Southampton; memb: Br Pharmacological Soc 1976, Assoc of Physicians GB & Ireland 1979, Scottish Soc of Physicians 1975; HonDSc Univ of Herts 2000, DSc (hc) Univ of Strathclyde 2001; FRCP, FRCPEd, FRCPGlas, FPPM, FFPH, fell American Coll of Clinical Pharmacology, hon fell Br Pharmacology Soc 2008; *Books* Clinical Pharmacy & Hospital Drug Management (with R M E Richards, 1982), Current Medicine – 2 (1990), Current Medicine – 3 (1991), Current Medicine – 4 (1994); *Recreations* hill walking, photography, bird-watching; *Clubs* Royal Commonwealth Soc, London; *Style—* Prof David Lawson, CBE; ✉ 5 Tannoch House, 138 Mugdock Road, Milngavie, Glasgow G62 8NP (☎ 0141 956 2766)

LAWSON, Hon Dominic Ralph Campden; s of Baron Lawson of Blaby, PC (Life Peer), *qv*, and his 1 w, Vanessa Mary Addison, *née* Salmon (d 1985); bro of Nigella Lucy Lawson, *qv*; *b* 17 December 1956; *Educ* Westminster, ChCh Oxford; *m* 1, 11 Sept 1982, Jane Fiona, da of David Christopher Wastell Whytehead, of W Dulwich, London; m 2, 30 Dec 1991, Hon Rosamond Mary Monckton (Hon Mrs Lawson, *qv*), only da of 2 Viscount Monckton of Brenchley, CB, OBE, MC, DL, FSA (d 2006); 2 da (Savannah Vanessa Lucia b 23 Dec 1992, Domenica Marianna Tertia b 1 June 1995); *Career* res The World Tonight Radio 4 1979–81; The Financial Times: joined staff 1981, energy corr 1983–86, columnist Lex 1986–87, columnist 1991–94; ed: The Spectator 1990–95 (dep ed 1987–90), The Sunday Telegraph 1995–2005; columnist: The Sunday Correspondent 1990, Daily Telegraph 1994–95, The Independent 2006–, Sunday Times 2008–; memb Press Complaints Cmmn 1998–2002; Harold Wincott Prize for financial journalism 1987; *Books* Korchnoi – Kasparov: The London Contest (with Raymond Keene, 1983), Britain in the Eighties (contrib, 1989), The Inner Game (1994, published in US as Endgame); *Recreations* chess; *Clubs* MCC; *Style—* The Hon Dominic Lawson

LAWSON, Elizabeth Ann; QC (1989); da of Alexander Edward Lawson (d 1995), of Croydon, Surrey, and Helen Jane, *née* Currie (d 1989); *b* 29 April 1947; *Educ* Croydon HS for Girls,

Univ of Nottingham (LLB); *Career* called to the Bar Gray's Inn 1969; currently head of chambers 1 Pump Court; recorder 1997–, dep High Court judge, dep district judge; chair Leeways Inquiry London Borough of Lewisham 1985, counsel Tyra Henry Inquiry 1987, represented social workers Sharon Campbell Inquiry 1987, chair Liam Johnson Inquiry London Borough of Islington 1989, counsel Victoria Climbie Inquiry 2001–02; chair Mental Health Review Tbnls; memb: Ctee Family Law Bar Assoc 1983– (sec 1994–95, chm 1995–97), Remuneration Ctee Bar Cncl, Review Ctee London Legal Services; sec St Paul's Bayswater United Reformed Church; The Times Woman Lawyer of the Year 2000; 1 Pump Court, London EC4Y 7AB; *Recreations* knitting, cake decoration; *Style*— Miss Elizabeth Lawson, QC

LAWSON, Lesley (Twiggy); da of William Norman Hornby, and Nell Helen, *née* Reeman; *b* 19 September 1949; *m* 1, 1977, Michael Whitney Armstrong (d 1983); 1 da (Carly); m 2, 1988, Leigh Lawson, the actor; *Career* actress, singer and dress designer; came to prominence in modelling career 1966–71; has been the recipient of many awards and honours; launched: Twiggy Skin Care range 2001, Twiggy London clothing for Home Shopping Network 2010, launched Twiggy collection for M&S (online clothing collection for Marks and Spencer) 2012–; *Theatre* incl: Cinderella 1976, Elvira in Blithe Spirit (Chichester) 1977, Captain Beaky 1982, My One And Only 1983–84, Noel & Gertie (Bay St Theatre NY) 1998, If Love Were All (Lucille Lortel Theatre NY) 1999, That Play I Wrote (Wyndhams Theatre London) 2002, Mrs Warren's Profession 2003; *Television* incl: Twiggy Series 1978, Twiggy And Friends 1980, Pygmalion 1981, Captain Beaky 1982, Little Match Girl 1986, Sun Child 1988, Sophie's World, The Young Charlie Chaplin 1989, Princesses (US pilot) 1991, Something Borrowed Something Blue (CBS) 1998, Twiggy's People 1998, Absolutely Fabulous 2001, Take Time With Twiggy 2001, America's Next Top Model 2005–08, Shakespeare Retold – The Taming of the Shrew 2005, Twiggy's Frock Exchange 2008; *Films* incl: The Boyfriend 1971, W 1975, There Goes The Bride 1979, Blues Brothers 1981, The Doctor And The Devils 1985, Club Paradise 1986, Madame Sousatzka 1988, Harem Hotel Istanbul 1988, Woundings 1998; *Recordings* incl: Here I Go Again, Please Get My Name Right, London Pride (Songs from the Brit Musicals), If Love Were All, Midnight Blue 2003, Gotta Sing, Gotta Dance 2009, Romantically Yours 2011; *Books* Twiggy (autobiography, 1975), An Open Look (1985), Twiggy in Black & White (autobiography, 1997), A Guide to Looking and Feeling Fabulous over Forty (2008), Twiggy: A Life In Photographs (2009); *Recreations* music, design, dressmaking; *Style*— Ms Twiggy Lawson; ✉ c/o PFD, Drury House, 34–43 Russell Street, London WC2B 5HA (☎ 0202 7344 1000, fax 0202 7836 9539); website www.twiggylawson.co.uk

LAWSON, Mark Gerard; s of Francis Lawson (d 2010), and Teresa, *née* Kane; *b* 11 April 1962; *Educ* St Columba's Coll St Albans, UCL (BA); *m* 1990, Sarah Gillian Jane, da of Alan John Gilbert Bull; 2 s (William Mark b 25 July 1992, Benjamin Gilbert Francis b 18 March 1999), 1 da (Anna Sarah b 15 March 1995); *Career* journalist; jr reporter and TV critic The Universe 1984–85, TV previewer The Sunday Times 1985–86, asst arts ed and TV critic The Independent 1986–89 (Parly sketchwriter 1987–88), chief feature writer The Independent Magazine 1988–95, TV critic The Independent on Sunday 1990–91; columnist and feature writer: The Independent 1993–95, The Guardian 1995–; freelance contrib to numerous pubns since 1984 incl: The Times, Time Out, The Listener, Mirabella, Vogue, New Statesman, The Tablet; writer and presenter of TV documentaries: Byline: Vote For Ron (BBC) 1990, J'Accuse: Coronation Street (Channel 4) 1991, The Secret Life of The Pope (BBC 2) 1996, The Clinton Complex (BBC 2) 1998; writer and presenter TV and radio progs: The Late Show (BBC 2) 1993–95, Late Review/Newsnight Review (BBC 2) 1994–2005, The Big Question (BBC 1) 1996–99, Vice or Virtue (BBC Radio 4) 1996–98, Burning for Atlanta (BBC Radio 4) 1996, A Brief History of The Future 1997, Front Row (BBC Radio 4) 1998–, Mark Lawson Talks To... (BBC 4) 2004–; script-writer: The Vision Thing (BBC TV) 1993, The Man who had 10,000 Women (BBC Radio 4) 2002, St Graham and St Evelyn, Pray for Us (BBC Radio 4) 2003, Absolute Power (BBC TV) 2003–05, The Third Soldier Holds his Thighs (BBC Radio 4) 2005, London, this is Washington (BBC Radio 4) 2006, Expand This (BBC Radio 4) 2007, Sex After Death (BBC Radio 4) 2007, The Number of the Dead (BBC Radio 3, 2009), The Power of Life and Death (BBC Radio 4) 2010; *Awards* British Press Award 1987, BP Arts Journalism Awards 1989, 1990 and 1991, TV-am Critic of the Year 1989, TV-am Broadcast Journalist of the Year 1990, Sony Radio Silver Award 1999, Cultural Commentator of the Year 2010; *Books* Bloody Margaret: Three Political Fantasies (1991), The Battle for Room Service (1993), Idlewild (1995), Conflicts of Interest: The Art of John Keane (1995), Going Out Live (2001), Enough is Enough (2005); contrib: House of Cards: A Selection of Modern Political Humour (1988), Fine Glances: An anthology of cricket writing (1990); *Recreations* television, watching football and cricket, red wine, reading; *Style*— Mark Lawson; ✉ e-mail mark.lawson.02@bbc.co.uk

LAWSON, His Hon Michael Henry; QC (1991); s of Dr Richard Pike Lawson, MC (d 2005), of Calne, Wilts, and Margaret Haines, *née* Knight (d 1990); *b* 3 February 1946; *Educ* Monkton Combe Sch Bath, Univ of London (LLB); *m* Ann Pleasance Symons, da of late John Guy Brisker, CBE, RD, RN; 2 da (Kate Alexandra b 13 Oct 1971, (Antonia) Sophia Louise b 27 Feb 1974); *Career* called to the Bar Inner Temple 1969 (bencher 1993); primarily in criminal advocacy practice, recorder of the Crown Court 1987 (asst recorder 1983–87), ldr SE Circuit 1997–2000, circuit judge (SE Circuit) 2004–16, ret; memb Bar Cncl 1997–2003; Liveryman Worshipful Co of Curriers 1982 (Master 2007, Ct Asst 2011–13, Sr Asst 2013–); *Clubs* Garrick; *Style*— His Hon Michael Lawson, QC; ✉ The Lewes Combined Court, 182 High Street, Lewes, East Sussex BN7 1YB

LAWSON, Nigella Lucy; da of Lord Lawson of Blaby, PC (Life Peer), *qv*, and Vanessa Mary Addison, *née* Salmon (d 1985); sis of Hon Dominic Ralph Campden Lawson, *qv*; *b* 6 January 1960; *Educ* Godolphin & Latymer Sch, Lady Margaret Hall Oxford (BA); *m* 1, Sept 1992, John Diamond (d 2001); 1 da (Cosima Thomasina b 15 Dec 1993), 1 s (Bruno Paul Nigel b 28 June 1996); m 2, Sept 2003 (m dis 2013), Charles Saatchi, *qv*; *Career* journalist and broadcaster; ed Quartet Books 1982–84; Sunday Times: asst on Arts & Review section 1984–86, dep literary ed 1986–88, arts writer 1988–89; restaurant columnist The Spectator 1985–96; columnist: Evening Standard 1989–94, The Times 1995–98, The Observer 1998–2001; food writer Vogue 1996–2002; TV shows on Channel 4: Nigella Bites 2000 and 2001 (won Television Broadcast of the Year at Guild of Food Writers Awards 2001), Forever Summer 2002; TV shows on BBC: Nigella Express 2007, Nigella's Christmas Kitchen 2008, Nigella Kitchen 2010, Nigellissima 2012; Author of the Year British Book Awards 2001; *Books* How to Eat (1998), How to be a Domestic Goddess (2000), Nigella Bites (2001), Forever Summer (2002), Feast (2004), Nigella Express (2007), Nigella Christmas (2008), Kitchen (2010), Nigellissima (2012); *Style*— Nigella Lawson; ✉ c/o Ed Victor Limited, 6 Bayley Street, Bedford Square, London WC1B 3HB (☎ 020 7304 4100, fax 020 7304 4111)

LAWSON, Sonia; da of Frederick Lawson (d 1968), of Castle Bolton, North Yorks, and Muriel Mary, *née* Metcalfe (both artists); *b* 2 June 1934, Darlington; *Educ* RCA (MA, postgrad travelling scholarship); *m* 14 Jan 1969, Charles William Congo; 1 da (b 29 May 1970); *Career* artist; part-time teacher: Harrow Sch of Art 1960, St Martin's, West Surrey Coll of Art, Royal Acad Schs 1975–2005; visiting lectr Royal Acad Schs 1985–2003; Rowney Drawing Prize 1984, Lorne Award 1987, Eastern Arts drawing prize (first prize 1984 and 1989); RA 1982, RWS 1985, Hon RWA 2005; *Solo Exhibitions* incl: Zwemmer Gallery London 1960, New Arts Centre London 1963, Queens Square Gallery Leeds 1964, Trafford Gallery London 1967, Billingham/Middlesbrough 1973, Harrogate Art Gallery 1979, retrospective Shrines of Life touring exhbn 1982–83, Central Art Gallery Milton Keynes 1982, Mappin Gallery Sheffield 1982, Cartwright Bradford 1982, Leicester Kimberlin and Hull Ferens 1983, Midnight Muse (City Art Gallery Manchester) 1987, Wakefield City Art Gallery 1988, Bradford Cartwright 1989, Boundary Gallery London 1989, 1995, 1998, 2000, 2003 and 2005, Univ of Birmingham 1994 and 2006, retrospective Dean Clough Halifax 1996, Shirehall Stafford 1999, Royal West of England Acad Bristol 2000, Carlow Arts Festival Eire 2001, Vertigo London 2002, Aylesbury Art Gallery & Museum 2006, Wakefield Art Gallery 2008, retrospective Mercer Art Gallery Harrogate 2015–16; *Group Exhibitions* incl: London Gp, Royal Acad, RWS, 25 Years of British Art (Royal Acad Jubilee) 1977, Fragments Against Ruin (Arts Cncl tour) 1981–82, Moira Kelly Fine Art (London 1982 and NY 1983), Tolly Cobbold Tour 1982–83 and 1985–86, Leeds Poly 'New Art' 1987, Manchester City Art Gallery 1988, London RCA Centenary 1988, Olympia, Islington, RCA and Bath Festivals 1989–2000, China Br Cncl Touring Exhbn 1989–90, Royal Inst of Fine Art Glasgow 1990, The Infernal Method etchings, Royal Acad London 1990, John Moores Liverpool 1991, Nielson & Wuethrich Inter Fine Art Thun Switzerland 1992, Mercury Gallery Duncan Campbell London 1992, Lamont, Connaught Brown 1994–97, Carlow Arts Festival Ireland; *Work in Collections* incl: Imperial War Museum London (BAOR cmmnd W Germany 1984), Arts Cncl GB, Sheffield Graves, Belfast Art Gallery, Univ of Leeds, Middlesbrough Art Gallery, Miny Works, Royal Acad and RCA Collections, Bradford, Huddersfield, Wakefield, Carlisle, Bolton and Rochdale Galleries, Univ Centre Birmingham (cmmnd 1994), St Peter's Oxford, various educn authorities and corp collections, Vatican Rome (cmmnd 1989), Lambeth Palace (cmmnd 1989), Chatsworth House collection, Univ of Queensland, Barclay Capital Paris, private collections in Europe, USA, Canada and Aust; *Publications* illustrator for: Look At It This Way (by James Kirkup, 1994), New Year's Eve (by Fay Weldon, 1995), Sonia Lawson Passions and Alarms (text by Nicholas Usherwood, 2014); *Recreations* cinema, reading, walking; *Clubs* Royal Over-Seas League, Arts, Dover Street; *Style*— Sonia Lawson, RA, RWS; ✉ Royal Academy of Arts, Piccadilly, London W1 (☎ 020 7300 5680, fax 020 7300 0837, e-mail art@sonialawson.co.uk, website www.sonialawson.co.uk)

LAWSON OF BLABY, Baron (Life Peer UK 1992), of Newnham in the County of Northamptonshire; Nigel Lawson; PC (1981); s of Ralph Lawson, and Joan Elisabeth, *née* Davis; *b* 11 March 1932; *Educ* Westminster, ChCh Oxford (scholar); *m* 1, 1955 (m dis 1980), Vanessa Mary Addison (d 1985), 2 da of Felix Addison Salmon, of Ham Common, Surrey; 1 s (Hon Dominic Ralph Campden, *qv*, b 1956), 3 da ((Hon) Nigella, *qv*, b 1960, Hon Thomasina Posy (Hon Mrs Hill) b 1961 d 1993, Hon Horatia Holly b 1966); m 2, 1980 (m dis 2012), Thérèse Mary Maclear, da of Henry Charles Maclear Bate, of Putney, London; 1 s (Hon Thomas Nigel Maclear b 1976), 1 da (Hon Emily Hero b 1981); *Career* Sub-Lt RNVR CO HMMTB Gay Charger 1954–56; memb editorial staff Financial Times 1956–60, city ed Sunday Telegraph 1961–63, special advsr to PM (Sir Alec Douglas-Home) 1963–64, columnist FT and broadcaster BBC 1965, ed The Spectator 1966–70, regular contrib to Sunday Times and Evening Standard 1970–71, The Times 1971–72, fell Nuffield Coll Oxford 1972–73; Parly candidate (Cons) Eton and Slough 1970, MP (Cons) Blaby 1974–92; oppn whip 1976–77, oppn spokesman on Treasy and Economic Affrs 1977–79, fin sec to the Treasy 1979–81, energy sec 1981–83, Chancellor of the Exchequer 1983–1989 (resigned); dir Barclays Bank 1990–98, chm Central Europe Trust Co Ltd 1990–2012, chm Oxford Investment Ptnrs 2006–13; pres Br Inst of Energy Economics 1994–2003; special advsr Cons HQ 1973–74; founding chm Global Warming Policy Fndn 2009–; memb Governing Body Westminster Sch 1999–2005; hon student ChCh Oxford 1996–; IEA Nat Free Enterprise Award 2008, Mousquetaire d'Armagnac 2010; Hon DSc Univ of Buckingham 2011; *Books* The Power Game (with Jock Bruce-Gardyne, 1976), The View From No 11 (memoirs, 1992, abridged and updated as Memoirs of a Tory Radical, 2010), The Nigel Lawson Diet Book (with Thérèse Lawson, 1996), An Appeal to Reason: A Cool Look at Global Warming (2008); *Clubs* Garrick, Beefsteak, Pratt's; *Style*— The Rt Hon the Lord Lawson of Blaby, PC; ✉ House of Lords, London SW1A 0PW

LAWTON, (Frederick) Anthony (Tony); s of Rt Hon Sir Frederick Horace Lawton (d 2001), and Doreen, *née* Wilton; *b* Bodmin, Cornwall; *Educ* Stonyhurst, Univ of Bordeaux (Certificat d'Études), CCC Cambridge; *m* 5 Sept 1964, Catherine Andrée, *née* Bellet; 3 da (Emilie b 18 June 1965, Marie-Josèphe b 11 Aug 1968, Sébastienne Agnès b 21 April 1970); *Career* articled to chief slr Br Railways Bd 1963–66, ptnr Grays Slrs 1967–2006 (conslt 2006–08); tstee Trustee Savings Bank of Yorkshire & Lincoln 1975–89; memb Ctee Conf of Slrs for Catholic Charities 1967– (memb 1967, chm 1998–2007); memb: Law Soc 1966, Yorks Law Soc 1967; *Recreations* history, gardening, travel; *Clubs* Yorkshire; *Style*— Tony Lawton, Esq; ✉ The Old Rectory, The Village, Skelton, York YO30 1XY (☎ 01904 470301, e-mail falawton@gotadsl.co.uk)

LAWTON, James Eric; s of Eric Lawton (d 2009), and Mary Frances, *née* Condon (d 2012); *b* 28 July 1943, Mold, Flintshire; *Educ* St Richard Gwyn Sch Flint; *m* 19 March 1966, Linda Anita, *née* Spence; 3 da (Jacinta Ann, Victoria Claire, Hannah Frances); *Career* jr reporter Flintshire Leader 1959–63, sport sub-ed Daily Telegraph 1963–64, sub-ed The Sun 1964–65, sports writer Daily Express 1965–79, chief sports columnist Vancouver Sun 1979–87, chief sports writer Daily Express 1987–2000, chief sports writer The Independent 2000–13; SJA Sports Journalist of the Year 1988, SJA Sports Columnist of the Year 2005, SJA Sports Feature Writer of the Year 2006, What The Papers Say Sports Writer of the Year 2007, Sports Journalist of the Year Br Press Awards 2010; *Books* Forever Boys (2015, Sunday Times Sports Book of the Year 2015); autobiographies: Malcolm Allison (1974), Tiger Williams (1984), Debbie Brill (1986), George Cohen (2003), Nobby Stiles (2004), Joe Jordan (2004), Ian St John (2005), Bobby Charlton Vol 1 (2007, Br Sports Autobiography of the Year 2007) and Vol 2 (2008), My World Cup Story – Bobby Charlton (2016); biographies: Lester Piggott (1980), Lennox Lewis (2000); All American War Game (1984); *Clubs* Br Sports Writers Foreign Dining; *Style*— James Lawton, Esq; ✉ c/o David Luxton, 23 Hillcourt Avenue, London N12 8EY (☎ 020 8922 3942)

LAWTON, Jeffrey; s of Harold Lawton (d 1975), of Oldham, and Edna, *née* Penney (d 1978); *b* 11 December 1938, Oldham; *Educ* Greenhill GS, Royal Manchester Coll of Music; *m* 26 Sept 1959, Ann Barbara, da of Alan Whitehead; 2 s (Andrew David b 19 Sept 1966, Robert Jeffrey b 7 May 1969), 1 da (Sara Jane b 17 Oct 1971); *Career* tenor; princ WNO 1982–87 (chorus 1981), freelance 1987–, artistic dir Civit Hills Opera Theatre 1995–2000, dir Manannan Opera Isle of Man 1995, dir of vocal studies and opera La Tour de France Festival 1995–99, prof Vocal Studies Dept RSAMD 1995–99, sr lectr RNCM (head of Sch of Vocal and Opera Studies 1999–2000); pres Manchester Wagner Soc, chief patron Oldham Choral Soc, chief patron Bury Choral Soc; has sung with various major Br orchs and conductors; appeared at various major festivals incl: Edinburgh, Llangollen, Salisbury, York, BBC Proms; Paul Harris fell; asst dist govr Rotary Dist 1280; fell Royal Northern Coll of Music 2009; *Performances* with WNO incl: Ringmaster in The Bartered Bride 1982, Tichon in Katya Kabanova 1982, Judge in Un Ballo in Maschera 1982, Large Prisoner in House of the Dead 1982, Laca in Jenufa 1984, Manolious in The Greek Passion 1984, title role in Siegfried 1985 and 1986, Siegfried in Götterdämmerung 1985, title role in Otello (in Brussels, Nancy and Paris) 1987 and 1990, Don José in Carmen 1987, Emperor in Die Frau ohne Schatten 1989, Luka in House of the Dead 1991, Aegisthus in Elektra 1992 and 1995, Tristan in Tristan und Isolde 1993; other operatic roles incl: Florestan in Fidelio (Opera North) 1988, Siegmund in Die Walküre (Cologne) 1988,

Siegfried in Götterdämmerung (Cologne) 1989, Erik in Der Fliegende Holländer (Opera North) 1989, title role in Otello (Lisbon) 1989 and (Covent Garden) 1990, Radames in Aida (Den Bosch Holland) 1991, Prince Shuisky in Boris Godunov (Opera North) 1992, Laca in Jenufa (New Israeli Opera) 1993, Captain in Wozzeck (Opera North) 1993, Aegisthus in Elektra (Covent Garden) 1994, Tristan in Tristan und Isolde (Scottish Opera, Lisbon and Mainz) 1994, Wird in Der Rosenkavalier (Covent Garden), Apollo in Daphne (Garsington) 1995, Aegisthus in Elektra (Canadian Opera Co) 1996, Laca in Jenufa (New Israeli Opera) 1996, Pedro in Indes de Castro (world premiere, Scottish Opera) 1996, title role in Tannhäuser (Opera North) 1997, President Mendez in Der Kuhhandel (Opera North) 2006, title role in Peter Grimes (Scottish opera); concert performances incl: Das Lied von der Erde (Paris, under Janovski, also broadcast on radio, BBC Proms 1995), Mahler Symphony No 8 (Turin, also televised), Tristan (Stuttgart 1997, Scottish Opera 1998, WNO 1999), Siegmund (Prague State Opera) 1998, Tristan (Lyric Opera Chicago) 1999, Tristan (Buenos Aires) 2000, Das Lied von der Erde (Buenos Aires) 2000, Siegmund in Die Walküre (BBC Scottish Symphony Orch) 2004, Zorn in Die Meistersinger von Nünberg (Edinburgh Festival) 2006; *Recordings* incl: The Greek Passion (under Sir Charles Mackerras) 1982, Panait and Adonis, Supraphon (with Brno State Philharmonic Orch), Siegfried and Götterdämmerung (Uner Sir Richard Armstrong), Tann Hauser (under Paul Daniel); *Clubs* Oldham Athletic FC; *Style*— Jeffrey Lawton, Esq; ✉ c/o Music International, 13 Ardilaun Road, London N5 2QR (☎ 020 7359 5183, fax 020 7226 9792)

LAWTON, Prof Sir John Hartley; kt (2005), CBE (1997); s of Frank Hartley Lawton (d 1982), of Leyland, Lancashire, and Mary, *née* Cuerden (d 2001); *Educ* Balshaw's GS Leyland, UC Durham (BSc, PhD); *m* 22 Oct 1966, Dorothy, da of Harold Grimshaw (d 1960), of Leyland Lancs; 1 da (Anna Louise b 1968), 1 s (Graham John b 1969); *Career* Univ of Oxford: departmental demonstrator in zoology 1968–71, lectr in zoology Lincoln Coll 1970–71, lectr in zoology St Anne's Coll 1970–71; Dept of Biology Univ of York: lectr 1971–78, sr lectr 1978–82, reader 1982–85, prof 1985–89; prof of community ecology and dir Centre for Population Biology Imperial Coll of Sci Technol and Med Univ of London 1989–99, adjunct scientist Inst of Ecosystem Studies Millbrook NY 1992–2000, chief exec NERC 1999–2005, chm Royal Cmmn on Environmental Pollution 2005–11; memb NERC (chm Terrestrial and Freshwater Sci and Technology Bd) until 1999, vice-pres RSPB 2000– (chm Cncl until 1998), vice-pres Br Tst for Ornithology 2000–07, pres Br Ecological Soc 2005–07 (hon memb 2009), pres Yorks Wildlife Tst 2014– (chm 2009–14); formerly memb: Cncl Freshwater Biological Assoc, Royal Cmmn on Environmental Pollution, Br Ecological Soc; WWF UK: tstee 2002–08, fell 2008–; patron Chartered Inst of Ecology and Environmental Mgmnt 2011; tstee York Museums Tst 2007– (chm Cncl 2012–); Japan Prize 2004, RSPB Medal 2011; Hon DSc: Lancaster Univ 1993, Univ of Birmingham 2005, Univ of York 2005, Univ of Aberdeen 2006, UEA 2006; fell ICSTM 2006; hon fell Royal Entomological Soc, FRS, Hon FZS, foreign memb Nat Acad of Sciences, foreign memb American Acad of Arts and Sciences, hon fell Instn of Environmental Sci 2011 (pres 2015–), hon fell Soc for the Environment 2013; *Books* Insects on Plants: Community Patterns and Mechanisms (1984), Blackwell Scientific Oxford (with T R E Southwood and D R Strong), The Evolutionary Interactions of Animals and Plants (ed with W G Chaloner and J L Harper, 1991), Linking Species and Ecosystems (ed with C G Jones, 1994), Extinction Rates (ed with R M May, 1995), Community Ecology in a Changing World (2000); *Recreations* bird watching, gardening, photography, hill walking, travel; *Style*— Prof Sir John Lawton, CBE, FRS; ✉ The Hayloft, Holburns Croft, Heslington, York YO10 5DP

LAWTON, Robert Noyes; CBE (1997), DL (2002); *Educ* Porchester Sch, Dorset Coll of Agric (NCA), Shuttleworth Coll of Agric (NDA), Wye Coll Centre for Euro Studies (advanced farm mgmnt); *Career* asst to Maj J B Schuster reorganising family estate in Oxon 1960–62, VSO asst mangr of large mechanised farming scheme in Basutoland Protectorate 1962–64, devpt offr and farm mgmnt conslt ICI Ltd 1964–69; chm Wessex Regnl Panel 1988–97 (advsr to min of agriculture); past chm Wiltshire Farming and Wildlife Advsy Gp; memb numerous agric ctees and advsy gps 1982–; govr: Royal Agric Coll 1996–, Silsoe Res Inst 1996–2002; High Sheriff Wilts 2000; Joseph Nickerson Husbandry Award 1982, Farmer of the Year 1993; FRAgS 1993, FIAgrE 2002; *Recreations* fly fishing, shooting, cross-country skiing, watercolour painting, military history, bee-keeping, book collecting (especially early agric publications); *Style*— Robert Lawton, Esq, CBE, DL

LAWTON, Rowan; *Career* literary agent; formerly with William Morris Endeavor and PFD, co-fndr (with Eugenie Furniss, *qv*) Furniss Lawton 2012–; *Style*— Ms Rowan Lawton; ✉ Furniss Lawton, 94 Strand on the Green, Chiswick, London W4 3NN

LAX, Prof Alistair; s of John Lax (d 1993), of Glasgow, and Isobel, *née* Coutts; *b* 30 March 1953, Glasgow; *Educ* Univ of Glasgow (BSc), ICRF (PhD); *m* 1 Sept 1975, Pauline, *née* Smith; 3 s; *Career* staff scientist Inst for Animal Health BBSRC 1979–96; King's Coll London: sr lectr 1996–2002, prof of cellular microbiology 2002–; *Books* Cellular Microbiology (jtly, 1999), Bacterial Protein Toxins (ed, 2005), Toxin (2005); *Style*— Prof Alistair Lax; ✉ King's College London Tower Wing, King's College London, Guy's Hospital, London SE1 9RT

LAY, David John; s of Walter Charles Frederick Lay (d 1984), and June Barbara, *née* Cadman (d 2003); *b* 15 August 1948; *Educ* Magdalen Coll Sch Oxford, CCC Oxford (MA); *m* 1 Sept 1973, Tamara Said, da of Said Pasha Mufti (d 1989), former PM of Jordan; 3 da (Sima b 1977, Maya b 1980, Lana b 1982), 1 s (Taimour b 1982); *Career* BBC radio news reporter 1974–79, presenter Twenty-four Hours BBC World Serv 1979–91, ed Oxford Analytica 1988–2000, md global risk assessments American Int Gp (AIG) 2000–13, sr dir global risk intelligence Starr Companies 2013–; sr assoc memb St Antony's Coll Oxford 1997–98, memb Sr Common Room CCC Oxford 1997–; *Recreations* foreign travel; *Style*— David Lay, Esq; ✉ 90 Coombe Lane West, Kingston upon Thames, Surrey KT2 7DB (☎ 020 8336 1325, e-mail davidjlay@hotmail.com); 2 Gold Street, Apartment 5108, New York, NY 10038, USA (☎ 00 212 430 5799)

LAY, Richard Neville; CBE (2001); s of late Edward John Lay, of Banstead, Surrey, and Nellie, *née* Gould; *b* 18 October 1938; *Educ* Whitgift Sch; *m* Jan 2003, Veronica Anne Jones, *née* Hamilton-Russell; 2 c by previous m (Melanie St Clair b 1965, Martin Richard Forbes b 1969); *Career* chartered surveyor; pres Royal Instn of Chartered Surveyors 1998–99, chm and tstee Portman Estate 1999–2016 (chm 1999–2015); ptnr Debenham Tewson & Chinnocks 1965–87, chm DTZ Holdings plc and subsid cos 1987–2000; dir London Bd RSA Gp 1968– (chm 2005–); tstee Tate Gallery Fndn 1988–94; chm: Market Requirements Ctee RICS (The Lay Report, 1991), Commercial Market Panel RICS 1992–96; dir Nat House Building Cncl 2000–07; co-chair Corby Regeneration Co Ltd 2003–06, chm North Northants Devpt Co Urban Regeneration Cos 2006–08; memb: Cncl Br Property Federation 1992–99, Bank of England Property Forum 1994–2000, Advsy Panel on Standards in the Planning Inspectorate 1996–2001, Bd of Coll of Estate Mgmnt 2000–04; chm Dept of Communities and Local Govt Commercial Property Gp 2004–10; chm London Underwriting Centre 2005–; surveyor to the Worshipful Co of Armourers & Brasiers 1983–98 (memb Ct 1998–, Master 2003–04); Property Personality of the Year 1999; FRICS; *Recreations* gardening, dogs; *Clubs* Hurlingham; *Style*— Richard Lay, Esq, CBE, FRICS; ✉ Meadow Cottage, Winderton, Banbury OX15 5JF (☎ 01608 685458, e-mail richard.lay@portmanestate.co.uk)

LAYARD, Baron (Life Peer UK 2000), of Highgate in the London Borough of Haringey; Prof (Peter) Richard Grenville; s of John Willoughby Layard (d 1974), and Doris, *née* Dunn (d 1973); *b* 15 March 1934; *Educ* Eton, Univ of Cambridge (BA), LSE (MSc); *m* 1991, Molly, *née* Reid (Baroness Meacher (Life Peer)), *qv*; *Career* 2 Lt 4 RHA 1953–54, RA 1952–54; sch teacher LCC 1959–61, sr res offr Robbins Ctee of Higher Educn 1961–64; LSE: dep dir Higher Educn Res Unit 1964–74, lectr 1968–75, head Centre for Lab Economics 1974–90, reader 1975–80, prof of economics 1980–, dir Centre for Econ Performance 1990–2003 (dir Well-being Prog 2003–); econ conslt Govt of Russian Fedn 1991–97; memb Univ Grants Ctee 1985–89, chm Exec Ctee Employment Inst until 1986 and chm 1987–91; conslt Dept for Educn and Employment 1997–2001; fell Econometric Soc, FBA; *Books* Microeconomic Theory (with A Walters, 1978, reissued 1987), How to Beat Unemployment (1986), Unemployment: Macroeconomic Performance and the Labour Market (with S Nickell and R Jackman, 1991), What Labour Can Do (1997), Tackling Unemployment (1999), Tackling Inequality (1999), What the Future Holds (ed, 2002), Happiness: Lessons from a New Science (2005, 2 edn 2011), A Good Childhood: Searching for Values in a Competitive Age (with J Dunn, 2009), Combatting Unemployment (with S Nickell, 2011), Thrive: The Power of Evidence-Based Psychological Therapies (with D M Clark, 2014); *Recreations* tennis; *Style*— Prof Lord Layard; ✉ London School of Economics and Political Science, Houghton Street, London WC2A 2AE (☎ 020 7955 7048, fax 020 7955 7595, e-mail r.layard@lse.ac.uk)

LAYDEN, Anthony Michael; CMG (2009); s of Sheriff Michael Layden, SSC, TD, and Eileen Mary Layden; *b* 27 July 1946, Edinburgh; *Educ* Holy Cross Acad Edinburgh, Univ of Edinburgh (LLB); *m* 1969, Josephine Mary, *née* McGhee; 3 s, 1 da; *Career* Lt 15 Scottish Volunteer Bn, Parachute Regt 1966–69; HM Dip Service: FCO 1968, MECAS Lebanon 1969, Jedda 1971, Rome 1973, FCO Middle East, Rhodesia, Personnel Ops Depts 1977–82, head of chancery Jedda 1982–85, FCO Hong Kong Dept 1985–87, cnsllr and head of chancery Muscat 1987–91, cnsllr (Econ and Commercial) Copenhagen 1991–95, dep head of mission Copenhagen 1994–96, head of W Euro Dept FCO 1996–99, ambass Morocco 1999–2002 (concurrently non-resident ambass to Mauritania), ambass to Libya 2002–06, spec rep for deportation with assurances FCO 2006–13; chm Br Moroccan Soc 2007–14, pres Soc for Libyan Studies 2009–12; *Recreations* sailing, walking, music, bridge; *Clubs* Travellers (chm 2010–14); *Style*— Anthony Layden, Esq, CMG; ✉ c/o Flat 76, South Block, 1B Belvedere Road, London SE1 7GD

LAYE, Michael George (Mike); s of George Edward Laye (d 2002), of North Lancing, W Sussex, and Audrey, *née* Ford; *b* 16 May 1948; *Educ* Henley GS Henley-on-Thames, Univ of Manchester (BA); *m* 1, 1968 (m dis 1972), Helen, *née* Capewell; m 2, 1982 (m dis 2006) Emily Louise, *née* Goodrum; 2 da (Maybelle Evelyn b 22 Aug 1983, Agnes Annie Webb b 23 May 1986), 1 step da (Selena Cleo b 8 Aug 1978); m 3, 1 July 2006, Sandra Ross; 1 s (Sam George Thomas Ross-Laye b 5 Sept 1994); *Career* actor/dir 1972–75, dir ICA Theatre 1975–77, freelance photographer 1977–2000; AFAEP: Merit Award 1987, Gold, Silver and Merit Awards 1988; chm Assoc of Photographers 1990 (memb Cncl 1987–90); fndr memb and communications offr The Digital Communications Group (UK) 1996–98; new media dir Contact Design and Mktg 1996–99; founded image-access.net 2000; *Recreations* walking, jazz, technology; *Style*— Mike Laye; ✉ Le Bourg, Monsac 24440, France (☎ 0844 351 1314); image-access.net, Kings House, 14 Orchard Street, Bristol BS1 5EH (e-mail mail@image-access.net)

LAYTON, Alexander William; QC (1995); s of Paul Henry Layton (d 1989), of London, and Frances Evelyn, *née* Weekes (d 1996); *b* 23 February 1952; *Educ* Marlborough, BNC Oxford (MA), Ludwig-Maximilians-Univ Munich; *m* 1988, Sandy Forshaw, *née* Matheson; 2 da; *Career* called to the Bar Middle Temple 1976 (bencher 2004), asst recorder 1998–2000, recorder 2000–, dep High Court judge; chm: Br German Jurists' Assoc 1988–93, Bar European Gp 2005–07; chm of tstees Br Inst of Int and Comparative Law 2005–11, tstee Acad of European Law; visiting prof KCL 2016–; memb Commercial Bar Assoc (COMBAR); FCIArb 2000; *Books* The Bar on Trial (contrib, 1977), European Civil Practice (co-author, 1989, 2 edn 2004), Practitioners Handbook of EC Law (contrib, 1998), Forum Shopping in the European Judicial Area (contrib, 2007), The Brussels I Review Proposal Uncovered (contrib, 2012), Extraterritoriality and Collective Redress (contrib, 2012), Forum Shopping in the International Commercial Arbitration Context (contrib, 2013); *Style*— Alexander Layton, Esq, QC; ✉ 20 Essex Street, London WC2R 3AL (☎ 020 7842 1200, fax 020 7842 1270, e-mail alayton@20essexst.com)

LAZAROWICZ, Mark; *b* 8 August 1953, Romford, Essex; *Educ* Univ of St Andrews (MA), Univ of Edinburgh (LLB); *m*; 4 c; *Career* MP (Lab) Edinburgh N and Leith 2001–15; memb Environmental Audit Ctee; memb Co-op Pty; *Style*— Mark Lazarowicz, Esq; ✉ House of Commons, London SW1A 0AA

LAZENBY, Terence Michael (Terry); MBE (2008); s of Ernest Lazenby (d 1990), and Joyce, *née* Spice (d 1987); *b* 29 November 1942; *Educ* King's Sch Macclesfield, Univ of Swansea (BSc), Stanford Univ (MSc), Cert Dip of Fin and Accounting; *m* 1971, Eleanor Jane, da of James Livingston Ritchie; 1 s (Simon James b 1975), 1 da (Sarah Jane b 1977); *Career* BP plc (formerly British Petroleum Co plc before merger 1998): univ apprentice 1961–64, technologist 1964–71, process engr 1971–77, engrg mangr Sullom Voe Project 1979–81, tech div mangr BP Developments Aust 1981–84, works gen mangr BP Chemicals Grangemouth 1984–88, dir of mfrg and supply BP Oil UK Ltd 1988–90, gen mangr BP Engrg 1990–92, mangr BP Research and Engrg Site 1993, chief engr BP Int 1994–99; chm: Br Pipeline Agency 1988–98, ACTIVE 1996–2002, Railtrack/Jarvis Alliance 2000–01, NTO Gp for Engrg 2000–09, UMITEK Ltd 2001–05, Portsmouth Water Ltd 2002–14, Engineering Construction Industry Trg Bd 2005–12; non-exec dir: Expo Int Group plc 2003–08, MTL Instruments Group plc 2002–08; assurance mangr Br Museum 2000–02; visiting prof of process integration UMIST; memb Senate Engrg Cncl 1996–98; govr and vice-chair Brooklands Coll Weybridge; Lt-Col (ELSC); FInstPet 1991, FIChemE 1992, FREng 1995; *Recreations* golf, swimming, gardening; *Style*— Terry Lazenby, Esq, MBE, FREng; ✉ Seamab, Woodland Drive, East Horsley, Surrey KT24 5AN (☎ 01483 284232, e-mail terrylazenby@terrylazenby.plus.com)

LE BRUN, Christopher Mark; s of John Le Brun, BEM, QSM, RM (d 1970), of Portsmouth, Hants, and Eileen Betty, *née* Miles; *b* 20 December 1951; *Educ* Southern GS Portsmouth, Slade Sch of Fine Art (DFA), Chelsea Sch of Art (MA); *m* 31 March 1979, Charlotte Eleanor, da of Gp Capt Hugh Beresford Verity, DSO, DFC, of Richmond, Surrey; 2 s (Luke b 1984, Edmund b 1990), 1 da (Lily b 1986); *Career* artist; prof of drawing Royal Acad Schs 2000–02, pres Royal Acad 2011–; awards and cmmns: prizewinner John Moores Liverpool Exhibitions 1978 and 1980, Calouste Gulbenkian Fndn Printmakers Commission Award 1983, designer Ballet Imperial Royal Opera House Covent Garden 1985; DAAD Fellowship Berlin 1987–88, Jerusalem Tst Cmmn Liverpool Cathedral 1996; tstee: Tate Gallery 1990–95, Nat Gallery 1996–2003, Dulwich Picture Gallery 2000–05, Royal Drawing Sch 2004–, Nat Portrait Gallery 2012–; patron: Turner's House Tst 2012–, Gainsborough's House Suffolk 2012–; pres Artists' General Benevolent Institution 2012–; hon memb Royal Birmingham Soc of Artists (RBSA) 2013; RA 1997, RI 2015, Hon RWS 2016; *Solo Exhibitions* incl: Nigel Greenwood Gallery London 1980, 1982, 1985 and 1989, Gillespie-Laage-Salomon Paris 1981, Sperone Westwater NY 1983, 1986 and 1988, Fruitmarket Gallery Edinburgh 1985, Arnolfini Gallery Bristol 1985, Kunsthalle Basel 1986, DAAD Galerie Berlin 1988, Galerie Rudolf Zwirner Cologne 1988, Art Center Pasadena 1992, LA Louver Los Angeles 1992, Marlborough Fine Art London 1994, 1998 and 2001, Astrup Fearnley MOMA Oslo 1995, Fitzwilliam Museum Cambridge 1995, Courtauld Gallery 1997, Marlborough Chelsea New York 2004, New Art Gallery Walsall 2008, Galerie Hohenthal und Bergen Berlin 2009, New Art Centre Salisbury 2010, One Canada Square London 2011, Friedman Benda New York 2014, Arndt Singapore 2016; *Group Exhibitions* incl: Nuova Imagine Milan Triennale 1980, Sydney Biennale 1982, Venice Biennale 1982 and 1984, New Art (Tate Gallery London) 1983, An International

Survey of Recent Painting and Sculpture (MoMA NY) 1984, The British Show (toured Australia and NZ) 1985, Paris Biennale 1985, San Francisco Biennale 1986, Falls the Shadow (Recent Br and Euro Art Hayward Gallery London) 1986, British Art of the 1980s (MoMA: Oxford, Budapest, Warsaw, Prague) 1987, Avant Garde in the Eighties (LA County Museum) 1987, Br Art of the 1980s (Liljevalchs Museum Stockholm) 1987, The British Picture (Louver Gallery LA) 1988, New British Painting (Cincinnati Museum and American tour) 1988–89, British Art Now (Setagaya Art Museum and Japanese tour) 1990–91, Contemporary British Art in Print (Scottish Nat Gallery of Modern Art and American tour) 1995–96, Encounters (Nat Gallery London) 2000, Contemporary Voices (MoMA NY) 2005, Morandi's Legacy (Abbott Hall Art Gallery Kendal) 2006, Frissiras Museum Athens 2006, Venice Now (Sotheby's London) 2007, Ebbsfleet Landmark Proposals (Bluewater) 2008, Paintings from the 80s (Tate London) 2008, Schlosspark Wendlinghausen Dorentrup 2009, Watercolour Tate Britain London 2011, Francis Bacon to Paula Rego (Abbott Hall Art Gallery Kendal) 2011, Encounter the Royal Academy in the Middle East Doha 2012, Das Ultimate Bild Raab Gallery Berlin 2013, I Cheer a Dead Man's Sweetheart (De La Warr Pavilion Brighton) 2014, Baratto (Galleria Bonomo Rome) 2014, Beyond Limits (Chatsworth) 2014, Don't Shoot the Painter (Galleria Reale Galleria d'Arte Milan) 2015, The Romantic Thread in British Art (Southampton City Art Gallery) 2016; *Books* Christopher Le Brun (2001), New Paintings (2014); *Style*— Christopher Le Brun, PRA; ✉ website www.christopherlebrun.co.uk; c/o Royal Academy of Arts, Piccadilly, London W1J 0BD

LE CARPENTIER, Francis Stewart; s of Frank Henry Le Carpentier (d 2001), of Worthing, W Sussex, and Elizabeth, *née* Stafford (d 1961); *b* 26 February 1949; *Educ* Royal Wolverhampton Sch; *m* 1, 2 July 1976 (m dis 1991), Nicole Madeleine Fischer Corderior, da of Willey Fischer, of Brussels; 1 s (Phillipe Alexandre), 1 da (Mercedes Elizabeth); 1 da from a previous relationship (Silke b 1971); m 2, 25 June 2014, Elisa Malavasi; 1 s (Francesco Giuseppe b 25 Aug 2014); *Career* official US Armed Forces 1969–74, served Europe and Far East; retail mangr until 1969, dir Int Property Developers 1974, chm and chief exec Paramount Property Group SA 1975–91; chief exec Explora Security Architects & Engrs Ltd & Inc (ops in Europe, N America, ME, Asia and Africa) 1991–; fndr Explora Fndn; FInstD 1989 (MInstD 1988); *Recreations* skiing, shooting (not animals), motorsports and powercraft racing; *Style*— Francis Le Carpentier, Esq

LE CARRÉ, John (pen name of David John Moore Cornwell); s of Ronald Thomas Archibald Cornwell, and Olive, *née* Glassy; *b* 19 October 1931; *Educ* Sherborne, Univ of Berne, Lincoln Coll Oxford (BA); *m* 1, 1954 (m dis 1971), Alison Ann Veronica Sharp; 3 s; m 2, 1972, Valerie Jane Eustace; 1 s; *Career* novelist; schoolmaster Eton 1956–58, British Foreign Serv 1960–64 (serv as second sec Bonn then political consul Hamburg); Grand Master Award Mystery Writers of America, Malaparte Prize Italy, Crime Writers' Assoc Diamond Dagger Award 1988, Goethe Medal 2011; subject of Time and Newsweek cover stories and work subject of many books; Hon DLitt: Univ of Exeter 1990, Univ of St Andrews 1996, Univ of Southampton 1997, Univ of Bath 1998, Univ of Oxford 2012; Hon Dr Berne Univ 2008; hon fell Lincoln Coll Oxford 1984; Commandeur d l'Ordre des Arts et des Lettres 2005; *Books* Call for the Dead (1961, filmed as The Deadly Affair 1967), A Murder of Quality (1962, TV film prize winner at Venice Prix Italia 1991), The Spy Who Came in From the Cold (1963, film, Somerset Maugham Award, Crime Writers' Assoc Golden Dagger Award, Best Mystery of the Year Mystery Writers of America Inc), The Looking Glass War (1965, film), A Small Town in Germany (1968), The Naïve and Sentimental Lover (1971), Tinker, Tailor, Soldier, Spy (1974, BBC TV series, film 2011), The Honourable Schoolboy (1977, James Tait Black Meml Prize, Crime Writers' Assoc Golden Dagger Award), Smiley's People (1980, BBC TV series), The Little Drummer Girl (1983, Warner Bros film), A Perfect Spy (1986, BBC TV series), The Russia House (1989, film, Nikos Kasanzakis Prize 1991), The Secret Pilgrim (1990), The Night Manager (1993, BBC TV series 2016), Our Game (1995), The Tailor of Panama (1996, film 2000), Single and Single (1999), The Constant Gardener (2001, film 2005), Absolute Friends (2004), The Mission Song (2006), A Most Wanted Man (2008, film 2014), Our Kind of Traitor (2010, film 2016), A Delicate Truth (2013); The Karla Trilogy (Smiley's People, Tinker, Tailor, Soldier, Spy and The Honourable Schoolboy) published in one volume as The Quest for Karla; *Style*— John le Carré, Esq; ✉ c/o Curtis Brown, Haymarket House, 28–29 Haymarket, London SW1Y 4SP (☎ 020 7393 4400, fax 020 7393 4401/2, e-mail cb@curtisbrown.co.uk)

LE GRAND, Sir Julian Ernest Michael; kt (2015); s of Roland John Le Grand (d 1976), of Taunton, Somerset, and Eileen Joan, *née* Baker (d 2006); *b* 29 May 1945; *Educ* Eton, Univ of Sussex (BA), Univ of Pennsylvania (PhD); *m* 19 June 1971, Damaris May, da of Rev Nigel Robertson-Glasgow, of Fakenham, Norfolk; 2 da (Polly b 1978, Zoe b 1981); *Career* lectr in economics: Univ of Sussex 1971–78, LSE 1978–85; sr res fell LSE 1985–87, prof of public policy Univ of Bristol 1987–92, prof of social policy LSE 1993–; sr policy advsr 10 Downing Street 2003–05; memb Avon Family Health Serv Authy 1990–95, non-exec dir Avon HA 1994–95, vice-chm Frenchay NHS Healthcare Tst 1996–99, cmmr Cmmn for Health Improvement 1999–2003; conslt: OECD, Euro Cmmn, WHO, World Bank, NAO, Dept of Health, HM Treasy, BBC; chm Health England Dept of Health 2006–, chm Social Care Practices Working Gp DfES 2006–07; ESRC: memb Social Affrs Ctee 1982–86, memb Research Grants Bd 1988–92; chm Mutuals Taskforce 2011–13; tstee Kings Fund; Hon DLitt Univ of Sussex; founding AcSS; Hon FFPHM, FBA 2012; *Books* The Economics of Social Problems (with R Robinson, 1976, 4 edn 2008), The Strategy of Equality (1982), Privatisation and the Welfare State (ed with R Robinson, 1984), Not Only the Poor (with R Goodin, 1987), Market Socialism (ed with S Estrin, 1989), Equity and Choice (1991), Quasi-Markets and Social Policy (ed with W Bartlett, 1993), Evaluating the NHS Reforms (ed with R Robinson, 1994), Learning from the NHS Internal Market (ed with N Mays and J Mulligan, 1998), Health Care and Cost Containment in the European Union (ed with E Mossialos, 1999), Motivation, Agency and Public Policy (2003), The Other Invisible Hand (2007), Government Paternalism (with Bill New, 2015); *Recreations* drawing, reading; *Style*— Sir Julian Le Grand; ✉ 7 Victoria Square, Bristol BS8 4EU (☎ 0117 973 0975, mobile 07771 985294); London School of Economics and Political Science, Houghton Street, London WC2A 2AE (☎ 020 7955 7353, fax 020 7955 7415, e-mail j.legrand@lse.ac.uk)

LE GRICE, (Andrew) Valentine; QC (2002); s of Charles Le Grice (d 1982), of Penzance, Cornwall, and Wilmay, *née* Ward (d 2007); *b* 26 June 1953; *Educ* Shrewsbury, Collingwood Coll Durham (BA); *m* 1, 17 Dec 1977 (m dis 2000), Anne Elizabeth, da of Philip Moss (d 2013); 2 s (Charles b 8 Oct 1984, Philip b 16 Aug 1986), 1 da (Alexandra b 24 Nov 1989); m 2, 1 May 2001, Jayne Elizabeth, da of late Dr Brian Sandford-Hill, and Eira Sandford-Hill (d 2014); 1 da (Blanche b 9 Oct 2002); *Career* called to the Bar Middle Temple 1977; MCIArb 2011; *Recreations* watching sport, throwing things away; *Clubs* Travellers; *Style*— Valentine Le Grice, Esq, QC; ✉ 1 Hare Court, Temple, London EC4Y 7BE

le JEUNE d'ALLEGEERSHECQUE, HE Susan Jane; CMG; *m* Stephane Herve Marie le Jeune d'Allegeershecque; 2 s (Pierre b 1993, Julien b 1995); *Career* diplomat; desk offr Nuclear Energy Dept FCO 1985–87, third then second sec chancery UKRep Brussels 1987–89, second sec Soviet Dept and desk offr for Baltic States FCO 1990–92, second sec press and economic Signapore 1992–95, head PMU2 Personnel Directorate FCO 1996–99; dep head of mission: Caracas 1999–2002, Bogota 2002–05; counsellor and consul-gen Washington 2005–07, dir HR FCO 2007–12, ambass to Austria and perm rep to UN 2012–; *Style*— HE Mrs Susan le Jeune d'Allegeershecque, CMG; ✉ c/o Foreign and Commonwealth Office (Vienna), King Charles Street, London SW1A 2AH

LE MARCHANT, Sir Francis Arthur; 6 Bt (UK 1841), of Chobham Place, Surrey; s of Sir Denis Le Marchant, 5 Bt (d 1987), and Elizabeth Rowena, *née* Worth; *b* 6 October 1939; *Educ* Gordonstoun, Royal Acad Schs; *Heir* kinsman, Michael Le Marchant; *Career* farmer and painter; solo exhibitions include Agnews, Sally Hunter Fine Art, Roy Miles 1996, Evansville Museum of Art Indiana 1998, Baring Asset Mgmnt at ING Bank 2005; mixed exhibitions include Royal Academy Summer Exhibitions, Leicester Galleries, Bilan de l'Art Contomerain Paris, Spink & Co 'Ten at Spink' '2261; *Clubs* Savile; *Style*— Sir Francis Le Marchant, Bt; ✉ c/o Savile Club, 69 Brook Street, London W1K 4ER (website www.francislemarchant.com)

LE MAY, Malcolm John; s of John Francis Le May, and Janet Bill; *b* 24 July 1958, Kent; *Educ* St Olave's and St Saviour's GS for Boys, UCNW Bangor; *m* 10 Sept 1983, Sarah, *née* McCormack; 3 s (Alexander Gilmour, Henry Graham, Oliver William); *Career* Arthur Andersen & Co 1979–83, Morgan Grenfell plc 1983–86, Drexel Burnham Lambert 1986–90, BZW Ltd 1990–95, UBS AG 1995–98, ING 1998–2001, Morley plc 2001–03, JER Partners 2003–09, ceo investment banking Matrix Gp 2009–; sr advsr to Ernst & Young 2011–; sr non-exec dir Provident Financial plc, non-exec dir Pendragon plc, chm Juno Wp; ACA 1982; *Recreations* shooting, tennis, sailing, golf, bridge; *Style*— Malcolm Le May, Esq; ✉ Upham House, Upham, Hampshire SO32 1JH

LE MÉTAIS, Dr Joanna Petra Fransisca Maria; *née* Bevers; da of Peter Joseph Bevers, of St Agnes, S Aust, and Geertruda Petronella, *née* van der Zanden; *b* 2 January 1949, Amsterdam; *Educ* Loreto Abbey Victoria Aust, Croydon Tech Coll, Gipsy Hill Coll Kingston upon Thames (CertEd, BEd), Université de Caen (Diplôme d'Études Françaises), Chartered Inst of Linguists (final level French), Brunel Univ (MA, PhD); *m* 2 Sept 1972 (m dis 1980), Michel Philippe Alfred Le Métais, s of Alfred Le Métais, of Vimoutiers, France; *Career* dep head Modern Languages Dept Redstone Sch Surrey 1974–76 (French teacher 1973–76), head Languages Dept Raynes Park HS 1976–82, pt/t adult educn teacher 1978–79, professional asst Educn Dept London Borough of Hounslow 1982–84; Nat Fndn for Educnl Research: dep head Info Dept and dir EPIC Europe (Educn Policy Info Centre for Europe) 1984–97, head Nat Unit EURYDICE (educn policy info network in the European Community) 1984–97, dir Int Centre 1997–2000, head Int Project Devpt 2000–04, dir Le Metais Consltg 2004–; conslt UNICEF Devpt and Implementation of a Nat Curriculum Framework for the Maldives 2009–11; external examiner: Univ of London 1977–81, SE Regnl Examination Bd 1977 and 1978; hon res fell Univ of Dundee 2006–11, pres Merton Branch Nat Assoc of Schoolmasters Union of Women Teachers 1980 (vice-pres 1979), tstee Inst of Linguists Educnl Tst 1988–90, memb Int Ctee Soc of Educn Offrs 1991–98, memb Exec Ctee UK Forum for Int Educn and Trg 1994–2004, memb Advsy Gp Teacher Mobility, Brain Drain, Labour Markets and Educnl Resources in the Cwlth 2003–06, quality assessor HEFCE 1995–96, project dir Int Review of Curriculum and Assessment Frameworks 1996–2003, memb Exec Ctee Br Assoc for Int and Comparative Educn 1998–2004; memb Editorial Advsy Bd Int Electronic Jl for Leadership in Learning 1997–, assoc conslt Qualifications and Curriculum Authy 2007–08; overseas expert Visiting Cmmn Netherlands 1992, attended UNESCO Int Forum for solidarity against intolerance Tbilisi Georgia 1995; life memb Sail Trg Assoc 1990–; Hon DEd Brunel Univ 2000; MIMgt 1985–89, MInstD 1989–95, FRSA 1979, FCIL 1986 (MIL 1978, memb Cncl 1987–90, chm Cncl 1988–90); *Publications* Communication and Culture: Foreign Languages in and out of the Curriculum (ed, 1988), The Impact on the Education Service of Teacher Mobility (1990), The Search for Standards (contrib, 1992), Performance-related Pay in Education (contrib, 1992), The Supply and Recruitment of Teachers (contrib, 1993), Teachers' Salaries in France, Germany and Scotland (1994), Effective Governors for Effective Schools (contrib, 1995), Legislating for Change: School Reforms in England and Wales 1979–1994 (1995), Values and Aims in Curriculum and Assessment Frameworks (1997), INCA: The International Review of Curriculum and Assessment Frameworks Archive (CD-Rom, jtly, 1998, published online 2000, 4 edn 2004), Values and Aims in Curriculum and Assessment Systems: a 16 nation review (in Curriculum in Context, 1998), Approaches to Comparology (1999), Strategic Market Research: A Study of Overseas Services (jtly, 1999), The Democratic Curriculum: Developments in England 1944–1999 (2000), School Curriculum Differences across the UK: Report to the British Broadcasting Corporation (jtly, 2001, also published online), International Developments in Upper Secondary Education: Context, Provision and Issues (2002, also published online), A Europe of Differences: Educational Responses for Interculturalism (ed, 2002), International Trends in Primary Education (2003, also published online), Secondary Education at the Crossroads: International Perspectives Relevant to Asia-Pacific Region (contrib, 2006), Curriculum Development Re-invented (contib, 2006), Encyclopedia of Europe 1914–2004 (contib 2006), Learning and Teaching for the 21st Century (contrib, 2007), Critique of The New Zealand Curriculum: Draft for Consultation (2007), QCA Thinking Primary Evidence Base (compiler, 2008), Development and Implementation of a National Curriculum Framework for the Maldives (jtly, 2011), Achieving Quality Education for All: Perspectives from the Asia-Pacific Region and Beyond (contrib, 2012); *Recreations* people, travel, pottery; *Style*— Dr Joanna Le Métais; ✉ Le Métais Consulting, 19 Geffers Ride, Ascot, Berkshire SL5 7JY (☎ 01344 622910, e-mail jlemetais@gmail.com)

LE PARD, Geoffrey; s of Desmond Allen Le Pard, of Sway, Lymington, and Barbara Grace, *née* Francis; *b* 30 November 1956; *Educ* Purley GS, Brockenhurst GS, Univ of Bristol (LLB); *m* 19 May 1984, Linda Ellen, da of Leslie Jones, of Costessey, Norwich; 1 s (Samuel William b 23 April 1990), 1 da (Jennifer Grace b 8 Feb 1993); *Career* slr specialising in commercial property law, property devpt, and landlord and tenant law; articled clerk Corbould Rigby & Co 1979–81, ptnr Freshfields 1987– (asst slr 1981–87); memb: City of London Slrs Co, Anglo American Real Property Inst; *Recreations* cycling, walking long distance footpaths, watching any sport, theatre, good food, gardening, being a dad; *Style*— Geoffrey Le Pard, Esq; ✉ Freshfields, 65 Fleet Street, London EC4Y 1HS (☎ 020 7936 4000)

LEA, Anthony William (Tony); s of George Frederick Lea (d 1995), and Elaine Constance, *née* Oman (d 1996); *b* 30 November 1948, Johannesburg, South Africa; *Educ* Michaelhouse Natal, Univ of the Witwatersrand Johannesburg (BA); *m* 2 Aug 1986, Clare, da of William Frederick Harries; 1 s (James Frederick b 1988), 1 da (Camilla Rose b 1990); *Career* Anglo American Gp: joined 1972, dir Anglo American Corporation of SA 1987–2005, fin dir Minorco SA, 1988–91, exec dir Minorco SA 1992–98, fin dir Anglo American plc 1998–2005; tstee RAF Benevolent Fund 2009; *Recreations* country pursuits; *Clubs* Reform, Boodle's, Inanda (Johannesburg); *Style*— Tony Lea, Esq

LEA, Prof Peter John; s of Dr Alan Joseph Lea (d 1983), of Tamworth, and Jessie, *née* Farrall (d 1997); *b* 1 December 1944; *Educ* Arnold Sch Blackpool, Univ of Liverpool (BSc, PhD, DSc); *m* 30 July 1965, Christine, *née* Shaw; 1 da (Julia b 5 Dec 1966); *Career* res fell Royal Soc 1972–75, princ scientific offr Rothamsted Experimental Station Harpenden Herts 1978–84 (sr scientific offr 1975–78); Lancaster Univ: prof of biology 1985–, head Div of Biological Scis 1988–91, dean 1994–96; chm Phytochemical Soc Europe 1988–94 (sec 1982–87), sec Soc Experimental Biology 1998–2001, pres Assoc of Applied Biologists 2006–08; FIBiol; *Books* incl: The Genetic Manipulation of Plants and its Application to Agriculture (with G R Stewart, 1984), The Biochemistry of Plant Phenolics (with C F van Sumere, 1986), Biologically Active Natural Products (with K Hostettmann, 1987), Methods in Plant Biochemistry (1989, 1993), The Biochemistry of Plants (with B J Miflin,

1990), Plant Biochemistry and Molecular Biology (with R C Leegood, 1993, 1998), Plant Nitrogen (with J F Morot-Gaudry, 2001), Functional Plant Genomics (with J F Morot-Gaudry, 2007); *Recreations* cricket, collecting wedgwood pottery; *Style—* Prof Peter Lea; ✉ The Old School, Chapel Lane, Ellel, Lancaster LA2 0PW (✆ 01524 751156); Lancaster University, Division of Biological Sciences, Bailrigg, Lancaster LA1 4YQ (✆ 01524 592104, fax 01524 843854, e-mail p.lea@lancaster.ac.uk)

LEA, Ruth Jane; CBE (2015); da of Thomas Lea, of Warburton, Cheshire, and Jane, *née* Brown (decd); *b* 22 September 1947; *Educ* Lymm GS, Univ of York (BA), Univ of Bristol (MSc); *Career* HM Treasy 1970–73, lectr in economics Thames Poly (now Univ of Greenwich) 1973–74, Civil Serv Coll 1974–77, HM Treasy 1977–78, CSO 1978–84, DTI 1984–87, Invest in Britain Bureau DTI 1987–88, Mitsubishi Bank 1988–93 (rising to chief economist), chief UK economist Lehman Brothers 1993–94, economics ed ITN 1994–95, head Policy Unit IOD 1995–2003, dir Centre for Policy Studies 2004–07, dir Global Vision 2007–10; non-exec dir Arbuthnot Banking Gp 2005–16 (economic advsr 2007–16); memb: RPI Advsy Ctee 1992–94, Nat Consumer Cncl 1993–96, Rowntree Fndn Income and Wealth Inquiry Gp 1993–94, Nurses' Pay Review Body 1994–98, Research Centres Bd ESRC 1996, Research Priorities Bd 1996–97, Statistics Advsy Ctee Office of Nat Statistics 1996–97, Nott Cmmn on the £ Sterling 1999; judge numerous awards on econ and business issues; author numerous research papers and articles on econ and business issues; memb Cncl Univ of London 2001–06, govr LSE 2003–08; Liveryman: Worshipful Co of Curriers, Worshipful Co of World Traders; Freeman City of London; Hon DBA: Univ of Greenwich, BPP Univ Coll, Univ of Chester 2015; memb: Royal Economic Soc 1994–2011 (memb Cncl 1995–2000), Soc of Business Economists 1998–2009; FRSA 1993, FSS 1996–2009; *Recreations* music, natural history and countryside, heritage, philately; *Clubs* Reform; *Style—* Miss Ruth Lea, CBE; ✉ 25 Redbourne Avenue, Finchley, London N3 2BP (✆ 020 8346 3482); Arbuthnot Banking Group, 7 Wilson Street, London EC2M 2SN (✆ 07800 608674)

LEA OF CRONDALL, Baron (Life Peer UK 1999), of Crondall in the County of Hampshire; David Edward Lea; OBE (1978); s of Edward Cunliffe Lea, of Tyldesley, Lancs; *b* 2 November 1937; *Educ* Farnham GS, Christ's Coll Cambridge (MA); *Career* asst gen sec TUC 1978–99; *Style—* The Lord Lea of Crondall, OBE

LEACH, Melanie; *Career* md Twofour Broadcast 2005–14, chief exec Twofour Gp 2014–; advsy chair Guardian Edinburgh Int Festival 2013–; First Woman of Media Real Business Awards 2014; *Style—* Ms Melanie Leach; ✉ Twofour Group, Kingsbourne House, 229–231 High Holborn, London WC1V 7DA

LEADBETTER, Dr Alan James; CBE (1994); s of Robert Pickavant Leadbetter (d 1989), and Edna, *née* Garlick; *b* 28 March 1934, Southport, Merseyside; *Educ* Univ of Liverpool (BSc, PhD), Univ of Bristol (DSc); *m* 23 Oct 1957, (Jean) Brenda, da of Percy Williams (d 1966); 1 s (Andrew Robert b 1 Aug 1964), 1 da (Jane b 22 Dec 1966); *Career* postdoctoral research fell Nat Res Cncl Canada Ottawa 1957–59; Univ of Bristol Sch of Chemistry: research asst 1959–62, lectr 1962–72, reader in physical chemistry 1972–74; prof of physical chemistry Univ of Exeter 1975–82; SERC: assoc dir Science Bd and head Neutron Div 1982–87, assoc dir and head Science Dept (Rutherford Appleton Lab) 1987–88, dir Daresbury Lab 1988–94, dir adjoint Institut Laue-Langevin 1994–99, pres Int Advsy Ctee Commisariat à l'Energie Atomique France (CEA) 2002–06, Evaluation Panels for Research Infrastructures and Marie-Curie actions of Framework Programmes of the EC 2003–07 and 2011–12; memb: Review Ctee Los Alamos Nat Lab USA 1999–2003, Tech Advsy Ctee Australian Nuclear Science and Technol Orgn (ANSTO) 2000–06; visiting prof De Montfort Univ 1994–2001, hon visiting prof Univ of Exeter 2002–05, Hon DSc De Montfort Univ 2000; FRSC, FInstP; *Publications* author of numerous articles in scientific jls; *Recreations* cooking, gardening; *Style—* Dr Alan Leadbetter, CBE

LEADER, Prof Zachary Anton; s of Anton M Leader (d 1988), and Rosalinde L, *née* Palca; *b* 1 December 1946, NY, USA; *Educ* Northwestern Univ (BA), Trinity Coll Cambridge (MA), Harvard Univ (AM, PhD); *m* 16 June 1969, Alice, *née* AuWerter; 2 s (Nicholas Max b 4 Oct 1979, Max Spencer b 10 March 1982); *Career* prof of Eng lit Univ of Roehampton (formerly Roehampton Inst of HE then Univ of Surrey Roehampton1993– (lectr then reader 1977–93); visiting prof: Université Rennes 2 1991, Div of Humanities and Social Sciences California Inst of Technol 1991–93, Ctee on Social Thought Univ of Chicago 2008; Dexter travelling scholar Harvard Univ 1973, Whiting Fndn fell Harvard Univ 1975, Andrew Mellon fellowship Huntington Library 1989 and 1991, Fletcher Jones Fndn fell Huntington Library 1997 and 2002, Leverhulme res fell 2002, Br Acad Res Leave Award 1984, Soc of Authors Authors' Fndn Award 1987, Br Acad res grant 2002; fell Guggenheim Fndn 2009, literature fell Centro Studi Ligure per le Arti e le Lettere Bogliasco Italy 2010, writing fell Civitella Ranieri Italy 2015; FRSL; *Publications* Reading Blake's Songs (1981), Writer's Block (1991), Revision and Romantic Authorship (1996), Romantic Period Writings (jt ed, 1999), The Letters of Kingsley Amis (2001), On Modern British Fiction (2002), Percy Bysshe Shelley: The Major Works (jt ed, 2003), The Life of Kingsley Amis (2006), The Movement Reconsidered: Essays on Larkin, Amis, Gunn, Davie and Their Contemporaries (ed, 2009), The Life of Saul Bellow: To Fame and Fortune 1915–1964 (2015), On Life Writing (ed, 2015); *Recreations* tennis, poker, film, watching sport; *Clubs* Garrick; *Style—* Prof Zachary Leader; ✉ 11 Brooksville Avenue, London NW6 6TH (✆ 020 8969 2763, fax 020 8967 1214); c/o The Wylie Agency, 17 Bedford Square, London WC1B 3JA (✆ 020 7908 5900, fax 020 7908 5901, e-mail mail@wylieagency.co.uk); Department of English, University of Roehampton, London SW15 5PH (✆ 020 8392 3000, fax 020 8392 3146, e-mail z.leader@roehampton.ac.uk)

LEADSOM, Rt Hon Andrea Jacqueline; PC (2016), MP; *née* Salmon; *b* 13 May 1963; *Educ* Univ of Warwick; *m* Ben Leadsom; 3 c; *Career* cncllr S Oxon DC 2003–07, MP (Cons) S Northants 2010–; sec of state for environment, food and rural affrs 2016–; *Style—* The Rt Hon Andrea Leadsom, MP; ✉ Office of Andrea Leadsom, MP, 4a Victoria House, 138 Watling Street East, Towcester, Northamptonshire NN12 6BT (website www.andrealeadsom.com); House of Commons, London SW1A 0AA

LEAF, Robert Stephen; s of Nathan Leaf, and Anne, *née* Feinman; *b* 9 August 1931; *Educ* Univ of Missouri (Bachelor of Journalism, MA); *m* 8 June 1958, Adele Renee; 1 s (Stuart b 4 June 1961); *Career* Burson-Marsteller International: joined 1957, vice-pres 1961, exec vice-pres 1965, pres 1968, chm 1985; chm Robert S Leaf Consultants Ltd 1997–; writer in various trade and business pubns for USA, Europe and Asia; speaker on PR mktg and communications in W and E Europe (incl Russia), Asia (incl China), Australia, N and S America; winner of first Chartered Inst of PR award for outstanding contributions to int public relations, selected by American Biographical Inst in 2013 as one of the great minds of the 21st century, selected by Int Biographical Centres as one of 2000 outstanding intellectuals of the 21st Century; memb: PR Consltg (former memb Bd), Int Advertising, Foreign Press; FIPR 1984 (MIPR 1973); *Books* The Art of Perception – Memoirs of a Life in PR; *Recreations* tennis, travel, theatre; *Clubs* Hurlingham; *Style—* Robert Leaf, Esq; ✉ 3 Fursecroft, George Street, London W1H 5LF (✆ 020 7262 4846)

LEAHY, Michael J; OBE (2004); *b* 7 January 1949, Pontypool; *m* Irene; 2 s (Sean, Greg); *Career* chargehand Cold Rolling Dept Panteg Works Richard Thompson & Baldwins Ltd 1965–77; Community (formerly Iron and Steel Trades Confedn (ISTC)): memb 1965–, organiser 1977–86, sr organiser 1986–92, asst gen sec 1993–98, gen sec 1999–2014, sec ISTC Superannuation Soc Ltd 1999–2004, sec ISTC Staff Pension Fund 2004–; pres Gen Fedn of Trade Unions 2001–02 (vice-pres 1999–2001, memb Exec Cncl 1996–2002, memb and tstee Educnl Tst), memb Gen Cncl TUC 1999– (memb Exec Ctee 2000–); memb Sheet Trade Bd 1966–77, memb Sandwell and Dudley Area Trg Bd Manpower Servs Cmmn 1986–88, memb Nat Trades Union Steel Co-ordinating Ctee 1992– (chm 1998–), memb Exec Cncl Confedn of Shipbuilding and Engrg Unions 1994–99, memb Euro Coal and Steel Community Consultative Ctee 1995–2002 (memb Sub-Ctee for Markets and Forward Studies 1995–2002), memb Nat Jt Industrial Cncl for the Slag Industry 1995–99, memb Exec Ctee Euro Metalworkers' Fedn 1999– (memb Industrial Policy Ctee 1999–, memb Steel Ctee 1999–), pres Iron, Steel and Non-Ferrous Metals Dept Int Metalworkers' Fedn 1999– (hon sec Br Section 1999–); Br Steel (now Corus Gp plc): memb Strip Trade Bd 1995–2000 (employees' sec 1998–2000), memb Long Products Jt Standing Ctee 1995–2000 (employees' sec 1998–2000), memb Jt Accident Prevention Advsy Ctee 1995–99, memb Advsy Ctee for Educn and Trg 1995–99, employees' sec Euro Works Cncl 1998–; memb Bd Unions Today Ltd 1999–2002, chm KSP (formerly Steel Partnership Trg Ltd) 2000–, memb European Economic and Social Ctee Consultative Cmmn on Industrial Change 2002–, memb Central Arbitration Ctee UK Steel Enterprise 2002– (memb Bd 2003–, non-exec dir 2011–), chair Trade Union Friends of Israeli (TUFI) 2014–; ldr Duke of Edinburgh Study Conference 1980; Bevan Fndn: chm 2000–02, memb Bd of Dirs 2002–, chm of tstees 2002–; memb Lab Pty 1966– (memb NEC 1996, memb Nat Policy Forum 1996–99, auditor 2002–); pres Welsh Abuse Tst 2005–; FRSA 2005; *Recreations* golf, rugby; *Style—* Michael Leahy, Esq, OBE

LEAHY, Sir Terence Patrick (Terry); kt (2002); s of late Terence Leahy, and Elizabeth Leahy; *b* 28 February 1956; *Educ* St Edward's Coll Liverpool, UMIST (BSc); *m* Aug 1985, Alison; 2 s (Tom b 9 Nov 1988, David b 1 June 1992), 1 da (Katie (twin) b 9 Nov 1988); *Career* Tesco: joined as mktg exec 1979, mktg mangr 1981, mktg dir Tesco Stores Ltd 1984–86, commercial dir fresh foods 1986–92, mktg dir 1992–95 (appointed to Bd Tesco plc), dep md 1995–97, chief exec Tesco plc 1997–2011; dir Liverpool Vision Regeneration Bd; chllr UMIST 2002–04, co-chllr Univ of Manchester 2004–; European Businessman of the Year Fortune Magazine 2004; Freeman City of Liverpool; *Recreations* sport, reading, theatre, architecture; *Style—* Sir Terry Leahy

LEAITHERLAND, Andrew; s of Arnold Terrence Leaitherland, and Jean Archer, *née* Fudge (d 2012); *b* 15 February 1969, Southampton, Hants; *Educ* Lancaster Univ (LLB), Univ of Leicester (LLM, Dip); *m* 26 June 1999, Rachael, *née* Mosley; 1 da (Grace Claire b 12 July 2001), 2 s (Harry William b 26 March 2003, Charlie Max b 16 May 2010); *Career* articled Field Cunningham and Co 1992–94, DWF 1994–96, Davies Arnold Cooper 1996–2000; DWF LLP: joined 2000–, ptnr and head of people 1999–2006, managing ptnr and ceo 2006–; Outstanding Achievement Award Lancaster Univ 2013; memb Law Soc 1996; *Recreations* golf, watching rugby, sailing, clay pigeon shooting; *Clubs* Mere Golf and Country; *Style—* Andrew Leaitherland, Esq; ✉ DWF LLP, 1 Scott Place, 2 Hardman Street, Manchester M3 3AA (e-mail andrew.leaitherland@dwf.co.uk)

LEAKE, Prof Bernard Elgey; s of Norman Sidney Leake (d 1963), and Clare Evelyn, *née* Walgate (d 1970); *b* 29 July 1932, Grimsby, Lincs; *Educ* Wirral GS Bebington, Univ of Liverpool (BSc, PhD), Univ of Bristol (DSc), Univ of Glasgow (DSc); *m* 23 Aug 1955, Gillian Dorothy, da of Prof Charles Henry Dobinson, CMG; 5 s (Christopher b 1958, Roger b 1959, Alastair b 1961, Jonathan b 1964, Nicholas b 1966); *Career* Leverhulme res fell Univ of Liverpool 1955–57, res assoc Berkeley California 1966, reader in geology Univ of Bristol 1968–74 (lectr 1957–68); Univ of Glasgow: prof 1974–97 (prof emeritus 1997), head Dept of Geology 1974–92, head Dept of Applied Geology 1989–92, hon keeper of geological collections Hunterian Museum 1974–97; currently hon res fell Cardiff Univ; author of over 160 res papers and maps, especially of Connemara Western Ireland; treas: Geological Soc London 1980–85 and 1989–96 (pres 1986–88), Geologists' Assoc 1997–2009 (hon life memb 2009, Foulerton Award 2009); memb Ct Univ of Cardiff 2000–14; Lyell Medal 1978; Gledden sr fell Univ of WA 1985, Erskine fell Univ of Canterbury NZ 1999, Leverhulme emeritus fell 2000–02, hon life fell Mineralogical Soc of GB 2004 (pres 1998–2000), hon life memb Liverpool Geological Soc 2007; FGS 1956, FRSE 1976; *Books* Catalogue of Analysed Calciferous Amphiboles (1968), The Geology of the Dalradian and associated rocks of Connemara, Western Ireland (1994), The Life of Frank Coles Phillips (1902–1982) and his role in the Moine petrofabric controversy (2002), The Life and Work of Professor J W Gregory FRS (1864–1932): Geologist, Writer and Explorer (2011), The Wyley History of the Geologists' Association in the 50 Years 1958–2008 (2013); *Geological Maps* Cashel (1969), Tayvallich (1972), Connemara (1981), South Mayo (1985), Central (2006), Western (2011), Galway Granite, Camus (2012), Joyce's Country (2014); *Clubs* Geological Soc; *Style—* Prof Bernard Leake, FRSE; ✉ School of Earth and Ocean Sciences, Cardiff University, Main Building, Park Place, Cardiff CF10 3AT (✆ 029 2087 6421, fax 029 2087 4326, e-mail leakeb@cardiff.ac.uk)

LEAKE, Christopher Jonathan Piers; s of Kenneth Piers Leake (d 1988), of Frodsham, Cheshire, and Sheila Mary, *née* Salt; *b* 17 May 1951; *Educ* St Olave's Sch York, St Peter's Sch York; *m* 1976, Carol Joan, da of Lawrence Miveld, of Hartford, Cheshire; 1 da (Claire Louise b 21 Oct 1978), 1 s (Gerard William b 13 Dec 1982); *Career* journalist; reporter W Cheshire Newspapers 1970–74, Express and Star Wolverhampton 1974–79 (reporter, industrial corr), The Daily Telegraph 1979–82 (Scottish corr, memb industrial staff), industrial and consumer affrs ed Mail on Sunday 1982–2001, UK communications dir Tesco Stores 2001–02, defence and home affrs ed Mail on Sunday 2002–; *Recreations* cycling, running, people, films; *Style—* Christopher Leake, Esq; ✉ The Mail on Sunday, Associated Newspapers plc, Northcliffe House, 2 Derry Street, Kensington, London W8 5TS (✆ 020 7938 7061, fax 020 7937 3829)

LEAMAN, Adrian John; s of Robert Edgar Leaman, and Rita, *née* Fricker; *b* 20 October 1946; *Educ* Tiffin Sch Kingston upon Thames, Univ of Sussex (BA); *m* Rita Harland, *née* Russell; 2 step c (Joseph Harland, Katie Harland (now Mrs Kelly)); *Career* researcher Science Policy Research Unit Univ of Sussex 1969–71, with RIBA 1971–78 (worked in Research Unit and ed Journal of Architectural Research), sometime teacher and researcher Bartlett Sch of Architecture and Unit for Architectural Studies UCL (co-fndr Space Syntax research programme), lectr Poly of N London 1978–86, md Building Use Studies Ltd (studying human behaviour in buildings) 1987– (joined 1986), dir of research Inst of Advanced Architectural Studies Univ of York 1993–97, sec and dir of educn The Usable Buildings Tst 2002–; visiting prof Univ of Delft Netherlands 1998, visiting fell School of Architecture Victoria Univ Wellington NZ 2002; FRGS 1983, FRSA 1994; *Style—* Adrian Leaman, Esq; ✉ Building Use Studies Ltd ✆ 01904 671280, e-mail adrianleaman@usablebuildings.co.uk, website www.usablebuildings.co.uk

LEAMAN, Richard Derek; CB (2010), OBE (1993); s of late Derek Leaman, of Torquay, Devon, and Jean, *née* Chapman; *b* 29 July 1956; *Educ* Torquay Boys' GS; *m* 1; 2 s (Adrian b 1977, Nicholas b 1980); m 2 (m dis 2016), Suzy, *née* Clarke; *Career* cmmnd RN 1975, early trg Baltic, Pacific and Caribbean, navigator HMS Crichton and HMS Birmingham, instr BRNC Dartmouth, Princ Warfare Offr Course 1982 (Edgerton Prize), Gunnery Offr HMS Glasgow, Anti-Air Warfare Course, operational duties HMS Birmingham and HMS Glasgow, staff appt trg offrs in air defence 1987, cmd HMS Dumbarton Castle 1988, Sr Warfare Offr HMS Ark Royal, promoted Cdr 1991, cmd HMS Cardiff 1991, served MOD 1995, promoted Capt 1996, cmd HMS Cumberland 1996, cmd RN Presentation Team, Higher Command and Staff Course 2000, dep dir responsible for warship procurement MOD, promoted Cdre 2000, dir of corp communications (Navy) 2000–02, Cdr UK Task Gp 2003–04, dir Higher Command and Staff Course 2004–05, promoted Rear Adm 2005, COS to CC MAR Naples 2005–07, DCOS NATO HQ Norfolk VA 2007–09, MOD 2009–10, ceo Guide Dogs for the Blind Assoc 2010–; tstee NCVO 2012; chm: ARNO 2013–16, RN Officers' Charity 2013–16; MIPR 2001, ACMI 2010; *Recreations* swimming, playing classical guitar, dog walking, theatre (attending and performing); *Clubs* Naval; *Style—*

Mr Richard Leaman, CB, OBE; ✉ Guide Dogs, Hillfields, Burghfield Common, Reading, Berkshire RG7 3YG (✆ 0118 983 8203)

LEAN, Prof Michael Ernest John; s of Maj John Holman Lean, of Suffolk and Cornwall, and Estelle Flower, née Oulton; b 16 March 1952; *Educ* Trinity Coll Glenalmond, Downing Coll Cambridge (MA), St Bart's Hosp Med Sch (MB BChir, MD (Cantab)); *Career* prof of human nutrition Univ of Glasgow, hon conslt physician Glasgow Royal Infirmary, dir Health Educn Bd for Scotland 1995–2003; chm Food Standards Agency Advsy Ctee on Res; memb: Diabetes UK, Nutrition Soc, Scottish Fiddle Orch, Le Clan des Gueux; weekly columnist Sunday Herald 2001–02; adjunct prof of human nutrition Univ of Otago; André Mayer prize 1986; FRCPEd, FRCPGlas; *Publications* over 400 scientific papers on nutrition and diabetes; *Recreations* violin, Scottish music, climbing, cross-country and hill running (winner Barmekin Hill Race 1991, 1992 and 1993, and Glenisla Games Hill Race 1996), fishing and mountaineering; *Clubs* Arctic, Alpine, Fiddle Force; *Style—* Prof Michael Lean; ✉ Hatton Castle, Newtyle, Angus PH12 8UN (✆ 01828 650404); Department of Human Nutrition, University of Glasgow, Glasgow Royal Infirmary, Glasgow (✆ 0141 201 8503, e-mail mike.lean@glasgow.ac.uk)

LEAPER, Prof David John; s of David Thomas Leaper, of Leeds, and Gwendoline, née Robertson; b 23 July 1947; *Educ* Leeds Modern GS, Univ of Leeds (MB ChB, MD, ChM); m Francesca Ann; 1 s (Charles David Edward), 1 da (Alice Jane Sophia); *Career* Univ of Leeds: house offr 1970–71, MRC res fell 1971–73, registrar in surgery 1973–76; Univ of London: CRC res fell, sr registrar in surgery 1976–81; conslt sr lectr in surgery Univ of Bristol 1981–95, prof of surgery at North Tees Gen Hosp 1995–2004; Hunterian prof of surgery RCS 1981–82, Zachary Cope lectr 1998, prof of surgery Hong Kong Univ 1988–90, emeritus prof of surgery Univ of Newcastle upon Tyne 2004–; visiting prof: Univ of Cardiff 2004–13, Univ of Southampton 2006–08, Imperial Coll London 2006–13; medical advsr: Renovo (UK) 2005–10, Arizant (USA), Inditherm plc (UK) 2004–06; memb Cncl and vice-pres RSM (surgery) 1982–88, fndr memb (pres 1999) Surgical Infection Soc of Europe, fndr memb European Wound Mgmnt Assoc 1990 (pres 1994), memb Ct of Examiners RCS 1992–98, memb Ctee Surgical Res Soc (UK) 1987–88, professorial memb Specialist Advsy Ctee, prog dir Higher Training Northern Deanery 2000–04, memb Bd European Tissue Repair Soc 2006–, chair Guidelines Devpt Gp (NICE) Surgical Site Infection 2007–08, chair EU Advsy Gp 2013; prof of clinical sciences Inst of Skin Integrity and Infection Control Univ of Huddersfield 2013–; medical advsr: Ethicon Johnson and Johnson 2007–, Altrazeal 2012–; expert memb Advsy Gp Antimicrobial Resistance and Healthcare Associated Infections 2007–13; FRCS 1975, FRCSEd 1974, FICA 1984, FRCS Glas 1998, FACS 1998, FLS 2010; *Publications* Your Operation (series), International Surgical Practice, Wounds: Biology and Management Oxford Handbooks Clinical Surgery, Operative Surgery and Operative Complications, Complete Revision for the Intercollegiate FRCS, An Introduction to Wounds, Wound Management: Changing Ideas on Antiseptics, Hospital Infection Control, Guidance on the Control of Infection in Hospitals; past memb Editorial Bd: Br Journal of Surgery, Surgery Research Cmmn, International Wound Jl, Wounds UK, Turkish Medical Jl, 195 papers listed on PubMed 2015 based on surgical infection and sepsis, wound healing, breast and colon cancer, medical education and computer aided diagnosis; *Style—* Prof David Leaper; ✉ 33 Peverell Avenue East, Poundbury, Dorchester, Dorset DT1 3RH

LEAPMAN, David; b 1 March 1959; *Educ* St Martin's Sch of Art, Goldsmiths Coll, Chelsea Sch of Art; *Career* artist; *Solo Exhibitions* Journeying in Search of Hidden Treasures (Ikon Gallery Birmingham) 1988, Galerie Raph Debarrn Paris 1993, Todd Gallery London 1988, 1990, 1992, 1994 and 1995, Hales Gallery London 1997, One in the Other (London) 1998, Beaux Arts London 2000, Habitat King's Road London 2000, Building Watertight Structures in Volcanic Pooles (Beaux Arts London) 2001, Precious Encounters (Beaux Arts London) 2002, Compliant Keeprs (Riverside Art Museum CA) 2008, Half Known Slow Burnt Layers (Brandstater Gallery La Sierra Univ CA) 2008, Whispered Sprinkle (CAS CA) 2008, Journeys to Recover your Future (Culver Center of the Arts Riverside CA) 2011; *Group Exhibitions* Young Blood (Riverside Studios London) 1983, Problems of Picturing (Serpentine London) 1984, Between Identity & Politics – A New Art (Gimpel Fils tour) 1996, Unheard Music (Stoke-on-Trent Museum) 1986, Small Scale (Lidewij Edelkoort Gallery Paris) 1986, Nature Morte (Edward Totah Gallery London) 1986, Impulse 8 (Galerie Lohrl Monchengladbach) 1986, Figuring Out the 80s (Laing Art Gallery & Museum Newcastle upon Tyne) 1988, New Paintings by David Leapman and Roy Voss (Curwen Gallery London) 1989, New Contemporaries (Institute of Contemporary Arts London) 1981, 1989, Aperto 90 (Venice Biennale Venice) 1990, Hyunsoo Choi et David Leapman (Galerie Gutharc Ballin Paris) 1993, Pet Show (Union Street Gallery London) 1993, In House Out House (Unit 7 Camberwell) 1993, Strictly Painting (Cubitt Street Gallery London) 1993, Moving into View (Arts Council touring exhbn) 1993–96, XXVIe Festival International de la Peinture (British Council) 1994, LandEscapes (Turin) 1994, John Moores Liverpool Exhibition 19 (Walker Art Gallery Liverpool, 1st prize winner) 1995–96, Being There II (Centrun Beeldende Kunst Rotterdam) 1996–98, Whitechapel Open (Whitechapel Art Gallery London) 1985, 1986, 1990, and 1996, The East Wing Collection (Courthauld Institute of Art London) 1996–98, WHAT (Trinity Buoy Wharf London) 1997, John Moores Liverpool Exhibition 20 (prize winner), The Art Works (Riverside California) 1998, The Jerwood Painting Prize (London) 1998, Recent Acquisitions (Beaux Arts London) 1999, Simmer (Beaux Arts London) 1999, Work on Paper (Stalke Gallery Copenhagen) 1999, Beaux Arts London 2000, 2001, 2002, 2003, 2004, 2005, 2006 and 2007, Discerning Eye (Mall Galleries London) 2000, Third Counter Callan, Hindle, Leapman and Seymour (7 Addington Square London) 2001, Cultural Ties (Kapil Jariwala-Westzone Gallery London) 2001, The Bigger Splash (Whitechapel Art Gallery at the London Art Fair) 2002, The Saatchi Gift (Talbot Rice Gallery Univ of Edinburgh) 2002, Fight Machester artists v London artists (LCCA London) 2002, Saatchi Gift to the Arts Cncl Collection (Usher Gallery Lincoln) 2002, Gifted (Arts Gallery London) 2004, Fine Arts Mostra (Br Sch at Rome) 2004, The Spiral of Time (Open Hand Open Space Reading) 2005 and (APT London) 2006, Cullterin Colours Roamin in Limbo (Keith Talent Gallery London) 2005, Ex Roma – Rome Scholars 1999–2004 (APT Gallery London) 2005, Moving Art (Artower London) 2005, Carter Presents pencil (a drawing show) (Jamie Robinson London) 2005, 40 Artists 40 Drawings (Drawing Gallery London) 2005, Jerwood Drawing Prize (Jerwood Space London and tour) 2006–07, Salon Connexions (Contemporary Art Projects London) 2006, 42 (Three Colts Gallery London) 2006, Pairs (Drawing Gallery London) 2006, John Moores Liverpool Exhibition 42 (Walker Art Gallery) 2006, Summer Sale (Foster Art London) 2006, Keith Talent LA Art Fair 2006, Fosterart Winter exhibition 2006, World Gone Mad (Limehouse Arts Fndn London, Herbert Read Gallery Canterbury and Castlefield Gallery Manchester) 2006, Lodestar (Terrace London) 2006, Driven (Fieldgate Street Gallery London) 2007, Oh Deborah (CAProjects London) 2007, Rebound (Quonset Hut Studios Riverside CA) 2010, Ricochet (Chip Projects London) 2010, 40 Artists 80 Drawings (Drawing Gallery Serpentine) 2010 and (Burton Art Gallery and Museum) 2011, Fate and Freewill (CAS Riverside CA) 2010, RCA Secret 2009 (RCA) 2010, Layers John Moores Contemporary Painting Prize Show (Seongnam Arts Center S Korea) 2010, Hang then decay...5th Terrace Annual (Terrace London) 2010, Doubt (CAS Riverside CA) 2012, Painting on Edge II (den contemporary LA) 2012, Painting on the Edge I (Autonomie LA) 2012, FlashFlOOd (Little Berlin Philadelphia) 2012, Monster Drawing Rally (Armory Center for the Arts Pasadena CA) 2013, Essential (Sweeney Art Gallery Riverside CA) 2013, Paradox Maintenance Technicians #2 (Torrance Art Museum CA) 2013, Theatrical

Dynamics (Torrance Art Museum CA) 2013, Max Attack (LA Mart) 2013; *Publications* Shark Infested Waters, The Saatchi Collection of British Art in the 90s; *Style—* David Leapman, Esq; ✉ c/o Beaux Arts, 22 Cork Street, London W1X 1HB (e-mail david.leapman@gmail.com, website www.davidleapman.com)

LEATES, Margaret; da of Henry Arthur Sargent Rayner, and Alice, née Baker; b 30 March 1951; *Educ* Lilley and Stone Girls' HS Newark, King's Coll London (LLB, LLM, AKC), Univ of Kent (MA); m 26 May 1973, Timothy Philip Leates; 1 s (Benjamin b 15 April 1982), 1 da (Lydia b 14 July 1983); *Career* admitted slr 1975; Parliamentary Counsel Office 1976–90, Parliamentary draftsman and conslt 1990–, draftsman Tax Law Rewrite 1996–2010; memb Law Soc; *Recreations* other people's gardens, hermeneutics, walking, the arts; *Style—* Mrs Margaret Leates; ✉ Crofton Farm, 161 Crofton Lane, Orpington, Kent BR6 0BP (✆ 01689 820192); Nyanza, 87 Bennells Avenue, Whitstable, Kent CT5 2HR (✆ 01227 272335)

LEATHAM, Lady Victoria Diana; DL (1993 Cambs); née Cecil; da of 6 Marquess of Exeter, KCMG (d 1981), and 2 w, Diana (d 1982), da of Hon Arnold Henderson, OBE (d 1933, 5 s of 1 Baron Faringdon, CH); b 1947; m 1967, Simon Patrick Leatham, DL; 1 s, 1 da; *Career* former dir Preservation Tst and Burghley House; presenter of tv progs on stately homes; lectr on antiques UK and overseas; Hon Dr of Arts De Montfort Univ Leicester 1994; Hon Col 158 (Royal Anglian) Regt 1996–2002; The Royal Logistics Corps (Volunteer); Master Drapers' Co City of London 2012–13; Hon DLitt Bishop Grosseteste Coll Lincoln 1999; *Books* Burghley – The Life of a Great House (1992); *Style—* The Lady Victoria Leatham, DL; ✉ Garden Farmhouse, Fotheringhay, Northants PE8 5HZ

LEATHER, Dame Susan Catherine (Suzi); DBE (2006, MBE 1994), DL (2009); da of Hugh Moffat Leather, and Catherine Margaret, née Stephen; b 5 April 1956, Kampala, Uganda; *Educ* St Mary's Sch Calne, Tavistock Sch, Univ of Exeter (BA, BPhil, CQSW), Univ of Leicester (MA); m 1986, Prof Iain Hampsher-Monk; 1 s, 2 da; *Career* sr res offr Consumers in Europe Gp 1979–84, trainee probation offr 1984–86, freelance consumer conslt 1988–97, chair Exeter and Dist NHS Tst 1997–2001, chair Human Fertilisation and Embryology Authy 2002–06; chair Charity Cmmn for England and Wales 2006–12; ex officio memb Human Genetics Cmmn 2002–06; chair: St Sidwell's Project Healthy Living Centre 1998–2001, Sch Meals Review Panel 2005, School Food Tst 2005–06, Cncl of Food Policy Advsrs 2008–10, Ethics Ctee RCOG 2011–14, Lankellychase Fndn 2012–, Plymouth Fairness Cmmn 2013–; dep chair Food Standards Agency 2000–02; memb: Bd Human Tissue Authy 2004–06, Cncl Univ of Exeter 2004–13, Bd UK Accreditation Serv 2006–15, Bd Consumer Focus 2008–13, State Honours Ctee 2008–14, Bd GMC 2013–; vice-pres Hospiscare 2012–, memb Bd SW Ministry Training Course 2014–, memb Bd StepChange 2015–, lay chapter Canon Exeter Cathedral 2015–, patron Donor Conception Network 2015–; Caroline Walker Tst Award (consumer category) 1993; Hon DLitt Univ of Exeter 2003, Hon DCL Univ of Huddersfield 2005, Hon LLD Univ of Leicester 2007, Dr (hc) Univ of Aberdeen 2007; FRCOG ad eundem 2004, Hon FRPSH 2006; *Publications* articles on consumer, food and health policy incl: Food and Low Income: a practical guide for advisers and supporters working with families and young people on low incomes (1994), Budgeting for Food on Benefits (1995), The Making of Modern Malnutrition (1996); *Recreations* keeping fit, walking, running; *Style—* Dame Suzi Leather, DBE, DL; ✉ 8 Clifton Hill, Exeter, Devon EX1 2DL (e-mail sleather01@live.co.uk)

LEATHERBARROW, Prof William John; s of William Leatherbarrow (d 1996), and Lily, née Halliday (d 1986); b 18 October 1947, Liverpool; *Educ* Liverpool Inst HS for Boys, Univ of Exeter (BA, MA); m 19 Oct 1968, Vivien Jean, née Burton; 1 s (James William b 28 April 1970), 1 da (Corin Jean (Mrs Robertson) b 15 Jan 1972); *Career* Univ of Sheffield: lectr in Russian 1970–89, sr lectr in Russian 1990–94, prof of Russian 1994–2007, dean Faculty of Arts 1997–99, chair Sch of Modern Languages 2001–04, emeritus prof 2007–; memb Br Assoc for Slavonic and East European Studies, memb Cncl Br Astronomical Assoc (pres 2011–13, vice-pres 2013–15); Hon DSc Univ of Sheffield 2016; *Books* incl: Fedor Dostoevsky (1981, CD-ROM 1993), A Documentary History of Russian Thought: From the Enlightenment to Marxism (jtly, 1987), Fedor Dostoevsky: A Reference Guide to the Literature (1990), Dostoevsky: The Brothers Karamazov (1992), Dostoevskii and Britain (ed, 1995), Dostoevsky's The Devils: A Critical Companion (ed, 1999), The Cambridge Companion to Dostoevsky (ed, 2002), A Devil's Vaudeville: The Demonic in Dostoevskii's Major Fiction (2005), A History of Russian Thought (jtly, 2010); also ed of critical edns of Dostoevsky; *Recreations* wine, cricket, walking, astronomy; *Style—* Prof William Leatherbarrow; ✉ Department of Russian and Slavonic Studies, University of Sheffield, Sheffield S10 2TN (e-mail w.leatherbarrow@shef.ac.uk)

LEAVER, Sir Christopher; GBE (1981), JP (Inner London); s of Dr Robert Leaver, and Audrey Kerpen; b 3 November 1937; *Educ* Eastbourne Coll; m 1975, Helen Mireille Molyneux Benton; 1 s (Benedict), 2 da (Tara, Anna); *Career* cmmnd RAOC 1956–58, Hon Col 151 (Gtr London) Tport Regt RCT (V) 1983–88, Hon Col Cmdt RCT 1988–91; chm Thames Line plc 1987–89, vice-chm Thames Water plc 1994–2000 (dep chm 1983–93, chm 1993–94); dir: Bath & Portland Group plc 1983–85, Thermal Scientific plc 1985–88, Unionamerica Holdings plc 1994–97; cncllr RBK&C 1971–74, Alderman Ward of Dowgate City of London 1974–2002 (memb Ct of Common Cncl 1973), Sheriff City of London 1979–80, Lord Mayor of London 1981–82; memb: Bd Brixton Prison 1975–78, Cmmn of Lt for City of London 1982–2002, Fin Ctee London Diocesan Fund 1983–86, Cncl Mission to Seamen 1983–93, Advsy Gp Royal Parks 1993–96; govr: Christs' Hosp Sch 1975–2002, City of London Girls' Sch 1975–78, City Univ 1978–2002 (chllr 1981–82), City of London Freemen's Sch 1980–81, Music Therapy Tst 1981–89; chm: Young Musicians' Symphony Orchestra Tst 1979–81, London Tourist Bd 1983–89, Eastbourne Coll 1988–2006; tstee London Symphony Orchestra 1983–90; vice-pres: Nat Playing Fields Assoc 1983–99, Bridewell Royal Hosp 1983–89; church warden St Olave's Hart St 1975–89, church cmmr 1982–93 and 1996–99; hon memb GSM 1982; Hon DMus City Univ 1982; Freeman Co of Watermen and Lightermen, Liveryman Co of Water Conservators; Hon Liveryman: Worshipful Co of Farmers, Worshipful Co of Environmental Cleaners; Master Worshipful Co of Carmen 1987–88; KStJ 1982; *Style—* Sir Christopher Leaver, GBE, JP; ✆ 01903 787495

LEAVER, Prof Christopher John; CBE (2000); s of Douglas Percival Leaver (d 1978), and Elizabeth Constance, née Hancock; b 31 May 1942; *Educ* Lyme Regis GS, Imperial Coll London (State Scholarship, BSc, ARCS, DIC, PhD), Univ of Oxford (MA); m 8 Oct 1971, Anne, da of Prof Hastings Dudley Huggins (d 1970); 1 s (Tristan), 1 da (Anya); *Career* Fulbright scholar Purdue Univ USA 1966–68, scientific offr ARC Plant Physiology Unit Imperial Coll London 1968–69; Univ of Edinburgh: lectr then reader 1969–86, SERC sr res fell 1985–90, prof of plant molecular biology 1986–89; Univ of Oxford: fell St John's Coll 1990–2008 (emeritus fell 2008–), Sibthorpian prof of plant sciences 1990–2007, head Dept of Plant Sciences 1991–2007, emeritus prof of plant science 2008–; Raine Medical Fndn visiting prof Univ of Western Aust 2002–15; author of over 160 pubns in int jls; chair: Scientific Advsy Bd IACR Rothamsted Research 1995–2000, Technol Transfer Advsy Gp 1995–2000, ITQB Advsy Ctee Univ of Lisbon 2000–07, Int Advsy Panel Graduate Sch for Integrative Sciences and Engrg Nat Univ of Singapore 2009–; advsr in biological sciences Carnegie Tst Univ of Scotland 2003–14; memb: Cncl AFRC 1990–94, Priorities Bd MAFF 1990–94, Cncl Euro Molecular Biology Orgn 1991–97 (chm 1997), ACOST 1992–93, Cncl Royal Soc 1992–94, External Scientific Advsy Bd Inst of Molecular and Cell Biology Univ of Oporto (chair 1999–), Exec Ctee Biochemical Soc (vice-chair 2002–05, chair 2005–07), GM Sci Review Panel DTI 2002–03, Sci Advsy Panel Royal

Instn of GB 2002–10, Scientific Advsy Bd Inst of Molecular and Cell Biology Singapore 2002–06, Exec Ctee Sense about Sci 2002–14 (also founding tstee), Ctee for Sr Academic Promotions in Biology, Sci and Clinical Med Univ of Cambridge 2003–08, Int Advsy Panel A*Star Grad Acad Singapore 2003–07, Ctee for Scientific Planning and Review Int Cncl for Science 2005–12, Int Networks Ctee 2005–15, Scientific Advsy Bd Plant Energy Biology ARC Centre of Excellence Univ of WA Perth 2006–14, Africa Exchange Ctee 2015–18; sr scientific advsr Biosciences for Farming in Africa (www.b4fa.org) 2011–; BBSRC: memb IMP Panel 1996–2005, memb Cncl 2000–03, chair Personal Merit Promotion Panel 2005–10; dir Isis Innovations Ltd 1996–2000; delg OUP 2002–07; tstee: John Innes Fndn 1987–2017 (memb Governing Body John Innes Centre 1984–2012), Nat History Museum London 1997–2006; T H Huxley Gold Medal Imperial Coll 1970, Tate and Lyle Award Phytochem Soc of Europe 1984, Humboldt Prize (Germany) 1997, Sibthorp Medal Univ of Oxford 2007; memb EMBO 1982, FRS 1986, FRSE 1987, memb Academia Europaea 1989, hon fell Royal Instn of GB 2002, inaugural fell American Soc of Plant Biologists (corresponding memb 2003); *Recreations* walking and talking in Upper Coquetdale; *Clubs* Queensland Club Perth Australia (hon memb 2011–); *Style—* Prof Christopher Leaver, CBE, FRS, FRSE; ✉ St John's College, St Giles, Oxford OX1 3JP

LEAVER, Colin Edward; s of Edward Roy Leaver, of Chichester, W Sussex, and Freda Eleanor, *née* Toogood; *b* 25 May 1958; *Educ* Haywards Heath GS, Lincoln Coll Oxford (MA); *m* 10 May 1986, Maria Victoria, da of John Hutton Simpkins, of Alicante, Spain; 2 da (Christina b 1987, Mónica b 1991), 1 s (James b 1989); *Career* Simmons & Simmons: articled clerk 1980–82, asst slr 1982–86, ptnr 1986–, based Hong Kong 1989–96, based London 1996–; *Recreations* sailing, philately, aviation; *Clubs* Royal Hong Kong Yacht; *Style—* Colin Leaver, Esq; ✉ Simmons & Simmons, CityPoint, One Ropemaker Street, London EC2Y 9SS (☎ 020 7628 2020, fax 020 7628 2070, e-mail colin.leaver@simmons-simmons.com)

LEAVER, Peter Lawrence Oppenheim; QC (1987); s of Marcus Isaac Leaver (d 1966), of London, and Lena, *née* Oppenheim (d 1984); *b* 28 November 1944; *Educ* Aldenham, Univ of Dublin; *m* 2 June 1969, Jane Rachel, o da of Leonard Pearl (d 1983), of London; 3 s (Marcus, James, Benjamin) 1 da (Rebecca); *Career* called to the Bar Lincoln's Inn 1967 (bencher 1995); recorder 1994–, dep judge of the High Court 1994–; memb Gen Cncl Bar 1987–90; chm: Bar Ctee 1989 (vice-chm 1988–89), Int Practice Ctee 1990; memb: Ctee on Future of Legal Profession 1986–88, Cncl Legal Educn 1986–90; dir Investment Mgmnt Regulatory Organisation Ltd 1994–2000, dep chm FSA Regulatory Decisions Ctee; chief exec FA Premier League 1997–99; memb Football Task Force 1997–99; former memb Court of Arbitration for Sport, pres Nat Anti-Doping Panel 2008–15, chm London Court of Int Arbitration 2010–15; former tstee The Free Representation Unit; *Recreations* sport, wine, theatre, opera; *Clubs* Garrick, MCC; *Style—* Peter Leaver, Esq, QC; ✉ 13 Clifton Gardens, London W9 1AL (☎ 020 7286 0208); 1 Essex Court, Temple, London EC4Y 9AR (☎ 020 7583 2000, fax 020 7583 0118, e-mail pleaver@oeclaw.co.uk)

LEBEDEV, Evgeny; *b* 8 May 1980; *Career* owner: Evening Standard Ltd 2009–, Independent Print Ltd 2010–; co-owner (with Sir Ian McKellen, CH, CBE, and Sean Mathias, *qqv*) The Grapes London; *Style—* Mr Evgeny Lebedev; ✉ Independent Print Ltd, Northcliffe House, 2 Derry Street, Kensington, London W8 5TT (Twitter @mrevgenylebedev)

LECCA, Marie-Jeanne; da of Mircea Lecca (d 1970), and Mona *née* Beller Cantacuzino (d 2007); *b* 31 January 1960; *Educ* Beaux Arts Inst Bucharest; *m* 2 Oct 1982, Dan Mihai Sandru, s of Vasile Sandru; *Career* set and costume designer; memb SBTD; patron Pro Patrimonio; *Theatre* incl: Yvonna, Princess of Burgundy (Mic Theatre Bucharest) 1984 (Best Scene Designer Assoc of Romanian Artists Prize), La Bete Humaine (Nottingham Playhouse) 1993, The Taming of the Shrew (RSC Stratford and Barbican) 1995, As You Like It (Nottingham Playhouse) 1997, Napoleon (Shaftesbury Theatre) 2000; *Opera* designs for ENO: The Stone Guest 1987, Pacific Overtures 1987, Falstaff 1989, Pelleas & Melisande 1990, The Adventures of Mr Brou?ek 1992 (transferred to Bayerische Staatsoper Munich 1995), Der Freischutz 1999, Nabucco 2000, Verdi Requiem 2000; other designs incl: Le Pre-aux-Clercs (John Lewis Partnership Music Soc) 1985, La Wally (Wexford Opera Festival) 1985, Iolanthe (Scottish Opera Glasgow) 1986, La Boheme (Eng Touring Opera) 1986, The Pirates of Penzance (d'Oyly Carte Opera Co London, UK and US tour) 1989, Carmen (Minnesota Opera) 1991 (transferred to Houston Grand Opera 1994, Seattle Opera 1995 and Teatro Regio Turin 1996), The Barber of Seville (Glimmerglass Opera) 1993–94, Cavalleria Rusticana and I Pagliacci (Berlin State Opera) 1996, The Nose (De Nederlandse Opera Amsterdam) 1996, La Maison des Morts (Opera du Rhin Strasbourg) 1996, Julietta (Opera North Leeds) 1997 (Martinu Fndn Medal, nomination Barclays Theatre Award 1998), Rienzi (Vienna State Opera) 1997, The Turn of the Screw (La Monnaie Brussels) 1998, Angel Magick (BBC Proms and Salisbury Playhouse) 1998, Salammbo (Bastille Opera Paris) 1998–2000, Katya Kabanova (Bayerische Staatsoper Munich) 1999, The Greek Passion (Bregenzer Festspiele and ROH) 1999–2000 (jt winner Olivier Award), Faust (Bayerische Staatsoper Munich) 2000, La Clemenza di Tito (Opera Nat du Rhin Strasbourg) 2001, Macbeth (Opernhaus Zurich) 2001, Therese Raquin (Dallas Opera) 2001, Jenufa (Vienna State Opera) 2002, Turandot (Salzburg Festival) 2002, Wozzeck (ROH) 2002 (jt winner Olivier Award), Wilhelm Tell (Bastille Opera Paris) 2003, West Side Story (Bregenzer Festspiele) 2003, Boccaccio (Volksoper Vienna) 2003, The Dwarf, Seven Deadly Sins (Opera North, jt winner South Bank Show Award), The Ring Cycle (ROH) 2004–07, Maskarade (Bregenzer Festspiele and ROH) 2005 (Opernwelt Magazine nomination for Costume Designer of the Year), Peter Grimes (Opernhaus Zürich) 2005, Magic Flute (Volksoper Vienna) 2005, Moses and Aron (Bayerische Staatsoper) 2006, Die Soldaten (Ruhr Triennale and Lincoln Center Festival) 2006–07, L'Étoile (Opernhaus Zürich) 2006, Khovanshchina (Welsh Nat Opera) 2007, La Juive (Opernhaus Zürich) 2007, Carmen (Bolshoi Opera Moscow) 2008, Tristan und Isolde (Oper Köln) 2009, Agrippina (Opernhaus Zürich) 2009, Krol Roger (Bregenzer Festspiele and Barcelona), Die Frau Ohne Schatten (Opernhaus Zurich), The Passenger (Bregenzer Festspiele, Teatr Wielki Warsaw and ENO) 2010–11, (Houston Grand Opera Lincoln Center Festival) 2014 and (Lyric Opera Chicago) 2015, Les Troyens (Deutsche Oper Berlin) 2010, Un Ballo In Maschera (Opernhaus Zurich) 2011, Festival Puccini Plus (Opéra National de Lyon) 2012, Knyaz Igor (Opern Haus Zürich) 2012, Lulu (Welsh Nat Opera) 2013, The Magic Flute (Bregenzer Festspiele) 2013–14, Mosé in Egitto and William Tell (Welsh Nat Opera) 2014 and (Teatr Wielki Warsaw and Grand Théâtre de Genève) 2015, Pelléas et Mélisande (Welsh Nat Opera) 2015, The Haunted Manor (Teatr Wielki Warsaw) 2015, Das Rheingold (Lyric Opera of Chicago) 2016; winner Prague Quadriennale Golden Tríga 2003 (jtly); *Dance* Roméo et Juliette (Theater St Gallen) 2015; *Television* The Big One 1991, Amahl and the Night Visitors 2001 (BAFTA nomination); *Recreations* cinema, photography, travel, gardening; *Style—* Mrs Marie-Jeanne Lecca; ✉ c/o Lynda Mamy, United Agents, 12–26 Lexington Street, London W1F 0LE (☎ 020 3214 0800, fax 020 3214 0801, website www.unitedagents.co.uk)

LECHLER, Prof Sir Robert Ian; kt (2012); s of Dr Ian Sewell Lechler (d 1972), and Audrey Florence, *née* Wilson (d 1979); *b* 24 December 1951; *Educ* Monkton Combe Sch, Univ of Manchester (MB ChB), Univ of London (PhD); *m* Valerie Susan, da of Harold Ord Johnston (d 1988); 2 s (Alastair Robert b 4 Feb 1980, Toby Ian b 23 Dec 1982), 1 da (Suzannah Jane b 24 Feb 1988); *Career* sr renal registrar Professorial Med Unit Hammersmith Hosp 1983–84 (renal registrar 1982–83), Wellcome Tst travelling fell Lab of Immunology Bethesda Maryland USA 1984–86; Imperial Coll Sch of Med at Hammersmith Hosp (Royal Postgrad Med Sch until merger 1997): sr lectr in immunology 1986–89, reader in immunology 1989–92, hon conslt in med 1989–94, prof of molecular immunology 1992–94, prof and dir of immunology 1994–2004, dean of campus 2001–04, head Div of Medicine 2003–04; Hammersmith Hosps Tst: conslt transplant physician 1986–2004, chief of immunology serv 1995–2004; KCL: prof of immunology 2004–, vice-princ for health 2005–, dean GKT Sch of Medicine 2004–05, dean Sch of Medicine and Dental Inst Guy's, King's Coll and St Thomas' Hosps 2005–; hon conslt Dept of Renal Medicine and Transplantation Guy's Hosp 2004–; dir Ruggero Cepellini Sch of Immunology Naples 2001–; chm: Scientific Advsy Bd Embryonic Stem Cell Int 2003–, Chairs and Prog Grants Ctte BHF 2003–; memb Scientific Ctee Inst de transplantation et de recherche en transplantation Nantes 2000–; int advsr to NIH Immune Tolerance Network 2000–, cncllr Int Xenotransplantation Assoc 2001–; memb Editorial Bd Transplantation Jl; memb: Renal Assoc 1980, Int Transplantation Soc 1987, Assoc of Physicians 1988; FRCP 1990 (MRCP 1978), FRCPath 1996, FMedSci 2000; *Recreations* classical music, theatre, family; *Style—* Prof Sir Robert Lechler; ✉ School of Medicine, King's College London, Hodgkin Building, Guy's Campus, London SE1 9RT

LEDERER, Helen; da of Peter Lederer, and Jeanne Lederer; *b* 24 September 1954; *Educ* Blackheath HS, Hatfield Poly (now Hatfield Univ), Central Sch of Speech & Drama; *m* Dr Chris Browne; 1 da (Hannah Louise b 28 April 1990); *Career* comedienne and actress; early work at the Comedy Store and similar venues; *Theatre* incl: Bunny in House of Blue Leaves (Lilian Bayliss Theatre), Educating Rita (with Julian Glover, *qv*), Doreen in Having A Ball (Comedy Theatre), Vagina Mologues (West End) 2002 (and V-Day Celebrations Albert Hall London), Full House (Palace Theatre Watford), The Hairless Diva (Palace Theatre Watford); *Television* appearances incl: The Young Ones, Girls on Top, The French and Saunders Show, Flossie in Happy Families (BBC 2), 5 series of Naked Video (writing and performing own material in between sketches, BBC 2), Wogan, Hysteria, The New Statesman, Bottom, Absolutely Fabulous (BBC), One Foot in the Grave (BBC), presented Butter Fingers (Taste CRN), occasional presenter Heaven and Earth Show (BBC 1), cmmd to write sitcom for BBC2 2001–02; *Radio* female actress in BBC Radio 4's In One Ear (Sony Award for Best Comedy); other radio work incl: writer and performer two series of Life With Lederer (Radio 4), short story readings (Radio 3 and 4), Comic Cuts (Radio 5), reg writer and performer of comic monologues Woman's Hour (Radio 4), wrote and featured in All Change (Radio 4, Pick of the Week) 2001; *Film* Solitaire for Two, Dance to your Daddy, Speak Like a Child (Screen Two); *Publications* Coping With Lederer, Single Minding (1995); contrib author in Girl's Night In/Big Night Out; author of numerous articles for New Woman, Options and She magazines, The Guardian; regular writer for Independent on Sunday LIFE and travel, Mail on Sunday travel, Woman and Home, EVE; *Recreations* cinema, reading, friends, pilates; *Style—* Ms Helen Lederer; ✉ c/o Elizabeth Ayto, Media Ambitions Ltd, Suite 2, Ground Floor, 127 Ladbroke Grove, London W11 1PN (☎ 020 7229 6610, e-mail elizabeth@mediaambitions.com)

LEDERER, Peter J; CBE (2005, OBE 1994); s of Thomas Francis Lederer, and Phoebe, *née* Blackman; *b* 30 November 1950, London; *Educ* City of London Sch, Middlesex Univ; *m* 10 Oct 1981, Marilyn Ruth MacPhail; *Career* Four Seasons Hotels Canada 1972–79, Wood Wilkings Ltd Toronto 1979–81, Plaza Hotels Ltd 1981–83; Gleneagle Hotels Ltd 1984–2014: gen mangr 1984–87, md 1987–2007, chm 2007–14; dir: Guinnes Enterprises 1987–2007, VisitBritain 2001–10, Royal Edinburgh Military Tattoo 2011–, Pod Global Solutions 2012–, The Hotel Management Co 2016–; pres Enable 2009–; chm: VisitScotland 2001–10, Hamilton and Inches Edinburgh 2010–, Taste Communications 2011–, Applecrate 2012–; patron Hospitality Industry Tst Scotland, patron Scottish Licensed Trade Assoc; Master Innholder; Freeman City of London, Liveryman Worshipful Co of Innholders; Hon DBA Queen Margaret Edinburgh, Hon DUniv Stirling Univ; CIMgt, FIoH, FSQA; *Style—* Peter J Lederer, Esq, CBE; ✉ 18 Great Stuart Street, Edinburgh EH3 7TN (☎ 07803 855421, e-mail pjlederer@icloud.com)

LEDGER, Christopher John Walton; JP (1993); s of Peter Walton Ledger, of Poundbury, Dorset, and Barbara Nancy, *née* Eve; *b* 5 February 1943, Banbury, Oxon; *Educ* The Nautical Coll Pangbourne; *m* 1, 21 April 1971 (m dis 1973); m 2, 19 Sept 1977 (m dis 2015), Gillian Penelope, da of Col Paul Heberden Rogers (d 1972); 1 da (Nicola Kate b 10 Aug 1978), 1 s (James Walton Herberden b 17 July 1981); *Career* cmmnd 2 Lt RM 1962, offr 43 Commando 1964, OC Recce Tp 45 Commando 1965–66, ATURM Poole 1966–67, OC HMS Bulwark 1967–69, Adj RM Poole 1969–72, ATT HQ CO Forces 1972–74; Shell UK Ltd: joined 1974, PA mangr Expro 1976–77, mangr Small Business Initiative Films and Educnl Serv 1978–81, dir of PA 1981–84, chief exec World Energy Business 1984–86; chief exec The Phoenix Initiative 1986–91; chm IDARAT ME LLC; ops dir IDARAT Maritime Ltd 2011–14, chief operating offr Idarat Resilience DMLC 2014–; chm FirstLight Tst 2014–15; Liveryman Worshipful Co of Grocers 1972; Queen's Commendation for Brave Conduct 1965; FRSA; *Recreations* sailing, history, photography; *Clubs* RMSC, RNSA, RNVR Yacht; *Style—* Christopher Ledger, Esq; ✉ Ridge Farm, King's Stag, Sturminster Newton, Dorset DT10 2AU (☎ 07946 476398 or 001 217 801 5999, e-mail cjwledger@gmail.com or cjwledger@icloud.com)

LEDINGHAM, Prof John Gerard Garvin; s of Dr John Ledingham (d 1970), of Ladbroke Square, London, and Dr Una Christina Ledingham, *née* Garvin (d 1965); *b* 19 October 1929; *Educ* Rugby, New Coll Oxford (MA, DM), Middx Hosp Med Sch Univ of London (BM BCh); *m* 3 March 1962, Elaine Mary, da of Richard Glyn Maliphant (d 1977), of Cardiff; 4 da (Joanna b 22 March 1963, Catherine b 19 May 1964, Clare b 10 Oct 1968, Sarah b 20 Nov 1971); *Career* Nat Serv 2 Lt RA 1949–50; registrar in med Middx Hosp London 1960–62 (house offr 1957–58), sr registrar Westminster Hosp London 1963–65, visiting fell Columbia Univ NY 1965–66, conslt physician United Oxford Hosps 1966–74; Univ of Oxford: May reader in med 1974–95, prof 1989–95, dir of clinical studies 1977–81 and 1991–95; fell New Coll Oxford 1974 (emeritus 1996–, hon fell 2000); contrib various med and science jls; tstee: Nuffield Tst 1978–2003, Beit Tst 1989–2008, Oxford Hospital Devpt Improvement Fund, Commonwealth Scholarships Cmmn 1992–98; chm Nuffield Oxford Hospitals Tst 1995–2005; examiner in med: Univs of Cambridge, Glasgow, Oxford, London, Southampton and Sheffield, Sultan Qaboos Univ, Royal Coll of Physicians, Royal Coll of Surgns of Ireland; former memb GMC; chm Med Research Soc 1988–91, memb Animal Procedures Ctee of Home Sec 1985–92, memb Supra-Regnl Servs Ctee Dept of Health 1983–86, censor RCP 1984–85, memb Nuffield Cncl on Bioethics 2000–03; former hon sec and hon treas Assoc of Physicians of GB and Ireland, former pres Br Hypertension Soc; Distinguished Friend of Oxford 2011; William Osler Memorial Medal 2000; FRCP 1971; *Books* Oxford Textbook of Medicine (ed with D J Weatherall and D A Warrell, 1983, 1987 and 1995), Concise Oxford Textbook of Medicine (ed with D A Warrell, 2000), We Hope to Get Word Tomorrow – The Garvin Family Letters 1914–1916 (ed, 2009); *Recreations* music, golf; *Clubs* Vincent's (Oxford); *Style—* Prof John Ledingham; ✉ 124 Oxford Road, Cumnor, Oxford OX2 9PQ (☎ and fax 01865 865806, e-mail jeled@btopenworld.com)

LEE, (Edward) Adam Michael; s of His Hon Judge Michael Lee, DSC, DL (d 1983), of Winchester, Hants, and Valerie Burnett Georges, *née* Drake-Brockman (d 1995); *b* 29 June 1942; *Educ* Winchester, ChCh Oxford (MA); *m* 5 July 1975, Carola Jean, da of Capt Frederick Le Hunte Anderson (d 1989), of Hungerford, Berks; 2 s (Frederick Edward Maconchy b 1977, (James) Michael Maconchy b 1981); *Career* called to the Bar Middle Temple 1964; cadet Glyn, Mills & Co 1964; Williams & Glyn's Bank: sr planner 1969, dep dir City Div 1974; local dir: Child & Co 1977–87, Holts Branches 1978–87, Drummonds 1985–87; asst gen mangr Royal Bank of Scotland 1985–87, gp devpt dir Adam & Co 1988–90; dir: Duncan Lawrie Tst Corp 1990–92, Trustee Resources 1993–

L

96, Minmet plc 1993–96, Crediton Minerals plc 1996–99; chm Unison International plc 1992–94; advsr Cncl Grange Park Opera 1998–; conslt to various cos; chm Explosion! The Museum of Naval Firepower Gosport 2000–03; sec and treas: Inverforth Charitable Tst 1990–2007, Matthews Wrightson Charity Tst 1990–2007; tstee Chelsea Opera Gp until 2015; chm Temple Bar Masters Assoc 2004–; memb Ct of Assts Worshipful Co of Dyers' 1998 (Liveryman 1984, Renter Warden 2002–03, Prime Warden 2003–04); FCIB 1981; *Recreations* opera, tennis, music, theatre, golf, food and wine, travel; *Clubs* Travellers, Rye Golf, Chatham Dining; *Style*— Adam Lee, Esq; ✉ Standen Hussey, Standen, Hungerford, Berkshire RG17 0RB (☎ 01488 681960, e-mail adam.lee22@sky.com)

LEE, Alan Peter; s of Peter Alexander Lee, of Sidmouth, Devon, and Christina, *née* Carmichael; *b* 13 June 1954; *Educ* Cavendish GS Hemel Hempstead; *m* 18 Oct 1980, Patricia Rosemary Drury, da of James Chesshire; 1 da (Victoria Helen b 22 Oct 1984), 1 s (James Patrick b 19 Feb 1987); *Career* sports writer; Watford Observer 1970–74, Hayter's Agency 1974–78; cricket corr: Mail on Sunday 1982–87, The Times 1988–99; covered England home test matches 1977–98; covered England tours: India and Aust 1976–77, Aust 1978–79, 1982–83, 1986–87, 1990–91, 1994–95, and 1998–99, W Indies 1981, 1986, 1990, 1994 and 1998, Pakistan 1983, India 1984–85, NZ 1988, 1992 and 1997; covered World Cups 1979, 1983, 1987, 1992 and 1996; racing correspondent The Times 1999–; highly commended Sports Magazine Writer of the Year 1987, shortlisted Sports Reporter of the Year 1999, Racing Journalist of the Year 2001 and 2004, Sports Journalist of the Year 2002; Specialist Sports Corr of the Year 2002; *Books* over 20 on cricket, racing and golf incl: A Pitch in Both Camps (1979), Jump Jockeys (1980), Lambourn (1982), Fred (biography of Fred Winter, 1991), To be a Champion (1992), Lord Ted (1995), Raising the Stakes (1996); *Recreations* National Hunt racing, tennis; *Clubs* Cricketers' Club of London, Cricket Writers'; *Style*— Alan Lee, Esq; ✉ 8 The Courtyard, Montpellier Street, Cheltenham, Gloucestershire GL50 1SR (☎ and fax 01242 572637); The Times, 1 Virginia Street, London E1 9XN (☎ 020 7782 5944, fax 020 7782 5211, mobile 078 8764 2255)

LEE, Anthony D M; *b* 15 August 1956, Singapore; *Educ* St Lawrence Coll Ramsgate, Chatham House Ramsgate, Thanet Tech Coll, Westminster Hotel and Catering Coll; *m*; 1 s; *Career* The Connaught London: receptionist 1979–80, chef de brigade 1980–82; receptionist The Crillon Hotel Paris 1982–84; The Connaught London: reception mangr 1985–88 (asst reception mangr 1984–85), house mangr 1988–2002 (incl takeover by Blackstone Gp), gen mangr 2002–10; gen mangr: May Fair Hotel 2010–13, Cafe Royal 2014–; memb: HCIMA, Amicale Internationale des Sous-Directeurs et Chefs de Réception des Grands Hôtels (AICR), Craft Guild of Chefs and Cookery and Food Assoc (ACFA), West One Mangrs' Assoc; awards for The Connaught incl: Travel and Leisure Top 30 Hotels in the World 2008, Best European Business Hotel of the Year Spears Wealth Management Magazine 2008, Conde Nast Traveller Gold List 2009 (Best for Location category); Helene Darroze at the Connaught awarded Michelin star 2009; *Recreations* sports incl tennis, sailing, music, design, current affairs, IT, travel, theatre and dining; *Style*— Anthony Lee, Esq; ✉ Cafe Royal Hotel, 68 Regents Street, London W1B 4DY

LEE, Gary; s of Victor Odu Silva, and Ronke Odu Silva; *b* London; *Educ* Trinity Catholic HS Woodford Green, Waltham Forest Coll; *Partner* Elianor Megan Wilson; 3 da (Quiana Wilson b 31 Jan 1989, Taquira Wilson b 2 June 1991, Khyra Wilson b 5 April 2000); *Career* head chef Bam-Bou 2002–07; exec chef The Ivy and Club at The Ivy 2007–; involvement with Solidarity Sports; 3 times Power List Top 100 Most Influential Black People in the Country; *Recreations* boxing, cycling; *Clubs* Gym Box, Gloves 'n' Doves; *Style*— Gary Lee, Esq; ✉ The Ivy, 1–5 West Street, London WC2H 9NQ (☎ 020 7557 6080, e-mail glee@the-ivy.co.uk, website www.the-ivy.co.uk)

LEE, Prof Dame Hermione; DBE (2013, CBE 2003); da of Dr Benjamin Lee, and Josephine Lee; *b* 29 February 1948; *Educ* Lycée de Londres, City of London Sch for Girls, Queen's Coll, St Hilda's and St Cross Colls Oxford (MA, MPhil); *m* 1991, Prof John Barnard, *qv*; *Career* instr William and Mary Coll Williamsburg USA 1970–71, lectr Univ of Liverpool 1971–77; Univ of York: lectr 1977–88, sr lectr 1988–90, reader 1990–93, prof of English 1993–98; Goldsmiths' prof of English Literature Univ of Oxford 1998–2008, fell New Coll Oxford 2008, pres Wolfson Coll Oxford 2008–; judge: Faber Prize 1981, Booker Prize 1981 and 2006 (chm of judges), W H Smith Prize 1987–92, Cheltenham Prize 1987, David Cohen Prize 1998; presenter: Book Four (Channel 4) 1982–86, Booker Prize (LWT) 1984–87; memb: Mgmnt Ctee Lumb Bank Arvon Fndn 1988–92, Arts Cncl Literature Panel 1998–2002; Rose Mary Crawshay Prize British Acad 1997; FRSL, FBA 2001; Hon DLitt: Univ of Liverpool 2002, Univ of York 2007, KCL 2013; hon fell St Cross Coll, St Hilda's Coll and New Coll Oxford 1998, fell American Acad of Arts and Scis 2003, hon fell Rothermere American Inst 2010; *Books* The Novels of Virginia Woolf (1977), Elizabeth Bowen (1981 and 1999), Philip Roth (1982), Willa Cather: A Life Saved Up (1989), Virginia Woolf (1996), Virginia Woolf's Nose: Essays on Biography (2005), Body Parts: Essays on Life-Writing (2005), Edith Wharton (2007), Biography: A Very Short Introduction (2009), Penelope Fitzgerald (2013, James Tait Black Prize 2014); editions and anthologies of: Kipling, Trollope, Woolf, Bowen, Cather; The Secret Self (short stories by women writers); *Clubs* Athenaeum; *Style*— Prof Dame Hermione Lee, DBE, FRSL, FBA; ✉ Wolfson College, Oxford OX2 6UD (☎ 01865 274101)

LEE, Howard Andrew Gabriel; s of Jack Lee, of Sydney, Aust, and Nora, *née* Blackburne; *b* 26 February 1953; *Educ* St Edward's Sch Oxford, Jesus Coll Cambridge (MA); *m* 16 Dec 1983, Jessica Lena, da of Robert Benton Bottomley; 2 da (Harriet Aimee b 29 January 1986, Rebecca Elizabeth b 9 March 1989), 2 s (James Jonathan b 2 June 1987, Jack b 17 Oct 1995),; *Career* with Charles Barker 1974–78, dep dir of info Nat Enterprise Bd 1978–80, public affairs exec British Telecom 1980–82; Valin Pollen: joined 1982, assoc dir 1983, dir 1984, int dir 1985, dir Investor Rels Div 1988, md Carter Valin Pollen Ltd 1988 (chief exec 1989), dir Valin International plc, dir Valin Pollen plc 1989 (chief exec 1990); Gavin Anderson & Company Ltd: chief exec 1991–97, head of Europe 1997–, chm London 2000–, exec vice-chm of gp 2000–04; fndr and chm Headland Consultancy 2004–; memb City & Financial Group IPR 1985, assoc memb Investor Rels Soc 1989; *Recreations* shooting, wine; *Clubs* Turf; *Style*— Howard Lee, Esq

LEE, James Giles; s of John Lee, CBE, and Muriel, *née* Giles; *b* 23 December 1942; *Educ* Trinity Coll Glenalmond, Univ of Glasgow, Harvard Univ; *m* 1966, Linn, *née* MacDonald; 2 da (Maggie b 1968, Katie b 1971), 1 s (John b 1974); *Career* ptnr McKinsey & Co 1969–80; dir S Pearson & Son 1981–84, dep chm Yorkshire TV 1982–85, chm Goldcrest Films and TV 1981–86, dir Boston Consulting Group Ltd 1987–92, md Lee & Co 1992–, dir Phoenix Pictures Inc 1995–2005; non-exec dir: Pearson Television Ltd 1993–2001, Nation Media Gp Kenya 2002–11; chm: Performing Arts Labs Tst 1990–98, Scottish Screen 1998–2002, Maidstone & Tunbridge Wells NHS Tst 2003–08, Bureau of Investigative Journalism 2009–; dir Film Cncl 1999–2005; Hon DLitt Caledonian Univ; *Recreations* photography, travelling, sailing; *Clubs* Reform, Harvard (NY); *Style*— J G Lee, Esq; ✉ Meadow Wood, Penshurst, Kent TN11 8AD (☎ 01892 870309, e-mail jas.lee@btinternet.com)

LEE, Jennifer Elizabeth; da of Ernest M B Lee, and Mary, *née* Fowlie; *b* 21 August 1956; *Educ* St Margaret's Sch for Girls Aberdeen, Edinburgh Coll of Art (DipAD), RCA (MA); *m* 29 March 1990, Jake Tilson, *qv*, s of Joe Tilson; 1 da (Hannah Lee Tilson b 26 May 1995); *Career* potter; artist in residence Shigaraki Ceramic Cultural Centre 2014 and 2015; *Solo Exhibitions* The Scottish Gallery Edinburgh 1981, Anatol Orient London 1984, Crafts Cncl Sideshow ICA London 1985, Rosenthal Studio-Haus London 1985, Craft Centre Royal Exchange Theatre Manchester 1986, Crafts Cncl Shop V & A 1987, Craft Centre and Design Gallery City Art Gallery Leeds 1987, Galerie Besson London 1990, 1992 and 1995, Graham Gallery NY 1991, Galleri Lejonet Stockholm 1993, Röhsska Museum of Arts and Crafts Göteborg 1993, Aberdeen Art Gallery 1994, Osiris Brussels 1994, Galerie Besson London 1995, James Graham and Sons NY 1996, Galerie Besson London 1997 and 2000, James Graham & Sons NY 1999, Frank Lloyd Gall LA 2002, Galerie Besson London 2003, Frank Lloyd Gallery Santa Monica 2005, 2009 and 2010, Liverpool Street Gallery Sydney 2006, Galerie Besson 2008, Liverpool Street Gallery Sydney 2010, Frank Lloyd Gallery Los Angeles 2012 Erskine, Hall & Co London 2013, Tado no yume deshouka, Jennifer Lee (Inst of Ceramic Studies Gallery Shigaraki Japan) 2015, Jennifer Lee (Gallery Sokyo Kyoto Japan) 2015; *Group Exhibitions* incl: Three Generations British Ceramics (Maya Behn Zürich) 1984, Jugend Gestaltet (Exempla Munich) 1985, Jugend Formt Keramik (Mathildenhöhe Award Darmstadt Germany) 1985, British Ceramic Art (Transform NY) 1985, Zeitgenössische Keramik Aus Grossbritannien (Keramik Studio Vienna) 1986, New British Design (Osaka and Tokyo) 1987, On a Plate (The Serpentine Gallery) 1987, British Ceramics (Marianne Heller Galerie Sandhausen Germany) 1987, The New Spirit (Crafts Cncl Gallery London and tour) 1987, Craft and Folk Museum (Los Angeles) 1988, Ton in Ton (Landesmuseum Germany) 1988, Christmas Exhibition (Galerie Besson London) 1988, Sotheby's Decorative Award Exhibition (Yorakucho Seibu Japan) 1988, Galleri Lejonet (Stockholm) 1989, L'Europe des Ceramistes (Auxerre France touring Spain, Austria, Hungary) 1989, The Royal Scottish Museum (Edinburgh) 1989, Lucie Rie, Hans Coper and their Pupils (Sainsbury Centre Norwich) 1990, Int Art Fair (Chicago) 1990, The Fitzwilliam Museum (Cambridge) 1991, British Ceramics (Int Art Fair Bologna Italy) 1991 and 1992, British Ceramics (Graham Gallery NY) 1991, Contemporary British Ceramics (Graham Gallery NY) 1992, Int Ceramic Art (Nat Museum of History Taipei Taiwan) 1992, Keramik aus Grossbritannien und Japan (Galerie Hinteregger Austria) 1992, Handbuilt Ceramics (Scottish Gallery Edinburgh) 1993, Towards the Future (Marianne Heller Germany) 1993, Visions of Craft (Crafts Cncl London) 1993, 20th Century European Ceramics (Los Angeles) 1993, Gallery Koyanagi Tokyo 1994, SOFA (Chicago) 1994 and 2002, The David Collection NY 1994, Wim Vromans Amsterdam 1995, James Graham & Sons NY 1995, Design im Wandel (Übersee Museum Bremen Germany) 1996, European Ceramics (Yufuku Gallery Tokyo) 1997, English Crafts (The Works Gallery Philadelphia) 1997, Gestaltendes Handwerk (Munich) 1998, Spirit of the Times (Bowes Museum Co Durham) 1998, Women in Europe (Galerie Marianne Heller Germany) 1998, Clay into Art (Metropolitan Museum of Art, NY) 1998, Current Context – new ways of seeing (Royal Museum, Edinburgh) 1999, Crafts Cncl 25th Anniversary Exhibition (V & A) 1999, Millennium Mugs (Galerie Besson London) 1999, Br Ceramics.2000.dk (Keramikmuseet Grimmerhus Denmark) 2000, Color and Fire: Defining Moments in Studio Ceramics 1950–2000 (Los Angeles County Museum of Art) 2000, Ceramic Biennale (Ichen World Ceramic Centre Korea) 2001, Poetics of Clay – An International Perspective, Philadelphia Art Alliance Philadelphia 2001, Bengt Julin's Ceramics, Gustavsbergs Porslinmuseum Sweden 2001, Modern Pots Ceramics from the Lisa Sainsbury Coll (Sainsbury Centre for Visual Arts UEA Norwich) 2001, Ceramic Modernism, The Gardiner Museum of Ceramic Art Toronto 2002, Vasen aus 10 Ländern (Bayerischer Kunstgewerbe-Verein Munich) 2002, British Ceramics (James Graham & Sons New York), British Cramics: Five Artists (Frank Lloyd Gallery Santa Monica CA) 2003, Constructed Clay (Galerie Besson London) 2003, SOFA (Chicago) 2003 and 2004, European Ceramics – Westerwald Prize (Keramik Museum Westerwald) 2004, Celebrating 30 Years Crafts Cncl (V&A) 2005, A Homage to Ruth Duckworth (Garth Clark Gallery NY) 2005, Modern Pots (Dulwich Picture Gallery) 2005, European Ceramics Biennale (Musée de l'Outil et de la Pensee Ouvriere Troyes) 2005, One Piece – One Artist (Galerie Marianne Heller Germany) 2005, Contemporary Potters (Galerie Besson London) 2005, Puur Klei (Pottenbakkers Museum Holland) 2006, Collect (V&A Museum London) 2006, Classic and Contemporary Ceramics (Galerie Besson London) 2006 and 2007, SOFA (NY) 2007, British Studio Ceramics 20th Century Transformations (Bucks County Museum) 2008, Twenty Years – Twenty Pots (Galerie Besson London) 2008, SOFA Chicago 2008, Beautifully Crafted (Nat Glass Centre Gateshead) 2008, SOFA NY 2009, U-Tsu-Wa (21–21 Design Sight Tokyo) 2009, Contemporary Studio Ceramics: The Dauer Collection (Calif State Univ) 2009, The CellMark Collection (Röhsska Museet Göteborg) 2009, Collect (Saatchi Gallery) 2010, Blue Chip Exhibition (Liverpool Street Gallery Sydney) 2010, Contemporary British Studio Ceramics: The Grainer Collection (Mint Museum of Craft and Design NC) 2010, Collect (Saatchi Gallery) 2011, Danese (NY) 2011, Int Masterworks (Yufuku Tokyo) 2012, The Nature of Things (New Art Centre Roche Court Sculpture Park) 2012, FIHOC part two, Frank's International House of Ceramics (Frank Lloyd Gallery LA) 2012, Galerie Besson, Retrospective of a Lifelong Passion (Officine Saffi Ceramic Arts Milan) 2012, Friendship Forged in Fire: British Ceramics in America (American Museum of Ceramic Art California) 2013, LSG 2013 (Liverpool Street Gallery Sydney) 2013, Classic & Contemporary (Erskine, Hall & Coe London) 2013, From the World II (Gallery Hu Nagoya Japan) 2013, International Ceramics (Verkehr Museum Shizuoka Japan) 2013, 2nd International Ceramic Art Festival (Sasama Japan) 2013, The Collector's Exhibition (Liverpool Street Gallery Sydney) 2014, Small is Beautiful (Frank Lloyd Gallery Santa Monica) 2014, British Ceramics from Bernard Leach to New Generation (Museum of Contemporary Ceramic Art Shigaraki Japan) 2014, Toward a DESIGN MUSEUM JAPAN (21_21 Design Sight Tokyo) 2014, Vessels, The Spirit of Modern British Ceramics (Mashiko Museum of Ceramic Art Japan) 2015, London Art Fair (Erskine, Hall & Coe London) 2015, International Ceramics (Erskine, Hall & Coe London) 2015, Many a Slip (Marsden Woo Gallery London) 2015, Summer Exhbn (Erskine, Hall & Coe London) 2015; *Collections* work in numerous public collections incl: V&A London, Royal Scottish Museum, Glasgow Museums and Art Galleries, Los Angeles Co Museum of Art, Leeds City Art Gallery, Contemporary Art Society, Crafts Cncl Collection, The Sainsbury Centre (Norwich), Fitzwilliam Museum Cambridge, Hawkes Bay Art Gallery NZ, Peters Fndn London, Buckinghamshire Co Museum, MIMA Middlesbrough, Thamesdown Collection Swindon, Hove Museum and Art Gallery, Norwich Castle Museum, Peter Siemssen Fndn Germany, Carnegie Museum of Art Pittsburgh, Aberdeen Art Gallery, Nat Museum of Sweden Stockholm, CellMark Göteborg Sweden, Trustees Savings Bank Collection, Europa Kunst Handwerk Landesgerwerbeamt Stuttgart, Röhsska Konstslöjdmuseet Göteborg, Scripps Coll Claremont Calif, Norwich Castle Museum, Hove Museum and Art Gallery, Bellerive Museum Zurich, Tochigi Prefectural Museum of Fine Arts Japan, Kunstsammlungen der Veste Coburg Germany, Museum für Kunst und Gewerbe Hamburg, Fitzwilliam Museum Cambridge, Long Beach Museum of Art Calif, Minneapolis Inst of Art, Philadelphia Museum of Art, Metropolitan Museum of Art NY, Museum of Contemporary Ceramic Art Shigarak, Mashiko Museum of Ceramic Art Japan, Crocker Art Museum Sacramento, British Museum London; *Awards* David Gordon Meml Tst Prize 1979, Andrew Grant Travelling Scholarship 1979, Allen Lane Penguin Book Award 1983, Mathildenhöhe Award Rosenthal Germany 1984, Jugend Gestaltet Prize Munich 1985, Crafts Cncl Grant 1987, Br Cncl Exhibitions Grant 1991, Bayerischer Staatspreis 1998, Crafts Cncl Outward Missions Grant 2002, Guest Artist Inst of Ceramic Studies Shigaraki Ceramic Cultural Centre Japan 2014 and 2015; *Style*— Ms Jennifer Lee; ✉ website www.jenniferlee.co.uk

LEE, Jeremy Charles Roger Barnett; s of Lt Cdr Charles Alexander Barnett Lee, RNR (d 1982), of Phyllis Kathleen Mary, *née* Gunnell (d 1986); *b* 10 July 1944; *Educ* Bristol

Cathedral Sch; *m* 4 April 1972 (m dis 1983), Patricia Margaret Drake, *née* Coleridge; 3 da (Veryan Georgina Coleridge b 1974, Isobel Mary b 1977, Caroline Sybella b 1978); *Career* RM: 2 Lt 1962, Troop Cdr 40 Commando serving in Malaya and Sabah 1964–65, Lt 1965, Co Cdr Sultan's Armed Forces Muscat and Oman 1967–69, Adj (later Co Cdr) 40 Commando 1972–74, serving in NI and Cyprus (during Turkish invasion), Capt 1973, invalided 1976; admitted solicitor 1978; sr ptnr Symes Robinson and Lee Solicitors (Exeter, Crediton and Budleigh Salterton) 1983–2013 (now consultant); Cons Pty: area treas Crediton 1980–88, chm Coldridge Brushford and Nymet Rowland Branch 1981–, pres Central Devon Cons Assoc 2014–; Br Red Cross: chm 125 Ctee 1995–, chm Invitation Events Ctee 1996–2001, pres Devon Red Cross 2016–; dir Solicitors Benevolent Assoc; trustee Hudson Memorial Trust Univ of Oxford 2004–; rugby: Capt RM 1971, RN 1971, Exeter FC 1965–67 and 1969–72, Harlequins FC 1967; memb: Anglo Omani Soc, Law Soc; ASBAH's Conversationalist of the Year 1990; Sultan's Bravery Medal 1968, Br Red Cross Cert of Commendation, Br Red Cross Badge of Honour for Distinguished Service; *Recreations* tennis, walking, gardening, conversation; *Clubs* Army and Navy, LTA, Farmers; *Style—* Jeremy Lee, Esq; ✉ Frogbury, Coldridge, Crediton, Devon EX17 6BW (☎ 01363 83484)

LEE, Jeremy James; s of Norman Lee, and Eileen, *née* Neave; *b* 21 October 1963, Dundee; *Educ* HS of Dundee; *Career* chef and food writer; chef: Old Mansion House Hotel Auchterhouse Angus Scotland, Bibendum, Alastair Little, Euphorium, Blue Print Cafe; chef patron Quo Vadis; food writer Guardian Weekend, conslt ed Saveur; *Recreations* eating, reading, film, music; *Clubs* Groucho, Union, Quo Vadis; *Style—* Jeremy Lee, Esq; ✉ c/o David Higham Associates, Lower John Street, London W1

LEE, Jessica Katherine; da of John Anthony Lee, of Devon, and Rosemary, *née* Checkley; *b* 7 April 1976, Nottingham; *Educ* Loughborough HS, Royal Holloway Univ of London, Coll of Law London (CPE); *Career* called to the Bar 2000; barr 42 Bedford Row London 2001–08, barr St Mary's Chambers Nottingham 2008–10; MP (Cons) Erewash 2010–15; FIBA 2003; *Clubs* Carlton; *Style—* Miss Jessica Lee; ✉ c/o Kathryn Clarkson, Jessica Lee MP's Office, House of Commons, London SW1A 0AA (☎ 020 7219 7067, e-mail kathryn.clarkson@parliament.uk)

LEE, Prof John Anthony; s of Cecil John Lee (d 1977), of Southsea, Hants, and Phyllis Gwendoline, *née* Fry (d 2004); *b* 18 March 1942; *Educ* The Portsmouth GS, Univ of Sheffield (BSc, PhD); *m* 17 April 1965, Barbara Lee, da of Thomas Harold Wright (d 1996); 2 s (Richard b 1968, Peter b 1971); *Career* Univ of Manchester: asst lectr in botany 1967, lectr 1970, sr lectr 1979, prof of environmental biology 1988–94, head Dept of Environmental Biology 1986–93; Univ of Sheffield: prof of environmental biology 1994–2005 (emeritus 2005–), chm Dept of Animal and Plant Sciences 1995–2002, Dean Faculty of Science 2002–05; dir Univ of Cumbria 2014–; ed The Journal of Ecology 1983–90, author of many scientific papers; pres: Br Ecological Soc 1996–97, Int Ecology Soc 1998–2009 (vice-pres 1989–95); memb: Soc for Experimental Biology, Nat Tst Cncl 1999–2009; hon memb Br Ecological Soc 2011; *Books* Yorkshire Dales (2015); *Recreations* theatre, Portsmouth FC, hill walking; *Style—* Prof John Lee; ✉ Department of Animal and Plant Sciences, PO Box 601, The University of Sheffield, Sheffield S10 2UQ (☎ 0114 222 0089, e-mail j.a.lee@sheffield.ac.uk)

LEE, Prof Mark Howard; s of Clifford Howard Lee, of Worcester, and Peggy Alice, *née* Osborne; *b* 9 April 1944; *Educ* Univ of Wales (BSc, MSc), Univ of Nottingham (PhD); *m* 24 July 1971, Elizabeth Anne, da of Rev Frank Andrew Willmot (d 1976), of London, 2 s (Matthew Peter Howard b 13 Oct 1976, Joseph Jonathan b 28 March 1979), 1 da (Bethan Louisa b 3 Jan 1984); *Career* lectr City of Leicester Poly 1969–74, prof of intelligent systems Univ of Wales Aberystwyth 1987– (lectr 1974–85, sr lectr 1985–87), visiting prof Univ of Auckland NZ 1988; FRSA, FIET, CEng, FLSW; *Books* Intelligent Robotics (1989), Intelligent Assembly Systems (ed with J J Rowland, 1995); *Recreations* mountaineering; *Style—* Prof Mark Lee; ✉ Department of Computer Science, Aberystwyth University, Aberystwyth, Ceredigion SY23 3DB

LEE, Michael James Arthur; s of Brian Arthur Frederick Lee (d 1983), of Newton Abbot, Devon, and Rachel Dorothy Strange, *née* Wickham (d 1992); *b* 22 June 1942; *Educ* Blundell's, Univ of Durham (LLB); *m* 1, 4 March 1974 (m dis 1984), Judith Mary, da of Humphrey David Oliver of Alresford Hants; 1 da (Henrietta Victoria b 4 Oct 1976); m 2, 18 March 1993, Caroline Mary, da of Duncan Hamilton (d 1994), of Marston Magna, Somerset; 1 da (Olivia Grace b 28 Feb 1994); *Career* admitted slr 1966, called to the Bar 2001; articled clerk Lovell White and King 1963–66 (asst slr 1966–67); legal asst New Scotland Yard 1967–69; Norton Rose: asst slr 1970–73, subsequently ptnr, sr litigation ptnr and managing ptnr Paris Office; currently barr 20 Essex Street; memb Int Bar Assoc; FCIArb; *Recreations* sailing, skiing; *Clubs* Tanglin (Singapore); *Style—* Michael Lee, Esq

LEE, Paul Anthony; DL; s of Wilfred Lee (d 1970), of Manchester, and Anne, *née* Molyneux; *b* 26 January 1946; *Educ* Central GS Manchester, Clare Coll Cambridge (MA, LLM); *m* 16 Sept 1977, Elisabeth Lindsay, da of Maj Geoffrey Robert Taylor, of Manchester; 2 s (Jonathan b 1980, William b 1985), 1 da (Antonia b 1983); *Career* admitted slr 1970; Addleshaw Goddard (formerly Addleshaw Booth & Co): ptnr 1973–, managing ptnr 1991–97, sr ptnr 1997–2010; dir: Leaf Properties 1986–, Barlows plc 1997–, Northern Ballet Theatre Ltd 1997–2004, Yorkshire Building Society 1998–2007 (vice-chm 2005–06), Royal Exchange Theatre Manchester 1985–2015 (chair 1998–2015), North West Business Leadership Team 2007– (dep chair 2007–09, chair 2009–12); non-exec dir Dewhurst Torvell & Co Ltd 2012–; chm: Bd of Govrs Chethams Sch of Music 1989–2013 (chair 1991–2005), NW Region CBI 1998–2000 (vice-chm 1997–98 and 2000–01, chm 1998–2000) NW Expansion Ctee The Prince's Tst 2001–06, memb Bd CBI 2004–12; chair Horserace Betting Levy Bd 2009–; govr Royal Northern Coll of Music 1991–2006, memb Bd of Govrs Univ of Manchester 2010–; feoffee Chethams Hosp and Library 1990 (chm of Feoffees 2005–); chair Opera North 2014–; High Sheriff Greater Manchester 2014–15; *Recreations* the arts, travel, tennis, wine, horse racing; *Clubs* Savile, Garrick, Real Tennis and Racquets (Manchester), Turf; *Style—* Paul A Lee, Esq, DL; ✉ Riverbank Cottage, 2 Stanton Avenue, W Didsbury, Manchester M20 2PG

LEE, Dr Phillip James; MP; *b* 1970, Bucks; *Educ* King's Coll London, Keble Coll Oxford, Imperial Coll London; *Career* former doctor; MP (Cons) Bracknell 2010–; *Style—* Dr Phillip Lee, MP; ✉ House of Commons, Westminster, London SW1A 0AA (e-mail leepa@parliament.uk)

LEE, Robin John; s of John Johnson Lee, of Dublin, and Adelaide Elizabeth, *née* Hayes; *b* 23 October 1952; *Educ* Wesley Coll Dublin, Trinity Coll Dublin (BA, MB BCh, MA, MD); *m* 23 Sept 1978, (Sylvia) Jane Lucette, da of Ernest Herbert Bodell, of Dublin; 2 da (Sarah b 31 Jan 1981, Victoria b 10 Feb 1992), 2 s (Charles, Christopher (twins) b 25 Dec 1982); *Career* sr registrar in otolaryngology: Royal Victoria Eye and Ear Hosp Dublin 1985, Federated Dublin Vol Hops 1986, Beaumont Hosp Dublin 1988; res fell Dept of Otolaryngology Head and Neck Surgery Univ of Iowa 1987, conslt ENT surgn Kettering Gen Hosp 1988–; memb Ctee Young Consultants in Otolaryngology Head and Neck Survery 1989–94; memb: BMA 1988, RSM 1988, Br Assoc of Otolaryngologists 1988, Irish Otolaryngological Soc 1983; FRCSI 1984, FRCS (ad eundem) 1999; *Style—* Robin Lee, Esq; ✉ Kettering General Hospital, Rothwell Road, Kettering, Northamptonshire NN16 8UZ (☎ 01536 492000 ext 2274, e-mail robin.lee@kgh.nhs.uk)

LEE, Simon Philip Guy; s of Philip Lee (d 2003), and Janet, *née* Laverty; *b* 4 March 1961, Reading, Berks; *Educ* Tonbridge Sch, Univ of Leeds (BA); *m* 1 Aug 1987, Fiona, *née* Andrews; 3 da (Rebecca b 2 Nov 1992, Alice b 23 Feb 1995, Beatrice b 12 Dec 1996); *Career* md NatWest Home Mortgage Corp USA 1993–95, md NatWest US Retail Banking 1995–96, chief exec NatWest Offshore 1996–98, dir of wholesale markets NatWest Gp 1998–2000, chief exec Affinitas Ltd 2001–03; RSA Insurance Gp plc: chief exec int businesses 2003–11, exec dir 2007–13, gp chief exec 2011–13; int advsr Fairfax Financial 2014–, global advsr SATMAP Inc 2015–; non-exec dir: Conister Tst plc 2002–06, TIA Technol 2014–; chm Osirium Ltd 2015–; dir Hilden Oaks Sch Tst Ltd 2001–09, chm Hospice in the Weald 2014–; *Recreations* cricket, golf, skiing, reading; *Clubs* Yellowhammers CC, Dragons CC, Chessmen CC, Royal Ashdown Forest Golf; *Style—* Simon Lee, Esq; ✉ Barnes Street House, Three Elm Lane, Golden Green, Tonbridge, Kent TN11 0LB (☎ 01732 851493)

LEE, Stewart; s of Graham Lee (d 2005), and Maureen Kemp, *née* Davis; *b* 5 April 1968, Wellington; *Educ* Solihull Sch, St Edmund Hall Oxford (BA); *m* 30 Nov 2006, Bridget, *née* Christie; 1 s (Luke Stagger b 24 April 2007); *Career* comedian, writer and dir; stand-up comedian 1987–, perfs incl Edinburgh Fringe (Tap Water Award 2004) and Montreal, Adelaide, Melbourne (Wood of Joy Award 2000) and Auckland festivals; contrib Culture Section Sunday Times 1995–; dir and co-writer Jerry Springer: The Opera (successively Battersea Arts Centre, Edinburgh Festival, RNT, Cambridge Theatre London and BBC2) 2001–05 (awards incl: Best Musical Evening Standard Theatre Awards 2003, Best Musical Olivier Awards 2004); television appearances incl: Stewart Lee's Comedy Vehicle (BBC) 2011 (Best Comedy Entertainment Prog and Best Male Television Comic Br Comedy Awards 2011, Best Comedy Prog 2012); Chortle Outstanding Contribution to Comedy Award 2006; memb: Nat Secular Soc, Br Humanist Assoc, Friends of Arthur Machen; *Books* The Perfect Fool (novel, 2001); contrib: Sit Down Comedy (2003), That Which Is Not Said (2006), Perverted by Language (2007), The Flash (2007); *Recreations* walking; *Style—* Stewart Lee, Esq; ✉ website www.stewartlee.co.uk

LEE, Prof Tak Hong; CBE (2012); s of Ming Lee (d 1991), and Maria, *née* Tseng; *b* 26 January 1951; *Educ* Marlborough, Clare Coll Cambridge (MA, MB BChir, MD, ScD, Eton Fives half blue), Guy's Hosp Med Sch; *m* 25 Aug 1980 (m dis 2010), Andrée, *née* Ma; 1 s (Adrian b 11 Aug 1984), 1 da (Jacqueline b 23 Feb 1987); *Career* clinical lectr Nat Heart and Lung Inst Brompton Hosp London 1980–82, research fell Harvard Med Sch 1982–84; UMDS Guy's Hosp London: lectr and hon sr registrar 1984–85, sr lectr and hon conslt physician 1985–88; Asthma UK prof of allergy and respiratory medicine KCL and hon conslt physician Dept of Asthma, Allergy and Respiratory Science Guy's Hosp London until 2011, dir MRC-Asthma UK Centre in Allergic Mechanisms of Asthma 2005–2011, dir Allergy Centre Hong Kong Sanatorium and Hosp 2012–; visiting prof: Univ of Calif San Diego 1989, Lion's Club of Tai Ping Shan Dept of Med Univ of Hong Kong 1990, RSM Fndn 1991, Woolcock Inst of Sydney Univ of Sydney 2009–; Pfizer visiting prof: Nat Jewish Hosp Denver 1997, Harvard Med Sch 2002 and 2006; visiting scholar Dept of Pharmacology Univ of Sydney 2009, hon clinical prof Univ of Hong Kong 2012–17; hon sec Clinical Immunology and Allergy Section RSM 1988–91; chm Jt Ctee on Immunology and Allergy RCP/RCPath 2000–04; memb: Nat Task Force on Asthma 1990– (chm Therapy Working Sub-Ctee 1991–96, chm Therapy Sub-Ctee 1996), Int Scientific Bd Pharmacia Allergy Research Fndn 1992–94, Specialist Register of Referees Hong Kong Univ and Polys Grants Ctee 1993–, Cncl Collegium Internationale Allergologicum 1994–97, JCHMT SAC for Clinical Immunology and Allergy RCP 1996–2000, Med Sub-Ctee Univ Grants Ctee Hong Kong 1997–2003, memb Cncl KCL 2010–11, memb Panel of Conslts Univ Health Service Univ of Hong Kong 2014–; MRC: memb Physiological Med and Infections Bd 1995–99, memb Health Services and Public Health Research Bd 1996–99; Nat Asthma Campaign: memb Research Ctee 1988–91 (chm 1990–91), memb Cncl 1990–91, vice-pres 1999–, chm Consultation on Basic Research Strategy 2001; advsr for allergic disorders Jt Formulary Ctee BMA and Pharmaceutical Soc of GB 1988–, advsr in allergy SE Thames Regn RCPath 1997– (advsr for SW Thames Regn 1998–); memb Editorial Bd: Clinical Immunotherapeutics 1993–96, Clinical and Experimental Allergy, Jl of Allergy and Clinical Immunology, Immunology, Allergology Int; Fogarty Int Research Fellowship Nat Insts of Health USA 1982, MRC Travelling Fellowship 1982, Saltwell Research Fellowship RCP 1983, T V James Fellowship BMA 1986; runner-up European UCB Research Award 1987, Doctor of the Year Research Award BUPA Med Fndn 1989, Pharmacia Int Scientific Research Award 1990; pres Br Soc for Allergy and Clinical Immunology 1996–99; memb: BSACI (pres 1996–99, memb Cncl 1988–2003), Br Thoracic Soc (memb Cncl 1994–98, memb Research Ctee 1995–98), Br Soc for Immunology, BMA, Med Research Soc, American Thoracic Soc, American Assoc of Immunologists, American Acad of Allergy and Immunology, Collegium Internationale Allergologicum; pres Hong Kong Inst of Allergy 2014–16; fell Hong Kong Coll of Physicians 1987, fell American Acad of Allergy, Asthma and Immunology 1989, FRCP 1989, FRCPath 1997, FMedSci 2000, FKC 2007; *Recreations* photography, tennis, swimming, flyfishing, golf, travel; *Clubs* RAC, Athenaeum, Hong Kong Jockey, Shek O Golf and Country, China, Chariot; *Style—* Prof Tak Lee, CBE; ✉ Allergy Centre, 9th Floor Li Shu Pui Block, HK Sanatorium and Hospital, 2 Village Road, Happy Valley, Hong Kong (☎ 00852 2835 8430, fax 00852 2892 7565, e-mail thlee@hksh.com)

LEE, Prof Thomas Alexander (Tom); s of Thomas Henderson Lee (d 1970), of Edinburgh, and Dorothy Jane Paton, *née* Norman (d 1990); *b* 18 May 1941; *Educ* Melville Coll Edinburgh, ICAS, Univ of Edinburgh, Inst of Taxation, Univ of Strathclyde (MSc, D Litt); *m* 14 Sept 1963, Ann Margaret, da of John Brown (d 1971), of Edinburgh; 1 s (Richard Thomas b 19 July 1968), 1 da (Sarah Ann (Mrs Birchall) b 17 August 1965); *Career* auditor J Douglas Henderson & Co and Peat Marwick Mitchell 1959–66, lectr Univ of Strathclyde 1966–69, lectr Univ of Edinburgh 1969–73, prof Univ of Liverpool 1973–76, prof of accountancy and finance Univ of Edinburgh 1976–90, Culverhouse endowed chair in accountancy Univ of Alabama 1991–2001 (now Culverhouse emeritus prof), hon prof of accounting Deakin Univ 1994–2001, hon prof of accounting Univ of Dundee 1995–2007, visiting prof of accounting Univ of Newcastle-upon-Tyne 2003–, hon prof of accounting and corporate governance Univ of St Andrews 2006–16 (lectr in accounting and corporate governance 2007–08); memb Exec Ctee AUTA (BAA) 1971–84, ed AUTA News Review 1971–75; ICAS: dir accounting and auditing res 1983–84, memb Cncl 1989–90, memb several ctees; memb Cncl Br Fin and Accounting Assoc 1973–77; ed Int Jl of Auditing 1995–2006, assoc ed Br Accounting Review 1993–97; memb Editorial Bd: Jl of Business Fin and Accounting 1976–82, Accounting Review 1977–80, Accounting and Business Research 1981–, Accounting, Auditing and Accountability Jl 1994–, Accounting Historians Jl 1995–, Accounting in the Public Interest 2000–; tstee Acad of Accounting Historians 1993–96 (vice-pres 1996–98, pres 1998–99, life memb 2010–); Burnum Distinguished Faculty Award Univ of Alabama 1998, Lifetime Achievement Award Br Accounting Assoc 2005, Accounting Hall of Fame Br Accounting Assoc 2005, Business Faculty Hall of Fame Univ of Alabama 2008; elder: Church of Scotland 1984–, Presbyterian Church USA 1992–; memb Academic Advsy Ctee ASC 1987–90; memb: ICAS 1964, IT 1966, AAA 1969, AAH 1974; *Books* incl: Company Auditing (1972), Income and Value (1974), Company Financial Reporting (1976), Cash Flow Accounting (1984), Towards a Theory and Practice of Cash Flow Accounting (1986), The Closure of the Accounting Profession (1989), Corporate Audit Theory (1992), Shaping the Accountancy Profession (1995), Seekers of Truth: The Founders of Modern Public Accountancy (2006), Scottish Chartered Accountants and the American Public Accountancy Profession (2006), Financial Reporting and Corporate Governance (2006); *Recreations* road running, cricket, history; *Style—* Prof Tom Lee

L

LEE OF TRAFFORD, Baron (Life Peer UK 2006), of Bowdon in the County of Cheshire; John Robert Louis Lee; DL (Gtr Manchester 1995); s of Basil Lee (d 1983), and Miriam Lee (d 1982); *b* 21 June 1942, Trafford, Gtr Manchester; *Educ* William Hulme GS Manchester; *m* 1975, (Anne) Monique, *née* Bakirgian; 2 da (Elspeth, Deborah); *Career* CA 1964, Henry Cooke Lumsden & Co Manchester stockbrokers 1964–66, founding dir Chancery Consolidated Ltd investment bankers 1974; MP (Cons): Nelson and Colne 1979–83, Pendle 1983–92 (Parly candidate (Cons): Manchester Moss Side Oct 1974, Pendle 1992); jt sec Cons Backbench Industry Ctee 1979–81, PPS to Min of State for Industry 1981–83, PPS to Sec of State for Trade and Industry 1983, Parly under sec of state MOD 1983–86, Parly under sec of state Dept of Employment 1986, min for tourism 1987–89, memb Select Ctee on Defence 1990–92; former Lib Dem spokesman on defence and tourism and asst whip House of Lords, memb Jt Ctee on the Nat Security Strategy 2010–14, chair All Pty Tourism Ctee; non-exec chm: Country Holidays Ltd 1989, Wellington Market plc 2006–; non-exec dir: Paterson Zochonis (UK) Ltd 1975–76, Paterson Zochonis plc 1990–99, Emerson Devpts (Hldgs) 2000–; chm Assoc of Leading Visitor Attractions (AVLA) 1990–, chair Museum of Science and Industry Manchester 1992–99, memb English Tourist Bd 1992–99; chair Christie Hosp NHS Tst 1992–98; Armed Forces Parl Tst Gvnr; chm tstees Withington Girls Sch; memb Refreshment Ctee House of Lords 2015–; vice-chm NW Conciliation Ctee Race Relations Bd 1976–77, chm Nat Youth Bureau 1980–83, vice-chair Lighter Evenings Experiment Gp 2006–; High Sheriff Gtr Manchester 1998–99; FCA; *Publications* Portfolio Man (2005), How to Make a Million – Slowly (2014); *Recreations* golf, stock market, salmon fishing, antiques; *Style*— The Lord Lee of Trafford, DL, FCA; ✉ House of Lords, London SW1A 0PW (☎ 020 7219 3949, e-mail leej@parliament.uk)

LEE-JONES, Christine; DL (Gtr Manchester), JP (Trafford 2008); da of George Pickup (d 1991), of Bolton; *b* 13 June 1948, Leeds; *Educ* Lawnswood HS Leeds, Univ of Wales (BEd), Univ of London (MA, Advanced Dip), Open Univ (Advanced Dip); *m* Aug 1972, Denys Lee-Jones, s of Robert Lee-Jones; 1 da (Amy b 31 Oct 1981); *Career* teacher tutor Inst of Educn Univ of London 1978–79, primary sch teacher Bethnal Green 1970–71, head of religious studies Archbishop Temple Sch Lambeth 1971–74, head of religious studies Archbishop Michael Ramsey Sch Camberwell 1974–82, sr lectr Woolwich Coll 1983–86, vice-princ Leyton Sixth Form Coll 1986–91, princ Eccles Sixth Form Coll Salford 1991–98, headmistress Manchester HS for Girls 1998–2008, educnl conslt 2009–; memb Cncl GSA, jt chair GSA/HMC Professional Devpt Ctee 2008; memb Gen Assembly Univ of Manchester (formerly memb Ct Victoria Univ of Manchester), govr Univ of Manchester 2010; non-exec dir Walton Centre for Neurology and Neurosurgery NHS Tst 2008–14; tstee: Gtr Manchester Police High Sheriff Tst 2011–, Genesis Breast Cancer Prevention Charity 2012–; volunteer Breast Cancer Care 2014; High Sheriff Gtr Manchester 2011–12; memb Manchester Literary and Philosphical Soc; FRSA 1999; *Recreations* theatre, travel, wine, tennis; *Style*— Mrs Christine Lee-Jones, DL; ✉ e-mail leejones13@me.com

LEE-POTTER, Dr Jeremy Patrick; s of Air Marshal Sir Patrick Lee Potter, KBE, MD (d 1983), of Wittersham, Kent, and Audrey Mary, *née* Pollock (d 2007); *b* 30 August 1934; *Educ* Epsom Coll, Guy's Hosp Univ of London (MB BS, DCP); *m* 26 Oct 1957, Lynda (d 2004), da of Norman Higginson, of Culcheth, Lancs; 2 da (Emma Clare, Charlotte Brodie (Charlie)), 1 s (Adam Brunton); *Career* Med Branch RAF 1960–68: sr specialist in pathology RAF Inst of Pathology and Tropical Med 1965–68, i/c Dept of Haematology 1966–68 (Sqdn Ldr); lectr in haematology St George's Hosp Med Sch Univ of London 1968–69, conslt haematologist Poole Hosp NHS Tst 1969–95; BMA: dep chm Central Conslts and Specialists Ctee 1988–90, chm Cncl 1990–93, vice-pres 1998–, chm Audit Ctee 1999–2002; memb: Standing Med Advsy Ctee 1990–93, GMC 1994–99 (dep chm Professional Conduct Ctee 1996–99), King's Fund Organisational Audit 1993–95, Clinical Disputes Forum 1998–99, Advsy Gp Cncl for Registration of Forensic Practitioners 1998–99; Engrg Cncl: memb Senate 2000–02, memb Bd for Engrs' Regulation 2001–02; pres Old Epsomian Club 2004–05; MRCS, LRCP 1958, DTM&H (Eng) 1964, FRCPath 1979; *Books* A Damn Bad Business: The NHS Deformed (1997); *Recreations* natural history, print, modern art, golf; *Clubs* Athenaeum, Parkstone Golf; *Style*— Dr Jeremy Lee-Potter; ✉ Icen House, Stoborough, Wareham, Dorset BH20 5AN (☎ 01929 556307)

LEECH, Prof Geoffrey Neil; s of Charles Richard Leech (d 1973), of Bredon, Worcs, and Dorothy Eileen Leech (d 1967); *b* 16 January 1936; *Educ* Tewkesbury GS, UCL (BA, MA, PhD); *m* 29 July 1961, Frances Anne, da of George Berman, MBE (d 1985), of Lancaster; 1 s (Thomas b 1964), 1 da (Camilla b 1967); *Career* Nat Serv SAC RAF 1954–56; Harkness fell MIT 1964–65, lectr English UCL 1965–69 (asst lectr 1962–64), visiting prof Brown Univ RI 1972, emeritus prof Lancaster Univ 2001– (reader in English language 1969–74, prof of linguistics and modern English language 1974–2001); memb: Cncl The Philological Soc 1979–83 and 1996–99, English Teaching Advsy Ctee The Br Cncl 1983–91, Academia Europaea 1990–, Norwegian Acad of Science and Letters 1993–; hon prof Beijing Univ of Foreign Studies China 1994–; hon fell UCL, hon fell Univ of Lancaster; Fil Dr Lund Univ Sweden 1987, DLitt Univ of Wolverhampton, DLitt Lancaster Univ; FBA 1987, hon doctorate Charles Univ Prague; *Books* English in Advertising (1966), Towards a Semantic Description of English (1969), A Linguistic Guide to English Poetry (1969), Meaning and the English Verb (1971), A Grammar of Contemporary English (with Randolph Quirk Sidney Greenbaum and Jan Svartvik, 1972), Semantics (1974), A Communicative Grammar of English (with Jan Svartvik, 1975), Explorations in Semantics and Pragmatics (1980), Studies in English Linguistics: For Randolph Quirk (ed with Sidney Greenbaum and Jan Svartvik, 1980), Style in Fiction: A Linguistic Introduction to English Fictional Prose (with Michael H Short, 1981), Semantics: The Study of Meaning (1981), Principles of Pragmatics (1983), A Comprehensive Grammar of the English Language (with Randolph Quirk Sidney Greenbaum and Jan Svartvik, 1985), An A-Z of English Grammar and Usage (1989), Spoken English on Computer (ed with Greg Myers and Jenny Thomas, 1995), Corpus Annotation (ed with Roger Garside and Anthony McEnery, 1997), Longman Grammar of Spoken and Written English (with Douglas Biber, Stig Johansson, Susan Conrad and Edward Finegan, 1999), An A-Z of English Grammar and Usage (with Benita Cruickshank and Roz Ivani?, 2001), Longman Student Grammar of Spoken and Written English (with Douglas Biber and Susan Conrad, 2002), Word Frequencies in Written and Spoken English (with Paul Rayson and Andrew Wilson, 2001), A Glossary of English Grammar (2006), Language in Literature: Style and Foregrounding (2008), Change in Contemporary English: A Grammatical Study (with Marianne Hundt, Christian Mair and Nicholas Smith, 2009), Selected Works on Applied Linguistics of Geoffrey Leech (2011), The Verb Phrase in English: Investigating Recent Language Change with Corpora (ed with Bas Aarts, Joanne Close and Sean Wallis, 2013), The Pragmatics of Politeness (2014); *Recreations* chamber music, playing the piano and the church organ, fell walking; *Style*— Prof Geoffrey Leech, FBA; ✉ Department of Linguistics and English Language, Lancaster University, Bailrigg, Lancaster LA1 4YL (☎ 01524 593036)

LEECH, John; *Educ* Manchester Grammar, Loreto Coll, Brunel Univ; *Career* cncllr (Lib Dem) Manchester City Cncl 1998–2008, MP (Lib Dem) Manchester Withington 2005–15; *Style*— John Leech, Esq; ✉ House of Commons, London SW1A 0AA

LEEDS, Archbishop (RC) 2012–; Most Rev Arthur Roche; s of Arthur Francis Roche, and Frances, *née* Day; *b* 6 March 1950; *Educ* Christleton Hall Chester, English Coll Valladolid Spain, Pontifical Gregorian Univ Rome (STL); *Career* ordained priest 1975, asst priest Holy Rood Barnsley 1975–77, sec to Bishop William Gordon Wheeler 1977–82, vice-chllr Dio of Leeds 1979–89, co-ordinator of Papal visit to York 1982, asst priest Leeds Cathedral 1982–89, fin admin Dio of Leeds 1986–90, parish priest St Wilfrid's Leeds 1989–91, spiritual dir Ven English Coll Rome 1992–96, gen sec Catholic Bishops' Conf of England and Wales 1996–2001, aux bishop (RC) of Westminster 2001–02, coadjutor bishop of Leeds 2002–04, bishop of Leeds 2004–12, appointed secretary to the Congregation of Divine Worship and Discipline of the Sacraments Vatican City 2012–; chm Int Cmmn for English in the Liturgy, chm Dept of Christian Life and Worship and memb Standing Ctee Catholic Bishops' Conf of England and Wales; hon ecumenical canon: Wakefield Cathedral 2006, Bradford Cathedral 2008; *Recreations* gardening, walking, travel; *Style*— The Most Rev the Archbishop Roche; ✉ Congregazione per il Culto Divino e la Disciplina de Sacramenti, 00120 Città del Vaticano, Italy

LEEDS, Bishop of (RC) 2014–; Rt Rev Marcus Stock; *Educ* Keble Coll Oxford (MA), Pontifical Gregorian Univ Rome (STL); *Career* asst priest Parish of our Lady and St Brigid Northfield 1988–91; parish priest: Parish of St Birinus Dorchester-on-Thames 1991–94, Parish of St Peter Bloxwich 1994–99, Parish of Sared Heart and St Teresa Coleshill 1999–2009; actg dir Catholic Educn Service 2011–13; gen sec Catholic Bishops' Conference of England and Wales 2009–14; *Books* Christ at the Centre (2005); *Style*— The Rt Rev the Bishop of Leeds

LEEDS, Lord Bishop of 2014–; Rt Rev Nicholas (Nick) Baines; s of Frank Baines, and Beryl Baines; *b* 13 November 1957, Liverpool; *Educ* Holt Comp Sch Liverpool, Univ of Bradford (BA), Trinity Coll Bristol (BA); *m* Linda; 2 s (Richard b 1981, Andrew b 1988), 1 da (Melanie b 1984); *Career* linguist specialist GCHQ Cheltenham 1980–84; asst curate St Thomas Kendal 1987–91, assoc min Holy Trinity Leicester 1991–92, vicar of Rothley 1992–2000, rural dean of Goscote 1995–2000, archdeacon of Lambeth 2000–03, bishop of Croydon 2003–11, bishop of Bradford 2011–14; non-exec dir The Ecclesiastical Insurance Gp 2002–10; memb Gen Synod C of E 1995–2005, chair Meissen Cmmn, chair Sandford St Martin Tst; memb House of Lords 2014–; Hon Doctorate Univ of Bradford 2013, hon fell Bradford Coll 2014, Hon DTheol Friedrich Schiller Univ Jena (Germany) 2014; *Books* Hungry for Hope? (1991, 2 edn 2007), Speedbumps and Potholes (2003), Jesus and People Like Us (2004), Marking Time (2005), Am Rande Bemerkt (2007), Scandal of Grace (2008), Finding Faith (2008), In höchsten Tönen (2009), Why wish you a merry Christmas? (2009); *Recreations* music, reading, sport, blogging; *Style*— The Rt Rev the Lord Bishop of Leeds; ✉ Hollin House, Weetwood Avenue, Leeds, West Yorkshire LS16 5NG (☎ 0113 284 4300, e-mail bishop.nick@westyorkshiredales.anglican.org, website www.westyorkshiredales.anglican.org, blog http://nickbaines.wordpress.com, Twitter @NickBaines)

LEEK, Anthony Thomas (Tony); s of Thomas Henry Howard Leek (d 1987), and Mary, *née* Curtis (d 2003); *b* 15 February 1947; *Educ* Forest Sch, Univ of Southampton (LLB); *Career* admitted slr 1975; ptnr: Austin Ryder & Co 1977–86, DLA Piper UK LLP (formerly DLA) 1987–; memb Law Soc; *Recreations* cricket, theatre, music; *Style*— Tony Leek, Esq; ✉ DLA Piper UK LLP, 3 Noble Street, London EC2V 7EE (☎ 020 7796 6216, fax 020 7796 6666)

LEEMING, His Hon Judge Ian; QC (1988); s of Flt Lt Thomas Leeming (d 1981), of Preston, Lancs, and Lilian, *née* Male (d 1993); *b* 10 April 1948; *Educ* Catholic Coll Preston, Univ of Manchester (LLB); *m* 26 May 1973, Linda Barbara, da of Harold Cook, of Walton-le-Dale, Lancs; 2 da (Lucinda b 1976, Angela b 1981), 1 s (Charles b 1985); *Career* called to the Bar Gray's Inn 1970, Lincoln's Inn (ad eundem); in practice at the Chancery and Commercial Bars Northern Circuit 1971–2006, recorder 1989–2006 (asst recorder 1986–89), circuit judge (Western Circuit) 2006–11 and (Northern Circuit) 2011–; actg deemster IOM 1998; legal advsr to GMC 2002; fndr memb Northern Soc of Cons Lawyers (vice-chm 1985–89), chm Heaton Cons Assoc 1986–88, lectr in law Univ of Manchester 1972–76; co dir; fell Soc for Advanced Legal Studies 1999; chartered arbitrator; FCIArb; *Publications* ed Equity and Trust chapters of Butterworths Law of Limitation; *Recreations* reading, walking, sports cars, family; *Style*— His Hon Judge Leeming, QC; ✉ Preston Crown Court, Openshaw Place, Ringway, Preston PR1 2LL

LEEMING, His Hon Judge Michael Peter George; *Career* called to the Bar 1983; asst recorder then recorder 2000, circuit judge (Northern Circuit) 2012–; *Style*— His Hon Judge Michael Leeming; ✉ Manchester Crown Court, Courts of Justice, Crown Square, Manchester M3 3FL

LEES, Prof Andrew John; s of late Lewis Lees, of Harrogate, N Yorks, and Muriel, *née* Wadsworth; *b* 27 September 1947, St Helens, Merseyside; *Educ* Roundhay Sch, Royal London Hosp Med Coll (MD); *m* 21 July 1973, Juana Luisa Pulin Perez-Lopez, da of late Juan Luis Pulin, of Geneva, Switzerland; 1 s (George Luis b 9 April 1975), 1 da (Nathalie Jasmine b 23 June 1976); *Career* prof of neurology Nat Hosp for Neurology and Neurosurgery and UCL Hosp; emeritus dir: Reta Lila Weston Inst of Neurological Studies, Sara Koe PSP Centre; visiting prof: Univ of Liverpool, UFMG Brazil, Hosp Sao Rafaele Salvador Bahia Brazil; past pres Int Movement Disorder Soc, former co-ed-in-chief Movement Disorders, former memb Cncl Acad of Medical Science; Lifetime Achievement Award American Acad of Neurology 2008, Assoc of Br Neurologists Medallist 2015; elected memb Acad of Nat de Medicina Brazil; FMedSci, FRCP; *Books* Parkinson's Disease – The Facts (1982), Tics and Related Disorders (1985), Ray of Hope – The Ray Kennedy Story (1993), The Hurricane Port A Social History of Liverpool (2011), Exploring the Victorian Brain, A Biography of Sir William Gowers (jtly, 2012), Liverpool, The Hurricane Port (2012), Alzheimer's, The Silent Plague (2012), Mentored by a Madman; The William Boroughs Experiment (2016); *Recreations* frequent visitor to Brazil, memb and hon med advsr to Liverpool FC; *Clubs* Groucho, London Library; *Style*— Prof Andrew Lees; ✉ Reta Lila Weston Institute of Neurological Studies, Institute of Neurology, UCL, 1 Wakefield Street, London WC1N 1PJ (☎ 020 7679 4246, fax 020 7278 4993, e-mail andrew.lees@ucl.ac.uk, Twitter @AJLees)

LEES, Prof Peter; CBE (1994); s of Harold Edward Lees (d 1943), of Farnworth, Lancs, and Gladys, *née* Miller (d 2003); *b* 15 July 1940; *Educ* Canon Slade GS, Chelsea Coll of Sci and Technol (BPharm), RVC London (PhD, DSc); *m* 3 Aug 1968, Mary Hogg, da of John Moffat; 1 s (Matthew Peter b 9 June 1975), 1 da (Katherine Mary b 30 March 1978); *Career* Royal Veterinary Coll: asst lectr in pharmacology Dept of Physiology 1964–66, lectr in vet pharmacology Dept of Physiology 1966–76, reader in vet pharmacology 1976–88, prof of vet pharmacology 1988–2005, head Dept of Vet Basic Scis 1991–96, dep princ and vice-princ for teaching 1997–2001, emeritus prof of vet pharmacology 2005–; ed Jl of Vet Pharmacology and Therapeutics 1983–93 and 2003–06; memb: Vet Products Ctee 1978–98, Mgmnt Ctee Home of Rest for Horses 1988–98, Panel Research Assessment Exercise (Agric, Food Sci and Vet Sci) 2001–05 and 2005–08; Peter Wilson Bequest Lecture Univ of Edinburgh 1989, Bogan Meml Lecture Univ of Cambridge 1990, Sir Frederick Smith Meml Lecture Br Equine Vet Assoc 1993; Ciba-Geigy Prize for res in animal health 1985, Open Award Equine Vet Jl 1985 and 1998, Victory Medal Central Vet Soc 1987, George Fleming Prize Br Vet Jl 1987, Amoroso Award Br Small Animal Vet Assoc 1988, Jl of Vet Pharmacology and Therapeutics Prize 1999, Fifth Schering Plough Animal Health and World Equine Vetinary Assoc Award for Applied Res 2001, Selbourne Award Assoc of Vet Teachers and Research Workers 2004, Br Pharmacological Soc plenary lectr to Indian Pharmacological Soc 2005, Centenary Prize Central Vet Soc 2006, Lloyd E Davis Award American Acad of Vet Pharmacology and Toxicology 2007; Dr (hc) Univ of Gent 1992; memb: Br Pharmacological Soc 1965–2009, Assoc for Vet Clinical Pharmacology and Therapeutics 1976–2009, European Assoc of Vet Pharmacology and Toxicology 1978–2009 (hon memb 1991, jr vice-pres 1991–97, pres 1997–2000, sr vice-pres 2000–06); hon assoc RCVS 1987, hon fell European Coll of

Vet Pharmacology and Toxicology 2000; FIBiol 1989; *Books* Pharmacological Basis of Large Animal Medicine (jtly, 1983), Veterinary Pharmacology, Toxicology and Therapy in Food Producing Species (jtly, 1988), Proceedings of the 6th International Congress of the European Association for Veterinary Pharmacology and Toxicology (co-ed, 1994), Handbook of Experimental Pharmacology: Comparative and Veterinary Pharmacology (co-ed, 2009); *Recreations* the works of Charles Dickens, Victorian and Edwardian history and literature, gardening; *Style*— Prof Peter Lees, CBE; ✉ Royal Veterinary College, Hawkshead Campus, North Mymms, Hatfield, Hertfordshire AL9 7TA (☎ 01707 666370, e-mail plees@rvc.ac.uk)

LEESON, Helen Victoria; da of Michael John Leeson (d 1988), and Lesley Case, *née* Tyler; *b* 8 February 1961; *Educ* Oakham Sch, Univ of Manchester (BSc), CIM (Dip); *m* 14 June 1996, John Sandom, s of Eric Sandom; 1 da (Emily b 24 Oct 1995), 1 s (James b 29 June 1998); *Career* grad trainee rising to sales exec Jefferson Smurfitt Gp plc 1982–86, account mngr, account dir then gp account dir Graphics Div Holmes & Marchant plc 1986–92, co-fndr The Sandom Partnership Ltd and LLS Holdings Ltd 1992–93 (estab Impackt Ltd and Distillery Ltd as gp subsidiaries); MCIM 1986; *Recreations* sport, tennis, riding, social activities, reading; *Style*— Ms Helen Leeson; ✉ Sandom Group, Old Brewery, 22 Russell Street, Windsor, Berkshire SL4 1HQ (☎ 01753 852488, fax 01753 857971, mobile 07850 776511, e-mail helen.leeson@sandomgroup.com)

LEESON, Sir Kevin James; KCB (2012), CBE (2003); s of A V Leeson, and I J Leeson, *née* Teal; *b* 11 June 1956; *Educ* Alcester GS, UMIST (BSc); *Career* joined RAF 1974, Dep ACOS HQ Strike Cmd 1996–98, RCDS 1999, dir Air Resources and Plans MOD 2000–04, ACDS (Logistic Ops) MOD 2004–07, ACDS (Resources and Plans) MOD 2007–09, chief of materiel (air), air memb for materiel and chief engr (RAF) MOD 2009–12, sr advsr Atkins Defence 2013; memb British Airways Bd Safety Review Ctee 2013–16; pres Combined Servs Winter Sports 2006–12, chm RAF Charitable Tst 2013, pres Royal Int Air Tattoo 2013; vice-patron Combined Services Winter Sports Assoc 2012; Liveryman Worshipful Co of Coachmakers and Coach Harness Makers 2016; CEng 1982, FIET 1997, FREng 2012; *Recreations* skiing; *Clubs* RAF; *Style*— Sir Kevin Leeson, KCB, CBE, FREng, CEng, FIET; ✉ RAF Charitable Trust, Douglas Bader House, Horcott Hill, Fairford, Gloucestershire GL7 4RB

LEFANU, Prof Nicola Frances; da of William Richard LeFanu (d 1995), and Elizabeth Violet Maconchy, DBE (d 1994); *b* 28 April 1947; *Educ* St Mary's Sch Calne, St Hilda's Coll Oxford (MA), Harvard Univ (Harkness fellowship), Royal Coll of Music, Univ of London (DMus); *m* 16 March 1979, David Newton Lumsdaine; 1 s (Peter LeFanu b 13 Nov 1982); *Career* composer (100 musical compositions); prof of music Univ of York 1994–2008; Hon DMus Univ of Durham, Hon DUniv Open 2004, Hon DMus Univ of Aberdeen 2006; FRCM, FTCL; *Recreations* conservation, natural history, feminism; *Clubs* Athenaeum; *Style*— Prof Nicola LeFanu; ✉ 5 Holly Terrace, York YO10 4DS (☎ 01904 651759, website www.nicolalefanu.com)

LEFEVER, Dr Robert M H; s of Henry Lefever (d 2001), and Evelyn, *née* Stewart (d 1996); *b* 20 March 1937, Kodaikanal, India; *Educ* Mill Hill Sch, CCC Cambridge, Middx Hosp; *m* 22 July 1961, Margaret, *née* Ellis; 1 da (Nicola b 24 Aug 1962) 2 s (Robin b 23 Aug 1966, Henry b 2 March 1968); *Career* GP in private practice, founding dir PROMIS Recovery Centre 1976–; Break Free From Addiction (2nd edn, 2008); *Recreations* opera, anitquarian books, mediaeval manuscripts; *Clubs* Garrick; *Style*— Dr Robert Lefever; ✉ 2A Pelham Street, London SW7 2NG (☎ 020 7584 6511, fax 020 7225 1147, e-mail k.stclair@promis.co.uk)

LEFÈVRE, Robin Charles; s of Jack Lefèvre, and Jean, *née* Syme; *b* 5 May 1947; *Educ* Irvine Royal Acad, The Royal Scottish Acad of Music and Dramatic Art; *m* 2 Oct 1970, Maureen, da of George Webster; 1 da (Laura b 15 Aug 1971); *Career* director; assoc dir Hampstead Theatre, prodns incl: Then and Now, Threads, Writer's Cramp, On the Edge, Fall, Bodies (transferred Ambassadors), Aristocrats (Evening Standard Best Play Award 1988, NY Drama Critics' Award for Best Foreign Play), Valued Friends (Long Wharf CT, Evening Standard Award), Give Me Your Answer Do, Disposing of the Body, Peggy for You, Peggy For You (also Comedy Theatre), Losing Louis; for Abbey Theatre Dublin incl: Someone Who'll Watch Over Me (also Hampstead, Vaudeville, and Broadway), The Cavalcaders (also Royal Court and Tricycle Theatre), The Bird Sanctuary, Translations, Observe the Sons of Ulster; for Gate Theatre Dublin: Private Lives, A Street Car Named Desire, Afterplay (also Gielgud Theatre), Pygmalion, Betrayal, Uncle Vanya, Glass Menagerie; for Donmar Warehouse: Three Days of Rain, Helpless, The Hotel in Amsterdam; other credits incl: Outside Edge (Queens), Rocket to the Moon (Apollo), Are You Lonesome Tonight? (Evening Standard Best Musical Award), Rowan Atkinson's New Review (Shaftesbury), The Entertainer (Shaftesbury), The Country Girl (Apollo), When We Are Married (NT), The Wexford Trilogy (Bush), Katherine Howard (Chichester Festival Theatre), Krapp's Last Tape (Pit and Ambassadors), The Homecoming (Comedy Theatre), Heartbreak House (Roundabout Theatre NY); television and film: Jake's Progress (by Alan Bleasdale), Self-Catering, A Piece of Monologue (by Samuel Beckett); *Style*— Robin Lefèvre, Esq

LEFF, Prof Julian Paul; s of Dr Samuel Leff (d 1962), of London, and Vera Miriam, *née* Levy (d 1980); *b* 4 July 1938; *Educ* Haberdashers' Aske's, UCL (BSc, MD); *m* 31 Jan 1975, Prof Joan Lilian Raphael-Leff, da of Jacob Raphael (d 1970), of Tel Aviv, Israel; 4 s (Michael b 1964, Alex b 1967, Jonty b 1976, Adriel b 1980), 1 da (Jessa b 1975); *Career* career scientist MRC 1972–2002, hon conslt physician Maudsley Hosp 1973–2002, clinical sub-dean Inst of Psychiatry 1974–79, hon sr lectr London Sch of Hygiene 1974–89, asst dir MRC Social Psychiatry Unit 1974–89, dir Team For Assessment of Psychiatric Servs (TAPS) 1985–2006, dir MRC Social and Community Psychiatric Unit 1989–95, prof of social and cultural psychiatry Inst of Psychiatry 1987–2002 (emeritus prof 2002–), inventor Avatar Therapy 2016; hon prof: Univ of Cape Town 2009–, UCL 2010–; Burghölzli Award 1999, The Marsh Award for Mental Health Work 2010; MRCP, Hon FRCPsych 2015; *Books* Psychiatric Examination in Clinical Practice (1978), Expressed Emotion in Families (1985), Psychiatry Around the Globe (1988), Family Work for Schizophrenia (1992), Principles of Social Psychiatry (1993), Care in the Community: Illusion or Reality? (1997), The Unbalanced Mind (2001), Advanced Family Work for Schizophrenia (2005), Social Inclusion of People with Mental Illness (2006); *Recreations* swimming, croquet, piano, silversmithing; *Style*— Prof Julian Leff; ✉ 1 South Hill Park Gardens, London NW3 2TD (e-mail julian.leff@kcl.ac.uk)

LEFROY, Jeremy John Elton; MP; *b* 30 May 1959; *Educ* Highgate Sch London, King's Coll Cambridge; *m* Janet; 2 c; *Career* cncllr Newcastle-under-Lyme Borough Cncl 2003–07, MP (Cons) Stafford 2010–; govr Friarswood Primary Sch; *Style*— Jeremy Lefroy, Esq, MP; ✉ House of Commons, London SW1A 0AA

LEGARD, Jonathan Antony; s of late Peter Herbert Legard, of Chester, and Brenda Valerie, *née* Kidd; *b* 17 July 1961; *Educ* Shrewsbury, Univ of Leeds (BA), Peterhouse Cambridge (Postgrad Cert in Educn); *m* 1996, Kate, *née* Chacksfield; 2s (Piers b 1999, Crispin b 2002), 1 da (Arabella b 2001); *Career* Cambridge Tutors Hong Kong 1984–85, Viper TV Chester 1986, BBC Radio Merseyside 1986–90 (reporter rising to prodr and presenter), reporter BBC Radio Sport 1990–; Radio 5 Live: sports news corr 1995–96, motor racing corr 1997–2004, football corr 2004–08; Formula 1 commentator BBC TV 2009–10, sports broadcaster and commentator FortyFiveMedia 2011–; *Recreations* golf, cycling, theatre, Chester FC; *Clubs* Delamere Forest Golf; *Style*— Jonathan Legard, Esq

LEGGATE, Philippa Margaret Curzon (Pippa); da of Thomas Frederick Ellis, OBE, and Rozanne Mary Laura Curzon, *née* Woods; *b* 15 August 1950; *Educ* Royal Sch Bath, Univ of York (BA), Univ of Bristol (PGCE), Univ of Bath (MEd); *m* 1980, David Ian Leggate; 1 da (Emily Laura Ellis b 28 Sept 1983); *Career* teacher VSO Br W Indies, history teacher Churchill Comp Sch Avon 1973–75; Bahrain Sch: history and social studies teacher 1975–76, co-ordinator British Curriculum and history teacher 1976–81, dep head 1981–83, pt/t conslt (set up and prepared introduction of Int Bacc prog) 1983–86, Int Bacc co-ordinator and history teacher 1986; head of history Muscat English Speaking Sch 1986–87, founding princ American-British Acad Oman 1987–91, regnl dir Africa and ME Int Bacc Orgn 1991–93 (Int Bacc UK dir), head Overseas Sch of Colombo Sri Lanka 1993–97, head Malvern Girls Coll 1997–2006, educational conslt CfBT Educn Tst 2006–; chm Boarding Schs Assoc (BSA) 2005–06; memb: MacMillan Nursing Assoc, CPRE and Royal Lifeboat Assoc, Assoc of Friends of Sri Lanka; govr: Tockington Manor Prep Sch, Westonbirt Schools, Int Sch Cape Town; assoc memb GSA 1997– (Int Bacc Exec Ctee 1993–97); *Recreations* reading, tennis, riding, walking, gardening, travel, sailing; *Clubs* Royal Over-Seas League; *Style*— Mrs Pippa Leggate; ✉ Church Farm House, Stinchcombe, Gloucestershire GL11 6BQ (☎ 01453 543039, e-mail pleggate@aol.com)

LEGGATT, Rt Hon Sir Andrew Peter; kt (1982), PC (1990); s of Capt W R C (Peter) Leggatt, DSO, RN (d 1983), of Odiham, Hants, and (Dorothea) Joy, *née* Dreyer (d 1992); *b* 8 November 1930; *Educ* Eton, King's Coll Cambridge (MA); *m* 17 July 1953, Gillian Barbara (Jill), da of Cdr C P Newton, RN (d 1970), of Petersfield, Hants; 1 s (Sir George Leggatt, *qv*, b 1957), 1 da (Alice (Mrs Alistair McLuskie) b 1960); *Career* cmmnd Rifle Bde 1949–50 and TA 1950–59; called to the Bar Inner Temple 1954 (bencher 1976); QC 1972, recorder of the Crown Court 1974–82, judge of the High Court of Justice (Queen's Bench Div) 1982–90, a Lord Justice of Appeal 1990–97; Chief Surveillance Cmmr 1998–2006; conducted Review of Tribunals 2000–01; chm Appeal Ctee Takeover Panel 2001–06; memb: Bar Cncl 1971–82 (chm 1981–82), Top Salaries Review Body 1979–82; pres Cncl of the Inns of Court 1995–97; hon fell American Coll of Trial Lawyers 1996; *Recreations* listening to music, personal computers; *Clubs* MCC; *Style*— The Rt Hon Sir Andrew Leggatt

LEGGATT, Hon Mr Justice; Sir George Andrew Midsomer Leggatt; kt (2012), QC (1997); s of Rt Hon Sir Andrew Leggatt, *qv*, and Gillian Barbara, *née* Newton; *b* 12 November 1957; *Educ* Eton, King's Coll Cambridge (MA), Harvard Univ (Harkness fell), City Univ (Dip Law); *m* 1987, Dr Stavia Blunt, *qv*; 1 s (Peter b 1990), 1 da (Elly b 1993); *Career* Bigelow teaching fell Law Sch Univ of Chicago 1982–83, called to the Bar Middle Temple 1983, assoc Sullivan & Cromwell NY 1983–84, in practice Brick Court Chambers 1985–, recorder 2002–; vice-chair Bar Standards Bd 2006–08, dep High Court judge 2008–12, judge of the High Court of Justice (Queen's Bench Div) 2012–; *Recreations* philosophy, cooking, visiting Greece; *Style*— The Hon Mr Justice Leggatt; ✉ The Royal Courts of Justice, Strand, London WC2 2LL

LEGGE, (John) Michael; CB (2001), CMG (1994); s of late Dr Alfred John Legge, of Guildford, Surrey, and late Marion Frances, *née* James; *b* 14 March 1944; *Educ* Royal GS Guildford, ChCh Oxford (MA); *m* 24 July 1971, Linda, da of late John Wallace Bagley, of Haywards Heath, W Sussex; 2 s (Christopher b 18 March 1975, Richard b 12 Nov 1978); *Career* MOD 1966–2001: asst private sec to Def Sec 1970, princ 1971, first sec UK Delgn to NATO 1974, asst sec 1978; Rand Corpn Santa Monica California 1982, asst under-sec of state for policy 1987, asst sec-gen for def planning and policy NATO 1988–93; dep under-sec of state: NI Office 1993–96, MOD 1996–2001; sec and dir of admin Royal Hosp Chelsea 2001–07; chm Civil Service Healthcare 2001–11; *Books* Theatre Nuclear Weapons and the Nato Strategy of Flexible Response (1983); *Recreations* golf, gardening, travel; *Style*— Michael Legge, Esq, CB, CMG; ✉ 53 St Mary's Road, Leatherhead, Surrey KT22 8HB

LEGGE-BOURKE, Dame the Hon (Elizabeth) Shân (Josephine); DCVO (2015, LVO); *née* Bailey; o child of 3 Baron Glanusk, DSO (d 1948), and Margaret (d 2002) (who later m 1 Viscount De L'Isle); *b* 10 September 1943; *m* 2 June 1964, William Nigel Henry Legge-Bourke (d 2009); 1 s, 2 da; *Career* lady-in-waiting to HRH The Princess Royal 1978–; pres Welsh Save the Children 1989–; chief pres for Wales St John Ambulance Bde 1990–94, pres Royal Welsh Agric Soc 1997; memb Brecon Beacons Nat Park Authy 1989–98, pres Nat Fedn of Young Farmers Clubs England and Wales 1998–2000, pres RFCA Wales 2013–; Hon Col Infrantry Battle Sch 2013–; High Sheriff Powys 1991–92, HM Lord-Lt Powys 1998–; *Style*— Dame the Hon Shân Legge-Bourke, DCVO; ✉ Gliffaes Fach, Crickhowell, Powys NP8 1RL (☎ 01874 730674)

LEGGE-BOURKE, Victoria Lindsay; LVO (1986); da of Maj Sir Harry Legge-Bourke, KBE, DL, MP (d 1973), and Lady Legge-Bourke (d 2007); *b* 12 February 1950, Witchford, Ely, Cambs; *Educ* Benenden, St Hilda's Coll Oxford; *Career* social attaché British Embassy Washington DC 1971–73, dir Junior Tourism Ltd 1974–81, lady-in-waiting to HRH The Princess Royal 1974–; special asst American Embassy London 1983–89, Price Investments Kansas City MO 1989–91, head of protocol American Embassy London 1991–94, exec dir Goldman Sachs International 1995–98, dir Lehman Brothers Ltd 1998–99, exec dir Goldman Sachs International 1999–2007, dir Torie's Tips Ltd 2007–; memb: Cncl The American Museum in Britain 1995–2007, Exec Bd LAMDA 2004–14; govr ESU 1996–99; tstee St Bride's Tom Olsen Tst 2003–; *Recreations* cooking, crosswords, music, reading, theatre; *Clubs* Grillions, The Pilgrims; *Style*— Miss Victoria Legge-Bourke, LVO; ✉ Bolfer Cottage, 14 Swanton Road, Gunthorpe, Norfolk NR24 2NS (☎ 01263 860937); 704 Keyes House, Dolphin Square, London SW1V 3NB (☎ 020 7798 8387, e-mail victoria@legge-bourke.com)

LEGH, Hon David Piers Carlis; DL (Derbys 2002); yr s of 4 Baron Newton (d 1992); *b* 21 November 1951; *Educ* Eton, RAC Cirencester; *m* 1974, Rev Jane Mary, da of John Roy Wynter Bee, of West End, Surrey; 2 da (Charlotte Mary b 1976, Katherine Anna b 1991), 2 s (Hugo Peter David b 1979, Thomas John Rowland b 1984); *Career* chartered surveyor; John German: ptnr 1984–99, managing ptnr 1991–95, sr ptnr 1995–99; sr ptnr Germans 1999–2000, ptnr Fisher German LLP 2000–12 (chm 2000–09, currently conslt); CLA: memb Cncl 1989–2005, chm Taxation Ctee 1993–97, pres Derbys Branch 2002– (chm 1992–94), chm E Midlands Region 2002–05 (vice-chm 2000–02); RASE: memb Cncl, rep Derbys 1986–91, nominated memb 1991–94; High Sheriff Derbys 2006–07; FRICS, MRAC (fell RAC 100 Club 2010); *Publications* 40 Years Owning a Rural Estate – a retrospective and the challenges ahead (2010); *Clubs* Farmers'; *Style*— The Hon David Legh, DL; ✉ Cubley Lodge, Ashbourne, Derbyshire DE6 2FB (☎ 01335 330297, fax 01335 330159, e-mail david.legh@cubleylodge.com); Fisher German, 2 Rutherford Court, Staffordshire Technology Park, Stafford ST18 0GP (☎ 01785 220044, fax 01785 220944, e-mail david.legh@fishergerman.co.uk)

LEGON, Prof Anthony Charles; s of George Charles Legon (d 2012), and Emily Louisa Florence, *née* Conner (d 1993); *b* 28 September 1941, Acton, Suffolk; *Educ* Coopers' Company Sch, UCL (BSc, PhD, DSc); *m* 20 July 1963, Deirdre Anne, da of Edgar Albert Rivers (d 1944); 1 da (Victoria May b 11 March 1977), 2 s (Anthony Daniel Charles b 14 Nov 1979, Edward James b 14 July 1989); *Career* Turner and Newall fell Univ of London 1968–70, lectr in chemistry UCL 1970–83 (reader 1983–84), prof of physical chemistry Univ of Exeter 1984–89, Thomas Graham prof of chemistry UCL 1989–90, prof of physical chemistry Univ of Exeter 1990–2005, prof of physical chemistry Univ of Bristol 2005–08 (sr research fell 2008–); sr fell EPSRC 1997–2002; Tilden lectr and medallist RSC 1989–90, Hassel lectr Univ of Oslo 1997, Spectroscopy Award Royal Soc of Chemistry 1998, Liversidge Award RSC 2012, Moscowitz meml lectr Univ of Minnesota 2012–13; in excess of 390 papers published; memb Physical Chemistry Sub-Ctee Chemistry Ctee SERC 1984–87, vice-pres Faraday Div RSC 2000–03; FRSC 1977, FRS

L

2000; *Recreations* watching soccer, reading; *Style*— Prof Anthony Legon; ✉ School of Chemistry, University of Bristol, Cantock's Close, Bristol BS8 1TS (☎ 0117 331 7708, fax 0117 925 0612, e-mail a.c.legon@bristol.ac.uk)

LEGRAIN, Gérard Marie François; s of Jean Legrain (d 1985), and Marie Hélène, *née* Merica (d 1962); *b* 16 April 1937; *Educ* Ecole St Louis de Gonzague, Sorbonne, Faculté de Droit, Sciences-Po, Ecole Nationale d'Administration Paris; *m* 1969, Katrin Ines, da of Harald Tombach, of Altadena, CA; 2 s (Philippe, *qv*, b 1973, Pierre b 1980), 1 da (Milli b 1976); *Career* Sub Lt 27 and 15 Bataillons de Chasseurs Alpins 1962; Citibank: Paris 1965, NY 1967, Mexico City 1969; exec dir Citicorp International Bank Ltd London 1972–74, md Int Mexican Bank Ltd London 1974–93; dir: Foreign Banks & Securities Houses Assoc 1991–93, Govett High Income Investment Tst 1993–2001, Govett Emerging Markets Investment Tst 1993–2001; hon treas: Société Française de Bienfaisance 1992–2013, Dispensaire Français 1992–2002; *Recreations* skiing, tennis; *Clubs* Brooks's, Hurlingham; *Style*— Mr Gérard Legrain; ✉ Hamilton House, 1 Temple Avenue, London EC4Y 0HA (☎ 020 7353 4212, e-mail gerard@legrain.eu)

LEGRAIN, Philippe; s of Gerard Legrain, *qv*, and Katrin Legrain; *b* 29 October 1973; *Educ* Westminster (scholar), LSE (BSc, ESRC scholar, MSc); *Career* economics corr then trade and economics corr The Economist 1997–2000, special advsr to the DG WTO 2000–01, ed World Link (World Economic Forum magazine) 2002; Britain in Europe: chief economist 2002–05, dir of policy 2004–05; contributing ed Prospect 2006–; visiting fell European Inst LSE 2007–10, princ advsr and head of analysis team Bureau of European Policy Advsrs European Cmmn 2011–14, visiting sr fell European Inst LSE 2014–; fndr Open Political Economy Network (OPEN) 2016–; writer: FT, The Guardian, The Times, Prospect, Wall St Jl Europe, New York Times, Project Syndicate, Foreign Policy, CapX; media commentator on globalisation, migration and European issues for BBC TV and radio; Highly Commended Young Financial Journalist of the Year Harold Wincott Press Awards 1999, shortlisted FT Business Book of the Year 2007; *Publications* Open World: The Truth about Globalisation (2002), Immigrants: Your Country Needs Them (2007), Aftershock: Reshaping the World Economic After the Crisis (2010), European Spring: Why Our Economies and Politics are in a Mess – and How to Put Them Right (2014); *Style*— Philippe Legrain; ✉ e-mail mail@philippelegrain.com, website www.philippelegrain.com, Twitter @plegrain

LEGRAND, Janet; da of Charles Legrand (d 2011), and Gladys Hannah, *née* Shadwell (d 2008); *b* 2 October 1958, London; *Educ* Green Sch for Girls London, Trinity Hall Cambridge (MA); *m* 2 Sept 1989, Neil Robert Tidmarsh; 1 da (Louise Olivia b 25 Nov 1994), 1 s (Oliver Richard b 10 July 1997); *Career* slr; ptnr Alsop Wilkinson 1991–96, ptnr Dibb Lupton Alsop 1996–99; DLA Piper: ptnr 1999–, memb Bd 1999–, head of specialist litigation 2008–09, chm and sr ptnr 2009–12, sr elected bd memb 2012–; Marshall Aid Commemoration cmmr 2013–; memb: Bd Leadership Fndn for HE 2013–, Audit Ctee Univ of Cambridge 2013–; chm Western Riverside Environmental Fund 1999–; memb: Advsy Bd New Perimeter 2009–, Bd PRIME 2012–; vice-chair Children's Soc 2013–; memb: Law Soc 1983, City of London Slrs' Co, City of London Law Soc; *Recreations* cinema, reading, walking, family; *Style*— Ms Janet Legrand; ✉ DLA Piper, 3 Noble Street, London EC2V 7EE (website www.dlapiper.com)

LEIGH, Adam Michael; s of (Harvey) Roy Leigh, of Manchester, and Susan, *née* Kelner; *b* 24 January 1967; *Educ* Stockport GS, Univ of Manchester (LLB); *m* 2 Sept 2000, Charlotte Kate Watson-Smyth; 2 s (Isaac Edward b 3 March 2001, Noah James b 25 August 2003); *Career* reporter Burton Herald & Post 1989–90, reporter Burton Mail 1990–92, copytaster and dep news ed Birmingham Post 1992–95; The Independent: sub-ed 1995, copytaster 1996, chief features sub-ed 1997–98; news ed Independent on Sunday 1998–99; The Independent: dep foreign ed 1999–2000, home ed 2000–03, exec ed (features) 2003–10, dep ed 2010–11; involved with: Nat Youth Theatre of GB 1981–87, Manchester Student TV 1985–89; *Clubs* Reform; *Style*— Adam Leigh, Esq

LEIGH, Bernard Malcolm; s of Lionel Leigh, of London, and Cecilia, *née* Ruderman; *b* 7 February 1950; *Educ* William Ellis GS, London Hosp Dental Inst Univ of London (BDS), Eastman Hosp Inst of Dental Surgery; *m* 25 Nov 1973, Yvonne Pamela, da of Leslie Wolfe; 2 da (Sara (Mrs Arieh Wagner) b 20 Nov 1974, Talia (Mrs Avi Smith) b 18 Oct 1980), 4 s (Daniel b 6 Nov 1976, Jeremy b 24 March 1979, Joshua b 25 July 1984, Avram b 27 July 1989); *Career* house offr London Hosp 1973; practised: City of London 1974–75, Hemel Hempstead 1976–82, London NW11 1976–84, Harley St 1982–2016, Devonshire Place 2016–; specialist in endodontics; hon clinical asst Dept of Cons Dentistry Inst of Dental Surgery Eastman Dental Hosp 1979–94; memb: Alpha Omega (Ctee 1984–88, chm 1999–2000), Br Endodontic Soc (Ctee 1981–82), Br Dental Assoc; *Recreations* music, computers, photography, writing; *Style*— Bernard Leigh, Esq; ✉ 8 Devonshire Place, London W1G 6HP (☎ 020 7637 2200, e-mail bmleigh@gmail.com)

LEIGH, David Irvine; s of Frederick Leigh (d 1980), of Glasgow, and Mary, *née* David; *b* 16 April 1944; *Educ* Mackintosh Sch, Edinburgh Coll of Art Heriot-Watt Univ (DA); *m* 30 Aug 1975, Lynda, da of Frank Thomas Taylor (d 1970), of Hawkhurst, Kent; 1 da (Claire Francesca b 1971), 1 s (Elliot b 1983); *Career* architect; ptnr R J Wood Chapman and Hanson 1974, chm and md Chapman and Hanson 1989–91 (dir 1981–91), chm and md Leigh Blundell Thompson chartered architects and interior designers 1991–94, princ architect E Sussex CC 1995–98, princ David I Leigh Chartered Architects 1999–; designed HQ bldgs for: Charrington & Co London 1978, R S Components Corby 1984, Electrocomponents Knightsbridge 1987, W M Lighting Northampton 1989; RIBA 1969; *Recreations* Arsenal FC, horse racing, travel, petanque; *Style*— David Leigh, Esq

LEIGH, Sir Edward Julian Egerton; kt (2013), MP; s of Sir Neville Egerton Leigh, KCVO (d 1994), and Denise Yvonne, *née* Branch; *b* 20 July 1950; *Educ* The Oratory Sch Berkshire, Lycée Français de Londres, Univ of Durham; *m* 25 Sept 1984, Mary, eldest da of Philip Henry Russell Goodman, of London, and Sophie (Sonia), o da of late Count Vladimir Petrovitch Kleinmichel, CVO; 3 s, 3 da; *Career* barr; memb Inner Temple; former: pres Durham Union Soc, chm Durham Univ Cons Assoc; Parly candidate (Cons) Middlesbrough 1974; MP (Cons): Gainsborough and Horncastle 1983–97, Gainsborough 1997–; hon dir Coalition for Peace through Security, chm Nat Cncl for Civil Defence 1980–83, memb House of Commons Select Ctee for Defence 1983–87, vice-chm and sec for Backbench Ctees on Agric Employment and Defence 1983–90, PPS to Min of State Home Office 1990–92, under-sec of state for Industry and Consumer Affairs DTI 1990–93, chm Public Accounts Ctee 2001–10 (memb 2000–01), co-chm, APPG on the Holy See 2010–, chm, APPG on France 2013–, chm Br-Italian Parly Gp 2015–, chm APPG on Russia 2015–; memb: House of Commons Agric Select Ctee 1995–97, House of Commons Social Security Select Ctee 1997–99, Speaker's Panel of Chairs 2010–, House of Commons Procedure Ctee 2016–; memb: Richmond Borough Cncl 1977–81, GLC 1977–81; veteran memb HAC 2003–; memb Cncl Lincoln Cathedral 2003–15, pres Catholic Union of GB 2014–; Knight of Honour and Devotion SMOM 1994, Chevalier Légion d'Honneur 2015; *Publications* Right Thinking (1976), The Nation That Forgot God (ed, 2008), Monastery of the Mind (2012); *Style*— Sir Edward Leigh, MP; ✉ House of Commons, London SW1A 0AA

LEIGH, Sir Geoffrey Norman; kt (1990); s of Morris Leigh, and Rose Leigh; *b* 23 March 1933; *Educ* Haberdashers' Aske's Hampstead Sch, Univ of Michigan; *m* 1, 1955 (m dis 1975), Valerie Lennard (d 1976); 1 s, 2 da; m 2, 1976, Sylvia Pell; 1 s, 1 da; *Career* chm of tstees The Leigh Academies Tst 2010–; chm Sterling Homes 1980–98 (md 1965–80), chm Allied London Properties plc 1987–98 (md 1970–87); dir Arrow Property Investments 2000–06; fndr and first pres Westminster Jr C of C 1959–63; underwriting memb Lloyd's 1973–97; special advsr Land Agency Bd Cmmn for New Towns 1994–96; chm Leigh Academies Tst 2008–; memb: Ctee Good Design in Housing 1978–79 (memb Ctee Good Design in Housing for Disabled 1977), British ORT Cncl 1979–80, Int Advsy Bd American Univ Washington 1983–97, Advsy Cncl Prince's Youth Business Tst 1985–2009, Main Fin Bd NSPCC 1985–2003 (hon memb Cncl 1995–), Governing Cncl Business in the Community 1987–2000, London Historic House Museums Tst 1987–98, Somerville Coll (Oxford) Appeal 1987–2006, Royal Fine Art Cmmn Art and Architecture Educn Tst 1988–2000, Per Cent Club 1988–2000, City Appeal Ctee Royal Marsden Hosp 1990–93, Review Body on Doctors' and Dentists' Remuneration 1990–93, Univ of Oxford Chllr's Ct of Benefactors 1991–, Emmanuel Coll Cambridge Devpt Campaign 1994–98, Wellbeing Cncl 1994–2009; chm St Mary's Hosp 150th Anniversary Appeal 1995–2009; cmmr and tstee Fulbright Cmmn 1991–99 (chm Int Advsy Bd 1995–); sponsor The Leigh City Technol Coll Dartford (chm of govrs 1988–2006, chm of tstees 2006–); fndr/sponsor Friends of the British Library 1987– (vice-pres 2000–); fndr Margaret Thatcher Centre Somerville Coll Oxford 1991; treas: Cwlth Jewish Cncl 1983–89, Cwlth Jewish Tst 1983–89; a treas Cons Pty 1995–98; Hampstead and Highgate Cons Assoc: patron 1991–95, pres 1994–97, vice-pres 1997–2005; vice-pres Conservatives Abroad 1995–; tstee: Margaret Thatcher Fndn 1991–2013, Industry in Educn 1993–98, Philharmonia 1992–2000; treas and tstee Action on Addiction 1991–2003; govr: Royal Sch Hampstead 1991–2003, City Lit Inst 1991–98; currently dir Palm Beach Civic Assoc and tstee Palm Beach United Way; hon memb Emmanuel Coll 1995, fndn fell Somerville Coll Oxford 1998; hon life memb The Conservative Med Soc 1998; Presidential Citation The American Univ 1987; Freeman City of London 1976; Liveryman: Worshipful Co of Furniture Makers 1987 (memb Ct of Assts 1992, honoris causa 2006), Worshipful Co of Haberdashers 1992; FRSA, FICPD; *Recreations* photography, reading, golf; *Clubs* Carlton (hon memb Political Ctee 2004), United and Cecil, Pilgrims, RAC, Wentworth, Palm Beach Country, Palm Beach Yacht, Palm Beach Ocean, Pilgrims USA; *Style*— Sir Geoffrey Leigh; ✉ 42 Berkeley Square, London W1J 5AW (☎ 020 7409 5054)

LEIGH, Prof Irene May; CBE (2012, OBE 2006); da of Archibald Allen, of Liverpool, and May Lilian, *née* Whalley; *b* 25 April 1947; *Educ* Merchant Taylors', London Hosp Med Coll (BSc, MB BS, MD, DSc); *m* 1 (m dis); 1 s (Piers Daniel b 24 June 1973), 3 da (Andrea Yseult b 11 Oct 1975, Miranda Chloe b 17 June 1982, Rosalino Clio b 12 Jan 1988); m 2, 30 Sept 2000, Dr John E Kernthaler; 3 step c (Jeremy b 15 Feb 1974, Simon Charles 8 June 1975, Sophie Margaret 15 June 1980); *Career* conslt dermatologist London Hosp 1983, hon dir ICRF Skin Tumour Unit 1986, prof of dermatology London Med Coll 1992–2002 (sr lectr 1987–92); Bart's and Royal London Sch of Med and Dentistry: asst warden research 1997–2002, prof of cellular and molecular medicine 2000–06, research dir 2002–05; vice-princ and head of coll Univ of Dundee; Hon DSc (Med) 1999; FRCP 1989, FMedSci 1999, FRSE 2009; *Books* Keratinocyte Handbook (1994); *Style*— Prof Irene Leigh, CBE; ✉ College of Medicine, Dentistry and Nursing, University of Dundee, Level 10 Ninewells Hospital and Medical School, Dundee DD1 9SY (☎ 01382 632763, fax 01382 644267)

LEIGH, Jonathan; s of Robert Montague Leigh, and Isabel Alexdrina, *née* Villiers; *b* 17 June 1952; *Educ* St George's Sch Windsor (chorister), Eton, Corpus Christi Coll Cambridge (choral exhbn, MA, cert of educn); *m* Emma Mary, da of Rear Adm Michael Kyrle Pope, CB, MBE, DL; 1 da (Isabel b 13 Jan 1985), 1 s (Charles b 4 May 1986); *Career* Cranleigh Sch: asst master 1976–83, housemaster 2+3 South House 1983–88, head of history 1988, second master 1988–92; headmaster Blundell's Sch 1992–2004, headmaster Ridley Coll Ontario 2005–12, master Marlborough Coll 2012–; chm: Small Schools Gp HMC 1999–2002, SW Div HMC 2000–01; dir: Abigail Au Pairs, Devon & Exeter Racecourse 2000–04 (vice-chm 2002–04), Highfield Sch Liphook 2000–; vice-pres Devon Playing Fields Assoc 1998; memb: Admiralty Interview Bd 1993, Advsy Cncl Devon Social Service Dept 1993–2001 (chm 1994–98), Cncl ISIS South West 1995–2001, Interviewing Panel ESU 1996, Bd Canadian Educnl Standards Inst 2008–11; advsr Vimy Fndn 2005–; govr: St Petroc's Sch Bude 1992–2004, Wolborough Hill Sch 1998–2000, Abbey Sch Tewkesbury 2000 (chm 2002–03), Cheam Sch 2013–; tstee: Tiverton Adventure Playground 1992–2004, Inner Cities Young Peoples Project 1996–99; FRSA 1994; *Recreations* singing, racing, 19th c Africa, painting, labradors; *Clubs* East India, Lansdowne; *Style*— Jonathan Leigh, Esq; ✉ The Master's Lodge, Marlborough College, Marlborough, Wiltshire SN8 1PA

LEIGH, Mark Andrew Michael Stephen (Bertie); s of Robert Arthur Leigh, and Shelagh Elizabeth Leigh; *b* 30 August 1946, Stockport, Cheshire; *Educ* St Christopher Sch Letchworth, UEA (BA); *m* 1975, Helen Mary; 1 s (Tobias Timothy Edwin b 1976), 1 da (Harriet Celia Kathleen b 1980); *Career* admitted slr 1976; Hempsons: joined as trainee, ptnr 1977–, sr ptnr 1998–; tstee NCEPOD 2005– (chair 2008–), pres Medico-Legal Soc 2006–08, chair Clinical Disputes Forum 2010–; govr City Lit Inst 2006–13, govr St Christopher's Sch 2012– (chair 2014); Hon FRCPCH 1997, FRCOG ad eundem 2003; *Publications* Dewhursts' Obstetrics and Gynaecology (contrib, 1997, 2007 and 2012), Roberton's Neonatology (contrib, 1997 and 2005), Rennie and Roberton's Textbook of Neonatology (2012); *Clubs* Reform; *Style*— Bertie Leigh, Esq; ✉ Hempsons, Hempsons House, 40 Villiers Street, London WC2N 6NJ (☎ 020 7839 0278, fax 020 7484 7566, e-mail mamsl@hempsons.co.uk)

LEIGH, Mike; OBE (1993); s of Alfred Abraham Leigh (d 1985), and Phyllis Pauline, *née* Cousin; *b* 20 February 1943; *Educ* Salford GS, RADA, Camberwell Sch of Arts and Crafts, Central Sch of Art and Design (Theatre Design Dept), London Film Sch; *m* 15 Aug 1973 (m dis 2001), Alison Steadman, the actress, da of George Percival Steadman; 2 s (Toby b 1978, Leo b 1981); *Career* dramatist, theatre/television and film director; assoc dir Midlands Arts Centre for Young People 1965–66, asst dir RSC 1967–68, lectr in drama Sedgley Park and De La Salle Colls Manchester 1968–69, lectr London Film Sch 1970–73; memb: Drama Panel Arts Cncl GB 1975–77, Dir's Working Pty and Specialist Allocations Bd 1976–84, Accreditation Panel Nat Cncl for Drama Trg 1978–91, Gen Advsy Cncl IBA 1980–82; chm of govrs London Film Sch 2001–; Hon MA Univ of Salford 1991, Hon MA Univ of Horthampton 2000, Hon DLitt Univ of Staffordshire 2000, Hon Dr Univ of Essex 2002; writer-dir: Nat Film Theatre Retrospectives 1979 and 1993, BBC TV Retrospective (incl Arena: Mike Leigh Making Plays) 1982, various US retrospectives incl MOMA NY 1992; writer-dir stage plays: The Box Play, My Parents Have Gone To Carlisle, The Last Crusade of the Five Little Nuns (Midlands Arts Centre) 1965–66, Nenaa (RSC Studio Stratford-upon-Avon) 1967, Individual Fruit Pies (E15 Acting Sch) 1968, Down Here And Up There (Royal Court Theatre Upstairs) 1968, Big Basil 1968, Glum Victoria And The Lad With Specs (Manchester Youth Theatre) 1969, Epilogue (Manchester) 1969, Bleak Moments (Open Space) 1970, A Rancid Pong (Basement) 1971, Wholesome Glory, Dick Whittington and his Cat (Royal Court Theatre Upstairs) 1973, The Jaws of Death (Traverse, Edinburgh Festival) 1973, Babies Grow Old (Other Place) 1974 (ICA) 1975, The Silent Majority (Bush) 1974, Abigail's Party (Hampstead) 1977, Ecstasy (Hampstead) 1979, Goose-Pimples (Hampstead, Garrick) 1981 (Standard Best Comedy Award), Smelling a Rat (Hampstead) 1988, Greek Tragedy (Belvoir St Theatre Sydney 1989, Edinburgh Festival and Theatre Royal Stratford East) 1990, It's A Great Big Shame! (Theatre Royal Stratford East) 1993; writer-dir BBC Radio play Too Much of A Good Thing 1979; writer-dir BBC TV plays and films: A Mug's Game 1972, Hard Labour 1973, The Permissive Society, Afternoon, A Light Snack, Probation, Old Chums, The Birth Of The 2001 FA Cup Final Goalie 1975, Nuts in May, Knock For Knock 1976, The Kiss of Death, Abigail's Party 1977, Who's Who 1978, Grown-Ups 1980, Home Sweet

Home 1982, Four Days In July 1984; writer-dir Channel 4 films: Meantime 1983, The Short And Curlies 1987; writer-dir feature films: Bleak Moments 1971 (Golden Hugo, Chicago Film Festival 1972, Golden Leopard Locarno Film Festival 1972), High Hopes 1988 (Critics' Prize Venice Film Festival 1988, Evening Standard Peter Sellers Best Comedy Award 1990), Life Is Sweet 1990 (winner American Nat Soc of Film Critics' Award, Cariddi D'Oro & Maschera di Polifemo Taormina Film Festival 1991), Naked 1993 (winner Best Direction Cannes Film Festival, 1993), Secrets and Lies 1996 (winner Palme D'Or, Inter Critics' Prize, Ecumenical Prize Cannes Film Festival 1996, 5 Oscar nominations incl Best Dir and Best Screenplay 1997, BAFTA Award for Best Original Screen Play 1997), Career Girls 1997, Topsy-Turvy 1999 (Evening Standard Best Film 2000), All or Nothing 2002, Vera Drake 2005 (3 Oscar nominations incl Best Dir and Best Screenplay), Happy-Go-Lucky 2008, Another Year 2010; Alexander Walker Special Award Evening Standard Br Film Award 2009; *Books* Abigail's Party (1983), Goose-Pimples (1983), Smelling A Rat (1989), Ecstasy (1989), Naked and Other Screenplays (1995), Secrets and Lies (1997), Career Girls (1997), Topsy-Turvy (1999), All or Nothing (2002); *Style*— Mike Leigh, Esq, OBE; ✉ c/o United Agents Ltd, 12–26 Lexington Street, London W1F 0LE (✆ 020 3214 0800, fax 020 3214 0801, website www.unitedagents.co.uk)

LEIGH, Ray Hugh; MBE (2001); s of Dennis Leigh, OBE (d 1989), of Mickleton, Glos, and Amy Dorothy, *née* Symes (d 2001); *b* 6 June 1928; *Educ* Morecambe GS, AA Sch of Architecture (AADipl); *m* 1952, Jean, da of Col J Wykes, OBE; 1 da (Sarah Jane b 1953), 2 s (Simon Christopher b 1955 d 1996, David William b 1962); *Career* chartered architect and designer; architectural practice 1952–67; Gordon Russell Ltd (furniture makers): exec dir i/c design 1967–71, md 1971–82, chm 1982–86, re-appointed dir following takeover 1991–94; independent furniture designer and design mgmnt conslt 1986–, chm Luke Hughes & Co (furniture makers) 1990–94; pres: Design & Industries Assoc 1996–99, Furniture Trades Benevolent Assoc 1997–; dir: British Furniture Manufacturers Exports Ltd 1970–93 (past chm), Lygon Arms Hotel Broadway 1970–86, British Furniture Manufacturers Ltd 1994–99; fndr chm Contract Design Assoc 1978–82, chm British Furniture Cncl 1995, memb Crafts Cncl 1977–83; chm: Furniture Industry Research Assoc 1980–86, Edward Barnsley Educnl Tst Furniture Workshops 1980–90, Gordon Russell Tst; pres Glos Guild of Craftsmen 1980–90, memb Furniture Economic Devpt Ctee NEDC 1987–88; fndr and tstee Gordon Russell Design Museum 2008–; memb Ct of Assts Worshipful Co of Furniture Makers (Master 1994–95, Achievement of the Year Award 2013); RIBA, FCSD, FRSA, Hon FRCA; *Publications* Drawn to Design, The Work of Sir Gordon Russell (2013), Two of a Kind, the Work of Prof R D Russell and Marian Pepler (2013), Advance the Product, the continuing adventure of Gordon Russell 1946–86 (2015); *Recreations* gardens, fell walking, painting, antiquarian books; *Style*— Ray Leigh, Esq, MBE; ✉ 5 The Green, Chipping Campden, Gloucestershire GL55 6DL (✆ 01386 840208, e-mail rayhleigh@talktalk.net)

LEIGH, (Richard) Rowley; s of Robert Arthur Leigh, of Chulmleigh, and Shelagh Elizabeth, *née* Ruddin; *b* 23 April 1950; *Educ* Clifton, Tiffin Boys' Sch, Christ's Coll Cambridge (exhibitioner); *m* 1, 1982, Sara Patricia, da of Peter George, the author; 2 da (Ruth Bronwen b 22 Aug 1985, Daisy Dorothy b 2 Oct 1988); m 2, 2002, Katharine Sylvia, da of John Chancellor, author and bibliographer; 1 s (Sidney Robert Chancellor b 22 Feb 1998); *Career* chef tournant Joe Allen Restaurant 1978–79, commis chef Le Gavroche 1979–81, various posts in Roux Restaurants including patisserie, butchery, buying, etc 1981–83, head chef Le Poulbot 1984–87 (sous chef 1983–84), head chef/ptnr Kensington Place 1987–2006, fndr Le Cafe Anglais 2007–; contrib Guardian 1996–, food writer Sunday Telegraph 1998–2004, food writer Financial Times 2004–; memb Académie Culinaire 1987; Glenfiddich Award for newspaper cookery writer of the year 1997, 2001 and 2006; *Publications* No Place Like Home (2000); *Recreations* reading, chess, music, golf; *Clubs* Groucho; *Style*— Rowley Leigh, Esq; ✉ 26 Spencer Road, London W3 6DW (✆ 020 8749 1452, e-mail rowleyleigh@hotmail.com); Le Cafe Anglais, 8 Porchester Gardens, London W2 4DB (e-mail rowley@lecafeanglais.co.uk, website www.lecafeanglais.co.uk)

LEIGH OF HURLEY, Baron (Life Peer UK 2013), of Hurley in the Royal County of Berkshire; Howard Darryl Leigh; s of Philip Mark Leigh (d 1987), of London, and Jacqueline, *née* Freeman; *b* 3 April 1959, London; *Educ* Clifton Coll Bristol, Univ of Southampton; *m* 14 Feb 1998, Jennifer, *née* Peach; 2 da (Olivia b 13 Jan 1999, Susannah b 28 Sept 2001); *Career* CA 1983; wlith Deloitte Haskins + Sells 1980–88, memb Bd Bolton Bldg Soc 1986–92, dir Cavendish Corporate Finance Ltd 1998–; memb Deregulation Taskforce DTI 1994–97; ICAEW: memb Cncl 1998–2004, chm Corporate Finance Faculty 1998–2004, memb (as alternate to ICAEW Pres) Takeover Panel Appeal Ctee 1998–; sr treas Cons Party 2005– (treas 2000–, chm Ldrs Gp 2010–); chm Westminster Synagogue 2001–11 (pres 2011–); tstee Jerusalem Fndn 1992– (chm 2016–), pres Inst for Jewish Policy Research (JPR) 2015–; memb Ct of Assts Worshipful Co of CAs 2003; memb Chartered Inst of Taxation 1985; *Recreations* running; *Clubs* Carlton; *Style*— The Lord Leigh of Hurley; ✉ Cavendish Corporate Finance LLP, 40 Portland Place, London W1B 1NB (✆ 020 7908 6000, fax 020 7908 6006, e-mail hleigh@cavendish.com)

LEIGH PEMBERTON, Jeremy; CBE (1992), DL (2004); s of Capt Robert Douglas Leigh Pemberton, MBE, MC, JP (d 1964), and Helen Isobel, *née* Payne-Gallwey (d 1985); bro of Baron Kingsdown, KG, PC (Life Peer), *qv*; *b* 25 November 1933; *Educ* Eton, Magdalen Coll Oxford (MA), INSEAD Fontainebleau (MBA); *m* 1, 30 May 1968 (m dis 1980), Mary, da of John Ames, of Boston, MA; 1 s (Richard b 13 Dec 1971); m 2, 3 June 1982, Virginia Marion, da of Sir John Curle, KCVO, CMG (d 1997); *Career* Nat Serv Grenadier Gds 1952–54, cmmnd 2 Lt 1953; Brooke Bond Liebig 1957–69 (rising to gp mktg controller), md W & R Balston Group 1973–74 (gp mktg controller and corporate planner 1970–73), dep chm Whatman plc (formerly Whatman Reeve Angel plc) 1990–94 (md 1974–89); chm: Mid Kent Holdings plc until 1998, Morgan Grenfell Equity Income Trust plc (renamed Deutsche Equity Income Trust plc) until 2003, JP Morgan Fleming US Discovery Investment Trust plc (formerly Fleming US Discovery Investment Trust plc) until 2004, Kent Co Crematorium plc 2010; dir: London & Manchester Group plc until 1998, Bailey Products Ltd until 1998, Kent TEC Ltd until 1994, Understanding Industry Trust Ltd until 2002, Savoy Hotel plc until 1998, The Learning and Business Link Co 1999–2001, ADL Partner Ltd 2002–09; chm: Tatem Ltd until 1999, Kent Economic Development Board until 1997, Business Link Kent Ltd until 1999 and 2003–, Claripoint Ltd 2000–07; CBI: former memb Nat Cncl, former memb Econ and Fin Policy Ctee, former memb Fin and Gen Purposes Ctee, fndr chm Kent Area Ctee (later chm SE Regnl Cncl); visiting prof in mktg INSEAD 1965–70; pres: INSEAD Int Alumni Assoc 1962–66, Kent branch Chartered Inst of Mktg 1988–92, Kent branch Inst of Mgmnt 1992–98; chm: The Haven Tst 1997–2006, D'Oyly Carte Charitable Tst 1998–; govr Kent Music Sch 1999–2010; tstee Lord Cornwallis Meml Fund; FCIM, FInstD, Hon FKC 2011; *Recreations* gardening, opera, fishing; *Style*—Jeremy Leigh Pemberton, Esq, CBE, DL; ✉ Hill House, Wormshill, Sittingbourne, Kent ME9 0TS (✆ 01622 884472, fax 01622 884784, e-mail jeremy.lp@btinternet.com)

LEIGH-PEMBERTON, Robin (Robert); *see:* Kingsdown, The Rt Hon Lord

LEIGH-SMITH, District Judge (Alfred) Nicholas Hardstaff; s of Lt-Col Alfred Leigh Hardstaff Leigh-Smith, TD, DL (d 1978), of Stanwell Moor, Middx, and Marguerite Calvert, *née* Calvert-Harrison (d 1983); *b* 21 December 1953; *Educ* Epsom Coll, Univ of Leeds (LLB); *m* Samantha Sian, *née* Morgan; 2 s (Thomas David b 29 June 2002, Henry Nicholas b 17 Dec 2003); *Career* called to the Bar Lincoln's Inn 1976; dep clerk: Bromley Justices 1985, Brent Justices 1989; clerk to the justices Cambridge and E Cambridgeshire Justices 1995–2001, in private practice New Walk Chambers Leicester 2001–04; asst stipendiary magistrate 1999–2000, dep district judge (Magistrates' Court) 2000–04, dist judge (Magistrates' Court) 2004–; *Recreations* church bellringing, rugby union football, clay pigeon shooting, reading, walking; *Style*— District Judge Leigh-Smith; ✉ The Hermitage, 23 Earning Street, Godmanchester, Huntingdon, Cambridgeshire PE29 2JD (fax 01480 435906); 3 & 4 John Street, Penmachno, North Wales (e-mail a.leighsmith@btinternet.com); The Magistrates' Court, Stuart Street, Luton, Bedfordshire LU1 5BL (✆ 01582 524200, fax 01582 524282)

LEIGHFIELD, John Percival; CBE (1998); s of late Henry Tom Dainton Leighfield, and late Patricia Zilpha Maud, *née* Baker; *b* 5 April 1938; *Educ* Magdalen Coll Sch Oxford (state scholarship), Exeter Coll Oxford (MA); *m* Margaret Ann, da of Charles Mealin; 1 s (Benjamin John b August 1968), 1 da (Rebecca Margaret b October 1970); *Career* with Ford Motor Co 1962–65, with Plessey Co 1965–72 (head of mgmnt info system 1970–72), with Br Leyland 1972–79 (IT dir Leyland Cars 1975–79), fndr and md ISTEL Ltd 1979–89, chm AT&T ISTEL (after AT&T acquired ISTEL) 1989–93, sr vice-pres and offr AT&T 1989–93; chm: RM plc 1993–2011, Birmingham Midshires Building Society 1996–99, Synstar plc 1998–2004; dir: TMA Ventures Ltd 1994–2002, IMPACT Programme Ltd 1998–2001, Halifax plc 1999–2001, KnowledgePool Ltd 2000–01, Getmapping plc 2005–; pro-chllr Univ of Warwick (chm Cncl 2002–11), hon prof and memb Advsy Bd Warwick Business Sch, visiting prof Warwick Manufacturing Gp; chm Alliance for Info Systems Skills; memb: Cncl of Computing Services and Software Assoc 1985–2002 (pres 1995–96), Bd of Intellect 2002–11; chm of govrs Magdalen Coll Sch Oxford 1995–2002, chm Advsy Cncl Oxford Philomusica 2002–11, chm of govrs WMG Acad for Young Engrs 2013–; Hon Dr: Univ of Central England, De Montfort Univ, Univ of Wolverhampton; Hon LLD Univ of Warwick; fndr memb, Liveryman and past Master Worshipful Co of Info Technologists, Freeman and Master Co of Educators 2007–; FInstD 1989, fell Inst for the Mgmnt of Info Systems 1990 (pres 2000–07), Hon FBCS 1991 (pres 1993–94), FRSA 1997, FIET 2007, FRGS 2011; *Publications* author of several papers on IT and on historical cartography; *Recreations* historical cartography, music, walking; *Clubs* RAC, Royal Fowey Yacht; *Style*— John Leighfield, Esq, CBE; ✉ 91 Victoria Road, Oxford OX2 7QG (e-mail john@leighfield.co.uk)

LEIGHTON, Sir John; kt (2013); s of Edwin Leighton (d 1982), and Norah Schwab, *née* Winterheim; *b* 22 February 1959, Belfast; *Educ* Portora Royal Sch Enniskillen, Univ of Edinburgh, Edinburgh Coll of Art (MA), Courtauld Inst of Art London (MA); *Partner* Gillian Keay; 1 da (Alexandra b 12 Nov 1989), 1 s (Frederick b 28 Oct 1992); *Career* lectr and tutor Dept of Humanities Edinburgh Coll of Art 1983–86, curator of 19th-century paintings National Gallery London 1986–97, dir Van Gogh Museum Amsterdam 1997–2006, DG National Galleries of Scotland 2006–; memb Bd De Pont Museum for Contemporary Art Tilburg 1998–, memb Supervisory Bd Mauritshuis 2009–; editorial advsr Amsterdam Univ Press 1998–2001, memb Steering Bd Apeldoorn Conference 1999–2006; Dr (hc) Univ of Edinburgh 2009; FRSE 2008; Chevalier Ordre des Arts et des Lettres; *Exhibitions* Edinburgh-Dublin 1885–1985 (Edinburgh Coll of Art) 1985, Jacques-Louis David: Portrait of Jacobus Blauw (National Gallery London) 1987, French Paintings from the USSR: Watteau to Matisse (National Gallery London) 1988, Caspar David Friedrich: Winter Landscape (National Gallery London) 1990, Art in the Making: Impressionism (National Gallery London) 1990–91, Corot (Manchester City Art Gallery and Castle Museum Norwich) 1991, Van Gogh to Picasso: The Berggruen Collection at the National Gallery (National Gallery London) 1991, Manet: The Execution of Maximilian (National Gallery London) 1992, Friedrich to Hodler: German, Austrian and Swiss Paintings from the Oskar Reinhart Foundation, Winterthur (National Gallery London, Alte Nationalgalerie Berlin, Los Angeles County Museum of Art, Metropolitan Museum of Art NY, Musée Rath Geneva) 1994, Seurat's Bathers (Nat Gallery London) 1997, Signac 1863–1935 (Grand Palais Paris, Van Gogh Museum Amsterdam, Metropolitan Museum of Art NY) 2001, Manet and the Sea (Art Inst of Chicago, Philadelphia Museum of Art, Van Gogh Museum Amsterdam) 2003–04; *Publications* Vincent van Gogh: Wheatfield with Crows (1999), 100 Masterpieces in the Van Gogh Museum (2002), Manet: Impressions of the Sea (2004), 100 Masterpieces from the National Galleries of Scotland (2015); also a number of exhibition catalogues; articles and reviews in various publications; *Style*— Sir John Leighton; ✉ National Galleries of Scotland, 73 Belford Road, Edinburgh EH4 3DS (✆ 0131 624 6508, website www.nationalgalleries.org)

LEIGHTON, Sir Michael John Bryan; 11 Bt (E 1693), of Wattlesborough, Shropshire; s of Col Sir Richard Tihel Leighton, 10 Bt, TD (d 1957), and Kathleen Irene Linda, *née* Lees (d 1993); *b* 8 March 1935; *Educ* Stowe, RAC Cirencester, Tabley House Agric Sch; *m* 1, 1974 (m dis 1980), Mrs Amber Mary Ritchie; m 2, 1991, Mrs Diana Mary Gamble; 1 da (Eleanor Angharad Diana b 20 Jan 1992); *Heir* none; *Career* photographer of wildlife; ornithologist; *Publications* Red Kites of the British Isles: 12 years' field studies diary (2008), collection of poems (2008), On the Marches (poetry, 2012), Your Yesterdays – Our Tomorrows (poetry, 2014); *Recreations* panel 'A' gun dog judge, cricket, tennis, golf, writing poetry, cooking; *Clubs* MCC; *Style*— Sir Michael Leighton, Bt; ✉ Loton Park, Alberbury, Shrewsbury, Shropshire SY5 9AJ (✆ 01743 884232)

LEINSTER, 9 Duke of (I 1766); Maurice FitzGerald; Premier Duke, Marquess and Earl in the Peerage of Ireland, also Baron of Offaly (I *ante* 1203 restored 1554), Earl of Kildare (I 1316), Viscount Leinster of Taplow (GB 1747), Marquess of Kildare, Earl of Offaly (both I 1761), and Baron Kildare (UK 1870); s of 8 Duke of Leinster (d 2004), and Anne, *née* Eustace Smith; *b* 7 April 1948, Dublin; *Educ* Millfield; *m* 19 Feb 1972, Fiona Mary Francesca, *née* Hollick; 1 s (Thomas, Earl of Offaly b 12 Jan 1974 d 1997), 2 da (Lady Francesca Emily Purcell b 6 July 1976, Lady Pollyanna Louisa Clementine b 9 May 1982); *Heir* n, Edward FitzGerald; *Career* landscape gardener and designer Maxwell Communication Corporation plc 1984–92; pres Oxfordshire Dyslexia Assoc 1978–2014; chm Thomas Offaly Meml Fund 1999–2015; *Recreations* fishing, shooting, riding, sailing, diving, DIY; *Style*— His Grace the Duke of Leinster; ✉ Courtyard House, Oakley Park, Frilford Heath, Oxfordshire OX13 6QW

LEINSTER, Prof Samuel John; s of late Victor Leinster, and Jemina Eileen Eva, *née* McGeown; *b* 29 October 1946, Belfast; *Educ* Boroughmuir Sr Secdy Sch Edinburgh, Univ of Edinburgh (BSc, MB ChB), Univ of Liverpool (MD); *m* 17 July 1971, Jennifer, da of James Woodward, of Wirral; 1 da (Angela b 1972), 3 s (Alistair b 1975, David b 1979, Benjamin b 1988); *Career* RAF Med Branch: PO 1969, Flying Offr 1971, Flt Lt 1972, MO 1972–77, Sqdn Ldr 1977, surgical specialist, ret 1977; lectr in surgery Welsh Nat Sch of Med 1978–81, sr lectr in surgery Univ of Liverpool and hon conslt surgn Liverpool HA 1982–90; Univ of Liverpool: reader in surgery 1990–93, prof of surgery 1993–2000, dir of med studies 1995–2000; dean of Sch of Med, Health Policy and Practice UEA 2001–11 (emeritus prof of medical educn 2011–); memb: BMA, Surgical Res Soc, Assoc of Surgns of GB and I, Assoc for the Study of Med Educn, Br Assoc of Surgical Oncology, Christian Med Fellowship, PLAB Bd GMC 2000–12; sr fell HE Acad; FRCS, FRCSEd, fell Acad of Med Educn; *Books* Systemic Diseases for Dental Students (with T J Bailey, 1983), Mammary Development and Cancer (with P S Rudland, D G Fernig and G G Lunt, 1997), Shared Care in Breast Cancer (with H Downey and T Gibbs, 2000), The Changing Face of Medical Education (with Penny Cavanagh and Susan Miles, 2011), The Changing Role of Doctors (with Penny Cavanagh and Susan Miles, 2013); numerous jl articles on medical educn and breast cancer; *Recreations* gardening, DIY, wood turning, active committed Christian; *Clubs* RAF; *Style—* Prof Samuel Leinster; ✉ University of East Anglia, Norwich NR4 7TJ (☎ 01603 593939, fax 01603 593752, e-mail s.leinster@uea.ac.uk)

LEITÃO, Robert Mark; s of Eduardo Francisco Felipe Leitão, of Portugal, and Brenda Miriam, *née* Jarman; *b* 28 June 1963; *Educ* St Julian's Sch Carcavelos Portugal, Oratory Sch Woodcote, Imperial Coll London (BSc); *m* 8 July 1995, Lucy Claire, *née* Birkbeck; 2 s (Felix Edward Oliver b 2 July 1998, Tobias Alexander Robert b 26 July 1999), 1 da (Hermione Sophie Isabel b 19 July 2003); *Career* KPMG 1985–89, Morgan Grenfell & Co Ltd 1989–98, head Global Advsy Rothschild 1998–; non-exec dir Manchester United plc 2012–; chm Pennies Fndn 2009–; ARSM 1984, ACA 1987; *Style—* Robert Leitão, Esq; ✉ Rothschild & Co, New Court, St Swithin's Lane, London EC4N 8AL (☎ 020 7280 5000, e-mail robert.leitao@rothschild.com)

LEITCH, Baron (Life Peer UK 2004), of Oakley in Fife; Alexander Park (Sandy) Leitch; s of Donald Leitch (d 1949), of Blairhall, Fife, and Agnes Smith, *née* Park (d 2006); *b* 20 October 1947; *Educ* Dunfermline HS; *m* 1 (m dis); 3 da (Hon Fiona b 1971, Hon Joanne b 1973, Hon Jacqueline b 1975); m 2, 29 Aug 2003, Noelle Dowd; 1 da (Hon Kathleen b 29 Oct 2007); *Career* chief systems designer National Mutual Life 1969, Hambro Life 1971 (bd dir 1981); Allied Dunbar plc: md 1988, dep chm 1990, chief exec 1993–96; chm Allied Dunbar Assurance plc 1996–98; chief exec: Br American Financial Services (UK and Int) Ltd 1996–98, Zurich Financial Services (UKISA) Ltd 1998–2001, Zurich Financial Services (UKISA/Asia Pacific) 2001–04; chm: Dunbar Bank 1994–2003, Eagle Star Holdings plc 1996–2004, Threadneedle Asset Management 1996–2004, ABI 1998–2000, Intrinsic Financial Servs 2005–, BUPA 2006– (dir 2005–), Scottish Widows 2007–; dir: BAT Industries plc 1997–98, United Business Media 2005–, Lloyds TSB 2005–, Paternoster 2006–; chm: SANE 1999–2000, Pensions Protection and Investment Accreditation Bd 2000–01, New Deal Task Force 2000–01, Nat Employment Panel 2001–07, Balance Charitable Fndn for Unclaimed Assets 2004–05, Leitch Review of UK Skills 2005; dep chm Business in the Community 1997–2004, vice-chm Cwlth Educn Fund 2002–, vice-pres UK Cares 2004; tstee: Nat Galleries of Scotland 1999–2003, Philharmonia Orch 2000–04; Prince of Wales Ambassador's Award for Charitable Work 2001; Freeman City of London 2002, memb Worshipful Co of Insurers 2002; MBCS 1966; *Recreations* antiques, football, antiquarian books, poetry; *Style—* The Rt Hon the Lord Leitch

LEITCH, Maurice Henry; MBE (1999); s of Andrew Leitch (d 1983), of Templepatrick, Co Antrim, NI, and Jean, *née* Coid (d 1973); *b* 5 July 1933; *Educ* Methodist Coll Belfast, Stranmills Trg Coll Belfast (teaching dip); *m* 1, 23 July 1956, Isobel, da of James Scott; 1 da (Bronagh b 17 Sept 1965), 1 s (Paul b 17 Feb 1967); m 2, 18 Nov 1972, Sandra, da of Alfred Hill; 1 s (Daniel b 29 April 1974); *Career* teacher Antrim NI 1954–60; BBC Radio: features prodr Belfast 1960–70, drama prodr London 1970–77, prodr Book at Bedtime 1977–89; author of several novels, TV screenplays, radio dramas, features and short stories; Guardian Fiction Prize 1969, Whitbread Fiction Prize 1981, Pye award for Most Promising Writer New to TV 1980–1981; memb Soc of Authors 1989; *Style—* Maurice Leitch, Esq, MBE; ✉ 6 Orestes Mews, London NW6 1AP

LEITH, Annie; *see:* Burgh, Anita, Lady; Anita Lorna

LEITH, Jake Quintin; s of Jack Leith (d 2010), and Louisa Teresa, *née* Quinn (d 2002); *b* 18 November 1958, Bushey, Herts; *Educ* Bushey Meads Sch, Herts Coll of Art & Design, Loughborough Coll of Art & Design (BA), Birmingham Inst of Art & Design (MA); *m* Jill Valerie Parker; 1 s (Alexander Jack b 22 April 2007); *Career* interior textile designer; export designer Textile Dept Everest Fabrics Ghaziabad India 1983–84, interior designer/textile advsr Europa Shop Equipment Ltd 1984–85, self-employed interior designer Fantasy Finishes 1985–86, sr ptnr The Jake Leith Partnership interior designers specialising in furnishing fabrics and wall-coverings 1986–; private and commercial cmmns; CSD: memb assessor Textiles/Fashion 1996–, tstee and memb Cncl 1998–, chair Textiles/Fashion Bd 2001–03, memb Ethics and Professional Practice Ctee 2004–, vice-pres 2004–07, pres 2011–13, imminent past pres 2014–; memb: Continual Professional Devpt Ctee 1995–97, Professional Standards Ctee 1995–98 (hon sec 2008–09, pres elect 2009–11, pres 2011–13, immediate past pres 2013–); external examiner, validator and advsr CHEAD 1997–, practicing assoc Acad of Experts 1998–2000; external examiner (Printed Textiles/Surface Decoration) Univ of E London 1998–2003, external examiner and consult (MA in design enterprise) Univ of Hull 2008–12; Loughborough Univ: ind assessor Multi-Media Textiles 1999–2000, internal examiner Furniture Design 2000–2002, co-ordinator and internal examiner Professional Business Studies 1999–2003; external advsr Utrecht Sch of Arts 2002–, external advsr Open Univ 2002–, external advsr Univ of Sussex 2005–, external assessor Manchester Met Univ 2013–; Univ of Brighton: internal examiner 2002–, visiting lectr 2002–03, area ldr business studies fashion and textiles 2003–, academic prog ldr fashion and textiles 2004–06 and 2011–13, course validator 2005–, business and professional practice ldr 2007–, memb Employability and Entrepreneurship Steering Ctee 2008– (princ lectr 2012–); memb Assoc of Degree Courses in Fashion and textile Design 2004–07, memb Colls Forum Steering Ctee British Fashion Cncl 2005–07; visual arts advsr Dacorum Borough Arts 1996–2004, judge Healey & Baker Fashion Awards 2002–06, external advsr South Coast Design Forum 2008–10, memb Nat Readers' Panel Queen's Anniversary Prizes for Higher and Further Educn 2009–, tstee Fashion Tst 2010–13, judge Sussex Fashion Awards 2011–13, tstee European Conference on e-Learning Ctee 2012–, delg Br Cncl Saudi Arabia, Nigeria and Morocco 2013; Freeman City of London, Liveryman Worshipful Co of Framework Knitters 2012; FCSD 1995 (MCSD 1983), FRSA 1996; *Recreations* classical guitar, printmaking, catamaran sailing, gardening, songwriting, good food, blues rock guitar; *Clubs* Sopwell House Country; *Style—* Jake Leith, Esq; ✉ The Jake Leith Partnership, 12 Midland Road, Hemel Hempstead, Hertfordshire HP2 5DJ (☎ 01442 247010, fax 01442 245495, e-mai jake@jlp.uk.com, website www.jakeleith.com)

LEITH, Prudence Margaret (Prue); CBE (2010, OBE 1989), DL (Gtr London 1998); da of Stewart Leith (d 1961), of Johannesburg, South Africa, and Margaret, *née* Inglis; *b* 18 February 1940; *Educ* St Mary's Sch Johannesburg, Univ of Cape Town, Sorbonne Paris (Cours de la Civilisation Francaise); *m* 1974, (Charles) Rayne Kruger (author); 1 s (Daniel b 1974), 1 da (Li-Da b 1974); *Career* restaurateur, caterer, author, journalist; fndr: Leith's Good Food 1961, Leith's Restaurant 1969, Prudence Leith Ltd 1972, Leith's Sch of Food and Wine 1975, Leith's Farm 1976; dir: Leith's Restaurant Ltd 1969–95, Prudence Leith Ltd 1972–94 (md), Br Transport Hotels Ltd 1977–83, BR Bd 1980–85 (pt/t), Safeway plc 1989–96 (formerly Argyll Group plc, joined gp as conslt to Safeway stores 1988), Halifax plc (formerly Leeds Permanent Building Society and Halifax Building Society until 1997) 1992–99, Leith's Ltd 1994–96 (chm), 3E's Enterprises Ltd 1994–2007 (chm), Whitbread plc 1995–2005, Triven VCT 2000–03, Forum for the Future 2000–03 (chm), Woolworths plc 2001–06, Omega plc 2004–09, Nations Healthcare 2006–07, Belmond (UK) Ltd 2006–15; chair School Food Tst 2007–10; memb Cncl Food From Britain 1983–87; chm: Restaurateurs' Assoc of GB 1990–94, Br Food Tst; vice-pres Royal Soc for the Encouragement of Arts, Manufactures and Commerce; team memb Opportunity 2000 Target; govr Ashridge Mgmnt Coll 1992–2007 (chm 2002–07); visiting prof Univ of N London 1993; appeared in: 26-part TV cookery series on Tyne-Tees TV, Best of Br BBC TV, The Good Food Show, Take 6 Cooks, Tricks of the Trade, Great British Menu; memb: Nat Trg Task Force Dept of Employment 1989–91, Centre for Tomorrow's Co 1990–2013, PO Stamp Advsy Ctee 1997–2003; hon fell Hotel Catering and Institutional Mgmnt Assoc 1986, hon fell Salford Univ 1992, hon fell City and Guilds of London Inst 1992–97, master Univ of North London 1997; Corning Award Food Journalist of the Year 1979, Glenfiddich Trade Journalist of the Year 1983, Veuve Clicquot Business Woman of the Year 1990; Freedom of the City of London 1994; Hon Dr: Univ of Greenwich 1996, Univ of Manchester 1996, Open Univ 1997, Oxford Brookes Univ 2000, City Univ 2005, Thames Valley Univ 2007; Hon DLitt Queen Margaret Coll Edinburgh 1997, Hon DLitt Univ of Warwick 2013; FRSA (chm RSA 1995–97), Hon FCGI; *Books* written 12 cookery books between 1972 and 1991 and five novels; Leaving Patrick (1999), Sisters (2001), A Lovesome Thing (2004), The Gardener (2007), Choral Society (2009), A Serving of Scandal (2010); Relish: My Life on a Plate (memoir, 2012), Food of Love: Laura's Story (2015); *Recreations* walking, flyfishing; *Clubs* Chelsea Arts; *Style—* Ms Prue Leith, CBE, DL; ✉ The Office, Chastleton Glebe, Moreton-in-Marsh, Gloucestershire GL56 0SZ (☎ 01608 674908, e-mail pmleith@prue-leith.com, website www.prue-leith.com)

LEMMON, Mark Benjamin; s of Edmund Lemmon (d 1984), of Great Bookham, Surrey, and Mary Patricia, *née* Bryan (d 2005); *b* 15 April 1952; *Educ* Wimbledon Coll, UCL (BA), LSE (MSc), Coll of Estate Mgmnt (Dip Property Investment (RICS) and Dip Arbitration); *m* 8 Aug 1980, Anna, da of Prof Tamas Szekely, of Budapest, Hungary; 3 da (Esther b 1981, Patricia b 1985, Bernadette b 1990); *Career* formerly with: Touche Ross, Grindlays Bank, Guinness Mahon, Hongkong and Shanghai Banking Corporation (sr corp mangr), HSBC Bank plc (dep chief exec project and export fin); currently exec vice-chm Mena Infrastructure Fun (GP) Ltd Dubai; dir ECGD; memb: Billingsgate Ward Club, Company of World Traders, Coopers, Hungarian Soc, English Speaking Union; Freeman City of London; FCA 1978, ATII 1979, ACIB 1982, FRSA, FCIArb 2011; *Recreations* squash, opera; *Clubs* Wimbledon Squash and Badminton, Old Wimbledonians, Wayfoong, Felpham Sailing, Star Gun, India, Royal Over-Seas League, Savage, Singhalese Sports, British (Bangkok), Foreign Correspondents (Thailand); *Style—* Mark Lemmon, Esq; ✉ 11 Crescent Road, Wimbledon, London SW20 8EX (☎ 00 97 1 56 480 1367, e-mail mark.lemmon@menainfrastructure.com)

LEMMY; *see:* Kilmister, Lemmy

LEMON, Jane Katherine; QC (2015); da of John Lemon, and Margaret, *née* Arber; *b* 19 September 1969, Clatterbridge, Cheshire; *Educ* King Edward VI HS for Girls, Jesus Coll Oxford (BA), Coll of Law (CPE); *m* 7 July 2006, Mark Hepburn; 2 s (Samuel, Nathaniel), 1 da (Niamh); *Career* called to the Bar 1993; memb: TECBAR, COMBAR; *Publications* contrib to pubns on construction contracts and professional negligence and liability; *Recreations* skiing, running; *Style—* Ms Jane Lemon, QC; ✉ Keating Chambers, 15 Essex Street, London WC2R 3AA

LENDRUM, Christopher John (Chris); CBE (2005); s of Herbert Colin Lendrum (d 2006), of St Neots, Cambs, and Anne Margaret, *née* Macdonell; *b* 15 January 1947; *Educ* Felsted Sch, Univ of Durham (BA); *m* 1 Aug 1970, Margaret Patricia, da of Joseph Ridley Parker; 1 s (Oliver David Ridley b 23 Sept 1976), 1 da (Victoria Alice b 11 Sept 1980); *Career* Barclays Bank plc: joined 1969, chief exec Corporate Banking 1996–2003, gp exec dir 1998–2004, chm Barclays Africa 2000–04, gp vice-chm 2004, chm Barclays Pension Fund Tstees Ltd 2005–11; non-exec dir: County Durham Community Fndn 2009–14, North East Finance Ltd 2009–, Motability Operations plc 2009–; govr Kent Coll 2000–08; memb Advsy Bd Nat Assoc of Citizens Advice Bureaux (NACAB) 2001–04, tstee CAB 2005–07; tstee: Aston Martin Heritage Tst 2003–10 (chm 2006–09), City of London Endowment Tst for St Paul's Cathedral 2007–16, The Alnwick Garden 2012–15, Tyne, Wear & Northumberland Community Fndn 2015–; govr Motability 2005–09; church warden St James Church Shilbottle 2013–; Freeman City of London 1999, Liveryman Worshipful Co of Woolmen 1999; Hon DLitt Univ of Durham 2008; FCIB 1992, CIMgt 2001; *Recreations* early motor cars, travel, gardening; *Clubs* RAC; *Style—* Chris Lendrum, Esq, CBE; ✉ Hazon House, Nr Guyzance, Morpeth, Northumberland NE65 9AT (☎ 01665 575846)

LENEY, Simon David; s of Colin Frank Leney, of E Sussex, and Patricia, *née* Easton; *b* 10 September 1952, Brighton; *Educ* Sherborne; *m* 6 Nov 1976, Jane, *née* Crouch; 2 s (George David b 16 Feb 1985, William James 6 Dec 1987); *Career* ptnr: Donne Mileham & Haddock 1980–94, Cripps Harries Hall LLP 1994–2015, Cripps LLP 2015–; memb: Law Soc 1977 (memb Private Client Ctee 2010–, chm Private Client Section 2012–15), Soc of Notaries Public 1989, Soc of Trust and Estate Practitioners 1991; MSI 1986; *Recreations* Porsche cars, rugby, house and garden; *Style—* Simon Leney, Esq; ✉ e-mail simon.leney@hotmail.co.uk; Cripps LLP, Wallside House, 12 Mount Ephraim Road, Tunbridge Wells TN1 1EG (☎ 01892 506005, e-mail sdl@cripps.co.uk)

LENG, James William (Jim); *b* 19 November 1945; *Career* ceo: Low & Bonar plc 1992–95, Laporte plc 1995–2001; non-exec dir: Pilkington plc 1998–2006, Corus Gp plc 2001–09 (chm 2003–09), IMI 2002–05, JPMorganFleming Mid Cap Investment Tst plc 2003–04, Hanson 2004–07; sr ind dir Alstom SA 2003– (chm Renumerations and Nominations Ctee), chm Doncasters Gp 2006–, dep chm Tata Steel India 2007–, TNK-BP 2009–; *Style—* J W Leng, Esq; ✉ 2nd Floor, 30 Millbank, London SW1P 4WY (☎ 020 7717 4554, fax 020 7717 4654)

LENIHAN, Conor Patrick; TD; s of Brian Lenihan (d 1995), and Ann, *née* Devine; *b* 3 March 1963, Dublin, Ireland; *Educ* Belvedere Coll, UC Dublin (BA), Dublin City Univ (Dip), INSEAD; *m* 10 Sept 1994, Denise, *née* Russell; 2 s (Brian, Jack) 1 da (Alex); *Career* political corr Irish News Westminster 1988, broadcast journalist Ind Radio News and 98FM 1990, mangr Radio Bohemia Prague 1992, sr exec Esat Digifone 1996, TD (Fianna Fáil) Dublin SW 1997–, min of state Dept of Foreign Affrs 2004–09, min of state Dept of Enterprise, Trade and Employment 2009–11; *Recreations* football, swimming, tennis, hill walking; *Clubs* Tallaght Athletic, Templeogue Tennis; *Style—* Conor Lenihan, Esq, TD; ✉ 93 St Stephen's Green, Dublin 2, Ireland (☎ 00353 1428 3555, e-mail lenihan.dublin@gmail.com)

LENMAN, Prof Bruce Philip; s of Jacob Philip Lenman (d 1986), of Aberdeen, and May, *née* Wishart (d 1976); *b* 9 April 1938; *Educ* Aberdeen GS, Univ of Aberdeen (MA, Forbes Gold Medal), St John's Coll Cambridge (MLitt, LittD); *Career* asst prof of history Victoria Univ 1963, lectr in Imperial and Commonwealth history Univ of St Andrews 1963–67, lectr Dept of Modern History Univ of Dundee 1967–72, reader in modern history Univ of St Andrews 1983–88 (lectr 1972–78, sr lectr 1978–83), James Pinckney Harrison prof Coll of William and Mary Virginia 1988–89, prof of modern history Univ of St Andrews 1992–2003 (reader 1989–92); Bird visiting prof Emory Univ Atlanta 1998; Br Acad fell Newberry Library Chicago 1982, John Carter Brown Library fell Rhode Island 1984, Cncl of Europe res fell 1984, Folger fell Folger Library Washington DC 1988–89 and 1997, Hill fell Huntington Library San Marino 2004; Weddell lectr Virginia Historical Soc 1991 (Mellon fell 1990); past pres Abertay Historical Soc; Scottish Arts Cncl Literary Award 1977 and 1980; FRHistS 1977, FRSE 2004; *Books* Dundee and its Textile Industry (1969), From Esk to Tweed (1975), An Economic History of Modern Scotland (1977), The Jacobite Risings in Britain (1980), Crime and the Law (ed, 1980), Integration and Enlightenment: Scotland 1746–1832 (1981), Jacobite Clans of the Great Glen (1984), The Jacobite Cause (1986), The Jacobite Threat: A Source Book (with John S Gibson, 1990), The Eclipse of Parliament (1992), Chambers Dictionary of World History (ed, 1993, 3 edn 2005), Colonial Wars 1550–1783 (2 vols, 2001), Enlightenment and Change (2009), Military Engineers and the Development of the Early Modern European State (2013); *Recreations* golf, curling, swimming, Scottish country dancing, badminton; *Clubs* Royal Commonwealth; *Style—* Emeritus Prof Bruce P Lenman; ✉ Apartment 4, 55 Victoria Place, Stirling FK8 2QT (☎ 01786 446090, e-mail bruceplenman@yahoo.co.uk)

LENNARD, Thomas William Jay; s of late Thomas Jay Lennard, MBE, of Falkirk, and Elizabeth Jemima Mary Patricia, *née* Poole; *b* 25 October 1953; *Educ* Clifton, Univ of

Newcastle upon Tyne (MB BS, MD); *m* 8 July 1978, Anne Lesley, da of Cyril Barber, of Ossett, W Yorks; 3 s (James Matthew Thomas b 1984, Jonathan Alexander Thomas b 1987, Oliver Thomas Jay b 1993); *Career* lectr in surgery Univ of Newcastle upon Tyne 1982–88, reader and conslt surgn Univ of Newcastle upon Tyne and Royal Victoria Infirmary Newcastle upon Tyne 1988–2002, prof of breast and endocrine surgery and head Sch of Surgical and Reproductive Scis Univ of Newcastle upon Tyne 2002–09, assoc dean of medicine Faculty of Medical Sciences Newcastle Univ 2014–; pres Br Assoc of Thyroid and Endocrine Surgns 2007–09, memb N of England Surgical Soc; FRCS 1980; *Books* Going into Hospital (1988); *Recreations* fly fishing, gardening; *Style*— Thomas Lennard, Esq; ✉ Ward 44, Royal Victoria Infirmary, Queen Victoria Road, Newcastle upon Tyne NE1 4LP (✆ 0191 282 4661)

LENNON, Aaron Justin; *b* 16 April 1987, Leeds, Yorkshire; *Career* professional footballer; clubs: Leeds United 2003–05, Tottenham Hotspur 2005–; England: 21 caps, debut v Jamaica 2006, memb squad World Cup 2006 and 2010; *Style*— Aaron Lennon, Esq; ✉ c/o Tottenham Hotspur Football Club, White Hart Lane, 748 High Road, London N17 0AP

LENNON, Neil Francis; *b* 25 June 1971, Lurgan, Co Armagh; *Career* football manager; player: Crewe Alexandra 1990–96 (147 appearances), Leicester City 1996–2000 (170 appearances, promoted to Premiership 1996, winners League Cup 1997 and 2000), Celtic 2000–07 (214 appearances, winners Scottish Premier League 2001, 2002, 2004, 2006 and 2007, Scottish FA Cup 2001, 2004, 2005 and 2007, finalists UEFA Cup 2003), Nottingham Forest 2007–08, Wycombe Wanderers 2008; NI: debut v Mexico 1994, 40 caps, ret from int football 2002; manager Celtic 2010– (winners Scottish FA Cup 2011 and 2013, winners Scottish Premier League 2012 and 2013); *Style*— Mr Neil Lennon; ✉ Celtic Football Club, Celtic Park, Glasgow G40 3RE

LENNOX; *see also:* Gordon Lennox

LENNOX-BOYD, Lady; Arabella Lennox-Boyd; *née* Parisi; da of Piero Parisi, of Rome; *b* 15 January 1938, Rome, Italy; *Educ* Greenwich Univ; *m* 1974, The Hon Sir Mark Lennox-Boyd; *Career* landscape designer; fndr Arabella Lennox-Boyd Landscape and Architectural Design, has designed gardens in the UK, Europe and other countries incl Russia, Ukraine, USA and Caribbean, ranging from small town gardens to large landscapes, projects incl roof garden at Number One Poultry London, Eaton Hall Cheshire and Nat Tst Gardens Ascott House and Sheringham Hall; formerly: tstee Kew Gardens, memb Historic Parks, memb Garden Panel English Heritage; currently: memb RHS Woody Plant Ctee, tstee Yorks Arboretum Tst, patron Painsill Park Tst, memb Cncl and Scientific Ctee Int Dendrology Soc, tstee Tree Register; 6 Gold Medals Chelsea Flower Show (incl Best Garden Award 1998); Hon Dr Greenwich Univ 2003, Premio Firenze Donna 2005, RHS Veitch Medal 2008; *Books* Traditional English Gardens (1989), Private Gardens of London (1993), Designing Gardens (2002); *Recreations* collecting rare trees, propagating, gardening, listening to music, cooking; *Style*— Lady Lennox-Boyd; ✉ Arabella Lennox-Boyd Landscape & Architectural Design, 1–5 Dells Mews, Churton Place, London SW1V 2LW (✆ 020 7931 9995, e-mail office@arabellalennoxboyd.com, website www.arabellalennoxboyd.com)

LENON, Barnaby John; s of Rev Philip John Fitzmaurice Lenon, of Dinton, Wilts, and Jane Alethea, *née* Brooke; *b* 10 May 1954; *Educ* Eltham Coll, Keble Coll Oxford (scholar, MA), St John's Coll Cambridge (univ prize for educn, coll prize, PGCE); *m* 27 August 1983, Penelope Anne, da of James Desmond Thain; 2 da (India Elizabeth Jane b 9 Nov 1989, Flora Catherine Dyne b 4 June 1992); *Career* teacher: Eton Coll 1976–77 and 1979–90, Sherborne Sch 1978–79; dep headmaster Highgate Sch 1990–94; headmaster: Trinity Sch of John Whitgift 1995–99, Harrow Sch 1999–2011; chm Ind Schs Cncl 2011–; dir Bd: Ofqual 2012–, Yellow Submarine Charity 2012–, Vocal Futures 2012–, New Schs Network 2014–; govr: John Lyon Sch, Orley Farm Sch, Wellesley House Sch, Aysgarth Sch, Francis Holland Schs, Papplewick Sch, Chelsea Acad, The Hall Sch, Swanbourne Sch, The Beacon Sch, Bellerbys Schs; chm of govrs London Acad of Excellence; FRGS 1987 (memb Cncl 1987–90 and 1998–2000, vice-pres 2009–12); *Books* Techniques and Fieldwork in Geography (1982), London (1988), London in the 1990's (1993), Fieldwork Techniques and Projects in Geography (1994), Directory of University Geography Courses 1995 (jt ed, 1995, 2 edn 1996), The United Kingdom: Geographical Case Studies (1995), Geography Fieldwork and Skills (2015), Cambridge AS and A-Level Geography (2016); *Recreations* writing, oil painting, deserts, rowing, athletics; *Style*— Barnaby J Lenon, Esq; ✉ 55 St John Street, Oxford OX1 2LQ (e-mail barnabylenon@ hotmail.co.uk, Twitter @barnabylenon)

LEONARD, His Hon Judge Anthony James; QC (1999); s of Hon Sir John Leonard (d 2002), and Lady Doreen Enid, *née* Parker (d 1996); *b* 21 April 1956; *Educ* Hurstpierpoint Coll, Inns of Court Sch of Law; *m* 4 June 1983, Shara Jane, da of John Macrae Cormack; 2 da (Olivia Mary b 13 Oct 1985, Stephanie Emma b 17 Jan 1989); *Career* short service ltd cmmn 1974–5, Maj 6/7 Queens Regt (TA) 1976–85; called to the Bar Inner Temple 1978 (bencher 2002); in practice SE Circuit, standing counsel to the Inland Revenue (SE Circuit) 1993–99, recorder 2000–09, circuit judge South Eastern Circuit 2009–; memb Criminal Bar Assoc 1979–09, vice chm Professional Practice Ctee 2006–08; dep chllr Diocese of St Edmundsbury & Ipswich 2009–, chllr Diocese of Ely 2012–, commissary to the Archbishop of Canterbury 2012–; Liveryman Worshipful Co of Plaisterers; *Recreations* opera, wine; *Clubs* Garrick; *Style*— His Hon Judge Leonard, QC

LEONARD, Brian Henry; CBE (2008); s of William Henry Leonard (d 1986), Bertha Florence, *née* Thomas (d 1977); *b* 6 January 1948; *Educ* Dr Challoner's GS, LSE; *m* 1975, Maggy, da of Charles Martin Meade-King; 2 s (Will Martin b 1 Jan 1977, James Henry b 20 July 1979); *Career* Heal & Son Ltd 1969–73, The Price Commission 1973–74; DOE: admin trainee 1974–77, HEO 1977–79, princ 1979–88, seconded to Circle 33 Housing Trust 1982–83, asst sec 1988–93, under sec and regnl dir of Northern Region 1993–94, regnl dir Govt Office for the South West 1994–97; dir Environmental Protection Strategy DETR 1997–98; DCMS: head of regions Tourism, Millennium and International Gp 1998–2001, head Tourism, Lottery and Regions Directorate 2001–02, head Tourism, Libraries and Communities Directorate 2002–04, then dir Industry; chief exec Sporta 2010–; non-exec dir Business in Sport and Industry (BISL) 2008–11, non-exec dir South West Screen 2008–11, memb UK Cncl for Child Internet Safety (UKCCIS) 2009–11; fell Hubert Humphrey Inst Minneapolis 1987–88; *Recreations* friends, games, pottering about; *Clubs* Marylebone Cricket; *Style*— Brian Leonard, CBE

LEONARD, (Douglas) Michael; s of Maj Douglas Goodwin Russell Leonard, IXth Jat Regt India (d 1942), and Kathleen Mary Leonard, *née* Murphy; *b* 25 June 1933, Bangalore, India; *Educ* Hallet War Sch Nainital India, Stonyhurst Coll (sch cert), St Martin's Sch of Art (NDD); *Career* artist; freelance illustrator 1957–72, painter 1972–; cmmnd by Reader's Digest to paint portrait of HM The Queen to celebrate her 60th birthday 1984 (presented to Nat Portrait Gallery 1986); *Solo Exhibitions* Fischer Fine Art London 1974, 1977, 1980, 1983 and 1988, Harriet Griffin NYC 1977, Stiebel Modern NYC 1992, Thomas Gibson 1993, 1997 and 2004, Forum Gallery NYC 1999 and 2009; *Retrospectives* Gemeentemuseum Arnhem 1977, Artsite Gallery Bath 1989, Michael Leonard: A Master of Ambiguity (Jonathan Edwards Coll Yale Univ) 2007; *Group Exhibitions* Fischer Fine Art London 1972, 1973, 1975, 1976, 1978, 1979, and 1981, Realismus und Realität (Darmstadt) 1975, John Moores Exhbns 10 and 11 Liverpool 1976 and 1978, Nudes (Angela Flowers Gallery London) 1980–81, Contemporary British Painters (Museo Municipal Madrid) 1983, The Self Portrait – A Modern View (touring) 1987–88, In Human Terms (Stiebel Modern NYC) 1991, Representing Representation (Arnot Art Museum Elmira NY) 1993, It's Still Life (Forum Gallery NYC) 1998, Still Life Painting Today

(Jerald Melberg Gallery Inc Charlotte NC) 1998, The Nude in Contemporary Art (The Aldrich Museum of Contemporary Art Ridgefield CT) 1999, Still Lifes (William Baczek Fine Arts Northampton MA), The Male Form in Contemporary Art (Art and Culture Center Hollywood, Florida), Between Earth and Heaven (MOMA Oostende) 2001, Artists of the Ideal (Galleria d'Arte Moderna Verona) 2002, What is Realism? (Albemarle Gallery London) 2005; *Public Collections* Museum Boymans-van Beuningen Rotterdam, Br Museum, V&A, Nat Portrait Gallery London, Ferens Art Gallery Hull, New Orleans Museum of Art, Fitzwilliam Museum Cambridge, Arnot Art Museum Elmira NY; *Books* Changing – 50 Drawings (intro by Edward Lucie-Smith, 1983), Michael Leonard – Paintings (foreword by Lincoln Kirstein, interviewed by Edward Lucie-Smith, 1985); *Style*— Michael Leonard, Esq; ✉ 3 Kensington Hall Gardens, Beaumont Avenue, London W14 9LS; www.michaelleonardartist.com

LEONARD, Nils; *m*; 3 s; *Career* designer Ammirati Puris Lintas 1993–97, designer TBWA 1996–97, head of art Rainey Kelly Campbell Roalfe 1998–2003, sr designer/art dir Abbott Mead Vickers BBDO 2003–05, head of art United 2005–07, exec creative dir then chief creative offr Grey London 2007–16 (chm 2014–16); campaigns incl: Spacechair (Toshiba), Louder (Lucozade), Kiss (Vodafone); Adweek Global Agency of the Year 2013, Cannes Black Lion; *Style*— Nils Leonard, Esq; ✉ Grey London, The Johnson Building, 77 Hatton Garden, London EC1N 8JS (website www.grey.co.uk)

LEONARD, Dr Robert Charles Frederick; s of André Lucien Maxime Leonard (d 1977), of Merthyr Tydfil, Wales, and Rosa Mary, *née* Taylor; *b* 11 May 1947; *Educ* Merthyr Tydfil Co GS, Charing Cross Hosp Med Sch (BSc, MB BS, MD); *m* 2 June 1973, Tania, da of Roland Charles Smith, and Keysoe, *née* North, of Louth, Lincs; 3 da (Victoria b 26 Sept 1974, Louisa b 26 Feb 1978, Emily b 18 Sept 1980); *Career* sr house offr: Charing Cross Hosp 1972, Hammersmith Hosp 1973; registrar Oxford Hosps 1974–76, res fell Leukaemia Res Fund 1976–79, lectr and sr registrar Newcastle Hosps 1979–82, fell Cancer Res Campaign 1981–82, res fell Dana Farber Cancer Inst Harvard Med Sch Boston 1982, conslt physician and hon sr lectr in clinical oncology Edinburgh 1983–2001, prof of cancer studies Univ of Wales Swansea 2001–, dir SW Wales Cancer Inst 2001–; memb: UKCCCR Breast Ctee, Br Breast Gp; memb Editorial Bd British Journal of Cancer; FRCPEd 1984, FRCP 1993, American Soc of Clinical Oncology; *Books* Understanding Cancer (1985), Serological Tumour Marks (1993), Breast Cancer: The Essential Facts (1995); author of over 300 scientific papers on cancer and related research; *Recreations* music, piano, soccer; *Style*— Robert Leonard; ✉ South-West Wales Cancer Institute, Singleton Hospital, Swansea SA2 8QA (✆ 01792 285300, fax 01792 285301, e-mail r.c.f.leonard@swansea.ac.uk)

LEONARD, Dr Rosemary; MBE (2004); da of Gordon Harris Leonard (d 1996), and Edna Alice, *née* Read; *b* 22 July 1956, London; *Educ* Dr Challoners HS Little Chalfont, Newnham Coll Cambridge (entrance exhibitioner, coll scholar, Johnson & Florence Stoney scholar, MA, MB, BChir), St Thomas' Hosp Med Sch; *m* 23 April 2011, Martin Pryor; 2 s from a previous relationship (Thomas O'Reilly b 26 Sep 1989, William O'Reilly b 28 Oct 1991); *Career* GP; ptnr in gen practice 1988–, resident GP Breakfast News (BBC) 1998; journalist Sun 1993–99, Daily Mail 1999–2002, GP contrib and columnist Daily Express and Sunday Express 2002–; GP rep Ctee of Safety of Medicines 2002–05, memb Human Genetics Cmmn 2006–08, non-exec memb Bd Health Protection Agency 2008–10, memb Advsy Panel on Cosmetic Interventions Dept of Health 2012–13; *Publications* 7 Ages of Woman (2007), Tales from the Surgery (2012), Doctor's Notes (2014); *Recreations* skiing, sailing, choral singing, arts and crafts movement, growing vegetables and delphiniums; *Style*— Dr Rosemary Leonard, MBE; ✉ c/o James Grant Management, 94 Strand on the Green, Chiswick, London W4 3NN (✆ 020 8742 4950, e-mail natalie@ jamesgrant.co.uk, website www.drrosemaryleonard.co.uk, Twitter @drrosemaryl)

LEONARD, Zach; *Educ* Harvard Univ (BA); *Career* account supervisor Chiat Day Advertising 1987–90, account supervisor Mullen 1990–92, dir mktg devpt Fidelity Investments 1992–94, vice-pres interactive programming Fidelity Investments US and Int 1994–99, ceo FTMarketWatch.com 1999–2001, chief operating offr FT.com 2001–04, Accenture 2005–06; News Int: digital publisher Times Media 2006–08, digital strategy and devpt 2008–09, md Milkround 2009–10; md digital Evening Standard and The Independent 2010–; dir Bd Contemporary Art Soc 2010–; *Style*— Zach Leonard, Esq; ✉ ESI Media, Northcliffe House, 2 Derry Street, Kensington, London W8 5TT (Twitter @digizach)

LEPPARD, Adrian; CBE (2016), QPM (2012); *Career* joined Surrey Police 1984, Dep Chief Constable Kent Police 2007–10 (former Asst Chief Constable), Cmmr City of London Police 2010–; *Style*— Adrian Leppard, Esq, CBE, QPM; ✉ City of London Police, 37 Wood Street, London EC2P 2NQ

LEPPARD, David George; s of John C Leppard, and Elizabeth, *née* Hapgood (d 1968); *b* 6 August 1957; *Educ* Hampton GS, Univ of Leicester (BA, Wallace Henry Prize), Univ of Oxford (DPhil); *Career* journalist; reporter The Times 1986; Sunday Times: reporter, dep Insight ed 1990–93, home affairs corr 1993–95, home affairs ed and dep news ed (investigations) 1995–96, ed Insight team 1996–2001, asst ed (home affairs) 2001–; *Awards* Br Press Awards: nominated Reporter of the Year 1990, 2007 and 2008, nominated Scoop of the Year 2001 and 2004, winner Specialist Writer of the Year 2004; Freedom of the Media Award 1995, nominated Scoop of the Year London Press Club Awards 2004; *Publications* On the Trail of Terror (1991), Fire and Blood (1993); *Recreations* reading and relaxing; *Style*— David Leppard, Esq; ✉ Sunday Times, 3 Thomas More Square, London E98 1ST (e-mail david.leppard@sunday-times.co.uk)

LEPPARD, Raymond John; CBE (1983); s of Albert Victor Leppard, and Bertha May, *née* Beck; *b* 11 August 1927; *Educ* Trinity Coll Cambridge; *Career* fell and lectr in music Trinity Coll Cambridge 1958–68, princ conductor BBC Northern Symphony Orch 1972–80, princ guest conductor St Louis Symphony Orch 1984–90, music dir Indianapolis Symphony Orch 1987–2001; Hon DUniv Bath 1972; Hon DMus: Indiana Univ 1991, Perdue Univ 1992; hon memb: RAM 1972, GSM 1984; Hon FRCM 1984; Commendatore al Merito Della Republica Italiana 1974; Monteverdi: Il Ballo Delle Ingrate (1958), L'Incoronazione Di Poppea (1962), L'Orfeo (1965), Cavalli: Messa Concertata (1966), L'Ormindo (1967), La Calisto (1969), Il Ritorno D'Ulisse (1972), L'Eqisto (1974), L'Orione (1983), Authenticity in Music (1988), Raymond Leppard on Music: An Anthology of Critical and Autobiographical Writings (1993), Music Made Me: Memoirs (2011); *Recreations* theatre, books, friends, music; *Style*— Raymond Leppard, Esq, CBE

LEPSCHY, Prof Giulio Ciro; s of Emilio Lepschy (d 1994), and Sara, *née* Castelfranchi (d 1984); *b* 14 January 1935; *Educ* Liceo Marco Polo Venice, Univ of Pisa (Dott Lett), Scuola Normale Superiore (Dip & Perf Sc Norm Sup); *m* 20 Dec 1962, Prof (Anna) Laura Lepschy, *qv*, da of Arnaldo Momigliano, Hon KBE (d 1987); *Career* Univ of Reading: lectr 1964–67, reader 1967–75, prof 1975–98, emeritus 2000; hon prof UCL 1998–; prof (status only) Univ of Toronto; pres MHRA 2001; Serena Medal Br Acad 2000; fell Accademia della Crusca 2009 (corresponding fell 1991); laurea (hc) Univ of Turin 1998; FBA 1987; *Publications* A Survey of Structural Linguistics (1970), The Italian Language Today (with A L Lepschy, 1977), Saggi di Linguistica Italiana (1978), Intorno a Saussure (1979), Mutamenti di Prospettiva nella Linguistica (1981), Nuovi Saggi di Linguistica Italiana (1989), Sulla Linguistica Moderna (1989), Storia della Linguistica (1990), La Linguistica del Novecento (1992), History of Linguistics (1994), L'amanuense analfabeta e altri saggi (with A L Lepschy, 1999), Mother Tongues and Other Reflections on the Italian Language (2002), Parole, parole, parole e altri saggi di linguistica (2007), Tradurre

L

e traducibilità (2009); *Style*— Prof Giulio Lepschy, FBA; ✉ Italian, SELCS, University College, Gower Street, London WC1E 6BT (e-mail g.lepschy@ucl.ac.uk)

LEPSCHY, Prof (Anna) Laura; *née* Momigliano; da of Arnaldo Dante Momigliano, Hon KBE (d 1987), of London, and Gemma Celestina, *née* Segre (d 2003); *b* 30 November 1933, Turin, Italy; *Educ* Headington Sch Oxford, Somerville Coll Oxford; *m* 20 Dec 1962, Prof Giulio Ciro Lepschy, FBA, *qv*, s of Emilio Lepschy, of Venice; *Career* jr fell Univ of Bristol 1957–59, lectr in Italian Univ of Reading 1962–68 (asst lectr 1959–62); UCL: lectr in Italian 1968–79, sr lectr 1979–84, reader 1984–87, prof 1987–; prof (status only) Univ of Toronto 2002–, hon visiting fell Univ of Cambridge 2003–, hon prof Univ of Bangor 2009–; vice-pres Associazione Internazionale Studi Lingua and Letteratura Italiana; Br Acad Serena Medal for Italian Studies 2009; memb: Soc for Italian Studies, Assoc for Study of Modern Italy, Pirandello Soc, Comparative Literature Assoc, Modern Humanities Research Assoc; hon fell Somerville Coll Oxford 2005; Commendatore della Repubblica Italiana 2004; *Books* Santo Brasca, Viaggio in Terrasanta 1480 (ed, 1967), The Italian Language Today (with G Lepschy, 1977), Tintoretto Observed (1983), Narrativa e Teatro fra Due Secoli (1984), Varietà linguistiche e pluralità di codici nel Rinascimento (1996), Davanti a Tintoretto (1998), L'amanuense analfabeta e altri saggi (with G Lepschy, 1999), Freud and Italian Culture (ed, with P Barrotta and E Bond, 2009), Le comunità immigrant nel Regno Unito: il caso di Bedford (ed, with A Ledgeway, 2011); *Recreations* theatre, art exhibitions; *Style*— Prof Laura Lepschy; ✉ Italian, SELCS, University College, Gower Street, London WC1E 6BT (e-mail a.lepschy@ucl.ac.uk)

LEREGO, Prof Michael John; QC (1995); s of Leslie Ivor Lerego (d 2001), and Gwendolen Frances, *née* Limbert (d 1990); *b* 6 May 1949; *Educ* Manchester Grammar, Haberdashers' Aske's, Keble Coll Oxford (open scholar, MA, BCL, Gibbs Prize in Law); *m* 24 June 1972, Susan, da of George Henry Northover (d 1969); 1 s (Colin Andrew b 8 Oct 1976 d 1977); 3 da (Louise Jane b 15 Feb 1979, Caroline Ruth, Victoria Ann (twins) b 26 Aug 1981); *Career* called to the Bar Inner Temple 1972 (bencher 2006); in practice 1972–2012, recorder 2002–15, jt head of chambers Fountain Court 2003–07; weekender The Queen's Coll Oxford 1972–78; memb: Jt Working Party of Law Soc & Bar on Banking Law 1987–91, Sub-Ctee on Banking Law Law Soc 1991–96; arbitrator: Modified Arbitration Scheme Lloyd's 1988–92, Arbitration Scheme Lloyd's 1993–2007; prof Univ of Law (formerly Coll of Law) 2009–13 (visiting lectr 2006–07, lectr 2007–08, sr lectr 2008–09); govr Wroxham Sch Potters Bar 1995–2004; FCIArb 1997 (ret), FHEA 2009; *Publications* Commercial Court Procedure (contrib, 2000), Encyclopaedia of Insurance Law (regulatory ed, 2007), Blackstone's Criminal Practice (contrib, 2008–16), The Law of Bank Payments (contrib, 4 edn 2010); *Recreations* watching sport; *Style*— Prof Michael Lerego, QC

LERENIUS, Bo Ake; Hon CBE (2005); s of Ake Lerenius of Sweden, and Elisabeth Lerenius; *b* 11 December 1946; *Educ* Westchester HS LA, St Petri Sch Malmo Sweden, Univ of Lund (BA); *Family* 1 s (Jockum), 1 da (Sarah); m, 23 Dec 2002, Gunilla; *Career* divnl dir Tarkett Swedish Match 1983–85, gp pres and ceo Ernstromgruppen 1985–92, pres and ceo Stena Line 1992–98, vice-chm Stena Line and dir of new business investments Stena AB 1998–99, gp chief exec ABP Holdings plc 1999–2007 (non-exec dir 2007–); non-exec chm Momentum Sweden 1999–2004, non-exec chm Mouchel 2009–11, chm Koole Tank Tport Rotterdam 2011–; non-exec dir: Inmarsat Ventures Ltd 2000–03, Group 4 Securicor plc 2004–, Land Securities 2004–, Thomas Cook Gp plc 2007–12; hon vice-pres Swedish C of C London, memb BV Soc; Hon DBA London Met Univ; *Recreations* golf, shooting, downhill skiing; *Clubs* Royal Bachelors (Gothenburg), RAC, Falsterbo Golf (Sweden); *Style*— Bo Lerenius, CBE

LERNER, Prof David Nicholas; s of Laurence David Lerner, of Sussex, and Natalie Hope, *née* Winch; *b* 16 January 1950; *Educ* Hove GS for Boys, Univ of Cambridge (MA), Univ of London (MSc), Univ of Birmingham (PhD, DSc); *m* Fiona Roubaix, da of Patrick Gillmore; 3 c (Rose b 1984, Robin b 1986, Roubaix b 1987); *Career* various appointments: Anglian Water Authy 1972–77, Binnie & Partners 1977–84, Univ of Birmingham 1984–94, Univ of Bradford 1994–97; prof Univ of Sheffield 1998–; FGS 1990, FICE 1995, FREng 2001; *Recreations* family; *Style*— Prof David Lerner; ✉ Department of Civil and Structural Engineering, University of Sheffield, Mappin Street, Sheffield S1 3JD (☎ 0114 222 5743, fax 0114 222 5701)

LESLIE, Dame Ann Elizabeth Mary; DBE (2007); da of late Norman Alexander Leslie, of Bourne End, Bucks, and late Theodora, *née* McDonald; *b* 28 January 1941, Rawalpindi, Br India; *Educ* Convent of the Holy Child Mayfield, Lady Margaret Hall Oxford (BA); *m* 15 Feb 1969, Michael Fletcher, s of Arthur George Fletcher; 1 da (Katharine Cordelia b 8 Sept 1978); *Career* broadcaster and journalist; staff Daily Express 1961–67, freelance journalist 1967–; memb NUJ; *Awards* commendation Br Press Awards 1980, 1983, 1985, 1987, 1991, 1995, 1996 and 1999, Women of the Year Award for Journalism and Broadcasting Variety Club 1981, Feature Writer of the Year Br Press Awards 1981 and 1989, Feature Writer of the Year What the Papers Say (BBC2/Granada) 1991, Media Soc Lifetime Achievement Award 1997, James Cameron Meml Award for International Reporting 1999, Gerald Barry Lifetime Achievement Award What the Papers Say (BBC2/Granada) 2001, London Press Club Edgar Wallace Award for Outstanding Reporting 2002, Foreign Corr of the Year What the Papers Say (BBC2/Granada) 2004, Int Media Cncl Award for Outstanding Contrib to Journalism 2012; *Books* Killing My Own Snakes (memoir, 2008); *Recreations* family life; *Style*— Dame Ann Leslie, DBE; ✉ Daily Mail, Northcliffe House, 2 Derry Street, London W8 5TT (☎ 020 7938 6000, e-mail ann.leslie@dailymail.co.uk and aemleslie@aol.com)

LESLIE, Charlotte Ann; MP; *b* 1978, Liverpool; *Educ* Balliol Coll Oxford; *Career* BBC TV Prodn 2002–03, special advsr on Educn to Cons Pty 2006–07, Nat Autistic Soc 2008, ed Crossbow Magazine Bow Gp until 2010, MP (Cons) Bristol NW 2010–; vice-chair Cons ME Cncl 2015–; Backbencher of the Year Spectator 2013; *Books* Towards a Royal College of Teaching (ed, 2013); *Publications* More Good School Places (jtly, 2005); *Style*— Miss Charlotte Leslie, MP; ✉ House of Commons, London SW1A 0AA

LESLIE, Christopher Michael (Chris); MP; s of Michael Leslie, and Dania Leslie; *b* 28 June 1972; *Educ* Bingley GS, Univ of Leeds (MA); *Career* research asst to Congressman Bernie Sanders US House of Representatives Washington DC 1992, research asst to Gordon Brown MP, *qv*, 1993, memb (Lab) Bingley City Bradford MDC 1994–98, researcher for Barry Seal, MEP, *qv*, 1996, MP (Lab): Shipley 1997–2005, Nottingham E 2010–; PPS to Lord Falconer of Thornton, *qv* (as Min of State Cabinet Office), 1998–2001, Parly sec Cabinet Office 2001–02, Parly under sec of state ODPM 2002–03, Parly under sec DCA 2003–05; dir New Local Govt Network 2005–; *Recreations* travel, film, tennis, golf; *Style*— Chris Leslie, Esq, MP

LESLIE, Ian James; s of James Beattie Leslie (d 1973), and Margaret Jean, *née* Ryan (d 2011); *b* 23 January 1945; *Educ* Brisbane Boys' Coll, Univ of Queensland (MB BS), Univ of Liverpool (MChOrth); *m* 1 Sept 1975, Jane Ann, da of Col (Allan) Rex Waller, MBE, MC (d 1985), of Waddesdon Manor, Bucks; 1 da (Charlotte Ann b 1978), 1 s (James Henry Rex b 1982); *Career* RAAF 1968–72 (flying offr 1968, Flt Lt 1969, Sqdn Ldr 1971); resident MO Royal Brisbane Hosp Aust 1969, MO RAAF 1970–72 (sr MO Vietnam 1971), teaching surgical registrar Princess Alexandra Hosp Brisbane 1973, registrar then sr registrar Nuffield Orthopaedic Centre Oxford 1974–77, lectr then sr lectr Univ of Liverpool 1978–81, conslt orthopaedic surgn Bristol Royal Infirmary and Avon Orthopaedic Centre, clinical sr lectr Univ of Bristol 1981–2011; treas Br Orthopaedic Research Soc 1988–90, pres Br Soc Surgery Hand 2000 (memb Cncl 1986–88 and 1996–2001), pres Br Orthopaedic Assoc 2005–06 (editorial sec 1990–92, hon sec 1994–95, memb Cncl 2003–05), chm Br Orthopaedic Jt Action Research Fund 2005–11; UK delegate SICOT 1996–, Br delegate Fedn European Soc Surg Hand 2001–03, invited memb Cncl RCS, chm Interface Ctee Hand Surgery RCS 2001–02; chm Bd of Mgmnt Jl of Hand Surgery (Br and Euro vol) 1996–2000; reviewer: Jl of Bone and Joint Surgery, Br Jl of Hand Surgery, International Orthopaedics, The Surgeon, Annals RCS; memb Editorial Bd Orthopaedics and Trauma; examiner Sicot Int Dip in Orthopaedic Surgery; former examiner: MChOrth Liverpool, RCS(Ed), FRCSEd(Orth); memb: Aust Orthopaedic Assoc, Br Orthopaedic Assoc, Br Soc Surgery of the Hand, BMA, World Orthopaedic Concern, Br Orthopaedic Research Soc; past memb Bd of Govrs Badminton Sch Bristol; FRCSEd 1974, MChOrth 1979, FRCS (ad eundem) 1995; *Books* Fractures and Discolations (contrib), Arthroscopy in Operative Orthopaedics (1979), Operative Treatment of Fractures in Children and Surgery of Wrist in Operative Orthopaedics (1989); *Clubs* Army and Navy; *Style*— Ian Leslie, Esq; ✉ Consulting Rooms, 1–5 Whiteladies Road, Clifton, Bristol BS8 1NU (☎ 0117 973 4509, e-mail leslie.surgery@gmail.com)

LESLIE, Prof Ian Malcolm; s of Douglas Alexander Leslie, and Phyllis Margaret, *née* Duncan; *Educ* Univ of Toronto (BASc, MASc), Univ of Cambridge (PhD); *m* 21 Dec 2013, Anne Elizabeth Willenbrock; *Career* Univ of Cambridge Computer Lab: lectr 1985–98 (asst lectr 1983–85), Robert Sansom prof of computer sci 1998–, head of dept 1999–2004; fell Christ's Coll Cambridge 1985– (pres 2014–); pro-vice-chllr (research) Univ of Cambridge 2004–09; contrib IEEE Jl on Selected Areas in Communications; MIEEE 1977, memb Assoc for Computing Machinery (ACM) 1983; FREng 2010; *Recreations* house renovation, scuba diving; *Style*— Prof Ian Leslie; ✉ University of Cambridge Computer Laboratory, William Gates Building, JJ Thomson Avenue, Cambridge CB3 0FD (☎ 01223 334607, e-mail ian.leslie@cl.cam.ac.uk)

LESLIE MELVILLE, (Ian) Hamish; o s of Maj Michael Ian Leslie Melville, TD, DL (d 1997), s of Lt-Col Hon Ian Leslie Melville (4 s of 11 Earl of Leven and 10 Earl of Melville), and Cynthia, da of Sir Charles Hambro, KBE, MC; *b* 22 August 1944; *Educ* Eton, ChCh Oxford (MA); *m* 1968, Lady Elizabeth Compton, yr da of 6 Marquess of Northampton (d 1978); 2 s (James b 1969, Henry b 1975); *Career* dir Hambros Bank Ltd 1975–82, fndr and chief exec Enskilda Securities Ltd 1982–87, chm and chief exec Jamestown Investments Ltd 1987–92; chm: Capel-Cure Myers Capital Management Ltd 1988–91, Dunedin Fund Managers Ltd 1992–95; md Credit Suisse Securities (Europe) Ltd 1998–; chm Mercantile Investment Tst plc; dir Persimmon plc; *Clubs* New (Edinburgh); *Style*— Hamish Leslie Melville, Esq; ✉ J.P. Morgan Asset Management, Client Administration Centre, 60 Victoria Embankment, London EC4Y 0JP

LESSER, Anton; s of late David Lesser, of Birmingham, and late Amelia Mavis, *née* Cohen; *b* 14 February 1952; *Educ* Moseley GS Birmingham, Univ of Liverpool (BA), RADA (Bancroft gold medal); *m* Madeleine Adams; *Career* actor; assoc artist RSC; *Theatre* for RSC incl: Richard in Henry VI, Dance of Death, Michael in Sons of Light, Romeo in Romeo and Juliet, Darkie in The Fool, Troilus in Troilus and Cressida (Stratford), Carlos Montezuma in Melons (The Pit), Bill Howell in Principia Scriptoriae (The Pit), Gloucester in Henry VI (Stratford and Barbican), title role in Richard III (Stratford and Barbican), Joe in Some Americans Abroad (Barbican), Bolingbroke in Richard II (Stratford), Forest in Two Shakespearian Actors (Stratford), Petruchio in The Taming of the Shrew, Ford in The Merry Wives of Windsor; other roles incl: Mark Antony in Julius Caesar (Tyne & Wear), Betty/Edward in Cloud Nine (Liverpool Everyman), Konstantin in The Seagull (Royal Court), Hamlet in Hamlet (Warehouse), Kissing God (Hampstead Theatre Club), Family Voices (Lyric Hammersmith), Feste in Twelfth Night (Riverside Studios), Stanley in The Birthday Party (RNT), Jack Rover in Wild Oats (RNT), Serge in Art (Wyndhams), William in Mutabilitie (RNT), Elyot Chase in Private Lives (RNT), Leo in The Lucky Ones (Hampstead Theatre Club); *Television* BBC incl: Orestes in The Oresteia, Philip in The Mill on the Floss, Abesey Ivanovich in The Gambler, Troilus in Troilus and Cressida, Trofimov in The Cherry Orchard, Edgar in King Lear, Wilheim Fliess in Freud, Willy Price in Anna of The Five Towns, Stanley in Stanley Spencer, Vincenzo Rocca in Airbase, Feste in Twelfth Night, Mungo Dawson in Downtown Lagos, Terell in Invasion Earth, Sir Pitt Crawley in Vanity Fair, Billy Blake in The Echo, Dr Andrew Ward in Pure Wickedness, Mr Merdle in Little Dorrit, The Hour; Channel Four incl: Cox in Good and Bad At Games, Valerie Chaldize in Sakharov, Mark Hollister in the Politician's Wife, Robert Schumann in Schumann; other prodns incl: Ken in The Daughters of Albion (YTV), London Embassy (Thames), Wiesenthal (TVS/HBO), The Strauss Dynasty (mini-series), David Galilee in Sharman, Vladic Mesic in Bodyguards, Ezra Jennings in The Moonstone, Dunn in Always Be Closing, Picard in The Scarlet Pimpernel, Councillor in Lorna Doone, Paul Valley in Swallow, Charles Dickens in Dickens, Stephen in Perfect Strangers; *Film* incl: The Missionary, Monseigneur Quixote, Moses, Fairytale, Esther Kahn, Jack and the Beanstalk, Charlotte Gray, Imagining Argentina, Miss Potter, Pirates of the Caribbean: On Stranger Tides; *Style*— Anton Lesser, Esq

LESSORE, John Viviand; s of Frederick Lessore (d 1951), of London, and Helen Lessore, OBE, RA, *née* Brook (d 1994); *b* 16 June 1939; *Educ* Merchant Taylors', Slade Sch of Fine Art London; *m* 1962, Paule Marie, da of Jean Achille Reveille (Officier de la Légion d'honneur, d 1967), of Paris; 4 s (Remi b 1962, Vincent b 1967, Timothy b 1973, Samuel b 1977); *Career* artist; co-fndr Prince's Drawing Sch 2000; tstee: Nat Gallery 2003–11, Arts Ctee Barts 2011–; Korn/Ferry Int Public Award 1st Prize 1991, Lynn Painter-Stainers 1st Prize and Gold Medal 2006; *Principal Exhibitions* incl: Beaux Arts Gallery 1965, New Art Centre 1971, Theo Waddington 1981, Stoppenbach & Delestre 1983 and 1985, Nigel Greenwood 1990, Theo Waddington and Robert Stoppenbach 1994, Solomon Gallery Dublin 1995, Theo Waddington Fine Art 1997, Miriam Shiell Fine Art Toronto 1997, Wolsey Art Gallery Christchurch Mansion Ipswich 1999, Ranger's House Blackheath 2000, Berkeley Square Gallery 2002, Annely Juda Fine Art 2004, Annandale Galleries Sydney 2005, Kings Place London 2013, Northumbria Univ Gallery London 2013, Thomas Williams Fine Art London 2013, Norwich University of the Arts (NUA) 2014/15, Norwich Castle 2014/15; *Works in Public Collections* incl: Leicester Educn Ctee, Arts Cncl Collection, Royal Acad of Arts, Tate Gallery, Swindon Museum and Art Gallery, CAS, Norwich Castle Museum, Br Cncl, Nat Portrait Gallery, Br Museum; *Style*— John Lessore; ✉ 44 Elm Grove, London SE15 5DE (e-mail john.lessore@gmail.com); c/o Jonathan Clark Fine Art, 18 Park Walk, London SW10 0AQ (☎ 020 7351 3555)

LESTER, Adrian Anthony; OBE (2013); *b* 14 August 1968; *Educ* RADA; *Career* actor; memb: Artistic Bd RNT, Bd RADA; memb: Amnesty Int, Greenpeace; patron Body & Soul; *Theatre* incl: Cory in Fences (Garrick) 1990, Paul Poitier in Six Degrees of Separation (Royal Court and Comedy Theatre) 1992 (Time Out Award), Anthony Hope in Sweeney Todd (RNT) 1994, Rosalind in As You Like It (Albery and Bouffes du Nord) 1995 (Time Out Award), Bobby in Company (Albery and Donmar) 1996 (Olivier Award), Hamlet in Hamlet (Bouffes du Nord, Young Vic and world tour) 2001, Henry in Henry V (RNT) 2003, Brink in Cat On A Hot Tin Roof (Novello Theatre) 2009–10, Othello (NT) 2013 (Best Actor Evening Standard Theatre Award 2013 (jtly with Rory Kinnear, OBE)); *Television* incl: Hustle (BBC), Beyond (Fox), Ballet Shoes, Bonekickers; *Film* incl: Primary Colours, Love's Labour's Lost, The Day After Tomorrow, Storm Damage, Spiderman 3, As You Like It, Scenes of a Sexual Nature, Doomsday; *Recreations* dance, martial arts, music; *Style*— Adrian Lester, Esq, OBE; ✉ c/o Tina Price Consultants, Bay Tree House, Haywards Lane, Child Oakford, Dorset DT11 8DX (☎ 01258 861221)

LESTER, Alexander Norman Charles Phillips (Alex); s of John Phillips Lester, of Walsall, W Midlands, and Rosemary Anne, *née* Edgely; *b* 11 May 1956, Walsall, W Midlands; *Educ* Denstone Coll, Birmingham Poly (Dip Communication Studies); *m* Kerry Marina;

2 step-c (Ella, Jamie); *Career* presenter/journalist: BBC local radio 1978–81, BBC Essex 1986–87; presenter: ind radio 1981–86, BBC Radio 2 and 4 1987– (incl Alex Lester Show); TV presenter The Boat Show (BBC 2) 1999; freelance announcer, voiceover artist and media trainer 1988–; memb Equity; patron: St Michaels Hospice St Leonards on Sea, Ambass Hosp Broadcasting Assoc, Hastings Winkle Club (fisherman's charity), Shrewsbury Int Cartoon Festival; pres SAFE Respite Care Beds; *Recreations* inland waterways, house restoration, travel, junk collecting, reading, flying; *Style—* Alex Lester, Esq; ✉ MPC Entertainment, MPC House, 15/16 Maple Mews, Maida Vale, London NW6 5UZ (☎ 020 7624 1184, fax 020 7624 4220, e-mail mpc@mpce.com)

LESTER, Anthony John; s of Donald James Lester (d 2006), of Wallingford, Oxon, and Edith Helen Hemmings (d 1982); *b* 15 September 1945, Oxford; *Educ* Gaveston Hall Nuthurst, St John's Coll Co Tipperary; *m* 2008, Elizabeth R Meek, MBE; *Career* ind fine art conslt, art critic, book reviewer and lectr; ed Watercolours, Drawings and Prints 1992–94; publisher and editorial dir Art Prices Review; fine art corr Antiques Trade Gazette and Antique Dealer and Collectors' Guide; gallery features ed Art in London 2007–; contribs to numerous magazines incl: Woman, Antique Collecting, Artists' and Illustrators' Magazine, Art Business Today, Limited Edition, The World of Antiques, The Speculator, Antiques and Decoration, The Collector, The Big Issue, Galleries, Miller's Magazine, Art and Artefact; featured in Farmers' Weekly, Radio Times, Sunday Express Magazine, British Midland Voyager Magazine; curator: Pure Gold (Mall Galleries) 2011, The Art of a Nation (Mall Galleries) 2015; regular broadcaster BBC TV: Antiques Roadshow 1986–89, Going for a Song 1999; judge: The Laing Art Exhbn 1997, Br Antiques and Collectables Awards 2002–, Watercolour C21 (RWS Open) 2003, GMAC Commercial Mortgage Europe Art Award 2004–; launched Anthony J Lester Art Critic Award 2005; selector The Discerning Eye 2002, gen valuer Flog It! (BBC) 2003–; chm Vetting Ctee 20/21 Int Art Fair London 2007–; memb: Int Assoc of Art Critics, Glass Circle, Glass Assoc, Academic Ctee Fedn of Br Artists, Critics' Circle; dep chm Exhibitions Ctee Fedn of Br Artists, patron Mall Galleries; Companion of the Pastel Soc; hon memb Royal Soc of Minature Painters; FRSA; *Books* The Exhibited Works of Helen Allingham (1979), The Stannards of Bedfordshire (1984), BBC Antiques Roadshow-Experts on Objects (contrib, 1987), George Large (1998), The Pastel Society 1898–2000 (contrib, 2000), Pure Gold: 50 Years of the FBA (2011), Rosa Sepple (2011), Art of the Real (2012), The Art of a Nation: Irish Works from the Allied Irish Banks and Crawford Art Gallery Collections (2015); *Recreations* travel, entertaining friends, charity work; *Clubs* Chelsea Arts (life memb); *Style—* Anthony J Lester, Esq, FRSA; ✉ Firle House, 75 Firle Road, Seaford, East Sussex BN25 2JA (☎ 01323 301755, mobile 07743 319522, e-mail anthonylester@fsmail.net)

LESTER, Charles Martin; s of Charles William Lester, of Banbury, Oxon, and Marjory Winnifred, *née* Pursail; *b* 20 March 1942; *Educ* N Oxfordshire Tech Sch, Oxford Coll of Technol, Gwent Coll of HE; *m* 16 March 1963, Patricia Caroline Lester, *qv*, da of Arthur Frederick Wake; 1 da (Georgina Caroline b 28 Oct 1964); *Career* research scientist ICI Fibres 1962–74, teacher of design craft and technol King Henry VIII Sch 1976–79, head Design Craft and Technol Dept Haberdashers' Monmouth Sch 1979–84, dir Charles & Patricia Lester Ltd (textile and fashion design co) 1984–; estab (with w) lifestyle shop incl fashion, textiles and interiors in Knightsbridge, London SW3, together developed unique method for finely hand pleating silk and decorating velvet and silks, developed original methods for structure of garments and interior pieces; estab couture house selling worldwide incl: Fortnum & Mason in London, Bergdorf Goodman, Neiman Marcus and Saks Fifth Avenue in US, other stockists in Germany, Italy, Hong Kong and Japan; additional products incl cushions, bedspreads, throws, unique silk tapestries, shawls and scarves; clients incl: HRH Princess Michael of Kent, Elizabeth Taylor, Barbra Streisand, Toni Braxton, Whitney Houston, Emma Kirkby; recreated Flaming June set for centenary of death of Lord Leighton (Leighton House) 1996; film work incl: costume designs for Wings of the Dove (Oscar nomination for costumes 1998), fabric for Hamlet, Greenfingers, Jack and the Beanstalk; theatre work incl all costumes for opera Iris (Holland Park Theatre 1997 and 1998, Teatro Grattacielo concert prodn Lincoln Centre NY 1998) and The Pearl Fishers (Opera Holland Park) 2002; featured in V&A Museum exhbn Cutting Edge 1997, solo exhbn Textile Experience (Leighton House) 1997; work featured in publications and collected in museums world-wide; Fit for Work Award (in recognition of commitment to the employment of disabled staff) 1985; *Recreations* Folly Fellowship, Steam Boat Association, rebuilding and restoring vintage boat, photography; *Style—* Charles Lester, Esq; ✉ Charles & Patricia Lester Ltd, The Workhouse, Hatherleigh Place, Union Road, Abergavenny, Monmouthshire NP7 7RL (e-mail cpl@charlespatricialester.com, website www.interior-design-world.com and www.charles-patricia-lester.co.uk)

LESTER, Michael; s of Jack Lester (d 1959), and Mary, *née* Sax (d 1987); *b* 10 March 1940; *Educ* Coopers' Company's Sch, New Coll Oxford (MA); *m* 17 Dec 1967, Pamela Frances Lester, da of Leopold Henry Gillis (d 1988); 1 da (Antonia b 1973), 1 s (James b 1976); *Career* Bigelow teaching fell Univ of Chicago Law Sch 1962–64, articled clerk and slr in private practice 1964–80; GEC plc: dir of legal affrs 1980–99, main bd dir 1983–99, vice-chm 1994–99; non-exec dir Premier Farnell plc 1998–; main bd dir BAE Systems plc 1999–; memb Law Soc, CCMI (CIMgt); *Style—* Michael Lester, Esq; ✉ 46 Sheldon Avenue, London N6 4JR (☎ 020 8340 7868); BAE Systems plc, Stirling Square, 6 Carlton Gardens, London SW1Y 5DA (☎ 01252 383904, fax 01252 383992)

LESTER, Patricia Caroline; MBE (1988); da of Arthur Frederick Wake, of NZ, and Dorothy Phyllis, *née* Flew; *b* 11 February 1943; *Educ* Thornton Coll, Oxford Coll of Technology; *m* 16 March 1963, Charles Martin Lester, *qv*, s of Charles William Lester; 1 da (Georgina Caroline b 28 Oct 1964); *Career* formerly employed as secretary St Anne's Coll Oxford then British steel Wales; textile, fashion and interior designer; fndr and currently dir Charles & Patricia Lester Ltd with husb, estab lifestyle shop incl fashion, textiles and interiors in Knightsbridge London; together developed unique method for finely hand pleating silk and decorating velvet and silks, developed original methods for structure of garments and interior pieces; estab couture house selling worldwide incl: Fortnum & Mason London, Bergdorf Goodman, Neiman Marcus and Saks Fifth Avenue US, other stockists in Germany, Italy, Hong Kong and Japan; additional products incl cushions, bedspreads, throws, unique silk tapestries, shawls and scarves; clients incl: HRH Princess Michael of Kent, Elizabeth Taylor, Barbra Streisand, Toni Braxton, Whitney Houston, Emma Kirkby; recreated Flaming June set for centenary of death of Lord Leighton (Leighton House) 1996; film work incl: costume designs for Wings of the Dove (Oscar nomination for costumes 1998), fabric for Hamlet, Greenfingers, Jack and the Beanstalk; theatre work incl all costumes for opera Iris (Holland Park Theatre 1997 and 1998, Teatro Grattacielo concert prodn Lincoln Centre NY 1998) and for The Pearl Fishers (Opera Holland Park 2002); featured in V&A Museum exhbn Cutting Edge 1997, solo exhbn Textile Experience (Leighton House) 1997; work featured in publications and collected in museums world-wide; Fit for Work Award (in recognition of commitment to the employment of disabled staff) 1985, Welsh Business Woman of the Year 1986 and 1987; *Recreations* gardening, painting, Folly Fellowship, Steam Boat Association; *Style—* Mrs Patricia Lester, MBE; ✉ Charles & Patricia Lester Ltd, The Workhouse, Hatherleigh Place, Union Road, Abergavenny, Monmouthshire (website www.interior-design-world.com and www.charles-patricia-lester.co.uk)

LESTER OF HERNE HILL, Baron (Life Peer UK 1993), of Herne Hill in the London Borough of Southwark; Anthony Paul Lester; QC (1975); s of Harry Lester (d 1984), of London, and Kate, *née* Cooper-Smith (d 2008); *b* 3 July 1936; *Educ* City of London Sch, Trinity Coll Cambridge (BA), Harvard Law Sch (LLM); *m* 29 July 1971, Catherine Elizabeth Debora, da of Michael Morris Wassey (d 1969), of London; 1 s (Hon Gideon b 1972), 1 da (Hon Maya b 1974); *Career* 2 Lt RA 1956; called to the Bar Lincoln's Inn 1963 (bencher 1985), memb NI Bar and Irish Bar; former recorder S Eastern circuit 1987; special advsr to: Home Sec 1974–76, Standing Cmmn on Human Rights in NI 1975–77; ind advsr to Justice Sec on aspects of constitutional reform 2007–09, cmmr Bill of Rights Cmmn 2011–; memb: House of Lord's Select Ctee on Euro Communities Sub-Ctee (Law and Institutions) 1996–2003 and 2004–07, Sub-Ctee on the 1996 Inter-Governmental Conf, Educn and Home Affairs, Parly Jt Human Rights Ctee 2001–; former memb Sub-Ctee on Social Affairs; pres Interights (Int Centre for Legal Protection of Human Rights) 1982–, chair Equal Rights Tst 2006–; chm Nat Ctee 50th Anniversary of UN Universal Declaration of Human rights 1998, memb Bd: Salzburg Seminar 1996–2000, Euro Roma Rights Center (co-chair 1999–2001); memb: Cncl JUSTICE 1977–, Advsy Bd Inst of European Public Law Univ of Hull, Advsy Ctee Centre for Public Law Univ of Cambridge 1999–, Int Advsy Bd Open Soc Inst 2000–, Ed Bd Public Law, Ed Bd Int Jl of Discrimination and the Law; ed-in-chief Butterworths Human Rights Cases, former chm and treas Fabian Soc, pres Lib Dem Lawyers' Assoc, co-fndr and former chm Runnymede Tst; hon visiting prof of law UCL; govr Br Inst of Human Rights, former chm and memb Bd of Govrs James Allen's Girls' Sch, former govr Westminster Sch; hon memb American Acad of Arts and Sciences 2002, memb American Philosophical Soc 2003; Chevalier de l'Ordre de la Legion d'Honneur 2009; *Books* Justice in the American South (1964), Shawcross and Beaumont on Air Law (ed jtly, 3 edn 1964), Race and Law (jtly 1972); conslt ed and contrib Constitutional Law and Human Rights in Halsbury's Laws of England (4 edn, 1973, re-issued 1996); contrib: British Nationality, Immigration and Race Relations in Halsbury's Laws of England (4 edn, 1973, re-issued 1992), The Changing Constitution (ed Jowell and Oliver, 1985, 7 edn 2010), Butterworths Human Rights Law and Practice (co-ed, 1999, 3rd edn 2009), Tolley's Discrimination Law (foreword, 2 edn 2011); *Recreations* walking, sailing, water colours; *Style—* The Lord Lester of Herne Hill, QC; ✉ Blackstone Chambers, Blackstone House, Temple, London EC4Y 9BW (☎ 020 7583 1770, sec 020 7404 4712, fax 020 7822 7350)

LESTER-DAVIS, Nick; s of Frank Lester (d 2000), and Eve, *née* Griffiths; *b* 20 March 1953; *Educ* UCL (BSc, DipArch); *m* 25 Aug 2006, Tom Davis (civil partnership converted 12 Aug 2014); *Career* exec dir Transport 2000 1980–84, sr policy offr Gtr London Cncl 1984–86, sr policy offr Assoc of London Authorities 1986–92, London parking dir Parking Ctee for London 1992–98, chief exec Transport Ctee for London 1998–2000; London Cncls (formerly Assoc of London Govt): dir of transport, environment and planning 2000–08, corporate dir of services 2008–; pres European Parking Assoc 2009–15; vice-chair European Road Traffic Res Ctee 2014–; FCILT 1985; *Style—* Nick Lester-Davis, Esq; ✉ London Councils, 59½ Southwark Street, London SE1 0AL

LETHBRIDGE, Prof Robert David; s of Albert Lethbridge (d 1988), and Muriel, *née* de Saram (d 2000); *b* 24 February 1947, New York; *Educ* Mill Hill Sch, Univ of Kent (BA), McMaster Univ (MA), St John's Coll Cambridge (MA, PhD); *m* 2 Jan 1970, Vera, *née* Laycock; 1 s (Jonathan b 23 Mar 1975), 1 da (Tamsin b 13 Jan 1979); *Career* Fitzwilliam Coll Cambridge: fell 1973–94 (Leathersellers' fell 1973–78), life fell 1994–, tutor 1975–92 (sr tutor 1982–92), master 2005–13, hon fell 2013–; lectr in French Univ of Cambridge 1985–94 (asst lectr 1980–85), prof of French language and lit Univ of London 1995–2005 (emeritus prof 2005–); Royal Holloway Univ of London: head Dept of French 1995–97, dean Grad Sch 1997–98, vice-princ (academic) 1997–2002, visiting prof 2003–05; dir Univ of London Inst in Paris (formerly Br Inst in Paris) 2003–05; provost Gates Cambridge Tst 2010–13; visiting prof: Univ of California at Santa Barbara 1986, Univ of Melbourne 2003; hon prof Queen Mary Univ of London 2003–05, hon prof Univ of St Andrews 2015–; memb Society of Dix-neuviémistes (hon pres 2001–06), Commandeur dans l'Ordre des Palmes Académiques (France) 2013; Maupassant: Pierre et Jean (1984), Zola and the Craft of Fiction (ed 1990), Artistic Relations, Literature and the Visual Arts in Nineteenth-Century France (ed 1994), editions of novels and short stories by Guy de Maupassant (2001 and 2016) and Emile Zola (1995, 2000 and 2001), 50 essays in learned jls and collective works; *Recreations* watching rugby, contemplating the sea; *Clubs* Oxford and Cambridge; *Style—* Prof Robert Lethbridge; ✉ e-mail rdl11@cam.ac.uk

LETHBRIDGE, Sir Thomas Periam Hector Noel; 7 Bt (UK 1804), of Westaway House, and Winkley Court, Somerset; s of Sir Hector Wroth Lethbridge, 6 Bt (d 1978), and Evelyn Diana, *née* Noel (d 1996); *b* 17 July 1950; *Educ* Milton Abbey, RAC Cirencester; *m* 1, 1976 (m dis), Susan Elizabeth, eldest da of Lyle Rocke, of Maryland, USA; 4 s (John Francis Buckler Noel b 1977, Edward Christopher Wroth b 1978, Alexander Ralph Periam b 1982, Henry Charles Hesketh b 1984), 2 da (Georgina Rose Alianore b 1980, Rachael Elizabeth Mary b 1986); m 2, 28 Feb 2007, Mrs Ann Marie Fenwick; *Heir* s, John Lethbridge; *Career* art dealer in sporting subjects of 1700 to date, int agent for distinguished retail names; *Style—* Sir Thomas Lethbridge, Bt; ✉ c/o Barclays Bank, 58 High Street, Newmarket, Suffolk CB8 8NH

LETLEY, Peter Anthony; s of Sidney Charles Letley (d 1978), of Woodbridge, Suffolk, and Ruby, *née* Berry (d 1994); *b* 11 November 1945; *Educ* Woodbridge Sch, St John's Coll Oxford (BA); *m* 21 March 1970, (Alice) Emma Campbell, da of late Lt-Col Campbell K Finlay, of West Ardhu, Isle of Mull; 1 s (Alfred Thomas b 4 Sept 1988); *Career* joined HSBC Group 1974; Wardley Ltd: head of Lending Dept 1974–78, dir overseas ops and dir 1978–82, jt md Aust 1982–83, chief exec Hong Kong International Trade Finance Ltd (London) 1983–86; fin dir James Capel Bankers Ltd 1986–87 (md 1987–88), fin dir HSBC James Capel & Co 1988–93 (dep chm 1993–97), dep chm HSBC Investment Banking Group Ltd 1993–99; CIBC World Markets plc: chief admin offr and chief fin offr 1999–2004, head of Europe 2004–08; gp ceo T Bailey Hldgs 2015–; chm Voiceability 2012–; *Recreations* theatre, gardening, reading; *Clubs* Hong Kong Jockey, Reform; *Style—* Peter Letley, Esq; ✉ 8 Avondale Park Gardens, London W11 4PH; West Ardhu, Dervaig, Tobermory, Isle of Mull, Argyll PA75 6QR

LETTE, Kathy; *m* Geoffrey Robertson, QC, *qv*; 1 s, 1 da; *Career* novelist; writer in residence Savoy Hotel London 2003; ambass: Plan, White Ribbon Alliance, Nat Autistic Soc; hon doctorate Solent Southampton Univ 2009, hon sr fell Regent's Univ London; *Books* Puberty Blues (1979), Hit and Ms (1984), Girls' Night Out (1988), The Llama Parlour (1991), Foetal Attraction (1993), Mad Cows (1996), Altar Ego (1998), Nip'n Tuck (2001), Dead Sexy (2003), How to Kill Your Husband and Other Handy Household Hints (2006), To Love, Honour and Betray – Till Divorce Us Do Part (2008), Men – A User's Guide (2010), The Boy Who Fell to Earth (2012), Love Is Blind- But Marriage is a Real Eye Opener (2013), Courting Trouble (2014); *Style—* Ms Kathy Lette; ✉ c/o Ed Victor, 6 Bayley Street, Bedford Square, London WC1B 3HB

LETTS, Dr Melinda Jane Frances; OBE (2003); da of Richard Francis Bonner Letts, of Cirencester, Glos, and Jocelyn Elizabeth, *née* Adami; *b* 6 April 1956, Cirencester, Glos; *Educ* Wycombe Abbey, Cheltenham Coll, St Anne's Coll Oxford (exhibitioner, MA), ChCh Oxford (MSt, DPhil); *m* 13 April 1991, Neil Scott Wishart McIntosh, s of William Henderson McIntosh; 1 s (Fergus George Christian b 15 Oct 1990), 1 da (Isobel Freya Johnstone b 15 Sept 1992); *Career* press and publicity offr Bubble Theatre Co 1980–81, research asst Sociology Dept Brunel Univ 1981–82, head orgn and admin CND 1982–84; VSO: head of admin 1985–86, prog funding mangr 1986–87, regnl mangr S Asia 1987–89; staffing mangr McKinsey & Co Inc 1989–91, chief exec Nat Asthma Campaign 1992–97 (dep dir 1991–92), chair Long-term Med Conditions Alliance (LMCA) 1998–2004 (tstee

L

1996–2004), chair Nat Strategic Partnersip Forum 2005–07; strategic conslt and coach, assoc conslt Compass Partnership 1998–2015; lectr Greek and Latin languages 2013–; dir Ask About Medicines 2003–09; chair Ctee on Safety of Medicines Working Gp on Patient Information 2003–05, tstee Parkinson's UK 2007– (vice-chair 2008–09, chair 2009–11); memb: NHS Modernisation Bd 1999–2003, Cmmn for Health Improvement 1999–2004, Cmmn for Healthcare Audit and Inspection 2003–04; former memb Bd New Opportunities Fund; tstee Gen Practice Airways Gp; former tstee: Nat Cncl for Vol Orgns, Charity Projects Comic Relief; former patron Men's Health Forum; MIMgt 1992, FRSA 1993; *Recreations* reading, yoga, gardening, crosswords; *Style*— Dr Melinda Letts, OBE

LETTS, Quentin Richard Stephen; s of late R F B Letts, and Jocelyn, *née* Adami; *b* 6 February 1963; *Educ* Haileybury, Bellarmine Coll Kentucky, Trinity Coll Dublin, Jesus Coll Cambridge; *m* 1996, Lois, *née* Rathbone; 1 s, 2 da; *Career* dustman and waiter 1981–84; ed: Oxon Magazine Oxford 1984–85, Mayday Magazine Dublin 1985–86, Filibuster Magazine Dublin 1986–87; journalist The Daily Telegraph 1988–95 (ed Peterborough Column), NY Bureau chief The Times 1995–97, freelance journalist 1997– (including parly sketch writer Daily Telegraph 1997–2000 and Daily Mail 2000–), theatre critic Daily Mail 2004–, writer Clement Crabbe column Daily Mail 2006–09, presenter What's the Point of? (BBC Radio 4) 2008–, presenter Panorama – May Contain Nuts (BBC1) 2009; judge Britain's Best Am-Dram (Sky Arts) 2013, BBC TV Celebrity Mastermind 2013–; dep church warden How Caple Church Herefordshire, govr Hereford Cathedral Perpetual Trust; Edgar Wallace Award London Press Club 2003, Feature Writer of the Year What the Papers Say Award 2007, Political Journalist of the Year Br Press Award 2009, Critic of the Year Br Press Award 2010, Sketchwriter of the Year Comment Award 2010, Columnist of the Year (Popular Papers 2014); *Publications* Fifty People Who Buggered Up Britain (2008), Bog Standard Britain (2009), Letts Rip! (2010), The Speaker's Wife (novel, 2015); *Recreations* singing hymns, watching cricket; *Clubs* Savile, MCC; *Style*— Quentin Letts, Esq; ✉ The Old Mill, How Caple, Herefordshire HR1 4SR (☎ 01989 740688)

LETWIN, Rt Hon Sir Oliver; kt (2016), PC (2002), MP; s of Prof W Letwin (d 2013), and Dr S R Letwin (d 1993); *b* 19 May 1956; *Educ* Eton, Trinity Coll Cambridge (MA, PhD); *m* 1984, Isabel Grace, da of Prof John Frank Davidson, FRS, *qv*; 1 s (Jeremy John Peter 5 July 1993), 1 da (Laura Shirley (twin) b 5 July 1993); *Career* visiting research fell Princeton Univ 1980–81, research fell Darwin Coll Cambridge 1981–82, special advsr Dept of Educn and Sci 1982–83, memb Prime Minister's Policy Unit 1983–86, md N M Rothschild and Sons Ltd 2003 (joined 1986, dir 1991–2003, non-exec dir 2005–10); MP (Cons) Dorset W 1997–; oppn frontbench spokesman on constitutional affrs 1998–99, shadow fin sec to the Treasy 1999–2000, shadow chief sec to the Treasy 2000–01, shadow home sec 2001–03, shadow sec of state for economic affrs and shadow chllr of the Exchequer 2003–05, shadow sec of state for environment, food and rural affrs 2005, min for govt policy 2010–15; chm Cons Pty Policy Review 2005–15; chllr Duchy of Lancaster 2014–; FRSA 1991; *Publications* Ethics, Emotion and the Unity of the Self (1984), Privatising the World (1987), Aims of Schooling (1988), Drift to Union (1990), The Purpose of Politics (1999); numerous articles in learned and popular jls; *Recreations* philosophy, walking, skiing, tennis; *Style*— The Rt Hon Sir Oliver Letwin, MP; ✉ House of Commons, London SW1A 0AA (☎ 020 7219 3000)

LEVAGGI, Peter; *b* 24 December 1965; *Educ* Univ of York (BA); *Children* 2 da (Hazel, Molly); *Career* admitted slr 1992, slr advocate; slr: Rochman Landau 1992–96, Charles Russell Slrs 1996–; memb: Property Litigation Assoc, Insolvency Lawyers Assoc; *Publications* Enforcement: A Guide to the New Law (2008), Property Insolvency Jordans (2009); *Style*— Peter Levaggi, Esq; ✉ Charles Russell, Buryfields House, Bury Fields, Guildford GU2 4AZ (☎ 01483 252525, fax 01483 252552, e-mail peter.levaggi@charlesrussell.co.uk)

LEVEAUX, David Vyvyan; s of Dr Michael Leveaux, of Derby, and Eve, *née* Powell; *b* 13 December 1957; *Educ* Rugby, Univ of Manchester (BA); *Career* director; assoc dir Riverside Studios 1981–85; artistic dir Theatre Project Tokyo (TPT) 1993–; *Theatre* Almeida: Betrayal 1991, No Man's Land 1992, Moonlight 1993; A Moon for the Misbegotten (Riverside Studios), Easter (Leicester Haymarket), Therese Raquin (Chichester) 1990, 'Tis Pity She's a Whore (RSC), The Father (RNT), Nine (Donmar Warehouse and Buenos Aires) 1996, Electra (Chichester Festival, UK tour and Donmar) 1997, Electra (McCarter Theater, Princeton) 1998, Jumpers (West End) 2003, Sinatra Live at the London Palladium 2006, A Doll's House (Tokyo) 2008, Three Sisters (Abbey Theatre Dublin) 2008, Rudolph (Vienna) 2008, The Real Thing (Donmar Warehouse/ Albery), Tales of Ballycumber (Abbey Theatre Dublin) 2009, Arcadia (Duke of Yorks Theatre) 2009; Berlin: The Dance of Death, Krapp's Last Tape; New York Broadway: A Moon for the Misbegotten (nominee Best Dir Tony Awards 1983/84), Anna Christie (nominee Best Dir and recipient Best Revival Tony Awards 1992/93), Electra (nominee Tony Award), Betrayal, The Real Thing (Best Revival Tony Award), Nine (Best Revival and nominee Outstanding Direction Tony Award), Jumpers (nominee Outstanding Direction Tony Award), Fiddler on the Roof, The Glass Menagerie 2005, Cyrano 2007; New York Off-Broadway: Messiah, Virginia; Tokyo: Les Liaisons Dangereuses, Madame de Sade 1990, Two Headed Eagle 1990, Lady from the Sea 1992; TPT: Therese Raquin 1993, Betrayal 1993, 'Tis a Pity She's a Whore 1993, Hedda Gabler 1994, Ellida 1994, The Two Headed Eagle 1994, The Ibsen Project 1994, The Changeling 1995, The Three Sisters 1995, two modern Noh plays 1995, Electra 1996, Macbeth 1996, Triumph of Love, Lulu, The Late Middle Classes (Donmar Warehouse) 2010; *Opera* The Turn of the Screw (Glasgow Tramway) 1996, The Marriage of Figaro (both Scottish Opera, 1995), Salome (ENO); *Style*— David Leveaux, Esq; ✉ c/o Simpson Fox Associates Ltd, 6 Beauchamp Place, London SW3 1NG (☎ 020 7434 9167, fax 020 7494 2887, e-mail david.bingham@simpson-fox.com)

LEVENE, Prof Malcolm Irvin; s of Maurice Mordechai Levene (d 2006), of Brighton, E Sussex, and Helen, *née* Kutner (d 1983); *b* 2 January 1951; *Educ* Guy's Hosp Med Sch (LRCP, MB BS, MD); *m* 1, 1972, Miriam Ann, *née* Bentley (d 1989); 3 da (Alysa b 20 Aug 1976, Katherine b 10 Jan 1979, Ilana b 13 Feb 1983); m 2, Susan Anne, da of Robert Cave; 1 da (Hannah Sophie b 2 Nov 1992), 1 s (David Jack b 18 May 1994); *Career* house surgn Royal Sussex Co Hosp Brighton March-Oct 1974, house physician Northampton Gen Hosp 1974, locum GP NSW Australia 1975–76, paediatric SHO Charing Cross Hosp 1976–77, registrar Derby Children's Hosp 1977–78, paediatric registrar Charing Cross Hosp 1978–79, hon sr registrar Hammersmith Hosp and Queen Charlotte's Hosp London 1979–82, research lectr in neonatal med Royal Postgrad Med Sch London 1979–82, hon conslt paediatrician Leicester Royal Infirmary and reader in child health Univ of Leicester Med Sch 1988 (sr lectr 1982–88); Univ of Leeds Med Sch: prof of paediatrics and child health, hon conslt paediatrician, dean of students 1989–2010, emeritus prof of paediatrics 2010; Scope (formerly The Spastics Soc): memb Med Advsy Ctee 1985–91, memb Combined Res Ctee 1986–91; memb Leicestershire Maternity Liaison Ctee 1984–88, chm Research Ctee Action Research 1993–96 (memb 1992–96), chm Centre for Reproduction, Growth and Devpt Research Sch of Med 1995–98; ed-in-chief Seminars in Neonatology, ed-in-chief Seminars in Total and Neonatal Medicine 1998–; memb Editorial Bd: Developmental Med and Child Neurology 1985–93, Jl of Perinatal Med 1987–, Neuropaediatrics 1992–; hon sec Div of Child Health Leicestershire DHA; Handcock prize RCS 1974, British Cncl travelling fellowship 1980, Michael Blecklow Meml prize BPA 1982, Ronnie MacKeith prize BPNA 1984, Guthrie medal BPA 1986, BUPA Nat Research award 1988, William Liley Medal 2009, James Spence Medal RCPCH 2010; memb: Neonatal Soc, RSM, Paediatric Research Soc, BPNA, British Assoc of Perinatal Med, Academic Bd Royal Coll of Paediatrics and Child Health 2002–; MRCS; FRCP, FMedSci 1999, fell Int Acad of Perinatal Medicine 2005; *Books* A Handbook for Examinations in Paediatrics (jtly, 1981), Ultrasound of the Infant Brain (jtly, 1985), Diseases of Children (jtly, 5 edn 1985), Current Reviews in Paediatrics (1987), Essentials of Neonatal Medicine (jtly, 1987, 2 edn 1993), Fetal and Neonatal Neurology and Neurosurgery (ed jtly, 1988, 4 edn 2009), Jolly's Diseases of Children (ed, 6 edn 1991), Paediatrics and Child Health (jtly, 1999 and 2006), MRCPCH Master Course (2007); author of numerous chapters in books and articles in learned jls; *Recreations* golf, gardening, music; *Style*— Prof Malcolm Levene; ✉ Acacia House, Acacia Park Drive, Apperley Bridge, West Yorkshire BD10 0PH (☎ 0113 250 9959); Academic Unit of Paediatrics, University of Leeds, D Floor, Clarendon Wing, Leeds General Infirmary, Leeds LS2 9NS (☎ 0113 292 3905, fax 0113 292 3902, e-mail medmil@leeds.ac.uk)

LEVENE OF PORTSOKEN, Baron (Life Peer UK 1997), of Portsoken in the City of London; Sir Peter Keith Levene; KBE (1989), JP (City of London 1984); s of Maurice Pierre Levene (d 1970), and Rose Levene (d 1991); *b* 8 December 1941; *Educ* City of London Sch, Univ of Manchester (BA); *m* 1966, Wendy Ann, da of Frederick Fraiman; 2 s, 1 da; *Career* chm United Scientific Holdings plc 1982–85 (md 1968–85), chm Defence Mfrs Assoc 1984–85, personal advsr to Sec of State for Defence 1984, chief of defence procurement MOD 1985–91, dir UK Nat Armaments 1988–91, chm European Nat Armaments Dirs 1989–90, personal advsr to Sec of State for the Environment 1991–92, personal advsr to Pres of the Bd of Trade 1992–95, efficiency advsr to the Prime Minister 1992–97, chm Defence Reform Gp MOD 2010–11; dep chm Wasserstein Perella & Co Ltd 1991–95, chm Docklands Light Railway 1991–94, chm and chief exec Canary Wharf Ltd 1993–96, sr advsr Morgan Stanley & Co Ltd 1996–98, dir Haymarket Group Ltd 1997–, chm Bankers Tst Int 1998–99, chm Investment Banking Europe Deutsche Bank 1999–2001, chm IFSL (formerly British Invisibles) 2000–10, vice-chm Deutsche Bank 2001–02, non-exec dir J Sainsbury plc 2001–04, chm General Dynamics UK Ltd 2001–, chm Lloyd's 2002–11, dir China Construction Bank 2006–12, chm NBNK Investments plc 2010–12, chm Starr Underwriting Agents Ltd 2012–, dir Groupe Eurotunnel SA 2012–, dir China Construction Bank Asia 2013–, chm Tikehau Investments Ltd 2013–; memb: Alcatel Chms Cncl 2000–03, Supervisory Bd Deutsche Börse AG 2004–05, Bd Total SA 2005–11; govr: City of London Sch for Girls 1984–85, City of London Sch 1985–, Sir John Cass Primary Sch 1985–93 (dep chm); vice-pres City of London Red Cross, memb Ct HAC, chm London Homes for the Elderly 1990–93, Hon Col Cmdt RLC 1993–2006 (RCT 1991–93); USA Insurance Leader of the Year 2010; common cncllr Ward of Candlewick 1983–84, Alderman Ward of Portsoken 1984–2005, Alderman Ward of Aldgate 2005–12; Sheriff City of London 1995–96; Lord Mayor of London 1998–99; Master Worshipful Co of Carmen 1992–93, Liveryman Worshipful Co of Information Technologists, Hon Liveryman Worshipful Co of Management Conslts 2004–; fell QMC London 1995, Hon DSc City Univ 1998, Hon DSc Univ of London 2005; KStJ 1998 (OStJ 1996), Cdr Ordre Nationale du Mérite (France) 1996, Knight Cdr Order of Merit (Germany) 1998, Middle Cross Order of Merit (Hungary) 1999, Hon Citizen City of Rio de Janeiro 2009; *Recreations* skiing, swimming, watching association football, travel; *Clubs* Guildhall, Walbrook, RAC; *Style*— The Lord Levene of Portsoken, KBE; ✉ 30 Fenchurch Avenue, London EC3M 5AD (☎ 020 7398 5087, e-mail peter.levene@starrcompanies.com)

LEVER, Prof Andrew Michael Lindsay; s of Ivor Lindsay Douglas Lever, and Sylvia Marion, *née* Tannock; *b* 23 June 1953; *Educ* Ripon GS, WNSM; *Career* various med posts 1978–82; MRC res fell 1983–84, Wellcome lectureship 1985–87, res fell Harvard Univ 1988–89, sr lectr St George's Hosp London 1989–1991; Univ of Cambridge: lectr and reader 1991–2000, fell Peterhouse 1993–, prof of infectious diseases 2000–; ed Jl of Infection 1996–2001, memb Gene Therapy Advsy Ctee; Croom lectr 1987 and 1992, Lennox K Black Prize 2001; Hon MD Univ of Cambridge 2001 (Hon MA 1998); FRCP 1993 (MRCP 1981), FRCPE 1993, FRCPath 1998 (MRCPath 1994), FMedSci 2000, FRSC 2006, FRSB 2011, FLSW 2012; *Publications* various scientific and clinical pubns on HIV and gene therapy; *Recreations* guitar, ornithology; *Style*— Prof Andrew Lever; ✉ University of Cambridge Department of Medicine, Addenbrooke's Hospital, Hills Road, Cambridge CB2 2QQ (☎ 01233 330191, fax 01233 336486, e-mail htb21@medschl.cam.ac.uk)

LEVER, Hon Bernard Lewis; His Hon Judge Lever; s of Baron Lever (Life Peer, d 1977), by his w Ray; n of Baron Lever of Manchester (Life Peer, d 1995); *b* 1 February 1951; *Educ* Clifton, The Queen's Coll Oxford (Neale exhibitioner, MA); *m* 1985, Anne Helen, da of Patrick Chandler Gordon Ballingall, MBE, of Seaford, E Sussex; 2 da (Helen Jane b 28 Sept 1986, Isabel Elizabeth Rose b 2 March 1991); *Career* called to the Bar Middle Temple 1975, practised Northern Circuit 1975–2001, recorder of the Crown Court 1995–2001, circuit judge 2001–; standing counsel to Inland Revenue (Northern Circuit) 1997–2001; co-fndr of SDP in NW 1981, Parly candidate (SDP) Manchester Withington 1983; *Recreations* walking, music, picking up litter; *Clubs* Vincent's (Oxford); *Style*— His Hon Judge Lever; ✉ Manchester Crown Court, Minshull Street, Manchester M1 3FS (☎ 0161 954 7500)

LEVER, Dr Sir (Tresham) Christopher Arthur Lindsay; 3 Bt (UK 1911), of Hans Crescent, Chelsea; s of Sir Tresham Joseph Philip Lever, 2 Bt, FRSL (d 1975), and Frances Yowart Parker, *née* Goodwin (d 1959); step s of Pamela, Lady Lever (d 2003), da of Lt-Col the Hon Malcolm Bowes-Lyon, former w of Lord Malcolm Avondale Douglas-Hamilton; *b* 9 January 1932; *Educ* Eton, Trinity Coll Cambridge (MA, PhD); *m* 1 (m dis); m 2, 1975, Linda Weightman McDowell, da of late James Jepson Goulden, of Tennessee, USA; *Heir* none; *Career* author; 2 Lt 17/21 Lancers 1950; Peat Marwick Mitchell & Co 1954–55, Kitcat & Aitken 1955–56, dir: John Barran & Sons Ltd (later plc) 1956–64; conslt: Zoo Check Tst 1984–91, Born Free Fndn 1991–2003; scientific advsr Galápagos Conservation Tst 2012–; memb: Cncl Soc for the Protection of Animals in N Africa 1986–88, Cncl Br Tst for Ornithology 1988–91, SOS Sahel Int (UK) 1995–2010; chm: African Fund for Endangered Wildlife (UK) 1987–90, Br Tst for Ornithology Nat Centre Appeal 1987–92, Ruaha Tst 1990–95, UK Elephant Gp 1991–92, UK Rhino Gp 1992–93; Int Tst for Nature Conservation: tstee 1980–92, vice-pres 1986–91, pres 1991–92; dir: World Society for the Protection of Animals 1998–2003, Earthwatch Inst Europe 2003–04; IUCN: memb Species Survival Cmmn 1988–, memb UK Ctee 1989–2011; memb Cncl of Ambass WWF (UK) 1999–2005, fell WWF-UK 2005; memb Editorial Bd Jl of Applied Herpetology 2005–09; patron: Rhino Rescue Tst 1985–2003 (tstee 1986–91), Lynx Educnl Tst for Animal Welfare 1991–2010, Respect for Animals 1995–2011; vice-patron Conservation Fndn 2005–06; hon life pres Tusk Tst 2004 (chm 1990–2004); hon life memb: Brontë Soc 1988, Soc for the Protection of Animals Abroad 2008, Butterfly Conservation 2014; HH Bloomer Award Linnean Soc of London 2014; FLS, FRGS, MBOU; *Books* Goldsmiths and Silversmiths of England (1975), The Naturalized Animals of the British Isles (1977, paperback edn 1979), Wildlife '80 – The World Conservation Yearbook (contrib 1980), Evolution of Domesticated Animals (contrib 1984), Naturalized Mammals of the World (1985), Beyond the Bars – The Zoo Dilemma (contrib 1987), Naturalized Birds of the World (1987), The Mandarin Duck (1990), They Dined on Eland – The Story of the Acclimatisation Societies (1992), The New Atlas of Breeding Birds in Britain and Ireland: 1988–91 (contrib, 1993), Naturalized Animals: The Ecology of Successfully Introduced Species (1994), The Introduction and Naturalisation of Birds (contrib, 1996), Naturalized Fishes of the World (1996), Stocking and Introduction of Fish (contrib, 1997), The EBCC Atlas of European Breeding Birds: Their Distribution and Abundance (contrib, 1997), The Cane Toad: The History and Ecology of a Successful Colonist (2001), The Migration

Atlas: Movements of the Birds of Britain and Ireland (contrib, 2002), Naturalized Reptiles and Amphibians of the World (2003), Biological Invasions: From Ecology to Control (contrib, 2005), Naturalised Birds of the World (2005), The Naturalized Animals of Britain and Ireland (2009), Silent Summer: The State of Wildlife in Britain and Ireland (contrib, 2010), Encyclopedia of Biological Invasions (contrib, 2011), The Mandarin Duck (2013); *Clubs* Boodle's, Swinley Forest Golf; *Style*— Dr Sir Christopher Lever, Bt; ✉ Newell House, Winkfield, Berkshire SL4 4SE (☎ 01344 882604, fax 01344 891744)

LEVER, Dr Eric G; s of Sam Lever (d 1978), and Freda, *née* Mann (d 2006); *b* 5 April 1947; *Educ* Quintin Sch, Univ of Birmingham (BSocSc), Trinity Coll Cambridge (MA, MB BChir), Univ Coll Med Sch, Univ of Chicago (Endocrinology Diabetes fell); *m* 26 Aug 1985, Nicola, da of Bernard Langdon; 4 s (Elliott b 21 Jan 1988, Michael b 2 May 1989, Charles b 27 June 1994, Simon b 22 March 1996); *Career* jr hosp dr appts 1975–88: UCH, Edgware Gen Hosp, Univ Hosp Nottingham, Royal Marsden Hosp, Hammersmith Hosp, KCH London, Billings Hosp Chicago; full-time private conslt in endocrinology diabetes and gen med Wellington Hosp and Hosp of St John and St Elizabeth 1988–; MRCP 1978; author of many papers on endocrinology and diabetes; *Recreations* art, music and the philosophy of ideas; *Style*— Dr Eric G Lever; ✉ Wellington Hospital, London NW8 9LE (☎ 020 7483 5148, fax 020 8371 8396, e-mail ericlever1@aol.com)

LEVER, Sir Jeremy Frederick; KCMG (2002), QC (England and Wales 1972, N Ireland 1988); s of Arnold Lever (d 1980), and Elizabeth Cramer, *née* Nathan (d 1993); *b* 23 June 1933; *Educ* Bradfield Coll, UC Oxford, Nuffield Coll Oxford, All Souls Coll Oxford (MA); *Partner* (civil partnership 2006), Brian Collie; *Career* 2 Lt RA (E African Artillery) 1952–53; called to the Bar Gray's Inn 1957 (bencher 1985); head of chambers 1989–96; sr dean All Souls Coll Oxford 1988–2011 (fell 1957–, sub warden 1982–84); visiting prof Wissenschaftszentrum Berlin für Sozialforschung 1999; memb: Arbitral Tbnl US/UK Arbitration concerning Heathrow Airport User Charges 1988–94, Ind Inquiry Univ of Portsmouth 1995; chm: Oftel Advsy Bd on Fair Trading in Telecommunications 1996–2000, Performing Right Soc Appeals Panel 1996–2002; non-exec dir: Dunlop Hldgs Ltd 1973–80, Wellcome Fndn Ltd 1983–94; memb Cncl and Ctee of Mgmnt Br Inst of Int and Comparative Law 1987–2004; pres Oxford Union Soc 1957 (tstee 1972–77 and 1988–2014); govr Berkhamsted Schs 1985–95; FRSA 1997; *Books* Chitty on Contracts (ed, 1961, 1968, 1972, 1977), Tort Law (co-author, 2000); *Recreations* music, ceramics; *Clubs* Garrick, Athenaeum; *Style*— Sir Jeremy Lever, KCMG, QC; ✉ Monckton Chambers, 1 Raymond Buildings, Gray's Inn, London WC1R 5NR (☎ 020 7405 7211, fax 020 7405 2084, e-mail chambers@monckton.com); All Souls College, Oxford OX1 4AL (☎ 01865 279379, fax 01865 279299)

LEVER, (Keith) Mark; s of Keith Lever (d 2002), and Rosemary Anne, *née* Wakeley; *b* 20 September 1960, Luton, Beds; *Educ* Wakeman GS Shrewsbury, Royal Holloway Coll London (BSc), Cranfield Univ (MBA); *m* 11 Nov 1989, Amanda Jane Sackville, *née* Davison; 4 s (William b 7 April 1994, Edward b 22 June 1997, Thomas b 4 Jan 1999, Joseph b 21 Feb 2002); *Career* ptnr and nat dir of HR and trg Kidsons Impey 1995; WRVS: dir of trg 1996, dir of strategic devpt 1999, chief exec 2002–07; dir Sackville Consulting 2007–, chief exec Nat Autistic Soc 2008–; MICAEW 1986, MCIPD 1987, MCIM 2001; *Recreations* golf, music, Chelsea FC, family, charity discos, cooking, tennis, long distance cycling; *Clubs* Harrow Golf, Wanborough Amateur Golf Soc, Wanborough Tennis; *Style*— Mark Lever, Esq; ✉ National Autistic Society, 393 City Road, London EC1V 1NG (☎ 020 7833 2299, fax 020 7833 9666, e-mail mark.lever@nas.org.uk)

LEVERETT, David; s of George Edgar Leverett, of Nottingham, and Doris, *née* Tebbit; *b* 12 January 1938; *Educ* John Player Sch Nottingham, Nottingham Sch of Art (NDD), Royal Acad Schs London (post grad dip, travelling scholar); *m* Sonia Loretta Wilhmena Holme; 2 s (Jason David b 2 June 1967, Simeon b 19 Jan 1970); *Career* artist; variously art teacher at instns incl: RCA, Dublin Coll of Art, Cooper Union NY; currently reg visiting lectr Slade Sch UCL; Sargant fell Br Sch at Rome 1990–91; poetry performance Running the Shadow (nat tour); *Solo Exhibitions* incl: Redfern Gallery London 1965, 1968, 1970, 1972, 1987 and 1990, Editions Alecto NY 1970, Studio La Citta Verona 1971, Galleria del Cavallino Venice 1972, Galerie Britta Herberle Frankfurt 1972, Ikon Gallery Birmingham 1973, ICA London 1974, Galleria G7 Bologna 1975, Gallery Desmos Athens 1975, Galerie Skulima Berlin 1975, Galleria Vinciana Milan 1976, Oliver Dowling Gallery Dublin 1977, Janus Suite Riverside Studios London 1979, Studio Gallery Palace of Culture Warsaw 1980, Gallery III Lisbon 1983, Bildornan Gallery Umea 1984, Curwen Gallery London 1985, Jersey Arts Centre St Helier 1986, Thumb Gallery London 1990 and 1992, Jill George Gallery London 1995, 1997 and 2001, Gallery In Collaboration Santa Monica 1996, Gallerie Maximillian Aspen 1998; *Group Exhibitions* incl: British Painting Monte Carlo 1966, British Painting and Sculpture (Whitechapel Gallery London) 1968, Play Orbit (ICA) 1969, British Drawing (Angela Flowers Gallery London) 1972, 6 Artists (Inglesi Galleria lo Spazio Berscia and Gallery Godel Rome) 1974, British Painting 1974 (Hayward Gallery) 1974, Empirica (Rimini City Museum) 1975, British Painting RA 1952–77 British Drawing from 1945 (Whitworth Art Gallery Manchester) 1979, Cralylus XV São Paulo 1979, Contemporary Choice 1979–81 (Contemporary Arts Soc and Serpentine Gallery London) 1982, One of a Kind (Maryland Inst Baltimore) 1983, Bradford Print Biennale Selection (V&A) 1986, Decade Exhbn Dublin 1986, Mediterranean Bienal graphic art Athens 1988, Ogle Fine Art 1989 and 1990, Thumb Gallery 1989, Int Art Fair Olympia 1990, Cabinet Paintings (Gillian Jason Gallery) 1991, Special Presentation (Merrill Chase Gallery Chicago) 1991, 1992 and 1995, Contraprint (Br Sch at Rome) 1991, Omphalos Series (Galleria Gianfranco Rosini Riccione) 1991, Cyril Gerber Gallery 1992, Cabinet Paintings (Hove Museum and Art Gallery and Glynn Vivian Art Gallery and Museum) 1992, Drawings 3 (Jill George Gallery London) 1995, Drawings (V&A) 1996, Small is Beautiful (Flowers East) 1998, Landmarks (Jill George Gallery) 1999, Mountain (Woverhampton Museum of Art) 1999, Galerie Maximillian Aspen 1999 Landscape (Flowers East) 1999, Scholar Fine Art London 2000, Editions Alecto 1960–1981 (Birmingham Museum and Art Gallery) 2000, A Fury for Prints (Whitworth Art Gallery Manchester) 2003, War and Peace (Flowers Central London) 2003; *Work in Public Collections* incl: Arts Cncl of GB, Br Cncl, V&A, Contemporary Arts Soc, Tate Gallery, Museum of Peace Hiroshima, Miny of Culture Athens, The State Collection Palace of Culture Warsaw, MOMA Sao Paulo, MOMA Campione, State Art Gallery NSW, Inst of Contemporary Graphics, MOMA Zagreb, Modern Art Gallery Koszalim, Umea Kommun, DOE, Reading Museum of Art, Nottingham City Museum, Univ of Liverpool, Univ of Warwick, British Rail Collection, London Press Exchange; *Publications* incl: A Possible Future – New Painting (1973), Colour in Painting – a European situation (1976), The Citadel (1994), The David Leverett Portfolio (1995), Dance Through the Labyrinth of Sand (1997), Between Night and Daylight (2001); *Style*— David Leverett, Esq; ✉ 132 Leighton Road, London NW5 2RG (☎ 020 7485 3317, e-mail david@ecoart.demon.co.uk, website www.ecoart.demon.co.uk)

LEVESON, Rt Hon Sir Brian Henry; kt (2000), PC (2006); s of Dr Ivan Leveson (d 1980), of Liverpool, and Elaine, *née* Rivlin (d 1983); *b* 22 June 1949; *Educ* Liverpool Coll, Merton Coll Oxford (MA); *m* 20 Dec 1981, Lynne Rose, da of Aubrey Fishel (d 1987), of Wallasey; 2 s (Andrew b 1983, James b 1989), 1 da (Claire b 1984); *Career* called to the Bar Middle Temple 1970 (bencher 1995), QC 1986; lectr in law Univ of Liverpool 1971–81, recorder of the Crown Court 1988–2000, dep High Court judge 1998–2000, judge of the High Court of Justice (Queen's Bench Div) 2000–06, presiding judge Northern Circuit 2002–05, Lord Justice of Appeal 2006–13, sr presiding judge for England and Wales 2007–09, pres Queen's Bench Div 2013–; chm: Criminal Justice Cncl 2008–11, Sentencing Cncl of England and Wales 2010–13, Inquiry into the Culture, Practices and Ethics of the Press 2011–12; chllr Liverpool John Moores Univ 2013– (hon fell 2012); memb: Cncl Univ of Liverpool 1983–92, Parole Bd 1992–95, Cncl UCS Hampstead 1998–2015 (chm 2009–15); fndn govr Liverpool Coll 2001, pres Merton Soc 2010–16; hon fell Merton Coll Oxford 2001; Hon LLD Univ of Liverpool 2007; *Style*— The Rt Hon Sir Brian Leveson; ✉ Royal Courts of Justice, Strand, London WC2A 2LL

LEVETE, Amanda; da of Michael Levete (d 2003), and Gina, *née* Seagrim; *b* 1955; *Educ* AA Sch of Architecture; *m* 2008, Ben Evans; 1 s from previous m; *Career* architect; in practice: Richard Rogers & Partners 1984–89, Future Systems 1989–2009 (with Jan Kaplicky, award-winning projects incl Hauer/King House 1994, West India Quay Bridge 1998, Media Centre Lord's Cricket Ground 1999 (Stirling Prize) and Selfridges Birmingham 2004); princ Amanda Levete Architects 2009– (award-winning projects incl 10 Hills Place 2009, Spencer Dock Bridge 2009, V&A Museum Exhibition Road and individual furniture pieces for Established & Sons); RCA: visiting lectr 1995–, external assessor 2004–08, visiting prof 2008–; tstee: Architecture Fndn 1997–2008, Artangel 2000–, Young Fndn 2009–; RIBA 1984; *Style*— Ms Amanda Levete; ✉ Amanda Levete Architects, 14a Brewery Road, London N7 9NH

LEVIEN, Robin Hugh; s of John Blomefield Levien, of Norwich, Norfolk, and Louis Beryl, *née* Squire; *b* 5 May 1952; *Educ* Bearwood Coll Wokingham, Central Sch of Art and Design (BA), Royal Coll of Art (MA); *m* 21 Aug 1978, Patricia Anne, da of Alan Newby Stainton; *Career* ceramics and glass designer; ptnr: Queensberry Hunt 1982–95 (joined 1977), Queensberry Hunt Levien (following name change) 1995–99, Studio Levien 1999–; mass market products for mfrs and retailers incl: Thomas China, Wedgwood, Ideal Standard, American Standard, Habitat, Dartington Crystal; major products incl: Trend dinnerware shape for Thomas China 1981 (Die Gute Industrieform Award Hanover 1982, Golden Flame Award Valencia 1983), Studio bathroom range for Ideal Standard 1986 (BT Prize BBC Design Awards 1987, runner-up DBA Design Effectiveness Awards 1989), Domi bathroom taps for Ideal Standard 1989 (runner-up Design Week Awards 1990), Symphony range of bathtubs for American Standard 1990 (Interior Design Product Award American Soc of Interior Designers 1991), Kyomi bathroom range for Ideal Standard 1996 (winner Design Week Award 1997), Home Elements kitchenware range for Villeroy and Boch 2003; lectr: RCA, Central St Martins Sch of Art and N Staffordshire Univ; visiting prof London Inst 1998; chm Product Design Panel Student Design Directions Awards RSA 1991–2000, memb Faculty of Royal Designers for Industry RSA; memb Friends of the Earth; fndr memb Brewcombe Woodland Tst, Cncl RCA 2001–; Hon Dr Staffordshire Univ 2006; FRSA, RDI 1995, life fell RCA 2013; *Recreations* 'Fulham Farmer' on 1952 Ferguson tractor, films, cooking; *Style*— Robin Levien, Esq, RDI; ✉ Studio Levien, 1 La Gare, 51 Surrey Row, London SE1 0BZ (☎ 020 7928 2244, fax 020 7928 2255, e-mail robin@studiolevien.com)

LEVIN, David Roger; s of Jack Levin (d 1995), of Durban, South Africa, and Elizabeth Isobel, *née* Robinson (d 1976); *b* 2 October 1949; *Educ* Kearsney Coll, Univ of Natal, Univ of Sussex; *m* 1977, Jean Isobel, da of Maj John Paxton-Hall; *Career* mangr Cutty Sark Hotel Natal 1971–73, asst master Whitgift Sch 1974–75, slr Radcliffe & Co 1976–78, asst master Portsmouth GS 1978–80, head of economics Cheltenham Coll 1980–93 (second master 1987–93), headmaster Royal GS High Wycombe 1993–99, headmaster City of London Sch 1999–; chm Supporting Local Schools Initiative in Lambeth 1999–2002, memb City of London Acad Steering Gp 2001–03; govr Canford Sch 1996–; memb Secondary Heads Assoc 1993; Freeman City of London 2001; FRSA 1992; *Recreations* long distance swimming (organised and participated in second-ever cross-channel swimming relay race 1987), surfing, military history, theatre, opera; *Clubs* East India; *Style*— David Levin, Esq; ✉ City of London School, Queen Victoria Street, London EC4V 3AL (☎ 020 7489 0291, fax 020 7329 6887, mobile 07947 429568, e-mail headmaster@clsb.org.uk)

L

LEVINSON, Hugh Alexander; s of Clive John Levinson, and Doris Frieda Levinson; *Educ* Hove Co GS for Boys, Blatchington Mill Sch, Emmanuel Coll Cambridge; *Career* teacher Kanto Gakuen Univ Japan 1985–87; trainee reporter BBC local radio 1987, reporter BBC Radio Merseyside 1987–90, sub ed The Japan Times Tokyo 1990–93, prodr The World at One (BBC Radio 4) 1993–97, prodr, reporter and ed BBC Radio world current affairs 1997–; *Recreations* conjuring, playing guitar, running (slowly); *Clubs* Magic Circle; *Style*— Hugh Levinson, Esq; ✉ BBC Broadcasting House, Portland Place, London W1A 1AA (☎ 020 3614 0967)

LEVINSON, Jan Matthew; s of David Levinson, of Israel, and Pearl Shein, *née* Rose, of Edinburgh; *b* 8 May 1968, Bury; *Educ* Manchester Grammar, Univ of Newcastle upon Tyne (LLB), Coll of Law Chester; *m* 17 Aug 1997, Jayne, *née* Flacks; 1 s (Joshua b 2 Nov 1999), 2 da (Cate, Anya (twins) b 28 Dec 2001); *Career* slr; ptnr Hammonds 1999–2003 (joined 1990), ptnr and head of commercial dispute resolution (N) DAC Beachcroft LLP 2003–; contrib: The Lawyer, Law Soc Gazette, The Times, BBC, ITV, Sky TV, Talksport, Manchester Evening News; hon slr Whitefield Hebrew Congregation; memb: Law Soc 1990, Commercial Litigation Soc, Property Litigation Assoc, British Assoc for Sport and the Law, Soc for Computers and the Law; *Recreations* travel, cycling, theatre, skiing, running; *Style*— Jan M Levinson, Esq; ✉ DAC Beachcroft LLP, 3 Hardman Street, Manchester M3 3HF (☎ 0161 934 3043, mobile 07803 599875 and 07834 308505, fax 0161 934 3743, e-mail jlevinson@dacbeachcroft.com, website http://uk.linkedin.com/pub/jan-levinson/14/398/879)

LEVINSON, Prof Stephen Curtis; *b* 6 December 1947; *Educ* King's Coll Cambridge (sr scholar, BA), Univ of Calif Berkeley (MA, Fulbright scholar, special career fell, PhD); *m* 18 Sept 1976, Penelope, *née* Brown; 1 s (b Oct 1980); *Career* teaching asst in linguistic anthropology Univ of Calif Berkeley 1972–73; Univ of Cambridge: asst lectr 1975–78, lectr in linguistics 1978–90, dir of studies archaeology and anthropology Emmanuel Coll 1978–80, Faculty Bd Archaeology and Anthropology Emmanuel Coll 1982–87, reader in linguistics 1991–94; prof Catholic Univ Nijmegen Netherlands 1995–, ldr Cognitive Anthropology Res Gp 1991–97 and dir Max-Planck-Inst for Psycholinguistics Nijmegen 1994–; Stanford Univ: visiting prof Linguistic Soc of America Linguistics Inst 1987, visiting assoc prof Dept of Linguistics 1987–88, convenor Research Seminar on Implicature Center for the Study of Language and Information 1987–88; memb editorial bd of numerous linguistics jls; memb High Table King's Coll Cambridge 1975–, Nijmegen lectr 1988, Stirling Prize American Anthropology Assoc 1992; memb: Scientific Ctee Fyssen Fndn Paris, Assoc of British Social Anthropologists, Linguistics Assoc of GB, American Anthropological Assoc, Linguistic Soc of America, European Assoc of Social Anthropologists, Academia Europaea; FBA; *Style*— Prof Stephen Levinson, FBA; ✉ Max Planck Institute, PB 310, NL 6500 AH Nijmegen, Netherlands (☎ 00 31 24 352 1911, fax 00 31 24 352 1300)

LEVINSON, Stephen Michael (Steve); s of Alfred Levinson (d 1976), of London, and Golda Levinson (d 1992); *b* 19 January 1949; *Educ* Kilburn GS, Univ of Newcastle upon Tyne (BA); *m* 23 Dec 1973, Vivien Elaine, da of Col James Grant; 1 da (Jemma Debra b 3 Nov 1976), 1 s (Thomas Alex b 13 July 1979); *Career* grad trainee Westminster Press Ltd 1970–71, industrial corr South Shields Gazette 1972–73 (educn corr 1971–72); economics corr: Press Association Ltd 1976–86 (sub-ed/copy taster 1973–76), The Independent 1986–88, BBC TV 1988–92, Channel Four News ITN 1993–98, fndr dir HBL Media Ltd 1998–; editorial managing dir: World Finance Magazine 1999–, World Finance Television 1999–, Congress TV 2003–, The Local Government Channel 2005–, WebsEdge TV 2006–; Industrial Soc Broadcasting Award 1995–96, Winott Fndn Broadcast Award 1998–99;

Style— Steve Levinson, Esq; ✉ HBL Media Ltd, Great Tichfield House, 14–18 Great Tichfield Street, London W1P 7AB (☎ 020 7612 1830, e-mail steve@hblmedia.com)

LEVISON, Jeremy Ian; s of Eric Levison (d 2001), and Sarah Levison (d 2006); *b* 3 February 1952, Ryde, IOW; *Educ* Charterhouse, Univ of Kent at Canterbury (BA); *m* 1 Feb 2002, Norma Miller; *Career* with Theodore Goddard 1974–80, ptnr Collyer Bristow 1980–98, founding ptnr Levison Meltzer Pigott 1998–; memb: Law Soc 1974, American Bar Assoc 1990, Resolution (formerly Slrs' Family Law Assoc); founding memb Int Acad of Matrimonial Lawyers (IAML) 1990; author of various articles in misc pubns; *Recreations* fine art, music, photography, cricket, fast cars, France, my wife!; *Clubs* Groucho; *Style—* Jeremy Levison, Esq; ✉ Levison Meltzer Pigott, 45 Ludgate Hill, London EC4M 7JU (☎ 020 7556 2400, fax 020 7556 2401, e-mail jlevison@lmplaw.co.uk)

LEVITT, Alison; QC (2008); *Career* called to the Bar Inner Temple 1988 (master of the bench 2009); memb 25 Bedford Row 1991–2009, recorder 2007, princ legal advsr to DPP 2009–14, ptnr Mishcon de Reya 2014–; chm Young Barristers' Cte Bar Cncl 1995, sec Criminal Bar Assoc 2006–07; *Style—* Ms Alison Levitt, QC; ✉ Mishcon de Reya, Summit House, Red Lion Square, London WC1R 4QD

LEVITT, Tom; s of John Levitt, and Joan, *née* Flood; *b* 10 April 1954; *Educ* Westwood HS Leek, Lancaster Univ (BSc), Univ of Oxford (PGCE); *m* 1983, Teresa, da of Waclaw and Halina Sledziewski; 1 da (Annie b 29 Nov 1983); *Career* science teacher: Wilts CC 1976–79, Glos CC 1980–91; supply teacher Staffs CC 1991–95, freelance research conslt sensory impairment and access to servs and info 1993–97, MP (Lab) High Peak 1997–2010; PPS to: Barbara Roche, MP 1999–2003, Baroness Amos 2003, Hilary Benn, MP 2003–07; memb House of Commons Select Ctee on: Standards and Privileges 1997–2003, Dept of Work and Pensions 2007–10; chm All-Pty Gp on Poland 1998–2000, co-chair All-Pty Minerals Gp 1998–2004, chm All-Pty Gp on the Voluntary Sector and Charities 2001–10 (jt vice-chm 1997–99), chair All-Pty Br-Swiss Parly Gp 2002–07; freelance conslt charity/business partnerships 2010–, dir Good Measures business consultancy 2011–; sec Future of Europe Tst 1997–99; cncllr: Cirencester PC 1983–87, Stroud DC 1990–92, Derbys CC 1993–97; chair Community Devpt Fndn 2004–10; assoc: Tomorrow's Co 2011–; memb: Lab Pty 1977–, Br Deaf Assoc (life memb), Ct Univ of Derby 1997–, League Against Cruel Sports, Amnesty International; tstee: RNID 1998–2003, Concern Worldwide (UK) 2011–15 (chair 2011–14), Coalition for Efficiency 2011– (chair 2013–), Work Fndn Alliance 2012–, Fair For You (chair 2015–); patron READ Int 2007–, patron Nat Assoc of Deafened People 2010–, non-exec dir Outreach Solutions 2013–; memb Br Humanist Assoc 2000–; hon degree Univ of Derby 2011; FRSA; *Publications* Sound Practice (for Local Govt Mgmnt Bd, 1995), Clear Access (for Local Govt Mgmnt Bd, 1997), Partners for Good: Business, Government and the Third Sector (2012), Welcome to GoodCo (2014, 2 edn 2015); *Recreations* cricket, theatre, walking; *Style—* Tom Levitt, Esq; ✉ website www.sector4focus.co.uk, Twitter @sector4focus

LEVY, Andrea; da of Winston Levy (d 1987), and Amy Levy (d 2015); *b* 7 March 1956, London; *Educ* Highbury Hill HS, Middx Poly (BA); *m* Bill Mayblin; 2 step da (Maya b 11 June 1976, Hannah b 21 April 1978); *Career* novelist; judge: Saga Prize 1996, Orange Prize for Fiction 1997, Orange Futures 2001; memb Soc of Authors; FRSL; *Books* Every Light in the House Burnin' (1994), Never Far from Nowhere (1996), Fruit of the Lemon (1999, Arts Cncl Writers' Award), Small Island (2004, Whitbread Novel Award and Whitbread Book of the Year 2004, Orange Prize for Fiction 2004, Best Book Eurasia Region Cwlth Writers' Prize 2005, Best Overall Book Cwlth Writer's Prize 2005, Orange Best of the Best Prize 2005, shortlisted Literary Fiction Award British Book Awards, Romantic Novelists' Assoc Award and Decibel Writer of the Year British Book Awards all 2005), The Long Song (2010, Walter Scott Prize for Historical Fiction 2010, shortlisted Man Booker Prize 2010), Six Stories and an Essay (2014); *Style—* Ms Andrea Levy; ✉ c/o David Grossman, David Grossman Literary Agency, 118B Holland Park Avenue, London W11 4UA (☎ 020 7221 2770, fax 020 7221 1445, website www.andrealevy.co.uk)

LEVY, Baron (Life Peer UK 1997), of Mill Hill in the London Borough of Barnet; Michael Abraham Levy; s of Samuel levy (d 1975) of London, and Annie, *née* Berenbaum (d 1987); *b* 11 July 1944, London; *Educ* Hackney Downs GS; *m* 20 Aug 1967, Gilda, da of late Benjamin Altbach (d 1972), of London, and Emilie, *née* Kohn (d 2005); 1 s (Daniel Edward b 17 June 1968), 1 da (Juliet Bella b 18 May 1970); *Career* CA 1966–73, fndr and owner MAGNET (record and music publishing gp of cos) 1973–88, in music and entertainment industry 1992–97, conslt to various int cos 1998–; PM's personal envoy until 2007, advsr in Middle East; vice-chm: Phonographic Performance Ltd 1979–84, Br Phonographic Industry Ltd 1984–87; fndr and former chm Br Music Industry Awards Ctee (now Music Industry Tst), patron Br Music Industry Tst 1995–; chm Int Standard Asset Mgmnt (ISAM) 2008–11; pres Jewish Care 1998– (chm 1992–97), pres Volunteering Matters (formerly CSV) 1998–; Jews Free Sch (JFS): govr 1990–95, pres 2001–; hon pres United Jt Israel Appeal 2000– (hon vice-pres 1994–2000, nat campaign chm Jt Israel Appeal (now UJIA) 1982–85); world chm Youth Aliyah Ctee Jewish Agency Bd of Govrs 1991–95; chm: Chief Rabbinate Awards for Excellence 1992–2007, Jewish Care Community Fndn 1995–2010, Fndn for Educn 1993–2006, Academies Sponsors Tst 2004–05; pres Specialist Schs and Acads Tst 2005–08; vice-chm Central Cncl for Jewish Social Servs 1994–2006, pres Jewish Lads' and Girls' Brigade 2006–, vice-pres Jewish Leadership Cncl 2010–11; memb: Keren Hayesod World Bd of Govrs 1991–95, World Bd of Govrs Jewish Agency (GB rep) 1990–95, World Cmmn on Israeli-Diaspora Relations 1995–, Advsy Cncl Foreign Policy Centre 1997–2006, Int Bd of Govrs Peres Center for Peace 1997–2009, NCVO Advsy Ctee 1998–, Community Legal Service Champions Panel 1999–2010, Hon Ctee Israel Britain and Cwlth Assoc 2000–11, Advsy Cncl Step Up to Serve Campaign 2013, World Bd of Dirs Int Peace Inst (IPI) 2014; chm Bd of Tstees New Policy Network Fndn 2000–07; memb Exec Ctee Chai-Lifeline 2001–02; tstee Holocaust Educnl Tst 1998–2007; patron: Prostate Cancer Charitable Tst 1997–2011, Friends of Israel Educnl Tst 1998–2011, Save a Child's Heart Fndn 2000–, Simon Marks Jewish Primary Sch Tst 2002–, Etz Chaim Sch, Mathilda Marks-Kennedy Sch; hon patron Cambridge Univ Jewish Soc 2002–; B'nai B'rith Award 1994, Friends of the Hebrew Univ of Jerusalem Scopus Award 1998, Israel Policy Forum (USA) Special Recognition Award 2003; Hon Dr Middlesex Univ 1999; FCA 1966; *Publications* A Question of Honour (2008); *Recreations* tennis, swimming; *Style—* The Rt Hon the Lord Levy; ✉ House of Lords, London SW1A 0PW (☎ 020 7487 5174, fax 020 7486 7919)

LEVY, Dr Paul; eld s of Hyman Solomon Levy (d 1980), of Lexington, Kentucky, USA, and Mrs Shirley Singer Meyers (d 1991); *b* 26 February 1941; *Educ* Univ of Chicago (AB), UCL, Harvard Univ (PhD), Nuffield Coll Oxford; *m* 1977, Penelope, da of Clifford Marcus (d 1952); 2 da (Tatyana b 1981, Georgia b 1983); *Career* journalist and lapsed academic; food and wine ed The Observer 1980–92, wine and food columnist (as Amy DeVine) You magazine The Mail on Sunday 1992–2013, sr contrib Europe, Arts and Leisure page Wall Street Journal 1993–2015; regular contrib: ArtsJournal.com, The Spectator, The Daily Telegraph, Oxford Dictionary of National Biography; frequent broadcaster on radio and TV; writer and presenter The Feast of Christmas (Channel 4) 1992 and 1993; national press specialist Writers' Commendations 1985 and 1987; tstee: Strachey Tst, Jane Grigson Tst until 2014; chair Oxford Symposium on Food and Cooking until 2015; memb: Circle of Wine Writers, Critics Circle (music, art, books and theatre sections); FRSL 1980; *Books* Lytton Strachey: The Really Interesting Question (ed, 1972), G E Moore and the Cambridge Apostles (1977, 3 edn 1989), The Shorter Strachey (ed with Michael Holroyd, 1980, 2 edn 1989), The Official Foodie Handbook (with Ann Barr, 1984), Out to Lunch (1986, new edn 2003), Finger-lickin' Good (1990), The Feast of Christmas (1992), The Penguin Book of Food and Drink (ed, 1996), Eminent Victorians, The Definitive Edition (ed, 2002), The Letters of Lytton Strachey (ed, 2005); *Recreations* being cooked for, drinking better wine, trying to remember; *Clubs* Groucho, Quo Vadis, Buckland; *Style—* Dr Paul Levy; ✉ Millwood Farm, Long Hanborough, Witney, Oxfordshire OX29 8BP (☎ 01993 881312, e-mail paullevy@paullevy.com, website www.paullevy.com)

LEVY, Russell Anthony; s of David Baynes Levy, of Sydney, Aust, and Gabrielle, *née* Baumgarten; *Educ* Hyde Park HS Johannesburg, Univ of the Witwatersrand (BA), Univ of Warwick (LLB, Maxwell Law Prize), Coll of Law London; *m* 1985, Sarah Anne Rogers; 2 s (Samora Roger b 10 Feb 1989, Max Antony b 24 July 1992); *Career* admitted slr 1984; head of clinical negligence Leigh Day; former sec Clinical Disputes Forum; chair Campaign for Freedom of Information; affiliated with Canon Collins Tst, tstee Africa Educnl Tst; *Recreations* wildlife; *Style—* Russell Levy, Esq; ✉ Leigh Day, 25 St John's Lane, London EC1M 4LB (☎ 020 7650 1200, fax 020 7253 4433, e-mail russ@leighday.co.uk)

LEW, Prof Julian David Mathew; QC (2002); s of Rabbi Maurice Abram Lew (d 1989), of London, and Rachel Lew, JP, *née* Segalov (d 1998); *b* 3 February 1948, Johannesburg, South Africa; *Educ* Univ of London (LLB), Catholic Univ of Louvain (Doctorate Int Law); *m* 11 July 1978, Margot Gillian, da of Dr David Isaac Perk (d 1994), of Johannesburg, South Africa; 2 da (Ariella b 1981, Lauren b 1983); *Career* called to the Bar Middle Temple 1970; admitted slr 1981, attorney at law NY 1985; ptnr Herbert Smith 1995–2005, barr and arbitrator 2005–; dir London Court of Int Arbitration 1986–2008 (memb Court 2001–07), UK memb Court of Int Arbitration Int C of C 2006–, memb Ct Singapore Int Arbitration Centre (SIAC) 2012–15, memb Int Advsy Bd Hong Kong Int Arbitration Centre (HKIAC); prof and head Sch of Int Arbitration Queen Mary Univ of London 1985–; hon fell Queen Mary Univ of London 2009; Freeman City of London; MCIArb 1976; *Books* Selected Bibliography on East West Trade Law (1976), Applicable in International Commercial Arbitration (1978), Selected Bibliography on International Commercial Arbitration (1979), Contemporary Problems in International Commercial Arbitration (ed, 1986), International Trade: Law and Practice (ed jtly, 1985, 2 edn 1990), The Immunity of Arbitrators (ed, 1990), Enforcement of Foreign Judgements (ed jtly, 1994), Comparative International Commercial Arbitration (jtly, 2003), Parallel State and Arbitral Procedures in International Arbitration (jt ed, 2005), Pervasive Problems in International Arbitration (jt ed, 2006), Arbitration Insights: Twenty Years of the Annual Lectures of the School of International Arbitration (jt ed, 2006), Arbitration in England (jt ed, 2012); *Recreations* tennis, reading, religion; *Style—* Prof Julian D M Lew, QC; ✉ 20 Essex Street, London WC2R 3AL (☎ 020 7842 1200, fax 020 7842 1270, e-mail jlew@20essexst.com)

LEWES, Bishop of 1997–; Rt Rev Wallace Parke Benn; s of William Benn (d 1956), and Lucinda Jane Benn (d 1985); *b* 6 August 1947; *Educ* St Andrew's Coll Dublin, UC Dublin (BA), Trinity Coll Bristol (DipTh awarded by Univ of London); *m* Lindsay Jane, da of Joseph Allan Develing; 1 da (Jessica Jane b 1983), 1 s (James William Thomas b 1987); *Career* ordained: deacon 1972, priest 1973; asst curate: St Mark's New Ferry Wirral Merseyside 1972–76, St Mary's Cheadle Cheshire 1976–82; vicar: St James the Great Audley Staffs 1982–87, St Peter's Harold Wood Essex 1987–97; pt/t hosp chaplain Harold Wood Hosp 1987–96; pres C of E Evangelical Cncl, pres Fellowship of Word and Spirit, memb Cncl REFORM, chm Bible by the Beach; *Publications* The Last Word (1996), Jesus Our Joy (2000); *Recreations* golf, reading, walking, keen rugby watcher and supporter; *Clubs* London Irish Rugby, National; *Style—* The Rt Rev the Bishop of Lewes; ✉ Bishop's Lodge, 16A Prideaux Road, Eastbourne, East Sussex BN21 2NB (☎ 01323 648462, fax 01323 641514, e-mail bishop.lewes@diochi.org.uk)

LEWIN, Christopher George; s of George Farley Lewin, of Ascot, Berks, and Hilda Mary Emily, *née* Reynolds; *b* 15 December 1940; *Educ* Coopers' Cos Sch Bow London; *m* 1 Nov 1985, Robin Lynn, da of Robert Harry Stringham; 2 s (Andrew Christopher Philip b 3 July 1987, Peter Edward James b 19 Oct 1990); *Career* actuarial asst: Equity & Law Life Assurance Society 1956–63, London Transport Bd 1963–67; Br Railways Bd: actuarial asst 1967–70, controller corp pensions 1970–80, seconded memb Fin Insts Gp DOE 1981–82, co-ordinator private capital 1980–88; pensions dir Associated Newspapers Holdings Ltd 1989–92, head of gp pensions Guinness plc 1992–98, head of UK pensions Unilever plc 1998–2003, pensions mangr EDF Energy plc 2005, chm ERM Gp 2008–; risk advsr Govt Actuary's Dept 2009–13; chm: Nat Fedn of Consumer Gps 1984–86, Jt Ctee on Corp Fin Inst and Faculty of Actuaries 1993–2001, working pty of actuaries and civil engrs (published RAMP (Risk Analysis and Management for Projects, 1998)) 1996–, Training Standards Initiative (pensions industry) 2004–06; chm tstees Marconi plc pension scheme 2004–05; memb: Cncl Occupational Pensions Advsy Service 1983–97, Cncl Nat Assoc of Pension Funds 1983–87 and 1995–2003 (hon treas 1997–99), STRATrisk Steering Gp 2003–, Investment Ctee The Pensions Tst 2004–11, Fin and Investment Bd of the Actuarial Profession until 2008, Risk Mgmnt Bd of the Actuarial Profession 2008–; public memb Network Rail 2012–15; reviewer Deregulatory Review of Private Pensions Dept for Work and Pensions 2007; govr: NIESR, Pensions Policy Inst; Joseph Burn Prize Inst of Actuaries 1962, Messenger and Brown Prize Inst of Actuaries 1968, Inst of Actuaries Prize for paper Capital Projects (jt author) 1995, Finlaison Medal Inst of Actuaries; govr Central Fndn Sch for Girls 2001–04, memb Upper Tweed Community Cncl 2011– (chm 2012–), memb Infinis Glenkerie Community Fnd 2013– (chm 2014–15); FIA 1964, FSS, FPMI; *Publications* Pensions and Insurance before 1800: A Social History (2003), From Sumer to Spreadsheets: The History of Mathematical Table Making (contrib, 2004), Sarum Chronicle (contrib, 2005), War Games and their History (2012); author of numerous articles in various actuarial jls 1970–; *Recreations* family life, old books and manuscripts relating to British social history, old board games; *Clubs* Argonauts (chm 1997–98), Gallio (chm 2005–06), Actuaries; *Style—* Christopher Lewin, Esq; ✉ e-mail thirlestane1903@aol.com

LEWIN, Lucille Patricia; da of Michael Witz (d 1969), of SA, and Elaine, *née* Hoffenberg (now Mrs Samuelson); *b* 27 July 1948; *Educ* Redhill Sch for Girls, Univ of Witwatersrand; *m* 1969, Richard Lewin, *qv*; 2 s (Joseph Michel b 1983, Jonathan Toby b 1988); *Career* fashion designer; design res Boston USA 1969–71, buyer Harvey Nichols 1973–76, fndr Whistles 1976–2001 (Br Design-led Retailer award Br Fashion Awards 1993 and 1995), creative dir Liberty 2002–03, currently co-fndr and creative dir Chiltern Street Studio; *Style—* Ms Lucille Lewin; ✉ Chiltern Street Studio, 78b Chiltern Street, London W1U 5AB (website www.chilternstreetstudio.com)

LEWINGTON, Richard; s of Ernest John (Jack) Lewington (d 1978), and Bertha Ann (d 1982); *b* 13 April 1948; *Educ* Orchard Secdy Modern Slough; *m* 25 March 1972, Sylviane, da of Armand Cholet; 1 s (Anthony b 13 May 1982), 1 da (Georgina b 7 Nov 1984); *Career* HM Dip Serv: joined 1967, f/t Russian language training 1971–72, third sec Ulaanbaatar 1972–75, second sec (Chancery/information) Lima 1976–80, second sec (commercial) Moscow 1982–83, first sec (commercial) Tel Aviv 1986–90; served FCO 1991–95, memb EC Monitoring Mission in Croatia and Bosnia 1991, dep high cmmr Valletta 1995–99, ambass to Kazakhstan 1999–2003 (concurrently non-resident ambass to Kyrgyzstan), ambass to Ecuador 2003–06; chief tech advsr EU Border Mgmnt and Drug Action Progs in Central Asia 2007–09, EU Monitor Mission Georgia 2011–12; memb Cncl Royal Soc for Asian Affrs 2009–; tstee Dorset Expeditionary Soc 2006–, memb Soc of Dorset Men 2006–; *Recreations* collecting old books and maps on Dorset, country walking, ipodding; *Style—* Richard Lewington, Esq

LEWINTON, Sir Christopher; kt (1993); s of Joseph Lewinton, and Elizabeth Lewinton; *b* 6 January 1932; *Educ* Acton Tech Coll; *Career* Lt REME; pres Wilkinson Sword USA 1960–70, chief exec Wilkinson Sword Group (acquired by Allegheny International 1978) 1970–85, chm Int Ops Allegheny International 1978–85; TI Group plc: chief exec 1986–98, chm 1989–2000; chm: CL Partners 2000–, Camper & Nicholsons Marina Investments Ltd 2008–; dir Messier-Dowty 1994–98; non-exec dir: Reed Elsevier 1993–99, WPP Group plc 1998–2003; memb Supervisory Bd of Mannesman AG 1995–99, memb Advsy Bd Morgan Stanley/Metalmark Capital 2001–, memb Exec Bd J F Lehman and Co 2001–; Hon DTech Brunel Univ; Hon FRAeS, CEng, FREng, FIMechE; *Recreations* golf, shooting; *Clubs* Boodle's, Sunningdale Golf, Royal Thames Yacht, MCC, Univ (NYC), Everglades (Palm Beach), Four Arts (Palm Beach); *Style*— Sir Christopher Lewinton; ✉ CL Partners, Fifth Floor, Cording House, 34–35 St James's Street, London SW1A 1HD (✆ 020 7201 5490, fax 020 7201 5499)

LEWIS, Alan Frederick; s of Frederick Lewis, of Belfast, and Veronica Selina, *née* McCleery; *b* 3 February 1950; *Educ* Boys' Model Sch Belfast, Queen's Univ Belfast; *Career* Pacemaker Press (picture agency) Belfast: joined 1971, photographer 1971, chief photographer 1973–76; with Daily Mail 1976–93, fndr Photo Press Picture Agency Belfast 1993–; fndr memb Belfast Press Photographers' Assoc 1979, chm NI Press Photographers' Assoc 2008–14 (hon memb 2016 for services to press photography); *Awards* NI Press Photographer of the Year 1975, NI Press Photographer of the Year 1977, Rothmans NI Photographer of the Year 1980, Carrolls Press Photographers' Assoc of Ireland News Picture of the Year 1980 and 1984, Nikon UK Photographer of the Year 1984, Kodak UK Photographer of the Year 1984, Northern Bank News Picture of the Year 1984, Northern Bank People Picture of the Year 1987, NI Sports Cncl Colour Picture of the Year 1991, Guinness Sports Picture of the Year 1994, NI News Photographer of the Year 2001, Vodafone Sports Photographer of the Year 2007, Individual Study Picture of the Year NI Press Photographers' Assoc 2016; *Books* A Day in the Life of Ireland (jtly, 1991), Out of the Darkness (jtly, 2007); *Recreations* fly fishing for trout and salmon; *Style*— Alan Lewis, Esq; ✉ e-mail alanlewis.pics@btinternet.com, website www.photopressbelfast.co.uk

LEWIS, Alastair Charles; *b* 6 August 1971, Chatham, Kent; *Educ* Univ of Leeds (BSc, PhD); *m* 1999, Prof Lucy Carpenter; 1 da (Josephine Lewis), 1 s (Finlay Lewis); *Career* currently prof of atmospheric science Univ of York; dir Nat Centre for Atmospheric Science; strategic technology advsr NERC 2007–13; advsr: DEFRA, MOD, UN Environment Prog, World Meteorological Orgn; author of more than 200 books, chapters and papers; Desty Meml Prize 2001, Philip Leverhulme Prize 2004; FRSC (SAC Silver Medal 2006, John Jeyes Award 2012); *Style*— Prof Alastair Lewis; ✉ Wolfson Atmospheric Chemistry Laboratories, Innovation Way, Heslington, York YO19 4RR

LEWIS, Andrew; *b* 1968; *Educ* Univ of N London, Mackintosh Sch of Architecture Glasgow; *Career* artist; work in Arts Cncl Collection; *Solo Exhibitions* Spatial Awareness Show (fig-1 London) 2000, Ark Royale with Cheese (Laurent Delaye Gallery London) 2001, Andrew Lewis: Systems (InIVA London) 2002, White Van Men (Galerie Serieuze Zaken Amsterdam) 2002, Photo Opportunities (The New Art Gallery Walsall) 2003–04; *Group Exhibitions* The Galleries Show (Royal Acad) 2002, Location UK (Gimpel Fils London) 2002; *Style*— Andrew Lewis, Esq; ✉ c/o Laurent Delaye Gallery, 11 Savile Row, London W1S 3PG (✆ 020 7287 1546, fax 020 7287 1562, e-mail office@laurentdelaye.com); c/o Hans Ulricht Obrist, Musée d'Art Moderne de la Ville de Paris, 11 Avenue du Président-Wilson, 75116 Paris, France (✆ 00 33 6 65 32 12 86)

LEWIS, Ben; s of Charles Lewis, and Joy, *née* Manné; *b* 7 November 1966, London; *Educ* St Paul's, Trinity Coll Cambridge (MA), Freie Universität Berlin (scholar); *Career* documentary film-maker, art critic and writer; prodr and writer MTV News 1990–98; art columnist Prospect magazine 2005–, art critic Evening Standard 2007–; documentaries incl: dir Leviathan (two series, BBC 2) 1997 and 1998, dir The Cost Race (BBC 2), Rover: Last Chance Saloon (Channel 4) 2000, dir The King of Communism 2001 (Grieson Award for Best Historical Documentary 2002), dir Baader Meinhof: In Love With Terror 2002, prodr, dir and presenter Art Safari (series 1 and 2) 2003–05 (Grimme Prize NRW Sonderpreis Kultur 2007, Bronze medal NY TV Festival 2007), prodr and dir Blowing Up Paradise: French Nuclear Testing 2004 (Environmental Award Grenoble Nature and Evironment Film Festival 2006, Special Just Prize Tahiti Film Festival 2007, Golden Panda Sichuan TV Festival China 2007), Hammer and Tickle: The Communist Joke Book 2006 (Best Documentary Zurich Film Festival 2006, nominated RTS Award); *Books* Hammer & Tickle: The Story of Humour Under Communism (2008); *Recreations* jazz, squash; *Style*— Ben Lewis, Esq; ✉ websites www.benlewis.tv, www.artsafari.tv and www.hammerandtickle.com

LEWIS, Ben; *Career* River Island: chief operating offr 2007–10, ceo 2010–; *Style*— Ben Lewis, Esq; ✉ River Island, Chelsea House, West Gate, London W5 1DR

LEWIS, Brandon Kenneth; MP; *b* 20 June 1971; *Educ* Univ of Buckingham (BSc, LLB), KCL (LLM); *Career* called to the Bar Inner Temple; cncllr Brentwood Borough Cncl 1998–2009 (ldr 2004–09), MP (Cons) Gt Yarmouth 2010–; parliamentary under-sec of state Dept for Communities and Local Govt 2012–14, min of state for housing and planning 2014–16, min of state for policing and the fire service 2016–; *Style*— Brandon Lewis, Esq, MP; ✉ 20 Church Plain, Great Yarmouth, Norfolk NR30 1NE (✆ 01493 854550, website www.brandonlewis.co); House of Commons, London SW1A 0AA (e-mail brandon.lewis.mp@parliament.uk)

LEWIS, (David) Byron; s of William Edward Lewis (d 1983), and Eiddwen, *née* Roberts (d 1996); *b* 14 February 1945, Swansea, W Glamorgan; *Educ* Gowerton GS Swansea; *m* 8 May 1969, Hilary Ann, *née* Morgan; 2 da (Elizabeth Holly (Mrs Hastie), Hanya Noelle (Mrs Harrison)); *Career* fin dir various private cos 1969–75, dir Christie-Tyler plc 1975–85, asst gp md Christie-Tyler plc 1985–91, md various subsids of Hillsdown Hldgs plc 1991–93, non-exec chm of various private cos 1993–2008; pres: W Glamorgan Cncl of St John, W Glamorgan SSAFA, W Glamorgan Area Scouts, W Glamorgan ABF; vice-pres RFCA Wales; chm W Glamorgan Magistrates Advsy Bd, chm W Glamorgan Joint Archives Service, county patron Royal British Legion; memb Ct Swansea Univ, memb Ct Cardiff Univ; hon fell Univ of Wales Trinity St David; High Sheriff W Glamorgan 2004–05, HM Lord-Lt W Glamorgan 2008–; Freeman City of London 1989; FCA 1968; CStJ 2008; *Recreations* sport, music, gardening; *Clubs* Army and Navy, Langland Bay Golf, Swansea Business; *Style*— D Byron Lewis, Esq; ✉ Bryn Newydd House, 1 Derwen Fawr Road, Sketty Green, Swansea SA2 8AA (✆ 01792 203012, mobile 07860 652962, e-mail byron.lewis@btinternet.com)

LEWIS, Charles William; s of Judge Peter Edwin Lewis (d 1976), and Mary Ruth, *née* Massey (d 2009); *b* 25 June 1954; *Educ* Eastbourne Coll, UC Oxford (MA); *m* 20 Sept 1986 (m dis 2008), Grace Julia Patricia, da of Alphonsus McKenna, of Dublin; 1 s (Hugo William Elliott b 4 April 1977), 2 da (Cliona Natasha b 14 July 1992, Helena Mary b 17 Feb 1994); *Career* called to the Bar Inner Temple 1977; accredited business coach 2013; *Recreations* skiing, bridge, golf, shooting, opera; *Clubs* MCC, East India, Northamptonshire County Golf, Northamptonshire County Cricket; *Style*— Charles Lewis, Esq; ✉ The Dower House, Church Walk, Great Billing, Northampton NN3 9ED; 36 Bedford Row, London WC1R 4JH (✆ 020 7421 8000, fax 020 7421 8080)

LEWIS, Chris Nigal; *b* 10 May 1961; *Career* former journalist, ceo and fndr LEWIS 1995–; fndr Kupambana charitable fndn; Freedom City of London; *Publications* The Unemployables, Brilliant Minds, Market Sense; *Recreations* reading, military history, woodland management, gardening, aviation, mountain biking, music, motorbikes, the visual arts and design; *Style*— Chris Lewis; ✉ LEWIS, Millbank Tower, Millbank, London SW1P 4RS (website www.lewispr.com); LEWIS, 575 Market Street, San Francisco, CA 94105, USA

LEWIS, Very Rev Christopher Andrew; *b* 4 February 1944; *Educ* Marlborough, Univ of Bristol (BA), Corpus Christi Coll Cambridge (PhD), Westcott House Theol Coll; *m* 1970, Rhona Jane, *née* Martindale; 1 da (Andrea b 20 Aug 1973), 2 s (Aidan b 5 Feb 1979, Hugh b 27 Sept 1986); *Career* served RN 1961–66; curate Barnard Castle 1973–76, priest-in-charge Aston Rowant and Crowell 1978–81, vice-princ Ripon Coll Cuddesdon 1981–82 (tutor 1976–81), vicar of Spalding 1982–87, canon residentiary Canterbury Cathedral 1987–94, dir of Ministerial Trg Dio of Canterbury 1989–94, dean of St Albans 1994–2003, dean of Christ Church 2003–14, ret; chm Assoc of English Cathedrals 2000–09; pro-vice-chllr Univ of Oxford 2010–14, ret; Hon DLitt Univ of Hertfordshire 1999; *Recreations* bicycles, guinea fowl; *Style*— The Very Rev Christopher Lewis; ✉ The Old Brewery, 16 Victoria Road, Aldeburgh, Suffolk IP15 5ED (✆ 01728 454263)

LEWIS, Hon Mr Justice; Sir Clive Buckland Lewis; kt (2013), QC (2006); *Career* called to the Bar Middle Temple 1987; recorder 2003, judge of the High Court of Justice (Queen's Bench Div) 2013–; presiding judge Wales 2016–, liaison judge Administrative Court in Wales 2016–; *Style*— The Hon Mr Justice Lewis; ✉ Royal Courts of Justice, Strand, London WC2A 2LL

LEWIS, Damian Watcyn; OBE (2014); *b* 11 February 1971, London; *Educ* Eton, GSM; *m* 4 July 2007, Helen McCrory, *qv*; 1 da (Manon Isabella Charlotte b 8 Sept 2006), 1 s (Gulliver Cameron b 2 Nov 2007); *Career* actor; *Theatre* incl: Hamlet, Little Eyolf (RSC), Cymbeline (RSC), Pillars of the Community (RSC), The Misanthrope (Comedy Theatre); *Television* incl: Band of Brothers 2001, The Forsyte Saga (ITV) 2002–03, Jeffrey Archer: The Truth 2003, Colditz 2005, Friends and Crocodiles 2005, Much Ado About Nothing 2005, Confessions of a Diary Secretary 2007, Life 2007–09, Stolen 2011, Homeland 2011–13 and 2014 (Outstanding Lead Actor in a Drama Series Emmy Award 2012, Best Performance by an Actor in a Television Series (Drama) Golden Globe 2013), Wolf Hall 2015; guest presenter Have I Got News for You; *Film* incl: Dreamcatcher 2003, Keane 2004, Nyfes (Brides) 2004, Chromophobia 2005, An Unfinished Life 2005, Stormbreaker 2006, The Situation 2006, The Baker 2007 (also prodr), The Escapist 2008, Your Highness 2011, The Sweeney 2012, Romeo and Juliet 2013, Our Kind of Traitor 2015, Queen of the Desert 2015; *Style*— Damian Lewis, Esq, OBE; ✉ c/o Markham & Froggatt Ltd, 4 Windmill Street, London W1T 2HZ

LEWIS, (Peter) Daniel Nicolas David; s of Maj Robert Cholmeley Lewis, TD (d 1993), of Shere, Surrey, and (Miriam) Lorraine, *née* Birnage (d 2000); *b* 14 October 1957; *Educ* Westminster Sch; *Career* Age Concern Westminster 1976–79, mangr London Business Sch Bookshop 1979–82, ptnr Burns Anderson Recruitment 1982–90, dir Smith & Manchester (clinical negligence specialists), currently md Longbridge Law; vice-pres and fell Inst of Recruitment Conslts 1990–95, treas and govr Abinger Hammer Village Sch Tst; *Recreations* dogs, being an expert on the Russian court 1900–17, exploring country house hotels; *Style*— Daniel Lewis, Esq; ✉ 4 Weston Yard, Albury, Surrey GU5 9AF (✆ 01483 202922); Longbridge Law, 3A London Wall Buildings, London EC2M 5SY (✆ 020 7464 1964)

LEWIS, David Edward; s of Edward Arthur Lewis (d 1992), of Pontypridd, and Nancy, *née* Williams (d 2008); *b* 26 March 1952; *Educ* Pontypridd Boys' GS, Univ of Exeter (LLB); *m* Susan Enid, da of James Eccleston; 2 s (Gareth Edward b 28 Feb 1986, Anthony David b 15 Jan 1990), 1 da (Alice Rebecca b 23 Nov 1987); *Career* Allen & Overy: articled clerk 1974–76, asst slr 1976–84, ptnr Tax Dept 1984–2007, conslt Tax Dept 2007–; memb Law Soc 1976; *Recreations* tennis, golf; *Clubs* RAC; *Style*— David Lewis, Esq; ✉ Allen & Overy, One Bishops Square, London E1 6AD (✆ 020 3088 3601)

LEWIS, David Gwynder; s of Gwynder Eudaf Lewis (d 1963), of Sketty, Swansea, and Gwyneth, *née* Jones (d 1979); *b* 31 August 1942; *Educ* Rugby; *m* 2 July 1966, Susan Joyce, da of Andrew Agnew, of Crowborough; 1 da (Alexandra b 1969), 1 s (George b 1972); *Career* Warrant Offr TA C Battery Hon Artillery Co; Hambros Bank Ltd: banker 1961–98, dir 1979–98, exec dir 1991–94, vice-chm 1994–98; chm Hambro Pacific Hldgs Ltd Hong Kong (md 1974–82), pres Hambro America NY 1982–85, dep chm Hambros Australia Ltd Sydney 1994–98, dir Hambros plc 1997; chm Hunters and Frankau Gp Ltd; tstee Gwasg Gregynog; ACIOB 1967; *Recreations* fishing, music, rare book collecting; *Clubs* Turf, RAC, Hong Kong, Royal Hong Kong Jockey, Shek O Country, MCC; *Style*— D G Lewis, Esq; ✉ 57 Victoria Road, London W8 5RH (✆ 020 7937 2277, fax 020 7376 9542)

LEWIS, David John; *b* 17 May 1939; *Educ* Grocers' Sch, Univ of London (BSc); *m* 1961; 4 c; *Career* chartered surveyor; Town & City Properties 1959–62, Maybrook Properties 1962–64, sr ptnr David Lewis & Partners 1964–93; dir: Cavendish Land Co 1972–73, Hampton Trust 1983–87, Mount Martin Gold Mines 1985–92, TBI plc 1995–2001; chm Molyneux Estates plc 1989–95; chm Jewish Blind Soc 1979–89, sr vice-pres Jewish Care 1992– (chm 1991–92), pres European Cncl Jewish Communities 1992–99, govr Oxford Centre for Hebrew & Jewish Studies 1992– (chm Library 1974–2011); tstee: Birmingham Museums Tst 2012–, Wiener Library 2012–; fndr govr Harris City Technol Coll 1991–2009; FRICS 1969 (ARICS 1961); *Recreations* art, music; *Clubs* Savile; *Style*— D J Lewis, Esq; ✉ Catherine House, 76 Gloucester Place, London W1U 6HJ (✆ 020 7487 3401, fax 020 7487 4211, e-mail david.lewis@catherinehouse.com)

LEWIS, Prof David Malcolm; s of Kenneth Stanley Lewis, and Kathleen Elsie, *née* Mann; *b* 24 May 1941; *Educ* Marling Sch Stroud, Univ of Leeds (BSc, PhD); *m* 14 Aug 1965, Barbara, da of Alfred Taylor (d 1965); 2 s (Stephen b 7 March 1967, Matthew b 15 April 1971), 1 da (Catherine b 5 May 1969); *Career* princ devpt offr Int Wool Secretariat 1965–78, sr res scientist CSIRO Geelong Aust 1978–79, princ devpt scientist IWS 1979–87; Univ of Leeds: prof and head of dept 1987–2004, head Resource Centre Sch of Physical Sciences 1997–2003, emeritus prof 2004–; chief scientific offr Perachem Ltd, research dir Inovink Ltd 2004–; hon visiting prof Xian Textile Inst PRC 1988, hon visiting prof Wuhan Inst of Science and Technology PRC 1999, hon visiting prof Heilangjiang Univ Harbin PRC; memb American Chemical Soc, memb and former chm WR Region Soc of Dyers and Colourists; pres Soc of Dyers and Colourists 1993–94; memb American Assoc of Textile Chemists and Colorists; author Wool Dyeing; Milson Medal for Innovation American Assoc of Textile Chemists and Colourists 2005, Olney Medal for Achievement American Assoc of Textile Chemists and Colourists 2009, Centenary Medal Soc of Dyers and Colourists 2015; Liveryman Worshipful Co of Dyers, Freeman City of London 1995; FRSC 1984, FRSA 1989; *Publications* The Coloration of Wool and Other Keratin Fibres (with John A Rippon, 2013); *Recreations* tennis, badminton, walking; *Style*— Prof David Lewis; ✉ Department of Colour Science, University of Leeds, Leeds LS2 9JT (✆ 0113 343 2931, fax 0113 343 2947, e-mail ccddml@leeds.ac.uk)

LEWIS, Denise; OBE (2001, MBE 1999); *b* 27 August 1972; *Career* athlete (heptathlon); memb Birchfield Harriers; achievements at heptathlon: Gold medal Cwlth Games 1994, second place Grand Prix 1995, winner European Cup 1995, seventh place World Championships Gothenburg 1995, second place Grand Prix 1996, Bronze medal Olympic Games Atlanta 1996, Silver medal World Championships Athens 1997, Gold medal European Championships Budapest 1998, Gold medal Cwlth Games Kuala Lumpur 1998, Silver medal World Championships Seville 1999, Gold Medal Olympic Games Sydney 2000; achievements at long jump: second National Championships 1994 and 1995, winner National Championships 1996, fifth place European Cup 1996; ret 2005; awards incl: Sunday Times International Performance of the Year 1994, Sunday Times Sportswoman of the Year 1994, Royal Mail Female Athlete of the Year 1996, BAF Female Athlete of the Year 1996, Athletic Writers Assoc Sportswoman of the Year 1996, Variety Club Sportswoman of the Year 1997, Daily Express Sportswoman of the Year 1997, voted 2nd BBC Sports Personality of the Year 1998, British Athletic Writers' Assoc British Athlete of the Year 2000; pundit BBC Sport 2009–; *Style—* Ms Denise Lewis, OBE

LEWIS, Derek Compton; s of Kenneth Compton Lewis (d 1982), and Marjorie, *née* Buick (d 2004); *b* 9 July 1946, Nottingham; *Educ* Wrekin Coll Telford, Queens' Coll Cambridge (scholar, MA), London Business Sch (MSc); *m* 1969, Louise; 2 da (Annabel Buick (Mrs Thomas) b 1983, Julia Mason b 1984); *Career* dir of finance Ford of Europe 1978–83, finance dir then chief exec Granada Gp plc 1984–91, DG HM Prison Service 1993–95; chm: Sunsail plc 1997–99, Patientline plc 1998–2006, Protocol Assocs 2002–09, JHP Gp 2008–12; dir: Protocol Assoc 2009–, learndirect 2012–13; pro-chllr Univ of Essex 1999–2009; chm: Drinkaware Tst 2008–14, Royal Mencap 2014–, Community Alcohol Partnerships 2014–; tstee WRVS 2007–14; *Publications* Hidden Agendas (1997); *Clubs* Caledonian; *Style—* Derek Lewis, Esq

LEWIS, Duncan; s of late Geoffrey Lewis, and Jean, *née* Daragon; *b* 28 April 1951; *Educ* John Fisher Sch Purley, Ecole St Louis de Gonzague Paris, Queens' Coll Cambridge; *Career* Nat Economic Devpt Office 1979–82, STC plc 1981–85, British Telecom plc 1985–90, Hawker Siddeley plc 1990–91, Cable & Wireless plc 1991–95, Granada Media Gp 1996, Equant NV 1997–2000, GTS Inc 2001–02, advsr The Carlyle Gp 2003–08, chief exec Vislink plc 2008–11; non-exec dir: Spirent Communications plc 2007–, euNetworks Ltd 2011–15, JQW Ltd; chm: nextiraOne NV 2011–, niuSolutions Ltd 2011–, Goldacre Ltd, Workshare Ltd; former chm: Apsmart Ltd, MPme Ltd; *Recreations* travel, reading, theatre; *Style—* Duncan Lewis, Esq; ✉ 4 Whitehall Court, London SW1A 2EP

LEWIS, Edward Trevor Gwyn; s of Rev Gwyn Lewis (d 1984), and Annie Millicent, *née* Thomas (d 2006); *b* 16 March 1948; *Educ* Ellesmere Coll, Lausanne Univ, KCL; *m* 6 April 1974, (Pamela) Gay, da of late Lt-Col Jimmy Wilson, DL, of Dorchester, Dorset; 3 da (Leone b 28 Feb 1975, Kim, Tamsin (twins) b 23 Jan 1979); *Career* called to the Bar Gray's Inn 1972, dep legal mangr Mirror Group Newspapers 1980–83, JP S Westminster Div 1981–84, prosecuting counsel Western Circuit DHSS 1985–2002, actg dist judge 1988–92, night lawyer: Daily Express, Sunday Express, The Sun; motoring corr: Penthouse Magazine, Country Magazine; commissioned by FT, Mail on Sunday and Evening Standard; *Recreations* riding my bike, opera, shooting, family, motor cars; *Clubs* Garrick; *Style—* Edward Lewis, Esq; ✉ 21 Wallgrave Road, London, SW5 0RF; 4 Breams Buildings, Chancery Lane, London EC4A 1HP (☎ 020 7092 1900)

LEWIS, Geraint; s of Melvyn Lewis (d 1992), and Mair Eluned, *née* Griffiths (d 1985); *b* 18 October 1954; *Educ* Bedwelty GS, Univ of Newcastle upon Tyne (BDS); *Career* photographer; graduated dental surgn Newcastle upon Tyne 1980, subsequently Dept of Oral Surgery London Hosp, in private practice until 1987; full time freelance photographer 1987–; worked with: Independent and Independent on Sunday, Royal Shakespeare Co, Daily and Sunday Telegraph, Evening Standard, RNT, Theatr Clwyd; dir photo gallery St Leonard's-on-Sea, former occasional lectr photojournalism course London Coll of Printing; exhbn of photographs: of Edinburgh Int Festival (Hampstead Theatre) 1993, of Israel (Lyric Theatre Hammersmith) 1993, of Poland (Polish Cultural Inst London) 1995 (also at Ty Llyen Gallery Swansea 1996), Polish Theatre (Moray House Edinburgh) 1996; highly commended Photography Award Br Arts Journalism Awards 1991 (nominated 1989); memb: Assoc of Photographers, Br Press Photography Assoc; *Recreations* cricket, football, cinema, photography; *Clubs* Archery Cricket, BFI, Photographers Gallery; *Style—* Geraint Lewis, Esq; ✉ mobile 07831 413452, e-mail geraint@geraintlewis.com, website www.geraintlewis.com

LEWIS, Gillian Margaret (Gill); da of Gwilym Thomas Lewis (d 1974), and Valerie, *née* Williams (d 1969); *b* 15 February 1944; *Educ* Howells Sch Llandaff (head girl), St Hilda's Coll Oxford (BA); *m* 1973, Anthony Joseph Lister (d 2000), s of late Walter Lister; 2 s (Timothy David b 1 Sept 1979, Adam Anthony b 30 Jan 1981); *Career* worked as advtg exec J Walter Thompson & Co and various sales and mktg appts in food industry 1967–74, gen mangr Europe Green Giant Co 1974–78, mgmnt conslt McKinsey & Co 1979–81, exec search conslt Fisher Dillistone & Associates 1981–86, dir of human resources and memb Gp Exec Ctee Courtaulds plc 1987–91, sr vice-pres human resources and corp affrs Nestlé SA Switzerland 1992–94; Heidrick & Struggles Exec Search Conslts: managing ptnr consumer practice 1995–98, managing ptnr HE/not-for-profit practice 2000–, sr ptnr English-speaking area 2001– (area managing ptnr 1998–2000); non-exec dir: Pearson plc 1992–2001, Zeneca Group plc 1993–96; memb Bd of Tstees NSPCC 1985–92 and 1997–2002; Veuve Clicquot UK Business Woman of the Year 1977; FIPD 1988, FRSA 1988; *Recreations* theatre, classical music, travel, good food; *Style—* Ms Gill Lewis; ☎ 020 7930 0793, fax 020 7075 4192, e-mail gmlewis@heidrick.com

LEWIS, Huw George; AM; s of David Lewis, and Marion, *née* Pierce, of Aberfan, Mid Glamorgan; *b* 17 January 1964; *Educ* Univ of Edinburgh (BSc), Open Univ (BA); *m* 1996, Lynne, *née* Neagle; 2 s (James b 25 June 2002, Samuel b 12 July 2008); *Career* teacher 1988–89 and 1990–94; researcher to Nigel Griffiths MP 1989–90, head of organisation and asst gen sec Wales Lab Pty 1994–99, memb Nat Assembly for Wales (Lab Co-op) Merthyr Tydfil & Rhymney 1999–, dep min for children Welsh Assembly 2009–; *Style—* Huw Lewis, Esq, AM; ✉ National Assembly for Wales, Cardiff Bay, Cardiff CF99 1NA (☎ 029 2089 8752 or 01443 692299 (Merthyr Tydfil and Rhymney office), e-mail huw.lewis@wales.gov.uk, website www.huwlewis.org and www.facebook.com/huwlewisam, Twitter @huwlewis)

LEWIS, Ivan; MP; s of Joel Lewis, and Gloria, *née* Goodwin; *Educ* William Hulme GS, Stand Coll, Bury Coll of FE; *m* 1990 (m dis), Juliette, da of Lesley Fox; 2 s (Ben b 5 Nov 1994, Harry b 26 June 1996); *Career* co-ordinator Contact Community Care Gp 1986–89; Jewish Social Services: social worker 1989–91, community care mangr 1991–92, chief exec 1992–97; MP (Lab) Bury S 1997–; formerly PPS to Rt Hon Stephen Byers MP, *qv*, sec of state for Trade and Industry; Parly under-sec of state DfES 2001–05, economic sec to HM Treasy 2005–06, Parly under sec of state Dept of Health 2006–08, Parly under sec Dept for Int Devpt 2008–09, min of state FCO 2009–10, shadow sec for culture, media and sport 2010–11, shadow sec of state for int devpt 2011–14, shadow Northern Ireland sec 2014–15; memb Bury MBC 1990–98 (chm Soc Servs Ctee 1991–95); former chm Bury MENCAP, chm Bury S Lab Pty 1991–96; *Recreations* football (Manchester City FC), reading, walking; *Style—* Ivan Lewis, Esq, MP; ✉ House of Commons, London SW1A 0AA (☎ 020 7219 6404)

LEWIS, Jacqueline; *née* Khoo; da of Raymond T T Khoo (d 2005), and Martta Maria Khoo; *b* 31 October 1962; *Educ* Trinity Coll Dublin (MB, BCh, BAO), RCS; *m* 20 June 1992, Jeremy Michael James Lewis; 2 da (Emily, Rebecca); *Career* house offr internship Dublin 1986–87, general and plastic surgical trg GB (Pan-Thames Plastic Surgery Trg Prog), France and Belgium 1987–2001; fell in breast surgery Institut Curie Paris, Royal Marsden Hosp London and Charing Cross Hosp London; memb: Br Assoc of Plastic Reconstructive and Aesthetic Surgns (BAPRAS), Br Assoc of Aesthetic Plastic Surgns (BAAPS), Br Assoc of Surgical Oncology (BASO), European Soc of Surgical Oncology (ESO); FRCS 1992 (Plas 1999); Royal Society of Medicine: Your Guide to Breast Cancer (2005); author of numerous articles in professional jls; *Recreations* photography, scuba-diving, sculpture; *Style—* Mrs Jacqueline Lewis; ✉ Total Practice Management, The General, Main Road, Boreham, Chelmsford CM3 3HJ (☎ 01245 234415, e-mail info@ tpm.org.uk and info@oncoplasticbreast.com)

LEWIS, Jane; *Career* designer; fndr and ceo Goat 2001–; *Style—* Ms Jane Lewis; ✉ Goat, 4 Conduit Street, London W1S 2DJ

LEWIS, His Hon Judge Jeffrey Allan; s of David Meyer Lewis (d 1969), and Esther Kirson (d 1995); *b* 25 May 1949; *Educ* Univ of the Witwatersrand (BA), UC Cardiff (PGCE), Univ of Leeds (LLB); *m* 18 May 1985, Elizabeth Ann, da of Geoffrey Threlfall Swarbrick; 1 da (Rachel Rose b 30 March 1986), 1 s (James David b 11 Aug 1988); *Career* teacher Hartridge HS Newport Gwent 1973–75; called to the Bar Middle Temple 1978, in practice NE Circuit 1978–2002, recorder 1997–2002 (asst recorder 1993–97), circuit judge (Northern Circuit) 2002–; pt/t chm Industrial Tbnls 1991–95; *Recreations* music, reading, skiing, gardening; *Style—* His Hon Judge Jeffrey Lewis; ✉ Manchester Crown Court, Minshull Street, Manchester M1 3FS (☎ 0161 954 7500)

LEWIS, Jeremy Morley; s of late George Morley Lewis, FRCS, of Seaford, E Sussex, and Janet, *née* Iles; *b* 15 March 1942; *Educ* Malvern Coll, Trinity Coll Dublin (BA), Univ of Sussex (MA); *m* 1968, Jane Petra, da of Thomas Anthony Freston; 2 da (Jemima b 5 June 1971, Hattie b 23 Sept 1975); *Career* author; advtg trainee Foote Cone & Belding 1960–61, publicity asst William Collins 1967–68, publicity manager Geoffrey Bles Ltd 1968–69, ed André Deutsch Ltd 1969–70, literary agent A P Watt 1970–76, ed Oxford University Press 1977–79, dir Chatto & Windus Ltd 1979–89, freelance writer and ed 1989–, dep ed London Magazine 1991–94, ed conslt Peters, Fraser & Dunlop 1994–2002, commissioning ed The Oldie 1997–2014, dep ed The Oldie 2014–, ed-at-large Literary Review 2004–; memb Ctee and sec R S Surtees Soc 1990–, memb Ctee Royal Literary Fund 2007–16; FRSL 1992; *Books* Playing For Time (1987), The Chatto/ Vintage Book of Office Life, or Love Among the Filing Cabinets (ed, 1992), Kindred Spirits (1995), Cyril Connolly: A Life (1997), Tobias Smollett (2003), Penguin Special: The Life and Times of Allen Lane (2005), Grub Street Irregular (2008), Shades of Greene: One Generation of an English Family (2010), David Astor: A Life in Print (2016); *Recreations* walking round Richmond Park, carousing with friends, re-reading Trollope, talking to the cat; *Clubs* Academy; *Style—* Jeremy Lewis, Esq; ✉ 3 Percival Road, London SW14 7QE (☎ 020 8876 2807, e-mail jeremy.lewis5@me.com); c/o Gillon Aitken Associates, 291 Gray's Inn Road, London WC1X 8QJ

LEWIS, John Henry James; OBE (2004); s of late Leonard Lewis, QC, of Newchapel, Surrey, and Rita Jeanette, *née* Stone (d 1994); *b* 12 July 1940; *Educ* Shrewsbury, UCL (LLB); *m* 30 Nov 1984, Susan Frances, da of Maj Robert Ralph Merton, of Burghfield, Berks; 2 da (Daisy Leonora Frances b 1 Jan 1985, Lily Charlotte Frances b 23 Feb 1986), 2 s (Barnaby Ralph James b 29 June 1989, Alfred Ralph James b 24 June 1992); *Career* admitted slr 1966; ptnr Lewis Lewis & Co 1966–82; conslt: Jaques & Lewis 1982–95, Eversheds 1995–; chm: Cliveden plc 1985–2002, Principal Hotels plc 1994–2001, Cons Party Tourism Task Force 2007–10, Photo-Me Int plc 20010–, Groucho Club 2008–15; vice-chm: John D Wood and Co plc 1989–98, Pubmaster Group Ltd 1996–2000; dir: GR (Holdings) plc, Prime People plc, Sloane Square Hotel Ltd, Blakeney Hldgs Ltd; BTA: memb Bd 1990–96, chm 1993; tstee: The Wallace Collection 1994–2004 (chm 1997–2004), Hertford House Tst – The Wallace Collection (chm 2004–14), The Watts Gallery until 2008, The Burlington Magazine Fndn until 2008, The Henry Moore Fndn until 2008; govr London Goodenough Tst for Overseas Graduates until 2008; chm: The Attingham Tst for the Study of Historic Houses and Collections 1998–, Public Monuments and Sculpture Assoc 2014–; Chevalier Wallace Collection; Freeman City of London, memb Worshipful Co of Gunmakers; *Publications* UK Tourism in a Competitive World (2010), British Tourism, Exploring Every Option for Growth (2012, revised edn 2016), Free Museums! (2012, revised edn 2016); *Recreations* sculpture, architecture, tennis; *Clubs* Brooks's, Garrick; *Style—* John Lewis, Esq, OBE; ✉ Shute House, Donhead St Mary, Shaftesbury, Dorset SP7 9DG (☎ 01747 828866, fax 01747 828821, e-mail mail@jhjlewis.com)

LEWIS, Jonathan; s of Henry Lewis, of London, and Jenny, *née* Cohen; *b* 2 November 1955; *Educ* St Paul's, Univ of Manchester (BA Econ); *m* 22 June 1980, Veronique; 3 da (Sara Giselle b 2 July 1983, Tanya Esther 4 May 1987, Gina Miriam Elisa 10 Sept 1999), 1 s (Joshua Prosper b 14 June 1985); *Career* D J Freeman: joined as trainee 1978, admitted slr 1980, ptnr 1982, memb Fin Ctee 1987–90, chief exec 1993–2001, head of property 2001–03; ptnr Olswang 2003– (head Int Real Estate Gp 2013–); memb Bd UK Jewish Film; Br under 20 sabre fencing champion 1973; memb Law Soc 1980; *Recreations* fundraising for charity, art, travel; *Style—* Jonathan Lewis, Esq

LEWIS, The Rt Hon, Dr Julian Murray; PC (2015), MP; s of Samuel Lewis (d 2008), and Hilda, *née* Levitt (d 1987); *b* 26 September 1951; *Educ* Dynevor GS Swansea, Balliol Coll Oxford (MA), St Antony's Coll Oxford (DPhil); *Career* research in strategic studies 1975–77 and 1978–81, sec Campaign for Representative Democracy 1977–78, research dir and dir Coalition for Peace Through Security 1981–85, dir Policy Research Associates 1985–; MP (Cons) New Forest E 1997– (Parly candidate Swansea W 1983); oppn whip 2001–02, shadow def min 2002–04 and 2005–10, shadow min for the Cabinet Office 2004–05; memb House of Commons: Select Ctee on Welsh Affairs 1998–2001, Select Ctee on Def 2000–01 & 2014–15, Intelligence and Security Ctee 2010–15; dep dir Cons Research Dept 1990–96, sec Cons Parly Def Ctee 1997–2001, vice-chm Cons Parly Foreign Affrs Ctee & Euro Affrs Ctee 2000–01, Exec 1922 Ctee 2001; Parly chm First Defence 2004–09; chm Defence Select Ctee 2015–; memb Armed Forces Parly Scheme: RAF 1998 and 2000, RN 2004, RCDS 2006, Army 2009; hon pres Br Military Powerboat Tst 2007–09 (tstee 1998–2001, hon vice-pres 2001–07); seaman RNR 1979–82; Trench Gascoigne essay prize RUSI 2005 and 2007, RCDS dissertation prize 2006; *Publications* Changing Direction: British Military Planning for Post-War Strategic Defence, 1942–1947 (1988, 2nd edn 2003), Labour's CND Cover-up (CCO, 1992), Who's Left? An Index of Labour MPs and Left-wing Causes, 1986–92 (CCO, 1992), What's Liberal? (CCO, 1996), Racing Ace: The Fights and Flights of 'Kink' Kinkead, DSO, DSC, DFC (2011); author of articles and pamphlets; *Recreations* history, films, music, photography, living in the New Forest; *Clubs* Athenaeum, Totton Conservative (hon pres 2001–15); *Style—* The Right Hon Dr Julian Lewis, PC, MP; ✉ House of Commons, London SW1A 0AA (☎ 020 7219 4179, website www.julianlewis.net)

LEWIS, Lynn Alexander Mackay; s of Victor Lewis (d 1982), journalist; *b* 23 August 1937; *Educ* Elizabeth Coll Guernsey, Trinity Kandy Sri Lanka; *m* 1959, Valerie Elaine, da of Harry Procter, journalist, of London; 1 da (Carol b 1959), 1 s (Lindon b 1961); *Career* reporter: Kentish Express 1954–57, Nottingham Evening Post 1959–61; fndr Corby News 1961, investigative reporter Sunday Mirror 1962–65 (subjects incl Profumo Affair, Kray Twins, Rachman Savundra), Rome bureau chief Sunday Mirror 1966–68, reporter LWT 1969, investigative reporter and presenter Nationwide (BBC TV) 1969–74 (subjects incl pyramid selling, Cottingley Fairies), fndr and md Nauticalia Gp (marine mktg, mail order and shops) 1974 (chm 1988–2012), ret 2013; publisher of Val Lewis's biography of Joanna Southcott 1998 and Ships' Cats in War and Peace 2001; chm: Marine Trades Assoc 1986–89, Shepperton C of C 2005–07; dir National Boat Shows Ltd 1988–94, dir Spelthorne C of C 1999–2000; Lord of the Manor of Shepperton-on-Thames; Queen's Award for Export 1998, Spelthorne Civic Award 2008; *Recreations* Thames boating, cricket; *Clubs* Shepperton Cricket (chm 1992–94); *Style—* Lynn Lewis, Esq; ✉ 381 Cromwell Tower, Barbican, London EC2Y 8NB (☎ 020 7628 6991)

LEWIS, Malcolm Neal; s of Neal Stanley Lewis, of Jersey, and Barbara Ann Lewis, *née* Able; *b* 20 August 1958; *Educ* Lancing, École Hoteliere de Lausanne (Dip); *m* 1, (m dis), Ragnhild Kjaernet; 1 s (David b 18 Aug 1984); *m* 2, Aug 1996, Florence Patricia Orr; 1 da (Sophie Louise b 2 March 2002), 1 s (James Malcolm b 10 Oct 2004); *Career* hotelier; receptionist Hotel Totem Flaine France 1977–78, École Hotelier de Lausanne 1978–81, chef Conaught Hotel London 1981–82, mangr and md Longueville Manor Hotel Jersey 1992–, chm Relais & Châteaux UK 2001–; pres Jersey Hospitality Assoc; *Recreations* tennis, boating, golf, reading; *Style*— Malcolm Lewis, Esq; ✉ Maison Catelain, La Route de la Francheville, Grouville, Jersey JE3 9UE; (☎ 01534 619448); Longueville Manor, Longueville Road, St Saviour, Jersey JE2 7WF (☎ 01534 725501, e-mail mlewis@longuevillemanor.com)

LEWIS, Mark; s of Brian Ellis Aaron Lewis, and Elaine, *née* Cohen; *b* 10 December 1964; *Educ* Middlesex Poly (BA); *Children* 4 da (Paisley, Emily, Tamara, Orli); *Career* admitted slr 1990; slr advocate (civl) 1996; ptnr George Davies Slrs Manchester 2001–09, Stripes Manchester 2009–10, formerly with Taylor Hampton, currently ptnr Seddons Slrs; memb: Law Soc, Lawyers for Media Standards, UK Lawyers for Israel; *Recreations* veteran cars, coats, cufflinks; *Clubs* Ivy; *Style*— Mark Lewis; ✉ Seddons, 5 Portman Square, London W1H 5NT (☎ 020 7725 8012, mobile 07508 008700)

LEWIS, Martin Steven; OBE (2014); s of Stuart Lewis, of Manchester, and Susan, *née* Tesciuba (d 1984); *b* 9 May 1972, Manchester; *Educ* LSE (BSc, gen sec Students Union), Cardiff Sch of Journalism (postgrad dip); *m* 31 May 2009, Lara, *née* Lewington; 1 da (Sapphire Susan b 1 Nov 2012); *Career* gen sec LSE Students' Union 1994–95; account exec Brunswick PR 1995–97, reporter/prodr BBC Business Unit 1998–99, business corr then money saving expert Simply Money TV 2000–01; columnist: Sunday Express 2001–05, The Guardian 2005–06, Sunday Times 2006–07, Sunday Post 2007–13, News of the World 2008–11, Daily Telegraph 2009–, Sunday Mirror 2014–; Money Saving Expert: This Morning (ITV1) 2003–05 and 2012–, GMTV and Daybreak 2006–; presenter: Make Me Rich (ITV1) 2005, It Pays to Watch 2008, The Martin Lewis Money Show (ITV 1) 2012–; reporter Tonight (ITV1) 2006; contrib: Vine Show (BBC Radio 2) 2005–, Radio 5 Consumer Panel 2010–; chm Independent Task Force on Student Finance Communication 2011–, memb Money Advice Service Panel 2015–, fndr and chair of tstees Money and Mental Health Policy Inst 2016–; chair MSE Charity 2008–; govr LSE 2009–; DBA (hc) Univ of Chester; *Books* The Money Diet (2004, 2 edn 2005), Thrifty Ways for Modern Days (2006), The Three Most Important Lessons (2008); *Recreations* trying to get my average Scrabble score above 410 (currently 406) and to run over 1,200 km per year, reading historic novels, very poor golf, anything with lists, watching athletics, supporting Manchester City; *Style*— Martin Lewis, OBE; ✉ website www.MoneySavingExpert.com

LEWIS, Martyn John Dudley; kt (2016), CBE (1997); s of Thomas John Dudley Lewis (d 1979), of Coleraine, NI, and Doris, *née* Jones; *b* 7 April 1945; *Educ* Dalriada GS Ballymoney, Trinity Coll Dublin (BA); *m* 1, 20 May 1970, Elizabeth Anne (d 2012), da of Duncan Carse, of Fittleworth, W Sussex; 2 da (Sylvie b 11 May 1975, Kate b 24 July 1978); m 2, 2 July 2012, Patsy St Clair Baker; *Career* TV journalist, presenter newsreader and businessman; presenter BBC Belfast 1967–68, journalist and broadcaster HTV Wales 1968–70, joined ITN 1970, set up and ran ITN's Northern Bureau Manchester 1971–78; newsreader and foreign corr ITN: News at Ten, News at 5.45 1978–86; ITN reporter 1970–86 incl: Cyprus War, Seychelles Independence, Fall of Shah of Iran, Soviet Invasion of Afghanistan, Vietnamese Boat People; co-presenter: ITV gen election programmes 1979 and 1983, ITV Budget programmes 1981–84, wrote and produced Battle for the Falklands video, presenter The Secret Hunters documentary (TVS); joined BBC as presenter One O'Clock News 1986, presenter Nine O'Clock News 1987–94, presenter Six O'Clock News 1994–99; host Today's the Day (series, BBC2) 1993–99; presenter: Crimebeat (series, BBC1) 1996, 1997 and 1998, Bethlehem Year Zero (ITV) 1999, Dateline Jerusalem (ITV) 2000, News '40 (ITV) 2000, Ultimate Questions (ITV) 2000–02, Agenda (The Wireless) 2012–; BBC documentaries: MacGregor's Verdict, Royal Tournament, Royal Mission Great Ormond Street – A Fighting Chance, Princess Anne – Save The Children, Help is There, Indian Summer, Fight Cancer, Living with Dying, The Giving Business, Health UK; presenter-in-chief The Medical Channel 2000; chm and fndr YouthNet (www.thesite.org) 1995–2014 (fndr at large 2014–), chm and fndr Global Intercasting Ltd 1999–2007, chm and co-fndr Teliris Ltd 2001–12, chm Nice TV Ltd 2005–12; TS Elite Gp: sr advsr 2012–14, dir 2013–, dir Performance Learning (subsidiary co) 2014–; dir IPSO 2014–; pres United Response 1988–; vice-pres: Help the Hospices, Marie Curie Cancer Care, Macmillan Cancer Support; tstee The Windsor Leadership Tst 2001–11, chm The Beacon Fellowship Charitable Tst 2005–08, chm NCVO 2010–, chm Families of the Fallen 2010–15, tstee Charities Aid Fndn 2010–, vice-pres EACH (East Anglia Children's Hospice); patron: Demelza House Children's Hospice 1996–, Dementia UK, Volunteering England until 2012 (merged with NCVO), Midmay Mission Hosp, Patchwork Fndn, Positive News 2013–, Do-It Tst 2014–; chm Main Award Ctee Queen's Award for Voluntary Service 2009–, perm dep chair Lord Mayor of London's Dragon Awards 2010–; memb: Cncl St George's House Windsor Castle 2009–12, Team London Advsy Bd 2013–; Freeman City of London 1989, Liveryman Worshipful Co of Pattenmakers; Hon DLitt Univ of Ulster 1994; FRSA 1990, memb BAFTA; *Books* And Finally (1984), Tears and Smiles – The Hospice Handbook (1989), Cats in the News (1991, ebook 2015), Dogs in the News (1992, ebook 2015), Go For It (annual, 1993–98), Today's the Day (1995), Reflections on Success (1997, ebook 2015), Seasons of Our Lives (1999, ebook 2015), Media Values (contrib, 2010); *Recreations* photography, good food, keeping fit, campaigning for solutions-driven journalism; *Clubs* Garrick; *Style*— Sir Martyn Lewis, CBE; ✉ c/o Anita Land (☎ 07837 764139 or 07899 792995, e-mail anita@anitaland.com)

LEWIS, (Patricia) Mary; da of late Donald Leslie Cornes, of Bayston Hill, Salop, and Eleanor Lillian, *née* Roberts; *b* Shrewsbury, Shropshire; *Educ* Stonehurst Sch Shrewsbury, St Margaret's Yeaton Peverey, Shrewsbury Sch of Art, Camberwell Sch of Arts and Crafts (BA), Central Sch of Art Middx Poly (postgrad); *m* 2, 7 Jan 1992, Robert Moberly, *qv*, s of Sir Walter Moberly, GBE, KCB, DSO (d 1973); 1 da (Scarlett Rose b 28 May 1992); *Career* graphic designer; creative dir and founding ptnr Lewis Moberly 1984–; responsible for: St Pancras Identity 2007, Gatwick Airport Identity 2010, Duchy Originals from Waitrose 2010, Moët & Chandon Identity; design conslt Marks and Spencer 1999–2015; awards incl: British Design and Art Direction Gold Award for Outstanding Design and 3 Silver Awards, Design Business Assoc Grand Prix for Design Effectiveness, Br Design and Art Direction President's Award for Outstanding Achievement, Pentawards USA Haraway Award 2012, Experiencia Gourmet Red Dot Award 2013; juror: BAFTA Graphic Design Awards, Millennium Products, Communication Arts Awards USA, Scottish Design Awards; chm: BBC Design Awards, pres Cannes Lion Design Jury 2013; speaker Design Thinkers Toronto 2014; work exhibited: London (V&A), Los Angeles, Japan, NYC, Paris, Moscow; pres Br Design and Art Direction 1995 (hon memb 1998); memb Wedgwood Design Policy Gp 1998–99, participant Creative Britain Workshops 1997; contrib Radio 4 Food Prog 1997; nominated Prince Phillip Designers Prize 2008; hon masters degree Univ of Surrey 2002; FRSA; *Books* Understanding Brands (co-ed); *Recreations* Shropshire Farm, British Eventing, South Shropshire Hunt; *Clubs* Br Eventing; *Style*— Ms Mary Lewis; ✉ Lewis Moberly, 33 Gresse Street, London W1T 1QU (☎ 020 7580 9252, e-mail hello@lewismoberly.com)

LEWIS, Emeritus Prof Mervyn Keith; s of Norman Malcolm Lewis (d 1982), and Gladys May Valerie, *née* Way (d 2012); *b* 20 June 1941; *Educ* Unley HS, Univ of Adelaide (BSc, PhD); *m* 24 Nov 1962, Kay Judith, da of Lt Royce Melvin Wiesner (d 1977), of Adelaide, Aust; 4 da (Stephanie b 1966, Miranda b 1967, Alexandra b 1969, Antonia b 1972); *Career* Elder Smith & Co Ltd 1957–58, Cwlth Bank of Aust 1959–64, assoc dean Univ of Adelaide 1981–83 (tutor and lectr 1965–84, sr lectr 1973–79, reader 1979–84), visiting scholar Bank of England 1979–80, conslt Aust Fin System Inquiry 1980–81, Midland Bank prof of money and banking Univ of Nottingham 1984–96, Nat Aust Bank prof in banking and finance Univ of S Aust 1996–2013 (adjunct prof 2013–16, emeritus prof 2016–) memb Multicultural Educn Ctee of S Aust 2000–02; series ed New Horizons in Money and Finance 2002–, series ed Studies in Islamic Finance, Accounting and Governance 2010–; visiting prof: of econs Flinders Univ of S Aust 1987–96, Wirtschaftsuniversität Wien 1987 and 1990–95, Int Teachers' Programme Bocconi Univ Milan 1988, Victoria Univ of Wellington 1991, Huazhong Univ of Science and Technol Wuhen 1998, Univ of Mauritius 2000–04 and 2009–11, Univ of Goettingen 2001, Euro Med Marseille 2007, Inaugural Securities Cmmn Univ of Malaya 2009, Catholic Univ of Leuven 2015; res assoc Center for Pacific Basin Monetary and Economic Studies Federal Reserve Bank of San Francisco 1991–96; memb Australian Research Cncl Asia Pacific Futures Research Network Islam Node 2005–, memb Australia and NZ Shadow Financial Regulatory Ctee 2010–; pres Cncl Kingston Coll of Advanced Educn 1978–79; jt winner Blake Dawson Waldron Prize for Business Literature 2005; elected fell Acad of the Social Sciences in Aust 1986 (emeritus fell 2016); *Books* Monetary Policy in Australia (1980), Australian Monetary Economics (1981), Monetary Control in the United Kingdom (1981), Australia's Financial Institutions and Markets (1985), Personal Financial Markets (1986), Domestic and International Banking (1987), Money in Britain: Monetary Policy, Innovation and Europe (1991), Current Issues in Financial and Monetary Economics (1992), The Australian Financial System (1993), Financial Intermediaries (1995, 2 edn 1996), Australian Financial System: evolution, policy and practice (1997), The Globalisation of Financial Services (1999), Monetary Economics (2000), Islamic Banking (2001), Public Private Partnerships: The Worldwide Revolution in Infrastructure Provision and Project Finance (2004), The Economics of Public Private Partnerships (2005), Reforming China's State-Owned Enterprises and Banks (2006), The Handbook of Islamic Banking (2007), Untangling the US Deficit: Evaluating Causes, Cures and Global Imbalances (2007), Islamic Finance (2007), An Islamic Perspective on Governance (2009), Global Finance After the Crisis: The United States, China and the New World Order (2013), Risk and Regulation of Islamic Banking (2014), Handbook of Islam and Economic Life (2014), Understanding Ponzi Schemes, can better financial regulation prevent investors from being defrauded? (2015), Financial Intermediaries: An Analysis of Essential Articles, Elgar Research Reviews in Economics (2016); *Recreations* rambling, tennis, music; *Clubs* East India; *Style*— Emeritus Prof Mervyn Lewis; ✉ Business School, University of South Australia, City West Campus, North Terrace, Adelaide, South Australia 5000 (e-mail mervyn.lewis@unisa.edu.au)

LEWIS, Rt Rev Michael; *see:* Cyprus and the Gulf, Bishop in

LEWIS, Paul; *b* 13 October 1981; *Educ* Fullbrook Comp Sch and Sixth Form Coll Surrey, King's Coll Cambridge (BA, pres Cambrige Univ Students Union 2002–03), Harvard Univ Grad Sch of Arts and Humanities; *Career* freelance journalist 2004–05, trainee reporter The Guardian 2005, reporter The Guardian 2006– (asst news ed 2008), reporter Washington Post 2007; Laurence Stern Fellowship 2007, Bevins Prize for outstanding investigative journalism 2009, Reporter of the Year Br Press Award 2010; *Style*— Paul Lewis, Esq; ✉ The Guardian, King's Place, 90 York Way, London N1 9GU (e-mail paul.lewis@guardian.co.uk)

LEWIS, Paul; s of William Denis Lewis, and Betty Blanche; *b* 22 April 1948, Cheshire; *Educ* Maidstone GS, Univ of Stirling; *m* 15 July 2014, Emma Lynch; *Career* journalist; presenter Money Box and Money Box Live (Radio 4) 2000– (former reporter), presenter Your Money (BBC World Service) 2012–; columnist: Saga Magazine, Radio Times, Money Marketing, Financial Times; regular guest: BBC Breakfast, News Channel, Radio Wales, Radio Ulster, PM, World at One, Today, You & Yours (Radio 4); Lifetime Achievement Award Assoc of Br Insurers 2006, Consumer Pension and Investment Journalist of the Year Aon 2006, Best Industry Commentator Daily Telegraph Wealth Management Awards 2008, Journalist of the Year Headline Money Award 2010, London Press Club Consumer Journalist of the Year 2010, Best Broadcast Journalist AIC Award 2011, Broadcast Journalist of the Year Headline Money Award 2011, 2013 and 2014, Voice of the Customer Award CII 2014, Money Marketing Finance Journalist of the Year Headline Money Awards 2014; Hon DUniv Essex 2013; *Books* Money Magic (2005), The Public Face of Wilkie Collins: The Collected Letters (jt ed, 2005), Live Long and Prosper (2006), Beat the Banks (2008), Pay Less Tax (2010); *Recreations* Wilkie Collins specialist (see Books); *Style*— Paul Lewis; ✉ e-mail paul@paullewis.co.uk, website www.paullewis.co.uk, blog www.paullewismoney.blogspot.com, Twitter @paullewismoney

LEWIS, Paul; CBE (2016); *Educ* Chetham's Sch of Music, Guildhall Sch of Music; *Career* pianist; reg performer of recital and chamber music, concerto soloist; Steinway & Sons 1000th registered Steinway Artist 1997, selected BBC's New Generation artist scheme1999, prof of piano Royal Acad of Music 2000–02; appeared at the Wigmore Hall 17 times 1999–2002, selected artist for Wigmore Hall in European Concert Halls Orgn's 'Rising Stars' Scheme 2002; recitals incl: Aldeburgh, Bath, Brighton, Cheltenham, Chester, Edinburgh, Lichfield Festival, Perth Festival, Schubertiade Schwarzenberg, Luzern Piano Festival, Klavier Festival Ruhr, Vancouver Chamber Music Festival, Queen Elizabeth Hall, Purcell Room, Queen's Hall Edinburgh, Turner Sims Concert Hall Southampton, many concerts for music clubs and socs; performed concertos with the RPO, London Philharmonic, Royal Liverpool Philharmonic, Bournemouth Symphony, City of Birmingham Symphony Orch, City of London Sinfonia, BBC Scottish Symphony, Hallé Orch, Scottish Chamber Orch, BBC Symphony Orch, BBC Nat Orch of Wales, Wiener Kammerphilharmonie, Kölner Kammerorchester; perfomed with conductors incl: Mark Elder, *qv*, Marin Alsop, Ivor Bolton, *qv*, Richard Hickox, *qv*, Emmanuel Krivine, Alexander Polianichko, Joseph Swensen, *qv*, Vassily Sinaisky, Gerard Schwarz; appeared as chamber musician with: Yo-Yo Ma, Michael Collins, *qv*, Ernst Kovacic, Quatuor Sine Nomine, Leopold String Trio, Haffner Wind Ensemble, Katherine Gowers, Adrian Brendel; presented Schubert Piano Sonata Series at numerous venues in UK and abroad 2002 (South Bank Show Classical Music Award 2003); other performances incl: Carnegie Hall NY 2002, Musikverein Vienna 2002, Concertgebouw Amsterdam 2002, Palais des Beaux Arts Brussels 2002, Tonhalle Zurich 2002, Chan Center Vancouver 2002, Risor Chamber Music Festival 2002, La Coruna Mozart Festival 2002, with the Hallé in UK and at Musikverein Vienna 2002, with the Seattle Symphony, BBC Proms (televised concert) with Bournemouth Symphony Orch 2002; *Recordings* incl: Schubert Sonatas D784 & D958 2002 (Diapason d'Or Choc de l'Année France 2002), Schubert Sonatas D959 & D960 2003, Mozart: Piano Quartets 2003; *Style*— Paul Lewis, Esq, CBE; ✉ c/o Ingpen & Williams Ltd, 7 St George's Court, 131 Putney Bridge Road, London SW15 2PA (☎ 020 8874 3222, fax 020 8877 3113)

LEWIS, Peter; *b* 16 April 1968, St Albans; *Educ* LLB; *Career* slr Allen & Overy 1991–95, Crisis 1997–99, ceo London Cycling Campaign 1999–2002, GLA 2002–08, chief exec London Voluntary Service Cncl 2008–11, chief exec Inst of Fundraising 2011–; tstee Street Doctors; memb ACEVO; *Recreations* cinema, skiing, tennis, walking; *Style*— Peter Lewis, Esq; ✉ Institute of Fundraising, Charter House, 13–15 Carteret Street, London SW1H 9DJ

LEWIS, Peter Edward; CB (2012); *Career* admitted slr 1981; West Midlands Prosecuting Slrs until 1986; CPS: joined 1986, chief crown prosecutor Notts 1999–2003, dir of business devpt 2003–07, ceo 2007–; *Style*— Peter Lewis, Esq, CB; ✉ Crown Prosecution Service, Rose Court, 2 Southwark Bridge, London SE1 9HS

L

LEWIS, Richard Alan; CBE (2013); s of Wilfred Lewis (d 1988), and Marian, *née* Eveleigh (d 1991); *b* 6 December 1954, London; *Educ* Goffs GS; *m* 5 June 2005, Jan, *née* Carter; 2 s (Nicholas b 19 Aug 1983, Alexander b 4 Nov 1985); *Career* professional tennis player 1969–87, team memb Davies Cup 1977–83; LTA: dir of nat training 1987–98, dir of tennis 1998–2000; conslt Merryck & Co 2000–02, chm Rugby Football League 2002–12, chief exec All England LTC 2012–; chair Sport England 2009–13; *Style*— Richard Lewis, Esq, CBE; ✉ The All England Club, Church Road, Wimbledon SW19 5AE (☎ 020 8971 2636)

LEWIS, Prof Richard Alexander; s of Harold Charles Lewis, of Whitbourne, Herefords, and Olwyn, *née* Witcombe; *b* 4 November 1949; *Educ* Buckhurst Hill Co HS, St Thomas' Hosp Med Sch Univ of London (DM, BSc, MB BS); *m* 26 May 1973, Dr Anne Margaret Lewis, da of Cdr Donald Maclennan, of Tong, Isle of Lewis; 2 s (Christopher b 1977, Peter b 1986), 1 da (Elizabeth b 1982); *Career* house physician St Thomas' Hosp London 1975, rotational SHO in med Southampton Gen Hosp and Dist Hosp 1976–77, rotational registrar in gen med St Richard's Hosp Chichester and St Thomas' Hosp London 1977–79, res fell Dept of Respiratory Med Unit One Univ of Southampton 1979–82, sr registrar in gen and thoracic med Southampton and Portsmouth Dist Hosp 1982–86; conslt physician specialising in diseases of the chest: Worcester and Dist HA Worcester Royal Infirmary 1986–, Worcester Acute Hosps NHS Tst 1993–2000, Worcs Acute Hosps NHS Tst 2001–12; hon sr research fell National Pollen Res Unit UCl Worcester 1999–, hon prof UC Worcester; vice-chm of govrs St Richard's Hospice Worcester, past pres Malvern Asthma Soc, vice-pres Friends of Worcestershire Royal Hosp; memb: Br Thoracic Soc, Euro Respiratory Soc, Christian Med Fellowship; MRCS, FRCP 1992 (LRCP, MRCP); *Books* contrib: Pharmacology of Asthma (1983), Drugs and the Lung (1984), Current Treatment of Ambulatory Asthma (1986), Difficult Asthma (1999); *Recreations* running, cycling, mountain walking, sailing, gardening, music, photography; *Clubs* Royal Lymington Yacht; *Style*— Prof Richard Lewis; ✉ Crews Court, Suckley, Worcester WR6 5DW (☎ 01886 884552)

LEWIS, Roger Charles; s of late Griffith Charles Job Lewis, and Dorothy, *née* Russ; *b* 24 August 1954; *Educ* Cynffig Comp Sch, Univ of Nottingham (BMus); *m* 1980, Dr Christine Trollope; 2 s; *Career* musician 1976–80, Avon Touring Theatre Co 1977–79, Birmingham Rep Theatre Studio 1978, Ludus Dance in Educn Co 1979, Scottish Ballet Workshop Co 1979, music offr Darlington Arts Centre 1980–82, presenter Radio Tees 1981–84, prodr Capital Radio 1984–85, head of music BBC Radio 1 1987–90 (prodr 1985–87), md Classical Div EMI Records 1995 (dir 1990–95), md EMI Premier 1995–97, pres Decca Records 1997–98, md and prog controller Classic FM 1998–2004, md ITV Wales 2004–06, gp chief exec Welsh Rugby Union and Millennium Stadium 2006–15, dir Br and Irish Lions 2014–15; dir: Cleveland Arts 1982–84, The Radio Corp Ltd 1999–2001, Digital One 2003–04; non-exec dir: Barchester Gp 2001–06, European Rugby Cup Ltd 2007–14, Celtic Rugby Ltd 2007–15, Racecourse Media Gp 2012–, European Professional Club Rugby (EPCR) 2014–15; non-exec dep chm Boosey and Hawke's 2004–06; chm: Classical Ctee BPI 1996–98, Tstees of the Ogmore Centre 1996–2007, Classic FM Charitable Tst 2000–04, Music and Dance Scheme Advsy Gp DFES 2000–04, Royal Liverpool Philharmonic 2003–06, Arts and Business Wales 2006, Int Advsy Bd Cardiff Univ Business Sch 2008–, Yes for Wales Referendum Campaign 2010–11, Churchill Lines Charitable Fund 2014–; chair Cardiff Capital Region 2013–15; pres Bromley Youth Music Tst 2000–06 (vice-pres 2006–); vice-pres: London Welsh Male Voice Choir 2004–; memb: Bd GWR Gp plc 1998–2004, Bd Liverpool European Capital of Culture 2003–06, Bd Wales Millenium Centre 2004–06, Wales Arts Review Panel 2006, Six Nations Cncl 2012–15, Advsy Bd D Group 2012–, Cardiff Capital Regn 2013–15, Cardiff Airport 2015–; tstee: Masterprize (int composers competition) 1995–2006, Masterclass Charitable Tst 2000–04, Inst of Welsh Affrs 2014–; hon fell Royal Welsh Coll of Music and Drama, hon memb Royal Coll of Music; Hon DLitt Univ of Nottingham, Hon DUniv Glamorgan; memb OStJ; *Awards* incl: Sony Award 1987–89, NY Grand Award Winner and Gold Medal 1987 (finalist 1989), finalist Monaco Radio Festival 1989, One World Broadcasting Tst award 1989, NTL Commercial Radio Programmer of the Year 2002, Lifetime Achievement Award Univ of Nottingham 2009; *Recreations* music, rugby, skiing, country pursuits; *Clubs* Wine Soc, Cardiff and County; *Style*— Roger Lewis, Esq, OStJ

LEWIS, Prof Roland Wynne; s of David Lewis (d 1958), and Mary Gladys, *née* Davies (d 1981); *b* 20 January 1940; *Educ* Amman Valley GS, UC Swansea (BSc, PhD, DSc); *m* 17 April 1965, Celia Elizabeth, da of Haydn Elgar Morris, of Ammanford, Dyfed; 2 da (Caroline b 16 June 1969, Angharad b 11 Feb 1973), 1 s ((David) Andrew b 4 March 1971); *Career* res engr ESSO Canada 1965–69, prof UC Swansea 1984– (lectr 1969–79, sr lectr 1979–82, reader 1982–84); chm Thermofluids Gp Nat Agency for Finite Element Methods and Standards; FICE 1991 (MICE 1973), FREng 1997, FLSW 2012; *Books* Civil Engineering Systems-Analysis and Design, Finite Elements in the Flow and Deformation of Porous Media, The Finite Element Method in the Static and Dynamic Deformation and Consolidation of Porous Media, The Finite Element Method in Heat Transfer Analysis; *Recreations* golf, photography, gardening; *Clubs* Clyne Golf (Swansea); *Style*— Prof Roland Lewis, FREng; ✉ Oakridge, 331 Gower Road, Killay, Swansea SA2 7AE (☎ 01792 203166); Mechanical Engineering Department, University of Wales Swansea, Swansea SA2 8PP (☎ 01792 295253, fax 01792 295705)

LEWIS, (David) Simon; OBE (2014); s of David Lewis, and Sally Elizabeth, *née* Valentine; *b* 8 May 1959; *Educ* Whitefield Sch, BNC Oxford, Univ of Calif Berkeley (Fulbright scholar, MA); *m* 1985, Claire Elizabeth, da of Eric Pendry, and late Jean Pendry; 2 s (Thomas Paul b 1989, Dominic William b 2000), 1 da (Olivia Rose b 1991); *Career* financial PR conslt Shandwick Consultants 1983–86, head of communications SDP 1986–87, head of PR S G Warburg Group 1987–92; dir of corporate affrs: NatWest Gp 1992–96, Centrica plc 1996–98, dir of corporate affrs and md Europe Centrica plc 1996–2004, on secondment as first communications sec Buckingham Palace 1998–2000, gp dir of corporate affrs Vodafone Gp 2004–09, dir of communications and PM's official spokesman PM's Office 2009–10, strategic communications advsr UK Trade & Investment 2010, ceo Assoc for Financial Markets in Europe (AFME) 2010–; pres IPR 1997; chm Fulbright Cmmn 2008–13 (patron 2013–), memb Chatham House N American Advsy Cncl and Acad Advsy Bd 2013–; chm Governing Cncl UC Sch 2015–; hon prof Cardiff Sch of Journalism 2000–, visiting fell Centre for Corporate Reputation Univ of Oxford 2007–; FRSA (chm), FCIPR (FIPR 1998); *Clubs* Reform; *Style*— Simon Lewis, Esq, OBE

LEWIS, Simon James; *b* 14 February 1958; *Educ* Holland Park Secdy Sch, Poly of Central London (BA); *m* 1, 4 March 1983, Milka Javiera, *née* Valenzuela; m 2, 8 Aug 2003, Susan Hogg; *Career* prodr: Central TV 1989–91 and 1993–94, Yorkshire TV 1992–93 and 1994–95; controller of drama: United Film & TV Productions 1995–97, Granada TV 1997–2000; prodr BBC TV 2000–; prodns incl: Boon (Central TV, 1989–91), The Darling Buds of May (Yorkshire TV, 1992–93), Sharpe (BAFTA nominated Best Drama Series, Central TV, 1994), A Touch of Frost (Yorkshire TV, 1994–95), No Child of Mine (Best Single Drama BAFTA Award 1998), Touching Evil (nominated BAFTA and RTS Best Drama Series 1998), Where The Heart Is (nominated RTS Best Drama Series 1998), Grafters, The Last Train, Butterfly Collectors, A+E, Tough Love, Little Bird, Born and Bred, The Eustace Bros, Death in Holy Orders, The Murder Room, Cherished, My Family and Other Animals, Five Daughters; *Style*— Simon Lewis; ✉ e-mail simon@opentvandfilm.com

LEWIS, Stephen John; s of late Douglas John Lewis, of Codsall, Staffs, and late Dorothy Pauline, *née* Shaw; *b* 8 March 1948, Wolverhampton; *Educ* Wolverhampton GS, Balliol Coll Oxford (BA); *Career* ptnr Phillips & Drew 1980–85, dir Securities Ltd 1985–88, md Fifth Horseman Publications Ltd 1988–92, dir The London Bond Broking Co Ltd 1992–96 (also chief economist); chief economist: Monument Securities Ltd (formerly Monument Derivatives Ltd) 1996–2006 and 2008–14, Insinger de Beaufort 2006–08, ADM ISI Ltd 2014–; memb: Securities Inst, Soc of Business Economists; *Recreations* antiquities, European philosophy; *Clubs* Reform; *Style*— Stephen Lewis, Esq; ✉ ADM ISI Ltd, 4th Floor, Millennium Bridge House, 2 Lambeth Hill, London EC4V 3TT (☎ 020 7716 8256, e-mail stephen.lewis@admisi.com)

LEWIS, Stephen Michael; s of Harry Lewis, of Stanmore, Middx, and Celia, *née* Softness; *b* 23 August 1949; *Educ* Orange Hill Co GS for Boys, St Catherine's Coll Oxford (open exhibition, BA), Univ of London (LLB); *m* 3 March 1974, Erica, da of Jacob Pesate; 2 da (Ann Marie b 25 April 1976, Francesca Rose b 2 Sept 1986), 1 s (Adrian William b 9 April 1979); *Career* mgmnt trainee Reed International 1970–71, articled clerk Clintons slrs 1971–74, legal asst Law Cmmn 1975–80, ptnr Clifford Turner (now Clifford Chance) 1985– (asst slr 1980–85); memb: Law Soc, Sub-Ctee on Insurance Law City of London Law Soc; *Recreations* music, reading, running, swimming, politics; *Style*— Stephen Lewis, Esq; ✉ Clifford Chance, 10 Upper Bank Street, London E14 5JJ (☎ 020 7006 1000, fax 020 7006 5555)

LEWIS, Stephen Richard; *b* 11 January 1959; *Educ* Deyes HS Maghull, Southport Coll of Art, Manchester Poly (BA), Jan Van Eyck Academie Maastricht; *Career* artist; visiting artist: Cyprus Sch of Art, Voss Sch Norway, Triangle Artists Workshop NY, Emma Lake Workshop Canada, Hardingham Sculpture Workshop UK; *Solo Exhibitions* incl: Francis Graham-Dixon Gallery 1988, 1990 and 1993, John Holden Gallery Manchester 1990, Christchurch Mansion Ipswich 1992, Galerie Schlassgoart Luxembourg 1996, Atrium Gallery London 1996; *Group Exhibitions* incl: New Contemporaries (ICA) 1979, Northern Young Contemporaries (Whitworth Gallery Manchester) 1979, The First Picture Show (Sainsbury Centre Norwich) 1980, Triangle Workshop Exhibition NY 1989, Kunst Europa (Kustverein Kirchzarten) 1991, Lancashire Contemporaries (Harris Museum Preston) 1992, Three Sculptors: Oleg Kudryashov, Stephen Lewis, Charles Quick (The Economist Building London) 1993, Three London Artists (Standoort Gallery Frankfurt) 1998, A Life Less Ordinary (Hammersons London) 2000; *Commissions* in London: Circumsphere River Thames Deptford 1999, Union Canal Project Southall 2001, Camden Plaques Camden Town 2002, Regent Quarter P&O Developments Sculpture Plaques Kings Cross 2003–04, Mumford Sculpture Greenwich 2004; *Work in Collections* incl: Simmons and Simmons London, Arbed Steel Co Luxembourg, Kunstlandschaft Germany; work in private collections in UK, Europe, USA and Canada;; *Style*— Stephen Lewis, Esq

LEWIS, Prof (Christopher) Terence; s of Dr C B Lewis (d 1980), and Rachel, *née* O'Connor (d 1956); *b* 24 May 1944; *Educ* UCL, Westminster Hosp Med Sch (MB BS, LRCP MRCS, FRCS); *m* 1975, Jill, da of Alan Weller; 2 da (Victoria b 1979, Abigail b 1981), 1 s (Freddie b 1985); *Career* conslt then sr const cardiothoracic surgn Royal London Hosp 1979–95, conslt cardiothoracic surgn St Bartholomew's Hosp London 1995–97, sr conslt cardiothoracic surgn SW Cardiothoracic Centre Derriford Hosp Plymouth 1997–2008, med dir Plymouth Hosp NHS Tst 2000–08; report on future of Papworth Hosp for Monitor 2014; dir: cardiac surgical research Royal London Hosp, Sir Henry Souttar Experimental Surgical Labs; UK rep European Initiative for the Devpt of Artificial Hearts 1985–92, memb Medical Engrg and Sensors Ctee Sci and Engrg Research Cncl 1992–96, regnl advsr Cardiothoracic Surgery for SW Region 2003–08 (for N Thames (E) 1992–95), med dir SW Advsy Ctee for Clinical Excellence Awards, chm Clinical Governance Steering Ctee Sperrin Lakeland Health and Social Servs Tst NI 2004–07; chm and fndr Project Equinox and The Good Companions Veterans and Medical Students Centre Plymouth 2013–; pres: Soc of Perfusionists of GB 2003–07, Plymouth Heartbeat; hon life vice-pres Heartswell SW; dir Heartswell House SW Carers Lodge 2006–12; chm Plymouth Marine Laboratories (tstee 2002–), tstee and dir St Luke's Hospice and Servs Plymouth 2008–12; Sir Clement Price Thomas Award RCS; govr Plymouth Univ 2009– (chm Medical Sch Bd 2012–); exec memb Soc of Cardiothoracic Surgeons of GB and I 1999–2003; Artificial Hearts (jtly); numerous pubns in int peer reviewed jls on various subjects connected with cardiothoracic surgery; *Recreations* fishing, sailing, shooting; *Clubs* Royal Fowey Yacht, Fowey Gallants Sailing, Army and Navy; *Style*— Prof Terence Lewis; ✉ Lifton Park, Lifton, Devonshire PL16 0DE (☎ 01566 784 659, e-mail terencelewis@hotmail.co.uk)

LEWIS, Thomas Warwick (Tom); s of Dr Edward Claude Lewis (d 2000), and Rosemary, *née* Batten (d 2004); *b* 5 April 1958, Reigate, Surrey; *Educ* Whitgift Sch, Westminster Coll (OND); *m* 13 June 1981, Rosemary Vivienne, *née* Hamley; 2 da (Anna Gwen b 28 May 1986, Ellen Rosemary b 19 Oct 1988); *Career* trainee mangr then asst food and beverage mangr The Dorchester London 1978–83, back of house mangr then food and beverage mangr Dukes Hotel London 1983–86, dep gen mangr The Lygon Arms Broadway 1986–88, dir and gen mangr The Feathers Hotel Woodstock 1988–97, gen mangr The Angel Hotel Midhurst 1997–99, hotel mangr Great Fosters Hotel Egham 1999–2002 and 2004–05, gen mangr Studley Priory Horton-cum-Studley 2002–04, gen mangr Le Manoir aux Quat'Saisons 2005–09, gen mangr Gilpin Lodge Kendal 2009–11, gen mangr Swinton Park Masham 2012–15, dir of operations Wildsmith Hotels 2015–; Master Innholder 2007; MHCIMA 1978, FIH 2007; *Recreations* swimming, music; *Style*— Tom Lewis, FIH, MI; ✉ Forest Side, Keswick Road, Grasmere, Cumbria LA22 9RN (☎ 01765 680900)

LEWIS, William; *b* 1969; *Educ* Univ of Bristol, City Univ; *Career* Telegraph Media Gp: ed-in-chief The Daily Telegraph, Sunday Telegraph and telegraph.co.uk 2006–10, gen mangr News International 2010–; ceo Euston Partners 2009–; Journalist of the Year Br Press Award 2010; *Style*— William Lewis, Esq

LEWIS-FRANCIS, Mark; MBE (2005); s of Shaun Lewis-Francis, and Hermine Francis; *b* 4 September 1982, Birmingham; *Career* athlete; memb Birchfield Harriers; achievements at 100m: World Youth Champion 1999, UK under 20 Champion 1999 and 2000, Silver medal European Jr Championships 1999, World Jr Champion 2000 (championship record), winner B race IAAF Grand Prix London 2000, winner Loughborough 2000 and 2002, semi-finalist IAAF World Championships 2001, European Jr Champion 2001, second place UK Championships 2001, winner European Cup Super League 2001, winner DVL Jr Gala Mannheim 2001, second place Penn Relays 2001, winner Talahassee 2001 and 2002, third place IAAF Grand Prix II Rieti 2002, fifth place IAAF Golden League Brussels 2002, UK Champion 2002, third place IAAF Golden League Paris 2002, second place IAAF Grand Prix II Sheffield 2002, second place Cwlth Games trials 2002, world ranking 8 Track and Field News 2002, second place IAAF Super Grand Prix Gateshead 2003, fourth place IAAF Golden League Paris 2003, winner IAAF Golden League Oslo 2003, winner European Cup 2003, winner IAAF Super Grand Prix Ostrava 2003; achievements at 60m: Bronze medal World Indoor Championships Lisbon (world jr record) 2001, second place Glasgow Indoor Match 2001, second place UK Indoor Championships 2002, second place Energizer Indoor Series Birmingham 2002, Silver medal European Indoor 2002, second place Glasgow Indoor Match 2003, third place Energizer Indoor Series Birmingham 2003, UK Indoor Champion 2003, fourth place World Indoor Championships Birmingham 2003, fifth place Birmingham Indoor Grand Prix 2004, Silver medal European Championships Barcelona 2010, Bronze medal Continental Cup Split 2010, Silver medal Cwlth Games Delhi 2010; achievements in

4x100m relay: World Jr Champion 2000 (European jr record), European Jr Champion 2001, Gold medal Olympic Games Athens 2004, bronze medal IAAF World Championships Osaka 2007; winner 200m Tallahassee 2002; Br Jr Male Athlete of the Year 2000 and 2001; *Style*— Mark Lewis-Francis, Esq, MBE; ✉ c/o Ricky Simms, PACE Sports Management, 6 The Causeway, Teddington, Middlesex TW11 0HE (☎ 020 8943 1072, fax 020 8977 6582, e-mail r.simms@pacesportsmanagement.com, website www.pacesportsmanagement.com)

LEWIS-JONES, Dr (Margaret) Susan (Sue); da of Ian Robert Munro Campbell, and Jean Douglas, *née* Ramsay; *b* 12 April 1948; *Educ* Tudor Grange Girls' GS Solihull, Univ of Liverpool Med Sch (MB ChB); *Career* medical and surgical house offr 1972–73, demonstrator in anatomy Univ of Liverpool 1973–74, GP 1974–77, medical registrar 1982, conslt dermatologist 1987– (registrar 1982–85, sr registrar 1985–87), hon lectr in dermatology Univ of Liverpool and Univ of Wales 1987–99, hon sr lectr Univ of Dundee; chm Br Soc Paediatric Dermatology 2000–04 (sec 1999–2000), convenor for dermatology RCPCH 2001–04, chair NICE Guidelines for childhood eczema 2005–07, pres Scot Dermatological Soc 2009–11 (sec 2001, pres elect 2007–09); chair Dermatological Cncl for Scotland 2009–11; currently memb: BMA, Br Assoc of Dermatologists, American Acad of Dermatology, Liverpool Med Inst; FRCP 1994 (MRCP 1982), FRCPCH 2004; *Recreations* walking, gardening, music; *Style*— Dr Sue Lewis-Jones

LEWISHAM, Archdeacon of; *see:* Hardman, Ven Christine Elizabeth

LEWISOHN, Oscar Max; s of Max Lewisohn (d 1973), of Copenhagen, Denmark, and Jenny Lewisohn (d 1984); *b* 6 May 1938; *Educ* Sortedam Gymnasium Copenhagen; *m* 1, 4 Aug 1962, Louisa Madeleine (d 1985), da of Henry Grunfeld, of London; 3 s, 1 da (Mark b 1963, Richard b 1965, Anita b 1967, James b 1970); m 2, 24 Oct 1987, Margaret Ann, da of Don Paterson (d 2013); 2 da (Jenny b 1989, Sophie b 1990); *Career* SG Warburg and Co Ltd 1962–95: exec dir 1969, dep chm 1987–94; dir SG Warburg Group plc 1985–95; chm Soditic Ltd 1996–; memb Advsy Bd Official Monetary and Financial Institutions Forum (OMFIF); tstee EORTC Cancer Research Fund AISBL, hon fell Cancer Research UK; govr Yehudi Menuhin Sch 2006–; hon memb Christ's Coll Cambridge; Liveryman Worshipful Co of Int Bankers, Freeman City of London 2005, Freeman Worshipful Co of Musicians; FRSA 1992, FCIB 2002; Knight Order of the Dannebrog 1 (Denmark); *Recreations* music; *Clubs* Garrick; *Style*— Oscar Lewisohn, Esq; ✉ Soditic Ltd, 12 Charles II Street, London SW1Y 4QU (☎ 020 7872 7090, fax 020 7872 7104, e-mail oscar.lewisohn@soditic.co.uk)

LEWISON, Rt Hon Lord Justice; Sir Kim Martin Jordan Lewison; kt (2003), PC (2011); s of Anthony Frederick Lewison (d 1993), and Dinora, *née* Pines (d 2002); *b* 1 May 1952; *Educ* St Paul's, Downing Coll Cambridge (MA, Betha Wolferstan Rylands Prize); *m* 1, 29 Sept 1979 (m dis 1998), Helen Mary, da of Josef Janecek (d 1980); 1 s (Joshua George b 1982), 1 da (Lydia Miriam b 1984); m 2, 15 Dec 2002, Sharon Moross; *Career* called to the Bar Lincoln's Inn 1975 (bencher 1998); QC 1991, recorder 1997–2003 (asst recorder 1993–97), dep judge of the High Court 2000–2003, judge of the High Court of Justice (Chancery Div) 2003–11, a Lord Justice of Appeal 2011–; memb Cncl: Lib Jewish Synagogue 1990–96, Leo Baeck Coll 1996–2001; govr Anglo-American Real Property Inst 1996– (chm 2002); tstee Centre for Jewish Educn 1999–2001; *Books* Development Land Tax (1977), Drafting Business Leases (2000), The Interpretation of Contracts (2011), Woodfall on Landlord and Tenant (gen ed); *Recreations* visiting France; *Style*— The Rt Hon the Lord Justice Lewison; ✉ Royal Courts of Justice, Strand, London WC2A 2LL

LEWITH, Prof George Thomas; s of Frank Lewith (d 1965), and Alice, *née* Schallinger; *b* 12 January 1950; *Educ* Queen's Coll Taunton, Trinity Coll Cambridge (MA), Westminster Hosp London (MB BChir), MD; *m* 7 May 1977, Nicola Rosemary, da of Bonham Ley Bazeley, DSC, of Stonehouse, Glos; 2 s (Thomas b 1981, Henry b 1986), 1 da (Emily b 1983); *Career* paediatric intern McMaster Univ Ontario 1974, jr positions Westminster Hosp and UCH 1974–78, GP Queensland Australia 1978, WHO studentship in acupuncture Nanjing Coll of Traditional Chinese Med 1978, lectr in general practice Dept of Gen Practice Univ of Southampton 1979–82, co-dir Centre for the Study of Complementary Med 1982–2005, prof Dept of Primary Care Univ of Southampton; visiting prof Univ of Westminster; formerly vice-chm Br Med Acupuncture Soc, memb numerous med orgns and ctees, author of numerous learned books and articles; MRCGP 1980, FRCP 1999; *Recreations* swimming, skiing, sailing, theatre; *Clubs* Royal Lymington Yacht, RSM; *Style*— Prof George Lewith; ✉ Swaywood House, Mead End Road, Sway, Lymington, Hampshire SO41 6EE (☎ 01590 682129, e-mail gl3@soton.ac.uk)

LEXDEN, Baron (Life Peer UK 2010), of Lexden in the County of Essex and of Strangford in the County of Down; Dr Alistair Basil Cooke; OBE (1988); s of Dr Basil Cooke, and Nancy Irene, *née* Neal; *b* 20 April 1945; *Educ* PhD; *Career* historical research and teaching Univs of Cambridge, Edinburgh and Belfast 1966–71, lectr and tutor in modern history Queen's Univ Belfast 1971–77; Cons Research Dept: political advsr on NI to Airey Neave 1977–79, asst then dep dir 1983–97; dir Cons Political Centre 1988–97, gen sec Ind Schs Cncl 1997–2004, conslt and ed in chief Cons Research Dept 2004–10, official historian and archivist Carlton Club 2007–, official historian Cons Pty 2009–, vice-chm Cons Policy Forum 2010–; *Style*— The Lord Lexden, OBE; ✉ House of Lords, London SW1A 0PW (website www.alistairlexden.org.uk)

LEY, Philip Edward Francis; s of Francis James Ley, of Abingdon, Oxon, and Alexandrina, *née* Moonie (d 1993); *b* 16 July 1960; *Educ* Ampleforth, Univ of Oxford (MA); *m* Feb 1994, Anna Elizabeth, da of David Tate; *Career* Unilever 1982–86: UCMDS trainee Lipton Export Ltd, brand mangr Lipton Yellow Label Tea ME and Scandinavia; Marketing Solutions 1986–87, Trowbridge Ley Partnership specialising in interior design in USA and men's clothing shops in UK 1987–89; Virgin Mastertronic/Sega Europe 1989–94: mktg mangr Sega Products until 1991, mktg dir UK (when Sega bought Virgin Mastertronic) 1991–93, Euro mktg dir 1993–94; mktg dir BSkyB 1994–96, fndr md Branded Ltd (communications agency) 1996–; Mktg Soc Marketeer of the Year 1993; memb Mktg Soc 1994; *Recreations* swimming, football, drumming, Manchester United supporter; *Clubs* The Electric; *Style*— Philip Ley, Esq; ✉ Branded Ltd, Albert Bridge House, 127 Albert Bridge Road, London SW11 4PL (☎ 020 7978 7780, fax 020 7801 9137, e-mail phil@branded.co.uk)

LEY, Shaun; s of Michael John Ley, and Rachel Diana, *née* Lock; *b* 14 June 1969, Lynton, Devon; *Educ* Ilfracombe Comp Sch, LSE (BSc); *Career* radio and television presenter; BBC: trainee 1990, subsequently prodr, reporter and presenter BBC West until 2001 (incl presenter Around Westminster (BBC2) and London political ed 1998–2001), lobby corr 2001–05; presenter: The World At One (Radio 4) 2005–07, The World This Weekend (Radio 4) 2007–14, Hardtalk (BBC World News), Dateline (BBC News Channel); *Style*— Shaun Ley, Esq; ✉ BBC Broadcasting House, Portland Place, London W1A 1AA (e-mail shaun.ley@bbc.co.uk)

LEY, Prof Steven Victor; CBE (2002); *Educ* Loughborough Univ (BSc, DIS, PhD), Univ of London (DSc); *m*; 1 c; *Career* post doctoral fell Ohio State Univ 1972–74; Imperial Coll London: post doctoral fell 1974–75, probationary lectr 1975–76, lectr 1976–83, prof of organic chemistry 1983–92, head of Dept 1989–92; BP (1702) prof of organic chemistry Univ of Cambridge 1992–, fell Trinity Coll Cambridge 1993–; chm Exec Ctee Ciba Fndn 1993–2004 (memb 1990–2004); memb: Newly Appointed Lectrs Grant Ctee Nuffield Fndn 1986–2004, Chemistry Leadership Cncl 2002–04; author of over 670 res papers and articles; Royal Soc of Chemistry: Corday Morgan medal and prize for 1980, Hickenbottom research fellowship 1981, Pfizer academic award 1983, Tilden lectr and medal 1988, award for organic synthesis 1989, Pedler lectr, medal and prize 1992, Simonsen lectr and medal 1993, 1992 natural products award 1994, pres Perkin Div Royal Soc of Chemistry 1993–96 (memb 1989–96), Flintoff medal 1995, Rhône-Poulenc lectr, medal and prize 1998, Haworth meml lectureship medal prize 2001, pres 2000–02, Robert Robinson Lectureship, Medal and Prize 2006; Pfizer academic award 1983, Dr Paul George Kenner prize and lectr Univ of Liverpool 1996, Janssen prize for creativity in organic synthesis Belgium 1996, Royal Soc Bakerian lectr 1997, Glaxo-Wellcome award for outstanding achievement in organic chemistry 1999, Royal Soc Davey medal 2000, Pfizer award for innovative science 2001, German Chemical Soc August-Wilhelm-von Hofman medal 2001, American Chemical Soc Ernest Guenther award 2003, Soc for Chemical Industry Messel medal 2004, Yamado Koga Prize (Japan) 2005, Nagoya Gold Medal Banyu Life Science Fndn Int Japan 2006, Thomson Scientific Laureate in Chemistry 2006, Award for Creative Work in Synthetic Organ Chemistry American Chemical Soc 2007, Paul Karrer Gold Medal Univ of Zürich 2007, SCI Innovation Award 2007, Société Française de Chimie Medal 2007, Hans Herloff Inhoffen Medal Helmholtz Zentrum für Infectionsforschung Germany 2008, Prous Institute-Overton and Meyer Award for New Technols in Drug Discovery European Fedn of Medicinal Chemistry 2008; Hon DSc: Loughborough Univ, Univ of Huddersfield, Salamanca Univ, Univ of Cardiff; memb: American Chemical Soc, Chemical Soc of Japan, Soc of Chemical Industry (London), Swiss Chemical Soc, Royal Inst London, American Assoc for the Advancement of Science, Int Soc of Heterocyclic Chemistry; CChem 1980, FRSC 1980, FRS 1990, fell Japanese Soc for the Promotion of Science 1993, FMedSci 2005; *Style*— Prof Steven Ley, CBE, FRS, FMedSci; ✉ website http://leygroup.ch.cam.ac.uk

LEYSHON, Robert Lloyd; s of Sqdn Ldr Mervyn Leyshon, of Pencoed, Mid Glamorgan, and Joan Hilton, *née* Lloyd (d 1950); *b* 12 February 1948; *Educ* Ogmore Vale GS, St Mary's Hosp (BSc, MB BS); *m* 16 July 1977, Catherine (Kay), da of Luther Edwards (d 1984); 1 s (Aled Lloyd b 18 Nov 1978), 1 da ((Catherine) Nia b 23 Feb 1980); *Career* house surgn and casualty offr St Mary's Hosp 1972–74, rotating surgical registrar Cardiff Hosp 1974–77, sr orthopaedic registrar Cardiff and Swansea Hosp 1979–83, sr lectr in orthopaedic surgery Welsh Sch of Med 1983–84, conslt orthopaedic surgn Swansea 1984–; author of papers on the use of carbon fibre as ligament replacement, research into post menopausal osteoporosis and reviews of hip prostheses in fractures of femoral neck, study into elbow replacement surgery in rheumatoid arthritis; past pres Welsh Orthopaedic Soc, treas Rheumatoid Arthritis Surgical Soc 2000, fndr memb Expert Witness Inst 1997, hon orthopaedic surgn Llanelli Scarlets Rugby 1988–2008; FBOA 1983, memb Euro Rheumatoid Arthritis Surgical Soc 1997, FRCS; *Recreations* skiing, rambling, gardening; *Style*— Robert Leyshon, Esq; ✉ 19 Westport Avenue, Mayals, Swansea SA3 5EA (☎ 01792 403003); St David's House, Sancta Maria Hospital, Ffynone Road, Uplands, Swansea SA1 6DF (☎ 01792 472922, fax 01792 466803)

LIANG, Prof (Wei) Yao; s of late Tien Fu Liang, of Singapore, and Po Seng Nio, *née* Lie; *b* 23 September 1940; *Educ* Pah Tsung Chinese HS Jakarta, Portsmouth Coll of Technol, Imperial Coll London (BSc, ARCS), Univ of Cambridge (PhD); *m* 17 Aug 1968, Lian Choo (decd), da of late Choong Sam; 3 da (Yifan, Chiafan, Hweifan); *Career* Univ of Cambridge: demonstrator in physics 1971–75, lectr in physics 1975–92, reader in high temperature superconductivity 1992–93, prof of superconductivity 1994–, dir Interdisciplinary Research Centre 1989–98; Gonville & Caius Coll Cambridge: Comyns Berkeley research fell 1968–71, fell 1971–93, coll lectr 1971–, dir of studies in natural sciences 1975–89, professorial fell 1994–, pres 2005–13, life fell 2007; visiting scientist Xerox Palo Alto Research Centre California 1975 and 1976; visiting prof: EPF Lausanne 1978, Acad Sinica Inst of Semiconductors Beijing 1983, Science Univ of Tokyo 2000, Univ of Tokyo 2001, Xiamen Univ 2001; hon fell St John's Coll Hong Kong Univ 2009–; fell American Physical Soc; CPhys, FInstP; *Books* Polarons and Bipolarons in High Temperature Superconductors and Related Compounds (ed with A S Alexandrov and E K H Salje, 1995), Fundamental Research in High Tc Superconductivity (jtly with W Zhou, 1999), High Temperature Superconductivity: Research and Application (jtly with D L Shi and W Zhou, 2008), A Portrait of Gonville & Caius College (jtly with Dan White, Christopher Brooke and Mick Le Moignan, 2008), Waterhouse and his Gate (jtly with Michael Prichard); *Recreations* music, conversation, photography; *Style*— Prof Yao Liang; ✉ Gonville and Caius College, Trinity Street, Cambridge CB2 1TA (☎ 01223 332425, e-mail wyl1@cam.ac.uk)

LICHFIELD, Rt Rev Jonathan Michael Gledhill; *b* 15 February 1949; *Educ* Strode's Sch Egham, Keele Univ (BA), Univ of Bristol (MA), Trinity Coll Bristol (BCTS); *m* 1971, Dr S Jane Gledhill; *Career* curate All Saints Marple 1975–78, priest i/c St George Folkestone 1978–83, vicar St Mary Bredin Canterbury 1983–96, rural dean Canterbury 1988–94, hon canon Canterbury Cathedral 1992–96, bishop of Southampton 1996–2003, bishop of Lichfield 2003–15; tutor/lectr: Canterbury Sch of Ministry 1983–94, SE Inst for Theol Educn 1994–96; chm: Anglican Old Catholic Int Consultative Cncl 1998–2013, Nat Coll of Evangelists 1998–2010; memb Meissen Cmmn 1993–96; Hon DUniv Keele 2007; *Style*— The Rt Rev Jonathan Gledhill; ✉ Bishop's House, 22 The Close, Lichfield, Staffordshire WS13 7LG

LICHFIELD, 6 Earl of (UK 1831); Thomas William Robert Hugh Anson; also Viscount Anson and Baron Soberton (both UK 1806); s of 5 Earl of Lichfield (d 2005), and Lady Leonora Mary, *née* Grosvenor, LVO, da of 5 Duke of Westminster, TD (d 1979); *b* 19 July 1978, London; *Educ* Harrow; *m* Dec 2009, Henrietta, da of 8 Marquess of Conyngham; 2 s (Thomas Ossian Patrick Wolfe, Viscount Anson b 20 May 2011, Hon Finnian Robert Leo Juliene Anson b 12 August 2014); *Heir* s, Viscount Anson; *Career* property conslt; *Recreations* fishing, travelling, sculpture; *Clubs* Whites; *Style*— The Earl of Lichfield

LICHT, Leonard Samuel; s of Bernhard Licht (d 1982), and Hilde, *née* Müller (d 2014); *b* 15 March 1945; *Educ* Christ's Coll Finchley; *m* 2 June 1973, Judith, da of Albert Grossman (d 1980); 1 s (Rupert b 27 July 1974), 1 da (Marina b 19 April 1976); *Career* investment banker; dir S G Warburg & Co Ltd 1982–85, vice-chm and founding dir Mercury Asset Mgmnt Gp plc 1986–92, chm Channel Islands and Int Investment Tst Ltd 1988–92, dep chm Jupiter Asset Mgmnt plc 1992–96, dir Falkland Islands Gp plc 1999–2009, chm HgCapital (HgInvestment Mangrs and HgPooled Mgmnt) 2001–07; non-exec dir Royal Free Hampstead NHS Trust 1990–97, special tstee Royal Free Hosp 1991–99, tstee Conservative & Unionists Agents Superannuation Fund 1999–2001; *Books* The Leonard Licht Collection of Great Britain Seahorses, The Leonard Licht Collection of Great Britain King Edward VII; *Recreations* philately, eating lunch with my wife; *Style*— Leonard Licht, Esq; ✉ c/o Susan Catt, The Key, 2nd Floor, 29 Ludgate Hill, London EC4M 7JR

LICKISS, Sir Michael Gillam; kt (1993); s of Frank Gillam, and Elaine Rheta, *née* Lefeuvre; *b* 18 February 1934; *Educ* Bournemouth GS, LSE, Univ of London (BSc); *m* 1, 1959 (m dis 1979), Anita; 2 s, 2 da; m 2, 1987, Anne; 1 s; *Career* articled clerk Bournemouth 1955–58, cmmnd Army 1959–62, chartered accountant in practice Bournemouth 1962–68; Grant Thornton (formerly Thornton Baker): Bournemouth office 1968–73, London office 1973–94, exec ptnr 1975–85, nat managing ptnr 1985–89, sr ptnr 1989–94; chm Accountancy Television Ltd 1992–94; non-exec dir United News and Media plc 1996–98, chm/dir various smaller cos; DTI inspr (jtly with Hugh Carlisle, QC) 1986–88; fndr pres Assoc of Accounting Technicians 1980–82; ICAEW: memb Cncl 1971–81 and 1983–94, pres 1990–91; chm: Somerset Economic Partnership 1993–98, EDEXCEL Fndn (formerly BTEC) 1994–2000, W of England Devpt Agency 1994–97, SW England RDA 1998–2002, Visit Britain (BTA) 2003–04, Theatre Royal Plymouth 2009–2016; memb: Cncl FEFC 1992–96, Ct of Govrs LSE 1993–2008, Senate Engrg Cncl 1995–98, Learning and Skills Nat Cncl 2001–03, Industrial Devpt Advsy Bd DTI 2000–02; tstee Jurassic

L

Coast World Heritage Site 2006–; lectr UK and overseas, author of numerous articles in learned jls; Liveryman Worshipful Co of Chartered Accountants; Hon DBA: UWE, Bournemouth Univ; Hon DEd Plymouth Univ 2006; hon fell LSE 2008 (emeritus govr 2009); FCA; *Recreations* walking in Lake District; *Clubs* RAC; *Style—* Sir Michael Lickiss; ✉ 5 Highcroft Court, Exeter EX4 4RW

LIDBETTER, Andrew William; s of William James Lidbetter (d 2005), and Margaret Ruth, *née* Smith; *b* 26 June 1965; *Educ* Eltham Coll, Worcester Coll Oxford (BCL, MA); *m* 7 Aug 1993, Elisabeth Jane, *née* Edser; 2 s (Michael William b 3 June 1996, Stephen Andrew b 11 March 2000); *Career* admitted slr 1990; Herbert Smith: articled clerk 1988–90, slr 1990–98, ptnr 1998–; memb: Administrative Law Bar Assoc, Assoc of Regulatory and Disciplinary Lawyers, Law Soc; *Books* Company Investigations and Public Law (1999), Blackstone's Civil Practice (contrib chapters on judicial review and human rights); *Style—* Andrew Lidbetter, Esq; ✉ Herbert Smith, Exchange House, Primrose Street, London EC2A 2HS (☎ 020 7374 8000, fax 020 7374 0888, e-mail andrew.lidbetter@herbertsmith.com)

LIDDELL, Alasdair Donald MacDuff; CBE (1997); s of Ian Donald Macduff Liddell, WS (d 1976), and Barbara Macduff (d 2001); *b* 15 January 1949; *Educ* Fettes, Balliol Coll Oxford (BA), Thames Poly (DMS); *m* 20 Feb 1976, Dame Jenny Abramsky, DBE, *qv*; 1 s (Rob b 22 Feb 1977), 1 da (Maia b 11 Dec 1979); *Career* admin (Planning and Policies) Tower Hamlets Dist 1977–79, area gen admin Kensington and Chelsea and Westminster AHA 1979–82, dist admin Hammersmith and Fulham HA 1982–84, dist gen mangr Bloomsbury HA 1985–88, regnl gen mangr E Anglian RHA 1988–94, dir of planning NHS Exec 1994–2000, ind conslt; chair NHS Innovation Challenge Prizes Expert Panel 2010–; dep chm HCL plc 2005–11; assoc King's Fund 2006–11, fell Young Fndn 2012–; *Recreations* skiing, personal computers, buying wine; *Style—* Alasdair Liddell, Esq, CBE; ✉ 3 Brookfield Park, London NW5 1ES (☎ 020 7813 1702, e-mail alasdair@aliddell.com)

LIDDELL, (Andrew) Colin MacDuff; WS (1980); *Educ* Cargilfield Sch Edinburgh, Fettes, Balliol Coll Oxford (BA), Univ of Edinburgh (LLB); *Children* 2 da (Iona Michelle b 1983, Bryony Marsali b 1985); *Career* slr; sr ptnr J & H Mitchell WS Pitlochry and Aberfeldy; accredited specialist in charity law 2001–; chm: Aberfeldy Highland Ball 2004–15, Pitlochry Highland Games 2004–13, Pitlochry Festival Theatre 2011–; tstee: Dunard Fund 1986–, Fndn Scotland (formerly Scottish Community Fndn) 2005–14, Peter Dixon Charitable Tst 2009–, New Sch Butterstone 2009–12, Royal HS Preservation Tst 2015–; patron Moulin & Pitlochry History Circle 1996–; commentator Pitlochry Highland Games; *Publications* Pitlochry: Heritage of a Highland District (1993, 2 edn 1994), Pitlochry: A History (2008); *Recreations* skiing, hill walking, photography, writing, Scottish history; *Style—* Colin Liddell, Esq, WS; ✉ J & H Mitchell WS, 51 Atholl Road, Pitlochry PH16 5BU (☎ 01796 472606, fax 01796 473198, e-mail j@hmitchell.co.uk)

LIDDELL OF COATDYKE, Baroness (Life Peer UK 2010), of Coatbridge in Lanarkshire; Rt Hon Helen Lawrie Liddell; PC (1998); da of late Hugh Reilly, of Coatbridge, Lanarkshire, and late Bridget, *née* Lawrie; *b* 6 December 1950; *Educ* Univ of Strathclyde (BA); *m* 22 July 1972, Dr Alistair Henderson, s of Robert Liddell, of Airdrie, Lanarkshire; 1 s (Paul b 1979), 1 da (Clare b 1985); *Career* head Econ Dept Scot TUC 1971–75 (asst sec 1975–76), economics corr BBC Scotland 1976–77, Scottish sec Lab Pty 1977–88, dir of public and corp affrs Scottish Daily Record and Sunday Mail Ltd 1988–92, chief exec Business Venture Prog 1993–94; Parly candidate (Lab) E Fife 1974; MP (Lab): Monklands E 1994–97, Airdrie and Shotts 1997–2005; economic sec to the Treasy 1997–98, min of state Scottish Office 1998–99, min for tport DETR 1999, min for energy and competitiveness in Europe DTI 1999–2001, sec of state for Scotland 2001–03; high cmmr to Australia 2005–09; non-exec dir: Scottish Prison Bd 1992–94, Central Scotland Broadcasting Ltd 1993–94, Visit Britain 2010–14, Br Australian Soc 2010, Offshore Renewable Energy Catapult 2012–16; chm Good Governance Gp (G3) Ltd; memb Nat Jt Cncl for Academic Salaries and Awards 1974–76, Cabinet rep Int Women's Year Ctee 1975, chair UN 50th Anniversary Ctee Scotland 1994–95; Hon LLD Univ of Strathclyde 2005; *Books* Elite (1990); *Recreations* writing, walking; *Style—* The Baroness Liddell of Coatdyke; ✉ House of Lords, London SW1A 0PW

LIDDELL-GRAINGER, Ian Richard Peregrine; MP; s of David Liddell-Grainger of Ayton (d 2007), and Anne, *née* Abel-Smith; *b* 23 February 1959; *Educ* Millfield; *m* 31 Oct 1985, Jill Nesbit; 1 s (Peter Richard b 6 May 1987), 2 da (Sophie Victoria b 27 Dec 1989, May Alexandra b 9 Sept 1993); *Career* MP (Cons): Bridgwater 2001–10, Bridgwater and W Somerset 2010–; memb: Scottish Affrs Ctee 2001–04, Public Administration Select Ctee 2001–10, EFRA 2002–05, Crossrail Select Ctee 2005–07, Environmental Audit Ctee 2006–10, Select Ctee on Statutory Instruments 2010–, Cncl of Europe 2010–, European Security and Defence Assembly Western EU 2010–; *Recreations* skiing, walking, garden; *Style—* Ian Liddell-Grainger, Esq, MP; ✉ House of Commons, London SW1A 0AA (e-mail ianlg@parliament.uk); Constituency Office, 16 Northgate, Bridgwater, Somerset TA6 3EU (☎ 01278 458383, website www.liddellgrainger.org.uk)

LIDDIARD, Michael Richard; s of Richard England Liddiard, CBE (d 1993) and Constance Lily, *née* Rook; *b* 15 November 1946; *Educ* Oundle, Univ of Exeter (BA), London Business Sch; *m* 14 March 1970, Judith Elizabeth Best, da of Wing Cdr Frederick John Edward Ison, DFC, RAF (d 1978); 1 s (James Stratton b 1973), 1 da (Amanda Brooke b 1975); *Career* C Czarnikow Ltd 1969–92: dir 1981, vice-chm 1983; dir C Czarnikow Sugar Ltd 1991–95, sr vice-pres C Czarnikow Sugar Inc NY 1995–99, currently conslt Agrilion Commodity Advisers (formerly Kingsman Americas); dir Lion Mark Holdings 1983–90; memb: Cncl Assoc of Futures Brokers and Dealers 1986–90, London Clearing House Bd 1987–91, World Sugar Ctee NY 1996–2000, ICE Sugar Arbitration and Coffee Control CITs 1996; Freeman City of London 1970, memb Ct of Assts Worshipful Co Haberdashers 1987 (Liveryman 1971); *Recreations* tennis, shooting, squash; *Clubs* RAC, Union (NY); *Style—* Michael Liddiard, Esq

LIDDLE, Baron (Life Peer UK 2010), of Carlisle in the County of Cumbria; Roger Liddle; *b* 14 June 1947, Carlisle, Cumbria; *Educ* Carlisle GS, Queen's Coll Oxford; *m* 30 July 1983, Caroline Agnes Morgan Thomson, *qv*, da of Lord Thomson of Monifieth, KT, PC, DL, FRSE (Life Peer); 1 s (Andrew b 29 Oct 1989); *Career* special advsr to PM 1997–2004, European Cmmn 2004–07, chm Cumbria Vision 2007–10 currently chm Policy Network; *Style—* The Lord Liddle; ✉ House of Lords, London SW1A 0PW

LIDINGTON, Rt Hon Dr David; CBE (2016), PC, MP; s of Roy Lidington, and Rosa Lidington; *b* 30 June 1956; *Educ* Haberdashers' Aske's, Sidney Sussex Coll Cambridge (MA, PhD); *m* 5 Aug 1989, Helen, da of late Lt-Col T F Parry; 4 s (Christopher David Parry b 4 June 1993, Thomas Stephen Anders b 21 March 1995, Edward Charles Panes, James Andrew Damant (twins) b 8 July 1997); *Career* with BP 1983–86, with RTZ Corporation 1986–87, special adviser to Rt Hon Douglas Hurd 1987–90, sr conslt Public Policy Unit 1991–92, MP (Cons) Aylesbury 1992– (Parly candidate (Cons) Vauxhall 1987); PPS to Home Sec 1994–97, PPS to ldr of HM's Oppn 1997–99; oppn spokesman on Home Affairs 1999–2001, oppn frontbench Treasy spokesman 2001–02, shadow min for Agric and Fisheries 2002, shadow sec of state for the Environment, Food and Rural Affrs 2002–03, shadow sec of state for NI 2003–07, shadow foreign office min 2007–10, min of state for Europe 2010–16, Lord Pres of the Cncl and ldr of the House of Commons 2016–; *Recreations* history, choral singing, reading; *Style—* The Rt Hon David Lidington, CBE, MP; ✉ House of Commons, London SW1A 0AA

LIDSTONE, John Barrie Joseph; s of Arthur Richard Francis Lidstone (d 1930), and Lilian May, *née* Teppett (d 1973); *b* 21 July 1929; *Educ* Presentation Coll Reading, Univ of Manchester, RAF Educn Officers' Course; *m* 1957, Primrose Vivien (d 2014), da of Vincent Russell (d 1947), of Derby, and Emily, *née* Macdonald (d 1995); 1 da (Susan Beverley (Mrs Page) b 1960); *Career* Nat Serv RAF 1947–48; English master Repton Sch 1949–52; Shell-Mex and BP and Assoc cos 1952–62, dep md Vicon Agricultural Machinery Ltd 1962–63, dir and gen mangr Marketing Selections Ltd 1969–72; Marketing Improvements Gp plc: joined 1965, dir 1968–, dir and gen mangr 1972–74, dep md 1974–88, dep chm 1988–89, non-exec dir 1989–93; non-exec dir: Kalamazoo plc 1986–91, North Hampshire Tst Co Ltd 1986–93, St Nicholas' School Fleet Educational Trust Ltd 1982–90 and 1995–96; memb: Chemical & Allied Products Industry Trg Bd 1975–79, UK Mgmnt Consultancies Assoc 1978–88 (chm 1986–87), Nat Inter-Active Video Centre 1988–90; ed Lidstorian 1985–88, mktg ed Pharmaceutical Times 1994–2006; voted top speaker on mktg in Europe 1974, Dartnell lecture tours USA 1978–82, sr visiting lectr Univ of Surrey 1990–2003; memb: Nat Exec Ctee CIM 1985–90, Ct of Assts Guild of Mgmnt Consultants 1993–99, BAFTA, Soc of Authors; Freeman City of London, Liveryman Worshipful Co of Marketors; FCMC, FCMI, FInstD, FCIM; *Films and Video* tech advsr and script writer: The Persuaders (1975), Negotiating Profitable Sales (1979), Training Salesmen on the Job (1981, won highest award for creative excellence at US Industrial Film Festival 1982), Marketing for Managers (1985), Marketing Today (1985), Reaching Agreement and Interviewing (1987, 1988); Training Salesmen on the Job (1975, 2 edn 1986), Recruiting and Selecting Successful Salesmen (1976, 2 edn 1983), Negotiating Profitable Sales (1977, made into two part film by Video Arts 1979), Motivating your Sales Force (1978, 2 edn 1995), Making Effective Presentations (1985), The Sales Presentation (jtly, 1985), Profitable Selling (1986), Marketing Planning for the Pharmaceutical Industry (1987, 2 edn 1999), Manual of Sales Negotiation (1991), Manual of Marketing (for Univ of Surrey, 1991), Beyond the Pay-Packet (1992), Face the Press (1992), Presentation and Media Relations Planning for the Pharmaceutical Industry (2003), How Did You Know All These People? (memoirs, 2013); contrib chapters to: The Best of Dilemma & Decision (1985), Marketing in the Service Industries (1985), Marketing Handbook (3 edn 1989), Gower Book of Management Skills (2 edn 1992), The Director's Manual (1992 and 1995), The Marketing Book (3 edn 1994), Ivanhoe Guide to Management Consultants (1994), International Encyclopedia of Business and Management (1996); author of the 1998 Churchill Soc Christmas Lecture 'The Reform of the Honours System'; expert evidence incl in House of Commons Public Administration Select Ctee 2004 report: 'A Matter of Honour: Reforming the Honours System'; articles contrib to: The Times and Sunday Times, Daily and Sunday Telegraph, FT, The Observer, Long Range Planning, International Management, Management Today, Marketing, Marketing Week, Evening Standard, The Independent, Yorkshire Post, Forbes Magazine; *Recreations* writing, cricket, golf (capt N Hants Golf Club 1992–93); *Clubs* Reform, North Hants Golf; *Style—* John B J Lidstone, Esq

LIDSTONE, Russ; s of Derek Lidstone (d 1998), and Rita, *née* Rustell; *b* 16 March 1970, Brixham, Devon; *Educ* Churston GS Devon, Univ of Keele (BA); *m* 1999, Amanda, *née* Rees; 1 da (Ella b 1998), 1 s (Harvey b 2001); *Career* ethnographic res Coca-Cola GB 1992–93, planner McCann-Erickson 1993–96, sr planner BDDH 1996–99, planner HHCL & Ptnrs 1999–2001, head of planning Lowe and Ptnrs 2001–05, head of planning JWT 2005–06, chief strategy offr Euro RSCG 2006–08, ceo Havas Worldwide London (formerly Euro RSCG London) 2008–15, Havas Worldwide Global Mgmnt; advsr D&AD; memb mgmnt team APG, memb Ctee IPA, mentor Mktg Acad; memb Mktg Gp of GB; *Awards* incl: Advertiser of the Year 2004, Cannes Lions Gold, The Independent Top 100 Inspirational Creative Leaders, Campaign Magazine Top 10 UK CEO, Drum magazine Top 50 Mobile Marketers, IPA Effectiveness, AME Effectiveness, Campaign Press, D&AD Creative and Mktg Soc awards; *Recreations* sport, gym, family; *Style—* Russ Lidstone, Esq; ✉ Havas Worldwide London, Cupola House, 15 Alfred Place, London WC1E 7EB (☎ 020 7257 6006, fax 020 7257 6012, e-mail russ.lidstone@havasww.com)

LIEBERMAN, Prof (Alexander) Robert; *b* 7 July 1942; *Educ* UCL (BSc, PhD, DSc); *m* 1, (m dis 1975); 2 s (Gerald b 1963, Nicholas b 1967); m 2, 1976, Dr Margaret Mary Bird; 2 da (Elizabeth b 1977, Georgina b 1979); *Career* UCL: asst lectr Dept of Anatomy 1965–68, lectr 1968–74, sr lectr 1974–76, reader 1976–87, dean Faculty of Life Sciences (biological and med) 1990–2004, vice-dean UCL Med Sch 1990–98, vice-dean Royal Free and UC Med Sch 1998–99, fell 2001; prof of anatomy (neurobiology) Univ of Aarhus Denmark 1983–85, prof of anatomy Univ of London 1987–2008 (emeritus prof 2009–); ed-in-chief Jl of Neurocytology 1986–2005 (jt ed 1972–85), Euro ed Jl of Electron Microscopy 1996–2002; memb: Scientific Advsy Panel The Brain Research Tst 1991–97, Scientific Advsy Bd CNRS/INSERM Unité de Recherches Neurobiologique Marseille 1990–96, Scientific Ctee R&D Directorate UCL Hosps Tst 1996–, Ctee of Mgmnt Eastman Dental Inst 1995–99, Sci Ctee Int Spinal Research Tst 1997–2004, Prize Ctee Kemali Fndn for Neuroscience 2006–11; govr Moorfields Eye Hosp NHS Tst 2004–08; tstee: Alzheimer Research Tst 1997–2009 (chm Scientific Advsy Ctee 2002–04), Alzheimer Brain Bank UK 2005–10; MD (hc) Charles Univ Prague 1998; FMedSci 1999; *Books* contrib: International Review of Neurobiology (1971), Essays On The Nervous System (1974), The Peripheral Nerve (1976), Neuron Concept Today (1976), Local Circuit Neurons (1976), Thalamic Networks for Relay and Modulation (1993), Progress in Neurobiology (1995), Progress in Brain Research (1998), Degeneration and Regeneration in the Nervous System (1999); *Recreations* cards, backgammon; *Style—* Prof Robert Lieberman; ✉ Department of Cell and Developmental Biology, University College London, Gower Street, London WC1E 6BT (☎ 020 7679 7769, fax 020 7679 7349, e-mail ucgarol@ucl.ac.uk)

LIEBERMAN, Dr Stuart; s of Jerome Leon Lieberman, of Miami, Florida, USA, and Libby, *née* Mizus; *b* 4 October 1942; *m* 1, 1965 (m dis 1981), Susan Joan Lieberman; 3 s (Samuel, Steven, Simon); m 2, 30 Oct 1986, Sybil Margaret Battersby, da of Joseph Heath, of Wallheath, Wolverhampton; 3 da (Abigail, Gemma, Mel); *Career* Capt USAF 1965–70; sr lectr and conslt psychiatrist St George's Hosp Med Sch 1975–92, conslt psychiatrist in psychotherapy Heathlands Mental Health Tst 1992–99, med dir Priory Hosp Woking 2000–01, conslt Warby Hospital 2003–; fndr memb and treas Inst of Family Therapy London 1976–79, fndr memb and sec Assoc for Family Therapy 1975–78 (chm 1998–2000); FRCPsych 1983; *Books* Transgenerational Family Therapy (1979); *Style—* Dr Stuart Lieberman; ✉ 13 Barnby Road, Knaphill, Woking, Surrey GU21 2NL (☎ 01483 481488)

LIFE, HE Vivien Frances; *m* Timothy Michael Dowse, CMG; 2 da (Rachel, Rebecca); *Career* diplomat; FCO: dep head EU Dept External 1996–97, dep head Latin America and Caribbean Dept 1997–99, head Consultancy Group FCO Services 1999–2003, head Strategy Group 2003–06, head External Relations Group Europe Directorate 2006–08, head of enlargement South-East and Wider Europe Group 2008–10, head Climate Change and Energy Dept 2010–12; ambass to Denmark 2012–; *Style—* HE Ms Vivien Life; ✉ Kastelsvej 36, 2100 Copenhagen, Denmark

LIFFORD, 9 Viscount (I 1781); (Edward) James Wingfield; DL (Hants 2004); also Baron Lifford (I 1768); s of 8 Viscount Lifford (d 1987), and (Alison) Mary Patricia, *née* Ashton; *b* 27 January 1949; *Educ* Aiglon Coll Switzerland; *m* 1976, Alison, da of Robert Law, of Withersfield, Suffolk; 2 da (Hon Annabel Louise b 1978, Hon Alice Mary b 1990), 1 s (Hon (James) Thomas Wingfield b 1979); *Heir* s, Hon Thomas Hewitt; *Career* dir Rathbone Bros plc 1996–2006, chm Rathbone Investment Mgmnt (CI) Ltd 2007–15; non-exec dir McKay Securities plc 2006–; Past Master Worshipful Co of Armourers and Brasiers; *Recreations* country sports; *Clubs* Boodle's, Pratt's; *Style—* The Rt Hon Viscount Lifford, DL; ✉ Field House, Hursley, Winchester, Hampshire SO21 2LE

LIFFORD, William Lewis (Will); s of George Edward Lifford (d 1993), and Madge Elizabeth, *née* Lewis (d 2012); *b* 14 January 1951; *Educ* Sevenoaks Sch, Univ of Bristol (BSc); *m* 20 Aug 1977, Susanne, da of Stanley Woof (d 1998); 2 s (David b 18 May 1984, Michael b 24 March 1986); *Career* Deloitte & Co London 1972–79 (qualified CA 1975); ptnr Grant Thornton 1982–2007 (UK sr audit ptnr 2002–07); chm Forum of Firms IFAC 2004–07; memb Audit Ctee Rural Payments Agency 2007–10, non-exec dir Entrust 2008–15; ind memb Agriculture and Horticulture Devpt Bd 2013–; govr Leeds Trinity Univ 2008–14, dir Connect Yorks 2009–13, chm Martin House Children's Hospice 2009–, tstee Axis Web 2011–16, ind memb Bd Yorkshire Housing 2015–; *Recreations* hill walking, photography, travel; *Style—* Will Lifford, Esq; ✉ 9 Rose Croft, East Keswick, Leeds LS17 9HR (☏ 01937 572473)

LIGENZA-MILDENHALL, Gabriela Maria; da of Tadeusz Ligenza, of Gdynia, Poland, and Gertruda, *née* Szydlowska; *b* 14 May 1959; *Educ* Acad of Fine Arts in Warsaw (MA, UNESCO award); *m* 1, 1978 (m dis), Count Andrzej Borkowski; 1 da (Alicja b 13 Oct 1980); m 2, 1988, Richard Mildenhall; 1 s (Oscar b 8 Nov 1988); *Career* collaboration with Akademia Ruchu visual avant garde theatre in Warsaw and participation in many Euro theatre festivals 1976–83; fndr Gabriela Ligenza (high fashion hat design) 1985–; designed own collections and collaborated with others incl: Missoni, Jasper Conran, Paul Smith, Roland Klein, Laura Ashley, Myrene de Premonville; *Clubs* Chelsea Arts; *Style—* Mrs Gabriela Ligenza; ✉ c/o Gabriela Ligenza Hats, 5 Ellis Street, London SW1X 9AL (☏ 020 7730 2200, e-mail ltc@gabrielaligenza.com, website www.gabrielaligenza.com)

LIGHTING, Jane; *b* 22 December 1956; *Career* fndr and md Minotar Int 1995–99, ceo Flextech 2002–03 (md Broadcast and Television 1999–2002), ceo Channel Five Broadcasting Ltd 2003–08; non-exec dir: Trinity Mirror 2008–, Paddy Power plc 2009–13, Countrywide plc 2014–; chm Br Television Distributors Assoc 1995–96, chair RTS 2006–08 (tstee 2008–), dir Edinburgh Television Festival 1998–2000, govr Nat Film and Television Sch 2001–07, memb Br Screen Advsy Cncl; FRSA, FRTS; *Recreations* painting, escaping to the country; *Clubs* Groucho; *Style—* Ms Jane Lighting; ✉ e-mail jane.lighting@gmail.com, website http://uk.linkedin.com/pub/jane-lighting/13/25a/588

LIGHTMAN, Brian; s of Ivor Lightman (d 2013), and Stella, *née* Blend, of Cardiff; *b* 15 June 1955; *Educ* Westminster City Sch, Univ of Southampton (BA, PGCE) Open Univ (MA); *m* 1981, Eva *née* Mohr; 4 da (Rebecca b 31 Oct 1982, Katya b 1 March 1986, Charlotte b 13 Nov 1987, Natalie b 30 June 1990); *Career* teacher Hazlewick Sch Crawley 1979–84, head Languages and Sixth Form Sondes Place Sch Dorking 1984–89, dep head St Martin's Sch Brentwood 1989–95, headteacher Llantwit Major Sch Vale of Glamorgan 1995–99, headteacher St Cyres Sch Penarth 1999–2010, gen sec Assoc of Sch and Coll Ldrs 2010–16 (hon treas 2003–06, pres 2007–08); currently freelance educn conslt and dir Lightman Consulting Ltd; FRSA; *Publications* listed at http://www.lightmanconsulting.co.uk/writing; *Recreations* music, reading, travel, walking; *Style—* Brian Lightman, Esq; ✉ 10 Quickthorns, Leicester, LE2 4EE (☏ 07977 541868, e-mail brian@lightmanconsulting.co.uk, Twitter @brianlightman)

LIGHTMAN, Prof Stafford Louis; s of Harold Lightman, QC (d 1998), and Gwendoline Joan, *née* Ostrer; *b* 7 September 1948; *m* 1977 (m dis), Susan Louise, da of John Stubbs, of London; 3 s (Sarne Louis b 1978, Joel David b 1979, Leon Alexander b 1982), 1 da (Elewys Gemma b 1987); *Career* prof of clinical neuroendocrinology Charing Cross Hosp London 1988–92, prof of medicine Univ of Bristol 1993–; ed Journal of Neuroendocrinology 1988–97; chm Pituitary Fndn 1996–2002; FRCP, FMedSci; *Books* Neuroendocrinology (ed with B J Everitt, 1986), The Functional Anatomy of the Neuroendocrine Hypothalamus (1992), The Management of Pituitary Tumours: A Handbook (ed with M Powell, 1996, 2 edn 2003), Horizons in Medicine: Vol 7 (ed, 1996), Endocrinology (with A Levy, 1997), Steroid Hormones and the T-Cell Cytokine Profile (with G Rook, 1997); *Style—* Prof Stafford Lightman; ✉ University of Bristol, Henry Wellcome Laboratories, Dorothy Hodgkin Building, Whitson Street, Bristol BS1 3NY (☏ 0117 331 3167, fax 0117 331 3169, e-mail stafford.lightman@bristol.ac.uk)

LIJN, Liliane; da of Herman Segall (d 1971), of Geneva, and Helena, *née* Kustanowitz; *b* 22 December 1939, NYC; *Educ* Sorbonne Paris, Ecole du Louvre Paris; *m* 1961 (m dis 1970), Takis Vassilakis, s of Athanasios Vassilakis; 1 s (Thanos Vassilakis b 17 April 1962); partner, Stephen Weiss; 1 s (Mischa Weiss-Lijn b 31 May 1975), 1 da (Sheba Weiss-Lijn b 24 Oct 1977); *Career* sculptor, poet and kinetic artist; experimented with fire and acids 1961–62, made and showed first kinetic poems Paris 1963–64, worked using natural forces Athens 1964–66, settled London 1966, numerous cmmns for large public sculptures 1971–, developed in collaboration with astronomer John Vallerga Solar Hills a large scale solar installation in the landscape, worked with NASA chemist to develop installations using aerogel 2005–09, solar beacon Golden Gate Bridge San Francisco 2012; memb Cncl of Mgmnt Byam Shaw Art Sch 1983–90, memb Artslab and Operalab 1999; artist in residence NaREC, AV Festival and Inspire Northumberland 2009, culture lab residency Univ of Newcastle 2010–11, artist in residence High-North Tromso Norway 2012–; *Awards* Arts Cncl Award 1976, Alecto Award (Bradford Print Biennale) 1976, Arts Cncl Publishing Award for Crossing Map 1981, Arts Cncl Bursary for holography 1982, London Production Fund Award 1996, Arts Cncl England Funding Award 2006, Gulbenkian Fndn Funding Award 2006; *Solo Exhibitions* incl: La Librairie Anglaise Paris 1963, Indica Gallery London 1967, Germain Gallery Paris 1972, Beyond Light (Serpentine Gallery London) 1976 (toured Durham LI Museum Durham, Mappin Gallery Sheffield and Walker Art Gallery Liverpool 1977), Circle of Light (Eagle Walk Gallery Milton Keynes) 1980, Aberdeen Art Gallery 1983, Paton Gallery London 1983, Heads (Galerie Peter Ludwig Cologne) 1985, Imagine the Goddess (Fischer Fine Art London) 1987, Poem Machines 1962–68 (Nat Arts Library, V&A) 1993, Her Mother's Voice (Eagle Gallery London) 1996, Koans (Shirley Day Ltd) 2000, Light and Memory (La Rocca Centro d'Arte Contemporanea Umbertide and Studio Nardi Florence) 2002, Works 1959–80 (Mead Gallery Coventry and Djanogly Gallery Nottingham) 2005, Stardust (Riflemaker Gallery London) 2008, Centrifugal (Royal Acad Schs Gallery London) 2008, Power Game (ICA London) 2009 and (BALTIC AV Festival Gateshead) 2010, Liliane Lijn Earth Art (Jewellery) (Willer Gallery London) 2009, Light Years (Sir John Sloane Museum and Riflemaker Gallery London) 2011, Caution Matter (with Jamie Allen, Anglia Ruskin Gallery Cambridge) 2012, Cosmic Dramas (MIMA Middlesbrough) 2012, Earth Body Art (Museo Civico di Santa Croce Umbertide) 2013, Early Work 1961–69 (RCM Galerie Paris) 2015; *Group Exhibitions* incl: Light & Movement (Musée d'Art Modern Paris) 1967, Kinetic Art (Kunstnishus Oslo, Helsinki and Gothenburg) 1969 (also at Hayward Gallery London 1970), Agam-Bury-Lijn-Soto-Takis Delson-Richter Galleries Tel Aviv 1973, Art of the Sixties (Tate Gallery London) 1976, British Sculpture in the 20th Century (Whitechapel Art Gallery) 1981, 20th Century Drawings & Watercolours (V&A) 1984, Tecnologia e Informatica (Venice Biennale) 1986, The Artist's Notebook (Galerie Bernard Jordan Paris, Galerie Akiyama Tokyo, Atelier Nishinomiya Nishinomya and Art Works LA) 1987, Chagall to Kitaj – Jewish Experience in 20th Century Art (Barbican Art Gallery London) 1990, The Sixties Art Scene in London (Barbican Art Gallery London) 1993, Art Unlimited (South Bank Centre touring exhbn) 1994, British Abstract Art – Sculpture (Angela Flowers Gallery) 1995, Rubies and Rebels (Barbican Gallery London) 1996, Chimériques Polymères (Musée d'Art Moderne et d'Art Contemporain Nice) 1996, Dream Machines (Arts Cncl touring exhbn) 2000, (S)cripturae (Galeria Civica Padova) 2001, Thinking Big Concepts for Twenty-First Century British Sculpture (Peggy Guggenheim Collection Venice) 2002, Editions Alecto: A Fury for Prints Artist's Multiples and Prints 1960–81 (Whitworth Art Gallery Univ of Manchester, Bankside Gallery London and City Art Gallery Edinburgh) 2003, Vaselle d'Autore per Il Vino Novello (La Vecchia Fornace Torgiano) 2003, Outside of a Dog (Baltic: The Centre for Contemporary Art Gateshead) 2003, Art and the Sixties: This was Tomorrow (Tate Britain London and Birmingham Museum and Art Gallery) 2004, A Summer of Love (Tate Liverpool) 2005, Describing Form (tour incl Henry Moore Inst and Tate Britain) 2005, Sixty Years of Sculpture in the Arts Cncl Collection (Longside Gallery Yorks Sculpture Park) 2006, Riflemaker becomes Indica (Riflemaker Gallery London) 2006, Magnetic Vision (Kinetica Museum London) 2006, Nyehaus Becomes Indica (Nyehaus Gallery NY) 2007, Zoo Art Fair (Riflemaker Gallery London) 2007, Recent Acquisitions Part II (Br Museum London) 2007, 100 Years 100 Artists 100 Works of Art (Art on the Underground London) 2008, Poor. Old. Tired. Horse. (ICA London) 2009, Pinch Pots and Pyramids (Kate Werble Gallery NY) 2009, Space-Time (Nat Glass Centre Sunderland) 2009, Inside Outside Show (Flat Time House London) 2009, The Brain Unravelled an exhibition in three disciplines: art, anthropology and neuroscience (Slade Research Centre London) 2009, AV Festival 10: Energy, All Art is, is rhythm (Hatton Gallery Newcastle upon Tyne) 2010, Beneath The Radar in 1970s London (England & Co London) 2010, Psychedelica (ICA London) 2011, Text, Light and Matternal Philosophy in Practice (Chelsea Coll of Art and Design) 2011, Signals and Indica (Tate Britain) 2011, Republic of the Moon/Moon Futures (FACT Liverpool) 2011, Ecstatic Alphabets/Heaps of Language (MoMa NY) 2012, Poetry, Language, Code (Anglia Ruskin Gallery Cambridge) 2012, Fourth Plinth Commission (St Martin-in-the-Fields London) 2013, Republic of the Moon (curated by The Arts Catalyst Bargehouse London) 2014, Caritas: Histoires, Paraboles et Rêves, Musée de Picardie Amiens) 2014, William S Burroughs, CAN YOU ALL HEAR ME? (October Gallery London) 2014, Graphic Constellations: Visual Poetry and the Properties of Space (Ruskin Gallery Cambridge) 2015, Images Moving Out Onto Space, (Tate St Ives) 2015; *Work in Public Collections* incl: Aberdeen Art Gallery, Art Inst of Chicago, Arts Cncl of GB, Bibliotecque Nationale Paris, Br Cncl, Br Museum, Contemporary Art Soc London, Derbyshire Museum Serv, Evelina Children's Hosp London, Fonds Nationale d'Art Contemporain Paris, Glasgow Museum Kelvingrove, Graves Art Gallery Sheffield, Henry Moore Fndn Leeds, Kunstmuseum Bern, MOMA NYC, Museum of NSW Sydney, Musée de la Ville de Paris, NY Public Library, Northampton Museum, Robert Mclaughlin Gallery Oshawa, Rutherston Collection City Art Gallery Manchester, Tate Gallery, Unilever plc, Univ of Warwick, V&A, Camden Public Library London, Govt Art Collection London, Joan Flasch Artists' Book Collection, Saint Thomas Hosp London; *Publications* incl: Six Throws of the Oracular Keys Paris (poems and drawings, 1982), Crossing Map (autobiographical sci fiction prose poem, 1983), A Symbolic Structure for the Turn of the Century (1988), Her Mother's Voice (artists' book/oral history, 1996), First Words (2000), Light and Memory (2002), Liliane Lijn: Works 1959–1980 (2005), Centrifugal (ed by Michael Petry, 2008), Stardust (2008), The Art of Not Making, The New Artist/Artisan Relationship (ed by Michael Petry, 2011); author of numerous articles for magazines and jls; *Videos* subject of: Liliane Lijn (2005), Let There Be Light (2008); *Recreations* swimming and gardening; *Style—* Ms Liliane Lijn; ✉ c/o Riflemaker Gallery, 79 Beak Street, London W1F 9SU (☏ 020 7439 0000, website www.riflemaker.org); studio: 93 Vale Road, London N4 1TG (e-mail liliane@lilianelijn.com, website www.lilianelijn.com)

LIKIERMAN, Prof Sir (John) Andrew; kt (2001); s of Adolf Likierman (d 1988), and Olga, *née* Heldenbusch (d 1978); *b* 30 December 1943; *m* 1987, Dr Meira, da of Joshua Gruenspan; 1 step da (Ruth Thompson b 1976), 1 step s (James Thompson b 1979); *Career* divnl mgmnt accountant Tootal Ltd 1965–68, lectr Dept of Mgmnt Studies Univ of Leeds 1972–74 (asst lectr 1968–69), Qualitex Ltd 1969–72 (md Overseas Div 1971–72), visiting fell Oxford Centre for Mgmnt Studies 1972–74, non-exec chm Ex Libris Ltd 1973–74, non-exec chm Economist's Bookshop Ltd 1987–91 (non-exec dir 1981–91); London Business Sch 1974–76 and 1979– (dean 2009–): dir Pt/t Masters Prog 1981–85, dir Inst of Public Sector Mgmnt 1983–88, prof of accounting and fin control 1987–93, dean of external affairs 1989–92, ex-officio govr 1990–93 (elected govr 1986–89), dep princ 1990–93, visiting prof 1993–2001, prof of mgmnt practice 2001–, acting dean 2007; asst sec Cabinet Office and memb Central Policy Review Staff 1976–79 (advsr 1979–82); HM Treasy: head of Govt Accounting Serv and chief accountancy advsr 1993–2004, dir of fin mgmnt, reporting and audit 1994–2000, princ fin offr 1995–2000, md of fin mgmnt, reporting and audit 2000–04; advsr House of Commons Select Ctees on: Treasy and Civil Serv 1981–91, Employment 1985–90, Tport 1981 and 1987–90, Social Servs 1988, Social Security 1991; memb Govt Inquiries on: N Sea Cost Escalation 1975, Future of Power Plant Mfrg Indust 1976, Int Comparisons with PO and British Telecom 1981, Accounting for Econ Costs and Changing Prices 1986, Professional Liability (chm) 1989; chm Nat Audit Office 2009–15; memb Editorial Bd Public Money and Management 1988– (chm 1988–93); dir: Bank of England 2004–08, MORI Ltd 2004–05 (chm 2005), Barclays plc 2004–13; chm Applied Intellectual Capital plc 2006–08; memb: Fin Ctee Oxfam 1974–84, Ctee on Med Costs Univ of London 1980–81, Current Affairs Advsy Gp Channel 4 1986–87, Audit Cmmn 1988–91, Ctee on Financial Aspects of Corp Governance 1991–95; memb Cncl: RIPA 1982–88, CIMA 1985–94 (pres 1991–92), Civil Serv Coll 1989–94, Defence Operational Analysis Centre 1992–93; observer: Accounting Standards Bd 1993–2004, Fin Reporting Cncl 1994–2004 (memb 1991–94), Tavistock and Portman NHS Tst Bd 2000–08, Steering Ctee Corp Governance of UN 2006; Non-Exec Dir of the Year Public and Not-for-Profit Organisations 2009; Freeman City of London; Hon DBA: Southampton Business Sch, Oxford Brookes Univ; Hon DPhil London Met Univ; CIMA (Gold Medal), FCMA, FCCA; *Books* The Reports and Accounts of Nationalised Industries (1979), Cash Limits and External Financing Limits (1981), Public Sector Accounting and Financial Control (jtly, 1983, 4 edn 1992), Structure and Form of Government Expenditure Reports (jtly, 1984, 1985, 1990, 1991 and 1992), Public Expenditure (1988), Accounting for Brands (jtly, 1989), Ethics and Accountants in Industry and Commerce (1990); *Recreations* cycling, ideas, architecture, wine; *Clubs* Reform; *Style—* Prof Sir Andrew Likierman; ✉ London Business School, Sussex Place, Regents Park, London NW1 4SA (☏ 020 7000 7012)

LILANI, Pinky; CBE (2016), DL (Greater London 2014); *b* 25 March 1954, Calcutta, India; *Career* owner Spice Magic Ltd; dir Blitz Communications Ltd 2012–; fndr and chm: Asian Women of Achievement Awards 1999–, Women of the Future Awards 2005–, Inspirational Women's Network 2007–, Global Empowerment Award 2008–; assoc fell Said Business Sch Oxford; *Books* Spice Magic Ltd (2001), Coriander Makes the Difference (2009); *Style—* Ms Pinky Lilani, CBE, DL; ✉ Spice Magic Ltd, 1A Furze Lane, Purley, Surrey CR8 3EJ

LILFORD, Prof Richard James; s of Maj Victor Lilford, and Eileen, *née* Gifford; *b* 22 April 1950; *Educ* St John's Coll Johannesburg, PhD; *m* 23 May 1981, Victoria Alice Lilford; 1 s (Peter), 2 da (Nicola, Philippa); *Career* formerly conslt obstetrician and gynaecologist Queen Charlotte's Hosp London, prof of obstetrics and gynaecology and chm Epidemiology Res Inst Univ of Leeds until 1995, dir of R&D NHS Exec W Midlands 1995–, prof of health servs research Univ of Birmingham 1995– (currently head Sch of Health and Population Scis and Birmingham Clinical Research Acad); MFPHM; FRCP, FRCOG; *Books* Basic Science for Obstetrics and Gynaecology (1984, 3 edn 1989), Prenatal Diagnosis and Prognosis (1990), Computing and Decision Suport in Obstetrics and Gynaecology (1991); *Recreations* flying, tennis; *Style—* Prof Richard Lilford; ✉ University of Birmingham, Department of Public Health and Epidemiology, Edgbaston, Birmingham B15 2TT (☏ 0121 414 6772, fax 0121 414 2752)

L

LILL, John Richard; CBE (2005, OBE 1978); s of G R Lill; *b* 17 March 1944; *Educ* Leyton County HS, Royal Coll of Music; *m* Jacqueline Clifton Smith; *Career* concert pianist; gave first recital aged nine, London debut playing Beethoven's Emperor (5th) Piano Concerto Royal Festival Hall 1962, first Br pianist to perform complete Beethoven Sonata Cycle (at the Queen Elizabeth Hall 1982, also at the Barbican Hall 1986 and Casals Hall Tokyo 1987); performed with orchs incl: LSO, LPO, CBSO, Royal Liverpool Philharmonic, BBC Welsh and Scottish Symphony Orchs, BBC Symphony, Hallé, Royal Philharmonic, Royal Scottish, Baltimore Symphony, Philadelphia, Cleveland, San Diego Symphony, Boston Symphony, NY Philharmonic, Leipzig Gewandhaus Orch, St Petersburg Philharmonic; worked with conductors incl: Sir Adrian Boult, Sir John Barbirolli, Seiji Ozawa, David Atherton, Eduardo Mata, Simon Rattle, Tadaaki Otaka, Rafael Frühbeck de Burgos, Andrew Davis, Walter Weller, James Loughran, Yuri Temirkanov, Kurt Masur; appeared at venues incl: Royal Festival Hall, Queen Elizabeth Hall, Konzerthaus Vienna, Hollywood Bowl, Le Châtelet Paris, Tanglewood, BBC Proms, Cardiff Festival, Swansea Festival; winner Moscow Int Tchaikovsky Competition 1970; *Recordings* incl: Beethoven Piano Concerto Cycle (with Scottish Nat Orch and Sir Alexander Gibson, and with CBSO and Walter Weller), Beethoven Sonata Cycle, Brahms Piano Concertos (with Hallé Orch and James Loughran), Tchaikovsky Piano Concerto No 1 (with LSO and James Judd), Prokofiev Sonatas, Rachmaninov complete works for piano (with BBC Nat Orch of Wales and Tadaaki Otaka); *Recreations* amateur radio, chess, computing; *Style—* John Lill, Esq, CBE; ✉ c/o Askonas Holt, Lincoln House, 300 High Holborn, London WC1V 7JH

LILLEY, Andrew; *Educ* Univ of Southampton (LLB); *Career* joined as articled clerk Freshfields 1985; Travers Smith: joined 1995, ptnr 1997–, managing ptnr 2010–; *Style—* Andrew Lilley, Esq; ✉ Travers Smith, 10 Snow Hill, London EC1A 2AL

LILLEY, Prof David Malcolm James; s of Gerald Albert Thomas Lilley, of Colchester, Essex, and Betty Pamela, *née* Dickerson; *b* 28 May 1948; *Educ* Gilberd Sch Colchester, Univ of Durham (BSc, PhD), Univ of London (MSc, E Stickings Prize); *m* 1981, Patricia Mary, da of Ronald Biddle; 2 da (Katherine Suzannah b 1982, Sarah Anne b 1985); *Career* res fell Univ of Warwick 1973–75, ICI res fell Univ of Oxford 1975–76, sr res investigator Searle Res Laboratories 1976–81; Univ of Dundee: lectr in biochemistry 1981–84, reader 1984–89, prof of molecular biology 1989–, dir Cancer Res UK Nucleic Acid Structure Res Gp 1993–; res fell Royal Soc 1983–90; visiting prof Xiamen Univ China 2013–; memb: Biochemical Soc 1974–, EMBO 1984–; memb Ctee: Br Soc for Cell Biology 1981–83, Tenovus Symposium 1981–88, Nucleic Acids and Molecular Biology Gp 1983–89, Biophysical Soc 1983–86; chair Nucleic Acid Gp 2005– (sec 1985–88); Colworth Medal 1982, G J Mendel Gold Medal Czech Acad of Sciences 1994, Prelog Medal for Stereochemistry ETH Zürich 1996, RSC Award in RNA and Ribozyme Chemistry 2001, RSC Interdisciplinary Award 2006, Khorana Prize 2016; FRSE 1988, FRS 2002, RNA Society Lifetime Service Award 2015; *Books* Nucleic Acids and Molecular Biology (jt ed); author of 360 scientific papers; *Recreations* foreign languages, running, skiing; *Style—* Prof David Lilley, FRS, FRSE; ✉ Cancer Research UK Nucleic Acid Structure Research Group, MSI/WTB Complex, University of Dundee, Dundee DD1 5EH (☎ 01382 384243, e-mail d.m.j.lilley@dundee.ac.uk)

LILLEY, Rt Hon Peter Bruce; PC (1990), MP; s of Arnold Francis Lilley, and Lilian, *née* Elliott; *b* 23 August 1943; *Educ* Dulwich Coll, Clare Coll Cambridge; *m* 1979, Gail Ansell; *Career* energy industries investment advsr; Parly candidate (Cons) Haringey Tottenham Oct 1974; MP (Cons): St Albans 1983–97, Hitchen and Harpenden 1997–; chm Bow Gp 1973–75, sec Cons Backbench Energy Ctee 1983–84, memb Treasy Select Ctee 1983–84, PPS to Min of State for Local Govt 1984, PPS to Rt Hon Nigel Lawson as Chllr of Exchequer 1985–87, econ sec to the Treasy 1987–89, fin sec to the Treasy 1989–90; sec of state: for Trade and Industry 1990–92, for Social Security 1992–97; shadow chllr of the Exchequer 1997–98, dep ldr Cons Pty 1998–99; Cons Pty leadership challenger 1997; chm Cons Pty on Globalisation and Global Poverty 2006–08, chm Jt Ctee of Lords and Commons on Financial Services Bill 2011, memb Select Ctee on Energy & Climate Change 2012–15, memb Environmental Audit Ctee 2015–; FInstPet 1978; *Books* Delusions of Incomes Policy (with Samuel Brittan), Do You Sincerely Want to Win – Defeating Terrorism in Ulster (1972), The End of the Keynesian Era (contrib, ed R Skidelsky, 1980), Thatcherism: The Next Generation (1989), Winning the Welfare Debate (1995), Patient Power (2000), Common Sense on Cannabis (2001), Taking Liberties (2002), Save Our Pensions (2003), ID Cards: Crisis of Identity (2004), Immigration: Too Much of a Good Thing? (2005), In It Together – the Attack on Global Poverty (2007), Paying for Success (2008), Markets in a State: Social Market and Financial Crisis (2011), What's Wrong with Stern's Review of Economics of Climate Change? (2012); *Style—* The Rt Hon Peter Lilley, MP; ✉ House of Commons, London SW1A 0AA

LILLEYMAN, Prof Sir John Stuart; kt (2002); s of Ernest Lilleyman (d 1992), and Frances, *née* Johnson (d 2011); *b* 9 July 1945; *Educ* Bart's Med Coll (MBBS); *Career* postgrad trg at Barts, Cardiff and Sheffield 1969–75, conslt in haematology Children's Hosp Sheffield 1975–95, Mark Ridgwell chair of paediatric oncology Bart's / Royal London Med Sch 1995–2004, medical dir National Patient Safety Agency 2004–07, ret; advsr National Research Ethics Service 2007–10, non-exec dir Medicines and Healthcare Products Regulatory Agency 2009–12; first Distinguished Serv Medal RCPath (for establishing UK system of pathology lab accreditation) 1991, personal chair in paediatric haematology Univ of Sheffield (in recognition of research work on childhood leukaemia) 1993; author of many pubns about childhood blood diseases; DSc (med) Univ of London 1996; pres: UK Assoc Clinical Pathologists 1998–99, RCPath 1999–2002, RSM 2004–06; Hon MD Univ of Sheffield 2003; FRCP 1986, hon fell Inst of Biomedical Science 1996, fndr FRCPCH 1997, FRCPEd 2000, Hon FFPathRCPI 2003, FMedSci 2007, hon FRSM 2007; *Style—* Prof John Lilleyman; ✉ 1 Hetton Hall Cottages, Chatton, Alnwick, Northumberland NE66 5SD (e-mail johnlilleyman@doctors.org.uk)

LILLIE, Stephen; *Career* diplomat; asst desk offr ME Dept FCO 1988–89, f/t Mandarin language training London and Hong Kong 1989–91, 2 then 1 sec (economic and political) FCO 1992–95; FCO: head of section EU Dept 1996–97, head of section Hong Kong Dept 1997–98, dep head China Hong Kong Dept 1998–99; consul-gen Guangzhou 1999–2003, counsellor (economic) and dir of trade and investment New Delhi 2003–06, head Far Eastern Gp FCO 2006–09, ambass to Philippines, Palau, Marshall Islands and Federated States of Micronesia 2009–13, dir Asia Pacific FCO 2013–; *Style—* Mr Stephen Lillie; ✉ Foreign & Commonwealth Office, King Charles Street, London SW1A 2AH

LILLYCROP, David Peter; *b* 12 June 1956; *Educ* Univ of Exeter (LLB), Coll of Law London; *m* 1983, Dr Kaye Smith; 2 s (Jonathan b Oct 1985, Christopher b Aug 1988), 1 da (Catherine b Jan 1994); *Career* called to the Bar Middle Temple 1978; legal advsr Mabey & Johnson Ltd 1978–82, gp co sec and legal advsr Mabey Holdings Ltd 1982–85, co sec and legal dir Quaker Oats Ltd 1985–89; TI Group plc: joined 1989, gp co sec 1991–2000, gen counsel 1997–2000, main bd dir 1998–2000; gen counsel and main bd dir Smiths Gp plc (following merger of TI Gp and Smiths) 2000–08, currently advsr Armstrong Bonham Carter; dist cncllr 1979–83; chm Bucks County Museum Tst; former chm of govrs Abingdon Sch, memb Cncl Wycombe Abbey Sch; former tstee Artificial Heart Fndn, former memb Cncl and Mgmnt Ctee Industry and Parliament Tst; FCMI; *Clubs* Arts, Halton Village Lawn Tennis; *Style—* David Lillycrop, Esq

LIM, Prof Chwen Jeng (CJ); *b* Malaysia; *Educ* Architectural Assoc; *Career* architect and academic; fndr and dir Studio 8 Architects Ltd 1994–; UCL: prof of architecture and urbanism The Bartlett 1993–, pro-provost 2008–11, prof of architecture and urbanism and vice-dean 2011–; visiting prof: Curtin Univ Perth Aust 1996, Stadelschule Frankfurt 1997 and 2000, GSA Mackintosh Sch of Architecture 2001–11, Technological Univ Lund Sweden 2001–12, Chiba Inst of Technol 2004, Royal Danish Acad of Fine Arts Copenhagen 2006, RMIT Australia 2012, Seoul Nat Univ Korea 2012, Aarhus Sch of Architecture Denmark 2012–; external examiner RIBA; chm Architecture/Planning Review Panel Royal Borough of Kensington and Chelsea, memb Architecture Design Review Panel London Borough of Newham; *Selected Exhibitions* ArchiLab: New Experiments 1950–2005 (Mori Art Museum Tokyo) 2004, Summer Exhibition Royal Acad 2005, 2006, 2007 and 2008, Virtually Venice (British Pavilion Venice Architecture Biennale) 2004 and (Fonds Regional d'Art Contemporian du Centre Orleans France) 2006, Future City (Barbican Arts Gallery) 2006, Emerging Talent, Emerging Technologies (World Art Museum Beijing) 2006, New Trends in Architecture in Europe and Asia Pacific (Art Front Gallery Tokyo) 2008, China Design Now (V&A, Guangming New City Hong Kong and Shenzhin Bi-City Biennale of Urbanism/Architecture) 2008, Seasons Through the Looking Glass (V&A) 2008, Drawing By Drawing (Danish Architecture Centre Copenhagen) 2012; *Awards* finalist: AJ/Bovis Land Lease Grand Architecture Prize 2006, President's Int Award for Research RIBA 2007, The Worshipful Soc Best Drawing Prize (for Royal Acad Summer Show) 2007, Iakov Chernikhov Int Prize for Architecture Russia 2007; 3rd prize 6th Schinkenchiku/Takiron Int Competition 1994, 1st prize UCL Cultural Centre Int Competition 1995, RIBA President's Medals Int Teaching Awards 1997, 1998 and 1999, 2nd prize Concept House 2000 Int Competition 2000, 1st prize Central Glass Int Competition Japan 2001 (for GlassHouse), hon mention Olympic Paris 2012 Landmark Int Competition 2002, Best Work First-time Exhibitor (for Royal Acad Summer Show) 2005 and 2006, The Worshipful Soc Best Drawing Prize (for Royal Acad Summer Show) 2006, Environmental Design Research Assoc USA Best Planning Award 2009; *Books* Sins and Other Spatial Relatives (2000), Realms of Impossibility: Air, Ground and Water: 3 Volumes (2002), How Green Is Your Garden (2003), Museums (2004), CJ Lim/Studio 8 (2005), Devices (2005), Virtually Venice (2006), Smartcities and Ecowarriors (2010), Short Stories: London in Two-and-a-Half Dimensions (2011), Food City (2014), Inhabitable Infrastructures: Urban future or science fiction? (2017); *Style—* Prof CJ Lim; ✉ Bartlett School of Architecture UCL, Wates House, 22 Gordon Street, London WC1H 0QB (☎ 020 7679 4842, website www.cjlim-studio8.com)

LIMB, Sue; da of Lewis Wilfred Limb and Margaret Winifred, *née* Andrew; *b* 12 September 1946; *Educ* Pate's GS for Girls Cheltenham, Newnham Coll Cambridge (scholarship, BA); *m* 1, 1970 (m dis 1979), Roy Sydney Porter; m 2, 1984 (m dis 1991), Jan Vriend; 1 da (Elisabeth Susanna b 18 Feb 1985); *Career* researcher Cambridge 1968–70, clerk Halifax Building Soc 1970, kitchen asst Corpus Christi Cambridge 1971, teacher of English and drama 1971–75; writer and broadcaster 1976–; columnist: Good Housekeeping 1986–91, The Guardian (under name of Dulcie Domum) 1988–2001; author of numerous articles, children's books, etc; memb Green Party, Euro Parly candidate (Green) Cotswolds 1989; *Books* Captain Oates – Soldier and Explorer (biography, with Patrick Cordingley, 1982, reprinted 1995), Up the Garden Path (novel and radio and TV series, 1984), Love Forty (novel, 1986), The Wordsmiths at Gorsemere (book and radio series, 1987), Love's Labours (novel, 1989), Me Jane (teenage novel, 1989), Big Trouble (teenage novel, 1990), Bad Housekeeping (1990), Sheep's Eyes and Hogwash (1992), Come Back Grandma (1993), Dulcie Dishes the Dirt (1994), Passion Fruit (1995), Enlightenment (1997), Girl, 15, Charming but Insane (2004), Girl (Nearly) 16: Absolute Torture (2005), Girl 16: Pants on Fire (2006), Ruby Rogers Is a Waste of Space (2006), Ruby Rogers: Yeah Whatever... (2006), Girl, 15, Flirting for England (2007), Zoe and Chloe: On the Prowl (2007), Ruby Rogers is a Walking Legend (2007), Ruby Rogers: Get a Life! (2007); *Recreations* muck-raking, mostly literal; *Style—* Ms Sue Limb; ✉ c/o United Agents Ltd, 12–26 Lexington Street, London W1F 0LE (☎ 020 3214 0800, fax 020 3214 0801, website www.unitedagents.co.uk); e-mail suelimb@btinternet.com, website www.suelimb.com

LIMEBEER, Prof David John Noel; s of Gerald John Limebeer (d 1988), and Joan Constance Limebeer (d 1997); *b* 31 July 1952; *Educ* Univ of the Witwatersrand (BSc), Univ of Natal (MSc, PhD), Univ of London (DSc); *Partner* Prof Suzanne Margaret Watt; *Career* asst engr Johannesburg City Cncl SA 1974–76, temp lectr Univ of Natal SA 1976–80, research assoc Univ of Cambridge 1980–84; Imperial Coll London: lectr 1984–89, reader 1989–93, prof of Control Engineering 1993–, head of Control Section 1996–99, head Electrical and Electronic Engrg Dept 1999–; sr motorcyclist instr IAM 1997; FREng 1997, FIEE 1994, FIEEE 1992; *Books* Linear Robust Control (co-ed 1995); *Recreations* motorcycling, antique lamp collecting, gym, table tennis; *Clubs* Middlesex Advanced Motorcyclists; *Style—* Prof David Limebeer, FREng; ✉ 4 Hollingbourne Gardens, Ealing, London W13 8EN (☎ 020 8998 5174, fax 020 8998 5174)

LIMERICK, 7 Earl of (I 1803); Edmund Christopher Pery; also Baron Glentworth (I 1790), Viscount Limerick (I 1800), Baron Foxford (UK 1815); s of 6 Earl of Limerick, KBE, DL (d 2003); *b* 10 February 1963; *Educ* Eton, New Coll Oxford, Pushkin Inst Moscow, City Univ; *m* 1, 21 July 1990 (m dis 2000), Emily, o da of Michael Gavin Lynam Thomas, of Worcester; 2 s (Felix Edmund, Viscount Pery b 16 Nov 1991, Hon Ivo Patrick b 26 Oct 1993); m 2, 13 July 2002 (m dis 2010), Lydia Ann Johnson; m 3, 1 July 2012, Kate Mary Inglis Hall; 1 s (Hon Basil Alexander b 5 Sept 2012), 1 da (Lady Phoebe Titania b 24 June 2014); *Heir* s, Viscount Pery; *Career* called to the Bar Middle Temple 1987; HM Dip Serv: FCO 1987–88, École Nationale d'Administration 1988–89, Quai d'Orsay 1990, second sec Dakar 1990–91, Amman 1991–92, resigned 1992; Clifford Chance slrs 1992–93, Freshfields slrs 1993–94, Milbank Tweed slrs Moscow 1994–96, dir Deutsche Bank AG Moscow, London and Dubai 1996–2004, Dubai International Capital 2005, ptnr Altima Partners LLP 2005–09, chm ESL UK Ltd 2010–13, chm Thermotec South East Ltd 2012–14; dir: Saddleback Corporation Ltd 2007–11, Chagala Gp Ltd 2009–13, Roxi Petroleum 2010–, Eagle iii Ltd 2016–; *Recreations* tennis, skiing, kitesurfing, wine; *Clubs* Sussex, Garrick; *Style—* The Earl of Limerick; ✉ Chiddinglye, West Hoathly, East Grinstead, West Sussex RH19 4QT (☎ 07852 942991, e-mail eclimerick@hotmail.com)

LINACRE, Nigel Guy Thornton; s of Vivian Thornton Linacre, of Edinburgh, and Joan Linacre; *b* 21 August 1957; *Educ* George Heriot's Sch, Imberhorne Sch, Univ of Reading (BA); *m* 1979, Sue, da of Ronald Farish; 2 da (Charlotte Lucy, Cordelia Mary), 2 s (Thomas Edward Benedict, George Henry Michael); *Career* account exec Charles Barker 1979–82, account mangr Collett Dickenson Pearce Financial 1982–85, advertising dir Boase Massimi Pollit Business 1985–87, exec dir Collett Dickenson Pearce Financial 1987–89, dir Charles Barker 1989–92, md Charles Barker Advertising 1989–92, dir Interactive Telephone Services 1992–95, dir ITS Group plc 1993–95, md Linacre Communications Ltd 1998–, chm SureTrack Monitoring plc 2007–11, dir Linacre Land 2007–11, dir Extraordinary Leadership 2008–, chm WellBoring 2011–, dir Lead-Now 2014–, dir Lead-Direct 2014–; exec coach Inside Out 2005–09; Parly candidate (Cons): Ealing Southall 1983, N Cornwall 1997; affiliate Centre for Leadership Studies 2012–; Freeman of Chippenham; *Books* Advertising For Account Handlers (1987), The Successful Executive (1997), Recipes for Happiness (2007), Why You Are Here – Briefly (2010), Knock Knock, Who's God? (2012), An Introduction to 3-Dimensional Leadership with Jefferson Cann (2012), The Other Side of You (2015), Why Men Can't Feel (2015), The Magic of Existence (2015), Leadership Paradoxes (co-ed, 2016); author of articles in European Jl and for the International Leadership Assoc among others, and occassional broadcasting; *Style—* Nigel Linacre, Esq; ✉ 51 St Mary Street, Chippenham, Wiltshire SN15 3JW (☎ 01249 654615, e-mail nigellinacre@hotmail.com, websites www.xleadership.com, www.leadnow.net, www.wellboring.org and www.whyyouareherebriefly.org, www.lead-direct.com)

LINAKER, Dr Barry David; s of Allan Lawrence Linaker (d 1973), and Gwendoline, *née* Higgs; *b* 7 April 1947; *Educ* Wigan GS, KCH Med Sch Univ of London (MB BS, MD); *m* 14 April 1973, Carol Yvonne, da of Lt Cdr John Michael Ogden, of Sunningdale, nr Ascot; 2 da (Emma b 1975, Amanda b 1979); *Career* MRC res fell and sr registrar in gastroenterology Univ Dept of Med Hope Hosp Manchester 1978–80, sr registrar in med Liverpool 1980–81, conslt physician and gastroenterologist Warrington Hosp 1981, ret from NHS; currently private conslt gastroenterologist North Cheshire Hosp; author of papers in various jls especially on mechanisms of histamine stimulated secretion in rabbit ileal mucosa in gut; memb: Br Soc of Gastroenterology, Liverpool Med Inst, N Eng Gastro Soc, Merseyside and N Wales Physicians; memb BMA, FRCP 1989; *Recreations* sailing, clay pigeon shooting, golf, reading, travel; *Clubs* Port Dinorwic Sailing; *Style—* Dr Barry Linaker

LINAKER, Lawrence Edward (Paddy); s of late Lawrence Wignall Linaker, and Rose, *née* Harris; *b* 22 July 1934; *Educ* Malvern; *m* 1963, (Elizabeth) Susan, *née* Elam; 1 s (Sam), 1 da (decd); *Career* with Esso Petroleum 1957–63; M & G Group plc: joined 1963, dep chm and chief exec 1987–94, chm M & G Investment Management Ltd 1987–94; chm Marling Industries plc 1996–97, non-exec chm Fisons plc 1994–95; non-exec dir: Securities Inst 1992–94, Lloyds TSB Group plc 1994–2001, Fleming Mercantile Investment Trust plc 1994–, SAUL Trustee Company 1994–99, Wolverhampton and Dudley Breweries plc 1996–2002; chm: Institutional Fund Managers Assoc 1992–94, YMCA Nat Coll 1992–2000, Fleming Technol Investment Trust 1997–2001; dir Childline 1992–2000 (treas 1994–2000); memb Cncl RPMS 1977–89; memb Governing Body: SPCK 1976–94, Malvern Coll 1989–2003, Canterbury Christchurch Coll 1992–98; memb Ct Imperial Coll London 1998–; tstee: Lloyds TSB Fndn for England and Wales 1994–2001, Carnegie UK Tst 1995–; *Recreations* music and gardening; *Clubs* Athenaeum, Brooks's; *Style—* Paddy Linaker, Esq; ✉ Swyre Farm, Aldsworth, Cheltenham, Gloucestershire

LINCOLN, Andrew (né Andrew James Clutterbuck); *b* 14 September 1973, London; *Educ* RADA; *Career* actor; *Television* incl: This Life 1996–97, Teachers 2001–03, Canterbury Tales 2003, Afterlife 2005–06, Wuthering Heights 2009, Strike Back 2010, The Walking Dead 2010–; *Film* incl: Love Actually 2003, Scenes of a Sexual Nature 2006, Made in Dagenham 2010; *Theatre* incl: Sugar (Bush Theatre), Hushabye Mountain (Hampstead Theatre and tour), Blue/Orange (NT and West End), Free (NT), The Late Henry Moss (Almeida), Parlour Song (Almeida) 2009; *Style—* Mr Andrew Lincoln; ✉ c/o Markham Froggatt and Irwin, 4 Windmill Street, London W1T 2HZ

LINCOLN, Bishop of 2011–; Rt Rev Christopher Lowson; s of George Frederick Lowson, of Lanchester, Durham, and Isabella Annie, *née* Spence; *b* 3 February 1953, Consett, Co Durham; *Educ* Newcastle Cathedral Sch, Consett GS, KCL (AKC), St Augustine's Coll Canterbury, Pacific Sch of Religion Berkeley CA (STM), Heythrop Coll London (MTh), Cardiff Law Sch (LLM); *m* 1976, Susan Mary, da of William James Osborne; 1 s (James b 1980), 1 da (Rebecca b 1982); *Career* ordained: deacon 1977, priest 1978; asst curate Richmond Surrey 1977–82, chaplain Avery Hill Coll of Educn 1982–85, vicar Holy Trinity Eltham 1983–91 (priest-in-charge 1982–83), chaplain to the Guild of St Bride Fleet Street 1983–, chaplain Thames Poly 1985–91, vicar Petersfield and rector Buriton Hants 1991–99, rural dean of Petersfield 1995–99, archdeacon of Portsdown 1999–2006; fndn tstee Gallipoli Meml Lecture Tst 1985–91, chm Portsmouth Diocesan Bd of Ministry, Bishop of Portsmouth's liaison offr for prisons 1999–2003, Bishop of Portsmouth's advsr to hosp chaplaincy 2003–06, archdeacon emeritus of Portsmouth 2006–, priest vicar Westminster Abbey 2007–11; dir Portsmouth Educn Business Partnership 1999–2006, visiting lectr Univ of Portsmouth 199–2006, memb Ecclesiastical Law Soc 1999–, die of miny Archbishops' Cncl of the C of E 2006–11; *Recreations* watching cricket, theatre; *Clubs* MCC, Athenaeum, RAC, Castle Hill (Lincoln); *Style—* The Rt Rev the Bishop of Lincoln; ✉ Bishop's Office, The Old Palace, Minster Yard, Lincoln LN2 1PU

LINCOLN, Prof Paul; OBE (2008); s of William Edward Lincoln, and Lucy Elizabeth Sillett; *b* 13 March 1955, Norwich, Norfolk; *Educ* Univ of Leicester (BSc), Univ of Birmingham (CertEd, Dip), Univ of Leeds (Dip); *Partner* Velena Gilfilian; 2 s (Aaron b 16 Nov 1996, Jordan b 20 Aug 1998); *Career* scientific researcher MAFF 1976, teacher 1976–80, health promotion offr Wolverhampton HA 1980–84, dir of health promotion servs Birmingham HA 1984–89, dir Health Educ Authy 1989–2000, ceo UK Health Forum (formerly National Heart Forum) 2000–; chair Public Health Guidance Review Ctee NICE, non-exec memb Bd Public Health England; visiting prof Chester Univ; Best Student Mgmnt Award DCMS; Hon MRCP, hon memb Assoc of Dirs of Public Health, professorial fell Royal Soc for Public Health; *Recreations* sport, art, antiques; *Style—* Professor Paul Lincoln, OBE; ✉ UK Health Forum, Fleetbank House, 2–6 Salisbury Square, London EC4Y 8JX (e-mail paul.lincoln@ukhealthforum.org.uk)

LINDLEY, Dr Bryan Charles; CBE (1982); s of Wing Cdr Alfred Webb Lindley (d 1988), of Lichfield, and Florence, *née* Pratten (d 1975); *b* 30 August 1932; *Educ* Reading Sch, UCL (BSc(Eng), PhD); *m* 2 May 1987, Dr Judith Anne Heyworth, da of Robert Heyworth, of Bramhall; 1 s ((John) Julian b 1960); *Career* Nat Gas Turbine Estab 1954–57, Hawker Siddeley Nuclear Power Co Ltd 1957–59, International Research and Development Company Ltd and CA Parsons Nuclear Res Centre 1959–65, mangr R&D Div CA Parsons & Co Ltd 1965–68, chief exec and md ERA Technology Ltd 1968–79 (concurrently chm ERA Patents Ltd and ERA Autotrack Systems Ltd), dir of technol Dunlop Holdings plc and dir Dunlop Ltd 1979–85, dir of technol and planning BICC Cables Ltd 1985–88, chm Optical Fibres, chief exec Nat Advanced Robotics Res Centre 1989–90, chm and chief exec Lord Lindley Associates 1990–; former chm: Dunlop Bioprocesses Ltd, Thermal Conversions (UK) Ltd, Soilless Cultivation Systems Ltd; dir: Thomas Bolton & Johnson Ltd 1985–88, RAPRA Technol Ltd 1985–97, Settle-Carlisle Railway Development Co 1991–93, J+B Imaging 1998–; chm N Lakeland Healthcare NHS Tst 1993–97; visiting prof Univ of Liverpool 1989–; memb: ACARD 1980–86, Materials Advsy Gp DTI 1984; fell UCL 1979; FIMechE 1968, FIET (FIEE 1968), FInstP 1969, FPRI 1980; *Recreations* music, photography, reading, travel, walking, skiing, sailing; *Style—* Dr Bryan Lindley, CBE; ✉ Lindenthwaite, Beacon Edge, Penrith, Cumbria CA11 8BN (☏ 01768 890652)

LINDLEY, Dr David; OBE (1998); s of William Lindley (d 1980), and Millicent, *née* Caine; *b* 26 June 1939; *Educ* Manchester Central GS, Univ of Salford (Gen Sir William Platt prize, BSc), Univ of Wales (PhD), Univ of Cambridge (Cert Advanced Engrg Design); *m* 14 July 1962, Dorothy, da of John Turnock; 3 s (Simon David b 11 April 1963 d 1993, Nicolas Rhys b 17 Nov 1964, Jonathan Peter b 3 Oct 1969), 1 da (Sarah Jane Kirsty b 31 Dec 1974); *Career* mangr Pump Experimental Dept Mather & Platt Ltd Manchester 1962–63 (apprentice 1955–62), head Turbo Machinery Aero-thermodynamics Dept CEGB 1967–70, sr lectr in mech engrg Univ of Canterbury NZ 1970–75, res fell UKAEA 1975–, mangr Energy Systems Gp Jet Propulsion Laboratory Caltech 1975–76, sr lectr Univ of Canterbury NZ 1976–78; Taylor Woodrow plc: joined 1978, md Wind Energy Gp Ltd 1979–91, dir of Taywood Engineering Ltd 1984–90, vice-pres US WEG Inc 1986–91, divnl dir Taylor Woodrow Construction Ltd 1987–91, memb Severn Tidal Power Gp Mgmnt and Supervisory Bd 1987–91, dir Taylor Woodrow Management and Engineering Ltd 1988–91; md National Wind Power Ltd 1991–96, chm Ocean Power Delivery Ltd 2002–05 (non-exec dir 2005–09), non-exec dir KP Renewables plc 2004–07; dir: Euro Wind Energy Assoc 1980–96 (pres 1986–89), British Wind Energy Assoc 1980–96 (chm 1982 and 1994); memb: Advsy Cncl for R&D for Fuel and Power 1986–92, Renewable Energy Advsy Gp 1991–92, Electrical Engrg Coll of Peers EPSRC 1993–96, Professional Bodies Advsy Gp Design Cncl 1995–99, Exec Bd Royal Acad of Engrg Educn Prog 2001–, Advsy Cncl SAM Private Equity Sustainability Fund II Switzerland 2006–; visiting prof: Loughborough Univ of Technol, De Montfort Univ 1994–2003, Univ of Nottingham 1997–2003; academician Russian Int Higher Educn Acad of Science; MASME, memb American Inst of Aeronautics and Astronautics, FIMechE, FRMetS, FREng 1993, FRSA; *Awards* incl: James Watt medal ICE 1987, Stephenson medal Univ of Newcastle 1989, Melchett medal Inst of Energy 1990, Industry Award BWEA 1995, President's Award BWEA 1996, EU and Univ of Florence Renewable Energy Res Award World Renewable Energy Congress 2006; *Recreations* walking, skiing, collecting, sailing, photography, reading, music; *Style—* Dr David Lindley, OBE, FREng, FRSA; ✉ Lindley Associates, Woodfield, Farm Lane, Jordans, Beaconsfield, Buckinghamshire HP9 2UP (☏ 01494 676570, e-mail davidlindleyobe@gmail.com)

LINDLEY, Richard Howard Charles; s of Lt-Col (Herbert) Guy Lindley (d 1976), of Winchester, Hants, and Dorothea Helen Penelope Hatchell (d 1996); *b* 25 April 1936; *Educ* Bedford Sch, Queens' Coll Cambridge (exhibitioner, BA, chm Film Soc); *m* 1, 1976 (m dis 1986), Clare Fehrsen; 2 c (Thomas Paul Guy b 29 Dec 1977, Joanna Frances Eleanor b 12 April 1979); m 2, 1999, Carole, da of Harry Stone and Kathleen Stone; *Career* Nat Serv: 2 Lt Royal Hampshire Regt, served Malaya Emergency; prodr TV commercials Foote Cone and Belding 1960–62, reporter presenter and newscaster Southern TV Southampton 1963–64, reporter ITN (in Vietnam, Nigeria, Zimbabwe, Egypt and Israel) 1964–72, reporter and presenter Panorama and Saturday Briefing BBC Current Affairs Gp 1972–88, sr prog offr IBA 1988, reporter and presenter This Week (Thames TV) 1989–92; presenter: ITN World News 1992–94, Special Reports ITN News at Ten 1995–99; pres The Media Soc 2002–03, chm Voice of the Listener and Viewer 2008–10; govr Royal Free NHS Tst; dir Lindley Stone Ltd; chm St Pancras Almshouses; *Books* Panorama – Fifty Years of Pride and Paranoia (2002), And Finally...? The News from ITN (2005); *Recreations* friends, food, familiar films; *Clubs* RTS; *Style—* Richard Lindley; ✉ 46 Oak Village, London NW5 4QL (☏ 020 7267 5870, e-mail linstone@btinternet.com)

LINDOP, Dr Michael John; s of Donald Frederick Lindop (d 2005), of Birmingham, and Phyllis Alice, *née* Burrows (d 1992); *b* 29 July 1942; *Educ* King Edward Sch Birmingham, Gonville & Caius Coll Cambridge (MA), Guy's Hosp (MB, BChir), FRCA 1971; *m* 16 Aug 1968, Kari, da of Per Brachel (d 1955), of Oslo, Norway; 3 da (Tanya b 1971, Michelle b 1973, Anne-Lise b 1978), 1 s (Tom b 1969); *Career* sr registrar Westminster Hosp 1969–74, instr Univ of Washington Seattle USA 1973, conslt in anaesthesia and intensive care 1974–, formerly dir anaesthesia servs Addenbrooke's Hosp; formerly examiner Royal Coll of Anaesthetists; pres Liver Intensive Care Gp of Europe 1996–2002; memb: Intensive Care Soc, Anaesthetic Res Soc; *Books* Anesthesia and Intensive Care for Organ Transplantation (ed with Dr J R Klinck, 1997); *Recreations* racquet control, weed control; *Style—* Dr Michael Lindop; ✉ Department of Anaesthesia, Box 93, Addenbrooke's Hospital, Cambridge CB2 2QQ (☏ 01223 217433, fax 01223 217223, e-mail mikelindop@doctors.org.uk)

LINDRUP, Garth; s of Viggo H Lindrup (d 1957), and Betty, *née* Ashworth (d 1995); *b* 10 September 1948, S Africa; *Educ* Wrekin Coll, Manchester Poly (BA), St John's Coll Cambridge (LLM); *m* 1991, Julie, *née* Topham; 2 s (Oliver b 11 Oct 1991, James b 22 June 1994); *Career* admitted slr 1975; articled clerk then asst slr Leak Almond & Parkinson 1973–77, sole practitioner 1978–79; Addleshaw Goddard (formerly Addleshaw Sons & Latham then Addleshaw Booth & Co): asst slr 1979–84, ptnr 1984–2004, conslt 2004–12 and 2014–; chm Law Soc European Gp 1994–95, hon lectr in law Univ of Manchester; memb: Competition Panel CBI, Competition Ctee ICC; memb: Law Soc 1975, Int Bar Assoc 1989, Ligue Internationale du Droit de la Concurrence 1985; FRSA; Butterworths Competition Law Handbook (ed, 1987–2010), Butterworths Public Procurement & CCT Handbook (ed, 1997), Butterworths PFI Manual (jt gen ed, 1998–2010), Solicitors in the Single Market (ed), Butterworths Expert Guide to the European Union (contrib), author of numerous articles in jls and other pubns; *Recreations* gardening, theatre, reading, fell walking; *Clubs* Manchester Tennis & Rackets; *Style—* Garth Lindrup, Esq; ✉ Garlin Associates Ltd, Wray, Lancaster LA2 8QT

LINDSAY, Andrew James Ronald; MBE (2001); s of Lt-Col S J Lindsay, of Acharacle, Argyll, and Ann, *née* Powell; *b* 25 March 1977; *Educ* Eton (scholar, capt of boats), BNC Oxford (scholar, BA, Rowing blue); *m* Lady Amy Jane, *née* Gordon; *Career* competitive career: jr int rower 1994 and 1995, pres OUBC 1998 (rowed in univ boat race 1997, 1998 and 1999), Gold medal men's eights Olympic Games Sydney 2000; memb Team of the Year BBC Sports Personality of the Year Awards 2000; currently chief operating offr and memb Exec Bd Telecom Plus plc; non-exec dir Ryness Electrical Supplies; tstee: Harry Mahon Cancer Research Tst, Dorney Rowing Lake; *Recreations* skiing, windsurfing, bagpipe playing; *Clubs* Vincent's (Oxford), Phoenix Soc (Oxford), Boodle's; *Style—* Andrew Lindsay, Esq, MBE; ✉ Invermoidart, Acharacle, Argyll PH36 4LR (☏ 07900 087595, e-mail alindsay@telecomplus.co.uk)

LINDSAY, HE Iain Ferrier; OBE (2002); James Lindsay, and Margaret Lindsay; *b* 9 March 1959, Falkirk; *Educ* John Lyon Sch, Edinburgh Acad, Univ of Glasgow; *m* Bridget; 1 s; *Career* diplomat; desk offr Aid Policy Dept FCO 1980–81, visa offr Warsaw then Doha 1982–83, asst mgmnt offr Tokyo 1983–86, third then second sec political Canberra 1986–89, Australia desk offr S Pacific Dept FCO 1989–91, head Baltic Unit Eastern Dept FCO 1991–94, first sec political Tokyo 1994–99, dep head S Asian Dept FCO 1999–2002, secondment as foreign policy advsr to Romanian Foreign Min Mircea Geoana 2003, dep head of mission and political counsellor Bucharest 2003–07, dep head of mission and dir trade and investment Hong Kong 2007–11, ambass to Bahrain 2011–15, ambass designate to Hungary 2015–; *Recreations* travel, cinema, history, sport (skiing, golf, cricket), Stenhousemuir FC; *Clubs* Caledonian; *Style—* HE Mr Iain Lindsay, OBE; ✉ c/o Foreign and Commonwealth Office (Budapest), King Charles Street, London SW1A 2AH

LINDSAY, 16 Earl of (S 1633); James Randolph Lindesay-Bethune; also Lord Lindsay of the Byres (S 1445), Lord Parbroath (S 1633), Viscount Garnock, and Lord Kilbirnie, Kingsburn and Drumry (both S 1703); s of 15 Earl of Lindsay (d 1989), by his 1 w, Mary, *née* Douglas-Scott-Montagu; *b* 19 November 1955; *Educ* Eton, Univ of Edinburgh (MA), Univ of Calif Davis; *m* 2 March 1982, Diana Mary, er da of Nigel Chamberlayne-Macdonald, LVO, OBE, of Cranbury Park, Winchester; 3 da (Lady Frances Mary b 1986, Lady Alexandra Penelope b 1988, Lady Charlotte Diana b 1993), 2 s (William James, Viscount Garnock b 1990, Hon David Nigel (twin) b 1993); *Heir* s, Viscount Garnock; *Career* involved with the environment and the food industry; vice-chm Inter-Parly Union Ctee on Environment 1994–95 (memb 1993), Parly under sec of state Scottish Office 1995–97; chm: Landscape Fndn 1992–95, Assured British Meat Ltd 1997–2001, Scottish Quality Salmon (SQS) 1998–2006, RSPB Scotland 1998–2003, Elmwood Coll Bd of Mgmnt 2001–09, UKAS (UK Accreditation Serv) 2002–, Moorland Forum 2007–, Greenfield Hldgs Ltd 2009–11, Br Polythene Pension Scheme Tstees 2009–; md MSCI (Marine Stewardship Cncl Int) 2001–04; non-exec dir: UA Gp plc 1998–2005, Scottish Resources Gp Ltd (formerly Mining (Scottish) Ltd) 2001–13, Scottish Agricultural College Ltd 2005– (dep chm 2006–07, chm 2007–), British Polythene Industries plc 2006–; pres: Int Tree Fndn 1995–2005 (vice-pres 1993–95 and 2005–), RSGS 2005–12 (vice-pres 2004–05 and 2012–), Nat Tst for Scotland 2012–; vice-pres: Royal Smithfield Club 1999–, RSPB 2004–, Trading Standards Inst 2011–; memb: Advsy Panel Railway Heritage Tst, Select Ctee on Sustainable Devpt 1994–95, World Resource Fndn 1994–98, Bd Cairngorms

Partnership 1998–2003, UK Roundtable on Sustainable Devpt 1998–2000, Sec of State's Advsy Gp on Sustainable Devpt 1998–99, Better Regulation Cmmn 2006–08 (dep chair 2007–08), Cmmn on Scottish Devolution 2008–, Risk and Regulation Advsy Cncl 2008–10; oppn spokesman House of Lords 1997; associateship RAS 2000–; Hon DUniv Glasgow 2012; hon fell Inst of Waste Mgmnt 1998–; *Books* Garden Ornament (jtly), Trellis (1991); *Clubs* New (Edinburgh); *Style*— The Rt Hon the Earl of Lindsay; ✉ Lahill, Upper Largo, Fife KY8 6JE

LINDSAY, Nigel Marc; *b* London; *Educ* Merchant Taylors', Univ of Birmingham (BA), Webber Douglas Acad (Amherst Webber scholarship); *m* 2006, Laura, *née* Evans; 2 da (Mia b 2000, Hope b 2002); *Career* actor; memb BAFTA 2006; *Theatre* incl: King Lear (Royal Court) 1993, Mugsy in Dealer's Choice (NT and Vaudeville Theatre) 1995, Blue Remembered Hills (NT) 1996, London Cuckolds (NT) 1998, The Real Thing (Donmar Warehouse, Albery Theatre and Ethel Barrymore Theater Broadway) 2000, Bedroom Farce (Aldwych Theatre) 2002, The Tempest (Old Vic) 2003, World Music (Sheffield Crucible) 2003, Ariel in The Pillowman (NT) 2003, William Morris in The Earthly Paradise (Almeida Theatre) 2004, Nathan Detroit in Guys and Dolls (Piccadilly Theatre) 2005, Moe Axelrod in Awake and Sing (Almeida Theatre; nomination Best Supporting Actor Whatsonstage Award 2008), Lenny in The Homecoming (Almeida Theatre) 2008, Under the Blue Sky (Duke of Yorks Theatre) 2008, Sucker Punch (Royal Court) 2010, Dr Harry Hyman in Broken Glass (Tricycle Theatre) 2010 (Best Supporting Actor in a Play Whatsonstage Award 2011), Shrek in Shrek the Musical (Theatre Royal) 2011 (nominations Best Actor in a Musical Olivier Award and Whatsonstage Award 2012), The Same Deep Water As Me (Donmar Warehouse) 2013, Bolingbroke in Richard II (RSC) 2013, Jack McCracken in A Small Family Business (NT) 2014, Speed-the-Plow (Playhouse Theatre) 2014; *Television* incl: Bye Bye Baby, Between the Lines, Dressing for Breakfast 1995–98, Brass Eye, A Dance to the Music of Time, The Armando Iannucci Shows, Midsomer Murders, Déjà Vu, I'm Alan Partridge, Murphy's Law, Tunnel of Love, OK Corral, Rome, Jam & Jerusalem 2006–08, Relief of Belsen, Spooks, Best of Men, George Gently, The Fear, Poirot, The Tunnel 2013, Foyle's War 2014, Death in Paradise 2016; *Film* incl: Rogue Trader, Mike Bassett: England Manager, Blackball, On A Clear Day, Scoop, Barry in Four Lions 2010 (nomination Best Comedy Performance in Film Br Comedy Award 2010), First Night, Breakfast with Jonny Wilkinson, Alpha Papa 2013, Access All Areas 2016; *Style*— Nigel Lindsay, Esq; ✉ c/o Hamilton Hodell, 20 Golden Square, London W1F 9JL (☎ 020 7636 1221, e-mail info@hamiltonhodell.co.uk)

LINDSAY, Robert (né Robert Lindsay Stevenson); s of late Norman Stevenson, and Joyce Stevenson; *b* 13 December 1949, Ilkeston, Derbys; *Educ* RADA; *m* 1, 1974 (m dis 1980), Cheryl Hall; m 2, 2006, Rosemarie Ford; 2 s (Samuel b 1999, James b 2003); 1 da from a previous relationship with actress Diana Weston (Sydney Laura b 1988); *Career* actor; *Television* incl: Get Some In! 1975–77, Citizen Smith 1977–80, Twelfth Night 1980, A Midsummer Night's Dream 1981, Seconds Out 1981–82, Cymbeline 1982, King Lear 1983, Much Ado About Nothing 1984, Confessional 1989, Nightingales (Channel 4) 1990–93, GBH 1992 (Best Actor BAFTA Award 1992), Jake's Progress 1996 (nominated Best Actor BAFTA Award 1996), Brazen Hussies 1996, Hornblower (ITV) 1998–2003, Fagin in Oliver Twist (ITV) 1999, My Family (BBC 1) 2000–11 (nominated Best Comedy Performance BAFTA Award 2002), Friends and Crocodiles (BBC 1) 2005, Tony Blair in A Very Social Secretary (Channel 4) 2005, Gideon's Daughter (BBC 1) 2005, Jericho (ITV) 2005, Tony Blair in The Trial of Tony Blair (Channel 4) 2007, Spy 2010–12, Atlantis 2013–15, Bull 2015, Galavant 2016; *Theatre* Me and My Girl 1984 (Best Actor in a Musical Tony Award, Best Actor in a Musical Laurence Olivier Award), Becket (Theatre Royal Haymarket) 1991 (Variety Club Best Theatre Actor), Cyrano de Bergerac (Theatre Royal Haymarket) 1992, Fagin in Oliver! 1997 (Best Actor in a Musical Laurence Olivier Award 1997), Richard III (Savoy Theatre) 1998, Power (NT) 2003, The Entertainer (Old Vic) 2007, Onassis (Novello) 2010, The Lion In Winter (Haymarket) 2011, Dirty Rotten Scoundrels (Savoy Theatre) 2014; *Film* Wimbledon 2006, Grace of Monaco 2013; *Books* Letting Go (autobiography, 2009); *Style*— Robert Lindsay; ✉ c/o Christian Hodell, Hamilton Hodell Talent Management, 20 Golden Square, London W1F 9JL

LINDSAY, Russell Grant (Russ); s of David Alexander Lindsay, of Catisfield, Hants, and Evelyn, *née* Birrell; *b* 12 July 1961; *Educ* Hardyes GS Dorchester; *m* 1, 15 June 1991, Caron Louisa Keating (d 2004); 2 s (Charlie b 1994, Gabriel Don b 1997); m 2, 4 Sept 2006, Sally Jennifer Meen; 2 da (Tilly Jennifer b 2008, Flora Lottie b 2010); *Career* began career as DJ/Radio/TV broadcaster, co-prodr of TV progs, theatre and radio shows incl: Schofield's Quest, Dr Dolittle and the All Star Cup; dir James Grant Management Ltd (fndr with Peter Powell, *qv* 1984); mgmnt for: Ant & Dec, Simon Cowell and Phillip Schofield; currently fndr Infinity Creative Media Ltd 2013–, exec prodr: The Classic Car Show, The Wine Show, The AA Show, The Luxury Lifestyle Show, Hope (HIV) Classic Rally; memb Bd Alchemy Global Hldgs LLC; memb Ctee Br Inspiration Awards, chm Media Sector Debrett's 500 2014; *Recreations* sport, art, leisure; *Clubs* MSA Competition Race Driving Licence, Celtic Manor Golf, St George's Hill Tennis; *Style*— Russ Lindsay, Esq; ✉ Infinity Creative Media Ltd, 8 Riverbank, Hampton Court, Surrey KT8 9BH (☎ 020 8979 7939)

LINDSAY-FYNN, Nigel; s of Sir Basil Lindsay-Fynn (d 1988), and (Marion) Audrey Ellen, *née* Chapman (d 1991); *b* 4 May 1942; *Educ* Charterhouse, Oriel Coll Oxford (MA); *m* 12 May 1971, Heleen Vanda Mary, da of Bill Willson-Pemberton, of London; 2 s (Piers b 1975, Charles b 1989), 2 da (Miranda b 1978, Eleanor b 1981); *Career* fin dir: IRG plc 1991–2000, Stanley Davis Gp Ltd 2000–, Brady & Co Law Searchers Ltd Ireland 2008–; chm The Crescent Tst Co (private equity portfolio mgmnt and trusteeship); treas Oriel Soc 1977–2002, pres Devon Co Agric Assoc 2007 (treas 1995–), tstee Exeter Cathedral Preservation Tst and other charities; Master Worshipful Co of Painter-Stainers 2005–06; *Recreations* playing the piano and composing, sailing, skiing; *Clubs* Garrick, Buck's, City Livery, Royal Yacht Squadron, Kildare St and Univ Dublin, Royal Irish Yacht, Irish Cruising, Kinsale Yacht, City Livery Yacht; *Style*— Nigel Lindsay-Fynn, Esq; ✉ Lee Ford, Budleigh Salterton, Devon EX9 7AJ (☎ 01395 445894, fax 01395 441100, e-mail crescent@leeford.co.uk); 74 Bedford Gardens, London W8 7EH (☎ 020 7229 1684); Sea House, Kinsale, Co Cork, Ireland (☎ 00 353 21 4777098)

LINE, Matthew John Bardsley; s of John Line, of London, and Jill, *née* Rowland; *b* 22 April 1958; *Educ* Chiswick Sch, Univ of Exeter (BA); *m* 1987, Elinor, da of Ian Fairhurst; 2 da (Flora b 21 March 1992, Nancy b 17 July 1995); *Career* actor 1982; asst publisher Shepheard-Walwyn Publishers 1984–87, prodn dir Concertina Publications 1988, freelance journalist 1987–92, ed Up Country 1992–93, ed Dialogue 1993–95, launch ed Colour 1995, gp ed home interest titles Redwood Publishing 1996–97, ed Homes & Gardens 1997–2002, chief exec The Prince's Fndn 2002–04, ed-in-chief National Magazines 2004–, launch ed new She 2005–06, editorial conslt Rich magazine 2006, editorial dir Craft Publishing 2007–10, md Craft London 2010–, md Rivington Bye 2015–; launched Homes & Gardens V&A Classic Design Awards 1999; memb Ctee BSME 2001–02; *Books* Homes & Gardens Book of Design (2001); *Recreations* family, philosophy, gardening; *Style*— Matthew Line, Esq; ✉ 3 Albemarle Way, London EC1V 4JB

LINEKER, Gary Winston; OBE (1992); s of Barry Lineker, of Wigston, Leicester, and Margaret Patricia Morris, *née* Abbs; *b* 30 November 1960; *Educ* City of Leicester Boys' GS; *m* 1, 5 July 1986 (m dis), Michelle Denise, da of Roger Edwin Cockayne, of Leicester; 4 s (George b 2 Oct 1991, Harry b 25 July 1993, Tobias b 3 Feb 1996, Angus b 5 Aug 1997); m 2, 2 Sept 2009, Danielle Bux; *Career* former professional footballer, currently journalist and broadcaster; clubs: Leicester City 1978–85 (215 appearances, 100 goals), Everton 1985–86 (57 appearances, 40 goals), FC Barcelona 1986–89 (140 appearances, 54 goals), Tottenham Hotspur 1989–92 (139 appearances, 80 goals, FA Cup winners 1991), Grampus 8 Nagoya, Japan 1993–94, ret 1994; England: debut 1984, 80 caps, 48 goals, capt 1990–92, memb squad World Cup Mexico 1986 (leading goal scorer) and Italy 1990, memb squad European Championships W Germany 1988 and Sweden 1992, ret 1992; PFA Player of the Year 1986, Football Writers' Assoc Player of the Year 1986 and 1992; memb Sports Cncl 1995–; host Gary Lineker's Football Night (BBC Radio 5) 1992, team capt They Think It's All Over (BBC 1) 1995–2003, presenter Match of the Day (BBC 1) 1999–; columnist The Sunday Telegraph 1998–2007; Best Presenter RTS Sports Awards 2002 and 2004, Sports Presenter of the Year TRIC Awards 2003, 2006, 2007 and 2009; Hon MA: Univ of Leicester 1992, Loughborough Univ 1992; *Recreations* cricket, golf; *Clubs* MCC, Groucho; *Style*— Gary Lineker, Esq, OBE

LING, Norman Arthur; s of William Arthur Ling (d 1998), and Helma, *née* Blum; *b* 12 August 1952; *Educ* Caldy Grange GS West Kirby, Univ of Sheffield (BA); *m* 12 May 1979, Selma, *née* Osman; *Career* employed in shipping industry 1975–78; FCO: joined 1978, second sec (commercial) Tripoli 1980–81, second rising to first sec Tehran 1981–84, dep consul-gen Johannesburg 1988–92, dep head of mission Ankara 1993–97, high cmmr to Malawi 2001–04, dir for change FCO 2005–07, ambass to Ethiopia, Djibouti and African Union 2008–11; *Recreations* walking, gardening, travel; *Style*— Mr Norman Ling

LINGARD, Brian Hallwood; s of Capt Abel Keenan Lingard, MC (d 1955), of Wanstead, London, and Elsie May Lingard, BEM; *b* 2 November 1926; *Educ* Stockport GS, Manchester Sch of Architecture (DA); *m* 20 July 1949, Dorothy Gladys Lingard, da of Capt Herbert Clay (d 1978), of Bramhall, Cheshire; 2 s (Christopher b 1951, Timothy b 1953), 1 da (Rebecca b 1960); *Career* RN 1944–46; served: HMS Wolverine, Gibraltar 1944–45; architect; commenced private practice 1950; ptnr: Brian Lingard & Partners 1972–93, Lingard Styles Landscape (landscape architects) 1975–, Gallery Lingard (architectural historians) 1982–98; professional awards incl: RIBA Regnl Award (Wales), DOE and RIBA Housing Medal (7 awards), Civic Tst (21 awards), The Times/RICS Conservation Award (2 awards), Prince of Wales Conservation Award (3 awards); vice-pres Architects Benevolent Soc 2002– (chm 1988–92); FRIBA 1957 (ARIBA 1949); *Books* The Opportunities for the Conservation and Enhancement of our Historic Resorts (1983), Special Houses for Special People (2004), Thrifty Homes for Thrifty People (2009), All the Rest of the Bricks and Mortar (2013); *Recreations* swimming, writing, old buildings; *Clubs* Carlton, RAC; *Style*— Brian Lingard; ✉ Le Bouillon House, St George's Esplanade, St Peter Port, Guernsey (☎ 01481 700244); Lingard Styles Landscape, 9 College Hill, Shrewsbury SY1 1LZ (☎ 01743 233961)

LINGARD, Joan Amelia; MBE (1999); da of Henry James Lingard (d 1963), and Elizabeth Cunningham Beattie (d 1948); *b* 8 April 1932; *Educ* Bloomfield Collegiate Sch Belfast, Moray House Coll of Educn Edinburgh; *m* Martin Birkhans; 3 da (Kersten, Bridget, Jennifer); *Career* author; cncl memb Scottish Arts Cncl 1980–85 (memb Lit Ctee 1980–85); hon fell Assoc of Scottish Literary Studies 2013; memb: PEN (hon pres Scottish PEN 2013), Soc of Authors (chm Scotland 1982–86), Bd Edinburgh Book Festival 1994–; 60 novels for adults and children incl *Adult Novels* Liam's Daughter, The Prevailing Wind, The Tide Comes In, The Headmaster, A Sort of Freedom, The Lord on Our Side, The Second Flowering of Emily Mountjoy, Greenyards, Sisters By Rite, Reasonable Doubts, The Women's House, After Colette, Dreams of Love, Modest Glory, The Kiss, Encarnita's Journey, After You're Gone; *Children's Novels* The Twelfth Day of July, Across The Barricades, Into Exile, A Proper Place, Hostages to Fortune, The Clearance, The Resettling, The Pilgrimage, The Reunion, Snake Among the Sunflowers, Frying As Usual, The Gooseberry, The File on Fraulein Berg, Strangers in the House, The Winter Visitor, The Freedom Machine, The Guilty Party, Rags and Riches, Tug of War, Glad Rags, Between Two Worlds, Hands Off Our School!, Night Fires, Lizzie's Leaving, Dark Shadows, A Secret Place, Tom and the Treehouse, The Egg Thieves, River Eyes, Natasha's Will, Me and My Shadow, Tortoise Trouble, The Sign of the Black Dagger, The Eleventh Orphan, The Chancery Lane Conspiracy, The Stolen Sister, What to Do About Holly, What Holly Did; *Awards* Scottish Arts Cncl bursary 1967–68, Buxtehuder Bülle Award for children's lit Germany 1986, Scottish Arts Cncl Award 1994, Scottish Arts Cncl Book Award 1999, shorlisted Saltire Soc Award; *Style*— Ms Joan Lingard, MBE; ✉ c/o David Higham Associates Ltd, 5–8 Lower John Street, Golden Square, London W1R 4HA (☎ 020 7437 7888, fax 020 7437 1072)

LINGENS, Michael Robert; s of Dr Friedrich Otto Lingens, of Hamburg, Germany, and Karin Weber; *b* 15 May 1957; *Educ* St Edmund's Sch Canterbury, Trinity Coll Oxford (MA); *m* 9 May 1992 (m dis 2008), Rachel, da of Charles Fay (d 1998), and Patricia Fay, OBE; 1 s (Matthew b 20 Sept 1995); *Career* admitted slr 1982, ptnr Charles Russell Speechlys (formerly Speechly Bircham, managing ptnr 1998–2013), chm Bow Group 1984–85; cncllr London Borough of Hammersmith and Fulham 1982–86; Parly candidate (Cons) Bolsover 1987; *Books* Beveridge and The Bow Group Generation, Winning on Welfare; *Recreations* real tennis, rackets, skiing; *Clubs* Queen's; *Style*— Michael Lingens, Esq; ✉ 49 Ashlar Court, Ravenscourt Park, London W6 0TU (☎ 07768 608783, e-mail michael.lingens@crsblaw.com)

LINGFIELD, Baron (Life Peer UK 2010), of Lingfield in the County of Surrey; Sir Robert George Alexander Balchin; kt (1993), DL (2001); s of Leonard George Balchin (d 1968), and Elizabeth, *née* Skelton (d 1997); the Balchin family settled in Surrey c 1190, Sir Roger de Balchen owning lands in both Normandy and Surrey, Adm Sir John Balchin (1669–1744) was Adm of the White and Governor of Greenwich RN Hosp; *b* 31 July 1942, Dulverton, Somerset; *Educ* Bec Sch, Univ of London, Univ of Hull and London; *m* 1970, Jennifer, OStJ, da of Bernard Kevin Kinlay (d 1975), of Cape Town; 2 s (Alexander Robert Christian George b 1975 d 1996, Hon Thomas Aubrey Bernard David (twin) b 1975); *Career* teacher 1964–69, res Inst of Educn Univ of Hull 1969–71, headmaster 1972–80; chm: Grant-Maintained Schs Centre (formerly Fndn) 1989–99, Centre for Educn Mgmnt (now CEFM) 1995–; DG St John Ambulance 1984–90 (asst DG 1982–84); fndr chm Balchin Family Soc 1993–; chm: Educn Cmmn 2003–10, Govt Review of Professionalism in Further Educn (Lingfield Report) 2012, Chartered Instn for Further Educn 2013–; chm Cadet Vocational Qualifications Organisation (CVQO) 2012–; memb: Surrey CC 1981–85, Funding Agency for Schs 1994–97; fndr pres English Schools Orch 1997–, pres League of Mercy 1999–, chm Maritime Heritage Fndn 2011–; chm ARNI Inst 2008–; memb Ct Univ of Leeds 1995–2001, memb Cncl Goldsmiths Coll London 1997–2005 (dep chm 1999–2005), pro-chllr Brunel Univ 2006–13; Hon Col Humberside and S Yorks ACF 2004–12; Imperial Soc of Knights Bachelor: memb Cncl 1995–, Knight Registrar 1998–2006, Knight Princ 2006–12, Knight Pres 2012–; Liveryman Worshipful Co of Goldsmiths 1987 (Freeman 1981), Worshipful Soc of Apothecaries 2013; Hon DLitt Univ of Hull 2006, Hon DEd Brunel Univ 2013; Hon FCP 1987 (FCP 1971), Hon FHS 1987, Hon FCGI 1997; KStJ 1984, Cdr's Cross (Pro Merito Melitensi SMOM) 1987, Grand Cross Order of Francis I 2014, Grand Cross Order of the Eagle of Georgia 2014; *Books* Choosing a State School (jtly, 1989); author of numerous articles on educn and politics; *Recreations* restoration of ancient house; *Clubs* Athenaeum; *Style*— The Lord Lingfield, DL; ✉ New Place, Lingfield, Surrey RH7 6EF; House of Lords, London SW1A 0PW

LINGWOOD, James Peter Boyce; MBE (2012); s of Robert Lingwood (d 1980), and Patricia Lingwood; *b* 28 May 1959; *Educ* Univ of Oxford, (BA, MPhil); *Partner* Jane Hamlyn; 2 da (Scarlett b 25 Aug 1990, Evie b 18 Nov 1994), 1 s (Louis b 14 Jan 1992); *Career* exhbns curator ICA London 1986–90, ind curator 1991–; exhbns curated incl: Juan Muñoz

(Tate Modern London) 2001, Douglas Gordon (Hayward Gallery London) 2002, Susan Hiller (Baltic Gateshead) 2004; co-dir (with Michael Morris, MBE): Artangel 1991–, Artangel Media Ltd 2000–; Artangel projects incl: House (Rachel Whiteread), Breakdown (Michael Landy), The Cremaster Cycle (Matthew Barney), Carib's Leap/ Western Deep (Steve McQueen); memb Int Advsy Bd: Museu Serralves Porto; tstee: Paul Hamlyn Fndn 2003–, Art Fund 2008–; *Publications* Juan Muñoz: Double Bind at Tate Modern (2001), Robert Smithson, Bernd and Hilla Becher: Field Trips (2001), Off Limits – 40 Artangel Projects (2002), Susan Hiller: Recall (2004); *Style*— James Lingwood, Esq, MBE; ✉ Artangel, 31 Eyre Street Hill, London EC1R 5EW (☎ 020 7713 1400, e-mail jl@artangel.org.uk)

LININGTON, Richard; s of Reginald Friend Linington (d 1981), of Birchington, Kent, and Gwendoline Florence Irene, *née* Amos (d 1986); *b* 31 March 1945; *Educ* Tonbridge, Birmingham Coll of Arts and Crafts (Dip Int Design); *m* 27 Sept 1969 (m dis 1994), (Hilary) Jane, da of Maj Ronald Jasper Lucas, of Chipping Campden, Glos; 2 s (Noel b 1971, Ben b 1975); *Career* designer; interior designer R Seifert and Ptnrs 1967–69, designer for architect Stephen Garrett 1969–72, assoc with Austin Smith Lord Architects 1972–79, princ Hurley Linington McGirr Design Ptnrshp 1979–87, ptnr Bloomer Tweedale Architects 1988–91, interior design mangr Austin-Smith Lord 1991–92, princ Linington – Architectural and Interior Design 1992–, design dir The Chadwick Group London 1994–96, ptnr PPML design practice 1996–; pres Int Fedn of Int Designers and Architects 1987–89 and 1991–93; FCSD 1987; *Recreations* music, gardening; *Style*— Richard Linington, Esq; ✉ Medlicott Manor Farm, Wentnor, Bishop's Castle, Shropshire SY9 5EL (☎ 01588 650185, e-mail linington31@gmail.com)

LINKLATER, Alexander Ragnar (Alex); s of Magnus Linklater , *qv*, and Baroness Linklater of Butterstone (Life Peer), *qv*; *b* 19 December 1968; *Educ* Glenalmond Coll Perthshire, Univ of Durham (BA), Univ of Glasgow; *Children* Eric (b 2001), Hugh (b 2005), Sula (b 2015); *Career* freelance journalist 1994–97; Glasgow Herald: feature writer 1997–98, architecture corr 1998–99, literary ed 1999–2000; dep arts ed Evening Standard 2000–01, assoc ed Prospect magazine, columnist The Guardian; judge Whitbread Novel of the Year Award 2000, books editor Ax:son Johnson Fndn 2005–, fndr Nat Short Story Prize 2006; ptnr and dir Buckny Hydro LLP 2012–; memb Partnership Bd New School Butterstone; Scottish Arts Writer of the Year 2000, Bank of Scotland Press award; fell Nat Endowment for Science, Technol and the Arts 2005–06; *Books* ed with Kurt Almqvist Ax:son Johnson Fndn series: On Russia (2009), The Idea of America (2010), On Capitalism (2011), Images of Sweden (2012), Politics and Ideology (2012), Images of Sweden II (2013), The Pursuit of Europe (2013), Civilisation (2014), Religion (2015), War (2016), Geopolitics (forthcoming); *Recreations* cinema, cricket, reading, walking; *Clubs* The Union, Soho; *Style*— Alex Linklater, Esq; ✉ e-mail alexlinklater@mac.com

LINKLATER, Prof Andrew; s of Andrew Linklater, and Isabella, *née* Forsyth; *b* 3 August 1949, Aberdeen; *Educ* Univ of Aberdeen (MA), Balliol Coll Oxford (BPhil), LSE (PhD); *m* Jane Christie, *née* Adam; *Career* lectr in political sci Univ of Tasmania 1976–81; Monash Univ: lectr in politics 1982–84, sr lectr in politics 1985–91, assoc prof 1992–93; prof of int rels Univ of Keele 1993–99, Woodrow Wilson prof of int politics Univ of Wales Aberystwyth 2000–; memb Learned Soc of Wales 2009; AcSS 2001, FBA 2005; incl: Men and Citizens in the Theory of International Relations (1982, 2 edn 1990), Beyond Realism and Marxism: Critical Theory and International Relations (1990), The Transformation of Political Community: Ethical Foundations of the Post-Westphalian Era (1998), The English School of International Relations: A Contemporary Assessment (jtly, 2006), Critical Theory and World Politics: Sovereignty, Citizenship and Humanity (2007), The Problem of Harm in World Politics: Theoretical Investigations (2011), Violence and Civilisation in the Western States-Systems (2016); *Recreations* the Turf, Australian aboriginal art, Wedgwood ware, woodland work, ECM recordings; *Style*— Prof Andrew Linklater; ✉ Department of International Politics, University of Wales, Aberystwyth, Ceredigion SY23 3FE (☎ 01970 621596, fax 01970 622709, e-mail adl@aber.ac.uk)

LINKLATER, Magnus Duncan; CBE (2013); s of Eric Robert Linklater, CBE, TD, and Marjorie MacIntyre (d 1997); *b* 21 February 1942; *Educ* Eton, Univ of Freiburg, Sorbonne, Trinity Hall Cambridge (BA); *m* 1967, Rt Hon Baroness Linklater of Butterstone (Life Peer), *qv*, da of Lt-Col Michael Lyle, OBE, JP, DL, of Riemore Lodge, Dunkeld; 2 s (Alexander, *qv*, b 1968, Saul b 1970), 1 da (Freya b 1975); *Career* journalist: Daily Express Manchester 1964–65, Evening Standard (ed Londoner's Diary) 1965–69, Sunday Times (ed Spectrum pages, ed Colour Magazine, asst ed News, exec ed Features) 1969–83; managing ed The Observer 1983–86; ed: London Daily News 1986–87, The Scotsman 1988–94; columnist: The Times 1994–, Scotland on Sunday 1998–2007; Scotland ed The Times 2007–12; presenter BBC Radio Scotland 1994–97; chm: Edinburgh Book Festival 1995–96, Scottish Arts Cncl 1996–2001, Little Sparta Tst 2001–, Horsecross Arts Co (Perth Concert Hall and Theatre) 2013–; pres Saltire Soc 2011–; Scottish Daily Newspaper Soc Lifetime Achievement Award 2005; Hon Dr of Arts Napier Univ, Hon LLD Univ of Aberdeen, Hon DLitt Univ of Glasgow, Hon DLitt Queen Margaret Univ; FRSE; *Books* Hoax – The Howard Hughes Clifford Irving Affair (with Stephen Fay and Lewis Chester), Jeremy Thorpe – A Secret Life (with Lewis Chester and David May), The Falklands War (with the Sunday Times Insight team), Massacre – the story of Glencoe, The Fourth Reich – Klaus Barbie and the Neo-Fascist Connection (with Isabel Hilton and Neal Ascherson), Not with Honour – the inside story of the Westland Affair (with David Leigh), For King and Conscience – John Graham of Claverhouse, Viscount Dundee (with Christian Hesketh), Anatomy of Scotland (co-ed), Highland Wilderness (photographs by Colin Prior), People in a Landscape – The New Highlanders (photographs by Craig Mackay), Concise History of Scotland (contrib); *Recreations* opera, fishing, book collecting; *Clubs* MCC; *Style*— Magnus Linklater, Esq, CBE; ✉ 71 Cumberland Street, Edinburgh EH3 6RD (☎ 0131 558 9616, e-mail magnus.linklater1@gmail.com)

LINKLATER OF BUTTERSTONE, Baroness (Life Peer UK 1997), of Riemore in Perth and Kinross; Veronica Linklater; da of Lt-Col Michael Lyle, OBE, JP, DL, of Riemore Lodge, Dunkeld, Perthshire, and Hon Elizabeth Sinclair; *b* 15 April 1943; *Educ* Cranborne Chase Sch, Sorbonne, Univ of Sussex, Univ of London (DipSocAdmin); *m* 1967, Magnus Duncan Linklater, *qv*, s of late Eric Robert Linklater; 2 s (Hon Alexander, *qv*, b 1968, Hon Saul b 1970), 1 da (Hon Freya b 1975); *Career* child care offr London Borough of Tower Hamlets 1967–68, co-fndr Visitors' Centre Pentonville Prison 1971–77, govr three Islington schs 1970–85, Prison Reform Tst project Winchester Prison 1981–82; The Butler Tst Prison Serv Annual Award Scheme: fndr, admin then conslt 1983–87, tstee 1987–2001, vice-pres 2001–; pres Crime Reduction Initiative 2007–; JP Inner London 1985–88; co-ordinator then tstee and vice-chm The Pushkin Prizes (Scotland) 1989–, pres Soc of Friends of Dunkeld Cathedral 1989–, fndr and chm The New Sch Butterstone 1991–2004 (pres 2004–); memb: Children's Panel Edinburgh South 1989–97, Ctee The Gulliver Award for the Performing Arts in Scotland 1990–96, Beattie Ctee (making recommendations on post sch provision for young people with special needs in Scotland) 1998–99, Advsy Bd Beacon Fellowship Charitable Tst 2003–, Cncl Winston Churchill Meml Tst 2005–; memb Maggie Keswick Jencks Cancer Care Centre 1997–2004; assessor to the chllr Ct Napier Univ 2001–04; tstee: Esmée Fairbairn Fndn 1991–, The Young Musicians Tst 1993–97, Univ of the Highlands & Islands 1999–2001, Riemore Tst 2007–; advsr Koestler Award Tst 2004–; patron: The Sutherland Tst 1993–2003, The Airborne Initiative 1998–2004, The Nat Schizophrenia Fell Scotland 2000–, Support in Mind Scotland (formerly Nat Family & Parenting Inst) 2002–, The Calyx – Scotland's Garden Tst 2004–08, Research Autism 2004–, Probation Bds Assoc 2005–, Action for Prisoners' Families 2005–, PUSH 2007–, Home-Start 2007–, Univ of St Andrews Med Campaign Ctee 2007–, Epilepsy Scotland 2009–; fndn patron Queen Margaret UC Edinburgh 1998; chm: Rethinking Crime and Punishment 2001–08, House of Lords All Pty Gp on Offender Learning and Skills 2005–06; memb Scot Ctee Barnado's 2001–04; sec Scottish Peers Assoc 2000–07; Parly candidate (Lib Dem) Perth and Kinross (by-election) 1995; pres Sova 2009–, patron Tacade 2009–; *Recreations* music, theatre, my family; *Style*— The Rt Hon the Baroness Linklater of Butterstone; ✉ 71 (1F2), Cumberland Street, Edinburgh EH3 6RD (☎ 0131 557 5705, fax 0131 557 9757, e-mail veronica.linklater@gmail.com)

LINLEY, Viscount; *see: Royal Family section*

LINNELL, Andrew John; s of late Cyril Barrie Linnell, of Newcastle-under-Lyme, Staffs, and Maureen, *née* Goodyear; *b* 28 June 1956; *Educ* Wolstanton GS, Univ of Salford (BSc), Keele Univ (PGCE), Mid Kent Coll of Further and Higher Educn (ACP); *m* 17 June 1989, Juliet, da of late Prof Oswald Hanfling; 1 da (Ruth Emily b 6 June 1990), 1 s (Simeon Jack b 14 July 1994); *Career* grad mgmnt trainee Royal Bank of Scotland plc 1977–78; geography teacher Howard Sch Gillingham 1979–84, youth tutor Rainham Sch for Girls and Howard Sch Rainham 1984–86, educn offr (community and youth) N Kent Area Educn Office 1986–89; Educn Dept Kent LEA: quality assurance conslt Mgmnt Review Team 1989–92, review mangr Local Mgmnt of Schs Scheme 1992; dep head teacher Sir Joseph Williamson's Mathematical Sch Rochester 1993–97, head master Reading Sch 1997–2005, headteacher Desborough Sch Maidenhead 2005–12, head of geography Prospect Sch 2012–16, geography teacher The Abbey Sch Reading 2016–; memb Cncl of Br Geography (COBRIG) 2016–; memb Ct Univ of Reading 1998–2010; FRGS 1983 (final assessor CGeog prog 2005–, memb Cncl 2005–09, vice-pres 2006–09, memb Cncl and vice-pres IBG 2013–15, chair Initial and Final Assessors' Ctees CGeog Scheme 2015–), CGeog 2002, FCP 2005 (MCP 1989); *Recreations* running, travelling, local history, reading, film, theatre; *Style*— Andrew Linnell, Esq; ✉ Prospect School, Cockney Hill, Tilehurst, Reading RG30 4EX (☎ 0118 959 0466)

LINNETT, Simon John Lawrence; s of Prof John Wilfrid Linnett (d 1975), and Rae Ellen Fanny, *née* Libgott; *b* 14 February 1954; *Educ* The Leys Cambridge, Balliol Coll Oxford; *m* 28 Nov 1987, Penelope Jane, da of Sir Charles William Willink, Bt; 2 s (John Lawrence Humfrey b 1991, Henry Simon Albert b 1993); *Career* NM Rothschild & Sons Ltd: joined 1975, mangr 1982, asst dir 1984, dir 1987, dir Exec Ctee 1989, md investment banking 1998; executive vice-chm Rothschild 2008–; chair Ind Transport Cmmn 2010–; chm: Advsy Bd Nat Railway Museum 2015–, Luton & Dunstable Univ Fndn Tst Hosp 2014–; tstee: Science Museum 2011–, Exbury Garden Tst 2013–; treas Queen Mary Univ of London 2010–; *Recreations* environmental issues, walking; *Clubs* Athenaeum, Bosham Sailing; *Style*— Simon Linnett, Esq; ✉ c/o N M Rothschild & Sons Ltd, New Court, St Swithin's Lane, London EC4N 8AL (☎ 020 7280 5062)

LINNEY, Piers; *Educ* Univ of Manchester (BA), Coll of Law London (LPC); *Career* slr S J Berwin 1995–97, corp fin Barclays de Zoete Wedd 1997, corp fin Credit Suisse 1997–2000; co-ceo Outsourcery plc 2007–; panel memb Dragons' Den (BBC) 2014–15; *Recreations* cinema, motorsport, mountain biking; *Style*— Piers Linney, Esq; ✉ website www.pierslinney.com, Twitter @pierslinney; Outsourcery plc, 10 Whitfield Street, Fitzrovia, London W1T 2RE

L

LINSCOTT, Gillian; da of Thomas Snow Linscott (d 1988), and Muriel Rosaline, *née* Fountain (d 1978); *b* 27 September 1944; *Educ* Maidenhead HS, Somerville Coll Oxford (MA); *m* 1988, Tony Geraghty; *Career* journalist: Liverpool Daily Post 1967–70, Birmingham Post 1970–72, The Guardian 1972–79, BBC 1979–90 (mainly as Parly journalist); freelance writer 1990–; author; memb Crime Writers' Assoc 1984; Crime Writers' Assoc Ellis Peters Historical Dagger 2000; *Books* A Healthy Body (1984), Murder Makes Tracks (1985), Knightfall (1986), A Whiff of Sulphur (1987), Unknown Hand (1988), Murder, I Presume (1990), Sister Beneath the Sheet (1991), Hanging on the Wire (1992), Stage Fright (1993), Widow's Peak (1994), Crown Witness (1995), Dead Man's Music (1996), Dance on Blood (1998), Absent Friends (1999), The Perfect Daughter (2000), Dead Man Riding (2002), The Garden (2002), Blood on the Wood (2003); writing as Caro Peacock: Death at Dawn (2007), Death of a Dancer (2008), A Corpse in Shining Armour (2010), When the Devil Drives (2011), Keeping Bad Company (2012), The Path of the Wicked (2013), Friends in High Places (2015); *Recreations* horse riding, gardening, hill walking; *Style*— Ms Gillian Linscott; ✉ Wood View, Hope under Dinmore, Leominster, Herefordshire HR6 0PP

LINSELL, Richard Duncan; s of Dr William Duncan Linsell, of Ipswich, and Margaret Sybil, *née* Burns; *b* 21 June 1947; *Educ* Mill Hill Sch, Jesus Coll Cambridge (MA); *m* 25 Oct 1986, Briony Margaret, da of Dr James Wright Anderton Crabtree, OBE, TD (Col and former QHP), of Devon; 1 da (Katherine Jemima Cory b 14 Oct 1987); *Career* admitted slr 1973; slr specialising in partnership and LLP law; ptnr: Mayer, Brown, Rowe & Maw LLP (formerly Rowe & Maw) 1976–2005, Addleshaw Goddard 2005–; currently chm Association Partnership Practitioners (APP); non-exec dir DHL International (UK) Ltd 1977–97, non-exec chm Jas Bowman & Sons Ltd 1991–99, non-exec dir Sunseeker International (Boats) Ltd; numerous pubns on matters affecting the regulated professions, in particular the law relating to limited liability partnerships; memb: Law Soc, Int Bar Assoc; *Recreations* collecting and consuming wine, music, golf, walking; *Style*— Richard Linsell, Esq; ✉ Addleshaw Goddard, 150 Aldersgate Street, London EC1A 4EJ (website www.addleshawgoddard.com)

LINSEY, Mark Raymond; s of Raymond Linsey, of Cambridge, and Lola, *née* Taylor (d 1993); *b* 15 March 1961, Cambridge; *m* 17 Oct 1998, Sarah, *née* Jones; 3s (Benjamin, Louis b 10 Dec 1997 (twins), Joshua b 12 Feb 2001); *Career* freelance series prodr until 1997 (progs incl The Lily Savage Show (BBC 1), You Bet (ITV 1), Something for the Weekend (Channel 4)), head of entertainment Tiger Aspect 1997–2001, md Zeal TV 2001–04, dir of entertainment Talent Television 2004–07; BBC: commissioning ed then exec ed entertainment commissioning 2007–08 (progs incl: Children In Need, The Royal Variety Performance, The Kids Are Alright, Hole In The Wall, The One And Only, Total Wipeout), acting controller entertainment commissioning 2008–09, controller entertainment commissioning 2009– (progs incl: Michael McIntyre's Comedy Road Show, The Apprentice, Top Gear, The Voice, Strictly Come Dancing, The Graham Norton Show); *Recreations* cinema, reading, skiing, travel, swimming; *Style*— Mark Linsey, Esq; ✉ BBC New Broadcasting House, Zone A, Floor 7, Portland Place, London W1A 1AA

LINTHWAITE, Peter John Nicholas; *b* 3 December 1956; *Educ* New Coll Oxford (MA); *m* 18 Sept 1982, Gillian Deborah, *née* Oblitas; 2 da; *Career* dir Murray Johnstone Private Equity Ltd 1990–95, md Murray Johnstone Asia Ltd 1995–2001, exec dir Royal London Private Equity Ltd 2001–05, ceo British Venture Capital Assoc (BVCA) 2005–07, managing ptnr 350 Investment Partners LLP (formerly CT Investment Partners LLP) 2008–, advsr Private Equity Royal London Asset Mgmnt 2010–, dir Maven Income & Growth VCT 2 plc 2015–; *Clubs* MCC; *Style*— Peter Linthwaite, Esq; ✉ Chadwick House, Birchwood Park, Warrington WA3 6AE

LINTOTT, Prof Andrew William; s of Ernest Roworth Carl Lintott, and Edith Eileen, *née* Garland; *b* 9 December 1936; *Educ* Tonbridge, Exeter Coll Oxford (MA, Arnold Ancient History Prize), Univ of London (PhD), Univ of Oxford (DLitt); *Career* 2 Lt RA 1958–60; asst lectr then lectr in classics KCL 1960–67, lectr then sr lectr in ancient history Univ of Aberdeen 1967–81; Worcester Coll Oxford: fell and tutor in ancient history 1981–2004, reader 1996, prof 1999–; visiting memb Inst for Advanced Study Princeton 1990–, Hugh Last fell Brit Sch Rome 1994–, visiting prof Univ of Texas at Austin 2002–; *Books*

Violence in Republican Rome (1968, 2 edn 1999), Violence, Civil Strife and Revolution in the Classical City (1982, reprinted 1987), Judicial Reform and Land Reform in the Roman Republic (1992), Imperium Romanum: Politics and Administration (1993), Cambridge Ancient History vol IX (ed with JA Crook and Elizabeth Rawson, 2 edn 1993), Cambridge Ancient History vol X (ed with Alan Bowman and Edward Champlin 1996), The Constitution of the Roman Republic (1999), The Roman Republic (2000), Cicero as Evidence: A Historian's Companion (2008), The Romans in the Age of Augustus (2010), Plutarch: Demosthenes and Cicero (2013); *Recreations* sailing, bridge; *Style—* Prof Andrew Lintott; ✉ Worcester College, Oxford OX1 2HB (✆ 01865 373551, fax 01865 278303, e-mail andrew.lintott@worc.ox.ac.uk)

LINTOTT, Lesley Joan; da of John Desmond Hutson (d 1979), of Durham, and Marion Hush, *née* Mallabar (d 1977); *b* 28 June 1950; *Educ* Washington Grammar Tech Sch, St Hilda's Coll Oxford (MA); *m* 19 Aug 1972, Christopher John Lintott, s of John William Lintott (d 1972); *Career* Penningtons Manches LLP (formerly Penningtons): articled clerk 1972–75, ptnr 1978, London admin ptnr 1990–96, head Private Client Dept 1995–2007, London managing ptnr 1996–97, nat managing ptnr 1997–2008, head Private Individuals Div 2007–10, head of private clients 2010–; Freeman: City of London Slrs' Co 1992, City of London 1995; memb: City of London Law Soc, Soc of Tsts & Estates Practitioners (STEP); *Books* Butterworths Wills, Probate & Administration Service (gen ed and revision ed, Wills Div); *Recreations* wine, art, music, cricket; *Clubs* Wine Soc Dining (vice-pres), Surrey CCC; *Style—* Ms Lesley Lintott; ✉ Penningtons Manches LLP, Abacus House, 33 Gutter Lane, London EC2V 8AR (✆ 020 7457 3000, fax 020 7457 3240,e-mail lesley.lintott@penningtons.co.uk)

LIPKIN, Dr Malcolm Leyland; s of Dr Reuben Lipkin (d 1944), of Liverpool, and Evelyne, *née* Urding (d 1982); *b* 2 May 1932; *Educ* Liverpool Coll, Royal Coll of Music London, Univ of London (BMus, DMus); *m* 5 Aug 1968, Judith Eda, da of Jacob Frankel (d 1968), of Port Elizabeth, South Africa, and Eileen, *née* Orr (d 1995); 1 s (Jonathan b 21 Sept 1970); *Career* lectr in music Dept of External Studies Univ of Oxford 1967–75, lectr Sch of Continuing Educn Univ of Kent at Canterbury 1975–96, lectr Centre for Continuing Educn Univ of Sussex 1994–2000; composer; premieres incl: Piano Sonata no 3 (Gaudeamus Fndn Int Music Week Holland) 1951, Piano Sonata no 4 (Cheltenham Festival) 1955, Piano Concerto (Cheltenham Festival) 1959, Violin Concerto no 2 (Bournemouth Symphony Orch) 1963, Sinfonia di Roma Symphony no 1 (Royal Liverpool Philharmonic) 1966, Psalm 96 for Chorus and Orch (John Lewis Partnership cmmn) 1969, Four Departures for Voice and Violin (Queen Elizabeth Hall London) 1972, Metamorphosis for Harpsichord (Purcell Room London) 1974, Clifford's Tower (Cheltenham Festival) 1980, Five Songs (BBC London) 1981, Harp Trio (Rye Festival) 1982, Naboth's Vineyard (Law Soc concerts) 1983, The Pursuit Symphony no 2 (BBC Philharmonic Manchester) 1983, Wind Quintet (BBC cmmn) 1986, Prelude and Dance in Memory of Jacqueline du Pré (City of London Festival) 1988, Piano Sonata no 5 (Gt Comp Festival) 1989, Piano Trio (Purcell Room London) 1989, Oboe Concerto (BBC cmmn) 1990, Variations on a Theme of Bartók for String Quartet (Newbury Spring Festival) 1992, Dance Fantasy for Solo Violin (Carl Flesch Int Violin Competition Cmmn London) 1992, Sun Symphony No 3 (BBC Philharmonic Manchester) 1993, Five Bagatelles (Wigmore Hall London) 1994, Second Violin Sonata (Green Room Cmmn Tunbridge Wells) 1998, From Across La Manche (Primavera Chamber Orch Cmmn Canterbury) 1998 (recorded by Royal Ballet Sinfonia 2006), Nocturne No 2 (Pianoworks Festival Blackheath) 1999, Nocturne no 5 for Piano (Tunbridge Wells Festival) 2005, Invocation for Double Bass and Piano (Swaledale Festival) 2015; CD Malcolm Lipkin The Symphonies (2015), made numerous other recordings, broadcasts and performances worldwide; memb Exec Ctee Composers' Guild of GB 1972–76; ARCM, LRAM; *Books* illustrated incl: Handel at Work (1963), A History of Western Music (1974), Casals and the Art of Interpretation (1976), The Nine Symphonies of Beethoven (1981), Tortelier – A Self-Portrait (1984), A Companion to the Concerto (1988); *Recreations* long country walks, travelling; *Style—* Dr Malcolm Lipkin; ✉ Penlan, Crowborough Hill, Crowborough, East Sussex TN6 2EA (✆ 01892 652454, e-mail mail@malcolmlipkin.co.uk, website www.malcolmlipkin.co.uk)

LIPMAN, Maureen Diane; CBE (1999); da of late Maurice Julius Lipman of Hull, and late Zelma Lipman (d 2003); *b* 10 May 1946; *Educ* LAMDA; *m* 18 Feb 1973, Jack Rosenthal, CBE (d 2004), s of Samuel Rosenthal (d 1964); 1 da (Amy b 7 June 1974), 1 s (Adam b 3 Oct 1976); *Career* actress; columnist: She Magazine (PPA Columnist of the Year Award 1991), Good Housekeeping 1991–96; Hon DLitt Univ of Hull 1994, Hon MA Univ of Salford 1995; *Theatre* 3 years NT incl Kathleen in A Long Day's Journey into Night; other credits incl: The Knack (Palace Theatre Watford), Molly in The Front Page (Old Vic), Miss Richland in The Good Natured Man, Celia in As You Like It (RSC); West End incl: Outside Edge, Messiah (both SWET Award nomination for Best Actress), Chapter Two (Lyric Hammersmith), The Meg and Mog Show (Arts Theatre), Kitty McShane in On Your Way Riley (Theatre Royal), lead role in Night and Day (Greenwich), See How They Run (Olivier Award for Best Comedy Performance and Variety Club Award), musical debut Ruth in Wonderful Town (Queen's Theatre, Variety Club Award and Olivier Award nomination), devised and appeared in one-woman show Re: Joyce (life of Joyce Grenfell, three seasons, West End and Long Wharf Theatre Connecticut) 1988–91, The Cabinet Minister (Albery) 1991, Lost in Yonkers (Strand Theatre) 1992, The Sisters Rosensweig (Old Vic) 1994; Mrs Malaprop in The Rivals (Manchester Royal Exchange), Live and Kidding (solo performance, Chichester, Leeds, tour and Duchess Theatre London, also on video), Oklahoma! (RNT 1998, Lyceum Theatre 1999), Peggy Ramsay in Peggy for You (Hampstead Theatre Club 1999 and The Comedy Theatre and tour 2000), Nina in Sitting Pretty (by Amy Rosenthal, Hypothetical Theatre NY and English tour) 2001, Mrs Meers in Thoroughly Modern Millie (Shaftesbury Theatre) 2003–04 (Olivier Award nomination for Best Actress in a Musical), Dim Sum in Aladdin (Old Vic) 2004, Martha in Martha, Josie and the Chinese Elvis (tour) 2007; *Television* incl: The Evacuees, Jane Lucas in Agony (BAFTA Award nomination for Best Comedy Performance), Smiley's People, The Evacuees, The Knowledge, Rolling Home, Maggie in Outside Edge (both BAFTA Award nomination for Best Actress), The Princess of France in Love's Labour's Lost, Absent Friends, Shift Work, lead in All At No 20 (Thames, TV Times Best Comedy Actress Award), Miss Minchin in The Little Princess (2 series, LWT), About Face (2 series, Central) 1989 and 1990, Enid Blyton in Sunny Stories (BBC2, Bookmark), Agony Again 1995, Shani in Eskimo Day 1996, Cold Enough for Snow 1997, Coronation Street 2002, Jonathan Creek 2002, The Fugitives 2005, In Search of Style (presenter), Art Deco, Sensitive Skin (Channel 4), The Wire in Dr Who (BBC) 2006; numerous guest appearances incl Have I Got News for You (BBC) 1994; *Film* incl: Up the Junction (debut), Gumshoe, Educating Rita (BAFTA Award nomination for Best Supporting Actress), Water (with Michael Caine), Carry On Columbus 1992, Captain Jack 1997, Solomon & Gaenor 1998, The Discovery of Heaven 2001, The Pianist 2001; *Radio* incl: When Housewives Had The Choice (2 series), The Lipman Test 1994, Choice Grenfell 1997; *Books* How Was it for You? (1985), Something to Fall Back On (1987), You Got an 'Ology? (with Richard Phillips, 1989), Thank You For Having Me (1990), When's It Coming Out? (1992), You Can Read Me Like a Book (1995), Lip Reading (1999), By Jack Rosenthal (2005), The Gibbon's In Decline But The Horse Is Stable (2006), Past-It Notes (2008); *Style—* Ms Maureen Lipman, CBE

LIPNER, Prof Julius Joseph; s of Vojtech Lipner (d 2008), and Sylvia, *née* Coutts; *b* 11 August 1946, Patna, India; *Educ* St Xavier's Sch Calcutta, St Joseph's Coll Darjeeling, Bridgewater Sch Salford, Pontifical Athenaeum Pune, Jadavpur Univ Calcutta, KCL (PhD); *m* 20 Feb 1971, Anindita, *née* Neogy; 1 da (Tanya Maria b 24 March 1972), 1 s (Julius Alan b 10 July 1975); *Career* lectr in Indian religion Univ of Birmingham 1973–74; Univ of Cambridge: lectr in Indian religion and the comparative study of religion 1975–99, dir Dharam Hinduja Inst of Indic Res 1995–99, reader in Hinduism and the comparative study of religion 1999–2003, chm Faculty Bd of Divinity 2003–06, prof in Hinduism and the comparative study of religion 2003–13, dir of research Faculty of Divinity 2013, prof emeritus in Hinduism and the comparative study of religion 2013–; fell: St Edmund's Coll Cambridge 1976–89, Clare Hall Cambridge 1990–2013 (vice-pres 2007–09, fell emeritus 2013–); visiting fell Viswabharati Univ India 1984; visiting prof: Univ of Calgary 1987, 1989 and 1996 (chair of Christian thought), Vanderbilt Univ Nashville 1992, Liverpool Hope UC 2003–04; hon prof Kurukshetra Univ India 1995–97, distinguished visiting fell Nanyang Technological Univ Singapore 2015–; memb Editorial Advsy Bd: Jl of Hindu-Christian Studies, Int Jl of Hindu Studies, Religions of South Asia, Jl of Hindu Studies; numerous named lectures; tstee: Spalding Trusts, Woolf Inst Cambridge, Ancient India and Iran Tst; tstee and chair Teape Tst; memb Br Assoc for the Study of Religions; Best Book in Hindu-Christian Studies 1997–1999 Soc for Hindu-Christian Studies (2000); MA by incorporation Univ of Cambridge 1975; FBA 2008; *Books* A Net Cast Wide: Investigations into Indian Thought in Memory of David Friedman (jt ed, 1986), The Face of Truth: A Study of Meaning and Metaphysics in the Vedantic Theology of Ramanuja (1986), Hindu Ethics: Purity, Abortion & Euthanasia (jtly, 1989), Hindus: Their Religious Beliefs and Practices (1994, 2 edn 2010), The Fruits of our Desiring: An Enquiry into the Ethics of the Bhagavadgita for Our Times (ed, 1997), Brahmabandhab Upadhyay: The Life and Thought of a Revolutionary (1999, Best Book in Hindu-Christian Studies 1997–1999 Soc for Hindu-Christian Studies USA 2000), The Writings of Brahmabandhab Upadhyay (jt ed, 1991, vol 2 2002), Anandamath, or The Sacred Brotherhood (translation and introduction, 2005, A K Ramanujan Prize for Translation S Asia Cncl American Assoc of Asian Studies 2008), Truth, Religious Dialogue and Dynamic Orthodoxy: Essays in Honour of Brian Hebblethwaite (ed, 2005), Debi Chandhurani, or The Wife Who Came Home (2009); *Recreations* reading, cricket, Indian and Western music, good food; *Style—* Prof Julius Lipner, FBA; ✉ Faculty of Divinity, University of Cambridge, West Road, Cambridge CB3 9BS

LIPPA, Domenic; s of late Marco Bruno Lippa, and Tessa, *née* Beecham; *b* 8 March 1962, London; *Educ* London Coll of Printing (BA); *m* 14 Sept 1991, Mo, *née* Coyne; 2 da (Edie b 28 Oct 1994, Flora b 25 April 2000), 1 s (Harry b 11 Feb 1997); *Career* owner/design dir Lippa Pearce Design 1990–2006, owner Pentagram Design Ltd 2006–; *Awards* numerous incl: D&AD, ADC, Cannes, Design Week, Creative Review; memb D&AD, Alliance Graphique Internationale (AGI); FRSA; *Recreations* cinema, music, reading, travel; *Clubs* ADC (Art Directors), TDC (Type Directors), Type Circle; *Style—* Domenic Lippa, Esq; ✉ Pentagram Design Ltd, 11 Needham Road, London W11 2RP (✆ 07900 581324, e-mail lippa@pentagram.com)

LIPPIETT, Rear Adm (Richard) John; CB (2004), CBE (2014, MBE 1979), DL (2014); s of Vernon K Lippiett (d 1982), and Katherine F I S, *née* Langston Jones; *b* 7 July 1949; *Educ* Brighton Hove and Sussex GS, BRNC; *m* 1976, Jennifer, da of Richard B R Walker; 1 da (Louisa b 1977), 2 s (Marc b 1979, Oliver b 1982); *Career* RN 1967; jr offr with: HMS Eastbourne, HMS Eagle, HMS Yarmouth, HMS Appleton 1968–72; Flag Lt to C-in-C Fleet 1973–74; served in HMS Achilles subsequently CO HMS Shavington 1976–77, PWO HMS Fife 1978–79, course offr Rowallan Young Officers' Leadership Course HMS Raleigh 1980–81, RNSC Greenwich 1981, exec offr HMS Ambuscade Falklands 1982–83, 2 i/c Polaris HQ 1984–86, CO HMS Amazon 1986–87, JSDC 1987, naval asst to First Sea Lord 1988–90, Capt 9 Frigate Sqdn and CO HMS Norfolk 1991–92, RCDS 1993, COS Surface Flotilla 1993–95, Cdre Sch of Maritime Operations HMS Dryad 1995–97, Flag Offr Sea Trg (FOST) 1997–99, COS to Commander Allied Naval Forces Southern Europe and sr Br Offr Southern Region 1999–2002, Cmdt Jt Servs Command and Staff Coll 2002–03; chief exec Mary Rose Tst 2003–15; tstee Naval Review 2003–13, vice-pres (RN) Combined Cadet Force 2004–15, patron Nautical Trg Corps 2007–; pres Ton Class Assoc 2007–, tstee Royal Mint Museum 2011–, govr Bedales Sch 2011–; yr bro Trinity House; Hon Dr: Southampton Solent Univ 2011, Univ of Portsmouth 2012; *Publications* Type 21 Frigate (1988), War & Peas: Intimate Letters from the Falklands War 1982 (2007); *Recreations* sailing, gardening, classical music, theatre, world travel as lecturer on maritime history; *Style—* Rear Adm John Lippiett, CB, CBE, DL; ✉ c/o The Mary Rose Trust, HM Naval Base, Portsmouth PO1 3LX

LIPSCOMB, Rev (Edwin) Paul; s of Dr A George J Lipscomb (d 1975), and Kathleen A Lipscomb (d 1993); *b* 9 September 1933; *Educ* Blackfriars Sch Laxton; *m* 17 June 1961, Pauline Ann, da of Capt Henry John Farrell Palliser (d 1937); 1 s (Christopher John Farrell b 1962), 1 da (Catherine Ann Farrell (Mrs Tony Payton) b 1965); *Career* Nat Serv The Green Howards 1952–54, TA The Green Howards 1955–61, ret as Capt; CA George A Touche & Co (now Deloitte & Co) 1955–62; fin dir: Biscuits Belin France (subsid of Nabisco) 1962–64, Levitt & Sons France 1964–65; Euro controller France Mead Corp 1965–68, mangr fin controls Belgium HQ ITT Europe 1968–72, divnl dir London HQ Rank Xerox 1972–75, exec vice-pres Amsterdam and London Cinema International Corp (now UIP) 1975–82, fin controller British Airways 1982–85, dir Borthwicks plc 1985–89, gp fin and prodn dir J W Spear & Sons plc 1989–96, chm Corgi Classics Ltd 1995–96; chm Standards Ctee and co-op memb Slough BC 1999–2011; tstee: Fortune Centre for Riding Therapy 1984–2014 (chm 2009–14), Life Opportunities Tst 1991–2013; ordained permanent deacon 1999, chm Diocesan Ecumenical Cmmn 2002–13; KHS; FCA, FCMI, AFST; *Recreations* travel, food and wine; *Clubs* Naval and Military, Savage; *Style—* The Rev Paul Lipscomb; ✉ c/o Naval and Military Club, 4 St James's Square, London SW1Y 4JU

LIPSEY, Baron (Life Peer UK 1999), of Tooting Bec in the London Borough of Wandsworth; David Lawrence; s of Lawrence Lipsey, and Penelope Lipsey; *b* 21 April 1948; *Educ* Bryanston, Magdalen Coll Oxford (Gibbs Prize, BA); *m* 1982, Margaret Robson; 1 da; *Career* journalist; research asst GMWU 1970–72, special advsr to Anthony Crosland MP 1972–77 (DOE 1974–76, FCO 1976–77), PM's Staff 10 Downing St 1977–79, journalist New Society 1979–80, economic ed Sunday Times 1982–86 (political staff 1980–82), ed New Society 1986–88, fndr and jt dep ed Sunday Correspondent 1988–90, assoc ed The Times 1990–92, political ed The Economist 1994–1998 (joined 1992); chm Impower plc 2001–03, non-exec dir LWT 2004–06; non-exec dir Personal Investment Authy 1994–2000, former memb Cncl ASA, former memb Advsy Panel CREST, former memb External Affrs Advsy Ctee ESRC, chair Make Votes Count 1999–2006, chm Social Market Fndn 2000–, chair Straight Statistics 2008–, chair Financial Servs Consumer Panel 2008–; memb: Exec Ctee Charter for Jobs 1984–86, Jenkins Ctee on the Electoral System 1998, Royal Cmmn on the Long-term Care of the Elderly 1998–99, Davies Panel on the BBC License Fee 1999, Cncl Advtg Standards Authy 1999–2005; non-exec dir Horserace Totalisator Bd 1998–2002, past chm Shadow Racing Tst, chm Br Greyhound Racing Bd 2004–08, conslt Greyhound Bd of GB 2009, tstee Retired Greyhound Tst; former visiting prof Dept of Public Policy Univ of Ulster, former visiting fell Dept of Health and Social Care LSE, currently visiting prof and memb Advsy Bd Centre for the Study of Gambling Salford Univ, visiting Parly fell St Anthony's Oxford 2016; memb Cncl Constitution Unit; chair Communications Advsy Ctee Hammersmith Women's Cancer Appeal, patron SOLLA, patron Glasbury Arts Festival, tstee Responsibility in Gambling Tst, chair Trinity Laban Conservatoire of Music and Dance, chair Sidney Nolan Tst; sec Streatham

Lab Pty 1970–72, chm Fabian Soc 1981–82, former memb Foresight Panel Lap Pty; *Books* Labour and Land (1974), The Socialist Agenda: Crosland's Legacy (co-ed Dick Leonard, 1981), Making Government Work (1982), The Name of the Rose (1992), The Secret Treasury (2000), Counter Coup (novel, 2009), In the Corridors of Power (autobiography, 2012); *Recreations* horse racing, greyhound racing, golf, opera; *Style*— The Rt Hon the Lord Lipsey; ✉ House of Lords, London SW1

LIPTON, Elliot Stephen; s of Sir Stuart Lipton, *qv*, and Ruth Kathryn, *née* Marks; *b* 17 March 1969; *Educ* BSc, MBA; *m*; 3 c; *Career* fndr First Base Ltd 2002; FRICS; *Style*— Elliot Lipton, Esq; ✉ First Base Limited, 33 Cavendish Square, London W1G 0DT (☎ 020 7851 5555, fax 020 7851 5599, website www.firstbase.com)

LIPTON, Prof Michael; CMG (2003); s of Leslie Lipton (d 1977), and Helen, *née* Janssen (d 2001); *b* 13 February 1937; *Educ* Haberdashers' Aske's, Balliol Coll Oxford (MA), MIT, Univ of Sussex (DLitt); *m* 9 Dec 1966, Merle, da of Charles Babrow (d 1979); 1 s (Emanuel b 1 March 1974); *Career* res offr with G Myrdal on Asian Drama 1960–61, fell All Souls Coll Oxford 1961–68 and 1982–84; Univ of Sussex: asst lectr 1961–62, lectr 1962–66, reader 1966–71, fell Inst of Devpt Studies and professorial fell 1971–94 (fell emeritus 2014–), prof of devpt economics and dir Poverty Research Unit 1994–97, research prof 1997–; employment devpt advsr Govt of Botswana 1977–78, sr policy advsr World Bank 1981–82, prog dir consumption and nutrition prog Int Food Policy Res Inst Washington DC 1988–89, conslt UN Human Devpt Reports on Poverty 1997, Consumption 1998 and Technol 2001, sr advsr World Bank, World Devpt Reports on Poverty 1990 and 2000–01; extensive research and consultancy on agric research and technol, rural employment, econs of population change and nutrition, poverty reduction and land distribution especially in India, Bangladesh, Sri Lanka, Botswana, Sierra Leone, South Africa and Romania, follow-up of impact of GM on developing countries 2002–03; ed Jl of Devpt Studies 1968–80, chm Br Assoc for South Asian Studies 1985–87; memb: Devpt Studies Assoc, Int Assoc of Agric Economists, Nuffield Cncl for Bioethics Working Parties on Genetically Modified Plants 1999 and 2003, Advsy Panel Int Development Enterprises 2002–, Programme Advsy Ctee HarvestPlus Biofortification Prog Consultative Gp for Int Agricultural Research 2003–, Advsy Gp Devpt Economics Growth Research Prog Overseas Devpt Inst and Dept for Int Devpt 2013–; numerous papers and pubns in jls; pres British Chess Problem Soc 1999–2000; memb Bd and Cncl Overseas Devpt Inst 2000–; Leontief Prize for advancing the frontiers of economic thought 2012; FBA 2006, fell Stellenbosch Inst of Advanced Studies 2011; *Publications* Chess Problems: Introduction to an Art (with R Matthews and J Rice, 1962), Assessing Economic Performance (1968), The Crisis of Indian Planning (with P Streeten, 1968), The Erosion of a Relationship: India and Britain since 1960 (with J Firn, 1975), Migration from Rural Areas: The Evidence from Village Studies (with J Connell, 1976), Why Poor People Stay Poor: Urban Bias and World Development (1977), Botswana: Employment and Labour Use (1979), New Seeds and Poor People (1989), Does Aid Work in India? (with J Toye, 1990), Including the Poor (with J van der Gaag, 1993), How Third World Households Adapt to Dietary Energy Stress (with P Payne, 1994), Successes in Anti-poverty (2 edn 2001), 'Quality of Life' and 'Poverty' in Asian Devpt Bank Emerging Asia (conslt and ed with Siddiqur Osmani and Arjan de Haan, 1997), Food and Nutrition Security: Why Food Production Still Matters in Food and Agric Organisation (2000), The Family Farm in a Globalizing World (2005), Land Reform in Developing Countries: property rights and property wrongs (2009), Farm Size (with R Eastwood and A Newell in Handbook of Agricultural Economics, 2010), The Persistence and Subsistence and the Wrong Counter-revolution: staples, self-provisioning and devpt (In Essays in Honour of Hans Binswanger, ed P Pingali, 2015); lead scholar Int Fund for Agric Devpt Report on Rural Poverty (2001); memb Editorial Bd: Jl of Devpt Studies, World Devpt; author of articles in learned jls; *Recreations* chess problems, music, play-going, poetry; *Clubs* Lansdowne; *Style*— Prof Michael Lipton, CMG, FBA; ✉ University of Sussex, Brighton BN1 9QN (direct ☎ 01273 682065, website www.michaellipton.net)

LIPTON, Sir Stuart Anthony; kt (2000); s of Bertram Green, of London, and Jeanette Lipton; *b* 9 November 1942; *Educ* Berkhamsted Sch; *m* 16 June 1966, Ruth Kathryn, da of Harry Marks (d 1986), of London; 2 s (Elliot Stephen, *qv*, b 17 March 1969, Grant Alexander b 20 Jan 1975), 1 da (Sarah Joanna b 15 June 1971); *Career* dir: Sterling Land Co 1971–73, First Palace Securities Ltd 1973–; jt md Greycoat plc 1976–83, chief exec Stanhope Properties plc 1983–95; Stanhope plc: chief exec 1996–2004, chm 2004–06; co-fndr and dep chm Chelsfield Ptnrs 2006–, ptnr Lipton Rogers Devpts LLP 2013–; chm Cmmn for Architecture and the Built Environment (CABE) 1999–2004; dir Nat Gallery Tst Fndn 1998–; dep chm Architecture Fndn 1992–99; advsr to: Hampton Site Co for Sainsbury Building Nat Gallery 1985–91, new Glyndebourne opera house 1988–94; property advsr DOE 1986–96; memb: Advsy Body Dept of Construction Mgmnt Univ of Reading 1983–91, Mil Bldgs Ctee MOD 1987–98, Cncl Br Property 1987–99, Governing Body Imperial Coll 1987–2001 (FIC 1998), Bd Royal Nat Theatre 1988–98, Royal Fine Art Cmmn 1988–99, Barbican Centre Advsy Cncl 1997–2005, English Partnerships Millennium Housing Tst Jury 1998–99, Bd Royal Opera House 1998–2006, Jury RIBA Gold Medal Award 1998 and 1999; tstee: Whitechapel Art Gallery 1987–94, Urban Land Inst Washington 1996–, Millennium Bridge Tst 1998–2002; Edward Bass visiting fell Yale Sch of Architecture 2006; govr LSE 2000–2006; Hon LLD Univ of Bath 2005, Hon DSc UCL 2009; hon bencher Inner Temple 2002–; memb Worshipful Co of Goldsmiths; Hon RIBA; *Recreations* architecture, crafts, art and technology, wine; *Style*— Sir Stuart Lipton

LISHMAN, (Arthur) Gordon; CBE (2006, OBE 1993); s of Dr Arthur Birkett Lishman, and Florence May Lishman; *b* 29 November 1947, Bolton; *Educ* Univ of Manchester (BA); *m* 1, 1968 (m dis 1972), Beverley Ann, *née* Witham; m 2, 1973 (m dis 1984), Stephanie Margaret, *née* Allison-Beer; 1 s, 1 da; m 3, 1988, Margaret Ann Brodie-Browne, *née* Long; 1 step da; *Career* Age Concern: field offr 1974–77, head of fieldwork 1977–87, ops dir 1987–2000, DG Age Concern England 2000–09, dir Age Concern Hldgs Ltd 1995–2009; sec-gen Eurolink Age 2001–, int vice-pres Int Fedn on Ageing 2001–11, memb Steering Gp Cmmn on Equalities and Human Rights 2004–06, memb Nat Stakeholder Forum Dept of Health 2006–09, chair Dept of Health Nutrition Action Plan Delivery Bd 2007–09, chair Audit Ctee Cmmr for Older People in Wales 2009–14; campaigner: age equality 1971–, homosexual law reform, homosexual equality; memb: Liberty, Fawcett Soc, Br Humanist Assoc, Friends of Ruskin's Brantwood, Lib Pty 1963–87, Lib Dem Pty 1987– (memb Fed Exec, former chair Burnley Lib Dems, pres NW Lib Dems), Royal Acad, Br Museum, ROH; chair Human Rights Ctee Liberal Int 2009–11, memb Cncl European Lib Dem and Reform Pty; govr Pensions Policy Inst 2002–; hon fell Univ of Central Lancs 2002; MCMI, FRSA; *Publications* Theory and Practice of Community Politics (jtly, 1980); *Recreations* reading, opera, travel; *Clubs* Nat Lib; *Style*— Gordon Lishman, Esq, CBE; ✉ 42 Halifax Road, Briercliffe, Burnley BB10 3QN (☎ 01282 421865, e-mail gordon@lishman.co.uk)

LISLE, 9 Baron (I 1758); (John) Nicholas Geoffrey Lysaght; s of 8 Baron Lysaght (d 2003), and Mary Louise Blackwell, *née* Shaw; *b* 20 May 1960; *Educ* Lingfield Sch; *Heir* bro, Hon David Lysaght; *Career* charity vol; *Recreations* avid horticulturalist, collector of books and Christmas tree decorations of the Victorian era and later; *Style*— The Rt Hon the Lord Lisle; ✉ 50 The Fairstead, Scottow, Norwich, Norfolk NR10 5AQ

LISNEY, Prof Stephen John William; s of Raymond Laurence Lisney, and Jean Avril, *née* Ladell; *b* 30 April 1951; *Educ* Queen Elizabeth's GS Barnet, Univ of Bristol (BSc, BDS, MA, PhD, Bristol Teaching Hosp's Gold medal, Colgate prize for dental research); *m* 4 Jan 1975, Sandra Jane, da of Bertram Henry Mears; 2 s (Thomas James b 27 May 1977, Robert William b 22 Aug 1981); *Career* MRC travelling fell 1978–79; Univ of Bristol: lectr in physiology 1980–89, sr lectr 1989–2000, head Dept of Physiology 1995–97, chm of Med Scis 1997–2000, dean Faculty of Med 2000–03, prof 2000–; non-exec dir N Bristol NHS Tst 2003–06; tstee BRACE Alzheimer's research charity 2009–; author/co-author of articles in scientific jls and books; memb Physiological Soc 1980; *Recreations* gardening, outdoor pursuits, collecting, printmaking; *Style*— Prof Stephen Lisney; ✉ Sunnyside Cottage, St John's Road, Clevedon, Somerset BS21 7TG (☎ 0117 928 7814, e-mail s.j.w.lisney@bris.ac.uk)

LISOGORSKAYA, Maria; *b* Moscow; *Educ* Univ of Cambridge; *Career* architect; founding dir Assemble 2010– (Turner Prize 2015), urban designer GLA 2011–12; assoc lectr Central St Martins 2013–; memb Bd and dir Blackhorse Workshop (www.blackhorseworkshop.co.uk); Winston Churchill Fellowship 2015; *Recreations* cinema, music, basketball, skiing, travel, walking, dancing; *Style*— Ms Maria Lisogorskaya; ✉ Instagram @marialisogorskaya

LISSACK, Richard Antony; QC (1994); s of Victor Jack Lissack (d 1981), of London, and Antoinette Rosalind Lissack (d 2006); *b* 7 June 1956; *Educ* Univ Coll Sch Hampstead; *m* 31 May 1986, Carolyn Dare Arscott, da of Gp Capt R H Arscott, CBE; 3 da (Holly Victoria Dare, Lucy Barbara Dare (twins) b 25 July 1994, Emily Jessica Dare b 28 Sept 1998); *Career* called to the Bar Inner Temple 1978 (bencher 2008–); asst recorder 1993–99, recorder 1999–, QC Eastern Caribbean 2002, foreign legal conslt NY 2007–, QC NI 2007–, admitted Dubai Int Financial Centre Courts 2008, dep High Ct judge 2010–; dir Kilmington Int Horse Trials 1997–, pres S & W Wilts Hunt 2002– (chm 1996–2002); memb Devpt Bd RADA 2009–, ambass ActionAid 2010–; *Books* Financial Services Law and Regulation (2011), Lissack on Bribery (2012), Public Inquiries (2012); *Recreations* riding and sailing too fast and falling off or falling in respectively; *Clubs* Soho House, Rock Sailing; *Style*— Richard Lissack, Esq, QC; ✉ Outer Temple Chambers, 222 Strand, London WC2R 1BA (☎ 020 7353 6381, mobile 07836 727162, fax 020 7583 1786, e-mail law@rlqc.com)

LISTER, Anthony Charles Bramham; s of David Bramham Lister (d 1980), and Monica Joan, *née* Russell (d 1991); *b* 31 August 1939; *Educ* Sutton Valence, Coll of Estate Mgmnt London; *m* 1 June 1963, Susan Kitty, *née* Funnell (d 2015); 3 s (Giles Anthony Bramham, Timothy Norman Bramham (twins) b 12 Jan 1966, Guy Bramham b 16 Oct 1968); *Career* equity ptnr Geering and Colyer Chartered Surveyors 1972–82, Black Horse Agencies 1982–90, dir Lister & Associates (commercial surveyors) 1991–2002, dir Kentstone Properties Ltd 2002–13; Freeman City of London 1961, Liveryman Worshipful Co of Leathersellers 1964 (Freeman 1961, memb Ct of Assts 1993–2015, Master 2004–05); FRICS 1970; *Recreations* sheep farming, golf, travelling; *Clubs* Rye Golf; *Style*— Anthony Lister, Esq; ✉ Dean Court Lodge, Westwell, Ashford, Kent TN25 4NH (☎ 01233 712924)

LISTER, Sir Edward; kt (2011); *b* 15 October 1949, London; *m* Eileen; 2 s (Matthew, Andrew), 1 da (Sophie); *Career* ldr Wandsworth BC 1992–2011, COS and dep mayor Policy and Planning GLA 2011–; *Recreations* walking, reading; *Style*— Sir Edward Lister; ✉ Greater London Authority, City Hall, The Queen's Walk, More London, London SE1 2AA

LISTER, John Thomas; MBE (2010); s of Albert William Lister (d 1978), and Joan Trenear, *née* Tarr (d 2013); *b* 26 November 1941; *Educ* Cardiff HS; *m* 1988, Mary; 2 s (Stephen b 29 July 1967, Andrew b 17 Sept 1975), 1 da (Victoria b 13 Nov 1979); *Career* athletics administrator; former int athlete Wales 1959–70 and Cardiff Amateur Athletic Club; events competed at: 110m hurdles, decathlon, long jump, high jump (former Welsh record holder); hon treas: Cardiff Amateur Athletic Club 1968–2006 (former pres and chm), AAA 1986–91, British Athletic Fedn 1991–96; memb Cncl European Athletic Assoc 1995–2007; qualified CA 1964, dir and shareholder Euro Investments Properties Ltd; *Books* Athletics in the UK – the rise and fall of the British Athletic Federation (2011); *Recreations* athletics; *Style*— John Lister, Esq, MBE

LISTER, Michael; s of late William Mayes Lister, and late Helen Tiernan, *née* Adams; *b* 1962; *Educ* Univ of Stirling, Ecole Normale d'Ille-et-Vilaine France; *Partner* Iain Black; *Career* lectr Scottish Coll of Textiles 1988–96, ind campaigner and promoter of the arts in Scotland and fundraiser for various artistic projects 1996–; memb Saltire Soc; non-professional lay memb Royal Scottish Soc of Painters in Watercolour, lay memb Soc of Scottish Artists, life memb Scottish Artists' Benevolent Assoc, Memb Scottish PEN; David Daiches: A Celebration of his Life and Work (jt ed); contrib to literary jls incl: Agenda, Chapman, Edinburgh Review, Edinburgh Star, Jewish Telegraph, Scottish Book Collector, textualities.net, TLS; contrib to various monographs; *Recreations* book collecting, book reviewing, collecting contemporary Scottish art; *Style*— Michael Lister, Esq; ☎ 07944 450481, e-mail mwwlister@googlemail.com

LISTER OF BURTERSETT, Baroness (Life Peer UK 2011), of Nottingham in the County of Nottinghamshire; Prof (Margot) Ruth Aline Lister; CBE (1999); da of late Dr Werner Bernard Lister, of Manchester, and late Daphne, *née* Carter; *b* 3 May 1949; *Educ* Moreton Hall Sch, Univ of Essex (BA), Univ of Sussex (MA); *Career* dir Child Poverty Action Gp 1979–87 (legal res offr 1971–75, asst dir 1975–77, dep dir 1977–79), prof and head of Dept of Applied Social Studies Univ of Bradford 1987–93, prof of social policy Loughborough Univ 1994–; Donald Dewar visiting prof of social justice Univ of Glasgow 2005–06, visiting prof of social policy Univ of Lincoln 2013–, hon prof Sch of Sociology and Social Policy Univ of Nottingham 2013–; tstee Friends of Citizens Advice Bureaux 1991–95, vice-chm NCVO 1991–93, chm Jt Univ Cncl Social Policy Ctee 1994–96, tstee Community Devpt Fndn 2000–, chm Compass Mgmnt Ctee 2011–; memb: Opsahl Cmmn NI 1992–93, Cmmn on Social Justice 1992–94, Cmmn on Poverty Participation and Power 1999–2000, Fabian Cmmn on Life Chances and Childhood Poverty 2004–06, Nat Equality Panel 2008–09, Jt Ctee on Human Rights 2012–15; founding Academician of Learned Societies for the Social Sciences 1999; Hon LLD Univ of Manchester 1987, Hon DLitt Glasgow Caledonian Univ 2012, Hon DUniv Essex 2012, Hon LLD Univ of Brighton, Hon DSc Univ of Lincoln 2013, Hon LLD Univ of Bath 2014, Hon DLitt Loughborough Univ 2015; FBA 2009; *Books* Supplementary Benefit Rights (1974), Welfare Benefits (1981), The Exclusive Society (1990), Women's Economic Dependency and Social Security (1992), Citizenship: Feminist Perspectives (1997, 2 edn 2003), Poverty (2004), Gendering Citizenship in Western Europe (jtly, 2007), Why Money Matters (jt ed), Understanding Theories and Concepts in Social Policy (2010); numerous articles, pamphlets and chapters in books; *Recreations* walking, tai chi, reading, music, films, watching tennis, mindfulness; *Style*— The Baroness Lister of Burtersett, CBE; ✉ House of Lords, London SW1A 0PW (☎ 020 7219 5353, e-mail listerr@parliament.uk)

LISTER-KAYE, Sir John Philip Lister; 8 Bt (UK 1812), of Grange, Yorkshire; OBE (2003); s of Sir John Christopher Lister Lister-Kaye, 7 Bt (d 1982), and his 1 w, Audrey Helen (d 1979), da of Edwin James Carter, of Westbury-on-Trym, Glos; descended from Sir John Kaye, of Almondbury, W Yorks, Col of Horse, created Baronet in 1641 by Charles I, also Lord Mayor of York; this Baronetcy became extinct on the death of the 6 Bt in 1809, but Sir John Lister-Kaye, natural s of the 5 Bt, was cr a Bt 1812 for services to George III; Sir John Lister-Kaye, 3 Bt, was groom-in-waiting to Edward VII; *b* 8 May 1946, Wakefield, Yorks; *Educ* Allhallows Sch; *m* 1, 1972 (m dis 1988), Lady Sorrel Deirdre Bentinck, da of 11 Earl of Portland; 1 s (John Warwick Noel Lister b 1974), 2 da (Amelia Helen, Melanie Jenifer (twins) b 1976); m 2, 17 Feb 1989, Lucinda Anne, eld da of Robin Law, of Withersfield, Suffolk, and formerly w of Hon Evan Baillie; 1 da (Hermione Anne Lucinda Lorne b 27 Sept 1990); *Heir* s, John Lister-Kaye; *Career* naturalist, author, lectr, farmer; dir of Aigas Field Centre Ltd 1977–; fndr dir Scottish Conservation Charity The

L

Aigas Tst 1980–; chm Scottish Advsy Ctee RSPB 1986–92; memb: Int Ctee The World Wilderness Fndn 1983, Scottish Ctee of Nature Conservancy Cncl 1990–91; chm: NW Region Nature Conservancy Cncl for Scotland 1991–92, NW Region Scottish Natural Heritage 1992–96, Home Grown Timber Advsy Ctee Forestry Cmmn 1994–96; tstee Environmental Training Organisation 1995–98, memb Advsy Cncl of Millennium Forest for Scotland 1996–2000; pres Scottish Wildlife Tst 1996–2001 (hon memb 2003); vice-pres: Assoc of the Protection of Rural Scotland 1998–, RSPB 2006–; dir Aigas Quest Ltd 1997–; Wilderness Soc Gold Award for Conservation 1984; Hon DUniv Stirling 1995, Hon DUniv St Andrews 2005; *Books* The White Island (1972), Seal Cull (1979), The Seeing Eye (1980), Ill Fares the Land (1994), One for Sorrow (1994), Song of the Rolling Earth (2003), Nature's Child (2004), At The Water's Edge (2010), Gods of the Morning (2015); *Recreations* breeding horses and Highland cattle, beach-combing and digger driving; *Clubs* Farmers', Royal Scots; *Style*— Sir John Lister-Kaye, Bt, OBE; ✉ House of Aigas, Beauly, Inverness IV4 7AD (☎ 01463 782729); Grange Estate Co Office (☎ 01463 782443, fax 01463 782097, e-mail jlk@aigas.co.uk)

LISTON, (Edward) Robin; s of David Joel Liston, OBE (d 1990), and Eva Carole, *née* Kauffmann (d 1987); *b* 30 October 1947; *Educ* Bryanston, Mercersburg Acad PA USA, Univ of Kent (BA); *m* 6 July 1969 (m dis 1987), Judith Margaret; 2 da (Rebecca b 1970, Victoria b 1974); *Partner* Maria José Lorca Garrido; *Career* dist ed Kent Messenger 1969–70, asst ed Benn Bros 1970–72; assoc dir: Forman House PR Ltd 1972–79, Welbeck PR Ltd 1981–84; dir: Carl Byoir Ltd 1984–86, Hill & Knowlton Ltd 1986–88; jt md Buckmans PR 1988–93, freelance consIt and travel writer 1993–; *Books* Travels with My Heart (2007), Bradt Guide to St Helena (2007), The Art of Flying Crooked (2009); *Recreations* music, films, railways, suburban architecture, Spanish politics and history; *Style*— Robin Liston, Esq; ✉ El Cortijuelo 1, La Atalaya, 29310, Villanueva de Algaidas, Provincia de Malaga, Spain (☎ 00 34 95 274 4239, e-mail robinliston@pobox.com)

LISVANE, Baron (Life Peer 2014), of Blakemere in the County of Herefordshire and of Lisvane in the City and County of Cardiff; Sir Robert James Rogers; KCB (2012), DL (Herefordshire 2015); s of Francis Barry Day Rogers (d 1993), and Jeanne Turner, *née* Prichard-Williams (d 2008); *b* 5 February 1950, Cardiff; *Educ* Tonbridge Sch (scholar), Lincoln Coll Oxford (scholar, Judd exhibitioner, Rhodes research scholar, MA); *m* 1981, Jane, *née* Perkins; 2 da (Catherine Elizabeth Prichard b 1983, Eleanor Frances Prichard b 1985); *Career* MoD 1971–72; House of Commons: asst clerk 1972, sr clerk 1977, clerk Select Ctee on Defence 1983–89, dep princ clerk 1985, clerk Private Members' Bills 1989–92, clerk Select Ctee on European Legislation 1992–98, princ clerk 1998, princ clerk of select ctees 1999–2002, sec House of Commons Cmmn 2002–04, clerk of the jls 2004–05, clerk of the Table Office 2005–06, clerk of legislation 2006–09, clerk asst of the House of Commons 2009, clerk of the House of Commons and chief exec House of Commons Service 2011–14; ind chm Standards Ctee Herefordshire Cncl 2002–09; chm Hereford Cathedral Perpetual Tst 2007–09; Liveryman Skinners' Co (Extra Memb Ct 2007–09); hon fell Lincoln Coll Oxford 2012; hon bencher Middle Temple 2013; churchwarden St Leonard's Church Blakemere, patron Herefordshire Headway; *Publications* How Parliament Works (jtly, 7 edn 2015), Order! Order! A Parliamentary Miscellany (2009), Who Goes Home? A Parliamentary Miscellany (2012); *Recreations* music, cricket, shooting, sailing, the natural world; *Clubs* Travellers; *Style*— The Lord Lisvane, KCB, DL; ✉ Blakemere House, Blakemere, Herefordshire HR2 9JZ

LITHGOW, Sir William James; 2 Bt (UK 1925), of Ormsary, Co Argyll, DL (Renfrewshire 1970); s of Sir James Lithgow, 1 Bt, GBE, CB, MC, TD, JP, DL (d 1952); *b* 10 May 1934; *Educ* Winchester; *m* 1, 1964, Valerie Helen (d 1964), da of Denis Herbert Scott, CBE (d 1958); m 2, 1967, Mary Claire, da of Col Frank Moutray Hill, CBE, of East Knoyle, Wilts; 1 da (Katrina Margaret b 5 Oct 1968), 2 s (James Frank b 13 June 1970, John Alexander b 8 Dec 1974); *Heir* s, James Lithgow; *Career* industrialist and farmer; Lithgows Ltd: dir 1954–, chm 1959–84 and 1988–99, vice-chm 1999–; chm: Hunterston Devpt Co Ltd 1987–, Scott-Lithgow Drydocks Ltd 1967–78, Western Ferries (Argyll) Ltd 1972–85; vice-chm Scott Lithgow Ltd 1968–78; dir: Bank of Scotland 1962–86, Landcatch Ltd 1981–96, Lithgows Pty Ltd 1972–; memb: Br Ctee Det Norske Veritas 1966–92, Exec Ctee Scottish Cncl Devpt and Indust 1969–85, Scottish Regnl Cncl of CBI 1969–76, Clyde Port Authy 1969–71, Bd Nat Ports Cncl 1971–78, W Central Scotland Plan Steering Ctee 1971–74, Gen Bd Nat Physical Lab 1963–66, Greenock Dist Hosp Bd 1961–66, Scottish Milk Mktg Bd 1979–83; chm Iona Cathedral Tstees Mgmnt Bd 1979–83, memb Cncl Winston Churchill Meml Tst 1979–83; hon pres: Students' Assoc, Mid Argyll Agric Soc 1976–99, West Renfrewshire Bn Boys Brigade 1962–2000, Inverclyde & District Bn Boys Brigade 1998–; memb Ct Univ of Strathclyde 1964–69; Hon LLD Strathclyde 1979, memb Queen's Body Guard for Scotland (Royal Co of Archers); *Recreations* rural life, invention, photography; *Clubs* Oriental, Western, Royal Scottish Automobile (Glasgow); *Style*— Sir William Lithgow, Bt, DL; ✉ Ormsary House, by Lochgilphead, Argyllshire (☎ 01880 770252); Drums, Langbank, Renfrewshire (☎ 01475 540606)

LITTLE, (Robert) Alastair; s of Robert Geoffrey Little, of Colne, Lancs, and Marion, *née* Irving; *b* 25 June 1950; *Educ* Kirkham GS, Downing Coll Cambridge (MA); *Family* 1 s ((Robert) George Tormod-Little), 1 da (Frederika Kirsten Tormod-Little); m, 2000, Sharon Jacob; 1 s (Alexander b 2004); *Career* self-taught chef; head chef Old Compton Wine Bar London 1974–76; chef/proprietor: Le Routier Wrentham Suffolk 1976–79, Simpsons Putney London 1979–81; chef: L'Escargot London 1981–82, 192 Kensington Park Road 1982–85; chef/proprietor Alastair Little: Frith Street 1985–2002, Lancaster Road 1996–2002; proprietor Tavola 2003–; Times Restaurant of Year 1993; memb Académie Culinaire; *Books* Keep It Simple (1993), Food of the Sun (1995), Italian Kitchen (1996), Soho Cooking (2000); *Recreations* reading, mycology, watching sport; *Style*— Alastair Little, Esq

LITTLE, (James) Allan Stuart; s of Robin Little, of Stranraer, and Elizabeth, *née* Clive; *b* 11 October 1959; *Educ* Stranraer Acad, Univ of Edinburgh (MA); *Partner* Sheena McDonald; *Career* broadcaster; with BBC Scotland 1983–85, reporter Today prog (Radio 4) 1988–90, reporter BBC News 1990–95, Africa corr BBC 1995–97 and 2000–01, Moscow corr BBC 1997–99, presenter Today prog (Radio 4) 1999–2002; Sony Radio Reporter of the Year 1992, Amnesty Int Reporter of the Year 1992, Bayeux War Corr of the Year 1994, Sony Documentary Gold Award 2000, Grierson Premier TV Documentary Award 2001; *Books* Death of Yugoslavia (1995); *Recreations* books, theatre, walking, talking, travel; *Style*— Allan Little, Esq; ✉ BBC Broadcasting House, Portland Place, London, W1A 1AA (☎ 020 8743 8000, e-mail allan.little@bbc.co.uk)

LITTLE, Amanda Penelope Wyndham; da of Capt Alec Haines Little, CBE, of Hants, and Pamela, *née* Bolt; *b* 19 January 1948; *Educ* Winchester/London; *Career* asst PR offr Milk Mktg Bd 1972–79; literary agent Bolt & Watson Ltd 1981–83, chm and literary agent Watson Little Ltd 1983–; memb Assoc of Authors' Agents; *Recreations* singing, music, books; *Style*— Ms Amanda Little

LITTLE, Anthony Richard Morrell (Tony); s of Edward Little (d 1990), and Rosemary Margaret, *née* Morrell; *b* 7 April 1954, Hillingdon; *Educ* Eton, CCC Cambridge (choral exhibitioner, MA), Homerton Coll Cambridge (PGCE); *m* 29 July 1978, Jennifer Anne, da of Cdr Patrick Greenwood, RN; 1 da (Sophie b 15 Jan 1985); *Career* asst master Tonbridge Sch 1977–82, head of English and boarding housemaster Brentwood Sch 1982–89; headmaster: Chigwell Sch 1989–96, Oakham Sch 1996–2002, Eton Coll 2002–15; chief academic offr GEMS Educn 2015–; govr: Northwood Coll 1990–97, St Albans Sch 1994–2014, Windsor Boys' Sch 2002–15, Oakham Sch 2009–, Sevenoaks Sch 2010–, London Acad of Excellence 2012–15, Holyport Coll 2013–15, Westminster Sch 2015–, Norwich 2016–; chm Mvumi Sch Tst (Tanzania) 2008–15, pres Int Boys' Schs Coalition 2012–15 (vice-pres 2009–12), hon pres Boarding Schs Assoc 2015–16; memb Cncl Brunel Univ 2013–16; FCP 1990, FRSA 1991; *Books* An Intelligent Person's Guide to Education (2015); *Recreations* music, literature, film, theatre, Norfolk; *Clubs* Leander; *Style*— Tony Little, Esq; ✉ e-mail tonyrlittle@icloud.com

LITTLE, Michael Robert; s of Robert William Little (d 1973), and Joan, *née* Brown; *b* 10 September 1949; *Educ* Blundell's; *m* 1, 16 June 1973 (m dis 1977), Susan Elizabeth, da of Desmond Richard Bowden (d 1972), of Ranby Hall, Lincoln; m 2, 18 July 1985 (m dis 1990), Ellen Louise, da of Winston Walker, of Welford-on-Avon, Warks; 1 s (Henry Robert William b 7 April 1986); m 3, 9 Aug 1991 (m dis 2004), Caroline Xania Garnham, *qv*; 1 s (Edward Charles Frank b 21 Nov 1992), 1 da (Georgia Elizabeth Medina b 10 Nov 1995); *Career* St Quintin Son and Stanley 1972–76; ptnr Molyneux Rose 1977–, chm Molyneux Rose Ltd 1987–; Master N Cotswold Hunt 1985–88; MCIArb 1980, FRICS 1981; *Recreations* hunting, shooting, squash; *Clubs* RAC; *Style*— Michael Little, Esq; ✉ The Lydes, Toddington, Gloucestershire (☎ 01242 621419); 104 Portsea Hall, Connaught Square, London W2; Molyneux Rose, 143 New Bond Street, London W1S 2TP (☎ 020 7409 0130, fax 020 7499 7636, e-mail michael.little@molyrose.co.uk)

LITTLE, Nigel Stuart; s of Edward Little (d 1963), and Josephine Little (d 1997); *b* 11 March 1954; *Educ* Queen Elizabeth I Sch (1563), Univ of London (BSc Hons); *m* 17 May 1986, Fiona Mary, da of Henry and Patricia Lee, of Foxes' Dale, Blackheath, London SE3; 2 s (Edward Oliver Henry b 11 Nov 1987, Oliver Nigel James b 10 Aug 1990); *Career* equity sales Kitcat & Aitken stockbrokers 1976–78, sr exec and head of Scottish and Irish sales James Capel & Co stockbrokers 1978–88, dir and head of sales (princ of global firm) Morgan Stanley investmt bankers 1988–89 (princ of global firm); memb Mgmnt and Stategic Bd NationsBanc Panmure Gordon (then takeover by WestLB) 1989–99, head of downstream investment banking Nomura Int 1999–2002, pres Canaccord Adams Investment Bank (UK/Europe) 2002–9, ret; currently sr advsr Smith and Williamson Corp Finance; Advisory Bd Memb of Kleinwort Benson Bankers 2011–12, memb of KBB Principal Investment team; Freeman City of London 1982; memb Int Stock Exchange 1982; memb Worshipful Company of Int Bankers (2009–); FBIM 1988, FCISI 2002, FSI; *Recreations* shooting, golf, racing, rugby; *Clubs* 67 Pall Mall; *Style*— Nigel Little, Esq; ✉ Walton Manor, Epping Upland, Epping CM16 6PH (☎ 01992 571355)

LITTLE, Ralf; *Career* actor; *Theatre* Love on the Dole (RNT), Presence (Royal Court, nominated Most Promising Performer Olivier Awards 2002), Notes on falling Leaves (Royal Court), Billy Liar (tour), In The Beginning (Westminster Abbey); *Television* incl: Heartbeat (YTV) 1995, 1999 and 2007, The Royle Family (BBC) 1998–2000 and 2006, Two Pints of Lager and a Packet of Crisps (BBC) 2001–06, Is Harry on the Boat? 2001, The Ralf Little Show 2002, Paradise Heights (BBC) 2002, Pear Shaped – North Face of the Eiger (BBC) 2002, The Eustace Bros 2003, Monkey Trousers 2005, Married, Single, Other (ITV) 2010; *Film* Al's Lads 2002, 24 Hour Party People 2002, Fat Slags 2004, Frozen 2005, The Waiting Room 2007; *Style*— Ralf Little, Esq

LITTLE, Tasmin Elizabeth; OBE (2012); da of George Villiers Little, the actor, of London, and Gillian, *née* Morris; *b* 13 May 1965; *Educ* Yehudi Menuhin Sch, Guildhall Sch of Music (Gold medal); *m* (m dis 2005); 2 c (Chloe b 25 Nov 2000, Ashley b 14 Aug 2002); *Career* violinist; debut Hallé Orchestra 1988; performed as soloist with orchs incl: LSO, NY Philharmonic, Cleveland, Philharmonia, Royal Philharmonic, Royal Liverpool Philharmonic, Hallé, BBC Symphony, Bournemouth Symphony, City of London Sinfonia, Gewandhaus, Berlin Symphony, Stavanger Symphony, Royal Danish; worked with conductors incl: Kurt Masur, Sir Simon Rattle, Vladimir Ashkenazy, Sir Charles Groves, Sir Charles Mackerras, Vernon Handley, James Loughran, Sir Edward Downes, Richard Hickox, Sian Edwards, Jan Pascal Tortelier, Jerzy Maksymiuk, Sir Yehudi Menuhin, Andrew Davis, Sir Peter Maxwell Davies; author of paper on Delius Violin Concerto for Delius Soc 1991; voted Woman of Tomorrow in the Arts Cosmopolitan Magazine 1990, Classic FM Gramaphone Award for Audience Innovation 2008 (for Naked Violin project); Hon D Litt Univ of Bradford 1996, fell Guildhall Sch of Music and Drama 1998; plays a 1757 Guadagnini; *Performances* in UK incl: world premieres of concertos by Robert Saxton, David Earl, Dominic Muldownie, Paul Barker and Stuart MacRae, Vivaldi Four Seasons (Royal Festival Hall and Barbican) 1990, Janácek Violin Concerto with Welsh Nat Opera Orch (BBC Proms debut) 1990, Dvorák Violin Concerto (BBC Proms) 1991, Delius Double Concerto (BBC Proms) 1992, Walton Concerto (BBC Proms) 1993, Elgar Concerto (BBC Proms) 1994, soloist Last Night of the Proms 1995, Sibelius Violin Concerto (BBC Proms) 1996, Prokofiev 2nd Concerto (BBC Proms) 1997, Britten Double Concerto (London Premiere) BBC Proms 1998, Last Night of the Proms in Hyde Park 1998; charity performances incl: Sutton Place for Dr Barnardo's, St James's Palace for Nat Children's Home Appeal 1989, Wigmore Hall for Jacqueline Du Prè Meml Appeal 1990, Gala Concert with Royal Liverpool Philharmonic Orch before HM The Queen 1991; overseas performances incl: Brahms Violin Concerto (Malta Festival) 1990, tour with Piers Lane to S America 1991, concertos and recitals in Paris, Vienna, Prague, Germany, Israel, Spain, Cyprus, Canada, Greece, Zimbabwe, Hong Kong, China, Sultanate of Oman, Scandinavia, USA (debut Cleveland Blossom Festival) 1997, four performances of Liegti with Simon Rattle in London, Vienna, Birmingham, Cambridge 2000, Brahms Concerto with Simon Rattle (Aix-en-Provence Festival) 2000, debut in Japan concerts in Tokyo and Nagoya 2000, seven concerts with Simon Rattle and Berlin Philharmonic 2003; TV appearances incl: Highway (ITV), Little by Little (documentary with father, Yorkshire TV), recorded two movements of Mendelssohn Concerto (HTV), Royal Liverpool Philharmonic Gala Concert for HM the Queen (Granada TV), The Lost Child (presenter BBC documentary for The Works) 1997, World War II 60th Anniversary Festival of Commemoration Horse Guards Parade in presence of HM The Queen, HRH The Duke of Edinburgh, HRH The Prince of Wales and HRH The Duchess of Cornwall (BBC1) 2005; *Recordings* incl: Bruch and Dvorák Violin Concertos (with Royal Liverpool Philharmonic under Vernon Handley, EMI Classics for Pleasure) 1990, George Lloyd Sonatas for violin and piano (with Martin Roscoe, Albany) 1990, Vaughan Williams The Lark Ascending (with BBC Symphony Orch under Andrew Davis, WEA, Gramophone award nomination) 1990, Delius Double Concerto (with Raphael Wallfisch and Sir Charles Mackerras, EMI Eminence, Gramophone award nomination) 1991, Delius Violin Concerto 1991, Robert Saxton Violin Concerto (Collins Classics), Brahms and Sibelius Violin Concertos, Virtuoso Violin Disc (EMI Eminence), Arvo Part Disc (EMI Eminence) 1994, Rubbra Violin Concerto (Conifer, Gramophone award nomination) 1994, Walton Violin Concerto (Decca) 1995, French Violin Sonatas (EMI Eminence) 1995, Bruch Scottish Fantasy and Lalo Symphonie Espagnole (EMI Eminence) 1997, Delius Violin Sonatas (BMG Conifer) 1997, Diapason d'Or Prize 1998, Gramophone Award Nomination 1998, Dohnanyi Sonata and Serenade (ASV), Elgar and Bax Sonatas (GMN), Finzi Violin Concerto (Chandos), Karlowicz and Moskowski Concertos (Hyperion), Partners in Time (BIS) 2009; *Recreations* theatre, languages, swimming, cooking; *Clubs* English Speaking Union; *Style*— Dr Tasmin Little, OBE; ✉ c/o Denise Kantor, Kantor Concert Managment, 67 Teignmouth Road, London NW2 4EA (☎ 020 8208 2480, fax 020 8208 2490, e-mail dkantor.kem@btinternet.com, website www.tasminlittle.org.uk)

LITTLECHILD, Prof Stephen Charles; s of Sidney Littlechild, of Wisbech, Cambs, and Joyce, *née* Sharpe; *b* 27 August 1943; *Educ* Wisbech GS, Univ of Birmingham (BCom), Stanford Univ, Northwestern Univ, Univ of Texas at Austin (PhD), UCLA; *m* 1 Aug 1975, Kate (d 1982), da of Charles T Pritchard; 1 da (Elizabeth b 1976), 2 s (Harry b 1978, Richard b 1980); *Career* Harkness fell Stanford Univ 1965–67, sr res lectr Grad Centre for Mgmnt Studies Birmingham 1970–72, prof of applied econs Aston Univ 1973–75, prof of commerce and head Dept of Industrial Econs and Business Studies Univ of Birmingham 1975–94 (on leave 1989–94, hon prof 1994–2004, emeritus prof 2004–), dir-gen Office of Electricity Regulation (Offer) 1989–98; sr research assoc Judge Inst of Mgmnt Studies Univ of Cambridge 2004–08 (princ research fell 2000–04), fell Judge Business Sch 2008–; visiting prof: NYU, Univ of Stanford, Univ of Chicago, Virginia Poly 1979–80; memb: Monopolies and Mergers Cmmn 1983–89, ACORD 1987–89, Postal Servs Cmmn (Postcomm) 2006–11; advsr UK Govt on privatisation of BT, water and electricity, advsr NZ Govt Inquiry into electricity industry 2000; Hon DSc Univ of Birmingham 2001, Hon DCivLaw UEA 2004; *Books* Operational Research for Managers (1977), Fallacy of the Mixed Economy (1978), Elements of Telecommunications Economics (1979), Energy Strategies for the UK (with K G Vaidya, 1982), Regulation of British Telecoms Profitability (1983), Economic Regulation of Privatised Water Authorities (1986), Austrian Economics (3 vols, ed, 1990), Operations Research in Management (with M F Shutler, 1991); *Recreations* genealogy; *Style—* Prof Stephen Littlechild; ✉ fax 01564 742793, e-mail sclittlechild@tanworth.mercianet.co.uk

LITTLEJOHN, Prof Gavin Stuart; *Educ* George Heriot's Sch Edinburgh, Univ of Edinburgh (BSc), Univ of Newcastle upon Tyne (PhD), Univ of Edinburgh (DSc); *m* 1966, Joan Margaret; 2 s (Iain, Andrew), 4 da (Joanna, Julie, Nicola, Alison); *Career* Cementation Co Ltd: sr geotechnical engr 1965–66, divnl liaison engr 1966–69, conslt Cementation Ground Engrg Ltd 1969–71; lectr Univ of Aberdeen 1971–76 (head Geotechnics Res Gp 1973–76); conslt Ground Anchors Ltd 1973–78; tech dir: The Cement Gun Co 1976–81, Losinger Systems (UK) Ltd 1979–84; dep md Colcrete Gp 1978–84 (tech dir 1976–84); conslt: Colcrete Ltd 1985–88, GKN Foundations Ltd 1988–90, Keller Colcrete Ltd 1990–92, Parsons Brinckerhoff & Morrison Knudsen 1992–94, AMEC Gp Ltd 1992–2010; dir COLROK Joint Venture Tarbela Dam Pakistan 1979–82; private conslt 1997–; Univ of Bradford: head Dept of Civil Engrg 1985–94, prof of civil engrg 1985–97, visiting prof 1998–2000, emeritus prof of civil engrg 2000–, memb Ct 2000–14; visiting prof Univ of Newcastle upon Tyne 1980–83; external examiner: Portsmouth Poly 1981–84, Univ of Glasgow 1982–87, Univ of Newcastle upon Tyne 1983–86, Univ of Edinburgh 1987–89, UMIST 1989–91, Univ of Nottingham 1991–93, Univ of Salford 1993–96; govr: Bradford GS 1985–87, Harrogate GS 1997–2000; chm: Working Gp on Pre-stressed Ground Anchorages Fédération Internationale de la Précontrainte 1983–96, Steering Gp on Site Investigation 1991–94, Organising Ctee for Int Conferences on Ground Anchorages ICE 1995–97 and 2006–08, Environmental Civil Engrg Ctee SERC 1993–94, Res Panel ISE 1993–94, Civil Engrg Panel for 1996 Res Assessment Exercise 1995–96; senator Engrg Cncl 1999–2001 (memb Bd for Engineers Regulation, memb Educn Ctee); memb: Cmmn on Practical Construction Fédération Internationale de la Précontrainte 1983–96, Engrg Res Cmmn SERC 1993–94, Cmmn on Rock Grouting Int Soc of Rock Mechanics 1989–95, Res Panel ISE 1991–93, Anchor Ctee Post Tensioning Inst USA 1992–2002, Teaching Quality Assessment Panel Scottish Higher Educn Funding Cncl 1993, Shaft Isolation Method Review Task Force UKAEA 1997, Expert Review Panel Hydro Tasmania 2000–02, Int Review Panel South Deep Gold Mine South Africa 2000–06; technical reviewer for BS8081:2015 BSI 2014–15; memb Ctee: Ground Improvement, Int Soc of Soil Mechanics and Fndn Engrg 1990–97, British Standards Inst 1990–2000, Working Gp on High Pressure Bulkheads S African Nat Standard 2006–; memb Cncl: ISE 1991–94, ICE 1989–91 and 1992–95; assessor of mature candidates ICE 1988–97; Honour of Grouting GREAT Int Conf Orgn for Grouting New Orleans 2012; FRSA, FREng 1993; *Style—* Prof G S Littlejohn, FREng; ✉ 31 Almsford Avenue, Harrogate, North Yorkshire HG2 8HD (☎ 01423 879430, fax 01423 872014, e-mail gslittlejohn@ntlworld.com)

LITTLEJOHN, Joan Anne; da of Thomas Littlejohn (d 1950), and Joan, *née* Wynn (Mrs Edward G Shepherd) (d 1999); *b* 20 April 1937; *Educ* Mary Datchelor Girls' Sch (Fitch Prizes for Musical Composition, Constance Webb Prizes for Piano, Donohue Essay Prize), Royal Coll of Music; *Career* freelance composer, poet, photographer and musicologist 1958–; postgrad study with Howells, Berkeley, Boulanger, Ruth Dyson and others; piano teacher Orpington GS 1958–59, admin staff Royal Coll of Music 1960–83, piano teacher Harrow 1972–73; asst to Br composers incl: Fricker, Howells, Hopkins, Poston; reassembled Howells Requiem 1980 and collated his MS sketches 1983; inducted memb Mozartgemeinde Vienna 1970s, memb Cncl Soc of Women Musicians 1970s, fndr memb Royal Coll of Music Staff Assoc 1976, chm Royal Coll of Music NALGO and London Music Colleges NALGO 1978–81, vice-chm Royal Coll of Music Local Jt Ctee 1978–81; creative works (music) incl: La Mascarade de Jean de la Fontaine, The Heights of Haworth, Poems from Palgrave, 4 Sea Songs (words by J M Ritchie), 4 Lieder von F Schnabl (cmmnd by Bertha Taylor-Stach and Austrian Inst London), London Street Cries (cmmnd by Beth Boyd), St Juliot Cornwall (words by Rachel Pearse), Dreams of Anubis, Settings of Blake, Burns, De La Mare, Shakespeare, Hardy, Herrick, choral scena The Bonny Earl of Murray (cmmnd by Antony Hopkins), Chimborazo (tribute to Christopher Palmer), Cecilia, A Tune for All Musicians, Bonny & Joe's Variations, The Sword and The Ploughshare (cmmnd by Hannah Francis), O Brignall Banks (cmmnd by Viola Tucker for Harrods Minstrels), Heraclitus (cmmnd by Doris Cole), The Sheepdog's Carol (cmmnd by Bow Primary School); creative works (poetry) incl: Poems for Free, In The Furrowed Field, Towards Exmoor, Bingo's Totleigh Diary, The Hearth, Hymn of the Interviewers, Grandad's Dinner, Autun, Legend; recorded 90 tunes for The Queen Mother's 90th Year; MSS and music deposited in The American Music Res Center Calif, BIRS London, Nat Library Vienna, Clarence House, Buckingham Palace and private collections, contrib (by invitation) to permanent exhibitions at The Int Museum of Peace and Solidarity Samarkand, contrib to Mary Datchelor Archives in the Pauline Holmes Collection Southwark Library; fndr dir The Joan Littlejohn Archive (collection of MSS, letters, diaries, genealogy, memorabilia of artists and personalities (destined for the nation) housed at The Devon Heritage Centre by arrangement with The Nat Heritage Meml Fund); memb: Br Fedn of Music Festivals, PRS, Brontë Soc, The Cinnamon Tst; UN Charter 50 patron 1994, fndr patron Dame Thora Hird Memorial Fund 2004; in life fell American Biographical Inst Research Assoc 1983; Patron's Fund Awards 1970 and 1972, RVW Tst Awards 1971 and 1976, Poetry Awards USA 1980s, recipient Howells' Composing Piano 1984, World Decoration of Excellence medallion American Biog Inst 1989, first recipient IBC Medal Collection 1989 (for most distinguished biographies), recipient Millenium Medal of Honour ABI 1998; GRSM, LRAM; *Publications* Howells Centenary (contrib), Poston Centenary (contrib), The Music of Herbert Howells (front cover photograph, 2013); *Recreations* animals especially dogs, psittacines and Dusty the cat; *Style—* Miss Joan Littlejohn; ✉ 49 Hamilton Lane, Exmouth, Devon EX8 2LW

LITTLEJOHNS, Douglas George; CBE (1991, OBE 1984); s of Gordon Augustus Littlejohns (d 1994), and Margaret Goudie, *née* Smith (d 1997); *b* 10 May 1946; *Educ* Borden GS, RNC Dartmouth, Univ of Reading (BSc), Univ of Warwick Business Sch (MBA); *m* 1, 14 Nov 1970 (m dis 1987), Fiona, *née* Hilton; 1 s (Andrew b 1974), 2 da (Imogen b 1978, Diana b 1979); m 2, 4 June 1988, Deborah Anne, da of Captain Angus Andrew Nicol (d 1971); *Career* served RN until 1994; CO: HMS Osiris 1975–76, HMS Sceptre 1981–83, HMS London 1987–89; PSO to CDS 1989–91, Capt RNEC Manadon 1992–94; halls md Earls Court and Olympia Ltd 1994–96, dep chm Beeton Rumford Ltd 1995–96, pres and ceo Red Storm Entertainment Inc 1996–2000, business conslt 2001–; Freeman City of London 1988, Younger Bro Trinity House 1989; CMath, FIMA 1995; *Recreations* golf, sailing, DIY, gardening, travel; *Clubs* RN 1765 and 1785, IOD, MCC; *Style—* Douglas Littlejohns, Esq, CBE; ✉ Hunters Ride, Brentor, Tavistock, Devon PL19 0NF (☎ 01822 810193)

LITTLEMORE, Christopher Paul; s of Frederick Percival Littlemore (d 2003), and (Edith) Marie, *née* Clarkson; *b* 8 March 1959; *Educ* Rugby, Univ of Manchester (BA, BArch), Univ of Bath (MSc); *m* 28 July 1984, Jane Evelyn, da of Derek Chalk (d 2007), of Broad Chalke, Wilts; 1 s (Andrew b 1987), 1 da (Katharine b 1989); *Career* architect Ellis Williams Manchester 1980–81, Pick Everard Leicester 1982; Charter Architects 1983–2006 (assoc dir 1987, dir 1989–2002, md 2002–08; ceo SMC Gp plc 2008, ceo Archial NORR (formerly Archial) 2009–; memb CBI 1995 (memb SW Regnl Cncl 2000–06, London Cncl 2012–, UK Construction Cncl 2012–); exhbns of oil paintings: Edwin Young Gallery Salisbury, Medeival Hall Salisbury, Sadler Gallery Wells; memb Farrant Singers Salisbury Cathedral; founding tstee CRESS charity providing relief and aid in S Sudan; RIBA 1984; *Recreations* shooting, mountaineering, fishing, oil painting, choral singing; *Clubs* Midland Assoc of Mountaineers, RAC; *Style—* Christopher Littlemore, Esq; ✉ Archial NORR, Tennyson House, 159–165 Great Portland Street, London W1W 5BP (☎ 0207 580 0400, fax 020 7580 6680, e-mail CPL@quantumgroup.org.uk and chris@cplarchitecture.com)

LITTLER, Brian Oswald; s of William Oswald Littler (d 1958), of London, and Mavis Pricilla, *née* Copping; *b* 22 November 1942; *Educ* St Dunstan's Coll, KCL (BDS, MB BS); *m* 19 Feb 1972, Susan Elizabeth, da of Arthur Stent, of Wonersh, Surrey; 1 s (Adam Oswald b 20 Oct 1975), 2 da (Elizabeth Ann b 30 May 1978, Bryony Susan Jayne b 24 Oct 1984); *Career* private conslt oral and maxillo-facial surgn to: The Thomas Rivers Med Centre, The London Ind Hosp, The Roding Hosp Redbridge; fell Br Assoc of Oral and Maxillo-Facial Surgns, FDS RCS 1969; *Recreations* sailing; *Style—* Brian Littler, Esq; ✉ Pentlow End, High Easter, Essex CM1 4RE (☎ 01245 231626)

LITTLER MANNERS, Judy; da of Sir Emile Littler (d 1985), and Lady Cora Littler, *née* Goffin; *b* 16 October 1952; *Educ* St Mary's Hall Brighton, Charters Towers Sch Bexhill-on-Sea, St Anne's Coll Oxford (MA); *m* 12 June 1982 (m dis 1990), David Peter Manners; 1 s (Max b 27 March 1983), 1 da (Marina b 6 Sept 1986); *Career* floor asst and asst floor mangr BBC Studio Mgmnt Dept 1975–78, prodn asst Drama in Europe Ltd and Derek Glynne Assocs 1978–79, producer MMA Presentations Ltd 1979–83, prop and chief exec Mum's The Word 1984–92; dir: The Night Company Ltd 1985–96, GR Productions Ltd 1985–96, British Amalgamated Theatres Ltd 1985–; non-exec dir Stratagem Group plc (formerly London Entertainments plc) 1987–93; vice-pres The Actors' Charitable Trust 2006– (hon treas1988–96), tstee The Emile Littler Fndn, patron Theatre in Trust; memb Bd of Mgmnt Royal Hosp and Home Putney 1992–95 (chm Forget-me-not Ball 1988–92); *Recreations* theatre, tennis; *Clubs* Hurlingham, Harbour; *Style—* Mrs Judy Littler Manners; ✉ c/o Goodman Derrick & Co, 10 St Bride Street, London EC4A 4AD

LITTLEWOOD, Anthony George (Tony); s of George Kershaw Littlewood, of Ashton-under-Lyne, Lancs, and Sarah, *née* Rogers; *b* 3 October 1949; *Educ* Audenshaw GS, Univ of Nottingham (BPharm); *m* 11 Dec 1982 (m dis 1992), Nikola Ann, da of Lance James du Lys Mallalieu (d 1973); 3 s (Russell b 1984, Guy b 1986, Harry b 1988); *Career* pharmacist; chm and md George Hinchliffe Ltd 1973–; chm Northern (chemists) Ltd 1981–, md Amchem (UK) Ltd 1995–; chm Local Pharmaceutical Ctee 1989–; non-exec dir Tameside Family Health Servs Authy 1990–; chm Hulme GS PTA 1998–, treas Christ Church Friezland 1998–, tstee Age UK 2002–, dir Centre Stage Concern 2003; fndr memb Aston Martin Heritage Tst, fndr and pres Saddleworth Classic and Rare Cars Enthusiasts (SCARCE) 2010–; MRPharmS 1972, MIMgt 1980; *Recreations* tennis, golf, travel, (collecting) photographic, classic cars, gardening, restoring old buildings, enjoying retirement and playing with grandchildren; *Clubs* Union (Ashton-under-Lyne), Henllys Hall Golf (Anglesey), Bentley Drivers, Alvis, Aston Martin, Jaguar Motor Clubs, Brooklands Soc, GRRC; *Style—* Tony Littlewood, Esq; ✉ Friezland Grange, Greenfield, Saddleworth OL3 7LQ

LITTLEWOOD, Mark; *Educ* Balliol Coll Oxford; *Career* formerly head of media Lib Dems and fndr Progressive Vision, currently DG IEA; *Recreations* Southampton FC; *Clubs* Reform; *Style—* Mark Littlewood; ✉ Institute of Economic Affairs, 2 Lord North Street, London SW1P 3LB

LITTLEWOOD, Prof Peter Brent; s of Horace Littlewood, and Edna May, *née* Cooper; *b* 18 May 1955; *Educ* St Olave's Sch Orpington, Trinity Coll Cambridge (BA), MIT (Kennedy Scholar), Cavendish Lab Univ of Cambridge (PhD); *m* Elizabeth, *née* Lamb; 1 s (Christopher), 1 da (Sophie b 2000); *Career* head Theoretical Physics Dept Bell Labs 1992–97 (joined 1980); Univ of Cambridge: fell Trinity Coll 1997–, prof of physics 1997–, head Dept of Physics 2005–; author of over 100 professional articles in the field of theoretical physics; fell American Physical Soc 1988, FRS 2007; *Recreations* squash, music; *Style—* Prof Peter Littlewood; ✉ Department of Physics, University of Cambridge, Cavendish Laboratory, Madingley Road, Cambridge CB3 0HE (☎ 01223 339991, fax 01223 337356, e-mail peter.littlewood@phy.cam.ac.uk)

LITTMAN, Jeffrey James; s of Louis Littman (d 1981), of Edmonton, Middx, and Sarah (Sadie), *née* Coberman (d 1974); *b* 19 February 1943; *Educ* Latymer Sch Edmonton, St Catharine's Coll Cambridge (MA); *m* 20 March 1975, Sandra Lynne, da of David Kallman (d 1975), of New York, USA; 2 da (Amanda, Léonie); *Career* called to the Bar: Middle Temple 1974, Gray's Inn (ad eundem) 1975; in private practice at Hendon Chambers specialising in real property, commercial law, insolvency and the law of slrs and costs; ldr Mgmnt Gp Dept of Computing and Control Imperial Coll London 1990–92, real property cnsl Welsh Nat Assembly 2008; memb: Chancery Bar Assoc, Professional Negligence Bar Assoc, Admin Law Bar Assoc, Public Access Bar Assoc, Wales Circuit Specialist Bar Assoc; writer, deviser and presenter of the course on civil procedure for TV Law 1993, presenter Seminars in Insolvency and Slr's Professional Negligence for Law Soc Continuing Professional Dept (Wales) 2004; author of articles in Legal News; *Recreations* history, Jewish studies; *Style—* Jeffrey Littman, Esq; ✉ Hendon Chambers, 25 Heriot Road, Hendon, London NW4 2EG (☎ 020 8922 6844, mobile 07939 092741, e-mail jeffreylittman@aol.com)

LITTON, Andrew; *Educ* Juilliard Sch NY; *Career* conductor; assoc conductor to Mstislav Rostropovich NSO Washington (formerly asst), debut with BBC Symphony Orch 1982, debut with RPO 1983; princ conductor and artistic advsr Bournemouth Symphony Orch 1988–94 (conductor laureate 1994–), music dir Dallas Symphony Orch 1994–2006 (dir emeritus 2006–), music dir Bergen Philharmonic 2002–06 (dir emeritus 2006–), artistic dir Minnesota Orch Sommerfest 2003–, music dir New York City Ballet 2015–; guest appearances with: all maj London orchs, English Chamber Orch, Scottish Chamber Orch, Royal Scottish National Orch, Oslo Philharmonic, Rotterdam Philharmonic, Stockholm Philharmonic, Orchestre Philharmonique de Monte Carlo, RAI Milan, RSO Berlin, l'Orchestre Suisse Romande, WDR Köln, Orchestre National de France, Czech Philharmonic, Chicago Symphony Orch, Los Angeles Philharmonic, Philadelphia Orch, Pittsburgh Symphony Orch and orchs of Minnesota, Montreal, Rochester, Toronto and Vancouver; opera debuts: Metropolitan Opera (Eugene Onegin, 1989), Royal Opera House (Trevor Nunn's Porgy and Bess, 1992), ENO (Falstaff, 1994); new prodn of Salome ENO 1996, new prodn of Britten's Billy Budd WNO 1998; *Recordings* incl: complete Tchaikovsky Symphonies (with Bournemouth Symphony Orchestra), all Rachmaninov Symphonies (with RPO), Mahler's Symphony No 1 and Songs of a Wayfarer, Elgar Enigma Variations, Walton symphonies and concertos, Bernstein The Age of Anxiety, Ravel and Gershwin piano concerti, Shostakovich Symphony No 10, Brahms Symphony No 1, recordings with Dallas Symphony Orch incl Shostakovich Symphony No 8, works by Schumann, Ives, Piston, complete cycle of Mahler Symphonies with the Dallas

L

Symphony Orch, complete Rachmaninoff Concertos (Classical Brits/BBC Critics Award); *Style—* Andrew Litton, Esq; ✉ website http://www.andrewlitton.com/contact.html

LIU, David Tek-Yung; s of Pro Liu Tsu-Shya, of Sydney, Aust, and Mabel King, *née* Liang (d 1977); *b* 26 April 1941; *Educ* All Saints Bathurst NSW Australia, Univ of Sydney (MB BS), Univ of Sussex (MPhil); *m* 28 July 1976, Pamela Margaret, da of Arthur Heptinstall, of Surrey, England; 1 da (Natasha b 9 Sept 1981); *Career* res fell Univ of Sussex, lectr and res lectr UCL, sr lectr and hon conslt Univ of Nottingham 1989–, conslt Univ of Malaya 1989–91; City Hosp Nottingham: dir Fetal Care Unit 1981–, clinical dir Obstetric and Gynaecology Dept 1993–; co-fndr Embrace 1991; memb: Nottingham Charity Appeal for Pre-Natal Diagnosis, Birmingham and Midland Obstetric and Gynaecological Soc, jt MRC-RCOG Ctee Chorion Villus Sampling; FRCOG 1986, FRCOG (Aust) 1992, DM Univ of Nottingham 1992; *Books* Thinking, Feeling (1987), Labour Ward Manual (1985, 3 edn 2001), Chorion Villus Sampling (1987), Practical Gynaecology (1988); *Recreations* gardening, water sports, writing; *Clubs* Nottingham County Sailing; *Style—* David Liu, Esq

LIVELY, Dame Penelope Margaret; DBE (2012, CBE 2002, OBE 1989); da of Roger Vincent Low, and Vera Maud Greer, *née* Reckitt; *b* 17 March 1933; *Educ* St Anne's Coll Oxford (BA); *m* 1957, Prof Jack Lively (d 1998); 1 s (Adam), 1 da (Josephine); *Career* writer; book reviews and short stories in numerous magazines, various TV and radio scripts; former chm Soc of Authors (memb 1973–); memb: PEN 1985–, Arts Cncl Lit Panel 1990–92, Bd The British Library 1993–99, Bd Br Cncl 1997–; Hon DLitt; FRSL; *Children's Books* Astercote (1970), The Whispering Knights (1971), The Wild Hunt of Hagworthy (1971), The Driftway (1972), The Ghost of Thomas Kempe (Carnegie medal, 1974), The House in Norham Gardens (1974), Going Back (1975), Boy Without a Name (1975), A Stitch in Time (Whitbread award, 1976), The Stained Glass Window (1976), Fanny's Sister (1976), The Voyage of QV66 (1978), Fanny and The Monsters (1978), Fanny and The Battle of Potter's Piece (1980), The Revenge of Samuel Stokes (1981), Fanny and the Monsters (three stories, 1983), Uninvited Ghosts (1984), Dragon Trouble (1984), Debbie and the Little Devil (1987), A House Inside Out (1987); *Non-Fiction* The Presence of the Past (1976), Oleander, Jacaranda: A Childhood Perceived (1994), A House Unlocked (2001), Ammonites and Leaping Fish: A Life in Time (2013); *Fiction* The Road to Lichfield (1977), Nothing Missing but the Samovar (Southern Arts Literary prize, 1978), Treasures of Time (Arts Cncl Nat Book award, 1979), Judgement Day (1980), Next to Nature, Art (1982), Perfect Happiness (1983), Corruption (1984), According to Mark (1984), Pack of Cards, stories 1978–86 (1986), Moon Tiger (Booker prize, 1987), Passing On (1989), City of the Mind (1991), Cleopatra's Sister (1993), Heat Wave (1996), Beyond the Blue Mountains (1997), Spiderweb (1998), The Photograph (2003), Making it Up (2005), Consequences (2007), How It All Began (2012); *Style—* Dame Penelope Lively, DBE; ✉ c/o David Higham Associates, 5–8 Lower John Street, Golden Square W1R 4HA (☎ 020 7437 7888)

LIVENS, Leslie John Phillip; s of Lt Leslie Francis Hugh Livens (d 1981), of London, and Betty Livens; *b* 13 December 1946; *Educ* Wimbledon County Secdy Sch; *m* 3 Aug 1968, Carole Ann, da of Henry William Todd, of London; 1 s (Stephen b 1970), 1 da (Clare b 1973); *Career* ed and conslt ed Taxation Practitioner (Jl of Inst of Taxation) 1974–84; former ed: Tax Planning International, Financial Times World Tax Report, Review of Parliament; managing ed Butterworths Tax Books 1977–81; Moores Rowland (formerly Nevill & Co): taxation conslt 1981–83, ptnr 1983–96, chm International Tax Group 1988–96; dir: Atlas Tst Co Ltd (Gibraltar) 1996–2008, CapitaX Ltd 2008–; CTA 1972, AITI 1983–2007; memb: Soc of Share and Business Valuers 1994–, Soc of Tst and Estate Practitioners 1995–; MRICS; *Publications* incl: Moores Rowland's Tax Guide (1982–87), Daily Telegraph Tax Guide (1987), Daily Telegraph Personal Tax Guide (1988), Debrett's International Offshore Finance (ed, 1992), Livens' Share and Business Valuation Handbook (1986–2009), Tolley's Tax Havens (2000); *Recreations* music, writing, walking, family; *Style—* Leslie Livens, Esq; ✉ 30 Ashley Court, Morpeth Terrace, London SW1P 1EN (☎ 020 7834 0809, e-mail leslie@capitax.net)

LIVERMAN, Prof Diana Margaret; da of John Liverman, of Oxford, and Peggy, *née* Earl (d 2005); *b* 15 May 1954, Accra, Ghana; *Educ* UCL (BA), Univ of Toronto (MA), UCLA (PhD); *Career* asst prof Univ of Wisconsin 1984–90, assoc prof Penn State Univ 1990–96, prof and dir Centre for Latin American Studies Univ of Arizona 1996–2003, prof of environmental science and dir Environmental Change Inst Univ of Oxford 2003–; chair US Nat Acad Ctee on Human Dimensions of Global Environmental Change 1995–99, co-chair Scientific Advsy Ctee Int Inst for Global Change Research 1998–2002, chair Global Environmental Change and Food Security Prog of IHDP/IGBP/WCRP 2006–; Mitchell Prize for Sustainable Devpt 1991; life memb Assoc of American Geographers 1977, FRGS 2005; People and Pixels (1998), World Regions in Global Context (co-author, 2005); *Style—* Prof Diana Liverman; ✉ Environmental Change Institute, Oxford University Centre for the Environment, South Parks Road, Oxford OX1 3QY (☎ 01865 275848, e-mail diana.liverman@eci.ox.ac.uk)

LIVERMORE, Karen; da of Joseph Livermore (d 1982), and Glenys, *née* Howard; *Educ* Grays Sch, Thurrock Coll; *Career* freelance journalist and stylist various cos; Daily Star: fashion ed 1989–95, womans ed 1995–97; ed: Essentials magazine 1997–2004, Family Circle 2004–; *Style—* Miss Karen Livermore; ✉ c/o Essentials, King's Reach Tower, Stamford Street, London SE1 9LS

LIVERPOOL, Archbishop of (RC) 2014–; Most Rev Malcolm Patrick McMahon; s of Patrick McMahon (d 1987), and Sarah, *née* Watson (d 1982); *b* 14 June 1949, London; *Educ* St Aloysius' Coll Highgate, UMIST (BSc, pres Students Union), Heythrop Coll Univ of London (BD, MTh); *Career* with London Transport 1971–76, joined Dominican Order 1976, ordained priest 1982, asst priest 1982–88, parish priest St Dominic's Newcastle upon Tyne 1989, prior St Dominic's Priory London 1989–92, prior provincial 1992–2000, bishop of Nottingham 2000–14; *Recreations* golf, reading novels; *Clubs* Notts Co Golf; *Style—* The Most Rev the Archbishop of Liverpool; ✉ Archbishop's House, 19 Salisbury Road, Cressington Park, Liverpool L19 0PH (☎ 0151 494 0686, e-mail archbishop.liverpool@rcaolp.co.uk)

LIVERPOOL, Bishop of 2014–; Rt Rev Paul Bayes; *Career* ordained 1979; asst curate St Paul's Church Whitley Bay 1979–82, univ chaplain London 1982–87, team vicar High Wycombe 1987–90, team rector High Wycombe 1990–94, team rector Totton 1995–2004 (area dean Lyndhurst 2000–04), nat mission and evangelism advsr Archbishops' Cncl 2004–10, hon canon Worcester Cathedral 2007–10, bishop of Hertford 2010–14; *Style—* The Rt Rev the Bishop of Liverpool

LIVERSEDGE, Richard Lorton; s of Lt-Col John Ridler Liversedge (d 1968), of Fawke House, Sevenoaks, Kent, and Grace Evelyn Liversedge (d 1982); *b* 31 August 1940; *Educ* Tonbridge, London Hosp Dental Sch (BDS), London Hosp Med Coll (MB BS); *m* 28 Oct 1972, Jennifer Jane, da of John Hurrel Robertson, of Johannesburg, South Africa; 1 s (Dominic b 1974), 2 da (Annabel b 1975, Belinda b 1979); *Career* registrar London Hosp 1970–72 (house surgn 1968–69), sr registrar Royal Dental Hosp and St George's Hosp 1972–77; conslt maxillo-facial surgn: Middx Hosp 1977–89, Barnet Gp of Hosps 1977–; responsible for various surgical instrument innovations; winter sportsman (luge); winner Br Luge Champs 1971; Winter Olympics: represented GB Grenoble 1968, capt Sapporo 1972, capt Innsbruck 1976; pres Br Racing Toboggan Assoc 1972–; chm Med Ctee Fedn Internationale de Luge de Course 1972–, memb Med Ctee Br Olympic Assoc 1976–; Freeman City of London 1968, Liveryman Worshipful Co of Skinners 1977; FDS RCSEd 1971, FDS RCS 1972; *Recreations* luge, Cresta run, moto polo; *Clubs* St Moritz Tobogganing; *Style—* Richard Liversedge, Esq; ✉ Oak Cottage, 117 Flaunden, Hertfordshire HP3 0PB (☎ 01442 833 047)

LIVERSIDGE, Michael John Howard; s of William James Howard Liversidge (d 1993), and Mary Kathleen, *née* Heddon (d 1973); *b* 29 August 1947, Nairobi, Kenya; *Educ* Prince of Wales Sch Nairobi, Abingdon Sch, Courtauld Inst of Art London (BA); *m* 1976, Stephanie Mary Leith, da of Prof Ross Macdonald; *Career* research asst Paul Mellon Fndn for Br Art London 1969–70; Univ of Bristol: lectr 1970–88, sr lectr in history of art 1988–2008, head History of Art Dept 1979–96, 2002–03 and 2004–06, dean Faculty of Arts 1996–2001 (dep dean 1983–85), emeritus dean of arts 2007–; Univ of Buckingham: academic advsr in art history 2011–, sr research fell Humanities Research Inst 2012–; visiting lectr Queens Univ Kingston Canada 1971, 1973 and 1977, visiting fell Yale Center for British Art Yale Univ 1978; memb Cncl Bristol and Gloucestershire Archaeological Soc 1980–2004 (vice-chm 1984–86, chm 1986–89), hon sec Friends of Bristol Art Gallery 1987–90, dir SW Museums Cncl (formerly Area Museums Cncl for the SW) 1994–2002 (memb Bd of Mgmnt 1985–2002); govr Dauntsey's Sch 1995–; tstee Theatre Royal Bristol 2000–08, memb Campaign Bd Children's Hospice SW 2004–08, govr Br Inst of Florence 2007–; memb Art Ctee RAI 2012; FSA 1982, FRSA 1983; *Books* Canaletto and England (1993), Imagining Rome. British Artists and Rome in the Nineteenth Century (1996); also author of numerous articles in publications such as The Burlington Magazine, Apollo, Antiquaries Journal and various exhibition catalogues; *Recreations* garden history; *Style—* M J H Liversidge, Esq, FSA; ✉ History of Art Department, University of Bristol, 43 Woodland Road, Bristol BS8 1UU (e-mail m.j.h.liversidge@bristol.ac.uk)

LIVERSIDGE, Pamela Edwards; OBE (1999), DL (1999); da of William H Humphries, of Bridgnorth, Salop, and Dorothy, *née* James; *b* 23 December 1949; *Educ* Bridgnorth GS, Aston Univ (BSc); *m* 1, 1971 (m dis 1981), Dr Dale S Edwards; m 2, 1991, Douglas B Liversidge; 2 step s (Mark b 28 Feb 1962, Andrew b 30 Nov 1963), 1 step da (Suzanne b 17 Dec 1968); *Career* GKN 1971–76: gp grad, prodn engr, special projects engr (Keeton Sons & Co Sheffield); G W Thornton (became Thornton Holdings plc) 1976–87: asst tech mangr, prodn control and customer liaison mangr, materials controller, precision forge and aerofoil products mangr, sales mangr, sales dir; East Midlands Electricity plc 1987–93: strategic planning mangr, divnl dir (responsible for corp planning); princ shareholder and md Scientific Metal Powders plc 1993–96; princ shareholder and md Quest Investments Ltd 1996–; chm Sheffield Business Link 1999–2001, dir Sheffield TEC 1999–2001, non-exec dir Chesterfield Royal FT Hosp 2006–12, dir Tool & Steel Products Ltd, non-exec dir Source Bioscience plc 2014–; memb Women into Sci and Engrg (WISE) Nat Coordinating Ctee; senator Engrg Cncl 1997–99; govr Sheffield Hallam Univ 1994–2006; visiting prof in industrial mfrg Univ of Sheffield 1997–99, special prof Univ of Nottingham 1998–2000; memb Chapter Sheffield Cathedral, memb Cncl C&G, non-exec dir Rainbow Seed Fund 2007–13; finalist Young Business Personality 1982, UK Business Pioneer Global Summit of Women 1998; High Sheriff of S Yorks 2004–05; Member Co of Cutlers in Hallamshire (Mistress 1998, Master 2011–12), Freeman City of London, Liveryman Worshipful Co of Engrs, Guardian Sheffield Assay Office 2005–; Hon DUniv Central England, Hon DSc Aston Univ, Hon DEng Univ of Bradford, Hon DEng Univ of Huddersfield, Hon DUniv Sheffield Hallam, Hon DEng Univ of Sheffield; CEng, FREng, FIMechE (pres 1997–98), FCGI, FRSA; *Recreations* golf, public speaking; *Clubs* Sicklehome, Hope Valley, Pelican Nest Golf, Naples (Florida), Lansdowne; *Style—* Mrs Pam Liversidge, OBE, DL, FREng; ✉ Quest Investments Ltd, Nicholas Hall, Thornhill, Hope Valley S33 0BR (☎ 01433 659874, fax 01433 659357, e-mail liversidge1@btconnect.com)

LIVESEY, Bernard Joseph Edward; QC (1990); s of Joseph Augustine Livesey (d 1965), of Hatch End, Middx, and Marie Gabrielle, *née* Caulfield (d 1999); *b* 21 February 1944; *Educ* Cardinal Vaughan Sch London, Peterhouse Cambridge (MA, LLB); *m* 25 Sept 1971, Penelope Jean, da of Samuel Walter Harper, of Fittleworth, W Sussex; 2 da (Sarah b 5 June 1973, Kate b 21 Aug 1977); *Career* called to the Bar Lincoln's Inn 1969 (bencher 1999); recorder 1987–2010, dep judge of the High Court 1998–2012; fell Int Acad of Trial Lawyers 1993; chm Cncl of Friends of Peterhouse 2002–10; *Style—* Bernard Livesey, Esq, QC; ✉ Hailsham Chambers, 4 Paper Buildings, Temple, London EC4Y 7EX (☎ 020 7643 5000, e-mail bernard.liveseyqc@hailshamchambers.com)

LIVESEY, Dr David Anthony; s of Vincent Livesey (d 1963), of Derby, and Marie, *née* Parr (d 1983); *b* 30 May 1944; *Educ* Derby Sch, Imperial Coll London (BSc Eng), Christ's Coll Cambridge (PhD); *m* 30 Dec 1967, Sally Anne, da (Alfred) Noel Vanston; 1 s (Nathaniel James b 14 May 1970), 2 da (Ruth Laura b 6 April 1973, Harriet Sarah b 24 Oct 1980); *Career* Univ of Cambridge: res offr Dept of Applied Economics 1969–75, univ lectr Dept of Engrg 1975–91, sec gen of the Faculties 1992–2003; res fell Peterhouse Cambridge 1971–74; Emmanuel Coll Cambridge: official fell 1974–91, bursar 1983–91 professorial fell 1992–2003, life fell 2003–, vice-master 2006–11; sec gen League of European Research Univs 2005–09; dir Cambridge-MIT Inst Ltd 1999–2000; non-exec dir Addenbrooke's NHS Tst 1992–99; tstee: Bedford Charity 2004–09, Citizens Advice 2005–11; govr Henley Mgmnt Coll 2005–07, govr St Mary's Univ Twickenham 2013–; ACGI; *Recreations* swimming, learning Welsh; *Style—* Dr David Livesey; ✉ 19 Glisson Road, Cambridge CB1 2HA (☎ 01223 364520); Emmanuel College, Cambridge CB2 3AP (☎ 01223 334243, fax 01223 334426)

LIVESEY, Rodger Charles; JP; s of Roland Livesey; *b* 19 June 1944; *Educ* Downing Coll Cambridge (MA); *m* 29 May 1972, Pat; 2 s (Matthew b 1974, Graham b 1979), 1 da (Caroline b 1977); *Career* md Security Pacific Hoare Govett Ltd 1976–88, Tokai Bank Europe plc 1988–2002, chm W Hampton Ltd 1987–; dir: Securities and Futures Authy 1994–99, Beds and Herts NHS Tst 1994–2000, UFJI plc 2002–; gen cmmr of tax; dir Eastern Arts Bd 1998–2001; govr Univ of Luton 1999–; Freeman City of London, Liveryman Worshipful Co of Actuaries; FIA; *Style—* Rodger Livesey, Esq; ✉ 60 West Common, Harpenden, Hertfordshire AL5 2LD (☎ 01582 767527)

LIVESEY, Tony; s of John Livesey, of Nelson, Lancs, and Jean, *née* Comber (d 1977); *b* 11 January 1964; *Educ* SS John Fisher and Thomas More HS Colne, Nelson and Colne Coll; *m* Barbara, *née* Maley; 1 da (Megan Maley b 23 Aug 1994), 1 s (Angus Maley b 23 May 1996); *Career* jr reporter Nelson Leader 1983–86, writer news and features Gulf News Dubai 1986–87, reporter Lancashire Evening Telegraph 1987–88; Sport Newspapers: successively sports reporter, sports ed, asst ed then dep ed Sunday Sport, launch ed News & Echo (since sold), managing ed Sunday and Daily Sport, ed Sunday Sport and gp managing ed 1993–95, gp ed-in-chief 1995–2006, md 1999–2006, presenter BBC Radio Lancashire 2006–10, presenter BBC Radio 5 Live 2010–; columnist News of the World 1999–2002; NW Young Journalist of the Year 1988; presenter Traitor (quiz show, BBC2); *Books* 10 Years of Sunday Sport (1996), Babes, Booze, Orgies and Aliens (1998), Stan the Man – A Hard Life in Football; also author of a series of short children's stories (1986–87); *Recreations* reading, writing TV scripts, watching Burnley FC (often from behind the seat), after dinner speaking; *Style—* Tony Livesey, Esq

LIVESLEY, Prof Brian; s of Thomas Clement Livesley (d 1980), and Stella Livesley (d 1980); *b* 31 August 1936; *Educ* King George V GS Southport, Univ of Leeds Med Sch (MB ChB, DHMSA, MD (Lond)); *m* 1, 1963, Beryl, *née* Hulme (d 1966); 1 s; m 2, 1969, Valerie Anne, *née* Nuttall; 2 da; *Career* house appts: Leeds Gen Infirmary 1961–62, Dist and Univ Hosps in Leeds, Manchester and Liverpool 1963–68; Harvey res fell King's Coll Hosp London 1969–72, conslt physician in geriatric med Lambeth, Southwark and Lewisham Health Authy 1973–87, Univ of London's prof of med in the elderly Imperial Coll Sch of Med at Chelsea and Westminster Hosp (Charing Cross and Westminster Med Sch until merger 1997) 1988–2001, emeritus prof Univ of London 2003–; clinical examiner in med Univ of London 1980–95 (sr clinical examiner 1990–95), examiner in med Worshipful Soc of Apothecaries 1987–94, examiner for dip in geriatric med RCP 1987–93, external examiner in med Royal Free and UC Sch of Med 1998–2001, external assessor RCP 2000–01; NW Thames regnl advsr on med for the elderly 1990–96, invited expert on the care of elderly persons for several Police Constabularies and HM Coroners' Officers 1999–2010, conslt forensic physician 2001–10; memb: Med Cmmn on Accident Prevention 1984–89 (chm Home and Family Safety Cmmn 1988–89), Br Acad Forensic Sciences 2002–09, Assoc of Forensic Physicians 2004–06; John Keats Meml Lectr 2009; govr: St Paul's Cray CE (controlled) Primary Sch Orpington 1986–87, Newstead Wood Sch for Girls Orpington 1987–92; Univ of London's Academic Cncl rep to Age Concern Bromley (chm 1992–93); memb Harris Manchester Coll Oxford 2012–; DG St John Ambulance 1994–96 (asst DG 1993–94); JP 1983–96; fell Hunterian Soc 2003–05 (lectr 2003); Liveryman Worshipful Soc of Apothecaries (Yeoman 1975, memb Ct of Assts 1990, Master 2005–06, chm Futures Ctee 2000–03, chm Academic Ctee 2001–03, Osler Lectr 1975, Gideon de Laune Lectr 2001 and 2016); memb BMA 1960, FRCP 1989 (MRCP), FRSM 1995; KStJ 1994 (OStJ 1992); *Publications* investigations into aspects of the history, pathophysiology, biochemistry, psychology, epidemiology, sociology and education in med and forensic med in our ageing society and palliative care for the dying, book reviewer for professional jls; *Recreations* family, Christian culture study, encouraging people to think; *Style*— Prof Brian Livesley; ✉ Wolfson House, Yarnells Hill, Oxford OX2 9BG (e-mail bl02@btinternet.com)

LIVINGSTON, Dorothy Kirby; da of late Albert Paulus Livingston, and late Margaret Alice, *née* Kirby; *b* 6 January 1948; *Educ* Central Newcastle HS, GDST, St Hugh's Coll Oxford (MA); *m* 11 Sept 1971 (m dis 2002), Julian, s of late Alfred Millar; 2 da; *Career* Herbert Smith Freehills LLP (formerly Herbert Smith): articled clerk 1970–72, slr 1972–80, ptnr 1980–2008, conslt 2008–; slr advocate (civil) 2005; memb: Law Soc 1979, City of London Slrs' Co 1979; chm Fin Law Ctee and memb Competition Law Ctee City of London Law Soc, memb Banking Liaison Panel 2009; *Publications* FT Law and Tax: Competition Law and Practice (1995), Euromoney: Leasing Finance (contrib, 3 edn 1997 and 4 edn 2003), Sweet & Maxwell: The Competition Act 1998: A Practical Guide (2001), Edward Elgar: Business Innovation and the Law: Perspectives from Intellectual Property, Labour, Competition and Corporate Law (contrib, 2013); *Recreations* gardening, photography, history; *Style*— Mrs Dorothy Livingston; ✉ Herbert Smith Freehills LLP, Exchange House, Primrose Street, London EC2A 2EG (☎ 020 7374 8000, fax 020 7496 0043, e-mail dorothy.livingston@hsf.com)

LIVINGSTON, Dr Martin Gerard; s of Arnold Louis Livingston, of Newton Mearns, Glasgow, and Joyce, *née* Sternstein; *b* 19 May 1953; *Educ* Hillhead HS Glasgow, Univ of Glasgow (MB ChB, MD); *m* 4 July 1974, Hilary Monica, da of Dr Basil Green, of Glasgow; 1 s (Richard Jack b 1983), 1 da (Judith Fiona b 1985); *Career* psychiatry rotation Southern Gen Hosp and Leverndale Hosp 1978–79; Univ of Glasgow: lectr Psychological Med Dept 1979–83, sr lectr and hon conslt psychiatrist 1983–98; conslt psychiatrist and hon clinical sr lectr Southern General Hosp Glasgow 1998–; regnl advsr on psychiatric rehabilitation 1987–, chm Glasgow Psychiatric Speciality Ctee 1989–92; chm: Mental Health Unit Audit Ctee, Mental Health and Community Servs Tst R&D Ctee; specialis advsr to GMC tribunals 2001–, pt/t cmmr Mental Welfare Cmmn 1994–97; memb: Collegium Internationale Neuropsychopharmacologicum (CINP), Euro Coll of Neuropsychopharmacology (ECNP), advocates discipline tribunal 2000–; FRCPsych 1994 (MRCPsych 1980); *Publications* Rehabilitation of Adults and Children with Severe Head Injury (contrib, 1989), CRAG/SCOTMEG Services for People Affected by Schizophrenia (1995); psychiatric advsr to Prescriber Jl; author of pubns on: rehabilitation in psychiatry, psychological impact of head injury and epilepsy on patients and their relatives, drug treatments in psychiatry; *Recreations* reading, photography, classical music; *Style*— Dr Martin Livingston; ✉ Department Psychiatry, Southern General Hospital, 1345 Govan Road, Glasgow G51 4TF (☎ and fax 0141 201 1947, e-mail mgl2w@udcf.gla.ac.uk

LIVINGSTON, Roderick George; s of Hugh Livingston (d 1981), of Streetly, and Rhoda Margaret, *née* Mathieson (d 2001); *b* 10 December 1944; *Educ* Shrewsbury, Univ of Aberdeen (BSc, Rowing blue), Univ of Exeter (ADPA), Univ of Western Ontario; *m* 23 Sept 1974, Willma, da of William Watt (d 1977), of Edinburgh; 2 s (Alastair Iain b 1 Sept 1976, Michael Andrew b 16 Jan 1981); *Career* admin asst UCW Aberystwyth 1970–72 (grad asst 1969–70), asst sec Univ of Dundee 1975–78 (sr admin asst 1972–75); Univ of Strathclyde: asst sec 1978–81, asst registrar 1981–85, sr asst registrar 1985–88, sr asst registrar and faculty offr 1988–2004, mangr Strathclyde Business Sch 2004–08, hon appointment 2008–; UCCA: memb Cncl of Mgmnt 1982–93, memb Statistics Ctee 1986–93, dir of co 1982–95, memb Exec Ctee 1988–94; UCAS (following merger of UCCA and PCAS): memb Jt Advsy Bd 1992–93, memb Bd of Dirs 1993–99; memb CVCP Steering Gp for the Review of the Nat Applications/Admissions Procedures 1994–99; vice-chm Glasgow Area Bd Young Enterprise Scotland 1993–2004 (chm 1999–2000, memb Scottish Cncl 1993–2004, Gold Award 1998); sec and treas Glasgow Quality Forum 1995–99 (sec 1994–95); memb Scot Univs Cncl on Entrance 1987–90; memb Undergrad Steering Ctee Assoc of Business Schs 1997–2006; vice-chm Glasgow Coll of Nautical Studies 2004–11 (memb 2001–11); memb Core Funding Ctee Scottish Further Educn Funding Cncl 2002–04; dir New Campus Glasgow 2008–10, tstee City of Glasgow Coll Fndn 2014–; convener Mil Educn Ctee Univs of Glasgow and Strathclyde 2005–11 (vice-convener 2004–05, memb 2000–), treas Cncl of Military Educn Ctees 2007– (memb Exec 2007–); memb Lowland Reserve Forces' and Cadets' Assoc 2006–; pres Univ of Aberdeen Athletic Assoc 1967–68; sec Abertay Historical Soc 1975–78; FSA Scot 1963, FRSA 1996, FCIS 1998 (ACIS 1972), FInstD 2000; *Recreations* castles, coins, rowing, sailing; *Clubs* Lansdowne, Leander, Royal Northern and Clyde Yacht; *Style*— Roderick Livingston, Esq; ✉ 51 Strathblane Road, Milngavie, Glasgow G62 8HA (☎ 0141 956 3851, e-mail roderick.livingston@btinternet.com); University of Strathclyde (e-mail r.livingston@strath.ac.uk)

LIVINGSTON OF PARKHEAD, Baron (Life Peer UK 2013), of Parkhead in the City of Glasgow; Ian Paul Livingston; *b* 28 July 1964; *Educ* Kelvinside Acad, Univ of Manchester (BA); *m* 1987; 1 s, 1 da; *Career* former appts: Arthur Andersen 1984–87, Bank of America 1987–88, 3i plc 1988–91; Dixons Group plc: joined 1991, chief fin offr (US) 1992–94, gp fin controller 1994–95, fin/systems dir 1995–97, gp fin dir 1997–2002; BT Gp plc: gp fin dir 2002–05, ceo BT Retail 2005–08, gp ceo 2008–13; min of state for trade and investment 2013–15; non-exec dir: Ladbrokes plc/Hilton Gp plc 2003–07, Celtic plc 2007–, Belmond Ltd; dep chm Dixons Carphone plc 2015–, chm Man Gp plc 2016–; ACA 1987; *Recreations* football, theatre; *Style*— The Lord Livingstone of Parkhead

LIVINGSTONE, Prof David N; OBE (2002); *b* 15 March 1953, Banbridge, NI; *Educ* Queen's Univ Belfast (BA, DipEd, PhD); *m*; 1 s, 1 da; *Career* research fell ESRC 1982–84; Queen's Univ Belfast: curator of maps 1984–89, reader Sch of Geosciences 1991–93 (lectr 1989–91), prof of geography and intellectual history (initially prof of geography) 1993–; visiting prof of geography and history of science Calvin Coll MI 1989–90, visiting prof of history Univ of Notre Dame IN 1995, visiting prof Regent Coll Vancouver 1997, 2000 and 2003, distinguished visiting prof of history and science Baylor Univ TX 2003–05, noted visiting scholar Univ of Br Columbia 1999; delivered numerous guest lectures at academic instns worldwide, organiser of confs; pres Geography Section BAAS 2005, vice-pres (research) RGS 2007–10; chair History and Philosophy of Geography Research Gp RGS (with IBG) 1995–98, co-fndr and jt sec Working Party on the History and Philosophy of Geography IBG 1981–84; memb: Ctee Study Gp on the History and Philosophy of Geography IBG 1984–94, Cmmn on the History of Geographical Thought Int Union of the History and Philosophy of Science and Int Geographical Union 1988–96, Nat Ctee for the History and Philosophy of Science Royal Irish Acad 1988–96, Nat Ctee for Geography Royal Irish Acad 1996–2003, Structures Review Ctee Br Acad 1997–98, Steering Ctee John Templeton Fndn Seminars on Science and Religion Univ of Oxford 1998–2001, Strategic Plan Ctee Royal Irish Acad 2000–02, Co-ordinating Ctee European Science Fndn Workshops on Science and Human Values 2000–03, Cncl Royal Irish Acad 2001–02, Cncl Br Soc for the History of Science 2009–; memb Editorial Bd: Annals of the Association of British Geographers 1990–93, Transactions of the Institute of British Geographers 1993–98, Ecumene 1993–99 (memb Advsy Bd 1999–), Isis 1995–97, The Cambridge History of Science CUP 1995–2002, Science and Christian Belief 1996–, Progress in Human Geography 1998–2002, History of Cartography Project Chicago Univ Press 2002–, Jl of Historical Geography 2003–; Charles Lyell lectr BAAS 1994–95, Admiral Black Award RGS 1997, Centenary Medal RSGS 1997, Templeton Fndn Lecture Series Award 1999, Br Acad Research Readership 1999–2001, Hettner Lectures Univ of Heidelberg 2001, Murrin Lectures Univ of Br Columbia 2002, Progress in Human Geography Lecture RGS-IBG Annual Conf 2005, Humboldt lectr UCLA 2007, Manley lectr Royal Holloway Univ of London 2007, Royal Irish Acad Gold Medal in Social Sciences 2008, Gunning lectr Univ of Edinburgh 2009, Gregory lectr Univ of Southampton 2010, Leverhulme Major Research Fellowship 2011–12 and 2013–15, Founder's Medal RGS 2011, Gifford Lectures 2014, Dudleian lectr Harvard Univ 2015; convocation speaker Gordon Coll MA 2000, memb Ct Univ of Ulster (Br Acad rep) 1996–2000; Hon DLitt Univ of Aberdeen 2013; memb Academia Europaea 2002, corresponding memb Int Acad of the History of Science 2011; FBA 1995, MRIA 1998, FRSA 2001, FAcSS 2002; *Publications* Nathaniel Southgate Shaler and the Culture of American Science (1987), Darwin's Forgotten Defenders (1987), The Behavioural Environment: Essays in Reflection, Application and Re-evaluation (ed with F W Boal, 1989), The Preadamite Theory and The Marriage of Science and Religion (1992), The Geographical Tradition: Episodes in the History of a Contested Enterprise (1992), What is Darwinism? And Other Writings on Science and Religion by Charles Hodge (ed with Mark A Noll, 1994), Human Geography: An Essential Anthology (ed with John Agnew and Alistair Rodgers, 1996), Them and Us? Attitudinal Variation among Belfast Churchgoers (with F W Boal and M Keane, 1997), Ulster-American Religion: Episodes in the History of a Cultural Connection (with R A Wells, 1999), Evangelicals and Science in Historical Perspective (ed with D G Hart and Mark A Noll, 1999), Geography and Enlightenment (ed with Charles Withers, 1999), Evolution, Scripture, and Science: Selected Writings of B B Warfield (ed with Mark A Noll, 2000), Science, Space and Hermeneutics (2001), Putting Science in its Place: Geographies of Scientific Knowledge (2003), Adam's Ancestors: Race, Religion and the Politics of Human Origins (2008), Geographies of Science (ed with Peter Meusburger and Heike Jöns, 2010), Geographies of Nineteenth Century Science (ed with C W J Withers, 2011), Dealing with Darwin (2014); numerous book chapters and articles; *Style*— Prof David Livingstone, OBE; ✉ School of Geography, The Queen's University of Belfast, Belfast BT7 1NN

LIVINGSTONE, Ian Lang; CBE (1998, OBE 1993); s of John Lang Livingstone (d 1998), of Motherwell, and Margaret Steele, *née* Barbour (d 1982); *b* 23 February 1938; *Educ* Hamilton Acad, Univ of Glasgow (BL); *m* 30 March 1967, Diane, da of Frank Hales (d 1989), of Lytham St Annes; 2 s (Andrew b 1968, Gordon b 1970); *Career* conslt slr, NP 1962, ptnr Ballantyne & Copland Slrs Motherwell 1963–89 (sr ptnr 1970–89, conslt 1989–); chm: Motherwell FC 1973–87, Lanarkshire Health Bd (now NHS Lanarkshire) 1993–2002 (memb 1988–), Lanarkshire Development Agency until 2000, Bowmere Properties Ltd, New Lanarkshire Ltd, House Sales (Motherwell) Ltd, Motherwell Coll Bd until 2011, Mansewood Factors Ltd, Kingdom F M Ltd 2008–, Bowmere Inc (USA), NL2017 Ltd until 2015; dir: Motherwell Enterprise Development Co 1983, Scotland West Bd TSB plc 1985, Fraser Tool Hire Ltd, James Hepburn Ltd until 2011, Kingdom FM Ltd; chm Scottish Local Authorities Remuneration Ctee until 2012; hon pres: Motherwell United YMCA, Motherwell Branch St Andrew's Ambulance Assoc, Lanarkshire C of C 2007–12; hon slr Dalziel HS Meml Tst, memb Dalziel HS Bd 1990–2011, govr David Livingstone Meml Tst 1988– (chm 2008–15); Dep Lord-Lt Lanarkshire 2008–15, DL Lanarkshire 2008–12; Hon DUniv West of Scotland 2008; *Recreations* golf, music; *Style*— Ian Livingstone, Esq, CBE; ✉ Roath Park, 223 Manse Road, Motherwell ML1 2PY (☎ 01698 253750, fax 01698 276730, e-mail ian@bowmere.com)

LIVINGSTONE, Marco Eduardo; s of Leon Livingstone, of London, and Alicia, *née* Arce Fernández; *b* 17 March 1952; *Educ* Univ of Toronto (BA), Courtauld Inst of Art (MA); *Partner* Stephen Stuart-Smith, *qv* (civil partnership 20 Jan 2006); *Career* asst keeper of Br art Walker Art Gallery Liverpool 1976–82, dep dir MOMA Oxford 1982–86, area ed 20th century The Dictionary of Art 1986–91 (dep ed 19th and 20th centuries 1987–91), UK advsr to Art Life Ltd Tokyo 1989–98; freelance writer, ed and exhbn organiser; exhbns organised incl: Patrick Caulfield retrospective (Liverpool and London) 1981, Jim Dine retrospective (Japanese tour) 1990–91, Pop Art (Royal Acad of Arts, touring Cologne, Madrid and Montreal) 1991, Tom Wesselmann retrospective (Japanese tour) 1993, Hockney in California (Japanese tour) 1994, Duane Hanson retrospective (Montreal Museum of Fine Arts) 1994, Jim Dine: The Body and its Metaphors (Japanese tour) 1996, The Pop '60s: Transatlantic Crossing (Lisbon) 1997, George Segal retrospective (Montreal Museum of Fine Arts, touring Washington, New York, Miami) 1997–98, R B Kitaj retrospective (Oslo, Madrid, Vienna, Hanover) 1998, Duane Michals: Words and Images (Montreal Museum of Fine Arts and Nat Gallery of Canada) 1998–99, David Hockney: Egyptian Journeys (Cairo) 2002, Pop Art UK: British Pop Art 1956–1972 (Modena) 2004, R B Kitaj: Portrait of a Hispanist (Bilbao) 2004, British Pop (Bilbao) 2005–06, Paula Rego (Madrid and Washington DC) 2007–08 and (Monterrey) 2010, David Hockney: A Bigger Picture (London, Bilbao and Cologne) 2012, Tom Wesselmann: A Retrospective (Montreal) 2012, Post Pop: East meets West (co-curator, London 2014); memb: Soc of Authors 1980, Association Internationale des Critiques d'Art (AICA) 1992; *Publications* Sheer Magic by Allen Jones (1979), David Hockney (1981, 3 edn 1996), Duane Michals (1985), R B Kitaj (1985, 2 edn 1992), David Hockney: Faces (1987), Pop Art (1990), Tim Head (1993), Jim Dine: Flowers and Plants (1994), Allen Jones Prints (1995), The Essential Duane Michals (1997), George Segal (1997), Jim Dine: The Alchemy of Images (1998), Patrick Caulfield (contrib, 1999), David Hockney: Space and Line (1999), Art: The Critics' Choice (contrib, 1999), Encounters: New Art from Old (contrib, 2000), D'Après L'Antigue (contrib, 2000), Enrico Baj (contrib, 2001), Kienholz Tableau Drawings (2001), Callum Innes: Exposed Paintings (2001), Langlands & Bell: Language of Places (2002), Maurice Cockrill (co-author, 2002), Clive Barker – Sculpture (co-author, 2002), Blast to Freeze – British Art in the 20th Century (contrib, 2002–03), Jim Dine: The Photographs So Far (contrib, 2003), David Hockney's Portraits and People (co-author, 2003, Sir Bannister Fletcher Award for Best Book on the Arts 2004), Red Grooms (co-author, 2004), Patrick Caulfield: Paintings (2005), David Hockney Portraits (contrib, 2006), Richard Woods (co-author, 2006), Tony Bevan (contrib, 2006), Gilbert & George: Major Exhibition (contrib, 2007), Gary Hume: Prints (2007), Seeing Double: The Poetic Focus of Claes Oldenburg and Coosje van Bruggen (2007), John Wesley (2008), Paula Rego: Human Cargo (2008), Colin Self: Art in the Nuclear Age (co-author, 2008), Jim Dine: Talking About Aldo (2008), David Hockney: Just Nature (contrib, 2009), Peter Blake: One Man Show (2009), Peter

L

Blake: Venice Fantasies (co-author, 2009), Peter Kinley (co-author, 2010), David Hockney: My Yorkshire (2011), Peter Blake: Paris Escapades (co-author, 2011), Paula Rego (contrib, 2012), David Hockney: A Bigger Picture (contrib, 2012), David Mach (2012), Pop Art Design (contrib, 2012), When Britain Went Pop – British Pop Art: The Early Years (contrib, 2013), Tom Wesselmann Still Life, Nude, Landscape: The Late Prints (2013), Shinro Ohtake (contrib, 2014), /touch: Figure Drawings by Allen Jones 1958–2012 (2014), Allen Jones (contrib, 2014), Hockney Printmaker (contrib, 2014); Post Pop: East meets West (contrib, 2014), Tom Wesselmann: A Line to Greatness (2015), Inside Out: Sculptures by Allen Jones (2015), Peter Blake: Portraits and People (2015), Jim Dine: About the Love of Printing (contrib, 2015), Michael Craig-Martin: Transience (contrib, 2015), Joe Tilson: The Stones of Venice (2016); *Style—* Mr Marco Livingstone; ✉ Flat 14, Spectrum Court, 2 Manor Gardens, London N7 6ER (☎ 020 7607 0282, e-mail marcolivingstone@aol.com); Plum Tree House, Huckers Lane, Selborne, Alton, Hampshire GU34 3JN (☎ 01420 511266); 1 Empire Square, London N7 6JN (☎ 020 7272 8727)

LIVINGSTONE-LEARMONTH, John Christian; s of Lt-Col Lennox John Livingstone-Learmonth, DSO, MC (d 1988), and Nancy Winifred, *née* Wooler (d 1989); *b* 30 October 1950; *Educ* Eton, Univ of York (BA); *m* 13 Dec 1986, (Elizabeth) Fiona, da of Arthur Ivor Stewart-Liberty, MC (d 1990), of The Lee, Bucks; 1 s (Edward Miles Christian b 22 Sept 1988), 1 da (Marina Francesca b 4 May 1991); *Career* SA mktg offr James Buchanan and Co 1975–83, sr ptnr Livingstone Communication 1987–, dir City Decisions Ltd 1990–95; distinguished visitor to Miami; memb Circle of Wine Writers; Citoyen d'Honneur of Châteauneuf-du-Pape, Chevalier de l'Ordre du Mérite Agricole; *Books* The Wines of the Rhône (1978, 3 edn 1992), The Wines of the Northern Rhône (2005, Louis Roederer International Wine Book of the Year 2006 and André Simon Award 2006), Gigondas (2011); *Recreations* the turf, vegetables, fishing, wine tasting and writing; *Clubs* Turf, Irish; *Style—* John Livingstone-Learmonth, Esq; ✉ Livingstone Communication (☎ 01424 844854)

LLANWARNE, Trevor; CB (2013); s of Douglas Llanwarne, and Margaret Llanwarne; *Educ* Forest Fields GS Nottingham, Christ Church Oxford (MA); *m* 1984, Margaret; 2 s (Thomas, Christopher), 1 da (Sarah); *Career* Sun Life Assurance Soc 1974–84, Pointon York Gp 1984–88; PricewaterhouseCoopers: joined 1988, ptnr 1992–, chief actuary pensions until 2008; govt actuary Govt Actuary's Dept 2008–14; FIA 1979; tstee Int Longevity Centre 2015–, various tstee and advsy appts in the investment, pensions and university arenas; *Publications* Government Actuary's Quinquennial Review of the National Insurance Fund (2010, 2014), Review of Certain Contracting Out Terms (jtly, 2011); *Recreations* major property conservation project, family history, bridge; *Clubs* Oxford and Cambridge; *Style—* Trevor Llanwarne, Esq, CB

LLEWELLYN, Carl; s of Eryl D Llewellyn, of Hundleton, Pembroke, and Jean, *née* Harries; *b* 29 July 1965; *Educ* Pembroke Secdy Sch; *Career* national hunt jockey; turned professional 1986, winner Apprentice Championship setting record of 41 winners, rode Grand National winner Party Politics 1992, rode Grand National winner Earth Summit 1998; rep Br Jump Jockeys Team: Australia 1987 (series winners), Russia 1992; trainer of Scottish Grand National winner Run for Paddy and Bet 365 Gold Cup winner Hennesy before retiring from training 2009; Pacemaker Jockey of the Year 1986–87; *Recreations* golf; *Style—* Carl Llewellyn, Esq; ✉ mobile 07836 783223, e-mail carlllewellyn1@gmail.com

LLEWELLYN, Prof David Thomas; s of Alfred George Llewellyn (d 1990), of Gillingham, Dorset, and Elsie Elizabeth, *née* Frith; *b* 3 March 1943, London; *Educ* William Ellis GS, LSE (BSc); *m* 19 Sept 1970, Wendy Elizabeth, da of Henry Cecil James, MM (d 1973); 2 s (Mark b 15 Aug 1972, Rhys b 18 Dec 1978); *Career* economist: Unilever NV Rotterdam 1964–65, HM Treasy 1965–68; lectr Univ of Nottingham 1968–73, economist IMF Washington 1973–76, prof of money and banking Loughborough Univ 1976– (head Dept of Economics 1980–90); chm Loughborough Univ Banking Centre 1985–2010; visiting prof: London Business Sch 1997–98, Swiss Banking Sch Zurich 2003–06, Cass Business Sch London 2003–13, IESE Business Sch Madrid 2005–08, Swiss Finance Inst 2006–09, Vienna Univ of Economics and Business 2007–13; dir London Bd Halifax Building Soc 1986–93, memb Academic Bd Sundridge Park Mgmnt Centre 1990–95, public interest dir Personal Investment Authy 1994–2000; memb Bd PIA Ombudsman Bureau; SUERF (Société Universitaire Européene Recheches Financières): memb Cncl 1998–, pres 2000–08; conslt economist: Butlers 1985–, Harlow Butler Ueda 1989–99, Garban Intercapital 1999–, ICAP 2000–13; conslt Reserve Bank of South Africa 2000–04; memb: Exec Bd Euro Fin Mgmnt Assoc, Financial Services Panel DTI Technol Foresight Prog 1992–2000, Task Force on Competition in South African Banking Industry 2003–04, Expert Panel on Banking Bank Indonesia, Consultative Gp on Governance in Supervisory Authorities IMF Washington, Credit Risk Consortium Harland Financial Solutions USA, Academic Bd Int Centre for Financial Regulation 2010–13; chair Banking Stakeholder Gp European Banking Authy 2013– (vice-chair 2011–13); former conslt The World Bank, OECD, regulatory authorities, building socs and banks; occasional memb Bank of England Panel of Academic Conslts; memb Int Advsy Bd: European Banking Report Italian Bankers' Assoc 1994–, Productivity Mgmnt Int 1995–2000, NCR Financial Solutions Gp 1996–2000; memb Editorial Bd: Banking World 1978–84, Jl of Retail Banking Int (NY), Jl of Fin Regulation and Compliance 2001–, Jl of Bank Regulation 2005–; managing ed Chartered Inst of Bankers Occasional Res Papers Series 1978–82; Bertil Danielsson Fndn visiting scholar Stockholm and Gothenburg Schs of Economics 1992; special advsr Jt Parly Ctee on the Fin Markets and Services Bill 1999; assoc memb Kellogg Coll Oxford 2009–; hon doctorate Loughborough Univ 2015; FCIB, FRSA, fell Chartered Inst of Finance 2000–; *Books* International Financial Integration (1980), Framework of UK Monetary Policy (1983), Regulation of Financial Institutions (1986), Evolution of British Financial System (1985), Reflections on Money (1990), Recent Developments in International Monetary Economics (1990), Surveys in Monetary Economics Vols 1 & 2 (with C Green, 1991), Competition or Credit Controls (Hobart Paper, 1991), The Economics of Mutuality and the Future of Building Societies (1997), Financial Regulation: Why, How and Where Now? (with Charles Goodhart, 1998), The New Economics of Banking (1999), Competitive Strategies in the New Economics of Retail Financial Services (2001), Financial Innovation in Retail and Wholesale Banking (2009), New Paradigms in Banking, Financial Markets and Regulation (2012), Future Risks and Fragilities for Financial Stability (2012), Fifty Years of Bank Business Models (2013), Markets for the Many: How Civic Finance Can Open Markets and Widen Access (with Adam Wildman, 2014), Viruous Banking: Placing Ethos and Purpose at the Heart of Finance (with Roger Steare and Jessica Trevellick, 2014); *Recreations* boating, cooking, DIY, gardening, travel; *Style—* Prof David T Llewellyn; ✉ 8 Landmere Lane, Ruddington, Nottingham NG11 6ND (☎ 0115 921 6071); Department of Economics, Loughborough University, Loughborough, Leicestershire LE11 3TU (☎ 01509 222700, e-mail d.t.llewellyn@lboro.ac.uk); Villa 10, Les Pins, Les Hauts du Golf, 760 Chemin de la Tire, Mougins, France

LLEWELLYN, Dr John; s of Sir (Frederick) John Llewellyn (d 1988), and Joyce, *née* Barrett (d 2001); *b* 13 September 1944; *Educ* Christchurch Boys' HS NZ, Scots' Coll Wellington NZ, Victoria Univ of Wellington NZ (BA), Univ of Oxford (DPhil); *m* 8 Dec 1990, Ruth, *née* Doncaster; 2 da, 3 s; *Career* researcher First National Bank of Boston 1966–67, research offr Dept of Applied Economics Univ of Cambridge 1970–74, fell St John's Coll Cambridge 1972–77, asst dir of research Faculty of Economics Univ of Cambridge 1974–77; OECD: head Economic Prospects Div 1978–86, dep dir Directorate for Social Affrs Manpower and Educn 1986–89, head Sec-Gen's Private Office 1989–94; Lehman Brothers: chief economist Europe and md 1995–96, global chief economist and md 1996–2006, sr economic policy advsr and md 2006–08; ptnr Llewellyn Consulting 2008–; advsr HM Treasy 2009–11; sec Degree Ctee Faculty of Economics Univ of Cambridge 1974–77, memb Bd of Graduate Studies Univ of Cambridge 1976–77, dir of studies St John's Coll Cambridge 1976–77; temp dir of research Centro de Investigación y Docencia Economicas Mexico City 1976–77, lectr Univ of Southern California Sch of Int Rels London 1976–77; memb Editorial Bd: OECD Economic Studies 1983–89, Economic Modelling 1983–93; memb: Conseil Scientifique Fondation Nationale des Sciences Politiques Paris 1986–94 (pt/t lectr in contemporary economic policy 1990–94), Comité Consultatif Observatoire Français des Conjonctures Economiques 1987–94, Pres of EC's Gp of Economic Analysis 2000–04, Cncl of Chatham House 2007–13, Cncl Nat Inst of Economic and Social Research 2010–, Advsy Panel Office for Budget Responsibility 2011–; dir Genesis Emerging Markets Fund 2009–, memb Advsy Bd Ondra Partners LLP 2009–14; tstee FIA Fndn for the Automobile and Society 2006–10; hon fell Univ of South Bank 1997; *Publications* Economic Forecasting and Policy – The International Dimension (with S J Potter and L W Samuelson, 1985), Economic Policies for the 1990s (ed with S J Potter, 1991), The Business of Climate Change (2007), The Business of Ageing (2008), The Ascent of Asia (2010), Conditions for Growth (2010), Europe Will Work (with Peter Westaway, 2011), Financing European Growth (with Bimal Dharmasena, 2012), UK Infrastructure (with Russell Jones, 2013), The Changing Face of Africa (with Ben Combes and Preston Llewellyn, 2013), UK Infrastructure: The Challenges for Investors and Policymakers (with Russell Jones, 2013), The Changing Face of the Oil Industry (with Betsy Hansen and Preston Llewellyn, 2013); author of numerous articles in economic jls and the press; *Recreations* writing, motor sport, photography, music; *Clubs* Athenaeum, RAC; *Style—* Dr John Llewellyn; ✉ Llewellyn Consulting, 1 St Andrew's Hill, London EC4V 5BY (☎ 020 7213 0300, e-mail john.llewellyn@llewellyn-consulting.com, websites www.llewellyn-consulting.com and www.llewellyn.co.nz)

LLEWELLYN, Laurence Richard; s of Illtyd Raymond Llewellyn (d 1991), of Slough, Berks, and Marjorie Patricia, *née* Weaver (d 1991); *b* 9 February 1948, Slough, Berks; *Educ* Abingdon Sch, UMIST (BSc), Cranfield Sch of Mgmnt (MBA), London Coll of Music (MMus); *m* 30 March 1970 (m dis 2007), Margaret, *née* Henry; 1 s (Dr Christopher Ian Henry Llewellyn b 14 Oct 1975), 1 da (Dr Clare Heidi Llewellyn b 29 Oct 1978); *Career* fin analyst Ford Motor Co 1968–72, Citibank: joined 1973, real estate and contracting head UK corporate bank 1977–81, credit supervisor and dep region head Levant & N Africa 1982–4, sr credit offr, country and regional mgmnt ME Africa Div 1981–86, head of institutional asset mgmnt UK and Europe 1988–92, head of retail asset mgmnt EMEA and Asia 1992–95, head European Div Investment Products and Distribution Gp 1995–98, head of wealth mgmnt EMEA 1998–2002; exec dir F&C Mgmnt Ltd 2002–05; chm: Taiwan Investment Co 2008–11, F&C Portfolios Fund 2008–14, Indian Investment Co 2008–14; fndr Bank T&D Wealth; prodr and music composer Degree of Difficulty (short film created for the Cultural Olympiad and exhibited on BBC Big Screens 2010–11); awarded Primrose Quartet Composition Prize 2007, jt winner Clothworkers Co competition for composition of their London Livery Co March 2008; vice-chm of govrs Hampton Sch 1999–2008; FCMA, CGMA, FRSA, memb BASCA; *Recreations* cycling, swimming, theatre, piano, guitar, music composition; *Style—* Laurence Llewellyn, Esq; ✉ e-mail laurence@llewellynweb.com

LLEWELLYN, Sir Roderic Victor (Roddy); 5 Bt (UK 1922), of Bwllfa, Aberdare, Glamorgan; 2 s of Sir Harry Llewellyn, 3 Bt, CBE (d 1999), and Hon Christine Saumarez (d 1998); *b* 9 October 1947, Crickhowell, Powys; *Educ* Shrewsbury, Aix-en-Provence, Merrist Wood Agric Coll (Nat Cert of Horticulture, Surrey Co Cert in Landscape Construction); *m* 1981, Tatiana Manora Caroline (Tania), da of Paul Soskin (d 1975), film producer; 3 da; *Career* landscape designer, author, lectr, journalist and presenter; gardening corr: (Daily) Star 1981–86, Oracle 1982–83, Mail On Sunday 1987–99; gardening presenter TV-am 1984; co-presenter: The Gardening Roadshow (LWT) 1992 and 1993, Grass Roots (Meridian TV) 1993–; presenter Roddy Llewellyn's Garden Guide (Granada Sky Breeze) 1997–99, gardening presenter This Morning (ITV) 1998–2000, Gardens of Wales (HTV) 2001 and 2002, co-presenter Turf Wars (Channel 4) 2004, co-presenter Best of Britain (Channel 4) 2004; guest appearances on Gardeners Question Time (BBC) 1994; regular contrib: Country Life; patron Southport Flower Show 1997–; garden dir Sudeley Castle Glos 2010–; Silver Gilt Medals Chelsea Flower Show and Hampton Court Flower Show 1988; assoc memb Inst of Horticulture (AIHort) 1995; *Books* Town Gardens (1981), Beautiful Backyards (1985), Water Gardens (1987), Elegance and Eccentricity (1989), Growing Gifts (1992), I Grew It Myself (1993), Roddy Llewellyn's Gardening Year (1997); *Recreations* walking, jig-saw puzzles, talking, philately; *Clubs* Chelsea Arts; *Style—* Sir Roderic Llewellyn, Bt; ✉ e-mail roddy.llewellyn@virgin.net, website www.roddyllewellyn.com

LLEWELLYN, Samson Evan (Sam); s of Bishop William Somers Llewellyn, and Innis Mary, *née* Dorrien Smith; *b* 2 August 1948, Tresco, Isles of Scilly; *Educ* Eton, St Catherine's Coll Oxford (MA); *m* 1975, Karen Margaret Wallace; 2 s (William David b 1978, Martin Stephen b 1980); *Career* author; bass guitarist Spread Eagle 1971–72, ed Pan/Picador 1973–76, sr ed McClelland & Stewart Toronto Canada 1976–79; columnist: Hortus, Broad Sheep, Classic Boat, Practical Boat Owner, Royal Yachting Assoc; ed The Marine Quarterly; *Books* Hell Bay (1980), The Worst Journey in the Midlands (1983), Dead Reckoning (1987), Great Circle (1987), Blood Orange (1988), Death Roll (1989), Pig in the Middle (1989), Deadeye (1990), Blood Knot (1991), Riptide (1992), Clawhammer (1993), Maelstrom (1994), The Rope School (1994), The Magic Boathouse (1994), The Iron Hotel (1996), Storm Force from Navarone (1996), The Polecat Café (1997), The Shadow in the Sands (1998), Thunderbolt from Navarone (1998), Wonderdog (1999), The Sea Garden (2000), The Malpas Legacy (2001), Nelson (2004), Little Darlings (2004), The Beaufort Scale (2004), Emperor Smith: The man who built Scilly (2005), Bad, Bad Darlings (2005), The Return of Death Eric (2005), Desperado Darlings (2006), The Haunting of Death Eric (2006), Eye of the Cannon (2007), Abbot Dagger's Academy and the Quest for the Holy Grail (2008), The Well Between the Worlds (2009), Darksolstice (2010), Black Fish (2010), The Minimum Boat (2010), Digging with the Duchess (2014); *Recreations* sailing, gardening, accompanying Mrs Llewellyn on the guitar and banjo; *Clubs* Royal Cruising; *Style—* Sam Llewellyn, Esq; ✉ Hope Farm, Lyonshall, Kington, Herefordshire HR5 3HT (e-mail sam@samllewellyn.com, websites www.samllewellyn.com and www.marinequarterly.com)

LLEWELLYN, Timothy Charles David (Tim); s of Charles Gordon Llewellyn (d 1940), of Cardiff, and Betty Ella, *née* Field; *b* 6 June 1940; *Educ* XIV Sch Bristol, Monkton Combe Sch; *m* Feb 1964 (m dis 1972), Geraldine, *née* McCallan; 1 s (Alun Brendan b 2 April 1965); 1 step da (Maccabee Szalwinska b 1978); *Career* reporter: Western Daily Press Bristol 1958–59, Barrie Examiner Barrie 1959–60, Toronto Telegram 1960–61; sub-ed: South Wales Echo Cardiff and Western Daily Press Bristol 1961, Press Assoc 1962–64, Globe and Mail 1964–66, Daily Sketch 1966; asst prodn team (Business Section) Sunday Times 1966, on staff prodn Times Business News 1967–71; BBC: chief sub/prodr 1971–73, newsroom 1973–76, corr Middle East 1976–80 and 1987–92 (East Africa 1980–82, foreign corr 1982–87); freelance 1992–; memb RUSI; *Recreations* permanent sloth punctuated by travel and desultory reading when unavoidable, talking; *Clubs* Travellers, Frontline; *Style—* Tim Llewellyn, Esq

LLEWELLYN, Timothy David; OBE (2007); s of late Graham David Llewellyn, and late Dorothy Mary Driver; *b* 30 May 1947; *Educ* St Dunstan's Coll, Magdalene Coll Cambridge; *m* 1, 8 Aug 1970, Irene Sigrid Mercy, da of Sigurd Henriksen, of Copenhagen, Denmark; 1 s (Kristian b 1975); m 2, 9 Sept 1978, Elizabeth, da of late Prof Mason Hammond, of Cambridge, Mass, USA; *Career* Sotheby's: dir 1974–94, md 1984–91, chief exec 1991–92, dep chm Sotheby's Europe 1992–94; dir The Henry Moore Fndn 1994–2007; chm: The Friends of the Courtauld Inst 1986–2002, The Henry Moore Sculpture Tst 1994–99; memb: incl Villa I Tatti The Harvard Univ Center for Italian Renaissance Studies 1990–2005, Bd The Courtauld Inst 1991–2001, Visual Art Advsy Ctee British Cncl 1995–2007, Cncl The Walpole Soc 1995–99, Cncl The Br Sch at Rome 2000– (chm 2013–); Miny of Culture and Fine Arts of the People's Republic of Poland Order of Cultural Merit 1986; tstee: Elgar Fndn 1991–99, Gilbert Collection Tst 1998–2001, Metropole Arts Tst 2004–, The Burlington Magazine 2006– (also dir, chm 2008–), Samuel Courtauld Tst 2007–15 (ret), Creative Fndn 2007–; fell the Ateneo Veneto Venice; Hon DLitt Southampton Solent Univ; *Books* Owen McSwiny's Letters 1720–1744 (2010); *Recreations* music, travel; *Clubs* Brooks's; *Style—* Timothy D Llewellyn, Esq, OBE; ✉ 3 Cranley Mansion, 160 Gloucester Road, London SW7 4QF (☎ 020 7373 2333)

LLEWELLYN SMITH, Caspar Michael; s of Prof Sir Christopher Llewellyn Smith, *qv*, and Virginia, *née* Grey; *b* 24 January 1971, Redwood City, CA; *Educ* Magdalen Coll Sch Oxford, Christ's Coll Cambridge (BA); *m* Zoe Moore; 1 s (Sam b 19 Sept 1998), 1 da (Esme b 24 Dec 2000); *Career* Daily Telegraph: editorial asst 1994–97, arts and books ed 1998–2001, asst ed Telegraph Magazine 2002–03; ed Observer Music Monthly 2004–; regular contrib: BBC World Serv, BBC Radio 6, Channel 5; Ed of the Year Record of the Day Awards 2007; *Publications* Pop Life: A Journey By Sofa (2002); *Style—* Caspar Llewellyn Smith, Esq; ✉ The Observer, 3–7 Herbal Hill, London EC1R 5EJ (☎ 020 7134 6000)

LLEWELLYN SMITH, Prof Sir Christopher Hubert (Chris); kt (2001); s of John Clare Llewellyn Smith (d 1990), and Margaret Emily Frances, *née* Crawford; *b* 19 November 1942; *Educ* Wellington, New Coll Oxford (BA, DPhil); *m* 10 Sept 1966, Virginia, *née* Grey; 1 da (Julia Clare b 2 Nov 1968), 1 s (Caspar Llewellyn Smith, *qv*, b 24 Jan 1971); *Career* Royal Soc exchange fell Lebedev Inst Moscow 1967–68, fell Theoretical Studies Div CERN Geneva 1968–70, res assoc Stanford Linear Accelerator Centre (SLAC) Stanford 1970–72, staff memb Theoretical Studies Div CERN Geneva 1972–74; Univ of Oxford: fell St John's Coll 1974–98, lectr 1974–80, reader 1980–87, prof 1987–98, chm of physics 1987–92, hon fell St John's Coll 2000–, hon fell New Coll 2002–, visiting prof 2004–, dir of energy research 2011–; DG CERN Geneva (on leave of absence from Oxford) 1994–98, provost and pres UCL 1999–2002, dir UKAEA Culham Div 2003–08; chm Consultative Ctee for Euratom on Fusion 2004–09, chair Cncl Int Tokamak Experimental Reactor (ITER) 2007–09, pres Cncl Synchrotron-light for Experimental Sci and Applications in the Middle East (SESAME) 2008–; FRS 1984; *Style—* Prof Sir Chris Llewellyn Smith, FRS; ✉ Theoretical Physics, 1–4 Keble Road, Oxford OX1 3NP (e-mail c.llewellyn-smith@physics.ox.ac.uk)

LLEWELLYN-JONES, HE Benedict; OBE; s of His Hon Christopher Llewellyn-Jones, QC, and Christine, *née* John; *b* 29 November 1976, Cardiff; *Educ* Jesus Coll Oxford (BA); *m* Laura, *née* Harries; 1 da (Grace b 2011), 1 s (Michael b 2015); *Career* diplomat; desk offr EU and Int Affrs Team Home Office 2000–01, second sec policing and drugs UK Perm Rep to EU Brussels 2002–04, first sec policing and organised crime UK Perm Rep to EU Brussels 2005–06, head Third Country Rels Team Home Office 2006, head Zimbabwe Team FCO 2007–08, dep head Climate Change and Energy Gp FCO 2009–11, high cmmr to Repub of Rwanda 2011–14 (concurrently ambass to Repub of Burundi), head of chancery Br High Commission Abuja Nigeria 2014–; *Clubs* Elizabethans, JCRFC; *Style—* Mr Benedict Llewellyn-Jones, OBE; ✉ c/o FCO, King Charles Street, London SW1A 2AH

LLEWELYN; see: Venables-Llewelyn

LLEWELYN-EVANS, Adrian; *b* 5 August 1953, Wales; *Educ* Glyn Sch Epsom, UC Durham (BA); *m* 1979, Catherine, *née* Forster; 3 s (Edward b 1986, Thomas, Hugh (twins) b 1988); *Career* slr Linklaters 1979–82, ptnr Burges Salmon 1984–2006, ind mediator 2009–; memb CIArb; *Recreations* fly fishing, gardening, hill walking; *Style—* Adrian Llewelyn-Evans, Esq; ✉ 1 St Cuthbert Street, Wells, Somerset BA5 2PQ (☎ 07891 862371, e-mail adrian@llewelyn-evans.co.uk)

LLOPIS RIVAS, Dr Ana María; da of Dr Álvaro Llopis, and Prof Regina Rivas; *b* 5 August 1950, Cumaná, Venezuala; *Educ* Univ Central de Venezuela, Univ of Maryland (Creole Fndn scholar), Princeton Univ, Univ of Calif at Berkeley (CONICIT scholar, MS, PhD); *m* Prof Félix Ynduráin Muñoz; 1 s (Jaime Yndurâin b 27 Sept 1983); *Career* asst rising to sr brand mangr Procter & Gamble 1978–83, sales, distribution and mktg mangr Playtex Int and Spain 1983–87, assoc gen mangr Banesto 1988–91, assoc gen mangr Schweppes 1992–93, chm Baitol SA 1993–95, ceo OpenBank Banco Santander 1995–2000, exec chm and ceo Viaplus 2000–01, ceo then exec chm Razona 2001–03, exec vice-pres financial and insur markets Indra 2002–05, exec dep chm José Félix Llopis Fndn 2005– (fndr and vice-chm 2003–); non-exec dir: Reckitt Benckiser plc 1998–2005, Net TV 2000–01, British American Tobacco plc 2003–, Supervisory Bd ABN AMRO Bank 2007; memb: Advsy Bd Watson Wyatt 2000–03, Editorial Advsy Bd Expansion 2004–05, Working Gp Spanish New Corp Governance Code 2005–06; former exec vice-pres Financial Execs Spanish Assoc; *Recreations* art, writing short stories, printmaking; *Style—* Dr Ana María Llopis Rivas

LLOYD, Prof Alan Brian; s of Howard Brinley Lloyd (d 1989), of Tredegar, Gwent, and Doris Marian, *née* Walsh; *b* 24 September 1941; *Educ* Tredegar GS, UC Swansea (BA), The Queen's Coll Oxford (MA, DPhil); *m* 1, 14 Aug 1965, Caroline Barclay (d 1984), da of Hon Julius McDonald Greenfield, CMG, of Rondebosh, South Africa; 2 s (Julian b 14 Aug 1966, Duncan b 19 Nov 1967), 1 da (Katherine b 28 Feb 1970); m 2, 30 Nov 1985, Patricia Elizabeth (d 2012), da of Patrick Cyril Ward, of Llandaff, Cardiff; *Career* Univ of Wales Swansea: asst lectr 1967, sr lectr 1977, reader 1983, prof 1988–, dean of arts 1991–93, pro-vice-chllr 1993–97, res prof 2006–; sometime chm Ctee of Egypt Exploration Soc, sometime memb Cncl Hellenic Soc, pres Egypt Exploration Soc 2011; FSA 1987; *Books* Herodotus Book II (1975–88); The Tomb of Hetepka (with G T Martin, 1978), Ancient Egypt (with B Trigger et al, 1983), Erodoto Le Storie Libro II (1989), Saqqara Tombs I, II and III (with W V Davies et al, 1984, 1990 and 2008), A Commentary on Herodotus Book I-IV (with David Asheri and Aldo Coriella, 2007), A Companion to Ancient Egypt (2010), Ancient Egypt: State and Society (2014); *Clubs* Oxford and Cambridge; *Style—* Prof Alan Lloyd; ✉ 3 Radyr Avenue, Mayals, Swansea SA3 5DU (e-mail alan.lloyd6@ntlworld.com)

LLOYD, Angus Selwyn; s of Selwyn Lloyd (d 1935), and Elaine Mary, *née* Beck (d 1992); *b* 12 July 1935; *Educ* Charterhouse; *m* 12 Jan 1961, Wanda Marian (d 1992), da of Raymond Davidson; 3 s (James, Christopher, Richard), 2 da (Virginia, Philippa); *Career* Nat Serv 1954–55, 2 Lt 15/19 King's Royal Hussars (serv Malaya 1955); dir: Nathaniel Lloyd & Co (printers) 1956–63, Oscar & Peter Johnson Ltd (fine art dealers) 1963–81, Sealproof Ltd (textile proofing) 1973–99; chm: Henri-Lloyd Ltd (textile mfrs) 1963–85, Craig-Lloyd Ltd (property) 1971–, Burlington Paintings Ltd (fine art/picture dealers) 1984–2011; tstee: Albany Piccadilly 1967–2011, Charterhouse in Southwark 1962–2003 (chm of tstees 1979–82); Freeman City of London, Liveryman Worshipful Co of Stationers and Newspaper Makers; *Recreations* golf; *Clubs* Royal St George's Golf (capt 1985), The Berkshire (capt 1978), Royal West Norfolk, Royal & Ancient, Swinley Forest, Walton Heath, PGA Nat (USA), Old Marsh Golf (USA), Hon Co of Edinburgh Golfers; *Style—* Angus Lloyd, Esq; ✉ West Court, Beech Avenue, Effingham, Surrey (☎ 01372 458111, e-mail lloydwanda@aol.com)

LLOYD, Anthony Joseph (Tony); MP; *b* 25 February 1950; *Educ* Univ of Nottingham, Manchester Business Sch; *m* Judith Lloyd; 3 da, 1 s; *Career* former university lectr; MP (Lab): Stretford 1983–97, Manchester C 1997–2012; oppn spokesman on: tport 1988–89, employment 1988–92, training (employment and educn) 1992–94, the environment and London 1994–97; min of state FCO 1997–99; cncllr Trafford Metropolitan Borough Cncl DC 1979–84; police and crime cmmr Gtr Manchester 2012–17, interim mayor of Gtr Manchester 2017–; *Clubs* West Indian Sports & SocialStanley Street Working Men's Social Higher Openshaw; *Style—* Tony Lloyd, MP; ✉ Greater Manchester Police and Crime Commissioner, GMP Openshaw Complex, Lawton Street, Openshaw, Manchester M11 2NS

LLOYD, Barbara Christine; da of Francis Kenneth Lloyd, of the Bahamas, and Herta Erica, *née* Menzler (d 1984); *b* 17 August 1946; *Educ* Putney HS for Girls, École Le Grand Verger Lausanne Switzerland, École Lemania Lausanne Switzerland, French Lycée London, Le Fleuron Florence Italy, Oskar Kokoschka Summer Acad Salzburg Austria; *Career* Marlborough Galleries 1967–90: shorthand typist and switchboard operator rising to registrar Marlborough Gallery NY, dir Marlborough Graphics 1979, subsequently dir Marlborough Fine Art London Ltd until 1990; responsible for exhibitions incl: all FIAC exhibitions Grand Palais Paris, Bill Brandt – A Retrospective, Brassai Secret Paris of the 30s, Irving Penn, Still Lives, Avigdor Arikha, Raymond Mason, Therese Oulton, Travelling Mason Retrospective; full time photographer 1990–; tstee: The Photographers Gallery London 1988– (chm 1994–97), Barry & Martins Tst London 1997–, Save A Child Tst Divyachaya, Bombay and Calcutta, Children of India 1995, Yorkshire Sculpture Park 1998–; memb Patrons of New Art Acquisitions Sub-Ctee Tate Gallery 1996–97; judge Kraszna-Krausz Fndn Photography Book Awards 1999 and 2000, advsr and judge Art in Prisons Koestler Award Tst; *Books* The Colours of India (1988), Reflections of Spain (1992), The Colours of Thailand (1997), Colours of Southern India (1999), Zent (2000), China: Travels Between the Yangtze and Yellow Rivers (2006); *Recreations* looking at and collecting art, opera, music, photography, reading, tennis, enjoying life; *Style—* Miss Barbara Lloyd; ✉ 23 Chepstow Villas, London W11 3DZ

LLOYD, Christopher; CVO; s of Rev Hamilton Lloyd, of Litchfield, Hants, and Suzanne, *née* Moon; *b* 30 June 1945; *Educ* Marlborough, ChCh Oxford (MA, MLitt); *m* 7 Oct 1967, (Christine Joan) Frances, da of George Henry Reginald Newth (d 1978), of Whitchurch, Hants; 4 s (Alexander b 1970, Benedict b 1972, Oliver b 1973, Rupert b 1980); *Career* asst curator pictures ChCh Oxford 1967–68; Dept of Western Art Ashmolean Museum Oxford: print room asst 1968, departmental asst 1969, asst keeper 1972–88; surveyor of the Queen's pictures 1988–2005; pres Nat Assoc of Decorative and Fine Arts Socs (NADFAS) 2007–14; tstee The Art Fund 2005–15, patron Living Paintings 2005–, govr Gainsborough's House 2005–13, memb Exhibitions Ctee Royal Acad of Arts 2008–15; fell Villa I Tatti Florence (Harvard Univ) 1972–73, visiting res curator early Italian painting Art Inst Chicago 1980–81; *Books* Art and Its Images (1975), A Catalogue of the Earlier Italian Paintings in the Ashmolean Museum (1977), Camille Pissarro (1980), A Catalogue of the Drawings by Camille Pissarro in the Ashmolean Museum (1980), The Journal of Maria Lady Callcott 1827–28 (1981), Camille Pissarro (1981), Dürer to Cézanne: Northern European Drawings from the Ashmolean Museum (1982), Impressionist Drawings from British Collections (1986), Catalogue of Old Master Drawings at Holkham Hall (1986), Studies on Camille Pissarro (ed and contrib, 1986), Woodner Collection Master Drawings (contrib, 1990), Henry VIII Images of A Tudor King (1990), The Queen's Pictures: Royal Collectors through the Centuries (1991), The Royal Collection. A Thematic Exploration of the Paintings in the Collection of Her Majesty The Queen (1992, revised paperback edn The Paintings in the Royal Collection (1999)), Italian Paintings before 1600 in the Art Institute of Chicago (1993), Gainsborough and Reynolds: Contrasts in Royal Patronage (1994), The Queen's Pictures. Old Masters from the Royal Collection (1994), Masterpieces in Little: Portrait Minitures from the Collection of Her Majesty Queen Elizabeth II (1996), The Quest for Albion: Monarchy and the Patronage of British Painting (1998), Arturo di Stefano (2001), Royal Treasures: A Golden Jubilee Celebration (contrib, 2002), Ceremony and Celebration: Coronation Day 1953 (2003), George III and Queen Charlotte: Patronage, Collecting and Court Taste (contrib, 2004), Enchanting the Eye: Dutch Paintings of the Golden Age (2004), Philip Morsberger: A Passion for Painting (2007), In Search of a Masterpiece (2011), Impressionism: Pastels, Watercolours, Drawings (2011), Impressionists on the Water (contrib, 2013), American Adversaries: West and Copley in a Transatlantic World (contrib, 2013), Degas: Drawings and Paintings (2014), Cézanne: Drawings and Watercolours (2015); *Recreations* real tennis, theatre, music; *Style—* Christopher Lloyd, Esq, CVO; ✉ Flat 4, Benacre Hall, Benacre, Beccles, Suffolk NR34 7LJ (☎ 01502 675535)

LLOYD, Prof David; s of Frederick Lewis Lloyd (d 1961), of Rhondda, Glam, and Annie Mary, *née* Wrentmore (d 1995); *b* 26 November 1940; *Educ* Porth Co GS for Boys, Univ of Sheffield (BSc, DSc), Univ of Wales Cardiff (PhD); *m* 5 April 1969, Margaret, da of Thomas John Jones, of Criccieth, Gwynedd; 2 s (Alun Lewis b 4 Aug 1970, Siôn Huw b 19 Sept 1973); *Career* MRC res fell Univ Coll of S Wales and Monmouth 1967–69 (ICI res fell 1964–67); Univ Coll Cardiff (now Cardiff Univ): lectr in microbiology 1969–76, sr lectr 1976, reader 1976–78, personal chair 1978–, head Dept of Microbiology 1982–87, established chair holder 1982–; memb: Biochemical Soc 1961, Ctee S Wales Cancer Res Campaign, Ctee of Welsh Scheme for Med and Social Sci Res, Soc of Gen Microbiology 1980; *Books* The Mitochondria of Micro-organisms (1974), The Cell Division Cycle: Temporal Organization and Control of Cellular Growth and Reproduction (1982), Ultradian Rhythms in Living Systems: A Fundamental Inquiry into Chronobiology and Psychobiology (1992), Flow Cytometry in Microbiology (1993), Microbiology Past, Present and Future (1994), Cellular and Metabolic Engineering (2002), Ultradian Rhythms from Molecules to Mind: a New Vision of Life (2008); author of more than 500 papers; *Recreations* music (especially opera); *Style—* Prof David Lloyd; ✉ Microbiology (BIOSI), Main Building, PO Box 915, Cardiff University, Cardiff CF10 3AT (☎ 029 2087 4772, fax 029 2087 4305, e-mail lloydd@cf.ac.uk)

LLOYD, (William) David; s of Hywel Lloyd, and Jean, *née* Davies; *b* 7 August 1955, Oswestry, Shropshire; *Educ* Shrewsbury; *m* 12 May 1979, Jennifer, *née* Tait; 2 s (James, Allan), 1 da (Zoë); *Career* ceo and chm Lloyd's (Animal) Feeds Ltd; FCA 1976; *Recreations* bibliophilia, music; *Style—* David Lloyd, Esq; ✉ Lloyd's (Animal) Feeds Limited, Morton, Oswestry, Shropshire SY10 8BH (☎ 01691 830741, fax 01691 831582)

LLOYD, David Alan; s of Dennis Herbert Lloyd, of Leigh-on-Sea, Essex, and Doris, *née* Renshaw; *b* 3 January 1948; *Educ* Southend HS; *m* 14 Dec 1972, Veronica Jardine, da of Maj Cochran Kirkwood MacLennan, MBE (d 1984); 1 s (Scott b 1975), 2 da (Camilla b 1979, Laura b 1981); *Career* former tennis player; memb Br Davis Cup Team 1973–82 (former capt), men's doubles semi-finalist Wimbledon (with J Paish) 1973; capt Br Davis Cup Team 1995–2000; chm David Lloyd Leisure plc 1982–96 (national chain of 16 health and fitness clubs, stock market flotation 1993, sold to Whitbread plc 1995), md Next Generation Clubs 1998–; non-exec dir: Clubhaus 1996–98, M V Sports & Leisure (formerly Snakeboard) 1996–2002, GV Incentives; tennis commentator ITV, Sky TV and BBC Radio; launched Slater Tennis Fndn (sponsorship and coaching scheme for young players) with J Slater 1986; owner and chm Hull City FC 1997–2002; former Entrepreneur of the Year; Freeman City of London 1985; *Recreations* golf; *Clubs* National Hunt Racing, Queenwood Golf, Loch Lomond Golf; *Style—* David Lloyd, Esq

L

LLOYD, Geoff; s of Geoff Lloyd Sr, and Rita Lloyd; *Educ* Ryles Park Co HS Macclesfield; *Career* writer and broadcaster; presenter Signal Radio Stockport 1992–96, prodn asst The Mrs Merton Show (Granada TV for BBC) 1995–96; presenter: Piccadilly Radio/Key 103 Manchester 1996–99, Virgin Radio 1999–, VH1/MTV Networks Europe 2001; columnist Manchester Evening News 1998–2001, head writer TFI Friday (Ginger Television for Channel 4) 2000, writer Comic Relief Red Nose Day 2001; EMAP Radio Award Best Daytime Show 1997 and 1998, Silver Award Best Daytime Music Programme Sony Radio Acad 1998, Gold Winner Music Programming Award Sony Radio Acad 2002, Bronze Award Radio Personality of the Year Sony Radio Acad 2008; *Recreations* travel, gastronomy, all types of music including piano playing; *Clubs* Arts Theatre; *Style*— Geoff Lloyd, Esq; ✉ c/o Alex Armitage, Noel Gay Artists, 19 Denmark Street, London WC2 (☎ 020 7836 3941)

LLOYD, Prof Sir Geoffrey Ernest Richard; kt (1997); s of William Ernest Lloyd (d 1975), of London, and Olive Irene Neville, *née* Solomon (d 1993); *b* 25 January 1933, London; *Educ* Charterhouse, King's Coll Cambridge (MA, PhD); *m* 14 Sept 1956, Janet Elizabeth, da of Edward Archibald Lloyd (d 1978), of Paris, France; 3 s (Adam b 1957, Matthew b 1962, Gwilym b 1963); *Career* Nat Serv Intelligence Corps 2 Lt/Actg Capt; Univ of Cambridge: fell King's Coll 1957–89, univ asst lectr in classics 1965–67, univ lectr 1967–74, sr reader 1974–83, prof of ancient philosophy and sci 1983–2000, master Darwin Coll 1989–2000; Bonsall prof Stanford Univ 1981, Sather prof of classics Univ of Calif Berkeley 1984; chm E Asian History of Sci Tst 1992–2002; hon fell: King's Coll Cambridge 1990, Darwin Coll Cambridge 2000; Hon LittD Univ of Athens 2003, Hon LittD Univ of Oxford 2011; hon foreign memb American Acad of Arts and Sciences 1995, memb Int Acad of the History of Sci 1997; fell Royal Anthropological Soc 1970; FBA 1983, FLSW 2015; *Books* Polarity and Analogy (1966), Aristotle The Growth and Structure of his Thought (1968), Early Greek Science (1970), Greek Science After Aristotle (1973), Hippocratic Writings (ed, 1978), Aristotle on Mind and the Senses (ed, 1978), Magic Reason and Experience (1979), Science Folklore and Ideology (1983), Science and Morality in Greco-Roman Antiquity (1985), The Revolutions of Wisdom (1987), Demystifying Mentalities (1990), Methods and Problems in Greek Science (1991), Adversaries & Authorities (1996), Aristotelian Explorations (1996), Greek Thought (ed, 2000), The Way and the Word (with N Sivin, 2002), The Ambitions of Curiosity (2002), In the Grip of Disease: Studies in the Greek Imagination (2003), Ancient Worlds, Modern Reflections (2004), The Delusions of Invulnerability (2005), Principles and Practices in Ancient Greek and Chinese Science (2006), Cognitive Variations: Reflections on the Unity and Diversity of the Human Mind (2007), Disciplines in the Making (2009), Being, Humanity and Understanding (2012), The Ideals of Inquiry (2014), Analogical Investigations (2015); *Recreations* travel; *Style*— Prof Sir Geoffrey Lloyd, FBA; ✉ 2 Prospect Row, Cambridge CB1 1DU (☎ 01223 355970, e-mail gel20@hermes.cam.ac.uk)

LLOYD, Dr Geoffrey Gower; s of William Thomas Lloyd (d 1979), and Anne, *née* Davies (d 1993); *b* 7 June 1942; *Educ* Queen Elizabeth GS Carmarthen, Emmanuel Coll Cambridge (MA, MB BChir, MD), Westminster Med Sch London, Inst of Psychiatry London (MPhil); *m* 19 Dec 1970, Prof Margaret Hazel Lloyd, da of Henry Doble Rose; 1 s, 2 da; *Career* sr registrar Maudsley Hosp London 1974–76 (registrar 1970–73), lectr Inst of Psychiatry and KCH Med Sch London 1976–79; conslt psychiatrist: Royal Infirmary Edinburgh 1979–85, Royal Free Hosp London 1985–2005 (chm Med Advsy Ctee 1996–98); med dir Grovelands Priory Hosp London 1997–2000; ed Jl of Psychosomatic Res 1986–93; pres Section of Psychiatry RSM 1995–96; Freeman City of London, Liveryman Worshipful Soc of Apothecaries; FRCPEd 1981, FRCPsych 1984 (chm Liaison Psychiatry Faculty and memb Cncl 2000–05), FRCP 1988; *Books* Textbook of General Hospital Psychiatry (1991), Handbook of Liaison Psychiatry (co-ed, 2007); *Recreations* golf, skiing, bridge, watching rugby football; *Clubs* Athenaeum, Hadley Wood Golf, Pennard Golf; *Style*— Dr Geoffrey Lloyd; ✉ e-mail ggll.gower@gmail.com

LLOYD, Her Hon Judge Heather Claire; da of John Lloyd, and Nancy Lloyd; *b* 16 May 1957; *Educ* St Edmunds Coll for Girls Liverpool, Univ of Liverpool; *m* P N D Kennedy; 2 s; *Career* Peel House Chambers Liverpool 1979–99, Chavasse Court Chambers Liverpool 1999–2007, recorder 1999 (asst recorder 1997), circuit judge (Northern Circuit) 2007–; *Style*— Her Hon Judge Heather Lloyd; ✉ c/o Northern Circuit Office, Young Street Chambers, 76 Quay Street, Manchester M3 4PR

LLOYD, Prof Howell Arnold; OBE (2004); s of John Lewis Lloyd (d 1971), of Llanelli, S Wales, and Elizabeth Mary, *née* Arnold (d 1986); *b* 15 November 1937; *Educ* Queen Elizabeth GS Carmarthen, UC Wales (BA), Jesus Coll Oxford (DPhil); *m* Sept 1962, Gaynor Ilid, da of Moses John Jones, of Mold, N Wales; 3 s (Jonathan, Timothy, Christian), 2 da (Susanna, Rebecca); *Career* fell Univ of Wales 1961–62; Univ of Hull: asst lectr in history 1962–64, lectr 1964–73, sr lectr 1973–82, reader 1982–85, prof 1985–, dean Sch of Humanities 1993–94, pro-vice-chllr then dep vice-chllr 1994–2003; visiting fell Clare Hall Cambridge 1983, fell commoner Churchill Coll Cambridge 1993; FRHistS 1975, Jubilee fell Historical Assoc 2014; *Books* The Gentry of South-West Wales, 1540–1640 (1968), The Relevance of History (with Gordon Connell-Smith, 1972), The Rouen Campaign, 1590–92 (1973), The State, France and the Sixteenth Century (1983), Charles Loyseau: A Treatise of Orders and Plain Dignities (ed, 1994), European Political Thought 1450–1700: Religion, Law and Philosophy (co-ed, 2007), The Reception of Bodin (ed, 2013); *Recreations* walking, swimming, travel; *Style*— Prof Howell A Lloyd, OBE; ✉ 23 Strathmore Avenue, Hull HU6 7HJ (☎ 01482 851146); Department of History, The University of Hull, Hull HU6 7RX (☎ 01482 465178)

LLOYD, His Hon Humphrey John; QC (1979); *b* 16 November 1939; *Educ* Westminster, Trinity Coll Dublin (MA, LLB); *m* 1969, Ann; 1 da, 1 s; *Career* called to the Bar Inner Temple 1963 (bencher 1985), recorder 1990–93, judge of Technology and Construction Ct (formerly official referee of the High Ct) 1993–2005; ed-in-chief: Building Law Reports 1977–93 (conslt ed 1993–98), The International Construction Law Review 1984–2015 (ed emeritus 2015–); conslt ed: Emden's Construction Law 1993–, Technol and Construction Law Reports 1999–; visiting prof Leeds Metropolitan Univ 2002–; chm ARB 2003–07 (memb 2001–07); hon prof Queen Mary Univ of London 1987–, hon fell American Coll of Construction Lawyers 1997–, hon fell Canadian Coll of Construction Lawyers 2002–, fell Int Acad of Construction Lawyers 2014–; Hon LLD Leeds Met Univ 2009; *Clubs* Reform; *Style*— His Hon Humphrey LLoyd, QC; ✉ Atkin Chambers, 1 Atkin Building, Gray's Inn, London WC1R 5AT (☎ 020 7404 0102, fax 020 7405 7456)

LLOYD, Dr (David) Huw Owen; s of Dr David Owen Lloyd (d 1984), of Denbigh, Clwyd, and Dilys Lloyd; *b* 14 April 1950, London; *Educ* Westminster, Gonville & Caius Coll Cambridge (MA, MB BChir), Guy's Hosp Med Sch London (DRCOG); *m* 1973, Dr Mary Eileen Pike, da of William Arthur George Pike; 3 da (Amy b 28 Dec 1976, Ceridwen b 4 April 1979, Bethan b 30 May 1986), 1 s (Dafydd b 17 July 1981); *Career* house surgn in orthopaedics Guy's Hosp 1974–75, house physician Beckenham Hosp 1975, SHO in psychiatry Joyce Green Hosp Dartford 1975, trainee GP Taunton 1976–79, princ GP Cadwgan Surgery Old Colwyn 1979–2012; memb Core Gp Wales Mental Health in Primary Care Network; memb N Wales Local Med Ctee; Faculty rep Welsh Cncl RCGP (former chm); memb PCC and reader St Cynbryd's Llanddulas, lay advocate (St Asaph Diocese) 2020 Vision, memb Governing Body Church in Wales; memb BMA; FRCGP 1991 (MRCGP 1979, Cert of Commendation 2014); *Recreations* music, gardening, cooking, walking; *Clubs* Colwyn Bay 41; *Style*— Dr Huw Lloyd; ☎ 01492 516909, e-mail dholloyd@yahoo.co.uk

LLOYD, Jeremy William; s of late Maj-Gen Richard Eyre Lloyd, CB, CBE, DSO, of Lymington, Hants, and Gillian, *née* Patterson; *b* 19 December 1942; *Educ* Eton, Pembroke Coll Cambridge (MA), Harvard Business Sch (MBA); *m* 2 Sept 1966, Britta Adrienne, da of Alfred de Schulthess, of Geneva, Switzerland; 3 da (Tara b 1971, Bettina b 1975, Antonia b 1985), 1 s (Adrian b 1979); *Career* called to the Bar Middle Temple; formerly with Hill Samuel & Co (corp fin), subsid dir London & Co Securities Bank 1971–72, md Manufacturers Hanover Property Services Ltd 1973–81, dir James Capel Bankers Ltd 1982–87, sr mangr Hongkong Bank and md HBL Property Finance Ltd 1982–98; *Recreations* tennis, skiing; *Style*— Jeremy Lloyd, Esq; ✉ 1 Lansdowne Rd, London W11 3 AL (☎ 020 7727 8944, e-mail jwl@lloydfamily.com)

LLOYD, Dr Jill Patricia; da of Peter Brown (d 1984), of Dublin, and Patricia Irene, *née* Tucker (d 2002); *b* 2 August 1955; *Educ* Courtauld Inst of Art (BA, PhD); *m* 1989, Dr Michael Henry Peppiatt, *qv*, s of Edward George Peppiatt; 1 da (Clio Patricia b 16 Feb 1991), 1 s (Alexander Michael b 23 April 1994); *Career* lectr in art history UCL 1981–88, ed-in-chief Art International (Paris) 1990–94, freelance writer and curator 1994–; regular contrib to: The Burlington Magazine, the TLS; articles on early 20th century and contemporary art; essays in exhibitions catalogues incl: Lovis Corinth (Tate Gallery) 1997, Per Kirkeby (Tate Gallery) 1998, L'École de Londres (Musée Maillol Paris) 1998, Austrian Expressionism (Musée Maillol Paris) 2001, Max Beckman (Tate Modern) 2003; awarded Paul Getty postdoctoral scholarship 1989; memb Int Art Critics' Assoc, memb Soc of Authors; FRSA; Order of Merit Germany; *Books* German Expressionism, Primitivism and Modernity (1991, Nat Art Book Prize 1992), Christian Schad and the Neue Sachlichkeit (2003), Kirchner the Dresden and Berlin Years (2003), Vincent van Gogh and Expressionism (2007), The Undiscovered Expressionist: A Life of Marie-Louise von Motesiczky (2007), Max Beckmann: Self-Portrait with Horn (2008), The Birth of the Modern: Style and Identity in Vienna 1900 (2011), Ferdinand Hodler: View to Infinity (2012); *Clubs* RAC, Philadelphia Racquet; *Style*— Dr Jill Lloyd; ✉ 56 St James's Gardens, London W11 4RA (☎ 07900 047250, e-mail j.lloyd@zen.co.uk)

LLOYD, John David; s of John Alfred Lloyd (d 1981), and Lilian Mary, *née* Griffiths (d 2001); *b* 1 September 1944; *Educ* SW Essex Sch of Art, London Coll of Printing (DipAD); *m* 24 May 1975, Julia Patricia, da of Geoffrey Ernest Maughan; 1 s (Adam John b 17 June 1978), 2 da (Elinor Jane b 27 May 1980, Anna Carol b 20 Dec 1981); *Career* apprentice lithographic artist Edwin Jones & Sons (printers) 1960–64; Allied International Designers: graphic designer 1968–75, jt head of graphic design 1972–75, corp identity projects incl ABN Bank, PRIBA Supermarkets (Belgium), Delta Group, Nicholas International and Meneba (Netherlands); Lloyd Northover (merged with Citigate Design 1993, Bass Yager LA 1997 and Marketplace Design 2006): fndr 1975, major corp identity projects incl Airport Express (Hong Kong), BAA, BNFL, British Biotech, Courtaulds, John Lewis, Land Tport Authy (Singapore), National Savings and Investments, Ordnance Survey, Partek (Finland), Taylor Woodrow, Tractebel (Belgium); currently designer, conslt, artist (painter) and writer; visiting lectr in typographic design London Coll of Printing 1970–72, chm Br Design Export Gp 1983–85; external assessor and course advsr: Information Graphics Trent Poly 1984–89, Media Design and Production London Coll of Printing 1989–97, Graphic and Media Design London Coll of Communication 2005–11; exhibitions of Lloyd Northover work: The Design Centre 1980–81, D&AD Assoc 1981–83, Art Directors' Club of NY 1988, London Coll of Communication 2005; frequent speaker on design and identity mgmnt at confs and seminars; Grand Prix in DBA/Mktg Design Effectiveness Awards for Courtaulds corp identity 1989, Int Gold Award for packaging design NY Art Dirs Club 1989; other design effectiveness awards: Amtico commercial interiors 1992, Partek corp identity 1998, JMC digital media 2001, National Savings and Investments digital media 2005; finalist: BRS corp identity 1994, AEA Technology corp identity 1995, Banner (HMSO) corp identity 1996; FCSD 1978, memb D&AD Assoc 1980, FRSA 2005; *Style*— John David Lloyd, Esq; ✉ Mitre Farm House, Fordcombe Road, Fordcombe TN3 0RT (e-mail john@johnlloyd.uk.com, website www.johnlloyd.uk.com)

LLOYD, Jonathan Salusbury; *Career* md Grafton Books 1986–91, md Trade Div HarperCollins 1991–93, gp md Curtis Brown 1995– (dir 1994–95, chm 2012–); pres Assoc of Authors' Agents 2000–02 (vice-pres 1997–99), chm Soc of Bookmen 2011–12; *Clubs* Garrick, RAC, MCC; *Style*— Jonathan Lloyd, Esq; ✉ Curtis Brown Group Ltd, Haymarket House, 28/29 Haymarket, London SW1Y 4SP (☎ 020 7393 4400, fax 020 7393 4401, e-mail jlloyd@curtisbrown.co.uk)

LLOYD, Mark; s of David Glyn Lloyd, and Harriet Joan, *née* Bowyer (d 2003); *b* 4 July 1967, Oswestry, Salops; *Educ* Rhyn Park Comp Sch St Martins, Oswestry Coll, Univ of Durham (MBA); *m* 19 March 2007, Shan, *née* Warren; 1 da, 1 s; *Career* Civil Service 1985–93, Powys TEC 1990–93, served on Lord Justice Scott's Inquiry into defence related exports to Iraq 1993, dir of educn and trg Central England TEC 1994–96, dep dep chief exec Bolton and Bury Chamber of Commerce, Trg and Enterprise 1996–99, chief exec County Durham TEC and Business Link 1999–2000; md Co Durham Devpt Co 2000–05; Durham CC: dir of economics, devpt and planning 2000–03, dep chief exec (policy and strategy) 2003–05, chief exec 2005–08; chief exec Cambridgeshire CC 2008–15, chief exec Local Govt Assoc 2015–; clerk Cambs Lieutenancy 2008–15; memb Assoc of County Chief Execs 2005–15 (chm 2012–13); *Recreations* cycling, running, travel; *Style*— Mark Lloyd, Esq; ✉ Local Government Association, Local Government House, Smith Square, London, SW1P 3HZ

LLOYD, Mark William; s of Keneth Charles Lloyd, of Pontycymmer, Mid Glam, and Ivy, *née* Jones; *b* 5 February 1963; *Educ* Ynysawdre Comp Sch, Swansea Coll of Art, North Essex Sch of Art; *m* Joanna Caroline, da of Daniel James Peter Ryan; 1 da (Emily Elizabeth b 22 Oct 1989), 1 s (William Henry b 15 Nov 1993); *Career* designer Michael Peters & Partners 1984–87, designer rising to asst creative dir Coley Porter Bell and Partners 1987–91, design dir Smith & Milton Ltd 1991–2002, creative dir Lloyd Ferguson Hawkins 1992–2005, currently creative dir Webb Scarlett deVlam; *Style*— Mark Lloyd, Esq; ✉ Webb Scarlett deVlam, 12 Junction Mews, London W2 1PN (website www.webbscarlett.com)

LLOYD, Sir Nicholas Markley; kt (1990); *b* 9 June 1942; *Educ* Bedford Modern Sch, St Edmund Hall Oxford (MA), Harvard Univ; *m* 1; 2 s, 1 da; m 2, 23 May 1979, Eve Pollard, *qv*; 1 s (Oliver b 6 Aug 1980); *Career* dep ed Sunday Mirror 1980–82; ed Sunday People 1982–84, dir Mirror Gp 1982–84, ed News of the World Jan 1984–85, dir News Gp Newspapers 1985–96, ed Daily Express 1986–96, presenter The Anne and Nick Show (with Anne Diamond) LBC 1996–99, chm Brown Lloyd James PR consultancy 1997–; *Style*— Sir Nicholas Lloyd; ✉ BLJ London, 15–17 Grosvenor Gardens, London SW1W 0BD (☎ 020 7932 1599, fax 020 7828 4920)

LLOYD, Prof Noel Glynne; CBE (2010); s of Joseph John Lloyd (d 1988), of Llanelli, and Gwenllian, *née* Davies; *b* 26 December 1946, Llanelli; *Educ* Llanelli GS, Queens' Coll Cambridge (MA, PhD); *m* 4 Aug 1970, Dilys June, *née* Edwards; 1 s (Hywel Glynne b 1976), 1 da (Carys Eleri b 1980); *Career* res fell St John's Coll Cambridge 1972–74; Aberystwyth Univ: lectr 1974–77, sr lectr 1977–81, reader 1981–88, prof 1988–, head Mathematics Dept 1991–97, dean of science 1994–97, pro-vice-chllr 1997–99, registrar and sec 1999–2004, vice-chllr 2004–11; memb Bd: Mid Wales TEC 1999–2001, QAA 2005–11, Univs and Colls Employers' Assoc (UCEA) 2005–11; memb Mid Wales Regnl Cttee ELWA 2001–04; chair HE Wales 2008–11; vice-pres Univs UK 2008–11; sec Capel y Morfa Aberystwyth 1989–2004; memb Editorial Bd Mathematical Proceedings Cambridge Philosophical Soc 1981–2008, ed London Mathematical Soc jl 1983–88; chair:

Church and Soc Dept Presbyterian Church of Wales until 2004 and 2014–, Fairtrade Wales 2011–, High Performance Computing Wales 2011–13; memb: Shadow Bd Jt Info Systems Ctee (formerly JISC, now co, Jisc) 2011–12 (memb Bd Jisc 2012–14), Cmmn on Devolution in Wales 2011–14, Judicial Appointments Cmmn 2012–, Bd of Tstees Musicfest Aberystwyth 2015–, Bd Hub Cymru Africa 2015–; hon memb Gorsedd of Bards 2013; FTCL 1965, FLSW 2011; Degree Theory (1978); numerous articles on nonlinear differential equations; *Recreations* music especially organ and piano; *Clubs* Oxford and Cambridge, Aberystwyth Music (pres 2011–); *Style—* Prof Noel G Lloyd, CBE; ✉ 44 Erw Goch, Aberystwyth, Ceredigion SY23 3AZ

LLOYD, Rt Hon Sir Peter Robert Cable; kt (1995), PC (1994); s of David Lloyd (d 1991), and his 1 w, late Stella Lloyd; *b* 12 November 1937; *Educ* Tonbridge, Pembroke Coll Cambridge (MA); *m* 1967, late Hilary Creighton; 1 s, 1 da; *Career* former mktg mangr United Biscuits; chm Bow Gp 1972–73, ed Crossbow 1974–76; MP (Cons) Fareham 1979–2001 (Parly candidate (Cons) Nottingham W Feb and Oct 1974); House of Commons: sec Cons Parly Employment Ctee 1979–81, vice-chm Euro Affrs Ctee 1980–81, PPS to Adam Butler as min of state NI 1981–82, memb Select Ctee on Employment 1982, PPS to Sir Keith Joseph as sec of state for Educn and Sci 1983–84, asst govt whip 1984–86, a Lord Cmmr of the Treasy (Govt whip) 1986–88, Parly under sec DSS 1988–89, Parly under sec Home Office 1989–92, min of state Home Office 1992–94, memb Select Ctee on Public Affrs 1996–97, vice-chm All-Pty Human Rights Gp 1996–2001, chm All-Pty Penal Affrs Gp 1997–2001, Parly advsr to the Police Fedn 1997–2001, memb House of Commons Cmmn 1998–2000, memb Treasy Select Ctee 1998–2000, chm Home Office Prisons Bds of Visitors Review Ctee 2000–01; vice-chm Br Section IPU 1994–99; chm NACRO Juvenile Remand Review Gp 1995–97, jt chm CAABU 1997–2001, pres Nat Cncl of Ind Monitoring Bds for Prisons 2003–07; chm: New Bridge 1994–2008, Arab-Br Centre 2001–03, London English Sch 2007–; *Style—* The Rt Hon Sir Peter Lloyd; ✉ 32 Burgh Street, London N1 8HG (☎ 020 7359 2871)

LLOYD, Phyllida Christian; CBE (2010); da of Patrick John Lloyd, of West Anstey, Devon, and Margaret, *née* Douglas-Pennant; *b* 17 June 1957; *Educ* Lawnside Sch Malvern, Univ of Birmingham; *Career* theatre, opera and film director; Arts Cncl trainee dir Wolsey Theatre Ipswich 1985 (prodns: Glengarry Glen Ross, Hard Times, Educating Rita), assoc dir Everyman Theatre Cheltenham 1986–87 (prodns incl Much Ado About Nothing, A Midsummer Night's Dream, Earth, Every Black Day, Woyzeck, Accidental Death of An Anarchist, Just Between Ourselves, and What the Butler Saw), assoc dir Bristol Old Vic 1989 (prodns: The Comedy of Errors, Dona Rosita The Spinster, A Streetcar Named Desire, Oliver Twist), Manchester Royal Exchange 1990–91 (prodns: The Winter's Tale, The School for Scandal, Death and the King's Horseman, Medea); RSC prodns: The Virtuoso 1991, Artists and Admirers 1992; Royal Court prodns incl: Six Degrees of Separation 1992, Hysteria 1993; RNT prodns: Pericles 1994, What the Butler Saw 1994, The Way of the World 1995, The Prime of Miss Jean Brodie 1998, The Duchess of Malfi 2003; Donmar Warehouse prodns: The Threepenny Opera 1994, Boston Marriage 2001, Mary Stuart 2005 (also Apollo Theatre), Julius Caesar (also St Ann's Warehouse NY) 2014, Henry IV (also St Ann's Warehouse NY) 2015, The Tempest (also St Ann's Warehouse NY) 2016; other credits incl: Dona Rosita (Almeida) 1997, Mamma Mia (worldwide), The Taming of the Shrew (Shakespeare's Globe), Wild East (Royal Court) 2005, The Fall of the House of Usher (Bregenz) 2006, Mary Stuart (Broadway) 2009 (nominated Best Dir Tony Award), Josephine and I (Bush Theatre and Public Theatre NY) 2015, Taming of the Shrew (Delacourte Theatre NY) 2016; operas: L'Étoile, La Bohème, Gloriana (ROH), Medea, Carmen, Albert Herring (Opera North), Macbeth (Opera National de Paris) 1999 (also ROH 2002), The Carmelites (ENO and WNO) 1999, The Handmaid's Tale (Royal Opera Copenhagen) 2000 and (also ENO 2003 and Canadian Opera Co Toronto 2004), Verdi's Requiem (ENO) 2000, The Rhinegold, The Valkyrie, Siegfried and Twilight of the Gods (ENO) 2004, Peter Grimes (Opera North) 2006; films: Gloriana – A Film 2000, Mamma Mia! 2008, The Iron Lady 2011; Cameron Mackintosh visiting prof Univ of Oxford 2006; *Style—* Ms Phyllida Lloyd, CBE; ✉ c/o Annette Stone, Arthouse, B7–3, 1 York Way, London N1C 4AT (☎ 020 3725 6893, e-mail annette@annettestone.com)

LLOYD, Richard; *b* 6 June 1970, Cardiff; *Educ* Aberdare Boys' Comp Sch, Univ of Aberystwyth, Coll of Law Chester; *m* Aug 1997, Rosemary; 3 s, 2 da; *Career* slr specialising in planning law, regeneration and compulsory purchase; slr then sr slr Edwards Geldard 1994–98 (articled clerk 1992–94), ptnr Eversheds 2003– (slr then assoc 1998–2003); legal assoc RTPI; memb: Law Soc 1992 (memb Specialist Planning Panel), Compulsory Purchase Assoc; *Recreations* listening to and playing music, cycling, football, reading (historical, political, biographical), family life; *Style—* Richard Lloyd, Esq; ✉ Eversheds LLP, Eversheds House, 70 Great Bridgewater Street, Manchester (☎ 07775 757827, e-mail richardlloyd@eversheds.com)

LLOYD, Robert Andrew; CBE (1991); s of Inspr William Edward Lloyd (d 1963), and May, *née* Waples; *b* 2 March 1940, Southend-on-Sea, Essex; *Educ* Southend HS, Keble Coll Oxford (MA), London Opera Centre; *m* 1, 1964 (m dis 1989), Sandra Dorothy, da of Douglas Watkins; 1 s (Marcus b 1965), 3 da (Anna b 1966, Candida b 1969, Alice b 1973); m 2, 1992, Lynda Anne Hazell, *née* Powell; *Career* freelance opera and concert singer (bass), writer and broadcaster; Instr Lt RN 1962–65, civilian tutor Bramshill Police Staff Coll 1966–68; princ bass: Sadler's Wells Opera 1969–72, Royal Opera 1972–83; performed at numerous int venues incl: Royal Opera House Covent Garden, La Scala Milan, Metropolitan Opera NY, Paris Opera, Munich, Vienna Staatsoper, San Francisco Opera; many performances at Salzburg Festival 1990–2013; performances incl: title role in André Tarkovsky prodn of Boris Godunov (Kirov Opera Leningrad), Simon Boccanegra (Metropolitan Opera), Magic Flute (Bastille Opera), Pelleas and Melisande (Metropolitan Opera), L'Incoronazione di Poppea (San Francisco), Faust (Dallas), created role of Tyrone in Hoddinot's Opera Tower 1999, title role in Don Quichotte (Chelsea Opera) 2012; sr artist Royal Opera House Covent Garden 2004–11; frequent broadcaster on radio and TV; memb: Exec Ctee Musicians' Benevolent Fund 1988–94, Conservatoires Advsy Gp HE Funding Cncl; pres Br Youth Opera 1989–94, pres Inc Soc of Musicians 2005–06, founding pres Highgate Opera Circle 2012–; visiting prof RCM 1998–, visiting coach Merola Prog San Francisco 2004; Charles Santley Award 1998, Foreign Singer of the Year Buenos Aires 1997, Chaliapin Memorial Medal 1998, hon fell Keble Coll Oxford 1990, hon fell Royal Welsh Coll of Music and Drama 2005; Hon RAM 1999; *Recordings* huge audio and video discography incl: Parsifal, Don Carlos, Entführung aus dem Serail, Magic Flute, Handel's Messiah, Dream of Gerontius, Fidelio, The Damnation of Faust, Verdi Requiem, The Coronation of Poppea, Samson and Dalilah 1999, Winterreise 1999, Don Quichotte (with Chelsea Opera) 2012; *Film* Parsifal (Artificial Eye), 6 Foot Cinderella (BBC), Bluebeard's Castle (BBC, Prix Italia 1989); *Recreations* sailing, hill walking; *Clubs* Highgate Literary and Scientific Instn, Colne Yacht, Royal Naval Sailing Assoc; *Style—* Robert Lloyd, Esq, CBE; ✉ c/o Askonas Holt, Lincoln House, 300 High Holborn, London WC1V 7JH

LLOYD, Simon Roderick; s of Desmond C F Lloyd (d 1978), and Amber, *née* Wallace-Barr; *b* 25 March 1947; *Educ* Wellington (BA); *m* April 1972, Susan Margaret, *née* Cuthbert; 1 da (Rebecca Catherine b 1976), 1 s (Andrew James Wallace b 1978); *Career* media planner/buyer Garland Compton Advertising 1966–74; Foote Cone & Belding Advertising: joined 1974, bd/media dir 1978–80, vice-chm 1980–84, md 1984–86, dir of media Euro Region 1986–88; vice-pres media Publicis FCB Europe (alliance of FCB and Publicis) 1989–2002, chm Optimedia Worldwide (network of media planning/buying specialist cos owned by Publicis Group); *Recreations* sailing, cricket, walking, dogs, travel, almost any new experience!; *Clubs* MCC, Royal London Yacht, Seaview Yacht (Isle of Wight); *Style—* Simon Lloyd, Esq; ☎ 020 8946 9083

LLOYD, Stephen Anthony Christopher; s of Edward John LLoyd, and Nuala, *née* Meenehan; *b* 15 June 1957, Mombasa, Kenya; *Educ* St George's Coll Weybridge; *Partner* Cherine Maskill; *Career* MP (Lib Dem) Eastbourne 2010–15, PPS to Rt Hon Edward Davey, MP, *qv*, sec of state Dept of Energy and Climate Change 2014–; memb Nat Liberal Club; business devpt dir West End Studios Ltd 2015–; *Recreations* cinema, motorsport, reading, travel; *Style—* Stephen Lloyd, Esq; ✉ 18 Bradford Street, Eastbourne BN21 1HZ (☎ 01323 747928, e-mail stephenlloydlibdem@hotmail.com); West End Studios Ltd, The Old Biscuit Factory, Finmere Close, Eastbourne BN22 8QN (website www.teamwestend.com)

LLOYD, Thomas Owen Saunders; OBE (2004), DL (Dyfed 2001); s of Maj John Audley Lloyd, MC (d 1999), of Court Henry, Carmarthen, and (Mary Ivy) Anna, *née* Owen; *b* 26 February 1955; *Educ* Radley, Downing Coll Cambridge (MA); *m* 7 Nov 1987, (Christabel) Juliet Anne (d 1996), da of Maj David Harrison-Allen (d 1976), of Cresselly, nr Pembroke; *Career* slr (not practising), author; Royal Cmmr on the Ancient and Historical Monuments of Wales 2010–, Wales Herald of Arms Extraordinary 2010–; chm: Historic Bldgs Cncl for Wales 1992–2004 (memb 1985–2004), Br Historic Bldgs Tst 1987–92, Pembrokeshire Historical Soc 1991–94, Buildings at Risk Tst 1992–2008, Carmarthenshire Antiquarian Soc 1999–2002 and 2009–11, Wales region HHA 2004–09, Picton Castle Tst 2006–10, Cambrian Archaeological Assoc 2007–08; chair Cathedrals and Churches Cmmn of the Church in Wales 2012–, vice-patron (Wales) War Memorials Tst; memb Cadw – Welsh Historic Monuments Advsy Ctee 1992–2004; tstee Architectural Heritage Fund 2006–13, vice-pres Friends of Friendless Churches 2010–; non-exec dir: Dyfed Family Health Servs Authy 1990–95 (chm Med and Dental Servs Ctees 1992–96), Wales Tourist Bd 1995–99; conslt Sotheby's (Wales) 1999–2013; High Sheriff Dyfed 2011–12; hon memb Royal Soc of Architects in Wales 1993; FSA 1991; *Books* The Lost Houses of Wales (1986, 2 edn 1989); The Buildings of Wales series: Pembrokeshire (co-author, 2004, 2 edn 2010), Carmarthenshire & Ceredigion (co-author, 2006); *Style—* Thomas Lloyd, Esq, OBE, DL, FSA; ✉ Court Henry, Dryslwyn, Carmarthen, SA32 8RU (☎ 01558 668252)

LLOYD, Tom; s of Sam Lloyd, of London, and Jane, *née* Watkins; *b* 18 September 1966, London; *Educ* Nottingham Trent Univ (BA), RCA (MA); *m* 19 Sept 1998, Polly Richards; 2 da (Molly Florence Gwendolen b 19 June 2001, Delilah Jocelyn Vera b 16 Jan 2004); *Career* early career as sr designer Pentagram London; co-fndr (with Luke Pearson, *qv*) PearsonLloyd 1997–; projects incl first class seat for Virgin Atlantic Airways 2001–03 and Westminster street light for Artemide 2001–04, other projects for clients incl Knoll International, Steelcase, Body Shop, Lufthansa, Modus, Fritz Hansen and Ideal Standard; architectural design: Duffer of St George 1997–2002, Levis/Dockers UK 2000, Carhartt 2000, TSE Cashmere 2000–02; exhbns: Architecture Fndn London 1999, Crafts Cncl London 2001, Stuttgart Design Centre 2001, MOMA NY 2001, Design Museum London 2001 and 2002, V&A 2002, Br Cncl China 2003, Br Embassy Tokyo 2004, ICFF NY 2005; visiting lectr: Ecole Cantonale d'Art de Lausanne, RCA; numerous awards incl FX Designers of the Year 2002, other awards from D&AD, Red Dot, IDEA, Baden-Württemberg, IF and Design Week; Royal Designer for Industry 2008; FRSA 2009; *Style—* Tom Lloyd, Esq; ✉ Pearson Lloyd, 117 Drysdale Street, London N1 6ND (☎ 020 7033 4440, fax 020 7033 4441)

L

LLOYD JONES, (Richard) David; s of Richard Francis Lloyd Jones (d 1976), and Hester, *née* Ritchie (d 1985); *b* 10 May 1942; *Educ* Edgeborough Sch, Bradfield Coll, AA Sch of Architecture (AADipl); *m* 1971, Linda Barbara, da of Duncan John Stewart; *Career* Stillman and Eastwick-Field Architects 1964, National Building Agency 1966–72, RMJM Ltd (previously Robert Matthew Johnson-Marshall & Partners) 1972–91 (dir 1986, chm Design Group 1987); projects incl: NFU Mutual and Avon Insurance Group HQ, Solar Offices Doxford International, Grange Park Opera House, Renewable Energy Systems Head Office and Visitor's Centre; dir Studio E Architects Ltd 1994–; UK rep Int Energy Agency Task 1995–2001; RIBA 1968 (memb London Regnl Cncl 1991–2001, memb Sustainable Futures Ctee 2004–), FRSA 1990; *Publications* Architecture and the Environment, Lawrence King (1999), BIPV Projects, DTI (2000); *Recreations* sculpture, painting, tennis, travelling; *Clubs* Architectural Assoc; *Style—* David Lloyd Jones, Esq; ✉ 24 Liston Road, London SW4 0DF; 28 Triqette Pupulyu, Ghammar, Gozo, Malta; Studio E Architects, Palace Wharf, Rainville Road, London W6 9HN (☎ 020 7385 7126, fax 020 7381 4995, e-mail david@studioe.co.uk)

LLOYD MOSTYN; *see also:* Mostyn

LLOYD OF BERWICK, Baron (Life Peer UK 1993), of Ludlay in the County of East Sussex; Sir Anthony John Leslie Lloyd; kt (1978), PC (1984), DL (E Sussex 1983); s of Edward John Boydell Lloyd, of Little Bucksteep, Dallington, E Sussex; *b* 9 May 1929; *Educ* Eton, Trinity Coll Cambridge; *m* 1960, Jane Helen Violet Shelford, MBE, DL, da of C W Shelford, of Chailey Place, Lewes, E Sussex; *Career* Nat Serv 1 Bn Coldstream Gds 1948; called to the Bar Inner Temple 1955 (treas 1999), QC 1967, attorney-gen to HRH The Prince of Wales 1969–77, ;judge of the High Court of Justice (Queen's Bench Div) 1978–84, Lord Justice of Appeal 1984–93, Lord of Appeal in Ordinary 1993–98; former memb Top Salaries Review Body; chm Security Cmmn 1992–99; memb Parole Bd 1983–84; vice-pres Corporation of the Sons of the Clergy 1996–2004; chm Glyndebourne Arts Tst 1975–94, dir Royal Acad of Music 1979–98; chm Chichester Diocesan Bd of Fin 1972–76; Master Worshipful Co of Salters 2000; hon fell Peterhouse Cambridge 1981 (fell 1953); Hon LLD: Queen's Univ Belfast 2005, Univ of Sussex 2006; *Clubs* Brooks's; *Style—* The Rt Hon Lord Lloyd of Berwick, PC, DL; ✉ Ludlay, Berwick, East Sussex (☎ 01323 870204); 68 Strand-on-the-Green, London W4 3PF (☎ 020 8994 7790)

LLOYD WEBBER, Baron (Life Peer UK 1997), of Sydmonton in the County of Hampshire; Sir Andrew Lloyd Webber; kt (1992); s of late William Southcombe Lloyd Webber, CBE, DMus, FRCM, FRCO, and late Jean Hermione, *née* Johnstone; *b* 22 March 1948; *Educ* Westminster, Magdalen Coll Oxford, Royal Coll of Music; *m* 1, 1971 (m dis 1983), Sarah Jane Tudor, *née* Hugill; 1 s, 1 da; m 2, 1984 (m dis 1990), Sarah Brightman; m 3, 1991, Madeleine Astrid, *née* Gurdon; 2 s, 1 da; *Career* composer; FRCM 1988; *Musicals* The Likes of Us 1965 (with lyrics by Tim Rice), Joseph and the Amazing Technicolor Dreamcoat 1968 (with lyrics by Tim Rice), Jesus Christ Superstar 1970 (with lyrics by Tim Rice), Evita 1976 (with lyrics by Tim Rice); Jeeves (with lyrics by Alan Ayckbourn) 1975, Tell Me On a Sunday (with lyrics by Don Black) 1980, Cats (based on poems by T S Eliot) 1981, Song and Dance (with lyrics by Don Black) 1982, Starlight Express (with lyrics by Richard Stilgoe and Charles Hart) 1984, The Phantom of The Opera (with lyrics by Richard Stilgoe and Charles Hart) 1986, Aspects of Love (with lyrics by Don Black and Charles Hart) 1989, Sunset Boulevard (with lyrics by Christopher Hampton and Don Black) 1993, By Jeeves (book and lyrics by Alan Ayckbourn) 1996, Whistle Down the Wind (with lyrics by Jim Steinman; premiere Washington DC Dec 1996, West End 1998), The Beautiful Game (book and lyrics by Ben Elton) 2000, The Woman in White (book by Charlotte Jones, lyrics by David Zippel) 2004, Love Never Dies (with lyrics by Glenn Slater) 2010, Stephen Ward (book and lyrics by Don Black and Christopher Hampton) 2013, School of Rock (book by Julian Fellowes, lyrics by Glenn Slater, premiere NY) 2015; prodr of many ventures incl: Joseph and the Amazing Technicolor Dreamcoat 1973 (also 1974, 1978, 1980 and 1991), Cats 1981, Song and Dance 1982, Daisy Pulls It Off 1983, On Your Toes 1984, Starlight Express 1984, The Hired

Man 1984, The Phantom of the Opera 1986, Café Puccini 1986, Lend me a Tenor 1988, Shirley Valentine 1989, Aspects of Love 1989, La Bête 1992, Sunset Boulevard 1993, By Jeeves 1996, Jesus Christ Superstar 1996 and 1998, Whistle Down the Wind 1996 and 1998, The Beautiful Game 2000, Bombay Dreams 2002, The Sound of Music 2006, The Wizard of Oz 2011; appeared in: How Do You Solve a Problem Like Maria? (BBC TV) 2006, Any Dream Will Do (BBC TV) 2007, I'd Do Anything (BBC TV) 2008, Your Country Needs You (BBC TV) 2009, Over The Rainbow (BBC TV) 2010, Superstar (ITV) 2012, 40 Musical Years (ITV) 2013; *Film Scores* Gumshoe 1971, The Odessa File 1974; *Compositions* Variations 1978, Requiem Mass 1985, Amigos Para Siempre (Friends for Life) – official Olympic theme for 1992; *Awards* incl: 6 Tony Awards, 3 Grammy Awards, 5 Olivier Awards, a Golden Globe, an Oscar, the Praemium Imperiale, Richard Rodgers Award, Critics' Circle Award for Best Musical 2000, Kennedy Centre Honour for Lifetime Contribution to American Culture 2006, Outstanding Contribution Classical BRIT Award 2008, fell BASCA 2012; *Publications* Evita (with Tim Rice, 1978), Cats – the book of the Musical (1981), Joseph and the Amazing Technicolor Dreamcoat (with Tim Rice, 1982), The Complete Phantom of the Opera (1987), The Complete Aspects of Love (1989), Sunset Boulevard – from movie to musical (1993); *Recreations* architecture, food, art; *Style*— The Lord Lloyd Webber; ✉ c/o The Really Useful Group Limited, 17 Slingsby Place, London WC2E 9AB (website www.andrewlloydwebber.com, Twitter @OfficialALW)

LLOYD WEBBER, Prof Julian; s of William Southcombe Lloyd Webber, CBE (d 1982), and Jean Hermione, *née* Johnstone (d 1993); bro of Baron Lloyd Webber (Life Peer), *qv; b* 14 April 1951; *Educ* Univ Coll Sch, Royal Coll of Music (ARCM), studied with Pierre Fournier (Geneva); *m* 1, 1974 (m dis 1989), Celia Mary, *née* Ballantyne; *m* 2, 1989 (m dis 1999), Zohra, *née* Mahmoud Ghazi; 1 s (David b 25 Feb 1992); *m* 3, 2001 (m dis 2007), Kheira, *née* Bourahla; *m* 4, July 2009, Jiaxin, *née* Cheng; 1 da (Jasmine Orienta b 14 June 2011); *Career* princ Birmingham Conservatoire 2015–, musician; UK debut Queen Elizabeth Hall London 1972, US debut Lincoln Centre NY 1980, debut with Berlin Philharmonic Orch 1984; has performed with orchestras worldwide and toured the USA, Canada, Germany, Holland, Africa, Bulgaria, China, Czechoslovakia, S America, Spain, Belgium, France, Scandinavia, Switzerland, Portugal, Australia, NZ, Singapore, Japan, Korea, Vietnam, Hong Kong and Taiwan; first recordings of works by: Malcolm Arnold, Benjamin Britten, Frank Bridge, Gavin Bryars, Frederick Delius, Philip Glass, Gustav Holst, Michael Nyman, Joaquin Rodrigo, Dimitri Shostakovich, Eric Whitacre, Ralph Vaughan Williams; artistic dir Cellothon '88 South Bank Centre London; chm Govt's In Harmony project 2008, pres Elgar Soc 2009, chair Sistema England 2011; govr South Bank Centre 2009; Best British Classical Recording (for Elgar Cello Concerto) 1987, Crystal Award World Economic Forum 1998, Red Award Classic FM 2005, Distinguished Musician Award Incorporated Soc of Musicians 2013; Hon Dr: Univ of Hull 2003, Thames Valley Univ 2004, Plymouth Univ 2014; FRCM 1994; *Books* incl: The Classical Cello (1980), The Romantic Cello (1981), The French Cello (1981), 6 pieces by Frank Bridge (1982), The Young Cellist's Repertoire Books 1, 2 & 3 (1984), Holst Invocation (1984), Vaughan Williams Fantasia on Sussex Folk Tunes (1984), Travels with My Cello (1984), Song of the Birds (1985), Recital Repertoire for Cellists (1986), Short Sharp Shocks (ed, 1990), The Great Cello Solos (1991), Cello Song (1993), The Essential Cello (1997), Cello Moods (1999), Married to Music (biography, 2001), Made In England (2003), Unexpected Songs (2007), A Tale of Two Cellos (2014), Vivaldi: Six Concertos for Two Cellos (2014); *Recreations* countryside (especially British), soccer (Leyton Orient); *Clubs* Chelsea Arts; *Style*— Prof Julian Lloyd Webber, FRCM; ✉ Birmingham Conservatoire of Music, Fletchers Walk, Birmingham, West Midlands B3 3HG (e-mail john@julianlloydwebber.com, website www.julianlloydwebber.com)

LLOYD-DAVIES, (Reginald) Wyndham; s of Dr Allan Wyndham Lloyd-Davies (d 1974), of Branksome Park, Dorset, and Muriel Constance, *née* Martin (d 1993); *b* 24 June 1934; *Educ* Rugby, Univ of London (MB, MS); *m* 1, 31 May 1958 (m dis 1981), Elizabeth Ann, da of Arthur Wesley Harding (d 1978); 2 da ((Susan) Vanessa Lloyd-Davies, MBE (Mil) b 1960 d 2005, Fiona Caroline b 1964); *m* 2, 20 Aug 1983, Jill Black, da of Austin Hemingsley (d 1969); *Career* res urologist San Francisco Med Center Univ of Calif 1969–70, conslt surgn Queen Victoria Hosp East Grinstead 1971–77, dep CMO Met Police 1983–98 (conslt surgn 1978–2003), sr conslt urologist St Thomas' Hosp London 1986–98 (MRC res fell Dept of Surgery 1965, sr surgical registrar in urology 1966–69, conslt urologist 1970–86), clinical dir urology and lithotripsy Guy's and St Thomas' Hosp Tst 1993–98 (urologist emeritus 1998–2004), surgn King Edward VII Hosp for Offrs London 1994–2004; memb Cncl RSM 1991–92; Urology Section RSM: memb Cncl 1975–87, treas 1983–87, pres elect 1990, pres 1991–92; author of numerous pubns on urological topics; late memb Bd Mgmnt London Mozart Players; Freeman City of London 1979, Liveryman Worshipful Soc of Apothecaries 1974; memb Br Assoc of Urological Surgns (memb Cncl 1980–83 and 1991–92); FRCS, FEBU, FRSM; *Recreations* shooting, fishing, stalking, music; *Clubs* Garrick; *Style*— Wyndham Lloyd-Davies, Esq; ✉ Flat 64 Darwin Court, Gloucester Avenue, London NW1 7BQ (📞 and fax 020 7419 6587)

LLOYD-JONES, David Mathias; s of Sir Harry Vincent Lloyd-Jones, and Margaret Alwyna, *née* Mathias; *b* 19 November 1934; *Educ* Westminster, Magdalen Coll Oxford (BA); *m* 23 May 1964, Anne Carolyn, da of Brig Victor Whitehead, of Montreal; 2 s (Gareth b 1966, Simon b 1968), 1 da (Vanessa b 1964); *Career* conductor; repetiteur with Royal Opera House Covent Garden 1959–60, chorus master and conductor New Opera Co 1961–64; freelance conductor engagements with: BBC, WNO, Scottish Opera; asst music dir Sadler's Wells and ENO 1972–78, artistic dir Opera North 1978–90; many opera and concert engagements abroad, numerous recordings of Br and Russian music; ed original version of Mussorgsky's Boris Godunov 1974, gen ed William Walton Edition 1995–2014; full score: Gilbert and Sullivan's The Gondoliers 1983, Berlioz's The Childhood of Christ 1999; trans: Eugene Onegin, Boris Godunov, The Queen of Spades, The Love forThree Oranges; Hon DMus Univ of Leeds; hon memb Royal Philharmonic Soc; *Style*— David Lloyd-Jones, Esq; ✉ 94 Whitelands House, Cheltenham Terrace, London SW3 4RA (📞 020 7730 8695)

LLOYD-JONES, Jonathan; s of Peter Lloyd-Jones (d 1990), and Margaret, *née* Marshall (d 2013); *b* 23 November 1954, Guildford, Surrey; *Educ* Sevenoaks Sch, Univ of Southampton (LLB); *m* 14 April 1984 (m dis 2015), Sarah Williams; 3 s (Thomas b 10 Feb 1986, Olly b 30 June 1987, Jamie b 25 Feb 1990); *Career* Stephenson Harwood 1977–80, Claude Hornby and Cox 1980–88, Blake Lapthorn 1988–2012 (chm 2005–11), ind mediator 2012–; chair of tstees The Art Room; memb Law Soc 1979; memb Scotch Malt Whisky Soc 1994; FRSA 2014; *Recreations* art, walking, family; *Style*— Jonathan Lloyd-Jones, Esq; ✉ e-mail lloydjonesjo@gmail.com

LLOYD-JONES, (Glyn) Robin; s of William Rice Lloyd-Jones (d 1980), and Esme Frances, *née* Ellis (d 2001); *b* 5 October 1934; *Educ* Blundell's, Selwyn Coll Cambridge (MA), Jordanhill Coll of Educn; *m* 30 July 1959, Sallie, da of Cdr John Hollocombe, RN (d 1981) and Kathleen, *née* Gregory (d 1964); 1 s (Glyn b 1962), 2 da (Kally b 1965, Léonie b 1969); *Career* educn advsr 1972–89; writer; pres Scot Assoc of Writers 1981–86, pres (Scot) PEN Int 1997–2000 (vice-pres 1991–97), co-ordinator Scottish Forum for Devpt Educn in Schools 1996–98; *Books* fiction incl: Where the Forest and the Garden Meet (1980), Lord of the Dance (winner BBC-Arrow First Novel competition, 1983), The Dreamhouse (1985), Fallen Angels (1992); other: Assessment from Principles to Action (with Elizabeth Bray, 1985), Better Worksheets (1986), Argonauts of the Western Isles (1989), Fallen Pieces of the Moon (2006), Red Fox Running (2007), The Sunlit Summer (2013, Saltire Society's Research Book of the Year); *Radio Drama* Ice in Wonderland

(Radio Times New Drama Script Award, 1992), Rainmaker (1995), The Sweet Especial Scene (2014); *Recreations* mountaineering, sea-kayaking, chess, photography; *Style*— Robin Lloyd-Jones, Esq; ✉ 26 East Clyde Street, Helensburgh G84 7PG (📞 01436 672010, e-mail robinlj34@gmail.com)

LLWYD, Elfyn; s of late Huw Meirion Hughes, and Hefina Hughes; *b* 26 September 1951; *Educ* Llanrwst GS, Ysgol Dyffryn Conwy, UCW Aberystwyth, Coll of Law Chester; *m* 27 July 1974, Eleri, da of Huw and Jane Lloyd Edwards; 1 s, 1 da; *Career* admitted slr 1977, pres Gwynedd Law Soc 1990–91; MP (Plaid Cymru): Meirionnydd Nant Conwy 1992–2010, Dwyfor Meirionnydd 2010–15; Parly ambass NSPCC; Parly friend of UNICEF; pres: Club memb Parly Select Ctee on Welsh Affrs 1992–2015 and 1998–2006, Parly whip (Plaid Cymru) 1995–99, Parly leader (Plaid Cymru) 1998; called to the Bar Gray's Inn 1997; govr Wesminster Fndn for Democracy 2001–05; memb Gorsedd of Bards; *Recreations* pigeon breeding, choral singing, rugby, fishing; *Clubs* Clwb Rygbi Bala Rugby (pres), Clwb Rygbi Dolgellau Rugby (pres), Estimaner Fishing (pres), Peldroed Llanuwchllyn Football (pres), Peldroed Betws-y-Coed Football (pres); *Style*— Elfyn Llwyd, Esq

LOACH, Kenneth Charles (Ken); s of John Loach (d 1973), of Nuneaton, Warks, and Vivien Nora, *née* Hamlin; *b* 17 June 1936; *Educ* King Edward VI Sch Nuneaton, St Peter's Coll Oxford (BA); *m* 17 July 1962, Lesley, da of William Leslie Ashton (d 1967); 3 s (Stephen b 1963, Nicholas b 1965 d 1971, James b 1969), 2 da (Hannah b 1967, Emma b 1972); *Career* film director; Golden Lion Award for Lifetime Achievement, Special Award for Contribution to British Film Evening Standard British Film Awards 1999; Hon DLitt Univ of St Andrews; ACTT; *Film* incl: Up The Junction 1965, Cathy Come Home 1966, Poor Cow 1967, Kes 1969, Family Life 1971, Days of Hope 1975, The Price of Coal 1977, The Gamekeeper 1979, Black Jack 1979, Looks and Smiles 1981, Which Side Are You On? 1984, Fatherland 1986, The View from the Woodpile 1988, Hidden Agenda 1990, Riff-Raff 1991, Raining Stones 1993 (Jury Prize Cannes Film Festival 1993, Best Film Prize Evening Standard Film Awards 1994), Ladybird Ladybird 1994 (Best Actress Award for Crissy Rock, Critics' Award for Best Film Berlin Film Festival 1994), Land and Freedom 1995, Felix 1995 (European Film of the Year Award 1995), Carla's Song 1996, The Flickering Flame (documentary) 1996, My Name is Joe 1998, Bread and Roses 2000, The Navigators 2001, Sweet Sixteen 2002, 11'09'01 2002, Ae Fond Kiss 2003, Tickets 2005, The Wind That Shakes the Barley 2006, It's a Free World 2007, Looking for Eric 2009, Route Irish 2010, The Angels' Share 2012; *Recreations* watching football; *Style*— Ken Loach, Esq; ✉ c/o Sixteen Films, 187 Wardour Street (2nd Floor), London W1F 8ZB

LOADER, Adrian; *b* 3 June 1948, Thessaloniki, Greece; *Educ* Univ of Cambridge; *m* 1975, Isa; 3 da; *Career* human resources Shell UK 1970–72, Shell Venezuela 1973–74, Shell Malaysia 1975–76, gp planning Shell Int 1977–78, Shell Honduras 1979–81, gen mangr Shell Uruguay 1982–84, admin mangr Shell Exploration and Prodn Aberdeen 1984–87, head Central Recruitment Shell Int 1987–89, chief exec Shell cos Philippines 1989–93, div head Central/East Europe and former Soviet Union 1993–95; Shell Oil Products: dir South Zone (Africa and Latin America) 1996–97, dir East Zone (Middle East and Far East) 1997–99, pres Shell Europe Oil Products 1999–2003; dir Strategic Planning, Sustainable Devpt and External Affrs Shell Int 2003–05, dir Strategy and Business Devpt Directorate Royal Dutch Shell 2005–07, pres and ceo Shell Canada 2007; chm Candax Energy Inc; non-exec dir: Alliance Unichem, Shell Canada Ltd, Holcim Ltd 2006–; FCIPD; *Recreations* skiing, scuba diving, wine, music; *Style*— Adrian Loader, Esq

LOADER, Prof Ian Spencer; *b* 2 April 1965, Harrow, Middx; *Educ* Univ of Sheffield (LLB), Univ of Edinburgh (MSc, PhD); *Career* lectr in law Liverpool Poly 1986–87; Centre for Criminology and the Social and Philosophical Study of Law Univ of Edinburgh: res asst 1988 and 1989, lectr in criminology and jurisprudence 1990–92; Univ of Keele: lectr 1992–99, sr lectr 1999–2002, reader 2002–04, prof of criminology 2004–05; prof of criminology and dir Centre for Criminology Univ of Oxford 2005–, professorial fell All Souls Coll Oxford 2005–; Jean Monnet fell Dept of Law European Univ Inst Florence 2004, visiting scholar Centre of Criminology Univ of Toronto 2003; ed Br Jl of Criminology 2006– (memb Editorial Bd 2001–), assoc ed Theoretical Criminology 1999–2002 and 2005– (book review ed 2002–05); memb Editorial Bd: Policing and Society 1998–, Int Political Sociology 2005–, Clarendon Studies in Criminology series 2005–; interviews and guest appearances on radio and TV; Radzinowicz Prize 2001; *Cautionary Tales: Young People, Crime and Policing in Edinburgh* (jtly, 1994), Youth, Policing and Democracy (1996, shortlisted Philip Abrams Meml Prize Br Sociological Assoc 1996), Crime and Social Change in Middle England: Questions of Order in an English Town (jtly, 2000), Policing and the Condition of England: Memory, Politics and Culture (jtly, 2003), Civilizing Security (jtly, 2007), Emotions, Crime and Justice (co-ed, 2007); contribs to edited books, jl articles, conf and res papers, res reports; *Style*— Prof Ian Loader; ✉ Centre for Criminology, University of Oxford, Manor Road Building, Manor Road, Oxford OX1 3UQ (📞 01865 274440, e-mail ian.loader@crim.ox.ac.uk)

LOADES, Prof David Michael; s of Reginald Ernest Loades, and Gladys Mary, *née* Smith; *b* 19 January 1934; *Educ* Perse Sch Cambridge, Emmanuel Coll Cambridge (MA, PhD, LittD); *m* 1, 18 Dec 1965 (m dis 1984), Ann Lomas, *née* Glover; *m* 2, 11 April 1987, Judith Ann, formerly Atkins; *Career* Nat Serv PO RAF 1953–55; lectr in political science Univ of St Andrews 1961–63, reader Univ of Durham 1977–80 (lectr in history 1963–70, sr lectr 1970–77), prof of history UCNW Bangor 1980–96; hon research prof Univ of Sheffield 1996–2008; dir Br Acad John Foxe Project 1993–2004; FRHistS 1967, FSA 1984; *Books* Two Tudor Conspiracies (1965), The Oxford Martyrs (1970), Politics and the Nation 1450–1660 (1974), The Reign of Mary Tudor (1979), The Tudor Court (1986), Mary Tudor – A Life (1989), Politics, Censorship and the English Reformation (1991), Revolution in Religion – The English Reformation 1530–1570 (1992), The Mid-Tudor Crisis 1545–1565 (1992), The Tudor Navy – An Administrative, Military and Political History (1992), Essays in European History 1453–1648 (1993), The Politics of Marriage: Henry VIII and his queens (1994), Essays on the Reign of Edward VI (1994), John Dudley: Duke of Northumberland (1996), Power in Tudor England (1996), Tudor Government (1997), England's Maritime Empire 1400–1600 (2000), Chronicles of the Tudor Queens (2002), Elizabeth I (2003), Intrigue and Treason: The Tudor Court 1547–1558 (2004), The Church of Mary Tudor (2006), Mary Tudor: A Tragical History (2006), Henry VIII: Court, Church and Conflict (2007), The Cecils: Privilege and Power behind the Throne (2007), The Princes of Wales: Royal Heirs in Waiting (2008), The Tudor Queens of England (2009), The Making of the Elizabethan Navy 1540–1590 (2009), The Fighting Tudors (2009), The Religous Culture of Marian England (2010), Henry VIII (2011), The Boleyns (2011), The Tudors (2012), Catherine Howard (2012), Jane Seymour (2013), Thomas Cromwell: Servant to Henry VIII (2014); *Style*— Prof David Loades, FSA; ✉ The Cottage, Priory Lane, Burford, Oxfordshire OX18 4SG (📞 01993 822625, e-mail davidloades22@btinternet.com)

LOBBAN, Peter William McDonald; OBE (2008); s of Christopher John Lobban, and May Margaret, *née* Robertson; *b* 8 August 1947, Nairn, Scotland; *Educ* Nairn Acad, Univ of Edinburgh (MA); *m* 7 Oct 1972, Elinor Joan, *née* Barkas; 1 s (James Mark b 10 July 1973), 1 da (Hannah May b 15 Sept 1975); *Career* sr res offr London Grad Sch of Business Studies 1969–76, head of econ policy CBI 1976–81, dep dir employment affrs CBI 1981–86, corp servs mangr Carrington site Shell Chemicals UK Ltd 1986–87, personnel dir Shell Chemicals UK Ltd 1987–90, dir HR Brunei Shell Gp 1990–92, dir HR and public affrs Shell Expro 1992–98, chief exec Construction Industry Trg Bd 1998–2008, chief exec ConstructionSkills 2004–08; chm Offshore Petroleum Industry Trg Orgn 1993–98, chm Sector Skill Alliance Scotland 2006–08, tstee BRE Tst; memb Bd Women in Sci, Engrg and Construction 2005–08, UK memb OECD Business and Industry Advsy Ctee 1979–82; author of articles published in learned jls; Liveryman Worshipful Co of Constructors 2009; *Style*— Peter Lobban, Esq, OBE; ✉ Greenbrook Lodge, 30 Dobbins Lane, Wendover, Bucks HP22 6DH (☎ 01296 624420, e-mail petlob@aol.com)

LOCATELLI, Giorgio; *b* 7 April 1963; *m* 5 Aug 1995, Plaxy, da of Clive Exton; 1 s (Jack Exton b 18 June 1988), 1 da (Margherita b 27 Jan 1996); *Career* chef and restaurateur; early work in N Italy and Switzerland, The Savoy (with Anton Edelmann, *qv*) 1986–90, Restaurant Laurent and La Tour D'Argent Paris 1990–92, head chef Olivo London 1992–95; prop: Zafferano London 1995, Spighetta London 1997, Spiga 1998, Locanda Locatelli 2002–; conslt: Refettorio at Crowne Plaza City Hotel, Cecconi's; *Television* Pure Italian (UK Food) 2002, Tony and Giorgio (BBC 2) 2003, Sicily Unpacked (BBC 2) 2012, Italy Unpacked (BBC 2) 2013; *Awards* for Zafferano: Best Italian Restaurant Carlton London Restaurant Awards 1997 and 1998, Restaurateur's Italian Restaurant of the Year Hotel and Restaurant Magazine 1998, 1999 and 2000, Michelin Star 1999; for Locanda Locatelli: Best New Restaurnat BMX/Squaremeal Award 2002, Best New Restaurant London Region Theme Bar and Restaurant Awards 2002, Best Italian Restaurant Restaurateur's Restaurant of the Year Awards 2002, 2003 and 2004, Best Italian Restaurant Carlton London Restaurant Awards 2003, Great Hotel Restaurants of the World Award Hotels Magazine 2003, 3 AA Rosettes 2003, Michelin Star 2003, 2004 and 2011; Best London Restaurant Theme Magazine Bar and Restaurant Awards (Cecconi's) 2001, voted Outstanding London Chef Moët & Chandon London Restaurant Awards 2001, Diploma di Buona Cucina Accademia Italiana della Cucina 2002, Premio Italia nel Mondo Fondazione Italia 2003, Int Five Star Diamond Award American Acad of Hospitality Sciences 2003; *Publications* Tony and Giorgio (2003), Made in Italy (2006), Made in Sicily (2011), Italy Unpacked (2014); *Style*— Giorgio Locatelli, Esq; ✉ Locanda Locatelli, 8 Seymour Street, London W1H 7JZ (☎ 020 7935 9088, fax 020 7935 1149, e-mail info@locandalocatelli.com, website www.locandalocatelli.com)

LOCHHEAD, Richard Neilson; MSP; s of Robert William Lochhead, and Agnes Robertson, *née* Neilson; *b* 24 May 1969; *Educ* Williamwood HS Glasgow, Univ of Stirling (BA); *m* 13 July 2002, Fiona Hepburn; *Career* fin trainee South of Scotland Electricity Bd 1987–89, office mangr for Alex Salmond MP, *qv*, 1994–98, economic devpt offr Dundee City Cncl 1998–99; MSP (SNP): Scotland North East (regnl list) 1999–2006, Moray 2006–; sec for rural affrs and the environment; *Recreations* reading fiction and history non-fiction, travel, cinema, listening to music; *Style*— Richard Lochhead, Esq, MSP; ✉ The Scottish Parliament, Edinburgh EH99 1SP (☎ 0131 348 5713, fax 0131 348 5737, e-mail richard.lochhead.msp@scottish.parliament.uk)

LOCK, David Anthony; QC (2011); s of late John Kirby Lock, and Jeanette Lock; *b* 2 May 1960; *Educ* Esher GS, Woking Sixth Form Coll, Jesus Coll Cambridge (MA), Poly of Central London (DipL), Inns of Court Sch of Law (Wilson scholar Gray's Inn); *m* Dr Bernadette, *née* Gregory; 1 s (Anthony), 2 da (Rebecca, Pippa); *Career* mgmnt trainee GEC Telecommunications 1982–83, barrister 1987–91,1992–97 and 2002–, MP (Lab) Wyre Forest 1997–2001; PPS: Lord Chancellor's Dept 1997–98, to Lord Chancellor and Parly sec at Lord Chancellor's Dept 1998–99; Parly sec Lord Chancellor's Dept 1999–2001; chm Serv Authorities for the Nat Criminal Intelligence Serv and Nat Crime Squad 2002–03; dir: Insolvency Management Ltd 2002–07, Lawbook Consultancy Ltd, Property Flow Ltd 2002–07; head Healthcare Practice Mills & Reeve slrs 2003–08, memb No 5 Chambers London, Birmingham and Bristol 2008–; Wychavon DC: memb 1995–97, chm Amenities and Econ Devpt Ctee, chm Wychavon Leisure Mgmnt Bd; memb: Br Student Debating Team 1985–86; *Recreations* family, paragliding, windsurfing, friends; *Style*— David Lock, Esq, QC

LOCK, David Peter; CBE (2007); s of Arthur Lovering Lock, of Kent, and Kathleen Barbara, *née* Nash (d 1961); *b* 12 March 1948; *Educ* Sir Roger Manwood's GS, Nottingham Coll of Art and Design/Trent Poly (Dip Town and Country Planning); *m* 19 Sept 1970, Jeanette Anita, da of Frederick Charles Jones; 3 da; *Career* area planning offr Leicester City Cncl 1970–73 (asst branch sec Leicester City Branch NALGO 1971–73), planning aid offr Town & Country Planning Assoc 1973–78, planning mangr Milton Keynes Devpt Corp 1978–81, assoc dir Conran Roche Ltd 1981–88, chm David Lock Associates Ltd 1988–2013 (strategic advsr 2013–), chief planning advsr DOE 1994–97, memb Bd Ebbsfleet Urban Devpt Corporation and Garden City 2015–; memb Editorial Bd: Town & Country Planning Jl 1973–2009, Built Environment Quarterly 1975–2010, Urban Design Quarterly 1996–2009; chm: Milton Keynes Urban Studies Centre Ltd 1982–87, City Discovery Centre Ltd 1985–2010 (pres 2010–), David Lock Associates (Australia) Pty Ltd 1998–2015, DLA Architects Practice Ltd 2001–15; dir: Rapid Tport Int plc 1997–2004, Integrated Tport Planning Ltd 1998–2010; visiting prof: town planning UCE Birmingham 1988–98, Centre of Planning Studies Sch of Business Univ of Reading 2002–10; external examiner 1985–89: CNAA, Jt Centre for Urban Design, Oxford Poly; memb Cncl: RTPI 1975–80, Town & Country Planning Summer Sch 1974–79; vice-pres Town & Country Planning Assoc 2008– (memb Cncl 1978–, vice-chm 1988–94 and 1998–2002, chm 2002–08); tstee Lady Margaret Patterson Osborn Tst 2000–; memb: Town & Country Planning Assoc 1969–2009; memb bd Ebbsfleet Dev Corp and Garden City 2015–, RTPI 1975; *Publications* incl: Control and Urban Planning (contrib, 1973), Planning Aid (jtly, 1974), Environmental Impact Assessment (contrib, 1975), People and their Settlements (contrib, 1976), Growth and Change in the Future City Region (contrib, 1976), Why the Poor Pay More (jtly, 1977), Planning and the Future (contrib, 1977), New Towns in National Development (contrib, 1980), The Office of the Future (contrib, 1981), Property and Technology: the needs of Modern Industry (jtly, 1983), Riding the Tiger: Planning the South of England (1989), Alternative Development Patterns: New Settlements (jtly, 1993), On Track (contrib, 1994), What Next after the Planning Green Paper? (2002), Ofplan (jtly, 2007), Best Practice in Sustainable Urban Extensions and New Settlements (jtly, 2007); *Recreations* history and geography, reading and research; *Style*— David Lock, CBE; ✉ David Lock Associates Ltd, 50 North Thirteenth Street, Central Milton Keynes, Buckinghamshire MK9 3BP (☎ 01908 666276, fax 01908 605747, e-mail dlock@davidlock.com)

LOCKE, Alasdair James Dougall; s of Donald Locke (d 2005), and Joan, *née* Foyster (d 2005); *b* 29 August 1953, Aldershot, Hants; *Educ* Uppingham, Wadham Coll Oxford; *m* 19 June 1993, Kathleen Anne, *née* Vincent; 2 s (Harry b 5 March 1995, George b 4 Aug 1997); *Career* Citibank 1974–78, Oceanic Finance Ltd 1979–81, dir Henry Ansbacher & Co 1982–87, dep chm and ceo Kelt Energy plc 1987–89, fndr and chm Abbot Gp plc 1990–2009; chm: NI Energy Holdings plc until 2008, First Property Gp plc, Argent Gp plc 2006–, Mecom Gp plc 2009–11, Motor Fuel Gp Ltd 2011–, Hardy Oil & Gas plc 2012–; Overall and Master Scot Entrepreneur of the Year 1999, Grampian Industrialist of the Year 2001, Entrepreneurial Exchange Hall of Fame 2003; *Recreations* shooting, skiing; *Clubs* Oxford and Cambridge; *Style*— Alasdair Locke, Esq; ✉ Glenrinnes Farms Ltd, Glenrinnes Lodge, Dufftown, Banffshire AB55 4BS (☎ 01340 820384, fax 01340 821077, e-mail alasdair.locke@glenrinnes.com)

LOCKET, David Frank; s of late Frank Barton Locket, and Phyllis Jesie, *née* Lawson; *b* 29 June 1940; *Educ* Haileybury and ISC, Battersea Coll of Technol; *m* 1966, (Ingegerd) Christina, da of Ake Bontell, of Sweden; 1 s (Martin Frank b 1970), 1 da (Annicka Louise b 1972); *Career* Savoy Hotel (Strand Hotels) London 1972–78, catering mangr Anchor Hotels London 1978–83; md LMS (Consultants) Ltd 1983–97, Locket Enterprises 1997–; clerk emeritus Master Innholders; Freeman City of London 1973, Liveryman Worshipful Co of Innholders; Master Innholder; *Recreations* veteran cars, fishing, clocks; *Style*— David F Locket, Esq; ✉ Pinecrest, Northdown Road, Woldingham, Surrey CR3 7AA (☎ 01883 653181, e-mail david@locket.info)

LOCKETT, Andrew; s of Terence Anthony Lockett, and Isobel Lockett (d 1997); *Educ* Hazel Grove HS Stockport, Lincoln Coll Oxford (scholar, BA); *Career* ed (social sciences) Croom Helm and Routledge Publishers 1986–89, literature ed (academic) OUP 1989–97, head BFI Publishing 1997–2003, reference dir Rough Guides 2003–; literature advsr Southern Arts 1995; *Books* Television Studies (assoc ed, 2002); *Recreations* soccer, travel; *Style*— Andrew Lockett, Esq; ✉ Rough Guides, 80 Strand, London WC2R 0RL (☎ 020 7010 3787, fax 020 7010 6787, e-mail andrew.lockett@roughguides.com)

LOCKHART; *see also:* Sinclair-Lockhart

LOCKHART, Dr Bill; OBE; s of Albert Lockhart, and Margaret, *née* Hagan; *b* 28 December 1947, Belfast; *Educ* Royal Belfast Academical Inst, Queen's Univ Belfast (BA), Aston Univ (PhD); *m* Audrey, *née* Buchanan; 3 s (Patrick, Fergus, Peter); *Career* chief exec Extern Orgn 1993–2004, chief exec Youth Justice Agency NI 2004–10, dir Lockhart Psychological Consulting Ltd 2010–; visiting scholar Univ of Cambridge 1991; AFBPsS 1981, registerd psychologist Health Professionals Cncl 2010; *Publications* Crime in Ireland 1945–1995 – Here be Dragons (jtly, 1997); *Recreations* rugby coaching, art, photography, Irish language, reading; *Clubs* IOD; *Style*— Dr Bill Lockhart, OBE; ✉ Fernwood, 10 Whinney Hill, Holywood BT18 0HW (☎ 028 9042 6825, mobile 07785 106890, e-mail bill@lockhartconsulting.co.uk, website www.lockhartconsulting.co.uk)

LOCKHART, Sheriff Principal Brian Alexander; s of John Arthur Hay Lockhart, and Norah, *née* Macneil, of Glasgow; *b* 1 October 1942; *Educ* Glasgow Acad, Univ of Glasgow (BL); *m* 1967, Christine Ross, da of James B Clark, of Ayr; 2 s, 2 da; *Career* slr; ptnr Robertson Chalmers & Auld 1964–79; Sheriff: N Strathclyde 1979–81, Glasgow and Strathkelvin 1981–2005; Sheriff Princ S Strathclyde Dumfries and Galloway 2005–15, temp High Court judge 2008–15, memb Sheriff Appeal Court 2015–; memb Parole Bd for Scotland 1997–2003; pres Sheriffs' Assoc 2004–05; *Recreations* fishing, golf, family; *Style*— Sheriff Principal Brian Lockhart; ✉ 18 Hamilton Avenue, Glasgow (☎ 0141 427 1921); Sheriff Court, Airdrie (☎ 01236 639170)

LOCKHART, Brian Robert Watson; s of late George Watson Lockhart, and late Helen, *née* Rattray; *b* 19 July 1944, Edinburgh; *Educ* George Heriot's Sch, Univ of Aberdeen (MA), Univ of Edinburgh (DipEd), Moray House Coll of Educn (CertEd); *m* 4 April 1970, Fiona Anne, da of late James Barclay Sheddon; 2 da (Joanne b 2 July 1973, Catriona b 24 May 1976), 1 s (Ross b 6 Feb 1979); *Career* George Heriot's Sch: history teacher 1968–72, princ teacher 1972–81; dep rector Glasgow HS 1981–96, headmaster Robert Gordon's Coll 1996–2004; chm Scottish Standing Ctee UCAS 2001–02 (memb 1994–, co-chm 1998–99); memb: Cncl Headteachers' Assoc of Scotland 1998–2004 (asst sec 1988–93), HMC 1996– (sec Scottish Div 2003, chm Scottish Div 2004), Higher Still Implementation Gp 1997–2000, Business Ctee Univ of Aberdeen 2001–12 (vice-convener 2006–10), Cncl St Margaret's Sch for Girls Aberdeen 2004–13, Bd Hutchesons' GS Glasgow 2005–12 (convener Educn Ctee 2010–12), Bd Voluntary Servs Aberdeen 2005–11; Univ of Aberdeen: memb Audit Ctee 2007–13, memb Remuneration Ctee 2010–12, memb Learning and Teaching Ctee 2010–12, convener Student Affrs Ctee 2010–12, gen cncl assesor Ct 2008–12, memb Exec Friends of Aberdeen Univ Library 2013–; tstee Robert Nicol Tst 2006– (convener 2014–); memb Bd of Govrs Lathallan Sch by Montrose; Burgess City of Aberdeen 1997; *Publications* The History of the Architecture of George Heriot's Hospital and School, 1628–1978 (article, 1978), Jinglin' Geordie's Legacy (2003), Robert Gordon's Legacy (2007), The Town School: A History of The High School of Glasgow (2010), Bon Record: A History of Aberdeen Grammar School (jtly, 2012), 'A Great Educational Tradition' A History of Hutchesons Grammar (2015); *Recreations* reading biographies, sport, films, politics, architecture, educational history; *Style*— Brian Lockhart, Esq; ✉ 80 Gray Street, Aberdeen AB10 6JE (☎ 01224 315776, e-mail brian.lockhart1@btinternet.com)

LOCKHART OF THE LEE, Angus Hew; recognised as Chief of the Name Lockhart by The Lord Lyon 1957; s of late Maj Simon Foster Macdonald Lockhart of the Lee, and Ella Catriona Gordon (d 2000); *b* 17 August 1946; *Educ* Rannoch Sch, N of Scotland Coll of Agric; *m* 1970, Susan Elizabeth, da of Hon William Normand (d 1967), s of Baron Normand (Life Peer, d 1962), and Hon Mrs William Normand; 1 s, 1 da; *Career* landowner and land manager; memb Standing Cncl of Scottish Chiefs; *Recreations* country pursuits; *Clubs* New (Edinburgh); *Style*— Angus Lockhart of the Lee; ✉ Newholm, Dunsyre, Lanark ML11 8NQ (☎ 01968 682254); Lee and Carnwath Estates, Estate Office, Dunsyre, Lanark (☎ 01899 810300)

LOCKHART-MUMMERY, Christopher John; QC (1986); s of Sir Hugh Evelyn Lockhart-Mummery, KCVO (d 1988), of Basingstoke, Hants, and Elizabeth Jean, *née* Crerar (d 1981); *b* 7 August 1947; *Educ* Stowe, Trinity Coll Cambridge; *m* 1, 4 Sept 1971 (m dis 1992), Hon Elizabeth Rosamund, da of Neil Patrick Moncrieff Elles, and Baroness Elles (Life Peer), *qv*, of London; 2 da (Clare b 1973, Alice b 1980), 1 s (Edward b 1975); m 2, 4 Feb 1993, Mrs Mary-Lou Putley; *Career* called to the Bar Inner Temple 1971 (bencher 1991); recorder of the Crown Court 1994–2004, dep judge of the High Court 1995–2004; former head of chambers; *Books* Hill and Redman's Law of Landlord and Tenant (specialist ed, 1973); *Recreations* fishing, opera; *Clubs* Garrick; *Style*— Christopher J Lockhart-Mummery, Esq, QC; ✉ Hookeswood House, Farnham, Blandford Forum, Dorset DT11 8DQ (☎ 01725 516259); 83 Abbotsbury Road, London W14 8EP (☎ 020 7603 7200); Landmark Chambers, 180 Fleet Street, London EC4A 2HG (☎ 020 7430 1221, fax 020 7430 1667)

LOCKLEY, Andrew John Harold; s of (Archdeacon) Dr Harold Lockley (d 2004), of Market Harborough, Leics, and Ursula Margarete, *née* Wedell (d 1990); *b* 10 May 1951; *Educ* Marlborough, Oriel Coll Oxford (Nolloth scholar, BA, MA); *m* 1, 14 Sept 1974 (m dis 2005), Ruth Mary, da of (Laurence) John Vigor, of Bath; 2 s (Thomas Andrew b 1978, Philip Jonathan b 1981), 1 da (Naomi Jane Ursula b 1987); m 2, 16 April 2005, Caryl Jane Berry, da of Denis Seymour, of Sheffield (d 2008); *Career* research scholar World Cncl of Churches 1973–75, trainee slr Messrs Kingsley Napley & Co London 1975–78; slr: Messrs Young & Solon London 1979–80, Messrs Meaby & Co London 1980–82; The Law Soc: sec Contentious Business Dept 1985–87 (asst sec 1982–85), dir of legal practice 1987–95, dir of corp and regnl affrs 1995–96; head of public law Irwin Mitchell 1996–2013, conslt Dept of Law Univ of Sheffield 1996–98, hon fell Univ of Sheffield 1999–2013; pt/t judge First Tier Tbnl – Health Educn and Social Care (formerly pt/t chm Special Educnl Needs and Disability Tbnl) 1996–, pt/t chair Doctors and Dentists Disciplinary Procedures Appeal Panels 2007–10, pt/t legal assessor GMC Fitness to Practise Panels 2007–, pt/t legal advsr Teaching Agency (formerly Gen Teaching Cncl) Professional Conduct Panels 2010–13, legally qualified chair Medical Practitioners Tbnl Service; dir Solicitors' Financial Services Ltd 1988–92, dir Solicitors' Property Centres Ltd 1997–2000 (chm 1998–2000), non-exec dir Legal Aid Agency 2013–; memb: Cmmn of Efficiency in Criminal Courts 1986–93, CITCOM Advsy Ctee 1988–90, IT and the Courts Ctee 1990–95, Justice Working Gp Civil Justice in an Age of Austerity 2014–15; chair Ind Policing Ethics Panel S Yorks 2014–; memb Editorial Advsy Bd Educn, Public Law and the Individual 2005–12; govr William Austin Sch Luton 1992–96; memb: Law Soc 1979, Justice, Amnesty Int; *Books* Christian Communes (1976), The Pursuit of Quality – a guide for lawyers (ed, 1993); *Recreations* growing fruit and vegetables, choral singing,

L

swimming, travel, walking, reading; *Style*— Andrew Lockley, Esq; ☎ 0114 234 2028, mobile 07889 023335, e-mail alockley1@yahoo.co.uk

LOCKLEY, Charles; s of John Edward Clare-Day, and Anne Francis, *née* Snell; *b* 22 February 1966; *Educ* Heathcote Sch Stevenage, Glasgow Poly; *Career* chef; asst chef airport restaurant Baden Baden 1983–87, second chef Clifton House Hotel Nairn 1987–91, second chef rising to head chef Restaurant No 1 and later Café No 1 Inverness 1992–97, head chef Boath House Auldearn 1997– (4 AA Rosettes, Michelin star 2009); work experience: Nico Ladenis 90 Park Lane London 1998, Foliage London 2005, Hibiscus Ludlow 2006; memb: Master Chefs of GB 2001–; Best Scottish Hotel Chef Scottish Chefs Assoc 2002, Scottish Chef of the Year Scottish Chef Awards 2009; *Style*— Charles Lockley, Esq; ✉ Boath House, Auldearn, Nairn IV3 5TE (☎ 01667 454896, e-mail charlielockley11@gmail.com)

LOCKS, Ian Roy; s of John Leonard Locks (d 1963), and Doreen Flower, *née* Bennett (d 1994); *b* 21 April 1941; *Educ* Felsted, SW Essex Poly (Dip Mgmnt Studies); *m* 10 Sept 1966, Valerie Jean, da of Edward George Surguy; 3 da (Katharine Elizabeth b 7 June 1968, Virginia Louise b 11 May 1970, Charlotte Claire b 22 May 1975); *Career* reporter and news ed W London and Essex 1958–64, sr editorial and mgmnt positions 1964–75 (incl editorial dir London, Middx and Essex Newspapers 1966–72), mangr regnl newspapers Printing and Publishing Trg Bd 1976–82, chief exec Assoc of Free Newspapers 1982–89, chief exec PPA 1989–2008; dir: Bd of Fin Advertising Standards Ctee 1989–2008, Audit Bureau of Circulation 1989–2008, Copyright Licensing Agency 1989–2009, Publishers Licensing Soc 1989–, Press Bd PCC 1991–2008, chm Trade Assoc Forum 2001–03; memb Cncl: Advertising Assoc 1982–2008, CBI Trade Assoc Cncl 2001–08; churchwarden St Bride's Fleet Street 2008–14; Freeman City of London, Master Worshipful Co of Stationers and Newspapermakers 2014–15; MInstD 1982, FCIM 2006, fell Inst of Assoc Mgmnt 2006; *Recreations* being a husband, father and grandfather, golf, tennis, walking, theatre, opera, travel; *Clubs* Theydon Bois Golf, Blackwater Sailing; *Style*— Ian Locks, Esq; ✉ 2 Potters Close, Loughton, Essex IG10 1JQ (e-mail i.locks@btinternet.com)

LOCKWOOD, David Stuart; s of Capt Ronald Arthur Lockwood, of Christchurch, Dorset, and Rachael, *née* Bamforth; *b* 15 May 1945; *Educ* Guthlaxton GS Leicester, Cambridge Sch of Art, Sch of Architecture Leicester, RIBA (DipArch); *m* 1, (m dis 1974); m 2, 25 May 1978 (m dis 2002), Marion Janice, da of Walter Glen Page (d 1974), of Sydney, Aust; *Career* Jr Ldrs Regt RE 1960–63, RE 1963–66; architect; John Whisson and Ptnrs Newmarket 1966–67, Heaton and Swales Bury St Edmunds 1967–70, Gordon White and Hood Leicester 1973–74, Ivan P Jarvis and Assoc Leicester 1974–76; Cecil Denny Highton and Ptnrs London: joined 1976, assoc 1979, equity ptnr 1983, gp ptnr 1990, dir 1995; sr vice-pres and dir of commercial architecture HOK Int Ltd 1995–2000, dir HOK sports, venue and entertainment architects 2000–01; md: Ellerbe Becket Ltd London and EBD Int Ltd 2001–03, DavidLockwood Consulting 2003–; RIBA chartered architect 1974, memb ARCUK 1974, RIBA client design advsr (CDA) 2005; Private House Sustainability and Environmental Award 2009; Freeman: Worshpiful Co of Chartered Architects 2000, City of London 2001; memb Assoc of Consultant Architects 2009; *Recreations* sailing, skiing, architecture, ballet, cycling, badminton; *Clubs* Corinthian Sailing; *Style*— David S Lockwood, Esq; ✉ DavidLockwood, Studio 4, 9 Albert Embankment, London SE1 7HD (☎ 020 7582 2325, mobile 07787 853011, e-mail david@david-lockwood.com)

LOCKWOOD, Rear Adm Roger Graham; CB (2005); s of Eric Garnett Lockwood (d 1985), and Nunda, *née* Doak; *b* 26 June 1950, Hitchin, Herts; *Educ* Kimbolton Sch, Univ of Warwick (BA); *m* 1 Sept 1984, Susan, *née* Cant; 3 s (Will b 18 Oct 1985, Robb b 30 Jan 1988, Andrew b 10 Sept 1995), 2 da (Rosie b 10 May 1991, Jennie b 19 May 2001); *Career* RN 1971–2005: jr offr appts 1971–84, JSDC 1985, Base Supply Offr HMS Dolphin 1985–87, Cdr RN Supply Sch 1987–89, Supply Offr HMS Ark Royal 1989–91, Dep Dir Naval Serv Conditions (Pay) 1991–93, RCDS 1994, Sec to Second Sea Lord 1995–96, Sec to First Sea Lord 1996–98, Cdre HMS Raleigh 1998–2000, COS to Second Sea Lord 2000–02, Sr Directing Staff (Navy) RCDS 2002–05; chief exec Northern Lighthouse Bd 2006–14; co sec Dunblane Devpt Tst 2005–07, cmmr Queen Victoria Sch Dunblane 2006–, chm Perth Sea Cadet Unit 2006–10; area vice-patron (Scotland) War Memls Tst 2007–, dir Scottish Shipping Benevolent Assoc 2009–12 (vice-pres 2010, pres 2011), tstee Merchant Navy Meml Tst (Scotland) 2009–16, tstee Bell's Nautical Tst 2015–, memb Cncl RNLI 2015–; assoc memb Hon Co of Master Mariners 2008–15; High Constable of the Port of Leith 2008–; *Recreations* family, reading the complete works of Charles Dickens, history – from BC to the modern day; *Clubs* New (Edinburgh); *Style*— Rear Adm Roger Lockwood, CB

LODDER, Peter Norman; QC (2001); *b* 3 February 1958; *Career* called to the Bar 1981 (Harmsworth Exhibitioner 1981, Jules Thorn Major Scholar 1982); asst recorder 1999, recorder 2000, sr circuit judge (SE Circuit) and resident judge Kingston Upon Thames 2015–; chm Criminal Bar Assoc 2008–09, chm Bar Cncl 2011; *Style*— His Hon Judge Lodder, QC

LODGE, Anton James Corduff; QC (1989); *Educ* Univ of Cambridge (MA); *Career* called to the Bar Gray's Inn 1966 (bencher 1997), recorder; *Style*— Anton Lodge, Esq, QC

LODGE, Prof David; s of Herbert Lodge, and Dorothy, *née* Moss; *b* 22 September 1941; *Educ* Weston Super Mare GS, Univ of Bristol (BVSc, PhD, DSc); *m* 1, 15 Feb 1964 (m dis), Susan, da of Sidney Hayling; 4 s (Marcus b 1964, Duncan b 1966, James b 1969, (Robert) Jolyon b 1971); m 2, 21 Oct 1995, Catherine Mary, da of Peter Sutton; 1 da (Josie Louise b 1993); *Career* jr fell and lectr Dept of Veterinary Surgery Univ of Bristol 1963–70, Wellcome Tst fell Dept of Physiology Animal Health Tst 1970–74; post doctoral res fell Aust Nat Univ 1974–79; Royal Veterinary Coll London: sr lectr 1979–84, prof of vet neuroscience 1984–91, prof of vet physiology and head of vet basic sciences 1989–91, research advsr CNS res Lilly Res Centre 1991–97; currently: visiting prof of vet physiology Univ of London, hon prof of physiology Univ of Cardiff, Benjamin Meaker visiting prof Univ of Bristol, dir of stroke research Eli Lilly & Co; ed Neuropharmacology 1992–; memb Ctee Physiological Soc 1983–87; MRCVS 1963, DVA 1969; *Books* Excitatory Amino Acid Transmission (1987), Excitatory Amino Acids in Health and Disease (1988), Ionotropic Glutanate Receptors as Therapeutic Targets (2002); *Recreations* rugby, running, skiing, coaching junior sport; *Style*— Prof David Lodge; ✉ Lilly Research Centre, Erlwood Manor, Windlesham, Surrey GU20 6PH (☎ 01276 483980, fax 01276 483525)

LODGE, Prof David John; CBE (1998); s of William Frederick Lodge, and Rosalie Marie, *née* Murphy; *b* 28 January 1935; *Educ* St Joseph's Acad Blackheath, UCL (BA, MA, John Oliver Hobbes scholar, John Morley medal, Quain Essay prize), Univ of Birmingham (PhD); *m* 15 May 1959, Mary Frances, da of Francis Jacob (d 1969); 1 da (Julia Mary b 1960), 2 s (Stephen David b 1962, Christopher Adrian b 1966); *Career* Nat Serv RAC 1955–57; asst British Cncl Overseas Students Centre London 1959–60; Dept of English Univ of Birmingham: asst lectr 1960–62, lectr 1962–71, sr lectr 1971–73, reader in English literature 1973–76, prof of modern English literature 1976–87, hon prof of modern English literature 1987–2000, emeritus prof of English literature 2001–; visiting assoc prof Univ of Calif Berkeley 1969, Henfield fell in creative writing UEA 1977, Whitney J Oates short term visiting fell Princeton Univ 1981, E J Pratt lectr Meml Univ of St John's Newfoundland 1985, Lansdowne scholar Univ of Victoria BC 1986, Regents lectr Univ of Calif Riverside 1989; chm Booker Prize Judges 1989; hon fell: UCL 1982, Goldsmiths Coll London 1992; Hon DLitt Univ of Warwick 1997, Hon DLitt Univ of Birmingham 2001; FRSL 1976; Chevalier de l'Ordre des Arts et des Lettres (France) 1997; *Novels* The Picturegoers (1960), Ginger You're Barmy (1962), The British Museum is Falling Down (1965), Out of the Shelter (1970), Changing Places: a Tale of Two Campuses (1975), How Far Can You Go (1980), Small World: an academic romance (1984), Nice Work (1988), Paradise News (1991), Therapy (1995), Home Truths: a novella (1999), Thinks... (2001), Author, Author (2004), Deaf Sentence (2008), A Man of Parts (2011); *Non-fiction* incl: Language of Fiction (1966), The Novelist at the Crossroads (1971), The Modes of Modern Writing (1977), Working With Structuralism (1981), Write On (1986), After Bakhtin (1990), The Art of Fiction (1992), The Practice of Writing (1996), Consciousness and the Novel (2002), The Year of Henry James (2006), Lives In Writing (2014), Quite a Good Year to be Born: a Memoir 1935–1975 (2015); *Stage and Screen* Between These Four Walls (with M Bradbury and J Duckett, 1963), Slap in the Middle (with M Bradbury, J Duckett and D Turner, 1965), Big Words – Small Worlds (Channel 4, 1987), Nice Work (BBC2, 1989), The Writing Game (Birmingham Rep 1990, adapted for Channel 4 1995), The Way of St James (BBC1, 1993), Martin Chuzzlewit (adapted from Charles Dickens' novel, BBC2, 1994), Home Truths (Birmingham Rep, 1998), Secret Thoughts (Bolton Octagon, 2011); *Style*— Prof David Lodge, CBE; ✉ c/o Curtis Brown, 28–29 Haymarket, London SW1Y 4SP

LODGE, Dr Denise Valerie; *Educ* Bury GS, Royal Holloway Coll London (BSc, PhD), Chelsea Coll London (MSc); *Children* 1 s, 1 da; *Career* teacher of biology, chemistry and PE, head of chemistry, head of sixth form and sr teacher (curriculum) Sir Roger Manwood's Sch Sandwich 1987–96, dep head Sheffield HS GDST 1996–99, headmistress Sydenham HS GDST 1999–2002, headmistress Putney HS GDST 2002–15; treas and memb Educn Research Ctee GSA 2003–07; memb Ct Imperial Coll London 2007–15; finalist Salters' Prize 1997, runner-up Tatler/HSBC Bank Best Headmistress of a Public Sch 2004; *Recreations* jazz, art, theatre, gym; *Style*— Dr Denise Lodge; ✉ e-mail contact@deniselodge.co.uk

LODGE, Jane Ann; da of John Humphrey Lodge (d 1984), of York, and Marian, *née* Smith; *b* 1 April 1955; *Educ* Mill Mount GS York, Univ of Birmingham (BSc); *m* 2 July 1983, Anthony (Tony) John Borton, s of Reginald Aubrey Borton (d 1980), of Rugby; 1 s (John Aubrey b 1988), 2 da (Emma Jane b 1990, Victoria Mary b 1992); *Career* Deloitte & Touche (formerly Touche Ross) Birmingham: trainee accountant 1973, qualified 1976, ptnr 1986–, ptnr i/c Allder Learning and Devpt 1999, office sr ptnr (Birmingham) 2000–02, practice sr ptnr (Midlands) 2002–05; UK mfrg industry ldr 2005–; memb: Ctee Birmingham and W Midlands Soc of Chartered Accountants 1987–96 (pres 1994–95), W Midlands Industrial Devpt Bd 1999–2004, W Midlands Regnl Cncl CBI 2001–, Bd Birmingham Forward 2001– (chm Business Growth Ctee 2002–04); memb Cncl Univ of Birmingham 1986–91 and 1993–2004 (pres Guild of Graduates 1987–88, memb Strategy Planning and Resources Ctee 1987–91, memb Audit Ctee 1997–), govr Arthur Terry Sch Sutton Coldfield Birmingham 1989–95; Midlands Businesswoman of the Year 2001, BWMSCA Lifetime Achievement Award 2003; FCA 1976; *Recreations* cookery, tapestry, golf; *Style*— Ms Jane Lodge

LODGE, Prof Juliet; da of Arthur Robert Mayer, of Islington, and Lenore Mayer; *b* London; *Educ* Coombe Co Girls' Sch, CNAA (BA), Univ of Reading (MA, MPhil, DLitt), Univ of Hull (PhD); *m*; 1 da (Keri-Michèle), 2 s (David, Christopher); *Career* lectr in European and int politics Univ of Auckland 1973–77, visiting fell Centre for Int Studies Dept of Int Relations LSE 1976–77; Univ of Hull: lectr in politics 1977–84, sr lectr in politics 1984–88, reader in EC politics 1988–91, prof of European politics 1991–96, Jean Monnet prof of European integration and co-dir EC Res Unit 1991–96; Univ of Leeds: dir Centre for Euro Studies 1996–2010, dir Jean Monnet European Centre of Excellence Inst of Communications Studies Univ of Leeds, currently sr analyst Saher; freelance journalist and broadcaster; NATO res fell 1992; visiting prof: Université Libre de Bruxelles 1992–95, Vrije Universitet Brussel 1995, Institut für Höhere Studien Vienna 1996; convenor UK Political Studies Assoc Study Gp on the EC 1980–, exec memb Univ Assoc for Contemporary European Studies 1988–94, dir Jean Monnet Gp of Experts on Enlargement and the 1966 Intergovernmental Conf; memb: Cncl for Europeanists NYC 1983–, Univs Assoc for Contemporary European Studies 1984–, Cncl European Consortium for Political Res (ECPR) 1985–96, Humberside TEC 1993–95, Team Europe, ESRC Postgrad Ctee, ESRC Research Bd, Nat Ctee of Women of Europe, Advsy Cncl Euro Movement, European Information Assoc, Privacy Expert Gp Biometrics Inst; conslt to EU Cmmn on Ethical Implications of Biometrics e-IDs and liberty; awards: UK Woman of Europe 1991–92, European Woman of Europe 1992, European Woman of Achievement Award 1992; hon pres Assoc for Euro and Int Co-ordination in Schs; FRSA 1992; *Books* The European Policy of the SPD (1976), The New Zealand General Election of 1975 (co-author, 1978), The European Parliament and the European Community (co-author, 1978), The European Community and New Zealand (1982), Direct Elections to the European Parliament: A Community Perspective (co-author, 1982), Democratic Legitimacy and the EC (1991), The EU and the Challenge of the Future (1993), The 1994 Euro-Elections (1995), 1999 Euro-Elections (2001), Election of the European Parliament 2004 (2004), Biometrics: Are you who you say you are? (2007), The 2009 Euro Elections to the European Parliament (2010); Institutional Implications of EMU and the Euro at the European and National Levels; Euratom and the IGC's (report for the European Parl, 1999 and 2002), reports to the European Parl on civil liberties, ethics, freedom of information, Europol, biometrics and e-governance 2005–10; ed numerous books and pubns on e-governance, ICTs, cross-border mgmnt and e-justice; *Recreations* art, writing, laughing; *Clubs* Club of Rhodes; *Style*— Prof Juliet Lodge; ✉ e-mail j.e.lodge@leeds.ac.uk

LODGE, HE Matthew James; *b* 3 June 1968, Crosby, Lancs; *Educ* Univ of Birmingham (BA); *m* Alexia; 2 s (James Pericles, Alexandros David); *Career* offr Royal Marines 1986–96; desk offr Bosnia Section Eastern Adriatic Dept FCO 1996–97, temp entry clearance offr Tbilisi and Yerevan 1997, second sec political/EU/press and public affrs Athens 1998–2000, second sec press and public affrs Paris 2001, UK rep to EU Brussels 2001–03, head Cyprus and Greece Section Europe Directorate FCO 2003–04, private sec/perm under sec FCO 2004–07, dep head of mission Baghdad 2007, head Afghanistan Gp FCO 2008–10, ambass to Finland 2010–13, ambass to Kuwait 2014–; non-exec dir FinnGuild 2014–; *Recreations* tennis, swimming, walking, cycling; *Clubs* In & Out; *Style*— Mr Matthew Lodge; ✉ website www.fco.gov.uk, Twitter @hmamatthewlodge, Instagram @hmamatthewlodge

LOEHNIS, Dominic (Dom); s of Anthony Loehnis, and Jennifer, *née* Anderson; *b* 31 August 1967, London; *Educ* Univ Coll Oxford (MA), INSEAD (MBA); *m* 2000, Tif, *née* Richards; 2 s (Freddie b 5 Aug 2003, Samuel b 23 Aug 2005), 1 da (Bay b 21 Dec 2007); *Career* journalist Sunday Telegraph 1990–92, special advsr Dept of Nat Heritage (DNH, later DCMS) 1992–94, new media devpt mangr Pearson plc 1994–97, assoc Booz Allen & Hamilton 1997–98, gen mangr AMFMi 1998–2000, fndr and md Monkey 2000–06, conslt Egon Zehnder 2006–; advsr to tstees of the P G Wodehouse Estate 2000–09; *Recreations* music, reading, skiing, travel, walking, cycling; *Clubs* Garrick, Soho House, Beefsteak; *Style*— Dom Loehnis, Esq; ✉ Egon Zehnder Ltd, Devonshire House, Mayfair Place, London W1J 8AJ (☎ 020 7943 1943, e-mail dom.loehnis@egonzehnder.com, website www.egonzehnder.com)

LOEWI, David Michael; s of Gerald Loewi (d 1977), and Angela, *née* Franklin; *b* 25 February 1959, Taplow, Berks; *Educ* Licensed Victuallers' Sch Ascot, Leighton Park Sch Reading, Oxford Brookes Univ; *Partner* Rolant Hergert; *Career* Hyatt Carlton Tower 1985–95 (dir of food and beverage 1991–95), gen mangr Mezzo 1995–96, md Conran Restaurants 1996–

2003 and 2005–06, fndr, co-owner and md CKL Restaurants 2003–04, co-owner and md D&D London 2006–; MHCIMA; *Recreations* food, music, walking in the Alps; *Style*— David Loewi, Esq; ✉ D&D London, 16 Kirby Street, London EC1N 8TS (☎ 020 7716 7804, fax 020 7716 7816, e-mail david@danddlondon.com)

LOFTHOUSE, Marjorie Helen; MBE (1990); da of Ronald Douglas Minns (d 1968), of London, and Marjorie May, *née* Axford (d 1989); *b* 3 March 1943; *Educ* City of Bath Girls' Sch, Co of Stafford Trg Coll; *m* Ken Stephinson (d 2012); 2 step da (Jacqueline, Joanne); *Career* broadcaster; formerly with HTV West; progs incl: Reports West, Here Today, Gallery; BBC: regular presenter of Pebble Mill at One (BBC 1), co-presenter Eating Out with Tovey (BBC 2), writer and narrator of many documentaries incl See for Yourself, presented The New Venturers series (BBC Scotland) 1990–91; radio: commenced broadcasting with Radio Metro Newcastle, presented Northern edn Woman's Hour (BBC Manchester and BBC Birmingham), developed Homing-In, created Vintage Cider (two part biography of Laurie Lee), presented Enterprise (BBC Radio 4), presented numerous features and documentaries, created Romantic Strings series (BBC Radio 2), own music prog Prelude (BBC Radio 4) 1989–95, presenter Business on the Move (BBC Radio 5); prodn work BBC Radio 4 incl: Feet First, Hair Today, The Long Sleep, Timpson's England, Norfolk Men, Free for All, This Stately Homes Business, The Big Day; presented Royal Show open air concert featuring Midland Concert Orch 1988, responsible for creating an annual competition to find Britain's most enterprising small businesses which were then featured on radio prog Enterprise 1984–91, voice-over artiste for corp and broadcast media trg; dir Stephinson Television; runner-up Sony Radio Awards for documentary Leslie 1986; pres Saddleworth Cancer Research Campaign, memb Bd Oldham Coliseum; *Books* The New Adventurers; *Style*— Ms Marjorie Lofthouse, MBE

LOFTHOUSE, Simon Timothy; QC (2006); s of Adam Lofthouse, of Salop, and Angela, *née* Manning; *b* 25 August 1966; *Educ* Fernwood Sch Nottingham, Beckett Sch Nottingham, UCL (LLB); *m* 1 Oct 1994, Sophia, da of Stefan Gawlik; *Career* called to the Bar Gray's Inn 1988 (bencher 2010); tenant Atkin Chambers 1989– (specialising in construction, int arbitration, professional negligence and energy law); recorder 2003–; articles ed Current Law 1989–94; memb Bar Professional Conduct Ctee 2002–05, prosecutor for Bar Standards Ctee 2006–08, chair Bar Standards Complaints Ctee 2011–15, memb Bd Bar Standards Bd 2011–15, memb Disciplinary Bd Inst and Faculty of Actuaries 2016–; memb: Technol and Construction Bar Assoc, Commercial Bar Assoc, Franco-British Lawyers Soc Ltd; accredited adjudicator, registed advocacy trainer; *Recreations* theatre, squash, travelling, opera; *Clubs* Reform; *Style*— Simon Lofthouse, Esq, QC; ✉ Atkin Chambers, 1 Atkin Building, Gray's Inn, London WC1R 5AT (☎ 020 7404 0102, fax 020 7405 7456, e-mail slofthouse@atkinchambers.com)

LOGAN, Andrew David; s of William Harold Logan, of The Leys, Witney, Oxford, and Irene May Logan; *b* 11 October 1945; *Educ* Lord Williams's Sch Thame, Burford GS, Oxford Sch of Architecture (DipArch); *Parnter* Michael Davis (civil partnership); *Career* artist and sculptor; medium mainly glass, worked in sculpture, jewellery, stage design, installation, interior design and performance; creator and artisitc dir The Alternative Miss World nos 1–12 1972–2009; opened Andrew Logan Museum of Sculpture Berriew 1991; jewellery collections for: Emmanuel Ungaro 2006, Swarovski Crystals 2007, Comme Des Gracons 2007, numerous collections with Zandra Rhodes; *Exhibitions* incl: Biba's Sculpture Garden 1974, Goldfield (Whitechapel Art Gallery) 1976, Egypt Revisited Sand and Light Spectacular (Super Tent Clapham Common) 1978, Trigon-Graz (Austria) 1979, Goddesses (Cwlth Inst London) 1983, Henley Arts Festival 1984, The Book Show (Cylinder Gallery London) 1984, Galactic Forest (Functional Art Gallery, LA, Chicago and Limelight Club NYC) 1985, Daily Mail Ideal Home (Earls Court London) 1986, Winged Pegasus (Living Art Pavilion Arts Cncl) 1986, Glass Sculpture Singapore 1986, Monuments and Music (Botanical Gardens Rome) 1987, London Capital of New Ideas (Moscow)1989, Avant Garde (Russia tour) 1989, Wings Over Waves (Angela Flowers Ireland) 1990, Untamed Fashion Assembly (Riga) 1990, An Artistic Adventure (MOMA Oxford, Flowers East Gallery and The Old Library Cardiff) 1991, Jewels of Fantasy (V&A) 1992, Millfield British 20th Century Sculpture (Somerset) 1992, LA Art Fair 1992, Bonham's Knightsbridge 1992, Cracked Mirrors – Very Nice (Festival Hall Craft Gallery London) 1993, Olympian Arts (CentrePoint London) 1993, Monuments of Hope and Joy (display of Pegasus I and II Heathrow Airport) 1993, The Elements (Concord Lighting London) 1993, Andrew Logan Museum of Sculpture Berriew (solo exhbn) 1994, Northern Centre for Contemporary Art 1994, 101 Chairs (South Bank Centre) 1994, Fabulous Fakes and Flying Carpets (Bluecoat Display Centre Liverpool) 1994, Pegasus and Jewels (Roscarbery) 1994, Elvis and Marilyn: 2 x Immortal (Boston MA and US tour) 1994, Shining Through (Crafts Cncl Islington) 1995, The Happy Heart Show (Manchester City Art Galleries) 1995, Int Jewellery Conf (Univ of Northumbria) 1996, Fluid (Manchester Rochdale Canal) 1996, Carnival (Sainsbury Centre Norwich) 1996, Moscow Art Fair 1996, Wings Over Waves (De La Warr Pavilion Bexhill on Sea) 1996, Museo del Vidrio (perm exhbn of sculptures, Monterrey) 1996, New Times, New Thinking (Crafts Cncl London) 1996, Men on Women (Denbighshire) 1997, Eyeworks (Crafts Cncl, London and tour) 1997, Portraits show (National Portrait Gallery) 1997, London Open House 1997, L'Age d'Or (Air Gallery London) 1997, Reflections of the Heart (Museo del Vidrio Monterrey) 1997, Love: Divine & Profane (American Visionary Art Museum Baltimore) 1998, Magic Moments (Ruthin Craft Centre Wales) 1998, Brit Figurative Art (Flowers East London) 1998, Britain in Russia (Ekaterinburg) 1998, Baku Azerbaijan 1998, Decadence (Crafts Cncl London) 1999, China Chic – East Meets West (Museum at the Fashion Inst of Technol NY) 1999, Br Cncl Vilnius 1999, Rebels, Pretenders, Imposters (Br Museum) 1999, Fashion Assembly (Riga) 1999, Forever Fantasy, Fantasy Forever (Riverside Studios London and Univ of Exeter) 1999, Sweet Sounds (Bourdelle Museum Paris) 1999, Modern British and Contemporary Art (Redfern Gallery London) 2000, Universe of Smiles (Hanover) 2000, The Queen, Rose Man & the Elements (Anglo-Italian Celebration Royal Albert Museum Exeter and Ruskin Gallery Sheffield) 2000, Glittering Glass (Cheltenham Museum and Gallery) 2000, Genius of Rome (Royal Acad of Arts) 2001, Pegasus I (Harley Gallery Worksop) 2001, The Mountain (Royal Acad of Arts Summer Exhbn) 2001, Adorn & Equip (Oriel Gallery Leicester) 2001 and (Edinburgh) 2002, Newtown Art Festival 2002, Ludlow Art Festival 2002, St Petersburg Festival 2002, model cow for Cow Parade Charity Auction London 2002, A&D Gallery London 2002, Icarus (Guy's Hosp London), About Face Art Fair (Maggie Hambling Croydon) 2002, Home is Where the Heart Is (Nehru Centre London) 2002, Alternative Miss World Filmshow 1972–2002 (Norwich Gallery) 2002 and (Margaret Gallery Univ of Herts) 2003, Uniververse of Smiles (Flowers W Gallery LA) 2003, The Heart of the Matter (About Face Theatre Co Leominster) 2003, Portraits & Jewellery (Stratos Gallery, Moscow) 2003, Llanwrtydd Wells Festival 2005, Jewellery & Fashion Performance Lithuania 2005, Newton Art Festival 2005, Pegasus I & Universe of Smiles (Sadlers Wells Theatre London) 2005, Gloves & Hats (Leicester City Gallery) 2005, Cosmic Egg & Frolics in the Ocean (American Visionary Art Museum Baltimore) 2005, Big Draw Show (Trafalgar Square London) 2005, Series Music, Fashion, Visual Arts & Literature Festivals (Andrew Logan Museum of Sculpture) 2005, Sir George Solti's portrait (ROH) 2005, Jaipur Heritage Festival 2006, Moscow Fashion Week 2006, Icarus (American Visionary Art Museum Baltimore) 2006, International Festival of Glass (Ruskin Glass Centre West Midlands) 2006, Homage to the New Wave (Hayward Gallery London) 2006, Big Draw (Somerset House London) 2006, Yoga Art Show London 2006, All That Glitters (Scream Gallery London) 2006, Sparkling Surfaces (Diggi Palace Jaipur) 2007, An Artistic Adventure (Br High Cmmn Delhi) 2007, Swarovski's Runaway Rocks (ACE Gallery Beverley Hills) 2007, Being Beauteous (White Space Gallery London) 2007, Panic Attack – Art in the Punk Years (Barbican Art Gallery London) 2007, Divine Alliances (Globe Gallery St Petersburg) 2007, Small is Beautiful (Flowers East London) 2007, solo show Rivington Gallery London 2007, Collect (V&A) 2008, An Artistic Adventure (solo show, New Ruthin Craft Centre and Arts Club Dover St) 2008, jt show with Jenny Runacre and Duggie Fields The Muse at 269 Gallery London 2008, The British Guide to Showing Off (Karlo Vi Vary Film Festival Czech Repub) 2011; *Work in Public Collections* Aust Gallery of Nat Art, National Portrait Gall London, Arts Cncl of GB, Warner Bros UK, Costume Inst Met Museum NY, Curzon Tussaud London, St Mary's Witney, Church Cleveland Jewellery Collection Cleveland Craft Centre Middlesbrough, Nat Museums & Galls on Merseyside, Museo del Vidrio Mexico, American Visionary Art Museum Baltimore, P&O Arcadia Cruise, ROH, Jersey Heritage Tst, Guys and St Thomas' Charitable Fndn, Andrew Logan Museum of Sculpture Grand Hyatt Hotels Mumbai, Peckham Housing Renewals Southwark Cncl, Swarovski Crystal, Her Majesty (portrait of The Queen) exhibited at Yale Centre for Br Art NY 2012, Clapham Library 2012, Hyatt Regency Chennai, Tate Liverpool 2013; work also held in numerous private collections; *Commissions* Millennium Pegasus (Dudley Sculpture Trail) 2001, Cosmic Egg (American Visionary Art Museum Baltimore) 2004, Two Cosmic Eggs (P&O super liner Arcadia) 2005, Cosmos Within (Grand Hyatt Hotel Mumbai) 2005, Wave (Guys and St Thomas Hosp Charitable Tst London) 2005, decorated a Vauxhall motor vehicle (Britain Int Motor Show) 2006, jewellery collection (Emmanuel Ungaro Paris) 2006, Teddy Noel Portrait (Jersey Museum) 2006, Bride of the Elements (Swarovski Crystals) 2007, Guitar (charity auction More London) 2007; *Collaborations* Wolfi (Ballet Rambert London) 1987, Bastet (Sadler's Wells Royal Ballet) 1988, jewelled sculptures for Magic Flute (San Diego Opera Co) 2001, designed spade (Unicorn Children's Theatre) 2004; *Books* An Artistic Adventure (2008); *Recreations* qualified yoga teacher; *Style*— Andrew Logan; ✉ The Glasshouse, Melior Place, London SE1 3SZ (☎ 020 7407 6575, fax 020 7403 6820, e-mail andrewdl@andrewlogan.com)

LOGAN, Sir David Brian Carleton; KCMG (2000, CMG 1991); s of Capt Brian Ewen Weldon Logan, RN (d 1995), of Linchmere, Surrey, and Mary, *née* Fass (d 1994); *b* 11 August 1943, Arbroath, Angus; *Educ* Charterhouse, UC Oxford (MA), Univ of Birmingham (DUniv); *m* 4 March 1967, Judith Margaret, da of Walton Adamson Cole (d 1963); 1 da (Joanna b 1968), 2 s (Matthew b 1970 d 1988, James b 1976); *Career* HM Dip Serv: third sec then second sec Ankara 1965–69, private sec to Parly Under Sec of State for Foreign and Cwlth Affrs 1970–73, first sec UK Mission to the UN 1973–77, FCO 1977–82, cnsllr, head of Chancery and consul-gen Oslo 1982–85, head of Personnel Ops Dept FCO 1986–88, sr assoc memb St Antony's Coll Oxford 1988–89, min and dep head of mission Moscow 1989–92, asst under sec of state (central and eastern Europe) FCO 1992–93, asst under sec of state (int security) FCO 1994–95, min Washington 1995–97, ambass Turkey 1997–2001; dir Centre for Studies in Security and Diplomacy and hon prof Sch of Social Sciences Univ of Birmingham 2002–07, chm Br Inst at Ankara 2006–; memb Int Advsy Cncl Thames Water 2002–06, non-exec dir European Nickel plc 2004–10, memb Supervisory Bd Efes Breweries Int 2004–07, ind dir Magnitogorsk Iron and Steel Co 2007–14; chm GAP Activity Projects 2002–07; sr fell Inst of Strategic Dialogue 2013–; *Recreations* music, reading, sailing, tennis; *Clubs* Royal Ocean Racing; *Style*— Sir David Logan, KCMG

LOGAN, Prof David Edwin; s of James Henry Logan and Mona Elizabeth Logan; *b* 27 August 1956, Belfast; *Educ* Sullivan Upper Sch Co Down, Trinity Coll Cambridge (MA, PhD); *m* 1981, Philippa Mary, *née* Walmsley; 2 da (Natasha, Georgina), 2 s (Crispin, Frederick); *Career* fell Christ's Coll Cambridge 1982–86, postdoctoral fell Univ of Illinois 1982–83; Univ of Oxford: lectr 1986–96, fell Balliol Coll 1986–2005 (emeritus fell 2005–), prof of chemistry 1996–2005, Coulson prof of theoretical chemistry 2005–, professorial fell Univ Coll 2005–; Marlow medal and prize RSC 1990, Corday-Morgan medal and prize RSC 1994, Tilden lectr and medal RSC 2007; MRSC 1989, foreign fell Nat Acad of Sciences India 2012; *Publications* numerous articles on theoretical chemistry and physics in scientific res jls; *Recreations* music, poetry, politics, gardening; *Style*— Prof David Logan; ✉ Physical and Theoretical Chemistry Laboratory, South Parks Road, Oxford OX1 3QZ (☎ 01865 275418, fax 01865 275410, e-mail david.logan@chem.ox.ac.uk)

LOGAN, Russell James Vincent Crickard; s of John Stuart Logan, of Kent, and Joan Ena, *née* Solly; *b* 5 October 1942; *m* 1978, Gillian Enid, da of Charles Redfern; *Career* studio mangr Forces Broadcasting Servs Cyprus 1960–62, freelance theatrical work 1963–67, systems analyst IBM 1967–70, sr project mangr Twinlock Computer Services 1970–71, memb Bd Book Club Associates 1977–79 (fulfillment mangr 1971), fndr and sr ptnr Business Aid 1979–2000; chm Database Mktg Ctee 1986–95, chm and organiser annual DMA Database Mktg Seminar 1986–95, speaker trade confs and educn courses, advsr Br companies and charities; chm Crime Writers' Assoc 2001–02; *Books* (all under pseudonym Russell James): Underground (1989), Daylight (1990), Payback (1991), Slaughter Music (1993), Count Me Out (1996), Oh No, Not My Baby (1999), Painting In The Dark (2000), The Annex (2002), Pick Any Title (2002), No One Gets Hurt (2003), Collected Stories (2007), The Maud Allan Affair (2008), Great British Fictional Detectives (2008), Great British Fictional Villians (2009), Pocket Guide to Victorian Writers & Poets (2010), Pocket Guide to Victorian Artists & Their Models (2011), Requiem for a Daughter (2011), The Exhibitionists (2012), Rafael's Gold (2013), Exit 39 (2014), The Newly Discovered Diaries of Doctor Kristal (2014), Stories I Can't Tell (2014), Victorian Romances (2015), When A Paperback Cost 6d (2015); also We Never Shall Marry (film script, 1998), The Break (film script, 1999); *Recreations* criminal research, travel to unlikely places, arts and culture of the 19th Century; *Clubs* Crime Writers' Assoc, Soc of Authors; *Style*— Russell Logan, Esq; ✉ Number 10, Lauriston Park, Cheltenham, Gloucestershire GL50 2QL (website: https://russelljamesbooks.wordpress.com)

LOGIE, Jamieson John; s of John Deas Logie, of St Andrews, and Jean Elizabeth, *née* Aitken; *b* 20 April 1961, Glasgow; *Educ* Univ of Glasgow (LLB), Univ of Dundee (DipLP); *m* 2 Aug 1986, Evelyn Mackenzie, *née* Brown; 2 s (Duncan Ross b 19 June 1988, James Cameron b 28 Dec 1989); *Career* slr; ptnr: Norton Rose 1992–99 (joined 1985), Sullivan & Cromwell LLP 2001– (joined 1999); memb: Law Soc Eng and Wales, Law Soc Scot, Int Bar Assoc; *Recreations* golf, skiing; *Clubs* Walbrook, New (St Andrews), Wisley Golf, George; *Style*— Jamieson Logie, Esq; ✉ Sullivan & Cromwell LLP, 1 New Fetter Lane, London EC4A 1AN (☎ 020 7959 8900, fax 020 7959 8950, e-mail logiej@sullcrom.com)

LOGIE, John Robert Cunningham; JP (Grampian, Higlands and Islands 2010); s of Norman John Logie, TD (d 1972), and Kathleen Margaret Cameron, *née* Neill (d 2013); *b* 9 September 1946; *Educ* Robert Gordon's Coll, Trinity Coll Glenalmond, Univ of Aberdeen (MB ChB, PhD); *m* 1, 1981, Sheila Catherine (d 2001), da of James Pratt Will (d 1957); 1 da (Joanna Catherine Neill b 1985), 1 s (David James Norman b 1989); m 2, 2004, Carol Joan, da of Gregor Macdonald; *Career* med trg Aberdeen Royal Infirmary 1970–81 (house offr, lectr, registrar, sr registrar), conslt gen surgn Raigmore Hosp Inverness 1981–2011; appointed med memb First-Tier Tribunal Social Entitlement Chamber 2013–; memb Cncl RSC (Ed) 1991–2002 (treas 2002–06, vice-pres 2006–09); FRCSEd 1974, FRCS 1975, FRCSGlas 1993; *Recreations* gardening, railway matters, ornamental waterfowl; *Clubs* Surgical Travellers; *Style*— John R C Logie, Esq, JP; ✉ The Darroch, Little Cantray, Culloden Moor, Inverness IV2 5EY (☎ 01463 792090); Raigmore Hospital, Inverness (☎ 01463 704000)

L

LOGIE, Dr Nicholas; *b* 12 May 1950; *Educ* Yehudi Menuhin Sch, Royal Coll of Music, Musikhochschule Detmold (German govt scholarship), Open Univ (BA, MA), Conservatorio Santa Cecilia Rome (Italian govt scholarship), Open Univ (PhD); *m*; 2 c; *Career* viola player; with Vienna Symphony Orch 1973–78, Chilingirian String Quartet 1978–81, freelance 1981–; princ viola Orch of the Age of Enlightenment; orch mangr: Kent Opera 1985–90, Glyndebourne Touring Opera 1990–2007; Royal Northern Coll of Music: sr lectr 1989–2000, dir of early music 1998–2000; numerous recordings; *Style*— Dr Nicholas Logie; ✉ Lotts End, Inkpen Lane, Forest Row, East Sussex RH18 5BQ (☎ 01342 825661, mobile 07713 742322, e-mail research.logie@gmail.com)

LOGSDAIL, (Christopher) Nicholas Roald; s of late John Logsdail, and Else, *née* Dahl; *b* 21 June 1945; *Educ* Bryanston, Slade Sch of Fine Art, UCL; *m* 1, 1968 (m dis), Fiona, *née* McLean; 1 s; m 2, 1985, Caroline, *née* Mockett; 2 s, 1 da; *Career* opened Lisson Gallery 1967; artists represented incl: Prof Richard Deacon, CBE, RA, Richard Wentworth, Tony Cragg, CBE, RA, Anish Kapoor, *qqv*, Julian Opie, Sol LeWitt, Ai Weiwei, Marina Abramovic, Ryan Gander; memb Soc of London Art Dealers; *Style*— Nicholas Logsdail, Esq; ✉ Lisson Gallery, 52–54 Bell Street, London NW1 5DA (☎ 020 7724 2739)

LOHN, Matthew Simon; s of Carl William Lohn (d 2005), and Ann Isobel, *née* Chattin (d 2012); *b* 19 November 1965, Brentwood, Essex; *Educ* Brentwood Sch, London Hosp Med Coll (BSc, MB BS), Coll of Law (CPE); *m* 18 July 1992, Johanna Gabriella Miranda, *née* Cornwell; 1 da (Beatrix Gabrielle Rose b 7 Feb 1998); *Career* slr; jr house offr Epsom Hosp 1991–92; Fieldfisher: joined 1994, ptnr 1999–, main bd memb 2004–12, managing ptnr 2011–13, chair Exec Ctee 2011–12, sr ptnr 2013–, chair Supervisory Bd; chair Regulatory Panel Chartered Institute of Public Finance and Accountancy 2016–; memb: Br Horseracing Authy Disciplinary Panel 2005–, Determinations Panel The Pensions Regulator 2013–, Dubai Healthcare City Authy Licensing Appeals Bd 2014–, Complaints Ctee Ind Press Standards Org 2014–; legal chair Nat Anti-Doping Panel 2010–; memb: GMC 1991, Law Soc 1994; *Recreations* gardening, tennis, shooting, fishing, horse racing; *Style*— Matthew Lohn, Esq; ✉ Fieldfisher, Riverbank House, 2 Swan Lane, London EC4R 3TT (☎ 020 7861 4000, fax 020 7488 0084, e-mail matthew.lohn@fieldfisher.com)

LOKER, John Keith; s of Denis Loker, of Pudsey, W Yorks, and Irene May, *née* Threapleton (d 1968); *b* 15 September 1938, Farsley, W Yorks; *Educ* Bradford Coll of Art and Design, RCA (Abbey minor travelling scholarship); *m* 1, 1961 (m dis 1970), Eva, da of Alfred Kalnins; 2 s (Daniel Valdis b 1962, Simon Andris b 1965); m 2, 13 Sept 1997, Emily Mayer (sculptor); *Career* artist; taught 1964–89: Manchester, Maidstone, Nottingham, Wolverhampton, Brighton, Portsmouth, Wimbledon, Chelsea, NE London, Middx; Nordstern Print Prize Royal Acad 1994; *Exhibitions* solo: studio exhbn London 1969, 1975, 1986 and 2001, Flowers Gallery 1970, 1973, 1975, 1978, 1980, 1982, 1983, 1985, 1988, 1990, 1992, 1993, 1994, 1995, 1998, 2001, 2009 and 2012, ICA 1970, Park Square Gallery Leeds 1975, 1978, Wetering Galerie Amsterdam 1978, 1980, 1982, 1986 and 1989, Arnolfini Gallery Bristol 1981, Newlyn Orion 1981, Cartwright Hall Bradford 1981, Newcastle Poly Gallery 1981, Galerie du Monde Hong Kong 1984, Watermans Arts Centre London 1992, Space is a Dangerous Country (Flowers Central Cork Street) 2016; numerous gp exhbns in UK and abroad; *Public Collections* Arts Cncl, Bradford City Art Gallery, British Cncl, Contemporary Art Soc, DOE, Dudley City Art Gallery, Ferens Art Gallery Hull, Hunterian Collection Glasgow, Leeds City Art Gallery, Manchester City Art Gallery, Power Inst of Fine Art Sydney, Rugby City Art Gallery, Tate Gallery, Van Reekumgalerie Apeldoorn, V&A, Wakefield City Art Gallery, Worcester City Art Gallery; *Commissions* Watmoughs Hldgs Bradford, Essex Gen Hosp, Stanhope Devpts for ITN Bldg (Norman Foster); *Publications* John Loker (monograph, 1981), Thriding (monograph, 1984), Littered Ways (suite of woodcuts and poem, 1986); *Recreations* harmonica player, cyclist; *Clubs* Chelsea Arts; *Style*— John Loker, Esq; ✉ Union Workhouse, Guilt Cross, Kenninghall, Norfolk NR16 2LJ (☎ 01953 681730, mobile 07881 584382, e-mail john@flyingbear.co.uk, website www.johnloker.co.uk); Flowers East, 82 Kingsland Road, London E2 8DP (☎ 020 7920 7777, fax 020 7920 7770, e-mail gallery@flowerseast.com, website www.flowerseast.com)

LOMAS, Derek Frank; s of Derek Edward James Lomas, of 3 Whitewood Cottages, Eynsford, Kent, and Pauline Lomas, *née* Clements; *b* 10 October 1960; *Educ* Dartford West Kent Secdy Boys Sch, Medway Coll of Art and Design (DATEC Dip Photography); *m* Sarah Ellen Kipps; 2 s (Edward, Jacob); *Career* freelance photographer (editorial photography, mainly still life work for magazines incl: Vogue, Tatler, Elle, Marie Claire) 1989–; *Awards* AFAEP award for non-commissioned still-life 1989; memb Photographers Assoc 1989; *Recreations* walking, cinema, cooking, photography; *Style*— Derek Lomas, Esq; ✉ Derek Lomas Photography (☎ 020 7622 0123)

LOMAS, HE Joanne (Jo); da of Geoffrey Lomas, and Judith Lomas, of Marlow, Bucks; *Educ* Univ of Bristol (BSc); *m* 25 May 2008, Christopher Finucane; 1 da (b 2010); *Career* diplomat; FCO: desk offr UN Dept 1993–95, Arabic language trg 1995–97, press offr/special asst to the dir Baghdad UNSCOM 1997, third sec Damascus 1997–2000, second sec UK Mission to the UN Geneva 2001–06, ldr Internal Communication Team 2006–08, head Global Response Centre 2008–10, dep head of mission Sarajevo 2011–15, high cmmr to Repub of Namibia 2015–; *Style*— Ms Joanne Lomas; ✉ Twitter @JoLomasFCO

LOMAX, Michael Acworth (Mike); s of Peter Francis George Lomax (d 1990), and Mary Rosamund Lomax (d 1993); *b* 9 January 1943; *Educ* Downside, Pembroke Coll Cambridge (BA); *m* 1, (m dis); 2 s; m 2, 1993, Margaret Ann Stone; *Career* account exec Sharps Advertising 1966–69, account mangr Foster Turner & Benson 1970–75 (dir 1972–75), dir Streets Financial 1975–84, jt md Charles Barker City 1984–87, chm First Financial Advertising/PR 1996–98 (md 1987–96); freelance mktg conslt 1998–; memb Nat Appeals Ctee Cancer Res Campaign 1974–90, nat chm Cancer Youth Action 1978–83, chm Mktg Ctee Cancer Res Campaign 1987–90; MIPA 1967; *Recreations* golf (capt Fin Advtg Golfing Soc 1989–90), cooking, hill walking, reading, opera; *Clubs* Roehampton; *Style*— Mike Lomax, Esq; ✉ First Finanical Advertising Ltd, One Red Lion Court, London EC4A 3EB

LOMAX, (Janis) Rachel; da of William Salmon, and Dilys Jenkins; *b* 15 July 1945; *Educ* Cheltenham Ladies' Coll, Girton Coll Cambridge (MA), LSE (MSc); *m* 1967 (m dis 1990), Michael Acworth Lomax; 2 s (Thomas b 1971, Daniel b 1973); *Career* HM Treasury: econ asst 1968–72, econ advsr 1972–78, sr econ advsr and asst sec 1978–86, princ private sec to Chancellor of the Exchequer 1985–86, under sec 1986–90, dep sec 1990–94; head Econ and Domestic Secretariat Cabinet Office 1994–95, vice-pres and COS World Bank Washington DC 1995–96; perm sec: Welsh Office 1996–99, DSS 1999–2001, DWP 2001–02, Dept for Tport 2002–03; dep govr (monetary policy) Bank of England 2003–08 (memb Monetary Policy Ctee 2003–08); non-exec dir: HSBC Hldgs 2008–, SAINTS, Reassurance Gp of America; pres IFS; memb Royal Econ Soc 1989–94; memb and chm UK Selection Ctee Harkness Fellowships; memb Bd RNT, memb Cncl Imperial Coll London, tstee Centre for Economic Policy Research; hon fell: LSE, Cardiff, UCW Swansea, Girton Coll Cambridge; Hon Dr: Univ of Wales, Univ of Glamorgan, Cass Business Sch City Univ, Glasgow Univ; *Style*— Ms Rachel Lomax

LOMBARD, Louise; *b* 13 September 1970; *Career* actress; *Theatre* Katerina in The Brothers Karamazov (Royal Exchange Manchester), Helen Hayle in On Approval (dir Sir Peter Hall), Hilary in Now You Know (Hampstead) 1995; *Radio* Twentieth Century Vampire (BBC Radio 5), La Vie de Boheme (BBC), Noel Coward's Private Lives (BBC); *Television* Evangeline in The House of Eliott (3 series, BBC) 1991–94, Anna in Chancer II (Central), Lucy in A Black Velvet Gown (Worldwide TV), Liz Shaw in Body Guards (Carlton) 1996–97, Lady Macbeth in Macbeth (BBC), Metropolis (ITV) 2000, War Stories 2003, Second Nature 2003, Sofia Curtis in CSI 2004–07, Judy's Got a Gun 2007, Blood Rush 2008; *Film* incl Lucy in Angels, Twice Upon A Time, Wax Doll – Aids and Drug Abuse, Gold in the Streets, Tale of the Mummy 1998, Hidalgo 2004; *Style*— Ms Louise Lombard

LOMBARDO, Marc; *Career* gp finance dir Blacks Leisure Gp plc 2008–2011, finance dir Joules 2011–; *Style*— Marc Lombardo, Esq; ✉ Joules, Joules Building, The Point, Rockingham Road, Market Harborough, Leicestershire LE16 7QU

LOMNICKA, Prof Eva Zofia; da of Adam Jan Lomnicki (d 2000), and Azdiz Josephine, *née* Szymanska; *b* 17 May 1951; *Educ* Girton Coll Cambridge (BA, MA, LLB, Chancellor's medal); *m* 1 Sept 1973, John Lewis Powell, QC, *qv*, s of Gwyn Powell; 2 da (Sophie Anna b 14 Feb 1980, Catrin Eva b 3 Jan 1982), 1 s (David John b 3 Feb 1985); *Career* called to the Bar Middle Temple 1974 (Harmsworth scholar, bencher); KCL: lectr 1975–90, reader 1990–94, prof of law 1994–; tstee Money Advice Tst 2007–12; FRSA; *Books* Encyclopedia of Consumer Credit (jt ed, 1976–), Encyclopedia of Financial Services Law (jtly, 1986–), Palmer's Company Law (contrib, 1986–), Modern Banking Law (jtly, 2 edn 1995, 3 edn 2002, 4 edn 2006, 5 edn 2012), The Financial Services and Markets Act 2000: An Annotated Guide (2002), The Law of Security and Title-based Finance (jtly, 2007, 2 edn 2012), Chitty on Contracts (contrib, 30 edn, 31 edn, 32 edn), Financial Services Law (contrib 2005, 2 edn 2013, 3 edn 2014); *Recreations* family, hill walking, music; *Style*— Prof Eva Lomnicka; ✉ School of Law, King's College London, Strand, London WC2R 2LS (☎ 020 7836 5454, fax 020 7848 2465, e-mail eva.lomnicka@kcl.ac.uk)

LOMONOSSOFF, Dr George Peter; s of George Lomonossoff (d 1954), and Gertrude Margaret, *née*, Winkworth (d 2010); *b* 15 August 1954; *Educ* Cambs HS for Boys, St John's Coll Cambridge (Lister scholar, MA, PhD); *m* 11 July 1987, Kim Susan (d 2004), da of late Remington Charles Chesher and late Betty Chesher, *née* Read; 1 da (Katherine Elizabeth Sumi b 26 Jan 1990), 1 s (Michael George Remington b 8 Nov 1993); m 2, 31 Dec 2014, Teresa Jean, *née* McInally; *Career* postdoctoral fell MRC Lab of Molecular Biology Cambridge 1979–80, memb of staff John Innes Inst 1981– (fell 1980–81); short term EMBO fell 1982 and 1990; Fulbright scholarship to Cornell Univ 1987–88; visiting scientist The Scripps Research Inst La Jolla 1998, hon prof Sch of Biological Sciences UEA 2008; achievements incl: determination of the genome structure of plant viruses, developing novel methods of producing virus resistant plants, and developing use of plant viruses as potential vaccines; numerous articles in scientific jls; BBSRC Innovator of the Year 2012, Colworth Prize lecture 2015; pres Int Soc for Plant Molecular Farming 2016–; memb: Soc for General Microbiology 1990, Assoc of Applied Biologists 2007; *Recreations* watching football, enjoying good food and drink; *Style*— Dr George Lomonossoff; ✉ Department of Biological Chemistry, John Innes Centre, Colney Lane, Norwich NR4 7UH (☎ 01603 450351, fax 01603 450045, e-mail george.lomonossoff@jic.ac.uk)

LONDON, Archdeacon of; *see:* Delaney, Ven Peter Anthony

LONDON, Prof Nicholas John Milton (Nick); s of Dr J M London, and Mrs Christine Keats; *Educ* Solihull Sch, Univ of Birmingham; *m* Susan, *née* Filer; 1 s (Ben b 22 Aug 1987), 1 da (Emily b 20 Feb 1989); *Career* trained in med and gen surgery Leicester hosps 1983–94, prof of surgery Univ of Leicester 1997–, assoc dean and head Leicester Medical Sch 2012; Hallet Prize RCS 1982, Hunterian prof RCS 1993, BUPA Fndn Res Dr of the Year 1994; FRCS 1986, FRCPEd 1999; *Publications* author of over 300 pubns in the areas of vascular surgery and related basic sci res; *Recreations* snowboarding, hiking, cycling; *Style*— Prof Nick London; ✉ Leicester Medical School, Centre for Medicine, University Road, Leicester LE1 7RH (☎ 0116 252 3022, e-mail sms16@le.ac.uk)

LONDON, Bishop of 1995–; Rt Rev and Rt Hon Richard John Carew Chartres; KCVO (2009), PC (1995); s of late Richard Arthur Carew Chartres, and Charlotte Ethel, *née* Day; *b* 11 July 1947; *Educ* Hertford GS, Trinity Coll Cambridge (MA), Cuddesdon Theol Coll, Lincoln Theol Coll (BD); *m* 1982, Caroline Mary, da of Sir Alan McLintock; 2 s (Alexander b 1986, Louis b 1991), 2 da (Sophie b 1988, Clio b 1993); *Career* master int sch Seville 1971, ordained 1973, curate Bedford St Andrew 1973–75, chaplain to the Bishop of St Albans 1975–80, Archbishop's chaplain 1980–84, vicar of St Stephen Rochester Row London 1984–92, bishop of Stepney 1992–95; six preacher Canterbury Cathedral 1991–96; London area dir of ordinands 1985–92, Gresham prof of divinity 1986–92; Prelate: of the Most Excellent Order of the British Empire 1996–, of the Imperial Soc of Knights Bachelor 1996–; dean of HM's Chapels Royal 1996–; chm: C of E Heritage Forum; ecclesiastical patron Prayer Book Soc, tstee St Catherine's Sinai Fndn, fndr and tstee St Ethelburga's Centre for Reconciliation and Peace; church cmmr; memb House of Lords 1996–; memb Central Ctee of the Conference of European Churches; hon bencher Middle Temple 1997; Liveryman: Worshipful Co of Merchant Taylors, Worshipful Co of Vintners; Hon Freeman: Worshipful Co of Weavers, Worshipful Co of Woolman; Freeman: Leathersellers Co, Drapers Co; Hon DD: Queen Mary & Westfield Coll, City Univ, Brunel Univ; Hon DLitt London Guildhall Univ; Ehrendomprediger vom Berliner Dom; FSA; *Publications* The History of Gresham College 1597–1997; *Style*— The Rt Rev and Rt Hon the Lord Bishop of London; ✉ The Old Deanery, Dean's Court, London EC4V 5AA (☎ 020 7248 6233, fax 020 7248 9721, e-mail bishop@londin.clara.co.uk)

LONDON, Timothy James (Tim); s of Jonathan London, and Jeanne, *née* Roche; *b* 24 June 1968; *Educ* Wells Blue Sch, Cardiff Univ (LLB); *m* 2 Dec 2003, Jane, *née* Haynes; *Career* slr; Eversheds 1990– (sr assoc 2008–); memb: Law Soc, Wales Commercial Law Assoc; *Publications* accredited author European Union Law of State Aid (2 edn by Kelyn Bacon); *Recreations* wine tasting, scuba diving, author food blog www.solicitingflavours.com; *Clubs* Jeroboam (Bristol); *Style*— Tim London, Esq; ✉ Eversheds LLP, 1 Callaghan Square, Cardiff CF10 5BT (☎ 029 2047 7530, fax 029 2046 4347, e-mail timlondon@eversheds.com)

LONEY, Francis Greville; s of Greville Groves Loney (d 1981), of Durban, South Africa, and Marjory Grace, *née* Redman (d 1995); *b* 11 December 1936, Pietermaritzburg, Natal, SA; *Educ* St Charles' Coll Pietermaritzburg, Regent St Poly London; *Career* freelance photographer 1966–; photographic career has covered all aspects of advtg and editorial photography incl fashion, beauty, interiors, still life, celebrities, CDs, books, magazine covers, theatre and corporate; *Recreations* theatre, ballet, cinema; *Style*— Francis Loney, Esq; ✉ Unit One, Quebec Wharf, 315 Kingsland Road, London E8 4DJ (☎ 020 7254 1199, mobile 07753 634443, e-mail francisloney@talktalk.net, website www.francisloney.co.uk)

LONG, Prof Adrian Ernest; OBE (2006); s of Charles Long (d 1985), and Sylvia Evelyn Winifred, *née* Mills (d 1974); *b* 15 April 1941; *Educ* Royal Sch Dungannon, Queen's Univ of Belfast (BSc, PhD, DSc); *m* 18 March 1967, Elaine Margaret Long, da of James Thompson (d 1980), and Muriel Margaret Hill (d 2004); 1 s (Michael b 22 Feb 1971), 1 da (Alison b 18 Dec 1972); *Career* bridge design engr Toronto Canada 1967–68, asst prof Civil Engrg Dept Queen's Univ Kingston Canada 1968–71; Queen's Univ Belfast: lectr Civil Engrg Dept 1971–75, prof of civil engrg 1976–2006, prof and head Civil Engrg Dept 1977–89, dean Faculty of Engrg 1988–91 and 1998–2002, dir Sch of the Built Environment 1989–98, prof emeritus 2006–; visiting prof RMC Kingston Canada 1975–76, ed Jl of Engrg Structures 1985–94, visitor Tport and Road Research Lab 1989–92, co-ordinator of research PSAM Sub-Ctee EPSRC 1990–94, memb Civil Engrg Panel Research Assessment Exercise 1996, 2001 and (chm) 2008; fell Tport Research Fndn 2005; inventor of Flexi Arch system for the rapid construction of arch bridges (62 bridges already constructed with spans from 4m to 16m); author of over 350 technical papers; 24 awards and medals incl: Royal Society/Esso Energy Award 1994, ICE/Royal Soc Ewing Medal 2009, ICE Gold Medal 2011; Hon DSc City Univ London 2007; FICE 1982 (chm NI Assoc 1985–86, memb Cncl 1989–92, vice-pres 1999–2002, pres 2002–03), FREng 1989, FIStructE 1989 (chm NI Branch 1993–94), FACI 1996, FIEI 1996, FICT 1997, FIAE 1998; *Recreations* walking, church activities, travel; *Style*— Prof Adrian Long, OBE, FREng; ✉ 29 Glen Ebor Park, Belfast BT4 2JJ; Civil Engineering Department, Queen's University, Belfast BT7 1NN (☎ 028 9097 6950, fax 028 9097 4278, e-mail a.long@qub.ac.uk)

LONG, Colin; s of Gordon Long, of Brighton, Sussex (d 1982), and Doreen, *née* Collins (d 1990); *b* 1946, Carshalton, Surrey; *Educ* Epsom Coll, Univ of Bristol (LLB); *m* 1979, Sheila, *née* Hughes; 1 da (Emily b 1983), 1 s (Charles b 1986); *Career* admitted slr 1970; asst slr Clifford-Turner 1970–73 and 1974–78, slr ICI plc 1973–74; ptnr: Bird & Bird 1978–90, Coudert Brothers 1990–98, Olswang 1998–2011; of Counsel Bird and Bird 2011–15; ind legal and regulatory conslt in communications 2015–; memb: Law Soc 1970, Int Bar Assoc 1986; Global Telecommunications Law and Practice (ed emeritus, 1988–); *Recreations* skiing, swimming, tennis; *Clubs* RAC, Hurlingham; *Style*— Colin Long, Esq; ✉ e-mail colin@colinlonglaw.com

LONG, Gulnara; *Educ* London Business Sch (MBA); *Career* founding ptnr Blackwood Realty Moscow 1992–98, mgmnt conslt London 2000–05, dir Property Vision HSBC Private Bank 2005–12, managing ptnr Property Vision LLP 2012–; *Style*— Mrs Gulnara Long; ✉ Property Vision, 8 Cromwell Place, London SW7 2JN

LONG, Martyn Howard; CBE (1991); s of Victor Frederick Long (d 1993), and Dorothy Maud, *née* Lawrence (d 1999); *b* 1 May 1933, Teddington, London; *Educ* UCS London, Merrist Wood Agric Coll Surrey; *m* 4 Oct 1958, Veronica Mary Gascoigne, da of James Edward Bates (d 1952); 4 da (Helen b 1959, Maria b 1961, Samantha b 1965, Rosalind b 1969); *Career* Nat Serv RAF 1952–54; farmer 1949–85, dir of family firm; memb: W Sussex AHA 1973–77, SW Thames RHA 1980–81; chm: Mid-Downs HA W Sussex 1981–94, Nat Assoc of Health Authorities 1988–90; vice-chm Nat Assoc of Health Authorities and Tsts 1990–93 (chm HA Ctee 1990–93), chm Sussex Ambulance Service NHS Trust 1995–98; chm East Grinstead Cons Assoc 1972–75; W Sussex CC: cncllr (Cons) 1973–93, chm Policy and Resources Ctee 1985–89, chm 1989–93; cncllr: E Sussex CC 1970–74, Cuckfield RDC 1972–74, Mid Sussex DC 1973–79; memb Assoc of CCs 1979–89, chm ACC Social Servs 1987–89; chm Br Homoeopathic Assoc 1993–95, memb Cncl and Instn King Edward VII Hosp Midhurst 1992–2006 (chm 2000–03), tstee Mobility Tst 1993–97, tstee Macular Soc (formerly Macular Disease Soc) 2012–, former health policy advsr to Sussex Health Care; tstee Culfrey Land Tst 2005; memb St Andrew's Church Potterhanworth PCC 2005–12 and 2016– (churchwarden 2007–12); Lincoln Dio: memb Diocesan Cncl, chm Clergy Housing Ctee 2005–12, memb Finance Exec 2005–12; assoc memb Inner Magic Circle; DL Sussex until 2003; *Recreations* magic (assoc memb Inner Magic Circle with Silver Star); *Clubs* Farmers'; *Style*— Martyn Long, Esq, CBE; ✉ e-mail martynlong@themagiccircle.co.uk

LONG, Naomi; *b* 13 December 1971, Belfast; *Educ* Bloomfield Collegiate Sch Belfast, Queen's Univ Belfast; *m* Michael; *Career* civil engr 1994–2003; cncllr (Alliance) Belfast City Cncl 2001–10, MLA (Alliance) Belfast E 2003–10, MP (Alliance) Belfast E 2010–15; dep ldr Alliance Pty 2006–; Lord Mayor of Belfast 2009–10; *Style*— Mrs Naomi Long; ✉ Alliance Party Headquarters, 88 University Street, Belfast BT7 1HE

LONG, Richard; CBE (2013); *b* 2 June 1945, Bristol; *Educ* Bedminster Down Sch, W of Eng Coll of Art Bristol, St Martin's Sch of Art; *Career* artist; works in numerous public collections; has created works and walks in landscapes worldwide; Hon DLitt Univ of Bristol 1995, Hon DLitt St Andrews Univ 2011; RA 2001; Chevalier de l'Ordre des Arts et des Lettres (France) 1990; *Solo Exhibitions* incl: Konrad Fischer Düsseldorf 1968, Whitechapel Art Gallery London 1971, MOMA NY 1972, Stedelijk Museum Amsterdam 1973, British Pavilion Venice Biennale 1976, Palacio de Cristal Madrid 1986, Solomon R Guggenheim Museum NY 1986, Tate Gallery London 1990, Hayward Gallery London 1991, Palazzo delle Esposizione Rome 1994, Setaguya Art Museum Tokyo 1996, Guggenheim Museum Bilbao 2000, Tate St Ives 2002, Tate Britain 2009; *Awards* Kunstpreis Aachen 1988, Turner Prize 1989, Wilhelm Lehmbruck-Pries Duisburg 1996, Praemium Imperiale (for sculpture) Tokyo 2009; *Publications* incl: South America (1973), Richard Long (text by Rudi Fuchs, 1986), Old World New World (1988), Nile, Papers of River Muds (1990), Walking in Circles (1991), Mountains and Waters (1992), From Time to Time (1997), Mirage (1998), Every Grain of Sand (1999), Richard Long – A Moving World (2002), Walking the Line (2002), Walking and Sleeping (2004), Heaven and Earth (2009); *Style*— Richard Long, Esq, CBE, RA; ✉ Lisson Gallery, 52–54 Bell Street, London NW1 5DA (☎ 020 7724 2739, websites www.richardlong.org and www.therichardlongnewsletter.org)

LONG, Dr Richard Glover; s of John Long (d 1978), of Higham, Kent, and Bridget, *née* Harrison (d 1999); *b* 13 August 1947; *Educ* Canford Royal Free Hosp Sch of Med (MB BS, MD); *m* 1, 12 Feb 1983, Anita Rosemary (d 2006), da of Kenneth Eaton Wilson, of Aldridge, West Midlands; 1 s (Charles Matthew b 1983 d 2000); *m* 2, 14 Oct 2011, Sajidah Asmat Hussain; 1 da (Tara Laila Bridget b 2005); *Career* hon sr registrar Hammersmith Hosp 1978–80, sr registrar St Thomas Hosp 1980–83, MRC travelling res fell San Francisco USA 1983, conslt gastroenterologist and clinical teacher Nottingham Hosp Med Sch 1983–2012; sr clinical examiner RCP 2007–12 (censor 2006–09); memb: Assoc of Physicians of GB and Ireland, Br Soc of Gastroenterology, American Gastroenterology Assoc, Med Res Soc; FRCP 1989; *Books* Radioimmunoassay of Gut Regulatory Reptides (jt ed with S R Bloom, 1982), Textbook of Gastroenterology and Liver Disease (jt ed with B B Scott, 2005); author of more than 100 clinical papers and book chapters; *Recreations* fly fishing, gardening; *Style*— Dr Richard Long; ✉ Coach House, Old Hall Drive, Widmerpool, Nottingham NG12 5PZ (☎ 0115 937 2467)

LONG, Hon Sarah Victoria; da of 4 Viscount Long; *b* 14 August 1958, Cookham, Berks; *m* 19 May 1990, George G Clegg Littler, *qv*, er s of George Clegg Littler, and Mrs Frithjof Meidell-Andersen; 1 s (Alexander George Richard b 17 Jan 1996), 1 da (Xenia Charlotte Marina b 15 April 1999); *Career* gallery owner and art conslt; dir Long & Ryle Ltd specialising in contemporary art; *Recreations* garden design, the music of John Tavener, literature; *Clubs* Chelsea Arts; *Style*— The Hon Mrs Sarah Long; ✉ Long & Ryle, 4 John Islip Street, London SW1P 4PX (☎ 020 7834 1434)

LONG, Dr Tracy Elisabeth; CBE (2016); *b* 4 June 1962, London; *Educ* Univ of London (BA), Henley Mgmnt Coll (MBA, APDMC, DBA); *m* 27 Aug 1998, Andrew Tuckey; 2 da (Eleanor Charlotte Rosemary b 5 June 1999, Florence Cecily Rose b 23 July 2002); *Career* fndr Boardroom Review 2004–; fndr: Avalon Prodns 1987–90, Classic FM 1990–94; dir: Baring Brothers 1994–96, BSkyB Ventures 1997–2000, Botts & Co 2000–03; non-exec dir: Kings Consort 2005–08, Lowland Investment Co 2004–09; non-exec dir and chair of ARC DCMS 2009–; memb Advsy Bd LSO 1996–2010, memb Devpt Bd RAM 2000–08, int dir Bd Carnegie Hall 2013–; tstee NESTA 2003–09, memb Cncl and Fndn Marlborough Coll 2013–, tstee Windsor Leadership Tst 2016–; Keith McMillan Prize for Research 2005; fell Cass Business Sch; Hon ARAM; *Publications* The Role of the Non-Executive Director (2005), Tales of Pride and Prejudice (2005), This Year's Model (2006), Diving For Pearls (2007), The Evolution of FTSE 250 Boards of Directors (2007), Sense, Sensibility and Intuition (2011), Board Evaluation, London Stock Exchange, Corporate Governance for Main Market and Aim Companies (2012), PLC Magazine (2014), Good Governance Institute (2015); *Recreations* music, travel; *Clubs* 5 Hertford Street; *Style*— Dr Tracy Long, CBE; ✉ Boardroom Review, 12 Horbury Mews, London W11 3NL (e-mail tlong@boardroomreview.com, website www.boardroomreview.com)

LONGAIR, Prof Malcolm Sim; CBE (2000); *b* 18 May 1941; *Educ* Morgan Acad Dundee, Queen's Coll Univ of St Andrews (James Caird travelling scholar), Univ of Cambridge (James Clerk Maxwell scholar, MA, PhD); *m* Deborah Janet; 1 s (Mark Howard b 13 Sept 1976), 1 da (Sarah Charlotte b 7 March 1979); *Career* lectr Dept of Physics and visiting asst prof of radio astronomy Calif Inst for Advanced Study Princeton 1978, exchange visitor to USSR Space Res Inst Moscow (on 6 occasions) 1975–79, regius prof of astronomy Univ of Edinburgh 1980–90, dir Royal Observatory Edinburgh 1980–90, Astronomer Royal for Scotland 1980–90; visiting lectr: Pennsylvania State Univ 1986 (in astronomy and astrophysics), Univ of Victoria Canada; Regents fellowship Smithsonian Instn at Smithsonian Astrophysical Observatory Harvard Univ 1990; emeritus Jacksonian prof of natural philosophy Univ of Cambridge (demonstrator Dept of Physics 1970–75, official fell and praelector Clare Hall 1971–80, emeritus professorial fell Clare Hall), dir of devpt Cavendish Laboratory; memb: IUE Observatory Ctee 1975–78, Working Gp Euro Space Agency 1975–78, Interdisciplinary Scientists for the Hubble Space Telescope 1977–, Anglo Aust Telescope Bd 1982–87, Space Science Programme Bd 1985–88; chm: Space Telescope Advsy Panel 1977–84, Astronomy II (AII) Ctee 1979–80 (memb 1977–78), Millimetre Telescope Users Ctee 1979–83, Space Telescope Science Inst 1982–84; author of numerous scientific papers, delivered numerous public lectures; Hon LLD Univ of Dundee 1982; FRAS, FRSE 1981, FRS 2004; *Books* Observational Cosmology (co-ed J E Gunn and M J Rees, 1978), High Energy Astrophysics (1981, Vol 1 1992, Vol 2 1994, Vol 3 2011), Alice and the Space Telescope (1989), The Origins of Our Universe (1990), Our Evolving Universe (1996), Galaxy Foundation (1998, 2 edn 2008), Theoretical Concepts in Physics (2003), The Cosmic Century: A History of Astrophysics and Cosmology (2006); *Recreations* music, opera, art, architecture, mountain walking; *Style*— Prof Malcolm Longair, CBE; ✉ Cavendish Laboratory, University of Cambridge, Cambridge CB3 0HE (☎ 01223 337429)

LONGCROFT, Anita Jane Henderson (Mrs James Longcroft); da of Kenneth Douglas Henderson Self (d 1998), of Norwich, and Hilda Oakley, *née* Cookson (d 1992); *b* 1 October 1950, Altrincham; *Educ* Newcastle upon Tyne Church HS, UEA (BA), Coll of Law; *m* 1, Sept 1977 (m dis 1989), Ian Symington; 1 s (Andrew b 17 June 1982); *m* 2, Aug 1993, James Longcroft (d 1994); 2 s (Charles b 10 Jan 1990, James b 16 Oct 1991); *Career* admitted slr 1977; Wartnabys 1977–79, full-time farmer Market Harborough 1979–80, legal advsr CLA 1980–83, Lovell White Durrant (latterly Lovells) 1983–91 (ptnr 1989–91), sole practitioner Symington & Co 1991–96, chief legal advsr CLA 1996–99, slr Thrings LLP (formerly Lee & Pembertons) 1999–; Liveryman City of London Slrs Co; various articles in legal press and in-house magazines; *Recreations* motorboating, skiing, property development; *Clubs* Little Ship, Nelson Boatowners, Bembridge Sailing, Hurlingham, Carnegie, RAC; *Style*— Mrs Anita Symington; ✉ Thrings LLP, Kinnaird House, 1, Pall Mall East, London SW1Y 5AU (☎ 020 7706 5600,e-mail asymington@thrings.com)

LONGDEN, Christopher John; s of John Stuart Longden (d 1994), of Sheffield, S Yorks, and Daisy, *née* Heath (d 2002); *b* 22 March 1955; *Educ* Granville Coll Sheffield, Blackpool Coll; *m* 31 March 1978, Carol, da of Bryan Pettinger; 2 s (Benjamin b 6 July 1981, James b 15 Feb 1984), 1 da (Jennifer b 31 March 1985); *Career* trainee mangr British Transport Hotels 1974–77, food and beverage mangr Hotel L'Horizon Jersey 1977–81, mangr Gleddoch House Hotel & Country Club Langbank 1981–85, md Gleddoch Hotels (incl Gleddoch House, Gleddoch Golf Club and Houstoun House Broxburn) 1985–91, exec gen mangr (pre-opening) Vermont Hotel Newcastle upon Tyne 1992–93, md Ballathie House Hotel Perthshire 2003– (gen mangr 1993–2003); Master Innholder 1986; Freeman City of London 1986; FHCIMA 1974; *Recreations* yacht racing; *Style*— Christopher Longden, Esq; ✉ Ballathie House Hotel, Kinclaven, by Stanley, Perthshire PH1 4QN (☎ 01250 883268, fax 01250 883396, e-mail longdenc@btconnect.com)

LONGE, Laurence Peter; s of Robert Longe, and Ellen Longe; *b* 9 January 1955; *Educ* St Thomas Aquinas' GS King's Norton; *m* 6 Sept 1980, Allyson Daphne, da of William Daniel Roberts; 1 s (Simon Laurence b 26 Nov 1986), 1 da (Rachel Allyson b 8 May 1992); *Career* Inland Revenue 1974–78, tax sr Dearden Farrow 1979–80, tax mangr KPMG Peat Marwick 1981–87; Baker Tilly: tax dir 1987–88, managing ptnr London Tax Dept 1988–91, managing ptnr Watford office 1991–96, nat managing ptnr 1996–; ATII 1981, ACA 1986; *Recreations* scuba diving, reading, family; *Style*— Laurence Longe, Esq; ✉ RSM UK Group LLP, 25 Farringdon Street, London EC4A 4AB (☎ 020 3201 8000, e-mail laurence.longe@rsmuk.com)

LONGHURST, Scott Robert James; s of Robert Longhurst, and Joan, *née* Gaunt; *b* 6 June 1967, London; *Educ* Dartford GS, Univ of Birmingham (Coopers & Lybrand Accounting Prize, KPMG Accounting Prize, BCom), Harvard Business Sch; *m* 1 Nov 1991, Karen Patricia, *née* Lyons; 2 s (Max b 11 Feb 1993, Henry b 22 May 1995), 1 da (Madeline b 7 Dec 1997); *Career* asst mangr Ernst & Young 1988–91, gp accountant global reporting, planning and analysis Shell Int Petroleum Co 1991–93, audit mangr Shell Cos Gtr China 1993–95, dep controller Shell Chemicals Europe 1995–97, chief financial offr oil products jt ventures Shell Saudi Arabia 1997–2000, vice-pres finance TXU Europe 2000–01, vice-pres corp planning TXU Corp 2001–02, chief financial offr and sr vice-pres Oncor Gp 2002–04, gp controller and chief accounting offr TXU Corp 2004, gp finance dir AWG plc 2004–; FCA 2002 (ACA 1991); *Recreations* travel, tennis, golf; *Style*— Scott Longhurst, Esq; ✉ AWG plc, Anglian House, Ambury Road, Huntingdon, Cambridgeshire PE29 3NZ (☎ 01480 323507, fax 01480 456018, e-mail scott.longhurst@awg.com)

LONGHURST, HE William Jesse (Bill); *Educ* King Edward VI GS Chelmsford, Univ of Sheffield (BA); *m* Kathryn Scheding; 3 da (b 1991, 1993, 2007), 1 s (b 2010); *Career* diplomat; joined FCO 1990, asst desk offr Economic Relations Dept FCO 1991, third sec (economic and trade policy) then second sec (political/info) Seoul 1992–95, first sec (commercial) Tokyo 1995–98, seconded as head Exports to Japan Unit Dept of Trade and Industry 1998–2001, first sec (finance and mgmnt reform) UK Mission to the UN NY 2001–06, Serbian language trg 2006–07, dep head of mission and consul gen Belgrade 2007–11, dep head ASEAN Dept FCO 2011–14, ambass to Cambodia 2014–; *Style*— HE Bill Longhurst; ✉ c/o FCO (Phnom Penh), King Charles Street, London SW1A 2AH

LONGLEY, Clifford; JP (Bromley 1998); s of Harold Anson Longley, of Purley, Surrey, and Gladys, *née* Gibbs; *b* 1940; *Educ* Trinity Sch Croydon, Univ of Southampton (BSc (Eng)); *m*; 3 c; *Career* journalist; reporter: Essex and Thurrock Gazette 1961–64, Portsmouth Evening News 1964–67; The Times: reporter 1967–69, asst news ed 1969–71, feature writer 1971–72, religious affairs corr and columnist 1972–87, ldr writer 1984–92, religious affairs ed and columnist 1987–92, asst ed (leaders) 1990–92; The Daily Telegraph: columnist 1992–2000, ldr writer 1992–95, religious affairs ed 1994–95; columnist and contributing ed The Tablet 1994– (actg ed 1996); conslt ed: The Common Good (Catholic Bishops Conf of Eng and Wales) 1996, Prosperity with a Purpose (Churches Together in Britain and Ireland) 2005; contrib: Thought for the Day (BBC Radio 4) 2002–, The Moral Maze (BBC Radio 4) 2004–; memb: Advsy Cncl Three Faiths Forum 1996–, Steering Ctee True Wealth of Nations project Univof Southern California 2006–; pres Bromley Neighbourhood Watch Assoc 2013; Univ of Oxford select preacher 1988, Hugh Kay meml lectr 1990; Br Press Awards Specialist Writer of the Year 1986, Gold medal Peace through Dialogue Int Cncl of Christians and Jews 2006; hon fell St Mary's Coll Univ of Surrey 1998; MLitt (Lambeth) 2012; FRSA 2013; *Books* The Times Book of Clifford Longley (1991), The Worlock Archive (1999), Chosen People (2002), The Babylon Conspiracy (2013); *Recreations* music, playing the piano, reading, student pilot; *Style*—

L

Clifford Longley, Esq; ✉ 24 Broughton Road, Orpington, Kent BR6 8EQ (☎ 01689 853189, fax 01689 811279, e-mail clifford.longley@ntlworld.com)

LONGLEY, James Timothy Chapman; s of Alan Timothy Chapman Longley, of York, and Avrill Ruth Nunn, *née* Midgley; *b* 21 May 1959; *Educ* Worksop Coll, Leeds Metropolitan Univ (BA); *Children* 1 s (Oliver b 13 Nov 2001); *Career* CA; Finnie and Co 1980–83, Arthur Andersen 1983–85, Creditanstalt-Bankverein 1985–88, Touche Ross and Co 1988–89, The Wilcox Group Ltd 1990, ptnr Dearden Chapman CAs; co-fndr: Bioprogress plc 1996–2002, Photobox Ltd 2000–06; dir: Plutus PowerGen plc, Papillon Hldgs plc, Extrajet Ltd, Eyeswide Ltd; FCA 1983; *Recreations* skiing, horse racing, tennis; *Clubs* Groucho, Hurlingham; *Style—* James Longley, Esq; ✉ Plutus PowerGen plc (☎ 020 3705 8350, e-mail jamestclongley@aol.com, website www.plutuspowergen.com)

LONGLEY, Michael; CBE (2010); *b* 1939, Belfast; *Educ* Royal Belfast Academical Instn, Trinity Coll Dublin; *m* Edna Longley, the critic; 3 c; *Career* poet and writer; sometime teacher Dublin, London and Belfast, combined arts dir Arts Cncl of NI until 1991; author of numerous scripts for BBC Schools Dept, regular broadcaster; work has been the subject of four films incl The Corner of the Eye (RTE, BBC and Channel 4); memb Aosdána, fndr memb Cultural Traditions Gp NI; FRSL; *Awards* Eric Gregory Award, British Airways Cwlth Poetry Prize, Whitbread Poetry Prize, T S Eliot Prize, Hawthornden Prize, Cholmondeley Award, Queen's Gold Medal for Poetry, Librex Montale Prize; other awards from Charitable Irish Soc of Boston, Irish American Cultural Inst and Ireland Funds of America; *Books* poetry collections: No Continuing City (1969), An Exploded View (1973), Man Lying on a Wall (1976), The Echo Gate (1979), Poems 1963–1983 (1985, re-issued 1991), Gorse Fires (1991), The Ghost Orchid (1995), Selected Poems (1998), The Weather in Japan (2000), Snow Water (2004), Collected Poems (2006); ed: Causeway (on the Arts in Ulster), Under the Moon, Over the Stars (children's verse), Selected Poems of Louis MacNeice, Poems of W R Rodgers, Selected Poems of John Hewitt, 20th Century Irish Poems; *Style—* Michael Longley, Esq, CBE, FRSL

LONGMAN, Peter Martin; s of Denis Martin Longman (d 2003), of Somerset, and Mary Joy Longman (d 1977); *b* 2 March 1946; *Educ* Huish's Sch Taunton, Univ Coll Cardiff (BSc), Univ of Manchester (Dip Drama); *m* 22 May 1976, Sylvia June, da of John Lancaster Prentice (d 2006), of E Sussex; 2 da (Tania Louise b 1978, Natalie Therese b 1981); *Career* housing arts offr Arts Cncl GB 1969–78 (Fin Dept 1968–69), dep dir Crafts Cncl 1978–83, dir and sec Museums & Galleries Cmmn 1990–95 (dep sec 1983–84, sec 1984–90); dir: The Theatres Trust 1995–2006 (tstee 1991–95, conslt 2006–08), Scarborough Theatre Tst 2005–11; conslt Charcoalblue LLP 2006–; a dir The Walpole Fndn 1997–2005, a dir Orange Tree Theatre Ltd 2004–10 (chm 2008–10); dep chm Textile Conservation Fndn 2000–11 (memb Cncl 1983–2013, chm 1998–2000); memb: Arts Centres Panel Gtr London Arts Assoc 1981–83, Bd of Caryl Jenner Prodns Ltd (Unicorn Theatre for Children) 1983–87, co-opted Bd Scot Museums Cncl 1986–95, British Tourist Authy Heritage Ctee 1991–95, Exec Ctee Cncl for Dance Educn and Trg 1996–97, Advsy Ctee Art in Churches 1996–98, Cncl Chichester Festival Theatre Tst 1998–2003, Restoration Ctee ENO 1999–2004; tstee Covent Garden Area Tst 2001–03; sec working pty reports on: Trg Arts Administrators Arts Cncl 1971, Area Museum Cncls and Servs HMSO 1984, Museums in Scot HMSO 1986, Act Now! Theatres Tst 2003; FRSA 1989, Hon FMA 1995; *Recreations* discovering Britain, listening to music, looking at buildings, studio ceramics; *Style—* Peter Longman, Esq; ✉ 37 Castle Road, Clevedon BS21 7DA (☎ 01275 544039)

LONGMORE, Rt Hon Lord Justice; Rt Hon Sir Andrew Centlivres; PC (2001); s of Dr John Bell Longmore (d 1973), and Virginia Albertina, *née* Centlivres (d 2012); *b* 25 August 1944; *Educ* Winchester, Lincoln Coll Oxford (MA); *m* 17 Oct 1979, Margaret Murray, da of Dr James McNair (d 1980), of Milngavie, Glasgow; 1 s (James Centlivres b 1981); *Career* called to the Bar Middle Temple 1966, bencher 1990; QC 1983, recorder of the Crown Ct 1992–93, judge of the High Court of Justice (Queen's Bench Div) 1993–2001, Lord Justice of Appeal 2001–; memb Bar Cncl 1982–85, chm Law Reform Ctee 1987–90; *Books* MacGillivray and Parkington Law of Insurance (co-ed, 7 edn 1981, 8 edn 1988, 9 edn 1997); *Recreations* fell-walking; *Style—* The Rt Hon Lord Justice Longmore; ✉ Royal Courts of Justice, Strand, London WC2A 2LL

LONGMORE, Prof Donald Bernard; OBE (1999); s of Bernard George Longmore (d 1992), of Sandwich, Kent, and Beatrice Alice, *née* Payne (d 1993); *b* 20 February 1928; *Educ* Solihull Sch (head of sch), Guy's Hosp Med Sch (Sailing blue, MB BS, LRCP), Baylor Univ Texas, Univ of Texas, The London Hosp; *m* 2 April 1956, Patricia Christine Greig, da of Arthur Hardman Spindler (d 1984), of Bray on Thames, Berks; 3 da (Annabel (Mrs Anthony Armstrong) b 1958, Juliet (Mrs Stephen Harris) b 1959, Susan (Mrs Richard Venn-Smith) b 1962); *Career* Guy's Hosp: house appts 1953, jr lectr in anatomy 1954; surgical resident Baylor Univ TX 1956–58, surgical registrar London Hosp 1958–59, sr registrar Middx Hosp 1960–61, lectr in surgery St Thomas' Hosp 1962–63, conslt Nat Heart Hosp 1963–83, dir Magnetic Resonance Unit Royal Brompton Hosp and Nat Heart Hosp 1983–93 (ret), cardiac surgn and memb Britain's first heart transplant team; fndr pres: Coronary Artery Disease Res Assoc (CORDA), Preventing Heart Disease and Stroke (formerly Heart); hon life pres Assoc of Dunkirk, memb Little Ships Restoration Tst, vice-pres Dunkirk Little Ships Restoration Tst 2009–; hon citizen State of Alabama 1994; personal chair Univ of London; Freeman Co of Worldtraders 1993; memb Br Inst Radiology; MRCS, FRCSEd, FRCR; *Books* over 250 scientific pubns incl: Spare Part Surgery (1968), Machines in Medicine (1969), The Heart (1970), The Current Status of Cardiac Surgery (1975), Modern Cardiac Surgery (1978), Towards Safer Cardiac Surgery (1981), A Witness Account of the Rise and Fall of the NHS (2013); *Recreations* sailing, skiing; *Clubs* Royal Yacht Sqdn, United Hosps Sailing, Rolls Royce Enthusiasts, Island Sailing; *Style—* Prof Donald Longmore, OBE; ✉ Whitemayes, 97 Chertsey Lane, Egham, Surrey TW18 3LQ (☎ 01784 452436); Slipway Cottage, The Parade, Cowes, Isle of Wight PO31 7QJ (☎ 01983 292816)

LONGSON, Dr Geoffrey John; s of late Arthur Walter Longson, and late Mary Margaret, *née* Pratt; *b* 1 August 1935; *Educ* Tiffin Sch Kingston upon Thames, Guy's Hosp Dental Sch (open scholar, LDS RCS (Eng), Newland Pedley prize), Univ of London BDS; *m* 1, Dianne Frances Isaac; 1 s (Mark Frazer), 1 da (Tanya Clare Marie); m 2, Heather Jane Sutherland; 1 da (Olivia Jane Scott); *Career* dental surgn; in private practice Harley St; fell: Int Acad of Implantology, Int Coll of Dentists, American Coll of Dentists; memb: American Acad of Gnathology, European Acad of Gnathology (pres); FRSM; *Style—* Dr Geoffrey J Longson; ☎ 07785 225075, e-mail doclongson@gmail.com

LONGTON, Carrie; da of Gordon Longton, and Sheila, *née* Morris (d 1991); *b* 21 May 1965; *Educ* St Anne's Coll Oxford (MA); *m* 30 Aug 1997, Philip Taylor; 2 da (Grace b 14 Dec 1998, Mimi b 16 Jan 2006), 1 s (Noah b 1 Aug 2001); *Career* Pebble Mill BBC 1986, Night Network ITV and After Dark Channel 4 1987–89, Clive James Progs 1989–2000, co-fndr Mumsnet 2000–; hon doctorate Univ of East London 2010; *Publications* Mums on Pregnancy (jt ed), Mums on Babies (jt ed), Mums on Toddlers (jt ed); *Style—* Ms Carrie Longton; ✉ Mumsnet, Studio 6, Deane House Studios, Greenwood Place, Highgate Road, London NW5 1LB (e-mail carrie@mumsnet.com, website www.mumsnet.com)

LONGWORTH, John; s of late Norman Longworth, and late Edith Longworth; *b* 14 May 1958, Bolton; *Educ* Smithills Moor GS Bolton, Univ of London, Univ of Salford (BSc, MSc); *m* 3 Sept 1983, Sheila, *née* McGivern; 1 da (Esther b 16 Jan 1991), 1 s (George b 24 July 1993); *Career* dir Trade Liaison CWS Ltd 1983–90, dir Operations Bd Tesco Stores Ltd 1991–2003, exec dir Asda Stores Ltd, Asda Fin Servs Ltd and McClaggan Property 2003–08, co-fndr and chm SVA Ltd 2010–15, DG Br Chambers of Commerce 2011–16, chair Vote Leave Business Cncl 2016–; non-exec dir Nichols plc 2011–; health and safety cmmr 1997–2003, memb Panel Competition Cmmn 2008–14; hon PhD BPP Univ; memb: ICSA (formerly ACIS) 1985, CIEH; *Publications* Product Due Diligence (1997); *Recreations* horse racing, motorsport, music, opera, skiing, walking, cycling, history; *Clubs* Reform; *Style—* John Longworth, Esq; ☎ 07775 876986, e-mail jjohnpaloma@btinternet.com)

LONSDALE, Anne Mary; CBE (2004); da of late Dr Alexander Menzies, of Harrow, Middx, and Mabel, *née* Griffiths; *b* 16 February 1941; *Educ* St Anne's Coll Oxford (BA (2), MA); *m* 1, 1962, Geoffrey Griffin (d 1962); m 2, 1964 (m dis 1994), Prof Roger Harrison Lonsdale; 1 s (Charles John b 1965), 1 da (Katharine Georgina b 1966); *Career* Univ of Oxford: Davis sr scholar and lectr in Chinese St Anne's Coll 1971–74, dir External Rels Office 1990–93; sec-gen Central Euro Univ Budapest, Prague and Warsaw 1993–96, pres New Hall (now Murray Edwards Coll) Cambridge 1996–2008, dep vice-chllr Univ of Cambridge 2000–08 (pro-vice-chllr 1998–2003, dep high steward 2010–), founding provost Nazarbayev Univ Kazakhstan 2010–12 (tstee 2013–); chair Camfed Int 2008–10; memb Bd: Open Soc Fndn 2010–; tstee: Inter-Univ Fndn 1988–, Cambridge Overseas Tst 1996–2004, Cambridge Cwlth Tst 1997–2004, Cambridge Euro Tst 1998–2006, Newton Tst 1999–2008, Moscow Sch of Social and Economic Sciences 1999–2008, Lead UK 1999–2008, CARA 2006– (chair 2010–), BACEE 2005–08, European Humanities Univ 2007–; Cavaliere dell'Ordine al Merito della Repubblica Italiana 1988, Officier dans l'Ordre des Palmes Académiques France 2002; *Recreations* modern and contemporary art; *Clubs* Athenaeum; *Style—* Mrs Anne Lonsdale, CBE; ✉ Murray Edwards Coll, Cambridge CB3 0DF (☎ 01223 762100)

LONSDALE, Charles; *b* 5 July 1965, Oxford; *m* 2011, Maria Sadoyan; *Career* second sec Budapest 1990–93, first sec Moscow 1998–2003, dep head Afghanistan Gp FCO London 2003–05, dep head Human Rights, Democracy and Governance Gp FCO London 2005–2008, ambass to Repub of Armenia 2008–12, dep head UK Delgn to OSCE Vienna 2012–; *Style—* Mr Charles Lonsdale

LONSDALE, Prof Roger Harrison; s of Arthur John Lonsdale (d 1977), of Hornsea, E Yorks, and Phebe, *née* Harrison (d 2004); *b* 6 August 1934; *Educ* Hymers Coll Hull, Lincoln Coll Oxford (BA, DPhil); *m* 1, 8 May 1964 (m dis 1994), Anne Mary, da of Alexander Charles Menzies, of Harrow, Middx; 1 s (Charles John b 5 July 1965), 1 da (Katherine Georgina b 16 Dec 1966); m 2, 20 Dec 1999, Nicoletta Momigliano, da of Massimo Momigliano, of Milan, Italy; *Career* Nat Serv navigator RAF 1952–54; English Dept Yale Univ 1958–60, fell and tutor in English literature Balliol Coll Oxford 1963–2000 (Andrew Bradley jr res fell 1960–63), prof of English literature Univ of Oxford 1992–2000 (reader in English literature 1990–92); FRSL 1990, FBA 1991; *Books* Dr Charles Burney: A Literary Biography (1965); ed: The Poems of Gray, Collins and Goldsmith (1969), Vathek (by William Beckford, 1970), Dryden to Johnson (1971), The New Oxford Book of Eighteenth Century Verse (1984), The Poems of John Bampfylde (1988), Eighteenth Century Women Poets (1989), Samuel Johnson's The Lives of the Poets (2006); *Recreations* music, book collecting; *Style—* Prof Roger Lonsdale, FRSL, FBA; ✉ Balliol College, Oxford OX1 3BJ

LOOMBA, Baron (UK Life Peer 2011), of Moor Park in the County of Hertfordshire; Rajinder Paul (Raj) Loomba; CBE (2008); s of Shri Jagiri Lal Loomba (d 1954), and Shrimati Pushpa Wati Loomba (d 1992); *b* 13 November 1943, Dhilwan, Punjab, India; *Educ* DAV Coll Jalandhar, State Univ of Iowa; *m* 1966, Veena; 2 da (Reeta (Mrs Sarkar) b 5 Dec 1966, Roma b 10 May 1969), 1 s (Rinku b 1 Oct 1970); *Career* fndr and exec chm Rinku Gp Ltd, fndr chm and md India First Ltd; memb Cncl RIIA 2002–09, memb Pres's Cncl London First 2004–06 (memb Bd 2000–04); fndr and chm The Loomba Fndn 1997–, vice-patron The Gates 1998–, fndr patron World Punjabi Orgn 2002–, patron Children in Need India 2002–13, tstee Maharajah Ranjit Singh Tst 2004–, vice-pres Barnardo's 2005–, vice-pres Safer London Fndn 2006–12, chm Friends of the Three Faiths Forum 2007–, memb Devpt Bd Oxfam 2008–, fndr and chm of tstees Shrimati Pushpa Wati Loomba Meml, fndr and chm of tstees British Indian Golden Jubilee Banquet Fund; Hind Rattan Award 1991, Int Excellence Award 1991, Asian of the Year UK 1997, Pride of India Gold Medal 1998, Into Leadership Award 2000, Judges' Special Commendation Worldaware Business Award 2001, Beacon Prize 2004, highly commended New Initiative Beacon Prize 2004, Neville Shulman Charity Cup 2005 and 2012, Priyadarshni Acad Global Award 2006, Asian Who's Who Charity of the Year Award 2006, NRI Inst of India Achievers Award 2008, Chief Min of Punjab Life Time Achievers Award; Freeman City of London 2000; memb Rotary Int (Paul Harris fell 2005); FRSA; *Publications* Invisible Forgotten Suffering (2010), A Hidden Calamity (2011); *Recreations* walking, reading, cooking; *Clubs* Rotary (London); *Style—* The Lord Loomba, CBE; ✉ c/o Safdar Shah (PA) (☎ 020 8102 0351, e-mail safdar@theloombafoundation.org); Rinku Group plc, Loomba House, 622 Western Avenue, London W3 0TF (☎ 020 8896 9922, fax 020 8993 2736, e-mail raj@loomba.com, website www.theloombafoundation.org)

LOOSE, Helen Jane Elizabeth; da of Peter Loose, of London, and Barbara Loose; *b* 1966, Solihull; *Educ* C of E Coll for Girls Edgbaston, Univ of Manchester; *Career* slr; articled clerk Freshfields 1990–93, Cameron Markby Hewitt 1995–97, ptnr and head Environment Gp Ashurst 2000– (slr 1997–2000); former memb Cncl and treas UK Environmental Law Assoc, non-exec dir London First, memb Cncl Princes Tst London Region; MInstD; A Practical Guide to Environmental Issues in Commercial Property Transactions (2006); author of numerous articles; *Recreations* opera, skiing, tennis; *Style—* Ms Helen Loose; ✉ Ashurst, Broadwalk House, 5 Appold Street, London EC2A 2HA (☎ 020 7638 1111, fax 020 7638 1112)

LOPEZ, His Hon Judge Paul Anthony; s of Anthony William Lopez, of Wolverhampton, and late Lillian, *née* Rowley; *b* 22 October 1959; *Educ* Pendeford HS Wolverhampton, Univ of Birmingham (LLB); *m* 3 Nov 1984, Diana Douglas, da of Douglas Black (d 1982); 2 da (Antonia Charlotte Elizabeth b 10 May 1991, Miranda Annabelle Lucy b 22 Nov 1993); *Career* called to the Bar Middle Temple 1982; tenant St Ives Chambers 1983–2014, treas St Ive's Chambers 1996–2008; recorder of the Crown Court 2001–, family and civil recorder 2003–, public law family recorder 2009, dep judge of the High Court of Justice (Family Div) 2013–14 and (Family and Queen's Bench Divs) 2014–, circuit judge (Midland Circuit) 2014–; memb: Midland Circuit, Family Law Bar Assoc, Birmingham Family Law Bar Assoc, Personal Injury Bar Assoc, Birmingham Medico-Legal Soc, Shropshire Child Care Gp; memb: Nelson Soc, 1805 Club; chm Bd St Dominic's Sch Brewood 2005–08; *Recreations* horse riding, history, working, collecting Nelson memorabilia; *Style—* His Hon Judge Lopez; ✉ 5 Rectory Drive, Weston-under-Lizard, Shropshire TF11 8QQ (☎ and fax 01952 850252, mobile 07850 898591); Wolverhampton Combined Court Centre, Pipers Row, Wolverhampton and Birmingham Civil and Family Justice Centre, Bull Street, Birmingham

LOPRESTI, Giacomo (Jack); MP; *b* 23 August 1969, Bristol; *Career* cncllr Bristol City Cncl 1999–2007, MP (Cons) Filton and Bradley Stoke 2010–; *Style—* Jack Lopresti, Esq, MP; ✉ House of Commons, London SW1A 0AA

LORD, (Charles) Edward; OBE (2011), JP (Central London, 2002); s of Charles Andrew Lord, and Vivienne Marie, *née* Fairbank (now Mrs Brittain); *b* 13 January 1972, Littleborough, Lancs; *Educ* Bury GS, Univ of Essex, BPP Law Sch (dip); *Partner* Dr Meg John Barker; *Career* various fundraising and communications roles 1994–98, dir John Moores Univ Tst 1998–2000, devpt dir City Univ 2000–02, princ Edward Lord Conslts 2002–15, dir Edward Lord Ltd 2015–; admitted to Middle Temple 2008; memb Ct of Common Cncl City of London 2001– (chm Licensing Ctee 2010–13, dep chm Social Investment Bd 2012–

13, dep chm London 2012 Ctee 2010–12, chm Standards Ctee 2013–16, dep chm Establishment Ctee 2015–); memb Lib Dems: dep party treas 2005–06, memb Fed Fin & Admin Ctee 2011–; Local Govt Assoc: memb Improvement Bd 2004–13, lead memb for equality and social inclusion 2004–13, memb Nat Exec 2008–12; London Cncls: memb Capital Ambition Bd 2010– (chm 2011–), memb Ldrs' Ctee 2011–; non-exec dir: Local Partnerships LLP (formerly 4ps) 2005–16 (chm 2005–12), London Strategic Housing 2006–09, Whittington Hosp NHS Tst 2007–10 (dep chm 2008–10), Parkwood Hldgs plc 2011–12, Social Investment Business Ltd 2013–; non-exec chm Megalith Realty Ltd; FA: chm London Inclusion Advsy Gp 2013–, memb Inclusion Advsy Bd 2013–14, chm Anti-Discrimination Disciplinary Cmmn 2013–; memb: Nat Exec NUS 1994–96, Cncl Coll of Optometrists 2000–03, Refugee Cncl 2004–05, Cncl for the Registration of Forensic Practitioners 2006–09, Conduct and Competence Ctee Nursing and Midwifery Cncl 2008–13; chm Sir John Cass's Fndn Sch 2001–03, memb Ct Univ of Essex 2011–, chm Gp Bd Amateur Swimming Assoc 2013–15, memb Community Advsy Bd Pride in London 2015– (dep chm 2016–); tstee: Br Youth Cncl 1995–97, City Parochial Fndn/Tst for London 2001–05 and 2015–, Anne Frank Tst 2006–09, Westminster Challenge 2006–10, St Andrew Holborn Charity 2009–14, City Bridge Tst 2010–, BiCon Continuity 2011–16, Albert Kennedy Tst 2012–13, BiUK 2013–; govr: GSMD 2002–09, Bury GS 2004–08, Christ's Hosp Fndn 2007–13, City of London Sch 2009–; Freeman Worshipful Co of Fletchers, Freeman Worshipful Co of Leathersellers, Liveryman Worshipful Co of Broderers; *Publications* Civic Ceremonial (co-ed, 2009); *Recreations* music, theatre, cinema, cricket and football (as a spectator), urban and country walking, gastronomy, current affairs, heritage, freemasonry; *Clubs* Guildhall (chm 2009–11), Rochdale Assoc Football, Soho House, Lord's Taverners, Middlesex CCC, MCC; *Style—* Edward Lord, Esq, OBE, JP; ✉ Members' Room, City of London Corporation, Guildhall, London EC2P 2EJ (e-mail city@edwardlord.org, website www.edwardlord.org, Twitter @EdwardLord)

LORD, Geoffrey; OBE (1989); s of Frank Lord (d 1978), of Rochdale, and Edith, *née* Sanderson; *b* 24 February 1928; *Educ* Rochdale GS, Univ of Bradford (MA); *m* 15 Sept 1955, Jean; 1 da (Karen Janet b 1959), 1 s (Andrew Nicholas b 1962); *Career* Midland Bank Ltd (AIB) 1944–58, Gtr Manchester Probation Serv 1958–77 (dep chief probation offr 1974–77); sec and treas Carnegie UK Tst 1977–93; fndr and vice-pres The Adapt Tst 1992–2007; chm of tstees Home Start UK 1995–97, chm Unemployed Voluntary Action Fund 1991–95, former chm Pollock Meml Missionary Tst, former vice-pres The Selcare Tst; tstee: Edinburgh Voluntary Orgns Tst 1997–2015, Nat Youth Orch of Scotland 1998–2013, The Playright Scotland Tst 1998–2007, Murrayfield Dementia Project 2006–13, Faith in Older People Ltd 2007–13, BSS Ltd 2009–15; memb Ctee Scottish Arts Cncl Lottery Ctee 1994–98, former pres Centre for Environmental Interpretation; hon fell Manchester Metropolitan Univ 1987; FRSA 1985; *Books* The Arts and Disabilities (1981), Access for Disabled People to Arts Premises – The Journey Sequence (jtly, 2003), Cathedrals for the Curious – An Introduction to Cathedrals, Minsters and Abbeys in Britain (2011); *Recreations* arts; *Clubs* New (Edinburgh); *Style—* Geoffrey Lord, Esq, OBE; ✉ 9 Craigleith View, Edinburgh EH4 3JZ

LORD, Jonathan George Caladine; MP; s of His Hon John Lord (d 1994), and June Ann, *née* Caladine; *b* 17 September 1962, Oldham, Lancs; *Educ* Shrewsbury Sch, Kent Sch CT USA, Merton Coll Oxford (MA); *m* 2000, Caroline, *née* Commander; 1 s (John Franklin Commander), 1 da (Katherine Isabelle Rosalie); *Career* dir Saatchi & Saatchi 1998–2000; MP (Cons) Woking 2010–; cncllr: City of Westminster 1994–2002 (dep ldr 1998–2000), Surrey CC 2009–11; chm Guildford Cons Assoc 2006–10; *Recreations* cricket, theatre, walking; *Style—* Jonathan Lord, Esq, MP; ✉ House of Commons, London SW1A 0AA (☎ 020 7219 6913, e-mail jonathan.lord.mp@parliament.uk)

LORD, Sir Michael Nicholson; see: Framlingham, Lord

LORENZ, Andrew Peter Morrice; s of Hans Viktor Lorenz (d 1985), and Catherine Jesse Cairns, *née* James; *b* 22 June 1955; *Educ* Stamford Sch, Worcester Coll Oxford (Open Exhibitioner, MA, sports and arts ed Cherwell); *m* 1 Sept 1988, Helen Marianne, da of Brig John Malcolm Alway; 2 s (James Andrew George b 13 Jan 1994, Harry Alexander Lewis b 8 June 1995); *Career* successively grad trainee, news reporter, labour reporter, educn corr then industrial corr The Journal Newcastle 1978–82, business corr The Scotsman 1982–86, dep city ed The Sunday Telegraph 1988–89 (City reporter 1986–88); Sunday Times: industrial ed 1989–91, assoc business ed 1991–94, dep business ed 1994–95, business ed 1995–2000; FTI Strategic Communications 2000– (currently sr md); *Books* A Fighting Chance – The Revival and Future of British Manufacturing Industry (1989), BZW: The First Ten Years (1996); *Recreations* cricket, rugby, football, film; *Style—* Andrew Lorenz, Esq; ✉ FTI Consulting, Holborn Gate, 26 Southampton Buildings, London WC2A 1PB

LORENZ, Anthony Michael; s of Andre Lorenz (d 1986), and Mitzi Lorenz (d 1999); *b* 7 December 1947; *Educ* Arnold House Sch, Charterhouse; *m* 1, 1 Feb 1986 (m dis), Suzanna Jane, da of Louis Solomon; 1 s (David Alexander b 5 June 1986), 1 da (Charlaine Alexandra b 15 Nov 1978); m 2, 30 Nov 1999 (m dis 2013), Jane Knights; *Career* former: sr ptnr Baker Lorenz Estate Agents, exec vice-chm Dunlop Heywood Lorenz; currently sr ptnr The Lorenz Consultancy; former chm Fundraising Ctee Multiple Sclerosis Soc; *Recreations* flying, polo, shooting, skiing; *Clubs* Hurlingham, Knepp Castle Polo, Cowdray Park Polo; *Style—* Anthony Lorenz, Esq; ✉ 24 Hanover Square, London W1S 1JD

LORIMER, Prof (Andrew) Ross; CBE (2004); *b* 5 May 1937; *Educ* Uddingston GS, HS of Glasgow, Univ of Glasgow (MD); *m* 1963, Fiona, *née* Marshall; *Career* conslt physician and cardiologist Royal Infirmary Glasgow 1972–2001; memb: Assoc of Physicians of the UK, Br Cardiac Soc; Hon DUniv Glasgow 2001; FRCP, FRCPI, FRACP, FACP, FCPS (Bangladesh), FRCPGlas (memb Cncl, pres 2000–03), FRCPEd, FMedSci, FFPH 2002, FRCS 2003, FRCSE 2003, FCPC(Ceylon) 2003, fell Coll of Physicians of South Africa (FCP(SA)) 2004, FRCSI 2005; *Books* Cardiovascular Therapy (1980), Preventive Cardiology (1990); *Style—* Prof Ross Lorimer, CBE; ✉ Woodlands Cottage, 12 Uddingston Road, Bothwell G71 8PH (☎ 01698 852156)

LORISTON-CLARKE, Anne Jennifer Frances (Jennie); MBE (1979); *née* Bullen; da of Lt Col John Fitzherbert Symes Bullen, RHA (d 1966), of Charmouth, Dorset, and Anne Harris St John (d 1963); *b* 22 January 1943; *Educ* privately; *m* 27 Feb 1965, Anthony Grahame Loriston-Clarke, s of Capt Geoffrey Neame Loriston-Clarke, CBE, RN; 2 da (Anne Frances b 19 Jan 1966, Elizabeth Jane b 27 July 1970); *Career* horse breeder, equestrian dressage; winner: City of London Cup for Best Rider 1953–56, Jr Jumping Championships Richmond Royal Horse Show 1955, Pony Club Horse Trials Championships; joined GB Dressage Team 1964; winner 6 World Cup qualifiers, Bronze medal World Dressage Championships (Goodwood) 1978; memb Br Olympic Team: Munich 1972, Montreal 1976, Los Angeles 1984, Seoul 1988; stud owner/mangr; developed The Catherston Stud, breeding competition Warmblood horses, pioneered the use of chilled and frozen semen in horses in the UK, international trainer and judge, author of 4 books and videos on dressage, longreining and training of young horses; chair Br Dressage 2007 and 2013, chair Sports Horse Breeding GB 2012; NPSDip, Duke of Edinburgh Gold Award, Animal Health Tst Special Award for Servs to the Equestrian Indust 2000; Br Horse Soc Queen's Award for Outstanding Services to Equestrianism 2006; Hon Freeman Worshipful Co of Saddlers 1981, Freeman Worshipful Co of Farriers 2001; fell Int Dressage Trainers Club 2010; FBHS; *Recreations* reading, writing, swimming, singing, walking the dog by bicycle; *Style—* Mrs Jennie Loriston-Clarke, MBE; ✉ Catherston Stud, Croft Farm, Over Wallop, Stockbridge, Hampshire SO20 8HX (☎ 01264 782716, fax 01264 782717, e-mail catherston@btconnect.com or jennielc@btconnect.com, website www.catherstonstud.com)

LOTAY, Avtar; *Educ* Univ of Bristol (BA, Dip Arch); *Career* architect; project offr Royal Coll of Art; Rogers Stirk Harbour and Partners (formerly Richard Rogers Partnership): joined 1986, assoc dir 1996–; *Projects* incl: Billingsgate Market, European Ct of Human Rights Strasbourg, Channel 4 TV HQ, St Katharine's Dock, Farnborough Air Terminal and Masterplan, Grosvenor Road Redevelopment, Scientific Generics Cambridge, King's Dock Liverpool, Lloyd's Register of Shipping, Antwerp Law Courts, One Hyde Park London, Barangaroo Sydney; *Style—* Avtar Lotay, Esq; ✉ Rogers Stirk Harbour and Partners, Thames Wharf, Rainville Road, London W6 9HA

LOTEN, Graeme Neil; s of Richard Maurice, of Portsmouth, and Brenda Ivy Elizabeth, *née* Shaw, of Portsmouth; *b* 10 March 1959; *Educ* Portsmouth GS, Univ of Liverpool (BA); *Career* HM Dip Serv: FCO 1981–83, UK delg to NATO Brussels 1983–86, Br Embassy Khartoum 1986–87, Br Embassy The Hague 1988–92, dep head of mission Br Embassy Almaty 1993–97, ambass to Rwanda 1998–2001 (concurrently accredited to Burundi), ambass to Mali 2001–03, ambass to Tajikistan 2004–09; Fondation Hirondelle Sierra Leone 2009–11, Fondation Hirondelle Democratic Repub of Congo 2011–12, exec dir NGO Imbabazi Rwanda 2013–15; *Recreations* tennis, travel, Portsmouth FC; *Style—* Mr Graeme Loten; ✉ e-mail graemeloten@gmail.com

LOTHIAN, 13 Marquess of (S 1701); Michael Andrew Foster Jude Kerr; PC (1996), QC (Scot 1996), DL (Roxburgh, Ettrick and Lauderdale, 1990); also Lord Newbottle (S 1591), Lord Jedburgh (S 1622), Earl of Lothian, Lord Ker of Newbattle (*sic*) (both S 1631), Earl of Ancram (1633), Viscount of Briene, Lord Ker of Newbottle, Oxnam, Jedburgh, Dolphinstoun and Nisbet (all S 1701), Baron Ker of Kersheugh (UK 1821), and Baron Kerr of Monteviot (Life Peer UK 2010), of Monteviot in Roxburghshire; s of 12 Marquess of Lothian (d 2004), and Antonella Reuss (Marchioness of Lothian, OBE) (d 2007), *née* Newland; *b* 7 July 1945; *Educ* Ampleforth, ChCh Oxford (MA), Univ of Edinburgh (LLB); *m* 1975, Lady Jane Fitzalan-Howard, da of 16 Duke of Norfolk, KG, GCVO, GBE, TD, PC (d 1975), and Lavinia, Duchess of Norfolk, LG, CBE (d 1995); 2 da (Lady Clare b 1979, Lady Mary b 1981); *Heir* bro, Lord Ralph Kerr; *Career* advocate (Scot) 1970; MP (Cons): Berwickshire and E Lothian Feb-Sept 1974, Edinburgh S 1979–87 (also contested 1987), Devizes 1992–2010; chm Cons Party in Scotland 1980–83 (vice-chm 1975–80), Parly under-sec Scottish Office (Home Affairs and Environment) 1983–87, Parly under sec NI Office 1993–94, min of state NI Office 1994–97, shadow Cabinet oppn spokesman for constitutional affrs 1997–98, chm Cons Pty 1998–2001 (dep chm 1998), shadow sec of state for Foreign and Cwlth Affrs 2001–03, dep ldr Cons Pty 2001–05, shadow sec of state for Int Affrs and shadow foreign sec 2003–05, memb Cons Pty Policy Bd 2001–05; memb Public Accounts Ctee 1992–93, memb Select Ctee on Energy 1979–83, memb Intelligence & Security Ctee 2006–10 and 2011–; chm: Global Strategy Forum, Gulf Policy Forum, Middle East Conslts (MEC) 2013–; chm Northern Corporate Communications Ltd 1989–91, memb Bd Scottish Homes 1988–90; chm Scottish Cncl of Ind Schs 1988–90; govr Napier Poly of Edinburgh 1989–90, pres Environmental Medicine Fndn 1988–92, chm Waverley Housing Tst 1988–90, pres Kennet and Avon Canal Tst 2009–11; Freeman City of Gibraltar 2011, Freeman of Devizes 2011; Grand Prior Military and Hospitaller Order of St Lazarus of Jerusalem (England and Wales) 2013–; GCLJ 2013; *Publications* numerous pamphlets; *Recreations* photography, folksinging, fishing; *Clubs* New (Edinburgh), Pratt's, Beefsteak, White's; *Style—* The Most Hon the Marquess of Lothian, PC, QC, DL; ✉ Monteviot, Jedburgh, Scotland TD8 6UQ

L

LOTT, Dame Felicity Ann Emwhyla; DBE (1996, CBE 1990); da of John Albert Lott, and Iris Emwhyla, *née* Williams; *b* 8 May 1947; *Educ* Pate's Girls GS Cheltenham, RHC Univ of London (BA), RAM (LRAM); *m* 1, 22 Dec 1973 (m dis 1982), Robin Mavesyn Golding; m 2, 19 Jan 1984, Gabriel Leonard Woolf, s of Alec Woolf; 1 da (Emily b 19 June 1984); *Career* opera singer, debut in The Magic Flute (ENO) 1975; pres Br Youth Opera; princ appearances: ENO, Glyndebourne, Covent Garden, WNO, Scottish Opera, Paris, Brussels, Hamburg, Chicago, Munich, NY, Vienna, Milan, San Francisco, Madrid; recordings for: EMI, Decca, Harmonia Mundi Chandos, Erato, Hyperion; Wigmore Medal 2010, ISM Distinguished Musician Award 2014; hon fell Royal Holloway Univ of London 1994, hon fell Guildhall Sch of Music and Drama 2014; Hon DMus Univ of Sussex 1989, Hon DLitt Loughborough Univ 1996, DMus (hc) Univ of London 1997, DMus RSAMD 1998, Hon DMus Univ of Leicester 2000, DMus (hc) Univ of Oxford 2001, hon doctorate Paris Sorbonne 2012; FRAM 1986, FRCM 2006; Chevalier de l'Ordre des Arts et des Lettres (France) 1992, Officier dans l'Ordre des Arts et des Lettres 2000, Chevalier de la Légion d'Honneur 2001, Bayerische Kammersängerin 2003; *Recreations* reading, gardening; *Style—* Dame Felicity Lott, DBE; ✉ c/o Askonas Holt, Lincoln House, 300 High Holborn, London WC1V 7JH (☎ 020 7400 1700, fax 020 7400 1799, website www.felicitylott.de)

LOUBET, Bruno Jean Roger; s of Clement Loubet, of Libourne Gironde, France, and Mauricette, *née* Lacroix (d 1989); *b* 8 October 1961; *m* 27 Dec 1983, Catherine, da of Jacques Mougeol; 3 da (Laeticia b 4 Aug 1985, Laura Claire b 8 April 1987, Chloé b 28 May 1998); *Career* lycée hotelier 1976–79; commis de cuisine: Hyatt Regency Brussels 1979–80, Restaurant Copenhague 1980–82; second maître Nat French Navy and chef to the Admiral TCD Ouragan 1982, commis chef Tante Claire London 1982; head chef: Gastronome One Fulham 1982–85, Le Manoir aux Quat'Saisons Great Milton 1985–86; chef mangr Petit Blanc Oxford 1986–88, chef Four Seasons Restaurant Inn On The Park 1988–93, chef/patron Bistro Bruno London 1993–96, opened L'Odeon London 1995, conslt Loubet Cuisine 1997–, devpt chef Gruppo Group 1998–, exec chef Isola 1999–2001, prop Bruno's Tables Toowong 2002–, exec chef Baguette Restaurant 2007–, chef-patron Bistrot Bruno Loubet 2010– (highest new entry Restaurant Magazine 2010), exec chef Grain Store King's Cross 2014– (Sustainable Restaurant of the Year 2014); Young Chef of The Year Good Food Guide 1985, Acorn Award Caterer & Hotelkeeper 1988, Michelin Star 1990, Chef of the Year Courier Mail 2004 and 2005; memb Académie Culinaire de France GB 1990; *Publications* Bruno Loubet: Cuisine Courante (1991), Bistrot Bruno: Cooking from L'Odeon (1995), Mange Tout (2014); *Recreations* gardening; *Style—* Bruno Loubet, Esq; ✉ BCL Cuisine, 81 Church Street, Langford, Bedfordshire SG18 9QA (☎ 07897 466539)

LOUDON, Alasdair John; WS (1987); s of John Duncan Ott Loudon, of Edinburgh, and Nancy Beaton, *née* Mann; *b* 7 April 1956, Edinburgh; *Educ* Edinburgh Acad, Univ of Dundee (LLB); *m* Angela Elizabeth Entwistle; 1 da (Susannah Mary b 8 Dec 1984), 2 s (Malcolm John William b 17 March 1986, Paul Durward Mann b 16 Feb 1989); *Career* slr; legal apprenticeship Tods, Murray & Jamieson 1978–80, ptnr Warner & Co Slrs 1982–92 (asst slr 1980–82), fndr and ptnr Loudons WS 1992–2001, ptnr Turcan Connell Slrs 2001–; pres Edinburgh Bar Assoc 1996–98; memb: Law Soc of Scot 1980, WS Soc; fell Int Acad of Matrimonial Lawyers; *Recreations* food and wine, golf, watching football; *Clubs* Bruntsfield Links Golfing Soc, Luffness New Golf, Royal Wimbledon Golf, Hon Co of Edinburgh Golfers; *Style—* Alasdair Loudon, Esq, WS; ✉ Turcan Connell, Princes Exchange, 1 Earl Grey Street, Edinburgh EH3 9EE (☎ 0131 228 8111, fax 0131 228 8118, e-mail ajl@turcanconnell.com)

LOUDON, George Ernest; *b* 19 November 1942; *Educ* Christlijk Lyceum Zeist Holland, Balliol Coll Oxford (BA), Johns Hopkins Univ Washington DC (MA); *m* Angela; 1 da (b 1970), 1 s (b 1972); *Career* fin analyst Lazard Frères & CIE Paris 1967–68, project mgmnt Ford Foundation NY and Jakarta 1968–71, project mgmnt McKinsey & Co Amsterdam 1971–76, memb Bd of MDs Amsterdam-Rotterdam Bank NV (Amro Bank) Amsterdam 1983–88 (gen mangr New Issue and Syndicate Dept 1976–83), dir Midland Bank plc

1988–92, chief exec Midland Montagu Ltd 1988–92 (chm 1991–92); chm: Altius Holdings Ltd 1999–2014, Pall Mall Capital Ltd 2001–14, Helix Assocs Ltd until 2005, GAM Diversity III 2005–, GAM Diversity Inc 2014–; dir GAM Diversity II 2013–; non-exec dir: Geveke NV (Netherlands) 1985–2001, Harrison/Parrott Ltd 1993–, Arjo Wiggins Appleton plc 1993–2000, M&G Group plc 1993–94, Global Asset Management Ltd 1994–99, CMG Ltd 1998–2002, LogicaCMG plc 2002–07, Evolution (formerly Beeson Gregory Group plc) 2001–04; former vice-chm: Amsterdam Stock Exchange, Samuel Montagu & Co Ltd; former treas Stichting 1986–88; memb Bd Trinkaus und Burkhardt (Germany), former chm and chief exec Euromobiliare (Italy); memb Cncl of Japan Festival 1990; memb: Acquisitions Ctee MMOMA City of Amsterdam, Bd of Tstees Netherlands Royal Coll of Art, van den Berch van Heemstede Stichting; former tstee Tate Fndn, former tstee London Library, former tstee South Bank Fndn, tstee and former dir Galapagos Conservation Tst, tstee Royal Botanic Gardens Kew 2007–15, memb Bd Fndn and Friends Royal Botanic Gardens Kew 2009–; *Books* Object Lessons (2015); *Style*— George Loudon, Esq; ✉ PO Box 34865, London W8 7WL

LOUDON, James Rushworth Hope; DL (Kent); s of Francis William Hope Loudon (d 1985), and Lady Prudence Katharine Patton, *née* Jellicoe (d 2000); *b* 19 March 1943; *Educ* Eton, Magdalene Coll Cambridge (BA), Stanford Business Sch (MBA); *m* 17 May 1975, Jane Gavina, *née* Fryett; 1 da (Antonia Louise Cameron b 1977), 2 s (Hugo John Hope b 1978, Alexander Guy Rushworth b 1980); *Career* fin dir Blue Circle Industries plc 1987–2001 (joined 1977); chm Caledonia Investments plc 2008–12 (non-exec dir 1995–2012); non-exec dir: Lafarge Malayan Cement 1989–2004, James Hardie Industries NV 2002–08; govr: Univ of Greenwich 2001–10 (dep chm), Royal Sch for Deaf Children 2002–05, Caldecott Fndn 2002–12, Kent, Surrey and Sussex Air Ambulance Tst 2005–, Canterbury Cathedral Tst 2005– (dep chm); High Sheriff Kent 2004–05; Hon DUniv Greenwich; *Recreations* golf, cricket, opera, skiing, cabinet making; *Clubs* MCC, Rye Golf, Royal St George's Golf, Swinley Forest Golf; *Style*— James Loudon, Esq, DL; ✉ Olantigh, Wye, Ashford, Kent TN25 5EW (☎ 01233 812294)

LOUDON, Prof Rodney; s of Albert Loudon (d 1965), and Doris Helen, *née* Blane (d 1980); *b* 25 July 1934; *Educ* Bury GS, BNC Oxford (MA, DPhil); *m* 6 June 1960, Mary Anne, da of Eugene Philips; 1 da (Anne Elizabeth b 1961), 1 s (Peter Thomas b 1964); *Career* postdoctoral fell Univ of Calif Berkeley 1959–60, scientific civil servant RRE Malvern 1960–65, Bell Laboratories Murray Hill New Jersey 1965–66, prof of physics Univ of Essex 1967–2007 (reader 1966–67, emeritus prof 2008–), BT Laboratories 1984 and 1989–95; visiting prof: Yale Univ 1975, Univ of Calif Irvine 1980, École Polytechnique Lausanne 1985, Univ of Rome 1988 and 1996, Univ Libre de Bruxelles 1990, Univ of Strathclyde 1998–2012, Univ of Erlangen 1999–2002; chm Bd of Eds Optica Acta 1984–87; Thomas Young Medal and Prize Inst of Physics 1987, Max Born Award of the Optical Soc of America 1992, Alexander von Humboldt Research Award 1998; fell Optical Soc of America 1994; FRS 1987; *Books* The Quantum Theory of Light (1973, 3 edn 2000), Scattering of Light by Crystals (with W Hayes, 1978), Introduction to the Properties of Condensed Matter (with D J Barber, 1989); *Style*— Prof Rodney Loudon, FRS; ✉ 3 Gaston Street, East Bergholt, Colchester, Essex CO7 6SD (☎ 01206 298550, e-mail loudr@essex.ac.uk)

LOUGHBOROUGH, Archdeacon of; *see:* Stanes, Ven Ian Thomas

LOUGHHEAD, Prof John; OBE (2011); *Educ* Imperial Coll London; *Career* former corp vice-pres of technol and intellectual property Alstom Paris, former exec dir UKERC, currently chief scientific advsr Dept for Business, Energy and Industrial Strategy; UK memb European Energy Research Alliance, memb European Advsy Gp on Energy, non-exec dir Miny of Defence R&D Devpt Bd, co-chair Energy Research Partnership, dir Carbon Mgmnt Canada, chair Engrg Policy Ctee Royal Acad of Engrg; hon prof Cardiff Univ; Freeman City of London; hon fell Queen Mary Univ of London, Hon DSc Keele Univ; CEng, FREng, FCGI, FIET (past-pres), FIMechE, FRSA; *Style*— Prof John Loughhead, OBE; ✉ BEIS, 1 Victoria Street, London SW1H 0ET

LOUGHREY, (Stephen Victor) Patrick; s of Eddie Loughrey (d 1979), and Mary, *née* Griffin; *b* 29 December 1955; *Educ* Loreto Coll Milford Donegal, Univ of Ulster (BA), Queen's Univ Belfast (MA, PGCE); *m* 4 July 1978, Patricia, da of Thomas Kelly (d 1984); 1 s (Stephen b 26 Dec 1980), 2 da (Joanne b 26 Feb 1982, Christine b 10 June 1985); *Career* teacher St Colm's HS Draperstown 1978–84; BBC Northern Ireland: joined as prodr 1984, head of educnl broadcasting 1988–91, head of programmes 1991–94, controller 1994–2000, dir Nations and Regions 2000–10; warden (vice-chllr) Goldsmiths Univ of London 2010–; FRSA; *Books* Ordnance Survey of Ballinascreen (ed, 1981), The People of Ireland (ed, 1988); *Recreations* talking; *Clubs* Athanaeum, Century; *Style*— Patrick Loughrey, Esq; ✉ Goldsmiths, University of London, New Cross, London SE14 6NW

LOUGHTON, David Clifford; CBE (2010); s of Clifford Loughton (d 1973) of Harrow, Middx, and Hazel Loughton; *b* 28 January 1954; *Educ* Roxeth Manor Sch Harrow, Technical Colls in Harrow, Watford and Southall; *m* 1986, Deborah, da of George Wellington; 1 da (Georgina Anna b 12 July 1987), 1 s (Theodore David b 12 July 1990); *Career* asst hosp engr Hillingdon Area HA 1974–76, hosp engr Herts Area HA 1976–78, dir and gen mangr Ducost Ltd 1978–83, divnl mangr GEC Electrical Projects 1984–86, chief exec Walsgrave Hosp NHS Tst (now Univ Hosps Coventry and Warwickshire NHS Tst) 1986–2002, devpt dir InHealth Gp of Cos 2002–04, chief exec Royal Wolverhampton Hosps NHS Tst 2004–; memb: Nat Cncl NHS Confederation 2007–, Advsy Bd NHS Nat Inst for Health Research 2007–; chm Coventry and Warwickshire Educn & Trg Consortium (NHS) 1996–; memb: Inst of Health Services Mgmnt; *Recreations* country pursuits; *Style*— David Loughton, Esq, CBE; ✉ The Royal Wolverhampton Hospitals NHS Trust, Hollybush House, New Cross Hospital, Wolverhampton WV10 0QP (☎ 01902 695951)

LOUGHTON, Timothy Paul (Tim); MP; s of Rev Michael Loughton, and Pamela, *née* Brandon; *b* 30 May 1962; *Educ* The Priory Sch Lewes, Univ of Warwick (BA), Clare Coll Cambridge; *m* Elizabeth Juliet, da of John B MacLachlan; 1 s (Hector b 14 Aug 1994), 2 da (Freya b 3 April 1996, Mathilda b 8 Dec 1997); *Career* dir Fleming Private Asset Management 1992–2000 (joined 1984), non-exec dir Netlink Internet Services 1995–99; MP (Cons) E Worthing and Shoreham 1997– (Parly candidate Sheffield Brightside 1992); oppn frontbench spokesman for the regions, urban regeneration, housing and poverty 2000–01, oppn frontbench spokesman on health 2001–07; shadow min for Children 2003–10, Parly under-sec for children and families 2010–12; memb: Environmental Audit Select Ctee 1997–2001, Finance Bill Standing Ctee 1997 and 1998, European Scrutiny C Standing Ctee 2000–01; chm All Pty Parly Gp on: Wholesale Financial Services and Markets 2005–10 (vice-chm 2003–05), the British Museum, Tibet, Wine and Spirits, Conception to Age Two – the first 1001 days; jt chm All Pty Gp on: Mental Health, Children, Mindfulness; vice-chm All Pty Gp on: Cardiac Risk in the Young 2009, Autism, Youth, Digital Crime, Missing Persons, Ethiopia, Child Protection, Looked After Children, Parents and Families; treas: Parly Maritime Gp until 2010, All-Pty Parly Gp Archaeology until 2010, All-Pty Parly Gp on Foetal Alcohol; sec All-Pty Parly Gp on: Switzerland, Young People & Social Technol; chm Conservative Disability Gp 1998–2006; memb: Centre for Policy Studies, Inst of Econ Affrs, Tibet Action (UK), Jt Ctee on Financial Services and Markets 1999; pres: Shoreham Cons Club; pres Ropetackle Centre Tst; patron: St Barnabas Hospice Worthing, League of Friends Worthing Hosp, League of Friends Southlands Hosp, Worthing Hockey Club, West Grinstead and Dist Ploughing and Agric Soc, Worthing Fairtrade Town, Electric Storm Youth; pres Southwick Camra Club; memb Ct Univ of Sussex; capt Lords and Commons Hockey team; MSI (Dip), FSA 2015; *Recreations* archaeology, skiing, tennis, hockey, wine; *Style*— Tim Loughton, Esq, MP; ✉ House of Commons, London SW1A 0AA (☎ 020 7219 4471, fax 020 7219 0461, e-mail loughtont@parliament.uk, website www.timloughton.com)

LOULOUDIS, Hon Mrs (Madeleine Mary); LVO (1997); *née* Dillon; 4 but 3 survg da (twin) of 20 Viscount Dillon (d 1979); *b* 29 October 1957; *m* 4 March 1989, Leonard Constantine Louloudis, o s of Constantine Louloudis; 1 s (Constantine Michael, *qv* (Olympic rower and GB World Champion) b 15 Sept 1991), 1 da (Theodora Catherine Lily b 6 July 1993); *Career* Lady in Waiting to HRH The Princess Royal 1997– (asst private sec 1988–97); *Style*— The Hon Mrs Louloudis, LVO; ✉ 66 Westbourne Terrace, London W2 3UJ

LOULOUDIS, Constantine; s of Leonard Constantine Louloudis, and Hon Madeleine Mary Louloudis, LVO, *née* Dillon, *qv*; *b* 15 September 1991, London; *Educ* Eton (King's scholar), Univ of Oxford (BA); *Career* rower; achievements incl: Gold medal (men's coxless four) World Jr Rowing Championships 2009, boat race wins (for Oxford) 2011, 2013, 2014 and 2015, Gold medal (men's coxless pair) World U23 Rowing Championships 2011, Bronze medal (men's eight) Olympic Games 2012, Gold medal (men's eight) World Rowing Championships 2014 and 2015, Gold medal (men's four) Olympic Games 2016; *Clubs* Oxford Univ Boat; *Style*— Constantine Louloudis, Esq

LOUSADA, Charles Terence; DL (2008); s of Charles Rochford Lousada (d 1988), and Elizabeth, *née* Shaw (d 2006); *b* 21 September 1938, Farnborough, Hants; *Educ* Cokethorpe; *m* 1962 (m dis 1974); 1 s (Simon Charles b 1963), 1 da (Elizabeth Natasha (Mrs Pollard) b 1964); *Career* office boy January's estate agents Cambridge 1953, prop estate agency 1965–74, md Lousada plc 1969–; dir Imperial Bathroom 1990–, dir 20 other property cos; farms in SA; tstee of several local charities; former chm Buy British campaign; High Sheriff Beds 1997–98; *Recreations* all country sports, helicopter pilot/owner; *Clubs* RAC, Kirtlington Polo; *Style*— Charles Lousada, Esq, DL; ✉ Lousada plc, Crawley Park, Husborne Crawley, Bedford MK43 0UU (☎ 01908 282860, fax 01908 282861, e-mail charles@lousada.com)

LOUSADA, Sandra Reignier; da of Sir Anthony Baruh Lousada (d 1994), of London, and his 1 w, Jocelyn Herbert (d 2003), da of late Sir Alan Herbert, CH; *b* 29 June 1938, Chiswick, London; *Educ* St Paul's Girls' Sch, Regent St Poly, Central St Martin's; *m* 1 Jan 1965, Brian Richards (d 2004), son of Alexander Hodgson Richards; 1 s (Sam b 12 June 1966), 1 da (Polly b 17 May 1968); *Career* asst photographer Scaioni Studios 1956–59; freelance photographer 1959–63; work for magazines incl: Queen Magazine, Tatler, Nova, Brides, Vogue, Elle (Paris), Marie Claire (Paris), Vanity Fair, Mademoiselle and Glamour Magazines (NYC); work for English Stage Co incl: John Osborne's Luther and Wesker Trilogy; film work incl: The Loneliness of the Long Distance Runner, Tom Jones, The Charge of the Light Brigade; travelled and worked in USA, Japan, India and Russia; joined Whitecross Studios 1963–81; advtg work for agencies incl: J Walter Thompson, Ogilvy Benson & Mather, Collett Dickinson & Pearce; chm Assoc of Photographers (AOP) 1998–99; editorial work for most main magazines and some publishers in London and New York; Susan Griggs Agency 1981–94, frequent travel to Europe and India; current photographic work incl portraits, children, crafts, fashion, health and beauty for number of London magazines, book publishers, design gps and advtg agencies; exhibition Nat Theatre Lyttleton Gallery 2009, exhibition Public Faces Private Places (Theatre Royal Plymouth) 2010, exhibition Nat Portrait Gallery 2012, Nat Portrait Garden Photographer in Focus; work for charities: Wellbeing (formerly Birthright), Great Ormond Street Hosp for Sick Children, Tommy Campaign, Peper Harow Fndn; chm Assoc of Photographers 1999; Silver Award Assoc of Photographers 1988, Sainsbury Baby Book Award 2001, Features Photographer of the Year Award Garden Writers' Guild 2003; *Publications* London's Parks and Gardens (2003), Hampstead Heath (2007), Public Faces Private Places (2009). London Light (2010), Regents Park (2010); *Style*— Ms Sandra Lousada; ✉ 49 Parkholme Road, London E8 3AQ (☎ 020 7249 4211, e-mail sandra@sandralousada.com); c/o Bo Steer (☎ 07711 007717, website www.sandralousada.com)

LOUVEAUX, Bertrand Jean-Philippe Francois; s of Xavier Louveaux, of Belgium, and Evelyne, *née* Carbonnelle; *b* 28 April 1967, Brussels; *Educ* Rugby, LSE (MSc); *m* 3 Sept 1994 Sarah Jane, *née* Bowen; 1 s (Tristan b 17 Nov 1997), 1 da (Amelie b 22 April 1999); *Career* slr; ptnr Slaughter and May 2001– (joined 1992); *Style*— Bertrand Louveaux, Esq; ✉ Slaughter and May, 1 Bunhill Row, London EC1Y 8YY (☎ 020 7090 4173, e-mail bertrand.louveaux@slaughterandmay.com)

LOVE, Andrew; s of James Love (d 1995), and Olive, *née* Mills (d 1997); *b* 21 March 1949; *Educ* Greenock HS, Univ of Strathclyde (BSc); *m* March 1983, Ruth Lesley, da of late Jack Rosenthal; *Career* sec CRS (London) Political Ctee 1985–92, parly offr Co-op Pty 1992–97; MP (Lab Co-op) Edmonton 1997–2015 (Parly candidate 1992); PPS to min of state Dept of Health and DTI 2001–05, PPS to Local Govt Min 2008–09; memb: Public Accounts Ctee 1997–2001, Deregulation Ctee 2000–01, Regulatory Reform Ctee 2001–05, Treasy Select Ctee 2005–15; chm All-Pty Parly Gp for Building Socs and Fin Mutuals 1997–2002, co-chair All-Pty Gp on Homelessness and Housing Need 2001–09, sec All-Pty Solvent Abuse Gp 1997–2001, co-chair All-Pty Sri Lanka Gp 2004– (sec 2000–04), chm All-Pty Small Businesses Gp 2005–10 (sec 1999–2005); vice-chm Backbench ODPM Ctee 2005–10, chm Backbench Treasy Ctee 2009–15; London Borough of Haringey: cncllr 1980–86, chm of fin 1984–85, chm of housing 1985–86; patron Beck House, patron HEAL Cancer Charity 2002–, vice-patron Helen Rollason Cancer Centre Appeal; memb: NE Thames RHA 1988–90, Unite, Fabian Soc, War on Want, Co-operative Gp; FCIS 2000, FRSA 2003; *Recreations* golf, opera, reading; *Style*— Andrew Love, Esq

LOVE, Kevin; s of Richard Love, of Bognor Regis, and Shirley, *née* Avery (d 1993); *b* 10 March 1977, Oxford; *Educ* Chichester HS; *Children* 1 s (Benjamin b 20 Sep 2004); *Career* chef El Raco de Can Fabes 1998, chef Royal Oak East Lavant, sous chef then head chef The Hinds Head Bray 2010– (2 AA Rosettes, Michelin Pub of the Year 2011, Michelin star 2013–); *Recreations* motorsport, skiing; *Style*— Kevin Love, Esq; ✉ The Hinds Head, High Street, Bray SL6 2AB (e-mail kevin@hindsheadbray.com, Twitter @KevinLoveHH)

LOVEDAY, Mark Antony; s of George Arthur Loveday (d 1981), and Sylvia Mary, *née* Gibbs (d 1967); *b* 22 September 1943; *Educ* Winchester, Magdalen Coll Oxford (MA); *m* 1981, Mary Elizabeth, da of John Tolmie; 1 s (Samuel George b 15 June 1982), 1 da (Lucy Sylvia Catherine b 9 Dec 1983); *Career* Cazenove & Co: joined 1966, corp fin ptnr 1974–94, sr ptnr 1994–2001; chm Foreign & Colonial Investment Tst plc 2002–10 (dir 2001–10), memb Stock Exchange and MSI 1974–2002; tstee Grosvenor Estate 1998–2008, chm Gosvenor Pension Plan 2008–15, chm Magdalen Coll Devpt Tst, dir Skinners Almhouse Charity; Waynflete fell Magdalen Coll, hon fell Trinity Laban Conservatoire of Music and Dance; Freeman City of London, Liveryman and Extra Memb Court Worshipful Co of Skinners; *Recreations* golf; *Clubs* Boodle's, Hurlingham, City Univ, MCC, Royal St George's; *Style*— Mark Loveday, Esq; ✉ 42 Royal Avenue, London SW3 4QF (☎ 020 7730 6335, e-mail loveday_mark@hotmail.com)

LOVEGROVE, Ross; s of Herbert William John Lovegrove, BEM, of Penarth, S Glamorgan, and Mary Eileen Lovegrove; *b* 16 August 1958, Cardiff; *Educ* St Cyres Comp Sch Penarth, Cardiff Coll of Art & Design, Manchester Poly (BA), RCA (MDes); *Partner* Miska Miller; 1 s (Roman S A Lovegrove); *Career* designer: Frogdesign Germany 1983–84 (projects incl: Apple Computers, Sony Walkman, AEG Telefunken and Louis Vuitton Luggage), Knoll International Paris 1984–86, Atelier De Nimes 1984, fndr ptnr Lovegrove & Brown 1986–90, fndr Lovegrove Studio X 1990– (clients incl: Knoll International, BA, Louis Vuitton, Hermes, Cappellini SPA, Connolly Leathers, London Underground, Apple Computers, Herman Miller, Luceplan, Driade Spa, Alessi Spa, Olympus Optical,

Samsonite, Tag Heuer, Peugeot, Acco USA); winner: Oggetti Per Domus award for the pocket disc camera and film cassette system 1984, first prize (product design) Creative Review Pantone Colour awards, winner of ID of N America Award by the IDSA 1993, jt winner CSD Minerva Awards for FO8 chair 1994, shortlisted to final five of the BBC Design Awards 1994, winner of Grunen Point Award Stuttgart Design Centre 1994; work featured in various jls incl: Axis, Form, Intramuros, Design Week, Blueprint, L'Architecture d'Aujourd'hui, Domus, Architectural Review, Sunday Times, Financial Times, ID Magazine, New Scientist, The Independent, Design Report, Interni Magazine, Washington Post, New York Times, Architektur und Wohnen; exhibitions incl: Mondo Materials (California) 1989–90, Synthetic Visions (V&A London) 1990, 91 Objects by 91 Designers (Gallery 91 NY) 1991, Conran Fndn Collection, curator of first permanent collection London Design Museum 1993, Industrial Elegance (Guggenheim Museum NY) 1993, Mutant Materials (MOMA NY) 1995, FO8 (Stockholm) 1996, Ross Lovegrove Objects (Tokyo, Cologne) 1996, Design Highlights from Great Britain (Danish Museum of Decorative Art) 1997; visiting lectr at: RCA London, Ecole Cammondo Paris, ADI Milan, Univ of Aberdeen, Domus Acad; TV and radio: Late Show BBC 2, The Changing Domestic Landscape (LBC Design Week interview with Ken Grange), Ross Lovegrove Industrial Designer (BBC Wales interview); *Books* Supernatural, The Work of Ross Lovegrove (2004, with essays by Greg Lynn, Tokujin Yoshioka and Cecil Balmond); *Style*— Ross Lovegrove, Esq; ✉ Ross Lovegrove Ltd, 21 Powis Mews, London W11 1JN (☎ 020 7229 7104, fax 020 7229 7032)

LOVELL, Alan Charles; DL (2012); s of William George Lovell (d 1984), of Andover, Hants, and Mary Kerr, *née* Briant (d 1970); *b* 19 November 1953, Winchester; *Educ* Winchester, Jesus Coll Oxford (MA, Lawn Tennis, Real Tennis and Rackets blues); *m* 10 July 1982, Hon Virginia, da of Baron Weatherill, PC, DL (d 2007); 2 da (Emma b 19 March 1985, Lucinda b 3 Oct 1986); *Career* articled clerk then CA Price Waterhouse 1976–80, The Plessey Company plc 1980–89; chief exec: Conder Group plc 1991–92 (fin dir 1989–91), Costain Group plc 1995–97 (fin dir 1993–95), Dunlop Slazenger Group 2004 (fin dir 1997–2003), Jarvis 2004–06, Infinis Ltd 2006–09, Tamar Energy 2011–13; chief advsr restructuring practice PricewaterhouseCoopers 2010–; dir of various NHS authorities and tsts 1990–2006; memb Cncl Lloyd's of London 2007–16, chm Assoc of Lloyd's Membs 2012–; chm Mary Rose Tst 2015–, tstee and memb Cncl Winchester Cathedral 2009–, chm Hampshire Cultural Tst 2014–, chm Consumer Cncl for Water 2015–; chair Univ of Winchester 2016–; High Sheriff Hants 2010–11; FCA 1989 (ACA 1979), FSA 2008; *Recreations* tennis, golf, gardening, forestry; *Clubs* All England Lawn Tennis, MCC, Queen's, Garrick; *Style*— Alan Lovell, Esq, DL; ✉ The Palace House, Bishop's Lane, Bishop's Waltham, Hampshire SO32 1DP (☎ 01489 892838, mobile 07767 874052)

LOVELL, Dr Christopher Roland; s of Graham Ernest Lovell (d 1990), and Marion Gladys (d 1984); *b* 29 April 1950; *Educ* Bristol GS, Univ of Bristol (MD); *Career* sr registrar and tutor in dermatology Inst of Dermatology London 1978–84, conslt dermatologist Bath Health Dist 1985–; ed Community Dermatology Jl; former hon treas Dowling Club (formerly hon sec and hon pres); former pres Clinical Soc of Bath (former hon sec); FRCP, FRSM (former pres Section of Dermatology); *Books* Plants and the Skin (1993), The Skin in Rheumatic Disease (with PJ Maddison and GV Campion, 1990); *Recreations* cultivation and preservation of rare bulbs, music (medieval and renaissance recorder player), choral singing (especially church music); *Style*— Dr Christopher Lovell; ✉ Royal United Hospital, Combe Park, Bath BA1 3NG (☎ and fax 01225 824524)

LOVELL, Margaret; *Educ* West of England Coll of Art Bristol, Slade Sch of Fine Art, Acad of Fine Art Florence; *m* with 2 da and 2 s; *Career Solo Exhibitions* Marjorie Parr Gall London, Park Square Gall Leeds, Fermoy Art Gall Kings Lynn, Mignon Gall Bath, Halesworth Gall Suffolk, City Art Gall Plymouth, Bruton Gall Somerset, The Arts of Living Bath, Armstrong Davis Gall Arundel, Minster Fine Art York; public commissions incl: sculpture at Grafham Water Hunts for Great Ouse Water Authy, sculpture for Barclays Bank Ltd Bristol, sculpture for City Museum & Art Gall Plymouth, sculpture Cadbury Heath Primary Sch Bristol, Unilever Growth Awards 2000 and 2003; work in public and private collections incl: Arts Cncl of Great Britain, Devon County Cncl, Leicestershire Educn Ctee, Univ of Southampton, Univ of London, Compton Acres Gardens Poole, Aldershot County HS, Godolphin & Latymer Sch; *Awards* Italian State Scholarship, Greek Govt Scholarship; memb RWA; FRBS; *Recreations* keeping sheep; *Style*— Ms Margaret Lovell; ✉ website www.margaretlovell.co.uk

LOVELL, Mary Sybilla; da of William George Shelton, and Mary Catherine Shelton; *Educ* Notre Dame Collegiate Liverpool, UCLA; *m* 1, 22 Oct 1960 (m dis 1977), Clifford C Lovell; 1 s (Graeme Robert b 1961); m 2, 11 July 1992, Geoffrey Alan Howard Watts (d 1995); *Career* author; fin controller Baron Instruments Ltd 1969–76; dir and co sec: Yachting Provence 1976–78, Baron Computers & Security Ltd 1978–80; mangr Tech Writing Div Tabs Ltd 1982–86; MFH New Forest Hounds 1987–89; vice-pres R S Surtees Soc 1981–; FRGS 1994; *Books* A Hunting Pageant (1980), Cats as Pets (1981), Boys Book of Boats (1982), Straight on yill Morning (1986), The Splendid Outcast (ed, 1987), The Sound of Wings (1989), Cast No Shadow (1992), A Scandalous Life (1995), A Rage to Live (1998), The Mitford Girls: The Biography of an Extraordinary Family (2001), Bess of Hardwick: First Lady of Chatsworth (2005); *Recreations* foxhunting, flying, sailing, travel, reading; *Clubs* Lansdowne, New Forest Hunt; *Style*— Mrs Mary S Lovell

LOVELL-PANK, Dorian Christopher; QC (1993); s of Christopher Edwin Lovell-Pank (d 1966), of Madrid, and Jean Alston de Oliva Day, *née* McPherson (d 1979), of Buenos Aires and Cape Town; *b* 15 February 1946; *Educ* Downside, Colegio Sarmiento Buenos Aires, LSE, Inns of Court Sch of Law; *m* 1983, Diana, da of late Michael Cady Byford, and late Sonia Byford, of Claret Hall, Clare, Suffolk; 1 da (Frederica Sonia b 2 May 1986), 1 s (Michael Christopher John b 20 June 1987); *Career* called to the Bar: Inner Temple 1971 (bencher 1998), Cayman Islands 2011, Gibraltar 2013; pupillage with Rt Hon Lord Brittan of Spennithorne, PC, QC, DL, *qv*, and Michael Worsley, QC, *qv*, criminal practitioner SE Circuit; jr Middx Bar Mess 1977–80, assist recorder 1985–89, recorder 1989–2006; memb Panel of Chm Police Appeal Tbnls 1991–; chm Bar Conf 1999; memb: Gen Cncl of the Bar 1989–92 and 1998–2005 (chm Int Rels Ctee 2001–05), Ctee Criminal Bar Assoc 1989–2006 (chm Int Rels Sub-Ctee 1993–2006), Int Bar Assoc 1993– (memb Cncl 2001–05), Human Rights Inst 1996– (memb Cncl 2000–04), American Bar Assoc (assoc) 1997–, Br Spanish Law Assoc 2001–, FCO Pro Bono Lawyers Panel 2002–; *Recreations* travel, reading, things latin; *Clubs* RNVR Yacht; *Style*— Dorian Lovell-Pank, Esq, QC; ✉ 6KBW, 21 College Hill, London EC4R 2RP (☎ 020 3301 0910, fax 020 3301 0911, e-mail clerks@6kbw.com or dorian.lovell-pank@6kbw.com, website www.6kbw.com)

LOVELOCK, Derek; *b* 1 January 1950, Banstead, Surrey; *Educ* Enfield Coll of Technol (BA); *Career* grad trainee buying team ldr Clockhouse Young Fashion C&A 1971–85, buying controller rising to md Richards then chief exec Mothercare and memb Main Bd Storehouse plc 1985–92, chief exec Sears Clothing and dir Main Bd Sears plc 1992–99, chief exec Mosaic Fashions 1999–2009; exec chm: Aurora Fashions 2009–, Karen Millen 2011–; non-exec chm Jacques Vert 2004–07; non-exec chm Richard House Children's Hospice Trading Co; *Style*— Derek Lovelock, Esq; ✉ Aurora Fashions, 69–77 Paul Street, London EC2A 4PN (☎ 020 7452 1814, fax 020 7452 1010)

LOVERING, John David; CBE (2016); s of John George Lovering (d 1990), and Ruby Beatrice, *née* Edwards (d 1978); *b* 11 October 1949, London; *Educ* Dulwich Coll, Univ of Exeter (BA), Manchester Business Sch (MBA); *m* 18 Dec 1971, Brenda Joan, *née* Wotherspoon; 2 s (Nicholas John b 5 Dec 1974, Matthew William b 1 April 1977), 1 da (Kate Victoria b 21 March 1985); *Career* corp devpt exec Spillers Ltd 1975–78 (also commercial mangr Int Div), head of strategy planning Lex Service Gp plc 1978–82, finance dir Grand Metropolitan Retailing then commercial dir GM Foods 1982–85, head of financial planning and strategy Imperial Gp plc 1985–86, finance dir Sears plc 1986–92 (also md int ops and chm Sears Financial Services), chief operating offr and memb Bd Tarmac plc 1993–95, managing ptnr Lovering & Lovering 1995–2014; chm: Hoogenbosch Beheer BV 1996–97, Birthdays Gp Ltd 1996–2002 (ceo 1996–98), Peacock Gp plc 1997–2004, Fired Earth Ltd 1998–2001, Odeon Cinemas Ltd 2000–03, Homebase Ltd 2001–02, Laurel High Street Ltd 2002–05, Debenhams plc 2003–10, Fitness First Ltd 2003–05, Somerfield Stores Ltd 2005–08, Mitchells & Butlers plc 2010–11, Maplin Electronics Ltd 2011–14, Jamella Ltd 2011–; vice-chm Barclays Capital 2007–08; non-exec dir AGA Food Services Ltd 2003–05, dir Montagu Private Equity Advsrs LLP 2011–14; chair: Retail Tst 2011–, Hastings Pier Charity 2012–, Retail Credit Union 2016–; tstee and dir Save the Children 1990–96, tstee Durrell Conservation Tst 2015–; memb: Ctee Prince's Tst Retail Leadership Gp 2009–11, Ctee Br Heart Fndn's Mending Broken Hearts Appeal 2010–14; ambass Woodland Tst 2014–; govr Dulwich Coll 2007–, dir Attwood Acads 2015–; *Recreations* sport, farming, music; *Clubs* Alleyn, Dale Hill; *Style*— John Lovering, Esq, CBE

LOVETT, Ian Nicholas; s of Frederick Lovett, of Croydon, Surrey, and Dorothy Evelyn, *née* Stanley; *b* 7 September 1944; *Educ* Selhurst GS, Univ of Wales (BA); *m* 3 May 1969, Patricia Lesley; 2 da (Emma b 1977, Sophie b 1979); *Career* chm: Dunbar Bank plc 2002–12 (ceo 1984–2004), Seven Investment Mgmnt Ltd 2009–; dir England and Wales Cricket Bd 2009–; FCIB 1982; *Recreations* cricket; *Clubs* MCC, Middlesex CCC (chm 2008–); *Style*— Ian N Lovett, Esq

LOVILL, Sir John Roger; kt (1987), CBE (1983), DL (E Sussex 1983); s of Walter Thomas Lovill, and Elsie, *née* Page; *b* 26 September 1929; *Educ* Brighton Hove and Sussex GS; *m* 1958, Jacqueline, *née* Parker; 2 s, 1 da; *Career* SG Warburg 1951–55, dep gen mangr Securicor 1955–60; chm: Sloane Square Investments 1960–98, Municipal Mutual Insurance 1993–2013 (dir 1984–2013), Prime Health Ltd 1993–94; memb E Sussex CC 1967–89 (leader 1973–77); Assoc of Co Cncls: memb 1973–89, leader 1981–83, chm 1983–86; pres Sussex Assoc of Local Cncls 1987–97; vice-pres: Lewes Cons Assoc 1986–94, Nat Assoc of Local Cncls 1991–94; chm: Brighton Pavilion Cons Assoc 1958–60, Sussex Police Authy 1976–79 (memb 1973–81), Local Authorities Conditions of Serv Advsy Bd 1978–83, Nationwide Small Business Property Tst 1989–95; *Recreations* opera, politics, marine paintings; *Style*— Sir John Lovill, CBE, DL

LOW; *see also:* Morrison-Low

LOW, Dr John; CBE (2008); *Educ* PhD; *Career* with: John Brown Engrg 1979–84, William McGeogh Birmingham 1984–87, Booker plc 1988–93, Bühler AG 1993–99, RNID 1999–2007 (chief exec 2002–07), chief exec Charities Aid Fndn 2007–; chm Disability Charities Consortium 2003–07; ind memb House of Lords Appointments Cmmn 2008–13; non-exec dir: ACEVO 2003–09 (chm 2005–09), Euclid Network of European Third Sector Leaders 2007–, CAF Bank Ltd 2007–, Charity Bank 2010–; ind memb Cncl City Univ London 2011–; deacon: Gilcomston Park Baptist Church 1977–84, Hertford Baptist Church 1991–2003 (treas 1994–2003); CEng, FIET, CCMI, FRSA; *Style*— Dr John Low, CBE; ✉ Charities Aid Foundation,10 St Bride Street, London EC4A 4AD (☎ 03000 123010, e-mail jlow@cafonline.org, website www.cafonline.org)

LOW, Robert Nicholas; s of Leslie Walter Low (d 1983), of Bath, and Agnes, *née* Walsh; *b* 15 August 1948; *Educ* St George's Coll Weybridge, Fitzwilliam Coll Cambridge (BA); *m* 1983, Angela, da of Monte Levin; 1 s (Daniel Reuben b 1 Oct 1984); *Career* journalist; teacher Univ of Chile La Serena 1970–72, journalist Birmingham Post and Mail 1973–77, successively sub-ed, reporter, dep managing ed, sports ed, managing ed news then assoc ed features The Observer 1977–93, freelance journalist and author 1993–94, Euro Bureau chief Reader's Digest 1998–2008 (sr ed then dep ed Reader's Digest Br edn 1994–98), conslt ed Standpoint 2008–; *Books* The Kidnap Business (with Mark Bles, 1987), The Observer Book of Profiles (ed, 1991), La Pasionaria: The Spanish Firebrand (1992), W G: A Life of W G Grace (1997), The Garrick Club: The Lawyers (2011); *Recreations* watching cricket, playing golf; *Clubs* Garrick, Middlesex CCC, RAC; *Style*— Robert Low, Esq; ✉ Flat 1, 59 Aberdare Gardens, London NW6 3AL (☎ 020 7624 9532, e-mail bob.low3@gmail.com)

L

LOW OF DALSTON, Baron (Life Peer UK 2006), of Dalston in the London Borough of Hackney; Colin MacKenzie Low; CBE (2000); s of Arthur Eric Low, and Catherine, *née*Anderson; *b* 23 September 1942, Edinburgh; *Educ* Worcester Coll for the Blind, The Queen's Coll Oxford (MA), Churchill Coll Cambridge (Dip Criminology); *m* 1969, Jill Irene Coton; 1 s (Peter James), 1 da (Philippa Frances); *Career* lectr in law Univ of Leeds 1968–84, dir Disability Resource Team 1984–94, sr res fell City Univ 1994–2000 (visiting prof 2001–11), vice-pres RNIB 2009– (memb Exec Cncl 1975–2009, vice-chair 1990–2000, chair 2000–09); pres: Nat Fedn of the Blind UK 1979–82 (memb Exec Cncl 1969–92, vice-pres 1977–79 and 1989–92), European Blind Union (EBU) 2003–11 (memb various cmmns 1996–2003), SKILL (Nat Bureau for Students with Disabilities) 2008–11 (fndr memb 1974, memb Cncl 1975–2003, vice-pres 2003–08), Disability Rights UK (formerly Disability Alliance) 2010–12 (fndr memb 1973–, vice-pres 1997–2010), Int Cncl for Educn of People with Visual Impairment (ICEVI) 2010– (memb Exec Ctee 1987–2010); disability rights cmmr 2000–02; chair Low Cmmn on the Future of Advice and Legal Support 2012–, chair ACEVO Cmmn on Third Sector Regulation 2014–15; memb: Special Educnl Needs Tbnl 1994–2007, Nat Disability Cncl 1996–2000, Disability Rights Task Force 1997–99, House of Lords Appts Cmmn 2013; tstee Snowdon Tst 2011–; Snowdon Award 1984; memb Cncl St Dunstan's 2000–09; hon fell The Queen's Coll Oxford 2008; *Recreations* music, wine appreciation; *Style*— The Rt Hon the Lord Low of Dalston, CBE; ✉ House of Lords, London SW1A 0PW (☎ 020 7291 4119); Royal National Institute of the Blind, 105 Judd Street, London WC1H 9NE (☎ 020 7391 2205, fax 020 7383 0508, e-mail colin.low@rnib.org.uk)

LOWCOCK, His Hon Judge Andrew Charles; s of Eric Lowcock, and Elizabeth, *née* Kilner; *b* 22 November 1949; *Educ* Malvern, New Coll Oxford (MA); *m* 1, 14 Aug 1976 (m dis 1985), Patricia Anne, da of Emlyn Roberts; m 2, 7 Sept 1985, Sarah Elaine, da of Robert Edwards; 2 s (Robert Charles b 24 Feb 1988, Edward George b 23 Jan 1990); *Career* called to the Bar Middle Temple 1973, in practice Northern Circuit 1974–2001, recorder 1997–2001 (asst recorder 1993–97), circuit judge 2001–; *Recreations* music (princ timpanist Stockport Symphony Orchestra), cricket, theatre; *Clubs* Nefyn Golf, Stockport Garrick Theatre, Lancashire CCC, MCC; *Style*— His Hon Judge Lowcock; ✉ The Crown Court, Minshull Street, Manchester M1 3FS

LOWCOCK, Mark Andrew; CB (2011); *Educ* Univ of Oxford (BA), Birkbeck Coll London (MSc); *Career* Dept for Int Devpt: joined 1985, private sec to Baroness Chalker (as Min for Overseas Devpt) 1992–94, dep head then head Rgnl Office for Central Africa 1994–97, head EU Dept 1997–99, head Regnl Office E Africa 1999–2001, dir fin and corp performance 2001–03, DG corporate performance and knowledge sharing 2003–06, DG policy and int 2006–08, DG country progs 2008–; memb CIPFA; *Style*— Mark Lowcock, Esq, CB; ✉ Department for International Development, 1 Palace Street, London SW1E 5HE

LOWE, (John) Christopher (Chris); s of Sir Edgar Lowe, KBE, CB (d 1992), and Mary McIlwraith, *née* Lockhart; *b* 25 January 1949; *Educ* Dragon Sch Oxford, Haileybury, Brasenose Coll Oxford (MA, CertEd); *m* 1975 (m dis), Judith Anne Fielding; 1 s (Alexander b 3 Oct 1978), 1 da (Rebecca Anne b 11 Nov 1980); *Career* BBC: grad journalist trainee 1972–74, newsroom reporter 1974–76, political corr local radio and regnl

TV 1976–81, news reporter network radio 1981–83, presenter Today (Radio 4) 1982–93, news reporter network TV 1983–86, presenter/reporter Newsnight (BBC2) 1986–89, presenter weekend TV news 1989–99, presenter PM (Radio 4) 1993–2000, currently presenter BBC News 24; other programmes presented incl: Talking Politics, Breakfast News, One O'Clock News, Six O'Clock News; vice-pres: Br Blind Sports, Middx Trust, Cricket Soc; chm Membership Middlesex CCC; former dir Ind Housing Ombudsman Service; *Recreations* sport (especially cricket, football and rugby), my children, a good book; *Clubs* Lord's Taverners, Middlesex CCC; *Style—* Chris Lowe, Esq; ✉ BBC Broadcasting House, Portland Place, London W1A 1AA

LOWE, Prof Christopher Robin; OBE (2011); s of Thomas Lowe (d 1971), of Maidenhead, Berks, and Hilda, *née* Moxham; *b* 15 October 1945; *Educ* Braywood C of E Sch, Windsor GS for Boys, Univ of Birmingham (BSc, PhD); *m* 14 Dec 1974, Patricia Margaret, da of late Albert Reed; 1 s (Alan Robert b 19 May 1979), 1 da (Andrea Elizabeth b 19 Oct 1981); *Career* postdoctoral res fell: Univ of Liverpool 1970–73, Univ of Lund Sweden 1973–74; sr lectr in biochemistry Univ of Southampton 1983–84 (lectr 1974–82), fell Trinity Coll Cambridge 1984, fndr dir Inst of Biotechnology Univ of Cambridge 1984–; prof of biotechnology Univ of Cambridge 1999–; dir: Affinity Chromatography Ltd 1988–99, Cambridge Sensors Ltd 1992–, Smart Holograms Ltd 2001–, Purely Proteins Ltd 2004–, Rebha Ltd 2007–, Psynova Neurotech Ltd 2007–, Paramata Ltd 2008, BioJo Ltd 2008–, Ceroma Ltd 2011; 375 research publications, 100 patents, memb 17 editorial bds; Pierce Award (for outstanding contributions to the field of affinity chromatography) 1989, Queen's Award for Technological Achievement 1996, Jubilee Medal Chromatographic Soc 2002, Henry Dale Prize and Medal Royal Instn 2003, Queen's Anniversary Prize for Higher and Further Educn 2007, BBSRC Commercial Innovator of the Year 2011; Most Entrepreneurial Scientist of UK 2006; fell Int Inst of Biotechnology 1987; FInstP 2003, FREng 2005, FRSC 2005; *Books* Affinity Chromatography (1974), An Introduction to Affinity Chromatography (1979), Reactive Dyes in Protein and Enzyme Technology (1987), Biosensors (1987); *Recreations* travel, antiques; *Style—* Prof Christopher Lowe, OBE; ✉ The Limes, Hempstead, Saffron Walden, Essex CB10 2PW (☎ 01799 599307); Institute of Biotechnology, University of Cambridge, Tennis Court Road, Cambridge CB2 1QT (☎ 01223 334160, fax 01223 334162, e-mail crl1@cam.ac.uk)

LOWE, Sir Frank Budge; kt (2001); s of Stephen Lowe, and Marion Lowe; *b* 23 August 1941; *Educ* Westminster; *m* 2 s (Hamilton Alexander, Sebastian Christopher), 1 da (Emma Rose); *Career* fndr and chm Lowe and Partners Worldwide 1981–2003; fndr first academy (Capital City Acad, chair of tstees 2000–); *Style—* Sir Frank Lowe

LOWE, John; *Educ* Chiswick Sch, Richmond upon Thames Coll, Oxford Brookes Univ (BA, Dip Arch); *Career* architect; Pascal & Watson 1983–86, Richard Rogers Partnership 1986–; *Projects* incl: American Airlines CIP lounge Gatwick Airport, refurbishment of Old Billingsgate Fish Market, Reuters Data Centre, Reuters Recreation, nine projects in Japan, Channel 4 TV HQ London, Heathrow Airport Terminal 1, Heathrow Airport Europier, VR Techno Centre Gifu Japan, Heathrow Airport Terminal 5, Skylight office Frankfurt Germany, Madrid Airport Spain, Nippon TV HQ Tokyo Japan; *Style—* John Lowe, Esq; ✉ Richard Rogers Partnership, Thames Wharf, Rainville Road, London W6 9HA (☎ 020 7385 1235, 020 7385 8409, e-mail john.l@rrp.co.uk)

LOWE, (David) Mark; s of Capt Francis Armishaw Lowe, CBE, DSC, RN (d 1981), and Jean Christine, *née* Coates; *b* 17 June 1948; *Educ* Monkton Combe Sch, Univ of Kent (BA); *m* 15 Nov 1975, Christine Anne Elizabeth, da of Mostyn Thomas (d 1991); 2 da (Rebecca b 22 Aug 1978, Jessica b 5 Nov 1981); *Career* admitted slr 1974; asst slr Kidd Rapinet Badge 1974–75, ptnr Kingsley Napley 1976–80, ptnr and head of Litigation Dept Field Fisher Waterhouse 1980–; fndr memb Euro Cncl LCIA 1987; memb: Soc of Construction Law, Int Cultural Exchange; supporting memb The London Maritime Arbitrators' Assoc; memb: British Polish Legal Assoc, Cwlth Lawyers' Assoc; ACIArb 1988; *Publications* Pollution in the UK (jtly with Franklin and Hawke, 1995); *Recreations* flying, music, squash, tennis; *Style—* Mark Lowe, Esq

LOWE, Mark Julian; s of Paul Lowe, of Bucks, and Jean, *née* Dolby; *b* 15 February 1950, Loughborough, Leics; *Educ* Balliol Coll Oxford (MA); *m* 20 Dec 1980, Zeinab, *née* Ibrahim Karam; 2 s (Omar, Khaled (twins) b 14 July 1982); *Career* dir Nomos Capital Ptnrs Ltd 1994–, owner Nomos Capital Int Ltd 1999–; *Style—* M J Lowe, Esq; ✉ Château de Grignon, 21150 Côte d'Or, France

LOWE, Michael Allan; s of William Henry Herbert (d 1946), of Salisbury, Rhodesia, and Katherine Zita (d 1973); *b* 22 September 1940; *Educ* Prince Edward Secdy Sch Harare, Univ of Cape Town (BArch), Washington Univ St Louis (MArch and Urban Design); *m* 4 Feb 1995, Marian Catherine; 1 s (William Michael b 11 March 1996); *Career* architect and urban designer; Spencer & Anthony Parker Architects 1957, W S Atkins Architects and Engineers 1962–63, F Lamond Sturrock Architect 1963–64, Victor Gruen Associates LA 1966–68, private practice in Cape Town 1970–78; Arup Associates: established Arup Urban Design 1978–2005, dir 1987–, conslt 2005–09; ind conslt architect and urban designer 2009–; projects for Arup incl: Zimbabwe Conf Centre Harare, IBM United Kingdom Ltd Havant, Eton Coll, Bedford HS, Clare Coll Cambridge, Stockley Park Heathrow, Closegate Newcastle upon Tyne, Great Common Farm Cambs, Olympia Quartier Berlin, Grande Porte des Alpes Lyon, Oxford Railway Station, Trawsfynydd Power Station competition, Stockley Business Park, Battersea Power Station, Stratford City, Spencer Dock Dublin, Bridge End Belfast, Canning Town, Lewisham Gateway, Heart of Doha Qatar (masterplan conslt); memb CABE Design Review Ctee 1999–2002; RIBA 1976, memb ARB 1980; *Publications* numerous papers and lectures on architecture and urban design; *Recreations* swimming, cycling, skiing; *Style—* Michael Lowe, Esq; ✉ Windmill Cottage, Duntisbourne Abbots, Cirencester, Gloucestershire GL7 7JN

LOWE, Peter; s of George William Lowe, and Anne Elizabeth, *née* Tilyard; *Educ* Univ of Leicester (MA); *Career* broadcaster; BBC: prodr, exec prodr; Carlton Television: controller community programmes, controller digital programmes; currently md Screenchannel Television Ltd; winner of more than 50 nat and int programme awards as prodr or exec prodr incl two RTS awards; memb: BAFTA, RTS; *Style—* Peter Lowe, Esq; ✉ Screenchannel Television Ltd, 45–46 Lower Marsh, Waterloo, London SE1 7RG (☎ 020 7207 5399, e-mail peterlowe@screenchannel.co.uk)

LOWE, Prof Philip David; OBE (2003); *b* 29 March 1950, Hull; *Educ* Univ of Oxford (MA), Victoria Univ of Manchester (MSc), Univ of Sussex (MPhil); *m* 1 Jan 1972, Veronica, *née* Gibbins; 1 da (Sylvia b 13 July 1979), 1 s (Oliver b 13 Feb 1985); *Career* UCL: lectr in countryside planning 1974–89, reader in environmental planning 1989–92, co-dir Rural Studies Research Centre 1990–92; Univ of Newcastle upon Tyne: Duke of Northumberland chair of rural economy 1992–, fndr Centre for Rural Economy 1992; research offr Union of Int Assocs Brussels 1973, visiting fell Science Centre Berlin 1983, research fell Woodrow Wilson Int Center for Scholars Washington DC 1985, visiting lectr Nat Agric Univ Wageningen Netherlands 1986; dir Rural Economy and Land Use (RELU) Prog of the UK Research Cncls 2003–13; conslt and a founding ed ECOS (Jl of Br Assoc of Nature Conservationists) 1980–88, Br ed Sociologia Ruralis (Jl of European Soc for Rural Sociology) 1983–90, memb Editorial Bd Jl of Environmental Planning and Mgmnt 1992–, European ed Progress in Rural Policy and Planning 1993–96, memb Editorial Bd Jl of Environmental Planning and Policy 1998–2007; expert advsr: House of Commons Select Ctee on the Environment 1996, House of Commons Environment, Tport and Regnl Affrs Ctee 1997–99; chm: Northumberland Rural Devpt Ctee 1996–99, England Market Towns Advsy Forum 2001–05, Vet and Vet Servs Working Gp DEFRA 2007–09, Scientific Ctee European Soc for Rural Sociology 2008–10; memb: Nat Policy Ctee CPRE 1992–98, Socio-Economic Advsy Panel English Nature 1994–2006, HEFCE Research Assessment Panel for Agric 1996, Agric Sub-Gp UK Round Table on Sustainable Devpt 1997–98, Ind Advsy Gp to Min of Agric, Fisheries and Food 1997–98, Mgmnt Ctee European COST Network on Rural Innovation 1998–2002, Bd Countryside Agency 1999–2006, Foresight Panel for Food Chain Office of Science and Technol 1999–2001, Economists Panel MAFF 1999–2001, Science Advsy Cncl DEFRA 2003–10, Scientific Advsy Bd MTT Agrifood Research Finland 2007–; Bertebos Prize Royal Swedish Acad of Agriculture and Forestry 2013, Queen's Anniv Prize for Innovation in Higher Education 2014; Hon DSci Univ of East Anglia 2014; AcSS 2009; *Recreations* cycling, cinema; *Style—* Prof Philip Lowe, OBE; ✉ Room 3.16, Agriculture Building, Centre for Rural Economy, School of Agriculture, Food and Rural Development, University of Newcastle upon Tyne NE1 7RU (☎ 0191 222 6887, fax 0191 222 5411, e-mail philip.lowe@ncl.ac.uk)

LOWE, Philip Martin; s of late Leonard Ernest Lowe, and late Marguerite Helen, *née* Childs; *b* 29 April 1947; *Educ* Reading Sch, St John's Coll Oxford (MA), London Business Sch (MSc); *m* 1, 1967 (m dis 1980), Gillian Baynton, *née* Forge; m 2, 1984, Nora Mai, *née* O'Connell; 2 s; *Career* Tube Investments Ltd 1968–73; EC: joined 1973, asst to DG XVIII Credit and Investments 1979–82, memb Cabinet of EC Pres Thorn 1982–85, memb Cabinet of Cmmr Alois Pfeiffer 1985–86, asst to DG XXII Co-ordination of Structural Instruments 1986–87, head of unit for structural funds 1987–89, chef de cabinet to Cmmr Bruce Millan 1989–91, dir of rural devpt DG VI Agric 1991–93, dir Merger Task Force DG IV Competition 1993–95, seconded as chef de cabinet to Neil Kinnock, *qv* (as Vice-Pres of the Cmmn) 1995–97, DG for Devpt 1997–2000, chef de cabinet to vice-pres Neil Kinnock 2000–02, DG for competition 2002–10, DG for energy 2010–; *Recreations* music, theatre, running, hill walking; *Style—* Philip Lowe, Esq

LOWE, Rt Rev Stephen Richard; *see:* Hulme, Bishop of

LOWE, Sir Thomas William Gordon; 4 Bt (UK 1918), of Edgbaston, City of Birmingham; QC (2008); s of Sir Francis Reginald Gordon Lowe, 3 Bt (d 1986), and Franziska Cornelia Lanier, da of Siegfried Steinkopf, of Berlin; *b* 14 August 1963; *Educ* Stowe, LSE (LLB), Jesus Coll Cambridge (LLM); *m* Mozhgan, da of H Asilzadeh; 1 s; *Heir* s, Theodore Lowe; *Career* called to the Bar Inner Temple 1985, in practice at Wilberforce Chambers; memb: Commerical Bar Assoc, Chancery Bar Assoc; *Style—* Sir Thomas Lowe, Bt, QC; ✉ 8 New Square, Lincoln's Inn, London WC2A 3QP (☎ 020 7306 0102, fax 020 7306 0095)

LOWE, Prof (Alan) Vaughan; QC (2008); s of Alan Lowe, and Pamela Lowe; *b* 1952, Smethwick, W Midlands; *Educ* Univ of Wales (LLB, LLM, PhD), Univ of Cambridge (MA), Univ of Oxford (MA), Membre de l'Institut de Droit Int; *m* Sally Lowe; *Career* called to the Bar Gray's Inn (bencher 2008); lectr and sr lectr: Univ of Cardiff 1973–78, Univ of Manchester 1978–88; reader in int law and fell CCC Cambridge 1988–99, Chichele prof of public int law and fell All Souls Coll Oxford 1999–2012 (emeritus 2012–); practising barr, memb Essex Court Chambers; arbitrator; sometime visiting prof: Univ of Thessaloniki, Univ of Helsinki, Tulane Univ New Orleans, Duke Univ NC; Order of the Rising Sun Gold Rays with Neck Ribbon Japan 2008, Cavaler of the Ordinul Nat Serviciul Credincios Romania 2009, Darjah Paduka Seri Laila Jasa Yang Amat Berjasa (Darjah Ke-Dua) Brunei 2010; *Publications* various books and articles on international law; *Recreations* music, walking, thinking; *Clubs* Oxford and Cambridge; *Style—* Prof Vaughan Lowe, QC; ✉ Essex Court Chambers, 24 Lincoln's Inn Fields, London WC2A 3EG (☎ 020 7813 8000)

LOWE, Veronica Ann; da of late Arthur Ernest Bagley, and Agatha Amy Annie, *née* Blackham (d 1978); *b* 29 June 1951, Birmingham; *Educ* King Edward VI GS for Girls Handsworth Birmingham, St Hugh's Coll Oxford (MA), Oxford Poly (Inst of Linguist exams), City of Birmingham Poly (slrs qualifying exams); *m* 2 Dec 1977, Ian Stanley Lowe, s of late Arnold Lowe; 1 da (Rhiannon Sara Amy b 21 Dec 1983); *Career* articled clerk with Messrs Ryland Martineau & Co (now Martineau Johnson) Birmingham 1976–78, admitted slr 1979, lectr in labour law Aston Univ 1978–80, slr in private practice 1980–86, asst area dir Legal Aid Area No 8 1986–88, memb Legal Aid Exec Bd Legal Aid Schem W Midland, E Midlands and E Anglia 1988–89, gp mangr (Midlands) Legal Aid Bd 1989–90, dir Slrs Complaints Bureau and memb Law Soc Mgmnt Bd 1990–96, chief exec Valuation Office Agency and memb Exec Bd Inland Revenue 1996–97; legal conslt to Warks CC, Oxford Brookes Univ and Pinsent Curtis 1998–2000; head of legal affrs EMEA Faulding Pharmaceuticals plc 2000–03, European legal affrs conslt Mayne Pharma plc (formerly Faulding) 2003–07; memb Bd European Generic Medicines Assoc 2002–07 (also memb Legal Affrs Ctee); pt/t immigration appeals adjudicator then immigration judge 2001–, judge in the SSCS First Tier Tbnl 2011–; conslt on immigration and asylum law Continuing Professional Devpt 2007–; memb Law Soc 1979; contrib to pubns on law for accountants and businessmen and articles on intellectual property law, generic medicines, ethics and professional conduct and European legislation; *Recreations* cooking, eating and drinking, travel, reading, talking, writing unfinished novels, home life; *Clubs* St Hugh's College Alumni Assoc (hon sec); *Style—* Mrs V A Lowe; ✉ e-mail veronica.lowe@auxilium.freeserve.co.uk

LOWE, (Alexander) Zane Reid; *b* 7 August 1973, Auckland, New Zealand; *m* Kara Jeanne Walters; *Career* DJ; former presenter Xfm, presenter Radio 1 2003–15, presenter Beats 1 (USA) 2015–; Music Broadcaster of the Year and Specialist Music Award Sony Radio Acad Awards 2006, Best Radio Show NME Award 2006, 2007 and 2008, Best TV Show NME Award 2006, 2007 and 2008, Music Radio Broadcaster of the Year Gold Award Radio Academy Awards 2014; *Recreations* music; *Style—* Mr Zane Lowe; ✉ c/o Money Talent Management, 42A Berwick Street, London W1F 8RZ (e-mail francis@moneymanagementuk.com); website www.zanelowe.com

LOWMAN, Ven David Walter; s of Cecil Walter Lowman, and Queenie Norah Lowman; *Educ* Crewkerne Sch, City of London Coll (Cert Civil Law), KCL (BD, AKC), St Augustine's Coll Canterbury; *Career* examiner Inland Revenue Estate Duty Office 1966–70; curate: St John Notting Hill 1975–78, St Augustine with St John Kilburn 1978–81; chaplain Church House Westminster 1981–86, selection sec, vocations advsr ACCM 1981–86, team rector Wickford and Runwell 1986–93, dir of ordinands Chelmsford Diocese 1993–2001, archdeacon of Southend 2001–13, archdeacon of Chelmsford 2013–16 (archdeacon emeritus 2016–); non-residentiary canon Chelmsford Cathedral 1993; memb Gen Synod C of E 1995–2005; govr Brentwood Sch, tstee Sons and Friends of the Clergy 2012; *Recreations* travel, good food and wine, opera, cricket; *Clubs* Essex; *Style—* The Ven David Lowman; ✉ 16 Kelvin Court, Fourth Avenue, Frinton on Sea, Essex CO13 9DT (☎ 01255 676793, mobile 07486 907780)

LOWNIE OF LARGO, Andrew James Hamilton; s of Dr Ralph Hamilton Lownie of Largo (d 2007), and Claudine, *née* Lecrocq; *b* 11 November 1961; *Educ* Fettes, Westminster, Magdalene Coll Cambridge (MA), Univ of Edinburgh (MSc), The Coll of Law Guildford; *m* 2 May 1998, Angela Caroline, da of Maj Peter Doyle; 1 s (Robert David Hamilton b 1999), 1 da (Alice Claudine Hamilton b 2001); *Heir* Robert Lownie of Largo, Younger; *Career* dir: John Farquharson Ltd literary agents 1986–88, Andrew Lownie literary agency 1988–, Denniston and Lownie Ltd 1991–93, Thistle Publishing; literary agent PEN 2001–05; journalist; contrib: Spectator, The Times, Scotland on Sunday; sec Biographers Club 1998–2008 (pres 2008–); tstee Iain MacLeod Award, former pres Cambridge Union Soc; Parly candidate (Cons) Monklands West 1992, vice-chm Cons Gp for Europe 1992–95; archives by-fell Churchill Coll Cambridge 2016; *Books* The Edinburgh Literary Guide, North American Spies, John Buchan – The Presbyterian Cavalier, John Buchan's Poems (ed), John Buchan's Complete Short Stories (ed), The

Scottish Shorter Fiction of John Buchan (ed), The Literary Companion to Edinburgh, Stalin's Englishman: The Lives of Guy Burgess; *Recreations* music, outdoor pursuits, history, travel, theatre; *Clubs* Beefsteak; *Style*— Andrew Lownie of Largo; ✉ 36 Great Smith Street, London SW1P 3BU (☎ 020 7222 7574, fax 020 7222 7576, e-mail lownie@globalnet.co.uk, website www.andrewlownie.co.uk)

LOWRY, Peter; s of Frederick George Lowry (d 1971), of Carlisle, and Dora, *née* Corkhill (d 1984); *b* 25 April 1938; *Educ* Gregg Sch Carlisle; *Career* served RAF (despatches, GSM (Malaya) 1960) 1956–65, Photographic Branch 1960–65; prop photographic business covering portraiture, weddings, industrial and commercial photography 1975–; exhibited Epcot Center USA 1991; served Admissions and Qualifications Bd: BIPP 1990–99, Dutch Inst of Professional Photography 1998–2000; memb Distinctions Panel RPS 1989–2001; Nat Portrait Photographer of the Year 1983, 1984 and 1989, Kodak Gold Award 1985, 1986 and 1987; hon fell Dutch Inst of Professional Photography 1998; FRSA 1985, FRPS 1988, FBIPP 1989; *Recreations* angling, cycling, walking; *Clubs* Avon Tributaries Angling Assoc, Golden Scale, Veteran-Cycle; *Style*— Peter Lowry, Esq; ✉ Little Thatch, Tynts Hill, Mells, Frome, Somerset BA11 3PU (☎ 01373 812716, mobile 07899 806115, e-mail email@peterlowry.com, website www.peterlowry.com)

LOWSON, Robert Campbell; s of George Campbell Lowson (d 1989), and Betty, *née* Parry (d 2006); *b* 7 March 1949; *Educ* Gravesend GS, BNC Oxford (BA); *m* 1973, Hilary May, da of Hubert Balsdon; 1 s (Andrew b 15 Nov 1980), 1 da (Judith b 18 Nov 1983); *Career* MAFF (now DEFRA): joined 1970, under sec Agricultural Inputs, Plant Protection and Emergencies Gp 1994–95, min (agric) UK Perm Representation to the EU 1995–99, dir of communications 1999–2001, dir Environment Strategy 2001–07, dir Regulation 2007, seconded to European Environment Agency 2007–11, conslt on space and research (incl for Technol Strategy Bd 2011–14); jt chair Cambridge for Europe Campaign 2015/16, tstee City of Cambridge Educn Fndn; FRSA; *Clubs* Athenaeum; *Style*— Robert Lowson, Esq

LOWTH, Simon Jonathan; s of Gerald Simon Lowth, of Ross-on-Wye, Herefords, and Ruth Elizabeth, *née* Carter; *b* 8 September 1961; *Educ* Gonville & Caius Coll Cambridge (MA), London Business Sch (MBA); *m* 1994, Helene, *née* Theodoly; 4 c (Manon b 29 Oct 2000, Faye, Grace (twins) b 10 Oct 2002, Marc b 20 Sept 2004); *Career* design engr Ove Arup & Ptnrs 1983–85, dir McKinsey and Co 1987–2003, exec dir corp strategy and devpt Scottish Power plc 2003–07, exec dir and chief fin dir AstraZeneca plc 2007–; *Style*— Simon Lowth, Esq

LOWTHER, Col Sir Charles Douglas; 6 Bt (UK 1824), of Swillington, Yorks; s of Lt-Col Sir William Guy Lowther, 5 Bt, OBE, DL (d 1982), and Grania Suzanne, *née* Douglas-Campbell (d 2001); *b* 22 January 1946; *Educ* Winchester; *m* 1, 1969 (m dis 1975), Melanie Pensée FitzHerbert, da of late Roderick Christopher Musgrave; m 2, 1975, Florence Rose, da of late Col Alexander James Henry Cramsie, OBE, of O'Harabrook, Ballymoney, Co Antrim; 1 s (Patrick William b 1977), 1 da (Alice Rose b 1979); m 3, 2006, Sarah Jane Davis; 2 s (Hugo Charles Sandy b 2008, George b 2012); *Heir* s, Patrick Lowther; *Career* served HM Forces 1965–93, Col; businessman and farmer; dir Chester Race Co 1995–, chm Bangor-on-Dee Racecompany 2002–; memb HM Body Guard of the Hon Corps of Gentlemen at Arms 1997, High Sheriff Clwyd 1997; *Recreations* field sports, racing, travel; *Clubs* Cavalry and Guards', Jockey (racing memb 1999); *Style*— Col Sir Charles Douglas Lowther, Bt; ✉ Erbistock Hall, Wrexham LL13 0DE

LOWTHER, James; s of George Hugh Lowther, of Holdenby House, Northampton, and Sheila Rachel Isabel, *née* Foster; *b* 27 January 1947; *Educ* Eton, Keble Coll Oxford (MA History); *m* Karen Healey, da of James Wallace; 3 da (Natasha Jane b 26 Nov 1988, Mamie Grace b 6 Aug 1994, Oona Aphrodite 6 March 2001), 1 s (James William Dolfin b 29 Dec 1991); *Career* Saatchi & Saatchi 1977–95 (creative dir and dep chm 1991–95); M&C Saatchi: fndr creative dir 1995–2000, chm 2000–04, founding ptnr 2004–; dir Children in Crisis; dir British Television Advtg Awards; memb: Historic Houses Assoc, Cncl for the Preservation of Rural England, Nat Tst, D&AD; *Awards* ITV Award for Best Cinema Commercial 1979 and for Best Commercial of the Year 1992, 3 times Best Black & White Press Advertisement Campaign Press Awards, 2 times Best Poster of the Year Campaign Poster Awards, 3 D&AD Silver Awards, 3 Silver and a Gold Cannes Int Advtg Festival, Ivor Novello Award (for composing advtg music for Schweppes), work incl in 100 Best Advertisements; *Books* The Copy Book (contrib), The 22 Irrefutable Laws of Advertising and When to Violate Them (contrib); *Recreations* listening to, playing and writing music; *Style*— James Lowther, Esq; ✉ M&C Saatchi Ltd, 34–36 Golden Square, London W1R 4EE (☎ 020 7543 4500, fax 020 7543 4535, e-mail jamesl@mcsaatchi.com)

LOWTHER, Merlyn Vivienne; *née* Humphrey; da of Norman Edward Douglas Humphrey, and Joan Margaret, *née* Hewitt; *b* 3 March 1954; *Educ* Manchester HS for Girls, Victoria Univ of Manchester (BSc), London Business Sch (MSc), Central Sch of Speech and Drama (MA); *m* 1 Nov 1975, David John Lowther; 1 s, 1 da; *Career* Bank of England: head Banking Div and dep chief cashier 1991–96, personnel dir 1996–98, chief cashier 1999–2004; non-exec dir: Schroders plc 2004–13, Co-operative Banking Gp 2011–14, ret; tstee: Henry Smith Charity, Winston Churchill Meml Tst; govr Manchester HS for Girls 2015–; Hon LLD Victoria Univ of Manchester 1999; FRSA 1996, FCIB 1999, CCMI 1999; *Recreations* theatre, singing, reading, family; *Style*— Ms Merlyn Lowther

LOYD, Jeremy Charles Haig; s of Geoffry Haig Loyd, of Herefords, and Patricia, *née* Maclean; *b* 4 July 1954; *Educ* Pangbourne Coll; *m* 1, 6 Oct 1983, Sally (d 2006), da of Duncan Robertson, TD, JP (d 1988), of Beadlam, N Yorks; m 2, 10 Jan 2009, Anne, da of Ian Fletcher of Invercargill, NZ; *Career* account exec Michael Rice and Co Ltd 1974–79; dir: RTI Productions Ltd 1976–80, Project Art Ltd 1978–2008, Carlton Television 1991–95, Carlton Music 1993–96; ceo Pickwick Group 1993–95, formerly md Capital Radio; dir: First Oxfordshire Radio Co 1988–2002, Hamden Entertainment (USA) 1992–2002, Channel KTV 1995–97, Enterprise Radio Holdings 1995–96, ITFC Ltd 1995–, Capital Radio Investments Ltd and Capital Enterprises Ltd 1989–91, Wren Orchestra of London Ltd 1989–91, Devonair Ltd 1989–91; chm Direct Home Entertainment Ltd 1993–95; formerly dep chm Blackwell Ltd; memb Bd of Advsrs Authentium (USA) 1995–2005; dir Marine Mgmnt Orgn 2010–, dir UCL Cancer Int Research Tst 2010–, dir Chelsea and Westminster Hosp 2011–; tstee Help A London Child 1987–91; assoc Marine Biology Lab/Woods Hole Oceanographic Inst; *Recreations* fishing, sailing; *Clubs* RNYS; *Style*— Jeremy Loyd, Esq

LOYN, David George; s of William George Grenville Loyn, and Elizabeth Margery, *née* Gent; *b* 1 March 1954; *Educ* Oundle, Worcester Coll Oxford (BA), Coll of Law London; *m* 1981, Estelle, da of Philip Daniel; 3 s (Thomas Jack b 18 Sept 1988, Christopher Mark b 19 Dec 1992, James Philip b 30 May 1995); *Career* reporter IRN/LBC 1979–87; BBC: joined 1987, S Asia corr 1993–97, foreign affrs corr 1997–; Sony Award for Radio Reporter of the Year 1985; RTS Awards: Journalist of the Year 1999, International News Reporter of the Year 1999; *Style*— David Loyn, Esq; ✉ BBC Foreign Affairs and Defence Correspondent, Broadcasting House, London W1A 1AA

LUBA, His Hon Judge Jan; QC (2000); s of Zenon Luba, and Marlene Luba; *b* 1957, London; *Educ* LSE (LLB), Univ of Leicester (LLM); *m* Adriana; 2 da; *Career* called to the Bar 1980 (bencher Middle Temple 2009); practising barr specialising in housing and social welfare law 1981–2015; recorder 2000–15, judge of the Employment Appeal Tbnl 2002–15, circuit judge (SE Circuit) 2015–; chair Ind Cmmn on the Future of Cncl Housing in the London Borough of Southwark 2012; chair Zacchaeus 2000 Tst 2014–16; *Publications* The Disabled Persons Handbook (1989), The Owner Occupier Handbook (1990), Rights Guide for Home Owners (co-author, 1990), Repairs: Tenants' Rights (co-author, 5 edn 2016), Housing and the Human Rights Act (2000), The Homelessness Act 2002 (co-author, 2002), Defending Possession Proceedings (co-author, 8 edn 2016), Housing Allocation and Homelessness (co-author, 4 edn 2016); *Recreations* walking; *Style*— His Hon Judge Luba, Esq, QC; ✉ County Court at Central London, Thomas More Building, Royal Courts of Justice, Strand, London WC2A 2LL

LUBBOCK, John David Peter; OBE (2015); s of Michael Ronald Lubbock, MBE (d 1989), and Diana Beatrix, *née* Crawley (d 1976); *b* 18 March 1945; *Educ* Radley, Royal Acad of Music (GRSM); *m* 12 Feb 1977 (m dis), Eleanor, *née* Sloan; 2 s (Daniel, Patrick); m 2, 13 July 1991, Christine Cairns, *qv*; 2 s (Adam Thomas b 28 Nov 1991, Alexander Michael b 30 June 1993); *Career* fndr and conductor Orchestra of St John's Smith Square; dir Music for Autism charity; tstee: Music of Life Fndn, Thomley Activity Centre, Clear Sky Fndn, My World; FRAM; *Recreations* tennis, racquets, Royal tennis; *Style*— John Lubbock, Esq, OBE; ✉ 7 Warborough Road, Warborough, Oxfordshire (☎ 01865 858210); Orchestra of St John's (website www.osj.org.uk); Music for Autism (website www.musicforautism.org.uk)

LUBRAN, Jonathan Frank; s of Prof Michael Lubran, of LA, Calif, and Avril Roslyn, *née* Lavigne; *b* 27 April 1948; *Educ* Bedales, Univ of Chicago (BA), Univ of Cambridge (Dip, PhD); *m* 2003, Clare, *née* Berry; *Career* investment advsr Crown Agents for Overseas Govts 1979–80; md: Royal Bank of Canada Investment Management International 1980–88, Bankers Trust Investment Management Ltd 1988–94, Foreign & Colonial Institutional 1994–2000; exec dir Schroder Investment Management 2000–03, dir Mellon Global Investments 2003–; former treas Crisis at Christmas, memb London Project Ctee Nat Art Collections Fund 1977–88, dep warden Guild of Benefactors CCC Cambridge 1996–; *Recreations* opera, theatre, antiques, swimming, photography; *Clubs* Brooks's, Hurlingham; *Style*— Jonathan Lubran, Esq; ✉ c/o Brooks's, St James's Street, London SW1A 1LN

LUCAS, Prof Alan; s of late Dr Saul H Lucas, and late Dr Sophia Lucas; *b* 30 June 1946; *Educ* Bedales, Clare Coll Cambridge (fndn scholar, BA), Oxford Med Sch (scholar, MB BChir), Univ of Cambridge (MD); *m* 1, 1967 (m dis), Sally, *née* Wedeles; m 2, 1978, Penny, *née* Hodgson; 1 s, 2 da; *Career* house physician, house surgn, SHO and registrar 1971–77; Wellcome research fell Dept of Paediatrics Univ of Oxford 1977–79, registrar in gen paediatrics John Radcliffe Hosp Oxford 1979–80; Dept of Paediatrics Univ of Cambridge: clinical lectr in paediatrics 1980–82, hon conslt 1982–95; head of infant and child nutrition MRC Dunn Nutrition Unit Cambridge 1982–96, MRC clinical prof and dir Childhood Nutrition Centre Inst of Child Health London 1996–, hon conslt in paediatric nutrition Gt Ormond St Hosp for Children London 1996–, chair in paediatric nutrition UCL 2001–; Univ of Cambridge: lectr Trinity Coll 1972–76, dir of med studies Peterhouse 1982–86, lectr in med sci 1982–90, fell Clare Coll 1982– (dir of studies in med 1982–97); coll lectr St Edmund Hall Oxford 1977–80; chm MRC Working Gp on Fluoride and Osteoporosis 1994; memb: DHSS Panel on Child Nutrition 1988–96, BPA Standing Ctee on Nutrition 1988–94, Working Gp on EEC Directive on Infant Formulae and Follow-up Milk 1988–, Academic Bd BPA 1989–94, Scientific Advsy Ctee Fndn for the Study of Infant Death 1992–94, MRC Physiological Med and Infections Bd 1992–96, MRC Steering Ctee Initiative in Fetal and Maternal Origins of Adult Disease 1993–, Central Research and Devpt Ctee Advsy Gp on Mother and Child Health 1994–95, MRC Physiological Med and Infection Bd (PMIB) 1995–96, Jt MRC/CCMRC (Cwealth Caribbean Medical Research Cncl) Working Gp (UK and Caribbean) 1995–, RCP Child Health Ctee on Nutrition 1996–2000; rep Health Services and Public Health Research Bd (HSPHRB) 1995–96, European rep Inst of Paediatric Nutrition USA 1995–, UK rep Int Inst of Paediatric Nutrition 2003–; delivered over 600 nat and int lectures 1980–, author of over 400 articles, books and papers in professional jls; Wellcome visiting prof in basic med sciences USA 1993–94; BPA Guthrie Medal 1982, James Spence Medal Royal Coll of Paediatrics and Child Health 2005 (for lifetime contribution to paediatric nutrition, notably the impact of early nutritian on long-term health and devpt); hon citizen Georgia 1994 (for educational services); FRCP 1991 (MRCP 1976), FMed Sci 2000, Hon FRCPCH 2005; *Style*— Prof Alan Lucas; ✉ Institute of Child Health, 30 Guilford Street, London WC1N 1EH (☎ 020 7905 2389, fax 020 7404 7109, e-mail a.lucas@ich.ucl.ac.uk)

LUCAS, Prof Arthur Maurice; AO (2005), CBE (2002); s of Joseph Alfred Percival Lucas (d 1985), of Colac, Victoria, and May Queen, *née* Griffin; *b* 26 October 1941, Moe, Victoria, Aust; *Educ* Univ of Melbourne (BSc, BEd), Ohio State Univ (PhD); *m* 1970, Paula Jean, da of Geoffrey Ross Williams (d 1991); 1 da (Elizabeth Karen b 1974), 1 s (Arthur David b 1975); *Career* science/biology teacher Educn Dept of Victoria 1964–66, sr demonstrator in biology Flinders Univ of S Australia 1969–70 (demonstrator 1967–68), pt/t res assoc ERIC Analysis Center Ohio State Univ 1970–72, fndn lectr Educn Unit Warrnambool Inst of Advanced Educn 1973; Flinders Univ of S Australia: lectr in science educn 1974–75, sr lectr 1976–80, chm Sch of Educn 1977–79; KCL: prof of science curriculum studies 1980–2003 (emeritus prof 2003–), asst princ 1988–90, chm Res Strategy Ctee 1991–93, vice-princ (academic affairs) 1991–93, actg princ 1992–93, princ 1993–2003; dep vice-chllr Univ of London 1997–2002; pres Soc for the History of Natural History 2006–09, vice-pres Cncl Zoological Soc of London 1993 (memb 1992–93); chm Med and Soc Panel Wellcome Fndn 1998–2002; memb: Exec Ctee Field Studies Cncl 1987–93, 1994–2000 and 2001–07, SE Thames RHA 1993–94, Ctee for Public Understanding of Sci (COPUS) 1993–96, Cncl Royal Instn of GB 1998–2004, Cncl Br Soc of History for Sci 1999–2002, Bd Quality Assurance Agency for HE 2001–08, Lord Chllr's Advsy Cncl on the Public Records and Archives 2006–15; tstee: Samuel Courtauld Tst 1997–2002, Wymondham Arts Forum 2013–15; chm Wymondham Arts Centre 2009–15; author and contrib to many pubns and jls in science educn, environmental educn, museum studies and history of science; fell Australian Coll of Educn 1995 (memb 1973), FSB (formerly FIBiol) 1981, FKC 1992; *Clubs* Athenaeum; *Style*— Prof Arthur Lucas, AO, CBE; ✉ c/o The Athenaeum, Pall Mall, London SW1Y 5ER

LUCAS, Dr Caroline; MP; *b* 9 December 1960; *m*; 2 c; *Career* Green Pty: joined 1986, nat press offr 1987–89, co-chair 1989–90, princ speaker (various occasions), co cncllr Oxfordshire CC 1993–97, MEP SE England 1999–2010, ldr 2008–12 and 2016–, MP (Brighton Pavilion) 2010–; memb Euro Parly Ctees on: Trade Industry Energy and Environment, Public Health and Consumer Policy; memb Palestinian Delegation, vice-pres Animal Welfare Intergroup, memb Intergroups on Peace Issues and Consumer Affairs, memb Environmental Audit Ctee; memb Advsy Bd Protect the Local, Globally, memb CND; *Publications* incl: Writing for Women (1989), The Trade Trap (with Belinda Coote, 1994), Reforming World Trade: The Social and Environmental Priorities (1996), Watchful in Seattle: World Trade Organisation Threats to Public Services, Food and the Environment (1999), The Euro or a Sustainable Future for Britain? A Critique of the Single Currency (with Mike Woodin, 2000), From Seattle to Nice: Challenging the Free Trade Agenda at the Heart of Enlargement (2000), Stopping the Great Food Swap: Relocalising Europe's Food Supply (2001), Time to Replace Globalisation (2001), Which Way for the European Union: Radical Reform or Business as Usual? (2001), Local Food: Benefits and Opportunities (with Andy Jones, 2003), Towards a GM free Europe: Halting the Spread of GMOs in Europe (2003), Global Warming, Local Warming: A Study of the Likely Impacts of Climate Change upon South East England (2004), Green Alternatives to Globalisation: A Manifesto (with Mike Woodin, 2004); *Style*— Dr Caroline Lucas, MP; ✉ House of Commons, London SW1A 0AA

L

LUCAS, Christine Frances; da of John Hennessy (d 1969), and Ellen Alice, *née* Jones (d 1994); *b* 26 May 1944; *Educ* Our Lady's Convent Sch Cardiff, Cardiff Coll of Art, Ravensbourne Coll of Art and Design, Leicester Coll of Art and Design (DipAD); *m* 24 April 1971, John Lucas, s of Victor Lucas; *Career* asst knitwear designer Jaeger Co London 1966–70, design conslt for various men's and women's knitwear, leisurewear, swimwear, and loungewear companies 1970–80; Windsmoor Group 1980–90: successively designer Windsmoor and Planet knitwear, design team ldr on new design collections, product mangr, design co-ordinator, fndr and merchandise dir Précis petite collection; design dir Viyella Retail Div 1990–2001, design dir Alexon and Alex & Co 2002–03, md Viyella 2004–09; hon sec Blockley Div Nat Assoc of Fine Arts Socs (Nadfas) 2011–15; Award for Excellence Coats Viyella Fashion Retail Div 1993; FRSA 2004; *Recreations* art, theatre, reading, travel, gardens, interiors; *Style*— Mrs Christine Lucas; ✉ Larkrise, Coneygree Fold, Chipping Campden, Gloucestershire GL55 6JL (☎ 01386 849272)

LUCAS, Christopher Tullis; CBE (1994); s of Philip Gaddesden Lucas, GM (d 1982), and Maise Hanson (d 1984); *b* 20 December 1937; *Educ* Winchester; *m* 14 July 1962, Tina, da of Dr E T Colville; 2 da (Katherine b 1964, Suzannah b 1966); *Career* Nat Serv 1956–58; CA (Scot) 1965, Thomson McLintock and Co 1958–66, chief exec ICEM Ltd 1966–72, IBA 1972–74, first md Radio Forth Edinburgh 1974–77, sec and dir RSA 1977–94, conslt and project ldr RSA 1995–99, fndr and dir Animarts 1999–2004, fndr and dir Eastfeast 2004–07 (chm Tstee Bd 2008–12), chm Wonderful Beast Theatre Co 2012–, chm Action Sax 2015–; *Recreations* staying alive; *Style*— Mr Christopher Lucas, CBE; ✉ The Clock House, Church Street, Saxmundham, Suffolk IP17 1ER

LUCAS, Sir Colin; kt (2002); s of Frank Renshaw Lucas, and Janine, *née* Charpentier; *b* 25 August 1940, Egypt; *Educ* Sherborne, Lincoln Coll Oxford (MA, DPhil); *m* 1, 1964, Christiane Berchon de Fontaine Goubert (m dis 1975); 1 s; m 2, 1990, Mary Louise Hume; *Career* lectr: Univ of Sheffield 1965–69, Univ of Manchester 1970–73; Univ of Oxford: fell Balliol Coll 1973–90, tutor for admissions 1978–81, tutor for graduates 1989–90, memb Governing Bd Assoc Examinations Bd 1982–90; Univ of Chicago: prof 1990–94, chm Dept of History 1992–93, dean Div of the Social Sciences 1993–94; Univ of Oxford: master Balliol Coll 1994–2001, fell All Souls Coll 2001–06, pro-vice-chllr 1995–97, vice-chllr 1997–2004; sec Rhodes Tst and warden Rhodes House Oxford 2004–09; chm Br Library 2006–10; visiting appts: asst prof Indiana Univ 1969–70, prof Univ of Western Ontario 1975, prof Univ of Lyon-II 1977–78, prof Smith Coll 1987, sr fell in Soc for the Humanities Cornell Univ 1989; Leverhulme Faculty fell 1977–78, Radcliffe Research fell 1984–86; memb Hong Kong Univ Grants Ctee 2003–14, memb Cncl Univ of Liverpool 2009–; govr: Ludlow Coll 1975–90, Bradfield Coll 1987–90 and 1994–2011 (warden 2007–11), Sherborne Sch 2002–06; chm Voltaire Fndn Fund Ctee 1994–97; Hon DLitt: Univ of Sheffield 2000, Univ of Western Australia 2000, Peking Univ 2002, St Francis Xavier Univ 2003, Oxford Brookes Univ 2004; Hon Dr Univ of Lyon-II France 1989, Hon Dr jur Univ of Glasgow 2001, Hon LLD Univ of Princeton 2002, Hon DCL Univ of Oxford 2003, Hon LLD Univ of Warwick 2006, Hon DUniv Heidelberg Univ 2013; hon fell: Lincoln Coll Oxford, Balliol Coll Oxford; FRHistS 1973; Officier de l'Ordre des Arts et des Lettres (France) 1990, Chevalier Ordre du Mérite 1994, Légion d'Honneur 1998 (Officier 2005); *Books* The Structure of the Terror (1973), Beyond the Terror (with Gwynne Lewis, 1983), The Political Culture of the French Revolution (ed, 1988), Rewriting the French Revolution (ed, 1991); *Publications* author of numerous learned articles on eighteenth-century France, principally the French Revolution; *Clubs* Reform, Vincent's (Oxford), Oxford and Cambridge; *Style*— Sir Colin Lucas; ✉ Turkey House, Pound Lane, Clanfield, Oxfordshire OX18 2QZ (☎ 01865 270902, fax 01865 270914, e-mail colin.r.lucas@gmail.com)

LUCAS, Helena Kate; MBE (2013); da of Geoffrey Lucas, of Reigate, Surrey, and Valerie, *née* Meredith; *b* 29 April 1975, Redhill, Surrey; *Educ* BEng; *m* 9 Oct 2010, Stephen Thomas; *Career* Paralympic yachtswoman; Design Dept Bowman Yachts 1996–98; sailing achievements incl: Bronze medal World Championships 2009, Bronze medal Hyeres Regatta 2011, Bronze medal World Championships 2011, Silver medal Princess Sofia Trophy 2012, Silver medal Hyeres Regatta 2012, Silver medal Skandia Sail for Gold 2012, Gold medal Paralympic Games 2012 (first Paralympic medal Britain has won in sailing), winner World Cup Series 2012, Silver medal 2.4mR Open World Championships 2013; nominated ISAF Sailor of the Year 2006 and 2012; dir Weymouth and Portland Sailing Acad; Gold memb RYA 1989; Hon DSc Univ of Winchester 2013, Hon Dr of Sport Southampton Solent Univ 2013, Hon Dr of Arts Bournemouth Univ 2013; MRINA 1996; *Recreations* cycling, skiing, windsurfing, cruising (sailing); *Clubs* Royal Southampton Yacht, Royal Dorset Yacht; *Style*— Ms Helena Lucas, MBE; ✉ website www.helenalucas.com, Twitter @hlucasgbr; c/o Into The Blue, 1 The Parade, Cowes, Isle of Wight PO31 7QJ

LUCAS, Ian; MP; *b* 1960, Gateshead, Tyne & Wear; *Educ* Newcastle Royal GS, New Coll Oxford; *Career* qualified slr 1985, ran slrs office 1989–92, former ptnr Stevens Lucas Slrs; MP (Lab) Wrexham 2001–; memb Transport Select Ctee 2003–05, PPS to Bill Rammell, MP (as Min of State for Lifelong Learning, Further and Higher Educn) 2005–06, PPS to Liam Byrne, MP (as Min of State Home Office) 2007–08, asst govt whip 2008–09, Parly under sec of state Dept for Business, Innovation and Skills 2009–10, shadow min for business, innovation and skills 2010–11, shadow min for culture, Olympics, media and sport 2011, shadow min for foreign affrs (with responsibility for Africa and ME) 2011–14, shadow min for defence 2014–; *Style*— Ian Lucas, Esq, MP; ✉ House of Commons, London SW1A 0AA

LUCAS, Jeremy Charles Belgrave; s of Percy Belgrave Lucas, CBE, DSO, DFC, of London, and Jill Doreen, *née* Addison; *b* 10 August 1952; *Educ* Stowe, Pembroke Coll Cambridge (MA); *m* 4 Sept 1976, Monica Dorothea, *née* Bell; 2 s (Christopher b 1981, Timothy b 1984); *Career* slr Denton Hall and Burgin 1974–78; merchant banker Morgan Grenfell & Co Ltd 1978–2005 (dir 1986–2005), sr conslt Adsatis 2005–; *Recreations* tennis, golf; *Clubs* Royal West Norfolk Golf; *Style*— Jeremy Lucas, Esq

LUCAS, Prof (William) John; s of Leonard Townsend Lucas, and Joan, *née* Kelly; *b* 26 June 1937; *Educ* Hampton GS, Univ of Reading (BA, PhD); *m* 30 Sept 1961, Pauline; 1 s (Ben b 28 June 1962), 1 da (Emma b 11 Dec 1964); *Career* asst lectr Univ of Reading 1961–64, visiting prof Univs of Maryland and Indiana 1967–68, reader in English studies Univ of Nottingham 1975–77 (lectr 1964–71, sr lectr 1971–75), dean Sch of Educn and Humanities Loughborough Univ 1979–82 and 1988–96 (prof of English and drama and head of dept 1977–88), currently research prof Dept of English and Media Studies Nottingham Trent Univ; Lord Byron visiting prof of English lit Univ of Athens 1984–85; advsy ed: Jl of European Studies, Victorian Studies, Critical Survey, Literature and History; gen and commissioning ed: Faber Critical Monographs, Merlin Press Radical Reprints; co-ed Byron Press 1965–82, publisher Shoestring Press 1994–; regular contribs incl: Times Literary Supplement, Times Higher Educational Supplement, London Review of Books, New Statesman, The Listener, Poetry Review, BBC (Radios 3 and 4), Essays in Criticism, Cahiers Victoriens & Edourdiens Stand; Aldeburgh Poetry Prize 1990; FRSA 1984; *Books* incl: Tradition and Tolerance in 19th Century Fiction (with David Howard and John Goode, 1966), The Melancholy Man: A Study of Dickens (1970 and 1980), Arnold Bennett: A Study of his Fiction (1974), The Literature of Change (1977), Moderns & Contemporaries (1985), Modern English Poetry: from Hardy to Hughes (1986), Modern English Poetry (1986), England & Englishness (1990), Dickens: The Major Novels (1992), John Clare (1994), Writing and Radicalism (1996), Starting To Explain – Essays on 20th Century British and Irish Poetry (2003), Robert Browning (2003), Shoestring's Commons (2009), All My Eye and Betty Martin (2010); poetry: About Nottingham (1971), A Brief Bestiary (1972), Chinese Sequence (1972), The Days of the Week (1983), Studying Grosz on the Bus (1989), Flying to Romania: A Sequence in Verse and Prose (1992), One for the Piano: Poems (1997), The Radical Twenties (1997), On The Track (2000), The Good That We Do (2001), Ivor Gurney (2001), A World Perhaps – New and Selected Poems (2002), The Long and the Short of It: Poems (2004), Flute Music: Poems (2007), 92 Acharnon Street (2007, Dolman Best Travel Book Award 2008), I, The Poet Egil (2008), All My Eye and Betty Martin (2009), Next Year Will Be Better: A Memoir of England in the 1950s (2010), Things to Say: Poems (2010), Waterdrops (novel, 2011), Poetry in English of World War 2 (2012), A Brief History of Whistling (2013), The Awkward Squad, Rebels in English Cricket (2015), Portable Property (poems, 2015), George Crabbe: A Critical Study (2015), The Plotting (2016); *Style*— Prof John Lucas; ✉ 19 Devonshire Avenue, Beeston, Nottingham NG9 1BS; Department of English and Media Studies, The Nottingham Trent University, Clifton Lane, Nottingham NG11 8NS (☎ 0115 941 8418, fax 0115 948 4266)

LUCAS, John Randolph; s of Ven Egbert de Grey Lucas (Archdeacon of Durham, d 1958), and Joan Mary, *née* Randolph (d 1982); *b* 18 June 1929; *Educ* Dragon Sch Oxford, Winchester, Balliol Coll Oxford (scholar, BA, John Locke Prize); *m* 17 June 1961, Helen Morar, er da of Adm Sir Reginald Portal, KCB, DSC (d 1983), of Marlborough, Wilts; 2 s (Edward b 1962, Richard b 1966), 2 da (Helen b 1964, Deborah b 1967); *Career* fell: Merton Coll Oxford 1953–56 and 1960–96, Corpus Christi Coll Cambridge 1956–59; memb Archbishops' Cmmn on Christian Doctrine; chm Oxford Consumer Gp; Gifford lectr (Edinburgh Univ) 1971–73; pres Br Soc for the Philosophy of Sci 1991–93; *Books* The Principles of Politics (1964), The Concept of Probability (1970), The Freedom of the Will (1970), A Treatise on Time and Space (1973), The Development of Mind (with AJP Kenny, HC Longuet-Higgins and CH Waddington) Democracy and Participation (1976), Freedom and Grace (1976), On Justice (1980), Space, Time and Causality (1985), The Future (1989), Spacetime and Electromagnetism (1990), Responsibility (1993), Ethical Economics (1997), The Conceptual Roots of Mathematics (1999), An Engagement with Plato's Republic (2003), Reason and Reality (2006), Economics as a Moral Science (2011), Heretical Orthodoxy: An Unreverent Reading of the Gospels and Acts (2015); *Recreations* walking and talking; *Style*— J R Lucas, Esq; ✉ Lambrook House, East Lambrook, South Petherton, Somerset TA13 5HW (e-mail john.lucas@merton.ox.ac.uk, web http://users.ox.ac.uk/~jrlucas)

LUCAS, Matt; *b* 5 March 1974, London; *Educ* Univ of Bristol; *Career* comedian, actor and writer; acted with Nat Youth Theatre, collaborated with comedy ptnr David Walliams, *qv* 1995–; columnist for Guardian 1999–2001; *Theatre* incl: Sir Bernard Chumley and Friends (Edinburgh Festival) 1995, 1996 and 1997, Troilus and Cressida 2000, Taboo (as Leigh Bowery) 2002, Little Britain Tour 2005–07, Prick Up Your Ears 2009, Les Miserables (Queens Theatre and 25th Anniversary Concert) 2011; *Television* incl: Shooting Stars 1993, It's Ulrika 1997, Sir Bernard's Stately Homes 1998, Bang, Bang, It's Reeves and Mortimer 1999, Rock Profile 1999, Da Ali G Show (writer) 2000, Little Britain (BBC 1 and HBO) 2003–08, Casanova 2004, Catterick (BBC 2) 2004, Wind in the Willows (BBC 1) 2007, Krod Mandoon and the Flaming Sword of Fire (BBC 2 and Comedy Central) 2009, Shooting Stars (BBC) 2009, Come Fly With Me 2011, The Matt Lucas Awards (BBC 1) 2012 and 2013, Portlandia 2012, Community 2013, Super Fun Night (USA) 2013, Man Seeking Woman (USA) 2014; *Radio* incl: Little Britain (BBC Radio 4) 2001 and 2002, presenter And The Winner Is (BBC Radio 2) 2010–12; *Films* incl: Plunkett & Macleane 1999, Shaun of the Dead 2004, Tweedledum and Twedledee in Alice and Wonderland 2010, The Infidel 2010, Bridesmaids, Gnomeo and Juliet, Small Apartments, In Secret 2013, Paddington 2014, Alice in Wonderland: Through the Looking Glass 2016; *Awards* for Little Britain incl: Silver Sony Radio Acad Award 2003, Gold Best Comedy Spoken Word Publisher Awards 2004, Best Comedy Performance and Best Entertainment RTS Awards 2004, Best Comedy Nat TV Awards 2004; British Comedy Awards: People's Choice Award 2004, Best Comedy Actor (joint with David Walliams) 2004, Best British Comedy 2004, Best TV Comedy 2005, Ronnie Barker Writer's Award 2005; BAFTA Awards: Best Comedy Series 2004 and 2005, Best Comedy Performance 2005; Best Comedy South Bank Show Awards 2005, Best Comedy Broadcast Magazine Awards 2005, Best TV Show NME Awards 2005, Best Comedy TRIC Awards 2005; *Style*— Matt Lucas, Esq; ✉ c/o Troika Talent, 10a Christina Street, London EC2A 4PA

LUCAS, His Hon Judge Noel John Mac; QC (2008); s of John Joseph Lucas (d 1964), and Aroosiak, *née* Sarkies (d 2006); *b* 5 December 1952, Asansol, India; *Educ* King's Sch Ely, Queen Mary Coll Univ of London (BSc), Inns of Court Sch of Law; *m* 20 Aug 1994, Sylvia, *née* Hagopian; 2 s (Haïg John b 24 Dec 2000, Raffi John b 21 July 2003); *Career* called to the Bar (Middle Temple) 1979, 187 Fleet Street 1981–2005, Red Lion Chambers 2005–14; asst recorder 1999, recorder 2000, circuit judge (South Eastern Circuit) 2014–; *Recreations* reading, sailing, skiing, walking, classic cars, motorcycling; *Style*— His Hon Judge Lucas, QC; ✉ Guildford Crown Court, Bedford Road, Guildford, Surrey GU1 4ST (☎ 01483 468500, e-mail HHJNoel.LucasQC@judiciary.gsi.gov.uk)

LUCAS, Peter William; s of William George Lucas (d 1993), of Bradford Abbas, Dorset, and Jose Mabel, *née* House (d 2002); *b* 12 April 1947, Sherborne, Dorset; *Educ* Foster's Sch Sherborne, Harrow Coll (DipM); *m* 10 June 1972, Gail (d 2000), da of John Small (d 1983), of Camberley, Surrey; 2 da (Zoe b 1978, Joanna b 1984), 1 s (James Peter William b 1981); *Career* mktg dir Lyons Tetley Ltd 1978–84, princ The Marketing Department 1984–2000, managing ptnr Mappin Parry Lucas 1988–91; dir: Custom Management (UK) Ltd 1990–92, Kingsbourne Ltd 1990–95, Orange Learning Ltd 1997–, Orange Logic Ltd 1998–2010, The Orange Simulation Co Ltd 1998–; md: Insight People Development Ltd 1997–2011, The Orange Group Ltd 1995–, Insight Training Ltd 2004–11, The Green (Burton) Mngment Co Ltd 2005–, STEMS by RP Ltd 2012–; dir Assoc of Cereal Food Mfrs 1981–84; chm: Bd Govrs Watlington CPS 1988–91, Watlington Primary Sch Tst 1990–99; FCIM 1987, MInstD 1989; *Recreations* shooting, fishing, sailing; *Clubs* Christchurch Sailing; *Style*— Peter Lucas, Esq; ✉ Sejant House, The Green, Burton, Christchurch BH23 7NZ

LUCAS, Robert R; s of John R Lucas, and Rosalind J W Lucas; *b* 28 August 1962, Lincoln; *Educ* Lincoln Christs Hosp Sch, Imperial Coll London (BEng); *m* 15 Sept 1989, Sara J Lowthorpe; 1 da (Darcey b 12 Jan 1999), 1 s (Bruno b 1 Jan 2002); *Career* GEC Marconi plc 1985–87, 3i plc 1987–96, managing ptnr CVC Capital Ptnrs Ltd 1996–; non-exec dir: IG Group Holdings plc 2003–10, AA Group 2004–07, Acromas (AA/Saga) 2007–, Merlin Entertainment Gp 2010–, Virgin Active 2011–; *Style*— Robert Lucas, Esq; ✉ CVC Capital Partners, 111 Strand, London WC2R 0AG

LUCAS, Sir Thomas Edward; 5 Bt (UK 1887), of Ashtead Park, Surrey, and of Lowestoft, Suffolk; s of Ralph John Scott Lucas (ka 1941), late Coldstream Gds, gs of 1 Bt, and Dorothy (d 1985), da of H T Timson; *b* 16 September 1930; *Educ* Wellington, Trinity Hall Cambridge (MA); *m* 1, 1958, Charmian Margaret (d 1970), da of late Col James Stanley Powell; 1 s (Stephen Ralph James b 1963); m 2, 1980, Mrs Ann J Graham Moore; *Heir* s, Stephen Lucas; *Career* engr, scientist, author, speaker and registered healer, strategic conslt and co dir 1958–; sr tstee Inlight and Truemark Tsts 1996–; *Publications* Handbook of Vacuum Physics Vol 1 Part 2 (1964); *Recreations* modern art, classic cars, cooking, Eastern energy medicine; *Style*— Sir Thomas Lucas, Bt; ✉ e-mail sirtomlucas@gmail.com

LUCAS OF CRUDWELL, 11 Baron (E 1663) and 8 Lord Dingwall (S 1609); Ralph Matthew Palmer; s of Anne Rosemary, Baroness Lucas of Crudwell (10 holder of the title) and Lady Dingwall (7 holder of the title in her own right) (d 1991), and Maj Hon Robert Jocelyn Palmer, MC (d 1991); *b* 7 June 1951; *Educ* Eton, Balliol Coll Oxford; *m* 1, 1978 (m dis 1995), Clarissa Marie, da of George Vivian Lockett, TD, of Stratford St Mary, Suffolk; 1 da (Hon Hannah Rachel Elise b 1984), 1 s (Hon Lewis Edward b 1987); *m* 2, 1995, Amanda Atha (d 2000); *m* 3, 2001, Antonia Vera Kennedy, da of late Anthony Benno Stanley Rubinstein, of London; 1 da (Hon Freya Anne b 2002); *Heir* s, Hon Lewis Palmer; *Career* S G Warburg & Co Ltd 1976–88; Lord in Waiting (Govt Whip) 1994–97, shadow Lords min for Int Devpt 1997–98; publisher: The Good Schools Guide 1998–, The Good Careers Guide 2013–; Liveryman Worshipful Co of Mercers; FCA 1976; *Style*— The Lord Lucas of Crudwell and Dingwall; ✉ House of Lords, London SW1A 0PW (e-mail lucasr@parliament.uk)

LUCE, Baron (Life Peer UK 2000), of Adur in the County of West Sussex; Sir Richard Napier; KG (2008), kt (1991), GCVO (2000), PC (1986), DL; s of Sir William Luce, GBE, KCMG (d 1977), and Margaret (d 1989), da of Adm Sir Trevelyan Napier, KCB; *b* 14 October 1936; *Educ* Wellington, Christ's Coll Cambridge; *m* 5 April 1961, Rose Helen, eldest da of Sir Godfrey Nicholson, 1 Bt (d 1991); 2 s (Alexander Richard b 1964, Edward Godfrey b 1968); *Career* Nat Serv Cyprus; dist offr Kenya 1960–62, former mangr Gallaher and Spirella Co (GB); Parly candidate (Cons) Hitchin 1970; MP (Cons): Arundel and Shoreham 1971–74, Shoreham 1974–92; PPS to Min for Trade and Consumer Affrs 1972–74, oppn whip 1974–75, oppn spokesman on foreign and Cwlth affrs 1977–79; FCO: Parly under sec 1979–81, min of state 1981–82 (resigned over invasion of Falkland Islands), re-appointed min of state 1983; min for the Arts and min of state Privy Cncl Office responsible for The Civil Serv Sept 1985–90, ret from Parl 1992; vice-chllr Univ of Buckingham 1992–97; govr and C-in-C Gibraltar 1997–2000; Lord Chamberlain to HM The Queen's Household 2000–06, High Steward Westminster Abbey 2011–; chm: Cwlth Fndn 1992–96, Atlantic Cncl of the UK 1992–97, Crown Nominations Cmmn for the See of Canterbury 2012; pres: Voluntary Arts Network 1992–2013 (founding patron 2013–), King George V Fund for Actors and Actresses 2007–12, Cwlth Youth Orch 2010–13; non-exec dir Meridian Broadcasting Ltd 1992–97, former non-exec dir Booker Tate Ltd; tstee Geographers A-Z Map Co; hon fell Christ's Coll Cambridge; *Publications* Ringing the Changes: A Memoir (2007); *Clubs* Royal Overseas League (pres 2003–), RAC; *Style*— The Rt Hon the Lord Luce, KG, GCVO, PC, DL; ✉ Dragon's Farmhouse, Cowfold, Horsham, West Sussex RH13 8DX (e-mail rrluce@hotmail.com); House of Lords, London SW1A 0PW

LUCIE-SMITH, (John) Edward McKenzie; s of John Dudley Lucie-Smith, MBE (d 1943), and Mary Frances Maud, *née* Lushington (d 1982); *b* 27 February 1933; *Educ* King's Sch Canterbury, Merton Coll Oxford (MA); *Career* Nat Serv RAF Flying Offr 1954–56; worked in advtg 1956–66, poet, art critic and freelance writer and photographer with contribs to The Times, Sunday Times, The Independent, The Mail on Sunday, The Listener, The Spectator, New Statesman, Evening Standard, Encounter, London Magazine, Illustrated London News, Art Review, La Vanguardia (Barcelona); photography exhbns in London, Rome, Barcelona, St Petersburg, Tel Aviv and Kuala Lumpur; FRSL; *Books* A Tropical Childhood and Other Poems (1961), A Group Anthology (ed with Philip Hobsbaum, 1963), Confessions and Histories (1964), Penguin Modern Poets 6 (with Jack Clemo and George MacBeth, 1964), Penguin Book of Elizabethan Verse (ed, 1965), What is a Painting? (1966), The Liverpool Scene (ed, 1967), A Choice of Browning's Verse (ed, 1967), Penguin Book of Satirical Verse (ed, 1967), Towards Silence (1968), Thinking About Art (1968), Movements in Art since 1945 (1969), British Poetry since 1945 (ed, 1970), Art in Britain 1969–70 (with P White, 1970), A Primer of Experimental Verse (ed, 1971), French Poetry: The Last Fifteen Years (ed with S W Taylor, 1971), A Concise History of French Painting (1971), Symbolist Art (1972), Eroticism in Western Art (1972), The First London Catalogue (1974), The Well Wishers (1974), The Burnt Child (1975), The Invented Eye (1975), World of the Makers (1975), How the Rich Lived (with C Dars, 1976), Joan of Arc (1976), Work and Struggle (with C Dars, 1977), Fantin-Latour (1977), The Dark Pageant (1977), Art Today (1977), A Concise History of Furniture (1979), Super Realism (1979), Cultural Calendar of the Twentieth Century (1979), Art in the Seventies (1980), The Story of Craft (1981), The Body (1981), A History of Industrial Design (1983), Art Terms: An Illustrated Dictionary (1984), Art in the Thirties (1985), American Art Now (1985), The Male Nude: A Modern View (with François de Louville, 1985), Lives of the Great Twentieth Century Artists (1986), Sculpture Since 1945 (1987), The Self Portrait: A Modern View (with Sean Kelly, 1987), Art in the 1980's (1990), Art Deco Painting (1990), Fletcher Benton (1990), Latin American Art of the Twentieth Century (1993), Art and Civilization (1993), Wendy Taylor (1993), Race, Sex and Gender: issues in contemporary art (1994), Frink: a portrait (with Elizabeth Frink, 1994), John Kirby (1994), American Realism (1994), Art Today (completely new version, 1995), Visual Art in the 20th Century (1996), Albert Paley (1996), Ars Erotica (1997), Lynn Chadwick (1997), Adam (1998), Zoo (1998), Women and Art (with Judy Chicago, 1999), Judy Chicago (2000), Flesh and Stone (photographs, 2000), Changing Shape (2001), Roberto Marquez (2001), Art Tomorrow (2002), Carlo Bertocci (2002), Stefano di Stasio (2002), Paola Gandolfi (2003), Alberto Abate (2003), Philip Pearlstein (2004), Carlos Ferns Barcla (2004), Ricardo Cinalli (2005), Elias Rivera (2006), Harry Holland (2006), Santiago Cardenas (2007), Kent Williams (2008), Lives of the Great Modern Artists (2009), The Glory of Angels (2009), The Face of Jesus (2011), Joe Machine (2013), Milos Sobaijc (2013), Jamaica in Black and White (2013), Jamil Naqsh: The Painted Word (2013); *Recreations* computers; *Style*— Edward Lucie-Smith, Esq; ✉ 104 West Kensington Court, Edith Villas, London W14 9AB (✆ 020 7603 2506, e-mail jemls_uk@ yahoo.com, website www.edwardlucie-smith.co.uk, Twitter @EdwardLucieSmit)

LUCK, Ralph David; OBE (2004); s of Bryan Spencer Luck, of Maidstone, Kent, and Betty Joan, *née* Wilson; *b* 27 March 1952, Maidstone, Kent; *Educ* Maidstone GS, Mid Kent Coll (DMS), Coll of Estate Mgmnt; *Career* sr devpt mangr Taylor Woodrow Property Co 1987–91, dir of devpt Chatham Maritime 1991–94; English Partnerships: dir London and South East 1994–97, dir of devpt for Greenwich Peninsula 1997–2003, dir London and Thames Gateway 2002–06; dir of property Olympic Delivery Authy 2006–13, dir of property and real estate devpt KCL 2013–14; chm Br Urban Regeneration Assoc 2004–07; FRICS 1976, FCMI 1981; *Recreations* sailing, cricket; *Clubs* various sailing clubs; *Style*— Ralph D Luck, Esq, OBE; ✆ 020 7848 7240, e-mail ralph.luck@kcl.ac.uk

LUCKETT, Dr Dominic Antony; s of Antony Luckett, of King's Lynn, Norfolk, and Moya, *née* Hinds; *b* 29 August 1966, Norwich; *Educ* Univ of Leicester (BA), Magdalen Coll Oxford (DPhil); *m* 17 Dec 2006, Cara, *née* Guthrie; 2 da (Charlotte b 17 Sept 2008, Jemima b 19 July 2013); *Career* head History and asst housemaster Harrow Sch, dep head Worth Sch, headmaster Mill Hill and chief exec Mill Hill Sch Fndn 2007–15, headmaster Sherborne 2016–; memb Cncl Univ of Leicester; FRSA 2007, FHA 2012; *Publications* incl various articles on early Tudor history; *Recreations* music, skiing, reading, clocks; *Clubs* Athenaeum; *Style*— Dr Dominic Luckett; ✉ Sherborne School, Abbey Road, Sherborne DT9 3AP (✆ 01935 810401, website www.sherborne.org)

LUCKHURST, Prof Geoffrey Roger; s of William Thomas Victor Luckhurst (d 1970), and Hilda Mary, *née* Flood (d 2001); *b* 21 January 1939; *Educ* Sir Joseph Williamson's Mathematical Sch Rochester, Univ of Hull, Univ of Cambridge; *m* 3 July 1965, Janice Rita, da of Colin Jack Flanagan (d 1995), of Romsey, Hants; 2 da (Nicola Jane b 25 Jan 1970, Caroline b 15 July 1972); *Career* Univ of Southampton: lectr 1967–70, reader 1970–

77, prof of chemistry 1977–2004 (emeritus prof 2004–), dep-dean of sci 2000–03, sr library curator 1996–, chm Advsy Bd Sch of Chemistry 2004–07; pres Int Liquid Crystal Soc 1992–96 (honoured memb), chm Br Liquid Crystal Soc 1994–2000; coordinator of EC TMR Network 1999–2002, co-ordinator INTAS Project 2000–02; Leverhulme emeritus fell 2004–07; G W Gray Medal Br Liquid Crystal Soc 2002, Fredericksz Medal and Dip Russian Liquid Crystal Soc 2007; hon memb Royal Irish Acad 2010; *Publications* Biaxial Nematic Liquid Crystals Theory Simulation and Experiment (ed with T J Sluckin, 2015); *Style*— Prof Geoffrey Luckhurst; ✉ Chemistry, University of Southampton SO17 1BJ (✆ 023 8059 3795, fax 023 8059 3781, e-mail gl@soton.ac.uk)

LUCKIN, (Peter) Samuel; s of Geoffrey Grimston Luckin (d 1986), of High Easter, nr Chelmsford, Essex, and Muriel Bessie, *née* Need (d 1962); *b* 9 March 1938; *Educ* Felsted; *Career* Nat Serv cmmnd Essex Regt 1956–58, platoon cdr BAOR; press aide for Rt Hon Edward Heath CCO 1960's, dep head of PR for Brewers' Soc 1970's, owner Sam Luckin Associates 1980–; freelance journalist; memb: Bd of Mgmnt Ashridge Mgmnt Coll Assoc 1982–85, Cncl IPR 1989–91 and 1992–95 (chm Membership Ctee 1991, memb Bd of Mgmnt 1991); FCIPR (FIPR 1990); *Recreations* , management development, watching first class cricket and rugby union; *Clubs* Farmers', MCC, Harlequins RFC; *Style*— Samuel Luckin, Esq; ✉ 4 Huggens College, College Road, Northfleet, Kent DA11 9DL (✆ and fax 01474 364440, e-mail samluckin@hotmail.com)

LUCKING, Her Hon Judge Adrienne Simone; QC (2014); da of Robert Dorrien Coombe, and Patricia Alice Maud Claxton, *née* Pardoe; *b* 28 October 1966, Leicester; *Educ* Prince William Sch Oundle, De Montfort Univ; *m* Andrew Duncan Collie; *Career* called to the Bar 1989; recorder 2009, circuit judge (Midland Circuit) 2015–; *Recreations* reading, rugby, national hunt racing, polo; *Style*— Her Hon Judge Lucking, QC

LUCRAFT, His Hon Judge Mark; QC (2006); s of the Rev C W Lucraft, and Ann Elizabeth, *née* Knight; *b* 28 December 1961, Essex; *Educ* Wood Green Sch, Univ of Kent (BA); *m* Fiona Carmel, *née* Ovington; 3 s; *Career* called to the Bar 1984; recorder 2003, circuit judge (South Eastern Circuit) 2012–; *Books* Archbold: Criminal Pleading, Evidence & Practice (contributing ed, 1996), Encyclopaedia of Road Traffic Law and Practice (jt ed, 2002), Fraud: Criminal Law and Procedure (jt ed, 2009), Halsbury's Laws of England, Road Traffic (conslt ed, 5 edn 2011), Crown Court Indes (jt ed, 36 edn 2016); *Recreations* cricket, classical music, gardening, good food and wine; *Clubs* MCC; *Style*— His Hon Judge Lucraft, QC; ✉ The Crown Court at Cambridge, 83 East Road, Cambridge CB1 1BT

LUCY; see: *Fairfax-Lucy*

LUDEMAN, Keith Lawrence; s of Joseph William Lawrence Ludeman, and Joan Violet, *née* Dopson; *b* 28 January 1950, London; *Educ* Univ of Newcastle (BA), Univ of Salford (MSc, DSc); *m* 26 Oct 1974, Diane June; 2 da (Emma, Claire); *Career* Gtr Manchester Tport 1974–82, sr tport offr Hong Kong Govt 1982–85, sr conslt MVA Consultancy 1985–86, md Burnley & Pendle Tport & Viscount Central 1986–88, md London General 1988–96; Go-Ahead Gp: md London Bus Div 1996–99, md Thameslink & Thames Trains 1999–2000, ceo rail 2000–06, gp ceo 2006–11; non-exec dir: ATOC Ltd 2003–, Inteserve plc 2011–; sr ind dir Network Rail 2011–14; chm: Bristol Water plc 2012–, Aspin Gp 2015–, TXM Plant 2016–; memb: Confedn of Passenger Tport 1997–2000, Br Tport Police Authy 2003–05; chm Assoc of Train Operating Companies 2003–05; dir and tstee London Transport Museum; Lifetime Contribution to Transport National Transport Award 2011; FRSA, FCILT, fell Instn of Railway Operators; *Recreations* sailing, scuba diving, swimming; *Clubs* RAC; *Style*— Keith Ludeman, Esq; ✉ e-mail ludemankd@aol.com

LUDER, Ian David; CBE (2010), JP (City of London, 2002); s of late Mark Luder, and Frances, *née* Stillerman; *b* 13 April 1951; *Educ* Haberdashers' Aske's, UCL (BSc); *m* 21 Aug 1999, Lin Jane *née* Surkitt; *Career* Arthur Andersen 1971–78: joined as articled clerk, subsequently tax sr then tax mangr 1975; ptnr: MacIntyre Hudson CA's 1980–88, Arthur Andersen 1989–2002, Grant Thornton 2002–09; chm Basildon and Thurrock Univ Hosps NHS Fndn Tst 2012–; cncllr Bedford BC 1976–1999; chm: Policy Ctee 1988–93, Planning & Transport Ctee 1995–1998; memb Ct of Common Cncl City of London 1998– (chm Fin Ctee 2003–06), Alderman Castle Baynard Ward 2005–, sheriff City of London 2007–08, Lord Mayor City of London 2008–09; non-exec dir Homerton Univ Hosp NHS Fndn Tst 2002–08; Liveryman: Worshipful Co fo Coopers, Worshipful Co of Tax Advsrs; FCA 1974, FTII 1974 (pres 1994–95), FRSA 1993; *Books* Tolleys Personal Tax and Investment Planning (ed), Simon's Taxes (contrib), Butterworths Tax and Remuneration Strategies; *Recreations* cricket, local politics, music; *Clubs* MCC, Bedford RUFC, East India; *Style*— Ian D Luder, Esq, CBE; ✉ c/o Members Room, City of London Corporation, Guildhall, London EC2

LUDER, (Harold) Owen; CBE (1986); s of Edward Charles Luder (d 1981), and Ellen Clara, *née* Mason (d 1986); *b* 7 August 1928; *Educ* Sch of Architecture Regent St Poly, Sch of Architecture Brixton Sch of Bldg; *m* 1, 29 Jan 1951 (m dis 1989), Rose Dorothy (Doris), *née* Broadstock (d 2010); 4 da (Jacqueline Kim b 3 May 1953, Kathryn Joy b 8 July 1954, Sara Jayne b 16 Oct 1966, Judith Amanda b 29 Jan 1968), 1 s (Peter Jonathan Owen b 6 Oct 1965 d 8 Dec 1965); *m* 2, 10 May 1989, Jacqueline Ollerton (d 2008); *Career* conscript RE and RA 1946–48; qualified architect 1954, started own practice Owen Luder Partnership 1957, withdrew 1987 to develop new consultancy Communication In Construction; designed many bldgs UK and abroad 1954–87 (incl Tricorn Portsmouth, Get Carter Car Park Gateshead, Taif City Hall Saudi Arabia, environmental conslt NCB – Belvoir coal mines 1975–87; non-exec dir Jarvis plc 1995–2003; various awards incl: RIBA Bronze Medal 1963 (for Eros House Catford 1963), RTPI Silver Medal (for regeneration of Br Rail Engrg Works Sheldon), Town Planning Assoc Silver Jubilee Medal (for study Housing Strategy for the 80s); audio biography included in British Library archive Architects' Lives 2016; memb UK Govt Mission to US Conference on Cities 1970 and US Congress Ctee of Urban Redevelopment 1967, Arkansas traveller USA 1971 (for advice on regeneration of Down Town Little Rock); columnist Building Magazine (Business Columnist of the Year 1985), contrib nat and tech press, radio and TV broadcaster; pres Norwood Soc 1981–92, pres RIBA 1981–83 and 1995–97 (hon treas 1975–78); chm ARB 2002–03 (vice-chm 1997–2002); vice-pres Membership Communications 1989–90; ARIBA 1954, FRIBA 1967, FRSA 1984, MBAE 1992; *Publications* Sports Stadia After Hillsborough (1991), Architects Guide to Keeping out of Trouble (1999, 4 edn 2012); *Recreations* writing, theatre, Arsenal FC, photography, writing poetry; *Style*— Owen Luder, Esq, CBE, PPRIBA; ✉ Owen Luder Consultancy, 702 Romney House, 47 Marsham Street, London SW1P 3DS (✆ 020 7222 0198, e-mail owenluder@dsl.pipex.com)

LUDFORD, Baroness (Life Peer UK 1997), of Clerkenwell in the London Borough of Islington; Sarah Ludford; da of Joseph Campbell Ludford, and Valerie Kathleen, *née* Skinner; *b* 14 March 1951; *Educ* Portsmouth HS for Girls, LSE (BSc, MSc), Inns of Court Sch of Law; *m* Steve Hitchins; *Career* barrister; called to the Bar Gray's Inn 1979; official Secretariat Gen and DG Competition EC 1979–85; Euro and UK policy advsr Lloyd's of London 1985–87, vice-pres corp external affrs American Express Euro 1987–90, Euro conslt 1990–99; MEP (Lib Dem) London 1999–2014 (contested Euro Parly constituency seat: Wight and Hampshire E 1984, London Central 1989 and 1994; contested UK Parly constituency seat: Islington N 1992, Islington S and Finsbury 1997); memb Lib Dem Pty, currently Lib Dem Parly spokesman on Europe; cncllr Islington BC 1991–99, vice-chair Lib Dem Fed Policy Ctee 1991–98, vice-pres Gay and Lesbian Lib Dems (DELGA), vice-chair Justice, patron Fair Trials Int; memb Cncl Federal Tst; memb: RIIA, Euro Movement; *Publications* The EU: From Economic Community to Human Rights

L

Community (article contrib to To the Power of Ten (G Watson & H Hazelwood (eds), 2000)); *Recreations* theatre, ballet, gardening; *Style—* The Baroness Ludford; ✉ House of Lords, London SW1A 0PW (e-mail ludfords@parliament.uk, Twitter @SarahLudford)

LUDLAM, Prof Christopher Armstrong; *b* 6 June 1946; *Educ* Univ of Edinburgh (BSc, MB ChB, PhD); *Career* research fell MRC Univ of Edinburgh 1972–75, sr registrar Univ Hosp of Wales Cardiff 1975–78, lectr in haematology Univ of Wales 1979; Dept of Med Univ of Edinburgh 1980–: conslt haematologist, dir Edinburgh Haemophilia Centre, prof of haematology and coagulation med; numerous publications on blood coagulation; FRCPE, FRCPath; *Style—* Prof Christopher Ludlam; ✉ 20 Tantallon Place, Edinburgh, Scotland EH9 1NB (☎ and fax 0131 667 6232, e-mail cal@ludlam.org.uk)

LUDLOW, Bishop of 2009–; Rt Rev Alistair James Magowan; s of late Samuel Magowan, and Marjorie Magowan; *b* 10 February 1955; *Educ* King's Sch Worcester, Univ of Leeds (BSc), Trinity Coll Bristol (DipHE), Univ of Oxford (MTh); *m* 1979, Louise, *née* Atkin; 2 da (Rachel, Susannah), 1 s (Andrew); *Career* curate St John the Baptist Owlerton 1981–84, curate St Nicholas Durham 1984–89, chaplain St Aid Coll Durham 1984–89, vicar St John the Baptist Egham 1989–2000, rural dean Runnymede 1993–2000, archdeacon of Dorset 2000–09; chair Guildford Diocese Bd of Educn 1996–2000; *Style—* The Rt Rev the Bishop of Ludlow; ✉ Bishop's House, Corvedale Road, Craven Arms, Shropshire SY7 9BT (☎ 01588 673571, e-mail bishopofludlow@btinternet.com)

LUETCHFORD, Robert Sellick; s of William Luetchford (d 1984), and Roma, *née* Lawrence; *b* 29 March 1949; *Educ* Harrow Co GS, Pembroke Coll Oxford (MA); *m* 7 Nov 1990, Nicola Christine, da of Michael Gilbert; *Career* International Computers Ltd 1971–74, Sperry Univac (UK) Ltd 1974–77; Plessey Co Ltd: Plessey Microsystems Ltd 1977–79, Plessey Corp Staff 1979–81, dir of planning and business devpt Plessey Office Systems Ltd 1981–84; Prudential Bache Securities: head of electronics res 1984–86, vice-pres 1986, sr vice-pres Corp Fin 1986; dir and controller Marshall Securities Ltd 1986–; fndr and non-exec dir Progressive Asset Management Ltd; *Recreations* opera, classical music, fly fishing; *Style—* Robert Luetchford, Esq; ✉ Marshall Securities Ltd, 145 St John Street, London EC1V 4QJ (☎ 020 7490 3788, fax 020 7490 3787)

LUFF, Sir Peter James; kt (2014); s of Thomas Luff (d 1963), and Joyce, *née* Mills (d 1985); *b* 18 February 1955; *Educ* Licensed Victuallers' Sch Slough, Windsor GS, CCC Cambridge (exhibitioner, MA); *m* May 1982, Julia Dorothy, da of Lt Cdr P D Jenks, RN; 1 da (Rosanna Amy b 29 Aug 1985), 1 s (Oliver Charles Henry b 10 Jan 1988); *Career* res asst to Rt Hon Peter Walker 1977–80, head of Private Office of Rt Hon Edward Heath 1980–82, asst md then md Good Relations Public Affairs Ltd 1980–87, special advsr to sec of state for Trade and Industry 1987–89, sr conslt Bell Pottinger Communications (formerly Lowe Bell Communications) 1989–90, co sec Luff and Sons Ltd Windsor 1980–87, asst md Good Relations Ltd 1990–92; MP (Cons): Worcester 1992–97, Worcestershire Mid 1997–2015 (Parly candidate (Cons) Holborn and St Pancras 1987); PPS to: min for Energy 1993–96, Lord Chllr 1996–97, min for Prisons 1996–97; oppn whip 2000–02, asst chief whip 2002–05; memb Commons Select Ctee on: Welsh Affrs 1992–97, Tport 1993, Agric 1997–2000 (chm), Information 2001–05, Admin 2003–05, Int Devpt 2014–15; chair Business, Innovation and Skills Select Ctee (formerly Trade and Industry and Business and Enterprise Ctee) 2005–10, Parly under sec of state for defence equipment, support and technol Miny of Defence 2010–12; jt sec Cons Backbench Ctee on Transport 1992–93, patron Cons Students 1994–98, chm Cons Parly Friends of India 2001–05; Industry and Parl Tst Fellowship 2009; FIPR, hon fell CIPR 2008; *Recreations* theatre, shooting, photography; *Style—* Sir Peter Luff; ✉ House of Commons, London SW1A 0AA; ☎ 01905 763952

LUKE, 3 Baron (UK 1929); Arthur Charles St John Lawson Johnston; s of 2 Baron Luke, KCVO, TD (d 1996), and Barbara (d 2006), da of Sir Fitzroy Hamilton Anstruther-Gough-Calthorpe, 1 Bt; *b* 13 January 1933; *Educ* Eton, Trinity Coll Cambridge (BA); *m* 1, 6 Aug 1959 (m dis 1971), Silvia Maria, da of Don Honorio Roigt, former Argentine ambass at The Hague; 2 da (Hon Rachel Honoria (Hon Mrs Parrack) b 1960, Hon Sophia Charlotte (Hon Mrs Kirk) b 1966), 1 s (Hon (Ian) James St John Lawson Johnston b 4 Oct 1963); m 2, 1971, Sarah Louise, da of Richard Hearne, OBE; 1 s (Hon Rupert Arthur b 1972); *Heir* s, Hon James Lawson Johnston; *Career* art dealer; co cncllr Beds 1966–70 (chm of Staffing Ctee 1967–70), High Sheriff Beds 1969–70, DL Beds 1989–2005; cdr St John Ambulance Bde Beds 1985–90 (cmmr 1972–85); pres Nat Assoc of Warehouse-Keepers 1960–78; memb Ct: The Drapers Co 1993– (jr warden 1993, 2nd master warden 1999–2000, master 2001–02), Corp of the Sons of the Clergy 1980–2005; sits as Cons House of Lords, oppn whip for culture media and sport and for defence 1997–2010, chm Works of Art Ctee House of Lords 2010–; KStJ 1990; *Recreations* shooting, fishing; *Clubs* MCC; *Style—* The Lord Luke; ✉ Camross Leys, 46 Main Street, Middleton, Leicestershire LE16 8YU (☎ 01536 772129, fax 01536 771198); London: ☎ 020 7219 3703, fax 020 7219 6069, e-mail lukea@parliament.uk

LUKE, Colin Rochfort; s of Donald Alfred Rochfort Luke, of Jersey, CI, and Mary Blanche, *née* Bennett; *b* 24 January 1946; *Educ* Bristol GS, Exeter Coll Oxford (MA, memb Univ fencing team, pres OU Film Soc, films ed Isis magazine); *m* 1, 1971 (m dis 1976), Sarah Moffat Hellings; m 2, 1978, Hon Felicity Margaret, da of Baron Crowther (Life Peer, d 1972); 2 s (Theodore Rochfort b 1979, Harley Rochfort b 1981), 1 da (Claudia Mary b 1983); *Career* director and producer; BBC: joined as trainee film ed 1967, film and studio dirs course 1969, prodr/dir 1969–79; formed own co Wobbly Pictures Ltd 1977 (renamed Mosaic Pictures Ltd 1989), freelance film dir 1979–, dir Document Films Ltd 1982, formed Document Television Ltd 1987, md Mosaic Films 1996–, formed Mosaic Films LLP 2007; Freeman City of Louisville Kentucky 1963; fndr memb BAFTA (dep vice-chm TV 1998–99), memb Bd Dirs UK; memb: PACT, RTS; *Television* progs for BBC 1969–79: The World About Us, The Romance of the Indian Railways (with James Cameron), A Desert Voyage (with Dame Freya Stark), Albion in the Orient (with Julian Pettifer), Black Safari, Take Six Girls-Israel, Taste for Adventure, Half Million Pound Magic Carpet, Diamonds in the Sky; as freelance dir/prodr: Nature Watch (ATV/TV) 1980, Towards an Unknown Land (with Dame Freya Stark) 1981, The Arabs (Channel 4) 1981, Britain at the Pictures (BBC) 1983, Duneriders (Channel 4) 1985, Heart of the Kremlin (Central/ITV Network) 1991, Will They Ring Tonight (BBC) 1993, A Change of Heart (BBC) 1993, Frontline Vietnam (Channel 4) 1993, The Making of Them (BBC) 1994, Apocalypse Then (BBC) 1994; exec prodr: Assignment Adventure (Channel 4) 1984–85 (winner numerous Adventure Film Awards), A Russia of One's Own (Channel 4) 1987, Frontline Doctors (BBC) 1991, Nomads (Channel 4) 1992, Captain Pedro and the Three Wishes (Channel 4), Ivanov Goes to Moscow (Channel 4) 1997, The Long Weekend (Channel 4) 1998, Return to Wonderland (BBC) 1999, Pakistan Daily (BBC) 2002, The Tube (Carlton) 2003; dir: The Golden Road (TBS) 1986–87, The Baltic Style (TBS) 1987, An Affair in Mind (BBC) 1987–88, The Princess's People (BBC) 1998; series ed: Voyager (Central/ITV Network) 1988–89, The World of National Geographic (Central) 1988–89, Classic Adventure (BBC) 1991–92; series dir Russian Wonderland (BBC) 1995, United Kingdom! (BBC) 1997, Unholy Land (Channel 4) 1998, EUtopia (BBC/Arte, winner Adolf Grimme Special Prize Germany) 2000; as prodr Quality Time (BBC) 1996 (winner of Best Documentary Award Broadcasting Press Guild Awards 1996), Birth of a Salesman (Channel 4) 1996, Think of England (BBC) 1999, The Tube Series 2 (ITV) 2004, The Tube Series 3 (ITV/Sky) 2005, Games in Athens (BBC) 2005; *Recreations* family, travel, cinema, politics; *Clubs* BAFTA; *Style—* Colin Luke, Esq; ✉ Mosaic Films Ltd, Shacklewell Studios, 28 Shacklewell Lane, London E8 2EZ (☎ 020 7923 2994, fax 020 7923 2994, e-mail info@mosaicfilms.com, website www.mosaicfilms.com)

LUKE, HE Robert Haydon Vernon (Rob); *m* Louise *née* Elwell; 1 da, 2 s; *Career* diplomat; grant scheme mangr Millennium Cmmn 1997–2000, desk offr Middle East Peace Process Section Nr East and North Africa Dept FCO 2000–01, secondment to Brazilian Diplomatic Inst 2002, second sec political/press and public affairs Brasilia 2002–05, head War Crimes Section Int Organisations Dept FCO 2005–08, secondment to French Immigration Miny 2008, cnsllr of justice and home affairs Paris 2009–12, high cmmr to Repub of Malta 2012–; *Style—* HE Mr Rob Luke

LUKE, (William) Ross; s of Maj Hamish Galbraith Russell Luke TD, JP (d 1970), and Ellen Robertson Boyd, *née* Mitchell; *b* 8 October 1943; *Educ* Stowe; *m* 16 May 1970, Deborah Jacqueline, da of Derek John Gordon; 3 da (Alison b 1973 d 1998, Kirstene b 1974, Victoria b 1978); *Career* CA 1968; sr ptnr Luke, Gordon & Co CAs; vice-pres London Scottish FC 1995– (hon sec 1988–92, hon treas 2006–11); Met Police Commendation 1983; *Recreations* rugby football, subaqua diving; *Clubs* Caledonian Soc of London; *Style—* Ross Luke, Esq; ✉ Luke, Gordon & Co (Chartered Accountants), 105 Palewell Park, London SW14 8JJ (☎ 020 8876 9228)

LUMB, David John; s of George Spencer Lumb (d 1988), and Margaret Minnie, *née* Spencer (d 1995); *b* 25 July 1950; *Educ* Abbeydale GS, Leeds Sch of Architecture (Dip Arch); *m* (m dis 2000), Judith Margaret, da of James Sewell; 1 s (Daniel James b 1978), 2 da (Amy Elizabeth b 1980, Rachel Lucy b 1984); partner, Ann Clare Lea; *Career* project architect Property Services Agency NE Region 1975–77; Fletcher Ross & Hickling: joined as architect 1977, assoc 1980–86, sr assoc 1986–88; md: Trevor Wilkinson Associates 1989–95 (joined as dir 1988), D Y Davies (York) 1995–96, ML Design Group (Northern) Ltd 1996–2006, Design Group Three Ltd 2003–09; dir: ML Design Group Ltd 1996–2003, Architecture 519 Limited 2009–14, Leeds Sustainable Devpt Gp CIC 2013–; ret 2014; vice-chm RIBA Companies Ltd 1995–97, pres West Yorkshire Soc of Architects 1997–98, memb Acad of Urbanism 2010–; corporate memb RIBA 1980–; *Awards* for Wistow Shaft site: Festival of Architecture Award 1984, Civic Tst Award 1986; White Rose Award (for Riccall and Stillingfleet Shaft sites) 1986, Concrete Soc Commendation (for Doncaster Crown Court) 1990, Craftmanship Award and Commendations (for York Crown Court) 1991; *Recreations* travelling, walking, reading; *Style—* David Lumb, Esq

LUMLEY, John Adrian; s of Thomas Lumley (d 1983), and Patience, *née* Henn Collins (d 1987); *b* 29 May 1942; *Educ* Eton, Magdalene Coll Cambridge (MA); *m* 1, 14 June 1969, Catita (d 2012), da of Hans Lieb (d 1959); 1 s (Joshua b 1970), 2 da (Eliza b 1973, Olivia b 1981); m 2, 9 March 2013, Susana Berenguer Monzon, da of Luis Berenguer (d 1979); *Career* Christie's (Christie, Manson & Woods Ltd); joined 1964, dir 1969–, jt dep chm 1993–96, jt vice-chm 1996–2004, hon vice-chm 2004–; dir Christie's Fine Art Ltd 1998–; memb Kent and E Sussex Regnl Ctee Nat Tst 1981–87; Liveryman Worshipful Co of Goldsmiths 1984; *Clubs* Brooks's; *Style—* John Lumley, Esq; ✉ Stonebridge Barn, Pluckley, Ashford, Kent TN27 9AN (☎ 01233 756249); Christie's, 8 King Street, London SW1Y 6QT (☎ 020 7839 9060)

LUMLEY, Karen Elizabeth; MP; *b* Barnsley, S Yorks; *m* Richard Lumley; 1 da, 1 s; *Career* MP (Cons) Redditch 2010–; *Style—* Mrs Karen Lumley, MP; ✉ House of Commons, London SW1A 0AA

LUMSDEN, Prof Andrew Gino Sita; s of Edward Gilbert Sita-Lumsden (d 1974), and Stella Pirie Lumsden (d 1980); *b* 22 January 1947; *Educ* Kingswood Sch Bath, St Catherine's Coll Cambridge (scholar, Frank Smart Prize for zoology, BA), Yale Univ (Fulbright scholar), Univ of London (PhD); *m* 21 Nov 1970 (m dis), Anne Farrington, da of Paul Donald Roberg (d 1996); 2 da (Ailsa b 6 Oct 1979, Isobel b 24 Aug 1981); m 2, 2 Feb 2002, Kathleen Marie, da of Roger Wets; *Career* Guy's Hosp Med Sch: jr lectr in anatomy 1970–73, lectr 1973–79, sr lectr 1979–87; prof of developmental neurobiology Univ of London 1989– (reader in craniofacial anatomy 1987–89, emeritus prof 2016–); int research scholar Howard Hughes Med Inst 1993–98, visiting prof Miller Inst Univ of Calif Berkeley 1994; memb European Molecular Biology Orgn 2008–; Royal Soc Prize for Neuroscience 2001; Liveryman Worshipful Co of Clockmakers; FRS 1994, FMedSci 1998, FKC 1999; *Publications* The Developing Brain (jtly, 2001), Principles of Development (jtly, 2016); 180 scientific papers; *Recreations* natural history, mechanical engineering, bridge; *Clubs* Athenaeum; *Style—* Prof Andrew Lumsden, FRS; ✉ 16 Elephant Lane, London SE16 4JD; Centre for Developmental Neurobiology, Kings College London, Guy's Hospital, London Bridge, London SE1 1UL (e-mail andrew.lumsden@kcl.ac.uk)

LUMSDEN, Andrew Michael; s of Sir David Lumsden, *qv*, of Winchester, Hants, and Sheila, *née* Daniels; *b* 10 November 1962; *Educ* Winchester (music scholar), RSAMD, St John's Coll Cambridge (organ scholar, MA); *Career* organist; chorister New Coll Oxford, asst to Dr George Guest St John's Coll Cambridge; asst organist Southwark Cathedral 1985–88, sub-organist Westminster Abbey 1988–92 (played for memorial services for Lord Olivier and Dame Peggy Ashcroft and 50th anniversary of Battle of Britain), organist and master of the choristers Lichfield Cathedral 1992–2002, organist and dir of music Winchester Cathedral 2002–, dir of music for funeral of Sir John Tavener 2013; reg broadcaster on BBC radio and television; performances incl: LPO, English Chamber Orch, Busoni's Doktor Faust ENO 1990, recitals at Sydney, San Francisco, Budapest and Harare, Bournemouth Symphony Orch, Florilegium, CBSO; recordings labels incl: Argo, Hyperion, Chandos, Virgin Classics, Nimbus; Nat Young Organist of the Year 1985, winner Manchester Int Competition 1986; Hon FRCO 2005 (ARCO 1979), Hon FGCM 2008; *Recreations* travel, wine, flying; *Style—* Andrew Lumsden, Esq; ✉ Cathedral Office, 9 The Close, Winchester SO23 9LS (☎ 01962 857200, fax 01962 857201)

LUMSDEN, Sir David James; kt (1985); s of Albert Lumsden (d 1985), and Vera, *née* Tate (d 1980); *b* 19 March 1928; *Educ* Dame Allan's Sch Newcastle upon Tyne, Selwyn Coll Cambridge (organ scholar, MA, MusB, PhD); *m* 1951, Sheila Gladys, da of George and Gladys Daniels; 2 s (Stephen, Andrew, *qv*), 2 da (Jennifer, Jane); *Career* asst organist St John's Coll Cambridge 1951–53, organist and choirmaster St Mary's Nottingham 1954–56, rector chori Southwell Minster 1956–59, fell and organist New Coll Oxford 1959–76, princ Royal Scottish Acad of Music and Drama Glasgow 1976–82, Royal Acad of Music London 1982–93 (prof of harmony 1959–61); fndr and conductor Nottingham Bach Soc 1954–59, conductor Oxford Harmonic Soc 1961–63, conductor Oxford Sinfonia 1967–70, choragus Oxford Univ 1968–72, organist Sheldonian Theatre Oxford 1964–76; Hugh Porter lectr Union Theological Seminary NY 1967, visiting prof Yale Univ 1974–75; pres: Incorporated Assoc of Organists 1966–68, Incorporated Soc of Musicians 1984–85, Royal Coll of Organists 1986–88; chm Nat Youth Orchestra 1985–93; hon fell: Selwyn Coll Cambridge 1986, KCL 1990, New Coll Oxford 1996; Hon DLitt Univ of Reading 1991; Liveryman Worshipful Co of Musicians; Hon FRCO 1976, Hon RAM 1978, FRCM 1980, FRNCM 1981, FRSAMD 1982, Hon GSM 1984, FLCM 1985, FRSA 1985, FRSCM 1987, Hon FTCL 1988; *Publications* An Anthology of English Lute Music (1954), Thomas Robinson's Schoole of Musicke, 1603 (1971); *Recreations* hill walking, reading, friends; *Style—* Sir David Lumsden; ✉ 26 Wyke Mark, Dean Lane, Winchester SO22 5DJ (☎ 01962 877807, e-mail lumsdendj@aol.com)

LUMSDEN, Edward Gabriel Marr (Eddy); s of late Edward Gabriel Lumsden, and Isobel, *née* Dyker; *b* 4 July 1946; *Educ* Hampton GS, Westminster Hotel Sch (Nat Dip Hotelkeeping and Catering); *m* 2 Sept 2000 (m dis 2013), Linda Mary Bachari; *Career* area mangr Truman Taverns 1980–81, dir and gen mangr Arden Taverns 1981–83, tied trade dir Drybroughs of Scotland 1983–86, innkeeper dir Truman Ltd 1986, innkeeper ops dir Watney Co Reid & Truman 1986–88, innkeeper dir Watney Truman 1989–91, md TW Guest Trust Ltd 1991–95, conslt to hospitality industry 1995–96 and 2003–; SFI Group plc: dir of ops 1996–98, dir of property 1998–2003; conslt to hospitality industry

2003–; memb Mensa; FHCIMA, FCFA, FRSH, FCMI, FBII, FInstD; *Recreations* travel, gastronomy, vintage motor cars, bridge; *Clubs* Rugby Club of London, Sherborne Bridge; *Style*— Eddy Lumsden, Esq; ✉ 6 Old Station Gardens, Henstridge, Templecombe, Somerset BA8 0PU (☎ 01963 364591)

LUMSDEN, Ian George; s of James Alexander Lumsden, MBE, of Helensburgh, Dunbartonshire, and Sheila, *née* Cross; *b* 19 March 1951; *Educ* Rugby, Corpus Christi Coll Cambridge (BA), Univ of Edinburgh (LLB); *m* 22 April 1978, Mary Ann, da of Maj Dr John William Stewart Welbon, of Cornwall; 1 s (Richard b 1984), 2 da (Sarah b 1986, Louise b 1989); *Career* ptnr Maclay Murray and Spens 1980– (trainee and asst slr 1974–78), asst slr Slaughter and May London 1978–80; memb: Law Soc of Scotland, Royal Faculty of Procurators; *Recreations* golf, shooting; *Clubs* New (Edinburgh), Prestwick Golf; *Style*— Ian Lumsden, Esq; ✉ The Myretoun, Menstrie, Clackmannanshire FK11 7EB (☎ 01259 761453); Maclay Murray and Spens, Quartermile One, 15 Lauriston Place, Edinburgh EH3 9EP (☎ 0131 228 7000, fax 0131 228 7001, e-mail ian.lumsden@mms.co.uk)

LUMSDEN, Prof Emeritus Keith Grant; s of Robert Sclater Lumsden (d 1964), of Bathgate, and Elizabeth, *née* Brow (d 1990); *b* 7 January 1935; *Educ* The Acad Bathgate, Univ of Edinburgh (MA), Stanford Univ (PhD); *m* 1, 21 July 1961, Jean Baillie (d 2005), da of Capt Kenneth Macdonald, MC (d 1962); 1 s (Robert Alistair Macdonald b 1964); m 2, 22 April 2009, Ruth Edith Reid; *Career* Stanford Univ: instr Dept of Econs 1960–63, assoc prof Graduate Sch of Business 1968–75 (asst prof 1964–67), prof of econs Advanced Mgmnt Coll 1971–90; currently affiliate prof of econs INSEAD France and dir and prof emeritus Edinburgh Business Sch Heriot-Watt Univ; res assoc Stanford Res Inst 1965–71, visiting prof of econs Heriot-Watt Univ 1969, academic dir Sea Tport Exec Programme 1984–96; dir: Stanford Univ Conf RREE 1968, Econ Educn Project 1969–74, Behavioral Res Laboratories 1970–72, Capital Preservation Fund Inc 1971–75, Nielsen Engineering Research Inc 1972–75, Hewlett-Packard Ltd 1981–92; memb: American Econ Assoc Ctee on Econ Educn 1978–81, Advsy Cncl David Hume Inst 1984–99; numerous articles in professional jls, creator of various software systems; Henry Villard Award 1994; FRSE 1992; *Books* The Free Enterprise System (1963), The Gross National Product (1964), International Trade (1965), New Developments in the Teaching of Economics, 1967), Microeconomics – A Programmed Book (with R E Attiyeh and G L Bach, new edn 1981), Economics – A Distance Learning Study Programme (1991, revised 2012); *Recreations* tennis, deep sea sports fishing; *Clubs* New (Edinburgh), Waverley Lawn Tennis, Squash, and Sports, Archerfield Links (Golf); *Style*— Prof Emeritus Keith Lumsden, FRSE; ✉ 40 Lauder Road, Edinburgh EH9 1UE (☎ 0131 667 1612); Edinburgh Business School, Heriot-Watt University, Riccarton, Edinburgh EH14 4AS (☎ 0131 451 3090, fax 0131 451 3002)

LUND, Dr Charles Ames; s of (Henry) Charles Lund (d 1980), of Bebington, Cheshire, and (Sophia) Violet Iris, *née* Ames (d 1976); *b* 18 August 1942; *Educ* Birkenhead Sch, Univ of Liverpool (MB ChB), Univ of Aberdeen (Dip Psychotherapy); *m* 14 Feb 1968, Pauline, da of Arthur Morris Hunter, of Ponteland, Newcastle upon Tyne; 2 da (Sonia b 1969, Kathryn b 1974); *Career* SHO and registrar in psychiatry Sefton Gen Hosp Liverpool 1968–71 (house offr 1967–68), sr registrar in psychiatry Royal Southern Hosp Liverpool 1971–72; Univ of Aberdeen: Rowntree fell in psychotherapy 1972–73, lectr Mental Health Dept 1973–78; conslt psychotherapist Newcastle upon Tyne 1978–2000, dir of Newcastle Psychotherapy Course 1984–89, examiner for Membership Examination of RCPsych 1990–95; memb Professional Conduct Panel Br Psychoanalytic Cncl 2007–13; author of pubns in psychotherapy trg, gp therapy and visual representation; memb BMA; FRCPsych 1987 (MRCPsych 1972); *Recreations* walking, gardening; *Style*— Dr Charles Lund; ✉ 92 Errington Road, Darras Hall, Ponteland, Newcastle upon Tyne NE20 9LA (☎ 01661 872018, e-mail charles@cplund.freeserve.co.uk)

LUND, Prof Raymond Douglas; s of Henry Douglas Lund, and Rose, *née* Morgan; *b* 10 February 1940; *Educ* Bablake Sch Coventry, UCL (Bucknill scholar, BSc, PhD); *m* 1963, Jennifer Sylvia, da of Meredith W Hawes; 2 s (Benjamin Isambard b 3 Jan 1971, Simon Meredith b 26 July 1974); *Career* asst lectr then lectr Dept of Anatomy UCL 1963–66, res asst anatomy Univ of Pennsylvania 1966–67, asst prof of anatomy Stanford Univ Calif 1967–68, asst prof then prof of anatomy and neurosurgery Univ of Washington 1968–79, prof and head Dept of Anatomy Med Univ of S Carolina 1979–83, prof and head Dept of Neurobiology, Anatomy and Cell Science Univ of Pittsburgh 1983–91, prof and head Dept of Anatomy Univ of Cambridge 1992–95, Duke-Elder prof of ophthalmology Inst of Ophthalmology 1995–2000, prof and dir of research Department of Ophthalmology and Visual Sciences University of Utah Health Sciences Center 2000–; memb Scientific Advsy Bd Fndn Fighting Blindness; memb: Soc for Neuroscience 1970–, Assoc for Res in Vision and Ophthalmology 1983–; Herrick award American Assoc of Anatomists, MERIT award NIH; fell Clare Coll Cambridge 1992–95; FRS, FMedSci 1998; *Books* Development and Plasticity of the Brain (1978); author/co-author of more than 400 papers, books, book chapters, and abstracts; *Recreations* chamber music (LRAM); *Style*— Prof Raymond Lund, FRS; ✉ Department of Ophthalmology and Visual Sciences, Moran Eye Center, University of Utah Health Sciences Center, 75 North Medical Drive, Salt Lake City, UT 84132, USA

LUND, Prof Valerie Joan; CBE (2008); da of George Andrew Lund, and Joan, *née* Henry (d 1984); *b* 9 May 1953; *Educ* Charing Cross Hosp Med Sch London (MB BS, MRCS LRCP), Univ of London (MS); *m* 2 July 2010, David John Howard; *Career* hon conslt: Royal Nat Throat Nose and Ear Hosp 1987–, Moorfields Eye Hosp 1990–, Univ Coll Hosp 2004–; Inst of Laryngology and Otology: lectr in rhinology 1986–87, sr lectr 1987–93, reader 1993–95, prof 1995–; memb working parties: Int Consensus in Sinusitis 1993, Int Consensus in Rhinitis 1993–94, RCSEd Guidelines in Endoscopic Nasal Surgery 1993, RCS Working Pty on Minimal Access Therapy 1993, WHO – Mgmnt of Rhinitis 2000, EAACI Taskforce on Rhinosinusitis; co-chm EPOS 2005, 2007 and 2012, co-chm Endoscopic Mgmnt of Sinonasal and Skull Based Tumours ERS Advsy Gp 2010; asst ed Jl of Laryngology and Otology, ed Rhinology; memb Editorial Bd: American Jl of Rhinology, Laryngoscope; Downs surgical travelling fell RSM 1985; European Rhinologic Soc: Special Prize 1986, Award of Merit 1996, Award of Excellence 1998; Lionel Colledge fell RCS 1986, Br Academic Conf in Otolaryngology Scientific Exhbn Award 1987, George Davey Howell Meml Prize Univ of London 1990, 2008 and 2015; McBride lectr Edinburgh 1993, Sir Arthur Sims travelling prof 2002, Guthrie lectr 2006, Leegaard lectr 2006, Bradshaw lectr 2006, Robert Owen lectr 2008, Semon lectr 2012, Franz Sacher Medal 2013, Stell lectr 2014, Stirk Adams lectr 2015; Hon MD Univ of Brighton 2016, Hon MD Univ of Sussex 2016; pres ENT-UK 2012–15; memb: BMA, RSM, European Rhinologic Soc (treas 1992, UK rep 2000, gen sec 2008–), Head and Neck Oncologists of GB, Euro Acad of Facial and Plastic Surgery (vice-pres UK 1993), Otorhinolaryngological Research Soc, Br Assoc of Otolaryngologists (pres 2012–), Collegium ORLAS 1990, American Rhinologic Soc 1992, American Triologic Soc 1993, German Acad of Science Leopoldina 2009; fell German ORL (Otorhinolaryngology) / HNS (Head and Neck Surgery) Soc 1999; FRCS 1982 (memb Cncl 1994, chm Educn Bd 1999 and 2002), FRCSEd 1993; *Books* Clinical Rhinology (with A Maran, 1990), Tumours of the Upper Jaw (with D F N Harrison, 1993), Nasal Polyps (with G Settipane 1997), Minimally Invasive Endonasal Sinus Surgery (with W G Hoseman, R K Weber and Keerl Rainer, 1999), Investigative Rhinology (with G Scadding, 2004), Scott Brown's Otorhinolaryngology (co-ed, 2008), Cummings Otolaryngology Head Neck Surgery (section ed, 2009, 2 edn 2012), Tumors of Nose, Paranasal Sinuses and Nasopharynx (with D J Howard and W I Wei, 2013); other pubns incl 300 peer-reviewed papers, 90 chapters and 30 monographs or supplements; *Recreations* cooking and eating; *Style*— Prof Valerie Lund, CBE; ✉ Professorial Unit, RNTNEH, 330 Gray's Inn Road, London WC1X 8DA (☎ 020 3456 5197, fax 020 7833 9480, e-mail v.lund@ucl.ac.uk)

LUNGHI, Cherie Mary; da of Allessandro Lunghi (d 1989), of London, and Gladys Corbett Lee (d 1996); *b* 4 April 1952; *Educ* Arts Educn Trust London, Central Sch of Speech and Drama; former partner, Roland Joffé, *qv*; 1 da (Nathalie-Kathleen Lunghi-Joffé b 26 Aug 1986); *Career* actress; *Theatre* Irena in The Three Sisters and Lisa in Owners (Newcastle) 1973–74, Kate Hardcastle in She Stoops to Conquer (Nottingham Playhouse) 1974, Laura in Teeth'n'Smiles (Royal Court) 1975, Holiday (Old Vic) 1987, Ruth in The Homecoming (Comedy Theatre) 1991; RSC 1976–80: Hero in Much Ado About Nothing, Perdita in The Winter's Tale, Cordelia in King Lear, Destiny, Bandits, Celia in As You Like It, Saratoga, Viola in Twelfth Night; National Theatre London: Arcadia, Uncle Vanya; Piscasso's Women (Ambassadors Theatre Gp) 2002; *Television* incl: The Misanthrope (BBC) 1978, 'Tis Pity She's a Whore (BBC) 1979, The Manhood of Edward Robinson (Thames) 1981, The Praying Mantis (Channel 4) 1982, Desert of Lies (BBC) 1983, Huis Clos (BBC) 1984, Much Ado About Nothing (BBC) 1984, Letters From an Unknown Lover (Channel 4) 1985, The Monocled Mutineer (BBC) 1985, The Lady's Not For Burning (Thames) 1987, The Manageress (Channel 4) 1988 and 1989, Put on by Cunning (TVS) 1990, Covington Cross (Reeves Entertainment and ABC TV), The Buccaneers (BBC), Hornblower 1999, David Copperfield 1999, A Likeness in Stone 1999, The Brief 2004; TV mini series: Master of the Game (US) 1983, Ellis Island (US) 1984, The Man Who Lived at The Ritz (US) 1988, The Strauss Dynasty (Austria) 1990, Little White Lies (BBC), Maloney (CBS TV), Guests of the Emperor (ABC TV), The Canterville Ghost (NBC TV), Master of the Game (CBS TV), Oliver Twist (CBS TV); *Radio* Alice in Alice in Wonderland (BBC) 1965, Hedvig in The Wild Duck (BBC) 1965; *Films* Excalibur 1980, King David 1984, The Mission 1985, To Kill A Priest 1987, Jack and Sarah 1995, Frankenstein 1995; *Recreations* drawing and painting, going to the cinema and theatre, reading, walking, mothering; *Style*— Miss Cherie Lunghi

LUNN, (George) Michael; s of John Lunn (d 1969), of Edinburgh, and May, *née* Hope (d 1971); *b* 22 July 1942; *Educ* Kelvinside Acad Glasgow, Univ of Glasgow (BSc), Heriot-Watt Univ (Dip Brewing); *m* 27 Aug 1971, Jennifer, da of John Burgoyne, of Glasgow; 3 s (Stuart b 17 Jan 1974, Jamie b 27 July 1978, Alexander b 18 March 1981); 1 da (Victoria b 11 Jan 1976); *Career* Lt RNR 1956–66; chm and chief exec The Whyte & Mackay Gp plc until 1995, dir Gallaher Ltd until 1995; dir Montrose Estates (1993) Ltd; chm: Wm Muir Ltd until 1995, Invergordon Distillers until 1995, Michael Lunn Assocs Ltd 1995–, The Unwins Wine Gp Ltd until 2005; non-exec dir Bernard Matthews Hldgs Ltd 2009–; former dir Cncl Scotch Whisky Assoc; former chm Glasgow Devpt Agency; memb: Inst of Brewing, Lord's Taverners, Keepers of the Quaich; *Recreations* golf; *Clubs* IOD, R&A Golf, New (Edinburgh), Buchanan Castle Golf; *Style*— Michael Lunn, Esq; ✉ Michael Lunn Associates Ltd, 4 West Grange, Grange, St Andrews, Fife KY16 8LJ (☎ 01334 470290, e-mail me@michaellunnassociates.com and michael.lunn@btinternet.com)

LUNN, Trevor; MLA; *b* 29 June 1946, Aylesbury, Bucks; *Educ* Belfast Royal Acad; *m* 26 Aug 1971, Laureen; *Career* cncllr Lisburn City Cncl 2001–11 (dep mayor 2005–06, mayor 2006–07), MLA (Alliance) Lagan Valley 2007–; former chm Alliance Pty, former pres Lisburn C of C; *Style*— Trevor Lunn, MLA; ✉ 12A Whinney Hill, Lisburn, Co Antrim BT28 3UZ (☎ 07968 154099, e-mail trevorlunn@ymail.com); 17 Graham Gardens, Lisburn, Co Antrim BT28 1XE (☎ 028 9267 1177); Northern Ireland Assembly, Parliament Buildings, Belfast BT4 3XX (e-mail trevor.lunn@mla.niassembly.gov.uk)

L

LUNT, Her Hon Judge Beverly Anne; da of Thomas Gordon Lunt (d 2007), of Huxley, Chester, and Mary, *née* Duff; *b* 8 March 1954, Rochester; *Educ* Oxford Poly (BA); *Career* called to the Bar Gray's Inn 1977; recorder 2000–04, circuit judge 2004– (currently sitting at Burnley and Preston Crown Courts); *Recreations* reading, theatre, cinema, entertaining, walking, supporting animal charities (RSPCA, WSPA, Battersea Dogs Home, Dogs Trust); *Style*— Her Hon Judge Lunt; ✉ Burnley Crown Court, Hammerton Street, Burnley BB11 1XD (☎ 01282 416899)

LUNT, Prof Ingrid Cecilia; da of Canon Ronald Lunt (d 1994), and Veslemøy, *née* Sopp Foss; *b* 16 May 1947; *Educ* King Edward VI HS for Girls, St Hugh's Coll Oxford (scholar, MA), UCL (MSc), Inst of Educn Univ of London (PhD); *m* 11 March 1989, His Hon Judge Julian Hall, *qv*; *Career* teacher Wanstead HS London 1973–78, educnl psychologist ILEA 1979–85; Inst of Educn Univ of London 1985–2005: appointed prof of educnl psychology 2001, dean of doctoral sch 2002–05; sr research fell and prof Univ of Oxford 2005– (vice-princ Green Templeton Coll 2011–15); affiliate: American Psychological Assoc, American Educnl Research Assoc; vice-pres Int Union of Psych Science 2004– (memb Exec Ctee 2000–); memb Editorial Bds: Psychology Teaching Review, Euro Psychologist; pres European Fedn of Psychologists' Assocs 1993–97, pres Br Psychological Soc 1998–99, vice-pres Int Union of Psychological cience 2004–08; CPsychol, FBPsS, FRSA, AcSS; *Publications* incl: Child Development: a first course (with K Sylva, 1982), Cognitive Development (contrib, 1983), Charting the Agenda: educational activity after Vygotsky (contrib, 1993), Working Together: inter-school collaboration for special needs (jtly, 1994), Professional Psychology in Europe: the state of the art (contrib, 1995), Psychology and Education for Special Needs: current developments and future directions (jt ed, 1995), Values in Special Education (contrib, 1997), A Century of Psychology. progress, paradigms and prospects for the new millennium (contrib, 1997), Professional Doctorates: Integrating professional and academic knowledge (with D Scott, A Brown and L Thorne, 2004), EuroPsy: Education and Standards for Professional Psychology (with J M Perio, Y Poortinga and R Roe, 2015), Lively Bureaucracy? the ESRC's Doctoral Training Centres and UK Universities (with L McAlpin and D Mills); *Recreations* playing music (piano, viola, flute and singing), walking and cross-country skiing, opera, gardening; *Style*— Prof Ingrid Lunt; ✉ Green Templeton College, 43 Woodstock Road, Oxford OX2 6HG (☎ 01865 421689, e-mail ingrid.lunt@gtc.ox.ac.uk)

LUPTON, Baron (Life Peer UK 2015), of Lovington in the County of Hampshire James Roger Crompton Lupton; CBE (2012); s of Alec William Lupton (d 1999), and Margaret Crompton Lupton; *b* 15 June 1955; *Educ* Sedbergh, Lincoln Coll Oxford (MA); *m* 23 July 1983, Béatrice Marie-Françoise, *née* Delaunay; 3 da (Annabelle, Victoria, Camilla), 1 s (Sam); *Career* admitted slr 1979; Lovell White & King 1977–79, S G Warburg & Co 1979–80; Baring Brothers & Co Ltd: joined 1980, dir 1986–98, dep chm Baring Brothers Int Ltd 1996–98; md Greenhill & Co Int 1998–; chm Greenhill Europe 2012–; chm Dulwich Picture Gallery 2005–12; co-treas Cons Pty 2013–2016; tstee Br Museum 2012–; memb Law Soc; *Recreations* opera, visual arts, shooting, skiing; *Clubs* Brooks's, 5 Hertford St; *Style*— The Lord Lupton, CBE; ✉ Greenhill & Co International, Lansdowne House, 57 Berkeley Square, London W1J 6ER (☎ 020 7198 7400, fax 020 7198 7501, e-mail jlupton@greenhill.com)

LUPU, Radu; CBE (2016); s of Meyer Lupu, and Ana, *née* Gabor; *b* 30 November 1945; *Educ* High Sch Brasov Romania, Moscow Conservatoire; *Career* concert pianist; London debut 1969, Berlin debut 1971, USA debut NY 1972; first prize: Van Cliburn Competition 1966, Enescu Competition 1967, Leeds Competition 1969; Abbiati Prize 1989 and 2006, Premio Internazionale Arturo Benedetti Michalangeli 2006; *Recordings* incl: Beethoven Piano Concertos (with Zubin Mehta and the Israel Philharmonic Orch), Mozart Sonatas for Violin and Piano (with Szymon Goldberg), Brahms Piano Concerto No 1 (with Edo de Waart and the London Philharmonic Orch), Mozart Piano Concerto K467 (with Uri

Segal and the Eng Chamber Orch), various Beethoven and Schubert Sonatas (incl B Flat Sonata D960, Grammy Award 1995), Mozart and Beethoven Wind Quintets in E Flat, Mozart Concerto for 2 Pianos and Concerto for 3 Pianos transcribed for 2 pianos (with Murray Perahia and the Eng Chamber Orch), Schubert Fantasie in F Minor and Mozart Sonata in D for 2 Pianos (with Murray Perahia), Schubert Piano Duets (with Daniel Barenboim), two disks of Schubert Lieder (with Barbara Hendricks), Schumann Kinderszenen, Kreisleriana and Humoresque (Edison Award 1996); *Recreations* chess, bridge, history; *Style*— Radu Lupu, Esq, CBE; ✉ c/o Barbara Golan, Stettbachstrasse 131H, 8051 Zurich, Switzerland (☎ 41 44 322 0704, fax 4144322 0724, email golan@bluewin.ch)

LUSBY, John Martin; s of William Henry Lusby (d 1990), of Hull, and Florence Mary, *née* Wharam (d 2010); *b* 27 April 1943; *Educ* Marist Coll Hull, Ushaw Coll Durham, Maryvale Inst Birmingham (DipTheol), Open Univ (MA); *m* 1966, (Mary) Clare, da of John Gargan (d 1957), of York; 1 s (James b 3 Sept 1969), 1 da (Sophie b 30 July 1973); *Career* entered NHS 1961; jr appointments: De la Pole Hosp Hull B Gp HMC 1961–66, County Hosp York A Gp HMC 1966–67, Kettering Gen Hosp Kettering and Dist HMC 1967–68; admin asst United Sheffield Hosps 1968–70, dep hosp sec E Birmingham Hosp E Birmingham HMC 1970–72, hosp sec Pontefract Gen Infirmary and Headlands Hosp Pontefract, Castleford and Goole HMC/Wakefield Area Health Authy 1972–74, area gen admin Kirklees AHA 1974–76; Merton, Sutton and Wandsworth AHA(T): asst dist admin (Patient Servs) 1976–79, dist admin Wandsworth and E Merton Dist 1979–81; area admin Doncaster AHA 1981; Doncaster HA: dist admin 1981–84, dist gen mangr 1984–90, exec dir 1990; Lothian Health Bd: gen mangr 1990–95, exec dir 1991–95 (memb 1990–91); chm Independent Review Panel NHS Complaints Procedure Northern and Yorkshire Region NHS Exec 1996–97; adjudicator (panel memb) Tbnls Serv Criminal Injuries Compensation Appeals Panel 1997–2008, memb First-tier Tbnl (Social Entitlement Chamber) 2008–09; tstee: Dementia Servs Devpt Centre Univ of Stirling 1991–95, The Scottish Dementia Appeal Tst 1994–95; memb: Scottish Cncl for Postgrad Med and Dental Educn 1992–95, Health Servs and Public Health Res Ctee (Scottish Office Home and Health Dept Chief Scientist Orgn) 1993–94, Scottish Implementation Gp Jr Doctors and Dentists' Hours of Work 1993–95, Jt Working Gp on Information Services NHS Scotland 1993–95, Catholic Theological Assoc of GB 1997–2008, Catholic Biblical Assoc of Great Britain 1998–, Catholic Inst for Int Relations 1999–2004, Soc for the Study of Theology 2000–08, European Soc for Catholic Theology 2004–08, Catholic Union of GB 2012–15; DipHSM 1972, MHSM (AHA 1972); *Recreations* music, reading, travel, the study of theology; *Clubs* Middlesex CC; *Style*— John Lusby, Esq; ✉ Flat A, Copper Beech, 31 North Grove, London N6 4SJ (☎ 020 8341 3426, mobile 07941 678056, e-mail john.lusby@sky.com)

LUSCOMBE, Prof David Edward; s of Edward Dominic Luscombe (d 1987), of London, and Nora, *née* Cowell (d 1995); *b* 22 July 1938; *Educ* Finchley Catholic GS, King's Coll Cambridge (MA, PhD, LittD); *m* 20 Aug 1960, Megan, da of John Richard Phillips (d 1967); 3 s (Nicholas b 1962, Mark b 1964, Philip b 1968), 1 da (Amanda b 1970); *Career* fell King's Coll Cambridge 1962–64, fell, lectr and dir of studies in history Churchill Coll Cambridge 1964–72; Univ of Sheffield: prof of medieval history 1972–95, Leverhulme personal research prof of medieval history 1995–2000, res prof of medieval history 2000–03, emeritus research prof of medieval history 2003–, head Dept of History 1973–76 and 1979–84, dean of Faculty of Arts 1985–87, pro-vice-chllr 1990–94, chm Humanities Research Inst 1992–2003 (Queen's Anniversary Prize for Higher and Further Educn 1998), dir of research Arts and Humanities Div 1994–2003; visiting prof: Royal Soc of Canada 1991, Univ of Connecticut at Storrs 1993, Japan Acad 1996; Leverhulme visiting European fell 1973, visiting fell All Souls Coll Oxford 1994; auditor Div of Quality Audit HE Quality Cncl 1994–95; pres Société Int pour L'Etude de la Philosophie Médiévale 1997–2002 (vice-pres 1987–97, hon pres 2002–); hon sec Cambridge Univ Catholic Assoc 1968–70; memb: Governing Body St Edmund's House Cambridge 1971–84, Ctee Ecclesiastical History Soc 1976–79, Cncl Royal Historical Soc 1981–85, Ctee Soc for the Study of Medieval Languages and Literature 1991–96, Jt Supervisory Ctee of Br Acad and OUP for Oxford Dictionary of Nat Biography 1992–99 (assoc ed 1993–2004), Cwlth Scholarship Cmmn 1994–2000, Cncl Worksop Coll and Ranby House 1996–2008; British Acad: Raleigh lectr 1988, memb Cncl 1989–97, pubns sec 1990–97, chm Medieval Texts Editorial Ctee British Acad 1991–2004, memb Humanities Research Bd 1994–96; gen ed Cambridge Studies in Medieval Life and Thought 1988–2004 (advsy ed 1983–88); tstee Church Burgesses Educnl Fndn Sheffield 2012–; Br Acad Medal 2014, J Franklin Jameson Award 2015; Hon LittD Univ of Sheffield; FRHistS 1970, FSA 1984, FBA 1986; *Books* The School of Peter Abelard (1969), Peter Abelard's Ethics (1971), David Knowles Remembered (jtly, 1991), Medieval Thought (1997, Portuguese translation 2000, Greek translation 2007), The Twelfth Century Renaissance: Monks, Scholars and the Shaping of the European Mind (in Japanese, 2000); co-ed: Church and Government in the Middle Ages (1976), Petrus Abaelardus 1079–1142 (1980), D Knowles, The Evolution of Medieval Thought (1988), Anselm: Aosta, Bec and Canterbury (1996), The New Cambridge Medieval History Vol IV c1024-c1198 pt 1 and 2 (2004), Peter Abelard Expositio in Hexameron (2004), Sententie Magistri Petri Abaelardi (2006), A Monastic Community in Local Society: The Beauchief Abbey Cartulary (2011), The Letter Collection of Peter Abelard and Heloise (2013), Rulership and Rebellion in the Anglo-Norman World, c.1066–1216 (2015); author of various articles and chapters in learned jls and books; *Recreations* family and grandchildren, using libraries, cooking for two, walking; *Style*— Prof David Luscombe, FBA; ✉ Department of History, University of Sheffield, Jessop West, 1 Upper Hanover Street, Sheffield S3 7RA

LUSH, Denzil Anton; s of Dennis John Lush, MBE, and Hazel June, *née* Fishenden (d 1979); *b* 18 July 1951, Southsea, Hants; *Educ* Devonport HS Plymouth, UCL (BA, MA), Coll of Law Guildford, CCC Cambridge (LLM); *Career* admitted slr England and Wales 1978, slr and NP Scotland 1993; ptnr Anstey Sargent & Probert Slrs Exeter 1985–95; Court of Protection: master 1996–2007, sr judge 2007–16; memb Master of the Rolls' Working Pty on Structured Settlements 2002; former memb: Mental Health and Disability Ctee Law Soc, Steering Gp on Advance Directives BMA; pt/t chm Social Security Appeals Tbnls 1994–96, judicial memb Soc of Tst and Estate Practitioners (STEP) 1996–; patron Slrs for the Elderly 2002–, tstee Action on Elder Abuse 2016–; tstee Pan-European Orgn of Personal Injury Lawyers (PEOPIL) Fndn 2004–06; Geoffrey Shindler Award for Outstanding Contrib to the Profession STEP Private Client Awards 2009, award in recognition of outstanding support provided to the Assoc of Contentious Trust and Probate Specialists (ACTAPS) 2015; hon memb Japan Adult Guardianhip Assoc 2013; FRSM 2001; *Books* Cohabitation Law, Practice and Precedents (1993, 5 edn 2012), Elderly Clients – A Precedent Manual (1996, 4 edn 2013), Cretney & Lush on Lasting and Enduring Powers of Attorney (7 edn 2013); contrib: Encyclopaedia of Forms and Precedents Vols 26 (Minors) and 31 (Powers of Attorney), Atkin's Court Forms Vol 26 (Mental Health), Butterworths Older Client Law Service, Butterworths Costs Service, Litigation Practice, Heywood and Massey Court of Protection Practice, Oxford Textbook of Old Age Psychiatry, Comparative Perspectives on Adult Guardianship, International Protection of Adults; *Recreations* supporting Plymouth Argyle FC, doing the 92, collecting commemorative pottery; *Clubs* Athenaeum; *Style*— Denzil Lush, Esq; ✉ 3 Pennsylvania Park, Exeter EX4 6HB (☎ 07340 278512, e-mail denzillush@gmail.com)

LUSH, Jane; *b* 10 August 1952; *Educ* Camden Sch for Girls; *m* 17 November 1974, Peter Tenenbaum; 1 da (Nancy b 28 August 1981), 1 s (Alex b 21 July 1987); *Career* BBC: dir Film...(with Barry Norman) 1979–81, prodr and dir 1981–90, head of devpt Features Dept 1990–95, head of TV devpt Features and Events Dept 1995–98, dep head of Features and Events 1995–98, head of Daytime TV 1998–2001, controller of entertainment commissioning 2001–05; co-fndr Splash 2005–; prodr and dir: Hitchcock 1981, Barbara Streisand A Film is Born 1982; prodr Show Business 1983; series prodr: Film...(with Barry Norman) 1984–88, Friday People 1985, Head Over Heels 1989; ed Holiday 1990–95; exec prodr: Redundant 1991, Sean's Shorts 1992, GOSH 1993, Your Place or Mine 1995, Money for Old Rope 1995, Big Kevin Little Kevin 1995, VetsWorld 1995, Martin Clunes Born to be Wild 1997–98; chair Caring for Kids; fundraiser Inst of Child Health Great Ormond Street Hosp; *Style*— Ms Jane Lush; ✉ Splash Media, 1 Bedford Avenue, London WC1B 3AU

LUSK, (Ormond) Felicity Stewart; da of Harold Stewart Lusk QC (d 2009), and Janet Kiwi, *née* Miller (d 2015); *b* 25 November 1955; *Educ* Marsden Collegiate Sch Wellington, Victoria Univ (BMus), Christchurch Teachers' Coll (Dip Teaching), Massey Univ (DipEd); *m* 1976 (m dis 1996); 2 s; *Career* head Music Dept: Wellington East Girls' Coll 1978–85, Aotea Coll 1986–89; Hasmonean HS London: head Music Dept 1990–92, dep head teacher 1993–96; headmistress Oxford HS GDST 1997–2010, head Abingdon Sch 2010–15, vice-pres Educn GEMS Dubai 2015–; ind memb Standards Ctee City of London Corp 2009–; memb Ct Oxford Brookes Univ 1999–2001, govr Guildhall Sch of Music and Drama 2000–09, memb Cncl Univ of Buckingham 2013–; Woolf Fisher fell (NZ) 1985; cncllr London Borough of Enfield 1990–94; memb: SHA 1993–99, GSA 1997, Forum UK 2008, HMC 2010–16; *Recreations* trekking, reading, theatre, travel, lhasa apso Dudley; *Style*— Miss Felicity Lusk; ✉ felicitylusk@hotmail.com

LUSTIG, Robin Francis; s of Fritz Lustig, and Susan, *née* Cohn; *b* 30 August 1948; *Educ* Stoneham Sch Reading, Univ of Sussex (BA); *m* 24 Feb 1980, Ruth, da of Dr W B Kelsey (d 1986), of London; 1 s (Joshua b 1982), 1 da (Hannah b 1985); *Career* journalist; Reuters: Madrid 1971–72, Paris 1972–73, Rome 1973–77; The Observer: news ed 1981–83, Middle East corr 1985–87, asst ed 1988–89; journalist and broadcaster 1989–, presenter The World Tonight (BBC Radio 4) and BBC World Service 1989–2012; Hon DLitt Univ of Sussex 2015; *Books* Siege: Six Days at the Iranian Embassy (jtly, 1980); *Style*— Robin Lustig, Esq; ✉ c/o Kate Moon Management Ltd, PO Box 648, Northampton NN6 9XT

LUTOSTAŃSKI, Matthew; s of Tadeusz Lutostanski (d 1986), and Maria Zuromska; *b* 22 July 1945, Tel Aviv, Israel; *Educ* Cardinal Vaughan Sch Kensington, City Univ (BA); *m* 1, 1969 (m dis 1979), Pamela Allport; 2 da (Alexandra Eleonora b 1973, Laura Maria b 1976); m 2, 1985 (m dis 2003), Carol Denley; 2 s (Sam Jonathan Tadeusz b 1988, Max Oliver George b 1989); *Career* advtg mangr Barclaycard 1967–73 (launched Britain's first credit card), head of advtg Barclays Bank (UK) 1986–93, fndr Generator Partnership 1993, subsequently jt chief exec Butler Lutos Sutton Wilkinson (following merger with Connell May Steavenson) until 1997, jt chief exec RPM3 (following merger with Cowan Kemsley Taylor) 1997–2000; chief exec Blu Orbit Int (London and NY) 2000, currently prop Ignite Retail Design Int; involved with: Tusk Force Charity (memb Advtg Ctee), Whale-Dolphin Preservation Soc (advtg fundraising campaigns), Elefriends Charity (advtg for new members), Rocks Lane Tennis Centre for Children, Anti Slavery International (advtg fundraising campaign); FInstM; *Recreations* tennis, skiing, football, squash, bridge; *Clubs* Queen's Tennis, Roehampton Tennis; *Style*— Matthew Lutostański, Esq

LUTYENS, Sarah Louise; *née* Cameron; da of Clive Bremner Cameron (d 1996), and Rosalind Louise, *née* Paget; *b* 12 February 1959, London; *Educ* Univ of Exeter (BA); *m* 1 Jan 1986, C Mark P Lutyens; 1 s (Arthur Eadred b 24 March 1997); *Career* literary agent Lutyens and Rubinstein 1993–; memb Assoc of Authors' Agents; *Style*— Ms Sarah Lutyens; ✉ Lutyens and Rubinstein, 21 Kensington Park Road, London W11 2EU

LUX, Jonathan Sidney; s of Martin Lux (d 1995), of Highgate, London, and Ruth, *née* Swager (d 1983); *b* 30 October 1951; *Educ* Abbotsholme Sch Rocester, Univ of Nottingham (LLB, exhibitioner), Université d' Aix-Marseille DES; *m* 3 Sept 1979, Simone, da of Shalom Itah, of Israel; 2 da (Ruth b 24 April 1981, Danielle b 24 Sept 1983), 1 s (Adam b 14 Jan 1986); *Career* admitted slr 1977, admitted slr Hong Kong 1986; Ince & Co: asst slr 1977–83, ptnr 1983–, mangr Hamburg branch office 2001–03 (also estab office); full time mediator on numerous panels; called to the Bar 2013, practising mediator, arbitrator and barr Stone Chambers Gray's Inn 2013–; hon consul to Cape Verde in London 2010; speaker at various maritime law confs and author of various articles 1983–; supporting memb London Maritime Arbitrators' Assoc; memb Int Bar Assoc (former chm Ctee A – Maritime and Tport Law), chm Ctee Corporate Social Responsibility; Global Shipping and Maritime Lawyer of the Year Who's Who Legal Award 2010 and 2011; Freeman of City of London, Liveryman of Worshipful Co of Solicitors; memb Law Soc 1977, FCIArb; *Books* The Law on Tug, Tow and Pilotage (jtly, 1982), The Law and Practice of Marine Insurance and Average (jtly, 1987), Classification Societies (1993), Alternative Dispute Resolution (2002), Bunkers (jtly, 2004), Corporate Social Responsibility (2005), Maritime Law Handbook, ADR Client Strategies (2008), Getting The Deal Through Shipping (2009, 2 edn 2012); contrib: Responsible Business: How to Manage a CSR Strategy Successfully (2010), Mediation Techniques (e-book, 2010), World Abritration Reporter (2 edn, 2010), Corporation Social Responsibility – The European Initiatives, Intro to Getting The Deal Through Mediation; *Recreations* single seater motor racing (holder of RAC nat racing licence), participated in 16,000 km Beijing to Paris rally 1997 (first in class and gold medal); *Clubs* Athenaeum; *Style*— Jonathan Lux, Esq; ✉ 7A The Grove, London N6 6JU (☎ 07876 232305, e-mail mediate@jonathanlux.co.uk); Stone Chambers, 4 Field Court, Gray's Inn, London WC1R 5EF (e-mail jonathan.lux@stonechambers.com)

LYALL, Dr Fiona Jane; MBE (1995), DL (Kincardine 1983); da of James Fraser (d 1984), and Christina Forbes (d 1983); *b* 13 April 1931; *Educ* Univ of Aberdeen (MB ChB, DPH); *m* 20 July 1957, Alan Richards Lyall, s of Alexander Lyall (d 1974); 1 da (Elizabeth Grace Hermione b 18 Oct 1958), 1 s (Peter James Fraser b 9 Oct 1961); *Career* GP Laurencekirk 1959–, dir Grampian TV plc 1980–; borough cncllr Laurencekirk, co cncllr Kincardineshire, regnl cncllr Grampian; *Recreations* skiing, provincial silver; *Style*— Dr Fiona Lyall, MBE, DL; ✉ Melrose Bank, Laurencekirk, Kincardineshire AB30 1FJ (☎ 01561 377220)

LYALL, John Adrian; s of Keith Lyall (d 1990), of Hadleigh, Essex, and Phyllis, *née* Sharps (d 1999); *b* 12 December 1949; *Educ* Southend HS for Boys, AA Sch of Architecture; *m* 25 May 1991, Sallie Jean, da of Frank and Noelleen Davies; 1 s (Adam John b 27 June 1997), 1 da (Madeleine Rose b 14 April 2000); *Career* architect and urban designer; architectural appts: Cedric Price 1969–70, Gerard Brigden 1970–71, Piano & Rogers 1973–74, Raymond J Cecil 1974–75, Page & Broughton/Planarc 1975–77, Bahr Vermeer & Haecker 1977–78, Rock Townsend 1978–79; in private practice Alsop Lyall and Störmer 1980–91, md John Lyall Architects 1991–; numerous arts-related and urban renewal projects incl: Dance East and Cranfields Mill Ipswich, Riverside Studios Hammersmith, Gallery 2000 Inverness, Perran Foundry Cornwall, St Anne's Wharf Devpt Norwich (incl costume museum), BR and underground station Tottenham Hale, The Corn Exchange and White Cloth Hall Leeds, The Crown Court Kirkgate, architect Crystal Palace Park regeneration 2000–01, New World Square, Liverpool Waterfront, Perth City Hall, Hammersmith Pumping Station, Goldsmiths Centre Clerkenwell, Olympic Pumping Station Stratford, Holborn Wharf Regeneration Chatham, various other urban design work and transport projects incl North Greenwich Jubilee Line Station; memb Design Panel: Cardiff Bay Devpt Corp 1989–2000, English Partnerships 1998–; vice-chair

Nat Design Review Panel CABE 2007–; vice-pres (Future Studies) RIBA 1997–2000; external examiner: Oxford Brookes Univ and Bartlett Sch of Architecture, Univ of Strathclyde; formerly: unit tutor AA and Greenwich Univ, visiting prof Ball State Univ Indiana, visiting lectr at other schs in UK, Ireland, USA, Bratislava and Moscow; chm RIBA Validation Task Force 2001, vice-chair RIBA Tst 2003–; conslt: CABE 2001–, Br Library 2003–05; memb Cncl Architectural Assoc 2005–; awards incl: William van Allen Medal for Architecure NY 1971, Leeds Award for Architecture 1990 and 1992, The Ironbridge Award (Br Archaeological Soc) 1990 and 1992, Design Week Award 1991, RIBA White Rose Award and Nat Award 1991, Europa Nostra Award 1991, RICS Urban Renewal Award 1995, Category and Regnl RIBA Award for N Greenwich Station 1999, Architectural Review/MIPIM Future Projects Award 2005, RICS Award for Cranfield Mills 2010, ICE CEEQUAL Award for Pudding Mill Pumping Station 2011; memb AA, RIBA, FRSA; *Publications* subject of: Architecture, Projects and Drawings of Will Alsop, Cliff Barnett and John Lyall (1984), New Buildings in Historic Settings (1998), John Lyall. Urban Regeneration: Context and Catalysts (1999); instigated and ed RIBA pubns: The Value of Design (2000), Tomorrow's Architect (2003); *Recreations* choral singing, fruit tree cultivation, supporting Tottenham Hotspur; *Clubs* Chelsea Arts; *Style*— John Lyall, Esq

LYALL GRANT, Sir Mark Justin; KCMG (2006, CMG 2003); s of Maj-Gen Ian Lyall Grant, MC, *qv*, of Chichester, W Sussex, and Mary Jennifer, *née* Moore; *b* 29 May 1956, London; *Educ* Eton (Newcastle scholar), Univ of Cambridge (scholar, MA), Université Libre de Bruxelles (Wiener-Anspach scholar, Licencié Speciale en Droit Européen); *m* July 1986, Sheila Jean, *née* Tresise; 1 s (Hallam b 3 Nov 1989), 1 da (Lucy b 28 Aug 1991); *Career* called to the Bar Middle Temple 1980 (bencher 2011); entered FCO 1980; posted: Islamabad 1982–85, Paris 1990–93, Pretoria 1996–98; dir for Africa FCO 2000–02, high cmmr to Pakistan 2003–06, political dir FCO 2007–09, UK perm rep to UN 2009–15, nat security advsr 2015–; *Recreations* golf, bridge, sailing, quizzes; *Clubs* RAC; *Style*— Sir Mark Lyall Grant, KCMG

LYCETT, Andrew Michael Duncan; s of Peter Norman Lycett (d 1979), and Joanna Mary, *née* Day (d 2005); *b* 5 December 1948; *Educ* Charterhouse, ChCh Oxford (MA); *m* 1981 (m dis 1989), Rita Diana Robinson; *Career* journalist and author; FRSL, FRGS; *Books* Gaddafi and The Libyan Revolution (with David Blundy, 1987), Ian Fleming (1995), From Diamond Sculls to Golden Handcuffs (1998), Rudyard Kipling (1999), Dylan Thomas – A New Life (2003), Conan Doyle: The Man Who Created Sherlock Holmes (2007), Kipling Abroad (2010), Wilkie Collins: A Life of Sensation (2013); *Recreations* travel, reading, cricket; *Clubs* RAC, Arts; *Style*— Andrew Lycett, Esq; ✉ 34 Torbay Road, London NW6 7DY (☎ 020 7328 4552, e-mail alycett@btinternet.com, website www.andrewlycett.co.uk)

LYCETT, Christopher Ronald (Chris); s of Eric Laybourn Lycett, MBE (d 1974), of the IOM, and Thelma, *née* George (d 1987); *b* 3 December 1946; *Educ* Archbishop Tenison's GS Croydon, Ramsey GS IOM; *m* 6 June 1970, Anne, da of Richard Charles Frank Geary; 2 s (Daniel Christopher Laybourn b 15 March 1971, Nicholas Richard Charles Geary (Charlie) b 23 Dec 1981), 1 da (Sarah Anne Marie b 30 April 1974); *Career* BBC Radio 1: studio engr responsible for sight and sound simulcasts, prodr 1975–87, ed mainstream progs 1987–2000, head of music 1990–94, exec prodr live music 1995–99, co-ordinator Special Event for Music Live 2000; fndr Broadcast Event Productions 2000–; work as prodr incl: Live Aid 1986 (Sony Award), Nelson Mandela Concert 1988, Walters Weekly arts prog (Broadcasting Press Guild Award), Prince of Wales 40th Birthday Party, Prince's Tst Anniversary Concert Wembley, Oasis at Knebworth (Sony Award), U2 live from Sarajevo, BBC Music Live Golden Jubilee events in Hyde Park, HDTV Relay of Live8 2005, Celebrate Success and Invest in Futures for Prince's Tst 2005–, West End Live, Regent Festival, The Big Diamond Jubilee Lunch, Piccadilly and Canary Wharf Olympics Big Screen; *Recreations* golf, walking, reading, theatre, music, cinema; *Style*— Chris Lycett, Esq; ☎ 020 7435 3326, mobile 07980 845655, e-mail chrislycett1@gmail.com, website www.chrislycett.com

LYDON, Prof Julie Elspeth; OBE (2014); da of Dennis John Hodges, of Wolverhampton, and Rosalind Nina Hodges (d 2012); *b* 14 June 1954, Builth Wells, Powys; *Educ* BA, MBA; *m* 23 March 1985, Stephen Leslie Lydon; 2 s (Benjamin Patrick b 30 April 1988, Thomas Joseph b 6 Feb 1992); *Career* asst vice-chllr UWE 2003–06; Univ of S Wales (formerly Univ of Glamorgan): joined 2006, dep vice-chllr, vice-chllr 2010–; *Style*— Prof Julie Lydon, OBE; ✉ University of South Wales, Pontypridd CF37 1DL (☎ 01443 428001)

LYE, Geoffrey Brian; s of James Douglas Lye, and Ruby Alma, *née* Cox; *b* 14 October 1949; *Educ* King Edward VI Sch Southampton, Gonville & Caius Coll Cambridge; *m* Linda May (m dis), da of George Arthur Muirhead; 2 da (Mary Elizabeth b 4 Sept 1975, Katherine Louise b 16 Nov 1978), 2 s (Charles Julian b 20 April 1982, Jonathan James b 29 Jan 1988); *Career* J Walter Thompson advtg agency 1972–74, General Foods 1974–80, gp dep chm Countrywide Porter Novelli Ltd 1980–97, chm BMP Countrywide 1997–99; dir SustainAbility Ltd 1995– (vice-chm 2004–09, chm 2009–); research fell Green Templeton Oxford 2005–; FRSA; *Style*— Geoffrey Lye, Esq

LYGO, Kevin; s of Adm Sir Raymond Lygo, KCB (d 2012), and Pepper, *née* Van Osten (d 2004); *b* 19 September 1957; *Educ* Univ of Durham (BSc); *Career* comedy scriptwriter (Not the Nine O'clock News, Two Ronnies, Three of a Kind) 1982, trainee (prodr Omnibus) BBC 1983–85; art dealer 1986–91; BBC: comedy prodr 1991–96, head of independent prodn 1996–97; head of entertainment Channel 4 1997–2001, dir of programmes Five 2001–03, dir of TV Channel 4 2003–10, md ITV Studios 2010–; *Recreations* tennis, Islamic art; *Style*— Kevin Lygo, Esq

LYLE, (Philip) Dominic; s of late Robert Lyle, and late Helena, *née* Perks; *b* 6 March 1949; *Educ* Stonyhurst, Alliance Française, Université de Lausanne; *m* 5 Sept 1992, Vyvyan Lynne, *née* Mackeson; *Career* sales and mktg mangr Europe Tate & Lyle Refineries 1976–79; Cameron Choat & Partners: joined 1979, dir 1985–90, md 1990–91; dir Countrywide Communications (London) Ltd 1992–94, md Countrywide Porter Novelli (Brussels) 1994–2000, chm European technol practice Porter Novelli (Paris) 2000–02, DG European Assoc of Communications Agencies (EACA) 2002–, vice-chm European Advertising Standards Alliance, treas European Digital Advertising Alliance; memb Mktg Soc, MIPR; *Recreations* opera, cooking; *Style*— Dominic Lyle, Esq; ✉ European Association of Communications Agencies, 152 Boulevard Brand Whitlock, B-1200 Brussels, Belgium

LYLE, Sir Gavin Archibald; 3 Bt (UK 1929), of Glendelvine, Co Perth; s of Capt Ian Archibald de Hoghton Lyle (ka 1942), and Hon Lydia, *née* Yarde-Buller (later Duchess of Bedford, d 2006), da of 3 Baron Churston; suc gf, Col Sir Archibald Moir Park Lyle, 2 Bt, MC, TD, 1946; *b* 14 October 1941; *Educ* Eton; *m* 1967 (m dis 1985), Susan (d 2011), o da of John Vaughan Cooper; 5 s (Ian Abram b 1968, Jake Archibald b 1969, Matthew Alexander b 1974, Joshua b 1979, Samuel b 1981), 1 da (Rachel b 1971); *Heir* s, Ian Lyle; *Career* estate mangr; farmer; co dir; *Style*— Sir Gavin Lyle, Bt; ✉ Glendelvine, Caputh, Perthshire PH1 4JN

LYLE, Richard; MSP; *b* 12 June 1950, Bothwellhaugh, Lanarkshire; *Educ* Bellshill Acad; *Career* formerly with RBS; SNP gp ldr: Motherwell DC and N Lanarkshire 1976–2011, Cosla 2007–09; cllr Motherwell DC 1976–96, cllr N Lanarkshire Cncl 1996–2012; MSP (SNP) Central Scotland 2011–; memb SNP 1966–; MICM; *Style*— Richard Lyle, Esq, MSP; ✉ The Scottish Parliament, Edinburgh EH99 1SP

LYLE, Robert Arthur Wyatt; s of Maj Robert David Lyle (d 1989), and Irene Joyce, *née* Penn-Francis (d 1984); n of Lord Wyatt of Weeford (Life Peer, d 1997); *b* 5 May 1952; *Educ* Eton, Oriel Coll Oxford (MA); *m* 1, 9 March 1991 (m dis 2002), Hon Teresa (Tessa) Ruth, da of Baron Mayhew (Life Peer, d 1997); 1 s (Christopher Robert David Wyatt b 12 Feb 1992); m 2, 25 Aug 2005, Lysanne Amanda Koetser, da of Brian Leonard Koester, of Nutbourne, West Sussex; *Career* dir: BPL Hldgs Ltd 1983–, NMG (Cornwall) Ltd 1992–, Commonwealth Disaster Mgmnt Agency Ltd 1999–; Cornwall Light and Power Co Ltd (first wholly private commercial wind farm in UK): fndr 1989, sold 2005; advsr Global Trade Insurance PTE Singapore; worldwide corr to China International Economic Consultants 1983–87, EC advsr to Russian Govt on investment insurance 1991–93; advsr to World Energy Cncl on trade and political risk insurance 2002–, advsr to African Trade Insurance (COMESA) 2003–10; dir Green Intelligence Pictures Ltd 2014–; BRCS: pres Cornwall Branch 1996–2001, vice-chm SW Regnl Cncl 1997–2001, vice-pres Overseas Territories 2002–, hon vice-pres Cornwall Branch 2002–; memb Advsy Ctee to the UK Natural Disaster Reduction Ctee 2000–, tstee and memb Cncl Int Social Service UK 2004–10, emeritus tstee China Oxford Scholarship Fund 2004–, memb Advsy Bd Ashmolean Museum Oxford 2005–, tstee Elgar Soc Edition 2005–07; exec prodr The Music for The Children's Party at the Palace 2006, dir The Music of the Great War 2014–; treas PCC St Keverne 1995–99, memb Upper Basildon PCC 1999–2002; Church Warden Aston Tirrold and Aston Upthorpe 2002–04, memb Bd Arab Int Women's Forum 2010–, pres Cwlth Beekeepers Assoc 2012–; one of four hereditary Lords of the Lizard; Liveryman Worshipful Co of Glass Sellers; FRSA, FRGS; *Recreations* art, architecture, music, travel, fishing, sailing; *Clubs* White's, Lansdowne; *Style*— Robert Lyle, Esq

LYNAM, Desmond Michael; OBE (2008); s of Edward Lynam, and Gertrude Veronica, *née* Malone; *b* 17 September 1942; *Educ* Varndean GS Brighton, Brighton Business Coll (ACII); *m* 1 1965 (m dis 1974), Susan Eleanor, *née* Skinner; 1 s (Patrick), 2 Rosemary Elizabeth *née* Diamond; *Career* in insurance and freelance journalism until 1967; local radio reporter 1967–69, reporter, presenter and commentator BBC Radio 1969–78, presenter and commentator BBC TV Sport 1978–99 (incl Grandstand, Match of the Day, Cwlth and Olympic Games, World Cup and Wimbledon); presenter: Holiday (BBC TV) 1988–89, How Do They Do That? (BBC TV) 1994–96, The Des Lynam Show (BBC Radio 2) 1998–99, ITV Sport 1999–2004, Des Meets... (BBC Radio Five Live) 2004–05, We'll Meet Again (BBC TV) 2005, The World's Greatest Sporting Legend (Sky One) 2005, Des at Wimbledon (BBC Radio Five Live) 2005, Are You Younger Than You Think? (BBC TV) 2005, Countdown (Channel 4) 2005–06, Sport Mastermind (BBC TV) 2008, Touchline Tales (BBC Radio 4) 2011–13; TV Sports Presenter of the Year (TV and Radio Industries Club) 1985, 1987, 1988, 1993 and 1997, Male TV Personality (Radio Times/Open Air) 1989, Sports Presenter of the Year (RTS Awards) 1994 and 1998, Richard Dimbleby Award (BAFTA) 1994, Broadcasting Press Guild Award for best performer (non-acting) 1996, BBC Viewers' Top Television Presenter on Auntie's All Time Greats a 60th Anniversary of the BBC 1996, Variety Club of Great Britain Media Award 1997, RTS Lifetime Achievement Award 2003; *Publications* Guide to Commonwealth Games (1986), The 1988 Olympics (1988), The Barcelona Olympics 1992 (with Caroline Searle, 1992), I Should Have Been at Work! (2005); *Recreations* golf, tennis, Brighton and Hove Albion FC, reading, theatre; *Style*— Desmond Lynam, Esq, OBE; ✉ c/o Jane Morgan Management Ltd, Argentum, 2 Queen Caroline Street, London W6 9DX (☎ 020 3178 8071, e-mail enquiries@janemorganmgt.com)

LYNCH, Holly; MP; *b* 1987, Halifax; *Career* MP (Lab) Halifax 2015–; *Style*— Ms Holly Lynch, MP; ✉ House of Commons, London SW1A 0AA

LYNCH, James; s of Ronald F T Lynch, and Joy Ann, *née* Berry, of Seend, Wiltshire; *b* 12 July 1956; *Educ* Devizes Sch, Swindon Coll (Dip Graphic Design); *m* 1977, Kate Mary, da of John Argent Armstrong; 2 s (Thomas Albert b 1978, Arthur James b 1982), 1 da (Alice Mary b 1980); *Career* artist; *Solo Exhibitions* incl: Linfield Galleries Bradford-on-Avon 1982 and 1983, Odette Gilbert London 1988, Maas Gallery London 1991, 1993, 1995, 1997, 1999, 2001, 2003 and 2006, Jonathan Cooper Park Walk Gallery London 2011 and 2014; *Group Exhibitions* incl: RA Summer Shows annually 1984–89, Royal Soc of Painters in Watercolour 1986, Agnews London 1989 and 1990, Discerning Eye Mall Gallery 1991, Galerie Michael Beverley Hills 2002; *Commissions* incl Nat Tst and Folio Soc (illustrations for Wind in the Willows 1994); *Public Collections* Chatsworth Collection, Nat Tst Fndn for Art, Wessex Collection; *Awards* Elizabeth Greenshields Fndn Award 1983, RA Pimms Prize 1986, winner Adams/Spectator Painting Award 1993; *Recreations* cycling, motorcycling, paragliding; *Style*— James Lynch, Esq; ✉ Four Chimneys, High Ham, Langport, Somerset TA10 9BB (☎ 01458 250367, website www.james-lynch.co.uk)

LYNCH, Jerome; QC (2000); s of Clifford James Lynch (d 1995), and Loretta Rosa, *née* Mazzolini (d 2004); *b* 31 July 1955; *Educ* Univ of Lancashire (BA); *m* 25 March 1983 (sep); 2 s (Oliver Jerome b 25 Oct 1986, Milo Sebastien b 11 Aug 2011); *Career* called to the Bar Lincoln's Inn 1983 (bencher 2008); co-presenter Nothing But The Truth (Channel 4) 1998–99, presenter Crime Team (Channel 4) 2002, presenter People's Court (ITV1) 2005; *Recreations* bad golfer, good skier, love wine; *Clubs* RAC; *Style*— Jerome Lynch, Esq, QC; ✉ Trott & Duncan, 17A Brunswick Street, Hamilton HM 10, Bermuda

LYNCH, John Stewart; OBE (2011); *Educ* Univ of London (BA); *m* 1984, Ewa Hawrylowicz; 2 s; *Career* researcher BBC Science 1976–80, prodr 1981–93, ed Horizon (BBC) 1994–98, dep head BBC Science 1998–2000, creative dir BBC Science 2000–05, head BBC Science 2006–10; chm World Congress of Science and Factual Prodrs Ltd 2006–; *Awards* Prix Italia, Banff Rockie, Paris Int Sci TV Festival Grand Prix, Quebec Int Scientific Film Festival Grand Prix, ABSW Sci Writers Award, Primetime Emmy, RTS and BAFTA (for Horizon and Walking With Dinosaurs); *Publications* Wild Weather (2002), Walking with Cavemen (2003), Earth: The Power of the Planet (2007), The Story of Science (2010); *Recreations* rest; *Style*— John Lynch, OBE; ✉ e-mail johnlynchmedia@gmail.com

LYNCH, Dr Michael Richard; OBE; s of Michael Lynch, and Dolores, *née* O'Neil; *b* 16 June 1965, London; *Educ* Bancrofts Sch Woodford Green, Christ's Coll Cambridge (MA); *m* 29 Sept 2001, Angela, *née* Bacares; 2 da (Esme Finola Maria b 15 June 2003, Hannah Deia b 27 Feb 2006); *Career* ceo and fndr Autonomy; non-exec dir: BBC, Blinkx plc; winner Electrical Engineer's medal for outstanding achievement, Entrepreneur of the Year CBI; *Recreations* breeding rare dogs; *Style*— Dr Michael Lynch, OBE; ✉ Cambridge Enterprise Ltd, University of Cambridge, Hauser Forum, 3 Charles Babbage Road, Cambridge CB3 0GT

LYNCH, Prudence; *née* Renny; da of Derek Renny (d 1970), and Hon Nicola, *née* Moncreiff (d 2003); *b* Dundee; *Educ* Blanchelande Coll Guernsey, Univ of St Andrews (MA), Goldsmiths Coll London (PGCE); *m* 22 Oct 1977, Paul Lynch; 2 s (James b 3 June 1980, Harry b 12 July 1983); *Career* teacher Heathfield Sch Pinner 1977–80, head of maths and IT Notting Hill & Ealing HS 1987–90, head of special needs Colet Court St Paul's Boys Prep Sch London 1990–98, head Notting Hill & Ealing Jr Sch 1998–2003, head Kensington Prep Sch 2003–; chair of govrs Grove Road Sch Hounslow; Best Headmistress of a Prep Sch Tatler 2006; memb: Psychological Soc 1976, ACT 1987, IAPS 2003, NAHT 2003; *Recreations* Arabic, singing, the sea, watching birds; *Style*— Mrs Prudence Lynch; ✉ Kensington Prep School, 596 Fulham Road, London SW6 5PA (☎ 020 7731 9300, fax 020 7731 9301, e-mail p.lynch@kenprep.gdst.net, website www.gdst.net/kensingtonprep)

LYNCH, Roderick Robertson (Rod); s of late Nanson Lynch, and late Catherine, *née* Robertson; *b* 22 May 1949; *Educ* Perth Acad, Univ of Dundee (MA); *m* 1972, Christina, da of William Williams; 2 s (James b 1975, Alexander b 1980); *Career* served RAC 1966–67; various positions British Airways 1971–89, md Air Europe 1989–91, dir Forte Hotels

1991–93, chief exec BBC Resources Directorate 1993–99, chief exec Olympic Airways Greece 1999–2000, chm and ceo GSS Ltd 2001–; memb Bd: CAA 1993–99, Nat Air Traffic Servs 1996–99; *Recreations* rugby, military history, music, aviation; *Clubs* Caledonian; *Style*— Rod Lynch, Esq

LYNCH, Her Hon Judge Sarah; *Career* admitted slr 1989; recorder 2008, circuit judge (North Eastern Circuit) 2012–; *Style*— Her Hon Judge Lynch; ✉ Leeds Combined Court Centre, The Court House, 1 Oxford Row, Leeds LS1 3BG

LYNCH-BLOSSE, Sir Richard Hely; 17 Bt (I 1622), of Castle Carra, Galway; s of Sir David Edward Lynch-Blosse, 16 Bt (d 1971), and Elizabeth, *née* Payne; *b* 26 August 1953; *Educ* Welwyn Garden City, Royal Free Hosp Sch of Med London (MB BS); *m* 1 (m dis), Cara Lynne, o da of George Longmore Sutherland, of St Ives, Cambs; 2 da (Katherine Helen (Katy) b 1983, Hannah Victoria b 1985); *m* 2, Jacqueline Hall, *née* Francis, o da of late Gordon Francis; *Heir* cous, David Lynch-Blosse; *Career* med practitioner, short serv cmmn with RAMC 1975–85; MO Oxfordshire Army Cadet Force; med referee S Oxfordshire Crematorium; pres Dorchester and District Branch Royal British Legion; memb Soc of Ornamental Turner; memb BMA; LRCP, MRCS, DRCOG, MRCGP 1984–2008, FRSM; *Recreations* archery, ornamental turning, precision engineering; *Clubs* RSM; *Style*— Sir Richard Lynch-Blosse, Bt; ✉ The Surgery, Clifton Hampden, Oxfordshire OX14 3EL

LYNDEN-BELL, Prof Donald; CBE (2000); s of Lt-Col Lachlan Arthur Lynden-Bell, MC (d 1984), and Monica Rose, *née* Thring; *b* 5 April 1935; *Educ* Marlborough, Clare Coll Cambridge; *m* 1 July 1961, Ruth Marion, da of Dr D N Truscott, of Ely; 1 da (Marion Katharine b 10 April 1965), 1 s (Edward Lachlan b 16 Dec 1968); *Career* res fell Clare Coll Cambridge and fell Cwlth (Harkness) Fund Caltech and Mt Wilson and Palomar Observatories 1960–62, dir of maths studies Clare Coll Cambridge and asst lectr Univ of Cambridge 1962–65, SPSO Royal Greenwich Observatory Herstmonceux 1965–72, visiting prof Univ of Sussex 1970–72, dir Inst of Astronomy Cambridge 1972–77, 1982–87 and 1992–95, prof of astrophysics Univ of Cambridge 1972–2001, prof fell Clare Coll Cambridge 1972–; Russell lectr American Astronomical Soc 2000; pres: Cambridge Philosophical Soc 1982–84, RAS 1985–87 (Eddington Medal 1984, Gold Medal 1993); featured in Star Men (film) directed by Alison Rose (DVD released 2016); Brower Prize American Astronomical Soc 1990; Bruce Gold Medal of the Astronomical Soc of the Pacific 1998, J J Carty Medal and Award of the US Nat Acad of Sciences 2000, First Kavli Prize for Astrophysics (jtly with Maarten Schmidt) 2008; Hon DSc Univ of Sussex 1987, Hon PhD Hebrew Univ of Jerusalem 2010, Hon Dr Charles Univ Prague 2012; hon memb American Astronomical Soc 2002–; hon fell Inter-Univ Centre for Astronomy and Astrophysics (IUCAA) Pune India 2004–; foreign assoc: US Nat Acad of Sci 1990, Royal Soc of SA 1994; hon memb Norwegian Acad of Science and Letters 2009; FRS 1978; *Recreations* hill walking; *Style*— Prof Donald Lynden-Bell, CBE, FRS; ✉ 9 Storey's Way, Cambridge CB3 0DP (☎ 01223 359557); Institute of Astronomy (Cambridge University), The Observatories, Madingley Road, Cambridge CB3 0DP (☎ 01223 337525, fax 01223 337523, e-mail dlb@ast.cam.ac.uk)

LYNDHURST, Nicholas; *Career* actor 1971–; *Theatre* incl: Harding's Luck (Greenwich), Trial Run (Oxford Playhouse), Black Comedy (tour), The Private Ear (tour), The Foreigner (Albery), Straight and Narrow (Wyndhams) 1992, The Dresser (Duke of York's) 2005, The Tempest (Haymarket) 2011; also appeared in Royal Variety Performance (Theatre Royal Drury Lane) 1986; *Television* incl: Davy in Anne of Avonlea, Peter in Heidi, Tom Canty and Prince Edward in The Prince and the Pauper, Tootles in Peter Pan, Raymond in Going Straight (BBC), Adam in Butterflies (BBC), Philip in Father's Day (Granada), Tim in Fairies (BBC), Philip in Losing Her, Dobson in To Serve Them All My Days (BBC), Wilson in Spearhead, Rodney in Only Fools and Horses (BBC, 10 series), The Two of Us (LWT, 5 series), The Piglet Files (LWT, 3 series), Goodnight Sweetheart (BBC, 6 series) 1994, Gulliver's Travels (Channel 4) 1996, Uriah Heap in David Copperfield 1999, Butterflies Reunion Special 2000, Thin Ice (BBC) 2000, Murder in Mind (BBC) 2003, After You've Gone (BBC, 3 series) 2007–, Rock and Chips (BBC) 2009, New Tricks (BBC) 2013–14; *Awards* Best Television Ad Award 1997 and 2000 (for WHSmith campaign), Most Popular Comedy Performer National Television Awards 1998 and 2000; *Recreations* surfing, flying, diving; *Style*— Nicholas Lyndhurst, Esq; ✉ c/o Chatto & Linnit Ltd, c/o Chatto & Linnit Ltd, World's End Studios, 132–34 Lots Road, London SW10 0RJ (e-mail info@chattolinnit.com)

LYNDON-SKEGGS, Andrew Neville; s of Dr Peter Lyndon-Skeggs (d 2002), of Preston Candover, Hants, and June Angela, *née* Reid (d 2014); *b* 10 January 1949, Hitchin, Herts; *Educ* Rugby, Magdalene Coll Cambridge (MA), La Sorbonne Paris; *m* 8 April 1972 (m dis); 2 da (Vanessa b 1975, Tessa b 1979); *Career* master and tstee Univ of Cambridge Drag Hunt 1968–71; chm Westbrook Property Developments Ltd 1981–, md and chief exec Town Pages Ltd and TownPagesNet.com.plc 1995–99, chm and chief exec TheGardenLine.com Ltd 2000–01; photographer ANLS Photography 2011–; mangr Collection Philippine de Lauwe 2014–; *Books* Images (2016); *Recreations* photography, stalking, hunting, fishing, skiing, gardening, travelling, navigating canals and rivers; *Clubs* Boodles, Cambridge Soc (Paris), British Luncheon Club (1916) Paris; *Style*— Andrew Lyndon-Skeggs, Esq; ✉ Westbrook House, Hampshire; Péniche La Béthanie, Paris (☎ 00 33 687 40 57 14, e-mail anls@lyndon-skeggs.com)

LYNE, Kevin Douglas; *Educ* Richard Hale Sch Hertford, Portsmouth Poly, Univ of Essex; *m* Anne Dabbadie-Lyne; 2 da; *Career* diplomat; Research and Analysis Dept FCO 1988–91, 2 sec chancery Santiago 1991–94, princ research offr and head Americas Research Gp FCO 1994–96, 1 sec Drugs and Int Crime Dept FCO 1996–98, 1 sec Human Rights Section UK Mission to UN Geneva 1998–2003, dep head of mission Rabat 2003–07, ambass to Montenegro 2007–09, research analyst FCO 2010, stabilisation planner ISAF Jt Command HQ Kabul 2011–12, diplomat Americas Directorate FCO 2012, stabilisation advsr N and W Africa Stabilisation Unit 2013–14; dir K Lyne Consulting France; *Recreations* fishing; *Style*— Mr Kevin Lyne

LYNE, Rt Hon Sir Roderic Michael John; KBE (1999), CMG (1992), PC (2009); s of late Air Vice-Marshal Michael Lyne, CB, AFC, DL, and Avril Joy, *née* Buckley; *b* 31 March 1948; *Educ* Highfield Sch Liphook, Eton, Univ of Leeds (BA); *m* 13 Dec 1969, Amanda Mary, da of Sir Howard Frank Trayton Smith, GCMG; 2 s (Jethro b 10 Nov 1971, Andrei b 31 May 1974), 1 da (Sasha b 7 Jan 1981); *Career* entered HM Dip Serv 1970, Br Embassy Moscow 1972–74, Br Embassy Senegal 1974–76; FCO: Eastern Europe and Soviet Dept 1976–78, Rhodesia Dept 1979, asst private sec to Foreign and Cwlth Sec 1979–82; UK mission to UN NY 1982–86, visiting res fell RIIA 1986–87, head of Chancery and head of Political Section Br Embassy Moscow 1987–90, head of Soviet Dept FCO 1990–91, head of Eastern Dept FCO 1992–93; private sec to PM 1993–96, dir Policy Devpt for CIS, Middle East and Africa British Gas plc 1996, UK permanent rep to UN and other int organisations in Geneva 1997–2000, HM ambass to Russia 2000–04; business conslt and lectr; special advsr: BP plc 2004–09, HSBC Gp 2004–07, JPMorgan Bank 2007–10; non-exec dir: Accor 2006–09, Aricom plc 2006–09, Peter Hambro Mining (subsequently Petropavlovsk plc) 2009–16, JPMorgan Bank Int 2013–; special rep ITE Gp plc 2005–10, memb Strategic Advsy Gp QucomHaps Hldgs Ltd 2005–, chm Int Advsy Bd Altimo 2006–07; visiting prof Faculty of Business and Law Kingston Univ 2005–11 (memb Bd of Govrs 2007–, chm 2011–13); memb: Trilateral Cmmn Task Force on Russia 2005–06 (co-author report Engaging with Russia: The Next Phase 2006), Bd Russo-Br C of C 2006–09, Exec Ctee UK/Russia Round Table 2006–08, Iraq Inquiry Ctee 2009–16; hon vice-pres GB-Russia Soc; memb Oxford Univ Task Force on Energy, the Environment

and Devpt 2006–07, chm Advsy Ctee Centre for East European Language Based Area Studies 2007–; tstee World Race Tst 2005–08, govr Ditchley Fndn 2005–11, memb Bd Int Early Music Tst St Petersburg 2007–10, dep chm Cncl Royal Inst of Int Affrs Chatham House 2009–16, patron Amur; Hon LLD Univ of Leeds 2002, Hon DBA Kingston Univ 2004, Hon DLit Heriot-Watt Univ 2004, Hon Dr Univ of Birmingham 2012; *Publications* Engaging with Russia: The Next Phase (Trilateral Cmmn, 2006) The Imaginary Curtain (in Russia: The Challenges of Transformation, Social Science Research Cncl 2011) Russia's Changed Outlook on the West (in The Russian Challenge, Chatham House 2015) Overcoming Enmity: The Evolution of British-Irish Relations in the 1990s (16th Stephen Roskill Memorial Lecture, Churchill Coll Cambridge 2016); *Recreations* sport, grandchildren; *Clubs* Travellers; *Style*— The Rt Hon Sir Roderic Lyne, KBE, CMG; ✉ 39 Richmond Park Road, London SW14 8JU (e-mail rmjlyne@gmail.com)

LYNER, Peter Edward; OBE (1991); s of Alfred Lyner (d 1997), of Belfast, and Doreen Mary, *née* Devenney (d 1994); *b* 13 October 1942; *Educ* Royal Belfast Academical Inst, Univ of London (DPA); *m* 1964, Anne, da of Frederick Rogers (d 1974); 1 da (Anna Elizabeth b 1967), 1 s (Patrick Edward b 1970); *Career* librarian Belfast Public Library 1960–70, freelance journalist Irish Times until 1970; British Council: librarian Sudan 1970–73, librarian Yugoslavia 1973–76, inspr Mgmnt Servs Dept 1976–79, asst dir of educn Nigeria 1979–82, Russian language trg Univ of Strathclyde 1982–83, asst cultural attaché Moscow 1983–87, Bulgarian language trg SSEES 1987, cultural attaché Bulgaria 1987–90, dir Br Cncl N Ireland 1990–, admin Encounter 1998–; ALA 1966, DPA 1967, MIMgt 1981; *Books* Consignment of Ore (under pseudonym Peter Warden, 1983); *Recreations* music, writing, reading; *Style*— Peter Lyner, Esq, OBE

LYNN, Jeffrey Anson; s of Frederick Lynn, and Ann, *née* Coleman, of Scottsdale, Arizona; *b* 4 July 1978, NY; *Educ* St Paul's Sch New Hampshire, Univ of Pennsylvania (BA), Univ of Virginia (JD), Univ of Oxford (MBA, BCL); *m* 24 Oct 2009, Lindsay Levkoff Lynn; 1 da (Hannah Lynn b 3 May 2016); *Career* researcher The Rt Hon Lord Strathclyde 2000, assoc Sullivan & Cromwell LLP 2004–08, co-fndr and ceo Seedrs 2009–; NY Bar 2004; founding chm The Coalition for a Digital Economy (COADEC) 2010–15, non-exec dir Companies House 2013–; *Recreations* skiing, scuba diving, boating, walking, travel; *Clubs* Carlton; *Style*— Jeff Lynn, Esq; ✉ Seedrs Limited, 201 Borough High Street, London SE1 1JA (website www.seedrs.com)

LYNN, Jonathan Adam; s of Dr Robin Lynn, of London, and Ruth Helen, *née* Eban; *b* 3 April 1943; *Educ* Kingswood Sch Bath, Pembroke Coll Cambridge (MA); *m* 1 Aug 1967, Rita Eleonora Merkelis; 1 s (Edward b 19 Oct 1973); *Career* director, writer and actor; Hon MA Univ of Sheffield, Hon PsyD American Behavioral Studies Inst; *Theatre* actor in repertory: Leicester, Edinburgh, Bristol Old Vic; West End (incl Fiddler on the Roof, 1967); artistic dir Cambridge Theatre Co 1977–81 (produced 42 prodns and directed over 20); London dir incl: The Glass Menagerie 1977, The Gingerbread Man 1977, The Unvarnished Truth 1978, Songbook 1979 (Olivier and Evening Standard Awards for Best Musical, re-titled The Moony Shapiro Songbook for Broadway Prodn 1981), Anna Christie (RSC) 1979, Arms and the Man 1981, Pass The Butler 1981, A Little Hotel On The Side (NT) 1984, Jacobowsky and the Colonel (NT) 1986, Three Men on a Horse (NT, Olivier Award for Best Comedy) 1987, Budgie 1988, Yes Prime Minister 2010–13 (co-writer and dir); company dir at NT 1986–87; *Television* as actor incl: Doctor in the House (series) 1970, The Liver Birds (series) 1972, My Brothers Keeper 1973 and 1974 (series, co-writer with George Layton), Barmitzvah Boy 1975, The Knowledge 1979, Outside Edge 1982, Diana 1984, as writer incl: Yes Minister 1980–82, Yes Prime Minister 1986–88 (with co-author Anthony Jay), BAFTA Writers' Award, Broadcasting Press Guild Award (twice), Pye Television Writers' Award (twice), Ace Award – best comedy writing on US cable TV, Special Award from The Campaign For Freedom of Information) and 2013 (co-writer, prodr and dir); TV dir: Smart Guys, Ferris Bueller (NBC TV pilots); *Film* as actor incl: Into The Night 1985, Three Men and A Little Lady 1990, Greedy 1993; screenplay The Internecine Project 1974; as dir: Micks People (also wrote) 1982, Clue (also wrote) 1986, Nuns On The Run (also wrote, Golden Cane Award at Festival de Comedie in Vevey) 1989, My Cousin Vinny 1991, The Distinguished Gentleman 1991 (Environmental Media Award, Political Film Soc Special Award), Greedy 1993, Sgt Bilko 1995, Trial and Error 1997, The Whole Nine Yards 2000, The Fighting Temptations 2003 (NAACP Image Award), Wild Target 2009; *Books* A Proper Man (1976), The Complete Yes Minister (1984), Yes Prime Minister vol 1 (1986), vol 2 (with Antony Jay, 1987), Mayday (1993), Comedy Rules (2011); *Plays* Yes Prime Minister (with Antony Jay, 2010), The Patriotic Traitor (2016); *Recreations* changing weight; *Style*— Jonathan Lynn; ✉ e-mail lofty.lynn@gmail.com, website www.jonathanlynn.com; c/o Alan Brodie Representation (☎ 001 7 253 6226, e-mail alan@alanbrodie.com)

LYNN, Bishop of 2011–; Rt Rev (Cyril) Jonathan Meyrick; s of Christopher Meyrick, and Isolde Meyrick; *b* 23 April 1952, Beaconsfield, Bucks; *Educ* Lancing Coll, St John's Coll Oxford (BA, MA), Salisbury and Wells Theological Coll; *m* 1984, Rebecca, *née* Keatley; 1 s, 2 da; *Career* ordained: deacon 1976, priest 1977; curate Bicester 1976–78, domestic chaplain to Bishop of Oxford 1978–81, tutor in Old Testament studies Barbados 1981–84, team vicar Taplow 1984–90, team rector Tisbury 1990–98, canon residentiary Rochester 1998–2005 (acting dean 2003–05), dean of Exeter 2005–11; memb House of Bishops 2012–; Hon DEd Plymouth Univ 2011; *Publications* Old Testament Syllabus for Developing Ministries Prog (2001), Cultural Diversity Guide (2001), Rochester Cathedral Guide (2004), A Carol of Hope (2008), The Church of the City (2008); *Recreations* acting, singing, punting, croquet, tennis; *Style*— The Rt Rev the Bishop of Lynn; ✉ The Old Vicarage, Priory Road, Castle Acre, King's Lynn, Norfolk PE32 2AA (☎ 01760 755553, e-mail bishop.lynn@dioceseofnorwich.org, website www.norwich.anglican.org)

LYNN, Prof Richard; s of Richard Lynn, and Ann Lynn; *b* 20 February 1930; *Educ* Bristol GS, King's Coll Cambridge (Passingham prize); *m* 1956 (m dis 1978), Susan Maher; 1 s, 2 da; *m* 2, 1989, Susan Lesley Hampson (decd); *m* 3, 2004, Joyce Walters; *Career* lectr in psychology Univ of Exeter 1956–67; prof of psychology: Dublin Economic and Social Research Inst 1967–72, Univ of Ulster 1972–96 (prof emeritus 1996–); currently head Ulster Inst for Social Research; awarded US Mensa award for Excellence (for work on intelligence) 1985, 1988 and 1993; *Books* Attention Arousal and the Orientation Reaction (1966), The Irish Braindrain (1969), The Universities and the Business Community (1969), Personality and National Character (1971), An Introduction to the Study of Personality (1972), The Entrepreneur (ed, 1974), Dimensions of Personality (ed, 1981), Educational Achievement in Japan (1987), The Secret of the Miracle Economy (1991), Dysgenics (1997, 2 edn 2011)), Eugenics: A Reassessment (2001), The Science of Human Diversity (2001), IQ and the Wealth of Nations (2002), Race Differences in Intelligence (2005), IQ and Global Inequality (jtly, 2006), The Global Bell Curve (2007), The Chosen People: Jewish IQ and Achievement (2011), Intelligence: A Global Construct (jtly, 2012); author of various articles on personality, intelligence and social psychology; *Recreations* DIY, bridge; *Clubs* Oxford and Cambridge; *Style*— Prof Richard Lynn

LYNN, Dame Vera Margaret; CH (2016), DBE (1975, OBE 1969); da of Bertram Welch, and Annie, *née* Martin; *b* 20 March 1917, East Ham; *Educ* Brampton Rd Sch East Ham; *m* 1941, Harry Lewis; 1 da (Virginia Penelope Ann); *Career* singer; with Ambrose Orch 1937–40, subsequently went solo, starred Applesauce (London Palladium) 1941, own radio show Sincerely Yours 1941–47; voted most popular singer Daily Express competition 1939, Forces' sweetheart WWII, toured Egypt, India, Burma 1944 (Burma Star 1985); subsequently: Tallulah Bankhead's Big Show (USA), London Laughs (Adelphi London), cabaret in Las Vegas, own TV show Vera Lynn Sings (BBC); numerous appearances over Europe, SA, Aust, NZ and Canada, 8 Command Performances, records incl Auf Wiedersehen (over 12 million copies sold), first British artist to top American Charts; pres: Aust Variety Ladies' Assoc, RAFA, Y-Care Int Fund for Africa, London Taxi Drivers' Benevolent Fund, Young Concert Artists' Assoc, Local Women's Br Legion; first woman pres Printers' Charitable Corp; vice-pres: Song Writers' Guild, Age Concern (memb Fund Raising Ctee); chm: Breast Cancer Tst Fund, Gilbert & Sullivan Tst Fund; vice-chm Stars Orgn for Spastics, life govr ICRF; Ivor Novello Award 1973, Show Business Personality Award Grand Order of Water Rats 1973, Music Publishers' Award and Songwriters of GB Award 1974 and 1975, Woman of the World Award 1987, int ambass Variety Club Int 1987 (Humanitarian Award 1985), BBC Woman of the Year 1994, Spirit of the 20th Century Award 2000, Lillian Keil Award for Outstanding Service to the Allied Cause by a Woman in WWII 2006, Nordoff Robbins Icon of the Century Award 2010; fndr Dame Vera Lynn Sch for Parents and Handicapped Children 1992, Master of Music City of London Univ 1992–; Freeman Cities of: London, Winnipeg, Melbourne, Cornerbrook, Nashville; Hon LLD Meml Univ Newfoundland; fell Univ of E London 1990; Cdr of Orange Nassau (Holland) 1976, OStJ 1998, Dutch War Veteran Medal 2010; *Books* Vocal Refrain (autobiography, 1975), We'll Meet Again (jtly, 1989), Unsung Heroines (1990); *Recreations* gardening, painting, needlework, knitting; *Style—* Dame Vera Lynn, CH, DBE, LLD, MMUS

LYNNE, Elizabeth (Liz); *b* 22 January 1948; *Educ* Dorking County GS; *Career* actress 1966–89, freelance speech and voice conslt 1989–92; Parly candidate (Lib Alliance) Harwich 1987; MP (Lib Dem) Rochdale 1992–97, MEP (Lib Dem) W Midlands 1999–2012; Lib Dem Shadow Sec of State Health and Community Care 1992–94, Lib Dem Shadow Sec of State Social Security and Disability 1994–97; vice-pres Employment and Social Affrs Ctee, memb delgn for relations with S Asia, submemb Regnl Affrs Ctee, memb Delgn Palestinian, vice-pres All-Pty Disability Intergroup, co-chair Parly Intergroup on Aging, vice-pres MEPs Against Cancer (MAC), pres Lib Dem Friends of Kashmir, co-chair European Forum for Manufacturing, co-fndr Independents Forum of Europe, pres Lib Dem Disability Assoc; shadow rapporteur Working Time Directive, rapporteur for European Year of Disabled People 2003, rapporteur EU Action Plan for Disabled People 2006–07, rapporteur Social Reality Stocktaking 2007, rappoteur Anti-Discrimination Stocktaking 2008; chair Indonesian Coordination Gp Amnesty Int 1972–79; vice-pres: Campaign to Protect Rural England (Staffordshire), Droitwich Canal Tst; patron: Jennifer Tst for Spinal Muscular Atrophy, Blue Eyed Soul Dance Co, Friends of the Montgomery Canal, George Coller Meml Fund, Tourism For All UK, Fedn of European Motorcyclists' Assocs, Worcestershire Lifestyles, Shropshire and Wrekin ME Support, Grown Up Congenital Heart Patient Assoc, Parkside Centre Tst, Mankind Initiative, S Andrew's Hospice, St Giles' Hospice; *Recreations* tennis, motorbiking; *Style—* Liz Lynne

LYON, Her Hon Judge Christina Margaret; da of late Edward Arthur Harrison, of Liverpool, and Kathleen Joan, *née* Smith; *b* 12 November 1952; *Educ* Wallasey HS for Girls, UCL (LLB, Maxwell Law prize); *m* 29 May 1976, His Hon Judge Adrian P Lyon, s of Alexander Ward Lyon, of London; 1 da (Alexandra Sophie Louise b 5 Jan 1984), 1 s (David Edward Arandall b 8 July 1985); *Career* tutor and sometime lectr in law Faculty of Law UCL 1974–75; slr Bell & Joynson Liscard Wallasey Merseyside 1975–77; lectr Law Faculty: Univ of Liverpool 1977–80, Univ of Manchester 1980–86 (sub-dean 1986); prof of law and head Sch of Law Keele Univ 1986–93; Univ of Liverpool: prof of common law and head Dept of Law 1993–97, dean Faculty of Law 1994–97, dir Centre for the Study of the Child, the Family and the Law 1994–2007 (hon dir 2007–), Queen Victoria prof of law 1998–2007 (emeritus prof 2007–); asst recorder of the Crown Court 1998–2000, recorder in HM Courts (crime and family) 2000–07, circuit judge (Northern Circuit) 2007–; ind chair Liverpool Early Years Devpt and Childcare Partnership 2001–; Dr Barnardos Res Fellowship 1987–91; chm and tstee Nat Youth Advocacy Serv 1998–2002; ed Journal of Social Welfare and Family Law 1984–, advsy ed Representing Children 1995–, ed Web Journal of Legal Issues 1995–, legal theory ed Amicus Curiae: The Jl of the Inst of Advanced Legal Studies 1998–; pres N Staffs RELATE (marriage guidance) 1987–93 (memb Nat Exec Ctee 1991–94), ind memb Merseyside Children's Secure Accommodation Panel 1988–93; memb ESRC Grants Bd 1988–91, memb Child Policy Review Gp NCB 1988–91, tstee, dir and chm IRCHIN 1988–98, tstee and dir Schs Cncls (UK) 1994–2003, vice-chair Merseyside Guardians ad Libem Ctee 1993–97; memb: Law Soc 1977, Soc of Public Teachers of Law 1977, Ctee of Heads of Univ Law Schs (memb Exec Ctee 1989–96); FRSA 1991; *Books* Matrimonial Jurisdiction of Magistrates Courts (1980), Cohabitation Without Marriage (1983), The Law of Residential Homes and Day Care Establishments (1984), Child Abuse (1990, 3 edn 2003), Atkins on Minors (1990), Butterworths Family Law Handbook (1991), Living Away From Home (1991), The Implications of the Children Act 1989 for Children with Disabilities (1991), Butterworths Law and Practice relating to Children (1992), Atkins on Infants (vols 1 and 2, 1992), The Law relating to Children (1993), Legal Issues Arising from the Care, Control and Safety of Children with Learning Disabilities who also Present Challenging Behaviour – Research Report and A Guide for Parents and Carers (1994), The Impact of the Law on Youth – The Years of Decision (1996), Butterworths Family Law Encyclopaedia (2005, also quarterly updates); contrib: The Impact of the Law on the Prevention of Child Abuse and Neglect in The National Commission of Inquiry Report into the Prevention of Child Abuse and Neglect 'Childhood Matters' (1996), Children Abused within the Care System in 'Child Protection and Family Support' (ed Parton, Routledge, 1997), Don't Forget Us (report for Mental Health Fndn, 1997), Children and the Law – Towards 2000 and Beyond. An Essay in Human Rights, Social Policy and the Law (1997), Effective Support Services for Children when Parental Relationships Break Down (1998), Loving Smack – Lawful Assault? (2000), A Trajectory of Hope (2000), Physical Interventions and the Law (2004), Breaking Down Walls (2004), A Parents' and Carers' Guide to Physical Intervention and the Law (2005); *Recreations* tennis, opera, theatre, foreign travel, writing; *Style—* Her Hon Judge Lyon; ✉ Preston Combined Court Centre, Ring Way, Preston, Lancashire PR1 2LL; The Liverpool Law School, University of Liverpool, Chatham Street, Liverpool L69 7ZS

LYON, George; MEP; s of Alister Lyon (d 1993), of Rothesay, Isle of Bute, and Mary, *née* McAlister (d 1998); *b* 16 July 1956; *Educ* Rothesay Acad, Nuffield Scholar 1987; *m* (sep 2002); 3 da (Lorna b 11 Oct 1984, Samantha b 20 Feb 1986, Amanda b 26 July 1990); *Career* farmer of family farms; dir Scottish Quality Beef and Lamb Assoc 1996–97; MSP (Lib Dem) Argyll & Bute 1999–2007, MEP (Lib Dem) Scotland 2009–; memb Nat Farmers Union of Scotland (held every office incl pres), assoc BVA; past chm Port Bannatyne Sch Bd; FRAgS; *Recreations* swimming, football, skiing, reading; *Clubs* Farmers; *Style—* George Lyon, Esq, MEP

LYON, John Macdonald; CB (2003); *b* 12 April 1948; *Educ* Univ of Cambridge (MA); *m*; 2 c; *Career* Home Office: joined 1969, asst sec Ctee on the Future of Broadcasting 1974–77, sec Inquiry into Prison Disturbances 1990–91, dir sentencing and correctional policy 1998–99, dir police policy 1999; DG Policing and Crime Reduction Gp 2000–03, DG Legal and Judicial Servs Gp Miny of Justice (formerly Dept for Constitutional Affrs) 2003–07, parly cmmr for standards House of Commons 2008–12; lay memb Bar Tbnls and Adjudication Service 2013–, expert adviser OSCE 2013; dir of strategy and implementation Woolf Inst Cambridge 2015–; Nat Tst: elected memb Cncl 2013–, chair Nominations Ctee Cncl 2014, chair Nominations Ctee Tstees 2015–; FRSA 2000; *Style—* John Lyon, Esq, CB

LYON, Thomas Stephen; s of Clifford Alexander Lyon (d 1962), and Felicia Maria Maximiliana, *née* Rosenfeld; *b* 26 November 1941; *Educ* Univ Coll Sch, Wadham Coll Oxford (MA), LSE (LLM); *m* 1971, Judith Elizabeth Jervis, da of Joseph Globe, of Toronto, Canada; 3 s (Edmund b 1971, Charles b 1973, Roger b 1974); *Career* slr; Woodham Smith Borradaile and Martin 1962–68, Berwin & Co 1968–70, Berwin Leighton 1970–2001, Berwin Leighton Paisner 2001–13; *Recreations* books, music, sailing, walking; *Clubs* Reform; *Style—* Thomas Lyon, Esq; ✉ 24 Denewood Road, Highgate, London N6 4AJ (☎ 020 8340 0846); Fernlea, Redmire, Leyburn, North Yorkshire (☎ 01969 622776)

LYON-DALBERG-ACTON; *see:* Acton

LYON-MARIS, Paul J; s of Peter David Lyon-Maris (d 2015), of W Sussex, and Sheila Margaret Ageless Wake (d 2016); *b* 7 June 1962; *Educ* Lancing; *Career* agent Independent Talent (formerly ICM); *Style—* Paul Lyon-Maris, Esq; ✉ Independent Talent, 40 Whitfield Street, London W1T 2RH

LYONS, Alastair David; CBE (2001); *b* 18 October 1953; *Educ* Whitgift Sch Croydon, Trinity Coll Cambridge (MA); *m* Shauneen, *née* Rhodes; 1 s (Edward Alexander Rhodes b 1982), 2 da (Lucy Jane b 1984, Tabitha Sallyanne b 1993); *Career* articled clerk rising to asst audit mangr Price Waterhouse & Co CAs 1974–79, corp finance mangr N M Rothschild & Sons Ltd 1979; H P Bulmer Holdings plc: gp treas 1979–82, gp financial controller 1983–88, fin dir H P Bulmer Drinks Ltd and actg gp fin dir 1988–89; divnl dir corp fin Asda Group plc 1989–90, fin dir Asda Stores Ltd 1990–91; National and Provincial Building Society: fin dir 1991–94, chief exec 1994–96, chm N&P Life Assurance Ltd and N&P Unit Trust Management Ltd; md Insurance Div Abbey National plc 1996–97; dir: Scottish Mutual Assurance plc 1996–97, Abbey National Life plc 1996–97, Commercial Union Underwriting Ltd 1996–97; chief exec National Provident Institution 1997–99; dir of corporate projects Natwest Gp 1999–2000; non-exec chm: Admiral Gp plc 2000–, In Retirement Services Ltd 2002–09, Legal Marketing Services Ltd 2002–, Health and Case Management Ltd 2003–08, Buy-as-you-View Ltd 2004–07, Highamgroup plc 2005–07, Cardsave Ltd 2008–10, Serco Gp plc 2010–15, Towergate Insurance Gp 2011–15, D?r Cymru Welsh Water 2016–; dep chm Bovis Homes 2008–, sr ind dir Pheonix Hldgs 2010–13; non-exec dir: Benefits Agency 1994–97, DSS 1997–2001, Dept for Work and Pensions 2001–02, Wishstream Ltd 2001–02, Dept for Tport 2002–05, Sesame Gp Ltd 2003–04; ATII, MCT; FCA; *Recreations* cycling, riding, hill walking, skiing, gardening, antiques; *Style—* Alastair Lyons, Esq, CBE; ✉ e-mail alastair_lyons@jaset.demon.co.uk

LYONS, Anthony; s of Alan Lyons, and Angela, *née* Collins; *b* 7 June 1967, London; *Educ* Mill Hill Sch; *m* 2 Sept 2001, Lucy, *née* Johnson; 1 da (Grace Ida Rose b 29 Aug 2003), 2 s (Edward Jack b 24 Oct 2005, Gabriel Joseph b 16 Feb 2007); *Career* Richman Conway Surveyors 1983–85, Davis Coffer Lyons 1985–2004, ceo Earls Court and Olympia 2004–08, ceo Matterhorn Capital Ltd 2008–; *Recreations* shooting, tennis, boating; *Clubs* Georges, Harry's Bar, Tramp, Annabel's; *Style—* Anthony Lyons Esq; ✉ Matterhorn Capital Ltd, 10 Gloucester Place, London W1U 8EZ (☎ 020 7908 3918, fax 020 7908 3920, e-mail anthony.lyons@matterhorncapital.co.uk)

LYONS, Dr Gerard; s of Francis Joseph Lyons (d 2004), and Anne, *née* Moran; *b* 31 March 1961, London; *Educ* Cardinal Vaughan Sch, Univ of Liverpool (BA), Univ of Warwick (MA), Univ of London (PhD); *m* 1 Sept 1990, Annette, *née* Lambert; 2 da (Emily-Anne b 10 June 1991, Marie-Louise Kezia b 17 Sept 1993), 1 s (Gerard Benedict Alfred Francis b 24 May 1997); *Career* economist Chase Manhattan 1985–86, chief UK economist Swiss Bank Corp 1986–90, chief economist and exec dir DKB Int and conslt Dai-Ichi Kangyo Bank Tokyo 1990–99, chief economist, gp head of global research and economic advsr to the Bd Standard Chartered 1999–2012, chief economic advsr to the Mayor of London 2013–; advsr Business Cncl for Britain 2007–08, memb Cncl Royal Economic Soc 2010–, memb Chatham House Task Force on Gold and the Int Monetary System 2011–12, inaugural chair CityUK Ind Economists Gp 2012–13, memb Global Agenda Cncls on Global Investment Flows 2009–10 and Banking and Capital Markets 2011–12 WEF, memb Expert Ctee Annual Fin Devpt Report WEF, memb Bd CityUK 2015–; memb Advsy Bd: Open Europe, Grantham Inst LSE and Imperial Coll 2008–, Official Monetary and Financial Insts Forum (OMFIF), Parker Fitzgerald 2014–, Warwick Business Sch 2014– (formerly memb Cncl); chair Steering Ctee Asia Study RIIA 2000–05, co-chair UK-Hong Kong Business Partnership 2006, memb Ctee Hong Kong Assoc 2007–, vice-chm 48 Gp Club 2009–, memb Cncl Royal Soc for Asian Affrs 2014–; former tstee Benenden Sch; fell Soc of Business Economists 2010–; FRSA 1993; *Publications* Report of the Commission on the £ Sterling (jtly, with Ruth Lea, 1999), The Qatar 2020 Report (2006), The Consolations of Economics (2014); *Recreations* cricket, reading, walking, football, ballet; *Clubs* London Capital; *Style—* Dr Gerard Lyons; ✉ The Mayor's Office, Greater London Authority, City Hall, The Queen's Walk, More London, London SE1 2AA (Twitter @DrGerardLyons)

LYONS, Jonathon Edward; s of Isidor Jack Lyons, *qv*, and Roslyn M Lyons, *née* Rosenbaum, of Canada; *b* 1 May 1951; *Educ* Carmel Coll; *Career* exec sales Alexandre Ltd Leeds 1968–71, chief exec John David Mansworld Ltd 1971–89, ptnr International Investments Ltd 1978–, chief exec H Alan Smith Ltd 1983–85, dir JLC Ltd London 1986, chm JE London Properties Ltd 1988–, private investment conslt Jonathon E Lyons & Co 1988–; dir: Britimpex Ltd Canada, Art Leasing Inc Canada, Johnson Fry plc (Jt Venture Property Div) 1994–96; memb Ctee: Cons Industrial Fund 1985–91, RMC, RAM; jt chm Hyde Park Ctee Central Br Fund 1975–80, tstee The Sir Jack Lyons Charitable Tst 1986–2000, tstee Drying Little Tears Switzerland Regine Sixt Children's Aid Fndn 2015–; rotarian Int Rotary Club 1995–, vice-pres Int Rotary Club of Westminster 1997– (past elect 1999–2000), jt exec chm Jewish Music Heritage Tst 1998–2010, hon jt vice-chm Jewish Music Inst at Sch of Oriental Arts & Studies; chm The Jewel Events Ltd (The Jewel of Jordan, The Jewel of Europe, The Jewel of China, The Jewel of the Cape, The Jewel of Monaco, The Jewel of Argentina, The Jewel That Is Cuba, ACM Monaco 2010, Gstaad Yacht Club 2010, Musquetaire d'Armagnac 2012, The Jewel of the Alps II Switzerland, The Jewel of Gstaad I, The Jewel of Bavaria Verona, The Jewel of the USA); int advsr Ronson plc 1999–; ptnr Leckhampton Estates 2010; patron Royal Acad of Arts; memb Renaissance Forum 2001, memb Club des Leaders Gstaad Switzerland 2013; FInstD, memb FIMBRA; *Recreations* classic car rallies, music, art; *Clubs* Carlton, IOD, Marks, Automobile Club de Monaco, Gstaad Yacht, Club des Leaders Gstaad, Les Amis Des Sommets de Gstaad; *Style—* Jonathon E Lyons, Esq; ✉ Chalet Emeraude E1, Rue des Chenolettes, 1660 Chateau d'Oex, Switzerland (☎ 00 4179 645 2207, e-mail embentley3uk@aol.com, website www.thejewelevents.com)

LYONS, (Andrew) Maximilian; s of Dennis John Lyons, CB, of Fleet, Hants, and Elizabeth Dora Maria, *née* Müller Haefliger; *b* 16 January 1946; *Educ* Queen Mary's GS Basingstoke, Brixton Sch of Bldg (Grad DipArch); *m* 18 June 1983, Katherine Jane (Kate), da of late Brig John Joseph Regan; 1 s (Shaun b 1984), 2 da (Rosalie b 1986, Charlotte b 1989); *Career* chm Lyons + Sleeman + Hoare architects 1977–; winner of numerous architectural design and environmental awards; tstee Lord Mayor Treloar Sch and Coll; RIBA 1974, FRSA 1993; *Clubs* RAC; *Style—* Maximilian Lyons, Esq; ✉ The Grange, 6 Old Park Lane, Farnham, Surrey GU9 0AH (☎ 01252 820082); Lyons + Sleeman + Hoare, Nero Brewery, Cricket Green, Hartley Wintney, Hook, Hampshire RG27 8QA (☎ 01252 844144, fax 01252 844800, e-mail maxlyons@lsharch.co.uk, website www.lsharch.co.uk)

LYONS, Roger Alan; s of Morris Lyons (d 1990), of Hove, and Phyllis, *née* Lebof (d 1989); *b* 14 September 1942, London; *Educ* Christ's Coll Finchley, UCL (BSc(Econ)); *m* Kitty, *née* Horvath; 2 da (Sarah b 1973, Hannah b 1982), 2 s (Gideon b 1975, Joshua b 1986);

L

Career ASTMS: regnl offr (North West) 1966–70, nat offr 1970–86, asst gen sec 1986–88 (until merger with TASS to form MSF); MSF: asst gen sec 1988–92, gen sec 1992–, jt gen sec amicus 2002–04; pres TUC 2003–04; conslt; advsr Business Services; former memb: TUC Gen Cncl, Confedn of Shipbuilding and Engrg Unions (pres 1999–2001), Design Cncl, Monopolies and Mergers Cmmn; UCL: fell 1996, former memb Cncl; memb: Central Arbitration Ctee 2002–12, Employment Appeals Tbnl 2003–12; fndr bd memb Univ for Industry/Learndirect; *Publications* contrib: Handbook on Industrial Relations (2004), Handbook on Management Development (2004), Free and Fair (2004); *Recreations* supporting Arsenal; *Style*— Roger Lyons, Esq; ✉ 22 Park Crescent, London N3 2NJ (✆ 020 8346 6843, mobile 07768 737475, e-mail rogerlyons22@hotmail.com)

LYONS, His Hon Shaun; CBE (2004); s of Jeremiah Lyons (d 1978), and Winifred Ruth, *née* Doble (d 2001); *b* 20 December 1942; *Educ* Portsmouth GS, Inns of Court Sch of Law; *m* 19 Dec 1970, Nicola Rosemary, da of Capt D F Chilton, DSC, RN; 1 s (Francis Daniel *b* 4 Jan 1972), 1 da (Victoria Clare *b* 26 Feb 1974); *Career* with RN 1961–92; Lt 1966, Lt Cdr 1974, called to the Bar Middle Temple 1975, Capt RN 1988 (Cdr 1981), chief naval judge advocate 1990–92, recorder of the Crown Court 1991–92 (asst recorder 1988–91), circuit judge (SE Circuit) 1992–2015, ret (sr circuit judge 2002–15), resident judge Wood Green Crown Court 1995–2016, chm Lord Chllr's Advsy Ctee on JPs for NW London 2004–08 (dep chm 1996–2004), ret; *Recreations* reading, gardening, walking, boating; *Clubs* Army and Navy, Royal Yacht Squadron; *Style*— His Hon Shaun Lyons, CBE; ✉ Wood Green Crown Court, Woodall House, Lordship Lane, London N22 4LF (✆ 020 8881 1400)

LYONS, Prof Terence John; s of Peter John Lyons (d 2003), and Christobel Valerie, *née* Hardie (d 2012); *b* 4 May 1953; *Educ* Univ of Cambridge (BA), Univ of Oxford (DPhil); *m* 30 Aug 1975, (Christina) Barbara, da of late Joseph Epsom; 1 s (Barnaby *b* 1981), 1 da (Josephine *b* 1983); *Career* jr res fell Jesus Coll Oxford 1979–81, Hedrick visiting asst prof UCLA 1981–82, lectr in mathematics Imperial Coll of Sci and Technol London 1981–85; Univ of Edinburgh: Colin MacLaurin prof of mathematics 1985–93, head Dept of Mathematics 1988–91; prof of mathematics Imperial Coll of Sci Technol and Med 1993–2000, Wallis prof of mathematics Univ of Oxford 2000–, dir Wales Inst of Mathematical and Computational Sciences 2007–11, dir Oxford-Man Inst of Quantitative Finance Univ of Oxford 2011–15; pres London Mathematical Soc 2013–; sr fell EPSRC 1993–98, fell Univ of Aberystwyth 2010, fell Univ of Cardiff 2012; Polya Prize London Mathematical Soc 2000, European Research Cncl Advanced Grant 2011, Humboldt Research Award 2014; Docteur (hc) Université Paul Sabatier Toulouse 2007; FRSE 1987, FRSA 1990, FIMA 1991, FRS 2002, FIMS 2004, FLSW 2011; *Recreations* cycling, writing software, family life; *Style*— Prof Terence Lyons, FRSE, FLSW, FRS; ✉ Mathematical Institute, University of Oxford, Andrew Wiles Building, Radcliffe Observatory Quarter, Oxford OX2 6GG (✆ 01865 616608, e-mail terry.lyons@oxford-man.ox.ac.uk)

LYSTER, Dr Simon; DL (Essex 2013); s of John Neal Lyster, and Marjorie Aird, *née* Everard; *b* 29 April 1952; *Educ* Radley, Magdalene Coll Cambridge (MA, PhD); *m* 1990, Sandra Elizabeth Charity; 2 c; *Career* admitted slr England and Wales 1978, qualified New York attorney-at-law 1979; slr Slaughter and May 1976–78, prog offr Defenders of Wildlife (USA) 1979–81, sec Falkland Islands Fndn 1982–86, treaties offr WWF International and head of conservation policy WWF UK 1986–95, DG The Wildlife Trusts 1995–2003, LEAD International (Leadership in Environment and Devpt): dir of devpt and progs 2003–05, ceo 2005–11; non-exec dir Northumbrian Water Ltd 2006–; chm World Land Tst 2014–, memb Bd Natural England 2014–; tstee: Conservation Int UK, Kilverstone Wildlife Charitable Tst, Rural Community Cncl of Essex 2013–; *Books* International Wildlife Law (1985); *Recreations* tennis, cricket, bird watching, golf; *Clubs* Queens; *Style*— Dr Simon Lyster, DL; ✉ Great Prestons Farm, Stock, Essex CM4 9RN (e-mail simonlyster1@gmail.com)

LYTTELTON, Hon Richard Cavendish; s of 10 Viscount Cobham, KG, GCMG, GCVO, TD, PC (d 1977); *b* 1949; *Educ* Eton; *m* 1971, Romilly, da of Michael Barker; 1 s (Thomas), 1 da (May); *Career* md EMI Finland 1977–80, dir int ops EMI Records (UK) Ltd 1980–83, gp md EMI South Africa 1984–86, pres Capital Records-EMI of Canada 1986–88, pres EMI Classics 1988–2006; chm English Touring Opera 2003–09, tstee EMI Archive Tst 2003, chm Musicians Benevolent Fund 2008–14, tstee EMI Music Sound Fndn 2009, memb Cncl Royal Coll of Music 2009, pres Royal Albert Hall 2010–11; Liveryman Worshipful Co of Musicians 2014; *Recreations* music, shooting; *Style*— The Hon Richard Lyttelton; ✉ 5 Queen's Gate Place Mews, London SW7 5BG

LYTTLE, Chris; MLA; *b* 1981, Belfast; *Educ* Queen's Univ Belfast, Univ of California Exchange Abroad Prog (Helen Ramsey Turtle fell conflict resolution), Harvard Univ (Frank Knox fell); *m* with children; *Career* MLA (Alliance) Belfast E 2010–; dep chairperson Ctee of the Office of the First and Dep First Min 2011–16; *Recreations* association football; *Style*— Chris Lyttle, Esq, MLA; ✉ Northern Ireland Assembly, Parliament Buildings, Belfast BT4 3XX (✆ 02890 472004, e-mail chris.lyttle@mla.niassembly.gov.uk, Twitter @Chris_Lyttle)

LYTTLETON, Trevor Michael; MBE (2007); s of David George Lyttleton, OBE (d 1990), and Perle, *née* Lyons (d 1991); *b* 23 April 1936, Leeds; *Educ* Clifton Coll (scholarship), King's Coll Cambridge (MA, LLM), Harvard Business Sch (instituted diploma); *m* 8 July 1984, Ziporah, *née* Abramovich; 2 da (Maya *b* 26 Sept 1973, Natalia *b* 10 April 1978), 1 s (Daniel *b* 15 Sept 1986); *Career* slr 1961–2013 (Freshfields 1961–63), md European Professional Servs 1963–65, fndr and chm Contact the Elderly 1965–2015; md Light Music Ltd 1972– (Grammy nomination for I Love a Film Cliché in A Day in Hollywood/A Night in the Ukraine 1979); memb Law Soc (later Slrs Regulation Authy); memb Slrs for the Elderly (patron 2014–); launched If Not Now, When? Golden Jubilee Appeal 2013; Queen's Diamond Jubilee Award for Volunteering 2013; Hon DHL Liverpool Hope Univ 2015; *Publications* series of articles on elderly isolation for Huffington Post, Elder Law, Solicitors Gazette and other legal journals and national press; *Recreations* music, opera, reading, travel, walking, composing music, encouraging the young to help the old and to combat their isolation with friendship and compassion; *Style*— Trevor Lyttleton, Esq, MBE; ✉ Flat 10, Newmount, 1 Lyndhurst Gardens, London NW3 5QA (✆ 07789 425973, e-mail trevor.lyttleton1@gmail.com)

LYTTON, 5 Earl of (UK 1880); Sir John Peter Michael Scawen Lytton; also Viscount Knebworth (UK 1880), 18 Baron Wentworth (E 1529), and 6 Bt (UK 1838); s of 4 Earl of Lytton; *b* 7 June 1950; *Educ* Downside, Univ of Reading; *m* 1980, Ursula, da of Anton Komoly, of Vienna; 1 da (Lady Katrina *b* 1985), 2 s (Philip Anthony Scawen, Viscount Knebworth *b* 7 March 1989, Hon Wilfrid Thomas Scawen *b* 8 Jan 1992); *Heir* s, Viscount Knebworth; *Career* Inland Revenue Valuation Office 1975–81, Permutt Brown & Co 1982–86, Cubitt & West 1986–87, sole principal John Lytton & Co (chartered surveyors) 1988–2015, Lawrence Foote and Ptnrs (London) Ltd (chartered quantity surveyors) 2014–; chm Leasehold Advsy Serv (LEASE) 1997–2000; pres: Horsham C of C 1995–2001 (chm 1983–85), Sussex Assoc of Local Cncls 1997–, Nat Assoc of Local Cncls 1999–2014 (currently vice-pres), Newstead Abbey Byron Soc; CLA: former memb Cncl and Exec, chm Sussex Branch 2003–05; memb RICS Boundaries and Party Walls Panel 1997–; co dir; elected hereditary Peer (ind crossbench) 2011–; chm Industry Consultative Ctee Univ of W London (Sch of Building); pres Inst of Heraldic and Genealogical Studies 2000–; Pyramus & Thisbe Club (party wall surveyors), hon fell and patron Chartered Assoc of Bldg Engrs 1997; FRICS, MCIArb, IRRV; *Recreations* DIY repairs, gardening, family history; *Style*— The Rt Hon the Earl of Lytton; ✉ Estate Office, Newbuildings Place, Shipley, Horsham, West Sussex RH13 8GQ (✆ 01403 741650)

M

MAAS, Robert William; s of Richard Felix Maas (d 1948), of London, and Hilda Rose, *née* Gietzen (d 2002); *b* 13 February 1943; *Educ* Gunnersbury GS; *Career* articled clerk Godwin & Taylor 1959–65, tax ptnr Stoy Hayward 1970–77 (tax sr 1965–70), proprietor Robert Maas & Co 1977–83; tax ptnr: Casson Beckman 1983–87, Blackstone Franks 1987–2013, consult CBW Tax 2013–; memb Editorial Bd Taxation; contrib of articles to various magazines and jls, lectr on a wide variety of tax topics; ICAEW: former chm Tech Ctee Tax Faculty, memb Tax Faculty Ctee; memb Cncl and chm Tech Ctee IIT; chm Small Practitioners Gp of Central London LSCA; FCA 1965, FTII 1965, FIIT 1997; *Publications* Tax Minimisation Techniques (4 edn, 1984), Taxation of Non-Resident Entertainers & Sportsmen (1987), Fringe Benefits (1987), Tax Planning for Entertainers (2 edn, 1987), Tax Planning for the Smaller Business (1990), Expat Investors Working and Retiring Abroad (1993), Taxation of Sportsmen and Entertainers (1993), Taxation of Employments (16 edn, 2014), Anti-Avoidance Provisions, Property Taxes 2015/16 (26 edn, 2015), Guide to Taxpayer Rights and HMRC Powers (4 edn, 2016); *Recreations* reading, walking, pubs, malt whisky, West Ham United, Chicago Cubs; *Clubs* Reform, St James's (Manchester); *Style*— Robert Maas, Esq; ✉ 76 Thirlmere Gardens, Wembley, Middlesex HA9 8RE (☎ 020 8904 0432); CBW Tax Ltd, 66 Prescot Street, London E1 8NN (☎ 020 7309 3800, e-mail robert.maas@cbw.co.uk)

MABEY, Richard Thomas; s of Thomas Gustavus Mabey (d 1963), and Edna Nellie, *née* Moore (d 1993); *b* 20 February 1941; *Educ* Berkhamsted Sch, St Catherine's Coll Oxford (MA); *Career* lectr in social studies Dacorum Coll of FE 1963–65, sr ed Penguin Books (Educn Div) 1966–73, freelance writer and broadcaster 1973–; columnist BBC Wildlife; reg contrib: Granta, New Statesman, The Guardian; Leverhulme res fell 1983–84 and 1993–94; memb: Cncl Botanical Soc of the British Isles 1981–83, Nature Conservancy Cncl 1982–86, Cncl Plantlife 1989–2000; vice-pres Open Spaces Soc 2002– (memb Advsy Cncl 1994–), pres Norfolk Naturalists Tst 2005–06; pres London Wildlife Tst 1982–92; dir: Common Ground 1988–, Learning Through Landscapes Tst 1990–2000; patron John Clare Soc; visiting fell Emmanuel Coll Cambridge 2014; Hon DSc Univ of St Andrews 1997, Hon DUniv Essex 2007, Hon DLitt Univ of E Anglia, hon doctorate Open Univ 2014; FRSL; *Awards* Times Educnl Supplement Information Books Award 1977, New York Acad of Sciences Children's Book Award 1984, Whitbread Biography Award 1986, British Book Awards 1996; *Television* wrote and presented: The Unofficial Countryside (World About Us, BBC2) 1975, The Flowering of Britain (BBC2) 1980, A Prospect of Kew (BBC2) 1981, Back to the Roots (C4) 1983, White Rock, Black Water (BBC2) 1986, Postcards from the Country (BBC2) 1996; *Books* incl: Class (ed, 1967), Behind the Scene (1968), The Pop Process (1969), Food for Free (1972), Children in Primary School (1972), The Unofficial Countryside (1973), The Pollution Handbook (1973), The Roadside Wildlife Book (1974), Street Flowers (1976), Plants with a Purpose (1977), The Common Ground (1980), The Flowering of Britain (with Tony Evans, 1980), In a Green Shade (1983), Cold Comforts (1983), Oak and Company (1983), Second Nature (ed, 1984), The Frampton Flora (1985), Gilbert White (1986), The Gardener's Labyrinth (ed, 1987), The Flowering of Kew (1988), Home Country (1990), Whistling in the Dark (1993), The Wild Wood (with Gareth Lovett Jones, 1993), Landlocked (1994), The Oxford Book of Nature Writing (ed, 1995), Flora Britannica (1996), Selected Writings (1999), Nature Cure (2005, shortlisted Whitbread Biography Prize, Ondaatje Prize and JR Ackerley Prize), Fencing Paradise (2005), Birds, Brittanica (jtly, 2005), Beechcombings (2007), Weeds (2010), A Brush with Nature (2010), The Barley Bird (2010, East Anglian Book Award), The Perfumer and the Stinkhorn (2011), Turned Out Nice Again (2013), Dreams of the Good Life (2014), The Cabaret of Plants: Botany and the Imagination (2015); *Recreations* early music, food; *Style*— Richard Mabey, Esq, FRSL; ✉ Sheil Land Associates, 52 Doughty Street, London WC1N 2LS (website www.richardmabey.co.uk)

MABEY, Simon John; *b* 29 September 1952; *Educ* City of London Sch, Clare Coll Cambridge (scholar, MA); *m* 9 May 1981, Carolyn Ann, *née* Crossman; 2 s (James b 1984, Richard b 1986), 2 da (Elizabeth b 1991, Victoria b 1993); *Career* CA Dixon Wilson & Co 1973–80; Smith & Williamson: joined 1980, ptnr 1981, currently sr tax ptnr; Westminster CC: memb 1982–90, chm Housing (private sector) Sub-Ctee and vice-chm Housing Ctee 1983–85, chm Social Servs Ctee 1985–89, Lord Mayor of Westminster (chm London Mayors' Assoc) 1989–90, dep high steward of Westminster 1989–90; Parly candidate (Cons) Knowsley North 1992, memb Cncl Assoc of Conservative Clubs Ltd 1993–2001; chm Bd of Tstees Charitable Tst City of Westminster 1989–90; Freeman City of London 1981, Liveryman Worshipful Co of Bakers 1981, hon memb Worshipful Co of Master Mariners 1989–90; ATII 1976, FCA 1981 (ACA 1976); *Clubs* Carlton (currently vice-pres Political Ctee); *Style*— Simon Mabey, Esq; ✉ Smith & Williamson, 25 Moorgate, London EC2R 6AY (☎ 020 7131 4000)

MAC NEICE, Rory John James; s of John Mac Neice, of Suffolk, and Pamela Mac Neice (d 1968); *b* 28 March 1968; *Educ* Kings Coll Taunton, Oxford Brookes Univ (LLB), Univ of Exeter; *m* 24 Aug 1999, Martha, *née* Maher; 1 s (Charlie b 1 Oct 2000), 1 da (Lily Anna b 20 Feb 2006); *Career* slr specialising in sports and bloodstock law; professional Nat Hunt jockey 1988–91, slr Burges Salmon 1998–2004, ptnr Ashfords 2004–; memb Law Soc; *Recreations* horse racing; *Style*— Rory Mac Neice, Esq; ✉ Ashfords, Ashford House, Grenadier Road, Exeter EX1 3LH (☎ 01392 334006, e-mail r.macneice@ashfords.co.uk)

MAC-FALL, Nigel James; s of Thomas Coulson Mac-Fall (d 1970), and Sylvia Dorothy, *née* Harriss (d 1987); *b* 27 April 1948; *Educ* Sch of Three Dimensional Design Ravensbourne Coll of Art and Design (BA), Sch of Furniture Design RCA (MA); *m* 1, 11 May 1974, Shirley Anne (d 1996), da of Ernest Chubb; 2 s (Julian James Chubb b 9 Jan 1976, Oscar Alexander James b 18 May 1981), 1 da (Rosina Sylvia Anne b 7 July 1977), 1 adopted da (Elaine Anne b 16 Aug 1968); m 2, 25 Sept 1997, Andrea Gudrun, da of Brian Fenwick-Smith; 3 s (Ambrose Brian James b 19 Oct 1998, Lucian Thomas James b 7 July 2001, Felix Henry James b 11 June 2004), 1 da (Vita Diemut Josephine b 26 June 2007); *Career* furniture and product designer Planning Unit Ltd 1972–75, sr designer Supplies Div Property Services Agency 1975–78, ptnr, dir and head Dept of Three Dimensional Design Minale Tattersfield & Partners Ltd 1978–97, fndr ptnr and chm Red Studio Ltd 1997– (specialising in innovative, conceptual and applied 3D design); FRSA 2005; *Recreations* family, making things, music, foreign travel; *Style*— Nigel James Mac-Fall, Esq; ✉ Red Studio Ltd, 6 Bedford House, The Avenue, Chiswick, London W4 1UD (☎ 020 8994 7770, e-mail nigel@red-studio.co.uk)

McADAM, Dr Elspeth Katharine; da of Prof Sir Ian McAdam decd, and Hrothgarde, *née* Gibson; *b* 16 October 1947, Kampala, Uganda; *Educ* Kenya HS, Newnham Coll Cambridge (MA), Middx Med Sch; *m* 1, 1970 (m dis 1981), Prof (John) David Seddon, s of Eric Seddon (d 1950); 2 s (Michael David Indra b 10 May 1974, James Alexander b 28 April 1976); m 2, 2000, Martin A Watson, s of Harry Watson (d 1998); *Career* conslt child and adolescent psychiatrist 1987–, systemic social constructionist conslt 1991–; conslt Swedish Mental Health Services 1991–, dir Informetrics-Systemic Organisational Consultancy; currently working freelance on community devpt in Africa and S America; FRCPsych 1997 (MRCPsych 1982); *Publications* Working Systemicly with Violence and Child Sexual Abuse (1992), Narrative Therapy in Asthma (1999); author of pubns in Cognitive and Systemic Therapies and articles on working with schs and communities and young people who misuse drugs; *Recreations* tennis, golf, ecology, bird watching, gardening; *Style*— Dr Elspeth McAdam; ✉ 49 Elm Quay Court, 30 Nine Elms Lane, London SW8 5DF (e-mail Elspeth_McAdam@compuserve.com)

McADAM, James; CBE (1995); s of John Robert McAdam (d 1975), and Helen, *née* Cormack (d 1981); *b* 10 December 1930; *Educ* Lenzie Acad; *m* 4 Oct 1955, Maisie Una, da of Ernest James Holmes (d 1947); 2 da (Catherine Tryphena b 1956, Fiona Jane b 1961); *Career* J & P Coats Ltd: joined 1945, various overseas assignments 1953–70; fin dir Coats Patons (UK) 1972–75; Coats Patons plc: dir 1975, chief exec 1985, chm 1986, dep chm and chief ops offr Coats Viyella plc (following merger) 1986–91; chm Signet Group plc 1992–2006 (ceo 1992–2000); non-exec dir: London PO 1985–87, Scotia Holdings plc (formerly Efamol Holdings plc) 1991–97; non-exec chm: F C Brown (Steel Equipment) Ltd 1991–2010, Bisley Office Equipment 1991–2010; chm: Br Clothing Industry Assoc 1991–2008, Br Knitting and Clothing Confedn 1991–2008, Apparel, Knitting and Textiles Alliance 1992–2008, Br Apparel and Textile Confedn 1993–2008; memb: Exec Ctee The Scottish Cncl Devpt and Industry 1989–99; FRSA, CIMgt, FInstD; *Recreations* theatre, travel; *Clubs* RAC, Farmers'; *Style*— James McAdam, Esq, CBE; ✉ Flat 143, 3 Whitehall Court, London SW1A 2EP

McADAM, John David Gibson; s of John and Sarah McAdam, of Bowness-on-Windermere; *b* 30 April 1948; *Educ* Kelsick GS Ambleside, Lakes Sch Windermere, Univ of Manchester (BSc, PhD); *m* 20 Jan 1979, Louise Mary; 1 da (Laura Sarah Louise b 2 June 1981), 1 s (David John James b 27 April 1984); *Career* Unilever plc: joined 1974, various mgmnt positions with Birds Eye Foods, gen mangr Birds Eye Wall's 1984–86, tech dir PPF Int 1986–87, sr vice-pres Quest 1987–90, memb bd Birds Eye Wall's 1990–93, chm and ceo Unichema Int 1993–97; ICI plc: chm and ceo Quest Int 1997–98, memb Exec Mgmnt Ctee 1997, chm and ceo ICI Paints 1998–2002, exec dir (memb plc bd) 1999–2008, ceo 2003–08; chm: Rentokil Initial plc 2008–, United Utilities plc 2008–; non-exec dir: Severn Trent plc 2000–05, J Sainsbury plc 2005– (sr dir), Rolls-Royce plc, Sara Lee Inc 2008–12; sr advsr TPG Capital 2008–16, sr advsr Royal Bank of Canada 2015–; medical research fell Univ of Manchester 1973–74; author of several scientific pubns; *Recreations* watching cricket, rugby and football, walking; *Style*— Dr John McAdam; ✉ United Utilities Gp Plc, 55 Grosvenor Street, London, W1K 3LJ

McADAM, Prof Keith Paul William James; DL (Herts 2012); s of Sir Ian William James McAdam, OBE, KB and (Lettice Margaret) Hrothgaarde, *née* Gibson (now Mrs Bennett); *b* 13 August 1945; *Educ* Prince of Wales Sch Nairobi, Millfield, Clare Coll Cambridge (MA, MB BChir, Cricket blue), Middx Hosp Med Sch; *m* 27 July 1968, Penelope Ann, da of Rev Gordon Charles Craig Spencer; 3 da (Karen Louise (Mrs Craig) b 1972, Ruth Alexandra Hrothgaarde (Mrs Hurst) b 1974, Dr Cheryl Felicity Dian (Mrs Conely) b 1977); *Career* house physician and house surgn Middx Hosp London 1969–70; SHO appts London: Royal Northern Hosp 1970–71, Brompton Hosp 1971–72, Royal Nat Hosp for Nervous Diseases 1972–73; lectr Inst of Med Res PNG 1973–75, Med Res Cncl travelling fellowship Nat Cancer Inst 1975–76, visiting scientist Nat Inst of Health Bethesda 1976–77, asst prof Tufts Univ Sch of Med 1977–81, assoc prof New England Med Centre Boston 1982–84, Wellcome prof of tropical medicine LSHTM 1984–2004 (emeritus prof 2004–), physician Hosp for Tropical Diseases Camden & Islington HA 1984–95, dir Medical Research Cncl Unit Fajara The Gambia 1995–2003, dir Infectious Diseases Inst and prof of med Faculty of Medicine Makerere Univ Uganda 2004–07, assoc int dir RCP 2009–13, int advsr for ECS Africa RCP London 2014–, co-fndr East, Central and Southern Coll of Physicians London 2014–; adjunct prof of medicine: Tufts Univ Sch of Med 2004–, Univ of Minnesota Sch of Med 2005–13; memb Med Advsy Bds: Br Leprosy Relief Assoc 1986–95, MRC 1988–93, Br Cncl 1988–93, Wellcome Trust 1985–90, Beit Trust 1990–95, The Leprosy Mission 1990–97; memb Academic Alliance for AIDS Care and Prevention in Africa 2006–, memb Int Bd of Dirs AMREF (African Medical and Research Fndn) 2010–15, memb Ctee on Clinical Trials during 2014–15 Ebola outbreak US Nat Acads of Sciences, Engineering and Medicine (NASEM) 2016–17; chief med offr conslt advsr 1989–95, expert advsr to House of Commons Soc Servs Ctee enquiry into AIDS 1987; Weber Parkes Prize RCP 1993; diplomate: American Bd of Internal med 1978, American Bd of Allergy and Clinical Immunology 1981; chm Redbourn900 2008–12; memb Bd of Tstees BBC Media Action 2013–; lay co-chair PCC Redbourn 2011–; fndr: Namweza 2010, Music for my Mind 2014; FRSTM&H 1973, FRCP 1985 (MRCP 1971), FWACP 1998; Presidential Award for Distinguished Serv to the People of Uganda 2006; *Publications* original articles in medical and scientific jls on tropical medicine topics incl leprosy, tuberculosis, malaria, AIDS, inflammation and amyloidosis; ed books on travel medicine, parasitology, tuberculosis and infectious diseases; *Recreations* cricket, tennis, skiing; *Clubs* MCC, Jesters; *Style*— Prof Keith McAdam, DL; ✉ Oakmead, 70 Luton Lane, Redbourn, Hertfordshire AL3 7PY (☎ and fax 01582 792833, mobile 07890 298514, e-mail keith.mcadam@lshtm.ac.uk)

MACAIRE, Robert Nigel Paul; CMG (2009); s of James Macaire, and Tatiana Macaire; *b* Farnham, Surrey; *Educ* Cranleigh Sch, St Edmund Hall Oxford; *m* Alice; 2 da; *Career* MOD 1987–90, Falkland Islands Dept FCO 1990, second sec (Know How Fund) Bucharest 1991–95, Near East and N Africa Dept FCO 1995–97, head Southern Africa Section then head Sierra Leone Unit Africa Directorate FCO 1997–98, first sec (Middle East and counter-terrorism) Washington DC 1998–2002, head Counter-Terrorism Policy Dept FCO 2002–04, political cnsllr New Delhi 2004–06, dir of consular servs FCO 2006–08, high cmmr to Kenya 2008–11; *Recreations* sailing; *Clubs* Royal Ocean Racing; *Style*— Mr Robert Macaire, CMG; ✉ c/o FCO, King Charles Street, London SW1A 2AH

McALEESE, Prof Mary Patricia; *née* Leneghan; da of Patrick Leneghan, and Claire, *née* McManus; *b* 27 June 1951; *Educ* St Dominic's HS Belfast, Queen's Univ Belfast (LLB), TCD (MA), Chartered Inst of Linguistics (Dip Spanish), NUI (MTh), Pontifical Gregorian Univ (Licentiate of Canon Law); *m* 1976, Martin McAleese; 2 da (Emma b 21 Sept 1982, Sara-mai b 6 April 1985), 1 s (Justin (twin) b 6 April 1985); *Career* barrister-at-law: Inn of Court NI 1974 (practising barrister 1974–75), Hon Soc of King's Inns Dublin 1978; Reid prof of criminal law, criminology and penology TCD 1975–79 and 1981–87, TV presenter/journalist RTE 1979–85, pt/t presenter EUROPA (monthly current affairs prog) RTE 1981–85; Queen's Univ Belfast: dir Inst of Professional Legal Studies 1987–97, pro-vice-chllr 1994–97; pres of Ireland 1997–2011; former non-exec dir: Viridian plc (formerly Northern Ireland Electricity plc), Channel 4 Television, Royal Gp of Hospitals Tst; fndr memb Campaign for Homosexual Law Reform (Dublin); chair EU Cmmn on Modernisation of HE; former fndr memb: Belfast Women's Aid, Irish Cmmn for Prisoners Overseas; former memb: Cncl of Social Welfare (Dublin), BBC Broadcasting Council for NI, Exec Ctee Focus Point for Homeless Young People (Dublin), Cmmn for Justice and Peace, Inst of Advanced Legal Studies, Irish Centre for European Law, Faculty of the Nat Inst of Trial Advocacy; hon pres NI Housing Rights Assoc; memb: Int Bar Assoc, European Bar Assoc, Inns of Court Northern Ireland, King's Inns (Dublin); chair Von Hugel Inst St Edmund's Coll Cambridge, patron Bob Hawke Inst Univ of S Australia; Silver Jubilee Commemoration Medal Charles Univ Prague, Great Gold Medal Comenius Univ Bratislava, American Ireland Fund Humanitarian Award, Tipperary Peace Prize, Gilbert Medal Universitas 21 2016; hon bencher: King's Inns, Inns of Court NI; hon fell: TCD, Liverpool John Moores Univ; professor emerita Queen's Univ Belfast, Burns Library scholar Boston Coll 2013, Farwell distinguished lectr Luther Coll Decorah Iowa 2015, distinguished Carmel and Martin Naughton fell Keough-Naughton Inst Univ of Notre Dame 2015, distinguished James J Clyne prof Law Sch Univ of Notre Dame 2015, distinguished visiting prof St Mary's Univ London; Hon LLD: NUI, Univ of Nottingham, Victoria Univ of Technol Aust, St Mary's Univ Halifax, Queen's Univ Belfast, Loyola Law Sch LA, Univ of Aberdeen, Univ of Surrey, TCD, Manchester Met Univ, Univ of Delaware, Univ of Bristol, Univ of Qld Brisbane, Harbin Inst of Technol, Shenzhen Univ, Univ of Chile, EHWA Univ Seoul, Villanova Univ Philadelphia, Notre Dame Univ, Univ of Edinburgh, St John's Univ NY, Univ of Otago NZ, Mount Holyoke Coll Springfield MA, Fordham Unv NY; Hon Dr of Humane Letters: Rochester Inst of Technol NY, Univ of San Francisco; hon doctorates: Dublin City Univ, UMass Lowell, Strathclyde Univ, St Andrews Univ 2013, Open Univ UK and I 2013, Univ of Massachusetts Lowell 2013, Univ of Strathclyde 2014, Univ of S Australia 2013; Hon DLitt Univ of Ulster; MIL 1994, MRIA, Hon FIEI, Hon FRCS, Hon FRCA, FRSA, Hon FRCPS, Hon fell Royal Soc of Edinburgh, fell Royal Edinburgh Acad 2013; *Publications* Reconciled Being: Love in Chaos (1997), Building Bridges: Selected Speeches and Statements (2011), Quo Vadis: Collegiality in the Code of Canon Law (2012); author (and co-author) of various books, articles, conference papers and dicussion documents; *Recreations* pursuing doctorate on children's rights in Canon Law, hiking; *Style—* Professor Mary McAleese

McALISTER, William Harle Nelson (Bill); s of Flying Offr William Nelson (d 1940), and Marjorie Isobel Nelson (d 2008); *b* 30 August 1940, Yorks; *Educ* St Edward's Sch Oxford, UCL (BA); *m* 1968 (m dis 1985), Sarah Elizabeth; 3 s (Daniel b 1969, Benjamin b 1977, Ned b 1985), 2 da (Leila b 1970, Alix b 1972); *Career* ind arts prodr; dir Almost Free Theatre 1968–72, dep dir Inter-Action Tst 1968–72, fndr dir Islington Bus Co 1972–77; dir: Battersea Arts Centre 1976–77, Sense of Ireland Festival 1980–; Bd dir London Int Theatre Festival 1983; chm for the Arts IT 82 Ctee 1982; co fndr Fair Play for Children 1974–75, advsr Task Force Tst 1972–74; tstee: Circle 33 Housing Tst 1972–75, Moving Picture Mime Tst 1978–80, Shape (Arts for the Disadvantaged) 1979–81; govr Holloway Adult Educn Inst 1974–76; dir: Inst of Contemporary Arts 1977–90, Creative Res Ltd 1988–91, Int House 1988–2004, Beaconsfield Gallery 1999–2003; cultural policy advsr Soros Fndns 1992–97, memb Cncl Africa Centre 1992–2000; memb: Ct RCA 1980–90, Bd World Circuit Arts 1995–2001, Hidden Art 2000–, Anglo-Polish Fndn 2004–; govr UCL Hospital Fndn Tst 2012–; Chevalier des Arts et Lettres; *Publications* Community Psychology (1975), EEC and the Arts (1978); also author of articles on arts policy; *Recreations* angling, tennis, travel, mycology; *Style—* Bill McAlister, Esq; ✉ 151C Grosvenor Avenue, London N5 2NH (☎ 07956 229796, e-mail bill.mcalister@gmail.com)

McALLISTER, Roderick Iain (Rod); s of Alastair Bruce McAllister, and Mary Delores, *née* Donnelly; *b* 1961, London; *Educ* Helston Sch, Girton Coll Cambridge, Univ of Liverpool; *m* Catherine Elizabeth, *née* Cummings; 1 s (Connor Bruce b 1999), 1 da (Innes May b 2003); *Career* founding ptnr King McAllister (projects incl: new studios and galleries Liverpool Sch of Architecture (RIBA Award 1989), Student Services Centre Univ of Liverpool (RIBA Award 1995)), princ McAllister Co (projects incl: Mellangoose Falmouth (RIBA Award 1999), Battersea Park Boat House (Building of the Year Royal Fine Art Cmmn Tst 2002), Battersea Park Pump House (Civic Tst Commendation 2006)), ptnr Sheppard Robson 2003–14 (projects incl: Small Animal Teaching Hosp Univ of Liverpool Sch of Veterinary Science (RIBA Award 2008, Civic Tst Award 2008), Active Learning Labs Dept of Engrg Univ of Liverpool, London Business Sch, Nelson Mandela Children's Hosp Johannesburg); lectr Liverpool Sch of Architecture, visiting prof Univ of Rome La Sapienza; tstee HE Design Quality Forum (HEDQF); Union Internationale des Architectes (UIA) Jeune Architects Grand Prix 1992; RIBA 1989, FRSA 2006; *Short Films* Revision 2010, Small Budget: Big Impact 2011, Out of the Box 2012, Resurrection 2013, SAW 2014, Centre Buildings 2015; *Recreations* sailing, skiing, tennis, travel; *Clubs* Chelsea Arts, Vout-O-Reenee's; *Style—* Rod McAllister, Esq; ✉ Twitter @rodmca

McALLISTER, Victor Lionel; s of late Victor Lionel McAllister, and late Ethel Caroline McAllister; *b* 9 October 1941; *Educ* Sydney GS Aust, UCH (MB BS); *m* 22 April 1965, Pamela, da of Dr Denis Joel Johnson, MBE, TD (d 1982); 1 s (Peter Victor Lionel b 1970), 1 da (Karen Ann b 1967); *Career* conslt in admin charge neuroradiology Regnl Neurological Centre Newcastle Gen Hosp 1974– (clinical dir of neurosciences); invited lectr: Europe, India, Singapore, Aust; sec and treas Br Soc of Neuroradiologists 1982–86 (pres 1996–98), memb Euro Soc of Neuroradiology, UK delegate (Br Soc of Neuroradiologists) to Euro Soc of Neuroradiology 1992–96; LRCP, MRCS, DMRD, FRCR; *Books* Subarachnoid Haemorrhage (1986), Pyogenic Neurosurgical Infections (1991); author of over 60 pubns on all aspects neuroradiology; *Recreations* travel, badminton; *Clubs* Ponteland Lions, '62 (radiological); *Style—* Victor McAllister, Esq

McALPINE, Angharad; *see:* Rees, Angharad Mary

McALPINE, Hon David Malcolm; 3 and yst s of Baron McAlpine of Moffat (Life Peer and 5 Bt; d 1990); *b* 8 October 1946; *m* 1, 1971 (m dis 1993), Jennifer Anne; 1 s (Robert Edward Thomas William b 1978), 2 da (Katherine Alexandra Donnison b 1972, Elizabeth Louise b 1973); m 2, 2005, Mrs Angharad Mary Cazenove (Angharad Rees, *qv*), da of late Prof Linford Rees, CBE; *Career* dir Sir Robert McAlpine & Sons; *Style—* The Hon David McAlpine

McALPINE, Joan; MSP; *b* 28 January 1964, Gourock, Renfrewshire; *Educ* St Columba's Secdy Sch Greenock, Univ of Glasgow (MA), City Univ London (Postgrad Dip); *m* (m dis) Patrick Mark Kane; 2 da; *Career* former journalist with Greenock Telegraph, The Scotsman and Sunday Times, ed Sunday Times Scotland 2000–01, dep ed The Herald 2001–07; currently columnist: The Scotsman, Daily Record; MSP (SNP) S of Scotland 2011–; *Books* A Time to Rage (jtly, 1994); *Style—* Ms Joan McAlpine, MSP; ✉ website www.joanmcalpinemsp.com; The Scottish Parliament, Edinburgh EH99 1SP

McALPINE, Hon Sir William Hepburn; 6 Bt (UK 1918), of Knott Park, Co Surrey; eld s of Baron McAlpine of Moffat (Life Peer and 5 Bt, d 1990), and his 1 w, Ella Mary Gardner, *née* Garnett (d 1987); *b* 12 January 1936; *Educ* Charterhouse; *m* 1, 1959, Jill Benton (d 2004), o da of Lt-Col Sir Peter Fawcett Benton Jones, 3 Bt, OBE (d 1972); 1 s (Andrew William b 1960), 1 da (Lucinda Mary Jane b 1964); m 2, 2004, Judith Mary, da of William H Sanderson (d 2004), and wid of Graham Nicholls (d 1991); *Heir* s, Andrew McAlpine; *Career* Life Guards 1954–56; dir: Sir Robert McAlpine Ltd 1952–2004, Newarthill plc 1977–2004, Turner & Newall plc 1983–91; chm: Railway Heritage Tst 1985–, Romney Hythe and Dymchurch Railway, Dart Valley Railway, Sir Walter Scott Tst Steamship, Cncl ZSL 2007–12; High Sheriff Bucks 1999–2000; Liveryman Worshipful Co of Carmen; FRSE 1978, FCILT; *Recreations* railways and transport preservation; *Clubs* Garrick, Caledonian; *Style—* The Hon Sir William McAlpine, Bt, FRSE; ✉ Fawley Hill, Fawley Green, Henley-on-Thames, Oxfordshire RG9 6JA (☎ 01491 637869, e-mail office@sirwmcalpine.com)

McANALLY, Vice Admiral John Henry Stuart; CB (2000), LVO (1982); s of Arthur Patrick McAnally (d 1983), and Mrs B H S McAnally (d 1999); bro of Mary McAnally (d 2016); *b* 9 April 1945, Epsom, Surrey; *Educ* Westminster, BRNC Dartmouth, Royal Naval Staff Coll, Royal Coll of Defence Studies, Higher Command and Staff Course; *Career* with RN; Lt 1967, navigating and ops offr 6 warships incl US destroyer and Australian aircraft carrier 1968–78 (CO HMS Iveston 1973–75), navigation subspecialisation course HMS Dryad 1971, Lt Cdr 1975, RN Staff Coll (Director's Prize) 1978, 2 i/c HMS Birmingham 1978–79, Cdr 1979, navigating commander HM Yacht Britannia 1980 and 1981, desk offr (size and shape of future RN) DN Plans MOD 1982–83, CO HMS Torquay and HMS Alacrity 1984–86, Capt 1987, Sixth Frigate Sqdn (CO HMS Ariadne and HMS Hermione) 1987–89, asst dir (role of future RN) DN Plans MOD 1989–91, RCDS 1992, Higher Command and Staff Course 1993, Cdre 1993, dir Naval Logistic Policy 1993, dir Naval Staff 1994–95, Rear Adm 1996, Flag Offr Training and Recruiting 1996–98, Vice-Adm 1998, Cmdt RCDS 1998–2000; pres Royal Naval Assoc 2001–, govr Portsmouth GS 1996–98, naval advsr Flagship Trg Ltd 2001–05, sr military advsr 2006–10, govr and tstee Corps Security Ltd 2010–; pres Int Maritime Confedn 2008–11; ind chm RO Selection Bds 2001–03, pres TS Barrosa 2001–, nat pres The Royal Naval Assoc 2001–, chm Naval & Military Club 2012–; memb: Naval Review 1964, US Naval Inst (prize memb) 1978, RUSI 1978, Hon Co of Master Mariners 2002–; Younger Brother Trinity House 1987–; FNI 2001–12, FRIN; *Recreations* golf, reading; *Clubs* Naval and Military (chm 2012–), National Liberal, Leckford, Liphook Golf, Royal Naval & Royal Albert Yacht (Portsmouth), Rye Golf; *Style—* Vice Admiral John McAnally, CB, LVO; ✉ c/o Naval and Military Club, 4 St James's Square, London SW1Y 4JU

MacANDREW, 3 Baron (UK 1959); Christopher Anthony Colin MacAndrew; er s of 2 Baron MacAndrew (d 1989); *b* 16 February 1945; *Educ* Malvern; *m* 1975 (m dis 2005), Sarah Helen, o da of Lt-Col Peter Hendy Brazier, of Nash Court Farmhouse, Marnhull, Dorset; 2 da (Hon Diana Sarah b 24 June 1978, Hon Tessa Deborah b 2 Aug 1980), 1 s (Hon Oliver Charles Julian b 3 Sept 1983); *Heir* s, Hon Oliver MacAndrew; *Career* farmer; tax cmmr 1996–2009; *Recreations* golf, tennis, cricket, football, rugby union, motor racing; *Style—* The Rt Hon Lord MacAndrew; ✉ 54B Sutherland Avenue, London W9 2QU

McANDREW, Geraldine (Gerri); *née* Baker; da of Arthur Baker (d 1982), and Norah McGuire (d 1955); *b* 11 November 1951, Dublin; *Educ* Univ of Herts (BA, CQSW), Univ of Sussex (Dip); *Children* 2 da (Cathryn, Madeleine); *Career* social worker: Hammersmith and Fulham 1975–79, Bronx NY 1979–81, Lambeth 1981–82; Hammersmith and Fulham: team mangr 1982–87, area mangr 1987–91; asst dir of social servs London Borough of Tower Hamlets 1991–92, asst dir of social servs (children and families) London Borough of Camden 1992–95, exec dir Fostering Network 1995–2003 (secondment Cabinet Office 2000), chief exec Buttle UK (formerly Frank Buttle Tst) 2003–; pres Int Foster Care Orgn 1997–2001, chair Nat Cncl of Voluntary Child Care Orgn 2001–03; tstee and chair: End Child Poverty 2003–10, Shaftesbury Homes & Arethusa 2005–; advsr on a number of govt gps in the four nations of the UK; Hon MLitt; *Recreations* music, singing, power walking, art; *Clubs* South London Theatre; *Style—* Gerri McAndrew; ✉ e-mail gerri@frankdixon.plus.com; Buttle UK, 15 Greycoat Place, London SW1P 1SB (☎ 020 7798 6230, e-mail gerrimca@buttleuk.org)

McANDREW, Ian Christopher; *b* 20 February 1953, Leeds; *Educ* Univ of Cambridge (MA); *m* 26 Aug 1978, Geraldine Baker; 2 da (Cathryn b 12 Jan 1985, Madeleine b 12 March 1989); *Career* Coopers & Lybrand 1975–88, fin and ops dir, co sec and compliance offr British and Commonwealth Merchant Bank plc 1988–92, fin dir Lawrence Graham 1992–2000, fin dir Clyde & Co 2001–; FCA (ACA 1978); *Style—* Ian McAndrew, Esq; ✉ Flat B, 27 Nevern Square, London SW5 9PD (☎ 020 8693 3592, e-mail ian.mcandrew@clyde.co.uk)

MacANDREW, Hon Nicholas Rupert (Nick); yr s of 2 Baron MacAndrew (d 1989); *b* 12 February 1947; *Educ* Eton; *m* 1, 1975 (m dis 1994), Victoria Rose Renton; 1 s, 2 da; m 2, 1998, Joy Elizabeth Meadows; *Career* Deloittes 1966–71, Schroders plc 1971–2002 (finance dir 1991–2002); non-exec dir: Wates Gp Ltd 2003–12, Jardine Lloyd Thompson Group plc 2005–14; chair of tstees Save the Children 2003–08; FCA 1971; *Clubs* MCC, Boodle's, Sunningdale Golf; *Style—* The Hon Nicholas MacAndrew; ✉ The Old Chapel, Greywell, Hook, Hampshire RG29 1BS (☎ 01256 702390)

McANDREW, Nicolas; s of Robert Louis McAndrew (d 1981), and Anita Marian, *née* Huband (d 1996, aged 100); *b* 9 December 1934; *Educ* Winchester; *m* 20 Sept 1960, Diana Leonie Wood (d 2015); 2 s (Charles Gavin b 14 Jan 1962, Mark James b 16 Feb 1964), 1 da (Fiona Catherine Mary b 16 June 1968); *Career* Nat Serv 1 Bn The Black Watch 1953–55 (active serv Kenya); articled clerk Peat Marwick Mitchell & Co 1955–61, qualified CA 1961; S G Warburg & Co Ltd: investment mangr 1962–69, chm Warburg Investment Management 1975–78 (md 1969–75); md: NM Rothschild & Sons Ltd 1979–88, Rothschild Asset Management Ltd 1979–88, Murray Johnstone Ltd 1988–99 (chm 1992–99); chm: Investec Extra Income Tst Ltd 1995–2002, Derby Tst 1999–2003, Martin Currie Enhanced Income Tst plc 1999–2005; dep chm Burn Stewart Distillers plc 1990–99; memb: Bd Highlands and Islands Enterprise 1993–97, North of Scotland Water Authy 1995–2002, Liverpool Victoria Friendly Soc 1995–2005; sr memb Ct of Assts Worshipful Co of Grocers (Master 1978–79); *Recreations* fishing, shooting, gardening; *Clubs* White's; *Style—* Nicolas McAndrew, Esq; ✉ Ard-na-Coille, Ruisaurie, By Beanly, Inverness-shire IV4 7AJ (☎ 01463 782524, e-mail kilcoy@btinternet.com)

McARDLE, John; s of John Joseph McArdle (d 1966), and Edeth, *née* Webster, of Liverpool; *b* 16 August 1949; *Educ* St Bede's Secdy Modern Sch, E15 Acting Sch Laughton; *Career* actor; various credits BBC Radio Manchester; also appeared in Horses for Courses (Br Film Sch); patron: Burnly and Rendle NSPCC, Bolton Octogon Theatre, Unity Theatre Liverpool, Liverpool Everyman Youth Theatre, E Lancs Hospice; completed Four Peaks Challenge for Wooden Spoon Soc 2009; hon memb NSPCC Cncl 1994, memb BAFTA; Best Actor Award RTS 2002; subject of This is Your Life 2003; *Theatre* began with various fringe cos in England and Wales; repertory: Liverpool Playhouse, Liverpool Everyman, Manchester Library Theatre, Contact Theatre, Forum Theatre, Oldham Coliseum, Bolton Octogan, Sheffield Crucible, Chester Gateway, Edinburgh Festival, Young Vic Theatre; The Arbour (RNT Studio) 1997, Snow White (pantomime, Theatre Royal Nottingham), Our Country's Good (Liverpool Playhouse) 2007, The Rise and Fall of Little Voice (English Touring Co Far East tour) 2008, Oh, What a Lovely War (Bolton Octogon) 2008, One Night In Istanbul (Liverpool Empire) 2009–10 and (Canal Theatre Dublin) 2010, Demolition Man (Bolton Octagon), Queen of the North (Bolton Octagon),

Brassed Off (nat tour) 2014; *Television* for BBC incl: Thacker, Underbelly, Gallowglass (Barbara Vine series), Spender, Bambino Mio (Screen One) 1994, Skallergrig (Screen One) 1994, Seaforth 1994, Rich Deceiver 1994, Throwaways (Sch TV) 1996, Born to Run 1996, Casualty 1997, City Central, Holby City, Out of Hours 1998, The Cazelet Chronicles 2001, Rough Aunty 2001, Silver Command (working title) 2001, The Bingo Club 2003, Casualty 2004, Holby City 2004, Merseybeat series II, III and IV, Dalziel and Pascoe, Busby Babes Story, The Muncih Disaster; for Granada incl: Coronation Street, Strangers, Kavanagh QC 1995, Prime Suspect V 1996, Metropolis 2000, My Fragile Heart 2000, Always and Everyone 2001, presenter Case Unsolved; other credits incl: Billy Corkhill in Brookside (Channel Four) 1986–91, Firm Friends (ITV), The Chief (police series, Anglia) 1994, Firm Friends II (Tyne Tees) 1994, Finney (ITV) 1994, Cracker (ITV) 1994, Wycliffe (HTV) 1995, Heartbeat (Yorkshire) 1995 and 2005, Its Not Unusual (Short and Curlies, Channel Four) 1995, In the Place of the Dead (LWT) 1995, And the Beat Goes On (Mersey) 1996, Family Ties (Channel Four) 1997, Lloyd's Bank Film Challenge 1997, Playing the Field (ITV) 1998, Where the Heart Is (ITV), Peak Practice (ITV) 2000–01, Active Defence (ITV) 2001, My Fragile Heart (Tiger Aspect) 2001, Through her Eyes (Channel 7 Australia) 2004, Foyles War (Bently Productions) 2004, prodr Demolition Dave (ITV) 2004–05, Heartbeat (ITV) 2005, The Bill (Talkback Thames) 2005, Mobile (ITV) 2007, Waterloo Road (BBC 1) 2010, Casualty, Doctors (ITV), Law and Order UK (ITV), Surviving Disaster (BBC 1), Blue Murder (ITV), All the Small Things (BBC 1), U B Dead (TV movie), Waking the Dead (BBC 1), The Case (BBC 1) 2012, Vera (BBC 1), Crime Stories (ITV), True Crime 2012, New Tricks (BBC 1) 2013; *Radio* The Circle (Radio 4), Stock 'So Good They Named it Once' (Radio 4); *Film* The Duke (writer and dir) 1999, There's Only One Jimmy Grimble 2000, Revengers Tragedy 2002, Function at the Junction (short film), Killing Joke, Charlie Noades 2008, The Caller, Lone Tomorrow, The Rochdale Pioneers, Friends of Money, Through Her Eyes 2009; *Recreations* windsurfing, fell walking; *Style*— John McArdle, Esq; ✉ c/o Roxane Vacca (☎ 020 7383 5971)

McARTHUR, (Allan Robin) Dayrell; s of Alan John Dennis McArthur (d 1988), and Pamela Mary, *née* Henderson (d 2007); *b* 28 June 1946; *Educ* Winchester; *m* 30 April 1977, Susan Diana, da of Christopher Cheshire, of Spain; 3 s (Alastair b 1979, Sam b 1981, Robert b 1985); *Career* Price Waterhouse 1965–69, McArthur Group Ltd 1969–2014 (md 1971–2011, chm 1987–2014); pres Nat Assoc of Steel Stockholders 1986–88, pres Fédération Européenne du Négoce d'Acier (European Steel Trades Fedn) 1992–94; govr UWE 1990–2004; chm Clifton Suspension Bridge Tst 2001–13; Master Soc of Merchant Venturers of Bristol 1989–90; *Recreations* tennis, golf, cricket, rackets, music, theatre, skiing; *Clubs* MCC, Tennis & Rackets Assoc, Bristol and Clifton Golf, Leatherjackets Golf, Downhill Only Ski; *Style*— Dayrell McArthur, Esq; ✉ Moorledge Farm, Chew Magna, Bristol BS40 8TL (e-mail dayrell.mcarthur@outlook.com)

McARTHUR, Douglas B; OBE (2001); *b* 17 March 1951; *Educ* Univ of Glasgow (BSc); *m* 14 Jan 2006, Miranda Kenett; 3 da by previous m (Vicki b 1977, Kate b 1980, Jill b 1984); *Career* mktg mgmnt positions 1973–83: Procter & Gamble, Scottish & Newcastle, Campbell Soups; dir Hall Advertising 1978–79, commercial dir Town Art & Design 1979–82, sales and mktg dir Radio Clyde 1983–84; dir 1985–92: Balgray Gp, Baillie Marshall Advertising; md and chief exec Radio Advertising Bureau 1992–2006, managing conslt Planning for Results 2006–; chm UKOnlineMeasurement Ltd 2009–; dir IMD plc 1999–2008; memb: Inst of Mktg 1979, MRS 1986, Mktg Soc 1992, Mktg Gp GB, Royal Instn; fell: CAM 1997, Radio Acad 1997; *Recreations* theatre, music, literature, swimming; *Clubs* 30 Club of London, Solus; *Style*— Douglas McArthur, Esq, OBE; ✉ Planning for Results, 73 Cromwell Tower, Barbican, London EC2Y 8DN (☎ 020 7628 2557, e-mail douglas@planningforresults.com, website www.planningforresults.com)

MacARTHUR, Dame Ellen Patricia; DBE (2005, MBE); da of Kenneth John MacArthur, and Avril Patricia MacArthur; *b* 8 July 1976; *Educ* Anthony Gell Sch Wirksworth; *Career* former professional offshore sailor; winner Class 2 Route du Rhum solo trans-atlantic race on 50' Kingfisher 1998, winner Open 60 Class Europe/New Man Star solo trans-atlantic race on 60' Kingfisher 2000, second overall Vendée Globe non-stop round the world race on 60' Kingfisher 2001, winner Class 1 (Open 60) Route du Rhum race on 70' Kingfisher 2002, attempted to set new Jules Verne non-stop round the world record 2003 (attempt aborted after losing mast of Kingfisher 2 in Southern Ocean), single-handed circumnavigation of the world on 60' B&Q 2005 (set world record time 71 days, 14 hours, 18 minutes); fndr Ellen MacArthur Tst, fndr Ellen MacArthur Fndn (promoting a circular economy); memb Club of Rome 2013; *Awards* YJA Young Sailor of the Year 1995, YJA Yachtsman of the Year 1999, Forum Int de la Course Océanique (FICO) World Champion 2001, Int Sailing Fedn (ISAF) World Champion Woman Sailor 2001; Légion d'Honneur 2008; *Publications* Taking on the World (autobiography, 2002), Race Against Time (2005), Full Circle (2010); *Recreations* sailing, walking, farming; *Style*— Dame Ellen MacArthur, DBE; ✉ c/o Natasha Fairweather, AP Watt, 20 John Street, 162–168 Regent Street, London, WC1N 2DR (☎ 020 7405 6774); Ellen MacArthur Foundation, The Sail Loft, Medina Road, Cowes, Isle of Wight PO31 7BX (☎ 01983 296 463, e-mail info@ellenmacarthurfoundation.org)

McARTHUR, Liam Scott; MSP; s of William (Bill) McArthur, of Sanday, Orkney, and Susan (Sue), *née* Scott; *b* 8 August 1967, Edinburgh; *Educ* Sanday Jr Secdy Sch, Kirkwall GS, Univ of Edinburgh (Football half blue, Sports Union Exec Award, MA); *m* 18 July 1998, Tamsin, *née* Bailey; 2 s (Calum Stanley Euan b 18 June 2000, Thomas Anton Mishael b 15 July 2003); *Career* researcher for Jim Wallace MP House of Commons 1990–92, stagiaire Directorate Gen 1A (External Rels) European Cmmn Brussels 1992–93, public affrs conslt EU 1993–98, public affrs conslt APCO UK 1998–2002, special advsr to Dep First Min of Scotland Scot Exec 2002–05, public affrs conslt Edinburgh 2005–07; MSP (Lib Dem) Orkney 2007–, spokesman on enterprise, energy and tourism Scot Parliament 2007–08, spokesman on rural affrs, environment and energy Scot Parliament 2008–; memb Finance Ctee Scot Parliament 2007–08, memb Rural Affrs and Environment Ctee Scot Parliament 2008–; dir Hearts and Balls, tstee Dug McArthur Tst Fund; *Style*— Liam McArthur, Esq, MSP; ✉ The Scottish Parliament, Edinburgh EH99 1SP (☎ 0131 348 5815, e-mail liam.mcarthur.msp@scottish.parliament.uk)

MacARTHUR CLARK, Dr Judy Anne; CBE (2004); *née* MacArthur; da of Archibald Alastair Cameron MacArthur (d 1990), of Manchester, and Elinore Muriel, *née* Warde Sandwich (d 2003); *b* 18 November 1950, Stoke-on-Trent; *Educ* Orton GS Peterborough, Univ of Glasgow Coll of Vet Med (BVMS), RCVS (Dip, election to specialist register), European Coll of Lab Animal Medicine (Dip); *m* 16 Feb 1991, David Wayne Clark, s of Robert Clark (d 1982), of Tell City, Indiana; 1 da (Sophie Katherine b 28 Aug 1991); *Career* gen vet practice Sussex 1973–74, vet advsr Univs Fedn for Animal Welfare 1974–76, pt/t hon lectr RVC London 1974–87, sr scientific offr 1976–82, head of lab animal science Searle R&D High Wycombe 1983–86, dir of lab animal sciemce Pfizer Central Research UK 1986–91, vet conslt JMC Consultancy 1991, vet dir BioZone Ltd Margate 1992–2005, vice-pres worldwide comparative medicine Pfizer Global R&D 2004–07; chief inspector Animals (Scientific Procedures) Inspectorate Home Office 2007–11, head Animals in Science Regulation Unit Home Office 2011–16; memb: Cncl Section of Comparative Med RSM 1979–87, Cncl Br Lab Animals Vet Assoc (BLAVA) 1979–89 (vice-pres and pres 1983–89), RCVS 1982– (vice-pres 1991–92, pres 1992–93, chm various ctees), Animal Procedures Ctee (APC) 1994–99, BBSRC 1996–99, Farm Animal Welfare Cncl (FAWC) 1993–2004 (chm 1999–2004, chm R&D Ctee 1994–98); memb: Technology Liaison Ctee Inst for Animal Health Compton 1994–98, Animal Production and Welfare Strategy Gp Silsoe Research Inst 1994–2003 (chm 1996–); chm Bill Hiddleston Award Fund Tstees 1985–92, vice-pres Inst of Animal Technol (IAT) 1991–; Winston Churchill travelling fell USA and Canada 1982, Victory Medal Central Vet Soc BVA 1992, Pres's Award Vet Mktg Assoc 1993; author of over 170 scientific papers, book chapters and invited keynote addresses to int conferences; hon memb Assoc of Vet Teachers and Research Workers; memb: BVA, LAVA, Fedn of Euro Lab Animal Science Assocs, Lab Animal Science Assoc, Univs Fedn for Animal Welfare, Vet Benevolent Fund; DVMS (hc) Univ of Glasgow 2001, Dip (hc) American Coll of Laboratory Animal Medicine 2007; MRCVS 1973, FRSM 1978, FRSB 1997, FRAgS 2002; *Recreations* company of family and friends; *Clubs* Farmers'; *Style*— Dr Judy MacArthur Clark, CBE; ☎ 01304 619665, mobile 07961 255676, e-mail judymacarthurclark@gmail.com

MACASKILL, Ewen; s of John Angus MacAskill, of Erskine, Renfrewshire, and Catherine, *née* MacDonald; *b* 29 October 1951; *Educ* Woodside Sch Glasgow, Univ of Glasgow (MA); *m* Anne, da of John Hutchison; 3 s (Robbie b 19 Nov 1981, Andrew b 27 July 1984, Jamie b 29 Aug 1988); *Career* reporter Glasgow Herald 1974–77; journalist: Nat Broadcasting Cmmn of Papua New Guinea 1978–79, Reuters 1980, Scotsman 1981–83, China Daily Beijing 1984, Scotsman 1985, Washington Post (reporter) 1986; political ed Scotsman 1989–96 (journalist 1987); The Guardian: chief political corr 1996–2000, diplomatic ed 2000–07, US bureau chief 2007–; Scotland's Young Journalist of the Year 1974, What The Papers Say Scoop of the Year (Guardian Team) 1999, Polk Award for reporting of Edward Snowden revelations 2014, Pulitzer Prize (Guardian Team) 2014, Emmy (Guardian Team) 2014; *Books* Always A Little Further (1983); *Recreations* mountaineering, theatre; *Clubs* Junior Mountaineering Club of Scotland, St Margaret's Film; *Style*— Ewen MacAskill, Esq; ✉ 11 Norman Avenue, St Margarets, Twickenham, Middlesex TW1 2LY (☎ 020 8891 0795); The Guardian, 90 York Way, London N1 9GU (☎ 020 7239 9579)

McASLAN, John Renwick; CBE (2012); s of Prof T Crawford McAslan (d 1985), and Jean *née* Wells Renwick (d 2009); *b* 16 February 1954, Glasgow; *Educ* Univ of Edinburgh (MA, DipArch); *m* 1981, Dava Sagenkahn; 2 da (Hannah b 1987, Flora b 1994), 1 s (Renwick b 1989); *Career* co-fndr: Troughton McAslan 1984, John McAslan & Partners 1996 (currently exec chm); estab John McAslan Family Tst 1997, chm Dundon Burgh Hall Tst; awards incl RIBA Award for Architecture, Royal Fine Art Cmmn Tst Award, British Construction Industry Award, Civic Tst Award, Japan Inst of Architects Award, Structural Steel Award, Concrete Society Award, Millennium Award, Brunel Award, World Architect of the Year 2009; RIBA, FICE, FRIAS, FRICS, FRSA; *Recreations* gardening, golf, opera, reading, travel, walking; *Clubs* Athenaeum, Caledonian; *Style*— John McAslan, Esq, CBE; ✉ 16 Hillsleigh Road, London W8 7LE; 7–9 William Road, London NW1 3ER (e-mail j.mcaslan@mcaslan.co.uk, website www.mcaslan.co.uk)

McATEER, Caroline; *Career* dir The Outside Organisation 1997–2003, dir CM Publicity 2003–07, dir The Sports PR Co 2007–; *Style*— Ms Caroline McAteer; ✉ The Sports PR Company, 10 Greek Street, London W1D 4DH (☎ 020 7434 3392, e-mail caroline@thesportsprcompany.com, website www.thesportsprcompany.com, Twitter @SportsPRCompany)

MACAULAY, Anthony Dennis; s of Dennis Macaulay, of Wakefield, W Yorks, and Frances, *née* Frain; *b* 15 November 1948; *Educ* Queen Elizabeth GS Wakefield, Keble Coll Oxford; *m* 7 Oct 1978, Dominica Francisca, da of Dr Henri Compernolle, of Bruges, Belgium; 1 s (Thomas b 29 March 1985), 2 da (Laura b 20 April 1983, Rosemary b 4 Oct 1987); *Career* admitted slr 1974; articled clerk/slr Biddle & Co 1971–75, asst slr Wilkinson Kimbers & Staddon 1975–77, ptnr Herbert Smith 1983– (asst slr 1977–83), sec to Panel on Take-overs and Mergers 1983–85; memb Law Soc; memb Worshipful Co of Slrs 1987; *Books* Butterworths Handbook of UK Corporate Finance (contrib, 1988), Palmer's Company Law (memb Ed Bd, 1998); *Recreations* tennis, skiing, music, cooking, family; *Style*— Anthony Macaulay, Esq; ✉ Exchange House, Primrose Street, London EC2A 2HS (☎ 020 7374 8000, fax 020 7374 0888, telex 886633)

M

MacAUSLAN, Harry Hume; s of John Mechan MacAuslan, and Helen Constance Howden, *née* Hume; *b* 2 October 1956; *Educ* Charterhouse, Univ of Manchester (BA); *m* 1981, Fiona Caroline, da of Brian Martin Boag; 1 da (Clare Emily b 5 Jan 1985), 2 s (Samuel Alexander b 9 Aug 1987, James Hume b 8 April 1989); *Career* advertising exec; mktg trainee De La Rue 1979–80; J Walter Thompson: joined as graduate trainee 1980, bd dir 1989–, head of account mgmnt 1993–96, dep chm 1996–2004; Leo Burnett: global dir 2004–06, vice-chm EMEA 2005–; non-exec dir Sadler's Wells Trust Ltd 1995–, chm Sadler's Wells Devpt Cncl 2003–07, govr Sadler's Wells 2005– (vice-chm 2009–); non-exec dir Perfect Pizza 2009–; tstee Mental Health Fndn 2008–, chm Russell Maliphant Dance Co 2010–; FRSA 2005; *Style*— Harry MacAuslan, Esq; ✉ Leo Burnett, Warwick Building, Kensington Village, Avonmore Road, London W14 8HQ (☎ 020 7071 1307, e-mail harry.macauslan@leoburnett.co.uk)

McAVAN, Linda; MEP; *Educ* Heriot-Watt Univ (BA), Université Libre de Bruxelles (MA); *Career* Euro policy expert Brussels 1984–91, European offr Coalfield Community Campaign 1991–95, princ strategy offr Barnsley Cncl 1995–98; MEP (Lab): Yorks S 1998–99 (by-election), Yorks and the Humber 1999–; European Parl: dep ldr EPLP 1999–2004, treas Party of European Socialists 2004–06, vice-pres (climate change portfolio) Party of European Socialists 2006–09, memb Environment, Public Health and Food Safety Ctee 2004–14, spokesperson for Socialist and Democrat Gp, chair Int Devpt Ctee 2014–, subst memb Fisheries Ctee 2014–; *Style*— Ms Linda McAvan, MEP; ✉ Labour Constituency Office, 79 High Street, Wath upon Dearne, South Yorkshire S63 7QB (☎ 01709 875665, fax 01709 874207, e-mail lindamcavan@lindamcavanmep.org.uk)

McAVOY, James; *b* 1979, Glasgow; *Educ* Royal Scottish Acad of Music and Drama; *m* Anne-Marie Duff, *qv*; 1 s (Andrew b 2010); *Career* actor; BAFTA Orange Rising Star Award 2006; *Theatre* incl: Breathing Corpses (Royal Court Theatre) 2005, Three Days Of Rain (Apollo Theatre) 2009; *Television* incl: Regeneration 1997, Lorna Doone 2000, Band of Brothers 2001, White Teeth 2002, State of Play 2003, Early Doors 2003, Shameless 2004–05 (nomination Best Newcomer British Comedy Awards), Macbeth 2005; *Films* incl: Swimming Pool 2001, Bright Young Things 2003, Wimbledon 2004, Inside I'm Dancing 2004 (Edinburgh Film Festival Audience Award), The Chronicles of Narnia: The Lion, the Witch and the Wardrobe 2005, Last King of Scotland 2006 (Best Actor: BAFTA Scotland 2007, nomination BIFA 2006, nomination European Award 2007, nomination BAFTA 2007), Starter for Ten 2006, Penelope 2006, Becoming Jane 2006, Atonement 2007 (Best Actor Award: London Film Critics Circle 2008, Empire 2008, Elle Style 2008, Richard Attenborough Film Award 2008, nomination BAFTA 2008, nomination Golden Globe Awards 2008), Wanted 2008, The Last Station 2009, X-Men: First Class 2011; *Style*— James McAvoy; ✉ c/o United Agents Ltd, 12–26 Lexington Street, London W1F 0LE (☎ 020 3214 0800, fax 020 3214 0801, website www.unitedagents.co.uk)

McAVOY, Baron (Life Peer UK 2010), of Rutherglen in Lanarkshire; Rt Hon Thomas McLaughlin McAvoy; PC (2003); s of Edward McAvoy (d 1985), and Frances McLaughlin McAvoy (d 1982); *b* 14 December 1943; *Educ* St Columbkilles Jr Secdy Sch; *m* 1968, Eleanor Kerr, da of William Kerr, of Rutherglen, Glasgow; 4 s (Thomas b 1969, Michael b 1971, Steven b 1974, Brian b 1981); *Career* regnl cncllr Strathclyde 1982–87; MP (Lab/Co-op): Glasgow Rutherglen 1987–2005, Rutherglen and Hamilton West 2005–10; oppn whip 1991–93 and 1996–97, comptroller of HM Household (Govt whip) 1997–2008, treas of HM Household and dep chief whip 2008–10; *Style*— The Lord McAvoy, PC; ✉ 9 Douglas Avenue, Rutherglen, Lanarkshire G73 4RA

McBAIN OF McBAIN, James Hughston; 22 Chief of Clan McBain (McBean); s of Hughston Maynard McBain of McBain (matriculated as Chief 1959, d 1977); *b* 1928; *Educ* Culver Mil Acad, Western Washington Coll, Univ of Arizona; *m* Margaret, *née* Stephenson; *Heir* s, Richard McBain; *Career* pres Scot Photo Shops AZ 1962–2001; *Books* History of the Clan McBain (MacBean) (2005); *Recreations* golf, Scottish history, Scottish country dancing; *Clubs* Royal Scottish Country Dance Soc; *Style*— James McBain of McBain

MACBETH, Dr Fergus Robert; s of Dr Ronald Graeme Macbeth (d 1992), and Margaret, *née* Macdonald (d 1983); *b* 5 January 1948; *Educ* Eton, Merton Coll Oxford, KCH Med Sch London (MA, BM BCh, DM), Univ of Stirling (MBA); *Career* conslt in radiotherapy and oncology Beatson Oncology Centre Glasgow 1988–96, dir Clinical Effectiveness Support Unit for Wales 1996–2001, conslt oncologist Velindre Cancer Centre Cardiff 1998–2008, dir Nat Inst for Health and Clinical Excellence 2008–13, assoc dir Wales Cancer Trials Unit 2013–; FRCR 1987, FRCPGlas 1989, FRCP 1997; *Style*— Dr Fergus Macbeth; ✉ Wales Cancer Trials Unit, Cardiff University, Heath Park, Cardiff CF14 4YS

McBRIDE, Angus; *b* 6 March 1965, London; *Educ* Kings Coll Taunton, UC Cardiff (J & R Corey scholarships); *Career* admitted slr 1991; Kingsley Napley 1999– (ptnr 2002–); memb: Law Soc 1991, London Criminal Courts Slrs Assoc 1999; *Recreations* music; *Style*— Angus McBride, Esq; ✉ Kingsley Napley LLP, Knights Quarter, 14 St John's Lane, London EC1M 4AJ (☎ 020 7814 1200 or 020 7814 1206 (direct), fax 020 7490 2288 or 020 7702 5146 (direct), e-mail amcbride@kingsleynapley.co.uk, website www.kingsleynapley.co.uk)

McBRIDE, Brian; *Educ* Univ of Glasgow (MA); *m* Linda; 2 da (Susan, Jennifer); *Career* joined Xerox 1977, subsequent positions with IBM, Crosfield Electronics, Madge Networks, Lucent and Dell Computers, md T-Mobile UK 2003–05, md Amazon.co.uk Ltd 2006–10, sr advsr Scottish Equity Ptnrs 2011–; chm: Asos plc 2012–, Wiggle.com 2015–; non-exec dir: SThree plc 2001–08, Celtic plc 2005–09, BBC 2012–14, AO.com plc 2014–; sr non-exec dir Computacenter plc 2011–15; memb Govt Digital Advsy Bd; *Recreations* golf, tennis, music; *Clubs* Camberley and District Social, Camberley Heath Golf; *Style*— Mr Brian McBride

McBRIDE, Dr Michael; *Educ* Queen's Univ Belfast (MB BCh, BAO), St Mary's Medical Sch and Imperial Coll London; *Career* Royal Hospitals: conslt physician 1994–2006, dir of educn 2002–02, medical dir 2002–06; chief medical offr for NI 2006–, chief exec Belfast Health and Social Care Tst 2014–; FRCP; *Style*— Dr Michael McBride; ✉ Department of Health, Social Services and Public Safety, Castle Buildings, Upper Newtownards Road, Belfast BT4 3SQ

McBRIEN, Michael Patrick; s of Leo Patrick McBrien (d 1969), and Elizabeth Rosemary, *née* Phillips (d 2005); *b* 4 July 1935; *Educ* Stonyhurst, St Thomas' Hosp Univ of London (MB BS); *m* 11 July 1964, Tessa Ann Freeland, da of Col Richard Bayfield Freeland (d 1980), of Beccles, Suffolk; 1 da (Emma b 12 March 1966), 2 s (James b 2 May 1968, Rowan b 6 May 1972); *Career* registrar in surgery: Southampton Hosp 1967–69, St Thomas' Hosp London 1969–70; sr registrar and lectr in surgery St Thomas' Hosp London 1970–73; sr conslt surgn: W Suffolk Gp of Hosps, St Edmund's Nuffield Hosp 1973–99, ret; Hunterian prof RCS 1974, clinical teacher and examiner in surgery Univ of Cambridge, lectr UEA, lectr skills courses RCS London, Cambridge and Norwich 2006–; external examiner in surgery: RCS(Ed), St Thomas' Hosp and KCH Univ of London, Royal Coll of Surgns of Sri Lanka, Royal Coll of Surgns in Cairo; RCS: sec Ct of Examiners 1992–99, memb Hospital Recognition Ctee 1992–2003, memb Educn Ctee Assoc of Surgns of GB and I; GMC assoc; med memb Pensions Appeal Tbnls 1996–2006; memb Panel Professional Linguistics AssesSment Bd (PLAB) GMC 2000–04, examiner PLAB OSCE (Objective Structured Clinical Examination) GMC 2001–06; nat dir Mannatech Inc; memb St Edmund's RC PC 2006–12; MS 1973; memb: BMA 1960–, RSM 1960; FRCS 1968; *Books* Postgraduate Surgery (1986); *Recreations* golf, shooting, bridge, skiing, travel, painting; *Clubs* RSM, MCC, Royal Worlington Golf, Emeriti CC; *Style*— Michael McBrien, Esq, MS, FRCS; ✉ Stanton House, Norton, Bury St Edmunds, Suffolk IP31 3LQ (☎ 01359 230832, e-mail mandtmcb2@btinternet.com)

McBRYDE, Prof William Wilson (Bill); s of William McBryde (d 1964), of Burntisland, Fife, and Marjory Wilson, *née* Husband (d 1991); *b* 6 July 1945, Perth, Scotland; *Educ* Perth Acad, Univ of Edinburgh (LLB, LLD), Univ of Glasgow (PhD); *m* 1, 4 Nov 1972 (m dis 1982), Elspeth Jean Stormont Glover; 1 da (Eileen b 23 Feb 1974), 1 s (Donald b 5 March 1976); m 2, 12 April 1986 (m dis 1999), Joyce Margaret, da of Rev James Marcus Gossip (d 1985), of Edinburgh; 1 da (Helen b 23 June 1988 d 2007); *Career* apprentice with Morton Smart Macdonald & Milligan WS 1967–70; admitted slr 1969; court procurator Biggart Lumsden & Co Glasgow 1970–72, lectr in private law Univ of Glasgow 1972–76, sr lectr in private law Univ of Aberdeen 1976–87, prof of Scots law Univ of Dundee 1987–99 (dean Faculty of Law 1989–90, dep princ Univ 1991–92, vice-princ 1992–94), prof of commercial law Univ of Edinburgh 1999–2005 (emeritus prof of commercial law 2005–), Van der Grinten prof of commercial law Univ of Nijmegen 2002–07; visiting prof L'Université de Paris V René Descartes 2000–05; dir Scot Univ Law Inst 1989–95; specialist Parly advsr to House of Lords Select Ctee on European Communities 1980–83; memb: Scot Consumer Cncl 1984–87, Scot Advsy Ctee on Arbitration 1986–2016, Insolvency Permit Ctee ICAS 1990–95, Advsy Panel on Security over Moveable Property DTI 1994–2016, consultant to Scottish Law Cmmn 1997–98; Hon Sheriff Tayside, Central and Fife Dundee 1991–; FRSE 1994; *Books* Bankruptcy (Scotland) Act 1985 (1986), The Law of Contract in Scotland (1987, 3 edn 2007), Petition Procedure in the Court of Session (2 edn, with N Dowie, 1988), Bankruptcy (1989, 2 edn 1995), Bankruptcy (Scotland) Act 1993 (1993), Principles of European Insolvency Law (jt ed, 2003); *Recreations* walking, photography; *Style*— Prof Bill McBryde, FRSE; ✉ Faculty of Law, The University of Edinburgh, Old College, South Bridge, Edinburgh EH8 9YL (☎ 0131 650 2038, fax 0131 650 6317)

McBURNEY, Simon; OBE (2005); *Educ* Univ of Cambridge; *Career* actor, writer and dir; co-fndr and artistic dir Complicité; artist associé Festival D'Avignon 2012; *Theatre* as dir for Compicité incl: Anything for a Quiet Life 1987, The Visit 1989, The Winter's Tale 1992, The Street of Crocodiles 1992 (also writer/adaptor; Barcelona Critics Award for Best Foreign Prodn 1993, Dublin Festival Award for Best Touring Prodn 1994), Out of a House Walked a Man... 1994, The Three Lives of Lucie Cabrol 1994 (Time Out Theatre Award 1994, Best Prodn of a Play Toronto DORA Award 1997), To The Wedding 1997 (also writer/adaptor), The Caucasian Chalk Circle 1997, The Chairs 1997, Mnemonic 1999 (Drama Desk Award for Unique Theatrical Experience 2001, Time Out Live Award for Outstanding Achievement 2001, Best New Play Critics' Circle Award 1999), Light 2000 (also writer/adaptor), The Noise of Time 2000, Strange Poetry 2004, The Elephant Vanishes 2004, Measure for Measure 2004, A Disappearing Number 2007 (Best New Play Laurence Olivier Award 2008, Evening Standard Award, Critics' Circle Award 2007), Shun-kin 2008 (Best Dir Yomiuri Theatre Award Grand Prize 2009), Endgame 2009 (also actor), A Dog's Heart 2010, The Master and Margarita 2011–12, The Encounter 2015–16; as dir on Broadway: The Resistable Rise of Arturo Ui 2002, All My Sons 2008; as writer/adaptor The Vertical Line 1999; *Film* as actor incl: The Manchurian Candidate 2004, Friends with Money 2006, The Last King of Scotland 2006, The Golden Compass 2007, The Duchess 2008, Body of Lies 2008, Jane Eyre 2011, Tinker, Tailor, Soldier, Spy 2011; as writer Mr Bean's Holiday 2007; *Television* as actor incl: Vicar of Dibley 1994–2004, Rev 2010–, The Borgias 2011–; *Awards* Perrier Award 1985 (with Complicité), Berlin Acad of Arts Konrad Wolf Prize for Outstanding Multi-disciplinary Artists 2008, Dirs' Guild Award for Outstanding Achievement in Theatre; *Publications* Who You Hear It From, essays by Simon McBurney (2012); *Style*— Simon McBurney, Esq, OBE; ✉ Complicité, 14 Anglers Lane, London NW5 3DG

McCABE, Bernice Alda; da of Alan Collis Wood, and Eileen May Wood; *Educ* Clifton HS Bristol, Univ of Bristol (BA, PGCE), Leeds Metropolitan Univ (MBA); *Career* teacher Filton HS Bristol 1974–81, head English Dept Cotham GS Bristol 1981–83, head English Faculty Collingwood Sch Camberley 1984–86, dep head Heathland Sch Hounslow 1986–90; headmistress: Chelmsford Co HS 1990–97, N London Collegiate Sch 1997–; dir HRH Prince of Wales Educn Summer Sch 2002–, co-dir The Prince's Teaching Inst and The Prince's Cambridge Prog for Teaching 2006–; exec Nat Grammar Schs Assoc 1995–97, memb Univs Sub-Ctee GSA/HMC 2001–08, memb Nat Curriculum Advsy Ctee 2010–, expert advsr Mayor of London's Schs Excellence Fund 2013–; govr Orley Farm Sch 1997–2001; friend: Royal Acad, Courtauld Inst of Art; memb: Tate Gallery, RSPB, Wildfowl and Wetlands Tst, Nat Tst; FRSA; *Recreations* family, reading, restoration of period home, cottage by the sea in Devon, gardening, art, watercolour painting, running, gym, walking, enjoying the countryside; *Clubs* Univ Women's, Lansdowne; *Style*— Mrs Bernice McCabe; ✉ North London Collegiate School, Canons Drive, Edgware, Middlesex HA8 7RJ (☎ 020 8951 6401)

MacCABE, Prof Colin Myles Joseph; s of Myles Joseph MacCabe, and Ruth Ward MacCabe; *b* 9 February 1949; *Educ* St Benedict's Sch Ealing, Trinity Coll Cambridge (MA, PhD), Ecole Normale Supérieure; *m*; 2 s, 1 da; *Career* research fell Emmanuel Coll Cambridge 1974–76, univ asst lectr in English Univ of Cambridge and coll lectr and fell King's Coll Cambridge 1976–81; Univ of Strathclyde: prof of English Univ of Strathclyde 1981–85, chm Dept of English Studies 1982–84, chm John Logie Baird Centre for Research in TV and Film 1985–91 (founding dir 1983–85), visiting prof in Prog for Literacy Linguistics 1985–91; prof of English Univ of Pittsburgh 1986– (distinguished prof of English and film 2002), prof of English Univ of Exeter 1998–2006; visiting fell Griffith Univ Brisbane 1981 and 1984, Mellon visiting prof Univ of Pittsburgh 1985, visiting prof Birkbeck Coll London 1992–2006; memb English Teaching Advsy Ctee Br Cncl 1983–85 (Br Cncl lectr Shanghai Foreign Language Inst 1984); Br Film Inst (BFI): head of prodn 1985–89, head of research 1989–98; prodr Minerva Pictures 1998–2005; ed Critical Quarterly 1987–; founding chm London Consortium 1995–2005 (assoc dir 2006–); *Books* James Joyce and the Revolution of The World (1979), Godard: Images, Sounds, Politics (1980), The Talking Cure: Essays in Psychoanalysis and Language (ed, 1981), James Joyce: New Perspectives (ed 1982), Theoretical Essays: film, linguistics, literature (1985), The BBC and Public Sector Broadcasting (jt ed, 1986), High Theory Low Culture: Analysing Popular Television and Film (ed, 1986), Futures for English (ed, 1987), The Linguistics of Writing (jt ed, 1988), Who is Andy Warhol (jt ed, 1997), Performance (1998), The Eloquence of the Vulgar (1999), Godard: A Portrait of the Artist at 70 (2003), T S Eliot (2006), The Butcher Boy (2007); *Recreations* eating, drinking, talking; *Style*— Prof Colin MacCabe

McCABE, John; CBE (1985); s of Frank McCabe (d 1983), and Elisabeth Carmen, *née* Herlitzius (d 1993); *b* 21 April 1939; *Educ* Liverpool Inst, Univ of Manchester (BMus), Royal Manchester Coll of Music (FRMCM), Hochschule für Musik Munich; *m* 1, (m dis 1973), Hilary Tann; m 2, 31 July 1974, Monica Christine, da of Jack Smith (d 1974); *Career* composer and pianist; res pianist Univ Coll Cardiff 1965–68, freelance music critic 1966–71, dir London Coll Music 1983–90; writer of operas, ballets, symphonies, concertos, choral and keyboard works, TV and film music; cmmnd works incl: Symphony No 4 Of Time and the River (BBC Symphony Orch and Melbourne Symphony Orch) 1995, Edward II (Stuttgart Ballet) 1995, Arthur Pendragon and Le Morte d'Arthur (Birmingham Royal Ballet) 2000–01, Symphony on a Pavane (London Philharmonic) 2007, Labyrinth (symphony, Royal Liverpool Philharmonic) 2008, Horn Concerto (David Pyatt, BBC NOW) 2007, Cello Concerto (Truls Mørk, Halle) 2008; numerous recordings incl 12 CD set complete piano works of Haydn; pres: Inc Soc Musicians 1982–83, Br Music Soc; memb Hon Cncl of Mgmnt RPS 1983–86, chm Assoc Professional Composers 1985–86, memb Gen Cncl and Donations Ctee Performing Rights Soc 1985–88; vice-pres: Malvern Music Club, Luton Music Club; memb: Wigmore Hall Board 1987–90, Mechanical Copyright Protection Soc; Hon DPhil Thames Valley Univ, Hon DMus Univ of Liverpool 2006; FLCM, FRCM, Hon RAM, FRNCM 1986, FTCL 1989; *Books* BBC Music Guide: Bartok's Orchestral Music (1974), Haydn's Piano Sonatas (1986), Gollancz Musical Companion (contrib, 1973), Novello Short Biography: Rachmaninov (1974), Alan Rawsthorne: Portrait of a Composer (1998); subject of Landscapes of the Mind: The Music of John McCabe (2008); *Recreations* cinema, books, cricket, golf, (watching) snooker; *Style*— John McCabe, Esq, CBE; ✉ c/o Novello & Co Ltd (Music Publishers), 14–15 Berners Street, London W1T 3LJ (☎ 020 7612 7400, fax 020 7612 7545)

McCABE, Michael Benedict; *b* 1 June 1965, Brighton, E Sussex; *Educ* Shoreham Coll, W Sussex; *Career* formerly mktg dir and subsequently also assoc prodr Mamma Mia! 1998–2004; prodr: Wicked (West End and UK/International tour) 2006, Spring Awakening (West End) 2009, How to Succeed (Broadway) 2011, Million Dollar Quartet (West End) 2011, Sweeney Todd (West End) 2012; assoc prodr Promises, Promises (Broadway) 2010; co-fndr Joe Public 2003, fndr Michael McCabe Productions 2004, co-fndr Andrews McCabe Productions 2015; mktg dir: Charlie and the Chocolate Factory, Wicked; tstee English Touring Theatre 2015; *Recreations* theatre, film, opera, reading, travel; *Clubs* Ivy, Hospital, Library; *Style*— Michael McCabe, Esq; ✉ Michael McCabe Productions, The Hub @ The Dutch House, 307–309 High Holborn, London WC1V 7LL (website www.michaelmccabe.net)

McCABE, Stephen James (Steve); MP; s of James McCabe, and Margaret, *née* McCrorie; *b* 4 August 1955; *Educ* Port Glasgow HS, Moray House Coll Edinburgh (qualification in social work, Dip Social Studies), Univ of Bradford (MA); *m* 1991 (m dis); *Career* generic social worker Wolverhampton 1977–79, social worker with young offenders Wolverhampton 1979–83, mangr The Priory Centre for Adolescents Newbury 1983–85, lectr in social work N Worcestershire Coll 1986–89, pt/t social worker child care team Solihull 1989–91, pt/t social policy researcher Br Assoc of Social Workers (BASW) 1989–91, social work educn advsr Central Cncl for Educn and Trg in Social Work (CCETSW) 1991–97, MP (Lab) Birmingham Hall Green 1997–; asst Govt whip 2006–; *Recreations* reading, cooking, hill walking, football; *Style*— Steve McCabe, Esq, MP; ✉ House of Commons, London SW1A 0AA (☎ 020 7219 4842/3509); Birmingham (☎ 0121 443 3878)

McCAFFER, Eur Ing Prof Ronald; s of John Gegg McCaffer (d 1984), and Catherine Turner, *née* Gourlay (d 1979); *b* 8 December 1943; *Educ* Univ of Strathclyde (BSc, DSc), Loughborough Univ (PhD); *m* 13 Aug 1966, Margaret Elizabeth, da of Cyril Warner; 1 s (Andrew b 29 April 1977); *Career* design engr Babtie Shaw and Morton 1965–67; site engr: The Nuclear Power Gp 1967–69, Taylor Woodrow Construction 1969–70; Dept of Civil Engrg Loughborough Univ of Technol: lectr 1970–78, sr lectr 1978–83, reader 1983–86, prof of construction mgmnt 1986–2009 (emeritus prof 2009–), head of dept 1987–93, dean Sch of Engrg 1992–97, dep vice-chllr 1997–2002, dir Strategic Business Partnerships, Innovation and Knowledge Transfer 2002–06; ed Engineering, Construction & Architectural Management 1994–2014, memb Engrg Construction Industry Trg Bd 1994–2003, memb Technical Opportunities Panel EPSRC 2000–04; chm: Loughborough University Enterprises Ltd 2002–06, Loughborough Innovation Centre Ltd 2002–06, Construction Industry Simulations Ltd 2007–; dir Imago Ltd 2003–06; memb Cncl Innovation East Midlands 2005–09; memb Bd of Tstees and advsr to Br Univ in Egypt 2005–10; memb Incorporation of Hammermen of Glasgow 2015–; FREng 1991, FRSE 2009, Eur Ing, FICE, FCIOB, MCMI until 2010, MASCE until 2010, memb Smeatonian Soc of Civil Engrs, fell Inst of Engrs and Shipbuilders in Scotland 2012; *Books* Modern

Construction Management (1977, 7 edn 2013), Worked Examples in Construction Management (1986), Managing Construction Equipment (1991), Estimating and Tendering for Civil Engineering (1991), International Bid Preparation (1995), International Bidding Case Study (1995), Management of Off-Highway Plant and Equipment (2002); website www.MERITgame.com (international business game supported by ICE, CIOB and Construction Industry Training Board now in its 27th year and used by CIOB for their Global Student Challenge); *Style*— Eur Ing Prof Ronald McCaffer, FREng, FRSE; ✉ Department of Civil Engineering, Loughborough University, Loughborough, Leicestershire LE11 3TU (☎ 01509 222600, mobile 07710 975495, fax 01509 223890, e-mail ronald@mccaffer.com, website www.mccaffer.com)

McCAFFERTY, Ian Alexander; s of William John Edward McCafferty, and Mary, *née* Cutts; *b* 1 July 1956; *Educ* Dulwich Coll, Univ of Durham (BA), Univ of Amsterdam Europa Instituut (Nuffic scholar, MA); *m* 27 Feb 1982, Susan Jean, *née* Craig; 2 s (Andrew b 3 May 1988, Alexander b 17 May 1991); *Career* economist Int C of C Paris 1979–83, head of statistics The Economist newspaper 1983–85, head of economic trends CBI 1985–88, chief int economist Baring Securities 1988–92, chief int economist NatWest Markets 1992–98, head of macroeconomics BP plc 1998–2001, chief economic advsr CBI 2001–12, memb Monetary Policy Ctee Bank of England 2012–; Hon DEcon Nottingham Trent Univ 2012; fell Soc of Business Economists 1985; FRSA 2007; *Recreations* cooking, rugby, golf, France; *Clubs* Sundridge Park Golf; *Style*— Ian McCafferty, Esq; ✉ Bank of England, Threadneedle Street, London EC2R 8AH (☎ 020 7601 3235, fax 020 7601 4610, e-mail ian.mccafferty@bankofengland.co.uk)

McCAHILL, His Hon Judge Patrick Gerard; QC (1996); s of John McCahill (d 1995), and Josephine, *née* Conaghan (d 2001); *b* 6 May 1952; *Educ* Corby GS, St Catharine's Coll Cambridge (scholar, MA), Univ of London (LLM), BSc (Open Univ); *m* 8 Sept 1979, Liselotte Gabrielle Steiner; 2 da (Gabrielle Marie b 29 Nov 1980, Claire Elizabeth b 17 Aug 1984); *Career* supervisor St Catharine's Coll Cambridge; called to the Bar: Gray's Inn 1975 (Bacon scholar, Atkin scholar, elected bencher 2014), King's Inns Dublin 1990; lectr St John's Coll Oxford 1975–78, asst dep coroner Birmingham and Solihull 1984–99, recorder of the Crown Court 1997–2001 (asst recorder 1993–97), circuit judge (Midland Circuit) 2001–07, specialist chancery circuit judge (Western Circuit) 2007–; memb: Mental Health Review Tbnl 1999–2007, Parole Bd 2004–07; FCIArb 1992; *Style*— His Hon Judge McCahill, QC; ✉ Bristol Civil Justice Centre, 2 Redcliff Street, Bristol BS1 6GR

McCAIL, Chad; *b* 1961, Manchester; *Educ* Univ of Kent (BA), Goldsmiths Coll London (BA); *Career* artist; *Solo Exhibitions* Collective Gallery Edinburgh 1998, Laurent Delaye Gallery London 1998 and 2000, Attitudes Geneva 1999, Snake (Laurent Delaye Gallery London) 2002, Chad McCail (Des Moines Art Center) 2003, Life Is Driven By The Desire For Pleasure (Fruitmarket Gallery Edinburgh, BALTIC Centre for Contemporary Art Newcastle) 2003 and (Banque du Luxembourg, Salon Museum of Contemporary Art Belgrade, MAMCO Geneva) 2004, Food, Shelter, Clothing, Fuel (Baltimore Museum of Art) 2004, Evolution Isn't Over Yet (Huddersfield City Art Gallery) 2005, We Are Not Dead (Gallery of Modern Art Glasgow) 2006, Edinbugh Printmakers Workshop 2008; *Group Exhibitions* Performance collaboration (CCA Glasgow) 1992, Installation (Cracker Factory Edinburgh) 1992, Billboard and Performance (Aerial, Edinburgh) 1994, Paintings (Out of the Blue Edinburgh) 1994, Drawings (The Virtuous Space Edinburgh) 1995, Drawings (The Bongo Club Edinburgh) 1996, Collective Gallery Edinburgh 1997, Insulator (Gasworks London) 1997, Out of the Blue (New Street Exhbn Space Edinburgh) 1997, Afternoon in the Park (Laurent Delaye Gallery London) 1997, Connected (Northern Gallery for Contemporary Art Sunderland) 1997, Canny (Archway London) 1998, Family Credit (Edinburgh Festival Exhbn Collective Gallery Edinburgh) 1998, Eurocentral (Transmission Gallery Edinburgh) 1998, Social Security, Seguridad Social (RCA and Ex-Teresa Arte Actual Mexico City) 1998, Surfacing: Contemporary Drawing (ICA London) 1998, Accelerated Learning (Duncan of Jordanstone Coll Dundee) 1999, Locale (City Art Centre Edinburgh) 1999, Evolution is not over yet (Fruitmarket Gallery Edinburgh) 1999, Sampling (Ronald Feldman Fine Arts NY) 1999, Melbourne Biennial 1999, Protest and Survive (Whitechapel Art Gallery London) 2000, Because a fire was in my head (S London Gallery) 2000, Becks Futures (ICA London and tour) 2000, Give and Take (Harris Museum and Art Gallery) 2000, Landscape (Br Cncl touring show) 2000, 2001 and 2002, British Art Show 5 (tour) 2000–01, Utopia Now! (Oliver Art Centre CCAC Inst San Francisco) 2001, Here + Now: Scottish Art 1990–2001 (Dundee Contemporary Arts, Generator Projects and McManus Galleries Dundee, Aberdeen Art Gallery and Peacock Visual Arts Aberdeen) 2001, Invitation á...Laurent Delaye Gallery invitée par la galerie Anton Weller (Galerie Anton Weller Paris) 2001, The Other Britannia (Tecla Sala Barcelona and tour) 2001, Utopia Now! (and Then) (Sonoma Co Museum Santa Rosa Calif) 2002, The Gallery Show (Royal Acad) 2002, Better Than The Real Thing (SMART Project Space Amsterdam) 2002, Micro/macro, Mucsarnok/Kunsthalle (Budapest) 2003, Ev+a (Limerick) 2005, Courage Is Stronger Than Fear (Wolverhampton Art Gallery) 2005, Wordwork (Aberdeen) 2005, Infrastructure (Studio Voltaire London) 2005, Eye on Europe: Prints, Books and Multiples 1960 to Now (MoMA NY) 2006, Normalisation (Rooseum Malmo) 2006, Cult Fiction (New Art Gallery Wallsal) 2007, After Neurath (Der Stroom Den Haag) 2007; *Work in Public Collections* Br Cncl Collection, Cake Fndn Zurich, Fonds Municipal d'Art contemporain de Genève, Mamco Geneva, Middlesbrough Art Gallery, Scottish Nat Gallery of Modern Art, City Art Centre Edinburgh, Musée d'Art Moderne Grand-Duc Jean Luxembourg, MOMA, NY Museum of Modern Art, Glasgow, Middlesborough Art Gallery, Birmingham Art Gallery, Wolverhampton Art Gallery, Grampian Hospitals Art Tst; *Publications* Active Genital (2002), Life Is Driven By The Desire For Pleasure (2003); *Style*— Chad McCail, Esq; ✉ Delaye Saltoun, 11 Savile Row, London W1S 3PG (☎ 020 7287 1546, e-mail info@delayesaltoun.com)

McCALL, Dame Carolyn; DBE (2016, OBE 2008); *b* 13 September 1961; *Educ* Univ of Kent (BA), Univ of London (MA); *Career* risk analyst Costain Gp plc 1984–86; The Guardian: planner 1986–88, advtg exec 1988–89, advtg mangr 1989–91, product devpt mangr 1991–92, display advtg mangr 1992, advtg dir Wired UK 1992–94, dep advtg dir 1994–95, advtg dir 1995–97, commercial dir 1997–98, dep md 1998–2000, ceo Guardian Newspapers Ltd 2000–06, ceo Guardian Media Gp plc 2006–10; ceo easyJet plc 2010–; non-exec dir: New Look Gp plc 1999–2004, Tesco plc 2005–08, Lloyds TSB 2008–09; chair Opportunity Now 2005–, tstee Tools for Schools (educnl charity) 2000–05; Veuve Clicquot Business Woman of the Year 2008; *Style*— Dame Carolyn McCall, DBE; ✉ easyJet plc, Hangar 89, London Luton Airport, Luton, Bedfordshire LU2 9PF

McCALL, Christopher Hugh; QC (1987); yr s of late Robin Home McCall, CBE, and late Joan Elizabeth, *née* Kingdon; *b* 3 March 1944; *Educ* Winchester, Magdalen Coll Oxford (BA); *m* 20 June 1981, Henrietta Francesca, 2 da of late Adrian Lesley Sharpe, of Trebetherick, Cornwall; *Career* called to the Bar Lincoln's Inn 1966 (bencher 1993); second jr counsel to Inland Revenue in chancery matters 1977–87, jr counsel to HM Attorney-Gen in charity matters 1981–87; tstee Br Museum 1999–2004; Lifetime Achievement Award Soc of Trust and Estate Practitioners 2015; *Recreations* mountains, music, travel, Egyptomania; *Clubs* Leander, Alpine; *Style*— C H McCall, Esq, QC; ✉ Sphinx Hill, Ferry Lane, Moulsford on Thames, Oxfordshire OX10 9JF (☎ 01491 652162); Maitland Chambers, 7 Stone Buildings, Lincoln's Inn, London WC2A 3SZ (☎ 020 7406 1200, e-mail cmccall@maitlandchambers.com)

McCALL, David Slesser; CBE (1988), DL (Norfolk 1992); s of Patrick McCall (d 1987), of Aberdeen, and Florence Kate Mary, *née* Walker (d 2002); *b* 3 December 1934; *Educ* Robert Gordon's Coll Aberdeen, Univ of Aberdeen; *m* 6 July 1968, (Lois) Patricia, da of Ernest Lonsdale Elder (d 1985), of Glasgow; *Career* CA 1958; Nat Serv RAF 1959–60; accountant Grampian TV Ltd 1961–68; Anglia Television: co sec 1968–76, dir 1970–2001, chief exec 1976–94, chm 1994–2001; chm: TSMS Ltd (airtime sales co) 1994–96, Greene King plc 1995–2005, 99.9 Radio Norwich (formerly Crown FM) 2005–13; fndr dir Channel 4 Television Co Ltd 1981–85; dir: British Satellite Broadcasting Ltd 1987–90, Independent Television News Ltd 1991–96, Hodder & Stoughton 1992–93, Cosgrove Hall Films Ltd 1993–96, Village Roadshow Ltd (Australia) 1994–96, Satellite Information Services 1994–96, United Broadcasting and Entertainment (formerly MAI Media UK Ltd) 1994–96, MAI plc 1994–96, Bernard Matthews plc 1996–2000, Anglo-Welsh Gp plc 1996–2000, Bakers Dozen Inns Ltd 1996–2006, Bernard Matthews Holdings Ltd 2002–13 (chm 2010); chm: ITV Assoc 1986–88, United Tstees Ltd 1997–, United Executive Tstees Ltd 1998–; hon vice-pres Norwich City FC 1988–93, dir Eastern Advsy Bd National Westminster Bank 1988–91, pres Norfolk and Norwich C of C 1988–90 (vice-pres 1984, dep pres 1986); chm: Norwich Playhouse 1992–98, The Forum Tst Ltd (formerly Norfolk and Norwich Millennium Bid Ltd) 1996–2005; UEA: treas 1995–97, chm Cncl 1997–2006; tstee CTBF 1995–2016 (pres 1998); RTS: fell 1988, vice-pres 1992–99, hon pres E Anglia Centre 1993; Hon DCL UEA 2005; MICAS 1958, CIMgt 1988, FRSA 1993; *Recreations* golf, tennis, skiing, soccer, travel; *Clubs* Garrick; *Style*— David McCall, Esq, CBE, DL, DCL; ✉ Woodland Hall, Redenhall, Harleston, Norfolk IP20 9QW (☎ 01379 854442)

McCALL, Davina; *b* 16 October 1967; *m* Matthew Robertson; 2 da, 1 s; *Career* TV personality, presenter and actress; formerly singer, booker Models One, restaurant mangr and singing waitress Paris; *Television* credits incl: Don't Try This At Home (3 series, ITV), Street Mate (Channel 4), Brit Awards 2000 (LWT), The British Fashion Awards (BBC), Big Brother (8 series, Channel 4), Oblivious (ITV), Closure (BBC), Comic Relief (BBC), The Vault (ITV), Popstars: The Rivals (ITV), Sam's Game (ITV), Brit Awards (ITV1), Reborn in the USA (ITV1), Love on a Saturday Night (ITV1), Davina (BBC), The BAFTAs (ITV1), Sports Relief (BBC1), Let's Talk Sex (Channel 4), Dead Set (E4), Got To Dance (Sky 1), Long Lost Family (ITV), The Million Pound Drop (Channel 4), Biggest Loser (ITV), Stepping Out (ITV1); *Style*— Ms Davina McCall; ✉ c/o James Grant Media Ltd, 94 Strand on the Green, Chiswick, London W4 3NN (☎ 020 8742 4950, fax 020 8742 4951)

McCALL SMITH, Prof Alexander; CBE (2007); *b* 24 August 1948; *Career* emeritus prof of med law Univ of Edinburgh and author; former vice-chm Human Genetics Cmmn; Author of the Year British Book Awards 2004, Author of the Year Booksellers Assoc 2004, Bollinger Everyman Wodehouse Prize for Comic Fiction 2015; Presidential Order of Meritorious Service (Botswana) 2010; *Legal Books* Law and Medical Ethics (1984), Butterworths Medico Legal Encyclopaedia (1987), The Criminal Law of Botswana (1992), Scots Criminal Law (1992), The Duty to Rescue (1994), Introduzione allo Studio del Diritto Penale Scozzese (1995), Forensic Aspects of Sleep (1996), Justice and the Prosecution of Old Crimes (2001), Errors, Medicine and the Law (2001); *Adult Fiction* Children of Wax (1989), Heavenly Date (1995), Lions and Anthropologists (1996), Portuguese Irregular Verbs (1997), The No 1 Ladies' Detective Agency (1998), Tears of the Giraffe (2000), Morality for Beautiful Girls (2001), The Kalahari Typing School for Men (2002), The Full Cupboard of Life (2003), The Sunday Philosophy Club (2004), In the Company of Cheerful Ladies (2004), 44, Scotland Street (2004), Espresso Tales (2005), Friends, Lovers, Chocolate (2005), Blue Shoes & Happiness (2006), Dream Angus (2006), The Right Attitude to Rain (2006), Love over Scotland (2006), The Good Husband of Zebra Drive (2006), The World According to Bertie (2006), The Careful Use of Compliments (2006), The Miracle at Speedy Motors (2008), La's Orchestra Saves The World (2008), The Comfort of Saturdays (2008), Corduroy Mansions (2009), The Lost Art of Gratitude (2009), Tea Time for the Traditionally Built (2009), The Double Comfort Safari Club (2010), The Dog Who Came In From The Cold (2010), The Importance of Being Seven (2010), The Charming Quirks of Others (2010), The Saturday Big Tent Wedding Party (2011), A Conspiracy of Friends (2011), The Forgotten Affairs of Youth (2011), Bertie Plays The Blues (2011), The Limpopo Academy of Private Detection (2012), The Uncommon Appeal of Clouds (2012), Sunshine on Scotland Street (2012), The Minor Adjustment Beauty Salon (2013), What W H Auden Can Do For You (2013), The Handsome Man's De Luxe Café (2014), Emma: A Modern Retelling (2014), A Work of Beauty (2014), The Novel Habits of Happiness (2015), The Woman Who Walked in Sunshine (2015), The Revolving Door of Life (2015), Chance Developments (2015); *Books for Children* incl: The Bubblegum Tree (2005), The Popcorn Pirates (2005), The Doughnut Ring (2005), The Spaghetti Tangle (2005), The Muscle Machine (2006), Teacher Trouble (2006), The Chocolate Money Mystery (2006), The Bursting Balloons Mystery (2006), The Joke Machine (2006), The Banana Machine (2006), Calculator Annie (2006), The Five Lost Aunts of Harriet Bean (2006), Precious and the Puggies (2010), Precious and the Monkeys (2011), Precious and the Mystery of Meerkat Hill (2012), Precious and the Zebra Necklace (2015), School Ship Tobermory (2015), Freddie Mole Lion Tamer (2016); *Clubs* Scottish Arts, New; *Style*— Prof Alexander McCall Smith, CBE; ✉ c/o David Higham Associates, 7th Floor, Waverley House, 7–12 Noel Street, London W1F 8GQ (☎ 020 7434 5900)

McCALLIN, Tanya Carel Pitcairn; da of Clement McCallin (d 1978), and Philippa, *née* Gurney; *b* 4 December 1949, Cambridge; *Educ* Univ HS Melbourne Aust, Central St Martins Sch of Art and Design; *m* 1986, Michael Blakemore, *qv*, s of Conrad Blakemore; 2 da (Beatie b 20 Aug 1981, Clemmie b 25 Nov 1984); *Career* designer; lectr and examiner in stage design, exhibitions in Manchester, London and Prague; memb: Equity, Soc of Brit Theatre Designers; FRSA; *Theatre* Hampstead Theatre London: Ancient Lights, Dusa, Fish, Stars and Vi (also West End, Paris and NY), Abigail's Party (also BBC); West End: Bodies, Exchange, Uncle Vanya, Ride Down Mount Morgan; NT: The Elephant Man, Who's Afraid of Virginia Woolf?, After the Fall; My Mother Said (Royal Court), Regent's Park Theatre London: Hamlet, Richard II; other credits incl: Fool for Love (Donmar Warehouse London), The Recruiting Officer (Chichester Festival Theatre); *Opera* ENO: The Barber of Seville (also Barcelona), Manon (also Dallas USA and NZ); Macbeth (Mariinski-Kirov Co, St Petersburg, Met and London), Rigoletto (ROH), Der Rosenkvalier (Scot Opera), Les Contes d'Hoffmann (Salzburg Festival Opera), Cosi fan Tutte (Opera Nat du Rhin), Le Nozze di Figaro (ROH), Semele (Theatre des Champs Elysees), Carmen (ROH, Astralian Opera), Manon (Liceu Barcelona and Chicago), The Turn of the Screw (St Petersburg and ENO), Manon (Valencia), Der Rosen Kavalier (ENO), La Traviata (Scottish Opera, Welsh Nat Opera, Grand Theatre Geneva, Liceu Barcelona, Teatre Real Madrid), Sweeney Todd (Theatre du Chatelet, Houston Grand Opera & San Francisco Grand Opera), La Traviata (Bolshoi Opera); *Recreations* fine arts, theatre, film, opera, travel, ceramics; *Style*— Ms Tanya McCallin, FRSA; ✉ Sam Lambourne, Performing Arts, 6 Windmill Street, London W1P 1HF (☎ 020 7255 1362, fax 020 7631 4631, e-mail richard@performing-arts.co.uk)

McCALLION, John; s of Robert Bernard McCallion, of London, and Patricia, *née* Furnston-Evans; *b* 4 November 1957; *Educ* Stanway Sch Colchester, Colchester Inst of Technol (HND Business and Mgmnt), Univ of Westminster (Postgrad Dip Mktg); *m* Kerry Jane; 1 s (James Elliot), 1 da (Harriet Laura); *Career* grad commercial mangr/buyer Marks & Spencer plc (Head Office) 1981–88, commercial mangr Texas Homecare plc 1988–90, sr mktg mangr Pizza Hut (UK) Ltd 1990–93, mktg dir Great Western Trains Co 1993–98, chief exec Merlin Investments Ltd 1998–2007, md Groundscope 2007–; memb: Mktg Soc, London Entrepreneurial Exchange, Pi Capital; Mentor of the Year Westminster Business Sch 2015; MCIM, MIDM; *Recreations* keeping fit, skiing, travel, private equity, golf; *Style*— John McCallion, Esq; ✉ Waterside House, 27 Wethered

M

Park, Pound Lane, Marlow, Buckinghamshire SL7 2BH (☎ 01628 478430, e-mail john.mccallion@btinternet.com); Groundscope, Birch House, Fairview Avenue, Staines upon Thames TW18 4AB (☎ 0845 680 4279, mobile 07970 164859, e-mail jmccallion@groundscope.co.uk)

McCALLISTER, John; MLA; *b* 20 February 1972; *m* Jane; 1 da (Molly), 1 s (Harry); *Career* MLA (UUP then Ind) S Down 2007–, dep ldr UUP 2010–13, UUP chief whip 2011–13, dep ldr NI21 2013–; *Clubs* Young Farmers' Clubs of Ulster (pres 2003–05); *Style*— John McCallister, Esq, MLA; ✉ 29a Central Promenade, Newcastle BT33 0AA (☎ 02843 727085); Northern Ireland Assembly, Parliament Buildings, Belfast BT4 3XX (e-mail john.mccallister@mla.niassembly.gov.uk)

McCANN, Christopher Conor; s of Noel McCann, and Katharine Joan, *née* Sultzberger; *b* 26 June 1947; *Educ* Downside, Clare Coll Cambridge (MA); *m* 1 June 1974, Merlyn Clare Winbolt, da of Dr Francis Lewis, of Bristol; 1 s (Edward), 2 da (Kate, Eleanor); *Career* Price Waterhouse and Co 1969–73, Barclays Merchant Bank 1973–82, sr vice-pres Barclays Bank plc NY 1983–87, vice-chm Bridgepoint Capital Ltd 1987–2002; chm: Numerica Gp plc 2001–05; non-exec dir Downing Protected VCTs; FCA 1972, ACIB 1978; *Recreations* skiing, sailing, travel, country pursuits; *Clubs* Carlton, Parkstone Yacht; *Style*— Christopher McCann, Esq; ✉ 10 Lonsdale Square, London N1 1EN (e-mail christopher.mccann@btinternet.com)

McCANN, Prof Hugh; s of Daniel McCann (d 1989), and Helen, *née* Mathieson; *b* 5 August 1954; *Educ* St Joseph's Acad Kilmarnock, Univ of Glasgow (BSc, PhD); *m* 23 July 1977, Margaret Frances, *née* McCulloch; 1 da (Louise b 27 July 1979), 2 s (Michael b 9 March 1982, Paul b 20 March 1987); *Career* researcher HEP Physics Deutsches Elektronen Synchrotron Hamburg 1979–83 and Victoria Univ of Manchester 1984–86, sr scientist Royal Dutch/Shell Gp, Thornton Res Centre 1986–96, prof of industrial tomography Univ of Manchester (formerly UMIST) 1996–2013 (head Dept of Electrical Engrg and Electronics 1999–2002, assoc dean (research) Faculty of Engineering and Physical Sciences 2010–13), prof of tomographic imaging and head Sch of Engrg Univ of Edinburgh 2013–; chm Virtual Centre for Industrial Process Tomography 2005–09; chm Ctee of UK Profs and Heads of Electrical Engrg 2003–05 (memb Ctee 2002–07); memb Ctee: Engrg Professors' Cncl 2003–05, EPSRC Peer Review Coll 2003–; external examiner electronic and electrical engrg Univ of Leeds 2004–07 and Imperial Coll London 2009–13; chm Strategic Advsy Team Capital and Equipment EPSRC 2014–; Arch T Colwell Merit Award Soc of Automotive Engrs 1994, Special Prize Euro Physical Soc 1995, Maurice Beck Prize World Cong Industrial Process Tomography 2007; chm IET Sch Ctee 2005–09 (memb 2002–10); parishoner St Vincent de Paul RC Church Bramhall; memb Lab Pty; MInstP 1987, CPhys 1987, FIEE 2000, CEng 2001, FREng 2009, FRSE 2013; *Publications* 106 jl pubns in sci and engrg, and many conf papers; *Recreations* theatre, listening to a range of music, golf; *Style*— Prof Hugh McCann

McCANN, Michael; s of Charles McCann (d 2002), and Bridget, *née* McGuigan; *b* 2 January 1964, Glasgow; *Educ* St Andrews RC HS; *m* 25 Feb 1989, Tracy Anne, *née* Thomson; 1 s (Jordan b 26 Dec 1991), 1 da (Erin b 11 Oct 1994); *Career* civil servant Overseas Devpt Admin 1982–92, sr full time official PCS Trade Union 1992–2008; cncllr S Lanarkshire Cncl 1999–2010, MP (Lab) E Kilbride, Strathaven and Lesmahagow 2010–15; *Recreations* golf, music; *Style*— Michael McCann, Esq; ✉ Constituency Office, Civic Centre, Andrew Street, East Kilbride G14 1AB (☎ and fax 01355 239642, website www.michaelmccann.org.uk), House of Commons, London SW1A 0AA (e-mail michael.mccann.mp@parliament.uk)

McCANNY, Prof John Vincent; CBE (2002); s of Patrick Joseph McCanny, of Ballymoney, Co Antrim, and Kathleen Brigid, *née* Kerr; *b* 25 June 1952, Ballymoney, Co Antrim; *Educ* Dalriada GS Ballymoney, Univ of Manchester (BSc), Univ of Ulster (PhD), Queen's Univ Belfast (DSc); *m* 7 July 1979, Mary Bernadette (Maureen); 1 s (Damian Patrick b 28 June 1983), 1 da (Kathryn Louise b 4 Feb 1986); *Career* lectr in physics Univ of Ulster 1977–78 (postdoctoral research fell Physics Dept 1978–79); Royal Signals and Radar Estab (RSRE): higher scientific offr 1979–82, sr scientific offr 1982–84, princ scientific offr 1984; Queen's Univ Belfast: IT research lectr Dept of Electrical & Electronic Engrg 1984–87, reader 1987–88, prof of microelectronics engrg 1988–, dir Inst of Electronics, Communications and IT 2000–, head Sch of Electronics, Electrical Engrg and Computer Science 2005–10, princ investigator Centre for Secure Information Technol (CSIT); dir Inst of Advanced Microelectronics in Ireland 1989–92, co-fndr and dir Audio Processing Technology Ltd 1989–96, co-fndr and tech dir Amplicon Semiconductor Ltd 1990–2004, non-exec dir Investment Belfast Ltd 1997–2002, non-exec dir Titan IC Systems Ltd 2009–; chm IEEE Signal Processing Soc Technical Ctee on the design and implementation of Signal Processing Systems 1999–2001; memb: IEEE Signal Processing Tech Directions Ctee 1999–2001, Royal Acad of Engrg Standing Ctee for Engrg 2001–04, Royal Soc Ctee on the future of HE in the UK 2003, Royal Soc Research Fellowships Panel A(ii) Chemistry and Engrg 2003–06, Royal Soc Sectional Ctee 4 2011–14 (chair 2005–06), Bd Ireland's Nat Tyndall Inst 2004–11, Sub-Panel 24 Electrical and Electronics Engrg UK HEFCE Research Assessment Exercise 2005–08, EPSRC ICT Strategic Advsy Team 2006–11, Int Advsy Bd German Excellence Initiative Centre for Ultra High Speed Mobile Inf and Communication Univ of Aachen 2007–12, Sub-Panel 13 Electrical and Electronics Engrg HEFCE Research Excellence Framework 2008–14, Int Ctee Royal Acad of Engrg 2009–13, Hooke Ctee Royal Soc 2010–13, Royal Soc Computing in Schs project 2010–11, UK Technol Strategy Bd Emerging Technologies and Industries Gp 2010–, UK Cyber Growth Partnership 2013–, Dowling Review on more effective collaborations between businesses and university researchers in the UK Royal Acad of Engrg 2015, ctee that produced Investing in Innovation Report Royal Acad of Engrg 2015, Assessment Panel US/Ireland Research Innovation Awards 2015–; chair Policy Ctee on Cybersecurity Research Royal Soc 2013–16 (policy report due to be published 2016); memb Cncl/tstee Royal Acad of Engrg 2008–11, memb Cncl Royal Irish Acad 2013–14; Royal Acad of Engrg Silver Medal (for outstanding and demonstrated personal contrib to Br Engrg leading to market exploitation) 1996, IEEE Millennium Medal for valued services and outstanding contributions 2000, Royal Dublin Soc/Irish Times Boyle Medal 2003, Br Computer Soc (Belfast Branch) IT Professional of the Year 2004, Faraday Medal Instn of Engrg and Technol 2006, Royal Irish Acad Cunningham Medal 2011, Queen's Anniversary Prize Centre for Secure Information Technol (CSIT) Queen's Univ Belfast 2015; CPhys 1982, CEng 1985, FIET 1992 (MIET 1985), FInstP 1992 (MInstP 1982), FREng 1995, FRSA 1996, FIEEE 1999 (MIEEE 1988, Sr MIEEE 1995), MRIA 2000, FRS 2002, FIEI 2006, FIAE 2006; *Publications* VLSI Technology and Design (jtly, 1987), Systolic Array Processors (jtly, 1989), VLSI Systems for DSP (jtly, 1991), Signal Processing Systems – Design and Implementation (jtly, 1997), System-on-Chip Architectures and Implementation for Private Key Data Encryption (jtly, 2003); 360 published tech papers in books, int jls and conf proceedings; 25 patents; *Recreations* golf, swimming, tennis, supporting Manchester United FC, supporting Ireland and Ulster rugby teams, watching sports (soccer, golf, rugby, cricket), listening to music, photography; *Clubs* Clandeboye Golf; *Style*— Prof John McCanny, CBE, FRS, FREng; ✉ The Institute of Electronics, Communications and Information Technology, Queen's University Belfast, Nothern Ireland Science Park, Queen's Road, Queen's Island, Belfast BT3 9DT (☎ 028 9097 1800, fax 028 9097 1802, e-mail j.mccanny@ecit.qub.ac.uk)

McCARTAN, Prof Eamonn Gerard; s of John McCartan (d 1978), of Belfast, and Margaret, *née* Barrett; *b* 23 January 1953; *Educ* St Joseph's Teacher Trg Coll Belfast (BEd), Queen's Univ Belfast (Dip Advanced Study in Educn) Univ of Ulster (Dip Mgmnt Studies), MBA; *m* 27 Dec 1976, Marian Francis, da of Patrick McFadden; 1 s (Kieran); *Career* PE teacher: St Mary's GS Belfast 1976–78, Sydney 1978–79, Christian Bros Secdy Sch Belfast 1979–80, St Mary's GS Belfast 1980–81; asst mangr Andersonstown Leisure Centre Belfast 1981–83, PA to asst dir of Leisure Servs Belfast CC 1983–84, asst dir of PE Queen's Univ Belfast 1984–94, chief exec Sports Cncl for NI 1994–; visiting prof Sch of Leisure and Tourism Univ of Ulster; dir: Chest Heart and Stroke Assoc, Odyssey Tst Co; chair Community Relations Cncl; memb Bd: Co-Operation Ireland, Odyssey Co; Hon DUniv Ulster; MCIM 1991, MIPD 1991; *Recreations* golf, basketball, gardening, current/political affairs; *Clubs* Malone Golf; *Style*— Prof Eamonn McCartan; ✉ Sport Northern Ireland, House of Sport, Upper Malone Road, Belfast BT9 5LA (☎ 028 9038 1222, fax 028 9068 2757, mobile 07860 331475)

McCARTER, Keith Ian; s of Maj Peter McCarter (d 1971), of Edinburgh, and Hilda Mary, *née* Gates (d 1996); *b* 15 March 1936; *Educ* The Royal HS of Edinburgh, Edinburgh Coll of Art (DA); *m* 5 Jan 1963, Brenda Maude Edith, da of James A Schofield (d 1974), of Langley, Bucks; 1 da (Alix-Jane b 1966), 1 s (Andrew Keith b 1968); *Career* Nat Serv RA 1954–56; sculptor; primarily involved in architectural and landscaped situations; numerous cmmns incl: Ordnance Survey HQ Southampton 1967, Lagos Nigeria 1974, Wingate Centre City of London 1980, Goodmans Yard City of London 1982, 1020 19th Street Washington DC 1983, American Express Bank City of London 1984, Guy's Hosp NCC London 1986, Royal Exec Park NY 1986, Evelyn Gardens London 1987, London Docklands 1988, Midland Bank London 1989, Vogans Mill London 1989, Moody Gardens Galveston Texas USA (with Sir Geoffrey Jellicoe), Abbey Rd London 1991, Monks Cross York 1992, John Menzies HQ Edinburgh 1995, Aldermanbury Bradford 1998, F I Gp Edinburgh 1999, Monks Cross York 2001, Univ Hosp Norwich 2001, Forth Quarter Devpt Edinburgh 2004, Riverside Devpt Greenock 2009; works in private collections world-wide; Sir Otto Beit medal RBS 1993; FRSA 1970, ARBS 1991; *Recreations* music, literature, beachcombing; *Clubs* Melrose RFC; *Style*— Keith McCarter, Esq; ✉ 10 Coopersknowe Crescent, Galashiels, Selkirkshire TD1 2DS (☎ 01896 751112, fax 01896 759010, e-mail keith@keith-mccarter.com, website www.keith-mccarter.com)

McCARTHY, Arlene; OBE (2015), MEP (Lab) North West England; da of John Joseph McCarthy, of Belfast, and June Florence McCarthy; *b* 10 October 1960; *Educ* The Friends' GS Lisburn, South Bank Poly (BA), Stuttgart Univ, Université de Clermont Ferrand, UMIST; *Career* researcher and press offr to ldr European Parly Lab Pty 1990–91; Freie Universität Berlin: lectr, DAAD scholar, guest res fell 1991–92; head of European affairs Kirklees MBC 1992–94; MEP (Lab): Peak District 1994–99, NW England 1999–; chair Internal Market and Consumer Protection Ctee 2006–09, vice-chair Economic and Monetary Affair Ctee 2009–, memb Delegation for Relations with SINEEA JPC, sub memb Delegation to the EU-Turkey JPC; fell Industry and Parl Tst 2005–06, grad Police Serv Parly Scheme (with Gtr Manchester Police) 2006; *Publications* Changing States (jt ed, 1996), The Socialist Way (contrib, 2013); *Recreations* swimming, dancing, travel, foreign languages and music, hill walking; *Style*— Arlene McCarthy, OBE, MEP; ✉ Express Networks, 1 George Leigh Street, Manchester M4 5DL (☎ 0161 906 0801, fax 0161 906 0802, e-mail arlene.mccarthy@easynet.co.uk)

McCARTHY, David; s of late John Francis McCarthy, and late Ivy Eileen, *née* Davies; *b* 27 January 1942; *Educ* Ratcliffe Coll, Univ of Birmingham (LLB); *m* 1, Rosemary Ruth, *née* Norman; 2 s (Gavin Stephen b 19 Feb 1972, Nicholas James b 17 May 1974); m 2, Judith Spencer, *née* Chester; *Career* slr; articled with Wragge & Co Birmingham, ptnr Clifford Chance (formerly Coward Chance) 1978–94 (joined 1976); conslt: Banco Ambrosiano Veneto SpA, Clifford Chance, Chiomenti Studio Legale, Banca Intesa SpA, Banca Nazionale del Lavoro, Banca di Roma SpA, Banca Popolare di Milano, Caboto Holding SIM SpA and other instns; *Recreations* fly fishing, cricket, history; *Clubs* Richmond Cricket, Loch Achonachie Angling, Ferrari Owners'; *Style*— David McCarthy, Esq; ✉ Inishbeg, Cavendish Road, St George's Hill, Weybridge, Surrey KT13 0JX

McCARTHY, Declan James John; s of Christopher Noel McCarthy, and Catherine Bernadette Temple, *née* Kinsella; *b* 11 February 1969, Oxford; *Educ* Wheatley Park Sch, Oxford Coll of FE (HND); *m* 3 Sept 2005, Jeanette, *née* Nunn; 2 da (Libby b 5 Sept 1997, Georgia b 11 Dec 2003), 1 s (Laurie b 29 June 2000); *Career* Ashmolean Museum: publishing asst 1989–97, mktg mangr 1997–2002, publishing mangr 2002–06, commercial mangr 2007–; sec, ed and memb Ctee Assoc for Cultural Enterprise, memb Museums Assoc 1991, memb Assoc for Cultural Enterprise (ACE) 2001; *Style*— Declan McCarthy, Esq; ✉ Publishing Department, Ashmolean Museum, Beaumont Street, Oxford OX1 2PH (☎ 01865 288070, fax 01865 278106, e-mail dec.mccarthy@ashmus.ox.ac.uk)

MacCARTHY, Fiona; OBE (2009); da of Lt-Col Gerald MacCarthy (d 1943), and Yolande, *née* de Belabre; *b* 23 January 1940; *Educ* Wycombe Abbey, Univ of Oxford (MA); *m* 19 Aug 1966, David Mellor, CBE (d 2009), s of Colin Mellor (d 1970); 1 s (Corin b 1966), 1 da (Clare b 1970); *Career* design corr The Guardian 1961–69, women's ed Evening Standard 1969–71, critic The Times 1981–92, The Observer 1992–99; RSA Bicentenary Medal 1987, Wolfson History Prize 1994, James Tait Black Biography Prize 2012; Hon DLitt Univ of Sheffield 1996, Hon Dr Sheffield Hallam Univ 2001; sr fell RCA 1997 (hon fell 1989); hon fell Lady Margaret Hall Oxford 2007, hon FRIBA 2012; FRSL 1997; *Books* All Things Bright and Beautiful (1972), The Simple Life: C R Ashbee in the Cotswolds (1981), British Design since 1880 (1982), Eric Gill (1989), William Morris: a Life for our Time (1994), Stanley Spencer, An English Vision (1997), Byron: Life and Legend (2002), Last Curtsey: The End of the Debutantes (2006), The Last Pre-Raphaelite: Edward Burne-Jones and the Victorian Imagination (2011), Anarchy and Beauty, William Morris and his Legacy 1860–1960 (2014); *Style*— Ms Fiona MacCarthy, OBE, FRSL; ✉ The Round Building, Hathersage, Sheffield S32 1BA (☎ 01433 650220, fax 01433 650944, e-mail fionamaccarthy@davidmellordesign.co.uk)

McCARTHY, Kerry; MP; *b* 26 March 1965; *Educ* Univ of Liverpool, City of London Poly, Goldsmiths Coll London; *Career* slr, political conslt; former Luton cncllr, legal advisor to Lab during 2001 election campaign; MP (Lab) Bristol E 2005–, shadow sec of state for environment, food and rural affairs 2015–; vice-chair Lab E of England Regnl Bd; memb: Lab Nat Policy Forum, Lab Economic Policy Cmmn, Unite, Howard League for Penal Reform; *Style*— Ms Kerry McCarthy, MP; ✉ House of Commons, London SW1A 0AA

McCARTHY, Rosalind Judith; DL (Kent 2009); da of Rev Cyril James Wilson, and Helen Frances, *née* Horton; *Educ* Folkestone Girls' GS, Univ of Leeds (BA); *Family* 1 s, 1 da; *Career* short term teaching posts: Priory Girls' Sch London 1965–66, Beaufoy Boys' Comp Sch London 1966–67, Lanfranc Secdy Sch Surrey 1966–67; teacher rising to head of dept Mungwi Secdy Sch for Boys Kasama Zambia 1967–69, supply and pt/t teaching 1972–75, head of religious educn St Leonard's Girls' Sch Hythe 1975–78, head of humanities Brockhill and St Leonard's Sch Hythe 1978–83, head of religious studies and head of house Ashford Sch 1983–89, head Cobham Hall 1989–2003; memb Govt Advsy Gp on State/Ind Sch Partnerships 1997–98; Boarding Schs Assoc: memb NEC and Jt Trg Ctee 1992–95, area co-ordinator 1992–94, vice-chm 1995–96 and 1997–98, chm 1996–97; GSA: co-opted rep Nat Cncl 1993, boarding rep Nat Cncl 1993–96, memb Boarding Ctee 1994–96; memb: SE Region Ctee ISIS 1991–94, Exec Ctee Kent Branch representing Ind Schs SHA 1992–94, Int Cncl Round Square Schs 1992–94, Folkestone Choral Soc, Sandgate Soc, Duke of York's Royal Mil Sch Dukies' Fndn 2010–; govr St Mary's Westbrook Sch Folkestone 2003–06, chm of HM cmmrs Duke of York's Royal Mil Sch 2008–10 (cmmr 2004–08), govr Northbourne Park Sch 2012–15; managing tstee Leney Tst 1995–2002, tstee Folkestone Academy 2013–; friend: Stour Music Festival, Primavera Chamber Orch,

Folkestone Book Festival, Cobham Hall Heritage Tst; *Recreations* travel, music, theatre, the Arts, family and friends; *Style*— Mrs Rosalind McCarthy, DL; ✉ Ullyett Cottage, Old School Mews, Sandgate Hill, Folkestone, Kent CT20 3ST (☎ 01303 246122)

McCARTHY, Suzanne Joyce; da of Leo Rudnick (d 1966), and Lillian Thal (d 1998); *b* 21 November 1948, Utica, NY; *Educ* NYU (BA), Univ of Cambridge (LLM), Univ of E London (MSc); *m* 25 Aug 1990, Brendan McCarthy; *Career* slr in private practice 1977–85, lectr in law Univ of Manchester 1986–89, various sr Civil Service appts 1989–; chief exec: Human Fertilisation and Embryology Authy 1996–2000, Financial Services Compensation Scheme 2000–04; Immigration Servs Cmmr 2005–15; chm Gen Chiropractic Cncl 2013–16, chm DePaul UK 2015–; memb: Bd RIBA Hldgs 2003–14, Determinations Panel Pensions Regulator 2005–13, Conduct Ctee CIMA 2006–08, Public Guardian Bd 2007–12, Exec Cncl British and Irish Ombudsman Assoc 2008–12, GMC 2009–12, Human Tissue Authy 2010–16, UK and Ireland Regulatory Body RICS 2012–16, Advsy Bd LSE Centre for Analysis and Regulation 2014–, Senet Gp 2015–, ASA 2015–, DePaul Int 2015–, Architects Registration Bd 2016–, Ind Advsy Panel Coll of Policing 2016–, Gender Equality Advsy Gp City Univ; memb and chair Code of Standards Ctee Fundraising Regulator 2016–; hon chm European Forum of Deposit Insurers 2008–; non-exec dir: Royal Brompton and Harefield NHS Tst until 2006, RIBA Bd 2003–14; independent appointed person Gtr London Authy 2012–; memb Bd of Tstees Univ of London 2008–16; memb Soc of West End Theatres 2002 Dance Awards Panel (Lawrence Olivier Awards); Freeman City of London 2006, Liveryman Worshipful Co of Ironmongers 2008 (Yeoman 2006); memb Assoc of Chartered Certified Accountants (memb Disciplinary and Regulatory Cmmn 2011–); *Recreations* dance; *Clubs* Athenaeum; *Style*— Mrs Suzanne McCarthy

McCARTNEY, Gordon Arthur; s of Arthur McCartney (d 1987), and Hannah, *née* Seel; *b* 29 April 1937; *Educ* Grove Park GS Wrexham; *m* 1, 23 July 1960 (m dis 1987), Ceris Isobel Davies; 2 da (Heather Jane b 11 April 1963, Alison b 6 Dec 1965); m 2, 26 March 1988, Wendy Ann Vyvyan, da of Sidney Titman; *Career* admitted slr 1959, chief exec Delyn Borough Cncl Clwyd 1974–81, sec Assoc of DCs 1981–91, co sec Local Govt Int Bureau 1988–91; dir National Transport Tokens Ltd 1984–91, md Gordon McCartney Associates 1991–, dir Leisure England Ltd 1993–; memb: Cmmn on the Legislative Process Hansard, Soc for Parly Govt 1991–93, Britain in Europe Cncl 2000–03; chm Local Govt Gp for Europe 1997–2005 (hon sec 2006–11), hon sec European Movement Local Govt Section 2011–; hon fell Inst of Local Govt Studies Univ of Birmingham; *Recreations* music, cricket; *Clubs* MCC; *Style*— Gordon McCartney, Esq; ✉ 21 Challenger Quay, Falmouth TR11 3YL (☎ 07951 703992, e-mail gordonmc@waitrose.com)

McCARTNEY, Jason Alexander; MP; *b* 29 January 1968, Harrogate, N Yorks; *Educ* Lancaster Royal GS, RAF Coll Cranwell, Leeds Trinity UC; *Career* RAF offr 1988–97, journalist BBC and ITV 1997–2008, sr lectr Leeds Met Univ 2008–10; MP (Cons) Colne Valley 2010–; memb Defence and Security Ctee NATO Parly Assembly, memb Culture, Media and Sport Select Ctee, memb 1922 Exec Ctee; *Recreations* Huddersfield Town AFC, Yorks CCC, Huddersfield Giants Rugby League; *Clubs* RAF; *Style*— Jason McCartney, Esq, MP; ✉ Upperbridge House, 24 Huddersfield Road, Holmfirth HD9 2JS (☎ 01484 688364); House of Commons, London SW1A 0AA (e-mail jason.mccartney.mp@parliament.uk)

McCARTNEY, Joanne; AM; da of Donald McCartney, and Patricia Marilyn McCartney; *b* 12 December 1966, Kendal, Westmorland; *Educ* Univ of Warwick (LLB), Univ of Leicester (LLM); *Career* called to the Bar Inner Temple 1990; cncllr London Borough of Enfield 1998–2006; GLA: memb London Assembly (Lab) Enfield and Haringey 2004–, chair Police and Crime Ctee 2012–16, memb Transport Ctee, memb Economy Ctee; dep mayor of London 2016–; *Style*— Ms Joanne McCartney, AM; ✉ GLA, City Hall, The Queen's Walk, London SE1 2AA (☎ 020 7983 5524, e-mail joanne.mccartney@london.gov.uk)

McCARTNEY, Karl Ian; JP, MP; s of John McCartney, of Birkenhead, Merseyside, and Brenda, *née* Weir; *b* 25 October 1968, Birkenhead, Merseyside; *Educ* Birkenhead Sch, Neston HS Cheshire, Willink Sch Berkshire, St David's UC Lampeter (BA), Kingston Business Sch (MBA); *m* May 1999, Cordelia Pyne; 2 s; *Career* MP (Cons) Lincoln 2010–; campaign dir Sir Keith Park Meml Campaign 2007– (dep chm 2010–); *Recreations* football, rugby, cricket, snowboarding, croquet, classic cars, green laning, hill walking; *Style*— Karl McCartney, Esq, JP, MP; ✉ House of Commons, London SW1A 0AA (☎ 020 7219 7221, e-mail karl.mccartney.mp@parliament.uk)

McCARTNEY, Sir (James) Paul; kt (1997), MBE (1965); s of late James McCartney, of Allerton, Liverpool, and late Mary Patricia, *née* Mohin; *b* 18 June 1942; *Educ* Liverpool Inst; *m* 1, 1969, Linda Louise (d 1998), da of late Lee Eastman, of New York City; 3 da (Heather b 1962, Mary b 1969, Stella b 1971), 1 s (James b 1977); m 2, 2002 (m dis 2008), Heather Mills; 1 da (Beatrice Milly b 2003); m 3, 2011, Nancy Shevell; *Career* musician and composer; first group The Quarry Men 1957–59, Beatles formed 1960, first maj appearance Litherland Town Hall 1960, Please Please Me first Br No 1 1961, She Loves You cemented their success 1963, I Want to Hold Your Hand became the biggest selling Br single ever with worldwide sales of 15,000,000; other songs (with John Lennon) incl: Love Me Do, Can't Buy Me Love, I Saw Her Standing There, Eight Days A Week, All My Loving, Help!, Ticket To Ride, I Feel Fine, I'm A Loser, A Hard Day's Night, No Reply, I'll Follow The Sun, Yesterday, Eleanor Rigby, Yellow Submarine, All You Need Is Love, Lady Madonna, Hey Jude, We Can Work It Out, Day Tripper, From Me To You, Get Back, Paperback Writer, Hello Goodbye, Let It Be, The Long And Winding Road; Beatles albums: Please Please Me 1963, With The Beatles 1963, A Hard Day's Night 1964, Beatles For Sale 1964, Help! 1965, Rubber Soul 1965, Revolver 1966, Sgt Pepper's Lonely Hearts Club Band 1967, Magical Mystery Tour 1967, The Beatles (White Album) 1968, Yellow Submarine 1969, Abbey Road 1969, Let It Be 1970; Beatles films: A Hard Day's Night 1964, Help! 1965, Yellow Submarine 1968, Let It Be 1970; played live for last time together on roof of the Apple building London 1969; Beatles disbanded 1970; formed MPL group of cos, formed Wings 1971, returned to live work 1972, own TV special James Paul McCartney 1973, honoured by the Guinness Book of Records (Triple Superlative Award for sales of 100,000,000 albums 100,000,000 singles and as holder of 60 gold discs) making him the most successful popular music composer ever 1979, Wings disbanded 1981, performed at Bob Geldof's Live Aid concert 1985 and for The Prince's Trust concert 1986; tours incl: UK and Europe 1972–73, UK and Aust 1975, Europe and USA 1976, UK 1979, Europe, UK, Canada, USA and Brazil 1989–90, World tour 1993; albums incl: McCartney 1970, Ram 1971, Wildlife 1971, Red Rose Speedway 1973, Band On The Run 1973, Venus And Mars 1975, Wings At The Speed Of Sound 1976, Wings Over America 1976, McCartney II 1980, Tug Of War 1982, Pipes Of Peace 1983, Give My Regards To Broad Street 1984, Press To Play 1986, All The Best! 1987, CHOBA B CCCP 1988, Flowers In The Dirt 1989, Unplugged 1990, Tripping the Light 1992, Off the Ground 1993, Paul is Live 1993, Flaming Pie 1997, Driving Rain 2001, Driving USA Tour 2002, Back In The US Tour 2002, Driving Mexico Tour 2002, Driving Japan Tour 2002, Back in the World (Live) 2003, 04 Summer Tour 2004, US Tour 2005, 09 Summer Tour 2009, Good Evening Europe Tour 2009, Up and Coming Tour 2010, On The Run Tour 2011–12; Wings films: Rockshow 1981, Give My Regards To Broad Street 1984, Rupert And The Frog Song 1984 (won Best Animated Film BAFTA); film scores: The Family Way 1967, Live And Let Die (title song, Oscar nomination for Best Song) 1973, Twice In A Lifetime (title song) 1984, Vanilla Sky (title song, Oscar nomination for Best Song) 2001; singles with Ringo Starr and George Harrison: Free as a Bird 1995, Real Love 1996; winner numerous Grammy awards incl Lifetime Achievement award 1990; Ivor Novello awards: best ever selling UK single (Mull Of Kintyre) 1977, Int Achievement 1980, Int Hit of the Year (Ebony And Ivory) 1982, Outstanding Contrib to Music 1989; PRS special award for unique achievement in popular music, Outstanding Contribution Brit Award 2008, MTV Ultimate Legend Award 2008, Gershwin Prize 2010, Kennedy Center Honor 2010, Songwriters' Songwriter NME Award 2014; Freeman City of Liverpool 1984; Hon DUniv Sussex 1988, Hon DMus Yale Univ 2008; *Books* Paintings (2000), Blackbird Singing: Poems and Lyrics 1965–1999 (2001), Wingspan (2002), High in the Clouds (2005); *Style*— Sir Paul McCartney, MBE; ✉ c/o MPL Communications Ltd, 1 Soho Square, London W1V 6BQ

McCAUGHAN, Conor; *b* Ballycastle, C Antrim; *Educ* Univ of Edinburgh (LLB); *Career* formerly agent ICM, co-fndr (with Melanie Rockcliffe and Michael Duff) and agent TROIKA 2005– (clients incl David Morrissey, David Walliams, *qqv*, and Michael Fassbender); *Style*— Conor McCaughan, Esq; ✉ TROIKA, 3rd Floor, 74 Clerkenwell Road, London EC1M 5QA

McCAUGHAN, Prof Daniel Vincent; OBE (1993); s of Vincent McCaughan (d 1984), and Elizabeth (Bessie, d 1974); *b* 1942, NI; *Educ* St Mary's GS Belfast, Queen's Univ Belfast (Sullivan and Lappin scholar, BSc, PhD, DSc); *m* Aug 1968, Anne Patricia, da of John Kinsella, and Mary Kinsella; 1 s (Gareth John b 1970); *Career* memb Tech Staff Bell Laboratories Inc NJ 1968–74, sr princ scientific offr RSRE Malvern 1974–81, asst dir GEC Hirst Res Centre Wembley 1981–86; tech dir: Marconi Electronic Devices Ltd and Electro-Optic Div EEV Ltd 1986–88, GEC Electronic Devices Ltd 1987–88; dir: NI Telecommunications Engrg Centre Northern Telecom (NI) Ltd 1988–93, External Affrs Nortel (NI) Ltd 1993–2000; chief scientist: Bell Northern Research 1995–96, Nortel Technology 1996–2000, Nortel Satellite Networks 1996–2000; pres and chief operating offr CDT Ltd 2000–01, managing ptnr McCaughan Associates 2001–, chief technol offr Trireme Systems NY 2002–08, chief technol advsr Kernel Capital Ptnrs Cork 2003– (ptnr 2011–), dir Chipsensors Ltd 2007–11, ptnr Kernel Capital NI 2013–; visiting prof, professorial fell and hon prof Queen's Univ Belfast 1982–, visiting prof UMIST 2002–; chm: Technol Bd for NI 1986–92, Bd Industrial Res and Technol Unit of Dept of Econ Devpt 1992–93, Tech Foresight Panel DTI 2001–02; co-chair (with Perm Sec) Home Office Science Advsy Ctee (HOSAC) 2006–09; memb Cncl Royal Acad of Engrg 1994–97, external bd memb DHSSPS(NI) 2006–10, pres NI Photographic Assoc 2010–12, memb Economic Strategy Ctee IOD; accredited sr imaging scientist 2009; FInstP 1975, CPhys 1975, SMIEEE 1990, FIET 1990, FInstD 1990, FREng 1992 (CEng 1990), FRAeS 1998, FIEI 1998, FIAcadE 2000, FRPS 2009; *Publications* tech chapters in numerous texts incl Handbook of Semiconductors; over 100 tech articles incl 20 patents; *Recreations* photography, antique glass, fungi, hiking, innovation; *Clubs* Physical Society; *Style*— Prof Daniel V McCaughan, OBE, FREng; ✉ Kernel Capital, Scottish Provident Building, 7 Donegal Square West, Belfast BT1 6JH (e-mail daniel.mccaughan@kernel-capital.com)

McCAUGHREAN, Geraldine Margaret; da of Leslie Arthur Jones (d 1980), and Ethel, *née* Thomas (d 2002); *b* 6 June 1951, Middx; *Educ* Enfield Co Sch for Girls, Christ Church Coll of Educn Canterbury (BEd); *m* 23 Nov 1988, John, s of William McCaughrean (d 1964), of Aughton, Lancs; 1 da (Ailsa b 12 Dec 1989); *Career* Thames Television Ltd 1970–77, Marshall Cavendish Partworks Ltd 1977–89 (sec, sub ed, staff writer); freelance writer 1989–; Br candidate Hans Christian Anderson Award 2004; hon fell Canterbury Christ Church Univ; memb Soc of Authors, fell English Assoc 2010; FRSL 2010; *Books* published in 59 other countries and 45 languages; incl: 1001 Arabian Nights (1982), The Canterbury Tales (1984), A Little Lower than the Angels (1987, Whitbread Children's Book of the Year, Katholischer Kindersbuchpreis Germany), A Pack of Lies (1988, Carnegie Medal, Guardian Children's Fiction Award), The Maypole (1989), St George and the Dragon (1989), El Cid (1989), The Story of Noah and the Ark (1989), My First Space Pop-Up Book (1989), My First Earth Pop-Up Book (1989), Fires' Astonishment (1990), Vainglory (1991), Greek Myths (1992), The Odyssey (1993), Gold Dust (1993, Beefeater/Whitbread Children's Book of the Year, shortlisted Smarties Book Award 1994), Stories from the Ballet (1994), Blue Moon Mountain (1994), Blue Moo (1994), Baabra Lamb (1994), Good Dog (1994), Gregorie Peck (1994), Stories from Shakespeare (1994), On the Day the World Began (1995), The Quest of Isis (1995), Wizziwig and the Singing Car (1995), Wizziwig and the Weather Machine (1995), Wizziwig and the Sweet Machine (1995), Wizziwig and the Crazy Cooker (1995), The Golden Hoard, Silver Treasure, Bronze Cauldron, Crystal Pool (1995–98), Cowboy Jess (1996), Cowboy Jess Saddles Up (1996), King Arthur and the Round Table (1996), Plundering Paradise (1996, Smarties Bronze Award, shortlisted Whitbread Children's Novel Award 1997), Lovesong (1996), Moby Dick (1996), God's People (1997), The Ideal Wife (1997), Princess Stories (1997), Forever X (1997, UKRA Award 1998, shortlisted Carnegie Medal 1998), Unicorns! Unicorns! (1997, shortlisted Kate Greenaway Prize 1998), Greek Gods and Goddesses (1997), Starry Tales (1998), Never Let Go! (1998), Casting the Gods Adrift (1998), Noah and Nelly (1998), Too Big! (1998), Hope on a Rope (1998), Aesop's Fables (1998), The Nutcracker (1999), The Hay Cart (1999), What Am I For? (1999), A Sheepless Night (1999), God's Kingdom (1999), The Stones are Hatching (1999), A Pilgrim's Progress (1999, Blue Peter Book of the Year), Roman Myths (1999), Britannia – 100 Stories from British History (1999, shortlisted Blue Peter Award (Facts Book) 2002), Beauty and the Beast (1999, shortlisted English 4–11 Award (picture books) 1999), Love and Friendship (2000), My First Book of Stories (2000), How the Reindeer Got Their Antlers (2000), Brave Magic (2000), The Great Chase (2000), Grandma Chicken-Legs (2000, shortlisted Blue Peter Award (Picture Book) 2002), The Kite Rider (2001, shortlisted Carnegie Medal 2001, Smarties Bronze Award 2002, Blue Peter Book to Keep Forever, shortlisted Angus Book Award 2002), Stop the Train (2001, Smarties Bronze Award, Highly Commended Carnegie Medal, shortlisted Stockton Children's Book of the Year 2003, shortlisted Nottingham Book Award 2003), Stories of Robin Hood (2001), Cat and Rat Fall Out (2001), My Grandmother's Clock (2002), Six Storey House (2002), Bright Penny (2002), Gilgamesh (2002), Showstopper! (2003), The Jesse Tree (2003, shortlisted Christian Children's Book Award 2004), Doctor Quack (2003, shortlisted Shorter Novel Portsmouth Book Award 2004), Dog Days (2003), Treasury of Fairy Tales (2003), Dancing the Night Away (2003), Hercules, Perseus, Odysseus, Theseus (2003), Jalopy (2003), The Questing Knights of the Faerie Queen (2004), Sky Ship (2004), Smile! (2004, Smarties Bronze Award 2004, shortlisted Shorter Novel Portsmouth Book Award 2005, shortlisted Braunston Children's Book Award 2005, shortlisted West Sussex Libraries Children's Book Award 2005), Not the End of the World (2004, Whitbread Children's Book of the Year 2004, shortlisted North East Book Award 2005), Fig's Giant (2005), Think Again (2005), Wenceslas (2005), The White Darkness (2005, shortlisted Whitbread Children's Book of the Year 2005, shortlisted Carnegie Medal 2005, shortlisted Calderdale Children's Book Award 2006, shortlisted LA Times Teenage Novel Award 2007, Michael L Printz Award for Teenage Novel (US) 2008), Peter Pan in Scarlet (2006, shortlisted Br Book Award 2006), Cyrano (2006), Father and Son (2006), Mo (2006, shortlisted Norfolk Shorts Award 2008), Noisy Neighbours (2006), The Nativity (2007), Tamburlaine's Elephants (2007, shortlisted UK Literacy Assoc Children's Book Award 2008), The Death Defying Pepper Roux (2009, shortlisted Carnegie Medal 2011), Pull Out All The Stops (2010), Monacello – The Little Monk (2011), Pittipat's Saucer of Moon (2012), Monacello – The Wish Bringer (2012), Go! Go! Chichico! (2013), The Positively Last Performance! (2013, shortlisted for UKLA Book Award), The Middle of Nowhere (2013, Young Adults Quills Historical Fiction Award 2014, Love Reading4Kids Book of the Year 2014, shortlisted Carnegie

M

Medal 2015, shortlisted Little Rebels Children's Book Award 2015, shortlisted Essex Book Award 2015, shortlisted Weald Library Award 2015); *Plays* Britannia on Stage (2000), Greeks on Stage (2002), Dazzling Medusa (Polka Theatre, 2005), Doctor Faustus (2006), Choose Me! (2013), The Escape (2013), Traffic Jam (2013), Three Mistakes and a Monster (2013), Tricked You! (2013), Seeing Things (performed in Warwickshire libraries, 2014); *Radio Play* Last Call (1991); *Recreations* theatre; *Style*— Ms Geraldine McCaughrean; ✉ c/o David Higham Associates, 7th Floor Waverley House, 7–13 Noel Street, London W1F 8GQ (✆ 020 7434 5900, fax 020 7437 1072, website www.geraldinemccaughrean.co.uk)

McCAUSLAND, Nelson; MLA; *b* 15 August 1951, Belfast; *Educ* Belfast Royal Acad, Worcester Coll Oxford, Queen's Univ Belfast; *m* 26 Oct 1974, Mary Elizabeth, *née* McWilliams; *Career* MLA (DUP) Belfast N 2003–; NI Assembly: min of culture, arts and leisure 2009–11, min for social devpt 2011–; *Style*— Nelson McCausland, Esq, MLA; ✉ Northern Ireland Assembly, Parliament Buildings, Belfast BT4 3XX

McCAVE, Prof (Ian) Nicholas; s of T T McCave (d 1941), and G M Langlois (d 1996); *b* 3 February 1941, Prestwick, Scotland; *Educ* Elizabeth Coll Guernsey, Hertford Coll Oxford (MA, DSc), Brown Univ Providence RI (Fulbright Scholar, PhD); *m* 3 April 1972, Susan Caroline Adams, da of G de P Bambridge; 3 s (Thomas b 1973, Robert b 1975, Geoffrey b 1978), 1 da (Elise b 1981); *Career* NATO res fell Netherlands Inst voor Onderzoek der Zee 1967–69, reader Sch of Environmental Sci UEA 1976–84 (lectr 1969–76), adjunct scientist Woods Hole Oceanographic Institution 1978–87, Woodwardian prof of geology Univ of Cambridge 1985–2008 (emeritus prof 2008–), head Earth Sciences Dept Univ of Cambridge 1988–98; fell St John's Coll Cambridge 1986–; pres Scientific Ctee on Oceanic Res of the Int Cncl of Science Unions 1992–96; Shepard Medal for Marine Geology US Soc for Sedimentary Geology 1995, Huntsman Medal for Oceanography Canada 1999, Leverhulme emeritus fell 2008–10, Lyell Medal Geological Soc London 2009; FGS 1963; *Books* The Benthic Boundary Layer (ed, 1976); *Style*— Prof Nicholas McCave; ✉ Department of Earth Sciences, University of Cambridge, Downing Street, Cambridge (✆ 01223 333400)

McCAWLEY, Leon Francis; s of Bernard McCawley, and Marian, *née* Sherwood; *b* 12 July 1973; *Educ* Chetham's Sch of Music Manchester, Curtis Inst of Music Philadelphia; *m* 3 June 1996, Anna H Paik; *Career* pianist; appeared with: CBSO under Sir Simon Rattle, BBC Philharmonic, LPO, RPO, Philharmonia, RLPO, Royal Scottish Nat Orch, Ulster Orch, BBC National Orch of Wales, Hallé; int orchestra appearances incl: Cincinnati Symphony, Dallas Symphony, Minnesota Orch, Philadelphia Orch, Malaysian Philharmonic, Austrian Radio Orchestra, Vienna Symphony Orchestra, Adelaide Symphony, Vienna Chamber Orch, Prague Symphony Orch; festival appearances incl: Spoleto, Edinburgh Int Festival, Brighton Festival, Helsinki, Bath and Cheltenham; debut BBC Proms with Bournemouth Symphony Orch 1995; int recital appearances: Berlin Philharmonie, Zurich Tonhalle, Vienna Musikverein, Kennedy Center, Washington DC, Festival Radio France, Deutschland Radio Berlin; UK recitals at Wigmore Hall, Purcell Room and Queen Elizabeth Hall, London; *Recordings* Barber: Solo Piano Music 1997, Beethoven: Sonatas and Variations 2001, Schumann: Piano Music 2003, Hans Gál: Complete Piano Music 2005, Mozart: Complete Piano Sonatas 2006, Ronald Corp: Piano Concerto 2010, Chopin: Piano Music 2010, Barber: Piano Music 2011, Brahms: Piano Music 2012, Beethoven: Choral Fantasy 2012, Schumann: Piano Music 2014, Rachmaninov: Complete Preludes 2015; *Awards* winner piano section BBC Young Musician of the Year 1990, young soloist of the year LPO/Pioneer 1990, first prize Ninth Int Beethoven Piano Competition (Vienna) 1993, second prize Leeds Int Piano Competition 1993; *Clubs* Garrick; *Style*— Leon McCawley, Esq; ✉ websites www.ikonarts.com and www.leonmccawley.com

McCLARKIN, Emma; MEP; *b* 9 October 1978, Stroud, Glos; *Educ* Stroud Girls HS, Bournemouth Univ; *Career* press offr Cons Party's East Midlands MEPs; MEP (Cons) East Midlands 2009–; govt rels exec Rugby Football Union; *Style*— Ms Emma McClarkin, MEP

McCLARTY, David; MLA; s of Douglas McClarty, and Helen, *née* Watts; *b* 23 February 1951; *Educ* Coleraine Academical Inst, Magee Coll Londonderry; *Career* fire insurance underwriter 1973–84, insurance conslt 1984–98; elected to Coleraine BC 1989, 1993, 1997, 2001 and 2005; mayor of Coleraine 1993–95; MLA (UUP then Ind) E Londonderry 1998–; chm West Bann Devpt; chm Bd of Govrs Christie Memorial Sch, memb Bd of Govrs Coleraine Academical Inst; Freeman City of London 1994; *Recreations* sport, reading, music, amateur dramatics, theatre, memb Killowen Parish Church choir; *Clubs* Ballywillan Drama, Royal Artillery Assoc (hon life memb); *Style*— David McClarty, Esq, MLA; ✉ Northern Ireland Assembly, Parliament Buildings, Stormont Estate, Belfast BT4 3XX (✆ 028 9052 0310, fax 028 9052 0309); 22 Slievebanna, Coleraine, Co Londonderry BT51 3JG (mobile 07771 605617, e-mail david.mcclarty.eld@gmail.com)

McCLEAN, Prof (John) David; CBE (1994), Hon QC (1995); s of Maj Harold McClean (d 1983), of Prestbury, Cheshire, and Mabel, *née* Callow (d 1981); *b* 4 July 1939; *Educ* Queen Elizabeth GS Blackburn, Magdalen Coll Oxford (MA, BCL, DCL); *m* 10 Dec 1966, Pamela Ann, da of Leslie Arthur Loader (d 1959), of Yeovil, Somerset; 1 s (Michael b 1969), 1 da (Lydia b 1972); *Career* Univ of Sheffield: lectr 1961–68, sr lectr 1968–73, prof 1973–2004, pro-vice-chllr 1991–96, emeritus prof 2004–; visiting lectr Monash Univ 1968 (visiting prof 1978); lay vice-pres Sheffield Diocesan Synod 1982–94; memb: Gen Synod 1970–2005, Crown Appts Cmmn 1977–87; vice-chm House of Laity 1979–85 (chm 1985–95); chllr: Dio of Sheffield 1992–2014, Dio of Newcastle 1998–2009; bencher Gray's Inn 2001; Hon LittD Univ of Sheffield 2012; FBA 2003; *Books* Criminal Justice and the Treatment of Offenders (jtly, 1969), Legal Context of Social Work (1975, 2 edn 1980), Defendants in the Criminal Process (jtly, 1976), Shawcross and Beaumont on Air Law (jtly, 4 edn, 1977, gen ed 2001–), Dicey, Morris and Collins, the Conflict of Laws (contrib, 10 edn 1980, 11 edn 1987, 12 edn 1993, 13 edn 1999, 14 edn 2006, 15 edn 2012), Recognition of Family Judgments in the Commonwealth (1983), International Judicial Assistance (1992, renamed International Co-operation in Civil and Criminal Cases, 2 edn 2002, 3 edn 2012), Mithani, Directors' Disqualification (contrib, 1998), Chitty on Contracts (contrib ed, 28 edn 1999, 29 edn 2004, 30 edn 2008, 31 edn 2012, 32 edn 2015), Tolley's Insolvency Law (contrib, 1999), Morris, Conflict of Laws (5 edn 2000, 6 edn jtly 2005, 7 edn jtly 2009, 8 edn jtly 2012, 9 edn jtly 2016), Transnational Organized Crime (2007); *Recreations* detective fiction; *Style*— Prof David McClean, CBE, QC; ✉ e-mail j.d.mcclean@sheffield.ac.uk

McCLEARY, (William) Boyd; CMG (2010), CVO (2004); s of Robert McCleary (d 1983), and Eleanor Thomasina, *née* Weir (d 1985); *b* 30 March 1949, Belfast; *Educ* Royal Belfast Academical Instn (High Hyndman scholar), Queen's Univ Belfast (BA); *m* 1, 1977 (m dis 1999), Susan Elizabeth Williams; 2 da (Alice Elizabeth b 23 Jan 1983, Katherine Eleanor b 3 Sept 1985); *m* 2, 2000, Jeannette Ann, *née* Collier; 1 da (Emily Hong-Hoa b 25 July 2001); *Career* asst princ then dep princ Dept of Agriculture NI 1972–75, first sec Agriculture then Chancery Br Embassy Bonn 1975–80, Western European Dept FCO 1981–83, European Community Dept FCO 1983–85, first sec, head of Chancery and consul Br Embassy Seoul 1985–88, asst head Far Eastern Dept FCO 1988–89, dep head of mission and dir of trade Br Embassy Ankara, cnsllr economic and trade policy Br High Cmmn Ottawa 1993–97, head Estate Dept FCO 1997–2000, consul-general and DG for trade and investment Dusseldorf Germany, dir global rollout for Oracle ERP system FCO 2005–06, high cmmr to Malaysia 2006–10, govr Br Virgin Islands 2010–14, ptnr The Ambassador Partnership 2014–; lay memb Special Immigration Appeals Cmmn

2015–, memb Cncl UK Overseas Territories Forum 2015–; mediator 39 Essex Chambers 2015–; memb Bd of Tstees SE Asia Rainforest Research Partnership 2015–; Hon LLD 2010; *Recreations* spending time with family, tennis, walking, reading; *Clubs* Royal Overseas League; *Style*— Mr Boyd McCleary, CMG, CVO

McCLELLAND, James Adrian; s of Rev James McClelland, of London, and Rev Anne, *née* Whitaker; *b* 8 September 1963, Padiham, Lancs; *Educ* Univ of Wales (BA, MA); *m* 1990, Deborah Anne, *née* Littler; 1 da (Eleanor May b 4 July 1991), 1 s (James Alexander b 21 Feb 1993); *Career* fndr Sustain' Magazine 1998; dir of sustainability McClelland Media Ltd 2004–, sr conslt Chelgate Ltd 2011–, media strategist Supply Chain Sustainability Sch 2014–; memb Advsy Bd (London) Sustainable Brands 2012–; commissioning ed and regular contrib special reports in The Times and Sunday Times newspapers 2012–; *Style*— James McClelland, Esq; ✉ The Giddings, Blackburn Road, Higher Wheelton, Chorley, Lancashire PR6 8JA (e-mail j.mcclelland@mcclellandmedia.co.uk, Twitter @sustmeme)

MACCLESFIELD, Archdeacon of; *see:* Gillings, Ven Richard John

McCLOSKEY, Jane; da of Brian McCloskey, of Wolverhampton, W Midlands, and Hilda, *née* Blunn; *b* 10 March 1966; *Educ* Wolverhampton Girls' HS, Univ of Birmingham (BA); *Career* various media projects 1984–86 incl: author of Into the Labyrinth for HTV West 1982, features writer for Select Magazine and Wolverhampton Post & Mail 1984–85; BBC 1986–92: researcher Pebble Mill at One, Pamela Armstrong and Reaching for the Skies (BBC 1 Network) 1986–87, successively asst prodr, studio dir then prodr Daytime Live (BBC 1 Network) 1988–90, prodr/studio dir Scene Today (BBC 1 Network) 1990, prodr People Today (BBC North), prodr/dir The Travel Show Guides (BBC North) and prodr BBC Election Night Special (BBC 1) and The Travel Show (BBC 2) 1991–92; freelance prodr 1993–94: series prodr Holiday Snaps and author of Holiday Snaps Brochure (GMTV), prodr Good Getaways (Carlton); head of features and prog devpt GMTV 1995–96 (head of features and entertainment 1994–95), dir of progs Westcountry Television 1996–2002, dir of progs West and Westcountry and controller South ITV 2002–, ed ITV Regnl Prodn Fund 2005–, regnl dir ITV West and Westcountry 2008–09, head of regnl and local progs BBC SW 2009–10, head of supplier mgmnt commissioning BBC 2010–; *Recreations* dog walking, cooking, gardening, good wine; *Style*— Miss Jane McCloskey

McCLOUD, Kevin; MBE (2014); *b* 8 May 1959; *Educ* Dunstable GS, CCC Cambridge; *Career* fndr and dir HAB Housing Ltd 2006; author, broadcaster and designer; television incl: Homefront (BBC), Grand Designs (Channel 4) 1999–, Don't Look Down (BBC 2) 2002, Demolition (Channel 4) 2005, The Big Town Plan (Channel 4) 2008, Grand Tour of Europe (Channel 4) 2009, Slumming It (Channel 4) 2010, Man Made Home (Channel 4) 2012 and 2013, Supersized Salvage (Channel 4) 2014; hon DUniv Oxford Brookes Univ, hon PhDUniv Plymouth Univ, hon fell Cardiff Univ; fell WWF; hon FRIBA, hon FSLL, hon FICF; *Books* The 43 Principles of Home (2010), The Best of Grand Designs (2012); *Style*— Kevin McCloud, Esq, MBE; ✉ c/o KBJ Management, 22 Rathbone Street, London W1T 1LA (✆ 020 7054 5999, email general@kbjmanagement.co.uk, website www.kbjmgt.co.uk)

McCLURE, Timothy Elston (Tim); s of Kenneth Elston McClure (d 1997), and Grace Helen, *née* Hoar (d 2011); *b* 20 October 1946, Woking, Surrey; *Educ* Kingston GS, St John's Coll Durham (BA), Ridley Hall Cambridge; *m* 1 Aug 1969, Barbara Mary, da of Ven George John Charles Marchant (d 2006); 1 s (Matthew Elston b 1 July 1970), 1 da (Naomi b 27 Nov 1973); *Career* curate Kirkheaton PC Huddersfield 1970–73, mktg mangr Agrofax Labour Intensive Products Ltd Harrow 1973–74, chaplain to Manchester Poly 1974–82, curate St Ambrose Chorlton-on-Medlock Manchester 1974–79, team rector Parish of Whitworth Manchester and presiding chaplain 1979–82, gen sec Student Christian Movement 1982–92, dir Churches' Cncl for Industry and Social Responsibility (ISR) Bristol 1992–99, hon canon Bristol Cathedral 1992–2012, bishop's social and industrial advsr 1992–99, Lord Mayor's chaplain 1996–99, archdeacon of Bristol 1999–2012 (ret), archdeacon for strategy delivery 2009–12; non-exec chm Traidcraft plc 1990–97 (non-exec dir 1983–97), chm Christian Conf Tst 1998–2003, chm Social Enterprise Works 2000–10; *Recreations* cooking, gardening, cider making, sailing, beekeeping, walking; *Style*— Mr Tim McClure; ✉ e-mail tim@mcclure.me.uk

McCLURE FISHER, David Anthony; s of Douglas McClure Fisher (d 1991), and Mary Margaret, *née* Haley (d 1996); *b* 4 March 1939; *Educ* Tonbridge; *m* 30 Dec 1961, Lesley Carol, da of William Henry Chester-Jones (d 1971); 1 s (Duncan b 1964), 1 da (Joanna b 1968); *Career* md: Hogg Automotive Insurance Services Ltd 1984–94, Greyfriars Administration Services Ltd 1984–94, Hogg Insurance Brokers Ltd; dir: Hogg Group plc 1990–94, Bain Hogg Ltd 1994–95, IMC Insurance Services Ltd 1995–96; chm Warranty Direct Ltd 1997–; FCII, FInstD, FCIS, FIMI; *Recreations* golf, bridge; *Clubs* Moor Park Golf, Phyllis Court; *Style*— D A McClure Fisher, Esq; ✉ 1 Wargrave Hall, High Street, Wargrave, Berkshire RG10 8DA (✆ 0118 971 9742, e-mail david@mcclure-fisher.co.uk)

McCLUSKEY, Baron (Life Peer UK 1976), of Church Hill in District of City of Edinburgh; John Herbert McCluskey; QC (Scot 1967); s of Francis John McCluskey (d 1961), of Edinburgh; *b* 12 June 1929; *Educ* St Bede's GS Manchester, Holy Cross Acad Edinburgh, Univ of Edinburgh (Vans Dunlop scholar, Harry Dalgety bursar, MA, LLB); *m* 1956, Ruth, da of Aaron Friedland, of Manchester; 2 s (Hon (John) Mark b 1960, Hon David Francis b 1963 d 2014), 1 da (Hon Catherine Margaret b 1962); *Career* advocate 1955, advocate-depute 1964, sheriff princ of Dumfries and Galloway 1973–1974, slr gen for Scotland 1974–79, senator of the Coll of Justice in Scotland 1984–2000; BBC Reith lectr 1986; chm: John Smith Memorial Tst 1997–2004, Age Concern Scotland 2000–01; Hon LLD Univ of Dundee 1989; *Books* Law, Justice and Democracy (1987), Criminal Appeals (1991, 2 edn 2000); *Style*— The Rt Hon the Lord McCluskey; ✉ House of Lords, Westminster, London SW1A 0PW

McCLYMONT, Gregg; s of Hugh Forbes McClymont, and Sheila, *née* McGalliard; *b* 3 June 1976, Glasgow; *Educ* Cumbernauld HS, Univ of Glasgow (MA), Univ of Pennsylvania (AM), St Hugh's Coll Oxford (MA), St John's Coll Oxford (DPhil); *Career* MP (Lab) Cumbernauld, Kilsyth and Kirkintilloch E 2010–15; head Retirement Savings Aberdeen Asset Mgmnt; fell St Hugh's Coll Oxford, visiting fell Nuffield Coll Oxford; *Publications* Twentieth Century British History Vol 19 (contrib, 2008), Cultures, Classes and Politics: Essays on British History (contrib, 2010), Pensions at Work that Work. Completing the Unfinished Pensions Revolution (with Dr Andy Tarrant, 2013); *Style*— Mr Gregg McClymont; ✉ 30 Park Way, Kildrum, Cumbernauld G67 2BU; House of Commons, London SW1A 0AA

McCOLL, HE Gen Sir John Chalmers; KCB (2008), CBE, DSO; *b* 17 April 1952; *Career* Dep Supreme Allied Cdr Europe 2007–11, Lt Govr of Jersey 2011–; *Style*— HE Gen Sir John McColl, KCB, CBE, DSO

McCOLL, Prof William Finlay; s of William McColl (d 1975), and Jeanie, *née* Lilley (d 1973); *b* 2 May 1952; *Educ* Univ of Strathclyde (BSc), Univ of Warwick (PhD); *m* Irene Ruth, *née* Houston; 2 s (Robert William b 23 July 1982, Iain Fraser b 29 June 1986), 1 da (Caroline Anna b 13 March 1985); *Career* SRC postdoctoral research fell 1976–77; lectr in computer science: Univ of Leeds 1977–80, Univ of Warwick 1980–85, Univ of Oxford 1985–96; prof of computing science Univ of Oxford 1996–; fell Wadham Coll Oxford 1985–, MA (by incorporation) Univ of Oxford 1985; *Recreations* skiing, scuba diving; *Style*— Prof William McColl; ✉ 24A Sunderland Avenue, Oxford OX2 8DX (✆ 01865 428346); Oxford University Computing Laboratory, Parks Road, Oxford OX1 3QD (✆ 01865 273829, e-mail wfm@comlab.ox.ac.uk)

McCOLL OF DULWICH, Baron (Life Peer UK 1989), of Bermondsey in the London Borough of Southwark; Ian McColl; CBE (1997); s of Frederick George McColl (d 1985), of Dulwich, and Winifred Edith, *née* Murphy (d 1984); *b* 6 January 1933; *Educ* Hutchesons' GS Glasgow, St Paul's, Univ of London (MB BS, MS); *m* 1, 27 Aug 1960, Dr Jean Lennox (d 2012), 2 da of Arthur James McNair, FRCS, FRCOG (d 1964), of London; 1 s (Dr the Hon Alastair James b 25 July 1961), 2 da (Dr the Hon Caroline Lennox b 19 Aug 1963, Hon Mary Alison b 9 Oct 1966); m 2, 2015, Dr Evy Lise Kaarvang, da of late Dr Kristian Kaarvang, and Mrs Evy Ugland Kaarvang, of Oslo; *Career* surgn to Bart's and sub dean Med Coll 1967–71, prof of surgery at Guy's Hosp 1971–99, dir surgery Guy's Hosp 1985–99, chm Dept of Surgery UMDS 1987–93; hon conslt surgn to British Army 1984–99; Parly private sec (Lords) to PM 1994–97, dep speaker House of Lords 1994–2002, oppn spokesman on health House of Lords 1997–2010; memb: Select Ctee on Euthanasia 1994–95, Select Ctee on Sci 2000–, Select Ctee on AIDs and HIV 2010–, Select Ctee on the Anti-Slavery Bill 2014; vice-chm Disablement Services Authy 1987–91; pres: Soc of Minimally Invasive Surgery 1991–94, Limbless Assoc (formerly Nat Assoc of Limbless Disabled), Assoc of Endo Surgns of Great Br and Ireland 1994–97, Leprosy Mission 1996–, Royal Med Fndn of Epsom Coll 2001–; vice-pres John Grooms Soc for the Disabled; dir Mercy Ships Int 1998–, chm Mercy Ships UK 2000–, vice-chm Int Bd Mercy Ships; chm Bd of Govrs Mildmay Mission Hosp 1994–2002 (pres 1985–94), chm James Allen's Girls' Sch 1998–2004; govr St Paul's Sch 2001–; memb: Cncl RCS 1986–94, Bd of Patrons RCS 1995–; Great Scot Award 2002, Nat Maritime Historical Soc Award USA 2002; Freeman City of London, Liveryman of Worshipful Soc of Apothecaries 1979, Middle Warden Worshipful Co of Barber Surgeons 1997 (Master 1999–2000, Upper Warden 1998, Liveryman 1986, dep Master 2000–01); FKC 2001, FRCS, FACS, FRCSEd, hon FDSRCS 2007; Order of Mercy 2007; *Books* Intestinal Absorption in Man (jtly, 1975), NHS Data Book (jtly, 1983); *Recreations* forestry, ornithology; *Style—* The Rt Hon the Lord McColl of Dulwich, CBE; ✉ House of Lords, London SW1A 0PW (☎ 020 7219 5141, e-mail mccolli@parliament.uk)

McCOMB, Dr Janet Mary; da of Samuel Gerald McComb, of Belfast, and Mary Clarke; *b* 22 August 1951; *Educ* Queen's Univ of Belfast (MB BCh, BAO, MD); *Career* clinical and research fell Harvard Med Sch and Massachusetts Gen Hosp 1983–86, conslt cardiologist Univ of Newcastle upon Tyne 1986– (sr lectr 1986–90); memb: Br Cardiac Soc, Br Pacing and Electrophysiology Gp, Assoc of Physicians; FRCP; *Style—* Dr J M McComb

McCOMB, Leonard; *b* 1930; *Educ* Manchester Sch of Art, Slade Sch of Art; *Career* artist; taught at various art colls (incl Oxford Poly, Royal Acad, Slade, Goldsmiths Coll London and John Cass) 1960–89, fndr Sunningwell Sch of Art 1977, fndr Vincent Soc of Drawing 1990; destroyed most of work up to 1976; cmmnd through Art for Work to paint 3 oil paintings of Kennecott Utah copper mines for RTZ London offices 1995; keeper of the Royal Acad 1995–; Hon Dr Oxford Brookes Univ 2004; RA 1990 (ARA 1987), fell Royal Soc of Painter Printmakers 1994, RP 2003, Hon RWS; *Exhibitions* incl: Human Clay (Arts Cncl) 1976, British Painting 1952–77 (Royal Acad) 1977, British Art Show (Arts Cncl touring exhbn), Venice Biennale – Painters of the 80's 1980, British Sculpture in the Twentieth Century (Whitechapel Art Gallery London) 1981, British Drawing Hayward Annual (Hayward Gallery) 1983, Leonard McComb Drawings, Paintings and Sculpture (Arts Cncl touring exhbn orgnd by MOMA Oxford) 1983, Hard Won Image (Tate Gallery) 1984, Human Interest: 50 Years of British Art (Corner House Manchester) 1985, Representation Abroad (Hirschhorn Museum Washington DC) 1986, Flowers in the Twentieth Century (Stoke on Trent City Museum touring exhbn) 1986, Large Watercolours and Drawings (Raab Gallery Berlin) 1986, Viewpoint Selection of British Art (MOMA Brussels) 1987, It's a Still Life (Plymouth City Museum and Art Gallery and tour) 1989, RA – Portraits Friends Room Exhbn 1989, various exhbns Gillian Jason Gallery London 1989–, Images of Paradise (Christie's London) 1990, The Discerning Eye (Mall Galleries London) 1992, The Sussex Scene (Hove and Eastbourne) 1993, Singer and Friedlander/Sunday Times watercolour competition (Mall Galleries) 1993, Drawings and Paintings (Browse & Darby London) 1993, Drawing on these Shores (mixed travelling exhbn) 1993–94, Browse and Darby Gallery London 1994, Open House exhbn (Kettles Yard Cambridge) 1995, The Pursuit of Painting (Irish MOMA Dublin) 1997, Portrait of Doris Lessing (Nat Portrait Gallery Coll) 1999, Leonard McComb Portraits (curated by David Cohen, NY Studio Sch) 2000, Between Earth and Heaven (MOMA Ostend) 2001, The Upright Figure (Turbine Hall Tate Modern) 2002, Leonard McComb Drawings, Paintings and Sculpture (Talbot Rice Gallery Edinburgh) 2004 (also at Wolsey Art Gallery Ipswich 2005), Dr Leonard McComb RA A Retrospective 1976–2006 Oils Watercolours Drawings Ceramics (43 Old Bond Street London) 2006, Sardines Swimming in the Sea (Ashmoleon Museum Oxford) 2008, Mosaic Design St Francis of Assisi (Westminster Cathedral) 2010, Mosaic Design St Anthony of Padua (Westminster Cathedral) 2010; *Public Collections* Arts Cncl, Birmingham City Art Gallery, British Cncl, Contemporary Arts Soc, Manchester Art Gallery, Swindon Art Gallery, Tate Gallery London, Univ of Cambridge, V&A, Worcester Museum and Art Gallery, Towner Art Gallery Eastbourne; cmmnd to produce tapestry design (woven at Edinburgh Weavers) for Boots Chemists Nottingham; *Awards* Jubilee Prize Royal Acad 1977, Korn Ferry Prize Royal Acad 1988, second prize Singer and Friedlander/Sunday Times watercolour competition 1993, second prize Singer & Friedlander/Sunday Times watercolour prize 1994, Sir Hugh Casson Prize for Drawing Royal Acad of Arts Summer Exhbn 2005, Turner Medal Watercolour Award Royal Acad Summer Exhibition 2007; *Clubs* London Sketch, Chelsea Arts; *Style—* Dr Leonard McComb, RA, RWS, RP, RE; ✉ Studio 4, 3 Stewarts Place, Blenheim Gardens, London SW2 5AZ (☎ 020 8671 5510)

McCOMBE, Rt Hon Lord Justice; Sir Richard George Bramwell McCombe; kt (2001), PC (2012); s of Barbara Bramwell McCombe, *née* Bramwell (d 1969); *b* 23 September 1952; *Educ* Sedbergh, Downing Coll Cambridge (MA); *m* 1 (m dis 1986), m 2, 1986 (m dis 2009), Carolyn Sara, da of Robert Duncan Birrell, of Limpsfield, Surrey; 1 s (Duncan b 4 April 1987), 1 da (Tamara b 20 Nov 1989); m3, 28 March 2013, Rt Hon Lady Justice Black, *qv*; *Career* called to the Bar Lincoln's Inn 1975 (bencher 1996); first jr counsel to Dir Gen of Fair Trading 1987–89 (second jr counsel 1982–87), DTI inspr into the affrs of Norton Group plc (with J K Heywood, FCA) 1991–92 (report published 1993), recorder of the Crown Ct 1996–2001 (asst recorder 1993–96), dep High Ct judge 1998–2001, QC 1989, judge of the High Ct of Justice (Queen's Bench Div) 2001–12, presiding judge Northern Circuit 2004–07, Lord Justice of Appeal 2012–; chm Assoc of High Ct Judges 2008–09, chm of tstees Royal Courts of Justice Citizens Advice Bureau 2013–; Attorney-Gen of the Duchy of Lancaster and Attorney and Serjeant within the County Palatine of Lancaster 1996–2001; memb: Senate Inns of Ct and Bar Cncl 1981–86, Bar Cncl Ctees 1986–89 (chm Young Barristers' Ctee 1983–84), Bar Representation Ctee Lincoln's Inn 1992–96, Bar Cncl 1995–97 (chm Int Rels Ctee 1997); head UK Delgn to the Cncl of the Bars and Law Socs of the EC 1996–98; pres Assoc of Lancastrians in London 2008; chm Oversight Ctee Royal Coll of Surgeons 2012–16; govr Sedbergh Sch 2002–13; Hon FRCS 2015; *Recreations* various sporting interests, flying aircraft; *Clubs* RAC, Garrick, MCC, Lancs CCC, Middx CCC, London Scottish FC; *Style—* The Rt Hon Lord Justice McCombe; ✉ Royal Courts of Justice, Strand, London WC2A 2LL

McCONNACHIE, (John Sneddon) Iain; s of John Meek McConnachie, of Sale, Greater Manchester, and Charlotte Sneddon, *née* Christie (d 1984); *b* 11 March 1956; *Educ* Sale GS, Lymm GS, Oxford Poly (HND), Huddersfield Poly (Dip Mktg Studies); *m* 9 June 1979 (m dis 1998), Shirley Diane, da of Norman George Burgess (d 1983); 1 da (Sara Anne b 2 Feb 1985); m 2, Hilary Diana Ohrstrand, da of Lewis Trevor Evans; *Career* mktg asst Zockoll Group 1977–78, asst advtg mangr Baxter Travenol 1978–79, American Express 1979–88 (mktg exec, mktg mangr, mktg dir), vice-pres sales and mktg Chase Manhattan Bank 1988–91, md Financial Marketing Consultancy Group 1991–92, head of direct distribution Legal and General plc 1992–93, md Financial Marketing Consultancy Group 1993–97, ptnr S2 Ltd 1997–99, managing ptnr Inst of Direct Marketing Consulting 1999–; md Europe Direct Entertainment 2005–, European direct mktg dir ACE INA Insurance; MInstM 1989; *Recreations* golf, photography, shooting; *Clubs* Castle Royle Golf; *Style—* Iain McConnachie, Esq; ✉ Somerford House, Somerford Place, Beaconsfield, Buckinghamshire HP9 1AZ (☎ 01494 671219, e-mail iain.mcconnachie@ace-ina.com)

McCONNELL, Carmel; MBE (2016); *Educ* Cass Univ London (MBA); *Career* fndr and ceo Magic Breakfast 2003–; *Style—* Ms Carmel McConnell, MBE; ✉ Magic Breakfast, One90 High Holborn, London WC1V 7BH

McCONNELL, Charlie Stephen; s of Charles Harold McConnell (d 1993), and Elsie Amelia, *née* Hogben (d 2004); *b* 20 June 1951; *Educ* BA, MPhil; *m* 28 April 1995 (m dis 2016), Natasha, *née* Smirnova; 1 adopted s (Timor b 1978), 1 da (Holly Isadora b 1995); *Partner* Iris Ella Steen; *Career* community devpt research practitioner and educationalist 1974–84, nat sec UK Consumers Congress 1984–88, European and public affrs dir Community Devpt Fndn 1988–93, ceo Scottish Community Educn Cncl 1993–2002, ceo Carnegie UK Tst 2003–08; vice-pres European Social Action Network 1991–93, sec-gen Int Assoc for Community Devpt 1998–2004, chair UK Nat Training Standards Orgn for Community Learning and Devpt 1999–2002, community devpt policy advsr Scottish Exec 2002–03, pres Int Assoc for Community Devpt 2014–16; Parly candidate 1983; FRSA 2000; *Publications* Community Worker as Politiciser of the Deprived (1977), Deprivation, Participation and Commmunity Action (et al, 1979), Community Education and Community Development (ed, 1982), Continuing Education in Scotland (ed, 1984), Consumer Action and Community Development (ed, 1988), Towards a Citizen's Europe (ed, 1990), Community Development in Europe (ed, 1992), Community Development and Urban Regeneration (ed, 1993), Community Education: The Making of an Empowering Profession (ed, 1995, 2 edn 1997), Community Education and Active Citizenship (ed, 1998), Lifelong Learning in Scotland (ed, 1998), Community Learning and Development: The Making of an Empowering Profession (ed, 2002), Finding my Voice: The Power of Community Education, Organisation and Development (2014); *Recreations* fell walking; *Style—* Charlie McConnell, Esq

McCONNELL, John; s of Donald McConnell (d 1982), and Enid, *née* Dimberline (d 1967); *b* 14 May 1939; *Educ* Borough Green Secdy Modern Sch, Maidstone Coll of Art (Nat Dip); *m* 1 March 1963, Moira Rose, da of William Allan Macgregor; 1 s (Sam b 20 Feb 1966), 1 da (Kate b 1 Feb 1969); *Career* designer; own practice 1963–74, co-fndr Face Photosetting 1967; ptnr Pentagram 1974–2005, ed Pentagram Papers 1975–2006; memb: PO Stamp Advsy Ctee, CNAA; D&AD Assoc President's Award for outstanding contrib to design 1985, special commendation Prince Philip Designer's Prize 2002; RDI 1987; *Books* Living By Design (jtly, 1978), Ideas on Design (jtly, 1986), Pentagram Book V (jtly, 1999); *Recreations* cookery, building; *Style—* John McConnell, Esq; ✉ McConnell Design Limited, 12 Orme Court, London W2 4RL

McCONNELL OF GLENSCORRODALE, Baron (Life Peer UK 2010), of the Isle of Arran in Ayrshire and Arran; Rt Hon Dr Jack Wilson McConnell; PC (2001); s of William Wilson McConnell, and Elizabeth, *née* Jack; *b* 30 June 1960; *Educ* Arran HS 1971–77, Univ of Stirling (BSc, DipEd) 1977–83; *m* 1990, Bridget; 1 s, 1 da; *Career* mathematics teacher 1983–92; Scottish Lab Pty: gen sec 1992–98, ldr 2001–07; cncllr Stirling DC 1984–93 (ldr 1990–92); MSP (Lab) Motherwell & Wishaw 1999–2011; Scottish Govt: finance min 1999–2000, educn, Europe and external affairs min 2000–01, first min 2001–07; PM's special rep on peacebuilding 2008–10; pres EU Regions with Legislative Powers 2004; memb Bd UK-Japan 21st Century Gp, ambass Action for Children UK; patron: Diana Awards, Positive Women; chairperson Radio Clyde Cash for Kids; *Recreations* golf, music, gardening; *Style—* The Rt Hon the Lord McConnell of Glenscorrodale; ✉ website www.jackmcconnell.org

McCONVILLE, Coline Lucille; *b* 21 July 1964; *Educ* Flensburg Gymnasium, Univ of NSW Law Sch (BJuris, LLB, Westgarth Middletons law scholar), Harvard Grad Sch of Business Admin (Harvard fell, Baker scholar, MBA); *m*; 2 c; *Career* sales mgmnt Australian Consolidated Press 1984–85, assoc conslt The L E K Partnership Munich 1989–92, sr assoc McKinsey & Co Ltd 1994–96, gp devpt dir More Gp plc 1996–98, chief exec (Europe) Clear Channel International Ltd 1998–; non-exec dir: HBOS plc 2000–09, Shed Media plc 2009–; *Recreations* cooking, entertaining, learning the piano, playing with my two children; *Style—* Mrs Coline McConville; ✉ e-mail cmcconville@hotmail.co.uk

McCORKELL, David William; DL (Co Antrim 2014); s of Col Sir Michael McCorkell, KCVO, OBE, TD, JP (d 2006), of Ballyarnett, Co Londonderry, and Aileen Allen, Lady McCorkell, OBE, *née* Booth (d 2010); *b* 26 February 1955, Londonderry; *Educ* Charterhouse; *m* 26 Sept 1981, Susan Mary, da of Desmond MacLellan Goodbody, of Kilcoursey, Clara, Co Offaly; 1 s (Christopher Desmond William b 4 May 1988), 1 da (Camilla Charlotte Elizabeth b 3 Jan 1986); *Career* served D (North Irish Horse) Squadron Royal Yeomanry 1976–78; Wm McCorkell & Co Ltd 1975–80, farmer 1980–86; Bell Lawrie: joined 1986, dir 1989–93, became part of Brewin Dolphin Hldgs plc 1993, dir Brewin Dolphin Ltd 2003–12, memb Bd Brewin Dolphin Hldgs plc 2006–12 (head of investment mgmnt 2007–12); non-exec dir Assoc of Private Client Investment Mangrs 2009–12; memb Quality Assurance Ctee Chartered Accountants' Regulatory Bd Ireland 2013–; tstee North Irish Horse Museum Collection 2011–, dir Irish Grouse Conservation Tst 2012–, memb Down Royal Racecourse Ctee 2014–, memb Funds and Appeals Ctee SSAFA (NI) 2015–; FCSI; *Recreations* country sports, golf, racing; *Clubs* Kildare Street and Univ (Dublin), Royal County Down Golf; *Style—* David McCorkell, Esq, DL FCSI; ✉ Ballymacbrennan House, 133 Saintfield Road, Lisburn, Co Antrim BT27 6YW

McCORMAC, Prof Francis Gerard (Gerry); s of Francis Gerald McCormac, and Jane Philomena Heaney (d 2013); *b* 1 August 1958, Belfast; *Educ* Ulster Polytechnic (BSc), Ulster Polytechnic and Univ of Southampton (PhD); *m* Sept 1982, Catherine Marie Louise Gormley; 3 s (Philip Gerald b March 1985, Brendan John b Aug 1988, James Michael b March 1990); *Career* post-doctoral research fell Univ of Michigan 1984–90, dir Carbon Dating Facility Queen's Univ Belfast 1990–2001, head Sch of Archaeology and Palaeoecology Queen's Univ Belfast 1997–2001, pro-vice chllr Queen's Univ Belfast 2001–10, princ and vice-chllr Univ of Stirling 2010–; memb: Univs Scotland, Univs UK, Carnegie Tst Univs of Scotland Exec Ctee, Scottish Ctee Univs and Colls Employers' Assoc, NI Ctee Inst of Directors, NI Economic Devpt Forum, NI Science and Industry Panel (MATRIX); memb Bd: NI Science Park, Business in the Community; FSA, FRSA; *Publications* Science and Stonehenge: Dating Stonehenge (with Bayliss and Bronk Ramsey, 1998), Anglo-Saxon Graves and Grave Goods of the 6th and 7th Centuries AD: A Chronological Framework (with Bayliss, Hines, Nielsen and Scull, 2013); *Style—* Prof Gerry McCormac; ✉ University of Stirling, Stirling FK9 4LA

McCORMICK, John; s of Joseph McCormick (d 1977), and Roseann, *née* McNamara (d 1976); *b* 24 June 1944; *Educ* St Michael's Acad Irvine, Univ of Glasgow (MA, MEd); *m* 4 Aug 1973, Jean Frances, da of William Gibbons, of Kirkintilloch, Glasgow; 1 da (Lesley Anne b 1978), 1 s (Stephen b 1980); *Career* teacher St Gregory's Secdy Sch Glasgow 1968–70, educn offr BBC Sch Broadcasting Cncl for Scotland 1970–75, sr educn offr Scotland 1975–82, sec and head of info BBC Scotland 1982–87, sec of the BBC 1987–92, controller BBC Scotland 1992–2004; chm: Edinburgh Int Film Festival 1996–2008 (memb Bd 1994–

M

96), Scottish Qualifications Authy 2004–09; memb Bd: Scottish Screen 1997–2003, Skillset 2001–04, Royal Scot Acad of Music and Drama 2003–08, Glasgow Sch of Art 2004–08, Scottish Opera 2005– (vice chair 2008–); non-exec dir Lloyds TSB Scotland 2005–09; vice-chm Youth-at-Risk Scotland 1985–92; memb: Glasgow Children's Panel 1972–77, Visiting Ctee Glenochil Young Offenders Instn 1979–85, Bd of Tstees Glasgow Science Centre 1999–2005, Bd Irvine Bay Urban Regeneration Co 2007–13, Bd Theatre Royal Glasgow 2010–; ind dir Glasgow Life 2013–; memb: Ct Univ of Strathclyde 1996–2002, Lay Advsy Ctee RCPEd 2010–15; electoral cmmr 2008–; Hon DLitt Robert Gordon Univ 1997, Hon LLD Univ of Strathclyde 1999; Hon DUniv: Glasgow 1999, Paisley 2003; FRTS 1998, FRSE 2003; *Style*— John McCormick, Esq

McCORMICK, Peter David Godfrey; OBE (2000); s of Ronald Godfrey McCormick (d 1994), of Leeds, and Paulina, *née* Salzman; *b* 27 June 1952, Leeds; *Educ* Ashville Coll Harrogate, KCL (LLB); *m* 16 May 1981, Kathryn, *née* Gill; 1 s (Guy James Godfrey b 16 Aug 1982), 1 da (Charlotte Alix b 25 Sept 1985); *Career* admitted slr 1976; ptnr Levi and Co 1978–83 (asst slr 1976–78), fndr and sr ptnr McCormicks Slrs 1983–; chm Premier League 2014–15; chm: Sport Resolutions (UK), Legal Advsy Gp Premier League, Football Bd Premier League; dir FA; memb: FA Cncl, Football Regulatory Authority, FA Int Ctee, Professional Game Bd, Professional Game Forum; memb Assoc of Regulatory and Disciplinary Lawyers; Yorkshire Lawyer of the Year 2000, Gen Practice and Niche Practice Lawyer of the Year 2000, Lifetime Achievement in Business Award Ackrill Media Gp Business Awards 2008; chm: Football Stadia Improvement Fund Ltd, Welcome to Harrogate Ltd (Visit Harrogate); chm Yorkshire Young Achievers Awards, vice-pres Outward Bound Tst; chm War Memls Tst; tstee: Helen Feather Meml Tst, Nat Media Museum, The Football Fndn, John Strutt Centre for Parrot Conservation, John Strutt Meml Fund; chm of tstees Yorkshire Young Achievers Fndn; *Publications* Sports Business (2005); author of numerous articles for legal and business jls and newspapers; *Style*— Peter McCormick, Esq, OBE; ✉ McCormicks, Wharfedale House, 35–37 East Parade, Harrogate, North Yorkshire HG1 5LQ (☎ 01423 530630, fax 01423 530709)

MacCORMICK, Sarah Jane; da of Donald MacCormick (d 2009), and Lis Forrester, of Chiswick, London; *b* 21 March 1970, Aberdeen; *Educ* Somerville Coll Oxford (BA); *Career* agent Conway van Gelder 1998–2002 (joined 1992), agent Curtis Brown 2002–; *Style*— Miss Sarah MacCormick; ✉ Curtis Brown Group Ltd, Haymarket House, 28–29 Haymarket, London SW1Y 4SP (website www.curtisbrown.co.uk)

McCORQUODALE, Ian Hamilton; er s of Hugh McCorquodale, MC (d 1963), and Dame Barbara Cartland, DBE (d 2000); half-bro of Raine, Countess Spencer, *qv*; *b* 11 October 1937; *Educ* Harrow, Magdalene Coll Cambridge; *m* 1, 1970 (m dis 1993), Anna, *née* Chisholm; 2 da (Iona b 1971, Tara b 1973); m 2, 2000, Bryony Brind, da of Maj Roger Michael Atchley Brind; *Career* former commercial and export mangr British Printing Corporation; ptnr Cartland Promotions 1976–, chm Debrett's Peerage Ltd 1981–97; *Recreations* fishing, shooting, gardening; *Clubs* Boodle's, White's; *Style*— Ian McCorquodale, Esq; ✉ The Home Farm, Camfield Place, Hatfield, Hertfordshire AL9 6JE (☎ 01707 642629, fax 01707 663041)

McCOSH, Prof Andrew Macdonald; s of Rev Andrew McCosh (d 1970), of Dunblane, and Margaret, *née* MacDonald (d 1968); *b* 16 September 1940; *Educ* Edinburgh Acad, Univ of Edinburgh (BSc), Univ of Manchester (MBA), Harvard Univ (DBA), Univ of Glasgow (MTh), Inst of Chartered Accountants (CA); *m* 1965, Anne, da of Nicholas Rogers; 3 da; *Career* assoc prof of accounting Univ of Michigan 1966–71; prof of mgmnt accounting Manchester Business Sch 1971–85, dean Faculty of Business Univ of Manchester 1979–83, prof of the orgn of industry and commerce Univ of Edinburgh 1986–95 (prof emeritus and univ fell in fin 1995–); Alvah Chapman prof of fin and ethics Florida Int Univ Miami 2000–, dir The Pilgrim Mutual Funds NY 1996–2002; MICAS 1963; *Books* Practical Controllership (1973), Management Decision Support Systems (1978), Developing Managerial Information Systems (1983), Organisational Decision Support Systems (1988), Financial Ethics (1999); *Recreations* fishing, climbing, golf; *Clubs* Royal Scots (Edinburgh), New (Edinburgh); *Style*— Prof Andrew McCosh; ✉ University of Edinburgh, 50 George Square, Edinburgh EH8 9JY (☎ 0131 650 4603, fax 0131 668 3053, e-mail a.mccosh@ed.ac.uk)

McCOSS, Dr Angus Murray; s of Leslie Hunter McCoss, of Kingsbarns, Fife, and Alison Gray, *née* Murray; *b* 13 November 1961, Broughty Ferry, Dundee; *Educ* Dundee HS, Univ of Dundee (BSc), Univ of Belfast (PhD); *m* 22 Aug 1984, Karen Anne, *née* James; 1 da (Fiona Ellen b 6 Oct 1988), 2 s (Fergus James b 8 Oct 1990, Calum Angus b 12 May 1993); *Career* Shell: exploration geologist The Netherlands, Syria, China and Oman 1987–98, exploration and prodn mangr Argentina 1998–2000, Brazil regnl business advsr and Americas regnl exploration vice-pres 2000–03, Nigeria exploration gen mangr 2003–06; gen mangr global exploration and exploration dir Tullow Oil plc 2006–; non-exec dir Ikon Science Ltd 2009; author of articles in Jl of Structural Geology 1986, 1987 and 1988; memb Chatham House Royal Inst of Int Affrs 2009; MInstD 2007, FRSA 2009; *Recreations* sailing, skiing, sabre; *Clubs* Heraldry Soc of Scotland, Nat Tst for Scotland; *Style*— Dr Angus McCoss; ✉ Tullow Oil plc, 9 Chiswick Park, Chiswick, London W4 5XT

McCOY, Sir Anthony Peter (A P); kt (2016), OBE (2010, MBE 2003); s of Peadar McCoy, of NI, and Claire McCoy; *b* 4 May 1974, Ballymena, NI; *m* Chanelle, *née* Burke; 1 da (Eve), 1 s (Archie); *Career* nat hunt jockey; winner: Cheltenham Gold Cup, Champion Hurdle, Queen Mother Champion Chase, Grand National; 19 times champion Nat Hunt Jockey, Jump Jockey of the Year 1995–2013; ridden over 4000 winners (a record for a jump jockey); subject of documentaries: The Real McCoy 2002, McCoy 2011; BBC Sports Personality of the Year 2010; Hon Dr Queen's Univ Belfast 2002; *Publications* McCoy: The Autobiography (2002), AP McCoy My Autobiography (2011), Taking the Fall (novel, 2013); *Recreations* football, golf; *Style*— Sir A P McCoy, OBE; ✉ Lodge Down Stables, Lambourn Woodlands, Hungerford, Berkshire RG17 7BJ (e-mail ap.mccoy@talk21.com)

McCOY, Hugh O'Neill; s of Hugh O'Neill McCoy, and Nora May, *née* Bradley; *b* 9 February 1939; *Educ* Dudley GS, Univ of London; *m* Margaret Daphne, da of Robert John Corfield; *Career* md Horace Clarkson plc, chm H Clarkson & Co Ltd until 1999, chm Baltic Exchange until 2001; past dir Benor Tanker Ltd Hamilton Bermuda, past dir Cammel Laird Holding plc; dir The Hadley Shipping Co 1999– (chm 2014–), former non-exec dir Gartmore Korea Fund plc; pres Inst of Chartered Shipbrokers 1992–94; specially elected memb Gen Cncl Lloyd's Register of Shipping; hon vice-pres Maritime Vol Serv; former memb: Cncl Mercy Ships, Mgmnt Ctee London Sea Cadets; govr Warley Sch; past chm Brentwood CAB; Freeman City of London, assoc memb Hon Co of Master Mariners, Liveryman Worshipful Co of Shipwrights; FICS; *Clubs* City, Royal Burnham Yacht; *Style*— Hugh O'Neill McCoy, FICS; ✉ 5 Heron Way, Hutton, Brentwood, Essex CM13 2LX

McCREA, Ian; MLA; s of Dr William McCrea, MP, *qv*, and Ann Shirley, *née* McKnight; *b* 12 June 1976, Magherafelt, Co Londonderry; *m* Wanita; 1 da (Natalia), 2 s (Lee, Alex); *Career* MLA (DUP) Mid-Ulster 2007–; *Style*— Ian McCrea, Esq, MLA; ✉ Northern Ireland Assembly, Room 313, Parliament Buildings, Belfast BT4 3XX

McCREE, Andrew Charles Gambon; s of Cyril Gerard Winifred McCree (d 1997), and Sheila, *née* Guthrie (d 1997); *b* 20 August 1957; *Educ* Mount St Mary's Coll, Fort Augustus Abbey Sch, Inst of Technol Glasgow; *m* 16 May 1980, Lesley Margaret, da of Leslie Eric Bromfield; *Career* Army 1975–76; grad trainee BP Oil Glasgow 1976–78; BP Petroleum Devpt: PR asst 1978–83, info offr 1983–84, press and info offr 1984–89; external affrs co-ordinator BP Exploration 1989–90, head of press and public affrs UKAEA 1990–93; AEA Technology: mangr public affrs 1993–94, gen mangr corp communications gp 1994–96, dir corp affrs 1996–97, exec dir corp affrs and HR 2000–02, gp md 2002–04, ceo 2005–; *Recreations* current affairs, conservation, sport; *Style*— Andrew McCree, Esq; ✉ 6 New Street Square, London EC4A 3BF (☎ 0870 190 2503, e-mail enquiry@aeat.co.uk, website wwww.aeat.co.uk)

McCREESH, Paul Dominic; s of Patrick Michael McCreesh, and Valerie Mary Bernadette Connors; *b* 24 May 1960; *Educ* Campion Sch Hornchurch, Univ of Manchester (BMus); *m* 1983, Susan Hemington Jones; 1 s (Samuel Adam b 19 Nov 1989), 1 da (Hannah Frances b 25 Jan 1994); *Career* conductor; fndr Gabrieli Consort & Players (choir and period instrument ensemble) 1982; *Performances* with Gabrieli Consort & Players: BBC Proms, Vienna Konzerthaus, Bergen Festival, Glasgow Mayfest, Lucerne Festival, Cité de la Musique Paris, Bremen Musikfest, Covent Garden Festival, Accademia Santa Cecilia Roma, South Bank Centre, Jerusalem Festival, Polish Radio, Styriate Graz, Palau de la Musica Barcelona, Flanders Festival, Utrecht Festival, Ludwigsbrugher Schlossfestspiele, Handelfestspiele Halle, BBC and City of London Festival, Lincoln Center NY, Concertgebouw Amsterdam, Symphony Hall Birmingham, Théâtre des Champs-Elysées, Théâtre du Châtelet Paris; others incl: Northern Sinfonia, Orch Regionale Toscana Florence, Netherlands Bach Soc, Netherlands Chamber Choir, opera and stage prodns in UK, France, Holland and USA, Handel & Haydn Soc Boston, WNO, Nat Symphony Orch Washington, San Francisco Symphony Orch, Norwegian Nat Opera, Minnesota Orch, Copenhagen Philharmonic, Deutsche Kammerphilharmonie, Orchestre Philharmonique de Radio France, KölnerRundfunk, Orquesta Ciudad de Granada; *Recordings* works by Gabrieli, Monteverdi, Purcell, Praetorius, Palestrina, Josquin, Victoria, Morales, Biber, Handel, Bach; exclusive contract with Deutsche Grammophon Archiv Produktion; *Awards* Edison Award 1991 and 1995, Gramophone Award 1990 and 1993, Deutschen Schallplatten Preis 1994, Diapason d'Or 1994, ABC Record of the Year 1990, Studio Prize Poland 1998, Danish Grammy 1998, John Owens Award Univ of Manchester 2002; *Recreations* children, walking, eating well; *Style*— Paul McCreesh, Esq; ✉ c/o Intermusica Artists Management Ltd, 16 Duncan Terrace, London N1 8BZ

McCRORY, Helen Elizabeth; da of Iain McCrory, of Scotland, and Ann Elizabeth, *née* Morgan; *b* 17 August 1968, London; *Educ* Int Sch Yaounde Cameroon, Int Sch Dar es Salaam Tanzania, Queenswood Sch Herts, Drama Centre London; *m* 4 July 2007, Damian Lewis, *qv*; 1 da (Manon Isabella Charlotte b 8 Sept 2006), 1 s (Gulliver Cameron b 2 Nov 2007); *Career* actress; fndr (with Michael Sheen) The Public prodn co (producing new work at Liverpool Everyman Theatre, Ambassadors London and Donmar Warehouse); theatre master Theatre Royal Haymarket; ambass: Princes Trust, Marie Curie; patron: Scene and Heard children's charity, Sir Hubert von Herkomer Arts Fndn; memb Equity 1991, memb and patron BIFA, memb SAG, ambass BFI; *Television* Full Stretch, The Entertainer, Dirty Old Town, Trial and Retribution, The Fragile Heart, Stand and Deliver, Split Second, In a Land of Plenty, Anna Karenina, North Square (Best Actress Award Critics Circle), Lucky Jim, Dead Gorgeous, Carla, Charles II (nominated LA Television Awards), Messiah, Frankenstein, Dr Who, The Garden, Peaky Blinders (seasons 1, 2 and 3), Penny Dreadful, Tommy Cooper – Not Like This, Like That, Leaving, Special Relationship, We'll Take Manhattan, Inside No. 9; *Theatre* Keely and Du (Olympia Theatre Dublin), Macbeth (Tricycle Theatre, Most Promising Newcomer Shakespeare Globe Awards), Rosalind in As You Like It (Wyndhams Theatre, nominated Best Actress Olivier Awards and Theatregoer Choice Awards), Pride and Prejudice (Royal Exchange Manchester), Venice Preserved (Royal Exchange Manchester), Les Enfants Du Paradis (RSC), Late Middle Classes (Donmar Warehouse); Almeida: Five Gold Rings, Platonov, The Triumph of Love, Rosemersholm; Donmar Warehouse: Old Times, Uncle Vanya (nominated Evening Standard Best Actress Award and New York Drama Desk Awards), Twelfth Night, How I Learned To Drive, In A Little World of Our Own, The Late Middle Classes; RNT: The Devil's Disciple, The Seagull, Trelawney of The Wells, Fuentovejuna, Blood Wedding (Best Actress Award Manchester Evening News), Medea, The Last of the Hausmans, The Deep Blue Sea; *Film* Streetlife (Best Actress: Welsh BAFTA, Monte Carlo Award), The Flemish Board, Interview With A Vampire, Witness Against Hitler, The James Gang, Dad Savage, Hotel Splendide, The Count of Monte Cristo, Charlotte Gray, Enduring Love, Casanova, The Queen (nominated Best Supporting Actress London Critics Circle), Becoming Jane, Flashbacks of a Fool, The Fabulous Mr Fox, Harry Potter and the Half Blood Prince, The Special Relationship, 4, 3, 2, 1, Harry Potter and the Deathly Hallows: Part 1, Harry Potter and the Deathly Hallows: Part 2, Hugo, Skyfall, Flying Blind, Little Chaos, Women in Black, Bill, Their Finest Hour and a Half; *Clubs* Soho House, London Library; *Style*— Mrs Damian Lewis, professionally known as Ms Helen McCrory; ✉ c/o Paul Lyon-Manis, Independent Talent Group Ltd, Oxford House, 76 Oxford Street, London W1D 1BS (☎ 020 7636 6565, fax 020 7323 0101); c/o Adam Issacs, Endevour, 9601 Wilshire Boulevard, 3rd Floor, Beverly Hills, CA 90210, USA (☎ 00 1310 248 2301, fax 00 1310 248 2020)

McCRUDDEN, Prof (John) Christopher; s of Gerard McCrudden, and Theodora McCrudden; *b* 29 January 1952; *Educ* Queen's Univ Belfast (LLB), Yale Univ (LLM), Univ of Oxford (MA, DPhil); *m* 1990, Caroline Mary, *née* Pannell; 1 s, 1 da; *Career* Univ of Oxford: lectr in law Balliol Coll 1976–77, jr res fell Balliol Coll 1976–80, fell Lincoln Coll 1980–2011, CUF lectr 1980–2011, reader in law 1996–99, prof of human rights law 1999–2011; William W Cook global prof of law Univ of Michigan Law Sch 1998–, prof of human rights and equality law Queen's Univ Belfast 2011–; Harkness fell 1974–76, visiting fell and lectr Yale Law Sch 1986, visiting sr fell PSI 1987–89, Leverhulme major research fell 2011–14, fell Straus Inst for the Advanced Study of Law and Justice NYU 2013–14, visiting fell Center for Constitutional Transitions NYU 2013–14, fell Wissenschaftskolleg zu Berlin 2014–15; visiting prof: Queen's Univ Belfast 1994–98, Univ of Texas Sch of Law 1996, Univ of Michigan Law Sch 1996–97; jt ed Law in Context series 1978–; memb Editorial Bd: Oxford Jl of Legal Studies 1983–, Int Jl of Discrimination and the Law 1996–, Jl of Int Econ Law 1998–2015; Expert Network on Application of Equality Directives EC 1986–, specialist advsr NI Affrs Select Ctee 1999; memb: Advsy Ctee ESRC Res Unit on Ethnic Rels 1982–85, Sec of State for NI's Standing Advsy Cmmn on Human Rights 1984–88, Public Procurement Implementation Gp NI Exec 2001, NI Public Procurement Bd 2002–08; called to the Bar: Gray's Inn 1996, Inns of Court NI 2006; non-resident tenant Blackstone Chambers; Hon LLD Queen's Univ Belfast 2006, Hon DCL Univ of Oxford 2016; Cert of Merit American Soc of Int Law 2008; FBA 2008; *Books* Regulation and Public Law (with R Baldwin, 1987), Women, Employment and European Community Law (ed, 1988), Fair Employment Handbook (ed, 1990, 3 edn 1995), Racial Justice at Work: the enforcement of the Race Relations Act 1976 in Employment (jtly, 1991), Equality in the Law between Men and Women in the European Community: United Kingdom (1994), Individual Rights and the Law in Britain (ed with G Chambers, 1994), Equality between Women and Men in Social Security (ed, 1994), Regulation and Deregulation (ed, 1998), Buying Social Justice (2007), Courts and Consociations (jtly, 2013), Understanding Human Dignity (ed, 2014), Reasoning Rights (jt ed, 2014); *Recreations* my family; *Style*— Prof Christopher McCrudden, FBA; ✉ School of Law, Queen's University, Belfast BT7 1NN (☎ 028 9097 3339, e-mail chris.mccrudden@qub.ac.uk)

McCRUM, Dr (John) Robert; s of Michael William McCrum (d 2005), of Cambridge, and Christine Mary Kathleen, *née* fforde; *b* 7 July 1953, Cambridge; *Educ* Sherborne, CCC Cambridge (scholar, MA), Univ of Pennsylvania (Thouron fell), Univ of Cambridge (PhD);

m 1, 1979 (m dis 1984), Olivia Timbs; m 2, 13 May 1995, Sarah Lyall; 2 da (Alice b 2 Feb 1997, Isobel b 5 May 1999); *Career* reader Chatto & Windus 1977–79, ed-in-chief Faber & Faber 1990–96 (editorial dir 1979–89); The Observer: lit ed 1996–2008, assoc ed 2008–; lit conslt to the Millennium Dome 1999–2000; patron Different Strokes, chm Norwich Writers' Centre; bye-fell Churchill Coll Cambridge 2001–03; Hon DLitt Univ of Heriot Watt Edinburgh 2011; *Books* In The Secret State (1980), A Loss of Heart (1982), The Fabulous Englishman (1984), The Story of English (non fiction, 1986, Peabody Award 1986, Emmy 1987), The World is a Banana (for children, 1988), Mainland (1991), The Psychological Moment (1992), Suspicion (1996), My Year Off (1998), Wodehouse: A Life (2004), Globish: How the English Language became the World's Language (2010), On Writing (e-book, 2012), On Reading (e-book, 2012), The 100 Best Novels in English (2015); *Style*— Dr Robert McCrum; ✉ 15 Bracknell Gardens, London NW3 7EE (☎ 07887 841966); The Observer, 90 York Way, London N1 9GU (☎ 020 3353 2000)

MacCUISH, Al; s of Donald Alec MacCuish, and Eleanor, *née* Blair; *b* 14 July 1971, Alexandria; *Educ* Hermitage Acad Helensburgh Scotland, Royal Scottish Acad of Music and Drama, Univ of Glasgow (MA); *m* 31 Dec 2011, Caroline Pay; 1 s (Buddy b 20 May; *Career* copywriter WCRS 1994–99, copywriter BMP DAB 1999–2001, creative dir Mother 2001–12, co-fndr and chief creative offr Sunshine 2012–; lectr D&AD; dir Bd London Philharmonic Orchestra; *Awards* numerous incl D&AD, One Show, BTAA (British Arrows), Cannes Lions; *Books* Operation Alphabet (Ministry of Letters) (2012), The Bee Who Spoke: The Wonderful World of Belle and the Bee (2014); *Recreations* cinema, fashion, music, opera, reading, sailing, skiing, travel; *Clubs* Soho House; *Style*— Al MacCuish, Esq; ✉ Sunshine, 8 Shepherdess Walk, London N1 7LB (e-mail al@thesunshinecompany.com, website www.thesunshinecompany.com)

McCULLOCH, Dr Andrew; s of Ian Robert McCulloch, and Marguerite Elizabeth McCulloch; *b* 21 April 1956, Woolwich, London; *Educ* Eltham Coll, Peterhouse Cambridge (MA), Univ of Southampton (PhD); *Partner* Louise Villeneau; 1 s, 1 da; *Career* Dept of Health: princ Policy Secretariat 1987–89, princ Child, Maternity and Prevention Div 1989–92, asst sec Gen Election Briefing Unit 1992, asst sec Mental Health and Community Care Div 1992–96; princ Andrew McCulloch Assocs 1996–2001, dir of policy The Sainsbury Centre for Mental Health 1996–2002, chief exec Mental Health Fndn 2002–13, chief exec Picker Inst Europe 2013–; Haringey Healthcare NHS Trust: memb Audit Ctee 1998–1999, non-exec dir 1998–2001, chair Mental Health Act Managers 1999–2001, chair R&D Ctee 1999–2001 (honorary non-exec 2002); Mental Health Media: memb Cncl (and tstee) 1997–2004, chair 1999–2002; memb: Sub-Gp on Employment NSF Standard 1 Taskforce 2001–2002, Workforce Numbers Advsy Gp 2002–04, Overarching Gp Women's Mental Health Task Force 2002–03, Ministerial Advsy Gp on Vulnerable Children 2004–05, Ministerial Advsy Gp on Mental Health 2007–09 and 2011–13, Mental Health Strategy Bd 2010–11, Public Mental Health Advsy Bd 2010–11; chair Children and Young People's Mental Health Coalition 2009–10, co-chair Future Visions Coalition 2009–12; expert advsr to Cncl of Europe 2007–08, mental health advsr to NESTA 2007–10; memb Comms Bd Br Psychological Soc 1999–2002, MIND Millennium Awards Assessment Panel 1997–1999; tstee UK Cncl for Psychotherapy 2009–12, patron Health Minds: Calderdale Wellbeing 2013–, vice-patron Family Action 2015–; winner Mental Health Achievement Awards 2002, President's Medal Royal Coll of Psychiatrists 2011, highly commended Emerald Literati 2012; govr Lea Valley HS Enfield 1992–95; life memb: Hawk and Owl Tst, Essex Naturalists' Tst; memb: Shakespeare's Globe 1000 Club, Tate Galleries, Dulwich Picture Gallery, NT, Charles Rennie Mackintosh Soc; fell RSPB; *Publications* Developing a National Mental Health Policy (2002); *Recreations* birdwatching, tennis, cinema, reading, bridge, travel, classical music, wine, writing; *Style*— Dr Andrew McCulloch; ✉ Picker Institute Europe, Buxton House, 3 West Way, Oxford OX2 0JB (e-mail andrew.mcculloch@pickereurope.ac.uk)

MACCULLOCH, Rev Prof (Sir) Diarmaid Ninian John; kt (2012); s of Rev Nigel J H MacCulloch, and Jennie, *née* Chappell; *b* 31 October 1951; *Educ* Stowmarket GS, Churchill Coll Cambridge (MA), Univ of Liverpool (Dip Archive Admin), Univ of Cambridge (PhD), Univ of Oxford (DipTh, DD); *Career* jr res fell Churchill Coll Cambridge 1976–78, approved lectr Univ of Cambridge 1977–78; tutor in history, librarian and archivist Wesley Coll Bristol 1978–90, pt/t lectr Univ of Bristol 1978–95, assoc scholar UEA 1984–87, fell St Cross Coll Oxford 1995– (sr tutor 1996–99), prof of the history of the church Univ of Oxford 1997–; ordained deacon 1987; pres Historical Assoc Bristol Branch 1994–95, pres Church of England Record Soc 2001–; co-ed Jl of Ecclesiastical History 1995–2014 (memb advsy bd 2014–); presenter: A History of Christianity (BBC 4 and BBC 2) 2009, How God Made the English (BBC 2) 2012, Sex and the Church (BBC 2) 2015; res fell Leverhulme Tst 1990–91, Wingate Scholar 1993–95, delivered Birkbeck Lectures Univ of Cambridge lent term 1998, delivered Gifford Lectures Univ of Edinburgh 2012; Liveryman Worshipful Co of Barbers; Hon DLitt Univ of E Anglia, Hon DD Virginia Theological Seminary, Hon DD Univ of the South, Hon DD Univ of St Andrews; FSA 1978, FRHistS 1982, FBA 2001; *Publications* The Chorography of Suffolk (ed vol 19, 1976), Suffolk and the Tudors: politics and religion in an English County 1500–1600 (1986, RHS Whitfield Prize 1987), The Reign of Henry VIII: Politics, Policy and Piety (ed, 1995), Thomas Cranmer: a Life (1996, Whitbread Biography Prize 1986, Duff Cooper Prize 1996, James Tait Black Meml Prize 1996), Tudor Church Militant: Edward VI and the Protestant Reformation (1999), Reformation: Europe's House Divided 1490–1700 (2003, Wolfson History Prize 2004, British Acad Prize 2004, Nat Book Critics Circle of the US Award for Non-Fiction 2005), A History of Christianity: The First Three Thousand Years (2009, Hessell-Tiltman Prize 2009, Cundill History Prize Montreal 2010), Silence: a Christian History (2013), All Things Made New: Writings on the Reformation (2016); author of numerous books, articles and textbooks on history, topography and archaeology, and theology and the Church; *Clubs* Athenaeum; *Style*— Rev Prof Diarmaid MacCulloch; ✉ St Cross College, Oxford OX1 3LZ (e-mail diarmaid.macculloch@stx.ox.ac.uk)

McCULLOCH, Ian; s of William Baxter McCulloch (d 1940), of Glasgow, and Elizabeth Harper (d 2001); *b* 4 March 1935; *Educ* Eastbank Acad Glasgow, Glasgow Sch of Art (DA); *m* 1959, Margery, da of James Palmer; 2 s (Neil b 1969, Euan b 1970); *Career* fine art fell Univ of Strathclyde 1994–2009 (lectr in fine art 1967–94), artist in residence Univ of Sussex 1976; SSA 1964, RSA 2005 (ARSA 1989); *Solo Exhibitions* incl: Artspace Galleries Aberdeen 1984, Camden Arts Centre 1986, Richard Demarco Gallery Edinburgh and tour 1986, Odette Gilbert Gallery London and tour 1987, Glasgow Print Studio 1989, The Return of Agamemnon and Other Paintings Aberystwyth Arts Centre, UC Wales Aberystwyth 1991, Aberdeen Art Gallery 1991–92, Relief Prints Peacock Printmakers Aberdeen 1994 (also tour), Recycled Lives: Paintings, Prints, Ceramics and Constructions 1997–2007 (Royal Scottish Acad Edinburgh) 2007, Trespassing: Paintings and Ceramics (Collins Gall Univ of Strathclyde) 2009; *Group Exhibitions* incl: Twentieth Century Scottish Painting (Arts Cncl of GB tour) 1963–64, Scottish Painters (Scottish Nat Gallery of Modern Art) 1964, Three Centuries of Scottish Painting (Nat Gallery of Canada Ottawa) 1968–69, New Tendencies in Scottish Painting (Demarco Gallery Edinburgh) 1969, Art Spectrum (Scottish Arts Cncl) 1971, Painters in Parallel (Scottish Arts Cncl) 1978, Stirling Smith Biennial 1985, Warwick Arts Tst (London) 1985, Reed Stremmel Gallery (San Antonia Texas) 1986, Chicago, LA and London Art Fairs 1986–88, Graven Image: Art, Religion and Politics (Harris Art Gallery Preston) 1988, Glasgow Printmakers (Berlin) 1988, John Moores Liverpool Exhbn 1989–90, New North (Tate Gallery Liverpool then tour) 1990, Unique and Original (Glasgow Print Studio then tour) 1992, Alter Ego/

Self Portrait (Glasgow Print Studio then tour) 1992, Scottish Painting (Flowers East Gallery London) 1993, Calanais (An Lanntair Gallery Stornoway and tour) 1995, Scottish Printmaking (Galerie Beeldspraak Amsterdam) 1995, Peacock 21 (Aberdeen Art Gallery) 1996, Day of the Dead (Galeria Otra Vez LA) 1996, Small is Beautiful (Flowers East Gallery London) 1996, Brave Art (Smith Art Gallery Stirling) 1996, Modern Scottish Graphics (Galerija Loskega Muzeja, Skofja Loka, Slovenia and tour) 1997, Scottish Spirit (Arthur Ross Gallery Univ of Pennsylvania and tour) 1998, Celtic Connections (Yorozu Tetsugoro Museum Japan) 1998, Scottish Painting (Albermarle Gallery London) 1999, On a Plate (Glasgow Print Studio) 1999, Liberation and Tradition: Scottish Art 1963–74 (Aberdeen Art Gallery and McManus Galleries, Dundee) 1999, Silver (Peacock Printmakers, Aberdeen) 1999, Connections (Royal Scottish Acad Edinburgh) 1999, Expressions: Scottish Art 1975–1989 (Aberdeen Art Gallery and McManus Galleries, Dundee, Dundee Contemporary Arts) 2000, Connections 2000 (Royal Scottish Acad, Edinburgh) 2000, The Dark Figure (Docherty Gallery Univ of NSW Sydney) 2001, Leabhar Mòr Book Exhibition and Tour (Stornoway Isle of Lewis) 2002–2003, Sons and Mothers Exhibition (Collins Gallery Univ of Strathclyde) 2003, Pittenweem Festival Exhibition 2004, Demarco European Art Fndn Skateraw 2006, Glasgow Gp Fiftieth Anniversary Exhibition Glasgow 2008; *Work in Public Collections* City Art Gallery Edinburgh, Univ of Glasgow, Univ of Liverpool, Univ of Strathclyde, Perth Town Cncl, Contemporary Arts Soc, Kelvingrove Art Gallery Glasgow, Dundee Art Gallery, Saatchi Collection London, Smith Art Gallery Stirling, Lillie Art Gallery Milngavie, Royal Scottish Acad Colls, Pallant House Gallery Chichester, murals cmmnd by Italian Centre Glasgow; *Awards* RSA travelling scholarship 1957–58, Scottish Arts Cncl Awards 1967 and 1972, first prize Stirling Smith Biennial 1985, winner Glasgow Int Concert Hall Mural Competition 1989–90, Gillies Award RSA 1999, Hope Scott Tst Award 2001; *Publications* Relief Print Illustrations in A Real Glasgow Archipelago (by Jack Withers, 1993), The Artist In His World, Prints 1986–97, with Eight Descriptive Poems by Alasdair Gray (1998), Images to Poems by Derick Thomson (Cencrastus magazine, 2005), The Drouth No 34 (contrib, 2009/10); *Style*— Ian McCulloch, Esq; ✉ e-mail mpm@waitrose.com, website www.royalscottishacademy.org

McCULLOCH, James Russell; s of late Dr John McCulloch, and late Laura Patricia, *née* Russell; *b* 19 November 1954; *Educ* Glasgow Acad, Univ of Stirling (BA); *m* 16 Oct 1980, Sally Lindsay, da of Benjamin Butters; 3 da (Lindsay Anne b 17 July 1984, Victoria Jayne b 6 June 1986, Caroline Fiona b 12 April 1989); *Career* CA; articled clerk Coopers & Lybrand Glasgow 1976–79, audit mangr Coopers & Lybrand Houston Texas USA 1979–82, ptnr Speirs & Jeffrey 1985–2016 (joined 1982, managing ptnr 2001–11, exec chm 2003–16); non-exec dir Seneca Global Income & Growth Tst 2015–; memb Stock Exchange 1985; memb Merchant House of Glasgow 1990; tstee Fndn Scotland 2011; MICAS 1979, CFCSI; *Recreations* golf, tennis, skiing, travel; *Clubs* Glasgow Academical, Pollok Golf, Prestwick Golf, Golf House Club Elie, Western Gailes Golf, Seniors Golfing Soc; *Style*— James R McCulloch, Esq; ✉ 2 Cypress Grove, Bridge of Weir, Renfrewshire PA11 3NJ (☎ 01505 610547, e-mail jamesrussellmcculloch@hotmail.com)

McCULLOCH, Ken; s of Archie McCulloch, of Glasgow, and Kathleen McCulloch; *b* 7 November 1948; *Educ* Gresham's; *Career* hotelier; mgmnt trg British Transport Hotels 1965–69, mgmnt Stakis Hotels 1969–74, dir Chardon Hotels 1974–76; proprietor: Le Provencal Glasgow 1976–, Charlie Parker's Glasgow 1976– and Edinburgh 1979–, Buttery Glasgow 1983–, Rogano Glasgow 1984–, One Devonshire Gardens 1986–, Malmaison 1994–98, Columbus Hotels 2001–; visiting prof Univ of Strathclyde Business Sch; Mktg Award (British Airways) BBC Scotland 1991, Best Hotel in Scotland (Book of the Best) 1992, County Restaurant of the Year (Good Food Guide) 1992 and 1993, UK Hotelier of the Year 1993, Egon Ronay Hotel of the Year 1994, Michelin Star 1996, Good Food Guide County Hotel of the Year 1997 (for Malmaison), Outstanding Achievement Award European Hotel Design Awards 2002; *Recreations* connoisseur of Scotland, cooking, Glasgow Rangers, motor racing; *Style*— Ken McCulloch, Esq

MacCULLOCH, Prof Malcolm John; s of William MacCulloch (d 1976), of Macclesfield, Cheshire, and Constance Martha, *née* Clegg; *b* 10 July 1936; *Educ* Kings Sch Macclesfield, Univ of Manchester (MB ChB, DPM, MD); *m* 1, 14 July 1962 (m dis 1975), Mary Louise, da of Ernest Sutcliffe Beton (d 1987), of Norwich, Norfolk; 1 s (Thomas Alistair b 1965), 1 da (Louise Elizabeth Mary b 1968); *m* 2, 24 Sept 1975, Carolyn Mary, da of Sqdn Ldr (William) Alan Walker Reid, of London; 2 da (Sarah Caroline b 1976, Sophie Isabel 1978); *Career* conslt child psychiatrist Cheshire 1966–67, lectr in child psychiatry and subnormality Univ of Birmingham 1967–70, sr lectr in psychiatry Univ of Liverpool 1970–75, sr princ med offr DHSS London 1975–79, med dir Park Lane Hosp Liverpool 1979–89, conslt WHO 1977–79, visiting prof of forensic psychiatry Toronto 1987–89, advsr in forensic psychiatry Ontario Govt 1987–92, emeritus prof of forensic psychiatry Univ of Wales Coll of Med Cardiff 2001– (prof of forensic psychiatry 1997–2001); ed Jl of Forensic Psychiatry and Psychology 2007– (ed-in-chief 2002–07), author of numerous pubns in professional jls; FRCPsych 1976; *Books* Homosexual Behaviour: Therapy and Assessment (1971), Human Sexual Behaviour (1980); *Recreations* music, golf, horse riding, inventing; *Style*— Professor Malcolm MacCulloch; ✉ 14 Tall Trees, Baunton Lane, Cirencester GL7 2AF (☎ 01285 642689)

McCULLOCH, Margaret; MSP; *née* Gorman; da of Joseph Gorman (d 2011), and Margaret, *née* Reid (d 2000); *b* 9 May 1952, Glasgow; *Educ* Glasgow Caledonian Univ (Postgrad Cert); *m* 1, 24 June 1972, William Cullen; 2 s (Paul b 27 Nov 1974, Gregg b 5 Dec 1976); m 2, 28 May 1993, Ian McCulloch; *Career* trg exec Univ of Strathclyde 1992–2009, owner Independent Training Consults Ltd 2009–10 (dir 2010–11); MSP (Lab) Central Scotland 2011–; *Style*— Margaret McCulloch, MSP; ✉ The Scottish Parliament, Edinburgh EH99 1SP (☎ 0131 348 6379, e-mail margaret.mcculloch.msp@scottish.parliament.uk, website www.margaretmcculloch.org and www.facebook.com/margaretmccullochmsp, Twitter @magmsp)

McCULLOUGH, Sir (Iain) Charles Robert; kt (1981); s of Thomas Warburton McCullough, CB, OBE (d 1989), and Lisette Hunter, *née* Gannaway (d 1980); *b* 31 July 1931, Glasgow; *Educ* Dollar Acad, Taunton Sch (Exhibitioner), Trinity Hall Cambridge (BA, MA); *m* 31 July 1965, Margaret Joyce Patey; 1 s (Angus Maxwell Thomas b 14 July 1966), 1 da (Flora Joyce McLean b 6 Jan 1988); *Career* called to the Bar Middle Temple 1956 (Blackstone Award, Harmsworth Law Scholar, N W Powell Prize), QC 1971, dep chm Notts Quarter Sessions 1969–71, recorder of the Crown Court 1971–81, judge of the High Court of Justice (Queen's Bench Div) 1981–98, surveillance cmmr 1998–2009, treas Middle Temple 2000; memb: Criminal Law Revision Ctee 1973–, Parole Bd 1984–86; visitor Loughborough Univ 2003–13; *Clubs* Garrick, Pilgrims; *Style*— Sir Charles McCullough; ✉ c/o Middle Temple Treasury, Temple, London EC4Y 9AT

McCULLOUGH, Dr John; s of Henry Christie McCullough (d 2007), and Jessie, *née* Niven (d 1978); *b* 23 March 1949; *Educ* Model Sch Belfast, Paisley Coll of Technol, Portsmouth Poly (MSc, PhD); *m* 25 March 1971, Geraldine Mabel, da of Gerald Thomas Gardner (d 2002); 2 da (Katherine b 1979, Eleanor b 1985), 1 s (Alexander b 1982); *Career* conslt engr (various appts in NI, England and Scot), expert witness in cases of litigation, arbitration and public inquiry in Scot, England and abroad, expert determination in Eastern Europe, appointed expert Arbitration Tribunal ICC; ptnr Hancox & Partners 1982–88; dir: Rendel Hancox Ltd 1988–91, Rendel Palmer & Tritton (Scot) Ltd 1991–97, Highpoint Rendel (Europe, Africa and ME) 1996–97; external conslt Cadogan Conslts 2009– (princ 1992–97, md 1997–2000, chm 2000–09), dir Cadogan Tietz 1999–2001 (conslt 2001–04); chm Scot Region Inst of Energy 1984–85; Freeman City of London, Liveryman

M

Worshipful Co of Engrs; CEng 1980, CSci 2005–14; FEI 1983, FIMechE 1986, Eur Ing 1988, MAE; *Recreations* music, cycling, reading, walking; *Style*— Dr John McCullough; ✉ Southpark, Kilmacolm, Renfrewshire PA13 4NN (☎ 01505 872895); Cadogans, Moncrieff House, 69 West Nile Street, Glasgow G1 2LT (☎ 0141 270 7060, fax 0141 270 7061, mobile 07712 199356, e-mail j.mccullough@cadogans.com, website www.cadogans.com)

McCUTCHEON, Prof John Joseph; CBE (1994); s of James Thomson McCutcheon (d 1964), and Margaret, *née* Hutchison (d 1984); *b* 10 September 1940; *Educ* Glasgow Acad, St John's Coll Cambridge (scholar, MA, Wright's prize), Univ of Liverpool (PhD, DSc); *m* 1978, Jean Sylvia, *née* Constable; *Career* actuarial student Scottish Amicable Life Assurance Soc 1962–65, conslt actuary Duncan C Fraser & Co 1965–66, demonstrator/ sr demonstrator Dept of Pure Mathematics Univ of Liverpool 1966–70, assoc prof Dept of Actuarial and Business Mathematics Univ of Manitoba 1970–72; Heriot-Watt Univ: sr lectr 1972–75, prof of actuarial studies 1975–2001 (emeritus 2001–), dean Faculty of Science 1995–98; FFA 1965 (pres 1992–94), FRSE 1993; *Publications* An Introduction to the Mathematics of Finance (with W F Scott, 1986); author of papers in mathematics, actuarial science and mortality studies; *Recreations* reading, opera, tennis, travel, occasional hill-walking; *Clubs* Woodcutters' Cricket; *Style*— Prof John McCutcheon, CBE, FRSE; ✉ 14 Oswald Court, Edinburgh EH9 2HY

MacDAID, Most Rev Liam Seàn; *see:* Clogher, Bishop of

McDERMID, Prof John Alexander; OBE (2010); s of John Alexander McDermid (d 1997), and Joyce Winifred, *née* Whiteley (d 1969); *b* 5 October 1952; *Educ* High Heaton GS, Univ of Cambridge (MA), Univ of Birmingham (PhD); *m* 29 March 1980 (m dis 2015), Heather Mair, *née* Denly; 2 da (Ailsa Gaynor b 26 Nov 1985, Catriona Isabel b 14 May 1993); *Career* student engr and research scientist MOD 1971–82, conslt then divnl mangr Systems Designers (now HP) 1982–87, prof of software engrg Univ of York 1987– (head Dept of Computer Science 2006–12); dir Origin Consulting 2003–12, chm Rapita Systems 2014–; non-exec dir: High Integrity Solutions 2002–08, York PRT 2004–06; author of six books and approximately 400 conf papers and jl articles; IEE Heaviside Premium 1982, BCS IT Award 1993; govr Pocklington Sch 1997–2004; Freeman City of London 2002, Liveryman Worshipful Co of Engrs 2002; FIEE 1975, FBCS 1982, FRAeS 1997, FREng 2002, FSaRS 2009; *Recreations* reading, music, badminton, walking; *Clubs* Athenaeum; *Style*— Prof John McDermid, OBE, FREng; ✉ Department of Computer Science, University of York, Deramore Lane, York YO10 5GH (☎ 01904 325419, fax 01904 325599, mobile 07802 234814 and 07818 418020, e-mail john.mcdermid@york.ac.uk)

McDERMOTT, Gerard Francis; QC (1999); s of Joseph Herbert McDermott, of Ashton-under-Lyne, and Winifred Mary, *née* Limon; *b* 21 April 1956; *Educ* De La Salle Coll Salford, Univ of Manchester (LLB), Coll of Law; *m* July 1992, Fiona, *née* Johnson, da of David Johnson, and Kay Johnson; *Career* called to the Bar Middle Temple 1978 (bencher 2005); recorder 1999–2015, dep High Court judge 2008–; attorney-at-law (NY) 1990, dir American Counsel Assoc 1998– (pres 2003–04); chm Young Barristers Ctee 1987, memb Gen Cncl of the Bar 1983–88, 1990–96, 1998–99 and 2003–07 (chm Int Rels Ctee 1999–2000), ldr European Circuit of the Bar 2006–09 (dep ldr 2003–05); fell American Bar Fndn; *Clubs* Athenaeum; *Style*— Gerard McDermott, QC; ✉ Outer Temple Chambers, 222 Strand, London WC2R 1BA (☎ 020 7353 6381, fax 020 7583 1786, gerard.mcdermottqc@outertemple.com or gerard@mcdermottqc.com, Twitter @mcdermottqc)

McDERMOTT, Jennifer; da of S K Harding, and E Harding, *née* Donkin; *b* 11 January 1957, Sunderland; *Educ* UCL (LLB); *Children* 1 s (Patrick Benedict), 1 da (Helen Frances); *Career* slr specialising in media and public law; Lovells (formerly Lovell White & King): articled clerk 1979–81, litigation assoc 1981–89, litigation ptnr 1989–2004; contentious ptnr Addleshaw Goddard 2004–07, commerical litigation ptnr Withers 2007–13; friend JUSTICE; *Style*— Mrs Jennifer McDermott; ✉ e-mail jenniferxmcdermot@me.com

McDERMOTT, Phelim Joseph; s of Edward William McDermott, and Stella Donovan; *b* 21 August 1963; *Educ* Manchester Grammar, Middlesex Poly (BA); *m* Matilda Leyser; 1 s (Riddley Wilbur); *Career* theatre dir and actor; co-fndr (with Julia Bardsley) and artistic dir dereck, dereck Prodns, shows incl Cupboard Man (performer, Fringe First Award), Gaudete (co-dir and performer, Time Out Dir's Award), The Vinegar Works, The Glass Hill and The Sweet Shop Owner (all dir); co-fndr (with Julian Crouch and Lee Simpson) and co-artistic dir Improbable 1996–, shows incl 70 Hill Lane (Time Out Best Fringe Show, Obie Award), Animo, Spirit, Cinderella, The Hanging Man, Theatre of Blood (NT) and Satyagraha (ENO) (all dir) and Shockheaded Peter (co-dir, Olivier Award for Best Entertainment, TMA Best Dir Award, South Bank Show Theatre Award nomination), Panic, The Still (performer and dir); other shows directed incl: The Ghost Downstairs (Leicester Haymarket), Dr Faustus and Improbable Tales (both Nottingham Playhouse), A Midsummer Night's Dream (English Shakespeare Co, TMA Best Touring Show Award), The Servant of Two Masters, The Hunchback of Notre Dame and The Government Inspector (all West Yorkshire Playhouse), Satyagraha (Met Opera), The Addams Family (Broadway, dir and designer, winner Drama Desk Award and Outer Critics Circle Award), Perfect American (premiere), Philip Glass (Teatre Real Madrid), Cosi Fan Tutte (ENO), Beauty and the Beast (Young Vic Theatre and Off Broadway), Metropolitan Opera 125th Anniversary Gala; memb: Bd Actors Centre, Faculty of the Michael Checkov Assoc, Bd Open Space Inst US; guest performer Comedy Store Players; involved with annual Devoted and Disgruntled event Open Space Facilitator; Hon Doctorate Univ of Middlesex 2007; NESTA fell (researching improvisation and conflict resolution) ACE Cultural Leadership Prog 2006; *Recreations* shamanism, newspaper animation, improvisation; *Clubs* Blacks, The Hospital; *Style*— Mr Phelim McDermott; ✉ Improbable, 3.18 Canterbury Court, 1–3 Brixton Road, London SW9 6DE (☎ 020 7240 4556, e-mail office@improbable.co.uk)

MacDONAGH, Lesley Anne; da of Arthur George Payne, and Agnes Dowie, *née* Scott; *b* 19 April 1952; *Educ* Queen Elizabeth I Sch Wimborne, Coll of Law Guildford and London; *m* 1, 1975 (m dis 1985), John Belton; 1 da; m 2, 1987, Simon Michael Peter MacDonagh; 3 s; *Career* admitted slr 1976; ptnr Lovells (formerly Lovell White Durrant) 1981–2006 (managing ptnr 1995–2005); non-exec dir: Bovis Homes Gp 2003–, Slough Estates plc 2007–; Law Soc: memb Planning and Environmental Ctee 1988–95, memb Cncl 1992–2001, memb Policy Ctee 1996–99, memb Audit Ctee 1999–2001; memb: Consultative Ctee Lands Tbnl 1991–95, Property Advsy Gp 1993–96; tstee Citizenship Fndn 1991–98, vice-chm Environmental Ctee Knightsbridge Assoc 1991–98; govr LSE until 2007; Liveryman Worshipful Co of Solicitors (memb Ct of Assts 1996–2006); *Recreations* family life, painting and drawing; *Style*— Mrs Lesley MacDonagh

McDONAGH, Martin; *b* 26 March 1970, Camberwell, London; *Career* playwright and screenwriter; *Plays* incl: The Leenane Trilogy (The Beauty Queen of Leenane 1996 (Most Promising Playwright Critics' Circle Theatre Award 1996), A Skull of Connemara 1997, The Lonesome West 1997), The Aran Islands Trilogy (The Cripple of Inishmaan 1996, The Lieutenant of Inishmore 2001, The Banshees of Inisheer), The Pillowman 2003 (Best New Play Laurence Olivier Award 2004), A Behanding in Spokane 2010; *Screenplays* Six Shooter (also dir) 2004 (Best Live Action Short Film Acad Award 2005), In Bruges (also dir) 2008 (Best Screenplay Br Ind Film Awards 2008, Best Film Script Irish Playwrights and Screenwriters Guild Award 2008, Best Screenplay Evening Standard Br Film Award 2009, Best Original Screenplay BAFTA 2009), Seven Psychopaths (also prodr and dir) 2012; *Style*— Mr Martin McDonagh; ✉ c/o Knight Hall Agency, Lower Ground Floor, 7 Mallow Street, London EC1Y 8RQ

McDONAGH, Siobhain; MP; *b* 20 February 1960; *Educ* Univ of Essex (BA); *Career* former housing devpt mangr Battersea Churches Housing Trust, MP (Lab) Mitcham and Morden 1997–; memb Social Security Select Ctee 1997–; *Recreations* music, reading, cooking; *Style*— Ms Siobhain McDonagh, MP; ✉ House of Commons, London SW1A 0AA (☎ 020 7219 4678)

MacDONALD, Angus; MSP; *b* Stornoway; *Educ* Grangemouth HS, Keil Sch Dumbarton, Coll of Estate Mgmnt; *m* Linda Macdonald; *Career* worked in family businesses: farming, wholesale and retail butchering, livestock auctioneering; MSP (SNP) Falkirk E 2011–; *Style*— Angus MacDonald, Esq, MSP; ✉ 2 York Arcade, Grangemouth, FK3 8BA

McDONALD, Antony Rycroft; s of Alexander McDonald, of Weston-super-Mare, and Cicely Elaine, *née* Hartley; *b* 11 September 1950; *Educ* Monkton Coombe Sch, Central Sch of Speech and Drama, Manchester Poly Sch of Theatre, Univ of Manchester, Motley Theatre; *Career* theatre designer and director; asst dir The Community and Schs; Co of The Welsh Nat Opera and Drama Co 1974–76; Best Costume Design Irish Times 2013, Best Costume Design Golden Mask Russia 2013; RDI 2004; work as dir and designer incl: Let's Make an Opera (Welsh Nat Opera) 1978, Jessonda (Oxford Univ Opera Soc) 1980, War Crimes (ICA) 1981, Degas (Ian Spink Dance Group and Channel 4) 1981, Carnival of the Animals (Second Stride) 1982, Dances from the Kingdom of the Pagodas (Royal Danish Ballet) 1982, Secret Gardens (Mickery Theatre Amsterdam) 1982, Insignificance (Royal Court) 1982, Mrs Gauguin, Hedda Gabler (Almeida) 1984, Tom and Viv (Royal Court) 1984 (also at Public Theatre NY 1985), Orlando (Scottish Opera) 1985, Midsummer Marriage (Opera North), Bösendorfer Waltzes (Second Stride, Munich New Dance Festival) 1986, Dancelines (Channel 4) 1986, A Streetcar Named Desire (Crucible Sheffield) 1987, The Trojans (WNO, Opera North and Scottish Opera) 1987, Billy Budd (ENO) 1988, Hamlet (RSC) 1988, Mary Stuart (Greenwich) 1988, Heaven Ablaze in his Breast (Second Stride), As You Like It (Old Vic) 1989, Beatrice and Benedict (ENO) 1990, Berenice (RNT) 1990, Mad Forest (Royal Court and NT Bucharest) 1990, Richard II (RSC) 1990, Benvenuto Cellini (Netherlands Opera) 1991, Lives of the Great Poisoners (Second Stride) 1991, Hamlet (American Repertory Theatre Cambridge MA) 1991, Marriage of Figaro (Aust Opera) 1992, The Seagull (American Rep Theatre Cambridge MA) 1992, Touch Your Coolness to My Fevered Brow (Dutch Nat Ballet) 1992, Euridice (Musica Nel Chiostro Italy) 1992, Why Things Happen (Second Stride) 1992, The Birthday Party (Glasgow Citizen's), Black Snow (American Rep Theatre Cambridge MA) 1992, Orlando (Aix-en-Provence Festival) 1993, Wallenstein (RSC) 1993, Escape at Sea (Second Stride) 1993, Cherubin (Royal Opera House) 1994, Fearful Symmetries (Royal Ballet) 1994, Francesca Da Rimini (Bregenz Festival) 1994, Pelleas and Melisande (Opera North) 1995, Nabucco (WNO) 1995, Ebony Concerto (Royal Ballet), Nabucco (ROH) 1996, Pelleas and Melisande (Minnesota Opera) 1996, Orlando (Brooklyn Acad of Music) 1996, Now Langorous – Now Wild (Royal Ballet) 1996, Ariadne auf Naxos (Bavarian State Opera) 1996, A Midsummer Night's Dream (Metropolitan Opera NY) 1996, The Country Wife (Glasgow Citizens) 1997, Samson and Dalila (Scottish Opera) 1997, Jenufa (Netherlands Opera) 1997, Snatched by the Gods/Broken Strings (Scottish Opera) 1998, Beatrice and Benedict (Santa Fe Opera) 1998, The Makropulos Case 1998, Cheating, Lying, Stealing (Royal Ballet) 1998, Der Zwerg and L'Enfant et Les Sortileges (Paris Opera) 1998, Endgame (Nottingham Playhouse) 1999, Aida (Scottish Opera) 1999, Ballo In Maschera (Bregentz Festival) 2000, Hidden Variables (Royal Ballet) 2000, The Merry Widow (Metropolitan Opera) 2000, Pélleas and Mélisande (ENO) 2000, Jenufa (Lyric Opera Chicago) 2000, Beatrice and Benedict (Netherlands Opera) 2001, La Bohème (Bregenz Festival) 2001, Dido and Aeneas/Acis and Galatea (Bavarian State Opera) 2001, Manouvre (ENB) 2002, Julietta (Paris Opera) 2002, Cheating, Lying Stealing (Royal Ballet) 2003, King Priam (Nat Reisopera Holland) 2003, Nathan The Wise (Minerva Theatre Chichester) 2003, The Nut Cracker (Scottish Ballet) 2003, Aida (Scottish Opera) 2003, Private Lives (Glasgow Citizens) 2003, The Tragedy of Fashion (Ballet Rambert) 2004, Wonderful Town (Grange Park Opera) 2004, Beatrice and Benedict (Santa Fe Opera) 2004, Pélleas and Mélisande (Bavarian State Opera) 2004, One Touch for Venus (set designer, Opera North) 2004, The Knot Garden (Scottish Opera) 2005, Manon Lescaut (designer, Vienna State Opera) 2005, Cinderella (designer, Scottish Ballet) 2005, The Cunning Little Vixen (designer, Netherlands Opera) 2006, Eugene Onegin (designer, ROH) 2006, Manon (Nat Reisopera Holland), Eugene Onegin (Finnish Opera), The Sleeping Beauty (designer, Scottish Ballet) 2007, Billy Budd (designer, Frankfurt Opera) 2007, Der Zareuitsch (Landestheater Niederbayern) 2008, Rusalka (Grange Park Opera) 2008, Pennies from Heaven (designer, Scottish Ballet) 2008, Carmen (designer, Scottish Ballet) 2009, Primadonna (designer, Manchester Festival) 2009, Das Rheingold (NAT Reisopera Holland) 2009, Maria Stuarda (Opera North) 2010, Primadonna (designer, Toronto Festival) 2010, Die Walküre (Nationale Reisoper) 2010, Billy Budd (designer, Nederlands Opera) 2011, Alice (designer, Scottish Ballet), 2011, Siegfried (Nationale Reisoper) 2011, L'Enfant et les Sortileges (Bolshoi Theatre Moscow) 2012, Queen of Spades (Grange Park Opera) 2012, Gotterdämmerung (National Reisoper) 2012, Lohengrin (WNO) 2013, The Importance of Being Earnest (opera, NI Opera) 2013, Lohengrin (Polish Nat Opera) 2014, Ein Reisen (ballet, designer, Vienna Staats Ballet) 2014, La Finta Giardineira (designer, Glyndebourne Opera) 2014, Tristan und Isolde (Opera du Rhin Strasbourg) 2015, Fiddler on the Roof (Grange Park Opera) 2015, The Bakkhai (designer, Almeida Theatre) 2015, Rusalka (Scottish Opera) 2016, A Midsummer Night's Dream (Hyogo Performing Arts Centre Japan) 2016; *Style*— Antony McDonald, Esq, RDI; ✉ Loesje Sanders, The Old Rectory, Church Road, Limpenhoe, Norwich NR13 3JB (☎ 01394 385260, e-mail antonymcdonald@mac.com, website www.loesjesanders.com)

MACDONALD, His Hon Judge Charles Adam; QC (1992); s of Alasdair Cameron Macdonald, of Glasgow, and Jessie Catherine, *née* McCrow; *b* 31 August 1949; *Educ* Glasgow Acad, New Coll Oxford (MA), Cncl of Legal Educn; *m* 17 June 1978, Dinah Jane, da of Ronald Manns, of Wargrave, Berks; 3 da (Kate, Anna, Elspeth); *Career* called to the Bar Lincoln's Inn 1972; practised in maritime and commercial law, recorder 1999–2005 (asst recorder 1996–99), circuit judge (SE Circuit) 2005–, tnbl judge First Tier Chamber (Health Educn and Social Care) 2009–13, memb Parole Bd 2010–13; Lloyd's salvage arbitrator 2000–05; *Publications* Butterworths Commercial Court and Arbitration Pleadings (2005); *Recreations* owns and breeds sport horses; *Style*— His Hon Judge Macdonald, QC; ✉ Maidstone Combined Court, Barker Road, Maidstone, Kent ME16 8EQ

MACDONALD, Chris; s of John Macdonald, of Oxford, and Cynthia, *née* Batts; *b* 13 March 1967, Oxford; *Educ* St Edward's Sch Oxford, Instituto Britannico de Firenze (Dip), Univ of Kent at Canterbury (BA); *m* 6 May 1995, Sarah, *née* Whitmore; 2 da (Georgina b 14 June 1996, Isadora b 15 May 2003), 1 s (Max b 31 Dec 1998); *Career* grad trainee DMB&B 1990–93, account dir and dir Lowe Howard-Spink 1993–97, head of account mgmnt Publicis London 1997–2000, managing ptnr RKCR/Y&R 2000–04, md McCann Erickson 2005–; memb: IPA, Mktg Soc; various industry awards incl IPA Effectiveness, Campaign Press and Poster awards and Cannes Silver; *Recreations* tennis; *Style*— Chris Macdonald, Esq; ✉ McCann Erickson, 7–11 Herbrand Street, London WC1N 1EX (☎ 020 7961 2115, e-mail chris.macdonald@europe.mccann.com)

MacDONALD, Dr (Isabelle Wilma) Claire; *née* Garland; da of William Garland (d 1972), and Barbara Sutherland, *née* MacDonald (d 2011); *b* 6 February 1951; *Educ* Hutchesons Girls GS, Univ of Glasgow (BSc, MB ChB); *m* 28 April 1977, David John MacDonald, s of Alastair J MacDonald (d 1991), of Glasgow; 2 da (Jennifer b 21 Aug 1979, Elizabeth b 6 Dec 1982), 1 s (Alastair b 31 July 1991); *Career* Victoria Infirmary Glasgow: house offr in surgery 1975–76, registrar in pathology 1977–79, sr registrar 1979–81; house offr in medicine Stirling Royal Hosp 1976, sr house offr in pathology Western Infirmary Glasgow 1976–77, lectr in pathology Univ of Aberdeen 1981–84; Pontefract Gen Infirmary: conslt histopathologist 1984–2013 (ret), chm Div of Pathology 1989–92, dir Functional Unit of Pathology 1992–99, dir Clinical Service Unit & Pathology Pinderfields & Pontefract NHS Tst 1999–2005, dir Pathology Mid Yorks NHS Tst 2005–09; CPA assessor; FRCPath 1994 (MRCPath 1982); *Recreations* swimming, reading; *Clubs* Caledonian Soc, Con; *Style—* Dr Claire MacDonald; ✉ 63 Ackworth Road, Pontefract, West Yorkshire WF8 3PG

MACDONALD, Euan Ross; s of Ian Somerled Macdonald (d 1958), and Elisabeth Barbara, da of Sir Denham Warmington, 2 Bt (d 1935); *b* 8 April 1940; *Educ* Marlborough, Trinity Coll Cambridge (BA), Graduate Sch of Business Columbia Univ NY (MBA); *m* March 1965, (Jacqueline) Anne Gatacre Evelyn-Wright; 4 s (Iain Graham b 12 Oct 1966, Russell Ross, James Curtis (twins) b 19 May 1969, Dougal Evelyn b 7 May 1974); *Career* Lazard Brothers & Co Ltd 1963–74, first gen mangr International Financial Advisers Kuwait 1974–79, dir gen Ifabanque SA Paris 1979–82, vice-chm S G Warburg & Co Ltd 1994 (dir 1982), chm Warburg Dillon Read (India) Bombay 1995–99, exec vice-chm HSBC Securities and Capital Markets India Private Ltd 1999–2001; head Corp Fin Advsy Team HSBC Republic London 2001–02; non-exec dir: Acrastyle Ltd 2004–08, Vedanta Resources plc 2005–16; vol teacher Westgate Sch Samburu Kenya 2008–09; tstee Cumberland Lodge 1995–2008; memb Worshipful Co of Clothworkers; *Style—* Euan Macdonald, Esq; ✉ Old Schoolhouse, Duisdale Beag, Isle of Skye IV43 8QU

MacDONALD, Hannah; da of Robert MacDonald (d 2001), and Vivien Rothwell; *b* 1971, London; *Educ* Wimbledon HS, Univ of Manchester (BA); *m* 14 Sept 2002, Paul Butterworth; 1 s (b 2006); *Career* former non-fiction ed Virgin Publishing and André Deutsch, subsequently joined Random House, currently sr publishing dir Ebury Press; memb Advsy Bd Kingston Univ Publishing MA; *Books* The Sun Road (2003, Betty Trask First Novel Award), Julianna Kiss (2006); *Recreations* travel, cooking, cinema; *Style—* Ms Hannah MacDonald; ✉ Ebury Press, Random House, 20 Vauxhall Bridge Road, London SW1V 2SA (☎ 020 7840 8400, e-mail hmacdonald@eburypublishing.co.uk); c/o Victoria Hobbs, AM Heath & Co Ltd, 6 Warwick Court WC1R SDT

McDONALD, Dr Henry; *Educ* Univ of Glasgow (BSc, DSc); *Career* engr Aerodynamics Dept Br Aircraft Corp 1960–65; United Technologies Research Centre CT: supervisor Theoretical Gas Dynamics Gp 1968–72 (research engr 1965–68), chief Gas Dynamics Section 1972–76; fndr, pres and ceo Scientific Research Assocs CT 1976–92, co-fndr Advanced Pulmonary Technologies Inc CT 1988–92, center dir NASA Ames Research Centre CA 1996–2002; memb: NASA/Rocketdyne Review Panel on Blade Cracking in the SSME Turbine 1986–87, US Air Force/Martin Marietta Special Review of Titian IV Test Failure 1991; chair: Space Shuttle Ind Assessment Team 2000, Review of the Aerodynamics Issues on the V-22 Osprey 2001; sr res fell Univ of Glasgow 1975–76, prof of mech engrg in residence Univ of Connecticut 1985–89, prof of mech engrg and asst dir Computational Sciences Pennsylvania State Univ Applied Research Lab 1991–97, prof of computational engrg Mississippi State Univ MS 1997–2002, distinguished prof and chair of excellence in engrg Univ of Tennessee at Chattanooga 2002–; visiting faculty memb Dept of Mechanical Engrg: Hong Kong Poly, Imperial Coll London; memb Advsy Ctee: Dept for Aeronautical Engrg Stanford Univ, Faculty of Engrg Univ of Calif Davis; memb: Bd of Dirs Connecticut Innovations, Govr's Advsy Cncl for High Technol CT 1989–90, Engrg Research Advsy Bd Mississippi State Univ 1996–2000, Sr Mgmnt Cncl NASA 1996–2002, Peer Ctee Aerospace Engrg Nat Acad of Engrg 2003–; assoc tech ed American Inst of Aeronautics and Astronautics (AIAA) Jl 1981–84; Small Business of the Year Award for High Technol CT 1989, NASA Outstanding Leadership Medal 1997 and 2000, NASA Gp Achievement Award (for Shuttle Ind Assessment Team) 2001, NASA Distinguished Service Medal 2001, Royal Aeronautic Soc Gold Medal 2009; Hon Dr Engrg Univ of Glasgow 1997; memb US Nat Acad of Engrg 2000, hon memb American Soc of Mechanical Engrgs 2001, hon fell American Inst of Aeronautics and Astronautics (AIAA), FRAeS, FREng 2003; *Style—* Dr Henry McDonald

MACDONALD, Hugh John; *b* 31 January 1940; *Educ* Univ of Cambridge (MA, PhD); *Career* lectr in music: Univ of Cambridge 1966–71, Univ of Oxford 1971–80; visiting prof of music Indiana Univ 1979, Gardiner prof of music Univ of Glasgow 1980–87, Avis Blewett prof of music Washington Univ St Louis 1987–2011; gen ed New Berlioz Edition 1967–2006; Szymanowski Medal (Poland); FRCM; Chevalier de l'Ordre National du Mérite (2015); *Books* Skryabin (1978), Berlioz (1982), Selected Letters of Berlioz (1995), Berlioz's Orchestration Treatise (2002), Beethoven's Century (2008), Music in 1853 (2012), Bizet (2014), The Bizet Catalogue (2014); *Style—* Hugh Macdonald; ✉ 18 Fishergate, Norwich NR3 1SE (☎ 01603 762477)

MACDONALD, Iain Lachlan; TD (1993); s of Angus Macdonald (d 2000), of North Uist, Scotland, and Elizabeth, *née* Reid; *b* 9 July 1955; *Educ* Allan Glen's Sch Glasgow, Univ of Glasgow (BArch, DipArch), Lanchester Polytechnic (MA), Domus Acad Milan (Master of Industrial Design); *m* 16 June 1984, Frances, *née* McKay; 2 s (Ruaridh b 1990, James b 1993); *Career* architect and planner; dir: IMA 1992–98 and 2012–, Aukett 1998–2004, YRM 2007–11; work exhibited: Europe, Asia and USA; winner Euro Medi-Park Competition 1992; formerly: Lt-Col Parachute Regt (V) 1980–95 (Lt 2 PARA 1982–83) RIBA, RIAS, MRTPI, FSIA; *Publications* Il Oggetto Neoclectico (1993), Architects Communicating Architecture (1997), Aukett (2001); *Recreations* drawing, bagpiping, cinema; *Clubs* Caledonian; *Style—* Iain Macdonald, Esq; ✉ Iain Lachlan Macdonald Architects, 28 Poland Street, London W1F 8QP (☎ 020 7494 9553, e-mail iain@ilmacdonald.com)

MACDONALD, Ian Alexander; QC (1988); s of Ian Wilson Macdonald (d 1989), of Gullane, E Lothian, and Helen, *née* Nicholson (d 1990); *b* 12 January 1939; *Educ* Glasgow Acad, Cargilfield Sch Edinburgh, Rugby, Clare Coll Cambridge (MA, LLB); *m* 1, 20 Dec 1968 (m dis 1977), Judith Mary, da of William Demain Roberts of Stockport, Cheshire; 2 s (Ian b 3 July 1970, Jamie b 25 Sept 1972); m 2, 12 Oct 1978 (m dis 1990), Jennifer, da of Roy Hall, of Grimsby, S Humberside; 1 s (Kieran b 17 Oct 1979); m 3, 31 Aug 1991 (m dis 2006), Yasmin Shahida, da of Mohammed Sharif, of Manchester; m 4, 27 Sept 2008, Brigid Mary, da of William Joseph Baillie; *Career* called to the Bar Middle Temple 1963 (Astbury scholar 1962–65, bencher 2002); jt head of chambers 1975–2002, lectr in law Kingston Poly 1968–72, sr legal writer and res conslt Incomes Data Servs 1974–80, pres Immigration Law Practitioners' Assoc 1984–, special advocate to Special Immigration Appeals Cmmn 1998–2004, memb Editorial Advsy Bd Immigration and Nationality Law and Practice Jl; memb: SE Circuit, Euro Law Assoc, Criminal Bar Assoc, Admin Law Bar Assoc, Inquiry into Disappearance of Gen Humberto Delgado 1965; chm: Ind Inquiry into Racial Violence in Manchester Schs 1987–88, Inquiry into Funding of Caribbean House Hackney 1989–90, Inquiry into Recruitment Fraud in Hackney 1995–96; Grande Oficial Ordem Da Liberdade (Portugal) 1995; *Books* Race Relations and Immigration Law (1969), Race Relations – The New Law (1977), The New Nationality Act (with N J Blake 1982), Murder in the Playground (1990), Immigration Law and Practice (8 edn 2010); *Recreations* swimming, watching football, reading; *Clubs* Cumberland Lawn Tennis; *Style—* Ian Macdonald, Esq, QC; ✉ Garden Court Chambers, 57–60 Lincoln's Inn Fields, London WC2A 3LS (☎ 020 7993 7600, fax 020 7993 7700 , e-mail info@gclaw.co.uk)

McDONALD, Dr Ian Archie; s of John Archie McDonald, and Thelma, *née* Seheult; *b* 18 April 1933, St Augustine, Trinidad; *Educ* Queens Royal Coll Trinidad, Clare Coll Cambridge (MA, capt lawn tennis team, pres Cambridge W Indian Soc); *m* 14 Sept 1984, Mary Angela, *née* Callender; 2 s (Jamie b 5 Feb 1983, Darren b 16 Dec 1988); 1 s from previous m (Keith b 15 May 1962); *Career* various positions in Guyana sugar industry 1955–76, dir of mktg and admin Guyana Sugar Corp 1976–99, ceo Sugar Assoc of the Caribbean 2000–; ed Kyk-Over-Al magazine 1984–, Sunday columnist Stabroek News Guyana 1986–, editorial asst W Indian Cmmn 1991–92; dir: Hand-In-Hand Fire and Life Insurance Gp 1990–, St Joseph's Mercy Hosp Guyana, Inst of Private Enterprise Devpt Guyana; memb Mgmnt Ctee Nat Art Collection Guyana; capt West Indies Davis Cup Tennis Team 1950s and 1960s; Guyana Sportsman of the Year 1957, Golden Arrow of Achievement (Guyana) 1986, Guyana Prize for Literature (Poetry) 1992 and 2004; Hon DLitt Univ of West Indies 1997; FRSL 1970; *Publications* The Humming-Bird Tree (novel, 1969, BBC film 1992, new edn 2004), Tramping Man (play, 1980), Mercy Ward (poems, 1988), Essequibo (poems, 1992), Heinemann Book of Caribbean Poetry (ed, 1992), Jaffo The Calypsonian (poems, 1994), Collected Poems of A J Seymour (ed, 2000), Between Silence and Silence (poems, 2003), Cricket at Bourda (cricket history), Selected Poems (2008), The Comfort of All Things (poems, 2012), A Cloud of Witnesses (essays, 2013), A Love of Poetry (essays, 2013); *Recreations* playing tennis, watching cricket, reading, enjoying my wife's beautiful garden; *Clubs* Georgetown Cricket, Georgetown, Hawks' (Cambridge), Int Lawn Tennis Club of GB; *Style—* Dr Ian McDonald; ✉ 16 Bel Air Gardens, Georgetown, Guyana (☎ 00 592 2268099, e-mail ianmcdonald74@gmail.com); 37 Sail Crescent, Vaughn, Ontario L6A 2Z4, Canada (☎ 00 1 905 303 0345)

MACDONALD, Prof Ian Robert; s of Robert Harold Macdonald (d 1972), of Sutton, Surrey, and Jannette Wilhelmina (d 2007), *née* Marang; *b* 4 May 1939; *Educ* Whitgift Sch, Univ of St Andrews (MA, Miller Prize), Univ of Aberdeen (PhD); *m* 21 April 1962, Frances Mary, da of James Ranald Alexander; 3 s (Bruce Ian b 10 May 1966, Andrew James b 14 April 1968, Graeme Alan b 6 Oct 1973); *Career* United Steel Cos Ltd 1961–64, postgraduate student 1964–65; Univ of Aberdeen: lectr in Spanish 1965–84, sr lectr 1984–90, prof in Spanish 1991–2001, convener Bd of Studies in Arts and Social Sciences 1989–92, dean Faculty of Arts and Divinity 1992–96, vice-princ 1995–97, sr vice-princ 1997–2001, research fell 2001–; memb AHRB 1999–2002 (chair Res Ctee 2000–02, memb Nominations Ctee 2002–04), memb Univ of the Highlands and Islands Project Academic Advsy Bd 1999–2001; convenor: Further Educn Professional Devpt Forum 1997–2001; tstee Aberdeen Int Youth Festival 1993–2001, govr Dick Bequest Tst 1991–96, govr Northern Coll of Educn 1999–2001; *Books* Gabriel Miró: His Private Library and His Literary Background (1975), Gabriel Miró, El Obispo Leproso (ed, 1993), Gabriel Miró, Epistolario (ed, 2009), Gabriel Miró: Su biblioteca personal y su circunstancia literaria (2010); *Recreations* walking, digging, literary research; *Style—* Prof Ian Macdonald; ✉ 9 Chemin de Montplo, 34310 Montouliers, France (☎ 00 33 467 89 54 73); School of Modern Languages, King's College, University of Aberdeen, Aberdeen AB24 3FX

McDONALD, James Oliver (Jim); CBE (2006), LVO (2002), KCSG (1996), JP (1989), DL (2003); s of Randal McDonald, and Jane, *née* McKeown; *b* 21 September 1937, Belfast; *Educ* St Mary's GS Belfast, Univ of Ulster (MSc); *m* 1960, Deirdre, *née* Kavanagh (d 2003); 1 s (Noel b 1962), 1 da (Jeanette b 1964); *Career* chm Royal Ulster Constabulary George Cross Fndn 2001–13; ind assessor of military complaints NI 1997–2007; chllr Papal Orders in Ireland; memb Victoria Cross and George Cross Assoc 2001–13; Knight Grand Cross of the Holy Sepulchre 2007; *Publications* contrib: Proceedings, Siochain, Garda Record; *Recreations* policing and military history; *Clubs* Civil Serv Ulster Reform; *Style—* Jim McDonald, Esq, CBE, LVO, KCSG, GCHS, JP, DL; ✉ Royal Ulster Constabulary GC Foundation, Brooklyn, 65 Knock Road, Belfast BT5 6LE

McDONALD, Prof Janet Brown Inglis; da of Robert Inglis Caldwell (d 1987), and Janet Gilbert, *née* Lindsay (d 1987); *b* 28 July 1941; *Educ* Hutchesons' Girls' GS Glasgow, Royal Scottish Acad of Music and Drama (pt/t), Univ of Glasgow (MA); *m* 1 July 1964, Ian James McDonald, s of James Murray McDonald (d 1947); 1 da (Katharine Lindsay b 14 April 1977); *Career* Univ of Glasgow: asst lectr Dept of English Literature 1965–66 (res fell 1963–65), lectr Dept of Drama 1968–79 (asst lectr 1966–68), prof of drama 1979–2005, dean of faculties 2006–; chair: Drama Ctee Scottish Arts Cncl 1985–88 (also memb Cncl), Drama Theatre Bd CNAA 1982–85, Performing Arts Bd CNAA 1989–91, Standing Ctee of Univ Depts of Drama 1982–85, Citizens' Theatre Ltd 1991–2005, Music and Performing Arts Res Bd Arts and Humanities Res Bd (AHRB); memb Creative and Performing Arts Advsy Panel Scottish Qualifications Authy (SQA) 2000–02, memb Bd AHRB 2002–04; govr RSAMD 1982–94 (memb Academic Bd 1994–2003), memb Ct Univ of Glasgow 1991–94, memb Cncl Royal Philosophical Soc Glasgow 2010–13 (vice-pres 2014–16, pres 2016–), memb Cncl Royal Glasgow Inst 2013–15; govr Merchants House of Glasgow 2002–08; FRSAMD 1992, FRSE 1991 (memb Cncl 1992–96, vice-pres Arts and Humanities 2005–08); *Publications* numerous monographs and articles on research interests incl nineteenth-century British theatre history and twentieth-century Scottish theatre; *Style—* Prof Janet McDonald, FRSE, FRSAMD; ✉ 4/1, 88 Victoria Crescent Road, Glasgow G12 9JL (☎ 0141 339 3193, e-mail chaika61@outlook.com)

MACDONALD, John Reginald; QC (1976); s of Ranald Macdonald, MBE (d 1959), and Marion Olive, *née* Kirkby (d 1981); *b* 26 September 1931; *Educ* St Edward's Sch Oxford, Queens' Coll Cambridge (MA); *m* 1958, Erica Rosemary, da of Lt-Col Eric Stanton (d 1987); 1 da (Hettie b 1962), 1 s (Toby b 1964); *Career* called to the Bar Lincoln's Inn 1955, bencher Lincoln's Inn 1985, in practice Chancery Bar specializing in human rights and constitutional cases; Parly candidate (Lib) Wimbledon 1966 and 1970, Parly candidate (Lib/Alliance) Folkestone & Hythe 1983 and 1987; chm: Lib Dem Lawyers 1991–93, Kent Opera 1996–2008; *Publications* The Law of Freedom of Information (2 edn 2009); *Recreations* cricket, theatre; *Clubs* MCC; *Style—* John Macdonald, Esq, QC; ✉ 12 New Square, Lincoln's Inn, London WC2A 3SW (☎ 020 7419 8000, fax 020 7419 8050)

MACDONALD, Julien; OBE (2006); *Educ* Brighton Univ (BA), RCA (MA); *Career* fashion designer; at coll worked for Koji Tatsuno, Alexander McQueen, and Karl Lagerfeld; former head knitwear designer Chanel Couture, Chanel mainline and Karl Lagerfeld collections (designed Chanel's best-selling outfit 1997); women's artistic dir House of Givenchy Haute Couture 2001–05; other projects incl: couture dresses for Harrods Christmas windows, tour outfits for the Spice Girls, outfits for Jennifer Lopez's Euro tour, uniforms for BA staff, outfits for Kylie Minogue's world tour, conslt and designer Marks & Spencer Autograph range, uniforms for staff at Bluewater shopping complex; Br Glamour Designer of the Year 2001; *Fashion Shows* Mermaids (launch of own label, Imagination Gallery London) 1997, Modernist (London Fashion Week) 1997, Alerairauh 1998, Metallurgical (restaged at NY Fashion Week) 1998, Snowbusiness 1999, Frock & Roll (Roundhouse) 1999, Modern Skins (London Fashion Week) 2000, Feeling Hot Hot Hot (Park Lane Hotel) 2000, ...I Haven't Stopped Dancing Yet (Grosvenor House Hotel) 2001, It's All in the Mix 2001, Rock Bitch (London Fashion Week tents) 2001, Super Paradise (Grosvenor House Hotel) 2002, Temptation (Roundhouse) 2003; *Style—* Julien Macdonald, Esq, OBE

MACDONALD, Dr Lewis; MSP; s of late Rev Roderick Macdonald, and late Margaret, *née* Currie; *b* 1 January 1957, Stornoway, Scotland; *Educ* Inverurie Acad, Univ of Aberdeen (MA, PhD); *m* Sandra, da of Sandy and Jo Inkster; 2 da (Sophie b 28 Dec 1991, Iona b 2 March 1998); *Career* Parly researcher to Frank Doran MP 1987–92 and 1997–99, shadow cabinet advsr to Tom Clarke MP 1993–97; Lab UK Parly candidate for Moray 1997, memb Exec Ctee Scot Lab Pty 1997–99; MSP (Lab): Aberdeen Central 1999–2011, NE Scotland 2011–; dep min for tport and planning 2001, dep min for enterprise, tport and lifelong learning 2001–03, dep min for enterprise and lifelong learning 2003–04, dep min for environment and rural devpt 2004–05, dep min for health and community care

2005–07; memb Cross-Pty Gps 1999–2001: Crofting, Gaelic in the Scot Parl, Oil and Gas, Strategic Rail Services for Scot, Media, Int Devpt, Agriculture and Horticulture; convenor Holyrood Progress Gp 2000–01; memb Grampian Regnl Equality Cncl, past memb Mgmnt Ctee Aberdeen CAB; memb Cross-Pty Gps 2007–: Oil and Gas (co-convener), Food (co-convener), Architecture the Built Environment, Construction, Diabetes, Human Trafficking; memb: Unite, Aberdeen Safer Community Tst, Co-operative Pty, Dons Supporters Together; *Recreations* walking, football, history; *Style*— Dr Lewis Macdonald, MSP; ✉ The Scottish Parliament, Edinburgh, EH99 1SP (☎ 0131 348 5915, e-mail lewis.macdonald.msp@scottish.parliament.uk, website www.lewismacdonald.info); Constituency Office, 80 Rosemount Place, Aberdeen AB25 2XN (☎ 01224 646333, fax 01224 645450)

McDONALD, Mark; MSP; *b* 1980, Inverurie, Aberdeenshire; *Educ* Univ of Dundee, Univ of Aberdeen; *Career* cncllr for Dyce, Bucksburn and Danestone Aberdeen City Cncl 2007–12; parly asst to: Richard Lochhead, MSP, *qv* 2003–06, Maureen Watt, MSP 2006–07, Nigel Don MSP, *qv* 2008–11; MSP (SNP): NE Scotland 2011–13, Aberdeen Donside 2013–; *Style*— Mark McDonald, Esq, MSP; ✉ The Scottish Parliament, Edinburgh EH99 1SP

McDONALD, Emeritus Prof Michael; s of Douglas Frederick McDonald (d 1999), and Joyce Mary Kathleen, *née* Burke (d 1977); *b* 10 December 1944; *Educ* Univ of Newcastle upon Tyne (BSc, Inst of Structural Engineers Prize), Univ of Southampton (PhD); *m* 1970, Millicent Elizabeth, *née* Agnew; 3 s (Robert Douglas b 1971, Duncan James b 1974, Alastair Michael b 1978); *Career* Univ of Southampton: Rees Jeffreys lectr in highway and traffic engrg 1971–86, sr lectr 1986–88, reader in transportation 1988–92, prof of transportation 1992–, dir Transportation Res Gp 1986–, head Dept of Civil and Environmental Engrg 1996–99; exec dir Roughton & Partners 1985–90; chm UK Universities Tport Studies Gp 1996–98, chair and fndr memb ITS UK 2004–07, vice-chm European Road Tport Research Advsy Cncl 2004–10, advsr to EU research progs, external advsr Road and Vehicle Safety Res DETR, visiting fell Tport Res Fndn, past chair ILT Road Pricing Working Pty; memb: Land Tport LINK Panel EPSRC, Built Environment Review Panel EPSRC, Tport Panel of the Technol Foresight Prog, TRF Nat Res Strategy Gp for Tport 1997–98, ICE Tport Editorial Panel, RAC Tech Ctee, Foresight Vehicle Telematic Thematic Gp; author of over 200 pubns; ITS UK Hills Rees Award for personal contribution to tport 2009, CIHT Award for Excellence within the transportation profession 2010; FICE; *Recreations* golf, fly fishing; *Style*— Emeritus Prof Michael McDonald; ✉ University of Southampton, Highfield, Southampton SO17 1BJ (☎ 02380 592192, fax 02380 593152, e-mail mm7@soton.ac.uk)

MACDONALD, Murdo James Stewart; *b* 25 January 1955; *Educ* Hammersmith Coll of Art, Univ of Edinburgh (class medal, Sinclair-McDonald scholar, univ bursary, Drever prize, MA, PhD); *Career* hon post-doctoral fell Univ of Edinburgh 1987–88, freelance art critic 1987–94, lectr Centre for Continuing Education Univ of Edinburgh 1990–97, prof history of Scottish art Univ of Dundee 1997; tstee Patrick Geddes Meml Tst 1996–2010 (assoc 2010–); Edinburgh Review ed 1990–94; memb: Assoc of Art Historians, Scottish Soc for Art History; FRSA 1998, FSA Scot 1999, HRSA 2009; *Publications* Scottish Art (2000); numerous articles, papers and reviews in learned jls; *Style*— Prof Murdo Macdonald; ✉ Duncan of Jordanstone College of Art and Design, University of Dundee, Perth Road, Dundee DD1 4HT (☎ 01382 345287, e-mail m.j.s.macdonald@dundee.ac.uk)

MACDONALD, Nigel Colin Lock; s of T W Macdonald, of Banstead, Surrey, and B E Macdonald, *née* Whitbourn; *b* 15 June 1945; *Educ* Cranleigh Sch; *m* Jennifer Margaret; 1 da (Genevieve Clare b 16 Dec 1985); *Career* articled clerk Thomson McLintock 1962–68, ptnr Ernst & Young (formerly Ernst & Whinney, previously Whinney Murray & Co) 1976–2003; chm James Lock & Co 1979–; dir British Standards Instn 1992–2004, accounting advsr Int Oil Pollution Compensation Fund 2002–11, dir CocaCola Hellenic 2005–; memb: Industrial Devpt Advsy Bd 1995–2001, Review Panel Fin Reporting Cncl 1990–2006, Electricity and Water Panels MMC 1998, Competition Cmmn 1999–2006; pres Inst of Chartered Accountants of Scotland 1993–94; tstee Nat Maritime Museum 2003–13, chm Royal Greenwich Museums Fndn 2014–, chm Awareness Fndn 2014–; MICAS 1968, FRSA 1993; *Recreations* cars, travel; *Clubs* RAC, City of London; *Style*— Nigel Macdonald, Esq; ✉ 10 Lynwood Road, Epsom, Surrey KT17 4LD (☎ 01372 720853 or 07793 823376, e-mail nigel.macdonald@ntlworld.com)

McDONALD, Patrick John; s of Patrick McDonald, of Hepscott Manor, Morpeth, Northumberland, and Margaret, *née* Price; *b* 26 September 1962; *Educ* Northumberland Co Coll (Int Schoolboys Rugby); *m* 4 Aug 1984, Claire Alison, da of Brian Kell; 2 s (Samuel Patrick Donovan b 29 June 1987, Nathanial John Ryan b 11 March 1991), 1 da (Lois Amelia Kelly b 15 May 1993); *Career* chef de partie Granby Hotel Northumberland 1980–83, chef de partie then sr sous chef Grosvenor House Hotel 1983–84, sous chef Dorchester Hotel 1984–85, head chef Manor House Hotel Castle Combe Wilts 1985–87; exec chef: Ettington Park Hotel Stratford upon Avon 1987–88, Charingworth Manor Hotel Glos 1988–89; dir Designer Dinner Parties Ltd 1990–, chef/patron Epicurean Restaurant (Stow on the Wold then Cheltenham) 1990–96, dir Epicurean Restaurants Ltd 1994–, chef conslt Harvey Nichols plc 1995–96, conslt chef/restaurant advsr to Sir Rocco Forte and chef dir/co-owner Les Saveurs Restaurant Mayfair 1996–98, chef/patron Epicurean Restaurant Pershore Worcs 1998–, gp exec chef City Inn Hotel Gp 1999–, md Epicurean Brasseries Ltd 2002– (incl Epic Bar Brasseries); chef/patron Paris Restaurant Patrick McDonald Birmingham 2003–, dir Ford McDonald Consultancy 2005–, owner Epicurean Restaurant 2006–, dir/co-owner Liberty Restaurants 2007–, dir/co-owner Food Inc Ltd 2008–, co-owner Obika Restaurant London, dir F&B UK Ltd; conslt chef: Newcastle United FC 1998–, Burj Al Arab Hotel 1999–, Worcester RFC 1999–, Pat McDonald Consultancy Ltd 1999–, Eden Project 2000–; conslt advsr to: Selfridges 2004–05, Park Plaza Hotels 2004–05, La Rinescente Milan 2005, Savoy Hotel Farimont 2008–; chef conslt advsr to London Capital Club; food and beverage dir Birmingham Mailbox 2002–04, food and beverage dir/conslt Tsvetnoy Food Market and Restaurants Moscow 2009–, food and beverage conslt Printemps Paris 2011–12, food and beverage conslt Intercontinental Hotels Europe 2013–14, Nespresso 2014–15, LVMH Gp, Fenwick Gp 2013–15; FRSA 2004; *Television* Recipe for Success 1999, If you can't stand the heat (Channel 4) 1999–, Carlton Food (Network TV) 2000; *Awards* AA Best Newcomer of the Year Award 1990, Master Chef 1990, Good Food Guide Restaurant of the Year 1990, two AA Rosettes 1991, Egon Ronay Star 1991, Ackerman Clover Award 1991, three AA Rosettes 1993, Egon Ronay Rgnl Dessert of the Year 1993, Courvoisier Guide one of finest restaurants in world (by Lord Lichfield) 1993, Michelin Star 1993, 1994, 1995, 1996, 1997, two Egon Ronay Stars 1994, Good Food Guide County Restaurant 1994, four AA Rosettes 1995, Michelin Red M 1995, Moet et Chandon Premier Crew Award (Harpers & Queen Front of House Award) 1999, Best Service Standards outside of London 1999, Michelin Bib Gourmand 2002, 2003, 2004 and 2005, 3 AA Rosettes 2004, 4 AA Rosettes 2005–06; *Books* Simply Good Food, Potato Dishes; *Recreations* shooting, fishing, artisan food production, bee-keeping, gardening; *Style*— Patrick McDonald, Esq; ✉ Ford McDonald Consultancy Ltd, 58 Grosvenor Street, Mayfair, London W1K 3HZ (☎ 07768 017282, e-mail patrick@fordmcdonaldconsultancy.com)

MACDONALD, Peter Cameron; DL (W Lothian 1987); s of Sir Peter George Macdonald, WS, JP, DL (d 1983), of Edinburgh, and Rachel Irene, *née* Forgan (d 1990); *b* 14 December 1937; *Educ* Loretto, E of Scotland Coll of Agric (Dip Agric); *m* 2 Aug 1974, Barbara Helen (d 2007), da of David Ballantyne (d 1997), of Peebles; 2 step s (David Drimmie b 1964, Patrick Drimmie b 1967); *Career* farmer 1961–96; chm J Dickson & Son Gunmakers 1997–99 (dir 1968–99); Scottish Landowners Fedn: memb Cncl 1976–2001, convener 1985–88, chm Countryside Review Gp 1988, vice-pres 1989–2001; Scottish Landowners Fedn rep: Standing Conf on Countryside Sports 1985–2004, Scottish Ctee Game Conservancy 1988–2001, Steering Ctee The Code of Good Shooting Practice 1990–2004, Ctee FACE (UK) 1991–2004; memb: Cncl Blackface Sheepbreeders Assoc 1970–74, Pentland Hills Rural Land Mgmnt Gp 1977–84, W Lothian Dist Countryside Ctee 1978–81, Forth River Purification Bd 1979–87, W Lothian Countryside Advsy Ctee; dir Royal Highland Agric Soc of Scotland 1985; vice-chm: Pentland Hills Regnl Park Consultative Ctee 1987–89, Pentland Hills Regnl Park Advsy Ctee 1989–95; *Recreations* fishing, shooting, golf; *Clubs* Hon Co of Edinburgh Golfers; *Style*— Peter Macdonald, Esq, DL; ✉ Waterheads Farmhouse, Eddleston, Peeblesshire EH45 8QX (☎ 01721 730229, e-mail pmacdonald63@hotmail.com)

MACDONALD, Roderick Francis; QC (Scot 1988); s of Finlay Macdonald (d 1991), and Catherine, *née* Maclean (d 1996); *b* 1 February 1951; *Educ* St Mungo's Acad Glasgow, Univ of Glasgow (LLB); *Career* admitted advocate 1975, advocate-depute (crown counsel) 1987–93, home advocate-depute (sr crown counsel) 1990–93; called to the Bar Inner Temple 1997; memb Criminal Injuries Compensation Bd 1995–, legal chm Pensions Appeal Tbnls for Scotland 1995–, memb Criminal Injuries Compensation Appeals Panel 1997–; *Style*— Roderick Macdonald, QC; ✉ 6A Lennox Street, Edinburgh EH4 1QA (☎ and fax 0131 332 72400); Advocates' Library, Parliament House, Edinburgh EH1 1RF (☎ 0131 226 5071, fax 0131 225 3642, e-mail rodmac@cwcom.net, telex 727856 FACADVG)

MacDONALD, Prof Ronald; OBE (2015); s of Duncan MacDonald (d 2010), and Effie, *née* MacRae (d 1982); *b* 23 April 1955; *Educ* Heriot-Watt Univ (BA), Univ of Manchester (MA, PhD); *m* 1 Nov 2002, Catriona, *née* Smith; *Career* teaching asst Univ of Manchester 1979–82, Midland Bank research fell in monetary economics Loughborough Univ 1982–84, lectr Economics Dept Univ of Aberdeen 1984–88 (sr lectr 1988–89), Robert Fleming prof of fin and investment Univ of Dundee 1989–91, prof of int fin Univ of Strathclyde 1992–2004; Univ of Glasgow: Bonar MacFie prof of economics 2005–06, Adam Smith prof of political economy 2006–; research fell CESifo Research Network Munich 2000–, int fell Kiel Inst of Economics 2006–; visiting prof: Economics Dept Queen's Univ Kingston Canada 1988, visiting prof Economics Dept Univ of NSW Sydney 1989 (visiting fell 1987), European Univ Inst Florence 1998 and 2000, Univ of Cergy-Pontoise Paris 1999, Zentrum für Europaische Wirschaftsforschung Mannheim 1999, Centre for Economic Studies Univ of Munich 1999; Bank of Valetta visiting prof of int fin Univ of Malta 1994 and 1995, visiting scholar Central Bank of Norway 2003, int fell Kiel Inst of World Economics; conslt and visiting scholar IMF Washington DC 1991–95 and 1997–2000, conslt Reserve Bank of NZ 2000, conslt European Central Bank 2001 and 2002, economist African Dept IMF 2003; assessor Cwlth Scholarship Cmmn 2002–; external examiner: Univ of Glasgow 1989–92, Univ of Liverpool 1990–92, Scottish Doctoral Prog 1990–, Dept of Banking and Fin City Univ Business Sch 1992–95, Birkbeck Coll London 1996–99, Loughborough Univ 1999, Maynooth Coll Ireland 2000–05, Univ of St Andrews 2007–; presented numerous papers at confs, univs, private sector fin instns and central banks in UK and overseas; assoc ed: Scottish Jl of Political Economy 1999–2000, Jl of Int Financial Markets, Institutions and Money 2001–, Economic Studies 2005–, Int Economic Jl 2005–, Economie Internationale 2005, Economics 2007–; regular referee of articles for learned jls; professional landscape photographer 2010–; memb: Royal Economic Soc, Scottish Economic Soc, Money Macro Finance Study Gp, Int Economics Study Gp; FRSE 2002; *Publications* International Money: Theory, Evidence and Institutions (with P Hallwood, 1986), Floating Exchange Rates: Theories and Evidence (1988), Exchange Rates and Open Economy Macroeconomics (ed with M P Taylor, 1989), Recent Developments in Australian Monetary Economics (ed with C P Kearney, 1991), The Economics of Exchange Rates, Vols 1 and 2 (ed with M P Taylor, 1992), International Money and Finance (with Paul Hallwood, 2 edn 1994, 3 edn 2000), Equilibrium Exchange Rates (ed with J Stein, 1999), Exchange Rate Modelling (with I W Marsh, 1999), Exchange Rate Economics: Theories and Evidence (2000), The Economics of Exchange Rates (ed, 2000), Central Europe Towards European Monetary Union (ed with Rod Cross, 2000), Exchange Rate Economics: Theories and Evidence (2007), Currency Union and Exchange Rate Issues (ed with A Al Faris, 2010), Credibility and the International Monetary Regime (ed with M Bordo, 2012); also author of conference papers, articles in books, refereed jl articles, discussion papers, mimeographs and book reviews; *Recreations* music, painting, photography, cycling, windsurfing; *Style*— Prof Ronald MacDonald, OBE; ☎ 0141 548 3861, fax 0141 552 5587

McDONALD, Sir Simon Gerard; KCMG (2014, CMG 2004), KCVO (2015); s of James B McDonald, of Ilkley, W Yorks, and Angela, *née* McDonald; *b* 9 March 1961, Salford; *Educ* De La Salle Coll GS Salford, Pembroke Coll Cambridge (MA); *m* 1989, Hon Olivia Wright, da of Baron Wright of Richmond, GCMG (Life Peer), *qv*; 2 s (Felix Dominic b 1990, Joachim James Patrick b 1994), 2 da (Matilda Dorothy b 1992, Adelaide Mary b 1996); *Career* diplomat; joined FCO 1982, Arabic language trg SOAS Univ of London 1984, third sec Jedda 1985, second sec Riyadh 1985–88, second sec Bonn 1988–90, first sec FCO 1990, private sec to perm under sec of state 1993–95, served Washington DC 1995–98, cnsllr, dep head of mission and consul-gen Riyadh 1998–2001, princ private sec to sec of state for Foreign and Cwlth Affairs 2001–03, ambass to Israel 2003–06, dir Iraq FCO 2006–07, PM's foreign policy advsr and head of foreign and defence policy Cabinet Office 2007–10, ambass to Germany 2010–15, permanent under-sec of state for foreign and Cwlth affrs and head Diplomatic Service 2015–; *Style*— Sir Simon McDonald, KCMG, KCVO

MacDONALD, (Dr) Stuart Wyllie; OBE (2006); s of Douglas MacDonald (d 1995), of Dundee, and Agnes, *née* Wyllie; *b* 8 September 1948; *Educ* Gray's Sch of Art Aberdeen (Dip Art), Aberdeen Coll of Educn (PGCE), Open Univ (Dip Educnl Mgmnt), Univ of Liverpool (PhD); *m* 25 Aug 1972, Catherine Elizabeth; 2 s (Duncan b 1977, Jamie b 1978), 1 da (Jennifer b 1980); *Career* head of art Forres Acad 1979–87, nat devpt offr for art and design 1983–85, sr advsr in art and design Strathclyde Regn 1991–96 (advsr 1987–91); educn dir: Glasgow Int Festival of Design 1996, Glasgow UK City of Architecture and Design 1996–98; dir Lighthouse (Scotland's Centre for Architecture, Design and the City) 1998–, head Gray's Sch of Art Robert Gordon Univ 2006–09; memb Design Cncl 2005–, tstee Scottish Architectural Educn Tst; fell Nat Soc for Educn in Art and Design 1991; FRSA 1996, Hon FRIBA 2004; *Recreations* painting; *Style*— Stuart MacDonald, OBE; ✉ 13 Woodside Crescent, Glasgow G3 7UL (☎ and fax 0141 332 0644)

McDONALD, Sir Trevor; kt (1999), OBE (1992); *b* 16 August 1939; *m*; 2 s, 1 da; *Career* television broadcaster; formerly local reporter and prog mangr with various local newspapers and radio stations WI, news presenter and interviewer Trinidad 1962–69, with BBC World Service 1969–73; ITN: reporter 1973–78, sports corr 1978–80, diplomatic corr 1980–82 (Channel Four News 1982–87), diplomatic ed Channel Four News 1987–89, news presenter News at 5:40 ITV and Channel Four News 1989–90, co-presenter News at Ten ITV 1990–92, sole presenter News at Ten ITV 1992–99, presenter ITV Evening News 1999–2001, presenter ITV News at Ten Thirty 2001–08, presenter ITV Tonight with Trevor McDonald 1999–, co-presenter ITV News at Ten 2008; reported from: USA, India, Pakistan, Hong Kong, Lebanon, Egypt, Syria, Uganda, Mexico, Argentina, Aust, NZ, Russia, Philippines, South Africa, Iraq, Mozambique, Zimbabwe, Cyprus; interviewed several leading international political figures incl: President Saddam Hussein, President Clinton, General Colin Powell, President Nelson Mandela, Chief Buthelezi, Asil Nadir; awards incl: BAFTA Award for Coverage of Philippines Elections 1985, Newscaster of the Year TRIC Awards 1993, 1997 and 1999, Most Popular Newscaster National TV Awards 1996, Gold Medal for Outstanding Contribution to TV News RTS 1998, BAFTA Richard Dimbleby Award for Outstanding Contribution to Television 1999; appointed chm Steering Gp for Better Use of English in Schools and the Workplace 1995–97, chm Nuffield Language Inquiry (a study into the learning of foreign languages) 1998–2000; chllr South Bank Univ 1999–; Hon DLitt: South Bank Univ 1994, Univ of Plymouth 1995, Univ of Nottingham 1997, Southampton Inst 1997; Hon LLD Univ of the West Indies 1996; Hon Dr: Open Univ 1997, Univ of Surrey 1997; fell Liverpool John Moores Univ 1998, fell BAFTA 2011; *Publications* author of biographies on Viv Richards and Clive Lloyd, Fortunate Circumstances (autobiography, 1993), Favourite Poems (ed, 1997), World of Poetry (1999); *Recreations* tennis, golf, cricket (memb Surrey CCC); *Style*— Sir Trevor McDonald, OBE; ✉ Independent Television News Ltd, 200 Gray's Inn Road, London WC1X 8XZ

MACDONALD LOCKHART OF THE LEE, Angus Hew; *see:* Lockhart of the Lee, Angus Hew

MACDONALD OF RIVER GLAVEN, Baron (Life Peer UK 2010), of Cley-next-the-Sea in the County of Norfolk; Sir Kenneth Donald John (Ken) Macdonald; kt (2007), QC (1997); s of Dr Kenneth Macdonald (d 1997), of Salisbury, Wilts, and Maureen, *née* Sheridan (d 2001); *b* 4 January 1953; *Educ* St Edmund Hall Oxford (BA); *m* 1980, Linda, da of Dr David Zuck; 1 da (Anna Maureen b 18 Nov 1981), 2 s (Edward Jonathan Kenneth b 23 March 1984, Theo Lindsay b 30 Sept 1993); *Career* called to the Bar Inner Temple 1978 (bencher 2003); specialising in criminal law; recorder of the Crown Court 2000, DPP 2003–08, dep High Court judge 2010–; visiting prof of law LSE 2009–; chair Criminal Bar Assoc 2003 (memb Exec Ctee 1997–, chm Educn Ctee 1999–, vice-chair 2002–03), vice-chair Bar Public Affairs Gp 2001–02; memb: Bar Cncl 2000, Treasy Counsel Selection Ctee (CCC), Sentencing Guidelines Cncl 2003–08, Criminal Procedure Rul Ctee 2003–08; tstee Index on Censorship 2009–12; warden Wadham Coll Oxford 2012–; *Recreations* twentieth century history, crime fiction, film noir; *Style*— The Lord Macdonald

MACDONALD OF SLEAT; *see:* Bosville Macdonald of Sleat

MACDONALD OF TRADESTON, Baron (Life Peer UK 1998), of Tradeston in the City of Glasgow; Angus John (Gus) Macdonald; CBE (1997), PC (1999); *Educ* Allan Glen's Sch Glasgow; *Career* marine engr 1956–63, journalist The Scotsman 1965–67, exec/presenter Granada TV 1967–85; Scottish Television plc: dir of progs 1986–89, md 1990–96, chm 1996–97, non-exec chm 1997–98; min for business and industry Scottish Office 1998–99, min for tport DETR 1999–2001, min for the Cabinet Office 2001–03, chllr of the Duchy of Lancaster 2001–03; chm: ITV Broadcast Bd 1992–94, Taylor & Francis 1997–98; memb Bd Bank of Scotland 1998, sr advsr Macquarie Gp 2004–16, memb Bd Scottish Power 2009–15; chllr Glasgow Caledonian Univ 2007–12, memb Cncl and Ct Univ of Sussex 2006–11; visiting prof of film and media studies Univ of Stirling 1985–98; fndr chm Edinburgh Int TV Festival 1976, chm Edinburgh Int Film Festival 1994–96, govr BFI 1997–98, govr Nat Film and TV Sch 1988–97; chm Cairngorms Partnership 1997–98, memb Bd Scottish Enterprise 1997–98; BAFTA Awards 1973 and 1997; Scottish Business Elite Award 1993 and 1998; Hon Dr: Univ of Stirling, Napier Univ, Robert Gordon Univ, Univ of Glasgow, Univ of Lincoln; *Books* Camera: Victorian Eyewitness; *Recreations* words, music, pictures, sports; *Style*— The Rt Hon Lord Macdonald of Tradeston, CBE

MacDONALD ROSS, George; s of John MacDonald Ross, CBE, of London, and Helen Margaret, *née* Wallace; *b* 11 November 1943; *Educ* Mill Hill Sch, St Catharine's Coll Cambridge (MA); *m* 24 June 1974, (Margaret) Lynne Ross, da of Elwyn Chubb, of Cardiff; *Career* asst lectr in philosophy Univ of Birmingham 1969–72; Univ of Leeds: res fell in history and philosophy of sci 1972–73, lectr in philosophy 1973–88, sr lectr 1988–2009, head of Dept of Philosophy 1990–93, dean Faculty of Arts 1991–93; vice-princ and academic dean Univ Coll Scarborough 1994–96 (hon fell 1996–); dir Philosophical and Religious Studies Subject Centre HE Acad 2000–09 (sr advsr 2009–); chm Nat Ctee for Philosophy 1985–94; memb: Ctee Br Soc for the History of Philosophy, Cncl Royal Inst of Philosophy, Ctee Leibniz-Gesellschaft; pres Leibniz Assoc; SAPERE; FHEA (nat teaching fell 2006); *Books* Leibniz (1984), Doing Philosophy (jtly, 2008), Starting with Hobbes (2009); *Recreations* conviviality, bricolage, walking; *Style*— George MacDonald Ross, Esq; ✉ 43 Grove Lane, Leeds LS6 4EQ (☎ 0113 294 7379, e-mail g.m.ross@leeds.ac.uk, website www.philosophy.leeds.ac.uk/GMR/index.html)

McDONNELL, Dr Alasdair; MP, MLA; s of Charles McDonnell, of Kilmore, Co Antrim (d 1996), and Margaret, *née* McIlhatton (d 1974); *b* 1 September 1949, Cushendall, Co Antrim; *Educ* St MacNissi's Coll Garron Tower, UC Dublin (MB BCh, BAO); *m* 6 Feb 1998, Olivia Nugent; 2 da (Dearbhla b March 1999, Aileen b Aug 2005), 2 s (Ruairi b Sept 2000, Oisin b Dec 2002); *Career* full time doctor 1975–2001 (jr hosp doctor 1975–79 (various posts in Belfast Hosps), GP Ormeau Health Centre 1979–2001), pt/t GP Ormeau Health Centre 2001–09; cncllr Belfast City Cncl 1977–2001, dep mayor Belfast 1995–96; memb NI Assembly 1998–, MP (SDLP) Belfast S 2005–; SDLP: spokesman on enterprise, trade and investment 1998–2003 and 2007–, spokesman for employment and learning 2003–07, dep ldr 2004–10; memb NI Forum for Political Dialogue; memb BMA; *Recreations* Gaelic sports; *Style*— Dr Alasdair McDonnell, MP, MLA; ✉ 120a Ormeau Road, Belfast BT7 2EB (☎ 028 9024 2474, fax 028 9043 9935); House of Commons, London SW1A 0AA (e-mail mcdonnella@parliament.uk)

McDONNELL, Charles Joseph (Charlie); *b* 1 October 1990, Bath; *Career* vlogger, musician and filmmaker; owner charlieissocoollike Youtube channel 2007–, creator and host Cereal Time Youtube channel 2015–; *Albums* incl: Chameleon Circuit (with Chameleon Circuit) 2009, This Is Me (solo) 2010, Still Got Legs (with Chameleon Circuit) 2011; *Short Films* incl: The Tea Chronicles 2013, Offline 2013, Strangers in a Bed 2014, Our Brother 2014; *Books* Fun Science: A Guide To Life, The Universe And Why Science Is So Awesome (2016); *Style*— Charlie McDonnell, Esq

McDONNELL, David Croft; CBE (2005), DL (Merseyside 2002); *b* 9 July 1943; *m* 9 Nov 1967, Marieke; 3 da (Emma, Sarah-Jane, Sophia); *Career* Bryce Hanmer & Co (became Thornton Baker 1964 then Grant Thornton 1985): ptnr 1972, nat managing ptnr 1989–2001, ceo worldwide 2001–09; chm Bd of Tstees National Museums Liverpool 1995–2005; pres Univ of Liverpool 2007–14 (pro-chllr 2015–); High Sheriff Merseyside 2009–10, Vice Lord-Lt Merseyside 2010–; hon fell Liverpool John Moores Univ 2002; FCA (ACA 1965); *Recreations* sailing, motor racing (spectating), walking; *Clubs* Athenaeum; *Style*— David McDonnell, Esq, CBE, DL; ✉ Burn Lea, The Serpentine, Grassendale, Liverpool L19 9DT

McDONNELL, Prof James Anthony Michael (Tony); s of Michael Francis McDonnell (d 2003), of Madeley, Cheshire, and Vera Phyllis, *née* Redding (d 1987); *b* 26 September 1938; *Educ* St Joseph's Coll Stoke on Trent, Univ of Manchester (BS, PhD); *m* 22 July 1961, Jean Mary, da of George Gordon (d 1976); 2 s ((Benedict) Michael b 27 Feb 1965, Roger James b 1 June 1971), 1 da (Louise Anne b 21 Aug 1962); *Career* res asst Nuffield Radio Astronomy Labs 1964–65, post-doctoral res assoc NASA Goddard Spaceflight Centre USA 1965–67; Univ of Kent: lectr in physical electronics 1967–72, sr lectr in electronics 1972–77, reader in space sciences 1977–85, prof of space physics and head of space sci 1985–; prof emeritus Open Univ 2007–; contrib to Planetary Science in Europe JAM McDonnell (Planetary and Interstellar Dust) 1980; various chapters of Advanced Space Res incl: Progress in Planetary Exploration 1981, Recent Researches into Solid Bodies and Magnetic Fields in the Solar System 1982, Cosmic Dust and Space Debris 1986; organiser and orater of welcome address Comet Nucleus Sample Return ESA Cornerstone Workshop Canterbury 1986; memb Ctee Space Astronomy and Radio Div SERC 1979–81; memb: UK Halley Watch Steering Ctee (later CHUKCC) 1983–87, Space Sci Prog Br Nat Space Centre 1988–; COSPAR: memb and sec Panel 3 C 1973–79, memb Sub-cmmn B1 ISC B 1982–86, exec memb ISC B 1984–88, chm ISC B 1988–, memb Organising Ctee IAU Cmmn 22 1979; memb: Meteoroid Shield Design Workshop ESA Comet Halley Mission 1981, ESA Lunar Polar Workshop 1981; govr Workshop on Planetology European Sci Fndn 1981, chm Organisation Ctee Symposium 6 COSPAR IAU IUTAM 1982, discipline specialist Int Halley Watch 1983, memb ESA NASA Primative Bodies Study Team 1984; conslt: space station design USRA 1985, Comet nucleus sample return CNSR 1985–87, CAESAR assessment study 1986, VESTA phase A 1987; memb: Solar System Working Gp 1988–90, Rosetta Mission Definition Team ESA 1988; co-investigator GIADA experiment ESA Rosetta Mission; minor planet Asteroid 9159 named in recognition of role in NASA Stardust mission detectors; FRAS, FBIS 1987; *Books* Cosmic Dust (ed and co-author with John Wiley, 1978); *Recreations* tennis, woodwork; *Style*— Prof Tony McDonnell; ✉ e-mail tony@unispacekent.co.uk

McDONNELL, John; MP; *Career* MP (Lab) Hayes and Harlington 1997–, shadow chllr of the Exchequer 2015–; *Style*— John McDonnell, Esq, MP; ✉ Constituency Office, Pump Lane, Hayes, Middlesex UB3 3NB (☎ 020 8569 0010, fax 020 8569 0109, website www.john-mcdonnell.net)

McDONNELL, Jonathan Robert; *b* 3 April 1957; *Educ* Oratory Sch Woodcote, Wadham Coll Oxford (MA); *Career* md I B Tauris & Co Ltd (publishers) 1991–, md Philip Wilson Publishers Ltd 2011–; *Style*— Jonathan McDonnell, Esq; ✉ I B Tauris & Co Ltd, 6 Salem Road, London W2 4BU (☎ 020 7243 1225, fax 020 7243 1226, e-mail jmcdonnell@ibtauris.com)

McDONOUGH, David Fergus; OBE (1998); s of late Alan James McDonough, and late Shirley Davis; *b* 7 June 1953, Eastbourne, Sussex; *Educ* Stowe, Merton Coll Oxford (MA); *m* 1, 1978, Caroline Eugénie, *née* Axford; m 2, 28 May 1992 (m dis), Mrs Vanessa E L Reeves, da of late Douglas Gent; *Career* special advsr to The Lord Feldman 1975–79, md McDonough Assocs Ltd 1979–90, dep chm Bell Pottinger Consultants (formerly Lowe Bell Consultants), chm Kiki McDonough Ltd, chm McDonough Assocs Ltd (The McDonough Partnership) 2003–, ptnr Norris McDonough LLP 2013–; co-fndr The October Club (chm 1988–98 and 2000–05, life pres 2005–), memb Bd of Regents Harris and hon fell Manchester Coll Oxford; cmmr Royal Hosp Chelsea 2008–14, dep chm Samaritans Advsy Bd; Freeman City of London, Liveryman Worshipful Co of Merchant Taylors; FRSA; OStJ 2002; *Recreations* politics, reading, music, theatre; *Clubs* White's, Garrick; *Style*— David McDonough, Esq, OBE; ✉ Norris McDonough LLP, 5–8 The Sanctuary, Westminster, London SW1P 3JS (☎ 020 7340 0380, website www.nmcdllp.com)

McDONOUGH, Roisín; *Career* chief exec Arts Cncl of NI; *Style*— Ms Roisín McDonough; ✉ Arts Council of Northern Ireland, 77 Malone Road, Belfast BT9 6AQ

McDOUGALL, Prof Bonnie S; da of William Morris McDougall (d 1990), and Ruth Constance, *née* Mather (d 1978); *b* 12 March 1941; *Educ* St George Girls' HS Sydney, Wollongong HS, Peking Univ, Univ of Sydney (MA, PhD, Univ medal); *m* Dec 1979, (Harry) Anders Hansson; 1 s ((Carl) Torkel b 30 April 1980); *Career* Univ of Sydney: Oriental librarian 1967–68, res fell 1970–71, lectr in Oriental studies 1972–76; Nuffield travelling scholar SOAS Univ of London 1975, assoc Harvard Univ 1979–80 (res fell 1976–79), ed and translator Foreign Languages Press 1980–83, English teacher Coll of Foreign Affairs Peking 1984–86; prof of modern Chinese: Univ of Oslo 1987–90 (sr lectr 1986–87), Univ of Edinburgh 1990–; visiting lectr Harvard Univ 1977, 1978 and 1979; advsr Assoc of Chinese Translators and Interpreters in Scotland 1993–; memb: Amnesty International 1987–, Edgar Wallace Soc 1988–94, PEN International 1989–92, Universities' China Ctee 1990– (memb Exec Cncl 1990–93), Cncl Br Assoc of Chinese Studies 1991– (pres 1995–97), Bd Euro Assoc of Chinese Studies 1992–, Exec Ctee Scots Australia Cncl 1994–95; *Books* The Introduction of Western Literary Theories into China 1919–25 (1971), Paths in Dream: Selected Prose and Poetry of Ho Ch'i-fang (ed, 1976), Mao Zedong's Talks at the Yan'an Conference on Literature and Art (ed, 1980 and 1992), Notes from the City of the Sun: Poems by Bei Dao (ed, 1983), Popular Chinese Literature and Performing Arts in the People's Republic of China 1949–79 (ed, 1984), Bodong (ed, 1985), Waves (ed, 1985), The August Sleepwalker (ed, 1988), The Yellow Earth: A Film by Chen Kaige (1991), The Literature of China in the 20th Century (with K Louie, 1997), Chinese Concepts of Privacy (co-ed, 2002), Love-Letters and Privacy in Modern China: The Intimate Lives of Lu Xua and Xu Guaugping (2002), Fictional Authors, Imaginary Audiences: Modern Chinese Literature in the Twentieth Century (2003); author of numerous papers in jls; *Recreations* travel, reading, walking; *Style*— Prof Bonnie S McDougall; ✉ Department of Chinese Studies, School of Languages and Cultures, A-18, The University of Sydney, Sydney NSW 2006, Australia

McDOUGALL, Douglas Christopher Patrick; OBE (2001); s of Patrick McDougall (d 1950), and Helen McDougall (d 1980); *b* 18 March 1944; *Educ* Edinburgh Acad, ChCh Oxford (MA); *m* 4 June 1986, Hon Carolyn Jane, da of Baron Griffiths, MC, PC (Life Peer) (d 2015), *qv*; 2 da (Fiona Maria b 1987, Mary Helen b 1990); *Career* sr ptnr Baillie Gifford & Co 1989–99 (investment mangr and ptnr 1969); chm IMRO 1997–2000 (non-exec dir 1987–); non-exec dir: Provincial Insurance plc 1989–94, Baillie Gifford Japan Tst plc 1989–99, Pacific Horizon Trust plc 1992–, Stramongate Assets plc 2003–11; chm: Institutional Fund Mangrs Assoc 1994–96, Assoc of Investment Tst Companies 1995–98, European Investment Tst Ltd (formerly Foreign and Colonial Eurotrust plc) 1999–, The Law Debenture Corp plc 2000–13 (non-exec dir 1998–2013), 3i Bioscience Investment Tst 2000– (dep chm 1999–2000), The Independent Investment Tst 2000–, The Scottish Investment Tst plc 2003–16 (non-exec dir 1998–2016); dep chm Sand Aire Ltd 1999–2003; non-exec dir: Sand Aire Ltd 1999–2003, The Monks Investment Tst plc 1999–, Herald Investment Tst plc 2002–16, Stramongate Assets plc 2003–; memb Investment Bd Univ of Cambridge 2005–11; hon student ChCh Oxford 2008; *Clubs* Brooks's, New (Edinburgh), Hon Co of Edinburgh Golfers; *Style*— Douglas McDougall, Esq, OBE; ✉ Linplum House, Haddington, East Lothian EH41 4PE (☎ 01620 810242)

MACDOUGALL, Patrick Lorn; s of James Archibald Macdougall, WS (d 1982), and Valerie Jean, *née* Fraser (d 2006); *b* 21 June 1939, Edinburgh; *Educ* schs in Kenya, Millfield, UC Oxford; *m* 1, 24 June 1967 (m dis 1982), Alison Noel, da of Herbert Charles Offer, MC (d 1991), of Cheshire; 2 s (Alasdair William Lorn b 1970, Thomas Hugh James b 1972); m 2, 15 April 1983, Bridget Margaret, da of Peter Scott Young (d 1988); 3 da (Laura Margaret Valerie b 1984, Nicola Elizabeth Bridget b 1987, Vanessa Emily Hope b 1990); *Career* called to the Bar Inner Temple 1962; mangr NM Rothschild & Sons 1967–70, chief exec Amex Bank (formerly Rothschild Intercontinental Bank) 1977–78 (exec dir 1970–77), exec dir Jardine Matheson Holdings 1978–85, chm West Merchant Bank Ltd (formerly Standard Chartered Merchant Bank) 1989–98 (chief exec 1985–97); non-exec chm Arlington Securities plc 1999–2005, chm China Private Equity Investment Hldgs 2008–13; dir: Global Natural Resources Inc 1994–96, Nuclear Electric plc 1994–96, National Provident Institution 1997–99; tstee SANE 2001– (chm 2002–06); FCA 1967, FRSA 1988; *Recreations* opera, bridge; *Clubs* Athenaeum, Hurlingham, Shek-O CC (Hong Kong); *Style*— Patrick Macdougall, Esq; ✉ 110 Rivermead Court, London SW6 3SB (☎ 020 7736 3506, fax 020 7731 8912)

McDOWALL, His Hon Judge Andrew Gordon; s of William C McDowall (d 1998), and Margery, *née* Wilson (d 1996); *b* 2 September 1948; *Educ* Glasgow Acad, The Queen's Coll Oxford (MA, BCL); *m* 21 Aug 1976, Cecilia, da of Harold Clarke; 1 s (Peter James b 7 May 1982), 1 da (Eleanor Katherine Louisa b 1 May 1985); *Career* called to the Bar 1972; circuit judge (SE Circuit) 1998–; memb London Orpheus Choir; *Recreations* squash,

M

reading, music, paranomasia; *Style*— His Hon Judge McDowall; ✉ c/o 1 King's Bench Walk, Temple, London EC4Y 7DB

McDOWALL, David Buchanan; s of Angus David McDowall (d 1957), and Enid Margaret, *née* Crook; *b* 14 April 1945; *Educ* Monkton Combe Sch, RMA Sandhurst, St John's Coll Oxford (MA, MLitt); *m* 19 April 1975, Elizabeth Mary Risk, da of Dr John McClelland Laird; 2 s (Angus b 1977, William b 1979); *Career* Subaltern RA 1965–70; Br Cncl (Bombay, Baghdad & London) 1972–77, UNRWA 1977–79; writer (for adults and children); *Books* Lebanon – A Conflict of Minorities (1983), The Kurds (1985), The Palestinians (children's book, 1986), The Palestinians (1987), The Spanish Armada (1988), An Illustrated History of Britain (1989), Palestine and Israel: The Uprising and Beyond (1989), The Kurds: A Nation Denied (1992), Europe and the Arabs: Discord or Symbiosis? (1992), Britain in Close-up (1993), The Palestinians: The Road to Nationhood (1994), A Modern History of the Kurds (1995, revised edn 2000), Richmond Park: the Walker's Historical Guide (1996, revised edn (Richmond Park: the Walker's Guide) 2006), Hampstead Heath: The Walker's Guide (jtly, 1998, revised edn 2006), The Thames from Hampton to Richmond Bridge (2002), The Thames from Richmond to Putney Bridge (2005), Windsor Great Park: The Walker's Guide (2007), Bute (2010), West Surrey: Walks into History (2013); *Style*— David McDowall, Esq; ✉ 13 Cambrian Road, Richmond, Surrey TW10 6JQ (☎ 020 8940 3911)

McDOWELL, Linda; CBE (2016); *Career* prof of Human Geography Univ of Oxford; vice-pres St John's Coll Oxford; *Publications* Working Bodies: Interactive service employment and workplace identities (2009), Working Lives: Gender, migration and employment in Britain, 1945–2007 (2013), Migrant Women's Voices (2016); *Style*— Prof Linda McDowell, CBE

McDOWELL, Prof Nicholas; s of Brian McDowell, of Belfast, and Margaret, *née* Whyte; *b* 16 March 1973, Belfast; *Educ* The Royal Belfast Academical Instn, Sidney Sussex Coll Cambridge (MA), Oriel Coll Oxford (MPhil, DPhil); *m* 20 July 2002, Dr Sally Faulkner; 2 s (Rowan b 26 Oct 2006, Cameron b 20 Feb 2009); *Career* res fell Fitzwilliam Coll Cambridge 1998–2000; Univ of Exeter: lectr 2001–05, sr lectr in English literature 2005–, assoc prof of English literature 2009–, prof of early modern literature and thought 2012–; visiting fell Centre for Research into the Arts, Social Sciences and Humanities Cambridge 2010–11; memb Inst for Advanced Study Princeton 2009–10; Philip Leverhulme Prize 2007, Irene Samuel Award Milton Soc of America for a distinguished collection of essays 2010, James Holly Hanford Award Milton Soc of America for a distinguished essay 2012, John T Shawcross Award Milton Soc of America for a distinguished edn 2014; Leverhulme Research Fellowship 2014–15; The English Radical Imagination: Culture religion and Revolution, 1630–1660 (2003), Poetry and Allegiance in the English Civil Wars (2008), The Oxford Handbook of Milton (2009), The Oxford Complete Works of John Milton Vol VI: Vernacular Regicide and Republican Writings (2013); *Style*— Prof Nicholas McDowell; ✉ Department of English, Queen's Building, Queen's Drive, University of Exeter, Exeter, Devon EX4 4QJ (☎ 01392 264269, e-mail n.mcdowell@exeter.ac.uk)

McDOWELL, Paul; s of Thomas Morris McDowell, and Christine Anne Burgess, *née* Moore; *b* 15 August 1962, Luton, Beds; *Educ* Queensbury Sch Dunstable, Univ of Central England (Dip), Fitzwilliam Coll Cambridge (MSt); *m* 14 July 2001, Janine Marcelle, *née* Morris; 2 s (Matthew b 10 April 1981, Kirk b 21 March 1984), 1 da (Joanna Louise b 3 Oct 1985); *Career* prison offr HM Young Offenders Inst Stoke Heath 1990–92, subsequently HMP Woodhill, HMP Wellingborough, HMP Gartree and HM Young Offenders Inst Feltham, seconded to Prison Min's Private Office Home Office 2000–01, dep govr HM Young Offenders Inst 2001–04, govr HMP Coldingley 2004–06, govr HMP Brixton 2006–09, chief exec Nacro 2009–14, chief inspector of probation 2014–15, criminal justice conslt 2015–; tstee Prison Radio Assoc; Hon DUniv Birmingham City Univ 2015; FRSA; *Recreations* Luton Town FC, Glastonbury Festival, music, family; *Style*— Paul McDowell, Esq; ✉ Twitter @paulmcdowell4

McDOWELL, Sidney; CBE; s of William Cameron McDowell, and Margaret, *née* Richmond; *b* 3 May 1942, Belfast; *Educ* Methodist Coll Belfast, Ruskin Coll Oxford; *m* 5 April 1966, Irish Hillock (d 1993); 3 s (Brian b 1970 d 2016, Niall b 1971, Michael b 1978); *Career* dep gen sec NI Public Service Alliance 1976–94, chm NI Housing Exec 1995–2004, chm Local Govt Staff Cmmn 1995–2005, chm Public Service Cmmn NI 2006–15; chm NI Region Nat House Building Cncl 2008–14, chm NI Assoc Care and Resettlement of Offenders 2011–, chm NI Co-Ownership Housing Assoc 2012–; formerly pres Citizens Advice NI, patron Cncl for the Homeless NI, chm Rethinking Construction Centre NI; memb Bd Lyric Theatre (formerly chm and vice-chm); Hon MCIH, hon fell Soc of Chartered Surveyors Ireland; *Recreations* theatre, opera, rugby; *Style*— Sidney McDowell, Esq, CBE; ✉ 23 Dalboyne Park, Lisburn, Co Antrim BT28 3BU (☎ 07540 635691, e-mail sidney.mcdowell@yahoo.co.uk)

MacDUFF, The Hon Mr Justice; Sir Alistair Geoffrey MacDuff; kt (2008), QC (1993); s of Alexander MacDonald MacDuff (d 1985), and Iris Emma, *née* Gardner (d 1997); *b* 26 May 1945; *Educ* Ecclesfield GS nr Sheffield, LSE (LLB), Univ of Sheffield (LLM); *m* 1, 27 Sept 1969, Susan Christine (d 1991), da of Ronald David Kitchener, of Salthouse, Norfolk; 2 da (Karen b 1971, Jennifer b 1972); m 2, 9 July 1993, Katherine Anne, da of late Dr John Buckley, of Frampton on Severn, Glos; 1 da (Rebecca b 1995), 1 s (George b 1997); *Career* called to the Bar Lincoln's Inn 1969, recorder of the Crown Ct 1987–97, circuit judge (Midland & Oxford Circuit) 1997–08, designated civil judge Birmingham 2000–, sr circuit judge 2002–08, judge of the High Court of Justice (Queen's Bench Div) 2008–; former chm local ward Lib Party; *Recreations* opera, theatre, golf, association football, travel; *Clubs* Hendon GC, Economicals AFC, Painswick RFC; *Style*— The Hon Mr Justice MacDuff

MacECHERN, Gavin MacAlister; s of late Dugald MacAlister MacEchern, and late Diana Mary, *née* Body; *b* 7 March 1944; *Educ* Tonbridge; *m* 1, 1972 (m dis 2002), Sarah Alison, da of late Eric and Cecil Walker, *née* Eaton-Evans; 3 da (Georgina b 1976, Tatiana b 1978, Christina b 1981); m 2, 2007, Caroline Valentine, da of late Maj William Riley, MC, and late Patricia, *née* Prioleau; *Career* admitted slr 1967; fndr shareholder and dir Arlington Securities plc 1975–94, fndr shareholder and chm Mansford Holdings plc 1995–2008, chm Heracles LLP 2009–16; *Recreations* racing, skiing, shooting, golf; *Clubs* Turf, New Zealand; *Style*— Gavin MacEchern, Esq; ✉ Langford Downs Farm, Nr Lechlade, Gloucestershire GL7 3QL

McELHONE, Natascha; *b* 14 December 1971, London; *Educ* LAMDA; *m* 1998, Dr Martin Kelly (d 2008); 3 s (Theodore b 2000, Otis b 2003, Rex b 2008); *Career* actress; *Theatre* incl: Richard III (Regent's Park), The Count of Monte Cristo (Manchester Royal Exchange), The Cherry Orchard (Haymarket Theatre Leicester), A Midsummer Night's Dream (Regent's Park London), Honour (West End) 2006, Fatal Attraction (Theatre Royal Haymarket) 2014; *Film* incl: Surviving Picasso 1996, The Devil's Own 1997, Mrs Dalloway 1997, The Truman Show 1998, What Rats Won't Do 1998, Ronin 1998, Love's Labour's Lost 2000, Contaminated Man 2000, Killing Me Softly 2002, Laurel Canyon 2002, FeardotCom 2002, City of Ghosts 2002, Solaris 2002, Ladies in Lavender 2004, Guy X 2005, Big Nothing 2006, The Secret of Moonacre 2008, The Kid 2010; *Television* incl: The Other Boleyn Girl 2003, Revelations 2005, Californication 2007–10; *Style*— Ms Natascha McElhone

McENTEE, John; s of Andrew Francis McEntee (d 1997), of Cavan, and Julia, *née* Cusack (d 2015); *b* 10 August 1952; *Educ* Poor Clares Convent Sch Co Cavan, De La Salle Sch Co Cavan, St Patrick's Coll Co Cavan; *m* 1976 (m dis 2003), Colette, *née* Fitzpatrick; 1 da (Laura b 1979), 2 s (Paul b 1981, Jack b 1989); *Career* journalist; trainee reporter The Anglo Celt 1970–72, reporter Dublin Evening Press 1972–73, reporter The Irish Press Group 1973–75, London corr The Irish Press Group 1975–88, dep ed Londoners Diary Evening Standard 1988–89, dep ed diary The Times 1989–91, feature writer Daily Express 1991; Sunday Express: royal corr 1992, media corr 1993, London section 1993, arts ed 1994; dep ed diary Express 1994–96; William Hickey: 1996–98, columnist 1998–2000; columnist Daily Mail 2002–08, writer Daily Mail 2010–, dep ed Ephraim Hardcastle 2015–; fndr Citizen Caine PR advice website 2010; memb Useless Information Soc 1997; supporter Goal; *Books* Biteback (autobiography, 2016); *Recreations* talking, thinking, lighting candles in churches; *Clubs* Reform, Gerry's, Capital; *Style*— John McEntee, Esq; ✉ e-mail jmcentee@live.co.uk; Daily Mail, 8 Derry Street, London W8 5TT (☎ 020 7938 6344)

McEVEDY, Allegra Sarah Bazzett; MBE (2008); *b* London; *Career* chef, cookery writer and broadcaster; co-fndr Leon Restaurants 2004–09; FRSA 2007; *Books* The Good Cook (2000), Allegra McEvedy's Colour Cookbook (2006, Chefs and Restuarants category winner Int Assoc of Culinary Professionals Cook Book Awards 2007), Leon Recipe Book (2008), Economy Gastronomy (2009); *Style*— Ms Allegra McEvedy, MBE; ✉ website www.allegramcevedy.com; c/o United Agents, 12–26 Lexington Street, London W1F 0LE (☎ 020 3214 0893, website www.unitedagents.co.uk)

McEVOY, Peter Aloysius; OBE (2003); s of Daniel Martin McEvoy, and Gladys Isabella Amelia McEvoy; *b* 22 March 1953; *Educ* Tudor Grange GS, Birmingham Coll of Law, Chester Coll of Law; *Career* amateur golfer; major tournament victories: Br Univs Stroke Play 1973, Leicestershire Fox 1976, Euro amateur championship 1977 and 1983, amateur champion 1977–78 (runner up 1987), Lytham Trophy 1978, Silver medal Open Championships 1978 and 1979, Scrutton Jug 1978, 1980 and 1985, Duncan Putter 1978, 1980 and 1987, Selborne Salver 1979 and 1980, English Open Amateur Stroke Play 1980 (tied, runner up 1978), Lagonda Trophy 1980, County Champion of Champions 1984, Berkshire Trophy 1985, Berkhamsted Trophy 1986, Hampshire Hog 1989; youth int 1974, England int 1976– (capt 1992–97), with Br team 1977–, capt GB and Ireland 1998–2001; memb team: Walker Cup 1977, 1979, 1981, 1985, 1989 (winners), 1999 (winners), 2001 (winners, first GB and I capt to win successive Walker Cups), Eisenhower Trophy 1978, 1980, 1984, 1986 and 1988, Fiat Trophy 1980; most successful English golfer (153 appearances), only player from any country to win a world individual title, play in a world championship winning team and captain a world championship winning team, only Br amateur to complete 72 holes in US Masters 1978; chm of selectors Walker Cup 2003 and 2005; Golf Writers Trophy 1978, Gerald Micklem Trophy 1999, Michael Williams Award Assoc of Golf Writers 2009; articled clerk Rees Edward Maddox & Co (Slrs) 1977–81, md Sporting Concepts Ltd 1981–; exec dir Power Play Golf 2009–; *Books* For Love or Money (2006); *Recreations* all sports; *Clubs* Royal & Ancient; hon memb: Copt Heath, Handsworth, City of Derry, St Annes, Chantilly (France), L'Ancresse (Guernsey), European, Nairn, Royal Troon, Filey, Tewkesbury Park, Rathsallagh GC; *Style*— Peter McEvoy, Esq, OBE; ✉ Sporting Concepts Ltd, Cider Mill House, Old Manor Lane, Tewkesbury, Gloucestershire GL20 7EA (☎ 01684 291345, fax 01684 273812, e-mail sportingconcepts@btconnect.com)

McEWAN, Ian Russell; CBE (2000); s of Maj David McEwan (d 1996), of Ash, Hants, and Rose Violet Lilian Moore; *b* 21 June 1948; *Educ* Woolverstone Hall Sch, Univ of Sussex (BA), UEA (MA); *m* 1, 1982 (m dis), Penelope Ruth, da of Dennis Allen, of Lewes, E Sussex; 2 s (William b 1983, Gregory b 1986), 2 step da (Polly b 1970, Alice b 1972); m 2, 1997, Annalena McAfee; *Career* author; began writing 1970; Shakespeare Prize 1999; Hon DLitt: Univ of Sussex 1989, UEA 1993, Univ of London 1998; FRSL 1982; *Books* First Love, Last Rites (1975), In Between The Sheets (1978), The Cement Garden (1978), The Comfort of Strangers (1981), The Imitation Game (1981), Or Shall We Die? (1983), The Ploughman's Lunch (1985), The Child in Time (1987), The Innocent (1990), Black Dogs (shortlisted Booker Prize, 1992), The Daydreamer (1994), Enduring Love (1997, shortlisted Whitbread Novel of the Year Award 1997, shortlisted Booker Prize 1998), Amsterdam (1998, winner Booker Prize 1998), Atonement (2001), Saturday (2005), Solar (2010, Bollinger Everyman Wodehouse Prize 2010); *Film* The Ploughman's Lunch (1983), Last Day of Summer (1984), Sour Sweet (1989), The Innocent (dir by John Schlesinger, 1993), The Good Son (1993); *Style*— Ian McEwan, Esq, CBE; ✉ c/o Jonathan Cape Ltd, 20 Vauxhall Bridge Road, London SW1V 2SA (☎ 020 7973 9730)

McEWAN, Mhairi; da of Edward McEwan, of Scotland, and Rose Helen, *née* Betts; *b* 5 July 1961; *Educ* Univ of Leicester (BSc, Faculty of Sci prize); *m* 25 June 1988, Phillip Keague (Phil) Bentley, *qv*, s of Alan William Bentley; 1 da (Naomi Frances b 22 Jan 1992), 1 s (Guy Edward Keague b 29 April 1994); *Career* Lever Brothers Ltd UK: brand mangr 1982–86, nat account exec (sales) 1986–88, Euro brand mangr 1988–89, market mangr Egypt Unilever Export Cairo 1989–92, Euro mktg mangr Lever Europe Paris 1992–94; vice-pres mktg (Europe) Pepsi-Cola International Ltd London 1995–96, vice-pres mktg Walkers Snacks Ltd (pt of Pepsi-Co) 1996–97; int mktg conslt 1998–; co-fndr and ceo The Brand Learning Partners Ltd 2000–, gp ceo and co-fndr Brand Learning Gp Ltd 2011; chm Mktg Gp of GB 2013 (memb Cncl 2011); fell Mktg Soc 2008, chartered marketer, FCIM 1995; *Books* The Growth Drivers (2011); *Recreations* sailing, skiing, walking; *Style*— Ms Mhairi McEwan; ✉ Brand Learning, Burgoine Quay, 8 Lower Teddington Road, Hampton Wick, Kingston KT1 4ER (☎ 020 8614 8150, fax 020 8255 9057, e-mail mhairi.mcewan@brandlearning.com, website www.brandlearning.com)

McEWAN, Hon Lord; Robin Gilmour McEwan; s of Ian Gilmour McEwan (d 1976), and Mary McArthur Bowman McEwan; *b* 12 December 1943; *Educ* Paisley GS, Univ of Glasgow (LLB, PhD); *m* 1973, Sheena, da of Stewart Francis McIntyre (d 1974); 2 da (Stephanie b 1979, Louisa b 1983); *Career* QC Scot 1981, Sheriff of Lanark 1982–88, Sheriff of Ayr 1988–2000, temp judge Court of Session and High Court of Justiciary 1991–2000, senator Coll of Justice 2000–; *Recreations* golf; *Clubs* New (Edinburgh), Hon Co of Edinburgh Golfers, Prestwick Golf; *Style*— The Hon Lord McEwan

McEWAN, Ross; *Career* Cwlth Bank of Australia 2002–12; RBS Gp: chief exec UK retail banking 2012–13, chief exec 2013–; *Style*— Ross McEwan, Esq; ✉ Royal Bank of Scotland Group, 280 Bishopsgate, London EC2M 4RB

McEWEN, Prof James; s of Daniel McEwen (d 1973), of Kinross, and Elizabeth Wells, *née* Dishington (d 1962); *b* 6 February 1940, Stirling; *Educ* Dollar Acad, Univ of St Andrews (MB ChB); *m* 24 Oct 1964, Elizabeth May, da of late Andrew Archibald; 1 s (Daniel Mark b 6 May 1966), 1 da (Ruth Elizabeth b 24 Jan 1968); *Career* various trg posts in hosp and general practice Dundee 1963–65, asst med offr of health Dundee 1965–66, lectr Dept of Social and Occupational Med Univ of Dundee 1966–74, sr lectr Dept of Community Health Univ of Nottingham 1975–81, chief med offr Health Educn Cncl 1981–82, prof of community med KCL and dir of public health Camberwell Health Authy 1982–89; Univ of Glasgow: Henry Mechan prof 1989–2000, prof of public health 2000–02, emeritus prof of public health 2002–; pres Faculty of Public Health Medicine RCP 1998–2001; chair: Public Health Register 2003–09, Pharmacy Healthlink 2004–07, Health Protection Advsy Gp Scotland 2005–13; chair Bd of Govrs Dollar Acad 2014–; chm Dunhill Medical Tst 2016–; Hon DSc Glasgow Caledonian Univ 2008; FMedSci, FFPH, Hon FFPHMI, FFOM, FRCP, FDS RCS; *Books* Coronary Heart Disease and Patterns of Living (jtly, 1979), Participation in Health (jtly, 1983), Measuring Health Status (jtly, 1986), Oxford Textbook of Public Health (jtly, 4 edn 2002); *Style*— Prof James McEwen; ✉ Auchanachie, Ruthven, Huntly AB54 4SS (☎ and fax 01466 760742, e-mail j.mcewen@tiscali.co.uk)

McEWEN, Prof Keith Alistair; s of George Charles McEwen (d 1979), and Marjorie Anne, *née* Field (d 1991); *b* 11 December 1944; *Educ* Dr Challoner's GS Amersham, Pembroke Coll Cambridge (MA, PhD); *m* 1, 12 April 1969 (m dis 1982), Anne (d 2015), da of Rupert Thompson (d 1980); 1 s (Carl Alistair b 1971), 1 da (Sarah Ruth b 1974); m 2, 20 May 1986, Ursula, da of Maximilian Steigenberger (d 1983); *Career* lectr in physics: Univ of Copenhagen 1970–73, Univ of Salford 1973–81; seconded as sr lectr to Institut Laue-Langevin Grenoble 1981–86, prof of experimental physics Birkbeck Coll London 1986–97, prof of physics UCL 1997–; CPhys, FInstP 1989; *Publications* 200 papers in physics research jls; *Recreations* music, opera, walking, skiing; *Clubs* Physical Soc; *Style*— Prof Keith McEwen; ✉ 90 Lydalls Road, Didcot, Oxfordshire OX11 7DT (✆ 01235 813284); Department of Physics and Astronomy, University College London, Gower Street, London WC1E 6BT (e-mail keith.mcewen@ucl.ac.uk)

MACEY, Roger David Michael; s of late Eric Hamilton Macey, and Margaret Maria, *née* Newman; *b* 15 November 1942; *Educ* St Mary's Coll Ireland; *m* 1, 1970 (m dis 1995), Julie Elizabeth, da of John Everard Mellors, of Mount Eliza, Melbourne, Aust; 2 s (Jonathan b 20 April 1973, Giles b 25 May 1976); m 2, 1996, Barbara; *Career* dir: Wm Brandts Sons & Co (insur) Ltd 1972–76, P S Mossé & Ptnrs Ltd 1977–83, Macdonagh Boland Group 1989; non-exec dir: J Jackson & Partners Ltd 1975–76, P S Mossé Life & Pensions 1977–83, George Miller Underwriting Agencies Ltd 1977–86; md Macey Williams Ltd 1976–94; chm: Macey Williams Insurance Services Ltd 1976–94, Macey Clifton Walters Ltd 1991–94, Conquest Security Services plc, K S Conquest plc, Aon Mergers and Acquisitions Gp UK; dir: Rollins Hudig Hall Ltd (following takeover of Macey Williams companies) 1994–96, Aon Risk Services Ltd (following name change) 1996–; memb Lloyd's 1974–; *Recreations* shooting, golf, tennis, horse racing; *Clubs* Turf, City of London, Mill Reef (Antigua); *Style*— Roger Macey, Esq; ✉ 62 Howards Lane, Putney, London SW15 6QD; Aon Mergers & Acquisitions, 8 Devonshire Square, London EC2M 4PL

McFADDEN, Andy; *b* Ireland; *Career* head chef L'Autre Pied 2011– (Michelin star); *Style*— Andy McFadden, Esq; ✉ L'Autre Pied, 5–7 Blandford Street, London W1U 3DB

McFADDEN, Rt Hon Patrick (Pat); PC, MP; *b* 26 March 1965, Paisley; *Educ* Holyrood Sch, Univ of Edinburgh; *Career* political sec PM's Office 2002–05, MP (Lab) Wolverhampton SE 2005–; Parly under-sec of state Cabinet Office 2006–07, min of state for employment rels and postal policy Dept for Business, Enterprise and Regulatory Reform 2007–09, min of state for business Dept of Business, Innovation and Skills 2009–10, shadow min for Europe 2014–16; memb: Community Union; *Style*— The Rt Hon Pat McFadden, MP; ✉ House of Commons, London SW1A 0AA

McFADYEN, Jock; s of James Lachlan McFadyen, of Carnoustie, Angus, and Margaret, *née* Owen; *b* 18 September 1950; *Educ* Renfrew HS, Chelsea Sch of Art (BA, MA); *m* 1, 1971 (m dis 1989), Carol Ann, *née* Hambleton; 1 s (James b 29 July 1972); m 2, 1991, Susie, *née* Honeyman; 1 da (Annie b 6 Feb 1993), 1 s (George b 23 June 1995); *Career* pt/t lectr Slade Sch of Art 1980–2005; designer The Judas Tree (Royal Opera House Covent Garden); RA 2012; *Exhibitions* 40 solo exhibitions since 1978 incl: Acme Gallery, Blond Fine Art, National Gallery, Scottish Gallery, Camden Arts Centre, Talbot Rice Gallery Edinburgh Festival 1998, Pier Arts Centre St Magnus Festival Orkney 1999, Agnews 2001, Roadworks (Scottish Gallery Projects Edinburgh Festival and Rude Wercs London) 2005, Pictures of Scotland (The Grey Gallery Edinburgh Festival) 2007, Kill Matthew Barney (The Grey Gallery London) 2008, Wolverhampton Art Gallery 2008, Clifford Chance London 2010, Bourne Fine Art Edinburgh Festival 2012, Fleming Collection London 2012, Fine Art Soc London 2012, Eleven Spitalfields 2012, Marsden Woo 2014; many mixed exhibitions in Europe and USA incl: A13 (Wapping Project), Hayward Annual, John Moore's, Royal Academy, British Art Show, New British Painting (USA), British Cncl touring shows, Reality, Endarkenment; *Works in Public Museums* incl: Tate Gallery, National Gallery (residency), V&A, Imperial War Museum, Kunsthalle Hamburg, Manchester, Birmingham, Glasgow, Govt Art Coll, Br Museum; *Commissions* incl: Arts Cncl purchase, National Gallery residency, Imperial War Museum Eastern Europe project; monograph written by David Cohen (2001); *Recreations* greyhounds, motorcycles; *Clubs* Vintage Japanese Motorcycle; *Style*— Jock McFadyen, RA; ✉ 15 Victoria Park Square, London E2 9PB (✆ 020 8983 3825, e-mail info@jockmcfadyen.com, website www.jockmcfadyen.com)

MACFADYEN, Matthew; *b* 17 October 1974, Gt Yarmouth, Norfolk; *Educ* RADA; *m* 2004, Keeley Hawes; 1 da, 1 s, 1 step-s; *Career* actor; *Theatre* incl: The Duchess of Malfi 1995, A Midsummer Night's Dream (RSC) 1996, Much Ado About Nothing 1998, The School For Scandal (RSC) 1998, Battle Royal (RNT) 1999, Henry IV (RNT) 2005, The Pain and the Itch (Royal Court Theatre) 2007, Private Lives (Vaudeville Theatre) 2010, Perfect Nonsense (Duke of York Theatre) 2013, Jeeves & Wooster (Duke of York's Theatre) 2013; *Television* incl: Wuthering Heights (ITV) 1998, Warriors (BBC 1) 1999, The Way We Live Now (BBC 1) 2001, Perfect Strangers (BBC 2) 2001, The Project (BBC 1) 2002, Spooks (BBC 1) 2002–04 and 2011, Secret Life (Channel 4) 2007 (Best Actor RTS Award 2007), Marple: A Pocket Full of Rye (ITV) 2008, Little Dorrit (BBC 1) 2008, Enid (BBC 4) 2009, Criminal Justice (BBC 1) 2009 (Best Supporting Actor BAFTA Television Award 2010), The Pillars of Earth (Channel 4) 2010, Any Human Heart (Channel 4) 2010, Ripper St (BBC 1) 2012–16, Ambassadors (BBC 2) 2013, The Enfield Haunting 2015; *Film* incl: Maybe Baby 2000, Enigma 2001, In My Father's Den 2004, Pride and Prejudice 2005, Middletown 2006, Death at a Funeral 2007, Frost/Nixon 2008, Robin Hood 2010, The Three Musketeers 2011, Anna Karenina 2012, Lost in Karastan 2014, The Von Trapp Family: A Life of Music 2015; *Style*— Mr Matthew Macfadyen; ✉ c/o Christian Hodell, Hamilton Hodell, 20 Golden Square, London W1F 9JL

McFALL OF ALCLUITH, Baron (Life Peer UK 2010), of Dumbarton on Dumbartonshire; John Francis McFall; PC (2004); *Career* former sch teacher; MP (Lab) Dumbarton 1987–2010; former oppn whip (with responsibility for foreign affrs, defence and trade and indust); a Lord Cmmr of HM Treasy (Govt whip) 1997–98, Parly under sec NI Office 1998–99; chair Treasy Select Ctee 2001–10; former memb Select Ctee: on defence, on Sittings of the House, on information; former dep shadow sec of state for Scotland; former memb: Parly & Scientific Ctee (hon sec), Exec Ctee Parly Gp for Energy Studies; vice-chm Br/Italian Gp; sec: Retail Indust Gp, Roads Study Gp; jt sec Br/Peru Gp; treas: Br/Hong Kong Gp, Scotch Whisky Gp; hon doctorate: Univ of Strathclyde 2010, Univ of Glasgow 2011, Univ of Stirling 2011; Hon DBA BSS Business Sch 2011; *Recreations* golf, running, reading; *Style*— The Rt Hon the Lord McFall of Alcluith; ✉ House of Lords, London SW1A 0PW

MACFARLANE, Prof Alan Donald James; s of Maj Donald Kennedy Macfarlane (d 1976), and Iris, *née* Rhodes James; *b* 20 December 1941; *Educ* Sedbergh, Worcester Coll Oxford (MA, DPhil), LSE (MPhil), SOAS Univ of London (PhD); *m* 1, 1966 (m dis), Gillian Ions; 1 da (Katharine b 1970); m 2, 1981, Sarah, *née* Tarring; *Career* Univ of Cambridge: lectr in social anthropology 1975–81, reader in hist anthropology 1981–, prof of anthropological science 1991–2009, emeritus prof 2009–; fell King's Coll Cambridge 1981– (sr res fell 1971–74); FRHistS 1967, FRAI 1970, FBA 1986; *Books* Witchcraft in Tudor and Stuart England (1970), The Family Life of Ralph Josselin (1970), Resources and Population (1976), The Diary of Ralph Josselin (ed, 1976), Reconstructing Historical Communities (1977), The Origins of English Individualism (1978), The Justice and the Mare's Ale (1981), A Guide to English Historical Records (1983), Marriage and Love in England (1986), The Culture of Capitalism (1987), Bernard Pignède, The Gurungs, A Himalayan Population of Nepal (ed and trans, 1993), The Savage Wars of Peace (1997), The Riddle of the Modern World (2000), The Making of the Modern World (2002), Glass: A World History (2002), Green Gold: The Empire of Tea (jtly, 2003), Letters to Lily: On How the World Works (2005), Japan Through the Looking Glass (2007), Reflections on Cambridge (2009), Dragon Days (jtly, 2012), Dorset Days (2012), The Invention of the Modern World (2014); *Recreations* gardening, second-hand book hunting, filming; *Style*— Prof Alan Macfarlane; ✉ 25 Lode Road, Lode, Cambridge CB5 9ER (✆ 01223 811976); King's College, Cambridge CB2 1ST (✆ 01223 331100, e-mail aml12@cam.ac.uk, website www.alanmacfarlane.com)

McFARLANE, Rt Hon Lord Justice; Sir Andrew Ewart McFarlane; kt (2005), PC (2011); s of Gordon McFarlane (d 1970), and Olive McFarlane (d 1991); *b* 20 June 1954; *Educ* Shrewsbury, Univ of Durham (BA, pres Student Union), Univ of Wales Cardiff (LLM); *m* 1981, Susanna Jane, *née* Randolph; 4 da (Laura b 29 Nov 1983, Mary b 19 Aug 1985, Iona b 27 Sept 1987, Philippa b 5 Nov 1991); *Career* called to the Bar Gray's Inn 1977; barr: 2 Fountain Court Birmingham 1978–93, One Kings Bench Walk Temple 1993–2005; QC 1998, recorder 1999–2005 (asst recorder 1995–99), judge of the High Court of Justice (Family Div) 2005–2011 (dep judge 2000–05), Midland Circuit Family Div liaison judge 2006–11, Lord Justice of the Court of Appeal 2011–; chair Family Law Bar Assoc 2002–03, memb Family Justice Review 2010–11, chm Bar Tribunal Appts Bd 2012–; pres Tribunals and chm Clergy Discipline Cmmn C of E 2014–; dep chllr Diocese of Wakefield 2004–07, chllr Diocese of Exeter 2005–; chair Hereford Cathedral Cncl 2016–; *Publications* Children: Law and Practice (co-author 1991), Child Care and Adoption Law (co-author, 2010), Family Court Practice (contrib to annual edns); *Recreations* family life, vegetables, bees, popular culture; *Clubs* Garrick; *Style*— The Rt Hon the Lord Justice McFarlane; ✉ Royal Courts of Justice, Strand, London WC2A 2LL

McFARLANE, Prof Angela; *Educ* Univ of Bristol (BSc, PhD); *Career* science teacher, dir Centre for Research in Educational ICT Homerton Coll Cambridge, dir for evidence and practice British Educnl Communications and Technol Agency (Becta), prof of educn and dir of learning technol Univ of Bristol 2000–, seconded as dir of public engagement and learning Kew Royal Botanic Gardens 2008–; *Books* Information Technology and Authentic Learning: Realising the Potential of Computers in the Primary Classroom (ed, 1996), ILS: A Guide to Good Practice (1999), A Digitally Driven Curriculum? (with David Buckingham, 2001), El aprendizaje y las techologias de la informacion (2001); *Style*— Prof Angela McFarlane; ✉ The Graduate School of Education, University of Bristol, 35 Berkeley Square, Bristol BS8 1JA

McFARLANE, John; OBE (1995); s of John McFarlane (d 1992), of Dumfries, Scotland, and Christina Campbell (d 1976); *b* 14 June 1947; *Educ* Dumfries Acad, Univ of Edinburgh (MA), Cranfield Sch of Mgmnt (MBA); *m* 1, 1970 (m dis 2005) Anne, da of Rev Fraser Ian MacDonald (d 1983), of Dumfries, Scotland; 3 da (Kirsty b 14 March 1976, Rebecca b 17 March 1979, Fiona b 18 March 1983); m 2, 2011, Anne, da of late James Scott and Mary Fyfe Marshall, of Sanquar, Scotland; *Career* Ford Motor Co 1969–74, Citicorp 1975–93 (md Citibank NA (UK), gp exec dir Standard Chartered plc 1993–97, ceo Australia & NZ Banking Gp Ltd Melbourne 1997–2007; chm: Aviva plc 2012–15, FirstGroup plc 2014–15, Barclays plc 2015–, TheCityUK 2015–; non-exec dir: London Stock Exchange 1989–91, Securities Assoc 1989–91, Auditing Practices Bd 1991–97, Fin Law Panel 1994–99, Capital Radio plc 1995–98, Royal Bank of Scotland 2007–12, National Westminster Bank 2007–12, Westfield Hldgs 2007–14, Old Oak Hldgs 2007–, Westfield Corp 2014–; chm Australian Bankers' Assoc; Distinguished Alumni Award Cranfield Sch of Mgmnt 2003; Australian Centenary Medal 2003; *Recreations* business education, art and music; *Style*— John McFarlane, Esq, OBE

MACFARLANE, John Foster; s of Alexander Macfarlane, and Agnes, *née* Thompson; *b* 1948, Glasgow; *Educ* Hillhead HS Glasgow, Glasgow Sch of Art; *Career* stage designer; Leverhulme Travelling Scholarship 1970, RSA Bursary 1970, Sam Mavor Bequest Scholarship 1970, Arts Cncl of GB Trainee Theatre Design Bursary 1972; fell Welsh Coll of Music and Dance; Chevalier de l'Ordre des Arts et des Lettres (France) 2002; *Designs for the Stage* incl: Othello (Ludlow Festival) 1974, Heroes (Royal Court) 1974, Miraculous Mandarin (Köln Tanz Forum) 1980, Forgotten Land (Stuttgart Ballet) 1981, Stravinsky's Firebird (Royal Danish Ballet Copenhagen) 1981, Stravinsky's Les Noces (Metropolitan Opera NY) 1982, Ravel's L'Enfant et les Sortileges (Holland Festival) 1984, Giselle (Royal Ballet London) 1985, Britten's Midsummer Night's Dream (Oper der Stadt Köln) 1988, The Nutcracker (Birmingham Royal Ballet) 1990, Benvenuto Cellini (Grande Théatre de Genève) 1992, Peter Grimes (Opera National La Monnaie Brussels) 1994, Swan Lake (Bayerisches Staatsballett Munich) 1994, Otello (Opéra National La Monnaie Brussels) 1997, Hansel and Gretel (WNO) 1998, Falstaff (Théatre Comunale La Monnaie Brussels) 1998, War and Peace (Bastille Paris) 2000, Agrippina (La Monnaie Brussles) 2000, Queen of Spades (WNO) 2000, Euryanthe (Glyndebourne) 2002, The Magic Flute (ROH) 2003, Trojans at Carthage (ENO) 2003; *Selected Exhibitions and Commissions* New Prints, Drawings and Sculpture (Akademia Salzburg) 1979, New Prints, Drawings and Paintings (Oriel Gall Cardiff) 1979, New Prints and Drawings (Andrew Knight Cardiff) 1984, Set and Costume Designs (Marina Henderson London) 1988, Set and Costume Designs (Marina Henderson London) 1991, Recent Paintings, Set and Costume designs (Marina Henderson London) 1993, New Paintings, Prints and Theatre Designs (Martin Tinney Cardiff) 1995; works in selected collections incl: Albertina Vienna, Welsh Arts Cncl, Kunsthalle Nuremberg, Glyn Vivian Art Gall Swansea, Nat Museum Wales, Hunterial Museum Glasgow; *Awards* nominated Olivier dance award for Nutcracker 1996, winner Olivier best opera award for Hansel and Gretel 2000, nominated South Bank Show best opera for Queen of Spades 2001, winner Olivier best opera production award for Lady Macbeth of Mtsensk 2004; *Recreations* playing piano, gardening; *Style*— John Macfarlane, Esq; ✉ c/o Gilly Adams, 25 Ilton Road, Cardiff CF23 5DU (✆ and fax 029 2049 4243)

MACFARLANE, Jonathan Stephen; s of William Keith Macfarlane (d 1987), and Pearl Hastings, *née* Impey; *b* 28 March 1956; *Educ* Charterhouse, Oriel Coll Oxford (MA), Univ of Surrey (BSc); *Career* admitted slr 1980; ptnr Macfarlanes 1985–2001 (specialising in corporate finance and M&A), currently dir The Professional Career Partnership; *Clubs* Leander, MCC; *Style*— Jonathan Macfarlane, Esq; ✉ The Professional Career Partnership, 52 Cornhill, London EC3V 3PD (e-mail jonathan.macfarlane@thepcp.com)

MACFARLANE, Nicholas Russel; s of John Macfarlane, DL, and Pamela, *née* Laing; *b* 21 February 1952; *Educ* Radley, Lancaster Univ (BA); *m* 25 July 1987, Elisabeth Anne, da of W David Crane, of Hallaughton; 1 s (James William Archibald b 7 Sept 1989), 1 da (Flora Emily Octavia b 11 Oct 1991); *Career* admitted slr 1977; ptnr Faithfull Owen & Fraser 1980 (amalgamated with Durrant Piesse 1985), currently conslt specialising in intellectual property law Hogan Lovells (after a series of amalgamations); Freeman Worshipful Co of Slrs; memb: Law Soc, Intellectual Property Lawyers Assoc; *Recreations* fishing, shooting, painting; *Clubs* Boodles, City of London, Royal W Norfolk Golf; *Style*— Nicholas Macfarlane, Esq; ✉ Hogan Lovells, Atlantic House, London EC1A 2FG (✆ 020 7296 2000, fax 020 7296 2001)

MACFARLANE, Prof Peter Wilson; CBE (2014); s of Robert Barton Macfarlane (d 1965), of Glasgow, and Dinah, *née* Wilson (d 2003); *b* 8 November 1942; *Educ* Hyndland Secondary Sch Glasgow, Univ of Glasgow (BSc, PhD, DSc); *m* 8 Oct 1971, Irene Grace, da of James Muir (d 1975), of Kirkintilloch; 2 s (Alan b 1974, David b 1977); *Career* Univ of Glasgow: asst lectr in med cardiology 1967–70, lectr 1970–74, sr lectr 1974–80, reader 1980–91, prof 1991–95, prof of electrocardiology 1995–2010 (emeritus prof 2010–); author and ed of various books and proceedings, res interest computers in electrocardiography, princ

M

author of electrocardiogram analysis programme marketed worldwide; pres Int Soc of Electrocardiology 2007–09, pres Bd Computing in Cardiology 2008–14, vice-pres Int Soc of Computerized Electrocardiology 2014–; chm Working Gp on Computers in Cardiology European Soc of Cardiology 2002–04, memb Br Cardiac Soc 1974; FBCS 1976, CEng 1990, FESC 1991, FRSE 1992, FRCP (Glasgow) 2001; *Books* An Introduction to Automated Electrocardiogram Interpretation (1974), Computer Techniques in Clinical Medicine (1985), Comprehensive Electrocardiology (1989, 2 edn 2011), 12-Lead Vectorcardiography (1995); *Recreations* jogging,; *Style*— Prof Peter Macfarlane, CBE, FRSE

MacFARQUHAR, Prof Roderick Lemonde; s of late Sir Alexander MacFarquhar; *b* 2 December 1930, Lahore, India; *Educ* Fettes, Keble Coll Oxford (BA), Harvard Univ (AM), LSE (PhD); *m* 1, 1964, Emily Jane (d 2001), da of Dr Paul W Cohen, of NY; 1 da (Larissa b 1968), 1 s (Rory b 1971); m 2, 2012, Dalena Wright; *Career* Nat Serv 2 Lt; China specialist Daily Telegraph 1955–61, ed The China Quarterly 1959–68, reporter BBC Panorama 1963–64, co presenter BBC World Serv 24 Hours 1972–74 and 1979–80; MP (Lab) Belper 1974–79; Harvard Univ: prof of govt 1984–2012 (ret), dir Fairbank Centre for E Asian Research 1986–92 and 2005–06, chair Govt Dept 1998–2004, Leroy B Williams research prof of history and political science 2013–; visiting prof Lee Kuan Yew Sch of Public Policy Nat Univ of Singapore 2005, Sin Wai-Kin distinguished visiting professor Hong Kong Univ 2015; fell: Research Inst on Communist Affairs and E Asian Inst Columbia 1969, RIIA 1971–74, Woodrow Wilson Int Centre for Scholars Washington DC 1980–81, American Acad of Arts and Sciences 1986–, Leverhulme Research Grant, Ford Fndn Research Grant, Rockefeller Fndn Research Grant; *Publications* incl: The Origins of the Cultural Revolution (3 vols), Mao's Last Revolution (jtly), The Politics of China (3 edn Sixty Years of the People's Republic of China), The Paradox of China's Post-Mao Reforms, The Cambridge History of China (vols 14 & 15, jt ed); *Recreations* reading, travel, listening to music; *Style*— Prof Roderick MacFarquhar; ✉ Fairbank Center, Harvard University, 1730 Cambridge Street, Cambridge, MA 02138, USA

McGAIRL, Stephen James; s of John Lloyd McGairl (d 1979), of Chichester, W Sussex, and Lucy Hudson; *b* 18 February 1951; *Educ* Chichester HS, Worcester Coll Oxford (MA); *m* 24 May 1975, Madeleine, da of Christopher William Talbot Cox (d 1964), of Sidlesham, W Sussex; 4 s (Sam b 1977, Thomas b 1978, Joe b 1983, George b 1986); *Career* admitted slr 1976, admitted Conseil Juridique 1988, avocat 1992; Legal and Parliamentary Dept GLC 1974–77; Freshfields (now Freshfields Bruckhaus Deringer): joined 1977, ptnr 1984, Paris office 1986–92, head Moscow office 1994–95; chm Legal Advsy Panel Aviation Working Gp, dir and tstee UK Fndn for Int Uniform Law; memb: Law Soc, City of London Slrs' Co, Société Française de Droit Aérien; *Publications* Aircraft Financing (co-ed and contrib 3 edn, 1998), Contract Practices under the Cape Town Connection (2004); contrib various professional jls relating to aviation, asset and project fin and business in CIS; *Recreations* sailing, opera; *Clubs* Cercle de l'Union Interalliée, RAC, Little Ship; *Style*— Stephen McGairl, Esq; ✉ 25 Ashley Gardens, London SW1P 1QD (✆ 020 7828 5889, e-mail mcgairl@btinternet.com)

McGANN, Paul; *Educ* Cardinal Allen GS Liverpool, RADA; *Career* actor; *Theatre* incl: Cain (Nottingham Playhouse) 1981, Oi For England (Royal Court Upstairs) 1982, Yakety-Yak (Half Moon and Astoria) 1982, The Genius (Royal Court) 1983, Loot (Ambassadors) 1984, A Lie of the Mind (Royal Court) 1987, Much Ado About Nothing (Horseshoe Theatre Basingstoke) 1996, Loot (Ambassadors) 1997, The Seagull (Liverpool Playhouse) 1998, A Lie of the Mind (Royal Court) 1999, The Little Black Book (Riverside Studios) 2003, Mourning Becomes Electra (Nat Theatre) 2003; *Television* Gaskin 1982, Give us a Break 1983, The Monocled Mutineer 1986, The Importance of Being Earnest 1986, Drowning in the Shallow End 1989, The Hanging Gale 1995, Dr Who (TV film) 1996, Forgotten 1999, Nature Boy 2000, Fish 2000, Hornblower 2000 and 2003, Sweet Revenge 2001, Blood Strangers 2002, The Biographer 2002, Lie with Me 2004, Kidnapped 2005, Marple 2006, If I Had You 2006, Tripping Over 2006, True Dare Kiss 2007, Collision 2009, Jonathan Creek 2010, Luther 2010–11, Waking The Dead 2011, New Tricks 2011, Ripper Street 2013, Moving On 2013, Doctor Who 2013, The Bletchley Circle 2014; *Films* Withnail and I 1986, Empire of the Sun 1987, Streets of Yesterday 1988, The Rainbow 1988, Dealers 1988, Paper Mask 1989, Afraid of the Dark 1990, Alien III 1991, Downtime 1996, Fairytale – A True Story 1997, Queen of the Damned 2000, My Kingdom 2000, Hotel 2000, The Biographer 2000, Listening 2003, Poppies 2006, Lesbian Vampire Killers 2009, Moving Target 2011; *Recreations* music, sport, travel; *Clubs* Liverpool FC; *Style*— Paul McGann, Esq

McGAREL-GROVES, Anthony Robin; s of Brig Robin Jullian McGarel-Groves, RM, OBE, of Lymington, Hants, and Constance Morton, *née* Macmillan; *b* 7 September 1954; *Educ* Eton, Univ of Bath (BSc); *m* 16 Dec 1978, Ann Candace (d 2006), da of Jack Dawes, of Ross-on-Wye, Herefords; *Career* Deloitte Haskins and Sells 1976–81, Kuwait Investment Office 1981–94, assoc dir Hambro's Fund Management plc 1994–97, Guinness Flight Hambro Asset Management plc 1997–1999, ptnr Mark Capital LLP 2001–07; memb: Faculty of Fin and Mgmnt, ICAEW; ACA; *Recreations* gardening, theatre, bridge, politics, vintage cars, old houses, countryside pursuits; *Style*— Anthony R McGarel-Groves, Esq; ✉ Clapton Revel, Wooburn Moor, Buckinghamshire HP10 0NH

McGARVEY, Seamus; s of Jimmy McGarvey (d 1981), and Peggy McGarvey (d 2012); *b* 29 June 1967, Armagh, NI; *Educ* Christian Brothers' GS Armagh, PCL (BA); *m* (m dis); *Career* photographer and cinematographer; solo exhibitions at City Centre Art Gallery Dublin: Armagh in a New Light 1984, Eternity Where? 1989; RPS Lumiere Award for contributions to the art of cinematography 2004; patron Edinburgh Int Film Festival; hon fell Edinburgh Coll of Art 2009; memb: BSC 1999, IATSE 600 (USA cinematography union) 1999, BAFTA 2000, AMPAS 2002, American Soc of Cinematographers 2008; *Television and Short Films* with Sam Taylor-Wood, *qv*: Sustaining the Crisis, Mute, Strings, Ascension, Pieta, Crying Men, Atlantic (nominated Turner Prize 1998), Breach, Third Party, Love You More; with Willie Doherty: Re Run (nominated Turner Prize 2003), Drive, Buried, Non Specific Threat, Ghost Story; documentaries incl: The Work of Angels, Space and Light; numerous pop promotions incl work for: U2, Elton John, Paul McCartney, Pet Shop Boys, P J Harvey, Coldplay, The Cure, Robbie Williams, Dave Stewart, Terry Hall, Orbital; *Film* Look Me in the Eye 1996, Butterfly Kiss 1997, The Slab Boys 1998, Harald 1999, Jump the Gun 1999, The Winter Guest 1999, The War Zone 2000, The Big Tease 2000, A Map of the World 2000, High Fidelity 2000, Enigma 2001, Wit 2001, The Hours 2002 (Evening Standard British Film Award for Technical Achievement 2004), The Actors 2002, Sahara 2004, Along Came Polly 2004, Destricted 2005, World Trade Center 2006, Charlotte's Web 2006, Atonement 2007 (Acad Award and BAFTA nominations and Irish Film and Television Acad Award), #1 Ladies Detective Agency 2007, The Soloist 2008, Nowhere Boy 2009, We Need To Talk About Kevin 2011, The Avengers 2012, Anna Karenina 2012 (London Film Museum Award For Technical Achievement London Evening Standard Br Film Award 2013 (jtly)); *Clubs* Chelsea Arts; *Style*— Seamus McGarvey

McGEE, Prof James O'Donnell; s of Michael McGee (d 1981), and Bridget Gavin (d 1982); *b* 27 July 1939; *Educ* Univ of Glasgow (MB ChB, PhD, MD), Univ of Oxford (MA); *m* 26 August 1961, Anne McCarron Lee, da of Patrick Lee, of Cardonald, Glasgow; 1 s (Damon-Joel b 1969), 2 da (Leeanne b 1962, Sharon b 1964); *Career* lectr then sr lectr in pathology Univ of Glasgow 1967–75, prof Univ of Oxford 1975– (former head Nuffield Dept of Pathology and Bacteriology), fell Linacre Coll Oxford 1975– (now emeritus), assoc fell Green Coll Oxford 1981–; dir UK Telepathology Co-ordinating Unit 1994–; distinguished visiting scientist Roche Inst of Molecular Biology Nutley NJ USA 1981 and 1989 (Med Res Cncl travelling fell 1969–70, visiting scientist 1970–71), Kattle Meml lectr Royal Coll of Pathologists 1981, guest lectr Royal Coll of Physicians of Ireland 1985, keynote lectr Med Res Inst SA 1994, special guest lectr Hellenic Pathology Congress Crete 1994; visiting prof: Univ of Baghdad 1976, Univ of Kuwait 1981 and 1983 (academic advsr 1984–), Univ of Witwatersrand SA 1994; academic advsr Hong Kong Medical Res Cncl 1990–; memb: Scientific and Grants Ctee Cancer Res Campaign UK 1978–93, Ctee on Safety of Meds Med Div UK 1984–90, Nat Cmmn (UK) Breast Screening Pathology 1989–; hon conslt Pathologist Oxford Health Authy 1975–; Bellahouston Gold Medal Univ of Glasgow 1973; FRCPath 1986 (MRCPath 1973), FRCP 1989; *Books* Biopsy Pathology of Liver (1980, 2 edn 1988), In Situ Hybridisation: Principles and Practice (1990, 2 edn 1999), Oxford Textbook of Pathology (vols 1, 2a and 2b, with P J Isaacson and N A Wright, 1992, Italian edn 1994 and 1996), Diagnostic Molecular Pathology (vols 1 and 2 with C S Herrington, 1992), The Macrophage (with C E Lewis, 1992), The NK Cell (with C E Lewis, 1992); *Recreations* talking with my family, swimming; *Style*— Prof James O'D McGee; ✉ John Radcliffe Hospital, Headington, Oxford OX3 9DU

McGEECHAN, Sir Ian Robert; kt (2010), OBE; s of Robert Matthew McGeechan (d 1969), and Hilda, *née* Shearer (d 1994); *b* 30 October 1946; *Educ* Moor Grange HS, West Park HS, Allerton Grange Comp, Carnegie Coll of Physical Educn; *m* 9 Aug 1969, Judith Irene, da of Thomas Fish (d 1976); 1 s (Robert James b 5 Nov 1978), 1 da (Heather Jane b 17 Aug 1983); *Career* rugby union player (fly-half) and coach; head of games Moor Grange HS 1968–72, head of humanities and year gp ldr Fir Tree Middle Sch 1972–90, trg mangr Scottish Life Assurance Company 1990–94; Hon MA Univ of Nottingham 1998, Hon Dr Leeds Metropolitan Univ 2004; *As Player* clubs: Headingley FC 1965–82 (300 appearances, capt 1972–73), Barbarians RFC 1973–78, Yorks CCC 1963–68 (played for second XI); Scotland: 32 caps, debut v NZ 1972, tour NZ 1975 (1 test appearance), capt 1977 and 1979, ret as player 1979; British and Irish Lions: toured South Africa 1974 (4 tests, won series 3–0, 1 drawn), toured NZ 1977 (4 tests); *As Coach* asst coach Scotland 1985–88, nat coach Scotland 1988–93 (Grand Slam winners 1990, fourth place World Cup 1991); dir: National Coaching Fndn 1995–, Northampton RFC 1996–99, English Premiership Rugby 1996–99, English Rugby Partnership 1996–99; technical and coaching conslt Scotland RFU 1997–98, nat coach Scotland 1999–2003, dir of rugby Scottish Rugby Union 2004–05, dir of rugby Wasps RFC 2005–09 (winners Heineken Cup 2007), performance dir Bath Rugby 2010–12; coach British and Irish Lions Aust 1989 (won series 2–1), NZ 1993 (lost series 1–2), South Africa 1997 (won series 2–1), and NZ 2005; coach World XV v NZ (for NZ rugby centenary) 1992; Rugby Writers Rubert Cherry trophy 1989, Coach of the Year Rugby World 1989 and 1990, Rugby Writers Pat Marshall trophy 1990, Coach of the Year Br Inst of Sports Coaches 1990 and 1993, inducted into Nat Coaching Fndn Hall of Fame 1999, Sport Scotland special millennium award for services to coaching 2000; *Books* Scotland's Grand Slam (with Ian Robertson and M Cleary), So Close to Glory (1993 (British Lions tour of NZ)), Heroes All (1997 (British Lions Tour to South Africa)); *Recreations* caravanning, hill walking, family life, sailing, cricket; *Style*— Sir Ian McGeechan, OBE

McGEEHAN, Prof Joseph Peter (Joe); CBE (2004); s of Joseph Patrick James McGeehan, of Liverpool, and Rhoda Catherine, *née* Sleight (d 1989); *b* 15 February 1946; *Educ* Bootle GS for Boys, Univ of Liverpool (BEng, PhD, DEng); *m* 3 Oct 1970, Jean, da of Alan Lightfoot (d 1969); 2 da (Kathryn Anne b 13 July 1978, Sarah Jane b 12 Feb 1981); *Career* sr scientist Allan Clark Research Centre (Plessey Group Ltd) 1970–72, lectr then sr lectr Sch of Electrical Engrg Univ of Bath 1972–85; Univ of Bristol: first dir Centre for Communications Res 1988– (estab 1987), head Dept of Electrical and Electronic Engrg 1991–98 (chair in communications engrg 1985–), dean Faculty of Engrg 1998–2003; md Telecommunications Research Lab Toshiba Research Europe Ltd 1998–2011 (sr gen advsr 2011–); sr ind dir Renishaw plc 2001–10; over 30 years' res in spectrum efficient modulation techniques and systems; memb various nat and int ctees CCIR 1980–, memb ctee studying comparative modulation schemes for mobile radio Home Office 1980–82, advsr to first MOD/DTI Defence Spectrum Review Ctee, memb Accreditation Ctee and Pool of Assessors IEE 1985–2000, sometime memb various res ctees EPSRC and DTI/EPSRC Link Mgmnt Ctee in Personal Communication Systems, memb Design and Technol Allice Home Office 2007–11; former dir Science Research Fndn (formed by Univs of Bristol and Bath); memb Women's Academic Initiative Bristol, memb int tech advsy panel Singapore's Centre for Wireless Communications (CWC) 2000–02, memb Industrial Bd Local Enterprise Partnership for Bristol and W of England 2010–, chair West of England Inward Investment Bd; Wolfson Fndn rep Bd of Govrs John Cabot City Technol Coll Bristol 1995–98; memb Soc of Merchant Venturers Bristol 2004–; former memb and treas Friends of Bath HS, govr Colston Sch Bristol 2008–; Mountbatten Premium (IEE) 1989, Neal Shepherd Award (IEEE, USA) 1990, Prince of Wales Award for Innovation 1992, Schlumberger Award 1992, winning finalist CBI/Toshiba Year of Innovation 1993, Motorola Research Fndn Award 1994; named sixth in silicon.com's World Agenda Setters list; FRSA 1989, FIEE 1992, FREng 1994; *Publications* Radio Receivers (contrib, 1986); over 400 academic papers; *Recreations* walking, music, cricket, cycling, theatre, reading, church; *Style*— Prof Joe McGeehan, CBE, FREng; ✉ Centre for Communications Research, Merchant Venturers Building, Woodland Road, Bristol BS8 1UB

McGEEVER, Brendan; s of Martin James McGeever, and Anne Marie, *née* Connolly; *b* 11 February 1958, Middlesbrough; *Educ* St Mary's Coll Middlesbrough, Univ of Birmingham (LLB); *m* 28 May 1983, Amanda Jane, *née* Groves; 2 s (Matthew b 3 Dec 1988, Dominic b 15 Aug 1993 (twin)), 2 da (Sinead b 29 June 1991, Roisin b 15 Aug 1993 (twin)); *Career* Gateley LLP 1984–2015 (ptnr 1986–2015), dir Gateley plc 2015–; memb: Inst for Turnaround (IFT), Law Soc 1981–; accredited mediator CEDR; *Recreations* golf, music, opera, travel; *Style*— Brendan McGeever, Esq; ✉ Gateley plc, 1 Paternoster Square, London EC4M 6DX

McGEOCH, Callum James Farquharson; s of Angus McGeoch, of Farnborough, Oxon, and Judy Ann Farquharson; *b* 6 September 1974, London; *Educ* Marlborough, Univ of Newcastle upon Tyne (BSc); *m* 2 April 2005, Sophia Fleur, *née* Parker; *Career* creative dir Livity; contrib ed: Dazed and Confused, Another Magazine, Another Man Magazine; publisher Live Magazine; contrib: The Independent, Rolling Stone, Friends of the Earth; juror: BAFTA Interactive Children's Award, Guardian MEGAS Awards, D&AD Student Awards; awarded Best Feature Pages Total Publishing Magazine Awards, Queen's Award for Enterprise Innovation, Mktg Agencies Assoc Agency of the Year 2013; *Publications* The Annual (2001), T (2004), T2 (2005); *Recreations* travel, music, cycling; *Style*— Callum McGeoch, Esq; ✉ Livity Ltd, Unit 11 Piano House, 9 Brighton Terrace, London SW9 8DJ (✆ 020 7326 5979)

McGEOUGH, Prof Joseph Anthony; s of Patrick Joseph McGeough (d 1982), of Stevenston, Ayrshire, and Gertrude, *née* Darroch (d 1975); *b* 29 May 1940; *Educ* St Michael's Coll Irvine, Univ of Glasgow (BSc, PhD), Univ of Aberdeen (DSc); *m* 12 Aug 1972, Brenda, da of Robert Nicholson, of Blyth, Northumberland; 2 s (Andrew b 1974, Simon b 1977), 1 da (Elizabeth b 1975); *Career* res demonstrator Univ of Leicester 1966, sr res fell Queensland Univ 1967, res metallurgist International R&D Ltd 1968–69, sr res fell Univ of Strathclyde 1969–72; Univ of Aberdeen: lectr 1972–77, sr lectr 1977–80, reader in engrg 1980–83; regius prof of engrg Univ of Edinburgh 1983–2005 (prof emeritus 2005–, hon professorial fell 2007–16), hon prof Nanjing Aeronautical and Astronautical Univ 1992–; visiting prof: Univ of Naples Federico II 1994, Glasgow Caledonian Univ 1997–2003, Tokyo Univ of Agric and Technol 2004, Monash Univ 2005; industrial fell SERC

Royal Soc 1987–89; chm Scottish Branch Inst of Mechanical Engrg 1993–95, chm Bd CIRP UK 2000–03; chm Int Conferences on Computer-Aided Prodn Engrg (CAPE) 1986–; ed-in-chief Processing of Advanced Materials 1991–94, CIRP ed Jl of Materials Processing Technology 1990–2008; various Scot Co AAA and universities Athletic Championship awards; pres Colinton Parish Church Literary Soc 2009–12; fell Int Acad for Production Engrg 1987, FRSE 1990, FIMechE (memb Cncl 2000–03, memb Tstee Bd 2004–10, vice-pres 2006–10), FREng 2008; *Books* Principles of Electrochemical Machining (1974), Advanced Methods of Machining (1988), section on Nonconventional Machining: Encyclopaedia Britannica (1987), entry on Mechanical Engineering, Encarta 99 Encyclopaedia (1999), Micromachining of Engineering Materials (ed, 2001), The Engineering of Human Joint Replacements (2012), entry on Electroforming, CIRP Encyclopaedia of Production Engineering (2014); *Recreations* hill walking, gardening; *Style*— Prof Joseph McGeough, FRSE, FREng; ✉ 39 Dreghorn Loan, Colinton, Edinburgh EH13 0DF (☎ 0131 441 1302); School of Engineering, University of Edinburgh, King's Buildings, Edinburgh EH9 3JL (☎ 0131 650 5682, fax 0131 650 6554, e-mail j.a.mcgeough@ed.ac.uk)

McGEOWN, Declan; s of Patrick McGeown, and Rosaleen, *née* Coleman; *b* 8 October 1971, Portadown, Craigavon; *Educ* Queen's Univ Belfast (BSc); *Career* mgmnt trainee NI Civil Serv 1996–2002; Dept for Social Devpt: Belfast Regeneration Office 2003–06, dir North Belfast Community Acton Unit 2006–08, Urban Regeneration Strategy Directorate 2008–; *Recreations* horse racing, distance running; *Style*— Declan McGeown, Esq; ✉ Department for Social Development Northern Ireland, Lighthouse Building, 1 Cromac Place, Gasworks Business Park, Belfast BT7 2JB (☎ 028 90 829362, e-mail declan.mcgeown@dsdni.gov.uk)

McGETTIGAN, Frank; OBE (2000); s of William McGettigan, and Elizabeth McGettigan; *b* 1951; *Educ* Cardinal Vaughan Meml Sch, Queen's Univ Belfast; *m*; 4 c; *Career* Channel Four Television: dir and gen mangr (and main bd dir) 1988–2000, md subsid 124 Facilities Ltd, chief exec Intelfax Ltd 2000–; chm SKILLSET (broadcasting industry trg orgn); dep chm Nat Film and TV Sch (and chm subsid Ealing Studios Ltd); *Style*— Frank McGettigan, Esq, OBE; ✉ e-mail frankmcgettigan@msn.com

McGHIE, Hon Lord; James Marshall; s of James Drummond McGhie (d 1970), and Jessie Eadie Bennie (d 1975); *b* 15 October 1944; *Educ* Perth Acad, Univ of Edinburgh; *m* 1968, Ann Manuel, da of Stanley Gray Cockburn (d 1982); 1 s (Angus b 1975), 1 da (Kathryn b 1983); *Career* admitted Faculty of Advocates 1969; QC (Scot) 1983, advocate-depute 1983–86, pt/t chm Med Appeal Tbnls 1987–92, memb Criminal Injuries Compensation Bd 1992–96, chm Scottish Land Court and pres Lands Tbnl for Scotland 1996–2014, pt/t judge Court of Session 2012–; *Recreations* golf, music, sailing, walking; *Style*— The Hon Lord McGhie; ✉ Parliament House, High Street, Edinburgh EH1 1RF (☎ 0131 225 2595)

McGILL, Ross Morrison; s of Hugh McGill (d 2004), and Sheila McGill; *b* 25 November 1973, Irvine, Aryshire; *Educ* Fleetwood Sixth Form, Goldsmiths Coll Univ of London (BAEd), Central Saint Martins (MA); *m* 10 April 2010, Jenni McGill; 1 s (Frederick Warbrook b 21 May 2011); *Career* head of design technol (VSO volunteer) St Thomas School Kano Nigeria 1997, technol teacher St Thomas More RC Sch 1997–2000, head of design technol Alexandra Park 2000–08, head of ICT Alexandra Park 2007–08, asst princ John Kelly Girls Technol Coll 2008–09, lead practitioner (Technol) Specialist Schs and Acads Tst (SSAT) 2009–10, asst princ Crest Girls' Acad 2008–11, asst vice princ Greig City Acad 2011–14, dep headteacher Quintin Kynaston 2014–; writer Guardian Teacher Network 2011–, writer Schools Week 2015–; Teacher of the Year in a Secondary School in London 2004, Best Education Blog UK Vuelio Blog Awards 2015; *Books* 100 Ideas for Secondary Teachers (2013), Teacher Toolkit: Helping You Survive Your First Five Years (2015); *Recreations* reading, travel, blogging/writing; *Style*— Ross McGill, Esq; ✉ Quintin Kynaston School, Marlborough Hill, London NW8 0NL (e-mail teachertoolkit@me.com, website www.teachertoolkit.me, Twitter @TeacherToolkit)

McGIMPSEY, Michael; MLA; *b* 1 July 1948; *Educ* Regent House GS Newtownards, Trinity Coll Dublin (BA); *m*; 1 s, 1 da; *Career* businessman; Belfast CC (Langbank Ward) 1993–2010; MLA (UUP) S Belfast 1998–; min for culture, arts and leisure 1999–2001, min for health, social servs and public safety 2007–11; *Recreations* reading, walking, gardening; *Style*— Michael McGimpsey, MLA; ✉ Ulster Unionist Constituency Office, Unit 2, 127–145 Sandy Row, Belfast BT12 5ET (☎ 028 9024 5801, e-mail michaelmcgimpsey@live.co.uk, website www.mmcgimpsey.org)

McGINLEY, Aideen; OBE (2000); da of Joseph Slevin (d 2008), and Terry Slevin (d 1972); *Educ* Salford Univ (BSc), Univ of Ulster (MSc); *m* James McGinley; 1 da (Laura b 1978), 2 s (Graeme b 1983, Connor b 1988); *Career* formerly: chief exec Fermanagh DC, Community Servs and Econ Devpt Strabane and Fermanagh, town planner Donegal; perm sec Dept of Culture, Arts and Leisure 1999–2005, perm sec Dept for Employment and Learning NI 2005–; currently chief exec Ilex Ltd; chair: NICS Centre for Applied Learning; memb: NI Ctee Br Cncl, NI Chief Execs Forum, Business in the Community, Fermanagh Tst; previous involvement in numerous UK and rgnl bodies incl: Univ for Industry, Nat Lotteries Charities Bd, Rural Devpt Cncl, NI Volutary Tst, Bank of Ireland, NI Millennium Co, Verbal Arts Centre, BBC Appeals Ctee, Omagh Fund, 2010 Steering Gp; memb NI women's team Habitat for Humanity Build Thailand 2004 and Chile 2006; Women of Inspiration Award 2007; Hon Doctorate Univ of Ulster 1998; hon memb Royal Soc of Ulster Architects 2004; *Style*— Mrs Aideen McGinley, OBE; ✉ Department for Employment and Learning Northern Ireland, Adelaide House, 39–49 Adelaide Street, Belfast BT2 8FD; Ilex Ltd, Exchange House, Derry BT48 7AS

McGINN, Conor; MP; *b* Co Armagh; *m* Kate; 1 s; *Career* MP (Lab) St Helen's North 2015–; *Style*— Conor McGinn, Esq, MP; ✉ House of Commons, London SW1A 0AA

McGINTY, Dr Lawrence Stanley; s of Lawrence McGinty, and Hilda, *née* Hardman; *b* 2 July 1948, Manchester; *Educ* Stand GS Manchester, Univ of Liverpool (BSc), Univ of Sheffield; *m* 26 March 2011, Kate Evans; *Career* asst ed Chemistry in Britain 1970–71, successively technol ed, health and safety ed, news ed New Scientist 1971–82, sci corr Channel 4 News 1982–87, health and sci ed ITN 1987–2014; memb: Assoc of Br Sci Writers 1971–, NUJ 1971–, Med Journalists Assoc 1982–; guest lectr: Ecole Polytechnique Paris, Soc for Radiological Protection, various other bodies; memb: Friends of Kew, Friends of the RA; Hon DLitt Univ of Liverpool 2012; Queen's Silver Jubilee Medal; Lifetime Achievement Award Assoc of Br Sci Writers 2014, Lifetime Achievement Award RTS 2015; *Recreations* walking, wine, football, supporting Manchester United FC, etchings; *Clubs* Royal Society of Medicine; *Style*— Dr Lawrence McGinty; ✉ Knight Ayton Management, 35 Great James Street, London WC1N 3HB (e-mail lawrence.smcginty@yahoo.com)

McGLADE, Prof Jacqueline Myriam; *née* Cox; *b* 30 May 1955; *Educ* UCNW (BSc), Univ of Guelph Canada (PhD), Univ of Cambridge (MA); *Children*; 2 da (Katie b 28 May 1982, Rhiannon b 1 April 1985); *Career* sr research scientist Fed Govt Canada 1981–87, research assoc Museum of Zoology Univ of Cambridge 1986–88, assoc prof Cranfield Inst of Technol 1987–88, Adrian fell Darwin Coll Cambridge 1987–90, dir and prof of Inst Theoretical Ecology FZ Jülich Germany 1988–92, prof of biological sciences Univ of Warwick 1992–98, dir NERC Centre for Coastal & Marine Sciences 1998–2000, NERC prof UCL 2000–03, prof of mathematical biology UCL 2003–; exec dir European Environment Agency 2003–13; memb: Br Ecological Soc 1992–, External Advsy Gp Environment, Energy & Sustainable Devpt (EU) 1998–2001, Bd Environment Agency 1998–2003; author of numerous papers and publications in learned jls; tstee: Earth Centre 1990–2003, Natural History Museum 2002–10; hon prof Univ of Warwick 1998, hon fell Univ of Wales 1999, Hon DSc Univ of Kent 2004; FRICS 1987, FRSA 1997, FLS 1998; Knight of the Order of St Charles Monaco; Advanced Ecological Theory (1999), The Gulf of Guinea Large Marine Ecosystem (2002); *Recreations* climbing, aviation, scuba-diving; *Style*— Prof Jacqueline McGlade; ✉ University College London, Gower Street, London WC1E 6BT

McGLONE, Heather Margaret; da of Eric Vickers McGlone, of Brighton, E Sussex, and Margaret Gavin Lamond, *née* Russell; *b* 15 February 1957; *Educ* N London Collegiate Sch, SCEGGS Sydney, Univ of Sydney, Univ of Sussex (BA), Université de la Sorbonne, City Univ London (Dip Journalism); *m* 3 Dec 1983, Louis Albert Francis Kirby, s of William Kirby, and Anne Kirby; 2 da (Clementine Margaret Allegra b 10 April 1987, Iona Alice Eliza b 17 Feb 1990); *Career* Western Morning News and Evening Herald 1981–83, freelance journalist 1983–86; The Express: dep woman's ed 1986–88, woman's ed 1988–91, features ed 1991–93, asst ed features 1993–94, assoc ed 1994, ed This Week magazine 1994–95, exec ed 1995; Daily Mail: commissioning ed Femail 1996–99, ed Weekend magazine 1999–2006, arts ed 2006–11, ed Weekend magazine and It's Friday! arts and entertainment section 2011–; *Recreations* theatre, ballet, art galleries, horse riding; *Clubs* Soho House; *Style*— Miss Heather McGlone; ✉ Daily Mail, Northcliffe House, 2 Derry Street, Kensington, London W8 5TT (☎ 020 7938 6000)

McGLONE, Patsy; MLA; *Career* cncllr Cookstown DC 1993–2009 (chm 2002–03 and 2005–06), MLA (SDLP) Mid-Ulster 2003–, dep ldr SDLP 2010–11, dep speaker NI Assembly 2016–; chair Ctee for Enterprise, Trade and Investment 2012–16, memb Ctee for Agriculture, Environment and Rural Affrs 2016–; *Recreations* music, walking, country sports; *Style*— Mr Patsy McGlone, MLA; ✉ Northern Ireland Assembly, Parliament Buildings, Belfast BT4 3XX (☎ 028 8675 8175, e-mail patsymcglonemla@yahoo.ie, Twitter @patsymcglone)

McGONAGLE, Declan George; s of Stephen McGonagle, and Margaret, *née* White; *b* 15 November 1952; *Educ* St Columb's Coll Derry, Coll of Art Belfast (BA, Higher Dip Painting); *m* 28 July 1980, Mary Bernadette (Moira), da of Anthony Carlin; 2 s (Declan b 26 Sept 1984, Paul b 2 March 1987); *Career* lectr in fine art Regnl Tech Coll 1976–78, organiser Orchard Gallery Derry 1978–84, dir of exhibitions ICA London 1984–86, visual arts organiser Derry 1986–90, dir Irish MOMA Dublin 1990–2001, dir City Arts Centre Civil Arts Inquiry 2001–04, chair of art and design and dir INTERFACE Research Centre Univ of Ulster 2004–; contributing ed Art Forum Magazine NY; Sunday Tribune Visual Arts Award 1987; *Recreations* politics, reading, piano; *Style*— Declan McGonagle, Esq; ✉ INTERFACE, School of Art and Design, University of Ulster, York Street, Belfast BT15 1ED (☎ 028 9026 7260)

McGOUGH, Roger Joseph; CBE (2004, OBE 1997); *b* 9 November 1937; *Educ* St Mary's Coll Liverpool, Univ of Hull (BA, CertEd); *Career* poet; fell of poetry Loughborough Univ 1973–75, writer in residence Western Aust Coll of Advanced Educn Perth 1986; pres The Poetry Soc 2012 (memb Exec Cncl 1989–93, vice-pres 1996); art installation Liverpool Doors (Museum of Liverpool) 2012; Signal Award 1984 and 1998, Cholmondeley Award 1998, Centre for Literacy in Primary Educn (CLPE) Poetry Award 2004 and 2005; hon prof Thames Valley Univ 1993, hon fell Liverpool John Moores Univ; Hon MA UC Northampton; Hon DLitt: Univ of Hull 2004, Univ of Roehampton 2006, Univ of Liverpool 2006, Open Univ 2009; Freeman City of Liverpool 2001; FRSL; *Publications* poetry: Summer with Monika (1967), The Mersey Sound (with Adrian Henri and Brian Patten, 1967), In the Glassroom (1976), Holiday on Death Row (1979), Waving at Trains (1982), Melting into the Foreground (1986), Selected Poems (1989), Blazing Fruit (1990), You At The Back (1991), Defying Gravity (1992), The Spotted Unicorn (1998), The Way Things Are (1999), Everyday Eclipses (2002), Wicked Poems (2002), Collected Poems (2003), Selected Poems (2006), That Awkward Age (2009), Mind the Gap (2010), As Far As I Know (2012), It Never Rains (2014); wrote and appeared in Thames TV prog Kurt Mungo BP and Me (BAFTA Award, 1984), wrote poems for and presented Channel Four TV prog The Elements 1992 (Royal Television Award); for children: The Great Smile Robbery (1983), Sky in the Pie (1983), The Stowaways (1986), Noah's Ark (1986), Nailing the Shadow (1987), An Imaginary Menagerie (1988), Helen Highwater (1989), Counting by Numbers (1989), Pillow Talk (1990), The Lighthouse That Ran Away (1991), My Dad's a Fire-eater (1992), Another Custard Pie (1993), Lucky (1993), Stinkers Ahoy! (1995), The Magic Fountain (1995), Sporting Relations (1996), The Kite and Caitlin (1996), Bad, Bad Cats (1997), Until I Met Dudley (1997), Good Enough to Eat (2002), What on Earth (2002), Moonthief (2002), The Bees Knees (2003), All the Best (2003), Dotty Inventions (2004), Daniel and the Beast of Babylon (2004), Slapstick (2008), I Never Liked Wednesdays (2015), If Only We Had a Helicopter (2015), Poetry Pie (2015); other work incl: Said and Done (autobiography, 2005), Moliere's Tartuffe (adaptation, 2008), The Hypochondriac (adaptation, 2009), The Misanthrope (adaptation, 2013); *Clubs* Chelsea Arts (chm 1984–86, tstee 1993–); *Style*— Roger McGough, Esq, CBE, FRSL; ✉ c/o United Agents Ltd, 12–26 Lexington Street, London W1F 0LE (☎ 020 3214 0800, fax 020 3214 0801, website www.unitedagents.co.uk); website www.rogermcgough.org.uk

McGOVERN, Alison; MP; *b* December 1980; *Educ* Wirral GS, UCL; *Career* MP (Lab) Wirral S 2010–; *Style*— Ms Alison McGovern, MP; ✉ House of Commons, London SW1A 0AA

McGOVERN, Prof Gerard Gabriel (Gerry); s of Patrick McGovern, and Philamina McGovern; *b* 23 September 1956, Coventry; *Educ* Binley Park Comp Sch Coventry, Lanchester Polytechnic Coventry, RCA; *m* 13 Nov 2014, Olga, *née* Khadzhi-Baronova; 2 da (Vanessa, Gabriella); *Career* designer Chrysler USA 1978–80, sr designer Peugeot/Chrysler Gp UK 1980–82, princ designer Austin Rover Gp UK 1982–99, sr designer Lincoln-Mercury USA 1999–2003, creative dir Ingeni 2003–04, dir of advanced design Land Rover 2004–06, memb Bd of Dirs Jaguar Land Rover, design dir and chief creative offr Land Rover 2006–; prof RCA; contrib: Interior Motives, GQ, Savile Row Style Magazine, Quattroruote, Bloomberg, The Director; Best Dressed Businessman GQ 2016; hon doctorate Coventry Univ; *Recreations* cinema, fashion, reading, travel, swimming; *Clubs* George (London); *Style*— Prof Gerry McGovern; ✉ Land Rover, Design Centre, Banbury Road, Gaydon, Warwickshire CV35 0BJ (☎ 01926 921161, e-mail gmcgovel@landrover.com)

McGOVERN, Sean; s of Thomas McGovern, of Coventry, Warks, and Margaret McGovern; *b* 31 May 1970; *Educ* Princethorpe Coll, Univ of Manchester (LLB); *m* 10 April 1999, Anita; 1 s (Thomas b 1 Sept 2000), 2 da (Amber, Madeleine (twins) b 18 May 2003); *Career* slr Clifford Chance 1992–96; Lloyd's of London: slr 1996–2000, head of legal 2000–02, dir and gen counsel 2002–, chief risk offr 2014–; memb Law Soc 1994; *Style*— Sean McGovern, Esq; ✉ Lloyd's of London, One Lime Street, London EC3M 7HA (☎ 020 7327 6142, fax 020 7327 5414)

McGOWAN, Alistair Charles; s of George (Mac) McGowan, and Marion McGowan; *b* 24 November 1964, Evesham, Worcs; *Educ* Evesham HS, Univ of Leeds (BA), Guildhall Sch of Music and Drama; *m* 2013, Charlotte Elizabeth Page; *Career* comedian, impressionist, actor, playwright and director; *Theatre* Kafka's Dick 1998, Endgame (Nottingham Playhouse) 1999, Art (Wyndham's Theatre) 2000, The Government Inspector (Chichester) 2005, Merry Wives the Musical (RSC) 2006, Little Shop of Horrors (Duke of York's) 2007 (nomination Olivier Award), The Mikado (Carl Rosa Opera) 2008, Cabaret (Lyric Theatre) 2008, Measure for Measure (tour) 2009, Cocktails With Coward/Sincerely Noel (Riverside Studios) 2010, Oleanna (Nottingham Lakeside) 2011, Pygmalion (Garrick) 2011 and (tour) 2014, An Audience with Jimmy Savile (Park Theatre) 2015, 4,000 Days (Park Theatre) 2016; as dir: Semi-Monde (Guildhall) 2008), The Mikado (Raymond Gubbay) 2010),

M

Priates of Penzance (Raymond Gubbay) 2011; as playwright Timing (King's Head Theatre) 2009, Erike Satie's Faction (writer/performer/pianist, St James Theatre) 2016; stand-up: The One and Many tour 2009, Not Just a Pretty Voice tour 2013, An Evening Shared with Jasper Carrott and Alistair McGowan 2015–16; *Radio* Weekending (BBC Radio 4) 1989–93, The Harpoon 1990–92, The Nick Revell Show 1991–93, The Game's Up 1995–97, Life, Death and Sex with Mike and Sue 1997–99, Elvenquest 2009–11, Continuity 2010, Look Away Now 2010, Fings Ain't Wot They Used Ter Be 2011, Kind Hearts and Coronets 2012, Three Pieces in the Shape of a Pear 2013 (writer and performer), Boswell's Lives (Radio 4) 2015, The Peregrinations of a Most Musical Irishman (Radio 4) 2016; *Television* Spitting Image (ITV) 1992–96, Preston Front (BBC1) 1994–97, Alistair McGowan's Big Impression (BBC1) 1999–2003 (Best Comedy Entertainment Prog Comedy Awards 2000, Comedy Award Variety Club Awards 2002, Best Entertainment Performance RTS Awards 2002, BAFTA Award for Best Comedy Programme 2003), Mayo 2006, Bleak House 2006, Who Do You Think You Are 2007, Live At The Apollo 2009, Leonardo 2011, You Cannot Be Serious 2012, The One Show 2013, Tonight at the Palladium (ITV) 2016; *Film* Driving Aphrodite 2009; *Video* Alistair McGowan's Football Backchat 1997, The Second Leg 1998; *Publications* A Matter of Life and Death/How To Wean A Man Off Football (with Ronni Ancona, 2009), Timing (2009); *Recreations* tennis, scrabble, piano playing, snooker, theatre; *Clubs* Roehampton, All England Lawn Tennis and Croquet (Wimbledon), BAFTA; *Style—* Alistair McGowan, Esq; ✉ website www.alistairmcgowan.co.uk; c/o Claire Comiskey, ARG, 4A Exmoor Street, London W10 6BD (☎ 020 7436 6400, e-mail comiskey@argtalent.com)

McGOWAN, Malcolm Russell; s of Bernard Earnest McGowan, and Gwendoline Blanche McGowan (decd); *b* 24 October 1955, London; *Educ* Emanuel Sch, Univ of Westminster (BA Arch, DipArch); *m* Katherine Antonia, *née* Murphy; 1 s (Alexander Jamieson b 15 Nov 1998), 1 da (Sophia Blanche b 24 Aug 2000); *Career* architect; Arhends Burton Koralek 1981–84, Richard Rogers 1985–89; Sheppard Robson (architects, planners and interior designers): joined 1989, assoc 1996–98, ptnr 1998–, managing ptnr 2005; projects incl: BBC W1 Broadcasting House, Barts Square for Helical Bar, Nelson Mandela Children's Hosp Johannesburg; ARB, RIBA; as rower: Silver medal (eight) Olympic Games Moscow 1980, fifth (eight) Olympic Games LA 1984; *Recreations* rowing; *Clubs* Leander, Crabtree, Home House; *Style—* Malcolm McGowan, Esq; ✉ Sheppard Robson, 77 Parkway, London NW1 7PU (☎ 020 7504 1700, fax 020 7504 1701, e-mail malcolm.mcgowan@sheppardrobson.com)

McGOWAN, Hon Mrs Justice; Dame Maura Patricia McGowan; DBE (2014); *Career* called to the Bar Middle Temple 1980; asst recorder 1997, recorder 2000, QC 2001, dep high court judge, judge of the High Court of Justice (Queen's Bench Div) 2014–; *Style—* The Hon Mrs Justice McGowan; ✉ Royal Courts of Justice, Strand, London WC2A 2LL

MacGOWAN, Walter John; s of James Thomas MacGowan, and Edith May MacGowan; *Educ* Burford GS, Forest GS; *Career* govr HMP Lincoln 1989–92, govr HMP Manchester 1992–95, dir HMP Buckley Hill 1996–97, dir HMP Wolds 1994–97, dir HMP Altcourse 1997, dir of ops Group 4 Prison Services 1997, md GEO Group UK Ltd 2003–11; Butler Tst award 1991; tstee Lower Moss Wood Animal Hosp; patron Apex Tst; memb: Nat Tst, Eng Heritage; *Recreations* reading (major interests history and RN), wine, travel; *Clubs* Kingston Wine Soc; *Style—* Walter MacGowan, Esq

McGRAIL, Prof Seán Francis; *b* 5 May 1928; *Educ* Univ of Bristol (Harry Crook scholar, BA), Inst of Archaeology Univ of London (PhD), Campion Hall Oxford (MA), Univ of Oxford (DSc); *m* 28 July 1955, (Ursula) Anne Yates; 3 da (Frances Joanna b 26 May 1956, Mary Ursula b 9 March 1960, Catherine Clare b 29 March 1963), 1 s (Hugh Fergus b 29 Jan 1958); *Career* RN: cadet to Lt Cdr (qualified as Master Mariner) 1946–68, pilot Fleet Air Arm 1952–68 (cmd 849 Sqdn 1962–63); Nat Maritime Museum: asst keeper (archaeology) Dept of Ships 1972, head Dept of Archaeology of Ships 1973–76, chief archaeologist and head Archaeological Research Centre 1976–86 (dep keeper 1976–80, keeper 1980–86); prof of maritime archaeology Inst of Archaeology Univ of Oxford 1986–93 (currently prof emeritus); visiting prof: Univ of Southampton 1991–, Danish Nat Museum's Centre for Maritime Archaeology Roskilde 1994, Centre for Maritime Studies Univ of Haifa Israel 1995; memb Cncl: Prehistoric Soc 1980–83, Soc of Antiquaries 1983–86; memb: Dept of Nat Heritage Advsy Ctee on Historic Wrecks 1975–98, Wardour Catholic Cemetery Tst 1976–2014 (treas 1999–2014), Exec Ctee Mary Rose Tst 1980–86, Egyptian Antiquity Orgn's Ctee on Establishment of a Nat Maritime Museum in Alexandria 1985–86, Academic Advsy Ctee of States of Guernsey Ancient Monuments Ctee 1985–, Editorial Bd Mary Rose Tst 1998–2002 and 2004–10; vice-chm Tst for Preservation of Oxford Coll Barges 1987–93; excavations on prehistoric and medieval sites (Norway, Denmark, Orkney, Ireland, Britain) 1974–94, maritime ethnographic fieldwork Bangladesh and India 1994–2001; FSA 1981, MIFA 1983; *Books* Sources and Techniques in Boat Archaeology (ed, 1977), Logboats of England and Wales (1978), Medieval Ships and Harbours in Northern Europe (ed, 1979), Rafts, Boats and Ships (1981), Aspects of Maritime Archaeology and Ethnography (ed, 1984), Ancient Boats in North-West Europe (1987, 2 edn, 1998), Seacraft of Prehistory (ed 2 edn, 1988), Maritime Celts, Frisians and Saxons (ed, 1990), Medieval Boat and Ship Timbers from Dublin (1993), Studies in Maritime Archaeology (1997), Boats of the World (2001, 2 edn 2004), Boats of South Asia (2003), Barland's Farm Romano-Celtic Boat (with N Nayling, 2004), Ancient Boats and Ships (2006), Early Ships and Seafaring (Vol 1 2014, Vol 2 2015); National Maritime Museum Archaeological Series (ed, 1977–86); *Style—* Prof Seán McGrail, FSA; ✉ Institute of Archaeology, 36 Beaumont Street, Oxford OX1 2PG (☎ 01865 278240)

McGRATH, Rev Prof Alister Edgar; s of Edgar Parkinson McGrath, of Co Down, and Annie Jane, *née* McBride; *b* 23 January 1953; *Educ* Wadham Coll Oxford (MA), Linacre Coll Oxford, Merton Coll Oxford (DPhil, BD, DD, DLitt), St John's Coll Cambridge; *m* 1980, Joanna Ruth, da of John Stuart Collicutt; 1 s (Paul Alister b 1981), 1 da (Elizabeth Joanna b 1983); *Career* curate St Leonard's Wollaton 1980–83, research lectr Univ of Oxford 1993–99, research prof of theol Regent Coll Vancouver 1993–98, princ Wycliffe Hall Oxford 1995–2004 (lectr 1983–95), prof of historical theology Univ of Oxford 1999–, prof of theology, ministry and educn KCL 2008–; Hon DD Virginia Theological Seminary 1996; FRSA 2005; *Books* Intellectual Origins of The Reformation (1987), The Genesis of Doctrine (1990), Encyclopaedia of Modern Christian Thought (1993), Christian Theology (1994), Foundations of Dialogue in Science and Religion (1998), In the Beginning (2001), A Scientific Theology (2002), The Twilight of Atheism (2004), Dawkins' God (2004), The Order of Things (2006), Christianity's Dangerous Idea (2007), The Open Secret (2008), Heresy (2009), A Fine-Tuned Universe (2009), Darwinism and the Divine (2011), C S Lewis – A Life (2013), The Intellectual World of C S Lewis (2013); *Recreations* walking, wines; *Style—* The Rev Prof Alister McGrath; ✉ Department of Education & Professional Studies, King's College London, Franklin-Wilkins Building (Waterloo Bridge Wing), Waterloo Road, London SE1 9NH (☎ 020 7848 3778, fax 020 7848 3182, e-mail alister.mcgrath@kcl.ac.uk)

McGRATH, Dr Anthony Charles Ormond; s of Patrick Anthony Ormond McGrath, MC, TD (d 1988), of Southwater, W Sussex, and Eleanor Mary Howard, *née* Horsman (d 2000); *b* 1949; *Educ* Worth Abbey Sch, Univ of Surrey (BSc), Open Univ (BA, MA), Univ of Sussex (PhD); *m* 20 July 1974, Margaret Mary, da of Capt William Arthur Usher, RN (d 1959), of Painswick, Glos; 1 s (Thomas), 1 da (Philippa); *Career* Deloitte Haskins & Sells 1971–76, Baring Brothers & Co Limited 1976–95, Baring Brothers Int Ltd 1995–97, Robert Fleming & Co Ltd 1997–2000, treas and tstee The King's Fund 2001–08; non-exec dir W & F C Bonham & Sons Ltd 1987–90; memb Nat Cncl CBI (memb Cos Ctee 1996–99), memb London Regnl Cncl CBI 1994–97; tstee English Nat Stadium Tst 1996–99, non-exec dir and tstee The Picker Inst 2006–08, tstee London Library 2014–; non-exec memb Br Standards Inst Quality Assurance Bd 1986–90; memb Ctee London HE Consortium 2001–03; FCA 1974; *Recreations* art history, gardening, music, walking (sometimes with a fly rod); *Style—* Dr Anthony McGrath; ✉ Town Place, Freshfield, Scaynes Hill, West Sussex RH17 7NR

McGRATH, Prof Elizabeth; da of Thomas McGrath, and Emilie, *née* Melvin; *b* 20 March 1945; *Educ* St Joseph's HS Kilmarnock, Univ of Glasgow (MA), Univ of London (PhD); *Career* curator Photographic Collection Warburg Inst London 1991–2010 (joined 1970); Durning Lawrence lectr UCL 1989, Slade prof Univ of Oxford 1990; ed Jl of the Warburg and Courtauld Insts 1977–; Hans Reimer prize Univ of Hamburg 1996; Mitchell Prize in the History of Art 1998, Eugène Baie Prize of Province of Antwerp 1999; hon fell Warburg Inst 2010–; memb Royal Flemish Acad of Arts and Sciences 2003; FBA 1998; *Books* Rubens: Subjects from History (1997), The Slave in Renaissance Art: From Renaissance Trophy to Abolitionist Emblem (with J M Massing, 2012), Rubens: Mythological Subjects, Achilles to the Graces (with G Martin et al, 2016); also author of articles in learned jls; *Style—* Prof Elizabeth McGrath, FBA; ✉ Warburg Institute, University of London, Woburn Square, London WC1H 0AB (☎ 020 7862 8949, fax 020 7862 8955, e-mail elizabeth.mcgrath@sas.ac.uk)

McGRATH, Prof (John Christie) Ian; s of late John (Jack) Christie McGrath, and late Margaret Gilmore Cochrane, *née* Murray; *b* 8 March 1949, Johnstone, Scotland; *Educ* John Neilson Instn, Univ of Glasgow (BSc, PhD); *m* 25 June 1970, Wilma (d 2007), da of late John Nicol; 1 s (Nicolas John b 13 Aug 1974), 1 da (Katie Isabella (Dr Gallacher) b 8 Jan 1981); *Career* Wellcome interdisciplinary res fell Dept of Pharmacology and Univ Dept of Anaesthesia Glasgow Royal Infirmary Univ of Glasgow 1973–75; Inst of Physiology Univ of Glasgow: lectr 1975–83, sr lectr 1983–88, reader 1988–89, titular prof 1989–91, head Dept of Physiology 1991–93, head of Biomedical Sci Gp 1991–93, regius prof 1991–2012, co-dir Clinical Research Initiative in Heart Failure 1994–99, head Div of Neuroscience and Biomedical Systems 1997–2004, head Div of Integrated Biology 2008–10, hon sr research fell and prof emeritus 2012–; hon sr princ research fell NeuroScience Australia 2008–, hon prof Univ of Sydney 2013–; chm Standing Ctee of Heads of UK Physiology Depts 2000–02; memb: SERC Case Panel 1981–82, Ctee Physiological Soc 1988–94 and 2004–10 (vice-chair 2004–06, chair 2006–08, pubns chair 2006–10), Cncl Biosciences Fedn 2007–10, UK RAE Panel 2008, Hong Kong RAE Panel 2014; memb Editorial Bd: Br Jl of Pharmacology 1984–91 and 2000–07 (sr ed 2001–07, ed-in-chief 2009–), Pharmacological Reviews 1989–98, Jl of Cardiovascular Pharmacology 1988–94, Jl of Vascular Res 1991–; Pfizer Award for Biology 1983; memb: Physiological Soc 1978, American Soc for Pharmacology and Therapeutics 1990, American Physiological Soc 1993, Soc for Neuroscience 2010–, Australasian Soc of Clinical and Experimental Pharmacologists and Toxicologists 2008– (hon memb 2012), Australasian Neuroscience Soc 2012–, Int Soc for Neurochemistry 2015–; fell Br Pharmacological Soc 2006 (memb 1975, Sandoz Prize 1980, J R Vane Medal 2011), FRSB 2014; *Publications* articles in academic jls; *Recreations* travel, cycling, running, eating and drinking, politics (memb Labour Party); *Style—* Prof Ian McGrath; ✉ West Medical Building, University of Glasgow, Glasgow G12 8QQ (☎ 0141 330 4483, fax 0141 330 5481, mobile 078 5050 2553, e-mail ian.mcgrath@glasgow.ac.uk)

McGRATH, Jim; *b* 22 May 1955; *Career* with Timeform Organisation 1974–2009; racing corr TV-AM 1983–89, ITV Racing 1981–85, C4 Racing 1985–; dir BHB 2004–07, ind dir BHA 2007–10; dir Newbury Racecourse 2015–; Horserace Writers and Photographers Assoc (HWPA): nominee Broadcasting Award 2002, nominee Specialist Award 2004; numerous videos, voice-overs and articles on horse racing; TV documentary Willie Carson: The People's Champion 1986; *Recreations* golf; *Clubs* Saints and Sinners; *Style—* Jim McGrath, Esq; ✉ Jim McGrath Racing, Suite 2B, Cartwright Court, Dyson Wood Way, Bradley Business Park, Huddersfield, West Yorkshire HD2 1GN (☎ 07768 312879, e-mail jimmcgrathracing@btconnect.com)

McGRATH, John Brian; *b* 20 June 1938, Ruislip; *Educ* Brunel Univ (BSc); *m* Sandy McGrath; 1 da (Lucy b 19 April 1969), 1 s (Paul b 17 Aug 1971); *Career* various appts with UKAEA, National Coal Board, Ford Motor Co, Jaguar Cars and Stone-Platt Ltd 1956–81, chief exec Compair Ltd 1984 (md Construction and Mining Div 1982–83); Grand Metropolitan group: gp dir Watney Mann & Truman Brewers Ltd 1985, chm and md Grand Metropolitan Brewing 1986, jt md responsible for GrandMet Brewing, International Distillers & Vintners Ltd, IDV UK and Heublein 1988–91, chm and chief exec International Distillers & Vintners Ltd 1992–95 (md and chief operating offr 1991–92), gp chief exec Grand Metropolitan plc 1996–97, gp chief exec Diageo plc (following merger with Guinness plc) 1997–2000; non-exec dir: Boots plc 1997–2003 (chm 2000–03), ITV plc (formerly Carlton Communications) 2003–08; chm Cicely Saunders Int 2002–; first chm The Portman Group (promoting responsible use of alcohol), chm The Scotch Whisky Assoc 1994–2000; govr Brunel Univ 2002–10, tstee Tetbury Hosp Tst 2013–; Freeman City of London; *Style—* John McGrath

McGRATH, Tom; CBE (2007, OBE 1997); s of John Edward McGrath (d 1996), and Elizabeth, *née* Cushway (d 2011); *b* 18 November 1944, Belfast; *Educ* Belfast HS, Belfast Inst of Further and Higher Educn; *m* 14 April 1973, Marjorie, *née* McCann; 2 da (Jane Elizabeth b 20 May 1979, Emma Victoria b 9 May 1983); *Career* md Marsh Inc 1993–2008, currently dir Thomas McGrath Professional Assocs Ltd; chm NI Tourist Bd 2002–08, chief cmmr NI Charity Cmmn 2009–; memb Professional Standards Bd Chartered Insurance Inst 2009–2015; memb CII Membship Appeals Ctee 2015–; professional witness in insurance matters, in UK and ROI, author of various articles on risk mgmnt for professionals and regular speaker at conferences; chm Consultative Forum Belfast Int Airport2012–; CII Exceptional Serv Award 2008; FCII, FInstAM; *Recreations* traditional jazz, military history; *Clubs* Army and Navy; *Style—* Tom McGrath, Esq, CBE; ✉ Hayfield, 44 Ballymartin Road, Templepatrick, Ballyclare BT39 0BS (☎ 028 9443 2325, mobile 07770 273857, e-mail tom@tommcgrath.co.uk)

McGRATH, William; *Career* fin dir Aggregate Industries 1992–97; Aga Rangemaster Gp plc: fin dir 1997–2001, chief exec 2001–; *Style—* William McGrath, Esq; ✉ Aga Rangemaster Group plc, Juno Drive, Leamington Spa, Warwickshire CV31 3RG

MacGREGOR, Alastair Rankin; QC (1994); s of Alexander MacGregor, and Anne, *née* Neil; *b* 23 December 1951; *Educ* Glasgow Acad, Univ of Edinburgh, New Coll Oxford (MA); *m* 21 Feb 1982, Rosemary Alison, da of Ralph Trevor Kerslake; 1 s (James b 13 June 1984), 1 da (Martha b 5 Jan 1989); *Career* called to the Bar Lincoln's Inn 1974, in practice London until 2004; cmmr Criminal Cases Review Cmmn 2004–13 (dep chm 2006–13), biometrics cmmr 2013–16; *Style—* Alastair R MacGregor, Esq, QC; ✉ Office of the Biometrics Commissioner, PO Box 72256, London SW1P 9DU (☎ 020 7035 5549, e-mail enquiries@biometricscommissioner.gsi.gov.uk)

McGREGOR, Alistair John; QC (1997); s of Lord McGregor of Durris (Life Peer, d 1997), and Nellie, *née* Weate; *b* 11 March 1950; *Educ* Haberdashers' Aske's, Queen Mary Coll London (LLB); *m* 14 Sept 1985, Charlotte Ann, da of Michael George East; 1 da (Emily Ann b 20 Feb 1987), 1 s (Alasdair Hugh b 17 March 1989); *Career* called to the Bar Middle Temple 1974; author of various articles in professional jls; memb: Nat Youth Orchestra of GB 1967–68, Nat Youth Jazz Orchestra of GB 1968–69; dir Forest Philharmonic Soc 1978–96; *Recreations* music, sport; *Clubs* Garrick; *Style—* Alistair McGregor, Esq, QC; ✉ 11 Kingâs Bench Walk, Temple, London EC4Y 7EQ

MACGREGOR, Elizabeth Ann; OBE (2011); da of late Rt Rev Gregor Macgregor, and Elizabeth Jean Macgregor; *b* 16 April 1958; *Educ* Stromness Acad Orkney, Univ of Edinburgh (MA), Univ of Manchester (post grad museums studies dipl); *Career* curator Scottish Arts Cncl Travelling Gallery 1980–84, art offr Arts Cncl of GB 1984–89, dir Ikon Gallery Birmingham 1989–99, dir Museum of Contemporary Art Sydney Aust 1999–; judge Turner Prize 1995; memb Bd: Public Art Devpt Tst, Biennale of Sydney 1999–2003, Chunky Move 2000–06, Australian Children's Music Fndn 2007–2011; memb Fndrs Bd Fauna and Flora Int Australia 2009–; chair Advsy Bd 1BBC Midlands 997–99, memb Advsy Bd Univ of Technology Sydney Business Sch 2012–; tstee Pier Art Centre Orkney; Australian Centenary Medal 2003, Equity Tstees Award for Significant Innovation 2007, Australian Veuve Clicquot Award 2008; memb: Visual Arts & Galleries Assoc 1985, The Lunar Soc 1991, Women in Business Assoc 1991; FRSA; *Style*— Ms Elizabeth A Macgregor, OBE

McGREGOR, Ewan; OBE (2013); s of James McGregor, and Carol McGregor; *b* 31 March 1971; *Educ* Morisson's Acad Perthshire, Guildhall Sch of Music and Drama; *m* Eve; 2 da (Clara Mathilde, Esther Rose), 1 adopted da (Jamyan); *Career* actor; Br Film Icon Award Empire Awards 2008; supporter: Children's Hospice Assoc, Meningitis Tst; ambass UNICEF; Hon DLitt Univ of Ulster 2001; *Theatre* incl: What the Butler Saw (Salisbury Playhouse), Little Malcolm and His Struggle Against the Eunuchs, Guys and Dolls (Piccadilly Theatre) 2005, Iago in Othello (Donmar Warehouse) 2007; *Television* incl: Lipstick on Your Collar (Channel Four), Scarlet and Black (BBC), Family Style (Channel Four), Kavanagh QC, Doggin' Around (Screen One), Cold War – Tales from the Crypt (HBO), ER (nominated Outstanding Guest Actor in a Drama Series Emmy Awards 1997), Long Way Round (factual travel series), Long Way Down (factual travel series) 2007, Cold Chain Mission (BBC 2); *Film* incl: Being Human, Shallow Grave (Best Film Dinard Film Festival 1994, BAFTA Alexander Korda Award for Outstanding British Film of the Year 1995, BAFTA Jt Best Actor Award, BAFTA Scotland Award for Best Feature Film), Blue Juice, The Pillow Book, Trainspotting, Emma, Brassed Off, Nightwatch, The Serpent's Kiss, A Life Less Ordinary, Curt in Velvet Goldmine, Star Wars: Episode I – The Phantom Menace, Star Wars: Episode II – Attack of the Clones and Star Wars: Episode III – Revenge of the Sith, Little Voice, The Eye of the Beholder, Rogue Trader, Moulin Rouge (Best British Actor Empire Awards 2002), Black Hawk Down, Big Fish, Robots, Valiant, Miss Potter, Stay, The Island, Cassandra's Dream, Deception, I Love You Phillip Morris, Angels & Demons, The Men Who Stare at Goats, Amelia, The Ghost, Nanny McPhee and the Big Bang, Beginners, Perfect Sense, Haywire, Salmon Fishing in the Yemen, The Impossible, Jack the Giant Slayer, Son of a Gun, Jane Got A Gun, Miles Ahead, Last Days in the Desert, Our Kind of Traitor, American Pastoral (also dir); *Style*— Ewan McGregor, OBE; ⊠ c/o Lindy King, United Agents, 12–26 Lexington Street, London W1F 0LE (✆ 020 3214 0800, fax 020 3214 0801, website www.unitedagents.co.uk)

MacGREGOR, Prof Graham A; s of Prof A B MacGregor (d 1964), and Sybil, *née* Hawkey (d 1974); *b* 1 April 1941; *Educ* Marlborough, Trinity Hall Cambridge (MA, MB BChir), Middx Hosp; *m* 2 Nov 1968, Christiane, da of Maurice Bourquin (d 1956), of Switzerland; 2 da (Annabelle b 16 Nov 1970, Vanessa b 6 April 1972), 1 s (Christopher b 5 Sept 1973); *Career* dir Blood Pressure Unit (former sr lectr) Charing Cross and Westminster Med Sch 1979–89, prof of cardiovascular med St George's Hosp Med Sch 1989–2009, prof of cardiovascular medicine Wolfson Inst of Preventive Medicine Barts and London Scho of Medicine; chm: Blood Pressure Assoc 1999–, Consensus Action on Salt and Health 1999–, World Action on Salt 2005–, Action on Sugar 2014–; FRCP 1982; *Books* Salt Free Diet Book (1985, 2 edn 1991), Hypertension in Practice (1987, 3 edn 1999), Salt Diet and Health: Neptune's Poisoned Chalice (1998), Fast Facts Hypertension (2015); *Style*— Prof Graham MacGregor; ⊠ Wolfson Institute, Charter House Square, London EC1M 6BQ (✆ 020 7882 6217, e-mail g.macgregor@qmul.ac.uk)

MacGREGOR, Ian Campbell; *b* 20 September 1961, Solihull; *Educ* Univ of Edinburgh (MA), Cardiff Univ (PGDip); *Career* reporter: Southern Evening Echo 1985, South West News Service Bristol; Press Assoc: court reporter, educn corr; Daily Express: educn corr, NY corr, dep news ed; Daily Mail: dep news ed, news ed; launch ed Metro 1999–2000, ed Scottish Daily Mail 2000–01, dep ed Evening Standard 2002–06, dep ed Daily Telegraph 2006–07, ed Sunday Telegraph 2007–14, ed Saturday and Sunday Telegraphs 2014–; editorial memb PCC 2008–; visiting prof of journalism Nottingham Trent Univ; *Style*— Ian MacGregor, Esq; ⊠ Daily Telegraph, 111 Buckingham Palace Road, London SW1W 0DT

MacGREGOR, Joanna Clare; OBE (2012); da of Alfred MacGregor, of North London, and Angela, *née* Hughes; *b* 16 July 1959; *Educ* South Hampstead Sch for Girls, New Hall Cambridge (BA), Royal Acad of Music (recital dip, Gold medallist), Van Cliburn Inst Texas (masterclasses with Jorge Bolet); *m* 19 Sept 1986, Richard Williams; 1 da (Miranda (decd)); *Career* pianist; appeared as soloist with RPO, LSO, Eng Chamber Orch (tours to Bermuda and USA incl Carnegie Hall), BBC Symphony Orch, BBC Orch Scot, City of London Sinfonia, Nat Youth Orch (Proms 1990), London Mozart Players, BBC Symphony Orch, Rotterdam Philharmonic, CBSO, Orch of St John's, Dutch Radio Orch, Berlin Symphony Orch, Chicago Symphony Orch, Sydney Symphony Orchestra; soloist Last Night of the Proms 1996; tours: Senegal, Sierra Leone, Zimbabwe, The Phillipines, Norway, New Zealand, South Africa, Sweden, Germany, Singapore, Australia; premiered works by Br composers incl: Michael Finnissy, Hugh Wood and Harrison Birtwistle; jazz collaborations incl: Django Bates, Iain Ballamy; recordings incl: American Piano Classics (1989), Satie Piano Music, Britten Piano Concerto (with Eng Chamber Orch and Steuart Bedford), Barber/Ives Sonatas, Scarlatti Sonatas, Bach Art of Fugue, Nancarrow Canons and pieces by Ravel, Bartók, Debussy and Messiaen; composer Br music for theatre and TV prodns incl: Cheek By Jowl, Oxford Stage Co, C4; organised Platform Festival of New Music ICA 1991–93; artistic dir SoundCircus Bridgewater Hall Manchester 1996; author of fantasy play based on Erik Satie's writings (BBC Entry Prix d'Italia 1990, Sony Awards entry 1991); prof of music Gresham Coll London 1998–2000; radio presenter BBC Radio 3; TV presenter: BBC Omnibus, BBC Masterclass, Young Musician of the Year, Strings Bow and Bellows (BBC series); fndr SoundCircus 1997 (record label, website www.soundcircus.com; recordings incl: John Cage Sonatas, Nikki Yeoh Piano Language, Lou Harrison Piano Concerto); South Bank Show award for classical music 2000; memb Arts Cncl of England 1998–; FRAM, FTCL, Hon FRAM; *Recreations* windsurfing; *Style*— Ms Joanna MacGregor, OBE

MACGREGOR, HE Dame Judith Anne; DCMG (2016, CMG 2012), LVO (1992); *née* Brown; *b* 17 June 1952, London; *Educ* Univ of Oxford; *m* 1982, John Malcolm Macgregor; 3 s, 1 da; *Career* diplomat; entered HM Dip Serv 1976, first sec (Chancery and info) Belgrade 1978–81, desk offr FCO 1981–83, head of recruitment FCO 1983–84, memb Planning Staff FCO 1985–86, on leave 1986–88, first sec (political and info) Prague 1989, on leave 1990–91, first sec (Chancery) Paris 1992, dep head Western European Dept FCO 1993–95, on leave 1995–2000, cnsllr and head Security Strategy Unit FCO 2001–03, FCO chair Civil Serv Selection Bd 2003–04, ambass to Slovakia 2004–07, dir Migration FCO 2007–09, ambass to Mexico 2009–13, high cmmr to South Africa and non-res high cmmr to Lesotho and Swaziland 2013–; *Recreations* walking, gardening, reading; *Style*— HE Dame Judith Macgregor, DCMG, LVO

MacGREGOR, (Robert) Neil; s of Alexander MacGregor, and Anna Neil; *b* 16 June 1946; *Educ* Glasgow Acad, New Coll Oxford, Ecole Normale Supérieure Paris, Univ of Edinburgh, Courtauld Inst of Art; *Career* memb Faculty of Advocates Edinburgh 1972, lectr in history of art and architecture Univ of Reading 1975–81, ed Burlington Magazine 1981–87, dir Nat Gallery 1987–2002, dir British Museum 2002–15; *Style*— Neil MacGregor; ⊠ The British Museum, Great Russell Street, London WC1B 3DG (✆ 020 7323 8000)

MacGREGOR, Susan Katriona (Sue); CBE (2002, OBE 1992); da of late Dr James MacWilliam MacGregor, and Margaret MacGregor; *b* 30 August 1941; *Educ* Herschel Sch Cape Town; *Career* programme presenter South African Broadcasting Corp 1962–67, BBC radio reporter (World at One, PM, World this Weekend) 1967–72; presenter BBC Radio 4: Woman's Hour 1972–87, Today 1984–2002, A Good Read 2003–10, The Reunion 2003– (Sony Gold Award 2007, Broadcasting Press Guild Prog of the Year Award 2015, Radio Production Awards Best News and Current Affairs Documentary 2015); memb Bd: John Ellerman Fndn 2003–12, Young Classical Artists' Tst 2002–11, Unicef UK 2003–13; Hon DLitt: Univ of Nottingham, Nottingham Trent Univ, Staffordshire Univ, London Metropolitan Univ; Hon LLD Univ of Dundee; hon fell Harris Manchester Coll Oxford; Hon MRCP, FRSA; *Books* Woman of Today: An Autobiography (2002); *Recreations* theatre, cinema, skiing; *Style*— Ms Sue MacGregor; ⊠ c/o Knight Ayton Management, 35 Great James Street, London WC1N 3HB (✆ 020 7831 4400)

McGREGOR, Wayne; CBE (2011); *b* 1970, Stockport; *Educ* Bretton Hall Coll, Univ of Leeds (BA), Jose Limon Sch NY; *Career* choreographer; fndr Wayne McGregor Random Dance Co 1992– (resident co of Sadler's Wells 2001–), choreographer in residence The Place Theatre London 1992, choreographer in residence Royal Ballet 2006–, represented GB in Bancs d'Essai Internationaux, SKITE Project Lisbon and European Choreographic Forum, prof of choreography Trinity Laban Conservatoire of Music and Dance 2014–; prodns for Company Wayne McGregor (formerly Wayne McGregor/Random Dance Co): The Millennarium (cmmned RFH) 1997 (Prix d'Auteur du Council General de Seine-Saint-Denis at Bagnolet 1998, L'Adami Prize for Performance Paris 1998), Sulphur 16 (cmmned RFH) 1998 (winner Ballett Int Choreographer In Residence Best Choreography Collaboration), Aeon (cmmned RFH) 2000 (nominated Benoise de la Danse 2002) 2000, digit01 (cmmned The Place) 2001, Nemesis (co-cmmned South Hill Park, Swindon Dance, Sadler's Wells, DanceEast) 2002, Alpha 2003, Polar Sequences 2003, Amu 2005 (nominated Critics' Circle Nat Dance Award for Best Choreography, Modern 2006), AtaXia 2005, Ossein 2005, Entity 2008, Dyad 1909 2009, FAR 2010, UNDANCE 2011, Big Dance Trafalgar Square 2012, Atomos 2013, Tree of Codes 2015; ind cmmns: Telenoia (Canary Wharf) 2000, Fleur de Peux (with Vivianna Durante, *qv*, Royal Ballet) 2000, Symbiont(s) (Royal Ballet Covent Garden) 2000 (nomination Best Choreography Critics' Circle Awards 2002), Velociraptor (Dance East/Bury Festival) 2001, Detritus (Rambert Dance Co) 2001, Castlescape (E London Dance) 2001, HIVE (Nat Youth Dance Wales (2001), Brainstate (Royal Ballet/Random Dance) 2001, Phase Space (Gothenberg Ballet/Random Dance) 2002, Game of Halves (Nat Youth Dance Wales) 2002, PreSentient (Rambert Dance Co) 2002, Binocular (Adam Cooper Dance Co) 2003, Xenathra (Dance Umbrella) 2003, Qualia (Royal Ballet) 2003, Nautilus (Stuttgart Ballet) 2003, 2 Human (English Nat Ballet) 2003, Eden/Eden (Stuttgart Ballet) 2005, Engram (Royal Ballet) 2005, Skindex (NDT1) 2006, Chroma (Royal Ballet) 2006 (nominated Olivier Award for Best New Dance Prodn 2007 and Outstanding Achievement in Dance 2007 (for choreography)), Eden/Eden (San Francisco Ballet) 2007, [memeri] (DANCE) 2007, Genus (Paris Opera Ballet) 2007, Renature (Nederlands Dans Theatre 1) 2008, Infra (Royal Ballet) 2008 (Best Classical Choreography Critics Circle Award), Dyad 1909 (Wayne McGregor Random Dance) 2009, Dyad (Australian Ballet) 2009, Limen (Royal Ballet) 2009, Outlier (NY City Ballet) 2010, Yantra (Stuttgart Ballet) 2010, Outlier 2010, L'Anatomie de la Sensation 2011, Live Fire Exercise 2011, Carbon Life 2012, Machina 2012, Amber 2013, Raven Girl 2013, Borderlands 2013, Tetractys 2014, Woolf Works 2015, Kairos 2015, Obsidian Tear 2016; site specific cmmns: CeBit Dances (Imagination/Ericsson Hanover), Dragonfly (Alternative Hair Show Drury Lane London), Slam (The Arches Glasgow), Match Half (Nottingham Forest Stadium), opening of World Disabled Games (Birmingham Int Stadium), Installation over 4 (Selfridges Gallery Window), Bio-logical (for Bodycraze at Selfridges London/Manchester), LOVE (Imagination Frankfurt), BodyScript (Connect at Sadler's Wells), Cybergeneration (Belfast Int Festival at Queens), Zero Hertz (Cork Opera House Ireland), Neurotransmission (Snape Maltings Concert Hall Aldeburgh), S.I.N (Shed O Docklands London), Dragonfly (Nat Glass Centre), Series (Houses of Parliament), Black on White (South Bank Centre Ballroom), Chameleon (Barbican), x2 (Royal Museum Edinburgh), Scottish Opera/Random Collaboration (GOMA Glasgow), Angel (Natural History Museum London), In:terplay (Bruce Nauman, Hayward Gall London), Pointe (Saatchi Gall London), Equation (Centre George Pompidu Paris), 11 Digital Mantras (The Roundhouse London), Sentient Net (The Gallert Sadler's Wells), Velociraptor (The Crypt Bury St Edmunds), Castlescape (Goresbrook Estate London), Amu@Durham (Durham Cathedral); *Theatre* A Little Night Music (RNT, Arts Fndn Fellowship 1994 and nomination Best Choreographer Olivier Awards 1996), Cleansed (Royal Court), Antony and Cleopatra (RNT), Woman in White (Palace Theatre) 2004–05, Cloaca (Old Vic) 2004, Alladin (Old Vic) 2004–05, You Can Never Tell (Peter Hall Co) 2005, Much Ado About Nothing (Peter Hall Co) 2006, Kirkou & Karaba (LLO Music and EMI) 2007, Ring Round the Moon (West End) 2008, Breakfast at Tiffany's (West End) 2009, Closer (Donmar Warehouse) 2015; *Opera* Rinaldo/The Mikado (Grange Park Opera), Salome (ENO), The Marriage of Figaro (Scottish Nat Opera), Orpheus et Eurydice (Scottish Nat Opera and Scottish Opera Go Round), Hansel and Gretel (Scottish Nat Opera), La Boheme (Scottish Nat Opera), The Midsummer Marriage (Chicago Lyric Opera), Did and Aeneas (La Scala), Dido and Aeneas/Acis and Galatea (Royal Opera) 2009, Didoand Aeneas (La Scala); *Television and Film* Redoxon commercial, Eurostar commercial, Physical Dysfunctional (BBC Knowledge), Horizone (Dance for Camera, BBC and ACE), Medusa (RaiUno Int), Bent (Channel 4 Films), Tomorrows World Live (cmmnd NESTA), The Last Siren (cmmnd RaiUno Italy), The Dancer's Body (BBC 2), Nemesis (BBC4/MJW), Symbiont(s) (BBC 2), Chrysalis (Arte), Dice Life (Channel 4), Dance USA (BBC 4), Harry Potter and the Goblet of Fire, Tremor (Channel 4); *Awards* Art Fndn fellowship, Lisa Ullmann travel scholarship 1997, nomination Outstanding Contribution to Dance Critics' Circle Awards 2001, nomination Award for Dance South Bank Show 2001, Outstanding Achievement in Dance Award Time Out Live awards 2001, Outstanding Choreography Award Time Out Live Awards 2003, Screen Choreography Award Monaco Dance Screen 2003, Laurence Olivier Award for Best New Dance Production, Laurence Olivier Outstanding Achievemtn in Dance for Choreography, Critics' Circle Award for Best Modern Choreography, South Bank Show Award, Best Classical Choreography Nat Dance Award for Woolf Works 2015, Best New Dance Production Olivier Award for Woolf Works 2016; *Style*— Wayne McGregor, Esq, CBE

MacGREGOR OF PULHAM MARKET, Baron (Life Peer UK 2001), of Pulham Market in the County of Norfolk; John Roddick Russell MacGregor; OBE (1971), PC (1985); s of late Dr N S R MacGregor, and Mary, *née* Roddick; *b* 14 February 1937, Glasgow; *Educ* Merchiston Castle Sch Edinburgh, Univ of St Andrews, KCL; *m* 1962, Jean Dungey; 2 da (Fiona b 1964, Catriona b 1969), 1 s (Ian b 1966); *Career* univ admin 1961–62; former chm: Fedn of Univ Cons and Unionist Assocs, Bow Gp; first pres Cons and Christian Democratic Youth Community; editorial staff New Society 1962–63, special asst to PM 1963–64, Cons Res Dept 1964–65, head of Ldr of Oppn's Private Office 1965–68; with Hill Samuel 1968–79 (dir 1973–79); MP (Cons) Norfolk S Feb 1974–2001, oppn whip 1977–79, a Lord Cmmr of the Treasy (Govt whip) 1979–81, Parly Under Sec for Trade and Industry incl responsiblity for small businesses 1981–83, Min of State for Agric

M

Fisheries and Food 1983–85, Chief Sec to the Treasy 1985–87, Min for Agric Fisheries and Food 1987–89, Sec of State for Educn 1989–90, Lord Pres of the Council and Leader of the Commons 1990–92, Sec of State for Transport 1992–94; chm House of Lords Economic Affrs Select Ctee 2010–14, chm Assoc of Cons Peers 2011–; non-exec dep chm Hill Samuel Bank 1994–96; non-exec dir: Associated British Foods plc 1994–2007, Slough Estates plc 1995–2006, Uniq plc (formerly Unigate plc) 1996–2005, London and Manchester Gp 1996–98; Friends Provident 1998–2007, Supervisory Bd DAF Trucks NV 2000–09; vice-pres: Assoc of County Cncls 1995–97, Local Govt Assoc 1997–99; memb: Cncl KCL 1996–2002, Ctee for Standards in Public Life 1997–2003; dep chm: Governing Bodies Assoc 1998–2002, Assoc of Governing Bodies of Ind Schs 2002–06; chm of tstees: Segro Pension Fund 2006–10, Br Energy Pension Fund 2007–14, Anglian Water Pension Fund 2009–12, Eggborough Power Ltd Pension Fund 2010–; chm St Andrews (Ecumenical) Tst 2006–12; High Steward Norwich Cathedral 2007– (memb Cncl 2002–, chm 2007–); Hon LLD Univ of Westminster 1995; MInstD (memb Cncl 1996–2005); FKC 1989; *Recreations* music (especially opera), gardening, travel, conjuring (memb Magic Circle 1989–); *Style*— The Rt Hon the Lord MacGregor of Pulham Market, OBE; ✉ House of Lords, London SW1A 0AA (☎ 020 7219 4439)

McGREGOR-JOHNSON, His Hon Judge Richard John; s of Maxwell McGregor-Johnson (d 1987), and Pamela, *née* Moy (d 2004); *b* 11 July 1950, Devizes, Wiltshire; *Educ* Dean Close Sch Cheltenham, Univ of Bristol (LLB); *m* 1974, Elizabeth, da of Sidney Weston; 1 s (James b 11 July 1978), 1 da (Caroline b 10 August 1980); *Career* called to the Bar Inner Temple 1973 (bencher 2001); in practice (specialising in criminal law) 1973–98, circuit judge 1998–, resident judge Isleworth Crown Court 2004–, sr circuit judge 2010–, hon recorder Royal Borough of Kensington and Chelsea 2011–; *Recreations* choral singing, sailing; *Style*— His Hon Judge McGregor-Johnson; ✉ The Crown Court, 36 Ridgeway Road, Isleworth, Middlesex TW7 5LP (☎ 020 8380 4500)

McGREGOR-SMITH, Baroness (Life Peer UK 2015), of Sunninghill in the Royal County of Berkshire Ruby McGregor-Smith; CBE (2012); *Career* qualified chartered accountant Stoy Hayward; with Serco Gp plc until 2002; Mitie Gp plc: gp fin dir 2002–05, chief operating offr 2005–07, chief exec 2007–; non-exec dir Michael Page Int plc; first Asian female chief exec of a FTSE 350 co; ACA; *Style*— The Baroness McGregor-Smith, CBE; ✉ Mitie Group plc, Ground Floor East, Cottons Centre, Cottons Lane, 47/49 Tooley Street, London SE1 2QG

McGRIGOR, Sir James Angus Rhoderick Neil; 6 Bt (UK 1831), of Campden Hill, Middx; MSP; s of Sir Charles Edward McGrigor, 5 Bt, and Mary Bettine, da of Sir Archibald Charles Edmonstone, 6 Bt (d 1954), of Duntreath Castle, Blanefield; *b* 19 October 1949; *Educ* Eton; *m* 1 (m dis), Caroline F, da of late Jacques Roboh, of Paris; 2 da (Sibylla b 1988, Sarah b 1989); m 2, 1997, Emma da of David L Fellowes of Cladich Argyll; 1 s (Alexander b 1998), 3 da (Violet b 2001, Rosanna b 2003, Davina b 29 Dec 2006); *Heir* s, Alexander McGrigor; *Career* farmer; memb Royal Company of Archers Queen's Body Guard for Scotland (Kentucky Col 2009); MSP (Cons) Highlands and Islands 1999–; *Recreations* fishing, shooting, travel, music, cinema; *Clubs* Chelsea Arts, White's, New; *Style*— Sir James McGrigor, Bt, MSP; ✉ Ardchonnel House, by Dalmally, Argyll PA33 1BW

McGROUTHER, Prof (Duncan) Angus; *b* 3 March 1946; *Educ* Univ of Glasgow (MB ChB, MD), Univ of Strathclyde (MSc); *Career* Cruden med res fell Bioengineering Unit Univ of Strathclyde 1972–73, sr registrar in plastic surgery Canniesburn Hosp Glasgow 1976–78 (registrar 1975–76), assistentarzt Klinikum rechts der Isar Munich 1978, hon clinical lectr Univ of Newcastle upon Tyne 1978–80; conslt plastic surgn: Northern RHA Shotley Bridge Gen Hosp 1979–80, Canniesburn Hosp Glasgow 1981–89; chm Div of Plastic and Maxillofacial Surgery 1986–, chair plastic and reconstructive surgery UCL (newly created, funded by Phoenix Appeal) 1989–2001; Univ of Manchester: fndr dept specialising in plastic and reconstructive surgery res, chair in plastic and reconstructive surgery 2001–; hon conslt surgn Univ Hosp of S Manchester; asst ed Journal of Hand Surgery 1987; examiner in anatomy Royal Coll of Physicians and Surgns of Glasgow; Br Assoc of Plastic Surgns: memb 1978, sec Sr Registrars Travelling Club 1978–79, memb Educn and Res Ctee 1982–84 (chm 1988–), memb Editorial Bd Br Journal of Plastic Surgery 1981–83, memb Cncl 1986–89; Br Soc for Surgery of the Hand: memb 1980, memb Cncl 1983–85, memb Editorial Bd 1983–85, pres 2011; Int Fedn of Socs for Surgery of the Hand: memb Flexor Tendon Injuries Ctee, memb Res Ctee, chm Dupuytren's Disease Ctee; tstee RESTORE Charity 1991–, memb Scientific Advsy Panel Healing Fndn 2000–11; advsr Changing Faces 1995–; Royal Soc Wolfson Personal Merit Award 2003; FRCS 1973 (memb Cncl and tstee 2010–), FRCSGlas 1973, Hon FRCSEd 1993, FMedSci 2005; *Publications* contrib: Cleft Lip and Palate, Oral Surgery (1986), Microanatomy of Dupuytren's Contracture, Dupuytren's Disease (1986), Dupuytren's Disease, Methods and Concepts in Hand Surgery (1986), Surgery of the Thumb (with D A C Reid, 1986), Principles of Hand Surgery (with F D Burke and P Smith, 1990), Dupuytren's Disease (1990), Current Surgical Practice (vol 6, 1992), Microvascular Surgery and Free Tissue Transfer (1993), Gray's Anatomy (38 edn, 1995), Bailey and Love's Short Practice of Surgery (22 edn, 1995), Green's Operative Surgery (5 edn, 2004); The Interactive Hand (teaching CD-ROM, BMA Award, Millennium Product); author of 190 papers on hand and limb reconstructive surgery and scientific studies in tissue repair and tissue engrg in relation to tendon healing, nerve repair, would healing and scar formation; *Recreations* skiing; *Style*— Prof D Angus McGrouther; ✉ The University of Manchester, Stopford Building, Oxford Road, Manchester M13 9PT (☎ 0161 275 1591, fax 0161 275 1813)

McGUCKIAN, Maeve (Medbh); da of Hugh and Margaret, of Belfast; *b* 1950; *Educ* Fortwilliam Convent GS Belfast, Queen's Univ Belfast (open scholar, BA, MA, Dip Ed, TC); *m* June 1977, John McGuckian, s of John McGuckian; 3 s (John Liam, Hugh, Fergus), 1 da (Emer); *Career* teacher of Eng Fortwilliam Convent Belfast and St Patrick's Coll Belfast, writer in residence Queen's Univ Belfast, lectr in Eng St Mary's Trg Coll Belfast, currently lectr Seamus Heaney Inst for Poetry Queen's Univ Belfast, visiting fell Univ of Calif Berkeley 1991, writer in residence New Univ of Ulster Coleraine 1995–98; Irish memb Aosdána, hon fell Inst of Irish Studies Queen's Univ Belfast, Hon DLitt Univ of Aberdeen 2008; *Awards* winner Nat Poetry Competition, Alice Hunt Bartlett Award, Rooney Prize for Lit, Gregory Award 1980, winner Cheltenham Poetry Prize, Irish-American Prize for Literature 1998, Tolman Cunard Prize for Best Single Poem 2002; *Books* incl: Single Ladies (1980), Portrait of Joanna (1980), The Flower Master (1982), Venus and the Rain (1984), On Ballycastle Beach (1988), Two Women – Two Shores (1988), Marconi's Cottage (1991), Captain Lavender (1994), Selected Poems (1997), Shelmalier (1998), Drawing Ballerinas (2001), The Face of the Earth (2002), Had I a Thousand Lives (2003), The Book of the Angel (2004), The Currach Requires No Harbours (2006); *Style*— Mrs Medbh McGuckian; ✉ c/o Henry Raddie, Downview Avenue, Antrim Road, Belfast BT15 4EZ

McGUFFOG, John Lee; s of Capt Donald McGuffog (d 1998), and Ethel Mary, *née* Lee (d 2000); *b* 18 August 1945; *Educ* Wallington GS; *m* 1, 1971 (m dis 1976), Patricia Anne White; m 2, 6 March 1978, Penelope Jayne, da of Philip Gordon Lee (d 1995); 1 da (Charlotte b 21 Feb 1979); *Career* surveyor 1963–, qualified chartered auctioneer 1968, chief surveyor Leonard W Cotton & Ptnrs 1969; Mann & Co (estate agents): joined 1972, dir 1975, chm commercial div 1985; main bd dir: Countrywide Surveyors Ltd 1988–, Douglas Duff Chartered Surveyors (formerly BBG Commercial then Countrywide Commercial) 1994–2007; conslt Morgan Smithyes 2008–15; memb Cranleigh and Dist Round Table 1978–86, chm Cranleigh and Dist 41 Club 1991–92, tstee and dir Cranleigh Village Hosp Tst until 2010; govr Farlington Sch Horsham 1993– (dep chm 2000–04, chm 2004–10); memb City Owls (promoted by Worshipful Co of Chartered Surveyors); FRICS 1976, MCIArb 1979; *Recreations* fishing; *Clubs* 41, SAA&IE Lunch Club; *Style*— John McGuffog, Esq; ✉ e-mail jlmcguffog@btinternet.com

McGUIGAN, Dr Daniel (Danny); s of Daniel McGuigan (d 2002), and Kathleen, *née* Connolly (d 2014); *b* 31 January 1954, Belfast, NI; *Educ* Christian Brothers Secondary Belfast, St Mary's Grammar Belfast, Queen's Univ Belfast (BSc, PGCE, DBA), Univ of Strathclyde (MBA, PhD); *m* 18 April 2006, Terry Daly; *Career* teacher St Louise's Coll 1978–79, sr duty offr British Midland Int 1979–80, exec trainer Siemens AG International Training Centre Munich 1981–82, trainer The British Cncl Munich 1981–82; md: Value Products Marketing Glasgow 1984–85, Scientific Instruments Glasgow 1985–86, Creative Business Services Ltd Glasgow 1986–94, Business Devpt Centre Glasgow 1994–; fndr and chm Strathclyde Business Sch MBA Alumni Assoc 1984–88; chm: Garrioch Residents Assoc 1994–2006, St Aloysius Parish Cncl Glasgow 1995–2006, Quest Scotland 1988–2002; fell Duke of Edinburgh's Int Award Fndn; memb: American Society for Training and Devpt, Assoc for Mangement Educ and Devpt (also chm); FRSA, FCIM, MIOD, MCMI; The Spirituality of Leadership 2008, Friendship at Work: An Exploration of the Views and Experiences of Senior Managers; *Recreations* soccer, golf, swimming, skiing, cycling; *Clubs* Carlton, RAC; *Style*— Dr Danny McGuigan; ✉ e-mail email@dannymcguigan.com, website www.dannymcguigan.com

McGUINNESS, Andrew; s of Gerald (d 2006), and Zita, *née* Mercer; *b* 22 April 1970, Southport; *m* 17 June 2000, Isabella, *née* Wesolowska; 2 da (Ella, Jessica b 25 June 2002 (twins)), 1 s (Alfie b 8 Sept 2005); *Career* account dir J Walter Thompson 1992–98, gp account dir M&C Saatchi Sydney 1998–2000, md TBWA 2001–02, ceo TBWA 2002–05, founding ptnr Beattie McGuinness Bungay (BMB) with Trevor Beattie, *qv* and Bill Bungay 2005–2014, ceo Freuds 2014–; chm Seven Dials PR 2013–; non-exec dir Chorion plc 2005–06, memb Bd The Marketing Soc 2008–10, chm Advertising Assoc 2009–12; FIPA; *Style*— Andrew McGuinness, Esq; ✉ Freuds, 1 Stephen Street, London W1T 1AL (☎ 020 3003 6300, e-mail andrew@freuds.com)

McGUINNESS, Anne Marie; da of Roland McGuinness, of Belfast, and Eileen, *née* Fitzpatrick; *b* 29 October 1954; *Educ* St Dominic's HS Belfast, Queen's Univ Belfast (MB BCh, BAO); *m* 10 March 1984, James William Park, s of James Boyd Park (d 1989), of Braintree, Essex; 2 s (Oscar Boyd b 1988, Hugo Blair b 1991); *Career* surgn in NI 1979–84, conslt Royal Free Hosp 1987–96, clinical dir in A&E UCH London 1996–; memb: BMA 1979, Br Assoc for Accident and Emergency Med 1986, Br Trauma Soc 1989, Br Assoc of Clinical Anatomists 1995; FMS (London) 1986, FRCSEd 1983, FCEM 2006; ind medicolegal conslt; overseas surveyor to the Leonard Cheshire Chair in Conflict Recovery, surveyor HQS 1996–, assessor CHI 2003, medical assessor Royal Pharmaceutical Soc 2007; *Publications* author of chapters in books and numerous articles and papers in learned jls on the subjects of head injury coma scales, trauma scoring models, plastic surgery and microvascular anatomy, and emergency med; *Recreations* writing, music, art; *Style*— Ms Anne McGuinness; ✉ Accident & Emergency Department, University College Hospital, Gower Street, London WC1E 6AU (☎ 020 7380 9768, fax 020 7380 9610, e-mail anne.mcguinness@uclh.nhs.uk)

McGUINNESS, Martin; MLA; *Career* MP (Sinn Féin) Ulster Mid 1997–2013, MLA (Sinn Féin) Ulster Mid 1998–; min for educn NI Assembly 1999–2007, dep first min of NI 2007–; *Style*— Martin McGuinness, Esq, MLA; ✉ c/o Parliament Buildings, Belfast BT4 3XX

McGUIRE, Rt Hon Dame Anne; DBE (2015), PC (2008); *Educ* Our Lady & St Francis Secdy Sch, Univ of Glasgow (MA), Notre Dame Teacher Trg Coll; *m* 1972, Len McGuire; 2 c; *Career* former teacher, depute dir Scottish Cncl of Voluntary Orgns until 1997, nat offr CSV 1988–93; MP (Lab) Stirling 1997–2015; asst Govt whip 1998–2001, a Lord Cmmr to HM Treasy (Govt whip) 2001–02, Parly sec Scotland Office 2002–05, min for disabled people and Parly sec Dept for Work and Pensions 2005–08, PPS to Rt Hon Ed Miliband, MP, *qv* (as Ldr of Oppn) 2010–11, shadow min Dept for Work and Pensions 2011–; *Recreations* cooking, reading, Scottish ceilidh music, watching football; *Style*— The Rt Hon Dame Anne McGuire, DBE; ✉ House of Commons, London SW1A 0AA (☎ 020 7219 3000); Constituency Office, 22 Viewfield Street, Stirling FK8 1UA (☎ 01786 446515, fax 01786 446513, e-mail mcguirea@parliament.uk)

McGUIRE, Prof William Joseph (Bill); s of John McMillan McGuire (d 1984), and Audrey, *née* Wade Owens; *b* 1 December 1954, Swansea; *Educ* St Michael's Coll Hitchin, UCL (BSc), CNAA (PhD); *m* Anna; 2 s (Fraser Robert John b 26 Nov 2003, Jake William Paul b 22 Feb 2009); *Career* volcanologist; lectr in igneous petrology and geochemistry W London Inst of HE (now Brunel Univ) 1981–90; Cheltenham and Gloucester Coll of HE: lectr 1990–93, sr lectr 1993–95, reader in volcanology 1995–97; prof of geophysical and climate hazards UCL 1997–2012 (emeritus prof of geophysical and climate hazards 2012–), co-dir UCL Environment Inst 2011–12; dir DisasterMan Ltd, conslt on natural hazards and climate change HSBC Gp 2006–; chair Volcanic Studies Gp Geological Soc of London 1993–96, UK nat corr Int Assoc of Volcanology and Chemistry of the Earth's Interior 1993–96, UK rep European Volcanology Project Ctee European Science Fndn, memb Cncl Geological Soc of London 1997–99; memb: UK panel Int Union of Geodesy and Geophysics 1993–95 (sec 1996–2000), UK Govt Natural Hazard Working Gp 2005, Science Media Panel Royal Instn 2002–, Lancet – UCL Cmmn on Climate Change and Global Health, UK Govt Science Advsy Gp Emergencies (Icelandic ash eruption) 2010, Advsy Bd Contraction and Convergence Fndn 2010–; dir Warm Wet and Windy Peak Climate Change and Eco Festival Cromford Derbyshire 2012–; memb Editorial Bd: Disasters, BBC Focus Magazine until 2011, Philosophical Transactions of the Royal Soc (Series A); memb Editorial Advsy Bd Versita Earth Sciences open access jls and books 2012–; presenter: Disasters In Waiting (BBC Radio 4) 2000, Scientists Under Pressure (BBC Radio 4) 2001; conslt Supervolcano (BBC1) 2005; annual science lectr Naural History Museum 2005, science advsr Footprint Friends 2009–; Roscoe Lecture (Liverpool John Moores Univ) 2012, Gregynog Lecture (Univ of Aberystwyth) 2012; memb: Assoc of Br Science Writers, American Geophysical Union, AAAS; FGS 1976, fell Royal Inst 2003; *Books* Monitoring Active Volcanoes: Strategies, Procedures, and Techniques (1995), Apocalypse: A Natural History of Global Disasters (1999), Italian Volcanoes (2001), Natural Hazards and Environmental Change (2002), Raging Planet (2002), A Guide to the End of the World: Everything You Never Wanted to Know (2002), Guide to Global Hazards (2003), World Atlas of Natural Hazards (2004), Surviving Armageddon: Solutions for a Threatened Planet (2005), Global Catastrophes: A Very Short Introduction (2005, fully revised new edn 2014), Seven Years to Save the Planet (2008), Waking the Giant: How a Changing Climate Triggers Earthquakes, Tsunamis and Volcanoes (2012), Climate Forcing of Geological Hazards (2013); *Recreations* pursuing the distant goal of self-sufficiency in fruit and veg, stroking cats Dave, Toby and Cashew, playing with sons Fraser and Jake, still worrying about the future of the planet; *Style*— Prof Bill McGuire; ✉ website www.billmcguire.co.uk; Department of Earth Sciences, University College London, Gower Street, London WC1E 6BT (☎ 020 7679 3449, fax 020 7679 2390, e-mail w.mcguire@ucl.ac.uk, website www.disasterman.co.uk); c/o Curtis Brown (e-mail rebecca@curtisbrown.co.uk and vanessa.fogarty@curtisbrown.co.uk)

McGURK, John Callender; s of John B McGurk (d 2005), and Janet, *née* Callender (d 1992); *b* 12 December 1952; *Educ* Tynecastle Secdy Sch Edinburgh; *m* 1984 (m dis 2005), Karen, da of Capt Peter Ramsay; 1 da (Chloe b 19 Aug 1991), 1 s (Josh b 13 Aug 1995); *Career* trainee journalist Scottish County Press 1970–74; reporter: Nottingham Evening Post

1974–75, Scottish Daily News 1975, Radio Clyde 1975–78; Sunday Mail: reporter 1978–85, news ed 1985–88, dep ed 1988–89; ed Sunday Sun Newcastle 1989–91, dep ed Daily Record 1991–94; ed: Edinburgh Evening News 1995–97, Scotland on Sunday 1997–2001 (UK Sunday Newspaper of the Year 1997, 1998 and 2000); ed dir The Scotsman Publications Ltd 2001–04, ed The Scotsman 2004–06, gp managing ed The Daily and Sunday Telegraph 2006; chm: Eds' Ctee, Scottish Daily Newspaper Soc 2001; memb PCC 2000–02; *Recreations* family, cinema, reading, dining out, travel; *Style*— John McGurk, Esq; ✉ e-mail jcmcgurk@blueyonder.co.uk

MACH, Prof David Stefan; s of Joseph Mach, of Methil, Fife, and Martha, *née* Cassidy; *b* 18 March 1956, Methil, Fife; *Educ* Buckhaven HS, Duncan of Jordanstone Coll of Art Dundee (Duncan of Drumfork travelling scholar, Dip Art, Post Dip Art, Pat Holmes meml prize, SED minor and major prizes), RCA (MA, Royal Coll drawing prize); *m* 25 Aug 1979, Lesley June, da of William Ronald White; 1 da (Jessie Hudson b 24 Aug 2002); *Career* professional sculptor 1982–; visiting prof of sculpture Edinburgh Coll of Art 1999–, prof of sculpture Royal Acad London 2000–, prof of inspiration and discovery Univ of Dundee 2004; exhibitions incl: British Sculpture' 83 (Hayward Gallery London) 1983, Fuel for the Fire (Riverside Studio London) 1986, A Hundred and One Dalmatians (Tate Gallery London) 1988, Five Easy Pieces (Barbara Toll Fine Art NY) 1989, Here to Stay (The Tramway Glasgow) 1990, Out of Order (Kingston upon Thames) 1990, David Mach Sculpture (Ujazdowski Castle Center for Contemporary Art Warsaw) 1993, Fully Furnished (Museum of Contemporary Art San Diego) 1994, David Mach New Drawings (Jill George Gallery London) 1995, David Mach (Galerie Andata/Ritorno Geneva) 1995, Train (Britain's largest contemporary sculpture, Darlington) 1997, Big Heids (M8 Motorway North Lanark) 1999, A National Portrait (The Dome at Greenwich) 1999, Hell Bent (Gallery of Modern Art Glasgow) 2002, Sculpture and collage (Forum Gallery NY) 2005, Iconography (Galerie Jerome de Noirmont Paris) 2007, collage shows Dubai, Hong Kong, Seoul and London 2008, Opera Gallery (London, Seoul, Paris and Geneva), Precious Light (Edinburgh City Art Centre) 2011 (Galway) 2012 and (Venice) 2013; video Clydeside Classic (Channel 4) 1990; one of two Br reps at São Paolo Biennale 1987, one of three Scottish reps at Venice Biennale 1990; nominated for Turner prize 1988; cmmns incl Peter Gabriel's US project 1992; tstee Nat Portrait Gallery 2006-' City of Glasgow Lord Provost Prize 1992; LLD (hc) Univ of Dundee 2002; RA 1998, Hon RSA 2004; *Publications* David Mach (2002), David Mach: Precious Light (2011); *Recreations* drummer The Voyeurs, tennis, skiing, reading; *Clubs* Chelsea Arts, Groucho, Dover St Art; *Style*— Prof David Mach; ✉ 8 Havelock Walk, Forest Hill, London SE23 3HG (☎ 020 8699 5659, e-mail davidmach@davidmach.com, website www.davidmach.com)

MacHALE, Joseph Patrick (Joe); s of Seamus Joseph MacHale (d 2006), and Margaret Mary, *née* Byrne (d 1982); *b* 17 August 1951; *Educ* Ampleforth, The Queen's Coll Oxford (MA); *m* 28 Feb 1981, Mary Ann, da of Rear Adm David Dunbar-Nasmith, CB, DSO; 3 s (Henry b 1983, Martin b 1986, Thomas b 1990), 1 da (Laura b 1985); *Career* with Price Waterhouse 1973–78, qualified CA 1976; joined J P Morgan Inc 1979, sr vice-pres Morgan Guaranty Tst 1986–89, md J P Morgan & Co Inc NY 1989–98, chief exec J P Morgan EMEA 1998–2001; advsr Abbot of Ampleforth 2007–; non-exec dir: Morgan Crucible plc 2003–08, Royal Bank of Scotland Gp plc 2004–13, Brit Insurance Holdings plc 2005–11, Huntsworth plc 2012–14; chm Prytania 2003–; chm Brendoncare Fndn 2013–; tstee Macmillan Cancer Support 2002–12 (treas 2002–10); FCA 1978; *Clubs* Brooks's, Vincent's; *Style*— Joe MacHale, Esq; ✉ The Old House, Wonston, Winchester, Hampshire SO21 3LS

McHARDY, David Keith; s of Charles Stuart McHardy (d 1956), and Mary Isabella, *née* Laverick; *b* 29 August 1950; *Educ* Lord Wandsworth Coll Long Sutton, PCL (now Univ of Westminster) (LLB); *m* Barbara Lillian, da of Donald Farley (d 1956); 2 s (Alexander b 27 Sept 1981, Nicholas b 31 July 1984), 1 da (Susannah b 6 June 1992); *Career* admitted slr 1978; ptnr: Hutchins & Co 1979–2000, Family Law Consortium 2000–03, Family Law Assoc LLP 2003–; Slrs Family Law Assoc: chm Legal Aid Working Pty 1987–89 (memb 1985–89), nat chm 1989–91, ed Review 1994–2003; memb Legal Aid Area Ctee Legal Aid Bd; memb: Law Soc, Justice; past chm Hackney and E London Family Mediation Serv; lectr; dep dist judge Princ Registry of the Family Div London; Lieutenant Baliff of the Royal Court of Guernsey 2003–; MCIA; *Recreations* tennis, golf; *Clubs* West Essex Golf (capt 1998–99, chm 1999–2009); *Style*— David McHardy, Esq; ✉ Family Law Associates LLP, 1 The Courtyard, Lynton Road, Crouch End, London N8 8SL (☎ 020 8340 7760, fax 020 8347 4227, website www.familylawassociates.co.uk)

McHARDY-YOUNG, Dr Stuart; s of John McHardy-Young (d 1974), of Twickenham, Middx, and Violet Collin; *b* 20 February 1936; *Educ* St Paul's, Guy's Hosp Univ of London (MD, MB BS), Stanford Univ; *m* 9 Sept 1961, Margaret Elizabeth, da of William Alan Cash (d 1949), of Eaglescliffe, Co Durham; 1 da (Catherine b 19 April 1978); *Career* post doctoral fell Stanford Univ Med Sch California 1967–68, sr lectr and hon conslt physician Guy's Hosp Med Sch 1970–72; conslt physician and endocrinologist: Central Middx Hosp 1972–, Royal Nat Throat Nose and Ear Hosp 1973–, Royal Masonic Hosp London 1982–96; subdean St Mary's Hosp Med Sch London 1983–88; hon clinical sr lectr UCL 1973–93; memb Br Diabetic Assoc, chm NW Thames Regnl Med Manpower Cmmn (memb Central Ctee), former univ memb Brent Health Authy; memb RSM; *Recreations* golf, travel, opera; *Clubs* Royal Mid-Surrey Golf; *Style*— Dr Stuart McHardy-Young; ✉ 20 Belmont Road, Twickenham, Middlesex TW2 5DA; 2 Hillview, Uploders, Bridport, Dorset (e-mail drsmchy@aol.com); Central Middlesex Hospital, London NW10

McHENRY, Rev Brian Edward; CBE (2008); s of Alexander Edward McHenry (d 1995), and Winifred Alice, *née* Wainford; *b* 12 December 1950, London; *Educ* Dulwich Coll, New Coll Oxford (MA), SE Inst for Theological Educn (dip), Canterbury Christ Church Univ (BA); *m* 19 Jan 1979, Elizabeth Anne, *née* Bray; 2 s (Thomas Edward b 12 March 1979, Joseph William b 9 Nov 1981); *Career* called to the Bar Middle Temple 1976; Treasury Slr's Dept 1978–92, legal advsr Monopolies and Mergers Cmmn 1992–96, slr to N Wales Tbnl of Inquiry into Child Abuse 1996–97, slr to BSE Inquiry 1998–2000, Treasury Slr's Dept 2000, chief legal advsr Competition Cmmn 2000–04, slr to OFT 2004–06, gen counsel to OFT 2006–08; memb Crown Appts Cmmn 1997–2002; memb Gen Synod C of E 1980–85 and 1987–2005, memb Archbishops' Cncl 1999–2005, vice-chm House of Laity 2000–05, hon lay canon Southwark Cathedral 2004–08, asst curate St Paul's Deptford 2008–11, vicar All Saints' Orpington 2011–; tstee Churches Conservation Tst 2008–13, memb Southwark Cathedral Chapter 2010–12, tstee Orpington Christian Counselling Service 2011–, chaplain Orpington Branch Royal Br Legion 2011–, vice-pres Churches Together in Orpington 2013–16; govr: Burwood Sch Orpington 2012–14, St Olave's Sch Orpington 2013–; *Recreations* swimming, walking, travel, history, Arsenal FC, classic detective fiction; *Style*— The Rev Brian McHenry, CBE; ✉ 1A Keswick Road, Orpington BR6 0EU (☎ 01689 824624, e-mail brian@mchenry.co.uk)

MACHIN, Derek Grenville; s of Eric Machin (d 1982), of Liverpool, and Vera, *née* Adams (d 2004); *b* 3 December 1948, Liverpool; *Educ* Liverpool Inst HS for Boys, Univ of Liverpool (MB ChB); *m* 3 Feb 1973, Dr Pamela Lesley Machin, *née* Halliday; 2 s (David Mark Grenville b 27 March 1980, Nigel Oliver Grenville b 14 Oct 1981); *Career* urologist; house offr Royal Southern Hosp Liverpool 1972–73, sr demonstrator Dept of Anatomy Univ of Liverpool 1973–75, surgical registrar Liverpool rotation 1975–77, middle grade gen surgical registrar St Catherine Hosp Birkenhead, Victoria Central Hosp Wallasey and Broadgreen Hosp Liverpool 1977–79, urological registrar Broadgreen Hosp Liverpool 1980–82; Royal Liverpool Hosp: Merseyside Assoc for Kidney Research research fell 1982–84, urological registrar 1984–85, urological sr registrar 1985–88; Univ Hosp Aintree: conslt urological surgn 1988–, clinical dir of urology 1993–; BMA: memb Cncl 1995–2008 and 2010–, chm Private Practice and Professional Fees Ctee 1995–97, memb Jt Conslts Ctee 1996–2004, chm Private Practice Ctee 1997–, dep chm CCSC Medical Mangrs Ctee 2007–10, dep chm BMA Pension Cmmn 2007–10; Central Conslts and Specialists Ctee: memb 1991–, dep chm 1998–2002, chm Surgical Specialities Sub-Ctee 1992–98, chm Surgical Specialties Sch 2010–12; author of papers on various urological topics and pain syndromes; FRCS 1977; *Recreations* reading, gardening, scuba diving, fine wines, good food; *Style*— Derek Machin, Esq; ✉ Department of Urology, Aintree University Hospital, Lower Lane, Liverpool L9 7AL (☎ 0151 529 3595, fax 0151 529 3772, e-mail derek.machin@aintree.nhs.uk)

MACHIN, Stephen James; s of Maj John Machin, of Sheffield, S Yorks, and Edna, *née* Young; *b* 9 November 1954; *Educ* King Edward VII Sch Sheffield, Univ of Cambridge (MA, LLB); *Children* 3 s (Alexander Peter b 22 April 1980, James Edward Spurway b 29 Dec 1995, Benedict Joshua Spurway b 30 Nov 2001), 2 da (Susannah Helen b 22 April 1982, Isabella Claire b 20 June 1999); *Career* admitted slr 1980, ATII 1982; ptnr: Ashurst Morris Crisp 1987–98, KPMG 1998–2010; *Recreations* golf, music, military history, riding, visiting Southern Africa; *Clubs* Carlton, Minchampton Golf; *Style*— Stephen Machin, Esq

MacHUGH, Linda; *b* Enniskillen, Co Fermanagh; *Educ* Trinity Coll Dublin (BA), Univ of Ulster (DipM); *Career* dir: Irish Linen Guild 1999–2004, NI Textiles and Apparel Assoc 2001–04, Urban Regeneration Strategy Dept for Social Devpt NI 2004–08; princ private sec to the First Min 2008–12, dir of local govt policy Dept of Environment 2012–; tstee Meningitis Research Fndn; *Style*— Mrs Linda MacHugh; ✉ Local Government Policy Division, 1 Causeway Exchange, Bedford Street, Belfast (e-mail linda.machugh@doeni.gov.uk)

McHUGH, Patrick; s of Capt B McHugh (d 1982), and Majorie Ann, *née* Mahoney; *b* 2 June 1952, Liss, Hants; *Educ* Mount St Mary's Coll, KCL (BSc(Eng)), Rose Bruford Coll (BA), Univ of N Glos (Dip Mgmnt Studies); *m* 31 Jan 1975, Henrietta Theresa Maria, da of Dr Hugh Francis Devlin; 1 s (Thomas Charles b 19 May 1981), 2 da (Alice Florence Henrietta Rose b 19 June 1984, Beatrice Lily Henrietta Rosamond b 8 Oct 1991); *Career* project engr (thermal, hydraulic and nuclear energy) CCM Sulzer (France) 1973–76, successively prodn control mangr, product gp mangr (diesel assembly and test), mktg mangr (Belgium) and prodn mangr (diesel assembly, test and press shop) R A Lister (Hawker Sideley Group) 1976–82; Coopers & Lybrand: successively conslt in mfrg and distribution mgmnt 1982–86, managing ptnr (engrg and technol industries) 1986–95; princ EDS 1995, vice-pres A T Kearney 1995–99, dir Strategic Partnership London Ltd 1996–2002, dir Gp e-Commerce J Sainsbury plc 2000–01, dir GlobalNetXChange 2000–01, chm Taste Network Ltd 2000–01, chm The Destination Wine Company 2001, chief exec Trinity Gp 2002–, chm B4baby 2002, chief exec Rangegate Mobile Solutions Ltd 2004–06; chm: Parametric Optimization Solutions Ltd 2005–08, ParOS plc 2006–, Worldlink Mobile plc 2009–, Gelaredan ac treow 2011–14, Bell Eudcn Services 2012–14; dir CCE Enterprises Ltd 2009–11, pres Bell Switzerland 2013–14; chm Media Group Action for Engrg Task Force 1993–95; memb: Inst Ops Mgmnt 1983–, Cncl Fndn for Sci and Technol 1991– (hon sec 2000–), Br Assoc for Sci and Technol 1992, Tomorrow's Company Enquiry 1992–95, City Values Forum 2010–15; fndr memb Guild of Mgmnt Conslts 1993; hon moorings offr Treaddur Bay Sailing Club 1991–98; pres Seabird Assoc 2004–05; pres Soc of Environmental Engrs 2003–11 (hon memb 2003–); fndr chm City Centre for Charity Effectiveness Tst 2004–11; chm La Nuova Musica 2014–; Liveryman: Worshipful Co of Mgmnt Conslts 2004 (Master 2002–03), Worshipful Co of Engrs 2004; CEng 1976, MIMgt 1978, FIMechE 1993, ACA 1994, FRSA 1991, FIMC 1997, CEnv 2010; *Books* Business Process Re-engineering (with H J Johansson, A J Pendlebury and W A Wheeler III, 1993), The Chain Imperative (with Paul Hannon, 1994), Beyond Business Process Reengineering (with Giorgio Merli and W A Wheeler III, 1995); *Recreations* sailing, opera; *Clubs* Trearddur Bay Sailing, Arts; *Style*— Patrick McHugh, Esq; ✉ Lia Fail, Ravenspoint Road, Trearddur Bay, Anglesey LL65 2AX (☎ 01407 861521, e-mail patrickmchugh1@aol.com)

M

McHUGH, Peter; s of Peter McHugh, and May, *née* Mannion (d 1997); *b* 25 October 1946; *Career* journalist; former newspapers incl: Hartlepool Daily Mail, Northern Echo, Newcastle Journal, Daily Mail, The Sun; ed TV-am 1982, head of current affairs Tyne Tees Television 1983, formerly ed The Time...The Place, dir of programmes GMTV 1993–2009, ceo Quiddity Prodns 2009–; *Recreations* journalism; *Style*— Peter McHugh, Esq

McHUGH, Spencer; *Career* planning dir Publicis Dialog 1999–2000, planning dir MBO 2000–02; Orange: head Digital Mktg 2003–08, head Brand Communications 2008–09, mktg dir 2012–16; mktg dir EE 2012–; tstee Plan UK 2012–

McILHENEY, Barry Wilson; s of David Parker McIlheney (d 1979), and Muriel, *née* Wilson (d 2008); *b* 13 May 1958; *Educ* Belfast Royal Acad, Trinity Coll Dublin (BA), City Univ (Dip Journalism); *m* 16 March 1991, Lola, da of Francis Borg (d 1999), and Jean, *née* Pukkey (d 1982); 1 s (Francis Salvador David b 5 June 1992), 1 da (Mary Sophia b 9 March 1996); *Career* reporter London Newspaper Group 1984–85, reviews ed Melody Maker 1985–86, ed Smash Hits 1986–88; managing ed: Empire 1992–94 (ed 1989–91), Premiere 1992–94; md EMAP Metro 1995–98, dir Délégué EMAP France 1999–2000, chief exec Emap élan network 2000–02, ed-in-chief Emap Consumer Media 2002–08, ed-in-chief Sport Media Gp 2008 (head of group editorial 2008–09), chief exec PPA 2010–; Feature Writer of the Year 1985, EMAP Ed of the Year 1987 and 1991, PPA Magazine of the Year 1991, PPA Consumer Magazine Ed of the Year 1993; memb BSME 1986; *Recreations* sport, cinema, travel, popular culture, history; *Clubs* Soho House, Hospital; *Style*— Barry McIlheney, Esq

McILLMURRAY, Prof Malcolm Barron; s of Joseph McIllmurray, and Margot, *née* Jordon; *b* 7 December 1945; *Educ* Taunton's Sch Southampton, London Hosp Med Coll (MB BS), Univ of Nottingham (DM); *m* 27 July 1968, Geraldine Mary, da of Dr Daniel Gerard O'Driscoll (d 1992); 2 da (Joanna Maria (Mrs Kelly) b 1969, Naomi Jane (Mrs Altham) b 1977), 2 s (Daniel Joseph Barron b 1971, Matthew James Barron b 1975); *Career* lectr in therapeutics Univ of Nottingham and hon sr registrar in gen med Nottingham City Hosp 1973–78, Macmillan conslt in med oncology and palliative care Royal Lancaster Infirmary and Westmorland Gen Hosp Kendal 1994–2006 (conslt physician and med oncologist 1978–94); med dir St John's Hospice Lancaster 1985–2002, non-exec dir Blackpool Teaching Hosps NHS Fndn Tst 2014–; med memb Tbnl Service 2007–14; Nat Lederle Bronze awarded to Lancaster Cancer Servs 1991, Ernest Finch lectr Univ of Sheffield 1992, Paul Harris fell Rotary Club of GB 1993; hon prof of biological scis Lancaster Univ; fndr tstee N Lancs and Lakeland Continuing Care Tst 1981–, fndr chm CancerCare – N Lancs and S Lakeland 1984–; govr Bentham Sch; hon fell Univ of Lancaster 2009; FRCP 1985 (MRCP); *Books* ABC of Medical Treatment (contrib, 1979), Essential Accident and Emergency Care (contrib, 1981); author of numerous articles in learned jls; *Style*— Prof Malcolm McIllmurray; ✉ Court House, Over Kellet, Carnforth, Lancashire LA6 1DL

McILRATH, Shaun Fulton; s of Dr Edwin Maynard McIlrath, and Ella Mary, *née* Fulton; *b* 30 January 1963; *Educ* Methodist Coll Belfast, Christ Church Coll, Univ of Kent at Canterbury (BA); *m* 2 Dec 1995, Lisa, da of Edward Snook; 1 s (Rufus Connor b 1997) 1 d (Lily Eve b 1999); *Career* scriptwriter BBC, RTE and ITV 1984–87, account exec The Moorgate Group plc 1988–91, copywriter FCB London 1991–93; creative dir: FCA London 1993–99, HHCL 2000, Heresy 2001– (also fndr), currently global chief creative offr Iris Worldwide; recipient of over 200 nat and int awards; voted UK's Most Innovative

Marketer 2002, Top 20 Most Creative People in Advertising Business Insider 2015; memb D&AD; *Recreations* spending time with family, fitness, food; *Clubs* The Irish; *Style*— Mr Shaun McIlrath

McILROY, Ian; *b* 28 December 1947; *Educ* Glasgow Sch of Art (DA); *m* Diane Elizabeth, *née* Murray; 1 s (Sean b 30 June 1983); *Career* designer; worked for: J & P Coats and William Collins 1972–79, Tayburn Design Group 1979–81; formed: McIlroy Coates 1981, EH6 Design Consultants 1992, Nevis Design Consultants 2001; independent design conslt 2003–; clients incl: Standard Life, The Nat Galleries of Scotland, The Design Cncl, The Clydesdale Bank; awards incl: Design Annual Award of Excellence 1984, D&AD Awards 1980, 1982, 1983 and 1990, Br Letterhead Awards 1981 and 1985, Scottish Designer of the Year runner up 1984, Scottish Annual Report prize 1988 and 1989, Lifetime Achievement Award for Design Scottish Design Award 2006; external degree course assessor graphic design Duncan of Jordanstone Coll of Art Dundee, visiting lectr Northumbria Univ; memb: D&AD Assoc 1980, RSA 1999; FCSD 1991; *Style*— Ian McIlroy, Esq; ✉ 26 Rintoul Place, Edinburgh EH3 5JF (☎ 0131 343 2795, e-mail ian.mcilroy@macunlimited.net)

McILVEEN, David; MLA; *Career* MLA (DUP) N Antrim 2011–; *Style*— David McIlveen, Esq, MLA; ✉ Northern Ireland Assembly, Parliament Buildings, Belfast BT4 3XX

McILVEEN, Michelle; MLA; *Educ* Methodist Coll Belfast, Queen's Univ Belfast (BSc, MSc, PGCE); *Career* cncllr Ards BC 2005–10, MLA (DUP) Strangford 2007–, junior min Office of the First Min 2015, min for regnl devpt 2015–16, min of agriculture, environment and rural affrs 2016–; dep chair Regnl Devpt Ctee 2009–11, chair Culture Arts and Leisure Ctee 2011–, chair Educn Ctee 2014–15; dir Ards Business Centre; govr: Castle Gardens Primary Sch, Killinchy Primary Sch, Nendrum Coll; *Style*— Michelle McIlveen, MLA; ✉ 7 The Square, Comber BT23 5DX (☎ 0289 1871441, e-mail mail@michellemcilveen.org.uk); Northern Ireland Assembly, Parliament Buildings, Belfast BT4 3XX (Twitter @MMcIlveenMLA)

MacILWAINE, David Robin; s of Robin MacIlwaine, and Anne MacIlwaine (d 1967); *b* 16 December 1947; *Educ* Rydens Sch Walton-on-Thames, Univ of Leicester (BA); *Partner*, Rose Gray; 1 s (Dante MacIlwaine Gray b 1973), 3 step c (Hester Gray b 1963, Lucy Gray b 1964, Ossie Gray b 1965); *Career* Christies Contemporary Art 1986–89, sculpture dir Berkeley Square Gallery 1989–96, ind art conslt 1996–, ptnr EXACT (exhbns in art and architecture) 1997–, creative dir Hubble Space Telescope Inc USA 1998–; *Recreations* sculpting; *Style*— David MacIlwaine, Esq; ✉ 7 Plympton Street, London NW8 8AB (☎ and fax 020 7258 1780)

McILWRAITH, Dr George Robert; s of Alexander Herd McIlwraith (d 1971), of Ruislip, Middx, and Kathleen Joan, *née* Heaton (d 1996); *b* 15 July 1941; *Educ* Merchant Taylors', Univ of St Andrews (MB ChB); *m* 24 July 1982, Isabel Margaret, da of Harry Jack Manwaring (d 1988), of Marden, Kent; 1 s (Harry Alexander b 1987); *Career* various jr appts in UK hosps; asst prof of internal med Pulmonary Div Univ of Michigan Med Sch 1979–80, conslt physician Maidstone Dist Hosps (merged forming Maidstone and Tunbridge Wells NHS Tst 2000) 1981–2007; author of pubns, chapters, papers and articles on cardiological and respiratory med matters; memb Br Thoracic Soc; FRCP 1988; *Style*— Dr George McIlwraith; ✉ Noah's Ark Farmhouse, East Sutton Road, Headcorn, Ashford, Kent TN27 9PS (☎ 01622 891278, e-mail mcilwraithgr@aol.com)

McINNERNY, Tim; s of William Ronald McInnerny, and Mary Joan, *née* Gibbings; *b* 18 September 1956; *Educ* Marling Sch Stroud, Univ of Oxford (BA); *Career* actor; *Theatre* performances incl: Lorenzaccio Story (Edinburgh Festival), Pygmalion (Glasgow Citizens), The Maid's Tragedy (Glasgow Citizens), Once A Catholic (Leicester Haymarket), Local Affairs, Hamlet, School for Scandal (Leicester Haymarket), Valued Friends (Hampstead), The Rocky Horror Show (Piccadilly), Romeo & Juliet (RSC), 'Tis Pity She's a Whore, Twelfth Night, Comedians (West Yorkshire Playhouse), Gaucho (Hampstead Theatre Co), Cloud 9 (Old Vic), The Provoked Wife (Old Vic), The Lady from the Sea (Almeida); Royal Exchange Manchester: The Misanthrope, PVT Wars, The Detective Story, One Flew Over The Cuckoos Nest, The Caretaker, Twelfth Night, The Unseen Hand, Lone Star, Othello (Globe) 2007, What the Butler Saw (Vaudeville) 2012; NT: The Government Inspector, Pravda, Hamlet, Mappa Mundi; *Television* incl: Blackadder, Blackadder II, Blackadder Goes Forth, Edge of Darkness, Sherlock Holmes, A Very British Coup, Shadow of the Noose, August Saturday, The Comic Strip Presents, The Great Kandinsky, The Vice, Longitude, Gunpowder, Treason and Plot, Miss Marple: Murder at the Vicarage, The Line of Beauty, Spooks, The Devil's Whore, The Bleak Old Shop of Stuff; *Films* Wetherby (Golden Bear Berlin Film Festival), Erik The Viking, 101 Dalmatians, Richard III (Golden Bear Berlin Film Festival), Fairy Tale – A True Story, Rogue Trader, Notting Hill, Blackadder Millennium, 102 Dalmations, My Napoleon, Emperor's New Clothes, Hot Dog, Casanova, Johnny English Reborn; *Recreations* acting, tennis, reading; *Style*— Tim McInnerny, Esq

McINNES, Prof Colin Robert; MBE (2014); s of Ian McInnes, of Glasgow, and Marion, *née* McDonald; *b* 12 February 1968, Glasgow; *Educ* Univ of Glasgow (BSc, PhD, DSc); *m* 7 March 1992, Karen, *née* McLaughlin; 3 s (Calum b 16 July 1996, Gregor b 15 April 1999, Ruaridh b 17 Aug 2001); *Career* lectr, reader and prof of space systems engrg Univ of Glasgow 1991–2004, prof of engrg science Univ of Strathclyde 2004–14, James Watt chair prof of engrg science Univ of Glasgow 2014–; Bruce-Preller Prize Lectureship RSE 1997, Pardoe Space Award RAeS 2000, Philip Leverhulme Prize Leverhulme Tst 2001, Ackroyd Stuart Prize RAeS 2004, Makdougall-Brisbane Prize RSE 2006, Leonov Medal 2007, Kelvin Prize RSE 2012; FRSE 2001, FREng 2003; *Publications* Solar Sailing (1999); contrib to numerous jls on space systems engrg; *Recreations* photography, hill walking, books; *Style*— Prof Colin McInnes, MBE, FREng, FRSE; ✉ School of Engineering, James Watt Building, University of Glasgow, Glasgow G12 8QQ (☎ 0141 330 8511, e-mail colin.mcinnes@glasgow.ac.uk)

MacINNES, Hamish; OBE (1980), BEM (1965); s of Duncan MacInnes (d 1987), of Gourock, Renfrewshire, and Catherine, *née* MacDonald (d 1967); *b* 7 July 1930; *Educ* Gatehouse of Fleet Public Sch; *Career* writer, mfr, film dir (Glencoe Productions Ltd); designer of mountain rescue equipment stretchers (used internationally), first all metal ice axe and terodactyl climbing tools; dep ldr Everest SW Face expedition 1975 (taken part in 20 other expeditions to various parts of the world), special advsr to BBC and feature films, author of 34 books; former pres Alpine Climbing Gp, fndr and former ldr Glencoe Mountain Rescue Team, hon memb Scottish Mountaineering Club, hon memb Alpine Club, former hon dir Leishman Rescue Laboratory; fndr and hon pres Search and Rescue Dog Assoc, patron Guide Dogs for the Blind, co-fndr Snow and Avalanche Fndn of Scotland (SAFOS); Scottish Award for Excellence in Mountain Culture, Scottish Sports Hall of Fame; Hon DSc: Univ of Aberdeen 1988, Heriot-Watt Univ 1992; Hon LLD: Univ of Glasgow, Univ of Dundee 2004; Hon DUniv Stirling 1997; *Style*— Hamish MacInnes, Esq, OBE, BEM; ✉ Tigh a'Voulin, Glencoe, Argyll PH49 4HX (☎ 01855 811258)

McINNES, Sheriff Principal John Colin; QC (Scot 1989), DL (Fife 1998); s of Ian Whitton McInnes (d 1976), of Cupar, Fife, and Lucy Margaret, *née* Wilson; *b* 21 November 1938; *Educ* Cargilfield Sch Edinburgh, Merchiston Castle Sch Edinburgh, BNC Oxford (BA), Univ of Edinburgh (LLB); *m* 6 Aug 1966, Elisabeth Mabel, da of late Hugh Royden, and Anne Neilson, of Kelso, Roxburghshire; 1 s (Ian b 1969), 1 da (Iona b 1972); *Career* 2 Lt 8 RTR 1956–58, Lt Fife and Forfar Yeo Scottish Horse TA 1958–64; advocate in practice Scottish Bar 1963–72, dir R Mackness & Co Ltd 1963–70, tutor Univ of Edinburgh 1964–72, chm Fios Group Ltd (continental quilt manufacturers) 1970–72; Parly candidate (Cons) Aberdeen N 1964; memb Ct Univ of St Andrews 1983–91, chm Fife Family Conciliation Serv 1988–90; vice-pres: Security Serv Tbnl 1989–2001, Intelligence Serv Tbnl 1994–2001, Cmmr for Northern Lighthouses 2000–06; chm Youth Ct Project Gp (Scot) 2002); memb: Information Technology Forum (Scotland) 1996–2000, Criminal Justice Forum (Scotland) 1996–2000, Judicial Studies Ctee (Scotland) 1997–2000, Efficiency Task Gp 1997–98, Investigatory Powers Tbnl 2000–; Sheriff: Lothians and Peebles 1973–74, Tayside Central and Fife 1974–2000; Sheriff Principal South Strathclyde, Dumfries and Galloway 2000–06; chm ctee to reform summary criminal justice in Scotland 2001–04, memb Parole Bd for Scotland 2005–11; pres The Sheriff's Assoc 1995–97; Hon LLD Univ of St Andrews 1994; *Books* Divorce Law and Practice in Scotland; *Recreations* fishing, shooting, skiing, photography; *Style*— Sheriff Principal John McInnes, QC, DL; ✉ Parkneuk, Blebocraigs, Cupar, Fife KY15 5UG

McINNES, Kenneth William; QPM (2002); s of William Lee McInnes (d 1980), of Alexandria, Dunbartonshire, and Jessie Harper, *née* Mathieson; *b* 15 January 1949; *Educ* Vale of Leven Acad, Univ of Glasgow (BSc); *m* 21 Nov 1970, Eileen, da of late William Lynch, of Clydebank, Dunbartonshire, and Mary Walls; 1 s (Kenneth b 1972), 1 da (Fiona b 1979); *Career* systems analyst Babcock & Wilcox 1970–73, City of Glasgow Police 1973–75, Strathclyde Police 1975–96 (divnl cdr Dumbarton 1992–96), HM Inspectorate of Constabulary 1997–98, Asst Chief Constable Lothian and Borders Police 1998–2000, Dep Chief Constable Fife Constabulary 2000–01, Asst Inspector of Constabulary 2002–; memb ACPOS 1998; former footballer: St Mirren FC, Scottish Police nat team; *Recreations* football; *Style*— Kenneth McInnes, Esq, QPM; ✉ HM Inspectorate of Constabulary, St Andrew's House, Regent Road, Edinburgh EH1 3DG (☎ 0131 244 5606, fax 0131 244 4131)

McINNES, Stuart Cameron; MBE (2006); *b* 30 December 1950, Edinburgh; *Educ* Univ of Hull (LLB), Univ of Madrid (LLM); *m* 3 June 1989, Caroline Lindsay, *née* Way; 1 s (Theodore Cameron b 19 March 1992); *Career* admitted slr 1981; conslt Squire Patton Boggs, arbitrator Ct of Arbitration for Sport (CAS); memb Law Soc of England and Wales 1981–; dir Br Show Jumping Assoc; chair Drug Abuse Resistance Educn (DARE) 1994–; *Recreations* motorsport, opera, reading, skiing, travel; *Style*— Stuart McInnes, Esq, MBE; ✉ Bay House, 5 Court Street, Nayland, Suffolk CO6 4JL (☎ 01206 264018); Squire Patton Boggs, 7 Devonshire Square, London EC2M 4YH (☎ 020 7655 1388, e-mail stuart.mcinnes@squirepb.com, website www.squirepb.com)

McINTOSH, Alisdair Douglas; s of Alexander McIntosh (d 2000), and Doreen Alexandra, *née* Dixon; *b* 19 July 1963, Addlestone, Surrey; *Educ* Strode's Sch Egham, Univ of Durham (BA), Univ of London (MA); *m* Sarah Mary Burnett; 1 da (Holly b 1999), 1 s (Hector b 2001); *Career* HM Treasy 1987–91, UK perm rep to EU Brussels 1991–96, European Cmmn 1996–99, Scottish Exec 1999–2009, dir Scotland Office 2009–; non-exec dir: Scottish Urban Regeneration Forum 2005–09, Real Life Options 2008–; *Recreations* hills, books, visual arts; *Style*— Alisdair McIntosh, Esq; ✉ 81 St John's Road, Edinburgh EH12 6NN; Scotland Office, Dover House, Whitehall, London SW1A 2AU (e-mail alisdair.mcintosh@scotlandoffice.gsi.gov.uk)

McINTOSH, David Angus; s of Robert Angus McIntosh, of Scotland, and Monica Joan Sherring, *née* Hillier; *b* 10 March 1944; *Educ* Selwood Co Sch Frome; *m* 14 Sept 1968, Jennifer Mary, da of Jack Dixon, of Mill Hill, London; 2 da (Sarah Alison b 1973, Louise b 1978); *Career* clerk Ames Kent & Rathwell Somerset, articled clerk Davies Arnold Cooper 1964, admitted slr 1968, sr ptnr Davies Arnold Cooper 1976–2006 (ptnr 1968, conslt 2006–); Int Bar Assoc: chm ctee on Consumer Affrs, Advtg, Unfair Competition and Product Liability, chm Disaster Litigation Worldwide Prog Strasbourg; Law Soc: memb various working parties on reform and admin of civil law, memb Jt Working Ctee of the Senate of the Bar and Law Soc (made recommendations to Lord Chllr on proposed US/UK Reciprocal Enforcements Convention and allied jurisdictional matters), memb Supreme Court Procedure Ctee 1994–, memb Cncl 1996–, chm Civil Litigation Ctee; US Int Assoc of Defense Counsel: memb Exec Ctee, memb Excess and Reinsurance Product Liability Litigation Ctee, memb Toxic and Hazardous Substances Litigation Ctee; memb Legal Servs Consultative Ctee Dept for Constitutional Affrs 2003–, chair Governance Bd Chartered Inst of Insurers 2006–; Freeman City of London, Liveryman Worshipful Co of Blacksmiths; pres Law Soc of England and Wales 2001–02, chm City of London Slrs' Co 2004–; memb: Int Bar Assoc, Law Soc, US Int Assoc of Defense Counsel, Def Res and Trial Lawyers Assoc of America, Professional Liability Underwriters Assoc, lay memb Cncl School of Pharmacy Univ of London 2003–04; CIArb, Notre Dame Law Sch accredited mediator; *Publications* regular contrib to legal, insurance, and pharmaceutical journals, memb Editorial Bd The Litigator; *Recreations* family, golf, fitness; *Clubs* Chigwell Golf, City Livery, Real Sotogrande Golf, Caledonian; *Style*— David McIntosh, Esq; ✉ Davies Arnold Cooper, 6–8 Bouverie Street, London EC4Y 8DD (☎ 020 7936 2222, fax 020 7936 2020)

McINTOSH, John Charles; CBE (2013, OBE 1996); s of Arthur McIntosh, and Betty, *née* Styche; *b* 6 February 1946, Walton-on-Thames, Surrey; *Educ* Ebury Sch, Shoreditch Coll, Univ of Sussex (MA); *Career* London Oratory Sch: asst master 1967–71, dep headmaster 1971–77, headmaster 1977–2007; chm Educn Ctee Ampleforth Coll 2007–10; visiting tutor Bucks Univ 2005–10; memb: Catholic Union of GB 1978–, Educn Gp Centre for Policy Studies 1982–99, Health Educn Cncl 1985–88, HMC 1986–2007, Educn Unit Advsy Cncl Inst of Econ Affairs 1988–95, Nat Curriculum Cncl 1990–93, Centre for Policy Studies 2006–, Nat Curriculum Review Advsy Ctee 2011–13, Teachers' Standards Review Ctee 2011–13, Bd Nat Coll for Sch Leadership 2012–14, Teaching Agency Advsy Ctee 2012–13; tstee The Oratory Oxford 2003–, chm of tstees London Oratory Sch Schola Fndn 2006–15, tstee English Schs Orch and Choir 2007–, dean Acad of St Cecilia 2007–, tstee W London Free Sch Multi-Acad Tst (hon patron 2014–); govr: St Philip's Prep Sch London 1985–2015 (chm of govrs 2007–15), More House Sch London 2008–11, W London Free Sch 2011–13; memb: Abbot of Ampleforth Advsy Bd 1997–2010, Acad Advsy Cncl Univ of Buckingham 2013–, Educn Ctee David Ross Educn Tst 2013–15, Interim Exec Bd Hurlingham & Chelsea Sch 2014–15, Interim Exec Bd Langford Sch 2014–15, Cncl Univ of Buckingham 2015– (vice-chm 2016–); advsr to the leader Hammersmith and Fulham LA, advsr W London Free Sch Steering Ctee 2010–11, DFE external advsr for free schs 2011–; chm: Bilingual Mgmnt Ctee Hammersmith and Fulham 2009–12, Mgmnt Intervention Bd St Francis of Assisi Sch Kensington 2013–15, Cmmn on Assessment Without Levels 2015; dir Hackney Free Sch Tst 2016–; Hon DLitt Univ of Westminster 2016; Hon FCP, FRSA, Hon FASC; KMCO 2012; *Recreations* playing the organ, ballet, opera; *Clubs* Athenaeum, Reform, House of St Barnabas; *Style*— John McIntosh, Esq, CBE; ☎ 07718 910888, e-mail cantemus@mac.com

MACINTOSH, Kenneth Donald; MSP; s of Farquhar and Margaret Macintosh, of Edinburgh; *b* 15 January 1962; *Educ* Royal HS Edinburgh, Univ of Edinburgh (MA); *m* Claire Kinloch, *née* Anderson; 2 s (Douglas b 1 May 1999, Lachlan b 23 March 2003), 4 da (Catriona b 30 May 2001, Annie b 2 Nov 2005, Isobel b 17 Nov 2007, Ruth b 11 April 2010); *Career* joined BBC 1987, sr broadcast news and current affairs journalist until 1999; MSP (Lab) Eastwood 1999–2016, MSP (Lab) W of Scotland 2016–; presiding offr Scottish Parl 2016–; *Recreations* sport (football, golf, tennis); *Style*— Ken Macintosh, MSP; ✉ Eastwood Parliamentary Office, 1 Spiersbridge Way, Thornliebank, East Renfrewshire G46 8NG (☎ 0141 620 6310, e-mail ken.macintosh.msp@parliament.scot, website www.kenmacintosh.scot, Twitter @KenMacintoshMSP)

McINTOSH, Sir Neil; kt (2000), CBE (1990), DL (Dumfriesshire 1998); *Educ* King's Park Sr Secdy Sch Glasgow; *m* Marie; 1 s (Neil), 2 da (Hazel, Lorna); *Career* early career in mgmnt servs and personnel: Honeywell Controls, Stewarts & Lloyds, Berks Oxford and Reading Jt Mgmnt Servs Unit, Lanark County Cncl, Inverness County Cncl; Highland

Regnl Cncl: personnel offr 1975–81, dir of manpower servs 1981–85; chief exec: Dumfries & Galloway Regnl Cncl 1985–92, Strathclyde Cncl 1992–96; head Convention of Scottish Local Authorities Consultancy 1996–99, chief counting offr for Scotland Scottish Parl Referendum 1997, chm Cmmn on Local Govt and the Scottish Parl 1999, memb UK Electoral Cmmn until 2008, advsr NI Review of Public Administration 2002–05, chm Judicial Appts Bd for Scotland 2002–08, Civil Serv cmmr 2008–; convenor Scottish Cncl for Voluntary Orgns 1996–2001, chm Nat Companies Contact Gp 1996–98, advsr Joseph Rowntree Fndn 2000–05 (chm Governance Ctee), memb Broadcasting Cncl for Scotland 2007–; tstee: National Museums of Scotland, Dumfries Theatre Royal 2003–06; non-exec dir BT Scotland 1998–2002; JP 1999–2007; Hon DHL Syracuse Univ 1993, Hon LLD Glasgow Caledonian Univ 1999; memb Chartered Inst of Secs, FIPD, FRSA; *Recreations* antique bottle collecting, dry-stane dyking, hill walking, curio collecting, local history; *Style*— Sir Neil McIntosh, CBE

McINTOSH, Dr Robert (Bob); CBE (2013); s of Robert H McIntosh, of Ayr, and Kathleen, *née* Frew; *b* 6 October 1951; *Educ* Linlithgow Acad, Univ of Edinburgh (BSc, PhD); *m* 23 Jan 2009, Linda, *née* Watt; *Career* Foresty Cmmn: asst dist offr Thetford Forest Dist 1973–75, asst dist offr Galloway Forest Dist 1975–78, silviculturist Northern Research Station 1978–84, dist mangr Kielder Forest Dist 1984–94, dir (ops) Forest Enterprise 1994–97, chief exec Forest Enterprise 1997–2003, dir Scotland Forestry Cmmn 2003–, dir environment and forestry Scottish Govt 2012–; contrib various articles to jls; FICFor 1975; *Recreations* farming, shooting, stalking; *Clubs* Farmers'; *Style*— Dr Bob McIntosh, CBE; ✉ East Brackley Grange, by Kinross KY13 9LU (☎ 01577 862057); Forestry Commission, 231 Corstorphine Road, Edinburgh EH12 7AT (☎ 0300 067 6456, e-mail bob.mcintosh@forestry.gsi.gov.uk)

McINTOSH, Thomas Lee; s of John Christian McIntosh (d 1967), of Washington DC, and Mildred White (d 1953); *b* 3 December 1938; *Educ* Juilliard Sch of Music (BSc, MSc); *m* 30 Sept 1982, Miranda Harrison Vincent, da of Vincent Booth Reckitt (d 1975), of Otley, W Yorks; *Career* conductor and music dir London City Chamber Orch 1973–; artistic dir: E Anglian Summer Music Festival 1978–, Penang Malaysia Music Festival 1986 and 1987, Opera Anglia 1989–, Artsanglia Ltd 1988–; princ guest conductor Canton Symphony Orch 1994; contributing ed eighteenth century symphonic music for Garland Symphony Series; Arrangements for Orch of the following: Valentine Waltzes (George Antheil), Rag Suite (various composers), Flower Rag Suite (Scott Joplin), Variations on Seven Japanese Folk Songs for Piano and Orchestra, Concerto for Piano (4 hands) and Orchestra 2007; FRSA; *Recreations* gardening, theatre; *Clubs* Civil Service; *Style*— Thomas McIntosh, Esq

McINTOSH OF HUDNALL, Baroness (Life Peer UK 1999), of Hampstead in the London Borough of Camden; Genista Mary McIntosh; *b* 23 September 1946; *Educ* Hemel Hempstead GS, Univ of York (BA); *m* 30 Jan 1971 (m dis 1990), Neil Scott Wishart McIntosh; 1 s (Hon Alexander b 22 Dec 1975), 1 da (Hon Flora b 25 April 1979); *Career* dir Marmont Management Ltd 1984–86; Royal Shakespeare Company: casting dir 1972–77, planning controller 1977–84, sr admin 1986–90, assoc prodr 1990; chief exec Royal Opera House 1997, exec dir Royal National Theatre 1997–2002 (also 1990–96), princ Guildhall Sch of Music and Drama 2002–03, tstee Southbank Sinfonia; memb Bd: The Roundhouse Tst, Nat Opera Studio, RSC; Hon DUniv York 1998, Hon DUniv Middlesex 2002, Hon DUniv City 2002; hon fell Goldsmiths Coll London 2003; FRSA; *Recreations* music, gardening; *Style*— The Baroness McIntosh of Hudnall

McINTOSH OF PICKERING, Baroness (Life Peer UK 2015), of Pickering of the Vale of York in the County of North Yorkshire Anne Caroline Ballingall McIntosh; da of Dr A B McIntosh, and G L McIntosh, *née* Thomson; *b* 20 September 1954; *Educ* Harrogate Coll, Univ of Edinburgh (LLB); *m* 19 Sept 1992, John Harvey; *Career* postgraduate studies Univ of Aarhus Denmark 1977–78, trainee EC Competition Directorate Brussels 1978, legal advsr Didier & Assocs Brussels 1979–80, trained Scottish Bar 1980–82, admitted Faculty of Advocates Edinburgh 1982, advocate Euro Community Law Office Brussels 1982–83, political advsr Euro Democratic Gp (EDG) Euro Parliament 1983–89; MEP (Cons): Essex N E 1989–94, Essex N and Suffolk S 1994–99; Br Conservative spokesman Euro Parliament: Tport Ctee 1992–99, Rules of Procedure Ctee 1992–94; memb Euro Parliament Delegation with: Norway 1989–94 (chm 1994–95), Poland 1994–97, Czech Rep 1997–99; memb: Social Affrs Ctee 1992–94, Women's Rights Ctee 1992–94, Euro Scrutiny Ctee, Euro Standing Ctee; substitute memb: Legal Affrs Ctee 1989–, Jt Parly Ctee with EEA 1995–; asst EDG whip 1989–92, elected to Bureau Br Section EPP 1994–; MP (Cons): Vale of York 1997–2010, Thirsk and Malton 2010–15 (Parly candidate (Cons) Workington 1987); shadow min for Culture Media and Broadcasting 2001–02, shadow min for Tport 2002–, shadow min for Environment and Tport 2003–; memb Select Ctee on Environment, Tport and the Regions (also Tport Sub-Ctee); memb Exec Cncl Br Conservative Assoc Belgium 1987–89; memb Yorks Agric Soc; memb Anglo-Danish Soc; exec 1922 Ctee; pres: Anglia Enterprise in Europe 1989–99, Yorkshire First Enterprise in Yorkshire 1998–; memb: Chllr's Cncl Anglia Poly Univ until 1999, Governing Bd Writtle Coll until 1999; *Recreations* swimming, reading, cinema; *Clubs* Royal Over-Seas League, RAC; *Style*— The Baroness McIntosh of Pickering; ☎ 01845 523835

McINTYRE, Blanche; *Educ* CCC Oxford (BA); *Career* director; *Theatre* incl: Accolade (Finborough Theatre) 2011 and (St James Theatre) 2014, When Did You Last See My Mother? (Trafalgar Studios) 2011, Foxfinder (Finborough Theatre) 2011, Angle Plays (Bush Theatre) 2012, The Only True History of Lizzie Finn (Southwark Playhouse) 2012, The Seagull (Headlong) 2013, The Birthday Party (Manchester Royal Exchange) 2013, Ciphers (Out of Joint) 2013, The Nutcracker (Nuffield Theatre) 2013, Tonight at 8.30 (Nuffield Theatre and Tour) 2014, The Comedy of Errors (Shakespeare's Globe) 2014, Arcadia (UK Tour) 2015, As You Like It (Shakespeare's Globe) 2015, The Oresteia (HOME Manchester) 2015, Two Noble Kinsmen (RSC) 2016, Noises Off (Nottingham Playhouse and Tour) 2016, Welcome Home, Captain Fox! (Donmar Warehouse) 2016; Critics' Circle Most Promising Newcomer 2011, Best Director TMA UK Theatre Awards 2013; *Style*— Ms Blanche McIntyre; ✉ c/o Giles Smart, United Agents Ltd, 12–26 Lexington Street, London W1F 0LE (☎ 020 3214 0800, e-mail gsmart@unitedagents.co.uk, website www.unitedagents.co.uk)

McINTYRE, Sir Donald Conroy; kt (1992), CBE (1985, OBE 1975); s of George McIntyre, and Hermyn, *née* Conroy; *b* 22 October 1934; *Educ* Mount Albert GS NZ, Auckland Teachers Trg Coll, Guildhall Sch of Music London; *m* 29 July 1961, Jill Redington, da of Norton Mitchell, DFC (d 1989), of Barnstaple, Devon; 3 da (Ruth Frances b 1965, Lynn Hazel b 1967, Jenny Jane b 1971); *Career* int opera singer, bass baritone; debut UK Welsh Nat Opera 1959; princ bass: Sadler's Wells Opera 1960–67, Royal Opera House Covent Garden 1967–, Bayreuth Festival 1967–84; frequent int guest appearances: Metropolitan (NY), Vienna, Munich, Hamburg, Paris, Buenos Aires, La Scala (Milan), Berlin, Sydney and more; princ roles incl: Wotan and Wanderer in The Ring, Dutchman in Flying Dutchman, Telramund in Lohengrin, Amfortas, Klingsor and Gurnemanz in Parsifal, Kurwenal in Tristan and Isolde, Hans Sachs in Die Meistersinger, Barak in Die Frau Ohne Schatten, Golaud in Pelleas and Melisande, Pizzaro and Rocco in Fidelio, Kasper in Der Freischütz, Scarpia in Tosca, title role in Macbeth, Nick Shadow in Rake's Progress, Count in The Marriage of Figaro, title role in Cardillac, Shakloviti in Khovanshchina; numerous concert appearances worldwide; appeared as: Hans Sachs in Die Meistersinger (first ever staged prodn of this opera in NZ) 1990, Balstrode in Peter Grimes (Munich) 1991–92, Boris in Lady Macbeth of Mtsensk 1993; video films incl: Der Fliegende Holländer 1975, Electra 1979, Bayreuth Centenary Ring 1981, Die Meistersinger 1984, Mandryka in Arabella (San Francisco), Baron Prus in The Makropulos Case (Toulouse and Brussels), Trulove in The Rake's Progress (Brussels); recording incl: Pelleas and Melisande, The Messiah, Beethoven's Ninth Symphony, Damnation of Faust, Il Trovotore, Oedipus Rex, The Ring, Parsifal; Fidelio Medal (Assoc of Int Dirs of Opera) 1989, NZ Commemoration Award 1990; life memb Auckland Choral Soc; *Recreations* swimming, tennis, farming, walking; *Style*— Sir Donald McIntyre, CBE; ✉ c/o Ingpen & Williams Ltd, 7 St George's Court, 131 Putney Bridge Road, London SW15 2PA (☎ 020 8874 3222, fax 020 8877 3113)

MACINTYRE, Donald John; s of Kenneth MacKenzie Campbell Macintyre (d 1988), and Margaret Rachel, *née* Freeman; *b* 27 January 1947; *Educ* Bradfield Coll, ChCh Oxford (BA), Univ Coll Cardiff (Dip Journalism); *Children* 1 s (James b 18 August 1979); *Career* journalist The Sunday Mercury 1971–75, industrial corr The Daily Express 1975–77, labour corr The Times 1977–83; labour ed: The Sunday Times 1983–85, The Times 1985–86, The Independent 1986–87; political ed: The Sunday Telegraph 1987–89, The Sunday Correspondent 1989–90, The Independent on Sunday 1990–93; The Independent: political ed 1993–96, chief political commentator 1996–, asst ed 2003–; *Books* Talking About Trade Unions (1980), Strike (co-author, 1985), Mandelson and the Making of New Labour (1999); *Style*— Donald Macintyre, Esq

MACINTYRE, Iain Melfort Campbell; s of late John Macintyre, of Edinburgh, and late Mary, *née* Campbell; *Educ* Daniel Stewart's Coll Edinburgh, Univ of Edinburgh (MB ChB, MD); *m* Tessa Lorna Mary, da of Rev Basil E R Millar; 3 da (Carol Anne Mary, Alison Jane, Lucy Nicola); *Career* trained in surgery Edinburgh and Durban SA; lectr in surgery: Univ of Edinburgh 1974–78, Univ of Natal SA 1978–79; conslt surgn with administrative responsibility Gen Surgical Unit Leith Hosp Edinburgh 1979–85, conslt surgn Gen Surgical and Gastro-Intestinal Unit Western Gen Hosp Edinburgh 1985–2002, conslt surgeon Edinburgh Royal Infirmary 2002–04; chm Lister Postgraduate Inst 1995–2000 (asst dir of studies 1991–95), Apothecaries' lectr in history of medicine Univ of Edinburgh 2006–; memb Nat Med Advsy Ctee 1991–94; vice-pres RCSEd 2003–06 (examiner 1979–2009, examiner Intercollegiate Bd in Gen Surgery 1994–99, memb Cncl 1990–2000, dir of Educn 1997–2000, hon sec 2001–03, vice-pres 2003–06); chm Surgeons Hall Tst 2004–07, pres Br Soc for the History of Med 2015–17; Cncl of Europe fell 1990, Continuing Med Educn fell in minimally invasive surgery 1992; Surgn to HM The Queen in Scotland 1997–2004; FRCSEd 1973, FRCPEd 1997; *Books* Venous Thrombo-Embolic Disease (ed with C V Ruckley, 1975), Endoscopic Surgery for General Surgeons (ed and contrib, 1995), Surgeons' Lives (ed with I F MacLaren, 2005), An Illustrated History of Scottish Medicine (jtly, 2011); *Recreations* reading, music; *Clubs* Moynihan Chirurgical, Aesculapians; *Style*— Mr Iain Macintyre; ✉ Royal College of Surgeons, Nicolson Street, Edinburgh EH8 9DW (☎ 0131 527 1600)

McINTYRE, Ian James; s of Hector Harold McIntyre (d 1978), of Inverness, and Annie Mary Michie (d 1979); *b* 9 December 1931; *Educ* Prescot GS, St John's Coll Cambridge (MA, pres Cambridge Union), Coll of Europe Bruges; *m* 24 July 1954, Leik Sommerfelt, da of Benjamin Vogt (d 1970), of Kragerø, Norway; 2 s (Andrew James, Neil Forbes), 2 da (Anne Leik, Katharine Elspeth); *Career* Nat Serv cmmnd Intelligence Corps; writer and broadcaster; BBC: current affrs talks prodr 1957–59, ed At Home and Abroad 1959–60, mgmnt trg organiser 1960–61, broadcasting contract 1970–76; controller: Radio 4 1976–78, Radio 3 1978–87; assoc ed The Times 1989–90; prog servs offr ITA 1961–62, dir of info and res Scot Cons Central Office Edinburgh 1962–70; author of book reviews for The Times, The Spectator and The Independent; contrib Oxford DNB; Parly candidate (Cons) Roxburgh, Selkirk and Peebles gen election 1966; *Books* The Proud Doers: Israel after Twenty Years (1968), Words: Reflections on the Uses of Language (1975), Dogfight: the Transatlantic Battle over Airbus (1992), The Expense of Glory: A Life of John Reith (1993), Dirt & Deity: A Life of Robert Burns (1995), Garrick (1999, Annual Book Prize Soc for Theatre Research), Joshua Reynolds: The Life & Times of the First President of the Royal Academy (2003), Hester: The Remarkable Life of Dr Johnson's 'Dear Mistress' (2008); *Recreations* walking, swimming, gardening; *Clubs* Cambridge Union; *Style*— Ian McIntyre, Esq; ✉ Spylaw House, Newlands Avenue, Radlett, Hertfordshire WD7 8EL (☎ 01923 853532, e-mail ian.mcintyre@waitrose.com)

McINTYRE, Keith Thomas; s of Gordon Leslie McIntyre, of Edinburgh, and Sheila, *née* McDonald; *b* 22 December 1959; *Educ* Trinity Acad Secdy Sch Edinburgh, Dundee Coll of Art (Drumfolk travelling scholar, Farquar Reid travelling scholar), Barcelona Paper Workshop; *m* 30 Dec 1983, Sheenagh Margaret Patience; 2 s (Lewis Cathcart b 22 Oct 1987, Casey John b 4 Sept 1991); *Career* artist; course ldr Fine Art Univ of Northumbria at Newcastle 1999–, visiting artist-in-residence Ludwig Fndn Havana Art Tst 1999, Louie A Brown Int Fell Valdosta State Univ Georgia 1997–98; solo exhibitions: Shore Gallery Leith 1982, 369 Gallery Edinburgh 1984 and 1986, Compass Gallery Glasgow 1985, Pittenweem Arts Festival Fife 1985, Raab Galerie Berlin 1987, Raab Gallery London 1988, The Paintings for Jock Tamson's Bairns (Tramway Theatre Glasgow and Raab Gallery London) 1990, Pittencrieff House Museum Dunfermline 1995, Northern Print Gallery N Shields 1996, Galerie Christian Dam Copenhagen 1996, Boukamel Contemporary Art London 1997, Valdosta State Univ Georgia 1998, GSU Gallery Statesboro Georgia 1998, Belenkey Gallery NY 1998, Harmonia Galerie Jyvaskyla Finalnd 2000, Galerie Habana Havana Cuba 2001, Indiana State Univ 2004; group exhibitions incl: Saltire Soc Edinburgh 1982, Clare Hall Cambridge 1984 and 1986, Five Contemporary Scottish Artists (Leinster Fine Art London) 1985, Open Circle (Schweinfurt Exhibition Germany) 1986, De Brakke Gallery Amsterdam 1987, The Lion Rampant: New Scottish Painting and Photography (Artspace San Francisco) 1988, Scottish Myths (Scot Gallery Edinburgh) 1990, Galerie Bureaux & Magasins Ostend Belgium 1991, Divers Memories (Pitt Rivers Museum Oxford), Premio Marco (MOMA Monterrey Mexico) 1997, Hibrida (Bradford Art Gallery) 2002, Hibrida II (Brno Museum of Art Czech Repub) 2005; public collections incl: Aberdeen Art Gallery, BBC, Dundee Coll of Commerce, Scot Nat Gallery of Modern Art, W Sussex CC; arts projects incl: visual dir Jock Tamson's Bairns (Tramway Theatre Glasgow) 1989–90, jt film venture (with Timothy Neat and John Berger) 1990; pt/t teacher in fine art Glasgow Sch of Art 1984–89, New Constellations (Baltic Centre for Contemporary Art Gateshead) 2004, keynote essay for Baltic Yearbook 2004; sr lectr in painting (now reader in art and interdisciplinary practices) Univ of Northumbria at Newcastle 1993–; artistic dir Songs for the Falling Angel (requiem for Lockerbie air crash victims, Edinburgh Int Festival) 1991, exhibition of paintings for Songs for the Falling Angel (Kelvingrove Art Gallery Glasgow) 1991/92; visual art dir: Rites (with Scottish Chamber Orch, Briggait Glasgow) 1993, Legend of St Julian (with Communicado, Traverse Theatre, Edinburgh Int Festival) 1993, Games (with Vocem and the Edinburgh Contemporary Art Trust) 1996, Mfalme Juha (with Parapanda Arts Tanzania) 2003, Heid (with Sounds of Progress and Parapanda Arts) 2006, Life Stories and Dreams (with Sounds of Progress and Scottish Nat Theatre Co) 2006, The Unconquered (with Stellar Quines Theatre Co) 2007; Hospitalfield scholar Arbroath 1981, RSA Carnegie 1982, RSA William Gillies 1983, Elizabeth Greenshields 1983, first prize Scottish Drawing Competition 1993, Arts Cncl Award 2004; *Style*— Keith McIntyre, Esq; ✉ Department of Fine Art, Squires Building, University of Northumbria at Newcastle, Sandyford Road, Newcastle upon Tyne NE1 8ST (☎ 0191 227 4935)

MACIVER, Archie Duncan; s of Iain Duncan Maciver, of Carloway, Isle of Lewis, and Christine, *née* Macarthur; *b* 13 December 1959, Glasgow; *Educ* Hutchesons GS Glasgow, Univ of Strathclyde (LLB, DipLP); *m* 15 July 1987, Pamela Anne, *née* Richardson; 2 da

(Victoria Elizabeth b 18 Nov 1989, Alexandra Christine b 30 May 1992); *Career* slr; Levy and McRae: trainee 1981–83, asst 1983–84, ptnr 1984–88; ptnr Brunton Miller 1988–; accredited specialist in licensing law Law Soc of Scotland; memb: Law Soc of Scotland; convenor Law Soc of Scotland Licensing Law Sub Ctee; *Recreations* golf, reading, quality family time; *Clubs* East Renfrewshire Golf; *Style*— Archie Maciver, Esq; ✉ Brunton Miller, 22 Herbert Street, Glasgow G20 6NB (✆ 0141 337 1199, fax 0141 337 3300, e-mail archiemaciver@bruntonmiller.com)

McIVER, Malcolm; OBE (1999); s of late Donald John McIver, and Jean Begg, *née* Macdonald (d 1958); *b* 9 March 1935; *Educ* The Nicolson Inst Stornoway, Univ of Glasgow (MA, LLB); *m* 15 April 1960, Margaret, da of Alexander Wilson Fox Elliot; 1 s (Calum Alexander b 10 July 1967); *Career* apprentice slr Baird Smith Barclay & Muirhead and Maclay Murray & Spens 1955–58; slr: Crawford Herron & Cameron 1958–59, Peter Morris & McTaggart 1959–60; ptnr: Crawford Herron & Cameron 1960–73, Bird Semple & Crawford Herron 1973–87; Bird Semple: ptnr 1987–97, sr ptnr 1991–97, conslt 1997–99; chm Sportech plc (formerly Rodime plc) 1991–2001; tutor in jurisprudence Univ of Glasgow 1960–85; chm Royal Scottish Acad of Music and Drama (now Royal Conservatoire of Scotland) 1993–98, dep chm Accounts Cmmn 1994–98 (memb 1988–98); formerly govr Pitlochry Festival Theatre; tstee: Tenovus Scotland, RSAMD Endowment Tst, Royal Conservatoire of Scotland Tst; memb Incorporation of Hammermen Glasgow; memb: Law Soc of Scotland 1958–2012; SSC, FRSA, FRSAMD; *Recreations* sailing, music; *Clubs* Glasgow Art; *Style*— Malcolm McIver, Esq, OBE; ✉ 29 Hughenden Lane, Glasgow G12 9XU (✆ 0141 339 8551)

MACK, Hazel Mary; *née* Perkins; da of Peter Nevard Perkins (d 1992), and Betty, *née* Walker (d 1998); *b* 4 April 1952, Derby; *Educ* Loughborough HS for Girls, Univ of Exeter (BA); *m* 19 May 1977, Brian Mack, s of Frank Mack (d 1982); *Career* co sec Morgan Grenfell & Co Ltd 1987–90 (joined 1980); Willis Gp: exec dir financial institutions 1990–95, dir Mergers and Acquisitions Practice 1995–2009, operations dir Finex Global 2009–13, ret; ACIS; *Recreations* cooking, gardening, walking, travel; *Style*— Mrs Hazel Mack; ✉ Pounce Hall Cottage, Sewards End, Saffron Walden, Essex CB10 2LE (✆ 01799 527740)

MACK, Prof (Brian) John; s of late Harold Brian Mack, of Belfast, and Joan Alexandra, *née* Kelly; *b* 10 July 1949; *Educ* Campbell Coll Belfast, Univ of Sussex (BA, MA), Merton Coll Oxford (DPhil); *m* 1976, Caroline Helen Claire, *qv*, da of Rev Dr Daniel T Jenkins; 1 da (Katy b 12 Oct 1985), 1 s (Samuel b 13 Feb 1989); *Career* Dept of Ethnography British Museum: research asst 1976–77, asst keeper 1977–91, keeper 1991–2004, sr keeper 1998–2002; prof of world art studies UEA 2004–, chm Sainsbury Inst for Art UEA 2011–15; visiting prof UCL 1997–2003; pres Br Inst in Eastern Africa 2005–11; memb: British Museum Res Bd, Advsy Cncl NACF, Bd W African Museums Programme, Bd for Academy Sponsored Insts and Socs British Academy, Bd of Visitors Pitt-Rivers Museum Oxford; tstee Horniman Museum and Gardens; govr Powell-Cotton Museum Kent; winner NACF Award for Images of Africa exhibition 1991; FRAI 1976, FSA 1994, FRSA 2005, FBA 2009; *Publications* African Textiles (with J Picton, 1979, 2 edn 1989, Craft Advsy Cncl Book of the Year), Zulus (1980), Culture History in the Southern Sudan (with P T Robertshaw, 1982), Ethnic Sculpture (with M D McLeod, 1984), Madagascar, Island of the Ancestors (1986), Ethnic Jewellery (1988), Malagasy Textiles (1989), Emil Torday and the Art of the Congo 1900–1909 (1990), African Textile Design (with C Spring, 1991), Masks, the Art of Expression (1994), Images of other Cultures (with K Yoshida, 1998), Africa, Arts and Cultures (2000), Museum of the Mind (2003), The Art of Small Things (2007), Preserving the Cultural Heritage of Africa (with K Yoshida, 2008), The Sea, A Cultural History (2011); also author of articles and reviews in learned jls; *Recreations* museums, galleries, walking; *Clubs* Aberdovey Golf (Gwynedd); *Style*— Prof John Mack, FBA; ✉ Sainsbury Research Unit, Sainsbury Centre for Visual Art, University of East Anglia, Norwich NR4 7TJ (✆ 01603 456161)

MACK, Lee (né McKillop); *Career* comedian; *Television* incl: Gas 1997–98, The Sketch Show 2001–04, They Think It's All Over 2005–06, Live at the Apollo 2005–10, Not Going Out 2006–, Would I Lie To You? 2007–, Have I Got News For You 2008–11, QI 2009–12, Never Mind the Buzzcocks 2010 and 2012, Lee Mack's All Star Cast 2011, 8 Out of 10 Cats Does Countdown 2013, Duck Quacks Don't Echo 2014, The Smiths 2014, The Feeling Nuts Comedy Night 2014; *Style*— Lee Mack, Esq

McKANE, Christopher Hugh; s of Leonard Cyril McKane, MBE (d 1997), and (Eleanor) Catharine, *née* Harris (d 2011); *b* 13 July 1946; *Educ* Marlborough, New Coll Oxford (MA); *m* 31 Oct 1970, Anna Rosemary, da of George Paul Henshell (d 1984); 3 da (Camilla b 1977, Sophie b 1979, Felicity b 1981); *Career* journalist: The Oxford Times 1968–71, The Birmingham Post 1971–74; The Times 1974–86; The Independent: dep home ed 1986–88, picture ed 1988–92, night ed 1992–94; The Times: rejoined 1994, night ed 1995–99, exec ed 1999–2007, dep managing ed 2007–11, ret; chm Charles Douglas-Home Memorial Tst 2013–; church warden St Bride's Fleet St 2002–10; Freeman City of London, Liveryman Worshipful Co of Stationers and Newspaper Makers (memb Ct of Assts 2000, Master 2010–11); *Recreations* bonsai, sweet wines, beekeeping; *Clubs* Saracens FC, Wynkyn de Worde Soc; *Style*— Christopher McKane, Esq; ✉ 36 Thornhill Square, London N1 1BE (020 7609 7811, e-mail christopher.mckane@gmail.com)

MACKAY, Andrew John (Andy); OBE (2006); s of John Mackay (d 1999), and Margaret, *née* Ogilvie (d 1996); *b* 28 July 1960, Cheltenham, Glos; *Educ* Clifton, Univ of Exeter (BA), Univ of Reading (MA), Univ of Durham (MBA); *m* 6 Oct 1990, Margaret Allport; 1 da (Isabel Margaret b 11 Aug 1996); *Career* British Cncl: asst dir Teaching Centre Cairo 1983–87, evaluation advsr 1988–89, dep dir Peru 1989–92, dir Dubai 1992–96, dir Barcelona 1996–2001, dir USA 2001–06; head of strategy and evaluation Communication Directorate FCO 2006–08; Br Cncl: head of corp affrs and sec 2008–13, dir of operations 2013–15, dir of Spain 2015–; FRSA 2002; *Recreations* cinema, literature, Hispanic cultures, walking; *Style*— Andy Mackay, Esq, OBE; ✉ British Council, 10 Spring Gardens, London SW1A 2BN (✆ 020 7930 8466, e-mail andy.mackay@britishcouncil.org)

MACKAY, Prof Angus Victor Peck; OBE (1997); s of Victor Mackay (d 1982), of Edinburgh, and Christine, *née* Peck (d 1985); *b* 4 March 1943; *Educ* George Heriot's Sch Edinburgh, Univ of Edinburgh (BSc, MB ChB), Univ of Cambridge (MA, PhD); *m* 1969, Elspeth Margaret Whitton, da of Thomas Norris; 2 s (Jason b 20 Nov 1970, Aidan b 31 March 1978), 2 da (Ashley b 20 June 1972, Zoe b 17 Jan 1983); *Career* undergraduate trg in pharmacology and med Univ of Edinburgh 1962–69, house offr Med/Surgical Professorial Unit Edinburgh Royal Infirmary 1969–70, graduate trg Univ of Cambridge 1970–73 (MRC jr res fell and supervisor in pharmacology Trinity Coll Cambridge and hon registrar Fulbourn Hosp Cambridge), MRC clinical res fell MRC Brain Metabolism Unit Edinburgh, hon registrar in psychiatry Royal Edinburgh Hosp and hon lectr Dept of Pharmacology Edinburgh 1973–76, hon sr registrar Edinburgh Royal Infirmary 1976, sr clinical scientific staff memb and latterly dep dir MRC Neurochemical Pharmacology Unit Cambridge and lectr in pharmacology Trinity Coll Cambridge, hon conslt Cambridge Area HA and hon lectr Dept of Psychiatry Cambridge 1976–80; currently: physician supt Argyll and Bute Hosp, conslt psychiatrist, dir of mental health services Argyll and Bute NHS Tst, chm Health Technol Board for Scotland, hon prof Dept of Psycological Med Univ of Glasgow 1980–; UK rep Conf on Psychiatric Hosp Orgn and Mgmnt WHO 1983; memb: Res Ctee Mental Health Fndn 1981–88, Working Gp on Guidelines for Clinical Drug Evaluation WHO 1984–89, Ctee on Safety of Meds Dept of Health 1983–, Faculty of Neuroscience Univ of Edinburgh 1999–; chm: Multidisciplinary Working Pty on Research into Care of the Dementing Elderly Chief Scientist Orgn 1986–87, Working Gp on Mental Illness Servs in Scotland CRAG/SCOTMEG 1992–96, External Reference Gp Scottish Health Dept 1996–, Working Gp on Scottish Health Technol Assessment 1999–2000, Advsy Bd on Regulation of Homeopathic Products; memb: NHS Policy Bd Scotland 1996–97, Mental Health Tbnl for Scotland, Bd Medicines and Healthcare Products Regulatory Agency 2002–14, Cmmn on Human Medicine 2012–14; author of over 80 pubns mainly on biological psychiatry; Keith Medal and Meml Lecture RSA 1974; FRCPEd 1989 (MRCP 1986), FRCPsych 1993 (MRCPsych 1976), TPsych 1995; *Recreations* sailing, rowing, rhododendrons; *Clubs* Ardrishaig Boat, American Rhododendron Soc; *Style*— Prof Angus Mackay, OBE; ✉ Tigh An Rudha, Ardrishaig, Argyll (✆ 01546 603272); Argyll and Bute Hospital, Lochgilphead, Argyll PA31 8LD (✆ 01546 602323, fax 01546 602606, e-mail angus.mackay@nhs.net); Health Technology Board for Scotland, Delta House, West Nile Street, Glasgow (✆ 0141 249 6665)

MACKAY, Charles Dorsey; CBE (2013); s of Brig Kenneth Mackay, CBE, DSO (d 1974), and Evelyn Maud, *née* Ingram (d 1982); *b* 14 April 1940, Congleton, Cheshire; *Educ* Cheltenham Coll, Queens' Coll Cambridge (MA), INSEAD (MBA); *m* 11 July 1964, Annmarie, da of Fritz Joder (d 1978); 2 s (Hugo b 1965 d 1981, Caspar b 1971), 1 da (Romola b 1966); *Career* The British Petroleum Co Ltd: commercial apprentice 1957–59, univ apprentice 1959–62, mktg asst 1962–63, sales supervisor Algeria 1963–65, commercial dir Burundi/Rwanda/Congo 1965–68, sponsored at INSEAD 1968–69; McKinsey & Co Inc London/Paris/Amsterdam/Dar es Salaam: conslt 1969–71, jr engagement mangr 1971–72, sr engagement mangr 1972–76; Pakhoed Holding NV Rotterdam: dir Paktrans Div 1976–77, chm 1977–81; Chloride Group plc: dir 1981–86, chm Chloride Overseas 1981–85, chm Chloride Power Electronics 1985–86; Inchcape plc: dir 1986–96, chm Inchcape (Hong Kong) Ltd 1986–87, chm and chief exec Inchcape Pacific Ltd (Hong Kong) 1987–91, gp chief exec 1991–96, dep chm 1995–96; chm Historic Royal Palaces 2006–15, chm Opera Holland Park 2015–; non-exec chm: DSL Defence Systems Ltd 1996–97, TDG plc 2000–08, Eurotunnel Gp 2001–2004 (non-exec dir 1997–2004, non-exec dep chm 1999–2001), Prodn Servs Network Ltd 2009–11; non-exec dep chm Thistle Hotels plc 1996–2003; non-exec dir: Union Insurance Society of Canton Ltd (Hong Kong) 1986–91, The Hongkong and Shanghai Banking Corporation Ltd (Hong Kong) 1986–92, HSBC Holdings plc 1990–98, Midland Bank plc 1992–93, British Airways plc 1993–96, Johnson Matthey plc 1999–2008; memb Supervisory Bd Gucci Group NV 1997–2001, memb Business Bd House of Habib 2007–; memb Bd INSEAD 2000–11 (memb Advsy Cncl 2011–); second vice-chm Hong Kong Gen C of C 1989–91 (memb 1987–91); memb: Gen Ctee Br C of C in Hong Kong 1987–91, Hong Kong Trade Devpt Cncl 1989–91, Bd Hong Kong Community Chest 1990–91; tstee Devpt Tst For The Mentally Handicapped 1993–; *Recreations* travel, restoring old buildings, fly fishing, skiing, opera, classical music; *Clubs* Brooks's, Hong Kong, Piscatorial Soc; *Style*— Charles Mackay, Esq, CBE; ✉ 4 Ormonde Gate, London SW3 4EU (✆ 020 7460 6034, mobile 07803 796295, e-mail charlesmackay8@gmail.com)

MACKAY, His Hon Judge David Ian; *b* 11 November 1945; *Educ* Birkenhead Sch, Brasenose Coll Oxford; *m* 1974, Mary Elizabeth; 2 da (Emily Jane b 1980, Harriet Louise b 1984), 1 s (James Hugh b 1981); *Career* called to the Bar Inner Temple 1969, circuit judge 1992, Official Referee's Business 1993–98, provincial judge Technol and Construction Court 1998–; chm of govrs Birkenhead Sch 1991–2001, chm Birkenhead Sch Fndn Tst 1998–2004; fell Soc for Advanced Legal Studies 2002; *Recreations* history, transport, travelling in France; *Clubs* Athenaeum (Liverpool); *Style*— His Hon Judge Mackay; ✉ Queen Elizabeth II Law Courts, Derby Square, Liverpool L2 1XA (✆ 0151 473 7373)

MACKAY, Derek; MSP; *b* 30 July 1977; *Career* cncllr Renfrewshire Cncl 1999–2011 (ldr 2007–11), MSP (SNP) Renfrewshire N & W 2011–, min for local govt and planning 2011–14, min for transport and the islands 2014–; *Style*— Derek Mackay, Esq, MSP; ✉ The Scottish Parliament, Edinburgh EH99 1SP

MacKAY, Prof Sir Donald Iain; kt (1996); s of William MacKay (d 1980), and Rhona, *née* Cooper; *b* 27 February 1937; *Educ* Dollar Acad, Univ of Aberdeen; *m* 31 July 1961, Diana Marjory, da of Maj George Raffan (d 1980); 2 da (Deborah Jane b 1964, Paula Clare b 1967), 1 s (Donald Gregor b 1969); *Career* prof of political economy Univ of Aberdeen 1971–76, professorial fell Heriot-Watt Univ 1982–91 (prof of econs 1976–81); chm: Pieda plc planning, economic and devpt conslts 1976–97, DTZ Pieda Consulting 1997–2002, Malcolm Gp plc 1998–2003, Scottish Mortgage Tst 2003–; dir Edinburgh Income and Value Tst 1999–; memb: Sea Fish Indust Authy 1981–87, S of Scot Electricity Bd 1985–88, Scot Econ Cncl 1985–; govr NIESR; FRSE 1987, FRSGS 1994; *Books* Geographical Mobility and the Brain Drain (1970), Local Labour Markets and Wage Structures (1970), Labour Markets Under Different Employment Conditions (1971), Men Leaving Steel (1971), The Political Economy of North Sea Oil (1975), British Employment Statistics (1977); *Recreations* tennis, golf, bridge, chess; *Style*— Prof Sir Donald MacKay, FRSE, FRSGS

MACKAY, Air Vice-Marshal (Hector) Gavin; CB (2002), OBE (1987), AFC (1982); s of John Maclean Mackay (d 1988), and Isobel Margaret, *née* Mackay (d 1988); *b* 3 October 1947, Inverness; *Educ* Dingwall Acad, Univ of Glasgow (BSc), RAF Coll Cranwell, RN Staff Coll Greenwich, RCDS; *m* 28 Aug 1971, Elizabeth Stark Bolton; 1 da (Aimi Elizabeth b 29 July 1973), 1 s (Graeme John b 26 Dec 1974); *Career* cmmnd RAF; instr Jet Provost RAF Linton-on-Ouse 1973–75, pilot (Hunter) 45/58 Sqdn, pilot (Harrier) 20 Sqdn RAF Wildenrath, served 3 (F) Sqdn RAF Gütersloh (promoted Sqdn Ldr), exec offr 1 (F) Sqdn RAF Wittering 1979–82, Harrier specialist Central Tactics and Trials Org, Wing Cdr 1984, Cdr Examining Wing Central Flying Sch RAF Scampton, served Concepts Studies and Operational Requirements MOD (promoted Gp Capt) 1987–90, Cdr RAF Gütersloh and RAF Germany Harrier Force 1991–93, dep dir Air Offensive MOD 1993–94, ACOS Ops NATO HQ Allied Air Forces Central Europe 1995–96, Cmdt Central Flying Sch Cranwell 1996–99, ldr Jt Force 2000 Implementation Team 1999–2000, AOC and Cmdt RAF Coll Cranwell 2000–02; sr mil advsr: Def Export Servs Orgn (DESO) MOD 2003–, UKTI Def and Security Orgn 2008–; Hon Air Cdre 2503 (Co of Lincoln) Sqdn RAuxAF Regt 2005; GAPAN: Liveryman 2002, Master Air Pilot 1998; memb Gaelic Soc of Inverness; Freeman City of London 2002; FRAeS 1997; *Recreations* flying, golf, walking; *Clubs* RAF; *Style*— Air Vice-Marshal Gavin Mackay, CB, OBE, AFC, FRAeS; ✉ Senior Military Advisor, Defence and Security Organisation, Ministry of Defence, Room 3/16 St Georges Court, 2–12 Bloomsbury Way, London WC1A 2SH

McKAY, Hilary Jane; da of Ronald Damms, of Boston, Lincs, and Mary Edith, *née* Hampton; *b* 12 June 1959; *Educ* Boston Girls' HS, Univ of St Andrews (BSc); *m* 13 Aug 1982, Kevin Kerr McKay; 1 s (James Rufus (Jim) b 8 Jan 1993), 1 da (Isabella Claire b 21 Dec 1996); *Career* writer; *Books* The Exiles series (3, 1991–93, jt winner Guardian Children's Fiction Award 1992, overall winner Smarties Prize for Children's Literature), Dog Friday (1994), The Amber Cat (1995), The Zoo in the Attic (1995), Saffy's Angel (2002, winner Whitbread Children's Book Award), Indigo's Star (2003), Permanent Rose (2005, shortlisted Whitbread Children's Book of the Year 2005); *Recreations* reading, gardening; *Style*— Mrs Hilary McKay

MACKAY, (Douglas) Ian; QC (Scot 1993); s of Walter Douglas Mackay (d 1982), of Inverness, and Carla Marie Anna, *née* Fröhlich (d 1974); *b* 10 August 1948; *Educ* Inverness HS, Univ of Aberdeen (LLB); *m* Susan Anne, da of William Nicholson; 1 da (Julie Anne b 2 Aug 1970), 2 s (Garry Ian b 28 July 1973, Andrew William Nicholas b 20 Feb 1986); *Career* admitted Faculty of Advocates 1980, chm Advocates Personal Injury Law Gp; *Recreations* Scottish art and antiques, travel, shooting and gundogs, mountaineering; *Style*— Ian Mackay, Esq, QC; ✉ St Ann's House, Lasswade, Midlothian EH18 1ND (☎ 0131 660 2634, fax 0131 654 1600, e-mail ian.mackay@compasschambers.com); Mount Pleasant Farm, by Fortrose, Ross-shire (☎ 01381 620888); c/o Advocates' Library, Parliament House, Edinburgh EH1 1RF (☎ 0131 226 5071)

MACKAY, Ian Stuart; s of Rev Gordon Ernest Mackay (d 1991), of Adelaide, Aust, and Sylvia Viola Dorothy, *née* Spencer (d 1975); *b* 16 June 1943; *Educ* Kearsney Coll Bothas Hill, Univ of London (MB BS); *m* 1, 11 May 1968 (m dis), Angela; 1 s (Angus b 1971), 1 da (Fiona b 1972); m 2, 4 Sept 1981, Madeleine Hargreaves, *née* Tull; 1 da (Antonia b 1982), 1 step da (Charlotte b 1971); *Career* conslt ENT surgn Charing Cross Hosp and Brompton Hosp, hon conslt King Edward VII Hospital for Officers, hon sr lectr in rhinology Inst of Laryngology and Otology, hon sr lectr Cardiothoracic Inst Univ of London; jt ed Rhinology Volume in Scott-Brown's Otolaryngology, contrib section on rhinoplasty to Smith's Operative Surgery; pres Br Assoc of Otolaryngologists 1999–2003, chm Fedn of Surgical Specialty Assocs 2001–03, chm Ind Doctors' Fedn 2012–; memb RSM, FRCS; *Style*— Ian S Mackay, Esq; ✉ 37A Devonshire Street, London W1G 6QA (☎ 020 7580 5070, fax 020 7323 5401, e-mail harleynoseclinic@btconnect.com)

MACKAY, Kenneth Finlay; s of Alexander Mackay, and Moira, *née* Finlay; *b* 29 May 1959; *Educ* Ballyclare Secdy Sch and HS, Canterbury Coll of Art (BArch), RCA (MA); *Career* architect; architect Rick Mather Architects 1983, design/project architect Jeremy and Fenella Dixon Architects 1983–85, design team leader Jeremy Dixon/BPD 1985–87, dir Harper Mackay Ltd 1987–2003, sr ptnr Mackay & Ptnrs LLP 2004–; clients incl: Anglia Television, Br Cncl, Japan Airlines, Carlton Communications plc, London Tport, M&C Saatchi, Polygram UK, Sony Music Entertainment, Tonbridge Sch, Virgin Media Gp, Bee Bee Developments, BBC, British Petroleum, Channel 4, Deloitte Consulting, Groupe Chez Gerard, Hilton Hotels plc, Horizon Serono Geneva, Ian Schrager Hotels, M & C Saatchi, McCann Erickson, N M Rothschild & Sons Ltd, Prudential Portfolio Mangrs, Sony Music Entertainment UK Ltd, Valtech Ltd, Workspace Gp; projects incl: Merck Serono Geneva 2007, Shropshire House London 2007, Gtr London House 2007, Baker St London 2007, Hotel K Nairobi 2007, hotel Southampton 2008, HSBC Geneva 2008, Old Street London 2008, Rosebery Ave London 2008, Berkeley Sq London 2008, Wigmore St London 2008, Citizen M London 2008, ChelloMedia London 2008, Clandon Park Surrey 2008, Central St Giles London 2008, private residence Parsons Green London 2009, private residence Highbury London 2011, wine bar London 2011, hotel London EC3 2012; work featured in exhbns incl: 40 under 40 (RIBA London) 1988, Art and Architecture of Gardens (RIBA Heinz Gall London) 1989, 12 Br Architects (Mackintosh Museum Sch of Art Glasgow) 1990, The Venice Biennale 1991, Summer Show (Royal Acad London) 1991, Wordsearch (MIPM 98 Cannes) 1998, New Br Architecture (The Architecture Centre London) 1998; dir Workdesign Fndn NY; RIBA 1991, FCSD 1992; *Awards* incl: RIBA portfolio prize 1980, heritage award Clifton Nurseries 1985 and 1987, Design Week Awards 1991, 1994, 1997, 1998, and 1999, D&AD Awards 1994, Minerva Awards 1994 and 1995, Birmingham Design Initiative Awards 1994, Br Cncl for Office award 1998 and 1999, FX Awards 1999, Best Hotel Design (St Martin's Lane) FX Awards 2000, Best Medium Office (Valtech) FX Awards 2001; *Recreations* skiing, diving, eating; *Clubs* Groucho, Shoreditch House, Paramount; *Style*— Kenneth Finlay, Esq

McKAY, Maura; da of Bernard Herron, and Tess, *née* Flynn; *b* 3 November 1962; *Educ* St Joseph's Convent GS Donaghmore Co Tyrone, Queen's Univ Belfast (LLB); *m* 31 Aug 1992, Trevor McKay; 2 da (Clare b 14 Oct 1993, Kiera b 9 April 1998); *Career* slr specialising in liquor licensing; slr then ptnr Shean Dickson Merrick 1986–; memb Law Soc of NI; *Recreations* music and dancing; *Style*— Mrs Maura McKay; ✉ Shean Dickson Merrick, 14/16 High Street, Belfast BT1 2BS

McKAY, Dr Sir Neil Stuart; kt (2009), CB (2001); s of Roy McKay (d 1989), and Alison Maud, *née* Dent; *b* 19 February 1952; *Educ* Dame Allan's Boys' Sch Newcastle upon Tyne; *m* 17 Aug 1978, Deirdre Mary, da of Patrick Francis McGinn; 2 s (Sean Francis b 6 Jan 1981, Joseph Anthony b 8 Oct 1983); *Career* clerical offr trainee Univ of Newcastle HMC 1970–72, asst hosp sec Dunston Hill Hosp Gateshead 1972–74, admin asst Gateshead AHA 1974–75, hosp admin Dryburn Hosp Durham 1975–76, commissioning offr St George's Hosp London 1978–80 (asst sector admin 1976–78), planning admin Wandsworth HA 1980–82, hosp admin Springfield Hosp London 1982–85, gen mangr Doncaster Royal Infirmary 1985–88, gen mangr Northern Gen Hosp Sheffield 1988–91, chief exec Northern Gen Hosp NHS Tst 1991–96, regnl dir Trent Regional Office NHS Exec 1996–2000, dep chief exec NHS Exec 2000, chief operating offr Dept of Health 2000–02, chief exec Leeds Teaching Hosps NHS Tst 2002–; DipHSM; Hon LLD Univ of Sheffield; *Recreations* family pursuits, reading, sport (including following Sunderland AFC); *Style*— Dr Sir Neil McKay, CB; ✉ Leeds Teaching Hospitals NHS Trust, Trust Headquarters, St James University Hospital, Beckett Street, Leeds LS9 7TF (☎ 0113 206 5835, fax 0113 206 7007, e-mail neil.mckay@leedsth.nhs.uk)

MACKAY, Prof Norman; CBE (1997); s of Donald Mackay (d 1937), of Glasgow, and Catherine, *née* Macleod (d 1957); *b* 15 September 1936; *Educ* Govan HS, Univ of Glasgow (MB ChB, MD); *m* 10 Feb 1961, (Grace) Violet, da of Charles McCaffer (d 1959), of Kilwinning; 2 da (Susan b 28 July 1962, Violet b 24 July 1964), 2 s (Ronald b 8 Sept 1967, Donald b 30 Dec 1970); *Career* hon conslt physician Victoria Infirmary Glasgow 1989–94 (conslt 1973–89), dean of postgrad med and prof of postgrad med educn Univ of Glasgow 1989–2001; Royal Coll of Physicians and Surgeons Glasgow: hon sec 1973–83, visitor 1992–94, pres 1994–97; hon sec Conf of Royal Med Colls and Faculties in Scotland 1982–91; pres Southern Med Soc 1989–90; memb GMC 1999–; Hon FACP, Hon FRACP, Hon FCPC, FRCP, FAMS, FRCPGlas, FRCPEd, FRCSEd, FRCGP, FCPSP, FCPS (Bangladesh), FRCS, FRCSI, FRCPI, FAMM; *Recreations* soccer, golf, gardening; *Style*— Prof Norman Mackay, CBE; ✉ 5 Edenhall Grove, Newton Mearns, Glasgow G77; Department of Postgraduate Medical Education, The University, Glasgow G12 8QQ (☎ 0141 339 3786, fax 0141 330 4526)

MACKAY, Peter; CB (1993); s of John Swinton Mackay, FRCS (d 1993), of Kinnoir, Aberdeenshire, and Patricia May, *née* Atkinson (d 1976); *b* 6 July 1940; *Educ* Glasgow HS, Univ of St Andrews (MA); *m* 29 Aug 1964, Sarah White, da of Reginald White Holdich (d 1992), of Cherry Burton, E Yorks; 1 s (Andrew), 2 da (Elspeth, Sally); *Career* teacher Kyogle HS NSW 1962–63; Scottish Office: joined 1963, ret as sec and chief exec Industry Dept 1995; exec dir Advanced Mgmnt Programme in Scotland 1995–97, non-exec dir British Linen Bank Group 1996–2000, dir Business Banking Div Bank of Scotland 1999–2001; chm: Pacific Horizon Investment Tst 2004–10 (dir 2001–04), Northern Lighthouse Bd 2005–07 (cmmr 1999–2008), Northern Lighthouse Heritage Tst 2013–; chm Local Govt Boundary Cmmn for Scotland 2007–13; memb: Univ Ct Napier Univ Edinburgh 1995–2004, Competition Cmmn (formerly Monopolies and Mergers) 1996–2002, Main Bd Scottish Natural Heritage 1997–2003; tstee Scottish Forestry Alliance 1999–2010, tstee Cairngorm Outdoor Access Tst 2009–13, dir Cairngorms Local Outdoor Access Forum 2014–; Hon LLD Robert Gordon Univ 1996; *Publications* Scottish Hill Tracks (lead ed, 2012); *Recreations* high altitudes and latitudes, mountains, sea canoeing, sailing, sculling; *Clubs* Loch Lomond Sailing; *Style*— Peter Mackay, Esq, CB; ✉ Silverwood, Dunachton Road, Kincraig, Inverness-shire PH21 1QE (☎ 01540 651745)

MacKAY, Prof Robert Sinclair; s of Donald Maccrimmon MacKay (d 1987), and Valerie, *née* Wood; *b* 4 July 1956; *Educ* Newcastle HS Newcastle-under-Lyme, Trinity Coll Cambridge (entrance and sr scholarships, Yeats Prize, Tyson Medal, MA), Plasma Physics Lab Princeton Univ (Fulbright Hayes Scholarship, PhD); *m* May 1992, Claude Noëlle, *née* Baesens; 1 s (Alexandre b 19 March 2002); *Career* research asst applied mathematics QMC 1982–83, prof invité Institut des Hautes Etudes Scientifiques France 1983–84; Univ of Warwick: successively lectr in mathematics, reader then prof 1984–95, dir of Mathematical Interdisciplinary Research 2000–; prof of nonlinear dynamics DAMTP Univ of Cambridge and fell Trinity Coll Cambridge 1995–2000; visiting prof Laboratoire de Topologie Univ de Bourgogne 1994–95, prof visiteur physique Université Libre de Brucelles 2010–11, Ordway distinguished visitor Univ of Minnesota 2012; Nuffield Fndn Science Research fell 1992–93, Stephanos Pnevmatikos Int Award for research in nonlinear phenomena 1993, Junior Whitehead Prize London Mathematical Soc 1994, Senior Whitehead Prize London Mathematical Soc 2015; memb: London Mathematical Soc 1990, FRS 2000, FInstP 2000 (MInstP 1993), FIMA 2003 (pres 2012–13); *Publications* Hamiltonian Dynamical Systems: a reprint selection (co-ed, 1987), Renormalisation in Area-preserving Maps (1993); and also author of over 135 learned papers in jls and 50 contribs to conf proceedings; *Style*— Prof Robert MacKay; ✉ Mathematics Institute, University of Warwick, Coventry CV4 7AL (☎ 02476 522218, fax 02476 524182, e-mail r.s.mackay@warwick.ac.uk)

MACKAY, Shena; da of Benjamin Carr Mackey, and Morag, *née* Carmichael; *b* 6 June 1944; *Educ* Tonbridge Girls' GS, Kidbrooke Comp; *m* 1964 (m dis), Robin Francis Brown; 3 da (Sarah Frances b 11 March 1965, Rebecca Mary b 21 Aug 1966, Cecily Rose b 15 May 1969); *Career* author; awarded: Arts Cncl grants 1970s, travelling scholarship Soc of Authors 1986, Fawcett Prize 1987, Scottish Arts Cncl Book award 1992 and 1994; judge: The Whitbread Prize 1998, The Macmillan Silver Pen for Fiction 1999, The Booker Prize 1999, The Macallan/Scotland on Sunday Short Story Competition 1999, John Llewellyn Rhys Prize; visiting prof Dept of English Middlesex Univ 2001–03; memb: PEN, London Arts Bd 1993–97, Soc of Authors, ALCS; FRSL 1999; *Books* Dust Falls on Eugene Schlumburger (1964), Toddler on the Run (1964), Music Upstairs (1965), Old Crow (1967), An Advent Calendar (1971), Babies in Rhinestones (1983), A Bowl of Cherries (1984), Redhill Rococo (1986), Dreams of Dead Women's Handbags (1987), Dunedin (1992), The Laughing Academy (1993), Such Devoted Sisters (ed, 1993), Collected Stories (1994), The Orchard on Fire (1996, shortlisted for Booker Prize), Friendship (ed, 1997), The Artist's Widow (1998), The Worlds Smallest Unicorn (1999), Heligoland (2003, shortlisted for Orange Prize and Whitbread Prize), The Atmospheric Railway: New and Selected Stories (2008); *Style*— Ms Shena Mackay, FRSL

MACKAY OF CLASHFERN, Baron (Life Peer UK 1979), of Eddracchillis in the District of Sutherland; James Peter Hymers Mackay; KT (1997), PC (1979); s of James Mackay (d 1958); *b* 2 July 1927; *Educ* George Heriot's Sch Edinburgh, Univ of Edinburgh, Trinity Coll Cambridge; *m* 1958, Elizabeth Gunn Hymers, da of D D Manson; 1 s (Hon James b 1958), 2 da (Hon Elizabeth Janet (Hon Mrs Campbell) b 1961, Hon Shona Ruth b 1968); *Career* advocate 1955, QC Scot 1965; sheriff principal Renfrew and Argyll 1972–74, dean Faculty of Advocates 1976–79 (vice-dean 1973–76); cmmr Northern Lighthouses 1975–84, pt/t memb Scottish Law Cmmn 1976–79, dir Stenhouse Holdings Ltd 1976–77, memb Insurance Brokers' Registration Cncl 1977–79; Lord Advocate of Scotland 1979–84, Lord of Session 1984–85, Lord of Appeal in Ordinary 1985–87, Lord Chllr 1987–97, Lord High Cmmr 2005–06, Lord Clerk Register 2007–; chm Cmmn in Law Reform in Mauritius 1997–98, chm Cmmn in Administration of Justice in Trinidad and Tobago 2000; Elder Bros Trinity House 1990; chllr Heriot-Watt Univ 1991–2005; hon pres Scottish Bible Soc 1997–; Hon LLD: Univ of Dundee 1983, Univ of Edinburgh 1983, Univ of Strathclyde 1985, Univ of Aberdeen 1987, Univ of St Andrews 1988, Univ of Cambridge 1989, Coll of William and Mary 1989, Univ of Birmingham 1990, Nat Law Sch of India 1994, Univ of Bath 1994, Univ of Glasgow 1999, De Montfort Univ 1999, Robert Gordon Univ 2000; Hon DCL: Univ of Newcastle upon Tyne 1990, Univ of Birmingham 1990, Univ of Leicester 1996, Univ of Oxford 1998; hon fell: Trinity Coll Cambridge 1979, Girton Coll Cambridge 1989, American Coll of Trial Lawyers 1990; Hon Freeman Worshipful Co of Woolmen; fell Int Acad of Trial Lawyers 1979, Hon FTII 1983, FRSE 1984, Hon FICE 1989, Hon FRCSEd 1989, Hon FRCPEd 1990, Hon FRCOG 1996; *Recreations* travel, walking; *Clubs* New (Edinburgh), Athenaeum, Caledonian; *Style*— The Rt Hon the Lord Mackay of Clashfern, KT, PC; ✉ House of Lords, London SW1A 0PW

M

MACKAY OF DRUMADOON, Baron (Life Peer UK 1995), of Blackwaterfoot in the District of Cunninghame; Donald Sage Mackay; PC (1996), QC (Scot 1987); s of Rev Donald George Mackintosh Mackay (d 1991), of Edinburgh, and Jean Margaret, *née* McCaskie, of Edinburgh (d 1994); *b* 30 January 1946; *Educ* George Watson's Boys Coll Edinburgh, Univ of Edinburgh (LLB, LLM), Univ of Virginia (LLM); *m* 5 April 1979, Lesley Ann, da of late Edward Waugh; 2 da (Hon Caroline b 7 Sept 1980, Hon Diana b 19 Aug 1982), 1 s (Hon Simon b 20 Jan 1984); *Career* apprentice slr Davidson & Syme CS Edinburgh 1969–71, slr Allan McDougall & Co SSC Edinburgh 1971–76, called to the Scottish Bar 1976, advocate depute 1982–85, memb Criminal Injuries Compensation Bd 1989–95, Slr Gen for Scotland 1995, Lord Advocate for Scotland 1995–97, oppn spokesman on constitutional affrs House of Lords 1997–2000, Senator Coll of Justice in Scotland 2000–13, master of the crossbench House of Lords 2013–; *Recreations* golf, Isle of Arran; *Style*— The Rt Hon Lord Mackay of Drumadoon, PC, QC; ✉ 39 Hermitage Gardens, Edinburgh EH10 6AZ (☎ 0131 447 1412, e-mail mackayd@parliament.uk)

MACKAY-DICK, Maj Gen Sir Iain; KCVO, MBE, DL (Gtr London 2011); *Educ* Sherborne, RMA Sandhurst, Staff Coll Camberley (psc, hcsc); *m* 1971, Carolynn, *née* Holmes; 3 da (Alexandra b 1972, Georgina b 1975, Olivia b 1979); *Career* cmmnd Scots Gds 1965, served as Platoon Cdr 1 Bn Scots Gds Borneo, platoon instr Gds Depot Pirbright 1967–69, Mortar Platoon Cdr 2 Bn Münster 1969–70, served Windsor and N Ireland 1970–71, Jr Div Staff Coll 1971, Adj 1 Bn 1971 (served Windsor, N Ireland and Germany), Co Cdr 2 Bn until 1974 (served Pirbright and N Ireland), Adj New Coll Sandhurst 1974–76, Army Staff Coll course 1976–78, Co Cdr 2 Bn Scots Gds Münster 1978–79, Bde Maj (COS) 3 Infantry Bde 1979–81, 2 i/c 2 Bn Scots Gds 1981–82 (served Falklands War), memb Directing Staff Army Staff Coll 1982–84, CO 2 Bn 1984–86 (served Cyprus), Cmdt Jr Div Staff Coll 1986–88, Higher Cmd and Staff Course Staff Coll 1989, Cdr 11 Armd Bde Minden 1989–91, Dep Mil Sec (A) MOD London 1991–92, GOC 1 Armd Div Germany 1992–93, Cdr Br Forces Falkland Is 1993–94, GOC London Dist and Maj Gen cmdg Household Div 1994–97; chm Guards Chapel Ctee 2011–; memb Governing Cncl Union Jack Club 2011–; clerk to the tstees and chief exec Morden Coll 1997–2011; Hon Col 256 City of London Field Hosp RAMC (v) 2000–07; tstee Falkland Islands Meml Chapel Pangbourne 2005; Freeman City of London 2000; MRUSI 1979–2006, FCMI (FIMgt) 1995–2011; *Recreations* military history, walking, all forms of sport incl tennis (represented Army), squash (Army squash champion 1971); *Clubs* Edinburgh Angus, Jesters, Guards Golfing Soc, Army Golfing Soc, Public Schools Old Boys LTA, Sherborne Pilgrims; *Style*— Maj Gen Sir Iain Mackay-Dick, KCVO, MBE, DL; ✉ c/o Lloyds TSB Bank plc, Cox's and King's, PO Box 1190, 7 Pall Mall, London SW1Y 5NA

McKEAN, Alastair; s of Jim McKean, and Sylvia, *née* Perrin; *b* 14 April 1979, Canterbury, Kent; *Educ* BA, BSc, PGCE; *m* 15 Aug 2009, Emily, *née* Heath; *Career* bench joiner 1996–99, Geography teacher 2004–07, Paralympic rower 2007–09 (achivements incl: World Rowing Champion 2005 and 2006, Silver medal World Rowing Championships 2007, Bronze medal mixed coxed four (with Naomi Riches, MBE, Victoria Hansford, James Morgan, *qqv*, and Alan Sherman) Paralympics Beijing 2008), competition mangr 2009–; *Recreations* rowing, athletics, cycling; *Clubs* Herne Bay Rowing; *Style*— Alastair McKean, Esq; ✉ The Canterbury High School, Canterbury, Kent CT2 8QA (☎ 01227 463971, e-mail amckeancm@yahoo.com)

McKEAN, Prof Charles Alexander; s of John Laurie McKean, of Glasgow, and Nancy Burns, *née* Lendrum; *b* 16 July 1946; *Educ* Fettes, Univ of Bristol (BA); *m* 18 Oct 1975, Margaret Elizabeth, da of Mervyn Yeo, of Cardiff; 2 s (Andrew Laurie b 1978, David Alexander b 1981); *Career* ed London Architect 1970–75; architectural corr: The Times 1977–83, Scotland on Sunday 1988–90; RIBA: London regnl sec 1968–71, Eastern regnl sec 1971–79, projects offr Community Architecture and Industrial Regeneration 1977–79; sec and treas RIAS 1979–94; Duncan of Jordanstone Coll Univ of Dundee: prof of architecture 1994–97, head of sch 1994–97, prof of Scottish architectural history Dept of History 1997–2012 (prof emeritus 2012–); dir Workshops and Artists Studios Ltd 1980–85; memb Exhibitions Panel Scottish Arts Cncl 1980–83, memb Advsy Cncl for the Arts in Scotland 1985–88, memb Cncl Architectural Heritage Soc of Scotland 1987–96, convenor Buildings Ctee Nat Tst for Scotland 1995–2003, memb Cncl Historic Environment Advsy Cncl for Scotland 2003–07, memb Scottish Ctee Heritage Lottery Fund 2003–09; sec to the RIAS Hill House Tst 1979–82, memb Environment and Town Planning Ctee The Saltire Soc 1984–85; chm Edinburgh World Heritage Tst 2006–12; tstee: Thirlestane Castle Tst 1983–93, Dundee City Arts Centre Tst 1995–97, St Vincent Street Church Tst 1996–99; former vice-chm Charles Rennie Mackintosh Soc, former memb Advsy Ctee Edinburgh Common Purpose; Architectural Journalist of the Year 1979 and 1983, RIBA Gordon Ricketts Award 1980, Building Journalist of the Year 1983, RSA Bossom Lecture 1986, RIAS Thomas Ross Award 1993, Nigel Tranter Award 2004; hon memb The Saltire Soc 1990, hon pres St Andrews Preservation Soc 2006–13, pres Scottish Castles Assoc; Hon DLitt RGU 1994; FRSA 1978, FSA Scot 1983, Hon FRIBA 1990, Hon FRIAS 1994, FRSE 1999, Hon FRSGS 2002, FRHistS; *Books* London 1981 (1970), Modern Buildings in London 1965–75 (with Tom Jestico, 1975), Living over the Shop (1976), Battle of Styles (with David Atwell, 1976), Funding the Future (1977), Fight Blight (1977), An Outine of Western Architecture (jtly, 1980), Architectural Guide to Cambridge and East Anglia since 1920 (1980), Edinburgh – an Illustrated Architectural Guide (1982), Dundee – an Illustrated Introduction (with David Walker, 1984), Stirling and the Trossachs (1985), The Scottish Thirties (1987), The District of Moray (1987), Central Glasgow (with Prof David Walker and Prof Frank Walker), Banff and Buchan (1990), For a Wee Country (1990), Edinburgh – Portrait of a City (1991), Dundee (with Prof D Walker, 1993), West Lothian (with Richard Jacques, 1994), Value or Cost (1993), Claim (1998), The Making of the Museum of Scotland (2000), The Scottish Château (2001), Battle for the North (2006), Lost Dundee (with P Whatley and K Baxter, 2008, 2 edn 2013); *Clubs* Scottish Arts; *Style*— Prof Charles McKean; ✉ 10 Hillpark Road, Edinburgh EH4 7AW (☎ 0131 336 2753); University of Dundee, Perth Road, Dundee DD1 4HN (☎ 01382 345738, e-mail c.a.mckean@dundee.ac.uk)

McKEAN, Lorne; da of Lt Cdr J A H McKean, RN (d 1981), and Beatrice Blanche Mowbray *née* Bellairs (d 1991); *b* 16 April 1939; *Educ* Elmhurst Ballet Sch, Guildford Art Sch, Royal Acad Schs; *m* 7 Nov 1964, Edwin John Cumming Russell, s of Edwin Russell; 2 da (Rebecca b 21 Jan 1966, Tanya b 25 April 1968); *Career* sculptor; public and large works include: A A Milne memorial London Zoo Bear Club, Arctic Terns Chester Zoo, Girl and the Swan Reading, 10' Horsham Heritage Sundial, Osprey Fountain Greenwich Connecticut USA, Great Swan Great Swan Alley EC2, Swan Fountain Horsham, Flight (27ft bronze) Norwich Union Leeds; equestrian and horse sculptures: HRH Prince Philip on his polo pony, HM The Queen's personal Silver Wedding gift to her husband, HRH The Prince of Wales on polo pony Pans Folly, John Pinches International Dressage Trophy, Galoubet French show jumping stallion, pony series for Royal Worcester Porcelain, racehorses Troy and Snurge, HRH The Duke of Edinburgh half lifesize bronze polo sculpture (Guards Polo Club Windsor) 2007; portraits include: the late Lord Salisbury (Hatfield House), Sir Michael Redgrave, HRH the late Prince William of Gloucester, the Earl of Lichfield televised for portrait series, HM The Queen, Drapers' Hall and RHHT; Best Sculpture Br Sporting Art Tst 2007; FRBS 1968; *Recreations* animals; *Clubs* Guards Polo; *Style*— Miss Lorne McKean; ✉ Lethendry, Polecat Valley, Hindhead, Surrey GU26 6BE (☎ 01428 605655)

McKEAN, Roderick Hugh Ross (Roddy); *b* 13 March 1956; *Educ* The HS of Dundee, Univ of Edinburgh (LLB); *Career* articled clerk Burness, WS 1978–80; admitted slr 1980; asst slr: Maclay Murray and Spens 1980–83, Lovell White & King 1984–88; ptnr Lovells 1988– (managing ptnr Asia 1996–2001); memb: Law soc, Law Soc of Scotland, Law Soc of Hong Kong; *Recreations* skiing, tennis, yachting, riding, golf; *Clubs* Royal London Yacht, Royal Corinthian Yacht, Royal Hong Kong Yacht, Woking Golf; *Style*— Roddy McKean, Esq; ✉ Lovells, Atlantic House, 50 Holborn Viaduct, London EC1A 2FG (☎ 020 7296 2000, fax 020 7296 2001)

McKECHIN, Ann; da of late William J McKechin, of Paisley, and Anne, *née* Coyle; *b* 22 April 1961; *Educ* Sacred Heart HS Paisley, Paisley GS, Univ of Strathclyde (LLB); *Career* slr; Kelvin Lab Pty: constituency sec Glasgow 1995–98, women's offr Glasgow 2000–01; MP (Lab): Glasgow Maryhill 2001–05, Glasgow North 2005–15; parly under sec of state Scotland Office 2008–10, shadow frontbench spokesperson Scotland Office 2010, shadow sec of state for Scotland 2010–11, memb Business, Innovation and Skills Ctee 2011–; memb Cncl World Devpt Movement 1998–2004, dir Mercy Corps Scot 2002–08, govr and vice-chair Westminster Fndn for Democracy 2012–15; memb Law Soc of Scot; *Recreations* dance, films, art history; *Style*— Ms Ann McKechin; ✉ e-mail mckechina@gmail.com, Twitter @AnnMckechin2

MACKECHNIE, John Allan; s of Allan Mackechnie (d 1986), and Christina Johan, *née* Mackenzie (d 1985); *b* 19 August 1949; *Educ* Hyndland Sr Secdy Sch, Glasgow Sch of Art (DA), Faculty of Art & Design Brighton Poly; *m* 28 June 1975, Susan Shirley, da of William Ian Burnett; 1 da (Kirsty Joanne Louise b 25 Feb 1978); *Career* printmaker; printmaking asst: Faculty of Art & Design Brighton Poly 1972–73, Faculty of Art & Design Newcastle Poly 1973–76; Glasgow Print Studio: etching technician 1978–79, workshop mangr 1980–82, dir 1983–; visiting lectr to art colls throughout UK; memb Soc of Scottish Artists 1984– (memb Ctee 1989), memb Advsy Bd Bradford Int Print Biennale 1990–91, memb Steering Ctee Glasgow Art Fair, memb Ctee Glasgow Visual Art Forum 1995–96, memb Jury World Print Festival 1998; advsr on printmaking to Northern Regn 1983–93, major contrib to Glasgow's year as 1990 European City of Culture through exhbns and artists exchanges and projects; organiser exhibitions: Slovenia 1997–98, India 1998; *Exhibitions* incl: Young Generation (Norrkoping Museum Sweden) 1974, Epinal Biennale France 1975, Bradford Int Print Biennale 1976, 30 Contemporary Printmakers (Arnolfini Gall Bristol) 1976, World Print Competition (MOMA San Francisco) 1977, Impressions (Scottish Arts Cncl tour) 1978, Scottish Print Open (touring UK and Aust) 1980, solo exhbn Third Eye Centre Glasgow 1981, solo exhbn Richard Demarco Gall Edinburgh 1981, Northern Printmakers (Gall F15 Norway) 1982, Ljubljana Print Biennale Slovenia 1983, New Scottish Prints (touring Scotland, USA and Canada) 1983, Photography in Printmaking Glasgow Print Studio 1983, solo exhbn Edinburgh Printmakers Workshop 1983, Scottish Prints Open tour 1984, Society of Scottish Artists 1984 and 1985, The Clyde Exhibition Glasgow Print Exhbn 1986, Urban Myth solo exhbn (Glasgow Print Studio) 1999, solo exhbn Eye 2 Gall Edinburgh 2000, solo exhbn RIAS Gall Edinburgh 2000, Expressions in Dundee Contemporary Art 2000, solo exhbn Rebecca Hossack Gallery London 2001; *Awards* Glasgow Educnl Tst award 1971, Northern Arts major award 1976 and 1978, Scottish Arts Cncl travel award 1982, Arts Cncl Incentive Funding award for Glasgow Print Studio 1989; *Public Collections* incl: Scottish Arts Cncl, Hunterian Museum & Art Gall, MOMA San Francisco, Norrkoping Museum Sweden, Aberdeen Art Gall, Br Cncl, V&A, Kelvingrove Museum and Art Gall; *Recreations* the visual arts, golf; *Style*— John Mackechnie, Esq; ✉ Glasgow Print Studio, 22 King Street, Glasgow G1 5QP (☎ 0141 552 0704, fax 0141 552 2919, e-mail john@mackechnie.demon.co.uk

McKEE, Prof (James Clark St Clair) Sean; s of James Roy Alexander McKee (d 1996), and Martha (Mattie) Beattie, *née* Chalmer; *b* 1 July 1945; *Educ* George Watson's Coll Edinburgh, Univ of St Andrews (class medal, Duncan medal, BSc), Univ of Dundee (PhD), Univ of Oxford (MA, DSc); *m* 2, 1996, Joyce Elizabeth, *née* Houston; *Career* National Cash Register fell Univ of Dundee 1970–72, lectr in numerical analysis Univ of Southampton 1972–75; Univ of Oxford: CEGB sr res fell 1975–79, co-ordinator univ consortium for industrial numerical analysis 1979–86; head of mathematics and statistics Unilever Research Colworth and prof of industrial mathematics Univ of Strathclyde 1986–88, prof of mathematics Univ of Strathclyde 1988–; fell Hertford Coll Oxford 1975–86; ed: Mathematical Engrg in Industry, Applied Mathematics and Computation, Applied Mathematical Modelling, Fasciculi Mathematici; Inst of Mathematics and its Application (IMA): fell, memb Cncl 1996–99, chm Scottish Branch 1997–99; fndr memb and memb Cncl Euro Consortium for Mathematics in Industry (ECMI), fndr memb Inst for Contemporary Scotland (fndr memb and memb Sci and Technol Cmmn); memb: US Soc for Industrial and Applied Mathematics, Edinburgh Mathematical Soc, Sociedade Brasilieira de Matemática Applicada e Computacional, American Mathematical Soc; homenagem Univ of Saõ Paulo 2003; ICMC Medal of Honour Univ of Saõ Paulo 2009; FRSE 1996; *Books* Industrial Numerical Analysis (1986), Vector and Parallel Computing (1989), Artificial Intelligence in Mathematics (1990); also author proceedings the Third European Conference on Mathematics in Industry (1990); *Recreations* golf, gardening, hill walking; *Clubs* Bonnyton Golf; *Style*— Prof Sean McKee, FRSE; ✉ Department of Mathematics and Statistics, University of Strathclyde, Glasgow G1 1XH (☎ 0141 548 3671, fax 0141 551 8657)

McKEE, William Stewart; CBE (2006); *Educ* Bangor GS, Queen's Univ Belfast (BSc), Ulster Poly (Dip Mgmnt Studies, MBA); *m* Ursula Catherine; 1 da (Catherine b 1 April 1987), 1 s (William b 27 June 1990); *Career* VSO teacher W Africa 1970–71, student Queen's Univ Belfast 1971–75, summer vacational student Conservation Branch NI Dept of the Environment 1973, 1974, 1975 and 1976, clerical offr Belfast City Cncl 1975–76, nat admin trainee NI Staffs Cncl for the Health and Social Servs 1976–78, sr admin offr Lisburn Health Centre and Dist Offices Eastern Health & Social Servs Bd 1978–79, units admin Daisy Hill Hosp Southern Health & Social Servs Bd 1979–82; Eastern Health & Social Servs Bd: units admin Ulster Hosp 1982–84, gp admin Musgrave Park Hosp 1984–88, gp admin Royal Gp of Hosps 1988–90, unit gen mangr Royal Gp of Hosps 1990–92, chief exec Royal Gp of Hosps and Dental Hosp NHS Tst 1992–; pres Inst of Healthcare Mgmnt; dir Belfast City Partnership Bd, dir NI Centre for Competitiveness; *Style*— William S McKee, Esq, CBE; ✉ Royal Group of Hospitals Trust, Royal Victoria Hospital, Grosvenor Road, Belfast BT12 6BA (☎ 028 9089 4755, fax 028 9024 0899)

McKELL, Iain Spiers; s of Joseph Duncan McKell, and Gwendoline Helen McKell; *b* 18 April 1957; *Educ* Clifton, Exeter Coll of Art and Design (SIAD Dip); *Career* fashion, advertising and editorial photographer since 1981, commercials director since 1993; subsequent experience in record sleeve photography 1982; working for for Italian Vogue, L'Uomo Vogue, i-D magazine and Harpers Bazaar, portrait cmmns for The Sunday Times and Observer magazines; memb: AFAEP, NUJ; subjects incl Madonna (her first magazine cover), Gilbert & George, Bob Hoskins, Sinead O'Connor, Boy George, Jilly Cooper, Tom Sharp, Jeremy Irons, Sir John Gielgud, Brad Pitt and Robert Carlyle; photographic advtg campaigns incl: Red Stripe 1986, Holsten Export 1988, Vladivar Vodka and Corona 1990, Levis (UK and Europe) 1991, Philip Morris (Germany) and Dunhill 1992; direction of Post Modern links for MTV (USA, UK and Europe) 1990; *Solo and Group Exhibitions* incl: Skinheads (Camera Obscura, Germany) 1981, Iain McKell Live (Open Day Studio Show) 1984, Iain McKell Live and Five Years of The Face (Photographers' Gallery) 1985, Fashion and Surrealism (V&A Museum) 1987, Creative Future Awards (cmmnd by Direction magazine) 1988 and 2000, BA sponsored exhbn (touring NY, Chicago, Los Angeles, Hong Kong, Tokyo and Sydney) 1989, Magnificent Seven 1992, Then & Now (Gallery Story London) 2001; *Awards* Bronze Arrow Award by BTAA and Clio USA-Europe for Fisherman's Friend commercial, BTAC Award for Sony Playstation commercial 1998; *Publications* Fashion Forever (2004); *Recreations* skiing, photography, drawing, writing; *Clubs* Soho House; *Style*— Iain McKell, Esq; ☎ 020 8968 8668

McKELLAR, Prof Quintin; CBE (2011); *Educ* PhD, DVM; *Career* scientific dir Moredun Research Inst 1997–2004, princ Royal Veterinary Coll Univ of London 2004–10, vice-chllr Univ of Herts 2011–; chair: Strategy Bd Regulatory Agency 2005–08, Scientific Advsy Ctee on Bovine Tuberculosis 2007–11; memb: Veterinary Products Ctee 1993–2001, Science Advsy Cncl Dept of Environment, Food and Rural Affrs 2011–14; memb Cncl: Royal Coll of Veterinary Surgeons 2004–10, Biotechnology and Biological Sciences Research Cncl 2005–11, Univ of London Sch of Pharmacy 2006–12; Wellcome Tst Medal for Veterinary Research 1993, Royal Agricultural Soc Bledisloe Award 2000, Saltire Soc Scottish Science Award 2001; *Recreations* rowing; *Clubs* Athenaeum, Leander; *Style*— Prof Quintin McKellar, CBE; ✉ Vice-Chancellor's Office, University of Hertfordshire, Hatfield, Hertfordshire AL10 9AB

McKELLEN, Sir Ian Murray; CH (2008), kt (1991), CBE (1979); s of Denis Murray McKellen (d 1964), of Bolton, Lancs, and Margery Lois, *née* Sutcliffe (d 1952); *b* 25 May 1939; *Educ* Wigan GS, Bolton Sch, St Catharine's Coll Cambridge (BA); *Career* actor and director since 1961; dir: Liverpool Playhouse 1969, Watford and Leicester 1972, A Private Matter (Vaudeville) 1973, The Clandestine Marriage (Savoy) 1975; assoc dir RNT; pres Marlowe Soc 1960–61, memb Cncl Equity 1971–72, Cameron Mackintosh prof of contemporary theatre Univ of Oxford 1991; Walpole Medal of Excellence 2003; Hon DLitt: Univ of Nottingham 1989, Univ of Aberdeen 1993; hon fell St Catharine's Coll Cambridge 1982; *Theatre* first stage appearance A Man for all Seasons (Belgrade Theatre Coventry) 1961, Arts Theatre Ipswich 1962–63, Nottingham Playhouse 1963–64, first London stage appearance A Scent of Flowers (Duke of York's) 1964 (Clarence Derwent Award); RNT incl: Much Ado About Nothing (also Old Vic) 1965, Venice Preserv'd 1984, Coriolanus 1984–85 (London Standard Award), Wild Honey (also Los Angeles & NY) 1986–87 (Olivier Award, Plays and Players Award), Kent in King Lear and title role in Richard III 1990 (Olivier Award (assoc prodr for world tour 1990–91)), Napoli Milionaria 1991, Uncle Vanya 1992, Richard III (also USA tour) 1992, An Enemy of the People 1997, Peter Pan 1997; RNT as assoc dir, prodr and performer: The Duchess of Malfi 1985, The Real Inspector Hound 1985, The Cherry Orchard (also Paris and Chicago) 1985, Bent (also Garrick) 1990; RSC incl: Dr Faustus (Edinburgh Festival and Aldwych) 1974, Marquis of Keith (Aldwych) 1974–75, King John (Aldwych) 1975, Too True to be Good (Aldwych and Globe) 1975, Romeo and Juliet 1976, The Winter's Tale 1976, Macbeth 1976–77 (Plays and Players Award 1976), Pillars of the Community 1977 (SWET Award), Days of the Commune 1977, The Alchemist 1978 (SWET Award), Iago in Othello (The Other Place, Stratford and Young Vic) 1989 (Evening Standard and London Critics' Award); prodr RSC tour 1978: Three Sisters, Twelfth Night, Is There Honey Still for Tea; Actors Company (fndr memb): Ruling The Roost 1972, 'Tis Pity She's a Whore (Edinburgh Festival) 1972, Wood-Demon (Edinburgh Festival) 1973, King Lear (Brooklyn Acad of Music, Wimbledon Theatre season) 1974; Acting Shakespeare 1977–90, tours incl: Israel, Norway, Denmark, Sweden, Spain, NYC (Drama Desk Award), San Francisco, Washington DC, Los Angeles, Olney, Cleveland, San Diego, Boston (Elliot Norton Award), Playhouse London; other roles incl: A Lily in Little India (St Martin's) 1965,

Man of Destiny/O'Flaherty VC (Mermaid) 1966, Their Very Own and Golden City (Royal Court) 1966, The Promise (Fortune, also Broadway) 1967, The White Liars/Black Comedy (Lyric) 1968, Richard II (Prospect Theatre Co) 1968, The Recruiting Officer 1970, Chips with Everything (Cambridge Theatre Co) 1970, Hamlet (Cambridge, UK and Euro tours) 1971, Ashes (Young Vic) 1975, Words, Words, Words (solo recital, Edinburgh and Belfast Festivals) 1976, Acting Shakespeare (Edinburgh and Belfast Festivals) 1977, Bent (Royal Court, Criterion) 1979 (SWET Award), Amadeus (Broadhurst) 1980–81 (Drama Desk, NY Drama League, Outer Critics' Circle and Tony Awards), Short List (Hampstead) 1983, Cowardice (Ambassadors) 1983, Henceforward (Vaudeville) 1988, A Knight Out (Lyceum Theatre, NYC, South Africa and UK tour, Vancouver) 1994–2002, Orpheus Descending (Broadway) 2001, Aladdin (Old Vic) 2004 and 2005, Waiting for Godot (nat tour, Theatre Royal) 2009; for West Yorkshire Playhouse: The Seagull 1998, Present Laughter 1999, The Tempest 1999; *Television* since 1966 incl: Loving Walter 1982 (RTS Performance Award), Walter and June 1983, Countdown to War 1989, And the Band Played On 1993 (Emmy nomination), Cold Comfort Farm 1994; appearences in: The Simpsons 2003, Coronation Street 2005, Vicious 2013; *Film* since 1968 incl: A Touch of Love 1968, Alfred the Great 1968, The Promise 1969, Priest of Love 1979, Scarlet Pimpernel 1982, Zina 1985, Plenty 1986, The Ballad of Little Jo 1992, I'll Do Anything 1992, Last Action Hero 1993, Six Degrees of Separation 1993, The Shadow 1993, Jack and Sarah 1994, Restoration 1995, Richard III 1996 (Evening Standard Best Film Award), Rasputin 1996 (Emmy nomination, Golden Globe Award for Best Supporting Actor), Bent 1997, Swept From the Sea 1997, Apt Pupil 1998, Gods and Monsters 1998 (Oscar nomination for Best Actor), X-Men 2000, The Lord of the Rings: The Fellowship of the Ring 2001 (Oscar nomination for Best Supporting Actor), The Lord of the Rings: The Two Towers 2002, The Lord of the Rings: The Return of the King 2003, X2 2003, Emile 2004, Asylum 2005, Neverwas 2005; *Style*— Sir Ian McKellen, CH, CBE; ✉ c/o Independent Talent, Oxford House, 76 Oxford Street, London W1N 0AX (✆ 020 7636 6565, fax 020 7323 0101); c/o ICM, 8942 Wilshire Boulevard, Beverly Hills, CA 90211–1934, USA (✆ 001 310 550 4000, fax 001 310 550 4100, website: www.mckellen.com)

McKELVIE, Christina; MSP; *b* 4 March 1968, Glasgow; *Educ* Anniesland Coll Glasgow, Cardonald Coll Glasgow, Univ of St Andrews; *Career* MSP (SNP): Central Scotland 2007–11, Hamilton, Larkhall & Stonehouse 2011–; *Style*— Ms Christina McKelvie, MSP; ✉ Barncluith Business Center, Townhead Street, Hamilton, ML3 7DP (✆ 01698 403311, fax 01698 403313, e-mail martha.mcallister@scottish.parliament.uk); The Scottish Parliament, Edinburgh EH99 1SP (e-mail christina.mckelvie.msp@scottish.parliament.uk)

McKENDRICK, Emma Elizabeth Ann; da of Ian Cameron Black, and (Patricia) Ann Black; *b* 24 June 1963, Perth, Scotland; *Educ* Bedford HS, Univ of Liverpool (BA), Univ of Birmingham (PGCE); *m* 19 Dec 1987, Iain Alastair McKendrick; 2 s (Fergus b 2002, Hamish b 2004); *Career* Royal Sch Bath: teacher of German 1986–88, head of sixth form and careers 1988–90, sixth form housemistress 1989–90, dep head 1990–93, headmistress 1994–97; headmistress Downe House 1997–; govr: Lambrook Sch, Sandroyd Sch Salisbury, Kings Sch Canterbury, Radley Coll 2008; memb: GSA 1994, BSA 1994, Educn Ctee GSA; FRSA 2004; *Recreations* travel, theatre, cinema; *Clubs* Lansdowne; *Style*— Mrs Emma McKendrick; ✉ Downe House, Cold Ash, Thatcham, Berkshire RG18 9JJ (✆ 01635 200286, fax 01635 204724, e-mail headmistress@downehouse.net)

McKENDRICK, Melveena; James Powell Jones, and Catherine Letitia Jones; *b* 23 March 1941; *Educ* Neath Girls' GS, Dyffryn GS Port Talbot, KCL, Girton Coll Cambridge; *m* Neil McKendrick , *qv*; 2 da (Olivia Sarah Katherine b 20 Nov 1970, Cornelia Alexandra b 6 Sept 1972); *Career* Girton Coll Cambridge: Jex-Blake research fell 1967, fell and lectr in Spanish 1970–99, tutor 1970–83, sr tutor 1974–81, dir of studies in modern languages 1984–95, professorial fell 1999–2008, life fell 2008–; Univ of Cambridge: lectr in Spanish Univ of Cambridge 1980–92, reader in Spanish literature and society 1992–99, prof of Spanish Golden Age literature, culture and society 1999–2008, pro-vice-chllr (educn) 2004–08, memb numerous bds and ctees; Br Acad: research readership 1990–92, memb Humanities Research Bd and Research Ctee of Br Acad 1996–98, chair Research Panel 2 (Other Languages and Literatures) 1996–98, memb AHRB, chair Research Panel 5 (Modern Languages and Lit) 1998–99; Lansdowne visitor Univ of Victoria BC 1997; conslt hispanic ed Everyman 1993–99; memb Editorial Bd: Donaire (the Spanish Embassy's scholarly jl) 1994–, Bulletin of Hispanic Studies 1998–; memb Advsy Bd Revista Canadiense de Estudios Hispánicos; LittD Univ of Cambridge 2002, Hon DLitt Univ of South Wales 2013; FBA 1999; *Publications* Ferdinand and Isabella (1968), A Concise History of Spain (1972), Woman and Society in the Spanish Drama of the Golden Age (1974), Cervantes (1980), Golden-Age Studies in Honour of Alexander A Parker (1984), Theatre in Spain 1490–1700 (1989), El mágico prodigioso (1992), Playing the King: Lope de Vega and the Limits of Conformity (2000), Identities in Crisis: Essays on Honour, Gender and Women in the 'Comedia'; also author of numerous articles, chapters and int conference papers; *Style*— Prof Melveena McKendrick, LittD, FBA; ✉ Girton College, Cambridge CB3 0JG (e-mail mcm1000@cam.ac.uk)

McKENDRICK, Neil; s of Robert Alexander McKendrick (d 1944), and Sarah Elizabeth, *née* Irvine (d 1996); *b* 28 July 1935; *Educ* Alderman Newton's Sch Leicester, Christ's Coll Cambridge (entrance scholar, Robert Owen Bishop Studentship, BA, MA); *m* 18 March 1967, Prof Melveena McKendrick, FBA, *qv*; 2 da (Olivia Sarah Katherine b 20 Nov 1970, Cornelia Alexandra b 6 Sept 1972); *Career* research fell Christ's Coll Cambridge 1958; Univ of Cambridge: asst lectr in history 1961–64, lectr in history 1964–95, chm Faculty of History 1985–87, reader in social and economic history 1995–2002; Gonville & Caius Coll Cambridge: fell 1958–96, lectr in history 1958–96, dir of studies 1959–96, tutor 1961–69, master 1996–2005; hon fell Christ's Coll Cambridge 1996; FRHistS 1971; *Books* Historical Perspectives (1974), The Birth of a Consumer Society: the Commercialisation of Eighteenth Century England (1983), Business Life and Public Policy (1986), The Birth of Foreign and Colonial: the world's first investment trust (1993), F & C: A History of Foreign and Colonial Investment Trust (1999); *Recreations* gardening, antiques, claret; *Clubs* Athenaeum, Bordeaux; *Style*— Neil McKendrick, Esq, FRHistS

McKENNA, Judge Alison; *Career* called to the Bar 1988; admitted slr 2003; fee-paid legal memb Mental Health Review Tbnl 2002, fee-paid tbnl judge of the first-tier (Health Educn and Social Care Chamber) 2008, pres Charity Tbnl 2008, princ judge First-tier Tbnl (Charity) 2009, judicial appts cmmr 2012–14, pres War Pensions and Armed Forces Compensation Chamber First-Tier Tbnl 2014–; *Style*— Judge McKenna

McKENNA, Geraldine Martina Maria; da of John McKenna (d 1988), and Mary McKenna (d 1995); *b* 9 August 1955, Omagh, NI; *Educ* Loreto Convent Omagh; *Career* British Airways NI 1976–81, Aer Lingus/Enterprise Travel FL 1981–84, Belfast City Airport 1984–87, InterContinental Hotel Corp London 1987–91, InterContinental Hotel Corp NY 1991–96; The Savoy Gp: dir of mktg 1996–2001, chief exec 2001–02; chief exec Maybourne Hotel Gp (formerly The Savoy Gp) 2002–06; ptnr Cedar Capital Ptnrs; advsr Fraser Giles Partnership; memb Br Airways Int Business Advsy Bd; Hon DHL Schiller Int Univ 2004; FRSA; *Recreations* sailing, horse riding, travel; *Style*— Ms Geraldine McKenna

McKENNA, His Hon Judge Martin Nicholas; s of Bernard Malcolm McKenna, of Lytham St Annes, Lancs, and Anne Rose *née* Orsman; *b* 19 November 1955; *Educ* Catholic Coll Preston, Univ of Birmingham (LLB), Lincoln Coll Oxford; *m* 1, 1979 (m dis 1995), Deborah Jane Scott; 2 da (Katherine Sophie (Katie), Charlotte Lucy (Charlie) (twins) b 13 Nov 1988); m 2, 1996, Sarah Louise, da of Alan Arthur Malden; 2 step da (Emma Louise b 15 July 1989, Annie Ruth b 12 June 1991); *Career* slr; Eversheds (formerly Evershed & Tomkinson): trainee 1978, slr 1980, assoc 1984–87, ptnr 1987–2000, head of litigation 1994–99; circuit judge (Midland Circuit) 2000–, sr circuit judge and designated civil judge for Birmingham 2008–; memb: Law Soc, Birmingham Law Soc, IPA, Assoc of Business Recovery Professionals, CEDR; *Recreations* sailing, skiing, rugby, cricket; *Clubs* East India; *Style*— His Hon Judge McKenna; ✉ c/o Midland Circuit Secretariat, The Priory Courts, 33 Bull Street, Birmingham B4 6DW (✆ 0121 681 3200, fax 0121 681 3202)

McKENNA, Prof Patrick Gerald (Gerry); DL (Co Londonderry 2002); s of Gerald Joseph McKenna (d 1989), of Benburb, Co Tyrone, and Mary Teresa, *née* Smyth (d 1989); *b* 10 December 1953; *Educ* St Patrick's Acad Dungannon, Univ of Ulster (BSc), Queen's Univ Belfast (PhD); *m* 10 Aug 1976, Phil, *née* McArdle; 2 s (Gerald John b 11 Sept 1980, James Philip b 23 March 1983); *Career* lectr in human biology and genetics New Univ of Ulster 1978–84; Univ of Ulster: sr lectr in biology 1984–88, dir Biomedical Sciences Research Centre 1985–88, prof and head Dept of Biological and Biomedical Sciences 1988–94, dean Faculty of Science 1994–97, pro-vice-chllr (research) 1997–99, vice-chllr and pres 1999–2006; subject advsr (biomedical sciences) Hong Kong Poly Univ 2010–, advsr to 6 UK univs on REF2014 2012–13; pres emeritus and hon exec sec Heads of Univ Centres of Biomedical Science 2011– (chair 1995–97); visiting prof: Univ of Malaya 1991, Univ Kebangsaan 1993, Univ of Calif Berkeley 1995; author of over 200 scientific pubns; chair: Audit Ctee NI Medical Physics Agency 1994–2001, NI Foresight Life and Health Technologies Panel 1996–2000, HE Funding Cncls Reseach Assessment Exercise Professions and Studies Allied to Medical Panel 2001–, Univs Ireland 2002–04, Ind Advsy Gp Doctoral Training Alliance (Univ Alliance) 2015–; coordinator RIA Review of HE funding in NI 2016; memb: Stormont All Pty Gp on Science and Technol 2012–, Heads of Univ Biosciences Exec Ctee 2013–, Int Advsy Bd Kufa Univ 2013–; Quality Assurance Agency (memb Biosciences and Biomedical Science Benchmarking Review Gps 2014–); memb Editorial Bd: Radiography 2004–, Br Jl of Biomedical Science 2006– (chair Review Working Gp 2014); chair: UUTECH Ltd 2002–04, UUSRP Ltd 2002–04; chair Servite Priory Library Ctee Mgmnt Bd 2010–, vice-chair Ulster Cancer Fndn 2000–04; Freeman Borough of Coleraine 2001; Hon DSc Nat Univ of Ireland 2001, Hon LLD Queen's Univ Belfast 2002; FIBMS 1982, FSB 1989 (memb Educn Policy Advsy Ctee 2014–), MRIA 2001 (memb North-South Standing Ctee 2012–, memb All Island and Int Task Force 2013–, memb Life and Medical Sciences Ctee 2014–, memb Council-nominated Members Ctee 2014–, memb Steering Gp on Optimal Govt Structures for HE and Research 2015); *Publications* over 200 incl books, scientific papers, reviews and reports; *Recreations* reading, the turf; *Clubs* Reform; *Style*— Prof Gerry McKenna, DL, MRIA; ✉ HUCBMS, c/o IBMS, 12 Coldbath Square, London EC1R 5HL (✆ 07766 745511, e-mail mckenna.gerry@rocketmail.com, website www.gerrymckenna.co.uk)

McKENNA, Paul William; s of William Joseph McKenna, of Enfield, Middx, and Joan Brenda, *née* Garner; *b* 8 November 1963; *Educ* St Ignatius Coll Enfield, PhD in clinical hypnosis; *Career* hypnotist, entertainer and television presenter; disc jockey: Radio Caroline 1984, breakfast show Chiltern Radio 1985–87, Capital Radio 1988–91, BBC Radio 1 1991–92; first hypnotic show 1986, appeared at numerous major venues incl Royal Albert Hall 1992, TV debut Paul McKenna's Hypnotic Show (special then series, Carlton) 1993, series The Hypnotic World of Paul McKenna (Celador Productions and Paul McKenna Productions for Carlton/ITV Network) 1994–, presenter Network First factual prog Paul McKenna's Hypnotic Secrets (Man Alive Group and Paul McKenna Productions for Carlton) 1995, series The Paranormal World of Paul McKenna (Man Alive Group and Paul McKenna Productions for Carlton) 1996, special The World's Funniest Hypnotist (ABC) 1996; also recorded set of audio and video hypnotherapy tapes; chm Br Cncl of Professional Stage Hypnotists 1990–92, memb Fedn of Ethical Stage Hypnotists (FESH); *Awards* TRIC Celebrity Award for New Talent of the Year 1994, Capital Radio Best London Show Award for Paul McKenna's Hypnotic Show 1994; *Books* The Hypnotic World of Paul McKenna (1993), Paul McKenna's Hypnotic Secrets (1996), The Paranormal World of Paul McKenna (1997), Change Your Life in Seven Days (2004), I Can Make You Thin (2005); *Style*— Paul McKenna, Esq; ✉ PO Box 5514, London W8 4ZY (website www.paulmckenna.com)

McKENNA, Virginia Anne; OBE (2004); da of Terence Morell McKenna (d 1948), and Anne-Marie (Anne de Nys, the music composer), *née* Dennis (who m (2) Jack Drummond Rudd and (3) Sir Charles Richard Andrew Oakeley, 6 Bt, and d 1993); *b* 7 June 1931; *Educ* Herschel Cape Town, Herons Ghyll Horsham, Central Sch of Speech and Drama; *m* 1 1954 (m dis 1957), Denholm Mitchell Elliot, CBE (d 1992), the actor; m 2, 19 Sept 1957, William Inglis Lindon (Bill) Travers, MBE (d 1994), the actor, s of William Halton Lindon Travers (d 1966); 3 s (William Morrell Lindon b 4 Nov 1958, Justin McKenna Lindon b 6 March 1963, Daniel Inglis Lindon b 27 Feb 1967), 1 da (Louise Annabella Linden b 6 July 1960); *Career* actress and writer; co-fndr The Born Free Fndn (formerly Zoo Check Charitable Tst) 1984; patron: Fitzroy, Plan International UK (formerly World Family), Children of the Andes 1991, Wildlife Aid 1991, The Surrey Badger Protection Soc 1996, Tayside Cat Shelter, Cinnamon Tst; Lifetime Achievement Wetnose Award 2011, Outstanding Contrib to Animal Welfare Br Animal Honours 2013; Hon DSc Nottingham Trent Univ 2012, Hon Dr of Arts Univ of Bedfordshire 2014; *Theatre* incl: season Old Vic 1955–56, The Devils 1961, Beggars Opera 1963, A Little Night Music 1976, The King and I (SWET Award for Best Musical Actress) 1979, Hamlet (RSC) 1984, The Best Christmas Present in the World (by and with Michael Morpurgo); *Television* incl: Romeo and Juliet (Best Actress Award ITV) 1955, Passage to India 1965, The Deep Blue Sea 1974, Cheap in August, The Scold's Bridle 1998, The Whistle Blower 2001; *Films* incl: The Cruel Sea 1952, A Town Like Alice 1954 (Academy Award for Best Actress), Carve Her Name With Pride (Belgian Prix Femina) 1957, Born Free (Variety Club Award for Best Actress) 1964, Ring of Bright Water 1968, Sliding Doors 1998, What Do You See? 2005, Home 2008, Golden Years 2016; *Books* On Playing with Lions (with Bill Travers), Some of my Friends have Tails, Beyond the Bars (jt ed and jt author), Headlines from the Jungle (anthology of verse, co-ed, 1990), Into the Blue (1992), Journey to Freedom (1997), Back To The Blue (1997), The Life in My Years (2009), Tonight the Moon is Red (poetry, 2014); *Audio books*: The Butterfly Lion (by Michael Morpurgo), Why The Whales Came (by Michael Morpurgo), The Secret Garden (2007), An African Love Story (2012); *Recreations* reading, travelling, gardening; *Style*— Miss Virginia McKenna, OBE; ✉ The Born Free Foundation, Broadlands Business Campus, Langhurstwood Road, Horsham, West Sussex RH12 4QP (✆ 01403 240170); Theatrical Agent: Geoff Stanton, Stanton Davidson Associates, RADA Studios, 16 Chenies Street, London WC1E 7EX (e-mail geoff@stantondavidson.co.uk); Literary Agent: Diana Tyler, MBA Literary and Script Agents, 62 Grafton Way, London W1T 5DW

MACKENZIE; *see also:* Muir Mackenzie

MACKENZIE, Prof Andrew Peter (Andy); s of Alexander Colin Mackenzie, of Dornoch, Sutherland, and Bridget Mary, *née* Gordon; *b* 7 March 1964, Elderslie, Strathclyde; *Educ* Univ of Edinburgh (BSc), Univ of Cambridge (PhD); *m* 17 May 1991, Olga Maria; 2 da (Lucia Cristina Maria b 8 Dec 1999, Katrina Maria b 25 March 2003), 1 s (Alexander Daniel (twin) b 25 March 2003); *Career* researcher CERN Geneva 1986–87; Univ of Cambridge: Katherine and Charles Darwin research fell Darwin Coll 1991–94, univ research fell 1991–93, Royal Soc univ research fell 1993–2001; reader Univ of Birmingham 1997–2001, currently prof and dir of research Sch of Physics and Astronomy Univ of St Andrews; visiting posts: Bariloche Univ 1995, Stanford Univ 2003, Kyoto Univ 2004, Cornell Univ 2006; Mott lectr Inst of Physics 1999, Daiwa-Adrian Prize

2004; FInstP 2002, FRSE 2004; *Recreations* golf, reading, mountain walking; *Style*— Prof Andy Mackenzie; ✉ School of Physics and Astronomy, The University of St Andrews, North Haugh, St Andrews KY16 9SS (☎ 01334 463108, fax 01334 463104, e-mail apm9@st-and.ac.uk)

MACKENZIE, Colin; s of Hector Colin Beardmore Mackenzie (d 1998), and Frances Evelyn, *née* Purkis (d 1996); *b* 4 November 1945; *Educ* Eastbourne Coll; *m* 19 Oct 1968, Fiona Maureen, *née* Barr; 2 da (Rebecca Ann b 7 April 1975, Elizabeth Fiona b 21 Dec 1976); *Career* chartered surveyor; Hampton & Sons: Mayfield E Sussex 1974–80, Sevenoaks Kent 1980–85, dir Country and Estates Depts 1987–98; ptnr Knight Frank Private Clients Buying Service 1998–2003; dir Colin Mackenzie Ltd 1995–; FRICS; *Recreations* country sports, vintage sports cars; *Style*— Colin Mackenzie, Esq; ✉ Bonischerch, Old Heathfield, East Sussex TN21 9AG (☎ 01435 866988, fax 01435 866662, e-mail cm@cmproperty.co.uk)

McKENZIE, Dr Dan Peter; CH (2003); s of William Stewart McKenzie, and Nancy Mary McKenzie; *b* 21 February 1942; *Educ* Westminster, King's Coll Cambridge (BA, MA, PhD); *m* 5 June 1971, Indira Margaret; 1 s (James Misra b 3 April 1976); *Career* Univ of Cambridge: sr asst in res 1969–75, asst dir of res 1975–79, reader in tectonics 1979–84, prof of earth sciences (currently emeritus) 1985–, Royal Soc prof of earth sciences 1996–2007; Balzan Prize of Int Balzan Fndn (with F J Vine and D H Matthews, 1981), Japan Prize Sci and Technol Fndn of Japan (with W J Morgan and X Le Pichon, 1990), Royal Medal of the Royal Soc 1991, Crafoord Prize of the Swedish Acad 2002, Copley Medal of the Royal Soc 2011; hon memb Japan Acad Tokyo 2014; Hon MA Univ of Cambridge 1966; memb Royal Soc 1976, foreign assoc US Nat Acad of Scis 1989; *Publications* author of various papers in learned journals; *Recreations* gardening; *Style*— Prof Dan McKenzie, CH; ✉ Bullard Laboratories, Madingley Road, Cambridge CB3 0EZ

MacKENZIE, Prof Donald; *Educ* Univ of Edinburgh (BSc, PhD); *Career* prof of sociology Univ of Edinburgh; ESRC professorial research fell 2004–08; FBA 2004; *Books* incl: Knowing Machines (1996), The Social Shaping of Technology (ed with Judy Wajcman, 2 edn, 1999), Mechanizing Proof: Computing, Risk and Trust (2001), An Engine, Not a Camera: How Financial Models Shape Markets (2006), Material Markets: How Economic Agents are Constructed (2009); *Style*— Prof Donald MacKenzie; ✉ School of Social and Political Science, The University of Edinburgh, Chrystal Macmillan Building, Edinburgh EH8 9LD

MacKENZIE, George Paterson; s of James Sargent Porteous MacKenzie (d 2000), and Flora Black Paterson (d 2012); *b* 22 September 1950, Lenzie, E Dunbartonshire; *Educ* George Watson's Coll Edinburgh, Leeds GS, Univ of Stirling (BA, MLitt), Moray House Coll of Educn; *m* 22 October 2005, Caroline Morgan; *Career* teacher of history Larbert HS 1974–75, research asst Scottish Record Office 1975–82, departmental records offr Gen Register Office for Scotland 1983–85, head Liaison Branch and Preservation Servs Branch Scottish Record Office 1986–94, dep sec-gen Int Cncl on Archives Paris 1995–96, head of external rels Nat Archives of Scotland 1997–2000, Keeper of the Records of Scotland (ceo Nat Archives of Scotland) 2001–12, Registrar Gen for Scotland (ceo Nat Records of Scotland) 2011–12, pres Scottish Records Soc 2014–; consultancy work on archives and records (particularly on preservation issues and the protection of archives in armed conflict) for UNESCO, World Bank and ICA; author of articles on archives and records in specialist pubns, numerous invited lectures and talks internationally; Int Inst for Conservation Award 2012; tstee Int Records Mgmnt Tst 2013–; chair Ancestral Tourism Steering Gp Scotland 2013–; FICA 2012; *Recreations* travel, cooking, reading; *Style*— George MacKenzie, Esq; ✉ Sheiling, Clachan Seil, by Oban PA34 4QZ (☎ 01852 300507, e-mail georgepmackenzie@gmail.com)

MACKENZIE, James; *Career* chef-proprietor Pipe and Glass Inn South Dalton Beverley 2006– (Michelin star 2010–, Michelin Pub of the Year 2012); *Books* On the Menu (2011); *Style*— James Mackenzie, Esq; ✉ The Pipe and Glass Inn, West End, South Dalton, Beverley, East Yorkshire HU17 7PN

MACKENZIE, Gen Sir (John) Jeremy George; GCB (1998, KCB 1992), OBE (1982), DL; s of Lt-Col John William Elliot Mackenzie, DSO, QPM (d 1990), and Valerie Margaret, *née* Dawes; *b* 11 February 1941; *Educ* Duke of York Sch Nairobi; *m* 12 April 1969, Elizabeth Lyon (Liz), da of Col George Leftwich Wertenbaker, USAF (d 1986); 1 s (Edward John George b 17 May 1976), 1 da (Georgina Elizabeth b 8 July 1978); *Career* cmmnd 1 Bn Queen's Own Highlanders 1961, CO Queen's Own Highlanders 1979–82, Cmd 12 Armd Bde (as Brig) 1984–87, Maj-Gen 1989, Cmdt Staff Coll Camberley 1989, GOC 4 Armd Div 1989–91, Lt-Gen 1991, cmd 1 British Corps Bielefeld 1991–92, cmd ACE NATO Rapid Reaction Corps (ARRC) 1992–94, Dep Supreme Cdr Allied Powers Europe (DSACEUR) 1994–98; govr Royal Hosp Chelsea 1999–2006; Lt Queen's Body Guard for Scotland (Royal Co of Archers) 1986–2016; Col Cmdt AGC 1992–98, Col The Highlanders Regt 1994–2001, Col Cmdt Army Physical Trg Corps 1999–2012; ADC Gen 1992–98; pres: Defence Deer Mgmnt 1996–2015, Combined Servs Winter Sports Assoc (life vice-pres); dir: Sirva plc 2003–08, Selex Communications Ltd 2004–13, Blue Hackle Security 2006, AC Cars Ltd 2012, UK Gear 2012–16, Secure Accommodation Worldwide Ltd 2014; sr mil advsr Beretta 2008–12; chm and owner Tantrax Int Ltd 2014; Cdr US Legion of Merit 1997 and 1999, Cross of Merit (Czech Rep) 1st Class 1998, Hungary Offrs Cross Order of Merit 1998, Order of the Madara Horsemen of Bulgaria 1st Class 1999, Gold Medal of the Slovenian Armed Forces 2002; *Recreations* shooting, fishing; *Clubs* Sloane; *Style*— Gen Sir Jeremy Mackenzie, GCB, OBE, DL; ✉ The Old Bell, 20 Long Street, Cerne Abbas, Dorset DT2 7JF

MacKENZIE, Prof John MacDonald; JP; s of Alexander MacKenzie (d 1987), and Hannah, *née* Whitby (d 1984); *b* 2 October 1943, Manchester; *Educ* Ndola Govt Sch Northern Rhodesia, Woodside Sch Glasgow, Univ of Glasgow (MA), Univ of Br Columbia (PhD); *Career* teaching asst and research fell Univ of Br Columbia 1964–68; Lancaster Univ: successively lectr, sr lectr and prof 1968–2002, princ County Coll 1976–81, dean of humanities and dean of educn 1989–97, prof emeritus 2002–; hon research prof: Research Centre for Irish and Scottish Studies Univ of Aberdeen 2001–, Research Centre for Environmental History Univs of St Andrews and Stirling 2001–; visiting prof Univ of Highlands and Islands 2016–; hon fell Scottish Centre of Diaspora Studies Univ of Edinburgh 2009–; Leverhulme Tst emeritus fell 2005–; historical advsr exhbn on David Livingstone Nat Portrait Gallery 1995–96, conslt curator exhbn on the Victorian Vision V&A 1997–2001; tstee Ruskin Fndn 1994–99; ed: Studies in Imperialism series Manchester Univ Press 1985–, Environment and History 2000–05; memb and chm Lancaster Bench 1990–2000; chm of govrs Morecambe HS 1981–85; hon fell Univ of Edinburgh 2006–; FRHistS 1984, FRSE 2003; *Books* The Partition of Africa (1983), Propaganda and Empire (1984), The Railway Station, a Social History (jtly, 1986), Imperialism and Popular Culture (ed, 1986), Imperialism and the Natural World (ed, 1990), Popular Imperialism and the Military (ed, 1992), Orientalism: History, Theory and the Arts (1995), David Livingstone and the Victorian Encounter with Africa (ed, 1996), The Victorian Vision (ed, 2001), Peoples, Nations and Cultures (ed, 2005), The Scots in South Africa (2007), Museums and Empire (2009), Scotland and the British Empire (ed, 2011), European Empires and the People (ed, 2011), Scotland, Empire and Decolonisation in the Twentieth Century (co-ed, 2015), Exhibiting the Empire (co-ed, 2015), Encyclopaedia of Empire (ed, 2016, 4 vols), Global Migrations: the Scots Diaspora since 1600 (co-ed, 2016); *Recreations* music, opera, deltiology, walking, travel; *Style*— Prof John MacKenzie; ✉ Old Bank House, Bank Street, Alyth, Perthshire PH11 8DB (☎ 01828 633469, e-mail john@dalmackie.com, website www.dalmackie.com)

McKENZIE, Julia Kathleen (Mrs Jerry Harte); da of Albion James Jeffrey McKenzie (d 1970), of Enfield, Middx, and Kathleen, *née* Rowe; *b* 17 February 1942; *Educ* Tottenham Co Sch, Guildhall Sch of Music and Drama; *m* 1972, Jerry Harte, s of Carl Harte; *Career* actress and director; Hon DLitt South Bank Univ 1999, Hon Dr Royal Acad of Music; FGSM 1985; *Theatre* West End and New York performances incl: Cowardy Custard, Miriam in Outside Edge, Lily Garland in On the Twentieth Century, Hobson's Choice, Schweyk in the Second World War, Miss Adelaide in Guys and Dolls (NT, Best Actress Variety Club Awards, Best Actress Soc of West End Theatre Awards, Olivier Award), Sally in Follies, The Witch in Into the Woods, Company, Promises Promises, Mame, Side by Side (by Sondheim); Alan Ayckbourn plays incl: Norman Conquests, Ten Times Table, Communicating Doors, Woman in Mind (Best Actress London Evening Standard Awards 1986); Mrs Lovett in Sweeney Todd (RNT, Olivier Award for Best Actress in a Musical) 1994, Royal Family 2001, Philadelphia Story 2005; theatre dir: Stepping Out (Duke of York's Theatre), Steel Magnolias (Lyric Theatre), Just So (Watermill Theatre Newbury), Merrily We Roll Along (staged concert, 1988), Putting it Together (NY and London), Little Night Music (Tokyo), Musical of the World (Denmark), Honk (NT, USA and Denmark, Best Musical Olivier Awards) 2000–01; *Television* incl: Fame is the Spur, Dear Box Number, Those Glory Glory Days, Blott on the Landscape, Absent Friends, Hotel du Lac, Adam Bede, Hester in Fresh Fields and French Fields (voted Favourite Comedy Performer TV Times Viewers' Poll 1985, 1986, 1987 and 1989), The Last Detective, Death in Holy Orders, Celebration 2006, You Can Choose Your Friends 2007, Cranford Chronicles 2007, Miss Marple in Marple 2008–, Cranford 2009, The Town 2013, Gangsta Granny (BBC) 2014, The Casual Vacancy (BBC) 2014; *Film* incl: Shirley Valentine, Old Curiosity Shop, Bright Young Things, Notes on a Scandal 2006; *Style*— Ms Julia McKenzie; ✉ c/o Roger Charteris, The Artists Partnership, 101 Finsbury Pavement, London EC2 (☎ 020 7439 1456, e-mail rogercharteris@artistspartnership.com)

McKENZIE, Kenneth Stevenson; *b* 18 June 1953; *Educ* Trinity Sch Croydon, Univ of Exeter; *m* 1985, Jane Helen Bowden; 2 da (Jennifer 1985, Alice b 1989), 1 s (James b 1987); *Career* admitted slr 1978; Davies Arnold Cooper (now DAC Beachcroft LLP): joined 1984, litigation ptnr 1986–, head of dispute resolution 2001–11; specialisms incl insurance, reinsurance and professional indemnity; author of numerous articles; memb Insurance Ctee City of London Law Soc; memb Law Soc 1978; *Style*— Kenneth McKenzie, Esq; ✉ DAC Beachcroft LLP, 1 Minster Court, Mincing Lane, London EC3R 7AA (☎ 020 7894 6480, e-mail kmckenzie@dacbeachcroft.com)

MacKENZIE, Madeleine; elder da of William Gordon MacKenzie, of Inverness, and late Veronica Dorothy Rachel MacKenzie; *b* 27 August 1963; *Educ* Inverness HS, Univ of Aberdeen (LLB, DipLP); *Career* trainee slr, slr then assoc Sutherland & Co Inverness 1986–90, asst Scottish Parly Counsel Lord Advocate's Dept London 1990–99, depute then Scottish Parly Counsel Edinburgh 1999–; *Recreations* bridge, reading, music, walking; *Clubs* Athenaeum, New (Edinburgh), Scottish Arts; *Style*— Miss Madeleine MacKenzie; ✉ Parliamentary Counsel Office, Victoria Quay, Edinburgh EH6 6QQ (☎ 0131 244 1667, e-mail madeleine.mackenzie@scotland.gsi.gov.uk)

McKENZIE, Master; Michael; CB (1999), QC (1991); s of Robert McKenzie (d 1992), of Brighton, E Sussex, and Kitty Elizabeth, *née* Regan (d 1985); *b* 25 May 1943; *Educ* Varndean GS Brighton; *m* 19 Sept 1964, Peggy Dorothy, da of Thomas Edward William Russell, of Heathfield, E Sussex; 3 s (Justin Grant b 31 May 1968, Gavin John b 28 April 1971, Jamie Stuart b 14 Jan 1977); *Career* called to the Bar Middle Temple 1970 (bencher 1993); dep clerk of the peace Middx QS 1970–72, dep courts admin Middx Crown Court 1972–73, courts admin NE Circuit (Newcastle) 1974–79, clerk of the Central Criminal Court and co-ordinator for taxation of crown court costs (s. eastern circuit) 1979–84, dep circuit admin SE Circuit 1984–86, asst registrar Court of Appeal (Criminal Div) 1986–88, Queen's Coroner and Attorney and Master of the Crown Office, registrar of Criminal Appeals and of Courts Martial Appeal Court and Master of the High Court of Justice (Queen's Bench Div) 1988–2003; memb Criminal Ctee Judicial Studies Bd 1988–2003, Br rep Int Judicial Conferences Washington, Sydney, Tasmania and Ottawa 1995–2000, Br rep The Great Debates on Judicial Reform Washington, NY, Boston and London 1997–2002, memb Ind Monitoring Bd Lewes Prison 2004–06, registrar Qatar Financial Centre Civil and Commercial Court and Regulatory Tbnl 2006–11; adjunct prof of law Wake Forest Univ Sch of Law NC 2001; Freeman City of London 1979; hon fell Univ of Kent 1991; FRSA 1990, memb NY Acad of Sci 1992, hon memb State Bar of Calif 1996 (visiting speaker 1995–2003); *Books* Butterworths Rules of Court (ed), Criminal Court Practice 1994–1997, A Review of the Working Methods of the European Court of Human Rights (with Lord Woolf, 2005); *Recreations* Northumbrian stick dressing, fell walking, shooting; *Style*— Master McKenzie, CB, QC, FRSA; ✉ Selwyns Wood House, Cross in Hand, East Sussex TN21 0QN (☎ 01435 862357)

MACKENZIE, Ruth; CBE (2013, OBE 1995); da of Kenneth Mackenzie, of Paris, and Myrna Blumberg, of London; *b* 24 July 1957; *Educ* South Hampstead HS, Sorbonne (dip), Newnham Coll Cambridge (MA); *Career* co fndr, dir and writer Moving Parts Theatre Co 1980–82, dir of Theatre in the Mill Univ of Bradford 1982–84, artistic dir Bradford Multicultural Festival Bradford Met Cncl 1983–84, drama offr with responsibility for theatre writing Arts Cncl of GB 1984–86, head of strategic planning South Bank Centre 1986–90, exec dir Nottingham Playhouse 1990–97, gen dir Scottish Opera 1997–99, special advsr to Sec of State of Culture, Media and Sport 1999–2002, dir Time/Room Prodns Ltd 2002–, artistic dir Chichester Festival Theatre 2002–06, gen dir Manchester Int Festival 2006–07, expert advsr to Dept of Culture, Media and Sport 2007–, dir of culture London 2012 2010–; consulting dramaturg Vienna Festival; visiting prof City Univ; memb Bd New Millennium Experience Co 1997–99; memb Exec Ctee Common Purpose 1993–97; memb Bd Arts Cncl Touring Panel 1992–99; memb Panel 2000 FCO 1998–99; memb QCA Ctee on Creativity 2000–; memb Chancellor's Forum London Inst 2001–; tstee Cass Sculpture Fndn 2005–07; govr: Trinity Coll of Music 2002–04, Royal Northern Coll of Music 2007; Hon DLitt: Nottingham Trent Univ, Univ of Nottingham; hon fell Univ of Nottingham; FRSA 1992; *Recreations* work; *Style*— Ms Ruth Mackenzie, CBE

MACKENZIE, Sheriff (Colin) Scott; DL (Western Isles 1974–2013); s of Colin Scott Mackenzie (d 1971), of Stornoway, Isle of Lewis, and Margaret Sarah Tolmie (d 1993); *b* 7 July 1938; *Educ* Nicolson Inst Stornoway, Fettes, Univ of Edinburgh (BL); *m* 1966, Christeen Elizabeth Drysdale, da of William McLauchlan (d 1968), of Tong, Isle of Lewis; *Career* admitted slr 1960; procurator fiscal Stornoway 1969–92, sheriff Grampian Highland and Islands at Kirkwall and Lerwick 1992–2003 (pt/t sheriff 2004–08, hon sheriff 2008–, re-employed ret sheriff 2010–13); memb Cncl Sheriffs' Assoc 2002–03; dir Harris Tweed Assoc Ltd 1979–95 clerk to the Western Isles Lieutenancy 1974–92, Vice Lord-Lt Western Isles 1984–92; memb Cncl Law Soc of Scotland 1985–92 (convenor Criminal Law Ctee 1991–92); kirk elder 1985, convener Church and Nation Ctee Presbytery of Lewis 1990–92; General Assembly of the Church of Scotland: convenor Study Gp on Young People and the Media 1991–93, memb Judicial Cmmn 2011–; FSA Scot 1995; *Publications* The Last Warrior Band: The Ross Mountain Battery at Gallipoli 1915 (2003), Shetland, Orkney and the Western Isles, a personal reflection (2010), The Overlooked Jewel in our Crown (2012), St Columba's Ui Church (2012), Gael Force on Gallipoli (2015); *Recreations* fishing, boating, travel, amateur radio (GM7 RD0), private flying; *Clubs* New (Edinburgh); *Style*— Sheriff C Scott Mackenzie, DL; ✉ Park House, Matheson Road, Stornoway, Isle of Lewis HS1 2NQ (☎ 01851 702008, e-mail colinsmackenzie@btinternet.com)

MACKENZIE, Ursula Ann; Ian Alexander Ross Mackenzie, of Great Massingham, Norfolk, and Phyllis, *née* Naismith; *b* 11 December 1951; *Educ* Malvern Girls' Coll, Westlake Sch for Girls LA (ESU exchange scholar), Univ of Nottingham (BA, PhD); *Children* 1 s (Matthew James Johnson b 18 Sept 1987); *Career* lectr in English and American literature Univ of Hong Kong 1976–79, International Scripts Literary Agency 1979–80, rights mangr Granada Publishing 1981–84; Transworld Publishers: editorial and rights mangr Bantam Press, editorial and rights dir 1985–88, publishing dir 1988–95, publisher of hardback books 1995–2000; Little, Brown Book Gp: publisher 2000–, ceo 2005–15, chair 2015–; chair Trade Publishers Cncl 2007–11; pres Publishers' Assoc 2012–13; *Style*— Ms Ursula Mackenzie; ✉ Little, Brown Book Group, Carmelite House, 50 Victoria Embankment, London EC4Y 0DY

MacKENZIE OF CULKEIN, Baron (Life Peer UK 1999), of Assynt in Highland Hector Uisdean MacKenzie; s of George Campbell MacKenzie (d 1986), and Williamina Budge, *née* Sutherland (d 1957); *b* 25 February 1940; *Educ* Nicolson Inst Stornoway, Portree HS Isle of Skye, Leverndale Sch of Nursing, W Cumberland Sch of Nursing (Lindsay Robertson Gold Medal, RGN, RMN); *m* 1961 (m dis 1991), Anna Roberston Morrison, da of George Morrison; 3 da (Catriona b 20 Aug 1961, Ishbel Georgina, Morag Sutherland (twins) b 23 April 1963), 1 s (David Hector b 15 Jan 1973); *Career* student nurse Leverndale Hosp Glasgow 1958–61, asst lighthousekeeper Clyde Lighthouses Trust 1961–64, staff nurse W Cumberland Hosp Whitehaven 1966–69 (student nurse 1964–66); COHSE: regnl sec Yorks and E Midlands 1970–74 (asst regnl sec 1969–70), national offr 1974–83, asst gen sec 1983–87, gen sec 1987–93; associate gen sec UNISON 1993–2000 (following merger of COHSE, NUPE and NALGO); pres TUC 1998–99 (memb Gen Cncl 1987–2000); co sec UIA (Insurance) Ltd 1996–2000; memb: Administrative and Clerical Staff Cncl NHS 1972–87, Professional and Technical Staff A Cncl (NHS), Nurses and Midwives' Negotiating Cncl 1979–91 (chm 1987–91); *Recreations* reading, aviation, travel, celtic music; *Style*— Lord MacKenzie of Culkein; ✉ House of Lords, London SW1A 0PW

MACKENZIE OF FRAMWELLGATE, Baron (Life Peer UK 1998), of Durham in the County of Durham; Brian Mackenzie; OBE (1998); s of Frederick George Mackenzie (d 1963), and Lucy, *née* Ward (d 1973); *b* 21 March 1943; *Educ* Eastbourne Boys' Sch, Univ of London (LLB), FBI Nat Acad Quantico USA (graduated 1985); *m* 1 (m dis 2009); 2 s (Hon Brian James b 21 March 1968, Hon Andrew Craig b 18 May 1971); m 2, 31 Dec 2009, Deborah, da of James Glaister; *Career* career police offr rising to chief superintendent Durham Constabulary (sometime head Durham drug squad and crime computer project team, also former advsr Home Office, govr Police Staff Coll Bramshill and memb Police Trg Cncl), ret 1998; special police advsr to Home Sec 1998–2001; patron Joint Security Industry Cncl 1999–; former vice-pres then pres Police Superintendents' Assoc; pres Assoc of Police and Public Security Suppliers 2000–, vice-pres Br Airlines Assoc (BALPA); *Publications* Two Lives of Brian (autobiography, 2004); *Recreations* swimming, music, after dinner speaking; *Clubs* Dunelm (Durham); *Style*— The Rt Hon the Lord Mackenzie of Framwellgate, OBE; ✉ House of Lords, London SW1A 0PW (☎ 020 7219 8632, fax 020 7219 1997, e-mail mackenzieb@parliament.uk)

MACKENZIE OF GAIRLOCH, John Alexander; DL (Ross, Cromarty, Skye and Lochalsh 1984); s of Brig William Alexander Mackenzie of Gairloch, DSO, OBE (d 1982), and Marjory Kythé, *née* Stirling (d 1988); *b* 27 May 1944, Muir of Ord, Ross-shire; *Educ* Gordonstoun; *m* 12 April 1969, Frances Marian, o da of Lt Col E S Williams, OBE (d 1963); 1 da (Kythé Caroline b 6 Feb 1974), 1 s (Duncan James b 10 April 1976); *Career* landowner; 2 Lt Queen's Own Highlanders 1962–65, James Buchanan & Co Ltd 1966–80, Gairloch and Conon estates 1980–, chm Black Isle Grain Ltd 1987–90; memb Red Deer Cmmn 1987–98, chm Highland Region Scottish Landowners Fedn 1990–95; *Style*— John Mackenzie of Gairloch, DL; ✉ Conan House, Conon Bridge, Ross-shire IV7 8AL (☎ 01349 861101)

McKENZIE OF LUTON, Baron (Life Peer UK 2004), of Luton in the County of Bedfordshire; William David (Bill) McKenzie; s of late George McKenzie, and Elsie May, *née* Doust (d 1979); *b* 24 July 1946, Reading; *Educ* Reading Sch, Univ of Bristol (BA); *m* Aug 1972, Diane Joyce, *née* Angliss; *Career* Price Waterhouse: joined London office 1973, ptnr 1980–86, joined Hong Kong office 1992, ptnr 1993–98, ptnr i/c Vietnam 1996–98; Parly under-sec (Lords) Dept for Work and Pensions 2007–10, min Dept for Communities and Local Govt 2009–10; memb Luton BC 1976–92 and 1999–2005 (ldr 1999–2003); Hon MBA Univ of Luton; FCA 1979; *Recreations* swimming, reading; *Style*— The Lord McKenzie of Luton; ✉ 6 Sunset Drive, Luton, Bedfordshire LU2 7TN (☎ and fax 01582 455384)

McKENZIE SMITH, Ian; CBE (2009, OBE 1992); s of James McKenzie Smith (d 1977), of Aberdeen, and Mary, *née* Benzie (d 1989); *b* 3 August 1935; *Educ* Robert Gordon's Coll Aberdeen, Gray's Sch of Art Aberdeen (DA, PGDip), Hospitalfield Coll of Art Arbroath; *m* 3 April 1963, Mary Rodger, da of John Fotheringham (d 1990); 1 da (Sarah Jane b 5 Jan 1965), 2 s (Patrick John b 8 Aug 1966, Justin James b 4 Feb 1969); *Career* artist; educn offr Cncl of Industrial Design Scottish Ctee 1963–68, dir Aberdeen Art Gallery and Museums 1968–89, city arts and recreation offr City of Aberdeen 1989–96; pres Royal Scottish Acad 1998–2007 (treas and dep pres 1990–91, sec 1991–98); memb: Scottish Arts Cncl 1970–77, Scottish Museums Cncl 1980–87, Nat Heritage Scottish Gp 1983–99, Nat Tst for Scotland Curatorial Ctee, Buildings Ctee Cncl Nat Tst for Scotland, Museums and Galleries Cmmn 1997–2001; memb Advsy Bd: Robert Gordon Univ 1992–95; memb Bd: RSA Enterprises 1972–, Scottish Sculpture Workshop 1979–2000, Aberdeen Maritime Museum Appeal 1981–98, Friends of the RSA, Grampian Hospitals Art Tst 1987–2000; tstee Nat Galleries of Scotland 1999–; chm: Marguerite McBey Tst 2002–, Patrick Allan-Fraser of Hospital Field Tst 2004–; external assessor: Glasgow Sch of Art 1982–86, Duncan of Jordanstone Coll of Art 1982–86; assessor Ruth Davidson Meml Tst, Morrison Portrait Award, Salvesen Art Tst, Noble Grossart Award, Royal Overseas League Scholarships; govr: Edinburgh Coll of Art, Robert Gordon Univ Aberdeen; fell Salzburg Seminar 1981, Hon LLD Univ of Aberdeen 1991, Hon DA Robert Gordon Univ 2000; Hon RA 1999, Hon RHA 1999, Hon RWA 2000, Hon RUA 2000; RSW 1981 (pres 1988–98), RGI 1999, FRSA 1973, FSS 1984, FMA 1987, FSA Scot 1970, FRSE 2003; *Work in Permanent Collections* Scottish Nat Gallery of Modern Art, Scottish Arts Cncl, Arts Cncl of NI, Contemporary Art Soc, Aberdeen Art Gallery and Museums, Glasgow Art Gallery and Museums, City Arts Centre Edinburgh, McManus Gallery Dundee, Perth Art Gallery, Abbott Hall Art Gallery Kendal, Hunterian Museum Glasgow, Nuffield Foundation, Carnegie Tst, Strathclyde Educn Authy, Lothian Educn Authy, Edinburgh District Cncl, Royal Scottish Acad, DOE, Robert Fleming Holding, IBM, Deutsche Bank, Grampian Hospitals Art Tst, RGU; *Awards* Inst of Contemporary Prints Award 1969, RSA Guthrie Award 1971, RSA Gillies Award 1980, ESU Thyne scholarship 1980, Sir William Gillies Award RSW 2008; *Clubs* Royal Over-Seas League, Scottish Arts (Edinburgh), Royal Northern (Aberdeen); *Style*— Dr Ian McKenzie Smith, CBE; ✉ e-mail i.mckenziesmith@btinternet.com

McKEON, Andrew John; s of Kenneth McKeon, of Manchester, and Maurine, *née* Ilsley; *b* 22 September 1955; *Educ* William Hulme's GS Manchester, St Catharine's Coll Cambridge (scholar, BA); *m* 1989, Hilary, da of Rev G Neville; 1 s (Christopher b 26 Feb 1990), 1 da (Sarah b 28 Nov 1991); *Career* DG of policy and planning Dept of Health 2002 (joined 1976), md health Audit Cmmn 2003–12, chief exec Nuffield Tst 2013–14 (tstee 2008–13, sr policy fell 2014–); non-exec dir NICE 2009–; adjunct prof Centre for Health Policy Inst of Global Health Innovation Imperial Coll London; *Style*— Andrew McKeon, Esq; ✉ Nuffield Trust, 59 New Cavendish Street, London W1G 7LP

McKEOWN, Prof Patrick Arthur (Pat); OBE (1991); s of Robert Matthew McKeown (d 1978), and Bessie Augusta, *née* White (d 1993); *b* 16 August 1930; *Educ* Cambridge GS, Bristol GS, Cranfield Inst of Technol (MSc); *m* 1954, Mary Patricia, da of Donald S B Heath, of Bristol; 3 s (Alistair Jonathan b 1957, Jeremy Patrick b 1960, Nicholas William b 1963); *Career* student apprentice Bristol Aircraft Co 1951–54 (nat state scholar 1954), Coll of Aeronautics Cranfield 1954–56, works and tech dir Société Genevoise d'Instruments de Physique 1964–68 (joined 1956), dir Cranfield Unit for Precision Engrg 1968–95, prof of precision engrg Cranfield Inst of Technol (now Cranfield Univ) 1974–95 (emeritus prof 1995), chm Cranfield Precision Engineering Ltd 1992–95 (fndr chm and chief exec 1987–92), dir Pat McKeown and Associates (conslts in advanced mfrg, precision engrg and nanotechnology) 1995–2003; non-exec dir: Control Techniques plc 1989–94, Cranfield Aerospace Ltd 2001–03; hon visiting prof Nanjing Aeronautical Inst People's Republic of China 1985, visiting prof of mechanical engrg Univ of Calif Berkeley 1994; int advsr GINTIC Inst of Mfrg Technol Singapore 1991–98; memb: Evaluation Ctee Nat Bureau of Standards USA 1980–86, Advanced Mfrg Technol Ctee DTI 1982–86, RCA Visiting Ctee 1984–87, UK Nanotechnology Strategy Ctee DTI/SERC 1987–94; pres: CIRP (int acad for prodn engrg) 1989–90, European Soc for Precision Engrg and Nanotechnology 1998–2000 (founding pres); Fulbright prof of mechanical engrg Univ of Wisconsin Madison 1982, F W Taylor medal USA Soc of Mfrg Engrs 1983, Thomas Hawksley Gold Medal IMechE 1987, Life Achievement Award American Soc for Precision Engrg 1998, Faraday Medal IEE 1999, Life Achievement Award European Soc for Precision Engrg and Nanotechnology 2002, Int Prize Japan Soc for Precision Engrg 2003, Georg Schlesinger Preis State of Berlin 2006, James Clayton Prize (2007) IMechE 2008, M Eugene Merchant Manufacturing Medal of ASME/SME (USA) 2009; Freeman City of London 2007, Liveryman Worshipful Co of Engrs 2008; Hon DSc: Univ of Connecticut 1996, Cranfield Univ 1996; fell Cranfield Univ 2011; FREng 1986, FIMechE, chartered fell American Soc of Mfrg Engrs; *Recreations* classical music, theatre, walking; *Style*— Prof Pat McKeown, OBE, FREng; ☎ 01234 267678, e-mail patmckeown37@gmail.com

McKERRELL OF HILLHOUSE, Charles James Mure; s of Capt Robert James Mure McKerrell of Hillhouse (d 1964), and Winifred Scott, *née* Walkinshaw (d 1997); matric arms Ct of the Lord Lyon 1973, recognised by the Lord Lyon as McKerrell of Hillhouse and Head of the Name by Interlocutor of Lord Lyon, also recorded arms Genealogical Office Dublin Castle and recognised as 15th Head of the Name by Chief Herald of Ireland; McKerrell of Hillhouse tartan and McKerrell of Hillhouse Dress tartan recorded by deed Court of the Lord Lyon 1982 and 2002; *b* 23 January 1941; *Educ* Cranleigh Sch; *m* 2 Jan 1991, May Weston Cochrane, NFNN, DLJ, FSAScot, da of Matthew Cochrane White (d 1967); *Career* fndr memb Heraldry Soc of Ireland, memb Bd Soc of Scottish Armigers; cmmnd Kentucky Col (hon ADC to the govr of Kentucky) 2012; memb: Royal Stuart Soc, Heraldry Soc of Scotland, Corona Legitima, Saltire Soc, Cncl Royal Celtic Soc; memb Bd and Cmmr EU Soc of Scottish Armigers; assoc memb Convention of the Baronage of Scotland; Freeman City of London 2000, memb Community Cncl Royal Burgh Lochmaben; FSA Scot; Guardian of the Nobiliary Fraternity of the Nia Naisc, OStJ, Knight Order of St Michael of the Wing, Knight Grand Cross of Justice of the Order of St Lazarus of Jerusalem, Hereditary Companion of The Companionate of the Royal House of O'Conor, Chevalier Grand Cross of the Patriarchal Order of St Ignace of Antioche, hon capt Canadian Bush Pilots Sqdn of Canada; *Style*— McKerrell of Hillhouse; ✉ Magdalene House, Lochmaben, Dumfries DG11 1PD (☎ 01387 810439)

McKERROW, June; da of late Alexander Donald McKerrow, and Lorna McKerrow; *b* 17 June 1950; *Educ* Brunel Univ (MPhil); *Children* 1 adopted da (Lucy b 17 July 1992); *Career* housing mgmnt in local govt and housing assocs 1967–80, dir Stonham Housing Assoc 1980–92; memb: Nat Cncl of Nat Fedn of Housing Assocs 1982–90, Br Cncl UN Int Year of Shelter for the Homeless 1987, Ctee English Rural Housing Assoc 1997–99, Bd Advance Housing and Support 2001–03; tstee and vice-chair Shelter 1985–93, fndr memb Homeless Int 1987–93, chair Housing Assocs Charitable Tst 1998–2002; tstee: Homeless Int 1988–93, Cherwell Housing Tst Oxford 1992–97, Charity Projects 1993–96, Comic Relief 1995–97, Winston's Wish 2002–04, Donnington Doorstep 2002–09, Change of Scene 2008–; patron Revolving Doors Agency 1993–99, non-exec dir Oxfordshire Mental Healthcare NHS Tst (formerly Oxfordshire Mental Healthcare NHS Tst) 2000–07, dir Soundabout 2003–11, mentor Prince's Tst 2011–; memb Ct Oxford Brookes Univ 2000–07; *Style*— Ms June McKerrow; ✉ e-mail june@junemckerrow.co.uk

MACKERSIE, Andrew James; s of John Anthony Mackersie, and Krystyna Anna, *née* Bragiel; *b* 16 November 1974; *Educ* St Benedict's Sch Ealing, St Peter's Coll Oxford (exhibitioner, MA), Merton Coll and Saïd Business School Oxford (MBA); *m* 2013, Daisy Alice Ricketts; 1 da (Elizabeth Mary Mackersie b 28 March 2016); *Career* House of Lords: clerk Parl Office 1997–2015, judicial clerk 1998–2001 and 2002–03, clerk Constitution Ctee 2001–02, clerk Legislation Office 2003–09, clerk Sub-Ctee on Lords' Conduct and head of strategy 2009–11; seconded to home civil service as princ private sec to Ldr of the House and Govt Chief Whip 2011–14; sec Assoc of Lord-Lts 2002–15; *Publications* contrib on judicial functions of House of Lords (now abolished) and peerages to various pubns incl: Halsbury's Laws of England, Atkin's Court Forms, Civil Procedure, Erskine May's Parliamentary Practice; *Recreations* horses, rural pursuits, buildings and how they work; *Clubs* Beefsteak, Brooks's; *Style*— Andrew Mackersie, Esq; ✉ 12 Hayles Street, London SE11 4SS

McKIBBIN, Dr Sir Malcolm; KCB (2016); *b* 20 November 1956, Belfast; *Educ* Univ of Southampton (BSc), Univ of Ulster (PhD, MBA); *m* Susan, 2 da (Christine, Jenny); *Career* civil servant; early career with Dept of the Environment then subsequently with Dept of Finance and Personnel (sometime dep sec i/c Central Procurement Div) and Dept of Regnl Devpt, chief exec Roads Service NI until 2007, perm sec Dept of Agriculture and Rural Devpt NI 2007–10, perm sec Dept for Regnl Devpt 2010–11, head NI Civil Service and perm sec Office of the First Min and Dep First Min and sec NI Exec 2011–; CEng, FICE; *Recreations* Tennis, Travel; *Style*— Dr Sir Malcolm McKibbin, KCB; ✉ Executive Office, Stormont Castle, Belfast BT4 3TT (☎ 028 9037 8131, fax 028 9037 8205, e-mail hocs@executiveoffice-ni.gov.uk, website www.executiveoffice-ni.gov.uk)

McKIDD, Kevin; s of Neil McKidd, of Elgin, and Kathleen, *née* Runcie; *b* 9 August 1973, Elgin, Moray; *Educ* Queen Margaret Coll Edinburgh; *m* 23 Jul 1999, Jane Parker; 1 s (Joseph George), 1 da (Iona Claire); *Career* actor; *Film* incl: Trainspotting 1996, Small Faces 1996, Hideous Kinky 1998, Dog Soldiers 2002, Nicholas Nickleby 2002, De-Lovely 2004, Kingdom of Heaven 2005, Hannibal Rising 2007, Made of Honor 2008, Percy Jackson & the Lightning Thief 2010, The Great Ghost Rescue 2011, Comes a Bright Day 2012, Brave 2012; *Television* incl: Anna Karenina 2000, The Virgin Queen 2005, Rome 2005–07, Grey's Anatomy 2008–, One Night in Emergency 2010, Seattle Grace: Message of Hope 2010; *Recreations* tennis, surfing; *Style*— Mr Kevin McKidd; ✉ c/o Independent Talent Group, 40 Whitfield Street, London W1T 2RH (Twitter @TheRealKMcKidd)

McKIE, Alastair John; WS; s of John Jack McKie, of South Queensferry, Flintshire, and Avril, *née* Quinton; *b* 15 June 1962, Ipswich, Suffolk; *Educ* Lornshill Acad Alloa, Univ of Dundee; *m* 6 Aug 2004, Dr Margaret McKinnon Mitchell; 1 da (Ava Lynne); *Career* admitted slr 1987; legal trainee Glenrothes Devpt Corp, with Kirkcaldy DC and Fife Cncl 1991–98, ptnr and head of planning and environment Anderson Strathern 1998–; accredited specialist in planning law Law Soc of Scotland; legal assoc RTPI; *Recreations* hill walking, fishing, tennis, dogs; *Clubs* Drummond Tennis; *Style*— Alastair McKie, Esq, WS; ✉ 3A Royal Crescent, Edinburgh EH3 6PZ; Anderson Strathern, 1 Rutland

Court, Edinburgh EH3 8EY (☎ 0131 625 7257, fax 0131 625 8030, e-mail alastair.mckie@andersonstrathern.co.uk)

MACKIE, His Hon David Lindsay; CBE (2004), QC (1998); s of Alastair Cavendish Lindsay Mackie, CBE, DFC, of London, and Rachel, *née* Goodson; *b* 15 February 1946; *Educ* St Edmund Hall Oxford (MA); *m* 1, 13 Feb 1971 (m dis 1986); 2 s (James b 1974, Edward b 1976), 1 da (Eleanor b 1978); m 2, 16 April 2015, Katherine Reece; *Career* admitted slr 1971, ptnr Allen & Overy 1975–2004 (head of litigation 1988–2004), recorder of the Crown Court 1992, dep judge of the High Court 1998, mercantile judge 2004–15; tstee RCJ Advice Bureau, a chm Financial Services and Markets Tribunal 2001, pres Financial Markets Tribunal Dubai Int Financial Centre 2014–; FCIArb; *Recreations* climbing; *Style*— His Hon David Mackie, CBE, QC

MACKIE, John David; CBE (2007); *b* 30 April 1953; *Educ* St Mary's GS Middlesbrough, Univ of Glasgow (BAcc); *m* 1982, Elaine, *née* Jackson; 2 da; *Career* numerous positions incl dj, lab asst and advtg salesman 1968–71, trainee mangr rising to gen mangr Woolco Dept Stores 1971–79, trainee accountant Arthur Andersen & Co 1982–85, investment dir 3i Gp plc 1985–89, fndr dir Morgan Grenfell Development Capital Ltd 1990–98 (bd memb Morgan Grenfell & Co (then Deutsche Morgan Grenfell) 1995–98), chief exec Br Venture Capital Assoc (BVCA) 2000–05; cnslt Technomark Medical Ventures 2000–03, ptnr Parallel Private Equity 2003–11; chm Henderson Private Equity Investment Tst plc 2006–13, chm Advsy Bd AESF 2007–, chm Advsy Bd Amadeus ECF 2008–, sr ind dir Mithras Investment Tst plc 2012–, dir Baronsmead VCT plc 2012–14, chm Advsy Bd AASF 2013–; supporter: Guide Dogs for the Blind Assoc, Br Lung Fndn; MICAS; *Recreations* family, books, cinema, theatre, wine; *Style*— John Mackie, Esq; ✉ e-mail johnmackie@hotmail.com

MACKIE, Dr Karl Joseph; CBE (2010); s of John Mackie, and Ethel, *née* Freeman; *Educ* Buckhaven HS, Univ of Edinburgh (MA), Univ of London (LLB), Univ of Nottingham (PhD), Open Univ (MBA), Univ of Edinburgh (DipEd); *m* 1, 1968 (m dis), Ann Douglas; 1 s (Alan), 1 da (Karen); m 2, 2001, Eileen Carroll; 1 step da (Jennifer); *Career* called to the Bar Gray's Inn 1982; research assoc Univ of Edinburgh 1971–72, lectr then sr lectr in law and social psychology Univ of Nottingham 1973–90, ptnr Network Associates Strategy Conslts 1985–90, chief exec CEDR 1990–; accredited mediator CEDR, chief adjudicator Ofsted Ind Adjudication Service, ombudsman NYSE Liffe 2011–14; memb: Panel of Ind Mediators and Arbitrators ACAS 1980–, Panel of Distinguished Neutrals CPR Inst NY, Singapore Commercial Mediation Panel; vice-chm Civil Mediation Cncl 2003–10; hon prof in alternative dispute resolution: Univ of Birmingham 1994–2001, Univ of Westminster 2004–09; special advsr to All Pty Parly Gp on Conflict; memb editorial ctees of various jls; memb: Educn Ctee Bar Assoc for Commerce, Finance and Industry 1987–90, Specialisation Ctee Law Soc 1989–92; chm Write Away 2003–06; CPsychol 1989; FCIArb 1992, FRSA 1993; *Publications* Learning Lawyers' Skills (jt ed, 1989), Lawyers in Business and the Law Business (1989), A Handbook of Dispute Resolution (ed, 1991), Commercial Dispute Resolution (jtly, 1995, 3 edn 2007), International Mediation: the art of business diplomacy (jtly, 2000, 2 edn 2006), The EU Mediation Atlas (co-ed, 2004); *Recreations* film, photography, writing; *Style*— Dr Karl Mackie, CBE; ✉ CEDR (Centre for Effective Dispute Resolution), International Dispute Resolution Centre, 70 Fleet Street, London EC4Y 1EU (☎ 020 7536 6000, fax 020 7536 6001, e-mail kmackie@cedr.com)

MACKIE, Prof Neil; CBE (1996); s of William Fraser Mackie (d 1979), of King's Gate, Aberdeen, and Sheila Roberta, *née* Taylor (d 1973); *b* 11 December 1946; *Educ* Aberdeen GS, Royal Scot Acad of Music and Drama (DipMusEdRSAMD, DipRSAMD), Royal Coll of Music (fndn scholar, ARCM); *m* 1973, Kathleen Mary, da of William Livingstone (d 1972); 2 da (Alison Kathleen b 1980, Elinor Sheila b 1983); *Career* international concert singer (tenor); Royal Coll of Music: prof of singing 1985–2008, head of vocal studies 1994–2006; prof Fine Arts Faculty Agder Univ Norway 2005–14, prof of singing Royal Acad of Music 2009–; artistic dir Mayfield Festival 2005–12; Gulbenkian fell, Caird scholar, Munster scholar; London recital debut Wigmore Hall 1972, London concert debut with Eng Chamber Orch under Raymond Leppard 1973; world premières incl: Unpublished Songs by Britten, Hans Werner Henze's Three Auden Settings, several Kenneth Leighton works incl Symphony No 3, many cmmnd works by Scottish composers; works especially written for him by Peter Maxwell Davies: The Martyrdom of St Magnus (title role), The Lighthouse (role of Sandy), Into the Labyrinth (solo cantata for tenor and orch), A Solstice of Light; hon memb Acad of Science and Letters Univ of Agder Norway 2012; Hon DMus Univ of Aberdeen 1993; FRSA 1991, FRSAMD 1992, FRSE 1996, FRCM 1996, Hon RAM 2011; CStJ 1996 (OStJ 1987); *Recordings* numerous on EMI, Decca, Philips, Chandos, Deutsche Grammophon, Unicorn-Kanchana, Somm, Accent, Collins, Abbey Records; *Awards* runner up Gramophone Solo Voice Recording of the Year for Britten Tenor, Horn and Strings (with Scottish Chamber Orch) 1989, Grammy Award 1993; *Recreations* reading, charity work and occasional gardening; *Clubs* Athenaeum, Royal Over-Seas League; *Style*— Prof Neil Mackie, CBE, FRSE; ✉ 70 Broadwood Avenue, Ruislip, Middlesex HA4 7XR (☎ 01895 632115, e-mail neilmackie@talktalk.net)

MacKIE-BLACK, Prof Rona McLeod; CBE (1999); da of Prof J Norman Davidson, FRS (d 1972), of Bearsden, Glasgow, and Morag, *née* McLeod; *b* 22 May 1940; *Educ* Laurel Bank Sch, Univ of Glasgow (MB ChB, MD, DSc); *m* 1, 1962 (m dis); 1 da (Alison b 1963), 1 s (Douglas b 1965); m 2, 1994, Prof Sir James Whyte Black, FRS, *qv*; *Career* hon conslt dermatologist Gtr Glasgow Health Bd 1978– (conslt dermatologist 1973–78); Univ of Glasgow: prof of dermatology 1978–2000, sr res fell Dept of Public Health and Health Policy 2000–; pres Br Assoc of Dermatologists, vice-pres Nat Eczema Soc; FRCPGlas 1978, FRSE 1983, FRCPath 1984, FRCP 1985, FIBiol 1988; *Books* Clinical Dermatology – An Illustrated Textbook (1981, 5 edn 2003), Eczema and Dermatitis (1983), Malignant Melanoma (ed, 1983), Current Perspectives in Immunodermatology (ed, 1984), Milne's Dermatopathology (ed, 1984), Clinical Dermatology An Illustrated Textbook (1994), Skin Cancer (1995); *Recreations* music especially opera, gardening, family; *Style*— Prof Rona MacKie-Black, CBE, FRSE; ✉ e-mail ronamblack@hotmail.com

McKILLOP, Prof James Hugh (Jim); s of Dr Patrick McKillop (d 1979), of Coatbridge, Strathclyde, and Dr Helen Theresa McKillop, *née* Kilpatrick (d 1998); *b* 20 June 1948; *Educ* St Aloysius' Coll Glasgow, Univ of Glasgow (BSc, MB ChB, PhD); *m* 17 Aug 1973, Caroline Annis, da of Charles Allen Oakley, CBE (d 1993), of Glasgow; 2 da (Beth b 1977, Jenny b 1981); *Career* Harkness fellowship Stanford Univ 1979 and 1980; Univ of Glasgow: lectr 1977–82, sr lectr 1982–89, Muirhead prof of med 1989–2011, assoc dean for med educn 2000–03, head Undergraduate Med Sch 2003–06, dep dean of medicine 2007–11; treas Scottish Soc of Experimental Med 1982–87; Br Nuclear Med Soc: memb Cncl 1985–94, hon sec 1988–90, pres 1990–92; Euro Assoc of Nuclear Med: memb Exec Ctee 1995–99, congress pres 1997, chm Educn Ctee 1998–2000, memb Strategy Ctee 2000–06; chm: Intercollegiate Standing Ctee on Nuclear Med 1995–98, ARSAC Ctee Dept of Health 1996–2004 (memb 1988–2007, vice-chm 1989–95), Scottish Med and Scientific Advsy Ctee 2001–08 (memb 1998–2008), MRCP Validation, Audit and Res Gp, NHS Educn Scotland Med Advsy Gp 2004–09, Scottish Dean's Med Curriculum Gp 2005–09, Br Polio Fellowship Expert Advsy Panel 2009–12; team leader GMC Quality Assurance of Basic Med Educn 2003–08, memb Cncl GMC 2009–, chair GMC Undergraduate Bd 2009–12, chair Review of Good Medical Practice 2010–12, chair Audit and Risk ctee 2015– GMC; vice-pres UEMS section of nuclear med 1998–2000, ed Nuclear Med Communications 1991–98; memb: MRCP Policy Cmmn 1998–2005, Scottish Bd for Academic Medicine 2006–11; vestry Sec St Mary's Episcopal Cathedral Glasgow 2011–; hon fell Acad of Medical Educators 2011; hon doctorate Örebro Univ 2011; FRCPGlas 1985, FRCPEd 1990, FRCP 1992, FRCR 1994, FMedSci 1998, Hon FAcadMedEd 2011; *Books* Atlas of Technetium Bone Scans (with D L Citrin, 1978), Imaging in Clinical Practice (with A G Chalmers and P J Robinson, 1988), Clinician's Guide to Nuclear Medicine: Benign and Malignant Bone Disease (with I Fogelman, 1991); *Recreations* football, cricket, opera, reading; *Style*— Prof Jim McKillop; ✉ Flat 1, 6 Kirklee Gate, Glasgow G12 0SZ (☎ 0141 339 7000, e-mail jim.mckillop@glasgow.ac.uk)

McKILLOP, Sir Thomas Fulton Wilson (Tom); kt (2002); s of Hugh McKillop, and Annie, *née* Wilson; *b* 19 March 1943; *Educ* Irvine Royal Acad, Univ of Glasgow (BSc, PhD), Centre de Mecanique Ondulatoire Appliquée Paris; *m* 1966, Elizabeth, *née* Kettle; 2 da, 1 s; *Career* research scientist ICI Corporate Laboratory 1969–75; ICI Pharmaceuticals: head of natural products research 1975–78, research dir France 1978–80, chemistry mangr 1980–84, gen mangr of Research Dept 1984–85, gen mangr of Devpt Dept 1985–89, tech dir 1989–94; ceo Zeneca Pharmaceuticals 1994–99; exec dir Zeneca Gp plc 1996–99, chief exec AstraZeneca plc 1999–2005; chm Br Pharma Gp 1994–2005; non-exec dir: Amersham International 1992–97, Nycomed Amersham plc 1997–2000, Lloyds TSB plc 1998–2004, BP plc 2004–, Royal Bank of Scotland 2005–06 (chm 2006–08); pro-chllr Univ of Leicester 1998– (memb Gen Cncl); tstee Darwin Tst of Edinburgh; world pres Soc of Chemical Industry 2004–, pres Science Cncl until 2007; memb: Royal Institution, RSC, ACS, Soc for Drug Research, Cncl for Industry and HE 2002–; Hon LLD: Victoria Univ of Manchester 1999, Dundee Univ 2003; Hon DSc: Univ of Glasgow 2000, Univ of Leicester 2000, Huddersfield Univ 2000, Nottingham Univ 2001, St Andrews Univ 2004, Univ of Salford 2004, Univ of Manchester 2005; Hon Dr Middlesex 2006, Hon Degree Univ of Paisley 2006, Hon Dr of Letters Heriot Watt Univ 2006; Hon Fell: Lancashire 2004, Icheme 2006, Manchester Interdisciplinary Biocentre 2006; FRS 2005; *Recreations* music, sport, reading, walking, carpentry; *Clubs* Wilmslow Golf; *Style*— Sir Tom McKillop

MACKINLAY, Craig; MP; s of Colin Francis Mackinlay, and Margaret Elizabeth; *b* 7 October 1966, Chatham, Kent; *Educ* Rainham Mark GS, Univ of Birmingham (BSc); *m* 11 June 2011, Katalin, *née* Madi; *Career* CA and chartered tax advsr; MP (Cons) Thanet S 2015–; memb Round Table Orgn 1990–2013; Freeman City of London; memb: ICAEW 1992, Chartered Inst of Taxation 1993; *Recreations* sailing, shooting, travel; *Clubs* Carlton, Castle (Rochester); *Style*— Craig Mackinlay, Esq, MP; ✉ House of Commons, London SW1A 0AA (☎ 020 7219 4442, e-mail craig@craigmackinlay.com, website www.craigmackinlay.com, Twitter @CMackinlay)

McKINLAY, Rebecca Kate; *née* Impey; da of Hugh Edward Impey (d 2002), and Rachel Rosemary, *née* Moody; *b* 6 February 1970; *Educ* Guildford HS, Univ of Hull (BA); *m* 18 Jan 1997, Jason McKinlay, s of John Walden McKinlay; 1 da (Charlotte Kate b 11 Feb 1999), 2 s (Thomas Edward Player b 28 July 2002, Maximilian Angus b 15 June 2004); *Career* account planner Hall Harrison Cowley 1992–93, head of mktg Club 18–30 1993–96, advtg and media mangr News Gp Newspapers News Int 1996–99, dir Haygarth Digital 2000–01 (account dir 1999–2000), gp mktg dir Haygarth 2001–05, fndr Ambition Communications 2005–; *Recreations* tennis, golf; *Clubs* RAC; *Style*— Mrs Rebecca McKinlay; ✉ Ambition, 26 Wadham Road, Putney, London SW15 2LR (☎ 020 8874 5520, e-mail rebecca@ambition-communications.co.uk)

McKINNEL, Rt Rev Nicholas Howard Paul; *see:* Plymouth, Bishop of

McKINNELL, Catherine; MP; *Educ* Sacred Heart Comp Sch Fenham, Univ of Edinburgh; *m* Rhys; 3 c; *Career* slr; MP (Lab) Newcastle N 2010–, shadow attorney general 2015–; *Style*— Ms Catherine McKinnell, MP; ✉ House of Commons, London SW1A 0AA

McKINNEY, Paul Benedict; s of James P McKinney, of Dumbarton, and Marie; *b* 21 May 1964; *Educ* St Thomas of Aquin's HS, United World Coll of the Atlantic (Int Bacc), UC Oxford (BA), Moray House Coll of Educn Edinburgh (PGCE); *Career* researcher and press offr to Gordon Brown, MP 1988–92, civil servant Scottish Office 1993; Scottish Television (now STV): researcher/reporter 1994, asst prodr news & current affairs 1994–96, chief news prodr 1996–99, head of news 1999–2000, head of news and current affairs 2000–; *Recreations* cinema, theatre, opera; *Style*— Paul McKinney, Esq

McKINNON, Prof Alan; s of Alexander Campbell McKinnon (d 1993), and Janet, *née* McPheat; *b* 19 September 1953; *Educ* Perth Acad, Univ of Aberdeen (MA, winner Royal Scottish Geographical Society medal), Univ of Br Columbia (MA, Canadian Commonwealth Scholarship), UCL (PhD); *m* 15 July 1983, Sabine, da of Werner Rohde; 2 s (Philip Alexander b 4 Dec 1985, Christopher Alan b 24 Aug 1988); *Career* lectr in geography Univ of Leicester 1979–87; Heriot-Watt Univ: lectr Dept of Business Organisation 1987–92, sr lectr 1992–94, reader 1994–95, prof of logistics 1995–2014, dir Logistics Res Centre 1998–2012, dir of research in Sch of Mgmnt and languages 2005–07, prof emeritus 2014–; head of logistics Kuehne Logistics Univ Hamburg 2012–15; visiting prof: Univ of Linkoping, Univ of Technology Mara (Malaysia), Dalian Maritime Univ (China), Cranfield Univ, Stellenbosch Univ, Central Univ of Finance and Economics Beijing; chm: Scottish Tport Studies Gp 1989–92, Foresight Retail Logistics Taskforce 2000–01, Tport Advsy Gp EU Horizon 2020 Research Prog 2014–16, Planning Ctee EU-US Symposium on the adaptation of transport systems to climate change; Euro ed Int Jl of Physical Distribution and Logistics Mgmnt 1990–95, ed-in-chief Tport Logistics Jl 1996–98; specialist advsr: House of Commons Scottish Affairs Ctee study of Future of Scotland's Tport Links with Europe 1992–93, Scottish Parl Local Govt and Tport Ctee Inquiry into Freight Tport in Scotland 2006; memb: Scottish Office's Nat Tport Forum 1998–99, Foresight Panel on the Built Environment and Tport 1999–2001, Cmmn for Integrated Tport Working Gp on lorry weight limits 1999–2000, Dept for Tport Freight and Logistics Research Gp 2003–09, World Economic Forum Global Agenda Cncl on the Future of Transportation 2008–10, Dept for Tport Low Carbon Tport Supply Chain Steering Gp 2010–11, World Economic Forum Global Agenda Cncl on Logistics and Supply Chain Systems 2010–, EU High Level Gp on Logistics 2012–; lead author of Transport chapter of Intergovernmental Panel on Climate Change's 5th Assessment Report 2012–; Herbert Crow Meml Award Worshipful Co of Carmen 2002, Sir Robert Lawrence Award Inst of Logistics and Tport 2003; FILT 1997, CFILT 2003, fell European Logistics Assoc 2015; *Publications* Physical Distribution Systems (1989), Transport Logistics (ed, 2002), Green Logistics (ed, 2010, 3 edn 2015), Supply Chain Innovation for Competing in Highly Dynamic Markets (ed, 2011); also articles in academic jls; *Recreations* piano playing, hill walking; *Style*— Prof Alan McKinnon; ✉ Kuehne Logistics University, Grosser Grasbrook 17, 20457 Hamburg (e-mail alancmckinnon@gmail.com, website www.alanmckinnon.co.uk and www.the-klu.org/mckinnon)

McKINNON, His Hon Judge Warwick Nairn; s of His Hon Judge Neil Nairn McKinnon, QC (d 1988), and Janetta Amelia, *née* Lilley (d 1989); *b* 11 November 1947; *Educ* KCS Wimbledon, Christ's Coll Cambridge (MA); *m* 29 July 1978, Nichola Juliet, da of David Alan Lloyd, of Limpsfield, Surrey; 1 s, 1 da; *Career* called to the Bar Lincoln's Inn 1970 (bencher 2010); ad eundum SE Circuit, recorder of the Crown Court 1995–98 (asst recorder 1991–95), circuit judge (SE Circuit) 1998–2010 (sr circuit judge 2010–), resident judge Croydon Crown Court 2006–, hon recorder Croydon 2008–; chm Essex Criminal Justice Strategy Ctee 1999–2001, IT liaison judge for Kent 2001–06, liaison judge and chm SE London region Area Judicial Forum 2006–13; *Publications* WordPerfect 5.1 for the Criminal Lawyer; *Recreations* travel, golf, gardening, painting, listening to and playing music; *Style*— His Hon Judge Warwick McKinnon; ✉ Croydon Crown Court, The Law Courts, Altyre Road, Croydon CR9 5AB

McKINSTRY, Dr Thomas Herbert (Tom); s of Ebenezer Herbert McKinstry (d 1977), and Margaret, *née* Eccles (d 2002); *b* 19 March 1943, Belfast, NI; *Educ* Belfast Royal Acad, KCL, Queen's Univ Belfast (MB, BCh, BAO); *m* 19 March 1967, Anna, *née* Miskimmin; 1 s (Caleb Eccles b 10 Sept 1968), 1 da (Zahra Hannah b 26 Aug 1978); *Career* registrar in psychiatry 1981–86, GP 1986–; chm E Dorset Div BMA 2005–12, former memb Cncl BMA, former chm Wessex and NI Junior Doctors Ctee; fell Belfast Royal Acad; Freeman City of London, Liveryman Worshipful Co of Gold and Silver Wyre Drawers; *Recreations* motor sport, theatre, rugby, polo, food and drink; *Clubs* Queen's Univ of London Assoc; *Style*— Dr Tom McKinstry; ✉ Toancaza, 17 St Cleeve Way, Ferndown, Dorset BH22 8LE (☎ 01202 855354)

MACKINTOSH, Sir Cameron Anthony; kt (1996); *b* 17 October 1946; *Educ* Prior Park Coll Bath, Central Sch of Speech and Drama (1 year); *Career* theatre producer; began work as cleaner, stagehand and later asst stage mangr Theatre Royal Drury Lane, work with Emile Littler (dep stage mangr 110 In The Shade, Palace Theatre) 1966 and Robin Alexandar 1967; chm Cameron Mackintosh Ltd 1981–, dir Delfont Mackintosh 1991–; owner: Prince Edward Theatre, Prince of Wales Theatre, Novello Theatre, Queen's Theatre, Gielgud Theatre, Wyndham's Theatre, Noel Coward Theatre, Victoria Palace Theatre; hon fell St Catherine's Coll Oxford 1990; *Theatre* London prodns incl: Anything Goes (Saville Theatre) 1969, Trelawny 1972, The Card 1973 (revived 1992 and 1994), Winnie the Pooh 1974 and 1975, The Owl and the Pussycat Went to See 1975, Godspell 1975, 1977 and 1978, Side By Side By Sondheim 1976–77, Oliver! 1977–80, 1983, 1994–98 and 2009–11, My Fair Lady 1979–81, Gingerbread Man 1979–84 (Christmas seasons), Oklahoma! 1980–81, TomFoolery (London and NY) 1980–82, Jeeves Takes Charge 1980–81, Cats (New London and worldwide) 1981–2002, Song & Dance (London and NY) 1982–86, Blondel 1983, Little Shop of Horrors 1983–85, Abbacadabra 1983, The Boyfriend 1984–85, Les Misérables (Barbican, Palace, Queen's and worldwide) 1985–, The Phantom of the Opera (Her Majesty's and worldwide) 1986–, Café Puccini 1986, Follies 1987–89, Miss Saigon (Theatre Royal Drury Lane and worldwide) 1989–99 and 2014–, Just So 1990–91, Five Guys Named Moe (Lyric, Albery and worldwide) 1991–95, Moby Dick 1992, Carousel (NT) 1992–94, Putting It Together (NY) 1993 and 1999, Martin Guerre 1996–98, The Fix 1997, Swan Lake (NY) 1998, Oklahoma! (NT) 1999, The Witches of Eastwick 2000–01, My Fair Lady (NT) 2001–03, Mary Poppins (London, NY and worldwide) 2004–08, Avenue Q 2006–10, Hair 2010, Betty Blue Eyes 2011, Barnum 2013; *Film* Les Miserables 2012; *Style*— Sir Cameron Mackintosh; ✉ Cameron Mackintosh Ltd, 1 Bedford Square, London WC1B 3RB (☎ 020 7637 8866, website www.cameronmackintosh.com)

MACKINTOSH, David; MP; s of Jamesa Mackintosh, and Dolores Mackintosh; *b* 2 April 1979, Northampton; *Educ* Durham Univ; *Career* County cncllr Northants 2009 (ldr, Northampton BC 2011–15), MP (Cons) Northampton S 2015–; tstee The KidsAid Fndn 2007–12; *Style*— David Mackintosh, Esq, MP; ✉ White Lodge, 42 Billing Road, Northampton, NN1 5DA (☎ 01604 633414, e-mail info@davidmackintosh.org.uk, website www.davidmackintosh.org.uk, Twitter @davidmackintosh); House of Commons, London SW1A 0AA

McKINTOSH, Peter Finlay; s of Peter McKintosh (d 2010), and Beryl McKintosh; *b* 22 January 1967, Liverpool; *Educ* Univ of Warwick, Bristol Old Vic Theatre Sch; *Career* set and costume designer; *Theatre* incl: Noises Off (Old Vic, West End and UK tour), Guys and Dolls, The Importance of Being Earnest, Hay Fever, Harvey, My Night with Reg, Dirty Rotten Scoundrels, Another Country, Viva Forever!, Relatively Speaking, The Winslow Boy, Love Story, Butley, The Birthday Party, Prick Up Your Ears, Donkeys' Years, Shirley Valentine, Educating Rita, Entertaining Mr Sloane, The Dumb Waiter, Fiddler on the Roof and A Woman of No Importance (all West End), The Home Place (Gate Theatre Dublin and West End), Brand (RSC and West End), Boston Marriage (Donmar Warehouse and West End), King John, The Merry Wives of Windsor, Pericles and Alice in Wonderland (all RSC), Our Country's Good, The Doctor's Dilemma, Honk! and Widowers' Housees (all NT), The Heretic (Royal Ct Theatre), The Knot of the Heart, House of Games, Waste, Cloud Nine and Romance (all Almeida Theatre), Splendour, Luise Miller, Serenading Louie, Be Near Me, The Chalk Garden, John Gabriel Borkman and The Cryptogram (all Donmar Warehouse), The Winslow Boy (Broadway), The 39 Steps (West End, Broadway and worldwide; Best Scenic Design and Best Costume Design Tony Award nominations 2008), Seven Brides for Seven Brothers, The Sound of Music, Hello, Dolly! (Open Air Theatre Regent's Park, Best Costume Design Olivier Award nomination 2010), Crazy for You (Open Air Theatre Regent's Park and West End, Best Costume Design Olivier Award 2012), The Wind in the Willows (UK tour), 42nd Street (Chatelet Paris); *Opera* incl: The Marriage of Figaro (ENO), world premiere of The Handmaid's Tale (Royal Danish Opera, Canadian Opera and ENO), The Silent Twins and Love Counts (both Almeida Theatre); *Style*— Mr Peter McKintosh; ✉ e-mail petermckintosh@mac.com; c/o Clare Vidal-Hall Agency, 57 Carthew Road, London W6 0DU (e-mail cvh@clarevidalhall.com)

MACKINTOSH, Steven; s of Malcolm Mackintosh, and Dorothy, *née* Parris; *Career* actor; *Theatre* credits incl: The Number of the Beast, A Midsummer Night's Dream (Bush Theatre), Comus (Ludlow Festival), Multiple Choice (Yvonne Arnaud Theatre), Brighton Beach Memoirs (NT/Aldwych), Entertaining Strangers (NT), Cymbeline (NT and tour), The Winter's Tale (NT and tour), The Tempest (NT and tour), Look Look (Aldwych), Cops (Greenwich Theatre), The Woman in Black (Fortune Theatre), My Zinc Bed (Royal Court Theatre), In a Dark Dark House (Almeida Theatre) 2009; *Television* credits incl: The Browning Version (BBC), The Luck Child (TVS), Newshounds (Working Title), Inspector Morse (Zenith), Six Characters in Search of an Author (BBC), The Buddha of Suburbia (BBC), Midnight Movie (BBC), Safe (BBC), A Dark Adapted Eye (BBC), Karaoke (Whistling Gypsy Prodns), Prime Suspect (BBC/Granada), Our Mutual Friend (BBC), Undercover Heart (BBC), Bad Blood (Carlton), Care (BBC, RTS Award Best Actor), The Other Boleyn Girl, England Expects, Mo, Criminal Justice (BBC), Luther (BBC), The Jury, Lost Christmas, Inside Men, What Remains, The Thirteenth Tale, From There to Here (BBC), A Song for Jenny (BBC) 2015, Lucky Man (Sky 1) 2016; *Film* credits incl: Prick Up Your Ears, Memphis Belle, London Kills Me, Princess Caraboo, The Return of the Native, Blue Juice, The Grotesque, Different for Girls, Twelfth Night, House of America, It's Good to Talk, Land Girls, Lock, Stock and Two Smoking Barrels, The Criminal, Far from China, The Tulse Luper Suitcases, Part 1: The Moab Story 2003, The Tulse Luper Suitcases, Part 2: Vaux to the Sea 2004, Underworld: Evolution 2006, First Born 2007, Underworld: Rise of the Lycans 2009, The Scouting Book for Boys, The Great Ghost Rescue, Elfie Hopkins, The Sweeney 2012, Kick Ass 2, Gold, Our Robot Overlords, Set Fire to the Stars 2014, Urban Hymn 2016, A Hundred Streets 2016; *Style*— Steven Mackintosh, Esq

MACKINTOSH OF HALIFAX, 3 Viscount (UK 1957); Sir (John) Clive Mackintosh; 3 Bt (UK 1935); s of 2 Viscount Mackintosh of Halifax, OBE, BEM (d 1980, whose f was head of the Mackintosh confectionery manufacturers), by his 2 w, Gwynneth, Viscountess Mackintosh of Halifax; *b* 9 September 1958; *Educ* The Leys Sch Cambridge, Oriel Coll Oxford (MA); *m* 1, 1982 (m dis 1993), Elizabeth, *née* Lakin; 2 s (Hon Thomas Harold George b 8 Feb 1985, Hon George John Frank b 24 Oct 1988); m 2, 1995, Mrs Claire Jane Wishart, yr da of Stanislaw Nowak; 1 da (Hon Violet Krystyna Jane b 5 Oct 2000); *Heir* s, Hon Thomas Mackintosh; *Career* chartered accountant; ptnr PricewaterhouseCoopers; pres OUCA 1979; FCA; *Recreations* cricket, golf, bridge; *Clubs* MCC, RAC, Beefsteak; *Style*— The Rt Hon the Viscount Mackintosh of Halifax; ✉ PricewaterhouseCoopers, 1 Embankment Place, London WC2N 6RH

McKITTERICK, Prof Rosamond D; da of Claude Anthony Pierce, and Melissa, *née* Heaney; *b* 31 May 1949; *Educ* Univ of Western Australia (Cwlth Univ scholar, Amy Jane Best Prize, BA), Univ of Munich, Univ of Cambridge (MA, PhD, LittD); *m* 15 May 1976, David John McKitterick; 1 da (Lucy Rosamond b 23 May 1983); *Career* temp tutor Dept of History Univ of Western Australia 1971; Univ of Cambridge: asst lectr 1979–85, lectr 1985–91, reader in early medieval Euro history 1991–97, prof (personal chair) in early medieval Euro history 1997–99, prof of medieval history 1999–; Newnham Coll Cambridge: fell 1977–97, research fell 1974–77, professorial fell 1997–2006, vice-princ 1996–98; Lady Margaret preacher Univ of Cambridge 1999, professorial fell Sidney Sussex Coll Cambridge 2007–, vice master Sydney Sussex Coll Cambridge 2013–, chair Faculty of Archaeology History and Letters Br Sch at Rome 2013–; Royal Historical Soc: memb Cncl 1990–98 and 2000–03, memb Publications Ctee 1992–95, Gen Purposes Ctee 1993–95, memb Editorial Bd Studies in History 1994–98, vice-pres 1994–98 and 2000–03; corresponding ed Early Medieval Europe 1999– (ed 1991–98), series ed Palaeography and Codicology, series ed Cambridge Studies in Medieval Life and Thought; memb Editorial Bd: Gazette du livre mediéval, Library History, Jl of Ecclesiastical History, Utrecht Studies in Medieval Literacy, Millennium Max Planck Institut für Rechtsgeschichte, Quaerendo; memb various learned socs incl: Ecclesiastical History Soc, Int Soc for Anglo Saxonists, Henry Bradshaw Soc (memb Cncl 1988–), French History Soc, Soc for Promotion of Byzantine Studies; Heineken Prize Laureate in History 2010; Hugh Balsdon fell Br Sch at Rome 2001–02, fell-in-residence Netherlands Inst of Advanced Studies 2005–06, Scaliger fell Univ Library Leiden Univ 2010, Lester K Little scholar in residence American Academy in Rome 2011; fell: Korrespondierendes Mitglied, Monumenta Germaniae Historica 1999–; corresponding fell Medieval Acad of America 2006–, korrespondierendes Mitglied im Ausland (phil-hist) Austrian Acad of Sciences 2006–; memb Academia Europaea 2011–; FRHistS 1980, FRSA 2001; *Books* The Frankish Church and the Carolingian Reforms 789–895 (1977), The Frankish Kingdoms under the Carolingians 751–987 (1983), The Carolingians and the Written Word (1989), Books, Scribes and Learning in the Frankish Kingdoms, Sixth to Ninth centuries (1994), Frankish Kings and Culture in the Early Middle Ages (1995), The Uses of Literacy in early mediaeval Europe (1990), Carolingian Culture: emulation and innovation (1994), The New Cambridge Medieval History, c.700-c.900 (1995), Edward Gibbon & Empire (with R Quinault, 1996), History and its Audiences (2000), The Short Oxford History of Europe: The early middle ages 400–1000 (2001), The Times Atlas of the Medieval World (2003), History and Memory in the Carolingian World (2004), Perceptions of the Past in the Early Middle-Ages (2006), Charlemagne: The formation of a European identity (2008), La Culture du Haut Moren Age: Une Question d'Elites Turnhout (jt ed, 2009), Ego Trouble: Authors and their Identities in the Early Middle Ages (jt ed, 2010), Rome Across Time and Space: Cultural Transmission and the Exchange of Ideas c 500–1400 (jt ed, 2011), Turning Over a New Leaf: Change and Development in the Medieval Manuscript (jtly, 2012), Old St Peter's, Rome (jt ed, 2013), 'Being Roman after Rome' themed edn Early Medieval Europe 22 (guest ed, 2014), The Resources of the Past in Early Medieval Europe (jt ed, 2015); also author of numerous book chapters and articles in learned jls; *Recreations* music, fresh air; *Style*— Prof Rosamond McKitterick; ✉ Sidney Sussex College, Cambridge CB2 3HU

McKITTRICK, David; s of Frey McKittrick (d 1987), of Belfast, and Rita, *née* Hegarty; *b* 10 August 1949; *m* 1978, Patricia, da of P J Hackett, of Coalisland, Co Tyrone; 2 da (Kerry b 1979, Julie b 1981); *Career* reporter East Antrim Times 1971–73; Irish Times: reporter Belfast 1973–76, Northern ed 1976–81, London ed 1981–85; journalist BBC Belfast 1985–86, Ireland corr The Independent 1986–; sometime Ireland corr: Sunday Times, Economist, Le Monde; contrib: Fortnight, Listener, New Statesman, Hibernia, Boston Globe, San Francisco Examiner, New York Times; numerous TV broadcasts; co-recipient Christopher Ewart-Biggs meml prize 1989, Irish media award for reporting on Ireland for a pubn abroad 1987, runner-up Reporter of the Year Br Press Awards 1987; memb: NUJ 1971, Exec Br-Irish Assoc; *Books* Despatches from Belfast (1989), Endgame (1994), The Nervous Peace (1996), The Fight for Peace (with Eamonn Maille, 1996); *Style*— David McKittrick, Esq; ✉ The Independent, 2 Derry Street, London W8 5TT (☎ 020 7293 2000, fax 020 7293 2435)

MACKNEY, Paul Leon John; s of Rev Leon E Mackney (d 1962), and Margaret *née* Dickinson (d 2004); *b* 25 March 1950, Lincoln; *Educ* Univ of Exeter (BA), Univ of Warwick (MA), Univ of Birmingham (CertEd), RSA (Dip); *m* 1, 20 Sept 1969 (m dis), Rosemary Angela Draper; 1 s (Sean Leon Mackney b 26 June 1972); m 2, 28 May 1982, Cherry Margot Sewell; 1 da (Ruby Yasmin Mackney Sewell b 21 April 1988); *Career* trainee probation offr 1971–73, gen studies lectr Poole Tech Coll 1974–75, English for Speakers of Other Languages (ESOL) organiser Hall Green Tech Coll 1975–79, trade union studies tutor Hall Green Coll 1980–85, head Birmingham Trade Union Studies Centre S Birmingham Coll 1986–92; NATFHE (univ and coll lectrs union): branch offr then Birmingham sec 1975–92, W Midlands regional official 1992–97, general sec 1997–2006; jt gen sec Univ and Coll Union (UCU) 2006–07, assoc dir (FE) NIACE 2008–; memb Gen Cncl TUC 2002–07, life memb Birmingham TUC (pres 1980–84); fndr memb Birmingham Campaign Against Racism and Fascism, vice-chair Coalition of Resistance 2010–, co-chair Greece Solidarity Campaign 2012–; former govr: Handsworth Coll, Bournville Coll; FRSA; *Publications* Birmingham and the Miners' Strike; *Recreations* music, guitar, singing; *Clubs* Birmingham Bread and Roses; *Style*— Paul Mackney; ✉ e-mail paulmackney@btinternet.com

McKNIGHT, Prof Eur Ing Dr James; *b* 21 April 1938; *Educ* Ayr Acad, Kilmarnock Slough and Barking Colls of Technol, Thurrock Tech Coll (HNC Business Studies), Mid Essex Mgmnt Coll (Dip Mgmnt Studies); *m* Susan; 1 da (Grace); *Career* Scottish Stamping and Engineering Co Ltd (GKN) 1954–63 (engrg apprentice, engrg draughtsman, asst to Forge Supt); Ford Motor Co 1963–77: successively resident engr Langley Truck Plant, project engr, princ engr then supervisor, mangr Advanced Truck Engrg; Leyland Vehicles Ltd 1977–87: chief engr Vehicle Engrg 1977–81, chief engr Test Ops Prototype 1981–83, controller Product Devpt Leyland Trucks 1983–84, chief engr Product Control 1984–85, product devpt dir Leyland Bus 1985–87, product devpt dir (following MBO) Leyland Bus Group Ltd 1987–88, product devpt dir Volvo Bus Ltd (Leyland Bus Ltd until 1991) 1988–95, chm Leyland Product Developments Ltd (formerly Volvo Bus Product Development) 1995–2004 (also md 1995–2001); visiting prof in mechanical engrg Univ of Leeds 1996–2003 (chm Industrial Advsy Ctee 1994–2002); course assessor Nat Dip in Engrg Scottish TEC 1978–86, memb Organising Ctee Int Symposium for Automated Testing of Automobiles 1981–86, memb Industrial Advsy Ctee Univ of Glasgow and Glasgow Sch of Art 1992–94; Instn of Mechanical Engrs: memb Qualifications Bd 1989–92 and 1994–96, chm Mechanical Pubns (MEP) Ltd, memb Cncl 1992–2001, memb Exec Ctee 1993–2001, vice-pres 1995–97, dep pres 1997–99, pres 1999–2000; SMMT: chm Heavy Commercial Vehicle Tech Ctee 1989–94, memb Engrg Ctee 1989–94; FISITA: memb Cncl 1992–2004, vice-pres 1994–98, pres 1998–2000; Engrg Cncl: senator 2000–02, memb Bd for the Engrg Profession 2000–02; memb Membership Ctee Royal Acad of Engrg 1998–2001; author of numerous papers in various professional jls; hon fell Bolton Inst 2000; Hon DEng Univ of Bolton 2010; Eur Ing, DMS, CEng, FIMechE (past pres 2000–), FISITA (past pres 2000–05), FCMI, FRSA, MSAE, FREng 1997; *Recreations* golf, rugby union; *Style*— Prof Eur Ing Dr James McKnight, FREng; ✉ 14 Furlong Lane,

M

Poulton-le-Fylde, Lancashire FY6 7HQ (☎ 01253 894070, mobile 07973 174777, e-mail jmcknight@fsmail.net)

McKNIGHT, Sam; *b* Irvine, Scotland; *Career* hair stylist; collaborations incl: Patrick Demarchelier, Nick Knight, Mario Testino, Karl Lagerfeld/Chanel, Vivienne Westwood, Balmain, Fendi, Tim Walker, Peter Lindbergh, Craig McDean; clients incl: Princess Diana, Cate Blanchett, Tilda Swinton, Lady Gaga, Kate Moss, Gisele Bundchen, Cara Delevingne; *Recreations* gardening, reading, walking; *Style*— Sam McKnight, Esq; ✉ c/o Premier Hair and Makeup, 8 Royalty Studios, 105–109 Lancaster Road, London W11 1QF

MACKRELL, Judith Rosalind (Mrs S P Henson); da of Alexander George Mackrell, of Surrey, and Margaret Elizabeth, *née* Atkinson; *b* 26 October 1954; *Educ* Sutton HS, Univ of York (BA), Univ of Oxford (DPhil); *m* Simon Peter Henson, s of Peter Henson; 2 s (Frederick Juan b 12 Feb 1990, Oscar Henson b 17 Dec 1992); *Career* pt/t lectr in English literature: Oxford Poly, Lincoln Coll Oxford, St Anne's Coll Oxford, City Lit London 1981–85; freelance dance writer 1984– (work published in Vogue, Tatler, Dance Theatre Journal); dance corr: The Independent 1986–94, The Guardian 1994–; broadcasts incl: Dance International BBC TV, South Bank Show, Radio 3, Radio 4 and World Service; hon fell Laban Centre London 1996; *Books* British New Dance (1991), Reading Dance (1997) A Life in Dance (with Darcey Bussell, 1998), Oxford Dictionary of Dance (with Debra Craine, 2000), Bloomsbury Ballerina: Lydia Lopokova, Imperial Dancer and Mrs John Maynard Keynes (2008), Flappers: Six Women of a Dangerous Generation (2013); *Recreations* family, travel, reading, food, music; *Style*— Ms Judith Mackrell

MACKRELL, Keith Ashley Victor; s of Henry George Mackrell (d 1967), of Romsey, Hants, and Emily Winifred Jesse Mackrell (d 1972); *b* 20 October 1932; *Educ* Peter Symonds Sch Winchester, LSE (BSc Econ); *m* 20 Feb 1960, June Mendoza; 3 da (Elliet b 1956, Kim b 1958, Lee b 1961), 1 s (Ashley b 1961); *Career* RAF Flying Offr 1953–55; dir: Cope Allman International 1977–86, Shell International 1977–91, Private Investment Corp for Asia (PICA) 1980–84, Shell Pensions Tst Ltd 1983–94, Rexam plc (formerly Bowater plc) 1991–97, Regalian Properties plc 1991–2001, Standard Chartered plc 1991–2002, Fairey Gp plc 1993–99, dep chm BG Gp plc (formerly British Gas plc) 1994–2005, Dresdner RCM Emerging Markets Tst plc 1998–2002, Gartmore Asia Pacific Tst plc (formerly Asia Recovery Tst plc) 1998–2004, Duke CE Ltd 2003–10 (vice-chm); govr LSE 1991–2009, pres emeritus Enterprise LSE; memb: Int Advsy Cncl East-West Centre Honolulu 1985; hon fell LSE; Hon LLD Nat Univ of Singapore; FInstD 1977, CIMgt; *Clubs* Hurlingham, Wimbledon; *Style*— Keith Mackrell, Esq; ✉ Duke CE Ltd, 165 Fleet Street, London EC4A 2DY (☎ 020 7936 6110)

McLACHLAN, John James; s of William McLachlan (d 1980), and Helen McLachlan (d 2000); *b* 28 August 1942; *Educ* Rock Ferry High GS; *m* 24 Sept 1966, Heather Joan, da of George Smith (d 1975), of Heswall; 1 da (Deborah b 19 Feb 1972), 1 s (Alexander b 4 Jan 1975); *Career* mgmnt accountant Norwest Construction 1966–67, investment analyst Martins Bank Trust Co 1967–69, investment res mangr Barclays Bank Trust Co 1969–71, dep investment mangr 1971–74, investment mangr British Rail Pension Fund 1974–83, dir pensions investment 1983–84, investment mangr Reed International plc 1984–88, investment dir United Friendly Insurance plc and United Friendly Group plc 1988–99; dir: United Friendly Unit Trust Managers Ltd 1993, United Friendly Asset Management plc 1993; Gp Investment Dir United Assurance Group plc 1996–99; former chm Investment Ctee Nat Assoc of Pension Funds; former memb: Panel on Take Overs and Mergers, Institutional Shareholders Ctee; former non-exec chm INVESCO Income Growth Trust plc; former chm GE Penson Plan (UK); FCA, FRSA; *Recreations* travel, watching cricket and soccer, reading; *Style*— John McLachlan, Esq; ✉ home ☎ 01732 762776, fax 01732 762355

McLACHLAN, Marjory Jane; da of Walter Alexander, and Kate, *née* Turnbull; *b* 15 February 1942, Falkirk; *Educ* St Leonard's Sch St Andrews; *m* 1 Sept 1962, Colin McLachlan; 2 da (Jane b 7 Aug 1966, Katy b 12 Aug 1968); *Career* DL Stirling and Falkirk 2000–05, Lord-Lt Stirling and Falkirk 2005–; supporter: Save the Children, Cancer Research, Barnardo's, Friends of Falkirk Hosps, Scottish Soc for Autism; *Recreations* curling, bridge, golf, travel, family; *Style*— Mrs Marjory McLachlan; ✉ 23 Majors Loan, Falkirk FK1 5QG (☎ and fax 01324 622633, e-mail marjmcl@aol.com)

MACLAREN, Deanna; *née* Bullimore; *b* 4 February 1944; *m* 1, 1965, Patrick Maclaren; m 2, 1974, Michael Godfrey; m 3, 1987, Nicholas Kent; *Career* author, journalist, broadcaster and public speaker; presenter The Single Life (Channel Four); *Books* Little Blue Room, The First of all Pleasures, Dagger in the Sleeve, Your Loving Mother, Ménage à Trois, Villa Fleurie, Strangers in a Garden, Azur Allure, In Bed with Mr Plantagenet, The Price of Love; non-fiction: The Single File, How to Live Alone and Like It; *Recreations* learning jazz piano; *Clubs* Chelsea Arts; *Style*— Ms Deanna Maclaren

McLAREN, Ian Alban Bryant; QC (1993); s of Alban McLaren (d 1972), and Doris Martha, *née* Hurst (d 2003); *b* 3 July 1940; *Educ* Sandbach Sch, Blackpool GS, Univ of Nottingham (LLB); *m* 7 Sept 1964, Margaret, da of Alfred George Middleton; 2 s (Andrew James b 28 Feb 1967, Mark Ian b 29 Aug 1968), 1 da (Rachel Margaret b 28 Dec 1970); *Career* called to the Bar Gray's Inn 1962 (entrance scholar, Mackaskie scholar, bencher 2004); law tutor Univ of Nottingham 1962–64, in practice at the Bar in Nottingham 1962–2009, recorder of the Crown Court 1996–2010 (asst recorder 1992), head Ropewalk Chambers 2000–06; pres Notts Medico-Legal Soc 1997–98, memb Standards Ctee Notts CC 2009–12; fell Inst Advanced Legal Studies; Hon LLD Nottingham Trent Univ 2005; *Recreations* wine, photography, gardening; *Style*— Ian McLaren, Esq, QC; ✉ Ropewalk Chambers, 24 The Ropewalk, Nottingham NG1 5EF (☎ 0115 947 2581, fax 0115 947 6532)

McLARTY, Stuart William; s of William Ross McLarty, of Pinjarra, Aust, and Evelyn May, *née* Parkhill; *b* 7 July 1960; *Educ* Hale Sch Perth, Curtin Univ Perth, South Bank Univ; *m* 7 April 1990, Christine, *née* Oborne; 3 s (Joshua William, Matthew David, Oliver Stuart); *Career* Aukett: joined 1985, associate 1990, asst dir 1995, dir 1997, marketing dir 2002, plc bd dir 2003, projects incl Doxford Int Business Park 1998 (BCO commendation) and MCI HQ 2001; founding dir De Novo Architecture Ltd 2004; govr St Luke's C of E Sch; RIBA 1990, ARB 1990; *Recreations* skiing, mountain biking, tennis, golf, cricket; *Clubs* Mortons Private Members, Wimbledon Minis RFC, Richmond Golf; *Style*— Stuart W McLarty, Esq; ✉ DN-A, 1 Castle Yard, Richmond, Surrey TW10 6TF (☎ 020 8332 3902, fax 020 8332 3901, e-mail stuart@mydn-a.com)

McLATCHIE, Cameron; CBE (1996, OBE 1988); s of Cameron McLatchie (d 1997), of Largs, and Maggie, *née* Taylor (d 2001); *b* 18 February 1947; *Educ* Ardrossan Acad, Univ of Glasgow (LLB, memb Scottish & British Junior Bridge Team); *m* 26 April 1973, (Helen) Leslie, da of Dr William R Mackie, of Largs; 2 s (Stuart b 19 April 1976, Fraser 4 Dec 1979), 1 da (Julie b 16 May 1985); *Career* British Polythene Industries plc (formerly Scott & Robertson plc): md 1983–88, chm and chief exec 1988–2003, chm 2003–; md Anaplast Ltd 1975–83, various positions with Thomas Boag & Co Ltd 1971–74, apprentice CA Whinney Murray & Co 1968–70; non-exec chm Hiscox Select plc 1993–98, non-exec dep chm Scottish Enterprise 1997–2000 (memb Bd 1990–95); non-exec dir: Motherwell Bridge Holdings Ltd 1993–97, Royal Bank of Scotland 1998–2002; memb: Advsy Ctee for Business and the Environment (ACBE-I) 1991–93, sec of state for Scotland's Advsy Gp on Sustainable Devpt (AGSD) 1994–95, Bd Scottish Environmental Protection Agency 1995–97; Hon DUniv Paisley 2000; CIMgt 1995; *Recreations* golf, bridge, gardening; *Clubs* West Kilbride Golf, Western Gailes Golf; *Style*— Cameron McLatchie, Esq, CBE; ✉ Ailsa, Summerlea Road, Seamill, Ayrshire KA23 9HP (☎ 01294 823650, fax 01294 822 853); British Polythene Industries plc, 96 Port Glasgow Road, Greenock PA15 2RP (☎ 01475 501000, fax 01475 743143, mobile 078 3670 1716, e-mail cameronmclatchie@aol.com)

McLAUCHLAN, Prof Keith Alan; s of Frederick William McLauchlan (d 1972), and Nellie, *née* Summers (d 1996); *b* 8 January 1936; *Educ* Queen Elizabeth's Hosp Bristol, Univ of Bristol (BSc, PhD, W E Garner prize for chemistry), Univ of Oxford (MA); *m* 23 Aug 1958, Joan Sheila, da of Howard Dickenson; 1 s (Gavin Ian b 4 June 1962), 1 da (Christine Anne b 4 Aug 1964); *Career* post doctoral fell Nat Research Cncl Ottawa 1959–60, sr res fell then sr scientific offr Nat Physical Laboratory 1960–65; Univ of Oxford: lectr 1965–94, reader in physical chemistry 1994–96, prof of chemistry 1996–2002 (now emeritus); fell Hertford Coll Oxford 1965– (now emeritus), Erskine fell Univ of Canterbury Christchurch 1997; visiting prof: Tata Inst Bombay 1986, Univ of Konstanz 1990, École Normale Supèrieure Paris 1998, Univ of Padua 1998, Univ of Chicago 1998; eminent scientist Inst of Physics & Chemistry Research Tokyo 2000–01; memb: Editorial Bd Chemical Physics Letters 1991–95, Exec Editorial Ctee Molecular Physics 1993–2002, Gen Bd Oxford 1993–97, Hebdomodal Cncl Oxford 1998–2000; pres Int EPR Soc 1993–96 (Silver Medal 1994, Gold Medal 2002), winner of Bruker Prize RSC 1997, Zavoisky Prize for EPR Kazan 2001; FRS 1992, fell Int EPR Soc 2005; *Books* Magnetic Resonance (1972), Molecular Physical Chemistry (2004); author of 180 pubns and reviews in scientific jls; *Recreations* walking, reading, listening to music, gardening; *Style*— Prof Keith McLauchlan, FRS; ✉ Hertford College, Catte Street, Oxford

McLAUGHLIN, Brian Finbar; s of Patrick William John McLaughlin, of Buncrana, Donegal, and Frances McLaughlin; *b* 21 August 1949, Portsmouth; *Educ* St Augustine's Abbey Sch Ramsgate; *m* 28 Sept 1968, Susan, *née* Middlemist; 2 da (Louisa Jane (Mrs Nicoll) b 27 Aug 1969, Katherine Francesca b 21 July 1987), 1 s (James William b 9 Dec 1973); *Career* HMV Gp plc: joined as first asst Portsmouth branch 1968, mangr Portsmouth 1971, mangr Leeds 1974, northern area mangr 1976, gen mangr of ops May 1980, ops dir and memb Bd HMV UK Nov 1980, oversaw launch of Oxford St branch (world's largest record store at the time) 1986, md HMV UK Ltd 1987–1996, md HMV Europe 1996–2001, acting md Waterstone's 2001, 2003–04 and 2004–06, chief operating offr 2001–05, non-exec dir 2006, conslt 2006–07; dir Pangbourne & Goring Properties Ltd 2006–, chm Starlight Events Ltd 2011–; chm Br Assoc of Record Dealers 1992–94 and 1998–2000, dir Music Industry Tst 2005–; chm Football Extravaganza 1996–, chm Footies Awards 2012–15; memb Music Industry Forum DCMS 1998; chm Fundraising Ctee Nordoff-Robbins Music Therapy Centre 2005–08, govr Nordoff Robbins Music Therapy 2006–15; govr BRIT Sch 2001; Strat Award Music Week Awards 1996, Man of the Year Music Industry Tsts 2001; *Recreations* family, music, movies, wine, Portsmouth FC, horse racing, reading; *Clubs* Royal Ascot Racing; *Style*— Brian McLaughlin, Esq

McLAUGHLIN, Christopher John; s of Patrick Thomas McLaughlin (d 1990), and Norah Mary, *née* Walsh; *b* 11 October 1955, London; *Educ* St Bonaventure's London, Harlow Tech Coll (NCTJ); *Partner* Katharine Walters; *Career* trainee reporter Barking Advertiser 1974–76, feature writer and local govt reporter Newham Recorder 1976–78, int ed and lobby corr Labour Weekly 1979–87, freelancer Mirror Gp 1981–85, political reporter, dep political ed, European ed The Scotsman 1987–95; dep political ed Mail on Sunday 1995–99, political ed Sunday Mirror 1999–2004, ed Tribune 2004–; political columnist Big Issue 2000–05; cncllr Newham Cncl 1978–82; memb NUJ 1974; *Recreations* swimming, walking, modern dance (viewing), reading; *Clubs* Soho House, Houses of Parl Sports and Social; *Style*— Christopher McLaughlin, Esq; ✉ Tribune, 9 Arkwright Road, London NW3 6AN (☎ 020 7433 6410, fax 020 7433 6419, e-mail mail@tribunemagazine.co.uk)

McLAUGHLIN, David; s of Terence McLaughlin, of Chesterfield, Derbys, and Margaret Lees, *née* Pears; *b* 2 April 1971, Shipston on Stour, Warks; *Educ* Lakes Sch Windermere, Kendal Coll; *m* 1 April 2000, Janette, *née* Hunt; 1 s (Callum b 6 Feb 2003), 1 da (Neve b 14 June 2006); *Career* chef; Wordsworth Hotel Grasmere 1988–93, Michael's Nook Grasmere 1993–2000, head chef Holbeck Ghyll Country House Hotel Windermere 2000– (Michelin star 2001–, Egon Ronay star, 3 AA Rosettes, Restaurant of the Year (Cumbria) Good Food Guide 2007); *Publications* 100 Best Risottos of the World (2007); *Style*— David McLaughlin, Esq; ✉ Holbeck Ghyll Country House Hotel, Holbeck Lane, Windermere, Cumbria LA23 1LU (☎ 01539 432375)

McLAUGHLIN, Niall; *Educ* UC Dublin; *m* Mary; 1 s (Diarmaid), 1 da (Iseult); *Career* Scott Tallon Walker Dublin and London 1984–89, fndr Niall McLaughlin Architects 1990–; visiting prof of architecture UCL; chair RIBA Awards Gp 2007–09; Young British Architect of the Year 1998, RIAI Best Building in the Landscape, RIBA Stephen Lawrence Award for the Best Building under £1 million, shortlisted Stirling Prize 2013 and 2015; *Style*— Niall McLaughlin, Esq; ✉ Niall McLaughlin Architects, Bedford House, 125–133 Camden High Street, London NW1 7JR

MacLAURIN, Brian David; s of Peter and Yvonne MacLaurin, of Kilmacolm, Scotland; *b* 7 December 1949, Renfrewshire; *Educ* Rannoch Sch, Sighthill Coll Edinburgh; *m* 1, 1974 (m dis 1983); 1 s (Peter b 17 Sept 1975), 1 da (Katie b 22 Feb 1978); m 2, 20 March 1987, Gill Elizabeth, *née* Ormston; 1 s (James b 10 Feb 1990), 1 da (Kirsten b 25 Jan 1994); *Career* journalist and TV presenter: Scottish TV plc 1971–73, ATV Network Ltd 1973–77; presenter and industrial ed ATV Network Ltd 1977–79; Scottish TV plc: head Press and PR Dept 1979–84, controller press & PR 1984–88; dir Media Relations Crown Communications Group plc 1988–92, md MacLaurin Communications Ltd 1992–96, chief exec MacLaurin Ltd 1996–2001; md hatch-group UK Ltd, dir hatch Int Ltd 2001–03, fndr Brian MacLaurin Associates Ltd (media consultancy, now MacLaurin Media Ltd) 2003; winner CIPR (formerly IPR) Industry & Commerce Award 1999 (for MacLaurin Ltd); memb RTS 1995; MInstD, MIPR 1996; pres: La Molazul community Puerto Andratx Mallorca 2007–09, Es Forti Community Puerto Andratx Mallorca 2014–; *Recreations* family, clay pigeon shooting, good food and friends; *Clubs* Ivy; *Style*— Brian MacLaurin, Esq; ✉ The Old Bakery, Esher Green, Esher, Surrey KT10 8AD; MacLaurin The Media Business, 26 Esher Green, Esher, Surrey KT10 8AD (e-mail brian.maclaurin@maclaurinmedia.com)

MACLAURIN, Robert Allister Charles; s of (Allister) James Maclaurin, and Mary, *née* Boniface; *b* 12 June 1961; *Educ* Edinburgh Coll of Art; *Career* artist; *Solo Exhibitions* incl: Mercury Gallery Edinburgh 1987, 369 Gallery Edinburgh 1989, Berkeley Square Gallery London 1990, 1997, 1999, 2001 and 2003, The Fruitmarket Gallery Edinburgh 1991, Benjamin Rhodes Gallery London 1991 and 1993, Edinburgh Printmakers Gallery 1993, Kirkcaldy Art Gallery & Museum 1994, Durham Art Gallery 1994, Glasgow Print Studio 1995, Compass Gallery Glasgow 1997, Niagara Galleries Melbourne 1998, Talbot Rice Gallery, Edinburgh Int Festival 1999, Open Eye Gallery Edinburgh 2005 and 2009, Osborne-Samuel Gallery London 2006 and 2008, Axia Modern Melbourne 2007, Penny Sch Gallery Maldon Australia Castlemaine State Festival 2007 and 2011, Castlemaine Art Gallery and Museum Australia 2008, Australian Galleries Melbourne 2012, Open Eye Gallery Edinburgh 2013 and 2016; *Group Exhibitions* incl: New Scottish Painting (Art in General NY) 1988, Chicago International Art Exposition 1988–91, Athena Awards Exhibition (Barbican Art Gallery London) 1988–89, International Weeks of Painting (Slovenia, touring exhibition of former Yugoslavia) 1989–90, Scottish Art Since 1900 (Scottish Nat Gallery of Modern Art Edinburgh, Barbican Art Gallery London) 1989–90, The Int FIAR Prize Exhibition (touring to Milan, Rome, Paris, London, LA, NY) 1991–92, Expressions: Scottish Art 1945–2000 (touring) 2000, Scottish Landscape (Scottish Gallery Edinburgh) 2001, En plein air (Geelong Gallery and Australian tour) 2003, Scottish Artists (Bohun Gallery Henley-on-Thames) 2005, 7 Artists (Uber Gallery St Kilda

Melbourne) 2005, Scots Abroad (Open Eye Gallery Edinburgh) 2007, Scottish Painters in Australia (Castlemaine Art Gallery and Museum Castlemaine State Festival) 2011; *Work in Collections* BUPA (UK), Edinburgh City Art Centre, Contemporary Art Soc, Scottish Nat Gallery of Modern Art, Flemings/Wyfold Fndn Collection, Coopers Lybrand Deloitte, Art in Healthcare Scotland, Nat Tst, Phillips Petroleum (London), The Standard Life Assurance Company, McKenna and Co, Gtr Manchester City Collection, Scottish Arts Cncl, Kirkcaldy Art Gallery & Museum, Unilever, Pearl Assurance, HM The Queen (Royal Collection), Tetrapak, Paris Banque, Anglo-American (London), Scottish Nat Portrait Gallery, Scottish Govt Collection, Pioneer International Australia, Castlemaine Art Gallery and Museum Australia; *Awards* Hospital Field House Painting Sch 1982, John Kinross scholar RSA Florence 1984, Turkish Govt scholar 1984–85, Br Cncl travel grant 1988, Scottish Arts Cncl bursary 1988, Durham Cathedral artist in residence 1993–94, Dunmoochin Fndn Studio 1995–96, Sir Robert Menzies fellowship 1995, First Prize Winner Noble Grossart Scot Painting Prize 1998, First Prize John Farrell Self Portrait Prize Castlemaine Art Gallery and Museum 2005; *Publications* featured in: The Dictionary of Scottish Painters, Scottish Art 1460–2000, A History of Scottish Art: The Fleming Collection, Scottish Painters in Australia; exhbn catalogues 1997–2008; *Style*— Robert Maclaurin, Esq; ✉ c/o Osborne-Samuel Gallery, London (e-mail robert@robertmaclaurin.com, website www.robertmaclaurin.com)

MacLAURIN OF KNEBWORTH, Baron (Life Peer UK 1996), of Knebworth in the County of Hertfordshire; Sir Ian Charter MacLaurin; kt (1989); s of Arthur George MacLaurin (d 1989), and Evelina Florence, *née* Bott (d 1970); *b* 30 March 1937; *Educ* Malvern Coll; *m* 1, 1960, Ann Margaret (d 1999), da of Edgar Ralph Collar (d 1968); 2 da (Fiona Margaret (Mrs Mason) b 1962, Gillian (Mrs O'Gorman) b 1964), 1 s (Neil Ralph Charter b 1966); m 2, 2002, Paula, da of Herbert Morris; *Career* Nat Serv RAF Fighter Cmd 1956–58; Tesco plc: first co trainee 1959, memb Bd 1970, md 1973, dep chm 1983, chm 1985–97; non-exec dir: Enterprise Oil plc 1984–90, Guinness plc 1986–95, National Westminster Bank plc 1990–96, Gleneagles Hotels plc 1992–97, Vodafone Group plc 1997– (dep chm 1998–2000, chm 2000–06), Whitbread plc 1997–2000 (dep chm 1999–2000), Evolution Gp plc 2004–11, Heineken NV 2006–10, Bath Rugby 2011–; chm: Food Policy Gp of the Retail Consortium 1980–84, UK Sports Cncl until 1997, England and Wales Cricket Bd 1996–2002, Chartwell Gp 2006–10; pres Inst of Grocery Distribution 1989–92; chm Cncl Malvern Coll 2002–15; memb Save The Children Fund Commerce and Industry Ctee, Stock Exchange Advsy Ctee 1988–91; chllr Univ of Hertfordshire 1996–2005; DL: Herts 1992–2007, Wilts 2007–12; Freedom City of London 1981, Liveryman Worshipful Co of Carmen 1982; hon fell Univ of Wales Cardiff; Hon DPhil Univ of Stirling 1987, Hon LLD Univ of Hertfordshire 1995, Hon DUniv Univ of Bradford 2001; FRSA 1986, FInstM 1987, Hon FCGI 1992; *Books* Tiger by the Tail (1998); *Recreations* cricket, golf; *Clubs* MCC, Royal & Ancient; *Style*— The Rt Hon Lord MacLaurin of Knebworth; ✉ Rowley Grange, Farleigh Hungerford, Bath BA2 7RS

MACLAY, Michael William; s of William Paton Maclay, and late Janette Kiddie Maclay; *b* 14 July 1953; *Educ* Churcher's Coll Petersfield, Trinity Coll Cambridge (sr scholar, MA), Univ of Freiburg; *m* Dec 1980, Elfi, da of Adam Lunkenheimer; 1 da (Catriona b 1983), 1 s (Christopher b 1986); *Career* FCO 1976, Br High Cmmn Lagos 1977–79, UK Mission to UN NY 1980–83, Southern Africa Dept FCO 1983–84, researcher, reporter and prodr Weekend World (LWT) 1984–88, policy ed The Sunday Correspondent 1988–90, prodr 'War in the Gulf' (LWT) 1991, asst ed The European 1991–93, special advsr to the Foreign Sec 1993–95, special advsr to Carl Bildt High Rep Bosnia 1995–97, dir Hakluyt and Company 1997–2002, exec chm Montrose Assocs 2003–; tstee Citizenship Fndn 1993–2014 (chm 2000–14); non-exec dir Open Broadcast Network (Bosnia) 1998–2000; sr advsr Club of Three 2006–15 (exec dir 2000–06, chm Steering Gp 2015–), memb Advsy Bd Br America Project 2005– (chm 2012–); *Publications* Multi-Speed Europe? (1992), Maastricht Made Simple (ed, 1993), Pocket History of EU (1998); *Clubs* Oxford and Cambridge, Garrick; *Style*— Michael Maclay, Esq; ✉ 10 Lammas Park Gardens, London W5 5HZ (☎ 020 8579 2739)

McLEAN, Alexander; s of Saint Aubyn McLean, and Lyn, *née* Jackson; *b* 9 April 1985, Kingston upon Thames; *Educ* Univ of Nottingham (BA, UK Graduate of the Year 2007), Univ of London (LLM); *m* 1 April 2011, Dr Hannah McLean, *née* Meadows; 1 s (Frederick b 9 Nov 2012); *Career* called to the Bar Lincoln's Inn 2010 (Lord Mansfield scholar); magistrate Nottingham Magistrates Ct 2006–; memb Commonwealth Magistrates and Judges Assoc; fndr African Prisons Project 2004–; prisons visitor UN 2010 and 2012; sr fell TED, Clore fell, Ashoka fell; Beacon Prize for Philanthropy; *Style*— Alexander McLean, Esq

McLEAN, Alison Mary; da of Leo McLean (d 1981), and Mollie, *née* Hackett (d 2003); *b* 16 December 1950; *Educ* Univ of Bristol (BA), LSE (DSA), Aston Univ (MSc); *m* 17 Jan 1976, Adrian While; 1 s (Benjamin b 24 June 1977), 2 da (Jennifer May b 11 April 1980, Eleanor Ruth b 20 July 1983); *Career* coordinator/team ldr Poole's Park Tenant Co-op 1975–78, recruitment prog coordinator Mozambique Info Centre 1978–80, community worker Islington Community Voluntary Serv Employment Unit 1981–83, rural devpt offr Leominster Marches Project 1987–89, community worker Hereford and Worcester Cncl 1989–92, rural devpt area project offr Malvern Hills DC 1992–95, project team mangr S Marches Partnership 1995–98, econ resources and policy mangr Herefordshire Cncl 1998–2001, policy and commissioning mangr Herefordshire Partnership 2001–03, dir rural regeneration zone Shropshire Co Cncl 2003–05, ind conslt 2005–, cmmr Cmmn for Rural Communities 2006–; memb Bd: Countryside Agency 2002–06, RegenWM 2002–05; vice-chm W Midlands Rural Affairs Forum 2005–; tstee Nat Heritage Memorial Fund 2008–; Rural Issues and an Enabling Church (1989), Progress in the Rural New Committment to Regeneration Pathfinders (2000); *Recreations* theatre, sailing, gardening; *Style*— Ms Alison McLean

MACLEAN, Prof Allan B; s of Bruce H Maclean, of Auckland, NZ, and Marie F, *née* Mackie; *b* 8 February 1947; *Educ* Univ of Otago (BMedSc, MB ChB, DipObst, MD); *m* Mary R, *née* Callanan; 2 da (Nicola b 19 March 1975, Fiona b 4 Aug 1977), 2 s (Simon b 16 April 1981, Allan b 10 Dec 1986); *Career* sr lectr Christchurch Clinical Sch of Med NZ 1980–85, sr lectr Dept of Midwifery Univ of Glasgow and conslt obstetrician and gynaecologist Queen Mother's Hosp and Western Infirmary Glasgow 1985–92, prof of gynaecology and head of dept Royal Free and UC Medical Sch 1992–; past pres Br Soc for the Study of Vulval Disease, pres Int Soc for the Study of Vulvo-Vaginal Disease; FRCOG 1990 (MRCOG 1978), FRCPEd 2006; *Books* Clinical Infection in Obstetrics and Gynaecology (1990), Hormones and Cancer (ed with PMS O'Brien, 1999), The Effective Management of Ovarian Cancer (ed with Martin Gore and Andrew Miles, 1999), Infection and Pregnancy (ed with L Regan and D Carrington, 2001), Disorders of the Menstrual Cycle (jt ed, 2000), Pain in Obstetrics and Gynaecology (jt ed, 2001), Incontinence in Women (co-ed, 2002), Maternal Morbidity and Mortality (jt ed, 2002), Rapid Obstetrics and Gynaecology (jt ed, 2003), Lower Genital Tract Neoplasia (jt ed, 2003); *Recreations* rowing and rugby, the life and works of Robert Burns; *Style*— Prof Allan Maclean; ✉ University Department of Obstetrics and Gynaecology, University College Medical School, Royal Free Campus, Rowland Hill Street, London NW3 2PF

McLEAN, Prof André Ernest Michael; s of Dr Fritz Fraenkel (d 1943), of Berlin, and Hildegard Maria, *née* Leo; *b* 5 January 1931; *Educ* Christ's Hosp, Univ of Oxford, UCL (BM BCh, PhD); *m* 1, Oct 1956 (m dis 1992), Dr Elizabeth Kathleen Hunter, da of Donald Hunter (d 1978); 2 s (Thomas b 1958, Adam b 1960), 2 da (Angela b 1961, Martha b 1965); m 2, Alison Lamb; 3 s (James, Andrew (twins) b 1992, Daniel b 1995); *Career* Colonial Med Serv 1960–63; assoc prof Chicago Med Sch 1964–65, memb scientific staff MRC Jamaica and Carshalton 1965–67, prof of toxicology Univ of London 1980–1996 (emeritus prof 1996–); author of papers on human malnutrition and relation between diet and toxicity of drugs and chemicals; chm Br Toxicology Soc 1987–88, former memb ctees on food additives, pesticides, and Ctee on Safety of Medicines for Dept of Health, currently conslt toxicologist on chemicals and pharmaceuticals; FRCPath; *Recreations* canoe, gardening; *Style*— Prof André McLean; ✉ *E-mail* andre.mclean@btinternet.com

McLEAN, Prof Bruce; *b* 1944, Glasgow; *Educ* Glasgow Sch of Art, St Martin's Sch of Art; *Career* artist; lectr Croydon Sch of Art 1976 (teacher of sculpture and three-dimensional studies 1966), co-fndr (with Mel Gooding) Knife Edge Press 1985, prof Slade Sch of Fine Art London 1998– (teacher 1985, currently head of grad painting); visiting prof Stadel Schüle Frankfurt 1999, visiting artist/advsr Rijkes Akademie das Bilden künst Amsterdam 1999; solo exhbns incl: Nova Scotia Coll of Art Gallery 1970, Tate Gallery 1972 and 1985, The Kitchen NY Rosi McLean 1978, Chantal Crousel Paris 1981 and 1982, Modern Art Galerie Vienna 1982, DAAD Gallery Berlin 1983, Whitechapel 1983, Gmyrek Galerie Düsseldorf 1985, 1991 and 1994, Arnolfini Gallery Bristol 1990, Harris Museum and Art Gallery Preston 1991, Berkeley Square London 1991, Miriam Shiell Fine Art Toronto 1991, William Jackson Gallery 1991, Droysen Berlin 1992, Scottish Gallery Edinburgh 1992, Norkoppings Kunstmuseum Sweden 1993, Kunstmuseum Soro Denmark 1993, Galerie Fortlaan 17 Ghent 1994, 1998, 2001 and 2006, Cornerhouse Manchester 1995, Ormeaum Baths Belfast 1996, Norwich Gallery 1996, Galerie se Bergen 1997, Talbot Rice Gallery Edinburgh 2000, Customs House Gateshead 2003, Chelsea Space London 2006; selected group exhibitions incl: Five Young Artists (ICA) 1965, The British Avant Garde (Cultural Centre NY) 1971, Lives and Annual Exhibition (Hayward) 1979, Performance Symposium (Centre Georges Pompidou) 1979, A New Spirit in Painting (Royal Acad) 1981, British Sculpture in the Twentieth Centre (Whitechapel) 1981, New Art (Tate) 1983, An International Survey of Recent Painting and Sculpture (MOMA NY) 1984, British Art in the Twentieth Century (Royal Acad) 1987, Twenty Years of British Sculpture (Lettovre) 1988, Great British Art Show (Glasgow) 1990, Contemporary Scottish Art Fair (Royal West of England Acad Bristol) 1991, The Sixties: The Art Scene in London (Barbican) 1993, RIBA London 1995, Out of Action: Between Performance and the Object 1949–79 (Museum of Contemporary Art LA) 1997, Sixty Years of Sculpture in the Arts Council Collection (Longside Gallery Yorks Sculpture Park) 2006, Importantn Mischief: British Sculpture from the 60s and 70s (Henry Moore Inst) 2006, Sculpture from St Martins Sch of Art from the 60s (Tate Britain London) 2007; numerous cmmns; performance artist and memb Nice Style 1965–; work in the collections of: Arts Cncl of GB, Br Cncl, Contemporary Arts Soc, Saatchi Collection, Nat MOMA Osaka, South Bank Centre, Canary Wharf, BR, Tate, Van Abbemuseum Eindhoven, V&A, Nat Museum of Scotland, Scottish National Modern Art Museum Edinburgh, Glasgow Museum and Art Galleries, Het Kruithaus Kunstmuseum Hergotenbosch, Laine Art Gallery, Tate Britain, Tate Modern, Tochigi Prefectural Museum of Fine Art Japan, Royal Museum of Scotland Edinburgh; Pratt Bequest for Scuplture 1965, Sainsbury Award for Sculpture 1966, Maj Arts Cncl of GB Award 1975, Arts Cncl Bursary 1978, DAAD fell Berlin 1981, John Moore Painting Prize 1985, Mercedes Benz Prize for Painting 1985, RTS Award for Prodn Design (for the Empress of Newfoundland) 1994; Hon Dip AA London 1997; *Style*— Prof Bruce McLean

MACLEAN, Colin William; OBE (2000); s of Percy Kenneth Maclean (d 1975), and Elsie Violet, *née* Middleton (d 1986); *b* 19 June 1938; *Educ* William Hulmes GS, Univ of Liverpool (MVSc, FRCVS, William Hunting awards); *m* 19 Sept 1959, Jacqueline Diana, da of Frederick Brindley; 2 da (Antonia Karen b 12 Feb 1962, Nicola Janine b 20 Dec 1963); *Career* vet surgn 1961–66; Unilever Ltd: chief vet advsr 1966–72, mangr pig breeding 1972–74, md Farm Mark Ltd and Masterbreeders Ltd 1974–80, gen mangr (South) BOCM Silcock Ltd 1980–83; dep md and dir product devpt Glaxo Animal Health Ltd 1983–88, DG Meat and Livestock Cmmn 1992–98 (tech dir 1988–92); chm: Royal Berks and Battle Hosps NHS Tst 2000–06, Royal Berks NHS Fndn Tst 2006–12; vice-chm Assoc of NHS Charities 2014–; non-exec dir Solutions for Public Health 2010–; fndr memb and pres Pig Vet Soc (memb 1966), past pres Br Cattle Vet Assoc; special tstee Moorfields Eye Hosp 2012–, chm My Cancer My Choices 2015–; memb: Royal Counties Vet Assoc 1975 (past chm), RASE 1988; *Recreations* squash, rugby, flying; *Clubs* Farmers'; *Style*— Colin Maclean, Esq, OBE

MACLEAN, Rt Hon David Jon; *see:* Blencathra, The Lord

McLEAN, Prof Iain; *b* 13 September 1946; *Educ* Royal HS Edinburgh, ChCh Oxford (exhibitioner, BA), Nuffield Coll Oxford (BPhil, DPhil); *Career* research fell Nuffield Coll Oxford 1969–71, lectr in politics Univ of Newcastle upon Tyne 1971–78, lectr (CUF) in politics Univ of Oxford 1978–91 (fell and praelector UC Oxford), prof of politics Univ of Warwick 1991–93, official fell in politics Nuffield Coll Oxford and prof of politics Univ of Oxford 1993–; dir of grad admissions Dept of Politics and Int Studies Univ of Warwick 1992–93, dir of grad studies in politics Univ of Oxford 1994–95, dir of research trg in politics Univ of Oxford 1996–99; visiting prof of politics: Washington & Lee Univ VA 1980, Univ of Warwick 1993–96, Univ of Newcastle upon Tyne 1996; visiting prof Dept of Political Science Stanford Univ 1990–91, academic visitor Dir's Section Research Sch of Social Sciences ANU 1996 and 2002, William H Orrick visiting prof Prog in Ethics, Politics and Economics Yale Univ 2001; jt ed Electoral Studies 1993–99; memb Editorial Bd: Electoral Studies, Br Jl of Political Science, Jl of Theoretical Politics; radio and TV commentator on UK politics; vice-pres for public policy British Academy; memb Tyne & Wear MCC 1973–79 (chm Economic Devpt Ctee 1976–78), memb Oxford City Cncl 1982–86 (ldr Alliance Gp); appeals dir Welshpool and Llanfair Light Railway Preservation Co Ltd (dir 1978–92 and 1999–); various offices Religious Soc of Friends; FBA, FRSE; *Publications* Keir Hardie (1975), Elections (1976), Why Electoral Reform? (pamphlet with P M Williams, 1981), Dealing in Votes (1982), The Legend of Red Clydesid (1983), Public Choice: an introduction (1987), Consumers' Guide to Tactical Voting (pamphlet, 1987), Democracy and New Technology (1989), Condorcet: foundations of social choice and political theory (trans and intro with F Hewitt, 1994), Classics of Social Choice (ed, trans and intro with A B Urken, 1995), Concise Oxford Dictionary of Politics (gen ed and contrib, 1996), A Mathematical Approach to Proportional Representation: Duncan Black on Lewis Carroll (with A McMillan and B Monroe, 1996), Fixing the Boundary: defining and redefining single-member electoral districts (ed with D Butler, 1996), The Theory of Committees and Elections by Duncan Black and Committee Decisions with Complementary Valuation by Duncan Black and R A Newing (ed with A McMillan and D Monroe, 1998), Aberfan: government and disasters (with M Johnes, 2000), Rational Choice & British Politics: an analysis of rhetoric and manipulation from Peel to Blair (2001), International Trade and Political Institutions Instituting Trade in the Long Nineteenth Century (with F McGillivray, R Pahre and C Schonhardt-Bailey, 2001), Adam Smith, Radical and Egalitarian (2006), What's Wrong with the British Consitution? (2009), Scotland's Choices (with J Gallagher and G Lodge, 2013), Legally Married (with S Peterson, 2013); also author of book chapters, website contributions, working papers, policy briefings, book reviews and numerous papers in refereed jls; *Recreations* mountaineering, skiing, choral music, narrow-gauge railway preservation; *Style*— Iain McLean; ✉ Nuffield College, Oxford OX1 1NF

McLEAN, Prof (William Henry) Irwin; s of Henry McLean, of Dervock, Ballymoney (d 1971), and Rosetta, *née* McAleese (d 1999); *b* 9 January 1963, Ballymoney, Co Antrim; *Educ* Queen's Univ Belfast (BSc, PhD, DSc); *Career* Dept of Medical Genetics Queen's Univ of

M

Belfast: research asst 1985–88, postdoctoral research asst 1988–91; research dir Ångström Laboratories 1991–92, postdoctoral research fell CRC Cell Structure Research Gp Univ of Dundee 1992–96, assoc prof Dept of Dermatology and Cutaneous Biology Jefferson Med Coll Philadelphia 1996–98; Human Genetics Unit Ninewells Med Sch Univ of Dundee: Wellcome Tst sr research fell, sr lectr and head of human genetics research 1998–2002, head of human genetics research 2002–08, prof of human genetics 2002–, head Div of Molecular Medicine 2008–; hon NHS clinical scientist 2000–06, hon NHS conlst clinical scientist 2006–; visiting prof of biochemistry Univ Tor Vergata Rome 2001–02, visiting prof Inst Medical Biology Biopolis Singapore 2008–; section ed Br Jl of Dermatology 2000–03, memb Editorial Bd Jl of Dermatological Science 2003–, assoc ed Jl of Investigative Dermatology 2003–07; memb Scientific Advsy Bd Br Skin Fndn 2001–07, chm Scottish Skin Biology Club 2004–08; fndr memb Med and Scientific Advsy Bd: Pachyonychia Project 2004–, Hidradenitis Suppurativa Fndn 2006–, Cancer Research UK Genomewide Assoc Studies Review Panel 2008–; regular reviewer for various learned jls, author of 176 peer-reviewed scientific papers in genetics, dermatology and ophthalmology, 5 patents, invited speaker at nat and int meetings and seminars; CERIES Dermatology Research Prize 2006, Times Higher Research Project of the Year 2006, Paul Unna Dermatology Prize 2006/7, Royal Soc Wolfson Research Merit Award 2007, American Skin Assoc Achievement Award 2009; FRSE 2005, FMedSci 2009; *Recreations* composing electronic music, reading, hill walking, geology, photography, astronomy; *Style*— Prof Irwin McLean; ✉ Epithelial Genetics Group, Division of Molecular Medicine, University of Dundee, Colleges of Life Sciences and Medicine, Dentistry & Nursing, Medical Sciences Institute, Dow Street, Dundee, DD1 5EH (☎ 01382 381048, fax 01382 386828, website www.mcleanlab.com)

McLEAN, John Talbert; s of late Talbert McLean, of Arbroath, and late Dorothy, *née* Gladhill; *b* 10 January 1939; *Educ* Reform Street Sch Kirriemuir, Arbroath HS, Univ of St Andrews, Courtauld Inst Univ of London (BA); *m* 1964, Janet Alison, da of Edward Backhouse Norman; *Career* teacher of art history: pt/t Chelsea Sch of Art 1966–74, UCL 1974–78; teacher of painting Winchester Coll of Art 1978–82, visiting tutor in painting at many art schs in GB, Canada and USA; over 40 solo exhibitions worldwide; paintings in public collections incl: Tate Gallery, Scot Nat Gallery of Modern Art, Arts Cncl of GB, Scot Arts Cncl, Br Cncl, DOE, Federated Union of Black Artists South Africa, Fitzwilliam Museum, Glasgow Museums and Galleries, Hunterian Collection Univ of Glasgow, City Art Centre Edinburgh, Whitworth Art Gallery Manchester, Boca Raton Museum of Art USA, Yale Center for British Art USA; paintings in corporate collections worldwide; maj work incl cmmn for three large paintings for Pollock Halls Univ of Edinburgh 1971, five large paintings for Scottish Equitable Edinburgh 1996 and three large paintings for Chelsea and Westminster Hosp 2007, two stained glass windows for Strawberry Hill 2010, three stained glass windows for Norwich Cathedral 2014; *Awards* Arts Cncl maj award 1980, Br Cncl travel award 1981, 1984, 1993 and 2000, Lorne award 1992/93, Critics award Edinburgh Festival 1994, Bryan Robertson Tst Award 2008 & 2015; *Publications* subject of John McLean (by Ian Collins, 2009); *Style*— John McLean, Esq; ✉ 704 Mountjoy House, Barbican, London EC2Y 8BP (☎ 020 7628 3073)

McLEAN, Katy; MBE (2014); da of Catherine Ann Ahmed, and David McLean, of South Shields; *b* 19 December 1985, South Shields; *Educ* Sunderland Univ (BA); *Career* teacher Bexhill Acad 2010–14; rugby union player (fly half); currently capt England (73 caps, winners World Cup 2014), memb Darlington Mowden Park Sharks; NE BBC Sports Personality of the Year 2014; *Style*— Ms Katy Mclean, MBE; ✉ c/o Rugby Football Union, Rugby House, Twickenham Stadium, 200 Whitton Road, Twickenham TW2 7BA (website www.katymclean10.com, Twitter @KatcyMc10)

MacLEAN, Rt Hon Lord; Ranald Norman Munro MacLean; PC (2001); s of John Alexander MacLean (d 1992), and Hilda Margaret Lind, *née* Munro (d 2003); *b* 18 December 1938; *Educ* Fettes, Univ of Cambridge (BA), Univ of Edinburgh (LLB), Yale Univ (LLM); *m* 21 Sept 1963 (m dis 1993), Pamela, da of Prof Allan Dawson Ross, of London (d 1982); 1 da (Catriona Joan b 1967), 3 s (Fergus Ranald b 1970, Donald Ross b 1972, 1 s decd); *Career* called to Scottish Bar 1964, QC 1977; advocate-depute 1972–75, home advocate-depute 1979–82, Senator of the Coll of Justice 1990–2005; chm: Ctee on Serious Violent and Sexual Offenders 1999–2000, Sentencing Cmmn for Scotland 2003–05, Billy Wright Inquiry Banbridge NI 2005–10, Vale of Leven Hosp Inquiry 2010–14; memb: Cncl on Tbnls 1985–90 (chm Scottish Ctee), Scottish Legal Aid Bd 1986–90, Sec of State for Scotland's Criminal Justice Forum 1996–2000, Parole Bd for Scotland 1998–2000 and 2003, Judicial Appts Bd for Scotland 2002–05; surveillance cmmr 2010–16; chm of govrs Fettes Coll 1996–2006; Hon LLD Univ of Aberdeen 2003; FRSE, FSA Scot; *Recreations* swimming; *Clubs* New (Edinburgh); *Style*— The Rt Hon Lord MacLean; ✉ 67/3 Grange Loan, Edinburgh, EH9 2EG; Court of Session, Parliament House, Parliament Square, Edinburgh EH1 1RQ

McLEAN, Vice Adm Rory Alistair Ian; CB, OBE; *b* 4 April 1950, Shoreham by Sea, West Sussex; *Educ* George Watson's Coll Edinburgh; *Career* joined RN 1968, pilot 1973, cmd HMS Lewiston, cmd HMS Upton, Exec Offr HMS Brazen, Cdr HMS Jupiter, Cdr HMS Charybdis, cmd HMS Fearless, cmd HMS Invincible, Dir of Navy Plans and Progs MOD 1997–2001, ACDS (Resources and Progs) 2001–04, DCDS (Health) 2004–; life memb United Servs Mess Cardiff, memb Capt Scott Soc, vice-chm Royal United Services Inst; Freeman City of London; *Recreations* golf, bowls, rugby, squash; *Style*— Vice Adm Rory McLean, CB, OBE

McLEAN, Prof Sheila Ann Manson; da of William Black (d 2003), of Dunblane, and Bethia, *née* Manson; *b* 20 June 1951; *Educ* Glasgow HS for Girls, Univ of Glasgow (LLB, MLitt, PhD); *m* 1976 (m dis 1987), Alan McLean; *Career* Area Reporter to the Children's Panel Strathclyde Regl Cncl 1972–75; Univ of Glasgow: lectr Dept of Forensic Medicine 1975–89, sr lectr Sch of Law 1989–90, Int Bar Assoc prof of law and ethics in med 1990–; dir Inst of Law and Ethics in Med Univ of Glasgow 1985– (co-dir with Prof K C Calman, *qv* 1985–87); rapporteur générale XXth Colloquy on Euro Law Cncl of Europe 1990; visiting researcher Univ of Otago New Zealand 1983; Sec of State appointee to UK Central Cncl for Nursing, Midwifery and Health Visiting; cmmnd by Dept of Health to review the consent provisions of the Human Fertilisation and Embryology Act 1990, specialist advsr to Jt Parly Ctee on the Human Tissue and Embryos Bill 2007, ethico-legal advsr Tenovus Scotland; chair Scottish Govt Working Gp on No Fault Liability for Medical Injury 2009–10; currently memb: BMA Ethics Ctee, Int Bioethics Ctee UNESCO, Advsy Ctee ESRC Genomics Policy and Research Forum, AHRC Peer Review Coll, Expert Panel on Assisted Dying Royal Soc of Canada 2009–10; former chair: Scottish Criminal Cases Review Cmmn, Scottish Office Steering Gp on Female Offenders, Scottish Exec Independent Ctee of Enquiry into Organ Removal and Rentention at Post-Mortem; former vice-chair Ctee Multi-Centre Research Ethics for Scotland; former memb: SHEFC, Advsy Gp to Data Protection Registrar on Biotechnology, Sectional Ctee Philosophy, Theology and Law Royal Soc of Edinburgh, UK Xeno Transplantation Interim Regulatory Authy, Policy Advsy Ctee Nuffield Cncl on Bioethics, Review Body on Doctors' and Dentists' Remuneration, MRC Genetics Advsy Ctee, Broadcasting Cncl for Scotland, Audit Ctee World Assoc of Medical Law, Ethics Ctee Int Fedn Obstetrics and Gynaecology; memb Editorial Bd: Int Jl of Medical Practice and Law, Medical Law Int, Bulletin of Medical Ethics, Jl of Law and Medicine; tstee: Scottish Civil Liberties Tst, Joyce Watson Meml Fund Re-Solv; Lifetime Achievement Award Scottish Legal Awards 2005; Hon LLD: Univ of Abertay Dundee 2002, Univ of Edinburgh 2002; FRSA 1996, FRSE 1996, FRCP (Edin) 1997, FRCGP 2003, FMedSci 2006; *Books* Medicine, Morals and the Law (co-author, 1983, reprinted 1985), A Patient's Right to Know: Information Disclosure, the Doctor and the Law (1989), The Case for Physician Assisted Suicide (jtly, 1997), Old Law, New Medicine (1999), Xenotransplantation: Law and Ethics (jtly, 2005), Modern Dilemmas: Choosing Children (2006), Disability and Impairment: Law and Ethics and the Beginning and End of Life (jtly, 2006), Assisted Dying: Some reflections on the need for law reform (2007); edited books: Legal Issues in Medicine (1981), Human Rights: From Rhetoric to Reality (co-editor, 1986), The Legal Relevance of Gender (jt ed, 1988), Legal Issues in Human Reproduction (1989), Law Reform and Human Reproduction (1992), Compensation for Personal Injury: An International Perspective (1993), Law Reform and Medical Injury Litigation (1995), Law and Ethics in Intensive Care (1996), Death, Dying and the Law (1996), Contemporary Issues in Law, Medicine and Ethics (1996), Legal and Ethical Aspects of Health Care (jtly, 2003); also author of numerous book chapters and articles in learned jls; *Recreations* playing guitar, singing, music, literature; *Style*— Prof Sheila McLean, FRSE; ✉ School of Law, The University, Glasgow G12 8QQ (☎ 0141 330 5577, fax 0141 330 4698, e-mail prof.s.mclean@law.gla.ac.uk)

MACLEAN, William James; MBE (2006); s of John Maclean (d 1962), Master Mariner, of Harbour House, Inverness, and Mary Isabella, *née* Reid (d 1978); *b* 12 October 1941; *Educ* Inverness Royal Acad, HMS Conway, Grays Sch of Art Aberdeen (DA); *m* 18 Aug 1968, Marian Forbes, da of David Leven, of Fife, Scotland; 1 da (Miriam b 1971), 2 s (John b 1973, David b 1981); *Career* schoolteacher (art) Fife County 1970–79; Univ of Dundee: prof of fine art Duncan of Jordanstone Coll 1981–, emeritus prof 2001; numerous exhibitions in UK and abroad, incl retrospective Talbot Rice Gall Edinburgh 1992; works in public collections incl: British Museum, Fitzwilliam Museum Cambridge, Scottish National Gallery of Modern Art Edinburgh, Kelvingrove Art Gallery Glasgow; memb: SSA, Royal Glasgow Inst of the Fine Arts; assoc Royal Scot Acad 1978; Scottish Educnl Tst award 1973, Scottish Art Cncl Visual Arts award 1979, Royal Scottish Acad Gillies award 1988; Hon DLitt Univ of St Andrews 2001, Hon DLitt Univ of Aberdeen 2009; hon fell Univ of the Highlands 2008; RSA 1991, RGI 1996, RSW 1997, FRSE 2010; *Style*— William Maclean, Esq, MBE

MACLEHOSE, Christopher C; CBE (2011); s of Alexander MacLehose, and Elizabeth, *née* Hope Bushell; *Educ* Shrewsbury, Univ of Oxford (MA); *Career* literary ed Scotsman Newspaper 1964–67; editorial dir Chatto & Windus 1973–79, ed-in-chief William Collins 1981–84, publisher Collins Harvill 1984–95, chm and publisher The Harvill Press 1995–2002 (publisher at large 2004–06), publisher MacLehose Press 2006–; *Recreations* gardening, wood, the sea, Vizslas; *Style*— Christopher MacLehose, Esq, CBE; ✉ Arundel House, 3 Westbourne Road, London N7 8AR

McLEISH, Alexander (Alex); s of Alexander N McLeish (d 1981), and Jane (Jean), *née* Wylie; *b* 21 January 1959; *Educ* Barrhead HS, John Neilson HS Paisley; *m* 8 Dec 1980, Jill Moira, da of Daniel Taylor, of Aberdeen; 2 s (Jon Alexander b 28 May 1981, Jamie Daniel b 6 Aug 1985), 1 da (Rebecca Lisa b 7 July 1989); *Career* football mangr and former professional footballer; Aberdeen FC: European Cup Winners' Cup medal, Super Cup medal, five Scottish Cup wins, two Scottish League Cup wins, three championship medals; transferred as player/mangr Motherwell FC 1994; mangr: Hibernian FC 1998–2001, Rangers FC 2001–06 (winners Scottish Premier League 2003 and 2005, winners Scottish FA Cup 2003, Scottish League Cup 2002), Birmingham City FC 2007–11 (winners League Cup 2011), Aston Villa FC 2011–12, Nottingham Forest 2012–13; Scotland: 77 full caps as player, mangr Scotland nat team 2007; involved in local charities; Dr (hc) Univ of Aberdeen 2008; *Books* Don of an Era (1988); *Recreations* tennis, cinema, golf; *Style*— Alex McLeish, Esq

McLELLAN, Prof David Thorburn; s of Robert Douglas McLellan (d 1973), and Olive May, *née* Bush; *b* 10 February 1940; *Educ* Merchant Taylors', St John's Coll Oxford (MA, DPhil); *m* 1 July 1967, Annie, da of André Brassart; 2 da (Gabrielle b 8 Nov 1968, Stephanie b 8 May 1970); *Career* Univ of Kent: lectr 1966–70, sr lectr in politics 1970–75, prof of political theory 1975–2002; prof of political theory Goldsmiths Coll London 2002–; visiting prof SUNY 1969, visiting fell Indian Inst of Advanced Study Simla 1970; *Books* The Young Hegelians and Karl Marx (1969), Marx before Marxism (1970), Karl Marx: The Early Texts (1971), Marx's Grundrisse (1971), The Thought of Karl Marx (1971), Marx (1971), Karl Marx: His Life and Thought (1973), Engels (1977), Karl Marx: Selected Writings (1977), Marxism after Marx (1980), Karl Marx: Interviews and Recollections (1983), Marx: The First Hundred Years (ed, 1983), Karl Marx: The Legacy (1983), Ideology (1985), Marxism: Selected Texts (ed, 1987), Marxism and Religion (1987), Simone Weil: Utopian Pessimist (1990), Unto Caesar: The Political Relevance of Christianity (1992), Religion in Public Life (ed, 1993), Politics and Christianity (1995), Political Christianity: A Reader (1997), Western Marxism (2004), Karl Marx: A Biography (2006), Marxism after Marx (2007); *Style*— Prof David McLellan

MACLELLAN, Ian David; s of Maj Henry Crawford Maclellan, MBE, TD, of Walton-on-the-Hill, Surrey, and Daphne Loya, *née* Taverner; *b* 21 February 1948; *Educ* Sherborne, Cranfield Business Sch (MBA); *m* 28 Sept 1974, Maja Ursula, da of Dr Hans Schaschek, of Weinheim, Germany; 1 da (Kirstin b 1980), 1 s (Henry b 1983); *Career* gp chief exec: Ibstock plc 1991–96, Cape plc 1998–2002; chm: Bristan Ltd 1997–2002, R A H Holdings Ltd 1999–2002, Farecla Products Ltd 2002–15, Swan Hill Gp plc 2003–04 (dir 1992–04), Celotex Gp Ltd 2005–10; tstee treas Br Horse Soc 2006–11; FCA; *Style*— Ian D Maclellan, Esq; ✉ Wormleighton Grange, Southam, Warwickshire CV47 2XJ (☎ 01295 770334)

McLELLAN, John; s of John McLellan, and Margaret, *née* Haviland; *b* 8 February 1962; *Educ* Hutchesons' GS Glasgow, Univ of Stirling (BA), Preston Poly; *m* 1993, Patricia; 1 da (Catriona b 10 March 1996), 2 s (Jamie b 8 April 2000, Fraser b 21 Sept 2004); *Career* journalist; reporter Chester Observer 1984–86, freelance 1986–87, reporter New Evening Mail 1987, dep ed Barrow News 1987–88, sports ed North West Evening Mail 1988–90, asst ed The Journal 1991–93 (asst news ed 1990–91), ed Edinburgh Evening News 1997–2002 and 2005–09 (dep ed 1993–97), ed Scotland on Sunday 2002–04, ed The Scotsman 2009–12, dir of communications Scottish Cons Pty 2012–13, dir Scottish Newspaper Soc 2013–; chm Editors' Ctee Scottish Daily Newspaper Soc 2001–03, memb Defence Press and Broadcasting Advsy Ctee 2006–12, memb Press Complaints Cmmn 2009–12, chm Editors' Ctee Scottish Newspaper Soc 2011–; hon prof Stirling Univ 2010–; *Awards* for Edinburgh Evening News: Scottish Daily Newspaper of the Year 1997, BT Scottish Daily Newspaper of the Year 1997 and 1998, Scottish Newspaper of the year 2001; For The Scotsman: Scottish Newspaper of the Year 2011; *Recreations* rugby, music; *Clubs* Royal Scots, Watsonian FC; *Style*— John McLellan, Esq

MACLENNAN, Prof Duncan; CBE (1997); s of James Dempster Maclennan (d 1968), of Mull, and Mary Mackechnie, *née* Campbell; *b* 12 March 1949; *Educ* Allan Glen's Secdy Sch Glasgow, Univ of Glasgow (MA, Silver Medal and univ essay prize Royal Geographical Soc, pres Geographical Soc, MPhil); *m* 1971 (m dis 1997, re-married 2005) Sharon M Chisholm; 1 s (John Campbell b 14 July 1975), 1 da (Marjory Kate b 21 Sept 1977); *Career* res fell Univ of Glasgow 1974–76, lectr in economics Univ of Aberdeen 1976–79; Univ of Glasgow: lectr in applied econ 1979–84, dir Centre for Housing Res 1984–96, prof of applied economics 1985–88, prof of urban studies 1988–90, Mactaggart prof of economics and finance 1991–2004; chief economist Govt of Victoria 2004–05, chief economist Infrastructure Canada 2005–09, dir Centre for Housing Research and prof of economics and geography Univ of St Andrews 2009–; Susman prof Wharton Business Sch Univ of Pennsylvania 1989, Regents prof Univ of Calif 1996, prof RMIT 2004–; dir ESRC Prog on Cities 1996–99, exec chm Joseph Rowntree Area Regeneration Steering Gp 1996–2000;

chm Care and Repair (Scotland) 1989–93; memb: Bd Scottish Homes 1989–99, European Urban Inst 1992–98, Co-ordinating Ctee European Housing Res Network 1989–98, bd Glasgow Alliance 1992–2002, Treasy Panel of Advisers on Public Policies 1996–99, Evidence Based Policy Fund (treas 2000); tstee David Hume Inst 1998–2005; economic advsr: housing Joseph Rowntree Fndn 1991–95, Duke of Edinburgh's second inquiry into British Housing 1990–91; special advsr to First Minister of Scotland 1999–2003; FRSA 1995, FRSE 1999, MCIH(Hon) 2002, MRTPI (Hon) 2002, AcSS 2010; *Books* Regional Policy: Past Experiences and New Directions (ed, 1979), Housing Economics (1982), Neighbourhood Change (1986), The Housing Authority of the Future (ed, 1992), Housing Finance (ed, 1993), Housing Policies for a Competitive Economy (1995), Fixed Commitments, Uncertain Incomes (1997), Changing Places, Engaging People (2001); *Recreations* walking, watching rugby, cycling; *Style*— Prof Duncan Maclennan, CBE; ✉ Centre for Housing Research, University of St Andrews, The Observatory, Buchanan Gardens, St Andrews KY16 9LZ (☏ 01334 461787, mobile 07540 668449, e-mail dm103@st-andrews.ac.uk)

MacLENNAN, Moray Alexander Stewart; s of Brig Donald Ross MacLennan, of Edinburgh; *b* 29 August 1961; *Educ* Fettes, Christ's Coll Cambridge (scholar, MA); *m* Wendy MacLennan; 1 da (Mia), 1 s (Kit); *Career* Saatchi & Saatchi Advertising: joined 1983, bd dir 1988, md 1994–95; M&C Saatchi Ltd: jt chief exec 1995, currently ceo Worldwide; *Recreations* golf, rugby, cooking; *Clubs* Muirfield, MCC, Groucho; *Style*— Moray MacLennan, Esq; ✉ M&C Saatchi, 36 Golden Square, London W1F 9EE

MacLENNAN OF MacLENNAN, Ruairidh Donald George; 35 Chief of Clan MacLennan; o s of Ronald George MacLennan of MacLennan (d 1989), 34 Chief of Clan MacLennan, and Margaret Ann, *née* MacLennan (d 1993); *b* 22 April 1977; *Educ* Fettes, Univ of Aberdeen (MA, Aberdeen OTC piper); *Career* rural surveyor CKD Galbraith Inverness; *Recreations* piping, canoeing, 51 Highland Regt TA; *Style*— The MacLennan of MacLennan; ✉ The Old Mill, Dores, Inverness IV2 6TR

MACLENNAN OF ROGART, Baron (Life Peer UK 2001), of Rogart in Sutherland; Robert Adam Ross Maclennan; PC; s of Sir Hector Maclennan (d 1978), by his 1 w, Isabel, *née* Adam; *b* 26 June 1936; *Educ* Glasgow Acad, Balliol Coll Oxford, Trinity Coll Cambridge, Columbia Univ NY; *m* 1968, Helen, wid of Paul Noyes, and da of Judge Ammi Cutter, of Cambridge, MA; 1 s, 1 da, 1 step s; *Career* called to the Bar 1962; MP (Lab until 1981, SDP 1981–88, then Lib Dem): Caithness and Sutherland 1966–97, Caithness, Sutherland and Easter Ross 1997–2001; PPS to Cwlth Affrs Sec 1967–69 and to Min without Portfolio 1969–70, oppn spokesman on Scottish Affrs 1970–71, on Def 1971–72, Parly under sec for prices and consumer protection 1974–79, memb Commons Public Accounts Ctee 1979–99, oppn spokesman on foreign affrs 1979–80, SDP spokesman on agric 1981–87, SDP spokesman on home and legal affrs 1983–87, ldr of the SDP 1987–88, Lib Dem spokesman on home affrs and nat heritage 1988–94, Lib Dem spokesman on constitutional affrs and culture 1994–2001, pres Lib Dems 1994–98, Lib Dem spokesman on Europe 2001–, alt memb representing UK Parly on Convention on Future of Europe 2002–03, memb House of Lords Select Ctee on the EU 2006–; Legion D'Honeur France; *Recreations* theatre, music and visual arts; *Clubs* Brooks's; *Style*— The Rt Hon the Lord Maclennan of Rogart, PC

MACLEOD, Chris; *Educ* Newcastle Business Sch, LSE; *Career* previous roles with: Saatchi & Saatchi, McCann Erickson, Collet Dickenson Pearce (roles incl chief exec and chm); TfL: joined 2007, currently mktg dir; fell Mktg Soc (former chm); *Style*— Chris Macleod, Esq; ✉ Transport for London, Windsor House, 42–50 Victoria Street, London SW1H 0TL

McLEOD, Emeritus Prof David; s of Norman McLeod (d 1985), and Anne McLeod (d 1994); *b* 16 January 1946, Burnley, Lancs; *Educ* The GS Burnley, Univ of Edinburgh (BSc, MB ChB, Ettles scholar); *m* 16 Dec 1967, Jeanette Allison; 1 s (Euan b 1972), 1 da (Seona b 1974); *Career* SHO and res fell Princess Alexandra Eye Pavilion Edinburgh 1970–72, conslt ophthalmic surgn Moorfields Eye Hosp 1978–88 (resident surgical offr 1972–75, fell in vitreoretinal surgery and ultrasound 1975–78), conslt advsr in ophthalmology to the RAF 1984–2003, prof of ophthalmology Univ of Manchester 1988–2006 (emeritus prof 2006–, head Dept of Ophthalmology 1988–98), hon conslt ophthalmic surgn Royal Eye Hosp Manchester 1988–; Duke-Elder lectr 1993, visiting prof UMIST 1996–2006; vice-pres Royal Coll of Ophthalmologists 1997–2001; FRCS 1974, FRCOphth 1988; *Recreations* walking, golf, dancing, grandchildren; *Clubs* Bramall Park Golf (Cheshire), Brookdale (Cheshire); *Style*— Emeritus Prof David McLeod; ✉ Langdale, 370 Chester Road, Woodford, Stockport, Cheshire SK7 1QG (e-mail david.mcleod@nhs.net)

MACLEOD, Dr Donald MacRae; s of Allan Martin MacLeod, of Glen House, Carloway, Isle of Lewis, and Margaret MacLeod; *b* 19 October 1956; *Educ* Nicolson Inst Stornoway, Univ of Aberdeen (MB ChB); *m* 19 April 1986, Moira Catherine, da of Thomas Anderson, of Marykirk; 1 s (Allan b 1987), 2 da (Alice b 1989, Elizabeth b 1992); *Career* lectr London Hosp Med Coll 1986–88, visiting assoc Duke Univ Med Centre Durham N Carolina USA 1988–89, conslt in anaesthetics Aberdeen Royal Infirmary 1989–; hon sr lectr Univ of Aberdeen; FFARCSI 1986; *Recreations* sailing, golf; *Clubs* Banff Sailing, Royal Aberdeen Golf; *Style*— Dr Donald Macleod; ✉ Westwood House, Kinellar, Aberdeen; Aberdeen Royal Infirmary, Aberdeen (☏ 01224 681818)

MACLEOD, Donald Walker; s of Ian M Macleod (d 1998), and Jean I W Macleod (d 1996); *b* 20 April 1953, Kirkintilloch, E Dunbartonshire; *Educ* Glasgow Acad, Univ of St Andrews (MA); *Children* 1 da (Flora Cecile b 11 Feb 1993); *Career* joined as presenter BBC Radio 3 1982, newsreader/reporter 60 Minutes (BBC 1) 1984; BBC Radio 3: presentation ed 1991–96, estab Through the Night 1996 (ed until 1998), writer and presenter Composer of the Week 1999–; *Recreations* cinema, gardening, music, opera, reading, walking; *Clubs* Scottish Arts, Athenaeum; *Style*— Donald Macleod, Esq; ✉ BBC Radio 3 Composer of the Week, BBC Wales, Cardiff CF5 2YQ (Twitter @donaldmacleod01)

McLEOD, Fiona; MSP; da of John McLeod (d 1989), of Glasgow, and Irene, *née* Robertson; *Educ* Bearsden Acad, Univ of Edinburgh, Univ of Glasgow (MA), Univ of Strathclyde (Dip Librarianship); *m* 24 July 1979, Dr Andrew David Rankine, s of Andrew Ballentine Rankine; 1 s; *Career* librarian: Balfron HS 1983–87, Glasgow North Coll of Nursing 1987–90, Marie Curie Cancer Care Centre Huntershill 1995–98; MSP (SNP): West of Scotland 1999–2003, Strathkelvin & Bearsden 2011–; former convenor Bearsden West Community Cncl; life memb Friends of Historic Scotland; MCILIP 1983; *Recreations* walking, volunteering; *Style*— Ms Fiona McLeod, MSP; ✉ The Scottish Parliament, Edinburgh EH99 1SP

McLEOD, Fraser Neil; s of James McLeod, of Cuffley, Herts, and Mary, *née* Yuill; *b* 13 July 1951; *Educ* Hertford GS, St Bartholomew's Hosp Med Coll (MB BS); *m* 16 April 1983, Angela Mary, da of Thomas Campbell, of Purley, Surrey; 1 s (David Paul Christopher b 13 Feb 1989), 1 da (Madeleine Kate b 17 June 1994); *Career* lectr in obstetrics and gynaecology and pioneer in test tube baby devpt Royal Free Hosp 1981–83, sr registrar in obstetrics and gynaecology Southmead Hosp Bristol 1983–85, conslt obstetrician and gynaecologist Frenchay and Southmead Hosps Bristol 1985–2015 (ret), trg prog dir in obstetrics and gynaecology Severn Deanery, currently conslt gynaecologist Spire Hosp Bristol; memb: British Menopause Soc, South West Obstetrical and Gynaecological Soc; founding memb Expert Witness Inst; local treas BMA, examiner RCOG, past sec Hey Groves Med Soc, fndr memb Br Soc for Gynaecological Endoscopy; capt: Medical Golf Soc, Nat Doctors Golfing Soc; FRCOG 1992 (MRCOG 1980), MRCS; *Recreations* golf, fine wine; *Clubs* Berkshire Golf; *Style*— Fraser McLeod, Esq; ☏ 0117 974 1396, fax 0117 973 3809, e-mail mcleodfraser@aol.com

MacLEOD, James Summers; s of Charles MacLeod (d 1982), and Margaret, *née* Summers (d 1986); *b* 3 August 1941; *Educ* Dumfries Acad, Univ of Glasgow (LLM); *m* 1, Sheila, da of George Stromier (d 2000); 1 da (Fiona b 1968), 2 s (Niall b 1971, Roderick b 1976); m 2, Rosemary Grant; *Career* CA (Scotland) 1965, CTA 1971; lectr Univ of Edinburgh 1965–68; lectr Heriot-Watt Univ 1968–71; Ernst & Young (formerly Arthur Young McClelland Moores & Co): joined 1971, ptnr 1973–98; dir Br Assets Tst plc, Scottish Investment Trust plc and other cos 1998–2014; hon prof Univ of Edinburgh; *Books* Taxation of Insurance Business (4 edn, 1999); *Recreations* bridge, piano, music, political biography; *Clubs* New; *Style*— James MacLeod, Esq

MACLEOD, Dr Malcolm Robert; s of Robin Macleod, of Inverness, and Mary, *née* Hossack; *b* 26 August 1965; *Educ* Loretto, Univ of Edinburgh (pres Students' Union, BSc, MB ChB, PhD); *m* 26 June 1992, Lindsay Dorothy Greig Thomson, da of James Thomson; 2 s (Calum Alexander Thomson b 10 Sept 1995, Magnus James Thomson b 27 Sept 2000); *Career* med house offr Eastern Gen Hosp Edinburgh; Western Gen Hosp Edinburgh: neurosurgical house offr, SHO in med 1992–94, hon clinical fell Dept of Clinical Neurosciences 1995–2000, specialist registrar Neurology 2001; currently head of neurology Forth Valley Royal Hosp; sr SHO Falkirk & District Royal Infirmary 1994–95, MRC clinical training fell Dept of Pharmacology Univ of Edinburgh 1995–98, research fell British Brain and Spine Fndn Dept of Molecular Endocrinology Univ of Edinburgh 1998–2000; currently prof of neurology and translational neuroscience Univ of Edinburgh; rector and chm Univ Ct Univ of Edinburgh 1994–97; MRCP 1994; *Recreations* juggling, hill walking, political history; *Style*— Dr Malcolm Macleod; ✉ e-mail malcolm@apoptosis.freeserve.co.uk

MacLEOD, Mary; OBE (2008); da of late James MacLeod, of Ullapool, Ross and Cromarty, and Effie, *née* Campbell; *b* 18 February 1948; *Educ* Ullapool Sch, Dingwall Acad, Univ of Edinburgh (MA, DSA, Dip Social Work); *m* 26 March 1979, Prof Dennis Walder; 1 da (Anna Ruth b 22 Sept 1984), 1 s (Rohan James b 19 June 1986); *Career* social worker Barnardo's Scotland 1972–75, sr social worker Lothian Region Social Work Dept 1975–78, lectr in social work Univ of Edinburgh 1978–79, lectr then sr lectr in social work Poly of N London 1979–91; ChildLine: dir of HQ counselling servs 1991–95, dir of policy, research and devpt 1995–99, dep chief exec 1999; chief exec Nat Family and Parenting Inst 1999–2009; memb: Bd Occupational Pensions Regulatory Authy 2002–05, Family Justice Cncl 2005–07, Advsy Bd Thomas Coram Research Unit, Ind Assessment Panel on Commercialisation and Children's Outcomes DCSF 2008–09, Exec Bd UK Cncl on Child Internet Safety 2008–12; chair Advsy Gp on Private Fostering Dept for Children, Schs and Families 2009–10, dep chair Cafcass; memb numerous univ research advsy ctees; author of articles on family policy and family servs; sr ind dir Gt Ormond St Hosp, non-exec dir Video Standards Cncl; chair Gingerbread 2010–13, vice-chair Internet Watch Fndn 2010–15, chair Ethics Ctee Internet Watch Fndn, tstee Columba 1400; Hon Dr Open Univ; *Style*— Mary MacLeod, OBE

MACLEOD, Mary; da of Rev Donald Beaton Macleod, and Una Maclean Macleod; *b* London; *Educ* Univ of Glasgow; *Career* sr exec Accenture 1990–2002, policy offr to HM the Queen Buckingham Palace 1998–99, chief of staff Global Operations ABN AMRO 2002–08, global head Transition and Communications RBS 2008–10; MP (Cons) Brentford and Isleworth 2010–15; PPS to the Policing and Justice Min 2010–12, culture sec 2012–14, min for women and equalities 2012–14, NI sec 2014–15; memb Home Affrs Select Ctee 2010, chm All-Pty Parly Gp for Women in Parliament 2010–15, PM's small business ambass 2012–15, memb No. 10 Policy Bd 2014–15, special advsr to Sec of State for Scotland 2015–; memb Cons Pty 1992–; memb Advsy Bd: Career Ready (formerly Career Acad UK) 2013–, Lewis PR 2014–, Kupambana Fndn 2014–; tstee: Holland Park Sch Tst 2010–, The Shelter Project Hounslow 2014–; pres Chiswick Royal Br Legion 2010–, patron London Women's Forum 2014–, friend RA, supporter London Air Ambulance; MCIPD, MCIM, FRSA; *Publications* Women on Boards: The Executive Pipeline (2011), Improving Parliament (inquiry report, 2014); *Style*— Ms Mary Macleod; ✉ e-mail mary.marymacleod@gmail.com

McLINTOCK, Michael George Alexander; s of Sir Alan McLintock, and Sylvia Mary, *née* Foster Taylor; *b* 24 March 1961; *Educ* Malvern Coll, St John's Coll Oxford (scholar, BA); *m* 1996, Nicola Fairles Ogilvy Watson; 2 da, 1 s; *Career* Morgan Grenfell & Co Ltd 1983–87, Baring Brothers & Co Ltd 1987–92; M&G Gp plc (acquired by Prudential 1999): PA to gp md 1992, head institutional and international desks until 1997, chief exec 1997–99; Prudential plc: chief exec M&G (formerly Prudential M&G Asset Mgmnt) 1999–, dir 2000–; dir: Close Brothers Gp plc 2001–08, Grosvenor Gp Ltd 2012–; tstee Grosvenor Estate 2008–; *Recreations* family, friends, good wine; *Clubs* Army & Navy, Boodle's, MCC (memb Finance Ctee 2005–); *Style*— Michael McLintock, Esq; ✉ Laurence Pountney Hill, London EC4R 0HH (☏ 020 7626 4588)

McLOUGHLIN, Jan; *née* McCreedy; *b* 12 September 1962; *Educ* BSc, MSc; *Career* PDSA: business devpt dir 2001–03, dir of veterinary services 2003–08, Director General 2008–; CBiol, MSB, FIoD; *Style*— Mrs Jan McLoughlin; ✉ PDSA, Whitechapel Way, Priorslee, Telford, Shropshire TF2 9PQ

McLOUGHLIN, Kevin; *b* 17 July 1952; *Educ* Xaverian Coll, Univ of Sheffield (MA), Univ of Salford (MA); *m* 16 Dec 1978, Sheila Mary McLoughlin; 1 s (Daniel b 27 July 1980), 1 da (Jessica b 14 Sept 1984); *Career* admitted slr 1978, slr advocate 2003; ptnr: DLA 1982–2005, Eversheds LLP 2005–07; called to the Bar Middle Temple 2007, practising barr Chambers of Keith Morton, QC 2007–; asst coroner: W Yorks (E) 2006–, S Yorks (W) 2008–, Gtr Manchester (W) 2009, Inner W London 2012–; tstee Instn of Occupational Safety and Health 2007–10; memb Coroners Soc 2006–; Chartered Safety and Health Practitioner (CMIOSH); *Style*— Kevin McLoughlin, Esq; ✉ 98 Riverdale Road, Ranmoor, Sheffield S10 3FD (☏ 0114 230 7350); chambers: Temple Garden Chambers, 1 Harcourt Buildings, Temple, London EC4Y 9BB (☏ 020 7583 1315, e-mail kevin.mcloughlin@tgchambers.com)

McLOUGHLIN, Rt Hon Sir Patrick; kt (2016), PC (2005), MP; *Career* MP (Cons) Derbyshire W 1986–; Parly under-sec of state: Dept of Tport 1989–92, Dept of Employment 1992–93, DTI 1993–94; a Lord Cmmr HM Treasy (Govt whip) 1995–97; oppn pairing whip 1997–98, oppn dep chief whip 1998–2005, oppn chief whip 2005–10, parly sec to the Treasy and chief whip 2010–12, sec of state for tport 2012–16, Chllr of the Duchy of Lancaster 2016–; *Style*— The Rt Hon Sir Patrick McLoughlin, MP; ✉ House of Commons, London SW1A 0AA (☏ 020 7219 3000)

McLUCAS, William Philip; s of James McLucas, of South Queensferry, and Jean Violet, *née* Stobie (d 1986); *b* 12 February 1955; *Educ* Daniel Stewarts Coll Edinburgh, Scottish Coll of Textiles Galashiels (now Heriot Watt Univ); *m* 25 March 1976, Blyth Agnes, da of late Thomas Russell McLaren; 1 s (James Thomas William b 19 June 1982), 1 da (Camilla Charlotte Blyth b 28 July 1984); *Career* investment analyst Scottish Amicable Life Assurance Soc 1967–77, moneybroker UDISCO Brokers Ltd 1977–78; stockbroker: Laurence Prust & Co (London) 1978–80, Jackson Graham Moore & Ptnrs (Sydney) 1980–84; chief exec Waverley Asset Mgmnt Ltd 1984–95, ceo Waverley Mining Finance plc 1995–98, pres and ceo Thistle Mining Inc (Canada) 1998–2004, pres and ceo Martina Minerals Corp 2010–14, pres and ceo Orex Exploration (Canada) 2014–; chm: Perseverance Corp Ltd (Aust), President Steyn Gold Mines (Free State) (Pty) Ltd (S Africa) 2002–04, Black Isle Resources Corp (formerly Luzon Minerals) 2005–15, Terra Nova Minerals (formerly Terra Nova Gold Corp) 2007–10; dir: Republic Gold Ltd (Aust)

2005–06, Longview Capital Ptnrs 2006–08, Willowstar 2006–09, Oriental Minerals 2007–08, Amur Minerals Corporation 2009–10, Adrok Ltd 2013–; memb: Assoc of Mining Analysts 1981, DHO 1994; *Recreations* skiing, sailing, travel; *Clubs* Down Hill Only; *Style*— William McLucas, Esq; ✉ 11/18 Western Harbour Breakwater, Edinburgh EH6 6PZ (☎ 07836 638912)

McLYNN, Francis James (Frank); *b* 29 August 1941; *Educ* John Fisher Sch Purley, Wadham Coll Oxford (open scholar, MA), UCL Inst of Latin American Studies (MA, PhD); *Career* author; asst dir Bogotá and Colombia Br Cncl 1969–71 (joined 1968), Parry fell Buenos Aires Argentina 1971–72, Alistair Horne res fell St Antony's Coll Oxford 1987–88, visiting prof Dept of Literature Univ of Strathclyde 1996–2001, professorial fell Goldsmiths Coll London 2000–02; Cheltenham Prize for Literature 1985; FRHistS 1987, FRGS 1987; *Books* France and The Jacobite Rising of 1745 (1981), The Jacobite Army in England (1983), The Jacobites (1985), Invasion: From The Armada To Hitler (1987), Charles Edward Stuart (1988), Crime and Punishment in Eighteenth Century England (1989), Stanley: The Making of An African Explorer (1989), Burton: Snow Upon The Desert (1990), Of No Country (1990), Stanley: Sorcerer's Apprentice (1991), From The Sierras To The Pampas (1991), Hearts of Darkness (1992), Fitzroy Maclean (1992), Robert Louis Stevenson (1993), Jung: A Biography (1995), Napoleon (1997), 1066: The Year of the Three Battles (1998), Villa and Zapata (2000), Wagons West (2002), 1759: The Year Britain Became Master of the World (2004), Lionheart and Lackland (2006), Heroes and Villains (2007), Marcus Aurelius (2009), The Burma Campaign (2010) Captain Cook (2011), The Road Not Taken (2012), Genghis Khan: The Man Who Conquered the World (2015); *Style*— Frank McLynn, Esq; ✉ c/o Random House, 20 Vauxhall Bridge Road, London SW1V 2SA

McMAHON, Prof April Mary Scott; *née* Dugan; da of Irene Dugan, *née* Grant (d 1985); *b* 30 April 1964, Edinburgh; *Educ* Univ of Edinburgh (MA, PhD); *m* 1984, Dr Robert McMahon; 2 s (Aidan b 15 Dec 1994, Fergus b 29 Aug 1996), 1 da (Flora b 21 Oct 1999); *Career* fell Selwyn Coll Cambridge 1988, lectr in phonology and historical linguistics Univ of Cambridge 1988–2000; Univ of Sheffield: chair of English language and linguistics 2000–04, head Sch of English 2002–04, head Dept of English Language and Linguistics; Univ of Edinburgh: Forbes chair of English language 2005–, vice-princ and head Coll of Humanities and Social Science 2008–, vice-princ planning, resources and research policy 2009–; vice-chllr Aberystwyth Univ 2011–16, dep vice-chllr Education Univ of Kent 2016–; pres Linguistics Soc of GB 2000–05; memb Cncl: AHRC 2005–, Br Acad 2007–; FRSE 2003, FBA 2005, FLSW 2012; *Books* Understanding Language Change (1994), Lexical Phonology and the History of English (2000), Change, Chance, and Optimality (2000), Time Depth in Historical Linguistics (ed with Colin Renfrew and R L Trask, 2000), An Introduction to English Phonology (2002), Language Classification by Numbers (with Robert McMahon, 2005), The Handbook of English Linguistics (ed with Bas Aarts, 2007), Evolutionary Linguistics (with Robert McMahon, 2012); *Recreations* walking, cooking, Scottish country dancing; *Clubs* Athenaeum; *Style*— Prof April McMahon; ✉ e-mail a.m.s.mcmahon@kent.ac.uk

McMAHON, Most Rev Malcolm Patrick; *see:* Liverpool, Archbishop of

McMAHON, Michael Joseph; MSP; s of Patrick Kane McMahon, of Newarthill, Lanarkshire, and Bridget McMahon, *née* Clarke; *b* 18 September 1961; *m* 16 April 1983, Margaret Mary, *née* McKeown; 2 da (Siobhan Marie, Mairead Ann), 1 s (Gerard Francis); *Career* welder Terex Equipment Ltd Motherwell 1977–92, freelance socio-political researcher 1996–99; MSP (Lab): Hamilton N & Bellshill 1999–2011, Uddingston & Bellshill 2011–; ministerial Parly aide to first min (Rt Hon Jack McConnell, MSP), convenor Public Petitions Ctee, shadow cabinet se for parly business; memb: Scottish Lab Pty, GMB; *Publications* CelticMinded 2; *Recreations* supporting Celtic FC, reading biographies and social histories, listening to jazz and soul music; *Style*— Michael McMahon, Esq, MSP; ✉ 7 Forres Crescent, Bellshill, Lanarkshire ML4 1HL; Parliamentary Advice Office, 188 Main Street, Bellshill, Lanarkshire ML4 1AE (☎ 01698 300223, mobile 07715 012463); The Scottish Parliament, Edinburgh EH99 1SP (e-mail michael.mcmahon.msp@scottish.parliament.uk)

McMAHON, Siobhan; MSP; *b* Bellshill, N Lanarkshire; *Educ* Glasgow Caledonian Univ (BA); *Career* former research asst to Rt Hon Jim Murphy, MP, *qv*, and Ken Macintosh, MSP, *qv*, MSP (Lab) Central Scotland 2011–; *Style*— Ms Siobhan McMahon, MSP; ✉ The Scottish Parliament, Edinburgh EH99 1SP

McMANUS, Prof John; s of Eric Stanley McManus (d 1986), of Harwich, Essex, and Jessie Amelia, *née* Morley (d 1991); *b* 5 June 1938; *Educ* Harwich Co HS, Imperial Coll London (BSc, PhD, Watts Medal), Univ of Dundee (DSc); *m* 31 July 1965, (Jean) Barbara (d 2007), da of David Kenneth Beveridge; 2 s (Steven b 21 Dec 1968, Neil b 21 July 1972), 1 da (Kay b 6 Dec 1974); *Career* lectr Univ of St Andrews 1964–67 (asst 1963–64); Univ of Dundee: lectr 1967–72, sr lectr 1972–80, reader 1980–88; Univ of St Andrews: reader 1988–93, prof 1993–2001, emeritus prof 2001–; memb Senate Univ of St Andrews (memb Ct 1991–95), former memb Senate Univ of Dundee; pres Estuary and Coastal Scis Assoc 1995–98 (tstee 2000–07); memb: Aquatic Atmospheric Physical Scis Ctee Natural Environment Research Cncl 1971–76, Bd SE Regn Nature Conservancy Cncl (Scotland) SE Region 1990–91, UNESCO Panel on Reservoir Sediment 1982–85, BSI Ctee on Sedimentation 1991–2001, Geological Conservation Review Panel Jt Nature Conservancy Cncl 1993–94; Scottish Natural Heritage: memb Bd SE Region 1991–97, memb Sci Advsy Bd 1992–97, memb Bd Eastern Areas 1997–99; chm Transactions Editorial Bd Royal Soc of Edinburgh 1996–99, memb E Area Bd Scottish Environment Protection Agency 2000–07; pres: Cupar Choral Assoc 1970–79, Cupar Amateur Opera 1979–91; memb E Fife Male Voice Choir, tstee FifeFolk Museum 2011; MInstEnvSci 1973–2001, MIGeol 1979, FRSE 1980, CGeol 1986, Hon FRSGS 2001, MIMM 2014; *Books* Developments in Estuary and Coastal Study Techniques (jt ed, 1989), Geomorphology and Sedimentology of Lakes and Reservoirs (jt ed, 1993), Mining between Ceres and St Andrews (2010), History of Coalmining in the East Neuk of Fife (2016); *Recreations* making music; *Style*— Prof John McManus, FRSE; ✉ Department of Geography and Geosciences, University of St Andrews, St Andrews, Fife KY16 9ST (☎ 01334 653546, e-mail jm@st-andrews.ac.uk)

McMANUS, Liz; TD (1992); da of Timothy O'Driscoll (d 1998), and Elizabeth, *née* McKay (d 2005); *b* 23 March 1947; *Educ* UC Dublin (BArch); *m* 26 Oct 1970, John McManus; 3 s (Luke b 9 Aug 1972, Ronan b 22 Dec 1973, Sam b 27 May 1976) 1 da (Emily b 2 Jan 1982); *Career* worked as architect in Derry NI, Galway, Dublin and Wicklow 1969–76, fiction writer and novelist 1981–92, newspaper columnist 1985–92, teacher of creative writing 1986–89; TD (Lab) Co Wicklow 1992–, min of state for housing and urban renewal 1994–97 (also chair Taskforce on Needs of Travelling People), dep ldr Irish Lab Party 2002; memb Irish Writers Union; Irish Pen, Henessy and Listowel Awards; author of short fiction in numerous anthologies; *Books* Acts of Subversion; *Recreations* walking, reading, writing; *Clubs* Bray Strollers Hill Walking; *Style*— Ms Liz McManus, TD; ✉ 1 Martello Terrace, Bray, Co Wicklow, Ireland (☎ 00 353 1 276 0583, fax 00 353 1 276 0584); Dáil Éireann, Kildare Street, Dublin 2, Ireland (☎ 00 353 1 618 3131, fax 00 353 1 618 4591, e-mail liz.mcmanus@oir.ie)

McMANUS, (Jonathan) Richard; QC (1999); s of Frank Rostron McManus, and Benita Ann, *née* Haughton; *b* 15 September 1958; *Educ* Neale-Wade Comp Sch, Downing Coll Cambridge (MA, Maxwell Law Prize 1979); *Career* called to the Bar 1982, jr counsel to the Crown (Common Law) 1992–99; *Books* Education and the Courts (1997, 2 edn 2004); *Recreations* travel, music, cricket, photography; *Style*— Richard McManus, Esq, QC; ✉ 4–5 Gray's Inn Square, Gray's Inn, London WC1R 5AH (☎ 020 7670 1518, fax 020 7242 7803, e-mail rmcmanus@4-5.co.uk)

McMASTER, Sir Brian; kt (2003), CBE (1987); *b* 1943; *Educ* Univ of Bristol (LLB), Strasbourg Univ, Arts Cncl of GB (Arts Admin); *Career* admitted slr; memb Int Classical Div EMI 1968–73, controller of opera planning ENO 1973–76, md WNO 1976–91, dir Edinburgh Int Festival 1991–2006; artistic dir Vancouver Opera 1984–89; Hon Dr: Univ of Bristol 1989, Univ of Edinburgh 1995, Heriot-Watt Univ 2000, Univ of Glasgow 2001, Napier Univ 2002, Open Univ 2004, Univ of Westminster 2006; *Style*— Sir Brian McMaster, CBE; ✉ Apartment 40, 1 Lambs Passage, London EC1Y 8AB (☎ and fax 0131 226 5520)

McMASTER, Paul; s of Dr James McMaster (d 1987), of Liverpool, and Sarah Lynne McMaster; *b* 4 January 1943; *Educ* Liverpool Coll, Univ of Liverpool (MB ChB), Univ of Cambridge (MA); *m* Aug 1969, Helen Ruth, da of Derek Bryce; 2 s (Michael Robert b 1971, Richard Benjamin b 1978), 1 da (Amanda Helen b 1974); *Career* conslt surgn; sr lectr dept of surgery Cambridge 1976–80, tutor Trinity Hall Cambridge 1978–80, dir Liver Transplant Services Queen Elizabeth Hosp Univ of Birmingham 1980–; currently chm MSF UK; memb: Cncl Nat and Int Transplantation Soc 1991–, Euro Soc Organ Transplantation (pres 1992–93); FRCS 1970; *Style*— Paul McMaster, Esq; ✉ Lilac Cottage, High Park, Ombersley Road, Droitwich, Worcestershire WR9 0RG (☎ 01905 776961, e-mail pl.mcmaster@virgin.net); The Liver Unit, The Queen Elizabeth Hospital, University of Birmingham, Edgbaston, Birmingham (☎ 0121 627 2413, fax 0121 414 8133)

McMEIKAN, Elizabeth; da of Dr Thomas Charles Dann, of Cambridge, and Jean, *née* Blackburn; *b* 15 March 1962, London; *Educ* King's HS for Girls Warwick, Jesus Coll Cambridge (exhibitioner, MA); *Children* 2 s (Cameron Eliot b 7 Oct 1995, Rory Thomas b 1 June 1997), 1 da (Sophie Gabriella b 4 Feb 1999); *Career* Colgate Palmolive 1984–89, Tesco plc 1989–2000 (devpt dir Tesco France 1994–95, md Tesco Express 1995–97, HR and change mgmnt dir Stores Bd 1997–2000); sr ind dir J D Wetherspoon plc 2005–; non-exec dir: Direct Wines Ltd 2006–15, Fresca Gp Ltd 2010, CH & Co Ltd 2011–, Unite plc 2014–, Flybe plc 2014–; chair Moat Homes Ltd 2013–, civil serv cmmr 2005–10; chair Membership Selection Panel Network Rail 2010–14, ind memb State Honours Ctee 2010–, lay memb Speaker's Ctee IPSA 2011–15; *Style*— Ms Elizabeth McMeikan; ✉ J D Wetherspoon plc, Wetherspoon House, Central Park, Reeds Crescent, Watford WD24 4QL

McMICHAEL, Prof Sir Andrew James; kt (2008); s of Sir John McMichael, FRS (d 1993), and Sybil Eleanor, *née* Blake (d 1965); *b* 8 November 1943; *Educ* St Paul's, Gonville & Caius Coll Cambridge (MA), St Mary's Hosp Medical Sch (MB BChir); *m* 12 Oct 1968, Kathryn Elizabeth, da of Capt Alexander Alfred Cross, MBE (d 1998), of Whittonditch, Wilts; 1 da (Fiona b 1971), 2 s (Hamish b 1973, Robert b 1982); *Career* Nuffield Dept of Med Univ of Oxford: Wellcome sr fell in clinical science 1977–79, lectr 1979–82, MRC clinical res prof of immunology 1982–98, dir MRC Human Immunology Unit 1998–2010, dir Weatherall Inst of Molecular Med 2000–12; fell Trinity Coll Oxford 1982–2000 (hon fell 2011–), fell CCC Oxford 2000–, hon fell Harris Manchester Coll 2009–; memb: Scientific Ctee Cancer Res Campaign 1986–88 and 1999–, Cell and Molecular Med Bd MRC 1994–99, Cncl Royal Soc 1997–98; FRCP 1985, FRS 1992; *Books* Monoclonal Antibodies in Clinical Medicine (ed, 1981), Leucocyte Typing III, White Cell Differentiation Antigens (ed, 1987); *Recreations* walking, reading; *Style*— Prof Sir Andrew McMichael, FRS; ✉ Nuffield Department of Medicine, NDM Research Building, Old Road Campus, Headington, Oxford OX3 7FZ

MACMILLAN, Prof (John) Duncan; s of Prof William Miller Macmillan (d 1974), and Mona Constance Mary, *née* Tweedie (d 2004); *b* 7 March 1939; *Educ* Gordonstoun, Univ of St Andrews (MA), Univ of London (Academic Dip), Univ of Edinburgh (PhD); *m* 5 June 1971, Vivien Rosemary, da of Canon W T Hinkley (d 1994); 2 da (Christina Rachel b 1973, Annabel Kate b 1976); *Career* Dept of Fine Art Univ of Edinburgh: lectr 1974–83, sr lectr 1983–88, reader 1988–94, personal chair history of Scottish art 1994–2001 (prof emeritus 2002–); dir Talbot Rice Gallery 1978–2004, curator Univ of Edinburgh Galleries and Collections 1988–2002; art critic The Scotsman 1994–2000 and 2002–; hon curator RSE 2008–12; Hon LLD Univ of Dundee; Hon RSA, FRSA, FRSE; *Books* Gavin Scobie (1984), Painting in Scotland – The Golden Age (1986), Scottish Art 1460–1990 (1990, Scottish book of the year Saltire Soc), Symbols of Survival – The Art of Will MacLean (1992), The Paintings of Steven Campbell (1993), Scottish Art in the Twentieth Century (1994), Eugenio Carmi (jtly with Umberto Eco, 1996), Elizabeth Blackadder (1999), F C B Cadell (jtly, 2011), Victoria Crowe (2012), Scotland's Shrine: The Scottish National War Memorial (2014); *Recreations* walking; *Style*— Prof Duncan Macmillan; ✉ 20 Nelson Street, Edinburgh EH3 6LJ (☎ 0131 556 7100, e-mail duncan.macmillan@ed.ac.uk)

McMILLAN, Fraser James John; s of John Wright McMillan, of Barrhead, E Renfrewshire, and Mary Wishart, *née* Nisbet; *b* 26 December 1967, Barrhead, E Renfrewshire; *Educ* Univ of Strathclyde (LLB, DipLP); *m* 14 June 1996, Amanda, *née* Tennant; 1 da (Sophie Anne b 6 July 2004), 1 s (Rory Charles b 3 Feb 2007); *Career* admitted slr Scotland 1991; trainee slr TC Young 1989–91, asst slr Bird Semple 1991–96, asst slr than assoc ptnr Dundas & Wilson CS: asst slr 1996–98; Pinsent Masons: sr assoc 1998–2000, ptnr 2000–, head of Scottish practice 2007–, head of Glasgow office 2012–, head of construction advsry and disputes grp 2014–; memb: Law Soc of Scotland 1991, Soc of Construction Law; *Recreations* travel, running; *Style*— Fraser McMillan, Esq; ✉ Pinsent Masons, 141 Bothwell Street, Glasgow G2 7EQ (☎ 0141 249 5403, fax 0141 248 6655, e-mail fraser.mcmillan@pinsentmasons.com)

MacMILLAN, Dr Margaret Olwen; OC; da of Robert Laidlaw MacMillan, and Eluned Jane Carey Evans; *b* 23 December 1943, Toronto, Canada; *Educ* Univ of Toronto (BA), St Hilda' Coll Oxford (BPhil), St Antony's Coll Oxford (DPhil); *Career* prof of history Ryerson Univ 1975–2002 (chair History Dept 1987–92); Univ of Toronto: prof of history 1999–, provost Trinity Coll 2002–07; co-ed Int Jl 1995–2003; speaker at numerous confs and lectures; pres Victorian Studies Assoc of Ontario 1991–93, memb Bd Ontario Heritage Fndn 1992–98 and 2003–05, nat bd memb Canadian Inst of Int Affrs 1995–2006, govr Canadian Cncl of Christians and Jews 2003–07, memb Bd Historica 2004–07; hon fell St Antony's Coll Oxford 2003 (sr assoc memb 1993, alumni rep for Canada 1994–97), hon fell St Hilda's Coll Oxford 2007; FRSL 2003; *Awards* Duff Cooper Prize for History or Biography 2002, Hessell-Tiltman Prize for History PEN UK 2002, Samuel Johnson Prize for Non-fiction 2002, shortlisted Westminster Prize for Military History 2002, Silver Medal Council on Foreign Relations Arthur Ross Book Award 2003, Canadian Booksellers Libris Award for Non-fiction Book of the Year 2003, Govr-Gen's Award for Non-Fiction 2003, shortlisted Gelber Prize 2004, shortlisted Charles Taylor Prize 2004; Warden St Antony's Coll Oxford 2007–; OC; *Publications* Women of the Raj (1988, new edn 1996), Canada and Nato: Uneasy Past, Uncertain Future (co-ed with Dr. David Sorenson, 1990), The Uneasy Century: International Relations 1900–1990 (co-ed with Arne Kislenko, 1996), Peacemakers: The Paris Conference of 1919 and Its Attempt to End War (2001, reissued as Paris, 1919: Six Months that Changed the World, 2002), Parties Long Estranged: Canadian-Australian Relations (co-ed with Francine Mckenzie and contrib, 2003), Seize the Hour: When Nixon Met Mao (2006), The Uses and Abuses of History (2009), The War That Ended Peace: How Europe Abandoned Peace For the First World War (2014), History's People: Personalities and the Past (2016); author of numerous articles and reviews in newspapers and learned jls; *Clubs* Toronto Lawn Tennis, Oxford and Cambridge; *Style*— Dr Margaret MacMillan, OC; ✉ St Antony's College, Oxford OX2 6JF

McMILLAN, Neil Macleod; CMG (1997); s of John Howard McMillan, CBE (d 1991), and Ruby Hassell, *née* Meggs (d 1994); *b* 21 October 1953, Sunbury on Thames, Surrey; *Educ*

Westminster City Sch, Univ of Exeter (BA), Univ of Kiel Germany, Univ of Regensburg Germany; *m* 1, 1978 (m dis 1985), Karin, *née* Lauritzen; m 2, 1994, Lena Madvig, *née* Madsen; 1 s (Christian Alexander Madvig b 29 March 1994); *Career* admin trainee Dept of Prices & Consumer Protection 1978, Steel Policy Dept of Indust 1979–80, Textile Trade Policy Dept of Trade 1981, private sec to Min for Industry and IT DTI 1982–84, advsr on telecomms reform Fed Miny of Research Bonn 1985, first sec UK Permanent Rep Brussels 1987–91, dir Int Communications Policy DTI 1991–98, dir EU Internal Trade Policy DTI 1998–2000; min and dep perm representative UK Mission Geneva 2001–05, dir Europe DTI 2005–06, dir and dep head European and Global Issues Secretariat Cabinet Office 2006–08, head Nabucco Political Strategy RWE Supply and Trading GmbH Brussels 2008–11, ptnr Brunswick LLP Brussels 2011–15, dir Advocacy Eurocommerce Brussels 2015–; chm: Euro Ctee on Telecomms Regulatory Affairs 1992–95, Euro Telecomms Office Copenhagen 1992–95, Basic Telecomms Negotiations World Trade Orgn Geneva 1994–97, ITU Telecoms Policy Forum 1998; memb Bd American C of C to EU 2013–; *Recreations* walking, reading, Medieval churches, languages; *Clubs* Athenaeum; *Style—* Neil McMillan, Esq, CMG

McMILLAN, Dr Nigel Charles; s of Ian McInnes McMillan (d 1980), and Joan Muriel McMillan, *née* Winchester (d 2009); *b* 13 May 1950; *Educ* Loretto, Univ of Glasgow (MB ChB); *m* 24 March 1976, Linda Jean Douglas, da of Sqdn Ldr Archibald McDougall (d 2004); 1 s (Christopher b 1978), 1 da (Lorna b 1981); *Career* GP S Glasgow 1976–78, conslt radiologist to Western Infirmary Glasgow 1983–2012 (registrar then sr registrar in radiology 1978–83), clinical dir diagnostic radiology West Glasgow Hosps Univ NHS Tst 1993–96; FRCR 1982, FRCPGlas 1997 (MRCPGlas 1995); *Recreations* Scottish country dancing, golf, curling; *Style—* Dr Nigel McMillan; ✉ 5 Woodburn Road, Glasgow G43 2TN (☎ 0141 637 1441, e-mail ncmcmillan@gmail.com)

McMILLAN, Stuart; MSP; *b* 6 May 1972, Barrow in Furness, Cumbria; *Educ* Univ of Abertay Dundee (MBA); *m* Alexandra, *née* McLaughlin; 2 da; *Career* MSP (SNP) W of Scotland 2007–; mgmnt bd memb Moving On Inverclyde Ltd; hon memb: Clydeside Action on Asbestos, Greenock and District Model Railway Club; ambass Ocean Youth Tst for Scotland; *Style—* Stuart McMillan, MSP; ✉ Parliamentary Office, 4 Argyle Street, Greenock, Inverclyde, PA15 1XA (☎ 01475 720930); Room 4.11, The Scottish Parliament, Edinburgh EH99 1SP

McMORROUGH, Fiona Mary; *b* 10 April 1964, Dublin, Ireland; *Educ* UCD (BA, MA); *Career* publicity dir/ dir Bd Virago 1995–96, publicity dir Bloomsbury Publishing 1996–97, fndr and ceo FMcM Communications 1998–; memb Bd English PEN 2006–10, co-fndr and tstee World Book Night 2010–14; Hospital Award for Creative Contribution to Books 2014, Bookseller 100 Most Influential 2014 and 2015, GQ Most Connected 2014; memb: CIPR, PRCA; *Clubs* Ivy, Groucho; *Style—* Ms Fiona McMorrough; ✉ FMcM Communications, The Mews, 1A Birkenhead Street, London WC1H 8BA (website www.fmcm.co.uk)

McMULLEN, Prof John; *Publications* Business Transfers and Employee Rights (1998–), Redundancy: Law and Practice (3 edn, 2011); *b* 29 March 1954; *Educ* Magnus GS Newark-on-Trent, Emmanuel Coll Cambridge (MA, PhD); *Career* admitted slr 1978; slr Rotheras 1978–80, fell, dir of studies, tutor and praelector Girton Coll Cambridge 1980–86 (lectr and bye-fell until 1993), ptnr Rotheras 1987–91, ptnr Simpson Curtis (later Pinsents then Pinsent Masons) 1991, currently ptnr Wrigleys Solicitors LLP; part-time prof of labour law Univ of Leeds 1994–2010, visiting prof of law Durham Univ, visiting prof Leeds Univ Business Sch; memb Exec Ctee and tstee Industrial Law Soc; FRSA, FCIPD, fell Soc for Advanced Legal Studies; *Recreations* cinema, opera, reading, travel, walking; *Style—* Prof John McMullen

McMURTRIE, Simon Nicholas; s of Anthony William Stratton McMurtrie, and Sally, *née* Bateson; *b* 20 February 1966; *Educ* Radley, Univ of Birmingham (BA); *Children* 1 da (Anna Charlotte b 22 Dec 1994), 1 s (Hugh William b 6 April 1998); *Career* exec: William Heinemann Ltd 1988, Mandarin Paperbacks 1989, Octopus Publishing 1990; publishing dir Mitchell Beazley and Miller's Publications 1991, publishing dir Reed Illustrated Books 1992–93, md De Agostini Editions 1993–95, chief exec De Agostini UK 1995–99, chief exec International Masters Publishers Ltd 1999–2005, exec conslt De Agostini Editore SpA 2005–08, md int Direct Wines Ltd 2007–08, group ceo Direct Wines 2008–15, md Thames CCS Ltd 2015–; non-exec dir and advsy conslt Harvard University Press 1989–2003, conslt Samlerhuset BV 2006, non-exec dir Folio Soc Ltd 2016–; dir Wine and Spirits Trade Assoc 2010–; chair: Riviera Travel 2014–, Oak Furniture Land 2015–, Family Bd Berry Bros & Rudd 2016–; Drinks Business Man of the Year 2011; Liveryman Worshipful Co of Vintners 2010; *Clubs* Garrick, Century; *Style—* Simon McMurtrie, Esq; ✉ e-mail simon.mcmurtrie@gmail.com

McMURTRY, Sir David Roberts; kt (2001), CBE (1994); *b* 5 March 1940, Ireland; *Career* chm and chief exec Renishaw plc 1973–; RDI 1989, FREng, FRS, CEng, FIMechE; *Style—* Sir David McMurtry, CBE, RDI; ✉ Renishaw plc, New Mills, Wotton-Under-Edge, Gloucestershire GL12 8JR

McNAB, Andy; *b* 28 December 1959; *Career* boy soldier Inf Jr Ldr's Bn 1976, Sgt 2 Bn Royal Green Jackets 1977–83, Staff Sgt 22 SAS 1983–93; lectr to UK and US security and intelligence agencies 1996–; Light Division Sword 1977; MM (1980), DCM (1991); *Film* scriptwriter: Bravo Two Zero 1996, Bomber 2003, A Simple Life 2005; tech advsr: Heat 1995, Bravo Two Zero 1996, Timewatch 1996, Ultimate Warrior 1997, Conduct Under Capture 2000, London 2005; *Books* Bravo Two Zero (1993), Immediate Action (1995), Remote Control (1997), Crisis Four (1999), Firewall (2000), Last Light (2001), Liberation Day (2002) Dark Winter (2003), Deep Black (2004), Boy Soldier (2005), Payback (2005), Aggressor (2005), Recoil (2006), Avenger (2006); *Style—* Andy McNab

McNAB, Angela; *Educ* St Martin's Sch, Nat Hosps Coll of Speech Scis, Open Univ, South Bank Univ (BA, MSc); *Career* led devpt of NHS sexual health and HIV strategy Dept of Health 1999, chief exec NE London PCT 2001–02, chief exec Human Fertilisation and Embryology Authy 2002–08, seconded as dir of public health performance and delivery Dept of Health 2007–08, chief exec NHS Luton and NHS Bedfordshire 2008–12, chief exec Kent and Medway Partnership 2012–16, ceo Camden and Islington Fndn Tst 2016–; *Style—* Ms Angela McNab; ✉ e-mail angela.mcnab@candi.nhs.uk

McNAB, Janice; *b* 1964, Aberfeldy; *Educ* Edinburgh Coll of Art (BA, Dip Painting), Glasgow Sch of Art (MFA), Hunter Coll NY (MFA exchange student); *Career* artist; *Solo Exhibitions* incl: Collective Gallery Edinburgh 1999, Laurent Delaye Gallery London 2001, doggerfisher Edinburgh 2001, The Greenock factory project (Tramway Glasgow) 2002, Galerie Volker Diehl Berlin 2002, Talbot Rice Gallery Univ of Edinburgh 2004, Drumcastle NTS/Iain Irvine Projects 2004; *Group Exhibitions* incl: Sick Building (Globe Collective Copenhagen) 1996, The Social Life of Stuff (Fly Gallery Glasgow) 1998, Sick Vitalists (Intermedia Glasgow) 1999, Anxiety (Collective Gallery Edinburgh) 1999, Evolution Isn't Over Yet (Fruitmarket Gallery Edinburgh, Lugar Comun Lisbon and The Dick Inst Kilmarnock) 1999, John, I'm Only Dancing (UH Galleries St Albans and Collective Gallery Edinburgh) 2000, 45th Salon de Mont Rouge (Galleries Mont Rouge Paris and ICA Lisbon) 2000, Art in the Home (Edinburgh and Yamaguchi) 2001, Here + Now (Dundee Contemporary Arts) 2001, Le mois de le photo (Galerie La Centrale Montreal) 2001, Tabu: Mavericks und Heisse Eisen (Kunsthaus Baselland Muttenz) 2002, The Gap Show (Musuem am Ostwall Dortmund) 2002, Sanctuary Goma Glasgow 2003, Now What? Bak Utrecht 2003, East Int Norwich 2004; *Awards* Glasgow City of Culture studio residency Vienna 1990, Wurlitzer Fndn of New Mexico studio residency 1998, Oppenheim-Downes Tst Award 1998, Hope Scott Tst Artists Award 1998 and 2001, Scottish Arts Cncl studio residency Amsterdam 2000, Br Cncl Artists Grant 2001; *Style—* Ms Janice McNab; ✉ Doggerfish Gallery, 11 Gayfield Square, Edinburgh EH1 3NT (☎ 0131 558 7110, e-mail enquiries@doggerfish.com)

McNALLY, Kevin Robert; s of Robert Gerard McNally, of Somerset, and Margaret June, *née* Sperring; *b* 27 April 1956; *Educ* Central GS Birmingham, RADA (Ronson Award, Bancroft Award); *Partner* Phyllis Logan; 1 s (David b 10 June 1996); another 2 c: 1 step s (Peter), 1 da (Rachel b 7 Nov 1988); *Career* actor; also writes for TV (with Bernard Dempsey); *Theatre* NT 1979–80: Lark Rise, The Passion, Dispatches, The Iceman Cometh; Loose Ends (Hampstead), Pistols and Airbase (The Arts), Andromache (Old Vic), Scenes from an Execution and Naked (with Almeida Co); West End theatre incl: Extremities (Duchess), Glengarry Glen Ross (Mermaid), Hidden Laughter (Vaudeville), Not Quite Jerusalem and Prayer For My Daughter (Royal Court), Dead Funny (Savoy) 1996, Plunder (Savoy) 1997, Naked (Playhouse) 1998, Lady in the Van (Queen's Theatre) 1999–2000, World Music (Donmar Warehouse) 2003, Boeing Boeing (Comedy Theatre) 2007, Ivanov (Wyndhams Theatre) 2008, Hamlet (Wyndhams and Broadhurst Theatres) 2009); *Television* for BBC incl: Poldark, I Claudius, Duchess of Duke Street, Diana, The Common Pursuit, Dad, Life on Mars, Spooks, Downton Abbey; also: Full Stretch (Meridian), Conspiracy, Shackleton, Demons, Law & Order, Wuthering Heights, Underworld (Channel 4); *Film* incl: The Spy Who Loved Me, The Long Good Friday, Enigma, Not Quite Jerusalem, The Berlin Affair, Cry, Freedom, Woody Allen's Scoop, Phantom of the Opera, De-Lovely, Pirates of the Caribbean I, II and III, Valkerie; *Clubs* Groucho, High Road House; *Style—* Kevin R McNally; ✉ c/o Hatton McEwan Management, PO Box 37385, London N1 7XF (e-mail kevinrmcnally@mac.com)

McNALLY, Peter Joseph Dean; s of Gp Capt Patrick John McNally, of Marlow, Bucks, and Mary Deane, *née* Outred; *b* 16 March 1933; *Educ* Stonyhurst; *m* 1, 1956 (m dis 1960), Mary B Gardiner; 1 da (Joanna b 1957); m 2, 3 March 1969 (m dis 1998), Edmée Maria, da of Egon Carmine, of Estaplatz, Vienna, Austria; 2 s (Alexis b 1970, Markus b 1972); m 3, June 1999, Beatrice, da of Rudi Blum of Zurich, Switzerland; *Career* exec dir: LWT 1969–93, LWT (Holdings) plc 1976–93; past non-exec dir: Hutchinson Ltd, Independent TV Publications Ltd, Arcadian International plc, The Listener Ltd, Johnson and Jourgeson Holdings plc; past chm Company of Designers plc; chm: Sunspot Tours Ltd 1994–2013, Mercury Direct; memb fundraising bd: Pearl Appeal Winged Fellowship, Evolution Appeal New Great Western Hosp Wiltshire; tstee Kimberley Falmouth Tst; amateur painter; exhbns at: The Osborne Studio Gallery London 1995 and 1997, The Malcolm Innes Gallery 2000; FCA (ACA 1955); *Recreations* fishing, shooting, skiing, tennis, bridge; *Clubs* Boodle's, Hurlingham; *Style—* Peter McNally, Esq; ✉ 16 Bolton Gardens, London SW5 0AJ (☎ 020 7370 2272); The Manor, Hannington Wick, Highworth, Wiltshire (☎ 01285 810152)

McNALLY, Baron (Life Peer UK 1995), of Blackpool in the County of Lancashire; Thomas (Tom) McNally; PC (2005); s of John Patrick McNally (d 1982), and Elizabeth May McNally (d 1982); *b* 20 February 1943; *Educ* Coll of St Joseph Blackpool, UCL (BSc); *m* 1, 1970 (m dis 1990), Eileen Isobel, da of Thomas Powell, of Dumfries; m 2, 1990, Juliet, da of George Lamy Hutchinson, of Swansea; 2 s (Hon John b 15 June 1990, Hon James George b 7 Aug 1993), 1 da (Hon Imogen b 28 Oct 1995); *Career* asst gen sec the Fabian Soc 1966–67, vice-pres NUS 1966–67, int sec Lab Party HQ 1969–74 (researcher 1966–67); political advsr: to Foreign and Cwlth Sec 1974–76, to PM (head of Political Office 10 Downing St) 1976–79, to Paddy Ashdown 1988–99; MP (Lab until 1981, whereafter SDP) Stockport S 1979–83; memb House of Commons Trade and Industry Select Ctee 1979–83; Lib Dem spokesman on Home Affairs in House of Lords 1998–2001, dep ldr Lib Dem House of Lords 2001–04, ldr Lib Dem House of Lords 2004–13, min of state for justice and dep ldr House of Lords 2010–13; memb House of Lords Select Ctee on: the Public Service 1997–98, Freedom of Information Act 1999; memb Jt Select Ctee on the Communications Bill 2002; chm Youth Justice Bd for England and Wales 2014–; public affrs advsr, head of public affrs Hill and Knowlton (UK) Ltd PR conslts 1987–93, vice-chm WeberShandwick UK PR conslts 1996–2004 (dir of public affrs 1993–96); memb Fed Exec Lib Dems 1987–99; fell UCL 1995; FCIPR, FRSA, Fell Inst of Telecommunications Professionals (ITP) 2015–; *Recreations* watching sport, reading political biographies; *Clubs* Nat Liberal; *Style—* The Rt Hon Lord McNally, PC; ✉ House of Lords, London SW1A 0PW (☎ 020 7219 5443, e-mail McNallyT@parliament.uk)

M

McNAMARA, Dr John Francis; s of Francis McNamara (d 1978), of Bolton, Lancs, and Olivia, *née* Whittingham (d 1982); *b* 18 July 1945; *Educ* Worsley-Wardley GS, Univ of Leeds, Univ of Greenwich (MA); *m* 19 Dec 1981, Olwen, da of Richard Fellows, of Altrincham, Cheshire; 1 s (James Declan b 23 Oct 1983), 1 da (Katherine Jane b 16 March 1985); *Career* sr MO Br Nuclear Fuels Risley Nuclear Power Centre 1979–83, occupational health physician City of Salford 1983–87, conslt physician in occupational med Cheshire and Wirral Partnership NHS Tst Chester 1986–2006, conslt occupational physician and dir of occupational med Univ Hosp of S Manchester 1992–2009; memb Med Appeals Tbnl, memb Criminal Injuries Appeals Tbnl 2010–; memb: BMA 1971, Soc of Occupational Med 1977, Cncl Assoc of Nat Health Occupational Physicians 1986; hon clinical lectr in occupational med Univ of Manchester 1993–; LLM Univ of Wales 1994; MRCS 1970, MRCGP 1975, MRCP (collegiate memb London) 1979 (LRCP 1970), FRCPGlas 1994, FRCPEd 1997, FFOM (RCP) 2002, FFFP (RCOG) 2005; *Books* The Patient with Respiratory Problems (contrib, 1989); *Recreations* travel, swimming, walking, maritime history, gym; *Style—* Dr John McNamara; ✉ Altrincham Medical Practice, Lloyd House, 7 Lloyd Street, Altrincham, Cheshire WA14 2DD (☎ 0161 928 2424, e-mail john.f.mcnamara@hotmail.com)

McNAMARA, Steve Shaun; s of Edward McNamara, of Hull, and Christine, *née* Bilton; *b* 18 September 1971; *Educ* South Holderness HS; *m* 15 July 1995, Michaela, da of Brian Jeffery; 1 da (Stacey b 19 July 1986); *Career* rugby league coach and former player; as player: Hull RLFC 1989–96, Bradford Bulls RLFC 1996–2000, Wakefield 2000, Huddersfield 2001–03; England schoolboy capt; GB: under 21s 5 appearances (capt twice), full debut v France 1991, memb touring team Australia and NZ 1992; as coach: Bradford Acad 2004–06, Bradford Bulls 2006–10, England 2010– (asst 2008–09); bricklayer 1987–92, commercial rep 1992–; *Recreations* golf and fishing; *Style—* Steve McNamara

McNAMEE, Dr Terence; s of Donald McNamee, and Joan, *née* Crawford; *b* 18 July 1969, Victoria, Canada; *Educ* Univ of Br Columbia Vancouver (BA), McGill Univ Montreal (MA), LSE (PhD); *m* 5 Aug 2000, Emily, *née* Outred; *Career* ed RUSI Jl 2002–, dir of publications RUSI 2003–; *Style—* Dr Terence McNamee; ✉ RUSI, Whitehall, London SW1A 2ET (☎ 020 7930 5854, e-mail terrym@rusi.org)

McNANEY, Annmarie; *Educ* Univ of Bristol (BA, PGCE); *Career* asst head Sixth Form Blackwell Sch; Chesham GS (formerly Chesham HS): head Sixth Form, asst head teacher, dep head teacher, head teacher 2015–; *Style—* Miss Annemarie McNaney

McNANEY, Peter Francis; CBE (2013); *b* 8 February 1959, Belfast; *Educ* Univ of Manchester (LLB, J G Lawson Prize), Univ of Ulster (Dip); *m* Karen, *née* McMillen; 2 da (Claire, Alice), 2 s (Christopher, James); *Career* grad recruit industrial rels offr 1980–82, asst slr Joseph O'Hara & Son 1983–85; Belfast City Cncl: asst slr 1985–88, sr slr 1988–91, asst town slr 1991–94, dir of legal servs 1994–2002, chief exec 2002–; Inst of Mgmnt Prize 1994; memb: Law Soc for NI, Soc of Local Authy Chief Execs; *Recreations* walking, sport, family time; *Style—* Peter McNaney, Esq, CBE; ✉ Chief Executive's Office, Belfast City Council, City Hall, Belfast BT1 5GS (☎ 028 9027 0202, fax 028 9027 0232, e-mail mcnaneyp@belfastcity.gov.uk)

McNAUGHT, Ian; s of Andrew Alan McNaught, and Janette, *née* Johnston (d 1989); *b* 19 May 1971, St Andrews, Fife; *Educ* Buckhaven HS, Glenrothes and Buckhaven Tech Coll; *m* 25 Feb 1995, Jo, *née* Maher; 1 da (Holly b 14 March 2001), 2 s (Stevie b 19 April 2003 d 2003, Jamie b 6 Aug 2004); *Career* commis chef Old Manor Hotel London Links 1988–89, pastry chef The Peat Inn St Andrews 1989–90, sous chef Ardnaisaig Hotel Kilchrenan 1990–91; Roman Camp Country House Hotel Callander: sous chef 1991–96, head chef 1996– (3 AA Rosettes 1999–); memb Master Chefs of GB 2001; Gold Medal The Salon Culinaire 1990 (Bronze Medal 1988); *Publications* Chefs of Distinction (contrib 2000, 2 edn 2002), Scotland on a Plate (contrib, 2001), Taste Scotland (contrib, 2006); *Recreations* golf, following Liverpool FC; *Style—* Ian McNaught, Esq; ✉ Roman Camp Country House Hotel, Callander, Perthshire FK17 8BG (☎ 01877 330003, fax 01877 330513, website www.romancamphotel.co.uk)

McNEANY, Kevin Joseph; s of Bernard Joseph McNeany, of Keady, Co Armagh, and Mary Christina, *née* McDonnell; *b* 10 April 1943; *Educ* St Patrick's Coll Armagh, Queen's Univ Belfast (BA), Univ of London, Univ of Manchester; *m* 1 Aug 1968 (m dis 1985), Christine, da of Stephen McNulty; 2 s (Matthew Ciaron b 1971, Myles Anthony b 1986); *Career* teacher: St Paul's Sch Lurgan Co Armagh 1964–66, Corpus Christi Sch Leeds 1966–68; lectr: Kitson Coll Leeds 1968–70, Southport Tech Coll 1970–73, Wythenshawe Coll Manchester 1973–77; co-fndr (with Christine McNeany 1972), exec chm Nord Anglia Education plc (formerly Nord-Anglia International) 2003–05 (chm and ceo 1977–2003), fndr and chm Orbital Educn Gp 2004–, exec chm Acorn Educn and Care Ltd 2005–10; fndr: Br Sch of Warsaw Poland 1992, Br Int Sch of Moscow 1994, English Sch Prague 1995, Br Sch of Kiev Ukraine 1997, Br Sch of Bratislava Slovakia 1997, Br Int Sch Shanghai China 2002, English Int Sch Moscow 2005, Br Int Kindergartens Seoul Korea 2006, Britannica Int Sch Shanghai 2013, Oryx Int Sch Doha State of Qatar 2016; *Recreations* walking, cycling; *Clubs* National Liberal; *Style—* Kevin McNeany, Esq; ✉ Ridge Park, 32 Bramhall Park Road, Bramhall, Cheshire SK7 3JN (☎ 0161 439 2563); Landmark House, Cheadle Hulme, Cheshire SK8 7BS (☎ 0161 475 6937, mobile 07802 740146)

MacNEIL, Angus; MP; *b* 21 July 1970; *Educ* Univ of Strathclyde (BEng), Jordanhill Coll (PGCE); *Career* former reporter BBC, teacher Eoligarry Sch Barra; MP (SNP) Na H-Eileanan An Iar 2005– (Parly candidate (SNP) Inverness 2001); chair Energy and Climate Change Select Ctee House of Commons; *Style—* Angus MacNeil, Esq, MP; ✉ House of Commons, London SW1A 0AA

McNEILL, James Walker; QC (Scot 1991); s of James McNeill, and Edith Anna Howie, *née* Wardlaw; *b* 16 February 1952; *Educ* Dunoon GS, Univ of Cambridge (MA), Univ of Edinburgh (LLB); *m* 1986, Katherine Lawrence, da of William Crocket McDowall; 2 s, 1 da; *Career* advocate 1978; standing jr counsel to: Dept of Tport in Scot 1984–88, Inland Revenue in Scot 1988–91; judge Courts of Appeal of Jersey and Guernsey 2006–; memb Bd of Scottish Int Piano Competition 2004–11, memb Cncl Cwlth Lawyers Assoc 2005–11, memb Judicial Appointments Bd for Scotland 2012–, chair Disciplinary Appointments Ctee Inst and Faculty of Actuaries 2013–; session clerk St Andrew's and St George's Parish Church Edinburgh 1999–2003, tstee and sec Edinburgh City Centre Churches Together 2012–; *Recreations* music, hill walking, skiing, cycling; *Style—* James McNeill, QC; ✉ 28 Kingsburgh Road, Edinburgh EH12 6DZ

McNEILL, Prof John; s of Thomas McNeill (d 1972), of Edinburgh, and Helen Lawrie, *née* Eagle (d 1984); *b* 15 September 1933; *Educ* George Heriot's Sch Edinburgh, Univ of Edinburgh (BSc, PhD); *m* 1, 29 July 1961 (m dis 1990), Bridget Mariel, da of Paul Winterton; 2 s (Andrew Thomas b 1964, Douglas Paul b 1966); m 2, 6 April 1990, Dr Marilyn Lois James; *Career* asst lectr then lectr Dept of Agric Botany Univ of Reading 1957–61, lectr Dept of Botany Univ of Liverpool 1961–69, sr res scientist Biosystematics Res Inst Canada Ottawa 1977–81 (res sci when formerly known as Plant Res Inst 1969–77), prof and chm Dept of Biology Univ of Ottawa Canada 1981–87, regius keeper Royal Botanic Garden Edinburgh 1987–89 (hon assoc 1998–), dir and pres Royal Ontario Museum Toronto Canada 1991–97 (assoc dir curatorial 1989–90, actg dir 1990–91, dir emeritus 1997–); concurrently dir George R Gardiner Museum of Ceramic Art Toronto and pres Royal Ontario Museum Fndn; prof Dept of Botany Univ of Toronto, adjunct prof Dept of Biology Univ of Ottawa 1991; nomenclature ed Taxon – Int Jl of Plant Taxonomy, Phylogeny and Evolution 2000–; pres: Biological Cncl of Canada 1986–87 (vice-pres 1984–86), Canadian Cncl of Univ Biology Chairmen 1984–85 (vice-pres 1983–84); chm: Int Organization for Plant Information 1997–2000 (vice-chm 1993–96), Flora North America Mgmnt Ctee 1998–2001; rapporteur-général Nomenclature Section XVII and XVIII Int Botanical Congress 1999–2011; treas Int Organization for Systematic and Evolutionary Biology 1996–2002; exec memb Int Union of Biological Sci 1985–88 and 1991–94, admin of fin Int Assoc of Plant Taxonomy 1987–93 (cncllr 1981–87 and 1993–2005); author of numerous scientific papers and reports; memb 15 scientific socs; *Books* Phenetic and Phylogenetic Classification (ed with V H Heywood, 1964), Grasses of Ontario (with W G Dore, 1980), The Genus Atriplex in Canada (with I J Bassett et al, 1983), International Code of Botanical Nomenclature (adopted 1981, jt ed, 1983), International Code of Botanical Nomenclature (adopted 1987, jt ed, 1988), Preliminary Inventory of Canadian Weeds (with C W Crompton, A E Stahevitch and W A Wojtas, 1988), Flora of North America (Vols 1 and 2I, jt ed, 1993, Vol 3, jt ed, 1997, Vol 22, jt ed, 2000, Vol 23, jt ed, 2003, Vol 26, jt ed, 2002), International Code of Botanical Nomenclature (adopted 1993, jt ed, 1994), International Code of Nomenclature for Cultivated Plants (jt ed, 1995 and 2004), International Code of Botanical Nomenclature (adopted 1999, jt ed, 2000), International Code of Botanical Nomenclature (adopted 2005, chair Editorial Ctee 2006), International Code of Nomenclature for Algae, Fungi and Plants (adopted 2011, chair Editorial Ctee 2012); *Style—* Prof John McNeill; ✉ Royal Botanic Garden, 20A Inverleith Row, Edinburgh EH3 5LR

McNEISH, Prof Alexander Stewart; s of Dr Angus Stewart McNeish (d 1964), and Minnie Howieson, *née* Dickson (d 1992); *b* 13 April 1938; *Educ* Glasgow Acad, Univ of Glasgow (MB ChB, MPhil), Univ of Birmingham (MSc), Univ of London (PhD); *m* 4 March 1963, Joan Ralston, da of William Hamilton (d 1970); 2 s (Alistair Stewart b 1964, Iain Alexander b 1968), 1 da (Fiona Hamilton b 1966 d 2004); *Career* fndn prof of child health Univ of Leicester 1976–80, Leonard Parsons prof of paediatrics and child health and dir Inst of Child Health Univ of Birmingham 1980–95 (dean Faculty of Medicine and Dentistry 1987–92), dir MRC Clinical Sciences Centre Royal Postgrad Med Sch London 1995–96, warden Bart's and the Royal London Med and Dental Sch and vice-princ Queen Mary & Westfield Coll London 1997–2000, emeritus prof in clinical sci Univ of London 2001–, hon prof Univ of Birmingham 2003–, hon fell Queen Mary and Westfield Coll 2007; memb Central Birmingham HA 1987–91, non-exec dir S Birmingham HA 1991–92, dir R&D W Midlands RHA 1992–95; pres European Soc for Paediatric Gastroenterology and Nutrition 1984–87; memb GMC 1985–95; hon fell Queen Mary Univ of London 2007; FRCP 1977, FRCPGlas 1985, FMedSci 1997; *Recreations* golf, music, gardening; *Clubs* Athenaeum, Blackwell Golf, Southerness Golf, Rye Golf; *Style—* Prof Alexander McNeish; ✉ 128 Westfield Road, Birmingham B15 3JQ (☎ and fax 0121 454 6081, e-mail asmcneish@btinternet.com); Drumbuie, Kirkbean, Dumfries and Galloway

McNICHOLAS, Bernard; s of Michael McNicholas (d 1962), and Mary, *née* Harwood; *b* 9 March 1941, London; *Educ* St James RC Sch Burnt Oak; *m* m 1, Patricia (d 1998); 3 da (Siobhan b 15 Oct 1965, Fiona b 31 Jan 1969, Lucy b 12 April 1974), 1 s (Sean b 17 Nov 1967); m 2, 18 March 2004, Pauline, *née* Mitchel; *Career* exec chm McNicholas Hldgs plc; AIB Businessman of the Year 1994; Hon LLD Galway Univ 2005; KSG 1999; *Recreations* golf, fishing, reading; *Style—* Bernard McNicholas, Esq; ✉ Windmill House, Windmill Lane, Arkley, Hertfordshire EN5 3HX; McNicholas Holdings plc, McNicholas House, Kingsbury Road, London NW9 8XA

McNICOL, Duncan; s of Alfred McNicol (d 1989), of Isle of Skye, and Joan, *née* Fox; *b* 18 March 1952; *Educ* Cranford Sch, London Coll of Printing (HND Creative Photography); *m* 21 June 1975, Margaret, da of Albert Frederick Bradberry; 2 s (Ross b 13 Nov 1979, Ewan b 27 June 1981); *Career* photographic asst 1973–76, own studio (advtg and design photography) 1976–; main advtg clients incl: Citroën, Rover, Barclays Bank, Nat Westminster, Kit Kat, Armitage Shanks, De Beers, Br Telecom, Royal Mail, Royal Insurance, Spanish Tourist Bd, Scottish Tourist Bd, Du Pont, Compuserve, Polaroid, BICC, Tarmac; pt/t photographic teacher London Coll of Printing 1976–79; memb Assoc of Photographers 1977, memb RPS; *Awards* Assoc of Photographers Awards 1987, 1989, 1995 and 1996, Assoc of Photographers Gold Award 1994, Communication Arts Award (USA) 1994, John Kobal Awards 1996; finalist: Epica Awards 1993, Cannes Ad Awards 1993; *Recreations* photography, walking, theatre, cycling, art galleries; *Style—* Duncan McNicol, Esq; ☎ 01798 869836, e-mail info@duncanmcnicol.com

McNICOL, Iain; s of James Iain McNicol, and Zoe *née* Coles (d 1997); *b* 17 August 1969; *Educ* Dundee Inst of Technol; *m* Sept 1995, Michelle, *née* Wright; 1 da (Scarlett, b March 2000), 1 s (Hamish, b April 2002); *Career* GMB: research, organisation and political offr 1997–98, regnl organiser Southern Region 1998–2004, nat political offr 2004–11; gen sec Lab Pty 2011–; tstee Polka Theatre; *Recreations* skiing, travel, karate (black belt); *Style—* Iain McNicol, Esq; ✉ The Labour Party, Labour Central, Kings Manor, Newcastle upon Tyne NE1 6PA (e-mail ian_mcnicol@labour.org.uk, Twitter @IainMcNicol)

MACNICOL, Malcolm Fraser; s of Rev Robert (Roy) Simson Macnicol (d 1986), of Edinburgh, and Eona Kathleen (d 2002); *b* 18 March 1943; *Educ* Royal HS Edinburgh (capt of sch, dux in English and biology), Univ of Edinburgh (BSc, MBChB), Stanford Univ CA, Harvard Univ MA, Univ of Western Aust, Univ of Liverpool (MChOrth); *m* 30 Sept 1972, Anne Morag; 1 da (Sarah Anne Marie b 1977), 2 s (Sean Malcolm Fraser b 1979, Calum Alexander Ruaridh b 1983); *Career* conslt orthopaedic surgn, regnl advsr in orthopaedic surgery S E Scot 1995–2002; sr lectr Univ of Edinburgh 1979–2005 (lectr 1976–79); chm Orthopaedic Specialists' Soc, treas Special Advsy Ctee in Orthopaedic Surgery; treas and memb Fin Ctee RCSEd; memb: Shaw Report team, Br Orthopaedic Res Soc, Br Orthopaedic Assoc (pres 2001–02), Br Assoc for Surgery of the Knee, Br Soc for Children's Orthopaedic Surgery, Cncl of Mgmnt and Editorial Bd Jl of Bone and Joint Surgery 1997–2002, Sub-Ctee Provision of Paediatric Surgery in Scotland 1997–99, Cncl British Orthopaedic Assoc 1998–2000 (chm Medicolegal sub ctee 1998–2003); hon med advsr Scottish Rugby Union 2003–07; patron Scottish Post-Polio Network 2004–; FRCSEd, FRCP, FRCS(Orth); *Books* Basic Care of The Injured Hand (1984), Aids To Orthopaedics (1984), The Problem Knee (1986, 3 edn 2011), Children's Orthopaedics and Fractures (1994, 3 edn 2009), Colour Atlas and Text of Osteotomy of the Hip (1995), Red Sandstone Buildings of Edinburgh (jtly, 2009); *Recreations* tennis, squash, painting; *Clubs* Scottish Arts, Robert Jones; *Style—* Malcolm Macnicol, Esq; ✉ Red House, 1 South Gillsland Road, Edinburgh EH10 5DE (☎ 0131 447 2694, e-mail mmacnicol@btinternet.com); New Royal Infirmary, Old Dalkeith Road, Edinburgh EH16 (☎ 0131 242 3494); Royal Hospital for Sick Children, Sciennes Road, Edinburgh EH9 (☎ 0131 536 0831), Murrayfield Hospital, 122 Corstorphine Road, Edinburgh EH12 6UD (☎ 0131 334 0363)

McNICOLL, Air Marshal Iain Walter; CB (2006), CBE (2000); s of Walter McNicoll (d 2013), and Maida Cameron, *née* Readdie (d 1987); *b* 3 May 1953, Dundee; *Educ* Dundee HS, Univ of Edinburgh (BSc); *m* 5 Sept 1980, Wendelien Henriëtte Maria, *née* van den Biggelaar; 2 da (Stephanie Henriëtte b 26 June 1983, Alexandra Frances b 10 April 1986), 1 s (Roderick Walter b 8 April 1989); *Career* cmmnd: RAFVR 1973, RAF 1975; offr and pilot trg 1975–77, Buccaneer S2B-XV Sqdn 1978–81 (qualified weapons instr 1979), Tornado GR1/4–45 (R) Sqdn 1982–85, 17 (Fighter) Sqdn 1985–86, 16 Sqdn 1986–89, RAF Staff Coll 1990, PSO to Dep C-in-C Strike Cmd 1991–92, OC 17 (Fighter) Sqdn 1992–95, MOD 1995–98, Station Cdr RAF Brüggen 1998–2000, Dir Force Devpt 2000–02, DG Jt Doctrine and Concepts 2002–05, AOC 2 Gp 2005–07, Dep C-in-C Ops Air Cmd 2007–10; assoc ptnr Defence Strategy and Solutions LLP 2010–11; dir: Jee Ltd 2009–16, Beech House Consulting Ltd 2012–16, NATS Hldgs Ltd 2013–; Queen's Medal 1977, QCVSA 1989; FRAeS 2001, FIoD 2015 (MIoD 2008), CDir 2010; *Clubs* RAF; *Style—* Air Marshal I W McNicoll, CB, CBE; ✉ e-mail iain_mcnicoll@hotmail.com

McNISH, Althea Marjorie; da of Joseph Claude McNish (d 1964), of Port of Spain, and Margaret Bourne (d 1977); *Educ* Port of Spain (by father and others), London Coll of Printing (NDD (Special), Illustration prize), Central Sch of Art and Crafts, Royal Coll of Art (DesRCA); *m* 20 Aug 1969, John Saul Weiss, s of Woolf Weiss (d 1994), of London; *Career* freelance designer 1957–; exhibitions incl: Inprint 1964–71, Design Cncl USA and Sweden 1969, London 1970 and 1975–80, USA 1972, Design-In (Amsterdam) 1972–74, The Way We Live Now (V&A London) 1978, Indigo Lille 1981–82, Cwlth Festival Art Exhibition (Brisbane) 1982, Textile hangings (Peoples Gallery London) 1982, Textile hangings (Magazine Workspace Leicester) 1983, Designs for British Dress and Furnishing Fabrics (V&A London) 1986, Make or Break (Henry Moore Gallery London) 1986, Surtex NY 1987, Ascher (V&A London) 1987, Caribbean Connection 2: Island Pulse, five Caribbean-born artists (Islington Arts Factory, London) 1996, Paintings and hangings (Hockney Gallery London) 1997, Transforming the Crown: African, Asian and Caribbean Artists in Britain 1966–1996 (Caribbean Cultural Center NY) 1997, Trinidad & Tobago Through the Eye of the Artist: from Cazabon to the Millennium (Commonwealth Inst London) 1997, gp exhbn Fine Arts Soc London 1998, gp exhbn 198 Gallery London 1998, Six into One: Artists from the Caribbean (Morley Gallery London) 1998, gp exhbn Studio Gallery Chelsea 2000, My World of Colour (Ohio Univ) 2003, Trade and Empire: Remembering Slavery (Whitworth Art Gallery) 2007; commissioned by Ascher and Liberty's 1957, designs for mfrs worldwide; visiting lectr: Central Sch of Art and Crafts and other colls, polys and univs (UK, USA, Italy, Germany, Slovenia)1960–; advsy tutor furnishing and surface design London Coll of Furniture 1972–90, external assessor for educnl and professional bodies incl CSD and CNAA 1966–, memb jury for Leverhulme scholarships 1968; judge: Portuguese textile design competition Lisbon 1973, Living Design Awards 1974, Carnival Selection Panels Arts Cncl of GB 1982–83; designer: murals for passenger cruise liner Oriana 1960, murals for hospitals and colls in Trinidad 1960–61, for Govt of Trinidad and Tobago in NY, Washington and London 1962, special features Daily Mail Ideal Home Exhibition 1966–78, for sec gen of the Cwlth 1975, bedlinen collection Courtaulds 1978, for BR Bd 1978–81, for London Office of High Cmmr of Trinidad and Tobago 1981, for Fede Cheti Milan 1987–91, murals and hangings for passenger liners Nordic Empress 1990 and Monarch of The Seas 1991; advsr on exhibition design for Govt of Trinidad and Tobago Cwlth Inst 1982–84; memb: Bd Design Cncl 1974–81, Selection Panels for Design Awards and Design Index 1968–80, Selection Panel Jubilee Souvenir 1976 and Royal Wedding Souvenir 1981, CNAA Fashion and Textiles Design Bd 1975–78, Governing Body Portsmouth Coll of Art 1972–81, London Local Advsy Ctee IBA 1981–90, Formation Ctee ILEA London Inst 1985; CSD: assessor and examiner 1966–, vice-pres 1977–78, memb Cncl and Ctees 1958–; Hon DFA Univ of Trinidad and Tobago 2006; FCSD, FSIA 1968 (MSIA 1960); Chaconia Gold Medal of the Repub of Trinidad and Tobago 1976, Scarlet Ibis Award of the Office of the High Cmmr for the Repub of Trinidad and Tobago London 1993; *Publications* textile designs produced in many countries and published in many jls and books incl: Decorative Art, Studio Books (1960, 1961 and 1962), Designers in Britain (1972), Did Britain Make It, Design Council (1986), Fabrics and Wallpapers (Bell and Hyman, 1986), Ascher (1987), English and American Textile from 1790 to the Present (1989), Fabrics and Wallpapers: Design sources and Inspirations (Ebury Press, 1991), The House of Liberty (Thames and Hudson, 1992), The Caribbean Artists Movement 1966–72 (New Beacon Books, 1992); *Recreations* skiing, travelling, music, gardening; *Clubs* Soroptimist; *Style—* Ms Althea McNish; ✉ website www.mcnishandweiss.co.uk

MacNULTY, Christine Avril; *née* Ralph; da of William Arthur Ralph (d 1975), of Egerton, Lancs, and Marjorie Holland, *née* Hale; *b* 22 April 1945; *Educ* Bolton Sch, Univ of London, George Washington Univ Washington DC; *m* 26 Aug 1972, (William) Kirk MacNulty Jr, s of Brig-Gen William K MacNulty; *Career* systems analyst Plessey Radar Ltd 1967–69, sr memb staff International Research & Technology Corporation 1969–72, ptnr Many Futures 1972–76, conslt Progs Analysis Unit 1976–78, program mangr Europe Strategic Environment Centre SRI International 1978–82, conslt Int Res Inst on Social Change 1982–84, md Taylor Nelson Applied Futures 1984–88, chief exec Applied Futures Ltd 1988–, pres Applied Futures Inc 1993–; lectr: Univ of Bradford, Admin Staff Coll, Ashridge Management Coll, Brunel Univ, The Industrial Soc, Nat Defense Univ, Naval War Coll, Air War Coll, Industrial Coll of the Armed Forces, NATO C2 Centre of Excellence; memb Inst for Transitional Dynamics; FRSA 1989; *Books* Industrial Applications of Technological Forecasting (jtly, 1971), The Future of the UK 2010 (jtly), Truth, Perception & Consquences (2007), Transformation: from the outside in or the inside out (2008); author of numerous articles on scenario devpt, social change and forecasting; *Recreations* sailing, cooking, philosophy, psychology, comparative mythology; *Style—* Mrs Christine MacNulty; ✉ 1600 South Eads Street, Apartment 504N, Arlington, VA 22202, USA (website www.applied-futures.com)

McNULTY, Dermot Anthony; s of William J McNulty (d 1970), of River Forest, Illinois, USA, and Margaret, *née* Reigh (d 1998); *b* 11 March 1949; *Educ* Marquette Univ USA (BA); *m* 11 June 1977, Paula, *née* Gaber; *Career* PR account dir Burson-Marsteller London 1977–81, sr vice-pres and md Burson-Marsteller Hong Kong 1981–87, exec vice-pres Burson-Marsteller NY 1987–89; exec vice-pres Shandwick North America NY 1989–90; Shandwick International plc: dir of int mktg 1990–91, chief operating offr 1991–94, chief exec 1994–98; with Burson-Marsteller 1998–2001 (pres and chief exec (Europe) 1999–2001), chm McNulty Consulting 2001–; *Recreations* golf, tennis, travel, reading; *Clubs* Naval and Military, Stoke Park, Hurlingham; *Style—* Dermot McNulty, Esq; ✉ McNulty Consulting (fax 001 804 4385982, e-mail dermotmcnulty@verizon.net)

McOWEN WILSON, Benjamin (Ben); *b* 23 January 1971, Northampton; *Educ* Univ of Nottingham (BSc), Br Psychological Soc (Dip); *m* Michelle Echeverria; 2 da (Lily, Anya); *Career* conslt Renaissance and Andersen Consulting 1994–99, ptnr and media head Spectrum Strategy Conslts 1999–2006; ITV plc: gp strategy dir 2006–07, md ITV Online 2007–10; dir EMEA YouTube 2010–; memb Bd Freesat plc 2007–10, chm Project Kangaroo 2008–10; memb RTS; *Recreations* cinema, reading, travel, walking, climbing and mountaineering; *Style—* Ben McOwen Wilson, Esq; ✉ YouTube, Google, Central St Giles, 1–13 St Giles High Street, London WC2H 8AG

McPARTLIN, Ant; OBE (2016); s of Raymond McPartlin, and Christine McPartlin; *b* 18 November 1975, Newcastle upon Tyne; *m* Lisa; *Career* actor and presenter; performed with Declan Donnelly, *qv*, as 'Ant & Dec' since 1993; jt winner (with Declan Donnelly):Best Double Act Carling Loaded Awards 2000, People's Choice Comedy Awards 2000, Entertainment Personality of the Year Nat TV Awards 2001, TV Personality of the Year Variety Club Awards 2002, TV Personality of the Year TRIC Awards 2002, 2007, 2013 and 2014, Special Recognition Award Nat TV Awards 2002, Best Entertainment Presenter Nat TV Awards 2001–08 and 2010–15, Most Popular Entertainment Presenter TV Choice Awards 2003, TV Personality Award GQ 2003 and 2004, Best Comedy Duo Loaded Awards 2003, Outstanding Contribution Award TV Choice Awards 2009, Most Popular Entertainment Presenters BAFTA 2010, Best Entertainment Performance RTS Award 2005 and 2011, Personality of the Year FreeSat Free TV Award 2012–14, Landmark Award: 25 Years in TV Nat TV Awards 2014, Best Entertainment Presenters Nat TV Awards 2014, UK TV Legends Nickelodeon Kids' Choice Award 2015; *Television* as actor incl: Byker Grove (as Duncan) 1989–93, A Tribute to the Likely Lads 2002; as presenter incl: The Ant & Dec Show 1995 (BAFTA, RTS Award), Ant and Dec Unzipped 1997 (BAFTA), SM:TV Live 1998–2001 (Best Entertainment Prog Children's BAFTAs 2000, Best Children's Show TV Quick Awards 2000 and 2001, Best Children's Entertainment Prog RTS Awards 2000, Best Children's Prog Broadcast Awards 2001, Best Children's Prog Indie Awards 2001, Best Presenters RTS Awards 2001, Kids Award Disney Channel 2001, TV Presenters of the Year RTS Awards 2002), CD:UK 1998–2001 (Best Teen Show TV Hits Awards 2000), Ant and Dec's Secret Camera Show 2000, Friends Like These 2000 (Bronze Rose Montreux Awards 2000), Slap Bang with Ant and Dec 2001, Pop Idol 2001 (Entertainment Prog of the Year TRIC Awards 2002, Best Entertainment Prog BAFTA Awards 2002, Golden Rose Montreaux Awards 2002, Best Entertainment Prog Nat TV Awards 2002), Brit Awards 2001 and 2015, Party in the Park 2001, Comic Relief: Say Pants to Poverty 2001, Record of the Year 2001 and 2002, Ant & Dec's Saturday Night Takeaway 2002– (Best Entertainment Prog TV Choice Awards 2003, 2004, 2007, 2008, 2009, 2010, 2013 and 2014, Best Entertainment Prog Nat TV Awards 2003, 2004 and 2007, People's Choice Best 2003 and 2006 and Comedy Entertainment Performance Comedy Awards 2003, Best Comedy Entertainment Performance and Best Comedy Entertainment Prog Comedy Awards 2004, Best Entertainment Presenter RTS Awards 2005, Best Entertainment Prog Broadcast Awards 2006, Best Prog Nat TV Awards 2010, Best Entertainment Prog Broadcast Awards 2006, 2014 and 2015, Entertainment Prog Br Acad TV Award 2014, Best Entertainment Performance 2014 and 2015 and Best Entertainment Programme BAFTA Television Awards 2010, 2014 and 2015), I'm a Celebrity, Get Me Out of Here! 2002– (Best Reality Prog TV Choice Awards 2003, 2004, 2012, 2013 and 2014, Lew Grade Award for Entertainment Prog or Series BAFTA Television Award 2005, Best Entertainment Performance BAFTA Television Award 2010, Best Entertainment Performance RTS Award 2011 and 2013, Best Reality TV Nat TV Award 2007 and 2012, TRIC Special Award TRIC Awards 2013, Best Entertainment Prog Nat TV Award 2011–15), Pride of Britain Awards 2003, Comic Relief: The Big Hair Do 2003, World Idol 2003, British Comedy Awards 2003 and 2004, Comic Relief: Red Nose Night Live 2005, Game Show Marathon 2005 (Most Popular Quiz Prog NTA Awards 2006), Soccer Aid 2006, All-Star Cup 2006, Pokerface 2006–07, Britain's Got Talent 2007– (Favourite Funny Person, Favourite TV Presenter and Favourite Family TV Show Nickelodeon Kids Choice Awards UK 2008, Best Talent Show TV Choice Awards 2009, 2011, 2013 and 2014), Wanna Bet 2008, Push The Button 2010 and 2011, Red or Black 2011 and 2012; *Films* incl Love Actually 2003, Alien Autopsy 2006; *Albums* with Declan Donnelly: Psyche 1994, Top Katz 1995, The Cult of Ant & Dec 1997; *Style—* Ant McPartlin, OBE; ✉ c/o James Grant Media Ltd, 94 Strand On The Green, Chiswick, London W4 3NN

McPARTLIN, Sheriff Noel; s of Michael Joseph McPartlin (d 1955), of Galashiels, and Ann, *née* Dunn (d 1978); *b* 25 December 1939; *Educ* Galashiels Acad, Univ of Edinburgh (MA, LLB); *m* 10 July 1965, June Anderson, da of David Anderson Whitehead, of Stirling (d 1961); 3 da (Alison b 1966, Diana b 1967, Julia b 1979), 3 s (Simon b 1970, Guy b 1972, Donald b 1982); *Career* slr 1964–76, advocate 1976; Sheriff: Grampian Highland and Islands at Peterhead and Banff 1983–85, Elgin 1985–2002 and 2008–, Lothian and Borders at Edinburgh 2002–08; *Recreations* country life; *Style—* Sheriff Noel McPartlin; ✉ Sheriff Court, Elgin

MacPHAIL, Sir Bruce Dugald; kt (1992); s of Dugald Ronald MacPhail; *b* 1 May 1939; *Educ* Haileybury, Balliol Coll Oxford, Harvard Business Sch; *m* 1, 1963, Susan Mary (d 1975), da of late Col T Gregory, MC, TD; 3 s; m 2, 1983, Caroline Ruth Grimston, o da of Capt Tatlock Hubbard, MC, RA, and former w of David Dangar Henry Honywood Curtis-Bennett; *Career* articled Price Waterhouse 1961–65, with Hill Samuel & Co 1967–69; fin dir Sterling Guarantee Trust 1969–74; md: Town & City Properties Ltd 1974–76, Sterling Guarantee Trust 1976–85, P&OSNCo 1985–2003 (dir 1983–2003); govr Royal Ballet Sch 1982–98; Univ of Oxford: tstee Balliol Coll 1991–, chm Cncl of Mgmnt Templeton Coll 1992–95 (memb 1986–95), chm Cncl Sch of Mgmnt Studies 1995–2001, Barclay fell Templeton Coll 1995–2013 (Barclay hon fell 2013–), chm Business Advsy Forum Saïd Business Sch 2001–07; non-exec dir: Chelsfield plc 1999–2004, Intelligent Engineering Ltd 2005–, Chelsfield Ptnrs 2006–, Scarborough Minerals 2006–08; life govr and memb Cncl Haileybury 1992–2004, tstee Sir Jules Thorn Charitable Trust 1994–; FCA; *Style—* Sir Bruce MacPhail; ✉ Thorpe Lubenham Hall, Market Harborough, Leicestershire LE16 9TR

McPHEE, George McBeth; MBE; s of late George Hugh McPhee, and of late Daisy, *née* Clyne; *b* 10 November 1937; *Educ* Woodside Sch, Royal Scot Acad of Music, Univ of Edinburgh (BMus); *m* 22 July 1961, Margaret Ann, da of Robert Scotland (d 1951); 1 s (Colin b 1964), 2 da (Catriona b 1966, Susan b 1969); *Career* asst organist St Giles' Cathedral Edinburgh 1959–63, dir of music Paisley Abbey 1963–, lectr in music Royal Scot Acad of Music and Drama 1963–2000, visiting prof of organ St Andrews Univ; numerous performances, recordings, broadcasts and appearances; special commissioner Royal Sch of Church Music, chm Paisley Int Organ Festival; pres Incorporated Society of Musicians 1999–2000, vice-pres RCO 2005–; Hon Doctorate Univ of Paisley 1997; memb ISM 1965, hon fell Royal Sch of Church Music 1991, hon fell Guild of Church Musicians 2006; *Recreations* golf; *Clubs* Royal Troon Golf; *Style—* George McPhee, Esq, MBE; ✉ 17 Main Road, Castlehead, Paisley PA2 6AJ (☎ 0141 889 3528, e-mail profmcphee@aol.com)

MACPHERSON, Angus John; s of late Lt Archibald Norman Macpherson, RN, and late Joan Margaret, *née* Backhouse; *b* 17 March 1953; *Educ* Stowe, Pembroke Coll Cambridge (MA); *m* 14 Aug 1982, Anne Louise Felicity, da of late Capt Edward Morton Barford; 2 da (Eloise Isobel b 5 Jan 1985, Myrtle Maud b 30 Jan 1991), 1 s (William Archibald b 19 March 1988); *Career* called to the Bar Inner Temple 1977, in practice SE circuit; *Recreations* tennis, Scottish history, cooking, wild flowers; *Clubs* Lansdowne; *Style—* Angus Macpherson, Esq; ✉ Orchard House, Longwood, Owslebury, Winchester, Hampshire SO21 1LB; Temple Garden Chambers, Temple, London EC4Y 9DA (☎ 020 7583 1315, e-mail angusmacpherson@tgchambers.com)

McPHERSON, Ian Andrew; QPM (2009); s of Ian Douglas McPherson (d 1976), of Preston, Lancs, and Mary Elizabeth, *née* Simpson; *b* 25 March 1961, Preston, Lancs; *Educ* Univ of Central Lancs (MBA), Fitzwilliam Coll Cambridge (Dip); *m* 1 April 1984, Wendy Jayne, *née* Spence; 1 s (Jack Alexander b 23 Aug 1992), 1 da (Olivia Jayne b 17 May 1995); *Career* Lancs Constabulary: joined 1979, various detective and uniform roles, chief supt in cmd of Pennine Div 1999–2001; asst chief constable Merseyside Police: Operational Policing 2001–05, Force Modernisation 2005; dep chief constable N Yorks Police 2005–06, chief constable Norfolk Constabulary 2006–09, asst cmmr (territorial policing) Met Police 2010–; Queen's Jubilee Medal, Queen's Long Service and Good Conduct Medal 2001; memb ACPO 2001; hon fell Univ of Central Lancs 2008; *Recreations* walking, reading, rugby; *Style—* Ian McPherson, QPM; ✉ Assistant Commissioner – Territorial Policing, Metropolitan Police Service, Room 1001, New Scotland Yard, 10 Broadway, London SW1H 0BG

MACPHERSON, Ishbel Jean Stewart; da of Sir Thomas Macpherson of Biallid, CBE, MC, TD, DL, *qv*, and Jean, *née* Butler Wilson; *b* 16 July 1960, London; *Educ* French Lycée, Wycombe Abbey, Fettes, Univ of Edinburgh (MA); *Career* grad trainee rising to dir of corp fin Barclays de Zoete Wedd 1983–94, head of smaller companies corp fin Hoare Govett Ltd 1994–99, head of UK mid market corp fin Dresdner Kleinwort Wasserstein 1999–2005; non-exec dir: MITIE Group plc 2005–09, GAME Group plc 2005–12, Hydrogen Gp plc 2006–12, Dignity plc 2009–, May Gurney plc 2010–13; chm: Speedy Hire plc 2011–14, Dechra Pharmaceuticals plc 2013–, Galliford Try plc 2014–, Bonmarché Holdings plc 2014–; govr Univ of Westminster 2000–07; *Recreations* riding, walking, having fun; *Style—* Miss Ishbel Macpherson; ✉ West Bradfield House, Bradfield, Devon EX15 2QY (☎ 01884 839875, e-mail email@ishbelmacpherson.co.uk)

McPHERSON, James Alexander Strachan; CBE (1982), JP (Aberdeenshire); s of Peter John McPherson (d 1953), and Jeannie Geddie, *née* Strachan (d 1969); *Educ* Banff Acad, Univ of Aberdeen (MA, BL, LLB); *m* 4 Aug 1960, Helen Marjorie, da of Capt Jack Perks, CBE, DSC, DL, RN (d 1973), of Kibworth, Beauchamp, Leics; 1 s (Ewan John b 1961), 1 da (Lesley Anne b 1963); *Career* Nat Serv cmmnd Lt RA 1952–54; slr Alexander George & Co Macduff, Banff & Buckie 1954–99, memb Macduff Town Cncl and Banff CC 1958–75, convener Banff CC 1970–75, provost of Macduff 1972–75, chm Public Protection Ctee Grampian Regnl Cncl 1974–86 (memb Cncl 1974–90); Lord-Lt of Banffshire 1987–2002, Hon Sheriff Grampian Highland and Islands at Banff 1972–; pres Banffshire Soc of Slrs 1977–80, vice-pres Scottish Highland Reserve Forces and Cadet's Assoc TAVRA 1987–2002; govr Scottish Police Coll 1974–86; dir: Banffshire Partnership, NE Scotland Preservation Tst; chm: Banff and Buchan JP Advsy Ctee 1987–98, Aberdeenshire JP Advsy Ctee 1998–2002; vice-chm Banff Preservation & Heritage Soc; fndr pres Talking Banffie and Turra Talk (talking newspaper for blind in NE Scotland); memb: Grampian Health Bd 1974–82, Police Advsy Bd for S 1974–86, Post Office Users' Nat Cncl for Scot 1976–80, Scottish Slr's Discipline Tbnl 1990–95, Ct Univ of Aberdeen 1993–97; elder and FWO treas Macduff Parish Church; FSA Scot 1974; *Recreations* reading, local history, swimming; *Clubs* Town and County (Banff), Duff House Royal Golf, Royal Northern & Univ (Aberdeen); *Style—* James McPherson, Esq, CBE, FSA; ✉ Dunalastair, Macduff, Banffshire AB44 1XD (☎ 01261 832377, fax 01261 832350)

MACPHERSON, Sir Nicholas Ian; GCB (2015, KCB 2009); s of Ewen Macpherson, of Attadale, Scotland, and Nicolette, *née* van der Bijl; *b* 14 July 1959; *Educ* Eton, Balliol Coll Oxford, UCL; *m* 1983, Suky, *née* Appleby; 2 s; *Career* econ CBI 1982–83, econ Peat Marwick Mitchell 1983–85; HM Treasury: joined 1985, princ private sec to Chllr of the Exchequer 1993–97, head Work Incentives Policy 1997–98, dir (welfare reform) Budget and Public Fin Directorate 1998–2001, md Public Services Directorate 2001–04, md Budget and Public Finance Directorate 2004–05, perm sec HM Treasy 2005–; non-exec dir HM Revenue and Customs 2005–07; visiting fell Nuffield Coll Oxford 2006–14, visiting prof KCL 2014–; *Clubs* Athenaeum, MCC; *Style—* Sir Nicholas Macpherson, GCB; ✉ HM Treasury, 1 Horse Guards Road, London SW1A 2HQ (☎ 020 7270 4360, e-mail action.permsec@hmtreasury.gsi.gov.uk)

MACPHERSON, (Philip) Strone Stewart; s of G P S Macpherson, CBE, TD (d 1981), and Elizabeth Cameron, *née* Smail (d 2004); *b* 21 July 1948; *Educ* Summer Fields Oxford, Fettes, Oriel Coll Oxford (MA), INSEAD (MBA); *m* 1981, Alexandra Grace, da of 5 Baron Northbrook, JP, DL (d 1991); 1 s (Philip Strone Alexander Stewart b 18 April 1985), 2 da (Temora Anne Stewart b 24 Jan 1988, Clementina Grace Stewart b 28 Sept 1989); *Career* trainee Bankers Tsts Co 1970–71, L Messel & Co stockbrokers 1971–74; Robert Fleming & Co Ltd: joined 1975, dir 1978–89, pres Robert Fleming Inc New York 1982–84; non-exec dir: Research Machines plc 1990–94, River and Mercantile Investment

M

Mgmnt 1993–96, River and Mercantile Tst plc 1979–96, Fleming Smaller Cos Investment Tst 1990–, AXA UK plc 1999–2008, Investment and Audit Ctee Kings Fund 1999–, British Empire Securities and General Tst plc 2002– (chm 2007–), Close Brothers Group plc 2003– (chm 2008–), Kleinwort Benson Private Bank 2003–10; Misys plc: non-exec dir 1989–91, exec dep chm 1991–2002, chm Misys Charitable Fndn 1999–2003; chm Tribal Gp plc 2004–09; chm Kings Fund Investment Ctee 2009–; tstee Oriel Coll: Devpt Tsts 1981–, Audit Ctee 2009–; govr Heriot-Watt Univ 2011–15; *Recreations* country pursuits, Scottish art, restoration of early motor cars; *Clubs* Caledonian; *Style*— Strone Macpherson, Esq; ✉ Close Brothers Group plc, 10 Crown Place, London EC2A 4FT

MACPHERSON, Tim John; s of Charles Jaffrey Macpherson, of Kingsbridge, S Devon, and Barbera, *née* Pratt; *b* 11 September 1962; *Educ* Kingsbridge Comp Sch, Kingsbridge Sixth Form Coll, S Devon Art Coll; *m* 29 May 1993, Lesley Ann, da of David Waters; 1 s (Isaac Jaffrey b 16 Nov 1996); *Career* asst photographer Prudence Cuming Associates fine art photographers Dover St London 1983–89, asst to Ben Rice people photographer London 1989–90, freelance asst photographer 1990–92 (worked with Jillian Edelstein, Dave Gamble, Frank Herholdt, Duncan McNicol, Bob Miller and Michael Joseph), photographer 1992–; editorial cmmns incl: Sunday Times, Observer, ES and GQ Magazines, Sunday Telegraph; other assignments for indust, design and advtg; memb Assoc of Photographers; *Exhibitions* Icons, Idols & Heroes 1992 and Portrait 1994 (Association Gallery), National Portrait Gallery; *Awards* Individual Image & Portfolio award Assoc of Photographers Assistants Awards 1991, Individual Image Silver medal RPS 135th Int Print Exhbn 1991, represented Britain at Kodak Euro Panorama of Young Photography Arles France 1992, winner Individual Image Assoc of Photographers Eleventh Awards 1993, American Communication Arts Award 1995 and 1997, winner of Individual Image Assoc of Photographers Fourteenth Awards 1997; *Recreations* travel, photography; *Style*— Tim MacPherson, Esq

MACPHERSON OF PITMAIN, (Michael) Alastair Fox; 17 Sr Chieftain of the Clan Macpherson; s of Stephen Marriott Fox (d 1971), of Surrey, and Margaret Gertude Macpherson of Pitmain; *b* 17 December 1944; *Educ* Haileybury, Magdalene Coll Cambridge (MA); *m* 10 June 1972, Penelope Margaret, da of Frederick William Birkmyre Harper (d 1977), of Oxon; 1 da (Isabella b 3 July 1973), 2 s (Alexander b 5 Feb 1976, Charles b 8 May 1980); *Heir* s, Alexander Macpherson, yr of Pitmain; *Career* admitted slr 1971; ptnr Ashurst Morris Crisp slrs 1974–2003, managing ptnr Ashurst Morris Crisp NY 2000–02; chm Maelor plc 1998–2006; non-exec dir: Smith & Nephew plc 1986–97, Johnson Fry plc 1987–89, Thomas Jourdan plc 1987–97; memb: Cncl White Ensign Assoc 1995–, Transatlantic Cncl of BritishAmerican Business Inc 2001–02; chm Clan Macpherson Assoc 1997–2000, pres Highland Soc of London 2008–12; memb Cncl: Nat Tst for Scotland 2004–07 (also London rep 2004–07), Nat Tst 2005–07; memb Exec Ctee Pilgrims Soc 2011–; tstee Bowel Cancer UK 2013–15; govr St Francis Sch Pewsey 2012–15; *Recreations* golf, shooting, rhododendrons; *Clubs* Boodle's, Royal St George's, MCC (memb Membership Ctee 2004–06); *Style*— Alastair Macpherson of Pitmain, Esq; ✉ Manningford Bruce House, Pewsey, Wiltshire SN9 6JW (✆ 01980 635482, e-mail mafmacpherson@aol.com); 8 Tedworth Court, 15–17 Tedworth Square, London SW3 4DR (✆ 020 7351 6772)

MACPHERSON-FLETCHER OF BALAVIL, Allan William; s of Rev John Fletcher (d 1990), of Edinburgh, and Elizabeth, *née* Stoddart (d 1966); nephew of Mrs H E Brewster-Macpherson of Balavil (d 1990); assumed additional surname of Macpherson 1990; *b* 27 July 1950; *Educ* Trinity Coll Glenalmond, Univ of Aberdeen (BSc); *m* 30 Oct 1976, Marjorie, da of George Daniel (d 1984), of Aberdeen; 1 s (James b 1979), 1 da (Elizabeth-Anne b 1978), 3 step s (Antony Sherlock b 1965, Michael Sherlock b 1966, Nicholas Sherlock b 1973); *Career* mangr McLaren Marine Queensland Aust 1973–75, proprietor Balavil Estate 1975–2015, dir Badenoch Land Management Ltd 1975–, mangr Bell-Ingram Sporting Dept 1987–89, sporting estate conslt Hamptons 1989–95 (dir E Midlands, Northern and Scottish region), Highland conslt Strutt and Parker 1996–; dir and govr Butterstone School Holdings Ltd 1988–93, ed Scottish and African Sporting Gazettes 1996–98, chm Highland Vernacular Bldgs Tst, pres Kingussie Sheep Dog Trial Assoc; memb Brenchley Vineyards Carriage Driving Team World Championships Poland 1995, Br nat champions Windsor 1995; memb: Northern Meeting Soc, Game Conservancy, the Highland Soc of London; *Recreations* shooting, stalking, fishing, skiing, travel; *Clubs* Not For Lunch; *Style*— Macpherson-Fletcher of Balavil; ✉ Croftcarnoch, Kingussie, Inverness-shire (✆ 01540 651296, mobile 07971 854088, e-mail balavil@aol.com); 13 Sandend, Portsoy, Banffshire PH21 1LU

McQUADE, Karen; *Career* former nat sales mangr Crown Foods Ltd, fndr The UK Foodhall Ltd 2007–; HSBC Start-Up Stars Award 2009, Every Woman Demeter Award 2009; *Style*— Ms Karen McQuade; ✉ The UK Foodhall, Greenfields, Foundry Lane, Welshpool SY21 7TR

McQUAY, Elizabeth; da of Thomas Alexander Ireland McQuay (d 1997), and Margaret Doreen, *née* Currie (d 1997); *b* 29 August 1953, Blackburn; *Educ* Harrogate Ladies Coll, LSE (BA), Coll of Law Chester; *m* 14 Sept 1979, Martin Kersh; 1 da (Georgia b 5 July 1990), 1 s (Freddie b 1 Oct 1994); *Career* admitted slr 1979; slr specialising in matrimonial law; trainee slr Forsyte Kerman 1977–79, registrar Attorney-Gen's Office Nairobi 1979–80, ptnr Gordon Dadds 1980–88, ptnr Winward Fearon 1988–93, sole practitioner 1993–; accredited mediator Family Mediators Assoc; memb: Law Soc, Slrs Family Law Assoc (memb Ctee 1988, memb London Regnl Ctee 1992); *Recreations* tennis; *Style*— Miss Elizabeth McQuay; ✉ The Old Rectory, Bletchingdon, Oxfordshire OX5 3DH (✆ 01869 351229, fax 01869 350231, e-mail law@elizabethmcquay.co.uk)

McQUEEN, Eric; *Career* former dir of field servs Scottish Ct Service, currently chief exec Scottish Cts and Tbnls Service; *Style*— Eric McQueen, Esq; ✉ Scottish Courts and Tribunals Service, Parliament House, Parliament Square, Edinburgh EH1 1RQ (e-mail pscourtservice@scotcourts.gov.uk)

MacQUEEN, Prof Hector Lewis; s of John MacQueen, of Damnaglaur, and Winifred MacQueen; *b* 13 June 1956; *Educ* George Heriot's Sch Edinburgh, Univ of Edinburgh (LLB, PhD); *m* 29 Sept 1979, Frances Mary, da of Robert Young, of Dalkeith; 1 da (Sarah b 1982), 2 s (Patrick b 1984, Jamie b 1987); *Career* Univ of Edinburgh: lectr in law 1979–91, assoc dean Faculty of Law 1987–90, sr lectr 1991–94, reader 1994, prof of private law 1994–, dean 1999–2003, dean of research Coll of Humanities and Social Science 2004–08; exec dir The David Hume Inst Edinburgh 1992–99 (chm 2012–15), dir AHRC Research Centre on Intellectual Property and Technol Law 2002–07; Scottish law cmmr 2009–; visiting prof: Cornell Univ 1991, Utrecht Univ 1997, Stetson Univ Coll of Law FL 2007–09, Lucerne Univ 2011; literary dir Stair Soc 1999–; ed Edinburgh Law Review 1996–2001; chair Scottish Records Advsy Cncl 2001–08; memb: DTI Intellectual Property Advsy Ctee 2003–05, DCA Advsy Panel on Public Sector Info 2004–11; vice-pres (humanities) RSE 2009–11; FRSE 1995, FBA 2006; *Books* New Perspectives in Scottish Legal History (ed, 1984), Centenary – Heriot's FP Cricket Club 1889–1989 (1989), Copyright, Competition and Industrial Design (1989, 2 edn 1995), The College of Justice and Other Essays by R K Hannay (ed, 1991), Studying Scots Law (1993, 4 edn 2012), Common Law and Feudal Society in Medieval Scotland (1993), Scots Law into the 21st Century (ed, 1996), Contract Law in Scotland (jtly, 2000, 3 edn 2012), Human Rights In Scots Law (jt ed, 2002), Unjustified Enrichment (2004, 3 edn 2013), Sale of Goods (jtly, 12 edn, 2010), European Contract Law: Scots and South African Perspectives (jt ed, 2006), Contemporary Intellectual Property: Law and Policy (jtly, 2007, 2 edn 2010), Gloag & Henderson's Law of Scotland (jt ed, 13 edn, 2012); *Recreations* cricket, things Scottish,

walking, golf, photography; *Clubs* Heriots FP Cricket; *Style*— Prof Hector MacQueen, FBA; ✉ Scottish Law Commission, 140 Causewayside, Edinburgh EH9 1PR (✆ 0131 668 2131, fax 0131 662 4900, e-mail hector.macqueen@scotlawcom.gsi.gov.uk)

McQUEEN, John; s of late Dr Leonard George McQueen, and late Mira Milstead, *née* Birch; *b* 20 May 1942, Walton-on-Thames, Surrey; *Educ* Rugby, Trinity Coll Cambridge, St Thomas' Hosp Med Sch (MA, MB BChir); *m* Dorothy, da of Gilbert Dyke; 5 da (Katy b 1968, Deborah b 1971, Philippa b 1977, Sarah b 1984, Laura b 1987); *Career* formerly sr registrar Queen Charlotte's Hosp and Chelsea Hosp then conslt obstetrician gynaecologist Bromley Hosps NHS Trust, ret from NHS; author of various papers on obstetrics, gynaecology and the menopause; memb Int Menopause Soc; Freeman City of London, Liveryman Worshipful Soc of Apothecaries; FRCS 1972, FRCOG 1985 (memb 1973); *Recreations* travel, golf; *Clubs* London Obstetric, Gynaecological Soc; *Style*— John McQueen, Esq; ✉ Downs View, Heritage Hill, Keston, Kent BR2 6AU (✆ 01689 859058, e-mail john@heritage-hill.demon.co.uk)

MacQUEEN, Prof John; s of William Lochhead MacQueen (d 1963), of Springboig, Glasgow, and Grace Palmer, *née* Galloway (d 1983); *b* 13 February 1929; *Educ* Hutchesons' GS, Univ of Glasgow (MA), Christ's Coll Cambridge (MA); *m* 22 June 1953, Winifred Wallace, da of Wallace McWalter (d 1979), of Calderwood, East Kilbride; 3 s (Hector b 1956, Angus b 1958, Donald b 1963); *Career* PO, Flying Offr RAF 1954–56; asst prof Washington Univ St Louis MO 1956–59; Univ of Edinburgh: lectr 1959–63, Masson prof 1963–71, dir Sch of Scottish Studies 1969–88, prof of Scottish lit 1971–88 (now emeritus), endowment fell 1988–92, hon fell Faculty of Arts 1992–95; Hon DLitt Nat Univ of Ireland 1985; FRSE 1992, FRAS 2004; *Books* St Nynia (1961, 2 revised edn 2005), Robert Henryson (1967), Ballattis of Luve (1970), Allegory (1970), Progress and Poetry (1982), Numerology (1985), The Rise of the Historical Novel (1989), Scotichronicon 3 and 4 (jtly, 1989), Humanism in Renaissance Scotland (ed, 1990), Scotichronicon 1 and 2 (jtly, 1993), Scotichronicon 5 and 6 (jtly, 1995), Place Names of the Rhinns of Galloway and Luce Valley (2002), Complete and Full with Numbers (2006), The Latin Poems of Archibald Pitcairne (jtly, 2009), Place-Names of the Moors and Machars (2008), Archibald Pitcairne, The Phanaticks (ed, 2012), Archibald Pitcairne, Tollerators and Con-Tollerators (ed, 2015); *Recreations* walking, reading, music, casual archaeology, astronomy; *Style*— Prof John MacQueen, FRSE; ✉ Slewdonan, Damnaglaur, Drummore, Stranraer, Wigtownshire DG9 9QN (✆ and fax 01776 840637, e-mail jackmacqueen@gmail.com)

MacQUITTY, (Joanna) Jane; da of William Baird MacQuitty (d 2004), of London, and Betty, *née* Bastin; *Educ* Benenden; *m* 12 Aug 1988, Philip Killingworth Hedges; 2 da (Alicia b 28 Dec 1990, Maya b 29 March 1994), 1 s (William b 11 June 1992); *Career* wine and food writer; with House & Garden 1975–82, ed Which? Wine Guide and Which? Wine Monthly 1982–84, wine ed Good Housekeeping 1984–2000; wine and drink corr The Times 1982–; wine lectr and judge 1982–; memb: Circle of Wine Writers 1977–, Soc of Authors 1982–; Glenfiddich Awards: Wine Writer of the Year 1981, Whisky Writer of the Year 1981; Special Award for Which? Wine Guide 1983, Journalist of the Year Portuguese Wine Awards 2014; patron Urology Fndn 2014–; *Publications* Which? Wine Guide (1983 and 1984), Jane MacQuitty's Guide to Champagne and Sparkling Wines (1986, 3 edn 1993), Jane MacQuitty's Guide to Australian and New Zealand Wines (1988); *Recreations* family, eating, drinking, talking, sleep; *Style*— Ms Jane MacQuitty; ✉ The Times Weekend, The Times, 1 London Bridge Street, London SE1 9GF

McRAE, Dame Frances Anne; DBE (2015, CBE 2004); *née* Cairncross; da of Sir Alexander Kirkland (Alec) Cairncross, KCMG, FBA (d 1998); *b* 30 August 1944; *Educ* Laurel Bank Sch Glasgow, St Anne's Coll Oxford (MA), Brown Univ RI (MA); *m* 10 Sept 1971, Hamish McRae, qv; 2 da (Isabella Frances b 28 July 1977, Alexandra Barbara Mary b 5 Dec 1979); *Career* staff memb: The Times 1967–69, The Banker 1969, The Observer 1970–73, The Guardian (economics corr 1973–81, ed women's page 1981–84); The Economist: Br ed 1984–89, environment ed 1989–94, media ed 1994–97, public policy ed 1997–98, mgmnt ed 1998–2004; rector Exeter Coll Oxford 2004–14; non-exec dir Prolific Group 1988–89, memb Bd Alliance & Leicester Building Society (then Alliance & Leicester plc, now Santander) 1990–2004; chair ESRC 2001–07, pres BAAS 2005–06, chair Exec Ctee Inst for Fiscal Studies 2008–15 (memb Cncl 1995–2001); memb: Economics Ctee SSRC 1972–76, Newspaper Panel Monopolies Cmmn 1973–80, Cncl Royal Economic Soc 1980–85, Inquiry into Br Housing 1984–85, Sch Teachers' Review Body 1992–93, Scottish Cncl of Economic Advsrs 2007–12, Advsy Bd Fndn for Effective Governance Ukraine 2007–13; hon treas Nat Cncl for One Parent Families 1980–83, tstee Kennedy Meml Tst 1974–89, govr NIESR 1995–2001, chair Devpt Tst Nat History Museum 2015–, interim dir NIESR 2015–16, tstee Nat History Museum 2016–; visiting fell Nuffield Coll Oxford 2001–04, chair Ct Heriot-Watt Univ 2015–, Woodrow Wilson visiting fell 2014–; High Sheriff Gtr London 2004–05; hon fell: St Anne's Coll Oxford, St Peter's Coll Oxford, Exeter Coll Oxford; FRSE, life fell RSA 2006, hon fell BAAS 2006; *Books* Capital City (with Hamish McRae, 1971), The Second Great Crash (with Hamish McRae, 1973), The Guardian Guide to the Economy (1981), Changing Perceptions of Economic Policy (1981), The Second Guardian Guide to the Economy (1983), Guide to the Economy (1987), Costing the Earth (1991), Green Inc (1995), The Death of Distance (1997, latest edn 2001), The Company of the Future (2002); *Recreations* home life; *Clubs* Lansdowne; *Style*— Dame Frances McRae, DBE

McRAE, Hamish Malcolm Donald; s of Donald Barrington McRae (d 1980), and Barbara Ruth Louise (Jasmine), *née* Budd (d 2003); *b* 20 October 1943; *Educ* Fettes, Trinity Coll Dublin (MA); *m* 10 Sept 1971, Dame Frances McRae, DBE, qv, da of late Sir Alexander Kirkland (Alec) Cairncross, KCMG, FBA; 2 da (Isabella Frances b 28 July 1977, Alexandra Barbara Mary b 5 Dec 1979); *Career* grad trainee Liverpool Post 1966–67, asst ed then dep ed The Banker 1967–72, ed Euromoney 1972–75, fin ed The Guardian 1975–89, business and city ed The Independent 1989–91 (assoc ed 1991–); Harold Wincott Young Fin Journalist of the Year 1971, Harold Wincott Fin Journalist of the Year 1979, David Walt Prize 2005, Business and Finance Journalist of the Year British Press Awards 2006, Best Communicator Business Journalist of the Year Awards 2007; *Books* Capital City: London as a Financial Centre (with Frances Cairncross, 1973, current edn 1991), The Second Great Crash: how the oil crisis could destroy the world economy (with Nihon Keisai Shimbun, 1975), Japan's Role in the Emerging Global Securities Market (1985), The World In 2020: Power, Culture and Property – a vision of the future (1994), Wake-up Japan! (with Tadashi Nakamae, 2000), What Works: Success in Stressful Times (2010); *Recreations* skiing and walking; *Style*— Hamish McRae, Esq; ✉ The Independent, 2 Derry Street, London W8 5HF (✆ 020 7005 2635)

McRAE, Steven James; s of Phillip McRae, of Sydney, Australia, and Dianne, *née* Austin; *b* 19 December 1985, Sydney, Australia; *Educ* St Paul's GS Sydney, Royal Ballet Sch London; *m* Elizabeth Harrod; *Career* ballet dancer; first soloist Royal Ballet Co 2006– (joined 2004), princ dancer 2009; guest appearances incl American Ballet Theatre, Australian Ballet, Queensland Ballet, Tokyo Ballet, Hong Kong Ballet, Nat Ballet of Canada, Nat Ballet of Romania, Nat Ballet of Portugal and int galas in Russia, Japan, Europe, USA, S America and Australia; *Performances* incl: Romeo & Des Grieux (Manon), Colas (La Fille Mal Gardée), Rhapsody, Oberon (The Dream), Prince (Sleeping Beauty, Cinderella, Nutcracker, Swan Lake), James (La Sylphide), Basilio (Don Quixote), Solar (La Bayadere); created roles in works by Wheeldon, McGregor, Scarlett, Tuckett, Brandstrup, Ratmansky, Dawson and Kobborg; *Awards* RAD Solo Seal Award, Adeline Genée Gold Medal RAD 2002, Prix de Lausanne 2003, Emerging Male Artist (Classical) Critics' Circle Dance Awards 2006, Int Rising Star Award 2006, nomination Olivier

Awards 2007, Best Male Artist (Critics' Circle Awards) 2012, Young Australian of the Year 2014; *Books* Dancer in the Fas Lane, Ballet Hero Fantasy (Japanese Manga); *Style*— Steven McRae, Esq; ✉ Royal Opera House, Covent Garden, London WC2E 9DD (☎ 020 7240 1200, Twitter @_stevenmcrae)

MacRAE, Stuart Campbell; s of Iain Maclean MacRae, and Ola Vean, *née* Sutherland; *b* 12 August 1976; *Educ* Charleston Acad Inverness, Univ of Durham (BA), Guildhall Sch of Music and Drama (MMus); *Career* composer in assoc BBC Scottish Symphony Orch (SSO) 1999–2003; concerts incl: Philharmonia Orch Music of Today 2000, Edinburgh Int Festival 2001, BBC SSO 2003; featured composer Spannungen Kammermusikfest 2003; compositions incl: Boreraig 1994 (revised 1995), The Witch's Kiss 1997, Landscape and the Mind: Distance, Refuge 1997, Piano Sonata 1998, Sinfonia 1998–99, Stirling Choruses 1999, Sleep at the Feet of Daphne 1999, Piano Quintet 1999, One Man In His Time 2000–01, Violin Concerto (premiered BBC Proms) 2000–01, Ancrene Wisse (premiered Huddersfield Contemporary Music Festival) 2002, 32 for Piano 2002, String Quartet 2002, Interact 2002–03, Motus 2003, Hamartia 2003–04; recordings incl: The City Inside, Salm 42, Piano Sonata; *Awards* BBC/Lloyds Bank Young Composer Award (for Boreraig) 1996, BBC Symphony Orch Composer's Forum 1997, citations Royal Philharmonic Soc Award for Large Scale Composition 2002 (Violin Concerto) and 2003 (Ancrene Wisse); *Recreations* walking, climbing, golf; *Style*— Stuart MacRae, Esq; ✉ c/o Novello & Co, 8/9 Frith Street, London W1D 3BJ (☎ 020 7434 0066, e-mail fiona.southey@musicsales.co.uk)

MacRITCHIE, Kenneth; s of Norman MacRitchie, of Glasgow, and Daveen, *née* MacMillan; *b* 3 September 1956, Glasgow; *Educ* Univ of Glasgow (LLB), Univ of Aberdeen (BD), Univ of Manchester (MA), Oriel Coll Oxford; *m* Brenda, *née* Sinclair; 2 da (Rowena, Arabella), 1 s (Cameron); *Career* slr; ptnr Clifford Chance 1991–93, managing ptnr London office Milbank Tweed Hadley and McCloy 1993–96, ptnr Shearman & Sterling 1996–2011 (managing ptnr 2002–08), gen counsel UK Green Investments Dept of Business, Innovation and Skills 2011–12, head Counterparty Body Dept of Energy and Climate Change 2013–14; non-exec dir Oxford Analytica Ltd Anoa Capital SA; chair Christians in Sport Thames Valley Partnership; memb: Law Soc, Law Soc of Scotland; *Recreations* Music, Skiing, Walking; *Style*— Kenneth MacRitchie, Esq; ✉ (☎ 07768 643951, e-mail kenneth@kmconsult.uk.uk)

MACRORY, Henry David; s of Sir Patrick Arthur Macrory (d 1993), of Walton-on-the-Hill, Surrey, and Marjorie Elizabeth, *née* Lewis; *b* 15 December 1947; *Educ* Westminster, Univ of Kent (BA); *m* 1, 4 April 1972 (m dis 2005), Janet Carolyn, da of Henry James Potts; 2 da (Julia b 1978, Caroline b 1980), 1 s (David b 1985); m 2, 28 June 2011, Frances Mary Smee; *Career* reporter Kent Messenger 1969–72; Sunday Express 1972–: reporter 1972–79, political columnist 1979–83, asst ed 1983, exec ed 1990, acting ed 1991, dep ed 1993; Daily Star: political ed 1993, exec ed 1996–2000; conslt Cons Pty 2000–2005, head of media Cons Pty 2005–10, special advsr 10 Downing St 2010–11, dep political dir Cons Pty 2011; *Books* One Family (2014); *Style*— Henry Macrory, Esq

MACRORY, Prof Richard Brabazon; CBE (2000), Hon QC (2008); s of Sir Patrick Arthur Macrory (d 1993), of Walton-on-the-Hill, Surrey, and Marjorie Elizabeth, *née* Lewis (d 1997); *b* 30 March 1950; *Educ* Westminster, ChCh Oxford (MA); *m* 6 Oct 1979, Sarah Margaret, da of Bernard Christian Briant, CVO, of Aldeburgh, Suffolk; 2 s (Sam b 1980, Robert b 1983); *Career* called to the Bar Gray's Inn 1974 (bencher 2010); legal advsr FOE Ltd 1975–78; Imperial Coll Centre for Environmental Technol 1980–94 and 1996–98; dir Environmental Change Unit Univ of Oxford 1994–95, supernumerary fell Linacre Coll Oxford 1996–, prof of environmental law UCL 1999–; Fernand Braudel sr fell European Univ Inst Florence 2009, sr global res fell Nyu Univ 2010; ed Jl of Environmental Law 1988–2007; standing counsel Cncl for Protection of Rural England 1981–92, first chm UK Environmental Law Assoc 1986–88 (hon patron 2007–), hon vice-pres Environmental Protection UK 2007–11; specialist advsr House of Commons Select Ctee on the: Environment 1982–97, Environment, Transport and the Regions 1997–; specialist advsr House of Lords Select Ctee on EC (Environment Sub Ctee) 1992 and 1996, ldr Cabinet Office Review on Regulatory Sanctions 2005–06; chm Steering Ctee European Environmental Advsy Cncls 2001–02; memb: UK Nat Advsy Ctee on Eco-labelling 1990–91, Royal Cmmn on Environmental Pollution 1991–2003, Expert Panel UK Inter-Agency Ctee on Global Environmental Change 1995–96, Bd Environment Agency 1999–2004, Eco Advsy Bd General Electric 2006–10, Sullivan Ctee on Access to Environmental Justice 2007–08; hon pres Nat Soc for Clean Air and Environmental Protection 2004–05; rapporteur UK Nat Biotechnology Conference 1997; chm Merchant-Ivory Film Prodns Ltd 1992–2005, chm Lady Sale Prodns LLP 2009–; Elizabeth Haub Prize for Environmental Law 2014; *Books* Nuisance (1982), Water Law: Principles and Practice (1985), Water Act 1989 (1989), Bibliography of European Community Law (1995), Principles of European Environmental Law (ed, 2004), Reflections on 30 Years of EU Environmental Law (ed, 2005), Regulation, Enforcement and Governance of Environmental Law (2008, 2 edn 2014), Carbon Capture and Storage – Emerging Legal and Regulatory Issues (ed, 2011), National Courts and EU Environmental Law (ed, 2013), First Afghan War (2016); author of articles in learned jls; *Recreations* conjuring, board games, films; *Clubs* Atheneum, Polish Hearth, Two Brydges; *Style*— Prof Richard Macrory, CBE; ✉ Faculty of Laws, University College London, Bentham House, Endsleigh Gardens, London WC1H 0EY (☎ 020 7679 1543, e-mail r.macrory@ucl.ac.uk); Brick Court Chambers, 7–8 Essex Street, London WC2R 3LD (☎ 020 7379 3550, fax 020 7379 3558)

McSHANE, Ian David; s of Henry McShane, of Manchester, and Irene, *née* Cowley; *b* 29 September 1942; *Educ* Stretford GS Leeds, RADA; *m* 1 (m dis), Suzan Farmer; m 2 (m dis), Ruth Post; 1 da (Kate b 18 April 1970), 1 s (Morgan b 7 July 1974); m 3, 30 Aug 1980, Gwendolyn Marie, da of Claude Humble; *Career* actor; memb: BAFTA, AMPAS, Screen Actors' Guild, Directors' Guild; *Theatre* West End: The Glass Menagerie 1965, Loot 1966, The Promise 1967, The Witches Of Eastwick 2000; Los Angeles: As You Like It 1979, Betrayal 1983, Inadmissible Evidence 1985, The Homecoming (Broadway) 2008; *Television* incl: Jesus of Nazareth, Wuthering Heights, Whose Life Is It Anyway?, Evergreen, The Letter, Marco Polo, AD, War and Remembrance, Dallas, Lovejoy, Columbo, The Young Charlie Chaplin, Madson, Trust, Deadwood, Trust, Kings, Pillars of the Earth; *Films* incl: The Wild and the Willing 1962, The Battle of Britain 1968, If It's Tuesday This Must Be Belgium 1969, Villain 1971, Sitting Target 1972, Cheaper to Keep Her 1977, Exposed 1984, Torchlight 1986, Sexy Beast 2000, Nine Lives 2005, Hot Rod 2007, We Are Marshall 2007, Death Race 2008, The Seeker 2008, 44' Chest 2009, Case 39 2009, Pirates of the Caribbean: On Stranger Tides 2011; *Style*— Ian McShane, Esq; ✉ c/o Independent Talent Group, 40 Whitfield Street, London W1T 2RH (☎ 020 7636 6565, fax 020 7323 0101)

McSHARRY, Brendan John; OBE (2012, MBE 1994); s of Charles Patrick McSharry (d 1976), and Emily Annie, *née* Poundall (d 1983); *b* 25 July 1949; *Educ* St James RC HS, Univ of Wales (BA), Univ of Exeter (PGCE), Univ of Leeds (MA), Univ of Cambridge (DTEFL); *Partner* Daniel Feng Fulong (civil partnership); *Career* exec offr staff trg Dept of Employment 1972–74, English teacher Folk Univ Örebro/Karlstadt 1975–77; British Council: English teacher Milan 1977–79, asst dir of studies Milan 1979–81, asst dir of teacher trg studies 1982–85, dir Chiang Mai Thailand 1985–87, dir of studies Baghdad 1987–89, mangr and ODA project mangr English teaching in secdy schs Quito 1989–92, dir Milan 1992–95, subsequently dir Yemen, dir Palestinian Territories and dir Bahrain, dir Iraq, dir Nepal 2012–15, currently dir Palestine and The Levant; speaker on educnl methodology at various int confs; memb Int Sonnenberg Assoc of GB 1973; *Recreations* reading, running (completed Singapore marathon 1984 and Stra Milano half marathon 1981 and 1994); *Style*— Brendan McSharry, Esq, OBE

McTAGGART, Anne; MSP; *b* 30 January 1970; *Career* MSP (Lab) Glasgow 2011–16; *Style*— Ms Anne McTaggart, MSP

MACTAGGART, Fiona Margaret; PC (2015), MP; da of Sir Ian Mactaggart (d 1987), and Rosemary, *née* Williams (d 1992); *b* 12 September 1953; *Educ* KCL (BA), Goldsmiths Coll London (Postgrad Teaching Cert), Inst of Educn Univ of London (MA); *Career* vice-pres and nat sec NUS 1978–81, gen sec Jt Council for the Welfare of Immigrants 1982–86, primary sch teacher 1987–92, univ lectr 1992–97, MP (Lab) Slough 1997–; PPS to sec of state for Culture, Media and Sport 1997–2001, Parly under sec of state Home Office 2003–06; memb Wandsworth Cncl 1986–90 (ldr of opposition 1988–90); *Recreations* walking, talking, arts, watching TV; *Style*— The Rt Hon Fiona Mactaggart, MP; ✉ House of Commons, London SW1A 0AA (☎ 020 7219 3416, fax 020 7219 0989, e-mail mactaggartf@parliament.uk)

MACTAGGART, Sir John Auld; 4 Bt (UK 1938), of King's Park, City of Glasgow; s of Sir Ian (John) Auld Mactaggart, 3 Bt (d 1987), and Rosemary, *née* Williams (d 1992); *b* 21 January 1951; *Educ* Shrewsbury, Trinity Coll Cambridge (MA); *m* 1, 1977 (m dis 1990), Patricia, yst da of late Maj Harry Alastair Gordon, MC; m 2, 18 May 1991 (m dis 2014), Caroline, yst da of Eric Charles Williams, of Esher, Surrey; 2 da (Kinvara May b 18 Feb 1992, Aphra Hope b 8 July 1999), 2 s (Jack Auld b 11 Sept 1993, Sholto Auld b 16 Dec 1996); *Heir* s, Jack Mactaggart; *Career* chm Western Heritable Investment Company; *Clubs* Boodle's; *Style*— Sir John Mactaggart; ✉ Ardmore House, Ardtalla Estate, Islay, Argyll PA42 7EF; 2 Babmaes Street, London SW1Y 6HD (☎ 020 7491 2948, fax 020 7808 3971)

McTAGUE, (George) Peter; s of George McTague, and (Eileen) Norah, *née* McCarthy; *b* 22 February 1951; *Educ* St Michael's Coll Leeds, The GS Harrogate; *m* 19 April 1980, Hilary Anne, da of Bernard Cheshire; 3 s (Richard William b 7 May 1982, Nicholas Michael b 22 Aug 1984, Patrick George b 15 Jan 1988); *Career* chain store mgmnt and personnel appts (latterly trg offr) The Littlewoods Organisation Ltd 1970–77; Stylo plc: gen mangr then commercial dir Stylo Barratt Shoes Ltd 1977–83, md Pennywise Discount Stores 1983–85; ops and property dir Comet Group plc 1985–91, dir Merry Hill Centre Mountleigh Group plc 1991–92, md NORWEB Retail 1992–96, devpt dir Comet Group plc 2001– (sales and property dir 1996–2001); conslt and property developer McTague Assocs 2001–03, non-exec dir PRG Powerhouse Ltd 2003–04, retail conslt and property developer 2004–; *Style*— Peter McTague, Esq; ✉ 3 Park Parade, Harrogate, North Yorkshire HG1 5AE

McTEER, Janet; OBE (2008); da of Alan McTeer, and Jean McTeer; *b* 5 August 1961; *Educ* Queen Anne GS for Girls York, RADA (Bancroft Gold Medal); *Career* actress; *Theatre* incl: The Grace of Mary Traverse (Royal Court) 1986, As You Like It, The Three Sisters, Cymbeline (all Manchester Royal Exchange) 1988–90, Much Ado About Nothing (Queen's) 1995, Uncle Vanya (RNT) 1995, Simpatico (Royal Court) 1996, A Doll's House (London and Broadway) 1997 (Olivier, Evening Standard and Tony Awards for Best Actress), The Duchess of Malfi (RNT), Mary Stuart (Donmar and West End) 2005, God of Carnage 2008; *Television* incl: The Governor (series I & II), Portrait of a Marriage, Precious Bane, Daphne, 5 Days, Sense & Sensibility; *Film* Tumbleweeds (Oscar nominated), King is Alive, Songcatcher, The Intended (also co-writer), Churchill at War; *Recreations* gardens, writing, cooking, people, life, love; *Style*— Ms Janet McTeer, OBE

McTIGHE, (Robert) Michael (Mike); s of late Glen McTighe, and Mary, *née* Saunders (d 2013); *b* 17 October 1953, West Midlands; *Educ* Stourbridge GS, UCL (BSc); 18 Aug 2013 Ms Terry Vega; 1 da (Stephanie Martha b 8 June 1984), 2 s (Henry Marcus b 3 April 1987, William Michael b 17 Sept 1992); *Career* GEC Machines Ltd 1975–76, Thorn EMI plc 1976–80; General Electric: UK manufacturing dir GE Medical Systems 1986–88, ultrasound and nuclear medicine business mangr GE-CGR 1988–90; European Cellular Subscriber Div Motorola Inc: gen mangr UK manufacturing ops 1990–91, dir European manufacturing ops 1991–92, gen mangr OEM markets 1992–93, gen mangr Area III 1993–94; dir of ops Asia Pacific Cellular Subscriber Div Motorola Inc 1994–95; Philips Electronics NV: md Philips Consumer Communications 1995–97, pres and chief exec Philips Consumer Communications LP 1997–98; self-employed conslt to cos incl Siemens AG 1998–99; Cable and Wireless plc: exec dir and chief exec global ops 1999–2001, exec dir strategy and business devpt 2001; chm and chief exec Carrier 1 International SA 2001–02; postal services cmmr 2010–11; former chm: Pace plc, Phyworks Ltd, Frontier Silicon Holdings Ltd, JJB Sports plc 2010–12, Volex Gp plc until 2013; chm Nujira Ltd until 2015; currently chm: WYG Gp plc (formerly White Young Green plc), Jerrold Hldgs Ltd 2010–, Gortmullan Hldgs Ltd (formerly Quinn Gp Holdco Ltd) 2012–, Arran Isle Ltd chm 2013–; special advsr Gen Atlantic LLP until 2012, sr ind dir Betfair Ltd until 2014; memb Bd Ofcom 2007–15; *Recreations* skiing, scuba diving, gardening; *Style*— Mike McTighe, Esq; ✉ Flat 1, 3 Eaton Place, London SW1X 8BN (☎ 020 7235 7223); Danesbury House, 4 Waverley Grove, Solihull, West Midlands B91 1NP (☎ 0121 704 1971); 11 Wilrich Glen Road, Morristown, New Jersey, 07960, USA (☎ +1 973 898 9050, mobile 07957 806158, e-mail mike@mctighe.net)

MACUR, Rt Hon Lady Justice; Rt Hon Dame Julia Wendy Macur; DBE (2005), PC (2013); da of Boleslaw Macur, and Betsy May Macur; *b* 17 April 1957; *Educ* Univ of Sheffield (LLB); *m* 1981; 2 s (Ben b 31 Dec 1991, Nicholas b 25 Jan 1995); *Career* called to the Bar Lincoln's Inn 1979; practising barr on Midland & Oxford Circuit 1979–2005, QC 1998, recorder of the Crown Court 1999–2005, judge of the High Court of Justice (Family Div) 2005–13, a Lady Justice of the Court of Appeal 2013–; *Style*— The Rt Hon Lady Justice Macur, DBE; ✉ c/o Royal Courts of Justice, Strand, London WC2A 2LL

McVAY, John Charles; s of John McVay, of Edinburgh, and Ruth, *née* Thomson; *Educ* Firhill Secdy Sch; *Partner* Ruth Buckingham; 3 s (Aidan McVay b 7 July 1996, Jamie McVay b 9 Feb 1998, Callum McVay b 22 Jan 2001); *Career* ind prodr 1983–85 and 1994–95; training mangr Edinburgh Video Training Co (EVTC) 1986–93; dir: Scottish Training Tst 1993–97, training Scottish Screen 1997–98, Research Centre for TV 1998–2001; chief exec Pact 2001–; fndr Edinburgh Video Course 1985; dir: Skillset, Independent Production Training Fund (IPTF); govr Nat Film Sch; FRTS 2001; *Recreations* fishing, gardening, reading; *Style*— John McVay, Esq; ✉ e-mail john@pact.co.uk

McVEY, Rt Hon Esther; PC (2014); da of James McVey, of Liverpool, and Barbara, *née* Corless; *b* 24 October 1967, Liverpool; *Educ* Belvedere Acad Liverpool, Queen Mary & Westfield Univ London (LLB), City Univ London, Liverpool John Moores Univ (MSc); *Career* dir J G McVey & Co (family construction business) 2000–06, md Making It (UK) Ltd 2002–10, fndr Winning Women 2003–10, MP (Cons) Wirral W 2010–15, min for disabled people and parly under sec of state Dept of Work and Pensions 2012–13, min for employment 2013–15; broadcaster: BBC, Channel 4, ITV; fndr If Chloe Can charity 2013; patron: Wirral Holistic Cancer Care, Full of Life, Wirral Fund for Children with Special Needs; North of England Excellence Award 2009 (for MSc on corporate governance); *Publications* If Chloe Can (2010), You Can (2013), If Chloe Can Too (2016), If Chloe Can in Politics (2016); *Style*— The Rt Hon Esther McVey; ✉ e-mail esther@esthermcvey.com

McVIE, Prof (John) Gordon; s of John McVie, of Haddington, Lothian, and Lindsaye, *née* Mair; *b* 13 January 1945, Glasgow; *Educ* Royal HS Edinburgh, Univ of Edinburgh (BSc, MB ChB, MD, Gunning Victoria Jubilee Prize in Pathology); *m* 1, 1967 (m dis 1996), Evelyn Strang; 3 s (Malcolm b 24 June 1971, Tammas b 7 Aug 1975, Douglas b 31 Jan

M

1978); m 2, 1998, Claudia Burke; *Career* house offr Royal Hosp for Sick Children and Royal Infirmary Edinburgh 1969–70; Univ of Edinburgh: MRC fell Depts of Pathology and Therapeutics 1970–71, temp lectr in Therapeutics 1971–73, lectr in Therapeutics 1973–76; hon sr registrar Lothian Health Bd 1971–76, CRC sr lectr in clinical oncology Univ of Glasgow 1976–80, hon conslt in med oncology Gtr Glasgow Health Bd 1976–80, clinical research dir The Netherlands Cancer Inst Amersterdam 1984–89 (head Clinical Research Unit, conslt physician and chm Div of Experimental Oncology 1980–84), DG Cancer Research Campaign London 1996–2002 (dir Scientific Dept 1989–96), DG Cancer Research UK 2002, dir Cancer Intelligence 2002–; chm ORIL Adelaide, chm Proton Ptnrs Int Ltd 2015–; hon conslt in Oncology Velindre Cancer Centre Cardiff; sr conslt European Inst of Oncology Milan 2003–15; visiting prof: Univ of Sydney NSW Aust 1983, Br Postgrad Med Fedn Univ of London 1990–96, Univ of Glasgow 1996–, Univ of Wales 2004–, Div of Cancer Studies KCL 2014–, Univ of Milan 2014–; clinical advsr Inst of Molecular Oncology Milan 2015–; visiting fell: Dept of Med Oncology Univ of Paris 1978, Netherlands Cancer Inst 1979; conslt in carcinogenesis of cytostatic drugs Int Agency for Research in Cancer WHO Lyon 1980, chm Int Union Against Cancer (UICC) Fellowships Prog 1990–, pres Euro Orgn for Research and Treatment of Cancer 1994–97 (memb Exec Ctee and Bd 1992–); ed-in-chief Euro Cancer News 1987–96, first Euro ed Jl of the National Cancer Inst 1994–, founding ed ecancermedicalscience.com 2007; author of numerous articles in scientific jls; Honeyman Gillespie lectr in oncology 1977; Hon DSc: Univ of Abertay Dundee 1996, Univ of Nottingham 1997, Univ of Portsmouth 1999, Edinburgh Napier Univ 2002, Univ of Ghent Belgium 2005, Univ of Bath 2014; FRCPEd, FRCPGlas, FRCP, FMedSci, FRCSEd; *Books* Cancer Assessment and Monitoring (with T Symington, 1979), Evaluation or Carcinogenic Risk of Chemicals to Man – Vol 26: Antineoplastic and Immunosuppressive Drugs (1981), Autologous Bone Marrow Transplantation and Solid Tumours (with I E Smith, 1984), Microspheres and Drug Therapy (with S S Davis, 1984), Clinical and Experimental Pathology and Biology of Lung Cancer (with D Carney, 1985); also author of book chapters and over 300 peer-reviewed articles; *Recreations* opera, music in general, walking, rugby, wine, cooking, family; *Clubs* IOD; *Style*— Prof Gordon McVie; ✉ Cancer Intelligence, 154 Cheltenham Road, Bristol BS6 5RL (☎ 0117 909 4608, fax 0117 909 4630, e-mail info@cancerintelligence.com); Scientific Directorate, Institute of Molecular Oncology, Via Adamello 16, 20139 Milan, Italy (☎ 0039 02 5748 9816, mobile 07785 325558, e-mail gordon@ecancer.org, website www.ecancer.eu); Division of Cancer Studies, Kings College London, Room 2.20A, New Hunt's House, Guy's Campus, London SE1 1UL (e-mail gordon.mcvie@kcl.ac.uk)

McWHIRTER, Prof John Graham; s of Francis David McWhirter (d 1982), of Newry, Co Down, and Elizabeth, *née* Martin (d 1984); *b* 28 March 1949; *Educ* Newry HS, Queen's Univ Belfast (fndn scholar, BSc, Purser research student, PhD); *m* 17 Aug 1973, Avesia Vivianne Wolfe; 1 da (Lindsey Joy b 17 Jan 1977), 1 s (Colin Francis b 13 Nov 1979); *Career* Defence Evaluation and Research Agency (DERA) Malvern: higher scientific offr 1973–77, sr scientific offr 1977–80, princ scientific offr 1980–86, sr princ scientific offr 1986–96, sr fell Signal Processing Gp 1996–2001; with Qinetiq Ltd 2001–07; visiting prof: Electrical Engrg Dept Queen's Univ Belfast 1986–, Sch of Engrg Univ of Wales Cardiff 1997–; distinguished research prof Univ of Cardiff 2007–; chm and proceedings ed IMA Int Conf on Mathematics in Signal Processing 1988, 1992, 1996, 2000, 2004, 2006 and 2008; pres IMA 2002–03 (vice-pres 1998–99), fndr memb Signal Processing Sub Gp IEE 1987–92, Euro Program chm Int Conf on Systolic Arrays 1989, memb IT Panel UK Technol Foresight Programme 1994, Euro Program chm Int Symposium on Computer Arithmetic IEEE 1995, memb EPSRC Peer Review Coll for IT (Communications) 1995–; author of over 200 research papers, inventor and co-inventor 30 UK, European, US and Canadian patents; Hon DSc: Queen's Univ Belfast 2000, Univ of Edinburgh 2002; CMath, FIMA 1988, FIEE 1994, FREng 1996, FRS 1999 (memb Cncl 2010–12), FInstP 1999; *Awards* Northern Ireland Info Technol Award Br Computer Soc (jtly with J V McCanny) 1987, J J Thomson Premium IEE (jtly) 1990, J J Thomson Medal IEE (for research on systolic arrays) 1994; *Recreations* swimming for exercise, building and flying radio controlled model gliders, walking, cycling for pleasure; *Clubs* Malvern Soaring Association; *Style*— Prof John McWhirter, FRS, FREng; ✉ School of Engineering, Cardiff University, Queen's Building, The Parade, Cardiff CF24 3AA (☎ 02920 870627, fax 02920 874716, e-mail mcwhirterjg@cardiff.ac.uk or mcwhirter@physics.org)

McWILLIAM, Sir Michael Douglas; KCMG (1996); s of Douglas McWilliam (d 1969), of Oakridge Lynch, Glos, and Margaret, *née* Leach (d 1992); *b* 21 June 1933; *Educ* Cheltenham Coll, Oriel Coll Oxford (MA), Nuffield Coll Oxford (BLitt); *m* 1, 1960, Ruth, da of Dr Friedrich Arnstein (d 2009); 2 s (Robert b 1962, Martin b 1964); m 2, 2010, Thalia Stone, da of Lt Col J L M B Gough; *Career* Treasy Kenya 1958–62, Samuel Montagu & Co 1962–66; The Standard Bank (subseq Standard Chartered Bank): joined 1966, a gen mangr 1973, gp md 1983–88; dir Sch of Oriental and African Studies Univ of London 1989–96; chm: Centre for Study of African Economies Oxford 1997–2012, Br Empire and Cwlth Museum 2006–08 (dep chm 2003–06), Cheltenham Festivals 2007–11 (dep chm 2006); memb Bd Cwlth Devpt Corp 1990–97, hon vice-pres Royal African Soc 1996– (memb Cncl 1979–91, vice-chm 1991–96, chm 1996–2004), vice-pres Royal Cwlth Soc 2003– (dep chm 1982–91, chm 1996–2002 and 2009); pres Cncl Cheltenham Coll 1988–92 (memb 1977–92); tstee David Vaisey Tst 2016–; memb Ct Hon Co of Glos 2013; hon fell SOAS 1997, hon fell Oriel Coll Oxford 2012; *Publications* The Development Business: A History of the Commonwealth Development Corporation (2001); *Clubs* The New Club (Cheltenham); *Style*— Sir Michael McWilliam, KCMG; ✉ Yew Tree Farm, Brimpsfield, Gloucestershire GL4 8LD (☎ 01452 862614)

MADDEN, Andrew John; s of Dennis Madden, and Jennifer, *née* Brown; *b* 29 October 1962, Birmingham; *Educ* Woodhouse Comp Sch Tamworth, Univ of Birmingham (LLB), Coll of Law Chester; *m* 15 Oct 1988, Vivienne, *née* Wakelam; 2 s (Scott b 8 July 1994, Richard b 14 March 2001); *Career* slr; trainee slr Duggan Lea & Co 1985–87, asst, assoc then ptnr Edge & Ellison 1987–96, ptnr Gateley (formerly HBJ Gateley Wareing) 1996–; non-exec dir Good Hope Hosp NHS Tst 2004–07, chair Birmingham Fundraising Ctee Charis; govr Midland Met Coll 2010–; memb Law Soc 1987; *Recreations* football (Birmingham City), cricket, ballet, golf; *Style*— Andrew Madden, Esq; ✉ Gateley plc, One Eleven, Edmund Street, Birmingham B3 2HJ (☎ 0121 234 0034)

MADDEN, Anne; *Educ* Wychwood Sch Oxford, Chelsea Sch of Art; *m* Louis le Brocquy; 2 s; *Career* artist; solo exhibitions: Leicester Galleries London 1959, 1961 and 1967, Dawson Gallery Dublin 1960, 1964, 1968, 1970 and 1974, New Gallery Belfast 1964, Oxford Gallery Oxford 1970, Gimpel Weitzenhoffer Gallery NY 1970, New Art Centre 1970, 1972, 1974, 1978 and 1990, Demarco Gallery Edinburgh 1971, Ulster Museum Belfast 1974, Galerie Darthea Speyer Paris 1976 and 1979, Galerie Le Dessin Paris 1978 and 1980, The Arts Cncl of NI Belfast 1979, Taylor Galleries Dublin 1979, 1982 and 1987, Fondation Maeght Saint-Paul France 1983, The Bank of Ireland Dublin 1984, Wexford Arts Centre Ireland 1984, Galerie Maeght Barcelona 1985, Galerie Joachim Becker Cannes 1985, Armstrong Gallery NY 1986, Galerie Jeanne Bucher Paris 1989, New Art Centre London 1990, The Kerlin Gallery Dublin 1990 and 1992, R H A Gallagher Gallery Dublin 1991, Crawford Municipal Gallery Cork 1992, Galerie Sapone 1993, The Kerlin Gallery Dublin 1995, Galerie Maeght Paris 1996, Château de Tours Municipal Art Gallery France 1997, Hugh Lane Municipal Gallery of Modern Art Dublin 1997, Butler Gallery Kilkenny 1998, Centre International d'Art Contemporain Carros 1998, Museum of Contemporary Art Oaxaza 2000, Taylor Galleries Dublin 2002, Gallery One Kilkenny 2003, New Art Centre Roche Court 2005, Centre Culturel Irlandais Paris 2005, Irish Museum of Modern Art Retrospective 2007, Flowers Gallery London 2009, Taylor Galleries Dublin 2010 and 2014; name given to Salle d'Honneur at Int Contemporary Arts Centre Carros, vaulted ceiling painting Empyrius inaugurated following year; group exhibitions: The Mirror and the Square (Burlington Galleries London) 1951, The Irish Exhibition of Living Art (Dublin) 1952, Art '65 (American Express Pavilion NY World Fair) 1965, Quatrième Biennale de Paris (representing Ireland) 1965, Modern Irish Painters (CIE Ulster Museum Belfast) 1966, Modern Irish Painting (Helsinki, Gothenburg, Norrköping, Stockholm) 1969, An Oireachtas Dublin 1970 and 1988, Les Abstractions Autour des Années 1970–80, The 8th International Biennial Exhibition of Prints Tokyo 1973, Irish Directions (touring) 1974–75, ICA Boston 1974–75, Salon de Montrouge (Paris) 1982, ROSC 84 (Dublin) 1984, Centre National d'Art Contemporain (CNAC) Nice 1985, A Propos de Dessin (Galerie Adrian Maeght Paris) 1987, Fonds Regional d'Art Contemporain Provence 1989, Modern Masters (Musée Jacquemart André Paris) 1989, The National Self Portrait Collection (Crawford Municipal Art Gallery Cork and Nat Gallery Dublin) 1990, Musée d'Art Moderne et d'Art Contemporain (MAMAC) Nice 1990; public collections possessing work incl: Contemporary Arts Society London, The Gulbenkian Fndn Portugal, The Arts Council of Ireland, The Arts Council of NI, The Arts Council of GB, Dublin City Gallery – The Hugh Lane, The J H Hirshhorn Museum and Sculpture Garden Washington DC, Contemporary Irish Arts Society, Musée d'Art Moderne de la Ville de Paris, La Fondation Maeght France, Musée Picasso Antibes, Foundation Van Gogh Arles France, Musée d'Art Moderne et d'Art Contemporain, Neuberger Museum New York, Smurfitt Foundation Dublin, Ulster Museum Belfast, Irish Museum of Modern Art Dublin, Limerick City Art Gallery Limerick 1991; subject of 60 min documentary Anne Madden Artist and Muse 2005; memb Aosdána; Hon LLD UCD 2005; Officier de l'Ordre des Arts et des Lettres 2008; *Books* Louis le Brocquy: Seeing His Way (1993), Anne Madden Painting and Reality: Irish Museum of Modern Art (2010); *Style*— Ms Anne Madden; ✉ e-mail info@anne-madden.com, website www.anne-madden.com

MADDEN, Deirdre; *b* 20 August 1960; *Educ* St Mary's GS Co Derry, Trinity Coll Dublin (BA), UEA (MA); *m* 1987, Harry Clifton; *Career* writer; fell Atelierhaus Worpswede 1993–94, writer in residence UC Cork 1994–95, writer fell Trinity Coll Dublin 1996–97; memb Aosdána 1997; *Awards* Hennessy Award for short fiction 1979, Arts Cncl of NI literature bursary 1987 and 1991, Rooney Prize for Irish Literature 1987, Somerset Maugham Award 1989, Soc of Authors Award 1992, Hawthornden fellowship 1993, Kerry Book of the Year Award 1997, shortlisted Orange Prize 1997, Ellis Dillon Award 2006, shortlisted Orange Prize 2009; *Books* Hidden Symptoms (1988), The Birds of the Innocent Wood (1988), Remembering Light and Stone (1992), Nothing is Black (1994), One by One in the Darkness (1996), Authenticity (2002), Snakes' Elbows (2005), Thanks for Telling Me, Emily (2007), Molly Fox's Birthday (2008), Jasper and the Green Marvel (2011), Time Present and Time Past (2013), All Over Irelands: New Irish Short Stories (ed, 2015); *Style*— Ms Deirdre Madden; ✉ c/o United Agents, 12–26 Lexington Street, London W1F 0LE (☎ 020 3214 0800, fax 020 3214 0801, website www.unitedagents.co.uk)

MADDEN, John Philip; s of William John Raleigh Madden, and Jean Elizabeth Hunt Mills; *b* 8 April 1949; *Educ* Clifton, Sidney Sussex Coll Cambridge (MA); *m* 1975, Penelope Jane, *née* Abrahams; *Career* film dir; artistic dir Oxford and Cambridge Shakespeare Co 1970–73, assoc prof Yale Sch of Drama 1977–80; hon fell Sidney Sussex Coll Cambridge 2000; Hon DLitt Univ of Portsmouth 2006; *Theatre* Wings, The Bundle, Measure for Measure, The Suicide, Terry by Terry, Grownups, Beyond Therapy, Salonika, Cinders, Between East and West, An American Comedy, Ivanov, Mrs Warren's Profession, Caritas, Proof; *Television* Poppyland, A Wreath of Roses, Sherlock Holmes, After the War, Widowmaker, Inspector Morse (four films), Prime Suspect: The Lost Child, Meat, Truth or Dare (BAFTA Scotland Award Best Single Drama 1997); *Radio* US Nat Public Radio: Wings (Prix Italia 1978), Star Wars, The Empire Strikes Back, Return of the Jedi; *Film* Ethan Frome 1992, Golden Gate 1994, Mrs Brown 1997, Shakespeare in Love 1998, Captain Corelli's Mandolin 2001, Proof 2005, Killshot 2006, The Debt 2009, The Best Exotic Marigold Hotel 2011; *Recreations* cooking, walking, sailing; *Style*— John Madden, Esq; ✉ c/o Jenne Casarotto, Casarotto Ramsay and Associates Ltd, Waverley House, 7–12 Noel Street, London W1F 8GQ

MADDEN, Nicholas Paul; s of Dr (Cyril) Paul Madden (d 1958), of Romford, Essex, and Barbara Joan, *née* Sykes (d 2003); *b* 12 June 1950; *Educ* Haileybury, Brasenose Coll Oxford (MA, BM BCh); *m* 11 Sept 1982, Su-Anna Margaret Boddy, *qv*; 1 s (Christopher Paul b 6 Feb 1987), 1 da (Katherine Anna b 15 Sept 1988); *Career* temporary lectr in anatomy Bart's Med Coll 1977–78, registrar in gen surgery and urology Luton and Dunstable Hosp 1980–82, registrar in paediatric surgery and urology Alder Hey Children's Hosp Liverpool 1982–85, res fell in paediatric surgery Inst of Child Health 1985–87, sr registrar paediatric surgn Leeds General Infirmary and St James's Univ Hosp Leeds 1987–91; conslt paediatric surgn/urologist: Chelsea and Westminster Hosp 1991–2014 (ret), St Mary's Hosp 1992–2013 (ret); BAPS Prize for Research 1987; memb: RSM 1991, British Assoc of Paediatric Surgns 1992 (prize 1987), European Soc for Paediatric Urology (ESPU) 1997, Br Assoc of Paediatric Urologists (BAPU) 1997 (pres 2008–10); vice-chair Paediatric Continence Forum 2014–; FRCS 1980; author of numerous pubns in med jls; *Recreations* skiing, swimming, watching cricket, golf and gardening; *Style*— Nicholas Madden; ✉ 15 Bridgefield Road, Sutton, Surrey SM1 2DG (e-mail nicholas.madden@nhs.net)

MADDEN, HE Paul Damian; CMG (2013); s of Antony Angus Thomas Madden, of Devon, and Doris May, *née* Brewer; *b* 25 April 1959, Honiton, Devon; *Educ* Marist Convent Sch Ottery St Mary, King's Sch Ottery St Mary, Gonville & Caius Coll Cambridge (MA), Univ of Durham Business Sch (MBA); *m* 30 Sept 1989, Sarah Pauline, *née* Thomas; 2 s (Sebastian Xavier Francis b 2 Oct 1991, Rupert Christian St John b 27 Dec 1992), 1 da (Francesca Imogen Zara b 7 June 1996); *Career* diplomat; DTI: joined 1980, private sec to Rt Hon David Trippier, MP (as Min for Small Business) 1984–85, private sec to Rt Hon Michael Howard, MP (as Min for Corporate Affrs) 1985–86, head of Japan desk 1986–87; joined FCO 1987, Japanese language trg SOAS Univ of London 1987–88, first sec Tokyo 1989–92, Environment, Science and Energy Dept FCO 1992–94, EU Dept (external) FCO 1994–96, first sec Washington DC 1996–2000, dep high cmmr Singapore 2000–03, head Public Diplomacy Policy Dept FCO 2003–04, md UK Trade and Investment 2004–06, high cmmr to Singapore 2007–11, high cmmr to Australia 2011–15, ambass to Japan 2017–; writer Alternate Serve (play performed at Sydney Short and Sweet Festival 2015); FRGS; *Publications* Raffles: Lessons in Business Leadership (2003); *Recreations* travel, family; *Clubs* Tanglin (Singapore), Australian (Sydney); *Style*— HE Mr Paul Madden, CMG; ✉ c/o FCO, King Charles Street, London SW1A 2AH

MADDERS, Justin; MP; *b* 22 November 1972, Manchester; *Educ* Univ of Sheffield; *m* Nicole Meardon; *Career* slr 1998–2015; cncllr Ellesmere Port and Neston BC 1998–2009 (ldr 2007–09), cncllr Cheshire W and Chester Cncl 2009–15 (ldr of the oppn 2011–14), MP (Lab) Ellesmere Port and Neston 2015–; *Recreations* football; *Style*— Justin Madders, Esq, MP; ✉ House of Commons, London SW1A 0AA (☎ 020 7219 6584, e-mail justin.madders.mp@parliament.uk, website www.justinmadders.com, Twitter @justinmadders)

MADDICOTT, Dr John Robert Lewendon; s of Robert Maddicott (d 1990), and Barbara, *née* Lewendon (d 1996); *b* 22 July 1943; *Educ* Cheltenham GS, King Edward's Sch Bath, Worcester Coll Oxford (MA, DPhil); *m* 1965, Hilary, da of Thomas Owen; 2 da (Philippa b 1968, Sarah b 1972); *Career* asst lectr Univ of Manchester 1967–69, fell and tutor in modern history Exeter Coll Oxford 1969–2006 (sub-rector 1988–90, emeritus fell 2006–); visiting prof Univ of South Carolina 1983, Raleigh lectr Br Acad 2001, Ford lectr British History Univ of Oxford 2004; jt ed English Historical Review 1990–2000; FRHistS, FSA, FBA 1996; *Books* Thomas of Lancaster, 1307–1322 (1972), The English Peasantry and the Demands of the Crown, 1294–1341 (1975), Law and Lordship: Royal Justices as Retainers in Thirteenth and Fourteenth Century England (1978), Simon de Montfort (1994), The Origins of the English Parliament 924–1327 (2010), Founders and Fellowship: The Early History of Exeter College, Oxford, 1314–1592 (2014); *Recreations* hill walking, book collecting, poetry; *Style*— Dr John Maddicott, FSA, FBA; ✉ Exeter College, Oxford OX1 3DP (fax 01865 279630)

MADDISON, Prof Peter John; s of John Maddison, of London, and Renée, *née* Le Mesurier; *b* 12 December 1945; *Educ* St Albans Sch, Pembroke Coll Cambridge, St Bartholomew's Med Sch (MA, MB BChir, MD); *m* 17 Feb 1968, Merle Chadburn, da of late Denby Bamford, CBE, of Little Barrow, Cheshire; 1 s (Christopher); *Career* fell in rheumatology and immunology SUNY Buffalo 1974–77, asst prof of med 1977–79, conslt rheumatologist Royal Nat Hosp for Rheumatic Diseases Bath 1979–88; Univ of Bath: prof of bone and joint med 1988–96, dean Sch of Postgraduate Med 1989–95; chm and res dir Bath Inst of Rheumatic Diseases until 1996, res and educn dir Royal Nat Hosp for Rheumatic Diseases 1991–92; conslt rheumatologist NW Wales NHS Tst 1996–2010; prof of joint and muscle disorders Bangor Univ 1999–2010 (prof emeritus 2010–), dir Bangor Inst for Clinical and Translational Research 2008–10; Greenberg scholar Oklahoma Med Res Fndn 1992–93, Heberden Roundsman British Soc for Rheumatology 1994; author of over 275 scientific articles, reviews and chapters; med sec Arthritis and Rheumatism Cncl 1990–93, chm Wessex R&D Grants Ctee 1993–96, memb Scientific Bd Nat Osteoporosis Soc, memb Cncl British Soc of Rheumatology 2003–06 (also chair Heberden Ctee), memb Educn Cmmn Arthritis Research Campaign 1999–2002; opened Peter Maddison Rheumatology Centre Llandudno Hosp 2013; FRCP 1986; *Books* Rheumatological Medicine (with P A Dieppe, M Doherty and D G Macfarlane, 1985), The Skin In Rheumatic Diseases (with C L Lovell and G Campion, 1989), Rheumatology Examination and Injection Techniques (with M Doherty, J D Perry, C W Hutton and B L Hazelman, 1992), Oxford Textbook of Rheumatology (ed with D A Isenberg, P Woo and D N Glass, 1993, 3 edn 2005); *Recreations* cooking, music, golf; *Style*— Prof Peter Maddison; ✉ Bryn Selar, Glan Conwy, Colwyn Bay LL28 5SL (☎ 01492 572126)

MADDOCK, Baroness (Life Peer UK 1997), of Christchurch in the County of Dorset; Diana Maddock; *b* 19 May 1945; *Educ* Brockenhurst GS, Shenstone Teacher Trg Coll, Portsmouth Poly; *m* 1, 1966, Robert Frank Maddock; m 2, 2001, Rt Hon Alan Beith, MP , *qv*; *Career* teacher Southampton 1966–69 and 1972–73, ESL teacher Extra Mural Dept Stockholm Univ 1969–72, Bournemouth Anglo Continental Sch of English 1973–76, city cncllr Southampton 1984–93; MP (Lib Dem) Christchurch 1993–97; former Lib Dem spokesperson on: housing, the family and women's issues; chair Br-Swedish All-Pty Gp, jt chair All-Pty Parly Gp for Building Societies and Financial Mutuals; vice-chair All-Pty Gp for the Roofing Industry, vice-chair All-Pty Univ Gp; former vice-chm All-Pty Parly: Warm Houses Gp, Homelessness and Housing Need Gp; sec Assoc Parly Renewable and Sustainable Energy Gp; housing spokesperson Lib Dems in House of Lords 1997–2004, pres Lib Dems 1998–2000, cncllr Northumberland 2005–08, cncllr Berwick-upon-Tweed Borough Cncl 2007–09, vice-pres Local Govt Assoc; memb Ctee on Standards in Public Life 2003–09; pres Nat Home Improvement Cncl, vice-pres Nat Energy Action, pres The Sustainable Energy Assoc (formerly Micropower Cncl); pres Anglo Swedish Soc; hon memb Chartered Inst of Housing; *Recreations* travel, music and reading; *Clubs* National Liberal, Northern Counties; *Style*— The Rt Hon Baroness Maddock; ✉ House of Lords, London SW1A 0PW

MADDOX, Brenda Power Murphy (Lady Maddox); da of Dr Brendan W Murphy, and Edith Giamperoli; *b* 24 February 1932; *Educ* Bridgewater HS MA, Radcliffe Coll (cum laude); *m* 1960, Sir John Maddox (d 2009); 1 s, 1 da, 1 step s, 1 step da; *Career* author and journalist; Patriot Ledger Quincy MA 1957–59, Reuters Ltd 1959–1960, The Economist 1962–72 and 1975–85 (latterly as Br ed then home affrs ed), media columnist Daily Telegraph 1987–1994, media columnist The Times 1994–97; vice-pres The Hay Festival, hon sec Kensington Soc 2012–; memb: Br Assoc of Science Writers (chm 1983–4), Broadcasting Press Guild (chm 1993–4); former non-exec dir London Broadcasting Co; former memb: UK Nat Cmmn for UNESCO, Mgmnt Ctee Soc of Authors, Royal Soc, Science in Society Ctee; Hon Phi Beta Kappa Harvard Univ 1978, Hon Dr Finch Univ 2004, Hon Dr Univ of Glamorgan 2005; FRSL 1994 (memb Cncl); *Publications* Beyond Babel: New Directions in Communications (1972), The Half-Parent (1975), Who's Afraid of Elizabeth Taylor? (biography, 1977), The Marrying Kind (1981), Nora: the Life of Mrs James Joyce (1988, LA Times Biography Prize 1988, Br Silver PEN Award 1989, Prix du Meilleur Livre Etranger 1990, adapted as film Nora 2000), D H Lawrence: The Married Man (1994, Whitbread Biography Award 1994), George's Ghosts: The Secret Life of W B Yeats (biography, 1999), Rosalind Franklin: the Dark Lady of DNA (2001, Marsh Biography Prize 2001, LA Times Science Prize 2002), Maggie: The First Lady (2003), Freud's Wizard: The Enigma of Ernest Jones (2006), George Eliot: Novelist, Lover, Wife (2009); author of reviews and articles for newspapers and magazines in GB and USA; *Recreations* gardening, cooking, exploring mid-Wales; *Clubs* Athenaeum; *Style*— Brenda Maddox; ✉ c/o A P Watt, 20 John Street, London WC1N 2DR

MADDOX, Bronwen Maria; da of John R Maddox (d 2009), and Brenda, *née* Murphy; *b* 7 May 1963; *Educ* St Paul's Girls' Sch London, Westminster, St John's Coll Oxford (BA); *Children* 1 da (Laura); *Career* venture capital analyst Charterhouse Bank 1985–86, Bd dir Kleinwort Benson Securities and head Media Res Team 1986–91; Financial Times: reporter 1991–94, leader writer 1994–96; The Times: US ed 1996–, foreign ed 1999–2006, chief foreign commentator 2006–; Br Press Award for Maxwell teams investigation; *Publications* In Defence of America (2008); *Style*— Ms Bronwen Maddox; ✉ c/o The Times, 1 Pennington Street, London E1 9XN

MADDOX, Air Vice Marshal Nigel David Alan; CBE (1999); s of Albert Maddox, of Hockley, Essex, and Beverley, *née* Brown (d 1997); *b* 1 April 1954, London; *Educ* Clark's Coll Southend-on-Sea, Westcliff HS, Open Univ (MBA); *m* 1 Sept 1979, Susan Armitage-Maddox, *née* Armitage; 1 da (Nicola Alexandra Beatrix b 16 June 1997); *Career* OC Ops Wing RAF Mount Pleasant Falkland Is, OC 12 Sqdn RAF Lossiemouth 1991–93, Asst Dir (W) Defence Commitments MOD 1993–95, sr RAF offr Germany and station cdr RAF Brüggen 1996–98, Air Cdre Maritime RAF Northwood 1999–2002, AOC No 2 Gp RAF High Wycombe 2002–05, Cmdt JSSC 2005–07, COS Ops Air Cmd 2007–09; Freeman City of London, Freeman Worshipful Co of Carmen; FRAeS; *Recreations* squash, golf; *Clubs* RAF; *Style*— Air Vice Marshal Nigel Maddox, CBE; ✉ Air Officer Commanding, No 2 Group, Group Headquarters, RAF High Wycombe, Buckinghamshire HP14 4UE (☎ 01494 496331)

MADDOX, Ronald Arthur; s of Harold George Maddox, and Winifred Maddox; *b* 5 October 1930; *Educ* Herts Coll of Art and Design, London Coll of Printing and Graphic Art; *m* 1, 1958, Camilla Farrin (d 1995); 2 s; m 2, 1997, Diana Goodwin; *Career* Nat Serv Air Miny Design Unit RAF 1949–51; graphic artist and art dir various advtg agencies London 1951–61, in private practice as artist, illustrator and conslt designer 1962– (cmmnd by nat and multinational cos, govt depts, local authys, TV and publishers); designer Br postage stamps and philatelic material 1972–; stamp issues designed incl: Village Churches, Historic Buildings, Urban Renewal, Industrial Archaeology; designer Landscape of Britain series Royal Mail aerogrammes, work widely reproduced as illustrations for books, calendars, prints and cards; exhibitions incl: Mall Galleries, Royal Acad, Bankside Galleries; works in the collections of: late HM Queen Elizabeth the Queen Mother, 10 Downing St, Sultanate of Oman, Nat Tst, PO, DOE, Barclays Bank, BP, Shell, John Laing, Mobil Oil; winner Prix de l'Art Philatelique 1987, Winsor and Newton RI awards 1981 and 1991, Rowland Hilder RI Award 1996 and 2000 (for outstanding landscape painting); memb Mgmnt Bd Fedn of Br Artists 1989–2004, memb Cncl Artists' Gen Benevolent Inst (AGBI) 2000 (hon sec 2002, chm 2010, chm/pres 2015); Royal Inst of Painters in Water Colours: memb 1959, vice-pres 1979, pres 1989–2014, hon PRI 2014; assessor: RSA Student Design Bursary Awards Postage Stamps 1981–99, Royal Acad Summer exhbn, Turner Watercolour Award 2003–07, Turner Watercolour Award RWS and RI 2008–12, Art Colls Illustration and Design Diplomas; patron: Danesbury/QVM Hospital Welwyn, Isabel Hospice Welwyn Garden City; tstee: Welwyn Scouts and Guides Assoc, Digswell Arts Tst; hon memb: Pastel Soc, Soc of Architect Artists, Fedn of Canadian Artists, United Soc of Artists, Soc of Graphic Artists, Wapping Gp of Artists, Campine Assoc of Watercolours Belgium; vice-pres Hertford Art Soc; Freeman City of London 2000, Hon Freeman Worshipful Co of Painter-Stainers 2000; Hon RWS 1990, Hon RBA 2002, FCSD, FSAI, FRSA, Hon Memb The Arts Club; *Recreations* compulsive drawing, walking, cycling, gardening; *Style*— Ronald Maddox, Esq; ✉ Herons, 21 New Road, Digswell, Welwyn, Hertfordshire AL6 0AQ (☎ 01438 714884)

MADDRELL, Geoffrey Keggen; OBE (2015); s of Capt Geoffrey Douglas Maddrell (d 1975), of Port Erin, IOM, and Barbara Marie Maddrell (d 2000); *b* 18 July 1936; *Educ* King William's Coll IOM, CCC Cambridge (MA), Columbia Univ NY (MBA); *m* 12 Oct 1964, Winifred Mary Daniel (d 2014), da of Frank Dowell Jones (d 1984), of St Asaph, Clwyd; 2 s (Paul b 1965, Michael b 1971), 1 da (Siân b 1966); *Career* Lt Parachute Regiment 1955–57; Shell Int Petroleum 1960–69; dir Bowater Corp 1978–86, chief exec Tootal Gp plc 1986–91; chm: Westbury plc 1992–2006, Ivory and Sime ISIS Tst plc 1993–2010, Glenmorangie plc 1994–2002, ProShare 1994–2003 (chief exec 1991–94), LDV Ltd 1995–2005, Unite Gp 1999–2009, Buildstore Ltd 1999–2008, Economic Lifestyle Property Devpt Co 2008–10, Human Recognition Systems Ltd 2009–15, F&C Select Tst plc; dir: Transport Development Gp plc 1992–97, Goldcrest Homes Ltd 2004–08; pt/t Civil Service cmmr 1992–96 and 2001–05; chm: Manchester TEC 1989–91, Phoenix High Sch 1994–97, Airborne Forces Charities 1996–2005, Uniaid 2003–07, Research Autism Tst 2003–; memb Bd of Govrs UMIST 1987–92; tstee Help the Aged 1983–86; *Recreations* running, golf; *Clubs* Serpentine Running, Castletown Golf; *Style*— Geoffrey Maddrell, Esq, OBE; ✉ 28 Sussex Street, London SW1V 4RL

MADDRELL, Prof Simon Hugh Piper; s of Hugh Edmund Fisher Maddrell (d 1969), farmer, and Barbara Agnes Mary, *née* Chamberlin (d 1996), photographer; *b* 11 December 1937, Selly Oak, Birmingham; *Educ* Peter Symonds' Sch Winchester, St Catharine's Coll Cambridge (scholar, MA, PhD), Gonville & Caius Coll Cambridge (ScD); *m* 1, Anna, *née* Myers; 1 da (Penelope Jane b 21 Feb 1962), 3 s (Robin Charles Fisher b 17 Jan 1965, Joseph Timothy b 19 June 1968, Samuel James b 2 Jan 1971); m 2, Katherine Mona, *née* Mapes; *Career* Nat Research Cncl of Canada postdoctoral research fell Dalhousie Univ Halifax Canada; Univ of Cambridge: SRC/NATO postdoctorate research fell Dept of Zoology 1964–65, fell and coll lectr Gonville & Caius Coll 1968–2006 (life fell 2006–), (open (prize) research fell 1964–68, also research assoc Univ of Massachusetts Amherst 1967), princ scientific offr ARC Unit of Invertebrate Chemistry & Physiology Dept of Zoology 1972–78 (sr scientific offr 1972, also research assoc Dept of Zoology Univ of Br Columbia 1974 and 1975), sr princ scientific offr (individual merit promotion) AFRC Unit of Insect Neurophysiology and Pharmacology Dept of Zoology 1978–90, hon reader in comparative physiology 1990–2003, hon prof of integrative physiology 2003–08, emeritus prof of integrative physiology 2008–; currently dir The Company of Biologists Ltd (fin sec 1965–2010); Centenary Year Scientific Medal Zoological Soc of London 1975; FRS 1981; *Publications* Neurosecretion (1979); *Recreations* swimming, gardening, art and architecture, wine, travel, photography, tree planting (chm Isle of Man Woodland Tst 2005–); *Clubs* Hawks (Cambridge); *Style*— Prof Simon Maddrell, FRS; ✉ Gonville & Caius College, Cambridge CB2 1TA (e-mail shpm100@cam.ac.uk)

M

MADELEY, Richard; s of Christopher Madeley (d 1977), and Mary Claire, *née* McEwan; *b* 13 May 1956; *m* 21 Nov 1986; Judith Finnigan, *qv*; 1 s (Jack b 19 May 1986), 1 da (Chloe b 13 July 1987); 2 step s (Thomas, Daniel (twins) b 2 March 1977); *Career* television presenter; reporter Brentwood Argus Newspaper 1972–74, news ed/asst ed East London Advertiser 1975–76, reporter/presenter/news prodr BBC Radio Carlisle 1976–78, reporter/presenter Border TV 1978–80, reporter/presenter YTV 1980–82; presenter: Granada TV 1982–2001, Cactus TV 2001–09 (Richard and Judy (Channel 4 then UKTV) until 2009, Br Book Awards (Channel 4) 2004–09); *Awards* RTS Team Award for This Morning 1994, Most Popular Daytime Programme National Television Awards 1998, 1999, 2000 and 2001; *Books* Fathers & Sons (2008); *Style*— Richard Madeley, Esq; ✉ c/o James Grant Management, 94 Strand on the Green, Chiswick, London W4 3NN (☎ 020 8742 4950, fax 020 8742 4951)

MAGAN OF CASTLETOWN, Baron (Life Peer UK 2011), of Kensington in the Royal Borough of Kensington and Chelsea; George Morgan Magan; s of Brig William Morgan Tilson Magan, CBE; *b* 14 November 1945; *Educ* Winchester; *m* 1972, Wendy Anne, da of Maj Patrick Chilton, MC; 2 s (Edward b 1975, Patrick b 1984), 1 da (Henrietta b 1977); *Career* merchant banker; Peat Marwick Mitchell 1964–70, Kleinwort Benson Ltd 1971–74, dir Morgan Grenfell & Co Ltd 1974–88, co-fndr and chm J O Hambro Magan 1988–96; chm: Hawkpoint Partners 1997–2001, Mallett plc 2001–08, Morgan Shipley Ltd Dubai 2001–, emuse Dublin 2004–; dir: Asprey plc 1980–96, Edmiston & Co 2001–13, Bank of Ireland 2003–09 (dep govr 2006–09), Allied Investment Partners Abu Dhabi 2007–12; dep treas Cons Pty 2002–03, pty treas and memb Bd Cons Pty 2003, dep chm Cons Pty Fndn 2009–13 (dir 2003–13); chm St George's Chapel Windsor Castle Devpt Appeal 2007–13, tstee Fndn of The Coll of St George Windsor Castle 2008–15; tstee: London Philharmonic Orch 1992–2006 (chm 1997–2006), ROH Covent Garden 1995–2001, Br Museum Devpt Tst 1999–2003; govr Stowe Sch 2001–16, chm Devpt Bd Royal Abert Hall 2014–, memb Works of Art Ctee House of Lords 2015–; FCA; *Clubs* Royal Yacht Sqdn, Turf, Boodle's, The Brook (NY), Kildare St and Univ (Dublin); *Style*— The Lord Magan of Castletown; ✉ House of Lords, London SW1A 0PW

MAGEE, Bryan; s of Frederick Magee; *b* 12 April 1930; *Educ* Christ's Hosp, Lycée Hôche Versailles, Keble Coll Oxford (MA), Yale Univ; *m* 1954 (m dis), Ingrid Söderlund; 1 da; *Career* author, critic and broadcaster; formerly: columnist The Times, drama critic The Listener; music critic for numerous pubns 1959–; Parly candidate (Lab) Mid Beds 1959 and 1960, MP Leyton 1974–83(Lab until 1982, Ind Lab 1982, SDP 1982–83); lectr in philosophy Balliol Coll Oxford 1970–71, visiting fell All Souls Coll Oxford 1973–74, hon sr fell in the history of ideas KCL 1984–94, visiting prof KCL 1994–2000, academic visitor LSE 1994–97; visiting fell: Wolfson Coll Oxford 1993–94 (visiting scholar 1991–93, life memb), New Coll Oxford 1995, Merton Coll Oxford 1998, St Catherine's Coll Oxford 2000, Peterhouse Cambridge 2001, Clare Hall Cambridge 2004 (life memb); elected to Sr Common Room St Antony's Coll Oxford 2009; visiting prof Univ of Otago NZ 2006, 2009 and 2012; memb Arts Cncl (chm Music Advsy Panel) 1993–94; memb Cncl: Critics' Circle 1970– (pres 1983–84), Ditchley Fndn 1982– (govr 1979–); judge: Evening Standard Opera Award 1973–84, Laurence Olivier Opera Award 1990–91 and 1993–95, Royal Philharmonic Soc Annual Opera Award 1991–2000; pres Edinburgh Univ Philosophy Soc 1987–88; Silver Medal RTS 1978; fell: Queen Mary & Westfield Coll London 1989

(QMC 1988), Royal Philharmonic Soc 1990; hon fell Keble Coll Oxford 1994; Hon DLitt Univ of Leicester 2005; *Books* Crucifixion and Other Poems (1951), Go West Young Man (1958), To Live in Danger (1960), The New Radicalism (1962), The Democratic Revolution (1964), Towards 2000 (1965), One in Twenty (1966), The Television Interviewer (1966), Aspects of Wagner (1968, revised edn 1988), Modern British Philosophy (1971), Popper (1973), Facing Death (1977), Men of Ideas (1978, re-issued as Talking Philosophy 2001), The Philosophy of Schopenhauer (1983, revised edn 1997), The Great Philosophers (1987), On Blindness (1995, re-issued as Sight Unseen 1998), Confessions of a Philosopher (1997), The Story of Philosophy (1998), Wagner and Philosophy (2000), Clouds of Glory: A Hoxton Childhood (2003, J R Ackerley Prize for Autobiography 2004), Growing Up in a War (2007), Ultimate Questions (2016); *Recreations* music, theatre; *Clubs* Garrick, Savile; *Style—* Bryan Magee, Esq; ✉ Flat 16, Ritchie Court, 380 Banbury Road, Oxford OX2 7PW; Curtis Brown, Haymarket House, 28–29 Haymarket, London SW1Y 4SP

MAGEE, Sir Ian Bernard Vaughan; kt (2006), CB (2002); s of Bernard Magee, and Wendy Magee; *b* 9 July 1946, Newcastle on Tyne; *Educ* St Michael's Coll Leeds, Univ of Leeds (BA); *m* 1 (m dis 1987); 1 s (Colin); m 2, Pam; 1 da (Sarah), 1 s (Edward); *Career* private sec to Min for Social Security 1976–78, seconded to Enterprise Unit Cabinet Office 1984–86, dep to Dir of Personnel DSS 1986–89, dir Southern Territory Benefits Agency 1990–93; chief exec Information Technology Services Agency 1993–98, chief exec Court Service Agency 1998–2003, chief exec (second permanent sec) ops DCA 2003–05; sr advsr Booz and Co 2006–11; chair Geographic Info Gp 2011–; sr fell Inst for Govt 2008–; *Recreations* sport, family, reading; *Clubs* MCC, RAC, Verulam Golf; *Style—* Sir Ian Magee, CB

MAGINNESS, Alban; MLA; s of Alphonsus Maginness (d 1999), of Belfast, and Patricia *née* O'Hara (d 2001); *b* 9 July 1950; *Educ* St Malachy's Coll, Univ of Ulster (BA), Queen's Univ Belfast (LLM); *m* 1 Aug 1978, Carmel, da of late Patrick McWilliams; 5 da, 3 s; *Career* barr-at-law Bar of NI 1976; Belfast CC 1985–2009, Lord Mayor 1997–98; Parly candidate Westminster General Election N Belfast 1997, 2001, 2005 and 2010, SDLP candidate European elections 2009; MLA (SDLP) N Belfast 1998–, chair SDLP Assembly Gp, chair Regnl Devpt Ctee, chair Enterprise Trade and Investment Ctee 2009–; memb Ctee of the Regions EU 2002–07, memb Assembly Cmmn 2007–09; govr Linenhall Library; *Recreations* walking, reading, theatre, Donegal; *Style—* Alban Maginness, Esq, MLA; ✉ 228 Antrim Road, Belfast BT15 4AN; Northern Ireland Assembly, Parliament Buildings, Stormont Estate, Belfast (☎ 028 9022 0520, fax 028 9022 0522)

MAGINNIS OF DRUMGLASS, Baron (Life Peer UK 2001), of Carnteel in the County of Tyrone; Kenneth Wiggins (Ken) Maginnis; s of Gilbert Maginnis (d 1974), of Dungannon, and Margaret Elizabeth Wiggins (d 1984); *b* 21 January 1938; *Educ* Royal Sch Dungannon, Stranmillis Teacher Trg Coll Belfast; *m* 1961, Joy Stewart, da of Herbert Moneymore (d 1976), and Jeannie Moneymore (d 2000); 2 s (Hon Stewart b 1963, Hon Steven b 1971), 2 da (Hon Gail b 1964, Hon Grainne b 1969); *Career* Ulster Special Constabulary 1958–65, UDR 1970–81 (RMA Sandhurst, Co Cdrs Course Warminster, Maj 1972); teacher: Cookstown Secdy Sch 1959–60, Drumglass Primary Sch Dungannon 1960–66; princ Pomeroy Primary Sch 1966–82; MP (UUP) Fermanagh and S Tyrone 1983–2001; memb: House of Commons Select Ctee on Def 1984–85, Southern Health and Social Servs Bd 1989–91, Armed Forces Bill 1990–91, Southern Health and Social Servs Cncl 1991–93, NI Affairs 1994–97; elected to NI Forum 1996–98; memb: Dungannon DC 1981–93 and 2001–04, NI Assembly 1982–86; memb Assembly's: Fin and Personnel Ctee (dep chm 1982–86), Security and Home Affairs Ctee (chm 1982–86); vice-pres UU Cncl, memb Exec UU Party (spokesman on defence, and home affrs); fndr Police Rehabilitation and Retraining Tst; fndr memb Prison Offrs Tst NI; chm Moygashel Community Devpt Assoc; *Publications* McGimpsey & McGimpsey v Ireland (1989), Witness for the Prosecution (1993), Disarmament – Pathway to Peace (1999); author of various articles in national newspapers; *Style—* The Rt Hon the Lord Maginnis of Drumglass

MAGNUS, Sir Laurence Henry Philip; 3 Bt (UK 1917), of Tangley Hill, Wonersh, Co Surrey; s of Hilary Barrow Magnus, TD, QC (d 1987), and Rosemary Vera Anne, *née* Masefield; suc unc, Sir Philip Magnus-Allcroft, 2 Bt (d 1988); *b* 24 September 1955; *Educ* Eton, ChCh Oxford (MA); *m* 1983, Jocelyn Mary, eldest da of Robert Henry Foster Stanton; 2 s (Thomas Henry Philip b 1985, Edmund Robert Hilary b 1991), 1 da (Iona Alexandra b 1988); *Heir* s, Thomas Magnus; *Career* Samuel Montagu & Co Ltd: gen mangr Singapore branch 1984–88, exec dir and dep head UK Corp Fin 1988–95; exec dir Phoenix Securities Ltd 1995–97, exec md investment banking Donaldson, Lufkin and Jenrette Inc 1997–2000, md investment banking Credit Suisse First Boston Inc 2000–01; Lexicon Partners: vice-chm 2001–10, chm 2010–11; dep chm Evercore Partners 2011–; non-exec dir: FIM Services Ltd 1997–, TT Electronics plc 2001–07, JP Morgan Income and Capital Tst plc 2001– (chm 2007–), Climate Exchange plc 2006–10, The Cayenne Tst plc 2006–15, Fidelity Japanese Values plc 2010–, Aggregated MicroPower plc 2010–, Pantheon Int Participations plc 2011–; non-exec chm Xchanging ins-sure Services Ltd 2001–09; tstee Eating Disorders Assoc (BEAT) 2005–13 (chm 2005–11), dep chm Nat Tst 2005–13 (chm Fin Ctee 2002–05 (memb 1997–2005), memb Cncl 2003–13), tstee Landmark Tst 2011–16, tstee All Churches Trust 2013–, chm Historic England (formerly English Heritage) 2013–, tstee English Heritage Tst 2014–, chm Windsor Leadership Tst 2015– (tstee 2006–), memb Sustainability and Review Panel English Churches and Cathedrals 2016–; *Recreations* fishing, reading, walking; *Clubs* Millennium, Brooks's, City of London, Beefsteak; *Style—* Sir Laurence Magnus, Bt; ✉ Flat 8, 44 Lower Sloane Street, London SW1W 8BP; Evercore Partners LLP, 15 Stanhope Gate, London W1K 1LN (e-mail laurie.magnus@evercore.com)

MAGONET, Rabbi Prof Jonathan David; s of Capt Alexander Philip Magonet (d 1978), and Esther, *née* Slonims (d 1972); *b* 2 August 1942, London; *Educ* Westminster, Middlesex Hosp Med Sch Univ of London (MB BS), Leo Baeck Coll (Rabbinic ordination), Univ of Heidelberg (PhD); *m* 10 May 1974, Dorothea Elsa Martha, da of Gerhardt Foth; 1 s (Gavriel b 4 May 1978), 1 da (Avigail b 28 April 1981); *Career* Leo Baeck Coll: lectr and head Dept of Bible Studies 1974–85, princ 1985–2005, prof of Hebrew and Biblical studies 1996–2005, emeritus prof of Bible 2005–; scholar in residence Dept of Jewish Educn Univ of Tel Aviv 1990–91; visiting prof: Kirchliche Hochschule Wuppertal 1992, 1993, 1995, 2004 and 2010, Carl von Ossietsky Univ Oldenburg 1999 and 2004, Universität Luzern 2003; Schalom ben Chorin prof of Jewish studies Univs of Wuerzburg and Augsburg 2008, research prof Seinan Gakuin Univ Japan 2010–15, visiting prof Doshisha Univ Kyoto Japan 2012; vice-pres World Union for Progressive Judaism 1985–2005; ed European Judaism 2004– (memb Editorial Bd 1978–, co-ed 1992–2004); Hon Dr: Kirchliche Hochschule Wuppertal 2005, Open Univ 2006, Hebrew Union Coll Jewish Inst of Religion 2007, Seinan Gakuin Univ Japan 2014; FRSA; Cross of the Order of Merit of the Federal Rep of Germany 1999; *Books* Form and Meaning: Studies in Literary Techniques in the Book of Jonah (1976), Forms of Prayer: Vol 1 Daily and Sabbath Prayerbook (co-ed with Lionel Blue, 1977, 8 edn 2008), Forms of Prayer: Vol III Days of Awe Prayerbook (co-ed with Lionel Blue, 1985), The Guide to the Here and the Hereafter (co-ed with Lionel Blue, 1988), A Rabbi's Bible (1991 and 2004 (as A Rabbi Reads the Bible)), How To Get Up When Life Gets You Down: A Companion and Guide (co-ed with Lionel Blue, 1992), Bible Lives (1992), The Little Blue Book of Prayer (co-ed with Lionel Blue, 1993), A Rabbi Reads the Psalms (1994 and 2004), Forms of Prayer: Vol II Pilgrim Festivals (co-ed with Lionel Blue, 1995), Kindred Spirits: A Year of Readings (co-ed with Lionel Blue, 1995), Jewish Explorations of Sexuality (ed, 1995), The Subversive Bible (1997), Mit Der Bibel Durch Das Jüdische Jahr (1998), The Explorer's Guide to Judaism (1998), Sun, Sand and Soul (co-ed Lionel Blue, 1999), Abraham-Jesus-Mohammed: Interreligiöser Dialog aus jüdischer Perspektive (2000), From Autumn to Summer: A Biblical Journey Through the Jewish Year (2000), Talking to the Other: Jewish Interfaith Dialogue with Christians and Muslims (2003), Seder Ha-t'fillot (ed), Seder Ha-t'fillot: Forms of Prayer for Jewish Worship Vol 1 (ed, 8 edn, 2008), Schabbat Schalom: Juedische Theologie – In Predigten entfaltet (2011), Rabbino Saishokaishak: Yudaiakuo to Kiristokuo no Taiwa (Japanese, 2012), Netsuke Nation: Tales from Another Japan (2013), A Rabbi Reads the Torah (2013); *Recreations* songwriting, performing; *Style—* Rabbi Prof Jonathan Magonet; ✉ Leo Baeck College, 80 East End Road, London N3 2SY (☎ 020 8349 5600, fax 020 8343 2558, e-mail jonathan.magonet@lbc.ac.uk or jonathan.magonet@gmail.com)

MAGORIAN, Michelle Jane; da of William Magorian, and Gladys Freda Evans (d 1975); *b* 6 November 1947; *Educ* Kilbreda Coll, Convent of the Cross, Rose Bruford Coll of Speech and Drama, L'Ecole Internationale de Mime Paris; *m* 18 Aug 1987 (m dis 1998), Peter Keith Venner, s of Albert Keith Venner; 2 s (Tom b 5 March 1989, George b 23 Sept 1993); *Career* writer, entertainer; in rep since 1970, one woman shows: touring Italy and UK 1980, The Pact 1993–, Food and Love – Play On! 1999, Life, Love and Second Helpings 2002; fell Rose Bruford Coll of Theatre and Performing Arts 2013; memb: Soc of Authors, PEN; Hon DLitt Univ of Portsmouth 2005; *Books* Goodnight Mister Tom (1981, lyrics for stage musical 1992, audio book 1997, broadcast Radio 5, TV film 1998, book and lyrics 2001, stage version won Olivier Award for Best Entertainment and Family 2013), Back Home (1985, made into TV films 1989 and 2001, dramatised for Radio 4 1995, audiobook 2001), Waiting For My Shorts To Dry (1989), Who's Going to Take Care of Me? (1990), Orange Paw Marks (1991), A Little Love Song (1991), In Deep Water (a collection of short stories, 1992, 3 dramatised for Radio 4 1999), Cuckoo in the Nest (1994), A Spoonful of Jam (1998), Hello Life! (book (jtly) and lyrics, 2001), Canapes for Company (book and lyrics, 2001, retitled Tinsel), Jump! (2002), Be Yourself (2003), Just Henry (novel, 2008, TV drama 2011, Costa Children's Book Award 2009), Impossible! (2014, nominated for the CILIP Carnegie Award 2016); short stories incl six anthologies; *Style—* Ms Michelle Magorian; ✉ c/o Claire Wilson, Rogers, Coleridge and White Literacy Agency, 20 Powis Mews, London W11 1JN (☎ 020 7221 3717, website www.michellemagorian.com)

MAGOS, Adam László; s of László Aurel Pal Magos, of London, and Eva Maria, *née* Benjamin; *b* 26 September 1953, Budapest; *Educ* Whitgift Sch Haling Park S Croydon Surrey, King's Coll London (BSc), King's Coll Hosp Sch of Med London (MB BS, MD, FRCOG); *m* Anne Cyprienne, *née* Coburn; 3 s (Tiarnan Adam b 5 Aug 1985, Siadhal László b 16 March 1987, Abban Zoltan b 24 April 1990); *Career* clinical lectr and hon sr registrar Nuffield Dept of Obstetrics and Gynaecology John Radcliffe Hosp Oxford 1986–90, sr lectr and hon conslt Academic Dept of Obstetrics and Gynaecology Royal Free Hosp Sch of Med 1990–91, conslt obstetrician and gynaecologist and hon sr lectr Univ Dept of Obstetrics and Gynaecology Royal Free Hosp 1991–, consult gynaecologist King Edward VII's Hosp for Offrs London 1992–2012; treas Br Soc for Gynaecological Endoscopy 1989–92; memb: Advsy Bd Euro Soc for Hysteroscopy 1990–96, Working Gp on New Technol in Endoscopic Gynaecological Surgery RCOG 1993–94, Editorial Bd Gynaecological Endoscopy 1993–2002 (ed 1990–93), MAS Training Sub-Ctee RCOG 1998–2001; author of over 250 pubns in peer review jls and chapters in books; Syntex Award (Int Soc of Reproduction Med) 1988; hon memb: Aust Soc of Gynaecological Endoscopy 1994, Egyptian Soc of Gynaecological Endoscopy 1996; memb: Blair Bell Research Soc 1982, Euro Soc of Hysteroscopy 1988, European Soc for Gynaecological Endoscopy 1995–; fndr memb: Br Soc for Gynaecological Endoscopy 1989, Soc of Minimally Invasive Therapy 1990; Cannell lectr Soc of Obstetricians and Gynaecologists of Canada 1999; awarded: the Dr Bhaneuben M Nanavati Golden Jubilee Oration Award in Bombay 1994, Veress Memorial Medal from the Hungarian Soc for Gynaecological Endoscopy 1997; FRCOG 1998, hon fell Br Soc for Gynaecological Endoscopy 2004; *Recreations* music, saxophone, jazz, computing, cooking; *Style—* Adam Magos, Esq; ✉ University Department of Obstetrics and Gynaecology, The Royal Free Hospital, Pond Street, Hampstead, London NW3 2QG (☎ 020 7431 1321, fax 020 7431 1321, e-mail adam.magos@gmail.com)

MAGUIRE, Adrian Edward; s of Joseph Maguire, of Kilmessan, Co Meath, and Philomena Maguire (d 1995); *b* 29 April 1971; *Educ* Kilmessan Nat Sch, Trim Vocational Sch; *m* 1995, Sabrina; 1 da (Shannon b 1996), 1 s (Finian b 1998); *Career* racehorse trainer and former jockey; achievements incl: champion pony race rider 1986, champion point-to-point rider 1990–91, champion conditional jockey 1991–92, ridden over 1000 winners; major races won: Cheltenham Gold Cup, Irish Grand Nat (youngest ever winning jockey), Galway Plate, Imperial Cup, Greenalls Gold Cup, Queen Mother Champion Chase (Cheltenham), King George VI Chase (Kempton Park), Triumph Hurdle and Cathcort Chase (both Cheltenham); records: most point-to-point winners in a season, most winners in a season for a conditional jockey (71) 1991–92; *Recreations* squash, watching TV; *Style—* Adrian Maguire, Esq

MAGUIRE, Dr Anne; da of Richard Patrick Maguire (d 1972), and Ruth Alice Maguire (d 1963); *Educ* Royal Free Hosp Sch of Med London (MB BS), CG Jung Inst Zurich (dip); *Career* dermatological trg St John's Hosp for Diseases of the Skin Guy's Hosp and UCH London 1956–64, in private practice Harley St; author of numerous papers in medicine and psychotherapy; Ratclyffe Crocker travelling fellowship Hosp Saint-Louis Paris; memb: Br Assoc of Dermatologists, Int Assoc of Analytical Psychologists; FRCP 1974 (MRCP 1956); *Books* Hauterkrankungen als Botschaften der Seele (1991, re-published in English as Skin Disease: A Message from the Soul, 2004), Vom Sinn der kranken Sinne (1993), The Seven Deadly Sins (published in German, 1996, re-published in English as Seven Deadly Sins: The Dark Companions of the Soul, 2004); *Style—* Dr Anne Maguire; ✉ 17 Wellington Street, St John's, Blackburn BB1 8AF (☎ 01254 59910); 10 Harley Street, London W1G 9PF (☎ 020 7467 8300)

MAGUIRE, Kevin; s of John Maguire, and Jennie Maguire; *b* South Shields, Tyne and Wear; *Educ* Harton, South Shields, York Univ, Cardiff Univ; *m* 1986, Emma Burstall; 2 s, 1 da; *Career* formerly: The Western Morning News, New Civil Engineer, Press Association, Daily Telegraph, The Guardian; currently assoc ed Daily Mirror; *Books* Great Parliamentary Scandals (with Matthew Parris, *qv*, 2004); *Recreations* sport, walking, pubs; *Clubs* Sunderland Association Football; *Style—* Kevin Maguire, Esq; ✉ Daily Mirror, 1 Canada Square, London E14 5AP

MAGUIRE, Máiread Corrigan; da of Andrew and Margaret Corrigan; *b* 27 January 1944; *Educ* St Vincent's Primary Sch Falls Road Belfast, Miss Gordon's Commercial Coll Belfast; *m* 1981, Jackie Maguire; 2 s (John Francis b 1982, Luke b 1984), 3 step c (Mark, Joanne, Marie Louise); *Career* initiator of Peace Movement in NI, jt fndr Community of the Peace People, chm Peace People 1980–81, hon life pres Peace People; winner numerous honours and awards; jt recipient Nobel Peace Prize 1976; winner: Norwegian People's prize, Carl-Von-Ossietzky medaille for Courage Berlin 1976; special honouree: UN Women of Achievement programme 1978, American Acad of Achievement; winner Pacem in Terris (Peace and Freedom award) Davenport Iowa 1990, Hon Dr Yale Univ; co fndr Ctee for the Administration of Justice, former volunteer Legion of Mary (work with prisons and prisoners); previously employed as confidential sec to md A Guinness Son & Co (Belfast) Ltd; *Recreations* swimming, music; *Style—* Mrs Máiread Corrigan Maguire; ✉ 224 Lisburn Road, Belfast BT9 6GE (office ☎ 028 9066 3465, fax 028 9068 3947, e-mail info@peacepeople.com, website www.peacepeople.com.)

MAGURRAN, Prof Anne; *Career* prof of ecology and evolution Univ of St Andrews; assoc ed Proceedings at the Royal Society: Biological Sciences 1998–2003, British Antarctic Survey Integrated Prog Review Ctee 2001–2006, Royal Soc Working Pty on Biodiversity Measurement 2002–2003, Awards Ctee Zoological Soc of London; Royal Society/Leverhulme Trust sr research fell 2002–2003; FRSE 2004; *Books* Measuring Biological Diversity (jt ed, 2004), Evaluating Ecology (2005); *Style—* Prof Anne Magurran; ✉ University of St Andrews Gatty Marine Laboratory, East Sands, St Andrews KY16 8LB

MAHAPATRA, Dr Sasi Bhusan; s of late Nila Kantha Mahapatra, and late Moti Mahapatra; *b* 2 November 1935; *Educ* BC HS Ranpur Orissa India, Ravenshaw Coll Cuttack Orissa India, SCB Med Coll and Utkal Univ Orissa India (MB BS, DPM); *m* 1 Oct 1963, Maureen Rose, da of late William Henry Piggott; 1 s (Timothy Martin, *qv*), 2 da (Sonjeeta Krishna, Rachelle Elizabeth); *Career* house offr and house surgn SCB Med Coll Cuttack Orissa 1958–59, med offr Manmunda Health Centre Orissa India 1959–61; sr registrar in psychiatry 1964–66: Runwell Hosp Wickford Essex (sr house offr and registrar 1961–64), St Clements Hosp, The London Hosp; conslt psychiatrist Univ of Leeds 1976– (lectr 1966–70, sr lectr and hon conslt 1970–76), conslt psychiatrist and sr clinical lectr St James's Hosp Univ Hosp 1976–94, dir of psychiatry servs Leeds Eastern HA 1986–90, med dir Harrogate Clinic 1990–2002, hon conslt psychiatrist Leeds Community and Mental Health Serv Tst Leeds 1994–, Lord Chllr's Medical Visitor 1995–2007, special visitor Ct of Protection 2007–; memb N Yorks Area HA 1971–76, sub dean RCPsych 1977–82; chm: NE Div RCPsych 1984–88, Sub Ctee of Overseas Psychiatry Trainees 1976–84; FRCP 1982, FRCPsych; *Books* Antidepressive Drugs – Side-Effects of Drugs (1972), Deafness and Mental Health (1972), Psychosomatic Aspects of Coronary Artery Disease – Psychosomatic Medicine (1973), Problems of Language in Examinations for Foreign Psychiatrists (1974), Short Term Effects of Antidepressive Drugs and Placebo (1975), Schizophrenic Language (ed, 1976), Handbook for Psychiatric Inceptors and Trainees (ed, 1980); *Recreations* cricket, gardening, sailing, music, skiing, photography; *Style—* Dr Sasi Mahapatra; ✉ 4 Holt Avenue, Adel, Leeds L16 8DH (☎ 01132 162757); Spire Leeds Hospital, Jackson Avenue, Roundday, Leeds LS8 1NT (☎ 0113 269 3939)

MAHAPATRA, Timothy Martin; s of Dr Sasi Bhusan Mahapatra, *qv*, and Maureen Rose, *née* Piggott; *b* 16 March 1964; *Educ* Leeds GS, Univ of Birmingham (BComm), Manchester Business Sch (MBA); *Children* 2 da (Isabella Priya, Sophia Beatriz); *Career* ptnr Arthur Andersen until 2002, currently md Global Financial Advsy Deloitte; FCA 1990; *Recreations* skiing, travel, motor and racing cars, boats; *Style—* Timothy Mahapatra, Esq; ✉ Deloitte & Touche LLP, Athene Place, 66 Shoe Lane, London EC4A 3BQ

MAHER, Ben; MBE (2013); *b* 30 January 1983; *Career* show jumper; winner: Hickstead Derby 2005, Bronze medal (team jumping) European Championships 2011, Gold medal (team jumping) Olympic Games 2012; *Style—* Mr Ben Maher, MBE

MAHER, Paul; s of Francis John Maher (d 2003), and Bridget Rita, *née* Dillon; *b* 30 July 1959, Harlesden, London; *Educ* Harrow HS, John Lyon Sch Harrow, Univ of Bristol (LLB); *m* 16 Feb 1990, Amanda; 1 s (Jamie b 17 March 1992), 2 da (Charlotte b 5 April 1994, Lara b 7 Oct 2003); *Career* Boodle Hatfield 1982–84, ICI 1984–90, Rowe & Maw 1990–2002, Mayer, Brown, Rowe & Maw LLP 2002–09, Greenberg Traurig Maher 2009–; memb Law Soc; *Recreations* football, running, squash, tennis, current affairs, music, reading, wine, politics; *Clubs* Mosimann's; *Style—* Paul Maher, Esq; ✉ Greenberg Traurig Maher, 7th Floor, 200 Gray's Inn Road, London WC1X 8HF (☎ 020 3349 8888, fax 020 7900 3632, e-mail maherp@gtmlaw.com)

MAHER, Stephen Francis; s of Francis John Maher, of Harrow, Middx, and Bridget Rita, *née* Dillon; *b* 19 February 1961; *Educ* The John Lyon Sch Middx, Balliol Coll Oxford (exhibitioner, MA, Coolidge Pathfinder award); *m* 23 Sept 1989, Sarah Jane, da of Adrian George Beckett; 2 da (Sophie Elizabeth b 10 March 1992, Beatrice Anna b 10 Feb 2001), 2 s (Edward Archie Francis b 3 Dec 1994, Frederick George b 7 Jan 1999); *Career* advtg grad account trainee Allen Brady & Marsh Ltd 1983; account mangr: ABM 1984–86, Abbott Mead Vickers SMS Ltd 1986–88; account dir AMV 1988–89; Simons Palmer Denton Clemmow & Johnson Ltd: account dir 1989–90, bd account dir 1990–93, head of account mgmnt 1993; ceo MBA 1994–; chm: Mktg Soc, fell and Cncl IPA, BAFTA Commercial Ctee; FRSA; *Recreations* music, guitar, skiing, football; *Style—* Stephen Maher, Esq; ✉ MBA, St Martin's Courtyard, 11 Slingsby Place, London WC2E 9AB (☎ 020 7309 7200, fax 020 7309 7201, e-mail stephen.maher@mba.co.uk, website www.mba.co.uk)

MAHER, Terence Anthony (Terry); s of Herbert Maher (d 1978); *b* 5 December 1935; *Educ* Xaverian Coll Manchester; *m* 1960, Barbara, da of Dr Franz Greenbaum (d 1961); 3 s (Nicholas b 1960, Anthony b 1962, Jeremy b 1964); *Career* with: Carborundum Co Ltd 1961–69, First Nat Fin Corp 1969–72; fndr, chm and chief exec Pentos plc 1972–93; chm: Dillons Bookstores 1977–93, Athena International 1980–93, Ryman 1987–93, Tempus Publishing Co Ltd 1994–98; fndr and chm: Maher Booksellers Ltd 1995–2008, Race Dynamics Ltd 1998–2008; fndr tstee Lib Dems 1988–2001, tstee Photographers' Gallery 1994–97, memb Advsy Cncl on Libraries 1996–98, led successful campaign to abolish price control on books; FCCA 1970 (ACCA 1960), FRSA 1988; *Books* Counterblast (co-author, 1965), Effective Politics (co-author, 1966), Against My Better Judgement (business memoir, 1994), Unfinished Business (fiction, 2003), Grumpy Old Liberal: a political rant (2005), What Would a Liberal Do? – A Polemic (2010), One of Lowry's Children (personal memoir, 2015); *Recreations* skiing, reading, walking, tennis, bridge; *Clubs* Savile, Portland; *Style—* Terry Maher, Esq; ✉ 27 Bryanston Square, London W1H 2DT (☎ 020 7723 4254)

MAHLOUDJI, Alidad; *see:* Alidad

MAHMOOD, Khalid; MP; *Career* MP (Lab) Birmingham Perry Barr 2001–; PPS to Tony McNulty MP 2004–; memb Broadcasting Select Ctee, chm Race Rels Ctee 1990–93; memb: AMICUS, Socialist Health Assoc, Socialist Educn Assoc; Lab Finance and Industry Gp: memb, exec memb Midlands branch; former advsr to: Pres Olympic Cncl Asia, Danish Int Trade Union; *Style—* Khalid Mahmood, Esq, MP; ✉ House of Commons, London SW1A 0AA

MAHONEY, Prof Craig; s of Bruce Mahoney (d 2008), and Vida, *née* Jordan (d 1994); *b* 13 April 1957, Burnie, Australia; *Educ* Tasmanian Coll of Advanced Educn, Univ of Birmingham, Queen's Univ Belfast (DPhil); *Children* 2 da (Ciara Mahoney b 28 July 1993, Ella Lewis-Mahoney b 21 Nov 2009), 2 s (Jordan Mahoney b 21 Dec 1994, Kadin Lewis-Mahoney b 18 Oct 2001); *Career* former founding dean Sch of Sport, Performing Arts and Leisure Univ Wolverhampton, dep vice-chllr Northumbria Univ until 2010, chief exec Higher Educn Acad 2010–13, princ and vice-chllr Univ of the W of Scotland 2013–; former chair Br Assoc of Sport and Exercise Sciences; CPsychol; *Style—* Prof Craig Mahoney; ✉ A314 Barbour Building, University of the West of Scotland, Paisley PA1 2BE (☎ 0141 848 3671, e-mail craig.mahoney@uws.ac.uk, website www.uws.ac.uk, Twitter @PrincipalUWS)

MAHY, Helen Margaret; CBE (2015); da of Donald Gregory Mahy, of Guernsey, and Mary Margaret, *née* Chapman; *b* 4 March 1961, Guernsey; *Educ* Guernsey Ladies' Coll, Univ of Manchester (R G Lawson scholar and prize, LLB), Inns of Court Sch of Law; *m* 17 Dec 1993, Mark Roy Hughes; *Career* called to the Bar Middle Temple 1982; insurance advsr Hogg Robinson 1982–87, dep head Commercial and Legal Dept Crown Agents 1987–93, Babcock King-Wilkinson Ltd 1993–97 (latterly commercial and legal dir), Babcock Int Gp plc 1997–2002 (latterly gen counsel and co sec), co sec Lattice Gp plc and National Grid Transco plc 2002–03, gp co sec and gen counsel National Grid plc 2003–13, chair The Renewables Infrastructure Gp plc 2013–; non-exec dir: AGA Rangemaster Gp plc 2003–09, Stagecoach Gp plc 2010–16, Bonheur ASA and Ganger Rolf ASA 2013–, SVG Capital plc 2014–, SSE plc 2016–; chair: GC100 Gp 2007 (vice-chair 2005–07), Obelisk Legal Support Services Ltd 2013–15; memb Bar Cncl 2005–07 (memb Gen Mgmnt Ctee 2005–06, co-chair Employed Barrs' Ctee 2006); chartered insurance practitioner 1996–2013, accredited performance coach Middlesex Univ 2010; ICSA Company Sec of the Year 2011; ACII 1985 (Arthur J Watson Award 1985); *Books* The Basil the Spaniel Books (2010–11); *Recreations* husband, my spaniel, sleeping, shooting, writing children's stories, collecting dolls, movies, opera, trying to finish writing my novel, travelling to weird places, learning Norwegian; *Style—* Ms Helen Mahy, CBE; ☎ 07500 706540, e-mail helenmmahy@gmail.com, website basilthespaniel.co.uk

MAHY, Peter Julian; s of Rodney Mahy (d 2006), and Karen, *née* Gillingham, of Guernsey; *b* 16 April 1971, Guernsey; *Educ* Guernsey GS, Univ of Sheffield (LLB), Darwin Coll Cambridge (MPhil), Univ of Northumbria (LPC); *m* 18 May 2006, Dr Nicola Jordan-Mahy; *Career* admitted slr; Howells Slrs 1996– (ptnr 2002–, currently head Civil Liberties Dept); memb Law Soc 1998; *Clubs* cycling, sailing; *Style—* Peter Mahy, Esq; ✉ Howells Solicitors, 15–17 Bridge Street, Sheffield S3 8NL

MAIDEN, Prof Martin David; s of Kenneth Henry Maiden, and Betty, *née* Liddiard; *b* 20 May 1957, Southampton; *Educ* King Edward VI Sch Southampton, Trinity Hall Cambridge (MA, MPhil, PhD); *m* 2005, Liliana Buruiana; 1 step-da; *Career* lectr in Italian Univ of Bath 1982–89, lectr in Romance philology Univ of Cambridge and fell Downing Coll Cambridge 1989–96, prof of Romance languages Univ of Oxford and fell Trinity Coll Oxford 1996–; conseiller to the Bureau de la Société Internationale de Linguistique et de Philologie Romanes 2001–; assoc memb Centre for Research on Language Contact York Univ Toronto 2006, membro associato Associazione Italiana di Romenistica 2006, memb Consiliu Director Dacoromania 2006, dir Oxford Research Centre for Romance Linguistics 2007, memb Collegio di Dottorato Facolti di Filologia Salvatore Battagla Université degli Studi Federico II Naples 2009–, chair Faculty Bd of Linguistics, Philology and Phonetics Univ of Oxfod 2013–16; conslt ed Revue Romane 2001–, conslt ed Current Issues in Linguistic Theory 2006; memb editorial bd: Bollettino Linguistico Campano 2001–, Legenda Publications 2002–, Diachronica 2003–; memb Comitato Scientifico Italian Jl of Linguistics 2007, memb Advsy Ctee Linguistica Ljubljana 2008; editorial advsr Troubador Pubns 2002–, delegate (with special responsibility for linguistics) Oxford Univ Press 2004–, jt series ed Oxford Guides to the World's Languages 2013–, memb Ed Bd Revue Roumaine de Linguistique 2015–; memb: Philological Soc 1981– (memb Cncl 2003–), Consejo Científico Aemilianense Spain 2003–, Consiliul Academic Philologica Jassyensia 2005–, Comitato Scientifico L'Italia Dialettale 2005–; vice-pres Società di Linguistica Italiana 2004–06, hon memb Asociatia Cultural? Alexandru Philippide Romania 2005–; fell Br Acad 2003; Dr (hc) Univ of Bucharest 2013; Commander Serviciul Credincios (Romania); *Books* Interactive Morphonology. Metaphony in Italy (1991), A Linguistic History of Italian (1995), The Dialects of Italy (co-ed with M Parry, 1997), Storia linguistica dell'italiano (1998), Reference Grammar of Modern Italian (with C Robustelli, 2000), The Early Textualization of the Romance Languages: recent perspectives (co-ed with M Zaccarello, 2004), Reference Grammar of Modern Italian (with C Robustelli, 2 edn, 2007), The Cambridge History of the Romance Languages I: Structures (co-ed with J C Smith and A Ledgeway, 2011), Morphological Autonomy: Perspectives from Romance Inflectional Morphology (co-ed with J C Smith, M Goldbach and M O Hinzelin, 2011), The Cambridge History of the Romance Languages II: Contexts (co-ed with J C Smith and A Ledgeway, 2013), The Boundaries of Pure Morphology (co-ed with S Cruschina and J C Smith), The Oxford Guide to the Romance Languages (co-ed, with A Ledgeway, 2016); *Recreations* travel, bicycling, Romanian culture and history; *Style—* Prof Martin Maiden; ✉ Trinity College, Oxford OX1 3BH (☎ 01865 270488, fax 01865 270575, e-mail martin.maiden@mod-langs.ox.ac.uk)

MAIDSTONE, Bishop of 2015–; Rt Rev Roderick Charles Howell (Rod) Thomas; *Career* ordained: deacon 1993, priest 1994; curate St Andrew's Church Plymouth 1995–99, priest-in-charge St Matthew's Church Elburton 1999–2005, vicar Elburton 2005–15; *Style—* The Rt Rev the Bishop of Maidstone

MAIN, Anne; MP; da of George Wiseman (d 1996), and Rita *née* Osborne; *b* Cardiff; *Educ* Univ of Swansea, Univ of Sheffield (PGCE); *m* 1, Stephen Tonks (decd); 1 s (Nick), 2 da (Claire, Jennifer); m 2, Andrew Main; 1 s (Alexander); *Career* MP (Cons) St Albans 2005–; cncllr (Cons) Beaconsfield Town Cncl 1999–2001, cncllr (Cons) S Bucks DC 2001–; *Style—* Mrs Anne Main, MP; ✉ House of Commons, London SW1A 0AA (e-mail maina@parliament.uk); Constituency Office ☎ 01727 825100, website www.annemain.com

MAIN, Prof Brian George McArthur; s of George McArthur Main, of Buckhaven, Fife, and Margaret Welsh, *née* Currie; *b* 24 August 1947; *Educ* Univ of St Andrews (BSc), Univ of Calif Berkeley (MBA, MA, PhD); *m* 4 July 1980, June Marks Lambert, da of James S Lambert; 2 s (Christopher b 23 June 1985, Simon b 4 July 1988), 1 da (Alice b 11 March 1992); *Career* prodn planning assoc and mangr Eli Lilly 1971–72, reader in economics Univ of Edinburgh 1983–87 (lectr 1976–83); prof of economics: Univ of St Andrews 1987–91, Univ of Edinburgh 1991–; dir David Hume Inst 1995–2005; memb Cncl Scottish Economic Soc 1982–91; FRSE 1998, acad fell CIPD 2012–; *Recreations* running, fishing; *Style—* Prof Brian Main, FRSE; ✉ University of Edinburgh Business School, Edinburgh EH8 9JS (☎ 0131 650 8360, e-mail brian.main@ed.ac.uk)

MAIN, Dr Monica Maitland; da of Kenneth Morrison (d 2006), and Gwynneth, *née* Austin; *b* 9 August 1952, Dingwall, Ross-shire; *Educ* Dingwall Acad, Univ of Aberdeen (MB ChB); *m* 12 July 1975, William George Main; 1 s (Robert Andrew Kenneth b 22 April 1980), 1 da (Jennifer Austin b 25 March 1983); *Career* med practitioner: Kingsmills Practice Inverness 1982–86, Brora 1992–2011; HM Lord-Lt Sutherland 2005–; DRCOG 1978, FRCGP 2011 (MRCGP 1979); *Recreations* curling, gardening; *Style—* Dr Monica Main; ✉ Ballamhor, 35 Golf Road, Brora, Sutherland KW9 6QS (☎ 01408 621234, e-mail pandorakw96@aol.com)

MAINE, John; *b* 31 October 1942, Bristol; *Career* sculptor; *Solo Exhibitions* incl: Dissenters Chapel Gallery London 2001, Howden Minster Yorks 2003, Islington Green Memorial 2006, Royal Acad of Arts London 2011, St Laurence Saxon Church Bradford-on-Avon 20120, Art on the Underground Green Park 2012, Salisbury Cathedral 2014, Pitmedden Garden 2015; RA 1995; *Style—* John Maine, Esq, RA; ✉ c/o Royal Academy of Arts, Burlington House, Piccadilly, London WIJ 0BD

MAINELLI, Alderman Prof Michael R; s of Michael R Mainelli, and Katherine E, *née* Smith; *b* 19 December 1958; *Educ* Harvard Univ (Martin Marietta scholar, BA), Trinity Coll Dublin, LSE (PhD); *Family* 1 s (Nicholas b 7 Oct 1989); m, 1996, Elisabeth, *née* Reuss; 2 da (Xenia b 2 Feb 1998, Maxine b 12 Sept 2000); *Career* researcher Harvard Laboratory for Computer Graphics and Spatial Analysis 1977–81; Petroconsultants Group: Geodat project dir Petroconsultants Ltd 1979–82, general mangr Petroconsultants (CES) Ltd 1982–85; pres ISF Inc 1985–86, sr mangr Arthur Andersen & Co Management Consultants 1986–87, ptnr (BDO Consulting) BDO Binder Hamlyn 1988–94, ptnr Arthur Andersen & Co 1994–95; dir: Whale Conservation Inst 1994–97, Z/Yen Gp 1995–, Comax Secure Business Services Ltd 1997–99, Eyebright plc 2002–2004; corp devpt dir Defence Evaluation & Research Agency (DERA) MOD 1995–97; chief scientist The Financial Laboratory 1995–98, princ advsr Long Finance and London Accord 2005–; cmmr London Waterways Cmmn GLA 2006–; chm: Jaffe Associates 1999–2003, CityAxis 2001–08; non-

M

exec dir: Sirius Minerals plc 2005–13, UK Accreditation Serv 2005–, Wishbone Gold plc 2012–, PCG Entertainment plc 2013–; Mercers Sch meml prof of commerce Gresham Coll 2005–09, visiting prof Dept of Mgmnt Info Systems and Innovation Gp LSE 2008–12, prof emeritus and fell Gresham Coll 2009–; memb: Strategic Planning Soc 1990–99 (dir 1995–98), Editorial Bd Jl of Strategic Change 1990–, Ed Bd Jl of Business Strategy, Advsy Bd City Univ Sch of Informatics 1999–2003, Professional Services Global Competitiveness Gp HM Treasy 2008–09, Advsy Panel Centre for Cities 2008–10, Corporate Governance and Risk Mgmnt Ctee ACCA 2009–, Professional and Business Services Cncl BIS 2009–, Governance, Risk and Performance Forum ACCA 2011–; int advsr Taoiseach's Office IFS Industry Advsy Ctee 2015–; author of numerous pubns in learned jls; Br Computer Soc IT Dir of the Year 2004/05, Gentiluomo Associazione Cavalieri di San Silvestro 2011, Consigliere del Senato Accademico L'Accademia Tiberina 2015–; chm Broad Street Ward Club 2004–05, chm Real Time Club 2009–10; tstee: Int Fund for Animal Welfare 2007–13, Gresham Cncl 2008–, Morden Coll 2015–; Alderman (Broad St Ward) City of London Corp 2013–; Liveryman Worshipful Co of World Traders 2006–, Freeman Co of Watermen & Lightermen 2013–, Hon Liveryman Co of Furniture Makers 2014–; MInstPet 1986, MInstD 1988, FIMC 1990, FCCA 1996, FCSI 1999, FBCS (MBCS 1989); *Publications* Clean Business Cuisine: Now and Z/Yen (2000), Information Technology for the Not for Profit Sector (2001), The Price of Fish: A New Approach to Wicked Economics and Better Decisions (2011, Finance, Investment & Economics Gold Prize Independent Publishers Book Awards 2012); *Recreations* sailing, bagpipes, skiing; *Clubs* Royal Corinthian Yacht, Harvard; *Style*— Alderman Prof Michael Mainelli; ✉ c/o Z/Yen Group Ltd, 90 Basinghall Street, London EC2V 5AY (☎ 020 7562 9562, fax 020 7628 5751, e-mail michael_mainelli@zyen.com); website www.lady-daphne.co.uk and www.zyen.com

MAINGARD DE LA VILLE-ÈS-OFFRANS, Sir (Louis Pierre) René; kt (1982), CBE (1961); s of Joseph René Maingard de la Ville-ès-Offrans (d 1956), and Véronique, *née* Hugnin (d 1969); *b* 9 July 1917; *Educ* St Joseph's Coll, Royal Coll of Mauritius, Business Trg Corp London; *m* 1946, Marie Hélène Françoise, da of Sir Philippe Raffray, CBE, QC (d 1975); 3 da (Catherine, Anne, Sophie); *Career* served WWII RAF Fighter Cmd 131 and 165 Sqdn 1939–45; chm De Chazal du Mée Assocs Ltd, chm and md Rogers & Co Ltd 1948–82; chm: Mauritius Steam Navigation Co Ltd 1964, Mauritius Portland Cement Co Ltd 1960–, Mauritius Molasses Co Ltd 1968–, United Docks Ltd 1960–; dir: Mauritius Commercial Bank Ltd 1956–, The Anglo-Mauritius Assurance Co; consul for Finland in Mauritius 1957–83; Order of the White Rose (Finland) 1973; *Recreations* golf, fishing, boating; *Clubs* Dodo, Mauritius Turf; *Style*— Sir René Maingard de la Ville-ès-Offrans, CBE; ✉ De Chazal Du Mée Associates Ltd, PO Box 799, Port Louis, Mauritius (☎ 2638549)

MAINI, Prof Philip Kumar; s of Panna Lal Maini (d 1972), and Satya Wati, *née* Bhandari; *b* 16 October 1959, Magherafelt, NI; *Educ* Balliol Coll Oxford (open exhibitioner, Mouat-Jones scholar, Prosser Prize, MA, DPhil); *Career* lectr in applied mathematics CCC Oxford 1984, SERC postdoctoral research asst Centre for Mathematical Biology Mathematical Inst Univ of Oxford 1985 and 1986–87, asst master Eton Coll 1986, lectr in applied mathematics Balliol Coll Oxford and jr research fell Wolfson Coll Oxford 1987–88, asst prof Dept of Mathematics Univ of Utah Salt Lake City 1988–90 (research visitor 1985), tutorial fell BNC Oxford 1990–2005, prof of mathematical biology and dir Centre for Mathematical Biology Univ of Oxford 1998– (lectr in mathematical biology 1990–2005), professorial fell St John's Coll Oxford 2005–; visiting scientist Los Alamos Nat Lab 1985, visiting conslt Dept of Applied Mathematics Univ of Washington Seattle 1993, visiting scholar Centre in Statistical Science and Industrial Mathematics Queensland Univ of Technol 1994, visiting scholar Sch of Mathematics and Statistics Univ of Sydney 1994 and 1995, visiting prof Williams Coll MA 1995, visiting prof IMA Univ of Minnesota 1998, Royal Soc-Mexican Acad of Sciences exchange visitor Univ Nacional Autónoma de Mexico 1998, mathematician-in-residence New Coll Univ of S Florida 1999, visiting fell Clare Hall Cambridge 2001, visiting fell Queensland Univ of Technol 2001 and 2003, prof Université Pierre et Marie Curie Paris VI 2002, foreign visiting fell Research Inst for Electronic Science Hokkaido Univ Sapporo 2002, visiting prof Nat Center for Theoretical Sciences Nat Tsing Hua Univ 2002, visiting prof Univ Degli Studi di Modena e Reggio Emilia and Univ Degli Studi di Ancona 2003, affiliated researcher Biocomplexity Inst Indiana Univ Bloomington 2005, hon guest prof Univ of Electronic Science and Technol Chengdu China 2005, visiting prof Dept of Mathematics Chinese Univ of Hong Kong 2005, adjunct prof Sch of Mathematical Sci Queensland Univ of Technol 2006–; memb: Co-ordination Ctee European Network on Dynamics of Complex Systems in Biosciences 1991–94, Mathematics Coll EPSRC 1994–2006, Advsy Bd Interdisciplinary Center for the Study of Biocomplexity Univ of Notre Dame 2003–, Cncl IMA 2004–07 (founding memb Ctee Forum on Mathematics in Med and Biology 1991–96 (sec 1991–96)), Scientific Advsy Bd Centre for Mathematical Medicine Fields Inst Toronto 2005–, Bd of Govrs Mathematical Biosciences Inst Ohio State Univ 2006–09; managing ed Bulletin of Mathematical Biology 2002–, ed-in-chief Jl of Nonlinear Science 2004–, assoc ed Cancer Research 2008–; memb Editorial Bd: FORMA 1994–, Mathematical Applied Med and Biology 1995–, Computational and Mathematical Methods in Medicine (formerly Jl of Theoretical Med) 1996–2012, Wiley Series in Mathematical and Computational Biology 1998, Chapman and Hall Mathematical Biology and Med Series 2001–09, Discrete and Continuous Dynamical Systems Series B 2001–04, World Scientific Lecture Notes in Complex Systems 2001–, Jl of Mathematical Biology 2002–, Springer Lecture Notes in Mathematics 2004–, Applied Mathematics Research Express 2004–06, Mathematical Biosciences and Engrg 2004–, Mathematical Models and Methods in Applied Sciences 2005–; memb: Br Soc for Developmental Biology 1988–, Soc for Mathematical Biology 1988– (memb Bd 1996–2000), Soc for Industrial and Applied Mathematics 1988– (memb Activity Gp on Life Sciences 2000–), European Soc for Mathematical and Theoretical Biology 1992– (memb Bd 1994–99), London Mathematical Soc 1992–, Physiological Soc 2004–06; Bellman Prize 1997, Royal Soc Leverhulme Tst sr research fell 2001–02; life memb Clare Hall Cambridge 2002; miembro correspondente Academia Mexicana de Crencias 2011; FIMA 2003, fell Soc for Industrial and Applied Mathematics 2012, FRSB 2013, FRS 2015; Experimental and Theoretical Advances in Biological Pattern Formation (ed, 1993), Mathematical Models for Biological Pattern Formation (jt ed, 2000), Morphogenesis and Pattern Formation in Biological Systems: Experiments and Models, Proceedings of Chubu 2002 Conference (ed, 2003), Multiscale Modeling of Developmental Systems (jt ed, 2007), Mathematical Biology (jt ed, 2009); author of over 300 research articles; *Recreations* travel, football; *Style*— Prof Philip K Maini; ✉ Wolfson Centre for Mathematical Biology, Andrew Wiles Building, Radcliffe Observatory Quarter, Woodstock Road, Oxford OX2 6GG (☎ 01865 283889, fax 01865 270515, e-mail maini@maths.ox.ac.uk)

MAINLAND, Kath; CBE (2014); *Career* chief exec Edinburgh Festival Fringe Soc 2009–16, exec dir Melbourne Festival 2016–; *Style*— Ms Kath M Mainland, CBE; ✉ Melbourne Festival, PO Box 10, Flinders Lane, Melbourne, Victoria 8009 Australia

MAIR, Alexander Stirling Fraser (Alistair); MBE (1987), DL (Perth and Kinross 1993); *b* 1935, Aberdeenshire; *Educ* Robert Gordon's Coll Aberdeen, Univ of Aberdeen (BSc), Open Univ (BA); *m*; 4 s, 1 da; *Career* short serv cmmn RAF 1960–62, tech offr Central Work Study Unit Air Miny; grad apprentice rising to shop control mangr and product centre mangr Rolls Royce Ltd Glasgow 1957–71, md Caithness Glass Ltd Wick 1971–75, mktg dir Worcester Royal Porcelain Co 1975–77; Caithness Glass plc: md 1977–91, cmmnd new factory Perth 1979, led MBO 1984, chm 1991–98, led second MBO 1993; non-exec

dir: Grampian Television 1986–2001, Crieff Hydro Ltd 1994–2003 (chm 1996–2003), Murray VCT 3 plc 1998–2006; CBI: memb Scot Cncl 1981–92, memb Cncl 1985–92, chm Scot 1989–91, memb Pres's Ctee 1990–91, chm Regnl Chairmen's Ctee 1990–91; pres Br Glass Manufacturers Confedn 1997–98 (dep pres 1995–96); govr Morrison's Acad Crieff 1985–2006 (chm 1996–2006), cmmr Queen Victoria Sch Dunblane 1992–97, memb Ct Univ of Aberdeen 1993–2010 (convenor FE Ctee 1998–2002, chllr's assessor and vice-chm 2000–10); chm: Crieff and Dist Aux Assoc (Richmond House) 1993–98, Perth (subsequently Ochil and S Perthshire) Cons & Unionist Assoc 1999–2009, Scot Ctee of Chairmen Higher Education Insts 2001–07; vice-chm Cons and Unionist Party Scotland 1992–93 (memb Scot Business Gp 1989–93); hon pres D of E Award Perth & Kinross Assoc 1993–; LLD Univ of Aberdeen 2004; FRSA 1986; *Recreations* reading, current affairs, gardening, walking; *Clubs* Royal Northern and University (Aberdeen); *Style*— Dr Alistair Mair, MBE, DL; ✉ Woodend, Madderty, Crieff, Perthshire PH7 3PA (☎ and fax 01764 683210)

MAIR, Avril; da of William Robert Mair, and Irene, *née* Nicol; *Educ* Buckie HS, Univ of Edinburgh (MA); *Career* journalist; clubs ed The List 1990–92, features ed Edinburgh Festival Times 1990–91; freelance contrib: Self Service, Raygun, Mixmag, The Herald On Sunday, Scotland On Sunday; i-D magazine: asst ed 1992–95, dep ed 1994–95, ed 1995–2004; former assoc ed Elle magazine, fashion features dir Harper's Bazaar 2013–; *Books* Smilei-D: Fashion and Style, The Best From 20 Years of i-D (2001); *Style*— Ms Avril Mair; ✉ Harper's Bazaar, Hearst, 72 Broadwick Street, London W1F 9EP

MAIR, Baron (life Peer UK 2015), of Cambridge in the County of Cambridgeshire; Prof Robert James Mair; CBE (2010); s of Prof (William) Austyn Mair, CBE, FREng, of Cambridge, and Mary Woodhouse, *née* Crofts; *b* 20 April 1950; *Educ* Leys Sch Cambridge, Clare Coll Cambridge (MA, PhD); *m* 19 Sept 1981, Margaret Mary Plowden, da of Rt Hon Sir Patrick O'Connor (d 2001); 1 da (Julia b 29 May 1984), 1 s (Patrick b 13 May 1986); *Career* asst engr (later sr engr) Scott Wilson Kirkpatrick & Partners London & Hong Kong 1971–82 (seconded to Univ of Cambridge researching tunnelling in soft ground 1976–79); dir Geotechnical Consulting Group (specialising in geotechnical engrg) 1983–; Royal Acad of Engrg visiting prof Univ of Cambridge 1997–; prof of engrg Univ of Cambridge 1998–; master Jesus Coll Cambridge 2001–11; chair Royal Soc/Royal Acad of Engrg Report on Shale Gas and Hydraullic Fracturing ('Fracking') 2012; Br Geotechnical Soc Prize 1981, ICE Unwin meml lectr 1992, Bishop Medal 1994, Sir Harold Harding meml lectr 1998, Gold medal ICE 2004, Singapore Public Service Medal 2011; fell St John's Coll Cambridge 1998–2001, fell Jesus Coll Cambridge 2011; Hon DSc Univ of Nottingham 2011; FICE 1990, FREng 1992 (sr vice-pres 2008–11), FRS 2007; *Publications* Pressuremeters : Methods and Interpretation (with D Muir Wood, *qv*, 1987); papers in jls on geotechnical engineering, particularly related to tunnelling; *Recreations* supporting QPR, sailing, tennis, golf, long walks; *Style*— Prof the Lord Mair, CBE, FRS, FREng; ✉ Department of Engineering, Trumpington Street, Cambridge CB2 1PZ (☎ 01223 332631, fax 01223 339713, e-mail rjm50@cam.ac.uk)

MAIRS, Raymond John; s of David Mairs (d 1991), of Co Antrim, and Susan Elizabeth, *née* Colvin (d 1978); *b* 15 August 1951; *Educ* Ballyclare HS, Queen's Univ Belfast (BSc, DipArch); *m* 6 Aug 1976, Carol Jean Ruth, da of Neville Arthur Ginn, of Co Antrim; 3 da (Rachel Ruth b 1981, Rebecca Ann b 1985, Jessica Elizabeth b 1989); *Career* architect, fish farmer; private practice 1978, ptnr Mairs & Wray 1979–92, Raymond J Mairs Chartered Architects 1992–; memb RSUA Housing Ctee 1985–86; chm: Br Trout Assoc 1988–90, Euro Gp of Fédération Européenne de la Salmoniculture 1988–93, Southern Trout Co-op Ltd 1993–95, Northern Ireland Seafoods Ltd 1997– (dir 1993–); dir NI Food and Drink Assoc 1996–2000; rapporteur Aqua-Culture Working Gp of Fisheries Advsy Ctee to Euro Cmmn 1989–92, vice-chm Health Promotion Agency N Ireland 1997–2000 (memb 1990–2000), memb BBC NI Agric Advsy Ctee 1994–; *Style*— Raymond J Mairs, Esq; ✉ Glen Oak House, Crumlin BT29 4BW (☎ 028 9442 3172, e-mail rjm@glenoak.co.uk)

MAIRS, Robin Gordon James; s of Gordon Mairs, and Elizabeth, *née* Waugh; *b* 10 April 1969, Northern Ireland; *Educ* Univ of Manchester (LLB), Univ of Cambridge (LLM); *m* 13 April 1998, Gaynor, *née* Crawford; 1 da (Beth b 30 April 1999), 1 s (Cameron b 24 March 2001); *Career* called to the Bar 1992, recorder 2009, fee-paid judge Health, Education and Social Care Chamber (Mental Health – Restricted Patients Panel) First Tier Tbnl 2011, circuit judge (NE Circuit) 2015–; *Recreations* rugby, history, food; *Style*— His Hon Judge Mairs; ✉ Leeds Combined Court Centre, 1 Oxford Row, Leeds LS1 3BG

MAITLAND, Lady (Helen) Olga; elder da of 17 Earl of Lauderdale (d 2008); *b* 23 May 1944; *Educ* Sch of St Mary and St Anne Abbots Bromley, Lycée Français de Londres; *m* 19 April 1969, Robin William Patrick Hamilton Hay, *qv*, s of William Reginald Hay, of Mapperley, Nottingham; 2 s (Alastair b 1972, Fergus b 1981), 1 da (Camilla b 1975); *Career* former trainee reporter: Fleet St News Agency, Blackheath and District Reporter; reporter and columnist Sunday Express 1967–91, freelance journalist 1991–, with Daily Mail 1998–2001; pres Defence & Security Forum 1992–; fndr and chm: Families for Defence 1983–; Parly candidate (Cons): Bethnal Green & Stepney 1987, Sutton and Cheam 2001; MP (Cons) Sutton and Cheam 1992–97; PPS to Rt Hon Sir John Wheeler as Min of State for NI 1996–97; former memb Select Ctees for: Educn, Health and Procedures; private membs bills: Prisoner's Return to Custody 1995, Offensive Weapons 1996; former sec to Cons Backbench: NI, Defence and Foreign Affrs Ctees, Yugoslav Parly Gp; public affrs conslt 2001–, ceo Int Assoc of Money Transfer Networks 2005–08, ceo Money Transfer Int 2008–; non-exec dir Earthport plc 2008–12; pres Algeria Br Business Cncl 2005–, chm Copenhagen Compliance UK 2016–; *Publications* Margaret Thatcher: The First Ten Years (1989), Faith in the Family (1997); contrib: Peace Studies in our Schools, Political Indoctrination in our Schools; *Recreations* theatre, travel; *Style*— The Lady Olga Maitland; ✉ 21 Cloudesley Street, London N1 0HX (☎ 020 7837 9212, e-mail olga.maitland@virgin.net)

MAITLIS, Emily; da of Prof Peter Michael Maitlis, FRS, *qv*, and Marion, *née* Basco; *b* 6 September 1970; *Educ* King Edward VII Sch Sheffield, Queens' Coll Cambridge (MA); *m* 21 Dec 2000, Mark Gwynne; *Career* documentary maker TVB Hong Kong 1992–96, hand-over prodn team Channel 4 1997, business corr NBC Asia 1997–98, business corr Sky News 1998–2000, presenter Sky News 2000–01, anchor BBC London News 2001–06, presenter Newsnight (BBC 2) 2006–; *Clubs* Soho House, Foreign Correspondents, Hong Kong; *Style*— Ms Emily Maitlis

MAITLIS, Prof Peter Michael; s of Jacob J Maitlis (d 1984), and Judith, *née* Ebel (d 1985); *b* 15 January 1933; *Educ* Hendon Co GS, Univ of Birmingham (BSc), Univ of London (PhD, DSc); *m* 19 July 1959, Marion da of Herbert Basco (d 1977); 3 da (Niccola b 1963, Sally b 1965, Emily, *qv* b 1970); *Career* asst lectr Univ of London 1956–60, Fulbright fell Cornell Univ 1960–61, res fell Harvard Univ 1961–62, prof McMaster Univ Hamilton Canada 1967–72 (asst prof 1962–64, assoc prof 1964–67), prof of inorganic chem Univ of Sheffield 1972–94 (research prof 1994–2002, now emeritus); fell Alfred P Sloan Fndn (USA) 1968–70, EWR Steacie Prize (Canada) 1971, RSC medallist (UK) 1981, Tilden lectr 1979, Sir Edward Frankland lectr (UK) 1984, RSC Mond lectr (UK) 1996–97, Gordon Stone lectr Univ of Bristol 2001, Paolo Chini lectr Italian Chem Soc 2001, Glenn T Seaborg meml lectr Univ of Calif at Berkeley 2004–05; Kurnakov Medal (Russian Acad of Sci) 1998; various offices in RSC (pres Dalton Div 1984–86), chm SERC Chemistry Ctee 1985–88, memb BBC Sci Consultative Gp 1988–93, foreign memb Accademia Lincei (Italy) 1999; FRS 1984 (memb Cncl 1991–93), FRSC; *Books* The Organic Chemistry of Palladium (Vols 1 & 2 1971), Metal Catalysis in Industrial Organic Processes (jtly, 2006),

Greener Fischer-Tropsch Processes (co-ed and co-author, 2013); res papers in various chemistry jls; *Recreations* travel, music, good company, dining; *Clubs* Royal Soc London; *Style—* Prof Peter Maitlis, FRS; ✉ Department of Chemistry, University of Sheffield, Sheffield S3 7HF

MAJEED, Ali Waqar; s of Haji Abdul Majeed, and Arshad Majeed; *b* 17 July 1959; *Educ* Cadet Coll Hasanabdal, King Edward Med Coll Lahore, Univ of Punjab (BSc, MB BS), Univ of Sheffield (MD); *m* Julia, da of Jonathan Hugh Dicks and Jennifer Lyn; 3 s (Adam Ali, Noah Ali, Jacob Ali); *Career* house offr Mayo Hosp Lahore 1984, demonstrator King Edward Med Coll Lahore 1985; SHO: Killingbeck Hosp Leeds 1986, St James's Univ Hosp Leeds 1986–87, Leicester Gen Hosp 1987–88, Leicester Royal Infirmary 1987–88; Peri-fellowship registrar Lincoln County Hosp 1988–89, res fell Univ Surgical Unit Royal Hallamshire Hosp Sheffield 1989–91, lectr in surgery and hon surgical registrar Chesterfield and N Derbys Royal Hosp 1993–94; Univ Surgical Unit Royal Hallamshire Hosp: lectr in surgery and hon sr registrar 1994–96, sr lectr in surgery and hon conslt surgn 1997–2003, conslt surgn 2003–, hon prof of surgery 2005–; Ronald Raven Travelling Fellowship Br Assoc of Surgical Oncology 1996, Dinwoody Travelling Fellowship Assoc of Surgns 2001, Sir Ernest Finch Travelling Fellowship 2001; Cutlers Prize 1992, Young Scientist Prize Euro Digestive Diseases Week Oslo 1994; FRCS 1989, FRCS(Gen) 1997; *Publications* author of numerous published book chapters, articles, papers and abstracts, mostly concerning the treatment of gallstones and colorectal liver metastases; *Recreations* photography, walking, gourmet food; *Style—* Ali Majeed, Esq; ✉ Department of Surgery, K Floor, Royal Hallamshire Hospital, Sheffield S10 2JF (☎ and fax 01142 712208)

MAJOR, Rt Hon Sir John; KG (2005), CH (1999), PC (1987); s of Thomas Major (d 1963), and his 2 w, Gwendolyn Minnie Coates (d 1970); *b* 29 March 1943; *Educ* Rutlish Sch; *m* 1970, Dame Norma Christina Elizabeth, DBE, da of Norman Wagstaff Johnson (ka 1945); 1 da (Elizabeth b 1972), 1 s (James b 1975); *Career* AIB banker and various exec posts in UK and overseas Standard Chartered Bank plc 1965–79; memb Lambeth Borough Cncl 1968–71 (chm Housing Ctee 1970–71), Parly candidate (Cons) St Pancras N (Camden) 1974 (both elections); memb Bd Warden Housing Assoc 1975–83; MP (Cons): Huntingdonshire 1979–83, Huntingdon 1983–2001; jt sec Cons Party Parly Environment Ctee 1979–81, pres Eastern Area Young Conservatives 1983–85; PPS to Mins of State Home Office 1981–83, asst Govt whip 1983–84, a Lord Cmmr of the Treasury (Govt whip) 1984–85, parly under-sec of state for social security 1985–86, min of state for social security DHSS 1986–87, chief sec to HM Treasury June 1987-July 1989, sec of state for foreign and Cwlth affrs July-Oct 1989, Chancellor of the Exchequer Oct 1989-Nov 1990, leader of the Cons Party, Prime Minister and First Lord of the Treasury 28 Nov 1990–97 (resigned as leader of Cons Pty June 1995, re-elected July); chm: European Advsy Cncl Emerson Electric Co 1999–2015, European Bd Carlyle Gp 2001–05 (memb 1998–2005), Advsy Bd Global Infrastructure Partners 2007–, Int Advsy Bd Nat Bank of Kuwait 2007–14, Campaign Bd KCL 2010–, Global Advsy Bd AECOM 2011–16; memb Cons Pty Advsy Cncl 2003–05; sr advsr Credit Suisse 2001–, memb European Bd Siebel Systems Inc 2001–03, non-exec dir Mayflower Corp plc 2000–03; chm Ditchley Cncl 2000–09, chm Queen Elizabeth Diamond Jubilee Tst 2011–; memb: Int Bd of Governors Peres Center for Peace Israel 1997–, Bd of Advisers Baker Inst Houston 1998–2005, InterAction Cncl Tokyo 1998–2008; hon pres Sight Savers Appeal 2001–; pres: Asthma UK 1998–, Br and Cwlth Cricket Charitable Tst 2002–; jt pres Chatham House London 2009–; vice-pres: Macmillan Cancer Relief 2001–, Inst of Sports Sponsorship 2001–, See Ability 2013– (patron Sight Pioneers 2006–13); patron: Mercy Ships, Prostate Cancer Charity, Support for Africa 2000, Atlantic Partnership 2001–, FCO Assoc 2001–, Professional Cricketers Assoc 2001–, Deafblind UK 2002–, Consortium for Street Children 2002–, 21st Century Tst 2002–, Goodman Fund Chicago 2002–, Norfolk Cricket Umpires and Scorers Assoc 2002–, Dickie Bird Fndn 2004–, Fndn for Peace 2004–, Margaret Thatcher Scholarship Tst 2012, Br Music Hall Soc 2012, Br Gymnastics 2013–, Ladybird Boat Tst 2014–, Cons Alumni 2014–, Oxford Univ Cons Assoc 2015–, Cromwell Museum Tst 2015–; ambass Chance to Shine 2005–, sr patron Bow Gp 2012–13 (pres 2012–14); vice-patron The Atlantic Cncl of the UK; hon cmmr Sir John A Macdonald Bicentennial Cmmn 2012–; hon bencher Middle Temple 1993; hon Freeman Merchant Taylor's Co 2002, Freedom of the City of Cork 2008, Elder Bro Corp of Trinity House 2013; Grand Cordon of the Order of the Rising Sun 2012; The Autobiography (1999), More Than a Game (2007), My Old Man (2012); *Recreations* music, theatre, reading, travel, cricket and other sports, opera; *Clubs* Carlton, Farmers', Buck's, Pratt's, Surrey CCC (pres 2000–02, hon life vice-pres), MCC (memb Ctee 2001–04, 2005–08 and 2009–12); *Style—* The Rt Hon Sir John Major, KG, CH; ✉ PO Box 38506, London SW1P 1ZW

MAJUMDAR, Bish; s of Pran Kumar Majumdar (d 1949), of Calcutta, and Sudha, *née* Sengupta; *b* 20 January 1944; *Educ* Univ of Calcutta (MB, BS), Univ of London (DLO); *m* 19 Jan 1979, Sutapa Majumdar, da of Kalyan Sengupta (d 1954); 2 da (Selina b 26 Jan 1983, Mita b 27 Nov 1985); *Career* registrar Dept of ENT Surgery: Univ Hosp of Wales 1974–76, W Infirmary Glasgow 1976–78; sr registrar: Sheffield Hosps 1978–80, Univ Hosps Nottingham 1980–82; conslt ENT surgn Derbys Royal Infirmary 1982–; clinical teacher otolaryngology Univ of Nottingham; Dep Lord-Lt Derbys 2011; memb: Portmann Fndn (Bordeaux), Res Soc, Br Assoc of Otolaryngology, Midland Inst of Otology; FRCSEd, FRCS, FRSM, FICS (USA); *Recreations* swimming, golf, travel; *Style—* Bish Majumdar, Esq; ✉ Beltoli, Malkin Lane, Mugginton, Ashbourne, Derbyshire DE6 4PL (☎ 01335 361123, e-mail beltoli@hotmail.co.uk); Derbyshire Royal Infirmary, Department of Otolaryngology, London Road, Derby (☎ 01332 254659)

MAK, Alan; *b* Nov 1983, York; *Educ* St Peter's Sch York, Peterhouse Cambridge (BA), Oxford Inst (MA); *Career* researcher Office of Ed Vaizey, MP 2006–07, slr Clifford Chance LLP 2007–14, small business owner 2014–15; MP (Cons) Havant 2015–; memb Law Soc of England and Wales 2009–; pres and tstee Magic Breakfast, fndr and chm Royal Br Legion Young Professionals' Bd, ambass One Young World; ECS Wade Prize for Administrative Law 2004; FRSA 2008; *Publications* Next Generation Vision for Financial Services; *Recreations* cinema, reading, sport, travel; *Style—* Alan Mak, Esq, MP; ✉ House of Commons, London SW1A 0AA (☎ 020 7210 3000, e-mail alan.mak.mp@parliament.uk, website www.alanmak.org.uk, Twitter @AlanMakMP)

MAKAROVA, Natalia; *b* 1940, Leningrad; *Educ* Vaganova Sch Leningrad; *m* 1976, Edward Karkar (who d 2013); 1 s (Andrei b 1 Feb 1978); *Career* ballet dancer and choreographer, also actress; with Kirov Ballet 1959–70, defected in London and joined American Ballet Theater (ABT) 1970 (but invited to dance with Kirov in Leningrad again in 1989, first ever Russian artistic exile so invited); guest artist with numerous int ballet cos incl: Royal Ballet, Paris Opera Ballet, National Ballet of Canada, Stuttgart Ballet, Royal Danish Ballet, English National Ballet (formerly London Festival Ballet), Béjart's Ballet of the 20th Century, Roland Petit's Ballet de Marseille, Hamburg Ballet; *Roles* with American Ballet Theater incl: debut in Giselle 1970, Tudor's Dark Elegies, Lilac Garden, Pillar of Fire and Romeo and Juliet, various by Balanchine, Robbins Neumeier, and Tetley, others incl: Rite of Spring (Tetley), Pas de Quatre (Dolin), La Bayadere (Makarova.Petipa), Miraculous Mandarin, The River (Ailey), Moors Pavanne (Limon), Raymonda, Concerto (Macmillan; & Nutcracker Works created for NM: Sacre du Printemps (Taras), I Vespri de Siciliani (dir by Callas in Turin 1973, choreography by Sege Lifar); Fellini (cr for Makarova & Babilee by Van Hoecke); other roles: Bach Sonata (Bejart), Neumeier's Illusions – Like Swan Lake; Cranko's Swan Lake; Le Jeune Home et La Mort (Petit); Proust Les Intermittence de Coeur (Petit); Cinderella (Ashton) Productions Staged; La BAyadere 2013 Stanislavsky & Nemirovich – Danchenko Theatre Moscow and the National Ballet of Kiev; with Royal Ballet incl: Swan Lake, Giselle, Sleeping Beauty, Les Sylphides, Manon, Song of the Earth, Concerto, Cinderella, A Month in the Country, Voluntaries, Dances at a Gathering, Serenade, Elite Syncopations, Rituals, Checkmate, Les Biches and Romeo and Juliet; works created for her incl: Robbins' Other Dances, Ashton's Rossignol, Tetley's Sacre du Printemps and Contradance, a MacMillan Pas de Deux with Donald MacLeary, Neumeier's Epilogue, Petit's Blue Angel, Bejart's Mephisto; others incl: Onegin (Evening Standard Award 1985), La Bayadère, The Firebird, Don Quixote, Coppélia, La Fille Mal Gardée, Notre Dame de Paris, Carmen, Cranko's Romeo and Juliet, La Sylphide, Jullitta Messina in Fellini (première, Rome Opera House) 1995; *Productions staged* The Kingdom of the Shades from La Bayadère (for American Ballet Theater) 1974; full length prodn of La Bayadère with reconstructed last act: ABT 1980, Royal Swedish Ballet and Royal Ballet 1989, Teatro Colon Buenos Aires 1992, La Scala Milan 1992, Ballet Santiago 1997, Finnish Nat Ballet 1997, Australian Ballet 1998, Teatro Municipal Brazil 2000, Neumeiers Hamburg Ballet 2002, Teatr Week Warsaw 2004, Ballet Corella Spain 2008, Tokyo Ballet 2009, Nat Ballet Sodre Uruguay 2012; Swan Lake: London Festival Ballet 1988, Teatro Municipal Brazil 2001, Perm Ballet Russia 2005, Nat Ballet of China 2006; Giselle (Royal Swedish Ballet) 2000, Sleeping Beauty (Royal Ballet) 2003, Shades: London Festival Ballet, Nat Ballet of Canada, San Francisco Ballet; Paquita: American Ballet Theatre, Korean Ballet, San Francisco Ballet; *Television* ballet prodns incl: Swan Lake, Giselle, Romeo and Juliet, La Bayadère, The Leningrad Legend, excerpt from Swan Lake in reunion with Kirov Ballet 1988; other dances, other progs and series: Ballerina (BBC) 1987, In a Class of Her Own (Channel 4), Assoluta (BBC), Natasha (BBC), Makarova Returns (documentary on return to the Kirov Ballet) 1989, Great Railway Journeys St Petersburg to Tashkent (documentary on the Bolshoi Express for BBC) 1994, Natalia Makarova Two Lives (Russian documentary); *Theatre* On Your Toes (musical comedy, Broadway, winner Tony award for best actress in a musical and seven other awards, later in West End, winner Olivier Award) 1983–84, Tovarich (Chichester Festival Theatre then West End) 1991, Two for the Seesaw (Moscow and St Petersburg) 1992, Misalliance (Chichester) 1997, Blithe Spirit (Palace Theatre Watford) 2000 *Awards* 1965 Gold Medal Varna Int Ballet Competition, 1969 Anna Pavlova Award, 1977 Dance Magazine Award, 1979 Mother of the Year Award, 1995 Positano Premia La Danza Lifetime Achievement Award, 2012 The Kennedy Centre Honours Lifetime Contribution Award, 2013 The Soul of Dance Award by Russian Ballet jnl & Min of Culture.; *Books* A Dance Autobiography (1979); chapter St Petersburg to Tashkent (in Great Railway Journeys, 1994); *Style—* Ms Natalia Makarova; ✉ c/o Dina Makaroff ☎ 16468 946977, e-mails dmakarova@aol.com

MAKEPEACE, John; OBE (1988); s of Harold Alfred Smith (d 1957), of Fenny Compton, Warks, and Gladys Marjorie, *née* Wright (d 1996); *b* 6 July 1939; *Educ* Denstone Coll; *m* 1 (m dis); m 2, 3 Dec 1984, Jennifer Moores, da of Harry Brinsden; *Career* furniture designer and maker; dir John Makepeace Ltd 1963–; fndr and dir: The Parnham Tst (charitable educnl tst) 1977–2000; memb Crafts Cncl 1972–77; tstee V&A 1987–91; sponsor Furniture Futures (V&A) 2009; *Exhibitions* incl: Arts Cncl Retrospective Touring Exhibition 2010–11, British Design 1948–2012: Innovation in the Modern Age (V&A) 2012; tstee Rycotewood Coll 1970–76; hon fell Arts UC Bournemouth 2009, fell Hereford Coll of Arts 2012 (hon fell 2013); Claxton Stevens Prize 1998 and 2009, Award of Excellence The Furniture Soc USA 2002, Prince Philip Designers Prize 2010 (special commendation), winner Prince Philip Designers Prize 2016; Liveryman Worshipful Co of Furniture Makers 1977 (Lifetime Achievement Award 2010); FCSD 1975, FRSA; *Publications* Makepeace: A Spirit of Adventure in Craft and Design by Prof Jeremy Myerson (1995), John Makepeace – Enriching the Language of Furniture (Arts Cncl Exhibition Catalogue, 2010); *Recreations* travel, contemporary applied arts and trees, gardening; *Clubs* Athenaeum; *Style—* John Makepeace, OBE; ✉ Farrs, Beaminster, Dorset DT8 3NB (☎ 01308 862204, e-mail info@johnmakepeacefurniture.com, website www.johnmakepeacefurniture.com)

MAKEPEACE, HE Richard Edward; CMG (2011); s of Edward Dugard Makepeace, and Patricia Muriel, *née* Malpas; *b* 24 June 1953, London; *Educ* St Paul's, Keble Coll Oxford; *m* 1980, Rupmani Catherine Pradhan; 2 s; *Career* served FCO 1976–77, 1985–89 and 1992–94; MECAS 1977–78; posted: Muscat 1979–80, Prague 1980–84, UKREP Brussels 1989–92, Cairo 1995–98; ambass to Sudan 1999–2002, ambass to United Arab Emirates 2003–06, consul-gen Jerusalem (Palestinian Territories) 2006–; *Recreations* travel, scuba diving; *Style—* HE Mr Richard Makepeace, CMG; ✉ c/o Foreign & Commonwealth Office (Jerusalem), King Charles Street, London SW1A 2AH

MAKGILL, Hon Diana Mary Robina; CVO (1990, LVO 1983, MVO 1971); da of 12 Viscount of Oxfuird (d 1986), and Anne Esther, *née* Bromley (d 1996); *b* 4 January 1930, London; *Educ* Strathcona Lodge Sch Vancouver Island; *Career* ceremonial offr Protocol Dept FCO 1961–90, protocol conslt 1990–; former pres Women of the Year Luncheon; memb Int Ctee Action on Addiction 1990–; conslt to Princess Helena Coll, govr St John and St Mary Primary Sch Hindon; hon steward of Westminster Abbey 1977–2002, memb Chalke Deanery Synod 1992–2002 and 2011–14, memb PCC St Mary's E Knoyle 2000–; pres Women's Branch Royal Br Legion E Knoyle, Sedgehill and Semley 2006–16 (now patron), chm SW Wilts Conservative Women's Ctee 2007–08, pres Wilts Branch Prayer Book Soc 2010–; Freedom of the City of London 1989; Jubilee Medal 1977; Order of Al Kawkab of Jordan 1966, Order of the White Rose of Finland 1969, Order of Star of Afghanistan 1971, Order of the Sacred Treasure of Japan 1971, Order of Independence of the UAE 1989; *Recreations* riding, reading, gardening, cinema, horse racing, shooting; *Style—* The Hon Diana Makgill, CVO; ✉ Clouds Lodge, East Knoyle, Wiltshire SP3 6BE (☎ and fax 01747 830260, e-mail dianamakgill@hotmail.com)

MAKHATELI, David; s of Nikoloz Makhatelli, of Denver, CO, and Marina, *née* Loladze; *b* 15 May 1975, Tbilisi, Georgia; *Educ* Tbsili V Chabukiani State Choreographic Inst, Royal Ballet Upper Sch; *m* 17 March 2007, Natalia, *née* Kremen; *Career* ballet dancer; Birmingham Royal Ballet 1994, Dutch Nat Ballet 1996–97, princ dance Houston Ballet 1997–2003; Royal Ballet: performances as guest dancer incl Des Grieux in Manon and Romeo in Romeo and Juliet 2003, first soloist 2003–07, princ 2007–; guest appearances in USA, Europe, Japan, Korea, Georgia, Panama and Russia; Prix de Lausanne (Espoire) 1992, first prize (jr div) Moscow Diaghilev Int Ballet Competition 1992, dip Paris Int Ballet Competition 1997; *Style—* David Makhateli, Esq; ✉ The Royal Opera House, The Royal Ballet, Covent Garden, London WC2E 9DD (☎ 020 7240 1200)

MAKIN, (Norman) Christopher; s of late Windsor Makin, and late Kathleen Mary, *née* Dyson; *b* 7 July 1943, Huddersfield, W Yorks; *Educ* King James GS Huddersfield; *m* 9 Aug 1969, Gillian, da of late Eric Reginald Mitton; 1 da (Rebecca Jane b 3 May 1977); *Career* chartered accountant; ptnr: Charles F Beer & Co 1971–87, Revell Ward Chartered Accountants 1987–97, Mazars Chartered Accountants (formerly Neville Russell) 1997–98, Bentley Jennison Chartered Accountants 1998–2003 (conslt in litigation support and mediation 2003–06), Chris Makin mediator 2006–; princ double bass: Leeds Symphony Orch, West Riding Opera; FCA 1969, FCMI 1978, FAE 1994, QDR 1998, MCIArb 2006; *Style—* N Christopher Makin, Esq; ✉ Well Cottage, 39 Water Royd Lane, Mirfield, West Yorkshire WF14 9SF; 3 Gray's Inn Square, London WC1R 5AH (☎ 020 7430 0333, fax 01924 494421, e-mail chris@chrismakin.co.uk, website www.chrismakin.co.uk)

MAKINSON, John Crowther; CBE (2001); s of Kenneth Crowther Makinson (d 1974), and Phyllis Georgina, *née* Miller; *b* 10 October 1954; *Educ* Repton, Christ's Coll Cambridge (exhibitioner, MA); *m* Virginia Clare, da of Dr John Macbeth; 2 da (Emma Violet b 13

M

April 1990, Lucy India b 3 Dec 1991); *Career* journalist Reuters (London, Paris and Frankfurt) 1976–79, ed Lex Column and head of companies section Financial Times 1979–86, vice-chm Saatchi & Saatchi (US) Holdings 1986–89, fndr ptnr Makinson Cowell investor relations conslts 1989–94, md The Financial Times Ltd 1994–96, fin dir Pearson plc 1996–2002, chm and ceo Penguin Gp 2002–; tstee Inst for Public Policy Research, tstee and chm Royal Nat Theatre; *Recreations* music, theatre, travel; *Clubs* Ivy; *Style*— John Makinson, Esq, CBE; ✉ Pearson plc, 80 Strand, London WC2R 0RL (☎ 020 7010 3030, fax 020 7010 6689, e-mail john.makinson@penguingroup.com)

MAKOWER, Andrew; s of Peter Makower, and Katharine, *née* Chadburn; *b* 5 October 1961; *Educ* St Paul's, Trinity Coll Cambridge (MA), Open Univ (MPA); *m*; 3 c; *Career* clerk House of Lords 1984–; *Style*— Andrew Makower, Esq

MALAHIDE, Patrick; *b* 24 March 1945; *Educ* Douai Sch, Univ of Edinburgh; *Career* actor; *Theatre* Bristol Old Vic incl: The Tempest, The Cherry Orchard, King Lear, Accidental Death of an Anarchist, Clandestine Marriage, Uncle Vanya; Birmingham Rep incl: The Crucible, The Wedding Feast; Traverse incl: The Android Circuit, Every Good Boy Deserves Favour; Royal Court incl: Operation Bad Apple, In the Ruins; other credits incl: Judgement (Liverpool), Cockups (Manchester Exchange), Map of the Heart (Globe), Mutabilitie (RNT), Hinterland (RNT), Embers (Duke of York's), Hamlet (RNT); *Television* incl: Minder, Black Adder, Pickwick Papers, The Russian Soldier, The December Rose, The Singing Detective, After the War, The Franchise Affair, Inspector Morse, Lovejoy, A Doll's House, The Blackheath Poisonings, The Secret Agent, Force of Duty, The Inspector Alleyn Mysteries, Middlemarch, Deacon Brodie, Longitude, All the King's Men, Victoria and Albert, Goodbye Mister Chips, In Search of the Brontës, Amnesia, Friends and Crocodiles, Elizabeth I, Five Days, Sensitive Skin, The Thirty Nine Steps, Game of Thrones, Endeavour, Hunted, The Paradise, New Worlds, Indian Summers, Luther; *Films* incl: The Killing Fields, Comfort and Joy, A Month in the Country, December Bride, A Man of No Importance, Two Deaths, Cutthroat Island, The Long Kiss Goodnight, US Marshals, Ordinary Decent Criminal, The World is not Enough, Billy Elliot, Quills, Captain Corelli's Mandolin, Sahara, Brideshead Revisited; *Screenplays* writer The Writing on the Wall (BBC) 1996, Pleas and Directions (BBC) 2002; *Recreations* sailing, walking; *Clubs* Royal Fowey Yacht; *Style*— Patrick Malahide, Esq; ✉ c/o Independent Talent Group, 40 Whitfield Street, London W1T 2RH(☎ 020 7636 6565)

MALBON, Vice Adm Sir Fabian Michael; KBE (2002); s of Rupert Charles Malbon (d 1989), and June Marion, *née* Downie (d 1981); *b* 1 October 1946, Southsea, Hants; *Educ* Brighton, Hove and Sussex GS; *m* 13 Dec 1969, Susan, *née* Thomas; 3 s (Timothy Fabian Charles b 22 April 1970, Benedict Rupert b 5 April 1972, Jonathon Howard b 11 July 1974); *Career* Offr under Trg 1965–69, Offr-of-the-Watch HMS Salisbury 1969–71, 1 Lt HMS Glasserton 1971–73, PWO course 1973–74, Staff Navigating Offr to Capt F6 HMS Andromeda 1975–77, Staff Navigating Offr Flag Offr Sea Training 1976–77, Navigating Offr HMS Antrim 1977–78, OIC Canadian Naval Navigation Sch Nova Scotia 1978–80, RN Staff Course 1981, Navigating Offr HMS Hermes 1981–82, CO HMS Torquay 1982–84, Directorate of Naval Logistic Planning MOD 1984, Cdr Sea Trg to Flag Offr Sea Trg 1985–87, CO HMS Brave 1987–88, dir Naval Serv Conditions 1988–91, RCDS 1991–92, CO HMS Invincible 1992–94, Asst COS to C-in-C Fleet 1994–95, dir of ops Jt HQ Land Command 1995–96, chief exec Naval Manning Agency and Naval Sec 1996–99, Dep C-in-C Fleet 1999–2001, dir Project TOPMAST 2001–02, warship trials master BAe Naval Systems 2002–05, Lt-Govr Guernsey 2005–11, C-in-C Guernsey 2005–11; pres Combined Cadet Force Assoc 2002–07, vice-pres Marine Soc and Sea Cadets 2007, pres Royal Naval Benevolent Tst 2007–12, pres/chm Union Jack Club 2011, tstee Chesil Tst 2013; *Recreations* sailing, fishing; *Clubs* RNSA; *Style*— Vice Adm Sir Fabian Malbon, KBE; ✉ e-mail yachtmaddie@gmail.com

MALCIC, Lawrence Michael; s of Lawrence Andrew Malcic, of St Louis, MO, and Marie Sprenger Malcic; *b* 22 September 1955; *Educ* Univ of Pennsylvania (BA, MArch); *m* 11 March 1995, Felicity Quevatre-Malcic, da of Leonard Quevatre; 2 s (Lawrence Justin b 13 Aug 1997, Luke Thomas b 12 Sept 1999); *Career* architect; architectural designer Robert L Boland Architects Inc St Louis 1978–79; Washington Univ St Louis: staff architect Urban Research and Design Center 1979–80, professional advsr for architecture and planning 1980–82, affiliate asst prof Sch of Architecture 1981–82, asst dean for planning and devpt Olin Sch of Business 1982–85; princ for design Gilmore, Malcic and Cannon Inc St Louis 1985–88, dir of design and sr vice-pres HOK Int Ltd London 1989–; visiting lectr in architecture Sch of Architecture and Environmental Design Univ of Texas 1987–88; architectural projects incl: Barclays Bank World HQ Canary Wharf, Cisco European HQ Amsterdam, Dexia Bank Tower Amsterdam, Forty Grosvenor Place London, Nortel Matra Campus Paris, NCR Netherlands HQ Amsterdam, Bow Bells House London, Darwin Centre Natural History Museum London, Washington Univ Plant Growth Lab St Louis, Ethyl Petroleum Research Lab St Louis, Passenger Terminal Amsterdam, VSM High Speed Rail Terminal St Petersburg, West India Quay Tower London, Metropole Hilton Hotel London, Taiz Hotel Yemen, St Barnabas Church Dulwich, Our Lady of Providence Church St Louis; planning project master plans incl: Oostelijke Handelskade (Eastern Docks) Amsterdam, Churchill Place Canary Wharf, Hof van Zuid (S Court), October Railway St Petersburg, Medun (Renault) Paris, Secheron Geneva, Washington Univ St Louis; AIA 1982; *Awards* incl: Medal of Honour Europa Nostra Awards 1997 and Special Commendation Obata Awards 1999 (both for FCO London), finalist Best Medium Sized Office FX Design Int Awards 1999 (for 216 Oxford St), Best Large Mixed-Use Scheme UK 1999 and Design Award Building Magazine 1999 (both for 02 Centre London), Commendation for Conversion/Restoration Environmental Awards Scheme 2000 (for Natural History Museum), Special Commendation Interior Design Times Gestetner Awards 2001 (for Goldings House Dept of Health London), finalist Best Large Office FX Design Awards 2001 and Special Commendation Times Gestener Awards 2001 (both for Cisco Bedfont Lakes Middx), Best Large Office Workplace FX Design Awards 2000 and Best Commercial Building SE Eng, Best Commercial Building Nat Award and Best of the Best all Categories and Regions Br Cncl for Offices Awards 2001 (all for Forty Grosvesnor Place), Commendation Innovation in Real Estate Corenet Global Awards 2003 (for both Darwin Centre Natural History Museum and Cisco European HQ Amsterdam); *Publications* author of various articles for jls incl Architects' Jl; *Recreations* travel; *Clubs* University (St Louis); *Style*— Lawrence Malcic, Esq; ✉ La Folie, Folie Lane, Vale, Guernsey GY3 5SE (☎ 01481 246444); HOK International Ltd, Qube, 90 Whitfield Street, London W1T 4EZ (☎ 020 7636 2006, fax 020 7636 1987, e-mail larry.malcic@hok.com)

MALCOLM, Christian Sean; *b* 3 June 1979, Cardiff; *Career* athlete; achievements incl: Silver medal (200m) Cwlth Games 1998, Bronze medal (4x100m relay) World Championships 2005, Bronze medal (4x100m relay) World Championships 2007, Bronze medal (200m) Cwlth Games 2010, Silver medal (200m) European Championships 2010; *Style*— Mr Christian Malcolm; ✉ c/o Nuff Respect, The Coach House, 107 Sherland Road, Twickenham, Middlesex TW1 4HB

MALCOLM, Dr Sir Noel Robert; kt (2014); *b* 26 December 1956; *Educ* Eton, Peterhouse Cambridge (BA), Trinity Coll Cambridge (MA, PhD); *Career* fell Gonville & Caius Coll Cambridge 1981–88; The Spectator: political columnist 1987–91, foreign ed 1991–92; political columnist Daily Telegraph 1992–95; visiting fell St Antony's Coll Oxford 1995–96, fell All Souls Coll Oxford 2002–; jt winner T E Utley Meml Prize for Political Journalism 1991; Liveryman Fishmongers' Co; FRSL 1997, FBA 2001; *Books* De Dominis 1560–1624 (1984), George Enescu: His Life and Music (1990), Bosnia: A Short History (1994), The Correspondence of Thomas Hobbes (1994), The Origins of English Nonsense (1997), Kosovo: A Short History (1998), Books on Bosnia: A Critical Bibliography (1999), Aspects of Hobbes (2002), JohnPell (1611–1685) (2004); *Style*— Dr Sir Noel Malcolm, FBA, FRSL

MALE, David Ronald; CBE (1991); s of Ronald Male (d 1963), of Worthing, W Sussex, and Gertrude, *née* Simpson (d 1946); *b* 12 December 1929; *Educ* Aldenham; *m* 6 June 1959, Mary Louise, da of Rex Powis Evans, of St Albans, Herts; 2 da (Sarah b 1962, Charlotte b 1966), 1 s (James b 1964); *Career* Nat Serv 2 Lt RA 1948–49; Gardiner & Theobald: ptnr 1960–79, sr ptnr 1979–91, conslt 1992–; RICS: memb Gen Cncl 1976–93, pres Quantity Surveyors Divnl Cncl 1977–78, pres 1989–90; memb: Bd of Dirs Building Centre 1970–80, Govt Construction Panel 1973–74; memb Econ Devpt Cncl for Bldg 1982–86, chm Commercial Buildings Steering Group 1984–88; MCC: memb Ctee 1984–95 and 1996–99, chm Estates Sub-Ctee 1984–94; govr: Aldenham Sch 1974–93, Downe House Sch 2000–07; pres Old Aldenhamian Soc 1986–89, non-exec dir London & Bristol Developments plc 1985–91; memb Bd of Mgmnt Macmillan Cancer Relief 1992–2000, memb Bd of Govrs The Wilson Centre Cambridge 1993–97; church cmmr 1989–93; Freeman City of London 1961, Liveryman Worshipful Co Painter-Stainers 1961–93, Past Master Worshipful Co of Chartered Surveyors (memb Ct of Assts 1977–90, Master 1984–85); ARICS 1954, FRICS 1964; *Recreations* opera, ballet, bridge; *Clubs* Boodle's, Garrick; *Style*— David Male, Esq, CBE; ✉ Manor Farmhouse, Benham Park, Marsh Benham, Newbury, Berkshire RG20 8LX (☎ 01635 522362, fax 01635 529046); 6 Bowland Yard, Kinnerton Street, London SW1X 8EE

MALEK, Ali; QC (1996); s of Ali Akbar Malek, and Irene, *née* Johnson; *b* 19 January 1956; *Educ* Bedford Sch, Keble Coll Oxford (MA, BCL); *m* Sept 1989, Francesca Shoucair; 2 da (Rokhsan Nesa b 18 July 1991, Mithra b 25 May 1993); *Career* called to the Bar Gray's Inn 1980 (Cynthia Terry Entrance Award, Malcolm Hilberry Award), specialist in commercial law; recorder 1998–; memb Commercial Bar Assoc; *Publications* Jack, Malek and Quest: Documentary Credits; *Recreations* running, skiing, golf, music; *Clubs* Vincent's (Oxford); *Style*— Ali Malek, Esq, QC; ✉ 3 Verulam Buildings, Gray's Inn, London WC1R 5NT (☎ 020 7831 8441, fax 020 7831 8479, e-mail amalek@3vb.com)

MALEK, Hodge Mehdi; QC (1999); s of late Ali Akbar Malek, and late Irene Elizabeth, *née* Johnson; *b* 11 July 1959; *Educ* Bedford Sch, Sorbonne, Keble Coll Oxford (MA, BCL); *m* m 1, 1986, Inez Dies Louise, *née* Vegelin Van Claerbergen; 2 s (Yousef Ali Louis, Cyrus Ali), 1 da (Leila); m 2, 2010, Azadeh; 1 s (Sam), 1 da (Yasmine Irene); *Career* called to the Bar Gray's Inn 1983 (scholarships: Atkin 1983, Birkenhead 1983, Band 1984; bencher 2004); in practice 1983–, recorder of the Crown Court 2004–; lectr regulation and civil procedure; memb: Customs and Excise Prosecution List (European) 1992–99, Supp Treasy Panel (common law) 1995–99, Commercial Bar Assoc (COMBAR), Admin Law Bar Assoc, Franco-British Lawyers Soc, Bar Sports Gp, Bar Disciplinary Tbnl 2001–11, Inns of Court Conduct Ctee 2010–; chm Competition Appeal Tbnl 2013–; memb Governing Cncl Royal Numismatic Soc 1991–94; Shamma Prize 1997; *Publications* Discovery (with Paul Matthews, 1992), Disclosure (with Paul Matthews, 2001, 4 edn 2011), Atkins Court Forms – Administrative Court, Disclosure, Financial Services and Human Rights vols (jtly, 2003–14), Information Rights (contrib, 2004), The Dabuyid Ispahbads and Early 'Abbasid Governors of Tabaristan (2004), Phipson on Evidence (ed, 18 edn 2013); articles in various jls; *Recreations* singing, skiing, swimming, history; *Style*— Hodge Malek, Esq, QC; ✉ 39 Essex Street, London WC2R 3AT (☎ 020 7832 1111, fax 020 7353 3978)

MALEM, Keir David; s of David Malem, of Greatstone, Kent, and Angela, *née* Wells; *b* 15 May 1965; *Educ* Southlands Comp Sch; *Career* fashion designer; fndr ptnr (with Patrick Whitaker, *qv*) Whitaker Malem 1988–; cmmns for: Givenchy Haute Couture 1997, Valentino Haute Couture 1997, Tommy Hilfiger Red Label 1998, Tommy Hilfiger 1999–2000, Hussein Chalayan collection 2009, Louise Goldin collection 2009, Giles Deacon collection 2010; launched new line of male and female leather torsos (with Adel Roostein) 1995; lectr in fashion various colls of art and design incl visiting lectr RCA 1999–2000; memb Br Cncl and Br Embassy mission to promote Br fashion, lecture and set Acad project Vilnius Lithuania; special assignments incl: body sculptures for re-opening of Bauhaus Dessau, outfit for Naomi Campbell in Vauxhall advertising campaign 1993, collaboration with sculptor Allen Jones 1999–, piece for permanent collection Museum of Leather Craft Northampton 2000, collection for Alma Home launch 2000, R&D for Gucci collection 2000, cmmn by Allen Jones for new sculpture Waiting on Table (exhibited Royal Acad Summer Exhbn), cmmn by Allen Jones for Kate Moss Project 2012; private cmmns for: Mick Jagger, Cher, Pamela Anderson, Gloria Estefan, Janet Jackson, Jerry Hall, Bono, George Michael, Madonna, Jon Bon Jovi, Spice Girls, Steven Tyler, Allen Jones (major sculpture cmmn 2008); film cmmns incl: Mortal Kombat 1995, The Changeling 1995, Die Another Day 2002, Tomb Raider 2 2003, Troy 2004, Aeon Flux 2005, Harry Potter and the Goblet of Fire 2005, Eragon 2006, Casino Royale 2006, Harry Potter and the Order of the Phoenix 2007, Batman: The Dark Knight 2008, Speed Racer 2008, Nottingham 2010, Clash of The Titans 2010, Captain America: The First Avenger 2011, Jack the Giant Killer 2012, Cloud Atlas 2012, 300 Battle of Artemesium 2013, 300: Rise of an Empire 2014, Jupiter Ascending 2015, Wonder Woman 2017; exhibitions: Unlaced Grace (Banbury Museum and nat tour) 1994–95, Inside Out (Design Museum London) 2000, Personal Space Br Cncl Show (and commn, NY, Milan, London) 2000, Art 2001 (with Jibby Beane, exhibited Chair sculpture) 2001, Tokyo Designers Weeks (Br Cncl exhibit Living Britain) 2001, Designing 007: Fifty Years of Bond Style (Barbican) 2012; new studio/residence Garden House (with Heyhurst & Co Architects, nominated RIBA Channel 4 Grand Designs House Of The Year 2016); *Books* Alexander McQueen (2015); *Recreations* film and soundtrack collecting, swimming, cooking, gardening; *Style*— Keir Malem, Esq; ✉ Whitaker Malem, The Garden Studio, 27 Buckingham Road, London N14 DG (☎ and fax 020 7923 7887, website www.whitakermalem.co.uk)

MALHOTRA, Seema; MP; da of S K Malhotra, of Hounslow, London, and Usha Malhotra; *b* 7 August 1972, Hammersmith, London; *Educ* Univ of Warwick; *m* 2005, Sushil Saluja; *Career* mgmnt conslt Accenture 1995–2003, sr mangr PricewaterhouseCoopers 2003–07, advsr to Rt Hon Harriet Harman, QC, MP (as Min for the W Midlands then Chair Cncl of Regnl Mins) 2007–09, advsr to Ian Austin, MP (as Min for the W Midlands) 2008–09, prog ldr Cross-Govt Prog to Increase Diversity in Public Appointments 2009–10, political advsr to Rt Hon Harriet Harman, QC, MP (as Acting Ldr of the Oppn) 2010, strategic prog advsr UKIE 2011, MP (Lab/Co-op) Feltham and Heston 2011–, PPS to Rt Hon Yvette Cooper, MP, *qqv* (as Shadow Home Secand Shadow Equalities Min) 2012–13, memb Justice Select Ctee 2012–13, oppn whip 2013–15, shadow chief sec to the treasy 2015–; current chair Parly Lab Pty BIS Gp, dir Fabian Women's Network, memb Exec Ctee Fabian Soc, tstee Swanswell; FRSA; *Publications* Dictionary of Labour Biography (contrib, 2001), From the Workhouse to Welfare (contrib, 2009); *Recreations* running, cinema, music, gardening, playing the guitar; *Style*— Ms Seema Malhotra, MP; ☎ 020 7219 8957, website www.seemamalhotra.com, Twitter @seemamalhotra1; House of Commons, London SW1A 0AA

MALIK, Hanzala; MSP; s of Mohammed Nanaz Malik, and Philomena Malik; *b* 1956, Glasgow; *Educ* Univ of Paisley (BSc); *m* Haleema; 1 s, 1 da; *Career* cncllr Glasgow City Cncl 1995–2012, MSP (Lab) Glasgow 2011–; chair W of Scotland Regnl Equality Cncl, dep convener European and External Relations Ctee, convener Cross-Party Gp on ME and S Asia; *Style—* Hanzala Malik, Esq, MSP; ✉ The Scottish Parliament, Edinburgh EH99 1SP (☎ 0141 218 4567, website www.hanzalamalik.org)

MALIK, HE Moazzam; s of Mohammed Amin Malik (d 1998), and Shamim Malik, of London; *b* London; *Educ* LSE (BSc), Univ of Oxford (MSc), ACCA (dip); *m* 1993, Rachel, *née* Richardson; *Career* diplomat; economist Nat Devpt Finance Corp 1988–89, researcher LSE 1990, sr advsr on monetary and foreign exchange policy Central Bank of Uganda 1991–94, conslt African Devpt Bank and EC 1994, conslt London Economics Ltd 1994–96, dir Global Trade Centre 1996–97, team ldr Int Economic Policy DFID 1997–99, md Autum Engrg Ltd 1999–2001; DFID: Pakistan prog mangr 2001–03, head Iraq Humanitarian Response Dept 2003, princ private sec to the Sec of State 2003–05, head White Paper Team: 'Eliminating World Poverty – Making Governance Work for the Poor' 2005–06, head Conflict Humanitarian & Security 2006–07, dir UN Conflict & Humanitarian Div 2007–10, dir Western Asia & Stabilisation Div 2010–13, actg DG Western Asia ME Humanitarian and Conflict 2013–14; ambass to Repub of Indonesia, Timor-Leste and ASEAN 2014–; *Style—* HE Mr Moazzam Malik; ✉ c/o FCO (Jakarta), King Charles Street, London SW1A 2AH (Twitter @MoazzamTMalik)

MALIK, Zubeida; da of Khurshid Ahmed, and Khalida Khurshid; *Educ* Univ of Southampton (BA, MA); *Career* reporter BBC Radio Oxford 1995, reporter BBC Thames Valley 1996, special corr Today prog BBC Radio 4 2000– (output ed 1997–2000), reporter Newsnight BBC; News Journalist of the Year BT Press and Broadcast Awards Radio 1997, Young Journalist of the Year Foreign Press Assoc Awards 2000, Radio News Journalist of the Year EMMA Awards 2001 and 2002, Media Personality Asian Women of Achievement 2002, Carlton TV Multicultural Award for TV and Radio 2003, Muslim News Journalist of the Year Award 2007; *Recreations* photography, reading, films; *Style—* Ms Zubeida Malik; ✉ c/o Today Programme, BBC Radio 4, New Broadcasting House, 03B Portland Place, London W1A 1AA (e-mail zubeida.malik@bbc.co.uk)

MALINOWSKI, Antoni Pawel; s of Wojciech Janusz Malinowski (d 1981), of Warsaw, and Krystyna G?ssowska (d 2004); *b* 13 June 1955, Warsaw; *Educ* Acad of Fine Art Warsaw, Chelsea Coll of Art; *Career* artist; *Solo Exhibitions* Künstlerhaus Hamburg 1985, The Drawing Room installation London 1986, Galerie Wilma Tolksdorf Hamburg 1987 and 1988, Life Drawing installation and performance Chisenhale Gallery London 1987, Provisional Statements on the Rights of the Citizen installation Angel Studios London 1988, Mario Flecha Gallery London 1989, The Showroom London 1990, Galeria Dziekanka Warsaw 1991, Galerie Marie-Louise Wirth Zürich 1993, Gimpel Fils Gallery London 1993 and 1995, Newlyn Art Gallery Penzance 1997, Camden Arts Centre London 1997, Angel Row Gallery Nottingham 1997, Oriel Mosyn Wales 1997, Royal Court Theatre: Related Work Gimpel Fils London 1999, De La Warr Pavilion Bexhill-on-Sea 2001, Echoing The Pavilion (The Architectural Assoc London) 2001, THRESHOLDscape (Gimpel Fils London) 2002, New Paintings (Gimpel Fils London) 2004, Bridging Lines (Studio Visconti and Assab One Milan) 2005, Prism of Time (In Situ Warsaw) 2006, Gimpel Fils London 2007, Meditation Museum Seoul 2007, The Polish Connection (Dulwich Picture Gallery London) 2009 and (Royal Castle Warsaw) 2010 , Teatrino (Contemporary Art Gallery) Opole 2010, Bridging Colours (Gallery 175 Seoul) 2011, Giardino Veneziano (Animali Domestici London) 2011, Spectral Flip (Aid and Abet Cambridge) 2012, Light Sensitive Installation (Museum of Cinematography Lodz) 2013; *Group Exhibitions* Open Futures (Ikon Gallery Birmingham) 1988, Syzygy (Mario Flecha Gallery London) 1988, Whitechapel Open London 1989, 1990 and 1992, What is a Gallery (Kettles Yard Cambridge) 1990, Drawing Show (Mario Flecha Gallery London) 1990, Jeste?my (Zach?ta Warsaw) 1991, New Voices (Br Cncl show Brussels) 1992, EC Young Painters (representing Britain, Seoul), Moving into View – Recent British Painting (Royal Festival Hall London) 1993, Recent CAS Art Aquisitions (MOMA Oxford) 1994, Recent Contemporary Art Soc Purchases (Butler Gallery Kilkenny Castle Ireland) 1995, London Stories (JE Gallery Winterthur Switzerland) 1995, The Subject of Art (NatWest Gp Art Collection London) 1997, What is a Photograph? (Five Years London) 1998, The Difference Between You and Us (Five Years London) 2001, Tracing the Land (Gimpel Fils London) 2004, Summer Exhbn Royal Acad London, Dis/Continuity of Line (Assab One Milan) 2005, Drawing Biennial Fundraiser (The Drawing Room London) 2009, In Space (Polonia Biennale Opole) 2010, Drawing Biennial (The Drawing Room London) 2011, Unearthed – creative remains (Carpenters Road Studios project) 2011, Collaborators 3 (ROOM London) 2012, Homenagem Shelagh Wakely (Museu do Açude Rio de Janeiro) 2012, Drawing Biennial (The Drawing Room London) 2013, Mobility of the Line (Brighton University Gallery) 2014, Conversation Pieces – A View from a Window (Camden Arts Centre London) 2014; *Work in Public Collections* Arts Cncl, Br Cncl, Tate Gallery, CAS, MOMA (Oxford); *Commissions* private cmmn for Palazzo Venice 1998, wall drawing Royal Court Theatre London 1998–2000, floor Canary Square London 1999–2000, painting installation Luxor Theatre Rotterdam 2002, artist/colourist to the redevelopment of BBC Broadcasting House 2003–05, Mosaic for the façade of the new building by Eric Parry Architects on Maddox Street London 2009, cb1 Cambridge façade Translucent Drawing intervention 2012; collaborations with Haworth Tompkins Architects: colour design for the façade and painterly interventions inside the Coin Street Neighbourhood Centre 2007, colour design for the foyer, wall and ceiling paintings at the Bush Theatre London 2011, ceiling paintings for the foyer of Everyman Theatre Liverpool 2013/14, Saturated Stairs Donmar Theatre Staircase 2014, Chichester Festival Theatre – painting interventions throughout the building 2014; *Publications* Antoni Malinowski (1997), Antoni Malinowski at The La Warr Pavilion (2001), Antoni Malinowski TRESHOLDscapes (2002), Antoni Malinowski New Paintings (2004), Antoni Malinowski – Dulwich Picture Gallery – The Polish Connection (2009), Antoni Malinowski – Light Sensitive Reflections (2013), Mobility of the Line – Art, Architecture, Design (contrib, 2013); *Style—* Antoni Malinowski, Esq

MALINS, Alderman Julian Henry; QC (1991); s of Rev Peter Malins, and Joan, *née* Dingley; *b* 1 May 1950; *Educ* Greenways Sch Codford St Mary, St John's Sch Leatherhead, BNC Oxford (MA, Boxing blue); *m* 1 July 1972, (Catherine) Joanna Wilson, da of John Henry Pearce; 3 da (Annabel b 1977, Cressida b 1979, Miranda b 1984); *Career* called to the Bar Middle Temple 1972 (bencher 1996); memb Ct Common Cncl; govr Museum of London; Alderman 2013–; Freeman City of London 1979; *Books* The Serpent's Dead – Revenge; *Recreations* conversation; *Clubs* Vincent's; *Style—* Alderman Julian Malins, QC; ✉ 115 Temple Chambers, Temple Avenue, London EC4Y 0DA (☎ 020 7583 5275, e-mail malins@btinternet.com, website www.malinschambers.com)

MALIPHANT, Russell Scott; s of Ralph Geoffrey Maliphant, and Patricia Anne, *née* Russell; *b* 18 November 1961; *Educ* Royal Ballet Sch, Rolf Inst of Structural Integration USA; *m* 12 Feb 2001, Dana, da of Theodore Fouras; 1 s (Jude Gabriel b 10 August 2000), 1 da (Aysa b 17 March 2003); *Career* choreographer and performer; with Sadlers Wells Royal Ballet 1982–88, freelance performer with DV8 Physical Theatre, Michael Clark & Co and Laurie Booth 1988–95, estab Russell Maliphant Co 1996; works created incl: Shift 1996, Unspoken 1996, Critical Mass 1998, Two 1998, Sheer 2001, Torsion 2002, One Part Two 2002, Broken Fall 2003, Choice 2003; toured worldwide incl Europe, India, Australia, Canada, Colombia and USA; maintains private practice of Rolfing Method of Structural Integration; represented GB The Int Bancs d'Essai 1995, fellowship Arts Cncl of England 2000–02; *Awards* Dance Umbrella Dance and Performance Award 1991, Time Out Award 1991, People's Choice Award Int Festival de Nouvelle Danse Montreal 2001, Time Out Live Award for Outstanding Collaboration 2002, South Bank Show Award for Dance 2003, Laurence Olivier Award for Best New Dance Publication (for Broken Fall) 2003; *Recreations* outdoor pursuits, parenting!; *Style—* Russell Maliphant, Esq; ✉ PO Box 43188, London E17 4XL (e-mail gwen@cueperformance.com, website www.russellmaliphantcompany.co.uk)

MALLABY, Sir Christopher Leslie George; GCMG (1996, KCMG 1988), GCVO (1992); s of Brig A W S Mallaby, CIE, OBE (ka 1945), and Margaret Catherine, *née* Jones; *b* 7 July 1936, Camberley, Surrey; *Educ* Eton, King's Coll Cambridge (BA); *m* 1961, Pascale, da of Francois Thierry-Mieg, of Paris; 1 s (Sebastian b 1964), 3 da (Emily b 1967, Julia b 1971, Charlotte b 1972); *Career* HM Dip Serv 1959–96: Moscow Embassy 1961–63 and 1975–77, first sec Berlin 1966–69, dep dir Br Trade Devpt Office (NY) 1971–74, head of Arms Control & Disarmament Dept 1977–79, then E Euro and Soviet Dept 1979–80, then Planning Staff FCO 1980–82, min Bonn 1982–85, dep sec Cabinet Office 1985–87, ambass Bonn 1988–92, ambass Paris 1993–96, ret; advsr then md UBS Investment Bank 1996–2006; dir: Sun Life & Provincial Holdings 1996–2000, Charter Pan-European Investment Tst 1996–2007, EDF Trading 1998–2003, Vodafone AG Germany 2000–10; advsr: RMC 1996–2000, BAe 1997–98, Herbert Smith 1997–2001; vice-chm Reuters then Thomson-Reuters Founders Share Co 1998–2013; chm: Primary Immuno-Deficiency Assoc 1996–2002 and 2005–06, Grossbritannien Institut of the Humboldt Univ Berlin 1997–2005, Cncl German Studies Inst Univ of Birmingham 1998–2005, Charitable Tst of European Orgn for Research and Treatment of Cancer 2000–14, Somerset House Tst 2002–06; tstee Tate Gallery 1996–2002; Hon LLD Univ of Birmingham 2004; Chllr Order of St Michael and St George 2005–11; Grand Cross of the Order of Merit (Germany) 1992, Grand Officier of the Legion d'Honneur (France) 1996, Commandeur de l'Ordre des palmes Académiques (France) 2004; *Recreations* grandchildren; *Clubs* Brooks's, Beefsteak, Grillion's; *Style—* Sir Christopher Mallaby, GCMG, GCVO; ✉ e-mail christopher.mallaby@tiscali.co.uk

MALLALIEU, Baroness (Life Peer UK 1991), of Studdridge in the County of Buckinghamshire; Ann Mallalieu; QC (1988); da of Sir (Joseph Percival) William Mallalieu (d 1980), and Harriet Rita Riddle; *b* 27 November 1945; *Educ* Holton Park Girls' GS, Newnham Coll Cambridge (MA, LLM); *m* 1979 (m dis 2007), as his 2 w, Sir Timothy Felix Harold Cassel, 4 Bt, QC, *qv*, eldest s of His Hon Sir Harold Felix Cassel, 3 Bt, TD, QC (d 2001); 2 da (Hon Bathsheba Anna b 1981, Hon Cosima Ione Harriet b 1984); *Career* called to the Bar Inner Temple 1970 (bencher 1992); recorder 1985–94; oppn spokesman on home affrs and legal affrs House of Lords 1991–97; chm: Independent Cncl of the Ombudsman for Corp Estate Agents 1993–2000, Suzy Lamplugh Tst 1996–2000; first woman pres Cambridge Union Soc 1967, hon fell Newnham Coll Cambridge 1991, pres Countryside Alliance 1998–; memb Br Horseracing Bd 2004–07, tstee Racing Welfare 2009–, pres The Horse Tst 2009, tstee Nat Assoc of Stable Staff 2009–; *Recreations* hunting, sheep, reading poetry, horse racing; *Style—* The Baroness Mallalieu, QC; ✉ House of Lords, London SW1A 0PW

MALLALIEU, Huon Lancelot; s of Sir (Edward) Lancelot Mallalieu, QC, MP (d 1979), and Betty Margaret Oxley, *née* Pride (d 1993); *b* 11 August 1946, Dublin; *Educ* Harrow, Trinity Coll Oxford (MA); *m* 11 Dec 1982, Fenella Jane, *née* Rowse; 1 da (Ilaira b 4 June 1988), 1 s (Joshua b 25 Sept 1990); *Career* cataloguer for Christie's 1969–73; writer and journalist 1973–; contrib: The Times, Country Life, Sunday Telegraph, Financial Times, Antiques Trade Gazette, The Oldie; ed Watercolours and Drawings Magazine 1986–91, property ed Country Life 1989–90, art market writer Country Life 1990–; Residential Property Journalist of the Year 1998; assoc ed Oxford DNB; memb: Cncl for the Care of Churches 1992–2001, Ctee London Library 1994–98, Advsy Ctee Lambeth Palace Chapel 1996–2001, Lambeth Palace Refurbishment Gp 2001–; visiting lectr City Univ 2006; FSA 2005, Hon RWS; *Books* incl: Crome, Cotman and The Norwich School (1974), The Dictionary of British Watercolour Artists (3 vols 1976, 1979, 1990, new edn 2002), How To Buy Pictures (1984), Understanding Watercolours (1985), The Illustrated History of Antiques (gen ed, 1991), Antiques Roadshow A-Z of Antiques Hunting (ed, 1995), Moving to the Country (2000), 1066 and Rather More (2009); *Recreations* walking, history, cartoons; *Style—* Huon Mallalieu, Esq, FSA

MALLALIEU, Robin; *Educ* Univ of Manchester (BA, BArch), RIBA; *m* Angela Brady , *qv*; 2 c; *Career* architect; dir Brady Mallalieu Architects Ltd 1987–; quinquennial inspr to C of E; *Awards* RIAI Award for house renovation in Islington London 1991, RIAI Award for office fitout for Groundwork Hackney London 1995, RIAI Award for Sch of Architecture Univ of North London 1997, RIAI Award for Barra plc Open Air Theatre 2005, RIAI Award for house in Knightsbridge London, RIAI Award for Mastmaker Road housing project 2010, Best New Housing Devpt Evening Standard 2010; *Books* Dublin: a guide to contemporary architecture (with Angela Brady, PPRIBA, 1997); *Style—* Robin Mallalieu, Esq; ✉ Brady Mallalieu Architects, 90 Queens Drive, London N4 2HW (☎ 020 8880 1544, e-mail bma@bradymallalieu.com, website www.bradymallalieu.com)

MALLET, Victor John; s of Philip Louis Victor Mallet, and Mary Moyle Grenfell, *née* Borlase; *b* 14 May 1960; *Educ* Winchester, Merton Coll Oxford (BA); *Career* journalist and author; with Reuters in London, Paris, Johannesburg and Cape Town 1981–86; Financial Times: Africa corr 1986–88, Middle East corr 1988–91, SE Asia corr 1992–94, dep features ed 1995–96, Southern Africa corr 1998–2001, Paris corr 2001–03, chief Asia corr 2003–06, Asia ed 2006–08, chief Madrid Bureau 2008–12, S Asia bureau chief 2012–; Society of Publishers in Asia Award for Opinion Writing 2005 and 2006; *Books* The Trouble With Tigers: the Rise and Fall of South East Asia (1999); *Recreations* sailing; *Style—* Victor Mallet, Esq; ✉ The Financial Times, 1 Southwark Bridge, London SE1 9HL (☎ 020 7873 3000, e-mail victor.mallet@ft.com)

MALLIN, Anthony Granville; s of Frederick Granville Mallin (d 1986), and Phyllis May Mallin; *b* 26 May 1955; *m* 1989, Marie-Louise; 2 da (Josephine Louise b 4 Dec 1990, Annabelle Marie b 18 Oct 1995), 1 s (Frederick Harry b 15 April 1993); *Career* former vice-chm Hambros Bank Ltd, dir Hambros plc 1995–2005; chief exec MRBS Capital Partners Ltd, currently fndr, ptnr and ceo Star Capital Partners; chm: Leaseurope 1998–99, Equipment Leasing Assoc 1992–, Finance & Leasing Assoc 1993–; dir East London Youth & Minorities Activities Ltd (charity); *Recreations* rowing, golf, opera; *Clubs* Lea Rowing (pres), Leander, Highgate Golf; *Style—* Tony Mallin

MALLINCKRODT, George Wilhelm; see: Von Mallinckrodt, Georg Wilhelm

MALLOCH-BROWN, Baron (Life Peer UK 2007), of St Leonard's Forest in the County of West Sussex; Rt Hon Sir George Mark Malloch-Brown; KCMG (2007), PC (2007); s of late George Malloch Brown; *b* 16 September 1953; *Educ* Magdalene Coll Cambridge (BA), Univ of Michigan (MA); *m* 1989, Patricia Anne Cronan; 3 da (Hon Madison Jane b 1992, Hon Isobel Anne b 1994, Hon Phoebe Victoria b 2001), 1 s (Hon George Philip b 1996); *Career* political corr The Economist 1977–79, UN High Cmmn for Refugees 1979–83, fndr and ed Economist Devpt Report 1983–86, int ptnr Sawyer-Miller Gp 1986–94, dir External Affrs World Bank 1994–96, vice-pres External Affrs and UN Affrs 1996–99, admin UN Devpt Prog 1999–2005, chief of staff UN 2005, dep sec-gen UN 2006, min for Africa, Asia and UN FCO 2007–09, vice-chm World Economic Forum 2010–; chm: EMEA FTI Consulting 2010–14, SGO Corp Ltd 2014–; Hon DLitt: Michigan State Univ 2002, Catholic Univ of Peru 2003, Pace Univ NY 2005, Walden Univ 2008; hon fell Magdalene Coll Cambridge 2005; *Publications* The Unfinished Global Revolution; *Style—* The Rt Hon Lord Malloch-Brown, KCMG; ✉ House of Lords, London SW1A 0PW

MALLYON, Catherine Rowena; *b* 1962, Cambridge; *Educ* Impington Village Coll, Cambs Coll of Arts and Technol, St John's Coll Oxford (MA); *Partner* Susan Foster; *Career* gen mangr Oxford Playhouse 1993–99, gen mangr arts and theatre Reading BC 1999–2005, dep chief exec Southbank Centre 2005–12, exec dir RSC 2012–; *Recreations* violin playing,

M

walking, surfing, skiing; *Style*— Ms Catherine Mallyon; ✉ Royal Shakespeare Company, Royal Shakespeare Theatre, Waterside, Stratford-upon-Avon, Warwickshire CV37 6BB

MALMESBURY, Archdeacon of; *see:* Hawker, Ven Alan Fort

MALONE, Gareth; OBE (2012); *b* 1975; *Educ* Bournemouth Sch, Univ of East Anglia, RAM; *Career* choirmaster and broadcaster; LSO 2001–09; hon doctorate UEA 2011; Freeman City of London 2010; FRAM 2013; *Television* incl: The Choir (BBC 2) 2006 (Best Feature BAFTA 2007), The Choir: Boys Don't Sing (BBC 2) 2008 (Best Feature BAFTA 2008, Constructed Factual Series RTS Award 2009), The Choir: Unsung Town (BBC 2) 2009 (Best Factual Prog Broadcasting Press Guild Awards 2010), How a Choir Works (BBC 4) 2009, Shanties and Sea Songs with Gareth Malone (BBC 4) 2010, The Big Performance (BBC) 2010–14, The Choir: Military Wives (BBC 2) 2011, Sing While You Work (BBC 2) 2012–13, It Takes a Choir (USA Network) 2013; *Recordings* incl: Wherever You Are (with the Military Wives, UK No. 1 single) 2011, In My Dreams (with the Military Wives, UK No. 1 album) 2012, Sing (with Gary Barlow, UK No. 1 single and album) Voices 2013 (tour 2014); *Books* Music for the People: A Journey through the Pleasures and Pitfalls of Classical Music (2011), Choir (2012); *Style*— Gareth Malone, Esq, OBE; ✉ c/o Curtis Brown Group Ltd, Haymarket House, 28–29 Haymarket, London SW1Y 4SP (website www.garethmalone.com, Twitter @garethmalone)

MALONE, Jo; *Career* early career: Pulbrook and Gould (florist), pt/t gardener; chairwoman and creative dir Jo Malone, opened first store London 1994, opened flagship store 1999, other stores incl Sydney and NY, over 300 concessions worldwide; *Style*— Ms Jo Malone

MALONEY, Michael Anthony Gerard; s of Gp Capt Gerard Maloney, of London, and Pamela Maloney; *b* 19 June 1957; *Educ* Ampleforth, LAMDA; *Career* actor; jt winner Alec Clunes Award LAMDA; *Theatre* RSC incl: Prince Hal in Henry IV Parts 1 and 2, Romeo in Romeo and Juliet, title role in Derek, Edgar in King Lear; other credits incl: Taking Steps (Lyric Theatre), William Blake in In Lambeth (Donmar Warehouse), Benjamin Britten in Once in a While the Odd Thing Happens (NT), title role in Peer Gynt (Cambridge), Two Planks and a Passion (Greenwich), Alice's Adventures Underground (RNT), Mouth to Mouth (Royal Court and Albery), title role in Hamlet (Greenwich, W Yorks Playhouse and nat tour); *Television* for BBC: Starlings (first prize Monte Carlo), Telford's Change, The Bell, Falkland in The Rivals, Relatively Speaking, Love On A Branch Line; other credits incl: Dominic in What if it's Raining, William Boot in Scoop, Prosper Proford in The Forsyte Saga, The Archbishop of Canterbury in The Six Wives of Henry VIII, Malvolio in Twelfth Night, Indiana Jones Chronicles, Sex & Chocolate, Macbeth, Children of the New Forest, Painted Lady, A Christmas Carol, The Swap, The Jury, Me and Mrs Jones, Believe Nothing; *Radio* Orsino in Twelfth Night, Brutus in Julius Caesar, title role in Alexander the Great, Konstantin in The Seagull, title role in Hitler, Lysander in A Midsummer Night's Dream, The Winslow Boy, Frankenstein, The Old Law, The Devil is an Ass, The Ambridge Chronicles, The Brothers Karamaov; *Film* incl: Dauphin in Henry V, Rosencrantz in Hamlet, Leonardo in La Maschera, Laertes in Hamlet, Michel in Bienvenue au Gite, Truly Madly Deeply, Ordeal By Innocence, Sharma and Beyond, In the Bleak Midwinter, Othello, American Reel, Sans Plomb, Hysteria; *Style*— Michael Maloney, Esq; ✉ c/o Markham & Froggatt Ltd, Julian House, 4 Windmill Street, London W1T 2HZ (☎ 020 7636 4412, fax 020 7637 5233)

MALPAS, Prof James Spencer; s of Tom Spencer Malpas (d 1972); *b* 15 September 1931; *Educ* Sutton Co GS, Bart's Univ of London, Univ of Oxford; *m* 1957, Joyce May, da of Albert Edward Cathcart (d 1962); 2 s (1 decd 2015); *Career* St Bartholomew's Hosp Univ of London: dean Med Coll 1969–72, conslt physician 1973–95, sr physician 1993–95, former dir Imperial Cancer Res Fund Unit of Med Oncology and prof of med oncology, currently emeritus prof of med oncology; treas then vice-pres Barts Med Coll 1987–95, special tstee Barts and the London Charitable Fndn 1999–2007, tstee Med Coll of St Bartholomew's Tst 1999–; academic registrar RCP 1975–80, pres Assoc of Cancer Physicians 1994–99; Master London Charterhouse 1996–2001; memb: Central Institutional Review Bd of Cancer Research Campaign 2001–04, Ctee Retired Fellows Soc RSM 2007– (treas 2008–12), Cncl RSM 2013–; fndr memb UK Children's Cancer Study Gp and Sick Children's Tst, tstee Mason le Page Charitable Tst 2001–14; Freeman City of London 1988; FRCP, FRCR, FRCPCH, patron Royal Institution; *Recreations* sailing, history, painting, travel; *Clubs* Little Ship; *Style*— Prof James Malpas; ✉ 253 Lauderdale Tower, Barbican, London EC2Y 8BY (☎ 020 7920 9337, e-mail jmalpas@aol.com)

MALSBURY, Angela Mary; da of late Reginald Malsbury, and Madge Meagan, *née* Stenson; *b* 5 May 1945; *Educ* Loughborough HS for Girls, Kibworth Beauchamp GS, Royal Coll of Music; *m* 1965, David Robin Pettit; 1 s (Timothy Nicholas David b 1967); *Career* clarinettist; Wigmore Hall debut 1968, Royal Festival Hall debut with London Mozart Players 1976; princ clarinettist London Mozart Players, prof of clarinet Royal Acad of Music; memb: Albion Ensemble, Primavera Ensemble, De Saram Clarinet Trio, London Winds, Musicians of the Royal Exchange; also plays with: Acad of St Martin in the Fields, London Sinfonietta, Nash Ensemble; Mozart Meml Prize, Hon RAM; *Recordings* incl: Mozart's 13 Wind Serenade (variously with London Mozart Players, Acad of St Martin's and Albion Ensemble), Mozart's Clarinet Quintet (with Coull Quartet), Mozart's Clarinet Concerto (with London Mozart Players), Prokovieff's Overture on Yiddish Themes, Mississippi 5 (with Albion Ensemble), A Trio of French Styles (with De Saram Trio), The Classical Harmonie (with Albion Ensemble); *Recreations* swimming, walking, cooking, art; *Style*— Ms Angela Malsbury; ✉ c/o Stephannie Williams Artists, 16 Swanfold, Wilmcote, Stratford-upon-Avon CV37 9XH (☎ 01789 266272, fax 01789 266467)

MALTBY, Colin Charles; s of George Frederick Maltby, MC (decd), and late Dorothy Maltby; *b* 8 February 1951; *Educ* George Heriot's Sch Edinburgh, King Edward's Sch Birmingham, ChCh Oxford (MA, MSc), Stanford Business Sch; *m* 1983, Victoria Angela Valerie, da of late Paul Guido Stephen Elton; 2 da (Lorna b 1976, Katherine b 1986), 1 s (Matthew b 1989); *Career* merchant banker; pres Oxford Union 1973, chm Fedn of Cons Students 1974–75; dir: Kleinwort Benson (ME) EC 1983–84, Kleinwort Benson Investment Mgmnt Ltd 1984–95, Banque Kleinwort Benson SA 1985–95 (chm 1993), Kleinwort Benson Group plc 1989–95, Fuji Investment Trust Mgmnt KK 1993–95, Abingworth BioEquities Fund Ltd 2010–, BACIT Ltd 2012–, Ocean Wilsons Hldgs Ltd 2013–, BH Macro Ltd 2015–; chief exec Kleinwort Benson Investment Mgmnt Ltd 1988–95; chm: Kleinwort Overseas Investment Trust plc 1992–96, Princess Private Equity Hldg Ltd 2007–09, BlackRock Absolute Return Strategies Ltd 2008–14, HarbourVest Senior Loans Europe Ltd 2010–14; chief investment offr Equitas Reinsurance Ltd 1996–2000, chief exec BP Investment Mgmnt Ltd 2000–07; non-exec dir: RM plc 1997–2000, H Young Holdings plc 1997–2001, CCLA Investment Mgmnt Ltd 1997–2003 (chm 1999–2003), BBGI SICAV SA 2012–; investment advsr Br Coal Staff Superannuation Scheme 2001–12, investment advsr British Airways Pension Schemes 2003–07; advsr Carbon Disclosure Project 2000–; memb: Tomorrow's Company Inquiry Team 1993–95, Funding Agency for Schools Finance Ctee 1996–99; fell Wolfson Coll Oxford 2002; FRSA, FRI, MSI; *Recreations* music, theatre, curiosity, the Alps; *Style*— Colin Maltby, Esq; ✉ 14 Chemin de la Gradelle, 1224 Chene-Bougeries, Switzerland (☎ 0041 22 860 0901)

MALTHOUSE, Kit; MP, AM; *b* 1966; *Career* qualified CA; memb Westminster City Cncl 1998–2006; GLA: memb London Assembly (Cons) West Central 2007–, dep mayor policing 2008–12, dep mayor business and enterprise 2012–; MP (Cons) Hamps NW 2015–; *Style*— Kit Malthouse, Esq, MP, AM; ✉ GLA, City Hall, The Queen's Walk, London SE1 2AA

MALTMAN, Christopher John (Chris); s of Robert John Maltman (d 2002), of Louth, Lincs, and Christine, *née* Lincoln; *b* 7 February 1970; *Educ* King Edward VI Sch Louth, Univ of Warwick (BSc), Royal Acad of Music (Dip RAM, LRAM, ARAM); *m* Leigh Woolf; 1 s (Maximus); *Career* opera singer; baritone; trained at Royal Acad of Music under Mark Wildman; princ operatic roles with: Met Opera NY, Royal Opera House, Glyndebourne Opera, Deutsche Staatsoper Berlin, Vienna Staatsoper, ENO, WNO, La Monnaie Brussels, Bayerisches Staatsoper Munich; worked under conductors incl: Sir Simon Rattle, Sir Colin Davis, Leonard Slatkin, Sir David Willcocks, Lord Menuhin; performed recitals at numerous venues incl: Wigmore Hall, Edinburgh Festival, Hohenems Schubertiade, Salzburg Festival, Lincoln Center NY, Carnegie Hall NY, Concertgebouw Amsterdam; *Recordings* with: BMG wth Placido Domingo, Decca, Deutsche Grammaphon, Erato, Colins Classics, Naxos, Hyperion; *Awards* winnner of Lieder Prize Cardiff Singer of the World 1997, Royal Philharmonic Soc Young Artist Award 1999 HM The Queen's Commendation for Excellence Royal Acad of Music; *Recreations* golf, fitness (gymnasium) cooking/food, watching sport of any kind; *Style*— Chris Maltman, Esq; ✉ c/o Askonas Holt, Lincoln House, 300 High Holborn, London WC1V 7JH

MALTZ, Dr Milton Beer; s of Prof Jayme Maltz, of Porto Alegre, Brazil, and Matilde, *née* Beer; *b* 2 October 1954; *Educ* Porto Alegre HS Brazil, Shawnee Mission S HS Kansas City (grad dip), Univ of Med Porto Alegre Rio Grande Do Sul Brazil (MD), Bart's Hosp Univ of London (Br Cncl scholar, dip gen med, MPhil), Univ of London and St Bartholomew's Med Coll; *Career* formerly casualty student offr Accident and Emergency Hosp Porto Alegre Brazil; Bart's London: sr house offr in gen med 1983–84, hon cardiac registrar Dept of Cardiology 1984–91, clinical asst in cardiology 1991–93; currently clinical asst in cardiology Royal Free Hosp and in private practice Harley St, chm Medical Centre Cardiac Research Ltd; med and nursing staff teacher for MB and GP trg on specialised courses, author of numerous med articles for learned jls, invited speaker at numerous int cardiac meetings; offr surgn St John Ambulance Prince of Wales District London; fell in gen med Univ of Med Porto Alegre Brazil 1984; *Books* The Clinical Evaluation on Angina Pectoris of a Calcium Antagonist – Tiapamil (thesis); *Recreations* tennis; *Clubs* Angela Bexton Tennis; *Style*— Dr Milton Maltz; ✉ 58 Harley Street, London W1G 9QB (☎ 020 7323 9292 and 020 7580 3145, fax 020 7323 4484)

MANACORDA, Francesco; s of Fabrizio Manacorda, and Simonetta Borgna Gajal de la Chenaye (d 1999); *b* 19 April 1974, Turin, Italy; *Educ* Univ of Turin, RCA (MA); *m* 2010, Rosalind Nashashibi; 1 da (Pauline b 2008), 1 s (Pietro b 2011); *Career* visiting lectr in exhibition history and critical theory RCA 2006–10, curator Barbican Art Gallery London 2007–09, dir Artissima Turin 2010–12, artistic dir Tate Liverpool 2012–; visiting prof Sch of Art and Design Liverpool John Moores Univ 2015–; *Style*— Francesco Manacorda, Esq; ✉ Tate Liverpool, Albert Dock, Liverpool L3 4BB

MANASSEH, Leonard Sulla; OBE (1982); *Educ* Cheltenham Coll, AA Sch of Architecture; *Career* pilot Fleet Air Arm 1943–46; asst architect CRE N London then Guy Morgan & Partners 1941, on teaching staff AA and Kingston Sch of Art 1941, asst architect Architects Dept Herts CC 1943–48, sr architect Stevenage Development Corporation 1948–50, winner Festival of Britain Competition 1950, fndr Leonard Manasseh & Partners 1950 (subsequently became Leonard Manasseh Partnership then, from 1994, LMP Architects Ltd); AA: on teaching staff Sch of Architecture 1951–59, memb Cncl 1955–66, pres 1964–65; memb Royal West of England Acad 1972– (pres 1989–94); memb Cncl: Industrial Design 1965–68, RIBA 1968–70 and 1976–82 (hon sec 1979–81), British Sch at Rome 1976–83, National Trust 1977–91; pres Franco-British Union of Architects 1978–79; chm Ctee Dulwich Picture Gallery 1988–93 (surveyor 1987–93), dep chm Chatham Historic Dockyard Tst 1991 (tstee 1984); RA nominee Bd of Govrs Dulwich Schools Fndn 1987–94; RA 1979 (ARA 1976), FRIBA 1964 (ARIBA 1941), FCSD 1965, FRSA 1967; membre de l'Academie d'Architecture de France; *Style*— Leonard Manasseh, Esq, OBE, RA, PPRWA, AADipl, FRIBA, FCSD; ✉ 6 Bacon's Lane, Highgate Village, London N6 6BL

MANCE, Baron (Life Peer UK 2005), of Frognal in the London Borough of Camden; Sir Jonathan Hugh Mance; kt (1993), PC (1999); s of Sir Henry Stenhouse Mance (d 1981), and Joan Erica Robertson, *née* Baker (d 2005); *b* 6 June 1943; *Educ* Charterhouse, UC Oxford (MA); *m* 26 May 1973, Dame Mary Howarth Arden, DBE (Rt Hon Lady Justice Arden), *qv*, da of Lt-Col Eric Cuthbert Arden (d 1973); 2 da (Hon Abigail b 1976, Hon Jessica b 1978), 1 s (Hon Henry b 1982); *Career* called to the Bar Middle Temple 1965, QC 1982, judge of the High Court of Justice (Queen's Bench Div) 1993–99, a Lord Justice of Appeal 1999–2005, a Lord of Appeal in Ordinary 2005–09, a Justice of the Supreme Court 2009–; dir Bar Mutual Indemnity Fund Ltd 1988–94; pres British Insurance Law Assoc 2000–02 (dep pres 1998–2000), chm various Banking Appeal Tbnls 1992–93; chm: Consultative Cncl of European Judges 2000–03 (memb until 2011), Bar Lawn Tennis Soc chair 2000–14, pres 2014–: Int Law Assoc 2009–, Lord Chllr's Advsy Ctee in Private Int law 2009–; memb: House of Lords EU Select Ctee 2007–09 (chair Sub-Ctee E), Judicial Integrity Gp, Panel set up under Article 255 of Treaty on Functioning of the EU, Senate European Law Inst 2011–; tstee European Law Acad 2003–11; High Steward Univ of Oxford 2012–; hon doctorate Canterbury Christ Church Univ 2013; hon fell: UC Oxford 2006, Liverpool John Moores Univ 2010, Wolfson Coll Oxford 2015; *Recreations* tennis, music, languages; *Clubs* Cumberland Lawn Tennis; *Style*— The Rt Hon Lord Mance, PC; ✉ UK Supreme Court, London SW1P 3BD

MANCHESTER, 13 Duke of (GB 1719); Alexander Charles David Drogo Montagu; also Baron Kimbolton (E 1620) and Earl of Manchester (E 1626, cr three days after Charles I's coronation); s of 12 Duke of Manchester (d 2002), and Mary Eveleen, *née* McClure; *b* 11 December 1962; *Educ* Geelong GS Victoria, Bancroft Jr HS CA, Kimbolton GS Cambs; *m* 21 Sept 2007, Laura Ann Smith, da of Francis Yoder, of Laguna Beach, CA; *Heir* s, Viscount Mandeville; *Career* pres Global Atlantic Investments 1983–, ceo International Security Tst 1990–; dir: Internal Security 1991–, Summit Investments 1994–, Royal Fidelity Tst 1996–; Hon Col Duke of Manchester Sealed Knot History Regt; *Style*— His Grace the Duke of Manchester; ✉ c/o British Consulate, 11766 Wilshire Boulevard, Los Angeles, California 90025-6538, USA

MANCHESTER, Bishop of 2013–; Rt Rev Dr David Stuart Walker; s of Fred Walker, and Joyce, *née* Garside; *b* 30 May 1957; *Educ* Manchester Grammar, King's Coll Cambridge (MA, Table Tennis capt), Queens' Coll Birmingham (DipTh); *m* Susan Ann, *née* Pearce; 1 s, 1 da; *Career* curate St Mary Handsworth 1983–86, team vicar Maltby 1986–91, vicar of Bramley and Ravenfield 1981–95, team rector Bramley and Ravenfield with Hooton Roberts and Braithwell 1995–2000, bishop of Dudley 2000–13; memb: Advsy Ctee for Relationships between Bishops and Religious Communities 2003– (chair 2008–), Gen Synod C of E 2005–, C of E Pensions Bd 2006–13 (vice-chair 2011–13), Archbishops' Cncl Remuneration and Conditions of Service Ctee 2010– (chair 2013–), C of E Ministry Cncl 2013–, Ethical Investments Advsy Gp 2014–; church cmmr 2013–, memb Church Cmmrs Pastoral Ctee 2014–15, memb Church Cmmrs Assets Ctee 2016–; chair S Yorks Housing Assoc 1995–2001, memb Cncl Nat Housing Fedn 1996–2002, memb Govt Policy Action Team on Housing Mgmnt 1998–2001, chair Housing Assocs Charitable Tst 2005–10, memb Bd Church Urban Fund 2008–15, chair Sandwell Homes 2011–12, visitor Soc of Ordained Scientists 2011–, memb Bd Wythenshawe Housing Gp 2014–, memb Gr Manchester Police and Ethics Ctee 2014–; FRSA 2007–16; *Publications* The Inclusivity of Rural Anglicanism: Theoretical and empirical considerations (doctoral thesis); *Recreations* cricket, hill walking, various needlecrafts, reading; *Style*— The Rt Rev the Bishop of Manchester; ✉ Bishopscourt, Bury New Road, Manchester M7 4LE

MANCROFT, 3 Baron (UK 1937); Sir Benjamin Lloyd Stormont Mancroft; 3 Bt (UK 1932); s of 2 Baron Mancroft, KBE, TD (d 1987); *b* 16 May 1957; *Educ* Eton; *m* 20 Sept 1990, Emma L, eldest da of Tom Peart, of Kensington; 1 da (Hon Georgia Esme b 25 April 1993), 2 s (Hon Arthur Louis Stormont b 3 May 1995, Hon Maximillian Michael b 3 Aug 1998); *Heir* s, Hon Arthur Mancroft; *Career* chm Inter Lotto (UK) Ltd 1995–, dep chm ROK Corp 2003–07, dir and sr vice-pres ROK Entertainment Gp Inc (USA) 2007–; chm: Inter Lotto (UK) Ltd 1996–2007, New Media Lottery Services plc (Repub of Ireland) 2006–09, Phoenix Gaming Ltd 2007–; dir St Martin's Magazines plc 1991–2008; vice-chm Phoenix House Housing Assoc 1990–96; patron: Patsy Handy Tst 1991–, Sick Dentists' Tst 1991–; chm: Addiction Recovery Fndn 1989–, Drug and Alcohol Fndn 1995–; vice-chm: Br Field Sports Soc 1992–2000, Parly All-Pty Misuse of Drugs Gp 1992–; exec: Assoc of Cons Peers 1989–94 and 1999–, Nat Union of Cons Assocs 1989–94; elected to sit in the House of Lords 1999–; hon sec Parly All-Pty Bloodstock and Racing Industries Ctee 1992–97; non-exec dir Countryside Alliance 2000– (dep chm 2005–); memb Exec Ctee Lotteries Cncl 1997–, chm Standing Conference on Country Sports 2006– (vice-chm 2000–06); jt master Vale of White Horse Hunt 1987–89; contrib articles to: Mail on Sunday, Sunday Express, The Guardian, Evening Standard, The Independent, The Field, Country Illustrated; regular appearances on TV and radio incl Newsnight, Panorama, Parliament Today, BBC Radio 4's Today prog, etc; tstee Mentor Fndn Int 1996–2000, chm Drug and Alcohol Fndn 1996–2007, chm Mentor Fndn UK 2000–07; patron: Osteopathic Centre for Children 1997–, Hepatitis C Tst 2006– (tstee 2000–06), Addiction Recovery Fndn 2008– (chm 1989–2001), Sick Dentists Tst, Exbourne Sch Tst, European Assoc for the Treatment of Addiction, Nelson House Tst; *Recreations* field sports, gardening, reading, travelling; *Style*— The Rt Hon the Lord Mancroft; ✉ House of Lords, London SW1A 0PW (✆ 020 7219 3000)

MANDELSON, Baron (Life Peer UK 2008), of Foy in the County of Herefordshire and of Hartlepool in the County of Durham; Rt Hon Peter Benjamin Mandelson; PC (1998); s of George Norman Mandelson (d 1989), and Hon Mary Joyce Mandelson, *née* Morrison (d 2006); *b* 21 October 1953; *Educ* Hendon Sr HS, St Catherine's Coll Oxford (BA); *Career* chm Br Youth Cncl 1977–80, cncllr Lambeth BC 1979–82, prodr Weekend World London Weekend TV 1982–85, dir of campaigns and communications Lab Pty 1985–90; MP (Lab) Hartlepool 1992–2004, oppn whip 1994–95, shadow Civil Service spokesman 1995–96, Lab Pty election campaign mangr 1996–97, min without portfolio Cabinet Office 1997–98, sec of state for trade and industry 1998–99, sec of state for NI 1999–2001, EU cmmr for external trade 2004–08, sec of state for business 2008–10; chm The Policy Network 2001–; *Publications* The Blair Revolution: Can New Labour Deliver (co-author, 1996), The Blair Revolution Revisited (2002); *Recreations* countryside, swimming, walking, travel and reading; *Style*— The Rt Hon the Lord Mandelson; ✉ House of Lords, London SW1A 0PW

MANDER, David Charles; s of Alan Mander (d 1998), of Warks, and Muriel Betty, *née* Whiteman (d 1975); *b* 16 April 1938; *Educ* Wrekin Coll, Univ of Birmingham (LLB); *m* Elizabeth Ann, da of late F W Thorn, of Warks; 2 s (Philip James b 1964, Nicholas David b 1967), 1 da (Charlotte Louise b 1972); *Career* slr; conslt Mander Hadley & Co Ltd – incorporating Browetts, Loughridge Bowler and N R Wilson Solicitors; dir Warks Law Soc Ltd 1969–2000; memb: Warks Law Soc (sec 1969–72, vice-pres 1997–98, pres 1998–99), Birmingham Law Soc 1972–80; memb Cncl Law Soc for constituency of: W Midlands W Mercia and Welsh Marches 1980–89, Coventry and Warks 1989–96; chm: Coventry Diocesan Tstees 1985–2016, Law Soc Indemnity Insurance Ctee 1986–87, Law Soc Trg Review Ctee 1994–96; dir: Solicitors Indemnity Fund Ltd 1987–2007 (chm 1987–89), Mander Property Investments Ltd 1991–2016, Legal Indemnity Operations Ltd 2004–07; former memb Ct Univ of Warwick, former tstee Spencers Charity (chm 1997–99); Freeman City of Coventry, memb Guild and Fellowship of Mercers; *Recreations* golf, music; *Style*— David C Mander, Esq; ✉ Whitestitch House, Great Packington, Meriden, Warwickshire CV7 7JE (✆ 01676 522362); Mander Hadley & Co Ltd, 1 The Quadrant, Coventry CV1 2DW (✆ 024 76631212, fax 024 7663 3131, e-mail davidandlibby@whitestitch.co.uk)

MANDER, Michael Stuart; s of James Charles Stuart Mander (d 1974), and Alice Patricia Mander (d 1964); *b* 5 October 1935; *Educ* Tonbridge, Hackley NY; *Career* dir: Times Newspapers Ltd 1971–80, Int Thomson Orgn plc 1983–86; chm Thomson Directories 1983–86, chm and chief exec Thomson Info Services Ltd 1985–86; dir: Hill Samuel & Co Ltd 1987–96, Close Brothers Corporate Finance Ltd 1996–99; chm: MAID plc 1988–97, Nat Readership Surveys Ltd 1990–93, The Dialog Corp plc 1997–99, Book Data Ltd 1997–2002, HS Publishing Gp 2000–01; dep chm Venda Ltd 2008–09; dir: Southnews plc 1989–2000, BLCMP (Library Services) Ltd 1993–99, TEMPUS Gp plc 1997–2000; pres Nat Advertising Benevolent Soc 1974–78; vice-pres: Periodical Publishers' Assoc, Inst of Directors 1997–2004 (memb Cncl 1974–, chm 1993–97); memb Nat Employers Advsy Bd for the Reserve Forces 1997–2005, memb Disciplinary Ctee ICA; tstee St Bride's Church Appeal, vice-patron Disabled Sailors Assoc 2008–, patron History of Advertising Tst; Liveryman Worshipful Co of Marketors; FCIM, FRSA, FCAM; *Recreations* sailing; *Clubs* Royal Southern Yacht, Buck's; *Style*— Michael Mander, Esq; ✉ Oddington Hill House, Oddington Road, Stow-on-the-Wold, Cheltenham, Gloucestershire GL54 1AL (✆ 01451 832522)

MANDL, Dr Anita Maria; da of Dr Bohumir Mandl (d 1941), and Hanna, *née* Ascher (d 1944 in Auschwitz); *b* 17 May 1926; *Educ* Dudley Girls HS, Birkbeck Coll London (BSc), Univ of Birmingham (PhD, DSc), Birmingham Coll of Art (pt/t); *m* April 1965, Dr Denys Arthur Jennings (d 1995); *Career* sculptor; research asst London Hosp 1946–47, asst lectr, lectr and sr lectr Univ of Birmingham 1948–62, reader in reproductive physiology 1962–65; set up sculpture workshop 1965, specialises in animal carvings and bronzes; fndr Otter Valley Assoc; RSMA 1971 (resigned 1994), RWA 1978, FRBS 1980; *Exhibitions* Royal Acad, John Davies Gall Moreton-in-Marsh, Wildlife Art Gall Lavenham, Sinfield Gall Burford, Bruton Street Gall London, Llewellyn-Alexander Gall London, F T Sabin Gallery London, Martin's Gall Cheltenham, Red Rag Gall Stow, Embankment Gall London 1982, Spring Exhibition RWA Bristol 1982, Guildford House Gall Guildford 1983, Czechoslovak Embassy London 1992, New Acad Gall London 1996, 2001, 2004, 2005, 2011 and 2015, Alresford Gall Hants 1996, 2000, 2004 and 2007, Falle Fine Arts Jersey 1997 and 2002, Gall Pangolin Chalford 2001 and 2008, Sinfield Gall Burford 2002–15, New Gall RWA Bristol 2004, Moncrieff-Bray Gall Petworth 2007–15, Wykeham Gall Stockbridge 2009–15, Jerram Gall Sherborne 2008–15, Russell Gall Putney 2014–15; *Publications* numerous papers in scientific journals, asst ed The Ovary (1962); *Recreations* gardening, swimming, walking, photography; *Style*— Dr Anita Mandl; ✉ 21 Northview Road, Budleigh Salterton, Devon EX9 6BZ (✆ and fax 01395 443227, e-mail anitajennings613@btinternet.com)

MANDUCA, Charles Victor Falzon Sant; s of Victor John Sant Manduca (d 1989), and Ethel Florence, *née* Johnson (d 1960); *b* 21 November 1954; *Educ* Harrow, UCL (LLB); *Children* 4 da (Alicia b 1988, Charlotte b 1992, Maria b 2002, Christina b 2005); 1 s (Alexander b 2010); *Career* admitted slr 1979; ptnr Lovells (formerly Durrant Piesse) 1983–2003; The ECU Gp plc: gen counsel 2006–09, chief exec 2009–10, chm 2010–11; ceo Woodsford Litigation Funding Ltd 2010–15; conslt: Jema Fund Management Ltd 2003–09, Titanium Capital 2006–08, Gerald Metals SA 2015–; Freeman Worshipful Co of Slrs 1988; memb Law Soc; *Recreations* golf, antique clocks; *Clubs* Wentworth Golf,; *Style*— Charles Manduca, Esq

MANDUCA, Paul Victor Falzon Sant; s of Victor Falzon Sant Manduca (d 1989), and Elisabeth, *née* Johnson (d 1960); *b* 15 November 1951; *Educ* Harrow, Hertford Coll Oxford (MA); *m* 1982, Dr Ursula, da of Edmund Vogt, of Bielefeld, Germany; 2 s (Mark b 1983, Nicholas b 1988); *Career* md TR Industrial and General plc 1986–88, chm TR High Income plc 1989–94, chm Touche Remnant Hldgs 1989–92 (vice-chm 1987–89), dep ceo Henderson Administration plc (following takeover of Touche Remnant) 1992–94, chm Gresham Trust 1994–99; ceo: Threadneedle Asset Management 1994–99, Rothschild Asset Mgmnt 1999–2002, Deutsche Asset Mgmnt (Europe) 2002–05; chm: Uniq Tstees Ltd 2005–09, Majid Al Futtaim Tst 2005–, Bridgewell Gp 2006–07, Aon UK Ltd 2008–12 (dir 2006–12), Microlease plc 2009–14, Prudential Gp plc 2012– (sr ind dir 2010–), Advsy Cncl TheCityUK 2015–; dir: Clydesdale Investment Trust 1987–88, Henderson Smaller Companies Investment Trust plc 1987–2006, Allied Dunbar Assurance plc 1994–99, Eagle Star Holdings 1994–99, MEPC plc 1999–2000 (taken over by GE Capital), Wolverhampton Wanderers FC Ltd 1999–2006, Development Securities plc 2001–10, Wm Morrison Supermarkets plc 2005–11, JP Morgan Fleming European Smaller Cos Investment Tst plc 2005–12, Kazmunaigaz plc 2006–12, Intrinsic Ltd 2006–12, Templeton Emerging Markets Investment Tst plc 2015 (chm 2015–); advsr Alexander Proudfoot 2010–12; chm Assoc of Investment Trust Cos 1991–93 (Takeover Panel 1991–93); memb: Investment Ctee Univs Superannuation Scheme 1993–2002, London Stock Exchange Institutional Investors Advsy Ctee 1998–2001; Freeman City of London 1988, Liveryman Worshipful Co of Bakers 1989; *Recreations* golf, squash, shooting; *Clubs* Wentworth, White's, Lansdowne; *Style*— Paul Manduca, Esq; ✉ 22 Rutland Gate, London SW7 1BB (✆ 020 7584 3987)

MANFORD, Bruce Robert James; s of late John Julian Manford, and Ruth, *née* Heldmann; *b* 21 March 1957, London; *Educ* Haberdashers' Aske's, Keele Univ (BA); *m* 1992, Frances, *née* Turay; *Career* admitted slr 1981; ptnr Lawrence Graham 1988–96, DG Cncl Oilinvest (Netherlands) Gp 1996–2009, gen counsel Libya Oil Hldgs Ltd 2009–; memb Law Soc 1981; *Clubs* RAC; *Style*— Bruce Manford, Esq; ✉ Libya Oil Holdings Limited, c/o Africana Corporate Services SARL AU, Casablanca Nearshore Park, 1100 Boulevard Al Qods, Shore 3, Plateau 202, Sidi Maarouf, Casablanca 20270, Morocco (✆ 00 212 529 044772, e-mail bruce.manford@oilibya.com)

MANFORD, Jason John; *b* 26 May 1981, Salford, Gtr Manchester; *m* 2007, Catherine; 3 da; *Career* comedian; host of radio breakfast show Xfm Manchester until 2008; stand-up incl: Jason Manford Live 2008, Off On Tour We Go 2010–11; television appearances incl: 8 Out of 10 Cats (team capt 2007–10), host Comedy Rocks 2010–11, co-presenter The One Show 2010, Would I Lie to You?, Live at the Apollo, Michael McIntyre's Comedy Roadshow, host Show Me The Funny; Best Breakthrough Act Chortle Award 2006; *DVDs* Live at the Manchester Apollo (2009), Jason Manford Live 2011 (2011); *Style*— Mr Jason Manford

MANGNALL, Richard Anthony; JP (S Westminster 1986–2004, City of Westminster 2005, SW Surrey 2006–10, Telford and S Salops 2010–12); s of late Col (Anthony) Derek Swift Mangnall, OBE, TD, of Chieveley, Berks, and (Cynthia) Mary, *née* Foster (later Lady FitzGerald); *b* 27 November 1942; *Educ* Douai Abbey; *m* 25 March 1975, Maureen Patricia, da of Lawrence Donnelly (d 1965), of Delhi, India; *Career* Sant & Co Loss Adjusters 1962–74, dir Tyler & Co (Adjusters) Ltd 1989–2000 (ptnr 1974–), conslt Marsh Private Client Services 2002–04, chm Proteus Open Space Mgmnt Ltd 1993–2010; pres: The Insurance Adjusters Assoc 1987–89 (assoc 1967, fell 1972), Chartered Inst of Loss Adjusters 1996–97; memb Ctee of Magistrates Inner London 1994–96; chm: S Westminster Bench 2002–04, City of Westminster Bench 2005; tstee Inner London Poor Box Tst 1994–2012; Freeman: City of London 1989, Worshipful Co of Fletchers 1989, Worshipful Co of Insurers 1997; FCILA 1992, FInstD, FRSA; *Recreations* shooting, sailing; *Clubs* Boodle's, Royal Southern Yacht; *Style*— Richard Mangnall, Esq; ✉ 36 Broad Street, Ludlow, Shropshire SY8 1NL (e-mail richard@mangnalls.com); 37 Westerhall Point, St David's, Grenada, West Indies

MANISTY, Edward Alexander; s of Henry Earle Manisty (d 1959), and Charlotte Evelyn Stephens, *née* Baird-Smith (d 2010); *b* 12 May 1941, Staplefield, W Sussex; *Educ* Wellington Coll, New Coll Oxford (MA); *m* 8 Nov 1967 (m dis 2015), Dr Dinah Lake Manisty, *née* Watson; 2 s (Alexander b 7 Dec 1968, Mark Edward b 6 Feb 1974), 1 da (Louisa (Mrs Trandafilovska) b 29 Sept 1971); *Career* admitted slr 1968, ptnr Stephenson Harwood 1971–92; Christie's (Christie, Manson & Woods Ltd): dir i/c Heritage and Taxation Dept 1992–2006, vice-chm 1999–2006, conslt 2006–08; conslt Farrer & Co 2006–15, conslt Shoosmiths LLP; dir Samuel Courtauld Tst 1995–2006; Liveryman Worshipful Co of Merchant Taylors 1974; *Publications* contrib: tech jls on taxation of chattels and heritage property 1993–2010, Tolley's Administration of Estates 1997–2005; *Recreations* classical music, reading; *Style*— Edward Manisty, Esq; ✉ 111 Ladbroke Road, London W11 3PR (✆ 020 7727 7724)

MANLEY, Charlotte Elizabeth; LVO (2003), OBE (1996); da of (John) Patrick Manley, MVO (d 2000), and (Ann) Priscilla, *née* Bunting; *b* 15 March 1957; *Career* RN 1976–96, joined Royal Household 1996, chapter clerk Coll of St George Windsor Castle 2003–, also extra equerry to HRH The Duke of York; *Style*— Miss Charlotte Manley, LVO, OBE; ✉ Chapter Office, Windsor Castle, Berkshire SL4 1NJ

MANLEY, Her Hon Judge Hilary; da of Peter Manley, and Alison, *née* Needham; *b* Sheffield; *Educ* UCL (LLB); *m* Jonathan Gregg; 1 da (Niamh Georgina b 2001); *Career* called to the Bar 1996; recorder 2012, circuit judge (Northern Circuit) 2014–; *Style*— Her Hon Judge Manley; ✉ c/o Manchester Crown Court, Courts of Justice, Crown Square, Manchester, Greater Manchester M3 3FL

MANLEY, HE Simon John; CMG (2009); s of James Frank Manley (d 2006), and Beryl Jean, *née* Owen (d 2012); *b* 18 September 1967, London; *Educ* Latymer Upper Sch, Magdalen Coll Oxford (BA), Yale Univ Grad Sch (MA); *m* 28 Aug 1996, Maria Isabel Fernandez Utgès; 3 da (Chiara b 29 Jan 2000, Melissa b 16 Jul 2001, Natasha b 22 April 2008); *Career* diplomat; UN Dept FCO 1990–93, seconded to DG for Competition European Cmmn 1993, second then first sec (political) UK Mission to the UN NY 1993–98, seconded to EU Cncl Secretariat's Asia Unit 1998–2002; FCO: head EU (Internal) Dept 2002–03, head EU Economic, Ireland & Central Europe Team 2003–06, head Counter Terrorism Policy Dept 2006–07, dir Defence and Strategic Threats 2007–11, dir Europe 2011–13, ambass to Spain and Andorra 2013–; Commander of Polish Order of Merit 2004; *Recreations* cinema, gardening, theatre; *Style*— HE Mr Simon Manley, CMG; ✉ c/o FCO (Madrid), King Charles Street, London SW1A 2AH (e-mail simon.manley@fco.gov.uk, Twitter @SimonManleyFCO)

MANN, Dr Anna; *Career* sr ptnr MWM Consulting; *Style*— Dr Anna Mann; ✉ MWM Consulting, 12 Charles II Street, London SW1Y 4QU

MANN, David William; s of William James Mann (d 1966), of Trimley Saint Mary, Suffolk, and Mary Ann, *née* Bloomfield (d 1987); *b* 14 June 1944; *Educ* Felixstowe Co GS, Jesus Coll Cambridge (MA); *m* 29 June 1968, Gillian Mary, da of Rev David Emlyn Edwards (d 1978), of Felixstowe, Suffolk; 2 s (Richard b 1972, Edward b 1975); *Career* computing systems conslt; CEIR (UK) Ltd (now EDS) 1966–69; Logica plc: joined on its formation 1969, mangr conslt 1971, mangr Advanced Systems Div 1972, dir Advanced Systems Gp 1976, md UK ops 1979, dep gp md 1982, md and chief exec 1987–93, dep chm 1993–94; chm Charteris plc 1996–2007 (dep chm 2007–14); non-exec dir: Industrial Control Services Gp plc 1994–2000, Druid Gp plc 1996–2000, Room Solutions Ltd 1996–2006, Eurolink Managed Services plc 1999–2000, Aveva Gp plc 1999–2010, Ansbacher Holdings Ltd 2000–04; non-exec chm: Cambridge Display Technology Ltd 1995–97,

M

Flomerics Gp plc 1995–2008, Velti plc 2006–14; pres Br Computer Soc 1994–95; memb Engrg Cncl 1993–95; chm Epping Forest Wine Soc 2005–12; Master Worshipful Co of Info Technologists 1997–98 (chm of tstees 2002–07, tstee 2007–11); chm Livery Past Masters' Assoc 1997–98 2006–09; CITP (Chartered IT Professional), CEng, FBCS; *Recreations* gardening, walking, skiing; *Clubs* Athenaeum (memb Wine Ctee 2010–16, memb Gen Ctee 2016–); *Style*— David Mann, Esq; ✉ Theydon Copt, Forest Side, Epping, Essex CM16 4ED (☎ 01992 575842, e-mail david@theydoncopt.com)

MANN, Fred; s of Andrew Lonsdale, of London, and Rosemary, *née* Stones; *b* 11 March 1972; *Educ* Camberwell Coll of Art, Univ of Brighton (BA); *Career* curator of exhibitions at Milch with Lisa Panting incl: New Installations Steve Farrer 1996, Behalter, Till Exit, Come, Kate Davis (touring) 1997, Wish You Were Here!, New Swiss Painting 1998, The New Contemporaries99; offsite curation: Retrospective: Jean Mark Proveur, Drawings: Kate Davis, Works: Keith Milow; teaching: Ruskin Coll of Art 1998–99, Univ of Brighton 1998–99, Goldsmiths Coll 1999; lectr at Serpentine Gall for exhibitions by Louise Bourgeois, William Kentridge, Jane and Louise Wilson 1998, Felix Gonzales Torres 1999; exhibitions: Take My Life (Milch) 1996, Furniture (Richard Salmon Gall London) 1999; various art direction and prodn for video and films incl work for: Guns 'n' Roses, Rage Against the Machine, Roger Corman, MTV and Derek Jarman; Metronome 1 in magazine format with Tracey Emin, *qv*, Gary Hume, Langlands and Bell and Susan Hiller; Rhodes & Mann Gall (representing 18 artists): launch of artists at Art2000 London Jan 2000, opened April 2000, 1st gp exhbn May 2000; memb The Furniture History Soc; *Publications* Behalter (1996), Kate Davis (1996), New Swiss Painting (1998), ashowabouttime (intro, 1999); *Style*— Fred Mann, Esq; ✉ FRED, 45 Vyner Street, London E2 9DQ

MANN, Geoffrey Horton; s of Stanley Victor Mann (d 1986), of Coventry, and Dorothy, *née* Horton (d 1964); *b* 12 May 1938; *Educ* Warwick Sch, Univ of Liverpool (BArch), RIBA (MCD); *m* 28 Dec 1963, Meg, da of Francis Richard Evans, of Denton, Manchester; 4 da (Katherine b 1964, Clare b 1966, Rachel b 1968, Shelley b 1972); *Career* architect; W S Hattrell & Ptnrs Manchester 1963–70, sr ptnr RHWL (Renton Howard Wood Levin Partnership) 1980– (joined 1970); responsible for: Arena 2001 Coventry, Dublin National Arena, St Katharine's Dock, County Hall, Ludgate, Commercial Union Tower, Orion House, Queensbury House, several new buildings in Moscow; memb: children's charities, Bodmin & Wenford Railway; ARCUK 1965, ARIBA 1965; *Recreations* Coventry City FC, railways; *Clubs* Coventry City; *Style*— Geoffrey Mann, Esq; ✉ Saughtree Railway Station, Roxburghshire; RHWL, 77 Endell Street, London WC2H 9AJ (☎ 020 7379 7900, fax 020 7836 4881)

MANN, Jessica D E (Jessica D E Thomas); da of Dr F A Mann, CBE (d 1991), of London, and Eleonore, *née* Ehrlich (d 1980); *b* 13 September 1937; *Educ* St Paul's, Newnham Coll Cambridge (MA), Univ of Leicester (LLB); *m* 1 July 1959, Prof A Charles Thomas, CBE (d 2016), s of D W Thomas (d 1959), of Cornwall; 2 s (Richard b 1961, Martin b 1963), 2 da (Susanna b 1966, Lavinia b 1971); *Career* writer and journalist; memb: Carrick DC 1972–78, Cornwall AHA 1976–78, Employment Tbnls 1977–2007, SW RHA 1979–84, Med Practices Ctee 1982–87, Cornwall FPC 1985–88; DOE planning inspector 1991–93; chair: Ofwat (SW) 1993–2001, Network 200 SW Ltd 1995–99; memb: Advsy Ctee England Ofcom, SW Arts Board, Detection Club, ForumUK, PEN; *Books* A Charitable End (1971), Mrs Knox's Profession (1972), The Only Security (1973), The Sticking Place (1974), Captive Audience (1975), The Eighth Deadly Sin (1976), The Sting of Death (1978), Deadlier than the Male (1981), Funeral Sites (1982), No Man's Island (1983), Grave Goods (1985), A Kind of Healthy Grave (1986), Death Beyond The Nile (1988), Faith Hope and Homicide (1991), Telling Only Lies (1992), A Private Inquiry (1996), Hanging Fire (1997), The Survivor's Revenge (1998), Under a Dark Sun (2000), The Voice from the Grave (2002), Out of Harm's Way (2005), The Mystery Writer (2006), Godrevy Light (jtly, 2009), The Fifties Mystique (2012), Dead Woman Walking (2013), The Stroke of Death (2016); *Style*— Ms Jessica Mann; ✉ Lambessow, St Clement, Cornwall TR1 1TB (☎ 01872 272980)

MANN, John; MP; s of James Mann, and Brenda Cleavin; *Educ* Univ of Manchester (BA); *Career* TUC Nat Trg Offr 1990–95, Nat Trade Union and Lab Pty liaison offr 1995–2000, head of research and educn AEU; MP (Lab) Bassetlaw 2001–; dir Abraxas Communications Ltd; MIPD 1992; *Recreations* football, cricket, hill walking; *Clubs* Manton Miners; *Style*— John Mann, Esq, MP; ✉ House of Commons, London SW1A 0AA (☎ 020 7219 8345)

MANN, Jonathan; QC (2015); *b* 19 June 1966, London; *Educ* Atholl GS, Univ of Essex, Inns of Court Sch of Law; *m* 16 Oct 2001, Pamela, *née* Reddy; 1 s (Kailen b 3 March 2004), 1 da (Safia b 15 Dec 2006); *Career* called to the Bar 1989; recorder of the Crown Court 2012; memb: Criminal Bar Assoc (treas 2008–10), Proceeds of Crime Lawyers Assoc, Assoc of Regulatory and Disciplinary Lawyers; reviewing lawyer Bar Pro Bono Unit; *Recreations* cinema, travel, walking; *Style*—Jonathan Mann, Esq, QC; ✉ Doughty Street Chambers, 54 Doughty Street, London WC1N 2LS (Twitter @jmbarrister)

MANN, Martin Edward; QC (1983); s of late S E and M F L Mann; *b* 12 September 1943; *Educ* Cranleigh Sch; *m* 1966, Jacqueline Harriette, *née* Le Maitre; 2 da; *Career* called to the Bar: Gray's Inn 1968 (Lord Justice Holker sr exhibitioner), Lincoln's Inn (ad eundum) 1973 (bencher 1991); dep judge of the High Court (Chancery Div) 1992–2016; memb Senate of the Inns of Court and the Bar 1979–82; chm: Bar Cncl Fees Collection Ctee 1993–95, Queen's Counsel Selection Panel 2013–; memb: Chancery Bar Assoc, Commercial Bar Assoc, Insolvency Lawyers Assoc, Pension Lawyers Assoc, European Circuit, Bar of the Eastern Caribbean Supreme Court; *Publications* What Kind of Common Agricultural Policy for Europe (jtly, 1975), Tolley's Insolvency Law (contrib), Palmer's Company Law Manual (conslt ed); *Recreations* many and various interests incl farming; *Clubs* Garrick; *Style*— Martin Mann, Esq, QC; ✉ 24 Old Buildings, Lincoln's Inn, London WC2A 3UP (e-mail martin.mann@xxiv.co.uk, website www.xxiv.co.uk)

MANN, Prof (Colin) Nicholas Jocelyn; CBE (1999); s of Colin Henry Mann (d 1987), of Mere, Wilts, and Marie-Elise, *née* Gosling (d 2001); *b* 24 October 1942, Salisbury, Wilts; *Educ* Eton, King's Coll Cambridge (MA, PhD); *m* 27 June 1964 (m dis 2003), Joelle, da of Pierre Emile Bourcart (d 1982), of Geneva; 1 da (Olivia Sophie b 1965), 1 s (Benedict Julian b 1968); m 2, 24 May 2003, Helen Margaret, da of Michael Anthony Stevenson, of Doncaster; 2 da (Clara Elizabeth b 2001, Verity Isabel b 2004); *Career* res fell Clare Coll Cambridge 1965–67, lectr Univ of Warwick 1967–72, visiting fell All Souls Coll Oxford 1972, fell and tutor Pembroke Coll Oxford 1973–90 (emeritus fell 1991, hon fell 2006), dir Warburg Inst and prof of the history of the classical tradition Univ of London 1990–2001, dean Sch of Advanced Study Univ of London 2002–07, pro-vice-chllr Univ of London 2003–07 (emeritus prof 2007–); memb Cncl: MOMA Oxford 1984–92 (chm 1988–90), Contemporary Applied Arts 1994–2006 (chm 1996–99), Br Acad 1995–98 and 1999–2006 (vice-pres and foreign sec 1999–2006), Royal Holloway Coll London 1996–98, RCA 2001–07; vice-pres ALLEA 2006–11; tstee: Cubitt Artists 1996–99, Learning Skills Fndn Research 2010–, Padworth Coll 2014–; Hon DLitt Univ of Warwick 2006; FBA 1992, fell Euro Medieval Acad 1993, fell Fondazione Lorenzo Valla 2007; *Books* Petrarch Manuscripts in the British Isles (1975), Petrarch (1984), A Concordance to Petrarch's Bucolicum Carmen (1984), Lorenzo the Magnificent: Culture and Politics (jtly, 1996), Medieval and Renaissance Scholarship (jtly, 1996), Giordano Bruno, 1583–1585: The English Experience (jtly, 1997), The Image of the Individual: Portraits in the Renaissance (jtly, 1998), Photographs at the Frontier. Aby Warburg in America, 1895–1896 (jtly, 1998), Carnets de Voyage (2003), Pétrarque: les voyages de l'esprit (2004), Britannia Latina: Latin in the Culture of Great Britain from the Middle Ages to the Twentieth Century (jtly, 2005), Francesco Petrarca, My Secret Book (ed and trans, 2016); *Recreations* yoga, poetry, sculpture; *Style*— Prof Nicholas Mann, CBE, FBA; ✉ 34 High Street, Axbridge, Somerset BS26 2AF (☎ 01934 732151, e-mail nicomann1304@gmail.com)

MANN, Scott; MP; s of Eugene Mann, and Peggy, *née* Bate; *b* 24 June 1977, Truro; *Educ* Wadebridge Comprehensive Sch; *m*; 1 da (Bethany; *Career* postman 1996–2015; MP (Cons) Cornwall N 2015–; *Style*— Scott Mann, Esq, MP; ✉ 10 Market House Arcade, Fore Street, Bodmin, Cornwall PL31 2JA (☎ 01208 74337, e-mail scott.mann.mp@parliament.uk, website www.scottmann.org.uk, Twitter @ScottMannMP); House of Commons, London SW1A 0AA

MANNERS, Crispin Luke; s of Norman Donald Manners (d 2001), and Noeline Mary, *née* Blake (d 1994); *b* 2 August 1957; *Educ* Ranelagh GS Bracknell, Bedford Coll London (BSc); *m* 18 Aug 1979, Judith Ann, da of Peter Simpson; 2 s (Matthew b 1 July 1981, Philip b 12 May 1985); *Career* salesman CPC UK Limited 1978–80; The Argyll Consultancies plc: exec asst to chm 1980, account dir 1984, md 1987, chief exec 1989–2007, dir 2007–11; dir Kaizo Ltd 2011–15, dir Nicorinse Ltd 2015–; chm Onva Consulting Ltd 2007–, chm Worldcom PR Gp EMEA 2007–09; chm PR Consits Assoc 2004–; tstee St Joseph's Hospice 2014–; FIPR, FInstD, fell PRCA; *Clubs* Surbiton Golf (memb Mgmnt Ctee); *Style*— Crispin Manners, Esq; ✉ Onva Consulting Ltd, 51 Court Farm Avenue, Epsom KT19 0HD (☎ 020 8224 7973, e-mail crispin.manners@onva.co.uk)

MANNERS, Debbie; da of Allan Snaith, and Sheila, *née* Macdonald; *Educ* UCL (BSc); *Children* 1 da (Ellen b 8 June 1994), 2 s (James b 1 Oct 1995, Alexander b 23 March 2002); *Career* formerly: chief operating offr Hat Trick Prodns, gp commercial dir RDF Media Gp, dir of rights and business affrs BBC; interim chief operating offr BBC Studios and Post Production 2011–12, ceo Keo Films 2012–, co-fndr Here Café Ltd 2013; chair PACT 2010–; *Clubs* Ivy; *Style*— Ms Debbie Manners; ✉ Keo Films, 9–10 Great Sutton Street, London EC1V 0BX

MANNERS, 6 Baron (UK 1807); John Hugh Robert (Willie) Manners; s of 5 Baron Manners (d 2008); *b* 5 May 1956; *Educ* Eton; *m* 1, 8 Oct 1983 (m dis 2005), Lanya Mary Patrica (Lala), da of late Dr H E Heitz, and Mrs Ian Jackson, and step da of late Ian Jackson; 2 da (Harriet Frances Mary b 29 July 1988, Catherine Mary Patricia b 18 Sept 1992); m 2, 24 Feb 2007, Juliet Elizabeth Anthea, da of David McMyn; 1 da (Virginia Constance Juliet b 21 Feb 2009), 1 s (John Alexander David b 22 Feb 2011); *Career* admitted slr 1980; ptnr Macfarlanes 1987–2014 (head of litigation 2000–08); *Recreations* gardening, shooting; *Clubs* Pratt's; *Style*— The Lord Manners; ✉ North Ripley House, Avon, Christchurch, Dorset BH23 8EP (☎ 01425 672249); (☎ 020 7831 9222, fax 020 7831 9607, e-mail willie.manners@gmail.com)

MANNING, Brittany; *Educ* Johnson and Wales Univ (BA); *m* Guy Manning, *qv*; *Career* pastry chef Per Se NY 2005–07, pastry chef and prop Red Lion Freehouse Wilts 2008– (Michelin star 2013–); *Style*— Mrs Brittany Manning; ✉ Red Lion Freehouse, East Chisenbury, Pewsey, Wiltshire SN9 6AQ

MANNING, Sir David Geoffrey; KCVO (2015, CVO 2007) GCMG (2008, KCMG 2001, CMG (1992)),; s of John Robert Manning, and Joan Barbara Manning; *b* 5 December 1949; *Educ* Ardingly, Oriel Coll Oxford (open history scholar, MA), Johns Hopkins Sch of Advanced Int Studies Bologna (postgrad scholar); *m* 1973, Dr Catherine Manning, da of Dr W Parkinson; *Career* HM Dip Serv: joined FCO 1972, third later second sec Warsaw 1974–76, second later first sec New Delhi 1977–80, E Euro and Soviet Dept FCO 1980–82, Policy Planning Staff FCO 1982–84, first sec (political internal) Paris 1984–88, cnsllr on loan to Cabinet Office 1988–90, cnsllr and head of Political Section Moscow 1990–93, head of Eastern (formerly Soviet) Dept FCO 1993–94, head of Policy Planning Staff FCO 1994–95 (concurrently Br rep on ICFY Contact Gp on Bosnia April-Oct 1994), ambass to Israel 1995–98, dep under sec of state FCO 1998–2000, UK perm rep UK Delgn NATO 2001, foreign policy advsr to PM (on loan to Cabinet Office) 2001–03, ambass to USA 2003–07, sr advsr to TRH Prince William and Prince Henry of Wales 2009–; non-exec dir: Lloyds TSB Group plc 2008–09, BG Gp plc 2008–16, Lockheed Martin UK 2008–; dir Gatehouse Advsy Ptnrs 2010–; memb Panel of Sr Advsrs Chatham House 2008–, tstee Turner Contemporary 2008–13, patron World Wide Volunteering 2009–, patron Afghan Connection 2008–, chair IDEAS LSE 2010–, tstee Royal Fndn 2010–, memb Cncl Lloyd's 2010–; Fulbright Cmmr 2009–15; Fisher Family Fell Harvard Kennedy Sch 2012; *Style*— Sir David Manning, GCMG, KCVO

MANNING, (Everard Alexander) Dermot Niall; s of Col Frederick Everard Beresford Manning, Indian Med Serv (d 1987), and Elizabeth Robina, *née* Webber (d 1999); *b* 20 February 1949; *Educ* Rossall Sch, The Middx Hosp Med Sch London (MB BS); *m* 1 Aug 1981, Ann Ming Choo, da of Pak Shoon Wong (d 1998), of Kuala Lumpur, Malaysia; 1 s (Edward b 1985), 1 da (Catherine b 1988); *Career* registrar in obstetrics and gynaecology: St Helier Hosp Carshalton 1981–83, The Middx Hosp London 1983–85; sr registrar in obstetrics and gynaecology Middx Hosp and Central Middx Hosp London 1985–87, conslt obstetrics and gynaecology Central Middx Hosp and hon clinical sr lectr Imperial Sch of Medicine 1987–; Br Soc for Colposcopy and Cervical Pathology FBI; FRCOG 1995 (MRCOG 1982), forum memb RSM 1985; *Recreations* photography, gemmology and jewellery; *Clubs* Wine Soc; *Style*— Dermot Manning, Esq; ✉ London North West Healthcare NHS Trust, Central Middlesex Hospital, Park Royal, London NW10 7NS (☎ 020 8453 2410, fax 020 8453 2408)

MANNING, Guy; *b* London; *m* Brittany Manning, *qv*; *Career* formerly: Chez Bruce Wandsworth, Per Se NY; currently chef patron Red Lion Freehouse Wilts (Michelin star 2013–); *Style*— Guy Manning, Esq; ✉ Red Lion Freehouse, East Chisenbury, Pewsey, Wiltshire SN9 6AQ

MANNING, Dr Jane Marian; OBE (1990); da of Gerald Manville Manning (d 1987), and Lily, *née* Thompson (d 1989); *b* 20 September 1938, Norwich; *Educ* Norwich HS, Royal Acad of Music (GRSM, LRAM, ARCM), Scuola Di Canto Cureglia Switzerland; *m* 24 Sept 1966, Anthony Edward Payne, s of Edward Alexander Payne (d 1958), of London; *Career* int career as soprano concert singer; London debut 1964, more than 300 world premieres, regular appearances in leading halls and festivals, Brussels Opera 1980, Scottish Opera 1978, numerous tours of Aust, NY debut 1981, first BBC broadcast 1965 (over 300 since), numerous recordings incl Messiaen Song Cycles; visiting prof: Mills Coll Oakland Calif 1981, 1983 and 1986, Royal Coll of Music 1995–, Kingston Univ 2007–11; hon prof Keele Univ 1996–2002; AHRC Creative Arts Research Fell Kingston Univ 2004–07, research fell Guildhall Sch of Music and Drama 2013–; visiting lectr: Harvard Univ, Stanford Univ, Princeton Univ, Yale Univ, Cornell Univ, Columbia Univ, Pennsylvania Univ, Univ of York, Univ of Cambridge, Univ of Durham; vice-pres Soc for the Promotion of New Music until 2009, chm Eye Music Tst, fndr and artistic dir Jane's Minstrels Ensemble 1988, tstee Help Musicians UK 1989–2014; received special award composers Guild of GB 1973, awarded Gold Badge of Merit Br Academy of Songwriters Composers and Authors (BASCA) 2013; Hon DUniv York 1988, Hon DMus Keele Univ 2004, Hon DMus Univ of Durham 2007, Hon DArts Kingston Univ 2013; memb: RPS, ISM, RSM 2012; FRAM 1984, FRCM 1998; *Books* New Vocal Repertory (1986, reissued 1993, Vol II 1998), A Messiaen Companion (contrib, 1995), Voicing Pierrot (2012), Cambridge History of Musical Performance (contrib, 2012), Vocal Repertoire for the 21st Century (2016); *Recreations* cinema, theatre, ornithology, reading; *Style*— Dr Jane Manning, OBE; ✉ 2 Wilton Square, London N1 3DL (☎ 020 7359 1593, e-mail janetone@gmail.com); 7 Park Terrace, Upperton Road, Tillington, Petworth, West Sussex GU28 9AE

MANNING, Patrick John Mannes (Paddy); s of late Col Francis James Manning, TD, of Wiveliscombe, Somerset, and late Sarah Margaret, *née* Jenkins; *b* 16 July 1940; *Educ* Downside, RMA Sandhurst; *m* 19 April 1986, Sally Gail, da of late Maj Jeremy Green; 1 da (Charlotte b 1987), 2 s (Francis James Daniel b 5 March 1990, Jeremy Patrick Augustus b 31 March 1992); *Career* Lt 4/7 Royal Dragoon Gds 1961–64, Royal Yeo 1965–72; stockbroker Laurence Keen & Gardner 1965–70; dir: Charles Barker City Ltd 1970–80, St James Public Relations Ltd 1984–98; chm The Paddy Manning Co 1998–; hon PR advsr Br Cwlth Ex-Servs League 1984–2004; *Recreations* country sports, opera, ballet, travel, book collecting; *Clubs* Cavalry and Guards'; *Style—* Paddy Manning, Esq; ✉ Eastwood Dairy Farm, Alverdiscot Road, Bideford, North Devon EX39 4PN (☎ mobile 07803 183622, e-mail paddy@pmanning.demon.co.uk)

MANNING, Paul; MBE (2009); *b* 6 November 1974, Sutton Coldfield; *Educ* Univ of Birmingham; *Career* track and road cyclist; memb Landbouwkrediet-Tönissteiner professional road cycling team; debut GB sr team 1999; achievements incl: winner individual pursuit Br Championships 2001, 2003, 2004 and 2005 (also winner points race 2005), Gold medal team pursuit World Track Championships 2005, 2007 and 2008 (Silver medal team pursuit 2000, 2001, 2003, 2004 and 2006, Bronze medal individual pursuit 2006), Gold medals individual pursuit and team pursuit Cwlth Games 2006 (Silver medal team pursuit and Bronze medal individual pursuit 2002), Gold medal team pursuit Olympic Games Beijing 2008 (Silver medal team pursuit Athens 2004, Bronze medal team pursuit Sydney 2000); *Style—* Paul Manning, Esq, MBE

MANNING, Peter; s of Harry Manning (d 2002), and Breda, *née* Carroll (d 1992); *b* 17 July 1956; *Educ* Chethams Hosp Sch of Music Manchester, Royal Northern Coll of Music (GRNCM, PPRNCM), Indiana Univ; *m* 1992, Marion, *née* Cookson; 3 s (Edward b 1983, Frederick b 1995, Orlando b 1997), 1 da (Isabelle b 1986); *Career* ldr LPO 1983–86, ldr Britten String Quartet 1986–96, ldr RPO 1997–99, concertmaster ROH 1999–; dir Soloists of Covent Garden; artistic dir and conductor The Manning Camerata, artistic dir and conductor Musica Vitae Sweden 2008–11, guest conductor Dallas Opera 2015–, artistic dir 3 Palaces Festival Malta 2016–, music dir Mozart KinderOrchester Salzburg Austria 2016–; int tours as soloist, dir and conductor; prof of new work Univ of Edinburgh and Royal Conservatoire of Scotland 2013–15; int fell Royal Conservatoire of Scotland; Hon RCM, FRNCM, FRSA; *Publications* Universal Edition Vienna Schnittke; *Recreations* sailing, fishing, mushroom hunting; *Clubs* Garrick; *Style—* Peter Manning, Esq; ✉ 52 Stockwell Park Road, London SW9 0DA (☎ 020 7733 5251, e-mail peter@manningcamerata.com)

MANNING-COX, Andrew Richard; s of Frederick Cox, of Kinver, Staffs, and Beatrice Maud, *née* Brown; *b* 23 April 1956; *Educ* Peter Symonds' Coll Winchester, Univ of Cambridge (MA); *m* 31 Oct 1987, Janet Elaine, da of Eric Binns, of Bramhall, Cheshire; 2 da (Octavia Freya, Verity Beatrice); *Career* admitted slr 1980; ptnr Wragge Lawrence Graham & Co 1985–, NP 1992, slr advocate 2002; accredited mediator 1996; memb Law Soc 1980, FCIArb 2002; *Recreations* riding, walking, country pursuits; *Style—* Andrew Manning-Cox, Esq; ✉ Wragge Lawrence Graham & Co LLP, 2 Snowhill, Birmingham B4 6WR (☎ 0121 393 0427, e-mail andrew.manningcox@wragge-LAW.com)

MANNINGHAM-BULLER, Baroness (UK Life Peer 2008), of Northampton in the Co of Northamptonshire; Hon Elizabeth Lydia Manningham-Buller; LG (2015), DCB (2005); da of 1 Viscount Dilhorne (d 1980); *b* 14 July 1948; *Educ* Benenden Sch, Lady Margaret Hall Oxford (MA); *Career* Security Serv: joined 1974, dep DG 1997–2002, DG 2002–07; sits in House of Lords as crossbench peer 2008–; govr Wellcome Tst 2008, chair Cncl Imperial Coll 2011–15, chair Wellcome Tst 2015–; Hon DUniv Open 2005, Hon DSc Cranfield Univ 2005, hon graduate Univ of Northampton 2008, Hon LLD Univ of St Andrews 2010, Hon LLD Univ of Leeds 2012, Hon DCL Univ of Oxford 2012; hon fell Lady Margaret Hall Oxford 2004, hon fell Cardiff Univ 2010; *Style—* The Baroness Manningham-Buller, LG, DCB; ✉ House of Lords, London SW1A 0PW

MANOR, Prof James Gilmore; s of James Gilmore Manor, of Lakeland, Florida, and Ann Jones Manor; *b* 21 April 1945; *Educ* Yale Univ (BA), Univ of Sussex (DPhil); *m* July 1974, Brenda, da of Sydney Cohen; 1 s (Hugh Benjamin b 16 March 1989); *Career* asst lectr Chinese Univ of Hong Kong 1967–69, tutor SOAS London 1973–75, asst prof Yale Univ 1975–76, lectr Univ of Leicester 1976–85, prof of government Harvard Univ 1985–87, fell Inst of Devpt Studies Univ of Sussex 1987, dir and prof of Cwlth politics Inst of Cwlth Studies Univ of London 1994–97, Inst of Cwlth Studies Univ of London; research fell: Australian Nat Univ 1974, MIT 1982; memb Senate Univ of Leicester 1980–84; memb Bd: Inst of Latin American Studies, British Documents on the End of Empire Project, Amsterdam Sch of Social Science Research, Centre for the Advanced Study of India Univ of Pennsylvania; conslt to: Ford Fndn, World Bank, OECD, UN Capital Devpt Fund, British, Dutch and Swedish govts; *Books* Political Change in an Indian State (1977), Transfer and Transformation: Political Institutions in the New Commonwealth (co-ed, 1983), Sri Lanka in Change and Crisis (ed, 1984), The Expedient Utopian: Bandaranaike and Ceylon (1989), States or Markets (co-ed, 1992), Rethinking Third World Politics (ed, 1992), Power, Poverty and Poison: Disaster and Response in an Indian City (1993), Nehru to the Nineties: The Changing Office of Prime Minister in India (ed, 1994); *Recreations* reading, theatre; *Style—* Prof James Manor

MANSEL, Prof Robert Edward; CBE (2006); s of Regnier Ranulf Dabridgecourt Mansel, and Mary Germaine, *née* Littlewood; *b* 1 February 1948; *Educ* Llandovery Coll, Charing Cross Hosp Med Sch (Morgan Evanson scholar, MB BS), Univ of London (MS); *m* 1987, Elizabeth Clare, da of Dr John Skone; 6 c; *Career* house surgn Charing Cross Gp London 1971, house physician St Mary's Hosp IOW 1972, SHO Charing Cross Hosp London 1972–74, sr registrar in surgery Princess Margaret Hosp Swindon 1974–76, sr registrar in surgery E Glamorgan Dist Gen Hosp 1978–79, prof of surgery Univ Hosp of S Manchester 1989–92; Univ of Wales Coll of Med: MRC res fell 1976–78, clinical lectr in surgery 1979–82, sr lectr in gen surgery and hon conslt 1983–89, head Univ Dept of Surgery 1992–2015, prof of surgery 1992–2015, chm (by election) Div of Hospital Based Specialities 2001–05, emeritus prof Cardiff Univ 2015–; lead cancer clinician for Wales 2006–; prog dir Welsh Higher Surgical Trg Ctee 1992–2000, non-exec dir Morgannwg HA 1996–2001; pres Br Assoc of Surgical Oncology 2004–05, sec Surgical Res Soc 1995–98 (chm Breast Surgns Gp, memb Screening Ctee), All Wales Breast Gp, surgical rep Welsh Nat Advsy Gp on Breast Screening, pres Welsh Surgical Soc 2010, pres European Soc of Breast Specialists 2014–17 (pres-elect 2012–13); memb: Scientific Ctee Cancer Res Campaign, Br Breast Gp, Med Faculty Res Ctee and Res and Devpt Ctee Univ of Manchester, Moore Working Pty (reviewing Manchester Med Sch), Speciality Review Panels London Cancer Services, Standing Ctee for Cancer RCS, UKCCR Breast Cancer Gp, Ntn Specialist Cancer Gp Welsh Govt 2010–14; Medical Practitioner Tribunal Service panellist 2012–; memb Editorial Bd Clinical Breast Cancer, memb Editorial Ctee Br Jl of Surgery; delivered numerous invited lectrs incl: Ivor Lewis Meml Lecture Rhyl 1990, Oscar Schuberth Annual Lecture Swedish Med Soc 1998, Welsh Livery Guild Annual Lecture 1998, Mary Breve Lecture Finnish Med Soc 1999, Turner Grey Meml Lecture Univ of Newcastle upon Tyne 2001; 30th Anniversary NHS Travelling Scholarship 1978, Hamilton Bailey Travelling Fellowship 1981, Churchill Meml Fellowship 1982, Surgical Res Soc/Br Jl of Surgery Travelling Fellowship 1982, UICC (Union International Contre le Cancer (Geneva)) and CRC (Cancer Research Campaign, now Cancer Research UK), UICC Int Fellowship 1982–83 (held at Univ of Texas), James IV Int Fellowship 1989 (memb 2000), Hunterian prof RCS 1989; Surgical Res Soc Patey Prize 1987, Br Assoc of Surgical Oncology Raven Prize 1988, Welsh Surgical Soc Registrar's Prize 1988 (jtly), Charles Gros Prize 1990; tstee Llandovery Coll 1996–2012; LRCP 1971, FRCS 1975 (MRCS 1971), FICS, Hon FRCSEd 2001; *Publications* author of 7 books and 400 papers; *Recreations* watching rugby, fishing, travel; *Style—* Prof Robert Mansel, CBE; ✉ Cardiff University School of Medicine, Heath Park, Cardiff CF14 4XN (☎ 029 2087 4000, fax 01600 551066, e-mail manselre@cf.ac.uk)

MANSELL, Mark; *Educ* KCL (LLB); *Career* admitted slr 1985; specialises in employment law; articled clerk Rowe & Maw until 1985, legal advsr Employment Affrs Directorate CBI 1985–87, ptnr Allen & Overy 1992– (asst slr 1987–91); memb: City of London Slrs' Co, Employment Lawyers Assoc, European Employment Lawyers Assoc; *Style—* Mark Mansell, Esq; ✉ Allen & Overy LLP, One Bishops Square, London E1 6AD (☎ 020 30 88 3663, e-mail mark.mansell@allenovery.com)

MANSER, (Peter) John; CBE (1992), DL (1999); s of Lt-Col Peter Robert Courtney Manser (d 1944), and Florence Delaplaine, *née* Ismay (d 1983); *b* 7 December 1939; *Educ* Marlborough; *m* 31 May 1969, Sarah Theresa Stuart (Tessa), *née* Todd; 2 da; *Career* CA; Robert Fleming group: with Brown Fleming & Murray 1959–66, dir Robert Fleming & Co Ltd 1967–75, md Jardine Fleming & Co Ltd 1975–79, chief exec Save & Prosper Group Ltd 1979–88, gp chief exec Robert Fleming Holdings Ltd 1990–97, chm Robert Fleming Holdings Ltd 1997–2000; chm: Delancey Estates 1997–2001, Intermediate Capital Gp plc 2001–10, Shaftesbury plc 2004–13, Hiscox Investment Mgmnt 2005–07, London Asia Chinese Private Equity Fund Ltd 2006–07, Strand Partners Ltd 2013–; dep chm Colliers CRE 2000–10; dir: Keppel Capital Holdings Ltd 1999–2001, SABMiller plc 2001– (chm 2013–15); dir Securities and Investments Bd 1986–93, chm London Investment Banking Assoc 1994–98; dep chm Cncl Marlborough Coll 2007–, chm Cncl Marlborough Coll Malaysia 2012–; chm Wilts Community Fndn 1997–2002; Freeman City of London, Liveryman Worshipful Co of Grocers; FCA 1976; *Recreations* gardening, shooting, walking; *Clubs* Boodle's, MCC; *Style—* John Manser, Esq, CBE; ✉ e-mail peterjohnmanser@yahoo.com

MANSER, Jonathan; s of Michael John Manser, of Chiswick, London, and Dolores Josephine, *née* Bernini; *b* 15 January 1955; *Educ* Westminster, Univ of Cambridge (MA, memb Boat Race crew 1976 and 1977), South Bank Poly (Dip Arch); *m* 1983, Sarah Christiane, da of Air Vice Marshal W V C Crawford-Compton, DSO, DFC; 2 da (Olivia Bianca Imogen b 1986, Claudia Augusta Marie-Claire b 1989); *Career* architect; Foster Associates 1974, Hulme Chadwick & Partners 1977–78, Renton Howard Wood Levine 1980–82, Chapman Taylor Partners 1982–83, self-employed sole practitioner 1983–85, dir The Manser Practice (formerly Manser Associates) 1986–; RIBA Award for Hilton Hotel Heathrow Airport, RIBA and Steel Award for Southampton Airport Terminal Building, RIBA Award for Artigiano HQ IOW, RIBA Award for Welch House IOW; also former int yachtsman; memb Br team: Onion Patch Cup 1978, Admiral's Cup 1979, Southern Cross Cup 1979; second place 6 metre class Euro Cup 1985, winner 6 metre class World Championships 1986; FRSA; *Clubs* Hawks' (Cambridge), Groucho, Archetypals; *Style—* Jonathan Manser, Esq, FRSA; ✉ The Manser Practice, Bridge Studios, Hammersmith Bridge, London W6 9DA (☎ 020 8741 4381, e-mail jonathanmanser@manser.co.uk)

MANSER, Michael John; CBE (1993); s of Edmund George Manser (d 1971), and Augusta Madge, *née* Bonell (d 1987); *b* 23 March 1929; *m* 1953, Dolores Josephine, da of Isadore Bernini; 1 s (Jonathan), 1 da (Victoria); *Career* chartered architect; Nat Serv RE, Staff Capt; chm The Manser Practice (founded as Michael Manser Associates 1961); memb Cncl: AA 1971–72, RIBA 1979–81 (pres 1983–85), RSA 1985–91; memb Design Policy Ctee London Transport 1990–96; awards incl: two Civic Tst Awards, Euro Heritage Year Award, DOE Commendation for Good Design in Housing, Steel Award and Steel Award Commendation, Harrow Heritage Tst Award, two RIBA Awards and two RIBA Regnl Awards, RCFA/Sunday Times Building of the Year Award, British Construction Industry Award; architectural corr The Observer 1961–65; fndr chm DOE/RSA Art in Architecture Awards 1989–91; chm: Art in Workplace Awards 1995–2001, RIBA Awards Gp 1999–, Nat Home Builder Design Awards 1999, Stirling Prize Award 2000, National Homebuilder Design Award 1999–, Annual RIBA Manser Medal Award for Best One off House in UK 2001–; chm Br Architectural Library Tst; memb: Cncl RSA 1986–91, Cncl Nat Tst 1992–95, Royal West of England Acad, RIBA Communications Ctee 1999, City of Westminster Public Art Panel 1999, Arts Advsy Ctee Chelsea and Westminster Health Charity; hon memb Royal Architectural Inst of Canada 1995–; Hon FRAIC; RA 1995 (Cncl 1997, Audit Ctee 1998, Architecture Ctee 1999, Building Ctee 1999, Renumeration Ctee 2000); *Recreations* home, garden, books, music, walks, boats; *Clubs* Brooks's, Arts, Farmers; *Style—* Michael Manser, Esq, CBE, RA; ✉ The Manser Practice, Bridge Studios, Hammersmith Bridge, London W6 9DA (☎ 020 8741 4381)

MANSER, Paul Robert; s of Bob Manser, and Margaret, *née* Rubinstein; *b* 27 March 1950; *Educ* Eltham Coll, Univ of Warwick (BA); *m* 28 July 1972, Lindy, da of Harry Myers; 2 s (Nicolas b 19 June 1981, Edward b 18 Feb 1983); *Career* admitted slr 1977: former ptnr Taylor Wessing, former gen counsel and dir Alta Advisers Ltd; memb Law Soc; *Publications* Tolley's Start-ups: Law and Business Handbook (2002); ed Int Company and Commercial Law Review 1997–2003; *Recreations* tennis, photography, music; *Style—* Paul Manser, Esq

MANSFIELD, Prof Averil O; CBE (1999); *b* 21 June 1937; *Educ* Blackpool Collegiate Sch, Univ of Liverpool (MB ChB, ChM); *m* Jack Bradley, FRCS (d 2013); *Career* formerly: lectr in surgery Univ of Liverpool, conslt surgn and hon sr lectr in surgery United Liverpool Hosps, conslt surgn Hillingdon and Hammersmith Hosps and St Mary's Hosp London, prof of vascular surgery Imperial Coll Sch of Med at St Mary's Hosp London, sr lectr in vascular surgery Royal Postgraduate Med Sch (Hammersmith Hosp), hon conslt in paediatric surgery/vascular surgery Hosp for Sick Children Great Ormond Street; postgraduate sub-dean St Mary's Hosp Med Sch 1987–91; currently emeritus prof; RCS: memb Cncl 1990–, Ct of Examiners (chm 1990–92), vice-pres 1998–2000; pres Section of Surgery RSM 1997–98; currently vice-pres Stroke Assoc, pres BMA 2009–10 (chm Bd of Science 2010–14); chm: Intercollegiate Bd in Gen Surgery 1992–95, Fedn of Surgical Speciality Assocs 1993–95; memb: Audit Ctee Euro Carotid Stroke Surgery Trial, Steering Ctee Asymptomatic Carotid Surgery Trial; Moynihan fell Assoc of Surgns of Great Britain and I, Hunterian prof, Arnott demonstrator, Bradshaw lectr and Kinmonth lectr RCS, Hon FRACS and Syme orator RACS 1996; memb: Assoc of Surgns of GB and I (pres 1992–93), Vascular Surgery Soc (pres 1996–97), Surgical Res Soc, Euro Soc of Vascular Surgery; fell Faculty of Medicine Imperial Coll London 2012; chm St Mary's Devpt Tst 2007–; Hon MD Univ of Liverpool 1994, Hon DSc Univ of Lancaster 2010; FRCSEd 1966, FRCS 1967, FRCPS 1998, Hon FACS 1998, FDSRCS 2003, FRCP 2005, Hon FRSM 2010; *Recreations* music, the Lake District; *Style—* Prof Averil O Mansfield, CBE; ✉ e-mail a.mansfield@imperial.ac.uk

MANSFIELD, David James; s of Wilfred Victor Leonard Mansfield (d 1972), and Helen, *née* Preston (d 2008); *b* 12 January 1954; *Educ* London Business Sch; *m* 15 Sept 1979, Alison Patricia, da of Gerald Frederick Hedley Pullin; 2 s (James William Robert b 1983, Edward Nicholas Jack (Ned) b 1994), 1 da (Clare Amy Frances b 1986); *Career* sales and sr mktg exec Scottish and Grampian TV 1977–80, mktg gp head and gen sales mangr Scottish TV 1981–84; Thames TV: mktg controller 1985–87, sales and mktg controller 1987–90, dep sales dir 1990–92; Capital Radio plc: gp commercial dir 1993–97, chief exec 1997–2005, subsequently chief exec GCap (following merger with GWR); non-exec dir: Ingenious Media plc 2006–13, Results Int LLP 2015–; non-exec chm: Rajar Ltd 2007, 1700 Gp plc 2008–10, 1801 Gp 2010–13, LoveliveTV Ltd 2010–, HelloU (formerly Student Aid) 2010–, Circus Street Ltd 2013–, Field & Flower Ltd 2014–; dir Carphone Warehouse

M

2005–10, non-exec dir Game Gp plc 2010–11, dir Drive Partnership Ltd 2011–, chm Music Festivals plc 2011–13, chm Field and Flower Ltd 2013–; former dir Bd Radio Advertising Bureau; visiting fell Univ of Oxford 2008–15, visiting prof Cass Business Sch 2015–; memb Radio Acad; *Recreations* fly fishing, contemporary music; *Clubs* Flyfishers, Soho House, The Ivy, Groucho, London Business Sch Enterprise 100; *Style*— David Mansfield, Esq

MANSFIELD, Guy Rhys John; QC (1994); 6 Baron Sandhurst (UK 1871); s of 5 Baron Sandhurst, DFC (d 2002), and Janet Mary, *née* Lloyd; *b* 3 March 1949; *Educ* Harrow, Oriel Coll Oxford (MA); *m* 1976, Philippa St Clair, da of late Digby Everard Verdon-Roe, of Le Cannet, France; 1 da (Hon Alice Georgina b 4 Feb 1980), 1 s (Hon Edward James b 12 April 1982); *Heir* s, Hon Edward James Mansfield; *Career* called to the Bar Middle Temple 1972 (Harmsworth exhibitioner, Winston Churchill pupillage award, bencher 2000), recorder of the Crown Court 1993–2012, dep High Court judge 2008–; chm Gen Cncl of the Bar 2005– (vice-chm 2004, chm Remuneration and Terms of Work Ctee 1998–99, memb Gen Mgmnt Ctee 1998–2005, chm Legal Services Ctee 2000–03); memb Cncl Justice 2006–, memb Queen's Counsel Complaints Ctee 2006–; *Publications* Financial Provision in Family Matters (contrib), Human Rights and the Common Law (contrib), Personal Injury Handbook (contrib); *Recreations* cricket; *Clubs* Leander, MCC, Reform; *Style*— Guy Mansfield, QC; ✉ 1 Crown Office Row, London EC4Y 7HH (☎ 020 7797 7500, fax 020 7797 7550, e-mail guy.mansfield@1cor.com)

MANSFIELD, Michael; QC; s of Frank Le Voir Mansfield (d 1960), of London, and Marjorie, *née* Sayer (d 1977); *b* 12 October 1941; *Educ* Highgate Sch, Keele Univ (BA); *m* 1, 28 Sept 1965 (m dis 1992), Melian, da of Lt Cdr Bordes; 3 s (Jonathan, Leo, Keiran), 2 da (Anna, Louise); m 2, 31 Dec 1992, Yvette Vanson; 1 s (Frederic); *Career* called to the Bar Gray's Inn 1967 (bencher 2007), estab chambers Tooks Court 1984; prof of law City Univ, visiting prof of law Univ of Westminster 2001–11; Hon LLD: South Bank Univ 1994, Keele Univ 1995, Univ of Hertfordshire 1995, Univ of Middx 1999; pres: Nat Civil Rights Movement (NCRM), Haldane Soc; hon fell Univ of Kent; memb TGWU, hon memb NUM; FRSA; *Books* The Home Lawyer (2003), Memoirs of a Radical Lawyer (2009); *Style*— Michael Mansfield, Esq, QC

MANSFIELD, Prof Roger; s of Arthur George Mansfield (d 1985), and Edith, *née* Leggett (d 1985); *b* 18 January 1942, Iver, Bucks; *Educ* Kingston GS, Gonville & Caius Coll Cambridge (BA), Wolfson Coll Cambridge (MA, PhD); *m* 24 July 1969, Hélène Marie Louise, da of René Rica, of Quimper, France; 2 da (Marie-Anne (Mrs Ian Mackie) b 1972, Stephanie (Mrs Matthew Cartwright) b 1977); *Career* student apprentice and res engr Stewarts and Lloyds Ltd Corby 1960–66; FME teaching fell Dept of Engrg Univ of Cambridge 1966–68, visiting lectr Yale Univ 1968–69, sr res offr London Business Sch 1969–73, lectr in industrial sociology Imperial Coll London 1973–76, prof of business admin Univ of Wales Cardiff Business Sch 1976–; head of dept: Business Admin and Accountancy UWIST 1977–85, Business and Economics UWIST 1985–87; dir Cardiff Business Sch 1987–2005, dep princ UWIST 1985–88, pro-vice-chllr Univ of Wales Cardiff 1996–2002, dean Sch of Healthcare Studies 2006–10; chm Br Acad of Mgmnt 1993–96, vice-chm Cncl of Univ Mgmnt Schs 1988–92; dir S Glamorgan Trg and Enterprise Cncl 1989–94; FRSA, CCMI, FLSW; *Books* Managers in Focus: the British Manager in the Early 1980s (with M J F Poole, 1981), Organizational Structures and National Contingencies (1983), Frontiers of Management Research and Practice (1989); *Recreations* gardening, opera, birdwatching; *Style*— Prof Roger Mansfield; ✉ Crowhurst, 64 Bishops Road, Whitchurch, Cardiff CF14 1LW (☎ 029 2061 7381, e-mail roger.mansfield@hotmail.co.uk)

MANSFIELD, Prof Terence Arthur (Terry); s of Sidney Walter Mansfield (d 1976), of Blackfordby, Leics, and Rose, *née* Sinfield (d 1979); *b* 18 January 1937, Ashby-de-la-Zouch, Leics; *Educ* Ashby-de-la-Zouch GS, Univ of Nottingham (BSc), Univ of Reading (PhD); *m* 1963, Margaret Mary, da of Henri Gerard James; 2 s (Timothy James b 1966, Michael Peter b 1968); *Career* research asst Univ of Reading 1961–65; Lancaster Univ: lectr 1965–71, reader 1971–77, prof 1977–, provost of science and engrg 1993–96, emeritus prof 2001–, hon fell 2007–; ed and chm Trustees of the New Phytologist 1979–2002; pres Shireshead and Forton Cricket Club 1993–2003; former dir Scottish Crops Research Inst; memb Soc for Experimental Biology 1962–, memb British Ecological Soc 1990; fell Soc of Biology 1984, FRS (memb Cncl 1990–92); *Books* Physiology of Stomata (1968), Effects of Air Pollution on Plants (1976), Plant Adaptation to Environmental Stress (1993); author of over 200 scientific papers; *Recreations* hill walking, music, cricket; *Clubs* Shireshead and Forton Cricket; *Style*— Prof Terry Mansfield, FRS; ✉ Department of Biological Sciences, Lancaster University, Lancaster LA1 4YQ (☎ 01524 791338, e-mail m.t.mansfield@btinternet.com)

MANSFIELD, Terence Gordon (Terry); CBE (2002); s of Archer James Mansfield (d 1990), and Elizabeth Sally, *née* Cox (d 1994); *b* 3 November 1938; *Educ* South West Essex Tech Coll; *m* 31 July 1965, Helen, da of Peter Maurice Russell; 2 da (Anna Helen b 18 September 1966, Victoria Sally b 12 October 1970); *Career* Nat Serv RAF 1959–61; Condé Nast 1961–66: asst advertisement mangr Photography Magazine, sales rep for several magazines incl House & Gardens, Wine & Food, Men in Vogue and Vogue; sr sales rep Queen Magazine 1966–69 (latterly advertisement mangr); National Magazine Co: joined 1969, advertisement mangr Harpers Bazaar 1969–70, assoc publisher Harpers & Queen 1973–74, advertisement dir Harpers & Queen 1974–75, publisher Harpers & Queen 1975–80, dep md 1980–82, md 1982–2002, pres and ceo 2002, ret 2003; chm: COMAG 1984–2002, Mobo Orgn; bd dir and vice-pres Hearst Corp until 2003 (conslt to Hearst Corp 2002–); chm Grad Fashion Week 2005–; tstee: NewstrAid Benevolent Soc, United World Coll (St Donat's Castle); chair of tstees Victim Support 2003–05; memb: Advsy Bd London Week of Peace, Campaign Bd Historic Royal Palaces; PPA Marcus Morris Award 2001; Freedom City of London 1989, Liveryman Worshipful Co of Stationers & Newspaper Makers; *Clubs* IOD, Hanbury Manor, RAF; *Style*— Terry Mansfield, Esq, CBE; ✉ 5 Grosvenor Gardens Mews North, Ebury Street, London SW1 0JP (☎ and fax 020 7565 6666, website www.terrymansfield.co.uk); The Hearst Corporation, Hearst Magazines UK, 72 Broadwick Street, London W1F 9EP (☎ 020 439 5000)

MANTEL, Dame Hilary Mary (Mrs Gerald McEwen); DBE (2014, CBE 2006); da of Henry Thompson (took name of step f, Jack Mantel), and Margaret Mary, *née* Foster; *b* 6 July 1952; *Educ* Harrytown Convent Romiley Cheshire, LSE, Univ of Sheffield (BJur); *m* 1972, Gerald McEwen, s of Henry McEwen; *Career* author; film critic The Spectator 1987–90, writer of columns and criticism in a wide range of newspapers and magazines 1987–; memb Public Lending Right Advsy Ctee 1997–2003; visiting prof Sheffield Hallam Univ 2006–09; memb Editorial Bd London Review of Books 2016–; govr RSC 2014–, patron Scene + Heard 2016–; Shiva Naipaul meml prize 1987, Winifred Holtby prize 1990, Cheltenham Festival lit prize 1990, Southern Arts lit prize 1991, Sunday Express Book of the Year Award 1992, Hawthornden Prize 1996, Mind Book of the Year Prize 2004, Yorkshire Post Fiction Prize 2006; for Wolf Hall: Man Booker Prize 2009, Walter Scott Prize 2010, Nat Book Critics Circle Fiction Award 2010, UK Author of the Year Galaxy Nat Book Award 2010; for Bring Up the Bodies: Costa Book Award 2013, Literary South Bank Award 2013; Hon DLitt: Univ of Sheffield 2005, Kingston Univ 2011, Univ of Cambridge 2013, LSE 2014, Univ of Oxford 2015, Oxford Brookes 2015; hon doctorate: Sheffield Hallam Univ 2009, Univ of Derby 2010, Univ of Exeter 2011, OU 2014; Hon DLitt: Bath Spa Univ 2013, Queen's Univ Belfast 2013; hon fell Royal Holloway Coll London 2008, hon fell KCL 2010; FRSL 1990 (vice-pres 2010); *Novels* Every Day is Mother's Day (1985), Vacant Possession (1986), Eight Months on Ghazzah Street (1988), Fludd (1989), A Place of Greater Safety (1992), A Change of Climate (1994), An Experiment in Love (1995), The Giant, O'Brien (1998), Giving Up The Ghost (memoir, 2003), Learning To Talk (short stories, 2003), Beyond Black (2005), Wolf Hall (2009), Bring Up The Bodies (2012), The Assasination of Margaret Thatcher (2014); *Recreations* watching cricket; *Style*— Dame Hilary Mantel, DBE, FRSL; ✉ c/o Bill Hamilton, 6 Warwick Court, Holborn, London WC1R 5DJ (☎ 020 7242 2811, fax 020 7242 2711)

MANTLE, Richard John; OBE (2013), DL; *b* 21 January 1947, London; *Educ* Tiffin GS, Ealing Coll; *m* 1970, Carol June *née* Mountain; *Career* personnel and industrial rels mangr Beecham Gp UK (now GlaxoSmithKline) 1968–72, assoc dir and personnel mangr J Walter Thompson & Co 1972–79, dep md ENO 1979–85, md Scottish Opera 1985–91, gen dir Edmonton Opera Canada 1992–94, gen dir Opera North 1994–; artistic dir Music for Life Southbank Fest 1992; chm: Negotiating Ctee UK Nat Opera 1982–91, Glasgow Cultural Forum 1990–91, Opera Ctee Theatre Mangrs Assoc 1996–; negotiating chair Professional Opera Cos of Canada 1992–94, sec Eurolyrica 1996–; tstee: Nat Opera Studio London 1985–91 and 1994–, Audiences Yorkshire 1996–2006; dir Walsingham Coll Tst Assoc Ltd 2003–; memb Arts Cncl of GB Touring Ctee 1986–91; Guardian Shrine of Our Lady of Walsingham Norfolk 1997–; hon doctorate Univ of Leeds 2009; *Recreations* travel, churches, food, wine (not making!), listening to and playing music; *Clubs* Savile; *Style*— Richard Mantle, Esq, OBE, DL; ✉ Opera North, Grand Theatre, 46 New Briggate, Leeds LS1 6NU (☎ 0113 243 9999, fax 0113 244 0418)

MANVILLE, Lesley; OBE (2015); *b* 12 March 1956, Brighton, E Sussex; *m* (m dis), Gary Oldman, *qv*; 1 s (Alfie); *Career* actress; memb BAFTA, memb Acad of Motion Pictures Arts and Sciences; *Theatre* incl: Chorus Girls (Theatre Royal Stratford East) 1981, Borderline (Royal Court) 1981, Top Girls (Royal Court and NY) 1982, Rita, Sue and Bob Too (Royal Court) 1982, Falkland Sound (Royal Court) 1983, Saved (Royal Court) 1984, The Pope's Wedding (Royal Court) 1984, Les Liaisons Dangereuses (RSC) 1985, Philistines (RSC) 1985, As You Like It (RSC) 1985, Serious Money (Royal Court) 1987, The Cherry Orchard (Aldwych) 1989, American Bagpipes (Royal Court) 1989, title role in Miss Julie (Greenwich Theatre) 1990, Three Sisters (Royal Court) 1991, The Wives' Excuse (RSC) 1994, His Dark Materials (Nat Theatre) 2005, Pillars of the Community (NT) 2005, The Alchemist (Nat Theatre) 2006, All About My Mother (The Old Vic) 2007, Some Girls (Gielgud Theatre) 2007, Her Naked Skin (Nat Theatre) 2008, Six Degrees of Separation (The Old Vic) 2010, Grief (Cottesloe Theatre) 2011, Ghosts (Almeida Theatre and Trafalgar Studios) 2013 (Best Actress Critics' Circle 2014, Best Actress Olivier Award 2014); *Television* incl: Emmerdale 1974–76, The Emigrants 1976, Grown-Ups 1980, The Firm 1989, Top Girls 1991, Soldier Soldier 1992, The Mushroom Picker 1993, Goggle Eyes 1993, Little Napoleons 1994, Tears Before Bedtime 1995, The Bite 1996, Holding On 1997, Real Women 1998–99, Other People's Children 2000, David Copperfield 2000, The Cazalets 2001, Bodily Harm 2003, North & South 2004, Cranford 2007, An Adventure in Space and Time 2013, Mayday 2013, Fleming 2014; *Film* incl: Topsy-Turvy 1999, Secrets and Lies 1996, All or Nothing 2002 (Br Actress of the Year Critics' Circle Award 2003), Vera Drake 2004, Sparkle 2007, A Christmas Carol 2009, Another Year 2010 (Br Actress of the Year London Critics' Circle Award 2011), Womb 2010, Ashes 2011, Spike Island 2013, Viaggio Sola 2013, Romeo and Juliet 2013, The Christmas Candle 2013, Molly Moon The Incredible Hypnotist 2014, Maleficent 2014, Mr Turner 2014; *Style*— Ms Lesley Manville, OBE; ✉ c/o A R G, 4a, Exmoor Street, London W10 6BD

MAR, Countess of (31 holder of S Earldom *ab initio*, before 1114); Margaret; also Lady Garioch (an honour originally held together with the ancient territorial Earldom of Mar; holder of Premier Earldom of Scotland by date (the oldest peerage in the Br Isles); the predecessors of the original Earls of Mar were Mormaers of Mar in pre-feudal Scotland, long before the term 'Earl' came to be used; maintains private offr-of-arms (Garioch Pursuivant); da of 30 Earl of Mar (d 1975), and Millicent Mary Lane, *née* Salton (d 1993); *b* 19 September 1940; *Educ* Lewes County GS for Girls; *m* 1, 1959 (m dis 1976), Edwin Noel of Mar (recognised in surname 'of Mar' by Warrant of the Lord Lyon 1969), s of Edwin Artiss; 1 da (Lady Susan Helen, Mistress of Mar b 31 May 1963); m 2, 1976, John (also recognised in the surname 'of Mar' by Warrant of Lord Lyon 1976), s of Norman Salton; m 3, 1982, John Henry Jenkin, MA(Cantab), LRAM, FRCO, ARCM, s of William Jenkin, of Hayle, Cornwall; *Heir* da, Mistress of Mar; *Career* British Telecom sales superintendent until 1982; farmer; dep speaker/dep chm House of Lords 1997–2007 and 2009–12, memb Delegated Powers and Regulatory Reform Ctee House of Lords 2013–; patron: Gulf Veterans' Assoc, Global Cabin Air Quality Exec 2007–, several ME charities; lay memb Immigration Appeals Tbnl 1985–2006; pres Three Counties Agric Soc 2003; chm Forward-ME 2009–; Laurent Perrier/Country Life Parliamentarian of the Year 1996, BBC Wildlife Magazine Green Ribbon Award 1997, Spectator Peer of the Year 1997, Dods Charity Champion Outstanding Achievement 2011; memb Specialist Cheese Makers Assoc; hon assoc: RCVS 2006, BVA 2006; *Recreations* gardening, painting, interior decoration, reading; *Clubs* Farmers; *Style*— The Rt Hon the Countess of Mar; ✉ St Michael's Farm, Great Witley, Worcester WR6 6JB (e-mail marm@parliament.uk)

MAR AND KELLIE, 14 and 16 Earl of (S 1565, 1619); James Thorne Erskine (Jamie); also Lord Erskine (S 1426), Baron Erskine of Dirletowne (*sic* as stated by The Complete Peerage, S 1604), and Viscount of Fentoun (S 1606), and Lord Dirletoun (S 1603); sits as Baron Erskine of Alloa Tower (Life Peer UK 2000), of Alloa, Clackmannanshire; also Hereditary Keeper of Stirling Castle; s of Maj the 13 Earl of Mar (and 15 of) Kellie, JP (d 1993), and Pansy Constance, OBE, JP, *née* Thorne (d 1996); *b* 10 March 1949; *Educ* Eton, Moray House Coll of Educn Edinburgh (Dip Social Work, Dip Youth and Co Work), Inverness Coll (Certificate in Bldg); *m* 1974, Mary Irene (Vice Lord-Lt Clackmannanshire 2007–14), yr da of Dougal McDougal Kirk (d 1992), of Edinburgh; 5 step c (1 decd); *Heir* bro, Hon Alexander Erskine; *Career* estate mangr; sits as a Scottish Lib Dem life peer in the House of Lords (hereditary 1994–99); Pilot Offr RAuxAF Regt 1979–82, Flying Offr 1982–86 (2622 Highland Sqdn), memb RNXS 1985–89; page of honour to HM The Queen 1962–63; community serv volunteer York 1967–68, youth and community worker Craigmillar 1971–73; social worker: Sheffield 1973–76, Elgin 1976–77, Forres 1977–78, Aviemore 1979, HM Prison Inverness 1979–81, Inverness West 1981, Merkinch 1982; supervisor Community Serv by Offenders Inverness 1983–87, former memb Visiting Ctee HM Young Offenders Inst Glenochil (no longer in existence since 2007); bldg technician 1989–91; project worker SACRO Central Intensive Probation Project Falkirk 1991–93; canoe and small boat builder 1993–94; chm Strathclyde Tram Inquiry 1996; cmmr Burrell Collection (lending) Inquiry 1997; contested Ochil Scottish Parly elections 1999, Mid-Scotland and Fife regnl list (Lib Dem); appointed to House of Lords Select Ctee on the Constitution 2001–05, memb Religious Offences Select Ctee 2002–03, asst whip 2003–07 and 2009–10, memb House of Lords Admin and Works Ctee 2004–08, asst tport spokesman 2005–, memb House of Lords Ad Hoc Ctee on the Barnett Formula 2008–09, memb Jt Ctee for Statutory Instruments 2008–13; memb Independence Convention 2004–; DL Clackmannan 1991–2014; *Recreations* open canoeing, Alloa Tower, hill walking, gardening, Church of Scotland, railways; *Clubs* Farmers'; *Style*— The Earl of Mar and Kellie; ✉ Hilton Farm, Alloa, Clackmannanshire FK10 3PS (☎ 01259 212438)

MARBER, Patrick; *b* 19 September 1964; *Educ* Wadham Coll, Univ of Oxford; *Career* writer, actor and director; memb English PEN; FRSL; *Theatre* as dir and/or writer: '1953' (Almeida), Dealer's Choice (RNT and Vaudeville, Evening Standard Award for Best Comedy 1995, Writer's Guild Award for Best West End Play 1995), Blue Remembered Hills (RNT), Closer (RNT, Lyric and Broadway, Evening Standard Best Comedy Award 1997, Critics' Circle Best Play Award 1997, Olivier Award for Best New Play 1998, NY

Drama Critics' Circle Award for Best Foreign Play), The Old Neighborhood (Royal Court at the Duke of Yorks), The Caretaker (Comedy), Howard Katz (RNT), After Miss Julie (Donmar Warehouse), Don Juan in Soho (Donmar Warehouse); *Television* as writer and actor for BBC2 incl: The Day Today, Paul Calf Video Diary, Knowing Me Knowing You, 3 Fights 2 Weddings and a Funeral (BAFTA Award); as writer and dir for BBC2 incl: The Curator, After Miss Julie; *Film* Closer (adaptation) 2004, Asylum 2005, Notes on a Scandal (adaptation) 2006 (Best Screenplay Br Ind Film Awards 2006); *Publications* Dealer's Choice (1995), After Miss Julie (1996), Closer (1997), Howard Katz (2001), The Musicians (2005), Don Juan in Soho (2006), Love You More (2008), Trelawny of the Wells (2013); *Clubs* Garrick; *Style—* Patrick Marber, Esq

MARBOUTY, Dominique Jean-Simon; *b* 9 June 1951, Tours, France; *Educ* Ecole Polytechnique, Ecole Nationale de la Météorologie, Université de Paris VI (dip); *m* Marié; 3 ch (b 1976, 1978 and 1981); *Career* meteorologist; researcher: Etablissement d'Etudes et de Recherches Météorologiques (EERM) Paris 1975–76, Centre d'Etudes de la Neige (CEN) 1976–77; head Centre d'Etudes de la Neige Grenoble 1977–84, regnl dir of meteorology Bordeaux 1984–89; Direction de la Météorologie Nationale: head Bureau de l'Exploitation 1989–91, dep dir 1992–93; dep DG Météo-France 1994–99; European Centre for Medium-Range Weather Forecasts (ECMWF): head of ops 1999–2004, dir 2004–; memb: Société Météorologique de France, RMetS, American Meteorological Soc; *Recreations* cinema, reading, running, skiing, hiking; *Style—* Mr Dominique Marbouty; ✉ 79 Alexandra Road, Reading, Berkshire RG1 5PS; European Centre for Medium Range Weather Forecasts, Shinfield Park, Reading, Berkshire RG2 9AX (☎ 0118 949 9001, fax 0118 986 8450, e-mail dominique.marbouty@ecmwf.int, website www.ecmwf.int)

MARCH, Lionel John; o s of Leonard March, and Rose March; *b* 26 January 1934; *Educ* Hove GS for Boys, Magdalene Coll Cambridge (state scholar, DipArch, MA, ScD); *m* 1 (m dis); 2 da (Candida b 1961, Talitha b 1966), 1 s (Ben b 1964); m 2, 23 July 1984, Maureen Mary Vidler; 1 step s (Ben b 1964), 2 step da (Anna b 1968, Sarah b 1969); *Career* Nat Serv Sub Lt RN 1953–55; Harkness fell (Cwlth Fund) Jt Centre for Urban Studies Harvard Univ and MIT 1962–64; Univ of Cambridge: res offr Estate Mgmnt Advsy Serv 1961–62, asst lectr Dept of Architecture 1966–67, dir Centre for Land Use and Built Form Studies 1969–73, lectr Dept of Architecture 1968–69 and 1973–76; prof Dept of Systems Design Faculty of Engrg Univ of Waterloo Ontario 1974–76, prof of design and head of design discipline Faculty of Technol Open Univ 1976–81, rector and vice-provost RCA London 1981–84, prof Grad Sch of Architecture and Urban Planning UCLA 1984–94 (vice-chm and head Architectural Prog 1985–90), prof emeritus of design and computation Sch of the Arts and Architecture UCLA 1994–2004; chm Bd of Dirs Applied Research of Cambridge Ltd 1969–73, vice-pres Applied Research of Cambridge (Canada) Ltd Toronto 1975–77, govr Imperial Coll of Science and Technol London 1981–84, memb Center for Medieval and Renaissance Studies UCLA 1992–; gen ed (with Sir Leslie Martin) Cambridge Urban and Architectural Studies 1970–, fndr ed Environment and Planning Series B Int Jl of Architectural and Design Science 1974–; FIMA 1979, FRSA 1979, FRCA 1981; *Books* Whitehall: A Plan for the Government and National Centre (with Sir Leslie Martin, 1965), The Geometry of Environment (with Philip Steadman, 1971), Urban Space and Structures (ed with Sir Leslie Martin, 1972), The Architecture of Form (ed, 1976), R M Schindler – Composition and Construction (ed with Judith Sheine, 1993), Architectonics of Humanism: Essays on Number in Architecture (1998), The Mathematical Works of Leon Battists Alberti (jt ed, 2010), Shape Grammars (ed, 2011); *Style—* Mr Lionel March; ✉ Spring Cottage, 20 High Street, Stretham, Cambridgeshire CB6 3JQ (☎ 01353 649880, e-mail lmarch@ucla.edu)

MARCH, Peter Reginald; s of Edwin Charles March (d 1987), of Bristol, and Alice Gladys, *née* Cave (d 1988); *b* 23 March 1940, Bristol; *Educ* Bristol GS, Redland Coll, Univ of Bristol (ACE, DipEd); *m* 25 Aug 1962, Christine Ann, da of Ernest William Clark (d 1973), of Poole, Dorset; 2 s (Andrew b 1965, Daniel b 1972), 2 da (Alison b 1967, Rachel b 1974); *Career* contrib ed Aircraft Illustrated 1968–2008; princ careers advsr Co of Avon 1974–87; managing ed RAF Benevolent Fund Publishing 1987–2004, RAF Charitable Tst Enterprises 2005–13; freelance aviation broadcaster; aviation correspondent HTV ITV West 1989–2007; chm Air Display Assoc UK 1994; managing ed: RAF Yearbook 1988–2010, USAF Yearbook 1989–2003; contrib ed Pilot Magazine 1998–; dir PRM Aviation Photo Library; *Books* 17+ Decisions – Your Choice Beyond School, Military Aircraft Markings (1978–2007), Preserved Aircraft (1980), Confederate Air Force (1991), Civil Airliner Recognition (1991, 1993, 1995, 1997 and 1999), Desert Warpaint (1991), Combat Aircraft Recognition (1991, 1998), Light Aircraft Recognition (1992, 1995 and 1997), Brace by Wire to Fly by Wire (1993 and 1998), International Air Tattoo 93 (1993), Royal Air Force Almanac (1994), International Air Tattoo 94 (1994), The Real Aviation Enthusiast II (1995), Hawk Comes of Age (1995), International Air Tattoo Silver Jubilee (1996), Sabre to Stealth (1997), abc Biz Jets (1997), Confederate Air Force – celebrating 40 Years (1997), Sabre to Stealth (1998), Eagles (1998), Freedom of the Skies (1999), Warplanes (2000), Directory of Military Aircraft of the World (2001), Wright to Fly (2002), The Concorde Story (2005), The Spitfire Story (2006), The Vulcan Story (2006), The Red Arrows Story (2006), Top Trumps Fighter Aircraft (2006), Top Trumps Airliners (2007), The Harrier Story (2007), The Hurricane Story (2007), The Stealth Story (2007), The Lancaster Story (2008), The Boeing 747 Story (2009), Boxkite to Concorde (2010), 50 Years of the Red Arrows (2014), Battle of Britain Yearbook (2015); *Recreations* private flying, photography; *Style—* Peter March, Esq; ✉ 25 Sabrina Way, Stoke Bishop, Bristol BS9 1ST (☎ 0117 968 5193, e-mail peter.march@blueyonder.co.uk)

MARCH AND KINRARA, Earl of; Charles Henry Gordon Lennox; o s and h of 10 Duke of Richmond and (4 Duke of) Gordon, *qv*; *b* 8 January 1955; *Educ* Eton; *m* 1, 1976 (m dis 1989), Sally, da of late Maurice Clayton, and Mrs Dennis Irwin; 1 da (Lady Alexandra b 1985); m 2, 30 Nov 1991, Hon Janet Elizabeth Astor, da of 3 Viscount Astor (d 1966); 3 s (Charles Henry, Lord Settrington b 20 Dec 1994, The Hon William b 29 Nov 1996, The Hon Frederick b 10 March 2000), 1 da (Lady Eloise b 10 Mar 2000); *Career* fndr: Goodwood Festival of Speed 1993, Goodwood Revival 1998; chm Goodwood Racecourse, chm Goodwood Gp of Companies; pres BARC, patron TT Riders Assoc; hon memb: BRDC, 500 Owners Club, Guild of Motoring Writers; *Clubs* Br Automobile Racing (pres); *Style—* Earl of March and Kinrara; ✉ Goodwood House, Chichester, West Sussex PO18 0PX

MARCHANT, Ian; s of Derek William Marchant, of Crawley, W Sussex, and Rosemary, *née* Bode; *b* 9 February 1961; *Educ* Trinity Sch Croydon, Univ of Durham (BA); *m* Elizabeth Helen; 1 da (Sarah Elizabeth b 4 Dec 1990), 1 s (James Richard b 18 Aug 1994); *Career* with Coopers & Lybrand 1983–92 (seconded Dept of Energy 1989–90); Scottish and Southern Energy plc (formerly Southern Electric plc): head of corp fin planning 1992–95, chief exec SE Power Generation 1995–96, gp fin dir 1996–2002, chief exec 2002–; non-exec dir John Wood Gp plc 2006–; chm UK Business Cncl for Sustainable Energy, memb Environmental Advsy Gp Ofgem, memb Energy Research Partnership; ACA 1983; *Recreations* golf, watching sport, travelling, reading; *Style—* Ian Marchant, Esq

MARCHANT, Paul; *Career* dir of womenswear, menswear and childrenswear Debenhams until 2005, New Look 2005–08 (chief operating offr 2008); Primark: chief operating offr 2008–09, chief exec 2009–; *Style—* Paul Marchant, Esq; ✉ Primark, PO Box 644, 47 Mary Street, Dublin 1, Ireland

MARCHANT, Peter James; s of Clifford James Marchant, of Bexhill, E Sussex, and Vivian Breta, *née* Sargent; *b* 7 September 1943; *Educ* Bexhill GS for Boys, Portsmouth Poly (HND); *m* 4 Oct 1969, Angela May, da of Walter Sydney Foster; 1 s (Christopher James b 28 Aug 1970), 1 da (Helen Elizabeth b 10 July 1973); *Career* engr BBC Engrg 1962–69, asst chief engr Centre for Educnl Television Overseas 1969; ITN: maintenance engr with special responsibility for intro of colour 1969–74, supervisory engr responsible for Television Standards conversion 1974–76, engrg mangr 1976–89, dep dir of engrg 1986–89; chief engr BBC Television 1989–94, chief engr (television) National Transcommunications Ltd (NTL) 1994–96, chief engr Channel Four Television Corporation 1996–2000, broadcast engrg conslt 2000–; CEng, FIET, FRTS; *Recreations* flying (PPL), languages, piano, rambling, skiing; *Clubs* RAF Henlow Flying; *Style—* Peter Marchant; ☎ 01462 459465, mobile 07968 730527, e-mail peter@pmarchant.co.uk

MARCHWOOD, 3 Viscount (UK 1945); Sir David George Staveley Penny; 3 Bt (UK 1933); also Baron Marchwood (UK 1937); s of 2 Viscount Marchwood, MBE (d 1979), and Pamela, *née* Colton Fox; *b* 22 May 1936; *Educ* Winchester; *m* 1, 1964, Tessa Jane (d 1997), da of Wilfred Francis Norris, of Lurgashall, W Sussex; 3 s (Hon Peter b 1965, Hon Nicholas b 1967, Hon Edward b 1970); m 2, 2001, Sylva, wid of Peter Willis Fleming; *Heir* s, Hon Peter Penny, *qv*; *Career* 2 Lt, Royal Horse Gds (The Blues) in UK and Cyprus 1955–57; former dir of various cos in Cadbury Schweppes Group; Moët Hennessy (UK) Ltd: md 1985–98, chm 1997–2002; dir other cos in Moët Hennessy Group; pres Royal Warrant Holders Assoc 2002–03; *Recreations* real tennis, shooting, racing, golf; *Clubs* Twelve, MCC; *Style—* The Rt Hon the Viscount Marchwood; ✉ Woodcock Farm, Chedington, Beaminster DT8 3JA (☎ 01935 891444)

MARCUS, Ian; s of Monty Marcus (d 1983), and Ruth, *née* Berman (d 1989); *b* 16 January 1959, Bournemouth, Dorset; *Educ* Westcliff Sch for Boys, Fitzwilliam Coll Cambridge (MA); *m* 29 April 1984, Beverley, *née* Silverman; 1 s (David b 9 Feb 1987), 1 da (Sophie b 28 May 1988); *Career* Bank of America 1981–86, UBS Phillips and Drew 1986–90, Natwest Markets 1990–97, Bankers Tst 1997–98, Deutsche Bank 1998–99, chm European Real Estate Investment Banking Credit Suisse 1999–2012; chm Evans Property Gp 2011–13, memb Advsy Bd Redevco BV, sr advsr Eastdil Secured, sr ind non-exec dir Secure Income REIT, non-exec dir Town Centre Securities plc; past chm Investment Property Forum, past pres Br Property Fedn, chm Bank of England Property Forum, chm Princes Regeneration Tst, memb Advsy Forum Dept of Land Economy Univ of Cambridge; Crown Estate cmmr; patron: Norwood, UJIA, Jewish Care; eminent fell RICS; *Recreations* rugby, golf, music concerts, Morris Minors; *Clubs* Saracens, Fitzwilliam Soc, OMTs; *Style—* Ian Marcus, Esq; ✉ Ian Marcus Consultants, Harewood, Priory Drive, Stanmore, Middlesex HA7 3HT (☎ 020 8416 3750, website www.ianmarcusconsultants.com)

MARCUS, Lucy P; *Educ* Wellesley Coll Mass (BA), Univ of Cambridge (MPhil); *m* 21 Aug 1996, Stefan Wolf; 1 s (Maximilian Alexander b 6 May 2006); *Career* formerly: Price Waterhouse E European Services Div Washington DC, US Treasy Dept Economic Policy Div, co-fndr and vice-pres of marketing & sales Invenio Boston, dir of marketing & business devpt for EMEA Infinity Financial Technologies (acquired by Sunguard), dir EMEA Operations BCWW Amsterdam; fndr and ceo Marcus Venture Consulting Ltd 1998–; non-exec chair Bd Mobius Life Sciences Fund 1999– (chair Investment Panel 1999–), memb Int Advsy Bd Intsituto de Empresa Business Sch Madrid 2002–, co-fndr and chair Leadership in Conflict 2008–, non-exec dir and chair Bd Audit Ctee BioCity Nottingham 2009–, non-exec bd dir and memb Control, Risk and Corp Governance Ctee Atlantia SpA 2013–; formerly: co-fndr, judge and chair Bd Aspen Inst Energy and Environment Awards, memb Bd Business Leadership Cncl Wellesley Coll Mass, chair Global Task Force on Building Women Leaders, fndr HighTech Women, non-exec dir and bd treas Br-American Project, various roles ISSA; prof of leadership and governance IE Business Sch 2011–; fell: Aspen Inst Henry Crown Fellowship Program, Br-American Project, BMW fndn Herbert Quandt Transatlantic Forum, Cncl of the US and Italy's Young Leaders columnist: Harvard Business Review, BusinessWeek, Huffington Post, CSR Newsire 2009–, Reuters 2011–, LinkedIn Global Thought Leadership/Influencer Program 2012–; host In The Boardroom with Lucy Marcus Reuters TV 2012–; Future Thinkers Award Thinkers 50 List, Global Leader for Tomorrow World Economic Forum, Rising Star of Corporate Governance Award Yale Univ 2011; *Publications* Women in the New Economy: A Regional Perspective (contrib, 2001), Conquering Carbon (foreword, 2009); articles published in The Independent, The Times, Mediaite, Management Today Magazine; *Style—* Ms Lucy Marcus; ✉ website www.marcusventures.com, Twitter @lucymarcus

MARCUS, Marshall; s of Hyman Marcus, and Betty, *née* Gaunt; *b* 29 January 1955; *Educ* Leeds GS, Royal Coll of Music (ARCM), The Queen's Coll Oxford (MA), Trinity Coll Cambridge (CertEd); *m* 1984, Annia Casagrande; 2 da (Gaia b 2 Dec 1986, Elena b 29 March 1989); *Career* memb BBC Symphony Orch 1977–79, concert master Orquesta Philarmonica de Caracas 1979–81, prof Orquesta Juvenil de Venezuela, ldr Orch of St John's Smith Square 1988–94, chief exec Orch of the Age of Enlightenment (OAE) 2003–06 (chm 1994–2003), head of music Southbank Centre 2006–11, fndr and dir Orquesta Barroca Juvenil Simon Bolevar de Venezuela 2011–12, ceo EU Youth Orch 2013–; fndr and chair Sistema Europe 2012–, fndr Sistema Africa 2012; exec dir Endymion Ensemble; performed in over 60 countries, appeared as a soloist in UK, Holland, Italy, Venezuela, Austria, Canada and USA; recordings with various London gps; violin teacher: Royal Coll of Music, Royal Acad of Music, Nat Youth Orch of GB, Univ of Bristol, Universidad de Valparaiso de Chile, Camerata de Caracas Venezuela, El Sistema Venezuela, Britten Pears Sch, Southbank Sinfonia; designer and ldr of creative music projects at primary schs, secdy schs and univs; advsr and tutor I Culture Orch 2011–12, advsr London Music Masters 2012–; former memb Bd Music Preserved, memb Br Cncl Arts and Creative Economy Advsy Gp 2012–, former memb Bd Assoc of Br Orchestras, former memb Bd Br Assoc of Concert Halls, memb Advsy Bd Sistema Global 2013–, former memb SphinxUK; former tstee Kings Place, tstee In Harmony Sistema England 2012–; vice-patron Kampala Music Sch Appeal 2011–; hon fell Worshipful Co of Musicians 2012–13; *Recreations* mountains, reading, jazz, skiing, the arts; *Style—* Marshall Marcus, Esq; ✉ European Union Youth Orchestra, 6A Pont Street, London SW1X 9EL (☎ 020 7235 7671, e-mail m.g.marcus@btinternet.com)

MARCUS, Steven David; s of Gerald Marcus (d 2008), and Joan Kasmir (d 2002); *b* 5 October 1951; *Educ* Merchant Taylors', Univ of Nottingham (BSc); *m* 5 Sept 1979, Madeleine, da of Godfrey Lee; *Career* Grant and Partners 1973–76 (jr negotiator, sr negotiator), Jones Lang Wootton 1976–78, assoc Allsop & Co 1978–84, ptnr then exec dir Druce & Co 1984–92 sr ptnr Marcus & Co 1992–; FRICS (prof assoc 1979); *Style—* Steven Marcus, Esq; ✉ Marcus & Co, Canons House, 7 Handel Close, Canons Drive, Edgware, Middlesex HA8 7QZ (☎ 020 8952 3636, fax 020 8952 6633)

MARENBON, Dr John Alexander; s of Arthur Marenbon (d 1984), of London, and Zena, *née* Jacobs; *b* 26 August 1955; *Educ* Westminster, Trinity Coll Cambridge (MA, PhD), Univ of Cambridge (LittD); *m* 1981, Sheila Margaret Mary, da of Arthur C Lawlor; 1 s (Maximus John Arthur b 10 Dec 1989); *Career* Trinity Coll Cambridge: research fell 1978–79, fell and dir of studies in English 1979–97, British Acad research reader 1991–93, fell in history of philosophy 1997–2004, sr research fell 2005–; hon prof of medieval philosophy Univ of Cambridge 2010–; guest prof Peking Univ 2016–17; memb Schs Examination and Assessment Cncl (SEAC) 1992–93; FBA 2009; *Books* From the Circle of Alcuin to the School of Auxerre (1981), Early Medieval Philosophy (1983), Later Medieval Philosophy (1987), Aristotle in Britain during the Middle Ages (1996), The Philosophy of Peter Abelard (1997), Routledge History of Philosophy III: Medieval Philosophy (1998), Aristotelian Logic, Platonism and the Context of Early Medieval

M

Philosophy in the West (2000), Poetry and Philosophy in the Middle Ages (ed, 2001), Peter Abelard: Collationes (ed with G Orlandi, 2001), Boethius (2003), Le Temps, la Prescience et les Futurs Contingents, de Boèce à Thomas d'Aquin (2005), Medieval Philosophy: An historical and philosophical introduction (2007), The Cambridge Companion to Boethius (ed, 2009), Aristotelian Logic, East and West 500–1500: On Interpretation and Prior Analytics on two traditions (jt ed, 2010), Methods and Methodologies: Aristotelian Logic East and West 500–1500 (jt ed, 2011), The Oxford Handbook of Medieval Philosophy (ed, 2012), Abelard in Four Dimensions: a twelfth-century philosopher in his time and ours (2013), Pagans and Philosophers: the problem of paganism from Augustine to Leibniz (2015), Medieval Philosophy: a very short introduction (2016); *Style*— Dr John Marenbon; ✉ Trinity College, Cambridge CB2 1TQ (✆ 01223 338524, e-mail jm258@cam.ac.uk)

MARGADALE, 3 Baron (UK 1964); Alastair John Morrison; DL (Wilts); s of 2 Baron Margadale (d 2003), and Clare, *née* Barclay; *b* 4 April 1958; *Educ* Harrow, RAC Cirencester; *m* 1 (m dis); 1 s (Hon Declan James b 1993), 1 da (Hon Nancy Lorna b 1995); m 2, 2 Sept 1999, Amanda, *née* Fuller; *Heir* s, Hon Declan Morrison; *Career* ran film catering and hotel business, upkeep of estates in Wilts and Islay; dir Salisbury Racecourse; involved with various charities; *Recreations* racing and breeding, shooting, hunting, fishing; *Clubs* White's, Turf, Caledonian, 5 Hertford Street; *Style*— The Rt Hon the Lord Margadale; ✉ Fonthill Estate Office, Fonthill Bishop, Salisbury, Wiltshire SP3 5SH (✆ 01747 820246)

MARGETTS, Sir Robert John (Rob); kt (2006), CBE (1996); s of John William (decd) and Ellen Mary Margetts (decd); *b* 10 November 1946; *Educ* Highgate Sch, Univ of Cambridge (BA); *m* Joan Sandra; 3 s, 1 da; *Career* ICI plc: joined as process design engr 1969, dir Agricultural Div 1982–85, dir Petrochemicals & Plastics Div 1985, dir Research & Operations Chemicals & Polymers Gp 1987, dir ICI Engrg 1987–89, gen mangr personnel 1989–90, chm and chief exec Tioxide Gp 1991–92, exec dir 1992–97, vice-chm 1998–2000, chm ICI Pension Fund Tstee Ltd 1994–2000; chm: Europe Huntsman Corp 2000–10, Ensus Ltd 2007–, Energy Technologies Inst LLP 2007–, Ordnance Survey 2008–16, Lythe Hill Park Ltd and Lythe Hill Park Properties Ltd 2015–; dep chm and sr ind dir OJSC Uralkali 2011–; non-exec dir: English China Clays plc 1992–99, Legal and General Gp plc 1996–2010 (vice-chm 1998–2000, chm 2000–10), Anglo American plc 1999–2010 (sr ind dir 2003–08), BOC Group plc 2001–06 (dep chm 2001–02, chm 2002–06), Falck Renewables plc 2007–10, Neochimiki SA 2008–10, Wellstream plc 2010–11, Huntsman Corp 2011–; vice-pres Royal Acad of Engrg 1994–97; chm: Action for Engrg 1995–97, NERC 2001–06, Govt Industry Forum Non-Food Uses of Crops 2001–04; dir Fndn for Science and Technology; tstee: Cncl for Industry and HE 2001–10 (memb 1992–), Brain Research Tst 2002–13; memb: CIA Cncl 1992–96 and 2001–, Bd CEFIC 1993–95 and 1998–2000, Cncl for Sci and Technol 1998–2007, Advsy Ctee on Business and the Environment 1999–2001, Technol Foresight Steering Gp, Economy and Science & Technol Honours Ctees 2005–12, Advsy Bd Teijin Ltd Japan 2004–06; govr memb Fin Ctee ICSTM 1991–2004; Hon Freeman Salters' Co, Freeman City of London 2004; memb Ct Univ of Surrey; Hon DEng Univ of Sheffield 1997, Hon DSc Cranfield Univ 2003; hon fell: Imperial Coll London 1999, Univ of Cardiff 2007, Inst of Energy 2008, Cncl for Industry and HE 2011; fell City and London Guilds 2001, FREng, FIChemE; *Recreations* sailing, skiing, tennis, watersports; *Style*— Sir Rob Margetts, CBE, FREng; ✉ c/o Cyrus Capital, 4 Cork Street, London W1S 3LB

MARGO, David Philip; s of Gerald Margo, of Bexleyheath, Kent, and Rene, *née* Goldstein; *b* 14 May 1951; *Educ* Chislehurst and Sidcup GS for Boys; *m* 14 Nov 1976, Lezley Susan (d 1991), da of Maurice and Helen Kaye, of Bournemouth, Dorset; 2 da (Jodi Rochelle b 1980, Kerri Miriam b 1984), 1 s (Alexi Nicholas b 1981); *Career* admitted slr 1975; ptnr: Forsythe Saunders Kerman (formerly Saunders Sobell Leigh & Dobin) 1975–98, Lawrence Graham LLP 1998–2007, founding ptnr David Margo Consulting 2007–11, founding ptnr Divorce Solutions (formerly The Divorce Consultancy) 2011–; *Recreations* bridge, travel; *Style*— David Margo, Esq; ✉ e-mail dm@divorcesolutions.co.uk, website www.divorcesolutions.co.uk

MARGOLIN, Daniel George; QC (2015); *b* 15 February 1972; *Educ* Balliol Coll Oxford (scholar, Coolidge Pathfinder), City Univ; *Career* called to the Bar Gray's Inn 1995 (Karmel Entrance Award, Prince of Wales scholar), jr counsel to the Crown 1999–2015; *Publications* contributing ed Mithani Directors' Disqualification; *Clubs* Buck's; *Style*— Daniel Margolin, Esq, QC

MARGOLYES, Miriam; OBE (2002); *b* 18 May 1941, Oxford; *Educ* Newnham Coll Cambridge; *Career* actress; BBC Drama Co; took Australian citizenship 2013; *Theatre* credits incl: The Threepenny Opera, 84 Charing Cross Road, The White Devil, Orpheus Descending (with Vanessa Redgrave, *qv*), She Stoops to Conquer (for Sir Peter Hall, *qv*), Gertrude Stein & Companion (fringe first Award 1986), Little Dorrit, The Killing of Sister George, Dickens' Women (world tour) 2012; *Television* numerous comedy & drama credits incl: The Girls of Slender Means, Blackadder, Old Flames, Cold Comfort Farm, The History of Man, Oliver Twist, The Lost Tribe, Life & Loves of a She-Devil, Frannie's Turn (USA), Vanity Fair, Supply and Demand, The Phoenix and the Carpet, Miss Fisher's Murder Mysteries, Plebs, Doc Martin; numerous guest appearances incl: Johnny Carson, Jay Leno, Terry Wogan, Michael Aspel; *Radio* and recordings incl: The Queen & I, Oliver Twist (Gramaphone Magazine's Best Audio Book 1994), Great Expectations (with Martin Jarvis, *qv*), A Christmas Carol; *Film* The Age of Innocence, Pacific Heights, Dead Again, I Love You to Death, As You Like It, The Fool, Ed & His Dead Mother, Stalin, Immortal Beloved, The Simon Wiesenthal Story, Balto, James and the Giant Peach, Romeo & Juliet, Different for Girls, The Nutcracker, Left Luggage, Fly's voice in Babe and Babe in the City, House, End of Days, Sunshine, Cats & Dogs, Harry Potter and the Chamber of Secrets, Life and Death of Peter Sellers, Being Julia, Chasing Liberty, Modigliani, Ladies in Lavender, Flushed Away, Happy Feet, How to Lose Friends & Alienate People, Harry Potter and the Deathly Hallows: Part 2, Legend of the Guardians: The Owls of Ga'Hoole (voice), The Wedding Video 2012, My Mother's Curse 2012; *Awards* LA Critics' Best Supporting Actress for Little Dorrit 1989, Sony Best Actress Award for The Queen & I 1993, BAFTA Best Supporting Actress for The Age of Innocence 1994, Talkies Best Performer 1997 (for Oliver Twist), Prix Jeunesse Best Children's Prog (0–6 fiction) 2000 (for The First Snow of Winter), Audiofile's Earphones Award 2001 (for A Christmas Carol), Best Supporting Actress in a Musical Theatregoers' Choice Award 2007 (for Wicked), Best Supporting Actress in a Play Theatregoers' Choice Award 2010 (for Endgame); *Books* Dickens' Women; *Recreations* politics, Italy, Charles Dickens, genealogy; *Style*— Ms Miriam Margolyes, OBE; ✉ c/o United Agents Limited, 12–26 Lexington Street, London W1F 0LE (✆ 020 3214 0800, fax 020 3214 0801, website www.unitedagents.co.uk)

MARGRIE, Prof Victor Robert; CBE (1984); s of Robert Margrie, of London, and Emily Miriam, *née* Corbett; *b* 29 December 1929; *Educ* Southgate Co GS, Hornsey Sch of Art (NDD, ATD); *m* 1, 1955 (m dis), Janet, *née* Smithers; 3 da (Joanna b 19 Oct 1959, Kate b 26 Dec 1961, Miriam b 10 Sept 1963); m 2, 2005, Rosemary, *née* Ash; *Career* studio pottery workshop 1952–71, pt/t teaching London Colls of Art and Design 1952–56, head of ceramics and sculpture Harrow Sch of Art 1956–71 (fndr studio pottery course 1963), sec Crafts Advsy Ctee 1971–77, dir Crafts Cncl 1977–84, prof RCA 1984–85, artist, critic and teacher 1985–, prof Univ of Westminster 1992–96; solo exhibitions Crafts Centre of GB (now Contemporary Applied Arts) 1964, 1966 and 1969, currently represented in Ashmolean Museum, V&A and other collections; external advsr: UWE Dept of Ceramics 1987–, Goldsmiths Coll London 1989–93, Sch of Fine Art Cardiff Inst of HE 1991–93, Recording the Crafts (formerly Nat Video and Electronic Archive of the Crafts) 1993–; memb: Advsy Cncl Victoria and Albert Museum 1979–84, Ctee for Art and Design CNAA 1981–84, Fine Art Advsy Ctee Br Cncl 1983–86, UK Nat Cmmn UNESCO 1984–85, Faculty of Visual Arts Banff Centre for the Arts Alberta 1988–, Bd Studies in Fine Art Univ of London 1989–94, Founding Ctee National Centre of Ceramic Art 1996–98; govr Loughborough Coll of Art and Design 1984–92, memb Craft Initiative Gulbenkian Fndn 1985–89; memb: Craftsmen Potters Assoc 1960–89, Int Acad of Ceramics 1971, FSIA 1974; *Books* contrib: Europaische Keramik Seit 1950–79 (1979), Oxford Dictionary of Decorative Arts (1975), Lucie Rie (1981), Tradition and Innovation: Five Decades of Harrow Ceramics (2012); assoc ed Studio Pottery 1993–2000, Ceramics in Society 2000–05; *Recreations* contemporary music; *Style*— Prof Victor Margrie, CBE; ✉ 15 Telegraph Street, Shroton, Iwerne Courtney, Dorset DT11 8QQ (✆ 01258 860944, e-mail margrie@me.com)

MARIGOLD, Peter John; s of David Frederic Marigold, and Loretta Anna Celestina Marigold; *b* 28 October 1974, London; *Educ* Southgate Sch London, Univ of Middx, Central St Martins (BA), Royal Coll of Art (MA); *Partner* Orly Orbach; 2 s (Kevin b 2000, Paul b 2002); *Career* designer; various freelance positions within prop, model costume and scenographic industry 1997–2000, year out in Brazil producing and selling coconut radios on Rio de Janeiro beach 1999–2000, fine art handler Br Cncl 2000–01, various freelance positions within scenographic industry 2001–04, dep master carpenter Mountview Acad of Theatre Studies 2004–05, estab own design studio specialising in interior design, manufactured furniture design and limited edn gallery pieces 2006–; exhibited: Paul Smith showroom Br Cncl Milan 2007, MOMA NY 2008; Esmee Fairbairn Fndn Award 2007, nominated Morgan Stanley Great Briton 2007 nominated Designs of the Year Design Museum London (for Make/Shift) 2008; *Recreations* much the same as what I do at work; *Style*— Peter Marigold, Esq; ✉ 11 South End Road, Hampstead, London NW3 2PT (✆ 07812 525245, e-mail info@petermarigold.com)

MARKESINIS, Prof Sir Basil Spyridonos; kt (2005), QC; s of Spyros Markesinis, former PM of Greece, and Ieta Markesinis; *b* 10 July 1944; *Educ* Univ of Athens (LLB, DIur), Univ of Cambridge (Yorke prize, MA, PhD, LLD), Univ of Oxford (DCL); *m* 5 Sept 1970, Eugenie, da of late George Trypanis; 1 da (Julietta b 6 July 1971), 1 s (Spyros George b 30 Jan 1976); *Career* asst prof Law Faculty Univ of Athens 1965–68; Univ of Cambridge: res fell Churchill Coll 1970–73, fell Trinity Coll and dir of studies in law 1974–86, univ lectr 1974–86; Denning prof of comparative law Univ of London 1986–93 (dep dir Centre for Commercial Law Studies Queen Mary & Westfield Coll), prof of European private law UCL 1993–95; Univ of Oxford: prof of European law 1995–99, fndr and dir Inst of European Law and Comparative Law 1995–2000, prof of comparative law 1999–2000, fell BNC 1999–2000; prof of common law and civil law UCL 2001–07 (fndr and chm Inst of Global Law UCL); prof of Anglo-American private law Univ of Leiden 1986–2000 (fndr and dir Leiden Inst of Anglo-American Law), Jamail Regents chair in law Univ of Texas at Austin 1998–2013; Francqui visiting prof Univ of Ghent 1989–90 and 2004–06; professore a contratto: Univ of Siena 1985–86, Univ of Rome 1996; visiting prof: Cornell Law Sch (fall terms) 1981–84, Univ of Paris I & II 1982–83, Univ of Michigan Ann Arbor (fall term) 1986, Univ of Texas at Austin (fall terms) 1985, 1987–94 and 1996 (Jamail Regents chair of law 1998–); Conseiller Scientifique du Premier Président de la Cour de Cassation France 2002–07; special advsr for European affrs Clifford Chance 1999–2002; called to the Bar Gray's Inn 1973 (bencher 1991), advocate to the Supreme Court Athens 1976–86; non-exec dir: Alexander S Onassis Fndn 2007–11, Alexander S Onassis Public Benefit Fndn 2007–11; Leverhulme fell 1981; Atkin lectr Reform Club 1989, Shimihzu lectr LSE 1991, Cohen lectr Hebrew Univ of Jerusalem 1993, Wilberforce lectr 1998, John Maurice Kelly meml lectr 2003, Eason-Weinmann lectr Tulane Law Sch 2005, Peter Taylor meml lectr Inner Temple 2006, Denning lectr Lincoln's Inn 2007; Humboldt Forschungspreise 1995, Silver Medal Univ of Leiden 1996, John Fleming Prize 2008; DIur (hc): Univ of Ghent 1992, Univ of Paris I (Panthéon-Sorbonne) 1998, Univ of Munich 1999, Univ of Athens 2007; memb: Int Acad of Comparative Law 1987–98, American Law Inst 1989, Institut Canadien d'Études Juridiques Supérieures 1990, Académie Internationale de Droit Comparé 2004; membre actif Cour d'Arbitrage et de Conciliation Paris 1991; corresponding memb: Unidroit 1992, Institut de France (Académie Sciences Morales et Politiques) 2004; foreign fell: Royal Belgian Acad 1990, Royal Netherlands Acad of Arts and Sciences 1995, Academia dei Lincei Rome 2005; fell Acad of Athens 1994; hon fell: Soc for Advanced Legal Studies 2000, Greek Archaeological Soc 2004; FBA 1997; Offr Ordre Nationale des Palmes Académiques (France) 1992, Cdr Order of Honour (Greece) 2000, Knight Grand Cross del Ordine al Merito (Republic of Italy) 2002 (Offr 1995, Knight Cdr 1999), Knight Cdr Order of Merit (Federal Repub of Germany) 2003 (Offr 1992, Cdr 1999), Commandeur dans l'Ordre National de la Légion d'Honneur 1995 (Chevalier 1995, Officier 2000), Knight Grand Cross Order of Merit (France) 2005; *Books* The Mother's Right to Guardianship According to the Greek Civil Code (1968), The Theory and Practice of Dissolution of Parliament (1972), The English Law of Torts – A Comparative Introduction (1976), An Outline of the Law of Agency (co-author, 1979, 4 edn 1998), Richterliche Rechtspolitik im Haftungsrecht (co-author, 1981), Tortious Liability for Unintentional Harm in the Common Law and the Civil Law Vol I and II (co-author, 1982), Tort Law (co-author, 1984, 7 edn 2012), La Réparation du Préjudice Corporel (co-author, 1985), The German Law of Torts – A Comparative Introduction (1986, 4 edn jtly with subtitle A Comparative Treatise, 2002, 5 edn 2014), The Gradual Covergence – Foreign Ideas, Foreign Influences on English Law on the Eve of the 21st Century (ed and contrib, 1994), Bridging the Channel (ed and contrib, 1996), The German Law of Contract and Restitution (co-author, 1997), Foreign Law and Comparative Methodology: A Subject and a Thesis (1997), Law Making, Law Finding, and Law Shaping. The Diverse Influences (ed and contrib, 1997), The Impact of the Human Rights Bill on English Law (ed and contrib, 1998), Protecting Privacy (ed and contrib, 1998), The Coming Together of the Common Law and the Civil Law (ed and contrib, 2000), Tortious Liability of Statutory Bodies (co-author, 2000), Always on the Same Path: Essays on Foreign Law and Comparative Methodology (2001), The British Contribution to the Europe of the Twenty-First Century: The British Academy Centenary Lectures (ed and contrib, 2002), Comparative Law in the Courtroom and the Classroom: The Story of the Last Thirty-Five Years (2003, trans in French, German, Italian and Chinese), Compensation for Personal Injury in English, German and Italian Law: A Comparative Overview (co-author 2004), The German Law of Contract. A Comparative Treatise (co-author, 2006), Judicial Recourse to Foreign Law: A New Source of Inspiration? (co-author, 2006, trans in Italian), Good and Evil in Art and Law (2007, Greek edn 2010, Chinese edn 2014), The Duality of Genius: Shades, blemishes and vices in the lives of great achievers (2008), Engaging with Foreign Law (2009); Greek edns: Shadows from America (2009), Communication and Substance in Diplomacy (2009), Writing for Myself (2011), Seven Ideas for the Revival of Greece (2011), The Greece of Crises (2011), The Legacy of the Greek Tragedy on Modern European Culture (Greek edn 2013, English and Chinese edns 2016), The Need for a New Foreign Policy and Military Dogma for Greece (2013), Mass Immigration, problems and opportunities (2016), Ancient Greek Thought, Insights for the General Reader (2016), Odysseus and his Creator: An attempt to analyse an unusual hero and a great poet (2016); author of numerous articles in US, Australian, Belgian, British, Canadian, French, German, Greek, Israel and Italian law jls; *Recreations* painting, music, archaeological digging, fundraising; *Style*— Prof Sir Basil Markesinis, QC, DCL, FBA; ✉ Middleton Stoney House, Oxford Road, Middleton Stoney, Bicester, Oxfordshire OX25 4TE (☎ 01869 343560, fax 01869 343562)

MARKHAM, Prof Sir Alexander Fred (Alex); kt (2008); *Career* hon consIt physician NHS Yorks, dir Molecular Medicine Unit St James's Univ Hosp, prof of medicine Univ of Leeds 1993–, chm Nat Cancer Research Inst, chief exec Cancer Research UK 2003–07; advsr: Dept of Health, MRC, Wellcome Tst; FMedSci; *Style*— Prof Sir Alex Markham

MARKHAM, Richard; s of Charles Roberts Markham, of Grimsby, Lincs, and Marion Edna, *née* Willows; *b* 23 June 1952; *Educ* Wintringham GS Grimsby, Royal Acad of Music, privately with Shirley Kemp and Max Pirani; *Career* concert pianist; London debut as soloist with Eng Chamber Orch under Raymond Leppard (Queen Elizabeth Hall) 1974, has toured internationally with David Nettle, *qv*, (Nettle-Markham Piano Duo), also with Raphael Wallfisch (cello) and Burlington Piano Trio; solo and piano duo performances at: Royal Festival Hall, Royal Albert Hall, Barbican Hall and at various major festivals incl BBC Proms; ARAM 1983; *Recordings* incl: works by Kabalevsky, Stravinsky and Rachmaninov (with Raphael Wallfisch, cello) 1976, Stravinsky's Rite of Spring and Petrushka (with David Nettle) 1984, Holst's The Planets 1985, Dyson's The Blacksmiths (with RCM Chamber Choir and RPO, 1987), Elgar's From the Bavarian Highlands 1987, Holst's Folksongs and works by Delius and Grainger 1988, Scenes from (Bernstein's) West Side Story (arranged and performed with David Nettle), Grainger's Fantasy on (Gershwin's) Porgy and Bess and Bennett's Four Piece Suite 1988, Rossini's Petite Messe Solennelle (with soloists Field, Owens, Barham and Tomlinson and CBSO chorus) 1990, South of The Border – Latin American Songs with Jill Gomez (with two pianos and NPO) 1990, Nettle and Markham in England 1993, Arnold's Concerto for Piano Duet 1993, Concerto for Two Pianos 1994, Nettle and Markham in France 1995, Brahms' Two-Piano Works 2006, Saint-Saens' Carnival of Animals and Poulenc's Babar the Elephant (with Jeremy Nicholas) 2007; *Awards* Nora Naismith Scholarship 1969–72, prizewinner Geneva Int Competition 1972, Countess of Munster Musical Tst Awards 1973 and 1974, Frederick Shinn Fellowship 1975, Gulbenkian Fndn Fellowship 1976–78, Music Retailers Assoc Award for Best Chamber Music Record 1985; *Recreations* travelling, theatre, playing cards, dining out, naturism; *Clubs* ISM; *Style*— Richard Markham, Esq; ✉ The Old Power House, Atherton Street, London SW11 2JE (e-mail richardpianouk@gmail.com, website www.nettleandmarkham.com)

MARKHAM, Sarah Anne Judith; da of Leonard Markham, of Tithe Farm, Renhold, Beds, and Margaret Elizabeth, *née* Joyce; *b* 25 July 1957; *Educ* Bedford HS, Oxford and County; *Career* Shuttleworth Coll staff 1981–88, Christie's Old Master Picture Dept 1988–93, Sotheby's Old Master Paintings Dept 1993–95, art dealer 1995–2001, Cheffins Fine Art 2001–; *Recreations* riding, travelling, wildlife conservation; *Style*— Mrs Nicholas Flynn; ✉ Cheffins Fine Art, Clifton House, Clifton Road, Cambridge CB1 7EA (☎ 01223 271937, e-mail sarah.flynn@cheffins.co.uk); School House, Renhold, Bedfordshire MK41 0LR (☎ 01234 870119)

MARKING, Giles; s of Frank I Marking, of Wareham, Dorset, and Anne, *née* Percival; *b* 26 December 1947; *Educ* Duncan Hall Norfolk, Architectural Assoc Sch of Architecture (AADipl), Univ of Washington (MArch); *m* 11 Sept 1971, (Margaret Judith) Stacy, da of Canon R Patteson Stacy-Waddy, of Hindhead, Surrey; 1 da (Havana b 6 March 1972); *Career* designer Francisco and Jacobus NY 1967–68, film designer Maizin Wycoff NY 1968–70, graphic designer Inst of Contemporary Arts 1971–74, lectr in architecture Univ of Washington 1975–76, md Fitch London 1976–2002, md Marking Design Ltd 2002–; visiting prof Univ Metropolitana Mexico City 1980; FCSD; *Books* Emergency Housing in Peru – Architectural Design; *Recreations* travel, sheep farming, India and cricket; *Style*— Giles Marking, Esq; ✉ The Manor, Toller Whelme, Beaminster, Dorset DT8 3NU (☎ 01308 862339, mobile 07715 379335, e-mail giles@markingdesign.com)

MARKS, Adam; *Career* slr; Taylor Wessing: head Real Estate Dept 2003–07, Int Mgmnt Bd 2006–07, UK sr ptnr 2011–; *Style*— Adam Marks, Esq; ✉ Taylor Wessing, 5 New Street Square, London EC4A 3TW

MARKS, David Joseph; MBE (2000); s of Melville Marks (d 1998), and Gunilla Marta, *née* Löven; *b* 15 December 1952; *Educ* Int Sch of Geneva, Kingston Poly Sch of Architecture, AA Sch of Architecture; *m* 17 July 1981, Julia Barbara Barfield, MBE, RIBA, *qv*, da of Arnold Robert Barfield; 1 s (Benjamin Jesse), 2 da (Maya Rosa Ray, Sarah Victoria Anna); *Career* architect; md Marks Barfield Architects 1989–, dir London Eye Co 1995–2006; Special Commendation Prince Philip Designers Prize 2000, Faculty of Building Trophy for Outstanding Work in the Field of Construction 2001, Pride of Britain Award for Innovation 2001; *Recreations* family, walking, skiing; *Style*— David Marks, Esq, MBE, RIBA; ✉ Marks Barfield Architects, 50 Bromells Road, London SW4 0BG (☎ 020 7501 0180, e-mail dmarks@marksbarfield.com)

MARKS, David Norman; s of Alex Marks, of London, and Edna, *née* Dufman; *b* 13 February 1953; *Educ* Orange Hill GS Edgware, LSE (BSc); *m* 22 June 1975, Selina Rachael, da of Michael Sharpe, of London; 2 s (Daniel b 1980, James b 1982); *Career* accountant; Arthur Andersen 1974–2002 (tax ptnr 1984), Deloitte & Touche 2002–05 (tax ptnr 2002), Apax Ptnrs 2005–; FCA 1978, CTA 1979; *Books* Practical Tax Saving (jtly, 1984), Tax Digest on Share Incentive Schemes for Institute of Chartered Accountants in England and Wales (1994), Profit-Related Pay (jtly, 1995); *Recreations* theatre, music; *Style*— David Marks, Esq; ✉ Apax Partners, 33 Jermyn Street, London SW1Y 6DN (☎ 020 7872 6362, fax 020 7666 6513, e-mail david.marks@apax.com)

MARKS, Laurence; s of Bernard Marks (d 1975), and Lily, *née* Goldberg (d 1969); *b* 8 December 1948, London; *Educ* Holloway County Sch London, Guildhall Sch of Music; *m* 1 June 1988, Brigitte Luise, da of Friedrich Ludwig Ernst Kirchheim; 1 step s (Daniel Joel Kahn b 28 Feb 1968); *Career* trainee journalist Thomson Regional Newspapers, reporter N London Weekly Herald, Sunday Times and current affrs prog This Week (Thames TV) until 1980, television scriptwriter 1980–; creator and writer (with Maurice Gran, *qv*): Holding the Fort 1979–82, Roots, Shine on Harvey Moon 1982–85 and 1995–, Roll Over Beethoven, Relative Strangers, The New Statesman 1987–91, Birds of a Feather (stage play) 1989, 2012 and 2013, Snakes and Ladders, So You Think You've Got Troubles, Get Back, Love Hurts 1991–93, Wall of Silence (film) 1993, Goodnight Sweetheart 1994–, Mosley 1997, Unfinished Business 1997, Starting Out 1999, Dirty Work 1999, Believe Nothing 2002, Playing God (stageplay) 2005, The New Statesman (stage play) 2006, My Blue Heaven (radio play) 2006, Me, My Dad and Moorgate (TV documentary) 2006, Dr Freud Will See You Now, Mrs Hitler (radio play) 2007, Mumbai Calling (TV comedy) 2007, Von Ribbentrop's Watch (radio play) 2008 and (stageplay) 2010, Dreamboats and Petticoats (stage musical) 2009, Save the Last Dance for Me (stage musical) 2012 and 2013, Love Me Do (radio play) 2012, Birds of a Feather (TV series) 2014 and (third series) 2016, Dreamboats and Miniskirts (stage musical) 2014, Love Me Do (stage play) 2014, Goodnight Sweetheart Revisited (TV) 2016, Save the Last Dance for Me (stage musical) 2016; fndr (with Maurice Gran and Allan McKeown *qv*) Alomo Productions 1988 (now part of Freemantle Television plc); pres Pipesmoking Cncl of Great Britain, Pipesmoker of the Year 1990; Freeman City of London 1992, Liveryman Worshipful Co of Tobacco Blenders and Briar Pipe Makers 1994; *Awards* Silver Medal Int Film and TV Festival NY for Relative Strangers 1985, Int Emmy for The New Statesman 1988, BAFTA Best Comedy Award for The New Statesman 1990, Mitsubishi TV Sitcom of the Year for Birds of a Feather 1991, Mitsubishi TV Drama of the Year for Love Hurts 1991, BAFTA Writer's Award (jtly with Maurice Gran) 1992, Berlin Film and TV Award 2007, Living Legends Award British Comedy Association 2015; *Books* Moorgate – The Anatomy of a Disaster (1976), Ruth Ellis – A Case of Diminished Responsibility (1977), Holding the Fort (with Maurice Gran, 1981), The New Statesman Scripts (with Maurice Gran, 1992), Dorien's Diary (with Maurice Gran, 1993), A Fan for all Seasons (1999); *Recreations* music (saxophone player), reading, English churches, tennis, medieval German, 18th and 19th century French literature, Chinese literature, the study of Freud, Jung and Breuer, British politics, The Peloponnesian War, mechanics of particles and molecular structures, the Chinese chemists and Oriental chemistry, the neuro-surgical work of Wilder Penfield, Br poetry, post-war German literature; *Clubs* Reform, Stone (Intelligence Squared), Arsenal Supporters', Cryptos; *Style*— Laurence Marks, Esq; ✉ Laurie Mansfield Associates, Suite 17, Adam House, 7–10 Adam Street, London WC2N 6AA (☎ 020 7520 9411)

MARKS, Prof Richard Charles; s of Maj William Henry Marks (d 1982), and Jeannie Eileen, *née* Piggott (d 1979); *b* 2 July 1945; *Educ* Berkhamsted Sch, QMC London (BA), Courtauld Inst of Art Univ of London (MA, PhD); *m* 19 July 1970, Rita, da of Charlie Spratley; *Career* researcher Corpus Vitrearum Ctee Br Acad 1970–73 (currently memb Ctee), asst keeper Dept of Medieval and Later Antiquities Br Museum 1973–79, keeper Burrell Collection and asst dir Glasgow Museums and Art Galleries 1979–85, dir Royal Pavilion Art Gallery and Museums Brighton 1985–92; prof of history of art and Centre for Medieval Studies Univ of York 1992–2008 (emeritus prof 2008–), hon prof of history of art Univ of Cambridge 2008–12, bye-fell Fitzwilliam Coll Cambridge 2009–; pres Int Bd Corpus Vitrearum 1995–2004, vice-pres Soc of Antiquaries 1991–94, memb Advsy Cncl Paul Mellon Centre for Studies in British Art; chm Stained Glass Advsy Gp and East Window Advsy Gp York Minster 2009–; FSA 1977; *Books* British Heraldry (jtly, 1978), The Golden Age of English Manuscript Painting (jtly, 1980), The Burrell Collection (jtly, 1983), Burrell: Portrait of a Collector (1983 and 1988), The Glazing of the Collegiate Church of the Holy Trinity Tattershall (1984), The Souvenir Guide to the Burrell Collection (1985), Sussex Churches and Chapels (jtly, 1989), Stained Glass in England during the Middle Ages (1993), The Medieval Stained Glass of Northamptonshire (1998), Gothic Art for England 1400–1547 (jtly, 2003), Image and Devotion in Late Medieval England (2004), Late Gothic England: Art and Display (ed, 2007), Studies in the Art and Imagery of the Middle Ages (2012); *Recreations* opera, parish churches, travelling in the Levant, cricket, equestrianism; *Clubs* MCC, North British Rowing, Athenaeum; *Style*— Prof Richard Marks; ✉ Hillcroft, 11 Stewkley Road, Soulbury, Bedfordshire LU7 0DH (e-mail rcm1@york.ac.uk or rcm41@cam.ac.uk)

MARKS, His Hon Judge Richard Leon; QC (1999); s of Harry Marks, and Denise, *née* Hilton; *b* 20 November 1953; *Educ* Clifton, Univ of Manchester (LLB); *m* 28 May 1987, Jane Elizabeth Tordoff; 1 da (Nicole Rebecca Tordoff b 15 Oct 1988), 1 s (Jacob Daniel Tordoff b 9 July 1999); *Career* called to the Bar Gray's Inn 1975 (bencher 2008), recorder (Northern Circuit) 1994 (asst recorder 1991), ldr Northern Circuit 2008–10, sr circuit judge Central Criminal Court 2012–; pres Mental Health (Restricted Patients) Review Tbnl 2000–15; Common Serjeant of London 2015–; *Style*— His Hon Judge Marks, QC; ✉ Central Criminal Court, Old Bailey, London EC4M 7EH

MARKS, Prof Ronald; s of Isadore Marks (d 1966), and Jessie Marks (d 1991); *b* 25 March 1935; *Educ* St Marylebone GS, Guy's Hospital Med Sch (BSc, MB BS); *m* 1 (m dis 1978); 2 da (Louise Anne b 17 March 1962, Naomi Suzanne b 1 Jan 1965); m 2, 11 Nov 1978, Hilary, *née* Venmore; *Career* MO short service cmmn 1960, med div Queen Alexander Mil Hosp 1961–63, specialist in dermatology Br Mil Hosp Munster W Germany 1963–65; sr lectr Inst of Dermatology and consIt dermatologist St John's Hosp for Diseases of the Skin London 1971–73; Univ of Wales Coll of Med Cardiff: sr lectr in dermatology Dept of Med 1973, reader 1977, personal chair in dermatology 1980, established chair in dermatology 1990–98 (prof emeritus 1998–); hon consIt in dermatology Univ Hosp of Wales 1973–98; clinical prof Dept of Dermatology and Cutaneous Surgery Univ of Miami Sch of Med 1995, hon prof of dermatology Besançon France 2010; author, ed, jt ed or contrib numerous papers in scientific jls, co-ed The Jl of Dermatological Treatment; lit award Soc of Cosmetic Chemists NY USA 1985; pres Br Cosmetic Dermatology Gp 1994, hon pres Int Soc for Bioengineering and the Skin, chm Int Soc for Stratum Corneum Research; Freeman City of Besançon 1983; FRCP 1977 (memb 1964), FRCPath 1985; *Publications* jt ed and/or contrib to numerous books incl: Common Facial Dermatoses (1976), Investigative Techniques in Dermatology (ed, contrib, 1979), Psoriasis (1981), Practical Problems in Dermatology (1983, 2 edn 1996), Acne (1984), Roxburgh's Common Skin Diseases (jtly, 1986, 16 edn 1993), Skin Diseases in Old Age (1987, 2 edn 1998), The Sun and Your Skin (1988), Acne and Related Disorders (jt ed, contrib, 1989), Retinoids In Cutaneous Malignancy (1991), Eczema (1992), Sun Damaged Skin (1992), The Environmental Threat to the Skin (1992), Clinical Signs and Procedures in Dermatology (1993), Skin Therapy (1994), Retinoids: a Clinicians Guide (1995), Emollients (1996), Photodamaged Skin: Clinical Signs, Causes and Management (1999), Facial Skin Disorders (2007); *Recreations* visual art of the 19th and 20th centuries; *Style*— Prof Ronald Marks; ✉ Cutest Systems Ltd, Abton House, Wedal Road, Cardiff CF14 3QX (☎ 029 204 5080, fax 029 2061 4688, e-mail skincarecardiff@aol.com)

MARKS, Emeritus Prof Shula Eta; OBE (1996); *née* Winokur; da of Chaim Winokur (d 1957), of Cape Town, South Africa, and Frieda, *née* Sack (d 2000); *b* 14 October 1936; *Educ* Univ of Cape Town (BA), Univ of London (PhD); *m* 31 March 1957, Prof Isaac Meyer Marks, s of Moshe Nahman Marks (d 1979), of Cape Town, South Africa; 1 da (Lara b 22 Jan 1963), 1 s (Rafi b 26 Jan 1965); *Career* Univ of London: lectr in history of Africa Inst of Cwlth Studies and SOAS (jtly) 1963–76, reader in history of Southern Africa 1976–84, dir Inst of Cwlth Studies 1983–93, prof of Cwlth history 1984–93, prof of history of Southern Africa SOAS 1993–2001 (prof emeritus 2001–, hon fell 2005), Douglas Southall Freeman prof Univ of Richmond VA 2005; consIt WHO 1977–80, chair World Univ Southern African Scholarships Ctee 1981–92, govr Inst of Devpt Studies Univ of Sussex 1988–91, chair Int Records Mgmnt Tst 1989–2004; vice-pres Royal African Soc 1999–2008; memb: Advsy Cncl on Public Records 1989–94, Cncl Soc for Protection of Sci and Learning (now Cncl for Assisting Refugee Academics (CARA)) 1983–2013 (chair 1993–2004), Governing Body Queen Elizabeth House Oxford 1991–94, Cwlth Scholarships Cmmn 1992–98, Humanities Research Bd 1997–98, AHRB 1998–2000, Cncl Canon Collins Tst 2004–14; Distinguished Africanist Award 2002; Hon DLitt Univ of Cape Town 1994, Hon DSocSci Univ of Natal 1996, Hon DLitt et Phil Univ of Johannesburg 2012; distinguished sr fell Sch of Advanced Study Univ of London 2002, hon prof Univ of Cape Town 2005; FBA 1995 (emeritus fell 2013), FRHistS 2000; *Books* Reluctant Rebellion: An Assessment of the 1906–08 Disturbance in Natal (1970), Economy and Society in Preindustrial South Africa (ed jtly, 1980), Industrialisation and Social Change in South Africa (ed jtly, 1982), Ambiguities of Dependence in South Africa: Class, Nationalism and the State in Twentieth Century Natal (1986), The Politics of Race, Class and Nationalism in Twentieth Century South Africa (ed jtly, 1987), Not Either an Experimental Doll: The Separate Worlds of Three South African Women (1987), Divided Sisterhood: Race Class and Nationalism in the South African Nursing Profession (1994), In Defence of Learning Academic Refugees: Their Plight, Persecution and Placement 1933–1980 (jt ed, 2012); *Recreations* theatre, cinema; *Style*— Emeritus Prof Shula Marks, OBE, FBA; ✉ School of Oriental and African Studies, Thornhaugh Street, London WC1H 0XG (☎ 020 7898 4612, fax 020 7898 4639, e-mail shula.e.marks@gmail.com)

MARKS, Susan E; *née* Jones; da of Edward George Howel Jones, of Wilmslow, Cheshire, and late Anne, *née* Sutcliffe; *b* 14 October 1956; *Educ* Wilmslow GS for Girls, Jesus Coll Oxford (MA, Rowing blue, Athletics half blue), Univ of Leicester (Advanced Cert Educnl

M

Mgmnt), Univ of Exeter (Cert in Theology); *Family* 3 da (Stephanie Jane b 8 Dec 1984 d 2002, Victoria Claire b 24 March 1986, Charlotte Anne b 11 July 1991), 1 s (Andrew Edward Gordon b 10 July 1993); *Career* corporate lending offr Chemical Bank 1978–81, real estate lending offr Bank of America 1981–88, property team mangr Kleinwort Benson 1988–89, vice-pres and head EMEA Airline Lending Div Bank of America 1990–91, full time mother 1991–95, head of economics and politics St George's Coll Weybridge 1995–2000, headmistress Tormead Sch Guildford 2001–10 (head of sixth form 2000–01), headmistress Withington Girls' Sch 2010–16; memb: Ind Schs Inspectorate 1998– (reporting inspector 2013–), GSA 2001–16 (hon treas 2007–12), HMC 2014–16; *Recreations* reading, painting; *Clubs* Lansdowne; *Style*— Mrs Susan Marks

MARKS, Victor James (Vic); s of Harold George Marks (d 1989), and Phyllis Joan, *née* Farthing; *b* 25 June 1955; *Educ* Blundell's, St John's Coll Oxford (BA, Cricket blue, Rugby Fives half blue); *m* 9 Sept 1978, Annabelle Margaret, *née* Stewart; 2 da (Amy Tamsin b 27 Nov 1979, Rosie b 8 Nov 1987); *Career* cricket correspondent; professional cricketer: Somerset CCC 1974–89 (capt 1988–89), 6 test matches England 1982–84 (35 one day ints 1980–88); teacher Blundell's 1978–80, cricket corr The Observer 1990–, contrib BBC's Test Match Special 1990–, assoc ed The Wisden Cricketer magazine (formerly The Cricketer, dir 1990–); cricket chm Somerset 1999–; *Books* Somerset CCC Scrapbook (1984), Marks out of XI (1985), TCCB Guide to Better Cricket (1987), Ultimate One Day Cricket Match (1988), Wisden Illustrated History of Cricket (1989), My Greatest Game – Cricket (with Bob Holmes, 1994); *Recreations* golf; *Style*— Vic Marks, Esq

MARKS OF HENLEY-ON-THAMES, Baron (Life Peer UK 2011), of Henley-on-Thames in the County of Oxfordshire; Jonathan Clive Marks; QC (1995); s of Geoffrey Jack Marks (d 2000), and Patricia Pauline, *née* Bowman (d 1995); *b* 19 October 1952; *Educ* Harrow, UC Oxford (BA); *m* 1, 18 Dec 1982 (m dis 1991), Sarah Ann Russell; 1 s (David b 1986), 1 da (Freya b 1988); m 2, 30 Oct 1993, Clementine Medina Cafopoulos, da of Panayiotes and Catherine Cafopoulos, of Athens; 2 da (Lara b 1996, Katya b 1998), 3 s (Alexander b 1999, Nicholas b 2001, George b 2006); *Career* called to the Bar Inner Temple 1975; in practice Western Circuit; visiting lectr in advocacy: Univ of Malaya Kuala Lumpur 1985 and 1989–91, Univ of Mauritius 1988, Sri Lanka Law Coll 1992; fndr memb SDP 1981, Euro Parly candidate for Cornwall and Plymouth 1984; Parly candidate: Weston-super-Mare 1983, Falmouth and Camborne 1987; memb Lib Dem Ctee for England 1988–89, chair Buckingham Constituency Lib Dems 2000–02, chm Lib Dem Lawyers Assoc 2001–07, memb Lib Dem Federal Policy Ctee 2004–10 and 2011–, co-chair Parly Ctee on Home Affairs, Justice and Equalities 2012–, memb Delegated Powers and Regulatory Reform Ctee House of Lords 2012–15, Lib Dem House of Lords spokesman on justice 2012–15, Lib Dem spokesman on justice 2015–; Freeman: City of London 1975, Worshipful Co of Pattenmakers (memb Ct of Assts 1998–2004); *Recreations* skiing, tennis, theatre, food, wine, travel; *Clubs* RAC, Boodle's; *Style*— The Lord Marks of Henley-on-Thames, QC; ✉ 4 Pump Court, Temple, London EC4Y 7AN (☎ 020 7842 5555, fax 020 7583 2036, e-mail jmarks@4pumpcourt.com); The House of Lords, London SW1A 0PW

MARKUS, Prof Hugh Stephen; s of Dr Andrew Markus, and Dr Patricia Markus; *b* 9 March 1960; *Educ* Clare Coll Cambridge (BA), Univ of Oxford (BM BCh); *m* 1994, Philippa, *née* Hird; 1 da (Helen b 2000), 1 s (Jonathan b 2003); *Career* reader in neurology GKT 1997–2000 (sr lectr in neurology 1994–97), fndn prof of neurology St George's Univ of London 2000–13, prof of stroke medicine and conslt neurologist Univ of Cambridge 2013–; FRCP 1999; *Publications* Stroke Genetics (ed, 2003), Stroke Medicine (2006), Handbook of Stroke Medicine (2010); papers on stroke research in scientific jls; *Style*— Prof Hugh Markus; ✉ University of Cambridge, Department of Neurology, R3, Box 83 Addenbrooke's Hospital, Cambridge CB2 0QQ (☎ 01223 586661, fax 01223 217909)

MARKWELL, Lisa; da of John Markwell, and Diane Markwell; *b* 23 April 1965, Buckinghamshire; *m* 3 July 1998 John Dempsey; 1 s (Peter b 13 May 1996), 1 da (Terri b 28 Jan 1999); *Career* magazine and features ed The Independent 1998–2004, features dir Easy Living 2004–08, exec ed The Independent and i 2008–13, ed The Independent on Sunday 2013–; Weekend Newspaper of the Year 2013 and 2014, Front Page of the Year 2014; *Recreations* food, films, fashion, fun, holidays, my children; *Clubs* Groucho; *Style*— Ms Lisa Markwell; ✉ Independent on Sunday, Northcliffe House, 2 Derry Street, London W8 5HF (☎ 020 36152038, e-mail l.markwell@independent.co.uk, website www.independent.co.uk)

MARLAND, Baron (Life Peer UK 2006), of Odstock in the County of Wiltshire; Jonathan Peter Marland; s of Peter Marland, and Audrey, *née* Brierley; *b* 14 August 1956; *Educ* Shrewsbury; *m* 1983, Penelope Mary, *née* Lamb; 2 s (Marcus, Hugo), 2 da (Allegra, Domenica); *Career* dir Lloyd Thompson plc 1982–97, dir Jardine Lloyd Thompson plc 1997–99; treas Cons Pty 2005–07, min for Dept of Energy and Climate Change 2010–12, min for Dept of Business, Innovation and Skills 2012, PM's trade envoy 2012–14; pres Salisbury Cons Assoc; chm Jubilee Holdings until 2011, former chm Janspeed Ltd, chm and tstee Harnham Water Meadows Tst 1990–2010; dir: Hunter Boot Ltd until 2010, WH Ireland until 2011, C&UCO Properties, Insurance Capital Partners Ltd, The Cricketer, Enterprise and Investment Co; chm: Commonwealth Enterprise and Investment Cncl Ltd, JP Marland & Sons Ltd, Tickets for Troops, The Churchill Soc UK, Ecoworld Mgmnt and Advsy Servs (UK) Ltd, Tricouni Brand Ltd; tstee: Atlantic Partnership, JP Marland Charitable Tst; memb Advsy Bd Peggy Guggenheim Museum Venice, pres Commonwealth Youth Orchestra 2014–16, patron Salisbury and S Wilts Sports Club, patron Wiltshire Churches; FRSA; Order of Merit of Malta 2015; *Recreations* enjoying every day to the full; *Clubs* MCC, Brooks's, Garrick; *Style*— The Rt Hon the Lord Marland; ✉ 78 Belgrave Road, London SW1V 2BJ (☎ 020 7752 0177)

MARLAND, Ross Crispian; s of John Marland (d 1988), and Sylvia, *née* Norris (d 2005); *b* 17 August 1940; *Educ* Stamford Sch, BRNC Dartmouth, UCL (LLM, Dip Air and Space Law); *m* 23 Oct 1965, (Daphne Mary) Virginia, da of Brig William Hugh Denning Wakely (d 1979); 1 s (Timothy b 27 July 1970), 1 da (Lavinia b 22 Sept 1974); *Career* graduated RNC Actg Sub Lt 1961, RAF 1963–79; called to the Bar Inner Temple 1975, in practice 1979–81; dir: International Insurance Services Ltd 1981–87, Airclaims Insurance Services Ltd 1987–91; mangr Tech Servs Div British Aviation Insurance Group 1991–97, ptnr Maxwell, Marland & Associates 1997–, conslt Clyde & Co 1997–2002, conslt LAD (Aviation) Ltd 2000–01; memb: Br Insurance Law Assoc, Air Law Gp Royal Aeronautical Soc, Bar Assoc Commerce Finance and Indust, Racehorse Owners' Assoc; Upper Freeman Guild of Air Pilots and Air Navigators 1999; MRIN 1973, MRAeS 1982, MCIArb 1999; *Recreations* salmon and trout fishing, equestrian sports; *Clubs* RAF; *Style*— Ross Marland, Esq; ✉ 84 East Hill, Wandsworth, London SW18 2HG (☎ 020 8874 5964, fax 020 8488 7487, e-mail mma2@dircon.co.uk); Place de l'Église, 64390 Laàs, Pyrénées-Atlantiques, France (☎ +33 559 385905, fax +33 559 385438, e-mail ross.marland@orange.fr)

MARLBOROUGH, 12 Duke of (E 1702); (Charles) James Spencer-Churchill; s of 11 Duke of Marlborough, JP, DL (d 2014) by his 1 w, *see* Mrs John Gough; *b* 24 November 1955; *Educ* Pinewood, Harrow, RAC Cirencester; *m* 1, 1990 (m dis 2001), Rebecca Mary, da of Peter Few Brown and Mrs John Winnington-Ingram; 1 s (George, Earl of Sunderland b 28 July 1992); m 2, 1 March 2002, Edla Griffiths, da of Alun Griffiths, of Monmouthshire; 1 da (Araminta Clementine Megan Cadogan Spencer-Churchill b 5 April 2007), 1 s (Caspar Ivor Ellis Spencer-Churchill b 17 Oct 2008); *Heir* s, Earl of Sunderland; *Career* insurance broker and helicopter pilot; freelance journalist for Sunday Times, Sunday Mail travel writer, Formula One hospitality and marketing co-ordinator; *Recreations* skiing, flying, shooting, fishing; *Clubs* Turf, Annabel's, White's; *Style*— His Grace the Duke of Marlborough; ✉ Blenheim Palace, Woodstock, Oxfordshire OX20 1PS (mobile 07785 795838); 16 Lawrence Street, London SW3 5NE (☎ 020 7351 2730); Woottondown Farmhouse, Wootton, Woodstock, Oxfordshire OX20 1AF (☎ 01869 331222, e-mail marlborough@blenheimpalace.com or duke@blenheimpalace.com)

MARLESFORD, Baron (Life Peer UK 1991), of Marlesford in the County of Suffolk; Mark Shuldham Schreiber; DL (Suffolk 1991); s of John Shuldham Schreiber, AE, DL (d 1968), of Marlesford Hall, Woodbridge, Suffolk, and Constance Maureen, *née* Dent (d 1980); *b* 11 September 1931; *Educ* Eton, Trinity Coll Cambridge (MA); *m* 1969, Gabriella Federica, da of Conte Teodoro Veglio di Castelletto d'Uzzone; 2 da (Hon Nicola Charlotte (Hon Mrs Stacey) b 8 Aug 1971, Hon Sophie Louisa (Hon Sophie Franklin) b 8 Sept 1973); *Career* Nat Serv Coldstream Gds, 2 Lt; Fisons Ltd 1957–63, Conservative Res Dept 1963–67, dir Conservative Party Public Sector Research Unit 1967–70, special advsr HM Govt 1970–74, special advsr to leader of the Opposition 1974–75, editorial conslt The Economist 1974–91 (Parly lobby correspondent); memb: EU Select Ctee 2003–07 and 2011–14, Economic and Financial Affrs Sub-Ctee 2000–05 and 2010–14, Home Affrs Sub-Ctee 2005–09; dir: Eastern Group plc 1989–95, Times Newspapers Holdings Ltd (ind nat dir) 1991–2014, Baring New Russia Fund 1997–2007; advsr: Mitsubishi Corporation International NV 1990–2003, John Swire & Sons 1992–2009; pres Suffolk Preservation Soc 1997–; memb: Countryside Cmmn 1980–92, Rural Devpt Cmmn 1985–93; chm CPRE 1993–98; *Clubs* Pratt's; *Style*— The Lord Marlesford, DL; ✉ Marlesford Hall, Woodbridge, Suffolk IP13 0AU; 5 Kersley Street, London SW11 4PR (e-mail marlesford@parliament.uk)

MARMOT, Prof Sir Michael Gideon; kt (2000); s of Nathan Marmot, of Sydney, Aust, and Alice, *née* Weiner; *b* 26 January 1945, UK; *Educ* Univ of Sydney (BSc, MB BS), Univ of Calif Berkeley (MPH, PhD); *m* 8 Sept 1971, Alexi, da of Bernard Ferster; 2 s (Andre b 1982, Daniel b 1986), 1 da (Deborah b 1992); *Career* Univ of Sydney: student fell in cardiovascular pharmacology 1965–66, res med offr Royal Prince Alfred Hosp 1969, fell in thoracic med 1970, travelling fell Postgrad Med Fndn 1971–72; lectr Dept of Biomedical and Environmental Health Sciences Univ of Calif Berkeley 1975–76, adjunct assoc prof Sch of Health Univ of Texas 1976, lectr then hon sr lectr in epidemiology LSHTM 1976–85, prof of epidemiology and public health UCL 1985– (also head of dept), prof of epidemiology LSHTM 1990–92, dir Int Centre for Health and Society UCL 1994–2005, adjunct prof Dept of Society, Human Devpt and Health Harvard Univ 2000–, dir Int Inst for Society and Health UCL 2005–, assoc in health policy and mgmnt Johns Hopkins Univ 2007–08, dir Inst for Health Equity UCL 2011–; hon conslt Med Div UCH and Bloomsbury Health Authy 1980–84, hon conslt in public health med Camden and Islington HA 1985–2004, hon conslt in public health med N Central London SHA 2004–06, hon conslt in public health med SHA for London 2006–; MRC research prof 1995, visiting fell Nat Centre for Social Research 2002, Charles M and Martha Hitchcock prof Univ of California Berkeley 2002, visiting fell commoner Trinity Coll Cambridge 2003, visiting prof Case Univ Ohio 2005, McLaughlin-Gallie visitng prof Royal Coll of Physicians and Surgns of Canada 2009; chair: Cmmn on Social Determinants of Health WHO, Scientific Reference Gp Dept of Health, R&D Ctee NICE; memb of numerous gps and ctees incl: Royal Cmmn on Environmental Pollution 1995–2002, Reference Gp on Inequalities Dept of Health; memb Editorial Bd: Epidemiologic Review, Jl of Cardiovascular Risk, Br Heart Jl, Psychological Medicine, Holistic Medicine, Addiction, WHO Bulletin; ldr writer The Lancet; tstee Br Heart Fndn; numerous named lectures incl: Geoffrey Rose meml lectr 1997, Redfern Oration Royal Australasian Coll of Physicians 2000, Lord Rayner lectr 2000, Beveridge lectr Royal Statistical Soc 2003, St Cyres lectr Br Cardiac Soc 2004, Harveian Oration RCP 2006, John F Wilkinson meml lectr Manchester Medical Soc 2007, R C Geary lectr Economic and Social Research Inst Dublin 2007, DARE lectr RCP 2007, Lewis A Conner meml lectr American Heart Assoc 2007; Medal European Soc of Cardiology 2000, Alumnus of the Year Sch of Public Health Univ of California Berkeley 2000, Patricia B Barchas Award American Psychosomatic Soc 2002, Bisset Hawkins Tst Medal RCP 2004, Alwyn Smith Prize Medal Faculty of Public Health 2004, Balzan Prize for Epidemiology 2004, Ipsen Fndn Longevity Award 2005, Jorma Rantanen Award (and lecture) 2006, Public Health Award BMA Book Awards 2006, Public Hero Award Centre for Disease Control Fndn 2007, William B Graham Prize for Health Servs Research 2008, Fèlix Restrepo SJ Medal of Honor Pontificia Universidad Javeriana Award 2015, Prince Mahidol Award for public health 2015, Centennial Winslow Medal Yale Sch of Public Health 2015, ?hsan Do?ramac? Family Health Prize WHO 2016, Distinguished Merit Gold Medal BMA Award 2017, Gold Medal RSM 2017; MD (hc): Univ of Sydney 2006, Université Libre de Bruxelles 2008, Univ of Athens 2009, Univ of Montreal 2009, Univ of Helsinki 2010, Univ of Stockholm 2010, TCD 2011, Universidad Peruana Cayetano 2011, Ghent Univ 2011 (nominated), Malmo Univ 2012, Middlesex Univ 2013, Lund Univ 2015, Univ of Ghent 2016, Norwegian Univ of Science and Technol 2016; Hon DSc Northumbria Univ 2012, Hon DCL Univ of Newcastle 2013, Hon Doctorate KU Leuven 2014; foreign assoc memb Inst of Med NAS 2002; FFPHM 1989 (MFPHM 1984), FRCP 1996, FMedSci 1998, fell Academia Europea 1998 (vice-pres and chair Behavioural Scis Section), hon memb Br Cardiac Soc 2005, Hon FBA 2008, fell European Soc of Cardiology, pres World Medical Assoc 2015–16 (pres-elect 2014), hon fell American Coll of Epidemiology 2015, hon FRCOG 2015, hon FRCPCH 2016, hon fell RSS 2016; *Books* Mortality of Immigrants to England and Wales (1984), Coronary Heart Disease Epidemiology (1992), Stress and the Heart (with S Stansfeld, 2002), Social Determinants of Health (with R Wilkinson, 1999), Status Syndrome (2004), The Health Gap (2015); numerous published articles and lectures; *Style*— Prof Sir Michael Marmot; ✉ Institute of Health Equity, Department of Epidemiology and Public Health, University College London, 1–19 Torrington Place, London WC1E 6BT (☎ 020 7679 1694, e-mail m.marmot@ucl.ac.uk)

MARNHAM, Patrick; *b* 1943, Jerusalem, Palestine; *Educ* Downside, CCC Oxford (MA, memb Univ of Oxford ski team); *Career* called to the Bar Gray's Inn 1966; reporter Private Eye 1966–76, asst features ed Daily Telegraph Magazine 1968–70, scriptwriter and presenter BBC TV and Granada TV 1968–71, literary ed The Spectator 1981–82, Paris corr The Independent 1986–92, Paris corr Evening Standard 1994–98; judge Duff Cooper Prize 2013–; winner Thomas Cook Travel Book Prize 1985, Marsh Biography Award 1991–92; FRSL 1988; *Books* Road to Katmandu (1971), Nomads of the Sahel (1977), Fantastic Invasion: Dispatches from Africa (1980), Lourdes: A Modern Pilgrimage (1980), The Private Eye Story (1982), So Far From God: A Journey to Central America (1985), Trail of Havoc (1987), The Man Who Wasn't Maigret: A Biography of Georges Simenon (1992), Crime and the Académie Française (1993), Dreaming with His Eyes Open: The Life of Diego Rivera (1998), The Death of Jean Moulin: Biography of a Ghost (2000), Wild Mary: A Life of Mary Wesley (2006), Snake Dance (2013), Army of the Night (2015); *Film Scripts* Snake Dance (2012); *Clubs* Academy; *Style*— Patrick Marnham, Esq; ✉ c/o Toby Eady Associates, 9 Orme Court, London W2 4RL (☎ 020 7792 0092)

MARPLES, Graham; s of Ronald Marples (d 1992), of Derby, and Catherine (d 1999); *Educ* Long Eaton GS, Univ of Durham Business Sch (MBA); *m* 1986, Christine, *née* Lane; 2 da (Alice b 1988, Charlotte b 2000), 1 s (James b 1990); *Career* journalist; reporter: Long Eaton Advertiser, Raymond's News Agency Derby, Teesside Evening Gazette; chief reporter Northern Echo Darlington, news ed Teesside Evening Gazette; Tyne Tees Television: newsroom journalist, news ed, prodr, sr prodr, managing ed news; *Awards* New York Television Festival Awards 1996 and 1998 for documentaries Climbing K2 and Back to K2, RTS Best Regnl News Magazine 1997 for North East Tonight (shortlisted 1998 and 1999); Soc of Editors 2000; *Recreations* rugby, running, real ale, travel, theatre; *Style—* Graham Marples, Esq

MARQUIS, Simon John; s of Henry Derek Marquis, of Harpenden, Herts, and Margaret, *née* Parish; *b* 3 May 1953; *Educ* Lancing, Peterhouse Cambridge (MA); *m* 1 May 1993, Nicola Jane Horner, da of Capt Richard Bates, RN; 1 s (Edward James Richard b 7 July 1994), 2 step da (Sophie, Clio); *Career* Benton & Bowles advtg 1975–80, Allen Brady Marsh advtg 1980–83, md Burkitt Weinreich Bryant Clients & Co Ltd 1990–92 (media dir 1983–90), editorial dir Marketing magazine 1993–98, chm ZenithOptimedia until 2006; chm Nat Readership Survey 2005–, chm Media Circle, non-exec dir St Ives; FIPA; *Recreations* golf, skiing, birds, drawing; *Style—* Simon Marquis, Esq

MARR, Andrew William Stevenson; s of William Donald Marr, and Valerie, *née* Stevenson, of Longforgan, Perthshire; *b* 31 July 1959, Glasgow; *Educ* Dundee HS, Craigflower Sch, Loretto, Trinity Hall Cambridge (MA, exhibitioner); *m* Aug 1987, Jackie Ashley, *qv*, da of Baron Ashley of Stoke, CH, PC (Life Peer), *qv*; 1 s (Harry Cameron b 5 July 1989), 2 da (Isabel Claire b 4 Oct 1991, Emily Catherine b 3 Nov 1994); *Career* trained TRN Newcastle upon Tyne 1981; The Scotsman: trainee 1982, gen reporter then business reporter 1983–85, Parly corr 1985–86; political corr and Whitehall corr The Independent 1986–87, political ed The Scotsman 1988, political ed The Economist 1989–92; The Independent: chief political commentator 1992–96, ed 1996–98, ed-in-chief 1998; columnist The Express and The Observer 1998–2000, political ed BBC 2000–05, presenter Sunday AM (BBC1) 2005–; Columnist of the Year Br Press Awards 1995, Creative Freedom Award 2000, RTS Specialist Journalist 2001, Hansard/Channel 4 Political Journalist 2000 and 2001, Voice of Listener and Viewer TV Journalist 2001, Broadcasting Press Guild TV Performer 2001, Richard Dimbleby Award Bafta TV Awards 2004; *Books* The Battle for Scotland (1992), Ruling Britannia (1995), The Day Britain Died (2000), The Making of Modern Britain (2010, Non-Fiction Book of the Year Galaxy Nat Book Award 2010); *Recreations* whining and dining; *Clubs* Buffers, St James's, Pinks, The Reaction; *Style—* Andrew Marr, Esq; ✉ BBC Westminster, 4 Millbank, Westminster, London SW1A

MARR, Lindsay Grigor David; s of Grigor Wilson Marr (d 1986), and Linda Grace, *née* Sergeant (d 2006); *b* 14 September 1955; *Educ* The Perse Sch Cambridge, Gonville & Caius Coll Cambridge (MA); *m* 23 Feb 1991, Susan Ann, *née* Scott; 1 s (Andrew b 1992); *Career* admitted slr 1981; Freshfields Bruckhaus Deringer: articled clerk 1979–81, asst slr 1981–87, ptnr 1987–2006, princ conslt 2006–12; seconded to LOCOG 2009–12; Freeman City of London Slrs' Co 1988; memb Law Soc, memb Int Bar Assoc; *Recreations* photography, music, sports and other outdoor pursuits; *Style—* Mr Lindsay Marr; ✉ 39 Broad Lane, Hampton, Middlesex TW12 3AL (e-mail lindsay.marr@mac.com)

MARRA, Jenny; MSP; *b* 6 November 1977, Dundee; *Educ* St John's HS Dundee, Univ of St Andrews, Emory Univ Atlanta; *Career* MSP (Lab) NE Scotland 2011–, shadow min for youth employment and shadow dep fin min, shadow cabinet sec for Health, Wellbeing and Sport; *Style—* Ms Jenny Marra, MSP; ✉ The Scottish Parliament, Edinburgh EH99 1SP

MARRE, Jeremy Peter; *b* London; *Educ* UCL (LLB), Slade Sch of Fine Art, RCA; *m* 2 July 1970, Diana, *née* Silman; 2 s (Oliver b 1981, Jesse b 1985); *Career* director, writer and producer; fndr Harcourt Films 1974; clients incl: Thames TV 1974, London Weekend TV 1975–79, BBC 2 1979–, Granada TV 1980, Open Road Films, Channel 4 1981–, BBC 1 1990–2005, ITV 1990–2005, ITV 1990–2005, BBC4 2007–; former memb Advsy Bd of Nat Sound Archive; memb: Directors UK, BAFTA; contrib: Times, Independent; custody visitor Mayor's Office for Policing and Crime; *Television* films incl: Artful Dodger (BBC 2) 2010, Elvis in Vegas (BBC 4) 2010, Reggae Britannia (BBC 4) 2010–11, Carlos Santana: Angels and Demons (BBC 4) 2011, Soul Ambassador – The Otis Redding Story (BBC) 2012, Voice of Africa (BBC 4) 2013, Key to the Highway (BBC) 2014, The Heart of the Country (BBC 4) 2014; *Awards* Golden Harp 1981, Golden Eagle 2001, nominated Grammy Award 2002, UNESCO Award 2011; *Books* Beats of the Heart (1985); *Recreations* cinema, music, reading, travel; *Style—* Jeremy Marre, Esq

MARRINER, Andrew Stephen; s of Sir Neville Marriner, the conductor; *b* 25 February 1954; *Educ* King's Coll Cambridge (chorister), King's Sch Canterbury, New Coll Oxford, Hochschule für Musik Hannover; *m* 1988, Elisabeth Anne, *née* Sparke; 1 s (Douglas Lawrence b 11 Oct 1989); *Career* solo chamber and orchestral clarinettist; freelance 1977–84, princ clarinet LSO 1985–, princ clarinet Acad of St Martin-in-the-Fields 1986–2008; solo and concert appearances at venues incl Royal Festival Hall, Barbican Hall, various in Paris, Berlin, Vienna, USA, Far East and Australia; concerto work with conductors incl Sir Neville Marriner, Valery Gergiev, Sir Colin Davis, Leonard Bernstein, Mstislav Rostropovich, Michael Tilson Thomas and Richard Hickox; Hon RAM 1994; *Recordings* with Acad of St Martin-in-the-Fields incl: Schubert Octet (Chandos), Beethoven Octet (Philips), Spohr Octet and Nonet (Philips), Mozart Divertimenti (Philips), Weber Concerti (Philips); others incl: Mozart Clarinet Quintet (Classics for Pleasure), Mozart Clarinet Concerto (CFP), Schubert Octet (with Chilingirian, EMI); *Recreations* family, cricket; *Clubs* Lord's Taverners; *Style—* Andrew Marriner, Esq; ✉ 67 Cornwall Gardens, London SW7 4BA; c/o Ingpen & Williams Ltd, 7 St George's Court, 131 Putney Bridge Road, London SW15 2PA (✆ 020 8874 3222, fax 020 8877 3113)

MARRIOTT; *see also:* Smith-Marriott

MARRIOTT, Jane; OBE (2004); da of Derek Marriott, and Pat Marriott; *b* Doncaster; *Educ* Danum Comp, Durham Univ (BA), Univ of Cambridge (MPhil); *Partner* Paul Lipscombe; *Career* diplomat; team ldr for nuclear non-proliferation FCO 2001–03, political advsr to Coalition Forces Al Amara 2003–04, political advsr to Combined Coalition Forces Kabul 2004, political-military team ldr and acting dep head Iraq Policy Unit FCO 2004–05, counsellor (political-military and economics) Baghdad 2005–06, dep head Afghan Gp FCO 2006–09, chief speechwriter Sec of State for Defence MOD 2009, sr political advsr to US Special Rep for Afghanistan and Pakistan Washington DC 2009, chargé d'affaires and dep head of mission Tehran 2010–11, dep dir (Americas, ME and Africa) Nat Security Secretariat Cabinet Office 2012–13, ambass to Yemen 2013–15; FCO dir Middle East and North Africa (MENAD) 2015–16, FCO dir International Counter Terrorism 2016–; *Style—* Ms Jane Marriott, OBE; ✉ Director International Counter Terrorism, c/o Home Office, 2 Marsham Street, Westminster, London SW1P 4DF

MARRIOTT, Michael; *b* 1963, Woolwich, London; *Educ* RCA; *Career* product designer; clients incl: 20/21, Arts Cncl of England, DIM, Möve, SCP, Topolski, Trico; exhibited worldwide; design installations incl: Mies Meets Marx/MMM (Geffrye Museum), Bring Me Sunshine (Tokyo Design Week), Economy of Means (Camden Art Centre); winner Jerwood Furniture Prize 1999; tutor of design products RCA; *Style—* Michael Marriott; ✉ Unit F2, 2–4 Southgate Road, London N1 3JJ (e-mail mm@michaelmarriott.com, website www.michaelmarriott.com)

MARRIS, Robert; s of Dr Charles Marris (d 1989), of Wolverhampton, and Margaret Marris, JP, *née* Crawley; *b* 8 April 1955; *Educ* Univ of British Columbia (BA, MA), Birmingham Poly (CPE, Law Soc Finals); *partner* Julia Pursehouse; *Career* truck driver Vancouver 1977–79, bus driver Vancouver 1979–82; articled clerk Wolverhampton 1985–87, slr Wolverhampton 1987–88, trade union slr Birmingham and Stoke-on-Trent 1988–2001; MP (Lab) Wolverhampton SW 2001–2010 and 2015–; trade union offr NUT 2011–13; memb Law Soc; *Recreations* talking, Wolves, Canadiana; *Style—* Rob Marris, Esq

MARRON, Peter Austin; s of Austin Marron, and Catherine, *née* Cassidy (d 2000); *b* 3 June 1944, Sunderland; *Educ* St Cuthbert's GS Newcastle upon Tyne, Univ of Liverpool (LLB), Coll of Law Guildford; *m* 17 March 1967, Christine, *née* Collins; 2 da (Kirsty b 6 March 1972, Sophie b 26 Feb 1975), 1 s (James b 11 Aug 1979); *Career* slr: IOW CC 1967–70, Leicester City Cncl 1970–72; slr and ptnr Gardiner & Millhouse 1972–78, fndr Marron Townsend (subsequently Marron Dodds, then Marrons, Slrs) 1978–2009, ret; memb: Law Soc 1970, CIArb 1991, RSA 1995, Soc of Advanced Legal Studies 1998, Int Bar Assoc 1996; legal assoc RTPI 1997; *Recreations* offshore sailing (RYA Ocean Yachtmaster 1994); *Clubs* Royal Yachting Assoc; *Style—* Peter Marron, Esq; ✉ The Hermitage, Church Lane, Lyddington, Oakham LE15 9LN (✆ 01572 822338)

MARSDEN, Gordon; MP; s of late George Henry Marsden, of Stockport, and late Joyce, *née* Young; *b* 28 November 1953; *Educ* Stockport GS, New Coll Oxford (scholar, MA, Gibbs prize in history), Warburg Inst Univ of London, Kennedy Sch of Govt Harvard Univ (Kennedy scholar in politics/int rels); *Career* tutor and lectr Open Univ 1977–97, public affrs/PR conslt 1980–85 (public affrs advsr Eng Heritage 1984–85), conslt ed New Socialist 1989–90, ed History Today 1985–97; MP (Lab) Blackpool S 1997– (Parly candidate (Lab) Blackpool S 1992); memb Commons Select Ctee Education and Employment 1998–2001 and 2005–07, PPS to Sec of State for Culture, Media and Sport 2003–05, PPS to Sec of State for Communities and Local Govt 2009–10, shadow min for communities and local govt 2010, shadow min for skills, further educn and regnl growth 2010–13, shadow min for transport 2014–15, shadow min for Univs, Further Educn and Skills 2015–; chair All-Pty Future of Europe Tst 2001–10, chair All-Pty Skills Gp, convenor Lab MPs Seaside and Coastal Towns Gp, co-chair All-Pty Osteoporosis Gp 2008–, co-chair All-Pty Arts and Heritage Gp 2015; chm Young Fabians 1979–80, chair Fabian Soc 2000–01; pres British Destinations 1998–; tstee: Dartmouth Street Tst 1997–2010 (chair 2010–), History Today Ltd 1997–2014, History of Parliament 1999–; memb Bd Inst of Historical Res 1994–2003; nat vice-chair Early Educn 2000–; visiting Parly fell St Antony's Coll Oxford 2003, Historical Assoc centenary fell 2006–07; *Books* The History Debate (contrib, 1990), Holland's War Against Hitler (contrib, 1991), Victorian Values? Personalities and Perspectives in Nineteenth-Century Society (2 edn, 1998), The English Question (contrib, 2000), Censorship: A World Encyclopedia (contrib, 2002), Nye Bevan in Eminent Parliamentarians, The Speaker's Lectures (contrib, 2012); *Recreations* swimming, choral and early music, theatre, medieval culture and travel; *Style—* Gordon Marsden, Esq, MP; ✉ House of Commons, London SW1A 0AA (✆ 020 7219 1262)

MARSDEN, Philip John; s of Christopher Marsden-Smedley, of Bristol, and Susan Penelope, *née* King; *b* 11 May 1961, Bristol; *m* 19 June 1999, Charlotte, da of Anthony Hobson; 1 da (Clio Tatyana b 4 Feb 2003), 1 s (Arthur James Anthony b 16 April 2005); *Career* author; Somerset Maugham Award 1994, Daily Telegraph/Thomas Cook Travel Book Award 1999; FRSL 1996; *Books* A Far Country: Travels in Ethiopia (1990), The Crossing Place: A Journey Among the Armenians (1993), The Bronski House (1995), The Spirit-Wrestlers (1998), The Main Cages (2002), The Chains of Heaven (2005), The Barefoot Emperor: An Ethiopian Tragedy (2007), The Levelling Sea: The Story of a Cornish Haven and the Age of Sail (2011), Rising Ground: A Search for the Spirit of Place (2014); *Style—* Philip Marsden, Esq, FRSL; ✉ c/o Gillon Aitken Associates, 18–21 Cavaye Place, London SW10 9PT (✆ 020 7373 8672); e-mail philip@philipmarsden.co.uk

MARSH, Colin; s of Leonard Roy Marsh (d 1960), and Ellenor Myra, *née* Clough; *b* 11 January 1953, Penshaw, Co Durham; *Educ* Washington GS, Durham Tech Coll, Dartington Coll of Arts (Dip), Rolle Coll Univ of Exeter, Inst of Educn (CertEd); *Children* 2 s (Oscar Jack b 15 Dec 1982, Archie b 2 Feb 1988); *Career* actor 1975– (incl with RSC and memb original cast Les Miserables); freelance contemporary dance mangr 1993–2002, prodr Punchdrunk Theatre Co 2002–; chair Protein Dance Co 2012–; hon tstee Brixton St Vincents Community Centre; memb Equity 1976; *Recreations* reading, walking, singing, writing; *Style—* Colin Marsh, Esq; ✉ 136 Benhill Road, London SE5 7LZ (✆ 020 7708 1844, e-mail colin@punchdrunk.org)

M

MARSH, David John; s of Harry Cheetham Marsh (d 1979), of Solihull, Warks, and Florence, *née* Bold (d 1990); *b* 2 November 1936; *Educ* Leeds GS, Merton Coll Oxford (MA); *m* 26 May 1962, Hilary Joy, da of Edwin Leslie Pitt (d 1993), of Tetbury, Glos; 2 da (Carole b 1963, Rowena b 1965), 1 s (Nigel b 1966); *Career* admitted slr 1961, ptnr Wragge & Co Slrs 1963–92, ptnr Lenchwick Management Services 1992–; dir: Marla Tube Fittings Ltd 1972–, Pacs Services Ltd 2006–, Cuddledry Ltd 2007–; chm Bd of Tstees: United Industries plc gp pension schemes 1992–2002, Neepsend plc gp pension scheme 1998–2004; memb Law Soc 1961; *Recreations* sport, travel, wine; *Style—* David Marsh, Esq; ✉ Lenchwick House, Lenchwick, Evesham, Worcestershire WR11 4TG (✆ and fax 01386 442451)

MARSH, Eric Morice; s of Frederick Morice Marsh (d 1970), of Carnforth, Lancs, and Anne, *née* Leigh (d 2003); *b* 25 July 1943; *Educ* The Abbey Sch Fort Augustus, Courtfield Catering Coll Blackpool (Nat Dip Hotelkeeping & Catering); *m* 2 Sept 1968, Elizabeth Margaret, da of John (Jack) Lowes, of Macclesfield, Cheshire; 2 s (Andrew Paul b 4 Aug 1969, Christopher Simon b 5 July 1974), 2 da (Erika Louise b 26 Oct 1971, Lucy Anne b 4 Aug 1982); *Career* student Hotel Sch 1960–63, stagiaire George V Hotel Paris 1964–65, trainee The Dorchester 1965–68, asst mangr Royal Lancaster 1969–73, dir and gen mangr Newling Ward Hotels Ltd 1973–75, tenant Cavendish Hotel Chatsworth Estate 1975–; md: Paludis Ltd (trading as Cavendish Hotel) 1975–, Cavendish Aviation Ltd, Eudaemonic Leisure Ltd (trading as George Hotel Hathersage) 1996–; chm Peak Leisure Mgmnt Ltd 2008–; dir Br Aerobatics Assoc; *Recreations* collection of fine art, aviation (aerobatics), distance running; *Style—* Eric Marsh, Esq; ✉ George Hotel, Hathersage, Derbyshire S32 1BB (✆ 01433 650436, fax 01433 650099, mobile 07770 860670, e-mail info@george-hotel.net, website www.george-hotel.net)

MARSH, Jeremy John Drysdale; s of Edward Marsh (decd), and Margaret, *née* Drysdale; *b* 11 May 1960; *Educ* Marlborough, West London Business Sch (BA), Harvard Business Sch (AMP); *m* Emma; 2 da (Georgina b 16 July 1990, Miranda b 13 Nov 1992); *Career* sales RCA Records 1983–84, product mgmnt Polygram records (artists incl: Brian Ferry, Roxy Music, Killing Joke, Level 42, Lloyd Cole) 1984–87, md AVL Virgin Label Div (artists incl: Neneh Cherry, Soul II Soul, Lenny Kravitz, T'Pau, Maxi Priest) 1987–90, md WEA Records (artists incl: Seal, Enya, Everything But the Girl, Madonna, REM, Prince) 1990–92, md RCA (artists incl: Robson and Jerome, M People, Take That, Annie Lennox) 1992–95, pres of music div BMG (UK) (artists incl: Natalie Imbruglia, Five, Whitney Houston, TLC) 1995–99, md Telstar Records (artists incl: Craig David, Mis-Teeq, The Hives, BBMak) 1999–2004, chm U-myx Ltd 2005–, dir Players Top 20 Ltd 2005–, md JML Ltd 2005–, vice-chm Warner Bros Records UK (artists incl: Michael Buble, Green Day, Muse, Katherine Jenkins) 2009–13, exec vice-pres International Warner Music UK (artists incl: Ed Sheeran, Coldplay, Enya) 2013–; co-chm Nordoff-Robbins Music Therapy Fund Raising Ctee; memb The Brits Ctee; *Recreations* golf, tennis, shooting; *Clubs* Groucho, Hurlingham, Royal Lymington Yacht, Sunningdale Golf, South Kensington Club; *Style—* Jeremy Marsh, Esq; ✉ Warner Music UK Ltd, 27 Wrights Lane, London W8 5SH (✆ 0207 368 3510, e-mail jeremy.marsh@warnermusic.com)

MARSH, Prof Sir John Stanley; kt (1999), CBE (1993); s of Stanley Albert Marsh (d 1973), and Elsie Gertrude, *née* Powell (d 1969); *b* 5 October 1931; *Educ* George Dixon GS Birmingham, St John's Coll Oxford (MA); *m* 20 Sept 1958, Kathleen Edith, da of Eric Arthur Casey (d 1982); 1 s (Peter b 1967), 1 da (Christine b 1969); *Career* Nat Serv RAF 1950–52; Univ of Reading 1956–77: res economist, lectr, sr lectr, reader; prof of agric economics Univ of Aberdeen 1977–84; Univ of Reading 1984–97: prof of agric economics 1984–97, dean agric 1986–89 dir Centre for Agric Strategy 1990–97 (now emeritus); author of numerous articles and pubns on agric related topics; pres Br Inst of Agricultural Conslts (BIAC) 1999–2009; sec Agric Economics Soc 1969–84; chm: Agric

Wages Bd 1990–99, Responsible Use of Resources in Agriculture and on the Land (RURAL) 1997–, Task Force on Pricing of Animal Medicines 2000–01, Task Force on Pricing of Inputs 2001, Centre for Dairy Information 2005–15; vice-chm Science Advsy Ctee Defra 2004–07; memb: Potato Mktg Bd 1979–84, SWP Food and Drink Mfrg 1990–92, Ctee Hunting with Dogs 2000; FRSA 1978, FRASE 1991, FRAgS 1993, CBiol, FIBiol; *Books* A Preliminary Study of the Small Dairy Farm and the Small Farm Scheme (1960), The National Association of Corn and Agricultural Merchants and the Merchant's Future (1967), A Future for European Agriculture (jtly, 1971), CAP: UK Priorities, European Opinion (1976), L'Ordre Alimentaire Mondial (contrib, 1982), The Human Food Chain (contrib, 1989), The Changing Role of the Common Agricultural Policy (jtly, 1991), GM Crops: The Scientists Speak (contrib, 2003); *Recreations* photography, caravanning, Methodist local preacher; *Clubs* Farmers'; *Style—* Prof Sir John Marsh, CBE; ✉ 15 Adams Way, Earley, Reading, Berkshire RG6 5UT (✆ 0118 986 8434, mobile 07909 913181, e-mail john.marsh27@ntlworld.com)

MARSH, Kevin John; s of John Marsh (d 1986), and Elizabeth Jill, *née* Johnson; *b* November 1954, Doncaster, Yorks; *Educ* Doncaster GS, ChCh Oxford (MA, chorister Exeter Coll), Salzburg Seminar; *m* 1 Dec 1979, Melissa Sue, *née* Fletcher; 1 s (John Frederick Alexander (Jack) b 1987), 1 da (Ellen Beatrice b 1990); *Career* joined BBC 1978; BBC Radio 4: ed PM 1989, ed World at One 1992, launched Broadcasting House 1998, ed Today 2002–06; exec ed BBC Coll of Jounalism 2006–11, dir OffspinMedia 2011–; memb Editorial Bd: Br Journalism Review, Jl of Applied Journalism and Media Ethics; visiting fell Bournemouth Univ 2006–, external examiner (MA TV journalism) Goldsmiths Coll London, tutor Geneva Centre for Security Policy 2007–, practitioner in residence Bournemouth Univ 2013–, course designer and teacher Birzeit Univ Palestine 2013–; conslt to Br Cncl 2013–; World Economic Forum Davos 2004, 2005 and 2006; Silver Sony Radio Award 1989, 1990 and 1991, Amnesty Int Radio Award 2000; alumnus Prince of Wales Sustainable Devpt Prog; memb Chatham House; patron St George's House Windsor; FRSA; *Publications* Stumbling Over Truth (2012), Dust (2015); contributions to books: An Essential Service in the Life of the Nation (in Web Journalism, a new form of citizenship, 2004), Can We Teach Trust (in Beyond Trust, 2008), Afghanistan, Truth and the Unexamined War (in Afghanistan, War and the Media, 2010), The Crystal Goblet (in Face the Future, 2011), Investigative Journalism, a craft in peril (in Investigative Journalism, Dead or Alive, 2011), The Arab Spring Did Not Take Place (in Mirage In The Desert, 2011), But What Comes After (in The Phone Hacking Scandal: journalism on trial, 2012), Secrets, Salience and Storytelling: the challenges of investigative journalism (2013); contributions to jls: Power But Scant Responsibility (British Journalism Review, 2004), Standing Up For Journalism, Standing Out From The Mob (British Journalism Review, 2010), Impartiality: impossibility or opportunity? (Journal of Applied Journalism and Media, 2011), The Illusion of Transparency (Political Quarterly, 2011), Stumbling Over Truth (British Journalism Review, 2012), The BBC, Trust and The Savile Affair (British Journalism Review, 2012); *Recreations* rugby, opera, living in France, cycling; *Clubs* RYA; *Style—* Kevin Marsh, Esq; ✉ c/o Biteback Publishing, 2 Albert Embankment, London SE1 7EP (website www.offspinmedia.co.uk and www.storycurve.blogspot.com)

MARSH, Dame Mary Elizabeth; DBE (2007); da of George Donald Falconer (d 1992), and Lesley Mary, *née* Wilson (d 1998); *b* 17 August 1946, Liverpool; *Educ* Birkenhead HS GPDST, Univ of Nottingham (BSc), Hatfield Poly (DipEd), London Business Sch (MBA); *m* 1968, Juan Enrique Marsh (d 1999); 4 s (Alexander b 18 April 1972, Tristan b 3 Dec 1973, George b 21 Aug 1976, Oliver b 29 Sept 1978); *Career* asst teacher Icknield HS Luton 1968–69, head of geography St Christopher Sch Letchworth 1969–71, full time mother 1972–80, dep head St Christopher Sch Letchworth 1980–90, head Queens' Sch Bushey 1990–95, head Holland Park Sch 1995–2000, dir and chief exec NSPCC 2000–08, founding dir Clore Social Leadership Prog 2008–; nat memb Learning and Skills Cncl 2005–10; non-exec dir HSBC Bank plc 2009– (memb Corporate Sustainability Ctee HSBC Hldgs plc 2009–); tstee Young Enterprise; chair Int Alumni Cncl and memb Governing Body London Business Sch 2010–; Hon LLD: Univ of Luton 2003, Univ of Nottingham 2005; FRSA; *Recreations* walking, swimming, music, reading, current affairs, good company; *Clubs* Reform; *Style—* Dame Mary Marsh, DBE; ✉ Level 14, 8 Canada Square, London E14 5HQ

MARSH, Prof Paul Rodney; s of Harold Marsh, of Bournemouth, and Constance, *née* Miller; *b* 19 August 1947; *Educ* Poole GS, LSE (BSc Econ), London Business Sch (PhD); *m* 13 Sept 1971, Stephanie, da of Mark Simonow, of London; *Career* systems analyst: Esso Petroleum 1968–69, Scicon 1970–71; Bank of England res fell London Business Sch 1974–85; Centre for Mgmnt Devpt London Business Sch: non-exec dir 1984–91, prof of fin 1985–2006 (emeritus prof 2006–), memb Governing Body 1986–90, faculty dean 1987–90, dep princ 1989–90, assoc dean Fin Programmes 1993–2004; non-exec dir: M&G Investment Mgmnt 1989–97, M&G Gp plc 1998–99, Hoare Govett Indices Ltd 1991–2011, Majedie Investments plc 1999–2006, Aberforth Smaller Companies Tst 2004–14 (chm 2010–14); juror FTSE Jury of Appeal 2012–; govr Examinations Bd Securities Inst 1994–2002; author of numerous pubns on corporate fin and investment mgmnt in: Jl of Finance, Jl of Business, Jl of Financial Economics, Harvard Business Review, Jl of the Institute of Actuaries, Research in Marketing, Long Range Planning, Financial Analysts Jl, Jl of Applied Corp Finance; memb CBI task force on city-industry relationships 1986–88; memb Exec Ctee Br Acad of Mgmnt 1986–89; memb: Euro Fin Assoc, American Fin Assoc; fell CFA Soc of the UK 2015–; *Books* The Numis Smaller Companies Index (annually, 1987–), Cases in Corporate Finance (1988), Managing Strategic Investment Decisions (1988), Accounting for Brands (1989), Short-Termism on Trial (1990), The Millennium Book: A Century of Investment Returns (2000), Triumph of the Optimists (2002), Global Investment Returns Yearbook (annually, 2001–); *Recreations* gardening; *Style—* Prof Paul Marsh; ✉ London Business School, Regents Park, London NW1 4SA (✆ 020 7000 7000, fax 020 7000 7001, e-mail pmarsh@london.edu)

MARSH, Ron J E; *Educ* BA; *Career* chief exec RPC Gp plc 1989–; *Style—* Ron Marsh, Esq; ✉ RPC Group plc, Sapphire House, Crown Way, Rushden, Northamptonshire NN10 6FB

MARSH, Russell; s of Victor Marsh (d 1979), and Angela Serle, *née* Page; *b* 30 May 1963, Alton, Hants; *Educ* Eggars GS Alton Hants, Basingstoke Technical Coll, Central Sch of Art (BA); *Partner* Marc David Linton (civil partnership 23 July 2011); *Career* casting dir Prada 1995–2012, freelance casting dir 2013–; work incl shows for: Céline, Christopher Kane, Jonathan Saunders, Victoria Beckham, Tommy Hilfiger, Dries van Noten; *Recreations* cinema, gardening, music, travel, walking; *Style—* Russell Marsh, Esq; ✉ Russell Marsh Casting, 29 Charlotte Road, London EC2A 3PB (✆ 020 7739 6811, e-mail russell@russellmarshcasting.com); c/o Beverley Streeter, Streeters London, 53–55 Scrutton Street, London EC2A 4PJ (✆ 020 7253 3949, e-mail beverley@streeterslondon.com, website www.streeterslondon.com)

MARSH, Thérèse Virginia (Terry); *née* Bell; da of late Rear Adm John Anthony Bell, CB, of Taunton, and late Eileen Joan, *née* Woodman; *b* 3 December 1946, Abroath; *Educ* St Joseph's Convent London, Norfolk Catholic HS Virginia, Gumley House Isleworth, Univ of Liverpool (BEd), Univ of Surrey (MSc); *m* 1968 (m dis 1980), Michael Frederick Marsh, s of late Francis Joseph Marsh; 2 da (Suzanna Joan (Mrs Ian Fry) b 14 Nov 1970, Caroline Margaret b 7 Jan 1972); *Career* mathematics teacher Trinity HS Trinidad 1970, princ Ifold Nursery Centre Sussex 1972–76, financial controller Marsh Developments Guildford 1976–77, assoc lectr in statistics Univ of Surrey 1977–78; BBC: researcher BBC Educn 1979–80, dir Playschool 1980–83, prodr BBC Computer Literacy Project BBC Continuing Educn 1984–89, exec prodr BBC School TV 1989–90, head of BBC School TV 1990–92, head bi-media BBC School Progs 1992–95; vice-pres programming Sci-Fi Europe 1995–97, conslt digital media strategy for various cos incl Granada, BBC Technol, Pearson and News Int 1997–; chief exec London Gifted and Talented 2004–05; dir WISE (Women into Sci, Engrg and Construction) 2006–10; memb: Steering Ctee TVYP Edinburgh Int TV Festival 1991–2004, Cncl RTS 2002–07; tstee Winchester Sci Centre and Planetarium 2010– (chair 2014–); FRTS, FRSA, MIET; *Recreations* community theatre, sculpture; *Style—* Ms Terry Marsh; ✉ e-mail terry@terrymarsh.tv, website www.terrymarsh.tv

MARSH, William Renold Arthur; s of Patrick Marsh, of London, and Ann, *née* Shell; *b* 12 March 1962, London; *Educ* Monkton Combe Sch Bath, Univ of Durham (BA), Coll of Law Guildford; *m* 20 June 1992, Dr Belinda Marsh, *née* Dawes; 3 s (Nicholas b 9 Dec 1992, James, Charles (twins) b 22 May 1996); *Career* slr; Osborne Clarke 1985–87 and 1988–90, Linklaters 1987–88; dir: CEDR 1990–2002, Conflict Mgmnt Int 2002–; ind mediator 2002–; memb: Advsy Bd Ukraine Business Mediation Centre, Advsy Bd UK Parliament's All-Pty Parly Gp on Conflict Issues, USA Int Mediator Panel, Ind Standards Cmmn Int Mediation Inst, PIM Sr Mediators; fndr memb Ind Mediators London; former mediation adviser to govts of Russia, Turkey, Romania, Slovakia and Bulgaria, former mediation adviser to EC, former mediation expert World Bank/IFC, mediator ICC Paris, mediation expert UN, mediator CPR Int NY, mediator Singapore Int Mediation Centre; special adviser on peace and reconciliation to Archbishop of Canterbury; former memb Advsy Bd Int Centre for Reconciliation Coventry Catheral; adjunct prof of law Shue Yan Univ Hong Kong; ed Kluwer Mediation Blog; memb Law Soc 1987, accredited mediator CEDR 1992, distinguished fell Int Acad of Mediators; The ADR Practice Guide: Commercial Dispute Resolution (jtly, 1995), Mediators on Mediation (2005); *Recreations* music, fishing, family; *Style—* William Marsh, Esq; ✉ Hurstwood Place, Hurstwood Lane, nr Haywards Heath, West Sussex RH17 7QY (✆ 01444 443848, fax 01444 443847, e-mail wm@billmarsh.co.uk); Conflict Management International, International Dispute Resolution Centre, 70 Fleet Street, London EC4Y 1EU (✆ 020 7917 6040, fax 020 7917 6041, e-mail info@cmi-consulting.com, website www.cmi-consulting.com)

MARSH-EDWARDS, Nadine Cecilia; da of Carlton Marsh-Edwards, and Frances, *née* Greenacre; *b* 27 October 1960, London; *Educ* Goldsmiths Coll Univ of London (BA); *m* 19 Aug 1994, Ronald Bailey; 2 da (Amber b 12 Dec 1995, Saffron b 19 May 1998); *Career* film and TV prodr; memb of Sankofa Film and Video 1983–91; fndr Xenos Pictures 1994, exec prodr Drama Dept BBC Scotland 1999–2006 exec prodr Leopradrama 2006–07, fndr Shimmer Prodns 2007–; films incl: Young Soul Rebels 1991, Bhaji on The Beach 1993, Hijack Stories 2002; memb Bd Film London 2006–; former memb Bd/Panel: Arts Cncl, Production Bd BFI, Advsy Panel Br Screen, Guiding Lights; memb BAFTA; awards incl: Berlin Bear 1989, Critics Prize Cannes Film Festival 1994, Best Short Venice 1997, Best Scottish TV Series BAFTA (for Sea of Souls) 2006; *Recreations* watching films, going to the theatre, travelling, meeting new people and having interesting conversations; *Style—* Ms Nadine Marsh-Edwards; ✉ Shimmer Productions, Unit 9, 34 Waterside, 44–48 Wharf Road, London N1 7UX (✆ 020 7734 3301, e-mail nadine.marsh-edwards@shimmerproductions.co.uk)

MARSHAL, Lyndsey; da of Abdul Baluch, and Sheila Handley; *Educ* Lostock HS, Shena Simon Coll, Welsh Coll of Music and Drama (BA); *Career* actress; *Theatre* Our Country's Good (Manchester Library Theatre) 1997, The Maids (Edinburgh Festival Theatre) 2000, Miss Julie (Hungarian tour) 2000, Top Girls (New Vic Theatre) 2000, Fire Face (Royal Court) 2000, Boston Marriage (Donmar Warehouse and New Ambassadors) 2001 and 2002 (nomination Best Supporting Actress Olivier Awards 2002), Redundant (Royal Court) 2001, Bright (Soho Theatre) 2002, A Midsummer Night's Dream (Bristol Old Vic) 2003 (TMA Award), The Crucible (Crucible Theatre Sheffield) 2004; nomination Best Newcomer Evening Standard Theatre Awards 2001, Best Newcomer Critics Circle Theatre Awards 2002; *Television* That's Not Me 1998, Peak Practice 2000, Midsomer Murders 2001, Sons and Lovers 2002, The Young Visitors 2003, Rome 2005–07, Green 2007, The Shadow in the North 2007, Kiss of Death 2008, 1234 2008, Marple: Murder Is Easy 2008, A Short Stay In Switzerland 2009, Being Human 2010; *Radio* Tess of the D'Urbervilles (BBC Radio 4) 2001, Holiday (BBC Radio 4) 2002, Bunn Eco (BBC Radio 4) 2002, Night Class (BBC Radio 4) 2002, Clear Water (BBC Radio 3) 2002, Before the Flood (BBC Radio 4) 2002, Heredity (BBC Radio 4) 2003, Lessons in Psychic Awareness (BBC Radio 4) 2004; *Film* The Hours 2001, Standing Room Only (short film) 2002, A Gathering Storm 2002, The Calcium Kid 2002, A Lonely War 2002, Frozen 2003, Festival 2004, Snuff Movie 2005; *Recreations* cinema, spending time with friends; *Style—* Miss Lyndsey Marshal

MARSHALL, Alexander John (Alex); QPM (2009); s of Clifford Marshall, and Patricia Marshall; *b* 7 December 1961, Barnet, London; *Educ* Univ of Cambridge (MSt); *Career* Thames Valley Police: asst chief constable 2004–06, acting dep chief constable 2006–07, dep chief constable 2007–08; chief constable Hants Police 2008–; *Style—* Alex Marshall, Esq, QPM; ✉ Hampshire Constabulary HQ, West Hill, Winchester, Hampshire SO22 5DB

MARSHALL, Andrew Paul; s of Michael David Marshall, of Lowestoft, Suffolk, and Doris Constance, *née* Greaves; *b* 27 August 1954; *Educ* Lowestoft Co GS, Borough Rd Coll Isleworth, Inst of Educn London (BEd); *Partner* Mark Laidler (civil partnership 10 April 2009); *Career* freelance screenwriter; contrib Week Ending (BBC Radio) during mid-1970's; memb BAFTA 1996, memb RTS 1996; work with David Renwick, *qv*: 47 episodes of The Burkiss Way (Radio 4); for LWT: End of Part One (Harlequin Award), Whoops Apocalypse (NY International Film and TV Festival Award, RTS Award 1981), Hot Metal (Emmy nomination); for BBC TV: Alexei Sayle's Stuff (3 series) 1989–91 (International Emmy, Broadcasting Press Guild Award, Writers' Guild Award), If You See God, Tell Him; others incl: The Steam Video Company (Thames), Whoops Apocalypse (film, ITC), Wilt (film, Rank/LWT); stage play Angry Old Men 1995; as solo writer: Sob Sisters (CTV) 1989, several episodes Poirot (LWT) 1991, 2point4 children (BBC, 8 series) 1990–99, Health & Efficiency (BBC) 1993–94, DAD (BBC) 1997–2000, Strange 2002–03 (BBC); various TV awards over many years; *Books* The Burkiss Way, Whoops Apocalypse; *Recreations* feature animation, architecture, modern art, classic television; *Clubs* Hospital; *Style—* Andrew Marshall, Esq; ✉ c/o Marc Berlin, Berlin Associates, 7 Tylers Gate, London SE1 3HX (✆ 020 7836 1112)

MARSHALL, Catriona Frances; da of Dr David Land, of Glasgow, and Moira McLean, *née* O'Neill; *b* 1 March 1967, Glasgow; *Educ* Univ of Dundee (LLB); *m* 3 Jan 2003, Mike Marshall; *Career* Mars Confectionery 1993–95, Asda Stores 1995–2003, trading and mktg dir Pets at Home 2003–10, ceo Hobbycraft 2011–; fndr Transforming Lives Charitable Fndn; *Recreations* tennis, running club, cycling events; *Style—* Mrs Catriona Marshall; ✉ Hobbycraft Trading Limited, 7 Enterprise Way, Aviation Park, Bournemouth International Airport, Christchurch, Dorset BH23 6HG (e-mail catriona.marshall@hobbycraft.co.uk)

MARSHALL, Prof Gordon; CBE (2003); *b* 20 June 1952; *Educ* Univ of Stirling (BA), Univ of Oxford (DPhil); *Career* research fell in sociology Nuffield Coll Oxford 1977–78, lectr in sociology Univ of Essex 1978–88 (sr lectr 1988–90), prof of sociology Univ of Bath 1990–93, official fell Nuffield Coll Oxford 1993–2000, chief exec ESRC 2000–02, vice-chllr Univ of Reading 2003–11, dir Leverhulme Tst 2011–; chm Higher Educn Statistics Agency (HESA) 2007–11; visiting prof: Univ of Uppsala 1989, Central European Univ Prague 1993, Univ of Stockholm 1996; Morris Ginsberg Fellowship in Sociology LSE 1985, Sir Norman Chester Visiting Fellowship Nuffield Coll Oxford 1991, Br Acad/Leverhulme Tst

Sr Research Fellowship 1992; Hon DUniv Stirling, Hon LLD Univ of Reading 2012; memb: Acad of Social Sciences 2000, Euro Acad of Sociology 2001, Royal Norwegian Soc for Sciences and Letters 2001; FBA 2000; *Publications* Presbyteries and Profits: Calvinism and the Development of Capitalism in Scotland, 1560–1707 (1980), In Search of the Spirit of Capitalism (1982), Social Class in Modern Britain (1988), In Praise of Sociology (1990), The Oxford Dictionary of Sociology (1994), Against the Odds? Social Class and Social Justice in Industrial Societies (1997), Repositioning Class: Social Inequality in Industrial Societies (1997); numerous book chapters and articles in jls; *Style—* Prof Gordon Marshall, CBE; ✉ The Leverhulme Trust, 1 Pemberton Row, London EC4A 3BG (☎ 020 7042 9877, fax 020 7042 9889, e-mail gmarshall@leverhulme.ac.uk)

MARSHALL, Prof (Ian) Howard; s of Ernest Ewart Marshall (d 1977), and Ethel, *née* Curran; *b* 12 January 1934; *Educ* Dumfries Acad, Aberdeen GS, Univ of Aberdeen (MA, BD, PhD), Univ of Cambridge (BA), Univ of Göttingen; *m* 1, 25 March 1961, Joyce Elizabeth (d 1996), da of Frederick John Proudfoot (d 1971); 1 s (Neil), 3 da (Morag, Aileen, Alison); m 2, 25 July 2011, Maureen Wing Sheung, da of Lim Chen Yeung (d 1978); *Career* asst tutor Didsbury Coll Bristol 1960–62, methodist min Darlington 1962–64; Univ of Aberdeen: lectr 1964–70, sr lectr 1970–77, reader 1977–79, prof 1979–99, dean Faculty of Divinity 1981–84, head Dept of Divinity with Religious Studies 1996–98, hon res prof of New Testament 1999–2007, prof emeritus 2007–; Hon DD Asbury 1996; *Books* Eschatology and the Parables (1963, 1978), Pocket Guide to Christian Beliefs (1963, 1978, 1989), The Work of Christ (1969, 1994), Kept by the Power of God (1969, 1975, 1995), Luke: Historian and Theologian (1970, 1989), The Origins of New Testament Christology (1976), New Testament Interpretation (ed 1977, 1979), The Gospel of Luke (New International Greek Testament Commentary, 1978), I Believe in the Historical Jesus (1977, 2002), The Epistles of John (New International Commentary on the New Testament, 1978), Acts (Tyndale NT Commentaries, 1980), Last Supper and Lord's Supper (1980), Biblical Inspiration (1982, 1995), 1 and 2 Thessalonians (New Century Bible, 1983), Christian Experience in Theology and Life (ed, 1988), Jesus The Saviour (1990), I Peter (IVP New Testament Commentary Series, 1991), The Theology of the Shorter Pauline Letters (with K P Donfried, 1992), The Acts of the Apostles (New Testament Guides, 1992), The Epistle to the Philippians (1993), Witness to the Gospel (ed with D Peterson, 1998), The Pastoral Epistles (1999), Moulton and Geden: Concordance to the Greek New Testament (ed, 2002), Exploring the New Testament, Volume 2: The Letters and Revelation (with S Travis and I Paul, 2002), Beyond the Bible (2004), New Testament Theology (2004), Aspects of the Atonement (2007), A Concise New Testament Theology (2008); *Recreations* reading, walking, gardening, music; *Style—* Prof I Howard Marshall

MARSHALL, Prof Mary Tara; OBE (1997); da of Percy Johnson Marshall, and April Johnson Marshall (d 1999); *b* 13 June 1945, Darjeeling, India; *Educ* Univ of Edinburgh (MA), LSE (Dip Social Admin), Univ of Liverpool (Dip Applied Social Studies); *Partner* Ronald Scott Smith; *Career* child care offr London Borough of Lambeth 1967–69, social worker Liverpool Personal Service Soc 1970–74, research project organiser Age Concern Liverpool 1974–75, lectr in applied social studies Univ of Liverpool 1975–83, dir Age Concern Scotland 1983–89, dir Dementia Services Devpt Centre Univ of Stirling 1989–2005, now emeritus prof; sessional inspr Scottish Care Inspectorate (formerly Scottish Social Work Inspection Agency) until 2016, currently sr conslt HammondCare; hon prof Univ of Edinburgh 2016–19; memb 21st Century Social Work Ctee 2004–06; former chair: Liverpool Housing Tst, Liverpool Cncl for Voluntary Services Welfare Orgns Ctee, Assoc of Chief Offrs of Scottish Voluntary Orgns, Exec Ctee Br Soc of Gerontology; former memb: Advsy Panel Centre for Policy on Ageing (also former govr), Royal Cmmn on Long Term Care of the Elderly, Modernisation Bd NHS in Scotland, Nat Care Standards Ctee, Bd Edinvar Housing Assoc; memb Bd Faith in Older People 2011–; Br Geriatrics Soc Medal for the Relief of Suffering 2008, Lifetime Achievement Award Faculty of Old Age Psychiatry RCPsych 2010; Hon DEd Queen Margaret UC Edinburgh, Hon DSc Univ of Edinburgh 2004, DUniv Stirling 2006; memb Br Assoc of Social Workers (BASW) 1971 (sometime memb Health and Handicap Advsy Panel); AcSS 2002, FRSE 2003; *Publications* Social Work in Action (jt ed, 1979), Teamwork: For and Against (jt ed, 1979), Loss (jt ed, 1983), Social Work with Old People (1983, 4 edn 2006), New Services for Old People (jtly, 1983), Social Work in the Eighties (jt ed, 1984), Guidelines for Social Workers Working with People with Dementia and their Carers (ed, 1988), Working with Dementia. Guidelines for Professionals (ed, 1990), Effective Management (jt ed, 1991), Dementia: New Skills for Social Workers (jt ed, 1993), Dementia Care (jtly, 1994), Social Work with Old People (jt ed, 1996), 'I Can't Place This Place At All': Working with People with Dementia and their Carers (1996), The State of Art in Dementia Care (ed, 1997), Past Trauma in Late Life: European Perspectives on Therapeutic Work with Older People (jt ed, 1997), Dementia and Technology (1997), Design for Dementia (jt ed, 1998), Facing our Futures: Discrimination in Later Life (jtly, 1998), Keeping in Touch: Ethical Dimensions (1998), A Guide to Using Technology within Dementia Care (ed, 2000), Food, Glorious Food, Perspectives on Food and Dementia (ed, 2003), Perspectives on Rehabilitation and Dementia (ed, 2005), Dementia: walking nor wandering (jtly, 2006), Social Work and People with Dementia (jtly, 2006), Time for Dementia (jt ed, 2010), Designing Balconies, Roof Terraces and Roof Gardens for People with Dementia (2010), Transforming the Quality of Life for People with Dementia through Contact with Nature (jt ed, 2011), Designing Mental Health Units for Older People (2014), Creating Culturally Appropriate Outside Spaces and Experiences for People with Dementia (with J Gilhard, 2014); author of numerous book chapters, articles, reports and published papers; *Recreations* bird watching, photography; *Clubs* Drumsheugh Baths; *Style—* Prof Mary Marshall, OBE; ✉ 24 Buckingham Terrace, Edinburgh EH4 3AE (☎ 0131 343 1732, e-mail mary@marymarshall7.wanadoo.co.uk)

MARSHALL, Sir Michael John; kt (2010), CBE (1999), DL (Cambs 1989); s of Sir Arthur Gregory George Marshall, OBE, DL (d 2007), and Rosemary Wynford, *née* Dimsdale (d 1988); *b* 27 January 1932; *Educ* Eton, Jesus Coll Cambridge (MA, Rowing blue, rep GB in European Championships 1954); *m* 1, 1960 (m dis 1977), Bridget Wykham Pollock; 2 s, 2 da; m 2, 1979, Sibyl Mary Walkinshaw, *née* Hutton; 2 step s; *Career* RAF pilot 1950–52; Marshall of Cambridge (Engineering) Ltd: joined 1955, dep chm and md 1964–90; chm and chief exec Marshall of Cambridge (Holdings) Ltd 1989–2012 (chm 2012–); dir Eastern Electricity Bd 1971–77; chm BL Cars Distributor Cncl 1977 and 1983 (memb 1975–84); vice-pres: IMI 1980–, Engrg Employers Fedn 1993–2003; chm Cambs Manpower Ctee 1980–83, chm Cambridge Olympic Appeal 1984, vice-chm Cambs Youth Involvement Ctee Silver Jubilee Fund 1977–78, memb Ely Cathedral Restoration Appeal Co Ctee 1987–2011 (vice-patron 2012–), pres Cambridge Soc for the Blind 1989–92, chm Prince's Tsts' Cambs Appeal Ctee 1991–92, pres Cambridge 99 Rowing Club 1996–2003, pres Addenbrooke's Charitable Tst 2000–, memb Bd Greater Cambridge Partnership 2002–11; chm: Civilian Ctee 104 (City of Cambridge) Sqdn ATC 1975–2013, Beds and Cambs Wing ATC 1987–2003 (hon pres 2008–); memb: Air Cadet Cncl 1994–2007, Cncl Air League 1995–2009 (chm 1998–2003, pres 2004–09, companion 2012–); hon vice-patron Royal Int Air Tattoo 2003–; Hon Air Cdre No 2623 (East Anglian) Sqdn RAuxAF 2003–; hon visiting prof Anglia Ruskin Univ 2009–11; chm Ct of Benefactors Cncl of Reference E Anglian Air Ambulance 2006–11, hon pres Cambridge Chariots of Fire Race 2007–, ambass World Land Tst 2009–, memb Prince's Charities Cncl 2009–; High Sheriff Cambs 1988–89, Vice Lord-Lt Cambs 1992–2006; Freeman City of London 1988, Liveryman Hon Co of Air Pilots (formerly Guild of Air Pilots and Air Navigators) 1989–; Hon DUniv Anglia Ruskin 2001, Hon DSc Kingston Univ 2014; fell Order of St Radegund Jesus Coll Cambridge 2007–; IEng, Licentiate Automobile Engr (LAE), FRAeS, FRSA, FIMI, CIMgt, FInstD; *Recreations* flying, friends, countryside, reading, lode walking; *Clubs* RAF, Hawks' (Cambridge), Air Squadron, Cambridge County, Leander (Henley-on-Thames), Eton Vickings; *Style—* Sir Michael Marshall, CBE, DL; ✉ Marshall of Cambridge (Holdings) Ltd, The Airport, Cambridge CB5 8RX (☎ 01223 373245/373825)

MARSHALL, Nigel Bernard Dickenson; s of Norman Dickenson Marshall (d 1958), of Lea, Lincs, and (Gertrude) Olga, *née* Pumfrey (d 1991); *b* 9 April 1935; *Educ* Rugby, Queens' Coll Cambridge (MA, LLM); *Career* slr Herbert Smith & Co London 1961–63; ptnr: Underwood and Co London 1964–90, Miller and Co Cambridge 1969–88; sole practitioner 1990–2006; clerk: St Edward's Parochial Charity Cambridge 1967–90, The Great St Mary's Charity Cambridge 1967–71, The Wray Jackenett Merrill & Elie Charity Cambridge 1971–72; sec Cambridge and Dist Trade Protection Assoc 1967–86; *Recreations* gardening, collecting; *Clubs* Boodle's, Oxford and Cambridge, Pitt (Cambridge), City Univ, Lansdowne; *Style—* Nigel Marshall, Esq; ✉ The Old Rectory, Lea, Gainsborough, Lincolnshire DN21 5JA

MARSHALL, Peter Joseph; s of Steve Marshall (d 1977), and Vera Marshall (d 2004); *b* 28 July 1952, Rhyl, Denbighshire; *Educ* Rhyl GS, De La Salle Coll Jersey, Birmingham Poly; *m* 3 Nov 1973, Carole, *née* McWhinney; 1 da, 1 s; *Career* student reporter Jersey Evening Post 1971–73, reporter Birkenhead News 1973–75, political ed Radio City 1975–78, reporter The World at One and The World This Weekend PM (BBC Radio 4) 1979–85, reporter BBC TV current affairs 1985–87, corr BBC Newsnight 1987–2013; freelance journalist and broadcaster 2013–; TV and radio documentaries, newspaper and magazine articles; reported from Europe, Asia, Africa, N and S America; covered over a dozen US presidential and congressional elections; *Recreations* football (Liverpool FC), music (Beatles, Bob Dylan, Super Furry Animals); *Clubs* Somali (Liverpool), Cadillac (Washington DC); *Style—* Peter Marshall, Esq

MARSHALL, Prof Robin; s of Robert Marshall (d 1944), and Grace Eileen, *née* Ryder (d 1999); *b* 5 January 1940; *Educ* Ermysted's GS Skipton, Univ of Manchester (BSc, PhD); *m* (m dis); 2 s, 1 da; *Career* DSIR fellowship 1965–67, research fellowship German Elektron Synchrotron DESY 1967–68, research scientist MIT 1968–70, research fellowship and princ scientific offr Daresbury 1970–78, princ scientific offr rising to sr princ Rutherford Appleton Lab 1978–1992, prof of physics Univ of Manchester 1992–; author of many scientific papers and books; dir and co sec Frontiers Science and Television Ltd; Max Born Medal and Prize German Physical Soc 1997; FRS 1995; *Recreations* writing and publishing books; *Style—* Prof Robin Marshall; ✉ Department of Physics and Astronomy, University of Manchester, Manchester M13 9PL

MARSHALL, Dr Rosalind Kay; da of Arthur Frederick Kay Robertson Marshall (d 1982), and Nan, *née* Duncan (d 1997); *Educ* Kirkcaldy HS, Univ of Edinburgh (MA, PhD); *Career* asst ed Dictionary of the Older Scottish Tongue 1970–71, freelance archivist 1971–73, head of archive Scottish Nat Portrait Gallery 1973–99, writer of historical books and articles 1973–; research assoc Oxford DNB 1998–; memb Cncl Scottish Record Soc 1996– (chm 2010–), memb Int Ctee Saltire Soc 1997–2004, chm Virtual Hamilton Palace Tst 2008– (vice-chm 2004–08); hon historian Edinburgh Incorporation of Bonnetmakers 2007–; FRSL 1974, FSA Scot 1983, FRSA 2000; *Awards* Sr Dobson Morpeth Prize in Scottish History 1966, Hume Brown Prize in Scottish History 1970, Jeremiah Dalziel Prize 1970, New Writing Award Scottish Arts Cncl 1974, R B K Stevenson Award Soc of Antiquaries of Scotland 1997; *Publications* The Days of Duchess Anne: Life in the Household of the Duchess of Hamilton, 1656–1716 (1973, new edn 2000), Mary of Guise (1977), Virgins and Viragos: A History of Women in Scotland 1080–1980 (1983), Queen of Scots (1986), Bonnie Prince Charlie (1988), Henrietta Maria: The Intrepid Queen (1990), Elizabeth I (1991), Mary I (1993), The Winter Queen (1998), John Knox (2000), Ruin and Restoration: St Mary's Church, Haddington (2001), Mary of Guise (2001), Scottish Queens 1034–1714 (2003), Queen Mary's Women (2006), St Giles': The Dramatic Story of a Great Church and its People (2009), Mary, Queen of Scots: Truth or Lies (2010), A Guide to the Memorials in St Giles' Cathedral Edinburgh (2011), Columba's Iona: A New History (2013), Mary, Queen of Scots: In my end is my beginning (2013); author of exhbn catalogues, numerous scholarly articles and reviews, incl more than 50 articles in Oxford Dictionary of National Biography (2004); *Recreations* gardening, reading, listening to music, cats; *Style—* Dr Rosalind K Marshall

M

MARSHALL, Steven; s of Victor Marshall (d 1992), and Kathleen Sarah, *née* Higginson (d 2010); *b* 11 February 1957, Isleworth, Middx; *Educ* Isleworth GS; *Career* BOC Gp plc 1977–82, Black & Decker Ltd 1982–84, Burton Gp plc 1984–87, dep finance dir and co sec Parkdale Holdings plc 1987–89, successively head of worldwide planning and analysis, gp investor rels dir and finance dir European Wines and Spirits Div Grand Metropolitan plc 1989–95, gp finance dir then gp chief exec Thorn plc 1995–99, gp finance dir then gp chief exec Railtrack Gp plc 1999–2002, exec chm Queens' Moat Houses plc 2003–04; non-exec chm: Delta plc 2005–10 (non-exec dir 2004–), Torex Retail plc 2007–, Balfour Beatty plc 2008–15 (exec chm 2014, non-exec dir 2004–8), Wincanton plc 2012–, Biffa Waste Mgmnt Ltd 2013–; non-exec dir: Southern Water plc 2005–10, Halma plc 2010–14; FCMA, CGMA, CCMI, memb CIMA Cncl 2013–; *Recreations* African travel and wildlife conservation, natural history; *Style—* Steven Marshall, Esq; ✉ Wincanton plc, Metheun Business Park, Chippenham, Wiltshire SN14 0WT (☎ 01249 710000, e-mail smatvh@gmail.com)

MARSHALL, Dr William Jasper; s of Edward Alwin Marshall (d 1986), of Tenterden, Kent, and Lorna Alice, *née* Jeffery (d 1988), of Bromley, Kent; *b* 1 April 1944; *Educ* St Dunstan's Coll, St Catherine's Coll Oxford (MA), Univ of London (PhD, MB BS, MSc); *m* 1 (m dis 1991), Anne Katharine Stewart; 2 da (Eleanor Ruth b 24 Nov 1970, Harriet Lorna Mary b 13 Aug 1973); m 2, Wendy Rowena French, *née* Morgan-Jones; *Career* sr lectr King's Coll Sch of Med and Dentistry 1980–98, reader and hon conslt in clinical biochemistry Guy's King's and St Thomas' Sch of Med 1998–2004 (chm MB BS Bd 1998–2004, sub-dean examinations), emeritus reader in clinical biochemistry KCL 2004–, conslt clinical biochemist and clinical dir of pathology The London Clinic; RCPath: asst registrar 1996–98, dir of pubns 1997–2001, treas 1998–2003; hon sec Inst of Biology 2007–09 (President's Medal 2009), hon treas Soc of Biology 2009–13; hon memb Assoc of Clinical Biochemists and Lab Medicine 2005 (chm Publications Ctee 1996–99, dir of finance 2012–); memb: BMA, Soc of Authors (chm Med Writers' Gp 1994–95 and 2008–09); Coll Medal RCPath 2004, IFCC/Beckman Coulter Award for distinguished contribution in educn 2005; FRCP 1993 (MRCP 1979), FRCPath 1992 (MRCPath 1980), FRCPEd 1996, FRSB 2009 (FIBiol 1999), FRSC 2009, FLS 2013; *Books* Clinical Chemistry (1988, 8 edn jtly, 2016), Clinical Chemistry, an Illustrated Outline (1991), Intensive Care and Clinical Biochemistry (jtly, 1994), Clinical Biochemistry: Metabolic and Clinical Aspects (jtly, 1995, 3 edn 2014), Primary Care and Laboratory Medicine (jtly, 1996), Nutrition and Laboratory Medicine (jtly, 2007), Clinical Cases in Laboratory Medicine (jtly, 2014); *Recreations* being outside, writing, gardening, visiting war graves; *Clubs* RSM; *Style—* Dr William Marshall; ✉ 1 Alleyn Crescent, London SE21 8BN (☎ 020 8761 3180, e-mail 1wjmarshall@doctors.net.uk)

MARSHALL-ANDREWS, Robert Graham; QC (1987); s of Robin Marshall-Andrews (d 1986), and Eileen Norah Marshall-Andrews (d 1996); *b* 10 April 1944, London; *Educ* Mill Hill Sch, Univ of Bristol (LLB); *m* Gillian Diana; 1 da (Laura b 1971), 1 s (Tom b 1973); *Career* called to the Bar Gray's Inn 1967 (bencher 1996); MP (Lab) Medway 1997–2010 (Parly candidate (Lab) Medway 1992); dep chair Theatre Cncl; tstee: George Adamson

Wildlife Tst, Geffrye Museum; former chm Grey Court Sch; fndr Old Testament Profits; winner Observer Mace Nat Debating Competition; *Books* Palace of Wisdom (novel, 1989), A Man Without Guilt (novel, 2002), Off Message (political memoir); *Recreations* sport, writing, reading, walking; *Clubs* Druidston (Pembrokeshire), Garrick; *Style*— Robert Marshall-Andrews, Esq, QC; ✉ Carmelite Chambers, 9 Carmelite Street, London EC4Y 0DR (☎ 020 7936 6300, fax 020 7936 6301)

MARSLAND, Prof David; s of Ernest Marsland (d 1991), of Leavesden Green, Herts, and Fay, *née* Savoury (d 1993); *b* 3 February 1939; *Educ* Watford GS, Christ's Coll Cambridge (scholar, BA, MA), LSE, Brunel Univ (PhD); *m* Dr Athena Leoussi-Marsland; 4 da; *Career* Dept of Sociology Brunel Univ 1964–88 (lectr, sr lectr, dir postgrad studies, prof assoc), prof of social res West London Inst of Higher Educn 1989–95, prof of social scis Brunel Univ 1995–2004, prof of sociology Univ of Buckingham 2004–; asst dir The Social Affairs Unit London 1981–89; dir Centre for Evaluation Research (CER) 1989–2004; special advsr to Parly Social Security Ctee 1993–95; memb: Social Scis Bd UNESCO 1983–86, Social Scis Ctee CNAA 1987–92; formerly memb EC Social Res Assoc and hon gen sec Br Sociological Assoc; first Thatcher Award winner for contribs to analysis of freedom 1991; memb: BSA 1964, SRA 1985; MIMgt 1987, FRSH 1990; *Books* Seeds of Bankruptcy (1988), Cradle to Grave (1989), Understanding Youth (1993), Work and Employment (1994), Self-Reliance (1995), Welfare or Welfare State? (1996); *Recreations* reading and writing poetry, music, theatre; *Style*— Prof David Marsland; ✉ University of Buckingham, Buckingham MK18 1EG (☎ 020 8572 7398)

MARSLEN-WILSON, Prof William David; s of David William Marslen-Wilson (d 1983), and Pera, *née* Funk (d 2005); *b* 5 June 1945; *Educ* St John's Coll Oxford (BA), MIT (PhD); *m* 1982, Lorraine Komisarjevsky Tyler; 2 da (Eliza and Lydia), 1 s (Jack); *Career* asst prof Dept of Behavioural Sciences Univ of Chicago 1973–78, scientific assoc Max-Planck-Institut für Psycholinguistik Nijmegen 1977–82, univ lectr Dept of Experimental Psychology Univ of Cambridge 1982–84, co-dir Max-Plank-Institut für Psycholinguistik Nijmegen 1985–87, sr scientist MRC Applied Psychology Unit Cambridge 1987–90, prof of psychology Birkbeck Coll London 1990–97, dir MRC Cognition and Brain Sciences Unit Cambridge 1997–, hon prof of language and cognition Univ of Cambridge 2002–; Sloan fell MIT 1980–81, visiting prof Univ of Southern Calif LA 1989–90, visiting prof Univ of Arizona 1994–95, hon dir Beijing Normal Univ 1995–, fell Birkbeck Coll London 2000–, fell Wolfson Coll Cambridge 2000–, Wei Lan visiting prof Chinese Univ of Hong Kong 2000; pres Experimental Psychology Soc 2008–10; fell Academia Europaea 1996, FBA 1996; *Publications* author of numerous articles in learned jls, conference proceedings and book chapters; *Style*— Prof William Marslen-Wilson, FBA; ✉ Medical Research Council, 15 Chaucer Road, Cambridge CB2 7EF (☎ 01223 355294, fax 01223 500250, e-mail william.marslen-wilson@mrc-cbu.cam.ac.uk)

MARSON, His Hon Judge Geoffrey Charles; QC (1997); *Career* called to the Bar Gray's Inn 1975; recorder 1995–2005 (asst recorder 1991–95), circuit judge (North Eastern Circuit) 2005–; *Style*— His Hon Judge Marson, QC; ✉ Leeds Combined Court Centre, 1 Oxford Row, Leeds LS1 3BG

MARSTON, (Jeffery) Adrian Priestley; s of Maj J E Marston, DSO, MC (d 1945), and Doreen, *née* Norris (d 1980); *b* 15 December 1927; *Educ* Marlborough, Magdalen Coll Oxford (MA, DM, MCh), St Thomas' Hosp Med Sch London; *m* 17 July 1951, Sylvie Colin; 1 da (Joanna b 24 Sept 1954), 2 s (John b 24 Feb 1960, Nicholas, *qv*, b 4 Jan 1963); *Career* Nat Serv Lt RAMC, then Capt 1954–57; surgical registrar and sr registrar St Thomas' Hosp 1960–65, sr lectr in surgery Middx Hosp Medical Sch (later Faculty of Clinical Science UCL) 1965–92; conslt surgn: The Middx Hosp 1968–92, Royal Northern Hosp 1970–85, UCH 1985–92; vice-pres RCS 1991–92, chm Senate of RCS Euro Ctee, memb Jt Conslts Ctee 1993–96; RSM: hon treas 1993–95, dean 1995–98, vice-pres 1998–2000; pres: Vascular Surgical Soc of GB and I 1985, Assoc of Surgns of GB and I 1986; memb d'honneur Association Française de Chirurgie 1986, socio de honor Asociación Espanola de Cirujanos 1987; Hon MD Nice 1986; FRCS 1958; Chevalier de l'Ordre National du Mérite de France; *Publications* Intestinal Ischaemia (1976), Contemporary Operative Surgery (1979), Visceral Artery Reconstruction (1986), Splanchnic Ischemia and Multiple Organ Failure (1989), Hamilton Bailey, a Surgeon's Life (1999), London Surprises (jtly, 2006); author of numerous papers on vascular surgery and gastroenterology; *Recreations* literature, languages, travel, music; *Clubs* Hurlingham; *Style*— Adrian Marston, Esq, FRCS; ✉ 4 Hereford Square, London SW7 4TS (☎ 020 7373 7678, e-mail adrimar@btinternet.com)

MARSTON, John James; MBE (2011); s of John Wilfred Marston (d 1984), and Elsie, *née* Shepherd (d 1978); *b* 19 February 1935, London; *Educ* Rugby, UMIST (BSc, Rugby maroon); *m* 29 Feb 1964, Mette; 1 da (Nicola Jane b 19 May 1968), 1 s (Andrew John b 26 March 1970); *Career* Costain: site engr 1957, runway engr Maldive Is 1958–59, special projects design engr 1960–61, site mangr 1961; W J Marston & Sons Ltd (family firm): joined as contracts mangr 1961, dir 1971, md 1978; chm: W J Marston Holdings Ltd 1980–2000, Marston Properties Holdings Ltd 2000–, Marston Hotel Holdings Ltd 2000–06; memb Cncl Nat Fedn of Building Trade Employees (chm Central and City of London 1976); memb Governing Body/ Corporation Hammersmith & W London Coll of FE 1970–2012, chm of govrs Granard Primary Sch 2003–12 (govr 1996–2014), church warden St Margaret's Church Putney 2007–13; MICE 1968, CEng 1990; *Recreations* sailing (skippered own yacht to Russia and back 1996, yacht deliveries UK to Majorca and France to Turkey, Atlantic ARC 2003), swimming; *Clubs* Shirley Wanderers RFC (tstee, chm 1976–86, pres 1996–99), Royal Harwich Yacht; *Style*— John Marston, MBE; ✉ Marston Properties Holdings Limited, 1 Mills Yard, London SW6 3AQ (☎ 020 7736 7133, fax 020 7731 8412, e-mail nicky@marstonproperties.co.uk)

MARSTON, Nicholas (Nick); s of (Jeffrey) Adrian Priestley Marston, *qv*, and Sylvie, *née* Colin; *b* 4 January 1963; *Educ* Westminster, Univ of Durham; *m* 1991, Rosalind Ellerton; *Career* literary and film agent A P Watt Ltd 1988–97, md Media Div Curtis Brown Gp Ltd 1997– (owning ptnr 2001–, chm 2012–); dir Touchpaper Television Ltd 2001–, md Cuba Pictures Ltd 2003–; exec prodr: MOJO 1997, Jonathan Strange & Mr Norrell (Cuba Pictures/BBC1) 2014, London Road (Cuba Pictures/NT/BBC Films/BFI) 2014, Coalition (Cuba Pictures/Channel 4) 2015 (Best Single Film RTS Awards), The Ones Below (Cuba Pictures/BBC Films) 2015; prodr: Boy A (Cuba Pictures/Channel 4) 2007 (4 BAFTA Awards), Broken (Cuba Pictures/BBC Films) 2012 (Grand Prix Odess Film Festival 2012, Best Film Br Independent Film Award 2012); course tutor ARISTA story ed workshop 1999–, tutor Guardian Masterclass 2012 and 2013; judge RTS Awards 1996 and 2000; memb BAFTA 1999–, Euro Film Acad 1999–; winner Vogue talent contest 1988; *Recreations* theatre, film, football, piano, German, tennis; *Clubs* Soho House; *Style*— Nick Marston, Esq; ✉ 57 Bromfelde Road, London SW4 6PP (☎ 020 7622 8851); Curtis Brown Group Ltd, Haymarket House, 28/29 Haymarket, London SW1Y 4SP (☎ 020 7393 4450, mobile 07768 356970, fax 020 7396 0110, e-mail nick@curtisbrown.co.uk)

MARTEN, (Richard) Hedley Westwood; s of Capt Lewis Westwood Marten, RA (ka 1944), and Kathleen, *née* Ogston (d 1988); n of Rt Hon Sir Neil Marten, MP, Min for Overseas Devpt 1979–83, gn of Sir Henry Marten, KCVO, Provost of Eton and personal tutor to HM The Queen, and descendant of Sir Henry Marten, republican statesman and signatory to the death warrant of Charles I; *b* 24 January 1943; *Educ* Winchester, Magdalene Coll Cambridge (MA); *m* 1971 (m dis 1983), Fiona Mary, da of George William Carter Sinclair, and sis of Sir Clive Sinclair, *qv*; 1 da (Laura b 19 April 1973), 2 s (Benedict b 9 Sept 1976, Alexander b 24 July 1978); *Career* called to the Bar Lincoln's Inn 1966 (bencher 2000); in practice Chancery Bar 1968–, Chancery Bar rep Bar Cncl 1990–95, memb Inst 1995–, head of chambers 1995–, pres Inst 2006; tstee King's Lynn Arts Centre Tst 2011–; *Publications* Contentious Probate Claims (co-author, 2003); *Recreations* playing the piano, exploring Greek islands, playing with my grandchildren; *Clubs* Brooks's, Butterflies Cricket, Academy; *Style*— Hedley Marten, Esq; ✉ Ingoldisthorpe Hall, King's Lynn, Norfolk PE31 6PF; Radcliffe Chambers, 11 New Square, Lincoln's Inn, London WC2A 3QB (☎ 020 7831 0081, fax 020 7405 2560)

MARTIN, Prof Benjamin Raymond (Ben); s of Adrian Sidney Martin, MBE, of Budleigh Salterton, Devon, and Joan Dorothy, *née* Mingo; *b* 9 August 1952, Fenny Bridges, Devon; *Educ* Blundell's, Churchill Coll Cambridge (Kitchener scholar, MA), Univ of Manchester (MSc, Rowing maroon); *m* 7 July 1973, Valerie Ann Martin, *qv*, da of William Herbert Bennett; 2 s (Paul Frederick b 3 June 1980, David Christopher b 10 Sept 1985), 1 da (Sarah Ann b 5 Dec 1982); *Career* VSO sci teacher Nigeria 1973–75; SPRU – Sci and Technology Policy Research: res fell 1978, lectr 1983, sr fell 1986, sr lectr 1990, prof 1996, dir 1997–2004; visiting lectr Imperial Coll London 1983–84, visiting fell Max-Planck-Inst Für Gesellschaftsforschung Cologne 1987, visiting prof Centre for Advanced Study Norwegian Acad of Scis 2007–08, visiting scholar Univ of Iceland 2009–12, assoc fell Centre for Science and Policy Univ of Cambridge 2010–, sr visiting fell Centre for Business Research Judge Business Sch Univ of Cambridge 2011–; memb: Steering Gp UK Technology Foresight Prog 1993–2000, Senate Univ of Sussex 1997–2004 (memb Cncl 1997–2002), Tech Opportunities Panel (TOP) EPSRC 2001–04, Royal Soc Fruits of Curiosity Advsy Gp 2009–10; specialist advsr House of Lords Select Ctee on Science and Technol 2009–10; ed Research Policy 2004–; Derek de Solla Price medal for sci studies 1997; *Publications* Foresight in Science (with J Irvine, 1984), Research Foresight (with J Irvine, 1989), Investing in the Future (with J Irvine and P A Isard, 1990), Equipping Science for the 21st Century (with J Irvine et al, 1997), The Political Economy of Science, Technology and Innovation (with A Nightingale, 2000), Creative Knowledge Environments (with S Hemlin and C M Allwood, 2004), Creativity and Leadership in Science, Technology and Innovation (with S Hemlin, C M Allwood and M M Mumford, 2013), The Future of Innovation Studies (with J Fagerberg and E S Andersen, 2013), The Triple Challenge for Europe: Economic Development, Climate Change and Governance (with J Fagererg and S Laestadius, 2015); *Recreations* indoor rowing (tenth place World Indoor Rowing Championships Boston 1998), skiing, reading, DIY, gardening, family – balancing demands of two professional careers and three children!; *Style*— Prof Ben Martin; ✉ 16 Longcroft Avenue, Banstead, Surrey SM7 3AE; SPRU – Science Policy Research Unit, University of Sussex, Falmer, Brighton BN1 9SL (☎ 01273 873562, e-mail b.martin@sussex.ac.uk)

MARTIN, Bonita Elizabeth (Bonnie); da of James William Martin, of London, and Barbara Margaret, *née* Walker; *b* 18 February 1959, Chiswick, London; *Educ* Lady Eleanor Holles Sch for Girls, Univ of Reading (BA), Univ of Nottingham, Coll of Law Guildford; *partner* John Grist-Taylor; 2 s (George Zachery, Oscar William); *Career* admitted slr 1985; articled clerk then asst slr Lewis Silkin 1983–87, asst slr Crossman Block & Keith 1987–90, ptnr Masons (latterly Pinsent Masons) 1992–2005 (asst slr 1990–92), ptnr Clarke Willmott 2005– (memb Bd 2011–); lectures to RICS, ARBRIX and Univ of Bristol; memb: ARBRIX, Town and Country Planning Assoc, Property Litigation Assoc, Bristol Property Agents Assoc, Nat Tst, WWF, RHS; memb Law Soc 1985; *Recreations* wine (WSET diploma in wine – pass with merit), walking, riding, films, skiing; *Style*— Miss Bonnie Martin; ✉ Clarke Willmott, 1 Georges Square, Bath Street, Bristol BS1 6BA (☎ 0845 209 1416, fax 0117 917 5594, e-mail bonnie.martin@clarkewillmott.com)

MARTIN, Charles David Zelenka; s of John Martin, and Joy Martin; *b* 2 February 1961, London; *Educ* Merchant Taylors', Univ of Bristol (LLB); *m* 1 Oct 1988, Sarah, *née* Wilson; 3 s (Ben b 22 Dec 1990, Harry b 13 Jan 1993, Alex b 1 Oct 1997); *Career* slr; Macfarlanes: joined 1983, ptnr 1990–, sr ptnr 2008–; *Recreations* food, skiing, running; *Style*— Charles Martin, Esq; ✉ Macfarlanes, 20 Cursitor Street, London EC4A 1LT

MARTIN, Chris; s of Michael Martin, of Kent, and Gillian Martin; *b* 1 November 1971, Nottingham; *Educ* Nottingham Trent Univ (BSc); *m* 18 Feb 2005, Debra; 1 s (Liam Goundry b 12 Aug 1992); *Career* Paralympic athlete; achivements incl: Gold medal IPC World Championship Brimingham 1998, Gold medal discus throw Paralympics Sydney 2000, Gold medal IPC World Championship Lille 2002, Silver medal discus throw Paralympics Beijing 2008; current Paralympic record holder 1996–; *Clubs* Mansfield Harriers Athletics; *Style*— Chris Martin, Esq

MARTIN, Claire; OBE (2011); da of David Godwin, and Carole *née* Mole; *Educ* Doris Holford Stage Sch Surrey, Carshalton Coll Surrey; *m* 18 Oct 2008, Philip Jackson; 1 da (Amelia Louise Sandie b 13 Aug 2002); *Career* jazz singer; co-presenter Jazz Line Up (BBC Radio 3); *Albums* The Waiting Game 1992, Devil May Care 1993, Old Boyfriends 1994, Off Beat 1995, Make This City Ours 1997, Take My Heart 1999, Perfect Alibi 2000, The Very Best of Claire Martin: Every Now and Then 2001, Toom Darn Hot 2002, Secret Love 2004, When Lights Are Low 2005, He Never Mentioned Love 2007, A Modern Art 2009, Too Much In Love To Care 2011, Say It Isn't So 2013, Time And Place 2014, We've Got a World that Swings (with Ray Gelato) 2016; formerly involved with Brighton Women's Centre; winner British Jazz Awards 1995, 1996, 2000, 2002, 2010, 2011; *Recreations* yoga, badminton; *Style*— Ms Claire Martin, OBE; ✉ 126 Valley Drive, Brighton, Sussex BN1 5FF (☎ 07973 349920, e-mail clairemartinjazz@btopenworld.com, website www.clairemartinjazz.co.uk); agent Jonathan Boddy, The John Boddy Agency, 10 Southfield Gardens, Twickenham TW1 4SZ (☎ 020 8892 0133)

MARTIN, David; *b* Southampton, Hants; *Educ* BA; *Career* qualified CA 1977; held finance and gen mgmnt positions before leading a MBO of a Midlands-based bus co in 1986; co-fndr British Bus (became one of the largest UK bus operators before selling this business to Arriva in 1996); Arriva plc: joined 1996, memb Bd 1998–, gp md ops and dep chief exec 2005–06, chief exec 2006–; FCMA, FCIT; *Style*— David Martin, Esq; ✉ Arriva plc, 1 Admiral Way, Doxford International Business Park, Sunderland SR3 3XP (☎ 0191 520 4000, fax 0191 520 4190)

MARTIN, David; s of Edward Sydney Morris Martin, of Exeter, and Dorothy Mary, *née* Cooper; *b* 11 February 1952; *Educ* Worthing HS for Boys, St John's Coll Cambridge; *m* 24 Aug 1991, Ruth Kathryn, da of Terence Colin Howells; 2 da (Abigail Ruth b 10 May 1994, Naomi Hope b 22 Feb 1997); *Career* ptnr Herbert Smith 1986– (asst slr 1979–86, tax slr 1979–); memb Religious Soc of Friends; *Recreations* reading, walking; *Style*— David Martin, Esq; ✉ Herbert Smith, Exchange House, Primrose Street, London EC2A 2HS (☎ 020 7374 8000, fax 020 7374 0888)

MARTIN, David Clifford; s of Rev John Bernard Martin (d 1986), and (Elizabeth) Alma, *née* Jones (d 2006); *b* 20 December 1956, Plymouth; *Educ* Chigwell Sch, UC Durham (BSc, PGCE); *m* 17 Dec 1988, Sally Elizabeth, *née* Bennett; 1 da (Elizabeth b 11 Feb 1990), 2 s (Andrew b 28 March 1992, Peter b 28 Sept 1993); *Career* teacher: Kenya 1978–79, Dronfield Derbys 1980–84; Microelectronics Educn Prog and TVEI 1984–87, European Educnl Software 1987–88; Br Cncl: educn advsr 1988–94, dep dir Nigeria 1994–98, dir Palestinian Territories 1998–2002, dir Central Africa 2002–06, dir Hungary 2007–09, dir Pakistan 2009–12, head of schs progs 2012–14, currently dir Maygrove Consulting, executive coach and educn conslt; govr Holy Trinity C of E Secdy Sch Crawley, tstee Lloyd Fndn, tstee Charles Wallace Pakistan Tst; *Recreations* music, gardening; *Style*— David Martin, Esq; ✉ Maygrove Consulting, 31 Oathall Rd, Haywards Heath, RH16 3EG; ☎ 07769 163353, e-mail davidc_martin@yahoo.co.uk

MARTIN, David MacLeod; s of Allan MacLeod Martin (d 1976), and Jessie Harris (d 1974); *b* 30 December 1922; *Educ* Govan HS, Glasgow Sch of Art (Dip Art); *m* 30 July 1951,

Isobel Agnes Fowlie (d 2000), da of George Frances Fowlie Smith (d 1972); 4 s (Brian b 4 Aug 1954, Allan b 26 Sept 1956, Kenneth b 21 July 1960, Derek b 30 Sept 1966); *Career* served WWII Sgt RAF 1943–46; teacher and princ teacher Hamilton GS 1973–83; painter 1983–; annual exhibitions: RSA, RSW, RGI (RA 1984); numerous group shows incl: Lynn Stern Assoc London, London 20th Century Art Fair, Miami Art Fair, Mall Galleries London 2000, RSA Gallery Edinburgh 2000, Richmond Hill Gallery 2001, 2003, 2004 and 2005, Affordable Art Fair London 2003, London Art Fair (with John Martin Gallery) 2015, Smithy Gallery Blanefield 2015 (two man show); one man shows: Glasgow, Edinburgh, Perth, Greenock & Stone Gallery Newcastle, Thackery Gallery London 1992 and 1994, Ferguson Fine Art Islington Art Fair 1994, Fosse Gallery Stow on the Wold 1995, John Martin of London 1995, 1997, 2000, 2002 and 2006, Richmond Hill Gallery 1997 and 2011, Wren Gallery Burford 1997, Art International NY 1998, featured artist Perth Festival Exhibition Perth Museum 1999, Roger Bilcliffe Gallery 2001, 2003, 2005, 2007, 2009, 2011 and 2014, Open Eye Gallery Edinburgh 2002, Edgar Modern Gallery Bath 2005, 2008–09 and (four works) 2015, Lemon St Gallery Truro 2007, 2008–09, 2011, 2013 and 2015, John Davies Gallery Moreton-in-Marsh 2007 and 2009, John Martin Gallery 2007–10, 2012, 2014 and 2015, Glasgow Art Fair 2009–10, Richmond Hill Gallery 2008–14, Contemporary Scottish Masters Manor House Gall Chipping Norton 2010, Purple Gallery Birmingham, Smithy Gallery Blanefield; work in numerous private and public collections incl: The Fleming Collection London, Credit Lyonnaise London, The Earl of Moray, late Lord Goold, Lord MacFarlane, Lady MacKay, Scottish Arts Cncl, Royal Bank of Scotland Collection; work cmmnd by Lord Bute for Bute Fabrics, featured artist in Perth Festival of the Arts 1999, special award of merit Robert Colquhoun Meml Art Prize Kilmarnock 1974, prizewinner Friends of the Smith Gallery Stirling 1981, May Marshall Brown Award RSW 1984, EIS Purchase Prize 1986, prizewinner Hamilton museum exhibition 1988, £1,000 prizewinner The Laing Collection Art Competition 1990 and 1993, David Cargill Award RGI 1995, RSW Cncl Award 2003; memb Cncl: RGI, RSW (past vice-pres); memb: SSA 1949 (hon memb 1992), RSW 1961, RGI 1981, Visual Arts Scotland (formerly SAAC) 1992; *Books* David M Martin, RSW, RGI (2011); included in Paintings from the Clydesdale Bank Collection (Patrick Bourne, 1990); *Recreations* gardening, period ship modelling, music, reading; *Style*— David M Martin, Esq; ✉ The Old Schoolhouse, 53 Gilmour Street, Eaglesham, Glasgow G76 0LG (✆ 01355 303308)

MARTIN, David Weir; MEP (Lab) Scotland; s of William Martin and Marion Weir; *b* 26 August 1954; *Educ* Liberton HS, Heriot-Watt Univ (BA, MA), Univ of Leicester (MA); *Career* former stockbroker's asst and animal welfare campaigner; memb Lab Pty 1975–, Lothian regnl cncllr Inch/Gilmerton 1982; MEP (Lab): Lothian 1984–99, Scotland 1999–; ldr Br Lab Gp European Parl 1987–89, vice-pres European Parl 1989–2004, memb International Trade Ctee; memb: TGWU, GMB, Fabian Soc; vice-pres Advocates for Animals; *Books* Traditional Industrial Regions of the European Community (report), Bringing Common Sense to the Common Market – A Left Agenda for Europe (pamphlet, 1988), The Democratic Deficit (chapter in A Claim of Right for Scotland, ed by Owen Dudley Edwards), European Union and the Democratic Deficit (pamphlet, 1990), Europe – An Ever Closer Union (1991), Refreshing the Parts (contrib), The Intergovernmental Conferences in the Context of Parliament's Strategy for European Union (4 reports on Maastricht), Towards a Wider, Deeper, Federal Europe (pamphlet, 1992), European Union – The Shattered Dream? (pamphlet, 1993), To be Efficient, the Commission Needs Major Reform (chapter in What Future for the European Commission, ed Giles Merritt, 1995), Power to the People (chapter in Changing States – A Labour Agenda for Europe, ed Glyn Ford, Glenys Kinnock, Arlene McCarthy, 1996), A Partnership Democracy for Europe (pamphlet, 1996); *Recreations* reading, sport; *Style*— David Martin, Esq, MEP; ✉ Unit 43, Midlothian Innovation Centre, Pentlandfield, Midlothian EH25 9RE (✆ 0131 440 9040, e-mail david@martinmep.com, website www.martinmep.com)

MARTIN, Geoff; *Career* chair and campaigns dir London Health Emergency, convenor London Region UNISON, head of press RMT, chair Health Emergency; dir Left Field Stage Glastonbury Festival; *Recreations* football, music, travelling; *Clubs* Sutton United FC; *Style*— Geoff Martin, Esq; ✉ London Health Emergency, London WC1N 3XX (✆ 020 8644 2965)

MARTIN, (Thomas) Geoffrey; OBE (2002); s of Thomas Martin (d 1973), Belfast, NI, and Sadie Adelaide, *née* Day (d 1991); *b* 26 July 1940; *Educ* Newry GS, Queen's Univ Belfast (BSc); *m* 6 July 1968, Gay Madeleine Annesley, da of Herbert Annesley Brownrigg, of Bognor Regis; 1 s (Thomas), 3 da (Bluebell, Poppy, Gabriella); *Career* pres NUS 1966–68, dir Shelter 1972–73, dip staff Cwlth Secretariat 1973–79, head Euro Cmmn Office NI 1979–85, head of Press and Info Serv EC SE Asia 1985–87, head of external relations Euro Cmmn Office London 1987–94, head Euro Cmmn Representation in the UK 1994–2002, Office of the Cwlth Sec Gen 2002–15; hon doctorate Univ of Plymouth; *Recreations* running; *Clubs* Travellers, RIIA; *Style*— Geoffrey Martin, Esq, OBE; ✉ e-mail tgmartin@ymail.com

MARTIN, Prof Geoffrey Almeric Thorndike; s of Albert Thorndike Martin (d 1947), and Lily, *née* Jackson (d 1964); *b* 28 May 1934; *Educ* Palmer's Sch Grays Thurrock, UCL (BA), CCC Cambridge, Christ's Coll Cambridge (MA, PhD, LittD); *Career* Lady Budge research fell in Egyptology Christ's Coll Cambridge 1966–70; UCL: lectr in Egyptology 1970–78, reader in Egyptian archaeology 1978–87, prof of Egyptology (ad hominem) 1987, Edwards prof of Egyptology 1988–93 (prof emeritus 1993); field dir: jt Egypt Exploration Soc and Leiden Museum expdn in Egypt 1975–98, jt Leiden Museum and Leiden Univ expdn in Egypt 1998 (hon dir 2001), Amarna Royal Tombs Project Valley of the Kings 1998–2003, Cambridge expdn to Valley of the Kings 2005, jt Cambridge expdn to Valley of the Kings and New Kingdom Research Fndn 2013; Christ's Coll Cambridge: hon keeper of the Muniment Rm 1997, fell commoner 1998, hon keeper of the Plate 2000–13, hon keeper of the Archives 2004; sr fell McDonald Inst for Archaeological Research Cambridge 2016; corresponding memb German Archaeological Inst 1982; FSA 1975; *Books* Egyptian Administrative and Private-Name Seals (1971), The Royal Tomb at El-Amarna (vol 1 1974, vol 2 1989), The Tomb of Hetepka (1979), The Sacred Animal Necropolis at North Saqqara (1981), Canopic Equipment in the Petrie Collection (with V Raisman, 1984), Scarabs, Cylinders and other Ancient Egyptian Seals (1985), The Tomb Chapels of Paser and Raia (1985), Corpus of Reliefs of the New Kingdom (vol 1 1987), Excavations in the Royal Necropolis at El-Amarna (with A El-Khouly, 1987), The Memphite Tomb of Horemheb (1989), The Hidden Tombs of Memphis (1991, German edn: Auf der Suche nach dem verlorenen Grab, 1994), A Bibliography of the Amarna Period (1991), The Tomb of Tia and Tia (1997), The Tombs of Three Memphite Officials (2001), Stelae from Egypt and Nubia in the Fitzwilliam Museum Cambridge (2005), Private Stelae of the Early Dynastic Period from the Royal Cemetery at Abydos (2011), The Tomb of Maya and Meryt Vol 1 (2012), Tutankhamun's Regent (2016); *Recreations* travel, English and European history, bibliography; *Style*— Prof Geoffrey Martin; ✉ Christ's College Cambridge, Cambridge CB2 3BU

MARTIN, Judge Geoffrey William; OBE (1992); s of late Bertie Philip Martin, of Suffolk, and Marion, *née* Bonney (d 1968); *b* 9 November 1935; *Educ* Framlingham Coll, St John's Coll Cambridge (MA); *m* 1, Patricia, *née* Jones; 2 da (Jane Elizabeth b 7 Dec 1960, Jill Marion b 9 June 1962); m 2, Marie Turner; *Career* dist offr and magistrate Tanganyika 1959–62, admitted slr 1966, private practice (litigation) 1966–77, registrar Co Court and dist 1977–86, puisne judge Tonga 1986–88, chief justice Tonga 1988–91, pt/t judge Vanuatu Court of Appeal 1988–95, pt/t judge Western Samoa Court of Appeal 1990, dist judge 1992–2003 (dep dist judge 2003–10), pt/t chief justice St Helena 1992–2006, pt/t judge of appeal Tonga 1994, pt/t judge Falkland Islands 1996, chief justice Turks and Caicos Islands 2004–05 (p/t judge and arbitrator 2005–12); memb: Law Soc, Cwlth Magistrates and Judges' Assoc; *Recreations* books, music, travel; *Clubs* Royal Over-Seas League; *Style*— Judge Geoffrey Martin, OBE; ✉ e-mail geoffwmartin@yahoo.co.uk

MARTIN, Glenn Philip; s of Walter Philip, and Eileen Denton, *née* Savage; *b* 11 February 1949; *Educ* KCS Wimbledon, Wadham Coll Oxford (BA); *m* 4 July 1970, Beryl, da of Albert Darby, of Sale; 3 s (Christopher, Alastair, Nicholas), 1 da (Sarah); *Career* dir of ops Swiss Bank Corporation 1995–96 (dir of banking ops 1990), chief info offr Salomon Smith Barney Europe 1996–2000, chief info offr Schroder Salomon Smith Barney 2000–01, chief technol offr Cazenove 2001–05, chief info offr JP Morgan Cazenove 2005, chief exec ShareMaestro Ltd 2007–; chm Reedham Park Sports Club Ltd, dir Reedham Park Tennis Club Ltd; *Publications* Personal Prosperity Plan, How to Value Shares and Outperform the Market (2011), 7 Successful Stock Market Strategies (2015); *Recreations* tennis, drumming; *Style*— Glenn Martin, Esq; ✉ Hatchetts, Westerham Road, Limpsfield, Surrey RH8 0SW (e-mail glennpmartin@sharemaestro.co.uk)

MARTIN, Iain James; s of John H Martin, of Paisley, Scotland, and Margaret, *née* Davison; *b* 2 October 1971; *Educ* Castlehead HS, Univ of Glasgow; *m* 2 April 2001, Fiona, da of James McJannet; *Career* journalist; reporter Sunday Times Scotland 1993–97, political ed Scotland on Sunday 1997–2000, political ed The Scotsman 2000–01, dep ed Scotland on Sunday 2001, ed The Scotsman 2001–04, ed Scotland on Sunday 2004–06; Telegraph Media Gp: dep ed Sunday Telegraph 2006, subsequently gp exec ed of politics, head of comment and community 2008–; fell Br American Project; *Clubs* Travellers, Beefsteak; *Style*— Iain Martin; ✉ Telegraph Media Group, 111 Buckingham Palace Road, London SW1W 0DT (✆ 020 7538 5000, e-mail iain.martin@telegraph.co.uk)

MARTIN, Dr Joan Eleanor; da of Herbert Martin (d 1995), of Belfast, and Sarah, *née* Neagle; *b* 25 March 1950, Belfast; *Educ* Univ of Warwick (MA), Univ of Ulster (DPhil); *m* 3 Jan 1987, Paul Lawson Hunt; 1 s (Timothy); *Career* occupational therapist KCL 1972–73, head of occupational therapy Atkinson Morleys Hosp London 1973–77, lectr and course dir in occupational therapy Univ of Ulster 1977–2000; memb: GMC 2003– (chair Fitness to Practice Reference Gp, memb Educn and Diversity and Equality Ctees), Gen Osteopathy Cncl 2014; memb: Appeals Serv NI 1994–, ARB 1999–2004, Review Panel RCS 2011, Advsy Bd Cncl of the Inns of Court 2012–, Advsy Bd Bar Tribunals & Adjudication Service 2014–, Panellists Appt Panel RCVS; fell Coll of Occupational Therapists 1981 (memb 1972); Eating Disorders, Food and Occupational Therapy (1998); *Recreations* travelling, cooking, craftwork, fair-weather gardening; *Style*— Dr Joan Martin; ✉ General Osteopathy Council, Osteopathy House, 176 Tower Bridge Road, London SE1 3LU

MARTIN, John Joseph Charles; s of Benjamin Martin (d 1987), and Lucille, *née* Miranda (d 1976); *b* 25 November 1940; *Educ* Latymer Upper Sch; *m* 1978, Frances, *née* Oster; 1 da (Lucy b 1980), 1 s (James b 1982); *Career* Illustrated Newspapers 1960–63, Planned Public Relations 1963–68, Martin Dignum Assocs 1969; Welbeck Golin/Harris Communications Ltd: joined 1969, dir 1972, chief exec 1984, chm 1988–97 (clients incl: Lever Brothers, McDonald's, ICI Dulux, Rowntrees, Govt of Bermuda, Brittany Ferries; devised Bottle Bank scheme for Glass Mfrs Fed); fndr John Martin Communications 1997–; portrait artist 2010, participant artist Lloyd's TSB The Art of Sport initiative, selected for Artist Magazine nat exhibition 2011, one-man show Garden Suburb Gallery 2011, winner Arts Depot Prize for Barnet artists 2013; FCIPR 1994 (MIPR 1968); *Recreations* tennis; *Style*— John Martin, Esq; ✉ 53 Hampstead Way, Hampstead Garden Suburb, London NW11 7DP (✆ 020 8455 8482, website www.hotpr.biz)

MARTIN, John Vandeleur; QC (1991); s of Col Graham Vandeleur Martin, MC, of Salisbury, Wilts, and Margaret Helen, *née* Sherwood; *b* 17 January 1948, York; *Educ* Malvern, Pembroke Coll Cambridge (MA); *m* 7 Dec 1974, Stephanie Johnstone, da of Maj Michael Johnstone Smith, MC, of Bedford; 2 s (Timothy b 1979, Nicholas b 1985), 1 da (Josephine b 1983); *Career* called to the Bar Lincoln's Inn 1972 (bencher 1999); in practice Chancery Bar: Northern Circuit 1973–81, London 1981–; dep judge of the High Court 1993–, judge Courts of Appeal Jersey and Guernsey 2007–; head of chambers Wilberforce Chambers 2010–; justice Cayman Islands Ct of Appeal 2013–; chm Disciplinary Appointments Ctee of the Actuarial Profession 2005–13; Freeman City of London 1969, Liveryman Worshipful Co of Drapers 1973; *Recreations* opera, being in Alderney; *Style*— John Martin, Esq, QC; ✉ Wilberforce Chambers, 8 New Square, Lincoln's Inn, London WC2A 3QP (✆ 020 7306 0102, fax 020 7306 0095)

M

MARTIN, Kevin Joseph; s of James Arthur Martin (d 1961), of Coventry, and Ivy Lilian, *née* Reeson (d 1986); *b* 15 June 1947; *Educ* Cotton Coll; *m* 7 Oct 1971, Maureen Dympna, da of Kevin James McCormack; 2 s (James Roland b 21 Oct 1975, Richard Thomas b 3 Oct 1977); *Career* admitted slr 1970, ptnr Mackintosh & Co Birmingham 1972–79 (joined 1970), fndr and sr ptnr K J Martin & Co 1979–2001, conslt Lodders (following merger) 2001–; Law Soc: memb Young Slrs' Gp 1978–82, memb Cncl 1996–, chm Compliance Bd 2001–03, memb Main Bd 2001–06, dep vice-pres 2003–04, vice-pres 2004–05, pres 2005–06; chm Will Certainty Ltd 2008–; co-proprietor (with wife) Davenport Lodge Sch Coventry 1986–2007; Freeman City of Coventry 1970; memb Law Soc 1970; *Recreations* golf, skiing, watching cricket, rugby, classical music, literature; *Clubs* Ladbrook Park Golf, Coventry and North Warwickshire Cricket, Drapers' (Coventry), RAC; *Style*— Kevin Martin, Esq; ✉ The Law Society, 113 Chancery Lane, London WC2A 1PL (✆ 020 7320 5602, fax 020 7320 5759, e-mail kevinj_martin@btinternet.com)

MARTIN, Kit; CBE (2012); s of Prof Sir John Leslie Martin, and Sadie, *née* Speight; *b* 6 May 1947; *Educ* Eton, Jesus Coll Cambridge (MA, DipArch); *m* 1, 24 Oct 1970 (m dis 1978), Julia Margaret, da of Dr Peter Dennis Mitchell, of Bodmin, Cornwall; m 2, 15 Sept 1980, Sally Martha, da of Sqdn Ldr Edwin Hector Gordon Brookes, AFC (d 1947), of Laxton, Northants; 1 da (Amy Victoria b 17 Sept 1992); *Career* ptnr Martin & Weighton 1969–76, chm Kit Martin Historic Houses Rescue Ltd 1974–; responsible for rescue, restoration and conversion of various important listed bldgs incl: Dingley Hall, The Hazells, Gunton Park, Cullen House, Keith Hall, Callaly Castle, Tyninghame House, Burley; memb Historic Bldgs Cncl for Scotland 1987–99; dir The Prince of Wales's Phoenix Tst 1997–2001, projects conslt The Prince's Regeneration Tst 2001–; tstee Save Europe's Heritage 1994–; Hon FRIBA; *Publications* The Country House – To Be or Not To Be, Jamaica's Heritage: An Untapped Resource, Silesia: The Land of Dying Country Houses; *Recreations* skiing, squash, private flying, landscape gardening; *Style*— Kit Martin, Esq, CBE; ✉ Park Farm, Gunton Park, Hanworth, Norfolk NR11 7HL (✆ 01263 761270)

MARTIN, Paul; MSP; Michael John Martin and Mary Martin; *b* 17 March 1967; *Career* researcher, cncllr Glasgow City Cncl 1993–99; MSP (Lab): Glasgow Springburn 1999–2011, Glasgow Provan 2011–; memb: Audit Ctee, Justice 1 Ctee, Cross-Pty Gp on Children and Young People, Cross-Pty Gp on Chronic Pain, Cross-Pty Gp on Tobacco Control; memb AEEU; *Recreations* football, golf, reading, walking; *Style*— Paul Martin, Esq, MSP; ✉ The Scottish Parliament, Edinburgh EH99 1SP (✆ 0131 348 5844, e-mail paul.martin.msp@scottish.parliament.uk, website www.paulmartinmsp.org.uk)

MARTIN, Dr Paul; *Educ* Christ's Coll Cambridge (MA, PhD); *Career* Harkness fell and postdoctoral scholar Dept of Psychiatry and Behavioral Sciences Stanford Univ 1982–84, jr lectr Univ of Cambridge 1984–86, fell Wolfson Coll Cambridge 1984–86 and 2001–04 (sr memb 2004–); civil servant MOD 1986–2000, dir of communication Cabinet Office 2000–01; science writer and conslt 2001–; *Books* Measuring Behaviour (with Patrick Bateson, 1993), The Sickening Mind (1998), Design for a Life (with Patrick Bateson,

1999), Counting Sheep (2002), What Worries Parents (with Kristina Murrin, 2004), Making People Happy (2005); *Style—* Dr Paul Martin

MARTIN, Prof Paul; *m* Jan; *Career* chief exec Highland Primary Care NHS Tst then dep chief exec (modernisation) Highland Direct Health Services 2002–04, chief nursing offr and interim dir of health workforce Health Directorates Scottish Govt 2004–09, currently dep princ Univ W of Scotland; *Publications* Family Health Nursing: A Response to the Global Health Challenges (jtly, in Jl of Family of Nursing and online 2013); *Style—* Prof Paul Martin

MARTIN, His Hon Judge Robert Ian; *Career* admitted slr 1974; circuit judge (Midland Circuit) 2007–; Appeal Tbnls: chm 1985–98, rgnl chm Mdland Region 1998, pres 2007–; *Style—* His Hon Judge Martin

MARTIN, Robert Logan (Roy); QC (Scot 1988, Eng and Wales 2008); s of late Robert Martin, MC, of Crosbie Wood, Paisley, and late Janet Johnstone, *née* Logan; *b* 31 July 1950; *Educ* Paisley GS, Univ of Glasgow (LLB); *m* 9 Nov 1984, Fiona Frances, da of John Roxburgh Bingham Neil, of St Ives, NSW; 1 s (Robert John Neil b 12 Aug 1987), 2 da (Camilla Nancy Neil b 25 Sept 1988, Phoebe Logan Neil b 2 Sept 1991); *Career* slr 1973–76, admitted to Faculty of Advocates 1976, memb Sheriff Courts Rules Cncl 1981–84, standing jr counsel to Dept of Employment (Scotland) 1983–84, advocate-depute 1984–87, admitted to Bar of NSW 1987, called to the Bar Lincoln's Inn 1990, called to the Bar of NI 2010, bencher Middle Temple 2011, judge of the Courts of Appeal of Jersey and Guernsey 2013–; dean Faculty of Advocates 2004–07 (vice-dean 2001–04); temporary sheriff 1988–90; pt/t chm Industrial Tbnls 1991–96, chm Scottish Planning, Local Govt and Environmental Bar Gp 1991–96, chm Police Appeals Tbnl 1997–, co-chair Forum for Barristers and Advocates 2002–06, co-chair Int Cncl of Advocates and Barristers 2004–08, memb Judical Appointments Bd for Scotland 2007–10, hon memb Australian Bar Assoc 2008; hon prof Univ of Glasgow 2006–; tstee Nat Library of Scotland 2004–07; govr Loretto 2002–12 (chm of govrs 2007–12); tstee Royal Coll of Obstetricians and Gynaecologists 2013–; hon sec Wagering Club 1982–91; Hon FRIAS 2009; *Recreations* shooting, skiing, modern architecture, vintage motoring; *Clubs* New (Edinburgh), Garrick; *Style—* Roy Martin, Esq, QC; ✉ Advocates' Library, Parliament House, Edinburgh (☎ 0131 226 5071); 6 Pump Court, Temple EC4Y 7AR

MARTIN, HE Simon Charles; CMG (2013); s of Nicholas Fearnley Martin (d 2005), and Patricia Margaret Martin, of Sutton Coldfield; *b* 15 May 1963, Beverley, Yorks; *Educ* King Edward's Sch Birmingham, Univ of Nottingham (BA); *m* 25 July 2015, Sophie Elisabeth, *née* Bridgford; 1 s (Alexander b 30 May 1996, Elyssia b 2 July 1998); *Career* diplomat; FCO: desk offr (for Zaire, Rwanda, Burundi and Sao Tome and Principe Central) African Dept 1984–85, South Africa sanctions desk offr Southern African Dept 1985–86, Burmese language trg then second sec and vice-consul Rangoon 1986–90, Gulf War Emergency Unit 1990–91, head Multilateral Section Drugs and Int Crime Dept 1991–93, head ME Terrorism and Lockerbie Section Security Coordination Dept 1993–95, Hungarian language trg then head Commercial Section Budapest 1995–2001, dep head Southern European Dept 2001–03; corporate relations advsr Unilever plc Africa Business Gp 2003–05, dep head of mission Prague 2005–09, dir Protocol and vice-marshal Diplomatic Corps FCO 2009–12, dep private sec to TRH The Prince of Wales and the Duchess of Cornwall Clarence House 2012–15, ambass to Bahrain 2015–; *Recreations* cinema, cricket, golf, motorsport, skiing, tennis, travel, running, cycling; *Style—* HE Simon Martin, CMG

MARTIN, Stanley William Frederick; CVO (1992, LVO 1981), JP (Inner London 1993–2000); s of Stanley Martin (d 1976), of Walmer, Kent, and Winifred Rose Kilburn (d 1976); *b* 9 December 1934; *Educ* Bromley GS, UC Oxford (MA, pres OU Law Soc 1957), Inner Temple (student scholar); *m* 3 Sept 1960, Hanni Aud, da of Aage Valdemar Johannes Hansen (d 1957), of Copenhagen, Denmark, and Oda Maja Valborg Nielsen (d 1989); 1 s (Nicholas b 1962), 1 da (Birgit b 1964); *Career* mil serv 2 Lieut RASC 1953–55; entered CRO 1958, asst private sec to Sec of State 1959–62; first sec: Canberra 1962–64, Kuala Lumpur 1964–67; Planning Staff and Personnel Dept FCO 1967–70, seconded to CSD (CSSB) 1970–71, asst marshal Dip Corps 1972–81, first asst marshal Dip Corps 1981–92, assoc head Protocol Dept FCO 1986–92, ret Dip Serv 1992, protocol advsr FCO 1993–; Extra Gentleman Usher to HM The Queen 1993–; visiting prof Univ of Westminster 1987– (hon fell 1998); freelance lectr 1993–; diplomatic conslt: Hyde Park Hotel 1993–99, Grosvenor House 1999–2002; advsr: The Consular Corps of London 1993–, London Mayors' Assoc 2004– (hon memb 2006); memb: Ctee London Diplomatic Assoc 1972–, Cncl The Oxford Univ Soc 1993–2002, Advsy Cncl Spanish Inst of Protocol Studies 1997–, Cwlth Observer Gp Guyana Elections 1997, Ctee European Atlantic Gp 2002–10, Pilgrims, Royal Historical Soc; tstee: The Attlee Fndn 1993–99, Toynbee Hall 1996–99, Jt Commonwealth Socs Tst 2005–10; patron Apex Tst 2002– (vice-patron 1995–2002); govr Goodenough Coll for Overseas Graduates 2005–10; Freeman City of London 1988; FRSA 1985; Companion Order of Distinguished Serv (Brunei) 1992; *Publications* Diplomatic Handbook (contrib, 2 edn 1977 to 8 edn 2004), Royal Service: History of Royal Victorian Order, Medal and Chain (jtly, Vol I 1996, Vol II 2001), The Order of Merit: One Hundred Years of Matchless Honour (2006), Honouring Commonwealth Citizens (contrib, 2007); also contrib to Jl of Orders and Medals Res Soc, Jl of Royal Over-Seas League, Bermuda Jl of Maritime History, Diplomat Magazine; *Recreations* collecting too many books, manuscripts and obituaries, historical research and writing, walking, siestas, watching old films in the afternoon, travelling by train; *Clubs* Royal Over-Seas League (memb Central Cncl 1982–2010, memb Exec Ctee 1993–2010, vice-chm 2002–05, chm 2005–10, vice-pres 2010–), Oxford and Cambridge, Danish; *Style—* Stanley Martin, Esq, CVO; ✉ 14 Great Spilmans, London SE22 8SZ (☎ 020 8693 8181)

MARTIN, Dr Stephen Alexander; MBE (1994); s of James Alexander Martin, of Bangor, Co Down, and Mamie, *née* Weir; *b* 13 April 1959; *Educ* Bangor GS, Univ of Ulster (BA); *m* 13 April 1987, Dorothy Esther Elizabeth, da of William Edwin Armstrong, of Belmont, Belfast; 1 s (Patrick Armstrong b 14 Nov 1991), 1 da (Hannah Rebecca b 18 Jan 1996); *Career* former hockey player; Bronze medal World Champions Trophy 1984 (vice-capt), Bronze medal Olympic Games LA 1984, Silver medal World Champions Trophy 1985, Gold medal Olympic Games Seoul 1988, sixth place Olympic Games Barcelona 1992 (capt); 94 caps GB 1983–92, 135 caps Ireland 1980–91 (capt 1984–85, European Cup 1983, 1987 and 1991, World Cup 1990, total 229 most capped player in GB and Ireland), World Champions Trophy 1984–92; Team Award BBC Sports Personality of the Year 1984 and 1988; played Ulster 1980–91; sports broadcaster; chief exec Olympic Cncl Ireland 2006–; dep chef de mission Team GB Olympic Games Salt Lake City 2002 and Olympic Games Athens 2004, Team Ireland official Olympic Games Turin 2006 and Olympic Games Beijing 2008; dep chef de mission Team Ireland: Olympic Games London 2012, European Games Baku 2015, Olympic Games Rio 2016; chef de mission Team Ireland Winter Olympic Games Sochi 2014; ambass London 2012 Olympic Games bid, Olympic torch relay runner London 2012; memb Bd Irish Sports Inst; memb: Br Assoc of Sports Med/Sci, Br Olympians Club, Br Inst of Sports Coaches; Hon DUniv Ulster 2001; *Recreations* hockey, golf; *Clubs* Bangor, Belfast YMCA, Holywood 87, Newry Olympic, Annadale Hockey, Donaghadee Golf, Lisnagarvey Hockey (hon life memb); *Style—* Dr Stephen Martin, MBE; ✉ 5 The Coaches, Brown's Brae, Holywood, Co Down BT18 0LE (☎ 028 9042 1338, e-mail stephen@olympicsport.ie, Twitter @samhockeygold)

MARTIN, Prof Stephen David; s of Bernard C Martin, and Anne Martin, of Yorks; *b* 8 January 1964, Saltburn, Yorks; *Educ* Newcastle Univ (MB BS); Khwanchai Martin; 2 s (Edward John b 2 April 1992, Richard Francis b 9 April 1994); *Career* Newcastle Nuffield Hosp: conslt in intensive care psychiatry 1995–98, conslt psychiatrist and head of research 1998–2001, conslt neuropsychiatrist 2003–; hon sr research fell Univ of Durham 1997–2000, visiting prof Univ of Sunderland 1999–2005, hon prof Univ of Chiang Mai 2006–; NHS UK Hospital Doctor Award (Psychiatry); dir S D Martin Ltd; solo flute broadcast on BBC Radio 3; MRCPsych 1992; *Publications* co-author of first study to prove brain changes in psychotherapy for depression (2001), contrib to scientific broadcasts and newspaper items, author of numerous papers on schizophrenia, functional neuroimaging in depression and psychotherapy; *Recreations* gardening, skiing, early music performance; *Style—* Prof Stephen Martin; ✉ Nuffield Health Hospital Newcastle-upon-Tyne, Clayton Road, Jesmond, Newcastle-upon-Tyne NE2 3JP

MARTIN, Stephen Graham Balfour; s of Graham Hunter Martin (d 1985), and Ragna, *née* Balch-Barth (d 2013); *b* 21 October 1939; *Educ* Tonbridge; *m* 1, 1966 (m dis 1969), Angela Wood; 1 s (Diccon Carl Henry b 1967); *m* 2, 1976, Elizabeth Mary, da of Dennis John Ward, of Chatteris, Cambs; 2 da (Charlotte Louise Elizabeth b 1978, Olivia Rose Ragna b 1993); *Career* chm and md: Intermail plc, Home Shopping Club Ltd; dir: Strategic Marketing Databases Ltd, Union Pen Co Inc, Royal Artillery Museum Ltd; Past Master Worshipful Co of Armourers and Brasiers; FIDM, DipDM, founder fell Inst of Direct Mktg; *Recreations* fishing, shooting, gardening, golf; *Clubs* Flyfishers', Norske; *Style—* Stephen Martin, Esq; ✉ Woodlands Farm House, Witcha, Ramsbury SN8 2HQ (e-mail stephen@balfourmartin.co.uk, website www.prayerhandles.co.uk)

MARTIN, Timothy Charles (Tim); s of Godfrey Martin (d 1975), of Findon, W Sussex, and Nancy Cordelia, *née* Orrom (d 1996); *b* 17 May 1951; *Educ* King's Coll Cambridge (MA); *m* 31 March 1984, Sarah, da of Arthur James Moffett, FRCS, of Cooksey Green, Worcs; 2 s (Alexander Dods b 19 Aug 1985, Charles Murray b 15 Jan 1988); *Career* admitted slr 1977, Allen and Overy 1975–79; dir (corp fin) Hill Samuel and Co 1986–87, dir Barclays de Zoete Wedd Ltd 1988–97, dir European utilities Credit Suisse First Boston 1997–99, head European utilities Flemings 1999–2000, dir JP Morgan Chase 2000–01; chief economist and dir of infrastructure and economic regulation Office of Rail Regulation 2001–05, dir UK Govt Investments 2005–; *Recreations* tennis, sailing, gardening, opera, collecting modern British pictures; *Clubs* Lansdowne; *Style—* Tim Martin, Esq; ✉ UK Government Investments, 1 Victoria Street, London SW1H 0ET (website www.gov.uk/government/organisations/uk-government-investments)

MARTIN, Valerie Ann (Val); da of William Herbert Bennett (d 1996), of Purley, Surrey, and Ann Georgina, *née* Hon (d 1977); *b* 15 October 1951; *Educ* King George V Sch Hong Kong, Girton Coll Cambridge (MA); *m* July 1973, Prof Benjamin Raymond Martin; 2 s (Paul b 3 June 1980, David b 10 Sept 1985), 1 da (Sarah b 5 Dec 1982); *Career* teacher VSO W Africa 1973–75, NHS nat mgmnt trainee Manchester 1975–77, asst sector administrator Univ Hosp S Manchester 1977–78, unit administrator New Cross Hosp London 1978–82, project mangr for reorganisation and merger of Guy's and Lewisham Health Dist 1982–83, dep unit general mangr Guy's Hosp London 1983–85, mangr Dist Industrial Servs Lewisham and N Southwark HA 1988–89, head Business Planning Unit Guy's Hosp 1989–90, project mangr for NHS Tst status application for Guy's and Lewisham NHS Tst 1990–91, gen mangr Lewisham and Hither Green Hosps 1991–93, chief exec Lewisham Hosp NHS Tst 1993–99, sr fell Leadership Devpt The King's Fund 2000–08 (leadership assoc 2008–); MHSM, FRSA; *Recreations* reading, swimming, trekking, enjoying life; *Style—* Mrs Val Martin; ✉ The King's Fund, 11–13 Cavendish Square, London W1M 0AN (☎ 020 7307 2650, fax 020 7307 2600)

MARTIN, Dr Vivian Max; s of Martin Martin, of Melbourne, Aust, and Rachel, *née* Godfrey; *b* 9 October 1941; *Educ* Monash Univ Aust (MB BS), RCP; *m* Dec 1967, Penelope Georgina, da of Leon Samuels; 2 s (Simon James b 22 Nov 1971, Nicholas Giles b 23 Dec 1973); *Career* jr RMO Launceston Gen Hosp Tasmania 1968, sr RMO Sutherland Dist Hosp Sydney 1969–70, sr RMO Queen Victoria Meml Hosp Melbourne 1970–71; SHO Royal Free Hosp 1972–73, registrar Whittington Hosp 1973–76; sr registrar UCH 1976–81; conslt rheumatologist: Cromwell Hosp 1982–, Manor House Hosp 1991–99, Princess Grace Hosp 2005–14; conslt physician PPP Med Centre 1985–94; memb: BMA, RSM, Br Soc for Rheumatology; MRCP; *Publications* author of articles in various learned journals; *Style—* Dr Vivian Martin; ✉ 121 Harley Street, London W1G 6AX (☎ 020 7486 2365, fax 020 7224 0034); Cromwell Hospital, Cromwell Road, London SW5 0TU (☎ 020 7460 2000, fax 020 7460 5555)

MARTIN, William Wylie Macpherson (Bill); MBE (2014); s of Ian Alistair Macpherson (d 1985), of Glasgow, and Lettia, *née* Wylie (d 2004); *b* 9 November 1938; *Educ* Govan HS Glasgow; *m* Janet Mary, da of Maj Bruce Anthony Olley (d 1981), and Jeanne, *née* Blackburn (d 2008); 1 s (Angus), 3 da (Meran, Alison, Melanie); *Career* songwriter: Puppet on a String (first Br songwriter to win Eurovision Song Contest), Congratulations, My Boy, The Water Babies, Shang-a-Lang and 50 other top ten songs; music publisher: Sky, Van Morrison, Bay City Rollers, BA Robertson, Billy Connolly; record producer: Billy Connolly, Bay City Rollers, Elkie Brooks; Variety Club Silver Heart award for servs to charity, inducted Govan HS Hall of Fame 2011, Johnnie Walker Blue Label Scot of the Year Award 2012; Freeman: City of London 1981, City of Glasgow 1987; Liveryman Worshipful Co of Distillers; *Recreations* golf; *Clubs* RAC (past capt Golf Club (1980)), Annabel's, St George's Hill Golf, MCC, Caledonian, Saints & Sinners; *Style—* Bill Martin, Esq, MBE; ✉ Flat 3, Stack House, Cundy Street, Belgravia, London SW1W 9JS (mobile 07850 845280, e-mail bill@billmartinsongwriter.com, website www.billmartinsongwriter.com)

MARTIN ALEGI, Lynda Margaret; da of George Watt (d 1990), and Dorothy May, *née* Humphreys; *b* 7 March 1952; *Educ* Woodford Co HS, Newnham Coll Cambridge (MA), Université Libre de Bruxelles – Institut D'Etudes Europèenes (License Spécial en Droit Europèen); *m* 6 Jan 1989, Peter Alegi; *Career* Baker & McKenzie: articled clerk 1975–77, asst slr 1977–81, ptnr 1981–2003, ptnr i/c EC, Competition and Trade Dept 1989–2003, memb Professional Devpt Ctee 1989–93, of counsel 2003–; memb: Competition Panel CBI 1990–, Law Ctee IOD 1993–95, Competition Ctee Int C of C UK 1995–; chair Competition Ctee Business and Industry Advsy Ctee OECD 2012–; ed Competition Law chapter Encyclopaedia of Information Technology Law (Sweet & Maxwell) 1989–; numerous articles and speeches on Euro and competition law issues; memb: Law Soc 1977, Slrs' Euro Gp 1977; *Recreations* Italian hill towns, wine and gardens; *Style—* Ms Lynda Martin Alegi; ✉ Baker & McKenzie LLP, 100 New Bridge Street, London EC4V 7JA (☎ 020 7919 1000, fax 020 7919 1999, mobile 07968 612556)

MARTIN OF SPRINGBURN, Baron (Life Peer UK 2009), of Port Dundas in the City of Glasgow; Rt Hon Michael John Martin; PC (2000); s of Michael Martin, and Mary Martin; *b* 3 July 1945; *Educ* St Patrick's Boys' Sch Glasgow; *m* 1966, Mary McLay; 1 s, 1 da; *Career* Rolls Royce (Hillington) AUEW shop steward 1970–74, trade union organiser 1976–79; MP: (Lab) Glasgow Springburn 1979–2000, (Speaker) Glasgow Springburn 2000–05, (Speaker) Glasgow NE 2005–09; PPS to Rt Hon Denis Healey MP 1980–83, chm Scottish Grand Ctee 1987–97, memb Speaker's Panel of Chairmen 1987–97, chm Administration Ctee 1992–97, memb Select Ctee on House of Commons Servs, dep speaker and first dep chm Way & Means 1997–2000, speaker House of Commons 2000–09; memb Coll of Piping, memb UNITE; *Recreations* playing and listening to the Scottish pipes, hill walking, folk music, local history; *Style—* The Rt Hon the Lord Martin of Springburn; ✉ House of Lords, London SW1A 0PW

MARTIN-JENKINS, David Dennis; eldest s of Lt-Col Dennis Frederick Martin-Jenkins, TD (d 1991), of Cranleigh, Surrey, and Dr Rosemary Clare Martin-Jenkins, *née* Walker (d 2000); *b* 7 May 1941, Glasgow; *Educ* Kingsmead, Meols, St Bede's Eastbourne,

Marlborough; *m* 24 June 1967, Anthea, da of Arthur Milton de Vinny (d 1983); *Career* dir: JW Cameron and Co Ltd 1972–82, Ellerman Lines plc 1974–82, Tollemache and Cobbold Breweries Ltd 1976–82; chm MN Offrs Pension Fund Investment Ctee 1976–82; dir: Primesight plc 1984–99, National Home Loans Holdings plc 1985–95, Capital and Regnl Properties plc 1986–95; chm: Paragon Gp plc Pension Fund 1991–2006, Electoral Reform Services Ltd 2001–06; tstee John Ellerman Fndn 1991–2009; treas Shipwrecked Mariners' Soc 1995–2006; FCA 1965; *Recreations* sport (Tranmere Rovers and Liverpool FCs), politics (Lib Dem), hill walking (climbed Mera Peak (21,200ft) Nepal 1986, Aconcagua (22,835ft) Argentina 1993, Pisco (18,867ft) Peru 1996), the countryside; *Clubs* Lancashire CCC; *Style—* David Martin-Jenkins, Esq; ✉ Jobson's Cottage, Jobson's Lane, Haslemere, Surrey GU27 3BY (☎ 01428 707294, fax 01428 708097)

MARTYR, Peter McCallum; s of John Walton Martyr, and Jean Wallace Robertson, *née* McCallum; *b* 31 March 1954; *Educ* Clifton, Univ of Wales (LLB); *m* 27 May 1978, Carol Frances, da of Donald Edgar Busby; 1 s (Luke b 26 Dec 1985), 1 da (Laura b 7 Nov 1988); *Career* admitted slr 1979, chief exec Norton Rose 2002– (ptnr 1985–, specialising in insurance, shipping and energy disputes); Freeman Worshipful Co of Solicitors 1979; *Recreations* skiing, collector's motor cars, music; *Style—* Peter Martyr, Esq; ✉ Norton Rose, 3 More London Riverside, London SE1 2AQ (☎ 020 7283 6000, fax 020 7283 6500)

MARVEN, Gary; s of Robert and Margaret Marven; *Educ* Bolton GS, Univ of Leeds; *Career* broadcaster; Granada plc 1996–98: commercial dir, business technol, sr fin exec; BBC 1998–2009: fin dir of prodn 1999–2009, chief operating offr factual and learning div 2000–09; ICA; *Recreations* squash, running, reading; *Style—* Gary Marven, Esq

MARWICK, Rt Hon Tricia; PC (2011), MSP; da of John (d 1995), and Mary, *née* Lynch (d 1994); *b* 5 November 1953; *m* 19 July 1975, Frank Marwick; 1 s, 1 da; *Career* public affairs offr Shelter Scotland 1992–99; elected memb SNP Nat Exec 1997–99; MSP (SNP): Scotland Mid & Fife 1999–2007, Fife Central 2007–11, Fife Mid & Glenrothes 2011–; presiding offr Scottish Parl 2011–; *Recreations* reading (anything), sport (watching); *Style—* The Rt Hon Tricia Marwick, MSP; ✉ The Scottish Parliament, Edinburgh EH99 1SP (☎ 0131 348 5680, e-mail presiding.officer@scottish.parliament.uk)

MARWOOD, Roger Paul; s of Kenneth Ian Marwood (d 1988) and Blanche Greenberg (d 1980); *b* 23 July 1947; *Educ* Cheltenham GS, Univ of London (MB BS, MSc, Water Polo double purple); *m* 21 Feb 1976, Suzanne Christine, da of Francis Brown; 1 s (Joseph Roger George b 31 Oct 1984), 2 da (Rebecca Alice Georgina b 25 March 1978, Sophie Christine Blanche b 30 Dec 1979); *Career* sr registrar in obstetrics and gynaecology St Mary's Hosp 1980–82 (registrar 1975–80); conslt in obstetrics and gynaecology Chelsea & Westminster Hosp 1982–2014, consl gynaecologist to King Edward VII Hosp 1985–2014; contrib to numerous jls on clinical obstetrics and gynaecology; pres Section of Obstetrics and Gynaecology RSM 2000–01, memb Cncl for London RCOG, memb Hosp Recognition Ctee RCOG; memb Worshipful Soc of Apothecaries 1985; FRCOG 1989 (MRCOG 1977); *Recreations* opera, skiing, sailing, swimming; *Clubs* Garrick; *Style—* Roger Marwood, Esq; ✉ 11 Chelsea Vista, London SW6 25D (☎ 020 7371 9504); Chelsea & Westminster Hospital, Fulham Road, London SW10 5NH (☎ 020 8746 8218, fax 020 8846 7998)

MARX, Clare Lucy; CBE (2007), DL (Suffolk, 2008); *Educ* Cheltenham Ladies Coll, UCL (MB BS); *m* 1989, Andrew W Fane, *qv*; *Career* consIt orthopaedic surgn St Mary's Hosp NHS Tst 1990–93, Ipswich Hospital NHS Tst: joined 1993, clinical dir trauma and orthopaedics 1994–98, chair Med Staff Ctee 2003–05, currently associate medical dir; chair Specialist Advsy Ctee in Orthopaedics Jt Ctee of Higher Surgical Trg RCS 2005–07 (memb 2000–09); memb Cncl Faculty of Medical Leadership and Mgmnt 2012; pres Br Orthopaedic Assoc 2008–09, pres RCS 2014–17 (memb Cncl 2009); author of numerous arthroplasty articles in scientific jls; Hon DSc Univ of Exeter 2016; ad hominen FRCSEd 2008, PRCS 2014 (FRCS 1981), FRCPEd 2015, Hon FRCPGlas 2015, hon fell Royal Australian Coll of Surgns (Hon FRACS) 2016; *Recreations* walking, with or without a dog, gardening, skiing, music, opera, Shakespeare; *Style—* Miss Clare Marx CBE, DL, PRCS; ✉ Office of the President, The Royal College of Surgeons of England, 35–43 Lincoln's Inn Fields, London WC2A 3PE (☎ 020 7869 6009, e-mail president@rcseng.ac.uk, website www.rcseng.ac.uk)

MARYON-DAVIS, Prof Alan Roger; s of Cyril Edward Maryon-Davis (d 1994), of Osterley, Middx, and Hilda May, *née* Thompson (d 1995); *b* 21 January 1943; *Educ* St Paul's, St John's Coll Cambridge (MA, MB BChir), St Thomas' Hosp Med Sch London, LSHTM (MSc); *m* 14 March 1981, (Glynis) Anne, da of Dr Philip Trefor Davies (d 1970) of Hartlepool, Cleveland; 2 da (Jessica b 1983, Elizabeth b 1985); *Career* med consIt, public health specialist, writer and broadcaster; clinical med 1969–74, community and preventive med 1974–, chief MO Health Educn Cncl 1984–87, hon sr lectr in community med St Mary's Hosp Med Sch London 1985–89, hon specialist in community med Paddington and N Kensington HA 1985–88, consIt in public health med W Lambeth HA (later Lambeth, Southwark and Lewisham HA) 1988–2002, dir of public health for Southwark 2002–07; KCL: sr lectr in public health med 1988–2007, hon prof of public health 2007–; vice-chair Nat Heart Forum 2005–13, chair Royal Inst of Public Health 2006–08 (vice-chair 2002–06), pres Faculty of Public Health 2007–10, chair Royal Soc for Public Health 2008–09, vice-chair Medical Journalists Assoc 2010–11, chair Best Beginnings 2011–16, vice-chair UK Health Forum 2013, chair Alcohol Research UK 2014–; regular med advice columnist Woman magazine 1988–2005, regular columnist Public Health News 2003–06, ed-in-chief Public Health Today 2010–; MRCP 1972, FFCM 1986, FRIPHH 1989, FRCP 2005, FRSH 2005, FFSEM 2007, hon FCMSA 2010, hon FRCGP 2011; *Radio* BBC Radio 4 series: Action Makes the Heart Grow Stronger 1983, Back in 25 Minutes 1984, Not Another Diet Programme 1985, Cancercheck 1988; *Television* BBC series: Your Mind in Their Hands 1982, Save a Life 1986, Bodymatters 1985–89; *Books* Family Health & Fitness (1981), Bodyfacts (1984), Diet 2000 (with J Thomas, 1984), How to Save a Life (with J Rogers, 1987), Pssst a Really Useful Guide to Alcohol (1989), Cholesterol Check (1991), The Good Health Guide (1994), Ruby's Health Quest (1995), The Body-Clock Diet (1996), Feeling Good (2007); *Recreations* relaxing in the Yorkshire Dales, singing in the group 'Instant Sunshine'; *Style—* Prof Alan Maryon-Davis; ✉ Friary Court, The Friary, Salisbury, Wiltshire SP1 2HU (☎ 01722 341786)

MASCHLER, Thomas Michael; s of Kurt Leo Maschler; *b* 16 August 1933; *Educ* Leighton Park Sch Reading; *m* 1970, Fay Goldie (the writer on restaurants Fay Maschler) (m dis), da of Arthur Coventry (d 1969); 1 s (Benjamin Joseph b 1974), 2 da (Hannah Kate b 1970, Alice Mary b 1972); m 2 1987, Regina Kaliniez; *Career* publisher; chm Jonathan Cape 1970– (editorial dir 1960, md 1966); prodn asst André Deutsch 1955, ed MacGibbon & Kee 1956–58, fiction ed Penguin Books 1958–60; *Recreations* tennis, skiing; *Style—* Thomas Maschler Esq; ✉ Jonathan Cape Ltd, Random House, 20 Vauxhall Bridge Road, London SW1V 2SA

MASEFIELD, Sir Charles; kt (1997); s of Sir Peter Masefield (d 2006), of Reigate, Surrey, and Lady Patricia Masefield; *b* 7 January 1940; *Educ* Eastbourne Coll, Jesus Coll Cambridge (MA); *m* 1970, Fiona Anne; 2 s (Ashley Charles b 1971, Fraser Graham b 1975); *Career* test pilot and sales exec Beagle Aircraft Ltd 1964–70, test pilot Hawker Siddeley Aviation (flying Nimrods, Victors, Vulcans) 1970–76; British Aerospace: dep chief test pilot Manchester 1976–78, chief test pilot Manchester 1978–80, project dir 1980–81, prodn dir Chadderton 1981–84, gen mangr Manchester 1984–86, pres BAe Commercial Aircraft Ltd 1990–93 (md 1986–90), sr vice-pres (commercial) Airbus Industries 1993–94, head Defence Export Services Orgn MoD 1994–98, vice-chm GEC plc 1998–1999, pres BAE Systems 2003–07 (gp mktg dir 2000–01, vice-chm 2002); chm: Microsulis Medical Ltd 2003–07, Helvetica Wealth Mgmnt 2004–13, Ioniq Capital Ptnrs 2013–16; memb Bd: Bank Piguet Geneva 2003–05, Qatar Fndn 2003–12, Epicure Berlin 2012–, Arab-Br Chamber of Commerce 2013–, Saudi-Br Jt Business Cncl 2014–; flying achievements: holder of existing London-NY record for bi-planes flying a 1935 DH90 dragonfly 1964, winner King's Cup Air Race flying P51-D Mustang 1967, Br Air Racing Champion 1968; pres RAeS 1994–95; memb Cncl: Air League, RAeS; Liveryman Guild of Air Pilots and Navigators; CEng 1986, FRAeS 1985, FIMechE 1986, (Hon FIMechE 2005); *Recreations* occasional golf; *Style—* Sir Charles Masefield; ✉ Old Hall, Markyate, Hertfordshire AL3 8AR (☎ 01582 849132, fax 01582 849134, e-mail charles.masefield@helvetica.com)

MASHAM OF ILTON, Baroness (Life Peer UK 1970), of Masham in the North Riding of Yorkshire; Susan Lilian Primrose Cunliffe-Lister (Susan, Countess of Swinton); DL (N Yorks 1991); da of Maj Sir Ronald Norman Sinclair, 8 Bt, and Reba Inglis, later Mrs R H Hildreth (d 1985); *b* 14 April 1935, Sinclair; *Educ* Heathfield Sch Ascot, London Poly; *m* 8 Dec 1959, 2 Earl of Swinton (d 2006); 1 s, 1 da (both adopted); *Career* sits as Independent peer in House of Lords; memb: All Party Parly Gps on Accident Prevention (vice-chair), Animal Welfare, Antibiotics (sec), Artrial Fibrilation, Autism, Civil Soc and Volunteering (treas), Clinical Psychology (chair), Complex Needs and Dual Diagnosis, Continence Care (treas), Dentistry, Drug Misuse (vice-chair), First Aid, Gardening and Horticulture, Headache Disorders (sec), Health (co-chair), Heart Disease (vice-chair), Hepatology (co-chair), HIV/AIDS (vice-chair), Horse (treas), Malaria and Neglected Tropical Disease, Men's Health (vice-chair), Muscular Dystrophy, Osteoporosis, Pancreatic Cancer, Pro-Life (vice-chair), Spinal Cord (treas), Stem Cell Transplant (vice-chair), Telehealth (vice-chair), Thrombosis, Tranquiliser Addiction, TB (vice-chair), Vascular Disease, Women's Sport and Fitness; memb: Bd of Visitors for Wetherby Borstal (now Young Offenders Inst) 1963–94, Yorks RHA 1982–90, Family Health Services Authy N Yorks 1990–96, Gen Advsy Cncl of BBC until 1991; chm: Home Office Ctee on Young People Alcohol and Crime, Cncl London Lighthouse; dir Assoc for the Prevention of Addiction; pres: N Yorks Red Cross 1963–88 (patron 1989–), Yorks Assoc for Disabled 1963–98, Spinal Injuries Assoc 1982–, The Psoriasis Assoc, The Registration Cncl of Scientists in Health Care, League of Friends of Harrogate Hosps, Inst of Welfare Offrs, Ripon St Cecilia Orch; vice-pres: Coll of Occupational Therapists Action for Dysphasic, Hosp Saving Assoc; chair Drug Misuse Gp, chair Disablement Income Gp, vice-chair Assoc of Health Gps; patron: Disablement Income Group, Adults (DIA), Int Spinal Res Tst; chair Phoenix House, chair Young Offenders Inst Wetherby 1963–94, pres, vice-pres and patron of numerous other orgns; Freeman Borough of Harrogate 1989; hon fell Bradford & Ilkley Community Coll 1988; Hon MA: York 1985, Open Univ 1985; Hon LLD: Univ of Leeds 1988, Teesside Univ 1993, UEA 2001; Hon DSc Univ of Ulster 1990, Hon DLitt Keele Univ 1993, Hon DCL UEA 2001; hon fell: Royal Coll of GPs 1981, Chartered Soc of Physiotherapy 1996; FRCN 2011; *Publications* Sue Masham, The World Walks By; *Recreations* swimming, breeding Highland ponies, gardening, farming; *Style—* Baroness Masham of Ilton, DL; ✉ Dykes Hill House, Masham, Ripon, North Yorkshire HG4 4NS (☎ 01765 689241, fax 01765 688184, e-mail susan@masham1935.fsnet.co.uk); 46 Westminster Gardens, Marsham Street, London SW1P 4JG (☎ 020 7834 0700)

MASKREY, Simeon Andrew; QC (1995); s of Norman Walter Maskrey, of Seaford, and Brenda, *née* Rose, of Market Harborough; *b* 17 May 1955; *Educ* King's Sch Grantham, Leicester Univ (LLB); *Family* 2 s, 1 da; *Career* pupil of Sir Lord Judge (former Lord Chief Justice) and Sir John Goldring (former Lord Justice of Appeal), recorder 1997– (asst recorder 1993–97), dep High Ct judge 2000–, Head of Chambers at 7 Bedford Row London; *Style—* Simeon Maskrey, Esq, QC; ✉ 7 Bedford Row, London WC1R 4BS (☎ 020 7242 3555, fax 020 7242 2511, e-mail clerks@7br.co.uk)

MASOJADA, Bronislaw Edmund (Bronek); s of Milek Edmund Masojada (d 2015), and Shirley Mary, *née* Johnston; *b* 31 December 1961; *Educ* Durban HS, Univ of Natal (BSc), Trinity Coll Oxford (Rhodes scholar, MPhil); *m* 1986, Jane Elizabeth Ann Lamont; 3 s (Adam Lamont b 14 Aug 1987, Dominik Edmund b 19 Nov 1995, Marek Roderick b 13 Oct 1999), 2 da (Michaela Jane b 11 March 1991, Lara Eva b 19 Oct 1993); *Career* Nat Serv South African Army Engrg Corps 1983–84; with McKinsey & Co Sydney, London and Tokyo 1989–93, md Hiscox Hldgs 1993–95, md Hiscox plc 1996–99, ceo Hiscox plc 2000–06, ceo Hiscox Ltd 2006; dep chm Cncl Lloyd's 2001–07, dir Xchanging Insure Services 2003–06, chm Insurance Intellectual Capital Initiative 2008–14; chm Lloyd's Underwriting Agents Assoc 2000 (memb Ctee 1993–98), memb Ctee Lloyd's Market Assoc 2000–01, memb Bd Assoc of Br Insurers 2012–, memb Bd Pool Re 2015–; pres Insurance Inst of London 2004–05; pres Lloyd's Croquet Soc 2004–12; tstee Lloyd's Tercentenary Research Fndn 2007–14 (chm 2008–14); Liveryman Worshipful Co of Insurers 2006–12 (Jr Warden 2012–13, Master 2013–14, Past Master 2014–); *Recreations* kite surfing, skiing, Caterham racing; *Style—* Mr Bronek Masojada; ✉ Hiscox plc, 1 Great St Helen's, London EC3A 6HX (☎ 020 7448 6012, fax 020 7448 6598, e-mail bronek.masojada@hiscox.com)

MASON, Col Colin Rees; OBE (2003), TD, DL; s of Clifford Harold Mason (d 1969), and Ann, *née* Jones (d 1986); *b* 19 August 1943; *Educ* Gwent Coll, St Julian's HS Newport, Univ of Wales Aberystwyth (BA), Magdalene Coll Cambridge (MPhil), Harvard Grad Sch of Business (OPM); *m* 22 Aug 1968, (Grace) Angela, da of Ernest Alan St Helier Tweney (d 1979); 1 s (Richard Colin St Helier b 12 Oct 1970), 1 da (Penelope Jane St Helier b 19 March 1974); *Career* former broadcaster; began in USA while postgrad researcher Rice Univ TX in 1960s; formerly with: Ulster TV, BBC Local Radio; Natural History TV Unit BBC until 1974, prog dir Swansea Sound 1974–79, asst md Standard Broadcasting 1979, fndr md Chiltern Radio plc 1980–95, dep chm Choice FM Group 1995–2004, md Chiltern Broadcast Management 1997–; dir Network News (Radio) Ltd 1991–96; Lt-Col Royal Regt of Wales (TA), served Gulf War 1991, CO Pool of Public Info Offrs TA 1990–93, 15 (UK) Psychological Ops Gp 1998–2003; served: Kosovo 1999–2000, Sierra Leone 2001, Macedonia 2001, Afghanistan 2002, Iraq 2003; Co Commandant 2000–2004; Hon Col 15 (UK) Psychological Ops Gp 2004–; dir Milton Keynes C of C and Industry 1984–91; High Sheriff Beds 2002; *Recreations* travel, rowing; *Clubs* Army and Navy, Reform; *Style—* Col Colin Mason, OBE, TD, DL; ✉ Hall End House, Hall End, Bedfordshire MK43 9HJ (☎ and fax 01234 766123, e-mail masonradio@aol.com)

MASON, David Gwyn; s of Gwyn Meirion Mason (d 2006), and Nansi Bronwen, *née* Roberts (d 1966); *b* 7 August 1949, Birkenhead, Cheshire; *Educ* Cheadle Hulme Sch, Univ of Liverpool (LLB); *m* 3 May 1980, Patricia Mary, *née* Gerrard; 3 da (Jennifer Mary b 11 Oct 1984, Emily Ann, Alice Wendy (twins) b 22 Feb 1987); *Career* slr; ptnr Park & Co slrs 1975–81, ptnr Birch Cullimore slrs 1983– (joined 1981); under sheriff: City of Chester 1990–2003, Cheshire 2003–; memb: Law Soc, Soc of Tst and Estate Practitioners, Agric Law Assoc; govr Queens Sch Chester; *Recreations* gardening, sport; *Clubs* Chester City, Deeside Ramblers Hockey; *Style—* David Mason, Esq; ✉ Cullimore Dutton, Friars, White Friars, Chester CH1 1XS (☎ 01244 356789, fax 01244 312582, e-mail david.mason@cullimoredutton.co.uk)

MASON, Edward Geoffrey; s of Robin Mason (d 1995), and Hon Elizabeth, *née* Eden; *b* 3 December 1961; *Educ* Oundle, Univ of Durham (BA, pres Union Soc); *m* 1 (m dis 2006); 1 da (Georgina b 1991), 1 s (Hector b 1994); m 2, 6 July 2012, Miranda Kate, *née* McLoughlin; *Career* managing ptnr Jones Mason Barton Antenen 1998–99, ceo Claydon Heeley Jones Mason 1999–2000 (md 1997–98); chm: Mango Event Mgmnt 2001–08, City Championships Ltd 2003–08; managing ptnr Mason Campbell Business Strategy ConsItg 2008–12 and 2014–, managing ptnr AGL Communications LLP 2012–13; non-exec dir

Fortnum & Mason plc 2004–07; judge and mentor Walpole Crafted Prog 2012–; assoc of faculty Moller Centre for Leadership Development Univ of Cambridge 2015–; FRSA 2003; *Recreations* sculpture, vintage cars; *Clubs* Brooks's, RSA; *Style*— Edward Mason, Esq; ✉ Claypits Hall, Foxearth, Sudbury, Suffolk CO10 7JD (e-mail ed.mason@masoncampbell.com, website www.masoncampbell.com)

MASON, Eileen Janet Vicky (Mrs Johnson); da of Garnald Percy Mason (d 1972), and June Barbara, *née* Lawrence (d 2010); *b* 13 October 1950; *Educ* Bluecoat Sch, Walsall Coll of Art, Sandwell Coll of Photography; *m* 1981, Bill Johnson; 2 da (Laura b 1979, Bobbie b 1985), 1 s (Martyn b 1983); *Career* trained as photographer Rubery Owen Co Ltd 1968–73, chief photographer Wolverhampton Educn Authy 1973–74, chief photographer Simon Livingstone Photography 1974–75, Eileen Mason Photography 1975–; memb Professional Photographers of America 1985, Craftsman with Distinction Guild of Wedding Photographers 1993; first woman to achieve fellowship of BIPP and MPA in wedding photography; hon fell Soc of Wedding and Portrait Photographers (SWPP); *Awards* Photographer of the Year Guild of Wedding Photographers (Nat Award) 1991, 1993 and 1995, British Inst Portrait Photographer of the Year (Midland region) 14 times 1976–95, Wedding Photographer of the Year 19 times 1976–2007, BIPP Midland Wedding Portfolio 1999, 2000 and 2001; FBIPP, FRPS, FMPA; *Recreations* theatre, music, comedy, movies (from old English black and white films to modern blockbusters), walking, French food and Indian curries; *Clubs* Walsall Rotary; *Style*— Eileen Mason; ✉ Eileen Mason Photography, 120 Lichfield Road, Rushall, Walsall, West Midlands WS4 1ED (☎ 01922 625229, fax 01922 613937, e-mail info@eileenmason.co.uk, website www.eileenmason.co.uk)

MASON, Prof Haydn Trevor; s of Herbert Thomas Mason (d 1973), and Margaret Ellen, *née* Jones (d 1973); *b* 12 January 1929; *Educ* Greenhill GS Tenby, Univ Coll of Wales Aberystwyth (BA), Middlebury Coll Vermont (AM), Jesus Coll Oxford (DPhil); *m* 1, 5 Feb 1955 (m dis 1982), Gretchen; 1 s (David b 24 March 1961), 1 da (Gwyneth b 8 April 1964); m 2, 14 Sept 1982, Adrienne Mary, da of Alfred Barnes, of Sutton Coldfield; 1 step da (Kate b 26 Nov 1968); *Career* Nat Serv 1951–53, 2 Lt RASC 1952; instr in French Princeton Univ USA 1954–57, lectr Univ of Newcastle 1960–63, reader Univ of Reading 1965–67 (lectr 1964–65), prof UEA 1967–79, prof Université de Paris-III (Sorbonne Nouvelle) 1979–81, prof Univ of Bristol 1981–94 (emeritus prof 1994–); distinguished scholar in residence Univ of Maryland USA 1986; pres: Assoc of Univ Profs of French 1981–82, Soc of French Studies 1982–84, Br Soc for Eighteenth Century Studies 1984–86 (hon fell 2006–), Int Soc for Eighteenth Century Studies 1991–95, Modern Humanities Research Assoc 1999; dir Voltaire Fndn Univ of Oxford 1977–97 (chm 1989–93), gen ed Complete Works of Voltaire 1998–2001; chm Clifton and Hotwells Improvement Soc 1994–98, ed Bristol Civic Soc Newsletter 2008–12; FLSW 2012–; Officier dans L'Ordre des Palmes Académiques 1985, Médaille d'Argent de la Ville de Paris 1989, Médaille de l'Académie Royale de Langue et de Littérature Française Belgium 1993; *Books* Pierre Bayle and Voltaire (1963), Voltaire (1975), Voltaire: A Biography (1981), French Writers and their Society 1715–1800 (1982), Cyrano de Bergerac: L'Autre Monde (1984), Voltaire: Candide (1992); ed: Marivaux: Les Fausses Confidences (1964), Voltaire: Zadig and Other Tales (1971), Essays Presented in Honour of W H Barber (with R J Howells, A Mason and D Williams, 1985), Myth and its Making in the French Theatre: Studies Presented to W D Howarth (with E Freeman, M O'Regan and S W Taylor, 1988), The Impact of the French Revolution on European Consciousness (with W Doyle, 1989), Voltaire: Candide (1995), Voltaire: Micromégas and Other Short Fictions (2002); *Recreations* crosswords, local history; *Style*— Prof Haydn Mason; ✉ 11 Goldney Avenue, Bristol BS8 4RA (☎ 0117 973 5767)

MASON, Martin Derrick; s of Derrick William Mason (d 2011), and Jean Margaret, *née* Pennicott (d 1999); *b* 22 February 1963, Sussex; *Educ* Chichester Sch for Boys; *m* 10 June 1994, Jacqueline, *née* Pratt; 1 da (Charlotte Isobel b 24 Nov 1996); *Career* sales dir John Smedley 1994–99, sales and mktg dir Pringle 1999–2003, mktg dir Mulberry 2003–06, chief exec Tanner Krolle 2006–07, chief exec Lulu Guinness 2008–13, chief exec Nicole Farhi 2014–15, md R E Tricker Ltd 2015–; memb: Br Fashion Cncl, Br Menswear Guild; PR Week Campaign of the Year (Pringle: Faldo to Beckham) 2002, winner HSBC Business Thinking 2012; *Recreations* painting, walking, travel, history; *Clubs* Lansdowne; *Style*— Martin Mason, Esq

MASON, Michael; s of Thomas and Janet Mason; *b* 1 June 1935, Lancs; *Educ* Ashton-under-Lyne Sch of Art, Manchester Regnl Sch of Art, Br Sch at Rome; *m* Barbara; 1 s, 1 da; *Career* sculptor; princ lectr in sculpture Manchester Metropolitan Univ 1982–96; fndr memb Partnership Environmental Art Studio, memb West Country Potters Assoc; sculpture fell Br Sch at Rome; FRBS; *Solo Exhibitions* Zaydler Gallery London 1969, 57 Gallery Edinburgh 1970, Heaton Park outdoor event Manchester 1972, West Park outdoor event Macclesfield 1972, The Anonymous Exhibition Oriel Gallery Univ of Wales 1974, Peterloo Gallery Manchester, Univ of Exeter, Royal Exchange Manchester 1977, Whitworth Art Gallery Univ of Manchester, Arts Centre Gallery Univ of Wales 1978, Serpentine London 1979, South Manchester Gallery 1985, Bury Metro Arts 1987, Galeria Bass Caracas, AVAF Caracas 1993, Mariners Gallery St Ives 1994, Scultpure Court Hanley Museum and Art Gallery Stoke-on-Trent 1997; *Group Exhibitions* G6 Salford City Art Gallery, Peterloo Gallery Manchester 1964, Here and Now Chester Cathedral 1965, Grosvenor Gallery Manchester 1968, V&A London 1970, Manchester City Art Gallery, Leeds City Art Gallery, Summer Show Piccadilly London 1971, Undercroft Gallery Manchester Poly 1973, Manchester Acad City Art Gallery 1974, 1991, 1992 and 1993, Br Sch at Rome 1976, Artists Market Gallery London 1979, Sculpture in the Botanic Gardens Edinburgh 1980, The British Art Show tour 1984, Red Rose Holden Gallery Manchester Poly 1985, Artizana Gallery Prestbury 1986, Hanover Gallery Liverpool 1987, Zagreb 3rd World Trienniale 1990, Fletcher Challenge Onehunga 1991, Zagreb 4th World Trienniale 1994, Warsaw Acad 1994, Galerie Vromans Amsterdam 1995, Sherborne Contemporary Arts 2002–03, Cultural Landscape Workshop Croatia, Mariner's Gallery St Ives 2004, Study Gallery Poole 2006, Bloomberg Arts 2006, Lighthouse Gallery Poole 2007, Royal West of England Academy 2008, Glastonbury Abbey 2015; *Commissions* incl: Cheshire County Cncl, Manchester City Cncl, St David's Church Hale, Severn Trent Water, Int Ring of Magicians, Hackney Empire, Shell UK, Royal Exchange Manchester, Prince of Wales Theatre Cardiff, Asociacion Venezolana de las Artes del Fuego; work in collections incl: Arts Cncl of GB, V&A, Aucklands Studios, Arte Feugo Caracas, Juan Carlos Lancara Caracas, Zagreb Gallery of Modern Art; *Awards* NW Arts ACGB, Royal Manchester Inst Haywards Prize, Titograd Prize Zagreb, Sculpture Prize Millfield 2008, Norweb Prize MC Acad; *Publications* River Earth and Sky, Degrees C; *Recreations* T'ai chi chuan, archery; *Style*— Michael Mason, Esq; ✉ e-mail mikem@madasafish.com

MASON, Paul; s of John Mason (d 1986), and Julia Wilkinson, *née* Lewis; *b* 23 January 1960, Leigh, Lancs; *Educ* Univ of Sheffield (BA), London Univ Inst of Educn; *m* Aug 1999, Pamela Jane Bruton; *Career* freelance journalist 1991–95, Reed Business Information 1995–2001 (dep ed Computer Weekly); Newsnight (BBC 2): business corr 2001–08, economics ed 2008–; economics ed Channel 4 News 2013–; visiting prof of economics Wolverhampton Univ 2012–; Wincott Prize for Business Journalism 2003, Workworld Broadcaster of the Year 2004, Diageo African Business Reporting Award 2007, RTS Specialist Journalist of the Year 2012; *Books* Live Working or Die Fighting: How the Working Class Went Global (2007), Meltdown – The End of the Age of Greed (2009), Why It's Kicking Off Everywhere: The New Global Revolutions (2012), Rare Earth: A Novel (2012), Lost Capitalism: A Guide to Our Future (2015); *Clubs* Frontline, Groucho; *Style*— Paul Mason, Esq; ✉ c/o Aitken Alexander, 18–21 Cavaye Place, London SW10 9PT (Twitter @paulmasonnews)

MASON, Prof Paul James; CB (2003); s of Charles Ernest Edward Mason, and Phyllis Mary, *née* Swan; *b* 16 March 1946; *Educ* Univ of Nottingham (BSc), Univ of Reading (PhD); *m* 1968, Mary, *née* Slaney; 1 da, 1 s; *Career* The Met Office: scientific offr 1967–71, sr scientific offr 1971–74, princ scientific offr 1974–79, head Meteorological Res Unit 1979–85, asst dir Boundary Layer Branch 1985–89, dep dir Physical Res 1989–91, chief scientist 1991–2003; dir NCAS/Univs Weather Research Network 2003–06; prof emeritus Dept of Meteorology Univ of Reading; chm Global Climate Observing Steering Ctee 2001–06; pres RMS 1992–94, memb Ed Bd Boundary Layer Meteorology 1988–2001; Buchan Prize RMS 1986, L G Groves Prize for Meteorology MoD 1980; FRS 1995; *Publications* scientific papers in meteorology and fluid dynamics jls; *Recreations* walking and exploring the countryside; *Style*— Prof Paul Mason, CB, FRS; ✉ Department of Meteorology, University of Reading, Earley Gate, PO Box 243, Reading RG6 6BB (☎ 01183 788957, fax 01183 788791, e-mail p.j.mason@reading.ac.uk)

MASON, Peter Edward; s of Arthur Edward Mason (d 2004), and Hazel, *née* Soulsby; *b* 3 December 1951, Stockton-on-Tees, Co Durham; *Educ* Grangefield GS for Boys Stockton-on-Tees, Oriel Coll Oxford (MA), Warwick Business Sch (Dip); *m* 3 Sept 1977, Sally Joanne Ashford; 1 s (Thomas Edward b 23 March 1989), 1 da (Sophie May Victoria b 9 April 1991); *Career* DTI: joined 1973, seconded to Panel on Take-overs and Mergers 1983–86, asst dir competition policy Office of Fair Trading 1989–92, head of design policy and mgmnt best practice 1992–94, dir of consumer safety and strategy 1995–2000, dir of coal 2000–03, dir of finance policy and support 2003–07; chief exec Nat Measurement Office (formerly Nat Weights and Measures Lab) 2007–14 (memb Steering Bd 2004–14), dir (International) Nat Measurement and Regulation Office (formerly Nat Measurement Office) 2014–16, head Int Legal Metrology Regulatory Delivery Dept of Business, Innovation and Skills 2016–; pres Int Ctee of Legal Metrology 2011–; tstee Coal Pension Schemes 2000–03; hon memb Chartered Trading Standards Inst 2014; *Recreations* music, reading, motorcycling; *Style*— Peter Mason, Esq; ✉ Regulatory Delivery, Department of Business, Innovation and Skills, Stanton Avenue, Teddington, Middlesex TW11 0JZ (☎ 020 8943 7211, fax 020 8943 7270, e-mail peter.mason@nmro.gov.uk)

MASON, Air Vice Marshal Richard Anthony (Tony); CB (1988), CBE (1982), DL (Glos 2002); s of William Mason (d 1971), and Maud, *née* Jenkinson (d 1978); *b* 22 October 1932; *Educ* Bradford GS, Univ of St Andrews (MA), Univ of London (MA), Univ of Birmingham (DSc); *m* 17 Nov 1956, Margaret Sneddon, da of Alexander McNab Stewart, MBE, of Burntisland, Fife, and Jean Young; 2 da (Alice Lindsay b 21 Sept 1957, Pamela Anne b 17 Aug 1959 d 1985); *Career* RAF: cmmnd 1956, USAF War Coll 1971, RAF Staff Coll 1972; dir: Defence Studies 1976–82, Personnel (Ground) 1982–84; Air Sec 1986–89 (dep 1985–86); Leverhulme Airpower res dir Fndn for Int Security 1989–94, memb Bd Brassey UK Ltd 1989–97; Univ of Birmingham: visiting sr fell 1989–96, prof of aerospace security 1996–98, dir Centre for Studies in Security and Diplomacy 1998–2001, prof Sch of Social Scis 2002–12; head SBAC Eurofighter Info Unit 1992–94; pres Cheltenham Branch RAF ASSOC 1987–2008; memb: IISS 1966–2006, RUSI 1966–2007; Hon Freeman Borough of Cheltenham 2001; Hon FRAeS 2006; *Books* History of RAF Staff College (1972), Readings in Airpower (1978), Airpower in the Next Generation (1979), The Royal Air Force Today and Tomorrow (1982), Airpower in the Nuclear Age (1983/5), British Airpower in the 1980s (1984), War in the Third Dimension (1986), The Soviet Air Force (1986), Airpower: an Overview of Roles (1987), To Inherit the Skies (1990), Air Power: A Centennial Appraisal (1994), Aerospace Power: Revised Roles and Technology (1998); author of many articles in int jls on defence policy and strategy; *Recreations* music, travel; *Clubs* RAF; *Style*— Air Vice Marshal Tony Mason, CB, CBE, DL; ✉ c/o Lloyds Bank, Montpellier, Cheltenham GL50 1SH

MASON, Prof Roger Maxwell; *b* 24 October 1940, Hull; *Educ* Welsh Nat Sch of Med UC Cardiff (MB BCh, PhD), Univ of London (MD); *m* 4 Aug 1978, Margaret Anne Phillipson; *Career* house physician Professorial Med Unit Cardiff Royal Infirmary 1965–66, house surgn St David's Hosp Cardiff 1966, MRC jr research fell Biochemistry Dept UC Cardiff 1966–69, lectr in biochemistry Univ of Nottingham Med Sch 1969–73, visiting scientist NIH Bethesda MD 1978–79, sr lectr in biochemistry Charing Cross Hosp Med Sch 1973–83; Imperial Coll Faculty of Med (Charing Cross and Westminster Med Sch until merger 1997): reader in biochemistry 1983–88, prof of biochemistry 1988–2003 (emeritus prof of renal medicine 2003–), head Dept of Biochemistry 1992–97, vice-chm Bio-Medical Sciences Div 1997–2000, head Molecular Pathology Gp 1997–2000; visiting prof Dogliotti Coll of Med Univ of Liberia (sponsored by Inter-Univ Cncl) 1977, guest worker Dept of Biochemistry Monash Univ Melbourne (Wellcome-Ramaciotti research travel grant) 1981; chm Research Sub-Ctee Arthritis Research Campaign 1998–2001; author of numerous scientific pubns on connective tissues and their diseases; Lettsomian lectr Med Soc of London 1995; Fell-Muir Award for Matrix Biology 2012; memb Br Soc Matrix Biology (chm 1992–96); FRSA, FRCP 2000; *Style*— Prof Roger Mason; ✉ Imperial College Kidney and Transplant Institute, Commonwealth Building, Room 5N8B, Hammersmith Hospital, Du Cane Road, London W12 0NN (☎ 07753 252149, fax 020 8383 2062, e-mail roger.mason@imperial.ac.uk)

MASON, Stephen Maxwell; s of Harold Geoffrey Mason (d 1986), and Ursula, *née* Habermann (d 2006); *b* 19 May 1949; *Educ* Bradford GS, Gonville & Caius Coll Cambridge (MA); *m* 27 March 1976, Judith Mary, da of Hebbert, of Ilkley; 2 da (Fiona b 1979, Nicola b 1985), 1 s (Alistair b 1981); *Career* slr; ptnr Travlaw LLP, ed Travel Law Quarterly; former chair Civil Justice Ctee Law Soc (memb 1997–); author of numerous articles on package holiday law including Holiday Law (jtly, 1995, 5 edn 2012), Alarms and Excursions (2010), The Medhotels Case – a heavyweight battle in four Titanic rounds (2014); *Recreations* writing, travel by train, directing plays (dir Pilot Theatre); *Clubs* Law Soc; *Style*— Stephen Mason, Esq; ✉ e-mail stephen@travlaw.co.uk

MASON, Tony; s of George Donald (d 1982), and Hattie, *née* Mockett (d 1986); *Educ* Lancaster Royal GS, MCAM, FIMI; *m* Susan; 1 da (Emma); *Career* early career training with various advtg and mktg agencies; former co-driver in Ford works team, winner numerous events incl RAC Rally (with Roger Clark) 1972 and Segrave Trophy 1975, later appointed competition co-ordinator with Ford, export dir Mill Accessory Group 1975, fndr own accessory co 1979, contracted to commentate on Lombard RAC Rally and joined Top Gear as a presenter (both with BBC) 1987, also contracted as occasional presenter for Channel 9 TV Aust, Sky and Discovery TV, fndr Tony Mason Motorsport (distributing motor sport products), regular contrib to numerous other pubns, fndr Tony Mason Associates (PR, TV and Motorsport consultancy) 1992; after dinner speaker (with over 1000 appearances, incl P & O Cruise Ships); *Books* author of 6 books incl: Rallying (with Stuart Turner), Mason's Motoring Mayhem! (autobiography, 2013); *Style*— Tony Mason, Esq; ✉ Tony Mason Associates, Maendy, Penrhos, Raglan, Gwent NP15 2LQ (☎ 07811 387267)

MASON, Tristan Lee Michael; s of late Michael Edward Mason, and Linda Jane, *née* Vatcher; *b* 14 November 1976, Bishops Stortford, Herts; *Educ* Monks Walk Sch Welwyn Garden City, Ware College, Cassio Coll Watford; *Career* trainee commis chef The Noke Hotel Thistle Gp 1995–97, head chef The Duck Public House and Restaurant 1997–98, jr sous chef Red Coats Farmhouse Hotel and Restaurant 1998–2000, sr chef de partie

The Mirabelle London 2000–02, jr sous chef The Greenhouse London 2002–03, private chef Herts 2003–04, head chef The Hare Restaurant Berks 2004–07 (1 Michelin Star, voted in the top 5 restaurants outside London by Harpers & Queen), head chef Orrery Restaurant London 2007–08 (1 Michelin Star, 3 AA Rosettes, voted in the top 10 London restaurants by Evening Standard), chef and prop Restaurant Tristan Horsham 2008– (Michelin star 2013–, 3 AA Rosettes 2014 and 2015); *Style*— Tristan Mason, Esq; ✉ Restaurant Tristan, Stans Way, East Street, Horsham, West Sussex RH12 1HU (☎ 01403 255688, e-mail info@restauranttristan.co.uk, website www.restauranttristan.co.uk)

MASON-WATTS, Christopher Nigel Stuart; s of Maj Ronald Henry Watts (d 1982), of Carlisle, Cumbria, and Eva Maria-Louise, *née* Gliese; *b* 6 March 1954; *Educ* Univ of Aberdeen (MA, LLM); *m* 24 Dec 1986, Nicola Clare, da of Wilfred Albert Mason, of Ashby-de-la-Zouch, Leics; 1 da (Poppy b 1988), 3 s (Billy b 1990, Joscelyn b 1991, Rollo b 1992); *Career* admitted slr 1980; dir Teifi Law Ltd; dir Mason-Watts Fine Art; former legal memb Mental Health Act Cmmn, pres Mental Health Review Tbnl, chm Mental Health Strategy and Review Ctee Warks HA 1993–96, memb Ceredigion Community Health Cncl 1996–2004, chm of govrs Sch Gp; *Recreations* music, opera, theatre; *Clubs* Lansdowne; *Style*— Christopher Watts, Esq; ✉ Noyadd Trefawr, Cardigan, West Wales SA43 2RF (☎ 01239 682608); 14 McCleods Mews, London SW7

MASSAM, (Arthur) David Wright; s of Arthur Greenwood Massam (d 1989), of Southport, Lancs, and Emily, *née* Wright (d 1945); *b* 18 November 1934; *Educ* King George V Sch Southport, Univ of Manchester (MPS), Univ of London (LLB); *m* 1957 (m dis 1970), Angela, da of Joseph Smith (d 1986), of Southport, Lancs; 1 da (Melinda Jane b 1958), 1 s (Nigel Robin b 1961); *Career* Nat Serv RAMC 1956–58; C F Thackray Ltd 1958–70; Datapharm Publications Ltd: exec dir 1980–92, dir 1993–97; sec Assoc of the Br Pharmaceutical Industry 1982–92 (joined 1970), dir Prescription Medicines Code of Practice Authy 1993–97 (conslt 1997–2015); former memb: Advsy Cncl on Misuse of Drugs, Poisons Bd, Standing Pharmaceutical Advsy Ctee; memb Hon Soc of the Inner Temple 1968; Freeman: Worshipful Soc of Apothecaries 1993, City of London 1994; FRPharmS 1980 (MPS 1956); *Recreations* history, reading; *Style*— David Massam, Esq; ✉ 80A Westbury Road, Finchley, London N12 7PD (☎ 020 8922 3249)

MASSARA, Paul Joseph; *b* 31 July 1965, Minehead, Somerset; *Educ* Kingston Univ (BSc), London Business Sch (MSc); *m* (m dis); 2 da (Josephine b 20 May 1995, Sophie b 8 Oct 1997); *Career* chief commercial operator Npower until 2012, formerly ceo RWE Npower, ceo Northstar Solar 2016–; exec memb Centrica 2000; Top 40 Under 40 Canada 2004; *Recreations* tennis, riding, cycling; *Style*— Paul Massara, Esq; ✉ e-mail p.massara@northstarsolar.co.uk

MASSER, David William; s of William Stanley Masser (d 1991), and Rose, *née* Lewis (d 2004); *b* 8 November 1948, London; *Educ* Trinity Coll Cambridge (MA, PhD); *m* 1, 1988, Hedda, *née* Freudenschuss (d 2009); *m* 2, 2015, Hedda, *née* Egerer; *Career* lectr Univ of Nottingham 1973–75, research fell Trinity Coll Cambridge 1975–76; Univ of Nottingham: lectr 1976–79, reader 1979–83; prof Univ of Michigan 1983–92, prof Univ of Basel 1992–2014; memb London Mathematical Soc 1974; FRS 2005; Elliptic Functions and Transcendence (1975); author of over 100 papers in mathematical jls; *Recreations* travelling to restaurants; *Style*— David Masser; ✉ Departement Mathematik und Informatik, Fachbereich Mathematik, Spiegelgasse I, 4051 Basel, Switzerland (☎ 0041 61 2671517, fax 0041 61 2672695, e-mail david.masser@unibas.ch); Nadelberg 17, 4051 Basel, Switzerland (☎ 0041 61 2620873)

MASSEY, Ray John Thomas; s of Kenneth Edwin Massey (d 1988), of Taunton, Somerset, and Dorothy May, *née* Brooks (d 2000); *b* 26 September 1951, Taunton, Somerset; *Educ* Ladymead Secdy Sch Taunton, Somerset Coll of Art, Medway Coll of Art and Technol; *m* (sep), Annie, da of Maurice Geay, of Pessac, France; 2 s (Jethro b 6 Jan 1978, Jean-Michel b 24 Feb 1983); 1 s (Joshua Thomas Kenneth Massey-Dearman b 30 Sept 2006) by Dr Vera Dearman; *Career* asst photographer 1970–71, freelance photographer 1972–; numerous exhbns incl: Assoc of Photographers London, JIP Arles France, IIP Ireland; life memb Assoc of Photographers; fell Royal Photographic Soc 2010; *Recreations* travel, swimming, photography; *Clubs* BSAC, Porsche Owners'; *Style*— Ray Massey, Esq; ✉ Camden Park Studios, The Church Hall, Camden Park Road, London NW1 9AY (☎ 020 7267 9550, e-mail ray@raymassey.com, website www.raymassey.com)

MASSEY, Raymond (Ray); s of David Massey, of Newcastle upon Tyne, and Elizabeth Irene, *née* Jeffrey (d 1987); *b* 7 June 1960; *Educ* Walbottle Grammar Northumberland, Univ of Warwick (Lord Rootes fndn scholar, Deutscher Akademischer Austauschdienst Stipendium, BA); *m* 1996, Elizabeth Kay, *née* Clinton; 2 s (Cameron b Oct 1997, Aidan b 22 July 2000); *Career* journalist and author; Coventry Evening Telegraph 1982–87 (reporter, industrial corr, feature writer and diarist, China corr); educn corr Press Assoc 1988–90 (news reporter 1987–); Daily Mail: educn corr 1990–95, motoring corr 1995–2000, tport ed 2000–; FRSA; *Books* Parent Power (1993); *Recreations* golf, travel; *Style*— Ray Massey, Esq; ✉ The Daily Mail, Northcliffe House, 2 Derry Street, London W8 5TT (☎ 020 7938 6102/6000, fax 020 7937 5287)

MASSEY, William Greville Sale; QC (1996); s of Lt Col Patrick Massey, MC (d 2002), of Liss, Hants, and Bessie Lee, *née* Byrne (d 1978); *b* 31 August 1953; *Educ* Harrow, Hertford Coll Oxford (MA); *m* 2 Dec 1978, Cecilia D'Oyly, da of Daniel Edmund Awdry, TD, DL, of Beanacre, Wilts; 3 s (Patrick William Edmund b 31 July 1983, Richard Daniel Hugh b 8 May 1985, Edmund Greville Robert b 12 June 1990); *Career* called to the Bar Middle Temple 1977 (bencher 2004); memb: Chancery Bar Assoc, Revenue Bar Assoc; govr Harrow Sch 2001–13 (vice-chm 2008–13), govr Summer Fields Sch Oxford 1996–2013; *Books* Potter and Monroe's Tax Planning with Precedents (jtly, 9 edn), Encyclopaedia of Forms and Precedents (contrib); *Recreations* skiing, gardening, music, chess; *Style*— William Massey, Esq, QC; ✉ Pump Court Tax Chambers, 16 Bedford Row, London WC1R 4EF (☎ 020 7414 8080, fax 020 7414 8099, e-mail wmassey@pumptax.com)

MASSEY OF DARWEN, Baroness (Life Peer UK 1999), of Darwen in the County of Lancashire; Doreen Elizabeth; da of Jack Hall (d 1989), of Darwen, Lancs, and Mary Ann, *née* Sharrock (d 1973); *b* 5 September 1938; *Educ* Darwen GS, Univ of Birmingham (BA, DipEd, vice-pres Student Union, Hockey and Cricket blues), Univ of London (MA); *m* Dr Leslie Massey, s of James York Massey, of Conisbrough, S Yorks; 3 c (Elizabeth Caitlin b 1969, Owen John b 1971, Benjamin James b 1973); *Career* family planner; grad serv overseas Gabon 1962–63, Springside Sch Philadelphia USA 1967–69, Pre-Sch Play Group Assoc 1973–77, Walsingham Sch 1977–83, advsr Inner London Educn Authy 1983–85, mangr Young People's Prog Health Educn Authy 1985–87, dir The Family Planning Assoc 1989–94 (dir of educn 1987–89); chair All-Pty Parly Gp for Children 2001–, vice-chair All Parly Cricket Gp; pres Brook Advsy Centres; memb: Select Ctee on Affordable Childcare 2014–15, EU Ctee 2015–, Parly Delgn to the Cncl of Europe 2015–; patron: Child Trafficking Unit Univ of Beds, Women and Children First, Amos Bursary 2015–, Maya Centre for Women; hon prof Nottingham Trent Univ 2016; FRSA; *Books* Sex Education: Why, What and How (1988), Sex Education Sourcebook (1994), Lovers' Guide Encyclopaedia (conslt ed, 1996); *Recreations* theatre, cinema, opera, reading, art and design, vegetarian cookery, travel, walking, pilates, swimming; *Clubs* Lady Taverners, Farmers'; *Style*— Baroness Massey of Darwen

MASSIE, Allan Johnstone; CBE (2013); s of Alexander Johnstone Massie, of Banchory, Aberdeenshire, and Evelyn Wilson, *née* Forbes; *b* 16 October 1938; *Educ* Drumtochty Castle, Glenalmond, Trinity Coll Cambridge (BA); *m* 22 June 1973, Alison Agnes Graham, da of Robert Scott Langlands, of Kelso, Roxburghshire; 2 s (Alexander, Louis), 1 da (Claudia); *Career* school master Drumtochty Castle 1960–71, TEFL Rome 1972–75; author, journalist and playwright; princ fiction reviewer The Scotsman 1975–, TV critic The Sunday Standard 1981–83; columnist: Glasgow Herald 1985–88, Sunday Times Scotland 1987–91 and 1997–, The Daily Telegraph 1991–, Daily Mail 1994–; winner: Frederick Niven Prize for the Last Peacock 1981, Fraser of Allander Award Critic of the Year 1982, Scottish Arts Cncl Book Awards 1982 and 1986, The Scotsman, Scottish Book of the Year 1990; tstee Nat Museum of Scotland 1995–98; memb Scottish Arts Cncl 1989; FRSL 1982, Hon FRIAS 1997; *Books* Change and Decay in All Around I See (1978), The Last Peacock (1980), The Death of Men (1981), The Caesars (1983), Portrait of Scottish Rugby (1984), One Night in Winter (1984), Augustus (1986), Byron's Travels (1987), A Question of Loyalties (1989), Glasgow (1989), The Hanging Tree (1990), Tiberius (1991), The Sins of the Father (1991), Caesar (1993), These Enchanted Woods (1993), The Ragged Lion (1994), King David (1995), Shadows of Empire (1997), Antony (1997), Nero's Heirs (1999), The Evening of the World (2001); *Plays* Quintet in October, The Minstrel and The Shirra (1989), First Class Passengers (1995); *Recreations* reading, watching rugby, cricket, walking the dogs; *Clubs* Academy, Selkirk RFC; *Style*— Allan Massie, Esq, CBE; ✉ Thirladean House, Selkirk TD7 5LU (☎ 01750 20393)

MASSIE, Amanda; *Educ* Univ of Bath (BSc); *m* Michael Sleet; *Career* gp co sec IMS and other insurance cos 1992–96; gp co sec, dir and memb Exec Mgmnt Bd: WS Atkins Gp plc 1996–2004, Mouchel Gp plc 2004–13, Hyperion Insurance Gp 2014–15; FCIS; *Style*— Ms Amanda Massie

MASSIE, Sir Herbert William (Bert); kt (2007), CBE (2000, OBE 1984), DL (2014); s of Herbert Douglas Massie, of Liverpool, and Joan Lucy, *née* Roberts; *b* 31 March 1949; *Educ* Sandfield Park Special Sch Liverpool, Portland Trg Coll for the Disabled Mansfield, Hereward Coll Coventry, Liverpool Poly (BA), Manchester Poly (CQSW); *m* 2007, Maureen Lilian Shaw; *Career* Wm Rainford Ltd 1968, West Cheshire Newspapers Ltd 1968–70, Liverpool Assoc for the Disabled 1970–72, Disabled Living Fndn 1977, dir The Royal Assoc for Disability and Rehabilitation (RADAR) 1990–99 (joined 1978), chm Disability Rights Cmmn 2000–07, cmmr Cmmn for Equality and Human Rights 2006–09, Cmmr for the Compact 2008–11; prop Bert Massie Ltd 2007–; chm Community Equipment Code of Practice Scheme CIC 2011–; non-exec dir Appleshaw Ltd 2007–09; memb: Mgmnt Ctee Disabled Drivers Assoc 1968–71, Careers Serv Advsy Cncl for Eng 1979–83, Exec Ctee OUTSET 1983–91, Access Ctee for Eng 1984–93, BR Advsy Gp on Disabled People 1986–94, Disabled Persons Tport Advsy Ctee 1986–2002, Nat Advsy Cncl on Employment of People with Disabilities 1991–98, Ind Cmmn on Social Justice 1993–94, DSS Panel of Experts on Review of Incapacity Benefit 1994, Cabinet Office Working Gp on Equal Opportunities in the Sr Civil Serv 1994–2000, Advsy Gp New Deal Taskforce 1997–2000, Bd Euro Disability Forum 1997–2000; pres Chester, Wirral and N Wales Gp Br Polio Fellowship 2011–; vice-pres: Fndn for Assistive Technol 2000–, Disabled Living Fndn, Royal Assoc for Disability Rights UK (formerly Disability and Rehabilitation 2009–, Muscular Dystrophy UK 2009–, Phab 2010–, Tourism for All 2012–; chm and tstee UK Assoc of Rights and Humanity until 2011; chm Volunteer Centre Liverpool 2012–16, chair Lab Pty Taskforce on Disability and Poverty 2013–14, tstee Liverpool Charity and Voluntary Service 2016–; vice-chm: Assoc of Disabled Professionals 1986–94 (memb Exec Ctee 1979–99), Vol Cncl for Handicapped Children 1985–93 (memb 1980–93), Tripscope 1989–2006 (memb 1986–2006); dep chm Nat Disability Cncl 1998–2000 (memb 1996–2000); tstee: BEAMA Fndn for Disabled People 1990–2000 (sec 1986–90), Ind Living Fund 1990–93, Habinteg Housing Assoc 1993–2009, Mobility Choice 1998–13, Inst for Employment Studies 2000–07, CSV 2001, The Brain Charity (formerly Merseyside Neurological Tst, then Neurosupport) 2004–, United Tsts 2006–08, RAISE 2008–, Local Solutions 2009–; govr: Pensions Policy Inst 2002–07, Motability 2002; patron: Heswall Disabled Children's Holiday Fund 2003–, Disability and Deaf Arts 2009–; UK nat sec Rehabilitation Int 1993–2000 (dep vice-pres for Euro 1996–2000); govr Liverpool John Moores Univ 2008–; Br Polio Fellowship Polio Person of the Last 70 Years 2009, Luke Fitzherbert Lifetime Achievement Award Third Sector Magazine 2010; memb Worshipful Co of Wheelwrights 2008 (Master Wheelwrights Award 2002), Freeman City of London 2008; hon fell Liverpool John Moores Univ 2002, Hon LLD Univ of Bristol 2005, Hon DUniv Staffs 2007, Hon LLD Univ of Liverpool 2013; FRSA 1988, MInstD 2001, FCGI 2009; *Publications* Work and Disability 1977 (with M Greaves, 1979), Employers Guide to Disabilities (with M Kettle, 1982, 2 edn 1986), Aspects of the Employment of Disabled People in the Federal Republic of Germany (1982), Day Centres for Young Disabled People (jtly, 1984), Travelling with British Rail (1985), Wheelchairs and their Use (with J Weyers, 1986), Choosing a Wheelchair (with J Male, 1990), Seat Belts and Disabled People (with J Isaacs, 1990), Social Justice and Disabled People (1994), Getting Disabled People to Work (2000), Employmentability 2010 (2010); *Style*— Sir Bert Massie, CBE, DL; ✉ 2 North Sudley Road, Liverpool L17 0BG (☎ 0151 727 3252, e-mail bert@massie.com)

MASSINGHAM, David Charles; s of Derek George Massingham (d 1976), and Margaret Catherine, *née* Callaghan (d 2007); *b* 26 June 1959; *Educ* Dame Alice Owens GS, Laban Centre for Movement and Dance (BA, Advanced Performance Certificate); *Career* choreographer and creative prodr; fndr/dancer Geographical Duvet 1984–86, dancer Transitions 1986, fndr dir/choreographer/dancer Adventures in Motion Pictures 1986–88, choreographer int course for choreographers and composers 1988, fndr David Massingham Dance 1989, choreographer in res Northern Arts 1995, currently dir DanceXchange Birmingham and artistic dir Bare Bones Dance Co, co-artistic dir Int Dance Festival Birmingham 2008; major works incl: Companion Pieces 1989, The Immortals 1990, Cradle 1994, Hinterland 1996, Untold 1998, The Elbow Room 2001, With the Company We Keep 2006; theatre incl: The Tempest (RNT), The Red Balloon (Birmingham Rep), Cabaret (Newcastle Live Theatre); Bonnie Bird Award 1992; *Recreations* motorcycling; *Style*— David Massingham, Esq; ✉ DanceXchange, Birmingham Hippodrome, Thorp Street, Birmingham B5 4TB (☎ 0121 689 3170, fax 0121 689 3179, e-mail david.massingham@dancexchange.org.uk)

MASTER, (Humphrey) Simon Harcourt; s of Humphrey Ronald Master, of Thetford, Norfolk, and Rachel Blanche, *née* Plumbly (d 1989); *b* 10 April 1944; *Educ* Ardingly, Univ de La Rochelle; *m* 3 May 1969, Georgina Mary, da of Sir Brian Caldwell Cook Batsford (d 1991), of Winchelsea, E Sussex; 2 s (Nicholas Harcourt b 1973, Matthew Harcourt b 1976); *Career* sr ed: Pan Books Ltd 1966–69, B T Batsford Ltd 1969–70; Pan Books Ltd: editorial dir 1970–73, publishing dir 1973–79, managing dir 1980–87; chief exec Random House UK Ltd 1987–89, exec vice-pres int Random House Inc 1989–91, dep chm Random House Group 1989–2004, exec chm Arrow Books 1990–92, exec chm Random House Gen Books Div 1992–2004 (non-exec dir 2004–11); non-exec chm London Book Fair 2006–12, memb Bd Br Book Acad 2006–; dir HMSO 1990–95; Publishers Assoc: memb Cncl 1989–95, vice-pres 1995–96, pres 1996–97 and 2001–02; *Recreations* reading, golf, classic cars, gardening; *Clubs* Groucho, Sherborne Golf; *Style*— Simon Master, Esq; ✉ Random House, 20 Vauxhall Bridge Road, London SW1V 2SA (☎ 020 7840 8400)

MASTERS, Blythe Sally Jess; *née* Levett; da of Gordon Robert Levett (d 2000), and Sally Elizabeth Ann, *née* Scott; *b* 22 March 1969, Oxford; *Educ* Ashford Sch for Girls, King's Sch Canterbury, Trinity Coll Cambridge (BA); *Children* 1 da (Honour Radegund b 3 Aug 1993); *Career* JPMorgan: currently memb Exec Mgmnt Ctee and CIB Operating Ctee, various former roles incl head of structured products 1991–2000, global head of credit portfolio and credit policy and strategy 2000–03, investment bank chief financial offr 2003–06, global head of commodities 2006–14; ceo digital Asset Holdings 2015–; non-

M

exec chm Santander Consumer USA 2015–; memb Bd: Breast Cancer Res Fndn, Global Fund for Women; former chair: Securities Industry and Financial Markets Assoc (vice-chair 2006–15), Global Financial Markets Assoc; *Recreations* equestrian; *Style*— Mrs Blythe Masters; ✉ Digital Asset Holdings, 96 Spring Street, 8th Floor, New York, NY 10012, USA (e-mail blythe@digitalasset.com)

MASTERS, Dr Christopher; CBE (2002); s of Wilfred Masters, and Mary Ann Masters; *b* 2 May 1947, Northallerton, Yorkshire; *Educ* Richmond GS, KCL (BSc, AKC), Univ of Leeds (PhD); *m* 1971, Gillian Mary; 2 da; *Career* research chemist Shell Research BV Amsterdam 1971–77, PA to md Shell Chemicals UK 1977–78, corp planner Shell UK 1978–79; Christian Salvesen plc: business devpt mangr 1979–81, dir of planning Merchants Refrigerating Co USA (following takeover by Christian Salvesen) 1981–83, md Christian Salvesen Seafoods 1983–85, md Industrial Servs Div 1985–89, main bd dir 1987–97, chief exec 1989–97; exec chm Aggreko plc (demerged from Christian Salvesen) 1997–2002; non-exec chm: Babtic Gp Ltd 2002–04, SMG plc 2004–07, Sagentia Gp plc 2006–10, Energy Assets Gp; non-exec dir: Scottish Opera 1994–99, Scottish Chamber Orch Tst 1994–2012, Wood Gp plc 2002–12, Alliance Tst plc 2002–12, The Crown Agents 2005–16, Speedy Hire plc 2011–15; chm: Scottish Higher Educn Funding Cncl 1998–2005, Festival City Theatres Tst 2002–13; ind co-chair Scottish Science Advsy Cncl 2011–16; Master Co of Merchants of the City of Edinburgh 2007–09, Lord Dean Guild of the City of Edinburgh 2009–11; memb Ct Univ of Edinburgh; Hon Dr: Strathclyde Univ 2006, Univ of St Andrews 2006, Univ of Dundee Abertay 2007, Univ of Edinburgh 2007; FRSE 1996; *Publications* Homogeneous Transition-metal Catalysis (1981); *Recreations* wines, music, opera; *Style*— Dr Christopher Masters, CBE, FRSE; ✉ 12 Braid Avenue, Edinburgh EH10 6EE

MASTERSON, David Napier; s of Philip Bursell Edwin Masterson (d 1985), of Upminster, Essex, and Pamela, *née* Napier; *b* 20 June 1959; *Educ* Brentwood Sch, City of London Poly; *Career* Kingston Smith LLP Chartered Accountants: trainee 1977–81, ptnr 1988–; memb Audit Registration Ctee ICAEW 1991–96; FCA 1991 (ACA 1981); *Recreations* golf, skiing; *Clubs* Greenford Rotary, Soc of Old Brentwoods; *Style*— David N Masterson, Esq; ✉ Kingston Smith LLP, Devonshire House, 60 Goswell Road, London EC1M 7AD (☎ 020 7566 4000, e-mail dmasterson@kingstonsmith.co.uk)

MASTERSON, (Margaret) Valerie (Mrs Andrew March); CBE (1988); da of Edward Masterson, and Rita McGrath; *Educ* Holt Hill Convent, studied in London and Milan on scholarship with Edwardo Asquez; *m* 1965, Andrew John March; 1 s ((Edward) Jason b 13 May 1969), 1 da (Caroline Louisa b 13 Aug 1973); *Career* opera and concert singer; debut Landestheater Salzburg; appearances with D'Oyly Carte Opera, Glyndebourne Festival Opera, ENO, Royal Opera House Covent Garden; has appeared at numerous major opera houses incl: Paris, Aix en Provence, Toulouse, NY (Metropolitan and Carnegie Hall), Munich, Madrid, Geneva, Barcelona, Milan, San Francisco, Chicago, Chile, Brazil; leading roles in: La Traviata, Le Nozze di Figaro, Manon, Faust, Alcina, Die Entführung, Julius Caesar, Rigoletto, Romeo and Juliet, Carmen, Count Ory, Mireille, Louise, Idomeneo, Les Dialogues des Carmelites, The Merry Widow, Xerxes, Orlando; recordings incl: La Traviata, Elisabetta, Regina d' Inghliterra, Der Ring des Nibelungen, The Merry Widow, Kismet, Song of Norway, Julius Caesar Scipione, several Gilbert and Sullivan; broadcasts regularly on radio and TV; hon pres Rossini Soc Paris, vice-pres Br Youth Opera, patron Mousehole Male Voice Choir 2002–; Soc of West End Theatre Award 1983; Hon DLitt 1999; FRCM 1992, Hon RAM 1993; *Style*— Ms Valerie Masterson, CBE; ✉ c/o Music International, 13 Ardilaun Road, Highbury, London N5 2QR

MASTERTON, Prof Gordon Grier Thomson; OBE (2008); s of Alexander Bain Masterton (d 1973), and Mary Low Grier, *née* Thomson (d 2003); *b* 9 June 1954, Charlestown, Fife; *Educ* Dunfermline HS, Univ of Edinburgh (Trevelyan scholar, ICE Prize, Lindsay Prize, Innes Prize, BSc), Open Univ (BA), Imperial Coll London (MSc, DIC); *m* 17 July 1976, Lynda Christine, *née* Jeffries; 1 s (Matthew Gordon Grier b 13 Sept 1983), 1 da (Natalie Elizabeth b 19 March 1986); *Career* Jacobs UK (formerly Babtie Gp): engr 1976–82, project engr 1982–91, dir responsible for bridge works 1991–95, estab Kuala Lumpur office 1995–96, dir i/c buildings and bridge works 1997–2001, md Facilities Business Centre 2001–02, md Environment Business Centre 2003–04, vice-pres environment 2004–09 (ret 2014); UK Govt project rep Crossrail 2009–13; many structural design projects incl: Buccleuch Street Bridge Dumfries (design commendation Saltire Awards 1986), A75 Annan Bypass (Annan River Bridge awarded design commendation Saltire Awards 1990) and Dumfries Bypass, A74 upgrade to D3 motorway; ICE: memb Cncl 1999–, vice-pres 2002–05, pres 2005–06, chm Glasgow & West of Scot Assoc 2000–01 (hon sec 1986–89), chm Structural and Buildings Bd 2000–02, memb Archive Panel 2001–05, memb Investigating Panel 2001–04, chm Working Gp on Registers Approved Lists and Licensing of Engrs, fndr memb Panel for Conservation Accreditation Register for Engrs, chm ICE Asia-Pacific Regnl Ctee 2007–13, chm Panel for Historical Engrg Works 2013–, chm Disciplinary Bd 2015–; chm: Professional Bodies Coll of Scot Construction Industry Gp 2001–04, Construction Industry Cncl 2010–12 (chm Health & Safety Ctee 2008–10), Constructionskills Scotland Industry Advsy Gp 2008–09, Scottish Panel RAEng 2012–; cmmr Royal Cmmn on the Ancient and Historic Monuments of Scotland (vice-chm 2008–15); memb: Wolfson Bridge Research Unit Advsy Ctee Univ of Dundee 1994–97, Structural Engrg Research Advsy Gp Univ of Dundee 1997–2002, ICE/IStructE Working Gp on Codes and Standards 1999–2000, ICE/IStructE Study Gp Safety in Tall Buildings 2001–02, Advanced Concrete and Masonry Centre Mgmnt Gp Univ of Paisley 2001–03, Master of Research Panel Univ of Dundee 2002–07, Cncl Royal Acad of Engrg 2008–11, External Affrs Ctee Royal Acad of Engrg 2012–, ICE/IstructE/HSE Standing Ctee on Structural Safety 2009–16; pt/t tutor Open Univ 1984–88, hon lectr Univ of Strathclyde 1991–94; visiting prof: Univ of Paisley 1998–2003, Glasgow Caledonia Univ 2011–, Univ of Edinburgh 2012–; chair Future Infrastructure Univ of Edinburgh 2015–; fndr and chm Scottish Engrg Hall of Fame 2011–, judge MacRobert Award 2012–; author and co-author numerous technical papers in engrg jls; television appearances: Life After People (History Channel), Engineering Empires: Britain (Discovery Channel), Thomas Telford: The Man Who Built Britain (Caledonian Television), Unbuilt Britain (Timeline Films); dir Thomas Telford Ltd; tstee: Forth Bridges Visitor Centre Tst 1988–2012, Scottish Lime Centre Tst 1998–2009; reader The Royal Anniversary Tst; Jr Members' Prize IStructE Scot Branch 1977, Harding Prize Br Tunnelling Soc 1981, Philip Gooding travelling scholar Concrete Soc 1982; Hon DTech Glasgow Caledonian Univ 2007, Hon DEng Heriot Watt Univ 2012; Liveryman Worshipful Co of Engrs 2008– (Ct Asst 2012–), memb Master Court Incorporation of Hammermen Glasgow 2015–; CEng 1980, MIWEM 1981, FICE 1993 (MICE 1980), FIStructE 1994, fell Inst of Engrs and Shipbuilders in Scotland 2001 (vice-pres 2008–10, pres 2010–12), FREng 2006, FRSE 2007; *Publications* CIRIA Reports: Piled Foundations in Weak Rock (with Wallace and Muir Wood, 1999), Concrete Mixes Planning and Design (with RA Wilson (1997); TRL Reports: A Literature Design Review of Crib Wall Systems (1995); The Popular Perception of the Civil Engineer (2000), Supreme Sacrifice: A Small Village in the Great War (with Walter Reid and Paul Birch, 2016); *Recreations* sailing, cycling, books, opera, engineering history, genealogy; *Clubs* Smeatonians; *Style*— Prof Gordon Masterton, OBE; ✉ Corrievreck, Montrose Terrace, Bridge of Weir, Renfrewshire PA11 3DH (☎ 01505 613503, e-mail themastertons@btinternet.com); e-mail (work) gordon.masterton@ed.ac.uk

MATES, James Michael; s of Rt Hon Michael Mates, and Mary Rosamund, *née* Paton; *b* Aug 1961; *Educ* King's Coll Sch, Marlborough, Farnham Coll, Univ of Leeds (BA); *m* Fiona Margaret, da of John Standish Bennett; 2 s (Leo James de Vars b 4 Nov 1991, Charles Michael John b 2 Nov 1997), 1 da (Flora Katherine b 3 March 1994); *Career* ITN: joined as grad trainee 1983, Tokyo corr 1989–91, N of England corr 1991–92, Moscow corr 1992–93, diplomatic ed 1993–97, Washington corr 1997–2001, sr news corr 2001–11, Europe ed 2011–; *Recreations* tennis, water sports, bridge; *Clubs* Portland, Garrick; *Style*— James Mates, Esq; ✉ e-mail james.mates@itn.co.uk

MATHER, Clive; s of Ronald Mather, and Ivy Mather; *b* 19 September 1947; *Educ* Warwick Sch, Lincoln Coll Oxford (MA); *m* 1976, Ann; 1 s, 2 da; *Career* Shell: joined 1969, early career UK, Brunei and Gabon, retail regnl mangr Shell UK 1984–86, dir of personnel and public affrs Shell South Africa 1986–91, dir of human resources and admin Shell UK and dir Shell Research Ltd 1991–95, chief information offr Shell Int 1995–97, dir (int) Shell 1997–99, chief exec Shell Services Int 1999–2002, chm Shell UK Ltd 2002–04, head of global learning 2002–04, chm/ceo Shell Canada 2004–07, dir Iogen Corp 2007–; chm Petroleum Employers' Cncl 1994, chm industry/govt Steering Gp on Corp Social Responsibility, cmmr Equal Opportunities Cmmn 1991–94; memb: Supervisory Bd Office of Govt and Commerce, Advsy Bd Relationships Fndn, President's Ctee CBI, memb UK Advsy Bd INSEAD; chm: IMD Business Cncl, Lensbury Ltd, Lambeth Educn Action Zone Forum 1998–; dep chm Windsor Leadership Tst, tstee Royal Anniversary Tst; *Recreations* sport, good food and wine; *Style*— Clive Mather, Esq

MATHER, Graham Christopher Spencer; er s of Thomas Mather, and Doreen Mather; *b* 23 October 1954; *Educ* Hutton GS, New Coll Oxford (Burnet law scholar, MA); *m* 1, 18 Sept 1981 (m dis 1995), Fiona Marion McMillan, er da of Sir Ronald Bell, QC, MP (d 1982); 2 s (Oliver James William b 20 June 1987, Alexander Richard Christopher b 30 March 1991); m 2, 17 July 1997, Geneviève Elizabeth, wid of James Seton Fairhurst; *Career* slr and subsequently consIt Cameron Markby 1978–80; IOD: asst to DG 1980–83, head of Policy Unit 1983–86; Inst of Econ Affrs: dep dir 1987, gen dir 1987–92; pres: European Policy Forum 1992–, European Media Forum 1997–2014, European Financial Forum 1999–, The Infrastructure Forum 2010–; visiting fell Nuffield Coll Oxford 1992–2000; vice-pres: Strategic Planning Soc 1993–99, Assoc of Dist Cncls 1994–99; Parly candidate (Cons) Blackburn 1983; MEP (Cons) Hampshire N and Oxford 1994–99; conslt: Tudor Investment Corporation 1992–2012, Elliott Assocs 2006–; radio and TV broadcaster, contributor to The Times and various jls; chm World Free Zone Convention 2000–; memb: Westminster City Cncl 1982–86, Cncl Small Business Research Tst, HM Treasy Working Pty on Freeports 1983, MMC 1989–94, Competition Appeal Tbnl 2000–12, Ofcom Consumer Panel 2004–08; non-exec dir Ofcom 2014–; *Clubs* Travellers, Naval; *Style*— Graham Mather, Esq; ✉ European Policy Forum, 49 Whitehall, London SW1A 2BX (e-mail graham.mather@epfltd.org)

MATHESON, Alexander (Sandy); CVO (2016), OBE (1990), JP (Western Isles 1972); s of Dr Alexander Matheson (d 1978), of Stornoway, Isle of Lewis, and Catherine Agnes, *née* Smith (d 1986); *b* 16 November 1941; *Educ* Nicolson Inst Stornoway, Robert Gordon Tech Coll Aberdeen; *m* 29 March 1965, Irene Mary, da of Alex Davidson; 2 s (Alexander b 2 Sept 1966, Donald Roderick b 9 Nov 1972), 2 da (Isobel Mary b 27 Nov 1969, Irene Louise Catherine b 26 March 1975); *Career* apprentice pharmacist Davidson & Kay Ltd (qualified 1965); Roderick Smith Ltd: superintendent pharmacist 1965–98, md 1967–82, chm 1967–; memb: Stornoway Town Cncl 1967–75 (provost 1971–75), Stornoway Tst Estate 1967–2009 (chm 1971–81), Stornoway Port Authy 1968–2010 (chm 1970–72 and 1991–2001), Ross and Cromarty CC 1967–75; fndr chm Western Isles Devpt Fund 1972–; memb: Western Isles Health Bd 1974–2001 (chm 1993–2001), Western Isles Cncl 1974–94 (convener 1982–90); pres Islands Cmmn of Conf Peripheral Maritime Regions of Europe 1987–91; dir Western Isles Enterprise 1991–95; chm Harris Tweed Authy (formerly Harris Tweed Assoc) 2001–08 (dir 1991–94, memb 1995–2008); chm Highlands and Islands Airports Ltd 2001–07; founding memb and chm Hebridean Men's Cancer Support Gp 2007–12; memb Stornoway Branch RNLI 1974–2004 (chm 1974–79 and 1994–2004); Hon Sheriff of the Western Isles 1972, HM Lord-Lt of the Western Isles 2001 (DL 1994, Vice-Lt 1994–2001); memb: Royal Soc of Health 1965, Inst of Pharmacy Mgmnt Int 1968; FRPharmS 1993 (MRPharmS 1965); *Recreations* local history, genealogy, European and Islands travel; *Style*— Sandy Matheson, Esq, CVO, OBE; ✉ 33 Newton Street, Stornoway, Isle of Lewis HS1 2RW (☎ 01851 702082, fax 01851 700415); Roderick Smith Ltd, 8–10 Cromwell Street, Stornoway, Isle of Lewis HS1 2DA (☎ 01851 702082, fax 01851 700415, e-mail sandy.matheson@tinyworld.co.uk)

MATHESON, Jamie Graham; s of James M Matheson (d 1985), and Marjorie Graham, *née* Todd; *b* 19 May 1954, Glasgow; *Educ* Loretto Sch Edinburgh; *m* 1 June 1990, Angela, *née* Thompson; *Career* Parsons & Co (latterly Allied Provincial Securities Ltd) 1972–96 (dir 1986–96); Brewin Dolphin Holdings plc: divnl dir Bell Lawrie 1996–2001, dir 2002–13 STV gp plc (formerly SMG plc) 2007–15, chartered FCSI 2010, chm Saracen Fund Mangrs 2014–; exec chm 2005–13; non-exec dir: Maven Income and Growth VCT 5 plc (formerly Bluehone AIM VCT 2 plc) 2000–13, SRH 2000–05, stv group plc (formerly SMG plc) 2007–, Latchways plc 2014–; dir HMS Victory Preservation Co 2012–; chm Beatson Cancer Charity 2014–; chm Glasgow Jr C of C 1984–85; deacon Incorporation of Bonnetmakers and Dyers of Glasgow 1986–87, precis Grand Antiquity Soc of Glasgow 1996–97; FSI 2000; OStJ; *Recreations* sailing, golf, field sports; *Clubs* Royal Yacht Squadron, Royal Thames Yacht, New (Edinburgh), Caldwell Golf, Clyde Cruising, W Kirkbride Golf, Western Gailes Golf; *Style*— Jamie G Matheson, Esq; ✉ Hallmoss, Dunlop, Ayrshire, KA3 4DT (☎ 01560 482002, e-mail jamie@hallmoss.com)

MATHESON, Michael; MSP; s of Edward Matheson, and Elizabeth, *née* Coyle; *Educ* John Bosco Secdy Sch Glasgow, Queen Margaret Coll Edinburgh (BSc), Open Univ (BA, Dip Applied Social Sciences); *Career* state registered occupational therapist; community occupational therapist: Highland Regnl Cncl Social Work Dept 1991–93, Stirling Cncl Social Work Services 1993–99; MSP (SNP): Scotland Central 1999–2007, Falkirk W 2007–; dep shadow min for justice and land reform 1999–2004, shadow min for culture and sport 2004–06, former memb Parly Enterprise and Culture Ctee, former memb Parly Justice Ctee, memb Glasgow Airport Rail Link Ctee 2006–07, former co-convenor Cross-party Gp on Malawi, former vice-convenor Cross-party Gp on Sport, former memb Parly Health and Sport Ctee, memb End of Life Assistance (Scotland) Bill Ctee 2010–11, former memb European and External Relations Ctee (dep convenor), min for public health 2011–14, cabinet sec for justice 2014–; state registered occupational therapist (Health Professions Cncl); memb Ochils mountain rescue team; *Recreations* mountaineering, travel; *Style*— Michael Matheson, Esq, MSP; ✉ 15A East Bridge Street, Falkirk FR1 1YD (☎ 0131 348 5671, fax 0131 348 6474, e-mail michael.matheson.msp@parliament.scot); Constituency Office ☎ 01324 629271, fax 01324 635576

MATHEW, Prof Christopher George Porter; s of Gother Donaldson Porter Mathew, QC (d 1984), of Port Elizabeth, South Africa, and Evelyn Mary, *née* O'Connor; *b* 7 September 1949; *Educ* St Andrew's Coll Grahamstown, Univ of Cape Town (BSc), Univ of London (PhD); *m* Denise, da of Charles Manning; *Career* sr biochemist Provincial Hosp Port Elizabeth 1972–77, PhD student Inst of Cancer Research London 1977–80, sr biochemist Univ of Cape Town 1981–82, specialist (med sci) Univ of Stellenbosch 1983–86, team ldr Inst of Cancer Research Sutton Surrey 1986–89, dir NHS Diagnostics DNA Lab 1989–98, prof of molecular genetics Guy's and St Thomas' Sch of Med London 1999–; Ranbaxy Sci Fndn visiting prof All-India Inst of Med Scis New Delhi 1995, distinguished prof of human genetics Sydney Brenner Inst Univ of the Witwatersrand Johannesburg 2015–; Distinguished Service Award Fanconi Anemia Research Fund 2001, Thomson Reuters global list of the most highly cited researchers of the past 11 years 2014; memb and chair Special Advsy Ctee (Genetics) RCP 1991–96; vice-chair Science Ctee Cancer Research UK 2008–11; FRCPath, FMedSci 2001; *Publications* Methods in Molecular Biology 9: Protocols in Human Molecular Genetics (ed, 1991); 260 research pubns; *Recreations* golf, cycling, theatre; *Clubs* Hampstead Golf; *Style—* Prof Christopher Mathew; ✉ Division of Medical Molecular Genetics, Guy's Hospital, London SE1 9RT (☎ 020 7188 3721, fax 020 7955 4644, e-mail christopher.mathew@kcl.ac.uk)

MATHEW, Robert Knox (Robin); QC (1992); s of Robert Mathew, TD, MP (d 1966), and Joan Leslie, *née* Bruce (d 1989); *b* 22 January 1945; *Educ* Eton, Trinity Coll Dublin (BA); *m* 13 Sept 1968, Anne Rosella, da of Brig Robert Elliott, RA; 1 da (Juliet Alexa Liberty); *Career* journalist 1967–75; called to the Bar 1974; *Recreations* country pursuits, racing; *Clubs* Boodle's; *Style—* Robin Mathew, Esq, QC; ✉ Church Farm, Little Barrington, Burford, Oxfordshire OX18 4TE (☎ 01451 844311); 3 Stone Buildings, Lincoln's Inn, London WC2A 3XL (☎ 020 7242 4937, e-mail rmathew@threestone.law)

MATHEWS, Arthur; s of James Mathews, and Joan, *née* Fallon; *Educ* Castleknock Coll, Coll of Mktg and Design Dublin; *Partner* Faith O'Grady; 1 da (Maud); *Career* writer; columnist: Irish Times, Big Issue; cartoonist: New Musical Express, Observer Sport magazine; *Television* credits with Graham Linehan incl: Paris, Father Ted (BAFTA 1996 and 1998, Writers Guild, RTS and Comedy awards), Big Train (Comedy Award), The Fast Show, Brass Eye, Jam, The All New Alexi Sayle Show, Toast of London (with Matt Berry, Golden Rose of Montreux 2014, BAFTA nominations 2014 and 2015); solo credits incl: Hippies, Big Train (series 2); *Theatre* I, Keano; *Radio* Luneen Live, The Golden Age, Men About The House; *Film* Wide Open Spaces; *Books* Well Remembered Days (2001), The Book of Poor Ould Fellas (with Declan Lynch), Angry Baby, Toast on Acting; *Recreations* history, football, TV documentaries, music, radio; *Style—* Arthur Mathews, Esq; ✉ c/o Katie Haines, The Agency, 24 Pottery Lane, London W11 4LZ

MATHEWS, HE Harriet; OBE (2005); *Career* diplomat; desk offr Central Africa Africa Directorate FCO 1997–98, press offr Press Office FCO 2003, head West Africa Section Africa Directorate FCO 2003–05, head Political and Press Section Tel Aviv 2005–08, head Rule of Law Afghanistan FCO 2008–09, head Energy Climate Change and Energy Dept FCO 2009–11, head East and West Africa Dept FCO 2012–14, head Ebola Task Force FCO 2014, ambass to Somalia 2015–; *Style—* HE Ms Harriet Mathews, OBE; ✉ c/o FCO (Mogadishu), King Charles Street, London SW1A 2AH

MATHEWS, Simon; s of Dennis Mathews (d 1986), and Simone, *née* Hayward (d 2008); *b* 24 July 1961; *Educ* Radley, Univ of Manchester (BA); *m* (m dis); 2 s (Gabriel b 3 April 1993, Donovan b 19 Dec 1995); *Career* Saatchi & Saatchi Garland Compton: media trainee 1981–82, media exec 1982–85, dep gp dir 1985–87; Young & Rubicam: asst media planning dir 1987–88, media planning dir 1988–89, jt media dir 1989–92, exec media dir 1993–94; chief exec Equinox Communications 1994–96, md Optimedia International (UK) 1996–2003, founding ptnr Rise Communications 2003–; *Recreations* sailing, scuba diving, skiing, wine collecting; *Style—* Simon Mathews, Esq; ✉ Rise Communications, Bramah House, 65–71 Bermondsey Street, London SE1 3XF

MATHEWSON, David Carr; s of H Douglas C Mathewson (d 1980), and Evelyn, *née* Carr; *b* 26 July 1947; *Educ* Daniel Stewarts Coll Edinburgh, Univ of St Andrews (BSc, capt athletics team), Wits Business Sch Johannesburg; *m* 23 Sept 1972, Janet, da of late James N McIntyre; 1 s (Ewan b 3 July 1981), 1 da (Emily b 4 Aug 1983); *Career* articled clerk Deloittes Edinburgh 1972, with Williams Glyn & Co London 1972–76, various sr appts Nedbank Group Johannesburg 1976–85; Noble Grossart Ltd merchant bankers: joined 1985, asst dir 1987–89, dir 1989–2000; also dir: Quicks Gp plc 1991–97, Martin Currie High Income Tst plc 1998–2005, Edinburgh UK Tracker Tst plc 1998–2011, Noble & Co Ltd 2003–07, Murray VCT plc 2004–06, Robertson Gp Ltd 2006–, Playtech Ltd 2010–13 (chief fin offr 2011–13), 24/7 Gaming Gp Hldgs plc 2013–, Rightster Gp plc 2013–, various private cos; chm: Geared Opportunities Income Tst plc 2000–06, Sportech plc 2002–06 (formerly Rodime plc, dir 1992–2002), Amazing Hldgs plc 2004–09, Asian Growth Properties Ltd 2006–09, Corsie Gp plc 2006–08, ifafa Tech Inc 2007–09, Macromac Gp plc 2013–15; conslt Andersen Corp Fin 2000–02, sr non-exec dir Rightster Gp plc 2013–; memb Bd of Tstees Royal Botanic Gardens Edinburgh 2001–09; memb Cncl St Leonards Sch 1999–2006, memb Bd New Park Sch St Andrews 2005–06; MICAS 1972; *Recreations* golf, shooting, gardening, family interests; *Clubs* New (Edinburgh), Desert Springs (Spain); *Style—* David Mathewson, Esq; ✉ 7 Melchbourne Park, Melchbourne, Bedfordshire MK44 1BD (☎ 00 34 950 069 140, e-mail davidmathewson@amitara.com)

MATHEWSON, Sir George Ross; kt (1999), CBE (1985); s of George Mathewson, of Perth, by his w Charlotte Gordon, *née* Ross; *b* 14 May 1940; *Educ* Perth Acad, Univ of St Andrews (BSc, PhD), Canisius Coll Buffalo NY (MBA); *m* 1966, Sheila Alexandra Graham, da of Eon Bennett (d 1975), of Bridge of Earn, Perth; 2 s; *Career* asst lectr Univ of St Andrews 1964–67; with Bell Aerospace (Buffalo, NY) in res and devpt and avionics engrg 1967–72, joined ICFC Edinburgh 1972 (area mangr Aberdeen 1974, asst gen mangr and dir 1979), chief exec and memb Scottish Devpt Agency 1981–87; The Royal Bank of Scotland Group plc: dir of strategic planning and development 1987–90, dep gp chief exec 1990–92, gp chief exec 1992–2000, exec dep chm 2000–01, chm 2001–06; chm Toscafund Ltd 2006–; dir: Scottish Investment Tst Ltd 1981–, IIF Inc 2001–06, Santander Central Hispano 2001–04; non-exec dir Stagecoach 2006–; pres Br Bankers Assoc 2002–04; Hon LLD Univ of Dundee 1983, Hon LLD Univ of St Andrews 2000, Hon DUniv Glasgow 2001, Dr (hc) Univ of Edinburgh 2002; FRSE 1988, FCIB (Scot) 1994, CEng, MIEE, CCMI (CIMgt); *Recreations* rugby, golf, business; *Clubs* New (Edinburgh); *Style—* Sir George Mathewson, CBE; ✉ The Royal Bank of Scotland Group plc, Gagarburn, Edinburgh EH12 1HQ

MATHEWSON, Dr Hew Byrne; CBE (2010); s of Alexander Mackechnie Mathewson, of Elie, Fife, and Dorothy Wightman, *née* Reid; *b* 18 November 1949; *Educ* HS of Glasgow, Univ of Glasgow (BDS), Univ of Wales Cardiff (LLM); *m* 1971, Lorna Anne Marshall, da of George S McConnachie; 1 da (Elizabeth b 1977), 1 s (Andrew b 1980); *Career* assoc dental surgn: Glidden and Archibald Wishaw 1974, Atkins & Cox Canterbury 1975–77; sr ptnr Mathewson Dental Practice Ltd Edinburgh 1977–; regnl gen practice vocational trg advsr for SE Scotland 1988–96, dental postgrad advsr for SE Scotland 1987–98, asst dir of dental studies Univ of Edinburgh 1987–99; BDA: memb Scottish Gen Dental Servs Ctee 1981–85 and 1991–2003 (chm 1991–97), pres E of Scotland branch 1985–86, Scottish sec 1985–90, chm Sick Dentist Mgmnt Gp 1990–97, memb Gen Dental Servs Ctee 1991–2003, memb Exec 1991–2003, vice-chm 2000–2003; chair GDC 2009 (memb 1996–, jt-chair Professional Conduct Ctee 2001–03, vice-chm Postgrad Sub-Ctee 2001–03, pres 2003–09); interim chair Bd Mental Health Tbnl Administration Scotland 2008–09, chair Scottish Dental Practice Bd 2012–; memb: Dental Ctee Scottish Cncl for Postgraduate Med and Dental Educn 1987–98 and 1999–2001, Cncl for the Healthcare Regulatory Excellence 2003–09 (vice-chair 2006–07), Cncl for the Registration of Forensic Practitioners 2007–10, UK Advsy Cncl on the Misuse of Drugs 2010–13; memb and chm various Scottish Dept of Health Working Parties; memb Editorial Bd British Dental Jl 1992–2003; pres Conference of Orders and Assimilated Bodies of Dental Practitioners in Europe (CODE) 2007–08, memb Medical and Dental Advsy Bd Wesleyan Assurance 2010–; lay memb Appeals Ctee ICAEW 2007–13; chm Peggy's Mill Assoc 1986–88; chair MS Soc Scottish Cncl 2012–15; memb: BDA 1970, Royal Odonto Chirurgical Soc of Scotland 1986, DGDP (UK) FGDP 1992, FDS RCSEd 1995, FDS RCS 2007; *Recreations* carpentry, walking, theatre, cinema, fishing; *Style—* Dr Hew Mathewson, CBE; ✉ St Johns Road Dental Practice, 176–178 St Johns Road, Edinburgh EH12 8BE (☎ and fax 0131 334 4350, e-mail hbm@blueyonder.co.uk)

MATHIAS, Prof Christopher Joseph; s of Lt Elias Mathias, and Hilda, *née* Pereira; *b* 16 March 1949, Mangalore, India; *Educ* St Aloysius Sch Visakhapatnam, St Joseph's Euro HS Bangalore, St John Med Coll Bangalore Univ (MB BS), Worcester Coll and Wolfson Coll Oxford (Rhodes scholar, DPhil), Univ of London (DSc); *m* Rosalind (Lindy), *née* Jolleys; 2 s (James, Timothy), 1 da (Sarah); *Career* med and surgical house offr 1971–72 and SHO (med) St Martha's Hosp Bangalore 1972, res offr and hon registrar Dept of Neurology Churchill Hosp Oxford 1972–76, clinical asst and res fell Nat Spinal Injuries Centre Stoke Mandeville Hosp 1973–76, SHO Dept of Med Royal Postgrad Med Sch Hammersmith Hosp 1976–77, registrar in med St Mary's Hosp Portsmouth and Dept of Renal Med Univ of Southampton 1977–79, Wellcome Tst sr res fell in clinical sci St Mary's Hosp Med Sch London 1979–84, hon conslt physician St Mary's Hosp London 1982–, Wellcome Tst sr lectr in med sci St Mary's Hosp Med Sch London and Inst of Neurology UCL 1984–92, hon conslt physician Nat Hosp for Neurology and Neurosurgery London 1985–, dir Neurovascular Med (Pickering) Unit St Mary's Hosp London 1987–2013, dir Autonomic Unit Nat Hosp for Neurology and Neurosurgery London 1989–2014, prof of neurovascular med Univ of London 1991–2013 (jtly with Imperial Coll London and Inst of Neurology/UCL), non-exec dir W London Mental Health Tst 2008–10, emeritus prof UCL 2014–; visiting prof: Academic Med Centre Univ of Amsterdam 1988, Nimmo visiting prof Univ of Adelaide 1996, Univ of Hawaii 1999, Univ of Adelaide Aust 2007, Univ of Hong Kong 2008; chm: Clinical Autonomic Res Soc of GB 1987–98 (fndn sec 1982–86), Res Ctee on Autonomic Disorders World Fedn of Neurology 1993–97 (memb 1989–93), MSA-Autonomic Gp Consensus Conf on MSA American Acad of Neurology 2007; memb: NW Thames Regnl Res Ctee 1987–93, Scientific Ctee Int Spinal Res Tst 1996–, Bd of Dirs American Autonomic Soc 1996–2004, NW Thames Regnl Advsy Ctee for Distinction Awards 1999–2001, task force American Spinal Injuries Assoc 2004–06, task forces European Fedn of Neurological Socs 2004–09, Sec of State for Transport Hon Med Advsy Panel on Driving and Disorders of the Nervous System 2004–09; conslt European Space Agency 1997–2000 (memb Jt European Space Agency/NASA Neuroscience Review Panel 1997); lead Task Force on Orthostatic Intolerance European Fedn of Neurological Socs 2008–; delivered numerous invited lectures at confs and symposia worldwide (incl: Br Peripheral Nerve Soc London 2008, 19th World Congress of Neurology Bangkok 2009, 12th European Fedn of Autonomic Socs 2010); fndr ed-in-chief Clinical Autonomic Research 1991–; memb Editorial Bd: Hypertension 1990–93, Functional Neurology 1990–2002, Jl of Pharmaceutical Med 1991–95, High Blood Pressure and Cardiovascular Med 1992–, Jl of Hypertension 1994–97, Parkinsonism and Related Disorders 1995–2005 and 2008–, Int Jl of Evidence Based Healthcare 2007–; pres European Fedn of Autonomic Socs 1998–2004; memb: Scientific Panel on the Autonomic Nervous System European Fedn of Neurological Societies 2004– (chm 1994–99), European Brain Cncl 2005–07; Shri K Gopalakrishna Endowment lectr Chennai 2006, Roche lectr Internal Medicine Assoc of Aust and NZ 2007, Northern Communities Health Fndn lectr Adelaide 2007, Chelsea Theapeutics lectr Vienna 2007, lectr Swiss Autonomic Soc 2008, G M Mascarenhas orator St John's Medical Coll N Atlantic Chapter FL 2008, Br Peripheral Nerve Soc London 2008, 19th World Congress of Neurology Bangkok 2009, 12th Euro Fedn of Autonomic Socs 2010, Chelsea Therapeutics lecture EFAS Autonomic Sch Lisbon 2011, Euro Fedn of Neurological Socs Stockholm 2012, American Rheumatological Congress Washington 2012, Hong Kong Neurological Soc 2012, RSM London 2013, Plenary Lecture jt meeting of the Int Soc of Autonomic Neuroscience and Euro Fedn of Autonomic Socs Germany 2013, ECN Mastocytosis Meeting London 2013, Autonomic Dysfunction in Parkinsons Disease Venice 2014, Austrian Neurological Soc Salzburg 2014, The Hot Topic Symposium RCP London 2014, 8th World Congress of NeuroRehabilitation Istanbul 2014, Ehlers Danlos Patient Awareness Day London 2014, Hypermobility Syndromes Assoc Burton-on-Trent 2014, Plenary lecture European Fedn of Autonomic Socs Malaga 2014, Streeten lecture American Autonomic Soc Puerto Rico 2014, Conclave lectures NIMHANS Bangalore 2015, 35th TS Srinivasan Endowment Oration Chennai 2015, Inaugural Congress Euro Acad of Neurology Berlin 2015, Int Congress RCPsych Birmingham 2015, Int Symposium Ehlers Danlos Soc NY 2016, RSM 2016, 7th Br Obesity and Metabolic Surgical Soc Cardiff 2016; govr Nat Soc for Epilepsy 2004–08; chm Dr P M Shankland (Pushpa Chopra) Charitable Tst Prize Fund 1998–2003; patron: Autonomic Disorders Assoc Sarah Matheson Tst 1997–2010, Syncope Tst (Stars) 2001–, Multiple System Atrophy Tst 2010–; founding tstee Autonomic Charitable Tst (ACT) 2012–; Prof Ruitinga Fndn Award 1988, 35th T S Srinivasan Gold Medal Award 2015; Dr (hc) Univ of Lisboa 2007; FRCP 1987 (LRCPE, LRCP Glasgow, MRCP 1978), FMedSci 2001; *Publications* Mild Hypertension: Current controversies and new approaches (jt ed, 1984), Concepts in Hypertension: a Festschrift for Professor Sir Stanley Peart (jt ed, 1989), Autonomic Failure: A textbook of clinical disorders of the autonomic nervous system (ed with Sir Roger Bannister, *qv*, 3 edn 1992, sr author 4 edn 1999 and 2002, sr author 5 edn 2013); also author of book chapters and scientific papers; *Recreations* gardening, watching cricket and football, observing human and canine behaviour; *Clubs* Athenaeum, Vincent's (Oxford), Royal Soc of Med; *Style—* Prof Christopher Mathias; ✉ Meadowcroft, West End Lane, Stoke Poges, Buckinghamshire SL2 4NE (fax 01753 645566); The Lindo Wing, Imperial College Healthcare NHS Trust, St Mary's Hospital, Praed Street, London W2 1NY; Autonomic and Neurovascular Medicine, Hospital of St John and St Elizabeth, St John's Wood, 60 Grove End Road, London NW8 9NH (e-mail profmathiasautonomic@gmail.com for personal and academic matters or autonomic.consulting@gmail.com for clinical matters)

MATHIAS, (Jonathan) Glyn; OBE (2016); s of Roland Mathias, of Brecon, and Mary Annie, *née* Hawes; *b* 19 February 1945; *Educ* Llandovery Coll, Jesus Coll Oxford (MA), Univ of Southampton (MSc); *m* Ann, *née* Hughes; 1 s (Mathew b 1971), 2 da (Megan b 1975, Hannah b 2001); *Career* reporter South Wales Echo 1967–70, reporter BBC Southampton 1970–73; ITN: political corr 1973, home affrs corr 1979–81, political ed 1981–86, asst ed 1986–91, controller of public affrs 1991–93, chief political corr 1993–94; political ed BBC Wales 1994–99; electoral cmmr 2001–08; memb Ofcom UK Content Bd 2011–15; chm Parly Lobby 1985; hon fell Univ of Wales Inst Cardiff (UWIC) 2004; *Books* Televising Democracies (contrib, ed Bob Franklin, 1992), Raising an Echo (2014); *Recreations* walking; *Clubs* Reform; *Style—* Glyn Mathias, Esq, OBE

MATHIAS, Julian Robert; s of Anthony Robert Mathias (d 1973), and Cecily Mary Agnes, *née* Hughes (d 2005); *b* 7 September 1943; *Educ* Downside, UC Oxford (MA); *m* 1996, Frances Bone, *née* Bartley, wid of Douglas Bone; *Career* mangr Hill Samuel and Co Ltd 1964–71, ptnr Buckmaster and Moore 1971–81, dir Foreign and Colonial Management Ltd 1981–95; *Recreations* wine tasting, bridge, golf, shooting; *Clubs* Boodle's; *Style—* Mr Julian Mathias; ✉ 8 Grove Court, Drayton Gardens, London SW10 9QY (e-mail jrm@julianmathias.co.uk)

MATHIAS, Prof Peter; CBE (1984); s of John Samuel Mathias (d 1960), and Marian Helen, *née* Love; *b* 10 January 1928; *Educ* Colston's Hosp, Jesus Coll Cambridge (MA), Harvard Univ, Univ of Oxford (LittD), Univ of Cambridge (DLitt); *m* 5 April 1958, (Elizabeth) Ann (d 2003), da of Robert Blackmore (d 1979); 2 s (Sam b 3 March 1959, Henry b 15 May 1961), 1 da (Sophie b 25 July 1964); *Career* Univ of Cambridge: res fell Jesus Coll 1952–55 (hon fell 1987), history lectr 1955–68, fell and dir of history studies Queens' Coll 1955–68 (tutor 1957–68, hon fell 1987), sr proctor 1965–66; Univ of Oxford: Chichele prof of econ history and fell All Souls Coll 1969–87, curator Bodleian Library 1972–87; master Downing Coll Cambridge 1987–95 (hon fell 1995); visiting prof: Toronto Univ 1961, Delhi Univ 1967, Univ of Calif Berkeley 1967, Pennsylvania Univ 1972, Columbia Univ

M

(Virginia Gildersleeve prof) 1972, Johns Hopkins Univ 1979, Natal Univ 1980, ANU 1981, Geneva Univ 1986, Leuven Univ 1990, San Marino Univ 1990, Waseda 1996, Osaka Gakuin Univ 1998, Bolzano 1999, Kansai 2006; hon pres Int Econ History Assoc 1978– (pres 1974–78); vice-pres: Royal Historical Soc 1975–80 (hon vice-pres 2001), Business Archives Cncl 1980–84 and 1995– (chm 1967–72, pres 1984–95), Int Inst of Econ History Datini Prato Italy 1987–99, Econ History Soc 1992– (pres 1989–92); hon treas: Econ History Soc 1967–88, Br Acad 1979–89; chm: Int Advsy Ctee Univ of Buckingham 1979–84, Advsy Panel for History of Med Wellcome Tst 1980–88, Friends of Kettle's Yard 1990–95, Nat Advsy Cncl Br Library 1994–2000 (memb Humanities and Social Scis Advsy Cncl 1990–94), Great Britain Sasakawa Fndn 1997– (pres 2005–11, hon pres 2011–), Advsy Bd of Central Euro Univ Press Budapest 2000–10; memb: Advsy Bd for the Res Cncls 1983–89, Round Table Cncl of Indust and Higher Educn 1989–93, Beirat Wissenschaftskolleg Berlin 1992–98; memb Syndicate Fitzwilliam Museum Cambridge 1987–, chm Fitzwilliam Museum Enterprises Ltd 1990–99; Hon LittD: Univ of Buckingham 1985, Univ of Hull 1992, Univ of Warwick 1995, De Montfort Univ 1995; Hon DLitt: Univ of Birmingham 1988, UEA 1999; Hon Dr: Russian Acad of Sciences 2002–, Kansai Univ Japan 2006, Keio Univ Japan 2008; memb: Econ History Soc 1951, Academia Europaea 1989; foreign memb: Royal Danish Acad 1982, Royal Belgian Acad 1988; FRHistS 1972, FBA 1977; Order of the Rising Sun (Japan) 2003; *Books* The Brewing Industry in England 1700–1830 (1959), English Trade Tokens (1962), Retailing Revolution (1967), The First Industrial Nation (1969, 1983), Science and Society (ed and contrib, 1972), The Transformation of England (1979), The First Industrial Revolutions (ed with J A Davis and contrib, 1989), Innovation and Technology in Europe (ed with J A Davis and contrib, 1991), L'Economia Britannica dal 1815–1914 (1994), Cinque lezioni di teoria e storia (2003), (UNESCO) History of Mankind Vol VI (ed, 2009); *Recreations* travel; *Style—* Prof Peter Mathias, CBE, FBA; ✉ 33 Church Street, Chesterton, Cambridge CB4 1DT (☎ 01223 329824)

MATHIAS, Sean Gerard; s of John Frederick Mathias (d 1983), of Swansea, and Anne Josephine Patricia, *née* Harding (d 2003); *b* 14 March 1956; *Educ* Bishop Vaughan Comp Swansea; *Career* director and writer; as playwright: Cowardice 1983, Infidelities (Edinburgh Fringe Festival (Perrier Pick of the Fringe Award), transferred to Donmar Warehouse and Boulevard Theatre) 1985, Prayer for Wings (Edinburgh Fringe Festival (Fringe First Award), transfered to Bush Theatre) 1985, Poor Nanny (King's Head) 1989, adapted The Lost Language of Cranes by David Leavitt (BBC, WNET Playhouse series USA (Golden Gate Award Best Television Drama, nominated Radio Times Best Screenplay 1992)); as dir: Acting Shakespeare (Ian McKellen's one-man show on Broadway), A Prayer for Wings (Bush Theatre) 1985, Infidelities (Donmar Warehouse and Boulevard Theatre) 1986, Exceptions (New End Theatre), The Bed Before Yesterday (int tour), Talking Heads (Theatre Royal) 1991, Noel and Gertie (nat tour and season at Duke of York) 1991, Ghosts (Sherman Theatre) 1993, Design for Living (Donmar Warehouse and Gielgud) 1994 (Evening Standard Award for Best Dir 1994 and Critics' Circle Award for Best Dir 1995), Indiscretions 1995 (Les Parents Terribles in UK (Barrymore Theatre NY, 9 Tony Award nominations incl Best Dir 1995, Fany Award for Best Dir)), Marlene (Lyric Shaftesbury) 1996 (nominated for two Olivier Awards); RNT: Bent 1991 (City Limits Best Revival of the Year Award), Uncle Vanya (5 Olivier Award nominations incl Best Dir 1992), Les Parents Terribles (Evening Standard Drama Award for Best Dir 1994 and Critics' Circle Award for Best Dir 1995, 7 Olivier Award nominations incl Best Dir 1994), A Little Night Music (4 Olivier Award nominations) 1995, Antony and Cleopatra 1998; other credits incl: Marlene (Cort Theatre Broadway) 1999 (nominated for 2 Tony Awards), Suddenly Last Summer (Comedy Theatre) 1999, Servicemen (New Group at St Clements NYC) 2001, Dance of Death (Broadhurst Theatre Broadway) 2001 (nomination Tony Award), The Elephant Man (Royale Theatre Broadway, 2 Tony Award nominations) 2002, Company (Sondheim Celebration at the Kennedy Center) 2002, Dance of Death (Lyric Theatre) 2003 (also at Sydney Festival 2004), Antigone (Grahamstown Festival and Baxter Theatre Cape Town) 2004, Aladdin (Old Vic) 2004, Shoreditch Madonna (Soho Theatre) 2005, Aladdin (Old Vic) 2005, The Cherry Orchard (Mark Taper Forum LA) 2006, Triptych (Market Theatre Johannesburg) 2007, Ring Round the Moon (Playhouse Theatre) 2008, Triptych (Southwark Playhouse) 2008, Heavenly Ivy (The Ivy Restaurant) 2010, The Syndicate (Chichester Theatre Festival and nat tour) 2011, Breakfast at Tiffany's (Cort Theatre Broadway) 2013, No Man's Land (Berkeley Rep CAL) 2013, Waiting for Godot and No Man's Land in Repertory (Cort Theatre Broadway) 2013, The Unbuilt City (NYSAF at Vassar) 2015; as artistic dir Theatre Royal Haymarket: Waiting for Godot 2009 (int tour 2010), Breakfast at Tiffany's 2009; *Films* Bent 1997 (premiered Official Cannes Film Festival winning La Prix de la Jeunesse); *Books* Manhattan Mourning (1988); *Style—* Sean Mathias, Esq; ✉ c/o St John Donald, United Agents, 12–26 Lexington Street, London W1F 0LE (☎ 020 3214 0800, fax 020 3214 0801, e-mail info@unitedagents.co.uk)

MATHIAS, Dr Tania; MP; da of Roger Wynn Mathias, and Vivienne Desiree Mathias; *Educ* St Paul's Girls' Sch, Univ of Oxford; *Career* MP (Cons) Twickenham 2015–; *Style—* Dr Tania Mathias, MP; ✉ House of Commons, London SW1A 0AA (Twitter @tania_mathias)

MATHIESON, Ian Douglas; s of Robert James Mathieson (d 1958), of Harrow, Middx, and Violet Lilian, *née* Jones (d 1981); *b* 1 October 1942; *Educ* Harrow Weald GS, Coll of Estate Mgmnt Univ of London (BSc), UCL (DipTP); *m* 19 Aug 1967, Lesley, da of Jack Stanley Glass, of Pinner, Middx; 2 s (Mark James b 1973, John Robert b 1977); *Career* chartered surveyor in local govt and private practice until 1973, md Commercial Union Properties Ltd 1984–99 (property investment mangr 1974–80, dir 1980–2000), dep md Commercial Union Asset Management Ltd 1987–99, md Morley Properties Ltd 1999–2000, dir Morley Fund Management 1999–2000; dir South Bucks NHS Tst 1993–2000, memb Wycombe Dist HA 1983–93; memb Teesside Devpt Corp 1990–98; Freedom City of London 1986; FRICS 1975 (ARICS 1967); *Clubs* RAC; *Style—* Ian Mathieson, Esq; ✉ Alloway, Maplefield Lane, Chalfont St Giles, Buckinghamshire HP8 4TY (☎ 01494 764820, e-mail ian.mathieson@alumni.insead.edu)

MATHIESON, John; s of Col A A Mathieson, MC, and Shirley, *née* Peal; *Educ* Uppingham, Bucks Coll of HE; *Career* cinematographer; dir of photography on feature films, commercials and music videos (incl Madonna, Tina Turner and Rolling Stones); memb: BSC, BECTU, Int Cinematographers Guild (IATSE); patron Learning for Life, memb Thorney Is Soc; Chevalier de l'Ordre des Arts et des Lettres (France) 1996; *Film* Pigulle 1993, Bye-Bye 1994, Love is the Devil 1998, Plunkett & Macleane 1999, Gladiator 2000 (Best Cinematography BAFTA Awards, AFI Award, Broadcast Film Critics Assoc Award, nomination Best Cinematography Oscars), Hannibal 2000, K-Pax 2002, Matchstick Men 2003, The Phantom of The Opera 2004 (nomination Best Cinematography Oscars), Kingdom of Heaven 2005, Flashbacks of a Fool 2008, Robin Hood 2010, Burke and Hare 2010, 47 Ronin 2013; *Recreations* skiing, diving, shooting; *Clubs* Royal Over-Seas League; *Style—* John Mathieson, Esq, BSC; ✉ 37 Talbot Road, London W2 5JH (☎ 020 7221 0476, fax 020 7243 4926); c/o Chris Smith, ICM, Oxford House, 76 Oxford Street, London W1D 1BS (☎ 020 7636 6565, fax 01844 261740); c/o Paul Hook, 8942 Wilshire Boulevard, Beverley Hills, CA 90211, USA (☎ 00 1 310 550 4474)

MATSON, Malcolm John; s of Gp Capt Jack Norman Matson (d 1991), and Wynne Ruth, *née* Parker (d 2000); *b* 4 October 1943; *Educ* Strode's Sch Egham, Trinity Coll of Music, Univ of Nottingham (BA), Harvard Univ (MBA); *m* 1, 1969 (m dis 1988), Judith Helen Wellby, da of Arthur Kenneth Colley (d 1986); 2 s (Thomas Daniel Blandford b 5 Feb 1975, Henry Samuel Quarrington b 21 Dec 1977), 1 da (Cecilia Elspeth Adean b 26 Feb 1980); m 2, 6 Aug 1991, Alexandra Mary, da of William Alexander Noble, MRCVS (d 2002); *Career* J Walter Thompson 1966–69, Winston Churchill fell 1969, mgmnt conslt 1972–84, gen commercial mangr Westland Helicopters Ltd 1978–81, conslt MMG Patricof (venture capital) 1982–84, fndr and chm Nat Telecable Ltd 1984–; fndr and chm: COLT Telecom 1988–92, Telecable One Ltd 1994, DataTrust Corp Ltd 1999–; chm: Chester Square Ltd 1994, Trinity Square Ltd; co-founder and chm Centre for Marketplace Theology, chief exec European Internet Capital plc 2000, md OpenPlanet Ltd 2004–, fndr and md Ebuild House Ltd 2015–; fndr The OPLAN Fndn; Freeman City of London 1967, elected alderman Ward of Bread Street City of London 1995, Liveryman: Worshipful Co of Coopers (Upper Warden 1991, Renter Warden 2001), Worshipful Co of Glass Sellers 1988; FIMgt 1982; *Recreations* music, motor cycling, thinking, chocolate; *Clubs* National; *Style—* Malcolm Matson, Esq; ✉ 77 Andrewes House, London EC2Y 8AY (☎ 020 7638 2344, e-mail cityman@city.co.uk); website www.oplan.org

MATTAR, Patrick; *b* St Asaph, Wales; *Educ* Solihull Sch (music scholar), Royal Acad of Music (Liszt scholar, LRAM), Inst of Educn (MA); *m* Andrea; 2 s; *Career* dep head Wetherby Sch 1998–2002, headmaster Norland Place Sch London 2002–; Tatler Prep Head of the Year 2010; FRSA; *Recreations* piano playing, cycling, food and wine; *Style—* Patrick Mattar, Esq; ✉ Norland Place School, 162–166 Holland Park Avenue, London W11 4UH

MATTHEW, Christopher Charles Forrest; s of Leonard Douglas Matthew (d 1984), of Wells-next-the-Sea, Norfolk, and Doris Janet Matthew (d 1988); *b* 8 May 1939; *Educ* King's Sch Canterbury, St Peter's Coll Oxford (MA); *m* 19 Oct 1979, Wendy Mary, da of Kenneth Henry Whitaker (d 1987), of Tilford, Surrey; 2 s (Nicholas b 1980, William b 1982), 1 step da (Charlotte b 1970); *Career* writer and broadcaster; columns incl: Punch, Vogue, The Daily Telegraph, The Observer, The Daily Mail; *Radio* chm: Something to Declare, The Travelling Show; presenter: Points of Departure, Invaders, Discursive Excursions, Plain Tales from the Rhododendrons, Cold Print, A Nest of Singing Birds; contrib: Fourth Column, Quote Unquote, Freedom Pass (with Alan Coren), Touchline Tales (with Des Lynam), Grey Shorts and Sandals (with Martin Jarvis); writer: A Portrait of Richard Hillary 1980, Madonna's Plumber 2003, Original Shorts 2005–11, A Nightingale Sang in Fernhurst Road 2007; *Television* scripts for The Good Guys (LWT/Havahall Pictures Ltd); *Theatre* Summoned by Betjeman; *Publications* The Times Travel Guide (ed 1972–74), A Different World: Stories of Great Hotels (1974), Diary of a Somebody (1978), Loosely Engaged (1980), The Long-Haired Boy (1980, adapted for TV as A Perfect Hero, 1991), The Crisp Report (1981), Three Men in a Boat (annotated edn with Benny Green, 1982), The Junket Man (1983), How to Survive Middle Age (1983), Family Matters (1987), The Amber Room (1995), A Nightingale Sang in Fernhurst Road (1998), Now We Are Sixty (1999), Knocking On (2001), Now We Are Sixty (and a Bit) (2003), Summoned by Balls (2005), When We Were Fifty (2007), The Man Who Dropped the Le Creuset on His Toe (2013), Dog Treats (2014); *Recreations* sailing, golfing, walking in the country with a dog, lunching with friends; *Clubs* Aldeburgh Golf, Slaughden Sailing, Chelsea Arts; *Style—* Christopher Matthew, Esq; ✉ c/o Jonathan Pegg Literary Agency, 32 Batoum Gardens, London W6 7QD (☎ 020 7603 6830, e-mail cmatt@onetel.com)

MATTHEW-WALKER, Robert; s of Samuel Walker (d 1964), of Eltham, and Mary Elizabeth Walker; *b* 23 July 1939; *Educ* St Olave's GS, Goldsmiths Coll, London Coll of Music, London Coll of Printing; *m* 27 Dec 1969, Lynn Sharon, da of Kenneth Herbert Alfred Andrews (d 1981), of Bromley, Kent; 1 s (Paul b 1971); *Career* Nat Serv RASC 1959–62; private composition study with W Darius Milhaud Paris 1962–63, co sec Thom and Cook Ltd 1963–70, head of Classical Dept CBS Records UK 1971–74, dir mktg CBS Records 1974, dir of masterworks Europe CBS 1974–75, head of Classical Dept RCA Records 1975–78, fndr Phoenix Records 1982–87; ed: Music and Musicians Int 1984–88, Musical Opinion, The Organ; editorial consltː Int Record Review, Musica Antiqua; dir classical music: Filmtrax plc 1986–88, AVM Records (UK) 1988–90, Allied West Entertainments Ltd 1989–91; md: Grayways Ltd 1989–91, Alfred Lengnick & Co Ltd 1989–91; first performances of compositions incl: Sonata for String Orch Tehran Orch 1976, Piano Trio Cardiff Festival 1978, Sinfonia Solemnis RNCM 1981, Sinfonia Magna For Organ Cologne Cathedral 1984, Christ On The Road to Emmaus City of London Festival 1988; prodr of over 120 records, awarded Grand Prix Du Disque of Académie Charles Cros Paris (for Sonatas for String Quartet by Brian Ferneyhough) 1980; memb PRS, pres E Lewisham Cons Assoc; *Books* incl: Rachmaninoff – His Life and Times (1980), Muhammad Ali – His Fights In The Ring (1978), Elvis Presley – A Study in Music (1979), Simon and Garfunkel (1984), David Bowie – Theatre of Music (1985), Madonna (1989), The Keller Column (1990), The Symphonies of Robert Simpson (1990), A Composer and the Gramophone – Alun Hoddinott on Record (1993), The Recordings of Edvard Grieg (1993), Edvard Grieg (1993), New World Music (1994), Heartbreak Hotel – The Life and Music of Elvis Presley (1995), Havergal Brian (1995), Cincinnati Interludes (1995), The Grieg Companion (ed, 1996–2008), Broadway to Hollywood (2001), Mahler's Das Lied von der Erde (2003), The String Quartets of Bela Bartok (3 edn, 2004), Sorrow, Tomorrow (2015); *Recreations* history, politics; *Style—* Robert Matthew-Walker; ✉ e-mail robertmw7@hotmail.co.uk

MATTHEWS, Belinda Mary; da of Maj-Gen Richard Eyre Lloyd, CB, CBE, DSO (d 1991), and Gillian, *née* Patterson (d 2006); *b* 26 June 1946, Worksop, Notts; *Educ* Downe House Newbury; *m* 29 Oct 1977, Dr Colin Matthews, OBE; 2 da (Jessica Ruth b 22 March 1972, Lucy Imogen b 2 July 1980), 1 s (Daniel John b 29 Sept 1978); *Career* Faber Music Ltd 1966–78; Faber and Faber Ltd: joined 1988, music books ed 1997, editorial dir 2003, memb Bd 2005–; dir Wandsworth Children's Opera Gp 1987–90, memb Bd London Sinfonietta 2010–; tstee David Tebbutt Tst 2012–; ALCM; *Recreations* piano, cello, reading, gardening; *Style—* Mrs Belinda Matthews; ✉ Faber and Faber Ltd, Bloomsbury House, 74–77 Great Russell Street, London WC1B 3DA

MATTHEWS, Christopher Wynne (Chris); s of Heilwynne James Matthews (d 1968), and Evelyn Christian, *née* Brodie; *b* 31 October 1955; *Educ* Royal HS Edinburgh, Univ of Newcastle upon Tyne (BA); *m* 11 Nov 2001, Sarah Fiona Watson-James; *Career* Arthur Andersen & Co 1977–82, fin dir Grass Roots Partnership 1982–85, Valin Pollen 1985–88, chief exec Shandwick Consultants 1993–97 (joined 1988), managing ptnr The Hogarth Partnership 1997–2010, managing ptnr Sutherlands 2010–; *Recreations* high-level walking, skiing, motorcycling; *Style—* Chris Matthews, Esq

MATTHEWS, Dr Colin Herbert; OBE (2011); s of Herbert Henry Matthews (d 1975), of London, and Elsie Lillian (d 2006); *b* 13 February 1946; *Educ* Univ of Nottingham (BA, MPhil), Univ of Sussex (DPhil); *m* 29 Oct 1977, Belinda Mary, da of Maj-Gen R E Lloyd, CB, CBE, DSO (d 1991), of Lymington; 2 da (Jessica b 1972, Lucy b 1980), 1 s (Daniel b 1978); *Career* composer; lectr Univ of Sussex 1971–72 and 1976–77; more than 100 compositions since 1968 incl: orchestral Fourth Sonata 1974, Night Music 1977, Landscape 1981, Cello Concerto 1984, Monody 1987, Cortège 1989, Broken Symmetry 1991, Memorial 1993, Cello Concerto No 2 1996, Renewal 1996, Unfolded Order 1999, Aftertones 2000, Pluto 2000, Continuum 2000, Horn Concerto 2001, Reflected Images 2003, Berceuse for Dresden 2005, Turning Point 2006, 24 Debussy Preludes 2006, Alphabicycle order 2007, Violin Concerto 2009, No Man's Land 2011, Grand Barcarolle 2011, String Quartet 4 2012, Traces Remain 2014, The Pied Piper of Hamelin 2015; assoc composer: London Symphony Orch 1991–99, Hallé Orch 2001–10 (composer emeritus 2011–); Prince Consort prof of composition Royal Coll of Music 2001–; S Nat Orch Ian

Whyte Award 1975, Park Lane Gp Composer Award 1983, Royal Philharmonic Soc Award 1996, Br Composer Award 2012 and 2013; dir Holst Estate and Fndn 1973–, memb Cncl and Exec Soc for Promotion of New Music 1981–93 and 1994–2002, tstee and music dir Britten Pears Fndn and exec dir Britten Estate 1983–99 (chm 2000–), memb Exec Cncl Aldeburgh Fndn 1984–93, patron Musicians against Nuclear Arms 1986–, fndr NMC Recordings 1988–, dir Performing Right Soc 1992–95, govr RNCM 2000–08, memb Cncl and Exec Royal Philharmonic Soc 2005–; distinguished visiting fell Univ of Manchester 2001–, visiting prof Univ of Nottingham; Hon DMus Univ of Nottingham 1998; FRNCM, FRCM, Hon RAM; *Style—* Dr Colin Matthews, OBE; ✉ c/o Faber Music Ltd, Bloomsbury House, 74–77 Great Russell Street, London WC1B 3DA (☎ 020 7908 5313, fax 020 7908 5339, e-mail promotion@fabermusic.co.uk)

MATTHEWS, Francis; s of Ronald Leslie Matthews, OBE, and Dorothy Olive Alice, *née* Mitchell; *b* 10 January 1953; *Educ* Harrow Co Sch for Boys, UC Oxford; *Partner* Philip Jon Plowman, OBE (civil partnership); *Career* assoc dir Chichester Festival Theatre 1983–87, fndr dir Cut & Thrust Theatre Co 1987–89, artistic dir Greenwich Theatre 1990–98; visiting dir Univ of South Florida; chair Mercury Musical Devpts 2016–; memb: Br Actors' Equity 1975, BAFTA, Nat Youth Theatre Assoc; FRSA; *Theatre* prodns for Greenwich incl: The Corn is Green (with Patricia Routledge), Cyrano de Bergerac (with Edward Petherbridge), The Government Inspector (with Timothy Spall), Caesar and Cleopatra (with Alec McCowen), The Adventures of Huckleberry Finn, Side By Side By Sondheim (with Dawn French); other credits incl: Rosencrantz and Guildenstern are Dead (RNT), A Midsummer Night's Dream (Albery Theatre), Arsenic and Old Lace (Strand Theatre), The Three Musketeers (North Shore Theatre Boston and Rose Theatre Kingston) 2010, Rose Tremain's Restoration (Salisbury Playhouse); *Opera* Fidelio (NI Opera), La Princesse Jaune (Buxton Opera) 2013, La Colombe (Buxton Opera) 2013, Tamerlano (Buxton Opera) 2016; *Television* prodr: Office Gossip (BBC), Gimme, Gimme, Gimme (Tiger TV, nominated Best Comedy BAFTA 2002 and Golden Globe Montreux 2002), My Dad's the Prime Minister (BBC), New Tricks (Wall to Wall) 2005–06, Ladies of Letters (Tiger Aspect) 2008–09 (nominated Best Comedy Br Comedy Award 2009), Benidorm (Tiger Aspect) 2011–12; *Publications* adaptations incl: The Prisoner of Zenda (1994), A Tale of Two Cities (1995), Northanger Abbey (1997), David Copperfield (1998); *Recreations* French Pyrenees, gardening, cooking, theatre, films; *Style—* Francis Matthews, Esq; ✉ c/o Maureen Vincent, United Agents, 12–26 Lexington Street, London W1F 0LE (☎ 020 3214 0800, website www.epicstoriesonstage.com)

MATTHEWS, Jeffery Edward; MBE (2004); s of Henry Edward Matthews (d 1960), and Sybil Frances, *née* Cooke (d 1951); *b* 3 April 1928; *Educ* Alleyn's Sch Dulwich, Brixton Sch of Building (NDD); *m* 12 Sept 1953, (Sylvia Lilian) Christine (d 1994), da of Cecil Herbert William Hoar (d 1974); 1 s (Rory b 1956), 1 da (Sarah Jane b 1958); *Career* graphic designer J Edward Sander 1949–52, pt/t tutor 1952–55, lettering and calligraphy assessor SIAD 1970–; designs for the PO: decimal 'To Pay' labels 1971, font of numerals for definitive stamps 1981, new range of colours for stamps 1987; stamps: United Nations 1965, British Bridges 1968, definitives for Scotland, Wales, NI and IOM 1971, Royal Silver Wedding 1972, 25th Anniversary of the Coronation 1978, London 1980, 80th Birthday of the Queen Mother 1980, Christmas 1980, Wedding of Prince Charles and Lady Diana Spencer 1981, Quincentenary of the College of Arms 1984, 60th Birthday of the Queen 1986, Wedding of Prince Andrew and Sarah Ferguson 1986, Order of the Thistle Tercentenary of Revival 1987, 150th Anniversary of The Penny Black 1990, self-adhesive definitives 1993, The Queen's Beasts 1998, Jeffery Matthews miniature sheet 2000, End of War miniature sheet 2005, Machin definitives 40th Anniversary miniature sheet 2007; also: first day covers, postmarks, presentation packs, souvenir books and posters; designer featured in film Picture to Post 1969; other work incl: title banner lettering and coat of arms Sunday Times 1968, cover design and lettering for official programme Royal Wedding 1981, The Royal Mint commemorative medal Order of the Thistle 1987, Millennium commemorative crown piece 1999/2000, End of War commemorative medal 2005, official heraldry and symbols HMSO, hand-drawn lettering COI, calligraphy, packaging, promotion and book binding designs, logotypes, brand images and hand-drawn lettering; work for various firms incl: Unicover Corp USA, Harrison & Sons Ltd, Metal Box Co, John Dickinson, Reader's Digest Association Ltd, Encyclopaedia Britannica International Ltd, ICI, H R Higgins (Coffee-Man) Ltd; designed stained glass window for Forest Hill Methodist Church (and accompanying film documenting the creative process) 2007; work exhibited in A History of Bookplates in Britain and at V&A Museum 1979; contrib Br Library's Oral History of the Post Office collection 2001; Royal Mail Rowland Hill Award for outstanding contribution 2004, Phillips Gold Medal for Stamp Design 2005; Citizen & Goldsmith of London (Freedom by patrimony) 1949; FCSD 1978, FRSA 1987; *Books* Designers In Britain (contrib 1964, 1971), 45 Wood-Engravers (contrib, 1982), Royal Mail Year Book (contrib, 1984, 1986, 1987, 1998), Queen Elizabeth II – A Jubilee Portrait in Stamps (contrib, 2002); *Recreations* furniture restoration, playing the guitar, gardening, DIY; *Style—* Jeffery Matthews, Esq, MBE

MATTHEWS, Prof John Burr Lumley (Jack); s of Dr John Lumley Matthews (d 1971), of Leamington Spa, and Susan Agnes, *née* Burr (d 1990); *b* 23 April 1935, Middx; *Educ* Warwick Sch, St John's Coll Oxford (MA, BSc, DPhil); *m* 28 July 1962, Jane Rosemary, da of Eric Goldsmith (d 1946); 1 s (Roderic John b 1964), 2 da (Susan Jane b 1966, Eleanor Mary b 1971); *Career* Nat Serv 15/19 King's Royal Hussars 1953–55 (served Germany and Malaya); sr scientific offr Oceanographic Laboratory Edinburgh 1964–67, visiting prof Univ of Br Columbia 1977–78, prof of marine biology Univ of Bergen 1978–84 (sr lectr 1967–78), hon prof Univ of Stirling 1988–; hon fell Scottish Assoc for Marine Science 1999– (dep dir 1984–88, dir 1988–96, sec 1988–99), dir Dunstaffnage Marine Laboratory NERC 1989–94; memb: Ctee for Scotland Nature Conservancy Cncl 1989–90, SW Region Bd Scottish Natural Heritage 1991–96 (dep chm 1994–96), Bd and Academic Cncl Univ Highlands Islands Project 1990–96, Sci Advsy Ctee Scottish Natural Heritage 1994–98; sec: Int Assoc of Biological Oceanography 1994–2000, MARS Network of Euro Marine Stations 1994–99; tstee: Int Sch Bergen 1980–84, Oban Hospice 1999–2005, Hebridean Whale and Dolphin Tst 2000–08 (chm 2001–08, patron 2009–), Nadair Tst 2003–07; pres Oban Rotary Club 1997–98; fndr fell Inst Contemporary Scotland; FRSE 1988, FRSA 1989; *Books* Freshwater on the Sea (jt ed), Aquatic Life Cycle Strategies (jt ed), Achievements of the Continuous Plankton Recorder Survey and a Vision for its Future (jt ed); author of numerous scientific articles in professional jls; *Recreations* gardening, 'Big History'; *Style—* Dr J B L Matthews, FRSE; ✉ The Well, 18 Manse Road, Milnathort, Kinross KY13 9YQ (☎ 01577 861066, e-mail matthews.oban@tiscali.co.uk)

MATTHEWS, John Waylett; s of Percy Victor Matthews (d 1970), and Phyllis Edith, *née* Waylett; *b* 22 September 1944; *Educ* Forest Sch; *m* 27 May 1972, Lesley Marjorie, da of Alastair Herbert Menzies Halliday; 2 s (Jonathan b 1975, Edward b 1977), 1 da (Anna b 1981); *Career* Dixon Wilson & Co 1962–69, NM Rothschild and Sons 1969–71, dir County NatWest Ltd 1971–88, dep ceo Beazer plc 1988–91 (dep chm 1982–91), ceo Indosuez Capital Ltd 1991–94; chm: Crest Nicholson plc 1996–2007, Mercury Holdings plc 1998–99, Media Systems Ltd 1999–, Regus Gp plc 2002–; dep chm Ludgate Group Ltd 1997– (chm 1991–97); non-exec dir: Ulster Investment Bank Ltd 1988–91, Mithras Investment Trust 1992–94, R W Baird 1995–2002, Perry Group plc 1997–2002, Rotork plc 1998–2008, SDL plc 2001–02, Allied Healthcare Inc 2002–03, Diploma plc 2003–, Center Parcs (UK) Gp plc 2003–, Minerva plc 2008–11; chm Cncl Forest Sch; FCA; *Recreations* golf, tennis, shooting, bridge; *Clubs* City of London, RAC, Crail Golfing Soc, The Club Pelican Bay (Naples, FL); *Style—* John Matthews, Esq

MATTHEWS, Paul Bernard; s of Leonard William Matthews, of London, and Noreen Elizabeth Matthews (d 1985); *b* 21 August 1955, Brentwood, Essex; *Educ* St Peter's Sch Bournemouth, UCL (Charlotte Ashby Prize, Andrews Prize, LLB), St Edmund Hall Oxford (BCL), Inns of Court Sch of Law, Univ of London (LLD); *m* 1986, Katie Bradford; *Career* called to the Bar Gray's Inn 1981 (Stuart Cunningham Mackaskie KC Award, Mould scholar); admitted slr: Eng and Wales 1987, Ireland 1997; slr-advocate Eng and Wales 2001; lectr in law UCL 1979–83 (pt/t tutor 1978–79), pt/t tutor St Edmund Hall Oxford 1979–80, barr in private practice 1982–84; Hopkins & Wood: legal asst 1984–87, ptnr 1987–92, conslt 1992–96; conslt slr Withers LLP 1996–15; HM coroner City of London 2002– (dep coroner 1994–2002), dep coroner Royal Household 2002–06, dep coroner ad hoc N London 2004–07; visiting lectr: City Univ 1981–84, UCL 1985–86, Inst de Droits des Affaires Univ d'Aix-Marseille 1991–99; visiting prof KCL 1995– (visiting sr lectr 1991–94), visiting prof Jersey Inst of Law 2009–12; dep Chancery master High Court 2008–15, recorder (civil) 2010–, Chancery master 2015–; memb Coroners Unit Resources Sub-Gp Home Office 2004–05, memb experts gp PRM III-IV EU 2005–08 and PRM III EU 2008–, specialist advsr House of Commons Constitutional Affrs Ctee 2006–08, coroner memb Review Bodies 2006–; dep chair Tst Law Ctee 2005– (memb Working Party on: Tstee Exoneration Clauses 1997–98, Tstee Indemnities 1998–99); vol N Islington Law Centre 1981–88; memb: Soc of Legal Slrs 1979–, Law Soc of Eng and Wales 1987– (memb Coroner's Courts and Inquests Working Party 2003–), Br Inst of Int and Comparative Law 1989–, Coroner's Soc of Eng and Wales 1994–, Soc of Tst and Estate Practitioners 1996–, Assoc of Contentious Tst Probate Specialists, Slrs' Assoc of Higher Court Advocates 2001–, Seldon Soc 2002–, Stair Soc 2003–, Assoc Il Tst in Italia; tstee David Isaacs Fund 2003–16; academician Int Acad of Estate and Tst Law 2004–; Liveryman City of London Slrs' Co 1992–; FRSA 1994, FRSM 2005; *Books* Jervis on Coroners (contrib, 10 edn 1986, 11 edn 1993, 12 edn 2002 and 13 edn 2014), The Jersey Law of Trusts (jtly, 1988, 3 edn 1994), The Jersey Law of Property (jtly, 1991), Disclosure (jtly, 1992, 4 edn 2012), A Guide to the Leasehold Reform, Housing and Urban Development Act 1993 (jtly, 1993), A Practitioner's Guide to the Trusts of Land and Appointment of Trustees Act 1996 (jtly, 1996), Butterworths Business Landlord and Tenant Handbook (co-ed, 1996, 6 edn 2012), Trusts: Migration and Change of Proper Law (1997), Hill and Redman's Law of Landlord and Tenant (contrib, 18 edn 1999), Trust and Estate Disputes (1999), Halsbury's Laws of England (author Mistake, 4 edn reissue 1999 and 2005, 5 edn 2010, ed Cremation and Burial, 4 edn reissue 2002, 5 edn 2010, ed Evidence, 4 edn reissue 2002 and ed Coroners, 4 edn reissue 2006, 5 edn 2010), Study Guide on the Law of Trusts (2009, 4 edn 2012), Underhill & Hayton's Law of Trusts and Trustees (jt ed, 19 edn 2016); author, co-author, book reviewer and ed of numerous articles in learned jls and professional pubns incl Law Soc's Gazette and Law Quarterly Review; *Recreations* reading, music, local history, cinema, languages; *Clubs* Athenaeum; *Style—* Paul Matthews, Esq; ✉ Royal Courts of Justice, Rolls Building, Fetter Lane, London EC4A 1NL; School of Law, King's College, Strand, London WC2R 2LS (☎ 020 7848 1176, e-mail paul.matthews@kcl.ac.uk)

MATTHEWS, Prof Paul McMahan; OBE (2008); s of Charles V Matthews, and Bernice Jacobson; *b* Chicago; *Educ* St Edmund Hall Oxford (BA), Univ of Oxford (DPhil), Stanford Univ Sch of Med (MD); *m* Catherine Comfort; 1 s (Ben), 1 da (Emily); *Career* intern (med) Stanford Univ Med Center 1986–87; McGill Univ Montreal: asst prof of neurology and neurosurgery and human genetics 1993–96, adjunct prof of neurology 1996–; Univ of Oxford: fell by special election St Edmund Hall 1997–, prof of neurology 1998– (reader 1995–98), head Dept of Clinical Neurology 2004–05, vice-pres Pharmaceuticals GlaxoSmithKline 2005–14, head GSK Clinical Imaging Centre 2005–11; dir Oxford Centre for Functional Magnetic Imaging of the Brain 1995–2005; prof of clinical neuroscience Imperial Coll London 2006–, head Div of Brain Sciences Imperial Coll London 2012–, Edmond and Lily Safra Chair Imperial Coll London 2014–; memb Advsy/Editorial Bd Nature Clinical Neurology, guarantor Brain; memb GMC 1995; FRCP(C) 1990, FRCP 2000, FMedSci 2014; *Awards* MRC (Canada) Clinician-Scientist Award 1990, Penfield-McNaughton Award 1990, Barbeau Prize for Neurosciences Research 1990, Baxter Award 1999; *Publications* Diagnostic Tests in Neurology (jtly, 1991), Metabolic Myopathies (jtly, 1995), Functional Magnetic Resonance Imaging: Methods for Neuroscience (jt ed, 2001), The Bard on the Brain (2003), The Memory Process (2010); author of numerous peer reviewed papers, invited reviews, chapters in books and letters; *Recreations* reading, walking; *Clubs* Athenaeum; *Style—* Prof Paul Matthews, OBE, FMedSci; ✉ Division of Brain Sciences, Imperial College London, Hammersmith Hospital, Du Cane Road, London W12 0NN (☎ 020 7594 2855, e-mail p.matthews@imperial.ac.uk)

MATTHEWS, Peter John; s of William John Matthews (d 1990), of Norwich, and Pamela Mary, *née* Butt; *b* 6 January 1945; *Educ* Uppingham; *m* 1 Nov 1969, Diana Joan, da of John Randell; 2 s (John Paul b 22 Dec 1972, Michael Robert b 1 Nov 1975); *Career* Arthur Guinness Son & Co Ltd 1963–77: information offr Guinness 1975–77, dir Guinness Publishing 1989–96 (gen mangr 1977–80, editorial dir 1980–84), ed Guinness Book of Records 1991–95 (sports ed 1982–91); media info mangr for athletics Olympic Games Atlanta 1996; chief announcer Athletics Commonwealth Games 1970 and 2002, athletics commentator IAAF 1991– (ITV 1985–97, BBC Radio 1975–85, Sky 2001–05); ed Int Athletics Annual 1985–, co-publisher Athletics Int 1993–; chm Nat Union of Track Statisticians, pres UK Counties Athletic Union 2009–; *Books* Guinness Book of Athletics Facts and Feats (1982), Official Book of the 1986 Commonwealth Games (1986), Guinness Encyclopaedia of Sports Records and Results (1987, 1990, 1993 and 1995), Cricket Firsts (with Robert Brooke, 1988), Who's Who in British Athletics (1990), Guinness International Who's Who of Sport (1993), All-Time Greats of British Sport (with Ian Buchanan, 1995), Whitaker's Almanack International Sports Records and Results (1998), Historical Dictionary of Track and Field (2012), World's Greatest in Athletics (with Richard Hymans, 2015); *Style—* Peter Matthews, Esq; ✉ 10 Madgeways Close, Great Amwell, Ware, Hertfordshire SG12 9RU (☎ 01920 870434, e-mail p.matthews121@btinternet.com)

MATTHEWS, Richard Burnell; s of Robert Matthews (d 2000), and Julia, *née* Watson (d 1993); *b* 10 December 1948, Romford, Essex; *Educ* Endsleigh Sch Colchester, North-East Essex Tech Coll Colchester; *m* 1 April 2011, Denette Wilkinson; 3 c from previous relationships (Merlin, Robert, Candice); *Career* fndr and former chm Oyster Marine (sold 2007); chm: Oyster Properties Ltd, Fox's Marina Ipswich Ltd, Gunfleet Marine Ltd; Queen's Award for Export 1991, Queen's Award for Int Trade 2000; former Br rep Offshore Racing Cncl; MInstD; *Recreations* yacht racing and cruising, golf, shooting, flying helicopters; *Clubs* West Mersea Yacht, Royal Ocean Racing (formerly Vice-Cdre), Royal Thames Yacht, Royal NZ Yacht Sqdn, Storm Trysail; *Style—* Richard Matthews, Esq; ✉ Oyster Properties Ltd, Fox's Marina, Ipswich, Suffolk IP2 8SA (☎ 01473 694730, fax 01473 694731, e-mail rm4421@me.com)

MATTHEWS, Her Hon Suzan Patricia; QC (1993); *Career* called to the Bar Middle Temple 1974; in practice in chambers: Bradford 1974–79, Guildford 1979–2003; recorder of the Crown Court 1995–2003 (asst recorder 1991–95), asst boundary cmmr 1992–2003, dep High Ct judge 1999–2014 (ret), dep circuit judge 2014–; chm: Ctees of Investigation MAFF 1994–2003, Richard Neale Inquiry 2003–04; rep London & SE Regn Gas Consumers Cncl 1987–96; memb: Criminal Injuries Compensation Appeals Panel 1996–2003 (dep chair

2002–03), Criminal Injuries Compensation Bd 1999–2000, Lord Chllr's Advsy Bd on Family Law 1997–2002; chm Disciplinary and Regulatory Ctees ACCA 2015–; FRSA; *Recreations* Farnham Competitive Music Festival; *Style—* Her Hon Suzan Matthews, QC; ✉ c/o Guildford Crown Court, Bedford Road, Guildford GU1 4ST (e-mail HHJudgeSuzan.MatthewsQC@judiciary.gsi.gov.uk)

MATTHEWS, Timothy John (Tim); s of Kenneth James Matthews, of Modbury, S Devon, and Vera Joan, *née* Fittall; *b* 24 June 1951; *Educ* Plymouth Coll, Peterhouse Cambridge (exhibitioner, BA); *m* Sally Vivien, da of William Tudor Davies; 2 s (Tom Alexander b 14 Sept 1984, James Osborn Louie b 5 Sept 1987); *Career* DHSS: admin trainee 1974, private sec to perm sec 1978–80, princ 1980–84; dist gen administrator Bloomsbury HA 1984–85, gen mangr The Middx Hosp Div Bloomsbury HA 1985–88, dist gen mangr Maidstone HA 1988–91, dist gen mangr W Lambeth HA and chief exec St Thomas' Hosp 1991–93, chief exec Guy's and St Thomas' Hosp NHS Trust 1993–2000, chief exec Highways Agency 2000–03, md Parsons Brinckerhoff Ltd 2003–08, chief exec Remploy 2008–14; dir: Focus Central London TEC 1997–2001, South Bank Careers 1997–2000, South Bank Employers Gp 1998–2000, John Laing plc 2004–07, Geoffrey Osborne Ltd 2011–; memb Cmmn for Integrated Tport 2000–03; chair: Univ of Coventry Social Enterprise CIC 2014–, Pursuing Independent Paths 2015–; govr Univ of Coventry 2010–; MHSM 1985, FIHT 2001; *Clubs* Surrey CCC; *Style—* Tim Matthews, Esq

MATTHIESEN, Patrick David Albert Francis Jonathan; s of Francis Matthiesen, and Olga, *née* Bode; *b* 1 March 1943, London; *Educ* Harrow, Oriel Coll Oxford (Briscoe Owen scholar, MA), Courtauld Inst of Art London; *m* 4 Oct 2002 (m dis 2009), Hiromi, da of Gen-Ichi Kaminishi, of Sendai Japan; 2 da (Alexandra, Takara-Julie (twins) b 17 April 2004); *Career* art dealer; supervisor of restoration sculpture project in Florence after floods 1966–67, supervisor in founding Conservation Inst for Sculpture in Venice in liaison with V&A 1968–69, ind art dealer 1970, assoc Queensbury Investments Ltd property developers 1970–71; P & D Colnaghi Ltd: assoc ind conslt 1972, i/c Research Dept 1972–73, gen mangr 1973–75, dir Old Master Paintings Dept 1976–77; fndr, chm and md Matthiesen Fine Art Ltd 1978–; exhibitions mounted and publications by Matthiesen Fine Art incl: Important Italian Paintings 1600–1700 1981, Early Italian Paintings and Works of Art 1300–1480 1983, From Borso to Cesare d'Este: School of Ferrara 1450–1628 1984, Around 1610: The Onset of Baroque 1985, Varlin 1985, Baroque III 1986, Paintings from Emilia 1500–1700 1987, The Settecento: Italian Rococo and Early Neoclassical Paintings 1700–1800 1987, A Selection of French Paintings 1700–1840 1989, Louis Léopold Boilly's 'L'Entrée du Jardin Turc' 1991, Fifty Paintings 1535–1825 1993, Paintings 1600–1912 1996, Gold Backs 1250–1480 1996, An Eye on Nature 1997, Collectanea: 1700–1800 1998, An Eye on Nature II – The Gallic Prospect 1999 and European Paintings 2001 (in association with Stair Sainty Matthiesen Inc), 2001: An Art Odyssey 2001, A Del Sarto Rediscovered 2002, Il Porto di Ripetta 2002, Chardin's Têtes d'Études au Pastel 2003, Virtuous Virgins 2004, Bertin's Ideal Landscapes 2004, Polidoro da Caravaggio 2005, Jacobello del Fiore 2007, Jacques Blanchard 2008, A Florentine Four Seasons 2009, Theodore Rousseau – A Magnificent Obsession 2009, The Mystery of Faith – Spanish Sculpture 1500–1750 2009, Révolution. République. Empire. Restauration 2010, James Ward – Lioness and Heron 2011, Luca Giordano's Liberation and Deliverance, Joseph Wright of Derby: Virgil's Tomb in Naples and The Grand Tour 2012, A Winning End-game: Earle Welby and his wife Penelope, Visions & Ecstasy: L B Castiglione's St Francis 2013, Fatal Attraction 2014, Juan de Sevilla 2015, Blasco de Grañén 2015, Paris Bordon 2015; paintings discovered/rediscovered incl: Gentile da Fabriano's Annunciation, Ribera's Prometheus, Caravaggio's St Francis, Tanzio da Varallo's Adoration, Domenichino's St Ignatius, Procaccini's Deposition, George de la Tour's The Meal of the Poor; advsr on valuation and purchase of Raphael's Madonna of the Pinks for HM Govt; chm and fndr The Matthiesen Fndn, hon sec Sparkman & Stephens Assoc 2002–08; *Recreations* gardening, J S Bach and eighteenth century and romantic music, travel, sailing, skiing, riding, good food and wine, opera, fine art, music sponsorship, eco-education projects; *Clubs* RAC, Sparkman and Stephens Assoc (hon life memb); *Style—* Patrick Matthiesen, Esq; ✉ Matthiesen Gallery, 7–8 Mason's Yard, Duke Street, London SW1 (☎ 020 7930 2437, fax 020 7930 1387, e-mail patrick@matthiesengallery.com, website www.thematthiesenfoundation.org and www.matthiesengallery.com)

MATTINGLY, Prof David John; s of Harold Mattingly, of Cambridge, and Erica, *née* Stuart; *b* 18 May 1958, Nottingham; *Educ* Lawnswood Sch Leeds, Univ of Manchester (BA, PhD); *m* 30 May 1981, Jennifer, *née* Warrell-Bowring; 2 da (Rebecca Jane b 5 March 1987, Susanna Frances b 27 Nov 1989), 1 s (Douglas Robert b 5 Nov 1993); *Career* Br Acad postdoctoral fell Univ of Oxford 1986–89, asst prof Dept of Classical Studies Univ of Michigan 1989–91; Sch of Archaeology and Ancient History Univ of Leicester: lectr 1991–95, reader 1995–98, prof of Roman archaeology 1998–, acting head of school 1998–99, 2002 and 2013–14, head of school 2015–19; research dir Coll of Arts, Humanities and Law Univ of Leicester 2009–12, site dir for Univ of Leicester AHRC Midlands3Cities Doctoral Training Partnership 2013; memb Research Assessment Exercise Panels for Archaeology and Classics 2008, memb Research Excellence Framework Panel for Geography and Archaeology 2014; chair of archaeology Br Sch at Rome 2015–19; chm Soc for Libyan Studies 1996–2001; James R Wiseman Book Award 2001, M Balmuth lectr 2006, T S Jerome lectr 2013, Antiquity Prize 2013; elected memb Academia Europaea 2013; FSA 1993, FBA 2003; *Books* 24 books and more than 230 articles and chapters incl: Town and Country in Roman Tripolitania. Papers in Honour of Olwen Hackett (jt ed, 1985), Libya. Research in Archaeology, Environment, History and Society 1969–1989 (jt ed, 1989), An Atlas of Roman Britain (jtly, 1990, revised edn 1993), Leptiminus (Lamta): A Roman Port City in Tunisia, Report no 1 (jtly, 1992), Tripolitania (1995), Farming the Desert. The UNESCO Libyan Valleys Archaeological Survey. Volume I, Synthesis (jtly, 1996), Farming the Desert. The UNESCO Libyan Valleys Archaeological Survey. Volume II, Gazetteer and Pottery (princ ed, 1996), Dialogues in Roman Imperialism. Power, Discourse and Discrepant Experience in the Roman Empire (ed, 1997), Life, Death and Entertainment in Ancient Rome (jt ed, 1999), Geographical Information Systems and Landscape Archaeology (jt ed, 1999), Economies beyond Agriculture in the Classical World (jt ed, 2000), Leptiminus (Lamta): Report no 2, The East Baths, Cemeteries, Kilns, Venus Mosaic, Site Museum and Other Sites (jtly, 2001), The Archaeology of Fazzan. Volume I, Synthesis (jtly, 2003), An Imperial Possession: Britain and the Roman Empire (2006), The Libyan Desert: Natural Resources and Cultural Heritage (jt ed, 2006), The Cambridge Dictionary of Classical Civilization (jt ed, 2006), The Archaeology of Fazzan Vol 2: Site Gazetteer, Pottery and Other Finds (jtly, 2007), Archaeology and Desertification: The Wadi Faynan Landscape Survey Southern Jordan (jtly, 2007), From Present to Past Through Landscape (jt ed, 2009), Imperialism, Power and Identity: Experiencing the Roman Empire (2010), The Archaeology of Fazzan Vol 3: Excavations carried out by C M Daniels (jtly, 2010), Imperialism, Power and Identity: Experiencing the Roman Empire (2011), Leptiminus (Lamta): A Roman Port City in Tunisia Report no 3 the Urban Survey (jtly, 2011), The Archaeology of Fazzan Vol 4 Excavations and Survey at Old Jarma (jtly, 2013), Frontiers of the Roman Empire: The African Frontiers (jtly, 2013); *Recreations* men's reading group, mediterranean cuisine, family; *Style—* Prof David Mattingly; ✉ School of Archaeology and Ancient History, University of Leicester, Leicester LE1 7RH (☎ 0116 252 2610, e-mail djm7@le.ac.uk)

MATTINSON, Deborah Susan; da of R R Mattinson, of Cheadle Hulme, Cheshire, and J M Mattinson; *b* 17 September 1956, Darlington, Co Durham; *Educ* Cheadle Hulme Sch, Univ of Bristol (LLB); *m* 1 July 1989, David Pelly; 1 da (Clara b 18 Sept 1990), 2 s (Theo b 10 Feb 1992, Francis b 19 April 1994); *Career* advtg account dir 1978–85, Gould Mattinson (political consultancy) 1985–89, GMA Monitor (research consultancy) 1989–92, jt ceo Opinion Leader Research 1992–2007; jt chair Chime Research Gp 2007–10, fndr dir BritainThinks (research and strategy consultancy) 2010–; tstee Dance Umbrella, chair The Young Women's Tst (formerly YWCA) 2012–; MMRS; *Books* Talking to a Brick Wall – how New Labour stopped listening to the voter and why we need a new politics (2010); *Recreations* reading, walking, relaxing with family; *Style—* Ms Deborah Mattinson; ✉ BritainThinks, Somerset House, Strand, London WC2R 1LA (☎ 020 7845 5880, e-mail dmattinson@britainthinks.com)

MATTISON, John Eric; s of Alfred James Mattison (d 1973), of Lingwood, Norfolk, and Mildred Edith, *née* Temperley (d 1974); *b* 12 August 1940; *Educ* City of Norwich Sch, LSE (BSc); *m* March 1964, Margaret Jane, da of Patrick Malervy; 3 s (John Patrick b 17 March 1965, James Gerard b 24 July 1966, Nicholas Frank b 30 Nov 1970); 2 da (Sally Jane b 22 March 1968, Catherine Temperley b 5 Sept 1975); *Career* financial journalist Investors' Chronicle, Evening Standard and Sunday Times 1962–70; dir: McLeish Associates 1970–80, Lopex Public Relations 1980–85, Hill & Knowlton 1985–88; chief exec Burson-Marsteller Financial 1988–93, dir Shandwick Consultants 1993–95; chm Mattison Public Relations 1995–; former memb Cncl CIPR; *Books* Bluffer's Guide to Finance (1968); *Recreations* golf, sailing; *Style—* John Mattison, Esq

MATTOCK, John Clive; s of late Raymond Jack Mattock, of Sidmouth, Devon, and Eva Winifred Zoë, *née* Ward; *b* 21 January 1944; *Educ* Dartford GS; *m* 1985, Susan, da of late Richard Clulow, of Harlow, Essex; 2 s (Anthony b 1986, Christopher b 1988); *Career* stockbroker; ptnr Fiske and Co 1975–88; dep chm: Carlisle Group plc 1985–90, Peak Tst Ltd 1988, Corporate Services Group plc 1989; dir: Stalwart Assurance Group plc 1986–89, Care First plc 1986–89, Seymour Pierce Gp plc 1991–2006, Dowgate Stockbrokers 2007– (chm 2008); FCA 1967; *Recreations* tennis, swimming administration; *Clubs* Bexley Lawn Tennis (vice-pres); *Style—* J C Mattock, Esq; ✉ Dowgate Stockbrokers, Talisman House, Jubilee Walk, Three Bridges, Crawley, West Sussex RH10 1LQ (☎ 01293 517744)

MAUD, Hon Sir Humphrey John Hamilton; KCMG (1993, CMG 1982); s of Baron Redcliffe-Maud (Life Peer; d 1982), and Jean, *née* Hamilton (d 1993); *b* 17 April 1934; *Educ* Eton, King's Coll Cambridge, Nuffield Coll Oxford; *m* 1963, Maria Eugenia Gazitua; 3 s; *Career* Nat Serv Coldstream Gds 1953–55; instr in classics Univ of Minnesota 1958–59; joined FO 1959, Madrid 1961–63, Havana 1963–65, FCO 1966–67, seconded to Cabinet Office 1968–69, Paris 1970–74, sabbatical at Nuffield Coll Oxford studying economics 1974–75, head of financial rels FCO 1975–79, min Madrid 1979–82, ambass to Luxembourg 1982–85, asst under-sec of state (int economic affairs and trade rels) FCO 1985–88, high cmmr to Cyprus 1988–90, ambass to Argentina 1990–93; Cwlth dep sec-gen (economic and social) 1993–99; chm: Emerging Markets Partnership-Financial Advisers 1999–2002, Cwlth Disaster Management Agency Ltd 1999–, Pall Mall Initiatives 2001–, Lyle and Partners 2011–; advsr to DG VIII European Cmmn 1999–2000; memb S Atlantic Council 2004–; chm CERES 2009–; memb Cncl RCM 1993–2002, dir Orch of St John's 1994–2000, tstee Parkhouse Award 1995–, tstee Prince Consort Fndn 2002–07, memb Ctee Queen's Medal for Music 2005–, chm of tstees Musequality 2007–; FRCM 2002; *Recreations* music ('cellist NYO 1949–52), golf, bird watching; *Clubs* Oxford and Cambridge, Garrick, Royal Mid-Surrey; *Style—* The Hon Sir Humphrey Maud, KCMG; ✉ 31 Queen Anne's Grove, Bedford Park, London W4 1HW (☎ 020 8994 2808, e-mail hmaud@cdma.org.uk)

MAUDE, Baron (Life Peer UK 2015) of Horsham, of Shipley in the County of West Sussex; Francis Anthony Aylmer Maude; PC (1992); yr s of Baron Maude of Stratford-upon-Avon, TD, PC (Life Peer; d 1993) and Barbara Elizabeth Earnshaw, *née* Sutcliffe (d 1997); *b* 4 July 1953; *Educ* Abingdon Sch, Corpus Christi Coll Cambridge (MA, Avory Studentship, Hulse Prize); *m* 1984, Christina Jane, yr da of A Peter Hadfield, of Copthorne, Shrewsbury; 3 da (Julia Elizabeth Barbara b 26 Dec 1986, Cecily Mary Anne b 29 July 1988, Lydia Helen Grace b 28 Feb 1996), 2 s (Henry Peter Angus b 10 Sept 1990, Alastair Timothy Charles b 17 March 1994); *Career* called to the Bar Inner Temple 1977 (Law scholarship, Forster Boulton Prize), barr in chambers of Sir Michael Havers, QC, MP (later Lord Havers); memb Westminster City Cncl 1978–84; MP (Cons): Warwickshire N 1983–92, Horsham 1997–2015; PPS to Hon Peter Morrison as min of state for Employment 1984–85, a Govt whip 1985–87; Parly under sec of state: corporate and consumer affrs DTI 1987–88, corporate affrs 1988–89; min of state FCO 1989–90, financial sec to the Treasy 1990–92; shadow culture sec 1997–98, shadow chllr of the Exchequer 1998–2000, shadow foreign sec 2000–01, chm Cons Pty 2005–07, shadow min for the Cabinet Office and shadow chllr of the Duchy of Lancaster 2007–10, min for the Cabinet Office and Paymaster Gen 2010–15, min for Trade and Investment 2015–16; chm HM Govt Deregulation Task Force 1994–97; advsr to Hongkong and Shanghai Banking Corp on bid for Midland Bank 1992, a dir of corporate finance (head of Privatisation Unit) Salomon Brothers International 1992–93, head of privatisation and an md Morgan Stanley 1993–97; non-exec chm: Prestbury Holdings plc 2002–, Incepta 2004–06; non-exec dir: Asda Group plc 1992–99, Brit Insurance 1994–99, Benfield Gp 1999– (dep chm 2003–); chm of govrs Abingdon Sch 1994–2003; *Recreations* skiing, cricket, music, opera; *Style—* The Rt Hon Lord Maude of Horsham; ✉ House of Commons, London SW1A 0AA (☎ 020 7219 3000)

MAUDSLAY, Richard Henry; CBE (2006); s of Cecil Winton Maudslay (d 1969), and Charity Magdalen, *née* Johnston (d 1995); *b* 19 November 1946; *Educ* Christ's Hosp, Univ of Edinburgh (BSc); *m* 3 Aug 1968, Rosalind Elizabeth, da of James Slater Seville; 2 da (Diana Elizabeth b 29 Jan 1973, Helen Catherine b 4 Sept 1974); *Career* grad trainee Scottish Electrical Trg Scheme 1968–69, systems analyst Parsons Peebles Ltd 1969–71, systems mangr Reyrolle Belmos Ltd 1971–72, systems and programming mangr Parsons Peebles Ltd 1972–74, prodn mangr Parsons Peebles Power Transformers 1974–78, general mangr Transformadores Parsons Peebles de Mexico 1978–85; md: NEI Parsons Ltd 1985–92, Rolls-Royce Industrial Power Group 1992–97 (memb Bd Rolls-Royce plc 1994–97); dep chm Hardy & Greys Ltd 1999–2013; non-exec dir: Domnick Hunter Gp plc 2000–05, N G Bailey Gp 2001–10; chm: NE Science and Industry Cncl 2004–08, Dstl (Defence Science and Technol Lab) MOD 2005–08, Nat Nuclear Lab 2009–15; cmmr Port of Blyth 2004–14; chm British Mexican Soc 2008–; FREng 1994, FIET; *Recreations* music, travel in Mexico; *Clubs* Royal Over-Seas League; *Style—* Richard Maudslay, Esq, CBE, FREng

MAULEVERER, (Peter) Bruce; QC (1985); s of Maj Algernon Arthur Mauleverer (d 1979), of Poole, Dorset, and Hazel Mary, *née* Flowers (d 1983); *b* 22 November 1946; *Educ* Sherborne, Univ of Durham (BA), Birkbeck Coll London (MA), Univ of Buckingham (MA); *m* 7 Aug 1971, Sara, da of Dr Michael Hudson-Evans, of St Maughans, Gwent; 2 s (Edward b 1972, Barnaby b 1974), 2 da (Harriet b 1977, Clementine b 1981); *Career* called to the Bar Inner Temple 1969 (bencher 1993); recorder of the Crown Court 1985–2004, dep judge of the High Court 1992–2004, head of chambers 1992–2000; hon sec gen Int Law Assoc 1986–93 (vice-chm 1993–2014, patron 2014–); vice-pres Int Social Science Cncl (UNESCO) 1998–2000; tstee: UNICEF UK 2002–08, Tavistock Centre for Couple Relationships 2005–, Jubilee Sailing Tst 2006–13 (chm 2010–13), MapAction 2010–13, The Listen Charity 2014–, Northwick Park Inst for Med Research 2015–; memb Knights of the Round Table 2015–; FCIArb 1997; *Recreations* sailing, skiing, opera, travel; *Clubs* Garrick, Royal Ocean Racing, Royal Yacht Squadron, Pilgrims; *Style—* Bruce

Mauleverer, Esq, QC; ✉ Eliot Vale House, 8 Eliot Vale, Blackheath, London SE3 0UW (☎ 020 8852 2070, fax 020 8852 4614, e-mail bruce@mauleverer.com)

MAUNDRELL, John William; s of Rev Canon Wolseley David Maundrell, of Chichester, W Sussex, and Barbara Katharine, *née* Simmons (d 1985); *b* 27 September 1955; *Educ* Winchester, Courtauld Inst of Art Univ of London (BA); *m* 31 Oct 1987 (m dis 2003), Hazel, da of Francis Walter Monck; 1 da (Alexandra Katharine b 30 Sept 1989), 1 s (William Frederick b 22 Nov 1991); m 2, 21 Feb 2004, Amanda, da of Christopher Horace Ireland; *Career* articled clerk Deloitte Haskins & Sells 1979–82, qualified chartered accountant 1982, asst dir County Bank Ltd/County NatWest 1986–87 (joined 1982), dir Gilbert Eliott Corporate Finance Ltd 1989–90 (asst dir 1987–89), dir Rea Brothers Limited 1991–93; co sec Hobson plc 1994–96, dir Utilitec plc (formerly Cruden Bay plc) 1996–97, dir Corporate Advsy Services 1998–, various public co directorships 1998–; ACA; *Recreations* mountaineering, swimming, tennis; *Style—* John Maundrell, Esq; ✉ Box Cottage, Hempstead, Saffron Walden, Essex CB10 2PD (☎ 01799 599268, e-mail jwmbox@aol.com)

MAURICE, Clare Mary; da of Antony Colin Deans Rankin (d 2000), of Manton, Wilts, and Barbara, *née* Vernon; *b* 25 February 1954; *Educ* Sherborne Sch for Girls, Univ of Birmingham (LLB); *m* 20 Dec 1980, Ian James Maurice, s of Douglas Creyke Maurice (d 1968); 2 da (Anna b 10 March 1987, Kate b 8 Oct 1989); *Career* admitted slr 1978; Allen & Overy: articled 1976, asst slr 1978, ptnr 1985–2009, head of private client dept 2002–09; ptnr Maurice Turnor Gardner LLP 2009–; dir: English Touring Opera 1995–2001, United Response in Business Ltd 1999–2001; chm Bart's and The London Charity 2001–09, chm SafeLives (formerly Coordinated Action Against Domestic Abuse) 2011–; tstee Childwick Tst 2013–, tstee The London Clinic 2015–; memb Int Acad of Estate and Trust Law, fell American Coll of Tst and Estate Counsel 2011; *Recreations* theatre, racing, travel; *Clubs* Reform; *Style—* Mrs Clare Maurice; ✉ 33 Norland Square, London W11 4PU (☎ 020 7221 0962)

MAURICE-WILLIAMS, Robert Stephen; s of Dr Hubert Cecil Maurice-Williams, OBE (d 1981), of Southampton, and Eileen Florence, *née* Lauder; *b* 14 June 1942; *Educ* Winchester, Pembroke Coll Cambridge (MA, MB BChir), St Thomas' Hosp Med Sch; *m* 9 Sept 1968, Elizabeth Anne, da of Dr Swithin Pinder Meadows, of London; 3 da (Francesca Clare Louise b 1971, Harriet Elizabeth Anne b 1974, Vanessa Christina Alice b 1982), 1 s (Julian Robert Cecil b 1979); *Career* registrar in neurosurgery Guy's Maudsley Neurosurgical Unit 1971–73, sr registrar in neurosurgery Bart's 1973–77, conslt neurosurgn Brook Hosp 1977–80, sr conslt neurosurgn The Royal Free Hosp 1980–2007 (emeritus conslt neurosurgn 2007–); papers on surgery and physiology of the central nervous system; ed Br Jl of Neurosurgery 1992–99, memb Ct of Examiners RCS 1992–99, pres Clinical Neurosciences Section RSM 2009–10; fell Hunterian Soc 1980; FRCS 1971, FRCP 1990 (MRCP 1973); *Books* Spinal Degenerative Disease (1981), Subarachnoid Haemorrhage (1988); *Recreations* walking; *Clubs* Athenaeum, Pitt (Cambridge); *Style—* Robert Maurice-Williams, Esq; ✉ c/o Neurosurgical Unit, Wellington Hospital, London NW8 9LE

MAVER, Prof Thomas Watt; *b* 10 March 1938; *Educ* Univ of Glasgow (BSc, PhD); *Career* Univ of Strathclyde: personal prof 1974–80, chair of computer-aided design 1980–2003, dir of grad sch Dept of Architecture and Building Science 1992–2002, vice-dean Faculty of Engrg 1996–2001, emeritus prof 2003–; research prof Glasgow Sch of Art 2006–; first hon cncl memb eCAADe; Royal Soc Esso Gold Medal, Distinguished Service Awards BEPAC and IBPSA, Lifetime Service Awards eCAADe and SIGRADI; Hon FRIAS, hon fell Design Research Soc; *Style—* Prof Thomas Maver; ✉ 8 Kew Terrace, Glasgow G12 0TD (☎ 0141 339 7185, e-mail t.w.maver@strath.ac.uk)

MAVROSKOUFIS, Dr Filippos; s of Simeon Mavroskoufis, of Thessaloniki, Greece, and Leontia, *née* Vassilakaki; *b* 15 August 1952; *Educ* Thessaloniki HS, Dental Sch Aristotelion Univ of Thessaloniki (DDS), UCL (MSc, PhD), Univ of Lund Malmö; *m* 25 May 1985, Janice Gibson, da of John Sailes Clark, and Margaret, *née* Fleming; 1 s (Simeon b 30 July 1985), 2 da (Antigoni b 15 July 1989, Elektra b 19 Aug 1991); *Career* UCH: registrar Prosthetics Dept Dental Sch 1977–78, registrar Community Med Dept 1978–79, involved in teaching of prosthetic dentistry and treating of patients Dental Sch 1977–83; in general practice: pt/t 1981–83, full-time 1983–; in Harley St 1988–; presented 3 scientific papers to dental confs of Euro Prosthodontic Assoc, published 6 scientific papers in dental jls of Europe and America; memb: Br Soc for Study of Prosthetic Dentistry 1977, Euro Prosthodontic Assoc 1977, Gen Dental Practitioners Assoc 1989, Hellenic Soc of Professional People and Scientists in GB, Hellenic Med Soc in GB, Macedonian Soc of GB (vice-pres 1996–99, pres 1999–2001 and 2011–15), Int Coll of Prosthodontists 1998; fell Int Coll of Dentists 2010; *Recreations* basketball, opera, stamp collecting, cooking, debating, skiing; *Clubs* Arsenal FC (gold memb); *Style—* Dr Filippos Mavroskoufis; ✉ 22 Mercers Road, London N19 4PJ (☎ 020 7272 5200); 44 Harley Street, London W1N 1AD (☎ 020 7580 5828, fax 020 7255 1492, e-mail fm@harleystreetsmile.co.uk, website www.harleystreetsmile.co.uk)

MAWER, Sir Philip John Courtney; kt (2002); *b* 30 July 1947; *Educ* Hull GS, Univ of Edinburgh (MA), Univ of London (External Dip Public Admin); *m* 1972, Mary Ann, *née* Moxon; 1 s, 2 da; *Career* sr pres Student Representative Cncl Univ of Edinburgh 1969–70; Home Office: joined 1971, private sec to Min of State 1974–76, princ 1976–83 (Nuffield and Leverhulme travelling fell 1978–79), sec Lord Scarman's Inquiry into Brixton Disturbances 1981, asst sec/head of industrial rels Prison Dept 1984–87, princ private sec to Home Sec 1987–89; under sec Cabinet Office 1989–90, sec gen Gen Synod C of E 1990–2002 (sec gen Archbishops' Cncl 1999–2002), Parly Cmmr for Standards 2002–07, PM's ind advsr on mins' interests 2008–11, ind reviewer House of Bishops' Declaration on Miny of Bishops and Priests 2014; chm All Churches Tst Ltd 2013–; non-exec dir Ecclesiastical Insurance Gp 2008–13 (dep chm 2009–13); chair Professional Regulation Exec Ctee Inst and Faculty of Actuaries 2009–13, memb Advsy Bd Notarial Profession 2013–16, memb Business Ctee Gen Cncl Univ of Edinburgh 2014; hon lay canon St Albans Cathedral 2003–12, canon provincial York Minster 2015; President's Award for Services to the Actuarial Profession 2012; Hon DLitt Univ of Hull 2006, Hon LLD Univ of Hertfordshire 2007; FRSA 1991–2007, Hon FIA 2014; *Recreations* family and friends; *Style—* Sir Philip Mawer; ✉ All Churches Trust Ltd, Beaufort House, Brunswick Road, Gloucester GL1 1JZ (☎ 01452 873189, website www.allchurches.co.uk)

MAWHINNEY, Baron (Life Peer UK 2005), of Peterborough in the County of Cambridgeshire; Sir Brian Stanley Mawhinney; kt (1997), PC (1994); s of Stanley Mawhinney; *b* 26 July 1940; *Educ* Royal Belfast Academical Inst, Queen's Univ Belfast (BSc), Univ of Michigan (MSc), Univ of London (PhD); *m* 1965, Betty Louise Oja; 2 s, 1 da; *Career* asst prof of radiation res Univ of Iowa 1968–70; lectr and sr lectr Royal Free Hosp Sch of Med 1970–84; memb: MRC 1980–83, Gen Synod 1985–90; pres Cons Trade Unionists 1987–90; Parly candidate (Cons) Stockton-on-Tees Oct 1974; MP (Cons): Peterborough 1979–97, Cambridgeshire NW 1997–2005; PPS to Barney Hayhoe (as Min of State Treasury) 1982–84, PPS to Rt Hon Tom King (as Sec of State for Employment then NI) 1984–86, Parly under sec of state NI Office 1986–90, min of state for NI 1990–92, min of state Dept of Health 1992–94, sec of state for tport 1994–95, chm Cons Pty 1995–97, Cabinet min without portfolio 1995–97, shadow home sec 1997–98; chm The Football League 2003–10 (hon pres 2010–13), dep chm England 2018 World Cup Bid 2009–10; Freeman City of Peterborough 2008; Hon LLD Queen's Univ Belfast 2008; hon MInstP; *Publications* In the Firing Line, Conflict and Christianity in Northern Ireland (with Ron Wells), Just a Simple Belfast Boy (2013); *Style—* The Rt Hon the Lord Mawhinney; ✉ House of Lords, London SW1A 0PW

MAWJI, Amin Mohamed; OBE (2012); *Educ* Aga Khan Sch, Queen's Coll Taunton, LSE; *m* Gulnar; 2 c (Sophia, Sameer); *Career* ptnr Arthur Andersen 1979–2002, ptnr Ernst & Young LLP 2002–13; pres H H Aga Khan Ismaili Cncl UK 2009–; *Publications* Programmed for Control; *Style—* Amin Mawji, Esq, OBE; ✉ Fircroft, 30 The Highway, Sutton, Surrey SM2 5QT

MAWREY, Richard Brooks; QC (1986); s of Philip Stephen Mawrey, of Benson, Oxon, and Alice Brooks, *née* Blezard; *b* 20 August 1942; *Educ* Rossall Sch, Magdalen Coll Oxford (Eldon law scholar, BA, MA), Gray's Inn (Albion Richardson scholar); *m* 18 Sept 1965, Gillian Margaret, da of Francis Butt (d 1985); 1 da (Eleanor Frances b 1977); *Career* barr; called to the Bar Gray's Inn 1964 (bencher 2004); lectr in law: Magdalen Coll Oxford 1964–65, Trinity Coll Oxford 1965–69; recorder of the Crown Court 1986– (asst recorder 1982–86), dep High Court judge 1994–; election cmmr 1994–; co-fndr and tstee Historic Gardens Fndn, chm Oxfordshire Gardens Tst; *Books* Computers and the Law (1988), Blackstone's Guide to the Consumer Credit Act 2006 (2006); *Recreations* opera, history, cooking; *Style—* Richard B Mawrey, Esq, QC; ✉ 2 Harcourt Buildings, Temple, London EC4Y 9DB (☎ 020 7583 9020, fax 020 7583 2686)

MAWSON, Baron (UK Life Peer 2007), of Bromley-by-Bow in the London Borough of Tower Hamlets; Rev Andrew Mawson; OBE (2000); *b* 8 November 1954; *Educ* Univ of Manchester (BA, MPhil); *m* 1975, Susan Barnes; 2 s, 1 da; *Career* min United Reform Church 1984; fndr, chief exec and pres Bromley-by-Bow Centre 1984, successively exec, dir and pres Community Action Network (CAN), fndr Stanton Guildhouse 1996, fndr Water City Gp, fndr and dir Andrew Mawson Partnerships; sits in House of Lords as crossbench peer 2007–; memb London Legacy Devpt Corp; *Publications* The Social Entrepreneur: Making Communities Work, St Paul's Way Transformation Project: Building the Road as we Walk it; *Style—* The Lord Mawson, OBE; ✉ Andrew Mawson Partnerships, Ground Floor, 46 Loman Street, London SE1 0EH (e-mail andrew@amawsonpartnerships.com); House of Lords, London SW1A 0PW

MAX, Robert Ian; s of Michael G Max, and Wendy, *née* Segal; *b* 7 February 1968; *Educ* St Paul's, Royal Acad of Music (GRSM, DipRam, LRAM), Royal Northern Coll of Music (postgrad dip), Juilliard Sch NY; *m* 21 March 1993, Zoë Solomon; 1 da (Sophie b 23 Aug 1997), 2 s (Noah b 29 Nov 1998, Hugo b 1 May 2002); *Career* cellist; plays 'Saveuse' Stradivarius cello of 1726; winner: Euro Music for Youth Cello Competition Brussels 1984, Int Young Concert Artists Tst competition (strings section) 1989; solo concert performances in UK, USA, Germany, Austria, Belgium, Denmark, Romania, Russia and France; as cellist of Barbican Piano Trio: recording for ASV 1989, 1994 and 2000, Guildmusic 2000, Black Box 2004, Dutton 2005; toured Denmark, Germany, France, Belgium, Italy, Bulgaria, USA, Russia, S America, Far East, Uzbekistan and UK; princ cello London Chamber Orch; guest princ cello: Royal Philharmonic Orch, Philharmonia, London Symphony Orch, Copenhagen Philharmonic Orch, Royal Northern Sinfonia, Bournemouth Symphony Orch; guest conductor: Kazakh State Philharmonic Orch, London Chamber Orch, BBC Concert Orch, Oradea Philharmonic Orch, Arad Philharmonic Orch, Covent Garden Chamber Orch, London Symphony Orch (conducting masterclass with Valery Gergiev 2010); broadcasts incl: BBC Radio 3, French TV and BBC World Service; chm Music Aid 1992–95; musical dir: Nonesuch Orch 1993–96, Zemel Choir 1994–98, Oxford Symphony Orch 2005–; conductor of symphony and string orchs Royal Holloway Univ of London 2001–14; conductor: Arad Philharmonic Orch Romania, Covent Garden Chamber Orch, London Symphony Orch (conducting masterclass with Valery Gergiev 2010), Sangat Chamber Music Festival Mumbai, Domaine Forget Chamber Music prog Canada; 2 recordings for Olympia, 1 recording for Chandos, 1 recording for MusicWorks; musical dir Pro Corda 1998–2000, chamber music coach MusicWorks; pres North London Festival of Music, Drama and Dance 2013–, artistic dir Frinton Festival 2014–; memb Int Bd of Govrs Jerusalem Acad of Music and Dance 2013–; memb Incorporated Soc of Musicians; hon prof Rachmaninov Inst Tambov Russia; author of articles for MusicTeacher, ESTA News and Views and Arco (chamber music journal); *Publications* Gordon Jacob Cello Octet and Suite for 8 Violins (ed), Davidov Hymn for Cellos for SJ Music (ed), Kouznetsov Suite for SJ Music (ed); *Recreations* cooking Indian food, reading, walking, skiing, clay pigeon shooting; *Style—* Robert Max, Esq; ☎ 020 8458 2839, e-mail robertmax3@gmail.com, website www.barbicanpianotrio.com, www.musicworks.info and www.frintonfestival.com

MAXLOW-TOMLINSON, Paul Christian; s of John Maxlow-Tomlinson, and Marjorie Maude, *née* Muhlenkamp; *b* 24 October 1931; *Educ* Cranleigh Sch, Trinity Coll Dublin, Wadham Coll Oxford (MA); *m* 1, 1 Nov 1959 (m dis 1962), Jeanette McDonald; m 2, 28 June 1969 (m dis 1994), Anne, da of Charles Trench Stewart; 1 da (Claudia Lucy b 6 March 1972), 1 s (Charles Henry b 29 July 1974); m 3, 6 Feb 1994, Julia, *née* Pipe-Wolferstan; *Career* cmmnd Queen's Royal Regt 1950–52; Mercantile Credit Co: Zimbabwe 1956–62, London 1962–63, NI 1963–64; Grand Circle Travel Co 1965–69; admitted slr 1971, former sr ptnr Stones Slrs joined 1972 (conslt 1997–99), former conslt: BNB plc, Stewarts Slrs, Lincoln's Inn Fields; arbitrator Int Court of Arbitration for Sport Lausanne 1994–2011, CAS arbitrator Commonwealth Games Manchester 2002; Br rep Legal Ctee Federation Internationale de Ski 1988–96, memb Sports Dispute Resolution Panel; chm Ski Club of GB 1982–87 (memb Cncl 1978–82), dir Br Ski Fedn 1982–87; memb: Devon Probation Ctee 1983–86, Exec Cncl Br Acad of Forensic Sciences 1987–90; fndr memb and chm Oakfields Project (ex-prisoners' hostel in Exeter), chm Prisoners Educn Tst 2001–06 (patron 2006–), chm Work This Way (Ford Prison) 2008–12; dir Omnijuris (consortium of Euro lawyers) 1992–95; hon slr Lord's Taverners 2001–05; memb Law Soc (memb Childrens Panel 1987–97); author of various articles and lectr on international skiing law; dep chm of govrs Sandroyd Sch 1984–2011, tstee Winchester Area Community Action 2007–11; *Recreations* skiing, shooting, fishing; *Clubs* Garrick, Ski Club of GB; *Style—* Paul Maxlow-Tomlinson, Esq

MAXTONE GRAHAM, Ysenda; *see:* Maxtone-Smith, Ysenda May

MAXTONE-SMITH, Ysenda May; da of Robert Mungo Maxtone Graham, of Sandwich, Kent; *b* 31 December 1962; *Educ* The King's Sch Canterbury, Girton Coll Cambridge (MA); *m* 14 Aug 1993, Michael James Smith (who upon marriage adopted by deed poll surname of Maxtone-Smith), s of David Smith, JP, of Keyworth, Notts; 3 s (Toby Robert b 2 July 1994, Charles Mungo b 8 Oct 1996, Francis James b 8 March 2002); *Career* as Ysenda Maxtone Graham: columnist for the Express on Sunday, freelance journalist writing for The Spectator, Sunday Telegraph, Evening Standard, Daily Mail, Church Times, Harpers and Queen, Tatler and others; *Books* The Church Hesitant, a Portrait of the Church of England Today (1993), Without a Guide (contrib, 1996), The Real Mrs Miniver (2001, shortlisted Whitbread Biography Award 2002), Mr Tibbits's Catholic School (2011), An Insomniac's Guide to the Small Hours (2012), Terms and Conditions: Life in British Girls' Boarding Schools 1939–1979 (2016); *Style—* Mrs Ysenda Maxtone-Smith; ✉ 1 Avalon Road, London SW6 2EX (☎ 020 7736 8710, e-mail ysenda@talk21.com)

MAXWELL, Donald; s of Kenneth M MacAlpine, of Perth, Scotland, and Margaret MacAlpine; *b* 12 December 1948; *Educ* Perth Acad, Univ of Edinburgh (MA); *m* Alison Norman; 1 da; *Career* baritone; Scottish Opera 1976–82: John Noble bursary, debut 1977, title role in Barbiere di Siviglia, Sharpless in Madama Butterfly, Enrico in Lucia di Lammermoor, Zurga in Les Pecheurs de Peries, Shiskov in From the House of the Dead; WNO 1982–85: Renato in Un Ballo in Maschera, Shishkov, Marcello in La Boheme, Don

M

Carlos in Ernani, Rigoletto, Iago in Otello, The Count in Le Nozze di Figaro, title role in Falstaff, Golaud in Pelleas and Melisande; freelance 1985–; ROH debut 1987; performances at ROH incl: Bartolo Barbière di Siviglia, Faninal Rosenkavalier, Kothner in Die Meistersinger von Nurnberg, Gunther in Götterdämmerung; ENO: title role in Il Barbiere di Siviglia, Wozzeck; Opera North: Germont in La Traviata, Pizarro in Fidelio, title role in Der Fliegende Holländer, Scarpia in Tosca; other performances incl: Berg's Lulu (BBC Proms) 1996, Don Alhambra in The Gondoliers (BBC Proms) 1997, First Night BBC Proms 1998; artistic dir Buxton Festival 1999, dir Nat Opera Studio 2001, dir of Opera Studies Royal Welsh Coll of Music and Drama 2004; numerous appearances in UK festivals and in foreign operas incl Paris, Vienna, NY, Tokyo, Milan, Buenos Aires, Amsterdam and Salzburg; regular contribs to radio and TV operas; memb Music Box; recordings incl: Carmina Burana, Kismet, Amahl and The Night Visitors, Sir John in Love, Midsummer Night's Dream, Noye's Fludde, The Song of Norway; Hon DMus Univ of Abertay Dundee; fell Royal Welsh Coll of Music and Drama (FRWCMD), fell Leeds Coll of Music (FLeedsCM); *Recreations* railways; *Style*— Donald Maxwell, Esq; ✉ Music International, 13 Ardilaun Road, Highbury, London N5 2QR (✆ 020 7359 5183, fax 020 7226 9792)

MAXWELL, Prof (James) Douglas; s of Henry Alastair Maxwell (d 1996), of Inverness, and Sheila Margaret, *née* Stewart (d 1957); *b* 15 September 1940; *Educ* Aberdeen GS, The HS of Glasgow, Univ of Glasgow (BSc, MB ChB, MD, Hunter medal), Univ of Calif; *m* 1, 1965 (m dis 1973), Gisela, *née* Michler; 1 s (Nicholas b 1969); m 2, 1976, Jane Elisabeth, *née* Sherwood; 1 da (Katherine b 1977), 1 s (Edward b 1979); *Career* jr med posts and McIntyre research scholarship Glasgow Royal Infirmary 1964–69, hon lectr Liver Unit KCH London 1969–72, research fell Depts of Med and Pharmacology Univ of Calif San Francisco 1972–74, conslt physician and sr lectr in med St George's Hosp and Med Sch London 1975–87; St George's Hosp Med Sch London: reader in med and dean of clinical studies 1987–97, prof of med 2003–, chair Accelerated Graduate Entry Programme (AGEP); dep dir Refugee Doctors Course 2005–06; clinical examiner Univ of London, Soc of Apothecaries and United Examining Bd; Winston Churchill Travelling Fellowship 1998; FRCPGlas, FRCP; *Publications* papers on gastroenterology, liver disease, vitamin D deficiency and tuberculosis; *Style*— Prof Douglas Maxwell; ✉ Dairy House, Milborne Wick, Sherborne DT9 4PW (✆ 01963 251093, e-mail jdmaxwell60@yahoo.co.uk)

MAXWELL, Glyn Meurig; s of Dr James Maxwell, and Mary Buddug, *née* Powell; *b* 7 November 1962; *Educ* Stanborough Sch Welwyn Garden City, Worcester Coll Oxford (exhibitioner, BA), Boston Univ Mass USA; *m* 1997, Hon Geraldine, *née* Harmsworth, da of 3 Viscount Rothermere (d 1998); 1 da (Alfreda b 1997); *Career* editorial asst W H Allen & Co plc 1989, poet and freelance ed/writer 1989–; writing fell Nanyang Technological Univ Singapore 1995, writer in residence Univ of Warwick 1997, visiting writer Amherst Coll Mass USA 1997–2000, adjunct prof: The New School NY 2002–, Columbia Univ NY 2002–, Princeton Univ NJ 2003–04; poetry ed The New Republic 2001–; contrib to various magazines and jls UK and USA incl: TLS, London Review of Books, Vogue, New Statesman, Spectator, The Independent, The Independent on Sunday, The Sunday Times, Poetry Review, The New Republic, The New Yorker, The New York Times, Atlantic Monthly, Manhattan Review, Massachusetts Review, Partisan Review; included on New Br Poets tour of UK 1990; third prize Nat Poetry Competition 1989, winner Eric Gregory Award 1991, Somerset Maugham Travel Prize 1992, shortlisted for Sunday Times Young Writer of the Year 1990 and 1992, winner E M Forster Prize American Acad of Arts and Letters 1997; FRSL; *Books* Tale of the Mayor's Son (Poetry Book Soc choice 1990, shortlisted for John Llewellyn Rhys Meml Prize 1990), Out of the Rain (Poetry Book Soc recommendation 1992, shortlisted Whitbread Poetry Prize 1992), Gnyss the Magnificent (1993), Blue Burneau (1994, shortlisted Whitbread First Novel Prize 1994), Rest for the Wicked (1995, shortlisted Whitbread Poetry Prize and T S Eliot Prize 1995), Moon Country (with Simon Armitage, 1996), The Breakage (1998, shortlisted for Forward Prize and T S Eliot Prize), The Boys at Twlilight: Poems 1990–95 (2000), Time's Fool (2001), The Nerve (2002); work incl in various anthologies incl: Poetry with an Edge (1988), Poetry Book Society Anthology (1988, 1990 and 1991), Soho Square (1991), New Writing (1991 and 1992), Penguin Modern Poets 3 (1995), British Poetry Since 1945 (1998), The Firebox (1998), Scanning the Century (1999), The Best of English Poetry (audio tape, 1999); *Plays* The Heart in Hiding (1995), Wolfpit (1996), Broken Journey (1999), Anyroad (2000), The Last Valentine (2000), The Only Girl In The World (2001), The Lifeblood (2001); *Style*— Glyn Maxwell, Esq, FRSL; ✉ c/o Micheline Steinberg Associates, 4th Floor, 104 Great Portland Street, London W1 (e-mail micheline@steinplays.com)

MAXWELL, James Rankin; s of John James Maxwell (d 1990), and Helen Morrison, *née* Tait (d 2006); *b* 20 April 1941; *Educ* HS of Glasgow, Univ of Glasgow (BSc, PhD), Univ of Bristol (DSc); *m* 1964, Joy Millar, da of John Hunter; 1 da (Jane b 5 Dec 1966), 1 s (Keir b 28 Dec 1970, d 1977); *Career* research asst Univ of Glasgow 1967, postdoctoral research chemist Univ of Calif Berkeley 1967–68; Univ of Bristol: postdoctoral fell 1968–69, research assoc 1969–72, lectr 1972–78, reader 1978–90, prof 1990–99 (now emeritus), head Section of Environmental and Analytical Chemistry 1991–99, sr research fell 1999–2010; J Klarence Karcher Medal Univ of Oklahoma 1979, Treibs Medal Geochemical Soc USA 1989, Interdisciplinary Award in Chemistry RSC 1994, jt geochemistry fell Geochemical Soc USA and Euro Assoc of Geochemistry 1996; FRS 1997; *Publications* author of over 250 papers in learned jls; *Recreations* walking, gardening, cooking; *Style*— Prof James Maxwell, FRS; ✉ School of Chemistry, University of Bristol, Cantock's Close, Bristol BS8 1TS (✆ 0117 954 6339, e-mail j.r.maxwell@bristol.ac.uk)

MAXWELL, His Hon John Frederick Michael; s of late Lt Frederic Michael Maxwell (RIN), of Sidcup, Kent, and late Mabel Doreen, *née* Turner; *b* 20 May 1943, Sidcup, Kent; *Educ* Dover Coll, New Coll Oxford (MA); *m* 1, 1964 (m dis 1986), Jennifer Mary; 1 da (Alice b 1966), 1 s (Edward b 1967); m 2, 1986, Jayne Elizabeth, da of George Douglas Hunter (d 1984), of Birmingham; *Career* called to the Bar Inner Temple 1965; practised Midland Circuit, recorder of the Crown Court 1995–2005, standing counsel to HM Customs & Excise for the Midland Circuit 1995–2005, standing counsel to Revenue & Customs Prosecutions Office 2005, circuit judge 2005–13; chm Birmingham Karma Ling Buddhist Centre; tstee: Rokpa Tst, Tara Tst (also chm), Solihull Symphony Orchestra; *Recreations* music, yachting; *Clubs* Royal Yachting Assoc, Old Gaffers Assoc; *Style*— His Hon John Maxwell; ✉ e-mail john@maxwell100.plus.com

MAXWELL, John Hunter; s of late John Hunter Maxwell, OBE, and Susan Elizabeth Una Smith; *b* 25 September 1944; *Educ* Melville Coll Edinburgh, Dumfries Acad, Univ of Edinburgh; *m* 1967, Janet Margaret, *née* Frew; 3 s; *Career* articled clerk T Hunter Thompson & Co CA 1962–67, qualified CA 1967, regnl dir (Far East) Rank Xerox Ltd 1967–83, gp fin controller Grand Metropolitan plc 1983–86, chief exec Provincial Group 1986–92, chief exec BPB Industries plc 1992–93, corp devpt dir Prudential Corporation plc 1994–96, DG Automobile Association 1996–2000; non-exec dir: Alliance & Leicester Building Society 1993–94, Wellington Underwriting 1999–2003 (chm 2000–03), Provident Financial plc 2000–, The Big Food Gp plc 2001–05, Parity Gp plc 2002–, Royal Sun Alliance Gp plc 2003–, Homeserve plc 2004–; chm: IAM 2002– (memb Cncl 1997–), DX Services plc 2005–06; dir Motor Sports Assoc 2007–; tstee Friends of UCL 1995–2002, govr Royal Ballet Sch; Freeman City of London 1998, Liveryman Worshipful Co of Coachmakers and Coach Harness Makers 1998–; CCMI, FRSA, FIMI; *Recreations* sailing, classic cars, motoring, travel, arts; *Clubs* Royal Thames Yacht, RAC (dir 2000); *Style*— John H Maxwell, Esq

MAXWELL, Liam; *Educ* Univ of Oxford (MA); *m*; 3 c; *Career* conslt Accenture 1991–93, IT mangr Office Angels 1994–97, European technol mangr Adecco 1997–2000, fndr and IT dir Huntress 2000–01, head of IT Capita Resourcing 2001–04, head of computing Eton Coll 2004–11, exec dir IT reform and dep Govt chief info offr Cabinet Office 2012, chief technol offr HM Govt 2012–16, nat technology advsr HM Govt 2016–; cncllr, cabinet memb for policy Royal Borough of Windsor and Maidenhead 2007–11; fndr Holypart Coll Berks 2014–; visiting prof in electronics and computer science Univ of Southampton 2014–; *Books* It's ours, why we not the government should own our data (2009), Better for Less (2010); *Style*— Liam Maxwell, Esq; ✉ Twitter @liammax

MAXWELL, Richard; QC (1988); s of Thomas Maxwell (d 1957), and Kathleen Marjorie, *née* Truswell (d 1979); *b* 21 December 1943; *Educ* Nottingham HS (scholar), Hertford Coll Oxford (state scholar and Baring scholar, MA); *m* 10 Sept 1966, Judith Ann, da of Hedley Vincent Iliffe, of Breaston, Derby; 2 da (Karen Laetitia b 1968, Catharine Antonia b 1969), 2 s (Richard Alexander b 1971, Thomas Daniel b 1973); *Career* called to the Bar Inner Temple 1968; recorder of the Crown Court 1992–, dep judge of the High Court 1998–; *Recreations* golf, fly fishing, watercolours, walking, malt whisky, wine; *Clubs* Darley Dale Fly Fishing, Peak Forest Angling, Beeston Fields Golf, Queen Anne's Bowling Green, Derwent Fly Fishing; *Style*— Richard Maxwell, Esq, QC; ✉ Ropewalk Chambers, 24 The Ropewalk, Nottingham NG1 5EF (✆ 0115 947 2581)

MAXWELL, Simon Jeffrey; CBE (2007); s of Frederic Norman Maxwell (d 2001), and Ruth Salinsky; *b* 1 May 1948, Birmingham; *Educ* Univ of Oxford (BA), Univ of Sussex (MA); *m* 1 Sept 1973, Catherine Elisabeth, *née* Pelly; 3 s (Daniel Julius b 8 April 1976, Oliver Conran b 10 Nov 1977, Dominic Giles b 4 Jan 1981); *Career* jr professional offr UNDP Nairobi 1970–72, asst resident rep UNDP New Delhi 1973–77, temp research offr Inst of Devpt Studies Univ of Sussex 1977–78, agricultural economist (farm systems) Centro de Investigacion Agricola Tropical (CIAT) Santa Cruz Bolivia Br Tropical Agric Mission ODA 1978–81, fell and head Food Security Unit Inst of Devpt Studies Univ of Sussex 1989–97 (prog mangr Poverty Reduction, Sustainable Devpt and the Rural Sector 1991–97); Overseas Devpt Inst: dir 1997–2009, sr res assoc 2009–; dir Simon Maxwell Ltd 2010–; pres Devpt Studies Assoc UK & Ireland 2001–05 (memb Cncl 1998–2005); memb: Oxfam Field Ctee for Latin America 1981–84, Ind Gp on Br Aid 1982–, UN Advsy Gp on Nutrition 1990–96, Prog Advsy Panel Fndn for Devpt Cooperation 1997–2009, Policy Advsy Cncl Inst of Public Policy Research 2009–; chair Humanitarian Global Agenda Cncl 2008–10 (vice-chair 2010–11); external examiner Wye Coll Univ of London 1995–98, govr Inst of Devpt Studies 1996–97, tstee Action for Conservation through Tourism (ACT) 1998–2002, patron One World Broadcasting Tst 1998–2009, tstee and memb Bd Fair Trade Fndn 2008–14, tstee Fundacion para las Relaciones Exteriores y el Dialogo Exterior (Madrid) 2011–15, memb Bd Int Food Policy Research Inst 2013–; chair European Think-Tanks Gp 2015–; hon fell Foreign Policy Assoc NY 2003–, forum fell World Economic Forum 2003–, emeritus fell Inst of Devpt Studies 2015–; *Publications* author, co-author or ed of numerous books, articles in books and jls, briefing papers, commissioned studies and reports; *Recreations* various; *Style*— Simon Maxwell, Esq, CBE; ✉ 20 West Drive, Brighton BN2 OGD (✆ 01273 686521, e-mail sm@simonmaxwell.eu, website www.simonmaxwell.eu)

MAXWELL, (William) Stewart; s of William Maxwell, and Margaret, *née* Torrance; *b* 24 December 1963, Glasgow; *Educ* King's Park Secdy Sch Glasgow 1976–81, Glasgow Coll of Technol (BA); *m* 2 Oct 1995, Mary, *née* Stevenson; 1 da (Catherine b 18 March 1998); *Career* Wilmax Ltd 1986–88 and 1991–92, admin offr Scottish Trg Fndn 1988–91; Strathclyde Fire Brigade: industrial trg mangr Trg Centre 1993–94, sr admin offr Central Command HQ 1994–2000, mgmnt info system project mangr Brigade Command and Control Centre 2000–03; MSP (SNP) West of Scotland 2003–16, shadow dep min for health 2004–06, shadow min for sport, culture and media 2006–07, min for communities and sport 2007–09; dep convener Justice 1 Ctee 2003–04; vice-pres EU Ctee of the Regions European Alliance Gp 2012–16; memb: Subordinate Legislation Ctee 2003–07, Justice 2 Ctee 2004–06, Enterprise and Culture Ctee 2006–07, Justice Ctee 2009–11; convener: Educn and Culture Ctee 2011–16, Referendum Bill Ctee 2012–16; hon vice-pres Royal Environmental Health Inst of Scotland (REHIS) 2006–; *Recreations* golf, photography; *Clubs* Whitecraigs Golf; *Style*— Stewart Maxwell, Esq; ✉ website www.stewartmaxwell.com

MAXWELL, Dr William Skene (Bill); s of Joseph Maxwell (d 2015), of Grandtully, Perthshire, and Sheena, *née* Sclanders (d 1960); *b* 14 November 1957, Edinburgh; *Educ* HS of Dundee, Univ Coll Oxford (MA), Univ of Edinburgh (PhD), Univ of Glasgow (MAppSci); *m* 21 Sept 1981, Margaret, *née* Warden; 2 da (Mhairi Louise b 26 March 1986, Alexandra Zoe b 11 Feb 1988); *Career* chartered psychologist; educnl psychologist Dumfries and Galloway Regnl Cncl 1984–90; Grampian Regnl Cncl: educnl psychologist 1990–92, princ educnl psychologist 1992–94; Scot Exec: HM inspr of schs 1994–2002, HM chief inspr of schs 2002–06, head of analytical servs (educn) 2006–08; HM chief inspr of educn and trg in Wales 2008–10, HM sr chief inspr IM Inspectorate of Educn in Scotland 2010–; chief exec Educn Scotland 2011–; AFBPsS 1984, FRSA 2012; *Recreations* mountaineering, rock and ice climbing; *Clubs* Alpine; *Style*— Dr Bill Maxwell; ✉ Education Scotland, Almondvale Business Park, Almondvale Way, Livingston EH54 6GA (✆ 01506 600200, e-mail bill.maxwell@educationscotland.gsi.gov.uk)

MAXWELL DAVIES, Sir Peter; CH (2014), kt (1987), CBE (1981); s of Thomas Maxwell Davies, and Hilda Maxwell Davies; *b* 8 September 1934, Manchester; *Educ* Leigh GS Salford, Univ of Manchester (MusB), Royal Manchester Coll of Music; *Career* composer and conductor; studied with Goffredo Petrassi in Rome 1957, dir of music Cirencester GS 1959–62, Harkness fell Grad Sch Princeton Univ (studying with Roger Sessions, Milton Babbitt and Earl Kim) 1962–64; fndr and co-dir (with Harrison Birtwistle) The Pierrot Players 1967–71, fndr and artistic dir The Fires of London 1971–87, fndr and artistic dir St Magnus Festival Orkney Islands 1977–86 (pres 1986–), artistic dir Dartington Hall Summer Sch of Music 1979–84, assoc composer/conductor Scottish Chamber Orch 1985–94, conductor/composer BBC Philharmonic Orch Manchester 1992–2001; assoc composer/conductor Royal Philharmonic Orch 1992–2000, composer laureate Scottish Chamber Orch 1994–, master of the Queens' music 2004; visiting Fromm prof of composition Harvard Univ 1985; pres: Schools Music Assoc 1983–, North of England Educn Conf Chester 1985, Composers' Guild of GB 1986–, Nat Fedn of Music Socs 1989–, Cheltenham Arts Festivals 1994–96, Soc for Promotion of New Music 1995–; major retrospective festival (28 works) South Bank Centre London 1990, Max: Peter Maxwell Davies – A Musician of Our Time (two week festival) South Bank Centre, Royal Acad of Music and Westminster Cathedral 2005; memb: Accademica Filarmonia Romana 1979, Bayerische Akademie der Schönen Künste 1998; hon memb: Guildhall Sch of Music and Drama 1981, Royal Philharmonic Soc 1987; hon fell: Royal Incorporation of Architects in Scotland 1994, Univ of Highlands and Islands 2004; Hon DMus: Edinburgh 1979, Manchester 1981, Bristol 1984, Open Univ 1986, Glasgow 1993, Durham 1994, Hull 2001, Kingston 2005; Hon LLD: Aberdeen 1981, Warwick 1986; Hon DLitt Salford 1999; Hon Dr Heriot-Watt Univ 2002; Freeman City of Salford 2004; Officier de l'Ordre des Arts et des Lettres (France) 1988; memb Royal Swedish Acad of Music 1993; hon memb RSA 2001; FRNCM 1978, hon RAM 1978, FRSAMD 1994, FRCM 1994, fell Br Acad of Composers and Songwriters 2005; *Awards* Cobbett Medal for services to chamber music 1989, First Award Assoc of British Orchs (ABO) 1991, Gulliver Award for the Performing Arts in Scotland 1991, Nat Fedn of Music Socs Charles Groves Award for outstanding contrib to Br music 1995, Royal Philharmonic Soc Award for large-scale composition (for Symphony No 5) 1995, Distinguished Musicians Award Inc Soc of Musicians 2001; *Works* incl Sonata (for trumpet and piano) 1955, Alma redemptoris mater (for ensemble) 1957, Five Motets (for SATB Soli, SATB Chorus and ensemble) 1959, O Magnum Mysterium (for SATB chorus) 1960, First Fantasia on an In Nomine of John Taverner (for orch) 1962, Second Fantasia on John Taverner's In Nomine (for orch) 1964, Revelation and Fall (for soprano and ensemble) 1966, Antechrist (for ensemble) 1967, Missa super L'Homme Armé (for speaker and ensemble) 1968, St Thomas Wake-Foxtrot for Orch 1968, Worldes Blis (for orch) 1969, Eight Songs for a Mad King (music theatre work for ensemble) 1969, Vesalii Icones – music theatre work (for dancer and ensemble) 1969, Taverner (opera in two acts) 1970, From Stone to Thorn (for mezzo soprano and ensemble) 1971, Stone Litany (for mezzo soprano and ensemble) 1973, Miss Donnithorne's Maggot (music-theatre work for mezzo-soprano and ensemble) 1974, Ave Maris Stella (for ensemble) 1975, Symphony No 1 1976, The Martyrdom of Saint Magnus (chamber opera) 1976, The Two Fiddlers (opera for children to perform) 1978, Le Jongleur de Notre Dame (music theatre work for juggle, baritone and ensemble) 1978, Salome (ballet in two acts) 1978, Black Pentecost (for mezzo-soprano, baritone and orch) 1979, Solstice of Light (for tenor, SATB chorus and organ) 1979, Cinderella (pantomime opera for children to perform) 1979, Symphony No 2 (for orch) 1980, Piano Sonata 1981, Brass Quintet 1981, Image, Reflection, Shadow (for ensemble) 1982, Sinfonia Concertante (for tenor and orch) 1983, Into the Labyrinth (for tenor and orch) 1983, The No 11 Bus (music theatre work for mime, singers and dancers and ensemble) 1984, Symphony No 3 (formorch) 1985, An Orkney Wedding with Sunrise (for orch) 1985, Violin concerto (for violin and orch) 1985, Strathclyde Concerto No 1 for oboe and orch 1986, Resurrection (opera) 1987, Strathclyde Concerto No 2 for Cello and orch 1988, Concerto for Trumpet and orch 1988, The Great Bank Robbery (music theatre work for children to perform) 1989, Symphony No 4 1989, Strathclyde Concerto No 3 for Horn, Trumpet and Orchestra 1989, Strathclyde Concerto No 4 for Clarinet and Orchestra 1990, Caroline Mathilde (ballet in two acts) 1990, Ojai Festival Overture (for orch) 1991, Strathclyde Concerto No 5 (for violin, viola and string orch) 1991, Strathclyde Concerto No 6 (for flute and orch) 1991, Strathclyde Concerto No 7 (for double bass and orch) 1992, The Turn of the Tide (for orch) 1992, Strathclyde Concerto No 8 (for bassoon and orch) 1993, A Spell for Green Corn: The MacDonald Dances (for orch) 1993, Symphony No 5 1994, Cross Lane Fair (for orch) 1994, Strathclyde Concerto No 9 (for six woodwind instruments and string orch) 1994, The Beltane Fire (choreographic poem for orch) 1995, The Three Kings (for chorus, orch and soloists) 1995, The Doctor of Myddfai (cmmnd Welsh National Opera 50th Anniversary season), Symphony No 6 (London premiere BBC Proms with RPO 1996), Strathclyde Concerto No 10: Concerto for orch 1996, Concerto for Piccolo 1996, Job – Oratorio (for chorus, orch and soloists) 1997, Mavis in Las Vegas – Theme and Variations (for orch) 1997, Orkney Saga I: Fifteen Keels Laid in Norway for Jerusalem-farers (for orch) 1997, The Jacobite Rising (for chorus, orch and soloists) 1997, Concerto for Piano 1997, Orkney Saga II: In Kirkwall, the first red St Magnus stones (for orch) 1997, A Reel of Seven Fisherman (for orch) 1998, Sea Elegy (for chorus, orch and soloists) 1998, Rome Amor Labyrinthus (for orch) 1998, Orkney Saga III: An Orkney Wintering – Stone poems in Orkahowe: 'great treasure...' (for alto saxophone and orch) 1999, Trumpet Quintet (for string quartet and trumpet) 1999, Mr Emmet Takes a Walk (music theatre work for soprano, baritone, bass and instrument ensemble) 1999, Horn Concerto 1999, Orkney Saga V: Westerly Gale in Biscay, Salt in the Bread Broken (for SATB chorus and orchestra) 2000, Symphony No 7 (for orch) 2000, Antarctic Symphony (Symphony No 8) (for orch) 2000, Canticum Canticorum (cantata for chorus, orch and SATB soloists) 2001, De Assumtione Beatae Mariae Virginis (for ensemble) 2001, Crossing Kings Reach (for ensemble) 2001, Mass (SATB chorus and organ) 2002, Naxos Quartet No 1 (string quartet) 2002, Piano Trio 2002, Naxos Quartet No 2 (string quartet) 2003, Naxos Quartet No 3 (string quartet) 2003, Naxos Quartet No 4: Children's Games (string quartet) 2004, Magnificiat and Nun Dimitis (SATB and organ) 2004, Naxos Quartet No 5 (string quartet) 2004, Hymn to Artemis Locheia (for clarinet quintet) 2004, The Fall of the Leafe (string orch) 2004, Naxos Quartet No 6 (string quartet) 2005, Commemoration Sixty (children's chorus, military band, military trumpets and trombones and orch) 2005, Beacons of Hope (Military Wind Band) 2005; *Style*— Sir Peter Maxwell Davies, CH, CBE; ✉ c/o Intermusica Artists' Management Limited, Crystal Wharf, 36 Graham Street, London N1 8GJ (☎ 020 7608 9900, fax 020 7490 3263, e-mail mail@intermusica.co.uk, website www.intermusica.co.uk)

MAXWELL MARTIN, Anna; *b* 1978, Beverley, Yorks; *Educ* Univ of Liverpool, LAMDA; *Partner* Roger Michell, *qv*; *Career* actress; *Theatre* incl: The Little Foxes (Donmar Warehouse) 2001, The Coast of Utopia (RNT) 2002, Honour (RNT) 2003, Three Sisters (RNT) 2003, His Dark Materials (Nat Theatre) 2004, Dumb Show (Royal Court Theatre) 2004, Other Hands (Soho Theatre) 2006, Cabaret (Lyric Theatre) 2007, The Female of the Species (Vaudeville Theatre) 2008, Measure For Measure (Almeida Theatre) 2010; *Television* incl: Bleak House 2005 (Best Actress BAFTA 2006), The Wind in the Willows 2006, White Girl 2008, Poppy Shakespeare 2008 (Best Actress BAFTA 2009), Freefall 2009, Moonshot 2009, Free Agents 2009, On Expenses 2010, Accused 2012; *Film* incl: Eddie Loves Mary 2002, Enduring Love 2004, The Other Man 2006, I Really Hate My Job 2007, Becoming Jane 2007; *Style*— Ms Anna Maxwell Martin; ✉ c/o United Agents, 12–26 Lexington Street, London W1F 0LE

MAXWELL-IRVING, Alastair Michael Tivey; s of Reginald Tivey (d 1977), of Warks, and Barbara Annie Bell Irving (d 1988); *b* 1 October 1935, Witham, Essex; *Educ* Lancing, Univ of London (BSc), Univ of Oxford, Univ of Stirling; *m* 21 Sept 1983, Esther Mary, da of Rev James Hamilton, formerly of Auchterhouse, Angus; *Career* chartered engr: English Electric Co 1960–64, Annandale Estates 1966–69, Weir Pumps Ltd 1970–91; quality conslt 1992–94; architectural and historical writer and archaeologist; sometime hon asst Royal Cmmn on Ancient and Historical Monuments Scotland; memb: Castle Studies Gp, Archaeology Scotland, Dumfries and Galloway Antiquarian Soc, Hawick Archaeological Soc, Stirling Field and Archaeological Soc, Clackmannan Field Soc, Friends of Alloa Tower, Friends of Sauchie Tower, Scottish Castles Assoc; fndr memb and sec BIM Central Scotland 1975–79, community cncllr Logie 1984–97, tstee Bonshaw Preservation Tst 2007–; Nigel Tranter Meml Award 2003; FSA Scot 1967, AMICE 1970, MIEE 1972, CEng 1973, MIMgt 1974, FSA 2001; *Publications* incl: Burke's Landed Gentry (contrib, 1968 and 2001), The Irvings of Bonshaw (1968), The Irvings of Dumfries (1968), Early Firearms and Their Influence on the Military And Domestic Architecture of the Borders (1974), Cramalt Tower (1982), Borthwick Castle (1982), Hoddom Castle (1989), Lochwood Castle (1990), The Castles of Buittle (1991), Torthorwald Castle (1993), Scottish Yetts and Window-Grilles (1994), The Dating of the Tower-houses at Comlongon and Elphinstone (1996), The Tower-houses of Kirtleside (1997), Kenmure Castle (1997), The Border Towers of Scotland: Their History and Architecture – The West March (2000), Lordship and Architecture in Medieval and Rennaissance Scotland (contrib, 2005), Family Memoirs (2007), Family Memoirs Supplement (2008), Reginald Tivey: A Celebration of his Art (2011), The Border Towers of Scotland 2: Their Evolution and Architecture (2014); *Recreations* architecture and history of the Border towers of Scotland, archaeology, family history and genealogy, art and architecture of Tuscany, horology, heraldry, photography, gardening; *Style*— Alastair Maxwell-Irving, Esq, FSA; ✉ Telford House, Blairlogie, Stirling FK9 5PX (☎ 01259 761721, e-mail a.maxwellirving@gmail.com)

MAY, Derwent James; s of Herbert Alfred May (d 1982), and Nellie Eliza, *née* Newton (d 1959); *b* 29 April 1930; *Educ* Strode's Sch Egham, Lincoln Coll Oxford (MA); *m* 22 Sept 1967, Yolanta Izabella, da of Tadeusz Sypniewski, of Lodz, Poland (d 1970); 1 s (Orlando James b 1968), 1 da (Miranda Izabella b 1970); *Career* theatre and film critic Continental Daily Mail Paris 1952–53, lectr English Univ of Indonesia 1955–58, sr lectr in English lit Univs of Warsaw and Lód? Poland 1959–63, ldr writer TLS 1963–65, lit ed The Listener 1965–86, lit and arts ed The Sunday Telegraph 1986–90, ed Élan (the arts magazine of the European) 1990–91, feature writer The Times 1993– (contrib of nature notes 1981–, European arts ed 1992), literary conslt The London Magazine 2010–; memb Booker Prize Jury 1978, memb Hawthornden Prize Ctee 1987– (chm 1997, 2004, 2010 & 2015); FRSL 1996; *Books* The Professionals (1964), Dear Parson (1969), The Laughter in Djakarta (1973), A Revenger's Comedy (1979), Proust (1983, reissued 2013), The Times Nature Diary (1983), Hannah Arendt (1986), The New Times Nature Diary (1993), Feather Reports (1996), Critical Times: The History of the Times Literary Supplement (2002), How to Attract Birds to Your Garden (2002), The Times: A Year in Nature Notes (2004), Wondering About Many Women (poems, 2011), Life on the Wing: A Bird Chronicle from the pages of The Times (2012); ed: Good Talk: An Anthology from BBC Radio (1968), Good Talk 2 (1969), The Music of What Happens: Poems from The Listener 1965–80 (1981); *Recreations* birdwatching, opera; *Clubs* Beefsteak, Garrick; *Style*— Derwent May, Esq, FRSL; ✉ 45 Burghley Road, London NW5 1UH (☎ 020 7485 2788)

MAY, Douglas James; QC (Scot 1989); s of Thomas May (d 1977), of Edinburgh, and Violet Mary Brough Boyd or May (d 1995); *b* 7 May 1946; *Educ* George Heriot's Sch Edinburgh, Univ of Edinburgh (LLB); *Career* advocate 1971, temp sheriff 1990–99, dep social security cmmr 1992–93, social security cmmr Child Support Cmmn 1993–, judge of the Upper Tbnl (Administrative Appeals Chamber) 2008–; memb Tbnls Procedure Ctee 2008–15; Parly candidate (C): Edinburgh E Feb 1974, Glasgow Cathcart 1983; capt Scottish Univs Golfing Soc 1990, pres Edinburgh Photographic Soc 1996–99, chm Contemporary Distinctions Panel Royal Photographic Soc 2010–; memb Faculty of Advocates, FRPS 2002; *Recreations* golf, photography, travel, concert going; *Clubs* Bruntsfield Links Golfing Soc, Merchants of Edinburgh Golf (capt 1997–99), Luffness New Golf; *Style*— Douglas May, Esq, QC; ✉ Office of the Upper Tribunal (Administrative Appeals Chamber), George House, 126 George Street, Edinburgh EH3 7PW (☎ 0131 271 4310)

MAY, Dr Geoffrey John; s of James Ebrey Clare May (d 1986), of London, and Eleanor Isobel, *née* Tate (d 1989); *b* 7 May 1948; *Educ* Eltham Coll London, Fitzwilliam Coll Cambridge (MA, PhD); *m* 5 Jan 1974, Sarah Elizabeth, da of Stanley George Felgate (d 1986), of Chislehurst; 2 s (Timothy b 1976, Daniel b 1980); *Career* Chloride Gp plc 1974–82, Hawker Siddeley Gp (BTR plc) 1982–90 and 1991–2000, dir Tungstone Batteries Ltd 1982–88, dir and gen mangr Hawker Fusegear Ltd 1988–90, dir Caparo Industries plc, md Barton Abrasives Ltd 1990–91, dir Hawker Batteries Gp 1991–2000, dir Invensys Power Systems 1998–2000, exec dir FIAMM SpA 2000–03, princ Focus Consulting 2003–; CEng 1978, FIM 1987; *Recreations* skiing, gardening, sailing; *Style*— Dr Geoffrey May; ✉ Troutbeck House, 126 Main Street, Swithland, Loughborough, Leicestershire LE12 8TJ (☎ 01509 890547, fax 01509 891442, e-mail g.j.may@btinternet.com)

MAY, Jane Veronica; da of Reginald Sydney Miller (d 1975), and Enid Brunt (d 1992); *b* 10 June 1956, Orpington, Kent; *Educ* Orpington Girls GS, Kingston Univ (BA); *m* 18 Sept 1982, Michael James May, s of Leslie Arthur May; 1 da (Anna Louise b 22 Aug 1991), 1 s (James Christopher b 18 March 1993); *Career* Freemans Mail Order 1978–93 latterly as customer servs dir, customer servs dir Thames Water 1994–2000; currently various non-exec roles and memb Ind Review Panel for HM Treasy; *Recreations* gardening, travel, reading; *Style*— Mrs Jane May

M

MAY, Peter N J; *Career* md Charterhouse Securities Ltd 1993–2000 (joined Charterhouse Bank 1982), chm MacArthur & Co Ltd 2000–; *Style*— P N J May, Esq

MAY, Stephen Richard (Steve); s of Robert May, ISM, and Vera *née* Edwards; *Educ* Lincoln GS, Durham Johnston Sch, Wyggeston Boys' GS Leicester, Univ of Leicester (BA); *m* 1993, Carol *née* Style; 1 da (Camilla Jayne b 1993), 1 s (James William b 1996); *Career* broadcaster; sports reporter: BBC Radio Leicester 1978–82, BBC Sport 1982–; sports presenter Today BBC Radio 4 1989– (featured in 2000 progs), football reporter Grandstand BBC1 1989–, sport presenter BBC Newsroom South East 1992–95, presenter BBC World Sport 1995–2000; author of various articles; *Recreations* cricket, swimming, football, family; *Clubs* Belgrave St Peters CC (sec 1984–99); *Style*— Steve May, Esq; ✉ c/o BBC Sport, MediaCityUK, Salford M50 2EQ (e-mail may.s@btinternet.com)

MAY, Rt Hon Theresa Mary; PC (2003), MP; da of Rev Hubert Brasier (d 1981), and Zaidee, *née* Barnes (d 1982); *b* 1 October 1956; *Educ* Wheatley Park Comp, St Hugh's Coll Oxford (MA); *m* 1980, Philip John May, s of John May (d 1999); *Career* with Bank of England 1977–83, Inter-Bank Research Organisation 1983–85, Association for Payment Clearing Services 1985–97 (head of Euro Affrs Unit 1989–96); cncllr London Borough of Merton 1986–94; Parly candidate: NW Durham 1992, Barking (by-election) 1994; MP (Cons) Maidenhead 1997–; oppn frontbench spokesman on educn and employment, disability issues and women 1998–99, shadow sec of state for educn and employment 1999–2001, shadow sec of state for educn and skills 2001, shadow sec of state for tport, local govt and the regions 2001–02, chm Cons Pty 2002–03, shadow sec of state for environment and transport 2003–04, shadow sec of state for the family 2004–05, shadow sec of state for culture, media and sport and the family 2005, shadow ldr of the House 2005–09, shadow min for women 2007–10, shadow sec of state for work and pensions 2009–10, min for women and equalities 2010–12, home sec 2010–16, ldr Cons Pty 2016–, prime minister and First Lord of the Treasury 2016–; *Recreations* walking, cooking; *Clubs* Maidenhead Conservative, Leander; *Style*— The Rt Hon Theresa May, MP; ✉ House of Commons, London SW1A 0AA (☎ 020 7219 5206)

MAY OF OXFORD, Baron (Life Peer UK 2001), of Oxford in the County of Oxfordshire; Prof Sir Robert McCredie May; OM (2002), kt (1996), AC (1998); s of Henry Wilkinson May, of Sydney, Australia; *b* 8 January 1936; *Educ* Sydney Boys' Sch, Univ of Sydney (BSc, PhD); *m* 3 Aug 1962, Judith, da of Jerome Feiner, of New York, USA; 1 da (Hon Naomi Felicity b 25 March 1966); *Career* Gordon Mackey lectr in applied mathematics Harvard Univ 1959–61 and 1966, prof of physics Univ of Sydney 1962–72, prof of astrophysics Caltech 1967; prof of plasma physics: UKAEA Lab Culham 1971, Magdalen Coll Oxford 1971, Inst for Advanced Study Princeton 1972, King's Coll Res Centre Cambridge 1976; visiting prof Imperial Coll London 1975–88, Class of 1877 prof of zoology Princeton Univ 1973–88, Royal Soc res prof Univ of Oxford and Imperial Coll London 1988–95 (leave of absence 1995–2000); chief scientific advsr to UK Govt and head of Office of Sci and Technol 1995–2000; pres British Ecological Soc 1991–93, pres Royal Soc 2000–05; memb: NRC, Sci-Advsy Cncl for WWF (US) 1978–88, Int Whaling Cmmn 1978–82, US Marine Animals Cmmn 1979–88, Governing Bd Soc of Conservation Biologists 1985–88, Advsy Bd Inst for Sci Info 1986–89, HSBC Corporate Sustainability Bd 2002–, UK Climate Change Ctee 2008–; chm Bd of Tstees Natural History Museum 1994–99 (tstee 1989–94); tstee: WWF (UK) 1990–94, Nuffield Fndn 1993–2008, Royal Botanic Gardens Kew and Wakehurst Place 1991–94; non-exec dir Dstl 2004–; contrib to various scientific jls incl Nature and Science; Rockefeller scholar Italy 1986; Weldon Medal in Biometrics Univ of Oxford 1980, MacArthur Award American Ecological Soc 1984, Zoological Medal Linnean Soc 1991, Marsh Award for Conservation Science Zoological Soc 1992, Frink Medal Zoological Soc of London 1996, Crafoord Prize Royal Swedish Acad of Sciences 1996, Balzan Prize 1998, The Blue Planet Prize 2001, Copley Medal Royal Soc 2007; Hon Degrees: City Univ London 1989, Uppsala Univ 1990, Yale

Univ 1993, Univ of Edinburgh 1994, Heriot-Watt Univ 1994, Univ of Sydney 1995, Princeton Univ 1996, Imperial Coll London 1996, Univ of Warwick 1997, Univ of Salford 1997, Univ of Kent 1997, ICL 1997, Brunel Univ 1999, Univ of Manchester 2001, Univ of Reading 2002, Univ of Nottingham 2002, Univ of Sussex 2003, ETH Zurich 2003, Univ of Sheffield 2004, Univ of York 2005, Queens Univ Belfast 2005, Univ of Lancaster 2006, Univ of Aberdeen 2006, UEA 2007, Univ of Oxford 2007; fell American Acad of Arts and Sciences 1977, corresponding fell Aust Acad of Sciences 1991, foreign memb US Nat Acad of Sciences 1994; FRS 1979 (pres 2000–05), hon fell Aust Acad of Technological Sci and Engrg 2001, Hon FREng 2005, Hon FRSE 2006, hon fell Acad of Med Sci 2007; various other hon fellowships of learned academies; *Books* Stability and Complexity in Model Ecosystems (1973, 2 edn 1974, re-issued 2000), Theoretical Ecology: Principles and Applications (ed 1976, 3 edn 2007), Population Biology of Infectious Diseases (ed with R M Anderson, 1982), Exploitation of Marine Ecosystems (ed, 1984), Perspectives in Ecological Theory (ed with J Roughgarden and S A Levin, 1988), Population Regulation and Dynamics (ed with M P Hassell, 1990), Infectious Diseases of Humans: Transmissions and Control (with R M Anderson, 1991), Large Scale Ecology and Conservation Biology (ed with P J Edwards and N R Webb, 1994), Extinction Rates (ed with J H Lawton, 1995), Evolution of Biological Diversity (ed with A Magurran, 1999), Virus Dynamics: Mathematical Principals of Immunology and Virology (with M A Nowak, 2000), SARS: A Case Study in Emerging Infections (ed with A McLean, J Pattison and R A Weiss, 2005); *Recreations* running, tennis; *Style—* The Rt Hon the Lord May of Oxford, OM, AC, FRS; ✉ Department of Zoology, University of Oxford, Oxford OX1 3PS (☎ 01865 271276, fax 01865 281060)

MAYALL, David William; s of Arthur William Mayall, of Derby, and Pamela, *née* Bryant; *b* 19 July 1957; *Educ* Repton, Univ of Cambridge (MA); *m* 22 June 1985, Wendy Madeleine, da of Peter Black of Douglas, IOM; 1 s (James b 13 April 1988), 1 da (Sophie b 31 May 1990); *Career* called to the Bar Gray's Inn 1979, pt/t special adjudicator 1993–; *Recreations* bridge, tennis, golf; *Style—* David Mayall, Esq; ✉ Lamb Chambers, Lamb Building, Temple, London EC4Y 7AS

MAYBURY, Neil Martin; s of Leonard Albert Maybury (d 1992), of Harborne, Birmingham, and Kathleen Margaret, *née* Howse (d 1982); *b* 25 August 1943; *Educ* King Edward's Sch Birmingham, Univ of Birmingham (LLB); *m* 10 May 1980, Sally Elizabeth, da of Kenneth Carroll, of Streetly, W Midlands; 3 s (Thomas Charles b 1983, Toby George b 1985, Henry Giles b 1992), 1 da (Natasha Poppy b 1987); *Career* admitted slr 1969; asst slr Clifford-Turner & Co London (now Clifford-Chance) 1969–72, ptnr Pinsent & Co (now Pinsent Masons) 1975–95, ptnr Dibb Lupton Alsop (now DLA) 1995–2000, ptnr Hammond Suddards Edge 2001–03, ptnr Maybury & Co 2003–; conslt Setfords 2012–; chm: Birmingham Rep Devpt Ctee 2000–02, Birmingham Business Focus 2002–, Gr Birmingham Monorail Co Ltd 2010–; memb Cncl Soc for Computers and Law 1979–88, memb Law Soc, chm Hood Down Club 1986–, memb Rgnl Cncl Arts Cncl of England 2010–14, lay Bd memb Telford & Wrekin NHS Clinical Commissioning Gp; *Books* Guide to The Electronic Office (with Keith James, 1988); *Recreations* tennis, flying, gardening, classic cars, skiing, classical music; *Clubs* Edgbaston Priory, Edgbaston Golf, Halfpenny Green Flying; *Style—* Neil Maybury, Esq; ✉ Maybury & Co, One Victoria Square, Birmingham B1 1BD (☎ 0121 632 2111, e-mail neil@sheinwood.com)

MAYER, Christine (Chris); CBE; *Career* joined Manchester Crown Court 1979 (subsequently various posts incl listing offr, court mangr and fin offr), courts administrator Lancs and Cumbria then Gtr Manchester and Manchester Central 1994–2001, circuit adminstrator Northern Circuit 2001–03; HM Courts Service: regnl dir North West 2003–08, chief exec 2008–; *Style—* Ms Chris Mayer, CBE; ✉ HM Court Service, 1st Floor, 102 Petty France, London SW1H 9AJ

MAYER, Prof Colin Peter; s of late Harold Charles and late Anne Louise Mayer, of London; *b* 12 May 1953; *Educ* St Paul's, Oriel Coll Oxford (MA), Wolfson Coll Oxford (BPhil), Harvard Univ (Harkness fell), Univ of Oxford (DPhil); *m* Annette Patricia, da of late Annesley Haynes; 2 da (Ruth Sarah b 21 Oct 1984, Hannah Claire b 21 July 1987); *Career* HM Treasy 1976–79, fell in economics St Anne's Coll Oxford 1980–86, prof of corporate finance City Univ Business Sch 1987–92, prof of economics and finance Univ of Warwick 1992–94, Peter Moores prof of mgmnt studies Univ of Oxford 1994–2006 and 2011–, professorial fell Wadham Coll Oxford 1994–2006 and 2011–, dir Oxford Financial Research Centre 1998–2006, dean Saïd Business Sch Univ of Oxford 2006–11, professorial fell St Edmund Hall Oxford 2006–11; chair: Advsy Bd Univ of Oxford Centre for Business Taxation 2012–, Humanities and Social Sciences Research Ethics Ctee Univ of Oxford 2014–, Mgmnt and Business Studies Gp Br Acad 2015–; ordinary memb Competition Appeal Tbnl 2011–; Houblon Norman fell Bank of England 1989–90; memb: Exec Ctee Royal Economic Soc 2002–06, Natural Capital Ctee 2012–, Int Advsy Bd Securities and Exchange Bd of India 2015–; chm OXERA Holdings Ltd 1987–2010, delg OUP 1996–2006, non-exec dir Aurora Energy Research Ltd 2013–; tstee Oxford Playhouse 2015–; fell European Corp Governance Inst; hon fell: St Anne's Coll Oxford, Oriel Coll Oxford; FBA, FRSA; *Books* The Economic Analysis of Accounting Profitability (jtly, 1987), European Financial Integration (jtly, 1991), Capital Markets and Financial Intermediation (jtly, 1993), Hostile Takeovers: Defence, Attack and Corporate Governance (jtly, 1994), Asset Management and Investor Protection (jtly, 2002), handbook of European Financial Markets and Institutions (jtly, 2008), Firm Commitment: Why the Corporation is Failing Us and How to Restore Trust in It (2013); *Recreations* piano playing, jogging, reading philosophy and science; *Style—* Prof Colin Mayer; ✉ Saïd Business School, University of Oxford, Park End Street, Oxford OX1 1HP (☎ 01865 288811)

MAYES, Ian; QC (1993); *b* 11 September 1951; *Educ* Highgate Sch (Fndn Scholar), Trinity Coll Cambridge (Hooper Prizeman); *Children* 2 s (Oliver Tobias b 31 Oct 1988, Theo Alexander b 9 Feb 1992); *Career* called to the Bar Middle Temple 1974 (Harmsworth scholar, bencher); recorder; Dept of Trade Inspection London Capital Group Ltd 1975–77, standing counsel to Inland Revenue 1983–93; chm Disciplinary Tbnl Lloyd's of London, memb Justice Ctee on Fraud; chm Art First; *Recreations* photography; *Clubs* Garrick; *Style—* Ian Mayes, Esq, QC; ✉ 3 (North) King's Bench Walk, Temple, London EC4Y 7HR (☎ 020 7797 8600, fax 020 7797 8699)

MAYFIELD, Sir Charlie; kt (2013); *Career* John Lewis Partnership: joined as head of business devpt 2000–01, devpt dir 2001–05, md John Lewis 2005–07, dep chm 2007, chm 2007–; *Style—* Sir Charlie Mayfield; ✉ John Lewis Partnership, Partnership House, Carlisle Place, London SW1P 1BX

MAYHEW, Charles; MBE (2005); *Educ* Wellington; *Career* co-fndr (with Sir Timothy Ackroyd, Bt, *qv*) Tusk Trust 1990 (chief exec 2002–); FRGS; *Style—* Charles Mayhew, Esq, MBE; ✉ Tusk Trust, 4 Cheapside House, High Street, Gillingham, Dorset SP8 4AA (☎ 01747 831005, e-mail info@tusk.org, website www.tusk.org, Twitter @mayhewcharlie)

MAYHEW, David; CBE (2011); *b* 20 May 1940; *Career* with Panmure Gordon 1961–69; Cazenove & Co: joined 1969, ptnr 1971–2001, dealing ptnr 1972, ptnr i/c Capital Markets Dept 1986–2001, chm Cazenove Gp Ltd (formerly Cazenove Gp plc) 2001–10, chm JPMorgan Cazenove 2005–11, chm Cazenove Capital Hldgs Ltd 2005–13; vice-chm J P Morgan; non-exec dir Rio Tinto plc and Rio Tinto Ltd 2000–10; tstee: Royal Anniversary Tst 2005–14, Wellcome Tst Ltd 2010–, Game & Wildlife Conservation Tst 2012–; chm Bd of Tstees Alzheimer's Research UK 2012–, Govt envoy for dementia 2016–; *Style—* Mr David Mayhew, CBE

MAYHEW, Jeremy Paul; s of Yon Richard Mayhew (d 2013), and Cora Angela, *née* Lamboll; *b* 1 February 1959; *Educ* Clifton, Western Reserve Acad Ohio (ESU scholarship), Balliol Coll Oxford (scholar, sec and treas Oxford Union), Harvard Business Sch (MBA); *Career* BBC TV: trainee asst prodr 1980–82, asst prodr Current Affrs 1982–84; ind prodr/dir (making documentary and current affrs progs for Channel 4) 1984–87, mgmnt conslt Booz Allen & Hamilton 1989–90, special advsr to Rt Hon Peter Lilley MP (DTI and DSS) 1990–93; head of BBC Strategy Devpt 1993–95; BBC Worldwide Ltd: dir New Media 1995–99, dir New Ventures and Strategy 1999–2001, bd dir 1997–2001; dir and head of strategy practice Human Capital (media strategy and res consultancy) 2001–02, ptnr Spectrum Value Ptnrs (formely Spectrum Strategy Consultants) 2003–08 (sr advsr 2002–03 and 2008–09); sr advsr: Oliver & Ohlbaum 2010–11, PwC 2012–; chm Bd Barbican Centre 2008–11; non-exec bd memb: Learning and Skills Devpt Agency 1999–2002, Strategic Rail Authy 2000–06, London Devpt Agency 2008–12; memb Cncl London C of C and Industry 1998–, memb (public rep) Evaluation Ctee ESRC 2011–14, memb UK Govt's Regulation Policy Ctee 2012–; non-exec advsr Mayor of London's Office for Policing & Crime (MOPAC) 2012–; constituency offr Hammersmith Cons Assoc 1990–93; memb: Cncl Bow Gp 1990–93, Ct City Univ 1996–; tstee: Hammersmith United Charities 1991–96, Br Friends of Harvard Business Sch 1993–, City Arts Tst 2001–, Thames Festival Tst 2004–08; pres Harvard Business Sch Club of London 1997 and 1998; govr: Sacred Heart Junior Sch 1990–96, City Literary Inst 1998–2002, London Guildhall Univ 2000–02, Clifton Coll 2000–, London Met Univ 2002–10; donation govr Christ's Hosp 1998–; Common Councilman Corp of London (Aldersgate Ward) 1996– (chm Educn Ctee 2005–06, chm Audit and Risk Mgmnt Ctee 2011–14, dep chm Policy & Resources Ctee 2013–, chm City Bridge Tst 2014–); Freeman City of London, Liveryman Worshipful Co of Loriners (asst Ct 2012–); memb RTS 1990–; govr Prior Weston Primary Sch (Islington) 2014–; tstee Crossrail art Fndn 2014–; cncl memb Heart of the City 2015; *Recreations* collecting political caricatures, theatre, cinema, arguing!; *Clubs* Reform, Guildhall; *Style—* Jeremy Mayhew, Esq; ☎ 07718 653215, e-mail jeremymayhew@btinternet.com; Members' Room City of London Corporation, PO Box 270, Guildhall, London EC2P 2EJ

MAYHEW JONAS, Dame Judith; DBE (2002); *b* 18 October 1948; *Educ* Otago Girls' HS NZ, Univ of Otago; *m* 2003, Christopher William Jonas, CBE; *Career* admitted: barr and slr NZ 1973, slr England and Wales 1993; lectr in law: Univ of Otago 1970–73, Univ of Southampton 1973–76 (also sub dean), KCL 1976–89 (also sub dean and dir Anglo French law degree Sorbonne); employment lawyer and dir of trg Titmuss Sainer Dechert 1989–94, employment lawyer and dir of educn and trg Wilde Sapte 1994–2000, special advsr Clifford Chance 2000–03, non-exec dir Merrill Lynch & Co Inc USA 2006–08 (advsr 2003–06), sr advsr Barclays Private Wealth 2012–13, special advsr Tishman Speyer 2013–; provost: King's Coll Cambridge 2003–06, Bishop Grossetest UC 2008–12; chllr Bishop Grossetest UC 2012–; Corp of London: memb Ct of Common Cncl and various Ctees (Finance, Housing, Social Services, Police) 1986–2004, chm Educn Ctee 1989–94 (memb 1986–2004), chm Policy & Resources Ctee 1996–2003 (dep chm 1993–96 and 2003–04); memb Leaders' and Educn Ctees Assoc of London Govt 1995–2003, city and business advsr to Mayor of London 2000–04; memb Bd: London Devp Agency (chair Private Investment Cmmn), Int Fin Servs London 2000–04, 4Ps; tstee Nat History Museum 1998–2006, chm ROH Covent Garden 2003–08, co-chair London NY Dialogue 2007–, co-chair Br Dutch Dialogues 2010–, tstee Imperial War Museum 2008–, chm New West End Co 2008–13, chm London and Ptnrs 2011–13, global tstee The Urban Land Inst 2013–; memb Bd Gresham Coll 1990–2009, chm of govrs Birkbeck Coll London 1993–2003, memb Ct and Cncl Imperial Coll London 2001–04, chm Ind Schs Cncl 2008–11, govr Westminster Sch 2008, govr Westminster Abbey Choir Sch 2008; fell: Birkbeck Coll, London Business Sch; Hon LLD: Univ of Otago 1998, City Univ 1999, London Met Univ 2003; hon fell Inst of CPD 2004, fell City and Guilds 2004; *Recreations* opera, theatre, old English roses, tennis, ballet; *Clubs* Guildhall; *Style—* Dame Judith Mayhew Jonas, DBE; ✉ 25 Victoria Square, London SW1W 0RB

MAYHEW OF TWYSDEN, Baron (Life Peer UK 1997), of Kilndown in the County of Kent; Sir Patrick Barnabas Burke Mayhew; kt (1983), PC (1986), QC (1972), DL (Kent 2001); s of (Alfred) Geoffrey Horace Mayhew, MC (d 1985), of Sevenoaks Weald, Kent, and Sheila Margaret Burke, *née* Roche; *b* 11 September 1929; *Educ* Tonbridge, Mons Officer Cadet Sch Aldershot, Balliol Coll Oxford (MA); *m* 15 April 1963, Rev Jean Elizabeth Mayhew, OBE, 2 da of John Gurney (d 2000), of Walsingham Abbey, Norfolk; 4 s (Hon James b 1964, Hon Henry b 1965, Hon Tristram b 1968, Hon Jerome b 1970); *Career* served 4/7 Royal Dragoon Gds, Capt (Nat Serv and AER); called to the Bar Middle Temple 1956, bencher 1982; Parly candidate (Cons) Camberwell and Dulwich 1970, MP (Cons) Tunbridge Wells Feb 1974–97; vice-chm Cons Home Affrs Ctee and memb Exec 1922 Ctee 1976–79, Parly under sec for employment 1979–81, min of state Home Office 1981–83, Slr-Gen 1983–87, Attorney-Gen 1987–92, sec of state for Northern Ireland 1992–97; chm PM's Advsy Ctee on Business Appointments 2000–08; non-exec Western Provident Assoc 1998–2007 (vice-chm 2000–07); *Recreations* country pursuits; *Clubs* Pratt's, Beefsteak, Garrick, Tunbridge Wells Constitutional; *Style—* The Rt Hon Lord Mayhew of Twysden, PC, QC; ✉ House of Lords, London SW1A 0PW (☎ 020 7219 3000)

MAYNARD, Emeritus Prof Alan; OBE (2009); s of late Edward Joseph Maynard, of W Kirby, Wirral, Merseyside, and late Hilda Marion, *née* McCausland; *b* 15 December 1944; *Educ* Calday Grange GS W Kirby Merseyside, Univ of Newcastle upon Tyne, Univ of York (BPhil); *m* 22 June 1968, Elizabeth Mary, da of Kevin Joseph Shanahan (decd), of Edinburgh; 2 s (Justin b 11 Feb 1970, John b 24 Oct 1971), 2 da (Jane b 31 July 1974, Samantha b 8 Nov 1976); *Career* asst lectr and lectr in economics Univ of Exeter 1968–71, prof of economics and founding dir Centre for Health Economics Univ of York 1983–95 (lectr in economics 1971–76, sr lectr and dir Graduate Prog in Health Economics 1976–83), sec Nuffield Provincial Hosps Tst 1995–96, prof of health economics Univ of York 1997–; adjunct prof Univ of Technol Sydney Aust; visiting lectr: Italy, NZ, Sweden; memb York Health Authy 1983–91, non-exec dir York NHS Tst Hosp 1991–97, chm York NHS Tst 1997–2010, chair Vale of York NHS Clinical Commissioning Gp 2012–15; conslt: DfID, World Bank, WHO; memb: ESRC 1983–86 (memb Human Behaviour and Devpt Ctee 1988–89), MRC Health Servs Res Ctee 1986–92; chm Evaluation Panel for Fourth Med and Health Res Prog Euro Cmmn 1990; memb Royal Society of Medicine; founding ed Health Economics 1992–, author of over 250 articles in jls; Hon DSc Univ of Aberdeen 2003, Hon LLD Univ of Northumbria 2006; William B Graham Prize 2015 (jtly); FMedSci 2000; *Books* Health Care in the European Community (1976), Public Private Mix for Health (ed with G McLachlan, 1982), Controlling Legal Addictions (ed with D Robinson and R Chester, 1989), Preventing Alcohol and Tobacco Problems (ed with P Tether, 1990), Competition in Health Care: Reforming the NHS (ed, with A J Culyer and J Posnett), Non Random Reflections on Health Services Research (ed, with I Chalmers, 1997), Being Reasonable about Health Economics (ed, with A J Culyer, 1997), Advances in Health Economics (ed, with A Scott and R Elliott, 2003), The Public-Private Mix for Health (ed, 2005); *Recreations* reading, walking, current affairs and cricket; *Clubs* RSM; *Style—* Emeritus Prof Alan Maynard, OBE; ✉ York Health Policy Group, Department of Health Sciences, University of York, Heslington, York YO10 5DD (☎ 01904 321333, e-mail alan.maynard@york.ac.uk)

MAYNARD, Dr Alice Mary; CBE (2015); da of Charles Rupert Gordon Maynard, of Wakefield, W Yorks, and Mary Ada Maynard; *b* 28 November 1957; *Educ* Univ of York (BA), Ashridge Business Sch (MBA), Cranfield Univ (DBA); *m* 1994 (m dis 2000); *Career*

Software devpt IT industry 1980–90, dir Equal Ability 1992–6, head if disability strategy Network Rail (Railtrack) 1998–2003, fndr and md Future Inclusion Ltd 2003–; memb Human Genetics Cmmn 2006–12; memb: Eastern Area Ctee Jephson Housing Assoc 2002–08, Ctee on Fuel Poverty 2016–; chair: Muscle Power! 2001–02, Employers Network on Disability for Milton Keynes and North Bucks 2003–05, Milton Keynes and North Bucks 2003–05, Milton Keynes Racial Equality Cncl 2006–07, Scope 2008–14, Swansea Charitable Tst 2015–; dir Assoc of Chairs 2013–16; Non-exec Dir of the Year (not-for-profit / public service orgn) Sunday Times 2014; DUniv (hc) Univ of York; MIOD; Chartered Dir; FRSA, FIoD; articles in various pubns incl: Counselling at Work, Therapy Weekly (1993–97); Adequate Technology (paper to Ecart III, 1995), The Way Forward: A development pack for organisations of disabled people (1996), COST 335 European Action Report (contrib, 1999), Breaking Down Bureaucratic Barriers (co-author, 2000), Transed (2007), Jl of Transport and Land Use (2009), Genetics, Disability and Bioethics (in Disabling Barriers, Enabling Environments by Swain et al 2014); *Style*— Dr Alice Maynard, CBE; ✉ Future Inclusion Ltd, PO Box 5672, Milton Keynes MK15 9WZ (✆ 01908 665850, fax 07043 017425)

MAYNARD, John David; s of Albert William Henry Maynard (d 1968), of Surrey, and Ellen Hughes-Jones (d 1970); *b* 14 May 1931; *Educ* Whitgift Sch, Charing Cross Hosp London (MB BS, Gold medal Clinical Medicine and Surgery), Univ of London (MS); *m* 1, 13 Aug 1955 (m dis 1971), Patricia Katharine, da of C W F Gray (d 1985), of Sutton, Surrey; 2 da (Sarah b 1956, Julia b 1962), 2 s (Andrew b 1959, Nicholas b 1962); m 2, 23 June 1972, Gillian Mary, da of H F Loveless, of Milford-on-Sea, Hants; 1 s (Timothy b 1976); *Career* Capt RAMC 1956; lectr in anatomy London Hosp 1958–59, sr conslt surgn Guy's Hosp London 1967–93, dir of the Pathology Museums of Guy's and St Thomas' Med Schs 1969–96, teacher Univ of London 1963–96, hon sr lectr in surgery Guy's Hosp 1992–96; hon conslt surgn St Luke's Hosp for the Clergy 1990–98; surgical tutor: RCS 1967–76, Guy's Hosp Med Sch 1967–76; sr examiner of surgery Univ of London 1962–85, examiner of surgery Soc of Apothecaries 1962–70; chm The Salivary Gland Tumour Panel England 1970–90, RCS advsr on surgical services to HM Prison Serv 1995–, memb Cncl RSM 1996–, surgical advsr to Dir of Museums Royal Coll of Surgns 1996–, vice-pres Grand Charity 2006– (memb Cncl and med advsr 1997–), memb Bd of Tstees Hunterian Collection at RCS 2006–; author of various papers on diseases of salivary glands; memb Soc of Expert Witnesses, memb Law Soc Directory of Expert Witnesses; Hunterian prof RCS 1963; Liveryman The Worshipful Soc of Apothecaries 1962; memb: BMA 1954, Med Soc of London 1961, The Chelsea Clinical Soc 1962; scientific FZS 1956; fell: Assoc of Surgeons 1967, Hunterian Soc 1985 (pres 2005); FRSM 1958, FRCS, fell Br Acad of Forensic Scientists 2006 (memb Cncl 2008); *Books* Surgery (jtly, 1974), Surgery of Salivary Glands in Surgical Management (1984, 1988), Contemporary Operative Surgery (1979), Carcinoma of Salivary Glands in Head & Neck Oncology (1991), Text Book and Colour Atlas of Diseases of Salivary Glands (contrib chapters on Parotid Surgery, 1995); *Recreations* golf, hill walking, photography; *Clubs* Savage; *Style*— John D Maynard, MS, FRCS; ✉ 14 Blackheath Park, London SE3 9RP (✆ 020 8852 6766); Mountsloe, Frogham, Fordingbridge, Hampshire SP6 2HP (✆ 0142565 3009, e-mail jmaynard@btopenworld.com)

MAYNARD, Paul Christopher; MP; *b* 1975, Cheshire; *Educ* Univ of Oxford; *Career* MP (Cons) Blackpool North and Cleveleys 2010–; *Style*— Paul Maynard, Esq, MP; ✉ House of Commons, London SW1A 0AA

MAYNE, Prof David Quinn; s of Leslie Harper Mayne (d 1963), and Jane, *née* Quin (d 1998); *b* 23 April 1930; *Educ* Christian Brothers Coll Boksburg, Univ of the Witwatersrand (BSc, MSc), Univ of London (PhD, DSc); *m* 16 Dec 1954, Josephine Mary, da of Joseph Karl Hess (d 1968); 3 da (Susan Francine b 9 March 1956, Maire Anne b 16 July 1957, Ruth Catherine b 18 April 1959); *Career* lectr Univ of the Witwatersrand 1950–54 and 1957–59, R&D engr Br Thomson Houston Co Rugby 1955–56; Imperial Coll London: lectr 1959–67, reader 1967–71, fell 2000; research fell Harvard 1971; Imperial Coll: prof of control theory 1971–91, head of Electrical Engrg Dept 1984–88; prof Dept of Electrical and Computer Engrg Univ of Calif Davis 1989–96 (prof emeritus 1996–); sr research investigator Imperial Coll London 1996– (prof emeritus Dept of Electrical and Electronic Engrg); hon prof Beihang Univ Beijing 2006; Heaviside Premium Award 1981 and 1985, Sir Harold Hartley Medal 1986, IEEE Control Systems Award 2009, IFAC (Int Fedn of Automatic Control) High Impact Paper Award 2011, IFAC Georgio Quazza Medal 2014; Hon DTech Univ of Lund 1995; hon fell Imperial Coll London 2000; FIEE 1980, FIEEE 1981, FRS 1985, FREng 1987, fell Int Fedn of Automatic Control 2006; *Books* Differential Dynamic Programming (1970), Model Predictive Control: Theory and Design (2009); *Recreations* walking, cross country skiing; *Style*— Prof David Mayne, FRS, FREng; ✉ Department of Electrical and Electronic Engineering, Imperial College London, London SW7 2BT

MAYO, Benjamin John; s of Dr Frank Mayo, OBE, of Fawley, Hants, and Gladys Margaret, *née* Mason; *b* 8 November 1944; *Educ* Churcher's Coll Petersfield, Univ of Birmingham (BSc); *m* 1973, Hon Christine Mary Plumb, da of Baron Plumb, DL (Life Peer), *qv*; 3 da (Katharine Elizabeth b 28 Jan 1977, Sarah Louise b 14 Nov 1979, Stephanie Caroline b 9 April 1983); *Career* ICI: joined 1966, process engrg mangr Plastics Div 1980–81, prodn mangr Dumfries Works 1982–83, works mangr Oil Works Billingham 1984–85, chief engr (NE) Engrg Dept Billingham 1986–87, ops dir ICI Imagedata 1988–90, research and technol dir ICI Films Wilton 1993–98 (ops dir 1991–92); tech dir European Process Industries Competitiveness Centre (EPICC) 1998–2002, dir Ben Mayo & Assocs 2002–; RAE visiting prof Sch of Engrg Univ of Warwick 2009–; memb EU Hydrogen and Fuel Cells Technol Platform 2003–, memb NE Energy Leadership Cncl 2007–; vice-pres Inst of Chemical Engrg 1998–2000 (memb Cncl 1990–93, chm Qualifications Bd); FIChemE 1990, FREng 1993; *Recreations* lawn tennis, real tennis, piano; *Style*— Benjamin Mayo, Esq, FREng; ✉ The Garth, Kirby Lane, Great Broughton, North Yorkshire TS9 7HH (✆ 01642 712214, e-mail ben.mayo@btinternet.com)

MAYO, His Hon Judge Rupert; *Career* called to the Bar 1987; recorder 2005, circuit judge (Midland Circuit) 2009–; justice of the Court of Appeal for St Helena, Ascension Island and Tristan da Cuna 2015–; *Style*— His Hon Judge Mayo; ✉ c/o Midland Circuit Office, Priory Courts, 33 Bull Street, Birmingham B4 6DW

MAYOR, (Frederick) James; s of Fred Hoyland Mayor (d 1973), and Pamela Margaret, *née* Colledge (d 1994); *b* 20 March 1949; *Educ* Charterhouse; *m* 1978, Viviane Martha Cresswell, da of John Leigh Reed (d 1982); 2 da (Louisa Harriett Cresswell b 1981, Alice Marina Pamela b 1984 d 2002); *Career* asst: Galerie Louise Leiris Paris 1968, Perls Galleries NY 1968, Impressionist Painting Dept Sotheby's London 1969, i/c Contemporary Painting Dept Parke-Bernet Inc NY 1969–72; The Mayor Gallery Ltd London: md 1973–, chm 1980–; memb Exec Ctee Soc of London Art Dealers 1981–88; *Recreations* cooking, painting and gardening; *Clubs* Brooks's, Buck's, Chelsea Arts, Shrewsbury Hunt, The Travellers (Paris); *Style*— James Mayor, Esq; ✉ The Mayor Gallery Ltd, 21 Cork Street, 1st Floor, London W1S 3LZ (✆ 020 7734 3558, fax 020 7494 1377)

MAYR-HARTING, Prof Henry Maria Robert Egmont; s of Herbert Mayr-Harting (d 1989), of Vienna, and Anna, *née* Münzer (d 1974); *b* 6 April 1936, Prague; *Educ* Douai Sch, Merton Coll Oxford (Amy Mary Preston Read scholar, MA, DPhil, DD); *m* 1968, Caroline Mary Humphries, da of Dr Thomas H Henry; 1 s (Felix b 1969), 1 da (Ursula b 1972); *Career* asst lectr and lectr in medieval history Univ of Liverpool 1960–68; Univ of Oxford: fell and tutor in medieval history St Peter's Coll 1968–97 (emeritus fell 1997–), lectr in medieval history Merton Coll 1976–97, Slade prof of fine art 1987–88, reader in medieval history 1993–97, regius prof of ecclesiastical history 1997–2003, lay canon Christ Church 1997–2003 (co-censor of degrees 2004–); corresponding memb Austrian Acad of Sciences 2001; visiting fell Peterhouse Cambridge 1983, Brown Fndn fell Univ of the South Tennessee 1992; Hon Dr: Lawrence Univ Wisconsin 1998, Univ of the South Tennessee 1999, Univ of East Anglia 2009; FBA 1992; *Books* The Acta of the Bishops of Chichester 1075–1207 (1965), The Coming of Christianity to Anglo-Saxon England (1972, 3 edn 1991), Ottonian Book Illumination: An Historical Study (2 vols, 1991, 2 edn 1999), Christianity: Two Thousand Years (ed with Richard Harries, 2001), Church and Cosmos in Early Ottonian Germany: The View from Cologne (2007), Religion and Society in the Medieval West 600–1200: Selected Papers (2010), Religion, Politics and Society in Britain 1066–1272 (2011); *Recreations* music (especially playing keyboard instruments), watching cricket; *Clubs* Athenaeum, Worcs CCC; *Style*— Prof Henry Mayr-Harting, FBA; ✉ St Peter's College, Oxford OX1 2DL; 29 Portland Road, Oxford OX2 7EZ (✆ 01865 515666)

MAYS, (Catherine) Jane; da of Michael Mays (d 1978), and Mary, *née* Poyntz Stewart (d 1995); *b* 30 May 1952; *Educ* Francis Holland Sch; *m* David John Bradbury, s of Vivian Bradbury; *Career* journalist; advtg account exec 1970–76, editorial asst Business Traveller 1976–80, freelance journalist Paris and NY 1980–85, sub ed arts page Daily Telegraph 1986–88, exec features ed Evening Standard 1988–92, literary ed Daily Mail 1992–; *Recreations* theatre, literature, food and wine, travel; *Style*— Ms Jane Mays; ✉ 21 Marsden Street, London NW5 3HE (✆ 020 7428 0444, e-mail davidjane.bradbury@blueyonder.co.uk); Daily Mail, Northcliffe House, 2 Derry Street, London W8 4TT (✆ 020 7938 6701, fax 020 7937 0332, mobile 07885 400928, e-mail jane.mays@dailymail.co.uk)

MCGRATH, Sir Harvey; kt (2016); *b* 23 February 1952; *Educ* St Catherine's Coll Cambridge (MA); *m* Allison McGrath; 1 s, 1 da; *Career* Chase Manhattan Bank 1974–80; Man Gp plc: joined 1980, subsequently treas, fin dir then pres Man Inc NY, gp ceo 1990–2000, chair 2000–07; chair Prudential plc 2009–12 (non-exec dir 2008–09); currently chair: Big Society Capital, Icould, Heart of the City, Prince's Teaching Inst; chair of govrs Birkbeck Coll Univ of London; dep chair London Enterprise Panel; former chair: London First, East London Business Alliance, Mayor of London's Skills and Employment Bd, London Devpt Agency; tstee: Mayor's Fund for London, New Philanthropy Capital, Frontline; *Recreations* music, reading, skiing, theatre; *Clubs* Reform; *Style*— Sir Harvey McGrath

MEACHER, Rt Hon Michael Hugh; PC (1997), MP; s of George Hubert Meacher (d 1969), of Berkhamsted, Herts; *b* 4 November 1939; *Educ* Berkhamsted Sch, New Coll Oxford; *m* 1, 1962 (m dis 1987), Molly Christine, da of William Reid, of Grayshott, Surrey; 2 s, 2 da; m 2, 1988, Lucianne, da of William Craven, of Gerrards Cross, Bucks; *Career* joined Lab Pty 1962, sec Danilo Dolci Tst 1964, lectr in social admin Univ of York 1966–69 and LSE 1970; MP (Lab): Oldham W 1970–97, Oldham W and Royton 1997–; Parly under sec of state: Dept of Industry 1974–75, DHSS 1975–76, Dept of Trade 1976–79; memb Treasy Select Ctee 1980–83, chm Select Ctee on Lloyd's Bill 1982, contested Lab dep leadership election 1983, elected to Shadow Cabinet 1983, memb NEC Oct 1983–; chief oppn spokesman on: health and social security 1983–87, employment 1987–89, social security 1989–92, devpt and co-operation 1992–93, Citizen's Charter 1993–94, tport 1994–95, employment 1995–96, environmental protection 1996–97; min of state for the environment: DETR 1997–2001, DEFRA 2001–03; candidate for Lab Pty leadership 2007; currently chair Parliamentary Gp for Reform of Parliamentary Procedure; author; *Books* Taken for a Ride (1972), Socialism with a Human Face (1982), Diffusing Power: the Key to Socialist Revival (1992), Destination of the Species: the Riddle of Human Existence (2010), The State We Need: Keys to the Renaissance of Britain (2013); ed and contrib: What the Three Parties Are Not Telling You: A Radical Way Out of Stagnation and Inequality (2014), What They Never Told You About Parliament and How it Should Be Put Right (2015); *Style*— The Rt Hon Michael Meacher, MP; ✉ 34 Kingscliffe Gardens, London SW19 6NR; House of Commons, London SW1A 0AA (✆ 020 7219 3000)

M

MEACHER, Baroness (Life Peer 2006), of Spitalfields in the London Borough of Tower Hamlets; Molly Christine Meacher (Lady Layard); da of late William Frederic Reid; *b* 15 May 1940; *Educ* Berkhamsted Sch for Girls, Univ of York (BSc), Univ of London (DipSoc, CQSW); *m* 1, 1962 (m dis 1987), Michael Hugh Meacher, *qv*, s of George Hubert Meacher (d 1969), of Berkhamsted, Herts; 2 s (Hon Christopher David b 1963, Hon Nigel Wentworth b 1964), 2 da (Hon Sally Elizabeth b 1966, Hon Roslyn Marie b 1971); m 2, 1991, Prof (Peter) Richard Grenville Layard (Baron Layard (Life Peer)), *qv*; *Career* Mental Health Act cmmr 1985–92, advsr to Russian Govt 1991–94; dep chm Police Complaints Authy 2000–02, chm Security Industry Authy 2002–04, chm E London and City NHS Fndn Tst 2004–13; sits in House of Lords as crossbench peer 2006–; chm All Pty Parly Gp for Drug Policy Reform 2011–; pres Haemophilia Soc 2013–, chm Dignity in Dying 2016–; *Style*— The Baroness Meacher; ✉ House of Lords, London SW1A 0PW

MEAD, Richard Barwick; s of Thomas Gifford Mead, MBE (d 2004), and Joyce Mary, *née* Barwick (d 1990); *b* 18 August 1947; *Educ* Marlborough, Pembroke Coll Cambridge (MA); *m* 25 June 1971, Sheelagh Margaret, da of James Leslie Thom; 2 s (Timothy b 1973, Rupert b 1977), 1 da (Nicola b 1975 d 1976); *Career* audit supervisor Arthur Young 1969–73, corporate fin exec Brandts Ltd 1973–75, dir and head Corporate Fin Dept Antony Gibbs and Sons Ltd 1975–83, dir corporate fin Credit Suisse First Boston Ltd 1983–85, ptnr and nat dir corporate fin Ernst & Young 1985–94, independent fin advsr to and non-exec dir of numerous companies 1994–2014; FCA 1972; *Books* Churchill's Lions (2007), General 'Boy' (2010), The Last Great Cavalryman (2012), The Men Behind Monty (2015); *Recreations* family, military history and biography, gardening; *Clubs* Oxford and Cambridge; *Style*— Richard Mead, Esq; ✉ Clayfurlong House, Kemble, Cirencester, Gloucestershire GL7 6BS (✆ 01285 770751)

MEADE, Stephen Thomas; s of P J Meade, and A E Meade, *née* Hughes, of Maidstone, Kent; *b* 15 October 1960; *Educ* Maidstone GS, St John's Coll Oxford (Heath Harrison scholar, gap year Vienna Univ, MA); *m* 16 Feb 1990, Donna Patricia Mary, *née* Ainsworth; 2 da (Gabriella Catherine, Chlöe Alice Elizabeth), 1 s (Ethan Alexander); *Career* advtg exec; McCormick-Publicis 1985–88, Publicis Conseil (Paris) 1988–89, Howell Henry Chaldicott Lury 1989–91; Publicis: bd dir 1994–2001, managing ptnr 1997–2001, client servs dir 1998–2001, head of brand devpt 2000–01; md Springpoint Brand Consultancy 2001–03; planning dir McCann-Erickson EMEA 2003–05, head of planning McCann London 2005–07, global strategic planning dir McCann 2007–10, fndr and chief exec McCann Enterprise 2010–; *Style*— Stephen Meade, Esq; ✉ McCann-Erickson, 7–11 Herbrand Street, London WC1N 1EX (✆ 020 7961 2570, e-mail stephen.meade@europe.mccann.com)

MEADEN, Deborah Sonia; da of Brian Douglas Meaden, and Sonia Irene, *née* Coneley (Sonia Meaden, OBE, *qv*); *b* 11 February 1959, Taunton, Somerset; *Educ* Godolphin Sch Salisbury, Trowbridge HS for Girls, Brighton Coll; *m* 13 Feb 1993, Paul Lawrence Farmer; *Career* ops dir Bryson Enterprises Leisure Ltd 1989–93, md Weststar Holidays Ltd 1995–99 (ops dir 1993–95), gp md TGGL Ltd 1999–2005; owner: Fox Brothers Ltd 2010–, Business Angel; memb SW Tourism advsy panel; judge Dragons' Den (BBC TV); chair NSPCC Child's Voice Appeal SW, tstee Roundhouse, patron Tusk Tst, tstee Design Cncl; ambass: WWF, Lend with Care; honorary doctorate: Univ of Staffs 2010, Univ of Exeter 2010; MInstD 2000, FRSA 2006; *Recreations* horse riding, travel, property devpt; *Style*— Mrs Deborah Meaden; ✉ Meadenspeak, The Granary, Bowdens Business Centre, Hambridge, Somerset TA10 0BP (✆ 01458 259371)

MEADES, Jonathan Turner; s of John William Meades (d 1981), of Salisbury, Wilts, and Marjorie Agnes (Bunty), *née* Hogg (d 1993); *b* 21 January 1947; *Educ* King's Coll Taunton, Univ of Bordeaux, RADA; *m* 1, 15 Sept 1980 (m dis), Sally Dorothy Renée, da of

Raymond Brown (d 1996); 2 da (Holly, Rose (twins) b 7 May 1981); m 2, 1 June 1988 (m dis), Frances Anne, da of Sir William Bentley (d 1998); 2 da ((Eleanor) Lily b 31 Dec 1986, (Evelyn) Coral b 15 April 1993); m 3, 1 May 2003, Colette Claudine Elizabeth, da of Michael Forder (d 2014); *Career* journalist, writer and TV performer 1971–; contrib to: Books and Bookman, Time Out, Curious, The Observer, Architects Jl, Sunday Times, Harpers & Queen, Literary Review, Tatler, A La Carte, The Times, The Independent, Sunday Correspondent, Evening Standard, magazines in Canada and USA; ed Event 1981–82, pt/t memb editorial staff Tatler 1982–87, restaurant critic The Times 1986–2001, columnist The Times 2002–05; TV series incl: The Victorian House 1987, Abroad in Britain 1990, Further Abroad 1994, Jerrybuilding 1994, Even Further Abroad 1997, Travels with Pevsner: Worcestershire 1998, Heart Bypass 1998, Victoria Died In 1901 and is Still Alive Today 2001, tvSSFBM 2001, Meades Eats 2003, Abroad Again in Britain 2005, Joebuilding 2006, Meades Abroad Again 2007, Magnetic North 2008, Jonathan Meades: Off Kilter 2009, Jonathan Meades On France 2011, The Joy of Essex 2013, Bunkers, Brutalism, Bloodymindedness 2014, Benbuilding: Mussolini, Monuments, Modernism and Marble 2016; Hon FRIBA; *Awards* Glenfiddich Awards 1986, 1990, 1995 and 1999, Essay Prize Paris Int Art Film Festival 1994, Glenfiddich Trophy 1999; *Books* This is Their Life (1979), An Illustrated Atlas of The World's Buildings (1980), Filthy English (1984), Peter Knows What Dick Likes (1989), Pompey (1993), The Fowler Family Business (2002), Incest and Morris Dancing (2002), The Times Restaurant Guide (2002), Museum Without Walls (2012), Pidgin Snaps (2013), An Encyclopaedia of Myself (2014), The Plagiarist in the Kitchen (2016); *Scripts* L'Atlantide (dir Bob Swaim, 1993); *Recreations* buildings, mushrooms, woods, sloth; *Clubs* Groucho, Academy; *Style—* Jonathan Meades, Esq; ✉ e-mail jtm.juvarra@orange.fr; c/o Anita Land, Anita Land Ltd, 10 Wyndham Place, London W1H 2PU (☎ 07836 764139 or 07899 792995, e-mail anita@anitaland.com)

MEADOWS, Prof (Arthur) Jack; s of Flt Sgt Arthur Harold Meadows (d 1971), and Alice, *née* Elson (d 1962); *b* 24 January 1934; *Educ* New Coll Oxford (MA, DPhil), UCL (MSc); *m* 6 Dec 1958, (Isobel) Jane Tanner, da of Stanley Charles Bryant (d 1937); 2 da (Alice b 1960, Sally b 1962), 1 s (Michael b 1962); *Career* Nat Serv Lt Intelligence Corps 1952–54; Univ of Leicester 1966–86: lectr, sr lectr, prof 1972–86, head Depts Astronomy and History of Sci; head Primary Communications Research Centre 1976–86, head Office Humanities Communication 1983–86, prof Dept of Info Sci Loughborough Univ 1986–2001 (dean Educn and Humanities 1991–94, pro-vice-chllr 1995–96); author of twenty books and approximately 300 research papers; hon vice-pres Library Assoc 1995; Hon DSc City Univ 1995; FInstP 1983, FLA 1989, FIInfSc 1987; *Recreations* sleeping; *Style—* Prof Jack Meadows; ✉ 47 Swan Street, Seagrave, Leicestershire LE12 7NL (☎ 01509 812557); Department of Information Science, Loughborough University, Loughborough, Leicestershire LE11 3TU (☎ 01509 635685, e-mail a.j.meadows@lboro.ac.uk)

MEADOWS, Pamela Catherine; da of late Sidney James Meadows, and Hilda Catherine Meadows; *b* 9 January 1949; *Educ* Kenya HS Nairobi, Univ of Durham (BA), Birkbeck Coll London (MSc); *m* 26 Aug 1975, Paul Andrew Ormerod; 1 s (Andrew Whitworth b 3 Sept 1982); *Career* research offr NIESR 1972–74 (research asst 1970–71); Home Office Economic Planning Unit: sr econ asst 1974–77, econ advsr 1977–78; Dept of Employment: econ advsr 1978–79, seconded to OECD 1979–80, econ advsr 1980–84, princ Manpower Policy Div I 1984–85, econ advsr Employment Market Research Unit 1985–87, head Economics Branch (sr econ advsr) 1988–90, head Educn and Skills Analysis Branch (sr econ advsr) 1990–91, head Labour Market Briefing and Labour Market Analysis Branch (sr econ advsr) 1991–92, chief econ advsr and dir Economics Research and Evaluation Div 1992–93; dir PSI 1993–98, chm Synergy Research Consulting Ltd 2004–; visiting fell NIESR 1998–, visiting prof Arbetslivsinstitutet Stockholm 1998–2000; memb: Editorial Bd Prospect, Guardian panel of economic advsrs, Cabinet Office Better Regulation Task Force 1997–2000; govr Birkbeck Coll London 1997–2000; *Publications* Young Men on the Margins of Work (2001), Beyond Employment (with Alain Supiot and others, 2001), Access to Financial Services (2000), Poverty Among Pensioners (2001), Early Retirement and Income in Later Life (2002), Recruitment and Retention of Childcare, Early Years and Playworkers: Research Study (jtly, 2003), Retirement Ages inthe UK (2003), Sure Start Local Programmes: Improving the Employability of Parents (with C Carbers, 2004), Economic Contribution of Older People (with W Cook, 2004), What Works with Tackling Worklessness? (2006), A Review of the Economic Impact of Employment Relations Services Delivered by ACAS (2007), Tracking Adult Basic Skills: Findings from longitudinal research (contrib, 2008); numerous articles in other pubns; *Style—* Ms Pamela Meadows; ✉ NIESR, 2 Dean Trench Street, Smith Square, London SW1P 3HE (e-mail pmeadows@niesr.ac.uk)

MEAKIN, Henry Paul John; s of Wing Cdr Henry John Walter Meakin, DFC and bar, RAF (d 1989), of Harare, Zimbabwe, and Elizabeth Wilma, *née* Fairbairns (d 2012); *b* 2 January 1944, Norfolk; *Educ* Plumtree Sch Rhodesia; *m* 2 Jan 1971, Vicki Lynn, da of Maurice James Bullus (d 1990), of Harrogate, N Yorks; 1 da (Katie b 1972), 2 s (Oliver b 1975, Harry b 1980); *Career* exec dir Pensord Press Ltd 1970–74; Aspen Communications plc: fndr dir, md 1975–91, chm 1991–97; fndr dir GWR Gp plc 1981–85; Classic FM plc: fndr chm 1991–93, dir 1993–2007; chm: GWR Gp plc 1986–2001, Aspen Gp Ltd 1999–2008; dir VERO Screening Ltd 2007; Companion Wine Guild of the UK; FRSA; *Recreations* tennis, golf, music; *Clubs* Mktg Gp of GB, Swinley Forest Golf; *Style—* Henry Meakin, Esq; ✉ Garsdon House, Garsdon, Malmebury, Wiltshire SN16 9NJ (☎ 01666 822800)

MEALE, Sir (Joseph) Alan; kt (2011), MP; s of Albert Henry Meale (d 1986), and Elizabeth, *née* Catchpole (d 1997); both parents trade union shop stewards; *b* 31 July 1949; *Educ* Univ of Durham, Ruskin Coll Oxford, Sheffield Hallam Univ; *m* 15 March 1983, Diana, da of Lt Cdr John Gillespy, RN (ret); *Career* nat employment devpt offr (Home Office funded) 1977–79, asst to Ray Buckton as Gen Sec ASLEF 1979–83, Parly and political advsr to Michael Meacher MP 1983–87; MP (Lab) Mansfield 1987–; oppn whip 1992–94, PPS to John Prescott: as Dep Ldr of Lab Pty 1994–97, as Dep PM 1997–98; under sec of state for the environment 1998–99; war graves cmmr 2003–10; memb Parly Select Ctees on: Euro Legislation 1988–90, Home Affrs 1990–92; chm PLP East Midlands and Central Groups 1988–95, chm Br Cyprus Ctee, chair Parly Racing and Bloodstocks Gp 2010–; former vice-chm Employment Ctee PLP; memb: War Pensions Bd 1990–95, SSAFA Bd 1990–94, Parly Ct of Referees 1997–, Cncl of Europe 2000– (pres Ctee on Environment, Agriculture, Local and Regnl Democracy 1997–, memb Bureau 2007–10, chair Local and Regnl Affrs 2010–), WEU 2000–; former exec memb Inter Parly Union; chair HOC Select Ctee Cross Rail 2006–09, exec memb Cwlth Parly Assoc (chm Cyprus Ctee 2003–); former sec All-Pty Parly Greyhound Gp; former treas Parly Football Ctee; founder, former chm and exec memb Parly Beer Industries Ctee; govt advsr on the racing industry and its needs 2002–10, advsr Tote Bd 2005–08; fell and postgrad Industry and Parly Tst; author; journalist of various publications; Hon Citizen of Morphou (Cyprus), Hon Citizen Mansfield Ohio (USA), Hon Senator Louisiana (USA); *Recreations* reading, writing, arts, politics, Cyprus, sports and Mansfield Town FC; *Clubs* Mansfield Labour, Bellamy Road and Mansfield Woodhouse Working Men's, Mansfield Town FC; *Style—* Sir Alan Meale, MP; ✉ House of Commons, London SW1A 0AA (☎ 020 7219 3000, e-mail enquiries@alanmeale.co.uk, website www.alanmeale.co.uk)

MEARS, Oliver; s of Martin Mears, of Haddiscoe, Norfolk, and Elisabeth, *née* Juen; *b* 5 February 1979, Norwich; *Educ* Norwich Sch, Lincoln Coll Oxford; *Partner* Suzy Flexer; 2 s (Theo b 18 Aug 2011, Ivor b 13 Nov 2013); *Career* fndr and artistic dir Second Movement 2004, artistic dir NI Opera 2010–; prodns with NI Opera incl: The Medium, Tosca (Best Opera Irish Times Theatre Award 2011), The Turn of the Screw, The Flying Dutchman, Noye's Fludde, Hansel and Gretel, L'Elisir D'Amore, Macbeth, Salome; other prodns incl: Albert Herring (Aldeburgh), The Bear (Nat Reisopera), The Magic Flute (Nevill Nolt Opera), Don Giovanni (Bergen Nat Opera); *Style—* Oliver Mears, Esq; ✉ Northern Ireland Opera, Grand Opera House, Great Victoria Street, Belfast BT2 7HR; c/o Loesje Sanders, Pound Square, North Hill, Woodbridge, Suffolk IP12 1UU (e-mail loesje@loesjesanders.co.uk, website www.loesjesanders.com)

MEARS, Patrick Michael; s of Alex Benjamin Albert Mears, of Henley-on-Thames, Oxon, and Moira Denise, *née* Buzetti; *b* 19 January 1958; *Educ* Henley GS, LSE (LLB); *m* 1, 27 Aug 1983, Carol Lucia (d 1987), da of Carl William Anders (d 1965); 1 da (Elizabeth Helen Carol b 8 Sept 1987); m 2, 7 Dec 1995, Rachel Elizabeth, da of Prof M S Anderson (d 2006); 1 s (Matthew Patrick b 16 Aug 1999); *Career* admitted slr 1982; Allen & Overy 1980–2012 (tax ptnr 1988–2011); chair General Anti-Abuse Rule (GAAR) Advsy Panel 2013–; chair LSE Alumni Assoc 2013–, memb Addington Soc, tstee Gingerbread 2012–; Freeman Worshipful Co of Slrs; memb Law Soc; *Publications* Tax Planning for International Mergers, Acquisitions, Joint Ventures and Restructurings – UK (2012); *Recreations* theatre, tennis, fine arts, bridge; *Clubs* Old Coll, Dulwich Sports; *Style—* Patrick Mears, Esq; ✉ 15 Burbage Road, Herne Hill, London SE24 9HJ

MEARS, Roger Malcolm Loudon; s of Dr Kenneth Patrick Geddes Mears (d 2001), and Dr Eleanor Mears, *née* Loudon (d 1992); *b* 15 February 1944, London; *Educ* City of London Sch, CCC Cambridge (MA, DipArch); *m* 4 Nov 1978, Joan Adams Speers; 3 da (Emily b 1981, Rebecca b 1983, Jessica b 1986); *Career* architect accredited in building conservation; ptnr Roger Mears Architects 1980–; work incl: Tudor House Cheyne Walk, The Ham Wantage, London houses and churches; memb Casework Panel London Diocesan Advsy Ctee; fndr chm Adfer Ban a Chwm; guardian SPAB 1996–2015; RIBA Specialist Conservation Architect (SCA), AABC; *Recreations* chamber music (viola player), watermills, walking, sculling (winner Henley Veterans' Regatta); *Clubs* Lea Rowing; *Style—* Roger Mears, Esq; ✉ Roger Mears Architects, 2 Compton Terrace, London N1 2UN (☎ 020 7359 8222, fax 020 7354 5208, e-mail rm@rmears.co.uk, website www.rmears.co.uk)

MEATH, Bishop (RC) of 1990–; Most Rev Michael Smith; s of John Smith, and Bridget Fagan, of Liss, Oldcastle, Co Meath; *b* 6 June 1940; *Educ* St Finian's Coll Mullingar, Lateran Univ Rome; *Career* ordained 1963; *Style—* The Most Rev Bishop of Meath; ✉ Bishop's House, Dublin Road, Mullingar, Co Westmeath, Ireland (☎ 00 353 44 934 2038, fax 00 353 44 934 3020, e-mail bishop@dioceseofmeath.ie)

MEDAWAR, Anthony Crosland (Tony); s of Nicholas Antoine Macbeth Medawar, QC, of London, and Joyce Catherine, *née* Crosland-Boyle; *b* 6 September 1962; *Educ* Univ of Kent; *m* 30 June 1990, Nicola, da of Alan Frank Seager; 1 s (Guy Richard Seager), 1 da (Lara Circe Seager); *Career* public servant; private sec to Sir Peter Gregson, GCB 1990–91, head Departmental Deregulation Unit DTI 1991–93, nat expert Competition Directorate Gen Euro Cmmn 1993–96, head Policy Unit Export Control Org DTI 1996–2000, dir Public Bodies Policy Cabinet Office 2000–02, dir Regnl Policy and Enterprise Govt Office for the SW 2002, dir regnl policy DTI 2003–06, dir of policy and external affrs London Devpt Agency 2006–12, sr assoc dir Onyx Communications 2012–, md PROveditor 2012–; memb Advsy Bd Crippen & Landru 2006–; chair and non-exec dir Theatre Peckham 2010–; *Publications* contrib: Crime and Detective Stories (CADS), Bottle Street Gazette, Sherlock Holmes Jl, The Armchair Detective, Tune in to Yesterday, Old-Time Detection, Railway Cuttings; ed various books; *Recreations* theatre, detective stories, amusing my wife; *Clubs* Noughts and Crosses; *Style—* Tony Medawar; ✉ 18 Soho Square, London W1D 3QL (e-mail tony@onyxcommunications.co.uk)

MEDD, Andrew; s of Robert Medd, of Warnford, Hants, and Sarah, *née* King; *b* 21 March 1966; *Educ* Winchester, New Coll Oxford; *m* 1 May 1993, Emma, *née* Fielding; 1 da (Issey Everett b 13 Oct 1994), 2 s (Finley Joe b 12 March 1998, Atticus Jay b 16 Aug 1999); *Career* SmithKline Beecham 1987–92, The Coca Cola Co 1993–97, ptnr Mother 1998–; *Recreations* family, surfing, dog walking; *Clubs* Soho House; *Style—* Andrew Medd, Esq; ✉ Mother, Biscuit Building, 10 Redchurch Street, London E2 7DD

MEDLAM, Charles Samuel; s of late Wilfrid Gaston Medlam, and late Virginia Medlam; *b* 10 September 1949; *Educ* Winchester, Salzburg Mozarteum, Vienna Acad, Paris Conservatoire; *m* 1979, Ingrid, da of Günther Seifert; 1 s (Lukas b 31 Dec 1985), 1 da (Hannah b 8 July 1988); *Career* dir London Baroque 1978–; ensemble has appeared at festivals and venues worldwide incl Salzburg, Bath, Innsbruck and Vienna; *Recordings* over 80 CDs of baroque chamber music for EMI, Harmonia Mundi (France) and Bis (Sweden), CD of French solo bass viol music for Cello Classics released 2010; *Recreations* literature, classics; *Style—* Charles Medlam; ✉ e-mail c.medlam@btinternet.com, website www.londonbaroque.com

MEDLAND, David Arthur; s of James William Medland (d 1986), and Merle Ermyntrude, *née* Rotchell (d 1994); *b* 23 September 1946; *Educ* St Paul's Sch Darjeeling India; *m* (m dis 1979); 1 s (Christopher James b 25 Dec 1968); *Career* CA; RSM Robson Rhodes: joined 1965, asst mangr 1973, mangr 1974, sr mangr 1976, ptnr 1979–2007, memb Exec Ctee 1990–92, seconded as asst dir Serious Fraud Office 1993–96; ptnr Grant Thornton UK LLP (following merger with RSM Robson Rhodes) 2007–10, ind conslt 2010–; FCA 1979 (ACA 1971); *Books* The Unlisted Securities Market – A Review; *Recreations* golf, music, theatre; *Style—* David A Medland, Esq; ✉ 2 Castleton Court, 4/5 Cleveland Gardens, London W2 6HA (☎ 020 7262 5806, e-mail damedland@aol.com)

MEDLYCOTT, Sir Mervyn Tregonwell; 9 Bt (UK 1808), of Ven House, Somerset; s of late Thomas Anthony Hutchings Medlycott (d 1970), 2 s of Sir Hubert Medlycott, 7 Bt, of Edmondsham House, Dorset, and Cecilia Mary Eden, da of late Maj Cecil Harold Eden, of Cranborne, Dorset; suc unc, Sir (James) Christopher Medlycott, 8 Bt (d 1986); *b* 20 February 1947; *Heir* none; *Career* genealogist; Somerset and Dorset Family History Soc: fndr 1975, hon sec 1975–77, chm 1977–84, pres 1986–; FSG (vice-pres 2014–); *Style—* Sir Mervyn Medlycott, Bt; ✉ The Manor House, Sandford Orcas, Sherborne, Dorset DT9 4SB (☎ 01963 220206)

MEEHAN, Prof Anthony Edward (Tony); s of late Edward Joseph Meehan, of Glasgow, and late Mary, *née* Whelan; *b* 24 August 1943, London; *Educ* St George's Westminster London; *m* 24 Oct 1975, Linda Jane, da of John Alexander Portugal Stone, of Vancouver Island, BC; 1 s (Michael Anthony b 1980), 1 da (Claire Louise b 1982); *Career* chm: Tony Meehan and Assocs Ltd 1976–, TMA Communications 1985–; chm: IPR Scottish Gp 1987–89 (chm Educn Ctee 1984–87, vice-chm 1985–87), SPRCA 1995–97; visiting prof Glasgow Caledonian Univ, fell Strathclyde Inst; memb Scottish Soc of Epicureans 1978–; dir Nat Piping Centre of Scotland 1998–2006; Freeman City of Glasgow; FRSA, FIPRA, FCIPR; *Clubs* Scottish Soc of Epicureans, BAFTA; *Style—* Prof Tony Meehan; ✉ Holnest Park House, Holnest, Sherborne, Dorset DT9 6HA (☎ 07768 850855, e-mail tmeehan@tmac.co.uk)

MEEK, Alison Fiona; da of Prof Ronald L Meek (d 1978), and Dorothea L, *née* Schulz; *b* 31 October 1959, Glasgow; *Educ* Beauchamp Coll Oadby, UCL (BA), Coll of Law London; *m* 1, 22 March 1991 (m dis 2002), Christopher Gayford; 1 s (William Augustus b 13 Oct 1992), 1 da (Katherine Elizabeth Dorothea b 19 May 1995); m 2, 21 April 2007, Sir Robert Francis, QC, *qv*; *Career* admitted slr 1986; asst slr: Herbert Smith (articled clerk 1984–86), Withers; ptnr: Boodle Hatfield 1997–2004, Speechly Bircham 2005–07, Harcus Sinclair 2007–; former memb: Wills and Equity Ctee Law Soc; A Practitioners' Guide to Contentious Trusts and Estates (jt author), International Trust Disputes (co-ed and contrib, 2012); contrib to professional jls; *Recreations* family, cooking, gardening, music; *Style*— Ms Alison Meek; ✉ Harcus Sinclair, 3 Lincoln's Inn Fields, London WC2A 3AA (☎ 020 7242 9700, e-mail alison.meek@harcus-sinclair.co.uk)

MEEKE, (Robert) Martin James; QC (2000); s of James Alexander Meeke, and Mildred Alverta Meeke; *b* 25 December 1950; *Educ* Allhallows Sch, Univ of Bristol (LLB); *m* Beverley Ann, *née* Evans; 1 s, 1da; *Career* called to the Bar Gray's Inn 1973; recorder 1995; *Style*— Martin Meeke, Esq, QC; ✉ Colleton Chambers, Colleton Crescent, Exeter EX2 4DG (☎ 01392 274898, fax 01392 412368)

MEERS, Jeffrey (Jeff); s of James Meers, of London, and Marie Ellen, *née* Hugkulstone; *b* 10 February 1953; *Educ* Ashford Co GS, Univ of Nottingham (BSc); *m* 7 Oct 2014, Sarah Jane; 2 s (James b 5 July 1982, David b 22 Oct 1983); *Career* psychologist RN (MOD) 1975–76; advtg exec: BMP and WCRS (award winning ads for Courage Best, John Smiths Yorkshire Bitter, Carling Black Label, BMW, Cadbury, Unisys, St Ivel, 3M, Nationwide); vice-chm Bozell Europe 1987–94, IPA Advtg Effectiveness Awards 1982 and 1994 Int Advtg Assoc (Global and Europe Awards); founding chm MAID (now Thomsons) 1985–93; worldwide pres IDG Global Solutions 1994–2000; fndr ceo: SPARZA, Software Div Officeshopper.com, Bright Station plc e-Commerce; fndr ceo: Cool Technologies, UKT&I Global Entrepreneurs Prog 2009–; dir: Logistics Int plc 2000–05; fndr: Koodos.com 2004–07, VC Finance, BusinessBook & socialICE.net Social Networks SaaS 2009–; business strategist Business Story Script Partnership Tim Hollins 2013– (clients incl Ernst & Young, Coca Cola and Ogilvy); chm Ashford Sports Club Ltd 1991–94; memb Mktg Soc, MIPA; *Books* Advertising Effectiveness (1982); commercial blog MeersNewsline (1986), New Product Development, MEERS on Social; *Recreations* golf, cricket and hockey (former Surrey Schs, Middx Colts Cricket Teams, Ashford Hockey Club and Surrey Youth Hockey, 1st XI Cricket and Hockey captain), skiing, opera; *Clubs* Surbiton Golf, VP Ashford Hockey; *Style*— Jeff Meers, Esq; ✉ 30 Upper Road, Wallington, Surrey SM6 8JY (e-mail jeffreymeers@gmail.com)

MEERS, Nicholas Raymond Beaghen (Nick); s of Peter Rupert Neame Meers (d 2000), of Cheltenham, Glos, and Rachel Barbara, *née* Beaghen (d 2015); *b* 16 May 1955; *Educ* Bryanston, W of England Sch of Art Bristol, Guildford Sch of Photography (Dip), W Surrey Coll of Art and Design; *m* 2001, Trudie Ballantyne; 1 da (Kirsty b 13 Nov 2004); *Career* photographer; numerous editorial and advtg cmmns (landscape, architectural, etc) 1978–; photographs have appeared on various book jackets, magazine front covers, calendars, postcards and in numerous magazines; lectr and teacher of photography; invited judge on many photo competitions incl: Fuji Dimensions, Nat Tst, Travel Photographer of the Year and others; currently photography and film-making of short clips; former memb: Assoc of Photographers, Int Assoc of Panoramic Photographers (IAPP); *Photographic Books* Amsterdam (1978), Paris (1978), California (1978), Los Angeles (1979), Orchids (Hawaii, 1979), Holland (1979), Wisconsin, USA (1979), Ohio, USA (1979), National Parks of California (1979), Israel the Promised Land (1980), Barbados (1980), Cayman Islands (1980), Bahamas (1980), Puerto Rico (1980), Parish Churches of England (1980), Senegal, West Africa (1981), Ivory Coast, West Africa (1981), Ireland and her People (1981), Ferrari (California, 1982), Porsche (California, 1982), The National Parks of Canada (1982), San Francisco (1983), Gardens of Britain (1985), New Shell Guide to South & Mid-Wales (with Wynford Vaughan-Thomas, 1986), New Shell Guide to the Channel Islands (1986), Christopher Wray's Guide to Decorative Lighting (with Barty Phillips, 1986), New Shell Guide to Oxfordshire & Berkshire (1987), The Spirit of the Cotswolds (with Susan Hill, 1987), New Shell Guide to Gloucestershire, Hereford & Worcester (1988), New Shell Guide to Sussex (1989), Enigmatic England (with Sue Seddon, 1989), Panoramas of English Gardens (with David Wheeler, 1990), Panoramas of England (with Adam Nicolson, 1991), Panoramas of English Villages (1992), Gardens of the National Trust (1996), A Year in the Garden (National Trust) 2001, Stretch, The World of Panoramic Photography (2003); *Recreations* panoramic photography, kite flying, astrocartography, videography; *Style*— Nick Meers; ✉ e-mail p@noramics.com, website www.nickmeers.com

MEGYERI, Matthias Aron; s of Josef Megyeri, of Stuttgart, Germany, and Erika, *née* Weber; *b* 13 November 1973, Stuttgart, Germany; *Educ* Nick Bollettieri Tennis Acad FL, State Coll of Design Centre for Art and Media Karlsruhe (Dip), Royal Coll of Art London (MA); *Partner* Juliane Otterbach; *Career* artist; fndr and ceo Megyeri & Ptnrs Ltd 2003–; artist in residence Akademie Schloss Solitude Stuttgart 2007–09, lectr Architectural Assoc; Focus Security Award Design Center Stuttgart 2007; *Collections and Installations* 51 Hoxton Square London 2004, Tokyo Hipsters Club 2005, Safety Nest SESC Pinheiros Sao Paulo 2006, Bank of America Tower public art installation NY 2006, Sweet Dreams Security products as part of perm collection of MoMA NY 2006; *Exhibitions* incl: Great Brits (Paul Smith Milan, Aoyama Tokyo, ICA Singapore, UTS Gall Sydney, RMIT Melbourne, Concert Hall Athens) 2005–07, Pop Noir: Critical Designs (Israel Museum Jerusalem) 2005–06, SAFE: Design Takes on Risk (MoMA NY) 2005–06, UK Jack, OK! (Colette Paris, Dover Street Market/Comme des Garcons London, Isetan Tokyo) 2006, Don't Panic! Emergent Critial Design (Architecture Fndn London) 2007, Fetish + Consumption (Akademie Schloss Solitude) 2008, Cantilever (Collyer Bristow Gallery London) 2008, 20,000 Images (Akademie Schloss Solitude) 2008; *Recreations* facade photography, tennis, lacrosse, parkour; *Style*— Matthias Megyeri, Esq

MEHTA, Bharat; CBE (2016, OBE 2000); s of Maganlal Jinabhai Mehta (d 1971), and Rattanben Mehta (d 2008); *b* 5 March 1956; *Educ* Shenfield Sch, Plymouth Poly (BA), UCL (MSc); *m* 29 Sept 1990, Sally Ann, da of Reginald Chambers; 2 c (Kriyaa Uma b 30 Sept 1991, Puja Kavita b 10 Nov 1993); *Career* research asst MRC UCH Med Sch 1979–80; community worker Pensioners Link 1981–83, policy offr NCVO 1983–87, princ offr for vol orgns London Borough of Waltham Forest 1987–89, chief exec National Schizophrenia Fellowship 1994–98 (dir of devpt 1989–94), chief exec Tst for London (formerly City Parochial Fndn) 1998–; dir Social Justice and Human Rights Centre 2011–; chair Resource for London 2011–15; memb Bd Joseph Rowntree Fndn 2003–13, memb Exec Ctee London Funders 2011–, memb Mental Health Fndn Cmmn on Ageing 2011–13, memb Bd London Emergencies Tst 2016–; non-exec dir N Middx UH NHS Tst 2005–09; patron Revolving Doors Agency; chm Bowes Primary Sch Governing Body 2000–05; fell Br American Project, Graduate of Common Purpose; FRSA 2003; *Recreations* hockey, squash, swimming; *Clubs* Southgate Adelaide Hockey (vice-pres 2002–, capt 2010–); *Style*— Bharat Mehta, CBE; ✉ Trust for London, 6 Middle Street, London EC1A 4PH (☎ 020 7606 6145, fax 020 7600 1866, e-mail info@trustforlondon.org.uk)

MEHTA, Bharat Himatlal; s of Himatlal Mehta, of Mombasa, Kenya, and Rasika Vora Mehta (d 1998); *b* 20 November 1952, Bombay, India; *Educ* MBA; *m* 22 July 1979, Renu; 2 s (Harshil b 26 Nov 1980, Ishil b 9 Oct 1987); *Career* prop Necessity Supplies 1987–; non-exec IMA Industries 2011; *Clubs* Lions (Acton branch); *Style*— Bharat Himatlal Mehta, Esq; ✉ IMA Industries Ltd, Atlantic House, Imperial Way, Reading RG2 0TD

MEIKLEJOHN, HE Dominic; OBE (2007); s of David Meiklejohn, and Eileen Hall; *b* 14 November 1967, London; *Educ* Merton Coll Oxford (BA); *m* 2008, Joanne, *née* Farrand; 1 da (Olivia b 12 Aug 2008); *Career* diplomat; European Community Dept FCO 1990–92, head Br Know-How Fund 1993–96, head India Team FCO 1998–99, first sec Warsaw 2000–03, dep head Environment Policy Dept FCO 2004, dep consul-gen Basra 2006–07, dep consul-gen NY 2008–12, high cmmr to Solomon Islands, Vanuatu and Nauru 2012–; *Recreations* cricket, football, travel; *Style*— HE Mr Dominic Meiklejohn, OBE; ✉ c/o BFPO 5612 (FCO) HA4 6EP

MELCHETT, 4 Baron (UK 1928); Sir Peter Robert Henry Mond; 4 Bt (UK 1910); but does not use titles; s of 3 Baron Melchett (d 1973, gs of 1 Baron, better known as Sir Alfred Mond, first chm of ICI and min of Health 1921–22); *b* 24 February 1948; *Educ* Eton, Pembroke Coll Cambridge, Keele Univ; *m* Cassandra Wedd; 1 da (Jessica Joan Mond Wedd, 24 April 1981), 1 s (Jay Julian Mond Wedd, 2 Sep 1983); *Career* sat as Lab peer in House of Lords; at LSE and Addiction Res Unit 1973–74; a lord in waiting (govt whip) 1974–75, Parly under-sec of state DOI 1975–76, min of state NI Office 1976–79; chm: Working Pty on Pop Festivals 1975–76, Community Industry 1979–85, Greenpeace UK 1986–88 (exec dir 1988–2000), Greenpeace Japan 1995–2001; policy dir Soil Assoc 2002–; memb: Greenpeace Int Bd 1988 and 2001, Govt Organic Action Plan Gp 2002–09, BBC Rural Affairs Ctee 2004–, DfES Sch Meals Panel 2005, DEFRA Rural Climate Change Forum 2009–11; pres Ramblers' Assoc 1981–84; hon dr of civil law Newcastle Univ 2013; *Style*— Peter Melchett

MELDING, David Robert Michael; AM; s of late David Graham Melding, of Neath, and Edwina Margaret, *née* King; *b* 28 August 1962; *Educ* Dwr-y-Felin Comp Sch Neath, Univ Coll Cardiff, Coll of William and Mary Va USA; *Career* memb Cons Research Dept 1986–89, dep dir Welsh Centre for Int Affairs 1994–96 (exec offr 1989–94), mangr Carers Nat Assoc in Wales 1996–99; memb Nat Assembly for Wales (Cons) South Wales Central 1999–, shadow min for economic devpt 2007–, dep presiding offr 2011–16, spokesperson for environment, sustainability, planning and housing 2016; *Publications* Will Britain Survive Beyond 2020? (2009), The Reformed Union: The UK as a Federation (2014); *Recreations* swimming, walking; *Style*— David Melding, Esq, AM; ✉ National Assembly for Wales, Cardiff Bay, Cardiff CF99 1NA (☎ 0300 200 7222)

MELDRUM, Sir Graham; kt (2002), CBE (1994), QFSM (1988); s of George Meldrum, and Agnes, *née* Gordon; *b* 23 October 1945; *Educ* Inverurie Acad; *m* 1963, Catherine Mary Elizabeth, da of Peter Meier; 1 s (Clive b 12 March 1972), 1 da (Jill b 29 Oct 1979); *Career* fireman rising to station offr London Fire Bde 1963–73, instr (asst divnl offr) Fire Serv Coll 1973–74, divnl offr III Hants Fire Serv 1974–76; Tyne & Wear Fire Serv: divnl offr II 1976–79, divnl offr I 1979–80, sr divnl offr 1980–83; W Midlands Fire Serv: asst chief offr 1983–84, dep chief fire offr 1984–90, chief fire offr 1990–98; HM Chief Inspr of Fire Servs (Home Office) 1998–2007, chm W Midlands Ambulance Serv NHS Tst 2007–; pres Chief and Asst Chief Fire Offrs' Assoc 1994–95; pres Fire Servs Youth Trg Assoc, pres The Fire Service Princes Tst Assoc, vice-pres Fire Servs Nat Benevolent Fund; vice-pres The Healing Tst; Hon DUniv UCE 1997; FIFireE 1994, CIMgt 1995; OStJ 1998; *Recreations* classic cars, motor boats; *Style*— Sir Graham Meldrum, CBE, QFSM; ✉ West Midlands Ambulance Service NHS Trust, Waterfront Business Park, Waterfront Way, Brierly Hill, West Midlands DY5 1LX

MELHAM, Prof Thomas Frederick; s of Frederick Elias Melham (d 1960), and Hildur Margaret Harms, *née* Lien; *b* 16 January 1960; *Educ* Univ of Calgary (BSc), Univ of Cambridge (PhD); *m* 16 Nov 2002, Karen Annette, *née* van der Meulen; *Career* research fell Gonville & Caius Coll Cambridge 1987–91; Univ of Glasgow: lectr 1993–97, sr lectr 1997–98, prof of computing science 1998–2002; Univ of Oxford: lectr in computer science 2002–04, tutorial fell in computation Balliol Coll 2002–, prof of computer science 2004–, praefectus of Holywell Manor 2010–, assoc head (research) MPLS Div 2012–15; memb EPSRC Peer Review Coll for IT/Computing 1997–; FRSE 2002, FBCS 2015, CEng 2015; *Publications* incl: Introduction to HOL: A theorem proving environment for higher order logic (ed with M J C Gordon, 1993), Higher Order Logic and Hardware Verification (1993); also various refereed pubns, invited papers and other pubns; *Recreations* music, philosophy; *Style*— Prof Thomas Melham; ✉ Balliol College, Oxford OX1 3BJ; Oxford University Department of Computer Science, Wolfson Building, Parks Road, Oxford OX1 3QD (☎ 01865 273824, fax 01865 273839, e-mail tom.melham@cs.ox.ac.uk)

M

MELLING, John Kennedy; o s of John Robert Melling (d 1948), of Westcliff-on-Sea, Essex, and Ivy Edith May, *née* Woolmer (d 1982); *b* 11 January 1927; *Educ* Thirsk Sch Westcliff, Westcliff HS for Boys; *Career* CA; lectr, author, broadcaster, playwright and historian; drama and literary critic: The Stage 1957–90, Fur Weekly News 1968–73; critic and contributor: Essex Countryside Magazine 1966–77, Evening Echo 1971–74, Crime Time 1996–2002; ed: The Liveryman Magazine 1970–75, The Farrier and his Craft 1981, Black Dagger series 1986–91, Murder in the Library 1986; book critic BBC 1984–85 and 1987; Crime Writers' Assoc: memb Ctee 1985–88, ed Handbook 1989; held master classes for Arts Cncl for Actors 2004–11; lectr on Liner QEII 1993; invited by BBC Radio to interview Alfred Hitchcock for retention in archives; CWA Award for Outstanding Servs; dip for 50 years' membership and support Craft Guild of Chefs/ Cookery & Food Assoc 2014; elected to US Chiefs of Police Nat Drug Task Force 1991, Medal of Honour and int life vice-pres American Fedn of Police, hon chief of police USA; govr Corp of the Sons of the Clergy; Westcliff Film and Video Club: first pres 1962–64, first hon life memb 1999; memb Worshipful Cos of Bakers, Farriers and Constructors, memb Ct of Assts Worshipful Co of Poulters 1974 (Master 1980–81, Father 2012); memb BAFTA 1960; FCA, FFB, FRSA, FTII, MCFA; Knight of the Grand Cross of the Order of St Michael the Archangel (OMAA), Knight of the Most Venerable and Holy Orthodox Order of Basil the Great of Russia; *Books* incl: Discovering Lost Theatres, Southend Playhouses from 1793, Discovering Theatre Ephemera, Discovering London's Guilds and Liveries, Alchemy of Murder, Gwendoline Butler: Inventor of the Women's Police Procedural, Murder Done To Death, Scaling the High C's (with John Brecknock), She Shall Have Murder, A Little Manual of Etiquette for Ladies, A Little Manual of Etiquette for Gentlemen, Social Development of Theatres (1987), Fantasy Games' Influence on the Young (1987), Twentieth Century Crime and Mystery Writers (contrib, 1991), The Oxford Companion to Crime and Mystery Writing (contrib, 1999), The Constructor's Company – Genesis and Growth (2006); *Plays* incl: George....from Caroline, The Gilded Cage, Murder at St Dunstan's, The Toast Is..., Old Christmas, The Gilbertian Consequences of Mr Sullivan; *Audiobooks and DVDs* incl The 39 Steps; *Recreations* reading, shooting, collecting theatre and crime ephemera, cinema, fashion, music; *Clubs* City Livery, Marylebone Rifle & Pistol; *Style*—John Kennedy Melling, Esq; ✉ 85 Chalkwell Avenue, Westcliff-on-Sea, Essex SS0 8NL; 44a Tranquil Vale, Blackheath, London SE3 0BD

MELLIS, Patrick David Barclay Nairne; s of Capt David Mellis, DSC, RN, and Anne Patricia, *née* Wingate-Gray (d 1994); *b* 14 May 1943; *Educ* Loretto, Univ of Glasgow (BSc); *m* 26 Nov 1969, Elizabeth Jane Workman, *née* Carslaw; 2 da (Rosemary Anne Nairne b 14 Nov 1975, Catherine Fiona Nairne b 25 April 1977), 1 s (Robert Barclay Nairne b 13 May 1980); *Career* student apprentice Alex Stephens & Sons (shipbuilders) Glasgow 1961–66 (design draughtsman 1966–68); naval architect: Litton Industries Mississippi USA 1968–70, A Darden & Sons (conslts) New Orleans USA 1970–72, International Offshore Services London 1972–74; project mangr P&O Three Quays 1974–83, marine dir Seaforth Maritime Ltd Aberdeen 1983–89, project mangr Saudi Arabian Oil Co Saudi Arabia 1990–96, md P&O Three Quays 1996–, md Three Quays International 2001–; memb Br Maritime League; memb Instn of Engrs and Shipbuilders in Scotland 1962, MRINA 1962, memb Soc of Naval Architects and Marine Engrs USA 1972; *Recreations* squash, golf, sailing; *Style*— Patrick Mellis, Esq

MELLISS, Simon Richard; s of Laurence Melliss, of Sherborne, Dorset, and Joan, *née* Franklin; *b* 2 July 1952, London; *Educ* Christ's Hosp, Univ of York (BA); *m* 4 Sept 1976, Jennifer Susan, *née* Webberley; 2 s (Oliver Simon b 31 Jan 1981, Dominic James b 1 June 1983); *Career* Whinney Murray & Co (later Ernst & Young) 1974–78, Reed Int plc 1978–88, fin controller Sketchley plc 1989–91; Hammerson plc: fin controller 1991–95, gp fin dir 1995–2011; memb Ctee of Mgmnt Hermes Property Unit Tst, non-exec dir: Assoc

British Ports Holdings plc 2006, Whitbread plc 2007–; treas and memb Cncl UCL 2012–; FCA 1978; *Style—* Simon Melliss, Esq

MELLITT, Prof Brian; s of John Mellitt (d 1990), of Preston, and Nelly, *née* Heaney (d 2002); *b* 29 May 1940; *Educ* Preston GS, Loughborough Univ (BTech), Imperial Coll London (DIC); *m* 30 Dec 1961, Lyn, da of Edward Waring, of Preston; 1 s (John Edward b 1967), 1 da (Anna Jane b 1969); *Career* design engr (Electric Traction) English Electric 1956–66, sr lectr Huddersfield Poly 1966–68, sr princ scientific offr Res Div British Railways Bd 1968–71; Univ of Birmingham: lectr 1971, sr lectr 1981, prof 1983, head Undergraduate Sch 1983, head Electrical Engrg and Electronics Dept 1985, dean Faculty of Engrg 1987–88, hon prof 1989; head Power Electronics and Traction Gp 1971–88 (conslt engr to various railways incl LUL, Hong Kong MTRC, Singapore MRTC, CIE, Metro Madrid), engrg dir London Underground 1989–95, dir engrg and prodn Railtrack plc 1995–99 (ret), pt/t engrg advsr Railtrack (UK) plc 1999–2000; hon ed IEE Proceedings – Electric Power Applications 1978–2009, ed IEE Proceedings Power Electronics 2009–; Leonardo da Vinci Award Italian Industrial Design Assoc 1989; chm Railway Forum 1998–2000; non-exec chm: Building Research Establishment 1998–2010, Metro Consulting 2000–02, SIRA Ltd 2001–06, Rail Personnel Int Hong Kong 2002–03; non-exec dir: Catalis Rail Trg Ltd 1998–2001, Jarvis plc 2002–08; rail conslt to NM Rothschild 1999–; Hon DTech Loughborough Univ 1991, Hon DSc Univ of Huddersfield 1997, Hon DEng Univ of Birmingham 1999; pres Welding Instn 2000–01; FIEE 1978 (vice-pres 1996–99, dep pres 1999–2001, pres 2001–02), FIMechE 1986, FIRSE 1984, FREng 1990; *Books* Computers in Railway Operations (ed, 1987), Computer Applications in Railway Operations (ed, 1990); *Recreations* bridge; *Clubs* Athenaeum; *Style—* Prof Brian Mellitt, FREng; ✉ The Priory, 36 Church Street, Stilton, Cambridgeshire PE7 3RF (☎ 01733 240573, fax 01733 240467, e-mail brianmellitt@msn.com)

MELLOR, The Rt Hon David John; PC (1990), QC (1987); s of late Douglas H Mellor; *b* 12 March 1949; *Educ* Swanage GS, Christ's Coll Cambridge (LLB); *m* 1974 (m dis 1996) , Judith Mary; 2 s (Anthony, Frederick); *Career* chm Univ of Cambridge Assoc 1970; called to the Bar Inner Temple 1972; Parly candidate (Cons) West Bromwich E Oct 1974, MP (Cons) Putney 1979–97; PPS to Francis Pym as Ldr of the House 1981; Parly under sec state: for energy 1981–83, Home Office 1983–86; min of state: Home Office 1986–87, FCO 1987–88, for Health 1988–89, Home Office 1989–90, Privy Cncl Office (min for the Arts) 1990; chief sec to the Treasury 1990–92, sec of state for Nat Heritage April-Sept 1992; advsr to major British and international cos 1992–; columnist: The Guardian 1992–95, Evening Standard (weekly football column), Sunday People (Man of the People column); arts and music critic Mail on Sunday 2000; contrib to various newspapers; host 6.06 phone-in show (Radio Five Live, BBC Radio Personality of the Year 1995 Variety Club Awards) 1992–; presenter: Vintage Years (BBC Radio 3), Across the Threshold (Classic FM), David Mellor Prog (BBC Radio 5), If You Liked That (Classic FM); judge: Sony Radio Awards 1993, Whitbread Literary Prize 1993, Sunday Express Award for Fiction; chm Panel of Judges Science Book Awards 1994; chm Sports Aid Fndn 1993–97, chm Football Task Force 1997–2000; pres Bournemouth Symphony Orch 2000–; govr Nat Youth Orchestra (memb cncl); tstee Fund for the Replacement of Animals in Medical Experiments (FRAME) 2004– (also co-patron); former dep chm London Philharmonic Tst, former memb Bd ENO; hon assoc BVA 1986; FZS; *Style—* The Rt Hon David Mellor, QC

MELLOR, Ian; s of Dr Michael James Mellor (d 2012), and Ruth Mary, *née* Alexander; *Educ* Bournemouth Sch (J J Dodds prize), Univ of Durham (BA); *Career* ICC Information Ltd 1989–91, asst ed Communicable Disease Report Public Health Lab Serv 1991–94; Martin Dunitz Ltd: ed 1994–97, jls mangr 1997–2001; special sales (jls) Informa plc 2001–06, head of business devpt IOP Publishing 2006–08, publications mangr Br Small Animal Veterinary Assoc 2008; *Recreations* oil painting, writing, badminton; *Style—* Ian Mellor, Esq; ✉ British Small Animal Veterinary Association, Woodrow House, 1 Telford Way, Waterwells Business Park, Quedgeley, Gloucestershire GL2 2AB

MELLOR, Dame Julie Thérèse; DBE (2006); da of Gp Capt Edward Vernon Mellor, of Oxford, and Patricia Ann, *née* Jenner-Baden (d 1994); *b* 29 January 1957, Bedford; *Educ* BNC Oxford (BA); *m* 23 Sept 1990, Nick Reed; 1 s, 1 da; *Career* teacher Inst for Educn and Research on Women and Work and Eleanor Emerson fell in labour educn Cornell Univ NY 1979–81, employee rels advsr Shell UK 1981–83, economic devpt offr London Borough of Islington 1983–84, dep head of contract compliance Equal Opportunities Unit and sr employment policy advsr GLC/ILEA 1984–89, HR mangr TSB Gp 1989–91, corp HR dir British Gas 1992–96, prop and princ conslt Julie Mellor Consits 1996–99, chair Equal Opportunities Cmmn 1999–2005, ptnr PricewaterhouseCoopers 2005–11, Parly and Health Service Ombudsman 2012–; cmmr Cmmn for Racial Equality 1996–2003; memb Bd Employers Forum on Disability 1995–2009, memb Bd Nat Consumer Cncl 2001–07, non-exec bd memb Dept for Innovation, Univs and Skills 2008–09; chair Fatherhood Inst 2005–08, memb Bd Green Alliance 2007–09, non-exec memb Bd Dept for Business, Innovation and Skills 2009–11; tstee Nesta 2011–; Hon Dr Anglia Poly Univ 2003; hon fell BNC Oxford 2003; FCGI 2003; *Recreations* theatre, travel, food; *Style—* Dame Julie Mellor, DBE

MELLOR, Kay; OBE (2009); *b* 1951, Leeds, Yorks; *Educ* Bretton Hall Coll, Univ of Leeds; *m* Anthony; 2 da (Gaynor Kay, Yvonne); *Career* screenwriter; fndr Yorkshire Theatre Co; Dennis Potter Award for Outstanding Writing for Television BAFTA 1997; *Television* script ed Albion Market, storyliner Coronation Street (ITV); writer: Climbing Out 1987, Children's Ward 1989–92, Brookside 1989, Families, Just Us 1990 (also actress, RTS Award for Children's Drama 1993, Writer's Guild Award 1994), Band of Gold 1995–97 (RTS Award, ITV Prog of the Year, 17th American Cable Ace Award), Girls' Night 1995 (Gracie Allen Award), Some Kind of Life (ITV) 1996 (Prix Niki Award), Jane Eyre 1997, Gold 1997, Playing the Field (BBC) 1998–2000 (also exec prodr), Fanny and Elvis 1999 (also dir, Dinard Audience Award, Fort Lauderdale Festival Award), Fat Friends 2000 (also exec prodr), A Good Thief 2002 (also actress), Between the Sheets (ITV) 2003, Gifted (ITV) 2003 (also actress and exec prodr), Strictly Confidential (ITV), The Chase 2006–07 (also exec prodr), A Passionate Woman (BBC) 2010, The Syndicate (BBC) 2012; *Plays* Place of Safety 1988 (NY Film and Television Award), In All Innocence (West Yorkshire Playhouse) 1991, A Passionate Woman (West Yorkshire Playhouse, Comedy Theatre and five nat tours) 1992, Queen (West Yorkshire Playhouse); *Style—* Ms Kay Mellor, OBE; ✉ c/o Sian Palfrey, Rollem Productions, 6 Weetwood Lane, Leeds LS16 5LS

MELLOR, Simon John; s of Raymond Mellor, and Phyllis, *née* Canter; *b* 10 September 1954, London; *Educ* Univ of Bristol (BSc); *m* 3 Feb 1990, (Carolyn) Mary, da of Ewen Langford; 2 da (Phoebe b 23 April 1991, Imogen b 12 July 1993), 2 step s (Dominic b 18 Nov 1975, Thomas b 23 June 1977); *Career* Saatchi & Saatchi Co plc: asst to chm 1976–78, corp devpt mangr 1978–84, assoc dir 1984–, dir Main Bd 1985, dep ceo Communications Div 1988, responsible for co's corp communication 1990, commercial dir Saatchi & Saatchi Advertising Worldwide 1991–94; gp commercial dir Blenheim Group plc 1994–96; managing ptnr: Mellor Watts 1996–2005, The Mellor Partnership 2005–; govr St Marylebone Sch for Girls; Freeman City of London, memb Worshipful Co of Clockmakers; *Recreations* theatre, cinema, soccer, cricket; *Style—* Simon Mellor, Esq; ✉ The Mellor Partnership, High Holborn House, 52/54 High Holborn, London WC1V 6RL (☎ 020 7692 0505, e-mail simon@mellorpartnership.com)

MELLORS, Prof Colin; s of George and Phyllis Mellors; *b* 2 June 1949; *Educ* Firth Park GS Sheffield, Univ of Sheffield (BA, MA), Univ of Bradford (PhD); *Career* tutor Univ of Sheffield 1971–73, lectr in politics Univ of Southampton 1973–74; Univ of Bradford: lectr 1974–84, sr lectr 1984–94, dean Faculty of Social Sciences 1992–94, prof 1994–, pro-vice-chllr 1994–2001; former tutor Open Univ and educn advsr NALGO; pro vice-chllr Univ of York 2006–, dir of HE strategy Yorkshire Forward (RDA) 2001–06, non-exec dir Corp Mgmnt Bd Govt Office for Yorkshire and Humber 2004–11; dep electoral cmmr and memb Boundary Ctee for England 2002–10, dep chair Local Govt Boundary Cmmn for England 2010–; dep chair of govrs Bradford GS; FHEA, FRSA; *Recreations* photography, fell walking; *Style—* Prof Colin Mellors; ✉ Innovation Centre, York Science Park, University of York, Heslington, York YO10 5DG

MELROSE, HE Dianna; *Career* dep head of policy planning staff FCO 1999–2000, head of policy staff FCO 2000–02, head Extractive Industries Transparency Initiative DFID 2002, head Int Trade Dept DFID 2003–06, head Enlargement & SE Europe Gp Europe Directorate FCO 2006–07, ambass to Cuba 2008–2012, high cmmr to Tanzania 2013–; *Style—* HE Ms Dianna Melrose; ✉ c/o FCO, King Charles Street, London SW1A 2AH

MELROSE, Margaret Elstob; DL (Cheshire 1987); da of Samuel Chantler Jackson (d 1978), of Prestbury, Cheshire, and Annie Young, *née* Arnot (d 1978); *b* 2 May 1928; *Educ* Howell's Sch Denbigh, Girton Coll Cambridge (Drapers' Co scholarship); *m* 19 June 1948 (m dis), Kenneth Ramsay Watson, s of late Albert Watson; assumed surname of Melrose by deed poll; 1 da (Joanne b 1953); *Career* vice-consul for the Lebanon for N England, Scotland and NI 1963–; Cheshire CC: cncllr (Cons) 1967–2001, Cons chief whip 1977–83 and 1994–2000, chm 1984–85 and 1986–87, 'father' of Cheshire CC 1997–2001, hon alderman 2001–09; hon alderman Cheshire East Unitary Cncl 2009–; cncllr: Macclesfield RDC 1968–74, Nether Alderley PC 1968–2004, Alderley Edge PC 2002–06; memb Cheshire Police Authy 1985–97; gen cmmr of taxes Salford and N Manchester 1985–2003; chm: NW Regnl Children's Planning Ctee 1977–81, Bd of Govrs Crewe and Alsager Coll of Higher Educn 1978–92, Tatton Park Mgmnt Ctee 1985–98, Manchester Airport Consultative Ctee 1986–2002, Cheshire Rural Community Cncl 1988–96; sch govr 1967–, pres Cheshire County Officers Golfing Soc 1984–87, vice-chm David Lewis Centre for Epilepsy 1993–98 (dir 1989–98), govr Manchester Met Univ 1993–99; vice-pres: Cheshire Agric Soc 1985– (lady patroness 1996–97), Ploughing and Hedgecutting Soc 1986–2004, Reaseheath Tst 1992–98, Tatton Constituency Cons Assoc 1999–2001 and 2004– (vice-chm 1995–99 and 2001–04); pres Macclesfield Constituency Cons Assoc 1988–95; memb: Runcorn New Town Devpt Corp 1975–81, Miny of Tport Sleep Research Steering Gp 1990–93, 1998–2001 and 2003–, ESU 1995–; N of England Woman of the Year 1985, Cheshire Woman of the Year 1986; *Recreations* sea and snow, horses, bridge, country life, golf, reading; *Style—* Mrs Margaret Melrose, DL; ✉ The Coach House, Stamford Road, Alderley Edge, Cheshire SK9 7NS (☎ 01625 585629, e-mail maggy@margaretmelrose.myzen.co.uk)

MELUA, Katie; *b* 16 September 1984, Kutaisi, Georgia; *Educ* Brit Sch for Performing Arts; *Career* singer and songwriter 2003–; highest selling female artist in Britain 2004 and 2005; albums: Call off the Search 2003, Piece by Piece 2005, Pictures 2007, The House 2010, Secret Symphony 2012; singles: The Closest Thing to Crazy 2003, Call Off the Search 2004, Crawling Up a Hill 2004, Nine Million Bicycles 2005, I Cried for You 2005, Spiders' Web 2006, If You Were A Sailboat 2007, Mary Pickford 2007, If The Lights Go Out 2008, Wonderful World 2008, Toy Collection 2008; Best Int Newcomer ECHO Awards (Germany) 2004, Biggest Selling Br Album World Music Awards, Best Female Artist Int Rock/Pop ECHO Music Award 2007; *Recreations* adrenaline sports; *Style—* Ms Katie Melua

MELVILLE, Prof Sir David; kt (2007), CBE (2001); s of Frederick George Melville (d 1981), and Mary, *née* Smith (d 2005); *b* 4 April 1944; *Educ* Clitheroe Royal GS, Univ of Sheffield (BSc, PhD), Columbia Univ NYC (NASA scholarship, Dip Space Physics); *Children* 2 da (Ruth Helen b 27 July 1971, Jane Cathryn b 17 Nov 1973), 1 s (Richard Sean b 20 Oct 1975); *Career* Univ of Southampton: ICI research fell 1968, lectr in physics 1968–78, sr lectr in physics 1978–84; Lancashire Poly: prof and head Sch of Physics and Astronomy 1985–86, asst dir 1986–89, vice-rector 1989–91, hon prof Univ of Central Lancs 1991–; dir Middlesex Poly 1991–92, vice-chllr Middlesex Univ 1992–96 (hon prof 1996–); chief exec Further Educn Funding Cncl 1996–2001; vice-chllr Univ of Kent 2001–07 (emeritus prof 2007–); visiting researcher: CNR Italy 1974 and 1976, ICI plc 1975; visiting prof: Univ of Parma Italy 1974–79, Oporto Univ Portugal 1984, Univ of Warwick 1997–2002; chm: HE Statistics Agency 2003–07 (memb Bd 2002–), Univ Vocational Awards Cncl 2003–08, HE South East 2003–06, Health and Safety Ctee Univs and Colleges Employers Assoc 2003–07, HE Race Consultation Project 2003–04, Lifelong Learning Sector Skills Cncl 2006–10 (memb Bd 2004–), Ctee of Inquiry into the Changing Learner Experience 2008–09, Kent Surrey and Sussex NHS Postgrad Deanery Bd 2011–13, Health Educn Kent Surrey and Sussex 2013–; memb: Cncl for Industry and HE 1993–2007, Cncl Inst of Employment Studies 1998–2001, Educn and Libraries Task Gp DfEE/DCMS 1999–2000, Bd HE Prospects 2002–07, Bd The Place 2002–08, Tomlinson Review of 14–19 Curriculum and Qualifications 2003–04, Fndn Degrees Task Force 2003–04, Qualifications and Skills Advsy Ctee QCA 2004–09, Foster Review of FE Colls 2005–06, Bd Edexcel 2005–11, Bd IFS Sch of Finance (formerly Inst of Financial Servs) 2005–11, DfES External Advsy Gp on 14–19 Diplomas 2005–07, HE Engagement Project Bd 2006–08, Bd K Coll (formerly W Kent Coll) 2008–13, Bd Network for Black Professionals 2010– (vice-chm 2014–15), Bd Pearson Educn Ltd 2011– (chm 2012–), HE Cmmn 2012–; bd memb British Non-Ferrous Metals Ltd 1987–92; chm Kent and Medway Learning and Skills Cncl 2006–07; vice-chm: CVCP 1995–96, Kent Public Serv Bd 2004–07, Kent Strategic Partnership 2003–07; memb: Kent Ambassadors 2002–08, Kent Partnership Bd 2003–07, Bd Medway Renaissance Partnership 2005–07, Thames Gateway Strategic Partnership 2007–10 (memb Exec Ctee 2008–10), Advsy Bd Black Leadership Initiative 2007–10, Thames Gateway Skills Envoy 2008–11, Bd London Southbank Univ 2009–13, Bd Manchester Met Univ 2011–; vice-chm of tstees Marlowe and Folkestone Acads 2005–09, tstee Learning from Experience Tst 1999–2009; patron: 157 Gp of FE Colls 2006–, Comprehensive Future 2007–, Thames Gateway Young Chamber 2009–, Faversham Festival 2011, Kent Law Campaign 2012–16, Faversham Creek Tst 2012–; vice-patron Disabled Sailors Assoc 2010–; Hon DSc Univ of Sheffield 1997, Hon DUniv Middlesex 1997, Hon DUniv Derby 2000, Hon DSc Univ of Southampton 2001, Hon DCL Univ of Kent 2008; FInstP 1978; *Publications* incl scientific pubns on solid state physics, biophysics and medical physics; *Recreations* sailing, golf; *Style—* Prof Sir David Melville, CBE; ✉ c/o Carol Hayward, Pearson plc, 80 Strand, London WC2R 0RW (Twitter @davidmelville)

MELVILLE, His Hon Judge (Richard) David Melville; QC (2002); s of Col Robert Kenneth Melville, of London, and Joan Emerton, *née* Hawkins (d 1996); *b* 22 April 1953; *Educ* Wellington, Pembroke Coll Cambridge (MA); *m* 31 Oct 1981, Catharine Mary, da of late Hon William Granville Wingate, QC, of Heathfield, E Sussex; 1 s (Thomas Wingate b 29 Aug 1985), 1 da (Emma Rose b 21 July 1987); *Career* called to the Bar Inner Temple 1975, recorder 2007–15, circuit judge (Western Circuit) 2015–; *Recreations* sailing; *Clubs* Royal Corinthian Yacht, Bar Yacht, Itchenor Sailing, West Wittering Sailing; *Style—* His Hon Judge Melville, QC; ✉ Plymouth Combined Court, Armada Way, Plymouth PL1 2ER

MELVILLE, Nigel Edward; s of Maj E K L Melville (d 1991), and P D Melville (d 1998); *b* 5 June 1945; *Educ* Sedbergh, Trinity Coll Oxford (MA), London Business Sch (MSc); *m* 15 Aug 1970, Maria Hadewij, *née* Van Oosten; 1 s (Christopher Patrick b 8 Dec 1978), 1 da (Sophie Olivia b 15 Dec 1980); *Career* with Baring Brothers rising to dir responsible for int corp fin 1974–95; currently: ptnr Melville Partners, chm Matrix Income and Growth

VCT, chm JPMorgan Fleming Chinese Investment Tst; FCA; *Recreations* tennis, golf, skiing, flying, cycling, opera, ballet; *Clubs* Hurlingham, Oriental, Boodle's, Hurlingham; *Style*— Nigel Melville, Esq; ✉ Melville Partners, 35 Kensington Place, London W8 7PR (☎ 020 7221 9175)

MELVILLE, Toby; s of George Melville, and Margaret, *née* Swabey; *b* 2 July 1970, Haslemere, Surrey; *Educ* Midhurst Sch, Wadham Coll Oxford (BA), Stradbroke Coll Sheffield (NCTJ); *Family* partner; 1 da; *Career* staff photographer: Bristol Evening Post and Western Daily Press 1994–98, Press Assoc 1998–2003; sr photographer Reuters 2003–; extensive travel in 5 continents covering news and sport incl Olympic Games 2000 and 2004 and World Cup 2002 and 2006; memb: Sustrans, Cyclists Touring Club, BPPA 2004; various photographic awards incl: UK Press Gazette Sports Regnl Photographer of the Year 1996 and 1998, UK Press Gazette Regnl Photographer of the Year 1997 and 1998, Nikon Sports Photographer of the Year 1998, Picture Ed's Sports Photographer of the Year 1998 and 2004, Nikon Photographer of the Year 1999, UK Sports Photographer of the Year 2000, Br Press Awards 2011, Specialist Sports Photographer of the Year 2011, finalist UK Sports Photographer of the Year 2011, finalist Photographer of the Year 2013; *Publications* contrib: Reuters: The Art of Seeing II (2004), Assignments (2006), Reuters: State of the World (2006), Reuters: State of the World III (2008), Reuters: State of the World IV (2010); *Recreations* ultra marathon runner, cycling, swimming, surfing, travel, arts; *Clubs* Serpentine Runners; *Style*— Toby Melville, Esq; ✉ c/o Reuters UK Picture Desk, The Reuters Building, 30 South Colonnade, Canary Wharf, London E14 5EP (☎ 020 7542 7949, fax 020 7542 6996, e-mail toby.melville@reuters.com)

MELVILLE-ROSS, Timothy David (Tim); CBE (2005); s of Lt Cdr Antony Stuart Melville-Ross, DSC, RN (ret) (d 1993), and Anne Barclay Fane, *née* Gamble (d 2013); *b* 3 October 1944; *Educ* Uppingham, Portsmouth Coll of Technol (Dip); *m* 19 Aug 1967 (m dis 2013), Camilla Mary Harlackenden, da of Lt-Col Richard Harlackenden Carwardine Probert, of Bures, Suffolk; 2 s (Rupert b 1971, James b 1972), 1 da (Emma b 1975); m 2, 17 May 2014, Irene Ruth Spellman; *Career* chief exec Nationwide Building Society 1985–94, DG IOD 1994–99; chm: Investors in People UK 1999–2006, DTZ plc 2000–11, Bank Insinger de Beaufort NV 2000–05, Manganese Bronze Holdings plc 2003–12 (dir 2000–03), Bovis Homes plc 2005–08 (non-exec dir 1997–2008), Royal London Mutual Insurance Society Ltd 2006–13 (dir 1999–2013, dep chm 2002–05); non-exec dir Monument Oil & Gas plc 1993–99 (dep chm 1997–99); pres Inst of Business Ethics 2013– (memb Advsy Cncl 1994–), memb Greenbury Ctee on executive remuneration 1995; chm Cncl Univ of Essex 2001–07, chair HEFCE 2008–, chm Homerton Univ Hosp NHS Fndn Tst 2013–; *Recreations* reading, walking, the countryside, family; *Style*— Tim Melville-Ross, Esq, CBE; ✉ 9 Maybury Mews, Stanhope Road, London N6 5YT (☎ 07850 875482)

MENAUL, Christopher; s of Stewart William Blacker Menaul (d 1987), and Helene Mary, *née* Taylor; *b* 25 July 1944, Cambridge; *Educ* Hurstpierpoint Coll, St Catharine's Coll Cambridge; *m* 4 Feb 1989, Kathleen Elizabeth Mackie, 1 s (Maximillian Bennett, b 1997), 1 da (Lucinda Helene b 1999); *Career* film and television drama director; credits incl: Precious Bane (BBC) 1989 (Public Jury Prize Best Fiction Film Télévision Rencontres Européennes de Reims 1990, nominated Best Single Drama RTS Awards 1989), Nice Work (BBC) 1989 (Best Drama Serial RTS Awards 1989, nominated BFI TV Award 1990), Prime Suspect (Granada) 1991 (Best Drama Serial BAFTA 1991, Best Drama Broadcasting Press Guild Awards 1991, Best Drama Serial RTS Awards 1991, Best Drama and Best Mini Film Awards Banff Festival 1992, Golden Plaque Chicago Int Film Festival), A Dangerous Man – T E Lawrence After Arabia (Enigma Films) 1992 (Int Emmy Best Drama 1992), Homicide (Baltimore Pictures/NBC) 1993, Fatherland (HBO) 1994 (Golden Globe nomination for Best Film), Feast of July (Merchant Ivory prodn) 1995, Bright Hair (Monogram/BBC) 1997, The Passion of Ayn Rand (Showtime) 1998, One Kill (Showtime/CBS) 1999, The Forsyte Saga (Granada) 2001, State of Mind (Monogram/ITV) 2002, Wall of Silence (Granada) 2003 (nominated Prix Italia 2004), Belonging (ITV) 2004 (Prix Special de la Mise en Scene Rheims 2006), Planespotting (ITV) 2005 (nominated Grierson Award 2005), Secret Smile (ITV) 2005, See No Evil (ITV) 2006 (Best Drama Award: RTS NW 2006, Broadcast 2007, South Bank Show 2007, Best Drama Serial BAFTA 2007), Above Suspicion (ITV) 2008, Zen Cabal (BBC/Mediaset) 2010, Combat Hospital (ABC/Shaw) 2011, First Night 2011 (feature film), Summer in February 2012 (feature film), The Suspicions of Mr Whincher (ITV 1) 2013, Ripper Street (BBC/Tiger Aspect) 2013, Chasing Shadows (ITV Studios) 2014, Killing Jesus (Scott Free/Nat Geographic) 2015 (nominated Best Movie Made for TV Emmy and Critics' Choice Awards); *Style*— Christopher Menaul, Esq; ✉ c/o Camille McCurry, United Agents, 12–26 Lexington Street, London W1F 0LE (☎ 020 3214 0800, fax 020 3214 0801, website www.unitedagents.co.uk)

MENDELOW, Prof (Alexander) David; s of Harry Mendelow, of Johannesburg, South Africa, and Ruby, *née* Palmer; *b* 19 May 1946; *Educ* Univ of the Witwatersrand (MB BCh, PhD); *m*; 3 da (Toni Andrea b 1969, Melissa Rose b 2004, Felicity May b 2007 (twin)), 3 s (Trevor Neil b 1971, Robert Kevin b 1974, Aaron Alexander b 2007 (twin)); *Career* registrar in neurosurgery Univ of the Witwatersrand and Johannesburg Hosp 1970–76, sr registrar Univ of Edinburgh 1977–79, sr lectr Univ of Glasgow 1980–86, prof of neurosurgery Univ of Newcastle upon Tyne 1987–; author of articles in scientific journals and books on head injury and stroke; convenor Br Neurosurgery Res Group, pres Euroacademia Multidisciplinaria Neurotraumatologica (EMN); pres Int Soc for Brain Oedema; memb: Expert Witness Inst, RSM, Soc of Br Neurosurgeons, Surgical Res Soc, American Assoc of Neurological Surgeons (AANS), Congress of Neurological Surgeons (CNS); FRCSEd 1974; *Books* Pyogenic Neurosurgical Infections (1991), Fibre Systems of the Brain and Spinal Cord (1997), Evidence Based Neurotrauma (2002), Critical Care of Stroke (2014), Stroke: Pathophysiology, Diagnosis and Management 6th Edition (2014); *Recreations* sailing, flying; *Style*— Prof A David Mendelow; ✉ Department of Neurosurgery, University of Newcastle upon Tyne, Regional Neurosciences Centre, Royal Victoria Infirmary, Newcastle upon Tyne NE1 4LP (☎ 0191 233 6161, fax 0191 282 4977); Newcastle Nuffield Hospital (☎ 0191 281 6131)

MENDELSOHN, Baron (Life Peer UK 2013), of Finchley in the London Borough of Barnet; Jonathan Neil Mendelsohn; *b* 30 December 1966; *m* Nicola Mendelsohn, CBE, *qv*; 4 c; *Career* advsr to Ldr of Oppn 1995–97, co-fndr LLM Communications 1997, dir of gen election resources Lab Pty 2007–10 (asst treas 2009–10), ptnr Oakvale Capital 2011–; co-pres Norwood 2015–; *Style*— The Lord Mendelsohn; ✉ House of Lords, London SW1A 0PW

MENDELSOHN, (Heather) Leigh; da of Maurice Raymond Mendelsohn (d 1989), and Hazel Francis, *née* Keable (d 1997); *b* 20 February 1946; *Educ* Fleetwood GS, Rothwell GS, Pudsey GS; *m* 27 Oct 2010, Paul Anthony Leppard; *Career* trainee journalist R Ackrill Ltd Harrogate 1965–69, dep ed Action Desk Western Mail Cardiff 1969–71, dep Women's Page ed Daily Record Glasgow 1971–73, fashion ed Reveille London 1973–74, contract foreign corr The Sun Amsterdam 1975, freelance TV current affairs researcher 1976, fndr dir Phoenix PR 1978–, fndr RivieraPress (press agency) 2006–, fndr www.cannestouristinformation.co.uk 2009; Parly candidate (Cons) London 2004; European Union of Women (exec int bd & web master); media trainer for emerging democracies; memb NUJ; *Recreations* social history, swimming, the good life; *Style*— Ms Leigh Mendelsohn; ✉ Phoenix Public Relations (mobile 07802 409956, e-mail phoenixpr07@gmail.com); RivieraPress, Golden Park, 14–16 rue Beaulieu, 06400, Cannes, France (☎ 00 33 493 688205, e-mail rivierapress@sfr.fr)

MENDELSOHN, Nicola; CBE (2015); *née* Clyne; da of Barry Clyne, and Celia Clyne; *b* Manchester; *Educ* Univ of Leeds (BA); *m* 7 Aug 1994, Jonathan, *qv* (now Lord Mendelsohn (Life Peer 2014)); 4 c (Gabi, Danny, Sam, Zac); *Career* dir BBH 1992–2004, dep chm Grey London 2004–08, ptnr and exec chm Karmarama 2008–13, vice-pres EMEA Facebook 2013–; pres IPA 2011–13, co-chair Creative Industries Cncl; co-pres Norwood; listed in Management Today's Top 35 Under 35 2005, Ad Age Woman to Watch 2011, Cosmetic Exec Women (CEW) Achiever Award 2011; memb: WACL, Mgmnt Gp of GB, CEW; *Style*— Lady Mendelsohn, CBE; ✉ Twitter @nicolamen

MENDELSON, Prof Maurice Harvey; QC (1992); s of late William Maizel Mendelson, and Anne, *née* Aaronson; *b* 27 August 1943, London; *Educ* St Marylebone GS, New Coll Oxford (MA, DPhil); *m* 26 Dec 1968, Katherine Julia Olga, da of late Bertalan Kertesz, of London; 2 da (Charlotte b 1 Nov 1972, Rachel b 15 Sept 1974); *Career* called to the Bar Lincoln's Inn 1965 (bencher), in practice 1971–; lectr in law KCL 1968–74, fell and tutor in law St John's Coll Oxford 1975–86, prof of int law UCL 1987–2001 (now emeritus); memb: American Law Inst, Exec Cncl Br Branch Int Law Assoc, Bd of Eds Br Year Book of Int Law; memb RIIA; FRGS; Officer Order of Valour of the Republic of Cameroon; *Publications* numerous articles and essays in learned jls; *Recreations* painting, the arts, swimming, tennis (real and lawn); *Clubs* Athenaeum; *Style*— Prof Maurice Mendelson, QC; ✉ Blackstone Chambers, Blackstone House, Temple, London EC4Y 9BW (☎ 020 7583 1770, fax 020 7822 7350, e-mail clerks@blackstonechambers.com)

MENDELSON, Paul Anthony; s of Monty Mendelson (d 1992), of Pinner, Middx, and Yetta, *née* Dresner; *b* 6 April 1951; *Educ* Royal GS Newcastle upon Tyne, Glasgow HS, Harrow Co GS, Emmanuel Coll Cambridge (MA); *m* 31 March 1974, Michal Zipora, da of Armand Safier; 2 da (Zoë Rachel b 17 April 1976, Tammy Polly b 3 Feb 1978); *Career* scriptwriter and prodr; articled Gasquet Metcalf & Walton slrs 1973, trainee copywriter rising to creative gp head Ogilvy & Mather advtg agency 1973–80, dep creative dir Wasey Campbell Ewald 1980–82, creative gp head Dorland Advertising 1982–88, creative dir Capper Granger 1988–90, full-time freelance TV writer 1990–; dir Full Moon Films Ltd; creator and writer: May to December (BBC comedy series, nominated Best Comedy Series BAFTA 1990), So Haunt Me (BBC comedy series), Under the Moon (BBC), My Hero (BBC comedy series), Neighbors From Hell (Dreamworks/Fox/TBS, creator and creative conslt); writer: Pigsty (BBC Children's TV), Losing It (ITV, nominated Televisual Best Writing Award 2007), Snap (BBC Radio 4), Dover (BBC Radio 4), A Meeting in Seville/I Am I Said/Fireworks at the Villa Lucia (BBC Radio 4), CS Forester's London Noir trilogy (BBC Radio 4), The African Queen (BBC Radio 4), Lost Souls/A Meeting in Seville/Losing Arthur/The McKenzie Friend/GSOH/Zenda (films in devpt); winner advtg awards incl: Cinema, TV and Best Radio Commercial and Best Radio Campaign (for Don't Drink and Drive), D&AD, Best Media Commercial Clio; judge on various panels incl London Int Advtg Awards, British Comedy Awards; memb Writers' Guild 1991; *Books* What IF? (novel); *Recreations* walking, theatre, collecting obscure Broadway musical recordings, Samaritans, carpentry, family; *Clubs* Groucho; *Style*— Paul A Mendelson, Esq; ✉ c/o Christine Glover, Casarotto Ramsay Ltd, Waverley House, 7–12 Noel Street, London W1F 8GQ (☎ 020 7287 4450, e-mail christine@casarotto.co.uk)

MENDES, Nuno; s of João Manuel Vidigal Durão Mendes (d 2011), and Odilia Da Silva Cameira, of the Algave, Portugal; *b* 8 April 1973; *Educ* California Culinary Acad; *Partner* Clarise Faria; 1 da (Orla Faria Mendes b 2011), 2 s (Noah Faria Mendes, Finn Faria Mendes b 2013 (twins)); *Career* chef owner: Bacchus, The Loft Project, Viajante (Michelin star 2011–), The Corner Room; chef dir: Chiltern Firehouse, Taberna do Mercado; creator: The Long Table, Craft by Nuno Mendes; *Recreations* cinema, motorsport, music, reading, tennis, travel, surfing, go-karting, table tennis, food writing; *Style*— Mr Nuno Mendes; ✉ e-mail nunoviajante@hotmail.com, website www.nunomendesholdings.co.uk, Twitter @nunoviajante

MENDES, Samuel Alexander (Sam); CBE (2000); s of James Peter Mendes, of London, and Valerie Hélène, *née* Barnett; *b* 1 August 1965; *Educ* Magdalen Coll Sch Oxford, Peterhouse Cambridge (scholar, BA); *m* May 2003 (m dis), Kate Winslet, *qv*; 1 s (Joe b 2003); *Career* theatre and film director; asst dir Chichester Festival Theatre 1987–88, artistic dir Chichester Festival Theatre Tent 1988, artistic dir Minerva Studio Theatre Chichester 1989 (prodns incl Summerfolk and Love's Labour's Lost), freelance dir, artistic dir Donmar Warehouse until 2002, co-fndr (with Caro Newling, and Pippa Harris, *qqv*) Neal Street Prodns 2003–; *Theatre* prodns incl: London Assurance (Chichester and Haymarket) 1989, The Cherry Orchard (Aldwych) 1989, Troilus and Cressida (RSC, Swan) 1990, Kean (Old Vic and Toronto) 1990, Plough and the Stars (Young Vic) 1991, The Alchemist (RSC, Swan) 1991, The Sea (RNT) 1991, The Rise and Fall of Little Voice (RNT and Aldwych, Olivier and Evening Standard Awards) 1992, Richard III (RSC regnl and world tour) 1992, Assassins (Donmar Warehouse, Critics' Circle Award) 1992, Translations (Donmar Warehouse) 1993, The Tempest (RSC, RST) 1993, Cabaret (Donmar Warehouse and Carlton TV, Gold Camera Award US Int Film Festival) 1993, The Birthday Party (RNT) 1994, Glengarry Glen Ross (Donmar Warehouse) 1994, Oliver! (London Palladium) 1994, The Glass Menagerie (Donmar Warehouse and Comedy, Critic's Circle Award) 1995, Company (Donmar and Albery, Critics' Circle Award) 1996, Habeas Corpus (Donmar Warehouse) 1996, Othello (RNT, Salzburg Int tour) 1997, The Fix (Donmar Warehouse) 1997, The Front Page (Donmar Warehouse) 1997, Cabaret (Roundabout Theatre NY, Tony Award for Best Revival of a Musical) 1998, The Blue Room (Donmar Warehouse) 1998, To The Greenfields Beyond (Domar Warehouse) 2000, Uncle Vanya (Donmar Warehouse) 2002, Twelfth Night (Donmar Warehouse) 2002, Gypsy (Broadway NY) 2003, Richard III (Old Vic) 2011; *Films* American Beauty 1999, Road to Perdition 2002, Jarhead 2005, Revolutionary Road 2008, Away We Go 2009, Skyfall 2012; *Awards* Hamburg Shakespeare Scholarship 1989, London Critics' Circle Most Promising Newcomer Award 1989, Olivier Award for Best Director (Company and The Glass Menagerie) 1996, Acad Award for Best Director and Best Film (American Beauty) 1999, numerous other awards for American Beauty, Hamburg Shakespeare Prize 2000, Olivier Awards for Best Revival and for Best Director (Uncle Vanya and Twelfth Night) 2003, Outstanding Br Film BAFTA (Skyfall) 2013, Best Film South Bank Award (Skyfall) 2013; *Recreations* watching and playing cricket; *Style*— Sam Mendes, CBE; ✉ c/o Neal Street Productions, 26–28 Neal Street, London WC2H 9QQ

MENDOZA, June Yvonne; AO (1989), OBE (2004); da of John Morton, and Dot, *née* Mendoza; *Educ* Lauriston Girls' Sch Melbourne, St Martin's Sch of Art; *m* Keith Mackrell; 1 s (Ashley), 3 da (Elliet, Kim, Lee); *Career* portrait painter; work for governments, regiments, industry, med, academia, theatres, literature and sport; exhibited in public and private int collections; portraits incl: HM The Queen, HRH The Prince of Wales, HRH The Princess of Wales, HM Queen Elizabeth The Queen Mother, The Princess Royal, Margaret Thatcher, John Major, Archbishops of Canterbury (Donald Coggan, Robert Runcie and George Carey), Corazón Aquino (former pres of the Philippines), Vigdis Finnbogadottir (former pres of Iceland), Ratu Sir Kamisese Mara (PM of Fiji), Sir John Gorton (former PM of Australia), Lee Kuan Yew (sr min Singapore); gp portraits incl: House of Commons in Session, Cncl Royal Coll of Surgns, Australian House of Representatives, Barber Surgeons (120 portraits); continuing series of musicians incl: Yehudi Menuhin, Georg Solti, Joan Sutherland, Charles Mackerras, Colin Davis, Sir Mark Elder; memb: Royal Soc of Portrait Painters, Royal Inst of Oil Painters; hon memb Soc of Women Artists; Hon DLitt: Univ of Bath 1986, Loughborough Univ 1994; Hon Dr

Open Univ 2003; Freeman City of London 1998; *Style*— Miss June Mendoza, AO, OBE; ✉ 34 Inner Park Road, London SW19 6DD (e-mail june@junemendoza.co.uk, website www.junemendoza.co.uk)

MENDOZA, Neil; *Educ* Haberdashers' Aske's, Oriel Coll Oxford; *Career* co-fndr (with William Sieghart) Forward Publishing 1986, chief exec Hammer Films 2000–07, currently chm Victoria Private Investment Office, dir Meira GTx 2015–; chm: Landmark Tst 2011–, Prince's Fndn for Children and the Arts 2013–; tstee: Soho Theatre 2007– (currently vice-chm), Shakespeare Schs Festival 2010–15; judge Laurence Olivier Awards 2010–11; non-exec dir Dept of Culture, Media and Sport 2016–, cmmr Historic England 2016–; *Clubs* Garrick, Portland, Army and Navy; *Style*— Neil Mendoza, Esq; ✉ 50 Albemarle Street, London W1S 4BD

MENEZES, Ivan; *Career* sr mgmnt positions Guinness; Diageo plc: chief operating offr N America then pres N America, chm Asia Pacific and chm Latin America and Caribbean, chief operating offr 2012–13, chief exec 2013–; memb Cncl Scotch Whisky Assoc; non-exec dir Coach Inc, memb Global Advsy Bd Kellogg Sch of Mgmnt Northwestern Univ; *Recreations* ;; *Style*— Ivan Menezes, Esq; ✉ Diageo plc, Lakeside Drive, Park Royal, London NW10 7HQ

MENKES-SPANIER, Suzy Peta; OBE (2005); da of Edouard Gerald Lionel Menkes (d 1943), and Betty Curtis, *née* Lightfoot (d 2014); *b* 24 December 1943; *Educ* Brighton & Hove HS, Newnham Coll Cambridge (MA); *m* 23 June 1969, David Graham Spanier (d 2000), s of Eric John Spanier (d 1973); 3 s (Gideon Eric Lionel b 26 Sept 1971, Joshua Edward Graham b 11 Nov 1973, Samson Curtis b 3 Oct 1978), 1 da (Jessica Leonie Salome b 24 May 1977 d 1977); *Career* jr reporter The Times London 1966–69, fashion ed The Evening Standard 1969–77, women's ed Daily Express 1977–80; fashion ed: The Times 1980–87, The Independent 1987–88, International Herald Tribune 1988–2014; ed International Vogue Condé Nast 2014–; Special Recognition Award Br Fashion Cncl 2013; Freeman of Milan 1987, Freeman of Florence 2015, Hon Citizenship of Seoul S Korea 2016; Hon FRCA 1999; Chevalier de la Legion d'Honneur (France) 2005, Fiorina d'Oro Florence 2015; *Books* The Knitwear Revolution (1983), The Royal Jewels (1985), The Windsor Style (1987), Queen and Country (1992); *Recreations* family life; *Style*— Mrs Suzy Menkes-Spanier, OBE; ✉ Condé Nast International, 25 Maddox Street, London W1S 2QN (e-mail suzy.menkes@condenastint.com, websites www.vogue.co.uk/person/suzy-menkes and www.suzymenkesvogue.com)

MENON, Prof David Krishna; s of Parakat Govindan Kutti Menon (d 1982), of India, and Violet Rebecca Menon (d 1999); *b* 21 August 1956; *Educ* Univ of Madras India (MB BS, MD), Univ of London (PhD); *m* 23 July 1988, Wendy, *née* Rutter; 1 s (Stephen Gareth b 11 April 1994); *Career* residency (internal med) Jawaharlal Inst Pondicherry India 1978–83, registrar (med) Professorial Med Unit Leeds Gen Infirmary 1984–86, SHO (anaesthetics) Leeds Gen Infirmary 1986–87, registrar (anaesthetics) Royal Free Hosp London 1987–88, MRC research fell Robert Steiner MR Unit Hammersmith Hosp London 1989–91; Univ of Cambridge: clinical lectr 1992–93, lectr in anaesthesia 1993–2000, princ investigator Cambridge Brain Repair Centre 1995–, princ investigator and co-chair Acute Brain Injury Prog Wolfson Brain Imaging Centre 1997–, Clinical Sch Faculty Bd 2000–, prof of anaesthesia 2001–, professorial fell in med scis Queens' Coll 2001–; Addenbrooke's Hosp Cambridge: lead conslt and dir of neurocritical care 1993–2001, first dir of neurointensive care 1997–2001, hon conslt Neurosciences Critical Care Unit and hon conslt anaesthetist 1993–; Br Oxygen prof Royal Coll of Anaesthetists 2006–; visiting prof: Univ of Washington St Louis 1998, Stroke Prog Univ of Alberta 2000, Dept of Neurosurgery Univ of Southampton 2002, Critical Care Unit Univ of Alberta at Calgary 2003; Charles Sherrington prof Royal Coll of Anaesthetists 1999–2000; co-chair European Brain Injury Consortium 2007–, sr investigator Nat Inst for Health Research UK 2009–; memb: Regnl Intensive Care Med Training Ctee 1998–, Strategic Regnl Intensive Care Review Gp 1999–, Regnl Anaesthetic Training Ctee, MRC Medical Advsy Bd 2000–, Nat Cncl Intensive Care Soc UK 2003–09 (memb Research Ctee 2002–), Founding Bd Faculty of Intensive Care Medicine 2010–; numerous invited lectrs, media appearances and public speeches; Royal Coll of Anaesthetists: Sir Robert Macintosh Medal 1988, Jubilee Fellowship Award 1998; Lewin lectr Univ of Cambridge 2000, Datex-Ohmeda lectr Assoc of Anaesthetists 2003, Laerdal Award Scandinavian Soc of Anaesthesia and Intensive Care 2013, Clover lecture Royal Coll of Anaesthetists 2014; FRCA 1988, FMedSci 1998, FRCP 1999 (MRCP 1984), fell Faculty of Intensive Care Medicine (FFICM) 2013; *Publications* author of textbooks, chapters and monographs, and numerous articles in jls; *Recreations* reading, basketball, cooking, lego; *Clubs* RSM; *Style*— Prof David Menon; ✉ Division of Anaesthesia, University of Cambridge, Box 93, Addenbrooke's Hospital, Cambridge CB2 2QQ (☏ 01223 217889, fax 01223 217887)

MENSCH, Louise Daphne; *née* Bagshawe; *b* 28 June 1971, London; *Educ* Woldingham Sch, ChCh Oxford; *m* 1, 2000 (m dis 2009), Anthony LoCicero; 3 c; m 2, 2011, Peter Mensch; *Career* author and politician; MP (Cons) Corby 2010–12; *Books* Career Girls (1995), The Movie (1996), Tall Poppies (1997), Venus Envy (1998), A Kept Woman (2000), When She Was Bad... (2001), The Devil You Know (2003), Monday's Child (2004), Tuesday's Child (2005), Sparkles (2006), Glamour (2007), Glitz (2008), Passion (2009), Desire (2010), Destiny (2011); *Style*— Mrs Peter Mensch; ✉ website www.louisemensch.com

MENTETH; *see:* Stuart-Menteth

MENZIES, Rt Hon Lord Duncan Adam Young; PC (2012); s of Douglas William Livingstone Menzies (d 1977), of Edinburgh, and Margaret Adam, *née* Young (d 2000); *b* 28 August 1953; *Educ* The Edinburgh Acad, Cargilfield Sch, Glenalmond Coll (scholar), Wadham Coll Oxford (scholar, MA), Univ of Edinburgh (LLB); *m* 31 March 1979, Hilary Elizabeth McLauchlan, da of Col T R R Weston, OBE, TD (d 2010); 2 s (Jamie Douglas Adam b 1985, Ruaraidh Duncan McLauchlan b 1988); *Career* admitted Faculty of Advocates 1978, standing jr counsel to Admiralty Bd 1984–91, QC (Scot) 1991, memb Faculty ADR Panel 1991–2000, temp sheriff 1996–97, advocate depute 1998–2000, home advocate depute 1998–2000, senator Coll of Justice (Lord of Session) 2001–; memb: Faculty Cncl 1998–2000, Judicial Cncl for Scotland 2007–12; chm Scottish Planning Local Govt and Environmental Bar Gp 1997–2001; Parly candidate (Cons): Midlothian 1983, Edinburgh Leith 1987; chm Ptarmigan Wines 1979–89; hon bencher Inner Temple 2013; Maître de la Commanderie de Bordeaux à Edimbourg; *Recreations* shooting, golf, wine, gardening; *Clubs* New (Edinburgh), Hon Co of Edinburgh Golfers, Saintsbury; *Style*— The Rt Hon Lord Menzies; ✉ Supreme Courts, Edinburgh EH1 1RQ

MENZIES, James; *Educ* Univ of London (BSc), Univ of Newcastle upon Tyne (MSc); *Career* fndr and ceo Salamander Energy plc 2005– (floated on the LSE 2006); *Style*— James Menzies, Esq; ✉ Salamander Energy plc, 4th Floor, 25 Great Pulteney Street, London W1F 9LT

MENZIES, Mark Andrew; MP; s of late Andrew Menzies, and Mary Isobel Menzies; *b* 18 May 1971, Irvine, Ayrshire; *Educ* Keil Sch Dumbarton, Univ of Glasgow (MA); *Career* grad trainee Marks & Spencer 1994–95, mktg mangr Asda Stores Ltd 1995–2007, head of local mktg W M Morrisons plc 2008–10; MP (Cons) Fylde 2010–, PPS to Min for Energy then Min for Int Devpt 2010–14; *Recreations* skiing, walking, cinema; *Style*— Mark Menzies, Esq, MP; ✉ House of Commons, London SW1A 0AA (☏ 020 7219 7073, fax 020 7219 2235, e-mail mark.menzies.mp@parliament.uk)

MENZIES, (Rowan) Robin; s of Capt George Cunningham Paton Menzies, DSO (d 1968), and Constance Rosabel, *née* Grice Hutchinson (d 2004); *b* 30 October 1952; *Educ* Stowe, Trinity Coll Cambridge (BA); *Career* ptnr Baillie Gifford and Co (investment mangrs); *Style*— Robin Menzies, Esq; ✉ Baillie Gifford and Co, 1 Greenside Row, Edinburgh EH1 3AN (☏ 0131 275 2000, fax 0131 275 3999, e-mail robin.menzies@bailliegifford.com)

MEON, Archdeacon of; *see:* Hancock, Ven Peter

MERCER, Prof Ian Dews; CBE (1996); s of Eric Baden Royds Mercer (d 1955), of Herongate, Wombourn, Staffs, and Nellie Irene, *née* Dews (d 1999); *b* 25 January 1933, Wolverhampton; *Educ* King Edward's Sch Stourbridge, Univ of Birmingham (BA); *m* 1, 7 July 1957 (m dis 1976), Valerie Jean, da of late Eric Hodgson; 4 s (Jonathan b 1958, Benjamin b 1961 d 1997, Thomas b 1963, Daniel b 1966); m 2, 10 Dec 1976, Pamela Margaret Gillies, da of late Maj Thomas Waldy Clarkson; *Career* Nat Serv Sub-Lt RNR 1954–56; warden Slapton Ley Field Centre Kingsbridge 1959–68, lectr St Luke's Coll Exeter 1968–70, co conservation offr Devon CC 1970–73, chief offr Dartmoor Nat Park Authy 1973–90, chief exec Countryside Cncl for Wales 1990–96; sec gen Assoc of Nat Park Authorities 1996–2001; prof of rural conservation practice Univ of Wales 1991–; pres: Devonshire Assoc 1983, Assoc of Countryside Rangers 1986–93, Field Studies Cncl 1986–2014, Devon Wildlife Tst 1986–; vice-pres Cncl for Nat Parks 2001–; chm: Regnl Advsy Ctee W England Forestry Cmmn 1987–90, Devon FMD Inquiry 2001, SW Forest Partnership 2002–08, Dartmoor Commoners Cncl 2004–13, chm Devon Rural Network 2005–08, SW Uplands Fedn 2006–, Public Inquiry into MSC Napoli Grounding 2008, Seale-Hayne Educnl Tst 2011–14; memb: England Ctee Nature Conservancy Cncl 1977–87, Gen Advsy Ctee BBC 1981–86, Inland Waterways Amenity Advsy Cncl 1995–2001, Devon and Cornwall Ctee Nat Tst 1996–2005, Rural Affrs Advsy Ctee BBC 1998–2002, Br Ecological Soc; hon fell and vice-pres Landscape Inst 1997–; govr: Univ of Plymouth 1996–2005, Stover Sch 1996–2005 (chm of govrs 2003–04); Hon LLD Univ of Exeter 1994, Hon DSc Univ of Plymouth 1995; memb Order of National Parks 2015; FRAgS 1996; *Books* Nature Guide to South West England, Conservation in Practice (contrib, 1973), Environmental Education (contrib, 1974), National Parks in Britain (contrib, 1987), Dartmoor (111 in New Naturalist series, 2009); *Recreations* golf, painting, birdwatching, watching sons play cricket; *Clubs* Symonds; *Style*— Prof Ian Mercer, CBE; ✉ Ponsford House, Moretonhampstead, Newton Abbot, Devon TQ13 8NL (☏ 01647 440612, e-mail ian.mercer@freeuk.com)

MERCER, Patrick; OBE (1997, MBE 1992), MP; s of Rt Rev Eric Arthur John Mercer, Bishop of Exeter, and Rosemary, *née* Denby; *b* 26 June 1956; *Educ* King's Sch Chester, Exeter Coll Oxford (MA, Boxing blue), RMA Sandhurst; *m* 1990, Catriona Jane, *née* Beaton; 1 s; *Career* Army Serv: trg team in Uganda post civil war 1986, fndr memb Province Exec Ctee NI 1992, instr Army Staff Coll Camberley 1994–95, CO 1 Bn Worcs and Sherwood Foresters Bosnia and Canada 1995–97, head of strategy Army Trg and Recruiting Agency 1997–98, nine tours NI (mentioned despatches 1983, gallantry commendation 1990); journalist Today (BBC Radio 4) 1999, freelance journalist 2000–01; memb KCL Mission to East Timor 2000; MP (Cons) Newark 2001–, PPS to Hon Bernard Jenkin, MP, *qv*, as shadow sec of state for Defence 2003, shadow min for Homeland Security 2003–07; memb Defence Select Ctee 2001–03; *Recreations* history, watercolour painting, country sports, writing; *Style*— Patrick Mercer, Esq, OBE, MP; ✉ House of Commons, London SW1A 0AA (☏ 020 7219 8225)

MERCER, (Andrew) Philip; s of Maj Laurence Walter Mercer (d 1951), of Huntingtower, Perthshire, and Josephine Madeline, *née* Moran (d 2001); *b* 24 August 1937, Cheltenham; *Educ* Stonyhurst, Univ of Edinburgh (BArch); *m* 2 Oct 1965, Alexandra Margaret, da of Capt John Cyril Dawson, of Sussex (d 2001); 2 da (Claudia Alexandra, Portia Andrea (twins) b 1977); *Career* architect; princ of architectural practice 1969– (specialising in planning and restoration in Central London and historic bldgs in Scotland); Knight of Honour and Devotion SMOM 2008; ARIBA 1970, RIAS 2013; *Recreations* music, travelling, gardening; *Clubs* New (Edinburgh), RIAS; *Style*— Philip Mercer, Esq; ✉ Studio 1, 79 Bedford Gardens, London W8 7EG (e-mail philip@mercer.uk.com); Via Dei Polacchi 42, Int 1, 00186 Rome, Italy; Hillslap Tower, Melrose TD1 2PA

MERCER, (Christine) Ruth; da of George Mercer, and Joan, *née* Stopforth; *Educ* Penwortham Girls' GS, Bedford Coll London (BA), Univ of Oxford (PGCE, Dip); *m* 1988, Colin Horsley; 2 c; *Career* teacher; successively head of years 8 and 9, head of years 10 and 11 and head of history and politics Notting Hill and Ealing HS 1986–98, dep headmistress Godolphin & Latymer Sch 1998–2002, headmistress Northwood Coll 2002–08, head mistress Godolphin & Latymer Sch 2009–; *Recreations* fell walking, reading, genealogy; *Style*— Mrs Ruth Mercer; ✉ The Godolphin and Latymer School, Iffley Road, Hammersmith, London W6 0PG (☏ 020 8741 1936)

MERCER, Dr Wendy Sara; da of Charles William Mercer (d 1976), of Castletown, Isle of Man, and Thelma Margaret Hawkins (formerly Mercer), *née* Higgins; *b* 23 December 1956; *Educ* Bedford Coll London (BA, MA), Univ of London (PhD), Sch of Educn Univ of Durham (PGCE), Heidelberg Univ; *Career* French teacher Greycoat Sch Westminster 1979–80, lectr Université de Paris X (Nanterre) 1981–83, visiting lectr in French Bedford Coll London 1983–84, visiting lectr Royal Holloway and Bedford New Coll London 1984–85 and 1988–91, pt/t visiting lectr in French Buckingham Univ 1984–85, lectr École Normale Supérieure Fontenay-aux-Roses 1985–87, pt/t chargée de cours Ecole Nationale de Statistique et d'Administration Economique 1985–87, pt/t res asst UCL 1987–88, British Acad Postdoctoral Res Fellowship RHBNC and UCL 1988–91, lectr Dept of French UCL 1991–; Medaille d'honneur Ville de Pontarlier 1992; *Books* Xavier Marmier (1808–1892) – Un Fils de Pontarlier Célèbre dans le Monde, Jane Osborn – Drama by Léonie d'Aunet (ed), Voyage d'une Femme au Spitzberg (ed, by Léonie D'Aunet); *Style*— Dr Wendy Mercer

MERCER NAIRNE, Joe; s of Robert Mercer Nairne, and Jane, *née* Gordon; *b* 20 June 1980, London; *Educ* Eton, St Hugh's Coll Oxford, Leith's Sch of Food and Wine; *m* 23 Sept 2006, Melissa, *née* Wakeley; 2 s (Fergus b 26 Sept 2009, Angus b 8 Aug 2013), 1 da (Florence b 17 April 2011); *Career* formerly: Carluccio's, The Savoy Grill, Chez Bruce, Rockpool Sydney; currently chef-prop Medlar Restaurant (Michelin star 2013–); memb Slow Food Orgn; *Style*— Joe Mercer Nairne, Esq; ✉ Medlar Restaurant, 438 Kings Road, Chelsea, London SW10 0LJ (☏ 020 7349 1900, e-mail joe@medlarrestaurant.co.uk, Twitter @joemnmedlar)

MERCER-NAIRNE, Lord Robert Harold; s of George John Charles Mercer-Nairne, 8 Marquess of Lansdowne, PC, JP (d 1999) and Barbara Dempsey Chase (d 1965) of Santa Barbara, CA; *b* 1947; *Educ* Gordonstoun, Univ of Kent at Canterbury (BA), Univ of Washington Grad Sch of Business Admin (MBA), PhD; *m* 1972, Jane Elizabeth, da of Lt-Col Lord Douglas Gordon; 2 s, 1 da; *Career* writer; md Blackman Martin Gp 1972–82, self-employed 1982–83, Univ of Washington 1983–89, managing tstee Meikleour Tst 1989–99; memb River Tay Flood Steering Gp 1990–94; elder Church of Scotland 1990–98; hon lectr Univ of Dundee 1992–97; Liveryman Worshipful Co of Fishmongers; FCMI; *Publications* In Malta (poetry, 2002), On Fire (poetry, 2004), The Letter Writer (fiction, 2004), Like No Other (fiction, 2005), Warlord (fiction, 2007), Notes: On the Dynamics of Man (non-fiction, 2010), The Storytellers: Metamorphosis (fiction, 2015); *Style*— Lord Robert Mercer-Nairne; ✉ Kinclaven Church House, Perth PH1 4QW

MERCHANT, Stephen James; *b* 24 November 1974, Bristol; *Educ* Univ of Warwick; *Career* comedy writer, actor and stand-up comedian; *Television* writer: Golden Years (Channel 4), Meet Ricky Gervais (Channel 4), The Office (BBC 2) 2001–03 (also co-dir, Best Situation Comedy BAFTA 2002, 2003 and 2004, Best TV Comedy Golden Globe 2004), Extras (BBC 2) 2005–07 (also co-dir and actor, Best TV Comedy Actor Br Comedy Award 2006, Best TV Comedy Golden Globe 2008), The Ricky Gervais Show 2010–, Life's Too

Short 2011 (also exec prodr, co-dir and actor); exec prodr: The Office (US version) 2005–, An Idiot Abroad 2010; *Radio* host Stephen Merchant Show (BBC 6 Music) 2007–09; *Film* actor: Cemetery Junction 2010 (also co-writer, co-dir and exec prodr), Tooth Fairy 2010, Hall Pass 2011, Gnomeo and Juliet 2011; *Style—* Mr Stephen Merchant; ✉ c/o United Agents Ltd, 12–26 Lexington Street, London W1F 0LE

MEREDITH, Christopher; s of Roger Meredith, of Northwich, Cheshire, and Gill, *née* Riley; *b* 29 June 1974, Warrington; *m* 24 June 2000, Linsey, *née* Stockdale; *Career* chef; commis chef The Grosvenor Chester 1993–94, first commis chef Paul Heathcotes 1994–95 (2 Michelin Stars, 4 AA Rosettes), chef de partie Arkle Restaurant The Grosvenor Chester 1995–96 (1 Michelin Star, 3 AA Rosettes); sr chef de partie: The Dorchester 1996–98, Hostellerie de Levernois Beaune France 1998, Michael's Nook Grasmere 1998 (1 Michelin Star, 4 AA Rosettes); sous chef: Pool Court and Brasserie 44 Leeds 1998–99 (1 Michelin Star), The Great Eastern Hotel 1999–2000, The Aubergine 2000–02 (1 Michelin Star, 4 AA Rosettes); head chef The Samling 2003–04 (1 Michelin Star, 3 AA Rosettes); exec chef: Gilpin Lodge 2004–08 (1 Michelin Star, 3 AA Rosettes), The Punch Bowl Inn Crosthwaite 2008–11 (Michelin Pub of the Year 2009), Coworth Park Ascot 2011–12; memb Acad of Culinary Arts, memb Lancs Educn Tst; Flavours of the North East (2004), Chefs of Distinction (2004); *Recreations* motorbike racing, fishing; *Style—* Christopher Meredith, Esq

MEREDITH, David Wynn; s of Rev John Ellis Meredith (d 1981), of Aberystwyth, Dyfed, and Elizabeth, *née* Jones; *b* 24 May 1941; *Educ* Ardwyn GS Aberystwyth, Normal Coll Bangor Gwynedd (Univ of Wales Teaching Dip); *m* 23 March 1968, Luned, da of Prof Emeritus Alun Llywelyn Williams, and Alis Llywelyn Williams; 3 c (Owain Llywelyn b 11 Feb 1969, Elin Wynn b 6 Jan 1971, Gruffydd Seimon Morgan b 7 Feb 1974); *Career* specialist teacher Welsh Cardiff Educn Authy 1961–65, mid-Wales mangr then advtg and sales exec Wales Tourist Bd 1965–68, head of press and PR HTV Cymru/Wales 1968–89, co-fndr dir Strata Matrix (PR co) 1989–90, estab David Meredith PR 1990–95, head of press and PR S4C Television 1995–2001; reg contrib to radio and TV in Wales; presenter in Eng and Welsh HTV: Pwy Fase'n Meddwl (quiz series), Gair o Wlad y Sais (lit prog), Arlunwyr (art series); memb: Royal Welsh Show Publicity Ctee 1969–2015, Mktg Bd Nat Eisteddfod of Wales 1990–2001, Cncl Nat Library of Wales 2002–07 (memb Advsy Ctee), Presbyterian Church of Wales Publicity Ctee, Welsh Academi; centenary offr Royal Welsh Agric Soc 2002–04; tstee Sir Kyffin Williams Tst 2009; RTS Award for Best Contrib to Television 1997–98, White Robe Gorsedd of Bards 2009; fell PR Soc of Wales 1984 (former chm), first BAFTA Cymru/Wales fell 2001; *Books* Michelangelo (Life and Work), Rembrandt (Life and Work), Congrinero (for children), Anturiaethau Fôn Fawr a Bili Bach (with Owain Meredith, with design and visuals by SEI), Pwy Fase'n Meddwl (autobiography, 2002), Kyffin in Venice: An Illustrated Conversation (with artist Sir Kyffin Williams RA, 2006), Bro a Bywyd – Kyffin Williams – His Life, His Land (2008), Obsessed – The Biography of Kyffin Williams (with John Smith, 2012); *Recreations* pottering on the farm, visiting art galleries and growing trees; *Style—* David Meredith, Esq; ✉ Ty'n Fedw, Cynllwyd, Llanuwchllyn, Bala, Gwynedd LL23 7DF (☎ 01678 540255, fax 01678 540530)

MEREDITH HARDY, Simon Patrick; s of Patrick Talbot Meredith Hardy (d 1986), of Bembridge, IOW, and Anne, *née* Johnson (d 1994); *b* 31 October 1943; *Educ* Eton; *m* 26 July 1969, Hon Joanna Mary, da of Baron Porritt, GCMG, GCVO, CBE (Life Peer); 2 s (Henry Patrick b 1975, George Peter b 1978); *Career* cmmnd LG 1964, ADC to HE The Govr-Gen of NZ 1967–68, left army 1969; stockbroker; formerly ptnr Wood Mackenzie & Co, dir NatWest Securities Ltd, dir Henderson Far East Income Tst plc, chm Framlington Income and Capital Trust plc; *Recreations* skiing, sailing; *Clubs* Household Division Yacht; *Style—* Simon P Meredith Hardy, Esq; ✉ 23 Baronsmead Road, London SW13 9RR (☎ 020 8748 1476)

MEREDITH-WINDLE, Glynis Margaret; da of Donald Charles Frank Windle (d 1978), of London, and Gwynneth Maud, *née* Meredith (d 1988); *b* 14 August 1951, Highgate, London; *Educ* Parliament Hill Sch for Girls (Hockey blue, hockey capt), Hendon Gp of Hosps Sch of Nursing (SRN), Central Sch of Counselling and Therapy (Cert Counselling); *Career* qualified SRN 1973, med ward sister (then yst in UK) 1974, sister various med and coronary care units NHS hosps 1974–80; Llewelyn-Davies Weeks: joined as nurse planning conslt 1980, pioneer of patient-focused healthcare in UK (in association with Booz Allen and Hamilton) 1989, assoc LDW 1992–95; independent conslt to Dept of Health and others as Meredith-Windle Associates Health Planning Consultancy 1996–; corp dir of healthcare planning HLM Architects 1998–2000; involved in devpt of evaluation tool for PFI hospital scheme for Dept of Health in assoc with DEGW 2001–02, launch of Archealth (consultancy for comprehension planning of health facilities) 2006; leading global health planner; fundraiser Sir Robert Mond Meml Tst for research into mental illness; memb Ed Advsy Bd Dept of Health NHS Estates 1999–; memb E & N Herts Acute Tst Cmmn for Patient and Public Involvement in Health (CPPIH); ARCN 1970, MIHSM 1989, MInstD 1996, sr assoc RSM 2014; *Publications* Working with Management Consultants (jtly, The Patient Focused Hopsital – facility and cost implications, Ward Planning – Kings Cross Station, Lighting the Way – Florence Nightingale the Visionary Planner; contrib to numerous professional jls; *Recreations* golf, cycling, badminton, theatre, opera, Cajun dancing; *Clubs* Champneys, Aldwickbury Golf; *Style—* Glynis Meredith-Windle; ✉ Archealth, 8 Dell Close, Harpenden, Hertfordshire AL5 4HP (☎ 01582 621539, e-mail glynis@archealth.com, website www.archealth.com)

MERRICKS, Walter Hugh; CBE (2007); s of Dick Merricks (d 1999), of Icklesham, E Sussex, and Phoebe, *née* Woffenden (d 1985); *b* 4 June 1945; *Educ* Bradfield Coll, Trinity Coll Oxford (MA); *m* 27 Nov 1982, Olivia, da of late Dr Elio Montuschi; 1 s (William b 1983), 1 da (Susannah b 1986), 1 step s (Daniel b 1971); *Career* admitted slr 1970, Hubbard travelling scholar 1971, dir Camden Community Law Centre 1972–76, lectr in law Brunel Univ 1976–81, legal affrs writer New Law J1 1982–85, dir of professional and legal policy Law Soc 1995–96 (head of communications 1985–95), Insurance Ombudsman 1996–99, chief ombudsman Financial Ombudsman Service 1999–; memb: Royal Cmmn on Criminal Procedure 1978–81, Ctee on Fraud Trials 1984–86, Human Fertilisation and Embryology Authy 2002–08; chm British and Irish Ombudsman Assoc 2001–02 (memb Exec Ctee 1997–99); pres British Insurance Law Assoc 2007–09 (vice-pres 2004–07), memb Law Soc 1970; The Achievement Award British Insurance Awards 2004; memb Worshipful Co of Insurers 1999; Hon Dr of Laws London Guildhall Univ 2001; Hon FCII 2005; *Style—* Walter Merricks, Esq, CBE; ✉ Financial Ombudsman Service, South Quay Plaza, 183 Marsh Wall, London E14 9SR (☎ 020 7964 1000, fax 020 7964 1001, e-mail enquiries@financial-ombudsman.org.uk)

MERRILL, Paul; s of Rupert Merrill, of Seale, Surrey, and Pauline Merrill; *b* 6 February 1968, Farnham, Surrey; *Educ* Woolmer Hill Secdy Sch, Godalming Coll, Loughborough Univ (BSc), Highbury Coll Cosham (NCTJ); *m* 4 July 2000, Ruth; 2 da (Eliza, Lois (twins) b and d 7 Dec 1997), 3 s (Joss b 12 May 1999, Louis b 25 Sept 2001, Barnaby b 27 Feb 2006); *Career* with Farnham Herald 1990–93; freelance journalist: The Sun, The Guardian, The Times; ed Chat 2001–03 (features ed 1997–98, asst ed 1998–2001), ed Zoo 2003–05, ed Zoo Aust 2005–11 (ed in chief 2007–11), ed in chief Ralph 2007–; memb: BSME, PPA; *Style—* Paul Merrill, Esq

MERRIMAN, Huw William; MP; s of Richard Merriman (d 2002), and Ann, *née* Offer; *b* 13 July 1973, Brackley, Northants; *Educ* Buckingham County Secdy Sch, Aylesbury Coll, Durham Univ (BA), Inns of Court Sch of Law; *m* 2001, Victoria, *née* Powdrill; 3 da (Amelia, Bethan, Holly); *Career* called to the Bar 1996; md Lehman Bros in Administration 2008; MP (Cons) Bexhill & Battle 2015–; *Recreations* gardening, cooking, beekeeping; *Clubs* Farmers, Bexhill Conservative; *Style—* Huw Merriman, Esq, MP; ✉ House of Commons, London SW1A 0AA (☎ 020 7219 8712, e-mail huw.merriman.mp@parliament.uk, website www.huwmerriman.org.uk, Twitter @HuwMerriman)

MERRIMAN, Dr Nicholas (Nick); s of Michael Merriman, of Sutton Coldfield, and Pamela, *née* Ford; *b* 6 June 1960, Sutton Coldfield; *Educ* King Edward's Sch Birmingham, St John's Coll Cambridge (Anglia Prize, BA), Univ of Leicester (Cert), Univ of Cambridge (PhD); *m* 1, 22 Oct 1993 (m dis 2008), Caroline Beattie; 2 s (Robert b 22 Feb 1997, Lucas b 23 Oct 2000); m 2, 29 May 2010, Maria Balshaw; *Career* hon curator Ely Museum 1984–86; Museum of London: curator of prehistory 1986–90, head Dept of Early London History and Collections 1990–97; Inst of Archaeology UCL: sr lectr in museum studies 1997–98, reader 1998–2005; UCL Museums and Collections: curator 1998–2004, dir 2004–05; dir Manchester Museum Univ of Manchester 2006–; chm Soc of Museum Archaeologists 1994–97, chm Int Cncl of Museums UK 2001–04, pres Cncl Br Archaeology 2005–08, chair Univ Museums Gp 2008–13, convenor Museums Assoc Ethics Ctee 2009–14, chair Collections Tst 2014–, chair Rothesay Pavilion Charity 2014–; fell Clore Leadership Prog 2004–06; AMA 1990, FSA 1994; Beyond the Glass Case: The Past, the Heritage and the Public in Britain (1991), The Peopling of London: Overseas Settlement from Prehistoric Times to Present (1993), Making Early Histories in Museums (1996), Public Archaeology (2004); *Recreations* cycling with my children, running; *Clubs* West Bromwich Albion FC; *Style—* Dr Nick Merriman; ✉ Manchester Museum, Oxford Road, Manchester M13 9PL (☎ 0161 275 2649, e-mail nick.merriman@manchester.ac.uk)

MERRYWEATHER, Col Roger; TD (1974, and clasp 1979), DL (Notts 1989); s of John Fletcher Merryweather (d 1989), and Kathleen Mary, *née* Conlon (d 1992); *b* 18 January 1939, Southwell, Notts; *Educ* Southwell GS; *m* 8 July 1967, Angela Joan, *née* Chatterton; 2 s (Graham Robert b 3 Sept 1969, Richard John b 8 Dec 1972), 1 da (Ruth Joanne b 27 Sept 1971); *Career* cmmnd Nat Serv Royal Corps of Signals 1959, served in BOAR then OC 2 Special Air Formation Signal Sqdn (later 616 Signal Troop Christmas Island); TA: cmmnd 1960, served with 46 (N Midland) Signal Reg then 38 Signal Reg (OC 87 (Nottingham) Signal Sqdn 1978–83); Notts ACF: Dep Cmdt 1984, Cmdt 1985–91, Hon Col 1994–2001; dir Henry Merryweather & Sons Ltd until 2005; memb: Newark DC 1976–83, Southwell Parish/Town Cncl 1976–2007 (chm 1981, 1982, 1985 and 1987); govr: Lowes Wong County Jr Sch Southwell 1977 (chm of govrs 1979–83), Lowes Wong County Infants Sch Southwell 1981 (chm of govrs 1989–2008); tstee Southwell Leisure Centre 1977 (chm 1983); memb: Army Benevolent Fund Ctee for Notts 1969– (chm 1993–2013), E Midlands TAVR/RFCA Notts Ctee 1978 (chm 1996–2005); pres Royal Soc of St George Notts 2003; vice-pres Notts County Royal Br Legion; High Sheriff Notts 2008–09; Liveryman Worshipful Co of Fruiterers 2010; *Style—* Col Roger Merryweather, TD, DL; ✉ Brinkley House, Brinkley, Southwell, Nottinghamshire NG25 0TP

MERSEY, 5 Viscount (UK 1916); Edward John Hallam Bigham; also 14 Lord Nairne (S 1681); s of 4 Viscount Mersey (d 2006); *b* 23 May 1966; *Educ* Eton, Balliol Coll Oxford, Ludwig Maximalian Univ Munich, Trinity Coll of Music London; *m* 2001, Caroline Clare, *née* Schaw Miller; 2 da (Hon Flora Diana Joan, Mistress of Nairne b 17 May 2003, Hon Polly Joanna Jean b 2006); *Heir* (to Viscountcy of Mersey) unc, Hon David Edward Hugh Bigham; (to Lordship of Nairne) da, Hon Flora Bigham, Mistress of Nairne; *Career* music composer; Culebra (CD featuring The Nairne Ballads performed by the Scottish Ensemble) 2014; *Style—* The Viscount Mersey; ✉ e-mail ned@oceanbloem.com, websites www.nedbigham.com, www.bignorpark.co.uk

MERTHYR, Barony of ; *see:* Lewis, Trevor

MESSERVY-WHITING, Maj-Gen Graham G; CBE (2003, MBE 1980); *b* 20 October 1946; *Educ* Lycée Français de Londres, Army Staff Coll, RAF Staff Coll, JSDC, RCDS; *m* 1 Feb 1969, Shirley, *née* Hitchinson; 1 s (Charles b 8 Sept 1972); *Career* cmmnd Intelligence Corps 1967; regtl duty incl: 1 KOSB and service in Germany, Libya, Cyprus and Hong Kong, cmd Intelligence and Security Gp Germany 1986–88; staff duty incl: plans offr N Ireland 1978–80, Secretariat of Chiefs of Staff MOD 1984–86, briefing offr to NATO Supreme Allied Cmd Europe 1988–91; mil advsr to Lord Owen as co-chm Int Conf on Former Yugoslavia 1992–93, promoted Brig 1993, res fell Centre for Def Studies KCL 1993, Dir Def Commitments Overseas (Far E and W Hemisphere) MOD 1994–95, Dep Dir and COS then Dir Western European Union PC 1995–98, asst dir operations GCHQ 1998–2000, promoted Maj-Gen 2000, COS European Union Military Staff 2000–03; Univ of Birmingham: dep dir Centre for Studies in Security and Diplomacy 2003–10, hon sr research fell Sch of Govt and Soc 2010–; has contributed extensively to pubns on European security and defence issues; memb War Pensions Appeals Tbnl 2005–; assoc fell Chatham House 2003–07; fell RUSI 1996–; *Recreations* working gundogs, bridge; *Clubs* Army and Navy; *Style—* Major-General G G Messervy-Whiting, CBE; ✉ e-mail g.messervywhiting@bham.ac.uk

MESTON, His Hon Judge; 3 Baron (UK 1919); James; QC (1996); s of 2 Baron Meston (d 1984), and Diana, Baroness Meston; *b* 10 February 1950; *Educ* Wellington, St Catharine's Coll Cambridge, Univ of Leicester; *m* 1974, Jean Rebecca Anne, yr da of John Carder, of Chalvington, E Sussex; 1 s (Thomas b 1977), 2 da (Laura b 1980, Elspeth b 1988); *Heir* s, Hon Thomas Meston; *Career* called to the Bar Middle Temple 1973; jr counsel to the Queen's Proctor 1992–96, recorder 1997–99, circuit judge (Western Circuit) 1999–; *Clubs* Hawks' (Cambridge); *Style—* His Hon Judge the Lord Meston, QC; ✉ Queen Elizabeth Building, Temple, London EC4Y 9BS

METCALF, Prof Sir David; kt (2013), CBE (2008); s of Geoffrey Metcalf (d 1983), and Dorothy Rosa, *née* Vecchia (d 2005); *b* 15 May 1942; *Educ* Univ of Manchester (MA), Univ of London (PhD); *m* 20 July 1968, Helen (d 2003), da of Percival Harnett; 1 s (Thomas b 25 Nov 1980); *Career* special advsr to Min for Social Security 1976–79; prof of economics Univ of Kent 1977–85, prof of industrial relations LSE 1985–2009 (emeritus prof 2009–); cmmr Low Pay Cmmn 1997–2007, chair Migration Advsy Ctee 2007–16, memb Sr Salaries Review Body 2009–15; memb Royal Econ Soc; *Books* Minimum Wage Policy in Great Britain (1981), New Perspectives on Industrial Disputes (1993), Trade Unions: Resurgence or Decline? (2005); *Recreations* watching Tottenham Hotspur FC, horse racing; *Clubs* MCC; *Style—* Prof Sir David Metcalf, CBE; ✉ London School of Economics and Political Science, Houghton Street, London WC2A 2AE (☎ 020 7955 7049, e-mail d.metcalf@lse.ac.uk)

METCALFE, Julian; OBE (2014, MBE 2000); s of David Metcalfe, and Alexa, *née* Boycun (d 1966); *b* 14 December 1959; *Educ* Harrow; *m* Melanie, da of John Michael Willson; 2 da (Celeste b 24 June 1987, Allegra b 31 Oct 1987), 2 s (Michael b 2 Feb 1993, Billy b 21 March 1995); *Career* co-fndr: Pret A Manger, itsu, Metcalfe's Food Co; *Clubs* White's, 5 Hertford St; *Style—* Julian Metcalfe, Esq, OBE; ✉ Pret A Manger, 1 Hudson's Place, London SW1V 1PZ (☎ 020 7827 8000, fax 020 7827 8787)

METCALFE, Stephen James; MP; *b* 9 January 1966; *m* Angela; 1 s (Thomas), 1 da (Katharine); *Career* cnclr Epping Forest DC until 2007, MP (Cons) Basildon S & Thurrock E 2010–; *Style—* Stephen Metcalfe, Esq, MP; ✉ House of Commons, London SW1A 0AA

METHAM, Patricia; JP; da of John (Jack) Andrews, and Jane Starrett Andrews; *Educ* Upper Chine Sch IOW, Univ of Bristol (BA); *Career* teacher Wimbledon HS 1975–82, fell Merton Coll Oxford 1981, head of sixth form and English Francis Holland Sch London 1982–87, head Farlington Sch 1987–92, head Ashford Sch 1992–97, headmistress Roedean Sch

M

1997–2002, princ Regent's Sch Thailand 2003–; chair Boarding Ctee GSA 1999–2001; govr: St Andrews Prep Sch Eastbourne, Cumnor House Sch, Newton Prep Sch; Ind Schs Examination Bd (vice-chm 1999), Boarding Sch Assoc (memb Exec Ctee 1999–2001); *Publications* ed of critical play texts (student edns): The Birthday Party (Pinter), The Caretaker (Pinter), The Importance of Being Earnest (Wilde), Lady Windermere's Fan (Wilde), A Streetcar Named Desire (Williams), The Father (Strindberg), Lear (Bond); *Recreations* theatre, choral singing, travel to archaeological and cultural centres (mainly Europe), good food and good wine; *Clubs* Univ Women's, Lansdowne; *Style*— Mrs Patricia Metham

METHERELL, Ian Patrick; s of Clarence George Metherell (d 1998), and Ethel Muriel, *née* Dyer; *b* 19 September 1943; *Educ* Bideford GS, Univ of Southampton (BA); *m* 7 April 1969, Louise Whitefield, da of James Edward Westwood (d 1986); 2 s (Andrew b 1977, Nicholas b 1981); *Career* PR conslt; chief exec MPR Leedex Group Ltd 1987–89, chm Proclaim Network Ltd 1991–98, chm EuroPR Ltd 1992–2007; dir: AS2 Ltd 1994–97, Communication Skills Europe Ltd 1997–2003, Aflame Ltd 2004–14; non-exec dir Mosaic Management Consulting Group 1984–88; treas PR Conslts Assoc 1987–89; memb Aylesbury Vale DC 1995–2007; chm Buckingham Constituency Lib Dems 2004–06 and 2009–10, chm Marsh Gibbon Parish Cncl 2011–; FIPR 1988; *Style*— Ian Metherell, Esq; ✉ 2 Forge Close, Marsh Gibbon, Buckinghamshire OX27 0HZ (☎ 01869 277620, e-mail ian@metherell.info)

METHUEN, Richard St Barbe; QC (1997); s of John Methuen, and Rosemary Methuen; *b* 22 August 1950; *Educ* Marlborough; *m* 18 May 1974, Mary Catherine Methuen; 2 da (Harriet b 10 May 1977, Alice b 20 Feb 1980), 1 s (David b 4 March 1982); *Career* called to the Bar Lincoln's Inn 1972; head of chambers 2000–05, recorder 2002–; arbitrator Untraced Drivers' Agreement 2001–; mediator 2005–; *Style*— Richard Methuen, Esq, QC; ✉ 12 King's Bench Walk, Temple, London EC4Y 7EL (☎ 020 7583 0811, fax 020 7583 7228, e-mail methuen@12kbw.co.uk)

METLISS, Jonathan Alexander; s of Cyril Metliss, and Anita, *née* Lander; *b* 12 June 1949; *Educ* Haberdashers' Aske's, Univ of Southampton (LLB); *m* 15 Dec 1974, Vivienne Hilary, da of Samuel Woolf; 1 s (Joshua b 25 Nov 1980), 2 da (Miriam b 4 Nov 1983, Elizabeth b 4 July 1988); *Career* slr; asst slr Nabarro Nathanson 1973–76, merchant banker Capel Court Corp Sydney Aust 1976–78, asst slr Berwin Leighton 1978–82, sr corp fin ptnr, head of Sports Business Gp and fndr memb SJ Berwin 1982–, conslt Shore Capital Gp plc, conslt Structadene Ltd; dir: London Freeholds plc, Interlaw Ltd 1993–, The Weizmann Inst Fndn, Southern Africa Business Assoc; British-Israel Chamber of Commerce (also memb Exec); chm British Friends of Haifa Univ, vice-chm Friends of the Weizmann Inst (UK); memb Exec: The Weizmann Inst Fndn, Israel-Britain Business Cncl; vice-pres Cwlth Jewish Cncl; jt sec and exec memb Inter-Parly Cncl Against Anti-Semitism, Parly Cncl Against Anti-Semitism; memb: Cons Friends of Isreal Tikkun SA, Exec Br Israel Communications and Res Centre (BICOM), Parkes Centre Devpt Bd Univ of Southampton, Advsy Bd Tel Aviv Univ Business Sch, Bd of Govrs Haifa Univ, Ctee on South African Trade (COSAT, a Br overseas trade bd business advsy gp), Govt Working Gp on Football Disorder, Trade Partners UK, African and ME Advsy Gp, Royal African Soc, Law Soc, Holborn Law Soc, Advsy Gp Kick It Out (football anti-racism orgn); advsy memb Trade Partners UK 2001–, memb Hong Kong UK Business Forum; memb: RHS, RSPB, Guild of Freemen of the City of London, Advsy Gp Kick It Out (Kick Racism Out of Fooball); MInstD; *Recreations* squash, soccer, cricket, travel, work Israel and S Africa, RHS; *Clubs* MCC, Arundel CC, Middx CCC, Sussex CCC, Surrey CCC, RAC, Saracens RC, Alcester RC, Middx Co RFU, Rugby, Broadgate, Mark's, Queen's, Lord Taverner's Primary; *Style*— Jonathan Metliss, Esq; ✉ SJ Berwin, 222 Gray's Inn Road, London WC1X 8HB (☎ 020 7533 2222, fax 020 7533 2000)

METTENHEIMER, Dr Konstantin; *b* 1955, Frankfurt, Germany; *Educ* Univ of Freiburg (Dr jur), Univ of Pennsylvania (MBA); *m* ; 3 c; *Career* Freshfields Bruckhaus Deringer LLP: ptnr 1990, regnl managing ptnr Germany, Austria and Central and Eastern Europe 2000–04, jt sr ptnr 2004–; memb: Union Internationale des Avocats, Int Fiscal Assoc, Bd Tstees Bucerius Sch, Common Purpose Germany; *Style*— Dr Konstantin Mettenheimer; ✉ Freshfields Bruckhaus Deringer LLP, 65 Fleet Street, London EC4Y 1HS (☎ 020 7427 3841, website www.freshfields.com)

METTER, Veronica Ann; da of Louis William Metter, of South Africa, and Valerie Phyllis, *née* Harris; *b* 9 January 1954; *Educ* Univ of the Witwatersrand (BA), Univ of London (BA); *Career* slr; ptnr Berwin Leighton (now Berwin Leighton Paisner) 1987–; memb Law Soc; *Recreations* theatre, tennis; *Style*— Miss Veronica Metter; ✉ Berwin Leighton Paisner, Adelaide House, London Bridge, London EC4R 9HA (☎ 020 7623 3144, telex 886420, fax 020 7623 4416)

MEWIES, Sandy; da of Tom Oldland (d 1990), and Margaret Owens (d 2006); *b* 16 February 1950, Wrexham; *Educ* Grove Park Girls' GS Wrexham, Open Univ (BA); *m* 17 July 1976, Paul Mewies; 1 s; *Career* journalist 1966–83, advsr Clwyd Community Care 1991–93, lay schs inspr 1993–2003, memb Nat Assembly for Wales (Lab) Delyn 2003–16; co cnllr Wrexham 1987–2004 (sometime mayor); former: dir Wales European Centre Brussels, former memb N Wales Probation Bd; hon fell Glyyndwr Univ; *Recreations* reading; *Style*— Mrs Sandy Mewies; ✉ National Assembly for Wales, Cardiff Bay, Cardiff CF99 1NA (☎ 0300 200 7315, fax 029 2089 8281, e-mail sandy.mewies@assembly.wales); Constituency Office, Unit 85, Greenfield Business Centre, Greenfield CH8 7GR (☎ and fax 01352 716897)

MEXBOROUGH, 8 Earl of (I 1766); John Christopher George Savile; also Baron Pollington (I 1753) and Viscount Pollington (I 1766); s of 7 Earl (d 1980; himself gs of the 4 Earl who, as Lord Gaverstock, featured in a minor role in Disraeli's Coningsby, and who, for the last seven and a half months of his life, enjoyed the distinction of being the last living ex-member of the unreformed House of Commons), and Josephine Bertha Emily, *née* Fletcher (d 1992); *b* 16 May 1931; *Educ* Eton, Worcester Coll Oxford; *m* 1, 1958 (m dis 1972), Lady Elisabeth Hariot Grimston, da of 6 Earl of Verulam; 1 s (John Andrew Bruce, Viscount Pollington b 1959), 1 da (Lady Alethea Frances Clare b 1963 d 1994); m 2, 1972, Catherine Joyce, da of James Kenneth Hope, CBE, DL, and formerly wife of 6 Baron Vivian (d 2004); 1 da (Lady Lucinda b 1973), 1 s (Hon James b 1976); *Heir* s, Viscount Pollington; *Career* late 2 Lt Grenadier Gds; MIMI; *Recreations* travel, motor cars, American popular music; *Clubs* White's, All England Lawn Tennis, Royal Air Sqdn; *Style*— The Rt Hon the Earl of Mexborough; ✉ Old Manor House, Helmsley, York YO62 5AB (☎ 01439 771387, e-mail jmexborough@hotmail.com)

MEYER, Lady; Catherine Irene; CBE (2012); *née* Laylle; da of Maurice Jean Damien Laylle, Légion d'Honneur, Croix de Guerre, and Olga, *née* Ilyina; *b* 26 January 1953, Baden-Baden, Germany; *Educ* French Lycée of London (Bacc), SSEES Univ of London (BA); *m* 1, 1984 (m dis); 2 s (Alexander Volkmann b 26 May 1985, Constantin Volkmann b 17 May 1987); m 2, 1997, Sir Christopher Meyer, KCMG, *qv*, s of Flt Lt Reginald Meyer (ka 1944); *Career* account exec: Merrill Lynch, Pierce, Fenner & Smith 1976–79, Dean Witter Reynolds Ltd 1979–80, E F Hutton Inc 1980–86; co-fndr Int Centre for Missing and Exploited Children (ICMEC) 1998, fndr PACT (now Action Against Abudction) 1999; co-chair Vote 2004; non-exec dir Liffe 2003–08; tstee London Mathematical Inst for Sciences (LIMS) 2012–14; Adam Walsh Rainbow Award, Women's Center Leadership Award; *Publications* Mechanism of Commodity Options on the London Metal Exchange (1980), Two Children Behind a Wall (1997), They Are My Children Too (1999); *Recreations* tennis, skiing, politics; *Clubs* Ivy, The Walbrook; *Style*— Lady Meyer, CBE; ✉ e-mail catmeyer18@mac.com; c/o PACT, 5/7 Vernon Yard, London W11 2DX (website www.actionagainstabduction.org)

MEYER, Sir Christopher John Rome; KCMG (1998, CMG 1988); s of Flt Lt Reginald Henry Rome Meyer (ka 1944), and Evelyn Landells, *née* Campani (decd); *b* 22 February 1944; *Educ* Lancing, Lycée Henri IV Paris, Peterhouse Cambridge (MA), Sch of Advanced Int Studies Bologna; *m* 1, 11 Dec 1976 (m dis), Françoise Elizabeth, da of late Air Cdre Sir Archie Winskill, KCVO, CBE, DFC, AE; 2 s (James b 21 March 1978, William b 20 June 1984), 1 step s (Thomas (Hedges) b 28 Aug 1972); m 2, 30 Oct 1997, Catherine Irene Meyer, *qv*, da of Olga and Maurice Laylle, Officier de la Légion d'Honneur; 2 step s (Alexander Volkmann b 26 May 1985, Constantin Volkmann b 17 May 1987); *Career* Dip Serv: third sec West and Central African Dept FO 1966–67, Russian language trg 1967–68, third (later second) sec Br Embassy Moscow 1968–70, second later first sec Madrid 1970–73, first sec E Euro and Soviet Dept FCO 1973–76, first sec planning staff 1976–78, first sec UK rep to Euro Community Brussels 1978–82, cnsllr and head of Chancery Moscow 1982–84, head News Dept and chief FCO spokesman 1984–88; visiting fell Center for Int Affrs Harvard Univ 1988–89; min (commercial) Washington 1989–92, min and dep head of Mission Washington 1992–93, chief press sec to the PM 1994–96, ambass to Germany 1997, ambass to USA 1997–2003; chm PCC 2003–09; co-writer and presenter: Mortgaged to the Yanks (BBC 2 and BBC 4) 2006, Corridors of Power (BBC Radio 4) 2006–07, How to Succeed at Summits (BBC Radio 4) 2006–07, Lying Abroad (BBC Radio 4) 2006–07, The Watchdog and the Feral Beast (BBC Radio 4) 2009, Getting Our Way (BBC 4) 2010, Networks of Power (Sky Atlantic) 2012; non-exec dir Arbuthnot Banking Gp, memb Int Advsy Bd BAB Inc, chm Advsy Bd Pagefield; memb Pilgrims Soc; hon fell Peterhouse Cambridge 2001, Morehead-Cain visiting prof Univ of N Carolina 2010, sr assoc fell RUSI 2013; memb Ct Worshipful Co of Stationers and Newspapermakers 2009, Freeman City of London 2009; *Publications* DC Confidential (2005), Getting Our Way (2010), Only Child (2013); *Recreations* reading, jazz; *Clubs* Garrick, Metropolitan (Washington DC), Walbrook, Ivy; *Style*— Sir Christopher Meyer, KCMG; ✉ Arbuthnot Banking Group plc, 7 Wilson Street, London EC2M 2SN (☎ 07789 462199)

MEYER, Julie; MBE; da of Delbert Meyer, and Lorna Sandberg; *b* 28 August 1966, Dearborn, MI; *Educ* South San Francisco HS, Valparaiso Univ Chicago (BA), INSEAD (MBA); *Career* fndr First Tuesday 1998 (sold 2000), fndr and ceo Ariadne Capital 2000–, fndr Entrepreneur Country 2009–, managing ptnr Ariadne Capital Fund 2011–; memb Sec of State Entrepreneurs Forum; memb Bd: INSEAD, Vestergaard Frandsen, Group Silverline; formerly memb Bd Medikidz, dir Bd Quill and Tagstar; Ernst & Young Entrepreneur of the Year, World Economic Forum Global Ldr of Tomorrow; *Publications* Welcome of Entrepreneur Country (2012); *Style*— Ms Julie Meyer, MBE; ✉ Ariadne Capital, 17–19 Cockspur Street, London SW1Y 5BL (e-mail julie@ariadnecapital.com, website www.ariadnecapital.com); www.follow-the-entrepreneur.com, www.entrepreneurcountry.com

MEYERS, Dr Jeffrey; s of Rubin Meyers, of NYC, and Judith Meyers; *b* 1939; *Educ* Univ of Michigan (BA, jr year at Univ of Edinburgh), Univ of Calif Berkeley (MA, PhD); *Career* writer; asst prof UCLA 1963–65, lectr Far East Div Univ of Maryland 1965–66, asst prof Tufts Univ Boston 1967–71, professional writer in London and Málaga 1971–75, prof Univ of Colorado 1978–92 (assoc prof 1975–78), Jemison prof Univ of Alabama 1992, professional writer 1992–; visiting prof: Univ of Kent Canterbury 1979–80, Univ of Massachusetts Amherst 1982–83; visiting scholar Univ of Calif Berkeley 1986–87 and 1992–94, Univ of Colorado research lectr 1988, Seymour lectures in biography Nat Library of Australia 2012; Award in Lit American Acad of Arts and Letters 2005; FRSL 1983; *Biographies* A Fever at the Core: The Idealist in Politics (1976), Married to Genius (1977), Katherine Mansfield: A Biography (1978), The Enemy: A Biography of Wyndham Lewis (1980), Hemingway: A Biography (1985), Manic Power: Robert Lowell and His Circle (1987), D H Lawrence: A Biography (1990), Joseph Conrad: A Biography (1991), Edgar Allan Poe: His Life and Legacy (1992), Scott Fitzgerald: A Biography (1994), Edmund Wilson: A Biography (1995), Robert Frost: A Biography (1996), Bogart: A Life in Hollywood (1997), Gary Cooper: American Hero (1998), Privileged Moments: Encounters With Writers (2000), Orwell: Wintry Conscience of a Generation (2000), Inherited Risk: Errol and Sean Flynn in Hollywood and Vietnam (2002), Somerset Maugham: A Life (2004), Impressionist Quartet: The Intimate Genius of Manet and Morisot, Degas and Cassatt (2005), Modigliani: A Life (2006), Samuel Johnson: The Struggle (2008), The Genius and the Goddess: Arthur Miller and Marilyn Monroe (2009), John Huston: Courage and Art (2011), Robert Lowell in Love (2016); *Literary Criticism* Fiction and the Colonial Experience (1973), The Wounded Spirit: A Study of 'Seven Pillars of Wisdom' (1973), A Reader's Guide to George Orwell (1975), Painting and the Novel (1975), Homosexuality and Literature 1890–1930 (1977), D H Lawrence and the Experience of Italy (1982), Disease and the Novel 1860–1960 (1985), The Spirit of Biography (1989), Hemingway: Life into Art (2000), Orwell: Life and Art (2010), Thomas Mann's Artist-Stories (2014); *Bibliographies* T E Lawrence: A Bibliography (1974), Catalogue of the Library of the Late Siegfried Sassoon (1975), George Orwell: An Annotated Bibliography of Criticism (1977); *Collections Edited* George Orwell: The Critical Heritage (1975), Hemingway: The Critical Heritage (1982), Robert Lowell: Interviews and Memoirs (1988), The Sir Arthur Conan Doyle Reader (2002), The W Somerset Maugham Reader (2004); *Original Essays Edited* Wyndham Lewis: A Revaluation (1980), Wyndham Lewis by Roy Campbell (1985), D H Lawrence and Tradition (1985), The Craft of Literary Biography (1985), The Legacy of D H Lawrence (1987), The Biographer's Art (1989), T E Lawrence: Soldier, Writer, Legend (1989), Graham Greene: A Revaluation (1990), Remembering Iris Murdoch: Letters and Interviews (2013), The Mystery of the Real: Letters of the Canadian Artist Alex Colville and Biographer Jeffrey Meyers (2016); *Recreations* tennis, travel, avoiding boredom; *Style*— Dr Jeffrey Meyers; ✉ 84 Stratford Road, Kensington, CA 94707, USA (e-mail vjmeyers@sbcglobal.net)

MEYERS, Jonathan Rhys; *b* 27 July 1977, Dublin; *Career* actor; *Theatre* Darkblood (RNT); *Television* Samson & Delilah 1996, Gormenghast 2000, The Magnificent Ambersons 2002 (Best Upcoming Young Actor in a Lead Role Venice TV & Film Festival), The Lion in Winter 2003, Elvis 2005, The Tudors 2007–10, Dracula 2013; *Film* The Disappearance of Finbar 1996, Michael Collins 1996 (Best Young Irish Actor 1998), The Maker 1997, Telling Lies in America 1997, B Monkey 1998, The Governess 1998, Velvet Goldmine 1998 (Special Jury Prize Cannes Film Festival 1999), Ride with the Devil 1999, The Loss of Sexual Innocence, Titus 1999, Prozac Nation 2001, Tangled, Happy Now 2001, Bend It Like Beckham 2002, The Tesseract 2003, Octane 2003, I'll Sleep When I'm Dead 2003, The Emperor's Wife 2003, Vanity Fair 2004, Alexander 2004, Match Point 2005, Mission Impossible III 2006, August Rush 2007, The Children of Huang Shi 2008, Shelter 2010, From Paris With Love 2010, Albert Nobbs 2011, The Mortal Instruments: City of Bones 2013; *Style*— Jonathan Rhys Meyers; ✉ c/o Independent Talent Group, Oxford House, 76 Oxford Street, London W1D 1BS

MEYRIC HUGHES, Henry Andrew Carne; s of Reginald Richard Meyric Hughes (d 1961), and Jean Mary Carne Brooke, *née* Pratt; *b* 1 April 1942; *Educ* Shrewsbury, Univ of Rennes, Univ of Munich, UC Oxford (BA), Univ of Sussex (MA); *m* 3 Aug 1968, Alison Hamilton, da of David Bruce Faulds (d 1976), of Chester; 1 da (Henrietta b 1971), 1 s (Steffan b 1975); *Career* Br Cncl: asst regnl dir W Berlin 1968–71, asst rep (arts) France 1971–73, asst dir and curator of permanent collection Fine Arts Dept 1977–79, regnl dir

N Italy Milan 1979–83, dir Visiting Arts Office GB and NI 1984–86, dir Fine Arts Dept 1986–92; dir (also i/c nat touring exhibitions and Arts Cncl Collection) Hayward Gallery London 1992–96; freelance curator/conslt 1996–; dir Riverside Tst 1986–94, memb Ct RCA 1986–92, hon memb SCR RCA 1988–; Int Assoc of Art Critics (AICA): pres UK section 1991–94, int pres 2002–08, hon int pres 2008–; pres Int Bd Manifesta Rotterdam 1996, Luxembourg 1998, Ljubljana 2000, Frankfurt 2002, Donostia-San Sebastian 2004, Nicosia 2006, Bolzano/Trento 2008; memb Bd: Watermans Arts Centre Brentford 1991–93, Academy Forum 1992–96, Inst for Int Visual Arts 1993–; The Br Sch at Rome: memb Faculty of Fine Arts 1988–92, memb Exhibitions Ctee 1996–98; memb: Bd Inst of Int Visual Arts (inIVA) 1986–, Slade Ctee Univ of London 1988–97, Advsy Gp Hayward Gallery London 1986–92, CIMAM (UNESCO), Internationale Kunstausstellungsleitertagung eV (IKT, memb Int Bd 1992–97), Mgmnt Ctee Matts Gallery London 1993–, Bd Göteborg Kunsthallen 1995–2000, Ctee E Europe Contemporary Art Network (SEECAN), Scientific Ctee Museum Moderner Kunst Stiftung Ludwig Wien 2000–01, Galleria d'Arte Moderna Bologna 2001–05, Scientific Ctee Archives de la Critique d'Art Rennes 2002–, Bd Dox Centre for Contemporary Art Prague 2004–, Bd Arnolfini Bristol 2006–14, Gp of Conslts Cncl of Europe Exhbns 2006–10; observer: Art Panel Scottish Arts Cncl, Visual Arts Panel Arts Cncl of GB 1986–92; adjudicator Claremorris Open Ireland 1987; jury memb: Turner Prize 1988, European Painting Prize Oostende 1990, ACC Euro Studios Prog Weimar 1998 and 2013, Biennale de Cetinje 2002, V Caribbean Biennial 2003, Gwangju Biennale 2004 (chair), Premio Furla Bologna 2005, Dakar Biennial 2006; Br cmmr Venice Biennale 1986–92 (Auerbach 1986, Cragg 1988, Kapoor 1990, Contemporary British Architecture 1991, Hamilton 1993), co-selector and catalogue contrib The Vigorous Imagination Edinburgh Festival 1987, chm Selection Ctee for Eighty (touring exhibition) Strasbourg 1988, chm of jury Contemporary View competition RCA 1990, chm of jury for the diploma exams Ecole Nationale Supérieure des Beaux-Arts Paris 2004, chm Organising Ctee John Moores Critics Award Shanghai and Liverpool 2012–; co-curator The Romantic Spirit in German Art 1790–1990 Edinburgh, London and Munich 1994–95, assoc curator The Age of Modernism Berlin 1997, co-curator Blast to Freeze: British Art in the 20th Century (Wolfsburg and Toulouse) 2002–03; curator: Cypriot Pavilion Venice Biennale 2003, Grenseløs/Boundless Oslo 2005–06, Plus que vrai Paris 2005; co-curator European Exhbn of Young Artists 2008–09, co-curator Prague Triennale 2008, co-curator XXX Cncl of Europe exhibition The Desire for Freedom: Art since 1945 Deutsches Historisches (Museum Berlin, Kumu Tallinn, Palazzo Reale Milan and MOCA Krakow 2012–13, then Macedonian Museum of Contemporary Art Thessaloniki and Art Gallery of Band H Sarajevo 2013–14); external examiner MA Curating course RCA 2011–13; numerous contributions to exhibition catalogues, translator of historical and art historical publications from French and German, author of articles on cultural policy and contemporary art; contributing ed Tema Celeste (Milan); contrib Times HE Supplement, reviews for The Burlington Magazine, Critique d'Art and others; Silver medal Czechoslovak Soc for Int Cultural Relations 1986; Officier de l'Ordre des Arts et des Lettres (France) 1997; Pour le mérite Federal Republic of Germany 2002; FRSA 1988; *Recreations* music, Europe; *Style—* Henry Meyric Hughes, Esq; ✉ 13 Ashchurch Grove, London W12 9BT (☎ and fax 020 8749 4098, e-mail henry.meyrichughes@tiscali.co.uk)

MEYRICK, (Cyril) Jonathan; *see:* Lynn, Bishop of

MICHAEL, Rt Hon Alun; PC (1998), JP (Cardiff 1972), MP; *b* 22 August 1943; *Educ* Colwyn Bay GS, Keele Univ; *m* 23 July 1966; 2 s, 3 da; *Career* journalist 1966–71, youth and community worker 1971–87, magistrate 1972– (chm Cardiff Juvenile Bench until 1987), memb Cardiff City Cncl 1973–89 (sometime chm: Planning Ctee, Fin Ctee, Econ Devpt Ctee, Performance Review Ctee); MP (Lab and Co-op) Cardiff S and Penarth 1987–, AM (Lab) Wales Mid & W 1999–2000; oppn whip 1987–88, shadow min for Welsh affrs 1988–92, shadow min for home affrs and for voluntary sector 1992–97; min of state Home Office 1997–98, sec of state for Wales 1998–99, first min Nat Assembly for Wales 1999–2000, min of state Rural Affrs 2001–06; chm Co-op Parly Gp 1990–92 (memb Nat Exec Ctee 1999–); variously: chm All-Pty Gp on Somalia, sec All-Pty Gp for Colleges, vice-chm British-German Parly Gp, chm All-Pty Gp on Alcohol Misuse, sec All-Pty Gp on Personal Social Services; chair Parly Hearings for Int Year of Vols 2001; chm Parly Friends of the Welsh National Opera, dep chm Cardiff Bay Opera House; former vice-pres YHA, former vice-pres Building Societies Assoc; FRSA 2003; *Recreations* long-distance running, hill walking, opera, music and reading; *Style—* The Rt Hon Alun Michael, MP; ✉ House of Commons, London SW1A 0AA (☎ 020 7219 5980, e-mail alunmichaelmp@parliament.uk); constituency office ☎ 029 2022 3533

MICHAEL, Anthony Colin; s of Edwin George Michael (d 1993), and Maureen Ellen, *née* McCabe; *b* 18 October 1958; *Educ* Erith GS, St Martins Sch of Art (BA); *Partner* Stephanie Joy Nash, *qv*; 2 s (Montgomery Louis Spencer b 6 May 1996, Nelson Bartholomew Edwin b 28 Nov 1998), 1 da (Astor Elizabeth Pearl b 8 Jan 2003); *Career* former gardener; self employed ptnr Michael Nash Associates 1984–; initially designers of record sleeves for artists incl Neneh Cherry, Fluke, Etienne Daho and Seal, subsequently cmmns for fashion designers Marc Jacobs, Jasper Conran, Issey Miyake, Jil Sander and Philip Treacy, etc, graphic designers for Harvey Nichols own brand food products 1992–, packaging designers for Egg (fashion retail outlet) 1994; *Awards* (for Harvey Nichols food packaging) Gold Award D&AD for the Most Outstanding Packaging Range 1993, Silver Award D&AD for the Most Oustanding Packaging – Individual Pack 1994, Art Dirs' Club of Europe Award 1994, CSD Minerva Award for Graphic Design 1994 and NY Festivals Gold Medal and Grand Award 1994, Silver Award D&AD for Compact Disk Packaging for Massive Attack 1995, Silver Award D&AD for Packaging UTH Retail Stores, D&AD Silver Award for John Galliano packaging; various others from music indust; memb AGI; *Style—* Anthony Michael, Esq; ✉ Michael Nash Associates, 9 Grafton Mews, London W1T 5HZ (☎ 020 7631 3370, fax 020 7637 9629, e-mail anthony@michaelnash.co.uk)

MICHAEL, George, né Georgios Panayiotou; *b* 25 June 1963; *Educ* Bushey Meads Sch; *Career* singer and songwriter; memb Wham! 1981–86; released first single Wham Rap! (Enjoy What You Do?) 1982; albums with Wham!: Fantastic (UK no 1) 1983, Make It Big (UK no 1) 1984, The Final (compilation, UK no 2) 1986; solo albums: Faith (UK no 1) 1987, Listen Without Prejudice, Vol 1 (UK no 1) 1990, Older 1996 (first album since legal dispute with Sony Music), Ladies and Gentleman: The Best of George Michael 1998, Songs from the Last Century 1999, Patience 2004, Twenty-Five 2006; singles incl: Careless Whisper (UK no 1) 1984, A Different Corner 1986, I Knew You Were Waiting (with Aretha Franklin) 1987, I Want Your Sex 1987, Hard Day 1987, Faith 1987, Father Figure 1988, One More Try 1988, Monkey 1988, Kissing a Fool 1988, Praying For Time 1990, Waiting For That Day 1990, Mother's Pride 1990, Freedom! '90 1990, Heal The Pain 1991, Don't Let The Sun Go Down On Me (with Elton John) 1991, Too Funky 1992, Jesus to a Child 1995, Fastlove (UK no 1) 1996, Star People '97, Outside (UK no 2) 1998, As (with Mary J. Blige) 1999, If I Told You That (with Whitney Houston) 2000, Freeek! 2002, Amazing 2004, Flawless (Go to the City) 2004, Round Here 2004, John and Elvis Are Dead (digital single) 2005, An Easier Affair 2006, This is Not Real Love (with Mutya Buena) 2006, December Song (I Dreamed of Christmas) 2008, True Faith 2011; awards incl: Songwriter of the Year Ivor Novello Awards 1985, 1990 and 1997, Best British Male Artist BRIT Award 1988, R&B Grammy Award 1988, Album of the Year (for Faith) 1989, two American Music Awards 1989, Video Vanguard Award MTV 1989, Best British Album of the Year Award BRIT Award 1991, Best Male Singer Rolling Stone Readers' Awards 1991; organised and headlined HRH The Princess of Wales's Concert of Hope 1993; *Books* Bare (autobiography, 1990); *Style—* George Michael, Esq

MICHAEL, Sir Jonathan; kt (2005); s of Prof Ian Michael, CBE (d 2014), and Molly, *née* Bayley (d 2007); *b* 21 May 1945; *Educ* Bristol GS, St Thomas' Hosp Med Sch London (MB BS); *m* 1, 1975 (m dis 1991), Jacqueline, *née* Deluz; 3 da (Susannah b 1977, Charlotte b 1981, Philippa b 1985), 1 s (Stephen b 1978); m 2, 17 Sept 2005, Karen, *née* Richards; *Career* conslt physician Queen Elizabeth Hosp Birmingham 1980–2000, chief exec Univ Hosp Birmingham NHS Tst 1996–2000, chief exec Guy's and St Thomas' Hosp NHS Tst 2000–07, dep md (healthcare) BT 2007–08, md BT Health 2008–10, ceo Oxford University Hosps NHS Tst 2011–15; FRCP 1985 (MRCP 1973), FKC 2005; *Style—* Sir Jonathan Michael; ✉ Beechlawn House, Hurtmore Road, Godalming, Surrey GU7 2RA (e-mail jonathan.michael@beechlawn.net)

MICHAEL, Sam; s of David Michael, of Aust, and Marion Michael; *b* 29 April 1971, Geraldton, Aust; *Educ* Univ of NSW (BE); *m* 28 Feb 1998, Vanessa, *née* Fielding; 1 da (Toni b 16 Aug 1999), 1 s (Jacques b 18 June 2001); *Career* design engr Team Lotus 1993–94, race engr Jordan Grand Prix 1995–2000; Williams F1: chief engr 2001–04, tech dir 2004–; *Recreations* running, surfing; *Style—* Sam Michael, Esq

MICHAEL, Simon Laurence; s of Anthony Denis Michael, of London, and Regina, *née* Milstone; *b* 4 January 1955; *Educ* King's Coll London (LLB); *Family* 2 da (Kay b 1988, Roxanne b 2001), 1 s (Alastair b 1990); *Career* called to the Bar Middle Temple 1978; tstee Road Victims Tst Beds and Herts; memb: Personal Injury Bar Assoc, Professional Negligence Bar Assoc; *Books* The Usurper (jtly, 1988), The Cut Throat (1989), The Long Lie (1991), The Brief (2015); *Recreations* travel, tennis, writing; *Style—* Simon Michael, Esq; ✉ No 5 Chambers, Steelhouse Lane, Birmingham B4 6DR (☎ 0121 606 0500, fax 0121 606 1501, e-mail slm@no5.com)

MICHAELS, Robert Stewart John; s of Alexander Michaels, of Stanmore, and Evelyn, *née* Susman; *Educ* Ravensfield Coll Orange Hill, St Martin's Sch of Art, Université d'Aix en Provence; *m* Marilyn, da of Edward Lee; 2 s (Mark John Louis, Daniel David); *Career* chm and md Robert Michaels Holdings plc 1974–2000; dir: Mardan Properties Ltd, John Crowther plc 1987, Robert Mark Ltd, Marongate plc, Twenty One Clothing Company Ltd, Independent Storage and Distribution Ltd, RMD Ltd; ptnr RMD Properties (London) LLP; memb Permanent Panel Nat Econ Devpt Office; cncllr (Cons) Knightsbridge Ward Westminster City Cncl 1990–94 (chm Investments Ctee, vice-chm Financial Mgmnt and Personnel Ctee, whip 1991), dir Westminster Enterprise Agency 1990–, vice-pres and memb Policy Gp Small Business Bureau 1991–, memb House of Lords Rural Economy Gp 1991; chm: Bd of Govrs Sussex House Sch, Cncl for Devpt Westminster Sch; Freeman City of London 1979, life memb Guild of Freemen City of London; Liveryman Worshipful Companies of: Horners, Farriers, Pattenmakers; FInstD 1980, memb Inst of Residential Property Mgmnt (MIRPM), ARICS, MCIH; *Recreations* family, reading, martial arts (kickboxing 1st Dan), cricket, racing cars; *Clubs* Carlton, MCC (life memb); *Style—* Robert Michaels, Esq; ✉ e-mail robertmichaels20@aol.com

MICHAELS-MOORE, Anthony; s of John Moore, of Grays, Essex, and Isabel, *née* Shephard; *b* 8 April 1957; *Educ* Gravesend Sch for Boys, Univ of Newcastle upon Tyne, St Mary's Teacher Trg Coll, RSAMD; *m* 16 Feb 1980, Ewa Bozena Maria, da of Stanislaw Migocki; 1 da (Kathryn Ashley Maria b 7 Feb 1987); *Career* baritone; teacher St John's CE Sch Crowborough 1979–84, opera course RSAMD 1984–85, professional debut Opera-go-Round Scottish Opera 1985; first Br winner Luciano Pavarotti/Opera Co of Philadelphia competition 1986; sung with orchs incl: Toronto Symphony, Scot Nat, The Philharmonia, Royal Philharmonic, LSO, CBSO, Vienna Philharmonic, BBC Symphony Orch (under Bernard Haitink, BBC Proms) 1997; *Roles* incl: Marcello in La Bohème Bohème (Opera North, Royal Opera House Covent Garden, ENO), Belcore in L'Elisir d'Amore, Dr Malatesta in Don Pasquale, (Royal Opera House), Ping in Turandot (Covent Garden), Forester in The Cunning Little Vixen (Covent Garden), Zurga in the Pearl Fishers (ENO debut 1987), Count Almaviva in The Marriage of Figaro (ENO, Bavarian State Opera), Figaro in The Barber of Seville (WNO debut 1990, Barcelona 1991, Royal Opera House 1993, Vienna 1995), Guglielmo in Cosi fan Tutte (USA debut Philadelphia 1988, Canadian Debut Canadian Opera Co 1991), Giorgio Germont in La Traviata (Opera North 1991), Marquis of Posa in Don Carlos (Opera North 1993 and Pittsburgh 1997), Licinius in La Vestale (La Scala Milan debut 1993), Lescaut in Manon Lescaut (Vienna Staatsoper debut 1994, Naples debut 1994), Sharpless in Madama Butterfly (Opèra Bastille debut 1994), Don Giovanni (Tel Aviv 1994), Hamlet Opera North 1995, Orestes in Iphigene en Tauride (Opera Bastille) 1995, Onegin in Eugene Onegin (Opera Bastille) 1995, Baron Scarpia in Tosca (Royal Opera House) 1996, Marcello in La Boheme and Silvio in Pagliacci (Met NY debut, 1996), Gérard in Andrea Chénier (Teatro Colon Buenos Aires debut, 1996), title role in Macbeth (Royal Opera House 1997), Rigoletto (Brussels 1999, Vienna 2000), Montforte in Sicilian Vespers (Vienna 2000), Iago in Otello (Paris 2001, Glyndebourne 2001), Ezio in Attila (Chicago 2001, ROH 2002); *Recordings* La Vestale (with La Scala under Riccardo Muti), The Fairy Queen (under Harnoncourt), Mendelssohn Die Erste Walpurgisnacht (with The Philharmonia), Orff Carmina Burana (with Vienna Philharmonic under Andre Previn), Gilbert & Sullivan Yeomen of the Guard, Szymanowski Stabat Mater (with The Philharmonia under Claus Peter Flor), Mercadante Orazi i Curiazi (Opera Rara recording), Opera Spectacular (with the Royal Philharmonic Orch), Die Fledermaus (video, with Royal Opera Co), Puccini Favourites (with Royal Opera Co), Lucia di Lammermoor (under Charles Mackerras), Falstaff (with Sir John Eliot Gardiner), Aroldo (with Fabio Luisi), La Favorite (with Marcello Viotti); *Recreations* clay pigeon shooting, football, cricket, swimming, Indian food; *Style—* Anthony Michaels-Moore, Esq; ✉ c/o IMG Artists, The Light Box, 111 Power Road, London W4 5PY

MICHEL, Keith; s of George Richard Michel (d 2005), and Winifred Eve Michel (d 1972); *b* 19 May 1948; *Educ* Bradfield Coll, Fitzwilliam Coll Cambridge (MA, Football blue, Oxbridge rep team Japan 1969, Univ Crusaders CC); *m* 16 Dec 1972, Rosemary Suzannah, da of Stanley Joseph Simons, of Southgate, London; 1 s (Edward b 30 April 1980); *Career* slr; articled clerk Coward Chance (now Clifford Chance) 1971–73, asst slr Clyde & Co 1973–75, ptnr Holman Fenwick & Willan 1978–2003 (joined as asst slr, conslt 2003–06); visiting prof of laws UCL 2006–; contrib to various legal pubns; memb Grasshoppers CC; tstee Univ of Cambridge FC; memb Law Soc 1973; *Books* Contraband (1988), Countdown (1991), Caracara (1995), Karakan (2000), War Terror and Carriage by Sea (2004), Corsair (2009); *Recreations* family life, sports, history, archaeology, wildlife conservation, photography, calligraphy; *Clubs* Hawks' (Cambridge); *Style—* Keith Michel, Esq; ✉ Thatchdale, Pennymead Drive, East Horsley, Surrey KT24 5AH (☎ 01483 283595, e-mail keith.michel@tiscali.co.uk)

MICHELL, Prof (Alastair) Robert; s of Dr Charles Francis Michell (d 1960), of London, and Eva, *née* Freyhan; *b* 28 December 1940; *Educ* Dulwich Coll, RVC London (BSc, BVetMed, PhD, DSc, MRCVS, pres RVC Students' Union); *m* 1963, Pauline, da of Frederick Arthur Mountford Selley (d 2007); 1 da (Tania Claire b 1968); *Career* Harkness fell (Cwlth Fund of NY) Rockefeller Univ, Nat Inst of Health and UCLA (Cedars Sinai Hosp) USA 1969–71, Beit meml research fell in med 1971–73, MRC research fell Nephrology Section Univ of Chicago Med Sch 1974–76; RVC London: lectr in physiology 1976–83, reader in med 1983–93, prof of applied physiology and comparative med 1993–; prof of comparative med Bart's 2001–; Evelyn Williams fell Univ of Sydney 2000; vice-chm Comparative Clinical Science Fndn 2001–; chm RCVS/BVA Jt Ctee on Continuing Professional Devpt 1988–92; pres: Euro Soc for Vet Nephrology 1985–88, Vet Research Club 1988–89, RVC Alumnus Assoc 1989–91, Assoc of Vet Teachers and Research Workers 1994–95; memb

M

Cncl: BVA 1983–85, 1988–92, 1995–99 and 2002–09, RVC 1986–94 and 1995–96, RCVS 1992–2004 (elected memb, pres 1999–2000), Comparative Med Section RSM (vice-pres 1992–94), Technol Foresight (Health Sciences Panel) 1995–99; memb: Advsy Cncl Campaign for Science and Engrg 2001–, Advsy Gp Fndn of New Vet Sch Univ of Nottingham 2003–05, Steering Gp Wellcome Tst Imerial Coll Research Project on History of Comparative Medicine, Steering Gp Dogs for the Disabled, Autism Project 2013, Health Professionals for Assisted Dying; appearances on: Dispatches (Channel 4) 1999, Comparative Medicine, Clinical Training (BBC Radio 4) 2000–01, Comparative Healthcare Delivery (BBC Radio 4) 2015; runner-up first Perspectives in Biology and Medicine writing award for young scientists 1975, Blaine award (Br Small Animal Vet Assoc) for outstanding contribs to the advancement of small animal med 1990, Weipers commemorative lectr 1991, Centenary Lecture (Central Vet Soc) 1991 and 1997, George Fleming prize (Br Vet Jl) 1992 and 2005, BVA Dalrymple-Champneys Cup and Medal 2007, BVA Chiron Award 2012; memb numerous professional bodies incl: Physiological Soc, Nutrition Soc, Assoc for Vet Clinical Pharmacology and Therapeutics, London Hypertension Soc, Renal Assoc, Consensus for Action on Salt and Hypertension, Central Vet Soc (pres 2002–03); tstee Hunterian Museum RCS; govr Addenbrooke's Hospital Fndn Tst 2004–12; lay memb RPharmS Assembly 2010–13 (memb Cncl, Privy Cncl rep 2002–10, hon memb), FRSM, FRSA; *Books* Renal Disease in Dogs and Cats: Comparative and Clinical Aspects (ed, 1988), An Introduction to Veterinary Anatomy and Physiology (jtly, 1989), Veterinary Fluid Therapy (jtly, 1989), The Advancement of Veterinary Science (ed, 4 vols, 1992), Clinical Biology of Sodium (1995), Veterinary Verse In Newer Veins (ed with E Boden, 1997); over 300 contributions to scientific and professional jls, mainly on fluids and electrolytes, notably renal function, hypertension and oral rehydration, and also on end-of-life issues; Speculum (monthly column in Veterinary Times, over 200 edns); *Recreations* music, theatre, tennis, travel, writing (including scientific journalism), choral singing; *Style*— Prof Robert Michell; ✉ Pine Croft, Upper Cleveley, Oxford OX7 4DX (e-mail bobmichell@hotmail.com)

MICHELL, Prof Robert Hall (Bob); s of Rowland Charles Michell, and Elsie Lorna, *née* Hall; *b* 16 April 1941; *Educ* Crewkerne Sch, Univ of Birmingham (BSc, PhD, DSc); *m* 1, 13 Jan 1967 (m dis 1971), June Mary, *née* Evans; *m* 2, 28 July 1992, Esther Margaret Oppenheim; 1 s (Ben *b* 1991), 1 da (Naomi *b* 1986); 1 s from a previous relationship (Jo *b* 1974); *Career* Harvard Med Sch 1966–68; Univ of Birmingham: res fell 1965–66 and 1968–70, lectr 1970–81, sr lectr 1981–84, reader in biochemistry 1984–86, prof 1986–87, Royal Soc res prof 1987–2006, emeritus prof of biochemistry 2006–; memb Editorial Bd: Jl of Neurochemistry 1974–78, Cell Calcium 1979–89, Biochemical Jl 1982–88 (ed Advsy Panel 1981–82), Current Opinion in Cell Biology 1988–95, Biological Sciences Review 1988–2006, Proceedings of The Royal Society of London 1989–97, Jl of Molecular Endocrinology 1991–99, Molecular Membrane Biology 1994–2000, Faculty of 1000 2004–13; fndn lectr RCPath 1989, Bertram Lewis Abrahams lectr RCP 1990, Wellcome visiting prof Univ of Vermont 1987, Royal Soc UK-Canada Rutherford lectr 1994, Morton Lecturer Biochemical Soc 2002; memb: Biochemical Soc (CIBA medal 1988), Br Nat Ctee for Pharmacology 1982–87, Br Nat Ctee for Biochemistry 1988–89, Physiological Systems and Disorders Res Bd MRC 1985–90, Int Rels Ctee Royal Soc 1991–94, Med and Scientific Advsy Panel Leukaemia Res Fund 1989–92, Advsy Bd Beit Meml Tst 1993–2006, Biochemistry Panel for 1996 and Biological Sciences Panel for 2001 and 2008 Research Assessment Exercises HEFCE, Sci Advsy Bd Babraham Inst 1997–2000, Sci Advsy Bd Lister Inst for Preventive Med 1998–2004, Human Frontiers Sci Programme Fellowships and Workshops Panel 1999–2001, Sci Advsy Bd Electromagnetic Fields (EMF) Biological Research Tst 2000–10 (tstee 2004–10); chm Systems Bd Grants Ctee MRC 1988–90; memb EMBO 1991; govr Cadbury Sixth Form Coll 1991–99 and 2003– (chair 2010–15); FRS 1986 (memb Cncl 1995–97), FMedSci 2002, hon memb Biochemical Soc 2010–; FRSB 2013; *Books* Membranes And Their Cellular Functions (with J B Finean and R Coleman, 1974, 3 edn 1984), New Comprehensive Biochemistry (contrib ed with J B Finean, 1981), Cell Calcium (contrib ed, 1982), Inositol Lipids and Transmembrane Signalling (ed with M J Berridge, 1988), Inositol Lipids and Cellular Signalling (ed with A H Drummond and C P Downes, 1989), Lipids: Biochemistry, Biotechnology and Health (with M I Gurr, J L Harwood, K N Frayn and D J Murphy, 2016); *Style*— Prof Robert Michell; ✉ 59 Weoley Park Road, Selly Oak, Birmingham B29 6QZ (☎ 0121 472 1356, mobile 07411 792640, e-mail r.h.michell@bham.ac.uk)

MICHELL, Roger; s of H D Michell, DFC, and J Michell, *née* Green; *b* 5 June 1956; *Educ* Clifton, Queens' Coll Cambridge (exhibitioner, BA); *m* 1, Kate Buffery (m dis 2002); 2 c (Harry *b* 6 Dec 1991, Rosanna *b* 17 March 1996); *m* 2, Anna Maxwell Martin, *qv*; 2 da (Maggie *b* 6 April 2009, Charlotte *b* 9 Oct 2011); *Career* director; Brighton Actors Workshop 1977, Thames TV training bursary Royal Court 1978–80, RSC 1985–91, Drama Director's Course BBC TV 1990; Judith E Wilson sr fell Trinity Coll Cambridge 1989; *Theatre* for RSC incl: Temptation, The Dead Monkey, Restoration, Some Americans Abroad, Two Shakespearean Actors, The Constant Couple, Hamlet, Merchant of Venice; for NT incl: The Coup, Under Milk Wood, The Homecoming 1997, Blue/Orange (also West End) 2000, Honour 2003, Landscape with Weapon; others incl: The Catch (Royal Court), The Key Tag (Royal Court), Private Dick (Edinburgh Festival and West End), Marya (Old Vic), My Night with Reg (Royal Court and West End), Some Sunny Day (Hampstead), Old Times (Donmar Warehouse) 2004, Betrayal (Donmar Warehouse) 2006, Female of the Species (Vaudeville) 2008, Rope (Almeida) 2009, Tribes (Royal Court) 2010, Farewell to the Theatre (Hampstead) 2011, Birthday (Royal Court) 2012; *Films* Downtown Lagos 1991, Buddha of Suburbia 1993, Ready When You Are Mr Patel 1995, Persuasion 1995, My Night with Reg 1996, Michael Redgrave – My Father 1997, Titanic Town 1997, Notting Hill 1998, Changing Lanes 2001, The Mother 2002, Enduring Love 2003, Venus 2005, Morning Glory 2010, Hyde Park on Hudson 2013, Le Week-End 2013, The Lost Honour of Christopher Jefferies 2014; *Awards* Buzz Goodbody Award RSC 1977, Edinburgh Fringe First Award 1977, Drama Desk nomination NY 1990, BAFTA nomination for Buddha of Suburbia; for Persuasion incl: BAFTA, RTS nomination; Critics' Circle Award; for Titanic Town: Grand Prix Festival de Laon, Ecumenical Prize Locarno, Trades Union Award, Emden; for Notting Hill: Evening Standard Peter Sellers Award, BAFTA Audience Award, Empire Magazine Award; *Style*— Roger Michell

MICHELS, Sir David Michael Charles; kt (2006); *b* 8 December 1946; *m* 15 Sept 1970, Michelle Ann; *Career* various sales and mktg positions rising to worldwide mktg dir Grand Metropolitan 1966–81; Ladbroke Group plc: sales and mktg dir hotels 1981–83, md Leisure Div 1983–85, md Ladbroke Hotels 1985–87; sr vice-pres sales and mktg Hilton International 1987–89, dep chm Hilton UK and exec vice-pres Hilton Worldwide 1989–91; chief exec: Stakis plc 1991–99, Hilton Int 1999–2000, Hilton Gp plc 2000–05; dep chm Marks and Spencer plc 2006–; non-exec dir: Arcadia Gp plc 2000–, British Land Co plc 2003–, EasyJet 2006–11; Hon DLitt Glasgow Caledonian Univ; FHCIMA; *Recreations* tennis, reading; *Clubs* Vanderbilt; *Style*— Sir David Michels

MICHIE, Prof David Alan Redpath; OBE (1997); s of James Beattie Michie (d 1960), and Anne Redpath, OBE (d 1965); *b* 30 November 1928; *Educ* Hawick HS, Edinburgh Coll of Art (DA); *m* 27 March 1951, Eileen Anderson (d 2003), da of James Temple Michie (d 1931); 2 da (Alison Jane *b* 1953, Lindsey Elizabeth *b* 1955); *Career* Nat Serv RA 1947–49; lectr in drawing and painting Grays Sch of Art Aberdeen 1957–61; Edinburgh Coll of Art: lectr 1961–74, vice-princ 1974–77, head Sch of Drawing and Painting 1982–90; prof of painting Heriot-Watt Univ 1988–91 (emeritus prof 1991–); visiting artist: Univ of the Arts Belgrade 1979, Univ of Calif Santa Barbara 1992; memb: Gen Teaching Cncl

for Scotland 1975–80, Edinburgh Festival Soc 1977–, Convocation and Ct Heriot-Watt Univ 1979–82, Cncl Br Sch in Rome 1980–85, Museums and Galleries Cmmn 1991–96, Scottish Int Educn Tst 2004–13, Nat Life Story Collection; hon fell Edinburgh Coll of Art 2009; memb SSA 1955, RSA 1972 (ARSA 1964), RGI 1983, FRSA 1990, FFCS 2000, RWA 1991–2000; *Solo Exhibitions* Mercury Gallery London 1966, 1969, 1971, 1974, 1980, 1983, 1992, 1996 and 1999, Mercury Gallery Edinburgh 1986, Lothian Region Chambers Edinburgh 1977, Scottish Gallery Edinburgh 1980,1994, 1998, 2003 and 2008, The Loomshop Gallery Lower Largo 1981 and 1987, Kasteel De Hooge Vuursche Baarn and Mia Joosten Gallery Amsterdam 1991, Scott Gall Hawick 2009, Scottish Arts Club 2010; *Group Exhibitions* incl: Fourteen Scottish Painters (Cwlth Inst London) 1963, Edinburgh Ten 30 Wales 1975, Contemporary Scottish Painting (The Alamo Gallery London) 1978, Contemporary Art from Scotland (touring) 1981–82, Works on Paper (Faculty of Fine Art Gallery Belgrade) 1986, Artists' Self Portraits (Tate Gallery London) 1989, Artist Families (Fine Art Soc Edinburgh) 1989, Guthrie Award Prize Winners Exhibition (Fine Art Soc Edinburgh and Glasgow) 1990, Art Studio Faculty Exhibition Univ of Calif Santa Barbara 1991, Scottish Art in the 20th Century (Royal W of England Acad Bristol) 1991, The Scottish Gallery – The First 150 Years (Edinburgh) 1992, The Edinburgh School (The Scottish Gallery) 1993, Contemporary Scottish Painting Hong Kong 1994 and 1996, Scottish Painters (Solomon Gallery Dublin) 1999, RSA members (Albemarle Gallery London) 1999, Les Belles Etoiles d'Ecosse (Napier Gallery St Helier) 2001, The Scottish Show (Thompson's Gallery London) 2001, Scottish Painting (Chelsea Gallery Palo Alto CA) 2005, Divided Selves (Talbot Rice Gallery Edinburgh and Fleming Gallery London) 2006, The Border Boys (Peebles) 2013, Anne Redpath and Family (Harwick) 2015; *Collections* incl: HM The Queen, Aberdeen Art Gallery and Museum, Aberdeen Asset Management, Barings Borders Museum Cncl Dumbarton Educnl Tst, Perth Art Gallery, Allied Lyons, James Capel, Edinburgh Educn Authy, Robert Fleming Holdings, Kirkcaldy Art Gallery, Glasgow Art Gallery and Museum, Kleinwort, Heriot-Watt Univ, Liverpool Univ, Nuffield Fndn, Queen Elizabeth Coll London, Robert Gordon Univ, Stirling Unv, Reading Art Gallery, NM Rothschild, RAC, Royal Scottish Acad, Royal W of Eng Acad, Scottish Life Assurance Co, Scottish Nat Gallery of Modern Art, Tate Gallery Archive, Turcan Connell; *Awards* Guthrie Award RSA 1964, David Cargill Prize RGI 1977, Lothian Region Award RSA 1977, Sir William Gillies scholarship RSA 1980, RGI Prize 1990, Cornelissen Prize RWA 1992; *Recreations* music, gardening; *Style*— Prof David Michie, OBE

MICHNA-NOWAK-SONDHI, Krysia Danuta; da of Sqdn Ldr Wladyslaw Jan Nowak (d 1982), and Henrietta Nowak (d 1994); *b* 18 March 1948; *Educ* Notre Dame GS Sheffield, Henry Hartland GS Workshop, Ealing Coll London (BA), Garnett Coll London (PGCE); *m* 17 Sept 2013, J C Sondhi; *Career* artist; Br Cncl lectr Poznan Univ Poland 1977 and 1978, lectr American Inst of Foreign Study in Paris, Florence, Rome, Amsterdam and Munich 1979–82; opened fashion co Lady Henrietta Ltd 1982–85; held pt/t positions at: The Drian Galleries London 1973, The Grabowski Gallery London 1973, Inst of Contemporary Art London 1973, 359 Gallery Nottingham 1974 (asst), Sheffield City Art Galleries 1975–87 (art educn offr); freelance interior designer for hospitals and clinics 1991–; arts advsr Northern Gen Hosp 1992–; Sheffield City Cncl: memb Cleansing Dept Keep Br Tidy 1985–87, Dept of Land and Planning A City Centre for People 1985–87, arts designer and advsr Arundel Gate Scheme 1985–87, public subway mural Hollywood Parade Sheffield; voluntary work: League of Friends N Gen Hosp 1979–82, sec Polish Med Aid Appeal Sheffield 1981, organiser charity fashion show for Ethiopia Graves Art Gallery Sheffield 1985, organiser designer fashion show Wentworth House 1987; pres Worksop Soc of Artists 1976, tstee York Arts Space Assoc 1986–87, fndr memb Anglo-Polish Soc Sheffield 1986–87, memb Open Learning Ctee BBC Radio Sheffield 1986–87, interior designer specialising in hosps and clinics 1990–96, arts advsr Northern Gen Hosp Sheffield 1991–93, memb Assoc of Polish Artists 1996, memb Printmakers Cncl; numerous paintings in public and private collections; *Solo Exhibitions* Drian Galleries, Waterloo Gallery, Stoke on Trent, Nottingham Playhouse, Crucible Theatre Sheffield, Philip Francis Gallery Sheffield, Worksop Library, Univ of Sheffield, New Work (Café des Arts Hampstead) 1997, Golfe de St Donat France 1999, Dragon International London 1999, Nice Airport 2000, Air Gallery London 2000, Letchworth Museum 2000, Seven Springs Gallery Ashwell 2000, Thomas Plunkett Fine Art St Albans 2000, St Raphael Gallery London 2001, Courtyard Arts Hertford 2001, The Old Laundry Gallery Wimpole Estate Cambs 2002, Hitchin Museum Herts 2002, Affordable Art Fair Battersea 2002, Boxfield Gallery Stevenage 2003, Letchworth Museum 2004, The Chapel Gallery Riseley 2005, Open Studios 2005, Letchworth Arts Centre Letchworth 2007, Ashwell Gallery Herts 2011; two person show Posk Gallery London 1997, two person show Hitchin Museum and Art Gallery 2007 (with Anne Songhurst); *Group Exhibitions* Seven Springs Gallery Ashwell 1999, Heiffer Gallery London 1999, Luton Museum 2000, Concourse Gallery Barbican 2000, The Place Arts Centre Letchworth 2000, Broughton House Gallery Cambridge 2000, Cambridge Contemporary Art Gallery 2000, McNeill Fine Art Gallery Radlett Herts 2000, Mayfest Exhibition Grosvenor Square London 2000, Thomas Plunkett Fine Art (with Richard Sorrel and Robin Hazlewood) 2002, Kaleidoscope Gallery London 2004, Marston Vale 2004, Sheridan Russell Gallery London 2005, Knowl Piece Gallery 2006 and 2007, Letchworth Arts Centre 2007, London Affordable Art Fair annually 2008–16, Benslow Music Centre Hitchin 2009, Letchworth Museum (exhbn with Anne Songhurst) 2010, Women in the Frame (Horsebridge Arts Centre Whitstable) 2010, BBH Print Soc 2011, Aceo Gallery Brighton 2012, Mixed Print Show (Art Nest Hitchin) 2013, 7 works taken to Poland for the Toru? Collection of Polish Émigré Art 2013, Seeart Tunbridge Wells 2014, 2015 and 2016, Edinburgh Corn Exchange Art Fair 2014 and 2015, Chelsea Art Fair 2015, Hampstead Art Fair 2015 and 2016, Cambridge Art Fair 2015 and 2016, mixed print exhbn Obsidian Gallery 2016; *Public Collections* hertford County Public Collection, Hitchin Museum; *Awards* shortlisted for Woman of the Midlands 1987, winner Dulux 2nd Nat Prize for Community Arts Project 1987, John West Memorial Award 2000; *Publications* Poland (contrib), The Planet of the Towers (illustrator, 1982), Sztuka Polska w Wielkies Brytanii 1940–2000 (2006), Squadron Leader Wladyslaw Jan Nowak (jtly, 2011), Squadron Leader Wladyslaw Jan Nowak (biography, 2012), The Diary of Wladyslaw Jan Nowak (in Polish and English, 2012); contrib article The Artist magazine 2004; *Recreations* painting, cooking, travelling, design (interior design and graphics), mural painting; *Style*— Miss Krysia D Michna-Nowak; ✉ Studio, 12 Knowl Piece, Wilbury Way, Hitchin, Hertfordshire; Keeble House, 309 Wedon Way, Bygrave, Baldock, Hertfordshire SG7 5DX (☎ 01462 893983, e-mail art@krysianowak.co.uk) website www.krysianowak.co.uk)

MIDDLEBURGH, Rabbi Dr Charles Hadley; s of Hyman Middleburgh (d 1987), and Elizabeth Middleburgh; *b* 2 October 1956; *Educ* Brighton Coll, UCL (BA, PhD), Leo Baeck Coll (ordained 1986); *m* 11 May 1984, Gill, *née* Blyth; *Career* lay reader Brighton & Hove Progressive Synagogue 1975–77, min Kingston Lib Synagogue 1977–83, rabbi Harrow & Wembley Progessive Synagogue 1983–97, exec dir Union of Lib and Progressive Synagogues 1997–2002, rabbi Dublin Jewish Progressive Congregation 2002–11, rabbi Progressive Jewish Forum Copenhagen 2003–05, rabbi Cardiff Reform Synagogue 2005–; Leo Baeck Coll: lectr in bible, Aramaic and practical rabbinics 1985–2001, lectr in Aramaic rabbinic literature and medieval bible commentaries 2003–09, sr lectr Bible and Liturgy 2010–, dir of Jewish studies 2011–14, dean 2014–; lectr in Jewish-Christian relations Irish Sch of Ecumenics TCD 2002–09; occasional broadcaster RTE, Radio Eireann, BBC Radio 4 and World Serv; FZS; *Publications* Union of Liberal and

Progressive Synagogues Daily, Sabbath and Festival Prayer Book (assoc ed, 1995), Union of Liberal and Progressive Synagogues High Holy Day Prayer Book (co-ed, 2003), Tefillot Ve-Tachanunim: Prayers in Times of Illness and Death (co-ed, 2006), High and Holy Days: A Book of Jewish Wisdom (co-ed, 2010), A Jewish Book of Comfort: Three thousand years of wisdom and experience (co-ed, 2014), Bright and Beautiful: Poems Inspired by the Natural World (2015); *Recreations* photography, birdwatching, studying animals, reading and writing poetry, playing the fool for my grandchildren; *Style—* Rabbi Dr Charles H Middleburgh; ✉ c/o Leo Baeck College, 80 East End Road, London N3 2SY (☎ 020 8349 5600, e-mail charles.middleburgh@lbc.ac.uk)

MIDDLETON, Edward Bernard; s of Bernard Middleton (d 1987), and Bettie Mabel, *née* Knight (d 2005); *b* 5 July 1948, London; *Educ* Aldenham; *m* 22 May 1971, Rosemary Spence, da of Maj Denis Frederick Spence Brown, MC, TD (d 1995), of Lincoln; 3 s (Nicholas b 1976, Simon b 1978, Hugo b 1982); *Career* sr Pannell Fitzpatrick & Co London 1971–73, mangr Pannell Bellhouse Mwangi & Co Nairobi 1973–75, ptnr PKF (UK) LLP 1979–2008 (mangr 1975–79, memb Bd 2005–08), dir PKF consultancy services 1996–2008; seconded to DTI as dir/under sec Industrial Devpt Unit 1984–86; memb Cncl Br Assoc of Hospitality Accountants 1997–2007; dir London Cremation Co plc 2011–; hon treas Hospitality Action 1992–2008, dir WCSM Educn Tst 2010–, tstee ResCu 2010–; memb Worshipful Co of Spectaclemakers 2005 (memb Ct 2008, tstee Worshipful Co of Spectaclemakers Charity 2009–12, Master 2015–16); FCA 1972; *Recreations* sailing, photography, travel, walking; *Clubs* Reform; *Style—* Edward Middleton, Esq; ✉ Barrans, Bury Green, Little Hadham, Ware, Hertfordshire SG11 2ES (☎ 01279 658684, e-mail ebmiddleton@btopenworld.com)

MIDDLETON, Rear Adm (John) Patrick Windsor; CB (1992); s of Cdr John Henry Dudley Middleton (d 1989), of Wimbledon, and Norna Mary Tessimond, *née* Hitchings (d 1996); *b* 15 March 1938, Valletta, Malta; *Educ* Cheltenham Coll, RNC Dartmouth, RN Engrg Coll Manadon Plymouth; *m* 31 March 1962, Jane Rodwell, da of Leslie Stephen Gibbs (d 1978), of Letchmore Heath, Herts; 1 s (Toby b 1963), 1 da (Isobel b 1965); *Career* entered RN 1954; served HMS: Lion 1962, Ambush 1965, Warspite 1969; Cdr 1973, NDC 1976, HMS Blake 1977, Capt 1981; CSO(E): Flag Officer Submarines 1981, Falklands 1983; Capt naval drafting 1984, dir in serv submarines 1987, Rear Adm 1989, CSO(E) Fleet 1989, CSO (Support) Fleet 1991, ret 1992; chm Conservation Direct 1993–94, sec Royal Cmmn for the Exhibition of 1851 1995–2002; chm CARE 1998–2007 (govr 1993–2007); Liveryman Worshipful Co of Armourers and Brasiers 1971 (memb Ct of Assts 1995–2015, Master 2001–02); MIMechE 1965, MIMarE 1965, FIMgt 1989; *Books* Admiral Clanky Entertains (2010); *Style—* Rear Adm Patrick Middleton, CB; ✉ Manora, Chilmark, Wiltshire SP3 5AH (☎ 01722 716231, e-mail mimanora@aol.com)

MIDDLETON, Peter; *Educ* Friends Sch Great Ayton, Nottingham Coll of Art; *Career* cinematographer; with BBC Film Dept Ealing Studios 1965–67, freelance dir of photography 1967–; work on TV and film incl: Jubilee, The Tempest, Body and Soul, Devil's Advocate, Call Red, Holding On, Painted Lady, Wuthering Heights, Cold Feet, The Alchemist, Trust, Extremely Dangerous, Last Christmas, Other People's Children, The Hunt, Whistleblower, The Jury, Foyle's War, Promoted to Glory, Henry VIII; BAFTA nominations: South Bank Show, Holding On 1996, Cold Feet 1997; memb BSC 1994; *Recreations* photography; *Style—* Peter Middleton, Esq, BSC; ✉ c/o United Agents, 12–26 Lexington Street, London W1F 0LE (☎ 020 3214 0800, fax 020 3214 0801, website www.unitedagents.co.uk)

MIDDLETON, Sir Peter Edward; GCB (1989, KCB 1984); *b* 2 April 1934; *Educ* Sheffield City GS, Univ of Sheffield (BA), Univ of Bristol; *m* 1, 1964, Valerie Ann, *née* Lindup (d 1987); 1 s (d 1991), 1 da; m 2, 20 Jan 1990, Constance Jean Owen, *née* Close; 2 step s, 1 step da; *Career* served RAPC 1958–60; HM Treasy: sr info offr 1962, princ 1964, asst dir Centre for Admin Studies 1967–69, private sec to Chllr of the Exchequer 1969–72, press sec 1972–75, head Monetary Policy Div 1975, under sec 1976–80, dep sec 1980–83, perm sec 1983–91; Barclays Bank plc: dep chm 1991–98, chief exec 1998–99, chm 1999–2004; chm Barclays Capital (formerly BZW) 1991–98 (non-exec dir 1998–89); chm: Camelot Gp 2004–11, Marsh Ltd 2005–13, Mercer Ltd 2009–14, Burford Capital 2009–, Hamilton Ventures 2010–, Hume Capital Securities plc 2014–15, The Resort Gp 2015–, Directa Plus 2015–; UK chm Marsh & McLennan Cos 2007–14 (memb Advsy Bd 2004–09); non-exec dir: Bass plc 1992–2001, CGU plc (following merger of General Accident and Commercial Union) 1992–98, United Utilities plc 1994–2007 (dep-chm 1994–99 and 2002–07, chm 1999–2001), Mobile TeleSystems OJSC 2005–08; memb Advsy Bd Financial Dynamics 2004–09, Fenchurch Advsy Ptnrs 2005–12, chm Advsy Bd Three Delta 2006–11, memb Advsy Panel ST Telemedia 2010–12; chm CEDR 2004–11; pres Br Bankers' Assoc 2004–06; visiting fell Nuffield Coll Oxford 1981–89, hon prof Mgmnt Sch Univ of Sheffield 2011–; dir: English Chamber Orch and Music Soc 1992–2001, Inst of Contemporary Br History 2001–04 (chm 1992–2001), Int Monetary Conf 2001–02; chm: Sheffield Urban Regeneration Co Ltd 'Sheffield One' 2000–06, Creative Sheffield 2006–11, Advsy Bd Burford Advsrs LLP 2008–09; tstee Philharmonia Tst Ltd 2012–; govr: London Business Sch 1984–90, Ditchley Fndn 1985, NIESR 1991–2006; memb: Cncl Manchester Business Sch 1985–92, Cncl Sheffield Univ 1991– (chllr 1999–2015), Exec Ctee Centre for Economic Policy Research 1991–, UK Advsy Bd Nat Economic Research Assoc 1991–2008, Int Advsy Panel Monetary Authy of Singapore 2002–05, Bd of Patrons European Assoc for Banking and Financial History; Cdre Civil Serv Sailing Assoc 1984–91; *Recreations* hill walking, music, outdoor sports; *Clubs* Reform; *Style—* Sir Peter Middleton, GCB; ✉ c/o Gill Herbert, Marsh & McLennan Cos, Tower Place East, London EC3R 5BU (☎ 020 7357 2673)

MIDGLEY, (David) William (Bill); OBE (2009); s of Norman Midgley (d 1995), of Huddersfield, and Margaret, *née* Alderson (d 1986); *b* 1 February 1942; *Educ* Huddersfield Coll of Technol, Newcastle Univ (MA); *m* 1, 19 Dec 1964, Anne Christine (d 1976), da of Charles Foreman, of Huddersfield; 1 s (Edward William b 1967), 1 da (Rachel Sarah b 1969); m 2, 10 June 1977, Ada Margaret, da of John Banks; 1 da (Louise Isobel b 1980); *Career* chief exec Newcastle Building Society 1986–98 (latterly exec vice-chm); pres Br C of C 2004–06, past pres NE C of C (Trade & Industry); chm Leazes Homes Ltd; dir: Photostuff Ltd, Personalised Greetings Cards Ltd; vice-pres Marie Curie Cancer Care, chair Tyne Metropolitan Coll, chm Theatre Royal Tst; patron: Downs Syndrome NE, Hindu Cultural Assoc, Asian Business Connections; FCIB, FRSA; *Recreations* golf; *Style—* Bill Midgley, Esq, OBE; ✉ 17 Beaumont Drive, Whitley Bay, Tyne & Wear NE25 9UT (☎ 0191 297 0401, fax 0191 251 1525); Leazes Homes Ltd, YHN House, Benton Park Road, Newcastle upon Tyne NE7 7LX (☎ 0191 278 8701)

MIDHA, Dr Arun Daniel; JP (Cardiff 1994); s of Rajendra Nath Midha (d 1983), of Campbellpur, India, and Olive Marion, *née* Wroe; *b* 24 April 1964; *Educ* Gowerton Comp Sch, Univ of Wales Swansea (BSc Econ, PhD), Exeter Coll Oxford (Dip), Univ of Wales Cardiff (MBA); *m* Aug 1991, Susan Margaret, da of John Rees Williams, of Caeo; 1 da (Sara Gwenan b 9 June 1997), 1 s (Elis Daniel b 30 May 2000); *Career* grad recruit Lloyds Bank plc 1988–89, commerce and industry advsr Health Promotion Authy for Wales 1990–94, prog mangr Public Health Med Specialist Registrar Trg Scheme Wales 1994–2001, dir of strategy and resources Sch of Postgrad Med and Dental Educn Cardiff Univ 2001–09; lay chair NHS Complaints Panel in Wales 1994–97, non-exec dir Welsh Servs NHS Ambulance Tst 2000–02; GMC: lay memb 2000–08, memb Educn Ctee 2001–, President's Advsy Ctee 2001–, tstee 2002–, treas 2003–, chair Resources Ctee 2003–; chair GB's Code of Conduct Panel Royal Pharmaceutical Soc 2005–, chair Renal Advsy Bd Wales 2006–08, external memb Audit, Risk and Quality Assurance Ctee Nursing and Midwifery Cncl 2009–, lay memb Health Professions Cncl 2009–, lay memb Advsy Ctee Clinical Excellence Awards Wales 2010–, memb Bd and tstee Acad of Medical Royal Colls 2011–, ind memb Nat Advsy Bd NHS Wales 2011–, ind memb Resources Ctee Wales Audit Office 2011–, lay memb Bar Standards Bd Bar Cncl 2011–, case examiner Royal Coll of Veterinary Surgeons 2012–, lay memb Gen Pharmaceutical Cncl 2016–, lay memb Ctee on Standards House of Commons 2016–; contrib to numerous jls; memb: Bd Welsh Language Bd 2000–10 (also memb Audit Ctee), Broadcasting Cncl for Wales 2006–08, Audience Cncl for Wales 2007–11, Postgraduate Medical Educn and Trg Bd 2007–10 (also memb Trg Ctee and Audit Ctee), HE Funding Cncl For Wales 2015–; chair Natural Resources Corporate Governance Ctee Welsh Govt 2012– (non-exec dir 2009–12); judge Queens Anniversary Prizes for Further and Higher Educn 2006–; referee Welsh Rugby Union 1992–2003, tstee and hon sec Welsh Rugby Charitable Tst; govr: Ysgol Pencae 2005–11, Ysgol Plasmawr 2008–; lay memb Cncl and memb Remuneration Ctee Swansea Univ 2011–12; JP Cardiff 1994–2004, High Sheriff S Glamorgan 2012–13; *Recreations* rugby, music, theatre, opera, family; *Style—* Dr Arun Midha

MIDLANE, Stephen Peter; s of Peter Alan Midlane (d 1986), of Pinner, Middx, and Muriel, *née* Young (d 2001); *b* 7 October 1951; *Educ* UCS London, Univ of Exeter, Univ of Birmingham; *m* 2013, Doris Settle; 1 s (Jonathan b 1980), 1 da (Becky b 1984); *Career* exec dir Polka Theatre for Children 1977–; memb Bd: Quicksilver Theatre for Children 1989–99, Yellow Earth Theatre 2004–10; Action for Children's Arts Membs' Award 2010, Love Wimbledon Business Improvement District 2012–; *Style—* Stephen Midlane, Esq; ✉ Polka Theatre for Children, 240 The Broadway, Wimbledon, London SW19 1SB (☎ 020 8545 8323, fax 020 8545 8365, e-mail stephen@polkatheatre.com)

MIDLETON, 12 Viscount (I 1717); Alan Henry Brodrick; also Baron Brodrick of Midleton (I 1715) and Baron Brodrick of Peper Harow (GB 1796); the full designation of the Viscountcy is Midleton of Midleton; s of Alan Rupert Brodrick (d 1972), and Alice Elizabeth, *née* Roberts; suc uncle 11 Viscount 1988; *b* 4 August 1949; *Educ* St Edmund's Canterbury; *m* 1, 1978 (m dis 2002), Julia Helen, da of Michael Pitt, of Lias Cottage, Compton Dundon, Somerton, Somerset; 2 s (Hon Ashley Rupert b 1980, Hon William Michael b 1982), 1 da (Hon Charlotte Helen b 1983); m 2, Maureen Susan, da of Joseph Sime, of Bessacarr, Doncaster; *Heir* s, Hon Ashley Brodrick; *Career* horologist; Keeper of Horology Gershom Parkington Collection Bury St Edmunds 1986–2002; conslt Vost's Auctioneers 1997–2000; memb Cncl and chm Br Horological Inst Museum Tst 1993–; chm Br Horological Inst 1998–2001 (vice-chm 1997–98); curator and librarian Br Horological Inst 2001– (pres 2015–); FBHI; *Recreations* bicycling, walking; *Style—* The Rt Hon the Viscount Midleton

MIDWINTER, Dr Eric Clare; OBE (1992); *b* 11 February 1932; *Educ* St Catharine's Coll Cambridge (BA, MA), Univ of Liverpool (MEd), Univ of York (DPhil); *Career* social historian and writer; academic appts 1955–68, dir of priority educnl project Liverpool 1968–75, head of Public Affrs Unit Nat Consumer Cncl London 1975–80, dir Centre for Policy on Ageing London 1980–91; chm: Advsy Centre for Educn 1976–80, London Regnl Passenger Ctee 1977–96, Health and Social Welfare Bd Open Univ 1983–90, Community Educn Devpt Centre 1994–2001; memb: Prince of Wales' Advsy Ctee on Disability 1990–95, Advsy Ctee on Telecommunications for Disabled and Elderly People (DIEL) 1990–96; visiting prof of educn Univ of Exeter 1992–2001; pres Assoc of Cricket Statisticians and Historians 1997–2004, chm Centre for Policy on Ageing 2003–09; Hon Dr Open Univ 1989; *Books* Victorian Social Reform (1968), Social Administration in Lancashire (1969), Old Liverpool (1971), Nineteenth Century Education (1970), Teaching in the Urban Community School (ed, 1972), Education for sale (1977), Make 'em Laugh: Famous Comedians and Their World (1979), W G Grace: His Life and Times (1981), The Wage of Retirement: the Case for a New Pensions Policy (1985), Caring for Cash: the Issue of Private Domiciliary Care (1986), Fair Game: Myth and Reality in Sport (1986), The Lost Seasons: Cricket in Wartime (1987), New Design for Old (1988), Red Roses Crest the Caps (1989), Creating Chances (1990), The Old Order (1990), Out of Focus (1991), Brylcreem Summer: the 1947 Cricket Season (1991), The British Gas Report on Attitudes to Ageing (1991), The Illustrated History of County Cricket (1992), Lifelines (1993), The History of Social Welfare in Britain (1994), First Knock; Cricket's Opening Pairs (1994), Surrey CCC: 150 Years – A Celebration (1995), Darling Old Oval: Surrey Cricket at the Oval (1995), State Educator: The Life and Enduring Influence of W E Forster (1995), Pensioned Off: Retirement and Income Examined (1997), The Billy Bunter Syndrome: Or Why Britain Failed to Create a Relevant Secondary School System (1998), Yesterdays: The Way We Were (1998), From Meadowland to Multinational: a Review of Cricket's Social History (2000), Yesterdays: Our Finest Hours (2001), Best-remembered: a Hundred Stars of Yesteryear (2001), Quill on Willow: Cricket in Literature (2001), As One Stage Door Closes – John Wade, Jobbing Magician (2002), Novel Approaches: a guide to the popular classic novel (2003), 500 Beacons: the USA Story (2004), Red Shirts and Roses: The Story of the Two Old Traffords (2006), The People's Jesters: Twentieth Century British Comedians (2006), Lord Salisbury (2007), Parish to Planet: How football came to rule the world (2007), George Duckworth: Warrington's Ambassador at Large (2008), An Outline of Political Thought and Practice (2008), I Say, I Say, I Say: The Double Act Story (2009), The Cricketer's Progress: Meadowland to Mumbai (2010), Britain's Story: A Overview of British History (2012), Guide to Cricket Lore (ed, 2014); *Recreations* writing, sport, theatre; *Clubs* MCC, Lancashire CCC, Savage; *Style—* Dr Eric Midwinter, OBE; ✉ Savage Club, 1 Whitehall Place, London SW14 2HD (☎ 020 7930 8118)

MIERS, Thomasina; da of Probyn Miers, and Niki, *née* Burrough; *b* 5 February 1976, Cheltenham, Glos; *Educ* St Paul's Girls' Sch, Univ of Edinburgh (MA); *m* Mark Williams; *Career* JWT 1998, digital strategist EHS Realtime 1999–2001, mangr and head of mktg Villandry 2002–04, mangr of cocktail bar Prima 2005, co-fndr Wahaca Restaurants, co-fndr DF/Mexico Restaurants; regular columnist Times on Saturday 2005–09, television presenter, campaigner (www.thepigidea.org); *Books* Soup Kitchen (2005), Cook (2006), Wild Gourmets (2007), Mexican Food Made Simple (2010), Wahaca – Mexican Food at Home (2012), Chilli Notes (2014); *Recreations* rifle shooting, tennis, swimming, dance; *Clubs* Quo Vadis, Hospital; *Style—* Miss Thomasina Miers; ✉ Wahaca, 117 Waterloo Road, London SE1 8UL (e-mail info@wahaca.co.uk, websites www.thomasinamiers.com and www.facebook.com/thomasinamiers, Twitter @thomasinamiers); Greene & Heaton, 37 Goldhawk Road, London W12 8QQ (☎ 020 8749 0315, fax 020 8749 0318, e-mail info@greeneheaton.co.uk)

MIFLIN, Dr Benjamin John (Ben); s of Stanley Benjamin Miflin (d 1971), of Lower Slaughter, Glos, and Kathleen Noel, *née* Davies (d 1999); *b* 7 January 1939; *Educ* Univ of Nottingham (BSc), Univ of Illinois (MS), Univ of London (PhD); *m* 3 Oct 1964, Hilary Frances, da of Wilfred Edward Newman; 3 da (Gail Kathryn b 12 Feb 1967, Clare Josephine b 2 Aug 1968, Johanna Frances b 8 May 1971); *Career* lectr in plant sciences Univ of Newcastle 1965–73, head Molecular Sciences Div Rothamsted Experimental Station 1983–85 (head Biochemistry Dept 1973–85), head of res devpt Ciba-Geigy Seeds 1985–93, dir Inst of Arable Crops Research 1994–99, chm Crop Evaluation Ltd 2000–09; visiting prof of plant sciences Univ of Nottingham 1981–85 and 1994–99, Lawes Tst sr fell 1999–2010; corresponding memb American Soc of Plant Physiologists; ed of several scientific books and author of over 100 scientific papers; *Recreations* photography, theatre, gardening; *Style—* Dr Ben Miflin

MIFSUD, Jean-Pierre; s of Ernest Xavier Mifsud (d 1954), of Port Fouad, Egypt, and Eugenie, *née* Grima; *b* 26 February 1944; *Educ* Coll des Frères St-Marie, Ealing GS; *m*

M

1, 1966, Carole, *née* Fearnhead (decd); 1 da (Amelia b 1 July 1974), 1 s (Dominic Xavier b 17 June 1977); m 2, 1983, Janet Elizabeth, da of Ernest Aubrey Dedman; 1 step da (Sarah Kathleen b 3 Jan 1970), 1 step s (Ross James b 21 Aug 1975); *Career* hotelier; hotel conslt and inspr hotels and restaurants AA until 1983 (joined 1970), prop: The Lake Country House and Spa Llangammarch Wells Powys 1983– (Johansens Restaurant of the Year 2005), Dinham Hall Hotel Ludlow 1994–2008, Northcote Manor Hotel Burrington Devon 2002–; Johansens Restaurant of the Year 1991–92, AA 3 Red Stars and 2 rosettes for food 1995, RAC Gold Ribbon, Good Hotel Guide Welsh Country House of the Year (César Award for Lake Country House Hotel) 1993, Pride of Britain Hotel; memb: Advsy Ctee Br Tourist Authy 1988–92; *Recreations* antique collecting, architectural renovation; *Style*— Jean-Pierre Mifsud, Esq; ✉ Lake Country House Hotel and Spa, Llangammarch Wells, Powys LD4 4BS (☎ 01591 620202, fax 01591 620457, e-mail info@lakecountryhouse.co.uk, website www.lakecountryhouse.co.uk)

MILANI, Roy; *Educ* Lycee Français de Londres, Univ of Swansea (BSc); *Career* cameraman Univ of London TV 1973–74, studio mangr BBC Radio 1974–76, vision mixer BBC Network TV 1978–82, sr prodr BBC Children's TV 1995–98 (asst prodr 1982–87, prodr 1986–95), head of factual progs and ed Newsround CBBC 1998–2001, head news and factual progs CBBC 2001–; *Awards* RTS Award 1994 and 1996, BAFTA Award 1994, 1996, 2000 and 2002, Prix Danube 1995, Prix Jeunesse (twice) 1996, Race in the Media Award 1996 and 2001, Broadcast Award 2002; *Style*— Roy Milani, Esq

MILBORROW, Ruan Leslie; s of Robert Leslie Milborrow (d 1986), of Wanstead, London, and Elizabeth Edith, *née* Cook (d 2006); *b* 11 July 1958; *Educ* Forest Sch, RAC Cirencester (MRAC, DipFM); *m* 2 Nov 2013, Debbie Anne Morris, da of Evan Morris, and Ruby Morris, both of South Cerney, Glos; *Career* sr art dir Yellowhammer Advertising Ltd 1984–91, creative dir Harari Page Ltd 1992–98, art dir Travis Sully Harari Ltd 1998–2001, creative ptnr cdp-travissully Ltd 2001–07, creative ptnr mr.h Ltd 2007–15; memb Devpt Bd Forest Sch 2005–15; *Awards* incl: D&AD, Creative Circle, Campaign Press, Campaign Posters and Aerials; Freeman City of London 1984; MIPA 1989; *Recreations* art, music, literature, theatre, association football; *Clubs* Goodwood Road Racing, Chelsea Arts; *Style*— Ruan Milborrow, Esq; ✉ 10 Edwards College, South Cerney, Cirencester, Gloucestershire GL7 5TR (e-mail r.milborrow@btinternet.com)

MILBURN, Rt Hon Alan; PC (1998); s of Evelyn Metcalfe; *b* 27 January 1958; *Educ* John Marlay Sch, Stokesley Comp Sch, Lancaster Univ (BA), Univ of Newcastle upon Tyne; *Partner* Ruth Briel; 2 s; *Career* co-ordinator Trade Union Studies Information Unit Newcastle upon Tyne 1984–90, sr business devpt offr N Tyneside Cncl 1990–92, MP (Lab) Darlington 1992–2010; shadow health spokesman 1995–96, shadow treasy spokesman 1996–97, min of state Dept of Health 1997–98, chief sec to Treasy 1998–99, sec of state for Health 1999–2003, Chllr of the Duchy of Lancaster (memb Cabinet) 2004–05; chm PLP Treasy Dept Ctee 1992–95, memb Public Accounts Ctee 1994–95; chair Social Mobility Cmmn 2016; chm Newcastle Central Constituency Lab Pty 1988–90, memb Exec Northern Region Lab Party 1990–92; co-ordinator Sunderland Shipyards Campaign 1988–89, pres NE Regn MSF 1990–92; *Recreations* cricket, football, music, cinema; *Style*— The Rt Hon Alan Milburn

MILBURN, Anthony; s of Lawrence Anderson Milburn (d 1958), of Halifax, and Constance, *née* Laskey (d 1985); *b* 3 August 1942; *Educ* Rastrick GS, Univ of Bradford (BTech), Univ of Birmingham (MSc); *m* 4 June 1983, Julia Margaret, da of Maj Charles Pierson Weeden (d 1996); 1 da (Catherine b 1986), 1 s (Richard b 1988); *Career* civil engr 1958–71, trg mangr National Water Cncl 1972–80, exec dir Int Assoc on Water Quality 1981–99, DG Int Water Assoc 1999–2002, chm and ceo Ambourne Environments 2002–, dir Dukeville Securities Ltd, fndr IWA Publishing Ltd; advsr to: UNESCO, World Water Assessment Prog; chm Pole Pole Fndn UK 2013–; memb Int Water Acad 1999, hon memb Int Water Assoc 2002; Freeman City of London, memb Worshipful Co of Water Conservators; Hon DEng Tech Univ of Istanbul 2001; MInstD (Dip Co Direction); FICE, FCIWEM 1972, fell Euro Acad of Sci and Arts 2000; *Books* Water Pollution Research and Control (ed, 1985, 1987, 1989, 1991), Water Quality Management (jt ed, 1993, 1995, 1997 and 1999); UN World Water Development Report (scientific ed, 2006); *Recreations* sailing, heritage transport, acting; *Style*— Dr Anthony Milburn; ✉ Amboume Environments, 34 Church Meadow, Surbiton, Surrey KT6 5EW

MILBURN, Sir Anthony Rupert; 5 Bt (UK 1905), of Guyzance, Parish of Acklington, Northumberland; s of Maj Rupert Leonard Eversley Milburn (d 1974, yr s of 3 Bt), and Anne Mary, *née* Scott-Murray (d 1991); suc unc, Sir John Nigel Milburn, 4 Bt (d 1985); *b* 17 April 1947; *Educ* Eton, RAC Cirencester; *m* 1977, Olivia, yst da of Capt Thomas Noel Catlow, CBE, DL, RN (ret), of Tunstall, Lancs; 2 s (Patrick Thomas b 1980, Edward Jake b 1987), 1 da (Lucy Camilla Anne b 1982); *Heir* s, Patrick Milburn; *Career* landowner; ARICS, MRAC; *Clubs* New (Edinburgh); *Style*— Sir Anthony Milburn, Bt; ✉ Bog House, Matfen, Newcastle-Upon-Tyne NE20 0RF (☎ 01661 855052, e-mail arm@armilburn.com)

MILDON, David Wallis; QC (2000); s of Arthur Mildon, and Iva, *née* Wallis; *b* 19 September 1955; *Educ* Emmanuel Coll Cambridge (MA, LLB); *m* 13 Aug 1983, Lesley Mary, *née* Richardson (d 2013); 1 da (Anne b 16 Dec 1986), 1 s (Peter b 25 Feb 1990); *Career* called to the Bar: Middle Temple 1980, Antigua and Barbuda 1990; practising barr, currently memb Essex Court Chambers; memb Ctee London Common Law and Commercial Bar Assoc 1999–; Agreements to Agree (2005), Property in Commingled Gas (2006), Gas Price Arbitrations, the adjustment phase (2014), Singapore Int Arbitration: Law and Practice, commencing an arbitration and the constitution of the tribunal (2014); *Recreations* music, sailing; *Clubs* Royal Solent Yacht; *Style*— David Mildon, Esq, QC; ✉ Essex Court Chambers, 24 Lincoln's Inn Fields, London WC2A 3ED (☎ 020 7813 8000, fax 020 7813 8080, e-mail dmildon@essexcourt.net)

MILDRED, Prof Mark; s of John Mildred (d 1996), of Usk, Gwent, and Eileen Smith (d 1969); *b* 16 September 1948; *Educ* Lancing, Clare Coll Cambridge (exhibitioner, MA); *m* 19 Oct 1974, Sarah Ruth, da of Harold Christopher Rackham (d 2007); 2 s (Joe b 13 July 1976, Tom b 16 May 1979); *Career* articled clerk B M Birnberg & Co 1973–75; ptnr: Messrs Mildred and Beaumont 1978–86, Pannone & Partners and Pannone Napier 1986–93, Evans Butler Wade 1993–95; prof of litigation Nottingham Law Sch 1995–, conslt in complex litigation matters 1995–; memb Legal Advsy Panel Nat Consumer Cncl 1987–2000, pt/t legal memb Family Health Services Appeal Authy 2002–; gen ed Civil Procedure Reports 2000–; chair Skipton Fund Appeals Panel 2006–, legally qualified memb Criminal Injuries Compensation Appeal Panel 2007–; non-exec dir Wandsworth Primary Care Tst 2003–11 (vice-chair 2005–11), chair Community Services Wandsworth 2009; memb: Law Soc 1975 (memb Consumer Law Ctee), Assoc of Personal Injury Lawyers 1990; tstee Trinity Hospice 2001–09, chair SW London Local Improvement Finance Tst 2005–11; *Books* 1989 Group Actions – Learning From Opren (Nat Consumer Cncl, 1989), Butterworths Product Liability and Safety Encyclopaedia (1992), Butterworths Clinical Negligence (contrib chapter on Class Actions, 3 edns), Product Liability: Law and Insurance (gen ed, 1994), Responsibility for Drug Induced Injury (1998), Product Liability in Comparative Context (contrib, 2005); *Recreations* singing, cooking, walking, racquet games; *Clubs* Scorpions; *Style*— Prof Mark Mildred; ✉ 67 Sisters Avenue, London SW11 5SW (☎ and fax 020 7228 1321, e-mail mild0000@aol.com)

MILES, Alastair Paul; s of John Charles Miles, of Harpenden, Herts, and Judith, *née* Baker; *b* 11 July 1961, Harrow; *Educ* St Marylebone GS London, Guildhall Sch of Music and Drama (Performer's Dip Flute), Nat Opera Studio; *m* Alison Jane, *née* Parry; 2 s (Jonathan Henry Alastair b 31 Oct 1991, Gregory Charles Frederick b 27 July 1995), 1 da (Felicity Miranda Jane b 11 Dec 1997); *Career* int operatic bass; operatic debut as Truelove in The Rake's Progress (with Opera 80) 1985; thereafter has performed a broad range of repertory at all the world's major opera houses incl: Covent Garden, La Scala Milan, Met NY, San Francisco, Vienna and Munich State Operas, ENP, Glyndebourne, Deutsche Oper Berlin, Netherlands Opera, Teatro Real Madrid, Paris Opera; given concert performances with numerous major orchs incl: LSO, London Philharmonic, Philharmonia, BBC Symphony, BBC Scottish, RPO, CBSO, Bournemouth Symphony and Bournemouth Sinfonietta, Ensemble d'Orchestre de Paris, Baltimore Symphony, NY Philharmonic, Atlanta Symphony, English Baroque Soloists, Concentus Musicus, London Classical Players, English Concert, Israel Philharmonic, Royal Scottish Nat Orch, Vienna Philharmonic, Boston Symphony; over 90 recordings for numerous labels; Decca/Kathleen Ferrier Prize 1986, Esso/Glyndebourne Touring Opera Award 1986, John Christie Award 1987; *Recreations* golf, cooking, flute playing, reading, decorative painting; *Clubs* Old Philologians; *Style*— Alastair Miles, Esq; ✉ website www.alastairmiles.com

MILES, Prof David; CBE (2016); s of Kenneth Douglas Miles, and Rebecca, *née* Owen; *b* 1959; *Educ* Univ of Oxford (BA, MPhil), Univ of London (PhD); *m* Faye Dimdore; 1 s (Oscar b 1994), 2 da (Georgia b 1999, Harriet b 2003); *Career* tutor in economics UC Oxford 1981–83, economist Bank of England 1983–89, research fell LSE 1988–89, reader in financial economics Univ of London 1989–93, economic advsr Bank of England 1993–94, chief UK economist Merrill Lynch 1994–96, prof of finance Imperial Coll London 1996–2004 (visiting prof of financial economics 2004–15), md and chief UK economist Morgan Stanley 2004–09, memb Monetary Policy Ctee Bank of England 2009–15; prof of financial economics Imperial Coll 2015–; non-exec dir FSA 2004–09; author The Miles Report on the UK mortgage market HM Treasy 2004; ed: Fiscal Studies, World Economics; *Books* Housing, Financial Markets and the Wider Economy (1994), Macroeconomics: Understanding the Wealth of Nations (co-author, 2001); *Recreations* cinema, squash, rugby, maths; *Style*— Prof David Miles, CBE; ✉ Bank of England, Threadneedle Street, London EC2R 8AH

MILES, James Archibald Robertson; s of Hamish Alexander Drummond Miles, of Edinburgh, and Jean Marie, *née* Smits; *b* 8 September 1961; *Educ* King Edward's Sch Birmingham, New Coll Oxford (BA Chinese); *m* 1 Aug 1992, Catherine Ruth, da of Trenwith John Wallis Sampson; 1 s (Alistair John Robertson b 10 June 1996), 2 da (Rachel Pamela Winifred b 15 Jan 1998, Kirsten Lily Wallis b 6 Nov 2000); *Career* business reporter South China Morning Post Hong Kong 1984; United Press International (UPI): Hong Kong reporter 1984–85, S Asia corr 1985–86, Beijing corr 1986–87; Beijing corr BBC Radio and Television 1987–94, Burton R Benjamin fell in broadcast journalism Michigan Univ 1994–95, Hong Kong corr BBC World Service 1995–97, sr Chinese affrs analyst BBC News 1997–2000, ed Strategic Comments and res fell for Asia The Int Inst for Strategic Studies 2000–01, Beijing corr The Economist 2001–14, China ed The Economist 2014–; Reporter of the Year Sony Radio Awards 1990, One World Broadcasting Award 1990; *Publications* The Legacy of Tiananmen, China in Disarray (Univ of Michigan Press, 1996); *Recreations* shooting, walking; *Style*— James Miles, Esq; ✉ The Economist, 25 St James's Street, London SW1A 1HG (☎ 020 7830 7000, e-mail jarmiles@usa.net)

MILES, (Henry) James Pearson; s of (Henry) Michael Pearson Miles OBE, *qv*, and Carol Jane Miles; *b* 24 September 1969, Hong Kong; *Educ* Wellington Coll, Manchester Coll Oxford (BA); *m* 8 Aug 1998, Laura Miles; 3s (Max, Rupert, Alfie), 1 da (Poppy); *Career* banker 1991–2000, co-fndr and md Liv-ex 2000–; *Recreations* cricket, golf, shooting, skiing, tennis; *Clubs* Boodles, Queens, Berkshire Golf, Trevose Golf; *Style*— James Miles, Esq; ✉ Liv-ex Ltd, Battersea Studios 2, 82 Silverthorne Road, London SW8 3HE

MILES, Jeremy Dylan; s of Hugh Miles (d 2005), and Pat Miles (d 2006); *b* 24 May 1955, Bromsgrove, Worcs; *Educ* Gordonstoun, Westminster; *m* 14 Feb 1981, Karina; 1 da (Tess b 7 Jan 1989); *Career* Abbott Mead Vickers BBDO: trainee account exec 1980–85, bd dir (Sainsbury's) 1985–84, bd dir (The Economist) 1985–99, bd dir (BT) 1994–99, bd dir (BT Global) 1995–99, vice-chm 1998–99; co-fndr and chm Miles Calcraft Briginshaw Duffy 1999–; memb: Marketing Soc 1985, Marketing Gp of GB 2001, Thirty Club 2005; *Awards* 9 Gold Campaign Awards, 24 Silver Campaign Awards, 8 D&AD Silver Pencils, Gold British Television Award, Gold IPA Effectiveness Award; *Recreations* travel, reading, ballet, watching sport, theatre and film; *Clubs* MCC, Reform, Harry's Bar, Annabel's, George; *Style*— Jeremy Miles, Esq; ✉ Miles Calcraft Briginshaw Duffy, 15 Rathbone Street, London W1T 1NB (☎ 020 7073 6900, e-mail milesj@mcbd.co.uk)

MILES, Prof John Richard; s of Thomas William Miles (d 1988), and Hilda Mary, *née* Davis (d 1994); *b* 22 June 1944, Oxford; *m* (m dis); *Career* designer and tutor; colourist designer and conslt Fidelis Furnishing Fabrics (later amalgamated with Tootals) 1969–74, work shown in prototype Exhibition at Design Council 1970; designer of fashion furnishings and household textiles for worldwide market 1969–; clients incl: Courtaulds, Heal's, Liberty's, Christian Dior, Yves Saint Laurent; set up own studio: Calver & Pound Designs 1973–77, Peppermint Prints 1977–81; design dir of home furnishings and apparel fabrics Courtaulds plc 1986–87 (design dir of home furnishings 1985–86); Next Interior: design mangr 1987, design and buying mangr 1987, gen mangr 1987–88; set up own studio Miles Whiston & Wright 1989–96, fndr John Miles Partnership 1996–2002; CNAA: chm Fashion and Textile Panel 1984–87 (memb 1978–81), memb Ctee for Art and Design 1984–87 and 1988–, specialist advsr to Ctee for Art and Design 1987; memb: Textile Ctee Design Centre Selection 1985–88 (memb Knitwear Ctee 1984–86), Selection Panel for Young Designers into Industry RSA 1987–89, Advsy Panel BFC 1994–97; sr lectr i/c of textiles St Martin's Sch of Art 1974–75, head of Fashion Dept and Textiles Course leader Brighton Poly 1979–85 prof of textiles and fashion RCA 1989–97, dir of product mktg Dollfus Mieg and Cie France 1997–2001, prof of design Univ of Southampton 2001–02, prof of fashion and textiles Bath Spa Univ 2002–, emeritus prof Bath Spa Univ 2013–; visiting prof Univ of Huddersfield 2010–, visiting prof Univ of Derby 2014; external examiner for various univs, dir of studies for various PhD students; co-fndr and conslt studio Claire and Lyn 1992, conslt studio Whiston and Wright 2014; memb Industrial Lead Body for Art and Design 1990–96, memb Res Assessment Panel Univ Funding Cncl 1992–; pt/t and visiting lectr; memb numerous academic ctees Brighton Polytechnic and RCA; internal and external assessor; memb Assoc of Heads of Degree Courses for Fashion and Textiles 1979–85; Hon Dr Univ of Southampton 1998; *Books* Textile Terms and Definitions (ed, 2014); *Recreations* gardening, cooking, theatre, films, reading, music; *Style*— Prof John Miles; ☎ 01529 488222, e-mail j.miles@bathspa.ac.uk

MILES, Keith Charles; OBE (1999); s of Leslie Maurice Miles, and Doris Ellen Wyard Miles; *b* 28 November 1941; *Educ* Owens Sch, Ljubljana Univ; *m* 20 Dec 1969, Slava, da of Joe Blenkus (d 1977), and Alojzija Blenkus; 1 s (Andrew Karel Scott b 1973 d 2002), 1 da (Jane Helena Louise b 1977); *Career* chartered accountant; dir of fin and ops Cable Authy 1985–88, dir of fin and admin Inst of Econ Affrs 1988–90, special advsr Putnam Hayes & Barlett 1989–90, co sec and gp fin dir Etam plc 1990–95; dir: Slovenia Trade and Investment Corporation Ltd 1996–2002, Bay Trading (Epcoscan Ltd) 1996–99, Lexecon Ltd 2000–05; only English memb Economic Advsy Cncl of the Cabinet of Repub of Slovenia 1990, hon sec-gen UK Representative Office Repub of Slovenia 1991–92, econ advsr in London Bank of Slovenia 1992–2001, rep Ljubljana Stock Exchange in UK 1995–2008, dir Sawston Hall Heritage 2009–14; memb Economic Devpt Cncl Repub of Slovenia 2005–08, memb Supervisory Bd Gorenje dd 2010–, memb Supervisory Bd Nova

Kreditna Banka Maribor dd 2012–15; chm British-Slovene Soc 1993–2012; memb Review Body for Nursing Staff, Midwives, Health Visitors and Professions Allied to Nursing 1996–99; cncllr Chiltern DC 2003–06; FRSA; *Publications* various articles on accountancy, free market economics and Central & Eastern Europe; reg contrib Finance (Slovene fin newspaper); *Recreations* skiing, reading, swimming; *Clubs* Royal Over-Seas League; *Style—* Keith Miles, Esq, OBE; ✉ 19 Elmtree Green, Great Missenden, Buckinghamshire HP16 9AF (✆ 01494 863128, e-mail kcmengland@gmail.com)

MILES, (Henry) Michael Pearson; OBE (1989); s of Brig H G P Miles (d 1966), of London, and Margaret, *née* Mounsey (d 1974); *b* 19 April 1936; *Educ* Wellington; *m* 25 Oct 1967, Carol Jane, da of Harold Berg (d 1955); 2 s (Henry James Pearson, *qv*, b 1969, Mark Edward Pearson b 1975), 1 da (Sasha Jane Pearson b 1971); *Career* Nat Serv cmmnd Duke of Wellington's Regt 1955–57; md John Swire and Sons (Japan) Ltd 1973–76; dir: Swire Pacific Ltd 1978–, Hongkong and Shanghai Banking Corporation 1984–88, John Swire & Sons Ltd 1988–; former chm: John Swire & Sons (Hong Kong) Ltd, Swire Pacific Ltd, Cathay Pacific Airways Ltd, Hong Kong Tourist Assoc; chm: Johnson Matthey plc 1998–2006 (dir 1990–2006), Schroders plc 2003–12, London Mining plc 2013–; dep chm Barings plc; also dir: BP plc 1994–2006, Portals plc, Thomas Cook Group, Fleming Far Eastern Investment Tst, Sedgwick Lloyd's Underwriting Agents, BICC 1996–2002; memb: Bd Navy Army and Air Force Inst, Int Advsy Bd Creditanstalt Vienna, Anglo-Taiwan Trade Ctee, China-Britain Trade Group (vice-pres 1996–); govr Wellington Coll 1990–2005; *Recreations* golf, tennis, shooting, family; *Clubs* Royal and Ancient, Berkshire Golf, Queen's, White's, Sunningdale; *Style—* Michael Miles, Esq, OBE

MILES, Nicholas Charles James; s of Kenneth Norman Miles, and Audrey Mary, *née* Rhodes; *b* 23 October 1958, Bombay, India; *Educ* Tonbridge Sch, Corpus Christi Coll Cambridge (MA); *m* 12-May-90; *Career* dir: BMP Business Ltd 1985–87, Lowe Bell Financial Ltd 1987–92; chief exec Financial Dynamics Ltd 1992–2001, chm Business Communications Int Gp 2001–02, fndr M: Communications 2002; performed in Death in the Aisles, Nightcap, Cambridge Footlights Revues 1979; *Recreations* gym, country pursuits, guitar; *Clubs* White's, Annabel's, Hurlingham; *Style—* Nicholas Miles, Esq; ✉ e-mail miles@mcomgroup.com or nick.cj.miles@gmail.com

MILES, Peter Thomas; s of Thomas Harry Miles (d 1968); *b* 1 August 1939; *Educ* Bromsgrove Sch; *m* 18 June 1971, Gail, da of Trevor Davies; 2 c (Juliet Elizabeth b 24 Sept 1972, Edward Thomas b 10 Feb 1975); *Career* chartered accountant; ptnr: Russell Durie Kerr Watson & Co 1968, Spicer & Pegler (following merger), Touche Ross 1990–96 (following merger, now Deloitte); chm Provincial Seals Ltd; FCA; *Recreations* fly fishing, golf, gardening; *Style—* Peter T Miles, Esq; ✉ The Old Barn, Cakebole, Chaddesley Corbett, Worcestershire DY10 4RF (e-mail peterthomasmiles@aol.com)

MILES, Dr Richard; *Educ* Univ of Liverpool (BA), Univ of Cambridge (PhD); *Career* sr lectr Dept of Classics and Ancient History Univ of Sydney; presenter Ancient Worlds (BBC 2) 2010; *Books* Constructing Identities in Late Antiquity (1999), Carthage Must Be Destroyed (2010), The Vandals (2010), Ancient Worlds: The Search for the Origins of Western Civilization (2010); *Style—* Dr Richard Miles; ✉ Department of Classics and Ancient History, Rm J6.08, A14 Quadrangle, University of Sydney, NSW 2006, Australia

MILES, Robert; QC; s of David and Marion Miles; *b* 29 November 1962; *Educ* ChCh Oxford (MA, BCL); *m* 1999, Lisabel, *née* Macdonald; *Career* called to the Bar Lincoln's Inn; *Style—* Robert Miles, Esq, QC; ✉ 4 Stone Buildings, Lincoln's Inn, London WC2A 3XT (✆ 020 7242 5524)

MILES, Dr Roger Tremayne; s of Lt Cdr Peter Tremayne Miles, RN (d 1995), of Maidenhead, Berks, and Christine, *née* Perks; *b* 9 March 1962; *Educ* Tonbridge, Trinity Coll Oxford (exhibitioner, MA), KCL (PhD), Univ of London (CertEd); *m* 28 May 1990, Deirdra Moynihan; 1 s, 2 da; *Career* bd dir OTG (Oxford Theatre Gp) Productions Ltd 1981–83, articled Price Waterhouse 1984, bd dir Charles Barker Ltd 1990–92, bd dir Georgeson and Company Ltd 1992–95, head of communications British Bankers' Assoc 1996–99, bd dir BBA Enterprises Ltd 1997–2000, bd dir The Entertainment Team Rides Ltd 1998–99, ptnr Regester Larkin – Reputation Risk Mgmnt 1999–2001, princ Repute 2002–04, risk communications advsr Civil Serv 2004–, assoc Hazards and Risk Research Gp KCL 2006–13, behavioural risk lead ThomsonReuters 2013–15, md Berkeley Research Gp 2015–; visiting lectr: ICC Commercial Crime Bureau 1999–2007, Cabinet Office Emergency Planning Coll 2000–10, Univ of London 2003–, Cranfield Univ/UK Defence Acad 2007–, Centre for Science and Policy Univ of Cambridge 2014–15, Judge Business Sch Univ of Cambridge 2015–; CMIPR 1991, MInstD 1994, FRSA 2001; *Books* The Behavioural Economics Guides (co-author, 2014 and 2015), Behavioural Risk: Catching the Careless Nudists (2015), Groupthink: Not What You Thought It Was (2015), Mortgage Markets: Squaring the Vicious Circle (co-author, 2015); *Publications* FT Operational Risk Handbook (contrib, 2011), Operational Risk: New Frontiers (2012), From Compliance to Coping: Experiences of Banks' Chief Risk Officers 2007–09 (PhD, 2012), Risk Culture White Papers (series, 2013–), When Compliance Becomes A Game (2014); *Recreations* fatherhood, music making, novels, new technologies, theatre, vintage technologies; *Clubs* RSA; *Style—* Dr Roger Miles

MILFORD, 4 Baron (UK 1939); Sir Guy Wogan Philipps; 4 Bt (UK 1919); QC (2002); s of 3 Baron Milford (d 1999), and Hon Mary (Mollie) Makins (now Viscountess Norwich), da of 1 Baron Sherfield; *b* 25 July 1961; *Educ* Eton (King's Scholar), Magdalen Coll Oxford (Roberts-Gawen Scholar, MA); *m* 1996, Alice Sherwood; 2 s (Hon Archie Sherwood b 12 March 1997, Hon Ben Aroya b 26 May 2000); *Heir* s, Hon Archie Philipps; *Career* called to the Bar Inner Temple 1986; *Style—* The Rt Hon the Lord Milford, QC; ✉ 68 Westbourne Park Road, London W2 5PJ (✆ 020 7229 1844, e-mail gmilford@outlook.com)

MILFORD, His Hon John Tillman; QC (1989); s of Dr Roy Douglas Milford (d 1982), of Strathtay, Perthshire, and Essie, *née* Rhind (d 1972); *b* 4 February 1946; *Educ* Hurstpierpoint Coll, Univ of Exeter (LLB); *m* 1975, Mary Alice, da of Dr Edmund Anthony Spriggs (d 1989), of Wylam, Northumberland; 3 da (Alice (Mrs Charles Bubear) b 1977, Sarah (Mrs James Gayner) b 1979, Emily b 1981); *Career* called to the Bar Inner Temple 1969 (bencher 1998); practising Newcastle upon Tyne 1970–2002, recorder of the Crown Court 1985–2002, head of Trinity Chambers Newcastle upon Tyne 1986–99, dep judge of the High Court 1994–2002, circuit judge (NE Circuit) 2002–16, ret, liaison judge to Northumberland and N Tyneside Magistrates 2003–12; chm Northumbria Area Judicial Forum 2004–12; co-chm for S Northumberland BFSS 1996–98, chm River Tyne Fishing Festival 1997, vice-chm Newcastle & District Beagles 1998–2005, regnl chm NE England Countryside Alliance 1999–2002 (co-chm S Northumberland 1998–99), chm Bywell Show 1999 and 2000; chm of tstees: Get Hooked on Fishing Charitable Tst 2004–10, Get Hooked on Fishing 2010–13; *Recreations* fishing, shooting, watching ballet, gardening; *Clubs* Northern Counties (Newcastle upon Tyne, chm 2003–07); *Style—* His Hon John Milford, QC; ✉ The Law Courts, The Quayside, Newcastle upon Tyne NE1 3LA

MILIBAND, Rt Hon David; PC (2005); s of Ralph Miliband (d 1994), and Marion *née* Kozak; bro of Edward Miliband, MP, *qv*; *b* 15 July 1965; *Educ* Haverstock Comp Sch, CCC Oxford (BA), MIT (MSc); *m* 1998, Louise Shackelton; 2 adopted s (Isaac, Jacob); *Career* Parly offr Nat Cncl for Voluntary Orgns 1987–88, research fell Inst of Public Policy Research 1989–94, head of policy Office of the Ldr of the Opposition 1994–97, head PM's Policy Unit 1997–2001; MP (Lab) South Shields 2001–13; min for schools DfES 2002–04, min of state Cabinet Office 2004–05, minister of communities and local govt 2005–06, sec of state for environment, food and rural affrs 2006–07, sec of state FCO 2007–10; sec Social Justice Cmmn 1992–94; *Publications* Reinventing the Left (ed, 1994), Paying for Inequality (co-ed, 1994); *Clubs* Whiteleas Social, Cleadon, South Shields Recreation, South Shields FC; *Style—* The Rt Hon David Miliband

MILIBAND, Rt Hon Edward (Ed); PC (2007), MP; bro of Rt Hon David Miliband, *qv*; *b* 24 December 1969, London; *Educ* Univ of Oxford, LSE; *m* 27 May 2011, Justine Thornton; 2 s (Daniel b 2009, Samuel b 2010); *Career* HM Treasy: special advsr to the Chllr 1997, took sabbatical to teach at Harvard Univ 2002–04, chm Cncl of Economic Advsrs 2004; MP (Lab) Doncaster N 2005–; min for the third sector Cabinet Office 2006–07, min for the Cabinet Office and for social exclusion and Chllr of the Duchy of Lancaster 2007–08, sec of state for energy and climate change 2008–10, ldr Labour Pty and HM Oppn 2010–15; memb TGWU; *Style—* The Rt Hon Ed Miliband, MP; ✉ House of Commons, London SW1A 0AA

MILL, Ian Alexander; QC (1999); s of Ronald MacLauchlan Mill (d 1984), and Thelma Anita, *née* Boliston; *b* 9 April 1958; *Educ* Epsom Coll, Univ of Cambridge (MA); *m* 13 June 1987, (Mary) Emma, da of Roger and Marian Clayden, of Los Gatos, CA; *Career* called to the Bar Middle Temple 1981; commercial barr specialising in entertainment and sports law 1982–; *Recreations* cricket, golf, good food and wine, travel; *Clubs* MCC; *Style—* Ian Mill, Esq, QC; ✉ Blackstone Chambers, Blackstone House, Temple, London EC4Y 9BW (✆ 020 7583 1770, fax 020 7822 7350)

MILL, Peter Stuart; s of Donald Norman Mill (d 1981), of London, and Heather Mary, *née* Lavelle; *b* 21 June 1957; *Educ* Claremont HS Kenton, Watford Coll of Technol (DipAD); *m* 4 Oct 1987 (m dis), Susan Ann, da of Dennis Austin Goode; 4 da (Helen Michelle b 23 Aug 1985, Hannah Catherine b 28 Dec 1988, Katie Heather b 15 June 1995, Rosie May Jennifer b 31 Oct 1998); m 2, March 2002, Jaqueline Ann, *née* Dougall; *Career* jr copywriter BBDO Advertising London 1975–76; copywriter: Fletcher Shelton Delaney 1976–78, Hall Advertising 1978–84; fndr ptnr and exec creative dir The Leith Agency 1984, sr ptnr new business 1995–2002; founding ptnr and dir 60 Watt 2003–, founding ptnr Planet Blog 2013; Silver Campaign Press Award, Campaign Poster Award, EPICA Award, Cannes Advtg Film Festival Silver Lion, Br TV Advtg Silver Award, Scottish Advtg Awards annually 1988–93, Roses Awards annually 1988–94; memb D&AD 1983–; *Style—* Peter Mill, Esq; ✉ Beechmount, Kingscavil, Linlithgow, West Lothian EH49 6NA

MILLAR; *see also:* Hoyer Millar

MILLAR, Darren David; AM; *b* 1976; *Career* memb Nat Assembly for Wales (Cons) Clwyd W 2007–, shadow min for environment 2007–09, shadow min for communities and local govt 2009–10, shadow min for economy and tport 2010–11, shadow min for health and older people 2011–16, shadow min for educn and children 2016–; chair: Public Accounts Ctee, Health, Wellbeing and Local Govt Ctee 2009–10; memb: Health and Social Services Ctee, Children Young People and Educn Ctee; FCMI, FRSA, FInstLM; *Style—* Darren Millar, Esq, AM; ✉ National Assembly for Wales, Cardiff Bay, Cardiff CF99 1NA (✆ 0300 200 7214, e-mail darren.millar@assembly.wales)

MILLAR, David William; s of Brig William Semple Millar, of Camberley, Surrey, and Maureen Heather, *née* Jones; *b* 30 January 1951; *Educ* Morrison's Acad, Univ of Edinburgh (BSc); *m* 3 Sept 1977, Daniele Yolande Germaine, da of Maurice Robert Ferreyrol; 1 s (Hamish Robert b 10 June 1983), 1 da (Pascaline Myrto b 10 Aug 1988); *Career* joined J Walter Thompson 1973, dir J Walter Thompson 1985–94, md JWT Direct 1990–94, head of communications strategy British Gas plc (now BG Group plc) 1995–97, head of corp mktg BG Group plc 1997–2003; memb Bd H&F Homes; MIPA 1982, FRSA 2000; *Recreations* golf; *Clubs* Hampton Court Palace Golf; *Style—* David Millar, Esq; ✉ Transpectra, 7 Flanchford Road, London W12 9ND (✆ 020 8749 2410)

M

MILLAR, Prof Sir Fergus; kt (2010); *b* 5 July 1935; *Educ* Edinburgh Acad, Loretto, Trinity Coll Oxford (BA), All Souls Coll Oxford (fell 1958–64, MA, DPhil, Conington Prize); *m* 1959, Susanna Friedmann; 2 s, 1 da; *Career* fell and tutor in ancient history The Queen's Coll Oxford 1964–76, prof of ancient history UCL 1976–84, fell Brasenose Coll Oxford 1984– (emeritus fell 2002–), prof of ancient history Univ of Oxford 1984–2002 (DLitt 1988), Sather prof of classical lit Univ of Calif Berkeley 2003; visiting appt Inst for Advanced Study Princeton 1968 and 1984; Br Sch at Rome: Balsdon sr fell 1983, memb Cncl 1989, vice-chm 1993, acting chm 1994–95, chm Cncl 1995–97, hon fell 2001; ed Jl of Roman Studies 1975–79; delg OUP 1989–95; pubns sec Br Acad 1997–2002; pres: Classical Assoc 1992–93, Soc for the Promotion of Roman Studies 1989–92 (chm Pubns Ctee 1980–89); foreign memb: German Archaeological Inst 1978, Bavarian Acad 1987, Finnish Acad of Science and Letters 1989, Russian Acad 1999, American Acad of Arts and Sciences 2003, Australian Acad of the Humanities 2009; sr assoc fell at Oxford Centre for Hebrew and Jewish Studies 1990; hon fell: Trinity Coll Oxford 1992, The Queen's Coll Oxford 1999; Hon DPhil Helsinki 1994; Hon DLitt: Univ of St Andrews 2004, Hebrew Univ Jerusalem 2012, Univ of Edinburgh 2012; Prize Cultori di Roma 2005, Kenyon Medal for Classical Studies Br Acad 2005; FBA 1976, FSA 1978; *Books* A Study of Cassius Dio (1964), The Roman Empire and its Neighbours (1967), E Schürer, A History of the Jewish People in the Age of Jesus Christ (175 BC-AD 135) I-III (ed with G Vermes and M D Goodman, 1973–87), The Emperor in the Roman World (31 BC-AD 337) (1977, 2 edn 1992), Caesar Augustus: Seven Aspects (ed with Erich Segal 1984), The Roman Near East (31 BC-AD 337) (1993), The Crowd in Rome in the Late Republic (1998), The Roman Republic in Political Thought (2002), The Roman Republic and the Augustan Revolution (jtly, 2002), Government, Society and Culture in the Roman Empire (jtly, 2004), The Greek World, the Jews and the East (jtly, 2006), A Greek Roman Empire: Power and Belief under Theodosius II, 408–450 (2006), Handbook of Jewish Literature from Late Antiquity 135–700 CE (with Eyal Ben-Eliyahu and Yehudah Cohn, 2012), Religion, Language and Community in the Roman Near East, Constantine to Mohammed (2013), Empire, Church and Society in the Late Roman Near East (2015); *Style—* Prof Sir Fergus Millar, FBA; ✉ Oxford Centre for Hebrew and Jewish Studies, Clarendon Institute Building, Walton Street, Oxford OX1 2HG (e-mail fergus.millar@bnc.ox.ac.uk)

MILLAR, Peter John; s of Norman Millar (d 1992), and Maureen Nelson, *née* McMaster (d 1998); *b* 22 February 1955; *Educ* Bangor GS Co Down, Magdalen Coll Oxford (MA); *m* 1981, Jacqueline Carol, *née* Freeman; 2 s (Patrick James Arthur b 1984, Oscar Alexander b 1987); *Career* Reuters corr: Brussels 1978–79, E Berlin 1981–83, Moscow 1983–85; journalist Daily Telegraph 1985–86, Euro corr Sunday Telegraph 1986–89, Central Euro corr Sunday Times 1989–90; The European: dep ed 1990–91, managing ed 1997–98; freelance columnist, broadcaster, literary translator and writer 1991–; contrib: Sunday Times, The Times, Daily Mail, The Guardian, The FT, BBC, Sky TV, German TV ARD and Westdeutsche Rundfunk; popular fiction critic The Times 1994–; Foreign Corr of the Year Granada TV What the Papers Say Awards 1989, commended Int Reporter Category Br Press Awards 1989; *Books* Tomorrow Belongs To Me (1991), Stealing Thunder (1999), Bleak Midwinter (2001), Schwarzer Winter, Hallowe'en Geschichten (2003), Gottes Feuer (2004), Eiserne Mauer (2005), Schwarze Madonna (2007), All Gone to Look for America (2009), 1989: The Berlin Wall – My Part in its Downfall (2009), The Black Madonna (2010), The Shameful Suicide of Winston Churchill (2011), Slow Train to Guantanamo (2013), Marrakech Express (2014); trans: The White Masai (2005), Return to Barsaloi (2006), Deal with the Devil (2007), Back from Africa (2007), The Murderer in Ruins (2015); *Recreations* cooking, skiing, painting; *Clubs* Groucho; *Style—* Peter Millar, Esq; ✉ Staddle Cottage, Bell's Lane, Hook Norton OX15 5LJ (website www.petermillar.eu)

MILLAR, (John) Richard; s of William Millar (d 1967), and Phyllis Millar (d 1996); *b* 16 February 1940; *Educ* Wellington, Coll of Law; *m* 2 Dec 1978, Rosemary, da of Thomas Hanson (d 1998); *Career* admitted slr 1963, sr ptnr Bischoff & Co 1990–93 (ptnr 1968–93), jt chm Frere Cholmeley Bischoff 1993–97 (conslt 1997–98), conslt Eversheds 1998–2006; memb Law Soc 1963–; tstee: Fidelity UK Fndn 2000–, St Ethelburga's Centre for Reconciliation and Peace 2002–15 (chm 2012–15); Freeman City of London, Liveryman City of London Solicitors' Co (Additional Asst 2006–08); *Recreations* sailing, gardening, barbershop singing; *Clubs* City of London, Little Ship; *Style—* Richard Millar, Esq; ✉ 15 Woodstock Road, London W4 1DS

MILLARD, Dennis Henry; s of Henry Edward Millard, of NY, and Edna Elizabeth, *née* Battale, of NY; *b* 28 February 1949; *Educ* Marist Brothers Coll, Univ of Natal, Univ of Cape Town (MBA, Gold Medal); *m* 22 March 1972, Paula Teresa Felicity, da of late William Coulter; 1 da (Lisa Catherine b 1972), 2 s (Sean Patrick b 1975, James Henry b 1988); *Career* audit clerk then audit sr H E Mattinson & Partners Chartered Accountants Durban 1967–73, mgmnt accountant then fin dir Hultrans Ltd Durban 1973–77, MBA 1978, gp mangr corp planning Huletts Corporation Durban 1979–80, gp mangr corp planning then fin dir Plate Glass Group Johannesburg 1980–93, fin dir Medeva plc London 1994–96, fin dir Cookson Group plc 1996–2005; chm and non-exec dir Smiths News plc 2006–, chm Halfords plc 2009–; non-exec dir: ARC Int plc 2001–03, Exel plc 2003–05, Xchanging Ltd 2005–13, Debenhams plc 2006–, EAG Ltd 2006–07, Premier Farnell plc 2007–15, Pets at Home plc 2014–; memb Economic Advsy Cncl CBI 1998–2002; chm of tstees Holy Cross Children's Tst; memb South African Soc of Chartered Accountants 1973; MInstD 1991; *Recreations* golf, surfing, cycling; *Clubs* Sunningdale Golf; *Style—* Dennis Millard, Esq; ✉ Halfords plc, Icknield Street Drive, Washford West, Reditch, Worcestershire B98 0DE (website www.halfords.com)

MILLER, Ambrose Michael; s of Ambrose Miller, of Bideford, Devon, and Margaret Dorothy, *née* Dennett; *b* 15 April 1950; *Educ* Radley, Magdalene Coll Cambridge, King's Coll London (BMus); *m* 4 April 1981, Celia Frances Sophia, da of Sir Desmond Arthur Pond (d 1986); *Career* mangr Royal Ballet Orchestra 1974–81, gen mangr Scottish Baroque Ensemble 1981–83, fndr and artistic dir European Union Chamber Orchestra 1983 (currently DG), artistic dir King's Lynn Festival 1998–, artistic dir Stratford on Avon Music Festival 2007–; Freeman City of London, Liveryman Worshipful Co of Musicians; *Recreations* cooking, reading; *Clubs* Royal Fowey Yacht; *Style—* Ambrose Miller, Esq; ✉ Hollick Farm, Yarnscombe, Devon EX31 3LQ (☎ 01271 858249, e-mail eucorchl@aol.com)

MILLER, Andrew; s of late Ernest Miller, and late Daphne Miller; *b* 23 March 1949, Isleworth; *Educ* Hayling Island Secdy Sch, Highbury Tech Coll, LSE; *m*; 2 s, 1 da; *Career* technician Geology Dept Portsmouth Poly, student LSE 1976–77, regnl offr MSF 1977–92, MP (Lab) Ellesmere Port and Neston 1992–2015; Team PPS to DTI 2001–05; dir Thornton Research Properties Ltd 2014–; chair: Regulatory Reform Select Ctee 2005–10, Parly Information and Communication Technologies Forum (PICTFOR, formerly Parly IT Ctee (PITCOM)) 2005–10 (vice-chair 2010–15), Sci and Technol Select Ctee 2010–15; chair Thornton Advsy Bd 2014–, chair Engagement Advsy Bd Grantham Centre for Sustainable Futures Sheffield 2015–, memb Advsy Bd UK Research Integrity Office 2015–; memb Science Policy Advsy Gp Royal Soc 2015–; *Style—* Andrew Miller, Esq; ✉ Hollytree Cottage, Commonside, Alvanley, Cheshire WA6 9HB (☎ 01928 722642, e-mail andrew.1949@outlook.com)

MILLER, (Dr) Andrew; *b* 29 April 1960, Bristol; *Educ* Univ of East Anglia, Univ of Lancaster (PhD); *Career* author; *Books* Ingenious Pain (1997, James Tait Black Meml Prize 1997, Premio Grinzane Carvour (Italy) 1998, Int IMPAC Dublin Literary Award 1999), Casanova (1998), Oxygen (2001), The Optimists (2005), One Morning Like a Bird (2008), Pure (2011, Best Novel and Book of the Year Costa Book Awards 2012); *Style—* Andrew Miller; ✉ c/o Ariella Feiner, United Agents, 12–26 Lexington Street, London W1F 0LE

MILLER, Ben; s of Michael Miller, and Marion Miller; *b* 24 February 1966, London; *Educ* Malbank Sch Nantwich, Chaffey Coll Calif, St Catharine's Coll Cambridge (MA); *m* 15 April 2004, Belinda Stewart-Wilson; 1 s (Jackson Blair b 7 July 2006); *Career* comedian and actor; Edinburgh Fringe (with Alexander Armstrong) 1994 and 1996 (nominated Perrier Comedy Award); *Television* Armstrong and Miller (Paramount Comedy Channel then Channel 4) 1997–2001, The Worst Week of My Life (BBC), The Worst Christmas of My Life (BBC) 2006, The Armstrong and Miller Show 2007– (Best Comedy Prog BAFTA Television Award 2010), Primeval (ITV 1) 2007–, Moving Wallpaper (ITV 1) 2008–09; *Radio* Armstrong and Miller (BBC Radio 4) 1998; *Film* The Parole Officer 2001, Johnny English 2003, Razzle Dazzle: A Journey Into Dance 2007; *Theatre* The Ladykillers (Gielgud Theatre) 2011–12; *Style—* Mr Ben Miller; ✉ c/o Independent Talent Group, Oxford House, 76 Oxford Street, London W1D 1BS

MILLER, Carolyn; CBE (2013); da of Norman Miller (d 2012), and Irene, *née* Hanger (d 2005); *b* 20 November 1951, London; *Educ* Univ of Southampton (BSc), City Univ London (DipTP); *Career* various local govt posts 1973–84, sr advsr Miny of Planning Nicaragua 1984–87; Save the Children: dir Mozambique/Angola 1987–89, head Southern Africa regnl office 1989–91, dir Asia, Latin American, Caribbean and Middle East 1991–96, dir of progs 1996–2001; dir Europe, Middle East and Americas DFID 2001–05, chief exec Merlin 2005–13; conslt 2013–; non-exec dir Oxford Policy Mgmnt 2015–; chair Int NGO Trg and Research Centre (INTRAC) 2015–; *Recreations* walking, cinema, theatre; *Style—* Ms Carolyn Miller, CBE; ✉ e-mail carolyn.millerpersonal@gmail.com, Twitter @carolynmil

MILLER, Sheriff Colin; s of James Miller (d 1980), and Isabella Millar Nicol Brown (d 1995); *b* 4 October 1946; *Educ* Paisley GS, Univ of Glasgow (LLB); *m* 28 Jan 1972, Joan Elizabeth, da of Robert Marshall Blyth; 3 s (James Douglas b 24 May 1973, Alasdair Robert b 7 July 1975, Euan Colin b 19 Jan 1977); *Career* legal apprentice Mitchells Johnston & Co Glasgow 1967–69, asst slr D S & W Semple Paisley 1969–70 (ptnr 1971), ptnr McFadyen & Semple Paisley 1971–91 (sr ptnr 1987–91); sheriff: for S Strathclyde Dumfries & Galloway at Hamilton 1991–95, at Ayr 1995–2010 and 2010–; dean Faculty of Procurators Paisley 1991; Law Soc of Scot: memb Cncl 1983–91, convener Conveyancing Ctee 1986–89, convener Judicial Procedure Ctee 1989–91, convener Rights of Audience in Supreme Courts Working Party 1990–91; *Recreations* family interests, walking, Clyde steamers, railways, motor vehicles and photography; *Clubs* Glasgow Art; *Style—* Sheriff Colin Miller; ✉ Sheriffs' Chambers, Sheriff Court, Wellington Square, Ayr KA7 1EE (☎ 01292 268474, fax 01292 292249)

MILLER, (Peter) David; s of John Morton Miller, and June Rosalind Withy, *née* MacLellan; *b* 4 February 1966, Edinburgh; *Educ* King's Sch Canterbury, Girton Coll Cambridge (BA); *m* 4 Dec 1999 (m dis), Kate, *née* Colquhoun; 2 s (Frederick David b 12 Dec 2000, William Arthur b 8 Aug 2003); *Career* literary agent; Rogers, Coleridge & White Ltd 1990– (dir 1997–); treas Assoc of Authors' Agents 1996–98; contrib: La Vanguardia, English Literature in Transition, The Conradian, TLS, Bookseller, Independent, Daily Telegraph; memb Joseph Conrad Soc of the UK; Orion Publishing Gp Literary Agent of the Year Br Book Industry Awards 2008; *Books* Today (2011), That Glimpse of Truth: the finest short stories ever written (ed, 2014); *Recreations* cooking, Conrad, Ibsen, music, mischief; *Style—* David Miller, Esq; ✉ Rogers, Coleridge & White Ltd, 20 Powis Mews, London W11 1JN (☎ 020 7221 3717, fax 020 7229 9084, Twitter @drearyagent)

MILLER, David James; s of James Samuel Miller, of Lymington, Hants, and Beryl Mary, *née* Jones; *b* 28 February 1952; *Educ* Stockport GS, Emmanuel Coll Cambridge (MA); *m* 17 Sept 1988, Sophie Kay Voss, da of Flemming Christian Rathsach, of Pindon Manor, Bucks; *Career* called to the Bar Middle Temple; dep chief exec Life Assurance & Unit Tst Regulatory Orgn 1986–89, dir legal & secretarial Royal & Sun Alliance Insurance Group plc 1989–99 (legal advsr and unit tst business mangr 1977–86); memb Ind Monitoring Bd Pentonville Prison (vice-chair 2009–10, chair 2011–13); *Books* Eureka (ed, 1973); *Recreations* travel, history of London; *Clubs* Oxford and Cambridge; *Style—* David Miller, Esq; ✉ 100 Rosebery Avenue, London EC1R 4TL (☎ 020 7833 3963)

MILLER, David John; OBE; s of Air Cdre John Douglas Miller, CBE (d 1998), of Guildford, Surrey, and Sybil Francis, *née* Powell; *b* 7 March 1947; *Educ* Dragon Sch Oxford, St Edward's Sch Oxford, Jesus Coll Cambridge (MA); *m* 24 Jan 1976, Maryrose, da of John Edgar Dulley; 3 s (Fergie b 8 June 1979, Bertie b 26 March 1981, Gregory b 28 Nov 1984); *Career* Joseph Sebag stockbrokers 1969–72; Robert Fleming Group: joined 1972, special advsr to Govt of Abu Dhabi 1975–78, Jardine Fleming Hong Kong 1979–81, Jardine Fleming Tokyo 1981–88, dir Robert Fleming Holdings until 1992; md State Street Global Advisors 1992–94, chief exec Wheelock NatWest Ltd Hong Kong 1994–97, md FBG Investment Ltd 1998–; chm Connect Mortgage Gp 2005–, dir Titus Int 2006–; *Recreations* golf, tennis, children; *Style—* David Miller, Esq, OBE

MILLER, Francis Edward; s of Alfred Lewis Miller (d 1971), and Emily Johannah, *née* Lark (d 1993); *b* 20 January 1940; *Educ* Brixton Sch of Building, Univ of Westminster; *m* 28 Nov 1964 (m dis 1987), Valerie, da of Sydney Victor Read (d 1985); 2 s (Richard Lewis b 7 Nov 1970, John Francis b 24 May 1976); *Career* jr quantity surveyor 1956, subsequently surveyor and mangr of bldg and civil engrg projects, commenced practice 1972 (specialising in resolution of disputes in bldg, civil engrg and process industries as conslt, conciliator, mediator, adjudicator and arbitrator); ed Arbitration – News and Views (CIArb) 1991–93; pres Law Alumni Assoc of Univ of Westminster 1997–99; memb Arbitration Panel: RICS 1975–94, CIArb; memb Worshipful Co of Arbitrators 1981 (memb Ct of Assts 1992–99); FRICS 1975–94, assoc Inst of Patentees and Inventors 1975–99, FCIArb 1975– (chartered arbitrator), FInstD 1979–91; *Books* Arbitration – Recommendations and Survey (1988), Building and Civil Engineering – Cost Value Comparison (1991), Arbitration – The Arbitrator and the Parties (1994), Civil Justice – Another Chance to Get it Right (1995), Disputes – The Avoidance and Resolution of Disputes (1995), Arbitration – The Arbitration Bill (1996), Arbitration – The Arbitration Act 1996 (trilogy of mock judgments) (1997), The Arbitration Act 1996 – The 46(1)(b) Brigade (1997), The Arbitration Act 1996 – Section 9 and Halki Shipping (1998), Disputes – the square root of disputes (1998), The Japanese Language – Where have all the Pronouns Gone? (2001), The Japanese Language – Millers Kanji Workbook (2002), Alphabet (A-Z) (2007); *Recreations* writing, walking, talking; *Style—* Francis Miller, Esq; ✉ 2 Wellington House, Auckland Close, Bexhill on Sea, East Sussex TN40 2FH (website www.yourhumblethinker.com)

MILLER, Rt Rev Harold Creeth; *see:* Down and Dromore, Bishop of

MILLER, Hugh; s of James Weir Miller (d 1991), of Wishaw, Scotland, and Alice, *née* Waddell (d 1990); *b* 27 April 1937; *Educ* Wishaw Acad, Wishaw HS, Stow Coll, Univ of Glasgow; *m* 18 May 1981, Annette Elizabeth, da of Albert John Slater; 3 c (by previous marriages) (Lesley b 1960, James b 1967, Rachel b 1972); *Career* author; asst to Dr John Grierson 1959, princ photographer Scottish TV 1961–62, co-owner Unique Magic Co London 1963–70; memb: Magic Circle 1965, Mark Twain Soc USA 1976; *Books* The Open City (1973), Ambulance (1975), The Dissector (1976), The Saviour (1977), Casualty (1981), Silent Witnesses (1984), An Echo of Justice (1990), Skin Deep (1991), Indelible Evidence (1991), Scotland Yard (co-author, 1993), Seaforth (1994), Unquiet Minds (1994), Proclaimed in Blood (1995), Prime Target (1996), Borrowed Time (1997), Forensic Fingerprints (1998), Secrets of the Dead (2000), Charlie's Case Notes (2000), More Secrets of the Dead (2001), Crimewatch Solved (2001), What the Corpse Revealed (2002), Mindset (2003), Dereliction Day (screenplay, 2005), Penumbra (2006), Legacy (2010), Sidekick (2011), A Pallid Grace (2013); *Recreations* travel, walking, reading; *Style—* Hugh Miller, Esq; ✉ 40 St John's Court, Warwick CV34 4NL (e-mail hugh448@btinternet.com); c/o Lucas Alexander Whitley Ltd, 14 Vernon Street, London W14 0RJ (☎ 020 7471 7900, fax 020 7471 7910)

MILLER, Ian Richard; s of Richard Miller, and Dawn Miller; *b* 1965, Ongar, Essex; *Educ* Brentwood Sch Essex, St Anne's Coll Oxford (MA); *m* 1987, Andrea, *née* Davies; *Career* Welsh Office: joined 1987, private sec to the Perm Sec 1989–91, grade 7 1991, grade 6 1998, grade 5 1999; Nat Assembly for Wales 1999–2000, head of finance Welsh Local Govt Assoc 2000–02, chief exec Denbighshire CC 2002–08, chief exec Wyre Forest DC 2009–; clerk N Wales Fire Authy 2002–08; memb Orders and Medals Res Soc; memb SOLACE 2002; *Recreations* collecting and researching medals; *Style—* Ian Miller, Esq; ✉ Wyre Forest District Council, Civic Centre, New Street, Stourport-on-Severn DY13 8UJ (☎ 01562 732700, e-mail ian.miller@wyreforestdc.gov.uk)

MILLER, James Francis Xavier; s of late Lt-Col John Francis Miller, and Barbara Mary Miller, *née* Cooke; *b* 3 March 1950; *Educ* Douai Sch, Merton Coll Oxford (MA); *m* 1976, Ruth Ellen Rowland, da of Canon C R Macbeth; 2 s (Tom b 4 March 1979, Richard b 2 Oct 1980); *Career* Winchester Coll: asst master 1972–89, head of economics 1978–82, housemaster 1982–89; headmaster Framlingham Coll 1989–94, headmaster Royal GS Newcastle upon Tyne 1994–2008; former chm Amazing Grades Ltd (formerly study-links.com); cncllr Winchester CC 1976–83 (chm Health and Works Ctee 1979–82); memb: Hereford Historic Churches Tst Ctee 2009–13, Eardisland Parish Cncl 2011–14; govr: King Edward's Sch and King Edward's HS Birmingham 2009–12, Hereford Sixth Form Coll 2009–; FRSA 1994; *Recreations* opera, crosswords, theatre, trying to play the sax less badly, malt whisky, bridge, photographing Herefordshire's historic churches; *Style—* James Miller, Esq; ✉ Orchard Cottage, Eardisland, Leominster, Herefordshire HR6 9BJ (☎ 01544 388454, e-mail jfxmiller@hotmail.com)

MILLER, James Lawson; s of David Wardrop Miller (d 1966), and Helen Frew, *née* Baxter (d 1952); *b* 26 January 1931; *Educ* The John Lyon Sch Harrow, St John's Coll Cambridge (MA); *m* 29 June 1957, Margaret Ann (d 2007), da of Beverley Robinson (d 1984); 2 s (David b 1958, Jeremy b 1959), 1 da (Jane b 1962); *Career* chartered builder, construction co chief exec; chm and dir: James Lawson Holdings Ltd, James Lawson Property Ltd 1965–; pres The Builders' Conference 1985; fell Chartered Inst of Building; *Books* Computer Aided Estimating (1977); *Recreations* duplicate bridge, Church of England activities, philosophy; *Clubs* Leander; *Style—* James L Miller, Esq; ✉ 40 North Park, Gerrards Cross, Buckinghamshire SL9 8JP

MILLER, Prof (Christopher) John; s of late Stanley Miller, of Henley-on-Thames, Oxon, and late Joan Beryl Gill; *b* 4 November 1941; *Educ* Bishop Vesey's GS Sutton Coldfield, Univ of Nottingham (BA, LLM); *m* 4 Sept 1964, Michèle Marie Juliette, da of late Raymond Michel Guérault, of Paris; 1 s (Mark), 1 da (Anne Marie); *Career* barr; lectr in law Univ of Durham 1966–70, reader in common law Univ of Leeds (lectr in law 1970–77), prof of law Univ of Warwick 1980–89 (reader 1979); Univ of Birmingham: prof of English law 1989–2003 (emeritus prof of law 2003–), dean Faculty of Law 1994–97; pt/t chm Social Security Appeals Tbnls and Disability Appeals Tbnls 1986–95; *Books* Contempt of Court (1976, 3 edn 2000), Product Liability (jtly, 1977, 2 edn 2004), Product Liability and Safety Encyclopaedia (1979–2014), Comparative Product Liability (ed, 1986), Business Law (jtly, 1991), Benjamin's Sale of Goods (jt ed, 1992, 9 edn 2014), Consumer and Trading Law: Text Cases and Materials (jtly, 1998); *Recreations* classical music, gardening, walking, sport; *Style—* Prof John Miller; ✉ Faculty of Law, Chancellor's Court, University of Birmingham, PO Box 363, Birmingham B15 2TT (☎ 0121 414 8113, fax 0121 414 3585, e-mail c.j.miller.law@bham.ac.uk)

MILLER, Sir Jonathan Wolfe; kt (2002), CBE (1983); s of Emanuel Miller, DPM, FRCP; *b* 21 July 1934; *Educ* St Paul's, St John's Coll Cambridge (MB BCh); *m* 1956, Helen Rachel Collet; 2 s, 1 da; *Career* television, theatre and opera director; stage dir London and NY 1965–67, res fell in history of med UCL 1970–73, assoc dir Nat Theatre 1973–75, visiting prof in drama Westfield Coll London 1977–, assoc prodr ENO 1980–, res fell in neuro-psychology Univ of Sussex 1981–83, artistic dir Old Vic 1988–90; memb Arts Cncl 1975–76, Silver medal Royal TV Soc 1981, Albert medal RSA 1990; curate exhibition Nat Gallery London 1998; From the Look of Things (lectures) 1995, River's lectr King's Coll Cambridge 1997; fell UCL 1981, hon fell St John's Coll Cambridge 1982, hon fell RA 1991; Hon DLitt: Univ of Leicester 1981, Univ of Cambridge 1996; FRCP 1997, FRCPEd 1998; *Stage* Nottingham Playhouse: School for Scandal 1968, The Seagull 1969, The Malcontent 1973; Old Vic: King Lear 1970, The Merchant of Venice 1970, Andromache 1988, One Way Pendulum 1988, Bussy D'Ambois 1988, The Tempest 1988, Candide 1988, King Lear 1989, The Liar 1989; The Tempest (Mermaid) 1970, Hamlet (Arts Theatre Cambridge) 1970; NT: Danton's Death 1971, School for Scandal 1972, Measure for Measure 1974, Marriage of Figaro 1974, The Freeway 1974; Chichester: The Taming of the Shrew 1972, The Seagull 1973; Greenwich: Family Romances 1974, The Importance of Being Earnest 1975, All's Well 1975, She Would If She Could 1979; Long Day's Journey Into Night (Haymarket) 1986; The Taming of the Shrew: (RSC Stratford) 1987, (Barbican) 1988; jtly adapted and directed The Emperor (Royal Court, televised 1988) 1987; A Midsummer Night's Dream (Almeida) 1996, She Stoops to Conquer (Gate Theatre London), As You Like It (Gate Theatre London), King Lear (Stratford Festival) 2002, King Lear (Lincoln Centre Theatre) 2004, The Cherry Orchard (Crucible Theatre Sheffield) 2007; *Television* ed BBC Monitor 1965, directed films for BBC TV 1966, The Body in Question (BBC series) 1978, exec prodr BBC Shakespeare series 1979–81; presenter: Madness series (ITV) 1991, Born Talking, Atheism: A brief history of disbelief (BBC) 2005; *Film* Take A Girl Like You 1970; *Opera* Arden Must Die (Sadler's Wells Theatre) 1974, The Cunning Little Vixen (Glyndebourne) 1975 and 1977; ENO: The Marriage of Figaro 1978 (directorial debut), The Turn of the Screw 1979, Arabella 1989, Otello 1981, Rigoletto 1982 and 1985, Don Giovanni 1985, The Magic Flute 1986, Tosca 1986 (transferred from Maggio Musicale Florence, subsequently revived Houston Grand Opera), The Mikado 1986, 1988, 1993 and 2001, The Barber of Seville 1987, The Turn of the Screw 1993, Rigoletto 1993, Rosenkavalier 1994 and 2003, Carmen 1995; Kent Opera: Cosi Fan Tutte 1975, Rigoletto 1975, Orfeo 1976, Eugene Onegin 1977, La Traviata 1979, Falstaff 1980 and 1981, Fidelio 1982, 1983 and 1988; Maggio Musicale Florence 1990–2001: Don Giovanni, Cosi Fan Tutte, The Marriage of Figaro, Idomeneo, Ariadne, La Boheme, Don Pasquale; Metropolitan Opera NY: Katya Kabanova, The Rake's Progress, Marriage of Figaro, Pelléas and Mélisande; Zurich Opera: Die Gezeichneten, Nabucco, Magic Flute, Die Sweigsamen Frau, Falstaff, Seraglio; other prodns incl: Fanciulla del West (La Scala), Figaro (Vienna State Opera), The Magic Flute (Israel Philharmonic prodn) and Roberto Devereux (Monte Carlo Opera) 1990–92, Manon Lescaut (La Scala) 1992, Maria Stuarda (Monte Carlo Opera), Capriccio and Falstaff (Deutsche Staatsoper Berlin) 1993, Bach's St Matthew Passion (Holy Trinity London) 1993, Anna Bolena (Monte Carlo Opera) 1994, Fedora (Bregenz Festival) 1993, L'incoronazione di Poppea (Glimmerglass Opera) 1994, Cosi fan Tutte (ROH, debut) 1995, Tamerlano (Glimmerglass Opera) 1996, Anna Bolena (Bayerische Staatsoper), I Puritani (Bayerische Staatsoper), Seraglio (Zurich Opera) 2003, Orfeo (Southbank Centre) 2003, L'Elisir d'Amore (Stockholm Opera) 2003, Falstaff (New Nat Theatre Tokyo) 2004, La Traviata (Lithuanian Opera) 2005, St Matthew's Passion (Brooklyn Acad of Music) 2006, L'Elisir d'Amore (NYC Opera) 2006, Don Giovanni (Palau des Arts Valencia) 2006, Rosenkavalier (New Theatre Tokyo) 2007; *Books* McLuhan (1971), Freud: The Man, His World, His Influence (ed, 1972), The Body in Question (1978), Subsequent Performances (1986), The Don Giovanni Book: Myths of Seduction and Betrayal (1990), Nowhere in Particular (1999); *Style*— Sir Jonathan Miller, CBE

MILLER, Jonny Lee; *b* 15 November 1972, Kingston, Surrey; *m* 1, 1996 (m dis 1999), Angelina Jolie; m 2, 2008, Michele Hicks; 1 s (Buster Timothy b 2008); *Career* actor; *Television* incl: Mansfield Park 1983, Itch 1989, Keeping Up Appearances 1990, Prime Suspect 3 1993, Cadfael 1994, Meat 1994, Dead Man's Walk 1996, Byron 2003, Canterbury Tales 2003, Smith 2006–07, Eli Stone 2008–09, Emma 2009, Dexter 2010, Elementary 2012–; *Films* incl: Dead Romantic, Hackers 1995, Trainspotting 1996, Afterglow 1997, Regeneration 1997, Plunkett & Macleane 1999, Mansfield Park 1999, Complicity 2000, Love, Honour and Obey 2000, The Escapist 2002, Mindhunters 2004, Melinda and Melinda 2004, Aeon Flux 2005, The Flying Scotsman 2006, Endgame 2009, Byzantium 2012, Dark Shadows 2012; *Theatre* Beautiful Thing (Bush Theatre) 1993, Festen (Almeida Theatre) 2004, Someone Who'll Watch Over Me (Ambassadors Theatre) 2005, After Miss Julie (Broadway) 2009, Frankenstein (NT) 2011 (Best Actor Olivier Award 2012 (with Benedict Cumberbatch)); *Style*— Mr Jonny Lee Miller; ✉ c/o 42, 20 Denmark Street, London WC2H 8NA

MILLER, Keith Manson; CBE (2005); s of John Manson Miller (d 1982), and Dolores, *née* McLauchlan (d 1970); *b* 19 March 1949, Edinburgh; *Educ* Loretto, Heriot-Watt Univ (BSc), Univ of Glasgow (Dip in Mgmnt Studies); *m* 10 Jan 1975, Lee, *née* Marshall; 3 da (Deborah b 19 April 1976, Lauren b 3 April 1978, Kathryn b 21 Oct 1980); *Career* The Miller Group Ltd (formerly James Miller & Partners Ltd): joined as dir Miller Mining 1975, gp bd dir 1976, md Miller Developments 1986, gp ceo 1994–2015; dir Edinburgh Int Festival 2014–; Scottish Business Achievement Award 2003, Ernst & Young Scottish Entrepreneur of the Year 2006; Hon DEng Napier Univ 2005; FCIOB 2003, FRICS 2010; *Recreations* sailing, ski-mountaineering, golf, shooting; *Clubs* RYS; *Style*— Keith Miller, Esq, CBE; ✉ Miller Investments Ltd, 93 George Street, Edinburgh, EH2 3ES (☎ 01312 401227, e-mail keith.miller@millerinvestments.co.uk)

MILLER, Malcolm Paul; s of Sidney John Miller (d 2001), and Daisy, *née* Bristow; *b* 31 May 1949, Hornchurch, Gtr London; *m* 1972, Geraldine Anne, *née* McKeating; 2 s (b 1978 and 1981); *Career* various posts incl fin and mgmnt accountant in health insurance BUPA 1971–84, fin controller BUPA Health Servs 1984–86, ops dir BUPA Health Servs 1986–91; The London Clinic: commercial dir 1991–94, chief exec 1994–2011; memb Ctee London C of C 1991–94; dir Bd: London Medicine 1995–2000, Ind Healthcare Assoc 1995–2003, Ind Healthcare Forum 2003–07; bd tstee and treas St Francis Hospice; memb Inst of Healthcare Mgmnt, MCMI, FRSM, FIoD; *Recreations* playing tennis at club level, golf, watching live sport, travelling, theatre, food and wines; *Clubs* MCC, RSM; *Style*— Malcolm Miller, Esq; ☎ 07775 567892, e-mail malcolmpmiller@me.com

MILLER, Rt Hon Maria; PC (2012), MP; *b* 1964, Wolverhampton; *Educ* Brynteg Comp Bridgend, LSE; *m* Iain; 3 c; *Career* joined Cons Pty 1983; account mangr Grey 1985–90, mktg mangr Texaco Ltd 1990–95, dir Grey 1994–99, dir Rowland/Saatchi 1999–2003; Parly candidate (Cons) Wolverhampton NE 2001, Parly spokesman Basingstoke 2003–05, MP (Cons) Basingstoke 2005–; shadow min for educn 2005–06, shadow min for family welfare 2006–07, shadow min for the family 2007–10, min for disabled people 2010–12, sec for culture, media and sport and min for women and equality 2012–14; *Style*— The Rt Hon Maria Miller, MP; ✉ House of Commons, London SW1A 0AA (e-mail millerm@parliament.uk)

MILLER, Michael Dawson; s of Cyril Gibson Risch Miller, CBE (d 1976), and Dorothy Alice, *née* North-Lewis (d 2002); *b* 12 March 1928; *Educ* Rugby; *m* 17 July 1954, Gillian Margaret, da of Dr Eric Gordon-Fleming (d 1948); 3 da (Caroline b 1957, Clare b 1961, Jane b 1961); *Career* Parachute Regt Regs 1946–48, TA 1949–55, HAC 1957–63; articled clerk 1949, in practice as slr 1954–55, ptnr Thos R Miller & Son 1962–90 (exec 1955–62, ptnr Bermuda 1969–90); dir: Shipowners Assurance Mgmnt Montreal 1973–84, AB Indemnitas Stockholm 1983–90, Thos Miller War Risks Services 1985–90; conslt Planning Bd for Ocean Shipping 1970–; Liveryman: Worshipful Co of Shipwrights 1977, Worshipful Co of Solicitors 1986; memb: Law Soc 1954, London Maritime Arbitrators' Assoc 1963; Silver medal Hellenic Merchant Marine Greece 1983; *Books* Marine War Risks (1, 2 and 3 edns, Br Insurance Law Assoc Prize 1991), Uncommon Lawyer, Wars of the Roses; *Recreations* going to sea on small ships, opera, history, reaching remote places, ancient civilisations, targeting intellectuals; *Clubs* Royal Ocean Racing, Royal Bermuda Yacht, Royal Thames Yacht, City, Hurlingham; *Style*— Michael Miller, Esq; ✉ 52 Scarsdale Villas, London W8 6PP (☎ 020 7937 9935); Dairy Cottage, Donhead, St Andrew, Wiltshire

MILLER, Dr (John) Paul; s of John Frederick William Miller (d 1961), and Edith Mary Miller (d 2004); *b* 10 July 1940; *Educ* Repton, Keble Coll Oxford (MA, DPhil, BM BCh), Univ of London (MSc), Guy's; *m* 19 Aug 1978, (Constance) Mary, da of Kenneth Anderson (d 1997); 1 da (Claire b 1981), 1 s (Christopher John Kenneth b 1984), 1 adopted s (Nicholas Francis Haynes b 1977), 1 adopted da (Jackie Marie Haynes b 1979); *Career* house physician Guy's 1968, house surgn Addenbrooke's Hosp Cambridge 1969, team leader Save the Children Fund Nigerian Civil War, sr house offr and registrar Hammersmith Hosp 1970–72, hon sr registrar St James's Hosp Leeds 1972–75, lectr med Univ of Leeds 1972–75, sr lectr med Univ of Manchester 1975–81, hon conslt physician Univ Hosp of S Manchester 1975–81, visiting prof med Baylor Coll Houston (MRC travelling fell) 1978–79, conslt gastroenterologist Univ Hosp of S Manchester 1981–2006 (clinical sub dean 1982–88); chm: Bd Faculty of Med, Dentistry, Nursing and Pharmacy Univ of Manchester 1997–2004, Cncl Med Protection Soc 1996–2003; pres Manchester Med Soc 2003–04 (chm Cncl 1997–2001), treas Br Atherosclerosis Soc 1997–2002; author of sci papers and reviews on: respiratory physiology, gastroenterology (especially peptic ulceration), disorders of lipoprotein metabolism; formerly: treas Br Hyperlipidaemia Assoc (now Heart UK), regnl advsr N W Reg RCP; currently memb Manchester Literary and Philosophical Soc; memb: Br Soc Gastroenterology, Assoc Physicians GB and Ireland; FRCP 1982, FACP; *Recreations* walking, cycling; *Clubs* RSM; *Style*— Dr Paul Miller; ✉ 1 Ballbrook Avenue, Manchester M20 6AB (e-mail jpmiller@btinternet.com)

MILLER, Richard Hugh; QC (1995); s of Sir Stephen James Hamilton Miller, KCVO (d 1996), and Lady Heather Miller; *b* 1 February 1953; *Educ* Charterhouse, Univ of Sussex (BSc); *Career* called to the Bar Middle Temple 1976 (bencher 2007, chm Finance Ctee and memb Exec Ctee 2012–); practising barr specialising in patent matters, head of chambers Three New Square IP 2012–; chm Intellectual Property Bar Assoc 2005–11 (vice-chm 2004–05), memb Bar Cncl 2006–11 (memb European Ctee 2005–11, memb Professional Practice and Ethics Ctee 2008–, co-chm 2009–11, memb Access to the Bar Ctee 2009–10); memb: Patents Sub-Gp Cncl of the Bars and Law Socs of Europe (CCBE) 2008–, Working Gp for Reform of the Patents County Ct (now Intellectual Property Enterprise Ct); observer memb Cncl (UK Gp) Int Assoc for the Protection of Intellectual Property (AIPPI) 2006–; *Books* Terrell on the Law of Patents (jt ed, 14, 15, 16 and 17 edns); *Recreations* travel, films; *Style*— Richard Miller, Esq, QC; ✉ Three New Square IP, 3 New Square, Lincoln's Inn, London WC2A 3RS (☎ 020 7405 1111, fax 020 7405 7800)

MILLER, Ronald Alan; s of Eric Norman Miller (d 1978), of London, and Rosemary, *née* Winter; *b* 10 March 1951; *Educ* Westminster, St Bartholomew's Hosp Med Sch London (MB BS, MS); *m* 1, 1975 (m dis 1995), Sarah Jane, da of Richard Griffiths Lumley, of Ross on Wye, Glos; 1 s (Mark Rudolph b 1979), 1 da (Rosalind Margaret Louise b 1982); m 2, March 1996, Linda Katheryn, da of Michael James Stanley Berriman, of Petersfield, Hants; 1 da (Georgina Megan Mallory Miller b 4 March 1999); *Career* Hunterian prof of surgery RCS 1985, Simpson Smith lectr Charing Cross Hosp 1986; currently: hon conslt urological surgeon London Urology Hosp St John and Elizabeth, conslt urological surgeon Wellington and Highgate Hosps, conslt urological advsr Centre for Health and Human Performance 2010–; md Urology Chambers Ltd 2011–; former postgrad dean Royal Northern Hosp; hon sr lectr: Inst of Urology, Royal Free Hosp, UCH; author of 200 papers on urological subjects; Cutler Prize RCS 1984, Prize of South German Urology Assoc 2014; sec N E Thames Advsy Ctee on Urology; chm NE Thames Urological Tumour Bd, chm Supervisory Bd Highgate Hosp LLP 2011; memb: Cncl Biological Engrg Soc, Instrument Ctee Br Assoc Urological Surgns, Steering Ctee Soc of Minimally Invasive Therapy (hon treas), Cncl Urological Section RSM, BAUS approved Expert Witness Register 2013; validated memb: Expert Witness Directory 2000, Expert Witness Register Legal Hub 2000; consulting ed: Endourology, Urology, Jl of Minimally Invasive Surgery, Jl of Day Surgery, Jl of Ambulatory Surgery; memb: BMA, RSM, Br Assoc Urological Surgns, American Urological Assoc, Endo Urology Soc, Minimally Invasive Soc; md Woolaston House Ltd 1999, chm Encyclomedia Ltd 2000; Order of Lenin; FRGS, MB BS 1974, MRCS LRCP 1974, FRCS England 1978, MS London 1986, MInstD; *Books* Percutaneous Renal Surgery (1983), Endoscopic Surgery (1986), Second Generation Lithotripsy (1987); *Recreations* riding, climbing, shooting, reading; *Style*— Ronald Miller, Esq; ✉ Urology Chambers Ltd, 17–19 View Road, London N6 4DJ (☎ 020 8341 3422, e-mail info@woolastonhouse.com, website www.woolastonhouse.com)

MILLER, Sir Ronald Andrew Baird; kt (1993), CBE (1985); *Educ* Daniel Stewarts Coll Edinburgh, Univ of Edinburgh (BSc); *Career* chm Dawson International plc 1982–1995; non-exec dir: Securities Trust of Scotland plc 1983–2001, Christian Salvesen plc 1987–97, Scottish Amicable 1987–97, Aggreko plc 1997–2002; vice-pres British Fashion Exports; dir Quality Assurance Agency for Higher Education 1997–2003; memb Scottish Higher Educn Funding Cncl 1992–95; chm Ct Napier Univ (now Edinburgh Napier Univ) 1998–2001, chm Edinburgh Napier Univ Devpt Tst; Freeman: City of London, Worshipful Co of Woolmen; Hon DSc Heriot-Watt Univ 1992, Hon Dr Napier Univ 2001; MICAS; *Recreations* golf, skiing, travel, gardening, art, music; *Clubs* Caledonian; *Style*— Sir Ronald Miller, CBE

MILLER, Dr Roy Frank; s of Thomas Richard Miller (d 1978), and Margaret Ann, *née* Tattum (d 2004); *b* 20 September 1935; *Educ* Wembley Co GS, Univ of Exeter (BSc), Univ of London (PhD); *m* 18 March 1961, Ruth Naomi, da of William Kenchington (d 1956); 1 s (Stephen b 1965); *Career* Royal Holloway Coll London: lectr in physics 1960, sr lectr 1972–81, vice-princ 1978, princ 1981–85; Royal Holloway and Bedford New Coll London (now Royal Holloway Univ of London): vice-princ 1985–98, hon research fell in physics 1998–, hon fell 2000–; res assoc Case Western Res Univ Cleveland Ohio 1968–69; chm Inst of Classical Studies Univ of London 1982–2001; tstee and govr Strode's Coll Egham 1981–; FInstP 1978, FRSA 1983–2004, CPhys 1986; *Recreations* music, climbing; *Clubs* Athenaeum; *Style*— Dr Roy Miller; ✉ Celyn, 3 Parsonage Road, Englefield Green, Egham, Surrey TW20 0JW (☎ 01784 432753)

MILLER, Sarah; da of John Harmsworth Miller, and Patricia, *née* Rhodes; *b* Cambridge; *Educ* Camden Sch for Girls, Wadham Coll Oxford (BA); *m* Deyan Sudjic; 1 da (Olivia); *Career* journalist; contributing ed Blueprint magazine and Wordsearch pubns (Eye magazine and Tate magazine) 1983–89, style ed Cosmopolitan 1984–85 (features asst 1983–84), co-ordinating ed Elle (Br launch) 1985–86, Look ed Sunday Times 1987–1989 (dep Look ed 1986–87), asst ed Sunday Times Magazine 1989–1992, assoc features ed Daily Telegraph 1992–94, arts ed Daily Telegraph 1994–95, features ed Saturday Telegraph Magazine 1995–97, ed-in-chief and founding ed Condé Nast Traveller 1997–2012, conslt launch ed Condé Nast Traveler China 2010–13 (conslt ed 2012–13), European ed Travel + Leisure 2013–; fndr and ceo Sarah Miller and Ptnrs (brand strategy and

M

content agency) 2012–; chairwoman BSME 2002; memb Cncl RCA; Ed of Year BSME 2000, 2001, 2003 and 2005, Consumer Lifestyle Magazine of the Year 2005 and 2007, Best Luxury Brand Luxuria 2009; *Books* Shangri-La at the Shard London (ed, 2015); *Recreations* arts, films, architecture, design, travel, literature; *Clubs* 67 Pall Mall; *Style*— Ms Sarah Miller; ✉ e-mail sarah@sarahmillerandpartners.com, website www.sarahmillerandpartners.com

MILLER, Sienna Rose; da of Edwin Miller, and Jo Miller; *b* 1981; *Educ* Heathfield Sch Ascot, Lee Strasberg Inst NY; *Career* actress; *Theatre* As You Like It (Wyndhams Theatre, West End) 2005, After Miss Julie (Broadway) 2009, Flare Path (West End) 2011; *Television* Bedtime 2002, Ken Eddie 2003–04, The Girl 2012; *Film* incl: Layer Cake 2004, Alfie 2004, Casanova 2005, Factory Girl 2006, Interview 2007, Camille 2007, Stardust 2007, The Mysteries of Pittsburgh 2008, The Edge of Love 2008, G I Joe: The Rise of Cobra 2009; *Awards* Environmental Media Awards Futures Award 2007, ShoWest Supporting Actress of the Year 2009; nomination: BAFTA Rising Star Award 2008, Best Supporting Actress Br Independent Film Award 2008 (for The Edge of Love), Best Female Lead Independent Spirit Award 2008 (for Interview), British Actress of the Year London Critics Circle Award 2008; *Style*— Ms Sienna Miller; ✉ c/o United Agents Ltd, 12–26 Lexington Street, London W1F 0LE (☎ 020 3214 0800, fax 020 3214 0801, website www.unitedagents.co.uk)

MILLER, Stephen Charles; s of Stanley Scott Miller (d 1996), and Madeline Ellice, *née* McGown; *b* 5 January 1965, Aberdeen; *Educ* Robert Gordon's Coll Aberdeen, Univ of Aberdeen (LLB, DipLP); *m* 1 Oct 1994, Paula Mary Nicola, *née* O'Reilly; 2 s (Matthew Whiteford b 24 March 1998, James Stanley b 4 July 1999), 1 da (Christina May b 21 Jan 2003); *Career* slr; ptnr: Harper Macleod 1994–2002, MacRoberts 2002–; ind legal chm Scottish Football Assoc, memb Sport Resolutions Panel of Arbitrators – Chairpersons; memb Law Soc of Scotland 1989; Sport and the Law: The Scots Perspective (jt author, 2001); *Recreations* cycling, golf, books, DJing; *Clubs* Bearsden Golf; *Style*— Stephen Miller, Esq; ✉ Rosslyn, 37 Drymen Road, Bearsden G61 2RA (☎ 0141 942 2976, e-mail stephen.miller321@btinternet.com); MacRoberts, 152 Bath Street, Glasgow G2 4TB (☎ 0141 332 9988, fax 0141 332 8886)

MILLER, Stuart James; s of Victor Albert Miller (d 2001), of Kent, and Valerie Deborah, *née* Powell; *b* 26 July 1967, Brentwood, Essex; *Educ* Ramsden Sch for Boys Orpington (head boy), Univ of Loughborough (BSc); *m* 1, 16 Dec 1995 (m dis 2014), Heather Claire, *née* Watson; 1 s (Augustus Horatio b 8 Jan 2002), 2 da (Florence Hebe b 26 Feb 2004, Natasha Grace b 12 Jan 2006); m 2, 9 Jan 2016, Zelga Simone, *née* Anderson; *Career* conslt Fin Servs Div Andersen Consulting 1990–94, co-fndr and ceo Octopus Information 1994–2000, co-fndr and ceo ByBox Hldgs Ltd 2000–; first prize World Music for Youth Championship Austria 1985, memb of UK's Top 40-under-40 UK entrepreneurs 2006, ranked 12th TechTrack 100 Sunday Times 2006, ranked as fastest growing technol co Deloitte Fast50 2007; co-author of several GB, Euro and US Patents; princ saxophonist for World Music for Youth champions Kerkrade 1984, Ramsden Sch for Boys created annual Stuart Miller Music Award 1985, fndr Loughborough Univ jazz orch, first entrepreneurial venture importing vintage saxophones to UK; memb Strategic Advsy Bd Loughbourgh Univ Business Sch, sector advsr for entrepreneurship Saïd Business Sch Univ of Oxford 2015–; former memb Bd Fredericks Fndn Oxon, former dep chm Oxon Business First; visiting prof Loughborough Univ; entrepreneur in res Glendonbrook Centre for Enterprise, chair Bd Lord Young's Small Business Charter 2016–; former govr Abingdon & Witney Coll; MCILT 2005; *Books* The Seven Conundrums of an Entrepreneur (2013); fndr www.mystreet.photography; *Recreations* playing the saxophone and teaching the saxophone in prisons, wine, recumbent racing (Kingcycle and Trice QNT), street photography; *Clubs* Ronnie Scott's Jazz, Br Human Powered Vehicle Assoc, Audax Club UK; *Style*— Stuart Miller, Esq; ✉ Merlin House, Grove Technology Park, Wantage, Oxon OX12 9FA (☎ 0800 678 1181, e-mail stuart.miller@bybox.com)

MILLER OF CHILTHORNE DOMER, Baroness (Life Peer UK 1998), of Chilthorne Domer in the County of Somerset; Susan Elizabeth Miller; da of Oliver Meddows Taylor (d 1984), and Norah, *née* Langham (d 1998); *b* 1 January 1954; *Educ* Sidcot Sch, Oxford Poly; *m* 1, 1980 (m dis 1998), John Christopher Miller; 2 da (Hon Charlotte Sarah b 24 May 1981 d 13 January 2001, Hon Madeleine Lucy b 3 Dec 1984); m 2, 1999, Humphrey Temperley; *Career* in publishing; formerly with David & Charles, Weidenfeld & Nicolson, Penguin Books; self employed bookseller Sherborne and Yeovil; ldr S Somerset DC 1996–98 (cncllr 1991–98), cncllr Somerset CC 1997–2005; Lib Dem spokesman in Lords Rural Affairs & Agriculture 1999–2007 (now Environment, Agriculture and Rural Affairs), memb Euro Sub-Ctee 1998–2002 and 2005–, spokesman Home Affairs 2007–10; dir Vignobles Temperley; chair: APPG Street Children, APPG Agroecology, APPG Food and Health, APPG Conservation & Wildlife, BTCV; patron: The Compassionate Friends, Josephine Butler Soc; memb: Lib Dems and Women Lib Dems, Devon Wildlife Tst; *Recreations* walking, reading, wine, friends; *Style*— The Rt Hon the Baroness Miller of Chilthorne Domer; ✉ House of Lords, London SW1A 0PW (e-mail millers@parliament.uk)

MILLER OF GLENLEE, Sir Stephen William Macdonald; 8 Bt (GB 1788), of Glenlee, Kirkcudbrightshire; s of Sir (Frederick William) Macdonald Miller of Glenlee, 7 Bt (d 1991), and (Marion Jane) Audrey, *née* Pettit; *b* 20 June 1953; *Educ* Rugby, St Bartholomew's Hosp (MB BS); *m* 1, 1978, Mary Carolyn (d 1989), o da of G B Owens, of Huddersfield; 1 s (James Stephen Macdonald b 1981), 1 da (Katherine Helen b 1983); m 2, 1990, Caroline Mary, da of Leslie A E Chasemore, of Shebbear, Devon, and widow of Harold Frederick Clark; *Heir* s, James Miller of Glenlee; *Career* GP Shebbear 1986–2012; memb Bd Northern Locality Devon Clinical Commissioning Gp 2013– (vice-chm 2014–); FRCS, FRCGP; *Style*— Sir Stephen Miller of Glenlee, Bt; ✉ Burrowland, Sandford, Crediton, Devon EX17 4EL

MILLER SMITH, Charles; s of William Smith, and Margaret Pettigrew Brownlie Wardrope; adopted gf's surname Miller Smith 1963; *b* 7 November 1939; *Educ* Glasgow Acad, St Andrews Univ (MA); *m* 1, 1964, Dorothy Agnes Wilson Adams (d 1999); 1 s, 2 da; m 2, 2004, Debjani Jash; *Career* Unilever plc: fin dir Vinyl Products 1970–73, head of planning 1974, fin dir Walls Meat Co 1976, vice-chm Hindustan Lever 1979–81, Speciality Chemicals Gp 1981, fin dir Bd 1989, exec Unilever Foods 1993–94; Imperial Chemical Industries: dir 1994–2001, chief exec 1995–99, chm 1999–2001; chief exec PPF Int 1983, chief exec Quest Int 1986, non-exec dir Midland Bank 1994–96, non-exec dir HSBC Hldgs plc 1996–2001; advsr Goldman Sachs 2002–05, sr advsr Warburg Puncus 2005–, sr advsr Deutsche Bank (RREEF Infrastructure) 2007–; chm: Scottish Power 2000–07 (chm Advsy Bd 2007–), Asia House 2007–09; dir Fritsource Solutions Ltd 2007– (chm Fritssource Solutions UK Ltd 2008–), memb Mngmnt Bd MOD 2002–07, memb Int Advsy Cncl Principal Financial 2008–; Hon LLD St Andrews Univ 1995; ACCA; *Recreations* reading, walking; *Clubs* National; *Style*— Charles Miller Smith, Esq

MILLETT, Prof Martin John; s of John Millett (d 2001), and Sybil Vera, *née* Paine (d 1987); *b* 30 September 1955; *Educ* Weydon Co Secdy Sch Farnham, Farnham Sixth Form Coll, Univ of London (BA), Merton Coll Oxford (DPhil); *m* Joanna Story; 1 da (Julia Maud b 31 Oct 2005), 1 s (Edward John b 22 Aug 2009); *Career* asst keeper of Archaeology Hants Co Museums 1980–81; Univ of Durham: lectr 1981–91, sr lectr 1991–95, prof of archaeology 1995–98; prof of classical archaeology Univ of Southampton 1999–2001; Univ of Cambridge: Laurence prof of classical archaeology 2001–, fell Fitzwilliam Coll 2001–, head Sch of Arts and Humanities 2014–; Royal Archaeological Inst: hon ed 1990–95, vice-pres 1998–2003; FSA 1984 (dir 2001–07, treas 2007–11), FBA 2006 (vice-pres 2010–14); *Publications* The Romanization of Britain (1990), Roman Britain (1995); *Recreations* wine, travel, food, outdoors; *Style*— Prof Martin Millett; ✉ Faculty of Classics, University of Cambridge, Sidgwick Avenue, Cambridge CB3 9DA (☎ 01223 335161, e-mail mjm62@cam.ac.uk)

MILLETT, Baron (Life Peer UK 1998), of St Marylebone in the City of Westminster; Peter Julian Millett; kt (1986), PC (1994); s of Denis Millett (d 1965), of London, and Adele Millett, *née* Weinberg (d 1997); *b* 23 June 1932; *Educ* Harrow, Trinity Hall Cambridge (MA); *m* 1959, Ann Mireille, da of David Harris (d 1980), of London; 3 s (Richard, Andrew, Robert d 1965); *Career* standing jr counsel to BOT and DTI 1967–73, QC 1973, bencher Lincoln's Inn 1980; memb Insolvency Law Review Ctee 1977–82, judge of the High Court of Justice (Chancery Div) 1986–94, a Lord Justice of Appeal 1994–98, a Lord of Appeal in Ordinary 1998–2004, non-permanent judge of the Court of Final Appeal Hong Kong 2000–; treas Lincoln's Inn 2004; hon fell Trinity Hall Cambridge 1994, hon fell Queen Mary's Coll London 2012; Hon LLD Univ of London 2000; Gold Bauhinia Star Hong Kong 2015; *Style*— The Rt Hon the Lord Millett, PC; ✉ 18 Portman Close, London W1H 6BR (☎ 020 7935 1152, fax 020 7935 1103); 38 Kewhurst Avenue, Cooden, East Sussex TN39 6BH (☎ 01424 842970)

MILLETT, Timothy Patrick; *b* 6 January 1951; *Educ* St Benedict's Sch Ealing, Wadham Coll Oxford (MA); *Career* called to the Bar Gray's Inn 1975; official of Court of Justice of the EU; legal sec to advocate general: Sir Gordon Slynn 1984–88, Francis Jacobs 1988–89; head div legal service Euro Parl 1998–2000; legal sec to judge Cunha Rodrigues 2000–10, currently dep registrar Court of Justice of the EU; *Books* The Court of First Instance of the European Communities (1990), Judicial Control in the EU (2004); *Style*— Timothy Millett, Esq; ✉ Court of Justice of the EU, Luxembourg L-2925 (☎ 00 352 4303 2358, fax 00 352 433766, e-mail timothy.millett@curia.europa.eu)

MILLHAM, David Harry; s of Harry Sidney Millham (d 1982), and Emily Harriet Millham, *née* Edwards (d 1998); *b* 20 June 1938; *Educ* William Morris Country Tech Coll Walthamstow, IMEDE Lausanne Switzerland; *m* 27 March 1965, Frances, da of Francis William DuBarry; 1 s (Alexander Gareth David b 20 March 1970), 1 da (Lisa Jane b 14 March 1967); *Career* Financial Times 1959–69 (new issues ed, gen fin news writer), The Times 1969–71 (new issues ed, contrib Fin Ed's Column), PR conslt ICFC 1971–74, dir Shandwick PR Company 1974–79; Shandwick Consultants: dep chm 1979–91, md Fin PR Div 1990–91; exec dep chm Streets International Ltd 1992, chm Millham Communications Ltd 1992–2001, chm DHM Associates 2002–; govr Columbus Sch and Coll Chelmsford; Freeman City of London 1988; *Recreations* watching football, gardening, reading, music; *Style*— David Millham, Esq; ✉ DHM Associates (☎ 01245 351276, mobile 07850 949324, e-mail dhmillham@aol.com)

MILLICAN, Peter; *Career* property developer; md Parabola Land Ltd, chief exec Kings Place; *Style*— Peter Millican, Esq; ✉ Central Square, Forth Street, Newcastle upon Tyne NE1 3PJ

MILLIGAN, Eric; JP (Edinburgh); *b* 27 January 1951; *Educ* Tynecastle HS, Napier Coll Edinburgh; *m* Janis; *Career* former printer; memb Edinburgh DC 1974–78, memb Lothian Regnl Cncl 1978–96 (chm Fin Ctee 1980–82 and 1986–90, convenor 1990–96), convenor City of Edinburgh Cncl 1995–96, Lord-Lt and Lord Provost City of Edinburgh 1996–2003, convenor Lothian Borders Police 2003–07; cncllr Stenhouse Div West Edinburgh; dir Edinburgh International Jazz and Blues Festival Ltd; Convention of Scottish Local Authorities 1980–82 and 1986–96; pres COSLA 1988–90; memb Lab Pty; Hon DBA Napier Univ 1999; Hon FRCSEd 2000; Hon Doc Heriot Watt Univ 2004; Chevalier dans l'Ordre National du Mérite France 1996, La Medaile de la Ville de Paris 2014; *Recreations* watching football and rugby as played by Heart of Midlothian FC and Boroughmuir RFC, listening to music, especially if sung by Sinatra; *Style*— Eric Milligan; ✉ The City of Edinburgh Council, City Chambers, High Street, Edinburgh EH1 1YJ (☎ 0131 200 2000)

MILLIGAN, Iain Anstruther; QC (1991); s of Maj Wyndham MacBeth Moir Milligan, MBE, TD (d 1999), and Helen Penelope Eirene, *née* Cassavetti (d 2002); *b* 21 April 1950; *Educ* Eton, Magdalene Coll Cambridge (exhibitioner, scholar (hc), MA); *m* 19 May 1979, Zara Ann Louise, da of Sir Alexander Cadwallader Mainwaring Spearman (d 1982); 2 da (Diana Rose b 1981, Evelyn Louise b 1983), 1 s (Ivar Francis b 1984); *Career* called to the Bar Inner Temple 1973; head of chambers 1999–2014; *Recreations* forestry, walking; *Style*— Iain Milligan, Esq, QC; ✉ 22 Edge Street, London W8 7PN (☎ 020 7492 4659); Dunesslin, Dunscore, Dumfries DG2 0UR (☎ 01387 820345); 20 Essex Street, London WC2R 3AL (☎ 020 7842 1200, fax 020 7842 1270)

MILLIGAN, John Andrew; s of Derek Milligan, and Dorothy, *née* Ward; *b* 2 November 1957, Halifax; *Educ* Univ of Reading (BSc); *m* 22 Aug 1981, Deborah Anne, *née* Long; 3 s (James David George, Alexander Thomas John, Thomas Arthur Edward); *Career* int dir Jones Lang LaSalle, owner and ceo Milligan; memb: Br Cncl of Shopping Centres, Int Cncl of Shopping Centres, Walpole Gp; FRICS; *Recreations* cinema, music, reading, tennis, travel, walking; *Clubs* RAC, Pall Mall; *Style*— John Milligan, Esq; ✉ Milligan Retail, 58 Grosvenor Street, London W1K 3JB

MILLING, Amanda Anne; MP; da of Humphrey Philip Milling, and Patricia Anne, *née* Kenyon; *b* 12 March 1975, Burton-upon-Trent; *Educ* Moreton Hall Sch, UCL (BSc); *Career* researcher SW1 Research 1997–99, dir Optimisa Research (formerly Quaestor Research) 1999–2014, MP (Cons) Cannock Chase 2015–; *Recreations* running; *Style*— Ms Amanda Milling, MP; ✉ House of Commons, London SW1A 0AA (e-mail amanda.milling.mp@parliament.uk, website www.amandamilling.com, Twitter @AmandaMilling)

MILLINGTON, Andrew; s of Walter Millington (d 1985), and Margaret, *née* Burley; *b* 28 June 1960; *Educ* Adwick Sch, UEA (BA); *m* 1989, Tamara, da of John Ingram; 1 s (Maximillian Isidore b 4 April 1991), 1 da (Anya Eve b 31 Dec 1992); *Career* gallery asst, journalist and PR exec 1981–89, account mangr Biss Lancaster 1989–92; dir: Christow Consultants 1992–95, Shandwick International 1995–; MIPR 1997; *Recreations* art, opera, theatre, friends; *Style*— Andrew Millington, Esq

MILLINGTON, Dr Gordon Stopford; OBE (1996); s of Percival Richard Millington (d 1981), of Killinchy, and Irene Ellen, *née* Forster (d 2012); *b* 29 June 1935, Belfast; *Educ* Campbell Coll, Queen's Univ Belfast (BSc); *m* 1, 30 April 1960, Margaret Jean (d 1999), da of Leslie Pegler (d 1964), of Croydon; 2 s (Mark Stopford b 28 Feb 1962, Gavin Paul b 11 Dec 1965), 1 da (Kathryn Margaret b 26 Feb 1964); m 2, Sept 2000 Norma Joan, *née*, Jordan; *Career* asst engr Sir William Halcrow & Partners 1957–59, Kirk McClure & Morton (engr 1959–66, ptnr 1966–87, sr ptnr 1988–98); chm: Amelwood Ltd, Stanwood Estates Ltd, NI Assoc ICE 1979–80; pres Belfast Rotary Club 1980–81; chm: Bd of Govrs Grosvenor HS 1983–90, NI Branch Inst of Highways and Transportation 1989–90, Structures and Building Bd ICE 1992–94, NI 2000 1992–2000; external examiner Cork Regnl Tech Coll; memb Exec Inst of Engrs of Ireland 1994–2000; dir: Ulster Orchestra Soc 1997–2000, Irish Engineering Publications 1997–99, Ormeau Baths Gall 1999– (chm 2000–03); pres Irish Acad of Engrg 2000–02; memb CBI – IBEC Tport Logistics Gp, memb Gen Consumer Cncl Energy Tport Gp 1998–2004; hon sec Mundell Fund 1998–2003; DSc (hc) Queens Univ of Belfast 2001; Hon FICE (vice-pres 1994–96, dep chm Disciplinary Bd 2004–), FIStructE, FIEI (vice-pres 1995–97, pres 1997–98), FIHT, MASCE; *Publications* The Rotary Club of Belfast...the second fifty years; *Recreations* yachting; *Clubs* Quoile Yacht; *Style*— Dr Gordon Millington, OBE; ✉ One Malone View Road, Belfast BT9 5PH (☎ 028 9061 1303, e-mail gordon.millington@ntlworld.com)

MILLNER, Etienne Henry de la Fargue; s of Guy Millner, of Cumbria, and Frances *née* Johnston (d 2000); *b* 15 January 1954; *Educ* Stowe, Goldsmiths' Coll Sch of Art (BA), Royal Acad Sch (postgrad cert); *m* 1987, Mary Elizabeth, da of Jack Castle; 2 da (Daisy b 1989, Polly b 1998), 1 s (William b 1991); *Career* figurative sculptor in plaster and clay for bronze working mainly in small and monumental portraiture; exhibitions incl: RA Summer Shows 1979, 1982, 1984, 1985, 1986 and 1988, National Portrait Gall (NPG) New Faces 1987, Art for Sale Whiteleys 1992, Chelsea Harbour 1993, Cadogan Contemporary Summer Show 1993, one-man show Cadogan Contemporary 1994, NPG 1994, Soc of Portrait Sculptors 1995–2010, Rye Festival 1997, Piers Feetham Gall Aldeburgh 1998, People's Portrait (touring exhibition) 2000–01, Alan Kluckow Gall Selected Portraits 2000; work in permanent collections incl: Wellington Coll 1993, NPG 1996, Harris Manchester Coll Oxford 1996, Arndean Gallery 1999–2002, Goodwood House, Longford Castle, Holdenby; Soc of Portrait Sculptors: memb Cncl 1996, vice-pres 2005, pres 2009; FRBS 1997 (ARBS 1992); *Recreations* walking, riding; *Clubs* Chelsea Arts; *Style—* Etienne Henry de la Fargue Millner, Esq; ✉ 5 Priory Grove, London SW8 2PD (☎ 020 7720 6695)

MILLS, Andrew; s of Robin Gerald Mills, of Benington, Herts, and Alice Daphne Mills; *b* 28 July 1958; *Educ* Haileybury (scholar), City Univ (BSc), RMA Sandhurst, City Univ Business Sch (now Cass Business Sch) (MBA); *m* 11 July 1987, Vanessa Anne, *née* Harford; 3 s (Charles b 6 Sept 1990, Thomas b 26 May 1993, Henry b 8 March 1995), 2 da (Alice b 27 Nov 1991, Lucinda b 5 Feb 1998); *Career* army offr 3 Bn Para Regt 1980–83; equity salesman Nat West Securities 1984–87, assoc dir of research BZW 1987–90, dir of corp affrs BET 1990–94, dir of investor rels/dir of corp affrs Kingfisher plc1994–2003; gp communications dir Rexam plc 2004–07, investor communications interim/consultancy 2008–; non-exec dir Farsight 1996–2002; fell Investor Rels Soc 1997 (non-exec dir 1994–97, chm 1997–99); Liveryman Worshipful Co of Merchant Taylors 1990; *Clubs* Naval and Military, Parachute Regt Assoc, Tadmarton Heath Golf; *Style—* Andrew Mills, Esq; ✉ St Michael's House, Aynho, Banbury, Oxfordshire OX17 3BG (e-mail armills@btopenworld.com)

MILLS, Angela Margaret; da of Dr Ronald Hubert Bonfield Mills (d 1989), and Audrey Vera, *née* Mountjoy; *b* 24 January 1948; *Educ* Vaynor and Penderyn Sch, Somerville Coll Oxford (MA, BM BCh), St Thomas' Hosp Med Sch; *Career* conslt gynaecologist; nat MO Family Planning Assoc 1983–88, hon lectr Dept of Obstetrics and Gynaecology Univ Coll Hosps London 1983–2002 (now hon sr lectr), currently emeritus conslt gynaecologist and hon sr lectr Univ Coll Hosps NHS Tst; formerly conslt gynaecologist United Elizabeth Garrett Anderson Hosp and Hosp for Women Soho; author of various pubns in jls; memb: Sub-Ctee RCOG on problems associated with AIDS in relation to obstetrics and gynaecology, Bd Faculty of Community Health 1991–94, Continuing Educn Sub-Ctee of Faculty of Community Health 1990–94, Bd Faculty of Family Planning and Reproductive Health Care 1994–96 (chm Clinical and Scientific Ctee 1994–98, examiner 1998–2005, chm Educn Ctee 2004–06), Professional Conduct Ctee GMC 2001–06, Ethical Ctee RCOG 2006–; chm London Soc Family Planning Doctors 1985–88, vice-chm Nat Assoc of Family Planning Doctors 1989–93, chm Women's Visiting Gynaecological Club 2003–, tstee Women's Health Concern until 2008; memb: Cncl Nat Assoc of Family Planning Doctors 1993–94, American Soc of Fertility and Sterility, Soc of Advancement of Contraception, Br Soc of Clinical Colposcopists, BMA; FRCOG 1993, MFPHM 1996; *Recreations* travelling, music, gardening; *Clubs* Network, RSM, Reform; *Style—* Miss Angela Mills; ✉ 80 Harley Street, London W1G 7HL (☎ 020 7637 0584, fax 020 7637 0242, website www.drangelamills.co.uk)

MILLS, Christopher Harwood Bernard; s of Cyril Bertram Mills (d 1991), and Marie Beatrice Louise Francoise, *née* Harwood (d 2002); *b* 5 November 1952; *Educ* Eton, Guildhall Univ; *m* 10 Oct 1987, Lynne Theresa, *née* Egan; 3 s (Charlie b 3 Sept 1988, Nicholas b 4 Aug 1990, Harry b 30 May 1994); *Career* Samuel Montagu Ltd 1970–85, ceo North Atlantic Smaller Companies Tst 1983–, dir Invesco MIM 1985–93, dir J O Hambro Capital Management Group Ltd 1993–2010, chm and ceo Harwood Capital Mgmnt 2010–; non-exec dir: Catalyst Media Group plc 2007–, Gleeson plc 2010, Indoor Bowling 2010–, Assetco plc 2011–, Bioquell 2012–, Cyprotex plc 2013–, EKF plc 2016–, Goals plc 2016–; awards incl Sunday Telegraph Investment Mangr of the Year 1993; *Recreations* shooting, diving; *Clubs* Whites, Annabel's, Harry's Bar, Hertford Street; *Style—* Christopher Mills, Esq; ✉ 10 Cliveden Place, London SW1W 8LA; Bradley Court, Chieveley, Berkshire RG18 9XZ; Harwood Capital Management, 6 Stratton Street, London W1J 8LD (☎ 020 7747 5600, 020 7747 5601, e-mail cmills@harwoodcapital.co.uk)

MILLS, Colin James Edmund; s of James Oliver Mills (d 1986), of Holcot, Northants, and Ada, *née* Cox (d 2001); *b* 28 November 1937; *Educ* Northampton GS, Leicester Sch of Architecture (DipArch); *m* 2 Sept 1961, Eileen Patricia (d 2013), da of Charles Frederick Swain (d 1986); 1 s (James b 1965), 3 da (Kathryn b 1967, Rosalind b 1969, Clare b 1982); *Career* chartered architect; ptnr Morrison & Partners 1970–77, dir Morrison Design Partnership 1977–86, princ Colin J E Mills 1986–2002; fndr chm Friends of Brodick Castle and Country Park 1996–98; ARIAS; *Books* The Nigel Tranter Bibliography (compiler 2003), The Vanished and Disappearing Churches of Arran, A Walk Around Arran with Colin Mills (2011); *Recreations* painting, ornithology, reading, history; *Style—* Colin Mills, Esq; ✉ Roadend, Shiskine, Isle of Arran KA27 8EW (☎ 01770 860448, e-mail colinmills474@btinternet.com)

MILLS, David John; s of John Mills (d 1958), and Violet, *née* Germaine (d 1970); *b* 9 February 1944; *Educ* Beal GS; *m* 27 March 1967, Lesley Jacqueline, *née* Wand; 1 s (Nigel John), 2 da (Penelope Jacqueline, Susan Jennifer); *Career* HSBC Bank: asst gen mangr mktg 1983–85, regnl dir 1985–87, IT dir 1987–89, direct banking dir 1990–93, chm First Direct 1990–93 and 2000–01, dir Midland General Ltd, Midland Unit Tst Mgmnt Ltd and Midland Bank Pension Tst Ltd 1993–94, gen mangr card services and mktg 1993–95, gen mangr business devpt and md personal fin services 1995–99, chm HSBC Life (UK) Ltd (formerly Midland Life Ltd) 1995–2001 (chief exec 1993–94), gen mangr personal banking 1999–2002, memb Asset & Liability Mgmnt and Exec Ctees 1995–2001, memb Chief Exec Ctee 2000–01; chief exec Post Office Ltd 2002–05, dir Royal Mail Holdings plc 2002–05, dir Royal Mail Gp plc 2002–05, chm Post Office Fin Services 2004–05; chm First Rate Travel Services Ltd 2002–04, dir First Rate Travel Services Holdings Ltd 2002–04; chm Mondex Int Ltd 1995–2001; dir: Mastercard/Europay UK Ltd 1990–94 (chm 1992–93), Euro Travellers' Cheque Int SC 1990–2001, Europay Int SA 1992–2001, European Payment Systems Services SA 1992–2001, Personal Investment Ombudsman Bureau Ltd 1995–2000, Personal Investment Authy Ltd 1995–2000, Maestro Int Inc 1995–2001, British Interactive Broadcasting (Market Contributions) Ltd 1995–2001, British Interactive Broadcasting Ltd 1995–2001, Camelot Gp plc 2003–05, Camelot Int Services Ltd 2003–05; chm: Foxdale Homes LLP 2006–10, The Move Factory Ltd 2007–10; sr ind dir: Cardpoint plc 2006–07, Payzone plc 2008–10, OneSavings Bank plc 2011–14; memb Cncl and Managing Ctee Assoc of Payment and Clearing Services (APACS) 1995–2000 (dep chm Card Payment Gp 1992–93 (memb 1990–92), chm Cash Services Gp 1995–2000); chm Employers Forum on Disability Ltd 2004–06 (dir 1993–2003), memb Nat Disability Cncl 1995–2000; tstee Royal Assoc for Disability Rights 2004–09, vice-pres Vitalise 2005–14; distinguished Sloan Fell London Business Sch; fell Inst of Fin Servs; *Recreations* family, wine, fishing, motorsport; *Clubs* RAC; *Style—* David Mills, Esq; ✉ e-mail david@davidjmills.com

MILLS, David John; s of Terence John Mills, and Geraldine Patricia, *née* Edwards; *b* 4 January 1963; *Educ* Wolverhampton GS, Gonville & Caius Coll Cambridge; *m* 27 July 1990, Janet Elizabeth, *née* Lazarus; 2 s (Frederick Lazarus b 26 April 1994, Albert Norman b 18 Nov 1995), 1 da (Matilda Rose Geraldine b 8 April 1998); *Career* ed The Artist's and Illustrator's Magazine 1986–89, managing ed Arts and Leisure The Sunday Times 1996– (dep arts ed 1989–90, arts ed 1990–96); *Recreations* cricket, music, squash, learning the violin; *Clubs* Groucho, Coolhurst Lawn Tennis and Squash Racquets; *Style—* David Mills, Esq; ✉ The Sunday Times, 1 London Bridge Street, London SE1 9GF (☎ 020 7782 5000)

MILLS, Gloria; CBE (2005, MBE 1999); *Educ* Open Univ (Cert, Dip, MBA); *Career* early career in law publishing, held various positions publishing unions Nat Soc of Operative Printers and Assts (NATSOPA) and SOGAT, sr nat offr and mangr Nat Union of Public Employees (NUPE) 1987–93; UNISON: dir of equal opportunities 1993–2006, nat sec equalities 2006–, memb Sr Mgmnt Gp; cmmr Cmmn for Racial Equality 2002–07; TUC: pres 2005–06, vice-pres 2006–07, memb Gen Cncl and Exec 1994–, memb European Ctee, Women's Ctee, Employment Appeals Tbnl and Race Rels Ctee; pres: Women and Gender Equality Ctee European Public Services Union Fedn 2010–, Women's Ctee European Trade Confedn 2015– (vice-pres 2009–15); vice pres European Trade Confedn 2015–; memb: Race Rels Forum Home Office 1998–2001, Lab Party Nat Policy Forum, Women's Ctee European Ctee 2000–, Editorial Advsy Bd Equal Opportunities Review 2002–, Gen Cncl ITUC 2006, Nat Race Advsy Gp FA 2007–, Advsy Ctee on Equal Opportunities European Cmmn 2011, Lab Pty Cmmn on Older Women 2012–, Mgmnt Ctee European Trade Union Inst 2015, Advsy Cncl Involvement and Partnership Assoc 2015; Public Servs Int: chair European Women's Ctee 2003–, vice-chair World Women's Ctee 2004–; Hon LLD Univ of Staffordshire 2006; MCIPD, FRSA, MCMI 2008; *Publications* various articles on gender equality and race equality, incl article on combating institutional racism in Industrial Law Jl; *Recreations* politics, football (Arsenal), cricket, reading; *Style—* Ms Gloria Mills, CBE; ✉ UNISON, 130 Euston Road, London NW1 2AY (☎ 020 7121 5409, e-mail g.mills@unison.co.uk)

MILLS, Dr Harold Hernshaw; CB (1995); s of Harold George Mills (d 1988), and Margaret Elliot Mills (d 2000); *b* 2 March 1938; *Educ* Greenock HS, Univ of Glasgow (BSc, PhD); *m* 1 Aug 1973, Marion Elizabeth, da of John Beattie (d 1999); *Career* cancer res scientist Roswell Park Meml Inst Buffalo NY 1962–64; lectr Univ of Glasgow 1964–69; princ Scot Home and Health Dept 1970–76, asst sec Scot Office 1976–81, Privy Cncl Office 1981–83, under sec Scot Devpt Dept 1984–88 (asst sec 1983–84), princ fin offr Scot Office 1988–92, sec Environment Dept Scot Office 1992–95, sec and head Devpt Dept Scot Office 1995–98; chm: Land Tst 1998–2014 (dir/tstee until 2015), Edinburgh World Heritage Tst 1999–2006, Caledonian MacBrayne Ltd 1999–2006, David MacBrayne Ltd 1999–2006, Caledonian MacBrayne Holdings Ltd 1999–2006, CalMac Ferries Ltd 2006; dir: Northlink Orkney and Shetland Ferries Ltd 2000–09, Northlink Ferries Ltd 2006–09; memb: Home in Scotland 1998–2004 (chm 2000–04), Home Gp Ltd 2000–04, Home Housing Tst 2000–04, Edinburgh City Centre Partnership 2002–05; memb Bd Queen Margaret UC Edinburgh 1998–2004; tstee: Scot Maritime Museum 1998–, Edinburgh Old Town and South Side Tst 2000–06; dir City of Adelaide Charitable Tst 2005–, dir/tstee Waterways Tst 2012–13, dir/tstee Scottish Waterways Tst 2012–14; *Style—* Dr Harold Mills, CB; ✉ 21 Hatton Place, Edinburgh EH9 1UB (☎ 0131 667 7910)

MILLS, Hayley Catherine Rose Vivien; da of Sir John Mills, CBE (d 2005), and Mary Hayley Bell, JP (d 2005); *b* 18 April 1946, London; *Educ* Elmhurst Ballet Sch, Institute Alpine Videmanette Switzerland; *m* 20 June 1971 (m dis 1977), Roy Boulting (d 2001); 1 s (Crispian Boulting Mills b 18 Jan 1973); has son by Leigh Lawson; 1 s (Jason (Ace) Lawson b 30 July 1976); partner Firdous Bamji; *Career* actress; patron: Mountview Theatre Sch, Jan de Vries Benevolent Tst, Only Make Believe NY, Shooting Star Children's Hospice, Gtr London Fund for the Blind, World Vision, Peta, Faculty of Integrated Medicine; patron: Integrated Health Tst, Pathfinder Dogs, Samantha Dickson Brain Tumour Tst, Mountview Theatre Sch, Jan de Vries Benevolent Tst, Only Make Believe NY, Shooting Star Children's Hospice, Gtr London Fund for the Blind, World Vision, Peta; tstee Anno's Africa, fndr memb and patron VIVA; serving sis OStJ 1999; *Theatre* incl: Peter Pan 1969, The Wild Duck 1970, Trelawney of the Wells 1972, The Three Sisters 1973, A Touch of Spring 1975, Rebecca 1977, My Fat Friend 1978, Hush of Hide 1979, The Importance of Being Earnest 1979, The Summer Party 1980, Tallys Folly 1982, The Secretary Bird 1983, Dial M for Murder 1984, Toys in the Attic 1986, The Kidnap Game 1991, The King and I (Gordon Frost Prodns Australia) 1991–92, Fallen Angels 1993, The Card 1994, Dead Guilty 1995–96, Brief Encounter 1996, The King and I (USA tour) 1997–98, Suite in Two Keys (NY) 2000, Vagina Monologues (NY) 2001, Little Night Music (USA) 2001, Wait Until Dark (USA) 2003, Humble Boy (UK) 2003, The Bird Sanctuary (USA) 2005–06, Two Can Play (USA) 2005, Ladies in Lavender 2012, Legends! 2015, Cinderella 2015; *Television* incl: Deadly Strangers 1974, Only a Scream Away 1974, two Loveboat Specials 1978, The Flame Trees of Thika 1980, Illusion of Life 1981, Amazing Stories 1986, Murder She Wrote 1986, Tales of the Unexpected 1987, Good Morning Miss Bliss 1988, Back Home 1989, Walk of Life 1990, Wild at Heart 2006–12, Midsomer Murders 2013, US Variety TV, The Danny Kaye Show, The Andy Williams Show, Moving On, Madge; *Films* incl: Tiger Bay 1959, Pollyanna 1960, Parent Trap 1961, The Castaways 1962, Whistle Down the Wind 1962, Summer Magic 1963, The Moonspinners 1964, The Chalk Garden 1964, That Darn Cat 1965, Sky West & Crooked 1965, The Truth About Spring 1965, The Family Way 1966, The Trouble with Angels 1966, Pretty Polly 1967, Twisted Nerve 1968, Take A Girl Like You 1970, Endless Night 1972, Mr Forbush and the Penquins 1972, What Changed Charlie Farthing 1975, The Diamond Hunters 1975, Parent Trap II 1986, Parent Trap III 1989, Parent Trap IV 1989, Appointment with Death 1988; *Books* My God (1988); *Recreations* reading, travel, walking; *Style—* Miss Hayley Mills; ✉ The Don Buchwald Agency, 10 East 44th Street, NY 10017, USA (☎ 00 1 212 867 1200, fax 00 1 212 972 3209); Chatto & Linnit Ltd, Worlds End Studios, 132–4 Lots Road, London SW10 0RJ (☎ 020 7349 7222)

MILLS, John Frederick; CBE (2008); s of Henry Alfred Mills (d 1973), and Jean Margaret Aitchison; *b* 6 September 1950; *Educ* Highgate Sch, The Queen's Coll Oxford, Merton Coll Oxford (Domus sr scholar, BLitt, MA); *m* 1974, Jean Marie, da of Aloysius Theodore Correia (d 1999); 1 s (Theodore b 1978), 3 da (Julia b 1980, Cecily b 1983, Claudia b 1983); m 2, 2003, Imogen Stephanie Nicholls; *Career* DTI 1974–: private sec to Min of State for Industry 1976–78, princ 1978–81, seconded as princ asst sec Govt of Hong Kong 1981–85, asst sec and head of Int Telecommunications Policy 1986–89, memb PM's Policy Unit 1989–92, under sec and dir of Consumer Affairs OFT 1992–95; chief exec: Cornwall CC 1995–99, Policy and Resources Dept States of Jersey 1999–2003; dir of rural policy DEFRA 2003–07; dir Cityshape plc 1991–2011; non-exec dir: Royal Cornwall Hosps NHS Tst 2007–09, Port of London Authy 2008–14; dep chm Ports of Jersey Ltd 2015–; memb Advsy Panel OFT 2001–03, memb State Membs Remuneration Review Body Jersey 2008– (chm 2015–), cmmr Cmmn for Rural Communities 2009–13, cmmr Jersey Financial Servs Cmmn 2009–14, income tax cmmr of appeal Jersey 2009–; govr Highgate Sch 1993– (chm and treas 1999–); *Style—* John Mills, Esq, CBE; ✉ Le Picachon, Les Varines, Jersey JE2 7SB (☎ 01534 732374)

MILLS, Sir Jonathan Edward Harland; kt (2013), AO (2011); s of Frank Harland Mills, and Elayne Mary Mills; *b* 21 March 1963, Sydney, Australia; *Educ* Univ of Sydney (BMus), RMIT Univ Melbourne (MArch); *Career* artistic dir Blue Mountains Festival 1988–90; RMIT Univ: composer-in-residence and research fell in environmental acoustics 1992–97, adjunct prof in environmental acoustics 1998–03; artistic dir Melbourne Festival 2000–01 (incl dir: Melbourne Millennium Eve Celebrations 1999, Fedn Festival 2001), composer-in-residence Bundanon Tst 2002, adjunct prof La Trobe Univ 2004–07, Vice-Chllr's professorial fell Univ of Melbourne 2006, dir Edinburgh Int Festival 2007–; artistic advsr: Brisbane Biennial Int Music Festival 1995–97, Melbourne Recital Centre and

M

Elisabeth Murdoch Hall 2005–; dir Alfred Deakin Innovation Lectures 2003–; visiting prof: Edinburgh Napier Univ, Univ of Edinburgh; cmmr Australian Heritage Cmmn 2002–04; chair: Review into the Australian Youth Orchestra & the Australian Nat Acad of Music Cwlth Govt 2004–05, Review of Opera Victorian Govt 2005; memb: Australian Int Cultural Cncl 1998–2003, Bd Synergy Percussion 2001–06, New Media Arts Bd Australia Cncl 2003–05, Bd Melbourne Recital Hall 2004–05, Australian Heritage Cncl 2004–06, Maj Performing Arts Bd Australia Cncl 2005–, Bd Arts Exhibitions Australia 2005–; artistic dir Seaborne Broughton & Walford Fndn 1988–; memb Jury: Pratt Prize for Musical Theatre 2002–, Ian Potter Fndn Music Cmmns 2003–05; patron Leigh Warren & Dancers 2001–; various works and performances for radio, film, theatre and concert incl: Ethereal Eye (electro-acoustic dance opera) 1996, The Ghost Wife (chamber opera) 1999–2002, Sandakan Threnody (for solo tenor, chorus and orchestra) 2001 (touring 2004–06, Prix Italia 2005), The Eternity Man (chamber opera) 2003; Genesis Prize Cmmn for Opera 2003; Centenary Medal Australia 2002; Hon DUniv Stirling, Hon DUniv Queen Margaret Univ 2009, Hon Dr Univ of Edinburgh 2012, Hon DLitt Univ of St Andrews, hon doctorate RMIT Univ Melbourne; FRSA, FRSE 2010; *Style*— Sir Jonathan Mills, AO; ✉ Edinburgh International Festival, The Hub, Castlehill, Edinburgh EH1 2NE (☎ 0131 473 2032, fax 0131 473 2002)

MILLS, Sir Keith Edward; GBE (2013), kt, DL; s of Edward James Mills (d 2002), of Brentwood, Essex, and Margaret Katherine, *née* Weber (d 1992); *b* 15 May 1950, Brentwood, Essex; *Educ* St Martins Sch Brentwood; *m* 31 Aug 1974, Maureen Elizabeth, *née* Simmons; 1 s (Alexander James Eaton b 5 May 1984), 1 da (Abigail Louisa Charlotte b 23 Nov 1988); *Career* ceo Mills Smith & Ptnrs Ltd 1984–89, ceo Air Miles UK Ltd 1988–92; chm and ceo: KEM Mgmnt Ltd 1994–, First Call plc 1999–2002; chm Loyalty Mgmnt Gp Ltd 2001–07; int pres and ceo London 2012 Ltd 2003–06, dep chm London Organising Ctee 2012 Olympic Games 2006–12; team princ Team Origin (Americas Cup team); chm: Sported Fndn, Invictus Games Fndn, 1851 Tst, Royal Fndn; Business Ldr of the Year London Business Awards 2005, Chief Exec Award for Mktg 2005, Sports Industry Personality of the Year 2005, Master Entrepreneur of the Year 2005; Hon PhD: Loughborough Univ 2006, Univ of Bath 2011, Anglia Ruskin Univ 2011, Univ of Essex 2013; fell Mktg Soc, life fell Inst of Direct Mktg; *Recreations* sailing, skiing, music, travelling; *Clubs* Royal Southern Yacht, Royal Thames Yacht, Royal Yacht Squadron, New York Yacht; *Style*— Sir Keith Mills, GBE, DL; ✉ KEM Management Ltd, 57 St James's Street, London SW1A 1LD (☎ 020 7389 1900, e-mail k.mills@kemmanagement.co.uk)

MILLS, Leif Anthony; CBE (1995); s of Victor William Mills (d 1967), and Bergliot, *née* Ström-Olsen (d 1989); *b* 25 March 1936; *Educ* Kingston GS, Balliol Coll Oxford (MA); *m* 2 Aug 1958, Gillian Margaret (d 2003), da of William Henry Smith (d 1966); 2 s (Adam, Nathanial), 2 da (Susannah, Harriet); *Career* 2 Lt RMP 1957–59; Nat Union of Bank Employees (then Banking Insurance and Fin Union) 1960–96: res offr 1960–62, asst gen sec 1962–68, dep gen sec 1968–72, gen sec 1972–96; Parly candidate (Lab): Salisbury gen election 1964, Salisbury by-election 1965; TUC: memb Non Manual Workers Advsy Ctee 1967–72, memb Gen Cncl 1983–96, chm Fin Servs Ctee 1983–90, chm Educn and Trg Ctee 1989–96, pres TUC 1994–95; memb: Manpower Econs Advsy Ctee on Equal Pay 1971, Ctee to Review the Functioning of Fin Instns (Wilson Ctee) 1977–80, Civil Serv Pay Res Unit Bd 1978–81, BBC Consultative Gp on Social Effects of TV 1978–80, Armed Forces Pay Review Body 1980–87, Monopolies and Mergers Cmmn 1982–91, Ctees TUC, Int Ctees FIET, Fin Reporting Cncl 1990–96, Nat Cncl for Vocational Qualifications 1992–96, Investors in People UK 1993–96, PIA Ombudsman Cncl 1994–2000, Cncl Consumers Assoc 1996–2002, Bd of Employment Tbnls Serv 1996–2001; chm: Cncl for Admin (formerly Admin Standards Cncl) 1997–99, Covent Garden Market Authy 1998–2005; tstee Civic Tst 1989–96, govr London Business Sch 1989–92, hon sec St John the Baptist PCC West Byfleet 1990–94; *Books* Frank Wild: A Biography (1999), Men of Ice (2008), The Redoubtable Mrs Smith (2010), The Adventures of Mrs Smith (2011); *Recreations* rowing, chess; *Clubs* Oxford and Cambridge, Weybridge Rowing (pres 2008–13); *Style*— Leif Mills, Esq, CBE; ✉ 1 Orchard View, High Street, Cuddesdon, Oxford OX44 9HP (☎ 01865 872022)

MILLS, Maureen; *b* Canada; *Career* fndr and dir Network London PR 1996– (PR specialists in top end restaurants and chefs in the UK); *Style*— Ms Maureen Mills; ✉ Network London, Mason's Yard, 34 High Street, Wimbledon Village, London SW19 5BY (☎ 020 8947 4474, mobile 07802 603627, fax 020 8947 4836, e-mail maureen@networklondonpr.com)

MILLS, Nigel; MP; *Educ* Loughborough GS, Univ of Newcastle; *Career* qualified CA; PricewaterhouseCoopers 1996–2008, Deloitte 2008–10; MP (Cons) Amber Valley 2010–; *Style*— Nigel Mills, Esq, MP; ✉ House of Commons, London SW1A 0AA

MILLS, Nigel Gordon; *b* 14 April 1955; *Career* Hoare Govett Ltd: joined as food mfrg sector investment analyst 1978, dir 1985–2005, joined Corp Fin Dept 1986, ceo 1994–2005; chm UK corp broking Citigroup 2005–; *Style*— Nigel Mills, Esq

MILLS, Russell Thomas; s of Sqdn Ldr Harry Wyndham Mills, DFM, RAF, ret (d 2011), and Mary, *née* Jeyes; *b* 22 November 1952; *Educ* Royal Alexandra & Albert Sch Reigate, Canterbury Coll of Art, Maidstone Coll of Art (BA), Royal Coll of Art (MA, travelling scholarship Berlin, Berger award); *m* 17 Aug 1974 (m dis 2005), Ann Elizabeth, *née* Symes; 1 s (Samuel Asher b 4 Aug 1992); *Career* artist, musician and prodr; lectr at numerous colls, univs and schs of art throughout Britain and USA; visiting prof: UWE, Glasgow Sch of Art; visiting lectr: Liverpool John Moores Univ, Manchester Metropolitan Univ, Salford Univ, Leeds Metropolitan Univ; external examiner: Univ of the Arts, Central St Martins, Hull Sch of Art, Univ of Lincoln; TV and radio appearances incl: London Weekend Show (ITV) 1977, Arena – Double Vision (BBC2) 1980; involved with: Grizledale Arts Hawkshead 2000–, The Armitt Trust Ambleside 2001–; *Solo Exhibitions* Fine Lines (The Thumb Gallery) 1980, ...returns an echo (Curwen Gallery and tour) 1983, Ciphers (Curwen Gallery and Metropole Arts Centre Folkestone) 1986, Enter the Silences (Parco Space 5 Tokyo) 1987, Silent Systems (Curwen Gallery) 1989, Planet and Glow-Worm (Visual Arts Museum NY) 1989, Sixteen Shimmers (Parco Space 5 Tokyo and Kirin Plaza Osaka) 1990, Within Without (Huntington Gallery Boston) 1991, The Possible Slow Fuse (Pentagram Gallery London) 1995, RSC Works (RSC Stratford-upon-Avon and Barbican) 1995, Trace Elements (Base Gallery Tokyo) 1998, Moth (The Lighthouse Glasgow) 2001, Extended Wings (Kendal) 2002, Cleave/Soft Bullets (Kendal) 2002; *Two-Person Exhibitions* Ember Glance (with David Sylvian, Tokyo) 1990, Earth Murmurs (with Ian Walton, Curwen Gallery) 1992, Between Two Lights (installation with Ian Walton, Charlotte Mason Coll Ambleside as part of Ambleside Mountain Festival) 1994, MW Undark (exhbn with Ian Walton, Zeffirellis Ambleside) 1994, Measured in Shadows (installation with Ian Walton, Tullie House Museum Carlisle) 1996 (also at Guinness Hopstore Dublin 1997), Looming (with Ian Walton, Eagle Gallery London) 1996, Nature's Teeth (with Ian Walton, The Samling at Dovenest Windermere) 1997, Spirit (with Ian Walton, Grizedale Forest Hawkshead, 1997), Ex Libris (with Ian Walton, Sun Street Studios, Lancaster Literature Festival, 1997), Filters: Past Presents (with Ian Walton, Gallery Al Ajibe, Arrecife, Lanzarote, 1997), The Gradual Instant (with Ian Walton, Dean Clough Galleries Halifax) 1998, Words and Images (The Samling at Dovenest Windermere) 1998, Still Moves (installation with Ian Walton in the Forest of Bowland, also guest speaker at accompanying conference in Ambleside) 1999, Sonic Boom: The Art of Sound (Hayward Gallery) 2000, Republic of Thorns (with Ian Walton, The Wordsworth Tst Grasmere) 2001, Black Ice (with Ian Walton, Buddle Arts Centre Gateshead) 2001, The Space of a Door (with Ian Walton, Futuresonic04 Urbis Manchester) 2004, Hold (Palazzo delle Papesse Centre for Contemporary Art Siena) 2004–05, Blue Tears (with Ian Walton and Mike Fearon, Silo Espaco Cultural Oporto) 2005, Dialogue Boxes (with Phil Mouldycliff, 20/21 Centre for Visual Arts Scunthorpe) 2006, Russell Mills and Ian Walton (Armitt Museum Ambleside) 2009, Forward to Far: From Schuritlers to Now (with Ian Walton, Avmitt Museum Ambleside) 2010 (co-curator), Bohemians in Exile: The Royal College of Art in Ambleside 1940–45 (Armitt Museum Ambleside) 2011, Sublime Transactions (Armitt Museum Ambleside) 2012; *Group Exhibitions* Cyprus Summer School 1972, Geek Work (Air Gallery and Greenwich Theatre Art Gallery) 1977, Contemporary British Illustrators (Belgrave Gallery) 1978, Shoes (Neal St Gallery) 1979, Five English Artists (Galerie Mokum Amsterdam) 1979, Summer Reflections (Thumb Gallery) 1981, Hayward Annual (Hayward Gallery) 1982, Images for Today (Graves Art Gallery Sheffield) 1982, Britain Salutes New York (Brooklyn MOMA NY) 1983, Out of Line (ICA) 1985, Ambit (Royal Festival Hall) 1985, Interaction (Camden Arts Centre) 1986, Critical Lines (Talbot Rice Gallery Edinburgh and Watershed Bristol) 1986, Art Meets Science (Smith's Gallery) 1986, Faber Artists (Cartoon Gallery) 1986, New British Design (Japan) 1987, Sydney Biennale (Art Gallery of NSW and Nat Gallery of Victoria) 1987 and 1988, Doobraak (Berlage Amsterdam) 1989, Pictures of Rock (European tour) 1990–91, The Art of Selling Songs (V&A) 1991, Art and Science (Plymouth City Museum and Art Gallery) 1991, Ember Glance (installation with Ian Walton and David Sylvian, Architectural Assoc London) 1993, Shelf Life (The Eagle Gallery London) 1994, Little Pieces from Big Stars (Flowers East Gallery London) 1994, Fuse (RCA) 1994, The Artists Bookfair Royal Festival Hall (with The Eagle Gallery London) 1995, Soundings: Sub Rosa (installation with Ian Walton and Hywel Davies, Green Park Station Bath as part of Bath Festival) 1995, Liquid Architecture (Brisbane and Melbourne) 2004, The Art of Lost Words (German Gymnasium, London and tour) 2009–11, Sedition: An Uprising of Cumbrian Artists (Tullic House Museum and Art Gallery) 2010; numerous RCA and Curwen Gallery exhibitions; *Work in Collections* Br Cncl, Br Museum, Kent CC, Reuters, V&A, Tate Gallery; *Commissions* Chatto & Windus Publishers, Decca Records, Polydor Records, Virgin Records, The Face, Harpers & Queen, The Sunday Times, Telegraph Magazine, Vogue, Nothing Records, BT, English Heritage, RSC, Fareham Town centre, Faber and Faber, Expo 2000, New Scientist, Cumbria Tourist Bd; *Awards* International Editorial Design Three Award of Excellence 1983, D&AD Silver Award 1984, Diamond Record Cover Award (with Dave Coppenhall) Diamond Awards Festival Antwerp Belgium 1989; *Albums* Undark (1996), Undark II: Pearl and Umbra (1999); many recordings with Dome, BC Gilbert and G Lewis, Bill Laswell, Nils Petler Molvaer, and for Unknown Public; *Publications* The Luftschifer Park Piece (1976), Evening Breakers (1977), More Dark than Shark (1986), Russell Mills/Ian Walton (1990), Ember Glance: The Permanence of Memory (1991), Looming (with Ian Walton, 1996), Trace Elements (1998), Sonic Boom (2000), Republic of Thorns (2001), Cleave/Soft Bullets (2002), Hold (2004), Blue Tears (2005), Forward to Far: From Schuritlers to Now (2010), Sublime Transactions (2012); *Recreations* music, reading, contemplating natural phenomena; *Clubs* Labour Pty, Chelsea Arts; *Style*— Russell Mills; ✉ e-mail mills@matter-shed.co.uk, website www.russellmills.com

MILLS-THOMAS, Aidan David; s of Lt Col (Frank) David Mills-Thomas (d 1994), and Margaret Alice, *née* Wallis; *b* 23 September 1949, Aldershot, Hants; *Educ* King's Sch Bruton, Coll of Law Guildford; *m* 2 Sept 1989, Alexa Nicole, *née* Peake; 1 da (Sophie Helene b 10 Nov 1990); *Career* admitted slr 1973; princ Mills-Thomas & Co, Slrs of London 1976–98; dir: Logsys Hldgs Ltd 1998–2001, Mercury Gp plc 2003–04; exec dir Ibis Project Servs Ltd 2005–10; non-exec dir Debrett's Ltd 2004–12; memb Law Soc; Freeman City of London, Liveryman Worshipful Co of Gold and Silver Wyre Drawers; Chevalier de Bretvin; *Recreations* game shooting, wine, history, walking, classic car racing; *Clubs* Oriental, Belsize Park RFC; *Style*— Aidan Mills-Thomas, Esq; ✉ 25 Priory Street, Cheltenham, Gloucestershire GL52 6DR (☎ 01242 515709, e-mail amillsthomas@gmail.com)

MILLWARD, Edwina Carole (Mrs David Bicker); da of Eric Millward, and Frances Morris, *née* Norton; *b* 20 September 1943; *Educ* Thornes House Sch Wakefield, Ilkley Coll of Housecraft, Univ of London (LLB); *m* 11 Nov 1972, David Charles Bicker, s of Arthur Charles Bicker; *Career* teacher 1965–67; admitted slr 1972; appointed by Lord Chllr to sit as dist judge in Co Court and Dist Registry High Court 1995; nat pres UK Fedn of Business and Professional Women 1985–87, pres Kent Law Soc 1994–95 (memb 1968–), pres Assoc of HM District Judges 2008; *Recreations* acting, swimming, needlework; *Clubs* Army and Navy, The Sloane; *Style*— Miss Edwina Millward

MILMAN, David Patrick; 10 Bt (GB 1800), of Levaton-in-Woodland, Devonshire; er s of Lt-Col Sir Derek Milman, 9 Bt, MC (d 1999); *b* 24 August 1945; *Educ* Univ of London (BEd, MA); *m* 1969, Christina, da of John William Hunt; 1 da (Katharine Jane b 1975), 1 s (Thomas Hart b 1976); *Heir* s, Thomas Milman; *Career* headteacher 1981, asst dir Sch Mgmnt South 1989, sr area advsr NW Kent 1993 (area advsr 1991); freelance educnl conslt 2000; *Books* Take a Look (1974/75), What Do You Think (1977), Senior Managers Personal Profile: Management Portfolio (jtly, 1991); *Style*— Sir David Milman, Bt; ✉ 71 Camden Road, Sevenoaks, Kent (e-mail dpmilman.sevenoaks@virgin.net)

MILMO, His Hon John Boyle; QC (1984); s of Dermod Hubert Francis Milmo (d 1973), and Eileen Clare, *née* White (d 1994); *b* 19 January 1943; *Educ* Downside, Univ of Dublin (MA, LLB); *Career* called to the Bar Lincoln's Inn 1966 (bencher 1992); recorder of the Crown Court 1982–2004 (dep circuit judge 1980–82), dep High Court judge 1993, circuit judge (Midland Circuit) 2004–13; head of chambers 1 High Pavement Nottingham 1990–2004; memb Gen Cncl of the Bar 1992–2002, memb Parole Bd 2005–15; *Clubs* United Services (Nottingham); *Style*— His Hon John Milmo, QC

MILNE, David Calder; QC (1987); s of Ernest Ferguson Milne, OBE (d 1995), of Walton Heath, Surrey, and Helena Mary, *née* Harkness (d 2007); *b* 22 September 1945; *Educ* Harrow, Univ of Oxford (MA); *m* 1 (m dis 1999); 1 da (Bryony b 1980); *m* 2, 1 Aug 2013, Amanda; *Career* CA 1969; articled to Whinney Murray & Co Chartered Accountants 1966–69, called to the Bar Lincoln's Inn 1970; recorder 1989–2006; tstee: Wildfowl and Wetlands Tst 2002–11, Br Tst for Ornithology 2009–12; hon fell Chartered Inst of Taxation 2009; FCA 1974; *Recreations* natural history, music, golf, rugby football; *Clubs* Garrick, Hurlingham, Gnomes, Walton Heath Golf; *Style*— David Milne, Esq, QC; ✉ Pump Court Tax Chambers, 16 Bedford Row, London WC1R 4EF (☎ 020 7414 8080, fax 020 7414 8099, e-mail dmilne@pumptax.com)

MILNE, Gordon Stewart; OBE (2002); s of Arthur Milne, OBE (d 1984), of Edinburgh, and Thomasina, *née* Gilroy (d 2002); *b* 1 October 1936; *Educ* Royal HS of Edinburgh, Leith Nautical Coll, Heriot-Watt Coll Edinburgh, Coll of Estate Mgmnt London; *m* 15 Oct 1960, Kathleen Mary; 2 s (Rhoderic Michael Steuart b 12 Feb 1965, Hector Arthur Steuart b 12 July 1966); *Career* local dir Guardian Royal Exchange Assurance 1979–92, md Scottish Metropolitan Property plc 1986–92 (dir 1969–92); memb Clyde Port Authy 1989–93; recently hon prof in land economy Univ of Aberdeen (visiting prof of land economy 1992–95); vice-pres Edinburgh Jr C of C 1968–69, DG Euro Conf of Jr C of C 1972; non-exec dir European Utilities Trust plc 1994–2006; memb NEDC Scot Strategy Planning Ctee 1974–76, former memb Exec Scot Devpt and Indust, dep chm Sec of State for Scot Scottish Valuation Advsy Cncl 1982–96; chm: The European Urban Inst 1995–2001, Local Govt Property Cmmn (Scotland) 1995–98, Sec of State for Scot Valuation and Rating Cncl 1996–2001; memb: Livingston Devpt Corp 1992–97, Capital Advsy Ctee

Scottish Higher Educn Funding Cncl 1993–95, Faculty of Advocates Disciplinary Tbn 1994–96, Gen Convocation Heriot-Watt Univ 1993–2007; fndr and tstee Merchant Navy Meml Tst Scotland, fndr and tstee Leith Tst; memb Hon Co of Master Mariners 2014–; FRICS 1964–2012, Hon FRIAS 1997–2012; *Recreations* travel, hill walking, music; *Clubs* Royal Scots; *Style*— Prof Gordon S Milne, OBE; ✉ Gean Cottage, 25 Dovecot Grove, Edinburgh EH14 2LU (✆ 0131 466 6396, e-mail gsmilne@live.co.uk)

MILNE, Dr Lisa; MBE; da of John Mione, and Gladys Mione; *b* 22 April 1971; *Educ* Royal Scottish Acad of Music & Drama; *Partner* (fiancé) Ian W Rose; *Career* soprano; memb of vocal staff RSC; Scottish Opera (contract princ) roles incl: Gianetta in L'Elisir d'Amore (debut), Dew Fairy in Hansel and Gretel, Coryphee in Alceste, Adele in Die Fledermaus, Adina in L'Elisir d'Amore, Zerlina in Don Giovanni, Susanna in Le Nozze di Figaro, Ilia in Idomeneo, Despina in Cosi Fan Tutte; other roles incl: Morgana in Alcina (ENO), Annchen in Der Freischütz (ENO), Servilia in La Clemenza di Tito (WNO), Gretel in Hansel and Gretel (Stuttgart Opera), Ilia in Idomeneo (Royal Danish Opera), Atalanta in Xerxes (Göttingen Handel Festival), title role in Theodora (Glyndebourne Festival Opera), title role in Rodelinda (Glyndebourne Festival Opera), Marzelline in Fidelio (Glyndebourne Festival Opera), Anna Trulove in The Rake's Progress (ENO), James McMillan's Parthenogenis (world premiere, The Cambridge Corn Exchange), Simon Holt's Sunrise, Yellow Noise (CBSO world premiere, under Sir Simon Rattle), Sophie in Der Rosenkavalier (Scottish Opera), title role in Alcina (ENO), Micaela in Carmen (Glyndebourne Festival Opera), Marzelline in Fidelio (Dallas Opera), Pamina in Die Zauberflöte (Glyndebourne Festival Opera); *Awards* Scottish Opera John Noble Bursary 1992, Maggie Teyte Prize 1993, Glyndebourne Festival Opera John Christie Award 1996, Royal Philharmonic Soc Young Artists Award 1998; Hon DMus: Univ of Aberdeen, Robert Gordon's Univ Aberdeen; *Recordings* incl: Ilia in Idomeno (EMI), Handel and Vivaldi Cantatas with King's Consort, Vaughan Williams' Serenade to Music, Xerxes, Ireland songs, Quilter songs, Hebridean folk songs; *Recreations* listening to the Beatles, Jacques Brel, Brian Jones, Prince and David Bowie, singing the Blues; *Clubs* Brian Jones Friends and Fans; *Style*— Dr Lisa Milne, MBE; ✉ e-mail lisa.milne@btinternet.com

MILNE, (Antony) Michael (Mike); s of Anthony Kenneth Milne, and Barbara, *née* King Chidley; *Educ* Westminster; *Career* computer animator; dir of production Electric Image Ltd 1984–91, head of graphics The Bureau Ltd 1991–92, dir computer animation Framestore Ltd (formerly Framestore-CFC Ltd) 1992–; animation dir: Walking with Dinosaurs (BBC TV series) 1999, Walking with Beasts (BBC TV series) 2001; visiting prof Bournemouth Univ 2003; D&AD Silver Award (Outstanding TV Graphics) 1984, BAFTA Innovation Award 2000, RTS Award for Best Visual Effects 2003; Emmy Awards: Best Visual Effects 2000, Best Animated Prog 2000, 2001, 2002, 2003 and 2006; Hon Dr of Arts Bournemouth Univ 2002; *Recreations* watching wildlife, reading evolutionary theory, visiting ancient ruins; *Style*— Dr Mike Milne; ✉ Framestore Ltd, 9 Noel Street, London W1F 8GH (✆ 020 7208 2600, fax 020 7208 2626, e-mail mike.milne@framestore.com)

MILNE, Nanette Lilian Margaret; OBE (1993), MSP; *Educ* Aberdeen HS for Girls, Univ of Aberdeen (MB ChB); *m*; 1 s, 1 da; *Career* various med appts rising to registrar 1965–73, pt/t researcher Genetics Dept Univ of Aberdeen 1978–80, MO (oncology) Aberdeen Hosps 1980–92; dir: Grampian Enterprise Ltd 1992–98, Aberdeen Countryside Project 1997–99; MSP (Cons) NE Scotland 2003–, shadow min for the environment 2007–10, currently shadow min for public health, former memb Public Petitions Ctee, currently memb Health and Sport Ctee; Cons Pty: joined 1974, various positions at branch, constituency and area level 1981–2002, vice-chm Scottish Cons Pty 1988–92, cncllr Aberdeen City/District Cncl 1988–99, Scottish Parly candidate Aberdeen S 1999, UK Parly candidate Gordon 2001; memb: Aberdeen and Grampian Tourist Bd 1992–95, Ct Univ of Aberdeen 1996–; tstee: Gomel Tst 1995–99, Aberdeen Int Youth Festival 1995–99 and 2000–; former JP (Aberdeen); FFARCS 1969; *Recreations* music, the countryside, hill walking, skiing, golf, gardening; *Clubs* Aberdeen Ladies Curling; *Style*— Mrs Nanette Milne, OBE, MSP; ✉ The Scottish Parliament, Edinburgh EH99 1SP

MILNE, Neil Morrison; s of Brig John Brebner Morrison Milne, OBE, and Marjory, *née* Duncan; *b* 24 June 1951; *Educ* Royal HS Edinburgh, Univ of Edinburgh (MA), Univ of Nottingham (MA); *m* 5 July 1996, Helen Grela; 2 da (Amelia Marjory Morrison Milne b 28 Sept 1997, Alexandra Lizzie Morrison Milne b 2 Dec 1998); *Career* Butler Till Ltd 1975–78, Standard Life Assurance Co 1978–81, sr mangr Euro Banking Co Ltd, exec dir York Trust Group plc 1984–90, managing ptnr Copernicus Capital Partners 1994–2007, managing ptnr Abris Capital Partners 2007–; *Recreations* tennis, skiing, reading; *Clubs* RAC; *Style*— Neil M Milne, Esq; ✉ York Trust Ltd, Smithfield House, 92 North Street, Leeds LS2 7PN (✆ 0113 222 3555, fax 0113 222 3550, e-mail n.milne@abris-capital.com)

MILNE-WATSON, Sir Andrew Michael; 4 Bt (UK 1937), of Ashley, Longbredy, Co Dorset; s of Sir Michael Milne-Watson, 3 Bt, CBE (d 1999); *b* 10 November 1944; *Educ* Eton; *m* 1, 1970, Beverley Jane Gabrielle, er da of late Philip Cotton, of Majorca; 1 s (David b 1971), 1 da (Emma b 1974); m 2, 1983, Mrs Gisella Stafford, da of Hans Tisdall, of London; 1 s (Oliver b 1985); *Heir* s, David Milne-Watson; *Career* dir Ogilvy & Mather 1970–82; chm: Phoenix Advertising 1982–86, Lewis Broadbent Advertising 1986–88, Minerva Publications Ltd 1988–90, GMW Fabrics 1989–; md ADR Associates Ltd 1993–2008; Liveryman Worshipful Co of Grocers; *Clubs* Garrick; *Style*— Sir Andrew Milne-Watson, Bt; ✉ 164 Rivermead Court, London SW6 3SF (e-mail mwandrew@globalnet.co.uk)

MILNER, Chris; s of John Milner, and Maureen, *née* Bullock; *b* 26 September 1973, Horsforth, Leeds; *Educ* City Univ of London (BA); *m* 18 Sept 2004, Alessia, *née* Piaggi; 1 s (Luca b 13 Jan 2008), 1 da (Serena b 9 Aug 2010); *Career* qualified actuary 1997; with Hewitts until 1999; Goldman Sachs: ldr Transition Mgmnt Gp Equities Div 1999–2003, estab Pensions Services Gp Investment Banking Div 2003–06, md 2004–, ldr Global Macro Structuring Team Securities Div 2006–11, ptnr 2008–, head of EMEA emerging market sales Securities Div 2011–, memb Securities Div Client and Business Standards Ctee and Firmwide Asset Liability Ctee; founding shareholder Cosaveli; *Recreations* motor racing, cycling, duathlons; *Style*— Chris Milner, Esq

MILNER, Prof (Arthur) David; s of Arthur Milner (d 1984), and Sarah-Ellen, *née* Gaunt (d 1965); *b* 16 July 1943; *Educ* Bradford GS, Lincoln Coll Oxford (open scholar, MA), Inst of Psychiatry London (Dip Psychology, PhD); *m* 24 July 1965, Christine, *née* Armitage; 2 s (Benedict Jon b 28 July 1966, Edward b 5 Oct 1969); *Career* res asst Univ of London 1966–70; Univ of St Andrews: lectr in psychology 1970–82, sr lectr 1982–85, chm Dept of Psychology 1983–88, reader 1985–90, prof 1990–2000, dean Faculty of Science 1992–94, head Sch of Psychology 1994–97; prof of cognitive neuroscience Durham Univ 2000–08 (emeritus prof 2008–), dir Durham Univ Neuroimaging Centre 2011–14, hon prof Univ of Edinburgh 2015–; Chichele lectr and visiting fell All Souls Coll Oxford 2006; memb: Int Neuropsychological Symposium 1971, Experimental Psychology Soc 1972 (hon fell 2009); tstee Dundee Science Centre 1998–2000; FRSE 1992, FRS 2011; *Books* The Neuropsychology of Consciousness (with Rugg, 1992), The Visual Brain in Action (with Goodale, 1995, 2 edn 2006), Comparative Neuropsychology (1998), Cognitive and Neural Bases of Spatial Neglect (with Karnath and Vallar, 2002), The Roots of Visual Awareness (with Heywood and Blakemore, 2003), Sight Unseen: The Neuropsychology of Unconscious Vision (with Goodale, 2004, 2 edn 2013); over 180 pubns in scholarly jls and edited books; *Recreations* walking, reading, writing, films, jazz; *Style*— Prof A D Milner, FRSE, FRS; ✉ Department of Psychology, Durham University, Science Laboratories, South Road, Durham DH1 3LE (✆ 0191 334 9148, fax 0191 334 3241, e-mail a.d.milner@durham.ac.uk)

MILNER, Joanne; *Career* with Arthur Andersen then RBS, investment dir Lloyds Devpt Capital (LDC) until 2012, ceo Debrett's Ltd 2012–16 (chm 2016–), ceo Garrard 2016–; chm and fndr Debrett's Fndn 2014–; *Recreations* motorsport, skiing, travel, ballet, running; *Style*— Ms Joanne Milner

MILNER, Prof John; s of James William Milner, of Derby, and Iris May, *née* Young; *b* 11 June 1946; *Educ* Bemrose GS Derby, Courtauld Inst of Art Univ of London (BA, PhD); *m* 1970, Lesley, da of late Denis Hill Marlow; 3 s (Henry George Marlow b 18 March 1971, Edward John b 16 July 1975, Michael James Denis b 21 April 1980); *Career* lectr Bournemouth and Poole Coll of Art and Hornsey Coll of Art London 1968–69; Dept of Fine Art Univ of Newcastle upon Tyne: lectr 1969, sr lectr 1979, reader 1985, head of dept 1985–91, prof of art history 1992–2004, prof emeritus 2004–; ind art historian, exhbn organiser and painter 2005–; dir Hatton Gallery Univ of Newcastle upon Tyne until 1991; memb Assoc of Art Historians; Leverhulme fellowship 1985 and 1993; AHRB Award 1992, Br Acad Award 2004; *Books* Symbolists and Decadents (1971), Russian Revolutionary Art (1979), Vladimir Tatlin and the Russian Avant-Garde (1983), The Studios of Paris, the Capital of Art in the Late Nineteenth Century (1988), Mondrian (1992), Dictionary of Russian Artists (1994), Kazimir Malevich and the Art of Geometry (1996), Art, War and Revolution: France 1870–1871 (2000), Kenneth Rowntree (2002); *Recreations* painting; *Clubs* Chelsea Arts; *Style*— Prof John Milner

MILNES COATES, Prof Sir Anthony Robert; 4 Bt (UK 1911), of Helperby Hall, Helperby, North Riding of Yorkshire; only s of Lt-Col Sir Robert Edward James Clive Milnes-Coates, 3 Bt, DSO, JP (d 1982), and Lady (Ethel) Patricia Hare, da of 4 Earl of Listowel; *b* 8 December 1948; *Educ* Eton, St Thomas' Hosp London (BSc, MB BS); *m* 1978, Harriet Ann, yr da of Raymond Burton, of Slingsby, N Yorks; 2 da (Sara b 1981, Sophie b 1984), 1 s (Thomas b 1986); *Heir* s, Thomas Milnes Coates; *Career* prof of med microbiology St George's, Univ of London; mayor Royal Borough of Kensington and Chelsea 2002–03; FRCPath, FRCP, MD; *Style*— Prof Sir Anthony Milnes Coates, Bt; ✉ Helperby Hall, Helperby, North Yorkshire YO61 2QP

MILROY, Lisa Katharine; da of Reginald Charles Milroy, of Canada, and Leona Vera, *née* Demchuk; *b* 16 January 1959, Vancouver; *Educ* Goldsmiths Coll Univ of London (BA); *m* 2 Sept 2011, Lewis Harold Biggs; *Career* artist; head of graduate painting Slade Sch of Fine Art UCL 2009–; guest advsr Rijksakademie van Beeldende Kunsten Amsterdam 1995–, artist tstee Tate 2012–; John Moores Painting Prize 1988, D&AD Silver Award 2000; RA 2006; *Solo Exhibitions* incl: Lisa Milroy (Tate Liverpool) 2001, Incident (New Art Centre Roche Court Wilts) 2006, Making Sense (IKON Gallery Birmingham) 2007, Improvisations (Royal West of England Acad Bristol) 2011, Act One, Seen Too (Bloomsbury Theatre London) 2012, Grosse Geister/ArtistRoom: Lisa Milroy (Kunstmuseum Bonn Germany) 2014, Out of Hand Laure Genillard Gallery London 2016; *Public Collections* incl: Tate, British Cncl, Arts Cncl, British Museum, Govt Art Collection, Met Museum of Art NY, Fukuoka Art Museum Japan, Nederlandsche Bank The Netherlands, Fonds National d'Art Contemporain France, Deutsch Bank Collection Germany, Calouste Gulbenkian Foundation Portugal; *Recreations* cinema, fashion, reading, travel, walking; *Style*— Ms Lisa Milroy

MILTON, Anne; PC (2015), MP; *b* 1955; *Educ* Haywards Heath GS, St Bartholomew's Hosp; *m* Graham Henderson; 4 c; *Career* former nurse; MP (Cons) Guildford 2005–; shadow min for culture and tourism 2006–07, shadow min for health 2007–10, Parly under-sec Dept of Health 2010–12, Lord Cmmr (Govt whip) HM Treasy 2012–14, vice chamberlain (Govt whip) HM Household 2014–15, treas HM Household (dep chief whip) 2015–; *Style*— The Rt Hon Anne Milton, MP; ✉ House of Commons, London SW1A 0AA (✆ 020 7219 8392, e-mail anne.milton.mp@parliament.uk)

M

MILTON, Dr Marcus Peter; s of Peter Maurice Milton (d 1979), and Eileen, *née* Browne (d 2006); *b* 2 December 1951; *Educ* De La Salle Coll Hove, Univ of Newcastle upon Tyne (BA), Tuebingen Univ (PhD); *m* Monika, *née* Geyer; 1 s (Patrick Lee b 4 March 1984), 1 da (Philippa Maren b 19 March 1986); *Career* trainer IBM Deutschland 1976–82 and 1984, lectr Univ of Zimbabwe 1982–84; Br Cncl: joined 1985, asst dir Tanzania 1986–89, asst regnl dir Southern Germany 1989–92, dep dir Sri Lanka 1992–94 (concurrently dep cultural attaché Br High Cmmn Colombo), head science and public affrs Germany 1994–98, dir Zimbabwe 2000–02 (dep dir 1998–2000), dir Burma 2002–06 (concurrently cultural attaché Br Embassy Rangoon); *Publications* articles on classical subjects in learned jls; *Clubs* Royal Over-Seas League; *Style*— Dr Marcus Milton; ✉ British Council, 10 Spring Gardens, London SW1A 2AH (e-mail marcus.milton@britishcouncil.org.mm)

MILWARD, Timothy Michael; s of Francis John Milward (d 1997), and Rosemary Gwendoline Milward (d 2005); *b* 24 March 1937, Chesterfield; *Educ* Rugby, Clare Coll Cambridge (MA, MB BChir); *m* 17 Jan 1970, Susan Isabel, da of Maj Glover Iggulden (d 1983), of Herne Bay, Kent; 4 da (Jessica b 24 Dec 1971, Caroline (Mrs Adrian West) b 15 June 1973, Ella (Mrs Michael Hamylton), Camilla (Mrs Edward Bond) (twins) b 21 Aug 1978); *Career* Nat Serv, midshipman RNR 1955–63, Lt in RNR; med trg St Thomas' Hosp London 1960–63, registrar in plastic surgery Canniesburn Hosp Glasgow 1971–72, sr registrar in plastic surgery QMH London 1972–76, Hand Surgery fell Louisville Kentucky 1975; conslt plastic surgn Leicester Royal Infirmary, Pilgrim Hosp Boston and Lincoln County Hosp 1976–2002 (emeritus 2002–); in private practice 2002–; assessor GMC 2004–10; pres: Br Assoc of Aesthetic Plastic Surgns 1987–89, Br Assoc of Plastic, Reconstructive and Aesthetic Surgns 1996; memb Cncl Br Soc for Surgery of the Hand 1982–83; FRCS 1966; *Recreations* squash, walking, tennis, silver beating; *Style*— Timothy Milward, Esq; ✉ Pine House, Gaddesby, Leicester LE7 4XE (✆ 01664 840213, fax 01664 840660)

MIMPRISS, Peter Hugh Trevor; CVO (2001); yr s of Hugh Trevor Baber Mimpriss (d 1990), and Gwyneth Mary, *née* Bartley (d 1982); *b* 22 August 1943; *Educ* Sherborne; *m* 1, 1971 (m dis 1992), Hilary Ann Reed; 2 da (Isobel b 19 Oct 1973, Victoria b 22 Feb 1979); m 2, 1992, Elisabeth Lesley Molle; *Career* admitted slr 1967; ptnr Allen & Overy 1972–2002, dir Edmond J Safra Philanthropic Fndn 2002–04, charities advsr to HRH The Prince of Wales 2004–06; chm Chariguard Group of Common Investment Funds 1994–2000; univ slr Univ of London 1995–2002; dir: Leeds Castle Fndn 1980–2006, Weston Park Fndn 1986–99, Chatham Historic Dockyard Tst 1988–2000, Prince's Youth Business Tst 1997–99, Lawcare Ltd 1997–2002, Prince's Tst 1998–2007, King George's Jubilee Tst 2000–06, The Queen's Tst (formerly The Queen's Silver Jubilee Tst) 2000–, Prince's Regeneration Tst 2002–08; chm Charity Law Assoc 1992–97; tstee: Inst of Philanthropy 2000–07, World Trade Center Disaster Fund 2001–07, Prince's Fndn for Children and the Arts 2004–08, Prince's Sch of Traditional Arts 2005–08, Autism Speaks 2005–08 (dep chm), Sir Edward Heath Charitable Fndn 2005–10, Jewish Museum 2006–11, John Ellerman Fndn 2009–13, St Helena Hospice 2012–14, Medical Detection Dogs 2015–; Hon DCL Univ of Durham 2003; *Recreations* walking, maritime history, vintage cars, collecting books; *Clubs* Athenaeum, Garrick; *Style*— Peter Mimpriss, Esq, CVO

MINFORD, Prof (Anthony) Patrick Leslie; CBE (1996); s of Leslie Mackay Minford (d 1970), and Patricia Mary, *née* Sale (d 2008); *b* 17 May 1943; *Educ* Wichester Coll, Balliol Coll Oxford, LSE (MSc, PhD); *m* 10 Feb 1970, Rosemary Irene, da of Gordon Hedley Allcorn; 2 s (Paul, David), 1 da (Lucy); *Career* econ asst UK Miny of Overseas Devpt 1965–67, econ advsr Malawi Miny of Fin 1967–69, asst on econ matters of fin dir Courtauld Co 1970–71, econ advsr Balance of Payments Div UK Treasy 1971–73 (delgn to Br Embassy Washington 1973–74), Hallsworth res fell Univ of Manchester 1974–75, ed NIESR

Economic Review 1975–76, Edward Gonner prof of applied economics Univ of Liverpool 1976–97, prof of applied economics Cardiff Business Sch 1997– (visiting prof 1993–97); memb: Monopolies and Mergers Cmmn 1990–96, HM Treasy independent panel of economic forecasting advisers 1992–96; *Books* Substitution Effects, Speculation and Exchange Rate Stability (1978), Unemployment: Cause and Cure (with D H Davies, M J Peel and A Sprague, 1983, 2 edn also with P Ashton, 1985), Rational Expectations and the New Macroeconomics (with D A Peel, 1983, 2 edn, sole author, as Rational Expectations Macroeconomics, 1992), The Housing Morass (with M J Peel and P Ashton, 1987), The Supply Side Revolution in Britain (1991), The Cost of Europe (ed/contrib, 1992), Markets not Stakes (1998), Britain and Europe: Choices for Change (with W Jamieson, 1999), Advanced Macroeconomics – A Primer (with D A Peel, 2002), Money Matters – essays in honour of Alan Walters (ed, 2004), Should Britain Leave the EU? An Economic Analysis of a Troubled Relationship (with V Mahambare and E Nowell, 2005, 2 edn, with S Gupta, V P M Le, V Mahambare and Y Xu, 2015), An Agenda for Tax Reform (2006), Breaking up is hard to do... Britain and Europe's dysfunctional relationship (contrib and ed, with J R Shackleton, 2016); *Style*— Prof Patrick Minford, CBE; ✉ Cardiff Business School, University of Cardiff, Aberconway Building, Colum Drive, Cardiff CF10 3EU (☎ 029 2087 5728, mobile 07778 005272, fax 029 2087 4419, e-mail minfordp@cf.ac.uk)

MINGHELLA, Loretta; OBE (2010); *Educ* Univ of Cambridge (BA); *Career* former head of enforcement law, policy and int co-operation FSA, chief exec Financial Services Compensation Scheme 2004–10, chief exec Christian Aid 2010–; *Style*— Ms Loretta Minghella, OBE; ✉ Christian Aid, 35 Lower Marsh, Waterloo, London SE1 7RL

MINGOS, Prof (David) Michael Patrick; s of Vasso Mingos (d 1962), of Athens, and Rose Enid Billie, *née* Griffiths; *b* 6 August 1944; *Educ* Harvey GS Folkestone, King Edward VII Sch Lytham, UMIST (Dept of Chemistry Prize, BSc), Univ of Sussex (DPhil); *m* 18 March 1967, Stacey Mary, da of Richard Joseph Fayrer Hosken; 1 da (Zoë Sarah *b* 14 Dec 1971), 1 s (Adam Toby Vasso *b* 2 Oct 1973); *Career* Fulbright fell Northwestern Univ 1968–70, ICI fell Univ of Sussex 1970–71, lectr QMC London 1971–76; Univ of Oxford: lectr in chemistry 1976–90, reader 1990–92, fell Keble Coll 1976–92, lectr Pembroke Coll 1977–92, univ assessor 1991–92; Sir Edward Frankland BP prof of inorganic chemistry Imperial Coll London 1992–99, dean Royal Coll of Science 1996–99, princ St Edmund Hall Oxford 1999–2009, emeritus prof of chemistry Univ of Oxford 2009–; memb: SERC, AFRC, ACOST, HEFCE, European Science Fndn Ctees; memb Editorial Bd: Transition Metal Chemistry, Advances in Inorganic Chemistry, Chemistry Soc Reviews, New Jl of Chemistry, Inorganic Chemistry; regnl ed Jl of Organometallic Chemistry, managing ed Structure and Bonding (also memb Editorial Bd); vice-pres Dalton Div RSC 1993–96; Corday Morgan Medal RSC 1980, Chemistries of Noble Metals Prize RSC 1983, Tilden lectr and Medal RSC 1988, Wilhelm Manchott Prize 1995, Michael Collins Award 1996, Lee Meml Lecture Univ of Chicago 1997, Alexander von Humbolt Stiftung Forschungs Preis 1999; govr Harrow Sch; fell by special election Keble Coll Oxford 1993 (hon fell 1999), distinguished prof Xi'an Petroleum Univ 1994, Univ of Auchland Fndn visitor 2000; hon fell St Edmund Hall Oxford 2009–; Hon DSc UMIST 2000, Hon DSc Univ of Sussex 2001; memb American Chemical Soc 1988; CChem, FRSC 1984, FRS 1992; *Books* Introduction to Cluster Chemistry (1990), Essentials of Inorganic Chemistry (I 1995, II 1998), Essential Trends in Inorganic Chemistry (1997), Structural and Electronic Paradigms in Cluster Chemistry (ed, 1997), Comprehensive Organometallic Chemistry III (ed-in-chief, 2007), Nitrosyl Complexes in Inorganic Chemistry, Biochemistry and Medicine, Structure and Bonding (ed and contrib, I Volume 153 and II Volume 154, 2014), Gold Clusters, Colloids and Nanoparticles, Structure and Bonding (ed and contrib, I Volume 161 and II Volume 162, 2014); *Recreations* tennis, cricket, walking, travelling; *Style*— Prof Michael Mingos, FRS; ✉ Inorganic Chemistry Laboratory, University of Oxford, Oxford OX1 3QR (☎ 01865 272316, fax 01865 272600, e-mail michael.mingos@seh.ox.ac.uk)

MINOGUE, Prof Kenneth Robert; s of Denis Francis Minogue (d 1988), and Eunice Pearl, *née* Porter (d 1949); *b* 11 September 1930; *Educ* Sydney Boys' HS, Univ of Sydney (BA), LSE (BScEcon); *m* 16 June 1954 (m dis 2000), Valerie Pearson, da of Frederick George Hallett (d 1974); 1 s (Nicholas Robert *b* 1955), 1 da (Eunice Karen Hallett *b* 1957); *Career* asst lectr Univ of Exeter 1955–56; LSE: asst lectr 1956, sr lectr 1964, reader 1971, prof of political science 1984–95; dir Govt and Opposition Centre for Policy Studies, chm Bruges Group 1991–93; tstee Inst for the Study of Civil Soc 2000–; pres Mount Pelerin Soc 2010; hon fell London Sch of Economics 2002; Centenary Medal (Australia) 2003; *Books* The Liberal Mind (1963), Nationalism (1967), The Concept of a University (1974), Alien Powers: The Pure Theory of Ideology (1985), Politics: A Very Short Introduction (1995), Conservative Realism: New Essays in Conservatism (ed, 1996), The Silencing of Society (1997), Waitangi Morality Reality (1998), The Servile Mind: How Democracy Erodes the Moral Life (2010); *Recreations* wine, women and song; *Clubs* Garrick; *Style*— Prof Kenneth Minogue; ✉ 43 Perrymead Street, London SW6 (☎ 020 7736 2380, fax 020 7371 9135); Department of Government, London School of Economics and Political Science, Houghton Street, London WC2A 2AE (fax 020 7371 9135, e-mail k.minogue@lse.ac.uk)

MINTER, Trevor John; OBE (1997), DL (Kent, 2002); s of John Minter, and Kathleen Edith, *née* Lee; *b* 19 August 1953; *Educ* Harvey GS Folkestone, Christ's Coll Finchley, Lancaster Univ (BA), RMA Sandhurst, Army Staff Coll; *m* 8 May 1976, Elizabeth Ann, da of Allan Kerry, and Vivian Kerry; 1 da (Alexandra Louise *b* 1 Dec 1978), 1 s (Edward Patrick George *b* 23 Nov 1980); *Career* cmmnd Royal Regt of Fusiliers 1973 (mentioned despatches 1989); CO 1 Bn 1993–96, cmd tour incl Bosnia (UN and NATO), staff appt HQ Br Forces Hong Kong 1986–88, Mil Asst to Chief of Defence Staff 1990–93, chief Jt Ops Centre SHAPE 1996–98, Cdr 2 (SE) Bde and 207th Dep Constable Dover Castle 1998–2001; Dep Col (Northumberland) Royal Regt of Fusiliers 1996–2002 (ret), Dep Col Tyne Tees Regt (TA) 1998–2002 (ret); currently with Roger De Haan Charitable Tst, project mangr Folkestone seafront redevelopment; former dir Kent Partnership Kent CC, dir Creative Fndn Folkestone, chm Shepway Sports Tst; former: offr Confederation of the Cinque Ports, pres Fusiliers Assoc of Northumberland, chm Fusiliers of Northumberland Benevolent Fund; former tstee: Fusiliers Museum of Northumberland, Adml Ramsay Meml Appeal, Folkestone GS for Girls, Fusiliers Aid Soc, Fusilier Fund; tstee: Marlowe Acad, Friends of the Folkestone and Marlowe Acad Tst; chm Shepway Sports Tst, patron Market Garden Veterans Assoc 1998–2001; pres Fusiliers Assoc SE Branch; non-exec dir: Marlowe Innovation Centre, Acad FM Folkestone, Acad FM Thanet, Folkestone Harbour Authy; Kent ambass; Col Royal Regt of Fusiliers 2007–12; Freeman City of London 1994; *Recreations* shooting, hill walking, history; *Style*— Trevor Minter, OBE, DL; ✉ c/o Strand House, 125 High Street, Sandgate, Folkestone, Kent CT20 3BZ

MINTO, Anne Elizabeth; OBE (2000); da of Robert Mitchell (d 1980), and Elizabeth Ann Geddes, *née* Rennie; *b* 29 May 1953, Aberdeen; *Educ* Ellon Acad, Univ of Aberdeen (LLB), Robert Gordon Univ Aberdeen (Dip); *Career* admitted slr 1977; NP 1978; with Shell UK Exploration and Production 1979–92, dep DG EEF 1993–98, gp HR dir Smiths Gp plc 1998–2002, gp dir HR Centrica plc 2002–11; non-exec dir: Shire plc 2010–, Tate & Lyle plc 2012, EXL Inc 2013, Ct Univ of Aberdeen; vice-chair Univ of Aberdeen Devpt Tst; FRSA 1988, FCMI (FIMgt 1998), FCIPD 2000, fell London City & Guilds 2009; *Recreations* travelling, opera; *Style*— Ms Anne Minto, OBE; ✉ e-mail anne.minto@outlook.com

MINTO, 7 Earl of (UK 1813); (Gilbert) Timothy George Lariston Elliot-Murray-Kynynmound; 10 Bt (S 1700); also Baron Minto (GB 1797) and Viscount Melgund (UK 1813); s of 6 Earl of Minto, OBE (d 2005); *b* 1 December 1953; *Educ* Eton, North East London Poly (BSc); *m* 30 July 1983, Diana Barbara, da of Brian S L Trafford, of Rudgwick, W Sussex; 3 s (Gilbert, Viscount Melgund *b* 1984, Lorne *b* and d 1986, Hon Michael *b* 1987), 1 da (Lady Clare Patricia *b* 1991); *Heir* s, Viscount Melgund; *Career* Lt Scots Gds 1972–76; worked in property devpt 1976–80, WH Smith 1983–95, chief exec Paperchase 1995–; memb Queen's Body Guard for Scotland (Royal Co of Archers); ARICS; *Clubs* White's, Shikar; *Style*— The Rt Hon the Earl of Minto

MINTON, Yvonne Fay; CBE (1980); da of Robert Thomas Minton (d 1974), of Sydney, Aust, and Violet Alice, *née* Dean (d 1997); *b* 4 December 1938; *Educ* Sydney Conservatorium of Music; *m* 21 Aug 1965, William Barclay, s of William Barclay (d 1964), of Scotland; 1 s (Malcolm Alexander *b* 1971), 1 da (Alison Elizabeth *b* 1973); *Career* mezzo-soprano; memb Royal Opera Covent Garden 1964–, guest memb Cologne Opera 1969–; guest singer: Aust Opera, Met Opera NY, Lyric Opera Chicago, San Francisco, Paris, Vienna, Bayreuth, Salzburg; Hon RAM; *Recordings* incl: Der Rosenkavalier, Marriage of Figaro, Parsifal, Tristan and Isolde, various song cycles; *Recreations* reading, gardening; *Style*— Ms Yvonne Minton, CBE; ✉ c/o Ingpen & Williams Ltd, 7 St Georges Court, 131 Putney Bridge Road, London SW13 2PA (☎ 020 8874 3222, fax 020 8877 3113)

MIQUEL, Prof Raymond Clive; CBE (1981); *b* 28 May 1931; *m*; *c*; *Career* Arthur Bell & Sons: joined 1956, md 1968–85, chm 1973–85; chm Wellington Importers Ltd USA 1984–85, Gleneagles Hotels plc 1984–85, chm and chief exec Belhaven plc 1986–88, dir Golf Fund plc 1989–94; chm and chief exec: Lees Foods plc 1992–2009, Lees of Scotland Ltd 1993–2009; visiting prof of business devpt Univ of Glasgow 1984–; chm Scottish Sports Cncl 1987–91, govr Sports Aid Fndn; memb: Sport and Recreation Alliance 1981–, Sports Cncl 1988–91; CCMI 1981; *Books* Business as Usual – The Miquel Way (biography, 2000, updated 2012); *Style*— Professor Raymond Miquel, Esq, CBE, CCMI; ✉ Whitedene, Caledonian Crescent, Gleneagles, Perthshire (☎ 07711 731827)

MIRO, Victoria; da of Montagu Cooper, and Jane Cooper; *Educ* Slade Sch of Fine Art; *Career* prop Victoria Miro Gallery 1985–; artists represented incl: Chris Ofili, Peter Doig, Isaac Julien, Doug Aitken, Grayson Perry, Inka Essenhigh, Ian Hamilton Finlay; tstee Little Sparta Tst; *Style*— Mrs Victoria Miro; ✉ Victoria Miro Gallery, 16 Wharf Road, London N1 7RW (☎ 020 7336 8109, e-mail victoria@victoria-miro.com)

MIRON, Stephen Gabriel; s of Roger Miron, and Jo Kaye, *née* Brass; *b* 8 May 1965, Kingston-upon-Thames; *Educ* Hampton Sch; *m* 1 May 2005, Suzanne, *née* Grover; 2 da (Georgia Emily *b* 8 March 2002, Anya Rose *b* 15 Nov 2004); *Career* commercial dir The Independent 1998–2001, md new ventures Associated Newspapers 2002–03, md Mail on Sunday and Mail Digital 2003–08, gp chief exec Global Radio 2008–; memb Advsy Bd Bartle Bogle Hegarty; fell Mktg Soc 2011–; *Recreations* golf; *Clubs* 30, MGGB, The George, Soho House, Ivy, Wisley, Arts, Beaverbrook; *Style*— Stephen Miron, Esq; ✉ Global Group, 30 Leicester Square, London WC2H 7LA (Twitter @stephenmiron)

MIRREN, Dame Helen; DBE (2003); *b* 26 July 1946; *Career* actress; fell BAFTA 2014; *Theatre* RSC 1970–72 incl: Troilus and Cressida, Two Gentlemen of Verona, Hamlet, Miss Julie, The Man of Mode; other credits incl: International Centre of Theatre Research (with Peter Brook, Paris, Africa/America tour) 1972–73, Macbeth (RSC) 1974, Teeth 'n' Smiles (Royal Court/Wyndhams) 1974, The Seagull (Lindsay Anderson Co) 1976, The Bed Before Yesterday (Lyric) 1976, Henry VI parts 1, 2 and 3 (RSC) 1977–78, Measure For Measure (Riverside) 1979, The Duchess of Malfi (Royal Exchange Manchester 1980, Roundhouse 1981), Faith Healer (Royal Court) 1981, Antony and Cleopatra (RSC) 1982–83, The Roaring Girl (RSC) 1983, Extremities 1984, Madame Bovary (Watford Palace) 1987, Two Way Mirror (Young Vic) 1988, Sex Please, We're Italian (Young Vic) 1991, The Writing Game (New Haven, Conn) 1993, A Month in the Country (Albery 1994 and Roundabout NY 1995, nominated for Best Actress Tony Award), Antony and Cleopatra, Collected Stories (Theatre Royal) 1999, Orpheus Descending (Donmar Warehouse) 2000, Dance of Death (Broadway) 2001, Mourning Becomes Electra (RNT) 2003–04, Phèdre 2009, The Audience 2013 (Best Actress Olivier Award 2013); *Television* for BBC incl: Cousin Bette (series) 1971, Miss Julie 1972, Jackanory 1973, Little Minister 1973, The Changeling (with Stanley Baker) 1974, The Apple Cart 1974, The Philanthropist 1975, Mussolini and Claretta Petacci 1975, The Country Wife 1976, Rosalind in As You Like It 1978, Blue Remembered Hills 1978, Oresteia in The Serpent Son 1978, A Midsummer Night's Dream 1981, Mrs Reinhart (with WNET/USA) 1981, After the Party 1982, Imogen in Cymbeline 1982; for ATV incl: Behind the Scenes 1971, Coffin for the Bride 1973, Quiz Kids 1978; for Granada The Collection 1976, DCI Jane Tennison in Prime Suspect I, II, III, IV and V 1990–96, VI 2003 and VII 2006 (BAFTA and BPG TV & Radio Best Actress Awards 1992, BAFTA Best TV Actress Award 1993, BAFTA Best TV Actress Award 1994, Emmy Award for Best Actress 1996); other credits incl: Bellamira (Thames) 1974, Coming Through (Central) 1985, Alma Rattenbury in Cause Celebre (Anglia) 1987, Red King, White King (HBO) 1988, Losing Chase 1996 (Golden Globe Award for Best Actress), Painted Lady 1998, dir Happy Birthday (US TV Film) 2000, Door to Door 2002, Georgetown 2002, Pride 2004, Elizabeth I 2005 (Best Actress in a Miniseries or TV Movie Golden Globe Awards 2007); *Films* Age of Consent 1969, Savage Messiah 1971, O Lucky Man 1972, Caligula 1976, Hussy 1979, The Long Good Friday 1979, Fu Man Chu 1980, Excalibur 1981, Cal 1983 (Best Actress Award Cannes Film Festival 1984), 2010 1984, White Knights 1984, Heavenly Pursuits 1985, Mosquito Coast 1986, Pascali's Island 1987, When the Whales Came 1988, Bethune, Making of a Hero 1988, The Cook, The Thief, His Wife and Her Lover 1989, The Comfort of Strangers 1989, Where Angels Fear to Tread, The Gift 1991, The Hawk 1992, Prince of Jutland 1993, Queen Charlotte in The Madness of King George 1994, Some Mothers Son 1995, Critical Care 1996, The Passion of Ayn Rand 1998 (Emmy Award Best Actress), The Killing of Mrs Tingle, Last Orders 2001, Gosford Park 2001 (Oscar nomination for Best Supporting Actress 2002), Calendar Girls 2003, The Clearing 2004, Raising Helen 2004, The Queen 2006 (Best Actress in a Drama Golden Globe Awards 2007, Best Actress in a Leading Role BAFTA Awards 2007, Best Actress Oscar 2007), National Treasure: Book of Secrets 2007, Inkheart 2008, State of Play 2009, The Last Station 2009, The Debt 2010, The Tempest 2010, Red 2010, Legend of the Guardians: The Owls of Ga'Hoole 2010, Brighton Rock 2011, Arthur 2011, The Door 2012, Hitchcock 2012; *Style*— Dame Helen Mirren, DBE; ✉ c/o Ken McReddie Associates Ltd, 11 Connaught Place, London W2 2ET

MIRRLEES, Prof Sir James Alexander; kt (1997); s of late Prof George B M Mirrlees; *b* 5 July 1936; *Educ* Trinity Coll Cambridge (BA, PhD), Univ of Edinburgh (MA); *m* m 1, 1961, Gillian Marjorie (d 1993); 2 da (Catriona, Fiona); *m* 2, 2001, Patricia; *Career* advsr MIT Center for Int Studies India Project New Delhi 1962–63, asst lectr rising to lectr in economics Univ of Cambridge 1963–68 (fell Trinity Coll Cambridge), advsr Pakistan Inst of Devpt Economics Karachi 1966–68, Edgeworth prof Univ of Oxford 1968–95 (fell Nuffield Coll Oxford), visiting prof Dept of Economics MIT 1968, 1970–71, 1976 and 1987; prof of political economy Univ of Cambridge 1995– (fell Trinity Coll); Ford visiting prof Dept of Economics Univ of Calif Berkeley 1986, visiting prof Dept of Economics Yale Univ 1989, asst editor Review of Econ Studies 1969–74 (memb Bd 1963–); Econometric Soc: fell 1970–, memb Cncl 1970–74 and 1976–, vice-pres 1980–82, pres 1983–84; memb Treasy Ctee on Policy Optimization 1976–78, co-editor Econometrica 1980–84; foreign hon memb: American Acad of Arts and Scis 1981, American Econ Assoc 1982; memb Cncl Royal Econ Soc 1982–, chm Assoc of Univ Teachers of

Economics 1983–87, vice-pres Atlantic Econ Soc 1986–87, pres Royal Econ Soc 1989–92, pres European Econ Soc 2000, foreign assoc US Nat Acad of Sciences 1999; Nobel Prize for Economics (jtly) 1996, Royal Medal Royal Soc of Edinburgh 2009; hon doctorate: Univ of Warwick, Univ of Portsmouth, Brunel Univ, Univ of Edinburgh, Univ of Oxford, Univ of Liège, Chinese Univ of Hong Kong, Univ of Macau, Peking Univ, Helsinki Sch of Economics; Hon FRSE 1998; FBA; *Publications* Manual of Industrial Project Analysis in Developing Countries Vol II (with I M D Little, 1969), An Exploration in the Theory of Income Taxation (Review of Eocnomic Studies, 1971), Optimal Taxation and Public Production (with P A Diamond, American Economic Review, 1971), On Producer Taxation (Review & Economics Studies, 1972), Notes on Welfare Economics, Information and Uncertainty (Essays in Equilibrium Behaviour under Uncertainty 1974), Arguments for Public Expenditure (Contemporary Economic Analysis 1979), The Economic Uses of Utilitarianism (Utilitarianism and Beyond 1982); *Recreations* reading detective stories, mathematics, playing the piano, travelling; *Style*— Prof Sir James Mirrlees, FBA; ✉ Trinity College, Cambridge CB2 1TQ (☎ 01223 339516, e-mail j.mirrlees@econ.cam.ac.uk)

MIRVIS, Rabbi Ephraim Yilzchak; *b* 7 September 1956, Johannesburg, SA; *Educ* Herzlia HS Cape Town, Univ of S Africa (BA), Machon Ariel (ordination); *Career* Chief Rabbi of Ireland 1984–92, Rabbi Western Marble Arch Synagogue 1992–96, Sr Rabbi Finchley Synagogue 1996–2013, Chief Rabbi of the United Hebrew Congregations of the Cwlth 2013–; pres Concl of Christians and Jews, associate pres Conference of European Rabbis; founding Rabbi and hon princ Sacks Morasha Primary Sch, pres London Sch of Jewish Studies; *Style*— Rabbi Ephraim Mirvis; ✉ Office of the Chief Rabbi, 305 Ballards Lane, London N12 8GB (e-mail info@chiefrabbi.org, website www.chiefrabbi.org)

MIRZA, Shazia; da of Mohammed Ayaz, and Sarwat, *née* Iqbal; *b* 3 October 1976, Birmingham; *Educ* Univ of Manchester (BSc), Rose Bruford Coll of Speech and Drama (Dip), Goldsmiths Coll Univ of London (PGCE); *Career* comedienne; TV and radio appearances incl: Have I Got News For You (BBC) 2001, Richard and Judy (Channel 4) 2002, 2005 and 2007, 60 Minutes (CBS) 2004, Mind Games (BBC 4) 2004, 28 Acts in 28 Minutes (BBC 3) 2005, The World Stands Up (Paramount Comedy) 2005, With Great Pleasure (Radio 4) 2005, Off the Page (Radio 4) 2007, F**k Off I'm a Hairy Woman (BBC 3) 2007, Last Comic Standing (NBC) 2008, Beautiful People (BBC 2) 2009, Muslim Driving School (voiceover, BBC 2) 2010, A Good Read (BBC Radio 4) 2010, The Wright Stuff (Channel 5) 2011; columnist: New Statesman 2006–, Asian Woman Magazine 2007–, The Guardian 2009–; Best New Act of the Year Hackney Empire 2001, Jongleurs Comedy Clubs/Metro Female Comedian of the Year 2002, Columnist of the Year PPA Award 2008, Asian Woman of the Year Arts & Culture Award 2010; publications written for: the Guardian, New Statesman, Financial Times, Woman's Weekly, Virgin Train's hotlin magazine; *Recreations* swimming, music; *Clubs* Soho House; *Style*— Miss Shazia Mirza; ✉ c/o Jonathan Brandstein, MBST Entertainment, Suite 200, 345 North Maple Drive, Beverley Hills 90210, USA (☎ 001 310 385 1756, website www.shazia-mirza.com)

MIRZOEFF, Edward; CVO (1993), CBE (1997); s of late Eliachar Mirzoeff, and Penina, *née* Asherov (d 2009); *b* 11 April 1936; *Educ* Hasmonean GS, The Queen's Coll Oxford (open scholar, MA); *m* 4 June 1961, Judith, da of Harry Topper; 3 s (Nicholas b 1962, Daniel b 1965, Sacha b 1969); *Career* market researcher Social Surveys (Gallup Poll) Ltd 1959–60, asst ed Shoppers' Guide Magazine 1962–63; BBC TV 1963–2000, freelance television conslt, exec prodr, prodr and dir 2000–; prodr and dir of many documentaries incl: Elizabeth R, Metro-land, A Passion for Churches, The Queen's Realm, The Front Garden, The Englishwoman and the Horse, Police – Harrow Road, The Regiment, Target Tirpitz, The Ritz, Torvill and Dean: Facing the Music, Treasures in Trust, John Betjeman – The Last Laugh; series prodr: Choice, Bird's-Eye View, Year of the French, In at the Deep End, Just Another Day, The Richard Dimbleby Lecture, A J P Taylor Lectures; ed 40 Minutes 1985–89; exec prodr of many documentary series since 1982 incl: Pandora's Box, The Ark, True Brits, Situation Vacant, The House, Full Circle with Michael Palin, The 50 Years War: Israel and the Arabs, Children's Hospital, Michael Palin's Hemingway Adventure, Queen Elizabeth the Queen Mother, The Lords' Tale, A Very English Village, The Lie of the Land; BAFTA Award for best documentary 1982, BAFTA Awards for best factual series 1986 and 1989, BFI TV Award 1988, Samuelson Award Birmingham Festival 1988, BAFTA Alan Clarke Award for outstanding contribution to television 1994, Int Emmy 1996, Broadcasting Press Guild Award 1996, Royal Philharmonic Soc Music Award 1996; BAFTA: memb Cncl 1988–99, vice-chm TV 1991–95, chm 1995–97, tstee 1999–2011; memb Bd Dirs and Prodrs Rights Soc 1999–2008; chm Grierson Tst 2002–06 (tstee 1999–2009, patron 2010–15); memb Cncl Salisbury Cathedral 2002–10; vice-pres Betjeman Soc 2006–; author of articles for pubns incl The Oldie and Standpoint; *Recreations* opera, lunching with friends; *Clubs* Garrick; *Style*— Edward Mirzoeff, Esq, CVO, CBE; ✉ 9 Westmoreland Road, London SW13 9RZ

MISHCON, Hon Jane Malca (The Hon Mrs Landau); da of Baron Mishcon (Life Baron); *b* 1950; *Educ* Univ of Oxford (MA); *m* 1, 1971 (m dis), Anthony Jay; 1 s (Adam), 1 da (Lucy); m 2, 30 Oct 1990, Edward Landau; *Career* called to the Bar Gray's Inn 1979, practising barr specialising in clinical and slrs' negligence; chair 8 ind inquiries into homicides by mentally disordered patients; memb Professional Negligence Bar Assoc; *Style*— Miss Jane Mishcon; ✉ Hailsham Chambers, 4 Paper Buildings, Temple, London EC4Y 7EX (☎ 020 7643 5000)

MISHCON, (Hon) Peter Arnold; er s of Baron Mishcon, QC, DL (Life Peer) (d 2006); *b* 1946; *Educ* City of London Sch, Birmingham Coll of Art, Poly of Central London (DipArch); *m* 1967, Penny Green; 1 s (Oliver b 1968), 3 da (Anna b 1972, Kate b 1973, Eliza b 1977); *Career* chartered architect and designer; princ Mishcon Associates 1976–; Housing Centre Trust Jubilee Award for Outstanding Achievement in Housing, Royal Borough of Kensington and Chelsea Environment Award, Times/RICS Conservation Award, Arango Design Fndn (USA) Award; chm Keniston Housing Association Ltd 1984–2001; RIBA, FRSA; *Recreations* Nelson boats, breakfast, fixing things; *Style*— Peter Mishcon; ✉ Mishcon Associates, Pembridge Studios, 27A Pembridge Villas, London W11 3EP (☎ 020 7229 9103, fax 020 7229 6744, e-mail peter@mish.com, website www.mishconarchitects.com)

MISKIN, Charles James Monckton; QC (1998); s of Nigel Monckton Miskin (d 2004), and Hilda Meryl, *née* Knight (d 1962); *b* 29 November 1952; *Educ* Charterhouse (Sutton prize), Worcester Coll Oxford (open exhbn, MA); *m* 1, 1982 (m dis), Kass, da of Ronald Booth; 1 s (Harry b 7 February 1983), 3 da (Cici b 11 May 1984, Julia b 19 November 1990, Flora b 10 November 1992); m 2, 2005, Angharad, da of Prof Brian Start; 1 s (Madoc), 2 da (Eluned, Yseult); *Career* called to the Bar Gray's Inn 1975 (bencher 2004), standing counsel to the Inland Revenue 1993–98, recorder of the Crown Court 1998– (asst recorder 1992–98), head of chambers 23 Essex St 2002–05; memb: SE Circuit, Criminal Bar Assoc, Justice; Liveryman: Worshipful Co of Armourers and Brasiers, Worshipful Co of Wax Chandlers; *Recreations* travel, history, opera, theatre (chm Bar Theatrical Soc 1986–), walking; *Clubs* Hurlingham, Travellers; *Style*— Charles Miskin, Esq, QC; ✉ 23 Essex Street, London WC2R 3AS (☎ 020 7413 0353, fax 020 7413 0374, e-mail clerks@23es.com)

MISRA, Prof Prem Chandra; JP (Glasgow 1985); s of Dr Man Mohan Lal Misra (d 1980), of Hardoi, India, and Vindhya Vasni De Vi (d 1970); *b* 24 July 1941; *Educ* KK Degree Coll Lucknow India (BSc), King George's Med Coll Lucknow India (MB BS), Royal Coll of Surgeons and Physicians Glasgow & Edinburgh (DPM); *m* 24 Jan 1970, Sandhya, da of Mr Manohar Lal Khanna, of Bombay, India; 2 da (Deepali b 1970, Nisha b 1980), 1 s (Vivek b 1975); *Career* demonstrator Dept of Human Physiology King George's Med Coll Lucknow India 1967, resident house surgn in gen surgery Royal Infirmary Wigan 1968–69, resident house physician in gen med Whelley Hosp Wigan 1969–70; Bolton Dist Gen Hosp Farnworth: resident sr house offr of gen psychiatry 1970–71, resident registrar of gen psychiatry 1971–73; Hollymoor Hosp Birmingham: sr psychiatric registrar 1973–76, conslt psychiatrist and sr clinical lectr Dept of Psychological Med Univ of Glasgow 1976–; memb Exec Ctee Strathclyde Community Relations Cncl 1981–87, pres Indian Assoc of Strathclyde, memb Bd of Dirs Scottish Refugee Cncl 1995–2001, govr Glasgow Caledonian Univ 1999–2006, lead conslt contact in Scotland Register of Psychiatrists with an Interest in Transcultural Issues RCP; American Gerontological Soc; fell: Indian Psychiatric Soc 1980–, RSM; memb American Psychiatric Assoc 1974–, chm Academic Ctee Br Soc of Med and Dental Hypnosis Scotland 1993–2006 (hon sec Div of Psychiatry 1980–95, pres 1987–89), memb Ethical Ctee (Eastern Dist Glasgow) 1980–93, life memb Scottish Assoc for Mental Health, fndr memb Glasgow Assoc for Mental Health; memb: Exec Ctee European Soc of Hypnosis, Int Soc of Hypnosis, Int Sci Ctee of Sexuality and Handicap in Paris, Exec Ctee Br Soc of Res on Sex Educn; media spokesperson (hypnosis, sexual disorders and phobia) Univ of Glasgow 1986–2006; mentor for newly arrived overseas doctors in Scotland Scottish Cncl for Postgrad Med and Dental Educn; hon prof Glasgow Caledonian Univ 2003; Award for Dedicated and Exceptional Service to Patients: Greater Glasgow Health Cncl, Indian Writers Assoc of Scotland, Med Assoc of Krakow; Asian Fedn of Sexology Hon (for pioneering health care contribution in developing new methods of hypnotherapy for psychosexual disorders), Lifetime Achievement Award in Medical Services Assoc of Indian Orgns of Scotland; FRCPsych (MRCPsych); *Books* Modern Trends in Hypnosis (ed with Waxman et al, 1985), author of 20 res papers on hypnosis and sexual disorders in med jls; *Recreations* classical music, walking in Scottish highlands, travelling to various countries in the world; *Style*— Prof Prem Misra; ✉ 21 Victoria Road, Lenzie, Glasgow G66 5AN (☎ 07775 687849, e-mail prof.p.misra@gmail.com)

MISSELBROOK, Peter; s of Dr D B Misselbrook (d 2005), and Anne, *née* Goodman; *b* 4 March 1953; *Educ* Winchester, Univ of Dundee (LLB); *m* 2 June 1979, Fiona Jane; 1 da (Katie); *Career* admitted slr 1978; trainee Maclay Murray & Spens, ptnr J & A Hastie SSC 1981–96, ptnr Tods Murray LLP 1996–2014 (chm 2002–04, exec ptnr 2004–08), conslt Shepherd and Wedderburn LLP 2014–; formerly: chm BASC, pres Fedn of Fieldsports Assocs of the EU (FACE), memb Firearms Consultative Ctee Home Office, memb Cncl and Exec RZS of Scotland; memb Law Soc of Scotland; moderator High Constables and Guard of Hon Holyrood House; *Recreations* shooting, fishing, stalking, hill walking, gardening, tennis, reading; *Style*— Peter Misselbrook, Esq; ✉ Baro Farmhouse, Haddington EH41 4PF; Shepherd and Wedderburn LLP, 1 Exchange Crescent, Conference Square, Edinburgh EH3 8UL (☎ 0131 473 5435, e-mail peter.misselbrook@shepwedd.co.uk)

MITCHARD, (Gerald Steven) Paul; QC (2008); s of Gerald Albert Mitchard, of Charlton, Wilts, and Janet Margaret, *née* Gregory; *b* 2 January 1952; *Educ* Taunton Sch, Univ of Oxford (MA); *m* 1, 28 June 1980 (m dis 1985), Shirley Anne Mitchard, *qv*, da of Dennis Robert Wilkins Chappell; m 2, 2 May 1987, Dorothy Neleitha, da of Leslie Grant, of Hornsey, London; 2 s (David Max Gregory b 10 Feb 1988, George Henry Steven b 2 Dec 1990); *Career* admitted slr England and Wales and slr-advocate (civil) 1974; asst slr Slaughter and May 1977–84; Simmons & Simmons: asst slr 1984–85, ptnr 1985–98, head of litigation 1994–98; ptnr Wilmer Cutler & Pickering 1999–2001; Skadden, Arps, Slate, Meagher & Flom UK LLP: head of Euro litigation and arbitration 2001–08, head of Asia litigation and arbitration 2009–14; careers dir Faculty of Law Chinese Univ of Hong Kong 2014–; qualified slr Hong Kong 1984 and Br Virgin Islands 2006; CEDR accredited mediator 1993; Liveryman City of London Solicitors' Co; memb: Law Soc 1977, American Bar Assoc, Int Bar Assoc, CPR's Panel of Distinguished Neutrals 1994; FCIArb 1993; *Recreations* reading, walking, scuba diving; *Clubs* Vincents, Oxford; *Style*— Paul Mitchard, QC; ✉ Faculty of Law, The Chinese University of Hong Kong, Shatin, New Territories, Hong Kong; (☎ 00852 3740 4840, e-mail paulm@cuhk.edu.hk)

MITCHARD, Shirley Anne; *née* Chappell; da of Dennis Robert Wilkins Chappell, and Joan Gladys, *née* Woolcott; *b* 15 February 1953, West Monkton, Somerset; *Educ* Weirfield Sch Taunton, Portsmouth Univ (BA); *m* 28 June 1980 (m dis 1985), (Gerald Steven) Paul Mitchard, *qv*; *Career* KPMG Peat Marwick 1975–81 (Tax Dept 1979–81), Tax Div Arthur Andersen & Co 1981–84 (sr mangr 1983), corp tax ptnr Clark Whitehill 1987–97 (joined 1985); BDO Stoy Hayward: corp tax ptnr 1997–2001, conslt Private Client Gp 2001–14; non-exec dir Cedar Int Ltd 2007–09; memb CISCO Tax Ctee 1999–2001; ACA 1978; *Recreations* the arts, gardening, cricket, property renovation; *Style*— Ms Shirley Mitchard; ✉ 40 Cavalry Square, London SW3 4RB (e-mail shirleymitchard@gmail.com)

MITCHELL, Rt Hon Andrew John Bower; PC (2010), MP; s of Sir David Bower Mitchell, DL, and Pamela Elaine, *née* Haward; *b* 23 March 1956; *Educ* Rugby, Jesus Coll Cambridge (MA); *m* 27 July 1985, Sharon Denise, da of David Benedict Bennett; 2 da (Hannah Katherine b 1987, Rosie Olivia Louise b 1990); *Career* 1 RTR (SSLC) 1975; pres Cambridge Union 1978, chm Cambridge Univ Cons Assoc 1977, chm The Coningsby Club (Cons Graduates) 1983–84; int and corp business Lazard Bros & Co Ltd 1979–87; Parly candidate (Cons) Sunderland S 1983; MP (Cons): Gedling 1987–97, Sutton Coldfield 2001–; sec One Nation Gp of Cons MPs 1989–92 and 2005–, a vice-chm Cons Pty 1992–93, asst Govt whip 1992–94, a Lord Cmmr and Govt whip 1994–95, Parly under-sec of state DSS 1995–97, shadow home affrs min 2004–05, shadow sec of state for int devpt 2005–10, sec of state for int devpt 2010–12, parly sec to the Treasy and chief whip 2012; dir: Lazard Bros 1997–2009, Miller Insurance Group 1997–2001, Financial Dynamics 1998–2002, CM Group 1998–2002; sr strategy advsr: Boots 1997–2000, Accenture 1997–2009; advsr to Bd Hakluyt & Co 1998–2001, sr advsr Investec 2013–, sr advsr Montrose Assocs 2013–; vice-chm Alexandra Rose Charity 1998–2010 (now tstee); memb: Cncl SOS Sahel 1990–2010, ESU Int Debating Ctee 1999–2010; tstee GAP Activity Projects 2000–06; pres Norman Laud Assoc 2000–12; Liveryman Worshipful Co of Vintners; *Recreations* skiing, sailing, reading; *Clubs* Cambridge Union Soc, Conservative Club Sutton Coldfield; *Style*— The Rt Hon Andrew Mitchell, MP; ✉ 30 Gibson Square, Islington, London N1 0RD (☎ 020 7226 5519); 8 Tudor Road, Sutton Coldfield (0121 355 5519)

MITCHELL, Andrew Robert; QC (1998); s of Malcolm Mitchell (d 1998), of Aldwick Bay, W Sussex, and Edna Audrey Cherry, of Boca Raton, Florida; *b* 6 August 1954; *Educ* Haberdashers' Aske's, Cncl of Legal Educn; *m* 1, 1982 (m dis 1990), Patricia Anne, *née* Fairburn; m 2, Carolyn Anne Blore; 1 s (Harry Aubrey b 8 March 1993), 1 da (Tiffany Rose b 26 Aug 1994); *Career* called to the Bar Gray's Inn 1976 (bencher 2005); memb Irish Bar, head of chambers 32 Furnival St 1991–2008, head of chambers Chambers of Andrew Mitchell QC 2008–; asst recorder of the Crown Ct 1995–99, recorder (crime and civil) 1999–; treas Gen Cncl of the Bar 2008–11, chm Proceeds of Crime Lawyers Assoc 2008–; memb: Criminal Bar Assoc, Justice; memb Cncl London Borough of Haringey 1984–94 (ldr oppn 1990 and 1991), Parly candidate (Cons) Islington S and Finsbury 1987; chm Bd of Govrs Highgate Primary Sch 1997–99; dir Lascalles de Mercardo 2009–12; chm Burn Stewart Distilleries Ltd 2010–13; *Publications* Confiscation (looseleaf, 1992, 3 edn 2002), Administrative Court law (co-author Proceeds of Crime chapter); *Recreations* playing tennis, watching football and cricket; *Clubs* RAC, MCC; *Style*— Andrew Mitchell,

M

Esq, QC; ✉ Chambers of Andrew Mitchell, QC, 33 Chancery Lane, London WC2A 1EN (☎ 020 7440 9950, fax 020 7430 2818, e-mail arm@33cllaw.com)

MITCHELL, Dr Charles James; s of Col P C Mitchell, MC, FRCPE, of Insch, Aberdeenshire, and Josephine Selina, *née* White; *b* 11 November 1946; *Educ* Trinity Coll Glenalmond, Univ of Edinburgh (BSc, MB ChB); *m* 21 Oct 1972, Elisabeth Bullen, da of Frank George Meakin, of Southfleet, Kent; 1 da (Alice b 1975), 1 s (Alexander b 1977); *Career* house physician Royal Infirmary Edinburgh 1971, SHO and registrar KCH London 1972–74, registrar Academic Dept of Med Royal Free Hosp London 1974–76, conslt physician Scarborough Health Authy (now York Teaching Hosp Fndn Tst) 1981–, hon conslt physician St James's Univ Hosp Leeds 1981–92 (lectr in med 1976–81); regnl advsr Royal Coll of Physicians 1994–97, sec Specialist Advsy Ctee General (Internal) Med 1999–2004; pres Pancreatic Soc of GB and Ireland 1992 (memb Ctee 1981–84), medical memb Appeals Panel PMETB (now GMC) 2005–, elected memb Cncl Royal Coll of Physicians of Edinburgh 2005–11; memb: Br Soc of Gastroenterology (memb Ctee 1987–90 and 1999–2002), Euro Pancreatic Club; chm Derwent Hunt 1998–2013; FRCPEd 1987, FRCP 1988; *Books* Pancreatic Disease in Clinical Practice (ed jtly and contrib, 1981), Textbook of Gastroenterology (contrib, 1992); *Recreations* field sports, piping, gardening; *Clubs* Royal Scot Pipers Soc, New (Edinburgh); *Style*— Dr Charles Mitchell; ✉ The Old Rectory, Ebberston, Scarborough, North Yorkshire YO13 9PA; Leafield, Dalton, Dumfriesshire; Department of Gastroenterology, Scarborough Hospital, Scarborough, North Yorkshire YO12 6QL (☎ 01723 368111, e-mail charles.mitchell@york.nhs.uk)

MITCHELL, His Hon Judge David Charles; s of Charles Mitchell (d 1982), and Eileen, *née* Aveyard (d 1990); *Educ* Batley Boys' GS, Queen Mary's Sch Basingstoke, Cavendish Sch Hemel Hempstead, St Catherine's Coll Oxford (MA); *m* 30 June 1973 (m dis 2013), Susan, *née* Cawthera; 1 da (Joanna b 4 Nov 1980), 1 s (Andrew b 31 July 1982); *Career* called to the Bar Inner Temple 1972 (scholar); barr: Bradford Chambers 1972–99, 6 Pump Court 1999–2001; recorder 1993–2001 (asst recorder 1989–93), circuit judge (SE Circuit) 2001–09 (sr circuit judge 2010–), designated civil judge: Kent (Canterbury) 2003–07, London 2008–; chm Mental Health Review Tbnl 2003–05, course dir Judicial Studies Bd Civil Refresher Course 2008–10, sr resident judge Central London Civil Justice Centre 2010–14; patron Salvation Army; *Recreations* hill walking, skiing, theatre, classical music, anything French; *Style*— His Hon Judge David Mitchell; ✉ Central London County Court, Thomas More Building, Royal Courts of Justice, Strand, London WC2A 2LL

MITCHELL, David James Stuart; s of Ian Douglas Mitchell, and Kathryn Grey, *née* Hughes; *b* 14 July 1974, Salisbury, Wilts; *Educ* Abingdon Sch, Peterhouse Cambridge (MA); *m* 17 Nov 2012, Victoria Coren; 1 da (Barbara Elizabeth June Mitchell b 20 May 2015); *Career* comedy writer and actor; *Television* Peep Show 2003– (Best TV Comedy Br Comedy Award 2006 and 2007, Best Comedy Actor Br Comedy Award 2007, Best Comedy Performance RTS Award 2008, Best Comedy Performance BAFTA 2009), Jam & Jerusalem 2006–09, That Mitchell and Webb Look 2006–10 (Best Comedy BAFTA 2007), team capt Would I Lie to You? 2007–, presenter The Bubble 2010, co-presenter 10 O'Clock Live 2011–, The Bleak Old Shop of Stuff 2011, Ambassadors 2013–, host Was It Something I Said 2013–, The Incredible Adventures of Professor Branestawm 2014; *Radio* That Mitchell and Webb Sound (BBC Radio 4) 2003–, The Unbelievable Truth (BBC Radio 4) 2006–; *Film* Magicians 2007; *Books* This Mitchell and Webb Book (2009), Back Story (2012), Thinking About It Only Makes It Worse (2014); *Clubs* BAFTA; *Style*— David Mitchell, Esq; ✉ c/o Michele Milburn, Milburn Browning Associates, The Old Truman Brewery, 91 Brick Lane, London E1 6QL (e-mail michele@milburnbrowning.com, Twitter @realdmitchell)

MITCHELL, David Stephen; s of Stan Mitchell, of Malvern, Worcs, and Jenny, *née* Cox; *b* 12 January 1969; *Educ* Univ of Kent (BA, MA); *m* 6 Oct 2001, Keiko, *née* Yoshida; 1 da (Hana May b 4 May 2002), 1 s (Noah Sean b 29 Sept 2005); *Career* author; named in Granta 20 List 2003; Hon PhD Univ of Kent, Hon PhD Univ of Worcester; *Publications* Ghostwritten (1999, John Llewelyn-Rhys Prize 1999), Number9Dream (2001, shortlisted Booker Prize 2001), Cloud Atlas (2004, Best Literary Fiction Br Book Awards, South Bank Show Literature Prize, Richard and Judy Best Read of the Year, shortlisted for six awards incl James Tait Black Award and Man Booker Prize), Black Swan Green (2006, longlisted Man Booker Prize), The Thousand Autumns of Jacob de Zoet (2010, shortlisted Commonwealth Writers Prize, Sir Walter Scott Prize for historical fiction, longlisted Man Booker Prize), The Reason I Jump (by Naoki Higashida, co-translator, 2013), The Bone Clocks (2014, World Fantasy Book Award, longlisted Man Booker Prize), Slade House (2015), From Me Flows What You Call Time (2016, to be published 2114); *Style*— David Mitchell, Esq; ✉ c/o Curtis Brown, Haymarket House, 28–29 Haymarket, London SW1Y 4SP (☎ 020 7396 6600, fax 020 7396 0110, e-mail jonnyp@curtisbrown.co.uk)

MITCHELL, His Hon Fergus Irvine; s of Sir George Mitchell, CB, QC (d 1978), and Elizabeth, *née* Leigh Pemberton (d 1989); *b* 30 March 1947; *Educ* Tiffin Boys' Sch Kingston; *m* 1 July 1972, Sally, yr da of late Sir Derrick Capper, QPM; 1 da (Rebecca Elizabeth b 22 March 1977), 1 s (Ewen George William b 15 Feb 1980); *Career* called to the Bar Gray's Inn 1971, head of chambers 1994–96, circuit judge (SE Circuit) 1996–2014; memb Gen Cncl of the Bar 1993–96 (memb Professional Conduct and Race Rels Ctees); chm Lord Chllr's Advsy Ctee SW London 2001–12; *Recreations* opera, military history; *Style*— His Hon Fergus Mitchell; ✉ Kingston Crown Court, 6–8 Penrhyn Road, Kingston upon Thames, Surrey KT1 2BB (☎ 020 8240 2500)

MITCHELL, Gary George; s of Charles Henry Mitchell, and Alexandra, *née* Moreland; *b* 3 May 1965, Rathcoole; *Educ* Rathcoole Secdy Sch; *m* 10 Jan 2004, Alison, *née* Butler; *Career* writer and dir; writer in residence National Theatre of GB and NI 1998–; *Theatre* Independent Voice 1993, Suspicious Minds 1993, Alternative Future 1994, That Driving Ambition 1995, In a Little World of Our Own 1997 (Best Drama Belfast Arts Awards, Irish Times Theatre Awards: Best Dir, Best Actor, Best Play), Sinking 1997 (Best Drama Belfast Arts Awards), Tearing the Loom 1998, As the Beast Sleeps 1998, Trust 1999 (Pearson Prize Best Play), Energy 1999, Marching On 2000 (nominated Best Play Theatre Mgmnt Award UK, nominated Best Play Irish Times), The Force of Change 2000 (jt winner George Devine Award, winner Evening Standard Charles Wintour Award Most Promising Playwright, nominated South Bank Show Award), Remorse 2002, Deceptive Imperfections 2003, Loyal Women 2003, Remnants of Fear 2006 (winner Outstanding Achievement in Culture and Arts Aisling Awards 2006); *Television* Made in Heaven (BBC2) 1996, Made in Heaven Unplugged (BBC2) 1996, Red, White and Blue (BBC1) 1998; *Radio* Radio 4: The World, the Flesh and the Devil 1991 (award winner Young Playwrights' Festival), A Tearful of Dreams 1993, Independent Voice 1993, Poison Hearts 1994, Mandarin Lime (with Jimmy Murphy) 1995; Dividing Force 1995: Useless Tools (episode one), Raising the Standard (episode two), Above the Law (episode three); Drumcree 1996, At the Base of the Pyramid 1997, The Force of Change 2001, Stranded (Radio 3) 1995, Loyal Women (BBC World) 2003, Just Cause (RTE Radio 1) 2008; *Film* An Officer from France (RTE) 1998, As The Beast Sleeps (BBC2) 2001, Suffering (short film) 2002 (Best Short Film Belfast Film Festival 2003); *Publications* Tearing the Loom and In a Little World of Our Own (one vol, 1998), Trust (1999), The Force of Change (2000), As the Beast Sleeps (2001), Loyal Women (2003); *Recreations* soccer, swimming, listening to The Ramones; *Style*— Gary Mitchell, Esq; ✉ c/o PFD, Drury House, 34–43 Russell Street, London WC2B 5HA (☎ 020 7344 1000, fax 020 7836 9543)

MITCHELL, Geoffrey Bentley; OBE (1999); s of Arthur Hale Mitchell (d 1990), and Eunice Bentley, *née* Wood (d 1989); *b* 20 June 1944; *Educ* Univ of Adelaide (BEcon); *m* 26 Jan 1967, Diedre Maria, *née* McKenna; 2 s (Mark James b 19 Oct 1971, Matthew Paul b 13 Oct 1973), 1 da (Melissa Kate b 22 Sept 1977); *Career* articled clerk Thomas Sara Macklin & Co Adelaide S Aust, lectr then sr lectr Univ of Adelaide 1966–77, reader The Flinders Univ S Aust 1977–81, sec gen International Accounting Standards Ctee 1981–85, tech dir ICAEW 1985–90; Barclays Bank plc: sr mangr 1991–93, head of accounting policies 1993–94, gp fin servs dir Chief Accountants Dept 1994–96, chief accountant 1996–2002, dir fin projects 2002–2006; non-exec dir Mizuho Int plc 2003–12 (chm Audit and Compliance Ctee 2006–12); chm EU Standards Advice Review Gp 2007–11; memb: Cncl ICAEW 2001–04 (memb Bd 2003–04), Audit Ctee RCA 2003–07 (chm Pension Tstees 2004–07), Audit Ctee The Law Soc 2004–07, Urgent Issues Task Force 2004–12, Audit and Compliance Ctee Euroclear UK and I Ltd (formerly CREST Co Ltd) 2006–12, Pension Tstees MCC 2006–13; Freeman City of London 1995; memb Inst of CAs in Aust 1966, FCA 1982; *Books* Principles of Accounting (Prentice Hall of Aust, 1981); *Recreations* tennis; *Clubs* Garrick, MCC, Adelaide; *Style*— Geoffrey Mitchell, Esq, OBE; ✉ 20 Swaylands, Penshurst, Tonbridge TN11 8DZ (e-mail gbmitchell101@aol.com)

MITCHELL, Geoffrey Roger; s of Horace Stanley Mitchell (d 1974), of Fordingbridge, and Madge Amy, *née* Rogers (d 1984); *b* 6 June 1936; *Educ* Exeter Cathedral Choristers' Sch, Brentwood Sch; *Career* Nat Serv leading coder educnl RN 1954–56; counter-tenor lay-clerk: Ely Cathedral 1957–60, Westminster Cathedral 1960–61; counter-tenor vicar-choral St Paul's Cathedral 1961–66, gen mangr John Alldis Choir 1966–2010, prof Royal Acad of Music and conductor Chamber Choir 1972–92, conductor New London Singers 1972–87, dir Geoffrey Mitchell Choir 1975–2010, choral mangr BBC 1977–92; conductor Trinity Coll Music vocal ensemble 1977–89, conductor London Festival Singers 1987–2010, guest conductor Camerata Antiqua Curitiba Brazil 1989–2000; Nat Fedn Cathedral Old Choristers' Assocs: vice-chm 1987–92, chm 1992–97, vice-pres 1997–, vice-chm 2010–14; Hon ARAM 1981, Hon FTCL 1989; *Recreations* food, collecting antiques and prints, swimming; *Clubs* Athenaeum; *Style*— Geoffrey Mitchell, Esq; ✉ 49 Chelmsford Road, Woodford, London E18 2PW (☎ 020 8491 0962, e-mail geoffrey-mitchell@ntlworld.com)

MITCHELL, Gregory Charles Mathew; QC (1997); s of John Mathew Mitchell, of Surrey, and Eva Maria Mitchell; *b* 1954; *Educ* Bryanston, Univ of London (BA, PhD), City Univ (Dip Law), Cncl of Legal Educn; *Children* 3 s (Frederick b 11 July 1992, George b 24 Jan 1996, Edmund b 16 Oct 2006), 1 da (Alice Isabel Maria b 19 Oct 2003); *Career* called to the Bar Gray's Inn 1979 (bencher); recorder of the Crown Court 2000–; *Recreations* skiing, tennis, scuba diving, powerboating and sailing; *Style*— Gregory Mitchell, Esq, QC; ✉ 3 Verulam Buildings, Gray's Inn, London WC1R 5NT (☎ 020 7831 8441, fax 020 7831 8479)

MITCHELL, Iain Grant; QC (1992); s of John Grant Mitchell (d 1990), of Perth, and Isabella, *née* Gilhespie (d 1997); *b* 15 November 1951; *Educ* Perth Acad, Univ of Edinburgh (LLB); *Career* called to the Bar Middle Temple 2012; apprentice Steedman Ramage & Co WS 1973–75, admitted Faculty of Advocates 1976, pt/t tutor in mercantile law Univ of Edinburgh 1975–80, temporary sheriff 1992–97; hon lectr Institut für Informations, Telecommunikations und Medienrecht Westfälische Wilhelms Universität Germany; local govt candidate (Cons) 1973–82; Parly candidate (Cons): Falkirk West 1983, Kirkcaldy 1987, Cumbernauld and Kilsyth 1992, Dunfermline East 1997, Edinburgh N and Leith 2001; Scottish Parly candidate: Dundee East 1999, Falkirk W 2003; Euro Parly candidate Scotland 1999; hon sec: Scottish Cons and Unionist Assoc 1993–98, Scottish Cons and Unionist Party 1998–2001; dir Cappella Nova Ltd 2008–, dir Animotion Art (London) Ltd 2014–; memb Strathclyde Cmmn 1997–98; chm Scottish Soc Computers & Law 2007–, UK rep IT Ctee CCBE 2011, memb IT Panel Bar Cncl of England and Wales 2011–, chm CCBE Working Pty on Surveillance 2015–, memb Privacy and Surveillance Working Gp Bar Cncl of Eng and Wales 2015–; ed Scottish Parl Law Review 1999–2005, jt ed E-Law Review 2001–05, jt ed Int Free and Open Source Software Law Review 2009–; memb: Exec Ctee Scottish Cncl Euro Movement 1992–, Central Advsy Ctee on Justices of the Peace 1999–2005; chm: Tst for Int Opera Theatre for Scotland 1984–, Scottish Baroque Ensemble Ltd 2001–03, Church of Scotland Church and Soc Cncl 2009; chm: Perthshire Public Arts Tst 2006–, N Queensferry Station Tst 2006–, N Queensferry Community Cncl 2013–; reader Church of Scotland 2005–; Liveryman Worshipful Co of Information Technologists; FSA Scot 1974, FRSA 1988, FFCS 2002; Electronic Evidence (contrib, 2007, 2 edn 2010), IFoss LRev Law Book (2010), Free and Open Source Software: Policy Law and Practice (contrib, 2013); *Recreations* music and the arts, photography, cinema, walking, travel, finding enough hours in the day; *Clubs* Scottish Arts; *Style*— Iain G Mitchell, Esq, QC; ✉ c/o Advocates' Library, Parliament House, High Street, Edinburgh EH1 1RF (☎ 0131 226 5071, fax 0131 225 3642, mobile 07739 638999, e-mail igmitchell@easynet.co.uk)

MITCHELL, Prof John Francis Brake; OBE (2001); s of Norman Brake Mitchell (d 1969) and Edith Alexandra Mitchell, *née* Reside (d 1997); *b* 7 October 1948, Belfast; *Educ* Down HS Downpatrick, Queens Univ Belfast (BSc, PhD); *m* 6 June 1973, Catriona; 1 s (Ewan Keith b 18 Nov 1976), 2 da (Mairi Ruth b 26 Nov 1978, Eileen Elizabeth b 27 Mar 1982); *Career* Met Office: research scientist 1973–77, forecaster 1977–78, head Climate Group 1978–88, head of modelling climate change 1988–2002, chief scientist 2002–07, dir of climate science 2007–08, princ research fell 2010–; visiting prof Sch of Maths, Physics and Meteorology Univ of Reading 2004–; chm World Climate Research Prog (WCRP) Jt Scientific Ctee-Climate Variability and Predictability Study (JSC-CLIVAR) Working Gp on Coupled Models 2001–08; memb: World Meteorological Orgn (WMO) Steering Gp on Global Climate Models 1990–94, WCRP-Int Geosphere-Biosphere Prog (IGBP) Paleoclimate Modelling Intercomparison Project Scientific Steering Ctee 1994–2001, WCRP CLIVAR Numerical Experimentation Gp II 1995–97, Euro-CLIVAR Ctee 1995–98, WCRP CLIVAR Scientific Steering Gp 1996–2000, WCRP JSC-CLIVAR Working Gp on Couple Models 1997–2000, Intergovernmental Panel on Climate Change Task Gp on Climate Impact Assessment 1997–2009, WMO Cmmn for Climatology Gp on Climate Change Detection 1998–99, IGBP Global Analysis Integration and Modelling Task Force 2001–04, UK Environmental Research Funders Forum 2002–07, UK Global Environmental Change Ctee 2002, NERC Nat Centre for Atmospheric Sciences Advsy Gp 2003, Scientific Advsy Panel UK Environment Agency 2003, Forum on Atmospheric Science and Technol NERC 2003, UK Inter-Agency Ctee on Marine Science and Technol 2003, Industrial Advsy Ctee Univ of Exeter 2003, Exec Cncl WMO 2005–08, NERC Cncl 2006–09; UK permanent rep to WMO 2005–08; hon visiting prof Univ of Exeter 2009–12; memb Editorial Bd Climate Dynamics 1994–, author of numerous articles in peer-reviewed jls; Symons meml lectr RMS 2003; LG Grove Prize for Meteorology Met Office 1984, Norbert Gerbier MUMM Int Award WMO (jtly) 1997 and 1998, Outstanding Scientific Paper Award Environmental Research Labs (jtly) 1997, Hans Oeschger Medal European Geophysical Union 2004, Symons Gold Medal RMS 2011; hon prof of environmental sciences UEA 2003; chartered meteorologist 2004; memb Academia Europaea 1998, fell Inst of Maths and its Applications 2003, FRS 2004; *Recreations* sport, outdoor activities, photography; *Style*— Prof John Mitchell, OBE, FRS; ✉ Met Office, Fitzroy Road, Exeter, Devon EX1 3PB (☎ 01392 884604, fax 01392 884400, e-mail john.f.mitchell@metoffice.gov.uk)

MITCHELL, Jonathan James; QC (Scot 1992); s of John Angus Macbeth Mitchell, of Edinburgh, and Ann Katharine, *née* Williamson; *b* 4 August 1951; *Educ* Edinburgh Acad, Marlborough, New Coll Oxford (BA), Univ of Edinburgh (LLB); *m* 28 Aug 1987 (m dis 2016), Melinda Jane, da of Michael McGarry; 1 da (Hannah Catriona McGarry b 1 March 1988), 1 s (Ewan Patrick Macbeth b 28 December 1992); *Career* apprentice Simpson & Marwick 1976–77, legal offr Citizens' Rights Office 1977, asst to Allan MacDougall 1977–78, admitted to Faculty of Advocates 1979, temp sheriff 1988–96, dep social security cmmr 1994–2002; *Books* Eviction and Rent Arrears (1994); *Clubs* Scotch Malt Whisky Soc; *Style*— Jonathan Mitchell, Esq, QC; ✉ Advocates Library, Parliament House, Edinburgh, EH1 1RF(☎ 0773 963 9343, e-mail jonathan.mitchell@advocates.org.uk, website www.jonathanmitchell.info)

MITCHELL, Jonathan Stuart; s of Rev Ronald Frank Mitchell, and Margery Mabel, *née* Callaghan; *b* 29 January 1947; *Educ* Mill Hill Sch, Trinity Coll Dublin (BA, MA); *m* 13 Oct 2012, Ute Bierbaum; 1 s (Christian Stuart b 21 Nov 1980), 1 da (Emily Katharina b 4 April 1982); *Career* Mktg Div Courtaulds Textiles 1969–72, PR John Laing 1972–73; called to the Bar Middle Temple; in practice SE Circuit 1974–; memb Int Criminal Bar 2003, fndr and memb Bd European Criminal Bar Assoc; memb Criminal Law Ctee Cncl of the Bars and Law Socs of Europe, memb Fair Trials Int Legal Experts Advsy Panel; Parly candidate (Lib Dem): Dulwich and W Norwood 2005 and 2010, Hornchurch and Upminster 2015; cncllr East Dulwich London Borough of Southwark 2006–14; hon alderman London Borough of Southwark 2015–; All-Pty Parly Ctee Burma Democracy Campaign; lectr Univ of Luxembourg 20108–14; memb Herne Hill Baptist Church; *Recreations* gardening, swimming, rowing, sailing; *Clubs* Thames Rowing; *Style*— Jonathan Stuart Mitchell, Esq; ✉ 35 Pickwick Road, Dulwich, London SE21 7JN (e-mail mitchbrief@hotmail.com); 25 Bedford Row, London WC1R 4HD (☎ 020 7067 1500, fax 020 7067 1572, e-mail clerks@25bedfordrow.com); ☎ 07506 461483

MITCHELL, Julian; s of late William Moncur Mitchell, and Christine Mary, *née* Browne (d 1994); *b* 1 May 1935; *Educ* Winchester, Wadham Coll Oxford (BA), St Antony's Coll Oxford; *Career* Nat Serv Sub Lt RNVR 1953–55; Harkness fell USA 1959–61, freelance writer 1962–; formerly: govr Chelsea Sch of Art, memb Lit Ctee English Arts Cncl, chm Drama Ctee Welsh Arts Cncl; curator Joshua Gosselin exhbn Chepstow 2003, curator The Wye Tour and its Artists Chepstow 2010; devised and narrated Adelina Patti – Queen of Song (1987); Wolfson Lectr 2003; FRSL 1985, FSA 2010; *Awards* incl John Llewelyn Rhys Prize 1965, Somerset Maugham Award 1966; *Books* Introduction (stories, 1960); novels: Imaginary Toys (1961), A Disturbing Influence (1962), As Far As You Can Go (1963), The White Father (1964), A Circle of Friends (1966), The Undiscovered Country (1968); Jennie, Lady Randolph Churchill (biography, with Peregrine Churchill, 1974); contrib: The Welsh History Review, The Monmouthshire Antiquary, Gwent County History; *Stage Plays* incl: A Heritage and its History (1965), A Family and a Fortune (1975), Half-Life (1977), Another Country (1981, Play of the Year), Francis (1983), After Aida (1986), Falling Over England (1994), The Good Soldier (2010), Family Business (2011), The Welsh Boy (2012); trans Pirandello's Henry IV (John Florio prize 1980), August (version of Chekhov's Uncle Vanya, 1994); *Television* incl: Elizabeth R (Emmy Award 1971), A Question of Degree, Rust, Jennie, Lady Randolph Churchill (series), Abide With Me (Int Critics Prize Monte Carlo and US Humanities Award 1977), The Mysterious Stranger (Golden Eagle Award 1983), Inspector Morse (RTS and Writers' Guild Awards 1991, 10 episodes), Survival of the Fittest, All the Waters of Wye (documentary), Consenting Adults (2007, Best TV Writing Scottish BAFTA); *Films* Arabesque (dir Stanley Donen, 1965), Another Country (dir Marek Kanievska, 1984), Vincent and Theo (dir Robert Altman, 1990), August (dir Anthony Hopkins, 1995), Wilde (dir Brian Gilbert, 1997); adaptations of books for screen incl: Persuasion, Staying On, The Good Soldier; *Other Publications* New Bats in Old Belfries (introduction, 2005), The Wye Tour and its Artists (catalogue, 2010), author of numerous reviews for magazines and newspapers; *Style*— Julian Mitchell, Esq; ✉ c/o United Agents, 12–26 Lexington Street, London W1F 0LE

MITCHELL, Prof Juliet Constance Wyatt; *b* 4 October 1940, Christchurch, NZ; *Educ* King Alfred Sch London, St Anne's Coll Oxford (exhibitioner, MA, state studentship); *Career* asst lectr Univ of Leeds 1962–63, lectr in English Univ of Reading 1965–71, trainee psychotherapist Paddington Centre for Psychotherapy 1975–77, sr psychotherapist Camden Cncl for Social Services 1976–78, psychoanalyst in private practice 1978–96; Univ of Cambridge: lectr in gender and soc, social and political sciences 1996–, convenor Sec-Gen's Working Pty for the Estab of Gender Studies in Cambridge Univ 1998–, prof of psychoanalysis and gender studies 2000–, head Dept of Social and Political Sciences 2002–03, fndr Centre for Gender Studies 2008–, sr research fell Dept of Human Geography 2008–; dir of prog for PhDs in theoretical psychoanalysis UCL 2010–; A D White prof-at-large (distinguished visiting professorship) Cornell Univ 1994–99 (also sometime visiting prof), visiting fell Social Science Res Unit Univ of London 1995–96, visiting prof Euro Univ Inst Florence 1996–97, visiting prof Central Euro Univ Budapest 1997–99, visiting prof Dept of Comparative Lit Yale Univ 1999, visiting Freud Archive prof Univ of Essex 2000– (visiting prof 1999); sometime visiting prof: SUNY, Washington Univ, Univ of Calif Santa Barbara, Univ of Calif Irvine, Stanford Univ, Austin Riggs Psychiatric and Psychoanalytical Trg Clinic, Intercollegiate Sch of Theory and Criticism Dartmouth Coll, Washington Inst of Psychiatry, Cornell Univ, Deakin Univ Aust, Princeton Univ 2011, Courtauld Inst of Fine Art 2012; Henry Luce visiting scholar Yale Univ, Sigma Chi Fndn – William P Huffman scholar in residence Miami Univ; Emeritus Leverhulme Fell 2013–; numerous named lectures; memb Bd of Gender Studies Central Euro Univ Budapest, hon memb Bd of Women's Studies Yale Univ; clincial work: Br Assoc of Psychotherapists, Lincoln Centre, London Centre for Psychotherapy, Guild of Psychotherapists, Arbours Fndn, Philadelphia Assoc, Addenbrooke's Hosp Cambridge; conslt psychoanalyst: Lima 1984, Brisbane 1988; fndr memb and devisor of educnl prog S of England Soc of Psychotherapists, mentor New Directions Prog Washington Psychoanalytic Fndn 1996–; sometime broadcaster and critic on TV and radio; memb Editorial Bd: Winnicott Studies, Gradiva, Common Knowledge, Gender and Psychoanalysis, Liverpool Studies in Language and Discourse, PsychCritique, Int Advsy Bd of Signs USA, Psychoanalytic Studies, Humanities Inst Stonybrook, Jl of the Inst for Psychological Study of the Arts, New Directions, Studies in Gender and Sexuality, Jl of Classical Sociology, New Left Review; memb: Br Psychoanalytical Soc 1988– (assoc memb 1978), Int Psychoanalytical Assoc 1988– (assoc memb 1978), Br Confedn of Psychotherapists 1996–; FBA; *Publications* Women: The Longest Revolution (1966), Women's Estate (1972, 2 edn 1986), Psychoanalysis and Feminism (1974, 2 edn 2000), The Rights and Wrongs of Women (jt ed, 1977), Daniel Defoe: Moll Flanders (ed, 1978), Feminine Sexuality: Jacques Lacan and the ecole freudienne (jt ed, 1984, reprinted 1996), Women: The Longest Revolution: essays on feminism, literature and psychoanalysis (1984), What is Feminism? (jt ed, 1986), The Selected Melanie Klein (ed, 1986, 2 edn 2000), Before I Was I: Psychoanalysis and the Imagination. The Work of Enid Balint (ed, 1992), Who's Afraid of Feminism? (jt ed and contrib, 1997), Mad Men and Medusas: Reclaiming Hysteria and the Effects of Sibling Relations on the Human Condition (2000), Siblings (2003); author of numerous chapters in books and articles in learned jls; *Recreations* swimming, seeing films, art galleries, reading; *Style*— Prof Juliet Mitchell; ✉ Jesus College, Cambridge CB5 8BL (☎ 01223 339696, fax 01223 339696, e-mail jcwm2@cam.ac.uk)

MITCHELL, Katie Jane; OBE (2009); da of Michael J Mitchell, of Marlborough, Wilts, and Sally, *née* Powell; *b* 23 September 1964; *Educ* Godolphin Sch Salisbury, Oakham Sch, Magdalen Coll Oxford; *Career* theatre dir; began career as prodn asst Kings Head Theatre Club 1986–87; asst dir: Paines Plough 1987, The Writer's Company 1988, RSC 1988–89; fndr own co Classic on a Shoestring (COAS) 1990; assoc dir: RSC 1996–98, Royal Court 2000–03, RNT 2003–; *Theatre* Gate Theatre London/COAS prodns incl: Vassa Zheleznova 1990, Women of Troy 1991, The House of Bernarda Alba 1992; RSC prodns incl: Dybbuk 1992, Ghosts 1993, Henry IV (part III) 1994, Easter 1995, The Phoenician Women 1995, The Mysteries 1997, Beckett Shorts 1997, Uncle Vanya 1998; RNT prodns incl: Rutherford and Son 1994, Machine Wreckers 1995, Oresteia 1999, Ivanov 2002, Three Sisters 2003, Ilanoy 2004, Dream Play 2005, Seagull 2006, Waves 2006, Attempts on Her Life 2006, Women of Troy 2007; WNO prodns incl: Don Giovanni 1996, Jenufa 1998, Katya Kabanova 2001, Jephtha 2003; Royal Court prodns incl: The Country 2000, Ashes to Ashes/Mountain Language 2001, Nightsongs 2002, Forty Winks 2004; other prodns incl: Arden of Faversham (COAS/Old Red Lion) 1990, Live Like Pigs (COAS/Royal Court) 1993, The Last Ones (Abbey Theatre Dublin) 1993, Widowing of Mrs Holroyd (BBC 2) 1995, Iphigenia at Aulis (Abbey Theatre Dublin) 2001; Jephtha (ENO) 2005; *Television* The Turn of the Screw (BBC) 2004; *Awards* Winston Churchill Memorial Tst Travel Fellowship 1989, Time Out Theatre Award (for Arden of Faversham, Women of Troy and Vassa Zheleznova) 1991, Prudential/Arts Cncl of GB Nomination for Contribution to Theatre 1995, Olivier Award nomination for Best Dir 1995, Evening Standard Award for Best Director (for The Phoenician Women) 1996; *Style*— Ms Katie Mitchell, OBE; ✉ c/o Leah Schmidt, The Agency, 24 Pottery Lane, Holland Park, London W11 4LZ (☎ 020 7727 1346, fax 020 7727 9037)

MITCHELL, Madeleine; *Educ* RCM (foundation scholar, Tagore Gold Medal, GRSM, ARCM), Eastman Sch of Music Univ of Rochester USA (Fulbright/ITT fell, MMus); *m* Zerlina; *Children* 1 da (Zarlina Vulliamy b 15 Dec 1998); *Career* concert violinist, performed as soloist and chamber musician in 50 countries, major festivals incl BBC Proms, numerous radio and television broadcasts worldwide; wide discography incl 2 albums of works written for her; prof RCM 1994– (memb Cncl 2013–16); dir London Chamber Ensemble, dir Red Violin Festival; memb ISM, FRSA; *Recreations* opera, art galleries; *Clubs* Consort; *Style*— Ms Madeleine Mitchell; ✉ e-mail mlmfrsa@aol.com, website www.classicalartists.com/madeleinemitchell, Twitter @MadeleineM_Vln

MITCHELL, Margaret; MSP; da of late John Aitken Fleming, and Margaret McRae, *née* Anderson; *b* 1952; *Educ* Coatbridge HS, Jordanhill Teacher Trg Coll (Cert), Hamilton Teacher Trg Coll (DipEd), Open Univ (BA), Univ of Strathclyde (DipLP, LLB); *m* 1978, Henry Thomson Mitchell; *Career* sch teacher primary and special educn N and S Lanarkshire 1974–91, co dir Fairfield Properties Ltd 1990–, special advsr to David McLetchie MSP and Lord James Douglas-Hamilton MSP 1999–2002, supply teacher N Lanarkshire 2002–03, MSP Central Scotland (Cons) 2003– (UK Parly candidate Hamilton 1992 and Cunningham North 1997, Scottish Parly candidate Hamilton South 1999 and 2003 and Hamilton, Larkhall and Stonehouse 2007, 2011 and 2016); convenor: Scot Parl Cross Party Gp on Dyslexia, Scot Parl Cross Party Gp Adult Survivors of Childhood Sexual Abuse, Scot Parl Cross Party Gp on The Caribbean; co-convenor Scot Parl Cross Party Gp on Taiwan; memb Scot Parl Cross Party Gp on: Recreational Boating and Marine Tourism, Tibet, Scotch Wisky; Scottish Cons Party: spokesman on women's issues 1997, chm Local Govt Advsy Ctee 1997–98, depute spokesman on educn 1999, justice spokesman 2003–07, convenor Equal Opportunities Ctee 2007–11, spokesman on local govt 2011–13, justice spokesman 2013–; memb: Cwlth Parly Assoc Scotland Branch Exec Ctee 2011–, Justice Sub-Ctee on Policing 2013–; cncllr and gp ldr Hamilton DC 1988–96; non-exec dir Stonehouse and Hairmyres NHS Hosp Tst 1992–95, memb Hamilton Crime Prevention Panel 1995–; *Recreations* photography, cycling, music; *Style*— Mrs Margaret Mitchell, MSP; ✉ The Scottish Parliament, Edinburgh EH99 1SP (☎ 0131 348 5639, e-mail margaret.mitchell.msp@scottish.parliament.uk)

MITCHELL, Baron (Life Peer UK 2000), of Hampstead in the London Borough of Camden; Parry Andrew Mitchell; s of late Leon Jack Mitchell, and Rose Mitchell; *b* 6 May 1943, London; *Educ* Christ's Coll GS Finchley, Univ of London (BSc), Grad Sch of Business Columbia Univ (MBA); *m* 1, 1972 (m dis 1986), Doreen Hargreaves; 1 da (Hon Charlotte Elise b 1978); m 2, 1988, Hannah, da of late Prof Jack Lowy, of Oxford; 2 s (Hon Oscar Jonathan, Hon Felix Joseph (twins) b 1988); *Career* chm United Leasing plc 1976–87, chm Syscap plc 1992–2006; chm: elearning Fndn 2006–11, Weizmann UK 2006–10, Coexistence Tst 2008–14; *Clubs* Players (NYC); *Style*— The Lord Mitchell; ✉ House of Lords, London SW1A 0PW

M

MITCHELL, Paul England; s of Ronald England Mitchell (d 2005), and Katia Patricia, *née* Hannay (d 2009); *b* 2 November 1951; *Educ* Canford Sch, Univ of Bristol (LLB); *Children* 1 da (Charlotte Daniele b 24 Sept 1986), 1 s (Mark England b 11 May 1989); *Career* articled clerk Joynson-Hicks 1974–76, ptnr Joynson-Hicks (now Taylor Wessing) 1978–2011 (conslt 2011–); chm Br Copyright Cncl 2005–13, tstee Copyright Soc USA 2009–12, dir PRS for Music 2015–; dir Ballet Rambert Ltd 2002–13, dir Roald Dahl Museum and Story Centre (chm 2014–), dir Dancers' Career Devpt, tstee Royal Ballet Benevolent Fund 2014–; Freeman City of London, memb Worshipful Co of Fishmongers; memb Law Soc; FRSA; *Recreations* family, theatre, food and wine; *Clubs* Garrick; *Style*— Paul Mitchell, Esq; ✉ Taylor Wessing, 5 New Street Square, London EC4A 3TW (☎ 020 7300 7000, fax 020 7300 7100, mobile 077 6776 1575, e-mail p.mitchell@taylorwessing.com)

MITCHELL, Sheila; da of George Bruce Mitchell (d 1999), and Mary, *née* McGinney (d 2008); *b* 20 May 1956, Milnthorpe, Cumbria; *Educ* Norte Dame HS Glasgow, Univ of Glasgow (MA), Napier Univ; *m* 30 May 1986, John Turner; 2 da (Juliet b 25 May 1989, Imogen b 19 July 1992); *Career* head of consumer mktg BT 1981–99, dir Turner Mitchell Mktg 1999–2002, mktg dir E Gov Unit Cabinet Office 2002–04, strategic mktg advsr Cabinet Office 2005–08, mktg dir Dept of Health 2008–13, mktg dir Public Health England 2013– (memb Mgmnt Bd 2015–); memb Mktg Gp of GB (MGGB); *Recreations* cinema, opera, travel, theatre, ballet; *Clubs* WACL; *Style*— Ms Sheila Mitchell; ✉ Public Health England, Wellington House, 133–155 Waterloo Road, London SE1 8UG (☎ 07930 300963, e-mail sheila.mitchell@phe.gov.uk, website www.phe.gov.uk)

MITCHELL, Prof Stephen; s of David Mitchell (d 1997), of Oxford, and Barbara Marion, *née* Davis; *b* 26 May 1948; *Educ* Magdalen Coll Sch Oxford, St John's Coll Oxford (MA, DPhil); *m* 1974, Matina Warren, *née* Weinstein; 3 s (Lawrence b 1982, Daniel b 1984, Samuel b 1985); *Career* temp lectr Univ of Bristol 1973–74, res lectr ChCh Oxford 1974–76; Univ of Wales Swansea: lectr 1976–83, sr lectr 1983–88, reader 1988–93, prof 1993–2001; Leverhulme prof of hellenistic culture Univ of Exeter 2002–11; visiting fell Inst for Advanced Study Princeton Univ 1983–84, Br Acad research reader Univ of Göttingen Ger 1990–92; memb Cncl Br Inst of Archaeology at Ankara 1974–99 and 2005– (hon sec 1984–85, 1995–99 and 2009–14), memb Cncl Roman Soc 1986–89 and 1992–95, corresponding memb German Archaeological Inst 1996–, memb Cncl Arts and Humanities Research Bd (AHRB) 1999–2001 (chm Postgrad Panel 1 1999–2002), pres Br Epigraphy Soc 1999–2001, memb Panel 57 Res Assessment Exercise 2001, memb Standing Ctee Cncl of Univ Classical Depts 2002–04, pres Assoc Int d'Épigraphie Grecque et Latine 2008–13; DTh (hc) Humboldt Univ Berlin 2006; FBA 2002 (memb Cncl 2006); *Publications* Anatolia: Land, Men and Gods in Asia Minor (2 vols, 1993), A History of the Later Roman Empire AD 284–641 (2007, 2 edn 2015), The Greek and Latin Inscriptions of Ankara (2012); *Style*— Prof Stephen Mitchell; ✉ c/o British Institute at Ankara, 10 Carlton House Terrace, London SW1Y 5AH (e-mail mitchank@gmail.com)

MITCHELL, Stephen Graham; s of Derek Mitchell, of Loughborough, and Margaret, *née* Rigden; *b* 14 July 1949; *Educ* Loughborough GS, Univ of Manchester; *m* 27 Aug 1977, Barbara Vina, da of Robert Henry Gilder; 1 da (Francesca b 6 Oct 1988), 1 s (Struan b 15 Aug 1990); *Career* with Thomson Regional Newspapers until 1974; BBC Radio: journalist 1974–91, managing ed BBC Radio News 1991–93, ed radio news progs 1993–97, dep head of news progs 1997–99, acting head of news progs 1999–2000, head of radio news 2000–07, head of BBC news progs and dep dir BBC News 2007–13; *Recreations* spending time with my family; *Style*— Stephen Mitchell, Esq

MITCHELL, Stuart Robert; s of Arthur Robert Mitchell, of Long Marston, York, and Margaret Patricia, *née* Marshall; *b* 22 December 1960; *Educ* Tadcaster GS, UMIST (BSc); *m* 27 July 1985, Tracey Victoria, *née* Webb; 1 da (Georgina Victoria b 31 Jan 1993), 1 s (Rory James b 2 Feb 1997); *Career* grad retail trainee J Sainsbury plc 1981–84, salesman Kalamazoo Business Systems 1984; Sainsbury's: trainee buyer 1984, sr mangr meat buyer 1989, vice-pres (store format) Shaw's Supermarkets USA 1993, dir of procurement, primary agric, strategy 1994, Bd trading dir 2000, md 2003–06 (asst md 2001–03); ceo Wilkinson 2007–12, ceo SIG plc 2012–; non-exec dir Enactus; memb Business in the Community; MInstD 2000; Liveryman Worshipful Co of Butchers; *Recreations* rugby, sailing, golf, cookery; *Clubs* RAC, Dorking Rugby Football (non-exec dir 2014–); *Style*— Stuart Mitchell, Esq; ✉ SIG plc, Signet House, 17 Europa View, Sheffield Busines Park, Sheffield S9 1XH

MITCHELL, Timothy James (Tim); s of Robert Sayers Mitchell, and Pamela, *née* Draisey; *b* 11 August 1965; *Educ* Westbourne Coll Penarth, Assoc of Br Theatre Technicians Paddington Coll; *m* (m dis); 2 s (Christopher, James); *Career* lighting designer and tech conslt, over 300 prodns worldwide; chief electrician Sherman Theatre Cardiff 1985–88 (electrician and projectionist 1982–83, dep chief electrician 1983–85), dep chief electrician and lighting designer Bristol Old Vic 1988–90; Birmingham Rep Theatre: head of lighting 1990–95, lighting conslt and designer 1995–2001, assoc artist; lighting conslt Sheffield Theatre 2001–, assoc lighting designer Chichester Festival Theatre 2009–, assoc artist RSC; memb: Assoc of Lighting Designers, United Scenic Artists Local 829 (USA); fell Royal Welsh Coll of Music and Drama (FRWCMD); *Theatre* Birmingham Rep: The Free State (also tour), My Best Friend (also Hampstead Theatre London), Paddy Irishman, Paddy Englishman, Paddy... (also Tricycle Theatre London), The Wind in the Willows, Absurd Person Singular, St Joan, The Threepenny Opera, Macbeth, The Atheist's Tragedy (Gold medal Prague Quadrennial 1995), Of Mice and Men, A View from the Bridge, Hamlet, The Doll's House (also tour); RNT: The Red Balloon, The Alchemist; Donmar Warehouse: A Lie of the Mind, Merrily We Roll Along; RSC: A Midsummer Night's Dream, Comedy of Errors, Women be Aware of Women, Oroonoko, The Winter's Tale, Romeo and Juliet, Macbeth, The Lieutenant of Inishmore, Jubilee, King John, Henry IV Parts I and II (Olivier Award nomination for Best Lighting Design 2002), Antony and Cleopatra, Much Ado About Nothing, Measure for Measure, Richard III, Titus Andronicus, King Lear, Othello (also Japan tour), The Tamer Tamed (Kennedy Center Washington and West End), The Taming of the Shrew (also at Kennedy Center Washington and West End), Hamlet, loves Labours Lost, Twelfth Night, Henry IV Parts I and II (Shakespeare Theater Washington, nominated Helen Hayes Award for Outstanding Lighting Design 2005); Crucible Theatre Sheffield: Edward II, High Society, Richard III, A Chorus Line, Sweet Charity, Lear, Ain't Misbehavin, Piaf, Cherry Orchard; Derby Playhouse: Danny Bouncing, Speaking in Tongues, Ain't Misbehavin', Les Liaisons Dangereuses, Our Boys; other credits incl: Two Pianos Four Hands (Comedy Theatre London), A Raisin in the Sun (Young Vic London), Pajama Game (Toronto and New Victoria Palace Theatre London), Speaking in Tongues, Alphabetical Order, Amongst Friends (Hampstead Theatre London), A Small Family Business, Cyrano De Bergerac, Oklahoma, Grapes of Wrath (Chichester Theatre), Hand in Hand (Hampstead Theatre London), Hamlet (Elsinore Denmark), Mahler's Conversation (Aldwych London), Noises Off (RNT, Piccadilly Theatre London, Broadway and tour), The Snowman (Peacock Theatre London), Sweet Panic (Duke of York's Theatre London), The Play What I Wrote (UK tour and Broadway), Of Mice and Men (West End), Hamlet (Sadlers Wells), A Small Family Business, When We Married (WYP), Benefactors (Albery Theatre London), Hamlet (WYP), Sleeping Beauty (Young Vic London), Winnie the Witch (nat tour), Anna Weiss (Whitehall Theatre London), Dames at Sea (Ambassadors Theatre London), Wodehouse on Broadway (BBC TV and Theatre Royal Plymouth), As You Like It (Wyndhams Theatre), Blood Wedding (Almeida), Brighton Rock (Almeida), Annie Get Your Gun (nat tour), Hamlet (Horripro, Japan and London), Dirty Dancing (London, Toronto and Hamburg), Enemies (Almeida), Big White Fog (Almeida), Into the Woods (ROH); *Opera and Dance* Covent Garden Festival: The King and I, The Gondoliers, A Midsummer Night's Dream; Kammeroper Vienna: The Marriage of Figaro, Requiem Ballet, Don Giovanni; Royal Coll of Music: Les Enfants Prodigues, Le Rossignol; other credits incl: On the Town (LSO, Barbican London, BBC TV), Prometheus (Berlin Philharmonic Orchestra), Carmen Negra (Icelandic Opera), Yeoman of the Guard (D'Oyly Carte), Die Fledermaus (WNO), Ariadne Auf Naxos (WNO, Boston Opera and Canadian Opera), St Davids Day Gala Concert (Channel 4/WNO), Hamlet (Northern Ballet, Knight of Illumination Award), Lady and the Fool (Birmingham Royal Ballet), Elektra (Mariinsky Theatre St Petersburg); *Recreations* reading, music; *Style*— Tim Mitchell, Esq; ✉ Glendun, Main Street, Offenham WR11 8RL (☎ 01740 620062, mobile 07976 273239, e-mail timmitchell@lightdesign.fsnet.co.uk); c/o Clare Vidal-Hall, 28 Perres Road, London W6 0EZ (☎ 020 8741 7647, fax 020 8741 9459)

MITCHELL, William; s of William Mitchell (d 1959), and Eileen, *née* King (d 1996); *b* 8 August 1944; *Educ* Campbell Coll Belfast, Oriel Coll Oxford (MA, Dip Social Studies); *m* 1, 1969, Pratima, *née* Bhatia; 1 da (Priya b 21 Feb 1971); m 2, 1993, Natalina, *née* Bertoli; 2 s (Luca b 4 May 1994, Rafael b 25 August 1997); *Career* dir of int divs and gp bd dir Oxford University Press UK 1970–85, exec ed Reference Publishing Oxford University Press USA 1985–88, exec dir Children's Publishing Reed Publishing Group UK 1988–89, md Children's Publishing Div and md Reference Div HarperCollins Publishers UK 1990–92, md JM Dent Ltd and dep gp md Orion Publishing Group Ltd 1992–93, md Bertoli Mitchell Specialist Publishing Brokers 1993–; *Recreations* normal; *Clubs* Groucho; *Style*— William Mitchell, Esq

MITCHELL-HEGGS, Dr Nita Ann; da of Maj (Dr) Lewis Posner (d 1975), and Olivia, *née* Jones (d 1999); *b* 6 June 1942; *Educ* N London Collegiate Sch, London Hosp Med Coll (MB BS, DCH); *m* 26 July 1967, Dr Peter Francis Mitchell-Heggs, s of Maj Francis Sansome Mitchell-Heggs (d 1986); 2 da (Emily b 2 July 1974, Sophie b 23 March 1977); *Career* formerly held posts in paediatrics, psychiatry, occupational med; former conslt occupational physician St George's Healthcare NHS Tst and sr lectr St George's Hosp Med Sch, currently in independent practice; medical panellist Nursing and Midwifery Cncl; FRCP, FFOM; *Publications* chapters and articles on mental health, occupational medical ethics etc; *Recreations* travel, skiing, theatre, opera; *Style*— Dr Nita Mitchell-Heggs; ✉ 70 Ridgway Place, London SW19 4SW

MITCHINER, Dr John Edward; s of late Geoffrey Morford Mitchiner, and Ursula Angela, *née* Adolph; *b* 12 September 1951; *Educ* Beaumont Coll, Univ of Bristol (BA), SOAS Univ of London (MA, PhD); *m* 1983, Elizabeth Mary Ford; *Career* HM Dip Serv; Cwlth research fell Visva Bharati Univ Santiniketan 1977–78, Bipradas Palchaudhuri fell Calcutta Univ 1978–79, joined FCO 1980, third then second sec (info) Istanbul 1983–85, FCO 1985–87, second sec (devpt) New Delhi 1987–91, second then first sec (political) Berne 1991–95, head Japan Section FCO 1995–96, ambass to Republic of Armenia 1997–99, dep high cmmr Calcutta 2000–03, high cmmr to Sierra Leone and ambass to Liberia 2003–06, ret; *Publications* Studies in the Indus Valley Inscriptions (1978), Traditions of the Seven Rsis (1982, 2 edn 2000) The Yuga Purana (1986, 2 edn 2002), Guru: the search for enlightenment (1992); contribs to learned jls; *Recreations* sheep farming, bridge, tennis, family history; *Clubs* Royal Asiatic; *Style*— Dr John Mitchiner; ✉ Bower Farm, Whitland SA34 0QX

MITCHINSON, David; s of Robert Stockdale Mitchinson (d 1988), of London, and Winifred May, *née* Earney (d 1975); *b* 8 December 1944; *Educ* Bath Acad of Art (Dip); *Career* designer; Kröller Müller Museum Otterlo 1967–68, Henry Moore 1968–77; The Henry Moore Fndn: joined 1977, keeper of graphics 1980–86, keeper of graphics and sculpture 1986–87, curator 1987–97 (organiser major exhbns 1982–95), head of collections and exhibitions 1998–2010; dir: Raymond Spencer Co 1989–90, HMF Enterprises Ltd 1991–2010; tstee Hat Hill Sculpture Fndn Goodwood 1994–2001, tstee Harlow Art Tst 2004–; Hon MA Univ of Herts 2007; *Publications* incl: Henry Moore Graphic Work 1973–86, Henry Moore: Unpublished Drawings (1972), With Henry Moore: The Artist at Work photographed by Gemma Levine (1978), Henry Moore Sculpture (1981), Life and Times, Henry Moore – A Short Biography (1984), Henry Moore: Life and Times (1995), Celebrating Moore (1998), Hoglands, the Home of Henry and Irina Moore (2007), Henry Moore Prints and Portfolios (2010), Calling, Cards and Cases (2012); *Style*— David Mitchinson, Esq; ✉ The Henry Moore Foundation, Dane Tree House, Perry Green, Much Hadham, Hertfordshire SG10 6EE (☎ 01279 843333, fax 01279 843647, e-mail curator@henry-moore-fndn.co.uk)

MITHANI, His Hon Judge Abbas; Hon QC (2009); *Educ* Newcastle Univ (LLD); *Career* circuit judge (Midland Circuit) 2006–; dep bankruptcy registrar until 2006; hon prof of law Univ of Birmingham 2000–15, visiting prof of law and memb Ct Newcastle Univ until 2012, visiting prof of law Kingston Univ Law Sch; Asian Jewel Award for Legal Excellence 2003, Soc of Asian Lawyers Lifetime Achievement Award 2009; *Books* Mithani on Directors' Disqualification, Encyclopaedia of Forms and Procedures, Atkin's Court Forms, Civil Court Service; *Style*— His Hon Judge Mithani, QC; ✉ c/o Midland Circuit Office, Priory Courts, 33 Bull Street, Birmingham B4 6DW

MITHEN, Prof Steven John; s of William Mithen, of Petersfield, Hants, and Patricia, *née* Caporn; *b* 16 October 1960, Ashford, Kent; *Educ* Slade Sch of Fine Art, Univ of Sheffield (BA), Univ of York (MSc), St John's Coll Cambridge (PhD); *m* 25 May 1985, Susan; 2 da (Hannah b 28 Jan 1988, Heather b 8 Aug 1994), 1 s (Nicholas b 26 May 1990); *Career* research fell in archaeology Trinity Hall Cambridge 1987–89, lectr in archaeology Univ of Cambridge 1989–91, research assoc in archaeology McDonald Inst for Archaeological Research Univ of Cambridge 1991–92; Univ of Reading: lectr in archaeology 1992–96, sr lectr in archaeology 1996–98, reader in early prehistory 1998–2000, prof of prehistory 2000–, head Sch of Human and Environmental Sciences 2003–, dean Faculty of Science 2008–10, pro-vice-chllr 2010–; British Acad Research Readership 2001–03; memb Cncl Prehistoric Soc of GB 1995–97; memb Editorial Bd: Cambridge Archaeological Jl 1994–, Jl of Social Archaeology 2000–, Jl of Cognition and Culture 2000–, Jl of Evolutionary Psychology 2000–; author of numerous articles and papers in learned jls; fell New England Inst for Cognitive Science 2001, fell Inst for Cultural Research 2003; FSA Scot 1993, FSA 1998, MRI 2003, FBA 2004; *Books* incl: Thoughtful Foragers: A Study of Prehistoric Decision Making (1990), The Prehistory of the Mind: A Search for the Origins of Art, Science and Religion (1996), After the Ice: A Global Human History, 20,000–5,000 BC (2003), The Singing Neanderthals: The Origins of Music, Language, Mind and Body (2005), To The Islands... (2010), Thirst: Water and Power in the Ancient World (2012); *Style*— Prof Steven Mithen; ✉ School of Human and Environmental Sciences, University of Reading, PO Box 227, Whiteknights, Reading RG6 6AB (☎ 0118 378 6102, fax 0118 931 0279, e-mail s.j.mithen@reading.ac.uk)

MITIUKOV, Ihor; *b* 27 September 1952, Kiev; *Educ* Kyiv State Univ, Inst of Economy Acad of Scis (PhD); *m* Anna; 1 da (Alexandra); *Career* Ukrainian diplomat; dep govr Ukrainia (bank) 1992–94, dep govr National Bank 1994, vice-PM for banking and fin 1994–95, special rep to EU Brussels 1995–97, min for fin 1997–2001, gen dir Fin Policy Inst 2002, ambass to the Ct of St James's 2002; non-exec dir Ferrexpo plc; pres Ukranian Nat Mortgage Assoc 2002; chair Nat Art Museum Devpt Fund; pres Ukranian Ski Fedn; *Recreations* tennis, skiing; *Style*— Mr Ihor Mitiukov; ✉ Ferrexpo plc, 2–4 King Street, London SW1Y 6QL

MITTAL, Aditya; s of Lakshmi Mittal, and Usha Mittal; *b* 22 January 1976; *Educ* Wharton Sch Univ of Pennsylvania (BSc); *m* Megha; 2 c; *Career* ceo and gp chief fin offr ArcelorMittal Europe (formerly Mittal Steel Co) 1997–; *Style*— Aditya Mittal, Esq; ✉ ArcelorMittal, Berkeley Square House, 7th Floor, Berkeley Square, London W1J 6DA

MITTLER, Prof Peter Joseph; CBE (1981); s of Dr Gustav Mittler (d 1962), of Leeds, and Gertrude Mittler (d 1987); *b* 2 April 1930, Vienna; *Educ* Merchant Taylors', Pembroke Coll Cambridge (MA), Univ of London (PhD); *m* 1, 2 April 1955 (m dis 1997), Helle, da of Dr Ernst Katscher (d 1980); 3 s (Paul b 1955, Stephen b 1959, Martin b 1964); m 2, 19 August 1997, Penelope Anastasia Platt, da of Lt Cdr John Brooke Westcott, RNVR, BEM (d 2009); *Career* Nat Serv Ordnance Corps 1949–50, RAMC 1950–80 (Capt Res); clinical psychologist 1954–63, lectr in psychology Birkbeck Coll London 1963–68, prof of special educn and dir Hester Adrian Res Centre 1968–82, dir Sch of Educn and dean Faculty of Educn Univ of Manchester 1991–94, emeritus prof of special educn 2000, hon res fell, fell Centre for Soc Policy Dartington 1995–, distinguished visiting prof Univ of Hong Kong 1997–98; former memb: Sch Examination and Assessment Cncl 1988–90, Prince of Wales Advsy Gp on Disability 1984–90; pres Int League of Socs for Persons with Mental Handicap 1982–86; tstee British Inst for Learning Disabilities 1995–2000 (chm 1995–97); hon fell Manchester Poly 1985; FBPsS 1966, CPsychol 1989; *Books* Psychological Assessment (1970), Study of Twins (1971), People Not Patients: Progress and Problems in Mental Handicap (1979), Advances in Mental Handicap Research (2 vols 1981, 1983), Parents, Professionals and Mentally Handicapped People (1983), Staff Training and Special Educational Needs (1988), Teacher Training for Special Needs in Europe (1995), Changing Policy and Practice for People with Learning Disabilities (1996), Working Towards Inclusive Education: Social Contexts (2000), Thinking Globally Acting Locally: A Personal Journey (2010), Overcoming Exclusion: Social Justice Through Education (2012); *Recreations* listening to music, Italy; *Style*— Prof Peter Mittler, CBE; ☎ 0161 434 5625, e-mail peter.mittler@manchester.ac.uk, website www.mittlermemoir.com

MOBERLY, Robert William Gardner; s of Sir Walter Hamilton Moberly, GBE, KCB, DSO (d 1973), and Gwendolen, *née* Gardner (d 1975); *Educ* Winchester, Lincoln Coll Oxford (BA, Capt of Boats, Desborough Medal); *m* 7 Jan 1992, (Patricia) Mary Lewis, *qv*, da of late Donald Cornes; 1 da (Scarlett Rose b 28 May 1992); *Career* 2 Lt Oxford and Bucks LI 1951–53, seconded to Northern Rhodesia Regt 1952, ADC to GOC E Africa (Sir Alexander Cameron) 1953; Beecham Foods Ltd 1960–63, Foote Cone & Belding Ltd (advertising) 1964–83 (dir 1979–83), fndr ptnr Lewis Moberly Ltd (design conslts) 1983 (md until 1998, chm 1998–); fndr memb DBA, memb Mktg Soc 1966, FRSA 1996; *Recreations* golf; *Clubs* Leander; *Style*— Robert Moberly, Esq; ✉ 24 Canonbury Park North, London N1 2JT (☎ 07785 316194); Whalleybourne Farm, Wrentnall, Pulverbatch, Shropshire SY5 8EB (☎ 01743 792878); Lewis Moberly Ltd, 33 Gresse Street, London W1T 1QU (☎ 020 7580 9252, fax 020 7255 1671, e-mail robert.moberly@lewismoberly.com website www.lewismoberly.com)

MODELL, David; *b* 21 February 1969; *Educ* William Ellis Sch, Barnet Coll of HE; *Family* 2 s (Louis b 15 Feb 1997, Theo b 9 Sept 2000), 1 da (Martha b 17 June 2003); *Career* photojournalist and film maker; fndr memb Int Photographer's Gp (IPG) 1995–; worked with: Time Out, City Limits, Sunday Telegraph, various colour supplement magazines, Independent on Saturday Magazine; photography for ad campaigns for cos incl Hugo Boss, IBM-Lotus, Arthur Andersen, AT&T and Ford 1992–; TV work: short TV documentaries Channel 4 News 1999; other Channel 4 documentaries: Young, Nazi and

Proud 2002 (winner three awards incl BAFTA for Best Current Affairs Prog of Year), Keep Them Out 2004, Being Pamela 2005, Mad About Animals 2006; Tory Story (2001); *Recreations* family life, carpentry; *Style*— David Modell, Esq; ✉ c/o Bonakdar Cleary, 35 Charles Square, London N11 6HT (☎ 020 7490 1133, fax 020 7490 1155, e-mail seamus@bonakdarcleary.com)

MODGILL, Vijay Kumar; s of Sansari Lal Modgill, of NZ, and Dwarka, *née* Devi (d 1978); *b* 1 September 1942; *Educ* Eastleigh Sch Nairobi, Leeds Univ Med Sch (MB ChB); *m* 14 Sept 1974, (Elizabeth) Margaret, da of John Harrop Lawton, CBE (d 1987), of Wakefield, W Yorks; 2 da (Victoria b 1977, Elizabeth b 1985), 1 s (Alexander b 1979); *Career* house physician Leeds Univ Med Sch 1967–68, registrar St James's Hosp Leeds 1968–70 (house surgn 1968), sr registrar Leeds and Bradford Hosps 1972, consult in vascular and gen surgery Halifax Gen Hosp 1975– (clinical tutor 1975–83); chm of Med Staff Ctee 1986–89, currently chm of Med Ctee of Elland BUPA Hosp; memb Vascular Soc of GB; memb Assoc of Surgns of GB, FRCS 1972, FRCSEd 1972; Renal Transplants; *Recreations* golf, cricket; *Clubs* Lightcliffe Golf (Halifax), Fixby Golf (Huddersfield), member of XL; *Style*— Vijay Modgill, Esq; ✉ Linden Lea, Cecil Avenue, Lightcliffe, Halifax, West Yorkshire (☎ 01422 202182); Halifax General Hospital, Salterhebble, Halifax, West Yorkshire (☎ 01422 357171); Elland BUPA Hospital, Elland Lane, Elland, Halifax, West Yorkshire (☎ 01422 375577)

MODOOD, Prof Tariq; MBE (2001); s of Mirza Sabauddin Modood, and Nafeesa Modood; *b* 4 October 1952, Karachi, Pakistan; *Educ* Univ of Durham (BA, MA), Univ of Wales Swansea (PhD); *m* 6 April 1979, Glynthea Margaret, *née* Thompson; 2 da (Ghizala-Ruth, Yasmin-Cariad); *Career* equal opportunity offr London Borough of Hillingdon 1987–89, princ employment offr Cmmn of Racial Equality 1989–91, Gwilyn Gibbon res fell Nuffield Coll Oxford 1991–92, Hallsworth res fell Univ of Manchester 1992–93, sr res fell Policy Studies Inst 1993–97, prof of sociology Univ of Bristol 1997–; dir Centre for the Study of Ethnicity and Citizenship Univ of Bristol 1999–; advsr Cmmn on the Future of Multi-Ethnic Britain Runnymede Tst 1997–2000; memb: Cmmn on National Security IPPR 2007–09, Nat Equality Panel 2008–10, IPPR Policy Advsy Cncl 2009–; tstee Young Fndn (formerly Inst of Community Studies) 2001–08; founding ed Ethnicities 1999–; AcSS 2004; *Books* Not Easy Being British (1992), Ethnic Minorities in Britain (co-author, 1997), Ethnicity, Social Mobility and Public Policy in the US and UK (co-ed, 2005), Multiculturalism (2007, 2 edn 2013), Multiculturalism Rethought (ed, 2015), Multiculturalism and Interculturalism (ed, 2016); *Recreations* badminton, cycling, swimming, films, theatre; *Style*— Prof Tariq Modood, MBE, AcSS; ✉ Centre for the Study of Ethnicity and Citizenship, University of Bristol, 11 Priory Road, Bristol BS8 1TU (e-mail t.modood@bristol.ac.uk, website www.tariqmodood.com)

MOFFAT, Alexander; OBE (2006); s of John Moffat (d 1956), of Cowdenbeath, Fife, and Agnes Hunter, *née* Lawson (d 1995); *b* 23 March 1943; *Educ* Daniel Stewart's Coll Edinburgh, Edinburgh Coll of Art (Andrew Grant scholar, Dip Art); *m* 1968 (m dis 1983), Susan Potten; 1 s (Colin b 1969); *Career* artist; photographer Scottish Central Library 1966–74, dir New 57 Gallery Edinburgh 1968–78; visiting lectr: Winchester Sch of Art 1973–74, Croydon Sch of Art 1974–75, RCA 1986–88; Glasgow Sch of Art: lectr in painting studios 1979–88, sr lectr in painting studios Glasgow Sch of Art 1988–92, head of painting and printmaking 1992–2005, chair Sch of Fine Art 1998–2000; external examiner: Canterbury Coll of Art (Kent Inst) 1988–91, N Staffs Poly Stoke 1989–92, Chelsea Coll of Art & Design (London Inst) 1997–2000, Gray's Sch of Art (RGU) Aberdeen 2002–05, Univ of Brighton 2003–07; sr external examiner Univ of the Highlands and Islands Project 2000–02; external expert Univ of London 1993–98; hon pres The Essential School of Painting 2014; Scottish Arts Cncl 1982–84 (memb Cncl, memb Art Ctee, chm Awards Panel), memb Bd Fruitmarket Gallery Edinburgh 1986–92, chm Bd ALBA magazine 1988–92; writer of numerous catalogue texts; memb Edinburgh Festival Soc; hon research fell Univ of Glasgow 2006, hon fell Assoc for Scottish Literary Studies 2011; RSA 2004 (chair Exhibitions Ctee 2007); *Solo Exhibitions* incl: A View of the Portrait (Scottish National Portrait Gallery) 1973, Gallery of the Press Club Warsaw 1975, Seven Poets (Third Eye Centre Glasgow and tour) 1981–83, Portrait Drawings (N E of Scotland Library and Museums Service) 1984, Portraits of Painters (Scottish Nat Gallery of Modern Art) 1988, Glasgow Art Gallery & Museum 1990, Pittencrieff House Museum Dunfermline 1991, Images From Three Decades (Open Eye Gallery Edinburgh) 2008, Town Hall Gallery Langholm 2012, Paintings as Arguments (Peacock Visual Arts Aberdeen) 2014; *Group Exhibitions* incl: Scottish Realism (Scottish Arts Cncl tour) 1971, The Human Clay (Hayward Gallery London and Scottish Nat Gallery of Modern Art) 1976, Three Painters (Midland Gp Gallery, Nottingham) 1978, Narrative Paintings (Arnolfini Bristol and ICA London) 1979, Private Views (Arts Cncl of GB and tour) 1982, In Their Circumstances (Lincoln Usher Gallery) 1985–86, Picturing People: Figurative Painting from Britain 1945–89 (Far East tour) 1989, Scottish Art since 1990 (Scottish Nat Gall of Modern Art) 1989–90, Turning the Century (Raab Gallery London & Berlin) 1990, The Discerning Eye (Mall Galleries London) 1990, The Line of Tradition (National Galleries of Scotland) 1993, The Scottish Renaissance (Hong Kong Land Co Hong Kong) 1996, Scotland's Art (City Art Centre, Edinburgh) 1999, Expressions (Aberdeen Art Gallery) 2000; *Work in public collections*: Scottish Nat Portrait Gallery, Scottish Nat Gallery of Modern Art, Arts Cncl of GB, Yale Center for British Art; *Portraits* Dr George Elder Davie 1999, Tom Fleming 2000, Robin Jenkins (Saltire Soc) 2002, Alasdair Gray 2010, Professor James Fraser (Univ of the Highlands and Islands) 2015; *Publications* Arts of Resistance: Poets, Portraits and Landscapes of Modern Scotland (jtly, 2008), Arts of Independence (with Alan Riach, 2014), Paintings as Arguments (2014); *Clubs* The Glasgow Art; *Style*— Alexander Moffat, Esq, OBE, RSA; ✉ 20 Haddington Place, Edinburgh EH7 4AF (☎ 0131 556 2731)

MOFFAT, Alistair Murray; *b* 16 June 1950; *Educ* Kelso HS, Univ of St Andrews (MA), Univ of Edinburgh (CertEd), Univ of London (MPhil); *m* Lindsay, *née* Thomas; 1 s, 2 da; *Career* organiser Edinburgh Festival Fringe 1976–81; Scottish Television: arts correspondent, prodr then controller of features 1981–90, dir of progs 1990–93, chief exec Scottish Television Enterprises 1993–99; rector Univ of St Andrews; *Books* The Edinburgh Fringe (1978), Kelsae: A History of Kelso from Earliest Times (1985), Remembering Charles Rennie Mackintosh (1989), Arthur and the Lost Kingdoms (1999), The Sea Kingdoms (2001), The Borders: A History of the Borders from Earliest Times (2002), Homing (2003), Heartland (2004), Before Scotland (2005), Tyneside (2005), East Lothian (2006), Fife (2007), The Reivers (2007), The Wall: Rome's Greatest Frontier (2008), Edinburgh: A Short History (2008), The Scots: A Genetic Journey (2010), The Faded Map (2011), The British: A Genetic Journey (2013), The Great Tapestry of Scotland (2013), The Great Tapestry of Scotland: The Making of a Masterpiece (2013), Hawick (2014), Bannockburn (2014); *Recreations* sleeping, supporting Kelso RFC; *Style*— Alistair Moffat; ✉ The Henhouse, Selkirk TD7 5EY (e-mail alistairmoffat@scottishborders.com)

MOFFAT, Sir Brian Scott; kt (1996), OBE (1982); s of Festus David Moffat (d 1995), and Agnes Scott Moffat (d 1991); *b* 6 January 1939; *Educ* Hulme GS Oldham; *m* 1964, Jacqueline Mary, *née* Cunliffe; 1 s (b 1969), 1 da (b 1974); *Career* chartered accountant Peat Marwick Mitchell 1961–68; British Steel Corp (subsequently British Steel plc): joined 1968, dir Assoc Products Gp 1973–76, dir Port Talbot Works 1976, md Finance 1986–91 (heavily involved in privatisation 1988), chief exec 1991–99, chm 1993–99; chm Corus Gp plc 1999–2003 (actg chief exec 2000–01); non-exec dir: Enterprise Oil plc 1995–2002, HSBC Holdings plc 1998–2008 (dep chm), Bank of England 2000–06, Macsteel Global BV 2003–12, Macsteel Holdings Luxemburg SARL 2012–; Hon DSc: Univ of Warwick 1998, Univ of Sheffield 2001; Inst of Materials Bessemer Gold Medal 1996; FCA 1961; *Recreations* farming, fishing, shooting; *Clubs* Fly Fishers; *Style*— Sir Brian Moffat, OBE; ✉ Springfield Farm, Earlswood, Chepstow, Monmouthshire NP16 6AT (e-mail sirbmoffat@btinternet.com)

MOFFAT, Dr David A; s of late James Graham Moffat, of Cambridge, and late Myra Constance, *née* Paul; *b* 27 June 1947; *Educ* St Nicholas' Sch Northwood, Univ of London (BSc, MB BS, MA, PhD); *m* 5 Dec 1970, Jane Elizabeth, da of Flt Lt David Dougherty Warwick, DFC, of Northwood Middx; 1 da (Claire b 29 Oct 1974), 2 s (Simon b 11 May 1976, Mark b 10 Oct 1979); *Career* sr registrar The London Hosp 1977–79, fell in otoneurosurgery Stanford Univ California 1979–80, consult ENT surgn Westminster Hosp London 1980, consult ENT surgn Addenbrooke's Hosp Cambridge and assoc lectr Univ of Cambridge 1981–, estab E Anglian and Supra Regnl Otoneurosurgical Serv base in Cambridge; past master Br Academic Conference in Otorhinolaryngology; past pres Br Skull Base Soc; memb: Med Defence Union, American Otological Soc, Politzer Soc; past chm Intercollegiate Faculty Bd, past memb SAC, past pres Otology Section RSM; Br rep IFOS (chair Otol/Neurotol Ctee); hon memb German ENT Assoc 2009; Dame Forth Forbes Meml Scholarship 1968, W J Harrison Prize 2000, Hunterian Medal RCS 2009, Gold Medal IFOS 2013, House-Hitselberger Lifetime Achievement Award American Neurological Soc 2015; LRCP, MRCS, FRCS; *Publications* 210 publications in peer-reviewed medical jls, 33 book chapters and 2 books; *Recreations* theatre, golf; *Clubs* Gog Magog, Royal Worlington Golf; *Style*— Dr David A Moffat, FRCS; ✉ Department of Otoneurological and Skull Base Surgery, Addenbrooke's Hospital, Hills Road, Cambridge CB0 2QQ (☎ 01223 586638, fax 01223 217559); Nuffield Health Cambridge Hospital, 4 Trumpington Road, Cambridge CB2 8AF (☎ and fax 01223 364114, secretary 01223 364114)

MOFFAT, Sheilagh; da of Alexander Findlay (d 1968), and Daphne Mary, *née* Ireland (d 1992); *b* 24 November 1948; *Educ* Bishops Coll Colombo Sri Lanka, Albyn Sch for Girls Aberdeen; *m* 11 Sept 1971, David Cunningham Moffat, s of James Cunningham Moffat; 1 da (Caroline Alexandra b 12 Jan 1981); *Career* chartered accountant; articled clerk Deloitte Plender Griffiths & Co London 1966–70, fndr own practice 1973; dir Mutual Accountants Professional Indemnity Co 1988–2005; memb Cncl ICAEW 1994–; pres: Warks Soc of chartered accountants 1990–91 and 2003–04; Birmingham & District Soc of chartered accountants 1999–2000 (GP bd rep 1992–97); practising assoc Acad of Experts 1996–; hon treas Warks Co Branch Br Red Cross Soc 1975–95; Freeman City of London 1999, Liveryman Worshipful Co of Chartered Accountants; FCA 1979 (ACA 1970); *Recreations* antiques, films, reading; *Clubs* Leamington Spa Regency Rotary (founding memb); *Style*— Mrs Sheilagh Moffat; ✉ Moffat Gilbert, 5 Clarendon Place, Leamington Spa, Warwickshire CV32 5QL (☎ 01926 334373, fax 01926 881464, e-mail moffat@btinternet.com)

MOFFAT, Steven; OBE (2015); *b* 18 November 1961, Paisley, Renfrewshire; *Educ* Univ of Glasgow (BA); *m* Sue Vertue, da of Beryl Vertue, OBE, *qv*; *Career* television script writer; dir Hartswood Films Ltd; RTS Judges Award 2011; BAFTA Special Award 2012; *Television* Press Gang (ITV) 1989–93 (Best Children's Prog BAFTA 1991, Best Children's Prog RTS Award 1991), Joking Apart 1991–95, Chalk 1997, Coupling (BBC) 2000–04 (Best TV Comedy Br Comedy Award 2003) and 2007–08, Jekyll 2007, Doctor Who (BBC) 2005–08 (Best Writer BAFTA 2008) and 2010–, Sherlock (BBC) 2010– (Best Drama Series RTS Award 2011 and 2013, Best Writer – Drama RTS Award 2013); *Style*— Steven Moffat, Esq, OBE; ✉ Berlin Associates, 7 Tyers Gate, London SE1 3HX

MOFFATT, Clive; s of Harold and Olive Moffatt; *b* 27 December 1948; *Educ* Thornes House Sch, LSE (BSc); *m* 1977, Kathleen, da of Robert Maguire; 1 s, 1 da; *Career* res economist to New Zealand Treasury 1972–75; consult economist and writer Economist Intelligence Unit Ltd London 1975–76, chief sub-ed (fin unit and CEEFAX) BBC 1976–78, business ed Investors Chronicle 1978–79, corporate affrs consult Guinness Peat Group plc 1979–81, chief exec Blackrod Ltd 1981–88, fndr and md Moffatt Associates (mgmnt and mktg consultancy) 1988–, fndr and md Nomadic Theatrical Productions Ltd (NTP); sr assoc consult Gas Strategies 2010–11, sr assoc consult Stag Energy 2012–, assoc consult Indepen, princ assoc JBP Energy; memb Inst of Risk Mgmnt, assoc memb Instn of Diesel and Gas Turbine Engrs (IDGTE); *Publications* Trends in Commercial Due Diligence (1999), A Risk Manager on Every Desktop (2000), Trends in the UK Telecoms Consultancy Market (2001), The World of Business Services – Some Personal Reflections (2002), EU Gas Market: Turning hopes into reality (2007), EU ETS Market: Firmer price expectations for Phase Two and beyond (2008), What's Missing from the Energy Bill? – New Power (2012), Reducing Investor Uncertainty in Energy (Conservative Home 2015); articles in professional journals; *Recreations* rugby, tennis, art, music, motorcycling, theatre; *Style*— Clive Moffatt, Esq; ✉ Suite 108, 95 Wilton Road, London SW1V 1BZ (☎ 07831 571776, e-mail clivem@moffatt-associates.com)

MOFFATT, Prof (Henry) Keith; s of Frederick Henry Moffatt (d 1974), and Emmeline Marchant, *née* Fleming (d 1997); *b* 12 April 1935; *Educ* George Watson's Coll Edinburgh, Univ of Edinburgh (BSc), Trinity Coll Cambridge (scholar, Ferguson scholar, BA, PhD, ScD, Smith's prize); *m* 17 Dec 1960, Katharine (Linty), da of Rev David Syme Stiven, MC, DD (d 1986); 2 s (Fergus b 1961 d 1987, Peter b 1962), 2 da (Hester b 1966, Penelope b 1967); *Career* Univ of Cambridge: asst lectr 1961–64, lectr 1964–76, prof of mathematical physics 1980–2002 (prof emeritus 2002–), head Dept of Applied Mathematics and Theoretical Physics 1983–91, dir Isaac Newton Inst 1996–2001; Trinity Coll Cambridge: fell lectr and dir Studies in Mathematics 1961–76, tutor 1970–74, sr tutor 1975, professorial fell 1980–; prof of applied mathematics Univ of Bristol 1977–80; professeur (temps partiel) en Mécanique Ecole Polytechnique Palaiseau 1992–99; sec IUTAM Congress Ctee 1984–92 (memb 1980–), memb Gen Assembly of IUTAM 1980–, memb Bureau of IUTAM 1992–2008 (pres 2000–04), Blaise Pascal Int Chair 2001–03; Panetti-Ferrari Int Prize and Gold Medal 2002, Euromech Fluid Mechanics Prize 2003, Sr Whitehead Prize of London Mathematical Soc 2005, Hughes Medal Royal Soc 2005, David Crighton Medal LMS and IMA 2009; Docteur (hc): Inst Nat Poly Grenoble 1987, Tech Univ Eindhoven 2006; Hon DSc: SUNY 1990, Univ of Edinburgh 2001, Univ of Glasgow 2007; foreign memb: Royal Netherlands Acad of Arts and Sciences 1991, Academia Europaea 1994, Officier des Palmes Académiques 1998, associé étranger Académie des Sciences (Paris) 1998, Accademia dei Lincei (Rome) 2001, Nat Acad of Sci USA 2008, Lisbon Acad of Sci 2010; FRS 1986, FRSE 1988, fell APS 2003, hon fell IMA 2007; *Books* Magnetic Field Generation in Electrically Conducting Fluids (1978), Topological Fluid Mechanics (ed, 1990), Topological Aspects of the Dynamics of Fluids and Plasmas (ed, 1992), Perspectives in Fluid Dynamics (ed, 2000), Tubes, Sheets and Singularities in Fluid Dynamics (ed, 2003), A Voyage through Turbulence (ed, 2011), Environmental Hazards: the Fluid Dynamics of Extreme Events (ed, 2011), Topological Fluid Dynamics: Theory and Applications (ed, 2013); Fundamental Problems of Turbulence (ed, 2014); *Recreations* breadmaking, French country cooking; *Style*— Prof Keith Moffatt, FRS, FRSE; ✉ Trinity College, Cambridge (e-mail hkm2@cam.ac.uk)

MOFFATT, Nigel; s of Ezra Moffatt, and Estella Moffatt; *b* 22 May 1954, Bethel Town, York, Jamaica; *m* Shirley; 3 da (Talita, Nicola, Dee), 1 s (Sean); *Career* playwright, singer/songwriter and poet; recorded Peace, Love and Harmony for Respond Records 1984, performed African Crisis and Poetry for Here and Now (Central TV) 1984, founded Writers' Gp Walsall 1984, runs Black Writers in Walsall project 2005, ed Multicultural magazine 2006, runs recording project in Walsall 2007 and The Drum Writers project 2008; currently filming and editing feature film The Trudy Allen Story (due for release

M

2016); writer in residence: Nat Theatre Studio 1985, Haymarket Theatre Leicester 1988, Shrewsbury Prison 1996–98; Winston Churchill travel fellowship 1989; advsr to W Midlands Arts; plays: Rhapsody in Black 'n' White (Nat Theatre Studio) 1985, Tony (Nat Theatre Studio 1985, Oval House 1987), Celebration (Royal Ct Theatre) 1986, Mamma Decemba (Temba Theatre Co and Birmingham Reperatory Co) 1987, Keeping Walsall Boxed In (W Midlands Arts Cncl) 1987, Opportunity (cmmnd by Br Film Inst) 1987, Prime Time (Haymarket Leicester) 1989, Beau Monde (Br Film Inst) 1990, Stop the Carnival (Cannon Hill Puppet Theatre) 1991, Musical Youth (Birmingham Reperatory Theatre) 2001, Mamma Decemba (Banana Boat Prodns NY) 2001, 2004, 2008 and 2012 (and a reading at the NT 2013), Gun Crime (Arts Cncl of England Bursary) 2004, Brotha 2013, Ordinary People 2016; radio plays: Lifetime (BBC) 1988, Lame Ducks (BBC) 1989, Selling Out (BBC) 1989, Wishful Thinking (BBC) 1990, Mamma Decemba (BBC) 1994, Wasteland (BBC) 1997, Fish Ain't Bitin' (BBC) 1998; TV: When Love Dies (Channel 4) 1989, Opportunity (BBC) 1992, Strange Fruit (BBC) 1993; films: Dinner 2008, Skins 2008, 10% 2008, Short Trousers 2012, Handsworth Revolution 2012, The Monologues 2016, Walsall Poetry Society 2016, The Trudy Allen Story 2016; albums: The Reggae Album 2010, State Bound 2013, Rainbow Mountain 2013; awards: Samuel Beckett Award for Mamma Decemba 1987, Giles Cooper Award for Lifetime 1987; Butler Tst Prison Service Annual Award; *Books* Lifetime (1988), Mamma Decemba (1988), Niggers (2008), Giro City (2011), Washed (2013), The Hairy Biker's Long Ride Home (2014), Jesus (2015), Friends Who Kiss (2016); *Recreations* tennis, football, walking, drawing, reading; *Style—* Nigel Moffatt, Esq; ✉ 44 Harrowby Place, Shepwell Green, Willenhall, West Midlands WV13 2RA (☎ 01902 632244, mobile 07760 846748, e-mail moffimedia@mac.com, website www.moffimedia.com)

MOFFITT, Prof Terrie E; *Educ* Univ of N Carolina Chapel Hill, Univ of Southern Calif (PhD); *Career* clinical trg UCLA Neuropsychiatric Inst, clinical psychologist, prof of social behaviour and devpt Inst of Psychiatry KCL; princ investigator MRC Environmetal-Risk Study (E-risk), assoc dir Dunedin Multidisciplinary Health and Devpt Research Unit Univ of Otago Med Sch; Distinguished Scientific Award for Early Career Contrib to Psychology American Psychological Assoc 1993, Wolfson Merit Award Royal Soc 2002, Stockholm Prize in Criminology 2007; FMedSci 1999, fell American Soc of Criminology 2003, FBA 2004; *Books* Sex Differences in Antisocial Behaviour: Conduct Disorder, Delinquency, and Violence in the Dunedin Longitudinal Study (jtly, 2001); *Style—* Prof Terrie E Moffitt; ✉ Box No P080, Social, Genetic and Developmental, Psychiatry Centre, Institute of Psychiatry, De Crespigny Park, London SE5 8AF

MOGER, Christopher Richard Derwent; QC (1992); s of the late Richard Vernon Derwent Moger, of Dartmouth, Devon, and late Cecile Eva Rosales, *née* Power; *b* 28 July 1949; *Educ* Sherborne, Univ of Bristol (LLB); *m* 1, 1974 (m dis 1991), Victoria, da of Arthur George Cecil Trollope, of Overton, Hants; 3 s (Robin b 1979, Sholto b 1981, Dominic b 1985); m 2, 1991, Prudence, da of Francis Anthony Leopold da Cunha, of Bowden, Cheshire; *Career* called to the Bar Inner Temple 1972 (bencher 2000); recorder of the Crown Court 1993–, dep judge of the High Court 1999–; cmmr Alderney Gambling Control Cmmn 2014–; *Recreations* fishing, tennis, walking; *Clubs* Garrick; *Style—* Christopher Moger, Esq, QC; ✉ 4 Pump Court, Temple, London EC4Y 7AN (☎ 020 7842 5555, fax 020 7583 2036, e-mail chambers@4pumpcourt.com)

MOGG, Baron (Life Peer UK 2008), of Queen's Park in the County of East Sussex; Sir John Frederick Mogg; KCMG (2003); s of Thomas W Mogg, and Cora M Mogg; *b* 5 October 1943; *Educ* Bishop Vesey's GS, Univ of Birmingham (BA); *m* 1967, Anne, *née* Smith; 1 da, 1 s; *Career* Rediffusion Ltd 1965–74; princ: Office of Fair Trading 1974–76, Dept of Trade 1976–79; first sec UK Permanent Rep 1979–82; DTI: asst sec Minerals and Metals Div 1982–85, princ private sec to Sec of State 1985–86, under sec European Policy Div 1986–87, under sec Industrial Materials Market Div 1987–89; dep head European Secretariat Cabinet Office 1989–90; European Cmmn: dep DG Industry and Internal Market (DG III) 1990–93, DG Internal Market 1993–2003; memb Gas and Electricity Markets Authy 2003, non-exec chair Ofgem 2003–13, chm European Regulators' Gp for Electricity and Gas 2005–11, memb Int Advsy Panel Singapore 2006–16, pres Cncl of European Energy Regulators, chair Bd of Regulators (Agency for the Cooperation of Energy Regulators), special advsr to pres Office for Harmonization in the Internal Market 2009–12, chair Int Confedn of Energy Regulators 2010–15, chair Advsy Bd EU Observatory on Infringements of Intellectual Property Rights 2012–, memb Advsy Cncl Electric Power Research Inst 2012–15, memb Bd Electric Power Research Inst 2015–; visiting prof Univ of Parma 2006–10; chair of govrs Univ of Brighton 2005–15, tstee Brighton Philharmonic Orchestra until 2012; memb House of Lords 2008–; *Style—* The Lord Mogg, KCMG

MOGGACH, Deborah; da of Richard Alexander Hough, and Helen Charlotte, *née* Woodyatt; *b* 28 June 1948; *Educ* Camden Sch for Girls London, Univ of Bristol (BA), Univ of London (DipEd); *m* 1971 (m dis), Anthony Austin Moggach; 1 s (Alexander b 1 Sept 1975), 1 da (Charlotte Flora b 9 May 1977); *Career* OUP 1970–72, journalist and teacher Pakistan 1972–74, full-time writer (for newspapers, magazines and TV) and novelist 1975–; Young Journalist of the Year 1975, Best Adapted TV Series Award Writer's Guild 1993, nomination BAFTA 2006; Hon DLitt Univ of Bristol; FRSL; *Novels* incl: You Must Be Sisters (1978), Close to Home (1979), A Quiet Drink (1980), Hot Water Man (1982), Porky (1983), To Have and To Hold (1986), Smile and Other Stories (1988), Driving in the Dark (1989), Stolen (1990), The Stand-In (1991), The Ex-Wives (1993), Changing Babies and Other Stories (1995), Seesaw (1996), Close Relations (1997), Tulip Fever (1999), Final Demand (2001), These Foolish Things (2004), In The Dark (2007), Heartbreak Hotel (2013); *Short stories* in various anthologies incl: Best Short Stories 1986, Best Short Stories 1988, The Best of Fiction Magazine (1986), The Woman's Hour Book of Short Stories (1990), Best Short Stories 1991; *Plays* Double-Take (produced 1990 and 1992); *Television* series: To Have and To Hold, Stolen, Goggle-Eyes (adaptation), Close Relations, Seesaw, Love in a Cold Climate (adaptation), Final Demand, The Diary of Anne Frank (adaptation); *Film* Pride and Prejudice; *Recreations* walking around London looking into people's windows; *Style—* Ms Deborah Moggach; ✉ c/o Curtis Brown Group Ltd, 28–29 Haymarket, London SW1Y 4SP (☎ 020 7396 6600, fax 020 7396 0110); c/o Rochelle Stevens & Co Ltd, 2 Terrett's Place, Upper Street, London N1 1QZ (☎ 020 7359 3500, fax 020 7354 5729); website www.deborahmoggach.com

MOGGRIDGE, Harry Traherne (Hal); OBE, VMH; s of Lt-Col Harry Weston Moggridge, CMG, Chevalier de la Legion d'Honneur (d 1961), of Tonbridge, Kent, and Helen Mary Ferrier Taylor (artist, d 1989); *b* 2 February 1936; *Educ* Tonbridge, AA (Leverhulme scholar, AADipl); *m* 1 Dec 1962, Catherine (Cass) Greville Herbert; 1 da (Harriet b 23 Sept 1965), 2 s (Geoffrey b 8 Sept 1967, Lawrence b 19 Feb 1970); *Career* Nottinghamshire CC 1960, asst to Sir Geoffrey Jellicoe 1960–63, site architect Sir William Halcrow & Partners Tema Harbour Ghana 1964–65, landscape asst GLC 1966–67, own landscape design practice, ptnr Colvin and Moggridge Landscape Consultants 1969–97 (ptnr with late Brenda Colvin, CBE, to 1981, continuing practice with Christopher Carter until 1997 (now conslt)), prof of landscape architecture Univ of Sheffield 1984–86; memb Cncl Landscape Inst 1970–83 (hon sec, vice-pres and pres 1979–81, delg to Int Fedn of Landscape Architects 1981–93 and 2001–06), chm The Landscape Foundation 1995–99, chm Penllergare Tst 2000–12; RHS Victoria Medal of Honour 1999, Landscape Inst President's Medal 2002; memb: Bd Landscape Res Gp 1983–88, Royal Fine Art Cmmn 1988–99, Nat Tst Architectural Panel 1990–2009; PPLI, FIHort, RIBA, FRSA; *Publications* author of numerous articles and chapters of books describing works or technical subjects; *Recreations* looking at pictures, gardens, buildings, towns, landscapes and people in these places, walking, theatre; *Clubs* Royal Soc of Arts, Farmers'; *Style—* Hal Moggridge, Esq, OBE, VMH; ✉ Colvin and Moggridge, Filkins, Lechlade, Gloucestershire GL7 3JQ (☎ 01367 860225, e-mail h.moggridge@colmog.co.uk)

MOHAN, Dominic James; s of Michael Mohan, and Deborah, *née* Vaughan; *b* 26 May 1969, Bath, Somerset; *Educ* Neale-Wade Sch March, Univ of Southampton (BA), Rutgers Univ NJ; *m* 31 Aug 1998, Michelle *née* Knee; 2 s (Gabriel b 10 Dec 1999, Huey b 28 March 2003), 1 da (Honor b 6 May 2009); *Career* reporter Sunday Mirror 1992–94, reporter News of the World 1994–95; The Sun: showbiz reporter 1996–97, dep showbiz ed 1997–98, showbiz ed and columnist Bizarre 1998–2003, asst ed and columnist 2003–04, assoc ed (features) 2004–07, dep ed 2007–09, ed 2009–13, asst to the CEO News Corp 2013–; DJ Virgin Radio 2002–04; conceived the idea of Band Aid and helped assemble the line-up with Bob Geldof and Midge Ure; Sony Gold Radio Award 2003, Hugh Cudlipp Award British Press Awards 2005 (nominated 2006); *Recreations* football (Bristol City and Arsenal), my children, music, film; *Clubs* Ivy, Soho House, Arsenal FC and Bristol City FC; *Style—* Dominic Mohan, Esq

MOHAN, Thomas Vincent; s of James Bernard Mohan, and Anna, *née* Quinn; *b* 9 July 1959; *Educ* Royal GS Newcastle upon Tyne, CCC Oxford (MA), organ scholar Westminster Cathedral and Countess of Munster Tst scholar; *m* 1999, Johanna, *née* Heckmann; *Career* music master Westminster Sch 1983–86; clerk House of Lords 1986–, clerk Euro Communities/Union Ctee 1996–2001, secondment to the Parly Assembly of the Cncl of Europe 1997–98, clerk Private Bills 2001–02, clerk Public and Private Bills 2002–11, dir of HR House of Lords 2011–; FRCO 1983; *Recreations* music, gardening, travel; *Style—* Thomas Mohan, Esq; ✉ House of Lords, London SW1A 0PW (☎ 020 7219 3186, e-mail mohant@parliament.uk)

MOIGNARD, Prof Elizabeth Ann; da of Lionel Arthur Moignard (d 2000), and Joan Pudsey, *née* Dawson (d 1982); *b* 3 January 1951, Poole, Dorset; *Educ* King's HS Warwick, St Hugh's Coll and Hertford Coll Oxford (sr scholar, Charles Oldham scholar, Thomas Whitcombe Greene scholar, MA, DPhil); *m* 22 July 1985, Alec Ernest Yearling; 1 step s (Simon Nicholas b 3 March 1977), 1 step da (Rebecca Kate b 13 June 1979); *Career* temp lectr in classical archaeology Univ of Newcastle upon Tyne 1977–78; Univ of Glasgow: lectr in Greek 1978–96, sr lectr in classics 1996–2000, dir Inst for Art History 1998–2005, prof of classical art and archaeology 2000–, dean Faculty of Arts 2005–09 (vice-dean 1999–2005); memb Academic Cncl Glasgow Sch of Art 1998–; quality assurance assessor Welsh HE Funding Cncl 1997, subject reviewer Quality Assurance Agency (QAA) 2000–, panel memb for Classics RAE (Research Assessment Exercise) 2001 and 2008, memb Peer Review Coll AHRC 2004–; chair Cncl Classical Assoc of Scotland 2003–05 (pres Glasgow and West Centre 2000–02), memb Strategic Advsy Bd Inst of Classical Studies 2005–; memb Ctee: Soc for the Promotion of Hellenic Studies 1987–90 and 2007–10, Scottish Hellenic Soc (Glasgow) 1992– (chm 1994–97); memb: British Sch at Athens, Classical Assoc, Assoc for Contemporary Jewellery, Scottish Art Historians' Forum; dir and tstee Scottish Mask and Puppet Theatre 2014–; James Knott Fellowship Univ of Newcastle upon Tyne 1978; FSA 2002, FRSE 2004; *Books* Corpus Vasorum Antiquorum: Great Britain – The National Museums of Scotland, Edinburgh (1989), Corpus Vasorum Antiquorum: Great Britain – The Glasgow Collections: The Hunterian Museum, The Glasgow Museum and Art Gallery, Kelvingrove, The Burrell Collection (1997), Greek Vases: An Introduction (2006), Corpus Vasorum Antiquorum: Great Britain – Aberdeen University, Marischal Collection (2006), Master of Attic Black-Figure Painting: the Art and Legacy of Exekias (2015); *Recreations* choral singing, walking, cooking, detective fiction; *Style—* Prof Elizabeth Moignard; ✉ Classics, School of Humanities, University of Glasgow, Glasgow G12 8QQ (☎ 0141 330 7361, fax 0141 330 4459, e-mail elizabeth.moignard@glasgow.ac.uk)

MOIR, Sir Christopher Ernest; 4 Bt (UK 1916), of Whitehanger, Fernhurst, Co Sussex; s of Sir Ernest Ian Royds Moir, 3 Bt (d 1998); *b* 22 May 1955; *Educ* KCS Wimbledon; *m* 1983, Vanessa, yr da of Victor Alfred Crosby, of Merton Park, London; 2 s (Oliver Royds, Alexander Victor (twins) b 1984), 1 step da (Nina Louise b 1976); *Heir* s, Oliver Moir; *Career* CA; *Style—* Sir Christopher Moir, Bt; ✉ Three Gates, 174 Coombe Lane West, Kingston upon Thames, Surrey KT2 7DE

MOIR, Judy; da of Dr Leon Nussbaum (d 1985), and Becky, *née* Abraham (d 2012); *b* 1 February 1957; *Educ* Townsend HS, Univ of Edinburgh (MA, Christie Bequest); *m* 6 Feb 1981, Neville Moir; 1 da (Helen Louise b 11 April 1986), 1 s (Stephen Leon William b 24 Dec 1988); *Career* freelance ed 1980–81, admin exec then dir Scottish Publishers Assoc 1981–86, freelance ed and book reviewer 1986–96 (worked for publishers incl: Mainstream, Canongate, Edinburgh Univ Press, Jonathan Cape, Transworld, Little Brown), pt/t lectr Napier Univ 1992–96, editorial and rights mangr Canongate Books 1996–99, editorial dir Canongate Books 2000–03, Scottish ed Penguin Books 2004–08, literary agent Judy Moir Literary Agency 2008–; dir Edinburgh Book Festival 2001–03, memb Bursary Panel Scottish Arts Cncl 1995–98, memb New Directions Lottery Ctee 1996–97; special advsr Lit Dept Scottish Arts Cncl 2008–13, chair Assoc of Scottish Literary Agents 2013–; shortlisted Ed of the Year Br Book Awards 2003; *Recreations* music, reading, travel; *Style—* Ms Judy Moir; ✉ Judy Moir Literary Agency, 4 Keith Terrace, Edinburgh EH4 3NJ (e-mail judy_moir@blueyonder.co.uk)

MOIR, Dr Lance Stuart; *b* 26 January 1957; *Educ* Cranfield Univ (PhD), Univ of Sheffield (BA); *Partner* Peter Capitano (civil partnership); *Career* account mangr Corp Banking Dept Grindlays Bank plc 1980–85, treas Br Home Stores plc 1985–86, head of corp finance and planning Storehouse plc 1988–90 (gp treas 1986–88), dir of corp finance Bass plc 1991–94, sr conslt MTM Partnership Ltd 1995–97, ind conslt 1995–97, finance dir First Choice Holidays plc 1997–98, sr lectr finance and accounting Cranfield Sch of Mgmnt 1998–2007, finance dir WIN plc 2007–; non-exec dir: Johnshaven Precision Engineering Ltd 1998–2005, Raft International Ltd 2000–06, Gartmore Global Tst plc 2007–; non-exec chm Thompson Dunn Ltd 2007–; ACIB 1983, FCT 1990, FRSA 2003; *Books* Introduction to Corporate Finance (memb Ed Panel), Managing Liquidity; *Recreations* singing, opera; *Style—* Dr Lance Moir; ✉ WIN plc, High Wycombe HP12 3YZ (☎ 01494 750500)

MOIZER, Prof Peter; s of Albert Moizer, of Blackburn, Lancs, and Kathleen, *née* Burton; *b* 6 October 1951, Blackburn, Lancs; *Educ* Queen Elizabeth's GS Blackburn, Merton Coll Oxford (MA), Victoria Univ of Manchester (MA, PhD); *m* 8 June 1989, Susan, *née* Hatch; 2 s (Mark b 1980, Richard b 1983), 1 da (Helen b 1994); *Career* auditor and asst mangr Price Waterhouse & Co 1974–79, lectr then sr lectr Victoria Univ of Manchester 1979–89, prof of accounting Univ of Leeds 1989–, dean Leeds Univ Business Sch 2008–; dir Weetwood Hall Ltd 2008–; reporting memb Competition Cmmn, memb of exec Assoc of Business Schools; advsr Gtr Manchester Pension Fund 1987–; sr moderator PS exams ICAEW 2003–; FCA; *Publications* The Audit Expectations Gap in the United Kingdom (1992), Resignations and Dismissals of UK Auditors (2004), Governance and Auditing (2005); *Recreations* theatre, opera, viola; *Clubs* Penn; *Style—* Prof Peter Moizer; ✉ Leeds University Business School, Maurice Keyworth Building, The University of Leeds, Leeds LS2 9JT (☎ 0113 343 4499, e-mail pm@lubs.leeds.ac.uk)

MOLDEN, Dr Nigel Charles; JP (Burnham 1991, Wycombe and Beaconsfield 1996, Bucks 2012); s of Percival Ernest Molden(d 2001), and Daisy Mary, *née* Currill (d 2009); *b* 17 August 1948; *Educ* City of Oxford HS, Univ of London (BSc), Brunel Univ (MSc), Fairfax Univ (PhD), Oxford Univ (Cert HE); *m* 14 Aug 1971, (Hilary) Julia, da of Frederick Withers Lichfield (d 1969); 3 s (Nicholas Stuart b 1974, Simon Charles b 1977, Alexander

Giles b 1983); *Career* Warner Brothers Records: label mangr 1976–77, gen mangr 1977–78; WEA Records: field promotion mangr 1972–75, int gen mangr 1978–80; chm Magnum Music Group Ltd 1985–97, jt chief exec TKO Magnum Music Ltd 1997–2002, chief exec Synergie Logistics Ltd 2002–; Beaconsfield town cncllr 1989–91, Chiltern dist cncllr 1991–95; chm: Beaconsfield Town Cons Assoc 1991–93, Seer Green & Jordans Cons Assoc 1991–94; magistrate Burnham/Wycombe and Beaconsfield Bench 1991–2013, dep chm Wycombe and Beaconsfield Bench 2003–09, memb Thames Valley Magistrates Courts Ctee (TVMCC) 2000–05 (chm Trg Sub-Ctee), chm HM Courts Bd for the Thames Valley 2007–10 (memb 2005–), memb HM Courts Bd for Beds, Herts & Thames Valley 2010–12; author of numerous articles; SPCP accredited mediator 2011; govr Royal GS High Wycombe 1989–93, partnership govr Claremont HS Harrow 2000 (chm of govrs 2006), CfBT govr Oxford Spires Acad 2011–, memb Ct Brunel Univ 2008, community govr Windmill Primary Sch 2013; chm Oxford Sch Old Boys Soc 1989–92 (pres 1993–96); fndr and tstee The Magnum Tst, tstee Oxford Past and Present Tst; Freeman City of London 1990, Liveryman Worshipful Co of Marketors 1989–2000; FIoD 1982, FIMgt 1987, FCIM 1988, FRSA 1995, Chartered Marketer 2001; *Recreations* rugby, Grand Prix speedway, guitar, ceramics; *Style—* Dr N C Molden, JP; ✉ Ashcombe House, Deanwood Road, Jordans, Buckinghamshire HP9 2UU (☎ 01494 678177, e-mail nigel.molden@hotmail.co.uk)

MOLE, His Hon David Richard Penton; QC (1990); s of late Rev Arthur Penton Mole, and late Margaret Isobel, *née* Heggie; *b* 1 April 1943; *Educ* Trinity Coll Dublin (MA), LSE (LLM); *m* 29 March 1969, Anu-Reet, da of Alfred Nigol; 3 s (Matthew David Penton b 20 Nov 1971, Joseph Tobias b 9 April 1974, Thomas Alfred William b 24 Aug 1978), 1 da (Susannah Juliet Martha b 5 July 1984); *Career* lectr City of London Poly 1967–74; called to the Bar Inner Temple 1970 (ad eundem Gray's Inn 1973); standing jr counsel to the Inland Revenue (Rating and Valuation) 1984–90, recorder of the Crown Court 1995–2002, circuit judge (SE Circuit) 2002–13, dep judge of the High Court 2004–10, judge Upper Tbnl 2009–13, dep judge Upper Tbnl 2013–15; jt head of chambers 4–5 Gray's Inn Square 2000–02; memb Parole Bd 2003–13, legal memb Lands Tbnl 2006–09; *Recreations* walking, drawing and painting, flying; *Style—* His Hon David Mole, QC

MOLL, Francis Raphael Anton; s of Frederick Charles Moll (d 1994), of Sheffield, S Yorks, and Anita Lilian, *née* Francis (d 1998); *b* 15 August 1947; *Educ* Repton, Birkbeck Coll London; *Career* Royal Free Hosp/Royal Free and UCL Med Sch: radiographer 1969–74, biomedical/ pathology photographer, imaging technologist and virtual learning developer 1974–2010, radiation protection supervisor 1987–2010; radiation protection supervisor PolyMASC Pharmaceuticals 1995–2000; memb: Anglian Water Customer Consultative Ctee (S Gp) 1984–89, Braintree and Bocking Civic Soc 1986– (chm 1988–94), Burma Action Gp UK 1996–, Racehorse Owners Assoc 2001–, The GB-China Centre, Asia House, Chopsticks Club, Scarborough CC, The Meridian Soc (dir 2014, sec 2015), SACU (Soc for Anglo-Chinese Understanding); racehorse owner in Ontoawinner partnership; churchwarden SS Peter and Paul Black Notley 1985–87; researching the life of Samuel Curtis, FLS (1779–1860), botanist and publisher, as a prelude to writing his biography; Freeman City of London, Liveryman Worshipful Soc of Apothecaries 1968; DSR 1969, AIMI 1986 (now MIMI), ARPS 1986; *Recreations* travel, studying China (the language, food, culture and people), reading, walking, photography, cinema, jazz; *Style—* Francis Moll, Esq; ✉ 10 Brook Close, Braintree, Essex CM7 2PY (☎ 01376 325974, mobile 07941 138572, e-mail francis.moll@uclmail.net)

MOLLAN, Prof Raymond Alexander Boyce; s of Alexander Mollan, of Belfast, and Margaret Emma Boyce (d 1984); *b* 10 August 1943; *Educ* Belfast Royal Acad, Queen's Univ (MB BCh, BAO, HD); *m* 1 Sept 1969, Patricia Ann Fairbanks, da of Alexander Scott (d 1961); 3 s (Ian Alexander b 1972, Andrew John b 1973, David William b 1975), 1 da (Susan Patricia b 1977); *Career* RNR 1968–84; trg grades: med 1964–69, obstetrics 1970–72, surgery 1972–74, orthopaedic surgery 1974–79; conslt orthopaedic surgn Ulster Hosp 1979–80; Queen's Univ Belfast: sr lectr in orthopaedic surgery 1980–84, prof of orthopaedic surgery 1984–95; currently orthopaedic surgn Green Park Trust Belfast; Br Orthopaedic Assoc: past chm Educn Ctee, past memb Cncl, past chm Info Technol Ctee; fndr memb and treas Br Hip Soc; memb: Irish, Edinburgh and English Coll of Surgns, BMA, Irish Orthopaedic Assoc; *Recreations* sailing, skiing; *Clubs* The Naval, Royal Ulster Yacht; *Style—* Prof Raymond Mollan; ✉ Department Orthopaedic Surgery, Musgrave Park Hospital, Belfast BT18 01ET (☎ 028 9066 9501, fax 028 9066 1112, telex 74487)

MOLLET, Richard James; s of Keith Mollet, and Helen, *née* Cowley; *b* 9 January 1970, Swansea; *Educ* Olchfa Comp Swansea, Worcester Coll Oxford (BA); *m* Sept 2000, Nicola, *née* Laffan; 3 s (Bryn b 2003, Aneurin b 2005, Dylan b 2008); *Career* offr RN 1988–96, public affrs conslt 1996–2005, public affrs dir BPI 2005–10, chief exec Publishers Assoc 2010–16; memb Bd: Publishers Licensing Soc, Copyright Licensing Agency, Book Industry Communication; tstee World Book Day; *Recreations* music, reading, skiing, tennis, football; *Clubs* Ivy; *Style—* Richard Mollet, Esq; ✉ The Publishers Association, 29b Montague Street, London WC1B 5BW

MOLLON, Prof John Dixon; s of Arthur Greenwood Mollon, of Scarborough, N Yorks, and Joyce, *née* Dixon; *b* 12 September 1944; *Educ* Univ of Oxford (BA, DPhil, DSc); *Career* Univ of Cambridge: lectr 1976–93, reader 1993–98, fell Gonville & Caius Coll 1996– (pres 2013–, dir of studies in psychological and behavioural sciences 2013–), prof of visual neuroscience 1998–2011, distinguished teaching fell 2011–15; chm Colour Gp of GB 1991–93, pres Int Colour Vision Soc 2011–; hon sec Experimental Psychology Soc 1974–78, pres Cambridge Philosophical Soc 2012–13; Rank Prize Funds Award for Work on Genetics of Colour Vision 1988, Edridge-Green lectr 1988, Champness lectr 1998, Newton Medal 1999, Kenneth Craik Award 2000, Tillyer Medal 2000, Verriest Medal 2005, Lord Crook Medal 2008; FRS 1999; *Books* The Senses (with H B Barlow, 1982), Colour Vision (with L T Sharpe, 1983), Normal and Defective Colour Vision (with J Pokorny and K Knoblauch, 2003); *Style—* Prof John Mollon, FRS; ✉ Gonville & Caius College, Cambridge CB2 1TA

MOLLOY, Francie; MLA; s of Arthur Molloy (d 1976), and Ann, *née* Daly; *b* 16 December 1950, Derrymagowan, Dungannon, Co Tyrone; *Educ* St Patrick's Intermediate Sch Dungannon, Feldon House Govt Trg Centre, Univ of Ulster; *Career* mechanical engr Ulster Plant/Powerscreen 1967–70; memb Dungannon Cncl 1985– (mayor 2001–02), MLA (Sinn Féin) Mid-Ulster 1989–, dep speaker NI Assembly 2007– (princ dep speaker NI Assembly 2011–); memb: NI Forum, NI Local Govt Asssoc, Office of the First Min and Dep First Min Ctee NI Assembly, Environment Ctee NI Assembly; *Style—* Francie Molloy, Esq, MLA; ✉ Derrymagowan, Dungannon, Co Tyrone (☎ 07801 418861); 9 The Square, Coalisland, Co Tyrone; Quarry Road, Gulladuff, Co Derry (☎ 028 8774 8689, e-mail francie.molloy@ireland.com)

MOLYNEUX, Her Hon Judge Anne; MBE (2015); da of late Robert Molyneux, and late Audrey, *née* Young; *b* 12 January 1959; *Educ* Southport HS for Girls, Univ of Sheffield (LLB), Chester Coll of Law; *m* 1, 30 May 1987 (m dis 2006), Joseph Jeremy Ogden, s of late Robert David Ogden; 1 da (Joanna Frances b 19 April 1988), 1 s (Henry Robert b 23 Dec 1989); m 2, 2 Sept 2006, George Jonathan Morris, s of late George Russell Morris and Dorothy Elizabeth, *née* Robb, of NZ; *Career* articled clerk Jacobson Ridley 1981–84; assoc ptnr Lawrence Messer & Co 1984–87; Masons: joined 1987, ptnr 1989–2003, head of property litigation 1992–2003; ptnr Sprecher Grier Halberstam 2003–07; recorder 2000–07, circuit judge (South Eastern Circuit) 2007–; judicial memb Parole Bd for England and Wales 2010–; speaker various confs; memb Law Soc; *Recreations* family, literature, walking; *Clubs* Ealing and Fulham Book, UK Assoc of Women Judges; *Style—* Her Hon Judge Molyneux, MBE

MOLYNEUX, Prof David Hurst; s of Reginald Frank Molyneux (d 1974), of Northwich, and Monica Foden Stubbs; *b* 9 April 1943; *Educ* Denstone Coll, Emmanuel Coll Cambridge (MA, PhD), Univ of Salford (DSc); *m* 1969, Anita Elisabeth, da of George Edgar Bateson; 1 da (Elisabeth Camilla b 18 Dec 1974), 1 s (Oliver James b 7 Jan 1978); *Career* lectr in parasitology Liverpool Sch of Tropical Med 1968–77 (seconded to Nigeria 1970–72, seconded to Burkina Faso as project mangr UN Devpt Prog/WHO 1975–77); Univ of Salford: prof of biology 1977–91, dean Faculty of Sci 1984–88, chm Dept of Biological Scis 1988–91; dir Liverpool Sch of Tropical Med 1992–2000, dir Lymphatic Filariasis Support Centre 2000–; Chalmers medal Royal Soc of Tropical Med 1986, Wright medal British Soc for Parasitology 1988, Mckay Medal American Soc of Tropical Med 2007; pres British Soc for Parasitology 1992–94, pres-elect Royal Soc of Tropical Med and Hygiene (vice-pres 1995–97); memb Bd JRS Biodiversity Fndn 1998–, memb Governing Bd Inst of Animal Health 2001–, memb Int Task Force for Disease Eradication 2001–; tstee National Museum and Galleries on Merseyside 1997–2000; Hon FRCP 2006; *Books* Biology of Trypanosoma and Leishmania (with R W Ashford, 1983), Human Parasitic Disease Control (guest ed, 2006); *Recreations* golf, antiques, African art; *Clubs* Delamere Forest Golf (capt 2007–08); *Style—* Prof David Molyneux; ✉ School of Tropical Medicine, Pembroke Place, Liverpool L3 5QA (☎ 0151 705 3291, fax 0151 709 0354, e-mail david.molyneux@liv.ac.uk)

MONAGHAN, Dr Paul; MP; *b* 11 November 1965, Montrose, Angus; *Educ* Univ of Stirling (BA, PhD); *m* Stephanie; 1 da (Sian); *Career* head of planning and devpt Northern Constabulary 2003–08, dir Highland Homeless Tst 2008–15, MP (SNP) Caithness, Sutherland & Easter Ross 2015–; dir MS Therapy Centre Inverness; memb Br Psychological Soc 1999, fell Inst of Leadership and Mgmnt 2007; *Recreations* reading, travel, cycling; *Style—* Dr Paul Monaghan, MP; ✉ House of Commons, London SW1A 0AA (e-mail paul.monaghan.mp@parliament.uk, website www.paulmonaghan.scot, Twitter @_PaulMonaghan)

MONBIOT, George; s of Raymond Monbiot, *qv*, of Burnham Market, Norfolk, and Rosalie Vivien Gresham Cooke, OBE, da of late R G Cooke, CBE, MP; *b* 27 January 1963; *Educ* Stowe, Brasenose Coll Oxford (open scholar, BA); *Career* investigative journalist, author and broadcaster; prodr natural history and environment progs BBC Radio 4 1985–87, prodr current affrs BBC World Service 1987, researching and writing book Poisoned Arrows: An Investigative Journey Through Indonesia 1987–89, researching and writing book Amazon Watershed (also series on Radio 4) 1989–91, fndr Forest Network (campaign to stop mahogany imports) 1989–91, researching and writing No Man's Land: An Investigative Journey Through Kenya and Tanzania (prodr and presenter No Man's Land series Radio 4) 1992–94, columnist The Guardian 1996–; presenter various programmes for BBC and C4; visiting fell Green Coll Oxford 1993–95, visiting prof of environmental sci Univ of E London 1995–99, hon prof of politics Keele Univ 1998–2000, visiting prof Dept of Philosophy Univ of Bristol 1999–2000, visiting prof Dept of Planning Oxford Brookes Univ 2003–08; fndr The Land is Ours Campaign 1995, co-fndr Rewilding Britain (charity) 2015–; patron: African Initiatives, Mikron Theatre; tstee: Naturesave Tst, African Initiatives, Advsy Cncl Environmental Law Fndn; radio production award Sony Awards 1987, Lloyd's National Screenwriting Award (for The Norwegian) 1987, United Nations Global 500 Award for outstanding environmental achievement 1995, named by Evening Standard as one of 25 most influential people in Britain 1996, named by Independent on Sunday as one of the 40 int prophets of the 21st century 1997, One World Nat Press Award 1998, Premio Mazotti Prize 2007, The Zoological Soc of London's Thomson Reuters Zoological Record Award 2013, Best General Book the Soc of Biology Book Awards 2014; Hon Dr: Univ of Essex 2007, Univ of St Andrews 2008; hon fell Sch of Journalism Univ of Cardiff 2007; *Books* Poisoned Arrows: An Investigative Journey Through Indonesia (1989), Amazon Watershed (Sir Peter Kent Award, 1991), No Man's Land: An Investigative Journey Through Kenya and Tanzania (1994), Captive State: The Corporate Takeover of Britain (2000), The Age of Consent: A Manifesto for a New World Order (2003), Heat: How to Stop the Planet Burning (2006), Bring on the the Apocalypse (2008), Feral: Searching for Enchantment on the Frontiers of Rewilding (2013, Orion Book Award for non-fiction 2015, Best General Book Soc of Biology Book Awards, ZSL Thomson Reuters Zoological Record Award), How Did We Get Into This Mess? Politics, Equality, Nature (2016); *Recreations* natural history, palaeontology, reading, gardening, ultimate frisbee, kayaking; *Style—* George Monbiot; ✉ website www.monbiot.com

MONBIOT, Raymond Geoffrey; CBE (1994, MBE 1981); s of Maurice Ferdinand Monbiot (d 1976), and Ruth Monbiot (d 1995); *b* 1 September 1937; *Educ* Westminster, London Business Sch; *m* 1961, Rosalie Vivien Gresham, OBE (1992), da of R G Cooke, CBE, MP (d 1970); 3 c (incl George Monbiot, *qv*, Eleanor Monbiot, OBE, and one of whom d 1997); *Career* with J Lyons & Co Ltd 1956–78, md Associated Biscuits Ltd 1978–82; chm: Campbell's UK Ltd 1982–88, Campbell's Soups Ltd 1983–88; pres Campbell's Frozen Foods Europe 1987–88, chm and md Rotherfield Management Ltd 1988–2010, vice-chm R & B Provisions Ltd 1990–95; dir: Pets Choice Ltd 1991–97, Paterson Bronte Ltd 1993–95, Arran Provisions Ltd 1993–95, Paramount Foods plc (formerly Canadian Pizza plc) 1996–98; chm Creative Food Systems Ltd 1997–2000; dep chm Cons Pty 2003–06; pres: S Oxon Cons Assoc 1980–92 (chm 1974–78), Cons Voluntary Pty 2000–01 (vice-pres 1997–2000), NW Norfolk Cons Assoc 2002–05; chm: Upper Thames Euro Constituency 1982–84, Oxon and Bucks Euro Constituency 1984–89, Cons Pty Nat Trade and Industry Forum 1988–96, Wessex Area Cons Pty 1995–98, Cons Pty Conf 2000, Cons Pty Nat Convention 2003–06; memb: Cons Pty NEC 1987–98, Cons Pty Fin and Gen Purposes Ctee 1989–93 and 1995–98, Cons Pty Bd 1998–2001 and 2003–06; memb: Cncl BIM 1981–84 (chm Westminster Branch 1978–82), Business Liaison Ctee London Business Sch 1984–88; chm Duke of Edinburgh Award for Industrial Projects Northants then Berks 1976–87; Prince Philip Cert of Recognition 1987; Freeman City of London 1990, Liveryman Worshipful Co of Butchers; *Books* How to Manage Your Boss (1980), One Hundred Not Out (2000), The Burnhams Book of Characters and Memories (2002), Characters of North Norfolk (2003), More Characters of North Norfolk (2006), Retirement is for Younger People – Life is too Short to Retire (2012), Characters of Fakenham (2016); *Recreations* writing, charity work, cooking; *Clubs* Farmers'; *Style—* Mr Raymond Monbiot, CBE; ✉ Eastgate House, Overy Road, Burnham Market, Norfolk PE31 8HH (☎ 01328 730928, mob. 07900 734558, e-mail rotherfieldmgmnt@btconnect.com)

MONCADA, Prof Sir Salvador; kt (2010); s of Salvador Moncada, of Tegucigalpa, Honduras, and Jenny Seidner (d 1985); *b* 3 December 1944; *Educ* Univ of El Salvador (MD), Univ of London (PhD); *Family* 1 da (Claudia Regina b 15 Nov 1966), 1 s (Salvador Ernesto b 6 May 1972 d 1982); m 2, HRH The Princess Maria Esmeralda de Belgique; 1 da (Alexandra Leopoldine b 4 Aug 1998), 1 s (Leopoldo Daniel b 21 May 2001); *Career* The Wellcome Res Laboratories: dir of Theraputic Res Div 1984–86, dir of res 1986–95; prof and dir Wolfson Inst for Biomedical Res UCL 1996–; memb Editorial Bd Proceedings Nat Acad of Sciences USA; recipient of numerous int med awards incl: Royal Medal, Prince of Asturias Prize, Amsterdam Prize; inventor of various patented pharmaceutical compositions; memb Br Pharmacological Soc 1974, memb Nat Acad of Scis 1994; FRS 1988, FRCP 1994, FMedSci 1998; *Books* Nitric Oxide from L-arginine: a bioregulatory system (1990), The Biology of Nitric Oxide (Parts 1–7, 1992–2000), Nitric Oxide and the

M

Vascular Endothelium (ed jtly, 2006); *Recreations* music, theatre, literature; *Style*— Prof Sir Salvador Moncada, FRS; ✉ e-mail s.moncada@ucl.ac.uk

MONCREIFFE OF THAT ILK, Hon Peregrine David Euan Malcolm; Baron of Moncreiffe and Easter Moncreiffe (both Scottish territorial baronies); 2 s of late Countess of Erroll (d 1978), and Sir Iain Moncreiffe of that Ilk, 11 Bt (d 1985); *b* 16 February 1951; *Educ* Eton, ChCh Oxford (MA); *m* 27 July 1988, Miranda Mary, da of Capt Mervyn Fox-Pitt, of Grange Scrymgeour, Cupar, Fife; 2 s (Ossian b 3 Feb 1991, Euan b 12 Sept 2000), 4 da (Idina b 3 Nov 1992, Eliza b 2 Feb 1995, Alexandra b 19 Nov 1996, Lily b 6 Nov 1998); *Career* Lt Atholl Highlanders 1974–2006; Slains Pursuivant 1970–78; investment banker; Credit Suisse First Boston 1972–82, Lehman Bros Kuhn Loeb/Shearson Lehman 1982–86, E F Hutton & Co 1986–88, Buchanan Partners 1990–99, former chm UA Gp plc; Royal Commissioner on the Ancient and Historical Monuments of Scotland 1989–94; memb Queen's Body Guard for Scotland (Royal Co of Archers); Freeman City of London, memb Worshipful Co of Fishmongers 1987; *Recreations* running, rowing, rustic pursuits, dance; *Clubs* Turf, White's, Pratt's, Puffins (Edinburgh), New (Edinburgh), Leander, Brook (NY); *Style*— The Hon Peregrine Moncreiffe of that Ilk; ✉ Highfield Place, La Pouquelaye, St Helier, Jersey JE2 3GG

MOND, Gary Stephen; s of Ferdinand Mond, of London, and Frances, *née* Henry; *b* 11 May 1959; *Educ* UCS Hampstead, Trinity Coll Cambridge (MA, Swimming blue); *m* 3 Feb 2001, Robyn, *née* Feinman; 1 da; *Career* chartered accountant 1981–84, Guinness Mahon & Co Ltd 1984–86, assoc dir Chancery Corporate Services Ltd 1986–89, Greig Middleton & Co Ltd 1989–91, fin business and trg conslt 1992–, conslt City Univ Business Sch 1992–97, md Redcliffe Training Assoc Ltd 1995–; memb ICAEW Corp Fin Faculty Exec 2003–08; Parly candidate (Cons) Hamilton Scot 1987, Parly candidate (Cons) Mansfield 1992, CPC chm Kensington and Chelsea Cons Assoc 1995–99, cncllr Royal Borough of Kensington & Chelsea 1996–2002, memb Cons Way Forward Exec 2004–07, memb Bd Cons Friends of Israel 2008–, memb Bd Jewish Nat Fund 2011–, memb Bd of Deputies of Br Jews 2011–; competitive butterfly swimmer: Nat Under 14 champion 1972, GB Int and Olympic trialist 1976, World Record holder long distance butterfly (six and a quarter miles) 1980; FCA 1995 (ACA 1985); *Recreations* swimming, theatre, chess; *Clubs* Coningsby; *Style*— Gary Mond, Esq; ✉ 1 Abbey View, London NW7 4PB (☎ 020 8959 4282, fax 020 7383 3507, e-mail garymond@redcliffetraining.co.uk)

MOND, Peter; *see:* Melchett, 4 Baron

MONDAY, Christopher Harry; s of Clifford Walter Monday (d 1992), and Isobel Phyllis Grace, *née* Lear (d 1992); *b* 1 June 1943; *Educ* Thornbury GS, Swansea Coll of Technol (Inst of Marine Engrs prize, OND), Riversdale Tech Coll, Bristol Coll of Technol (HNC Mech Engrg); *m* 21 Oct 1967, Heather, da of William Bengree Burgess; 1 s (Richard Paul b 13 Oct 1976); *Career* Shell Oil Co: apprentice 1959–64, fifth engr offr 1964–65; sub assembly supervisor Automatic Handling Ltd 1965–68, sr tech engr (tech engr 1968–70) Rolls Royce Aero Engines Ltd 1970–76; NNC Ltd: res engr 1976–77, site rep 1977–81, section head (Electronics) 1981–87, sr section head 1987–90, gp head 1990–92, tech sales exec 1992–94; dir Community Integrated Care Ltd 1989–94, md CTSS Ltd 1990–99; CIC Ltd: former head of tech servs, former head of IT and communications, head of IT and compliance and asst dir 2003–08, ret; chm Inst of Tech Engrs 1983–85, memb Engrg Cncl 1988–94, memb Cncl Instn of Engrg and Technol 2006–09; hon treas Instn of Incorporated Engrs 1999–2006; *Recreations* DIY (built my own house), travel, badminton, fanatic supporter of American football; *Style*— Christopher Monday, Esq; ✉ The Dairy, Bradley Hall, Bradley Lane, Frodsham, Cheshire WA6 7EP (☎ 01928 733221, e-mail chris_monday@hotmail.com)

MONDS, Prof Fabian; CBE (1997); s of Edward James Monds, and Mary Bridget Monds; *b* 1 November 1940, Omagh, Co Tyrone; *Educ* Christian Brothers GS Omagh, Queen's Univ Belfast (BSc, PhD); *m* 1967, Eileen Joan Graham; 2 da; *Career* formerly provost Magee Coll and pro-vice-chllr for planning Univ of Ulster, held positions at Purdue Univ and Queen's Univ Belfast; fndr ptnr: Medical and Scientific Computer Services Ltd, Western Connect Ltd; BBC: memb Bd of Govrs 1999–2006, nat govr for NI 1999–2006; chm: Invest NI 2000–05, Centre for Trauma and Transformation Omagh, Omagh Enterprise Co 2008–14; co-chair US-Ireland R&D Partnership 2005–13; vice-chair NW Regional Coll 2007–15; CCMI; *Books* An Introduction to Mini and Micro Computers (with R A McLaughlin, 1981, 2 edn 1984), The Business of Electronic Product Development (1984); *Recreations* general aviation; *Style*— Prof Fabian Monds, CBE, CCMI

MONEY, Julian David Kyrle; s of Robert Washborn Money (d 1986), of Truro, Cornwall, and Brenda, *née* Mitchell; *b* 28 July 1959; *Educ* Blundell's, St Austell Sixth Form Coll, Falmouth Art Sch, Kingston Poly (BA); *m* 1992, Katharine Pethick; 1 s (Freddy Bob b 29 April 1987), 1 da (Tabitha Lily b 27 March 1989); *Career* designer specialising in packaging systems; fndr (with w) Pethick & Money 1984 (design consultancy specialising in graphics for corp identities, packaging and multi-media clients); clients incl: Marks & Spencer, Tesco, Boots, J Sainsbury, Alfred Dunhill, Mont Blanc, Walt Disney, Jaeger, CBRE; created M-Pak packaging system and FFW flexible food wrap; founded RAP Ltd (Rapid Action Packaging) manufacturing packaging for quick service restaurant indust; clients incl: Pret, MacDonalds, Starbucks, Nero, Costa, Boots, Tesco, Asda, Wild Bean Café, KFC, Greggs, Abrakebabra Ireland; winner BBC Design Award and BBC Technol Award 1996; *Recreations* sailing, tennis, squash, fishing, golf, film, gardening; *Style*— Julian Money, Esq; ✉ 8 Sydney Road, Richmond, Surrey TW9 1UB (☎ 020 8948 3184); RAP Ltd (☎ 020 8392 8320, fax 020 8392 3821, e-mail julian.money@rapuk.com)

MONK, Prof Anthony John (Tony); s of John Andrew Monk, and Dorothy Marjorie, *née* Pettifer; *b* 11 September 1936; *Educ* Windsor County Boys' Sch, UCL (Dip Arch, Alfred Bossom Atelier Prize), Yale Univ (Henry Fund fell, ESU scholar, MArch); *m* 1964, Ann Monk, JP; 1 s (Craig Antony b 1973), 1 da (Jane Elizabeth b 1977); *Career* jt winner Paisley Civic Centre architecture competition 1963; fndr ptnr Hutchison Locke & Monk (architects) 1964–88, fndr and non-exec dir Acton Housing Assoc 1969–74, md HLM Architects Ltd 1988–91, non-exec dir Building Centre London 1991–96, prof of architecture Univ of Luton 1994–2001 (Pr lectr 1994, head of architecture 1994–97), architectural advsr Lottery Awards Panel Sports Cncl 1995–98, chm BDA Awards Panel 2000; govr Frimley Health NHS Fndn Tst 2015–16; negotiator RIBA Part I exemption for BSc(Hons) Architecture 1993; memb Expert Witness Inst 2004; RIBA 1961, ARIAS 1967, FFB 1968, MBAE 1994; *Awards* Paisley Civic Centre Civic Tst Award 1968, Civic Tst Commendation Darville House Windsor 1983, Civic Tst Award and Brick Devpt Assoc Award Chariott House Windsor 1985, Building Magazine Premier Practice Award (nationwide competition) HLM Architects 1991, DOE Housing Project Design Award Cromwell House Mortlake 1992, winner St Albans Ryder competition 1995; *Publications* The Art and Architecture of Paul Rudolph (1999), Hospital Builders (2004), HLM 50+ towards a social architecture (2016); author of numerous publications featuring architectural projects; *Recreations* cricket (pres Windsor Cricket Club 2000–16), golf; *Clubs* MCC, Wentworth; *Style*— Prof Tony Monk; ✉ Millrun, White Lilies Island, Mill Lane, Windsor, Berkshire SL4 5JH (☎ 01753 861917, mobile 07816 241387, website www.tonymonk.com); Edgington Spink and Hyne, Meridian House, 2 Russell Street, Windsor, Berkshire SL4 1HQ (☎ 01753 857092, fax 01753 857096)

MONK, David; *Educ* Glyn GS Epsom; *m*; 2 c; *Career* The News (Portsmouth) 1978–86, Today 1986–95, Daily Mail 1996–99; Metro: asst ed 1999–2004, dep ed 2004–; *Recreations* Writing about the cruise industry; *Style*— David Monk, Esq; ✉ Metro, Associated Newspapers Limited, Northcliffe House, 2 Derry Street, London W8 5TT (Twitter @dcmonk)

MONK, Stuart John; s of John Monk (d 1989), and Margaret, *née* Holmes (d 2009); *b* 7 August 1949, Epping, Essex; *Educ* Durham Johnson Grammar Tech; *m* 2 June 1979, Jennifer, *née* Spink; 1 da (Jane b 4 Nov 1980), 1 s (Stephen b 19 March 1983); *Career* articled clerk King Hope & Co 1969–71; self employed 1972–, currently md Jomast Ltd; *Recreations* tennis, golf; *Style*— Stuart Monk, Esq; ✉ Jomast Limited, Oriel House, Bishop Street, Stockton-on-Tees TS18 1SW (☎ 01642 674203, fax 01642 618153, e-mail stuart@jomast.co.uk)

MONK BRETTON, 3 Baron (UK 1884); John Charles Dodson; DL (E Sussex 1983); s of 2 Baron, CB, JP, DL (d 1933), by his w Ruth (herself da of Hon Charles Brand and gda of 1 Viscount Hampden and 23 Baron Dacre); *b* 17 July 1924; *Educ* Westminster, New Coll Oxford; *m* 1958, Zoë Diana, da of Ian Douglas Murray Scott (d 1974); 2 s; *Heir* s, Hon Christopher Dodson; *Career* took Cons whip in House of Lords; retired farmer; *Style*— The Rt Hon the Lord Monk Bretton, DL; ✉ Chemin de La Becque 24, CH 1814, La Tour de Peilz, Switzerland

MONKMAN, Prof Andrew Paul; *b* 6 September 1963; *Educ* QMC London (BSc, PhD); *m* Sophia Carmen; 1 da (Mischa Cornelia b 23 Nov 1993), 1 s (Maximillian Cyrus b 9 Feb 1997); *Career* Sch of Engrg and Applied Science (now Dept of Physics) Univ of Durham: lectr Applied Physics Gp 1988–97, promoted to readership 1997, promoted prof 2002, dir Photonic Materials Inst 2004–; EPSRC: memb Materials Coll, memb Photonics Panel (chm Oct 2001 meeting); Swedish Fndn for Int Co-operation in Research and HE (STINT) fell Swedish govt 1998 (held at Univ of Linkoping), Leverhulme fell 2002–03; guest lectr and speaker at confs and symposia; author of numerous books contribs and peer-reviewed papers; fndr memb Northern Dales Branch Int Wine and Food Soc; memb American Physical Soc; CPhys, FInstP; *Recreations* classical, jazz and rock music, hill walking, skiing, football, motor sport, driving, cooking, being a father; *Style*— Prof Andrew Monkman; ✉ Organic Elecroactive Materials Research Group, Department of Physics, University of Durham, Science Laboratories, South Road, Durham DH1 3LE (☎ 0191 374 2406, fax 0191 374 3848, mobile 07714 066462, e-mail a.p.monkman@durham.ac.uk)

MONKS, John; *Educ* Univ of Nottingham (BA); *Career* jr mangr Plessey Co Ltd 1967–69; TUC: joined 1969, head Orgn and Industrial Rels Dept 1977, dep gen sec 1987–94, gen sec 1994–2003; gen sec European TUC 2003–; memb: ACAS 1979–95, ESRC 1988–91, Learning and Skills Cncl 2000–04; visiting prof Manchester Business Sch; *Style*— John Monks, Esq; ✉ ETUC, ITU House, Boulevard du Roi Albert II 5, B-1210 Brussels, Belgium

MONKS, John Christopher; *Educ* Liverpool Poly, RCA (MA); *Career* artist; visiting artist Garner Tullis Workshop Santa Barbara California 1987, British Council artist in residence British Inst Madrid 1990; numerous solo exhibitions incl: Evidence 1989 and New Work 1990 (both Paton Gallery London), John Monks, Paintings 1990–93 (Manchester City Art Galleries) 1994, Beaux Arts 1996 and 1997, Peter Findlay Gallery NYC 1999, Recent Works Clare Hall Coll Cambridge 2009; work in group exhibitions incl: New Contemporaries (ICA London, prizewinner) 1976, Three College Show (RCA) 1979, Alternative Tate (Paton Gallery London) 1982, Artists for the 1990s (Paton Gallery) 1984, Monotypes (Paton Gallery) 1986, Birthday Offering (five years of Paton Gallery) 1986, Six Figurative Painters (Paton Gallery) 1987, 20 British Artists (London, Glasgow, NY) 1988, Metropolitan Museum of Art (NY) 1988, Recent Work (Paton Gallery) 1990, The New British Painting (Queen's Museum NY) 1990, Paton Gallery 1993, Beaux Arts London 1994, Artists of Fame and Promise (Beaux Arts) 1995; work in collections incl: Metropolitan Museum of Art (NY), Contemporary Art Society (London), Gulbenkian Foundation (Lisbon Portugal), Arts Council (GB), British Institute (Madrid), Manchester City Museum, Yale Center for British Art (Conn USA), Unilever plc, Ocean Trading and Transport plc; one-man shows incl: Peter Findlay NY 2004 and 2006, Artificial Light (Long & Ryle London) 2005 and 2007, Barber Inst of Fine Arts Birmingham 2013–14; awarded British Council grant for working visit to NY 1990; guest lecture tour of American Art Centres Spring 1992; guest speaker: Tate Gallery 1993, Sch of The Art Inst Chicago 1997 and 2007, NY Studio Sch NY 1998; *Publications* subject of John Monks Paintings (monograph, 2008); *Style*— John Monks, Esq; ✉ c/o Long & Ryle, 4 John Islip Street, London SW1P 4PX

MONKS, Baron (Life Peer UK 2010), of Blackley in the County of Greater Manchester; John Stephen Monks; s of Charles Edward Monks (d 1970), and Bessie Evelyn Monks; *b* 5 August 1945; *Educ* Ducie Tech HS Manchester, Univ of Nottingham (BA); *m* 18 July 1970, Francine Jacqueline, da of Franciscus Hendrikus Schenk, of 187 Forest Row, Tunbridge Wells, Kent; 2 s (Matthew b 1973, Daniel b 1975), 1 da (Catherine b 1981); *Career* jr mangr Plessey Radar 1967–69; TUC: asst Orgn Dept 1969–74 (asst sec 1974–77), head Orgn and Industl Rels Dept 1977–87, dep sec gen 1987–93, sec gen 1993–2003; gen sec European Trade Union Confederation 2003–11; memb Cncl: ACAS 1979–95, ESRC 1988–; vice-chair Learning and Schs Cncl 2001–04; tstee Nat Museum of Labour History 1988–; govr: LSE, Hedgehill Sch; *Recreations* squash, music, swimming; *Clubs* Tulse Hill and Honor Oak Squash; *Style*— The Lord Monks; ✉ House of Lords, London SW1A 0PW

MONKS, Sandra Elizabeth; TD; da of George Jagger (d 1993), and Maisie Campbell, *née* Watson (d 1998); *b* 27 March 1945; *Educ* Grove Acad Broughty Ferry, Santa Ana Jr Coll UCLA; *m* 1965 (m dis 1970), Terence John Monks; *Career* civil servant Dept of Educn 1962–66, insurance exec International Group Plans Inc Washington DC 1966–68; D C Thomson & Co Ltd 1970–: sub-ed Romeo magazine, sub-ed Jackie magazine, chief sub-ed Jackie, ed Jackie, ed Annabel magazine, ed My Weekly magazine, fiction and rights ed; Maj RCS (TA) 39th (City of London) (V) (SC), ret; *Recreations* Territorial Army, horse riding, swimming, sailing; *Style*— Ms Sandra Monks, TD; ✉ My Weekly Magazine, Albert Square, Dundee DD1 9QJ (☎ 01382 575888, fax 01382 322214, e-mail smonks@dcthomson.co.uk)

MONMOUTH, Dean of; *see:* Fenwick, Very Rev Dr Richard David

MONRO, Brig the Hon Hugh Brisbane Henry Ewart; CBE ((Mil) 2003, MBE (Mil) 1988); s of Baron Monro of Langholm (Life Peer) (d 2006), and Elizabeth Anne, *née* Welch; bro of Maj-Gen the Hon Seymour Monro, CBE, LVO, *qv*; *b* 4 March 1953, Edinburgh; *Educ* Trinity Coll Glenalmond; *m* Catriona Elizabeth, da of Rev and Mrs Ronald Torrie; 3 da (Flora, Clare, Ailsa); *Career* cmmnd Queen's Own Highlanders 1972; last CO 1 Bn Queen's Own Highlanders 1993–94, first CO 1 Bn The Highlanders 1994–95, Col MOD 1995–98, Bde Cdr 52 Lowland Bde 1998–2001, Col The Highlanders 2001, Cmdt Sch of Infantry 2001–05, Dep Commanding Gen Multi Nat Security Transition Corps Iraq 2006–07; sr assoc Exclusive Analysis Ltd 2007–09; HM chief inspector of prisons for Scotland 2009–13; Brig Queen's Body Guard for Scotland (Royal Co of Archers); *Recreations* golf, country sports; *Clubs* Northern Meeting, New (Edinburgh), Caledonian; *Style*— Brig the Hon Hugh Monro, CBE

MONRO, Dr Jean Anne; *b* 31 May 1936; *Educ* St Helen's Sch Northwood, London Hosp Med Coll (MB BS); *m* 1 (widowed); 2 s (Alister, Neil); m 2, 1993 (widowed); *Career* house offr London Hosp 1960; W Herts Hosp Gp: SHO geriatric med 1962 (paediatrics 1961), registrar 1963, med asst 1967–79; hon clinical asst Nat Hosp for Nervous Diseases London 1974–84, assoc physician Edgware Gen Hosp 1979–82, clinical allergist Humana Hosp Wellington London 1982–84, Allergy and Environmental Med Clinic Hemel Hempstead 1984–88, Breakspear Hosp for Allergy and Environmental Med Abbots Langley 1988–93, Breakspear Hosp Hemel Hempstead 1993–, visiting physician in environmental med Fachkrankenhaus Nordfriesland Schleswig-Holstein 1993–2010; med dir Allergy and Environmental Med Dept (ltd co 1986–91) located at: Nightingale Hosp London 1984–86, Lister Hosp London 1986–89, Hosp of St John and St Elizabeth London 1989, Middlesex Hosp 1989–90, London Welbeck Hosp 1990–91; author of numerous pubns on allergy and nutrition related topics; formerly med journalist contributing to Hospital Doctor, Doctor and other jls; memb Bd Inst of Functional Med 1994–; former memb Sub-Ctee of Central Ctee for Hosp Med Servs; diplomate Int Bd of Environmental Med; memb: American Coll of Occupational and Environment Med, Soc of Occupational Med (GB), RSM, Hunterian Soc, Br Soc of Immunology; fell American Acad of Environmental Med; MRCS, LRCP, FAAEM, MACOEM; *Books* incl: Some Dietary Approaches to Disease Management (1974), Chemical Children (jtly, 1987), Handbook of Food Allergy (contrib, 1987), Food Allergy and Intolerance (contrib), Immunology of Myalgic Encephalomyelitis (contrib, 1988), Breakspear Guide to Allergies (contrib, 1991), Blanc Vite (contrib, 1998), Electromagnetic Environments in Buildings (contrib, 2004); *Style—* Dr Jean Monro; ✉ Breakspear Medical Group, Hertfordshire House, Wood Lane, Hemel Hempstead, Hertfordshire HP2 4FD (☎ 01442 261333, fax 01442 266388, website www.breakspearmedical.com)

MONRO, Maj Gen the Hon Seymour Hector Russell Hale; CBE (1996), LVO (2010), DL (2011); s of Baron Monro of Langholm, PC, AE (Life Peer) (d 2006), and Elizabeth Anne, *née* Welch; bro of Brig the Hon Hugh Monro, CBE, *qv*; *b* 7 May 1950; *Educ* Glenalmond Coll, RMA Sandhurst (Sword of Honour), Canadian Staff Coll Toronto, Army Staff Coll, Aust Coll of Defence and Strategic Studies (ACDSS) Canberra; *m* 16 April 1977, Angela, da of Wing Cdr Barney Sandeman; 3 s (Harry Seymour Edward b 29 Nov 1979, Alexander Hector Barney b 6 Sept 1981, Robert John Ewart b 15 Dec 1983); *Career* instr Army Staff Coll Camberley 1986–89, CO 1 Bn Queen's Own Highlanders (Germany, Belfast, the Gulf) 1989–91, Gen Staff MOD 1991–93, Cdr 39 Infantry Bde NI 1994–95, Pres Regular Commissions Bd Westbury 1996–97, Dep Chief Jt Ops Bosnia 1997, Dir of Infantry HQ Infantry 1998–2001, ADC 1998–2001, Dep Cdr NATO Rapid Reaction Corps (Italy) Milan 2001–03; dir Atlantic Salmon Tst 2004–08; Hon Air Cdre 2622 (Highland) Sqdn RAuxAF 2008–; adjutant Queen's Body Guard for Scotland (Royal Co of Archers) 2000–09; vice-pres Royal Br Legion Scotland; chm: Highlands and Islands Bd Prince's Tst Scotland 2004–07, Highland Heritage Appeal 2007–13, Findhorn, Nairn and Lossie Fisheries Tst 2008–15, Highland Military Tattoo 2013–; dir Cairngorm Mountain Ltd 2009–14; convenor Northern Meeting Soc 2009–12, pres Brisbane Observatory Tst 2011–, pres Forres Pipe Band 2012–; *Recreations* stalking, shooting, fishing, golf, conservation, photography, reading, rugby, travel, vintage cars; *Clubs* New (Edinburgh); *Style—* Maj Gen the Hon Seymour Monro, CBE, LVO, DL; ✉ Kirkton, Dallas, Moray IV36 2RZ (e-mail seymourmonro@gmail.com)

MONROE, Alexander John (Alex); s of William Stuart Monroe, of Suffolk, and Peggy-Ann, *née* Parish; *b* 27 June 1963; *Educ* Ipswich Sch for Boys, Ipswich Art Sch, Sir John Cass Sch of Art (BA); *m* m 25 July 1998, Denise Elizabeth, *née* Hill; 3 da (Verity Alice b 19 Oct 1997, Constance Bella b 3 April 1999, Liberty Grace b 28 June 2001); *Career* jewellery designer/mfr (estab 1987); exhibitions incl: Jablonex Int Jewellery Fair Czechoslovakia 1987, Br Designer Show London 1987 and 1990, Pret à Porter NY 1988, Fish and Foul (Hibiscus Gallery) 1989, A Beast of an Exhibition (Hollyhouse Gallery) 1989, London Works 1991, Sundials in the Study London 1991, London Works (Smiths Gallery London) 1991, The Who's Who Exhibition London 1992, London Designer Show 1992, Crafts in Performance (Crafts Cncl) 1993, Premier Classe 1993; work cmmnd by: Br Museum, BBC, World Gold Cncl, Browns (London), Barneys (NYC); work in the collections of: Sedgwick collection, Sainsbury private collection; Prince's Tst bursary 1987, Design Centre selection 1988, Gtr London Arts bursary (to make sundials) 1991; pt/t tutor Camden and Central London Insts and lectr Croydon Coll, London Enterprise Agency and Battersea Adult Educn 1988; memb Br Sundial Soc 1992–; *Publications* A Guide to Sundials with Special Reference to Portable Dial and Navigational Equipment (1990); *Recreations* sailing; *Style—* Alex Monroe, Esq; ✉ 9A Iliffe Yard, London SE17 3QA (☎ 020 7703 8507)

MONSON, (John) Guy Elmhirst; s of Maj the Hon Jeremy Monson (d 2007), and Patricia Mary Monson; *b* 11 September 1962; *Educ* Eton, Univ of Oxford (BA); *m* 17 March 1995, Lady (Olivia) Rose Mildred FitzRoy, da of 11 Duke of Grafton, KG (d 2011); 2 da (Olivia Effie Fortune b 8 Dec 1995, Leonora Grace b 19 Aug 1999); *Career* Sarasin Investment Management Ltd: joined 1984, dir 1989–, chief investment offr 1993–2007, ceo 2007, managing ptnr 2008–; chief investment offr Bank Sarasin Gp 1997–, ptnr Bank Sarasin & Co 2001; memb IMRO; *Recreations* flying; *Clubs* White's, Pratt's; *Style—* Guy Monson, Esq; ✉ Sarasin and Partners, Juxon House, 100 St Paul's Churchyard, London EC4M 8BU (☎ 020 7038 7000, fax 020 7038 6850, e-mail guy.monson@sarasin.co.uk)

MONSON, Prof John Patrick; s of Joseph Patrick Monson (d 1973), and Margaret, *née* Connor (d 2004); *b* 11 July 1950; *Educ* Guy's Hosp Sch of Med (MB BS, MD), St George's Hosp, Royal London Hosp; *m* Eva Helena, *née* Lind; 2 s (Kevin b 8 Dec 1977, Andrew b 6 Jan 1981); *Career* reader in endocrinology London Hosp Med Coll 1994–95 (sr lectr 1982–94), reader in med Dept of Endocrinology Bart's 1995–99, prof and head clinical endocrinology Bart's and the Royal London Sch of Med and Dentistry 1999–2005, currently emeritus prof Queen Mary Univ of London and hon conslt physician St Bartholomew's and The Royal London Hospitals; memb: Soc for Endocrinology 1983, American Endocrine Soc 1995, Assoc of Physicians; FRCP, FRCPI; *Publications* Challenges in Growth Hormone Therapy (1999); author of numerous papers and articles on diabetes and endocrinology with particular reference to pituitary disease; *Recreations* theatre, film, music, skiing; *Clubs* Savile; *Style—* Prof John Monson; ✉ 70 Landmann Point, 6 Peartree Way, London SE10 0GW (☎ 020 3725 9434, e-mail johnmonson@aol.com)

MONTAGUE, Sir Adrian Alastair; kt (2006), CBE (2001); s of Charles Edward Montague (d 1985), of Sevenoaks, Kent, and Olive, *née* Jones (d 1956); *b* 28 February 1948; *Educ* Mill Hill Sch, Trinity Hall Cambridge (MA); *m* 1, May 1970 (m dis 1982), Pamela Joyce (d 2000); 2 da (Emma b 1974, Olivia b 1980), 1 s (Edward b 1977); m 2, 8 Nov 1986, Penelope Jane Webb; 1 s (William b 1988); *Career* Linklaters & Paines: asst slr 1973–74, asst slr Paris 1974–77, asst slr London 1977–79, ptnr 1979–94; dir and head of project fin Kleinwort Benson Ltd 1994–97, co head global project fin Dresdner Kleinwort Benson 1997, chief exec Private Fin Initiative Taskforce HM Treasy 1997–2000, dep chm Partnerships UK plc 2000–01, sr int advsr Société Générale 2001–04, chair Michael Page International plc 2002–11 (dir 2001–), dep chm Network Rail 2001–04, chm British Energy 2002–, chm Cross London Rail Links 2004–; dir CellMark AB, chm Friends Provident 2005– (dir 2004–), chm Infrastructure Investors Ltd 2005–; memb Law Soc; *Books* Joint Ventures (ed with C G E Nightingale, 1989); *Style—* Sir Adrian Montague, CBE

MONTAGUE, Sarah Anne Louise; da of late Lt-Col John Anthony Montague, and Mary Theresa, *née* O'Malley; *Educ* Blanchelande Coll, Univ of Bristol (BSc); *m* 2002, Sir (Richard) Christopher Brooke, Bt; 3 da (Hope Mary, Florence Faith Harriet, Carola Irene Charity), 1 step-da (Tabitha Elizabeth); *Career* broadcaster; stockbroker and eurobond dealer Natwest Capital Markets 1987–89; reporter Channel Television CI 1991–94, Reuters Television 1994–96, Sky News 1996–97, BBC radio and TV presenter 1997–, currently presenter Today Prog (Radio 4); also presented: Newsnight (BBC 2), news bulletins (BBC 1 and BBC News 24), Hardtalk (BBC World); *Style—* Ms Sarah Montague; ✉ BBC Broadcasting House, Portland Place, London W1A 1AA (☎ 020 3614 1222, e-mail sarah.montague@bbc.co.uk)

MONTAGUE-MASON, Perry; s of Arthur John Mason (d 1991), of Brighton, and Lily Beulah, *née* Montague (d 2013); *b* 12 November 1956, Shepherd's Bush, London; *Educ* St Marylebone GS, Royal Acad of Music; *m* December 2013, Fiona Suzanne, *née* Duff; 1 da (Jemima Montague-Mason), 3 step da (Sally Lawrence-Archer, Olivia Armon, Aiden Grayling-Duff); *Career* memb BBC Concert Orch 1976–80, guest princ London Philharmonic Orch; guest ldr: BBC Concert Orch, Ulster Orch, New Symphony Orch, New Sadler's Wells Opera Orch; co-ldr London Chamber Orch; ldr Mantovani Orch 1983–91, ldr and artistic dir Nat Symphony Orch 1992–2001; ldr many major West End musicals incl Phantom of the Opera; session violinist with numerous musical acts incl Oasis, Bjork, Elton John, Spice Girls, Adele, Jamiroquai, Diana Ross, Jimmy Page, Coldplay, Emeli Sandé, Mick Jagger, The Verve, Paul McCartney, Joni Mitchell, Bryan Ferry, Amy Winehouse, Stevie Wonder, Take That, Eric Clapton and Rod Stewart 1994–; ldr recording orchestras for many film soundtracks incl: Gladiator, Bridget Jones's Diary, The Book of Eli, The Bourne Ultimatum, Broken Embraces, Iron Man, Gosford Park, Kung Fu Panda, Wilde, Love Actually and How to Train Your Dragon; ARAM, FRSA; *Recreations* skiing, scuba diving, ornithology; *Style—* Perry Montague-Mason, Esq

MONTEITH, Brian; s of Donald Mcdonald Monteith, of Edinburgh, and Doreen Campbell, *née* Purves; *b* 8 January 1958; *Educ* Portobello HS, Heriot-Watt Univ; *m* 1 Sept 1984 (m dis 2009), Shirley Joyce, da of Peter Marshall; 2 s (Duncan Peter, Callum Douglas (twins) b 13 April 1988); m 2, 18 Dec 2010, Jacqueline Moira, da of Christopher Anderson; 3 step-da (Emma Jacqueline Lockett, Katy Anna Lockett, Amy Elizabeth Lockett); *Career* nat chm Cons Students 1982–83, nat chm Scot Youngs Cons 1987–88; account exec Michael Forsyth Assoc London 1983–84 and 1985–86, Dunseath Stephen PR Edinburgh 1984–85, md Leith Communications Ltd 1986–91, PR dir Forth Marketing 1991–95, dir Communication Gp Scotland 1995–97, prop Dunedin PR 1997–99; MSP (Cons until 2005, then Ind) Scotland Mid and Fife 1999–2007; spokesman educn, culture and sport 1999–2003, spokesman fin, local govt and public servs 2003–05, convenor Audit Ctee Scot Parl 2003–07; fndr Cons Against Apartheid 1988, fndr Tuesday Club 1996; fndr and campaign mangr No No Campaign 1997, chm English Speaking Union Scotland 2009–; columnist: Edinburgh Evening News 2001–, The Scotsman 2009–; ed: ThinkScotland.org 2009–, TheFreeSociety.org 2013–; int PR conslt Botswana, Pakistan, Nigeria, Trinidad & Tobago, Tunisia 2007–; *Books* Paying the Piper (2007), The Bully State (2009), The Full Monty (2009, 4 edn 2014), ThinkScotland (2012); *Recreations* Hibernian FC, Richard Wagner, fine dining; *Style—* Brian Monteith, Esq; ✉ La Pastrié, Trévien, 81190 Tarn, France

MONTGOMERIE, Colin; OBE (2005, MBE 1998); s of James Montgomerie, sec of Royal Troon Golf Club; *b* 23 June 1963; *m* 1, June 1990 (m dis 2006), Eimear, *née* Wilson; 2 da (Olivia Rose b March 1993, Venetia Grace b Jan 1996), 1 s (Cameron Stuart b May 1998); m 2, April 2008, Gaynor Knowles; *Career* professional golfer; amateur victories: Scottish Amateur Stroke-play Championship 1985, Scottish Amateur Championship 1987; tournament victories since turning professional 1987: Portuguese Open 1989, Scandinavian Masters 1991, 1999 and 2001, Dutch Open 1993, Volvo Masters 1993 and 2002, Spanish Open 1994, English Open 1994, German Open 1994 and 1995, Trophee Lancome 1995, Alfred Dunhill Cup 1995 (individual), Dubai Desert Classic 1996, Irish Open 1996, 1997 and 2001, European Masters 1996, Sun City Million Dollar Challenge 1996, European Grand Prix 1997, King Hassan II Trophy 1997, World Cup (Individual) 1997, Andersen Consulting World Champion 1997, PGA Championship 1998, 1999 and 2000, German Masters 1998, British Masters 1998, Benson and Hedges International Open 1999, Standard Life Loch Lomond Invitational 1999, Int Open Munich 1999, World Matchplay Championships Wentworth 1999, French Open Paris 2000, Skins Game USA 2000, Ericsson Australian Masters 2001, TCL Classic 2002, Macau Open 2003, Cartex Masters Singapore 2004, Dunhill Links Championship 2005, UBS Hong Kong Open 2006, European Open Ireland 2007; US Open: third 1992, second 1994,1997 and 2006; second The Open R&A 2005; US PGA 1995 (second); Tournament Players Championship 1996 (second); team memb: Eisenhower Trophy (amateur) 1984 and 1986, Walker Cup (amateur) 1985 and 1987, Alfred Dunhill Cup 1988, 1991, 1992, 1993, 1994, 1995 (winners), 1996, 1997, 1998, 1999 and 2000, World Cup 1988, 1991, 1992, 1993, 1997, 1998, 1999, 2006, 2007 and 2008 (winners), Ryder Cup 1991, 1993, 1995 (winners), 1997 (winners), 1999, 2002 (winners), 2004 (winners), 2006 (winners) and 2010 (capt, winners), UBS Cup 2003 and 2004, Seve Trophy 2000, 2002, 2003, 2005 and 2007; Henry Cotton Rookie of the Year 1988, winner European Order of Merit 1993, 1994, 1995, 1996, 1997, 1998, 1999 and 2005, Coach of the Year BBC Sports Personality of the Year 2010; *Books* The Real Monty: The Thinking Man's Guide To Golf; *Recreations* motor cars, music, DIY; *Style—* Colin Montgomerie, Esq, OBE; ✉ c/o IMG, McCormack House, Hogarth Business Park, Burlington Lane, London W4 2TH

MONTGOMERY, Alexander Jamieson (Alex); s of Walter Montgomery, of Eastbourne, and Helen, *née* Jamieson; *b* 12 August 1943; *Educ* Hyndland Sr Sch Glasgow; *m* 9 June 1970, Anne, da of James Robertson; 2 da (Helen Robertson b 16 June 1972, Katie Elizabeth b 24 Jan 1974); *Career* sports writer; various jobs Glasgow 1959–61, football reporter Sunday Post and Weekly News Glasgow/Newcastle/Manchester 1963–68, news reporter Sunday Express 1968, sports reporter Hayter's Sports Agency 1968–70, sports reporter Daily Mail 1970–71; The Sun: football reporter 1971–83, chief football writer 1983–92, football feature writer 1992–93; chief football news reporter Today 1993–95, chief football reporter News of the World 1996, formerly with Mail on Sunday; chm Football Writers' Assoc 1994–95 (vice-chm 1993); *Publications* numerous football-related books on subjects incl Terry Venables, Martin O'Neill, Charlie George and John Hartson; *Recreations* sport, music; *Clubs* Royal Cwlth; *Style—* Mr Alex Montgomery; ✉ 36 Downside Close, Eastbourne, East Sussex BN20 8EL (mobile 07785 250439, e-mail alexjmontgomery@gmail.com)

MONTGOMERY, Archdeacon of; *see:* Griffith, Ven David Vaughan

MONTGOMERY, Clare Patricia; QC (1996); da of Dr Stephen Ross Montgomery, of Bath, and Ann Margaret, *née* Barlow; *b* 29 April 1958; *Educ* Millfield, UCL (LLB); *m* 14 Dec 1991, Victor Stefan Melleney; 2 da (Natasha b 27 Dec 1994, Anna b 3 June 1997); *Career* called to the Bar Gray's Inn 1980, recorder 1999–, dep judge of the High Court 2003–, judge Court of Appeal of Jersey and Guernsey; capt Br Women's Foil Team 1992–96; *Style—* Miss Clare Montgomery, QC; ✉ Matrix Chambers Gray's Inn, London WC1R 5LN (☎ 020 7404 3447, fax 020 7404 3448, e-mail claremontgomery@matrixlaw.co.uk)

MONTGOMERY, David; *b* 8 February 1937, Brooklyn, NYC; *Educ* Midwood HS, Juilliard Sch of Music; *m* 1 (m dis); 2 da; m 2, 1982, Martine King; 1 s, 1 da; *Career* former musician; professional photographer 1964–; worked for: Jocelyn Stevens at Queen Magazine, The Sunday Times Magazine, Vogue, Tatler, Harpers & Queen, Rolling Stone, New York Times; has photographed: HM Queen Elizabeth II, HM Queen Elizabeth The Queen Mother, Lord Home, Lord Callaghan, Sir Edward Heath, Lady Thatcher, King Hussein of Jordan, The Duke and Duchess of York plus innumerable personalities; winner many int awards; visiting prof Univ of East London 2007–; *Recreations* gardening, photography, contemporary guitar; *Style—* David Montgomery, Esq; ✉ c/o M & M Management, Studio B, 11 Edith Grove, London SW10 (☎ 020 7823 3723, e-mail martine@mmmanagement.com)

M

MONTGOMERY, David John; s of William John Montgomery, and Margaret Jean, *née* Flaherty; *b* 6 November 1948; *Educ* Bangor GS, Queen's Univ Belfast (BA); *m* 1, 1971 (m dis 1987), Susan Frances Buchanan, da of James Francis Buchanan Russell, QC; *m* 2, 1989 (m dis 1997), Heidi, da of Dr Edward Kingstone, of McMaster, Ontario; *m* 3, 1997, Sophie, formerly w of 3 Earl of Woolton, *qv*, and da of 3 Baron Birdwood, *qv*; 1 s (b 15 July 2001); *Career* asst chief sub ed Daily Mirror 1978–80 (sub ed 1973–78), chief sub ed The Sun 1980–82, asst ed Sunday People 1982–84, ed News of the World 1985–87, ed and md Today 1987–91 (Newspaper of the Year 1988); md News UK 1987–91; chief exec Mirror Group plc 1992–99; dir: News Group Newspapers 1986–91, Satellite TV plc 1986–91, London Live Television 1991–99, Caledonian Newspaper Publishing Ltd 1992, Newspaper Publishing 1994–98, Donohue Inc 1992–95, Scottish Television 1995–99, Press Assoc 1996–99; chm: TRI-MEX Gp Ltd 1999–2002, MECOM Gp plc 2000–11, YAVA 2000–02, Integrated Educn Fund Devpt Bd NI 2000, African Lakes plc 2000–07, Campaign for Peace and Democratic Reconstruction for NI 2002, Team Northern Ireland 2002, West 175 Media Inc 2002–06, Berliner Verlag (Germany) 2005–09, Media Gp Limburg (Netherlands) 2006–11, Royal Wegener (Netherlands) 2009–11, Local World Ltd 2012–16; dir National World 2016–; *Style*— David Montgomery, Esq; ✉ 15 Collingham Gardens, London SW5 0HS (✆ 07720 289131, e-mail montymedia.m@gmail.com)

MONTGOMERY, Rev Prof John Warwick; Baron of Kiltartan and Lord of Morris, Comte de St-Germain de Montgommery; s of Maurice Warwick Montgomery (d 1993), and Harriet Genevieve, *née* Smith (d 1986); *b* 18 October 1931; *Career* academic, barr (Middle Temple, Lincoln's Inn, US Supreme Court Bar and Paris Bar), theologian; ordained to ministry Lutheran Church 1958; certified fraud examiner 2008; assoc prof Dept of History Wilfred Laurier Univ Ontario 1960–64, prof of history, prof of Christian thought and dir European Seminar Prog Trinity Evangelical Divinity School Illinois 1964–74, prof of law and theology Sch of Law George Mason Univ Virginia 1974–75, theological conslt Christian Legal Soc 1975–76, dir of studies International Inst of Human Rights Strasbourg 1979–81; fndr dean, prof of jurisprudence and dir European Prog Simon Greenleaf Sch of Law California 1980–88, distinguished prof of theology and law Faith Evangelical Lutheran Seminary Washington State 1989–91; Univ of Beds: princ lectr in law 1991–92, reader in law 1992–93, prof of law and humanities 1993–97, prof emeritus 1997–; distinguished prof of apologetics and law and vice-pres of academic affairs (UK and Europe) Trinity Coll and Theological Seminary Indiana 1997–2007, distinguished prof of law Regent Univ Virginia 1997–99, distinguished res prof of philosophy and Christian thought Patrick Henry Coll Virginia 2007–14, hon prof Lavengamalie Coll Tonga 2010–, distinguished res prof of philosophy Concordia Univ Wisconsin 2014–; sr counsel European Centre for Law and Justice Strasbourg 1997–2001; visiting prof: Concordia Theological Seminary Illinois 1964–67, De Paul Univ Chicago 1967–70, Concordia Univ Irvine California 2006; hon pres Academic Bd Int Inst for Religious Freedom Germany 2005–; memb: ALA, European Acad of Arts, Sciences and Humanities, Lawyers' Christian Fellowship (hon vice-pres 1995–2010), National Conference of Univ Profs, California, Virginia, DC and Washington State Bar Assocs, Int Bar Assoc, World Assoc of Law Profs, American Soc of Int Law, Union Internationale des Avocats, Assoc Française des Docteurs en Droit, American Historical Assoc, Presbyterian Historical Soc (NI), Heraldry Soc, Soc of Genealogists, Tyndale Fellowship, American Theological Library Assoc, Evangelical Theology Soc, Tolkien Soc, C S Lewis Soc, Creation Research Soc, Stair Soc (Scotland), Int Wine and Food Soc, Chaîne des Rôtisseurs, Académie Internationale des Gourmets et des Traditions Gastronomiques, Club Prosper Montagné Paris, Soc des Amis des Arts Strasbourg, Sherlock Holmes Soc; fell: American Scientific Affiliation, Trinity Coll Indiana, Victoria Inst London (hon vice-pres 2004–), Soc for Advanced Legal Studies; Freeman City of London, Freeman and Liveryman Worshipful Co of Scriveners; FRSA; *Publications* books incl: Slaughter of the Innocents (1981), The Marxist Approach to Human Rights: Analysis and Critique (1984), Human Rights and Human Dignity (1987), Evidence for Faith: Deciding the God Question (1991), Giant in Chains: China Today and Tomorrow (1994), Law and Morality: Friends or Foes (1994), Jésus: la raison rejoint l'histoire (1995), Christians in the Public Square (with C Cranfield and D Kilgour, 1996), Conflicts of Law (1997), The Transcendental Holmes (2000), The Repression of Evangelism in Greece (2001), Christ Our Advocate (2002), History, Law and Christianity (2002), Heraldic Aspects of the German Reformation (2003), The Church: Blessing or Curse? (2004), Tractatus Logico-Theologicus (5 edn, 2012), Christ as Centre and Circumference (2012), The Libraries of France at the Ascendancy of Mazarin (2015), Fighting the Good Fight: A Life in Defense of the Faith (2015); conslt ed (religion and law) Amicus Curiae: Journal of the Society for Advanced Legal Studies 2010–; author of articles in numerous learned jls; *Films* incl: Is Christianity Credible? (1968), In Search of Noah's Ark (1977), Defending the Biblical Gospel (1985); *Recreations* 16th and 17th century rare books, antique Citroën cars, Macintosh computers; *Clubs* Athenaeum; *Style*— The Rev Prof John Warwick Montgomery; ✉ No 9, 4 Crane Court, Fleet Street, London EC4A 2EJ (✆ 020 7583 1210); 2 rue de Rome, 67000 Strasbourg, France (✆ 00 33 3 88 61 08 82)

MONTGOMERY, Kenneth; OBE (2010); s of Thomas Montgomery, and Elizabeth, *née* McBride; *b* 28 October 1943, Belfast; *Educ* Royal Belfast Academical Inst, RCM; *m* 31 Aug 2002, Jan Van Dooren; *Career* musical dir Bournemouth Sinfonietta 1973–75, musical dir Glyndebourne Touring Opera 1975, princ conductor Dutch Radio Symphony Orch 1975, artistic and musical dir Opera Northern Ireland 1985, dir of opera studies Royal Conservatory The Hague 1991, acting music dir Santa Fe Opera House 2008, princ conductor Ulster Orch; hon doctorate Queen's Univ Belfast 2010; *Style*— Kenneth Montgomery, Esq, OBE; ✉ c/o François Rousseau, Le Bureau, 20 Rue Milton, F-75009, Paris, France (✆ 0033 1 4536 7936, fax 0033 1 7118 1142, e-mail frousseau@fr-lebureau.com)

MONTGOMERY, Richard John; s of Basil Richard Montgomery, of Tonbridge, Kent, and Mary Elizabeth, *née* Goddard; *b* 5 May 1955; *Educ* Tonbridge, Univ of Newcastle upon Tyne (MB BS); *m* 3 July 1982, Angela, da of John Todd, of Newcastle upon Tyne; 1 s (Duncan Richard b 16 Nov 1991), 3 da (Clare Louise b 20 Sept 1987, Esme Helen b 16 Feb 1993, Eleanor Frances b 29 Nov 1995); *Career* surgn; demonstrator in anatomy Univ of Newcastle Med Sch 1979–80; post grad trg Northern Region: surgery 1980–83, orthopaedic surgery 1983–88; orthopaedic research fell Mayo Clinic Rochester Minnesota USA 1986–87, conslt in traumatic and orthopaedic surgery N and S Tees Health Dist 1989–91, conslt in traumatic and orthopaedic surgery S Tees Health Dist 1991–, regnl speciality advsr in trauma and orthopaedic surgery Northern Deanery 2008–11, dir of professional affrs for NE England RCS 2011–12; hon clinical lectr Faculty of Med Univ of Newcastle upon Tyne 1996–; Univ of Teesside: hon lectr Sch of Human Studies 1996–, visiting fell Sch of Health and Social Care 2002–; memb: Panel of Examiners Intercollegiate Speciality Bd for Trauma and Orthopaedic Surgery 2002– (hon sec 2011–), Cncl RCS(Ed) 2011–; memb: Br Soc for Children's Orthopaedic Surgery (hon treas 2006–09), Br Limb Reconstruction Soc (hon treas 2002–08, pres 2008–10), Br Orthopaedic Assoc (memb Cncl 2009–11), BMA; FRCSEd 1983 (memb Panel of Examiners 2001–06); *Recreations* sailing; *Style*— Richard Montgomery, Esq; ✉ The James Cook University Hospital, Middlesbrough, Teesside TS4 3BW (✆ 01642 850850)

MONTGOMERY, HE Susannah; *m* Andrew James; *Career* diplomat; vice-consul Almaty 1996, second sec political Moscow 1997, acting head of mission Minsk 1998, second sec political UK Mission to the UN NY 1999–2000, secondment to Dept for Int Devpt 2001, operations mangr Finance Directorate FCO 2002–04, head of nuclear safety Science and Environment Team Moscow 2004–05, strategic policy advsr Policy Planners FCO 2005–07, head Europe Prog Team FCO 2007–08, high cmmr Gambia 2008–09, advsr Parly Relations Team 2010, communications mangr Paris 2011, ambass to the Slovak Repub 2011–; *Style*— HE Ms Susannah Montgomery; ✉ British Embassy, Panska 16, 811 01 Bratislava, Slovak Republic

MONTGOMERY OF ALAMEIN, 2 Viscount (UK 1946); David Bernard Montgomery; CMG (2000), CBE (1975); o s of 1 Viscount Montgomery of Alamein, KG, GCB, DSO (d 1976), and Elizabeth, *née* Hobart (d 1937); *b* 18 August 1928; *Educ* Winchester, Trinity Coll Cambridge; *m* 1, 27 Feb 1953 (m dis 1967), Mary Raymond, yr da of Sir Charles Connell (d 1973); 1 s, 1 da; *m* 2, 30 Jan 1970, Tessa, da of Lt-Gen Sir Frederick A M Browning, GCVO, KBE, CB, DSO (d 1965), and Lady Browning, DBE (Daphne du Maurier, the writer, d 1989), and former w of Maj Peter de Zulueta; *Heir* s, Hon Henry Montgomery; *Career* sat as Cons peer in House of Lords 1976–99, elected ind (crossbench) peer 2005–2016; dir Yardley International 1963–74, md Terimar Services Ltd (overseas trade consultancy) 1974–2000, chm Baring Puma Fund 1991–2002; memb Editorial Advsy Bd Vision Interamericana 1974–94; cncllr RBC&K 1974–78; chm: Hispanic and Luso Brasilian Cncl Canning House 1978–80 (pres 1987–94), Antofagasta (Chile) and Bolivia Railway Co and subsids 1980–82; vice-pres Brazilian C of C GB 1983– (chm 1980–82), chm European Atlantic Group 1992–94 (pres 1994–97); non-exec dir: Korn/Ferry Int 1977–93, Northern Engrg Industries 1980–87; patron D-Day and Normandy Fellowship 1980–94, Eighth Army Veterans Assoc 1984–2002; patron Restaurateurs Assoc of GB 1990–99 (pres 1982–90); pres: Centre for International Briefing Farnham Castle 1983–2003, Univ of Cambridge Engrgs Assoc 2001–06; Anglo-Argentine Soc 1976–87, Redgrave Theatre Farnham 1978–90, Anglo-Belgian Soc 1994–2006; Liveryman Worshipful Co of Mercers; Gran Oficial Orden Bernardo O'Higgins (Chile) 1989, Gran Oficial Orden Libertador San Martin (Argentina) 1992, Grande Oficial Orden Nacional Cruzeiro do Sul (Brazil) 1993, Encomienda Orden de Isabel la Catolica (Spain) 1993, Commanders Cross Order of Merit (Germany) 1993, Encomienda Orden del Aguila Azteca (Mexico) 1994, Commander Order of Leopold II (Belguim) 1997, Gran Cruz Orden de San Carlos (Colombia) 1998, Gran Ofical Orden del Libertador (Venezuela) 1999; *Books* The Lonely Leader – Monty 1944–45 (with Alistair Horne, 1994); *Clubs* Garrick, Canning; *Style*— The Rt Hon Viscount Montgomery of Alamein, CMG, CBE; ✉ 2/97 Onslow Square, London SW7 3LU (✆ 020 7589 8747)

MONTROSE, 8 Duke of (S 1707); Sir James Graham; 11 Bt (S 1625), of Braco; also Lord Graham (S 1445), Earl of Montrose (S 1505), Marquess of Montrose (S 1644, new charter granted 1706), Marquess of Graham and Buchanan, Earl of Kincardine, Viscount Dundaff, Lord Aberuthven, Mugdock and Fintrie (all S 1707), Earl Graham and Baron Graham (GB 1722); also Hereditary Sheriff of Dunbartonshire; s of 7 Duke of Montrose (d 1992), and his 1 w, Isobel Veronica, *née* Sellar (d 1990); *b* 6 April 1935, Salisbury, Rhodesia; *Educ* Loretto; *m* 1970, Catherine Elizabeth MacDonnell (d 2014), yst da of Capt Norman Andrew Thompson Young (d 1942), Queen's Own Cameron Highlanders of Canada; 1 da (Lady Hermione Elizabeth b 1971), 2 s (James Alexander Norman, Marquess of Graham b 1973, Lord Ronald John Christopher b 1975); *Heir* s, Marquess of Graham; *Career* farmer and landowner; Capt Queen's Body Guard for Scotland (Royal Co of Archers) 2006–14 (Ensign 2001–03, Lt 2003–06); sits as Cons in House of Lords (elected hereditary peer 1999–), former oppn whip, oppn spokesman for Scottish affrs until 2010; memb Cncl NFU of Scotland 1981–86 and 1987–90 (vice-chm Loch Lomond and Trossachs Working Pty 1991–93), pres Royal Highland and Agricultural Soc of Scotland 1997–98, hon pres Nat Sheep Assoc 2010–; chm Buchanan Community Cncl 1982–93; FRAgS 2012 (ARAgS 2009); OStJ 1978; *Clubs* Royal Scottish Pipers' Soc, Royal Highland Agric Soc, The Farmers; *Style*— His Grace the Duke of Montrose; ✉ Montrose Estates Ltd, Buchanan Castle, Drymen, Glasgow G63 0HY (✆ and fax 01360 870382); House of Lords, London SW1A 0PW (✆ 020 7219 3000, fax 020 7219 5979, e-mail montrosej@parliament.uk)

MOODY, Prof (Anthony) David; s of Edward Tabrum Moody, of Dunedin, NZ, and Nora, *née* Gordon; *b* 21 January 1932; *Educ* St Patrick's Coll Wellington, Canterbury Coll Univ of NZ (MA), Univ of Oxford (MA); *Career* Shirtcliffe fell Univ of NZ 1953–55, asst info offr UNHCR Geneva 1957–58, sr lectr Univ of Melbourne 1958–64, Nuffield Fndn travelling fell 1965, memb Dept of English and Related Literature Univ of York 1966–99 (emeritus prof 2000–); fell English Assoc (FEA); *Books* Virginia Woolf (1963), Shakespeare: 'The Merchant of Venice' (1964), 'The Waste Land' In Different Voices (ed, 1972), Thomas Stearns Eliot: Poet (1979 and 1994), At the Antipodes: Homage to Paul Valèry (1982), News Odes: The El Salvador Sequence (1984), The Cambridge Companion to T S Eliot (ed, 1994), Tracing T S Eliot's Spirit: Essays (1996), Ezra Pound: Poet, A Portrait of the Man and His Work – Vol 1, the Young Genius 1885–1920 (2007), Ezra Pound to His Parents: Letters 1895–1929 (jt ed, 2010), Ezra Pound: Poet – Vol 2, The Epic Years 1921–1939 (2014), Ezra Pound: Poet – Vol 3, The Tragic Years 1939–1972 (2015); *Recreations* listening, looking, hill walking; *Style*— Prof A David Moody; ✉ Church Green House, Old Church Lane, Pateley Bridge, North Yorkshire HG3 5LZ

MOODY, Lewis Walton; MBE (2004); *b* 12 June 1978, Ascot, Berks; *Educ* Oakham Sch; *Career* rugby union player (flanker); with Leicester Tigers RUFC until 2010 (winners Madrid Sevens 1997, winners four successive Premiership titles 1999–2002, winners Heineken Cup 2001 and 2002, winner Guinness Premiership 2007, winner EDF Cup 2007), Bath Rugby 2010–; England: 56 caps, debut v Canada 2001, ranked no 1 team in world 2003, winners Six Nations Championship 2003 (Grand Slam), winners World Cup Aust 2003, finalists World Cup France 2007; memb Br & I Lions tour squad NZ 2005 (2 Test caps); Zurich England Young Player of the Season 2001/02; *Style*— Mr Lewis Moody, MBE

MOODY, Nicola; *Educ* Saffron Walden Co HS, Cambridge Coll of Arts and Educn, Univ of York (BA), Middlesex Poly (Dip Film and TV); *Career* researcher rising to dir BBC Manchester 1987–88, documentaries dir Diverse Productions 1988, dir, prodr and dep ed (documentaries and feature) BBC TV London 1988–94, ed Reportage BBC Manchester 1994–96, exec prodr factual series 1995–97, commissioning exec then head of factual commissioning Ind Commissioning Gp BBC London 1997–2000, controller factual commissioning BBC TV 2000–03, acting controller BBC4 2003, cmmr documentaries and contemporary factual BBC TV 2003–05, dir of factual progs Optomen TV 2005–; memb RTS 1999; *Recreations* writing, film, walking; *Style*— Ms Nicola Moody

MOODY, Philip Edward; s of Frederick Osborne Moody, and Hilda Laura, *née* Frost; *b* 27 July 1954, Chippenham, Wilts; *Educ* Bentley GS Calne; *m* 1 (m dis 2008); *m* 2, 26 Dec 2014, Marjorie Ann Readman; *Career* CA; articled clerk Monahan & Co Chippenham 1972–82; Solomon Hare: fndr ptnr Chippenham 1983–88, sr ptnr and lead corporate finance ptnr Bristol 1989–2005, managing ptnr Bristol 2005–07; dir Centaur Grain Ltd 1990–2008, corp devpt dir Dairy Farmers of Britain Ltd 2003–08, head of corp fin Smith & Williamson 2005– (dir 2005–14), dir Food & Farming Fndn Ltd, dir Grand Central Railway Co Ltd 2007–11; chm: Oakfield Grove Properties Ltd 1996–, Berry Gardens BV 2006–08; non-exec dir: Locker Gp Pty Ltd 2003–06, Openfield Gp Ltd 2008–, Dawnfresh Holdings Ltd 2014–; govr Royal Agricultural Univ 2007–, govr Bolton Wanderers Free School 2015; FCA 1990 (ACA 1980), ATII 1982; *Recreations* Formula 1, walking, photography, snooker, cricket; *Style*— Philip Moody, Esq; ✉ Smith & Williamson, Portwall Place, Portwall Lane, Bristol BS1 6NA (✆ 07836 360084, e-mail philip_moody@btinternet.com)

MOODY-STUART, Sir Mark; KCMG (2000); s of Sir Alexander Moody-Stuart, and Judith, *née* Henzell; *b* 15 September 1940, Antigua; *Educ* Univ of Cambridge (BA, PhD); *m* Judy; 3 s, 1 da; *Career* Royal Dutch/Shell Group: joined Shell Internationale Petroleum Maatschappij BV as geologist 1966, worked as geologist in Spain, Oman and Brunei 1966–72, chief geologist Australia 1972–76, i/c North Sea oil exploration teams 1976–78, servs mangr Brunei 1978–79, mangr Western Div Shell Petroleum Development Co of Nigeria 1979–82, gen mangr Shell Group of Cos Turkey 1982–86, chm and chief exec Shell Cos in Malaysia 1986–90, gp exploration and prodn coordinator 1990–94, dir Shell International Petroleum Co 1991–2001, a gp md 1991–2001, chm Shell Transport and Trading Co plc 1997–2001 (an md 1991–97), non-exec dir 2001–05; chm: Anglo American plc 2002–09, Hermes EOS 2009–16; dir Accenture 2001–15, non-exec dir HSBC Holdings plc 2001–10, non-exec dir Saudi Aramco 2007–; chm Business Action for Sustainable Devpt 2001–02, co-chm G8 Renewable Energy Taskforce 2000–01, memb UN Sec Gen's Advsy Cncl for the Global Compact 2001–04, vice-chair UN Global Compact Bd and chm Global Compact Fndn 2006–, chm Innovative Vector Control Consortium 2008–, hon co-chm International Tax and Investment Center 2011–; pres Liverpool Sch of Tropical Med 2001–08, chm Int Advsy Cncl SOAS 2004–09; govr Nuffield Hosps 2000–08; author of articles in scientific and other jls; FGS (pres 2002–04), FRGS; *Books* Responsible Leadership – Lessons from the Front Line of Sustainability and Ethics (2014); *Recreations* sailing, travel; *Clubs* Travellers; *Style—* Sir Mark Moody-Stuart, KCMG; ✉ 9 Gun House, 122 Wapping High Street, London E1W 2N

MOON, Madeleine; MP; da of Albert Edward Ironside, and Hilda, *née* Greener; *b* 27 March 1950, Sunderland; *m* 2 June 1983, Stephen John Moon; 1 s (David Stephen b 16 May 1984); *Career* social worker Care Standards Inspectorate until 2005; former Mayor Porthcawl, cncllr Porthcawl 1992–, rep Bridgend CBC on Sports Cncl for Wales and Tourism S and W Wales Ctee, nat chair Br Resorts Assoc 1999–2001; MP (Lab) Bridgend 2005–; *Style—* Mrs Madeleine Moon, MP; ✉ House of Commons, London SW1A 0AA

MOON, Richard John; *b* 3 January 1959, London; *Educ* Chase Sch Enfield, Wadham Coll Oxford (MA), LSE (PhD); *m* Sandra Sheila Francis Eddis (d 2009); 1 s, 1 da; *Career* diplomat; joined FCO 1983, 2 sec political Jakarta 1984–88, EU Dept (Internal) FCO 1988–90, head of section Security Policy Dept FCO 1990–92, first sec political affrs Rome 1993–95, first sec economic and EU affrs Rome 1995–97, dep head EU Directorate (External) FCO 1997–99, finance cnsllr then memb UN Advsy Ctee on Administrative and Budgetary Questions UKMIS NY 1999–2004, UK dep perm rep Orgn for Economic Co-operation and Devpt Paris 2005–07, ambass to Latvia 2007–09, FCO 2009–11, memb UN Advsy Ctee on Administrative and Budgetary Questions UKMis NY 2011–16, dep ambass Br Embassy Kabul 2016–; *Recreations* history of art, marathon running; *Style—* Mr Richard Moon; ✉ FCO, King Charles Street, London SW1A 2AH

MOONCEY, His Hon Judge Ebraham Mohamed; s of late Mohamed Gantawalla-Patel, and Amina Patel; *b* Jogwad, Gujarat, India; *Educ* Stoneygate Coll Leicester, Linwood Secondary Modern Leicester, Gateway Sixth Form Leicester, Kingston Poly (LLB), Inns of Court Sch of Law London (Bar Finals); *m*; *Career* called to the Bar Gray's Inn 1983; recorder 2004–09, circuit judge 2009–; memb Ctee Cncl of Circuit Judges 2014–; tutor judge The Judicial Coll 2016–; *Recreations* tennis, gardening; *Style—* His Hon Judge Mooncey; ✉ c/o Midland Circuit Secretariat, The Priory Courts, 33 Bull Street, Birmingham B4 6DW

MOONEY, Bel; da of Edward Mooney, and Gladys, *née* Norbury; *b* 8 October 1946; *Educ* Aigburth Vale Girls' HS Liverpool, Trowbridge Girls' HS, UCL (BA); *m* 1, 1968 (m dis 2006), Jonathan Dimbleby, *qv*, s of Richard Dimbleby, CBE (d 1965); 1 s (Daniel Richard b 1974), 1 da (Katharine Rose b 1980); m 2, 2007, Robin Allison-Smith; *Career* asst to the ed then contributing ed Nova magazine 1971–75, freelance contrib (The Guardian, The Times, The Observer, New Statesman, Sunday Times, Daily Express, Daily Mail amongst others) 1972–; columnist: Cosmopolitan, The Mirror, Sunday Times, The Listener, The Times, Daily Mail 2007–; TV presenter 1980–86 (Mothers by Daughters (C4), Fathers by Sons (C4), Dora Russell (BBC2), Ellen Wilkinson (BBC2)), presenter Radio 4 1985–2002 (Women: Equal Sex?, American Authors, Turning Points, A Perspective for Living, Devout Sceptics); ed Proof Magazine 2000–01; dir Friends of Great Ormond Street 1993–97, dir Theatre Royal Bath 2009–14; Hon DLitt Univ of Bath 1998; fell UCL 1994, hon fell Liverpool John Moores Univ 2002; *Non-Fiction Books* The Year of the Child (1979), Differences of Opinion (1984), Bel Mooney's Somerset (1989), Perspectives for Living (1992), Devout Sceptics (2003), Small Dogs Can Save Your Life (2010), LifeLines: Words to Help You Through (2015); *Novels* The Windsurf Boy (1983), The Anderson Question (1985), The Fourth of July (1988), Lost Footsteps (1993), Intimate Letters (1997), The Invasion of Sand (2005); *Children's Books* Liza's Yellow Boat (also illustrated by the author, 1980), I Don't Want To! (1985), The Stove Haunting (1986), I Can't Find It! (1988), It's Not Fair (1989), A Flower of Jet (1990), But You Promised! (1990), Why Not? (1990), I Know! (1991), I'm Scared (1994), The Voices of Silence (1994), I Wish! (1995), Why Me? (1996), I'm Bored (1997), Joining the Rainbow (1997), The Green Man (1997), It's Not My Fault (1999), So What! (2002), Kitty's Friends (2003), Mr Tubs is Lost! (2004), Who Loves Mr Tubs? (2006), Big Dog Bonnie (2007), Best Dog Bonnie (2007), Bad Dog Bonnie (2008), Brave Dog Bonnie (2009), Busy Dog Bonnie (2009), Bright Dog Bonnie (2010); *Satire* Father Kissmass and Mother Claws (with Gerald Scarfe, 1985); *Anthology* From This Day Forward (1989); *Recreations* literature, art, music, friends, churches; *Style—* Ms Bel Mooney; ✉ e-mail bel.mooney@dailymail.co.uk, website www.belmooney.co.uk

MOONEY, Kevin Michael; s of John Fergal Mooney (d 1984), and Bridget Mooney (d 1986); *b* 14 November 1945, Hammersmith, London; *Educ* Cardinal Vaughan Sch Kensington, Univ of Bristol (LLB); *m* 1 May 1972, Maureen; 2 s (Christopher James b 9 Aug 1974, Benjamin John b 7 Sept 1976), 1 da (Charlotte Elizabeth b 28 March 1979); *Career* admitted slr 1971; Simmons & Simmons: slr 1971–73, ptnr 1973–, memb Bd 1999–2005; memb Advsy Bd European Patent Lawyers Assoc (past pres); *Recreations* farming in Majorca, supporting QPR FC; *Style—* Kevin Mooney, Esq; ✉ Simmons & Simmons, CityPoint, One Ropemaker Street, London EC2Y 9SS (☏ 020 7628 2020, fax 020 7628 2070, e-mail kevin.mooney@simmons-simmons.com)

MOONIE, Baron (Life Peer UK 2005), of Bennochy in Fife; Dr Lewis George Moonie; *b* 25 February 1947; *Educ* Grove Acad Dundee, Univ of St Andrews (MB ChB), Univ of Edinburgh (MSc); *m*; 2 c; *Career* jr med posts 1970–75, DPM 1975, sr med advsr and clinical pharmacologist in the pharmaceutical indust in Holland, Switzerland and Edinburgh 1976–80, conslt in public health Fife Health Bd 1984–87 (trainee in community med 1980–84), MP (Lab) Kirkcaldy 1987–2005; memb Treasy Select Ctee 1988–89; oppn spokesman: trade and industry 1989–92, science and technol 1992–94, industry 1994–95, nat heritage 1995–97; Parly under-sec of state MOD 2000–; memb Liaison Select Ctee 1997–; non-exec dir AEA Technology 2004–; MFCM 1984, MRCPsych 1979; *Style—* The Rt Hon the Lord Moonie; ✉ House of Lords, London SW1A 0PW

MOONMAN, Prof Eric; OBE (1991); s of Borach Moonman (d 1953), and Leah, *née* Bernstein (d 1959); *b* 29 April 1929; *Educ* Christ Church Southport, Univ of Manchester (MSc), Univ of Liverpool (Dip Social Sci); *m* m 1 (m dis); 2 s (Daniel b 10 July 1965, Joshua b 27 Jan 1972), 1 da (Natasha b 19 April 1968); m 2, 11 Feb 2001, Gillian Louise, da of Joseph Mayer, and Muriel Mayer; *Career* Nat Serv Kings Liverpool Regt 1951–53; human rels advsr Br Inst Mgmnt 1956–62, leader of Stepney Cncl 1958–62, memb Tower Hamlets Cncl 1963–67; MP: Basildon 1966–70, Billericay 1974–79; govr BFI 1978–83, dir Gp Rels Educn Tst 1979–88, chm Islington HA 1980–90, memb Bloomsbury and Islington DHA 1990–93; HM treas Toynbee Hall 1979–93, sr vice-pres Bd of Deps of Br Jews 1986–91 and 1994–2000, visiting prof of health mgmnt City Univ 1990–2005; dir Natural History Museum Tst 1990–92, chair Friends of Natural History Museum 2007–11; chm Essex Radio 1991–2001; consIt Int Red Cross Namibia and Zimbabwe 1992–95, chair Continuing Care Appeals Panel City of Liverpool 1996–2005, memb Advsy Bd Centre for Counter Terrorism Studies, Potomac Inst Washington; tstee Everton FC Former Players Fndn, exec Assoc of Former MPs 2009–; FIMgt 1959; *Books* The Manager and the Organisation (1961), Communications in an Expanding Organisation (1970), Reluctant Partnership (1971), Alternative Government (1984), Violent Society (1987), Learning to Live in the Violent Society (2006); *Recreations* cinema, theatre, football; *Style—* Prof Eric Moonman, OBE; ✉ 1 Beacon Hill, London N7 9LY (☏ 01704 551325)

MOOR, Jonathan Edward; CBE (2011); s of Rev David Drury Moor (d 2005), and Evangeline Margaret, *née* White (d 1994); *b* 23 June 1964, Bournemouth, Dorset; *Educ* Canford Sch Wimborne, Univ of Kent at Canterbury (BA); *m* 30 June 1990 (m dis 2015), Sara Louise, *née* Stratton; 3 da (Sophia b 5 March 1992, Olivia b 5 Nov 1993, Serena b 8 March 1999); *Career* Touche Ross & Co 1985–91; Audit Cmmn: various roles 1991–2000, fin dir 2000–03; Dept for Tport: dir of strategy and resources 2003–06, dir of airports strategy 2006–09, DG for civil aviation 2009–13, DG resources and strategy 2013–; non-exec memb Audit and Risk Ctee DEFRA, chm Evaluation and Audit Advsy Ctee Int Civil Aviation Org; vice-pres European Civil Aviation Conf; FCA 2001 (ACA 1989), CPFA 2016; *Recreations* family, travel, DIY; *Style—* Jonathan Moor, Esq, CBE; ✉ Department for Transport, Zone 4/26, Great Minster House, 33 Horseferry Road, London SW1P 4DR (☏ 020 7944 4597, e-mail jonathan.moor@dft.gsi.gov.uk, website www.dft.gov.uk)

MOOR, Hon Mr Justice; Sir Philip Drury Moor; kt (2011), QC (2001); s of late Rev David Moor, and Evangeline, *née* White; *b* 15 July 1959; *Educ* Canford Sch, Pembroke Coll Oxford; *m* 18 July 1987, Gillian Elizabeth, *née* Stark; 2 da (Alice Elizabeth b 24 May 1992, Emily Ruth b 9 Sept 1995); *Career* called to the Bar Inner Temple 1982 (bencher 2004, chm Scholarship Ctee 2010–12); recorder of the Crown Court 2003–11, head of chambers 1 Hare Court 2007, judge of the High Court of Justice (Family Div) 2011– (dep judge 2009–11), liaison judge for Wales Family Div 2012–; chm Family Law Bar Assoc 2004–05 (vice-chm 2002–2003, actg treas 2000–01); memb: Gen Cncl of the Bar 1987–89, 2004–05 and 2009, Cncl of Legal Educn 1988–91 (memb Bd of Examiners 1989–92), Phillips Ctee on Financing Pupillage 1989, Professional Standards Ctee 2002–03 (vice-chm 2003); tstee Gingerbread 2010–11; govr Royal Russell Sch Croydon 2009–; hon fell Pembroke Coll Oxford 2013; *Books* contrib to Family Law; *Recreations* cricket, association football; *Clubs* MCC; *Style—* The Hon Mr Justice Moor; ✉ Royal Courts of Justice, Strand, London WC2A 2LL

MOORCOCK, Michael John; s of Arthur Edward Moorcock, of Worthing, W Sussex, and June, *née* Taylor; *b* 18 December 1939; *Educ* Michael Hall Sch Forest Row, Pitman's Coll Croydon; *m* 1, 25 Oct 1962 (m dis 1978), Hilary Denham Bailey; 2 da (Sophie Elizabeth b 3 Sept 1963, Katherine Helen b 5 Sept 1964), 1 s (Max Edward b 24 Feb 1971); m 2, 7 May 1978 (m dis 1983), Jill Riches; m 3, 23 Sept 1983, Linda Mullens Steele; *Career* author 1956–; ed: Tarzan Adventures 1957–, Fleetway Publications 1959–, Liberal Party 1961–, New Worlds 1964–; awards incl: August Derleth Award (four times, 1971–75), Nebula Award 1968, World Fantasy Award 1979, Guardian Fiction Prize 1977, World Fantasy Lifetime Achievement Award 2000, Prix Utopia 2004, Bram Stoker Award 2005, SF Grand Master 2008; memb: Womankind Worldwide, Amnesty Int, PEN Int Royal Overseas League, Soc of Authors; *Books* over 80 books incl: Byzantium Endures (1981), The Laughter of Carthage (1984), Mother London (1988), Jerusalem Commands (1992), Blood (1994), Fabulous Harbours (1995), The War Amongst the Angels (1996), Tales from the Texas Woods (1997), King of the City (2000), London Bone (2001), The Dream Thief's Daughter (2002), The Skrayling Tree (2003), The Lives and Times of Jerry Cornelius (2003), Wizardry and Wild Romance (2004), The Vengeance of Rome (2006), The Metatemporal Detective (2007), Modern Times 2.0 (2008), The Best of Michael Moorcock (2009), The Coming of the Terraphiles (2010), The Sunday Books, W.M. Peake (2011), Curare! (2012), The Whispering Swarm (2014); omnibus novels reissued 1992 and 1993: Von Bek, The Eternal Champion, Corum, Sailing to Utopia, The Nomad of the Time Streams, The Dancers at the End of Time, Elric of Melniboné, The New Nature of the Catastrophe, The Prince with the Silver Hand, Legends from the End of Time, Stormbringer, Earl Aubec, Count Brass, Gloriana, The Brothel in Rosenstrasse, Behold the Man, Breakfast in the Ruins, Jerry Cornelius Quartet, A Cornelius Calendar; The Michael Moorcock Collection (collected edn of all fantastic ficition, 2013–15); ed of numerous anthologies, collections and short stories; *Recreations* camel racing, mountaineering; *Style—* Michael Moorcock, Esq; ✉ Old Circle Squared, PO Box 1230, Lost Pines, Texas 78602, USA (e-mail corneliusjcx@aol.com); Chez Agence Hoffman, 77 boulevard St Michel, 75005 Paris, France

MOORE, Prof Adrian William; s of Victor George Moore, of Wilmslow, Cheshire, and Audrey Elizabeth, *née* Wallis; *b* 29 December 1956, Kettering, Northants; *Educ* Manchester Grammar, King's Coll Cambridge (MA), Balliol Coll Oxford (BPhil, John Locke Prize, DPhil); *Career* lectr UC Oxford 1982–85, jr research fell King's Coll Cambridge 1985–88, tutorial fell St Hugh's Coll Oxford 1988–, prof of philosophy Univ of Oxford 2004– (lectr 1988–2004); memb: Editorial Ctee European Jl of Philosophy 2003–14, Exec Ctee Mind Assoc 2005–14, Exec Ctee Br Philosophical Assoc 2005–11, Cncl Royal Inst of Philosophy 2008–11, Exec Ctee Aristotelian Soc 2013–16; pres Aristotelian Soc 2014–15; Leverhulme maj research fell 2006–09; Meaning and Reference (ed, 1993), Infinity (ed, 1993), Points of View (1997), The Infinite (1990, 2 edn 2001), Noble in Reason, Infinite in Faculty: Themes and Variations in Kant's Moral and Religious Philosophy (2003), Bernard Williams: Philosophy as a Humanistic Discipline (ed, 2006), The Evolution of Modern Metaphysics: Making Sense of Things (2012), Contemporary Kantian Metaphysics: New Essays on Space and Time (co-ed, 2012); *Recreations* lifelong Manchester City FC supporter; *Style—* Prof A W Moore; ✉ St Hugh's College, Oxford OX2 6LE (☏ 01865 274953, fax 01865 274912, e-mail adrian.moore@philosophy.ox.ac.uk)

MOORE, Austin; s of Michael Moore, of Whatton, Notts, and Shirley, *née* Hutchins; *b* 5 February 1963, Leeds; *Educ* Leeds GS, Univ of Manchester (LLB); *Children* 2 da (Lucy Ann b 19 March 1994, Sarah Elizabeth b 4 Oct 1995), 1 s (James Augustin b 29 Sept 1998); *Career* admitted slr 1992; slr specialising in corporate law and corporate finance; ptnr HBJ Gateley Wareing; memb Cncl Notts Law Soc 1998–, memb Law Soc; chm Notts Multiple Sclerosis Soc 1996–2000; *Publications* The Owner-Managed Business, Business Sale; *Recreations* drums and music; *Clubs* Nottingham; *Style—* Austin Moore, Esq; ✉ 177A Melton Road, West Bridgford, Nottingham NG2 6JL (☏ 0115 846 5007, e-mail austin_moore4@hotmail.com); HBJ Gateley Wareing LLP, City Gate East, Tollhouse Hill, Nottingham NG1 5FS (☏ 0115 983 8216, fax 0115 983 8201, e-mail amoore@hbj-gw.com)

MOORE, Brian; *m* ; 2 s; *Career* joined Police Serv 1975, served with Lancs Constabulary and Met Police Serv, dep chief constable Surrey Police, chief constable Wilts Police 2008–12, head UK Border Force 2012–; *Style—* Brian Moore, Esq

MOORE, Prof Brian Cecil Joseph; *b* 10 February 1946; *Educ* Sir Walter St John's GS Battersea, St Catharine's Coll Cambridge (exhibitioner, MA), Univ of Cambridge (PhD); *m* Dr Hedwig Gockel; *Career* lectr in psychology Univ of Reading 1971–73, Fulbright-

M

Hays sr scholar and visiting prof Dept of Psychology Brooklyn Coll City Univ NY 1973–74, lectr in psychology Univ of Reading 1974–77; Univ of Cambridge: lectr in experimental psychology 1977–89, reader in auditory perception 1989–95, prof of auditory perception 1995–; fell Wolfson Coll Cambridge 1983–; Univ of Calif Berkeley: visiting researcher 1985, visiting prof Dept of Psychology 1990; visiting conslt prof Dept of Bioengineering Univ of Ulster 1991–93; pres Assoc of Independent Hearing Healthcare Professionals; memb: Experimental Psychology Soc, Cambridge Philosophical Soc, Br Soc of Audiology, American Speech-Language-Hearing Assoc, Audio Engrg Soc, American Auditory Soc, Assoc for Research in Otolaryngology; memb Editorial Bd: Int Jl of Audiology, Jl Audiology and Neuro-otology, Hearing Research; sometime memb various MRC ctees and advsy gps 1979–95 (incl Hearing Research Ctee 1986–94); T S Littler prize Br Soc of Audiology 1983 and 2006, Silver Medal Acoustical Soc of America 2003, Int Award in Hearing American Acad of Audiology 2004, Award of Merit Assoc for Research in Otolaryngology 2008, Hugh Knowles Prize for Distinguished Achievement 2008, T S Littler Lectureship Br Soc of Audiology 2013, Gold Medal Acoustical Soc of America 2014; hon doctorate Adam Mickiewicz Univ Poland; fell Acoustical Soc of America 1985, Van Houten fell Inst for Perception Research Eindhoven 1994, hon fell Belgian Soc of Audiology 1997, hon fell Br Soc of Hearing Aid Audiologists 1999, FMedSci 2001, FRS 2002, fell Audio Engrg Soc 2016; *Books* An Introduction to the Psychology of Hearing (1977, 6 edn 2012), Frequency Selectivity in Hearing (ed, 1986), Auditory Frequency Selectivity (jt ed, 1986), Hearing (ed, 1995), Perceptual Consequences of Cochlear Damage (1995), Cochlear Hearing Loss (1998, 2 edn 2007), New Developments in Hearing and balance (jt ed, 2002), The Perception of Speech: from Sound to Meaning (jt ed, 2008), Basic Aspects of Hearing: Physiology and Perception (jt ed, 2013) Auditory Processing of Temporal Fine Structure: Effects of Age and Hearing Loss (2014); also author of numerous book chapters, papers and articles in learned jls; *Recreations* playing guitar; *Style—* Prof Brian Moore; ✉ Department of Experimental Psychology, University of Cambridge, Downing Street, Cambridge CB2 3EB (☎ 01223 333574, fax 01223 333564, e-mail bcjm@cam.ac.uk, website http://hearing.psychol.cam.ac.uk)

MOORE, Charles Hilary; s of Richard Gillachrist Moore, and Ann Hilary, *née* Miles; *b* 31 October 1956; *Educ* Eton, Trinity Coll Cambridge (BA); *m* 1981, Caroline Mary (former fell Peterhouse Cambridge), da of Ralph Lambert Baxter, of Etchingham Sussex; 2 c (William, Katharine (twins) b 1 April 1990); *Career* journalist and author; editorial staff Daily Telegraph 1979, ldr writer Daily Telegraph 1981–83, asst ed and political columnist The Spectator 1983–84, ed The Spectator 1984–90, weekly columnist The Daily Express 1987–90, fortnightly column Another Voice The Spectator 1990–95, dep ed The Daily Telegraph 1990–92, ed The Sunday Telegraph 1992–95, ed The Daily Telegraph 1995–2003, gp consltg ed The Telegraph Gp 2004–, weekly columnist The Daily Telegraph and The Spectator 2004–; chm Policy Exchange 2005–; memb Cncl Benenden Sch 2000–09, tstee T E Utley Meml Fund, chm Rectory Soc; Hon DLitt Univ of Buckingham 2007; *Publications* 1936 (ed with C Hawtree, 1986), The Church in Crisis (with A N Wilson and Gavin Stamp, 1986), A Tory Seer – The Selected Journalism of T E Utley (ed with Simon Heffer, 1989), Margaret Thatcher: The Authorised Biography Vol I: Not for Turning (2013); *Clubs* Beefsteak, White's; *Style—* Charles Moore, Esq

MOORE, Charlotte; *Career* BBC: commissioning exec for documentaries 2006–09, commissioning ed of documentaries 2009–12, acting controller BBC Daytime TV 2013, controller BBC 1 2013–; *Style—* Ms Charlotte Moore; ✉ BBC Broadcasting House, Portland Place, London W1A 1AA

MOORE, Christopher M; o s of Sir Harry Moore, CBE (d 2001); *b* 1 December 1944; *Educ* Winchester, Pembroke Coll Cambridge (MA); *m* 2 Sept 1972, Charlotte C, da of J Glessing, of Montague, Hankham, E Sussex; 3 s (Tercel R, Wilaf M, Frederic C); *Career* investment banking/venture capital/businessman; Price Waterhouse 1966–70, Robert Fleming inc 1970–72, Lazards 1972–73; dir: Jardine Fleming and Co Ltd 1973–76, Robert Fleming and Co Ltd 1978–95, Robert Fleming Holdings Ltd 1986–95, Stop Loss Mutual Insurance Association Ltd 1992–2000, Income & Growth VCT plc 2001–10, Matrix Income & Growth VCT plc 2005–10, Matrix Income & Growth 3 VCT plc 2005–10; chm: Fleming Ventures Ltd 1992–2003, Moore Corporation 1995–, Calderburn plc 1996–99, Mobeus Income & Growth 4 VCT plc 2002–; sr advsr to Chm Lloyd's of London 1996–2000; chm Fight for Sight 2006–14; vice-chm Bletchley Park Tst; memb Hon Co of Air Pilots; FCA; *Recreations* agriculture, books, country sports, flying, music, tennis; *Clubs* Farmers', Leander, Pratt's, Royal Air Squadron, White's; *Style—* Christopher Moore, Esq; ✉ Thornborough Grounds, Buckingham MK18 2AB (☎ 01280 812170)

MOORE, Debbie; OBE (2010); *Children* 1 da (Lara b 1973); *Career* former fashion model; fndr and chm Pineapple Dance Studios 1979 (which joined unlisted securities market 1982, reprivatised 1988), 1 Pineapple centre with 10 studios opened in Covent Garden London 1979, fashion designer of Pineapple branded dance, fashion and casual wear for Pineapple shops and various outlets and catalogues; licensing deals covering eyewear, swimwear, lingerie, footwear, toiletries and exclusive clothing ranges; Dance Masterclass (home exercise video series) launched 2002; Pineapple Dance Studio documentary (Sky 1) 2010; Business Woman of the Year 1984; Hon MA Univ of Creative Arts 2011; *Books* Pineapple Dance Book (1983, paperback 1985), When A Woman Means Business (1989); *Style—* Ms Debbie Moore, OBE; ✉ Pineapple Holdings Ltd, 7 Langley Street, London WC2H 9JA (☎ 020 7379 8090, fax 020 7240 4537, e-mail mail@pineapple.uk.com)

MOORE, Fionna Patricia; MBE (2013); da of Maj Samuel James Moore, and Margaret Patricia Moore, *née* Boyd; *b* 18 May 1950, Jos, Nigeria; *Educ* Croydon HS for Girls (GPDST), UCL (BSc), UCH Med Sch (MB BS); *m* 12 April 1980, Richard Philip Ward; 2 s (Jonathan b 1982, Patrick b 1988), 2 da (Victoria b 1975, Jennifer b 1985); *Career* registrar in gen surgery St James and St George's Hosps 1980–81, Bayer res fell UCH 1981–83 (registrar in surgery 1978–80), sr registrar in accident and emergency med Ealing Central Middx and Hammersmith Hosps 1983–85; conslt in accident and emergency med: UCH and Middx Hosp 1985–94, John Radcliffe Coll Oxford 1994–96, Hammersmith Hosp NHS Tst 1996–; Imperial Coll Healthcare Tst 2008–; currently med dir London Ambulance Service; memb RSM, FRCS, FRCSEd, FFAEM, FCEM, FIMC, RCS(Ed); OStJ; *Recreations* reading, music, walking; *Style—* Dr Fionna Moore, MBE

MOORE, Henrietta; DBE (2016); da of Stephen Andrew Moore, of Yorkshire, and Josephine Anne Jane Mary Moore (d 1993); *b* 18 May 1957, Saunderton; *Educ* Durham Univ (BA), Newnham Coll Cambridge (PhD); *Career* social anthropologist; LSE: dir Gender Inst 1994–99, govr 1999–2005, dep dir for research and external relations 2002–05, dir Culture and Knowledge Prog Centre for Global Governance 2005–11; William Wyse chair of social anthropolgy Cambridge 2008–14, currently dir Inst for Global Prosperity and chair Culture, Philosophy and Design UCL; memb Global Food Security Prog Advsy 2015–, memb Scientific Advsy Cncl Dept of Environment, Food and Rural Affrs UK 2016–; pres Cncl Br Inst Eastern Africa 2016–; tstee Barbican Arts Centre 2011–; FRSA 2000, FAcSS 2001, FBA 2007; *Publications* Feminism and Anthropology (1988), Cutting Down Trees: Gender, Nutrition and Change in the Northern Province of Zambia 1890–1990 (with M A Vaughan, 1994, winner Herskovits Prize for the Best Book Published on Africa 1995), A Passion for Difference: Essays in Anthropology and Gender (1994), Space, Text and Gender: An Anthropological Study of Marakwet of Kenya (2 edn with new introduction and conclusion, 1996), The Subject of Anthropology: Gender, Symbolism and Psychoanalysis (2007), Still Life: Hopes, Desires and Satisfactions (2011); *Recreations* gardening, opera, travel, walking; *Clubs* Groucho; *Style—* Prof Dame Henrietta Moore, DBE; ✉ UCL Institute for Global Prosperity, The Bartlett, UCL Faculty of the Built Environment, Gower Street, London WC1E 6BT (☎ 020 7679 2000, website www.henriettalmoore.com, Twitter @MooreHL)

MOORE, Jane; da of Prof John Moore, of Oxford, and Patricia, *née* Richardson; *b* 17 May 1962; *Educ* Worcester Girls' GS, South Glamorgan Inst of HE Cardiff (Dip); *Career* journalist; trainee reporter Solihull 1981–83, news reporter Birmingham Post and Mail 1983–86, freelance reporter The People 1986–, pop columnist The Sun 1986–87, freelance researcher Thames News 1987–88; Today: feature writer 1988, Royal corr 1989, dep news ed 1989, feature ed 1990; features ed The Mirror 1993–95, women's ed and columnist The Sun 1995–99; columnist The Sun 2000–, writer The Sunday Times 2000–, columnist GQ 2008–; co-presenter: Loose Women (ITV) 2000–, Crimewatch Daily (BBC) 2001; regular presenter on This Morning (ITV) 2002–; presenter Breakfast Show LBC Radio 2003–04; authored documentaries: The Beckhams (Sky One) 2004, Spoilt Children (Channel 4) 2004, Mothers Who Leave (Sky One) 2004, Supermarket Secrets (Channel 4) 2005, Dispatches (What's Really in Your Christmas Dinner?) 2005, (Fast Food) 2006, (Obesity, Wine) 2007, (Supermarket Labelling, Cervical Cancer Vaccine) 2008, (Government Waste) 2009, (Banking Crisis) 2009 and (Debt Collectors) 2009, What's In Your..? (BBC 2) 2010, Wonderstuff (BBC 2) 2011, Dispatches: 5-A-Day (2012), Dispatches: Weightwatchers (2013); Grumpy Old Women 2005–06; *Novels* Fourplay, The Ex Files, Dot. Homme, The Second Wives Club, Perfect Match, Love Is On The Air; *Recreations* photography; *Style—* Ms Jane Moore; ✉ The Sun, 1 London Bridge Street, London SE1 9GF (☎ 020 7782 4000, fax 020 7782 4063, e-mail jane.moore@the-sun.co.uk); literary agent: Jonathan Lloyd, Curtis Brown, Haymarket House, 28–29 Haymarket, London SW1Y 4SP

MOORE, John Edward; s of late Sqdn Ldr Joseph Enos Moore (d 1995), of Marlow, Bucks, and Audrey Sheila, *née* Matthews (d 1997); *b* 15 November 1947; *Educ* Royal GS High Wycombe, Univ of London (LLB); *m* 1, 12 April 1971 (m dis 1998), Diana, da of John Horend Dixon, MBE, of Ealing; 3 s (James b 1974, Alexander b 1976, Thomas b 1988); m 2, 1 May 1999, Lucy, da of George Tsourous, of N Wales; 1 da (Matilda b 2000), 1 s (Henry b 2004); *Career* civilian gliding instr RAF(VR)T 1967–77; admitted slr 1973; Macfarlanes: joined 1979, head property dept 1986–94, currently ptnr in charge healthcare; lectr and author of articles on agric law, public and private sector partnerships, commercial property, and property jt ventures; memb: Agric Law Assoc, City of London Slrs Co, Law Soc; *Recreations* flying; *Style—* John Moore, Esq; ✉ Messrs Macfarlanes, 10 Norwich Street, London EC4A 1BD (☎ 020 7831 9222, fax 020 7831 9607, telex 296381)

MOORE, Dame Julie; DBE (2012); da of Edward James Moore, of Liverpool, and Kathleen Mary, *née* Downey; *b* 18 August 1958, Liverpool; *Educ* BSc, MA; *Partner* Lesley Ann Pattenson (civil partnership 8 July 2006); *Career* clinical posts Leeds 1980–89, nurse mgmnt Leeds 1989–93, gen mgmnt 1993–2002; Univ Hosp Birmingham NHS Fndn Tst: exec dir of operations 2002–06, chief exec 2006–; hon prof Univ of Warwick 2013; memb: Ct Univ of Birmingham, Faculty Advsy Bd Univ of Warwick Medical Sch; FRSA; *Recreations* music, opera, reading, cycling, travel, walking; *Style—* Dame Julie Moore, DBE; ✉ THQ, PO Box 9551, Mindelsohn Way, Edgbaston, Birmingham B15 2PR (☎ 0121 371 4311, e-mail julie.moore@uhb.nhs.uk, website www.uhb.nhs.uk, Twitter @ceojuliem)

MOORE, Dr Kevin Charles; s of Dr Donald Charles Moore (d 1989), and Nellie Partington (d 1985); *b* 25 January 1941; *Educ* Giggleswick Sch, Univ of Manchester Med Sch (MB ChB); *m* 23 Feb 1972, Jillian Margaret, da of Frank Bromley (d 1984); 1 da (Alison b 1972); *Career* conslt anaesthetist Oldham 1973–2001, chm Med Staff Ctee Oldham 1981–85, chm Rochdale Private Surgical Unit 1983–88, dir Highfield Private Hosp Rochdale 1988–91; vice-pres Int Laser Therapy Assoc 1988–94, treas Br Med Laser Assoc 1987–98, treas World Assoc of Laser Therapy 1994–2011; memb Oldham HA 1987–90, pres Oldham Medical Soc 2002–03, pres Saddleworth Rotary Club 2006–07, pres Royal Soc of St George Halifax branch 2006–08; chm: Governing Cncl Dr Kershaw's Hospice Oldham 1992–2008 (memb 1982–92, med dir 1994–2008), Med Advsy Ctee BMI, Highfield Hosp 1991–97, Highfield M R Scanning plc 1992–99; pres Dr Kershaw's Hospice 2013–; Paul Harris fellowship Rotary Int 2008; FFARCS 1972; *Recreations* horse riding, carriage driving; *Style—* Dr Kevin Moore; ✉ Sherwood House, Field Lane, Wroot, Doncaster DN9 2BN (☎ 01302 775189, e-mail kevincmoore@outlook.com); Department of Anaesthesia, The Royal Oldham Hospital, Rochdale Road, Oldham, Lancashire OL1 2JH (☎ 0161 627 8828)

MOORE, Martin Luke; QC (2002); s of Brig Peter Moore, DSO**, MC, and (Enid) Rosemary, *née* Stokes; *b* 25 April 1960, Aldershot, Hants; *Educ* Winchester, Lincoln Coll Oxford; *m* 21 Sept 1985, Caroline Mary, *née* Mason; 3 da (Alexandra Emily b 1989, Laura Charlotte b 1991, Serena Frances b 1995); *Career* called to the Bar Lincoln's Inn 1982; barr specialising in company law; memb Erskine Chambers 1983–; memb: Commercial Bar Association, Chancery Bar Assoc, Insolvency Lawyers' Assoc, SE Circuit; *Recreations* equestrianism; *Clubs* Naval and Military; *Style—* Martin Moore, Esq, QC; ✉ Erskine Chambers, 33 Chancery Lane, London WC2A 1EN (☎ 020 7242 5532, website www.erkine-chambers.co.uk)

MOORE, Rt Hon Michael Kevin; PC (2010); s of Rev W Haisley Moore, and Jill, *née* Moorhead; *b* 3 June 1965; *Educ* Strathallan Sch, Jedburgh GS, Univ of Edinburgh (MA); *m* 2004, Alison Louise, *née* Hughes; 1 da (Ella); *Career* research asst to Archy Kirkwood, MP 1987–88, Coopers & Lybrand Edinburgh 1988–97; MP (Lib Dem): Tweeddale, Ettrick and Lauderdale 1997–2005, Berwickshire, Roxburgh and Selkirk 2005–15; memb Scottish Affrs Select Ctee 1997–99, Lib Dem spokesman on tport then on Scotland until 2001, dep Lib Dem spokesman for foreign affrs 2001–05, Lib Dem defence spokesman 2005–06, Lib Dem foreign affrs spokesman 2006–07, Lib Dem int devpt spokesman 2007–10, Lib Dem spokesman on Scotland and NI 2008–09, sec of state for Scotland 2010–13; dep ldr Scot Lib Dem Pty 2003–10; govr and vice-chm Westminster Fndn for Democracy 2002–05, memb Cncl RIIA 2004–10; govr Ditchley Fndn 2010–; memb: Amnesty Int, Charter 88, ICAS 1991–; *Recreations* jazz, film, music, hill walking, rugby; *Style—* The Rt Hon Michael Moore; ✉ House of Commons, London SW1A 0AA (☎ 020 7219 2236, fax 020 7219 0263, e-mail michaelmooremp@parliament.uk, website www.michaelmoore.org.uk)

MOORE, Mike; s of Jack Francis Moore, BEM, of Epsom, Surrey, and Joan Florence, *née* Walker; *b* 6 January 1954; *Educ* Bideford Sch of Art and Design, Reading Sch of Art and Design; *m* Helen; 1 s (Harry b 13 July 1990), 1 da (Sophie b 28 June 1992); *Career* photographer: Thomson Regnl Newspapers 1976–79, London Evening Standard 1980–85, The Today Newspaper 1986–93, Daily Mirror 1993–; *Awards* Midland Bank Press Awards commendation 1977 and 1978, World Press Photo Fndn Gold Medal 1978, Br Press Awards commendations 1981 and 1991, Ilford Press Awards commendation 1984 and 1991, Royal Photographer of the Year 1987, Press Photographer of the Year 1987, Kodak Press Awards commendation (two) 1991, Nikon Press Awards commendation 1991, News Photographer of the Year 1991, Gulf War Medal 1991, Photographer of the Year (UK Press Gazette) 1997, Royal Photographer of the Year and Feature Photographer of the Year (UK Picture Eds' Guild) 1997, Photographer of the Year (Amnesty Int) 2000, World Press Award 2004; *Books* Desert War (1991); *Style—* Mike Moore, Esq; ✉ The Daily Mirror Picture Desk, 1 Canada Square Canary Wharf, London E14 5AP (☎ 020 7293 3851, mobile 07710 613936)

MOORE, Nicholas Alan (Nick); s of Dr John M Moore (d 2005), and Jill, *née* Maycock (d 1995); *b* 16 July 1962; *Educ* Rugby, Magdalene Coll Cambridge (MA); *m* 3 October 1987,

Jane, *née* Clarke; 2 da (Natasha Louise b 24 Sept 1992, Charlotte Sarah b 24 Jan 1996); *Career* various copywriting positions 1985–89, dep creative dir Wunderman London 1989–92; creative dir: Sutch Webster WMGO 1992–95, Barraclough Hall Woolston Gray (latterly Proximity London) 1995–2000, TBWA/GGT 2000–04; exec creative dir TEQUILA/London 2005–06, chief creative offr Wunderman NY 2006–14, exec creative dir Roar 2014–; full memb D&AD, MIDM; awards: BDMA, DMA, Caples, Echo, Cannes, Effies, Webby; *Recreations* wine, family, garden, poetry, sailing; *Style*— Nick Moore, Esq; ✉ Roar, 375 Hudson Street, 12th Floor, New York, NY 10014, USA (☎ 00 1 212 804 4145, e-mail nicholas.moore@roargroupe.com)

MOORE, Nigel Sandford Johnson; s of Raymond Johnson Moore (d 1977), and Lucy Mary, *née* Kirby (d 2000); *b* 12 April 1944; *Educ* Radley; *m* 16 Aug 1969, Elizabeth Ann, da of Joseph Henry Bowker (d 1986); 2 da (Louise b 20 Feb 1974, Rachel b 1 March 1977), 1 s (Peter b 9 Jan 1983); *Career* Buckley Hall Devin & Co 1962–68; Ernst and Young 1968–2003: Sydney Aust 1969–71, ptnr UK 1973–2003, human resources ptnr 1973–81, mktg dept 1983–86, managing ptnr London Office 1986–88, dir of client servs Europe 1988–90, regnl managing ptnr Eastern Europe 1990–96, dir Int Lending Orgns 1994–96, dir Energy Servs Gp 1996–2003; chm JKX Oil and Gas plc; non-exec dir: Hochschild Mining plc; FCA 1977; *Recreations* theatre, golf, tennis, travel; *Clubs* City of London, IOD, The Pilgrims; *Style*— Nigel Moore, Esq; ✉ Vinesgate, Brasted Chart, Westerham, Kent TN16 1LR (☎ 01959 564510, e-mail nigel.moore6@btinternet.com)

MOORE, Dr Philip John; s of late Cecil Moore, and late Marjorie, *née* Brewer; *b* 30 September 1943; *Educ* Maidstone GS, RCM; *Children* 1 s (Thomas), 2 da (Sophie, Bianca); *Career* asst music master Eton 1965–68, asst organist Canterbury Cathedral 1968–74, organist and master of the choristers Guildford Cathedral 1974–82, organist and master of the music York Minster 1983–2008 (organist emeritus 2008–), organist St Michael and All Angels Barton le Street 2008–; memb: RCM Union 1962, Br Acad of Composers and Songwriters 1987, Performing Rights Soc 1988; Cranmer Award for Worship from the Archbishop of Canterbury 2016; BMus (Hons) Dunelm, Dr (hc) Univ of York; FRCO 1962 (pres 2015–17), GRSM, ARCM, FRSCM, FGCM; memb Order of St William of York, fell Acad of St Cecilia; *Publications* composer of choral music, organ music, songs, chamber works and orchestral works; *Recreations* collecting Imari and old fountain pens, malt whisky, cooking, gardening, log fires; *Style*— Dr Philip Moore; ✉ Rectory Cottage, Barton le Street, Malton YO17 6PN; c/o Val Withams, Choral Connections, 28 Wright's Lane, Prestwood, Great Missenden, Buckinghamshire HP16 0LH (☎ 01494 866389, e-mail val@choralconnections.com)

MOORE, Philip Wynford; TD (1993); s of Cecil Philip John Moore, of Potters Bar, Herts, and Christine Margaret Moore; *b* 5 January 1960, Welwyn Garden City, Herts; *Educ* St Albans Sch, Clare Coll Cambridge (MA); *m* 29 April 1995, Amanda; 2 da (Georgina Emily b 7 Feb 1998, Victoria Lucy b 16 Feb 2000); *Career* Coopers & Lybrand (now PricewaterhouseCoopers): ptnr i/c UK life actuarial servs 1989–95, ldr of insurance consulting practice E Asia 1995–98; finance dir and actuary NPI 1998–2000, corp dir of finance and head of M&A AMP (UK) plc 2000–03; Friends Provident plc: gp finance dir 2003–06, gp chief exec 2007; interim chief finace offr HM Revenue and Customs 2008, gp finance ptnr and chief risk offr Pension Corporation LLP 2008–10, gp finance dir Liverpool Victoria Friendly Soc 2010–; non-exec dir F&C Asset Mgmnt plc 2005–07, non-exec dir and chm Audit Ctee RAB Capital plc 2009–11; Towergate Partnership Co Ltd: non-exec dir 2011–15, chair Audit Ctee 2011–15, sr ind dir 2013–15; non-exec dir and chair Audit Ctee Towergate Insurance Ltd 2015–; tstee Childhood Eye Cancer Tst 2007–13 (chm 2008–13), tstee and chm Fin Ctee Royal Br Legion 2014–; govr Aylward Acad 2011– (chair Achievement and Standards Ctee 2014–15, chair Student Wellbeing Ctee 2015–,vice-chm Governing Bd 2016–); Freeman City of London, Liveryman Worshipful Co of Actuaries; FIA 1988; *Recreations* running, skiing, travel; *Clubs* HAC; *Style*— Philip Moore, Esq, TD; ✉ Liverpool Victoria Friendly Society, County Gates, Bournemouth BH1 2NF (☎ 01202 542323, e-mail philip.moore@lv.com)

MOORE, Richard Hobart John deCourcy; s of Hobart Harold deCourcy Moore (d 1981), and Elizabeth Helen, *née* Tod (d 2016); *b* 31 August 1949; *Educ* Stowe; *m* 30 April 1977, Lucy Annabelle, da of Victor Sefton-Smith (d 2007), and Babette, *née* Salt (Lady Millais) (d 2014); 1 s (Francis Richard Hobart deCourcy b 25 June 1985), 1 da (Natasha Elizabeth Victoria deCourcy b 1 Nov 1993); *Career* Moore Stephens: articled clerk 1968–72, CA 1972, ptnr 1975–, sr ptnr 1989–, chm Moore Stephens Int 2004–; cmmr Royal Hosp Chelsea 2006–12; Freeman City of London 1974, Liveryman Worshipful Co of Vintners, Liveryman Worshipful Co of Shipwrights (memb Ct of Assts); FCA 1979 (ACA 1972); *Recreations* real tennis, cricket; *Clubs* MCC, Boodle's, Queen's, Hurlingham; *Style*— Richard Moore, Esq; ✉ 11 Chelsea Park Gardens, London SW3 6AF (☎ 020 7352 7594); Moore Stephens, 150 Aldersgate Street, London EC1A 4AB (☎ 020 7334 9191)

MOORE, HE Richard Peter; s of John Robert Moore, of Addlestone, Surrey, and Norah Patricia (Pat), *née* Buckley; *b* 9 May 1963, Tripoli, Libya; *Educ* St George's Coll Weybridge, Worcester Coll Oxford (exhibitioner, BA), John F Kennedy Sch of Govt, Harvard (Kennedy Scholar), Stanford Exec Prog; *m* 3 Aug 1985, Margaret Patricia Isabel (Maggie), *née* Martin; 1 s (Jack Rigney b 5 July 1989), 1 da (Olivia Maureen Amelia b 11 Jan 1992); *Career* diplomat; joined FCO 1987, third sec Hanoi 1988, second sec (political) Ankara 1990, consul (political and press) Istanbul 1991–92, desk offr Iran FCO 1992–95, first sec Islamabad 1995–98, section head Security Policy Gp FCO 1998–2001, counsellor Kuala Lumpur 2001–05, dep dir of ME FCO 2005–08, dir of progs and change FCO 2008–10, dir of Europe, Latin America and globalisation FCO 2010–14, ambass to Turkey 2014–; *Recreations* golf; *Clubs* Vincent's, MCC; *Style*— HE Mr Richard Moore; ✉ British Embassy, ?ehit Ersan Caddesi 46/A, Çankaya 06680, Ankara, Turkey (☎ 00 90 312 455 3320, e-mail richard.moore@fco.gov.uk, Twitter @UKAmbRichard)

MOORE, His Hon Judge Robert Jeffery; *Career* circuit judge (North Eastern Circuit) 1995–, ethnic minorities liaison judge S Yorks and Humberside 1998–2004, memb Examinations and Interview Panel Judicial Appointments Cmmn 2008–10; *Style*— His Hon Judge Moore; ✉ The Law Courts, 50 West Bar, Sheffield S3 8PH

MOORE, Prof Robert Samuel; s of late Douglas Kenneth Moore, of Rhos-on-Sea, and late Kathleen Phyllis Moore; *b* 3 June 1936; *Educ* Beckenham and Penge Co GS, RNC Dartmouth, Univ of Hull (BA), Univ of Durham (PhD); *m* 16 Aug 1969, Lindy Ruth, da of late Sir Alan Parker, of Shenstone, Sutton-cum-Beckingham; 1 s (David Kenneth b 1974), 1 da (Heloise Kathryn b 1976); *Career* RN 1952–61; sociology lectr Univ of Durham 1965–69, sr lectr in sociology Univ of Aberdeen 1970–75, reader in sociology 1975–77, prof of sociology 1977–89, Eleanor Rathbone prof of sociology Univ of Liverpool 1989–2001 (emeritus prof 2001–); vice-pres Aberdeen City Anti Apartheid, chm Grampian Community Relations Cncl until 1989, tstee N Wales Regnl Equality Network; memb: Univ and Coll Union, CND, Br Sociological Assoc 1964–, Br Assoc 1965–; FRSA, FAcSS; *Books* Race, Community and Conflict (with John Rex, 1967), Pitmen, Preachers and Politics (1970), Slamming the Door (with Tina Wallace, 1975), Racism and Black Resistance in Britain (1975), The Social Impact of Oil (1982), Women in the North Sea Oil Industry (with Peter Wybrow, 1985), Ethnic Statistics and the 1991 Census (1995), Positive Action in Action: equal opportunities and declining opportunities in Merseyside (1997), Globalisation and the New City (ed with M Cross, 2002), Community Health and Wellbeing (jt ed, 2007); *Recreations* gardening, photography; *Style*— Prof Robert Moore; ✉ The University of Liverpool, Eleanor Rathbone Building, Bedford Street South, Liverpool L69 7ZA (☎ 01352 714456, fax 01352 714456, e-mail rsmoore@liverpool.ac.uk)

MOORE, Sir Roger George; KBE (2003, CBE 1999); *b* 14 October 1927; *Educ* Battersea GS, RADA; *m* 1 (m dis 1953), Doorn van Steyn; m 2 (m dis 1969), Dorothy Squires; m 3 (m dis), Luisa Mattioli; 2 s, 1 da; m 4, Kristina Tholstrup; *Career* actor; chm Stars Organisation for Spastics 1973–76, UNICEF special ambass 1991–; *Television* Ivanhoe 1958, The Alaskans 1959, Maverick 1960, The Saint 1962–68, The Persuaders 1972–73, The Muppet Show 1980, The Wedding of Prince Andrew and Sarah Ferguson (ABC-TV) 1986, Happy Anniversary 007 (ABC-TV) 1987, The Dame Edna Experience Christmas Show (LWT) 1987, James Bond - 30th Anniversary (LWT) 1992, The Man Who Wouldn't Die (Universal) 1992, Best Ever Bond 2002; *Film* extra in Caesar and Cleopatra 1945, Trottie True 1949, The Last Time I Saw Paris 1954, Interrupted Melody 1955, The King's Thief 1955, Diane 1956, The Miracle 1959, Gold of the Seven Saints 1961, Rachel Cade 1961, Rape of the Sabines 1961, No Man's Land 1961, Crossplot 1969, The Man Who Haunted Himself 1970, Gold 1974, That Lucky Touch (Who Needs Friends?) 1975, Shout at the Devil 1975, Street People (Sicilian Cross) 1975, Sherlock Holmes in New York 1976, Wild Geese 1977, Escape to Athena 1978, North Sea Hi-jack 1979, The Sea Wolves 1979/80, Sunday Lovers 1980, The Cannonball Run 1980, Curse of the Pink Panther 1982, The Naked Face 1983, Bed & Breakfast 1989, Bullseye 1989, Fire, Ice and Dynamite 1990, The Quest 1995, cameo role Spiceworld The Movie 1997, The Enemy 2001, Boat Trip 2002; as Cdr James Bond: Live and Let Die 1973, The Man with the Golden Gun 1974, The Spy Who Loved Me 1976, Moonraker 1978, For Your Eyes Only 1980/81, Octopussy 1982, A View to a Kill 1984; *Awards* nominated: Golden Globe World Film Favourite Award (USA) 1980, Man of the Year Award Friars Club of NY 1986, Bambi Lifetime Achievement Award (Germany) 1990; *Publications* James Bond Diary (1973), My Word Is My Bond (2008), Bond On Bond (2012), Last Man Standing (2014); *Style*— Sir Roger Moore, KBE

MOORE, Rowan William Gillachrist; s of Richard Gillachrist Moore, of Battle, E Sussex, and Ann Hilary, *née* Miles; *b* 22 March 1961; *Educ* Westminster, St John's Coll Cambridge (BA, DipArch); *m* 3 Aug 1991, Elizabeth Black Treip; 2 da (Helena Rose Rebecca, Stella Hannah Hilary); *Career* ptnr Zombory-Moldovan Moore Architects 1990–2005; dir Architecture Fndn 2002–; architecture critic Daily Telegraph 1993–98, architecture critic Evening Standard 1998–, ed Blueprint 1994–97; *Books* Vertigo, The Strange New World of the Contemporary City (1999), Building Tate Modern (2000), The New Art Gallery Walsall (2003); *Style*— Rowan Moore, Esq; ✉ Architecture Foundation, 2a Kingsway Place, Sans Walk, London EC1R 0LS (☎ 020 7253 3334, fax 020 7253 3335, e-mail rowan@architecturefoundation.org.uk)

MOORE, Stephen; s of Stanley Moore (d 1992), of Highgate, London, and Mary Elisabeth, *née* Bruce-Anderson (d 1978); *b* 11 December 1937; *Educ* Archbishop Tenison's GS London, Central Sch of Speech and Drama (Lawrence Olivier Award); *m* 1, Barbara Mognaz; 3 c (Robyn, Guy, Hedda); m 2, Celestine Randall; 1 da (Charlotte); m 3, Beth Morris; m 4, Noelyn George; 1 da (Sophie Martha George-Moore); *Career* actor; prof stage debut 1959 as 1st Immigration Officer in A View from the Bridge (Theatre Royal Windsor), London stage debut 1959 as William in As You Like It (Old Vic Theatre Co); many radio plays, dramas and short stories incl The Hitch Hiker's Guide to the Galaxy; *Theatre* numerous appearances; Old Vic Theatre Co 1959–61 incl: A Midsummer Night's Dream, Dr Faustus, Twelfth Night, The White Devil, Saint Joan, Romeo and Juliet, Mourning Becomes Electra; Theatre Royal Windsor 1959–1968 incl: Pride and Prejudice, Present Laughter, An Ideal Husband, The Importance of Being Ernest; Mermaid Theatre 1962–67 incl: The Plough and the Stars, The Good Soldier Schweyk, The Trojan Wars, The Fight for Barbara; Royal Court 1963–72 incl: Julius Caesar, Ojections to Sex and Violence, Action, Treats; Colchester Rep Co 1967–68 incl: A Day In The Life of Joe Egg, Spring and Port Wine (also dir), Forget-Me-Not Lane; Bristol Old Vic 1969–71 incl: Major Barbara, Macbeth, A Streetcar Named Desire, Woyzeck, The Iceman Cometh, Who's Afraid of Virginia Woolf; RSC 1973–86 incl: Section Nine, Peter Pan, Henry VIII, Twelfth Night, All's Well That Ends Well, Poppy, Mother Courage, A Penny for a Song; RNT 1977–1998 incl: Bedroom Farce, State of Revolution, Plenty, The Romans in Britain, The Life of Galileo, Love for Love, The Threepenny Opera, Dalliance, A Small Family Business, Sister Feelings, The Shaughraun, Peer Gynt, Piano, An Enemy of the People, The Cherry Orchard, The President of an Empty Room, The Hot House 2007; West End appearances incl: Hughie and Others (Duchess) 1963, It's a Two Foot Six Inches Above The Ground World (Wyndham's) 1970, Treats (Mayfair) 1976, New Found Land (Arts Theatre) 1977, Bedroom Farce (Prince of Wales, also Broadway) 1978, The Hardshoulder (Aldwych) 1983, Paris Match (Garrick) 1989, Reflected Glory (Vaudeville) 1992, Disposing of the Body (Hampstead) 1999, The Cherry Orchard (National Theatre) 2001, My Fair Lady (Theatre Royal Drury Lane) 2003, Festen (Lyric) 2004–05, The History Boys (Wyndham's) 2006–07, The Hothouse (Nat Theatre) 2008; *Television* debut in 1962 as Georges in Dinner With the Family (BBC); since then over 200 appearance incl: Three Men in a Boat, Brideshead Revisited, The Secret Diary – The Growing Pains of Adrian Mole, Rock Follies, Middlemarch, Solo, Just Between Ourselves, Small World, Soldiers Talking Cleanly, Love on A Gunboat, Just William, The Last Place on Earth, Love on a Branchline, The Beat Goes On, The Queen's Nose (4 series), The Missing Postman, Leprechauns, Silent Witness, Ready When You Are Mr McGill, Foyles War, The Brief; guest appearances with Fry and Laurie, Dawn French, Emma Thompson, Rowan Atkinson, Lenny Henry, Alexei Sayle and Harry Enfield; *Film* roles incl: Young Man in The White Bus, Major Steele in A Bridge Too Far, Michael in White Bird, Guy in Diversion, Howard in Singleton's Pluck, Mr Jolly in Clockwise, Roscoe in Under Suspicion, MacKenzie in Brassed Off; *Awards* winner of SWET Award (now known as The Olivier Award) for Best Actor in a Revival for A Doll's House (RSC) 1982; 1983 SWET Award nominations incl: Best Actor in a Musical, Best Supporting Actor, Best Actor in a Revival; Tony Award nomination for Broadway prodn of All's Well That Ends Well 1983; *Recreations* supporter Chelsea FC, motor cycling, music, computing; *Style*— Stephen Moore, Esq; ✉ c/o Markham & Froggatt Ltd, Julian House, 4 Windmill Street, London W1P 1HF (☎ 020 7636 4412, fax 020 7637 5233, e-mail stephenhimself@gmail.com, website www.stephenmoore.uk.com)

MOORE, Terence (Terry); CBE (1993); s of Arthur Doncaster Moore, and Dorothy Irene Gladys, *née* Godwin; *b* 24 December 1931; *Educ* Strand Sch Univ of London (BScEcon), Harvard Business Sch; *m* 17 Sept 1955, Tessa Catherine, da of Ernest Walter Wynne; 2 s (Simon Jeremy b 1961, Adam Gavin b 1965), 1 da (Anna Louise b 1968); *Career* Nat Serv Army; mktg, fin and economics appts Shell International 1948–64, economist Locana Corp 1964–65; Conoco Ltd: economist, mangr econ planning, gen mangr and dir 1965–74, dep md Mktg Ops 1974–79, md Supply and Trading 1979–86, gp md/ceo 1986–95, conslt 1995–; non-exec dir John Fisher plc 1998–2003; pres Oil Industries Club 1989–90 and 2003–09; dir and hon sec Inst Petroleum 1995–2003; dir Conoco Pension Fund Ltd 1995–2003; govr Greenwich Theatre 1992–98; ACII, AICS, FInstPet 1996, FEI 2003; *Recreations* theatre, reading, music; *Style*— Terry Moore, Esq, CBE; ✉ 67 Merchant Court, Thorpes Yard, 61 Wapping Wall, London E1W 3SJ (☎ and fax 020 7481 0853, e-mail t.moore@talktalk.net)

MOORE, Maj Gen W H (Bill); CBE; *b* 24 February 1958, Pembroke; *Educ* Ipswich Sch, Univ of Salford; *m* Jane; 2 s; *Career* operational experience incl: NI, Falklands Campaign, Iraq, Sierra Leone, UN serv; cmd 7 Para RHA 1996, Col Force Devpt 1998, Higher Command and Staff Course 2000, ACOS (Ops) Sierra Leone 2001, cmd 19 Mech Bde 2001, cmd Jt Task Force Sierra Leone (Operation Keeling) 2003, cmd 19 Mech Bde Iraq 2003, DEC Ground Manoeuvre MOD 2004, DG logistics, support and equipment 2007,

M

dep commanding gen Multi Nat Corps Iraq 2009, dir Battlespace Manoeuvre and master gen of the ordnance 2010; chief exec Portman Estate 2011; Hon Col 7 Para RHA; CCMI; *Recreations* cycling, skiing, walking, gym; *Clubs* Home House, Special Forces; *Style*— Bill Moore, CBE; ✉ The Portman Estate, Ground Floor, 40 Portman Square, London W1H 6LT (e-mail bill.moore@portmanestate.co.uk)

MOORE OF LOWER MARSH, Baron (Life Peer UK 1992), of Lower Marsh in the London Borough of Lambeth; John Edward Michael Moore; PC (1986); s of Edward O Moore, of Brighton; *b* 26 November 1937; *Educ* Licensed Victuallers' Sch Slough, LSE (BSc, chm Cons Assoc 1958–59, pres Students' Union 1959–60); *m* 1962, Sheila Sarah (d 2008), da of Richard Tillotson, of Illinois, USA; 1 da (Hon Stephanie b 1968), 2 s (Hon Martin b 1970, Hon Richard b 1972); *Career* Nat Serv Royal Sussex Regt Korea 1955–57; worked in banking and stockbroking and took part in Democratic politics in Chicago 1961–65; cncllr (Cons) London Borough of Merton 1971–74, MP (Cons) Croydon Central Feb 1974–92; vice-chm Cons Pty 1975–79, Parly under sec Energy 1979–83, econ sec Treasy June-Oct 1983, fin sec Treasy (responsibilities incl taxation and privatisation) 1983–86; sec of state for: Tport 1986–87, Health and Social Servs 1987–88, Social Security 1988–89; chm: Dean Witter International Ltd 1975–79 (dir 1968–79), Credit Suisse Asset Management 1992–2000 (dir 1991–2000), Energy Saving Trust Ltd 1992–95 (pres 1995–2001), Rolls-Royce plc 2003–05 (dir 1994, dep chm 1996–2003, chm 2003–05); dir: Gartmore Investment Management Group Ltd 1990–91, Monitor Company Inc USA 1991–2005 (chm Monitor Europe 1991–), Swiss American Corporation 1992–96, GTECH Corporation 1992–2001, Blue Circle Industries plc 1993–2001, Camelot Holdings Ltd 1993–94, Camelot Group plc 1994–98, Central European Growth Fund plc 1995–2000, BEA Associates 1996–98, TIG Holdings Inc 1997–99, Private Client Bank Zurich 1999–2004; memb: Advsy Bd Marvin & Palmer Associates Inc USA 1989–2014 (dir 1994–2014), Supervisory Bd ITT Automotive Europe GmbH 1994–97, Advsy Bd Sir Alexander Gibb & Co 1990–95; memb Cncl IOD 1991–2002; memb Ct of Govrs LSE 1977–2002; *Recreations* sport; *Clubs* RAC; *Style*— The Rt Hon Lord Moore of Lower Marsh, PC

MOORE-BICK, Maj-Gen John D; CBE 1997 (OBE 1991), DL; s of John Ninian Moore-Bick (d 2001), and Kathleen Margaret, *née* Beall (d 2003); bro of Martin James Moore-Bick (Rt Hon Lord Justice Moore-Bick), *qv*; *b* 10 October 1949; *Educ* Univ of Oxford (MA); *m*; 1 da; *Career* early serv with Royal Marines, Germany, Falkland Islands, Norway and NI, Führungsakademie der Bundeswehr 1979–82, asst to chm NATO Mil Ctee Brussels 1987–89, Regtl Cdr Germany and Gulf War 1989–91, Branch Col MOD 1991–94, Higher Command and Staff Course 1994, chief engr NATO Implementation Force Bosnia 1994–96, dir Princ MOD Directorate 1997–99, ldr study team Defence Postgrad Acad 1999, mil advsr to High Rep Bosnia and Herzegovina 2000; formerly: GOC UK Support Command Germany, special defence advsr to Govt of Serbia and Montenegro; Hon Col 39 Regt Royal Signals 2001–06, Col Cmdt RE 2002–12, Hon Col Sussex ACF 2007–; gen sec Forces Pension Soc 2007–15; chm Skinners' Sch 2005–15, govr Plumpton Coll 2016–; Master Skinner 2008–09; FICE 1997, FCIL 2005; *Style*— Maj-Gen John Moore-Bick, CBE, DL

MOORE-BICK, Rt Hon Lord Justice; Rt Hon Sir Martin James Moore-Bick; kt (1995), PC (2005); s of John Ninian Moore-Bick (d 2001), and Kathleen Margaret, *née* Beall (d 2003); bro of Maj-Gen John Moore-Bick, CBE, , *qv*; *b* 6 December 1946; *Educ* The Skinners' Sch Tunbridge Wells, Christ's Coll Cambridge (MA); *m* 3 Aug 1974, Tessa Penelope, da of George Michael Gee; 2 da (Catherine b 1977, Elizabeth b 1977), 2 s (Christopher b 1980, Matthew b 1983); *Career* called to the Bar Inner Temple 1969 (bencher 1992, reader 2014, treas 2015), recorder of the Crown Court 1990–95, judge of the High Court of Justice (Queen's Bench Div) 1995–2005, Lord Justice of Appeal 2005–, dep head of civil justice 2007–12; chm Legal Servs Consultancy Panel 2005–09, vice pres Court of Appeal (Civil Division) 2014–; hon fell Christ's Coll Cambridge 2009; *Recreations* music, literature, gardening; *Style*— The Rt Hon Lord Justice Moore-Bick; ✉ Royal Courts of Justice, Strand, London WC2A 2LL

MOORE-GILLON, Dr John Christopher; *b* 2 January 1953, London; *Educ* Tiffin Sch, St Catharine's Coll Cambridge, St Thomas' Hosp Med Sch; *m* 1980, Victoria Kirby, FRCS; 1 s (Edwin b 1984), 2 da (Olivia b 1986, Claudia b 1994); *Career* conslt physician: Dept of Respiratory Med St Bartholomew's Hosp 1988–2010, King Edward VII's Hosp for Offrs 2005–; physician emeritus St Bartholomew's Hosp 2010–; vice-pres Br Lung Fndn 2008– (chm 1994–99, pres 2001–08), hon sec Br Thoracic Soc 1992–94; Master Worshipful Soc of Apothecaries 2014–15; *Publications* author of book chapters, invited review articles and original scientific papers on respiratory medicine; *Recreations* music, theatre; *Clubs* Trygone, Athenaeum, Garrick; *Style*— Dr John Moore-Gillon, MA, MD, FRCP; ✉ 37 Devonshire Street, London W1G 6QA (✆ 020 7935 1977, e-mail susan.katz@btconnect.com)

MOOREHEAD, Caroline; OBE (2005); *b* 28 October 1944; *Educ* French Lycées London and Rome, Sorbonne, Univ of London (BA); *m*; 2 c; *Career* child psychologist Rome 1967–68, reporter Time Magazine Rome 1968–69, feature writer Daily Telegraph Magazine 1969–70, features ed TES 1970–73, specialist in human rights and feature writer The Times 1973–88, human rights corr and feature contrib The Independent 1988–93; contribs and reviews for TES, TLS, London Review of Books, Spectator, New Statesman, New Society, Listener, Literary Review, Sunday Telegraph, Harpers, Departures, Traveler (US); memb: Wolfenden Ctee on Voluntary Work 1977, London Library Ctee 1990–94, Human Rights Mission Eminent Persons to Moscow 1990, Exec Ctee PEN 1993–96 (memb Writers in Prison Ctee 1989–96), Cncl RSL 1995–, Cncl Soc of Authors 1996–, Ctee Redress Tst; tstee and memb Cncl Index on Censorship 1990–, tstee Br Inst of Human Rights, conslt various refugee ctees, judge various literary and human rights prizes; FRSL; *Television* script writer: Forty Minutes Troublesome People (also presenter, BBC) 1987, Prisoners of Conscience (also assoc prodr, two 10-part series BBC) 1988–91, Children and Human Rights (UN film), Human Rights, Human Wrongs (also prodr 1992–); *Books* trans of novel and 3 art books from French and Italian 1967–70, Fortune's Hostages (1980), Sidney Bernstein: A Biography (1983), Freya Stark: A Biography (1985), Troublesome People (1987), Beyond the Rim of the World: The Letters of Freya Stark (ed, 1988), Betrayed: Children in Today's World (1989), Bertrand Russell: A Life (1993), The Lost Treasures of Troy (1994), Dunant's Dream: War, Switzerland and the Red Cross (1997), Iris Origo, Marchesa of Val D'Orcia (2000), Martha Gellhorn: A Life (2003), Human Cargo: A journey among refugees (2005), The Collected Letters of Martha Gellhorn (ed, 2006), Dancing to the Precipe: Lucie de la Tour du Pin and the French Revolution (2008), A Train in Winter: A Story of Renaissance, Friendship and Survival (2011); *Pamphlets* incl: Working Children (Anti-slavery Soc, 1987), Children of Namibia (Oxfam, 1988), A Guide to Human Rights (BBC, 1992); *Style*— Ms Caroline Moorehead, OBE, FRSL; ✉ c/o Clare Alexander, Aitken Alexander, 18–21 Cavage Place, London SW10 9PT

MOORHOUSE, Barbara; da of Andre Moorhouse, and Rosalind Moorhouse; *b* 21 November 1958; *Educ* Prince Henry's HS Evesham, St Catherine's Coll Oxford (BA); *m* 2001; *Career* co accountant T I Gp plc and Northern Foods 1981–86, European fin dir Courtaulds plc 1986–90, regulatory dir South West Water plc 1990–95, dir of European fin Johnson Controls Inc 1996, dir of gp fin Morgan Sindall plc 1997–98, interim exec appointments Jigsaw plc, Energis plc and Mandex Int 1998–2000, gp fin dir Kewill Systems plc 2000–02, chief fin offr Scala Business Solutions NV 2003–05, DG of fin and commerce Miny of Justice (formerly Dept for Constitutional Affrs) 2005–07, DG Corporate Resources Gp Dept for Transport 2007–09, dir of finance Westminster City Cncl 2009–; memb Governing Cncl CIMA 1996–2002, non-exec dir and chair Audit Ctee Child Support Agency 2003–06, memb Financial Reporting Review Panel 2004; assoc memb ACT; fell CIMA; *Recreations* horse riding, ballroom dancing, walking, skiing; *Style*— Ms Barbara Moorhouse

MOORHOUSE, His Hon Judge M G C; *Career* circuit judge (North Eastern Circuit) 2001–; *Style*— His Hon Judge Moorhouse; ✉ Teesside Crown Court, Russell Street, Middlesbrough TS1 2AE

MORAES, Claude; MEP; s of Mr H I Moraes, and Theresa, *née* Aranha; *b* 22 October 1965; *Educ* St Modan's HS Stirling, Univ of Dundee (LLB), Birkbeck Coll London (MSc), LSE; *m* Bharti, *née* Patel; 1 s (Anish b 21 May 2010); *Career* political advsr to Dr John Reid MP and Paul Boateng MP House of Commons 1987–89, nat offr TUC 1989–92, rep Euro TUC, dir JCWI 1992–; chief exec Immigrants' Aid Tst, cmmr Cmmn for Racial Equality 1998–99; Parly candidate (Lab) Harrow West 1992; MEP (Lab) London 1999–; dep ldr Lab MEPs in the European Parl 2009–, Socialist and Democrats Gp spokesperson on justice and home affrs European Parl 2009–14, chair Civil Liberties, Justice and Home Affrs Ctee European Parl 2014–; former vice-pres Educn Action International, former memb Cncl Liberty (NCCL), former tstee Toynbee Hall East London; FRSA 1998; *Publications* Social Work and Minorities: European Perspectives (co-author, 1998), The Politics of Migration (co-author, 2003), Immigratie e Italiani (co-author, 2004), Perspectives on Migration (contirb, 2005), Roma: A European Minority (co-author, 2011), The European Union after the Treaty of Lisbon (co-author, 2013); articles on human rights and European issues in journals and newspapers; *Recreations* film (memb BFI), Scottish literature, chess, listening to BBC Radio 4, BBC London Radio and the World Service; *Style*— Claude Moraes, MEP; ✆ 020 7609 5005, e-mail office@claudemoraes.com, website www.claudemoraes.com, Twitter @ClaudeMoraesMEP

MORAN, Andrew Gerard; QC (1994); s of Francis Michael Moran (d 1979), of Widnes, and Winifrede, *née* Plant (d 1971); *b* 19 October 1953; *Educ* West Park GS St Helens, BRNC Dartmouth, Balliol Coll Oxford (BA); *m* 17 Feb 1977, Carole Jane, da of James Sullivan; 6 s (Michael b 1978, James b 1980, Peter b 1984, Kevin b 1987, John b 1989, Matthew b 1995), 1 da (Claire Louise b 1982); *Career* Univ Cadetship RN, Offr and Merchant Navy Deck Offr 1972; called to the Bar Gray's Inn 1976 (bencher 2005), dep High Ct judge; recorder of the Crown Ct; arbitrator Singapore Chamber of Maritime Arbitration; chm Disciplinary Tribunal Int Petroleum Exchange; memb Commercial Bar Assoc; *Recreations* travel, sport, walking, sailing; *Style*— Andrew Moran, Esq, QC; ✉ 7 Harrington Street, Liverpool L2 9YH (✆ 0151 242 0700); Stone Chambers, 4 Field Court, Gray's Inn, London WC1R 5EF (✆ 020 7440 6900); St John's Building, 24A-28 St John Street, Manchester M3 4DJ (✆ 0161 214 1500, e-mail agmqc@aol.com)

MORAN, Brendan John; s of Peter Moran, of Kilmihil, Co Clare, and Teresa, *née* Morrissey (d 1959); *b* 21 July 1957; *Educ* Laken Nat Sch, Christian Brothers Sch Kilrush, UC Cork (MCh, MB BCh, BAO); *m* 4 May 1985, Dr Karina Kirby; 1 s (Shane b 14 Jan 1986), 1 da (Suzanne b 28 June 1987); *Career* sr registrar: Basingstoke Dist Hosp 1993–94, Royal Hants County Hosp 1994–95, Univ of Southampton Hosps 1995; conslt surgn N Hants Hosp Basingstoke 1995–, dir UK Pseudomyxoma Nat Referral Centre; memb Bd and Ctee: Assoc of Coloproctology of GB and I, Assoc of Surgns of GB and I, Nutrition Soc, Section of Surgery RSM, Section of Coloproctology RSM (memb Cncl), Surgical Assoc for Clinical Research in Europe (SACRE); tstee: Wessex Cancer Tst, Kingston Tst; numerous contribs to nat and int meetings 1994–, numerous lectures 2002–; accredited clinical nutritionist 1991; Espen-Abbott Fellowship European Soc of Parenteral & Enteral Nutrition 1989, Alfano Award for Colorectal Cancer Surgery American Soc of Abdominal Surgns 2002; European Sch of Oncology colorectal fellowship 1994, RSM Section of Coloproctology travelling fellowship 1992 and 1995, European travelling fell Br Jl of Surgery 1995, Assoc of Coloproctology of GB & I American travelling fell 2000; FRCSI 1984, FRCSI (Gen) 1995, FRCS 1997; reg reviewer: The Br Jl of Surgery, Techniques in Coloproctology, Colorectal Disease, Cancer, Gut; author of numerous chapters and articles in various pubns; *Style*— Brendan Moran, Esq; ✉ The North Hampshire Hospital, Basingstoke, Hampshire RG24 9NA

MORAN, Catherine Elizabeth (Caitlin); da of John Moran, of Brighton, and Margaret, *née* Hite; *b* 5 April 1975, Brighton, E Sussex; *Educ* home schooled; *m* 27 Dec 1999, Peter Paphides; 2 da (Dora b 5 Feb 2001, Eavie b 12 Aug 2003); *Career* columnist The Times 1992–; Observer Young Journalist of the Year 1990, Columnist of the Year Br Press Award 2010, Critic of the Year and Interviewer of the Year Br Press Awards 2011, BSME Magazine Columnist of the Year 2011, BSME Columnist of the Year 2013; *Books* The Chronicles of Narmo (1991), How To Be A Woman (2011, Galaxy Book of the Year 2011, Non-Fiction Book of the Year Irish Book Award 2011), Moranthology (2012), How To Build A Girl (2014); *Recreations* hair biggening, Cava, The Struggle, Twitter; *Style*— Ms Caitlin Moran; ✉ The Times, 1 Pennington Street, London E1 9XN (Twitter @caitlinmoran); literary agent Georgia Garrett (e-mail georgia@rcwlitagency.com); screenwriting agent Nick Marston at Curtis Brown

MORAN, Dr Christopher John; s of Thomas Moran (d 1977), and Iva Mary, *née* Alcock (d 1989); *b* 16 January 1948, London; *Educ* Owens GS; *m* 1981 (m dis 1999), Helen Elisabeth Taylor; 2 s (Charles, Jamie (twins) b 31 Jan 1988); *Career* chm Christopher Moran Gp of Cos 1970–; chm: Co-operation Ireland (GB) 2004–, Co-operation Ireland 2006–; chm: Cncl of Christians and Jews Exec Ctee 2003– (vice chm 2008–), Finance Bd LSO 2004–, Prince's Charities Cncl 2009–; memb Advsy Cncl LSO 2008–; dir C&UCO Properties Ltd 2006– (chm 2011–); tstee: UCL Hosps Charitable Fndn 1999– (chm 2003–), Mary Rose Tst 2004–, LSO Endowment Tst 2007–; memb: Consultative Ctee Dulwich Picture Gallery 1993–96, Advsy Bd Thames 1994–97; Hon LLD Ulster Univ; FRSA 2005; *Recreations* architecture, opera, art, politics, country pursuits; *Style*— Dr Christopher Moran; ✉ c/o Crosby Hall, Cheyne Walk, London SW3 5AZ (website www.christophermoran.org)

MORAN, HE David John; *b* 22 August 1959; *m* 1993, Carol Ann Marquis; *Career* diplomat; exec offr Office of Telecommunications (Oftel) DTI 1985, entered FCO 1985; ODA: higher exec offr Zimbabwe Africa Gen Section 1985–86, higher exec offr Finance Dept 1986–87, spokesman News Dept 1987–88; second sec Nairobi 1988–91, head IMF/Debt Section Economic Relations Dept FCO 1991–93, first sec (Know How Fund) Moscow 1993–96; FCO: head France and Switzerland Section Western European Dept 1996–98, head Justice and Home Affrs Section EU Dept (Internal) 1998–99, head Charter of Rights Section EU Dept (Internal) 1999–2000; dep perm rep UK Delgn to OECD Paris 2001–05, ambass to Uzbekistan 2005–07, cnsllr HR Directorate 2007–08, seconded to Cabinet Office 2008–09, ambass to Kazakhstan 2009–12 (non-resident ambass to Kyrgyzstan 2009–12), chargé d'affaires to Georgia 2013, ambass to Switzerland and non-resident ambass to Liechtenstein 2014–; *Style*— HE Mr David Moran; ✉ c/o Foreign & Commonwealth Office, King Charles Street, London SW1A 2AH

MORAN, Dylan; *Career* comedian, actor, writer and performer; weekly columnist The Irish Times 1995–96; *Live Performances* incl: Edinburgh Festival 1996, 1998 and 1999 (Perrier Award 1996), Gurgling for Money (UK tour) 1997, Murphy's Cat Laughs (Kilkenny Festival) 1997, Hay Literary Festival 1997 and 2001, Black Books (Channel 4 Sitcom Festival) 1998, Just for Laughs (Montreal Comedy Festival) 1998, Vancouver Comedy Festival 1998, Ready, Steady...Cough (UK tour) 2000, Monster (UK tour) 2003, Monster II (UK and USA tours) 2004, Like Totally (UK tour) 2006, Aust and NZ tours 2006 and 2007, What It Is (UK tour) 2008 and (Australia and NZ tour) 2009; *Television* How Do You Want Me 1998 and 1999, Black Books 2000 and 2001 (Bronze Rose of Montreux for Best Sitcom 2001, BAFTA Best Sitcom 2001), Black Books 3 2004; *Film* Notting Hill 1999, The Actors 2003, Shaun of the Dead 2004, A Cock and Bull Story 2005, Run Fat Boy Run 2007, A Film With Me In It 2008; *Style—* Dylan Moran, Esq; ✉ c/o PBJ and JBJ Management, 22 Rathbone Street, London W1T 1LA (☎ 020 7287 1112, fax 020 7287 1191)

MORAN, Dr John Denton; RD (1977); s of Paul Francis Moran (d 1989), of Marine Gate, Brighton, and Mary, *née* Denton (d 1997); *b* 3 November 1940; *Educ* Downside, Univ of London, St George's Hosp London (MB BS), Guy's Hosp London (LDS, RCS, DFFP, Dip), Univ of Surrey (Dip, MSc); *m* 16 June 1973, Jane, da of Gen Sir Malcolm Cartwright-Taylor, KCB (d 1969); 2 da (Iona b 16 Sept 1973, Louise b 18 March 1975), 1 s (Paul b 29 Jan 1976); *Career* RNR: Surgn Sub Lt (dental) 1962, Surgn Lt (dental) 1964, Surgn Lt Cdr (dental) 1969, dental offr HMS Centaur RN 1965, med and dental offr White City and Jamaica Rd RMR, resigned 1979; dental house surgn Bart's 1964, med house surgn ENT Dept St George's Hosp Tooting 1970, med house physician Christchurch and Boscombe Hosps Bournemouth 1971, GP Brandon Manitoba Canada 1972, private dental practice Harley St 1973–, medical dir Holistic Medical Clinic 19 Wimpole St London 1998–; hon conslt dental surgn to retired RN offrs 1999–2006; MO: Margaret Pyke Centre 1974, Marie Stopes 1978–96, Menopause Clinic 1979–96; memb Ctee Br Soc for Ecological Medicine (BSEM); Freeman City of London 1979, Liveryman Worshipful Co of Barber Surgns 1980; memb BMA, FRSM; *Publications* Actions and Uses of Phytoestrogens in the Menopause (2005), The Cancer Revolution (Patricia Peat, one of 37 contribs); *Recreations* golf, shooting, skiing, walking, bridge, music, reading, travel; *Clubs* RAC, Royal Ashdown; *Style—* Dr John Moran, RD; ✉ The Red Cottage, Back Lane, Fairwarp, East Sussex TN22 3BL (☎ 01825 712006, e-mail john.555moran@btinternet.com)

MORAN, Michael Edward (Mike); s of Edward Moran, of Barkingside, Essex, and Iris Jean, *née* Munn; *b* 16 February 1960; *Educ* Buckhurst Hill Co HS, Ealing Coll of HE (BA, Dip MRS); *m* 1, 8 Dec 1984 (m dis 2000), Sonya Caroline; 1 s (Oliver Eduard b 1 Jan 1989), 2 da (Rebecca b 15 April 1991, Gabriella b 27 Sept 1992); m 2, 15 April 2000, Janet Mary; 1 da (Gina Elizabeth b 6 April 2001), 1 s (Sean Edward b 27 June 2005); *Career* Ford Motor Company Ltd 1982–96: sales and after sales experience Ford of Britain 1982–89, mangr of trg Ford of Europe Brussels 1989–90, fleet sales/mktg Ford of Britain 1990–93, dir of sales and mktg Ford of Spain Madrid 1994–96; mktg dir Toyota (GB) plc 1996–99, commercial dir Toyota (GB) plc 1999–2003, worldwide dir of marketing and strategy RWE Thames Water plc 2003–04, chm RWE España 2003–04, dir ESSBIO Chile 2003–04, fndr and managing ptnr The Orchard Consultancy Ltd 2004–09, md CBS Outdoor Ltd 2010–11, chief operating offr Arena Media 2012–15, ceo Best&Final Ltd 2015–; non-exec chm MOOH Gp Ltd 2012–14; memb MRS 1982, GMP, ASA 2000; FRSA, fell Marketing Soc, FIMI; *Recreations* golf, motor sports; *Clubs* Solus, GRRC; *Style—* Mike Moran, Esq

MORAN, Simon; *Educ* Univ of Sheffield; *Career* md SJM Concerts, dir Academy Music Gp; promotes tours for artists incl: Take That, Coldplay, One Direction, Beyoncé, Arctic Monkeys, Stone Roses, Peter Kay; Hon DMus Univ of Sheffield 2013; *Recreations* music, super league rugby; *Clubs* Warrington Wolves (rugby super league); *Style—* Simon Moran, Esq; ✉ SJM Ltd, 5th Floor, 61 Mosley Street, Manchester M2 3HZ

MORAN, Tom; s of Michael Moran, and Brigid Gillick; *b* 16 November 1955, Dublin; *Educ* UC Dublin (BA, MA, DipEd), Inst of Public Administration Dublin (Cert); *m* 1979, Elizabeth, *née* O'Byrne; 4 s (Andrew, Conor, Declan, Barry); *Career* secdy sch teacher 1978–80, administrative offr then asst princ offr Irish Dept of Agriculture 1980–89, agriculture attaché to France and OECD Irish Embassy Paris 1989–92; Irish Dept of Agriculture: asst sec gen 1992–2005, sec gen 2005–; *Style—* Tom Moran, Esq; ✉ Department of Agriculture, Fisheries and the Marine, Agriculture House, Kildare Street, Dublin 2, Ireland (☎ 0035 3 607 2184)

MORBEY, Gillian Ann; OBE (1995); *née* Kay; *b* 11 June 1953, Glasgow; *Educ* Univ of Strathclyde (BA); *Career* RGN; NHS 1971–81, fndr Sense Scotland 1985 (chief exec 1985–2010), ceo Sense and Sense Int 2010–; vice-chair and chairperson Glasgow Cncl for the Voluntary Sector 1989–95, memb All Pty Disability Gp 1994, ministerial appointment tstee Family Fund Tst 1995–97 (vice-chair 1997–2001), memb Nat Disability Cncl 2000, pres Deafblind Int 2011–; Scottish Social Entrepreneur of the Year 2005, Anne Sullivan Macy Medal 2015; FRSA; *Recreations* walking, gardening, reading; *Style—* Ms Gillian Morbey, OBE; ✉ Sense, 101 Pentonville Road, London N1 9LG (website www.sense.org.uk)

MORCOS, Prof Sameh Kamel; *b* 19 April 1949; *Educ* Maronite Sch Cairo, Univ of Cairo (MB BCh); *m* ; 3 da; *Career* radiologist; pre-registration house jobs Cairo Univ Teaching Hosps 1971–72, resident in gen surgery and orthopaedics Benha Gen Hosp Egypt 1972–73; SHO: in orthopaedics and casualty Bedford Gen Hosp England 1973, in casualty Noble's Hosp IOM 1973–74, in orthopaedics Queen Mary's Hosp for Children Carshalton Surrey 1974–75, in orthopaedics Rowley Bristow Orthopaedic Hosp Pyrford Surrey and St Peter's Hosp Chertsey Surrey 1975–76, in surgical rotation Taunton and Somerset Hosps 1976–78; sr registrar in radiodiagnosis Sheffield Teaching Hosps 1981–83 (registrar 1978–81), conslt radiologist Northern Gen Hosp Sheffield UK 1983–2011, ret; chm Medical Staff Ctee Sheffield Teaching Hospitals 2008–10; Univ of Sheffield: hon reader 2003–05, prof 2005–11, emeritus prof 2011–; recipient: Graham-Hodgson scholarship RCR 1987, Flude meml prize BIR 1993, Nuclear Electric Research travel bursary 1994, Barclay's prize BIR 1997, Barclay's medal BIR 2004; assoc ed Br Jl of Radiology (BJR) 2002–10, dep ed European Radiology 2008–10, author of numerous articles in learned jls; European Soc of Urogenital Radiology (ESUR): sec and treas 2000–04, pres elect 2004–06, pres 2006–08, past pres 2008–10; memb BMA (chm Sheffield Div 1991–92); hon fell Overseas Doctors Assoc 1988 (memb Nat Exec Ctee 1982–93), chm Sheffield Dist Div of Radiology 1992–95; ECF MG (USA) 1974, FRCS (Glasgow) 1978, DMRD (London) 1981, fell Faculty of Radiologists RCS (Dublin) 1982, FRCR (London) 1982; *Publications* New Techniques in Uroradiology (2006), Imagining the Genitourinary Tract: A Problem-orientated approach; *Style—* Prof Sameh Morcos; ✉ e-mail morcsk2@aol.com

MORDAUNT, Penelope Mary (Penny); MP; da of John Edward Patrick Mordaunt, and Jennifer, *née* Snowden (d 1988); *b* 1973; *Educ* Oaklands RC Comp Sch, Univ of Reading; *Career* MP (Cons) Portsmouth N 2010–; parly under-sec of state Dept for Communities and Local Govt 2014–15, min of state for the Armed Forces 2015–; *Recreations* artist, amateur astronomer; *Style—* Ms Penny Mordaunt, MP; ✉ House of Commons, London SW1A 0AA

MORDAUNT, Terence Charles; s of Archibald Raleigh Mordaunt (d 1995), of Reigate, Surrey, and Diana Patricia, *née* Gresty (d 1994); *b* 22 May 1947; *Educ* Wells Cathedral Sch; *m* 3 April 1973 (m dis 1993); 1 da (Sharon b 13 May 1975), 1 s (Jonathan b 29 June 1978); partner, Julia Grassick; *Career* navigation offr master mariner Merchant Navy 1965–73, operations mgmnt Saguenay Shipping 1974–76, distribution mangr Alcan UK 1976–82, mktg dir Port of Tyne 1982–83, commercial dir Bellway plc 1983–87, founded First Corporate Consultants 1987, purchased Port of Bristol 1991, chm Bristol Port Co 1991–; chm Pendennis Shipyard (Hldgs) Ltd, past chm UK Major Ports Gp; memb: Nautical Inst, Inst of Chartered Shipbrokers, Soc of Merchant Venturers; past tstee SS Great Britain Tst; patron Outward Bound; Hon LLD Univ of Bristol; *Recreations* sailing, hill walking, gardens; *Style—* Terence Mordaunt, Esq; ✉ The Bristol Port Company, St Andrew's House, St Andrew's Road, Avonmouth, Bristol BS11 9DQ (☎ 0117 982 0000, fax 0117 982 5931, e-mail exec@bristolport.co.uk)

MORDEN, Jessica; MP; *b* 29 May 1968; *Educ* Croesyceiliog Comp, Univ of Birmingham; *Career* MP (Lab) Newport E 2005–; general sec Welsh Lab Pty; memb GMB; *Style—* Jessica Morden, MP; ✉ House of Commons, London SW1A 0AA (☎ 020 7219 6213, e-mail mordenj@parliament.uk)

MORE NISBETT, Patrea Evelyn; da of David Agar MacDonald (d 1967), of Dorset, and Elisabeth May, *née* Ferguson (d 2014); *b* 2 March 1944; *Educ* Cranborne Chase, Sorbonne, House of Citizenship Bucks; *m* 2 March 1968, George Alan More Nisbett, s of Surgn Cdr John Graham More Nisbett (d 1991), of Mid Lothian; 3 s (William David Hamilton b 1979, Alexander Talbot John b 1982, Charles Neilson George b 1984); *Career* writer and broadcaster; Harpers and Queen Magazine, contrib Sloane Ranger Handbook, assoc ed The Good Schools Guide; *Style—* Mrs Patrea Evelyn More Nisbett; ✉ 43 Godfrey Street, London SW3 3SX (mobile 077 6742 1046, e-mail patrea@morenisbett.com); The Drum, Gilmerton, Edinburgh EH17 8RX

MORE-MOLYNEUX, Michael George; s of Maj James More-Molyneux, OBE, DL (d 2013), and Susan, *née* Bellinger; *b* 3 September 1951; *Educ* Milton Abbey, RAC Cirencester (DipAg, Dip Advanced Farm Mgmnt); *m* July 1980, Sarah, da of Christopher Westmacott (d 1998); 3 s (Alexander b 1982, Christopher b 1985 d 1997, Tristram b 1986), 1 da (Katrina b 1983); *Career* Loseley Dairy Products: managing ptnr 1980–87, chm 1988–91; currently chm Loseley Park Farms; memb Bd Visit Surrey; vice-pres: Shooting Star CHASE, Surrey branch SSAFA-Forces Help; tstee Loseley and Guildway Charitable Tst, patron Disability Challengers, dir and tstee Yvonne Arnaud Theatre; memb Bd HHA, lay canon Guildford Cathedral; High Sheriff Surrey 2000, DL Surrey 2000, Lord Lt Surrey 2015; *Recreations* art galleries, skiing, countryside, travel; *Style—* Michael More-Molyneux, Esq; ✉ Estate Office, Loseley Park, Guildford, Surrey GU3 1HS (☎ 01483 405114, fax 01483 302036, e-mail pa@loseleypark.co.uk)

MOREHEN, Prof John Manley; JP (Notts, 1991); s of Harry Morehen (d 1953), and Gertrude Rhoda, *née* Fann (d 1980); *b* 3 September 1941, Gloucester; *Educ* Crypt GS Gloucester, Clifton Coll Bristol, Royal Sch of Church Music Croydon, New Coll Oxford (Margaret Bridges Organ Scholar, MA), Coll of Church Musicians Washington DC (Ralph H Lane Memorial Scholar), King's Coll Cambridge (PhD); *m* 26 July 1969, Marie Catherine, *née* Jacobus; 1 s (Simon James b 30 Sept 1974), 1 da (Catherine Louise b 19 April 1976); *Career* musicologist, organist and conductor; asst dir of music St Clement Danes Church and Hampstead Parish Church London and keyboard player Hampstead Choral Soc, Martindale Sidwell Choir and London Bach Orchestra 1964–67; lectr Coll of Church Musicians Washington Cathedral American Univ Washington DC US 1967–68, sub-organist St George's Chapel Windsor Castle 1968–72; Univ of Nottingham: music lectr 1973–82, sr lectr 1982–89, prof of music 1989–2002, head Sch of Humanities 1998–2001, emeritus prof of music 2002; memb panel Humanities Res Bd 1994–97, subject assessor music HEFCE 1994–95, music advsr Cwlth Scholarship Cmmn 1996–2000, pres Inc Soc of Musicians 2003–04; numerous broadcasts as organist, speaker and conductor; recital tours of Europe, N America and Aust; numerous presentations on computer applications in music at conferences in the UK, US, Canada, France and the Netherlands; Freeman City of London 1991, Liveryman Worshipful Co of Musicians 1991 (Master 2012–13); DLitt Univ of Nottingham 2005; FRCO (chm), Hon FGCM 2004; *Publications* critical edns of music by English and Italian composers of the 16th and 17th centuries, contributions to The New Grove Dictionary of Music (1980 and 2004 editions) and to scholarly journals; *Original Compositions* incl Five Ceremonial Fanfares for Brass and carols for choirs; *Recreations* collecting English domestic silver, indulging in nostalgia; *Clubs* Athenaeum, Nottingham and Notts United Services; *Style—* Prof John Morehen, JP; ✉ Chestnut Barn, Syerston Hall Park, Newark, Nottinghamshire NG23 5NL (☎ 01636 525068, e-mail john@morehen.fsworld.co.uk); Music Department, University of Nottingham, University Park, Nottingham NG7 2RD (e-mail john.morehen@nottingham.ac.uk, website www.morehen.com)

M

MOREIRA MORÁN, HE Julio; *b* 29 July 1945, Montevideo, Uruguay; *Educ* Univ of Uruguay, Intitut d'Etudes Politiques Paris; *m* Ana Maria Medina-Novoa; 1 s (Matías b 31 July 1985); *Career* Uruguayan diplomat; consular directorate offr Miny of Foreign Affrs 1977, desk offr Directorate for Int Orgns Miny of Foreign Affrs 1978, consul and head of consular affrs Paris 1978, perm delegate UNESCO Paris 1978–83, desk offr Economic Bilateral Relationships Dept for Europe Miny of Foreign Affrs 1983–86, counsellor and head of consular affrs Mexico 1986–, dep rep Organismo para la Proscripción de las Armas Nucleares en América Latina Mexico 1986–89, desk offr Cabinet Sistema Económico Latinoamericano Caracas 1989, COS of the Under Sec of State Office Miny of Foreign Affrs 1990–93, min counsellor France 1993–98, dep dir of protocol and State Ceremonial Directorate Miny of Foreign Affrs 1998–2002, ambass to Sweden 2002–2007 (concurrently non-resident ambass to Finland 2003–07 and non-resident ambass to Norway, Denmark, Estonia and Latvia 2006–07), dep dir Regnl Directorate for Europe Miny of Foreign Affrs 2007, dep DG Directorate for Political Affrs Miny of Foreign Affrs 2008, ambass to the Ct of St James's 2009– (concurrently ambass to Ireland 2010–); Commendatore of the Order of Merit (Italy), Insignia of the Order Mexicana del Aguilla Azteca (Mexico); *Recreations* art and antiques, music; *Clubs* Travellers, Canning; *Style—* HE Mr Julio Moreira Morán; ✉ Embassy of Uruguay, 125 Kensington High Street, London W8 5SF (☎ 020 7937 4170, website www.mree.gub.uy)

MORELAND, Her Hon Judge Penelope Jane; *Career* called to the Bar 1986; recorder 2003, circuit judge (North Eastern Circuit) 2012–; *Style—* Her Hon Judge Moreland; ✉ Newcastle-upon-Tyne Combined Court Centre, The Law Courts, The Quayside, Newcastle-upon-Tyne NE1 3LA

MORELAND, Robert John; s of Samuel John Moreland, MC, TD (d 1998), and Norah Molly, *née* Haines (d 1980); *b* 21 August 1941; *Educ* Glasgow Acad, Dean Close Sch Cheltenham, Univ of Nottingham (BA), Univ of Warwick; *Career* civil servant Canada 1966–72, mgmnt conslt Touche Ross & Co 1974–; MEP (EDG) Staffs 1979–84; memb Econ and Social Ctee of Euro Community 1986–98 (chm Section on Regnl Policy and Town Planning 1990–98); Westminster City Cncl: cncllr Knightsbridge Ward 1990–98, dep chief whip 1991–93, chief whip 1993–94, chm of the environment 1994–95, chm of planning and the environment 1995–97; dep chm London Research Centre 1996–98, chm London Europe Soc 2000– (dep chm 1997–2000), cncllr Gloucester City Cncl 2001–02, treas European Movement 2003–08, dep chm Cons Gp for Europe 2006–09; memb Waterways Partnership for Severn and South Wales 2012–; tstee Albert Meml Tst 1996–2000, chm of govrs Archbishop Tenison's Secdy Sch 2003–11 (govr 1993–); *Books* Transport for Europe (jtly 1983), The European Union and Global Climate Change (jtly with The Rt Hon J S Gummer, MP, 2000); *Recreations* swimming, skiing, golf, watching cricket; *Clubs* MCC, Glos CCC; *Style—* Robert Moreland, Esq; ✉ 3 The Firs, Heathville Road, Gloucester GL1 3EW (☎ 01452 522612); 7 Vauxhall Walk, London SE11 5JT (e-mail r.moreland@virgin.net)

MORENO, Glen Richard; s of John Richard Moreno (d 2003), and Ellen Oberg Moreno; *b* 24 July 1943, San Jose, CA; *Educ* Stanford Univ (BA), Harvard Law Sch (JD); *m* 26 March 1966, Cheryl Eschbach; *Career* sr positions in Europe and Asia incl gp exec dir and memb Policy Ctee Citigroup 1969–87, pres Fidelity International 1987–91 (dir 1987–), non-exec chm Pearson plc 2005–15, non-exec chm Virgin Money plc 2015–; acting chm UK Fin Investments 2009, dep chm Lloyds Banking Gp 2010–12, dep chm Fin Reporting Cncl 2010–14, sr advsr HSBC 2014; sr ind non-exec dir Man Gp plc 1994–2009; govr Ditchley Fndn; *Recreations* cattle breeding, wine making, shooting, fishing; *Clubs* Farmers', In & Out, Corinthian Yacht; *Style—* Glen Moreno, Esq; ✉ Neala, 100 Neala

Lane, Madison, Virginia 22727, USA (☎ 00 1 540 948 4529, e-mail grmoreno@msn.com); 3 Whitehall Court, London SW1A 2EL (☎ 020 7930 9103); Virgin Money plc, 1 Eagle Place, London SW1Y 6AF (☎ 020 7111 0071)

MORETON, Cole; s of Arthur Moreton, and Marion Moreton; *b* 18 June 1967, Walthamstow, London; *Educ* Univ of Middx (BA); *m* 1 Sep 1990, Rachel, *née* Cole; 2 s, 2 da; *Career* Walthamstow Guardian newspaper 1983–87, writer (specialising in relief and devpt, Africa and Asia) and musician 1987–89, with Church Times and freelance writer for national newspapers 1992–96, chief feature writer Express Magazines 1996–97, successively feature writer, asst ed then exec ed Independent on Sunday 1997–2009, freelance author, journalist and broadcaster Mail on Sunday, The Guardian, Sunday Times and others 2009–; two times judge British Press Awards; shortlisted: John Llewellyn Rhys Prize 2000, Team of the Year British Press Awards 2002 and 2006, Interviewer of the Year Br Press Awards 2008 and 2009; memb: NUJ 1983, Soc of Authors 2000; Hungry for Home (2000), My Father Was A Hero (2004), Is God Still An Englishman? How Britain lost its faith (but found new soul) (2010); *Recreations* walking by the sea, music, reading, writing, playing; *Clubs* Authors, Arts; *Style*— Cole Moreton, Esq; ✉ e-mail colemoreton@mac.com, website www.colemoreton.com; c/o Elizabeth Sheinkman, Curtis Brown Ltd, Haymarket House, 28–29 Haymarket, London SW1Y 4SP (e-mail elizabeth@curtisbrown.co.uk)

MOREY-BURROWS, Linda; *Career* interior designer; fndr and md MoreySmith 1993– (leading architectural design practice with portfolio of commercial workplace, development, leisure and residential projects); clients incl: Coca-Cola, Red Bull, Sony, Primark; *Style*— Ms Linda Morey-Burrows; ✉ MoreySmith Ltd, 24 Marshalsea Road, London SE1 1HF

MORGAN, Alan William; s of Alfred Charles Morgan, ISO (d 2003), of Stoke Bishop, Bristol, and Eliza Dora, *née* Sproul-Cran (d 2004); *b* 4 October 1951; *Educ* Clifton (scholar), Trinity Coll Oxford (exhibitioner, MA), Harvard Business Sch (MBA); *m* 17 Oct 1981, Janet Cullis, da of late Rainier Campbell Connolly, FRCS; 2 s (Campbell b 1983, Edward b 1986), 1 da (Georgina b 1988); *Career* called to the Bar Middle Temple 1974; Brandts 1974–76, Harvard Business Sch 1976–78, McKinsey & Co 1978–2006 (ptnr 1984, head UK Fin Servs Practice 1986–96, dir 1991, head Euro Fin Services Practice 1996–2001 (co-head 1993–96), head ME Fin Servs Practice 2001–06), co-fndr and chm MMC Ventures (Venture Capital) 1999–, fndr and chm Adfisco (fintech investor) 2010–; non-exec dir: KB European Private Bank, City of London Sinfonia 2007–; tstee Clifton Coll Devpt Tst 2010–, tstee Riverside Studios Tst 2013–; visiting fell Nuffield Coll Oxford 2005–13; govr St Paul's Sch London 2003–10; memb Cncl Clifton Coll Bristol 2002–11; FRSA; *Recreations* horse racing, golf, theatre, books, walking; *Clubs* Brooks's, Hurlingham, Queenwood, 67 Pall Mall, The Links (New York); *Style*— Alan Morgan, Esq; ✉ Adfisco, 22 Adam and Eve Mews, London W8 6UJ (e-mail alan.morgan@adfisco.com)

Morgan, Anne Yvette; JP (1980), DL (Mid Glamorgan); da of Evan Morgan Davies, of Bridgend, Mid Glamorgan, and Yvonne Davies; *b* 1939; *Educ* Bridgend Girl's GS, Univ Coll Cardiff; *m* 1963, Derek William Charles Morgan; *Career* personnel mangr Ilford-ICI Ltd; cncllr: St Brides Major Community Cncl 1974–79, Merthyr Mawr Community Cncl 1979–; charity/tstee work with orgns incl: Br Red Cross, Barnardo's, Community Fndn in Wales, Soroptimist Int, Teenage Cancer Tst, Women's Aid; sch govr: Penybont Welsh Medium Sch, Oldcastle Jr Sch, Brackla Primary Sch; High Sheriff Mid Glamorgan 2008–09; *Recreations* music, entertaining; *Clubs* Soroptimist; *Style*— Mrs Anne Y Morgan, JP, DL; ✉ Erw Graig, Merthyr Mawr, Bridgend, Mid Glamorgan CF32 0NU

MORGAN, Most Rev Dr Barry Cennydd; *see:* Wales, Archbishop of

MORGAN, Beth; da of Derick Morgan, of Harrow, and Rhona, *née* Wills; *b* 27 September 1981, Harrow, Middx; *Educ* BSc; *Career* cricketer; with clubs: Gunnersbury WCC, Middx WCCC; England: debut v Holland 1999, memb Ashes-winning side 2005 and 2008, memb touring squad Aust and NZ 2008, memb World Cup-winning side 2009; memb Coaches Assoc (level II coach); *Style*— Ms Beth Morgan; ✉ The England and Wales Cricket Board, Lord's Cricket Ground, London NW8 8QZ

MORGAN, Vice Adm Sir (Charles) Christopher; KBE (1996); s of Capt Horace Leslie Morgan, CMG, DSO, RN (d 1973), and Kathleen Hilda, *née* Bellhouse (d 1972); *b* 11 March 1939; *Educ* Clifton; *m* 14 Feb 1970, Susan Caroline, da of William Sturge Goodbody (d 1962); 3 da (Kirsty Joanna b 26 Aug 1970, Victoria Kate b 26 Nov 1972, Juliet Anne b 5 Dec 1978); *Career* initial trg BRNC Dartmouth 1957–59, served HMS Paladin first Cod War Iceland 1959–60, Amphibious Warfare Sqn Persian Gulf 1960–62 (incl Kuwait crisis 1961), 2 i/c HMS Woolaston 1962–64 (incl Brunei rebellion and Indonesia confrontation), Flag Lt to C-in-C Home Fleet 1964–66, i/c HMS Greatford 1966 (active serv Singapore), Specialist Navigation Course HMS Dryad 1966–67, exchange serv Royal Australian Navy 1967–69, Sqn Navigation Offr to Capt F4 HMS Juno 1970–72, Advanced Navigation Course 1973, Flag Navigating Offr to FOF1/FOF2 HMS Tiger and Blake 1973–76, Cdr i/c HMS Eskimo 1976–78, attended Nat Def Coll 1978–79, Cdr Sea Trg Portland 1979–81, Capt Operational Requirements Div MOD 1981–83, RCDS 1984, Capt 5 Destroyer Sqn (i/c HMS Southampton) 1986–87, on staff of JSDC 1987–89, Rear Adm Naval Sec 1990–92, Vice Adm 1992, Flag Offr Scotland, Northern England and NI (FOSNNI) 1992–96, ret; DG UK Chamber of Shipping 1997–2002, dir CM Shipping Consultants 2002–10; govr: Clifton Coll 1993–, Tancred's Charities 1997–; pres RN Lawn Tennis Assoc 1990–96, vice-pres RN Rugby Union 1993–96, chm Navy Club 1998–2001 (ctee memb 1990–96), chm The Royal Navy Benevolent Society for Officers 1998–2006 (tstee 1996–), memb Nat Cncl RNLI 2003–09, chm N Devon Bubbly Charity 2005–14, memb Campaign Bd Sailors' Soc 2006– (ambass 2010); Yr Bro Trinity House 1977, elected Honourable Co of Master Mariners 1999, Freeman Citizen and Master Mariner of London 1999, Liveryman Worshipful Co of Shipwrights 2000; FIMgt 1980, FRIN 1996 (MRIN 1990); *Recreations* family, golf, tennis, wine, gardening, reading; *Clubs* Army and Navy, Royal N Devon Golf, Sherborne Golf; *Style*— Vice Adm Sir Christopher Morgan, KBE; ✉ c/o Lloyds Bank Ltd, 75 Cheap Street, Sherborne, Dorset DT9 3BD

MORGAN, (Frederick) David; OBE (2008), DL (Gwent 2008); s of Frederick Barlow Morgan (d 1976), and Caroline, *née* Constable (d 1999); *b* 6 October 1937, Tredegar; *Educ* Thomas Richards Tech Sch Tredegar, Henley Mgmnt Coll; *m* 27 Feb 1960, Ann, da of Spencer Cruickshank; 1 s (William Jonathan b 11 Aug 1969); *Career* chm: Glamorgan CCC 1994–98, First Class Forum (ECB) 1997–2002, ECB 2003–07; pres Int Cricket Council 2008–10 (dir 2003–); commercial dir European Electrical Steels 1991–2000; pres MCC 2014–; memb Exec Ctee Friends of St Woolos Cathedral, memb Newport Devpt Bd, vice-pres Friends of Newport Cathedral Choir; Chllr's Medal Univ of Glamorgan 2004; hon fell Univ of Wales Newport 2011; *Publications* Morgan Review of the Business of Domestic Cricket in England and Wales (2012); *Recreations* wine, cricket, church liturgy and music, travel; *Clubs* MCC (pres 2014/2015), Glamorgan CCC (pres 2013/2017), Worcester CCC, Surrey CCC (hon life vice-pres); *Style*— David Morgan, Esq, OBE, DL; ✉ e-mail fdm53a@gmail.com

MORGAN, David Treharne; MBE (2003), TD (1983); s of Maj Hugh Treharne Morgan, OBE, TD (d 1996), of Crowborough, E Sussex, and Betty Gladys Boys, *née* Schreiber; *b* 21 October 1941; *Educ* Dragon Sch Oxford, Winchester, Innsbruck Univ; *m* 7 July 1973, Heather, da of William Thomson (d 1953), of Steilston House, Dumfries; 1 da (Claire b 2 Aug 1979); *Career* TA; joined HAC 1964, cmmnd 2 Lt 1975, transferred RCT 1977, Lt Movement Control Offr 1977, Capt 2 i/c 282 MC Sqdn 1979, Maj Cmdg 281 MC Sqdn 1984, Lt Col Liaison Offr to MOD (Netherlands) 1988, Lt Col Liaison Offr All Arms Liaison Unit RLC until 1996, ret; admitted slr 1970; ptnr: R A Roberts 1973–83, Wright Son & Pepper 1987–2000; practising as David T Morgan Slrs 2000–06, conslt RadcliffesLeBrasseur 2006–13; pres Holborn Law Soc 1998–99, pres Fedn of European Bars (memb Cmmn on Ethics) 2002–03, memb Cncl Law Soc of Eng and Wales 2005–15; pres North Norfolk Railway plc 2010– (dir 1969–2010, chm 1973–92 and 2001–10); chm Maritime Heritage Tst (formerly Heritage Afloat), chm Great Central Railway plc, dir and dep pres Heritage Railway Assoc; West Somerset Railway plc: dir 1981–2009, chm 1982–87, vice-pres 2012–; dir The Solent Steam Packet Ltd, dir Boiler Engrg Skills Trg Tst Ltd 2011–; former dir Eden Valley Railway Tst (until 2001), pres Fedecrail (European Fedn of Museum and Tourist Railways) 1992, dep pres Transport Tst (former chm), memb Railway Heritage Ctee 1996–2000, vice-pres Severn Valley Railway, pres World Assoc of Tourist Trams and Trains (WATTRAIN), tstee and vice-chm Cutty Sark Tst 1992–2015, memb Industrial & Engrg Ctee Europa Nostra 2012–; Distinguished Service Medal Barcelona Bar 2011; Freeman City of London 1982, Liveryman Worshipful Co of Glaziers; memb Law Soc 1970, FInstD, MCIT; *Recreations* cinema, opera, sailing, heritage railways, maritime heritage; *Clubs* Norfolk; *Style*— David Morgan, Esq, MBE, TD; ✉ 12 Cheyne Gardens, London SW3 5QT (☎ 020 7352 6077, mobile 07703 319212, e-mail davidtmorgan21@hotmail.com and davidtmorgan@outlook.com)

MORGAN, His Hon Judge David Wynn; s of late Arthur Islwyn Lewis Morgan, and Mary, *née* Wynn; *b* 18 April 1954, Newport, Monmouthshire; *Educ* Kingswood Sch Bath, Balliol Coll Oxford (BA); *m* 25 Sept 1982, Marian Elena, o da of late David Richard Lewis; 1 da (Catherine Lowri b 1 July 1986), 1 s (Huw Alexander b 4 June 1988); *Career* called to the Bar Gray's Inn 1977, in practice 1978–2000, recorder of the Crown Court 1995–2000, circuit judge (Wales & Chester Circuit) 2000–; memb Parole Bd 2002–09; *Recreations* walking, opera, reading, Pembrokeshire; *Style*— His Hon Judge David Wynn Morgan; ✉ The Law Courts, Cathays Park, Cardiff CF10 3PG (☎ 029 2067 8730, fax 029 2041 4445, e-mail j11dwm@aol.com)

MORGAN, Prof Derec Llwyd; s of Ewart Lloyd Morgan (d 1970), and Margaret, *née* Jones (d 1984); *b* 15 November 1943; *Educ* Amman Valley GS, UCNW Bangor (BA), Jesus Coll Oxford (DPhil), Univ of Wales (DLitt); *m* 1965, Jane, da of Richard Edwards; 1 da (Elin b 17 Dec 1966); *Career* research fell Univ of Wales 1967–69, lectr UCW Aberystwyth 1969–74; UCNW Bangor: sr lectr then reader 1975–89, dir Research Centre Wales 1985–89; UCW Aberystwyth: prof of Welsh 1989–95, vice-princ 1994–95, vice-chllr and princ 1995–2004; sr vice-chllr Fed Univ of Wales 2001–2004; non-exec dir: Royal Mail for Wales and the Marches 1996–2000, Menter a Busnes 1997–2000; memb: Gen Advsy Cncl BBC 1984–90, Broadcasting Cncl for Wales 1990–95, Bd of Celtic Studies Univ of Wales 1990–95, Ct and Cncl Nat Library of Wales 1995–2007, Governing Body Inst of Grassland and Environmental Research 1995–2004, Ind Television Cmmn 1999–2003, Governing Bd Royal Welsh Coll of Music and Drama 2000–03, Pantyfedwen Tst 2001– (chm Exec Ctee 2011–); Royal Nat Eisteddfod of Wales: chm Cncl 1979–82 and 1985–86, pres Ct 1989–93, tstee and managing bd memb 2015–17; chm Exec Ctee Nat Eisteddfod Ynys Môn 1983 and 2017; chm Celtic Film and Television Festival 2000; chm: Kyffin Williams Tst 2006–, Anglesey Welsh Language Forum; chm Rowntree Cmmn on Rural Housing in Wales 2007–08; Welsh Arts Cncl Literature Prize 1971, Ellis Jones Griffith Prize 1982; hon fell Univ of Wales Bangor 1996, hon fell Jesus Coll Oxford 1999 (supernumerary fell 1997–98 and 2003–04); Hon DUniv Wales 2006; hon memb Gorsedd of the Bards 1999, founding FLSW 2010 (also memb Cncl 2010–12); *Publications* Y Tân Melys (1966), Pryderi (1970), Barddoniaeth Thomas Gwynn Jones: Astudiaeth (1972), Kate Roberts (1974, 2 edn 1991), Cerddi '75 (ed, 1975), Iliad Homer (1976), Adnabod Deg (ed, 1977), Gwna yn Llawen, Wr Ieuanc (1987), Y Diwygiad Mawr (1981, trans, The Great Awakening in Wales, 1988, reprint 1999), Williams Pantycelyn (1983), Pobl Pantycelyn (1986), Glas y Nef: Cerddi ac Emynau John Roberts Llanfwrog (ed, 1987), Cefn y Byd (1987), Emynau Williams Pantycelyn (ed, 1991), Meddwl a Dychymyg Williams Pantycelyn (ed, 1991), Charles Edwards (1994), Y Beibl a Llenyddiaeth Gymraeg (1998), John Roberts Llanfwrog: Pregethwr, Bardd, Emynydd (1999), Nid hwn mo'r llyfr terfynol: Hanes Llenyddiaeth Thomas Parry (2004), Kyffin: A Celebration (2007), Tyred i'n Gwaredu (2010), Y Brenhinbren: Bywyd a Gwaith Thomas Parry 1904–1985 (2013), Emlyn Hooson: Essays and Reminiscences (ed, 2014); *Recreations* gardening, cricket, Swansea City FC, reading; *Clubs* Premier, Glamorgan CCC, Llangefni RFC; *Style*— Prof Derec Llwyd Morgan; ✉ Carrog Uchaf, Tregaian, Anglesey LL77 7UE

MORGAN, Derek William Charles; OBE (1997), DL (Mid Glamorgan 1992); s of Thomas Brinley Morgan (d 1978), of Neath, and Brenda Vanessa, *née* Megraw (d 1992); *b* 28 November 1934; *Educ* Neath GS, Univ of Nottingham (BA); *m* 17 Aug 1963, Anne Yvette, da of Evan Morgan Davies (d 1977), of Bridgend; 2 da (Si?n, Louise); *Career* Nat Serv RE 1956–58; mangr Littlewoods Ltd 1958–61, plant mangr Ilford Ltd 1961–67, dir PA Consulting Group 1967–90, dir Business Action Team (Birmingham) Ltd 1988–90, chm API 1991–2003, dir Moulded Foams (Wales) Ltd 1991–99, HSBC Venture and Enterprise Funds (Gen Ptnr Wales) Ltd 1999–; non-exec dir: Morganite Electrical Carbon Ltd 1982–2003, Corgi Toys Ltd 1987–89; memb: Neath Devpt Partnership 1981–88, Welsh Health Common Servs Authy 1982–90, Mid Glamorgan HA 1987–92, Wales Regnl Cncl CBI 1987–97, Birmingham Chamber of Industry and Commerce 1987–90, BT Advsy Forum for Wales 1991– (chm), Cncl Univ of Wales Coll of Med 1995–99; dir Wales Mgmnt Cncl 2000–02; chm: Ogwr Partnership Tst 1988–95, Artificial Limb and Appliance Serv Ctee for Wales 1988–90, PA Pension Scheme 1988–2002, Mid Glamorgan Educn Business Partnership 1989–95, Welsh Wildlife Appeal 1989–93, Bridgend & Dist NHS Tst 1992–95, Prince's Youth Business Tst S Wales 1993–2000, Princess of Wales Hosp Brigend Macmillan Cancer Appeal 1993–96, Univ Hosp of Wales Healthcare NHS Tst 1995–99, Technology Means Business-Wales@TEB 1999–2001, Business in Focus/Cardiff and Vale Enterprise Tst Ltd 1999–, Br Heart Fndn Cardiff 2000–01; vice-chm Mid Glamorgan TEC1990–95; govr: UC Swansea 1982–98, Univ of Wales 1997–, Howell's Sch Llandaff 2000–; pres Cardiff C of C and Industry 1990–91, chm St David's Hall and New Theatre Tst 1990–98, memb All Wales e-Crime Steering Gp 2005–, chm ESU S Wales 2006–; High Sheriff Mid Glamorgan 1988–89; Freeman City of London 1986, Liveryman Worshipful Co of Tin Plate (Wire) Workers 1986, Liveryman Welsh Livery Guild 1993; Hon Dr Univ of Glamorgan 1995; FIMC 1976, CIMgt 1996 (FIMgt 1979); *Recreations* walking, wine, reading, cricket; *Clubs* Cardiff and Co (Cardiff); *Style*— Derek Morgan, Esq, OBE, DL; ✉ Erw Graig, Merthyr Mawr, Bridgend CF32 0NU

MORGAN, Gareth Dylan; s of Dr Edward Morgan, of Codsall, S Staffs, and Enfys Magdalene Grace, *née* Jones; *b* 11 September 1968, Aberystwyth; *Educ* Victoria Univ of Manchester (BSc); *m* 1, 1999 (m dis 2004), Helen Louise; 1 da (Katherine Grace b 28 April 2001); m 2, 2010, Sandra Cristina Campos; 1 da (Jocelyn Faith b 25 Aug 2005); *Career* with Army Weapons Div British Aerospace 1987–91, reporter Mercury Press Agency 1992–93, reporter then chief reporter Daily Star 1993–99, reporter Sunday Mirror 1999, asst ed Daily Star 2000–03, ed Daily Star Sunday 2003–13, dir of digital content Express Newspapers 2013–14, ceo Gluball Ltd 2015–; *Recreations* rugby, beer, chips and gravy; *Style*— Gareth Morgan, Esq; ✉ HTH Arts Centre, The Broadway, Crouch End, London N8 9JJ (e-mail gareth@gluball.com)

MORGAN, Howard James; s of late Thomas James Morgan, of N Wales, and late Olive Victoria, *née* Oldnall; *b* 21 April 1949, Denbigh, N Wales; *Educ* Fairfax HS Sutton Coldfield, Univ of Newcastle upon Tyne (MA); *m* 1, 27 Aug 1977 (m dis), Susan Ann, da of Alexander Sandilands; 2 s (Alexander James b 26 May 1985, Rupert Thomas Oldnall b 23 March 1991), 1 da (Romilly Grace Victoria b 27 March 1989); m 2, 4 June 2004, Sarah Jane, da of Roger Milligan; 2 s (Perseus Aubrey William Roger (twin) b 27

Sept 2001, Samuel Ronald Mackenzie b 10 Sept 2005), 1 da (Velvet Rose Luna Talullah Vanda (twin) b 27 Sept 2001); *Career* artist; numerous Royal and private cmmns incl: Philip Larkin, Univ of Hull, HM The Queen, HM The Queen of the Netherlands (Unilever Tricentennial celebrations), HRH Prince Michael of Kent (for Mark Masons), TRH The Prince and Princess of Hanover, Dame Antoinette Sibley NPG, Mr and Mrs Neill McConnell (USA) 1992, Chelsea Arts Club (for Absolut Vodka) 1994, Lady Bell, Mr & Mrs Nick Mason 1996, Mr & Mrs Matt Handbury 1996, Mr & Mrs Shaun Woodward 1997, Sarah Von Hallé 1998, Mr and Mrs Bernard Carl 1998, Marqués de Caltójar Tulio O'Neill Castrillo 1999, Mrs J L Thornton 1999, Mr and Mrs Mike Cottman family and friends 2001, children of Christopher Carter, children of Barbara Winkworth, black and white picture of Fleur Gibbs, three portraits for Rt Hon the Lord Magan of Castletown, Garvin Brown of Jack Daniels, Walid Abu Zalaf, Lord Douro (painting of the Battle of Waterloo, displayed by Charlie Mackinnon 2015); perm display of work Nat Portrait Gallery including: Paul Maurice Dirac, Herbert Howells, Francis Crick and Tom Stoppard; Portrait Painting Prize RSPP 2004; memb RSPP 1986; *Subject Work* incl: Shanty Pictures (In Plymouth Towne, A Drop of Nelson's Blood... and Mingulay) 1990–91, Golden Gate Quartet 1994, Monticello watercolours of Jefferson's House (for Civilization magazine) 1994, Snow White Triptych, Cinderella Triptych 1995, Ladies in Hats 1996–98, Mozart Opera pictures (Figaro, Magic Flute, Cosi Fan Tutte, Don Giovanni) 1999–2000, Strauss's Der Rosenkavalier 1999, Dinner Party 1999, Theseus and Ariadne Triptych 2001, The Quiet American 2002, Mozart's Requiem 2012, The Third Man; *Exhibitions* incl: Anthony Mould 1983, Claridges 1984, Richmond Gallery 1986–87, 1988, 1989, 1990, 1991 and 1995 (including Difficult Red, Le Soirée du Comte Fredériqúe de la Chasseur, Dinner Party-Tiananmen Square, etc), Cadogan Contemporary Watercolours 1988, 1989, 1990, 1991 and 1995, Thomas Agnew 1989, 1996 and 1998, Park Walk Gallery (lithography) 1990, Leighton House Exhibition 1993, Sara Stewart watercolours 1998, Opera pictures 2001, Eaton Gallery (studio party) 2003, David Messum Cork Street 2006, Sarah Stewart Cork Street 2008, second OK Corral picture Laine Oppenheim, Agnews 2011, watercolours shown with William Thuillier Old Bond Street 2013, Wooden Wife and Mozart's Requiem (with Sarah Stewart) Duke Street 2014; interview given to RTL Netherlands 2014, Daily Mail profile 2014, Country Life article 2015 (on Marlborough's March to the Danube with appraisal by Robert Hardy); *Books* Raising of the Light House; *Recreations* riding, 1938 Citroën, books, cricket, music, opera, reading; *Clubs* Chelsea Arts, Beefsteak; *Style*— Howard Morgan, Esq; ✉ Studio 401 1/2, Wandsworth Road, Battersea, London SW8 2JP (☎ 07892 773870, e-mail howard@howard-morgan.co.uk, website www.howard-morgan.co.uk); Studio R1 The Old Imperial Laundry, 71 Warriner Gardens, London SW11 4XW; 12 Rectory Grove, Clapham Old Town, London SW4 0EA (Twitter @howardjmorgan1)

MORGAN, James Anthony; s of Anthony Handley, of Deal, Kent, and Teresa Morgan; *b* 29 April 1978, Dover, Kent; *Educ* Castle Community Coll Deal, South Kent Coll, Univ of Kent, Open Univ; *Children* 2 da (Lily Florence b 29 May 2004, Scarlett Alice b 23 Feb 2007); *Career* Paralympic rower; achievements incl: South Coast Sr 4 rowing champion 1997, Nat Indoor Rowing champion LTA 2007, Bronze medal mixed coxed four (with Alastair McKean, Naomi Riches, MBE, Victoria Hansford, *qqv*, and Alan Sherman) Paralympics Beijing 2008; engrg maintenance mangr Pfizer Inc 1997–2011, contract mangr Norland Managed Services 2013–14 (engrg mangr 2011–13), contract mangr CBRE 2014–16, area gen mangr CBRE 2016–; *Recreations* rowing, cycling, reading, golf; *Clubs* Deal, Walmer and Kingsdown Amateur Rowing (capt 2002–05 and 2010), Folkestone Rowing; *Style*— James Morgan, Esq; ✉ Contract Manager, CBRE, 20 Lower Corniche, Hythe, Kent CT21 5TP (e-mail jamesam1978@googlemail.com)

MORGAN, Dr Janet; *see:* Balfour of Burleigh, Lady

MORGAN, John C; *Career* formerly with BP (latterly pres BP Exploration Alaska); non-exec chm Venture Production Co plc (dir 1998–), non-exec dir John Wood Gp plc 1998–; *Style*— John Morgan, Esq; ✉ Venture Production plc, Crimon Place Wing, King's Close, 62 Huntly Street, Aberdeen AB10 1RS (website www.vpc.co.uk)

MORGAN, John Christopher; s of Ieuan Gwyn Jones Morgan, of Winchester, and late Gwen, *née* Littlechild; *b* 31 December 1955; *Educ* Peter Symonds Coll Winchester, Univ of Reading (BSc), Open Univ (MBA); *m* 1 Sept 1984, Rosalind Jane, da of John Kendrew; 2 s (James b 1986, Charles b 1988), 1 da (Anna b 1989); *Career* Morgan Sindall Gp plc: chief exec 1977–2000, exec chm 2000–12, chief exec 2012–; FRICS; *Recreations* sailing; *Clubs* Mudeford Sailing, Beaulieu River Sailing; *Style*— John Morgan, Esq; ✉ Morgan Sindall Group plc, Kent House, 14–17 Market Place, London W1W 8AJ

MORGAN, John White; s of John White Morgan (d 1973), of Bridge of Allan, and Catherine, *née* Halliday (d 2000); *b* 11 March 1946, Glasgow; *Educ* Greenock Academy; *m* Morag Nicol, da of William McFarlane; 2 da (Megan Sarah b 14 Sept 1973, Erika Catherine b 11 Jan 1977); *Career* md: Simpson & Gemmell 1972–78, Woolward Royds 1978–80, Morgan Associates 1980–89; chief exec The Morgan Partnership 1999–2001 (md 1990–93, chm and md 1993–99), chm and chief exec Merle Ltd 2001, sr ptnr Stirling 1314 LLP 2013–, dir of business devpt Ferguson Marine 2014–; memb Incorporation of Maltmen; MInstM 1980; *Recreations* internet gallery, chess sets, Highland Games, Robert Burns, Town of Stirling, football, public speaking; *Clubs* Old Manor Burns (chm); *Style*— John W Morgan, Esq; ✉ 21 Claremont Drive, Bridge of Allan, Stirling FK9 4EE (☎ 0141 242 1800, mobile 07050 172007, e-mail john.morgan@merleagency.com)

MORGAN, Julie; AM; *Career* MP (Lab) Cardiff N 1997–2010, memb Nat Assembly for Wales (Lab) Cardiff N 2011–; *Style*— Ms Julie Morgan, AM; ✉ National Assembly for Wales, Cardiff Bay, Cardiff CF99 1NA

MORGAN, Baron (Life Peer UK 2000), of Aberdyfi in the County of Gwynedd; Prof Kenneth Owen; s of David James Morgan (d 1978), of Aberystwyth, and Margaret, *née* Owen (d 1989); *b* 16 May 1934, Wood Green, London; *Educ* Univ Coll Sch, Oriel Coll Oxford (MA, DPhil, DLitt); *m* 1, 4 Jan 1973, Jane (d 1992), da of Jessica Keeler, of Wrexham; 1 s (Hon David Keir Ewart b 4 July 1974), 1 da (Hon Katherine Louise b 22 Sept 1977); m 2, 25 April 2009, Elizabeth, da of Derek and Marie-Magdelaine Gibson, of Bordeaux, France; *Career* lectr in history Univ Coll Swansea 1958–66 (sr lectr 1965–66), visiting fell American Cncl of Learned Socs Univ of Columbia NY 1962–63, fell and praelector in modern history and politics The Queen's Coll Oxford 1966–89, lectr Univ of Oxford 1967–89 and 1995–; vice-chllr Univ of Wales Aberystwyth 1989–95, sr vice-chllr Univ of Wales 1993–95, research prof Univ of Wales Aberystwyth 1995–99; visiting prof: Columbia Univ 1965, Univ of Cape Town 1997, Univ of the Witwatersrand 1997–2000, Univ of Bristol 2000, King's College London 2011–; visiting lectr Univ of Texas Austin 1994, 1999, 2007, 2010 and 2014; hon prof Univ of Swansea 1999–; BBC political commentator on elections, radio and TV 1964–79; ed: Welsh History Review 1965–2003, 20th Century British History 1994–99; memb: Lab Pty 1955–, Bd Celtic Studies 1972–2003, Welsh Political Archive 1985–, Cncl Nat Library of Wales 1989–95, Lords Select Ctee on the Constitution 2001–04, Fabian Soc Ctee on the Monarchy 2002–03, Jt Select Ctee on the Constitutional Renewal Bill 2008; vice-pres Hon Soc of Cymmrodorion; hon bard Gorsedd of Nat Eisteddfod of Wales 2008, Lifetime Achievement Gold Medal Hon Soc of Cymmrodorion 2009, Lifetime Achievement Award Parliamentary History and Archives 2014, Welsh Parliamentarian of the Year Award 2014; hon fell Univ of Wales Swansea 1985, supernumerary fell Jesus Coll Oxford 1991–92; hon fell: The Queens' Coll Oxford 1992, Univ of Wales Cardiff 1997, Trinity Coll Carmarthen 1998, Oriel Coll Oxford 2003; Hon DLitt: Univ of Wales 1997, Univ of Glamorgan 1997, Univ of Greenwich 2004; FRHistS 1964, FBA 1983, fell Inst of Welsh Affrs 2013; *Books* Wales in British Politics 1868–1922 (1963, 3 edn 1980), David Lloyd George – Welsh Radical as World Statesman (1963, 2 edn 1964), Freedom or Sacrilege? (1966), Keir Hardie (1967), The Age of Lloyd George (1971, 3 edn 1983), Lloyd George – Family Letters 1885–1936 (1973), Lloyd George (1974), Keir Hardie – Radical and Socialist (1975), Consensus and Disunity – the Lloyd George Coalition Government 1918–1922 (1979), Portrait of a Progressive – the Political Career of Christopher, Viscount Addison (with Jane Morgan, 1980), Rebirth of a Nation – Wales 1880–1980 (1981), David Lloyd George 1863–1945 (1981), Welsh Society and Nationhood – Historical Essays (jt ed, 1984), The Oxford Illustrated History of Britain (ed, 1984, latest edn 2009), Labour in Power 1945–1951 (1984), Labour People – Leaders and Lieutenants, Hardie to Kinnock (1987), The Oxford History of Britain (ed, 1988, latest of many edns 2010), The Red Dragon and the Red Flag – The Cases of James Griffiths and Aneurin Bevan (1989), The People's Peace – British History since 1945 (1990, latest edn 2001), Modern Wales, Politics, Places and People (1995), Young Oxford History of Britain and Ireland (ed, 1996), Callaghan: A Life (1997), Crime, Protest and Police in British Society (jt ed, 1999), The Twentieth Century (2001), The Great Reform Act (2001), Michael Foot: A Life (2007), Ages of Reform (2011), David Lloyd George (ed, 2013), Reolution to Devolution (ed, 2014), My Histories (ed, 2015); *Recreations* architecture, music, sport, travel, cinema, cricket, opera, reading, French culture; *Clubs* Reform; *Style*— Prof the Rt Hon the Lord Morgan, FBA; ✉ The Croft, 63 Millwood End, Long Hanborough, Witney, Oxfordshire OX29 8BP (☎ 01993 881341)

MORGAN, Marilynne Ann; CB (1996); da of J Emlyn Williams (d 1984), and Roma Elizabeth, *née* Ellis (d 1992); *b* 22 June 1946; *Educ* Gads Hill Place Sch, Bedford Coll (BA); *m* 26 Sept 1970, Nicholas Alan Morgan, eld s of Rear Adm Sir Patrick Morgan, KCVO, CB, DSC (d 1989); *Career* called to the Bar Middle Temple 1972 (bencher 2002, Lent reader 2012); DHSS: legal asst 1973, sr legal asst 1978, asst slr 1982, princ asst slr (grade 3) 1985–91; DOE: dep slr 1991–92, slr and legal advsr (grade 2) 1992–97, sr dir Legal and Corp Servs Gp 1996–97; the slr DWP (formerly DSS) and Dept of Health 1997–2004, head Law and Special Policy Gp DWP (formerly DSS), non-exec dir Treasy Slr's Dept 2004–12; contrib articles to learned jls; chm: Legal Section First Div Assoc 1984–86 (vice-chm 1983–84), Departmental Task Force 1994–95; memb Gen Cncl of the Bar 1986–92, hon legal advsr Civil Serv Sports Cncl 2006–; tstee/dir Alzheimer's Soc 2003–09, tstee/dir Alzheimer's Brain Bank UK 2006–11; memb Appeal Ctee Bucks Historic Churches Tst 2007–, chm Friends of Bucks' Historic Churches 2008–; *Books* Halsbury's Laws of England (contrib 4 edn), Vaughan's Law of the European Communities (contrib, 1990); *Recreations* homely pursuits; *Clubs* Univ Women's; *Style*— Mrs Marilynne A Morgan, CB; ✉ c/o The University Women's Club, 2 Audley Square, South Audley Street, London W1K 1DB

MORGAN, Neil Christopher; s of Ernest Morgan, of Morriston, Swansea, and Myra, *née* John; *b* 28 January 1967, Morriston, Swansea; *Educ* Ystalyfera Comp Swansea, Aberystwyth Univ (LLB), Coll of Law Chester; *Children* 1 da (Emily Ceri b 13 Dec 1999), 1 s (Daniel William b 1 Oct 2004); *Career* slr specialising in property dispute resolution, commercial litigation and social housing; articled clerk Edwards Geldard Slrs 1989–91, asst slr Hugh James Jones & Jenkins 1991–96, ptnr and head Property Dispute Resolution and Social Housing Hugh James Slrs 1996–2014, ptnr Darwin Gray Slrs 2014–; memb Property Litigation Assoc; author of various articles in the legal press; memb Law Soc 1991; *Recreations* most sports, especially football; *Style*— Neil Morgan, Esq; ✉ Darwin Gray Solicitors, Helmont House, Churchill Way, Cardiff CF10 2HE (☎ 029 2082 9138, fax 029 2082 9101, e-mail nmorgan@darwingray.com)

MORGAN, Rt Hon Nicky; PC (2014), MP; *b* 10 October 1972, Kingston upon Thames; *Educ* Surbiton HS, St Hugh's Coll Oxford; *m*; 1 s; *Career* MP (Cons) Loughborough 2010–, Govt whip 2012–13, economic sec to the Treasy 2013–14, fin sec to the Treasy 2014, min for women 2014, sec of state for educn and min for women and equalities 2014–; *Publications* Ombudsmen -Time for Reform, Battle of Cotes Bridge; *Style*— The Rt Hon Mrs Nicky Morgan, MP; ✉ House of Commons, London SW1A 0AA

M

MORGAN, Hon Mr Justice; Sir Paul Hyacinth; kt (2007); s of Daniel Morgan (d 1977), of Londonderry, and Veronica Mary, *née* Elder (d 2000); *b* 17 August 1952; *Educ* St Columbs Coll Londonderry, Peterhouse Cambridge (scholar), Lincoln's Inn (Hardwicke scholar, Droop scholar); *m* 19 April 1980, Sheila Ruth, da of Arthur Reginald Harvey; 3 s (Daniel Arthur b 17 Oct 1982, Edwin Hugh Rory b 22 Oct 1985, Leo Robert b 26 Sept 1987); *Career* called to the Bar Lincoln's Inn 1975 (bencher 2001), joined chambers of Ronald Bernstein QC at 11 King's Bench Walk Temple (which removed to Falcon Chambers), QC 1992, judge of the High Court of Justice 2007– (dep High Court Judge 2001–07); dep chm Agricultural Land Tbnl 1999–2007; *Publications* incl: Megarry on Rent Acts (jt ed, 11 edn 1988), Woodfall on Landlord and Tenant (jt ed, 28 edn 1994), Fisher & Lightwood's Law of Mortgage (jt ed, 14 edn 2014), Gale on Easements (jt ed, 19 edn 2012); *Style*— The Hon Mr Justice Morgan; ✉ Royal Courts of Justice, Rolls Building, Fetter Lane, London EC4A 1NL

MORGAN, Paul William David; s of Evan John Morgan (d 1987), and Sonia Myfanwy Morgan, of Blackwood, Gwent, S Wales; *b* 12 November 1948; *Educ* Pengam GS, Ealing Sch of Business (BA); *m* 29 Dec 1988, Linda Anne, *née* Jenner; 2 s (Matthew John b 9 Feb 1989, Alexander David b 25 July 1994); *Career* brand mangr: Res Projects Smiths Industries 1971–72 (mktg trainee Clock and Watch Div 1967–71), Snacks Div United Biscuits 1972–74; RHM Foods: brand mangr 1975–77, sr brand mangr 1977–79, mktg mangr 1979–81, sr mktg mangr 1981–84; The Brand Development Company: mktg dir 1984–86, jt managing ptnr 1986–89, md 1989–; memb: Mktg Soc 1987, Market Research Soc 1995; *Recreations* sport, reading, music; *Clubs* Brentham Lawn Tennis, Ealing RFC, Beaconsfield Tennis; *Style*— Paul Morgan, Esq; ✉ Rose Cottage, Andrew Hill Lane, Hedgerley, Buckinghamshire SL2 3UL; The Brand Development Company, 50 Long Acre, London WC2E 9JR (☎ 020 7497 9727, fax 020 7497 3581)

MORGAN, Peter William Lloyd; MBE (2003); s of Matthew Morgan (d 1974), and Margaret Gwynneth Morgan (d 2005); *b* 9 May 1936; *Educ* Llandovery Coll, Trinity Hall Cambridge (MA); *m* 18 April 1964, Elisabeth Susanne, da of William Edward Davis; 3 da (Justine Elisabeth b 9 Aug 1965, Penelope Susanne b 4 March 1967, Gabrielle Margaret b 11 Sept 1969); *Career* IBM: joined 1959, sales dir London 1971, gp dir mktg IBM Europe, Middle East and Africa (Paris based) 1975, dir IBM UK 1983–87, dir IBM UK Holdings 1987–89; DG Inst of Directors 1989–94; chm: South Wales Electricity plc (Swalec) 1996 (non-exec dir 1989–95), NPI (formerly National Provident Institution) 1996–99 (non-exec dir 1990–95, dep chm 1995), Pace Micro Technology plc 1996–2000, Baltimore Technologies plc 2000–2003 (dep chm 1998–2000); non-exec dir: Oxford Instruments plc 2000–09, Hyder Consulting plc 2002–09; public memb Network Rail 2012–15; memb Economic and Social Ctee European Community 1994–2002 and 2006–15; memb Lloyd's 1987 (memb Cncl 2000–09), dir Assoc of Lloyd's Membs (ALM) 1997–2015; Master Worshipful Co of Information Technologists 2002; *Books* Alarming Drum (2005); *Recreations* gardening, wine, history, overseas travel, watching Welsh rugby, dog walking; *Clubs* Oxford and Cambridge; *Style*— Peter Morgan, Esq, MBE; ✉ Fairwood, Grayswood Road, Haslemere, Surrey GU27 2BU (☎ 01428 642757, e-mail petermorgan@cleeves2.demon.co.uk)

MORGAN, Piers; s of Anthony Glynne Pughe-Morgan, and Gabrielle Georgina Sybille, *née* Oliver; *b* 30 March 1965; *Educ* Chailey Sch, Lewes Priory Sixth Form Coll, Harlow Journalism Coll; *m* 1, 13 July 1991 (m dis 2008), Marion Elizabeth, da of Niall Shalloe; 3 s (Spencer William b 26 July 1993, Stanley Christopher b 18 June 1997, Albert b 11 Dec 2000); m 2, 24 June 2010, Celia Walden, *qv*; 1 da (b Nov 2011); *Career* reporter Surrey and S London Newspapers 1987–89, showbiz ed The Sun 1989–94; ed: News of the World 1994–95, The Mirror 1995–2004; co-prop Press Gazette 2005–06; presenter: Morgan and Platell (Channel 4) 2004–05, You Can't Fire Me I'm Famous (BBC 1) 2006–07, Piers Morgan's Life Stories (ITV 1) 2009–, Piers On (ITV 1) 2009–, When Piers Met... (ITV 1) 2009–, Piers Morgan Live (CNN) 2011–14, Good Morning Britain (ITV 1) 2015–, Killer Women (ITV 1) 2016–; judge: America's Got Talent (NBC) 2006–10, Britain's Got Talent (ITV 1) 2007–10; *Books* Private Lives of the Stars (1990), Secret Lives of the Stars (1991), Phillip Schofield – To Dream a Dream (1992), Take That – Our Story (1993), Take That – On The Road (1994), The Insider (2005), Don't You Know Who I Am? (2007), God Bless America (2009), Shooting Straight (2013); *Recreations* cricket, Arsenal FC; *Clubs* Newick Cricket; *Style*— Piers Morgan, Esq; ✉ c/o John Ferriter, The Alternative Company (e-mail john.ferriter@thealternativeco.com)

MORGAN, Rebecca; da of Alec H Carter, and June E, *née* Cavie; *b* 8 September 1967; *Educ* Queen Mary and Westfield Coll Univ of London (BA, Old English Prize), Univ of London (Dip); *m* 25 Sept 1993, Nicholas M Morgan; *Career* Bartle Bogle Hegarty: account dir 1993–96, head of account mgmnt 1996–98, planning dir 1998–2000, planning gp head 2000–04; global head of mktg communications BT 2004–06, chief strategy offr Lowe London 2006–; author of numerous articles in mktg press; APG Bronze Award 2003; memb: IPA 2000, APG 2000; *Recreations* running, skiing, eating, travelling, interiors; *Style*— Mrs Rebecca Morgan; ✉ Lowe, 60 Sloane Avenue, London SW3 3XB (☎ 020 7894 5000, e-mail rebecca.morgan@loweworldwide.com)

MORGAN, Robin Richard; s of Raymond Morgan, and Jean Edith Bennett; *b* 16 September 1953; *Educ* King Edward VI GS Stourbridge; *m* 31 July 1977 (m dis 2000), Ruth Winefride Mary; 2 s, 1 da; *Career* journalist and author; County Express Stourbridge 1971–73, Evening Echo Hemel Hempstead 1973–78; Sunday Times: reporter 1979–83, dep news ed 1983–85, ed Insight 1985–87, features ed 1987–89; ed Sunday Express 1989–91, ed Sunday Times Magazine 1991–93, editorial dir designate Reader's Digest 1993–95, ed Sunday Times Magazine 1995–, contrib ed GQ 1999–; Campaigning Journalist of the Year 1983 (commended 1982); *Books* The Falklands War (co-author, 1982), Rainbow Warrior (co-author, 1986), Bullion (co-author, 1988), Manpower (ed, 1988), Ambush (co-author, 1989), 1000 Makers of the Cinema (co-ed), Sinatra: Frank and Friendly (ed, 2007), Eltonography (ed, 2008); *Recreations* US politics, modern American literature, travel, cinema; *Style*— Robin Morgan, Esq; ✉ Sunday Times, 1 Pennington Street, Wapping, London E98 1ST (☎ 020 7782 7380)

MORGAN, Prof Rodney Emrys (Rod); s of William Emrys Morgan (d 1976), of Ystalfera, Glamorgan, and Jesmine Lilian, *née* Reed; *b* 16 February 1942; *Educ* Haberdashers' Aske's, Paston GS, Univ of Southampton (BSc, Dip Social Studies); *m* 19 August 1966, Karin Birgitta, da of Folke Mortimer Lang, of Växjö, Sweden; 3 s (Magnus Rodney b 4 Oct 1968, Tobias Mortimer b 26 Feb 1970, Benjamin Emrys Folke b 20 July 1972); *Career* sr lectr in criminology Univ of Bath 1981–89 (lectr 1972–81), prof of criminal justice Univ of Bristol 1990–2001 (prof emeritus 2001–, dean Faculty of Law 1992–95), HM chief inspr Probation Serv for Eng and Wales 2001–04, chair Youth Justice Bd for Eng and Wales 2004–07, Home Office advsr to criminal justice inspectorates 2007–11; visiting fell Univ of Oxford 1985–87; visiting prof: Univ of W Australia 1991, Harvard Univ 1996, LSE 2007–, Univ of Cardiff 2008–13, Univ of Sussex 2012; assessor to Lord Justice Woolf's inquiry into prison riots 1990–91; expert advsr to: Amnesty Int on custodial conditions 1986–, Cncl of Europe on custodial conditions 1989–; memb: ind inquiry into role and responsibilities of the police 1993–95, Avon and Somerset Police Authy 1997–2001, Parole Bd 1998–2001, memb Daniel Morgan Ind panel 2014–, numerous ctees concerned with criminal justice policy; chm Bath Philharmonia 2008–15; tstee: Police Fndn 2005–, Dance United 2006–14, Bath Festivals Tst 2008–13, Cumberland Lodge Advsy Bd 2011–16; memb Br Soc of Criminology; JP City of Bath 1974–95; Hon LLD: Univ of West of England 2005, Univ of Bath 2007; *Books* A Taste of Prison (1976), The Future of the Prison System (1980), Prisons and Accountability (1985), Coming to Terms with Policing (1989), The Oxford Handbook of Criminology (1994, 5 edn 2012), The Politics of Sentencing Reform (1995), The Future of Policing (1997), Preventing Torture (1998), Protecting Prisoners (1999), Combating Torture (2001), The Handbook of Probation (2007); memb editorial ctees of various learned jls; *Recreations* sailing, theatre, gardening, music; *Style*— Prof Rod Morgan; ✉ e-mail karin.rod@freeuk.com

MORGAN, Sadie; da of late Jack Morgan, and Caroline Darke; *b* 28 September 1969; *Educ* Kingston Poly (BA), RCA (MA); *Partner* Alex de Rijke; 2 da (Ava de Rijke b 4 April 1997, Inez de Rijke b 17 Aug 1999); *Career* founding dir dRMM Architects 1995–; projects incl: Television Centre White City London, Clapham Manor Primary Sch London, Arthouse King's Cross London, Trafalgar Place Elephant & Castle London, Athletes' Village Stratford London, York Road Opportunity Area Maidenhead, 51–54 Fenchurch Street London; design chair HS2 *Awards* BD Best New Architectural Practice Award 2004, Next Generation Award Architecture Fndn 2005, BD Architect of the Year 2013, Education Architect of the Year 2013, Schueco Gold Architect of the Year 2013, Housing Architect of the Year 2015, CBI First Women Award (Built Environment) 2015, numerous RIBA, BCSE, Civic Tst and New London (NLA) awards for individual projects; Architectural Assoc: hon treas Cncl 2009–12, pres 2013–15, chair Past Presidents' Advsy Cncl 2013–15; *Recreations* sailing, cycling; *Style*— Ms Sadie Morgan; ✉ dRMM Architects, Magdalen House, 136–148 Tooley Street, London SE1 2TU (☎ 020 7803 0777, e-mail roslyn@drmm.co.uk, website www.drmm.co.uk, Twitter @drMMArchitects)

MORGAN, Sir Terry Keith; KBE (2016, CBE 2009); s of Keith Morgan (d 1985), of Cwmbran, Gwent, and Ivy Margaret, *née* Went (d 2012); *b* 28 December 1948; *Educ* Croesycelliog Secdy Modern, Newport & Monmouth Tech Coll (HND), Univ of Birmingham (MSc); *m* 22 Aug 1970, Ann Elizabeth, da of Kingsley Jones; 1 da (Rebecca Elizabeth b 24 April 1978), 1 s (Rhys Keith b 16 June 1980); *Career* Lucas Girling: craft apprentice 1965–68, student apprentice 1968–72, prodn engr 1972–78, prod engr 1978–80; res mangr Leyland Vehicles 1980–83, mfrg mangr Leyland Bus 1983–85; Land Rover Ltd: prodn dir Range Rover 1985–87, prodn ops dir 1987–89; Rover Group: ops dir 1989–90, md Land Rover Vehicles 1991–94; md Royal Ordnance Div British Aerospace Defence Ltd 1994–96, dir of personnel British Aerospace plc 1997–2001, gp managing dir ops BAE Systems, ceo Tube Lines 2002–09, non-exec chm Crossrail 2009–; non-exec dir NAAFI 2000–, non-exec dir MITIE, chm Ricardo plc 2014–; chm: Central England Training & Enterprise Cncl, Solihull Chamber of Commerce and Industry, Manufacturing Technol Centre 2010–16, Nat Coll for High Speed Rail; memb: Bd Investors in People UK, Solihull Health Authy, Exec Industrial Soc, Qualification Curriculum Authy (QCA) 2001–; Silver Medal Inst of Mgmnt; MIMfgE 1975, FIEE 1994, FREng 1995; *Recreations* golf, rugby, gardening; *Clubs* Copt Heath Golf; *Style*— Sir Terry Morgan, KBE, FREng; ✉ 51 Lady Byron Lane, Knowle, Solihull, West Midlands B93 9AX (☎ 01564 777560)

MORGAN, Dr Thomas Clifford Naunton; s of Sir Clifford Naunton Morgan (d 1986), and Ena Muriel, *née* Evans (d 1993); *b* 9 March 1948; *Educ* Harrow, St Bartholomew's Hosp Med Sch London (MB BS); *m* 15 June 1974, Dr Rosemary Naunton Morgan, da of Maj Arthur William Hayward Bradstreet (d 1987), of Buxted, E Sussex; 3 da (Nicola Anne b 3 Dec 1977, Katherine Lucy b 24 Aug 1981, Louise Polly b 8 Oct 1985); *Career* house surgn 1974; conslt radiologist W Middx Univ Hosp 1988–2011, clinical dir of radiology Surrey and Sussex NHS Tst 2012–; Freeman City of London 1974, Liveryman Worshipful Co of Barbers 1974; memb: BMA, MDU; LRCP, FRCS 1978 (MRCS), FRCR 1987; *Recreations* shooting, tennis, windsurfing; *Clubs* Roehampton; *Style*— Dr Thomas Naunton Morgan; ✉ 3 Campion Road, Putney, London SW15 6NN (☎ 020 8789 5211, mobile 07721 401237, tom.nauntonmorgan@btinternet.com)

MORGAN, Prof (David) Vernon; s of David Vernon Grenville Morgan (d 1941), and Isobel Lovina, *née* Emanuel (d 1996); *b* 13 July 1941; *Educ* Llanelli Boys' GS, Univ of Wales Aberystwyth (BSc), Gonville & Caius Coll Cambridge (PhD), Univ of Leeds (DSc); *m* 31 July 1965, Jean, da of Francis Anderson (d 1979); 1 da (Suzanne b 22 Jan 1969), 1 s (Dyfrig b 3 Sept 1973); *Career* Cavendish Laboratory Cambridge: Univ of Wales fell 1966–68, Harwell fell 1968–70; Univ of Leeds: lectr 1970–77, sr lectr 1977–80, reader 1980–85; Univ of Wales Cardiff: prof of microelectronics 1985–, head Sch of Electrical & Systems Engrg 1992–94, head Cardiff Sch of Engrg 1995–2002, distinguished research prof 2002–; visiting prof Cornell Univ 1978 and 1979; vice-pres IOP 1992–96; IEE: chm Books Publication Ctee, memb Accreditation Ctee; memb MOD Electronic Materials and Devices Ctee; hon fell Univ of Wales Aberystwyth 2006; FIEE, FInstP, FCGI 1988, FREng 1996, FLSW 2011; Papal Cross Pro Ecclesia et Pontifica 2004; *Books* Introduction to Semiconductor Microtechnology (1983), Gallium Arsenide for Device and Integrated Circuits (1986); *Recreations* golf, hill walking; *Style*— Prof Vernon Morgan, FREng; ✉ Cardiff School of Engineering, Queen's Building, PO Box 925, University of Wales, Cardiff CF2 1XH (☎ 029 2087 4424, fax 029 2087 4292)

MORGAN, Zoe Jeanette; *née* Knight; da of Malcolm Knight, and Jeanette, *née* Mitchelson; *b* 28 January 1963, Ipswich, Suffolk; *Educ* Felixstowe Coll, Braintree Coll of FE (vice-pres student union and govr), Univ of Newcastle upon Tyne (BSc); *m* James Neale Morgan; *Career* dir of mktg Hasbro 1993–94, dir of mktg and merchandise Boots plc 1994–99, mktg dir Boots plc 2000–02, gp mktg dir HBOS Retail 2003–04, gp dir of mktg The Co-operative Gp 2004–07; fndr The Good Care Gp 2008–; non-exec dir: Kind Consumer 2009–, Burbidge 2011–16, Moss Bros 2012–, Finsbury Foods 2016–; tstee Compassion in World Farming 2007–11; memb: Industry and Parly Tst 1997, Women's Advtg Club of London (WACL) 2001; *Recreations* woodlands and wildlife preservation; *Clubs* Farmers; *Style*— Mrs Zoe Morgan

MORGAN OF DREFELIN, Baroness (Life Peer UK 2004), of Drefelin in the County of Dyfed; Delyth Jane Morgan; *b* 1962; *Educ* Bedford Coll London, UCL; *Career* campaigns co-ordinator Shelter 1987–89, dir Working for Childcare 1989–92, Nat Asthma Campaign 1992–96, chief exec Breakthrough Breast Cancer 1996–2005; Baroness-in-waiting 2007–08, Parly under sec of state Dept for Innovation, Univs and Skills 2008, Parly under sec Dept for Children, Schs and Families 2008–10; chm Dept of Health Primary Task Gp on Patient Choice, memb NHS Nat Cancer Taskforce, memb Exec Cncl Assoc of Med Research Charities; patron Breast Cancer Campaign; *Style*— Baroness Morgan of Drefelin; ✉ House of Lords, London SW1A 0PW

MORGAN OF ELY, Baroness (Life Peer UK 2011), of Ely in the City of Cardiff; (Mair) Eluned Morgan; AM; da of Canon Bob Morgan, and Elaine, *née* Evans; *b* 16 February 1967; *Educ* Ysgol Gyfun Gymraeg Glantaf, United World Coll of the Atlantic (scholar), Univ of Hull (BA); *m* 18 May 1996, Rev Dr Rhys Jenkins; 1 s (Arwel b 15 April 2001), 1 da (Gwenllian b 10 July 2003); *Career* stagiaire Euro Parl 1990, S4C 1991, Agenda TV 1992, TV documentary researcher BBC Wales 1993; MEP (Lab): Wales Mid and W 1994–99, Wales 1999–2009; AM (Lab) Mid and W Wales 2016–; dir of nat devpt SSE Wales 2010–, shadow min for Wales and Foreign Affairs House of Lords 2013–, shadow whip; hon distinguished prof Cardiff Univ 2010; *Style*— The Baroness Morgan of Ely, AM; ✉ website www.elunedmorgan.com, Twitter @eluned_morgan

MORGAN OF HUYTON, Baroness (Life Peer UK 2001), of Huyton in the County of Merseyside; Sally Morgan; da of Albert Edward Morgan; *b* 28 June 1959; *Educ* Belvedere Girls' Sch Liverpool, Univ of Durham (BA), Univ of London (PGCE, MA); *m* 1984, John Lyons; 2 s; *Career* secdy sch teacher 1981–85; Lab Pty: student organiser 1985–87, sr targeting offr 1987–93, dir of campaigns and elections 1993–95; head of pty liaison for ldr HM Oppn 1995–97, political sec to PM 1997–2001, min of state Cabinet Office 2001, dir of govt relations PM's Office 2001–05; non-exec dir Carphone Warehouse plc, memb Advsy Bd Virgin Hldgs; chair Ofsted 2011–14, memb Advsy Panel Inst of Educn; advsr to Bd ARK; chair Future Leaders Charity; *Style*— The Baroness Morgan of Huyton; ✉ e-mail morgan@parliament.uk

MORGAN WILLIAMS, Hugh Richard Vaughan; OBE; s of Hugh Morgan Williams (d 1980), of Canford Magna, Dorset, and Jean, *née* Crocker (d 1967); *b* 29 January 1953; *Educ* Aiglon Coll Switzerland, Canford Sch, Grey Coll Durham (BA); *m* 1982, Anna Louise, da of Peter Terry; 3 da (Sophie b 1984, Madeleine b 1987, Keira b 1998), 1 s (Oliver b 1991); *Career* trainee journalist Metro Radio Newcastle 1974–75, journalist LBC 1975–81, news ed Radio Tees 1981–85, fndr dir rising to chm Canford Gp plc 1985–2012; non-exec dir Nstar Finance 2008–09; chm: NE Regnl Investment Fund Ltd 1999–2009, Galaxy Radio NE 1999–2003, Capital NE 2002–, NE Economic Forum 2006–, Northern Way 2009–11, NE Access to Finance 2009–12; fndr dir Minster Sound Radio; CBI: regnl chm (NE) 1995–98, chm Small and Medium Enterprises Nat Cncl 2004–06, memb Econ Affrs Ctee; chm Small and Medium Enterprises Ctee Business Europe; memb Bd One NE 1998–2001; chm Nat Language Trg Orgn 1998–2003, govr Centre for Info on Language Trg (CILT) Nat Centre for Languages 2003–, memb Govt Steering Gp for Languages, cmmr IPPR Higher Educn Report 2013; currently chair Northumberland Tyne and Wear NHS Mental Health Tst, chair ARCC (community rehabilitation co) Durham and Tees Valley 2015–16; tstee: Int Centre for Life Newcastle 2001–10, Cowesby Tst; memb Bd Univ of Durham 2006–; chm Queen Mary's Sch Topcliffe; runner-up NE Businessman of the Year, semi-finalist Entrepreneur of the Year, Smaller Companies Export Award, DTI Languages for Export Award (twice), FT Exporter of the Year; FInstD; *Publications* Variations on a Recipe (series of cookery books, 1980), Improving Regional Competitiveness – The Business Agenda for the North (1996), Nuffield Languages Inquiry (co-author, 2001); *Recreations* skiing, tennis, reading, theatre, opera; *Clubs* Northern Counties; *Style*— Hugh Morgan Williams, Esq, OBE; ✉ e-mail hugh.morgan_williams@onyxnet.co.uk

MORGAN-OATES, Fay (Mrs Roger Oates); da of Phillip Hughes Morgan, of Goodwick, Pembrokeshire, and Iris Friend, *née* John; *b* 18 December 1946; *Educ* Bishopswood Secdy Sch, Hornsey Coll of Art (DipAD), RCA (MDes); *m* 31 July 1976, Roger Kendrew Oates, *qv*, s of William Oates; 1 s (Daniel Morgan Oates b 25 Jan 1979); *Career* textile designer; set up own studio London 1970–75, dir Weavers Workshop Edinburgh 1973–75, pt/t lectr Goldsmiths Coll London 1975–79, memb Governing Body Herefordshire Coll of Art and Design 1989–95; Morgan Oates Partnership at the House in the Yard Ledbury 1975–86, Morgan & Oates Ltd 1986–97 (designing for own label and clients incl Ralph Lauren, Christian Dior, Sonia Rykiel, Donna Karan and Laura Ashley), sr ptnr Roger Oates Design Associates 1987–98, dir Roger Oates Design Co Ltd 1998–; work in exhibitions incl: The Craftsman's Art (V&A Museum) 1973, The House in the Yard Textiles from the Workshop of Fay Morgan and Roger Oates (Welsh Arts Cncl Cardiff and tour) 1978, Tufted Rugs (Environment London) 1980, Texstyles (Crafts Cncl London and tour) 1984–85, Design Awards (Lloyd's Building London) 1988; awarded: USA ROSCOE award 1984, British Design award 1988, Duke of Edinburgh's certificate for services to design, Weavers Co Silver Medal 2011 (with Roger Oates); contrib various TV prodns, IdFX Magazine Decorex Award Best Contempory Product 1998; FRSA; *Books* Clothes Without Patterns (1977); *Style*— Mrs Fay Morgan-Oates; ✉ Roger Oates Design Company Ltd, The Long Barn, Eastnor, Ledbury, Herefordshire HR8 1EL (☎ 01531 632718, fax 01531 631361, e-mail fmorgan@rogeroates.com, website www.rogeroates.com); Roger Oates

Design, 1 Munro Terrace, Cheyne Walk, London SW10 0DL (☎ 020 7351 2288, fax 020 7351 6841)

MORGANS, (John) Barrie; *b* 9 November 1941; *Educ* Dyffryn GS Port Talbot, Swansea Tech Coll; *m*; 1 s, 2 da; *Career* fin mangr British Steel until 1964 (joined 1957), fin mangr British Rail 1965–67; IBM: cost accountant then pricing mangr 1967–71, fin mangr Southern Area IBM Europe Paris 1971–73, controller IBM UK Ltd 1975–78, dir of fin 1978–86, dir of fin and planning 1986–92, dir of quality and mgmnt servs 1992–95, chief exec IBM UK Ltd 1995–96, chm and chief exec IBM UK Ltd 1996–97, dir IBM United United Kingdom Holdings Ltd until 1997; non-exec chm: Plasmon plc 1990–2006, Azlan Gp plc 1997–, Telemedic Holdings plc, IBM Pensions Trust Ltd; non-exec dir: Legal & General Gp plc 1997–2006, Psion plc 1998–2001, 1... Ltd 2000–; chm of govrs Chichester Coll of Technol; FCCA, FRSA; *Recreations* good wine, food, skiing, travel; *Style*— J Barrie Morgans, Esq

MORGENSTERN, Philip Louis; s of Maurice Joseph Morgenstern (d 1966), and Celia, *née* Hausmann (d 1999); *b* 15 January 1932; *Educ* St Paul's, Univ of London (BA); *m* 1961, Estelle Pamela, da of Jakoba Erenberg; 2 da (Ava Miriam b 18 Oct 1963, Deborah Sarah b 15 April 1972), 2 s (Neil Hardy Iain b 31 March 1965, Matthew Joseph b 6 Jan 1968); *Career* Nicholson Graham & Jones: articled clerk 1954, ptnr 1962, sr ptnr 1981–95; sec GB-Sasakawa Foundation 1986–97; tstee: Inst of Jewish Studies 1989 (chm 1999–2013, emeritus pres 2013–), Jewish Law Publication Fund 1990–2012, Kessler Fndn 1993–2011; Freeman City of London; *Recreations* hermeneutic and rhetorical exegesis of ancient texts, music, art history; *Style*— Philip Morgenstern, Esq; ✉ c/o K&L Gates LLP, 1 New Change, London EC4M 9AF (☎ 020 7648 9000, fax 020 7648 9001)

MORIARTY, Hon Mr Justice Michael Anthony; s of Dr James Moriarty (d 1975), of Belfast and Dublin, and Nora, *née* Diamond (d 1992); *b* 10 August 1946, Belfast; *Educ* Blackrock Coll Dublin, UC Dublin (BCL, Dip European Law), King's Inns Dublin; *m* 1980, Mary Irvine; 1 s (Mark b 1 Oct 1983), 2 da (Clare b 31 Aug 1986, Aoife b 2 Aug 1988); *Career* called to the Bar: King's Inns Dublin 1968, Middle Temple London 1981; barr-at-law 1968–82, sr counsel 1982–87, circuit judge 1987–96, judge of the High Court of Ireland 1996–; chm Lord Mayor's Cmmn on Crime in Dublin 1995, chm and sole memb Tbnl of Inquiry into Payments to Charles Haughey and Michael Lowry 1997; *Recreations* music (especially opera), sport (especially cricket), wine; *Clubs* Fitzwilliam Lawn Tennis (Dublin), Pembroke Cricket (Dublin); *Style*— The Hon Mr Justice Michael Moriarty; ✉ The High Court, Four Courts, Inns Quay, Dublin 7, Ireland; Tribunal of Inquiry, Upper Yard, Dublin Castle, Dublin 2, Ireland

MORIARTY, Stephen; QC (1999); s of George William Moriarty, and Dorothy Violet, *née* Edwards; *b* 14 April 1955; *Educ* Chichester HS for Boys, BNC Oxford (BA, Proxime Accessit Prize 1977, BCL 1978, Vinerian Scholarship 1978); *m* 1989, Dr Susan Clare Stanford; *Career* Univ of Oxford: fell and tutor in law Exeter Coll 1979–86, lectr in law 1979–86; memb Middle Temple 1976 (bencher 2009), called to the Bar 1986, practising barr 1987–; chm Commercial Bar Assoc 2011–13; *Recreations* theatre, opera, cycling; *Clubs* Reform; *Style*— Stephen Moriarty, Esq, QC; ✉ Fountain Court Chambers, Temple, London EC4Y 9DH (☎ 020 7583 3335, fax 020 7353 0329, e-mail sm@fountaincourt.co.uk)

MORISON, Hugh; CBE (2002); s of Archibald Ian Morison, of Felpham, W Sussex, and Enid Rose, *née* Mawer; *b* 22 November 1943; *Educ* Chichester HS for Boys, St Catherine's Coll Oxford (MA); *m* 1, 1971 (m dis 1993), Marion, da of Fred Aubrey Smithers, of Lincoln; 2 da (Emma b 1972, Lucy b 1975); m 2, 1993, Ilona, da of Sandor Roth, of Budapest; *Career* Civil Serv SO 1966–93: under sec Scottish Home and Health Dept 1984–88, Industry Dept for Scotland 1988–93; chief exec Scotch Whisky Assoc 1994–2003; pres European Confedn of Spirits Producers 2001–03, chm Scottish Business and Biodiversity Gp 1999–2003; non-exec dir Praban Na Linne Ltd 2005–06; memb: Health Appointments Advsy Ctee (Scotland) 1994–2000, Exec Ctee Barony Housing Assoc Ltd 1996–2010 (chm 2005–09); chm Letterfearn Moorings Assoc 2001–; govr Univ of the Highlands and Islands 2004–13; *Recreations* hill walking, sailing, literature, archaeology, playing the euphonium; *Clubs* New (Edinburgh); *Style*— Hugh Morison, Esq, CBE; ✉ 12 Sunbury Place, Edinburgh EH4 3BY (☎ 0131 225 6568, e-mail hugh.morison@at-inform.com)

MORITZ, Sir Michael; KBE (2013); *b* Cardiff; *Educ* Univ of Oxford; *Career* venture capitalist; early career as journalist (incl head San Francisco bureau Time magazine late 1970s) then held various positions with Time Warner and founded Technologic Ptnrs, with Sequoia Capital 1986–; currently dir: Flextronics, Google, Saba Software; formerly founding dir: Agile Software, Global Center, LinkExchange, eGroups, NeoMagic, Quote.com, Visigenic, CenterRun, PayPal, Yahoo!; hon student ChCh Oxford; *Style*— Sir Michael Moritz, KBE; ✉ Sequoia Capital, 3000 Sand Hill Road, Building 4, Suite 180, Menlo Park, CA 94025, USA

MORLAND, Miles Quintin; s of Cdr Henry Morland, RN, and Vivienne Yzabel Suzanne Nicholson Walters, *née* Hogg; *b* 18 December 1943, Vizagapatam, India; *Educ* Radley, Lincoln Coll Oxford; *m* 10 March 1972 (m dis 2003), Guislaine, da of Guy Vincent Chastenet de la Maisoneuve; 2 da (Katherine Natasha b 29 Aug 1973, Georgia Susanna b 18 Dec 1976); *Career* md The First Boston Corp 1983–89; chm Blakeney Management 1990–, chm and fndr DPI 2008, chm and fndr Miles Morland Fndn 2013–; dir SABMiller plc 1999–2015; *Publications* The Man Who Broke Out of the Bank (1992), Cobra in the Bath (2015); *Recreations* visiting places where you can't drink the tapwater; *Clubs* Leander, Boodle's, Pratt's, Passing Clouds; *Style*— Miles Morland, Esq; ✉ Jubilee House, 2 Jubilee Place, London SW3 3TQ

MORLEY, HE David; *m* Jacqueline (Jacki), *née* Wells; *Career* diplomat; FCO: joined 1973, commercial attaché Kaduna 1984–88, desk offr CCD 1988–91, mgmnt offr Moscow 1991–93, sanctions enforcement then desk offr Bosnia 1993–95; dep high cmmr Mbabane 1995–99, first sec (information) UK Del NATO 1999–2001; FCO: head Export Licensing Team NPD 2001–03, head Prisoner Policy Team Consular Directorate 2003–05, head Strategy Team Consular Directorate 2005–07; administrator Tristan da Cunha 2007–11, high cmmr to The Gambia 2011–; *Style*— HE Mr David Morley; ✉ c/o FCO (Banjul), King Charles Street, London SW1A 2AH

MORLEY, David Howard; s of Glyn Morley, of Ludlow, Shropshire, and Yvonne, *née* Auvache; *b* 21 September 1956; *Educ* Queens Park HS Chester, St John's Coll Cambridge; *m* 4 Sept 1982, Susan Diana, da of Denis C Radcliffe, of Huxley, nr Chester, Cheshire; 2 s (William b 27 Jan 1987, Thomas b 13 April 1989), 2 da (Emma b 20 May 1985, Rachael b 11 Jan 1992); *Career* admitted slr 1982; Allen & Overy: ptnr 1988–, global head of banking practice 1998, managing ptnr 2003–08, sr ptnr 2008–; memb Law Soc; *Style*— David Morley, Esq; ✉ Allen & Overy, One Bishops Square, London E1 6AD (☎ 020 3088 2551, e-mail david.morley@allenovery.com)

MORLEY, Paul Robert; s of Leslie Ronald Morley (d 1977), and Dilys, *née* Young; *b* 26 March 1957; *Educ* Stockport GS, Stockport Coll of Technol; *partner* Elizabeth Levy; 1 da (Madeleine Amber b 7 January 1992); *Career* writer NME 1976–83, dir Zang Tuum Tumb Records, A&R and art dir Frankie Goes to Hollywood (incl Relax, biggest selling single of 1980s), fndr memb Art of Noise, conslt Island Records 1990–92 (exec prodr Vic Reeves, *qv*, no 1 single Dizzy); contrib ed: Blitz Magazine 1983–87, Esquire Magazine 1991–99; TV critic: New Statesman 1987–89, The Guardian 1991–94, GQ Magazine 1998–99; regular contrib to nat newspapers, TV documentaries and radio arts progs; co-fndr Service prodn co 2002; conslt Palm Pictures 2002–; hon memb Peter Cook Appreciation Soc; *Television* fndr presenter The Late Show (BBC2) 1989–91, writer and presenter The Thing Is...(Channel 4) 1989–92, panellist Newsnight Review (BBC2) 2001–, writer and dir arts documentaries for BBC, ITV and Channel 4 (incl Omnibus on Reeves and Mortimer); *Publications* Ask: The Chatter of Pop (1986), Nothing (2000); contrib: Faber Book of Pop, The Penguin Book of Rock and Roll Journalism; *Recreations* listening, looking, reading, philosophy, hotels, internet, music, waiting; *Style*— Paul Morley, Esq; ✉ David Goodwin Associates, 55 Monmouth Street, London WC2H 5DG (☎ 020 7240 9992, fax 020 7395 6110, e-mail assistant@davidgodwinassociates.co.uk)

MORONY, Elizabeth Rachel Anne; *née* Gent; da of Eric Gent, and Monica, *née* Jukes; *b* 2 May 1968; *Educ* Chislehurst and Sidcup GS, Wadham Coll Oxford (MA); *m* 8 May 1993, Matthew Morony; 2 s (George Lovett b 21 Feb 1997, Henry Thomas b 10 June 1999); *Career* slr; ptnr Clifford Chance 2000–; *Recreations* tennis, gardening, family; *Clubs* Roehampton Tennis, Arts; *Style*— Mrs Elizabeth Morony; ✉ Clifford Chance LLP, 10 Upper Bank Street, London E14 5JJ (☎ 020 7006 1000, fax 020 7006 5555, e-mail elizabeth.morony@cliffordchance.com)

MORPETH, Iain Cardean Spottiswoode; TD (1991); s of Sir Douglas Spottiswoode Morpeth, TD, of Shamley Green, Surrey, and Anne Rutherford, *née* Bell; *b* 28 December 1953, Edinburgh; *Educ* Fettes, Univ of Bristol (LLB); *m* 30 June 1979, Angela Susan, da of Sir Thomas Gordon Devitt, 2 Bt (d 1995), of Colchester, Essex; 3 s (Richard Douglas Gordon b 18 Nov 1985, Duncan Hugh Sinclair b 1 Dec 1987, James Rutherford Thomas b 17 Oct 1992), 1 da (Catherine Louise Nicholl b 10 Feb 1990); *Career* admitted slr 1978, ptnr Clifford Chance 1988–2011, ptnr Ropes & Gray 2012–; memb: Law Soc, Int Bar Assoc; Liveryman Worshipful Co of Slrs 1993; *Publications* Property Joint Ventures, Structures and Precedents (contrib); *Recreations* fishing, skiing, Alpine climbing; *Style*— Iain Morpeth, Esq; ✉ Ropes & Gray, 60 Ludgate Hill, London EC4M 7AW

MORPHET, John Charles; s of William Morphet (d 1999), and Peggy, *née* Maddock (d 1999); *b* 22 November 1954, Preston; *Educ* Bentham GS; *m* 15 June 2013, Donna Jane; 3 s (Matthew b 7 May 1974, James b 21 Aug 1977, William b 7 Dec 1989), 2 da (Rebecca b 9 Dec 1986, Madison b 20 Aug 2003); *Career* worked on family estate; fndr: South Lakeland Caravans 1988, South Lakeland Caravans Ltd 1996, Lake District Leisure Pursuits Ltd 2002, Pure Leisure 2004 (including Royal Westmoreland, Barbados, Spain and Cyprus lodge devpts); Fast Track 100 Award for 4 years; *Recreations* golf, farming, fishing; *Style*— John Morphet, Esq; ✉ Bishops Court, Kirkmichael, Isle of Man (☎ 01824 871106, e-mail jmbishopscourt@manx.net)

MORPHY, Leslie Ann; OBE (2010); *Career* formerly: head of research and devpt Basic Skills Agency, UK dir of progs and policy The Prince's Tst; chief exec Crisis 2006–; *Style*— Ms Leslie Morphy, OBE; ✉ Crisis, 66 Commercial Street, London E1 6LT

MORPURGO, Michael Andrew Bridge; OBE (2006, MBE 1999); s of Tony Van Bridge (d 2005), and Catherine, *née* Cammaerts; step s of Jack Morpurgo (d 2002); *b* 5 October 1943, St Albans; *Educ* King's Sch Canterbury, RMA Sandhurst, KCL; *m* Clare Lane; 2 s (Sebastian b 1964, Horatio b 1967), 1 da (Rosalind b 1968); *Career* writer; early career as primary sch teacher, fndr (with wife) Farms for City Children 1976–; children's laureate 2003–05, Author of the Year 2005; Chevalier des Arts et des Letteres (France) 2004; incl: It Never Rained: Five Stories (1974), Living Poets (1974), Long Way Home (1975), Thatcher Jones (1975), The Story-Teller (1976), Friend or Foe (1977), Do All You Dare (1978), What Shall We Do with It? (1978), All Around the Year (with Ted Hughes, 1979), Love at First Sight (1979), That's How (1979), The Day I Took the Bull by the Horn (1979), The Ghost-Fish (1979), The Marble Crusher and Other Stories (1980), The Nine Lives of Montezuma (1980), Miss Wirtle's Revenge (1981), The White Horse of Zennor: And Other Stories from below the Eagle's Nest (1982), War Horse (1982), Twist of Gold (1983), Little Foxes (1984), Why the Whales Came (1985), Words of Songs (libretto, music by Phyllis Tate, 1985), Tom's Sausage Lion (1986), Conker (1987), Jo-Jo, the Melon Monkey (1987), King of the Cloud Forests (1988, Prix Sorciere (France) 1993), Mossop's Last Chance (with Shoo Rayner, 1988), My Friend Walter (1988), Albertine, Goose Queen (with Shoo Rayner, 1989), Mr. Nobody's Eyes (1989), Jigger's Day Off (with Shoo Rayner, 1990), Waiting for Anya (1990, shortlist Carnegie Medal 1991), And Pigs Might Fly! (with Shoo Rayner, 1991), Colly's Barn (1991), The Sandman and the Turtles (1992), Martians at Mudpuddle Farm (with Shoo Rayner, 1992), The King in the Forest (1993), The War of Jenkins' Ear (1993), Arthur, High King of Britain (1994, shortlist Carnegie Medal 1995), Ghostly Haunts (ed, 1994), Snakes and Ladders (1994), The Dancing Bear (1994), Blodin the Beast (1995), Muck and Magic: Tales from the Countryside (ed, 1995), Mum's the Word (with Shoo Rayner, 1995), Stories from Mudpuddle Farm (with Shoo Rayner, 1995), The Wreck of the Zanzibar (1995, Whitbread Children's Book Award 1995, shortlist Carnegie Medal 1996), Beyond the Rainbow Warrior: A Collection of Stories to Celebrate 25 Years of Greenpeace (co-ed, 1996), Robin of Sherwood (1996), Sam's Duck (1996), The Butterfly Lion (1996, Gold Award Nestlé Smarties Book Prize 1996), The Ghost of Grania O'Malley (1996), Farm Boy (1997), Cockadoodle-doo, Mr Sultana! (1998), Escape from Shangri-La (1998), Joan of Arc (1998), Red Eyes at Night (1998), Wartman (1998), Animal Stories (ed, 1999), Kensuke's Kingdom (1999, Red House Children's Book Award 2000, Prix Sorciere (France) 2001), The Rainbow Bear (1999), Wombat Goes Walkabout (1999, Prix Sorciere (France) 1999), Billy the Kid (2000), Black Queen (2000), Dear Olly (2000), From Hereabout Hill (2000), The Kingfisher Book of Classic Boy Stories: A Treasury of Favourites from Children's Literature (ed, 2000), The Silver Swan (2000), Who's a Big Bully Then? (2000), More Muck and Magic (2001), Out of the Ashes (2001, shortlist WH Smith Award for Children's Literature 2002), Toro! Toro! (2001), Because a Fire Was in My Head: 101 Poems to Remember (ed, 2002), Cool! (2002, shortlist Blue Peter Book Award: The Book I Couldn't Put Down 2003), Mr. Skip (2002), The Kingfisher Treasury of Classic Stories (co-ed, 2002), The Last Wolf (2002, Bronze Award Nestlé Smarties Book Prize 2002), The Sleeping Sword (2002), Gentle Giant (2003), Private Peaceful (2003, shortlist Carnegie Medal 2003, shortlist Whitbread Children's Book Award 2003, Red House Children's Book Award 2004), Cock Crow (co-ed, 2004), Cockadoodle-doo Mr Sultana! (with Holly Swain, 2004), Orchard Book of Aesop's Fables (ed, 2004), Sir Gawain and the Green Knight (2004), War: Stories of Conflict (ed, 2005); *Style*— Michael Morpurgo, Esq, OBE; ✉ c/o David Higham Associates, 5–8 Lower John Street, Golden Square, London W1F 9HA (www.michaelmorpurgo.org)

MORPURGO DAVIES, Prof Anna Elbina Laura Margherita; Hon DBE (2001); da of Augusto Morpurgo (d 1939), and Maria, *née* Castelnuovo (d 1991), of Rome; *b* 21 June 1937, Milan, Italy; *Educ* Liceo-Ginnasio Giulio Cesare Rome, Univ of Rome (MA); *m* 8 Sept 1962 (m dis 1978), John Kenyon Davies, s of Harold Davies; *Career* assistente in classical philology Univ of Rome 1959–61, jr fell Center for Hellenic Studies Washington DC 1961–62, lectr in classical philology Univ of Oxford 1964–71, fell St Hilda's Coll Oxford 1966–71, prof of comparative philology Univ of Oxford 1971–2004 (Diebold prof of comparative philology 2003–04, prof emeritus 2004–), fell Somerville Coll Oxford 1971–2004 (emeritus fell 2004–); visiting prof: Univ of Pennsylvania 1971, Yale Univ 1977, Univ of Calif Berkeley 2006 and 2007; Collitz prof Linguistic Soc of America 1975, Semple lectr Univ of Cincinnati 1983, TBL Webster prof Stanford Univ 1988, Jackson lectr Harvard Univ 1990; Sather prof of classical literature Univ of Calif Berkeley 2000; delegate OUP 1992–2004; pres Br Philological Soc 1976–80 (hon vice-pres 1980–); foreign hon memb American Acad of Arts & Sciences 1986, corresponding memb Oesterreichische Akademie der Wissenschaften (Wien) 1988, hon memb Linguistic Soc of America 1993, memb Academia Europaea 1989, foreign memb American Philosophical Soc 1991, corresponding memb Académie des inscriptions et belles-lettres, Institut de France 1992,

M

Bayerische Akademie der Wissenschaften 1998, foreign memb Accademia dei Lincei 2010; Premio Linceo per la Linguistica Accademia dei Lincei 1996; hon fell St Hilda's Coll Oxford 1972; Hon DLitt: Univ of St Andrews 1981, Univ de Nancy 2009; FSA 1974, FBA 1985; *Books* Mycenaeae Graecitatis Lexicon (1963), Studies in Greek, Italic and Indo-European Linguistics offered to L R Palmer (ed with W Meid, 1976), Linear B/A 1984 Survey (ed with Y Duhoux, 1985), La Linguistica dell' Ottocento (1996), Nineteenth Century Linguistics (1998), A Companion to Linear B Vol I-II (ed with Y Duhoux, 2008–11); numerous articles in Br and foreign periodicals; Festschrift: Indo European Perspectives, Studies in honour of Anna Morpurgo Davies (ed by J H W Penney, 2004), A Companion to Linear B Vol I-II-III (ed with Y Duhoux, 2008); *Style*— Prof Anna Morpurgo Davies, DBE, FSA, FBA; ✉ 22 Yarnells Hill, Oxford OX2 9BD; Somerville College, Oxford OX2 6HD (e-mail anna.davies@some.ox.ac.uk)

MORRELL, Peter John; s of Arthur Markham Morrell (d 1984), of Oxford, and Geraldine Doris, *née* Harvey (d 1992), of Devon; *b* 28 February 1931; *Educ* numerous schs (latterly Worthing HS), Kingston upon Thames Coll of Art (NDD), RCA (life drawing and life painting prizes, ARCA); *m* 1, 1958, Yvonne Nichol; m 2, 1964, Margaret Froud; 1 s (Steven b 1967), 1 da (Nicola b 1971); m 3, 1981, Helene Halstuch, of New York; *Career* artist; pt/t lectr in fine art painting: Maidstone Coll of Art 1961–62, Sir John Cass Sch of Art 1962–65, Hornsey Coll of Art 1962–70, St Martin's Coll of Art 1969–70, Central Sch of Art and Design 1970–92; instigated summer schs at Central Sch of Art and Design 1986; numerous solo and gp exhbns, work in numerous private and public collections; work purchased by the Arts Cncl since 1964; memb London Gp 1990–; RWS 1983; *Awards* Br Cncl Prize 1955, Arts Cncl Prize 1959, Prix de Rome in Painting 1959; *Style*— Peter Morrell, Esq; ✉ 19 Tremeadow Terrace, Hayle, Cornwall TR27 4AF (☎ 01736 755051, website www.petermorrell.co.uk)

MORRICE, Graeme; *b* 23 February 1959, Edinburgh; *Educ* Broxburn Acad, Napier Univ; *Career* MP (Lab) Livingston 2010–15; *Recreations* literature, art, music; *Style*— Graeme Morrice, Esq; ✉ Constituency Office, Geddes House, Kirkton North Road, Livingston, West Lothian EH54 6GU; House of Commons, London SW1A 0AA (e-mail graeme.morrice.mp@parliament.uk, website www.graememorricemp.co.uk)

MORRILL, Rev Prof John Stephen; s of William Henry Morrill, of Hale, Cheshire, and Marjorie, *née* Ashton; *b* 12 June 1946; *Educ* Altrincham GS for Boys, Trinity Coll Oxford (MA, DPhil); *m* 27 July 1968, Frances Dreda Mary, *née* Mead (d 2007); 4 da (Rachel Clare (Mrs Finch) b 18 Jan 1973, Ruth Mary b 11 Nov 1978, Naomi Catharine (Mrs McCulloch) b 27 May 1981, Clare Margaret b 27 Nov 1983); *Career* research fell Trinity Coll Oxford 1970–74; lectr in history: St Catherine's Coll Oxford 1973–74, Univ of Stirling 1974–75; Univ of Cambridge: lectr in history 1975–92, reader in early modern history 1992–98, prof of Br and Irish history 1998–; fell Selwyn Coll Cambridge 1975– (sr tutor 1987–92, vice-master 1994–); ordained to the permanent diaconate RC diocese of East Anglia 1996; Br Acad: chair Public Understanding and Activities Ctee 1997–, memb Cncl 1999–, vice-pres 2001–; AHRB: convenor History Panel 1999–2002, tstee 2000–03, memb Bd 2000–04; Ford's lectr in Br history Univ of Oxford 2006; centenary fell Historical Assoc 2006; hon fell Trinity Coll Oxford 2006; Hon DLitt UEA 2002, Hon DUniv Surrey 2002; FRHistS 1977 (vice-pres 1992–96), FBA 1996, Hon MRIA 2010; *Publications* author and ed of 18 books on Br and Irish history principally concerning the 16th and 17th centuries, and author of more than 60 essays and articles; *Recreations* classical music, travel, malt whisky; *Style*— Rev Prof John Morrill; ✉ 1 Bradfords Close, Bottisham, Cambridgeshire CB25 9DQ (☎ 01223 811822); Selwyn College, Cambridge CB3 9DQ (☎ 01223 335895, fax 01223 335837, e-mail jsm1000@cam.ac.uk)

MORRIS; *see also:* Temple-Morris

MORRIS, Abigail; da of Geoffrey Morris, and Audrey, *née* Wolfson; *Educ* Woodhouse Sch Finchley, Camden Sch, Sidney Sussex Coll Cambridge (MA); *m* David Evans; 3 da; *Career* fndr and artistic dir Trouble & Strife Theatre Co 1984–90, artistic dir Soho Theatre Co 1992–, artistic dir of team which designed, raised money for and built new Soho Theatre and Writers' Centre Dean Street (opened 2000); Judith E Wilson visting fell in drama Univ of Cambridge 1990–91; ceo Jewish Museum London 2012– (introduced prog of temporary exhbns on topics such as Kitaj, menswear, blood and Judith Kerr); *Productions* for Trouble & Strife Theatre Co: Present Continuous, Now and at the Hour of our Death (co-author), Next to You I Lie (co-author); Soho Theatre Co prodns incl: Tulip Futures, Kindertransport (also Manhattan Theatre Club and West End), Rock Station (Cockpit Theatre), The Station, Be My Baby, Stop Kiss, Navy Pier, Kiss Me Like You Mean It, Office (also Lyceum Theatre Edinburgh), Protection, Wrong Place, Colder than Here, A Night at the Dogs; freelance credits incl: Leave it to Me (Arts Theatre), Noyes Fluddle (Albert Hall), Julius Caesar Jones (Sadler's Wells Theatre); *Awards* Fringe First 1986 and 1987, Time Out Award 1988 and 1993, London Fringe Award 1994, Empty Space Award 1996; *Recreations* swimming, running, family, watching football, Jewish Learning; *Clubs* Cally Masters, Tri London; *Style*— Ms Abigail Morris; ✉ c/o Jewish Museum, Raymond Burton House, Albert Street, London NW1 7NB

MORRIS, Alfred Cosier; CBE (2003), DL (Glos 2002); s of Stanley Bernard Morris (d 1970), of Anlaby, E Yorks, and Jennie, *née* Fletcher (d 1994); *b* 12 November 1941; *Educ* Hymers Coll Hull, Lancaster Univ (MA); *m* 26 Sept 1970, Annette, da of Eamonn and May Donovan, of Cork, Ireland; 1 da (Jessica b 24 April 1980); *Career* articled clerk Oliver Mackrill 1958–63, co sec fin controller and dir various cos 1963–71, sr Leverhulme res fell in univ planning and orgn Univ of Sussex 1971–74, visiting lectr in fin mgmnt Univ of Warwick 1973, gp mgmnt accountant Arthur Guinness Ltd 1974–76, sr mgmnt consIt Deloitte Haskins & Sells 1976–77, fin advsr subsids of Arthur Guinness 1977–80, acting dir South Bank Poly 1985–86 (dep dir 1980–85), dir Bristol Poly 1986–92, vice-chllr UWE 1992–2005, vice-chllr Univ of Wales Lampeter 2008–09, vice-chllr London Met Univ 2009–10; strategic advsr Kaplan (Washington Post Co) 2010–11, chm Higher Education Assocs Ltd 2011–; memb: HE Quality Cncl 1992–94, HE Funding Cncl for Wales 1992–2000, FE Funding Cncl for England 1997–99; advsr House of Commons Select Ctee on Educn Sci and Arts 1980–83; chm Audit Ctee e-Universities Holding Co 2002–06; dir Bristol and West plc (formerly Bristol and West Building Soc) 1992–2002; chm: Bristol Old Vic Tst 1992–94, Patrons of the Bristol Old Vic Ltd 1993–2008, N Bristol NHS Tst 2006–08; memb: SW Arts 1994–2000, SW E RDA 1998–2002, Gtr Bristol Fndn 1999–2003 (chm 1999–2000); pres Dolphin Soc 2008; tstee: Bristol Old Vic Theatre Sch 2006–10, Bristol Charities 2006–, Trinity of David Tst 2009–10 (chair); patron: Davar 1999–2011, Fast Track Tst 2000–11; pres City Acad Bristol 2003–05; fell Humberside Coll; Hon LLD: Univ of Bristol, UWE, Univ of Glos; High Sheriff Glos 2006–07; FCA 1963 (memb Cncl 2007–11), FSS, hon fell RWA 2001; *Books* Resources and Higher Education (jt ed and contrib, 1982); *Recreations* tennis, windsurfing, sailing; *Clubs* Salcombe Yacht; *Style*— Alfred Morris, Esq, CBE, DL; ✉ 81a Fore Street, Salcombe TQ8 8BY (e-mail alfred.morris@btinternet.com)

MORRIS, Prof Alun Owen; OBE (2000); s of Arthur Morris (d 1969), of Ruthin, and Jennie, *née* Owen (d 1993); *b* 17 August 1935, Ruthin; *Educ* Brynhyfryd Sch Ruthin, UCNW Bangor (BSc, PhD); *m* 1, 16 April 1960, Margaret Erina (d 1987), da of Rev William Jones, of Caernarfon; 2 da (Lowri b 1962, Angharad b 1971), 1 s (Iwan b 1964); m 2, 11 April 1992, Mary, da of Moses Jones, of Aberystwyth; *Career* Univ of Wales Aberystwyth: asst lectr 1959–61, lectr 1961–66, sr lectr 1966–69, prof 1969–2000, vice-princ 1986–90, emeritus prof 2000–; London Mathematical Soc: memb Cncl 1974–78, jt ed 1983–88, vice-pres 1993–94, treas 1994–2002; chm Higher Educn Section Jt Mathematical Cncl 1993–95, memb Mathematics Ctee UGC 1986–89, advsr to Univ Funding Cncl 1989–93; memb: London Mathematical Soc 1960, American Mathematical Soc 1962; FLSW 2013; *Books* Linear Algebra – An Introduction (1978, 2 edn 1982); *Style*— Prof Alun Morris, OBE, FLSW; ✉ Hiraethog, Cae Melyn, Aberystwyth, Ceredigion SY23 2HA (☎ and fax 01970 623464, e-mail alun@morus25.fsnet.co.uk); Institute of Mathematics and Physics, Aberystwyth University, Aberystwyth, Ceredigion SY23 3BZ

MORRIS, Amanda Claire; da of David Ellis, and Shirley, *née* Springate; *b* 2 December 1962, Haslemere, Surrey; *Educ* Horsham HS for Girls, Collyers Sixth Form Coll, Univ of Warwick (LLB), Guildford Coll of Law, Nottingham Law Sch (Dip); *m* 29 May 2004, Michael Crehan; *Career* slr Thomas Eggar Verrall Bowles 1992–97, ptnr Sherwin Oliver 1999–2001 (sr slr 1997–99), ptnr Blake Lapthorn (formerly Blake Lapthorn Tarlo Lyons) 2001– (head of real estate dispute resolution 2008–); memb Law Soc 1994; Neighbour Disputes: A concise guide to the law and practice (2006); *Recreations* amateur dramatics and operatic singing, vintage car touring and trials, skiing, mountain biking; *Clubs* Vintage Sports Car, Ulster Vintage Car, Petersfield Hilights Soc, Petersfield Operatic Soc; *Style*— Ms Amanda Morris; ✉ Blake Lapthorn Tarlo Lyons, Harbour Court, Compass Road, North Harbour, Portsmouth PO6 4ST (☎ 023 9222 1122, fax 023 9222 1124, e-mail amanda.morris@bllaw.co.uk)

MORRIS, Andrew; *Educ* Architectural Association (Dip Arch), Croydon Technical Coll (ONC/HNC); *Career* architect; architectural asst: Dept of the Environment 1969–72, H G Huckle & Partners Architects 1972–75; Crysalis Architects 1980–81, consIt to Alan Stanton Architects 1981–82; Richard Rogers Partnership: consIt 1981–82, joined 1982, job architect (on Richard Rogers' house) 1983–85, dir 1994–, sr dir 2000–; dir: Reading Construction Forum, Design and Build Fndn; *Projects* incl: Coin Street London, Lloyds of London, Centre Commercial St Herblain Nantes France, Reuters, Blackwall Yard London, Royal Docks London, Christopher Columbus Centre Baltimore USA, Harbour Place Seattle USA, Channel 4 TV HQ London, Heathrow Terminal 1 Airside devpt, Euopier devpt Heathrow Airport; Transbay Bus Terminal San Francisco, Antwerp Law Courts Belgium, National Assembly for Wales Cardiff, Cabinteely residential scheme Dublin, Jotel Hesperia L'Hospitalet de Llobregat Catalunya, Grand Canal Docks/Barrow Street Dublin, Las Arenas retail Barcelona, Ian Research Inst Headquarters Dublin, Barcelona Business Park, Paddington Waterside & Grand Union building London, Tower Bridge House London, New Wembley Masterplan London, Fourth Grace Liverpool, Mossbourne Community Acad London, Tower Bridge House London, Fairfield Halls masterplan, Pirelli site redevelopment Southampton, Woolston Shipyard masterplan Southampton, ARU site Chelmsford, NEO Bankside London, Riverside South Canary Warth, Chiswick Park, Bracknell masterplan, Newington First Base London, cb1 Cambridge Station redevelopment, LIFT White City London, Wood Wharf London, One Hyde Park London, Marconi site masterplan Chelmsford, Transbay Tower and Terminal competition San Francisco, Deptford Rise London, redevelopment of Chelsea Barracks London, Marine Hotel Salcombe, Sea Container's House London, o2 Skywalk London, St Lawrence Market North, Law Courts and market toronto, Riverlight London, Eastbury House London, Guys and St Thomas's Cancer Treatment Centres London, Burlington Gate London, New Global Centre for Social Sci LSE London, Macallan Distillery Scotland; co-dir responsible for design co-ordination and mgmnt of consIt team on: Heathrow Terminal 1 Airside and Europier schemes, redevelopment of Lloyds Register of Shipping, office devpt 88 Wood St London, Designer Retail Outlet Centre Ashford Kent, Millennium Experience Greenwich, Terminal 5 Heathrow Airport, Europe House/K2 St Katherine Docks London, San Francisco Bus Terminal, Elan HQ Dublin; *Style*— Andrew Morris, Esq

MORRIS, Andrew Bernard; s of Samuel Cyril Morris, and Golda, *née* Berkowitz; *b* 16 October 1952; *Educ* Christ's Coll GS, Coll for the Distributive Trades (HND Business Studies), Harvard Business Sch (Mgmnt Prog); *m* 29 June 1976, Jennifer Amanda, da of late Arthur Leslie Maizner; 2 da (Amy Louise b 10 June 1979, Sophie Victoria b 5 Oct 1981), 1 s (Ben Oliver b 24 Sept 1987); *Career* apprentice rising to sales role City Industrial Ltd (family shopfitting co) 1973–76, jt md Jontique (City Industrial subsid) 1976–80, sales and mktg dir City Industrial Ltd 1981–85, md Business Design Centre 1989–99 (bd dir 1986–89), chief exec Earls Court & Olympia 1999–2004, chief-exec NEC Gp Ltd 2004–06, chm Brand Events Ltd 2007–; dir Short List Media; chief exec Acad for Chief Execs; chm Sony World Photography Awards, dir Ingenious Media Live VCT; *Recreations* family, contemporary art, running, cycling, tennis, leadership; *Clubs* Home House; *Style*— Andrew B Morris; ✉ 5 Ruskin Close, London NW11 7AU (☎ 020 8209 0241, e-mail andrew@andrewbmorris.com)

MORRIS, Anne Marie; MP; da of late John Backes, and Margaret Agg; *b* 5 July 1957, London; *Educ* Hertford Coll Oxford, Coll of Law London, Open Univ (MBA); *Partner* Roger Kendrick; *Career* admitted slr 1982; trainee slr Withers 1981–83, corp fin lawyer Norton Rose 1983–85, corp, commercial and banking lawyer Crossman Block 1985, asst fin lawyer Sinclair Roche & Temperley Singapore 1986–88, corp fin lawyer Allen & Overy 1988–90, head of educn and trg Allen & Overy 1990–93, dir of professional and business devpt Baker & McKenzie 1993–95, dir of mktg and business devpt Simmons & Simmons 1995–97, mktg dir tax and legal servs Europe Middle East and Africa PricewaterhouseCoopers 1997–99, global mktg dir assurance and advsy business servs Ernst & Young 1999–2000, global mktg dir corporate fin Ernst & Young 2001–02, global mktg dir Linklaters 2002–05, md Manteion Ltd 2005–; non-remunerated dir: Small Business Bureau, Genesis Initiative; memb Ctee and chm Nat Legal Educn & Trg Gp 1990–94, memb Lord Chcllr's Advsy Ctee on Legal Educn 1992–93, specialist assessor law HE Funding Cncl 1992–93, memb Ctee Nat Professional Servs Mktg Gp 1994–97, memb Bd European Mentoring and Coaching Cncl 2008–09; cncllr W Sussex CC 2005–07, vice-chm County Local Ctee Mid Sussex 2006–07, shadow cabinet and now memb Assembly Sr Cncl for Devon 2007–10; MP (Cons) Newton Abbot 2010–, co-fndr and chair All-Pty Parly Gp for Micro Businesses 2011–15, vice-chair All-Pty Parly Gp for Entrepreneurship 2011–15, memb Work and Pensions Select Ctee 2012–15, chair All-Pty Parly Gp for Small Business 2014–15, PPS to Nick Boles, MP, *qv*, min of state for skills and Jo Johnson, MP, *qv*, min of state for universities and science 2015–; Cons small business ambass for the SW 2013–, tstee LawWorks 2012–15; govr: Rydon Sch Kingsteignton 2010–, Newton Abbot Coll 2010–12; FRSA 2000, MInstD 2001 (memb Devon and Cornwall Branch Ctee), FCIM 2002; *Recreations* horse riding, clay pigeon shooting, rowing, theatre, opera; *Style*— Anne Marie Morris, MP; ✉ House of Commons, London SW1A 0AA (e-mail annemarie.morris.mp@parliament.uk, website www.annemariemorris.co.uk)

MORRIS, Prof Anthony Isaac; s of Moshe Morris (d 1991), of Manchester, and Betty, *née* Harris (d 1977); *b* 18 August 1946; *Educ* Salford GS, Univ of Manchester (BSc, MSc, MB ChB, MD); *m* 16 Sept 1972, (Joan) Sheila, da of Eric Broadhurst (d 1970); 2 s (Daniel b 19 Feb 1976, David b 2 Aug 1978); *Career* sr house offr Manchester Royal Infirmary 1971–72 (house offr 1970–71), med registrar Whittington and UCH London 1972–74, lectr in med Univ of Manchester 1974–79, res fell in hepatology Univ of Pittsburgh USA 1978–79, sr lectr in med Univ of Liverpool 1979–85, consIt physician and gastroenterologist 1985–, past clinical dir of gastroenterology 1995–2002; dir endoscopy trg Mersey Sch of Endoscopy (Nat Endoscopy Trg Centre) and Royal Liverpool Hosp; past chm Jt Advsy Gp on Gastrointestinal Endoscopy; hon prof Dept of Medicine Univ of Liverpool, visiting prof Liverpool John Moores Univ; past pres Br Soc of Gastroenterology (educn offr and past vice-pres Endoscopy); FRCP 1985 (MRCP 1972);

Books ECG'S for Examinations (1975), Illustrated Case Histories in Gastroenterology (1994), Clinician's Manual on Gastro-Oesophageal Reflux Disease (1994); 102 papers and chapters and 70 abstracts on various gastrointestinal subjects; *Recreations* narrowboating, music, travel; *Style—* Prof Anthony Morris; ✉ 42 Birchdale Road, Appleton, Warrington WA4 5AW; 52 Link Unit, Royal Liverpool University Hospital, Prescot Street, Liverpool L7 8XP (✆ 0151 706 3554, e-mail tony.morris@rlbuht.nhs.uk)

MORRIS, His Hon Judge Anthony Paul; QC (1991); s of Isaac Morris Morris (d 1966), and Margaret Miriam, *née* Hassan; *b* 6 March 1948; *Educ* Manchester Grammar, Keble Coll Oxford (MA); *m* 26 Sept 1975, Jennifer Morys (Jennie), da of Maurice George Foley (d 1962); 2 s (Guy b 1977, Charles b 1980); *Career* called to the Bar Gray's Inn 1970 (bencher 2001), recorder of the Crown Court 1988–2003, circuit judge (SE Circuit) 2003–; *Recreations* travel, the arts, sport incl cycling across Europe, visiting 'the theatre of dreams'; *Style—* His Hon Judge Morris, QC; ✉ Central Criminal Court, Old Bailey, London EC4M 7EH

MORRIS, Candida Frances (Candy); CBE (2010); da of Philip John Butcher (d 2001), and Faith Layland, *née* Parker; *b* 3 February 1956, W Kilbride; *Educ* Manchester HS for Girls, St Hilda's Coll Oxford (scholar, MA), Inst of Health Service Mgmnt (Dip); *m* 26 Oct 1985, Stanley David Morris; *Career* nat administrative trainee NW Regnl HA 1977–80, dep hosp administrator Fairfield Gen Hosp 1980–83, dep sector administrator S Trafford Hosp 1983–84, princ asst administrator rising to asst unit gen mangr Stepping Hill Hosp 1984–89, unit gen mangr Grimsby HA 1989–92; chief exec: Scunthorpe and Goole Hosps Tst 1992–2000, W Sussex HA 2000–02, E Surrey HA 2001–02, Kent and Medway Strategic HA 2002–06, NHS SE Coast 2006–13; md candymorrisconsulting 2013–; frequent speaker at healthcare confs; *formerly:* memb Lord Chllr's Humberside Advsy Sub-Ctee on Magistrates, memb N Lincs Partnership, govr John Leggott Sixth Form Coll; FCMI, fell Inst of Leadership and Mgmnt; *Recreations* travel, puzzles, good company; *Style—* Mrs Candy Morris, CBE; ✉ 170 Comptons Lane, Horsham, West Sussex RH13 6DA (✆ 01403 264739, mobile 07850 814786, e-mail candymorris@candymorrisconsulting.co.uk or candymorris@btinternet.com, Twitter @candymorris3)

MORRIS, Christopher (Chris); s of John Morris, and Maria Morris; *b* 9 March 1960, Bristol; *Educ* Lincoln Coll Oxford; *m* 1 Sept 1984, Stefania Morris; 2 da, 1 s; *Career* head of real estate Freshfields Bruckhaus Deringer LLP (joined 1982, ptnr 1991–); memb City of London Slrs Co; memb Law Soc; *Style—* Chris Morris, Esq; ✉ Freshfields Bruckhaus Deringer, 65 Fleet Street, London EC4Y 1HS (✆ 020 7832 7494, fax 020 7108 7494, e-mail chris.morris@freshfields.com, website www.freshfields.com)

MORRIS, David Scott; s of John Hilary Morris (d 1994), of Bow Brickhill, Bucks, and Frances Deans, *née* Cooper (d 1995); *b* 20 December 1940; *Educ* Westmont Sch IOW, Royal Liberty GS Romford; *m* 23 Oct 1965, Jennifer Lois, da of Alan George Skinner (d 1986), of Sydney, Aust; 1 da (Catriona Lucy Scott b 1967); *Career* admitted slr 1965; HM coroner: for Huntingdon 1987–99, for Beds 1992–2013, for S and W Cambs 1999–2015; asst coroner Cambs and Peterborough 2015–; judge Mental Health Review Tbnl 1989–2013; pres: Milton Keynes and Dist Law Soc 1985–86, Beds Law Soc 1987–88, Berks, Bucks and Oxon Inc Law Soc 2003–04, E Anglian Coroners Soc 2003–07; memb Law Soc; FInstD, FRSM; *Recreations* travel, gardening, cycling, walking; *Clubs* Carlton; *Style—* David S Morris, Esq; ✉ The Old Vicarage, Granborough, Buckinghamshire MK18 3NT (✆ 01296 670217, fax 01296 670543, e-mail davidsmorris40@gmail.com); Coroners Office, Lawrence Court, Princes Street, Huntingdon PE29 3PA (✆ 03450 451364, fax 01480 372777)

MORRIS, David Thomas; MP; s of Capt Alan Lewis Morris, and Vera, *née* White (d 2013); *b* 3 January 1966, Leigh, Lancs; *m* (m dis); 2 s (Thomas, Robert); *Career* commerical property investor 1995–2010; MP (Cons) Morecambe and Lunesdale 2010–2; Honourable Co of Master Mariners 2014; *Style—* David Morris, Esq, MP; ✉ c/o Emma Smith, House of Commons, London SW1A 0AA (✆ 020 7219 7234, e-mail emma.smith@parliament.uk, website www.davidmorris.org.uk)

MORRIS, Sir Derek James; kt (2003); s of Denis William Morris, and Olive Margaret, *née* Collison; *b* 23 December 1945, Harrow, Middlesex; *Educ* Harrow County GS, St Edmund Hall Oxford (MA), Nuffield Coll Oxford (DPhil); *m* 4 Oct 1975, Susan Mary, da of Walter Whittles; 2 s (Alastair Henry Whittles b 14 Nov 1981, Roderick William Tudor b 6 July 1984); *Career* research fell Centre for Business and Industrial Studies Univ of Warwick 1969–70; Univ of Oxford: fell and tutor Oriel Coll and CUF lectr in economics 1970–98, Sir John Hicks research fell 1991–92, reader in economics 1996–98, chm Competition Cmmn (formerly Monopolies and Mergers Cmmn) 1998–2004, provost Oriel Coll 2004–13; chm of tstees OUP Pension Fund 2006–, non-exec chm Lucida plc 2012–14; economic dir NEDO 1981–84, dir and chm Oxford Economic Forecasting Ltd 1984–98, (memb 1991, dep chm 1995–98), chm Morris Review of Actuarial Profession 2004–05, memb Ctee on Standards in Public Life 2008–14; Snr Conslt Frontier Econs 2012–; visiting prof Univ of Calif Irvine 1986–87; hon fell: St Edmund Hall Oxford, hon fell Oriel Coll Oxon, TCD; Hon Dr: UC Dublin, UEA, Cranfield Univ; memb Royal Economic Soc 1985–; *Books* The Economic System in the UK (ed, 1977, 3 edn 1985), Industrial Economics: Theory and Evidence (1979), Unquoted Companies (1984), Strategic Behaviour and Industrial Competition (ed), Industrial Economics and Organisation (1991), State Owned Enterprises and Economic Reform in China 1979–87; *Recreations* skiing, walking, history, watching rugby; *Clubs* Reform, Oxford and Cambridge; *Style—* Sir Derek Morris; ✉ Oriel College, Oxford OX1 4EW (✆ 01865 276543)

MORRIS, Dr Desmond John; s of Capt Harry Howe Morris (d 1942), and Dorothy Marjorie Fuller, *née* Hunt (d 1996); *b* 24 January 1928; *Educ* Dauntsey's Sch West Lavington, Univ of Birmingham (BSc), Univ of Oxford (DPhil); *m* 1952, Ramona Joy, da of Windsor Baulch, of Marlborough, Wiltshire; 1 s (Jason b 1968); *Career* zoological res worker Univ of Oxford 1954–56, head of Granada TV and Film Unit at Zoological Soc of London 1956–59, curator of mammals at Zoological Soc of London 1959–67, dir Inst of Contemporary Arts 1967–68, res fell Wolfson Coll Oxford 1973–81; TV series: Zootime (weekly) 1956–67, Life (fortnightly) 1965–6, The Human Race 1982, The Animals Roadshow 1987–89, The Animal Contract 1989, Animal Country 1991–96, The Human Animal 1994, The Human Sexes 1997; one man (paintings) shows: Swindon Art Centre 1948, London Gallery 1950, Ashmolean Museum Oxford 1952, Stooshnoff Fine Art London 1974, Quadrangle Gallery Oxford 1976, Lasson Gallery London 1976, Public Art Gallery Swindon 1977 and 1993, Galerie d'Eendt Amsterdam 1978, Mayor Gallery London 1987, 1989, 1991, 1994, 1997, 1999, 2002 and 2004, Shippee Gallery New York 1988, Keats Gallery Knokke 1988, Galerie Michele Heyraud Paris 1991, Public Art Galleries Stoke and Nottingham 1996, Charleston Gallery Sussex 1997, Buxton Public Art Gallery 1997, Clayton Gallery Newcastle 1998, Keitelman Gallery Brussels 1998, Van der Velde Gallery Antwerp 1998; Art Consultancy Witteveen Amsterdam 1999 and 2002, Galerie Pack-Huys Meckelen 2001, MOMA Ostend 2002, Solomon Gall Dublin 2003, Mayor Gallery London 2004 and 2008, Art Consultancy Witteveen Amsterdam 2005, Guillermo de Osma Galeria Madrid 2005, Alexander Clayton Art Stratford-upon-Avon 2005, Gallery Pack-Huys Mechelen 2006, Said Business Sch Oxford 2007, Taurus Gallery Oxford 2007, 2008, 2009, 2010, 2011, 2012, 2013, 2014 and 2015, Williamson Art Gallery and Museum Birkenhead 2008, Witteveen Gallery Amsterdam 2008, Verbeke Fndn Belgium 2010, ISPA Gallery Lisbon 2012, O3 Gallery Oxford 2015; Hon DSc Univ of Reading; hon fell ZSL, hon fell Linnean Soc; *Books* The Reproductive Behaviour of the Ten-spined Stickleback (1958), The Story of Congo (1958), Curious Creatures (1961), The Biology of Art (1962), Apes and Monkeys (1964), The Big Cats (1965), The Mammals, a

Guide to the Living Species (1965), Men and Snakes (with Ramona Morris, 1965), Men and Apes (with Ramona Morris, 1966), Men and Pandas (with Ramona Morris, 1966), Zootime (1966), Primate Ethology (ed, 1967), The Naked Ape (1967), The Human Zoo (1969), Patterns of Reproductive Behaviour (1970), Intimate Behaviour (1971), Manwatching, a Field-guide to Human Behaviour (1977), Gestures, their Origins and Distribution (jtly, 1979), Animal Days (autobiography, 1979), The Soccer Tribe (1981), Inrock (fiction, 1983), The Book of Ages (1983), The Art of Ancient Cyprus (1985), Bodywatching, a Field-guide to the Human Species (1985), The Illustrated Naked Ape (1986), Catwatching (1986), Dogwatching (1986), The Secret Surrealist (1987), Catlore (1987), The Animals Roadshow (1988), Horsewatching (1988), The Animal Contract (1990), Animalwatching (1990), Babywatching (1991), Christmas Watching (1992), The World of Animals (1993), The Naked Ape Triology (1994), The Human Animal (1994), The Illustrated Catwatching (1994), Bodytalk: a World Guide to Gestures (1994), Illustrated Babywatching (1995), Illustrated Dogwatching (1996), Catworld, a Feline Encyclopedia (1996), The Human Sexes (1997), Illustrated Horse Watching (1998), Cool Cats (1999), Body Guards (1999), The Naked Eye (2000), Dogs: A Dictionary of Dog Breeds (2001), People Watching (2002), The Nature of Happiness (2004), The Naked Woman (2004), Watching: Encounters with Humans and Other Animals (2006), Fantastic Cats (2006), The Naked Man (2008), Baby: the Amazing Story of the First Two Years of Life (2008), Planet Ape (2009), Owl (2009), Child: How Children Think, Learn and Grow in the Early Years (2010), Monkey (2013), The Artistic Ape; Three Million Years of Art (2013), Inrock; The Illustrated Edition (2013), Leopard (2014), Headworks; Collected Poems (2014), Bison (2015), The Boats of Malta, the Art of the Fishermen (2016), The Soccer Tribe; Revised Edition (2016); *Recreations* book collecting, archaeology; *Style—* Dr Desmond Morris; ✉ website www.desmond-morris.com; c/o Jonathan Cape, 20 Vauxhall Bridge Road, London SW1V 2SA; literary agent Silke Bruenink (e-mail silke@silkeagency.de), gallery agent Mark Spence (enquiries@taurusgallery.com)

MORRIS, Edward (Ed); *b* 13 July 1967, London; *m* ; 2 c; *Career* previously with agencies incl TBWA, appointed creative dir Lowe London 2004 (exec creative dir until 2008, currently conslt); worked on numerous accounts incl: Levi's, The Guardian, Harvey Nicholls, Volkswagen, Hellmans, Tesco, Stella Artois, Innocent Drinks, Sony Playstation; numerous awards incl: Cannes Silver Lion, Best Creative Director of the Year Campaign Magazine 2006, Pres's Award Creative Circle 2006; *Style—* Ed Morris, Esq; ✉ Lowe London, 60 Sloane Avenue, London SW3 3XB (✆ 020 7984 5410, fax 020 2984 5012, e-mail ming.brookes@loweworldwide.com)

MORRIS, Frances; *Career* Tate: joined 1988, head Displays Tate Modern 2000–06, dir Collection for Int Art Tate Modern 2006–16, dir Tate Modern 2016–; *Style—* Ms Frances Morris; ✉ Tate Modern, Bankside, London SE1 9TG

MORRIS, Frank; s of Michael Joseph Morris (d 1981), of Uttoxeter, Staffs, and Mary Agnes, *née* Lavin (d 2006); *b* 13 July 1948; *Educ* St Joseph's Coll Stoke-on-Trent, Imperial Coll London (BSc, full colours, Union Gen Award for social activities); *m* 1, 6 Sept 1969 (m dis 2003), Ann Jeanette, da of Robert McIlquham; 1 s (David John b 21 Jan 1972); *m* 2, 19 Sept 2009, Linda Mary, da of Lewis Gilbey; *Career* asst exec engr PO Research Station Dollis Hill London 1967–74, exec engr PO Engineering 1974–79, design and devpt dir Kent Process Control Luton 1983–89 (design mangr 1979–83), associate director and manager of consulting practice Cambridge Consultants Ltd 1995–2001 (divnl mangr 1990–95); fndr Vecta Consulting Ltd 2001–; govr The Highfield Sch Letchworth 1986–98 (chm of govrs 1988–95), dir Letchworth Community Educn Tst 1997–98; cncllr Cottenham PC 2014– (chair 2015–); assoc City and Guilds of London Inst, chartered electrical engr, FIET, sr memb Instrument Soc of America; *Recreations* Argentine tango; *Style—* Frank Morris, Esq; ✆ 07768 713084, e-mail frank.morris@vecta5.com, website www.vecta5.com

MORRIS, Grahame Mark; MP; s of Richard Morris (d 1989), and Constance May, *née* Carter; *b* Easington, Co Durham; *Educ* Peterlee GS; *Career* MP (Lab) Easington 2010–; shadow sec of state for communities and local govt and shadow min for the constitutional convention 2016–; *Style—* Grahame Morris, Esq, MP; ✉ House of Commons, London SW1A 0AA

MORRIS, Harvey James; s of Kenneth Montague Morris (d 1969), and Mary, *née* Hutchison (d 1992); *b* 3 April 1946; *Educ* Wilson's GS Camberwell, Queens' Coll Cambridge (BA, MA); *m* 1976 (sep 1991), Sarah Margaret Perry; 2 s (Jack b and d 1981, Joseph b 1983), 1 da (Rose b 1985); *Career* gen reporter: Walthamstow Guardian 1969–71, East Anglian Daily Times Ipswich 1971–72; sub ed Associated Press London 1972–73; Reuters 1973–86: news ed Latin America 1976–79, chief corr Teheran 1979–80, actg chief corr Beirut 1980, dip corr 1981–83, energy corr 1984, political corr 1984–86; The Independent: asst foreign ed 1986–88, Middle East ed 1988–90, dep foreign ed 1990–92, foreign ed 1992–94; ed Geneva Post Switzerland 1994–95; sr ed Bloomberg News London 1995–97, devpt manager Latin American Newsletters 1997–; fndr ed Tower Magazine on-line 1996–; FT: Sunday news ed 1997, currently chief corr Jerusalem; *Publications* No Friends But the Mountains: The Tragic History of the Kurds (co-author, 1992); *Style—* Harvey Morris, Esq

MORRIS, Ingrid Mary; da of Robert W Morris, and Edith, *née* Bundy; *b* 10 October 1945; *Educ* Nat Cathedral Sch for Girls Washington DC, Herts and Essex HS Bishop's Stortford, Architectural Assoc Sch of Architecture (AADipl, SADG); *Children* 1 s (Anthony Robert Vasiles Polydorou b 4 Aug 1981, architect); *Career* architect; estab Bone & Morris Architects private practice with Jeanne Bone 1976 (formerly asst for McNab and Jamieson 1968–69, Piano and Rogers 1972–74), sole prop Bone & Morris Architects and Interior Designers 1976–; memb Co of Women in Architecture 1974–76; visiting lectr: Royal Univ of Malta 1974–77, Univ of Queensland 1982; memb Cncl Architectural Assoc 1985–1999 (hon librarian 1985–97), RIBA rep on ARCUK Educn Ctee 1987, RIBA assessor RIBA Housing Awards Northern Region 1988; external examiner: Architectural and Engrg degree course Univ of Westminster 1993–95, Part III courses Univ of Westminster and Univ of North London 1996–98, Univ of Plymouth 1996–2000, UCL 2001–; memb AA, RIBA; *Recreations* swimming, skiing, painting; *Clubs* Architecture, Chelsea Arts; *Style—* Miss Ingrid Morris; ✉ Bone & Morris Architects and Interior Designers, 1 Park Hill, Old Harlow, Essex CM17 0AE (✆ 01279 42739, e-mail ingrid_morris@talktalk.net or ingrid.morris@virginmedia.com)

MORRIS, Jack Anthony; CBE (2016, OBE 2005); s of Samuel Cyril Morris, of London, and Golda, *née* Berkovitch, of London; *b* 23 June 1956; *Educ* Christ's Coll GS; *m* 1 Nov 1983, Susan Anne, da of Harry Lee, of London; 1 da (Emily Kate b 14 May 1985), 2 s (Robert Edward b 27 May 1987, Harry Samuel b 18 March 1993); *Career* chm: Business Design Centre Gp Ltd 1992– (dir 1982–91), Business Design Centre Ltd 1992– (dir 1982–91), Portland Design Assocs Ltd 1992–2005 (dir 1988–91), Upper Street Car Park Ltd 1992– (dir 1981–91), North London Area CBI 1994–99 (memb London Region Cncl 1993–99), Clifton House Islington Ltd 2007–15, City North Islington Hldgs Ltd 2009–, Islington Business Bd 2009–, Islington Giving Appeal 2010–; dir: Earls Court & Olympia Gp Ltd 1999–2004, Upper Street Events Ltd 2010–14; tstee: The Morris Charitable Tst 1989– (chm), Islington Building Preservation Tst 1997–2008, Anne Frank Tst UK 2000–04; special advsr to Bd City and Inner London North TEC 1993–95; memb: Mayor of London's Skills and Employment Bd 2006–11, Ministerial Advsy Panel on Further Educn and Skills Dept for Business, Innovation and Skills 2006–14, London Cncls Young People's Educn and Skills 2010– (co-vice-chm), London Enterprise Panel 2012–; govr: North London Coll 1992–93, City & Islington Coll 1992–2014, London Met Univ 1996–

99; chm City & Islington Coll 1996–2014 (vice-chm 1992–96); Beacon Fellowship for Philanthropy 2013; freeperson London Borough of Islington 2003; Hon DSc City Univ London 2007; FInstD 1988, FRSA 2007; *Recreations* cycling, classic cinema and film music, piano, contemporary art, collecting vintage radios, Spanish culture, charity and voluntary work; *Style—* Jack Morris, CBE; ✉ Business Design Centre, Upper Street, Islington, London N1 0QH (☎ 020 7359 3535, fax 020 7226 0590)

MORRIS, Dr Jackie Evelyn; da of Prof Norman Morris (d 2008), and Lucy, *née* Rivlin; *b* 26 June 1948; *Educ* Camden Sch for Girls London, St Mary's Hosp Med Sch Univ of London (MB BS); *m* 1974, Dr Martin Howard Seifert (d 2013); 1 da (Victoria Charlotte b 1975), 1 s (Benjamin William D'Avigdor b 1978); *Career* house appts St Mary's Hosp and Hillingdon Hosp Uxbridge, subsequently SHO (rotation med) Central Middx Hosp 1972–74, med registrar St Mary's Hosp Paddington 1974–75, pt/t sr registrar in geriatric med UCH London 1975–79; conslt physician: St Mary's Hosp 1979–85, Royal Free Hosp 1985–2004 (seconded Dept of Health 1992–94); hon conslt physician UCH 2007–10; Frohlich visiting prof UCLA 1987, hon research assoc Dept of Primary Care and Popluation Health Faculty of Biomedical Sciences UCL Medical Sch, hon sr fell Sch of Community and Health Sciences City Univ London 2011–; Br Geriatrics Soc: hon dep sec and sec 1984–89, chair Primary and Continuing Care Special Interest Gp 2001–05, chair Policy Ctee 2005–07, chair Behind Blosed Doors Campaign 2006–, conslt physician, dignity champion; RSM: pres Geriatrics and Gerontology Section 1996 (hon sec 1991–94), dep chm RSM Academic Bd 1997–2000; expert assessor GMC; pres Central London Branch Parkinson's Disease Soc 1991–, chm Age Concern London 1994–97; memb Editorial Bd: Br Jl of Hosp Med 1984–90, RSM Jl 1992–96; examiner RCP Dip in Geriatric Med 1996–; memb: Disability Living Allowance Bd 1994–95, Arthritis Care Services Ctee 1994–95, N Thames Geriatric Trg Ctee (chm Educn Sub-Ctee 1996–2004), RCP UK GP Steering Gp 2012–; tstee: Age Concern Westminster 2004–12, British Inst of Human Rights 2007–12; FRCP 1990, FRSA 2002; articles on community problems of elderly people; *Recreations* reading, friends, music, children, cooking; *Style—* Dr Jackie Morris; ✉ 35 Murray Mews, London NW1 9RH

MORRIS, James George; MP; *b* 4 February 1967, Nottingham; *Educ* Univ of Birmingham (BA), Cranfield Sch of Mgmnt (MBA); *m* Anna; 2 c; *Career* MP (Cons) Halesowen and Rowley Regis 2010–; *Style—* James Morris, Esq, MP; ✉ House of Commons, London SW1A 0AA

MORRIS, (Catharine) Jan; CBE (1999); *b* 2 October 1926; *Educ* Univ of Oxford (MA); *Career* author; memb Gorsedd of Bards Nat Eisteddfod of Wales; fell yr Academi Gymreig; Hon DLitt: Univ of Wales, Univ of Glamorgan; hon fell: UCW Aberystwyth, UCW Bangor; hon student ChCh Oxford; Hon FRIBA, FRSL; *Books* Coast to Coast (1955), Sultan in Oman (1957), Coronation Everest (1958), Venice (1960), Spain (1964), Oxford (1965), The Pax Britannica Trilogy (1973–78), Conundrum (1974), The Venetian Empire (1980), The Matter of Wales (1984), Last Letters from Hav (1985), Among the Cities (1985), Manhattan '45 (1987), Hong Kong (1988), Pleasures of a Tangled Life (1989), Sydney (1992), O Canada! (1992), A Writer's House in Wales (1992), A Machynlleth Triad (1993), Fisher's Face (1995), 50 Years of Europe (1997), Lincoln (1999), Trieste and the Meaning of Nowhere (2001), A Writer's World (2003), Hav (2006), Contact! (2009); The Oxford Book of Oxford (ed, 1978), Travels with Virginia Woolf (ed, 1993); 6 books of collected travel essays; *Style—* Ms Jan Morris, CBE, FRSL; ✉ Trefan Morys, Llanystumdwy, Gwynedd LL52 0LP (☎ 01766 522222, e-mail jan.morris1@yahoo.com)

MORRIS, (Mary) Jane; da of William John Morris, and Mary Marguerita, *née* Morgan, of Downton-on-the-Rock, Herefordshire; *b* 10 March 1969, Belfast; *Educ* Malvern Girls Coll, Central St Martin's (BA), City Univ (postgrad); *Partner* William Duberley; *Career* artist 1991–95, writer and journalist 1996–, ed IAM Magazine 1998–99, ed and head of publications Museums Jl Museums Assoc 1999–2005, managing ed The AA Newspaper 2005–08, news ed Art World Magazine 2007–08, ed The Art Newspaper 2008–; memb Judging Ctee European Museum of the Year Award 2005–08; *Style—* Ms Jane Morris; ✉ The Art Newspaper, 70 South Lambeth Road, Third Floor, London SW8 1RL (☎ 020 7739 9122, e-mail j.morris@theartnewspaper.com, website www.theartnewspaper.com, Twitter @maryjanemorris)

MORRIS, John Paul; s of Herbert Edward Morris (d 1975), and Iolande Maria, *née*Perugini; *b* 17 January 1954, Stepney, London; *Educ* Richard Challenor Secdy Modern Surrey; *Partner* Tracey Honeysett; 3 s (Simon James b 25 Sept 1984, Matthew John b 20 May 1986, Nathan Alexander b 31 Dec 1998); *Career* restaurateur; asst gen mangr Lord's Cricket Ground 1978–80, gen mangr Oval Cricket Ground 1980–82, fndr Capital Catering Ltd 1982–2000, prop Drakes on the Pond Abinger Hammer 2000– (head chef 2007–); 1 Michelin Star 2008–10; *Recreations* running, sports; *Style—* John Morris, Esq; ✉ Drakes on the Pond, Dorking Road, Abinger Hammer, Surrey RH5 6SA (☎ 01306 730957, fax 01306 731174, e-mail honeysett573@aol.com)

MORRIS, Judith Anne; da of Harold Morris (d 1986), of London, and Eve, *née* Sutton; *b* 23 August 1948; *Educ* Buckingham Gate Sch, Camden HS for Girls, City Univ London (BSc, MSc); *Career* sr sessional optometrist Contact Lens Dept Moorfields Eye Hosp London 1971–94; Inst of Optometry London: sr lectr 1983–91, dir 1991–2001, head of contact lenses 2001–; sr lectr in contact lens educn City Univ 2001–15, module lead Moorfields-UCL Higher Qualifications 2015–; hon life memb Br Contact Lens Assoc (pres 1983–84, ed jl of Br Contact Lens Assoc 1984–89), hon life fell Coll of Optometrists (memb Cncl and examiner 1980–2006, pres 1989–90), EMEA pres Int Assoc of Contact Lens Educators 1998–; elected memb Gen Optical Cncl 1997–2006; memb Lambeth Southwark and Lewisham FPC 1988–90; Freeman City of London 1972, Liveryman Worshipful Co of Spectacle Makers 1992; FBCO 1971; *Publications* The Contact Lens Manual (4 edn); *Recreations* theatre, ballet, bridge; *Style—* Miss Judith Morris

MORRIS, Mali; *b* 5 February 1945; *Educ* Univ of Newcastle upon Tyne (BA), Univ of Reading (MFA); *Career* artist; more than 30 solo shows since 1979, recently in London, NY and Tokyo; many gp exhbns incl: Whitechapel Gall, Serpentine Gall, Barbican, Hayward Gall; int shows: France, Belgium, Luxembourg, Netherlands, Cyprus, USA, Eastern Europe, Canada, Brazil, Botswana, Japan; public collections incl: Arts Cncl England, Br Cncl, Contemporary Art Soc, Nat Museum Wales, The Whitworth Art Gallery Manchester, Lloyd's of London, Nat Museum Gaborone; lectured and examined widely incl: Chelsea Coll of Art and Design, Univ of the Arts London, RCA, Slade Sch of Art; cmmn Stage-Set Ledbury Poetry Festival 2009, tstee Poetry London; chair Selection Panel Jerwood Contemporary Painters 2009; judge/mentor Jerwood Painting Fellowships 2012–13; RA 2010; *Awards* Hatton scholar 1968, Arts Cncl Award 1976, GLAA Major Award 1979, Elephant Tst Award, Lorne Award 1994–95, Daiwa Award 2000, Br Cncl Travel Awards 2000, prizewinner Creekside Open 2007, prizewinner Royal Acad Summer Exhibition 2008; various research awards 1983–2005; *Publications* Mali Morris Paintings (1994), Mali Morris Recent Paintings (2002), Mali Morris New Paintings (2008); *Style—* Mali Morris, RA; ✉ website www.malimorris.co.uk

MORRIS, Martin John; s of Norman Ernest Morris, and Margaret Joan Morris; *Educ* Dauntsey's Sch West Lavington, St Luke's Coll Exeter (BEd), Open Univ (BA); *Career* teacher and sports coach Sedbergh Sch 1978–89 (master i/c cricket 1981–89), Master of Fryer and teacher Leighton Park Sch Reading 1989–95 (also i/c cricket), headmaster Catteral Hall Sch Giggleswick 1995–2000, headmaster Kingham Hill Sch 2000–08, headmaster Queen Elizabeth Hosp Jr Sch 2008–; memb IAPS 1995–2000 (memb Sports and Recreation Ctee), memb Ctee SHMIS 2000–08, memb IAPS Sports Ctee 2009–; govr Dormer House Sch Moreton-in-Marsh until 2000; memb: RSPB, Christians in Sport, Fell-Runners Assoc; MInstD 2001; *Recreations* sport, particularly cricket, rugby, hockey, golf, road, cross and fell-running, bird watching, walking; *Clubs* Bristol Phoenix CC (vice-chm); *Style—* Martin Morris, Esq

MORRIS, Nigel; s of Donald Morris (d 1991), and Peggy (d 1971), *née* McKay; *b* 30 March 1958, London; *Educ* Lancaster Univ (BA); *m* 19 Dec 1998, Jane, *née* Rayment; 2 s (Leon b 5 Oct 1999, Jago b 29 Sept 2001); *Career* commercial dir knitwear coats Viyella 1985, mktg dir Light & Coley 1989; Aegis plc: mktg dir BBJ 1992, vice-pres Carat Int 1999, ceo Isobar 2003–; chm: Farfar Sweden 2007–, Clownfish Marketing 2008–; fndr memb Digital Mktg Gp; Top Ten Global Marketers Ad Age 2004, fourth in Digital Power Fifty Revolution Magazine 2006 and 2008; memb Mktg Soc, MIPA; *Recreations* all sports, writing, music, horse racing; *Clubs* Hospital; *Style—* Nigel Morris, Esq; ✉ Isobar, Parker Tower, 43–49 Parker Street, London WC2B 5PS (☎ 020 7550 3204, fax 020 7550 3322, e-mail nigel.morris@isobar.net)

MORRIS, Dr Norma Frances; *née* Bevis; da of Henry Albert Bevis (d 1984), of Chadwell Heath, Essex, and Lilian Eliza, *née* Flexon (d 1993); *b* 17 April 1935; *Educ* Ilford Co HS, UCL (BA, MA, George Smith prize), Univ of Twente Netherlands (PhD); *m* 14 July 1960, Samuel Francis Morris (d 2015), s of Samuel Morris (d 1969), of London; 2 da (Jane Albertine b 1965, Anne Caroline b 1970), 1 s (John Stephen b 1967); *Career* TEFL Paris 1956–57, asst lectr Univ of Hull 1959–60; MRC: various admin appts 1960–76, estab offr 1976–78, head of accommodation and industrial liaison 1978–84, head of fin 1984–89, admin sec 1989–95; research fell UCL 1995–; chm Gen Chiropractic Cncl 1998–2002; memb and dep chm Nat Biological Standards Bd 1990–98, memb Bd Campaign for Sci and Engrg (CaSE) 2002–14; memb: Int Sociological Assoc, Br Sociological Assoc, Br Acupuncture Accreditation Bd 2004–14 (chm Accreditation Sub-Ctee 2010–14); tstee Patient's Assoc 2004–06; FRSM; articles in academic jls on sci and health policy; *Recreations* canoeing and sea kayaking, opera, edible fungi; *Clubs* Hampton Canoe, Portsmouth and District Canoe; *Style—* Dr Norma Morris; ✉ e-mail normorris@gmail.com; Department of Science and Technology Studies, University College London, Gower Street, London WC1E 6BT (☎ 020 7679 3703, fax 020 7679 2328, e-mail norma.morris@ucl.ac.uk)

MORRIS, Paul Christopher Early; s of Christopher John Morris (d 2014), and (Alice) Ruth, *née* Early (d 1997); *b* 21 September 1950; *Educ* Westminster Abbey Choir Sch, Westminster, UCNW Bangor (BA); *m* 1991, Rosemary Kinross; 2 s (Nicholas Paul Makumbi b 16 Oct 1992, Benedict Patrick Mulira b 31 Oct 1994); *Career* organist and choirmaster Christ Church Llanfairfechan N Wales 1970–73; admitted slr 1978, ptnr Winckworth Sherwood (formerly Winckworth & Pemberton) 1981– (asst slr 1978–81, sr ptnr 2003–10); slr: Southwark Diocesan Bd of Fin, London Diocesan Fund; registrar: Diocese of Southwark, Diocese of London; chapter clerk Southwark Cathedral; Freeman City of London 1984; Liveryman: Worshipful Co of Wheelwrights 1984–2012, Worshipful Co of Weavers 1993; *Recreations* music; *Clubs* Athenaeum, Oriental; *Style—* Paul Morris, Esq; ✉ Winckworth Sherwood, Minerva House, 5 Montague Close, London SE1 9BB (☎ 020 7593 5000, fax 020 7248 3221)

MORRIS, Paul David; s of Reginald Morris (d 1981), of Leicester and IOM, and Patricia, *née* Sayle (d 1999); *b* 10 September 1955; *Educ* Ramsey GS IOM, Univ of Sheffield (LLB); *m* 28 Aug 1982, Joy Anne, *née* Turner; *Career* admitted slr 1997, advocate Manx Bar 1981; sr ptnr Morris Maddrell 1985–99, ptnr Dickinson Cruickshank 1999–2009 (sr ptnr 2005–09); Appleby (as result of merger with Dickinson Cruickshank): ptnr 2009–11, sr counsel 2011–; non-exec dir Isle of Man Bank Ltd 2012–; chm Interception of Communications Tribunal 2010–; memb: IOM Law Soc 1981 (pres 2001–03), Law Soc of Eng and Wales 1997, Criminal Injuries Compensation Tbnl 2009–, Panel of Acting Deemsters Isle of Man High Court 2012; tstee Manx Aviation Preservation Soc; cmmr Isle of Man 2014–; *Recreations* golf, cricket, aviation, archaeology, reading, walking; *Clubs* MCC, Ramsey Golf (pres 2008–10); *Style—* Paul Morris, Esq; ✉ Appleby, 33–37 Athol Street, Douglas, Isle of Man IM1 1LB

MORRIS, Peter John; OBE (2008); s of Eric Charles Morris, and Joan Morris, of Carmarthen; *b* 29 April 1958; *Educ* Queen Elizabeth GS Carmarthen, Univ of Exeter (BA), Poly of Central London (MBA); *m* Angela, da of Michael Sadlo; 1 s (Alexander b 6 May 1991), 1 da (Sarah b 10 Aug 1993); *Career* gen mgmnt posts NHS SW and SE England 1980–86; assoc mangr Leicester Royal Infirmary: Accident and Trauma Unit 1986–89, Med Unit 1989–91; assoc gen mangr Univ Hosp of Wales Cardiff 1991–94, dir of business and contracting Northern Gen Hosp NHS Tst 1994–98, chief exec The Ipswich Hosp NHS Tst 1998–2002, chief exec Univ Hosp of S Manchester NHS Fndn Tst (formerly S Manchester Univ Hosps NHS Tst) 2002–09, chief exec Barts and The London NHS Tst 2009– (joined as interim chief exec); FHSM 1988; *Recreations* golf, sailing; *Clubs* Bramhall Park Golf; *Style—* Peter Morris, Esq, OBE

MORRIS, Richard Francis Maxwell; s of Maxwell Morris (d 1996), of Pulborough, W Sussex, and Freda, *née* Abelson (d 1981); *b* 11 September 1944; *Educ* Eton, New Coll Oxford (MA), Coll of Law London; *m* 1, 1974 (m dis 1978), Sarah Quill; m 2, 1983, Marian Sperling; 2 da (Harriet b 1984, Jessica b 1986); *Career* slr Farrer & Co 1967–71, dep head Sterling Banking Dept Grindlay Brandts Ltd 1971–75, gen mangr Corp Fin S G Warburg & Co Ltd 1975–79; Hodder & Stoughton Holdings Ltd: fin dir then md Educational & Academic Publishing 1979–89, jt md 1989–91; chief exec Associated Board of the Royal Schools of Music 1993–09 (special envoy for China 2010–11); dir: Southern Radio plc (formerly Invicta Sound plc) 1984–92, The Lancet Ltd 1986–91; md Edward Arnold (Publishers) Ltd 1987–91; co-fndr and tstee Mayor of London's Fund for Young Musicians 2011–; memb: Governing Body Kent Opera 1985–90, Exec Ctee Music Educn Cncl 1995–2008 (chair 1998–2001), Devpt Bd Arvon Fndn 2008–, GLA Steering Gp on Music Educn 2010–; fndr Almaviva Opera 1989; tstee: Cncl for Dance Educn and Trg 1999–2005, Magma Poetry 2014–15 (assoc 2010–14), Music Preserved 2010–14, Music Mark 2014–; govr: Kent Music Sch 2001–14, The Yehudi Menuhin Sch 2004– (dep chair 2010–11, chair 2011–); Hon RCM, Hon RNCM, Hon FRAM; *Publications* The Nibelung Ballad (2013), One Crazy Day (2013), Sextet (2014), Hell-Bent (2014); *Recreations* music, dance, golf, poetry, visual arts; *Clubs* Athenaeum; *Style—* Richard Morris, Esq; ✉ Holdfast House, Edenbridge, Kent TN8 6SJ (☎ 01732 862439, e-mail richard@richardmorris.org.uk)

MORRIS, Prof Richard Graham Michael; CBE (2007); s of Robert Walter Morris (d 2004), and Edith Mary, *née* Bundy (d 1996); *b* 27 June 1948; *Educ* St Alban's Sch Washington DC, Marlborough, Univ of Cambridge (BA), Univ of Sussex (DPhil); *m* 1, 18 May 1985 (m dis), Hilary Ann, da of Ian D Lewis; 2 da (Louise Edith b 4 June 1988, Josephine Claire b 26 March 1991); m 2, 24 Oct 2015, Monica, da of Jesus Munoz; 1 s (Adrian b 27 Dec 2011); *Career* Addison-Wheeler res fell Univ of Durham 1973–75, sr scientific offr British Museum 1975–77, res Science and Features Dept BBC TV 1977, lectr Univ of St Andrews 1977–86; Univ of Edinburgh: reader 1988–93, prof of neuroscience and dir Centre for Neuroscience 1993–97, chm Dept of Neuroscience 1998–2002, dir Centre for Cognitive and Neural Systems, Royal Soc/Wolfson prof of neuroscience 2006–; head of neuroscience and mental health Wellcome Tst 2007–09 (sr advsr 2009–11); MRC res fell 1983–86, visiting prof MIT 1991, adjunct prof Univ of Trondheim 2001–, Caro Almela prof of neuroscience Inst for Neurosciences Alicante 2013–, visiting prof Nat Centre for Biological Sciences Bangalore 2013–; Segerfalk lectr Univ of Lund 1991, BNA Decade of Int Brain lectr 1998, Zotterman lectr Karolinska Inst 1999, Edwards lectr Univ of Seattle 2002, American Alumnus lectr Univ of St Andrews 2003, Presidential Lecture Soc for Neuroscience 2009, Public Lecture on Neuroscience Kavil Prize Ceremony Oslo 2014; pres

Fedn of European Neuroscience Socs 2006–08 (pres Tst 2013–); memb: MRC Neurosciences Grants Ctee 1981–85, MRC Neurosciences Bd 1993–97, MRC Strategy Developments Gp 2000–03, Editorial Advsy Bd Trends in Neurosciences, Editorial Bd Learning and Memory, Experimental Psychology Soc (hon sec 1985–89), Brain Res Assoc (chm 1994–98), European Neuroscience Assoc, European Brain and Behaviour Soc; pres Fedn of European Neuroscience Tst 2012–, Carol Almela Chair of Neurobiology Inst of Neuroscience Alicante 2015–; memb Bd of Reviewing Eds Science Magazine 2007–; Henry Dryerre Prize RSE 2000, BNA Neuroscientist of the Year Award 2003, Feldberg Prize and Lecture 2006, IPSEN Prize 2013, Royal Medal RSE 2014, Brain Prize 2016; FRSE 1994, FRS 1997 (chair Hooke Ctee 2013–18), FMedSci 1998, FAAAS 2004, fell American Assoc for the Advancement of Science 2005, fell Norwegian Acad of Science and Letters 2006; *Publications* Parallel Distributed Processing: Implications for Psychology and Neurobiology (ed, 1990), Neuroscience: Science of the Brain (1994, 2 edn 2003), Long-term Potentiation (ed, 2004), The Hippocampus Book (ed, 2007); academic papers on memory and its brain mechanisms; *Recreations* sailing; *Clubs* Royal Yachting Assoc, Port Edgar Sailing; *Style*— Prof Richard Morris, CBE, FRS; ✉ Centre for Cognitive and Neural Systems, University of Edinburgh, 1 George Square, Edinburgh EH8 9JZ (☎ 0131 650 3520, fax 0131 651 1835, e-mail r.g.m.morris@ed.ac.uk)

MORRIS, Richard Nicholas; s of Rev D S Morris, and Mrs V A Morris; *b* 3 March 1967, Warrington, Cheshire; *Educ* Queen Elizabeth's Hosp Bristol, St Catharine's Coll Cambridge (MA); *m* ; 3 da; *Career* advertising exec; DDB London 1988–2009 (latterly rgnl dir (advertising) DDB Europe); Identica: md 2009–12, ceo 2012–; *Recreations* skiing, gardening, politics, writing, walking; *Style*— Richard Morris, Esq; ✉ Identica, 101 New Cavendish Street, London W1W 6XH

MORRIS, Prof Robert John (Bob); *b* 12 October 1943; *Educ* Acklam Hall GS Middlesbrough, Keble Coll Oxford (BA), Nuffield Coll Oxford (DPhil); *m* Barbara Anne; 1 s (George b 1969), 1 da (Helen b 1971); *Career* Univ of Edinburgh: lectr in economic history 1968–80, sr lectr 1980–91, prof of economic and social history 1991–2009, prof emeritus 2009–; ed Book of the Old Edinburgh Club 2014–; pres European Assoc of Urban Historians 2000–02; FRHistS 1990; patron Thoresby Society (Leeds); *Books* Cholera (1974), Class and Class Consciousness in the Industrial Revolution (1976), Class, Sect and Party 1820–1850 (1988), Men, Women and Property in England 1780–1870 (2004), Scotland 1907, Valentine and Sons Photographers (2007), Book of the Old Edinburgh Club (ed), and various other pubns; *Recreations* growing vegetables, planting an orchard of old apple varieties; *Style*— Prof Bob Morris; ✉ School of History and Classics and Archeology, University of Edinburgh, William Robertson Wing, Old Medical School, Teviot Place, Edinburgh EH8 9AQ (☎ 0131 650 6693, e-mail rjmorris@ed.ac.uk)

MORRIS, Robert Vernon (Robin); MBE (2014); s of Harold Vernon Morris, MRCVS (d 1986), of Hereford, and Dorothy Agnes, *née* Foulkes (d 1994); *b* 27 May 1932; *Educ* St Mary's Coll Bitterne Park Southampton, LSE (LLB); *m* 19 Sept 1959, Patricia Margaret, da of Thomas Norman Trevor (d 1968), of Gloucester; 3 s (Nicholas b 1960, Timothy b 1963, James b 1965), 1 da (Sally b 1970); *Career* Nat Serv 1956–58, Intelligence Corps GCHQ Cheltenham; slr Supreme Court 1957, sr ptnr Rowberry Morris Glos (and assoc offices), conslt slr Madge Lloyd and Gibson (Gloucester and Newent offices) 2010; chm: Social Security Appeal Tbnl (Wales and SW) 1980–99, Glos Legal Assoc 1985–88, Child Support Appeal Tbnls (Wales and SW) 1993–99; legally qualified panel memb Appeals Serv 1999–2006; chm House of Tailor of Gloucester plc 2006–; sec Glos Historic Bldgs 1980–, pres Glos Rotary Club 1981–82, chm Glos Civic Tst 1983– (Queen's Award for Voluntary Service 2013), cdr St John Ambulance Glos 1988–94; chm: Cncl Order of St John Glos 1994–98, Order of St John Visitation Ctee 1998–2000; memb: Chapter Gen Order of St John 1996–2000, Priory Chapter of England and the Islands 2001– (alternate memb Glos 2000), Law Soc; Paul Harris fell 2005, Sapphire Paul Harris fell 2015; KJStJ 1996 (OStJ 1986, CStJ 1991); *Recreations* jogging, inner city conservation; *Clubs* LSE, Army and Navy; *Style*— Robin Morris, Esq, MBE; ✉ The Court House, Church Street, Newent, Gloucestershire GL18 1AB (☎ 01531 822526, mobile 07074 301903); 22–24 Church Street, Newent, Gloucestershire GL18 1PP (☎ 01531 820088, fax 01531 821120, e-mail robin.morris@madgelloyd.com)

MORRIS, His Hon Judge Sean Robert; *Career* called to the Bar Lincoln's Inn 1983, barr (NE Circuit) 1983–2008, recorder 2003–, circuit judge (Midland Circuit) 2008–, hon recorder of Lincoln and resident judge Lincoln Crown Court 2010–; *Recreations* skiing, walking, military history; *Style*— His Hon Judge Sean Morris; ✉ The Crown Court, The Castle, Lincoln LN1 3GA

MORRIS, Simon James; s of Kenneth Stapleton Morris, of Cape Town, South Africa, and Grace, *née* Skitmore; *b* 24 January 1958; *Educ* Aberdour Sch, Whitgift Sch, Gonville & Caius Coll Cambridge (MA), Birkbeck Coll London (PhD); *Career* admitted slr 1982; ptnr CMS Cameron McKenna LLP (formerly Cameron Markby Hewitt) 1988–; memb Cncl London Topographical Soc 1983–; cmmr Jersey Financial Services Cmmn 2015–; FRGS 2013, FSA; *Books* Financial Services: Regulating Investment Business (1989, 2 edn 1995), Highgate Archway: Gateway to the City (with Towyn Mason, 2000), Financial Services Regulation in Practice (2016); *Recreations* history of London; *Style*— Simon Morris, Esq; ✉ CMS Cameron McKenna LLP, 78 Cannon Street, London EC4N 6AF (☎ 020 7367 3000, fax 020 7367 2000, e-mail simon.morris@cms-cmck.com)

MORRIS, HE Timothy Colin; s of Major Anthony Morris, and Sheila Morris; *b* 17 September 1958, Harrogate; *Educ* Queen's Coll Oxford (BA); *m* Patricia Tena; 3 s; *Career* diplomat; Mexico and Central American Dept FCO 1981–82, Japanese language trg 1982–84, second sec (commercial) Tokyo 1984–87, Southern Africa Dept FCO 1987–89, head Exports to Japan Unit DTI 1989–91, first sec and head of political section Madrid 1991–96, dep head UN Dept FCO 1996–98, cnsllr (trade and investment) Tokyo 1998–2002, dep head of mission Lisbon 2003–05, head Int Orgns Dept FCO 2005–08, ambass to Morocco and Mauritania 2008–12, Sahel coordinator FCO 2012–13, UK special envoy for South Sudan 2014, temp head of mission Kinshasa 2014–15, ambass to South Sudan 2015–; *Recreations* music, literature; *Clubs* Oxford and Cambridge; *Style*— HE Mr Timothy Morris; ✉ c/o Foreign and Commonwealth Office, King Charles Street, London SW1A 2AH

MORRIS, Tom; OBE (2016); s of Dr Michael Morris, and Dr Rosemary, *née* Parrington; *b* 22 June 1964, Stamford, Lincs; *Educ* Pembroke Coll Cambridge (fndn scholar, MA); *m* 4 June 2011, Kate McGrath; 1 da (Hannah Katinka b 11 Sept 1999), 1 s (Jack b 15 Aug 2012); *Career* freelance writer, prodr, broadcaster and dir 1990–; artistic dir BAC 1995–2004, assoc dir Nat Theatre 2004–, artistic dir Bristol Old Vic 2009–; work as dir incl: Othello Music, Trio, Oedipus, All That Fall, Unsung, Macbeth (with Corin Redgrave), Disembodied (with David Glass), Newsnight The Opera, War Horse (Nat Theatre and Lincoln Center NYC, Best Director Tony Award 2011), Every Good Boy Deserves Favour (Nat Theatre); at Bristol Old Vic: Juliet and Her Romeo, Swallows and Amazons, A Midsummer Night's Dream; The Death of Klinghoffer for ENO and Met Opera NYC; writing incl: Ben-Hur, Jason and the Argonauts, World Cup Final 1966 (with Carl Heap), The Wooden Frock, Nights at the Circus, A Matter of Life and Death (with Emma Rice); tstee: Complicité, Punch Drunk Theatrical Events, JMK Tst, Arts Patrons Tst; *Recreations* cricket, singing; *Style*— Tom Morris, Esq, OBE; ✉ Bristol Old Vic, King Street, Bristol BS1 4ED (e-mail directorsoffice@bristololdvic.org.uk)

MORRIS, Prof Trevor John; s of Peter Morris, of E Grinstead, and Dorothy, *née* Haines; *b* 13 July 1955; *Educ* Drayton Manor GS, Univ of Exeter (BA); *m* 21 May 1982, Claire, *née* Laven; 2 da (Olivia b 27 Oct 1988, Flora b 22 August 1991); *Career* asst to mktg dir Fenwick of Bond Street 1977–79, mktg servs mangr OEM plc 1979–81; The Quentin Bell Organisation: campaign dir 1982–84, md 1984–, chm 1998–; chm Good Relations Gp 2000–, chm QBO Bell Pottinger 2002; visiting prof Univ of Westminster 2005–, prof Richmond Univ 2014–; *Publications* Public Relations for Asia (jtly, 2007), Public Relations for New Europe (jtly, 2008), PR: A Persuasive Industry? (jtly), PR Today (jtly, 2011); *Recreations* reading, theatre, football; *Clubs* 2 Brydges Place; *Style*— Prof Trevor Morris; ✉ Richmond University, Queens Road, Richmond, Surrey TW10 6JP (☎ 07771 810984, e-mail trevor.j.morris@btinternet.com)

MORRIS OF ABERAVON, Baron (Life Peer UK 2001), of Aberavon in the County of West Glamorgan and of Ceredigion in the County of Dyfed; Sir John Morris; KG (2003), kt (1999), PC (1970), QC (1973); s of late D W Morris, of Talybont, Cardiganshire, and late Mrs M O A Morris (later Mrs Lewis); *b* 1931; *Educ* Ardwyn Aberystwyth, Univ Coll of Wales Aberystwyth, Gonville & Caius Coll Cambridge, Acad of Int Law The Hague; *m* 1959, Margaret, da of Edward Lewis, OBE, JP, of Llandysul; 3 da; *Career* served Royal Welch Fusiliers and Welch Regt; called to the Bar Gray's Inn 1954 (Holker sr exhibitioner 1955–58), bencher 1985; legal advsr Farmers' Union of Wales 1955–57, recorder of the Crown Court (SE Circuit) 1982–97; MP (Lab) Aberavon 1959–2001, Parly sec Miny of Power 1964–66, jt Parly sec for tport 1966–68, min for defence (equipment) 1968–70, sec of state for Wales 1974–79, oppn spokesman on legal affrs and shadow attorney-gen 1979–81 and 1983–96; attorney-gen 1997–99; memb: UK Delgn Consultative Assembly Cncl of Europe and WEU 1963–64, N Atlantic Assembly 1970–74; chllr Univ of Glamorgan 2001–13; Lloyd George Meml Lecture 2008; pres London Welsh Assoc 2001–09, patron London Welsh Lawyers Assoc; HM Lord-Lt Dyfed 2003–06; Hon LLD Univ of Wales 1983, Hon LLD Univ of S Wales 2013; hon fell: Gonville & Caius Coll Cambridge, UC Aberystwyth, UC Swansea, Trinity Coll Carmarthen, St David's UC Lampeter; *Publications* 50 Years in Politics and the Law (2011), The Development by Attorney Generals of the Doctrine of Armed Intervention Without Security Council Authorization to Avert an Overwhelming Humanitarian Catastrophe (2011); *Style*— The Rt Hon the Lord Morris of Aberavon, KG, PC, QC

MORRIS OF BALGONIE, Yr Stuart Gordon Cathal; s of Raymond Stanley Morris of Balgonie and Eddergoll, and Margaret Newton Morris, *née* Stuart; matriculated arms (Morris of Balgonie and Eddergoll quartered with Stuart) Court of the Lord Lyon Edinburgh 1987, tartan Morris of Balgonie; *b* 17 April 1965, Aberfeldy, Perthshire; *Educ* Bell-Baxter HS, Elmwood Coll, Univ of Birmingham; *m* 20 April 2013, Kelly Dianne Holley-Whittaker; *Career* historian, armorist, author; Scottish Castles Assoc: fndr memb, memb Cncl 1996–2010, sec 1997–2003, chm 2003–05, vice-chm 2005–08; fndr memb Heraldry Soc of Scotland, memb The Stewart Soc 1981 (memb Cncl 1998–2006 and 2010–), memb Ctee Markinch Heritage Gp 2004– (vice-chm 2007–), memb Cncl Royal Celtic Soc 2009–, memb Sons of Confederate Veterans 2012–; Lt Col and ADC to HE the Govr of the State of Georgia 1991–2012, Col Commonwealth of Kentucky 1999; dir: Balgonie Castle Enterprises, Theobald-Hicks, Morris & Gifford 2001–05; chm Central Fife Branch Order of St John 2007–, fndr Tay Rail Bridge Disaster Meml Tst 2010 (chm 2010–12), memb Highland Reserve Forces and Cadets Assoc (HRFCA) 2015–; Freeman City of London 2001, Liveryman Worshipful Co of Meadmakers 1982; FSA Scot 1983, FRSA 1990 (assoc 1986); Cdr Order of Polonia Restituta 1990, Companion Order of Malta, Grand Cross Order of the Eagle of Georgia 2010, OStJ 2011 (SBStJ 2003, area chm for Fife 2015–), Cross of Merit Second Class Red Cross of the Repub of San Marino 2012, Grand Offr Order of St Agatha Repub of San Marino 2012, memb Order of Stars and Bars 2012 (first in UK); *Recreations* archery, heraldry, genealogy, historical researching, painting; *Clubs* Royal Scots (Edinburgh); *Style*— Stuart Morris of Balgonie; ✉ Balgonie Castle, by Markinch, Fife KY7 6HQ (☎ 01592 750119, e-mail sbalgonie@yahoo.co.uk, website www.balgoniecastle.co.uk)

MORRIS OF BOLTON, Baroness (Life Peer UK 2004), of Bolton in the County of Greater Manchester; Patricia Morris; OBE (1997); da of James Sydney Whittaker (d 1994), and Alice, *née* Redington (d 2004); *b* 16 January 1953, Bolton, Lancs; *Educ* Bolton Sch Girls' Div, Clifton Coll of Educn, Didsbury Coll of Educn; *m* 1978, His Hon Judge William Patrick Morris; 1 s (Hon Jonathan William Basil b 1983), 1 da (Hon Katharine Elizabeth b 1985); *Career* PA to the Northern Regnl Dir Slater Walker Ltd 1974–75, PA to the Chevalier Dr Harry D Schultz 1975, fund mangr PPS 1975–77, tech analyst Foster & Braithwaite 1977–78, tech analyst Charlton, Seal, Dimmock & Co 1979–83, policy and political advsr to Cons MEP 1999–2001, vice-chm Cons Pty 2001–05; sits as Cons in House of Lords 2004–, oppn whip 2004–, oppn spokesman on children, families and women 2005–, oppn spokesman on educn and skills 2006–; Parly candidate (Cons) Oldham Central & Royton 1992; memb Ctee Patrons and Assocs of Manchester City Art Galleries 1982–94, memb Manchester North Valuation and Community Charge Tbnl 1988–92, chm Bolton Cancer Res Campaign 1992–95, govr and tstee Bolton Sch 1992–, dep chm Salford Royal Hosps NHS Tst 1993–97, memb Bd of Mgmnt Bolton Lads' & Girls' Club 1994–97 (dir 1997–2002), advsr to Abbot of Ampleforth 1998–2004, pres Nat Benevolent Instn 2006–, patron Oxford Parent Infant Project (OXPIP) 2006–, tstee The Disability Partnership 2007–, co-chair Women in Public Policy 2007–; *Recreations* reading, football, country pursuits, cinema; *Clubs* Special Forces; *Style*— The Baroness Morris of Bolton, OBE; ✉ House of Lords, London SW1A 0PW (☎ 020 7219 3000)

MORRIS OF HANDSWORTH, Baron (Life Peer UK 2006), of Handsworth in the County of West Midlands; Sir William Manuel (Bill) Morris; kt (2003), DL (Staffs 2008); *b* 19 October 1938, Jamaica; *Educ* Mizpah Sch Jamaica, Handsworth Tech Coll; *m* Minetta (d 1990); 2 s (Garry, Clyde); *Career* arrived in UK from Jamaica 1954, joined Hardy Spicers c1955, memb TGWU 1958, shop steward 1963, memb TGWU Gen Exec Cncl 1971–72; TGWU (employed): Nottingham/Derby dist organiser 1973–76, Northampton dist sec 1976–79, nat sec Passenger Servs Trade Gp 1979–86, dep gen sec 1986–91, gen sec 1991–2003; memb Exec Bd Int Transport Workers' Fedn 1986–2003, memb Gen Cncl and Exec Ctee TUC 1988–2003, pres TUC 2000–01, memb Cncl ACAS 1997–2003; non-exec dir Bank of England 1998–2006; chm Morris Inquiry 2004; past chm Conf Arrangements Ctee Lab Pty; memb: Cmmn for Racial Equality 1977–87, Prince of Wales Youth Business Tst 1987–90, Employment Appeals Tbnl 1988–2009, Economic and Social Affrs Ctee EC 1990–92, New Deal Taskforce 1997–99, Royal Cmmn on Reform of House of Lords 1999, Cmmn for Integrated Tport 1999–2005, ARB 2001–05, Panel of Mergers and Takeovers 2005–; vice-chair Jamaica Nat Money Services 2007–12; memb Gen Advsy Bd: IBA 1981–86, BBC 1987–88; non-exec dir ECB 2004–15; tstee Performance Birmingham 2008–15; chllr: Univ of Technol Jamaica 2000–10, Staffordshire Univ 2004–11; chm Midland Heart Housing Assoc 2007–14; hon degrees: Southbank Univ, Open Univ, Leeds Metropolitan Univ, Univ of Westminster, Greenwich Univ, Teesside Univ, Thames Valley Univ, UC of Northampton, Staffordshire Univ, Middlesex Univ, Univ of Warwick, Univ of Birmingham, Univ of Luton, Univ of Technol Jamaica, Univ of Nottingham, Hull Univ; FRSA, FCGI; OJ 2002; *Recreations* family life, walking, gardening, music; *Style*— The Rt Hon the Lord Morris of Handsworth, OJ, DL; ✉ House of Lords, London SW1A 0PW (website www.billmorris.info)

MORRIS OF YARDLEY, Baroness (Life Peer UK 2005), of Yardley in the County of West Midlands; Estelle Morris; PC (1999); da of late Rt Hon Charles Morris, former MP, and Pauline Morris; *b* 17 June 1952; *Educ* Whalley Range HS, Coventry Coll of Educn; *Career* teacher Sidney Stringer Sch and Community Coll 1974–92; cncllr Warwick DC 1979–91 (ldr Lab Gp 1982–89); MP (Lab) Birmingham Yardley 1992–2005; oppn whip 1994–95, oppn spokesperson on educn 1995–97, Parly under-sec of state (school standards) DfEE

M

1997–98, min of state for school standards 1998–2001, sec of state for educn and skills 2001–02, min of state for the arts 2003–05; *Style—* The Rt the Lady Morris of Yardley, PC

MORRISON, Anne Catherine; da of George Charles Morrison (d 1993), and Persis Mae, *née* Ross; *b* 18 August 1959, Belfast, NI; *Educ* Richmond Lodge Sch Belfast, Churchill Coll Cambridge (MA); *m* 1989, Robert John Jarvis Johnstone, s of Robert Johnstone (d 1974); 1 da (Alice Emily b 21 May 1993); *Career* BBC TV: trainee 1981–83, researcher and dir Documentary Features Dept 1983–87, prodr Holiday 1987–88, series prodr Crimewatch UK 1988–90, chief asst Documentary Features Dept 1990–92, exec prodr Taking Liberties and Rough Justice 1992, dep head Features Dept 1992–94, head Features Dept 1994–96; BBC Prodn: head Consumer and Leisure Dept 1996–98, head Features and Events Dept 1998–2000, controller Leisure and Factual Entertainment 2000–01, controller General Factual Gp 2001–03, controller Documentaries and Contemporary Factual 2003–06, controller Network Production 2006–09, dir BBC Acad 2009–14; chm BAFTA 2014– (memb Bd of Tstees, chair Learning and Events Ctee), memb Bd London & Ptnrs 2015–; tstee Charleston Tst 2015–; FRSA; *Recreations* reading, films, theatre, dancing; *Style—* Ms Anne Morrison

MORRISON, Professor (Philip) Blake; s of Arthur Blakemore Morrison (d 1991), of Skipton, N Yorks, and Agnes, *née* O'Shea (d 1997); *b* 8 October 1950; *Educ* Ermysted's GS Skipton, Univ of Nottingham (BA), McMaster Univ (MA), UCL (PhD); *m* 1976, Katherine Ann, da of Robert C Drake; 2 s (Seth Nicholas b 1981, Gabriel Eli b 1989), 1 da (Aphra Grace b 1984); *Career* various pt/t teaching posts 1976–81 (Open Univ, Goldsmiths Coll London, Furzedown Coll), poetry and fiction ed TLS 1978–81, dep literary ed Observer 1981–86 (literary ed 1986–89); Independent on Sunday: literary ed 1990–94, staff writer 1994–95; prof of creative and life writing Goldsmiths Coll London 2003–; poet; chm Poetry Book Soc 1984–87, memb Mgmnt Bd Poetry Soc 1980–83; FRSL 1990; *Awards* Eric Gregory Award, Somerset Maugham Award, Dylan Thomas Meml Prize, EM Forster Award, Volvo/Waterstone's Award for Non-Fiction 1993, J R Ackerley Prize 1994; *Books* The Movement (1980), Dark Glasses (1984), The Ballad of the Yorkshire Ripper (1987), The Yellow House (children's book, 1987), And When Did You Last See Your Father? (memoir, 1993), The Cracked Pot (play, 1996), As If (non-fiction, 1997), Too True (stories and essays, 1998), Dr Ox's Experiment (libretto, 1998), Selected Poems (1999), The Justification of Johann Gutenberg (2000), G (libretto, 2002), Things My Mother Never Told Me (non-fiction, 2002), Oedipus (trans, 2003), Antigone (trans, 2003), The Man With Two Gaffers (play, 2006), South of the River (novel, 2007), Elephant & Castle (libretto, 2007), Lisa's Sex Strike (play, 2007), The Last Weekend (novel, 2010), We Are Three Sisters (play, 2011), A Discoverie of Witches (poems, 2012), This Poem...(pamphlet, 2013), Shingle Street (poems, 2015); *Recreations* tennis, football, running; *Style—* Professor Blake Morrison; ✉ c/o United Agents, 12–26 Lexington Street, London W1F 0LE (☎ 020 3214 0800, fax 020 3214 0801, website www.unitedagents.co.uk)

MORRISON, Colin; s of Percy Morrison (d 1985), of London, and Elfrieda Edith, *née* Swann (d 1998); *b* 15 October 1950, London; *Educ* Royal Wanstead Sch, Stanford Univ; *m* 6 Dec 1985, Mary, *née* Ratcliffe; 2 da (Emily Louise b 12 Nov 1986, Kate Elizabeth b 15 Dec 1989); *Career* dep ceo Reed Publishing Gp 1979–91, dir Emap plc 1991–95, ceo Australian Consolidated Press Ltd and dir Publishing & Broadcasting Ltd 1995–99, md Axel Springer Int and dir Axel Springer TV 1999–2001, chief operating offr and md Future plc 2001–03, ceo ACP-NatMag and dir ACP Media (UK) Ltd 2004–08; dir GRB Entertainment Inc 2000–01; chm: Royal Pharmaceutical Soc Publishing 2003–13, Globelynx Network Ltd 2010–15, RCN Publishing Ltd 2011–12, Great Golf Media Ltd 2015–, Jacobs Media Gp Ltd 2009–, SBTV News 2016–; non-exec dir: Centaur Media plc 2004–14, Br Nat Formulary 2004–13, eQuoteCentral Ltd 2009–10, IPCN Ltd (Creating in China) 2008–13, Jacobs Media Ltd 2009–; strategic conslt to media, news and info cos UK and Asia Pacific 2008–; chm Magazine Publishers of Australia 1995–99, dir Periodical Publishers' Assoc 1989–95 and 2001–03; ed Flashes and Flames MediaBlog www.flashesandflames.com 2011–; chm Royal Nat Children's Fndn (incl Royal Wanstead Children's Fndn and Jt Educn Tst) 2001–16, govr Royal Wanstead Sch Fndn, memb Pathfinder on Vulnerable Children Dept for Children, Schs and Families 2005–09, chm Boarding Sch Partnerships (Dept for Educn) 2016–; memb Stanford Univ Alumni; Freeman City of London 2005, Liveryman Worshipful Co of Stationers and Newspaper Makers 2005; FRSA, fell Industry and Parl Tst, fell Aust Inst of Mgmnt; *Books* Nowhere Else (1986); blogger Huffington Post 2013–; *Recreations* tennis, magazines, movies, music, football (Spurs); *Clubs* Groucho, RAC, 1920, Cook Soc, Savile; *Style—* Colin Morrison, Esq; ✉ 41 The Downs, Wimbledon, London SW20 8HG (☎ 020 8944 2819, e-mail morrisoncolin@gmail.com, www.flashesandflames.com)

MORRISON, Fiona Jane; da of John Black (Ian) Morrison (d 1994), and Marion Lilian Morgan (subsequently Mrs Bicknell; d 2011)); *b* 2 May 1957, Stevenage, Herts; *Educ* Dauntsey's Sch Devizes, Selwyn Coll Cambridge (MA, Rowing blues, pres Cambridge Univ Women's Boat Club); *m* 14 July 1984, Dr Eivind James Dullforce (d 2006); *Career* Lane Clark & Peacock LLP: actuarial trainee 1979–82, staff actuary 1982–84, ptnr 1984–; Inst of Actuaries: memb Cncl 2001–07 and 2008–, memb Pensions Bd 2001–08 (dep chm 2006–08), chm Pensions Guidance Ctee 2002–06 (memb 1996–2006), hon sec 2004–06, memb Regulation Bd 2008–, President's Award 2012, pres-elect 2014–15, pres 2015–; chm Staple Inn Actuarial Soc 2008–10; pres Selwyn Coll Alumni Assoc 2012–13; Liveryman Worshipful Co of Actuaries, tstee Co of Actuaries Charitable Tst 2004–12 (Ct Asst 2012–); FIA 1984; *Recreations* ski touring, rowing; *Clubs* Lansdowne, Leander, Oriental; *Style—* Miss Fiona Morrison; ✉ Lane Clark & Peacock LLP,95 Wigmore Street, London W1U 1DQ (☎ 020 7439 2266, fax 020 7439 0183, e-mail fiona.morrison@lcp.uk.com)

MORRISON, Frances Margaret (Fran); da of Lt Cdr W Morrison, OBE, VRD, of Helensburgh, Scotland, and Hilary Morrison; *Educ* Queen's Park Sch Glasgow, Univ of St Andrews (MA); *m* 1984 (m dis); 2 s; *Career* broadcaster and media conslt, tobacco and oil industry communications mangr; news and current affrs reporter/presenter BBC Radio and TV, first woman presenter of BBC TV's Newsnight at its launch 1979; reporter/presenter BBC TV: Nationwide 1981–83, 60 Minutes 1983–84; reporter BBC TV Watchdog 1984–85, reporter various documentary progs BBC TV 1978–86, presenter various arts and music progs BBC TV 1978–86; reporter/presenter Thames TV, Channel 4, Sky TV and BBC Radio Womans Hour 1986–91; media conslt 1986–91, freelance journalist 1978–91, head of media rels and communications Shell UK Ltd 1991–99; British American Tobacco plc: mangr external communications 1999–2000, head corp communications 2000–10; Freeman City of London 2013, Liveryman Worshipful Co of Tobacco Blenders and Tobacco Pipe Makers 2013; FRSA 1992; *Recreations* reading, theatre, visual arts; *Style—* Ms Fran Morrison; ✉ c/o The RSA, 8 John Adam Street, London WC2N 6EZ (☎ 020 7451 6827)

MORRISON, Sir (Alexander) Fraser; kt (1998), CBE (1993); s of late Alexander Ferrier Sharp Morrison, and Catherine Colina, *née* Fraser; *b* 20 March 1948; *Educ* Tain Royal Acad, Univ of Edinburgh (BSc); *m* 23 Sept 1972, Patricia Janice, da of late Peter David Murphy; 1 s (Alexander Peter b 13 Jan 1974), 2 da (Claire Catherine b 6 June 1975, Sarah-Jane b 21 Aug 1977); *Career* Morrison Construction Group: dir 1970–76, md 1976–84, chm and md 1984–96, exec chm 1996–2000; dir: Shand Ltd 1978–89, Alexander Shand Holdings Ltd 1982–86; chm: Teasses Capital Ltd 2003–, Ramco Hldgs Ltd 2005–12/13; dep chm Clydesdale Bank plc 1999–2004 (non-exec dir 1994–99), memb Bd Yorkshire Bank plc 1999–2004; FCEC: chm Scotland 1991–92, chm 1993–94, vice-pres 1994–96; dir Chief Execs Orgn 2003–13; chm: Highlands and Islands Enterprise 1992–98 (dir 1991–92), Univ of Highlands and Islands Project 1997–2001; Hon DTech 1995 and 1997; Hon DUniv Open 2000; CEng, MIHT, FRSA 1990, FICE 1993, FScotvec 1994, FCIOB 1995; *Recreations* golf, skiing, shooting, opera, art; *Style—* Sir Fraser Morrison, CBE; ✉ Teasses House, Leven, Fife KY8 5PG (☎ 01334 828048, fax 01334 828 049)

MORRISON, Graeme Alexander; s of Kenneth Morrison, of Hong Kong, and Isabel, *née* Lobo; *b* 17 October 1982, Hong Kong; *Educ* Dollar Acad; *Career* rugby union player (centre); with Glasgow Warriors 2003–; Scotland: 23 caps, debut 2004; *Style—* Mr Graeme Morrison; ✉ c/o Glasgow Warriors, Firhil Stadium, Firhill Road, Glasgow G20 7AL

MORRISON, Graham; OBE (2016); s of Robert Morrison (d 2000), and Robina Sandison, née Wilson; *b* 2 February 1951, Kilmarnock; *Educ* Brighton Coll, Jesus Coll Cambridge (MA, DipArch, Brancusi award); *Children* 1 da (Laura b 16 Sept 1981), 1 s (Alan b 6 Nov 1984); *Career* architect; co-fndr (with Bob Allies, *qv*) Allies and Morrison 1983 (Architectural Practice of the Year Award Building Awards 2004 and 2015); architects to Royal Festival Hall 1994–98; other projects incl: The Clove Bldg (RIBA Award 1991), Pierhead Liverpool 1995, Sarum Hall Sch (RIBA Award 1996), Nunnery Square Sheffield (RIBA Award 1996), Rosalind Franklin Bldg Newnham Coll Cambridge (RIBA Award 1996), Br Embassy Dublin (RIBA Award 1997), Abbey Mills Pumping Station Stratford (RIBA Award 1997), Rutherford Info Servs Bldg Goldsmiths Coll London (RIBA Award 1998), Blackburn House London (RIBA Award 2000), Blackwell House Cumbria (RIBA Award 2003), extension to Horniman Museum London (RIBA Award 2004), 85 Southwark Street London (Building of the Year Award RIBA London 2004, Corporate Workplace Building Br Cncl for Offices Awards 2004), Fitzwilliam Coll Gatehouse and Auditorium (RIBA Award 2005), BBC Media Village White City (RIBA Award 2005), Girton Coll Library (RIBA Award 2006), Girton Coll Library and Archive, The Finlay Building Merton Coll, Royal Festival Hall (finalist RIBA Nat Award and Stirling Prize, Design for London Public Space RIBA Award, RIBA Award), Royal Observatory Greenwich (RIBA Award), Paradise Street Liverpool One (RIBA Award 2009), Charles Street Car Park Sheffield (RIBA Award 2009), One Vine Street The Quadrant Regent Street (RIBA Award 2009), Bankside 123 (RIBA Award 2010), Highbury Square (RIBA Award 2010), masterplan London 2012 (RIBA Award 2013), Rambert Dance Co London (RIBA Award 2014), Ash Court Girton Coll Cambridge (RIBA Award 2014), St Thomas the Apostle Coll London (RIBA Awards 2015); Masterplanning Architect of the Year Building Design Awards 2007, Public Building Architect of the Year Building Design Awards 2007, Architect of the Year Building Design Awards 2007; exhibitions: New British Architecture (Japan) 1994, Retrospective (USA Schs of Architecture) 1996–98; memb: Nat Cncl RIBA 1992–95 (dir RIBA Jl 1994–98), Architecture Advsy Ctee Arts Cncl of England 1997–98, Royal Fine Art Cmmn 1998–99, CABE Design Review Ctee 2000–04, London Advsy Ctee English Heritage 2001–13, English Heritage's CABE and Urban Panel 2009–12, English Heritage Advsy Ctee 2013–, South Downs Nat Park Design Review Panel 2014; cmmr English Heritage 2011–; external examiner Univ of Portsmouth 2003–05, visiting prof Univ of Nottingham 2004–05; RIBA 1976; *Publications* Allies and Morrison (Univ of Michigan Architectural Papers, 1996), Allies and Morrison 1 (2011), The Fabric of Place (2014); *Recreations* blues music; *Style—* Graham Morrison, Esq, OBE; ✉ Allies and Morrison, 85 Southwark Street, London SE1 0HX (☎ 020 7921 0100, fax 020 7921 0101, e-mail gmorrison@alliesandmorrison.com)

MORRISON, Sir Howard Andrew Clive; KCMG (2015), CBE (2007, OBE 1988), QC (2001); s of Howard Edward Morrison (d 1986), and Roma, *née* Wilkinson (d 1998); *b* 20 July 1949, Kent; *Educ* Univ of London (LLB), Inns of Court Sch of Law; *m* 1980, Kathryn Margaret, *née* Moore; 1 da, 1 s; *Career* called to the Bar: Gray's Inn 1977 (bencher 2008), Fiji 1988, Eastern Caribbean 1990; VSO: vol Ghana 1968–69, desk offr Zambia and Malawi 1975–76; practising barr Midland and Oxford Circuit 1977–85, resident magistrate then chief magistrate Fiji and sr magistrate Tuvalu 1985–87, locum attorney-gen Anguilla 1988–89, practising barr Midland and Oxford Circuit 1989–2004, def barr UN War Crimes Tbnls The Hague and Arusha 1998–2004, circuit judge 2004–, sr judge Sovereign Base Areas Cyprus 2007, judge Special Tbnl For Lebanon 2009, perm judge UN Int Criminal Tbnl for Former Yugoslavia 2009–, UK judge Int Criminal Court 2011–, Appeals Div judge Int Criminal Court 2015–; lectr in int law, advocacy teacher/trainer Gray's Inn 1994, Holding Redlich distinguished visiting fell Monash Univ 2007, hon prof of law Univ of Leicester 2012, sr fell Lauterpacht Centre for Int Law Univ of Cambridge 2013; memb Advsy Bd Jl of Int Criminal Law, memb Advsy Bd Int Criminal Law Network 2013; Bar Cncl: memb Race Rels Ctee 1996–2002, memb Equal Opportunities Ctee 2002–03; Hon LLD Univ of Leicester 2014; memb: Int Bar Assoc, Cwlth Judges and Magistrates Assoc, Br Inst for Int and Comparative Law; Subalt Queen's Regt and Parachute Regt (TAVR); FRGS 1991; *Publications* various articles and chapters, mainly on international criminal and humanitarian law and human rights law; *Recreations* travel, scuba diving, sailing, flying; *Clubs* Portsmouth Offshore Gp, Societeit de Witte (The Hague), Royal Over-seas League; *Style—* Sir Howard Morrison, KCMG, CBE, QC; ✉ 36 Bedford Row, London WC1R 4JH (☎ 020 7421 8000)

MORRISON, Hon Hugh; s of 2 Baron Margadale (d 2003), of Wilts, and Clare, *née* Barclay; *b* 7 November 1960, London; *Educ* Eton, Ealing Coll of HE (BA); *m* 1, Jan 1986 (m dis), Jane, *née* Jenks; 1 s (Geordie Anthony b 29 Sept 1989), 1 da (Amber Belinda b 14 Sept 1993); m 2, Aug 2004, Mary Dorothy Wordsworth, *née* Drysdale; *Career* racehorse trainer 1997–, horses trained incl Pastoral Pursuits (champion sprinter 2005), Alcazar (Group One winner) and Sakhee's Secret (champion sprinter 2007); dir Islay Estates Co Ltd 1989; *Recreations* country sports; *Clubs* White's, Turf; *Style—* The Hon Hugh Morrison; ✉ Summerdown, East Ilsely, Newbury, Berkshire RG20 7LB (☎ 01635 281678, fax 01635 281746, e-mail hughie@hughiemorrison.co.uk)

MORRISON, (William) Ivan; s of William Morrison, of Coleraine, NI, and Wilhelmina, *née* Stirling; *b* 15 March 1949; *Educ* Royal Sch Dungannon, Univ of Glasgow (BVMS, PhD); *m* 14 March 1974, Sheila Jean, da of James Orr; 3 s (Liam James b 17 Aug 1974, Neil Ivan b 29 May 1977, Euan Thomas b 22 Oct 1979), 1 da (Karen Sarah b 3 Nov 1982); *Career* Int Lab for Research on Animal Diseases Nairobi: postdoctoral research fell 1975–77, scientist 1978–85, sr scientist and prog leader 1985–89; head Div of Immunology and Pathology Inst for Animal Health 1990–2002, prof of immunology Royal (Dick) Sch of Vet Studies Univ of Edinburgh 2002–; visiting prof: Univ of Glasgow 1996, Univ of Bristol 1999; scientific advsr to: Wellcome Tst, DFID (formerly ODA), DEFRA (formerly MAFF), Horserace Betting Levy Board; MRCVS 1972, FRCPath 1996 (MRCPath 1986), FRSE 1997; *Awards* Pfizer Award 1990, Wellcome Tst Medal for Vet Research 1991, Distinguished Vet Immunologist Award American Assoc of Vet Immunologists 1994, RASE Bledisloe Award 2001; *Publications* The Ruminant Immune System in Health and Disease (ed, 1986), Cell-Mediated Immunity in Ruminants (jtly ed, 1994); author of over 200 articles in scientific jls; *Style—* Professor Ivan Morrison, FRSE; ✉ The Roslin Institute, Royal (Dick) School of Veterinary Studies, The University of Edinburgh, Easter Bush, Roslin, Midlothian EH25 9RG (☎ 0131 651 9247, e-mail ivan.morrison@roslin.ed.ac.uk)

MORRISON, James; *b* 13 August 1984, Rugby, Warks; *Career* singer and songwriter; *Albums* Undiscovered 2006 (UK no 1), Songs for You, Truths for Me 2008 (UK no 3), The Awakening 2011 (UK no 1); *Singles* incl: You Give Me Something 2006, Wonderful World 2006, The Pieces Don't Fit Anymore 2006, You Make It Real 2008, Broken Strings 2008, Please Don't Stop the Rain 2009, I Won't Let You Go 2011, Up 2011; *Style—* Mr

James Morrison; ✉ c/o Paul McDonald, Closer Artists, Matrix Complex, 91 Peterborough Road, London SW6 3BU

MORRISON, James Fyffe Thomson; s of John Morrison (d 1952), and Margaret Morrison (d 1984); *b* 11 April 1932; *Educ* Hillhead HS Glasgow, Glasgow Sch of Art (DA), Jordanhill Coll of Educn; *m* 12 April 1955, Dorothy Jean Allison, da of James Barclay McCormack; 1 s (John Coull b 25 Aug 1959), 1 da (Judith Kate b 10 Aug 1961); *Career* oil and watercolour painter; travels and paints extensively in the Arctic, Southern Africa and France; visiting artist Hospitalfield House 1962 and 1963, head of dept Duncan of Jordanstone Coll of Art 1978–87 (lectr 1965–78); presenter Scope (BBC) 1976–, writer and presenter A Scottish Picture Show (STV) 1988; memb: Soc of Scottish Artists 1963 (Cncl 1964–67), Bd of Govrs Duncan Jordanstone Coll of Art 1988–; Torrance Award RGI 1958, Arts Cncl Travelling Award 1968; Hon DUniv Stirling 1986; RSW 1968, RSA 1992 (ARSA 1973); *Solo Exhibitions* McClure Gallery 1959, Scottish Gallery 1959, 1989, 1992, 1994, 1997, 1999 and 2002, Reid Gall 1962, Vaughan Coll Leicester 1968, Richard Demarco Gallery 1968, Compass Gallery 1970, Galleria Vaccarino 1971, Steiger Gallery 1973, Düsseldorf Kunstmesse 1974, Edinburgh Festival Exhbn (Scottish Gallery) 1978, Thackeray Gallery 1979, 1981, 1985, 1995, 1997 and 2000, Fine Art Soc 1986, Waddington and Sheill Gallery 1987, Perth Festival Exhbn (Perth Museum and Art Gallery) 1988, Talbot Rice Gallery (Univ of Edinburgh) 1995, Macaulay Gallery 1989, William Hardie Gallery 1990, Riverside Gallery 1991; *Work in Various Collections* incl: Duke of Edinburgh, Scottish Arts Cncl, Aberdeen Art Gallery, Dundee Museum and Art Gallery, Kelvingrove Art Gallery and Museum, Perth Museum and Art Gallery, Bank of Scotland, Univ of Edinburgh, Tayside Educn Ctee, British Linen Bank, Grampian Television, Clydesdale Bank, Univ of Glasgow, BBC, Low and Bonar plc, Glaxo Wellcome, Conoco, SISIS Equipment Ltd, IBM, Robert Fleming Holdings Ltd; numerous works in private collections in USA, Britain, Canada and Europe; *Publications* Aff the Squerr (2 edn 1990), Paris in Winter (1992); *Recreations* playing the recorder in a chamber group; *Style*— James Morrison, RSA; ✉ Craigview House, Usan, Montrose, Angus, Tayside DD10 9SD (☎ and fax 01674 672639); The Scottish Gallery, 16 Dundas Street, Edinburgh

MORRISON, Jasper; s of Alec Morrison, and Dinah, *née* Herbert; *b* 11 November 1959, London; *Educ* Bryanston, Kingston Poly, RCA; *m* 2004, Ruth, *née* Donaghey; *Career* designer; opened: Office for Design London 1986, Paris studio 2002; designs for leading Italian mfrs incl: Alessi, Cappellini, Flos, Vitra, Rosenthal, Rowenta; designer Hannover Tram for Üstra 1997, furnished public spaces in Tate Modern London 2000; Designer of the Year Paris Design Fair 2000; RDI 2001; *Publications* Designs, Projects & Drawings 1981–89 (1990), A World Without Words (ed, 1992, 2 edn 1998), A Book of Spoons (ed, 1997), A Tram for Hanover (1998), International Design Yearbook (ed, 1999), Everything but the Walls (2002 and 2006), Super Normal (2007); *Style*— Jasper Morrison, Esq; ✉ Jasper Morrison Ltd, 24b Kingsland Road, London E2 8DA (e-mail mail@jaspermorrison.com)

MORRISON, John; *b* 6 March 1949; *Educ* St Edward's Coll Liverpool, St Catherine's Coll Oxford (BA); *m* 29 Feb 1980, Judith, *née* Lee; 1 s (Nicholas b 1981), 1 da (Joanna b 1984); *Career* news trainee BBC 1971, scriptwriter ITN 1973, prog ed Channel 4 News 1982, features ed The Independent 1986, ed Newsnight BBC 1987, ed Assignment BBC 1990, ed Six O'Clock News BBC 1993–95, managing ed BBC News 1995–96, ed BBC TV News 1996–97, exec ed Core News BBC TV 1997–99, head of ops BBC World Service News 1999–2000, ed BBC World Service News and Current Affairs 2000–02; Morrison Media Consultants 2002–, specialist ptnr Pagefield 2011–; *Style*— John Morrison

MORRISON, Ven John Anthony; s of Leslie Claude Morrison (d 1967), of Hastings, E Sussex, and Mary Sharland (d 1997), da of Sir Frank Newson-Smith, 1 Bt (d 1971); *b* 11 March 1938; *Educ* Haileybury, Jesus Coll Cambridge (MA), Lincoln Coll Oxford (MA), Chichester Theol Coll; *m* 20 July 1968, Angela, da of Jonathan Eric Bush (d 1978), of Leatherhead; 2 s (Dominic b 19 June 1970, Nicholas b 11 May 1974), 1 da (Philippa b 26 March 1972); *Career* ordained deacon Birmingham 1964, priest 1965; curate: St Peter Birmingham 1964–68, St Michael-at-the-North Gate Oxford 1968–74; examining chaplain to Bishop of Oxford 1973–86; chaplain Lincoln Coll Oxford 1968–74, vicar Basildon Berks 1974–82, rural dean Bradfield 1978–82, vicar Aylesbury 1982–90, rural dean Aylesbury 1985–89; archdeacon: of Buckingham 1990–98, of Oxford 1998–2005; canon residentiary of Christ Church Oxford 1998–2005, archdeacon and canon emeritus 2005–; RBI county chaplain: Bucks 1990–98, Oxon 1998–2007; St John Ambulance chaplain: Bucks 1990–98, Oxon 1998–2007; memb Gen Synod C of E 1980–90 and 1998–2000, treas Corp of Sons of the Clergy 2002–08 (sr treas 2005–08); Ct Asst Worshipful Co of Spectacle Makers 1994–2013 (Master 2006–07); *Recreations* growing tomatoes and other things; *Clubs* Leander, Vincent's (Oxford); *Style*— The Ven John Morrison; ✉ 39 Crown Road, Wheatley, Oxford OX33 1UJ (☎ 01865 876625, e-mail morrison039@btinternet.com)

MORRISON, Hon (Dame) Mary Anne; GCVO (2013, DCVO 1982, CVO 1970); does not use style of Dame; da of 1 Baron Margadale (d 1996); *b* 17 May 1937; *Educ* Heathfield Sch Ascot, abroad; *Career* woman of the bedchamber to HM The Queen 1960–; *Style*— The Hon Mary Morrison, GCVO

MORRISON, Michael John; s of John Percy Morrison, JP, and Kathleen Morrison; *b* 31 March 1939; *Educ* Fettes, St Catharine's Coll Cambridge (MA, LLB); *m* 11 Sept 1965, June; 1 s (Nicholas James b 21 Dec 1967), 1 da (Louise Charlotte b 23 June 1971); *Career* admitted slr 1965; ptnr Parker Garrett 1969–82; sr ptnr: Taylor Garrett 1988 (ptnr 1982–88), Taylor Joynson Garrett 1989–99; chm: Yuills Ltd 1975–, Bride (Exel) Ltd 1997–, Skelton Gp Ltd 2000–; dir: Leif Hoegh UK Ltd 1978–, Norwegian American Cruises UK Ltd 1980–87; memb Law Soc; *Recreations* golf, squash; *Clubs* Moor Park Golf, Melton Mowbray GC; *Style*— Michael Morrison, Esq; ✉ Yuills Ltd, 104 Park Street, London W1K 6NF (☎ 020 7499 8447)

MORRISON, Sheriff Nigel Murray Paton; QC (Scot 1988); s of David Paton Morrison (d 1968), of Edinburgh, and Dilys Morrison (d 1995); *b* 18 March 1948; *Educ* Rannoch Sch; *Career* called to the Bar Inner Temple 1972, admitted to Scot Bar 1975; asst ed Session Cases 1976–82, asst clerk to Rules Cncl 1978–84, clerk of faculty Faculty of Advocates 1979–86, standing jr counsel to Scot Devpt Dept (planning) 1982–86, temp sheriff 1982–96, Sheriff of Lothian and Borders 1996–, dir of Judicial Studies 2000–04, pres Sheriffs' Assoc 2011–13 (vice-pres 2009–11), temp judge Court of Session and High Court of Justiciary 2013–, appeal sheriff Sheriff Appeal Court 2015–; chm Social Security Appeal Tbnl 1982–91, counsel to Sec of State under the Private Legislation Procedure (Scot) Act (1936) 1986–96, first counsel to Lord Pres of Court of Session 1989–96 (jr and second counsel 1984–89); chm Med Appeal Tbnl 1991–96; tstee Nat Library of Scotland 1989–99; memb Faculty of Advocates; *Publications* contrib to: Stair Memorial Encyclopaedia of the Laws of Scotland, Macphail on Sheriff Court Practice (2 edn); princ author Green's Annotated Rules of the Court of Session; ed Sentencing Practice; *Recreations* being taken for walks by my dogs, music, riding, Scottish country dancing, visiting Italy; *Clubs* New (Edinburgh); *Style*— Sheriff Nigel Morrison, QC; ✉ Sheriff's Chambers, Sheriff Court House, 27 Chambers Street, Edinburgh EH1 1LB (☎ 0131 225 2525, fax 0131 225 4422)

MORRISON, Richard Duncan; s of Donald Melville Morrison, and Winifred Mary, *née* Stocks; *b* 24 July 1954; *Educ* Univ Coll Sch, Magdalene Coll Cambridge (MA); *m* 1, 1977 (m dis 2011), Marian, da of Joseph Plant; 2 s (Philip b 1984, Edmund b 1988), 1 da (Katharine b 1985); m 2, 2013, Anna Louise Elisabeth, da of Leonard Tilbrook; *Career* asst ed Classical Music Magazine 1977–84, dep ed Early Music Magazine 1985–89; The Times: music critic 1984–89, dep arts ed 1989–90, arts ed 1990–99, columnist 1999–, chief culture writer 2012–; FRSA 1995; *Recreations* walking, playing the organ; *Style*— Richard Morrison, Esq; ✉ 8 Avenue Road, London N6 5DW (☎ 07770 381928); The Times, 3 Thomas More Square, London E98 1TT (☎ 020 7782 5038, fax 020 7782 5748, e-mail richard.morrison@thetimes.co.uk)

MORRISON, Prof Ronald; s of David Morrison, of Airdrie, and Catherine, *née* Turner (d 1958); *b* 15 April 1946; *Educ* Eastbank Acad, Univ of Strathclyde (BSc), Univ of Glasgow (MSc), Univ of St Andrews (PhD); *m* 17 Oct 1975, Ann Margaret, da of Alistair MacDonald, of Edinburgh; 1 s (David b 1979), 1 da (Catriona b 1981); *Career* prof of software engrg Univ of St Andrews 1985– (sr res fell 1971–72, lectr 1972–84, reader 1984–85); pres Scottish Cross Country Union 1986–87, pres Scottish Athletics Fedn 1997–99 (vice-pres 1995–97); MBCS, CEng, FRSE; *Books* Davie & Morrison Recursive Descent Compiling (jtly, 1981), Cole & Morrison Introduction to S-Algol Programming (jtly, 1982), Sommerville & Morrison Software Development with Ada (jtly, 1987), Atkinson, Burneman & Morrison Data Types and Persistence (1988), Hull, Morrison, Stemple Database Programming Languages (1989), Albamo, Morrison Persistent Object Systems (1993), Morrison, Kennedy Advances in Databases (1996), Morrison, Jorden & Atkinson Advances in Persistent Object Systems (1998); *Recreations* golf, athletics, cross-country running; *Clubs* St Andrews Golf, Fife Athletic, Grail Golfing Soc; *Style*— Prof Ronald Morrison; ✉ School of Computer Science, University of St Andrews, North Haugh, St Andrews, Fife KY16 9SS (☎ 01334 463254, fax 01334 463278, e-mail ron@dcs.st-and.ac.uk)

MORRISON, Stephen Roger (Steve); s of Hyman Michael Morrison, and Rebecca, *née* Zolkwer; *b* 3 March 1947; *Educ* Univ of Edinburgh, Nat Film Sch; *m* 1979, Gayle Valerie, *née* Broughall; *Career* Granada Television: joined to set up Northern Documentary Unit 1974, subsequently prodr/dir World in Action, head of regnl progs then head of features and documentaries until 1987, dir of progs 1987–92, md 1993–94; md: Granada Broadcasting 1992, LWT 1994–96; dep chief exec TV Div Granada Group plc 1995, ceo Granada Media plc 1996–2001 (chief operating offr 1996), ceo Granada plc 2001–02; chm Granada Sky Broadcasting 1996–2002; chief exec Granada Film (fndr mid 1980s); Granada network credits incl: The Spanish Civil War, Disappearing World, China, Scully (comedy-drama), The Road to 1984, 28-Up (fourth Seven-Up series); Granada film credits incl: prodr The Magic Toyshop and The Fruit Machine, exec prodr My Left Foot (two Oscars), The Field (Oscar nomination) and Jack & Sarah; chm North West Vision 2003–, chief exec All3Media 2003–; memb Bd: British Screen Advsy Cncl, Edinburgh Int Film Festival; govr NFTS; dir British Screen Finance; FRTS 1998; *Recreations* reading, films and theatre, talking and dining, touring delicatessens; *Clubs* Garrick; *Style*— Steve Morrison, Esq

MORRISON, Susan; da of Glen Wilkinson, and Eileen Iris, *née* Greenwood; *b* 1 July 1960; *Educ* Balderstone HS Rochdale, Loughborough Univ (BSc); *m* (m dis); 1 da; *Career* joined Prison Serv 1981; served at: HMP Holloway, HM YOI Glen Parva, HMP Liverpool N Regnl Office 1981–90; head of residence HMP Leeds 1990–93, secondment to area mangr's office 1993–94, head of throughcare HMP Styal 1994–99, dep govr HMP Manchester 1999–2001, govr HMP Buckley Hall 2001–; Butler Tst Award for outstanding contribution to the quality of prison care 1997; *Recreations* gardening, cooking, singing, theatre, swimming; *Style*— Mrs Susan Morrison; ✉ HMP Buckley Hall, Buckley Hall Road, Rochdale, Lancashire OL12 9DP (☎ 01706 514300)

MORRISON-BELL, Sir William Hollin Dayrell; 4 Bt (UK 1905), of Otterburn Hall, Elsdon, Northumberland; s of Capt Sir Charles Reginald Francis Morrison-Bell, 3 Bt (d 1967), and Prudence Caroline, *née* Davies; *b* 21 June 1956; *Educ* Eton, St Edmund Hall Oxford; *m* 6 Oct 1984, Cynthia Hélène Marie, yr da of Teddy White, of Switzerland; 1 s (Thomas Charles Edward b 13 Feb 1985); *Heir* s, Thomas Morrison-Bell; *Career* solicitor; legal advsr for Air Products plc; farmer; *Style*— Sir William Morrison-Bell, Bt; ✉ 28 Batoum Gardens, London W6 7QD (☎ 020 7602 1363; Highgreen, Tarset, Hexham, Northumberland (☎ 01434 240223); Air Products plc, Hersham Place, Molesey Road, Walton on Thames, Surrey KT12 4RZ

MORRISSEY, David Mark; *b* 21 June 1964, Liverpool; *Educ* RADA; *m* Esther Freud, *qv*; *Career* actor, dir and prodr; co dir On The Corner Prodns; patron: Merseyside Unity Theatre, Merseyside Fact Centre; *Theatre* credits incl: King John (RSC), Peer Gynt (RNT), Much Ado About Nothing (Queen's), Three Days of Rain (Donmar); *Television* credits incl: Framed, Finney, The One That Got Away, Holding On (nominated BAFTA Award), Our Mutual Friend, Big Cat, Pure Wickedness, Sweet Revenge (dir), State of Play (nominated BAFTA Award), Murder, Linda Green, The Deal (RTS Award), Blackpool, Cape Wrath, Sense and Sensibility, One Summer, Red Riding, Five Days, Mrs Mandela, True Love, The Hollow Crown, The Walking Dead, The Driver (also prodr); *Film* Drowning By Numbers, Waterland, The Commissioner, Hilary and Jackie, Fanny and Elvis, The Suicide Club (dir only), A Secret Audience (dir only), Some Voices, Born Romantic (dir only), Bring me your Love (prodr and dir), Captain Corelli's Mandolin, Out Of Control, This Little Life (dir only), Passer-By (dir only, nominated Best New Dir BAFTA Awards)), The Reaping, The Other Boleyn Girl, The Waterhorse, Nowhere Boy, Welcome to the Punch, Don't Worry About Me (writer and dir); *Recreations* cinema, golf, horse racing, motorsport, music, reading, travel; *Clubs* Soho House, One Alfred Place, Garrick; *Style*— David Morrissey, Esq; ✉ Tubedale Films, c/o Barley Mow Centre, 10 Barley Mow Passage, Chiswick, London W4 4PH (☎ 020 8994 6477)

MORRISSEY, Helena Louise; CBE (2012); *Educ* Univ of Cambridge; *m* Richard; 9 c; *Career* chief exec Newton Investment Mgmnt Ltd 2001– (joined 1994); fndr 30% Club, chair Investment Action 2014–; *Style*— Mrs Helena Morrissey, CBE; ✉ Newton Investment Management Ltd, Mellon Financial Centre, 160 Queen Victoria Street, London EC4V 4LA

MORRISSEY, Michael Peter; s of Peter Anthony Morrissey (d 2007), of Langshott Wood, Surrey, and Sheila Margaret, *née* Berrett (d 1984); *b* 15 August 1959; *Educ* Worth Sch Sussex, RMA Sandhurst; *m* 30 May 1987, Sally-Anne, da of Derek Harris (d 1996), of St Buryan, Cornwall; 3 da (Rosie Henrietta b 16 Aug 1990, Olivia Mary b 27 March 1996, Francesca Sophie b 26 Oct 1998), 1 s (Hugo William b 18 March 1993); *Career* enlisted 1977; Irish Guards: cmmnd 2 Lt 1978, Lt 1980, Capt 1983, Maj 1988, Co Cmd 1 Irish Guards; serv: Cyprus, Kenya, NI, Belize, Canada, Germany; Thornton Management Ltd London 1989–91, Mercury Asset Management 1991–2002, dir Mercury Investment Services 1994–2002, dir Mercury Fund Managers 1998–2002, Liontrust Asset Mgmnt 2002–12, dir Liontrust Investment Funds Ltd 2002–12, ptnr Smith & Williamson 2012–; dir Investment Ctee Forces Pension Soc 2012–, tstee Combat Stress 2014–; *Recreations* shooting, rugby, cricket; *Clubs* Cavalry and Guards, MCC; *Style*— Michael Morrissey, Esq; ✉ Home Farm, Kineton, Guiting Power, Gloucestershire GL54 5UG; Smith & Williamson, 25 Moorgate, London (☎ 020 7131 4693, e-mail mickey.morrisey@smith.williamson.co.uk)

MORROCCO, Leon; s of Alberto Morrocco (d 1998), and Vera Cockburn, *née* Mercer; *b* 4 April 1942; *Educ* Duncan of Jordanstone Coll of Art Dundee, Slade Sch of Art, Edinburgh Coll of Art; *Career* lectr in painting Edinburgh Coll of Art 1965–68, Academia di Brera Milan (Italian Govt scholarship) 1968–69, lectr in painting Glasgow Sch of Art 1969–79, head Dept of Fine Art Chisholm Inst Melbourne 1979–84, lectr in drawing Ballarat Univ Coll Victoria 1991–92; ARSA 1971, RGI 1996; *Solo Exhibitions* Douglas and Foulis Gallery Edinburgh 1965, French Inst Gallery Edinburgh, Traverse Theatre Gallery Edinburgh 1965, The Scottish Gallery Edinburgh 1971 and 1975, The Loomshop Gallery Edinburgh 1973, Univ of St Andrews 1976, Stirling Gallery 1978, Greenock Arts Centre 1978, Univ of Strathclyde 1978, Glasgow Sch of Art 1979, Stuart Gertsman Galleries Melbourne 1982, Australian Galleries Melbourne 1984, 1986, 1992 and 2003, Bonython-

M

Meadmore Gallery Sydney 1988, Australian Galleries Sydney 1989 and 2003, Portland Gallery London 1991 and 1993, Roger Billcliffe Fine Art Glasgow 1993, 1994 and 1998, Open Eye Gallery Edinburgh 1993, 1995, 1997, 2001, 2003 and 2005, Loomshop Gallery Fife 1994, John Martin of London 1996, 1998, 2000 and 2003, Scottish Painting (Chelsea Gallery Palo Alto) 2005, Salon d'Automne Paris 2005, Havana (John Martin Gallery London) 2006, Lalique NY 2007, The Sketchbooks of Leon Morrocco (Open Eye Gallery Edinburgh) 2007; *Work in Collections* HRH Princess Margaret, The Scottish Nat Gallery of Modern Art, Univ of Liverpool, Univ of Strathclyde, Scottish Arts Cncl, Scottish Educn Dept, Leeds Art Gallery, Lillie Art Gallery, Australian Govt Collection, Queensland Govt Collection, United Distillers plc, Touche-Ross plc; *Awards* Andrew Grant Travelling Scholarship 1965, Royal Scottish Acad Latimer Award 1970, Guthrie Award 1971, Royal Bank of Scotland Painting Award 1999; ARSA 1972, RGI 1995; *Style—* Leon Morrocco, RSA, RGI; ✉ 99 St James's Lane, Muswell Hill, London N10 3RJ (✆ 020 8883 3774)

MORROW, His Hon Graham Eric; QC (1996); s of George Eric Morrow, of Liverpool, and Freda, *née* Duckett; *b* 14 June 1951; *Educ* Liverpool Coll, Univ of Newcastle upon Tyne (LLB); *m* 31 Jan 1987, Rosalind Nola, da of Samuel Ellis; 1 s (Philip Ellis *b* 24 July 1987), 2 step da (Erika Suzanne Patrick *b* 11 May 1971, Lisa Danielle Patrick *b* 6 Oct 1973); *Career* called to the Bar Lincoln's Inn 1974, recorder 1997–2006, circuit judge (Northern Circuit) 2006–16; fndn memb Liverpool Coll; tstee Royal Sch for the Blind Liverpool; *Recreations* skiing, swimming, walking, cycling; *Style—* His Hon Graham Morrow, QC; ✉ e-mail graham.morrow@btconnect.com

MORROW, Baron (UK Life Peer 2006), of Clogher Valley in the County of Tyrone; Maurice George Morrow; MLA; *b* 1948; *Educ* Dungannon Secdy Sch, Dungannon Technical Coll; *Career* MLA (DUP) Fermanagh and South Tyrone 1998–, cncllr Dungannon and South Tyrone Borough Cncl; min for social devpt NI Exec 2000–01; sits in House of Lords as crossbench peer 2006–; *Style—* The Lord Morrow, MLA; ✉ House of Lords, London SW1A 0PW

MORSE, Christopher George John (Robin); s of John Morse, of Swansea, and Margaret, *née* Maliphant; *b* 28 June 1947; *Educ* Malvern Coll, Wadham Coll Oxford (MA, BCL); *m* 26 March 1983, Louise Angela, da of Ronald Stott (d 1974), of Mirfield, W Yorks; 1 s (Richard *b* 24 May 1985); *Career* called to the Bar 1971; visiting prof: John Marshall Law Sch Chicago 1979–80, Leuven Univ 1982; King's Coll London: lectr in law 1971–88, reader in law 1988–92, prof of law 1992–, dean and head of Sch of Law 1992–93 and 1997–2002, FKC 2000; *Books* Torts in Private International Law (1978), The Conflict of Laws (ed, 11 edn 1987, 12 edn 1993, 13 edn 2000, 14 edn 2006, 15 edn 2012), Benjamin's Sale of Goods (ed, 3 edn 1987, 4 edn 1992, 5 edn 1997, 6 edn 2002, 7 edn 2006), Public Policy in Transnational Relationships (1991), Chitty on Contracts (ed, 27 edn 1994, 28 edn 1999, 29 edn 2004, 30 edn 2008, 31 edn 2012); *Recreations* travel, Swansea City AFC; *Style—* Prof Robin Morse; ✉ School of Law, King's College, London WC2R 2LS (✆ 020 7836 5454, fax 020 7873 2465)

MORSE, David Thomas; s of Thomas Walter Morse (d 1984), of London, and Emily Annie, *née* Garrett (d 2003); *b* 10 November 1943; *Educ* Royal Ballet Sch (White Lodge); *m* 9 Oct 1971, Marion, da of Charles Arnold Browell Tait, OBE; *Career* ballet dancer; with the Royal Ballet 1961–65; princ character artist Birmingham Royal Ballet (formerly Sadler's Wells Royal Ballet) 1989–2011, concurrently video archivist 1998–2011; roles with co incl: the Rake in The Rake's Progress, Jasper in Pineapple Poll, Hilarion in Giselle, Polchinelle in Meadow of Proverbs, Punch in Punch and the Street Party, The Dago and Popular Song in Façade, Bootface in The Lady and the Fool, Widow Simone and Alain in La Fille Mal Gardée, Carabosse in The Sleeping Beauty, Henry Hobson in Hobson's Choice, Dr Coppelias in Coppélia, Lord Capulet in Romeo and Juliet, the Merchant in Beauty and the Beast, Kostchei in The Firebird; choreography incl the works Pandora and Birdscape for Sadler's Wells; ret 2011, appearances as guest artist 2011–; awarded Polish ballet's bicentennial medal of honour; *Recreations* photography, reading, music; *Style—* David Morse, Esq; ✉ Birmingham Royal Ballet, Birmingham Hippodrome Theatre, Thorp Street, Birmingham B5 4AU (✆ 0121 245 3500)

MORSE, John Frederick; s of late Leonard John Morse, and late Flossie, *née* Bishop; *b* 4 September 1944, Swansea; *Educ* Bishop Gore GS Swansea, Coll of Law Guildford; *m* 13 July 1970, Andrea, *née* Morris; 1 s (James Edward *b* 25 Oct 1971), 2 da (Rachel Jane *b* 7 March 1973, Natalie Alexandra *b* 17 March 1975); *Career* admitted slr 1967; fndr and sr ptnr John Morse Slrs 1971–; chair Gwalia Housing Tst 2010–; memb: Law Soc 1967–, Swansea and Dist Law Soc 1967– (pres 1999); *Recreations* golf, horse racing, skiing; *Clubs* Royal Porthcawl Golf, Langland Bay Golf, Beechwood (Swansea), Bristol Channel Yacht; *Style—* John Morse, Esq; ✉ Blaen Coed, Cilonnen, Gower, Swansea SA4 3UP (✆ 01792 872307); John Morse Solicitors, St Helen's House, 156 St Helen's Road, Swansea SA1 4DG (✆ and fax 01792 648111, fax 01792 648028, e-mail mail@johnmorse.co.uk)

MORT, District Judge Paul Collins; s of James Mort, and Myrtle Kathleen Mort; *Educ* Bootham Sch York, Univ of Manchester (LLB), Coll of Law Guildford; *m* Karen Mort; 2 da (Georgina, Henrietta); *Career* asst slr 1974–76, partner in private practice 1976–2000, district judge (NE Circuit) 2000–, nominated judge of the Ct of Protection; *Recreations* riding, travel, the arts, jazz, swimming; *Clubs* Reform; *Style—* District Judge Mort

MORTENSEN, Neil James McCready; s of Peter John McCready Mortensen, of Laleham, Middx, and Rhoda, *née* Bamber; *b* 16 October 1949; *Educ* Hampton Sch, Univ of Birmingham (MB ChB), Univ of Bristol (MD); *m* 16 June 1973, Jane Alison, da of Lt-Col Paul Baker, of Shortlands, Kent; 2 da (Gemma *b* 1977, Chloe *b* 1981), 1 s (James *b* 1979); *Career* conslt sr lectr Univ of Bristol and Dept of Surgery Bristol Royal Infirmary 1983–86, conslt surgn John Radcliffe Hosp Oxford 1986–, reader in surgery Univ of Oxford 1994–2000, prof of colorectal surgery Univ of Oxford 2000–, fell Green Coll Oxford 2005– (memb 1987), memb Intercollegiate Bd in Gen Surgery 2003–10; memb: Ctee Surgical Section Br Soc of Gastroenterology 1987–1995, Cncl Br Soc of Gastroenterology 1992–97; pres Assoc of Coloproctology Great Britain and Ireland 2002–03 (memb Cncl 1995–99), pres Coloproctology Section RSM 2003–04, hon treas Surgical Res Soc; ed-in-chief Colorectal Disease 2014– (co-ed 1985–94), assoc ed Dis Col Rect, ed-in-chief Bulletin; chair Br Jl of Surgery Soc 2004–13 (treas 1996–2004), memb Editorial Ctee Br Jl of Surgery; FRCS 1980 (memb Cncl 2013–, tstee Bd 2016); *Books* Colo Rectal Cancer (1989), An Atlas of Rectal Ultrasound (1991), Restorative Proctocolectomy (1993), Challenges in Inflammatory Bowel Disease (2001, 2 edn 2006), Anorectal and Colonic Diseases (2009); *Recreations* tennis, farming; *Style—* Neil Mortensen, Esq; ✉ Department of Colorectal Surgery, Churchill Hospital, Oxford OX3 7LE (✆ 01865 235613)

MORTIMER, Dr Andrew Joseph; s of Stanley Joseph Mortimer (d 1960), and Grace Wilkinson, *née* Armorey (d 2006); *b* 11 October 1948; *Educ* Barnard Castle Sch, Univ of Newcastle upon Tyne (BSc, MB BS, MD); *m* 1, 30 June 1973 (m dis 2003), Janet Mary, da of Kenneth Harry Levis (d 1993); 3 s (Sam *b* 3 Feb 1975, Tom *b* 21 April 1978, Joe *b* 25 Aug 1989); *m* 2, 20 Sept 2004, Susan Howard; *Career* SHO in obstetrics and gynaecology Hexham Gen Hosp 1974–75 (house offr in med and surgery 1973–74), vocational trainee in family med Musgrove Park Hosp Taunton 1975–78; Nuffield Dept of Anaesthetics Radcliffe Infirmary Oxford: SHO in anaesthesia Jan-July 1979, registrar in anaesthesia 1979–80, MRC research trg fell Dec 1980–84; sr registrar Oxfordshire RHA 1984–87 (hon sr registrar 1980–84), conslt anaesthetist (with special interest in intensive care) S Manchester Univ Hosps NHS Tst 1987–, hon clinical lectr Univ of Manchester 1988–; memb: Multi-Centre Research Ethics Ctee 1997–2000, Steering Ctee Nat Confidential Enquiry into Patient Outcome and Death 1998–2001, Steering Ctee of Serious Hazards of Transfusion 1999–, Steering Ctee Nat Comparative Audit of Blood Transfusion RCP 2004–, NW Region Clinical Excellence Awards Ctee 2008–13; Royal Coll of Anathaesthetists: elected memb Cncl 1997 and 2003–07, chm Examinations Ctee 2002–04, Final FRCA 2002–04, jt treas and chm Finance Ctee 2002–05; invited lectr at home and abroad; memb Health Fndn 2000–05; DObstRCOG, FRCA; *Books* A Handbook of Clinical Anaesthesia (ed Section on Vascular Anaesthesia, 1996), Guide to the Final FRCA (ed); author of numerous papers in learned jls; *Recreations* running, skiing, mountain biking, swimming; *Style—* Dr Andrew Mortimer; ✉ Department of Anaesthesia, University Hospital of South Manchester, Baguley House, Southmoor Road, Wythenshawe, Manchester M23 9LT (✆ 0161 291 6420, fax 0161 291 6421, e-mail marie.oliver@uhsm.nhs.uk)

MORTIMER, Prof Ann Margaret; da of late Harry Mortimer, and Muriel, *née* Wood; *b* 11 May 1957; *Educ* Heckmondwike GS, Univ of Leicester (MB ChB, BSc, MD), Univ of Leeds (MMedSc); *Family* 2 s (Benjamin Hugo, Jeremy Alexander), 1 da (Lucille Jacinthe); *Career* lectr in psychiatry Univ of Leeds 1986–88, conslt psychiatrist St Luke's Hosp Huddersfield 1988, sr lectr in psychiatry Charing Cross and Westminster Med Sch (Univ of London) 1991–95, foundation chair in psychiatry Postgraduate Med Sch Univ of Hull 1995–2012, emeritus prof NAViGO and Univ of Hull 2012–; FRCPsych 1999 (MRCPsych 1985); *Books* Managing Negative Symptoms of Schizophrenia (2001), Therapeutic Strategies in Schizophrenia (jtly, 2011); numerous other pubns on schizophrenia; *Recreations* gardening, shooting, skiing, playing the piano; *Clubs* Humberside Shooting, North Cotes Butts Rifle; *Style—* Prof Ann M Mortimer; ✉ c/o Mrs Julie Branton, Holly Lodge Cottage, Main Street, Brantingham, Brough, East Yorkshire HU15 1QG (e-mail julie@simongriff.karoo.co.uk)

MORTIMER, Emily; da of Sir John Mortimer (d 2009), and Penelope Mortimer; *b* 6 October 1971; *Educ* St Paul's Girls' Sch London, Lincoln Coll Oxford (BA); *m* Alessandro Nivola; 1 s (Sam *b* 2003), 1 da (May *b* 2011); *Career* actress; *Television* The Glass Virgin 1995, Sharpe's Sword 1995; *Silent Witness:* Heartstones 1996, Lord of Misrule 1996; A Dance to the Music of Time 1997, Midsomer Murders 1998, Coming Home 1998, Cider with Rosie 1998, Noah's Ark 1999, The Newsroom 2012, *Films* Ghost and the Darkness 1996, The Last of the High Kings 1996, The Saint 1997, Elizabeth 1998, Notting Hill 1999, Love's Labour's Lost 1999, Scream 3 1999, Killing Joe 1999, The Kid 2000, The 51st State 2001, Lovely & Amazing 2001, A Foreign Affair 2003, Nobody Needs to Know 2003, The Sleeping Dictionary 2003, Young Adam 2003, Bright Young Things 2003, Dear Frankie 2004, Match Point 2005, The Pink Panther 2006, Chaos Theory 2007, Lars and the Real Girl 2007, Transsiberian 2008, Redbelt 2008, City Island 2009, The Pink Panther 2 2009, Harry Brown 2009, Shutter Island 2010, Leonie 2010; *Style—* Ms Emily Mortimer; ✉ c/o Independent Talent, Oxford House, 76 Oxford Street, London W1D 1BS

MORTIMER, Robert (Bob); *b* 23 May 1959; *Career* comedian, part of comedy duo with Vic Reeves, *qv*; *Television* Vic Reeves Big Night Out 1990 and 1991, Weekenders (both Channel 4) 1992, The Smell of Reeves and Mortimer (3 series, BBC) 1993, 1995 and 1998 (BAFTA Award for Originality 1992, Best Live Performance British Comedy Awards 1992, Best Comedy Series British Comedy Awards 1994), A Night in with Vic and Bob (Boxing Day Special) 1993, Shooting Stars 1995, 1996, 1998, 2002 and 2003 (Best Entertainment Prog RTS Award 1996, Silver Rose of Montreux 1996, BAFTA Award for Best Light Entertainment 1997), A Nose Through Nature 1995, It's Ulrika (BBC) 1997, Families at War (BBC) 1998 and 1999, Bang Bang, It's Reeves and Mortimer (BBC) 1999, Randall and Hopkirk (Deceased) (BBC1) 2000 and 2001, Surrealissimo – The Trial of Dali (BBC 2 and BBC 4) 2002, Celebrity Boxing (BBC 2) 2002, Celebrity Mastermind (BBC 2) 2002, Catterick (BBC 3) 2004, All Star Comedy Show (ITV) 2004; *Film* Churchill: The Hollywood Year 2003; *Tours* Vic Reeves Big Night Out 1990 and 1991, The Smell of Reeves and Mortimer 1994, The Smell of Reeves and Moritmer: The Weathercock Tour 1995, Shooting Stars (nat tour) 1996, Shooting Stars/Fast Show Live (Labatt's Apollo) 1998; *Video* Shooting Stars – Unviewed & Nude 1996, Shooting Stars – Unpicked and Unplucked 1997; *Recordings* Dizzy (single, UK no 1), I Will Cure You (album), I'm A Believer (single), Let's Dance (single, with Middlesbrough FC); *Books* Big Night In (1991), Smell of Reeves and Mortimer (1993), Shooting Stars (1996); subject of Reeves & Mortimer (by Bruce Dessau, 1998); *Style—* Bob Mortimer; ✉ c/o PBJ and JBJ Management, 22 Rathbone Street, London W1T 1LA (✆ 020 7287 1112, fax 020 7287 1191, e-mail general@pbjmgt.co.uk, website www.pbjmgt.co.uk)

MORTIMER, Tim; *b* 6 December 1957; *Educ* West of England Coll of Art (BA Graphic Design, DipAD); *m* Virginia Lana; *Career* account mangr Boase Massimi Pollit 1979–83, account dir/assoc dir KMP/KHBB 1983–86, account dir FCO 1986–88; Generator: joined as bd account dir 1988, md 1989, md Advertising Options 1994–95, fndr ptnr Mortimer Whittaker O'Sullivan 1995–; *Recreations* fitness and Formula 1; *Style—* Tim Mortimer, Esq

MORTIMORE, Prof Peter John; OBE (1993); s of late Claude Mortimore, of Richmond, Surrey, and Rose, *née* Townsend; *b* 17 January 1942; *Educ* Chiswick GS, Univ of London (BSc, MSc, PhD); *m* 19 April 1965, Jo Marie, da of Michael Hargaden (d 1986), of Monmouth, Gwent; 3 da (Joanna *b* 1966, Rebecca *b* 1967, Claudia *b* 1968); *Career* teacher secdy sch 1964–73; res offr Inst of Psychiatry 1975–78, memb HMI 1978, dir of research and statistics ILEA 1979–85, asst educn offr (sec) ILEA 1985–88, prof and dir Sch of Educn Lancaster Univ 1988–90; Univ of London: prof of educn 1990–, dir Inst of Educn 1994–2000 (dep dir 1990–94), pro-vice-chllr 1999–2000; prof of pedagogy Inst of Philosophy, Pedagogy and the Study of Religions Univ of Southern Denmark 2008; conslt OECD 2003–05; memb: Br Psychological Soc, Assoc for Child Psychology and Psychiatry, Br Educnl Research Assoc, American Educnl Research Assoc; fell Birkbeck Coll London 2001; Hon DLitt 1998, Hon PhD 2008; FBPsS 1988, FRSA 1990, FCP 1994, AcSS 2000; *Books* Fifteen Thousand Hours (co-author, 1979), Behaviour Problems in Schools (1984), Helpful Servant not Dominating Master (1986), School Matters (1988), The Primary Head (1991), The Secondary Head (1991), Managing Associate Staff (1993), Planning Matters (1995), Living Education (1997), Forging Links (1997), The Road to Improvement (1998), Understanding Pedagogy (jtly, 1999), Culture of Change (jtly, 2000), Improving School Effectiveness (jtly, 2001), An Education System for the 21st Century: Which Way Forward? (2006), Education under Siege (2013); writer Opinion Columns Guardian Education 2007–10; *Recreations* music, theatre, walking; *Style—* Prof Peter Mortimore, OBE; ✉ c/o Institute of Education, University of London, 20 Bedford Way, London WC1H 0AL (✆ 020 7612 6004, fax 020 7612 6089)

MORTIMORE, Simon Anthony; QC (1991); s of Robert Anthony Mortimore (d 1995), and Katharine Elizabeth, *née* Mackenzie Caine (d 1986); *b* 12 April 1950; *Educ* Westminster, Univ of Exeter (LLB); *m* 26 March 1983, Fiona Elizabeth, da of Bernard Maurice Jacobson (d 1988); 1 da (Laura Alexandra *b* 21 Feb 1985), 1 s (Edward Robert *b* 20 Jan 1988); *Career* called to the Bar Inner Temple 1972; dep bankruptcy registrar High Court 1987–99; CEDR accredited mediator 1997–; memb ACCA Disciplinary and Regulatory Ctee 2003–07; chm Peasmarsh Chamber Music Festival Tst 2012–, dir Opera Rara 2015–; *Publications* Bullen Leake & Jacobs Precedents of Pleading (contrib 13 edn, 1990), Insolvency of Banks – Managing the Risks (contrib, 1996), Company Directors (conslt ed, 2009, 2 edn 2013); *Recreations* golf; *Clubs* Hurlingham, Royal St George's Golf, Rye Golf, Brooks's; *Style—* Simon Mortimore, Esq, QC; ✉ 3–4 South Square, Gray's Inn, London WC1R 5HP (✆ 020 7696 9900, fax 020 7696 9911)

MORTON, Ralph Nicholas; s of John Frank Morton, and Nancy Margaret, *née* White; *b* 19 September 1958; *Educ* Alleyn's Sch Dulwich, Westfield Coll Univ of London (BA); *m* 26 May 1984, Alison Ellenor, da of Robert George Sharpe (d 1987); 1 s (Matthew

James b 25 May 1992), 1 da (Sarah-Ellen b 25 Feb 1996); *Career* Autosport 1982–86, What Car? 1986–94 (ed 1992–94), ed-in-chief Haymarket motoring special projects 1994–98; fndr: Mortonmedia 1998–, Business Car Manager 2006, Business Vans 2008; editorial dir Business Car Manager Ltd; ed: www.businesscarmanager.co.uk, www.businessvans.co.uk, www.leasingbrokernews.co.uk, Car & Van Funding magazine; memb Ctee Guild of Motoring Writers 1993–98; Business Writer of the Year Guild of Motoring Writers Award 2009, Business Writer of the Year (commended) Guild of Motoring Writers Award 2010; *Recreations* swimming, tennis, running, theatre; *Clubs* Harlequins RFC; *Style—* Mr Ralph Morton; ✉ e-mail editor@businesscarmanager.co.uk, website www.businesscarmanager.co.uk

MORTON, Robert Edward; s of Charles Morton, and Yvonne, *née* Galea; *b* 20 May 1956; *Educ* Canford Sch, Oriel Coll Oxford (MA); *m* 12 Dec 1981; 2 da (Caroline b 13 Aug 1983, Georgina b 21 Jan 1985); *Career* res analyst: Simon & Coates 1978–83, de Zoete & Bevan 1983–86 (ptnr 1986); dir and head Conglomerates and Support Services Res Teams: Barclays de Zoete Wedd 1986–92; dir Charterhouse Securities 1992–99; exec dir and head Support Services Team WestLB Panmure 1999–2003, head Support Services Team Investec Securities 2004–12, investment banker Espirito Santo Investment Bank 2012–13, investment banker Liberum Capital 2013–; MSI; *Recreations* squash, music, sailing, reading, theatre, tennis; *Clubs* RAC, Hurlingham; *Style—* Robert Morton, Esq; ✉ e-mail robertmorton@btinternet.com

MORTON, Samantha-Jane; da of Peter Morton, and Pamela Mallek; *b* 13 May 1977, Nottingham; *Children* 2 da (Esmé Creed-Miles b 5 Feb 2000, Edith Holm b 4 Jan 2008), 1 s (Theodore Holm b 31 March 2014); *Career* actress, director and writer; hon assoc London Film Sch; ambass Save the Children UK; Hon DLitt Nottingham Trent Univ 2011; *Theatre* Star-Gazey Pie and Sauerkraut (Royal Court) 1995, Ashes and Sand (Royal Court) 1995; *Television* incl: Boon 1986, Soldier Soldier 1991, Cracker 1993, Band of Gold 1995, Jane Eyre 1997, The History of Tom Jones 1997, Emma 1997, Max & Ruby 2002, Longford 2006 (Best Supporting Actress in a Series, Mini-series or Movie Golden Globe 2008), Cider With Rosie, The Last Panthers; dir The Unloved 2009; *Films* incl: The Future Lasts a Long Time 1996, Under the Skin 1997, This is the Sea 1998, Pandaemonium 1999, Sweet and Lowdown 1999 (nomination Best Supporting Actress Acad Awards), Jesus' Son 1999, Dreaming of Joseph Lees 1999, The Last Yellow 1999, Eden 2000, Morvern Callar 2002, Minority Report 2002, In America 2002 (nomination Best Actress Acad Awards), Code 46 2003, Enduring Love 2004, The Libertine 2004, River Queen 2004, Lassie 2005, Expired 2006, Mr Lonely 2006, Elizabeth: The Golden Age 2007, Synecdoche, New York 2008, The Daisy Chain 2008, The Messenger 2009, John Carter of Mars 2012, The Harvest 2013, Miss Julie 2014; *Style—* Ms Samantha Morton

MORTON, Wendy; MP; *b* 9 November 1967, Northallerton, N Yorks; *m* David Morton; *Career* MP (Cons) Aldridge-Brownhills 2015–; *Style—* Mrs Wendy Morton, MP; ✉ House of Commons, London SW1A 0AA (website www.wendymorton.co.uk, Twitter @morton_wendy)

MOSBACHER, Michael Oliver; s of Ottmar Mosbacher (d 2001), and Renate Mosbacher (d 1998); *b* 14 July 1972, NY; *Educ* St Edward's Oxford, Collingham London, Univ of Exeter (BA, MA); *m* 22 Feb 2003, Amanda; 2 s (Toby b 2009, Sebastian b 2012); *Career* Social Affairs Unit: prog offr 1996–2001, dep dir 2001–04, dir 2004–; managing ed Standpoint magazine 2008–; *Publications* Another Country (ed, 1999), Marketing the Revolution: The New Anti-Capitalism and the Attack upon Corporate Brands (2002), Understanding Anti-Americanism (contrib, 2004), numerous articles in Standpoint magazine; *Recreations* perusing auction catalogues and polling websites, failing to put the children to bed, dinner; *Style—* Michael Mosbacher, Esq; ✉ Standpoint Magazine, 11 Manchester Square, London W1U 3PW (☎ 020 7563 9845, e-mail mmosbacher@standpointmag.co.uk)

MOSELEY, Dr Ivan Frederick; s of Frederick Clarence Moseley (d 1994), and Edith Sophia, *née* Smith (d 1987); *b* 29 May 1940, Isleworth, Middx; *Educ* Latymer Upper Sch, St Mary's Hosp Med Sch Univ of London (BSc, MB BS, DMRD, MD), Centre for the Study of Philosophy and Health Care UC Swansea (PhD), Royal Northern Coll of Music (MMus), Royal Holloway Univ of London (PhD); *m* 22 April 1967, Mary Cheyne Thomson, da of George Malcolm (d 1991), of Royston, Cambs; 1 da (Hannah b 1968), 1 s (James b 1978); *Career* house offr: St Mary's Hosp Paddington 1965–66, Whittington Hosp 1967; SHO: Royal Marsden Hosp 1967–68, London Chest Hosp 1968; sr registrar in radiology Bart's 1970–72 (registrar 1968–70), clinical assoc fell Mount Zion Hosp and postdoctoral scholar Univ of Calif San Francisco 1972–73; consultant radiologist: National Hosp Queen Sq London 1975–2000 (sr registrar 1973–75, dir of radiology 1994–2000), Wellington Hosp London 1975–87, Moorfields Eye Hosp London 1984–2000 (dir of radiology 1987–2000), London MRI Centre 1987–2010; hon conslt Royal Surrey Co Hosp Guildford 1988–92; Br Cncl visiting prof Université de Nancy 1978; visiting prof: Univ of Calif San Francisco 1982, Univ of Hong Kong 1988, Univ of Auckland 1988, Univ of Sydney 1995; Br rep Euro Union of Med Specialists 1988–2000; Wellcome Tst scholar Univ of West Indies Jamaica 1964, CIBA/INSERM scholar Hôpital Lariboisière Paris 1974, Euro Soc of Neuroradiology prize 1976; ed Neuroradiology 1993–2005; memb: Br Soc of Neuroradiologists 1975 (sec 1986–90, pres 1998–2000), European Soc of Neuroradiology 1976 (chair Cncl of Nat Delegates 1997–2000), BIR 1978, European Soc for Philosophy of Med and Health Care 1992; hon memb Japanese Soc of Neuroradiology 2002; memb: Southwold Sailors Reading Room Assoc 1997–, Turner Soc (sec 2003–10); FFR 1972, FRCR 1975, FRSM 1980 (pres Section of Clinical Neurosciences 1999–2000), FRCP 1985 (MRCP); *Books* Computer Tomographie des Kopfes (contrib, 1978), Computerized Tomography in Neuro-Ophthalmology (contrib, 1982), Diagnostic Imaging in Neurological Disease (1986), Magnetic Resonance Imaging in Diseases of the Nervous System (1988), The English and the Bulls (2009), Turner and Music (2015), ""... to die in the skin of a rich man"" (2016); *Recreations* music, wine, bullfighting, graphic arts; *Clubs* Club Taurino of London (sec gen 1985–90, pres 1990–2003 and 2006–10); *Style—* Dr Ivan Moseley; ✉ 65 St Mary's Grove, London W4 3LW (☎ 020 8995 5668)

MOSELY, Judith; *née* Harland; *b* 27 August 1964, Durham; *Educ* St Hugh's Coll Oxford (MA); *m* Andrew Miles Mosely; *Career* Int Div Nat West Bank 1986–87, Hambros Bank 1987–90, md mining finance Société Générale 1990–2011, business devpt dir (mining) Rand Merchant Bank 2011–; non-exec dir BlackRock World Mining Tst plc 2014–; tstee Earthwatch Inst 2011–; Freeman City of London, memb Worshipful Co of Fanmakers; *Recreations* opera, reading, sailing, travel; *Clubs* Oxford and Cambridge; *Style—* Mrs Judith Mosely

MOSES, Colin John; *b* 13 September 1962; *Educ* Woodhouse Grove Sch Bradford, Univ of Sheffield (BArch, DipArch); *Career* dir RMJM Ltd until 2010, dir MosesCameronWilliams 2010–; *Style—* Colin Moses, Esq; ✉ MosesCameronWilliams, Oast House, Malting Lane, Cambridge CB3 9HF

MOSES, Geoffrey Haydn; s of Canon Haydn Moses (d 1983), of Llanelli Vicarage, Dyfed, and Beryl Mary, *née* Lloyd); *b* 24 September 1952; *Educ* Ystalyfera GS, Emmanuel Coll Cambridge (BA, Cricket blue), KCL (PGCE); *m* 24 July 1981, Anne Elizabeth, da of Harry Mason; 1 s (Timothy b 1 Dec 1994), 1 da (Lucy b 27 Nov 1996); *Career* bass; princ singer WNO 1978–82; *Performances* Barber of Seville (WNO 1978, Scottish Opera 1984, Hamburg State Opera 1984), Tales of Hoffman (Royal Opera House Covent Garden) 1981, Don Giovanni (Glyndebourne Touring Opera 1982, Kent Opera 1983), Madame Butterfly (Opera North) 1983, Arabella (Glyndebourne Festival Opera) 1983, Simon Boccanegra (Belgian Opera) 1983, Salome (Netherlands Opera) 1988, Falstaff (WNO 1988–92, touring NY, Paris, Milan and Tokyo), La Favorita, Tristan & Isolde, Eugene Onegin and Lucia di Lammermoor (all WNO 1993), Peter Grimes (Glyndebourne Festival) 1994; concerts and recitals at: Gothenburg, Frankfurt Alte Oper, Royal Festival Hall, Royal Albert Hall; debut Deutche Opera Berlin (I Puritani) 1991, debut Opera de Nancy (Somnambula) 1991, Hong Kong Festival (Marriage of Figaro) 1991, Faust Nabucco (ENO) 1996, Die Meistersingers (Covent Garden) 1997, debut Rape of Lucretia (Caen) 1998, La Traviata (tour to Baden Baden with Govent Garden) 1998, debut Peter Grimes (Strasbourg) 1999, world premier The Last Supper (Berlin Staatsoper) 2000, Verdi Requiem (Berlin Philharmonie) 2000, A Midsummer Night's Dream (Glyndebourne Festival Opera) 2001, debut Seville (Collatinus in Rape of Lucretia) 2002, debut La Fenice Venice (Midsummer Night's Dream) 2004, Glyndebourne Festival 2006, Rocco in Fidelio (Dublin) 2006, Gremin in Eugene Onegin (English Touring Opera) 2007, Raimondo in Lucia di Lammermore (Dublin) 2007; *Recreations* walking, cricket, reading, wine; *Style—* Geoffrey Moses, Esq; ✉ Music International, 13 Ardilaun Road, London N5 2QR

MOSESSON, John Gunnar; s of Torsten Johannes Mosesson (d 1974); *b* 9 July 1938; *Educ* Frensham Heights Sch, Keele Univ (BA), Royal Coll of Music (ARCM); *m* 1, 1968 (m dis 1980), Jennifer Davies; 1 da (Gaël b 1970), 2 s (Dargan b 1972, Truan b 1976); m 2, 1985 (m dis 1990), Ruth Marland; m 3, 1990, Baroness Anne, da of Baron Jack Anstruther Carl Knutson Bonde; 1 da (Cecilia b 1991); *Career* John Laing R&D 1959–61, Keele Univ 1961–65; chm The Mosesson Gp; dep chm Green Resources Development Ltd Beijing 2000–, chm Stramit Int; tstee Britten in Oxford; *Recreations* music, tennis, golf; *Style—* John Mosesson, Esq; ✉ e-mail john@mosesson.co.uk

MOSEY, Roger; s of late Geoffrey Swain Mosey, and late Marie, *née* Pilkington; *b* 4 January 1958; *Educ* Bradford GS, Wadham Coll Oxford (MA), INSEAD (AMP); *Career* with Pennine Radio Ltd Bradford 1979–80; BBC: reporter BBC Radio Lincolnshire 1980–82, prodr BBC Radio Northampton 1982–83, prodr The Week in Westminster BBC Radio 4 1983–84, prodr Today 1984–86, prodr BBC New York Bureau 1986–87, ed PM 1987–89, ed The World at One 1989–93, ed The Today Programme 1993–96, exec ed Radio 4 current affairs progs 1996, controller Radio 5 Live 1996–2000 (acting dir of continuous news 1999–2000), head of TV news 2000–05, dir BBC Sport 2005–09, dir London 2012 2009–13, editorial dir 2013; master Selwyn Coll Cambridge 2013–; author of book reviews for The Guardian and contrib to The Guardian, The Times, The New Statesman and The Spectator; memb: RTS, BAFTA; One World Broadcasting Tst Award 1990, Br Environment and Media Award 1990, 1991 and 1995, Sony Gold Award 1994, Broadcasting Press Guild Radio Prog of the Year 1995, Best Speech-Based Breakfast Show Sony Radio Awards 1995, Voice of the Listener & Viewer Award for Outstanding Radio Prog 1996, Sony Gold Award Station of the Year (Radio 5) 1998, RTS Award for London 2012; chair Cncl Bishop Grosseteste Univ Lincoln 2013–, Centre for Family Res Cambridge 2014–; syndicate of Fitzwilliam Museum 2015–; memb Bd Invictus Games 2014; hon doctorate: Univ of Lincoln 2011, Univ of Bradford 2013; fell Radio Acad 1999, FRTS 2013; *Books* Getting Out Alive: News, Sport and Politics at the BBC (2015); *Recreations* cinema, reading political biographies and thrillers, watching football, walking with a basset hound; *Clubs* Oxford and Cambridge; *Style—* Roger Mosey, Esq; ✉ Selwyn College, Cambridge, CB3 9DQ (☎ 01223 335890, e-mail master@sel.cam.ac.uk)

MOSIMANN, Anton; OBE (2004), DL (Gtr London 2011); s of Otto Albert Mosimann (d 1996), and Olga, *née* Von Burg (d 1966); *b* 23 February 1947; *m* 13 April 1973, Kathrin, da of Jakob Roth; 2 s (Philipp Anton b 1975, Mark Andreas b 1977); *Career* chef; apprentice Hotel Baeren Twann Switzerland 1962–64, commis entremétier Palace Hotel Villars 1964–65, commis garde-manger Cavalieri Hilton Rome 1965, commis saucier Hotel Waldhaus Sils-Maria Switzerland 1965–66, chef tournant/chef saucier/sous chef Queen Elizabeth Hotel Montreal 1966–67, chef de froid/sous chef Canadian Pavilion EXPO '67 Montreal; chef tournant: Palace Hotel Montreux 1969, Palace Hotel St Moritz 1969–70; exec chef Swiss Pavilion Expo 70 Osaka Japan 1970, chef entremétier Palace Hotel Lausanne 1970–71; sous chef: Palace Hotel Lucerne summer seasons 1971–73, Kulm Hotel St Moritz winter seasons 1972–73 and 1973–74 (chef restaurateur 1971–72); commis pâtissier Palace Hotel Gstaad 1974–75, dir of cuisine Dorchester London 1986–88 (maître chef des cuisines 1975), chef patron Mosimann's London 1988–; chm: Mosimann's Ltd, Mosimann's Party Service 1990–, The Mosimann Acad 1995–, Créative Chefs 1996–; frequent TV and radio appearances incl: Anton Goes to Switzerland (BBC) 1985 (Glenfiddich Award), Anton Mosimann – Naturally (Channel 4) 1991 and 1994, co-presenter My Favourite Nosh (BBC) 1996, Natürlich, Leichtes Kochen (Swiss TV) 1997, Mosimann's Culinary Switzerland (Swiss TV) 1998; Royal Warrant Holder for Catering to HRH Prince of Wales 2000, pres Royal Warrant Holders Assoc 2006; memb Int Advsy Bd Ecole Hoteliere Lausanne 2012; hon prof Thames Valley Univ, invited as guest speaker Oxford Union 1997; winner of numerous gold medals and awards worldwide incl: Chef of the Year 1985, Restaurauteur of the Year 2000, ICD Lifetime Achievement Award 2010, Carl-Friedrich von Rumohr-Ring Awrad Gastronomische Akademie Deutschlands EV 2013, Lifetime Achievement Award Hotelympia 2016; Freeman City of London 1999; Hon Dr Culinary Arts Johnson and Wales Univ SC, Hon DSc Bournemouth Univ 1998; hon memb: World Assoc of Chefs Socs 2008, Cercle des Chefs de Cuisine Berne 2008, Club Chefs des Chefs 2008; Diciple d'Escoffier of GB 2008; La Croix de Chevalier du Mérite Agricole, Officier National Ordre du Merite Agricole (France) 2006; *Books* Cuisine à la Carte (1981), The Great Seafood Book (1985), Cuisine Naturelle (1985), Anton Mosimann's Fish Cuisine (1988), The Art of Anton Mosimann (1989), Cooking with Mosimann (1989), Anton Mosimann – Naturally (1991), The Essential Mosimann (1993), Mosimann's World (1996), Mosimann's Fresh (2006), 25 Years of Mosimann's (2013); *Recreations* participating in classic car rallies around the world from his first, Peking to Paris 2007, to others in the Alps, Eastern Europe and South America, collecting antiquarian cookery books, enjoying fine wine, passionate about food and travel; *Clubs* Reform, Garrick; *Style—* Anton Mosimann, Esq, OBE, DL; ✉ Mosimann's, 11B West Halkin Street, Belgrave Square, London SW1X 8JL (☎ 020 7235 9625, fax 020 7245 6354, e-mail amosimann@mosimann.com)

MOSLEY, Max Rufus; 4 s (but only 2 by his 2 w, Diana (Hon Lady Mosley)) of Sir Oswald Mosley, 6 Bt; *b* 13 April 1940; *Educ* ChCh Oxford (sec Oxford Union 1960); *m* 1960, Jean Marjorie, er da of James Taylor; 2 s (Alexander b 1970 d 2009, Patrick b 1972); *Career* called to the Bar Gray's Inn 1964; dir March Cars Ltd, co-fndr March Grand Prix Team; former Formula Two racing driver; chair Mfrs Cmmn Fedn Internationale du Sport Automobile (FISA) 1986–91; pres: FISA 1991–93, FIA 1993–2009 (memb Fndn Bd of Tstees 2001–14, chair Fndn Progs Ctee 2001–14, hon pres 2009–, memb Senate 2009–14); legal advsr to Formula One Constructors Assoc; chair European New Car Assesment Prog 1997–2004, chair Global New Car Assessment Prog 2011–; Supervisory Bd ERTICO Intelligent Transport Systems Europe: vice-chair 1999–2001, chair 2001–04, pres and spokesperson 2004–07, hon memb 2007–; hon pres: European Parl Automobile Users Gp 1994–99, Nat Road Safety Cncl Armenia 2005; co-fndr EU Cmmn: eSafety Forum 2003, CARS 21 High Level Gp 2005–09; fndr memb Institut du Cerveau et de la Moelle épinière France 2005; patron eSafety Aware 2006–09; Gold medal Castrol/Inst of the Motor Industry 2000, Gold medal Quattroruote Premio Speciale per la sicurezza stradale (Italy) 2001, Der Goldene VdM-Dieselring (Germany) 2001; hon pres Nat Road Safety Cncl of Armenia 2006; Hon DCL Univ of Northumbria 2005; Order of Merit (Italy) 1994, Order of Madarski Kannik, First Degree (Bulgaria) 2000, Order of Merit (Romania) 2004, Huesped Ilustre de Quito (Ecuador) 2005, Chevalier de la Légion d'Honneur (France) 2006, Commandeur de l'Ordre de Saint Charles (Monaco) 2006; *Books* Formula One and

M

Beyond; *Recreations* snowboarding, walking; *Style*— Mr Max Mosley; ✉ 7 Bd des Moulins, MC 98000, Monaco

MOSLEY, Nicholas; *see:* Ravensdale, 3 Baron

MOSLEY, Stephen James; *b* 22 June 1972, Solihull, W Midlands; *Educ* King Edward's Sch Birmingham, Univ of Nottingham (BSc); *m* Caroline; *Career* cncllr Chester CC 2005–09 (dep ldr 2007–09), MP (Cons) City of Chester 2010–15; *Style*— Stephen Mosley, Esq; ✉ House of Commons, London SW1A 0AA

MOSS, Prof (Jennifer) Ann; *née* Poole; da of John Shakespeare Poole (d 1945), and Dorothy Kathleen Beese, *née* Sills (d 1988); *b* 21 January 1938, Solihull; *Educ* Barr's Hill GS Coventry, Newnham Coll Cambridge (MA, PhD); *Children* 2 da (Imogen b 1963, Abigail b 1965); *Career* asst lectr UC of North Wales 1963–64; Univ of Durham: resident tutor and pt/t lectr Trevelyan Coll 1966–79, univ lectr in French 1979–85, sr lectr 1985–88, reader 1988–96, prof of French 1996–2003; FBA 1998; *Books* Ovid in Renaissance France (1982), Poetry and Fable (1984), Printed Commonplace Books and the Structuring of Renaissance Thought (1996), Latin Commentaries on Ovid from the Renaissance (1998), Les recueils de lieux communs: apprendre à penser à la Renaissance (2002), Renaissance Truth and the Latin Language Turn (2003); *Recreations* grandchildren, C of E licensed reader (ret), research on Thomas Traherne; *Style*— Prof Ann Moss, FBA; ✉ 10 Tudor Grange, 114 Westcombe Park Road, London SE3 7RZ (☎ 020 8858 4628, e-mail ann.moss@btinternet.com)

MOSS, His Hon Judge Christopher John; QC (1994); s of John Gordon (Jack) Moss (d 1984), of Kingston upon Thames, Surrey, and Joyce Mirren (Joy), *née* Stephany (d 2003); *b* 4 August 1948; *Educ* Bryanston, UCL (LLB); *m* 1, 11 Dec 1971 (m dis 1987), Gail Susan, da of late Frederick Pearson; 2 da (Melanie Jane b 17 Feb 1975, Rebecca Caroline b 1 Sept 1980), 1 s (Nicholas John b 17 Sept 1977); m 2, 31 March 1988 (m dis 1997), Tracy Louise, da of Geoffrey Levy; 1 s (Aaron Geoffrey b 2 Oct 1989), 1 da (Liberty Michele b 10 April 1992); m 3, 9 July 1999, Lisa Annette, da of Barry O'Dwyer; 2 da (Caitlin Philomena Joy b 5 March 2001, Mirren Lisa b 3 March 2003); *Career* called to the Bar Gray's Inn 1972; recorder of the Crown Court 1993, circuit judge (SE Circuit) 2002–; memb Criminal Bar Assoc 1980–; *Recreations* playing the piano and piano accordion; *Style*— His Hon Judge Moss, QC; ✉ Central Criminal Court, Old Bailey, London EC4M 7EH (☎ 020 7248 3277)

MOSS, David John; s of John Henry Moss (d 2003), and Doris Fenna (d 2005); *b* 23 May 1947; *Educ* Sevenoaks Sch, St John's Coll Cambridge (MA), Central London Poly (DMS); *m* 24 May 1975, Susan Elizabeth, da of Reginald Victor Runnalls (d 1982); 3 s (Oliver Richard, Benjamin Roland (twins) b 21 April 1976, Jonathan Edward b 1 Dec 1980); *Career* mgmnt accountant Philips 1970–73 (mgmnt trainee 1968–70), asst fin offr St Thomas' Hosp 1973–74; dist fin offr: Enfield 1974–79, E Dorset 1979–85; unit gen mangr: Poole Gen Hosp 1985–88, Southampton Gen Hosp 1988–90; gen mangr Southampton Univ Hosps 1990–93, chief exec Southampton Univ Hosps NHS Tst 1993–2004; chm UK Univ Hosps Forum 2001–03, memb Audit Cmmn 2001–07, dep dir of workforce Dept of Health 2003–07; chm of govrs Ferndown Upper Sch 2009–; memb CIPFA 1979, memb Inst of Healthcare Mgmnt 1979, FCMA 1981, FRSA 1994, FCMI (FIMgt 1984); *Books* Managing Nursing (co-author, 1984); *Recreations* history, golf, walking, opera, tennis, cricket; *Style*— David Moss, Esq; ✉ 41 Pinewood Road, Ferndown, Dorset BH22 9RP (e-mail davidmoss56@hotmail.com)

MOSS, David Reginald (Dave); s of Frank Moss, and Iris, *née* Thornton; *b* 11 March 1949; *Educ* Stockport Sch, Faculty of Art and Design Liverpool Poly (DipAD, RSA bursary); *m* 10 Aug 1971, Pauline Althea, da of Edward Scott Jones; 3 s (Robin James b 10 Nov 1973, Andrew Thornton, Laurence Scott (twins) b 20 Sept 1978); *Career* visualiser Clough Howard & Richards 1971–73; Brunning Advertising Liverpool: sr visualiser 1973–74, art dir 1974–75, creative controller 1975–76, creative dir 1977; exec prodr Five Cities Films 1977–79, bd account dir Michael Bungey DFS Liverpool 1979–85, account dir Brunning Advertising Yorkshire 1985–86; fndr dir: Quadrant Advertising and Marketing 1986–98, Insite-Webmedia 1998–2001; chm PSA Films 2001–13; *Recreations* photography, blues guitar; *Style*— David Moss; ✉ 18 Menlove Gardens South, Liverpool L18 2EL (☎ 07919 264028, e-mail dave@psafilms.co.uk)

MOSS, Gabriel Stephen; QC (1989); *b* 8 September 1949; *Educ* Univ of Oxford (Eldon scholar, MA, BCL); *m* 1979, Judith; 1 da; *Career* called to the Bar Lincoln's Inn 1974 (Hardwicke and Cassel scholarships, bencher 1998); in practice specialising in business and fin law, dep judge of the High Court 2001–; fndr memb Bd Insolvency Res Unit KCL (now at Univ of Sussex) 1991–; called to the Bar Gibraltar and E Caribbean Supreme Court; memb: Editorial Bd Insolvency Intelligence 1991– (chm 1994–), Insolvency Law Sub-Ctee of the Consumer and Commercial Law Ctee Law Soc 1991–, Insolvency Ctee of Justice 1993–, Advsy Ed Bd Receivers Administrators and Liquidators Quarterly 1993–, Insolvency Lawyers' Assoc 1999–, UK Insolvency Serv Review Panel (considering changes to Eng Law and practice in the light of EU Insolvency Regulation) 2000–, Editorial Bd Int Insolvency Review 2000–, Int Insolvency Inst 2001–; Insol Europe: assoc memb 1996–2001, memb 2001–; formerly: lectr Univ of Connecticut Law Sch, pt/t lectr/tutor Univ of Oxford, LSE and Cncl of Legal Educn; visiting prof in corporate insolvency law Law Faculty Univ of Oxford 2011; fell Soc of Advanced Legal Studies Inst of Advanced Legal Studies Univ of London 1998; *Books* Rowlatt on Principal and Surety (jt ed, 4 edn 1982, 5 edn 1999, 6 edn 2011), Law of Receivers of Companies (jtly, 1986, 5 edn 2011), Insolvency of Banks (jt author of chapter 6, Cross-Border Issues, 1996), Cross-Frontier Insolvency of Insurance Companies (jtly, 2001), The EC Regulation on Insolvency Proceedings (jtly, 2002, 3 edn 2016), EU Banking and Insurance Insolvency (jtly, 2006); *Recreations* foreign travel, tennis; *Style*— Gabriel Moss, Esq, QC; ✉ 3–4 South Square, Gray's Inn, London WC1R 5HP (☎ 020 7696 9900, fax 020 7696 9911, e-mail clerks@southsquare.com)

MOSS, Kate; da of Peter Edward Moss, and Linda Rosina, *née* Shephard; *b* 16 January 1974, Croydon; *Educ* Riddlesdown HS Croydon; *m* 2011, Jamie Hince; 1 da from a previous relationship (Lila Grace b 29 Sept 2002); *Career* fashion model; first appeared on cover of British Vogue 1993, first cover girl of Russian Vogue; exclusive worldwide contract with Calvin Klein 1992–2000 (campaigns incl: Calvin Klein Obsession fragrance 1993, CK One fragrance 1994); various worldwide campaigns incl: Dolce & Gabbana, Katherine Hamnett, Versace and Versace Versus, Yves Saint Laurent, Louis Vuitton, Gucci, Rimmel London, Celine; appeared in the film Unzipped 1996; Fashion Personality of the Year British Fashion Awards 1995, Model of the Year British Fashion Awards 2001; *Books* Kate (1995); *Style*— Miss Kate Moss; ✉ c/o Storm Model Management, 5 Jubilee Place, London SW3 3TD (☎ 020 7352 2278)

MOSS, His Hon Judge Peter Jonathan; s of Capt John Cottam Moss (d 1997), and Joyce Alison, *née* Blunn (d 1977); *b* 29 March 1951; *Educ* Charterhouse; *m* (m dis 2003), Rosanne Marilyn, da of late Alexander James Houston, of Emsworth, Hants; 3 s (Alexander b 28 Oct 1981, Ben b 14 Nov 1983, Patrick b 22 April 1987); *Career* called to the Bar Lincoln's Inn 1976; asst recorder 1999, recorder 2000, circuit judge (SE Circuit) 2004–; memb Mental Health Review Tbnl 1994–; Freeman City of London 1985, Liveryman Worshipful Co of Clockmakers 1987; *Recreations* golf, windsurfing, skiing, cricket, fishing, motorcycling, fun; *Clubs* New Zealand Golf, MCC; *Style*— His Hon Judge Peter Moss; ✉ Guildford Crown Court, Bedford Road, Guildford, Surrey GU1 4AS

MOSS, Stephen Raymond; s of Raymond Moss, and Catherine, *née* Croome; *b* 30 July 1957; *Educ* Hartridge HS Newport, Balliol Coll Oxford (BA), Univ of London (MA); *m* 1984, Helen Mary Bonnick; 1 s (Timothy b 1986); *Career* worked previously in magazine and book publishing; The Guardian: sometime dep arts ed and dep features ed 1989–95, literary ed 1995–98, feature writer 1999–; *Recreations* cricket, chess, riding; *Style*— Stephen Moss, Esq; ✉ c/o The Guardian, 90 York Way, London N1 9GU (☎ 020 7278 2332, fax 020 7239 9935, e-mail stephen.moss@guardian.co.uk)

MOSS, Sir Stirling; kt (2000), OBE (1957); s of Alfred Moss, and Aileen Moss; *b* 17 September 1929; *Educ* Haileybury and ISC; *m* 1, 1957 (m dis 1960), Kathleen, da of F Stuart Molson, of Canada; m 2, 1964 (m dis 1968), Elaine, da of A Barbarino, of New York; 1 da; m 3, 1980, Susan, da of Stuart Paine of London; 1 s; *Career* racing driver 1947–62; learnt to drive aged 6, built own Cooper-Alta 1953, Br Nat Champion 1950–52, 1954–59 and 1961; winner: Tourist Trophy 1950–51, 1955 and 1958–61, Coupe des Alpes 1952–54, Alpine Gold Cup 1954, Italian Mille Miglia 1955 (only Englishman to win); competed in 529 races, rallies, sprints, land speed records and endurance runs, completed 387 and won 211; Grand Prix and successes incl: Targa Florio 1955, Br 1955 and 1957, Italian 1956–57 and 1959, NZ 1956 and 1959, Monaco 1956 and 1960–61, Leguna Seca 1960–61, US 1959–60, Aust 1956, Bari 1956, Pesara 1957, Swedish 1957, Dutch 1958, Argentinian 1958, Moroccan 1958, Buenos Aires 1958, Melbourne 1958, Villareal 1958, Caen 1958, Portuguese 1959, South African 1960, Cuban 1960, Austrian 1960, Cape Town 1960, Watkins Glen 1960, German 1961, Modena 1961; Driver of the Year 1954 and 1961, holder of 1500cc World speed record driving MG EX181 at 240mph; md Stirling Moss Ltd; dir: Designs Unlimited Ltd, SM Design & Interior Decorating Co; former dir of racing Johnson's Wax; judge: Miss World (4 times), Miss Universe 1974; former demonstrator Dunlop Rubber Co (travelled across India and Malaysia); conslt incl work for: Ferodo Opel Germany and Chrysler Aust; has given numerous lecture tours across US and in UK, NZ, Aust and Hong Kong; *Books* Stirling Moss's Book of Motor Sport (1955), In the Track of Speed (1957), Stirling Moss's Second Book of Motor Sport (1958), Le Mans (1959), My Favourite Car Stories (1960), A Turn at the Wheel (1961), All But My Life (1963), Design and Behaviour of the Racing Car (1964), How to Watch Motor Racing (1975), Motor Racing and All That (1980), My Cars, My Career (1987), Fangio, A Pirelli Album (1991), Great Drives in the Lakes (1993), Motor Racing Masterpieces (1994), All My Races (2009), My Racing Life (2015); *Recreations* historic motor racing, cruising, work, model making, designing; *Clubs* Br Racing Drivers', Br Automobile Racing, Br Racing and Sports Car, Road Racing Drivers of America, 200mph, RAC, International des Anciens Pilotes des Grand Prix; chm or pres of 36 motoring clubs; *Style*— Sir Stirling Moss, OBE; ✉ 46 Shepherd Street, London W1J 7JN (☎ 020 7499 3272, e-mail stirlingmossltd@aol.com)

MOSS, Tim; CBE (2016); *Educ* Univ of Cambridge, Swansea Univ (MBA); *Career* chief exec and registrar of companies for England and Wales 2012– (joined 2002); *Style*— Tim Moss, Esq, CBE; ✉ Companies House, Crown Way, Cardiff CF14 3UZ

MOSSE, Katharine Louise (Kate); OBE (2013); da of Richard Hugh Mosse (d 2011) and Barbara Mary, *née* Towlson; *b* 20 October 1961; *Educ* Chichester HS for Girls, New Coll Oxford (MA); *Partner* Greg Charles Mosse, *né* Dunk; 1 da (Martha b 25 Feb 1990), 1 s (Felix b 8 Oct 1992); *Career* publisher 1985–92, broadcaster 1988–; co-fndr Orange Prize for Fiction (now Baileys Women's Prize for Fiction; chair Judging Panel 1996, hon dir 1998–); memb various arts ctees incl Arts for Everyone (A4E) Panel Arts Cncl of England; former dep dir Chichester Festival Theatre; former presenter Readers and Writers Roadshow, regular host on BBC television and radio; judge of various literary/cultural awards incl: Arts & Business FT Sponsor of the Year Award 1999, Orange Prize for Fiction 1996, Aventis Science Prize; European Woman of Achievement for the Arts 2000, Spirit of Everywoman Award 2011; *Books* Becoming a Mother (1993 and 1997), The House: A Year in the Life of the Royal Opera House Covent Garden (1996), Eskimo Kissing (novel, 1996), Crucifix Lane (novel, 1998), Labyrinth (novel, 2005), Sepulchre (novel, 2007), The Winter Ghosts (novel, 2009), Chichester Festival Theatre at Fifty (non-fiction, 2012), Citadel (novel, 2012), The Mistletoe Bride and Other Haunting Tales (short stories, 2013); *Recreations* theatre, literature, classical music, swimming, politics, walking; *Clubs* Union; *Style*— Mrs Kate Mosse, OBE; ✉ e-mail enquiries@lawagency.co.uk, website www.katemosse.co.uk

MOSTYN, Hon Mr Justice; Sir Nicholas Anthony Joseph Ghislain Mostyn; kt (2010); of Jerome Mostyn, of Salisbury, Wilts, and Mary Learoyd, *née* Medlicott; *b* 13 July 1957; *Educ* Ampleforth, Univ of Bristol (LLB); *m* 1981 (m dis 2012), Lucy Willis; 3 s (Henry b 1987, Gregory b 1995, Charlie b 1998), 1 da (Daisy b 1989); *Career* called to the Bar Middle Temple 1980 (bencher 2005), QC 1997, recorder 2000 (asst recorder 1997), dep judge of the High Court 2000, judge of the High Court (Family Div) 2010–; Knight of Honour and Devotion SMO Malta 2003; *Publications* Child's Pay (1993, 3rd edn 2002), At a Glance (22 edn 2013); *Recreations* Southampton FC, Wagner, skiing; *Clubs* MCC; *Style*— The Hon Mr Justice Mostyn; ✉ Royal Courts of Justice, Strand, London WC2A 2LL

MOTHERWELL, Bishop of (RC) 2014–; Rt Rev Joseph Anthony Toal; s of Patrick Toal, and Mary Toal; *b* 13 October 1956, Inverness; *Career* ordained: as deacon 1979, as priest 1980, as bishop 2008; parish priest: St Michael's Ardkenneth 1986–91, St Kieran's Campbeltown 1991–93, St Mary's Benbecula 1991–99; Royal Scots Coll Salamanca Spain: joined as spiritual dir 1999, rector 2005–08; bishop of Argyll and the Isles 2008–14; *Style*— The Rt Rev the Bishop of Motherwell; ✉ Diocesan Office, Coursington Road, Motherwell ML1 1PP

MOTION, Sir Andrew; kt (2009); s of Lt-Col A R Motion, of Braintree, Essex, and C G Motion (d 1982); *b* 26 October 1952; *Educ* Radley, UC Oxford; *m* 1985, Jan Dalley, *qv*, da of C M Dalley, of Maldon, Essex; 2 s (Andrew Jesse b 26 July 1986, Lucas Edward b 19 May 1988), 1 da (Sidonie Gillian Elizabeth (twin) b 19 May 1988); *Career* Poet Laureate 1999–2009; currently prof of creative writing Royal Holloway Univ of London; formerly: poetry ed Chatto & Windus, ed Poetry Review; freelance writer; prizes incl: Avon Observer prize 1982; memb Arts Cncl of England (currently chm Lit Panel); Hon DLitt: Univ of Hull, Univ of Exeter, Brunel Univ, Anglia Poly Univ, Open Univ, Sheffield Hallam Univ; hon fell UC Oxford; FRSL 1984, FRSA 2000; *Poetry* incl: The Pleasure Steamers (1978), The Penguin Book of Contemporary British Poetry (ed with Blake Morrison, 1982), Dangerous Play (John Llewelyn Rhys prize, 1984), Natural Causes (Dylan Thomas prize, 1988), Love in a Life (1991), Salt Water (1997), Selected Poems (1998), Public Property (2002); *Writings* incl: The Lamberts (Somerset Maugham award 1987), Philip Larkin: A Writer's Life (Whitbread award for biography, 1993), Keats (1997), Wainewright the Poisoner (2000), The Invention of Dr Cake (2003); *Style*— Sir Andrew Motion, FRSL

MOTSON, John Walker; OBE (2001); s of Rev William Motson (d 1992), of Worthing, W Sussex, and Gwendoline Mary Motson (d 1991); *b* 10 July 1945; *Educ* Culford Sch Bury St Edmunds, NCTJ (Cert); *m* 1976, (Jennifer) Anne, da of Cyril Jobling (d 1991), and Marion Jobling; 1 s (Frederick James b 4 Feb 1986); *Career* football commentator and reporter; news and sports reporter Barnet Press 1963–67, sports writer and sub ed Morning Telegraph Sheffield 1967–68, freelance BBC Radio Sheffield 1968, presenter, reporter and commentator (football, boxing, tennis) BBC Network Radio Sports Dept 1968–71, football commentator and reporter BBC TV (incl Match of the Day, Sportsnight, Grandstand and other outside broadcasts) 1971–; major events as commentator: all World Cups 1974– (incl finals 1982–, commentator on record sixth World Cup Final Germany 2006), all Euro Championships 1976– (incl finals 1980–), FA Cup Final annually 1977– (commentator on record 25th FA Cup Final BBC 2004); writer and narrator over 20 football videos for BBC Enterprises 1987–, also numerous club histories and Match of the Day compilations; voted nation's favourite commentator Carling-Net website 1998; *Books* Second to None: Great Teams of Post-War Soccer (1972), The History of the European Cup (with John Rowlinson, 1980), Match of the Day: the Complete Record (1992, reprinted 1994), Motty's Diary (1996), Motty's Year 2004 (2004), Motson's National Obsession (2004), Motson's FA Cup Odyssey (2005), Motson's World Cup Extravaganza (2006), Motty – 40 Years in the Commentary Box (2009); *Recreations* running (half marathons and 10km races), reading novels, theatre, cinema, watching sport; *Style—* John Motson, Esq, OBE; ✉ c/o Jane Morgan Management, Argentum, 2 Queen Caroline Street, London W6 9DX (☎ 020 3178 8071)

MOTT, Philip Charles; QC (1991); s of Charles Kynaston Mott (d 1981), of Taunton, Somerset, and Elsa, *née* Smith (d 2000); *b* 20 April 1948; *Educ* King's Coll Taunton, Worcester Coll Oxford (MA); *m* 19 Nov 1977 (m dis 2011), Penelope Ann, da of Edward Caffery; 2 da (Sarah b 1981, Catherine b 1983); *Career* called to the Bar Inner Temple 1970 (bencher 2006); practising Western Circuit 1970–, recorder of the Crown Court 1987–, dep judge of the High Court 1998–, ldr Western Circuit 2004–07; Mental Health Tbnl judge Restricted Patients Panel 2000–; memb: Bar Legal Services Ctee 2004–05, Advocacy Trg Cncl 2004–12, Bar Carter Response Gp 2005–07; vice-chm Bar Policy & Res Gp 2006–07; *Recreations* the countryside, growing trees, sailing; *Clubs* Bar Yacht, Percuil Sailing; *Style—* Philip Mott, Esq, QC; ✉ Outer Temple Chambers, 222 Strand, London WC2R 1BA (☎ 020 7353 6381, fax 020 7583 1786, e-mail philip.mottqc@outertemple.com)

MOTT, Susan Jane (Sue); da of Dennis Charles Mott, and Jean, *née*, Taylor; *Educ* Woodhouse GS London, Univ of Nottingham (BA); *Children* 1 s (Tom), 1 da (Jeannie); *Career* journalist; trainee Hull Daily Mail 1979–81, freelance journalist NY Daily News and San Francisco Chronicle 1982–85; sports feature writer: The Australian 1985–86, Sunday Times 1986–94, Daily Telegraph 1994–; sport corr BT Sport 2013–; TV presenter On the Line (BBC) 1987–91; Sports Feature Writer of the Year 1995 (highly commended 1999 and 2001), highly commended UK Press Awards 1999; *Publications* Girl's Guide to Ball Games (1996, shortlisted William Hill Sports Book Awards); *Recreations* Arsenal FC, tennis; *Clubs* Henham Tennis, Dover Street Wine Bar; *Style—* Ms Sue Mott

MOTT, Toby Victor; s of James Mott, of London, and Patricia, *née* Stark; *b* 12 January 1964; *Career* artist, designer and sometime punk historian; founding memb Grey Orgn (artists' gp) 1983–90, curator of exhbns Coins Coffee Shop London 1996–, curator and dir Mott Collection; dir DEF COM Ltd 1998– (supplying products incl fashion, homeware and stationery, under Toby Pimlico and Toby Studio brands); involved with numerous charities; *Solo Exhibitions* Jean Louis Pierson Gallery San Francisco 1993, Survey (Thomas Solomon's Garage LA) 1993, Lost in Music (Tri Gallery LA) 1995, Maureen Paley Interim Art London 1995, London 1997 (Maureen Paley Interim Art London) 1997, Totally London (designed London bus for mayor Ken Livingstone) 2004; *Group Exhibitions* Riot Furniture (Furniture of the Twentieth Century NY) 1991, Casual Ceremony (White Columns NY) 1991, Scraping By (Project Box LA) 1994, Elements of Mystery, Motifs of Lunacy (PS1 Museum NY) 1994, Given Space (Canute's Pavillion Ocean Village Southampton) 1994, Candy Man II (Building C – Tower Bridge London) 1994, House of Styles (Tri Gallery LA) 1995, Action Station, Exploring Open Systems (Santa Monica Museum of Art) 1995, Greatest Hits (Tri Gallery LA) 1995, Sick (152c Brick Lane London) 1995, Affinità (Castello di Rivara Torino) 1996, Loosy (Galerie Philippe Rizzo Paris) 1996, Flag (Clink Street London) 1996, Some Drawings: from London (Princelet Street London) 1996, Vocimiecontemporanee (Sala 1 Rome) 1997, Host (Tramway Glasgow) 1998, The Road (Espace Culturel François Mitterand Beauvais) 1998, The Forest (Tabernacle London) 1998, Klega's Flat (Sali Gia Gallery London) 1999, Temple of Diana (Blue Gallery London) 1999, Big Blue, Century City (Tate Modern) 2001, Copy (Roth Horowitz NY) 2002, Let There Be Light (B&B Italia London) 2003, Sirreal (Redux Gallery London) 2004; The Mott Collection exhibns: Loud Flash: British Punk on Paper (MUSAC Spain and Haunch of Venison London) 2010, Crass: Selections from the Mott Collection 2011, Dazed Live (The Tramshed London) 2011, Loud Flash: British Punk on Paper (Honor Fraser LA) 2011, We Have Our Own Concept of Time and Motion (Auto Italia South East London) 2011, Nothing in the World but Youth (Turner Contemporary Margate) 2011, We are the Writing on the Wall (MoMA PS1 NY Art Book Fair) 2011, JUBILEE, 2012: Sixty Punk Singles (The Vinyl Factory London) 2012, KRAFTWERK. 45RPM (The Vinyl Factory London) 2012, David Bowie – Nacht Musik (The Vinyl Factory London) 2012, American Hardcore 1978–90 (The Vinyl Factory London) 2013, The Mott Collection in Print: In Italy (ONO Arte Contemporanea Bologna) 2013, Loud Flash at CCAD (Columbus College of Art & Design Ohio) 2013, Where Have All the Boot Boys Gone? (London College of Communication) 2013, Skinhead: An Archive (Ditto Press London UK) 2014–15, Punk in Print 1976–80: The Complete Mott Collection and Skinhead: An Archive (LA Art Book Fair Museum of Contemporary Art LA) 2015; *Publications* Loud Flash: British Punk on Paper (contrib, 2 edns 2010, 1 edn 2011), Crass 1977–1984 (contrib, 2011), 100 Fanzines/10 Years of British Punk (contrib, 2011), Nothing in the World But Youth (contrib, 2011), Jubilee 2012 Sixty Punk Singles (2012), Kraftwerk 45rpm (2012), David Bowie Nacht Musik (2013), American Hardcore 1978–1990 (2013), Loud Flash: British Punk on Paper (2013), Esopus 20: Special Collections (contrib, 2014), Skinhead: An Archive (2014), Punk in Print 1976–80: The Complete Mott Collection (2015); *Recreations* poetry, long country walks, gardening; *Style—* Toby Mott, Esq; ✉ Toby Mott, 22 Notting Hill Gate, Suite 467, London W11 3JE (e-mail tobymott@yahoo.co.uk)

MOTTERSHEAD, Christopher Alan Leigh (Chris); s of Alan Mottershead, and Elvene Mottershead; *b* 24 September 1958; *Educ* Cowbridge Sch, Univ of Warwick (BA); *m* Vivienne; 3 da (Olivia b 25 Oct 1992, Lily b 20 July 1994, Holly b 25 April 1996), 1 s (Joseph b 14 Dec 1998); *Career* grad trainee Wales Gas 1980–84, prodn control mangr, accounts mangr and fin accountant Business Forms Div Burroughs Machines Ltd 1984–86, fin controller Sterilin/Motil Plastics Ltd 1987–88, fin dir Avon Inflatables Ltd 1988–90, gp fin dir Aspro Travel & Inter European Airways 1990–93; Airtours plc: md Airtours Holidays 1998–2000 (fin dir 1993–97, dep md and fin dir 1997–98), pres and ceo N American Leisure Gp 2000–01; md TUI UK (Thomson Holidays, Lunn Poly, Travelhouse and Portland) 2001–04, gp ceo Travelzest plc 2005–09, chief operating offr TUI Canada 2009, md TUI Russia & CIS 2010–14, commercial dir Thomas Cook UK 2015–; ACMA 1985; *Style—* Chris Mottershead, Esq

MOTTERSHEAD, Derek Stuart; s of Alan Mottershead (d 1954), of Blackpool, and Irene, *née* Huyton; *b* 2 September 1947; *Educ* Royal Masonic Sch Bushey, Univ of Manchester (BSc); *m* 1, 1 Sept 1969 (m dis 1988), Jean, da of James Arthur Wright, of Nelson, Lancs; 3 da (Gillian b 30 May 1964, Sarah b 11 April 1972, Lucy b 17 Feb 1982); m 2, 5 June 1993, Jacqui, da of Michael Martin, of Aspley Guise, Beds; *Career* mktg dir Pretty Polly Ltd (winner Br Mktg awards 3 consecutive years) 1976–80, Euro mktg dir Lee Apparel UK Ltd (subsid Vanity Fair Corp America) 1980–82, mktg dir Lee Cooper Ltd 1982–84, md All-time Sportswear UK Ltd 1984–87, md Prontaprint plc 1987–92 (chm Prontaprint Communications Ltd, md Prontaprint International Ltd, jt gp md Continuous Stationery plc), jt md Prontaprint Group plc 1992–93, chm and md Prontaprint Ltd, chm and md The Franchise Option 1993–, md Bang and Olufsen UK Ltd 1994–; chm Br Franchise Assoc 1992–93, vice-pres Br Small Business Bureau; memb: Br Inst of Mktg, IOD; *Recreations* private aviation, golf, shooting; *Style—* Derek Mottershead, Esq; ✉ Bang and Olufsen UK Ltd, Unit 630, Wharfedale Road, Winnersh, Wokingham, Berkshire (☎ 0118 969 2288, fax 0118 969 3388, e-mail dmt@bang-olufsen.dk)

MOTTRAM, Sir Richard Clive; GCB (2006, KCB 1998); s of John Mottram (d 1991), of Chislehurst, Kent, and Florence Bertha, *née* Yates (d 2007); *b* 23 April 1946; *Educ* King Edward VI Camp Hill Sch Birmingham, Keele Univ (BA); *m* 24 July 1971, Dr Fiona Margaret Mottram, da of Keith David Erskine (d 1974) and Audrey, *née* Skinner (d 2003); 3 s (Keith b 1974, David b 1981, Thomas b 1985), 1 da (Ruth b 1977); *Career* Home Civil Serv, assigned MOD 1968, Cabinet Office 1975–77, private sec to Perm Under Sec of State MOD 1979–81, private sec to Sec of State for Def 1982–86, asst under sec MOD 1986–89, dep under sec (policy) MOD 1989–92; perm sec: Office of Public Service and Science 1992–95, MOD 1995–98, DETR 1998–2001, DTLR 2001–02, Dept for Work and Pensions 2002–05; perm sec Intelligence, Security and Resilience Cabinet Office and chair Jt Intelligence Ctee 2005–07; pres Cwlth Assoc for Public Admin and Mgmnt 2000–02 (vice-pres 1998–); chm: Amey plc 2008–, Defence Science and Technol Lab 2008–14; memb Int Advsy Bd GardaWorld 2008–15, tstee Royal Anniversary Tst 2010–; visiting prof Dept of Govt LSE 2008–; govr Ashridge Business Sch 1998–2015; Hon DLitt Keele Univ 1996; *Publications* The New Protective State (contrib, 2007); *Recreations* theatre, cinema; *Style—* Sir Richard Mottram, GCB; ✉ e-mail rcmottram@googlemail.com

MOULD, Christopher Peter; s of Peter Sidney Mould (d 1998), of Pembrokeshire, and Phyllida Charlotte Elaine, *née* Ormond; *b* 30 November 1958; *Educ* Royal GS High Wycombe, Magdalen Coll Oxford (BA), LSE (MSc); *m* 18 Aug 1979, Angela Geraldine, da of Roger Ellis Druce; 4 da (Hannah Elizabeth b 26 Dec 1984, Verity Ruth b 20 June 1986, Alicia Ellen Joy b 27 April 1990, Madeleine Grace b 4 June 1993); *Career* fund raiser LEPRA 1982, planning asst NE Thames RHA 1982–83, planning mangr Southend Health Authy 1983–86, hosp mangr Southend Hosp 1986–88, gen mangr Community and Mental Health Servs S Beds Health Authy 1989–91 (gen mangr Mental Health 1988–89), chief exec S Beds Community Health Care NHS Tst 1991–92, dist gen mangr Salisbury Health Authy and chief exec Salisbury Health Care 1992–94, chief exec Salisbury Health Care NHS Tst 1994–98 and 1999–2001, prog dir Prog Cmmn for Strategic Change in Wiltshire and Swindon (health care) 1998–99 (on secondment); dir Nat Police Trg 2001–02, chief exec Centrex (Central Police Trg and Devpt Authy) 2002–03; conslt in strategy and organizational change; chair and memb various police ctees and bds until 2004; chm Healthwork UK (Health Care National Trg Orgn) 1998–2001, chm FranchisingWorks Ltd 2011–, non-exec dir The Together Group 2013–; prog dir: Postgrad Medical Educn and Trg Bd 2004–05, V (Nat Youth Vol Charity) 2006–07; ptnr Shaftesbury Partnership 2010– chm Fndn Redlynch C of E Primary Sch 2005–06 (govr 1994–2002); tstee Ffald y Brenin Tst 1994–, tstee and exec chm Trussell Tst 2004–, fndr and chm Fndn for Social Change and Inclusion Bulgaria; appraisal fellowship Nuffield Prov Hosps Tst, 4th prize RIPA/Hay Award for Managerial Innovation 1989, Charity Times Charity of the Year 2012, Third Sector Britain's Most Admired Charity 2013 (both with Trussell Tst), overall winner Charity Awards 2016; MHSM, DipHSM; *Publications* chapter in Public and Third Sector Leadership: Experience Speaks (2014); *Recreations* jazz guitar, hockey, running, Christian preaching; *Style—* Chris Mould, Esq; ✉ 96 Harnham Road, Salisbury SP2 8JW (☎ 01722 333937, mobile 07881 624887, e-mail chris@chrismould.co.uk)

MOULE, John Stuart; *b* 29 May 1971, Shrewsbury, Salops; *Educ* Lady Margaret Hall Oxford (scholar); *Career* Dean Close Sch Cheltenham 1993–98, head of history and housemaster Stowe 1998–2005; Bedford Sch: vice master 2006–08, head master 2008–14; warden Radley College 2014–; *Recreations* theatre, cricket, theology; *Clubs* East India; *Style—* John Moule, Esq; ✉ The Warden's House, Radley College, Abingdon, Oxfordshire OX14 2HT

MOULTON, Jonathan Paul (Jon); s of Douglas Cecil Moulton (d 1992), of Stoke-on-Trent, and Elsie Turner Moulton (d 1984); *b* 15 October 1950; *Educ* Hanley HS, Lancaster Univ (BA); *m* 13 Aug 1973, Pauline Marie, da of Stanley Dunn, of Stoke-on-Trent; 1 da (Rebecca Clare b 1978), 1 s (Spencer Jonathan b 1980); *Career* mangr Coopers & Lybrand 1972–80; Citicorp Venture Capital: dir NY 1980–81, gen mangr London 1981–85, managing ptnr Schroder Ventures 1985–94; dir Apax & Co 1994–97, managing ptnr Alchemy Partners 1997–2009, chm A G Stanley plc 1997–98; non-exec dir: Haden MacLellan Holdings plc 1987–2000, Appledore Holdings Ltd 1990–93, Ushers Holdings plc 1991–98, R J B Mining plc 1992–94, Unicorn Abrasives plc 1995–97, Prestige Holdings Ltd 1995–99, United Texon plc 1995–98, Brands Hatch Leisure Holdings plc 1995–98, Phoenix IT Services Ltd 1997, USM Group Holdings Ltd 1997–2000, Wardle Storeys plc 2000–01, Aardvark TMC Ltd 2001–04, Datapoint 2001–09, Cedar plc 2002–09, Better Capital PCC Ltd, BACIT, Collabrium Capital Ltd 2011–, Verdi Semiconductor Ltd 2011–, Omnico Gp Ltd 2011–, Greensphere Mgmnt Ltd 2013–, Gardner Aerospace Hldgs Ltd 2014–; chm: British Allergy Fndn 1996–99, Airborne Systems Gp Ltd 2001–09, Riverdeep 2003–04, Tattershall Castle Group Ltd 2005–09, CedarCrestone Inc 2005–09, FinnCap Ltd 2010–, Centre for Policy Studies Ltd 2010–, Channel Islands Stock Exchange, Better Capital GP & 12 GP Ltd; dep chm Parker Pen Ltd 1986–97; dir Geo Systems 2008–09; tstee UK Stem Cell Fndn 2005–, tstee J P Moulton Charitable Fndn, memb Advsy Gp Gt Ormond St Children's Charity, memb Advsy Bd Rgnl Growth Fund; Corporate Finance Qualification (ICAEW); FCA 1983, FIMgt, fell Soc of Turnaround Professionals; *Recreations* chess, fishing; *Style—* Jon Moulton, Esq

MOUNFIELD, Dr Peter Reginald; s of Reginald Howard Mounfield (d 1969), of Benllech, Gwynedd, and Irene, *née* Williams (d 1992); *b* 15 February 1935; *Educ* Canon Slade GS Bolton, Univ of Nottingham (BA, PhD); *m* 12 Sept 1959, Patricia, da of Ernest John Jarrett (d 1991); 2 s (John, David); *Career* asst lectr then lectr Dept of Geography and Anthropology Univ Coll of Wales Aberystwyth 1958–68, lectr then sr lectr Univ of Leicester 1968– (head Dept of Geography 1988–91); visiting assoc prof Dept of Geography and Regnl Planning Univ of Cincinnati Ohio USA 1966–67, sr Fulbright scholar 1966–67, sr visiting res fell Jesus Coll Oxford 1988; *Books* World Nuclear Power (1991), Victoria County History of Northamptonshire (Industry and Transport) (contrib footwear and leather chapters, 2007); *Recreations* lawn bowls, gardening, bridge; *Clubs* RGS; *Style—* Dr Peter Mounfield; ✉ Department of Geography, University of Leicester, University Road, Leicester LE1 7RH (☎ 0116 252 3840, fax 0116 252 3854, e-mail themounfields@btinternet.com)

MOUNSEY-HEYSHAM, Giles Herchard; s of Maj Richard Herchard Gubbins Mounsey-Heysham (d 1960), of Castletown, Rockcliffe, Carlisle, and Mrs Isobel Margaret Rowcliffe (d 2008); *b* 15 August 1948; *Educ* Gordonstoun, RAC Cirencester; *m* 24 April 1982, Penelope Auriol, da of William Anthony Twiston-Davies (see Debrett's Peerage and Baronetage, Archdale, Bt); 3 s (Toby b 23 Jan 1984, Benjamin b 3 March 1986, Rory b 2 Feb 1989), 1 da (Anna b 29 May 1991); *Career* chartered surveyor; Smiths Gore 1970–72 and 2008– (ptnr), Cluttons 1973–2008 (ptnr 1976); memb Ct of Assts Worshipful Co of Grocers; FRICS 1982 (memb 1972); *Recreations* music, walking, travelling, motorbiking, golf; *Clubs* Boodle's, Pratt's; *Style—* Giles Mounsey-Heysham, Esq; ✉ Castletown Estate Office, Rockcliffe, Carlisle CA6 4BN (☎ 01228 674792, fax 01228 674464)

MOUNTBATTEN, Lord Ivar Alexander Michael; DL (Devon); yr s of 3 Marquess of Milford Haven, OBE, DSC (d 1970), and Janet, Marchioness of Milford Haven; *b* 9 March 1963, London; *Educ* Gordonstoun, Middlebury Coll Vermont USA (BA); *m* 23 April 1994 (m dis 2011), Penelope Ann Vere, da of Colin Thompson, of Warminster, Wilts; 3 da (Ella Louise Georgina b 20 March 1996, Alexandra Nada Victoria b 8 May 1998, Louise Xenia Rosie b 30 July 2002); *Career* Monarch Resources Venezuela 1987–88; dir: Delta Minerals Corp Bermuda 1988–, AEI Redifusion 1995–98, AEI Music Inc 1998–2001; md Crown

M

Self-Storage Ltd 1999–2011; chm Int Corporate Protection Ltd 2000–03; chm Regain, The Tst for Sporting Tetraplegics 1997– (tstee 1994–97); hon pres: Haverhill RNA 1996–, 1451 (Haverhill) Squadron ATC 1996–; tstee Coldharbour Mill Museum 1998–2006, tstee The C Group (subsidiary of RMCTF) 2010–; *Recreations* skiing, windsurfing, flying, shooting; *Style*— The Lord Ivar Mountbatten, DL; ✉ Bridwell Park, Uffculme, Devon EX15 3BU (☎ 01884 840890, fax 01884 840950)

MOUNTFORD, Margaret Rose; da of James Ross Gamble, of Holywood, NI, and Kathleen Margaret, *née* Stevenson; *b* 24 November 1951; *Educ* Strathearn Sch Belfast, Girton Coll Cambridge (MA), UCL (MA); *Career* admitted slr 1976, ptnr Herbert Smith 1983–99 (latterly jt head of corp finance); non-exec dir Georgica plc, former non-exec dir Amstrad plc; appearances as memb of the bd The Apprentice (BBC2) 2005–09; Liveryman Worshipful Co of Solicitors; memb Law Soc; *Recreations* travel, opera, wine; *Style*— Ms Margaret Mountford

MOUNTFORD, Philip; *b* 26 February 1965; *Career* mgmnt trainee rising to buying and merchandise dir Simpson Piccadilly 1984–96, retail dir (Europe and UK) Daks Simpson Gp 1996–97, sales and mktg dir Nautica Europe 1997–99, md Wholesale Div (UK and Scandinavia) Gianni Versace 1999–2002, chief exec Moss Bros Gp plc 2004– (gp trading dir 2002–04); *Style*— Philip Mountford, Esq; ✉ Moss Bros Group plc, 8 St Johns Hill, London SW11 1SA

MOUNTFORD, Roger Philip; s of Stanley W A Mountford (d 1984), of Leatherhead, Surrey, and Evelyn Mary Richardson (d 1979); *b* 5 June 1948; *Educ* Kingston GS, LSE (BSc), Stanford Grad Sch of Business (Sloan fell, MS); *m* 24 July 1981, Jane Rosemary, da of Rev Canon Eric Edwin Stanton, hon Canon of Canterbury (d 1984); 3 da (Laura Jane b 1983, Annabel Louise b 1985, Nicola Mary b 1989); *Career* PA to Rt Hon Edward Heath 1969–70 and during 1970 and 1974 gen elections, nat chm Fedn of Cons Students 1970–71; merchant banker; Hambros Bank Ltd 1971–98 (dir 1984–98); md: Hambro Pacific Ltd Hong Kong 1983–89, SG Hambros 1998–2000; chm: Civil Aviation Authy Pension Scheme 2003–15, LSE Enterprise Ltd 2004–14, Hg Capital Tst plc 2005– (non-exec dir 2004–), The Housing Finance Corp 2007–13, Dover Harbour Board 2011–12 (non-exec dir 2001–11), Allied Domecq Pension Fund 2013–; non-exec dir: Thames Valley Housing Assoc 2001–07, Civil Aviation Authy 2003–13, High Speed Two (HS2) Ltd 2015–; govr and chm of fin Cobham Hall 1995–2004, govr LSE 2006– (memb Cncl 2014–, chm Finance Ctee 2016–); memb: C of E Pensions Bd 2012–, Finance Advsy Ctee Westminster Abbey 2013–; Freeman City of London 1974, Liveryman Worshipful Co of Stationers and Newspaper Makers 1992; FRSA 2014; *Recreations* opera, music, theatre; *Clubs* Carlton, Hong Kong, Royal Hong Kong Jockey, London Capital (hon bd of advsrs); *Style*— Roger Mountford, Esq; ✉ Hookstile House, Godstone, Surrey RH9 8JH (☎ 01342 893198)

MOUNTFORD, (John) Toby; s of John Dennis Mountford, of Thames Ditton, Surrey, and Wendy, *née* Gowlland; *b* 4 November 1954; *Educ* Wellington, Univ of Durham (BSc); *m* 18 Oct 2003, Carolina, *née* Van Oordt; 2 s (Benjamin Alexander b 13 March 2006, Teddy Emmanuel b 6 Jan 2012); *Career* articled clerk then chartered accountant Price Waterhouse London 1976–80, mgmnt accountant Int Div Beecham Pharmaceuticals 1980–81, fin PR dir Streets Financial Ltd 1981–87, dir Citigate Dewe Rogerson (formerly Citigate Communications Ltd) 1987–2014, sr dir Citigate Dewe Rogerson; ACA 1980; *Books* Practice Development – A Guide to Marketing Techniques for Accountants (1985); *Recreations* skiing, walking, swimming, theatre; *Clubs* Hurlingham; *Style*— Toby Mountford, Esq; ✉ Citigate Dewe Rogerson Ltd, 3 London Wall Buildings, London Wall, London EC2M 5SY (☎ 020 7638 9571, fax 020 7628 3444, e-mail toby.mountford@citigatedr.co.uk)

MOURBY, Adrian Roy Bradshaw; s of Roy Mourby (d 2011), and Peggy, *née* Bradshaw (d 2013); *Educ* King Edward VI Camp Hill Sch Birmingham, Univ of Wales (BA), Univ of Bristol Film Sch (postgrad); *m* 1, 19 July 1980 (m dis 1998), Katharine Mary, da of John Richard Trevena Nicholas (d 1971), of West Penwith, Cornwall; 1 da (Miranda Jane b 1987), 1 s (John James b 1990); m 2, 20 March 2004, Kathryn du Bois, da of Martin Connor Miller, of Washington State, USA; *Career* BBC TV and Radio prodr 1979–92; currently writer and prodr; columnist Times Educnl Supplement 1998–2002, regular contrib Independent on Sunday, int architectural corr Opera Now 1998–2012; writer: 8 broadcast plays, numerous radio talks, two Radio 4 comedy series Whatever Happened to...?, Silkies, Men of Letters, Mr Handel & Mr Congreve (stageplay, Valletta) 2002 (also Buxton 2003); writer, prodr and presenter of BBC independent documentary Nimrod, contrib talks and entertainments to Radio 3 Proms 1994–97 and Christmas on Radio 4 1993, 1995 and 1997, prog essayist Covent Garden, ENO and WNO 1996–, co-artistic dir Celebrating Handel 2002, co-artistic dir Oxford Millennium Opera 2004–; opera prodr: Semele (Malta), Cosi fan tutte (Oxford Millennium Opera) 2004, The Grave's a Fine and Pleasant Place 2005 (with Ian Hogg), Marriage of Figaro (Oxford and Blewbury Festival) 2006; dramaturg Idomeneo (Wiener Staatsoper) 2014–15; creator Tristan & Matilda (cartoon series) 2003–08; contributing ed Famous Hotels, currently hotel historian; *Awards* Smith-Kline Award for Radio Journalism 1983, commendation Sony Radio Awards 1985, BAFTA/Cymru Best English Drama Award 1991, Celtic Film Festival Best Short Drama Award 1994, Sony Silver Award for Radio Writing 1995; others from Francisco Film Festival 1993 and NY Int Radio Festival 1994; Canadian Travel Awards 1998, Puccini Journalism Award 2007, Best Travel Article in a Magazine Award 2013; *Books* We Think the World of Him (novel, 1996), The Four of Us (novel, 1997), Whatever happened to....? (1998), Wishdaughter (novel, 2004), AA Spotlight on Venice (2007), AA Spotlight on Brussels (2008); *Recreations* eating, drinking, talking, architecture, travel, opera, films, cats; *Clubs* British Guild of Travel Writers; *Style*— Adrian Mourby; ✉ 24 Cox's Ground, Oxford OX2 6PX (e-mail mail@adrianmourby.com)

MOUSLEY, His Hon Judge Timothy John; QC (2003); *Career* called to the Bar 1979; asst recorder 1998, recorder 2000, circuit judge (Western Circuit) 2013–; *Style*— His Hon Judge Mousley, QC; ✉ Swindon Combined Court, The Law Courts, Islington Street, Swindon SN1 2HG

MOUTAFIAN, Princess Helena; MBE (1976); da of Prince Alexei Gagarin (d 1938), and Countess Ana Phillipovitz (d 1944); *b* 2 May 1930; *m* 14 Jan 1955, Artin Moutafian (d 1992), s of Nikogos Moutafian (d Armenia 1914); 2 s (Nicholas b 6 Nov 1958, Mark b 21 Dec 1960); *Career* vice-pres Help the Aged (pres Ladies' Ctee), fndr pres Anglo-Russian Children Appeal, hon vice-pres Women's Cncl, life patron NSPCC; patron: Inst for Complementary Natural Medicine, Young ME Sufferers Tst, Hampsted Town Hall; patron emeritus Cwlth Countries League; vice-pres Byron Soc; awarded Silver Medal of Grollo d'Ore for paintings of Venice; fell Soil Assoc; FRGS 1964, FRZS; Croix de Chevalier (Ordre de la Courtoisie Française) 1976, Etoile Civique (Grande Médaille de Vermeil de la Ville de Paris) 1977, Freedom City of Paris 1977; DStJ 1990, Russian decoration for service to children's charity; *Recreations* painting, writing; *Clubs* ESU; *Style*— Princess Helena Moutafian, MBE; ✉ 18 Burgess Hill, Hampstead, London NW2 2DA (☎ 020 7435 2104)

MOUTRAY, Stephen William; MLA; s of William Moutray (d 1984), and Lena, *née* Campbell (d 1990); *b* 25 February 1959, Enniskillen, Co Fermanagh; *Educ* Lurgan Jr HS, Lurgan Coll; *m* 1 June 1985, Myrtle, *née* Taylor; 1 da (Grace b 17 Aug 1987), 2 s (Philip b 6 Sept 1991, Kyle b 7 Nov 1995); *Career* memb DUP 1979– (memb Party Exec), cncllr Craigavon Borough Cncl 2001– (currently gp ldr), MLA (DUP) Upper Bann 2003–; *Recreations* swimming, walking, golfing; *Style*— Stephen Moutray, Esq, MLA; ✉ DUP Advice Centre, 50A High Street, Lurgan, Craigavon, BT66 8AU (☎ 028 38 310088, fax 028 38 310099, website www.stephenmoutray.co.uk)

MOUTREY, David John; s of John Thomas Moutrey (d 2001), and Jean, *née* Beck, of Billingham, Teeside; *b* 13 February 1958, Sedgefield, Durham; *Educ* Univ of Leeds (BEd), Open Univ (MBA); *m* 23 Nov 1984, Lindsey, *née* Howarth; 1 da (Anna), 1 s (Robert); *Career* drama teacher South Chadderton Sch 1981–84, theatre mangr Abraham Moss Centre Theatre 1984–90, dir Arts About Manchester 1991–98, dir and ceo HOME (formerly Cornerhouse and Library Theatre Co) 1998–; Theatre Award Manchester Evening News 1994; tstee Abandon Normal Devices Festival Ltd; memb: BAFTA, CMI, RSA; *Recreations* cinema, music, reading, travel, walking, theatre; *Style*— David Moutrey, Esq; ✉ HOME, 2 Tony Wilson Place, First Street, Manchester M15 4FN (☎ 0161 228 7621, e-mail dave.moutrey@homemcr.org, website www.homemcr.org, Twitter @DaveMoutrey)

MOVERLEY SMITH, Stephen Philip; QC (2002); s of Philip Smith, of Llanrwst, N Wales, and Carol, *née* Moverley; *b* 10 January 1960, Frimley, Surrey; *Educ* Reading Sch, Pembroke Coll Oxford (MA); *m* 8 Sept 1990, Caroline, *née* Topping; 3 s (Benjamin b 25 Sept 1995, Rupert, Theodore (twins) b 5 Dec 1997); *Career* called to the Bar: Middle Temple 1985, Eastern Caribbean Supreme Court 1995; practising barr specialising in int company and commercial litigation, currently memb of chambers 24 Old Buildings; jr counsel to the Crown (Chancery) 1992–2001; *Style*— Stephen Moverley Smith, Esq, QC; ✉ 24 Old Buildings, Lincoln's Inn, London WC2A 3VP (☎ 020 7691 2424, fax 0870 460 2178, e-mail sms@xxiv.co.uk)

MOWAT, David John; MP; *b* 20 February 1957, Rugby, Warks; *Educ* Imperial Coll London; *m* Nicky; 1 s (Andrew), 3 da (Laura, Emma, Victoria); *Career* CA; industry global managing ptnr (energy) Accenture 2001–04; MP (Cons) Warrington S 2010–; *Style*— David Mowat, Esq, MP; ✉ House of Commons, London SW1A 0AA

MOWAT, Magnus Charles; s of John F M Mowat, MBE (d 1988), of Ellesmere, Shropshire and Elizabeth Rebecca, *née* Murray (d 1977); *b* 5 April 1940; *Educ* Haileybury; *m* 27 April 1968, Mary Lynette St Lo, da of Alan D Stoddart (d 1994), of Cothelstone, Somerset; 3 s (Charles b 15 April 1969, Alexander b 7 June 1970, Hugh b 27 June 1973); *Career* CA; Peat Marwick Mitchell & Co 1959–67, Hill Samuel & Co Ltd 1968–70, ptnr Illingworth & Henriques Stockbrokers 1970–84, dir Barclays de Zoete Wedd Ltd 1984–90; chm: Woodard Schools Taunton Ltd 2005–10, Aardvark E M Ltd 2005–11; Hon DLitt Univ of Salford 2011; FCA 1964; *Recreations* shooting, thinking about the future, music; *Clubs* East India, Somerset Dining; *Style*— Magnus Mowat, Esq; ✉ Glebe Farmhouse, Brompton Ralph, Taunton, Somerset TA4 2RY (☎ 01984 656 824)

MOWAT, Her Hon Mary Jane Stormont; da of late Duncan Mackay Stormont Mowat, and late Jane Archibald Mowat, *née* Milne; *b* 7 July 1948; *Educ* Sherborne Sch for Girls, Lady Margaret Hall Oxford (MA), Inns of Court Sch of Law; *m* Prof the Hon Nicholas Michael John Woodhouse, s of 5 Baron Terrington; 1 s (Thomas Duncan b 4 Feb 1987); *Career* called to the Bar Inner Temple 1973; circuit judge (SE Circuit) 1996–2014, ret; *Recreations* music, walking, riding, reading; *Style*— Her Hon Mowat; ✉ Oxford Combined Court Centre, St Aldates, Oxford OX1 1TL

MOWSCHENSON, Terence Rennie; QC (1995); s of Henry Mowschenson (d 1994), and Hanny Mowschenson (d 1992); *b* 7 June 1953; *Educ* Peterhouse, Queen Mary Coll London (LLB), Exeter Coll Oxford (BCL); *m* 10 Oct 1992, Judith Angela, da of Christopher Strang; *Career* called to the Bar Middle Temple 1977 (bencher 2003); memb Chambers of Edward Nugee QC, asst recorder 1995–2000, recorder 2000–, dep judge of the High Court 2003; chm: Financial Services and Markets Act Tbnl 2001, Pensions Tbnl 2004; chm Barristers' Benevolent Assoc 1999–, memb Chancery and Commercial Bar Assocs; FCIArb 1991; *Recreations* opera; *Clubs* RAC; *Style*— Terence Mowschenson, Esq, QC; ✉ Wilberforce Chambers, 8 New Square, Lincoln's Inn, London WC2A 3QP (☎ 020 7306 0101, fax 020 7306 0095)

MOXHAM, Prof John; s of Wilson Moxham (d 1949), and Marie, *née* Blande; *b* 9 December 1944; *Educ* Prince Henry's GS Evesham, LSE (BSc), UCH (MB BS, MD); *m* 4 June 1978, Nicola Dawn, da of (Alec William) Larry Seaman; 3 da (Jessica Hannah b 4 May 1980, Madeleine Emily b 15 Dec 1985, Rose Harriet b 20 Dec 1988); *Career* conslt physician King's Coll Hosp 1982, dean Faculty of Clinical Med King's Coll Sch of Med and Dentistry 1997–98, subsequently dean King's Denmarkhill Campus; currently dir of clinical strategy King's Health Partners; author of numerous papers, chapters and reviews on respiratory physiology; FRCP 1987 (MRCP 1975); *Recreations* my wonderful daughters; *Clubs* The Lord Lyndhurst; *Style*— Prof John Moxham

MOXON, Prof (Edward) Richard; s of Gerald Richard Moxon, CBE (d 1980), and Margaret, *née* Forster Mohun; *b* 16 July 1941; *Educ* Shrewsbury, St John's Coll Cambridge (BChir); *m* 20 Oct 1973, Marianne, da of Prof George Graham; 2 s (Christopher Alan b 1978, Timothy Stewart b 1987), 1 da (Sarah Graham b 1981); *Career* sr house offr Hosp for Sick Children 1969, res fell Children's Hosp Med Centre Boston USA 1971–74 (asst resident paediatric 1970), asst prof of paediatrics Johns Hopkins Univ Hosp Baltimore USA 1974–78 (assoc prof and Eudowood chief of paediatric infectious diseases 1978–84), prof of paediatrics Univ of Oxford 1984–; *Recreations* sport, music, literature; *Style*— Prof Richard Moxon; ✉ Department of Paediatrics, John Radcliffe Hospital, Headington OX3 9DU

MOXON BROWNE, Robert William; QC (1990); s of late Kendall Edward Moxon-Browne, and Sheila Heron, *née* Weatherbe; bro of Prof Edward Moxon-Browne, *qv*; *b* 26 June 1946; *Educ* Gordonstoun, Univ Coll Oxford (BA); *m* 26 June 1968, Kerstin Elizabet, da of Oscar Warne; 1 da (Emily Kendall b 20 Oct 1973), 1 s (James Weatherbe b 7 April 1977); *Career* called to the Bar Gray's Inn 1969, in practice specialising in commercial and insurance law on Western Circuit and in London, recorder 1991–, dep judge of Technol and Construction Ct 1992–, dep judge of the High Court 1998; *Recreations* theatre, gardening, cooking; *Style*— Robert Moxon Browne, Esq, QC; ✉ 2 Temple Gardens, London EC4Y 9AY (☎ 020 7583 6041, fax 020 7583 2094)

MOXON-BROWNE, Prof Edward; s of Kendall Edward Moxon-Browne, and Sheila Heron, *née* Weatherbe; bro of Robert Moxon Browne, QC, *qv*; *b* 28 January 1944, Halifax, NS, Canada; *Educ* Gordonstoun, St Andrews Univ (MA Medieval History), Univ of Pennsylvania (MA Int Rels); *Career* lectr in int rels US Int Univ 1970–72, lectr, sr lectr then reader in political sci Queen's Univ of Belfast 1973–91, Jean Monnet chair of Euro integration Univ of Limerick 1992–; Univ of Limerick: dir Centre for European Studies, memb Bd Centre for Criminal Justice; memb Editorial Bd: Regional and Federal Studies, Contemporary Politics; external examiner: Queen's Univ of Belfast, South Bank Univ; memb: RIIA, Int Studies Assoc, Euro Community Studies Assoc; *Books* Nation, Class and Creed in Northern Ireland (1983), Political Change in Spain (1989), European Terrorism (ed, 1993), The Police, Public Order and the State (co-author, 2 edn, 1996), A Future for Peacekeeping (ed, 1997), Who are the Europeans? (ed, 1999); also author of numerous contrib to various learned pubns; *Style*— Prof Edward Moxon-Browne; ✉ University of Limerick, Limerick, Ireland (☎ 00 353 61 202202, fax 00 353 61 330316, e-mail edward.moxon-browne@ul.ie)

MOYES, David William; *b* 25 April 1963, Glasgow; *m* Pamela; 1 s (David), 1 da (Lauren); *Career* football mangr and former player; player: Celtic 1980–83, Cambridge United 1983–85, Bristol City 1985–87, Shrewsbury Town 1987–90, Dunfermline Athletic 1990–93, Hamilton Academical 1993, Preston North End 1993–98; mangr: Preston North End 1998–2002 (champions Div Two 2000), Everton 2002–13 (LMA Mangr of the Year 2003 and 2005), Manchester United 2013–14; *Style*— Mr David Moyes

MOYES, James Christopher (Jim); *b* 29 April 1943; *Educ* Maidstone Coll of Art, Univ of Kent (BA), Slade Sch of Fine Art London (MA); *m* 1, 1969 (m dis 1981), Elizabeth McKee;

1 da (Sara Jo b 1969); m 2, 1987 (m dis 2000), Joanna Margaret, da of Col David E G Price (decd); 2 da (Beatrice Oliphant b 1987, Clementine b 1990); *Career* laboratory asst and quality control technician Watneys Laboratories 1959–64, merchant marine 1964–66, artist and gallery asst 1971–, fndr Momart plc (int fine art serv co, Royal Warrant holder), estab Momart fellowship (artist in residence Tate Gallery Liverpool), former dir Momart Ltd (Royal Warrant reassigned); lectr in art handling techniques; practising artist in all media; former memb Ctee Contemporary Art Soc; *Recreations* art exhibitions and other arts related activities; *Style—* Jim Moyes, Esq; ✉ Unit 4, Ropewalk Mews, 118 Middleton Road, London E8 4LP (☎ 020 7241 4007, fax 020 7241 3172); Studio (☎ 020 7241 4007, fax 020 7241 3172)

MOYLAN, Daniel; s of James Moylan, and Susan Moylan; *b* 1956; *Educ* St Philip's GS Edgbaston, Queen's Coll Oxford; *Career* FCO 1979–82, County Bank Ltd 1982–86, vice-pres Security Pacific Hoare Govett Ltd 1986–87, prop Egan Assocs; memb Royal Borough of Kensington and Chelsea Council 1990– (dep ldr 2000–11), dep chair Transport for London 2009–12 and 2016 (memb Bd 2008–), chm London Legacy Devpt Corporation 2012, chm Crossrail 2 Ltd 2016–; *Style—* Daniel Moylan, Esq; ✉ 55 Broadway, London SW1H 0BD

MOYLE, Andrew; s of Peter Moyle, of Sydney, Aust, and Anne, *née* Mavin; *b* 28 May 1964, Aust; *Educ* Univ of Melbourne (LLB, BComm); *m* 26 Feb 1994, Julie A, *née* Duffey; 2 da (Eliza b 23 June 1997, Alice b 15 Aug 2002), 1 s (Sam b 6 April 2000); *Career* slr; ptnr: Freehill Hollingdale and Page 1996, Shaw Pittman 1996–2003; Latham and Watkins: ptnr 2003–, managing ptnr 2006–; memb Law Soc; *Recreations* skiing; *Clubs* Australia; *Style—* Andrew Moyle, Esq; ✉ Latham and Watkins, 99 Bishopsgate, London EC2M 3XF (☎ 020 7710 1000, fax 020 7374 4460, e-mail andrew.moyle@lw.com)

MOYLE, Robert; s of Maj T G Moyle (d 2005), of Old Dalby, Leics, and Maureen Gertrude, *née* Pickett; *b* 31 January 1952, Leamington Spa, Warks; *Educ* Uppingham, Univ of Birmingham (BSc); *m* 10 Aug 1985, Alexandra Elizabeth Foster, *née* Holmden; 2 da (Kate Elizabeth Foster b 5 Aug 1988, Elizabeth Rolfe b 18 Aug 1991); *Career* North Midland Construction plc 1973– (currently exec chm); memb E Midlands Advsy Bd BITC; CEng 2008, FICE 2008; *Recreations* opera, shooting, gardening, supporting Leicester Tigers; *Style—* Robert Moyle, Esq; ✉ Old Dalby Wood House, Lawn Lane, Old Dalby, Melton Mowbray, Leicestershire LE14 3NB (☎ 01509 880305); North Midland Construction plc, Nunn Close, The County Estate, Huthwaite, Sutton-in-Ashfield, Nottinghamshire NG17 2HW (☎ 01623 515008, fax 01623 440071, e-mail robert.moyle@northmid.co.uk)

MOYNIHAN, 4 Baron (UK 1929); Sir Colin Berkeley Moynihan; 4 Bt (UK 1922); s of 2 Baron Moynihan, OBE, TD (d 1965), and June Elizabeth, *née* Hopkins (d 2012); suc half-bro 3 Baron (d 1991), (claim to barony admitted by Ctee for Privileges House of Lords 1997); *b* 13 September 1955; *Educ* Monmouth, UC Oxford (MA, Rowing and Boxing double blue, pres Oxford Union); *m* 7 March 1992, Gaynor-Louise, only da of Paul G Metcalf, of Healing, S Humberside; 2 s (Hon Nicholas Ewan Berkeley b 31 March 1994, Hon George Edward Berkeley b 4 June 1995), 1 da (Hon India Isabella Sarah b 2 Sept 1997); *Heir* s, Hon Nicholas Moynihan; *Career* personal asst to chm Tate & Lyle Ltd 1978–80, mangr Tate & Lyle Agribusiness 1980–82, chief exec Ridgways Tea and Coffee Merchants 1980–83, MP (Cons) Lewisham E 1983–92, jt md Independent Power Corp plc and affiliates 1996–2001, dir Rowan Gp of Companies 1996–2015, exec chm and md Consort Resources Gp of Companies 1999–2003, chm Clipper Windpower Europe Ltd 2001–07, chm Spectron Gp plc 2004–05, chm Pelamis Wave Power Ltd 2005–11, chm Hydrodec plc 2012–, dir Aquantis Inc 2012–, dir Ecomerit Technologies LLC 2012–, chm Buckthorn Capital LLP 2014–; chm BOA 2005–12, memb Organising Ctee London 2012 Olympics 2005–12; political asst to Foreign Sec 1983, PPS to Rt Hon Kenneth Clarke as Min of Health and PMG 1986–87, Parly under-sec of state DOE and min for sport 1987–90, Parly under-sec of state Dept of Energy 1990–92, oppn sr spokesman on foreign and Cwlth affrs House of Lords 1997–2000, a shadow min for sport 2003–05; chm: All-Pty Gp on Afghanistan 1984, Govt Inner City Working Gp on Sport and Recreation 1988, Govt Review Gp on Sport for the Disabled 1989, Govt Renewable Energy Advsy Gp 1991–97; vice-chm Cons Backbenchers Sports Ctee; memb: Bow Gp 1978 (chm Bow Gp Industry Ctee 1985–87), Paddington Cons Mgmnt Ctee 1980–81, Exec Bd European Olympic Ctees 2005–13, Int Olympic Ctee's Int Relations Cmmn 2008–, House of Lords Select Ctee on Olympic and Paralympic Legacy 2013–14, House of Lords Select Ctee on the Arctic 2014–15, House of Lords Select Ctee on Delegated Powers and Regulatory Reform 2015–; sec: Major Spectator Sports Ctee CCPR 1979–87, CCPR Enquiry into Sponsorship of Sport 1982–83, Cons Foreign and Cwlth Affairs Ctee 1985; memb Sports Cncl 1982–85, govr Sports Aid Fndn (London and SE) 1980–82; steward British Boxing Bd of Control 1979–87; tstee: OUBC 1980–83, Sports Aid Tst 1983–87; fndr memb Worldwatch Inst Europe 1991; dir Canterbury Festival 1999–2001; rowing achievements incl: Gold medal World Championships 1978, Silver medal Olympic Games Moscow 1980, Silver medal World Championships 1981; Freeman City of London 1978, Liveryman Worshipful Co of Haberdashers (memb Ct of Assts); *Recreations* collecting Nonesuch books, music, sport; *Clubs* Leander, Vincent's (Oxford), Club at the Ivy; *Style—* The Lord Moynihan; ✉ House of Lords, London SW1A 0PW (e-mail moynihanc@parliament.uk)

MOYNIHAN, Sir Daniel; kt (2012); s of Edmund Moynihan (d 1992), and Bridget Moynihan (d 2006); *b* London; *Educ* UCL (BSc), Inst of Educn London Univ (PGCE, MA, EdD); *m* 1 Aug 1987, Jane, *née* Iles; 1 da (Sarah b 17 Aug 1989), 1 s (Thomas b 3 April 1992); *Career* head teacher Valentines HS Redbridge 1998–2004, princ Harris City Acad Crystal Palace 2004–07, ceo Harris Fedn 2005–; chm UK Educn Honours Ctee Cabinet Office 2016–; *Books* Economics – A Complete Course for IGCSE and O-Level (jtly, 2007), Complete Economics for Cambridge IGCSE and O-Level (jtly, 2012); *Recreations* cinema, music, reading, walking, politics; *Style—* Sir Daniel Moynihan; ✉ Harris Federation, 4th Floor Norfolk House, Wellesley Road, Croydon CR0 1LH

MOYNIHAN, Jon; OBE (1994); s of Sir Noel Moynihan (d 1993), of Herstmonceux, E Sussex, and Margaret, *née* Lovelace (d 1989); *b* 21 June 1948, Cambridge; *Educ* Balliol Coll Oxford (MA), N London Poly (MSc), MIT (SM); *m* Dec 20 1980, Patricia Underwood, *née* Gilbert; *Career* worked for War on Want and Save the Children India and Bangladesh 1971–72; Roche Products 1972–76, McKinsey & Co Amsterdam 1977–79, Strategic Planning Assocs Washington DC 1979–81, First Manhattan Gp NY 1982–92; exec chm PA Consltg Gp (formerly ceo rising to chm and ceo) 1992–2014; chm: Cubiks 1998–2005, Ubinetics Ltd 1999–2005, Meridica Ltd 2000–05, ImPAct Execs 2002–03, Procserve Ltd 2006–15; Aegate Ltd: chm 2003–10, non-exec dir 2011–; managing ptnr IPEX Capital LLP 2008–; chm Balliol Campaign Bd 1994–2009, chm Helen Bamber Fndn until 2009, tstee Chelsea Festival until 2010; Royal Albert Hall: memb Cncl 2012–, pres 2015–; memb: Dean's Cncl Sloan Sch MIT until 2011, Dean's Business Advsy Forum Saïd Business Sch until 2008, Bd Business for Britain 2013–; distinguished friend of Oxford 2010–, memb Ct Imperial Coll 2015–; fndn fell Balliol Coll Oxford, fell Gray's Inn 2012; *Clubs* Travellers, MCC, Carlton, Academy; *Style—* Jon Moynihan, Esq, OBE; ✉ 41 Chelsea Square, London SW3 6LH

MUCKLE, Prof David Sutherland; s of John Leslie Muckle, and Ruth, *née* Sutherland; *b* 30 August 1939; *Educ* Univ of Durham (MB BS), Univs of Oxford and Newcastle upon Tyne (MS MD); *m* Christine; 2 da (Carolyn Jane b 22 July 1964, Deborah Christine b 17 July 1966); *Career* research assoc Univ of Durham 1963; orthopaedic surgn: Radcliffe Infirmary Oxford, Nuffield Orthopaedic Centre and Univ of Oxford 1970–77, Cleveland AHA 1977–95; held various visiting professorships in Japan, Caribbean and USA 1977–82, visiting prof Univ of Teesside 1994; examiner RCS(Ed) 1989–; med advsr to the FA, UEFA, FIFA, Nat Rehabilitation Centre and FA Sch of Excellence; MO: UEFA Nations Cup Final Gothenburg 1992, Euro 96 Final Wembley 1996; formerly dep chm and fndr Medical Ctee the FA; DSc research at Univ of Oxford, Durham Univ and Teesside Univs leading to discovery of the use of anti-inflammatory agents in soft tissue trauma based on original biochemical and biomechanical investigations 2010; winner President's Prize in Orthopaedic Research 1973–74, Child of the Year Award 1987 and 1993, runner-up Jacksonian Prize in Surgery RCS 1972; author of over 200 articles incl Comparative Study of Ibuprofen and Asprin in Soft Tissue Injuries 1974 (reprinted 1974–88, over 100,000 copies); over 500 worldwide lectures incl NY Acad of Science, Nat Insts of Health and RSM; memb: Br Orthopaedic Research Soc 1973, Br Orthopaedic Assoc 1974, Girdlestone Orthopaedic Soc of Oxford; Hon Dip Sports Med The Scottish Royal Colls 1997, Hon Dr Professional Achievement Univ of Teesside 2014; FRCS, FRCSEd, FRGS; *Books* On Distant Fells, a story of the Great War (2014); *Non-Fiction Publications* A Doctor's Look at Life and History (1970), Sports Injuries (1971), Football Fitness and Injuries (1974), Femoral Neck Fractures (1977), Injuries in Sport (1977), Get Fit for Soccer (1981), An Outline of Orthopaedic Practice (1985), An Outline of Fractures and Dislocations (1985), Dickens by Charles Dickens – a biography (2010); *Novels* The Sower Went Forth Sowing (2002); A Country Doctor: Vol 1 – On Distant Fells (2003), Vol 2 – The Holly Blue (2003), Vol 3 – A Child at War (2003); A Highland Story – Written on Glass (2005); *Poems* The Call of Dusk (2002), Such Happiness is Life (2002), Endangered Species (2004); *Recreations* natural history, classical English literature, sport in general, breeding rare farm animals, fell walking, astronomy, ornithology; *Style—* Prof David S Muckle; ✉ Park View Medical Clinic, Middlesbrough TS4 2NS (☎ 01642 242357)

MUCKLOW, Rupert Jeremy; s of Albert Mucklow, and Gillian, *née* Bullock; *b* 27 April 1963, Stourbridge, W Midlands; *Educ* Millfield (head boy, rugby capt), Boston Univ (BSc); *m* 18 Sept 1993, Diana, *née* Mullett; *Career* surveyor; Chesshire Gibson 1986–88, Grimley J R Eve 1988–90, A & J Mucklow Gp plc: investment surveyor 1990–96, md 1996–2004, chm 2004–; memb Investment Property Forum; *Recreations* golf, horse racing, sailing; *Clubs* Blackwell Golf; *Style—* Rupert Mucklow, Esq; ✉ A & J Mucklow Group plc, 60 Whitehall Road, Halesowen, West Midlands B63 3JS

MUDDIMAN, Noel; CBE (1992, OBE 1985); step s of Arthur George Muddiman (d 1976), and s of Flora May, *née* Holdsworth (d 2010); *b* 17 December 1943; *Educ* Borden GS, RMA Sandhurst; *m* 25 Oct 1969, Patricia Anne, *née* Sevage; 2 s (Andrew Robert b 1 April 1973, Matthew b 21 July 1980); *Career* served Army until 1995 (joined 1963), CO 25 Regt Royal Corps of Transport; head of Personnel and Logistics Falkland Is 1985–86, princ logistic planner Br Forces Germany 1987–90, cdr Tport and Movements BAOR 1990–92, cdr Logistic Support Gp (Middle East) March-Aug 1991, RCDS 1992, cmdt Army Sch of Mechanical Tport 1992–95, ret Army (with rank of Brig) 1995; dir CF Solutions Ltd 2004–, dir Metropole Search Partners 2013–; memb Motability (charity) 2004– (dir 1995–2004); Freedom of Oerlinghausen (Germany) 1984, Norwegian Gulf Medal (with Clasp) 1992; *Books* Blackadder's War (jtly, 1995); *Recreations* gardening, photography, philately; *Clubs* RASC/RCT Officers' (chm Luncheon Club 2015–), Movement Control Officers'; *Style—* Noel Muddiman, Esq, CBE; ✉ c/o Motability, Warwick House, Roydon Road, Harlow, Essex CM19 5PX (☎ 01279 303414, fax 01279 632002)

MUDIE, Colin Crichton; *b* Edinburgh; *Educ* Scotland and England; *m* Rosemary Horder; 1 s (Colin Maxwell); *Career* naval architect and yacht designer; design apprentice: British Power Boat Co Hythe Southampton, Laurent Giles & Partners yacht designers Lymington; fndr independent design firm (partnerd by w): Westminster London 1958–68, Lymington 1968–2013; designs incl sail trg vessels, special reproduction, expedition and exploration boats, power boats, sailing yachts, motor cruisers, motor sailers, workboats, pilot boats and dinghies; design work incl: TS Royalist (23 metre brig for Sea Cadet Corps) 1971, STS Lord Nelson (43 metre barque for the Jubilee Sailing Tst) 1986, STS Young Endeavour (35 metre brigantine – official gift of the British nation to Australia to mark the 1988 Bicentennial) 1987, HMRB Zinat al Bihaar (50 metre dhow (Baghla)) 1988, KLD Tunas Samudera (35 metre brigantine for the Royal Malaysian Navy) 1989, Aileach (12 metre birlinn which re-enacted Lord of the Isles voyages 1991 and 1992) 1991, Matthew (reconstruction of vessel which retraced John Cabot's 1497 historic voyage from Bristol to Newfoundland in 1997) 1995, INV Tarangini (43 metre barque for Indian Navy) 1995; Dunbrody, built in Ireland (36 metre reproduction of an 1845 barque) 1998, Jockey Club Huan (40 metre Chinese junk) 2005; for Tim Severin: Brendan (11 metre curragh) 1975, Sohar (20 metre dhow) 1980, Argo (16.5 metre galley) 1984; Winston Churchill fell 1968, Lloyd's Award (for best design and construction for the sail trg brig Royalist) 1971, RINA Small Craft Medal (for outstanding contribs to the Small Craft Indust) 1984, INV Sudarshini (43m barque – sister ship to Tarangini – for the Indian Navy) 2012, Br Design Cncl Award (for sail trg barque Lord Nelson) 1993; past memb: Hovercraft Ctee CAA Air Requirements Bd, Marine Technol Ctee and Mech and Electrical Engrg Requirements Bd Dept of Indust, Mary Rose Structure Advsy Panel, Steering Ctee Yacht and Boat Design Course Southampton Inst of HE; a life vice-pres RNLI; RDI 1995, CEng, FRINA, Hon FRIN, FRSA; *Books* Motor Boats and Boating, Power Boats, Sopranino (with Patrick Ellam), The Story of the Sailing Ship (with Rosemary Mudie), Power Yachts (with Rosemary Mudie), The Sailing Ship (with Rosemary Mudie), Sailing Ships; also author of various conf papers and pubns; *Recreations* sailing, model boats, books; *Clubs* Royal Lymington Yacht, Ocean Cruising, Square Rigger; *Style—* Colin Mudie, Esq; ✉ Bywater Lodge, Undershore Road, Lymington, Hampshire SO41 5SB

MUDIE, George; *Career* MP (Lab) Leeds East 1992–2015; formerly treas HM Household (dep chief whip), Parly under sec Dept for Educn and Employment 1998–; *Style—* George Mudie, Esq; ✉ House of Commons, London SW1A 0AA (☎ 020 7219 3000)

MUEHLE, Henrik; *b* 15 June 1968; *Educ* Usdorfschool Frechen Germany, Commercial Sch Bergisch-Gladbach Germany, Tech Sch for Hotel Business Garmisch-Partenkirchen Germany; *Career* mgmnt trainee Hotel and Casino Imperial Palace Annecy 1991–1992, front office mangr Millennium Hotel Charles-de-Gaulle Paris 1993–94 (reception mangr 1992–93), front of house mangr Hotel Copthorne Windsor 1994–96, front office mangr Holiday Inn Republique Paris 1996–97, ops mangr Hotel L'Horizon Jersey 1998–2000, dep gen mangr Tylney Hall Hotel Rotherwick 2000–02, gen mangr The Capital Hotel Knightsbridge 2002–; PDP Yield Mgmnt Cornell Univ 1999; *Awards* for Tylney Hall: IIP achieved June 2000, Golden Ribbon 2000 and 2001, Hotel of the Year 2000, Southern England Hotel of the Year 2002, SEB England 2002, Michelin Award 5 Black Houses 2002; for The Capital: 2 Michelin Stars, Golden Ribbon 2002, runner-up Hotel of the Year 2002/2003 LTB, RAC 5 Star Townhouse Award 2003/2004, AA 5 Red Star Townhouse Award 2003/2004; *Style—* Henrik Muehle, Esq; ✉ The Capital Hotel, 22–24 Basil Street, Knightsbridge, London SW3 1AT (☎ 020 7591 1207)

MUGGERIDGE, Rev Sara Ann (Sally); da of John Raymond Muggeridge, MBE, FICE, CEng (d 2001), and Sylvia, *née* Jenkins; niece of Malcolm Muggeridge (d 1990), the journalist and author; *b* 10 September 1949; *Educ* South Hampstead HS, Westfield Coll, Univ of London (BA), Henley Mgmnt Coll (MBA), South East Inst of Theological Educn (Fndn Degree), Canterbury Christ Church Univ (Fndn Degree); *m* 19 July 1969, Lt Richard David Williams; 2 da (Philippa Ann b 1973, Georgina Elizabeth b 1977), 1 s (Jonathan Roland b 1982); *Career* mktg mangr BT plc 1985–91; Cable & Wireless plc: mktg dir Mercury Communications 1991–93, mgmnt devpt dir 1993–96, HR dir Asia 1996–99; mgmnt devpt

M

dir Pearson plc 1999–2003, chief exec Industry and Parliament Tst 2003–10, dir Total Upstream UK Ltd 2010–15; pres CIM Singapore 1996–98, exec vice-pres CIM UK 1999–2004, memb Senate CIM 2007–13; memb Chartered Dir Ctee IOD 2006–; memb Cncl Univ of Kent 2006–12; int pres Malcolm Muggeridge Soc; memb House of Laity Gen Synod, licensed reader C of E 2013, church cmmr C of E 2014; ordained: deacon 2015, priest 2016; curate St Stephen Walbrook 2015–; Voluntary Sector Achiever Woman of the Year Awards 2007, Achievement Award and hon life memb Acad of Mktg 2013, The Int Alliance for Women (TIAW) World of Difference 100 Award 2015; Freeman City of London, Master Worshipful Co of Marketors 2013–14; FCIM 1988, FRSA 1995, fell IPT 1995, chartered fell CIPD, FIoD 2011; *Recreations* jogging, cycling, country walks, grandchildren; *Clubs* Farmers, Kennel, City Livery; *Style—* The Rev Sally Muggeridge; ✉ The Old Farm House, Pike Road, Tilmanstone, Kent CT15 4DJ (☎ 01304 831964, e-mail sally@sallymuggeridge.com); St Stephen Walbrook, 39 Walbrook, London EC4N 8BN (☎ 020 7626 9000, e-mail curate@ststephenwalbrook)

MUGHAL, Dr Hamid Ghafoor; OBE (2014); *Career* dir of new product progs BMW Gp until 2001, dir of global manufacturing Rolls-Royce plc (joined 2001); pro-chllr and memb Cncl Univ of Nottingham 2008–; FREng; *Style—* Dr Hamid Mughal, OBE; ✉ Rolls-Royce, 65 Buckingham Gate, London SW1E 6AT (e-mail hamid.mughal@rolls-royce.com)

MUGHAL, Sajda; OBE (2015); *b* Nairobi, Kenya; *Educ* BA; *Career* community and women's rights activist; md JAN Tst 2007–; Int World of Difference Award 2012, GG2 Leadership Award for Spirit in the Community 2012, highly commended for public service Women of the Future Awards 2012, finalist Young Achiever British Muslim Awards 2013, winner Excellence in the Community Muslim News Awards 2013, finalist Asian Women of Achievement Awards 2014, finalist Asian Achievers Awards 2014, Top 1000 Most Influential Londoners (Campaigners) Evening Standard 2014; *Publications* Consent Matters – Towards effective prevention of forced marriages within the Pakistani community in the UK (2012), Internet Extremism – Working Towards A Community Solution (2013); *Recreations* cinema, fashion, music, reading, travel; *Style—* Ms Sajda Mughal, OBE; ✉ JAN Trust, 8–10 Bedford Road, London N22 7AU (☎ 020 8889 9433, e-mail sajda@jantrust.org, website www.jantrust.org, Twitter @SajdaMughal)

MUIR, Gregor; *Career* fndr Lux Gallery London 1997, curator Tate 2001–, dir Hauser & Wirth 2004–11, exec dir Inst of Contemporary Arts 2011–; *Style—* Gregor Muir, Esq; ✉ Institute of Contemporary Arts, 12 Carlton House Terrace, London SW1Y 5AH

MUIR, Jim; s of John Muir-Long Muir (d 1963), and Constance Jeannie, *née* Gilmour; *b* 3 June 1948; *Educ* Sedbergh, Univ of Cambridge (BA, Wright Prize); *m* 1, 1968, Carleen, *née* Batstone; 2 s (Judd b 1970, Joseph b 1972); m 2, 1986, Joumana, *née* Sayegh; 2 da (Shona b 1986, Diyala b 1992); *Career* ed Frank Cass & Co publishers 1970–74, Beirut corr Inter Press Service (IPS) 1975–78, freelance corr in Beirut for BBC and others 1978–80, freelance corr in Cyprus for BBC, Sunday Times, Daily Telegraph, Christian Science Monitor, National Public Radio (US) and Middle East International 1980–95 (covering Lebanon and Middle East, also covering Afghanistan and Bosnia 1993–94), BBC Middle East corr based Cairo 1995–99, BBC Tehran corr 1999–2004, BBC special corr in Middle East (based Beirut) 2004–; *Recreations* ornithology, squash, travel, hill walking; *Style—* Jim Muir, Esq; ✉ PO Box 24446, Nicosia 1704, Cyprus (e-mail jim.muir@bbc.co.uk)

MUIR, Dr Keith William; s of William John Muir, and Jean Bulloch, *née* Shanks; *b* 8 March 1967, London, Ontario, Canada; *Educ* Univ of Aberdeen (MB ChB, MD), Univ of Glasgow (MSc); *Career* conslt neurologist S Glasgow Univ Hosps NHS Tst 1999–2001; Univ of Glasgow: sr lectr in neurology 2001–, prof of clinical imaging 2009–; memb Assoc of Br Neurologists 2000; MRCP 1992, FRCPGlas 2002; *Style—* Dr Keith Muir; ✉ Institute of Neurological Sciences, Southern General Hospital, Glasgow G51 4TF (☎ 0141 201 1100, fax 0141 201 2510)

MUIR, Dr Richard Ernest; s of Kenneth Richard Muir, of Birstwith, Harrogate, and Edna Violet, *née* Huggall; *b* 18 June 1943; *Educ* Univ of Aberdeen (MA, PhD); *m* 13 Oct 1978, Nina Bina-Kumari, da of Indrajit Rajpal; *Career* lectr in geography Trinity Coll Dublin 1970–71, lectr and sr lectr in geography Cambridge Coll of Art and Technol 1971–80, freelance author and photographer 1981–94, sr lectr in geography UC of Ripon and York St John 1994–2001; co-fndr and ed LANDSCAPES jl 2000–, ed Nat Tst Histories, ed Countryside Cmmn Nat Parks; hon research fell in Geography and Environment Univ of Aberdeen 2001–; Yorks Arts Literary Award 1982–83; hon life memb Yorks Dales Soc 2005; various articles in Observer, Sunday Times, Geographical Magazine, NY Times; memb: FOE, CPRE, Yorks Dales Soc; *Books* Modern Political Geography (1975), Geography Politics and Behaviour (1980), The English Village (1980), Riddles in The British Landscape (1981), The Shell Guide to Reading The Landscape (1981), The Lost Villages of Britain (1982), History From The Air (1983), Visions of The Past (with C Taylor, 1983), The National Trust Guide to Prehistoric and Roman Britain (with H Welfare, 1983), A Traveller's History of Britain and Ireland (1984), The Shell Countryside Book (with E Duffey, 1984), The National Trust Guide to Dark Age and Medieval Britain (1985), The National Trust Guide to Rivers of Britain (with N Muir, 1986), Landscape and Nature Photography (1986), Old Yorkshire (1987), Hedgerows (with N Muir, 1988), The Countryside Encyclopaedia (1988), Fields (with N Muir, 1989), Portraits of the Past (1989), Barleybridge (1990), Castles and Strongholds (1990), The Dales of Yorkshire (1991), The Villages of England (1992), Coastlines (1993), Political Geography: A New Introduction (1997), The Yorkshire Countryside: A Landscape History (1997), Approaches to Landscape (1999), New Reading the Landscapes (1999), Landscape Detective (2001), Landscape Encyclopaedia (2004), Ancient Trees, Living Landscapes (2005), Be Your Own Landscape Detective (2007), How to Read a Village (2007), Woods, Hedgerows and Leafy Lanes (2008), Britain's Lost Villages (2010), Elegy for the Dales (2010); *Recreations* historical and environmental issues relating to British landscape, landscape and wildlife photography; *Style—* Dr Richard Muir; ✉ Lane End Cottage, Bempton Lane, Flamborough, East Yorkshire YO15 1QS

MUIR WOOD, Prof David; s of Sir Alan Marshall Muir Wood, FREng, FRS, and Winifred Leyton, *née* Lanagan; *b* 17 March 1949, Folkestone, Kent; *Educ* Royal GS High Wycombe, Peterhouse Cambridge (MA, PhD); *m* 7 Sept 1978, Helen Rosamond, *née* Piddington; 2 s (Alan Jamie b 8 May 1980, Andrew Peter b 25 May 1982); *Career* William Stone research fell Peterhouse Cambridge 1973–75, Royal Soc research fell Norwegian Geotechnical Inst Oslo 1975, lectr Univ of Cambridge and fell Emmanuel Coll Cambridge 1975–87; Univ of Glasgow: prof of civil engrg 1987–95, head of dept 1991–93, dean of engrg 1993–94; Univ of Bristol: prof of civil engrg 1995–2009, head Dept of Civil Engrg 1997–2002, dean of engrg 2003–07, emeritus prof of civil engrg 2009–; prof of geotechnical engrg Univ of Dundee 2009–14 (emeritus prof 2014–), prof affilierad of geotechnical engrg Chalmers Univ of Technol Gothenburg 2014–; MTS visiting prof of geomechanics Univ of Minnesota 2000, Fndn for Promotion of Industrial Science visiting prof Univ of Tokyo 2003, Japan Soc for the Promotion of Sci visiting prof Nagoya Inst of Technol 2008, professor affilierad of geotechnical engrg Chalmers Univ of Technol Gothenburg Sweden 2014–; visiting prof: Politecnico di Milano 2014, Dresden Technical Univ 2015, Univ of Innsbruck 2016; conslt: Geotechnical Consulting Gp 1983–, Babtie Gp Glasgow 1997–2006 (Royal Soc industry fell 1995–96); chm Scottish Geotechnical Gp 1991–93; hon ed Géotechnique 1991–93, elder Cairns Church of Scotland Milngavie 1993–98, elder Monikie and Newbigging Murroes and Tealing Church of Scotland 2011–; British Geotechnical Soc Prize (with C P Wroth, 1978), 20th Bjerrum lectr Norway 2005, 19th Prague Geotechnical lectr 2011; memb Smeatonian Soc of Civil Engrs 2010; FICE 1992, FREng 1998, FRSE 2012; *Books* Pressuremeter testing: Methods and Interpretation (with R J Mair, *qv*, 1987), Soil behaviour and critical state soil mechanics (1990), Geotechnical Modelling (2004), Piled Foundations in Weak Rock (with J A Gannon, G G T Masterton and W A Wallace, 1999), Soil Mechanics: a one-dimensional introduction (2009), Civil Engineering: a very short introduction (2012); also author of numerous learned articles in professional jls; *Recreations* music, opera, travel; *Style—* Prof David Muir Wood, FREng, FRSE; ✉ Kirklands, Kirkton of Monikie, Broughty Ferry, Angus DD5 3QN (☎ 01382 370685, e-mail d.muirwood@dundee.ac.uk)

MUIRHEAD, Alastair William (Sandy); s of William Calliope Muirhead, OBE (d 1983), and Joan Andrade, *née* Sutherland; *b* 12 September 1953; *Educ* Tonbridge, St John's Coll Oxford (MA); *m* 19 April 1980, Linda Anne, da of Robert Johnson, of Wakefield; 3 da (Joanna b 19 Feb 1983, Nicola b 12 March 1985, Catriona b 16 Aug 1989); *Career* Price Waterhouse 1976–80, Saudi International Bank 1980–84; md: Charterhouse Bank Ltd 1984–96, DLJ Euro Investment Banking Gp; dir D L J Phoenix Private Equity Ltd 1996–2001; ptnr: The Phoenix Partnership 1996–99, Phoenix Equity Ptnrs 2001–; non-exec dir: Amazon Gp Ltd 2008–, Karma Communications Hldgs Ltd 2011–16, Key Retirement Gp 2013–, Bridge Leisure Hldgs 2015–; tstee RHS 2007– (treas 2013–); ACA; *Recreations* fly fishing, gardening, hill walking; *Clubs* London Capital, Hankley Common; *Style—* Sandy Muirhead

MUIRHEAD-ALLWOOD, Sarah Kathryn; formerly William Forster Gillespie Muirhead, name changed by deed poll to Muirhead-Allwood 1956; name changed by statutory declaration 1996; c of Maj W R Muirhead (d 1946), and Joyce, *née* Forster; *b* 4 January 1947; *Educ* Wellington, St Thomas' Hosp Med Sch (BSc, MB BS, LRCP); *m* 1983; 2 s (William Ritchie b 12 Sept 1984, James Miles b 3 July 1986); *Career* St Thomas' Hosp: house surgn 1971–72, SHO 1972–73, anatomy demonstrator 1973; SHO Stoke Mandeville Hosp 1973–74; registrar: UCH 1974–77, Charing Cross Hosp 1977–78; sr registrar 1978–84 (Queen Mary's Hosp Roehampton, Westminster Hosp, Royal Nat Orthopaedic Hosp, UCH); conslt orthopaedic surgn: Whittington Hosp 1984, Royal Nat Orthopaedic Hosp 1991, King Edward VII's Hosp for Offrs; hon sr clinical lectr UCL 1984; hon conslt: St Luke's Hosp for the Clergy 1984, Hosp of St John and St Elizabeth; memb: Br Orthopaedic Assoc 1980, BMA 1983, Br Hip Soc 1989, European Hip Soc 1993; FRCS; *Books* contrib: Joint Replacement – State of the Art (1990), Recent Advances in Orthopaedic Surgery (1991), Grays Anatomy (1995); *Recreations* sailing, golf; *Style—* Miss Sarah Muirhead-Allwood; ✉ The London Hip Unit, 4th Floor, 30 Devonshire Street, London W1G 6PU (☎ 020 7908 3709, fax 020 7636 5758, e-mail londonhip@aol.com, website www.londonhip.com)

MUKHERJEE, His Hon Judge Avik; s of Sourin Mukherjee (d 1984), and Rina, *née* Sodhi (d 2016); *b* 27 February 1967, Bolton; *Educ* Trent Polytechnic (LLB), Inns of Court Sch of lAW; *m* 2002, Rosaline, *née* Kings; 1 s (Barny b 16 Feb 2007); *Career* called to the Bar 1990; recorder 2009, circuit judge (Midland Circuit) 2015–; *Recreations* cinema, music, running; *Style—* His Hon Judge Mukherjee

MUKHERJEE, Neel; *Educ* Jadavpur Univ Calcutta (BA), Univ Coll Oxford (MA), Pembroke Coll Cambridge (PhD), UEA (MA); *Career* writer; *Books* Past Continuous (2008), A Life Apart (2010), The Lives of Others (2014, shortlisted Man Booker Prize 2014, shortlisted Costa Best Novel Award 2015, winner Encore Award 2015); *Style—* Mr Neel Mukherjee

MULDOON, Prof Paul Benedict; s of Patrick Muldoon (d 1985), and Brigid, *née* Regan (d 1974); *b* 20 June 1951; *Educ* St Patrick's Coll Armagh, Queen's Univ Belfast (BA); *Career* prodr Arts Progs (Radio) BBC Northern Ireland (sr prodr 1978–85), TV prodr BBC Northern Ireland 1985–86, Judith E Wilson visiting fell Univ of Cambridge 1986–87, creative writing fell UEA 1987, pt/t teacher Writing Div Sch of the Arts Colombia Univ 1987–88, pt/t teacher Creative Writing Prog Princeton Univ 1987–88, writer in residence 92nd Street 'Y' New York 1988, Roberta Holloway lectr Univ of Calif Berkeley 1989, visiting prof Univ of Massachusetts Amherst 1989–90; Princeton Univ: lectr 1990–95, dir Creative Writing Prog 1993–2002, prof 1995–98, Howard G B Clark prof in the Humanities 1998–; fell Hertford Coll Oxford 1999–2004, prof of poetry Univ of Oxford 1999–2004; memb Aosdána (Irish Acad of Artists); memb: American Acad of Arts and Sciences 2000, American Acad of Arts and Letters 2008; FRSL 1981, *Awards* Eric Gregory Award 1972, Sir Geoffrey Faber Meml Award 1980 and 1991, John Simon Guggenheim Meml Fellowship 1990, shortlisted Aristeion Euro Translation Prize 1994, shortlisted Forward Poetry Prize 1994, T S Eliot Prize 1994, American Acad of Arts and Letters Award for Literature 1996, Pulitzer Prize for Poetry 2003; *Poetry* Knowing My Place (1971), New Weather (1973), Spirit of Dawn (1975), Mules (1977), Names and Addresses (1978), Immram (1980), Why Brownlee Left (1980), Out of Siberia (1982), Quoof (1983), The Wishbone (1984), Selected Poems 1968–83 (1986), Meeting the British (1987), Madoc: A Mystery (1990), Selected Poems 1968–86 (1987 and 1993), Incantata (1994), The Prince of the Quotidian (1994), The Annals of Chile (1994), New Selected Poems 1968–94 (1996), Kerry Slides (1996), Hay (1998), Poems 1968–98 (2001), Moy Sand and Gravel (2002), Horse Latitudes (2006), Maggot (2011); *Drama* Monkeys (TV play, BBC 1989), Shining Brow (opera, 1993), Six Honest Serving Men (play, 1995), Bandanna (opera, 1999); *Childrens* The Last Thesaurus (1995), The O-O's Party (1981 and 1997), The Noctuary of Narcissus Batt (1997); *Edited* The Scrake of Dawn (1979), The Faber Book of Contemporary Irish Poetry (1986), The Essential Byron (1989), The Faber Book of Beasts (1997); *Other Work* To Ireland, I (criticism, 2000); numerous recordings and readings, anthologies and translations and interviews and criticisms; *Style—* Prof Paul Muldoon, FRSL

MULGAN, Dr Geoffrey J (Geoff); CBE (2004); *b* 28 August 1961; *Educ* Univ of Oxford (BA), PCL (PhD); *m* Rowena Young; 1 s, 1 da; *Career* investment exec Greater London Enterprise Bd 1984–86, Harkness fell MIT 1986–88, lectr Poly of Central London and memb Comedia consulting gp 1988–90, policy advsr to Gordon Brown MP 1990–92, fell BFI 1992–93, fndr and dir Demos (independent think-tank) 1993–97, memb PM's Policy Unit 1997–2000, dir Performance and Innovation Unit (PIU) Cabinet Office 2000–02, dir PM's Strategy Unit 2001–04, head of policy PM's Office 2003–04, dir The Young Fndn 2004–11, chief exec Nesta 2011–; advsr to PM of Australia; chair Carnegie Inquiry into the Future of Civil Society, chair Studio Schs Tst 2012–; co-chair Digital, Creative, Science and Technol Working Gp London Enterprise Panel (appointed by the Mayor of London) 2013–; visiting prof: UCL, LSE, Melbourne Univ, Chinese Executive Leadership Acad; sr visiting scholar Harvard Univ 2016–; dir/tstee: Political Quarterly, Work Fndn, Design Cncl, Health Innovation Cncl; *Books* Saturday Night or Sunday Morning (with Ken Worpole, 1987), The Question of Quality (ed, 1990), Communication and Control (1991), The Hollywood of Europe (ed BBC monograph series, 1993), Reconnecting Taxation (with Robin Murray, 1993), Politics in an Antipolitical Age (1994), Connexity (1997), Good and Bad Power (2006), The Art of Public Strategy (2009), The Locust and the Bee (2013); *Style—* Dr Geoff Mulgan, CBE

MULGREW, John; OBE; *Career* previously head teacher, dir of educnl and social servs E Ayrshire Cncl, chair Learning and Teaching Scotland 2006–10 (also chair Remuneration Ctee), pres Assoc of Dir of Educn in Scotland 2000; former memb: Determined to Succeed Gp, Smith Gp; memb: Jt Bd Scottish Arts Cncl and Scottish Screen, Scottish Opera, Arts Tst of Scotland, Project Scotland; *Style—* John Mulgrew, Esq, OBE

MULHALL, HE Daniel; *Career* Irish diplomat; third sec: Headquarters (Economic Div) 1978, Headquarters (Development Cooperation Div) 1979, Embassy of Ireland New Delhi 1980–83, Headquarters (Political Div) 1983–87; first sec: Embassy of Ireland Vienna 1987–89, Headquarters (Economic Div) 1989–90, Permanent Representation of Ireland to the EU

Brussels 1990–94, on secondment to the Forum for Peace and Reconciliation 1994–95, Headquarters (Press Section) 1995; counsellor Headquarters (Press Section), consul gen Consulate Gen of Ireland Edinburgh 1998–2001, ambass to Malaysia, Laos, Thailand and Vietnam 2001–05, asst sec Headquarters (EU Div) 2005–09, ambass to Berlin 2009–13, ambass to the Ct of St James's 2013–; *Style*— HE Daniel Mulhall; ✉ Embassy of Ireland, 17 Grosvenor Place, London SW1X 7HR

MULHOLLAND, Greg; MP; *b* 31 August 1970; *Educ* Univ of York (BA, MA); *Career* account handler sales promotion and events 1997–2002, cncllr (Lib Dem) Headingley 2003–05, MP (Lib Dem) Leeds NW 2005–; *Style*— Greg Mulholland, MP; ✉ House of Commons, London SW1A 0AA (website www.gregmulholland.org)

MULHOLLAND, John; *Educ* Dublin City Univ, Calif State Univ; *Career* media ed The Guardian 1994–98; The Observer: dep ed 1998–2008, ed 2008–; asst ed The Guardian 2015–; *Style*— John Mulholland, Esq; ✉ The Observer, Kings Place, 90 York Way, London N1 9GU

MULHOLLAND, John Peter Patrick; s of John Llewellyn Mulholland (d 1989, eld s of Hon Alfred John Mulholland, himself s of 1 Baron Dunleath), and Helen, *née* Moss (d 1993); *b* 2 September 1929; *Educ* Berkhamsted Sch, SSEES Univ of London (BA), Trinity Coll Dublin (BL), RAC Cirencester (Dip Advanced Farm Mgmnt); *m* 15 Dec 1973, Rosemary Kathleen Vaughan, da of Charles Hawkins, MC, of Cirencester, Glos; 2 s (John Charles b 1975, James Patrick b 1977); *Career* freelance journalist 1955–: Latin American corr News Chronicle 1959–61, prog organiser BBC External Serv 1963–69, numerous articles on fin and tax; called to the Bar: Middle Temple 1969, King's Inns Dublin 1975; in practice: Southampton and London 1969–, Repub of Ireland 1975–; sr lectr in law Royal Agric Coll 1980–88; memb: Chancery Bar Assoc 1970, Lincoln's Inn 1971; MRAC 1980, ACIArb 1992; *Books* Practical Puppetry (1961), Brazil 1968 (1968), Ploughing of Rights of Way (jtly, 1988), The Northern Dilemma (2006); *Recreations* hunting, shooting, equestrian sports; *Style*— John Mulholland, Esq; ✉ 21a Wixs Lane, London SW4 0AL

MULLEE, HE Patrick; *m* Joanna, *née* Johnson; 2 da (Kate, Hannah); *Career* Western European Dept FCO 1974–76, policy planning staff FCO 1985–88, vice consul San Jose 1988–91, 2 sec Bridgetown 1991–95, Eastern Caribbean Desk FCO 1995–97, dep head Personnel Mgmnt Unit FCO 1997–2000, dep head of mission and consul Quito 2000–03, HR mangr Directorate Gen for Defence and Intelligence FCO 2003–07, ambass to Uruguay 2008–12, ambass to Ecuador 2012–; *Recreations* mountains, golf, football; *Clubs* Barbados Wanderers; *Style*— HE Mr Patrick Mullee; ✉ c/o FCO (Quito), King Charles Street, London SW1A 2AH

MULLEN, Larry, Jr; s of Larry Mullen, of Dublin, and Maureen Mullen; *b* 31 October 1961; *Educ* Mount Temple Sch; *Partner* Ann Acheson; *Career* drummer and fndr memb U2 1978– (with Bono, The Edge, and Adam Clayton, *qqv*); first U2 release U23 (EP) 1979; *Albums* Boy 1980, October 1981, War 1983 (entered UK chart at no 1), Under A Blood Red Sky 1983 (live album), The Unforgettable Fire 1984 (entered UK charts at no 1), Wide Awake in America 1985, The Joshua Tree 1987 (entered UK charts at no 1, fastest selling album ever in UK, Album of the Year Grammy Awards 1987), The Joshua Tree Singles 1988, Rattle & Hum 1988 (entered UK charts at no 1), Achtung Baby 1991, Zooropa 1993 (no 1 in 18 countries, Best Alternative Album Grammy Awards 1993), Pop 1997 (no 1), The Best of 1980–1990 1998, All That You Can't Leave Behind 2000 (no 1, Best Rock Album Grammy Awards 2002), The Best of 1990–2000 2002, How To Dismantle An Atomic Bomb 2004 (Album of the Year and Best Rock Album Grammy Awards 2006), U218 Singles 2006, No Line on the Horizon 2009; *Singles* incl: Fire 1981, New Year's Day (first UK Top Ten hit) 1983, Pride (In the Name of Love) 1984, Unforgettable Fire 1985, With or Without You 1987, I Still Haven't Found What I'm Looking For 1987, Where The Streets Have No Name 1987 (Best Video Grammy Awards 1989), Desire (first UK no 1 single) 1988 (Best Rock Performance Grammy Awards 1989), Angel of Harlem 1988, When Love Comes to Town 1989, All I Want Is You 1989, Night & Day (for AIDS benefit LP Red Hot & Blue) 1990, The Fly (UK no 1) 1991, Stay 1993, Discotheque (UK no 1) 1997, Staring at the Sun 1997, Sweetest Thing 1998, Beautiful Day (UK no 1) 2000 (Record of the Year, Song of the Year and Best Rock Performance by a Duo or Group with Vocal Grammy Awards 2001), Stuck in a Moment You Can't Get Out Of 2001 (Best Song by a Pop Duo or Group Grammy Awards 2002), Elevation 2001 (Best Rock Performance by a Duo or Group with Vocal Grammy Awards 2002), Walk On 2001 (Record of the Year Grammy Awards 2002), Electrical Storm 2002, Vertigo (UK no 1) 2004 (Best Rock Performance by a Duo or Group with Vocal, Best Rock Song and Best Short Form Music Video Grammy Awards 2004), Sometimes You Can't Make It On Your Own (UK no 1) 2005 (Song of the Year, Best Rock Duo or Group Vocal and Best Rock Song Grammy Awards 2006), City of Blinding Lights 2005 (Best Rock Song Grammy Awards 2006), All Because of You 2005, the Saints are Coming 2006, Window in the Skies 2007, Get on Your Boots 2009, Magnificent 2009, I'll Go Crazy If I Don't Go Crazy Tonight 2009, Ordinary Love 2013 (Best Original Song – Motion Picture Golden Globe Award 2014); *Film* Rattle & Hum 1988; *Tours* incl: UK, US, Belgium and Holland 1980, UK, US, Ireland and Europe 1981–83, Aust, NZ and Europe 1984, A Conspiracy of Hope (Amnesty International Tour) 1986, Joshua Tree tour 1987, Rattle & Hum tour 1988, Zoo TV tour (played to 5 million people) 1992–93, Popmart Tour 1997–98, Elevation 2001 tour 2001, Vertigo tour 2005; also appeared at: Live Aid 1985 (Best Live Aid Performance Rolling Stone Readers' Poll 1986), Self Aid Dublin, Smile Jamaica (Dominion Theatre, in aid of hurricane disaster relief) 1988, New Year's Eve concert Dublin (broadcast live to Europe and USSR) 1989; performed at venues incl: Wembley Stadium, Madison Square Garden NY, Longest Day Festival Milton Keynes Bowl, Croke Park Dublin, Sun Devil Stadium AZ; *Awards* Best Band Rolling Stone Readers' Poll 1986 (also jt winner Critics' Poll), Band of the Year Rolling Stone Writers' Poll 1984, Best International Act BPI Awards 1989 and 1990, Best Live Act BPI Awards 1993, Best International Group Brit Awards 2001, Outstanding Contribution to the Music Industry Brit Awards 2001, Outstanding Song Collection Ivor Novello Awards 2003, Golden Globe Award (for Hands that Built America) 2003, Oscar nomination (for Hands that Built America) 2003; *Publications* U2 by U2 (2006); *Style*— Larry Mullen, Jr; ✉ c/o Regine Moylett Publicity, 2C Woodstock Studios, Woodstock Grove, London W12 8LE (☎ 020 8749 7999)

MULLEN, Dr Richard; s of Dr Richard W Mullen, of Paterson, NJ, and Eleanor Wild Mullen; *b* 25 May 1945; *Educ* Seton Hall Univ (BA), Fordham Univ (MA), St Edmund Hall Oxford (DPhil); *Career* tutor in history and politics Univ of Oxford and Univ of London 1969–78, literary ed Christian World 1978–79, historical advsr CBS TV 1981, author numerous historical and literary features for BBC Radio 1981–, ed Contemporary Review 1991–2012; edited: The Pamphleteer 1813–28 (29 vols, 1978), Frances Trollope Domestic Manners of the Americans (1984), Malachi's Cove and Other Stories and Essays by Anthony Trollope (1985); BBC documentaries and features incl progs on Queen Victoria, Anthony Trollope, Charles Lamb, John Galsworthy, William Pitt, Lord Palmerston, Scott Fitzgerald, Edward Fitzgerald; Weaver fellowship 1972; naturalised British subject 2006; *Books* Victoria: Portrait of a Queen (with James Munson, 1987), Anthony Trollope: A Victorian in His World (1990, winner Yorkshire Post Book of the Year award 1991), The Sayings of Anthony Trollope (1992), Anthony Trollope: A Pocket Anthology, Birds of Passage: Five Englishwomen in Search of America, The Penguin Companion to Trollope (with James Munson), The Smell of the Continent: The British Discover Europe 1814–1914 (with James Munson); *Recreations* music, walking, reading, golf, Scottish history; *Clubs* Toastmaster Int; *Style*— Dr Richard Mullen; ✉ 2 Butts Road, Horspath, Oxfordshire OX33 1RH (☎ 01865 874286, e-mail richardmullen@contemporaryreview.co.uk)

MULLIGAN, David; *Educ* Rickmansworth Sch, Emmanuel Coll Cambridge (BA); *Career* Ernst and Young 1991–96, Smiths Gp plc 1996–97; Morgan Sindall plc: fin controller 1997–2004, fin dir 2004–; AMCT 2000, FCA 2005 (ACA 1995); *Clubs* MCC (assoc memb); *Style*— David Mulligan, Esq; ✉ Morgan Sindall plc, Kent House, 14–17 Market Place, London W1W 8AJ

MULLIN, Geoffrey Kenneth (Geoff); s of Kenneth Mullin (d 1986), of Garstang, Lancs, and Lily, *née* Butcher (d 1976); *b* 11 September 1942; *Educ* Burnage GS for Boys Manchester, Royal Victoria Coll of Music (Dip); *m* 1, 5 Dec 1970 (m dis 1989), Caroline Moira, da of William Frederick Irving Stephenson (d 1988), of Henley, Oxon; 1 da (Crystal b 1973); m 2, 8 July 1999, Lesley, da of Anthony McCann (d 1979), of Didcot, Oxon; *Career* schoolteacher 1960–61, civil servant 1962–64, professional musician, singer, songwriter with recordings for DECCA and CBS 1964–68; advertising mangr and journalist 1968–70: Record Mirror, Music Week, Billboard; freelance prodr with BBC 1970–73, record prodr for various artists incl Marmalade and the Troggs 1970–73; prodr BBC Radio Two 1973–94: Simon Bates 1973–74, Jack Jackson, Terry Wogan 1975–79, David Hamilton 1979–80, Kenny Everett 1980–83, Sounds of the Sixties (Keith Fordyce) 1983–84, Ken Bruce 1985–86, Your Hundred Best Tunes (Alan Keith) 1987, Anne Robinson, Michael Aspel, The Earl Spencer, Wally Whyton, Maureen Lipman, Sue Cook, Brian Blessed and Anna Raeburn 1988–90, Jimmy Young, Terry Wogan and Glen Campbell's A to Z of Country Music 1991, Brian Hayes Breakfast Show 1992, Country Music Assoc Awards Show 1992, Radio 2 Country Season 1992, Buddy Concert for Nat Music Day 1992, Michael Aspel Xmas Special 1992, Wake Up to Wogan 1993, Elizabeth Power 1993, Beatles Day with George Martin 1993, Sarah Kennedy 1993, Country Style (BBC World Serv) 1993, Michael Aspel Sunday Show 1994 (Gold Sony Radio Award, Best Breakfast Show for Non-Contemporary Music 1994); head of music Melody FM (formerly Melody Radio) 1994–97: VJ Day Music Thames Relay 1995, Ella Fitzgerald Special Tribute (with David Jacobs, CBE); head music policy BBC Radio 2 1997–2001; music radio conslt 2001–; judge: Ivor Novello Awards 1983, Sony Awards 1995, Brit Awards 1998, Song for Europe 1998; memb: Ctee Music and Radio Conf 1995, 1996 and 1997, Radio Acad; *Recreations* badminton, skiing, reading, travel, music, films, theatre, croquet, bowls; *Style*— Geoffrey Mullin, Esq; ✉ 3 Maurice Way, Marlborough, Wiltshire SN8 3LG (☎ 01672 519889, e-mail geoffmullin@btinternet.com)

MULLIN, Roger; MP; *Career* MP (SNP) Kirkcaldy and Cowdenbeath 2015–; *Style*— Roger Mullin, Esq, MP; ✉ House of Commons, London SW1A 0AA (e-mail roger.mullin.mp@parliament.uk)

MULLIN, Prof Tom; s of Joseph Michael Mullin (d 1991), and Elsie, *née* Fynney; *b* 5 September 1949, Broxburn, Lothian; *Educ* Napier Coll Edinburgh, Univ of Edinburgh (PhD); *m* 21 Nov 1970, Sylvia Janet; 1 da (Zoe Elizabeth b 26 April 1971), 1 s (Graham b 7 Sept 1974); *Career* scientific asst then scientific offr Naval Construction Research Establishment 1966–75, postdoctoral research asst Imperial Coll London and Univ of Oxford 1979–82, research fell Clarendon Lab Univ of Oxford 1982–91, research fell Wolfson Coll Oxford 1987–91 (jr research fell 1982–87), univ lectr in physics and fell Linacre Coll Oxford 1991–96, prof of physics Schuster Lab Univ of Manchester 1996–, dir Manchester Centre for Nonlinear Dynamics 2002–; sr fell ESPRC 2002– (advanced fell 1982–87); memb: Mathematics Coll EPSRC, UK Panel Int Union of Theoretical and Applied Mechanics (IUTAM); memb Editorial Bd Proceedings of the Royal Society A; several invited lectures; author of numerous articles; FRSE 2004, fell APS 2005; *Recreations* cycling, fell walking, music; *Style*— Prof Tom Mullin; ✉ Department of Physics and Astronomy, University of Manchester, Manchester M13 9PL (☎ 0161 275 4070, fax 0161 275 4056, e-mail tom.mullin@man.ac.uk)

MULLINER, Stephen Nigel; s of Dr Gerald Norman Mulliner (d 2001), and Kathleen Wilma, *née* Ritchie (d 2012); *b* 4 September 1953; *Educ* Downside, Emmanuel Coll Cambridge (MA, LLB), Inns of Court Sch of Law; *m* 18 Aug 1979, Sarah Lucinda, da of Lt-Col John Arthur Speirs, of Coombe Bissett, Wilts; 2 s (Andrew b 1983, Jonathan b 1985), 2 da (Lucy b 1983, Charlotte b 1989); *Career* called to the Bar 1978; assoc dir Swiss Bank Corporation Investment Banking Ltd 1987–89, gen mangr Tokai International Ltd 1989–91, gen mangr Arbitrage and Derivatives Dept Tokai Capital Markets Ltd 1991–98, exec dir Tokai Derivative Products Ltd 1995–98, md Witherden Financial Services Ltd 1999–, latterly head of performance mgmnt Old Mutual plc 2001–06; non-exec chm JS Real Estate plc (formerly James Smith Estates plc) 1989–2007 (non-exec dir 1988); Assoc Croquet: Br Open Doubles champion 1980, 1981, 1984, 1986, 1988, 1994, 1997, 2000 and 2010, President's Cup winner 1981, 1983, 1986, 1987 and 1992, Br Men's champion 1985 and 1986, World Invitation Singles champion 1986, 1987, 1988 and 2001, Br Open Croquet champion 1988, 1990 and 2000, NZ Doubles champion 1990, Euro Open champion 1993, 1994, 1995, 1998, 1999, 2000, 2003, 2004, 2005, 2008, 2009, 2011 and 2013, 2nd World Championships 1997 and 2008, Australian Doubles champion 2007, Australian Open champion 2009, NZ Open champion 2009, US Nat champion 2011, US Nat Doubles champion 2011, World champion 2016; Golf Croquet: Br Open champion 2000, 2001, 2010, 2011, 2012, 2013 and 2016, Euro Open champion 2007, 2009, 2013 and 2015; vice-pres Croquet Assoc 2002– (chm 1990–92), sec gen World Croquet Fedn 2013– (memb Mgmnt Ctee 2010–13); *Books* The World of Croquet (1987), Play The Game – Croquet (1989); *Recreations* croquet, golf, tennis, real tennis, running; *Style*— Stephen Mulliner, Esq

MULLINS, Andrew; *b* 21 March 1964, London; *Educ* Cranbrook Sch, Univ of Bristol (BSc); *m* Lucinda, *née* Nelson; 2 s (Benjamin b 16 Dec 1995, Charles b 28 Jan 1999); *Career* mktg mangr UK detergents Lever Brothers 1993–95, md UDV Amsterdam, global brand dir gin portfolio and global innovations dir UDV Diageo 1995–2001, mktg dir and gen mangr News Int 2001–07, md Evening Standard 2007–14, md The Independent 2010–14, ceo ESTV 2013–14, ceo Knowledge and Networking Div Informa plc 2014–; non-exec dir: Which? 2011–16, ESL, ESTV and IPL 2014–; *Recreations* golf, cycling, skiing; *Clubs* Band of Brothers; *Style*— Andrew Mullins, Esq; ✉ KNect House, 30–32 Mortimer Street, London W1W 7RE

MULLINS, Anthony Roy (Tony); s of Royston George Mullins, and Evelyn Hilda Mullins; *b* 20 September 1939; *Educ* Loughton Sch, SW Essex Tech Coll, London Sch of Printing; *m* 1, 1964 (m dis 1995), Patricia Janet Stone; 2 s (John b 1969, Benjamin b 1973), 1 da (Nicola b 1971); m 2, Julie Elizabeth, da of Dr and Mrs Peter Hacking; *Career* art asst Sunday Times Magazine 1962–64, art ed The Observer Magazine 1967–76, art dir The Observer Newspaper 1976–95 (Focus Newspaper of the Year Design Award 1995), art dir The Design Desk 1995–; *Recreations* theatre; *Style*— Tony Mullins, FISTD; ✉ 27 Holmes Road, Salisbury, Wiltshire SP1 3DF (e-mail tonym29@btinternet.com)

MULLINS, Charlie; OBE (2016); *b* 28 October 1952, London; *Educ* Tower Bridge Comp (left without qualifications); *Children* Scott, Samm, Lucy, Alice; *Career* formerly self-employed plumber and heating engr, fndr and md Pimlico Plumbers 1979–; patron Women on the Tools (WOTT); *Television* appearances incl: The Secret Millionaire (Channel 4), Show Me Your Money (Channel 4), Young Plumber of the Year (BBC), Posh Plumbers (BBC 1); *Books* Bog-standard Business – How I took the plunge and became The Millionaire Plumber (autobiography, 2015); *Recreations* tennis, boxing; *Style*— Charlie Mullins, Esq, OBE; ✉ c/o Pimlico Plumbers Ltd, Pimlico House, 1 Sail Street, London SE11 6NQ (☎ 07956 555555, e-mail charlie@pimlicoplumbers.com, website www.pimlicoplumbers.com, Twitter @PimlicoPlumbers)

M

MULLINS, Sam; *Educ* Bishop Wordsworth Sch Salisbury, Pembroke Coll Oxford (MA), Univ of Leicester; *Career* curator Market Harborough Museum 1982–87, dir St Alban's Museums 1987–94, dir London Transport Museum 1994–; vice-pres Assoc of Ind Museums; memb Bd: Museums Prize Tst, SS Great Britain, Royal Logistics Corps Museum; FMA, FRSA, FSA; *Books* Talking Shop (1994), Underground (2012); *Recreations* house and garden, music; *Style*— Sam Mullins, Esq; ✉ London Transport Museum, 39 Wellington Street, London WC2E 7BB

MUMFORD, Prof David; *b* 11 June 1937, Three Bridges, W Sussex; *Educ* Harvard Coll (BA), Harvard Univ (PhD); *Career* Harvard Univ: instr and research fell in mathematics 1961–62, asst prof 1962–63, assoc prof 1963–67, prof 1967–77, Higgins prof of mathematics 1977–97, chm Dept of Mathematics 1981–84; prof Div of Applied Mathematics Brown Univ 1996–2007; visiting prof: Univ of Tokyo 1962–63, Tata Inst of Fundamental Research 1967–68 and 1978–79, Inst des Hautes Etudes Scientifiques Paris 1976–77, Inst Henri Poincare Paris 1998; Nuffield prof Univ of Warwick 1970–71, Rothschild prof Isaac Newton Inst Univ of Cambridge 1993; pres Int Mathematical Union 1995–98 (vice-pres 1991–94); Fields medal Int Congress of Mathematics Vancouver 1974, Shaw Prize 2006, Wolf Prize 2008, Nat Medal of Science 2009; Hon DSc: Univ of Warwick 1983, Norwegian Univ of Science and Technol 2000, Rockefeller Univ 2001;hon doctorate Brown Univ 2011; fell Nat Acad of Sciences 1975, hon fell Tata Inst of Fundamental Research 1978, MacArthur Fndn fell 1987–92, foreign memb Accademia Nazionale dei Lincei Rome 1991, hon memb London Mathematical Soc 1995, fell American Philosopical Soc 1997, foreign memb Royal Soc 2008; *Publications* Lectures on Curves on Surfaces (jtly, 1964), Geometric Invariant Theory (1965, 3 edn jtly) 1994), Abelian Varieties (1970, 2 edn 1974), Toroidal Embeddings I (jtly, 1973), Curves and their Jacobians (1975), Smooth Compactification of Locally Symmetric Varieties (jtly, 1975), Algebraic Geometry I: Complex Projective Varieties (1976), Tata Lectures on Theta (jtly, Part I 1982, Part II 1983, Part III 1991), Filtering, Segmentation and Depth (jtly, 1993), Two and Three Dimensional Patterns of the Face (jtly, 1999), Mathematics: Frontiers and Perspectives (contrib, 2000), Indra's Pearls (jtly, 2002), Pattern Theory (jtly, 2010); writer of numerous articles on algebraic geometry and on vision; *Style*— Prof David Mumford; ✉ website www.dam.brown.edu/people/mumford

MUMFORD, Peter Taylor; *s* of John Stanley Mumford, and Doreen, *née* Taylor; *b* 12 December 1946; *Educ* Rutlish GS, Wimbledon Sch of Art, Central Sch of Art; *m* 1, late Mary Davida Beckett; 3 *s* (Daniel b 1972, Luke b 1975, Samuel b 1982); *m* 2 (m dis), Tana Marie Lester; 1 *da* (Théa Rose b 1995); *m* 3, 2009, Alexandra Thompson; *Career* director and lighting designer; extensive work throughout Britain and Europe in dance, drama and opera; chm Assoc of Lighting Designers, memb United Scenic Artists (USA); *Theatre* most recent designs for Opera North incl: Madam Butterfly and Peter Grimes (Met Opera House NY), Vincent In Brixton, The Merchant of Venice, The Rose Tattoo, All's Well That Ends Well, The Hothouse (Nat Theatre), The Seagull (Royal Court and Broadway), A View From The Bridge (Duke of York's Theatre), Fiddler On The Roof and Carousel (Savoy Theatre), The Ring Cycle (also dir, Leeds and Southbank London) 2016; for RNT designs incl: Volpone, Mother Courage, Richard II, Stanley (also Broadway), The Invention of Love; for Birmingham Royal Ballet designs incl: Nutcracker Sweeties, Carmina Burana, Edward II (also Stuttgart Ballet); for RSC designs incl: Learned Ladies, Wallenstein, Ion, Goodnight Children Everywhere, Henry V, Camino Real; other designs incl: The Dolls House (Thelma Holt Prodns and Broadway), The Marriage of Figaro (Sydney Opera House), Mr Wordly Wise, Fearful Symmetries, Two Part Invention (all Royal Ballet), Symphony in C, Simon Boccanegra (both Munich Opera), The School for Wives, The Winter Guest (both Almeida Theatre), The Strip (Royal Court Theatre Upstairs); *Television* credits as dir incl: Swan Lake (1996, Adventures in Motion Pictures for BBC (winner The Crystal Award and Emmy nomination 1997)), Sound on Film (1996, The Music Practice/Andy Sheppard for BBC/ ACE), Dance for the Camera III (BBC/ACE), Natural Selection (BBC Wales), White Bird Featherless (Siobhan Davies Dance Co for BBC), White Man Sleeps (winner Dance Screen Best Studio Adaptation) and Wyoming (both Siobhan Davies Dance Co for Channel Four), Heaven Ablaze in His Breast (for BBC 2 (winner Opera Screen/London Dance and Time Out Performance Award)), Dancehouse (1990, 12 pt series for BBC 2 (Special Jury mention at Dance Screen and Video Dance Grand Prix and NY Film Festival Finalist Award)), 48 Preludes and Fugues (dir 24 short films, lighting dir for remaining 24 films, BBC 2); *Awards* first lighting designer to win Olivier Award for Outstanding Achievement in Dance 1995 for lighting the Royal Ballet's Fearful Symmetries and Siobhan Davies Dance Co's The Glass Blew In, Olivier nomination RNT (Volpone, Richard II and Mother Courage) 1996, Olivier nomination Hamlet and Private Lives (RSC) 2000, winner Irish Times Award for Best Lighting Design for Iphigenia (Abbey Theatre Dublin) 2001, winner Olivier Award for Best Lighting Designer for Bacchai (NT) 2003, Best Lighting Design Helpman Award for King Kong 2013, Best Lighting Design Green Room Award for King Kong 2013, Best Drama Lighting Design Knight of Illumination Award 2011, nominated Best Lighting Design Olivier Award for Ghosts 2014; *Publications* Lighting Dance 1993; *Recreations* fishing; *Style*— Peter Mumford; ✉ e-mail mumf1@mac.com, website www.petermumford.info

MUMMERY; *see also:* Lockhart-Mummery

MUMMERY, Rt Hon Sir John Frank; kt (1989), PC (1996), DL (Kent 2007); *s* of late Frank Stanley Mummery (d 2002), of Bridge, Kent, and Ruth, *née* Coleman (d 2001); *b* 5 September 1938; *Educ* Oakleigh House, Dover Co GS, Pembroke Coll Oxford (MA, BCL); *m* 11 March 1967, Elizabeth Anne Lamond, da of Dr Glyn Lackie (d 1985), of Edinburgh; 1 *da* (Joanna b 1968), 1 *s* (David b 1974); *Career* Nat Serv Border Regt RAEC 1957–59; called to the Bar Gray's Inn 1964 (bencher 1985, treas 2005); counsel attorney gen in charity matters 1977–81, jr treasy counsel Chancery 1981–89, recorder 1989, judge of the High Court of Justice (Chancery Div) 1989–96, a Lord Justice of Appeal 1996–2013; pres: Employment Appeal Tbnl 1993–96, Security Services Tnbl 2000–13, Intelligence Services Tbnl 2000–13, Investigatory Powers Tbnl 2000–13, Cncl of the Inns of Court 2000–03; memb Legal Advsy Cmmn of Gen Synod of C of E 1988–2015, chm Clergy Discipline Cmmn 2004–13, pres Clergy Discipline Tbnl 2004–13, judge Court of Ecclesiastical Causes Reserved 2006–, dep chm Takeover Appeal Bd 2014–, review of Competition Appeal Tribunal Rules 2014–16, memb Ecclesiastical Rules Ctee 2015–; chm of tstees CAB Royal Courts of Justice 2003–13; govr Inns of Court Sch of Law 1996–2001; chm Charity Law Unit Univ of Liverpool; tstee Wye Rural Museum Tst 2007–; hon pres of employment Law Bar Assoc until 2013, hon pres Charity Law Assoc until 2015, hon memb Soc of Legal Scholars; hon fell: Pembroke Coll Oxford 1989, Soc for Advanced Legal Studies, Oxford Intellectual Property Research Centre; Hon LLD: De Montfort Univ, City Univ; Hon DUniv: Canterbury Christ Church Univ, Univ of Derby; *Books* Copinger and Skone James on Copyright (jt ed 13 edn, 1991); *Recreations* walks with family, friends and alone; *Style*— The Rt Hon Sir John Mummery, DL; ✉ Hogarth Chambers, 5 New Square, Lincoln's Inn, London WC2A 3RJ

MUNASINGHE, (Leelananda) Sepala; *s* of Lairis Appu Munasinghe (d 1992), of Kurunegala, Sri Lanka, and Joslyn, *née* Samarasinghe (d 1990); *b* 2 January 1937; *Educ* Trinity Coll Kandy Sri Lanka; *m* 21 May 1964, Dorothea Brunhildis, da of Wilhelm Karger (d 1968), of Ostbevern, Germany; 2 *da* (Karin b 1965, Gitanjali b 1968); *Career* called to the Bar Lincoln's Inn 1963; advocate Supreme Court of Ceylon 1964, attorney at law Supreme Court of Sri Lanka 1972, law reporter Court of Appeal Criminal Div All England Law Reports 1974–83; chm: Social Security Appeals Tbnl 1986–99, Disability

Appeals Tbnl 1991–99 (both UK); asst cmmr Parly Boundary Cmmn for England 1992–95, special adjudicator Immigration Appeals Authy 1995–98; lectr in law Friedrich Ebert Stiftung Colombo Sri Lanka 1966–70, lectr in law Isleworth Poly 1973–84, examiner in law Associated Examination Bd 1983; presenter and broadcaster Sri Lanka Broadcasting Corp 1970–71; govr Waldegrave Sch for Girls 1980–83, memb Birmingham City Cncl Public Inquiry into Handsworth Riots 1986; *Recreations* cooking, reading, travelling; *Clubs* Capri (Colombo); *Style*— Sepala Munasinghe, Esq; ✉ 50 Impasse des Deportes, 34370 Maraussan, Languedoc, France

MUNDAY, Peter James; *s* of Frederick Lewis James Munday (d 1987), of Esher, Surrey, and Lily Charlotte Rebecca, *née* Fowler (d 1998); *b* 31 October 1938; *m* 1 (m dis 1984), Inger Kristina Fagersjo; 1 *da* (Lisa Kristina b 1975); *m* 2, 22 Dec 1984, Linda Ann (Lin), da of Leslie Breckon (d 2006); 2 *da* (Emma Sophie b 1986, Zara Jane b 1989); *Career* Nat Serv RCS 1957–59; admitted slr 1968, NP 1975–2009; sr ptnr Mundays 1976–2007 (ptnr 1968–2007); pres Cicero League of Int Lawyers; former tstee: Princess Alice Hospice Esher, Esher War Meml Property Fund, Bright Futures Tst; Freeman City of London, Liveryman Worshipful Co of Bakers; memb: Law Soc 1968, Notaries Soc 1975; *Recreations* hockey, cricket, football; *Clubs* MCC, Clandon Regis Golf; *Style*— Peter Munday, Esq; ✉ Pinewood Lodge, Warren Lane, Oxshott, Surrey KT22 0ST (✆ 01372 843078, mobile 07710 900359, e-mail pjmunday@hotmail.co.uk, website www.ciceroleague.com)

MUNDELL, Rt Hon David Gordon; PC (2010), MP; *s* of Dorah Mundell; *b* 27 May 1962; *Educ* Lockerbie Acad, Univ of Edinburgh (LLB), Univ of Strathclyde (MBA); *m* (m dis); 2 *s* (Oliver Gordon Watson b 1 Dec 1989, Lewis Kenneth David b 16 Dec 1994); 1 *da* (Eve Margaret b 21 Aug 1991); *Career* sr corp lawyer Biggart Baillie and Gifford Slrs Glasgow 1989–91, gp legal advsr BT Scotland 1991–98, head of national affairs BT Scotland 1998–99; MSP (Cons) Scotland S 1999–2005, MP (Cons) Dumfriesshire, Clydesdale and Tweeddale 2005–, shadow sec of state for Scotland 2006–10, parly under-sec for Scotland 2010–15, sec of state for Scotland 2015–; House of Commons: memb Select Ctee on Scottish Affrs 2005–10; memb: Law Soc of Scotland, Law Soc of England and Wales; *Recreations* family and friends, cycling, travel; *Style*— The Rt Hon David Mundell, MP; ✉ House of Commons, London SW1A 0AA

MUNDY, Prof Anthony Richard (Tony); *s* of Peter Gordon Mundy, of London, and Betty, *née* Hall; *b* 25 April 1948, London; *Educ* Mill Hill Sch, St Mary's Hosp Medical Sch London and Univ of London (MB BS, MS); *m* 20 Sept 1975 (m dis 1992), Marilyn June, da of Edward Ashton, of South Ockendon, Essex; 1 *da* (Emily b 1977), 1 *s* (Harry b 1986); partner, Debra Ann, da of late Owen Hendley; 1 *da* (Katie b 1995); *Career* trg in gen surgery and urology Guys Hosp London, CO and conslt surgn Force Base Hosp Muscat Oman 1977–78, conslt urological surgn Lewisham Hosp 1981–86, sr lectr in urology Inst of Urology and UMDS 1981–91; prof of urology Univ of London at Guy's Hosp and Inst of Urology 1991–, clinical dir of urology and nephrology UCL Hosps 1994–2000, dir Inst of Urology and Nephrology 1996–2008, med dir UCL Hosps 2000–; conslt urological surgn: Guy's Hosp 1981–99, St Peter's Hosps UCL Hosps 1986–; visiting conslt urologist St Luke's Hosp Malta (now Mater Dei Hosp) 1984–; hon conslt urological surgeon Nat Hosp for Neurology and Neurosurgery 1995–; chm Specialist Advsy Ctee in Urology 1996–99, hon civilian conslt urological surgn RN 2000–08; pres Br Assoc of Urological Surgns 2006–08 (vice-pres Cncl 2004–06, pres Cncl 2006–08), memb Cncl RCS 2000–10, memb Exec Ctee Euro Assoc of Urology 1994–2001, memb Exec Ctee Br Jl of Urology, Urological Res, memb Jt Ctee on Higher Surgical Trg 1996–99, memb Bd Euro Urological Scholarship Fndn 1996–99, memb Scientific Ctee Br Urological Fndn 1996–99, fndn memb Soc of Genito-Urinary Reconstructive Surgeons, examiner and memb Intercollegiate Bd FRCS (Urology) 1994–2000; Sir Ernest Finch visiting prof Sheffield 1994, hon prof of medicine Univ of Crete 2009–; Bodo von Garelts lectr Stockholm 1995, C E Alken lectr Dusseldorf 1999, Ian Aird lectr Imperial Coll London 1999, Grey Turner lectr Newcastle 1999, Rovsing lectr Copenhagen 2000, Moynihan lectr RCS and ASGBI 2009; St Peter's Medal Br Assoc of Urological Surgeons 2002, Hunterian Oration RCS 2007; Hon PhD Univ of Crete 2009; convener and fndr memb Urological Research Soc and Assoc of Academic Urologists; hon memb Urological Soc of Australia, Germany, Holland, Malaysia and Singapore and South Africa; FRCS 1975, FRCP 1996 (MRCP 1974), Hon FRACS 2013; *Books* Urodynamics – Principles Practice and Application (1984, 2 edn 1994), Scientific Basis of Urology (1986, 3 edn 2010), Current Operative Surgery-Urology (1988), The Neuropathic Bladder in Childhood (1990), Urodynamic and Reconstructive Surgery of the Lower Urinary tract (1992), Succeeding as a Hospital Doctor (2000, 3 edn 2007), Operative Techniques for the Trainee in Urology (2009); author of 276 pubns on lower urinary tract function and dysfunction and reconstructive urology; *Recreations* food, wine, history; *Style*— Prof Tony Mundy; ✉ UCL Hospitals, 2nd Floor Central, 250 Euston Road, London NW1 2PG (e-mail tony.mundy@uclh.nhs.uk)

MUNDY, Toby; *b* 11 November 1968, London; *Educ* Univ of London (BA, MA); *m*; 2 *c*; *Career* editorial dir Weidenfeld and Nicolson 1997–2000, fndr and ceo Atlantic Books 2000–; *Clubs* Union, Century; *Style*— Toby Mundy, Esq; ✉ Atlantic Books, Ormond House, 26–27 Boswell Street, London WC1N 3JZ (✆ 020 7269 1611, e-mail tobymundy@atlantic-books.co.uk)

MUNIR, Dr (Ashley) Edward; *s* of Hon Sir Mehmed Munir, CBE (d 1957), and Lady Vessime Munir, *née* Ziai (d 1979); *b* 14 February 1934; *Educ* Brentwood, St John's Coll Cambridge (MA), King's Coll London (MPhil, PhD); *m* 6 June 1960, Sureyya, da of Shukri Dormen, of Istanbul, Turkey; 1 *s* (Simon b 24 Oct 1964); *Career* called to the Bar Gray's Inn 1956; crown counsel 1960–64, legal asst Govt Legal Serv 1964, under sec MAFF 1982, resumed practice at the Bar 1993; *Books* Perinatal Rights (1983), Fisheries after Factortame (1991), Mentally Disordered Offenders (1993); *Recreations* walking, playing the double-bass, listening to music; *Clubs* Oxford and Cambridge; *Style*— Dr Edward Munir; ✉ 5 St Andrew's Hill, London EC4V 5BY (✆ 020 7332 5400, fax 020 7489 7847)

MUNKENBECK, Alfred Hedges III; *s* of Alfred Hedges Munkenbeck Jr, of Old Greenwich, CT, and Adelaide Celina, *née* Rickert; *b* 26 March 1947, USA; *Educ* Le Rosey Rolle Switzerland, The Canterbury Sch New Milford CT, Dartmouth Coll Hanover NH (BA), Harvard Univ (MArch); *m* (m dis); 1 *da* (Chloe Adelaide b 25 June 1993), 2 *s* (Alfred Hedges IV b 30 Oct 1995, Finn John b 6 May 1998); *Career* architect; worked with James Stirling Architects on Stuttgart Contemporary Art Museum 1977–80, urban design conslt for Yanbu and MOIT new towns, Umm al Qura Univ and Royal palaces Saudi Arabia 1980–85; sr ptnr Munkenbeck & Ptnrs 1985–; projects incl: office buildings at 45 Gee St EC1, 11 Leadenhall St City of London and 87 Lancaster Rd Notting Hill, Roche Court Art Gallery, Mount Stuart Visitor Centre, Jerwood Space Rehearsal Studios, Grand Rapids Art Museum MI, 43 The Bishops Avenue London, apartment buildings at Gainsborough Studios Hackney and Paddington Basin, Jerwood Space Rehearsal Studios; lectr in architectural design: Univ of Cambridge, Kingston Univ, AA; assessor Civic Trust Awards, chm RIBA E London Awards, chm Royal Borough of Kensington and Chelsea Architects Appraisal Panel, memb RIBA Urbanism and Planning Gp; RIBA 1980; RFAC Building of the Year commendation 1992 and 1999, Kensington and Chelsea Environmental Award 1992, Civic Trust Award 1999, RIBA Stephen Lawrence Award 1999; *Recreations* skiing, sailing, sandcastles; *Clubs* Architecture, Shoreditch House; *Style*— Alfred Munkenbeck, Esq

MUNN, Prof Charles William; OBE (2005); *s* of David Shearer Munn (d 1968), of Glasgow, and Elizabeth McCowan, *née* Renfrew (d 2001); *b* 26 May 1948, Glasgow; *Educ* Queens Park Secdy Sch Glasgow, Univ of Strathclyde (BA), Univ of Glasgow (PhD), Jordanhill

Coll of Educn (CertEd); *m* 1 Sept 1973 (m dis 2009), Andrea, da of David Cuthbertson and Violet Cuthbertson; 1 s (David Stuart b 19 Aug 1977), 1 da (Kirsten Elizabeth b 8 April 1981); m 2, 6 Dec 2013, Rev Frances Jean Ruthven, da of James Ruthven, and Phyllis Jean Ruthven; *Career* clerk and teller various Glasgow branches British Linen Bank 1964–67, student 1967–75, lectr Dept of Finance and Accountancy Glasgow Coll of Technol (now Glasgow Caledonian Univ) 1975–78, lectr then sr lectr Dept of Econ History Univ of Glasgow 1978–88, chief exec Chartered Inst of Bankers in Scotland 1988–2007; pres The European Bank Training Network 2003–05 (chm Professional Standards Ctee 1998–2003), chm Quality Assurance Agency for HE (Scotland) 2003–07 (memb UK Bd 2003–07, chm Audit Ctee 2005–07), exec i/c Ctee of Scottish Clearing Bankers 2003–07, chm Bd Customer Contact Assoc 2006–08, chm Church of Scotland Special Cmmn on the Purpose of Economic Activity 2010–12; memb: Scottish Qualifications Authy 1997–2001, Bd Chartered Insurance Inst 2007–13, Bd European Financial Planning Assoc, Professional Standards Bd Chartered Insurance Inst 2013–; visiting prof Univ of Paisley 2000–06; hon prof: Sch of Accountancy and Fin Univ of Dundee 2002–, Univ of Glasgow 2007–, Univ of Stirling 2007–15; FCIBS 1993; *Books* The Scottish Provincial Banking Companies 1747–1864 (1981), Banking in Scotland (1982), The Clydesdale Bank: The First 150 Years (1988), Ethics, Integrity and Reputation (with N Gallagher, 2001), Airdrie Savings Bank: A History (2010), Investing for Generations (2012); *Recreations* reading, writing, golf; *Clubs* New Golf (St Andrews), Aberdour Golf; *Style*— Prof Charles W Munn, OBE; ✉ 118 Dover Park, Dunfermline, Fife KY11 8HX (e-mail charles.munn@btinternet.com)

MUNN, Prof Robert William; s of William Anderson Munn (d 1989), and Kathleen Maud, *née* Bishop (d 1981); *b* 16 January 1945, Bath, Somerset; *Educ* Huish's GS Taunton, Univ of Bristol (BSc, PhD), Victoria Univ of Manchester (DSc); *m* 24 June 1967, Patricia Lorna, da of Robert William Moyle (d 1965); 1 s (Nicholas b 1971), 1 da (Philippa b 1974); *Career* postdoctorate fell Nat Res Cncl of Canada 1968–70, ICI postdoctoral fell Univ of Edinburgh 1970–71, visiting fell ANU 1982; UMIST (now Univ of Manchester): lectr 1971–80, reader 1980–84, prof of chemical physics 1984–, vice-princ 1987–90, dean 1994–99; vice-pres for teaching and learning Univ of Manchester 2004–07, conslt Finchwood Academic 2008–; co-ordinating ed Jl of Molecular Electronics 1985–91, assoc ed Advanced Materials for Optics and Electronics 1992–2000, numerous pubns in scientific jls; chair Chester Diocesan Advsy Ctee 2009–; FRSC 1987, FInstP 1987, FHEA 2007; *Books* Molecular Electromagnetism (with A Hinchliffe), Magnetism and Optics of Molecular Crystals (with J W Rohleder); *Recreations* singing; *Style*— Prof R W Munn; ✉ e-mail bobmunn@btinternet.com

MUNN, Simon; s of Dave Munn, and Sue, *née* Ash; *b* 31 January 1968, Aylesbury, Bucks; *m* Michele Hooker; 2 s (Luke b 13 July 1988, Henri b 27 June 2007), 1 da (Terri b 10 Oct 1994); *Career* wheelchair basketball player (forward); currently with MK Aces; memb GB squad: Paralympics Barcelona 1992, Paralympics Atlanta 1996 (Silver medal), Paralympics Sydney 2002, Athens 2004 (Bronze medal), Paralympics Beijing 2008 (Bronze medal); memb: UK Sport, GB Wheelchair Basketball Assoc; *Style*— Simon Munn, Esq

MUNRO, Sir Alan Gordon; KCMG (1990, CMG 1984); s of Sir Gordon Munro, KCMG, MC, and Lilian Muriel, *née* Beit; *b* 17 August 1935; *Educ* Wellington, Clare Coll Cambridge (MA); *m* 1962, Rosemary Grania, da of Cdr N A Bacon; 2 s (twins), 2 da; *Career* HM Dip Serv: consul-gen Rio de Janeiro 1974–77, head of East African Dept FCO 1977–78, head of Middle East Dept 1979, head of Personnel Operations Dept 1979–81, dir of ME Def Sales MOD 1981–83, ambass to Algeria 1984–87, dep under sec of state FCO 1987–89, ambass to Saudi Arabia 1989–93; vice-chm Bd British Red Cross 1994–2002, advsr Tate & Lyle plc, non-exec dir Middle East International Ltd, dir Schroder Asseily Ltd 1993–2003; vice-chm Arab-Br C of C; chm: Beit Tst for Central Africa, Red Cross Order of St John Ctee, Saudi-Br Soc, Soc for Algerian Studies; MIPM; *Books* An Arabian Affair (Arab Storm): Politics and Diplomacy Behind the Gulf War (1996 and 2006); *Recreations* Middle East travel, conservation, history, gardens; *Clubs* Travellers; *Style*— Sir Alan Munro, KCMG

MUNRO, Colin Andrew; CMG (2002); s of Capt Frederick Bertram Munro (d 1963), and Jane Eliza, *née* Taylor (d 1998); *b* 24 October 1946; *Educ* George Watson's Coll Edinburgh, Univ of Edinburgh (MA), KCL (MA); *m* 1967, Ehrengard Maria, da of Rudolf Heinrich (d 1981); 2 s (Peter b 25 Dec 1967, Richard b 27 Jan 1978); *Career* asst princ Bd of Inland Revenue 1968–69, third sec FCO 1969–71, third then second sec Bonn 1971–73, second then first sec Kuala Lumpur 1973–77, FCO 1977, private sec to Min of State 1979–80, head of Chancery Bucharest 1981–82, FCO 1983, dep head Western Euro Dept 1985, dep head of mission E Berlin 1987–90, consul-gen Frankfurt 1990, head OSCE Cncl of Europe Dept 1993–97, ambass to Croatia 1997–2000, dep high rep Bosnia and Herzegovina (based in Mostar) 2001, RCDS 2002, UK perm rep to Orgn for Security and Co-operation in Europe (OSCE) 2003–07, int relations conslt 2007–; assoc Ambassador Partnership LLP 2009–; *Publications* contribs to journals of Prince Albert Society, Coburg, Vienna Univ and German Historical Inst London, Collective Security: The OSCE and the European Experience (in Korea and E Asia: The Stony Road to Collective Security, ed Frank Rüdiger and John Swenson-Wright); *Recreations* history, sports especially hockey, cricket, golf, skiing; *Clubs* Reform, Rotary Wien Nord Ost, Royal Selangor (Kuala Lumpur); *Style*— Colin A Munro, Esq, CMG

MUNRO, Prof Colin Roy; s of James Smith Munro (d 1970), and Isabel, *née* Thomson (d 1993); *b* 17 May 1949; *Educ* Aberdeen GS, Univ of Aberdeen (LLB), Open Univ (BA); *m* 10 April 1976, Ruth Elizabeth, da of Dr Thomas Leonard Cheesbrough Pratt; 1 s (Philip Edward b 12 Dec 1980), 1 da (Sally Joanna b 22 Sept 1982); *Career* lectr in law: Univ of Birmingham 1971–72, Univ of Durham 1972–80; reader in law and dean Sch of Law Univ of Essex 1984–85 (sr lectr 1980–84), prof of law Univ of Manchester 1985–90 (dean Faculty of Law 1986–88), prof of constitutional law Univ of Edinburgh 1990–2009 (dean Faculty of Law 1992–94, prof emeritus 2009–); visiting faculty: Univ of Hong Kong 2003–, Inst of Law Jersey 2010–; memb: Scottish Media Lawyers Soc 1995–, Consultative Cncl Br Bd of Film Classification 2000–11, Advtg Advsy Ctee 2005–09; *Books* Thalidomide: The Legal Aftermath (with H Teff, 1976), Television, Censorship and the Law (1979), Studies in Constitutional Law (1987, 2 edn 1999), Sentencing, Judicial Discretion and Training (with M Wasik, 1992), Devolution and the Scotland Bill (with C Himsworth, 1998), The Scotland Act 1998 (with C Himsworth, 1999, 2 edn 2000); *Recreations* sport, film and theatre, beer and skittles; *Style*— Prof Colin Munro; ✉ University of Edinburgh, Old College, South Bridge, Edinburgh EH8 9YL (☎ 0131 650 2008, fax 0131 662 0724, e-mail colin.munro@ed.ac.uk)

MUNRO, Dr Dowling Donald; s of John Munro (d 1980), of Great Missenden, Bucks, and Etta Mansfield, *née* Cottrell (d 1992); *b* 29 May 1931; *Educ* Merchant Taylor's Sch Crosby, Royal Free Hosp Sch of Med London (MD); *m* 1, 7 Sept 1962, Pamela Grace (d 1977); 2 da (Fiona b 1964, Janet b 1966); m 2, 22 March 1980, Isabella Sinclair, da of Alexander Baillie Macdonald (d 1954), of Lanarkshire; 2 step da (Jane Tillotson b 1964, Helen White b 1967); *Career* Capt RAMC Cyprus; US public health res fell in dermatology Western Reserve Univ of Cleveland OH 1964; conslt dermatologist: Bart's 1968–93, Harley Street 1968–2000; civilian conslt dermatologist RN 1981–; asst surgn St John Ambulance Buckinghamshire 1997–2003; pubns in med jls incl British Jl of Dermatology; *Books* Steroids and the Skin (ed, 1976); *Recreations* horticulture, ornithology; *Clubs* RSM; *Style*— Dr Dowling D Munro; ✉ 18 Upper Hollis, Great Missenden, Buckinghamshire HP16 9HP (☎ 01494 864683)

MUNRO, Prof Eileen Margaret; CBE (2012); da of Patrick Higgins (d 1972), and Margaret Higgins (d 1985); *b* 21 October 1950, Cirencester, Glos; *Educ* Univ of Exeter (BA), Univ of Southampton (CQSW), LSE (MSc, PhD); *m* 1974 (m dis 1999), Alexander Munro; 3 da (Penny b 1979, Kate, Alice b 1981 (twins)); *Career* prof of social policy LSE; Hon DLitt Tavistock Inst Univ of E London 2012; *Publications* Child Protection (2007), Effective Child Protection (2008); numerous articles in professional jls; *Style*— Prof Eileen Munro, CBE; ✉ Department of Social Policy, LSE, Houghton Street, London WC2A 2AE

MUNRO, Neil; s of Neil Munro, and Alexina Munro; *b* 18 March 1952, Stornoway, Scotland; *Educ* Nicolson Inst Stornoway, Univ of Edinburgh (MA); *m* 1, 1982 (m dis), Anne; m 2, 2007, Eilish; 2 s; *Career* journalist; West Highland Free Press: reporter 1974, ed 1974–75; TES Scotland: reporter 1975–77, dep ed 1977–2001, ed 2001–11, managing ed 2011–; *Recreations* cycling, walking, reading, swimming; *Style*— Neil Munro, Esq; ✉ Torlundy House, 26 Milton Road East, Edinburgh EH15 2NJ (e-mail neil.munro@tesglobal.com)

MUNRO, Robert Malcolm; s of Malcolm William Munro (d 1975), of Chelmsford, and Sheila Mary, *née* Lamont (d 1983); *b* 16 May 1937; *Educ* Trinity, Mid-Essex Tech Coll, Manchester Business Sch; *m* 25 March 1961, Irene Mavis (Freeman City of London), da of late William David Percy, of Chelmsford; 2 s (Nigel Robert b 1964, Philip Spencer b 1966); *Career* branch mangr Lloyds & Scottish Finance Ltd 1958–68, asst gen mangr ELCO (Hambros Bank) 1968–72, md Williams & Glyn's Leasing Co Ltd 1972–80, assoc dir Nordic Bank Ltd 1980–81, md Nordic Leasing Int Netherlands 1981–83, exec dir The Union Discount Company of London plc 1983–90, banking and leasing conslt Munro Associates 1990–; chm: Int Ctee ELA 1976–81, VRL Publishing Ltd 1993–2003, Field Solutions Ltd 2002–, Park Finance Gp Ltd 2002–06; dep chm Mid Essex Hosp Servs NHS Tst 1992–98; memb: Mgmnt Ctee ELA 1973–90, Cncl LEASEUROPE 1976–81; Freeman City of London; FIoD; *Books* The Leasing Handbook (with D R Soper, 1992); *Recreations* tennis, golf, music, theatre; *Style*— Robert Munro, Esq

MUNRO, Her Hon Judge Sarah Belinda MacLeod; QC (2002); *Career* called to the Bar 1984; asst recorder 1998, recorder 2000, circuit judge (Western Circuit) 2011–; *Style*— Her Hon Judge Munro, QC; ✉ Portsmouth Combined Court Centre, The Courts of Justice, Winston Churchill Avenue, Portsmouth PO1 2EB

MUNT, Tessa; *née* Vasey; da of Paul M Vasey, and Jean Irene McMillan; *b* 16 October 1959; *Educ* Reigate County Sch for Girls, Sutton HS for Girls Surrey; *m* 1992, Martin Munt; 1 step da (Sarahjane b 1986), 1 da (Emma b 1993), 1 s (Harry b 1994); *Career* MP (Lib Dem) Wells 2010–15; *Clubs* Farmers'; *Style*— Ms Tessa Munt; ✉ Kelson House, Kelson Farm, Plud Street, Wedmore, Somerset BS28 4BH (☎ 01934 440639)

MURCH, Fiona Margaret; *see:* Stourton, Fiona Margaret

MURDIN, Prof Paul Geoffrey; OBE (1988); s of Robert Samuel Frederick Rodham Murdin, and Ethel, *née* Chubb; *b* 5 January 1942; *Educ* Trinity Sch of John Whitgift, Wadham Coll Oxford (BA), Univ of Rochester NY (PhD); *m* 8 Aug 1964, Lesley Carol, da of Frederick Milburn; 2 s (Benedict Neil b 1966, Alexander Nicholas b 1970), 1 da (Louisa Jane b 1974); *Career* princ scientific offr Royal Greenwich Observatory 1974–75 (sr res fell 1971–74), princ res scientist Anglo-Australian Observatory 1975–78; Royal Greenwich Observatory: princ scientific offr 1978–81, sr princ scientific offr and head La Palma Ops Dept 1981–87, head Astronomy Dept 1987–91, dep dir 1990–91 and 1993–94; dir and head Royal Observatory Edinburgh 1991–93; head of Astronomy Div Particle Physics and Astronomy Res Cncl 1994–2001, dir Sci and Microgravity Br Nat Space Centre 1994–2001; sr memb Wolfson Coll Cambridge 1996–, sr fell Inst of Astronomy Cambridge 2001–; visiting prof Liverpool John Moores Univ 2002–; pres Euro Astronomical Soc 1994–97; memb: Bd of Tstees Nat Maritime Museum 1990–2001, Int Astronomical Union, Academia Europaea; FRAS (memb Cncl 1994–2001 and 2013–16, vice-pres 2000–01, treas 2001–12, Award for Services to Astronomy 2012), FInstP; *Books* Astronomers Telescope (1962), Radio Waves From Space (1964), New Astronomy (1978), Catalogue of the Universe (1979), Colours of the Stars (1984), End in Fire (1990), Encyclopedia of Astronomy and Astrophysics (2001), Firefly Encyclopedia of Astronomy (2004), Full Meridian of Glory (2008), Secrets of the Universe (2009), De Astronoom en de Gazelles (2011), Mapping the Universe (2011), A Discovery of New Worlds (2012), Are We Being Watched? (2013), Planetary Vistas (2015), Rock Legends (2016); *Style*— Prof Paul Murdin, OBE; ✉ Institute of Astronomy, Madingley Road, Cambridge CB3 0HA (☎ 01223 337548, fax 01223 337523, e-mail paul@murdin.com)

MURDOCH, Andrew James; s of James Clive Leonard Murdoch (d 1981), and Adela Marjorie, *née* Gepp; *b* 16 November 1949; *Educ* Charterhouse, Pembroke Coll Cambridge (MA); *m* 1972, Lynn Hilary, da of Vernon Cecil Thompson; 1 s (Simon Scott b 16 April 1976), 1 da (Hilary Caroline Noel b 17 Dec 1979); *Career* architect; HKPA 1973–78, Eric Lyons Cunningham Partnership 1978–79, Cambridge Design 1979–80, John S Bonnington Partnership 1980–84, Aukett Fitzroy Robinson (formerly The Fitzroy Robinson Partnership then Fitzroy Robinson) 1984– (currently dir); RIBA; *Recreations* painting, golf; *Clubs* Royal Ashdown Forest Golf; *Style*— Andrew Murdoch, Esq

MURDOCH, David; *b* 17 April 1978, Lockerbie, Scotland; *Career* curler; achievements incl: Gold medals European Championships 2003, 2007 and 2008, Silver medal European Championships 2006, Gold medals World Championships 2006 and 2009, Bronze medals European Championships 2005 and 2013, Silver medals World Championships 2005 and 2008, Bronze medals World Championships 2010 and 2013, Silver medal Winter Olympic Games 2014; *Style*— David Murdoch, Esq; ✉ c/o British Curling, The Royal Caledonian Curling Club, Cairnie House, Ingleston, Newbridge, Midlothian EH28 8NB

MURDOCH, Elisabeth; da of Rupert Murdoch, *qv*, and Anna Maria, *née* Torv; *Educ* Vassar Coll Poughkeepsie NY; *Children* 3 da (Anna, Cornelia, Charlotte), 1 s (Samson); *Career* Nine Network Australia: presentation and promotions asst 1990–91, researcher and prodr 1991–93; mangr of programming and promotion Fox TV LA 1993, prog dir KSTU Fox 13 Salt Lake City 1993–94, dir of prog acquisitions FX Cable Network LA 1994–95, pres and ceo EP Communications 1995–96 (Peabody Award for Broadcast Excellence 1995); BSkyB Ltd: general mangr Broadcasting Dept 1996, dir of programming 1996–98, md Sky Networks 1998–2000; chm and chief exec Shine Ltd 2001–; *Style*— Ms Elisabeth Murdoch

MURDOCH, His Hon Gordon Stuart; QC (1995); s of Ian William Murdoch (d 1978), and Margaret Henderson McLaren, *née* Scott (d 1974); *b* 7 June 1947; *Educ* Falkirk HS, Sidney Sussex Coll Cambridge (MA, LLB); *m* 27 Dec 1976, Sally Kay, da of Henry Cummings, of Ludlow, Salop; 2 s (Thomas b 1979, Alexander b 1982); *Career* called to the Bar Inner Temple 1970; recorder of the Crown Court 1995–2002 (asst recorder 1991–95), circuit judge (SE Circuit) 2002–15; *Recreations* music, walking; *Style*— His Hon Gordon Murdoch, QC

MURDOCH, John Derek Walter; s of James Duncan Murdoch, OBE (d 1979), and Elsie Elisabeth, *née* Hardman (d 1989); *b* 1 April 1945; *Educ* Shrewsbury, Magdalen Coll Oxford (BA), KCL (MPhil); *m* 1, 9 Sept 1967 (m dis 1986), Prudence Helen, da of late Brig WR Smijth-Windham, CBE, DSO, of Pitney, Somerset; 1 s (Thomas Duncan b 1970), 2 da (Clarissa Helen b 1972, Rosamond Elsie b 1977); m 2, 9 Nov 1990 (m dis 2007), Susan Barbara, da of late Alan Lambert, of Little Bookham, Surrey; m 3, Allison Browne, da of Louis Freeman, of Fresno, CA; 2 da (Margaret Deborah Browne b 2005, Charlotte Anthea Elizabeth b 2009), 1 s (James Oliver Louis b 2008); *Career* asst keeper Dept of Art City Museum and Art Gallery Birmingham 1969–73; V&A: dep keeper Dept of Paintings 1977–85 (asst keeper 1973–77), keeper dept of prints drawings photographs and paintings 1986–89, asst dir in charge of collections 1989–93; dir Courtauld Inst Galleries 1993–2002, dir Huntington Art Collections Calif 2002–; tstee: The William

M

Morris Gallery Walthamstow 1975–2002 (dep chm 1997–2002), Wordsworth Library and Museum Dove Cottage 1982–2002; *Books* David Cox (1970), Byron (1974), Forty-Two English Watercolours (1977), The English Miniature (1981), Discovery of the Lake District (1984), Painters and The Derby China Works (1987), Seventeenth Century Miniatures in the Collection of the V&A (1997); *Style*— John Murdoch, Esq

MURDOCH, Dr Peter Stevenson; s of John Duncan Murdoch, TD (d 1988), and Zoe Mann, *née* Hannay (d 1987); *b* 16 October 1950; *Educ* Haileybury, Guy's Hosp Med Sch (MB BS); *m* 28 Dec 1974, Sarah, da of Tor Ingemar Lundegard; 2 s (Neil b 1976, John b 1979); *Career* med supt Presbyterian Jt Hosp Uburu Nigeria 1975–81, sr registrar in geriatric med Royal Victoria Hosp Edinburgh 1981–82; conslt physician in geriatric med: Falkirk and Dist Royal Infirmary 1983–2010, Stirling Royal Infirmary 2005–11; NHS Forth Valley: assoc medical dir 2011–13, interim medical dir 2013–14, ret; tstee Dementia Servs Devpt Tst; Hon DUniv Univ of Stirling 2006; FRCPEd 1987, FRCPGlas 1993; *Style*— Dr Peter Murdoch; ✉ 4 Abercromby Place, Stirling, Falkirk FK8 2QP (☎ 01786 473087 or 01324 566000, e-mail murdochps@btinternet.com)

MURDOCH, (Keith) Rupert; AC (1984); only s of Sir Keith Murdoch, sometime chm and md The Herald & Weekly Times Ltd, Melbourne Herald, Sun-News Pictorial, Weekly Times (d 1952), by his w Dame Elisabeth Murdoch, AC, DBE (d 2012); *b* 11 March 1931; *Educ* Geelong GS, Worcester Coll Oxford (MA); *m* 1, 1956 (m dis); 1 da (Prue); m 2, 1967 (m dis 1999), Anna Maria, da of J Torv, of Scotland; 2 s (Lachlan Murdoch, James Murdoch), 1 da (Elisabeth Murdoch, *qv*); m 3, Wendi Deng; 2 da (Grace Helen b 2001, Chloe b 2003); *Career* publisher; chm and ceo News Corporation, chm and pres News America Publishing Inc, chm and ceo 20th Century Fox until 1996 (currently dir); dir: News International, HarperCollins Publishers Ltd 1989–, British Sky Broadcasting plc 1990–2007; UK newspapers owned incl The Sun and The Times; hon fell Worcester Coll Oxford 1982–; *Style*— Rupert Murdoch, AC; ✉ c/o News America Inc, 1211 Avenue of the Americas, New York 10036, USA; Times Newspapers Limited, PO Box 495, Virginia Street, London E1 9XY

MURDOCK, Christopher; s of Dr Charles Rutherford Murdock (d 1968), and Eirene Nolan, *née* Baird (d 2001); *b* 15 August 1946, Belfast; *Educ* Brackenber House Belfast, Portora Royal Sch Enniskillen; *m* 31 Jan 1970, Dorothy Rosemary Richardson; 2 s (Christopher Jeremy b 1973, Antony John b 1975), 1 da (Rosemary Sarah Alexandra b 1980); *Career* joined NHS 1965, asst dist admin offr Armagh and Dungannon Dist 1974–75, dist personnel offr S Belfast Dist 1975–76, asst dist admin offr E Belfast and Castlereagh Dist 1976–84; gp admin Purdysburn Unit of Mgmnt 1984–89, sr mangr Eastern Health and Social Services Bd 1989–98; Fold Housing Assoc: memb Bd 1998–2013, chm Care Services Ctee 1999–2012 (memb 1999–2013), chm Audit Ctee 2001–07, vice-chm Bd 2003–13; dir Fold Housing Tst and Shepherdcare Ltd 1998–2013, non-exec dir Fold Housing Assoc (Ireland) 2002–13, memb Bd Craigowen Housing Assoc 2013–; chief exec (on consultancy basis) The Commandery of Ards in NI of the Most Venerable Order of the Hospital of St John of Jerusalem and St John Ambulance in NI 2001, tstee and dir (training and marketing) The Commandery of Ards in NI of the Most Venerable Order of the Hospital of St John of Jerusalem and St John Ambulance in NI 2005–; commercial mangr: Eventing Ireland N Region 2000–02, Necarne Int Horse Trials 2000–03; MIHM, DipHSM, MCMI; CStJ 2015 (OStJ 2006); *Recreations* photography and video, Donegal (Inishowen), wines; *Clubs* IEC Wine Society, NI Wine and Spirit Inst; *Style*— Christopher Murdock, Esq; ✉ Fairmount, 42 Comber Road, Hillsborough, Co Down BT26 6LW (e-mail c.murdock@btinternet.com); Ballybrack Lodge, Moville, Co Donegal, Ireland

MURE, Kenneth Nisbet; QC (Scot 1989); s of late Robert Mure, and Katherine Mure; *b* 11 April 1947; *Educ* Glasgow HS, Univ of Glasgow (MA, LLB); *Career* admitted to the Scots Bar 1975, called to the English Bar Gray's Inn 1990; lectr in Law Faculty Univ of Glasgow 1971–83; temp sheriff Scotland 1982–99, tbnl judge (tax and social entitlements) 2000–; CTA (Fellow) 1971; *Style*— Kenneth Mure, Esq, QC; ✉ Advocates' Library, Edinburgh EH1 1RF

MURFITT, Her Hon Judge Catriona Anne Campbell; da of Dr Alfred Ian Campbell Murfitt (d 1983), and Anne, *née* Ritchie (d 1998); *b* 16 January 1958; *Educ* St Mary's Sch Ascot, Leicester Poly Sch of Law (BA); *Career* called to the Bar Gray's Inn 1981; in practice South Eastern Circuit 1982–2007, recorder South Eastern and Western Circuit 2000–07 (asst recorder 1998–2000), circuit judge (South Eastern Circuit) 2007–; FRSA; *Recreations* skiing, gardening, art, sacred choral music; *Style*— Her Hon Judge Murfitt; ✉ Chelmsford County Court, Priory Place, New London Road, Chelmsford CM2 0PP

MURISON, Krissi; da of Ian Murison, of Aberdeen, Scotland, and Lynn, *née* Hetherington; *b* 14 October 1981, Oxford; *Educ* The Abbey Sch Reading, Bristol Univ (BA); *m* 31 Oct 2009, Oliver Hodge; *Career* dep ed NME 2007–09 (joined as jr staff writer 2003), music dir Nylon NY 2009, ed NME 2009–12, Sunday Times 2012–; *Style*— Ms Krissi Murison; ✉ The Sunday Times, 3 Thomas More Square, London E98 1XY

MURNAGHAN, Dermot John; s of Vincent Patrick George Murnaghan, of Chipping Norton, Glos, and Wendy, *née* Bush; *b* 26 December 1957; *Educ* Sullivan Upper Sch Holywood Co Down, Univ of Sussex (BA, MA), City Univ (Postgrad Dip Journalism); *m* Maria, da of Patrick Keegan; 3 da (Kitty Niamh b 13 March 1992, Molly Josephine b 1 May 1997, Alice Aoife b 20 Jan 1999), 1 s (Jack Patrick b 15 Feb 2002); *Career* reporter: Coventry Evening Telegraph 1984–85, The Business Programme (Channel 4) 1985–88; corr/presenter Euro Business Channel 1988–89, presenter Channel 4 Daily 1989–90, newscaster ITN 1990–2002, presenter The Big Story (ITV) 1993–2002, presenter Breakfast (BBC 1) 2002–07, host Eggeheads, Celebrity Eggheads and Are You An Egghead? 2003–, presenter Sky News 2008–, presenter Murnaghan (Sky) 2011–; *Documentaries* A Whale of a Mess (Channel 4), Against the Odds (Channel 4); *Recreations* racing, tennis, running, theatre, cycling; *Style*— Dermot Murnaghan, Esq; ✉ KBJ Management, 5 Soho Square, London W1D 3QA (☎ 020 7434 6767, fax 020 7287 1191, e-mail general@kbjmgt.co.uk)

MURPHY, Anna Gabrielle; da of Peter Murphy, and Rosemary, *née* Atkinson; *b* 10 January 1972, Clevedon, Somerset; *Educ* Pembroke Coll Oxford (MA); *Career* Sunday Telegraph: ed Stella Magazine 2005–, exec ed (features) 2007–; *Style*— Ms Anna Murphy; ✉ The Sunday Telegraph, 111 Buckingham Palace Road, London SW1W 0DT

MURPHY, Prof Brian; s of James Murphy (d 1987), of Huddersfield, and Winifred Helen, *née* Ellis (d 1990); *b* 20 May 1940; *Educ* Rotherham GS, Lancaster Univ (MSc), Open Univ (BA); *m* 18 Dec 1982, Vivienne; *Career* rating and auditing asst Rotherham Co Borough 1956–61, accountancy and auditing asst Castleford BC 1961–63, head of Accountancy Section West Riding CC 1963–64, sr accountant Oxford CBC 1964–66, lectr in management accountancy Worcester Tech Coll 1966–69; Univ of Huddersfield (formerly Huddersfield Poly): sr lectr in management accountancy 1969–70, princ lectr 1970–71, head of Accountancy Div 1971–72, head Dept of Accountancy and Fin 1972–87, prof (for life) 1987–; md BWD Rensburg Unit Tst Mangrs Ltd 1988–96; dir: Conscious Visions Ltd 1997–, Conscious Properties Ltd 1999–; former dir Clifton Language Servs Ltd; former dir and co sec: Double M Construction Ltd, Daleside Devpts Ltd; lectr, examiner and conslt 1997–; rotarian 1978–; memb: Inst of Public Finance and Accountancy 1963, Chartered Inst of Cost and Management Accountants 1971; fell Assoc of Certified Accountants 1982; CISI 1992; *Books* Management Accounting (3 edn, 1986); *Recreations* shooting, classic cars, cycling; *Clubs* Penine Rotary 1977–; *Style*— Prof Brian Murphy; ✉ fax 01484 300786

MURPHY, Brian Arthur; s of Arthur Albert Murphy (d 1982), and Constance Margaret, *née* Young (d 2001); *b* 3 May 1951; *Educ* Emanuel Sch London, Keble Coll Oxford (BA); *m* 30 April 1977, Jane (d 2005), da of John Champion Stevenson, of Atherstone, Warks; 1 s (Giles b 10 March 1980), 1 da (Leila b 14 June 1982); *Career* slr, dep head legal servs Allied Lyons plc 1982, counsel Ashurst Morris Crisp 1989; Freeman City of London, Liveryman Worshipful Co of Founders; memb Law Soc 1976; *Clubs* Ski Club of GB; *Style*— Brian Murphy, Esq; ✉ The Old Rectory, Little Brickhill, Buckinghamshire MK17 9NA (☎ 020 7638 1111, fax 020 7638 1112)

MURPHY, Catherine; TD; da of Colm Murnane (d 1996), of Dublin, and Eileen, *née* Byrne; *b* 1 September 1953, Dublin; *Educ* Dominican Convent Ballyfermott, Coll of Commerce Rathmines, Institute of Public Administration Ireland (Dip); *m* 27 Aug 1974, Derek Murphy; 1 s (Alan b 2 Aug 1977), 1 da (Yvonne b 25 March 1980); *Career* town cncllr Leixlip 1988–2005, co cncllr Kildare 1991–2005, TD (Ind) Co Kildare 2005–; *Recreations* researching genealogy, sport (spectator); *Style*— Ms Catherine Murphy, TD; ✉ 49 Main Street, Leixlip, Co Kildare, Ireland (☎ 00 353 1624 3052, fax 00 353 1624 7276, e-mail catherine.murphy@oir.ie); Dáil Éireann, Leinster House, Kildare Street, Dublin 2, Ireland (☎ 00 353 1618 4411, fax 00 353 1618 4507)

MURPHY, Conor; MP; *Educ* St Colman's Coll, Univ of Ulster, Queen's Univ Belfast; *m* Catherine; 1 s, 1 da; *Career* cncllr Newry and Mourne DC 1989–97; memb NI Assembly 1998–2012 (ldr Pty Gp), MP (Sinn Féin) Newry and Armagh 2005– (Parly candidate (Sinn Féin) Newry and Armagh 2001); *Style*— Conor Murphy, Esq, MP; ✉ House of Commons, London SW1A 0AA

MURPHY, Baroness (Life Peer UK 2004), of Aldgate in the City of London; Prof Elaine Murphy; *née* Lawson; da of Roger Lawson (d 1978), of Nottingham, and Nell, *née* Allitt; *b* 16 January 1947; *Educ* West Bridgford GS Nottingham, Univ of Manchester Med Sch (MB ChB, MD), Univ of London (PhD); *m* 1, 1969 (m dis 2001), John Matthew Murphy, s of Daniel Murphy (d 1975), of Ilford, Essex; m 2, 2001, Michael Alfred Robb; *Career* psychiatric trg London Teaching Hosps, subsequently research registrar Bedford Coll London, conslt psychiatrist NE Thames RHA 1981–83, prof of old age psychiatry Univ of London 1983–96; vice-chm Mental Health Act Cmmn 1987–94; chm: City and Hackney Community Servs NHS Tst 1995–98, E London and the City HA 1998–2002, NE London SHA 2002–06; chm Cncl St George's Univ of London 2006–10; crossbench peer House of Lords 2004–; Dr (hc): Univ of Stirling 1993, City Univ 2006, Univ of London 2007; FRCPsych; *Books* After the Asylums (1991), Dementia and Mental Illness in Older People (1986 (as Dementia and Mental Illness in the Old), 2 edn 1993), The Falling Shadow (with Blom-Cooper and Hally, 1995); *Recreations* Italy, Norfolk, social history; *Style*— The Rt Hon the Baroness Murphy; ✉ House of Lords, London SW1A 0PH

MURPHY, Emma Catherine; da of James Murphy, and Rita Murphy; *b* 20 August 1975, Lancaster; *Educ* Queen Elizabeth Sch Kirkby Lonsdale Cumbria, Univ of Central Lancashire (NCTJ pre-entry to journalism); *Partner* Bernard Cole (d 2014); *Career* reporter Blackpool Gazette 1995–98, Granada TV Manchester 1998–2004; ITN: London gen reporter 2004–06, North of England corr 2006–11, Europe corr Brussels 2011–14, London sr corr 2014–; *Awards* RTS Home News Award 2005/06, RTS Int Coverage (jtly, for ITN's coverage of Haiti Earthquake) 2009/10 and (jtly, for ITN's coverage of Ukraine crisis) 2014/15; *Style*— Ms Emma Murphy; ✉ ITV News, 200 Gray's Inn Road, London WC1X 8XZ (Twitter EmmaMurphyITV)

MURPHY, Ian Patrick; QC (1992); s of Patrick Murphy (d 2013), and Irene Grace, *née* Hooper; *b* 1 July 1949; *Educ* St Illtyd's Coll Cardiff, LSE (LLB); *m* 31 Aug 1974, Penelope Gay, da of Gerald Hugh-Smith (d 1965), of Hove, E Sussex; 2 da (Anna b 1982, Charlotte b 1984); *Career* chartering clerk Baltic Exchange 1970–71; called to the Bar Middle Temple 1972 (bencher 2001); recorder of the Crown Court 1990– (asst recorder 1986–90); *Recreations* golf, skiing, rugby and cricket; *Clubs* Royal Porthcawl GC, Cardiff County; *Style*— Ian Murphy, Esq, QC; ✉ Chambers, Farrar's Building, Temple, London EC4Y 7BD (☎ 020 7583 9241)

MURPHY, Rt Hon Jim; PC; *b* 23 August 1967; *Educ* Milnerton HS Cape Town; *m*; 3 c; *Career* pres: NUS Scotland 1992–94, NUS 1994–96 (concurrently dir Endsleigh Insurance Services); special projects mangr Scottish Lab Pty 1996–97; MP (Lab) Eastwood 1997–2015; PPS to Rt Hon Helen Liddell, MP, *qv*, 2001–02, asst Govt whip 2002–03, Lords Cmmr (Govt Whip) 2003–05, Parly sec Cabinet Office 2005–06, min of state Dept for Employment and Work Reform 2006–07, min of state for Europe FCO 2007–08, sec of state for Scotland 2008–10, shadow sec for defence 2010–13, shadow sec of state for int devpt 2013–; memb Public Accounts Select Ctee 1999–2001; chm Lab Friends of Israel 2001–02; *Books* The 10 Football Matches that Changed the World ... And the One that Didn't; *Recreations* sport, cinema, travelling around Scotland; *Style*— The Rt Hon Jim Murphy; ✉ House of Commons, London SW1A 0AA (☎ 020 7219 3000, e-mail jimmurphymp@parliament.uk); constituency ☎ 0141 620 6310

MURPHY, Joe; s of J F Murphy (d 2001), and Iris, *née* Dove, of Plungar, Leics; *b* 20 September 1964, Sleaford, Lincs; *m* 2 Feb 1997, Joy Copley; 1 da (Laura b 2 Sept 1999); *Career* Mail on Sunday: political corr 1991–93, political ed 1993–99; political ed Sunday Telegraph 1999–2002; Evening Standard: Whitehall ed 2002–04, political ed 2004–; *Style*— Joe Murphy, Esq; ✉ The Evening Standard, 2 Derry Street, London W8 5EE

MURPHY, Prof Sir Jon; kt (2014), QPM (2007); *Educ* Univ of Liverpool, Univ of Cambridge (Dip); *Career* Merseyside Police 1975–2001, Asst Chief Constable Nat Crime Squad 2001–04, Dep Chief Constable Merseyside Police 2004–07, ldr Tackling Gangs Action Prog 2007–08, nat co-ordinator for serious and organised crime 2008–10, Chief Constable Merseyside Police 2010–16, ret; prof of advanced policing studies Liverpool John Moores Univ 2016–; *Style*— Prof Sir Jon Murphy, QPM; ✉ LJMU, Redmonds Building, Brownlow Hill, Liverpool L3 5UG (☎ 0151 231 4828, e-mail j.m.murphy@ljmu.ac.uk)

MURPHY, Liz; da of James Murphy (d 1981), and Elizabeth, *née* Mair (d 2007); *b* 14 November 1959; *Educ* Sacred Heart HS Paisley, St Margaret's Secdy Sch Paisley, Napier Coll of Commerce (NCTJ Proficiency Cert, ESSO Student Journalist of the Year Special Prize, NCTJ Year Prize); *m* 19 Sept 1992, Steven Le Comber, s of Peter Le Comber; 2 da (Rachel b 1997, Eleanor b 2000); *Career* reporter and features writer Paisley Daily Express 1978–83; features writer: Evening Express Aberdeen 1983–85, Woman's Own London 1985–87; features ed Best 1988–90 (dep features ed 1987–88), assoc ed Me 1990, dep ed Best 1990–92, ed TV Times 1994–99, freelance showbusiness writer and editorial conslt 1999–2001, project ed Bauer 2001–02, conslt Good Housekeeping 2002, ed Sky The Magazine 2002–04, editorial conslt 2005–08, assoc ed House Beautiful 2008–; Young Journalist of the Year for 1984 Scottish Press Awards 1985; memb BSME 1994; *Recreations* tennis, pilates, writing, sch govr; *Style*— Ms Liz Murphy; ✉ mobile 07889 152808, e-mail lizcmurphy@gmail.com

MURPHY, Michael; s of Francis Murphy (d 1989), and Dorothy Byrne, *née* Kenny (d 1998); *b* 12 February 1954; *Educ* Lourdes Secdy Sch Glasgow, Napier Coll Edinburgh; *m* (m dis); 2 s ((Michael) Stuart b 1984, Lewis Kwong Sang b 1995), 1 da (Kimberley Jane b 1987); *Career* journalist Johnston Newspaper Gp 1972–76, press offr Greater Glasgow Passenger Transport Gp 1976–78, PRO Ind Coope Scotland 1978–93, md PR Consultants Scotland; ceo Shandwick Hong Kong Ltd 1994–98, chief exec Shandwick Asia 1995–98, chief exec Shandwick Europe 1998–2001, dep ceo Shandwick Int 1999–2001, chief exec Hatch-Group 2001–03, ceo Trimedia Int 2004–09, ceo Grayling 2009–13, sr advsr and non-exec dir Michael Murphy And Ltd 2013–15; govr London Met Univ 2014–; hon degree Leeds Met Univ 2011; FIPR, FSA Scot; *Recreations* keeping fit, reading; *Style*— Michael Murphy, Esq; ☎ 07785 116018, e-mail michael@michaelmurphyand.com, website wwwmichaelmurphyand.com, Twitter @MichaelMurphyPR

MURPHY, Michael; MBE (2014); *b* 25 January 1965; *Educ* Harvard Univ Grad Sch of Business Admin; *m*; 2 da; *Career* gen mangr SE London & Kentish Mercury Gp 1984–93, gp advertisement mangr Oxford & County Newspapers 1993–95, md Free Press Gp 1995–96; FT Gp: dir FT UK 1996–98, worldwide commercial dir 1998–99, md FT Business 1999–2002, md FT.com 2000–01, chief operating offr FT 2001–02; ceo Friends Reunited 2003–08; non-exec chm: DLG 2008, Instant Offices 2010–12, Trurating 2014–; chm Quidco.com 2008–12; non-exec dir: Datamonitor plc 2003–07, Multimap 2006–07, Racing Post 2008–, Sussex Place Ventures 2014–; *Recreations* golf, swimming, football; *Style*— Michael Murphy, Esq, MBE; ✉ e-mail michael@murphymail.co.uk

MURPHY, Prof Michael Furber; s of Arthur Furber Murphy (d 1989), and Dr Jean Marjorie Frazer; *b* 2 May 1951; *Educ* Malvern Coll, St Bartholomew's Hosp (MB BS, MD); *m* 1 Sept 1984, Dr (Elizabeth) Sarah Green, da of Prof L L Green, of Eastbury, Berks; 1 s (James Nicholas Furber b 16 March 1993), 1 da (Anna Cordelia Furber b 16 May 1995); *Career* house physician St Bartholomew's Hosp 1974; sr house offr in med: St Leonard's Hosp, Brompton Hosp and Nat Heart Hosp 1975–78; St Bartholomew's Hosp: registrar in haematology 1978–79, sr registrar 1979–84, sr lectr and hon conslt 1985–96; lead conslt and clinical dir Nat Blood Serv Oxford and conslt haematologist John Radcliffe Hosp Oxford 1996–, prof of blood transfusion Univ of Oxford 2004–; sec Br Ctee for Standards in Haematology 1992–95, sec Nat Blood Transfusion Ctee 2002–15; memb Blood Transfusion Task Force Br Ctee for Standards in Haematology 1995–2001; scientific memb Biomedical Excellence for Safer Transfusion Research Collaborative 1999– (chair 2014–), memb Bd American Assoc of Blood Banks 2010– (sec 2014–16); Kenneth Goldsmith award Br Blood Transfusion Soc 1994; FRCP 1993 (MRCP 1976), FRCPath 1994 (MRCPath 1982, memb Cncl 2006–08), FFPath 2015; *Books* Practical Transfusion Medicine (co-ed, 2001, 2005, 2009 and 2013); *Publications* original articles and reviews on clinical aspects of transfusion medicine; *Recreations* surfing, golf, wine tasting; *Style*— Prof Michael Murphy; ✉ National Blood Service, John Radcliffe Hospital, Headington, Oxford OX3 9BQ (☎ 01865 447902, fax 01865 447915, e-mail mike.murphy@nhsbt.nhs.uk)

MURPHY, Shaun Peter; s of Tony Murphy, of Stanwick, Northants, and Jean, *née* Fulham; *b* 10 August 1982, Harlow, Essex; *Educ* Huxlow Sch Irthlingborough, educn at home; *m* 16 July 2005, Clare Louise, *née* Llewellyn; *Career* professional snooker player 1998–; winner: Benson & Hedges Championship 2000, Embassy World Championship 2005, Malta Cup 2007 and 2008; ranked 3 in the world 2007/08; memb: World Snooker Assoc, World Professional Billiards and Snooker Assoc (WPBSA); World Snooker Young Player of the Year 2001, World Snooker Newcomer of the Year 2001; *Recreations* golf, piano, tennis, ten pin bowling, cars, cinema; *Clubs* 147 Snooker (Sheffield), Sitwell Golf; *Style*— Shaun Murphy, Esq; ✉ Champions UK plc, Meadow End, Leake Road, Costock, Loughborough LE12 6XA (☎ 01509 852927, fax 01509 853378, e-mail info@championsukplc.com); c/o Brandon Parker (☎ 07799 474147, e-mail brandon.p@ntlworld.com)

MURPHY, Stuart; s of David Murphy, and Patricia, *née* Downing; *b* 6 November 1971, Leeds; *Educ* St Mary's Sch Menston Ilkley, Clare Coll Cambridge (MA); *m* (m dis 2006); 2 s (Maximilian Raphael b 4 Sept 2000, Joshua David Murphy b 4 March 2002); *Career* early positions as researcher then asst prodr BBC 1995, series prodr MTV 1996, prodr The Big Breakfast (Planet 24) 1996, strategic devpt mangr Ind Commissioning Gp BBC 1997, broadcast devpt exec BBC 1997, channel ed UK Play 1997–99, head of programming BBC Choice 1999–2001, controller BBC Choice 2001–03, controller BBC Three 2003–05 (also memb BBC TV Mgmnt Bd), creative dir RDF Media 2006, creative dir Twofour Broadcast 2006–08, Sky 1 2009–10, dir of commissioning Sky Entertainment 2010–12, launched Sky Atlantic 2011–, dir of entertainment channels Sky 2012–; memb Bd Nickelodeon 2013, memb Bd Jaunt (San Francisco) 2014; *Recreations* boxing, travel, my kids, gardening, theme parks; *Clubs* Ivy; *Style*— Stuart Murphy, Esq; ✉ Sky TV, Grant Way, Isleworth, Middlesex TW7 5QD

MURPHY OF TORFAEN, Baron (Life Peer UK 2015) of Torfaen, of Abersychan in the County of Gwent; Rt Hon Paul Peter Murphy; PC (1999); s of Ronald Murphy, and Marjorie Murphy (d 1984); *b* 25 November 1948; *Educ* St Francis RC Sch Abersychan, W Monmouth Sch Pontypool, Oriel Coll Oxford (MA); *Career* lectr in history and politics Ebbw Vale Coll of Further Educn 1971–87; memb Torfaen Borough 1973–87, MP (Lab) Torfaen 1987–2015; oppn spokesman on: Welsh affrs 1988–94, NI 1994–95, foreign affrs 1995, defence 1995–97; min of state NI Office 1997–99, sec of state for Wales 1999–2002 and 2008–09, sec of state for NI 2002–2005, min of state Digital Inclusion 2008–09; chair: Intelligence and Security Ctee 2005–08, Cross-Departmental Ctee on IT and Info Security 2008, Ctee on Local Govt and Regions 2008; hon fell Oriel Coll Oxford 2000, hon fell Glyndwr Univ; Hon DUniv Univ of S Wales 2014; *Recreations* classical music, cooking; *Style*— The Rt Hon the Lord Murphy of Torfaen; ✉ House of Commons, London SW1A 0AA

MURPHY-O'CONNOR, His Eminence Cardinal Cormac; s of Dr George Patrick Murphy-O'Connor (d 1960), and Ellen Theresa, *née* Cuddigan (d 1971); *b* 24 August 1932; *Educ* Prior Park Coll Bath, The Ven English Coll Rome, Gregorian Univ Rome (PhL, STL); *Career* ordained to RC Priesthood 1956; asst priest: Corpus Christi Parish Portsmouth 1956–63, Sacred Heart Parish Fareham 1963–66; private sec and chaplain to Bishop of Portsmouth 1966–70, parish priest Parish of Immaculate Conception Southampton 1970–71, rector Venerable Eng Coll Rome 1971–77, bishop of Arundel and Brighton 1977–2000, archbishop of Westminster 2000–09 (archbishop emeritus 2009–); chm: Bishops' Ctee for Europe 1978–83, Ctee for Christian Unity 1983–99, Dept for Mission & Unity of Bishops' Conf of England and Wales 1993–2000; jt chm of Anglo-Roman Catholic Int Cmmn (ARCIC-II) 1983–2000; pres: Catholic Bishops' Conf of England and Wales 2000–09, Congregation for Bishops 2010–13, Congregation for Evangelisation of Peoples 2010–13; Hon DD Lambeth 1999; *Books* The Family of the Church (1984), At the Heart of the World (2004), The Human Face of God (2004), Faith in Europe? (ed, 2005), Memoirs – An English Spring (2015); *Recreations* music, sport; *Style*— His Eminence the Cardinal Archbishop Emeritus of Westminster; ✉ St Edward's, 7 Duke Avenue, Chiswick, London W4 2AA (fax 020 8742 1145, e-mail cardinalmoc@rcdow.org.uk)

MURRAY, Andrew; *m* Anna Murray; *Career* political corr Morning Star 1978–84, dir of communications TGWU 1994–98 and 2003–10, currently COS Unite; chair Stop the War Coalition until 2011 (dep pres 2011–), memb Gen Cncl TUC 2011–; *Books* Flashpoint: World War III (1997), Off the Rails (2001), Stop the War (2005), History of the TGWU (2008); *Style*— Andrew Murray, Esq; ✉ Unite, Unite House, 128 Theobald's Road, Holborn, London WC1X 8TN

MURRAY, Andrew (Andy); OBE (2013); s of William Murray, and Judy, *née* Erskine; *b* 15 May 1987, Glasgow; *Educ* Dunblane HS, Schiller Int Sch Barcelona; *m* 11 April 2015, Kim Sears; *Career* tennis player; joined ATP tour 2004; tournament wins: SAP Open San José 2006 and 2007, St Petersberg Open 2007 and 2008, Doha 2008 and 2009, Marseille 2008, Cincinnati Masters 2008, Madrid Masters 2008, Miami Masters 2009, Canada Masters 2009, Aegon Championships 2009, Rotterdam 2009, Valencia 2009, US Open 2012, Wimbledon 2013, Wimbledon 2016; Gold medal Olympic Games 2012 and 2016; finalist: Bangkok 2005, Washington 2006, Doha 2007, Metz 2007, US Open 2008, Indian Wells 2009, Australian Open 2010; ranked 3 in the world 2015; doubles wins: Valencia Open 500 2010, Rakuten Japan Open Tennis Championships 2011 (both with bro, Jamie Murray); Silver medal (mixed doubles, with Laura Robson) Olympic Games 2012; BBC Young Sports Personality of the Year 2004, BBC Scotland Sports Personality of the Year 2005, BBC Sports Personality of the Year 2013; *Style*— Mr Andy Murray, OBE; ✉ c/o 19 Entertainment, Unit 33, Ransomes Dock Business Centre, 35–37 Parkgate Road, London SW11 4NP (☎ 020 7801 1919, e-mail sharon.ely@19.co.uk, website www.19.co.uk and www.andymurray.com)

MURRAY, Dr Andrew Christopher; s of Andrew Murray (d 1984), and Bridget, *née* Geraghty; *b* 9 June 1955; *Educ* Bishop Ullathorne Comp Sch, Queens' Coll Cambridge (BA), Univ of Warwick (PGCE), Boston Univ (MA), Univ of Manchester (PhD); *m* July 1984, Valerie, *née* Clark (d 2005); 2 s (Edward b 1987, Richard b 1994), 2 da (Katherine b 1989, Elizabeth b 1991); *Career* lectr in history Univ of Botswana 1984–88; Br Cncl: asst dir Malawi 1988–92, asst dir Romania 1992–95, asst dir Poland 1995–99, dir Br Cncl Seminars 1999–2004, mangr Knowledge and Learning Prog 2004–05; UK Change Prog: mangr 2005–09, regnl head Europe and Americas overseas ops 2009–; FRSA 2001; *Books* A Historical Dictionary of Botswana (1989), People's Rights: The Case of Bayei Separatism (1990); *Recreations* tennis, squash, supporting Coventry City FC; *Style*— Dr Andrew Murray; ✉ British Council, 10 Spring Gardens, London SW1A 2BN (☎ 020 7389 4413, e-mail andrew.murray@britishcouncil.org)

MURRAY, His Hon Judge Anil Peter; s of Thomas Edward Murray (d 2016), and Margaret, *née* Snowball; *b* 25 November 1966, Sunderland; *Educ* Univ of Hull (LLB); *m* 22 Dec 1991, Elizabeth, *née* Tansey; 2 da (Kathryn, Josephine b 22 Dec 1991 (twins)); *Career* called to the Bar 1989; recorder 2012, circuit judge (Northern Circuit) 2015–; *Clubs* Whitby Yacht; *Style*— His Hon Judge Murray

MURRAY, Braham Sydney; OBE (2010); s of Sam Goldstein, and Gertie Murray; *b* 12 February 1943, London; *Educ* Clifton, UC Oxford; *m* (m dis) Johanna Bryant; 2 s (Jake, Joe); *Career* artistic dir Century Theatre 1965–67, founding dir '69 Theatre Co 1968–75, founding artistic dir Royal Exchange Theatre Co 1975–2012; memb NW Arts Bd 1994–2000, Hon BA Manchester Met Univ 1996, Hon BA Univ of Central Lancs 2008; *Theatre* Royal Exchange Theatre Co: The Dybbuk, Riddley Walker, The Nerd, Leaping Ginger, Andy Capp, The Three Musketeers, Court in the Act!, Your Home in the West (Mobil Prize), The Odd Women, The Brothers Karamazov, Hamlet, Maybe (with Vanessa Redgrave, *qv*), Smoke, The Count of Monte Cristo, Unidentified Human Remains and the True Nature of Love, Private Lives, Miss Julie, The Candidate, Peer Gynt, Bats (co-writer), Snap-Shots, The Ghost Train Tattoo, Snake in Fridge (world premiere), Loot, Hedda Gabler, Time and the Conways, Othello, Cold Meat Party, Hobson's Choice, The Happiest Days of Your Life, Antony and Cleopatra, The Glass Menagerie; '69 Theatre Co (all prodns transferred to London): Charley's Aunt, Mary Rose, Endgame, Erb, Catch My Soul, She Stoops to Conquer; West End: The Good Companions (with Judi Dench, *qv*, and John Mills), The Black Mikado, The Cabinet Minister, Lady Windermere's Fan; other prodns incl: Hang Down Your Head and Die (Oxford, West End and Broadway), Uncle Vanya (Circle in the Square Theatre NY) 1995, Resurrection (world premiere Houston Grand Opera, Boston and Calif) 1999, Talking Heads (Aust tour) 2007, Skellig (world premiere The Sage) 2008, The Glass Menagerie (with Brenda Blethyn, OBE, *qv*) 2008, True Love Lies (world premiere) 2009, Haunted (world premiere, NY and Sydney, with Brenda Blethyn) 2009, The Bacchae 2010.5@50 (world premiere) 2011, Wonderful Town (in collaboration with the Halle Orchestr), Kill Me Now (Park Theatre) 2015, The Tempest (Singapore Repertory Theatre) 2015; *Books* The Worst It Can Be Is A Disaster (autobiography), How To Direct A Play (2011); *Recreations* food, wine, reading, Spurs; *Style*— Braham Murray, Esq, OBE; ✉ agent Penny Wesson (☎ 020 7722 6607, e-mail penny@pennywesson.com)

MURRAY, Colin Keith; s of Brig George Murray, CBE, DSO, MC (d 1983), and Betty, *née* Wheeler (d 1982); *b* 18 June 1932; *Educ* Wellington; *m* 1 Feb 1964, Precelly, da of Col David Davies-Scourfield, MC (d 1998); 1 s, 2 da; *Career* Seaforth Highlanders and 1 Bn King's African Rifles 1950–52, TA 1952–64; CT Bowring & Co Ltd 1953–63, R J Kiln & Co Ltd 1963–95 (chm 1985–95); memb Cncl Lloyd's 1983–86 and 1989–92 (dep chm 1989–90), chm Lloyd's Volunteer Forces Fund 1990–95; dir Kiln Capital plc 1994–98, tstee Equitas Holdings Ltd 1996–2001; pres Youth Clubs Hants and IOW 1996–2006, chm Trust in Children 1994–2004, chm Friends of Music in Winchester 2000–11, dir St Joseph's Soc 1985–2006, chm Cuidich'n Righ Dinner Club 2005–09, govr St John the Baptist Primary Sch Andover 2001–11; Lt City of London 1993; High Sheriff Hants 2002–03; Liveryman Worshipful Co of Insurers; *Recreations* music, bridge, gardening, fishing; *Clubs* Boodle's, Flyfishers', The City; *Style*— Colin Murray, Esq; ✉ The Long House, Hurstbourne Priors, Whitchurch, Hampshire RG28 7SB (☎ 01256 892606)

M

MURRAY, Dale; CBE (2013); *b* New Zealand; *Career* technol entrepreneur and angel investor; BellSouth NZ (now Vodafone NZ), co-fndr Omega Logic 1999–2005; advsr Bd: Seedrs, Centre for Entrepreneurs; non-exec dir: Sussex Place Ventures, BIS; Br Angel Investor of the Year UK Business Angels Assoc 2011; memb NZ Inst of Chartered Accountants 2013, FCA; *Style*— Ms Dale Murray, CBE; ✉ website www.dalemurray.net, Twitter @dalejmurray

MURRAY, Sir David Edward; kt (2007); s of David Ian Murray (d 1975), and Roma Murray (d 2013); *b* 14 October 1951; *Educ* Fettes, Broughton HS; *m* 1, 22 July 1972, Louise Violet (decd); 2 s (David Douglas b 1973, Keith Andrew b 1975); m 2, 3 June 2011, Kae Alexandra Tinto; *Career* fndr and chm Murray International Holdings and subsidiaries 1976–2015, chm Glasgow Rangers Football Club plc 1988–2002 and 2004–09 (hon chm 2002–04), chm Murray Capital Ltd 2012–; estab The Murray Fndn 1996 (Queen's Award for Voluntary Serv 2006); chm UK 2000 Scotland 1987–88, govr Clifton Hall Sch 1987–89; commercial devpt conslt Scottish Rugby Union 1997–2006; Hon Dr of Business Heriot-Watt Univ 1986, Hon DUniv Edinburgh 2008; Chevaliers Du Tastevin 2006; *Recreations* collecting and producing wine, watching sport; *Style*— Sir David Murray; ✉ 26 Charlotte Square, Edinburgh EH2 4ET (☎ 0131 243 2100, fax 0131 243 2101)

MURRAY, Diana Mary; *née* Collyer; da of Keith Gordon George Collyer, of Sale Green, Worcs, and (Joyce) Mary, *née* Cottrell; *b* 14 September 1952, Birmingham; *Educ* King Edward VI Camphill Sch for Girls Kings Heath, Univ of Cambridge (MA); *m* 14 Feb 1987, Robin Francis Murray; 2 da (Katharine Mary b 4 June 1988, Clare Frances b 6 Oct 1989); *Career* Royal Cmmn on the Ancient and Historical Monuments of Scot: res asst 1976–83, head Nat Monuments Record of Scot (NMRS) Recording Section 1983–90, curator Archaeology Record 1990–95, curator depute NMRS 1995–2004, sec (chief exec) 2004–15; sr exec Historic Environment Scotland 2015–; chm Inst of Field Archaeologists 1995–96 (sec Scot Gp 1985–92, hon sec 1993–95); memb: Cncl Soc of Antiquaries of Scot 1984–87, Exec Ctee Cncl for Scot Archaeology 1993–96, Cncl Nat Tst for Scot 2003–08 (non-exec dir 2004 and 2008–10), Cncl Soc of Antiquaries of London 2004–07, Bd Nat Tst for Scotland 2008–13; tstee: Scot Waterways Tst 2012–, Scot Seabird Centre 2013–, Royal botanic gdns of Edinburgh 2013–, Scot int Educn tst 2015–; ldr E Lothian Young Archaeologists Club 1998–2001; memb Dirleton Sch Bd 1995–96 and 2001–03, chm Dirleton Village Assoc 1996–2001; JP E Lothian 2000–07; FSA Scot 1977, MIFA 1984, FSA 1986, MInstD 2012, FRSE, FSGS; specialist pubns on archaeology and heritage info data mgmnt; *Recreations* choral singing, gardening; *Clubs* Scotch Malt Whisky Society (SMWS); *Style*— Mrs Diana Murray; ✉ The Rowans, 15 Manse Road, Dirleton, East Lothian EH39 5EL (e-mail diana.murray@rowanberry.co.uk); Royal Commission on the Ancient and Historical Monuments of Scotland, John Sinclair House, 16 Bernard Terrace, Edinburgh EH8 9NX (☎ 0131 662 1456, fax 0131 662 1477, e-mail diana.murray@rcahms.gov.uk)

MURRAY, Dr Elaine Kildare; MSP; da of Kenneth Gordon Murray, of Edinburgh, and Patricia Murray, *née* Kildare; *b* 22 December 1954; *Educ* Mary Erskine Sch, Univ of

Edinburgh (BSc), Univ of Cambridge (PhD); *m* 1986, Jeff Leaver, s of John Leaver (decd); 2 s (Alex b 6 Jan 1986, Richard b 20 Dec 1989), 1 da (Elspeth b 4 Jan 1988); *Career* postdoctoral res fell: Cavendish Lab Cambridge 1979–82, Royal Free Hosp London 1982–83; sr sci offr Inst of Food Res Reading 1984–87; asst to Alex Smith MEP 1989–93, cncllr Strathclyde Regnl Cncl 1994–96, cncllr South Ayrshire Cncl 1995–99 (convenor Educnl Services Ctee); MSP (Lab): Dumfries 1999–2011, Dumfriesshire 2011–; shadow min for enterprise 2007–08, Lab spokesperson on the environment 2008–11, shadow min for housing and transport 2011–; vice-convenor Finance Ctee 2007–08 and 2011–12, convenor Cross Pty Gp on Civil Nuclear Energy 2007–11, convenor Cross Pty Gp on Sci and Technol 2007–, vice-convenor Cross Pty Gp on Animal Welfare 2007–12, memb Rural Affrs and Environment Ctee 2008–11, co-convenor Cross Pty Gp on Life Scis 2008–11, memb Infrastructure and Capital Investment Ctee 2012–; assoc lectr Open Univ Scotland 1992–99; *Recreations* reading, cooking, gardening, music; *Style*— Dr Elaine Murray, MSP; ✉ The Scottish Parliament, Holyrood, Edinburgh EH99 1SP (☎ 0131 348 5826, fax 0131 348 5834, mobile 07919 392049, e-mail elaine.murray.msp@scottish.parliament.uk); 5 Friar's Vennel, Dumfries DG1 2RQ (☎ 01387 279205, fax 01387 279206)

MURRAY, (Ian) Gordon; s of William Gordon Murray (d 1984), and Rosemary Morrison, *née* Irvine; *b* 18 June 1946; *Educ* Glenwood HS Durban, Natal Tech Coll (Dip Mech Engrg, Arthur May prize); *m* 4 June 1970, Stella Lynne, da of Victor Gane; 1 s (Christopher Dylan b 23 Jan 1978); *Career* motorsport designer; design draughtsman South Africa 1964–69, moved to England 1969; Brabham: design draughtsman 1970–73, chief designer 1973–74, tech dir 1974–86; tech dir: McLaren International 1986–90, McLaren Cars Ltd 1990–2004 (also dir TAG McLaren Gp 1990–2004); ceo and technical dir Gordon Murray Design Ltd 2007–; achievements as designer: 51 grand prix wins, 4 World Drivers' Formula One Championships, 2 World Constructors' Formula One Championships, McLaren F1 (fastest road car in the world), McLaren F1 GTR (winner Le Mans 1995, Global Endurance GT series, European Endurance GT series, GT World Championship 1996, All Japan GT Championship 1996, GT Class 24 hr Le Mans 1997); winner various awards for motorsport design; memb: South African Inst of Mech Engrs, Inst of Engrg Designers; hon prof Durban Inst of Technol; *Recreations* motor sport, music, art; *Style*— Gordon Murray, Esq; ✉ Gordon Murray Design Limited, Wharfside, Broadford Park, Shalford GU4 8EP

MURRAY, Ian; MP; s of James Brownlie Murray, and Lena Christina Buchan Skeldon; *b* 10 August 1976, Edinburgh; *Educ* Univ of Edinburgh; *Career* MP (Lab) Edinburgh S 2010–, Parly private sec to Shadow Sec of State for Culture, Media and Sport 2010–11, shadow min for employment relations, consumer and postal affrs 2011–12, shadow min for trade and investment 2012–15, shadow sec of state for Scotland 2015; *Recreations* supporter Heart of Midlothian FC; *Style*— Mr Ian Murray, MP; ✉ Constituency Office: 31 Minto Street, Edinburgh EH9 2BT; House of Commons, London SW1A 0AA

MURRAY, James David George; s of George Murray, and Susan, *née* Tullis; *b* 11 February 1970, Newcastle upon Tyne; *Educ* Shiplake Coll Henley-on-Thames, Cambridge Business Studies Coll; *m* 7 Oct 2006, Natasha, *née* Forrest-Hay; 1 s (George Anthony James b 13 Nov 2007), 2 da (Bronte Katherine Grace b 9 July 2009, Ottilie Beatrice Natasha b 22 Feb 2012); *Career* trainee engr Lamont Telecommunications 1989–90, trainee project mgmnt/sales Rapid Telecom 1990–92, Lynton Europe Ltd 1992–94; Alternative Networks plc: co-fndr and ceo 1994–2013, exec chm 2013–; Young Entrepreneur of the Year regnl and nat winner 2005; *Recreations* cars, supporting Newcastle United FC; *Style*— James Murray, Esq; ✉ Alternative Networks plc, Chatfield Court, 56 Chatfield Road, London SW11 3UL (☎ 0870 190 7006, fax 0870 190 7602, e-mail jmurray@alternativenetworks.com)

MURRAY, Janice; *née* Blair; da of Harold Blair, and Irene Nancy Robertson; *b* 15 August 1957, Newcastle upon Tyne; *Educ* Univ of Warwick (BA), Univ of Leicester (PGCert); *m* 1, 1982, late Terence Christopher Murray; 2 s (Thomas Michael b 1986, Stephen Patrick b 1988); m 2, 2004, David John Stockdale; *Career* dep head Nat Railway Museum 2002–08, ceo Royal Armouries 2008–10, DG Nat Army Museum 2010–; memb Ctee Br Friends of Normandy, memb Bd Icomam; AMA, FRSA; *Books* The Miles Tae Dundee (1991), Glorious Victory (1997), Dundee at Work (2000); *Recreations* hardy plants, church architecture, 20th century glass; *Clubs* Sloane, Army & Navy; *Style*— Mrs Janice Murray; ✉ National Army Museum, Royal Hospital Road, Chelsea, London SW3 4HT (☎ 020 7881 2402)

MURRAY, Dame Jennifer Susan (Jenni); DBE (2011, OBE 1999); da of Alvin Bailey, of Barnsley, S Yorks, and Winifred, *née* Jones; *b* 12 May 1950; *Educ* Barnsley Girls' HS, Univ of Hull (BA); *m* 1, (m dis), Brian Murray; partner, David Forgham-Bailey; 2 s (Edward Louis b 1983, Charles Edgar b 1987); *Career* prodr and presenter BBC Radio Bristol 1973–76, presenter and reporter BBC TV South 1977–82; presenter: Newsnight (BBC TV Lime Grove) 1983–85, Today (BBC Radio 4) 1986–87, Woman's Hour (BBC Radio 4) 1987–, This Sunday (Granada TV), Turning World (BBC Radio 4) 1998–2001, The Message (BBC Radio 4) 2001–; documentary films for TV incl: The Duchy of Cornwall, Everyman, Stand by Your Man, Breaking the Chain, Here's Looking At You; contrib: The Guardian, The Independent on Sunday, Daily Mail, The Observer, The Times, The Express and various magazines; columnist Manchester Evening News; trg public speaking presentation; non-exec dir The Christie Manchester; vice-pres FPA, memb Bd The Women's Library; hon degrees from various univs; *Books* The Woman's Hour, Is It Me, or Is It Hot in Here?, That's My Boy!, Memoirs of a Not So Dutiful Daughter; *Recreations* horses, books, swimming, the children; *Style*— Dame Jenni Murray, DBE; ✉ Woman's Hour, BBC Broadcasting House, London W1A 1AA (☎ 020 7580 4468); agent Speakeasy (☎ 0116 240 4101), literary agent Barbara Levy (☎ 020 7435 9046)

MURRAY, John Joseph; s of Kevin Thomas Murray (d 2000), of Bridge of Weir, Renfrewshire, and Mary, *née* Leahy (d 1973); *b* 10 May 1953; *Educ* Fort Augustus Abbey Sch, Glasgow Coll of Technol, Univ of Leeds (LLB), Coll of Law Guildford; *Career* admitted slr 1979; articled clerk Smallpeice & Merriman 1977–79, ptnr Nabarro Nathanson 1986–2007 (asst slr 1979); chm Tax and Legislation Sub-Ctee 1994–97, memb Ctee Assoc of Pensioneer Trustees 1991–97 and 2003–05, memb Pensions Ctee Assoc of Corp Tstees 2000–07, memb Ctee Assoc of Member-Directed Pension Schemes 2005–06; memb Law Soc; memb: American Civil War Round Table (UK), Western Front Assoc, Cedar Creek Brigade (USA) 2010; memb Isle of Man Victorian Soc, memb Friends of Manx Nat Heritage, memb Isle of Man Family History Soc; FRSA 2005; *Publications* Encyclopedia of Forms and Precedents (5 edn), contrib Vol 31 Pensions, Pensions Law Handbook (contrib, 2000, 6 edn 2004); articles in Pensions World, Pension Dimension, Journal of Pensions Management and Marketing, Professional Pensions, Crossfire, Journal of Isle of Man Family History Soc, Isis; *Recreations* military history research, watching rugby, playing golf; *Style*— John Murray, Esq; ✉ Inglenook, 1 Marathon Road, Douglas, Isle of Man IM2 4HN

MURRAY, Jorian Mark; s of Michael Murray (d 2005), of London, and Rosemary, *née* Weber (d 1991); *b* 1 September 1961, London; *Educ* Westminster City Sch, Univ of London (BA), Harvard Business Sch (AMP); *m* 2 Sept 1989, Deborah, da of Geoff Scott; 2 s (Joseph b 22 July 1994, George b 21 Jan 2001), 1 da (Eleanor b 29 Jan 1997); *Career* Lasky's Hi-Fi 1986, Publicis 1988, successively account dir, head of dept and md DDB London 1992 (IPA Effectiveness Agency of the Year 1992–2006), bd account dir 1998, founding ptnr Dye Holloway Murray LLP 2007, chm Arnold Amsterdam 2010, fndr Senex 2014; memb Mktg Soc 2002; MIPA 1989, MInstD 2007; *Recreations* cinema, cricket, gardening, music, cycling, reading, travel, watching and playing football (season ticket Arsenal FC), gym, dog walking; *Clubs* Home House; *Style*— Jorian Murray, Esq; ✉ Dye Holloway Murray LLP, 14 Newburgh Street, London W1F 7RT (☎ 020 7494 9600, e-mail jorian@dhmlondon.com)

MURRAY, Kevin Ian; s of Ian Campbell Murray (d 1994), and Shirley Esme Gladys Maud, *née* Edwards; *b* 9 June 1954, Rhodesia; *Educ* Hyde Park HS Johannesburg; *m* 4 Feb 1978, Elisabeth Anne Mary, da of Maj-Gen William Leonard Whalley, CB; 1 s (Jason Nicholas b 14 Aug 1979), 1 da (Kirstin Leigh b 27 Jan 1981); *Career* Nat Serv SA Inf 1971–72, active serv (annual civilian force tours of duty) Transvaal Scot Regt 1972–82; The Star Johannesburg 1973–81, gp pubns ed and PR exec Barlow Rand Ltd Johannesburg 1981–82, managing ed Leadership SA magazine rising to dir of mktg and advtg Churchill Murray Publications 1982–85, md Kestrel Publications rising to md Shearwater Communications Services 1985–88, PR mangr Bayer UK Ltd rising to gp PR mangr all Bayer plc cos in UK 1988–92, dir of corp communications UKAEA and dir of corp affrs/memb Mgmnt Ctee AEA Technology 1992–96, dir of communications British Airways plc 1996–98, sr conslt rising to chm Bell Pottinger Communications 1998–, chm PR Div Chime Communications plc 2003–12, chm Good Relations Gp 2012–; dir Frilford Heath Golf Club Ltd 2016–; FCIPR, MInstD, CCMI 2014; *Publications* The Language of Leaders (2011), Communicate to Inspire (2014), Blood of the Rose (2014); *Recreations* golf, film, writing, travel; *Clubs* RAC, Frilford Heath Golf; *Style*— Kevin Murray, Esq

MURRAY, Neil Alastair Charles; s of Alastair Richardson Murray, of Wimbledon, London, and Patricia Stella Ray, *née* Jones; *b* 25 February 1954; *Educ* King George V Sch Hong Kong, Univ of Southampton (LLB), City Univ (MA); *m* 1 Sept 1984 (m dis 1998), Patricia Susan, da of John Herbert Mulholland, of Connecticut, USA; 1 s (James b 4 July 1987), 1 da (Stephanie b 18 June 1989); *Career* admitted slr 1980; Boodle Hatfield & Co London 1978–80, Legal Dept ICI 1980, Norton Rose 1980–85, ptnr Travers Smith Braithwaite (now Travers Smith LLP) 1987–2010 (joined 1985), ptnr Stephenson Harwood LLP 2010–; Freeman Worshipful Co of Slrs, Liveryman Worshipful Co of Chartered Surveyors 2013; memb Law Soc; *Recreations* music, golf, skiing, fitness; *Style*— Neil Murray, Esq; ☎ 07733 327358, e-mail neil@neilmurray.net; Stephenson Harwood LLP, 1 Finsbury Circus, London EC2M 7SH (☎ 020 7809 2516, fax 020 7003 8609, e-mail neil.murray@shlegal.com, website www.shlegal.com)

MURRAY, Nicholas Julyan Edward; s of Sir (Francis) Ralph Hay Murray, KCMG, CB (d 1986), of Whaddon Hall Mews, Whaddon, Bucks, and Mauricette, *née* Countess von Kuenburg (d 1996); *b* 7 March 1939; *Educ* Bedford Sch, English Sch Cairo, Univ of St Andrews (MA); *m* 14 July 1973, Caroline Anne, da of Capt A McClintock, of Glenbower, Coolbawn, Nenagh, Co Tipperary, Ireland; 1 da (Anstice Aileen Thérèse b 22 Jan 1981); *Career* S H Benson Ltd 1962–71 (dir 1968), dir Ogilvy Benson & Mather Ltd 1971–72, md Murray Parry & Ptnrs 1972–81, dir Woodyer Hutson Chapman 1981–86, md Conzept Int Mgmnt Business Devpt Conslts 1986–97, chief exec Galileo Brand Architecture Ltd 1997–; memb and professional advsr Bd of Trade (missions Tokyo 1968, San Francisco 1969); chm Friends of the Vale of Aylesbury 1987–92 (memb ctee 1975–, vice-chm 1985); FInstD; *Books* Chronicle of the Villages of the Vale of Aylesbury (1986); *Recreations* sailing; *Clubs* Sussex Yacht, Lough Derg Yacht; *Style*— Nicholas Murray, Esq; ✉ 38 Perrers Road, London W6

MURRAY, Nigel Patrick; MBE (2013); s of Matthew Murray (d 2007), and Rosemary, *née* Boyles; *b* 22 May 1964, Leamington Spa, Warks; *Partner* Sylvia Talyor; *Career* Paralympic boccia player; achievements incl: Gold medal individual event Paralympics Sydney 2000, Gold medal mixed team (with David Smith, Dan Bentley and Zoe Robinson, *qqv*) Paralympics Beijing 2008, Silver medal individual event Paralympics Beijing 2008, Bronze medal mixed team medal mixed team (with David Smith, Dan Bentley and Zoe Robinson, *qqv*) Paralympic Games 2012; patron: Whitnash Charitable Tst, Kenilworth Phab; local govt offr Warks CC 1981–2011; *Style*— Nigel Murray, Esq, MBE; ✉ 45 Montgomery Road, Whitnash, Leamington Spa, Warickshire CV31 2TG; c/o British Paralympic Association, 40 Bernard Street, London WC1N 1ST

MURRAY, Norman Loch; s of Thomas Loch Murray, of Troon, Ayrshire, and May Fox, *née* Davidson; *b* 17 March 1948; *Educ* George Watson's Coll Edinburgh, Heriot-Watt Univ (BA), Harvard Grad Sch of Business Admin (PMD); *m* 17 March 1973, Pamela Anne, da of George Low; 2 s (Niall, Andrew); *Career* qualified CA 1976; Scottish and Newcastle Breweries plc Edinburgh 1971–73, Arthur Young & Co Edinburgh 1973–77, Peat Marwick Mitchell & Co Hong Kong 1977–80, The Royal Bank of Scotland plc Edinburgh 1980–85, dir Charterhouse Development Capital Ltd 1985–89; Morgan Grenfell Development Capital Ltd: dep chief exec 1989–96, chief exec 1996–98, chm 1996–98; dir: Morgan Grenfell Development Capital France SA 1995–98, Morgan Grenfell Asset Mgmnt 1996–98, Deutsche Morgan Grenfell Devpt Capital Italy SA 1996–98, Deutsche Morgan Grenfell Private Equity Asia Fund Ltd 1997–98; chm Cairn Energy plc 2002– (dir 1999–2002); non-exec dir: Burn Stewart Distillers plc 1988–90, Taunton Cider plc 1991–92, Bristow Helicopter Group Ltd 1991–96, EuroDollar (Holdings) plc 1993–94, Glasgow Income Tst 1999–2003; dir: Penta Capital Ptnrs Ltd 2000–07, Robert Wiseman Dairies plc 2003–, Greene King plc 2004–; chm Ind Ctee Audit Firm Governance Gp, chm and govr Investment Ctee St Columba's Hospice Edinburgh; chm Br Venture Capital Assoc 1997–98 (memb Cncl 1992–98), pres Inst of Chartered Accountants of Switzerland 2006–07 (memb Cncl 1992–98 and 2004–07, convenor Fin and General Purposes Ctee); hon prof Heriot-Watt Univ 2008; memb Co of Merchants of City of Edinburgh; FRSA; *Books* Making Corporate Reports Valuable (jtly, 1988); *Recreations* squash, golf, climbing; *Clubs* Luffness New Golf, Watsonian, Harvard Business School, Royal Hong Kong Yacht; *Style*— Norman Murray, Esq

MURRAY, Peter; CBE (2010, OBE 1996); *b* 1941, Middlesbrough; *Educ* Teesside Coll of Art, Univ of Leeds; *Career* teacher and curator; exhibited extensively until 1975 (paintings, drawings and prints in several public and private collections); taught in general, further and higher educn, lectr/visiting tutor to colls, polys and univs throughout Britain and abroad, formerly princ lectr responsible for postgrad studies Bretton Hall Coll W Yorks; fndr and exec dir Yorkshire Sculpture Park (pioneering the siting and exhibiting of sculpture in the open air) 1977–; organised maj open air exhibitions incl: Henry Moore and Landscape (largest ever open Henry Moore exhibition), Scultura – Carving from Carrara, Massa and Pietrasanta 1988, Emile Antoine Bourdelle – Pioneer of the Future 1989, Contemporary Stone Carving from Zimbabwe, Lynn Chadwick 1991–92, Phillip King, Barry Flanagan 1992, Jorgen Haugen Sorenson Retrospective and Fritz Wotruba 1993, Elizabeth Frink Meml 1994, Ed Paolozzi 70th Birthday Exhbn 1994, Kan Yasuda 1994; organiser and dir first Open Air Sculpture Symposium in Britain 1983, made presentations at Int Sculpture Confs USA 1982, Japan 1984 and San Francisco 1994; sponsored by: French Govt to visit Paris and northern France 1984, Canadian Govt to visit Canada 1981 and 1986, Br Cncl to visit India 1988, Zimbabwe 1990, Thailand 1991, N America 1992, 1993 and 1994, Germany 1993 and Austria 1993; estab: Artist Residences, Public Sculpture Workshops, Educn and Outreach Prog, Access Sculpture Trail at Yorks Sculpture Park; author of reviews for arts jls, contrib to several Radio and TV progs incl Review of Jacob Epstein exhibition BBC Radio 4 Kaleidoscope 1987, contrib to catalogues for exhibitions for other galleries and organisations nationally and internationally; hon fell RCA 1989; *Publications* incl: Sculpture Parks in Britain (Studio International, 1983), Sculpture Parks – Origins & Aims (Arts Review Yearbook, 1983), Zimbabwe Carving (Arts Review Yearbook, 1990); *Style*— Peter Murray, Esq, CBE;

✉ Yorkshire Sculpture Park, Bretton Hall College, West Bretton, Wakefield, West Yorkshire WF4 4LG (☎ 01924 830579)

MURRAY, Peter Gerald Stewart; s of Stewart Hay Murray (d 1988), and Freda, *née* Woodland (d 2000); *b* 6 April 1944; *Educ* King's Coll Taunton, Royal West of England Acad Sch of Architecture, Univ of Bristol, AA Sch of Architecture London; *m* Jane Rosetta, da of Alexander Wood; 2 s (Rupert Hay b 28 May 1969, William Alexander b 21 April 1972), 2 da (Sophie Elizabeth b 12 Oct 1977, Alice Adelaide b 31 Aug 1981); *Career* freelance journalist and designer 1967–70 (design corr for Nova Magazine, Domus, Town Magazine); Architectural Design magazine: art ed 1970–72, tech ed 1972–74; ed Building Design 1974–79, ed RIBA Jl and RIBA Transactions 1979–84, md RIBA Magazines Ltd 1979–84, fndr Wordsearch Ltd 1983, launched Blueprint magazine 1983; fndr: Blueprint Monographs book series 1986, Blueprint Extras book series 1989, Eye Magazine, The Int Review of Graphic Design 1990, Design Review (jl of the Chartered Soc of Designers) 1991; publisher Tate Magazine and Perspectives Magazine 1993; fndr Wordsearch Communications 1995; architectural advsr St Hugh's Coll Oxford 1996; dir London Architecture Biennale 2004 and 2006, fndr dir New London Architecture 2005–, dir London Festival of Architecture 2008 and 2010, chm The London Soc 2013–; ed Pidgeon Digital 2007–; lectr in architecture and design, visiting prof IE Univ Madrid 2011–; RIBA: ex officio memb Policy Ctee 1978–83, memb Events Ctee 1978–83, Library Ctee 1981–83, Mktg Ctee 1985–87, Br Architectural Library Ctee 2001–04; Architectural Assoc: memb Cncl 1987–90, hon sec 1989–90; exhibitions at the Royal Academy: New Architecture – The Work of Foster Rogers Stirling 1986, Living Bridges: Inhabited Bridges Past, Present and Future 1996, Beyond Minimalism – The Work of Tadao Ando 1998; chm Int Building Press 1976–78 (pres 1978–83); sec Architecture Club 1978–; memb Bedford Park Soc Ctee 1998 (hon sec and dep chm 2000–), memb Royal Acad Architecture Ctee 1997–; tstee: Bannister Fletcher 1984–86, Article 25, Cycle to Cannes; chm BBC Design Awards Panel 1994; memb Selection Panel: Nat Portrait Gall extension 1987, Inland Revenue HQ Nottingham 1991, The Crown Estate 1995, Br Cncl for Offices Awards 1998; D&AD Silver Medal 1973, Publisher of the Year PPA 1991, Property Mktg Awards 1993, 1994, 1995, 1998 and 1999, Debrett's 500 2014; Master Worshipful Co of Chartered Architects 2015–16 (Renter Warden 2013–14, Upper Warden 2014–15); FRSA 1989, Hon FRIBA 1999; *Books* A Village in Wiltshire (1975), The Lloyds Building (1980), Ove Arup & Partners (1981), SOM: Reality before Reality (1982), YRM: On Making a Building (1983), BDP: Expressing Corporate Personality (1983), Modern Architecture in Britain (1984), Harry Seidler: Towers in the City (1985), Contemporary British Architects (1993), Living Bridges: The Inhabited Bridge Past, Present and Future (1996), New Urban Environments (1998), Understanding Plans (1998), New Architects (1998), The Saga of Sydney Opera House (2003), Architecture and Commerce (2004), A Passion to Build (2011), The Great Estates (2013), London's Growing Up (2014), Manser Houses (2015); *Recreations* cycling, painting, looking at architecture, wood turning; *Clubs* Architecture, Athenaeum; *Style—* Peter Murray, Esq; ✉ Wordsearch, 85 Clerkenwell Road, London EC1R 5AR (e-mail pgsmurray@mac.com)

MURRAY, Rob; s of Prof John Murray, of Botley, Hants, and Jeanne, *née* Faith (d 1998); *b* 29 November 1963, Bristol; *Educ* Exeter Coll Oxford (scholar, BA), Vrije Univ Brussels (Flemish Govt scholar, LLM); *m* 28 Dec 1990, Sarah, *née* Giles; 1 s (Tom b 21 April 1995), 1 da (Gracie b 18 March 1997); *Career* admitted slr 1989; slr Commercial Dept then EC Unit Clifford Chance 1989–96 (articled clerk 1987–89), ptnr and head of EU/competition Bond Pearce 1996–2000, dir EU/Competition Gp and Legal Risk Mgmnt Gp KLegal 2000–02, ptnr and head EU/Competition Gp DLA 2002–04, currently ptnr Mishcon de Reya; memb Competition Cmmn Reporting Panel 2005–; md Foreverafter Ltd 2004–, dir Cornelia Properties Ltd 2004–; memb Law Soc; *Style—* Rob Murray, Esq; ✉ Mishcon de Reya, Summit House, 12 Red Lion Square, London WC1R 4QD

MURRAY, Sir Robin MacGregor; kt (2011); s of James Alistair Campbell Murray (d 1979), of Glasgow, and Helen, *née* MacGregor (d 1992); *b* 31 January 1944; *Educ* Royal HS Edinburgh, Univ of Glasgow (MB ChB, MD), Univ of London (MPhil, DSc); *m* Shelagh, da of Frank Harris; 1 s (Graham Keith b 8 Feb 1972), 1 da (Claire Alison b 22 May 1978); *Career* SHO and registrar: Dept of Med Univ of Glasgow 1969–72, Maudsley Hosp 1972–76; Inst of Psychiatry: sr lectr 1978, dean 1982, prof of psychological med 1989–99, prof of psychiatry 1999–2009, prof of psychiatric research 2009–; visiting fell Nat Inst of Mental Health Washington 1976, pres Assoc of European Psychiatrists 1995–96; FRS 2010; *Style—* Sir Robin Murray; ✉ Division of Psychological Medicine, Institute of Psychiatry, DeCrespigny Park, London SE5 8AF (☎ 020 7703 6091)

MURRAY, Samantha Elizabeth; *b* 25 September 1989, Preston, Lancs; *Educ* Univ of Bath (BA); *Career* athlete (modern pentathlon); achievements incl: Silver medal (team) World Championships 2010, Gold medal (team) and Bronze medal (individual) World Championships 2012, Bronze medal (individual) World Cup 2012, Silver medal Olympic Games 2012 (youngest ever female Olympic athelete in the history of modern pentathlon); *Style—* Miss Samantha Murray; ✉ e-mail samantha.murray89@gmail.com, website www.samanthamurray.co.uk, Twitter @_samanthamurray; c/o Liz Box, Professional Sports Group (☎ 07702 884009, e-mail liz@profsports.com)

MURRAY, Sheryll; MP; *b* 4 February 1956, Millbrook, Cornwall; *Educ* Torpoint Community Sch; *m* Neil Murray (d 2011); 1 da (Sally), 1 s (Andrew); *Career* MP (Cons) SE Cornwall 2010–; *Style—* Mrs Sheryll Murray, MP; ✉ Office of Sheryll Murray, MP, Windsor Place, Liskeard, Cornwall PL14 4BH (☎ 01579 344428, e-mail sheryll@sheryllmurray.com, website www.sheryllmurray.com); House of Commons, London SW1A 0AA (☎ 020 7219 7148, e-mail sheryll.murray.mp@parliament.uk)

MURRAY, Simon Anthony; s of Dr Frank Murray (d 1962), and Rosemary de Meza, *née* Williams (d 1997); *b* 31 August 1951; *Educ* St Andrews HS Malawi, Hampton GS, Welbeck Coll, Imperial Coll London (Unwin Medal); *m* 1983 (m dis 2004), Lindsay; 3 c (Maxim b 1986, Jenevora b 1988, Calum b 1992); *Career* dir Ove Arup & Partners 1990–94, md gp technical services BAA plc 1994–98, dir major projects and investment Railtrack plc 1998–2001, conslt 2001–; non-exec dir: Ascot Authy (Holdings) Ltd 2000–06, Manchester Airport Developments Ltd 2002–04; chm: Construction Round Table 1997, Geoffrey Osborne Ltd 2003–; memb EPSRC, FCGI 1999, FICE 2001 (MICE 1978); *Recreations* reading, keeping fit; *Style—* Simon Murray, Esq; ✉ 150 Langton Way, London SE3 7JS (☎ 020 8858 2235, e-mail samurray1951@aol.com)

MURRAY, Susan E; *b* 1957; *Career* Colgate Palmolive UK Ltd 1979–82, General Foods (UK) Ltd 1982–89, Duracell 1989–92, IDV Ltd 1992–98, pres and ceo Pierre Smirnoff Co Ltd 1995–98, Littlewoods Stores Ltd 1998–2004; non-exec dir: Enterprise Inns 2004–14, Imperial Tobacco Gp 2004–14, chm Farrow and Ball 2007–14, Compass Gp 2007–, Pernod Ricard 2010–14; former non-exec dir: Wm Morrisons 2005–10, Aberdeen Asset Mgmnt, SSL Int; non-exec dir and memb Cncl Advtg Standards Authy, memb Complaints Panel Portman Gp; chm Int Centre for Alcohol Policies; memb: Women in Advertising and Communications, Forum UK; FRSA; *Recreations* walking, music, theatre; *Style—* Mrs Susan Murray

MURRAY, Thomas Kenneth (Tom); WS (1982); s of Charles Murray, of Edinburgh, and Audrey, *née* Haddon; *b* 25 June 1958; *Educ* Sedbergh, Univ of Dundee (LLB); *m* 12 Sept 1986, Sophie, da of Alexander Mackenzie; 3 da (Millie b 21 Sept 1989, Katie b 20 March 1991, Flora b 30 Dec 1993); *Career* slr; ptnr Gillespie Macandrew 1983–; chm Br Hallmarking Cncl 2004–11 (memb 1991–); memb Charity Law Ctee Law Soc of Scotland; chm Trefoil House 2002–08, dir MercyCorps 2008–; Purse Bearer to Lord High Cmmr to Gen Assembly Church of Scotland 2003–, memb Queen's Body Guard for Scotland (Royal Co of Archers), deacon Incorporation of Goldsmiths City of Edinburgh; tstee Scottish Nat War Meml 2010–; *Recreations* fishing, golf; *Clubs* New (Edinburgh), Hon Co of Edinburgh Golfers; *Style—* Tom Murray, Esq, WS; ✉ Gillespie Macandrew LLP, 5 Atholl Cresent, Edinburgh EH3 8EJ (☎ 0131 225 1677, fax 0131 225 4519, e-mail tom.murray@gillespiemacandrew.co.uk)

MURRAY WELLS, Jamie; *b* 21 March 1983, London; *Educ* Harrow, Univ of the West of England; *Career* fndr Glasses Direct 2004–13, industry head of retail Google 2013–; enterprise advsr to private and public sector; memb Chllr George Osborne's New Enterprise Cncl 2008–11, fndr StartUp Britain 2012; UK Shell Livewire Young Entrepreneur of the Year 2005, Queen's Award for Enterprise Promotion 2009; *Style—* Mr J N Murray Wells, OBE; ✉ Google UK, Central St Giles, 1 St Giles High Street, London WC2H 8AG; (☎ 07789 557540)

MURRAY-LYON, Dr Iain Malcolm; s of Ranald Malcolm Murray-Lyon (d 1970), of Edinburgh, and Jennipher, *née* Dryburgh (d 2003); *b* 28 August 1940; *Educ* Loretto, Univ of Edinburgh (BSc, MB ChB, MD); *m* 7 Nov 1981, Teresa Elvira, da of Antonio Gonzalez Montero, of Buenos Aires; 1 da (Caroline Claire b 1982), 1 s (Andrew Malcolm b 1984); *Career* hon sr lectr Liver Unit KCH 1972–74; conslt physician and gastroenterologist: Charing Cross Hosp 1974–2002, Chelsea Westminster Hosp 1993–; hon conslt physician: Hosp of St John & St Elizabeth 1976–2003, King Edward VII Hosp for Offrs 1990–; author of over 150 pubns in the areas of liver disease and gastroenterology; former: censor Royal Coll of Physicians, chm Liver Section Br Soc of Gastroenterology, sec Br Assoc for Study of the Liver (memb); Liveryman Worshipful Soc of Apothecaries; FRCP 1980, FRCPE 1980; *Recreations* golf, skiing, tennis; *Clubs* Brooks's, Hurlingham; *Style—* Dr Iain Murray-Lyon; ✉ Flat 4, 30 Bramham Gardens, London SW5 0HF (☎ 020 7370 2221); 116 Harley Street, London W1G 7JL (☎ 020 7935 6747/4444, fax 020 7935 7017, e-mail i.m-lyon@lonclin.co.uk)

MURRAY-PHILIPSON, Robin Hylton; OBE (2002), DL (Leics 1994); s of Hylton Ralph Murray-Philipson, MP (d 1934), and Monica Lloyd, *née* Beasley-Robinson (d 1994); *b* 5 June 1927; *Educ* Eton; *m* Oct 1954, Catherine Cornelia (Nini), da of late Brig Robert Tilney, CBE, DSO, TD, DL; 3 da (Cornelia b 1955, Suzie b 1961, Kate b 1963), 1 s (Hylton b 1959); *Career* Lt Grenadier Guards 1945–48; owner: Executive Travel Ltd 1957–75, Executive Helicopters Ltd 1960–64; dir: Helicopter Sales Ltd 1960–70, Trans World Helicopters Ltd 1967–72; md Serenissima Travel Ltd 1973–86; pt/t Marie Curie Cancer Care 1986–94 (patron Marie Curie Cancer Care Leics 1994–98); jt rep The Art Fund (formerly National Art Collections Fund) (Leics and Rutland) 1986–99; vice-pres Young Leics (formerly Leics Clubs for Young People); fndr Leics and Rutland Crimebeat Ltd (now Warning Zone Ltd) 1993 (chm 1993–2007), memb Ctee Leics Crimestoppers 1996–2010, memb Ctee National Crimebeat 1997–2010; High Sheriff Leics 1993–94; *Recreations* tennis, travel; *Clubs* White's; *Style—* Robin Murray-Philipson, Esq, OBE, DL; ✉ The Garden House, Blaston, Market Harborough, Leicestershire LE16 8DE (☎ 01858 555233, e-mail nini.blaston@btinternet.com); 31 Astell Street, London SW3 3RT (☎ 020 7352 1250)

MURRAY-SMITH, Prof David James; *b* 20 October 1941; *Educ* Aberdeen GS, Univ of Aberdeen (BSc Eng, MSc), Univ of Glasgow (PhD, DSc); *m* Effie, *née* Macphail; 2 s (Roderick William b 1969, Gordon David b 1972); *Career* engr Inertial Systems Dept Ferranti UK Edinburgh 1964–65; Univ of Glasgow: asst 1965–67, lectr 1967–77, sr lectr 1977–83, reader 1983–85, prof of engrg systems and control Dept of Electronics and Electrical Engrg 1985–2005, dean Faculty of Engrg 1997–2001, prof emeritus 2005–; FIET; *Publications* Continuous System Simulation (1995), Modelling and Simulation of Integrated Systems in Engineering (2012); over 200 jl and conference papers; *Recreations* railway history, photography; *Style—* Prof David Murray-Smith; ✉ School of Engineering, University of Glasgow, Rankine Building, Glasgow G12 8LT (☎ 0141 330 6125, e-mail david.murray-smith@glasgow.ac.uk, website http://glasgow.academia.edu/davidmurraysmith)

M

MURRELL, David Brian; s of William Percy John Murrell (d 1988), of Minehead, Somerset, and Muriel Mary Elizabeth, *née* Stevens (d 1988); *b* 7 February 1946; *Educ* Taunton Sch; *m* 29 Nov 1969, Sheila Mary, da of Lt Alured Francis Fairlie-Clarke (d 1984), of Norton Fitzwarren, Somerset; 1 s (Alan b 1970), 2 da (Deborah b 1972, Julia b 1974); *Career* qualified as CA with Amherst and Shapland of Minehead 1967; KPMG: joined London office 1968, ptnr 1981–99, head of UK and global media and entertainment industry practice 1984–99, chm UK and Euro info communications and entertainment practice 1994–97, chm UK and global mktg 1995–97, chm UK alumni programme 1993–99; dir Renscombe Properties Ltd 2000–, sr ind dir Chrysalis plc 2003–11 (non-exec dir 2000–03); sr ptnr: Target Films 2000–03, Jasper Films 2001–; chm City Boardroom 2000–06; barker Variety Club, pres Cinema and TV Benevolent Fund 2007–10 (dir 2003–); mentor ICAEW 2010–; memb: BAFTA, RTS, Mktg Soc; FCA 1978 (ACA 1968), fell Radio Acad; *Publications* author of numerous articles on finance and tax in leading media and entertainment industry trade magazines; *Recreations* golf, photography, classic car trials, racehorse owning; *Clubs* Old Tauntonians Golfing Soc, Wooden Spoon Soc, Soho House, Motor Cycling, St George's Hill Lawn Tennis, Variety Club Golf Soc, LWT Golf Soc (capt 2014–15), Chartered Accountants Golf Soc, Silvermere Golf, Hospital; *Style—* David Murrell, Esq; ✉ Cinema and Television Benevolent Fund, 22 Golden Square, London W1F 9AD (☎ 07710 962148)

MURRELL, Prof John; MBE (2004); s of George Henry Murrell (d 1993), and Anne, *née* Rock (d 1933); *b* 12 December 1933; *Educ* Lawrence Sheriff Sch Rugby, Coll of St Mark and St John London (CertEd), Birkbeck Coll London (BA), Chelsea Coll London (MEd); *m* 14 May 1960, Anne Amy Helen, *née* Prees; 1 s (Richard Anthony), 1 da (Laura Helen); *Career* Nat Serv RAF 1952–54, VRT RAF 1960–67; mathematics teacher 1958–68; Homerton Coll Cambridge: lectr 1968, sr lectr 1970, princ lectr 1975, dir of postgrad studies 1976, George Peabody prof of educn and human devpt (jtly with George Peabody Coll) 1992–2001, postgrad tutor 2001–04, emeritus fell 2010, sometime sec to Coll Cncl; Faculty of Educn Univ of Cambridge: memb Faculty Bd, memb Degree Ctee Faculty Bd, examiner in educational theory, teaching practice and res methods; George Peabody Coll Nashville USA: visiting scholar 1984, visiting lectr summer sch 1986, scholar in residence 1990; trg conslt Judicial Studies Bd and Lord Chllr's Dept 1994–, conslt Advsy Cncl Industrial Soc 2020 Vision Project 1996–98, conslt Local Advsy Ctee BBC 1996–2000, trg conslt GMC 1997–2000; designed and taught courses on trg and educn, delivered numerous guest lectures; former chm Cambridge and Huntingdon Nurse Educn Ctee, former memb Working Parties of the Lord Chancellor's Office, former memb Educn Ctee School of Physiotherapy Addenbrooke's Hosp Cambridge; memb Regnl Cncl Duke of Edinburgh's Award 1992–2003, memb Working Pty of the Lord Chllr's Office on Equality in the Lay Magistracy and the Gen Cmmrs of Income Tax 2000–; inaugural Hon MEd Univ of St Mark and St John Plymouth 2013; *Publications* Nurse Training: An Enterprise in Curriculum Development at St Thomas' Hospital London (with Hazel O Allen, 1978), Handbook for the Training of Magistrates (jtly, 1989), Tribunals Training Handbook (2005); numerous essays, articles and research papers published in learned jls; *Recreations* golf, fly fishing, Anglo-American history; *Clubs* RAF, Victory Services; *Style—* Prof John Murrell, MBE; ☎ 01223 354042, e-mail jm150@hermes.cam.ac.uk

MURRISON, Dr Andrew William; MP; s of late William Gordon Murrison, RD, and Marion, *née* Horn; *Educ* Harwich County HS, The Harwich Sch, Univ of Bristol (MB ChB, MD), Univ of Cambridge (DPH); *m* Jennifer Jane, *née* Munden; 5 da; *Career* MO (Surgeon Cdr) RN 1981–2000 (recalled 2003), former princ MO HM Naval Base Portsmouth, conslt occupational physician 1996–99, locum conslt occupational physician Glos Royal Hosp

2000–01; MP (Cons): Westbury 2001–10, SW Wilts 2010–; shadow health min 2003–07, shadow defence min 2007–, PPS to Health Sec 2010–, PM's special rep for First World War Centenary Commemoration 2011–, min for int security strategy 2012–14, NI Office min 2014–15, trade envoy to Morocco and Tunisia 2016–; chm All Pty Morocco Gp 2010–12, memb Jt Select Ctee on Nat Security Strategy; Gilbert Blane Medal 1996; hon research registrar Southampton Gen Hosp 1990–93; memb Faculty of Occupational Med RCP 1996 (assoc 1993); *Publications* Fighting Fit (2010), A Better Deal for Military Amputees (2011), Tommy This an' Tommy That: The Military Covenant (2011); various biomedical pubns; *Recreations* sailing, skiing; *Style*— Dr Andrew Murrison, MP; ✉ House of Commons, London SW1A 0AA; Constituency Office, 1 Holloway House, Epsom Square, White Horse Business Park, Trowbridge BA14 0XG (☎ 01225 358584)

MURTON, Dr John Evan; s of Anthony Stewart Murton, of Cowbridge, Vale of Glamorgan, and Marion Elizabeth, *née* Heale; *b* 18 March 1972, Aldershot, Hants; *Educ* Cowbridge Comp Sch, Sidney Sussex Coll Cambridge (scholar (twice), MA), Darwin Coll Cambridge (PhD, Audrey Richards UK African Studies Assoc Prize), Univ of Nairobi; *m* 19 Dec 1998 (m dis 2015), Sarah Elizabeth, *née* Harvey; 2 s (Theodore Harvey b 28 Nov 2002, Raphael Dominic b 28 Nov 2006), 1 da (Annabella Grace b 14 Oct 2004); *Career* diplomat; teacher Kawondera Secdy Sch Zimbabwe 1990–91, UN Dept FCO 1997–98, Japanese language trg FCO 1998–2000, second sec then first sec Br Embassy Tokyo 2000–04, dep dir Sec Gen's Private Office NATO Brussels 2004–07, high cmmr to Republic of Mauritius 2007–10 (concurrently non-resident ambass to Madagascar and Comoros), head East Asia and Pacific Dept FCO until 2013, currently dep high cmmr Nairobi and UK perm rep to the UN in Nairobi; *Recreations* hiking, skiing, cooking; *Style*— Dr John Murton; ✉ British High Commission, Upper Hill Road, Nairobi

MUSCATELLI, Prof Vito Antonio (Anton); s of Ambrogio Muscatelli, of London, and Rosellina, *née* Defonte; *b* 1 January 1962, Bari, Italy; *Educ* HS of Glasgow, Univ of Glasgow (MA, PhD, Logan Prize); *m* 1986, Elaine, *née* Flood; 1 da (Anna Rosa b 1990), 1 s (Ambrogio Roberto b 1999); *Career* Univ of Glasgow: lectr 1984–90, sr lectr 1990–92, prof of economics 1992–94, Daniel Jack prof of economics 1994–2007, dean Faculty of Social Sciences 2000–04, vice-princ (strategy and budgeting then strategy and advancement) 2004–07; princ and vice-chllr Heriot-Watt Univ 2007–09, princ and vice-chllr Univ of Glasgow 2009–; research fell CES-info Research Inst Munich 1999–; visiting prof: Univ of Parma 1989, Catholic Univ Milan 1991 and 1997–98, Univ of Bari 1995–2004, Univ of Pavia 1997–98, Tel-Aviv Univ 2001, Univ of Brescia 2003–04; guest prof Nankai Univ China 2014–; chair: Universities Scotland Res and Knowledge Exchange Ctee 2007–08 and 2012–14, Strategic Advsy Bd Scottish Res Partnership in Engineering 2007–10, Cmmn of Urban Economic Growth for the new Glasgow City Region 2015–; convener Universities Scotland and vice-pres Universities UK 2008–10, dir Russell Gp of Univs 2009–, dir Universitas 21 Gp of Univs 2009–, dir Nat Centre for Univs and Business 2013–, dir Univs Superannuation Scheme Bd 2015–; advsr House of Commons Treasy Select Ctee 2007–10; memb: Advsy Panel of Economic Conslts to Sec of State for Scotland 1998–2000, Economics and Econometrics Panel HEFCE Research Assessment Exercise 2001 and 2008, Cncl Royal Economic Soc 2002–07, Research Grants Bd ESRC 2002–07, Scottish Funding Cncl Res and Knowledge Transfer Ctee 2004–08, SFC Knowledge Transfer Innovation Gp 2005–08, Bd Glasgow City Mktg Bureau 2009–, Bd Scottish Funding Cncl 2012–, Cncl of Economic Advsrs Scottish Govt 2015–; dir Beatson Inst 2015–; ed Scottish Jl of Political Economy 1990–2003; memb Bd of Govrs HS of Glasgow 2000–, dir GU Hldgs 2004–07; tstee Council for Advancement and Support of Education (CASE) 2013–, chair Glasgow and Clyde Valley Cmmn on Urban Economic Growth 2015–; hon pres David Hume Inst 2015–; Hon LLD McGill Univ 2012; FRSA 1995, FRSE 2003, AcSS 2004; Commendatore Repub of Italy 2009; *Books* Macroeconomic Theory and Stabilisation Policy (jtly, 1988), Economic and Political Institutions in Economic Policy (ed, 1996), Fiscal Policies, Monetary Policies and Labour Markets: Key Aspects of European Macroeconomic Policies after Monetary Unification (jt ed, 2003), Macroeconomic Policy Making in the EMU (2004); *Recreations* football, music, literature; *Style*— Prof Anton Muscatelli; ✉ Univ of Glasgow, Glasgow G12 8QQ (☎ 0141 330 5995)

MUSGRAVE, Mark Jonathan; s of Sir (Frank) Cyril Musgrave, KCB (d 1986), of Flixton, Suffolk, and Jean Elsie, *née* Soulsby (d 1993); *b* 6 October 1952; *Educ* Haileybury; *m* 1 Sept 1979, Belinda Joan, da of John Hugh Clerk (d 1976), of Kingston, Jamaica; 2 s (William b 1984, George b 1988), 1 da (Chloe b 1987); *Career* admitted slr 1977; Speechly Bircham: ptnr 1981–2012, personnel ptnr 1988–91, dep managing ptnr 1989–90, fin ptnr 1992–95, managing ptnr 1995–98; conslt Charles Russell Speechlys 2012–; dir Devoran Trustees Ltd 1991–2013; memb: Law Soc 1977, Justinians 1989–2001, New England Co 1993–2001; tstee and treas Nat Brain Appeal 1999–; *Recreations* sport, gardening, travel; *Style*— Mark Musgrave, Esq; ✉ 15 Hotham Road, London SW15 1QL; Charles Russell Speechlys, 5 Fleet Place, London EC4M 7RD (☎ 020 7203 5000)

MUSGRAVE, Olivia Mirabel; *b* Dublin, Ireland; *Educ* City and Guilds of London Inst; *m* 22 May 2004, John Gardiner (Lord Gardiner of Kimble (Life Peer), *qv*); *Career* sculptor; Royal Soc of Br Sculptors Fedora Gleichen Award, Rodney Burns Drawing Award; pres Soc of Portrait Sculptors 2014; *Solo Exhibitions* incl: John Martin of London 1997, Sculptures 2000–2002 (John Martin of London) 2002, Recent Work (John Martin Gallery) 2004, Taking Flight (John Martin Gallery) 2006, Jorgensen Fine Art Dublin 2008, The Seven Deadly Sins & Other Sculptures (John Martin Gallery) 2009; *Group Exhibitions* incl: The Discerning Eye (The Mall Galleries) 1989, 1995 and 2002, Sculptor's Drawings (Stephen Bartley Gallery) 1991, Royal Acad Summer Exhibition 1992 and 1994, Young British Sculptors (Beaux Arts Gallery Bath) 1996, Royal West of England Acad Bristol 2003, The Stuff of Magic (John Martin Gallery) 2004, Royal Hibernian Acad Summer Exhibition 2007, London Art Fair John Martin Gallery 2008; *Style*— Ms Olivia Musgrave

MUSHIN, Alan Spencer; s of Dr Louis Mushin (d 1984); *b* 31 January 1938; *Educ* Haberdashers' Aske's, London Hosp Med Coll (MB BS); *m* 27 Feb 1972, Joan Carolyn, da of Dr Simon Behrman, of London; 1 da (Rosalind b 1974), 1 s (James b 1976); *Career* conslt ophthalmic surgn: Moorfield Eye Hosp London, Royal London Hosp and Queen Elizabeth Hosp for Children; sec European Paediatric Ophthalmology Soc; Freeman City of London; fell American Acad of Ophthalmology; FRSM, FRCS, FRCOphth, FRCPCH; *Publications* papers on paediatric ophthalmology; *Recreations* photography, philately, gardening; *Clubs* Savage; *Style*— Alan S Mushin, Esq; ✉ 935 Finchley Road, London NW11 7PE (☎ 020 8455 7212); 82 Harley Street, London W1G 7HN (☎ 020 7580 3116, fax 020 7580 6998, e-mail almushin@hotmail.com)

MUSKERRY, 9 Baron (I 1781); Sir Robert Fitzmaurice Deane; 14 Bt (I 1710); s of 8 Baron Muskerry (d 14 Oct 1988), and Betty Fairbridge, *née* Palmer (d 20 Aug 1988); *b* 26 March 1948; *Educ* Sandford Park Sch Dublin, Trinity Coll Dublin (BA, BAI); *m* 1975, Rita Brink, of Pietermaritzburg, South Africa; 2 da (Hon Nicola b 1976, Hon Catherine b 1978), 1 s (Hon Jonathan Fitzmaurice b 1986); *Heir* s, Hon Jonathan Deane; *Career* shipyard mangr Dorbyl Marine, dir Dorbyl Marine Ltd; md: Stride Ltd, Bridco Ltd; currently md Elgin Brown and Hamer (Pty) Ltd; *Style*— The Rt Hon Lord Muskerry; ✉ 29 Winston Road, Kloof, 3610, South Africa (e-mail rfd@iafrica.com)

MUSTERS, Patrick Havelock Auchmuty; s of Patrick Thorvald Auchmuty Musters, DFC, RA (d 2003), of Rutland, and Nancy Stella, *née* Havelock-Allan (d 2015); *b* 20 July 1952, Kuala Lumpur, Malaya; *Educ* Allhallows Sch Lyme Regis, Univ of London; *m* 1991 (m dis 1996), Lavinia Stephanie, *née* Moore; *Career* admitted slr 1977, appointed Higher Court advocate 1994; fndr Twitchen & Musters (now BTMK LLP) 1981–; freelance criminal and regulatory law conslt, serious and complex crime and fraud specialist; memb: Law Soc, Br Acad of Forensic Sciences, London Criminal Courts Slrs Assoc; costs and funding adjudicator Legal Aid Agency; Law Soc's Handbook on Road Traffic Offences; *Recreations* cricket, golf, rugby, skiing, other people's fine wine; *Clubs* Royal Cinque Ports Golf, Law Soc Golf (capt 2011–12); *Style*— Patrick Musters, Esq; ✉ e-mail phamusters@sky.com

MUSTOE, Nicholas (Nick); s of Raymond Mustoe, of Claygate, Surrey, and Maureen, *née* Pringle; *b* 7 July 1961; *Educ* Wimbledon Coll, Esher Coll, Coll of Distributive Trades; *Career* dir Lowe Howard Spink (advtg agency) 1984–93, fndr Mustoe Merriman Herring Levy Ltd 1993 (merged with Geronimo PR agency 2008 to form Kindred, currently ceo); chm Kempton Park Racecourse; dir: ABC Connection, Premaitha plc; dep chm Starlight Children's Charity; *Recreations* National Hunt racing, squash; *Style*— Nick Mustoe, Esq

MUSTON, (Frederick Charles) Lee; s of Howard Alfred Paul Muston, and Rose Amelia Muston, of Chaddesden, Derby; *b* 13 September 1943; *Educ* Bemrose GS, Bishop Lonsdale Coll, Open Univ (BA, CertEd); *m* 20 Aug 1966, Irene Mary, *née* Barker; 1 s (Nicholas John b 17 Oct 1971), 1 da (Jena Victoria b 20 Dec 1973); *Career* asst teacher Darwin Co Secdy Sch Breadsall Derby 1965–67, head Liberal Studies Dept Spondon House Sch Derby 1967–70, head Humanities Dept Cranbourne Sch Basingstoke 1970–74, dep headmaster Larkmead Sch Abingdon 1974–80, headteacher Middleton Park HS Leeds 1980–84, headteacher Fakenham HS 1984–2001, chair N Norfolk PCT 2002–; *Recreations* rugby, cricket, poetry, cooking; *Style*— Lee Muston, Esq; ✉ Kelling Hospital, High Kelling, Norfolk (☎ 01263 710611)

MUTHALAGAPPAN, Kumar; OBE (2009); s of Muthu Muthalagappan, and Meena Muthalagappan; *b* 2 June 1960, India; *Educ* Univ of Warwick (BSc); *m* 23 March 1988, Kannahi; 1 da (Seetha), 2 s (Deva, Dharma); *Career* KPMG 1983–96, fndr and md Paramount Hotel Collection 1994–, md MeDiNova Clinical Research & Medical Services 2011–; chm City of Birmingham Symphony Orch 2007–12; memb Bd: Belgrade Theatre 2000–04, Heart of England Tourist Bd 2000–04, Visit Britain 2002–10, Advantage W Midlands 2009–12, Olympic Delivery Authy 2006–, Age UK 2012–; memb Fundraising Bd Alexandra Palace 2010–; memb Cncl Univ of Warwick 2007–10; FCA; *Style*— Kumar Muthalagappan, Esq, OBE; ✉ 149 Warwick Road, Kenilworth, Warwickshire CV8 1HY (e-mail kumar@muthalagappan.com)

MUTTER, David Goodwin; s of Alexander Mutter, and Elizabeth, *née* Gillespie; *b* 27 December 1965, Glasgow; *Educ* Royal Environmental Health Inst of Scotland (Cert); *Career* chef; trainee chef then sous chef Dornoch Hotel 1983–88, sous chef Copthorne Hotel Aberdeen 1988–90; head chef: St Olives Court Town House Exeter 1990–94 (RAC Merit for Food), Gerard's Brassiere London 1994–95, Darroch Learg Hotel Aberdeenshire 1995– (3 AA Rosettes); memb Fedn of Chefs of Scotland 1997; Craft Trainer Award 1996, Scottish Hotel Chef of the Year Scottish Chef Awards 2005; MCFA 1997, fell Master Chefs of GB 2004; *Recreations* travelling, cinema; *Style*— David Mutter, Esq; ✉ Darroch Learg Hotel & Restaurant, Braemar Road, Ballater, Aberdeenshire, Scotland AB35 5UX (☎ 01339 755788, e-mail dg.mutter@btinternet.com)

MUTTRAM, Roderick Ian; s of Wilfred Reginald Muttram DSC RN (d 1977), and Dorothy May, *née* Best (d 1977); *b* 15 January 1952; *Educ* St Bartholomew's GS Newbury, Abingdon Coll of Technol (ONC), Reading Tech Coll (HNC), Victoria Univ of Manchester (BSc), Manchester Poly (DMS); *m* 10 Aug 1974, Jane Elisabeth, *née* Sinkinson; 4 da (Claire Sarah-Jane b 10 Dec 1985, Jennifer Karen-Anne b 20 April 1988, Rebecca Helen-Louise b 22 Feb 1990, Caroline Laura-Elisabeth b 16 July 1992); *Career* asst scientific offr UK AEA 1969–76, dep chief engr Chloride Lorival Ltd 1978–80 (project engr 1976–78); Ferranti Instrumentation Ltd: asst project engr design 1980–82, gp ldr electronic design 1982, asst chief engr 1982–83, chief engr 1983–86, gen mangr Weapons Equipment Div 1986–89, dir gp engrg and quality 1989–90; dir and gen mangr Defence Systems Div Thorn EMI Electronics Ltd 1990–93, dir safety and standards Railtrack plc 1997–2000 (dir electrical engrg and control systems 1994–97), chief exec Railway Safety 2000–03, dir AEIF 2001–03 and 2004–06, ind engrg and safety conslt 2003; Bombadier Transportation (UK) Ltd: vice-pres technol, rail controls and communications networks and railway standards and regulations 2003–04, vice-pres project mgmnt and ops improvement 2004–07, vice-pres quality and safety 2007–10, pt/t princ engineering specialist (internal conslt) 2010–12; dir and prop Fourth Insight Ltd 2012–; chm Supervisory Bd European Rail Research Inst Dutch Research Fndn, chm Bd Rail Industry Trg Cncl (RITC) Ltd 2001–03, vice-chm European Rail Research Advsy Cncl (ERRAC) 2004; visiting prof Int Advsy Bd Beijing Jiatong Tech Univ 2013–; Liveryman Worshipful Co of Engrs 2005 (Freeman 2004); CEng, MIMgt 1980, FIET (FIEE 1994), FIRSE 1995, MCIT 1998, FREng 2002, FIoD 2008 (MInstD 1994); *Recreations* rifle shooting, DIY, vehicle restoration; *Style*— Roderick I Muttram, Esq, FREng; ✉ Fourth Insight Ltd, The Cottage, The Street, Ewhurst, Cranleigh, Surrey GU6 7QA (☎ 07919 305076, e-mail rmuttram@aol.com or fourthinsight@aol.com)

MUTTUKUMARU, Christopher; CB (2006); s of late Maj-Gen Anton Muttukumaru, OBE, ADC, of Canberra, and Margaret Vasanthi, *née* Ratnarajah; *b* 11 December 1951; *Educ* Xavier Coll Melbourne, Jesus Coll Oxford (MA); *m* 15 May 1976, Ann Elisabeth, da of Dr and Mrs John Tutton; 2 s (Timothy b 27 June 1982, Nicholas 25 March 1984); *Career* called to the Bar Gray's Inn 1974 (bencher 2011), practised at the Bar 1976–83; Treasy Slrs Dept (TSD) 1983–88, law officers' dept 1988–91, head of employment litigation section TSD 1991–92, sec to Sir Richard Scott's Inquiry into exports of defence and defence related equipment to Iraq 1992–96, dep legal advsr Min of Defence TSD 1996–98, memb UK delegation to diplomatic conf on establishment of the International Criminal Ct, legal advsr to DCMS TSD 1998–99, dir Legal (Commercial, Environment, Housing and Local Govt) DETR 1999–2001, dir Legal (Tport) DTLR 2001–02, legal advsr and legal services dir Legal DfT 2002–13; memb Editorial Advsy Bd Nottingham Law Jl; memb Advsy Bd City Univ Law Sch; Hon LLD City Univ 2012; *Publications* contrib to learned jls and books incl: The Quality of Fairness is not Constrained (1996), The International Criminal Court, The Making of the Rome Statute (1999); *Recreations* reading, music of Anne Sofie von Otter, running, sunflowers, photography; *Style*— Christopher Muttukumaru, Esq, CB

MYDDELTON, Prof David Roderic; s of Dr Geoffrey Cheadle Myddelton, and Jacqueline Esther, *née* Nathan; *b* 11 April 1940; *Educ* Eton, Harvard Business Sch (MBA); *m* 28 April 1986 (m dis 1998), Hatherley Angela d'Abo; 1 step da (Louisa b 1974), 1 step s (Charles b 1975); *Career* CA 1961; lectr fin and accounting Cranfield 1965–69, lectr accounting London Business Sch 1969–72, prof of fin and accounting Cranfield Sch of Mgmnt 1972–2005 (emeritus prof 2005–); chm Inst of Economic Affrs 2001–15; ACIS 1966, FCA 1971; *Books* The Power to Destroy (1969, 2 edn 1994), The Meaning of Company Accounts (1971, 8 edn 2005), On A Cloth Untrue (1984), The Economy And Business Decisions (1984), Essential Management Accounting (1987, 2 edn 1992), Accounting and Financial Decisions (1991), Managing Business Finance (2000), Unshackling Accountants (2004), They Meant Well: Government Project Disasters (2007), Margins of Error in Accounting (2009); *Recreations* crossword puzzles, jigsaw puzzles; *Clubs* MCC, Reform; *Style*— Prof D R Myddelton; ✉ 20 Nightingale Lodge, Admiral Walk, London W9 3TW (☎ 020 7286 9945)

MYERS, Andrew; s of Gordon Elliot Myers, CMG, and Wendy Myers; *b* 1964; *Educ* Haberdashers' Aske's, UC Oxford; *m* 1993, Dr Kathryn Myers; *Career* slr Travers Smith Braithwaite 1991–2001, ptnr Howes Percival until 2008, ptnr Denton Wilde Sapte (now Dentons) 2008–12, ptnr Stephenson Harwood 2012–; Alfred Syrett Prize 1991; memb

Law Soc 1993; *Style—* Andrew Myers, Esq; ✉ Stephenson Harwood LLP, 1 Finsbury Circus, London EC2M 7SH (☎ 020 7809 2275, e-mail andrew.myers@shlegal.com)

MYERS, Bernard Ian; s of Edward Nathan Myers (d 1985), and Isabel Violet, *née* Viner (d 2000); *b* 2 April 1944; *Educ* Hendon Co GS, LSE (BSc Econ); *m* 17 Sept 1967, Sandra Hannah, da of Samuel Barc (d 1980); 2 da (Lara b 1969, Lyndsey b 1974), 1 s (Andrew b 1972); *Career* accountant 1962–72, merchant banker 1972–; directorships incl: Shield Tst Ltd 1976–96, N M Rothschild & Sons Ltd 1976–97 (md gp fin and overseas 1988–96), Rothschilds Continuation Holdings AG 1983–99, Rothschilds Continuation Ltd 1984–, Smith New Court plc 1985–95, Rothschild North America Inc 1987–99, Industrial Dwelling Soc (1885) Ltd 1997–, Fairacre Property Holdings Ltd 1999–2004, Rothschild Group Companies (non-exec); chm: Lambert Fenchurch plc 1998–99, Rothschild Tst Co Ltd 1998–2005, Enable Hldgs Ltd 2005–11, Norwood Ravenswood 2008–13; non-exec dir Moss Bross Group plc 2001–09; FCA 1968; *Recreations* opera, golf, theatre; *Style—* Bernard I Myers, Esq; ✉ Rothschilds Continuation Ltd, New Court, St Swithin's Lane, London EC4N 8AL (☎ 020 7280 5031, e-mail bernie.myers@rothschild.com)

MYERS, Ian David; s of Stuart Charles Myers, of Oxshott, Surrey, and Enid, *née* Alexander; *b* 3 August 1954; *Educ* Latymer Upper Sch, Pembroke Coll Oxford (MA); *m* 1976, Helen Rosemary, *née* Bennett; 1 da (Anastasia Tiffany b 2 July 1979), 2 s (Nikolai James Elliot b 23 April 1982, Anatoly Cornelius Constantine Wreyland b 18 Dec 1987); *Career* White Weld & Co London 1977–78 (NY office 1976–77), dir PaineWebber Inc 1989–2000, chm PaineWebber International (UK) Ltd 1990–2000 (joined 1978, dir 1987), md UBS Warburg 2000–2003, md SG Cowen 2003–; *Style—* Ian Myers, Esq; ✉ Cowen International Limited, 11th Floor, 1 Snowden Street, London EC2A 2DQ

MYERS, Sidney Albert; s of Gordon Myers, of London, and Leonora, *née* Wilson; *b* 21 May 1958, London; *Educ* St Paul's, Worcester Coll Oxford (BA); *m* 2 April 1995, Lorraine, *née* Viner; 1 da (Rosine Alex b 26 Nov 1996), 1 s (Samuel Edward b 1 July 1999); *Career* Allen & Overy LLP: articled clerk 1982–84, assoc 1984–90, ptnr 1991–2008, head Regulatory Investigations Gp 1998–2008; ptnr Financial Regulatory Practice Berwin Leighton Paisner LLP 2009–; memb Lawyers Consultative Gp FCA, memb Advsy Bd Financial Services Lawyers Assoc 2006; memb Law Soc 1984; *Recreations* family, sport; *Clubs* MCC, RAC; *Style—* Sidney Myers, Esq; ✉ Berwin Leighton Paisner LLP, Adelaide House, London Bridge, London EC4R 9HA (☎ 020 3400 4847, fax 020 3400 0000, e-mail sidney.myers@blplaw.com)

MYERSCOUGH, Ishbel; da of Henry Ferdinand Myerscough (d 2006), and Elizabeth Crichton, *née* Fraser; *b* 5 November 1968; *Educ* Highbury Hill HS, City of London Sch for Girls, Glasgow Sch of Art (BA), Slade Sch of Art (postgrad with distinction); *m* 17 March 2001, Cormac John Alexander; 2 s (Herbert Henry b 17 Aug 2001, Fraser Ian b 1 May 2004), 1 da (Isabella Elizabeth Maeve b 30 Aug 2007); *Career* artist; cmmns incl portraits of: Helen Mirren for the Nat Portrait Gallery, Graham Gooch for the MCC, Sir Peter Strawson for the Nat Portrait Gallery 2005, George Benjimen 2006, Sir Willard White for the Nat Portrait Gallery 2009; *Exhibitions* incl: Van Gogh Self-Portrait Exhbn (Burrell Collection Glasgow) 1990–91, RSA Student Exhbns Edinburgh 1990 and 1991, Nat Portrait Gallery Portrait Competition Exhbn 1990, 1991, 1992 and 1995, one man show Turtle Quay Art Centre London 1992 and 1996, RGI 131st Annual Exhbn McLellan Gallery Glasgow 1992, ROI annual show Mall Gallery London 1994, Treasures of the Nat Portrait Gallery (touring show Japan) 1995–96, Group Realist Show Berlin 1995, British Figurative Art (pt 1) Flowers East 1997, one man show Cork Street Gallery London 2000, Being Present (Jerwood Space London) 2004, group show Her House (curated jtly with Chantal Joffe Hoxton London) 2008, one man show Flowers Gallery Cork Street London 2011, Spitfire Pilot Portraits (RAF Museum) 2013, Self (Turner Contemporary Margate) 2015, The Last of the Tide: portraits of D-Day veterans (Buckingham Palace) 2015, Friendship Portraits (jt exhbn with Chantal Joffe, Nat Portrait Gall) 2015; *Awards* incl: John and Mabel Craig Bequest 1990 and 1991, Elizabeth Greenshields Fndn award 1991, 1993 and 1999, first prize in Hunting/Observer plc Prize for Art 1992, Nat Portrait Gallery BP Portrait Awards 1st prize 1995 (commended 1991 and 1993, 3rd prize 1992), National Westminster Bank prize for Art 3rd prize, Rootstein Hopkins Travel award to NY 1996, Robert and Susan Summers Connecticut residency 1996 and 1997; *Style—* Miss Ishbel Myerscough; ✉ 73 Colebrooke Row, London N1 8AA (☎ 020 7354 9511, e-mail ishbelmyerscough@gmail.com)

MYERSCOUGH, Morag Crichton; da of Henry Ferdinand Myerscough and Elizabeth Crichton Myerscough, of London; *b* 3 December 1963; *Educ* Highbury Hill HS, St Martin's Sch of Art (BA), Royal Coll of Art (MA); *Career* graphic designer; sr designer Lamb & Shirley 1988–90, independent designer 1990–93 (incl 6 months in Milan at Studio De Lucchi), fndr designer/dir Studio Myerscough 1993–; clients incl: Barbican Centre (Barbican Foyer Signale 2001–), Architecture Fndn, Derwent Valley Hldgs plc, Design Museum, Cmmn for Architecture and the Built Environment (CABE), RIBA, GLA, Design Cncl, Sci Museum, Br Cncl, Arts Cncl, British Land Company plc; external examiner MA Communications Central St Martins; graphic design conslt Conran Design Partnership 1996–; exhbns incl: Memphis Remembered (Design Museum) 2001, Rock Style: Fashion, Attitude & Style (Barbican) 2001, Architectural Odyssey (RIBA) 2001, Web Wizards (Design Museum) 2002, London Living City (RIBA); touring exhbns incl: Curation/Design 'Millennium Products' (Br Cncl and Design Cncl), 12 for 2000 (Br Cncl), Design Against Crime (Design Cncl) 2001, Expo E3 – 'State of Play' British Pavilion (Br Cncl LA) 2003, Hometime (Br Cncl China tour) 2003–04, European Design Biennial (Design Museum) 2003–04; owner 'Her House' Gallery 2002–; launched Hel Lamp (with Luke Morgan) and other products; lectr/judge: Germany, Norway, Canada, Switzerland, UK; Silver Award D&AD 1998, Design Week Award 2003; *Publications* incl: Myerscough Caravan (2003); *Style—* Ms Morag Myerscough

MYERSON, Prof Jeremy; *b* 6 August 1956; *Educ* Univ of Hull, RCA (MA); *Career* writer, speaker, academic and activist in design; with The Stage 1970s, design journalist 1980s, fndr ed Design Week 1986–89, ind author, researcher and curator in design 1990s; dir Helen Hamlyn Centre for Design RCA 1999–2015 (Helen Hamlyn prof of design 2008–); dir Innovation RCA 2004–09; FRSA; *Exhibitions* curator: Doing a Dyson (Design Museum London) 1996, Look Inside: New British Interiors for People (Br Cncl touring show) 1998, Rewind: 40 Years of Design and Advertising from the D&AD (V&A) 2002; *Publications* Gordon Russell: Designer of Furniture (1992), Design Renaissance (ed, 1994), New Public Architecture (1996), Making the Lowry (2000), The 21st Century Office (2003), New Demographics New Workspace (2010), Life of Work (2014); *Recreations* jazz, football, architecture; *Style—* Prof Jeremy Myerson; ✉ Helen Hamlyn Centre of Design, Royal College of Art, Kensington Gore, London SW7 2EU (☎ 07973314984, e-mail jeremy.myerson@rca.ac.uk)

MYERSON, Dr Keith Roger; s of Alexander Myerson, and Maxine, *née* Pearson; *b* 1 February 1950, Liverpool; *Educ* Quarry Bank HS Liverpool, Univ of Liverpool (MB, ChB); *m* 18 Dec 1981, Stella, *née* Brooks; 1 da (Alice Heather b 3 May 1984), 1 s (Peter Edward b 19 March 1986); *Career* house offr St Helen's Hosp Lancs 1973–74, SHO in clinical measurement Middx Hosp 1976–77, SHO in anaesthetics Plymouth 1977–78, registrar in anaesthetics Southampton 1979–81, sr registrar Bristol and SW region 1981–87, sr registrar Flinders Univ Adelaide 1982–83, conslt in anaesthesia and intensive care med Eastbourne Dist Gen Hosp 1987–2010, ret; sr perf assessor GMC; memb Postgrad Medical Educn and Trg Bd Workplace Based Assessment Ctee 2004–05, chm Assessment Ctee Acad of Royal Med Colls 2006–; memb Cncl Royal Coll of Anaesthetists 2003– (chair Clinical Question Gp, ed Bulletin 2004–, chm Communications Ctee 2006–); *Recreations* music, sailing, skiing; *Clubs* Kellog's Noddy; *Style—* Dr Keith Myerson

MYKURA, Hamish Finlayson; s of Walter Mykura (d 1988), and Alison, *née* Edmond; *b* 28 March 1962, Edinburgh; *Educ* George Heriot's Sch Edinburgh, Univ of Aberdeen (MA), Univ of Manchester (PhD); *m* 26 July 1997, Janey, *née* Walker; 2 da (Anna, Ingrid (twins) b 20 March 2000); *Career* prodn trainee BBC 1989–91, documentaries prodr BBC Radio 1991–92, prodr and dir BBC TV 1992–2000, dir Blakeway Productions 2000–01; Channel 4: commissioning ed for history 2001–03, head of history, science and religion 2003–07, head of specialist factual progs 2007, head of documentaries and More4 2008–12; exec vice-pres and head of int content Nat Geographic Channel 2012–; FRSA; *Recreations* skiing, hill walking, travel writing; *Clubs* West Hoathly; *Style—* Hamish Mykura, Esq; ✉ National Geographic Channels International, 10 Hammersmith Grove, London W6 7AP (☎ 020 7471 7601, e-mail hamish.mykura@fox.com)

MYLNE, Nigel James; QC (1984); s of Maj Harold James Mylne (10 Royal Hussars, d 1942), and Dorothy Evelyn Hogg, *née* Safford (d 1985); *b* 11 June 1939; *Educ* Eton; *m* 1, 4 April 1967 (m dis 1978), Julie Felicity Selena, da of Cdr Christopher Phillpotts, RN (d 1982); 1 da (Jessica b 1968), 2 s (Jonathan b 1969, Dominic b 1972); m 2, 18 Jan 1980 (m dis 1997), Mrs Judy Camilla Wilson, da of Maj Francis Gawain Hamilton Monteith (d 1975); 1 s (James b 1981); m 3, 18 Dec 2009, Susan, Lady Walker, da of Maj Derek Stuart Holmes; *Career* Nat Serv 2 Lt 10 Royal Hussars; called to the Bar Middle Temple 1963 (bencher 1995); recorder of the Crown Court 1983–, head of chambers 1997–99, pres Mental Health Review Tbnl 1999–, immigration judge 2005– (immigration adjudicator 1997–2005); Liveryman Worshipful Co of Haberdashers; *Recreations* beekeeping; *Clubs* Pratt's; *Style—* Nigel Mylne, Esq, QC; ✉ Langleys, Brixton Deverill, Wiltshire BA12 7EJ (☎ 01985 840351,e-mail nigelmylne@btinternet.com)

MYNERS, Baron (Life Peer UK 2008), of Truro in the County of Cornwall; Paul Myners; CBE (2003); *b* 1 April 1948; *m* 1995, Alison A I Macleod; 1 s (Bartholomew Piers Trevelyan b Feb 1996), 1 da (Talitha Phoebe Molly b April 1998); *Career* with N M Rothschild 1974–85 (latterly bd memb), chief exec and exec chm Gartmore Investment Management plc 1987–96 (joined as chief exec 1985), with NatWest Gp (following acquisition of Gartmore) 1996–2000 (exec dir 1997–2000), chm Gartmore plc 2000–01; non-exec chm: Guardian Media Gp plc 2000–, Marks and Spencer plc 2004–06 (non-exec dir 2002–06), Land Securities Gp plc 2007– (non-exec dir 2006–), Aspen Insurance Holdings Ltd; non-exec dir: PowerGen plc until 1996 (sometime non-exec dep chm), English & Scottish Investors Ltd, Orange plc, Bank of NY, mmO2 2001–; led HM Treasy's Review of Institutional Investment, chm Low Pay Cmmn 2006–, chm Personal Accounts Delivery Authy 2007–; former chm Assoc of Investment Cos, chm Investment Ctee Lloyd's of London; memb: City Disputes Panel, Financial Reporting Cncl, Ct of Dirs Bank of England 2005–; memb Advsy Bd: London Symphony Orch, Nat Maritime Museum Cornwall; tstee: Royal Acad, Glyndebourne, Tate (chair 2004–); FRSA; *Style—* The Lord Myners, CBE

MYNORS, Sir Richard Baskerville; 2 Bt (UK 1964), of Treago, Co Hereford; s of Sir Humphrey Charles Baskerville Mynors, 1 Bt (d 1989); *b* 5 May 1947; *Educ* Marlborough, Corpus Christi Coll Cambridge; *m* 1970, Fiona Bridget, da of late Rt Rev George Edmund Reindorp; 3 da (Alexandra Fiona (Mrs Stephen Herbert) b 1975, Frances Veronica (Mrs Michael Tomlinson-Mynors) b 1978, Victoria Jane (Mrs Michael Orsmond) b 1983); *Heir* none; *Career* schoolmaster and asst dir of music King's Sch Macclesfield 1970–73; dir of music: Wolverhampton G S 1973–81, Merchant Taylors' Sch Crosby 1981–88, Belmont Abbey Sch Hereford 1988–90; landowner and freelance musician 1990–; fell Woodward Corporation (Midland Div) 1995–2012; *Recreations* gardening, DIY, organ building; *Style—* Sir Richard Mynors, Bt; ✉ Treago, St Weonards, Hereford HR2 8QB (☎ and fax 01981 580208, e-mail fionamynors@btinternet.com)

M

N

NAGELSZTAJN, Michael James; s of Chajm Nagelsztajn, of Newcastle upon Tyne, and Cecelia, *née* Cooney; *b* 13 April 1955; *Educ* St Mary's Tech Sch Newcastle upon Tyne, Univ of Sheffield (BA, Dip Arch); *m* 16 Oct 1976, Judith, *née* Jennings; 2 s (Adam b 19 March 1982, Peter b 22 June 1985), 1 da (Hannah b 14 March 1989); *Career* fndr ptnr NSP Architects Nottingham 1988–89, project dir Benoy Ltd 1989–2000, dir S-P Architects 2000–, dir i/c media village for Olympic Games Athens 2004, dir Leonard Design Architects 2008–; projects in India, Spain, Kenya, Malaysia and UK; memb BCSC; memb Nottingham Ambassadors; memb ARB 1985, RIBA 1985; *Recreations* food and wine, keep-fit, football and rugby; *Style—* Michael Nagelsztajn, Esq; ✉ 16 Hillcrest Gardens, Burton Joyce, Nottingham NG14 5DE (☎ 0115 9314283, mobile 07989 555109); Leonard Design Architects, Albion House, 5–13 Canal Street, Nottingham NG1 7EG (☎ 0115 9450080, e-mail miken@leonarddesignarchitects.com)

NAHUM, Peter; s of Denis E Nahum, and Allison Faith, *née* Cooke; *b* 19 January 1947; *Educ* Sherborne; *m* 29 Aug 1987, Renate Angelika, da of Herr Ewald Meiser, of Germany; *Career* dir Peter Wilson's Sotheby's 1966–84; regular contrib as painting expert Antiques Roadshow 1980–2002 (discovered lost Richard Dadd painting 1986, subsequently sold to Br Museum); currently art dealer and publisher The Leicester Galleries Bloomsbury Square London, also website and web portal builder (created Online Galleries); chm Contemporary Arts Tst 2015–; *Books* Prices of Victorian Painting Drawings and Watercolours (1976), Monograms of Victorian and Edwardian Artists (1976), Cross Section, British Art in the 20th Century (1988), British Art From the 20th Century (1989), Burne-Jones, The Pre-Raphaelites & Their Century (1989), Burne-Jones: A Quest for Love (1993), Fairy Folk in Fairy Land (1997), Pre-Raphaelite. Symbolist. Visionary (2001), Medieval to Modern (2003), My Secret Book From the World of Tolkien (2007); *Recreations* gardening, sailing, photography, theatre, travel, walking, horse trekking, museums and galleries; *Style—* Peter Nahum, Esq; ✉ c/o Renate Nahum, 5 Bloomsbury Square, London WC1A 2TA (e-mail peternahum@leicestergalleries.com, website www.leicestergalleries.com)

NAIDU, Logan; *Educ* Univ of Birmingham; *Career* analyst J P Morgan 2000–01, corporate finance TMT PricewaterhouseCoopers 2001–03, fndr and ptnr The Cornell Partnership 2005–12, owner and memb Bd CityButler 2008–, ceo Dartmouth Ptnrs 2012–; investor Diginius 2015–; *Recreations* reading, tennis; *Style—* Logan Naidu, Esq; ✉ Dartmouth Partners, 12 Appold Street, London EC2A 2AW

NAIPAUL, Sir Vidiadhar Surajprasad (Vidia); kt (1990); *b* 1932; *Educ* UC Oxford (BA); *m* 1, 1955, Patricia Ann Hale (d 1996); 1 da (Maleeha Maria b 1979); m 2, 1996, Nadira Khannum Alvi; *Career* author; awards incl: David Cohen British Literature Prize 1993, Nobel Prize for Literature 2001; Hon DLitt: Univ of Cambridge 1983, Univ of London 1988, Univ of Oxford 1992; CLit 1994; *Books* The Mystic Masseur (winner of John Llewelyn Rhys Memorial prize, 1958), A House for Mr Biswas (1961), In A Free State (winner of Booker prize, 1971), A Bend in the River (1979), The Return of Eva Peron (1980), Among the Believers (1981), The Enigma of Arrival (1987), A Turn in the South (1989), India: A Million Mutinies Now (1990), A Way in the World (1994), Beyond Belief (1998), Half a Life (2001); *Style—* Sir Vidia Naipaul; ✉ c/o Andrew Wylie Agency, 17 Bedford Square, London WC1B 3JA (☎ 020 7908 5900)

NAIRN, Andrew; s of Capt Andrew Nairn, MC (d 1971), of Glasgow, and Margaret Cornfoot, *née* Turner (d 1972); *b* 31 July 1944, Glasgow; *Educ* Strathallan Sch; *m* 1, 1970 (m dis 1983), Susan Anne, da of Richard Alphonse Napier (d 1997); 1 da (Penelope Margaret b 1976), 1 s (Jonathan Richard b 1981); m 2, 1983, Glynis Vivienne, *née* Sweet; 1 step s (Barnaby Craggs b 1971), 1 step da (Charlotte Craggs b 1974); *Career* trainee chartered accountant Thomson Jackson Gourlay and Taylor 1962–67; Baker Tilly: joined 1967, ptnr 1970–2004, London region managing ptnr 1990–93, conslt 2004–09; England and Wales area sec and treas ICAS until 1999; dir Booker Prize Trading Ltd 2002–, co sec and dir Colebream Estates Ltd 2004–; tstee Caza Azul Tst 2003–09; dep chm Dulwich Cons Assoc 1978; MICAS; *Recreations* fly fishing, golf; *Clubs* Garrick, Union Soc of the City of Westminster (hon sec 1995–2008, chm 2005–06), Society of Bookmen (hon sec 2004–07); *Style—* Andrew Nairn, Esq, CA; ✉ 86 Douglas Lane, Grimsargh, Preston, Lancashire PR2 5JF (☎ 01772 705117, mobile 07939 042573, e-mail andrew@nairn.me.uk)

NAIRN, Nicholas (Nick); s of James and Irene Nairn, of Lochend House, Port of Mentieth, Stirling; *b* 12 January 1959; *Educ* McLaren HS, Glasgow Nautical Coll; *m* 1, 30 Jan 1986 (m dis), Fiona, da of Hector Macdonald; m 2, 16 June 2001, Holly, da of Rodger Anderson; 1 da (Daisy Skye b 27 Sept 2002), 1 s (Callum James Roger b 16 May 2004); *Career* served Merchant Navy 1976–83 (third navigating offr 1980–83); fndr, chef and formerly dir Braeval restaurant by Aberfoyle Stirling 1986–97 (renovation 1984–86), fndr, chef and dir Nairns (Glasgow) 1998–2003, fndr Nairns Cook Sch 2000–, fndr Nairns Anywhere 2000–, owner Nick Nairn Enterprise 1995–; chef conslt Tesco; conslt: Foodfest Scottish Exhbn Centre 2001 and 2002, Aquascot Seafarms, Weber Barbecues, Royal Bank of Scotland, Salton Europe, Scottish Exec Healthy Eating Campaign; launched Baxter's with Nick Nairn range of sauces 2000, launched Nick Nairn Cookware (Best Cookware and Bakeware Housewares Industry Awards 2002); television: Ready Steady Cook (BBC2) 1995–, Wild Harvest with Nick Nairn (BBC2) 1996, Who'll do the Pudding? (BBC1) 1996, Wild Harvest 2 with Nick Nairn (BBC2) 1997, Island Harvest (BBC2) 1998 (Silver Ladle for Best TV Show Jacobs Creek World Food Media Awards), Celebrity Ready Steady Cook (BBC1) 1998–, Back to Basics with Nick Nairn (Carlton) 2000, Kitchen Invaders 2000, So You Think You're A Good Driver (BBC1) 2002, Nick Nairn and the Dinner Ladies (BBC Scotland) 2003, Eating in the Sun (BBC 2) 2006, finalist Taste the Nation (ITV) 2008, winner Great British Menu (cooked main course for Queen's 80th birthday); regular contrib: Food and Drink, Masterchef, Junior Masterchef and Carlton Daily, Good Food Live, Saturday Kitchen; columnist and contrib: Sunday Mail 1997–2000, BBC Good Food Magazine 1997–, Sunday Herald 2000–01, Sunday Herald Magazine 2000–, Scots Magazine 2000–03; fndr memb: Scottish Chefs' Assoc 1993 (memb Advsy Bd), Scottish Martell Cordon Bleu Assoc 1994; memb Masterchefs of GB 1992; hon pres Scottish Chefs Nat Cookery Centre; patron Queen Margaret Univ Coll; DUniv Stirling 2007; *Awards* Scottish Field/Bollinger Newcomer of the Year 1987, Acorn award Caterer and Hotelkeeper Magazine 1988, Scottish Field/Carlton Best Restaurant in Category 1988, Michelin Red M award 1990, Scottish Field/Charles Heidsieck Scottish Restaurant of the Year 1990, Good Food Guide County Restaurant of the Year 1991, Michelin Star 1991–, 3 AA Rosettes 1991–, Macallan/Decanter Scottish Restaurant of the Year 1992, Scottish Field/Bowmore Restaurant of the Year 1992, 4/5 Good Food Guide 1996, Thistle Award Scottish Tourist Board 1998, Michelin Bib Gourmand 1998, Glenfiddich Spirit of Scotland Award 2000, Personality of the Year Food Processing Awards 2002; *Books* incl: Wild Harvest with Nick Nairn (1996), Wild Harvest 2 (1997), Meat, Poultry and Game (1997), Nick Nairn Cooks The Main Course (with video, 1998), Island Harvest (1998), Nick Nairn Cooks Desserts (with video, 1998), Tower Pressure Cooker recipe Book (1999), Nick Nairn Top 100 Salmon Recipes (2002), New Scottish Cookery (2003), Nick Nairn's Top 100 Chicken Recipes (2004), Fish 'n' Tips (2006), Nick Nairn Cook Sch (2008); contrib to numerous cookery books; *Recreations* hill walking, mountain biking, windsurfing, wine, eating in!; *Style—* Nick Nairn, Esq; ✉ Nick Nairn Enterprise, Port of Menteith, Stirling FK8 3JZ (☎ 01877 389909 fax 01877 389901, e-mail info@nairncookschool.co.uk, website www.nairnscookschool.com and www.nicknairn.tv)

NAIRN-BRIGGS, Very Rev George Peter; DL (West Yorkshire 2006); s of Fredrick Nairn-Briggs (d 1980), and Gladys Lilian Nairn-Briggs (d 1999); *b* 5 July 1945; *Educ* Slough Tech HS, KCL (AKC), St Augustine's Coll Canterbury; *m* 1968, Candida, da of William Vickery; 1 da (Rebekah b 1970), 1 s (Edmund b 1972); *Career* local authy housing 1963–64, press offr MAFF 1964–66; ordained: deacon 1970, priest 1971; curate: St Laurence Catford 1970–73, St Saviour Raynes Park 1973–75; vicar: Christ the King Salfords 1975–81, St Peter St Helier 1981–87; Bishop's advsr for social responsibility Wakefield 1987–97, canon residentiary Wakefield Cathedral 1992–97, provost of Wakefield 1997–2000, dean of Wakefield 2000–07, emeritus dean 2007–; dep prolocutor Convocation of York 1995–2006; memb Gen Synod C of E 1980–2007 (memb Bd for Social Responsibility 1985–2001, memb Panel of Chm 1997–2004), memb C of E Marriage Law Working Gp 2003–07; chm Churches Regnl Cmmn for Yorkshire and the Humber 1998–2002, memb Exec Assoc of English Cathedrals 2000–07, church cmmr 2004–07; memb: Wakefield City Centre Partnership 1995–2006, Wakefield Standards Ctee 1999– (ind chair 2004), Wakefield Local Strategic Partnership 2001–03, Yorks Regnl Cultural Consortium 2002–07, Mid-Yorks Hosp Tst Bd 2002–04; chair Community Fndn for Wakefield District 2011–12; fndn govr Cathedral Sch 1997–2007, govr Bretton Hall Coll 1999–2001, govr Wakefield Coll 2002–06; chm various local charitable trusts; Freeman City of Wakefield; *Publications* Love in Action (1986), Serving Two Masters (1988), It Happens in the Family (1992); *Recreations* reading, buying antiques, travel; *Style—* The Very Rev George Nairn-Briggs, DL, AKC; ✉ Abbey House, 2 St James Court, Wakefield WF2 8DN (☎ 01924 291029, mobile 07770 636840, e-mail nairnbriggs@btinternet.com)

NAIRNE, Alexander Robert (Sandy); CBE (2011); s of Rt Hon Sir Patrick Dalmahoy Nairne, KCB, MC, of Chilson, Oxon, and Penelope Chauncy, *née* Bridges; *b* 8 June 1953; *Educ* Radley, UC Oxford (MA, memb Isis Boat Crew); *partner* Prof Sylvia Elizabeth Tickner, FBA (Lisa); 1 s (Kit b 1984), 1 da (Eleanor b 1987); *Career* asst dir: MOMA Oxford 1974–76, Modern Collection Tate Gallery London 1976–79; dir of exhibitions ICA London 1980–84, freelance curator and writer 1984–87, dir of visual arts Arts Cncl of GB London 1987–92, sr research fell Getty Grant Prog 1992–93; Tate Gallery: dir of public and regnl servs 1994–98, dir of nat progs 1998–2001, dir progs 2001–02; dir Nat Portrait Gallery 2002–15; chair Fourth Plinth Commissioning Gp 2003–08, Maggie's Art Grp 2012–, Clore Cultural Leadership Prog Bd 2014–; memb: Exec Ctee Art Galleries Assoc 1976–81, Exec Ctee Gtr London Arts 1983–86, Art and Architecture Advsy Panel RSA 1990–95, Fabric Advsy Ctee St Paul's Cathedral 1997– (chair 2011–), Bank Note Advsy Ctee; advsr Works of Art Ctee Br Library 1989–91; govr Univ of Middx 1996–2003 (dep chair 1999–2001); memb Cncl: Br Sch at Rome 2001–10, RCA 2001–10; Hon Dr: Middx Univ 2005, De Montfort Univ 2008, Univ of London 2012, Norwich Univ of the Arts 2015; hon fell UC Oxford 2006, sr fell Royal Coll of Art 2010; FSA 2011; *Books* British Sculpture in the Twentieth Century (jt ed, 1981), Picturing the System (jt ed, 1981), State of the Art (1987), Thinking About Exhibitions (jt ed, 1996), The Portrait Now (2006), Art Theft and the Case of the Stolen Turners (2011), The 21st Century Portrait (2013); *Recreations* racing punting, competitive croquet; *Clubs* Chelsea Arts, Leander (Henley); *Style—* Sandy Nairne, Esq, CBE; ✉ e-mail: sandynairne43@gmail.com

NAIRNE, Andrew; s of Sir Patrick Nairne, of Oxon, and Penelope Chauncy, née Bridges; bro of Sandy Nairne, *qv*; *b* 10 February 1960, Guildford, Surrey; *Educ* Radley, Univ of St Andrews; *m* 1 July 1995, Nicola Dandridge; 2 s (Matthew b 5 Oct 1996, Patrick b 29 April 1998); *Career* asst curator Kettle's Yard Cambridge 1984, dep dir Ikon Gall Birmingham 1985, exhbns dir Centre for Contemporary Arts (CCA) Glasgow 1986–92, visual arts dir Scottish Arts Cncl 1992–97, dir Dundee Contemporary Arts 1997–2001, dir Modern Art Oxford 2001–08, exec dir arts Arts Cncl England 2008–11, dir Kettle's Yard Cambridge 2011–; visiting fell Nuffield Coll Oxford 2003–09; FRSA; *Recreations* running; *Style—* Andrew Nairne, Esq; ✉ 15 Grazebrook Road, London N16 0HU

NAISH, John Alexander; s of William Henry Naish (d 1987), and Elizabeth Lyon (d 1993); *b* 12 April 1948, Bristol; *Educ* Queen Elizabeth's Hosp Bristol, Dr Challoner's GS Amersham, City of London Coll (BA); *m* 18 Sept 1982, Bonnie Kam Pik, da of Pham Tak, of Hong Kong; 2 s (William b 3 April 1987, Henry b 3 Aug 1989); *Career* dir Hill Samuel Bank Ltd 1985–93, dir Investment Banking Asia Pacific NatWest Markets 1994–97, sr conslt Penna 1997–2014; exec dir Willis 1997–2014; memb Cncl Japan Soc 1998–2005; FCIB 1983; *Recreations* golf, astronomy, music; *Clubs* Oriental, Royal Over-Seas League, Tokyo; *Style—* John Naish, Esq; ✉ 39 Hamble Court, 1 Broom Park, Teddington TW11 9RW (e-mail johnnaish@btinternet.com)

NANDY, Lisa Eva; MP; da of Dipak Nandy, of Nottingham, and Luise, *née* Byers; *b* 9 August 1979, Manchester; *Educ* Univ of Newcastle upon Tyne (BA), Birkbeck Coll London (MSc); *Career* researcher to Neil Gerrard, MP 2001–03, policy researcher Centrepoint 2003–05, policy advsr Children's Soc 2005–10; cncllr Hammersmith and Fulham 2006–10, MP (Lab) Wigan 2010–, shadow sec of state for energy and climate change 2015–; dir Lyric Hammersmith 2006–10; *Recreations* theatre, rugby league; *Style—* Lisa Nandy, MP; ✉ House of Commons, London SW1A 0AA (e-mail lisa.nandy.mp@parliament.uk); Office of Lisa Nandy, MP, Elizabeth House, The Pier, Pottery Road, Wigan WN3 4EX (☎ 01942 242047)

NAPIER, Christopher Lennox; OBE (2016); s of Capt Lennox William Napier, DSO, DSC, RN (d 2001), and Elizabeth Eve, *née* Lindsay (d 1996); *b* 5 December 1944; *Educ* Sherborne, Britannia RNC Dartmouth; *m* 1971, Susan Margaret, da of Ian McLauchlan (d 1985); 1 s (James b 1972), 1 da (Georgina b 1976); *Career* joined BRNC Dartmouth

1962, qualified submarines 1966, ret as Lt Cdr 1976; Clifford Turner: articled clerk 1976–78, admitted slr 1979, slr 1979–83, ptnr 1983–87; ptnr Clifford Chance 1987–99; civil mediator 1999–; tstee Hants CPRE; vice-pres Petersfield Soc; Freeman City of London, Liveryman City of London Slrs' Co; memb Law Soc; FRSA; *Recreations* walking, reading, golf, sailing; *Style—* Christopher Napier, OBE; ✉ Kimpton House, Durford Wood, Petersfield, Hampshire GU31 5AS (☎ 01730 893272, e-mail christopher.napier@btinternet.com)

NAPIER, Iain John Grant; *b* 10 April 1949, Rothesay, Bute; *m*; 3 c; *Career* Whitbread plc 1972–77, Ford Motor Co 1977–89 (latterly fleet sales dir Ford of Britain), Bass plc 1989–2000 (positions incl chief exec Bass Brewers and Bass International Brewers 1996–2001), vice-pres UK and Ireland and memb Exec Ctee Interbrew SA 2000–01, chief exec Taylor Woodrow plc 2002–06; non-exec chm: Imperial Tobacco Gp plc 2007–14 (non-exec dir 2000–, jt vice-chm 2004–06), McBride plc 2007–, John Menzies plc 2010– (non-exec dir 2008–); non-exec dir: Perry Gp 1996–2001, Henderson Investors plc 1997–99, St Modwens Properties plc 2001–02, BOC Gp plc 2004, Collins Stewart plc 2007–09, Molson Coors Brewing Co USA 2008–, W M Grant & Sons (Distillers) Ltd 2009–; FCMA, CGMA; *Recreations* rugby, walking; *Style—* Iain J G Napier, Esq; ✉ Castlehill, Rockcliffe, Dalbeattie, Kirkcudbrightshire DG5 4QG

NAPIER, John; s of James Edward Thomas Napier, and Florence Emma, *née* Godbold; *b* 1 March 1944; *Educ* Hornsey Coll of Art, Central Sch of Art & Crafts; *m* 1 (m dis 1985), Andreane Neofitou; 1 s (Julian b 1965), 1 da (Elise b 1968); m 2 (m dis 1995), Donna King; 1 s (James b 1984), 1 da (Jessica b 1988); m 3, 21 June 2014, Caroline McGee; *Career* set designer; assoc designer RSC; hon fell London Inst 2001; RDI 1996; *Theatre and Film* 150 film, musical and theatrical prodns incl: The Ruling Class 1968, The Fun War 1968, Muzeeka 1968, George Frederick 1968, Turista 1968, Cancer 1969, Isabel's a Jezebel 1969, Mister 1970, The Foursome 1970, The Lovers of Viorne 1970, Lear 1970, Jump 1971, Sam Sam 1971, Big Wolf 1971, The Devils (ENO) 1972, Equus (NT) 1972, The Party 1972, Knuckle 1973, Kings & Clowns 1974, The Travelling Music Show 1974, Hedda Gabler (RSC) 1974, Much Ado About Nothing 1975, The Comedy of Errors (RSC) 1975, King Lear (RSC) 1975, Macbeth (RSC) 1975, A Midsummer Night's Dream 1976, As You Like It 1976, The Merry Wives of Windsor 1977, Twelfth Night 1977, Three Sisters 1977, Once in a Lifetime 1977, Lohengrin (Royal Opera House, SWET Award), The Greeks (RSC) 1979, Nicholas Nickleby (RSC, SWET and Tony Awards) 1979, Cats (Tony Award) 1980, Henry IV Parts I and II 1981, Peter Pan (RSC) 1981, Idomeneo (Glyndebourne) 1982, Macbeth (Royal Opera House) 1983, Starlight Express (Tony Award 1987) 1984, Les Misérables (Tony Award 1987) 1985, Time (Dominion) 1986, Captain EO (Disney film starring Michael Jackson) 1987, Miss Saigon 1989, Siegfried and Roy (The Mirage Las Vegas) 1989, Children of Eden 1990, Hook (Steven Spielberg film) 1991, Trelawny of the Wells (RNT) 1993, Sunset Boulevard 1993 (Tony Award 1995), Burning Blue (Haymarket (Olivier Award for Best Set Design 1996)) 1995, The Tower (Almeida) 1995, Who's Afraid of Virginia Woolf? (Almeida and Aldwych) 1996, Jane Eyre (Toronto) 1996, Jesus Christ Superstar (Lyceum) 1996, An Enemy of the People (RNT) 1997, Peter Pan (RNT) 1997, Martin Guerre (UK tour) 1998, Candide (RNT) 1999, Jane Eyre (NY) 2000, Nabucco (Met Opera) 2001, South Pacific (RNT) 2001, Skellig 2003, Aladdin 2004 and 2005, Equus 2007 and (NY) 2008, Disconnect 2010, Birdsong 2010, Don Giovanni (WNO) 2011; *Exhibitions* incl: Stages – Beyond the Fourth Wall (exhbn of fine art, Towner Art Gallery Eastbourne) 2015–16; *Recreations* photography; *Style—* John Napier, Esq; ✉ c/o Macnaughton Lord Representation, 2nd Floor, 16 Crucifix Lane, London SE1 3JW (☎ 020 7407 9201, website www.johnnapierstages.com)

NAPIER, John Alan; s of William Arthur Napier, of Sudbury, and Barbara Eileen, *née* Chatten (d 1962); *b* 22 August 1942; *Educ* Colchester Royal GS, N E Essex Tech Coll, Emmanuel Coll Cambridge (BA); *m* 1, 24 June 1961 (m dis), Gillian Joyce, *née* Reed; 2 s (Stephen Paul b 1 Dec 1961, Russell John b 15 Sept 1965), 1 da (Karen Clare b 3 Oct 1963); m 2, 12 March 1992, Caroline Mary Elizabeth, da of Charles Jarvis; 1 da (Amelia Caroline b 17 Sept 1992); *Career* jr and middle mangr Int Publishing Corp and Reed Int 1960–69, md Index Printers 1969–72, md QB Newspapers 1972–76, exec dir (Aust) James Hardie Industries 1976–86, gp md AGB plc 1986–90, md Hays plc 1991–98; chm: Booker plc 1998–2000, Kelda Gp plc 2000–08, Royal & Sun Alliance Insurance Gp plc 2003–12, Aegis Gp plc 2008–13; former bd memb Yorkshire Forward; chm Yorks and Humber Rural Affrs Forum 2000–; *Recreations* rural matters, outdoor activities, people and philosophy; *Style—* John Napier, Esq; ✉ Aegis Group plc, 10 Triton Street, Regent's Place, London NW1 3BF

NAPIER, (Thomas) Michael; CBE (2005), Hon QC; s of Montague Keith Napier (d 1975), and Mary, *née* Mather (d 1954); *b* 11 June 1946; *Educ* Loughborough GS, Hulme Hall Univ of Manchester (open exhibition, First XV Rugby); *m* 27 Dec 1969, Denise Christine; 2 da (Holly Danielle b 26 June 1973, Amy Abigail b 9 June 1975), 1 s (Frederick John b 31 Oct 1980); *Career* articled clerk Malcolm H Moss Moss Toone & Deane Loughborough 1968–70, asst slr W H Thompson Manchester 1970–72, sr ptnr Irwin Mitchell Sheffield, Leeds, Birmingham, Newcastle upon Tyne, Manchester, Glasgow, Malaga, Madrid, Bristol and London 1983–2012 (ptnr Sheffield 1973), jt sr ptnr Pannone Napier 1985–94; conslt 2012–; former chm Harbour Litigation Funding Ltd (currently sr ind non-exec dir); visiting prof of gp litigation and disaster law Nottingham Law Sch 1992–; pro bono envoy to Attorney-Gen 2002–; former editorial conslt: Personal Injury Compensation, Medical Law Review; Mental Health Act Cmmn: cmmr 1983–92, jt vice-chm 1985–88, chm NE region 1985–89; former pres S Yorks Medico-Legal Soc, memb Governing Bd Assoc of Trial Lawyers of America 1990–97, memb Cncl Law Soc 1993– (pres 2000–01), pres Assoc of Personal Injury Lawyers 1994–96, memb Legal Servs Bd 2009–10, assessor Lord Justice Jackson's Review of the Costs of Civil Litigation; memb: Cncl JUSTICE 1995–2010, Civil Justice Cncl 1998–2008; chm Hosp Advsy Ctee Rampton Hosp 1992–96; tstee Thalidomide Tst until 2014 (vice-chm); Freeman Co of Cutlers in Hallamshire 1992, Liveryman City of London Slrs Co 2008–; Hon LLD Univ of Sheffield, Hon LLD Nottingham Law Sch; hon bencher Gray's Inn; memb Law Soc 1970; *Books* Conditional Fees, A Survival Guide (Napier and Bawdon 1995), Compensation for Psychiatric Injury (Napier and Wheat 1995); *Recreations* mountain biking in Norfolk; *Clubs* Athenaeum; *Style—* Michael Napier, Esq, CBE, QC; ✉ Windmill Hill, Great Walsingham, Norfolk (☎ 01328 820213, website www.michaelnapier.com)

NAPIER, Robert Stewart; CBE (2011); s of Andrew Napier (d 1967), and Lilian V, *née* Ritchie (d 2000); *b* 21 July 1947; *Educ* Sedbergh, Sidney Sussex Coll Cambridge (MA), Harvard Business Sch (AMP); *m* 17 Dec 1977, Patricia Gray Stewart; 1 da (Catriona Rose Stewart b 1984); *Career* Rio Tinto Zinc Corp 1969–73, Brandts Ltd 1973–75, Fisons Ltd 1975–81; Redland plc: fin dir 1981–87, gp md 1987–97, chief exec 1991–97; chief exec WWF-UK 1999–2007; chm: English Partnerships 2007–08 (non-exec dir 2004–08), Met Office 2006–, Homes and Communities Agency 2008–; non-exec dir: United Biscuits (Holdings) plc 1992–2000, Rentokil Initial plc 1996–99, Anglia Water Services Ltd 2002–; pres Nat Cncl of Building Materials Prodrs 1996–99; *Style—* Robert Napier, Esq, CBE

NAQVI, Dr Nayyar; OBE (2004); s of Syed Tassawar H Naqvi (d 1965), and Aquila, *née* Raza (d 1990); *b* 17 May 1945, Rampur, India; *Educ* MB BS; *m* 28 Oct 1970, Nasreen, *née* Khan; 2 da (Nitha, Zahra); *Career* house physician/surgeon New Cross Hosp Wolverhampton 1968–69, sr house physician Wigan Royal Infirmary 1970–71, medical registrar Wigan Royal Infirmary 1971–75, cardiology registrar Wythenshawe Hosp Manchester 1976–77, Kleinwort research fell St Thomas Hosp London 1977–78, hon sr registrar cardiology St Thomas Hosp London 1978–79, conslt cardiologist Wrightington, Wigan and Leigh NHS Fndn Tst 1979–; author of numerous pubns; Wigan Life Award 2011, awarded star on the Wigan Walk of Fame 2013; govr Winstanley Coll Lancs 2014–; memb Br Cardiac Soc 1984, FRCPE 1986, FESC 1990, FRCP 1995, FACC 2004; *Recreations* golf, gardening, music, reading; *Clubs* Wigan Golf, Arley Hall, Haigh, Finchley Golf; *Style—* Dr Nayyar Naqvi, OBE; ✉ Zenith, 7 Meadowfield, Lostock, Bolton BL6 4PA (☎ 01204 492514, e-mail nayyar.naqvi@btinternet.com); Department of Cardiology, Royal Albert Edward Infirmary, Wigan Lane, Wigan WN1 2NN (☎ 01942 822542, e-mail nayyar.naqvi@wwl.nhs.uk)

NAQVI, Syed (Zakir Husain) Haider; s of Dr Ather Husain Naqvi (d 1954), and Saghir Fatima, *née* Rizvi (d 1997); *b* 14 October 1949; *Educ* Karachi Univ (BCom, MA Econ); *m* Marja-Liisa, da of Paavo Ilmari Nyyssönen, of Sorsakoski, Finland; 2 da (Chantal Samreen b 1980, Sabrina Yasmin b 1986); *Career* chartered accountant; internal auditor Philip Industries (UK) Ltd 1975–77, gp fin controller London Export Corporation (Holdings) Ltd 1977–78, ptnr Haider Naqvi & Co Chartered Accountants 1978–; fndr HELPs Group; FCA 1973, FCCA, FCIS 1974; *Recreations* Urdu poetry, snooker, chess; *Style—* Syed Haider Naqvi, Esq; ✉ Corner Cottage, 75 Lake View, Canons Drive, Edgware, Middlesex HA8 7SA (☎ 020 8958 8015, fax 020 8958 8535, e-mail hnco786@aol.com)

NAREY, Sir Martin James; kt (2013), DL (N Yorks 2015); s of John Narey, and Ellenor Narey; *b* 5 August 1955; *Educ* Sheffield Poly (BA); *m* 1978, Jan Goudy; 1 s, 1 da; *Career* prison govr at various establishments 1982–91; Home Office: private sec to min of state 1991–92, Criminal Policy Dept 1992–96; Reviewer of Delay in the Criminal Justice System 1996–97; HM Prison Service: head of security policy 1997–98, dir of regimes 1998–99, DG/ceo 1999–2003; second perm sec Home Office 2002–05, chief exec Nat Offender Mgmnt Service 2004–05; chief exec Barnardo's 2005–11, govt advsr on adoption 2011–13, govt advsr on children's social care 2013–; conslt and writer; memb ASA Cncl 2011–, chair Portman Gp 2012–, chair The Brain Tumor Charity 2015–; visiting prof Sheffield Hallam Univ, visiting prof Durham Univ 2012–; Gold medal Chartered Mgmnt Inst 2003; Hon Dr: Sheffield Hallam Univ 2003, Teesside Univ 2007, Manchester Metropolitan Univ 2011; *Publications* review of delay in criminal justice system (1997), report on an investigation at the Maze Prison (1998), report of the Ind Cmmn on Social Mobility (Liberal Democrat Pty 2009), A Blueprint for the Nation's Lost Children (The Times 2011), Making the Education of Social Workers Effective (Dept for Education 2013); numerous articles for The Guardian, The Times, The Telegraph and New Statesman; *Recreations* planning holidays, watching Middlesbrough FC; *Style—* Sir Martin James Narey, DL; ✉ e-mail nareymartin@gmail.com

NARGOLWALA, Kaikhushru Shiavax; s of Shivax D Nargolwala (d 1986), and Dhun S Nargolwala; *b* 22 April 1950; *m* 8 July 1973, Aparna, da of M G Kaul; *Career* CA Peat Marwick Mitchell & Co UK 1970–76; Bank of America: various mgmnt roles in UK 1976–84, head of US High Technology Industry Gp 1984–89, sr vice-pres and sr credit offr Asia 1990–93, gp exec vice-pres and head of Asia Wholesale Banking Gp 1993–95; gp exec dir Standard Chartered Bank 1999–2007 (gp head of corp banking sales 1998–99), Credit Suisse Asia Pacific: ceo 2008–10, chm 2010–; non-exec dir Tate & Lyle 2004–; ACA 1975, FCA 1981; *Recreations* reading, music, technology; *Clubs* Tower (Singapore), Tanglin (Singapore), Oriental (London); *Style—* Kai Nargolwala, Esq

NARULA, Prof Antony Ajay Pall (Tony); s of Yash Pall Narula (d 2003), and Prakash, *née* Varma; *b* 14 November 1955, Burma; *Educ* Epsom Coll, Trinity Hall Cambridge (MA), Univ of London (MB, BChir); *m* Aug 1985, Charlotte, *née* Beech; 1 da (Alexandra), 2 s (Maximilian, Henry); *Career* conslt surgn: Univ Hosp Leicester 1989–2001, St Mary's Hosp London 2001–14, ret; hon prof Middlesex Univ 2003–; memb Cncl RCS (treas 2008–13); pres ENT-UK 2015–18; NHS Beacon Award 1999; FRCS 1984, FRCSEd 2001; Clinical ENT: an illustrated textbook (1992, 2 edn 1999); *Clubs* RAC, Carlton; *Style—* Prof Tony Narula; ✉ London Reach House, Wargrave, Berkshire RG10 8HL (e-mail ent@narula.org.uk or secretary@narula.org.uk, website www.tonynarula.com or www.ent-surgeon-london.com)

N

NASEBY, Baron (Life Peer UK 1997), of Sandy in the County of Bedfordshire; Rt Hon Michael Wolfgang Laurence Morris; PC (1994); s of late Cyril Laurence Morris; *b* 25 November 1936, Bickley, Kent; *Educ* Bedford Sch, St Catharine's Coll Cambridge (MA); *m* 1960, Ann Phyllis, da of Percy Appleby (d 1973); 2 s (Hon Julian b 1961, Hon Jocelyn b 1972), 1 da (Hon Susannah b 1965); *Career* Nat Serv pilot offr RAF and NATO Wings; dir Benton & Bowles (advertising agency) 1971–81, fndr proprietor AM International Public Affairs Consultants 1976–92; Parly candidate (Cons) Islington N 1966, MP (Cons) Northampton S Feb 1974–97; PPS to Min of State NI Office 1979–81, chm Ways and Means Ctee and dep speaker 1992–97; memb: Public Accounts Ctee 1979–92, Cncl of Europe and WEU 1983–91, Speaker's Panel of Chairmen 1984–92; chm Br-Sri Lanka Parly Gp 1975–2015; chm: PSP Euro Med Charity 1993–2001, Tunbridge Wells Equitable Friendly Soc 1998–2005, Northants Victoria Co History 1994–2008; former chm: Br Singapore Parly Gp, Br Malaysia Gp, Br Burma Gp, Br-Maldives Parly Gp; former vice-chm Br-Indonesia Gp; former treas: Br-Thailand Gp, Br-Asian Gp; chm Invesco Recovery Tst 1998–2011, non-exec dir Mansell plc 1998–2003, non-exec dir City Disputes Panel Ltd 2015–; fndr prop Julius International Consultants 1997–2008; jt patron Naseby Battlefield Project Tst 2006–14; chm Bedford Sch 1989–2002 (govr 1982–2002); hon fell in history Univ of Nothampton; chm Confradia del Vino Chileno; Chamberlain Ordre des Coteaux de Champagne, Chevalier Confrérie des Chavaliers du Tastevin, Sri Lanka Ratna (Titular) 2005, Bernardo O'Higgins Medal Chile 2013; *Recreations* cricket, golf (pres Parly Golf Soc), tennis, heritage, forestry, budgerigars; *Clubs* Carlton, John O'Gaunt Golf, Port Stanley Golf, MCC, Northampton CCC (pres), All England Lawn Tennis, Lord's Taverners, La Commanderie de Bordeaux a Londres; *Style—* The Rt Hon the Lord Naseby, PC; ✉ Caesar's Camp, Sandy, Bedfordshire SG19 2AD (☎ 01767 680388)

NASH, Prof Anthony Aubrey; s of Alfred Nash (d 1967), of Coalville, Leics, and Mabel Evelyn, *née* Garrett; *b* 6 March 1949; *Educ* Newbridge Secdy Modern Coalville, Loughborough Coll, Queen Elizabeth Coll London (BSc), Univ of Birmingham (MSc, PhD); *m* 1979, Marion Eileen, da of Eric James Bazeley; 4 da (Laura Amy b 25 Feb 1980, Ruth Ellen b 23 Jan 1983, Esther Jane b 29 April 1985, Hannah Bethan b 24 Feb 1990); *Career* lectr Dept of Pathology Univ of Cambridge 1989–94 (research assoc 1977–84), prof and head Dept of Vet Pathology Univ of Edinburgh 1994–; Eleanor Roosevelt fell 1989–90; memb: Cncl of Soc for Gen Microbiology 2001–, BBSRC 2002–, Soc for Gen Microbiology, Br Soc of Immunology; FMedSci 1999, FRSE 2005; *Books* Mims Pathogenesis of Infectious Disease (1995); *Style—* Prof Anthony Nash; ✉ Department of Veterinary Pathology, University of Edinburgh, Summerhall, Edinburgh EH9 1QH (☎ 0130 650 6164, fax 0130 650 6511, e-mail tony.nash@ed.ac.uk)

NASH, Christopher Arthur Haseltine; s of Arthur Edward Nash, and Patricia, *née* Haseltine; *b* 16 August 1955; *Educ* Eastbourne GS, Eastbourne Coll of Art and Design, Univ of Bristol (BA, DipArch), Royal Western Acad Sch of Arch; *m* 1981, Sarah Patricia, *née* Woodgate; 1 s (Edward Thomas Woodgate b 1990), 1 da (Poppy Margot Lillian b 1992); *Career* architect; Form Structures Ltd Bristol 1976–77, Rock Townsend London 1978–81; Grimshaw Architects LLP (formerly Nicholas Grimshaw & Partners Ltd): dir 1992–2007, ptnr 2007–, dir various projects incl new airside centre for Zürich Airport, Euro Inst of Health and Med Sciences Univ of Surrey, RAC Regnl Control Centre Bristol, UK Pavilion Expo 92, and Cutty Sark Conservation Project; memb Architectural Ctee Steel Construction Inst; numerous public lectures at home and abroad; assessor: Civic Tst Awards 1993–2006, Corus Students' Competition 1994–2009, Structural Steel Awards

2005–; memb ARCUK 1981, RIBA 1981, MInstD 1996; *Recreations* sailing (yachtmaster); *Clubs* Seahorse Sailing, Royal Yachting Assoc, Cruising Assoc; *Style*— Christopher Nash, Esq; ✉ Grimshaw Architects LLP, 57 Clerkenwell Road, London EC1M 5NG (☎ 020 7291 4141, fax 020 7291 4194, e-mail chris.nash@grimshaw-architects.com)

NASH, David Harwood; s of Victor Nash, of Welwyn, Herts, and Anne, *née* Richardson; *Educ* St Albans Sch; *m* 1, Susan Margaret (d 1991), da of John Charlesworth Haldane; 1 s (James Harwood), 2 da (Charlotte Louise Harwood, Annabel Haldane); m 2, 10 Sept 2004, Valerie Conroy Scott; *Career* ptnr: Binder Hamlyn 1966–76, Pannell Kerr Forster (and predecessor firms) 1977–91, Nash & Co, chartered accountants 1991–; dir: Pelham Investment Property plc 1990; Liveryman Worshipful Co of Farriers; FCA; *Recreations* skiing, sailing, tennis; *Clubs* Royal Thames Yacht, MCC, Harlequin Football; *Style*— David Nash, Esq; ✉ Highclose Farm, Hungerford, Berkshire RG17 0SP (☎ 01488 680616, fax 01488 680643)

NASH, David John; s of Herbert John Nash, of Swanage, Dorset, and Daphne Diana, *née* Wedekind; *b* 12 May 1942; *Educ* Ashdown House, Marlborough, Université de Neuchâtel; *m* 1, 1966, Judith, *née* Small; 1 da (Sarah b 30 Jan 1970); m 2, 1986, Lucy Mitchell-Innes, 2 da (Josephine Clare b 14 Nov 1987, Isobel Daphne 16 April 1990); *Career* Sotheby's: London 1961–63, asst rep NY 1963–66 dir 1966–78, dir Painting Dept Sotheby's USA 1978–89, sr vice-pres and worldwide dir of Impressionist and Modern Painting Dept 1989–96; dir Mitchell-Innes & Nash Fine Art Consultants and Dealers 1996–; memb Art Advsy Panel US Internal Revenue Serv 1984–; *Style*— David Nash, Esq; ✉ 1060 Fifth Avenue, New York City, New York 10128, USA; Mitchell-Innes & Nash, 1018 Madison Avenue, New York City, New York 10075, USA (☎ 00 1 212 744 7400)

NASH, Prof David John; OBE (2004); s of Lt-Col W C E Nash (d 1984), of Maentwrog, N Wales, and D L Nash (d 1994); *b* 14 November 1945; *Educ* Brighton Coll, Kingston Coll of Art, Chelsea Sch of Art; *m* 1972, Claire, da of Walter Langdown; 2 s (William b 1973, Jack b 1977); *Career* artist; sculpture, environmental projects and works on paper exhibited worldwide; exhibitions incl: David Nash (Tate St Ives) 2004, Monumental Sculpture (Mannheim Museum) 2009, David Nash (Yorks Sculpture Park) 2010–11, David Nash – A Natural Gallery (Kew) 2012–13; work in over 100 public collections incl: Tate Gallery London, Guggenheim Museum NY, Metropolitan Museum of Art Tokyo; Hon Dr of Art and Design Kingston Univ 1999, Hon Dr of Humanities Univ of Glamorgan 2002; hon fell Univ of Wales Cardiff 2004; RA 1999; *Books* Forms into Time (1996, reprinted 2001), The Sculpture of David Nash (1996, reprinted 1999), Black and Light (2001), The Return of Art to Nature (2003), David Nash (2007), David Nash at Yorkshire Sculpture Park (2010), David Nash – A Natural Gallery (2013); *Style*— Prof David Nash, OBE, RA; ✉ c/o Annely Juda Fine Art, 23 Dering Street, London W1S 1AW (☎ 020 7629 7578)

NASH, George; *b* 2 October 1989, Guildford, Surrey; *Educ* Winchester Coll, St Catharine's Coll Cambridge; *Career* rower; achievements incl: Gold medal (fours) World Rowing Junior Championships 2007, memb Cambridge crew Oxford v Cambridge Univ Boat Race 2010, 2011 and 2013 (pres Cambridge Univ Boat Club 2013), Silver medal (fours) World Rowing U23 Championships 2010, Gold medal (coxless pair) World Rowing U23 Championships 2011, Bronze medal (coxless pair) Olympic Games 2012, Gold medal (eights) World Rowing Championships 2013, Gold medal (fours) World Rowing Championships 2014, Gold medal (eights) World Rowing Championships 2015, Gold medal (fours) Olympic Games 2016; *Clubs* Molesey Boat; *Style*— George Nash, Esq

NASH, Baron (Life Peer UK 2013), of Ewelme in the County of Oxfordshire; John Alfred Stoddard Nash; s of Lewis John Alfred Maurice Nash, and Josephine Karen, *née* Stoddard (d 1962); *b* 22 March 1949; *Educ* Milton Abbey, CCC Oxford (MA); *m* 6 Aug 1983, Caroline Jennifer, da of Geoffrey Hamilton Paul (d 1985); 1 da (Josephine b 1984), 1 s (Charles b 1985); *Career* asst dir Lazard Brothers and Co Ltd 1975–83, md Advent Ltd 1987 (joined 1983), chm British Venture Capital Association 1988–89, chm Sovereign Capital Ptnrs LLP 1989–2010; non-exec dir Dept for Educn 2010–13, Parly under sec of state for schools 2013–; chm: Pimlico Acad, Future Charity, Future Acads Tst; *Recreations* golf; *Clubs* Athenaeum, Turf; *Style*— The Lord Nash; ✉ e-mail nash.ps@education.gsi.gov.uk

NASH, Pamela; da of David Nash, and Kathleen *née* McGuinness (d 2002); *b* 24 June 1984, Bellshill, N Lanarkshire; *Educ* St Margaret's HS N Lanarkshire, Univ of Glasgow (MA); *Career* parly researcher to The Rt Hon Dr John Reid until 2010, MP (Lab) Airdrie & Shotts 2010–15, PPS to Vernon Coaker (as Shadow Sec of State for NI) 2010–13, Margaret Curran, (as Shadow Sec of State for Scotland) 2011–12 and Jim Murphy, *qqv* (as Shadow Sec of State for Int Devpt); memb Scottish Youth Parliament for Airdrie and Shotts 2007–09; *Style*— Miss Pamela Nash; ✉ e-mail pamela@pamelanash.com

NASH, Ronald Peter; CMG (2004), LVO (1983); s of John Henry Nash, and Jeanie Carmichael, *née* McIlwraith; *Educ* Harefield Secdy Modern Sch, Southall Grammar Tech Sch, Southall GS, Univ of Manchester (BA); *Career* entered HM Dip Serv 1970; served: Moscow, Vienna, New Delhi, Colombo; ambass to Nepal 1999–2003, ambass to Afghanistan 2002–03, high cmmr to Trinidad and Tobago 2004–06, ambass UK co-chair UK-Turkmen Trade and Industry Cncl 2010–; MCIL 1995; *Recreations* tennis; *Clubs* Royal Scots (Edinburgh); *Style*— Mr Ronald Nash, CMG, LVO; ✉ 175 Hivings Hill, Chesham, Buckinghamshire HP5 2PN

NASH, Stephanie Joy; da of Alfred Raymond Nash (d 1973), and Mary, *née* Spencer; *b* 20 March 1959; *Educ* Oldfields Hall Sch for Girls Uttoxeter, Sch of St Mary & St Anne Abbots Bromley (Duke of Edinburgh Gold award), St Martin's Sch of Art (BA); *Partner* Anthony Colin Michael, *qv*; 2 s (Montgomery Louis Spencer b 6 May 1996, Nelson Bartholomew Edwin b 28 Nov 1998), 1 da (Astor Elizabeth Pearl b 8 Jan 2003); *Career* Island Records: graphic designer 1981–86, art dir 1986–88; full-time ptnr Michael Nash Associates 1988– (fndr ptnr 1984); initially designers of record sleeves for artists incl Neneh Cherry, Fluke, Etienne Daho and Seal, subsequently cmmns for fashion designers Marc Jacobs, Jasper Conran, Issey Miyake, Jil Sander and Philip Treacy, etc, graphic designers for Harvey Nichols own brand food products 1992–, packaging designers for Egg (fashion retail outlet) 1994; memb AGI, FRSA; *Awards* (for Harvey Nichols food packaging) Gold Award D&AD for the Most Outstanding Packing Range 1993, Silver Award D&AD for the Most Outstanding Packaging – Individual Pack 1994, Art Dirs' Club of Europe Award 1994, CSD Minerva Award for Graphic Design 1994 and NY Festivals Gold Medal and Grand Award 1994; Silver Award D&AD for Compact Disc Packaging for Massive Attack 1995, Silver Award D&AD for Packaging Range for UTH Menswear 2001, Silver Award D&AD for John Galliano Packaging; various music industry awards; *Style*— Miss Stephanie Nash; ✉ Michael Nash Associates, 9 Grafton Mews, London W1T 5HZ (☎ 020 7631 3370, fax 020 7637 9629, e-mail stephanie@michaelnash.co.uk)

NASH, Dr Timothy Paul (Tim); s of Flt Lt Laurence Nash (d 1970), and Margaret Ellen, *née* Davis (d 1985); *b* 13 August 1946; *Educ* Changi GS, Andover GS, UCH Med Sch London (MB BS); *m* 18 Oct 1969, Bridget Eleanor, da of William Albert Harrison, of Tonbridge; 3 da (Deborah b 23 Feb 1972, Rebecca b 24 April 1974, Juliette b 3 April 1980), 1 s (Matthew b 2 Dec 1981); *Career* conslt in anaesthetics and pain mgmnt Basingstoke and N Hants Health Authy 1976–94, conslt in pain medicine The Walton Centre for Neurology and Neurosurgery Liverpool 1995–2006 (dir 1998–2002), Mersey regnl advsr in Pain Mgmnt Royal Coll of Anaesthetists 2002–07; hon sr lectr Univ of Liverpool 1999– (hon clinical lectr 1995–99, dir Pain Studies 1997–2006), visiting prof Kwong Wah Hosp Hong Kong 1999; ed Frontiers of Pain 1988–92, asst ed The Pain Clinic 1989–95; pres The Pain Soc 1994–97 (fndr ed IPS Forum 1982–85, sec 1985–88); chm: Pain Speciality Working Gp NHS Clinical Terms Project 1992–95, Task Force on Educnl Standards (memb Cncl), European Fedn of Chapters, Int Assoc for the Study of Pain 1995–99 (also memb task forces on taxonomy and data retrieval); memb Cncl Nat Back Pain Assoc 1994–2000; tstee Pain Relief Fndn 2007–; contrib World of Pain (TV documentary) 2002; memb: BMA, RSM, Assoc of Anaesthetists; hon memb The Pain Soc; FFARCS 1974, fell Faculty of Pain Medicine of the Royal Coll of Anaesthetists; *Publications* contrib to: Pain (1985, 1986, 1993 and 2002), Chronic Non-Cancer Pain (1987), The Pain Clinic (1987, 1990, 1992 and 2001), British Medical Journal (1988, 1998), British Journal of Hospital Medicine (1991), Medicine International (1991 and 1995), International Journal of Pain Therapy (1993), Read Codes (3 version, 1994), Anaesthesia Review 12 (1995), Management of Pain – A World Perspective (1996, 1998), Health and Healing the Natural Way: Managing Pain (1998), Acta Neurologica Scandinavia (1999), Pain Digest (1999), Prescriber (1999), Alternative Answers: Pain (1999), Clinical Pain Management (2002 and 2008), Palliative Medicine (2003), British Journal of Anaesthesia (2005), Journal of Pain Symptom Management (2006), Oxford Pain Management Library: Neuropathic Pain (2006), Palliative Medicine (2008); *Recreations* music, reading, hiking, badminton, cricket, art; *Style*— Dr Tim Nash; ✉ Pain Relief Foundation, Clinical Sciences Centre, University Hospital Aintree, Lower Lane, Fazakerley, Liverpool L9 7AL (☎ 0151 529 5820, fax 0151 529 5821, e-mail timothy.nash2@btinternet.com)

NATHAN, Dr Anthony Wayne; s of Murray Nathan (decd), of London, and Pamela Simone, *née* Spack; *b* 10 September 1952; *Educ* Haberdashers' Aske's, Middx Hosp Med Sch (MB BS, MD); *m* 11 July 1975, Alison Jane, da of late John Dick Campbell; 1 da (Emma Michelle b 4 March 1979), 1 s (Mark b 9 Feb 1981); *Career* house physician Middx Hosp London 1975–76, house surgn in neurosurgery The Royal Infirmary Sheffield Feb-July 1976, SHO in gen med and clinical pharmacology Hammersmith Hosp London 1976–77, SHO in cardiology Brompton Hosp London Feb-July 1977, SHO in renal and transplant med Guy's Hosp London 1977–78, registrar in gen med Royal Free Hosp London March 1978–79; Bart's: registrar in cardiology 1979–81, hon sr registrar in cardiology 1981–87, conslt cardiologist 1987–; conslt cardiologist Barts & the London NHS Tst, currently conslt cardiologist Watford Gen Hosp; former sec Br Pacing and Electrophysiology Group, former sr ed Jl of Electrophysiology; currently contrib papers to various other learned jls; Int Cardiac Pacing Soc Award for Scientific Excellence 1983; memb: Br Cardiac Soc, Br Cardiovascular Interventional Soc, Br Med Laser Assoc, Br Pacing and Electrophysiology Gp, Euro Laser Assoc, Int Soc for Heart Transplantation, N American Soc of Pacing and Electrophysiology (memb Advsy Cncl); hon memb Spanish Soc of Cardiology, fndr fell Euro Soc of Cardiology, Fell American Coll of Cardiology, FRCP 1992; *Recreations* sailing, skiing, football, theatre, modern British art; *Style*— Dr Anthony W Nathan; ✉ Spire Bushey Hospital, Heathbourne Road, Bushey, Hertfordshire WD23 1RD (☎ 020 8420 4471, fax 020 8420 4472); (e-mail anthony.nathan@spirehealthcare.com)

NATHAN, Ian L B; s of Christopher Nathan, of Stevenage, and Patricia, *née* Lowe; *b* 17 July 1969; *Educ* John Hampden GS High Wycombe, UC Cardiff (BSc), Watford Coll (Dip Publishing); *Career* freelance film journalist and broadcaster 1990–94; Empire: staff writer 1994–95, reviews ed 1995–96, features ed 1996, ed 1996–99, assoc ed 1999–, awards prodr 1999–, Empire TV prodr 1999–, nominated for PPA Consumer Magazine of the Year 1998; contrib: The Times, Arena, Mail on Sunday, Q; *Recreations* travelling, sport, literature; *Style*— Ian Nathan, Esq; ✉ Endeavour House, 189 Shaftesbury Avenue, London WC2 4JG (☎ 020 7859 8612, fax 020 7859 8613, e-mail ian.nathan@emap.com and ilbn_uk@yahoo.co.uk)

NATHAN, Janet; *b* 31 March 1938, London; *Educ* St Martin's Sch of Art London; *m* 1999, Patrick Caulfield; *Career* artist; *Solo Exhibitions* Newcastle Poly Art Gallery 1979, Air Gallery London 1981, Ikon Gallery Birmingham 1982, Ferens Art Gallery Hull 1982, Riverside Studios London 1983, Howard Gardens Gallery Cardiff 1983, Mappin Art Gallery Sheffield 1984, Windsor Old Ct Windsor 1986, Warwick Arts Tst London 1988, Hampstead Theatre 1991, The Gallery at John Jones 1992, Chelsea Arts Club London 1993, Reed's Wharf Gallery London 1995, Concourse Gallery Barbican Centre London 1997, Metropole Arts Centre Folkestone 1997, Graves Art Gallery Sheffield 1997, Gardner Arts Centre Brighton 1997, The Customs House South Shields 1997, Tiempos Modernos Madrid 1997, British Airways Terminal 1 1999–2002, Aalders Gallerie France 2006, Redfern Gallery London 2008, Tiempos Modernas Madrid 2011, Aldeburgh Arts Festival Campden Gallery Glos 2011, The Stone Gallery London 2012, Ventnor Arts Club Isle of Wight 2013, Redfern Gallery 2013, Tiempos Modernos 2014; *Group Exhibitions* incl: The British Art Show (Arts Cncl touring, Arnolfini Bristol, Newcastle upon Tyne and Mappin Art Gallery Sheffield), Painted Constructions (ICA London) 1980, Royal Acad Summer Exhbn 1980–2002, Art and the Sea (Third Eye Centre Glasgow 1981 and ICA London 1982), 10 London Artists (Scandinavian tour) 1983, Coloured Constructions (Ikon Gallery Birmingham and touring), Whitechapel Open Exhbn 1983 and 1984, Leicestershire Exhbn (annually) 1983–93, TWSA Touring Exhbn 1984, The London Group (Morley Coll and RCA) 1984–2000, Crawford Centre for the Arts (Univ of St Andrews) 1985, Scarborough Festival 1985, Art on a Plate (Serpentine Gallery London) 1987, John Moores 15 Exhbn 1987, London Group Members Exhbn 1981–93, London Group (RCA) 1990, Riverside One London 1990, The Discerning Eye (invited by Sir Roger de Gray, PRA) Exhbn London 1990, Redfern Gallery London 1992, Leicestershire Exhbn 1993, London Group (London Inst and Barbican) 1993, Bruton Street Gallery 1993, RGI Glasgow 1993, Summer Exhbn (William Jackson Gallery) 1994, London Group 1994, 1995, 1996, 2000, 2003, 2004 and 2005, Contemporary British Artists (Smiths Galleries London and Business Design Centre London) 1995, John Moores 19 Exhbn 1995, Cross Currents (Reeds Wharf and Barbican) 1996, Angela Flowers Small Works 1997, RCA Br Art Fair 1998, Olympia Art Fair 1999, Aalders Gallery France 2000, Walk Gallery 2003, RA Summer Exhbn 2004, 2005 and 2006, Extra Sensory Material (Bonhams London) 2006, Deutsche Bank London 2007, Merrier Art Gallery London 2007, Bridge Art Fair London 2007, Arts Club London 2007, Royal Acad Summer Exhbn 2008, London Group 2009, London Group 2010 and 2011, Royal Acad 2011, Martins Gallery Cheltenham 2012, Advanced Graphics London 2012, Monttisfort Abbey Hampshire 2013, Pitzhanger Manor Museum 2013, Brighton Museum 2014, Royal Acad 2014, London Group 2014, Combines Exhbn 2015, Discerning Eye Exhbn 2015, Redfern Gallery Summer Exhbn 2016; *Work in Collections* Walker Art Gallery Liverpool, ICI HQ Millbank, Exchange House Broadgate, Leics Educn Authy, HRH The Princess Margaret, Lord Snowdon, Lonrho Group, Smiths Industries, Unilever House, Pentland Industries, Coopers & Lybrand, Chelsea and Westminster Hosp, Arts Cncl of GB, Br Cncl, Br Acad, BBC Nat Collection, Tate Gallery Cawder Castle, private collections in Britain, America and Europe; *Style*— Ms Janet Nathan; ✉ 19 Belsize Square, London NW3 4HT (☎ 020 7431 1188, e-mail janet@janetnathan.com, website www.janetnathan.com); Redfern Gallery, Cork Street, London W1

NATHAN, Peter Geoffrey; OBE (1999), DL (Gtr London 1991); s of Maj Cyril H Nathan, FCA (d 1977), of Chiddingfold, Surrey, and Violet, *née* Simon (d 1974); *b* 27 July 1929; *Educ* Summer Fields, Charterhouse, Oriel Coll Oxford (MA), Univ of Paris (Dip Etudes de Civilisation Française); *m* 14 May 1970, Caroline Monica, da of Lt Cdr Anthony C Mullen, RINVR (d 1991); 2 da (Arabella, Venetia), 2 s (Hugo, Anthony); *Career* writer RN 1948–49; admitted slr 1958; Herbert Oppenheimer Nathan & Vandyk 1954–88 (ptnr 1959–88); conslt: Boodle Hatfield 1988–92, Wood & Awdry 1992–2000; govr Sports Aid

Fndn Ltd 1999–2002, hon pres Sports Aid London 2003–15 (chm 1999–2002); London Playing Fields Soc: chm 1984–97, vice-pres 1997–, dep chm Peter May Meml Appeal 1995–97; vice-pres Croydon Playing Fields Soc 1996–; Nat Heritage Sec's ministerial nominee London Cncl for Sport and Recreation 1992–95; tstee Oriel Coll Devpt Tst until 1996 (patron 1996–), chm Oriel Law Soc until 1996, chm Oriel Law Fellowship Appeal until 1996; chm Chiddingfold Branch of Farnham Cons Assoc 1965–70; memb: Community Health Cncl for Kensington, Chelsea and Westminster representing Royal Borough of Kensington and Chelsea 1974–78, Cncl British Heart Fndn 1976–93, Cncl Anglo-Swiss Soc 1988–2005, Ct City Univ 1989–93, Livery Consultative Ctee Corp of London 1994–97; successively memb Post Office User Area Cncls for City of London and London W2-W14 1988–93; chm Butterflies CC 1986–93 (hon treas 1961–86); recipient Nat Playing Fields Assoc Pres's Cert for servs to the playing fields movement 1992; Freeman City of London 1961, Master Worshipful Co of Gold and Silver Wyre Drawers 1989 (Past Master Emeritus, chm Tercentenary 1993 Exhbn Ctee); hon memb Geographical Assoc; memb Law Soc; *Recreations* sport, reading, wine, art, music; *Clubs* MCC, Vincent's (Oxford), Jesters; *Style—* P G Nathan, Esq, OBE, DL; ✉ Kites Nest House, Bourton, Dorset SP8 5AZ

NATHAN, Philip Charles; MBE (2001); s of Denis William Nathan (d 2006), and Grace Pauline, *née* Brennan; *b* 11 May 1951; *Educ* Alexandra Park Sch; *m* Heidi-Anne; 2 da (Francesca, Hannah); *Career* stockbroker; dir Charles Stanley & Co Ltd; Lions Clubs Int: former pres Rayleigh, South Woodham Ferrers Essex, dist govr E Anglia 1995–96, chm Cncl of Govrs Br Isles and Ireland 1996–97, int dir 1999–2001, Int Bd appointee 2002–03; formerly chm MedicAlert Fndn UK & Ireland (now ret), currently memb Exec Ctee MedicAlert Int Fndn, chm: Music & The Deaf until 2013, A Gift for Living, Lion Cubs Int Central and Eastern Europe Initiative 2013–; dir Bd: Special Olympics GB, Lions Lifeskills Ltd; memb: Stock Exchange Veterans' Club Ctee (charity steward), Stock Exchange Benevolent Fund Ctee, Lime Street Ward Club; Freeman City of London; FCSI, FIoD; *Clubs* City of London, Lime Street Ward; *Style—* Philip C Nathan, Esq, MBE, FCSI, FIoD; ✉ Charles Stanley & Co Ltd, 25 Luke Street, London EC2A 4AR (☎ 020 7667 2266, fax 020 7149 6947, mobile 077 8538 0069, e-mail phil.nathan@charles-stanley.co.uk)

NATHAN, Sara Catherine; OBE (2008); da of Derek Maurice Nathan (d 2008), and Mary Catherine, *née* Lavine; *b* 16 February 1956, Epsom, Surrey; *Educ* Wimbledon HS, New Hall Cambridge (BA, vice-pres Cambridge Union), Stanford Univ (Harkness fell); *m* 15 July 1984, Malcolm John Singer, dir of music Yehudi Menuhin Sch, s of Gerald Singer, of Finchley, London; 1 da (Rachel Fonya b 23 Jan 1989), 1 s (Jonathan Joseph b 5 June 1991); *Career* BBC: news trainee 1980–82, prodr/sr prodr BBC News and Current Affrs (on News, Newsnight, Breakfast Time and The Money Programme) 1982–87, output ed Breakfast News and Newsnight 1989–92, results ed Gen Election 1992, asst to Jenny Abramsky as ed News & Current Affrs Radio/controller Radio 5 Live 1992–93, ed The Magazine (Radio 5 Live) 1994–95; ed Channel Four News ITN 1995–97, freelance journalist 1998–; ed: TUC Live '98 (BBC2) 1998, The State of Israel (Channel 4) 1998; media columnist The Scotsman 1999–2000; ind editorial advsr BBC Tst 2009–; chair Animal Procedures Ctee 2006–12; Slrs Regulation Authy: memb Bd 2010–14, chair Standards Ctee 2011–14; Public Appointments Assessor 2012–; tbnl chair Nursing and Midwifery Cncl 2012–; memb Cmmn on Youth Crime and Anti-Social Behaviour and chair Custody Sub-Ctee 2008–10; memb: Human Fertilization and Embryology Authy 1998–2005, Bar Cncl 1998–2004, BAFTA, Radio Authy 1999–2003, Gambling Review Body 2000–01, Criminal Injuries Compensation Appeal Panel 2000–06, Regulatory Decisions Ctee FSA 2001–07, Bd Ofcom 2002–07, Judicial Appts Cmmn 2006–12, Bd Assoc of TV On Demand 2010–12; chair Children's First Cmmn Lambeth 2000–02; cmmr Marshall Scholarships 2002–06; memb Phonepay Plus (formerly Ind Ctee for the Supervision of Standards of Telephone Info Servs (ICSTIS)) 2002–08; chair Churchfield Community Assoc 2009–12; tstee Why Me? 2010–; *Recreations* theatre, cinema (film and television voting member of BAFTA), running Acton bookswap, community activism: Playing Out and street parties; *Clubs* BAFTA; *Style—* Ms Sara Nathan, OBE; ☎ 020 8992 2318, e-mail sara@natsing.co.uk

NATKIEL, Rod; s of Daniel Natkiel (d 1986), and Marjorie Jessie, *née* Pinkham (d 1988); *b* 30 January 1952; *Educ* Kingston GS, Univ of Bristol (BA), Univ of Birmingham (MBA); *m* 6 Nov 1976, Janet Ruth; 2 s (Rory b 29 Aug 1978, Alastair b 6 March 1981); *Career* Arts Cncl Bursary trainee dir 1976, assoc dir and resident musical dir Contact Theatre Manchester 1975–78, dir/prodr BBC TV Light Entertainment Dept Scotland 1978–84, freelance exec prodr/dir in entertainment, drama, news and current affairs 1984–92, prodn exec Birmingham Media Devpt Agency 1992–93, head of network TV BBC Midlands and East (Pebble Mill) 1992–96, head of network prodn BBC Birmingham 1996–99, md and head of prodn Rod Natkiel Associates 1999–; visiting prof of television studies Univ of Central England 1993–99; chm: Variety Club Midlands 1997–2000, W Midlands Arts 1997–2002; memb Arts Cncl of England 1997–98; tstee Variety Club of GB 1999–; chair Screen W Midlands 2001–03; *Recreations* squash, cricket, cinema, theatre, DIY; *Style—* Rod Natkiel, Esq; ✉ Rod Natkiel Associates Ltd, 5 Vesey Road, Sutton Coldfield, West Midlands B73 5NP (☎ 0121 355 2197, fax 0121 355 8033, e-mail rod@rodnatkiel.co.uk)

NAUGHTIE, (Alexander) James; s of Alexander Naughtie (d 1973), and Isabella, *née* Milne (d 1994); *b* 9 August 1951; *Educ* Keith GS, Univ of Aberdeen (MA), Syracuse Univ NY (MA); *m* 1986, Eleanor, *née* Updale; 1 s (Andrew b 22 Sept 1987), 2 da (Catherine b 24 Feb 1989, Flora b 25 Jan 1991); *Career* journalist: The Press and Journal 1975–77, The Scotsman 1977–84; chief political corr The Guardian 1984–88; presenter: The World at One (BBC Radio) 1988–94, BBC Proms 1991–, Today Programme (BBC Radio) 1994–, Book Club (BBC Radio) 1998–; contrib to newspapers and magazines; Laurence Stern fell The Washington Post 1981, Sony Radio Personality of the Year 1991; memb Cncl Edinburgh Int Festival 2003–; Hon LLD Univ of Aberdeen 1991, Hon LLD Univ of St Andrews 2001, Hon DUniv Stirling 2001, Hon Dr Napier Univ 2002, Hon Dr Glasgow Caledonian Univ 2002; *Books* The Rivals (2001), The Accidental American (2004); *Recreations* books, opera; *Clubs* Travellers, Garrick; *Style—* James Naughtie; ✉ The Today Programme, BBC Broadcasting House, Portland Place, London W1A 1AA (fax 0181 772 0694, e-mail james.naughtie@bbc.co.uk)

NAUNTON, William; *Career* admitted slr 1992; Eversheds LLP: ptnr 1999–, head Eversheds Real Estate Gp 2003–; ✉ Eversheds LLP, One Wood Street, London EC2V 7WS (☎ 020 7919 4627)

NAWAZ, His Hon Judge Amjad; *Educ* Aston Univ; *Career* called to the Bar Lincoln's Inn 1982 (Hardwicke scholar, Droop scholar); recorder 2002, circuit judge (Midland Circuit) 2008–; *Recreations* cricket, squash, tennis, reading, hill walking; *Style—* His Hon Judge Nawaz; ✉ c/o Midland Circuit Office, Priory Courts, 33 Bull Street, Birmingham B4 6DW

NAWAZ, Maajid; *b* Rochford; *Educ* SOAS (BA), LSE (MSc); *m* Oct 2014, Rachel Maggart; *Career* founding chm Quilliam 2008–, author 2012–, columnist Daily Beast; prisoner of conscience Amnesty Int 2002; assoc fell Nat Secular Soc; parly candidate (Lib Dem) Hampstead and Kilburn 2013–; *Books* Radical: My Journey from Islamist Extremism to a Democratic Awakening (autobiography, 2012), Islam – The Future of Tolerance (2015); *Recreations* cinema, fashion, music, travel; *Style—* Maajid Nawaz, Esq; ✉ Quilliam Foundation, PO Box 60380, London WC1A 9AZ (☎ 020 7182 7280, e-mail information@quilliamfoundation.org, websites www.quilliamfoundation.org, www.maajidnawaz.com, Twitter @maajidnawaz)

NAYLER, Georgina Ruth; da of late Dennis Nayler, and Yvonne Dorothy, *née* Loader; *b* 16 March 1959; *Educ* Brentwood Co HS, Univ of Warwick (BA); *Partner* Simon Stillwell; 1 s, 1 da; *Career* Nat Heritage Memorial Fund: joined 1982, asst dir 1986, dep dir 1988, dir 1989–95; dir The Pilgrim Trust 1996–; memb Historic Buildings Cncl for Scotland 1990–96; tstee: Charlotte Bonham-Carter Charitable Tst 2008–, Pitzhanger Manor Tst 2013– (dep chair 2014–); *Recreations* gardening; *Style—* Miss Georgina Nayler; ✉ The Pilgrim Trust, 55a Catherine Place, London SW1E 6DY

NAYLOR, Douglas Rodger (Doug); s of Leslie Naylor, of Manchester, and Isabella Graham Barclay, *née* McLaughlan; *b* 31 December 1955; *Educ* Chethams Hosp Sch of Music Manchester, Univ of Liverpool; *m* 7 June 1986, Linda Jane, da of Dr Richard Arthur de Keler Glover; 2 s (Richard Duncan Glover b 20 Nov 1986, Matthew Lawrence b 9 Jan 1990); *Career* screenwriter, producer and director; writer for series incl: Son of Cliche (BBC Radio 4, Sony Award for Best Comedy, Ondas Award), Carrott's Lib (BBC TV, BAFTA Award), Three of a Kind (BBC TV, BAFTA Award), Spitting Image (a head writer and prodr, ITV, Montreux Rose and International Emmy awards); co-creator, prodr and writer (with Rob Grant): Red Dwarf (6 series, BBC2, various awards incl International Emmy for Best Popular Arts Prog 1994, British Comedy Awards Best Sitcom on BBC 1994), Red Dwarf VII and VIII (writer and exec prodr), The 10%ers 1993–94 (2 series Carlton TV/ITV Network, Silver Medal NY Festival), Red Dwarf Back to Earth (writer, dir and exec prodr), Red Dwarf X (writer, dir and exec prodr), Over To Bill 2014 (writer, dir and exec prodr, BBC1 Comedy Playhouse); co-fndr Grant Naylor Productions Ltd; memb: Performing Rights Soc, BAFTA; *Books* Red Dwarf: Infinity Welcomes Careful Drivers (with Rob Grant, 1989), Red Dwarf: Better than Life (with Rob Grant, 1990), Red Dwarf: Last Human (1995); *Recreations* film and theatre, reading, golf; *Style—* Doug Naylor, Esq; ✉ Grant Naylor Productions Ltd, Shepperton Studios, Studios Road, Shepperton, Middlesex TW17 0QD (☎ 01932 592175)

NAYLOR, Sir Robert Antony; kt (2008); s of Francis Thomas Naylor, of Reading, and Kathleen Mary, *née* Donellan; *b* 13 November 1949; *Educ* Salesian Coll Oxford, Presentation Coll Reading, Univ of London (BSc); *m* 9 Nov 1974, Jane Karen, da of Charles Evans; 1 s (James Richard), 1 da (Victoria Jane); *Career* grad mgmnt trainee NW Thames RHA 1972–74, hosp sec Nat Hosp for Nervous Diseases London 1974–77, sector admin Kent AHA 1977–79, dist admin Enfield DHA 1979–84, gen mangr E Birmingham Hosp 1986–90, chief exec Birmingham Heartlands Hosp NHS Tst 1991–2000, chief exec UCL Hosps 2000–; AHSM; *Recreations* golf, scuba diving; *Style—* Sir Robert Naylor; ✉ 4 Chester Terrace, Regent's Park, London NW1 4ND; University College London Hospitals, 2nd Floor Central, 250 Euston Road, London NW1 2PG

NAYLOR, Prof (Andrew) Ross; s of Robert Charles Naylor, and Patricia Mary, *née* Goodall; *b* 22 March 1958, Chester; *Educ* Merchiston Castle Sch Edinburgh, Univ of Aberdeen (first bursar, MB ChB, MD); *m* 1982, May Bruce, *née* MacPherson; 1 s (Iain Bruce), 1 da (Sarah May); *Career* basic surgical trg Aberdeen and Edinburgh Royal Infirmary 1981–91, higher surgical trg Leicester Royal Infirmary 1991–93; conslt vascular surgn: Aberdeen Royal Infirmary 1993–95, Leicester Royal Infirmary 1995–; Hunterian prof of surgery RCS 2002, prof of surgery Univ of Leicester 2003 (reader in surgery 2002); memb Editorial Bd: Br Jl of Surgery 2000–05, Jl of Vascular Surgery 2003–08, European Jl of Vascular and Endovascular Surgery 2006– (assoc ed 2008–10, sr ed 2010–13, ed in chief 2013–); memb: R&D Ctee UK Stroke Assoc 1993–2002, Cncl Vascular Soc of GB and I (pres 2011–12), Cncl European Soc of Vascular Surgery 2010–; Wilfred Card Medal 1990, Gore European Pioneer in Vascular Surgery 2012; memb: GMC 1981–, European Vascular Soc 1990–, Vascular Surgical Soc 1990–, Medical and Dental Defence Union of Scotland 1991–, Br Vascular Fndn 1994–98; FRCSEd 1986, FRCS 1994; *Publications* Carotid Artery Surgery: A Problem-Based Approach (ed), Vascular Surgery: Principles and Practice (ed, with S Wilson, J C Jiminez and FJ Veith, 2016); 69 book chapters, 440 publications; *Recreations* skiing, road cycling; *Style—* Prof Ross Naylor; ✉ Vascular Surgery Group, Division of Cardiovascular Sciences, Leicester Royal Infirmary, Leicester LE2 7LX (☎ 0116 258 7768, fax 0116 258 5029)

NAYLOR-LEYLAND, Sir Philip Vyvian; 4 Bt (UK 1895), of Hyde Park House, Albert Gate, Co London; s of Sir Vivyan Edward Naylor-Leyland, 3 Bt (d 1987), and Hon Elizabeth Anne Marie Gabrielle Fitzalan-Howard (d 1997), da of 2 Viscount Fitzalan of Derwent; *b* 9 August 1953; *Educ* Eton, Sandhurst, New York Univ, RAC Cirencester; *m* 1980, Lady Isabella Lambton, 5 and yst da of Antony Claud Frederick Lambton (6 Earl of Durham, who disclaimed his peerage 1970); 4 s (Thomas Philip b 1982, George Antony b 1989, Edward Claud b 1993, William Rufus Luke b 1999), 2 da (Violet Mary b 1983, Beatrix Rose Elizabeth b 1998); *Heir* s, Thomas Naylor-Leyland; *Career* Lt LG (ret); pres National Coursing Club 1988–, chm Peterborough Royal Foxhound Show Soc 1995– (vice-chm 1989–95); dir: Milton (Peterborough) Estates Co, Nantclwyd Farms Ltd, Talbot Hotel Malton; jt master Fitzwilliam (Milton) Hunt 1987–; *Recreations* hunting, coursing, shooting, golf; *Clubs* White's, The Air Squadron, Sunningdale Golf; *Style—* Sir Philip Naylor-Leyland, Bt; ✉ Milton, Peterborough, Cambridgeshire PE6 7AA; Nantclwyd Hall, Ruthin, Denbighshire LL15 2PR

NEAL, Prof Alan Christopher; s of Harold Joseph Neal, of Bath, and Gladys May, *née* Lovelock; *b* 9 January 1950; *Educ* City of Bath Boys' Sch, Univ of Warwick (LLB), LSE (LLM), Univ of Stockholm Sweden (DGLS); *m* 1, 30 July 1981 (m dis 2011), Alessandra, da of Dr Alessandro Tadini (d 1974), of Lucca, Italy; 1 s (James Alexander b 1984), 1 da (Francesca Jane b 1986); m 2, 31 March 2012, Pauline, da of Derek Livesey (d 1997), of Blackburn, and widow of William Upton (d 1979) and John Davenport (d 2007); *Career* called to the Bar Gray's Inn 1975; in practice Midland & Oxford Circuit; pt/t Employment Judge 1995–, convenor Euro Assoc of Labour Court Judges 1996–, scientific dir The International Journal of Comparative Labour Law and Industrial Relations 1996– (ed-in-chief 1984–95); prof of law Univ of Leicester 1988–2000 (lectr 1976–86, sr lectr 1986–88); Univ of Warwick: prof of law 2000–, dir Employment Law Research Unit 2002–; visiting prof: Salford Univ 1992–2005, Vienna Wirtschaftsuniversität 1992–93, Univ of Paris I (Sorbonne) 1993–96, Univ of Paris II (Panthéon-Assas) 2003–, Univ of Strasbourg III (Robert Schuman) 2004–05, Univ of Trento 2004–05, Zhejiang Univ (China) 2007–, Beijing Jiao Tong Univ China 2008–; ind int expert ILO (Ukraine) 2002, ind int expert China Miny of Labour and Social Security (Beijing) 2005–07, standing high-level ind expert Lab Law and Social Security Law Inst Peking Univ China 2012–; *Books* Law and the Weaker Party (ed, 5 vols 1981–92), A Perspective on Labour Law (1982), Collective Agreements and Collective Bargaining (1984), Arbejdsretlig Terminologi Dansk-Engelsk (1984), How to Study Law (6 edns, 1986–2010), Comparative Labour Law: Anglo-Soviet Perspectives (1987) European Communities Health and Safety Legislation (1992), Developing the Social Dimension in an Enlarged European Union (1995), Fundamental Social Rights at Work in the European Community (1999), European Labour Law and Social Policy (1999, 2nd edn 2002), European Social Policy and the Nordic Countries (2000), The Changing Face of European Labour Law and Social Policy (2004), The Changing Institutional Face of British Employment Relations (2006), Cross-Currents in Modern Chinese Labour Law (2013); *Recreations* hockey (formerly Somerset and Warwickshire), skiing, music; *Clubs* Royal Over-Seas League; *Style—* Prof Alan C Neal; ✉ School of Law, The University of Warwick, Coventry CV4 7AL (☎ 024 7652 3205 (direct) and 024 7652 3098 (sec), fax 024 7652 4105, e-mail alan.neal@warwick.ac.uk)

NEAL, Dr Anthony James; *b* 18 October 1961; *Educ* Roan GS for Boys London, St Thomas' Hosp Med Sch London (MB BS, MD); *m*; 3 c; *Career* house surgn St Thomas' Hosp London, house physician Queen Mary's Hosp Sidcup, SHO (vocational trg scheme in gen

N

med) Colchester gp of hosps 1986–88, SHO (radiotherapy and oncology) Essex Co Hosp Colchester 1988, lectr and hon registrar in med oncology Royal London Hosp 1988, registrar in gen med Newham gp of hosps 1989, registrar in radiotherapy and oncology Royal London Hosp1989–92, clinical res fell Inst of Cancer Res and hon sr registrar Royal Marsden NHS Tst 1993–94, sr registrar in clinical oncology Royal Marsden NHS Tst 1994–96 (conslt 1996–99), hon sr lectr Inst of Cancer Res 1996–2000, conslt in clinical oncology Royal Surrey Co Hosp Guildford, recognised teacher Univ of London 1996–2000, clinical tutor Univ of London and Royal Marsden Hosp 1999, RCR tutor St Luke's Cancer Centre Guildford 2000–; memb: American Soc of Clinical Oncology, Euro Soc of Therapeutic Radiology and Oncology (ESTRO), Br Oncological Assoc, Med Protection Soc; MRCP 1988, FRCR 1992; *Awards* ICI Travel Award 1993, runner up Finzi Jr Radiologist Prize RSM 1993, ESTRO Philips Fellowship 1994 (funded study at Dept of Radiation Oncology Univ of Michigan), ESTRO Travelling Grant 1994, Amgen-Roche Jr Investigator Award 1994, Br Oncological Assoc Award 1994, Pfizer Academic Travel Award 1994, ESTRO Varian Physics Res Award 1994, Lilly Oncology Award 1995; *Publications* Clinical Oncology – Basic Principles and Practice (with P J Hoskin); *Recreations* photography, tennis, golf, computing and IT, personal fitness training, family-orientated activities; *Style—* Dr Anthony Neal; ✉ St Luke's Cancer Centre, Royal Surrey County Hospital, Guildford, Surrey GU2 5XX (☎ 01483 406767, fax 01483 406813, e-mail anthony.neal@nhs.net)

NEAL, Prof David Edgar; CBE (2014); s of Norman Neal, of Ripon, N Yorks, and Beth Neal; *b* 9 March 1951, Otley, Yorkshire; *Educ* Prince Henry's GS Otley, UCL, UCH Med Sch (BSc, MB BS), Univ of London (MS); *m* 27 July 1972, Deborah Mary, *née* Heyworth; 3 da (Rebecca b 29 June 1976, Emily b 17 June 1978, Miriam b 22 August 1980); *Career* house physician and surgeon W Suffolk Hosp, Bury St Edmunds Hosp and Stoke Mandeville Hosp 1975–76, SHO UCH 1977, registrar in gen surgery and urology Kettering Hosp 1977–79, surgical registrar Gen Infirmary Leeds 1979–80, clinical lectr in gen surgery Univ Dept of Surgery Gen Infirmary Leeds 1982–83; Univ of Newcastle upon Tyne: Leech-Green first asst in urology (hon sr registrar) Dept of Surgery 1983–88, sr lectr in urological surgery (hon conslt urologist) Dept of Surgery (also at Dept of Urology Freeman Hosp) 1988–92, head Dept of Surgery 1992–98, head Sch of Surgery 1992–98, head Sch of Surgical and Reproductive Sci 1992–98, dir of research Faculty of Med 1998–2001, prof of surgery and hon conslt urologist Dept of Surgery the Med Sch (and Newcastle upon Tyne Hosps NHS Tst) 1992–2002, chm Jt Research Exec (also at Newcastle upon Tyne Hosps NHS Tst) 2000–02; prof of cancer research (surgical oncology) Addenbrooke's Hosp Univ of Cambridge 2002–; chm Urological Site Specific Gp W Anglia Cancer Network 2003–, advsr Nat Dir of Cancer Services 2003–; sr vice-pres Global Research (Academic) Elsevier plc 2014–, prof of surgical oncology Univ of Oxford 2015–; currently sr visiting fell and prof emeritus of surgical oncology Univ of Cambridge and hon conslt urological surgn Cambridge Univ Hosps NHS Tst; memb: Cncl RCS, American Assoc of Genito-urinary Surgns (overseas memb) 1998–, Clinical Standards Gp for Urological Cancers 2003–, CR UK Health Policy Advsy Gp 2003–; St Peter's Medal Br Assoc of Urological Surgns 2001; FRCS 1980, FRCSEd (ad hominem) 1994, FMed Sci 1998; *Publications* author of over 580 pubns in academic jls (480) and books; *Recreations* motor cycles, guitar playing; *Style—* Prof David Neal, CBE; ✉ 3 Pemberton Terrace, Cambridge CB2 1JA (☎ 07850 570698, e-mail den22@cam.ac.uk); Nuffield Department of Surgery, University of Oxford, Room 6603, Level 6, John Radcliffe Hospital, Headley Way, Headington, Oxford OX3 9DU (☎ 01865 617126)

NEAL, Gub Matthew Michael; s of Michael David Neal, and Barbara Lisette, *née* Carter; *b* 24 January 1959; *Educ* Eton, Univ of Exeter (BA), Univ of Calif Berkeley (postgrad directing course, exchange scholarship); *m* 1991, Anna, da of Glynne Price (d 2004); 2 s (William b 8 Nov 1993, Isaac b May 1998), 1 da (Phoebe Agnes b 1 March 1996); *Career* prodr London Int Festival of Theatre 1981–84, floor mangr BBC TV 1985–87, script ed BBC TV 1987–89, television drama prodr 1989–; fndr Gub Neal Productions Ltd 1995, controller of drama Granada TV 1995–97, head of drama Channel 4 1997–2000, fndr Box TV Ltd 2000–09, co-fndr Artists Studio 2009–; prodr films and series incl: Medics (Granada TV) 1990, The Cloning of Joanna May (Granada) 1991, Angels (Granada) 1991, The Humming Bird Tree (BBC Films) 1992, Cracker (Granada) 1993, Bad Boys (BBC Films) 1994; exec prodr: Hillsborough (Granada) 1996, Moll Flanders, Prime Suspect V; other credits incl: Sunday (Channel 4) 2001 (winner Grand Prix Italia), Swallow (Channel 4) 2001, Trust (BBC 1) 2002, Gunpowder Treason and Plot (BBC 2) 2003; memb: BAFTA, Equity; *Awards* Best Film Award (for The Humming Bird Tree) Rheims TV Festival 1993; for Cracker: RTS Award for Best Series 1994, American Cable Ace Award 1995, BAFTA Best Series nomination 1994, Prix Italia nomination 1995; US Emmy Best Mini Series (for Prime Suspect V); *Recreations* walking, motorbiking, skiing, cycling, art history, photography; *Clubs* Teatro; *Style—* Gub Neal, Esq

NEAL, Harry Morton; CBE (1991); s of Godfrey French Neal (d 1985), and Janet Bryce Morton (d 1960); *b* 21 November 1931; *Educ* Uppingham, Imperial Coll London (BSc), City and Guilds Coll; *m* 1954, Cecilia Elizabeth, da of Col Mervyn Crawford, DSO (d 1977); 1 s (Michael b 1956), 3 da (Camilla (Mrs Edward Cottrell) b 1960, Carolyn (Mrs Rupert Ryle-Hodges) b 1961, Alexandra (Mrs Rupert Asquith) b 1967); *Career* Flying Offr RAF 1953; Harry Neal Ltd (bldg and civil engrg contractors): md 1963–86, chm 1985–2010; dir: Connaught Hotel Ltd 1966–97 (chm 1980–94), Savoy Hotel 1982–93; chm: St Anselm Devpt Co Ltd 1985–2013; memb Lloyd's; vice-pres C&G 1999–2004 (memb Cncl 1970–2004, chm Cncl 1979–91); pres: City and Guilds Coll Assoc 1994–95, City and Guilds Assoc 2006–09; memb: Technician Educn Cncl 1982–83, Business and Technology Educn Cncl 1983–94, Ct City Univ 1982–91, Mgmnt Ctee Courtauld Inst of Art 1983–99, Delegacy St Mary's Hosp Med Sch 1993–97; memb Bd of Govrs: Willesden Tech Coll 1983–86, Imperial Coll London 1988–2001, Francis Holland Sch 1988–2006 (vice-chm 1996–2005); memb Ct Univ of Herts 2006–; tstee: Buckminster Estate 1969–2005, Samuel Courtauld Tst 1989–2006, HRH Prince of Wales Inst of Architecture 1991–99 (memb Bd of Advsrs 1993–99); pres Middx W Co Scout Cncl 1983–2007; pres Herts Agric Soc 2004; High Sheriff Herts 1999–2000; fell Univ of Herts 2015; Liveryman Worshipful Co of Carpenters (Master 1997); hon fell Courtauld Inst of Art 2007–; FIC, FCGI, FCIOB, FRSA; Chevalier de Tastevin 1981; *Recreations* gardening; *Style—* Harry Neal, Esq, CBE; ✉ Great Sarratt Hall, Sarratt, Hertfordshire WD3 4PD

NEAL-STURGESS, Prof Clive; s of Albert Neal, and Violet Neal; *b* 13 April 1942; *Educ* Higham Lane Secdy Modern Nuneaton, King Edward VI GS Nuneaton, Nuneaton Tech Coll (ONC), Lanchester Poly Coventry (BSc), Univ of Birmingham (PhD, Avery Res Prize); *m* Ellen Neal-Sturgess; *Career* project engr Clarkson International 1965–67; Univ of Birmingham: sr lectr Dept of Mechanical Engrg 1985–89 (Chubb res fell 1971–73, lectr 1973–85), Jaguar prof of automotive engrg Sch of Manufacturing & Mechanical Engrg 1989–2005 (dir of res 1990–92, dir Automotive Engrg Centre 1992–93 and 1997–, dir of undergrad studies 1993–97, jt head 2001–), emeritus prof 2005–; chm Materials Gp IMechE 1986–92, res grant assessor FORESIGHT EPSRC and Australian Res Cncl, QAA specialist assessor 1996–98, chm Birmingham Centre Automobile Div IMechE 2000–; external examiner: Dept of Engrg Univ of Reading 1990–93, Mech Engrg Univ of Mauritius 1995–99, Univ of Hertfordshire 1999–2003, Univ of Northumberland 2004–08, Caledonian Coll Oman 2005–; memb: BCFG Ctee 1980–85, Res Policy Ctee IMechE 1986–2000, Technical Policy Bd IMechE 1986–92, Cncl Inst of Metals 1989–91, Parly Advsy Ctee on Transport Safety 1990–, Br Cncl LINK Co-ordinator Univ of Mauritius 1995–2000, Euro Tport Safety Cncl, Qualifications Panel IMechE 2000–, Engrg Integrity Soc, Engrg Professors Cncl, Oman Accreditation Cncl; town cllr Alcester 2011– (mayor 2015–16); liaison offr Engrg Cncl; CEng 1981, FIMechE 1987 (MIMechE), FIM 1995, FRSA; *Publications* author/co-author of over 180 papers and 3 books; *Recreations* golf, renovating a Tudor grade II listed building; *Clubs* Royal Over-Seas League; *Style—* Prof Clive Neal-Sturgess; ✉ e-mail clivenealsturgess@gmail.com; School of Engineering, The University of Birmingham, Edgbaston, Birmingham B15 2TT (☎ 0121 414 4144, fax 0121 414 3688, e-mail c.e.n.sturgess@bham.ac.uk, website www.neal-sturgess.com)

NEALE, Frank Leslie George; s of Hugh Neale, and Mona, *née* Clarkson; *b* 25 August 1950; *Educ* King Henry VIII Sch Coventry, St John's Coll Cambridge (MA), Manchester Business Sch (MBA), Open Univ (BA); *m* 16 June 1976, Helen, da of Ronald Carter; 3 s (Michael James b 29 May 1979, Jeremy John Simon b 20 Jan 1985, Rory William b 1 Jan 1989); *Career* Econ Intelligence Unit 1973–77, PA Mgmnt Conslts 1977–83, Citicorp Venture Capital 1983–88, ptnr IRRfc; dir: Northern 2 VCT plc, Garrets Int Ltd 2013–16, FutureLearn Ltd; former vice-chm Cncl Br Venture Capital Assoc; chair W Herts Coll; FRSA; *Recreations* ballet, swimming, reading; *Clubs* Watford FC; *Style—* Frank Neale, Esq; ✉ 53 The Avenue, Watford, Hertfordshire WD1 3NJ (☎ 07710 960902)

NEALE, Mark; CB (2010); s of Sir Alan Neale (d 1995), and Joan, *née* Frost (d 2003); *b* 7 July 1957; *Educ* Highgate Sch, The Queen's Coll Oxford (BA); *m* 27 Aug 1988, Xanthe, *née* Lunghi; 1 da (Catherine b 25 Jan 1994), 1 s (Daniel b 22 Dec 1996); *Career* civil servant; head: Assessment Div DfE 1991–95, Spending Div HM Treasy 1995–98, Structural Unemployment Policy Div DfEE 1998–2000; fin dir Employment Serv 2000–01, dir for children and housing DWP 2001–03, DG security, int and organised crime Home Office 2003–05, DG budget, tax and welfare HM Treasy 2005–10, chief exec Financial Services Compensation Scheme 2010–; *Style—* Mark Neale, Esq, CB; ✉ Financial Services Compensation Scheme, 10th Floor, Beaufort House, 15 St Botolph, London EC3A 7QR (website www.fscs.org.uk)

NEAME, Gareth Elwin; OBE (2016); s of Christopher Elwin Neame (d 2011), and Heather Marilyn, *née* Wade; *b* 8 March 1967, Beaconsfield, Bucks; *Educ* Univ of Birmingham (BA); *m* 1995 (m dis 2001), Karen Elizabeth, *née* Hughes (d 2010); *Career* tv prodr and exec; head of drama BBC 2000–04, md Carnival Film & Television Ltd 2004–; credits incl: Downton Abbey, The Last Kingdom, The Last Honour of Christopher Jefferies, Turks & Caicos, Salting the Battlefield, The 7.39, Murder on the Home Front, The Hollow Crown, Page Eight, The Philanthropist, Harley Street, Midnight Man, The Old Curiosity Shop, Whistleblowers, Empathy, Life Line, Sea of Souls, Hotel Babylon, 20,000 Streets Under the Sky, Rome, New Tricks, Hustle, Fingersmith, The Rotters Club, The Grid, Outlaws, Conviction, Bodies, Gunpowder Treason and Plot, The Hound of the Baskervilles, Tipping the Velvet, Spooks, Murder, Clocking Off, The Missing Postman, The Woman in White; ambass GREAT Britain Campaign 2014–; David L Wolper Award for Outstanding Prodr Prodrs Guild of America 2012; *Recreations* travel, arts, literature, film and television, countryside, fine wine; *Clubs* Savile; *Style—* Gareth Neame, Esq, OBE; ✉ Carnival Film & Television, 55 New Oxford Street, London WC1A 1BS (website www.carnivalfilms.co.uk)

NEAME, Robert Harry Beale; CBE (1999), DL (Kent 1992); s of Jasper Beale Neame (d 1961), and Violet Evelyn, *née* Cobb (d 1976); The Neame family have been resident in E Kent and can be traced back 500 years; *b* 25 February 1934; *Educ* Harrow; *m* 1, 1961, Sally Elizabeth, *née* Corben; 2 s (Jonathan, Richard (decd)), 2 da (Charlotte, Sarah); *m* 2, 1974, Yvonne Mary, *née* Mackenzie; 1 da (Moray); *Career* cmmnd 17/21 Lancers 1953–55 (army racquets champion 1954); chm Shepherd Neame Ltd 1971– (joined 1956, dir 1957, mktg dir 1961), former dir and chm Faversham Laundry Co, regnl dir National Westminster Bank plc 1982–92; dir: Kent Econ Devpt Bd 1984–89, Folkestone Racecourse 1984–99 (chm 1989); local dir Royal Insurance (UK) Ltd 1971–2000; non-exec dir Merrydown Cider 1997–2004; memb Faversham CC 1965–89, ldr Kent CC 1982–84; High Sheriff Kent 2001–02; vice-pres SE Eng Tourist Bd 1990– (chm 1979–90), chm Int Union of Local Authorities 1986–89, chm Kent Ambassador 2002–; memb: Rural Devpt Ctee SEEDA 1999–, Assoc of Brewing; pres Kent CCC 2003; Master Worshipful Co of Brewers 1999–2000; *Recreations* shooting, riding, cricket, golf, squash, racquets; *Clubs* MCC, I Zingari, Butterflies, Escorts, Jesters, Band of Brothers, Press, Royal St George's, Free Foresters; *Style—* Robert Neame, Esq, CBE, DL; ✉ Dane Court Farmhouse, Kits Hill, Selling, Faversham, Kent (☎ 01227 752284); c/o Shepherd Neame Ltd, 17 Court Street, Faversham, Kent ME13 7AX (☎ 01795 532206)

NEARY, Martin Gerard James; LVO (1998); s of Leonard Walter Neary (d 1996), of Walton-on-Thames, Surrey, and Jeanne Marguerite, *née* Thébault; *b* 28 March 1940; *Educ* City of London Sch, Chapel Royal Choir, Gonville & Caius Coll Cambridge (organ scholar, MA); *m* 22 April 1967, Penelope Jane, da of Sir Brian Warren (d 1996), of London, and Dame Josephine Barnes, DBE (d 1999); 2 da (Nicola b 1969, Alice b 1972), 1 s (Thomas b 1974); *Career* prof of organ Trinity Coll London 1963–72, organist and master of music St Margaret's Westminster 1965–71; conductor: Twickenham Musical Soc 1966–72, St Margaret's Westminster Singers 1967–71, Waynflete Singers 1972–87, RSCM Millennium Youth Choir 1999–2001, Paulist Choristers of California 1999–2003, English Chamber Singers 1999–; organist and master of the music Winchester Cathedral 1972–87, organist and master of the choristers Westminster Abbey 1988–98, lectr in church music Royal Acad of Music 1989–96, dir of music First Congregational Church LA 2001–02, artistic dir LA Bach Festival 2002; guest conductor: Academy of Ancient Music, Bournemouth Symphony Orchestra, English Chamber Orchestra, London Symphony Orchestra, Winchester Baroque Ensemble 1982–87, Westminster Baroque Ensemble 1988, Brandenburg Orchestra 1991; chief guest conductor Grand Rapid Choir of Men and Boys; 12 foreign tours with Winchester Cathedral Choir 1978–87, toured America (thrice), France (twice), Germany, Hungary, Switzerland, Norway, Russia and Ukraine with Westminster Abbey Choir 1988–97; dir Southern Cathedrals Festival 1972, 1975, 1978, 1981, 1984 and 1987; many organ recitals and broadcasts in UK, Europe, America, Aust, NZ, Korea and India, has conducted premières of music by many Br composers especially Jonathan Harvey and John Tavener, numerous recordings incl Purcell Music for Queen Mary; pres: Cathedral Organists' Assoc 1985–88, Royal Coll of Organists 1988–90 and 1996–98, Organists Charitable Tst 1988–, John Carpenter Club 1997–98; chm Herbert Howells Soc 1993–, music advsr John Lyon's Charity 2004–; fell Salzberg Global Seminar 2011; Grammy Award nomination 1996; hon citizen Texas 1971; Hon DMus Univ of Southampton 1997, Lambeth Doctorate of Music 2012; Hon FTCL 1969, Hon RAM 1988; FRCO 1963, FRSCM 1997; Knight of the Order of St Lazarus of Jerusalem (KLJ) 2001; *Books* Early French Organ Music (ed 2 vols, 1975), Organists Charitable Tst Little Organ Book (ed, 2010); several compositions incl May The Grace (for Royal Golden Wedding), O Worship the Lord, All Saints Mass 2004, Mass of the Redeemer 2010, and numerous arrangements of carols and hymns; *Recreations* watching cricket, concerts and opera, family; *Clubs* Garrick, Middx CCC; *Style—* Dr Martin Neary, LVO; ✉ 13 Parkwood Road, Wimbledon SW19 7AU (☎ 020 3016 7439, e-mail martin@mneary.co.uk)

NEATE, Francis Webb; s of Francis Webb Neate (d 1982), of Kew, Surrey, and Fiona L M, *née* O'Brien (d 2003); *b* 13 May 1940; *Educ* St Wilfrid's Sch Seaford, St Paul's, BNC Oxford (BA), Univ of Chicago Law Sch (JD); *m* 25 Aug 1962, Patricia Anne, da of Anthony Vincent Hugh Mulligan (d 1984); 2 da (Polly b 1966, Emily b 1973 d 2007), 2 s (Vincent b 1968, Patrick b 1970); *Career* assoc Davis Polk & Wardwell NY 1963; admitted slr 1966; Slaughter and May: articled clerk 1964–66, asst slr 1966–71, ptnr 1972–97; gp legal advsr Schroders plc 1997–2004, of counsel Kirkland & Ellis Int LLP 2004–09; pres Int Bar Assoc 2005–06; memb Law Soc; *Recreations* cricket, reading, family; *Clubs* MCC, Berkshire CCC (pres), Richmond CC, Falkland CC, Oxford Univ CC (pres); *Style—* Francis Neate, Esq; ✉ 2 Daylesford Avenue, London SW15 5QR

NEATH, Gavin Ellis; CBE (2007); s of Ronald William Neath (d 2002), of Portsmouth, and Frances Gillian, *née* Davis; *b* 5 April 1953, Mbulu, Tanzania; *Educ* Warwick Sch, Univ of Manchester (BA), Univ of Warwick (MSc), Stanford Univ; *m* 6 Jan 1979, Ann Elizabeth; 3 da (Gemma Louise b 1983, Georgia Beatrice b 1986, Nancy Sian b 1990); *Career* Unilever: joined as grad trainee 1977, various sales and mktg roles Lever Bros UK 1977–85, mktg dir Lever France 1985–90, category dir laundry Lever Europe 1990–94, md Lever Ponds SA 1994–98, chm Unilever Bestfoods UK 1999–2004, chm Unilever UK 2004–; pres Food and Drink Fedn 2005–; *Recreations* theatre, cinema, squash, tennis; *Clubs* St Margarets Film (hon sec); *Style—* Gavin Neath, Esq, CBE

NEAVE, Prof Guy Richard Irvine; s of Lt Cdr Arundel Richard York Neave, DSC (d 1977), and Barbara Marie, *née* Liardet (d 1979); *b* 27 December 1941; *Educ* Kings Sch Worcester, Univ of London (BA, PhD); *m* 6 Dec 1986, Martine Gabriele Thérèse, da of Claude Herlant, of Woluwe Saint Pierre, Belgium; 2 c (Joel, Magali (twins) b 3 Aug 1988); *Career* lectr in history Wales 1967–69, research fell Univ of Edinburgh 1969–75, prof of comparative and gen educn Amsterdam 1978–80, directeur de recherche Paris 1981–85 (maitre de recherche 1975–78), prof of comparative educn Univ of London 1986–90, prof Centre for Higher Educn Policy Studies Univeriteit Twente Enschede 1998–2006 (prof emeritus 2006–), dir of research CIPES Matosinhos Portugal 2006–; hon vice-pres Soc for Research in Higher Educn, foreign memb Nat Acad of Educn USA 1999–, pres Euro Assoc for Institutional Research 2001–03; jt ed European Jl of Educn 1980–91, fndr ed Higher Educn Policy 1988–2006; fell Cwlth of Aust Fellowship 1993; FRSA 1987; *Books* How They Fared (1975), An Improper Sixth Year (jtly, 1976), Modèles d'Egalité (1976), The EEC And Education (1985), La Communidad Europea Y La Educación (1987), Prometheus Bound (jtly, 1991), The Teaching Nation (1992), Encyclopedia of Higher Education (jt ed-in-chief, 4 vols, 1992), Government and Higher Education Relationships across Three Continents: The Winds of Change (jtly, 1994), The Complete Encyclopedia of Education (CD-Rom, jt ed-in-chief, 1999), Higher Education and the Nation-State (jtly, 2001), Abiding Issues, Changing Perspectives: Visions of the University across a Half Century (ed, 2001), La Universidad Contemporanea: historia y politicas, Barcelona (2001), Higher Education in Portugal 1974–2009 a Nation a Generation (jt ed, 2011), The Evaluative State, Institutional Autonomy and Re-engineering Higher Education in Western Europe: The Prince and His Pleasure Basingstoke/New York (2012); *Recreations* jogging, bricolage, building model warships in 1/96th scale; *Clubs* Anglo-Belgian; *Style—* Prof Guy Neave; ✉ 31 Square Saint Germain, F78100 Saint Germain En Laye, France; Centro de Investigacao de Politicas de Ensino Superior (CIPES), Rua de 1 Dezembro 399, 4450–227 Matosinhos, Portugal (☎ 00351 229 398790, fax 00351 229 398799)

NEBHRAJANI, Sharmila; OBE (2014); da of Vir Tirathdas Nebhrajani, of London, and Jayantee, *née* Chanda; *b* London; *Educ* St Anne's Coll Oxford (MA); *Family* 1 s, 1 da; *Career* strategy conslt Coopers & Lybrand 1988, strategic planning mangr Cable & Wireless plc 1993, asst dir Media Corp Fin Gp Price Waterhouse 1995; BBC: sr strategy advsr 1996, head of corporate planning 1997–2002, chief operating offr Future Media and Technol 2002–09; exec dir of finance and performance NHS Sussex 2009–11, chief exec Assoc of Medical Research Charities 2011–14, chair Human Tissue Authy 2014– (memb 2004–07); dir of external affrs Medical Research Cncl 2015–; dep chair Human Fertilisation and Embryology Authy 1998–2007, charity cmmr 2007–13; memb: Olympic Lottery Distributor 2004–07, Ind Audit Ctee Inst of Cancer Research 2010–14, Bd Pension Protection Fund 2012–, Bd Parly and Health Service Ombudsman 2013–14; gen memb Cncl Univ of Sussex 2012–; Yale world fell 2007; memb ICAEW 1991; *Style—* Ms Sharmila Nebhrajani, OBE; ✉ HTA, 151 Buckingham Palace Road, London SW1

NEEDHAM, Andrew James (Andy); s of Paul Needham, and Sandra, *née* Mylne; *b* 25 August 1971; *Educ* Castle Hall GS Mirfield, Huddersfield Tech Coll; *Career* chef; Savoy Hotel London 1988–91, Le Pré Catalan Paris 1992–93, La Cinlianella Lumbardia Italy 1993–94, Aubergine 1994–95, Zafferano 1995– (1 Michelin star 2001–); *Style—* Andy Needham, Esq; ✉ Zafferano, 15 Lowndes Street, Belgravia, London SW1X 9EY

NEELY, William Robert Nicholas (Bill); s of William John Neely (d 1960), and Lucy Patricia, *née* Larney (d 2000); *b* 21 May 1959; *Educ* St Malachy's Coll Belfast, Queen's Univ Belfast (BA); *m* 5 June 1988, Marion, da of John Kerr; 2 da (Sarah Caroline Kerr b 20 June 1989, Emma Sophie Kerr b 6 May 1998); *Career* reporter News & Current Affairs BBC: NI 1981–87, London 1987–88; reporter/presenter Sky News 1989; ITN: reporter 1989–90, Washington corr 1991–96, Europe corr 1997–2002, int ed 2002–14; chief global corr NBC News 2014–; RTS News Award 1999 and 2001, Monte Carlo TV Award 1999, BAFTA TV News Awards 2009, 2010 and 2011, Emmy Int News Award 2009, RTS Int News Award 2011, Broadcast Journalist of the Year London Press Club 2013, Peabody Award Univ of Georgia 2014; *Recreations* wine, poetry, competitive running, triathlon; *Style—* Bill Neely, Esq

NEHME, Dr Jean; s of George Nehme, and Alina, *née* Chalhoub; *b* 21 July 1984, Zahlé, Lebanon; *Educ* BSc, Univ of London (MB BS), Imperial Coll London (MSc); *Career* registrar plastic surgn Royal Free Hosp; co-fndr and ceo Touch Surgery 2010–; entrepreneur Blueprint Health LLC 2013; hon research fell Imperial Coll London 2011–; MRCS; *Recreations* reading, tennis; *Style—* Dr Jean Nehme; ✉ Touch Surgery, Lower Ground Floor, 17–18 Haywards Place, London EC1R 0EQ (020 3217 2090, website www.touchsurgery.com)

NEIGHBOUR, Dr Roger Harvey; OBE (2011); s of late Kenneth George Neighbour, and late Eileen Nora, *née* Roberts; *b* 9 June 1947, Berkhamsted, Herts; *Educ* Watford GS for Boys, King's Coll Cambridge (MA), St Thomas' Hosp Medical Sch (MB BChir), Watford Vocational Trg Scheme; *Career* princ in gen practice Vine House Health Centre 1975–2003; trainer in gen practice 1977–94, course organiser Watford Vocational Training Scheme 1979–86; pres RCGP 2003–06, MRCGP examiner 1984– (convenor Panel of MRCGP examiners 1997–2002); columnist: Educn for Gen Practice 1990–2001, Br Jl of Gen Practice 2002–03; author of numerous articles in medical trade jls and papers on vocational trg, family therapy, the MRCGP examination, medical assessment, foetal memory and Franz Schubert; RCGP: George Abercrombie Award 2001, Richard Scott lectr 2001, George Swift lectr 2001; Hon DSc Univ of Hertfordshire 2004; inaugural fell Assoc of Course Organisers 1988; DObstRCOG 1975, FRCGP 1987 (MRCGP 1975), Hon FRCP 2004; The Inner Consultation (1987, 2 edn 2004), The Inner Apprentice (1992, 2 edn 2004), The MRCGP Examination (contrib, 2000), The Successful GP Registrar's Companion (co-author, 2003), The Management Handbook for Primary Care (contrib, 2004), I'm Too Hot Now (2005), The Inner Physician (2016); *Recreations* playing the violin, the music of Schubert, France, writing, armchair philosophy, trying to give up golf; *Style—* Dr Roger Neighbour, OBE; ✉ Argowan, Bell Lane, Bedmond, Hertfordshire WD5 0QS; Apartment 26, La Falaise d'Hacqueville, 52 rue Saint Gaud, 50400 Granville, France

NEIL, Alex; MSP; s of Alexander Neil (d 2001), of Ayr, and Margaret Neil (d 1977); *b* 22 August 1951; *Educ* Dalmellington HS, Ayr Acad, Univ of Dundee (MA); *m* 1978, Isabella, *née* Kerr; 1 s (Michael b 1 Dec 1979); *Career* project ldr Manpower Service Cmmn Project Univ of Glasgow 1977–79; Digital Equipment Corp Ayr and USA: mktg rep 1979–80, mktg and admin mangr 1981–82, logistics mangr 1982–83; mktg mangr Future Technology Systems Beith 1983, dir Cumnock and Doon Enterprise Tst (CADET) 1983–88, chief exec The Prince's Scottish Business Tst (PSYBT) 1988–90, dir Development Options Ltd 1988–89, md EES Consultants Ltd 1990–95; freelance advsr econ and business 1995–; MSP (SNP): Scotland Central 1999–2011, Airdrie & Shotts 2011–; oppn spokesperson on Social Security 1999–2000, chm Enterprise and Lifelong Learning Ctee 2000–03, memb Standards Ctee 2003–04, min for housing and communities Scottish Parl 2009–12, sec for health and wellbeing 2012–; *Recreations* golf, reading, travel; *Style—* Alex Neil, Esq, MSP, MIED; ✉ The Scottish Parliament, Edinburgh EH99 1SP (☎ 0131 348 5703, mobile 07899 876139, e-mail alex.neil.msp@scottish.parliament.uk)

NEIL, Andrew Ferguson; s of Maj James Neil (d 1987), and Mary, *née* Ferguson (d 1993); *b* 21 May 1949; *Educ* Paisley GS, Univ of Glasgow (MA); *Career* Cons Res Dept 1971–72, UK ed The Economist 1982–83 (UK and US corr 1973–81), ed The Sunday Times 1983–94, exec chm Sky TV 1988–90, exec ed Fox News (New York) June-Dec 1994, freelance broadcaster, writer, lectr and media conslt 1995–, columnist The Sunday Times and Daily Mail 1995–96, contrib ed Vanity Fair 1994–, publisher ed-in-chief and chief exec Press Holdings Ltd (The Scotsman, Scotland on Sunday, Edinburgh Evening News, Scotsman.com) 1996–2006, chief exec then chm The Spectator and Apollo 2004–; chm: World Media Rights 2005–, ITP Dubai 2006–, PFD 2008–10; co-presenter: The Midnight Hour (BBC 2) 1994–98, Conference Talk (BBC 2) 1996–99, Thursday Night Live (Carlton TV) 1997–2000, Despatch Box (BBC 2) 1998–2002; presenter: The Andrew Neil Show (BBC 2) 1995–96, The Sunday Breakfast Programme (BBC Radio 5 Live) 1998–2000, The Daily Politics (BBC 2) 2003–, This Week with Andrew Neil (BBC 1) 2003–, Straight Talk with Andrew Neil (BBC News 24) 2006–10, The Sunday Politics (BBC 1) 2012–; Political Journalist of the Year 2013; lord rector Univ of St Andrews 1999–2002; FRSA 1997; *Books* The Cable Revolution (1982), Full Disclosure (autobiography, 1996), British Excellence (1998); *Recreations* dining out in London, NY, Dubai and Côte d'Azur, cycling; *Clubs* RAC; *Style—* Andrew Neil, Esq; ✉ Glenburn Enterprises, 8 Cadogan Square, London SW1X 0JU (☎ 0845 299 7225, e-mail afneil@icloud.com)

NEIL, Prof James Charles; s of Charles Neil (d 1960) and Margaret, *née* Bishop (d 2003); *b* 6 January 1953; *Educ* Allan Glen's Sch Glasgow, Univ of Glasgow (BSc, PhD); *m* 1975, Una Anne Dunlop, *née* Murray; 2 da (Ailsa b 1981, Lucy 1986), 1 s (Charles b 1983); *Career* Univ of Southern Calif 1979–81, Beatson Inst for Cancer Research 1987–1992, prof of virology and molecular oncology Univ of Glasgow 1992–; memb: Soc of Gen Microbiology 1975, Human Genome Orgn 1996; Lievre fell American Cancer Soc 1981; FRSE 1997; *Publications* author of numerous papers and articles in scientific jls and books on virology; *Recreations* music, racket sports; *Style—* Prof James Neil, FRSE; ✉ University of Glasgow, Molecular Oncology Laboratory, Institute of Comparative Medicine, Bearsden, Glasgow G61 1QH (☎ 0141 330 2365, fax 0141 330 2271, e-mail j.c.neil@vet.gla.ac.uk)

NEILAND, Prof Brendan Robert; s of Arthur Neiland (d 1990), and Joan Agnes Bessie, *née* Whiley; *b* 23 October 1941; *Educ* Lowestoft Co GS Birmingham, St Philips GS Birmingham, St Augustine's Seminary Co Cavan Eire, Birmingham Coll of Art (dip), RCA (MA); *m* 1970, Hilary Vivienne, da of late Morris Salter; 2 da (Naomi b 23 Aug 1974, Lucy 17 Feb 1977); *Career* artist; gallery artist: Angela Flowers Gallery 1970–78, Fischer Fine Art 1978–92, Redfern Gallery 1992–; pt/t teaching: Manchester Art Coll 1969–73, Brighton Art Coll 1983–; prof Univ of Brighton 1996–; keeper Royal Acad of Arts 1998–2004; co-operated in making of video Commissioned Art and Professional Practice (dir Gavin Nettleton 1991); lectr Buildings Within Buildings, Reflections on Paintings RIBA 1989; artist in residence Nan Yang Univ Singapore 2014; hon doctorate De Montfort Univ 2013; hon fell Royal Soc of Painters and Etchers 1998; FRSA 1996; *Solo Exhibitions* Flowers Gallery 1971–72 and 1974–76, Fischer Fine Art 1979–84 and 1987–91, Tate Gallery 1988, RIBA Galleries 1989, Redfern Gallery London 1993, 1997 and 2006, touring show (Gardner Art Centre Brighton, Milton Keynes Exhbn Gallery, N Centre for Contemporary Art Sunderland, Stafford Art Gallery, Grundy Art Gallery Blackpool) 1992–, Reading Coll Reading 1993, Friends Room RA 1997, Brighton Univ 1997, Loughborough Univ 1998, Keele Univ 1998, retrospective Turlej Gallery Krakow 2006, retrospective Sharjah Museum UAE 2006, Night Day (Redfern Gall London) 2008, Neiland at 70 (Redfern Gallery) 2011, 45 Park Lane 2013, Searcys at the Gherkin 2013, The Light Fantastic Redfern Gallery 2014, Neiland in Singapore Galerie Belvedere Singapore 2015; *Group Exhibitions* Bradford Int Print Biennale 1970, 1972, 1974, 1976, 1982 and 1986, From Britain '75 Helsinki Finland 1975, Arts Cncl Coll Hayward 1976, Eight British Realists Meisel Gallery NYC 1983, Pintura Británica Municipal Museum Madrid 1983, Images et Imaginaires d'Architecture Centre Georges Pompidou Paris 1984, Artists in National Parts V&A and touring UK and USA 1988, Printmaking from Britain Moscow 1989, The New Patrons NACF Christie's London 1992, RA Summer Exhbn 1979–81 and 1986–92, five paintings for InterCity 225 (later used for posters) 1990–91, This Could Happen To You Ikon in the 1970s (Ikon Gallery Birmingham) 2010, Blake, Neiland and Faine (New Walk Gallery Leicester) 2011 and others; *Commissions* incl: A T Kearney, Aukett, BAA, BMW Gp, Univ of Brighton, CapitaLand Singapore, English Heritage, Enron, Great Western, Intercity, Loughborough Univ, Mazda, Nat Bank of Dubai, Rolls Royce, Rover, Royal Mail, Scot Rail, Waterloo Int; *Awards* CAS Purchase Prize Northern Young Contemporaries 1968, Arthur Tooth's Prize Young Contemporaries 1969, Silver Medal RCA 1969, Minton Scholarship 1969, Arts Cncl Minor Award 1972, John Moores XI Prizewinner 1978, scholar Crabtree Fndn 1982, Daler Rowney Award RA Summer Exhbn 1989; *Publications* Brendan Neiland at 70 (2012); *Recreations* listening to the Radio 4 cricket commentary, drinking fine wines; *Clubs* Chelsea Arts; *Style—* Prof Brendan Neiland; ✉ 2 Granard Road, London SW12 8UL (☎ and fax 020 8673 4597, e-mail brendan.neiland@yahoo.com, website www.brendanneiland.com); c/o Redfern Gallery, 20 Cork Street, London W1X 2HL (☎ 020 7734 1732/0578, fax 020 7494 2908)

NEILL, John Mitchell; CBE (1994); s of Justin Bernard Neill, and Johanna Elisabeth, *née* Bastiaans; *b* 21 July 1947; *Educ* George Heriott Sch Edinburgh, Univ of Strathclyde (BA, MBA, DBA); *m* 24 May 1975, Jacqueline Anne, da of Phillip Brown (d 1985); 2 s (Richard John b 19 July 1979, Alexander James b 4 Nov 1982); *Career* mktg mangr Europe AC Delco 1972–73 (planning mangr 1969–71), sales and mktg dir British Leyland Parts & KD Div 1976 (merchandising mangr 1974–75); md: Leyland Car Parts Div 1977–78, BL Components 1979–80, Unipart Group 1981–82; gp md Unipart Gp Ltd 1983–86, chm and gp chief exec Unipart Gp of Cos 1987–; dir BITC 1992–; non-exec dir: Charter Int plc 1994–2012, Bank of England 1996–2003, Royal Mail Hldgs plc 2003–07, Rolls-Royce plc 2008–15; chm Atlantis Resources Ltd 2013–; SMMT: memb Cncl, memb Exec Ctee, dir Industry Forum, pres 2000–01 (also sometime vice-pres); vice-pres: Inst of Motor Industry, BEN; memb: Cncl Business in the Community Bd, Alumni Bd Univ of Strathclyde; tstee Nat Motor Museum 1992–99; FInstM; *Recreations* tennis, skiing, motorsport; *Style—* John M Neill, Esq, CBE; ✉ Unipart Group, Unipart House, Cowley, Oxford OX4 2PG (☎ 01865 778966, fax 01865 383790)

NEILL, Robert James MacGillivray (Bob); MP; s of John MacGillivray Neill, of Ilford, Essex, and Elsie May, *née* Chaston; *b* 24 June 1952; *Educ* Abbs Cross Sch Hornchurch Essex, LSE (LLB); *Career* called to the Bar: Middle Temple 1975, King's Inns Dublin 1992; memb: Havering London Borough Cncl 1974–90 (chief whip), GLC for Romford (Cons) 1985–86; GLA: memb London Assembly (Cons) Bexley and Bromley 2000–08, ldr Cons Gp 2000–02, chair Planning and Spatial Devpt Ctee 2001–02; MP (Cons) Bromley and Chislehurst 2006–, shadow min for London 2007–09, shadow min for local govt 2008–10, Parly under-sec of state Dept for Communities and Local Govt 2010–12, vice-chm Cons Pty 2012–15, chm Justice Select Ctee House of Commons 2015–; first ldr London Fire & Civil Defence Authy 1985–87, oppn spokesman Fire and Public Protection Ctee Assoc of Met Authorities; chm Gtr London Cons Political Centre 1990–93; Nat Union of

N

Cons & Unionists Assocs: dep chm Gtr London Area 1993–96, chm Gtr London Area 1996–98, regnl chm Gtr London Conservatives 1996–99; memb UK delgn Ctee of the Regions EU 2000–08, memb Parly Assembly Cncl of Europe 2012–15; *Recreations* sailing, travel, opera; *Clubs* Carlton; *Style*— Bob Neill, Esq, MP; ✉ House of Commons, London SW1A 0AA (✆ 020 7219 8169, fax 020 7219 8089, e-mail bob.neill.mp@parliament.uk)

NEILL, Robert Moore; s of Charles Neill (d 1991), of Donaghadee, NI, and Elizabeth Ida, *née* Moore; *b* 16 September 1950; *Educ* Campbell Coll Belfast, Queen's Univ Belfast (LLB); *Career* admitted slr: England and Wales 1976, Hong Kong 1987; Herbert Smith: articled clerk 1974–76, ptnr 1984–2004, sr litigation ptnr Hong Kong Office 1987–90; accredited mediator Centre for Dispute Resolution; *Recreations* sailing, tennis, theatre, travel; *Clubs* RAC, Royal Hong Kong Yacht; *Style*— Robert Neill, Esq

NEILL, Rose Mary Margaret; da of Roger Henry James Neill (d 1979), and Doreen Elizabeth, *née* Morrice (d 2016); *b* 29 November 1958; *Educ* Mount Sch York, City and E London Coll; *m* 1, 22 Feb 1985 (m dis 1997), (Robert) John Magill, s of Thomas Stewart Magill (d 1987); 2 s (Roger Thomas b 23 June 1986, Henry Harley Peter b 11 Sept 1988); m 2, 23 Dec 2000, Ivan Wilson, s of Richard Wilson; *Career* television newscaster, sports presenter and gen prog presenter; Ulster TV Ltd 1978–86; BBC Belfast 1986–2008: co presenter main evening news prog, newscaster and writer for other daily bulletins; UTV 2008–: co-presenter UTV Live at 6 and gen newscaster, presenter Titanic documentary; regular broadcaster Pick of the Week radio prog, host of hour long chat show BBC Radio, writer and presenter various TV documentaries, travel corr; involved in annual Children in Need TV presentation and Royal Dublin Horse Show; memb Ctee NI Mother and Baby appeal, hon patron Ulster Cancer Res Campaign, chm Riding for the Disabled Killinchy; *Recreations* hunting, skiing (water and snow), sailing, travelling, tennis; *Clubs* Royal Ulster Yacht, Strangford Lough Yacht, E Down Fox Hounds, Windsor Lawn Tennis; *Style*— Miss Rose Neill; ✉ UTV Newsroom, Ormeau Road, Belfast BT7 1EB (✆ 028 9032 8122, e-mail rose.neill@u.tv)

NEILL, (James) Ruary Drummond; s of Thomas Neill (d 1969), and Elsie Margaret Wilson, *née* Sharp; *b* 9 January 1959; *Educ* Gresham's, Univ of London (BA); *m* 5 Sept 1987, Hilary Jane Vipan, da of Peter Harvey Bourne; 1 da (Georgina Kim Jane b 13 Feb 1990), 1 s (Tom Callum Ruary b 21 Jan 1993); *Career* Chartered Bank Abu Dhabi UAE 1981–83, Chartered Bank Hong Kong 1983–85, Rowe & Pitman then Warburg Securities London 1985–88; Schroder Securities Ltd: joined 1988, dir 1990–94, head of int sales Asian Div 1993–94; md Schroder Securities (Hong Kong) Ltd 1990–93, md UBS 2003–14 (exec dir 1994–2003); memb Advsy Cncl SOAS China Inst Univ of London; fndn govr Albury Primary Sch 1999–2003, assoc tstee and chm Investment Ctee Great Ormond St Children's Charity 2014–; *Recreations* shooting, farming, reading; *Clubs* Travellers; *Style*— Ruary Neill, Esq; ✉ c/o Travellers Club, 116 Pall Mall, London SW1Y 5EP

NELIGAN, His Hon John Oliver; s of Desmond Neligan (d 1993), of NZ, and Penelope Anne, *née* Mason (d 1996); *b* 21 June 1944, Horsham, Sussex; *Educ* Brickwall Sch Northiam; *m* May 1971, Mary Brigid, *née* Daniel; 2 da (Fiona Claire b Oct 1974, Caroline Mary b Jan 1977), 1 s (Andrew James b Jan 1978); *Career* admitted slr 1969, called to the Bar Middle Temple 1975; in practice Western Circuit 1975–96, recorder 1994–96, circuit judge (Western Circuit) 1996–2014; legal memb Mental Health Review Tbnl 2001–11; *Recreations* walking, gardening, painting; *Style*— His Hon John Neligan; ✉ c/o Exeter Crown and County Courts, Southernhay Gardens, Exeter EX1 1UH

NELMES, Dianne Gwenllian; da of late James Allen Nelmes, and Celandine, *née* Kimber; *Educ* The Holt Girls' GS Wokingham, Univ of Newcastle upon Tyne (BA, DCL); *m* 17 May 1986, Ian McBride, s of Robert McBride; *Career* pres Newcastle Univ Students' Union 1973–74, graduate trainee Thomson Newspapers 1974–78 (variously sr news reporter, municipal corr and property reporter The Journal Newcastle), regional journalist and on-screen reporter/presenter BBC TV North East 1978–83; Granada Television: dep news ed Granada News 1983, researcher World in Action 1984; prodr/dir Brass Tacks BBC News & Current Affrs 1987–88; rejoined Granada Television as launch ed This Morning 1988, exec prodr Entertainment Dept 1989–92; dir of news and current affrs Meridian Broadcasting (from start of franchise) 1992; Granada Television: rejoined Granada as exec prodr World in Action 1992, head of factual progs 1993–94, controller of factual progs 1994–95, dir of programming Granada Satellite Television 1995–97; ITV: controller of daytime progs 1998–2000, controller of documentaries and features 2000–03; dir daytime and lifestyle programming Granada 2003–, md Liberty Bell Prodns 2008–12; visiting prof of media and journalism Univ of Newcastle upon Tyne 2008–11 (memb Cncl 2015–); trustee Refuge, lay tstee NUS 2012; Hon DCL Univ of Newcastle upon Tyne 2011; memb BAFTA, FRTS, FRSA; *Recreations* canal boating, walking, mountain trekking; *Style*— Ms Dianne Nelmes

NELSON, Andy; *Educ* Eastbourne GS, Univ of Oxford (MA); m; 3 s; *Career* mgmnt conslt Accenture 1980–87, Price Waterhouse 1989–93, head of trading systems and dir computer services Adsa Stores Ltd 1993–97, chief info offr GE Capital Global Consumer Services 1998–2001, gp dir for strategic change and IT Royal and Sun Alliance 2003–06, chief info offr Miny of Justice 2009–13, Govt chief info offr 2012–13, chief info offr Dept of Work and Pensions 2013–; *Style*— Andy Nelson, Esq; ✉ Department for Work and Pensions, Caxton House, Tothill Street, London SW1H 9NA

NELSON, David Brian; s of Victor Harry Nelson (d 1987), of Leicester, and Edna Mary, *née* Elliot (d 1987); *b* 15 April 1951; *Educ* Longslade Sch Birstall, Loughborough Coll of Art, Hornsey Coll of Art (DipAD), Royal Coll of Art (MA, travelling scholar Northern Italy); *m* 13 Aug 1977, Caroline Georgette, da of John Weston Evans; 2 da (Aimee Jacqueline b 17 Oct 1979, Bibiana Christina b 9 Nov 1983); *Career* architect; dir Foster + Partners (formerly Sir Norman Foster & Partners) 1984– (joined 1976), dep chm 2004–, jt head of design 2007–; former projects incl: Hongkong and Shanghai Bank 1979–85 (latterly project ldr), American Air Museum Duxford Cambridge (winner of the BSkyB/Royal Fine Art Cmmn Bldg of the Year award and RIBA Stirling Prize for Architecture 1998), Millennium Tower 1989, Century Tower Tokyo 1991, Bilbao Metro System Spain 1995, ptnr i/c Canary Wharf Station (Jubilee Line) 1999 and Reichstag New German Parliament Berlin, Clark Center Stanford Univ, Technology Centre McLaren UK, Petronas Univ Malaysia 2004, Supreme Ct Singapore 2005, Repsol HQ Madrid, 126 Philip Street Sydney, Regent Place Sydney; Hon FRIBA 2002; *Style*— David Nelson, Esq; ✉ Foster + Partners, Riverside Three, 22 Hester Road, London SW11 4AN (✆ 020 7738 0455, fax 020 7738 1107/1108, website www.fosterandpartners.com)

NELSON, Dr Elizabeth Hawkins; OBE (1997); da of Harry Dadmun Nelson (d 1965), of Summit, NJ, and Gretchen, *née* Hawkins (d 1984); *b* 27 January 1931; *Educ* Hanover HS NH, Middlebury Coll VT (BA), Inst of Psychiatry Univ of London (PhD); *m* 1, 1960 (m dis 1972), Ivan Piercy; 1 da (Catherine b 15 Sept 1961), 2 s (Christopher b 5 March 1963, Nicholas b 3 Aug 1965); m 2, 26 July 1975 (m dis 1998), Claude Jacob Esterson, s of Elias Esterson; *Career* fndr dir and chm Taylor Nelson Group 1965–92; chm Addison Consultancy Group plc 1989–91, chm Taylor Nelson AGB 1992, chief exec Princess Royal Tst for Carers 1992–96; chair: Stargate Capital Investment Gp Ltd 2004–07, Q Research 2006–10, Fly Research Ltd 2009–; non-exec dir: The Royal Bank of Scotland plc 1987–97, Bright Talk Ltd 2004–06; pres World Assoc of Public Opinion Res 1990–92; chair: UK Ecolabelling Bd 1992–98, Univ of Roehampton (formerly Roehampton Inst) 1996–2001, Richmond, Twickenham, Roehampton Healthcare NHS Tst 1997–99, SW London Community NHS Tst 1999–2002, Exec Ctee Well Being RCOG 2002–04; vice-chair and memb Cncl Open Univ 1992–2001, dir US Open Univ 1998–2001; memb: Pay Review Body Doctors and Dentists 1992–97, Consumer Ctee Meat and Livestock Cmmn 1998–2005, Cncl City & Guilds 1998–2009, Quality Assurance Agency 1999–2003, Cncl Market Research Soc 2012– (dir Bd 2011–); exec chm Fly Research Ltd 2010–; tstee: Immigrant Advsy Service 2005–11, Genetic Alliance 2008–13, Tavistock Inst 2008–13; patron: Jeans for Genes 2008–, Family Planning Assoc 2007–11; govr Wimbledon Sch of Art; memb: First Forum (UK), Int Women's Forum UK; Int Women's Forum Women Who Make a Difference 2010, CBI/Lloyds Bank First Women's Award 2011; Hon DSc City Univ 1993, Hon Dr Open Univ 2003, hon fell City & Guilds 1994, hon fell Univ of Roehampton 2003; FRSA; *Recreations* bridge, choral singing, opera; *Style*— Dr Elizabeth Nelson, OBE; ✉ 57 Home Park Road, Wimbledon, London SW19 (✆ 020 8946 2317, car 07885 546905, e-mail liznlson53@gmail.com)

NELSON, Fraser; *b* 14 May 1973; *Educ* Nairn Acad, Dollar Acad, Univ of Glasgow, City Univ; *m* Sept 2006, Linda Nelson; *Career* The Times: business journalist 1995–2000, Scottish political correspondent 2000–01; political ed The Scotsman 2001–06; The Spectator: political ed 2006–09, gen ed 2009–; Editor's Editor of the Year 2013, Political Journalist of the Year 2013; *Style*— Fraser Nelson, Esq; ✉ The Spectator, 22 Old Queen Street, London SW1H 9HP

NELSON, Hon James Jonathan; yr s of 2 Baron Nelson of Stafford (d 1995); *b* 17 June 1947; *Educ* Ampleforth, McGill Univ Montreal (BCom); *m* 18 Nov 1977, Lucilla Mary, da of Roger Gopsill Brown, of Albrighton, Salop; 3 da (Camilla Amy b 1982, Lara Kitty b 1986, Eloise Violet b 1988); *Career* commercial banking offr Morgan Guaranty Tst Co of New York 1969–73, dir Foreign & Colonial Management Ltd 1974–2001, md and dir Foreign & Colonial Ventures Ltd 1985–2001, ptnr Graphite Captial 2001–07, chm PRI Gp 2002–03, chm PIFC Group 2002–07; non-exec dir: Intermediate Capital Group plc 2001–, Henderson Smaller Companies Investment Trust 2002–; chm Br Venture Capital Assoc 1999–2000; Freeman City of London 1986, Liveryman Worshipful Co of Goldsmiths 1989; *Recreations* golf, tennis, skiing, shooting, fishing; *Clubs* Boodle's, Hurlingham, New Zealand; *Style*— The Hon James Nelson

NELSON, Emeritus Prof Dame Janet Laughland (Jinty); DBE (2006); da of William Wilson Muir (d 1965), and Elizabeth Barnes, *née* Laughland (d 1991); *b* 28 March 1942; *Educ* Keswick Sch Cumbria, Newnham Coll Cambridge (BA, PhD); *m* 1965 (m dis 2010), Howard George Horatio Nelson; 1 da (Elizabeth Muir b 1972), 1 s (William Horatio b 1974); *Career* King's Coll London: lectr 1970–87, reader 1987–92, prof 1992–2007, emeritus prof 2008–, dir Centre for Late Antique and Medieval Studies 1994–2000; pres Ecclesiastical History Society 1993–94 (memb 1969–), pres Royal Historical Soc 2000–04, vice-pres Br Acad 1999–2001; memb: Confraternity of St James 1990–; corresponding fell Medieval Acad of America 2000–, fell KCL 2001–; FRHistS 1981, FBA 1996, FSA 2014; *Books* Politics and Ritual in the Early Middle Ages (1986), The Annals of St Bertin (1991), Charles the Bald (1992), The Frankish World (1996), Rulers and Ruling Families in Early Medieval Europe (1999), Rituals of Power (ed, with F Theuws, 2000), The Medieval World (ed, with P Linehan, 2001), Courts, Elites and Gendered Power in Early Medieval Europe (2007), Reading the Bible in the Middle Ages (ed, with D Kempt, 2015), Ravenna: Change and Exchange (ed, with J Herrin, 2016); *Recreations* music, walking, spending time with grandchildren Elias, Ruth, Martha and Dorie; *Style*— Emeritus Prof Dame Jinty Nelson, FBA; ✉ 71 Oglander Road, London SE15 4DD; Department of History, King's College London, Strand, London WC2R 2LS (e-mail jinty.nelson23@gmail.com)

NELSON, John Frederick; *b* 26 July 1947; *Educ* Marlborough; *m*; 3 c; *Career* Kleinwort Benson: joined (corp fin) 1971, a vice-pres Kleinwort Benson Inc NY 1973–75, dir Kleinwort Benson Ltd 1980–86; Lazard Brothers & Co Ltd: md 1986–98, vice-chm 1990–98; chm Credit Suisse First Boston Europe Ltd 1999–2002; non-exec chm Hammerson plc 2005–13 (non-exec dir 2004–13), dep chm and sr ind dir Kingfisher plc 2002–11; non-exec dir: Woolwich plc 1998–2000, BT Gp plc 2002–08, JPMorgan Cazenove Hldgs Ltd and Cazenove Gp Ltd 2008–10; chm London Investment Banking Assoc (LIBA) 2001–02, chm Lloyd's of London 2011–; dir ENO 2002–10, tstee Nat Gallery 2010–, chm Chichester Harbour Tst 2013–; FCA (ACA 1970); *Style*— John Nelson, Esq

NELSON, John Graeme; s of Charles Nelson (d 1985), and Jean, *née* Blackstock; *b* 19 June 1947; *Educ* Aylesbury GS, Slough GS, Univ of Manchester (BA); *m* 19 June 1971, Pauline Viola, da of Stanley Arthur Dickinson (d 2002), of Hayes, Kent; 2 s (Andrew b 1973, Ian b 1976 d 2007), 1 da (Clare b 1979); *Career* BR: management trainee Western Region 1968–71, asst station mangr Liverpool St 1971–73, area passenger mangr Shenfield 1973–77, passenger sales offr Leeds 1977–79, passenger mangr Sheffield Div 1979–81, PA to chief exec BRB 1981–82, parcels mangr Southern Region 1982–84, nat business mangr Red Star Parcels 1984–87, gen mangr Eastern Region 1987–92, dir InterCity E Coast Main Line 1991–92, md Network SouthEast 1992–94, md British Rail South and East 1994–97, mgmnt conslt First Class Partnerships 1997– (chm 2000); monthly contrib Transit Magazine 1999–2009; dir: First Class Insight Ltd 1997–2002, Renaissance Trains Ltd 1999–, Hull Trains 1999–; memb Bd: M40 Trains 1998–2002, Laing Rail 2002–06, Wrexham Shropshire and Marylebone Railway 2006–09, Tracsis plc 2007–, YourRail Ltd 2007–10; chm: N Yorks Ambulance Serv NHS Tst 1997–99, Tees E and N Yorks Ambulance Serv NHS Tst 1999–2002, ctee advising Govt on use of defibrillators in public places 1999–2001; memb Advsy Bd: Nat Railway Museum 2006–, Yorks Rail Acad 2007–09; former memb: London Regnl Cncl CBI, Cncl London C of C, Br Tport Police Ctee; *Recreations* piano, football, painting, psephology; *Style*— John Nelson, Esq; ✉ First Class Partnerships, 148 Lawrence Street, York YO10 3EB (✆ 01904 870792, e-mail fcp@easynet.co.uk)

NELSON, Dame Nicola; DBE (2014); *b* 9 December 1971, Newcastle upon Tyne; *Educ* BEd, MEd; *Children* 1 s (Benjamin Nelson-Taylor b 8 Jan 2002); *Career* sr teacher Shiremoor Primary Sch 1992–2003, exec headteacher Newcastle City Cncl 2003–, currently exec headteacher Beech Hill Primary and Walbottle Village Primary; nat ldr of educn Nat Coll for Leadership of Schs and Children's Services 2010–, tstee Schools North East; memb NAHT; *Recreations* cinema, opera, reading, travel; *Clubs* Heaton Harriers; *Style*— Dame Nicola Nelson, DBE

NELSON, Nigel David; s of David Gordon Nelson (d 1978), and Iris May, *née* Phillips (d 2001); *b* 16 April 1954; *Educ* Sutton Valence; *Children* 3 s (Marcus, Dominic, Hallam), 2 da (Nicolette, Cordelia); *Career* reporter: Kent Evening Post 1972–75 (crime reporter 1973–75), Daily Mail 1975–79 (royal reporter 1978, New York corr 1978–79); freelance US corr 1979–82, feature writer Sunday Mirror 1982–86, political ed Sunday People 1986–, political ed Sunday Mirror 2015–; book reviewer Tribune, diary columnist Politics First, newspaper reviewer Sky News and BBC News; memb NUJ; *Books* The Porton Phial (1991), William Blake: Songs of Innocence and of Experience (introduction, 2015); *Recreations* writing; *Clubs* Parliamentary Sports; *Style*— Nigel Nelson, Esq; ✉ The Sunday People, 1 Canada Square, Canary Wharf, London E14 5AP (✆ 020 7293 3490, e-mail nigel.nelson@people.co.uk)

NELSON, Prof Philip Arthur; s of David Nelson, of Kings Somborne, Hants, and Brenda, *née* Sneath; *b* 22 June 1952; *Educ* Colchester Royal GS, Univ of Southampton (BSc, PhD); *m* 4 Aug 1979, Jennifer, *née* Mills; 2 s (Benjamin b 23 April 1983, Samuel b 14 Sept 1985); *Career* research devpt and consltg engr Sound Attenuators Ltd Colchester 1978–82; Inst of Sound and Vibration Research Faculty of Engrg and Applied Sci Univ of Southampton: lectr 1982–88, sr lectr 1988–94, prof of acoustics 1994–, dir 2001–05; chief exec Engrg and Physical Sciences Research Cncl 2014–; pro vice-chllr Univ of Southampton 2005–13; dir: Adaptive Audio Ltd, Opsodis Ltd, Univ of Southampton Science Park Ltd; conslt: Br Aerospace, Lotus Engrg, Short Bros, Tek Gp Ltd, EA

Technol Ltd, Yamaha Corp, Ultra Electronics, Rolls-Royce plc; memb Cncl Inst of Acoustics 1991–2000, pres Int Cmmn for Acoustics 2004–07 (UK rep 1998–), memb CBI SE Regnl Cncl; keynote lectr at int confs in Tokyo, Yokohama, Blacksburg, Chicago, Liverpool, Atlanta, Eindhoven, Copenhagen, Hawaii and Paris; Tyndall Medal Inst of Acoustics (jtly) 1992, Rayleigh Medal Inst of Acoustics 2002; distinguished corresponding memb Int Inst of Noise Control Engrs 1995; fell Acoustical Soc of America 2002 (memb 1990), CEng 1992, FIMechE 1997 (MIMechE 1993), FIOA 1997, MIEEE, FREng 2002; *Publications* Active Control of Sound (with S J Elliott, 1992), Active Control of Vibration (with C R Fuller and S J Elliott, 1996); author of more than 120 sci pubns in refereed jls, and more than 200 other pubns; *Recreations* golf; *Clubs* Hockley Golf; *Style*— Prof Philip Nelson, FREng; ✉ 3 Montfort Heights, Halterworth Lane, Romsey, Hampshire SO51 9LP (☎ 01794 515936); Institute of Sound and Vibration Research, University of Southampton, Highfield, Southampton SO17 1BJ (☎ 023 8059 2259, fax 023 8059 5409, e-mail p.a.nelson@soton.ac.uk)

NELSON, Richard William; s of Cyril Aubrey Nelson (d 1971), and (Gillian) Mary Withers; *b* 14 June 1950, Nottingham; *Educ* Nottingham HS, Univ of Bristol (LLB); *m* 29 April 1978, Elizabeth Mary, *née* Cope; 1 s (William Henry b 18 Nov 1987), 1 da (Charlotte Louise b 11 March 1990); *Career* admitted slr 1975; asst slr J & A Bright Richards & Flewitt, slr Freeth Cartwright & Sketchley 1977–83 (ptnr 1980–83), sr ptnr and fndr Nelson Johnson & Hastings Slrs 1983–2003, princ Richard Nelson Business Defence Slrs 2003– (fndr and sr memb Medic Assistance Scheme); dir: Homeland Videos Ltd, Evocell Ltd, Stellarview Ltd, North Lodge Enterprises Ltd, Cradleland Ltd; former govr Trent Coll, former dir Industrial Automation and Trent College Ltd, former dir Trent College Trading Ltd; sec Serious Fraud Assoc, fndr memb Complex Crime Practitioners Gp, memb Criminal Business Ctee Notts Law Soc, memb Slrs Assistance Scheme, pres Notts Law Soc 2014–15 (former vice-pres), memb Lord Chllr's Advsy Cncl on Criminal Justice; fndr: Lawyers Defence Gp; former vice-chair Notts Hospice; memb Law Soc 1975; FRSA; *Recreations* sport (rugby and fishing in particular), comedy, gardening; *Style*— Richard Nelson, Esq; ✉ Priory Court, 1 Derby Road, Nottingham NG9 2TA (e-mail richardnelson@richardnelsonllp.co.uk)

NELSON, Trevor; MBE (2002); *b* 7 January 1964, Hackney, London; *Educ* Central Foundation Boys Sch Islington London; *Career* DJ and radio and television presenter; Best DJ MOBO Award 1996, 1997, 2008 and 2009; *Radio* DJ Kiss (then pirate radio station) 1986; Kiss FM: daytime presenter 1990–92, Street Soul Chart and Classic Cut Show 1992–96; BBC Radio 1: presenter Rhythm Nation 1996–, presenter Soul R&B Chart Show 1997; presenter breakfast show 1Xtra 2007–, presenter BBC Radio 2 2008–; *Television* presenter The Lick (MTV) 1998–2009; *Style*— Trevor Nelson, Esq, MBE; ✉ BBC Radio 2, Western House, 99 Great Portland Street, London W1W 7NY (Twitter @djtrevornelson); c/o Money Management (☎ 020 7287 7490, e-mail jessica@moneymanagementuk.com)

NELSON-JONES, Rodney Michael; s of Dr Archibald Nelson-Jones (d 1995), and Constance Vera, *née* Riley (d 1996); *b* 11 February 1947; *Educ* Repton, Hertford Coll Oxford (MA); *m* 21 Sept 1988, Kusum, da of Babulal Keshavji, of Derby; 1 s; *Career* admitted slr 1975; Prothero & Prothero 1973–77, L Bingham & Co 1977–83, ptnr i/c Personal Injury Litigation Dept Field Fisher Waterhouse 1983–2012; memb: M1 Air Crash Steering Ctee 1989–93, FOCIS; Assoc of Personal Injury Lawyers (APIL) Award for Outstanding Achievement 2002; *Books* co-author: Product Liability – The New Law Under The Consumer Protection Act 1987 (2 edn 1988), Personal Injury Limitation Law (1994, 2 edn 2007), Medical Negligence Case Law (2 edn 1995), Schedules of Loss (2002, 3 edn 2010); sole author: Computing Personal Injury Damages (1997, 4 edn 2001), Multipliers (1998), Butterworths Personal Injury Damages Statistics (1999, 12 edn 2010), Butterworths Monthly Multiplier Tables (2006); contrib: Butterworths Personal Injury Litigation Service (1988), Structured Settlements – A Practical Guide (1993, 2 edn 1997), The Medical Accidents Handbook (1998); *Periodicals* Personal Injury Interest Calculation (annually, 1980–2010), Nelson-Jones and Nuttall's Tax and Interest Tables (5 edn 1992), Special Damages Statistics (1994, 5 edn 1998); *Recreations* classical music, tennis, travel; *Clubs* Campden Hill Lawn Tennis; *Style*— Rodney Nelson-Jones, Esq; ✉ 36 Pattison Road, London NW2 2HH (e-mail rodneylknj@gmail.com)

NEOFITOU, Andreane (Andy); *Career* costume designer; *Theatre* Les Miserables (25th anniversary prodn on Broadway and tour, performances at O2 Arena, tours of US, UK and Europe, Tony nomination for Best Costumes), Miss Saigon (London prodn 2014, original London prodn and worldwide), Grease (West End and tour), The Far Pavilions (West End), Martin Guerre (West Yorkshire Playhouse, UK and US tours), The Baker's Wife (West End), Jane Eyre (Toronto and Broadway), Timon of Athens (Young Vic), Peter Pan (RNT), Miss Julie (Athens), Nabucco (Met Opera NY), Gone With The Wind (West End); RSC prodns incl: Nicholas Nickleby, Fair Maid of the West, The Merchant of Venice, The Changeling, Peter Pan, Hedda Gabler; *Films* Still Life, Rosencrantz and Guildenstern are Dead; *Style*— Ms Andy Neofitou; ✉ c/o Stella Richards Management, 42 Hazlebury Road, London SW6 2ND (☎ 020 7736 7786)

NEOPTOLEMOS, Prof John Phitoyiannis; *b* 30 June 1951; *Educ* Owen's GS N London, Churchill Coll Cambridge, Guy's Hosp London (MA, MB BChir), Univ of Leicester (MD); *m* 2 Feb 1974, Linda Joan, da of Richard Blaylock, of Kenton, Newcastle upon Tyne; 1 s (Ptolemy b 11 Aug 1978), 1 da (Eleni b 12 May 1981); *Career* Guy's Hosp London 1976–77, Leicester Royal Infirmary 1978–84 and 1986–87, UCSD San Diego 1984–85, sr lectr then reader Univ Dept of Surgery Birmingham and conslt surgn City Hosp 1987–94, prof of surgery Queen Elizabeth Hosp Birmingham 1994–96, prof of surgery and head Div of Surgery and Oncology Univ of Liverpool Royal Liverpool Univ Hosp 1996–, head Sch of Cancer Studies Univ of Liverpool 2005–; Hunterian prof of surgery RCS 1987–88; scientific contribs to aetiology, diagnosis and treatment of diseases of the pancreas, bilary tree and liver;; chm: European Study Gp for Pancreatic Cancer 1991–, NCRI Pancreas Cancer Subgroup 2004–; memb: Ctee Surgical Research Soc 1994–98, World Cncl Int Hepato-Pancreato-Bilary Assoc 1995–98, Scientific Ctee United European Gastroenterology Fedn 2002–06 (memb Cncl 1997–2002); pres: Pancreatic Soc of GB and I 1994–95 (memb Ctee 1987–90), Int Assoc of Pancreatology 2000–02 (memb World Cncl 1996–2004); sec European Pancreatic Club 1996–2002 (memb Cncl 1995–2002), treas European Digestive Surgery 1997–2004; Rodney Smith prize 1987, Moynihan travelling fell Assoc of Surgns of GB and I 1988; FRCS, FMedSci 2007; *Recreations* latin and ballroom dancing, squash; *Clubs* Heswell Squash (memb ctee 1999–2004); *Style*— Prof John P Neoptolemos; ✉ Division of Surgery and Oncology, The Duncan Building, Daulby Street, Liverpool L69 3GA (☎ 0151 706 4175, fax 0151 706 5798, e-mail j.p.neoptolemos@liv.ac.uk)

NESBITT, Michael (Mike); MLA; *b* 11 May 1957, Belfast; *Educ* Campbell Coll Belfast, Univ of Cambridge; *m* 1992, Lynda Bryans; 2 s; *Career* began broadcasting career as sports reporter BBC NI, presenter Good Morning Ulster (BBC Radio Ulster) 1986–90, presenter and reporter UTV 1992–96, co-presenter UTV Live (UTV) 1996–2006, co-presenter Sunday Morning (Anglia TV) 1999–2001; commissioner of victims and survivors NI Assembly 2008–10, MLA (UUP) Strangford 2011–, ldr UUP 2012–; *Style*— Mike Nesbitt, Esq, MLA; ✉ Northern Ireland Assembly, Parliament Buildings, Belfast BT4 3XX

NESBITT, Prof Robert William; s of Thomas Dodgson Nesbitt (d 1977), of Blyth, Northumberland, and Mary Florence Nesbitt (d 1983); *b* 26 September 1936; *Educ* Blyth GS, Univ of Durham (BSc, PhD); *m* 24 Oct 1959, Catherine, da of Peter Robertson (d 1976), of Blyth, Northumberland; 3 da (Carolyn Anne b 1960, Joanne Louise b 1964, Jacqueline Clare b 1969); *Career* geologist Greenland Geological Survey 1958–59; Univ of Adelaide: lectr 1962–68, sr lectr 1968–72, reader 1972–80; visiting res fell Yale Univ 1968, visiting prof Université de Rennes 1979–92, dean of sci Univ of Southampton 1987–90 (prof of geology 1980–); subject advsr Univ Funding Cncl 1985–93; hon corr Geological Soc of Australia, chm Ctee of Heads of Geoscience Dept 1992, memb Cncl Geological Soc London 1994–97; FGS (Aust) 1976, FGS 1980; *Recreations* golf; *Style*— Prof Robert Nesbitt; ✉ School of Ocean and Earth Science, Southampton Oceanography Centre, University of Southampton, Empress Dock, Southampton SO14 3ZH (☎ 023 8059 2037, fax 023 8059 3052)

NESBITT, Simon John; QC (2015); s of Henry Nesbitt (d 1999), and Elizabeth Nesbitt; *b* 27 September 1966, Belfast; *Educ* Pembroke Coll Oxford (MA); *Partner* Simon Buxton (civil partnership 2007); *Career* trainee slr Lovell White Durrant 1992–94, admitted slr 1994, assoc Lovells 1994–2002, admitted avocat à la cour (France) 1997, ptnr Hogan Lovells 2002–15 (global co-head Int Arbitration 2013–15); called to the Bar 2015; FCIArb 2006; *Recreations* sailing, horse riding; *Style*— Simon Nesbitt, Esq, QC; ✉ 7 Stone Buildings, London WC2A 3SZ (☎ 020 7406 1200, e-mail snesbitt@maitlandchambers.com)

NETHERCOT, Prof David Arthur; OBE (2006); s of Arthur Owen Martin Nethercot (d 1980), and Dorothy May, *née* Bearman (d 1996); *b* 26 April 1946; *Educ* Minchenden GS, Univ of Wales (BSc, PhD, DSc, Page prize and medal); *m* 3 Aug 1968, Hedd Dwynwen, da of John Byron Evans; 2 da (Susanna Kate b 29 Dec 1971, Emily Victoria b 4 March 1975); *Career* ICI fell Univ of Wales 1970–71, lectr and reader Univ of Sheffield 1971–89; Univ of Nottingham: prof of civil engrg 1989–99, head of dept 1994–99; Imperial Coll London: prof of civil engrg 1999–2011, head Dept of Civil and Environmental Engrg 1999–2011, dep princ Faculty of Engrg 2008–12, prof emeritus and sr research investigator 2011–; visiting prof: Japan Soc for Promotion of Science Univ of Nagoya 1980, Swiss Federal Inst of Technology Lausanne 1990; chm and memb Ctee: BSI, EPSRC, IABSE; memb Cncl Steel Construction Inst 1992–2009, chm Jt Bd of Moderators 1996–98 (memb 1993–99); FIStructE 1989 (memb 1976, memb Cncl 1986–89 and 1991–96, vice-pres 2000–03, pres 2003–04); FREng 1993 (memb Cncl 2000–03), FICE 1995, FCGI 2001, FRSA 2002, foreign fell Acad of Technical Sciences and Engrg Australia 2010, foreign memb Nat Acad of Engrg USA 2015; *Awards* ICE: Miller Prize 1971, Telford Premium 1991; IStructE: Oscar Faber Bronze medal 1989, Murray Buxton Prize 1992, Henry Adams dip 1994, 1998 and 2006, Charles Massonet Prize ECCS 2008, Gold Medal IStructE 2009, Lynn Beedle Prize SSRC 2015; *Books* Design for Structural Stability (1985), Limit States Design of Structural Steelwork (2001); author of over 400 papers on structural engineering; *Recreations* sport; *Style*— Prof D A Nethercot, OBE, FREng; ✉ 132 Queens Road, London SW19 8LS (☎ 020 8542 2349); Department of Civil and Environmental Engineering, Imperial College London, Imperial College Road, London SW7 2A2 (☎ 020 7594 6097, fax 020 7594 6042, e-mail d.nethercot@imperial.ac.uk)

NETHERTON, Derek Nigel Donald; s of John Gordon Netherton, of London, and Beryl Agnes, *née* Freeman; *b* 4 January 1945; *Educ* Charterhouse, King's Coll Cambridge (MA); *m* 1, 1978 (m dis 1998), Jane, *née* Corkill; 4 s (Charles b 1981, George b 1984, Patrick, David (twins) b 1987); m 2, 2003, Elizabeth, *née* Green; 3 step s (Alexander b 1988, Rupert b 1991, Freddie b 1994); *Career* dir J Henry Schroder 1981–96; non-exec dir: St James's Place Capital 1996–2012, Next 1996–2008, Hiscox plc 1999–2006, Canada Life Ltd 2012–, Irish Life 2013–; chm: Greggs plc 2002–13, Opera North 2010–14; FIA; *Recreations* bridge, opera, smallholding farming (pigs and sheep); *Style*— Derek Netherton, Esq

NETTEL, Julian Philip; s of Leopold Nettel (d 1990), and Clare, *née* Carter (d 2000); *b* 23 October 1953; *Educ* Sutton GS, Univ of Bristol (BA); *m* 9 Aug 1980, Caroline Gillian, *née* Mawhood; 2 s (Thomas Alexander b 7 July 1984, Edward Philip b 17 May 1987); *Career* hosp sec Westminster Hosp 1983–86, gen mangr Whittington Royal Northern Hosps 1986–1990, divnl mangr King's Coll and Dulwich Hosps 1990–93, exec in res Univ of Ottawa Ontario 1992–93; chief exec: Ealing Hosp NHS Tst 1994–99, St Mary's NHS Tst London 1999–2007, Barts and the London NHS Tst 2007–09; md NHS Inst for Innovation and Improvement 2011–12, interim chief exec Great Ormond St Hosp 2014, interim chief exec Moorfields Eye Hosp NHS Fndn Tst 2015–16; tstee Wimbledon Coll of Art; *Recreations* painting, jazz, cricket, golf, cycling; *Clubs* Roehampton, Royal Thames Yacht, Wimbledon Park Golf; *Style*— Julian Nettel, Esq; ✉ website www.artbyjuliannettel.com

N

NETTLE, David Richard; s of Gerald Nettle, of Redruth, and Viola, *née* Tregenza; *b* 10 June 1956; *Educ* Redruth GS, Royal Coll of Music; *m* 2015, Christo Stoman; *Career* concert pianist, conductor and teacher; worldwide appearances with Richard Markham, *qv*, as Nettle-Markham Piano Duo: North American debut 1979, London debut (Wigmore Hall) 1982, Far East tour 1983, Middle East tours 1983 and 1985, African and Aust tours 1992/93, regular US tours, frequent performances at princ Euro festivals incl BBC Proms, major two piano works dedicated to them by Kenneth Leighton, Robert Walker and Hendrik Hofmeyr (Concerto for 3 Pianos and Orch) 2004; professional conducting debut with CPO 2007; *Recordings* incl: The Rite of Spring and Petrushka (1984), The Planets (1985), Dyson's The Blacksmiths (1987), Delius and Grainger Folksongs (1988), Rossini's Petite Messe Solennelle (1990), Carnival of the Animals (1991), Nettle & Markham in England (1993), Arnold-Piano Duet Concerto (1993), Nettle & Markham in America (1994), Arnold-2 Piano Concerto (1994), Nettle & Markham in France (1996), Complete 2-Piano Works of Brahms (2006); *Awards* Norris prize 1977, Music Retailers' Assoc Award Award for best chamber music record 1985; *Recreations* travel, cooking, wining and dining, gardening, photography, languages, writing; *Style*— David Nettle, Esq; ✉ The Old Power House, Atherton Street, London SW11 2JE (☎ 020 7738 2765, e-mail nettleandmarkham@gmail.com, website www.nettleandmarkham.com)

NETTLES, John; OBE (2010); *Career* actor; early stage work incl plays at Royal Court, Traverse Theatre Edinburgh and Theatre 69; *Repertory* Northcott Theatre Exeter: Jimmy Porter in Look Back in Anger, Feste in Twelfth Night, Vladimir in Waiting For Godot, Mompesson in Roses of Eyam, Tranio in The Taming of the Shrew; Bristol Old Vic: Thersites in Troillus and Cressida, Sganarelle in Don Juan, Harold in The Philanthropist, Joey in Butley, Alwa in Lulu, Ed in Entertaining Mr Sloane; Crucible Theatre Sheffield: Charles Surface in School for Scandal; Derby Playhouse: Leonard in Time and Time Again, Brian in A Day in the Death of Joe Egg; RSC: Florizel in A Winter's Tale, Thersites in Troilus and Cressida, Maxwell in Destiny, Godber in That Good Between Us, Kung Tu in The Bundle, Von Lieres in A Miserable Death, Detective in The Factory Birds, Priest in Frozen Assets, Bassanio in The Merchant of Venice, Lucio in Measure For Measure, Thompson in The Churchill Play, Harry Thunder in Wild Oats, Alexei Tourbin in The White Guard, Ernest in Once in a Lifetime, La Ronde, The Hollow Crown (USA tour), Leontes in The Winter's Tale, Page in The Merry Wives of Windsor, Caesar in Antony and Cleopatra, Merecraft in The Devil is an Ass, Julius Caesar; *Other Theatre* incl: Lord Foppington in The Relapse (Old Vic), title role in Butley (Fortune Theatre); *Pantomine* Abanazar in Aladdin (Theatre Royal Bath), Sheriff of Nottingham in Babes in the Wood (Palace Theatre Manchester), Bluebeard the Pirate in Robinson Crusoe (Theatre Royal Plymouth and New Theatre Cardiff), King Rat in Dick Whittington (Palace Theatre Manchester, Wimbledon and Leeds); *Television* LWT incl: Black Beauty, Holding On; BBC incl: The Liver Birds, The Merchant of Venice, Bergerac, Bergerac Special, Hands Across the Sea; other credits incl: Submarine (narrator, series), A Family at War, Dickens of London, Boon (guest lead role), Midsomer Murders; *Books* Nudity in a Public Place (semi-autobiographical, 1991); *Style*— John Nettles, Esq, OBE; ✉ c/o

Saraband Associates, 265 Liverpool Road, London N1 1LX (☎ 020 7609 5313, fax 020 7609 2370)

NETTLETON, Charles; s of Travers Dering Nettleton, and Margrit, *née* Schill; *Educ* Dover Coll, Peterhouse Cambridge (exhibitioner, MA); *Career* William Collins Publishers 1980–86; Hodder & Stoughton Publishers: sales and mktg dir H & S 1991–93, dep md Headline 1993–96, md religious books 1996–2002, md children's books 2002–06, operations dir Working Partners 2006–; *Recreations* family, singing, mountain biking; *Style*— Charles Nettleton, Esq

NEUBERG, Roger Wolfe; s of Klaus Neuberg (d 2013), and Herta, *née* Hausler (d 1986); *b* 24 May 1941, Wellington, New Zealand; *Educ* Hendon Co GS, Middx Hosp Med Sch (MB BS), De Montfort Univ Leicester (LLM); *m* 16 Aug 1964, Ruth Denise, da of Manning Ephron (d 1984), of Bournemouth; 2 s (Guy b 1966, Kim b 1967); *Career* emeritus conslt obstetrician and gynaecologist; registrar Middx Hosp and Hosp for Women; sr registrar: John Radcliffe Hosp Oxford and Royal Berkshire Hosp; conslt and dir of infertility servs Leicester Royal Infirmary until 2007; clinical memb HFEA 2006–09; ALSO(UK) (Advanced Life Support Obstetrics): chm 2006–09, obstetrician memb Exec Ctee, tstee; fndr and dir Infertility Guidance Serv 2009–, vasectomy surgn Marie Stopes Int 2011–, community first responder E Midlands Abulance Service 2014–; memb: Br Fertility Soc, Assoc of Broadcasting Drs; LRCP 1965, MRCS 1965, FRCOG 1983; *Books* So You Want to Have a Baby (1985, 4 edn 1996), Infertility (1991, 2 edn 1994), Obstetrics: A Practical Manual (1995); *Recreations* aikido, gardening; *Clubs* Rotary (Oadby); *Style*— Roger Neuberg, Esq; ✉ 9 Barrington Road, Stoneygate, Leicester LE2 2RA (☎ 07711 067969 e-mail roger@neuberg.co.uk)

NEUBERGER, Prof James Max; s of Prof Albert Neuberger, CBE (d 1996), of London, and Lilian Ida, *née* Dreyfus; *b* 4 November 1949; *Educ* Westminster, ChCh Oxford (MA, BM BCh, DM); *m* 14 Sept 1979, Belinda Patricia, da of Patrick Joseph Keogh, of Manchester; 2 s (Oliver b 1980, Edmund b 1984), 2 da (Francesca b 1982, Octavia b 1988); *Career* sr lectr in med KCH London 1980–86, conslt physician Queen Elizabeth Hosp Birmingham 1986– (assoc med dir for R&D), hon prof of med Univ of Birmingham 1999; medical dir Organ Donation and Transplantation NHS Blood and Transplant 2009–16; chair Ctee on Safety of Blood Tissues and Organs; FRCP 1991 (MRCP 1977); *Books* Liver Annual (1988), Immunology of Liver Transplantation (1993), Liver Transplantation (1994), Alcohol and Liver Disease (2016); *Recreations* fishing, gardening, reading; *Style*— Prof James Neuberger; ✉ Allerton House, North Street, Winchcombe, Gloucestershire GL54 5PS (☎ 01242 609526); Queen Elizabeth Hospital, Edgbaston, Birmingham B15 2TH (e-mail jamesneuberger@hotmail.co.uk)

NEUBERGER, Baroness (Life Peer UK 2004), of Primrose Hill in the London Borough of Camden; Rabbi Julia Babette Sarah Neuberger; DBE (2004); *née* Schwab; da of Walter Manfred Schwab (d 1996), of London, and Alice, *née* Rosenthal (d 2001); *b* 27 February 1950; *Educ* S Hampstead HS for Girls, Newnham Coll Cambridge, Leo Baeck Coll London; *m* 17 Sept 1973, Anthony John Neuberger, s of Prof Albert Neuberger, CBE (d 1996), of London; 1 da (Hon Harriet b 16 June 1979), 1 s (Hon Matthew b 2 July 1981); *Career* rabbi S London Liberal Synagogue 1977–89, visiting fell King's Fund Inst 1989–91, visiting and Harkness fell Harvard Med Sch 1991–92, chair Camden and Islington Community Health Servs NHS Tst 1992–97, chief exec The King's Fund 1997–2004, sr rabbi W London Synagogue 2011–; fell King's Fund Coll London 1992–97, chllr Univ of Ulster 1994–2000; memb: HFEA 1990–95, Ethics Ctee BMA 1992–94, GMC 1993–2001, MRC 1995–2000, Library Cmmn 1995–97, Ctee on Standards in Public Life (Wicks Ctee) 2001–04; Civil Service cmmr 2001–02; chair Cmmn on the Future of Volunteering 2006–08, PM's volunteering champion 2007–09, chair Responsible Gambling Strategy Bd 2008–12, Advsy Panel Judicial Diversity 2009–10, chair One Housing Gp 2009–12, chair Review of the Liverpool Care Pathway 2013; vice-pres Patients' Assoc 1992–97; memb Cncl: UCL 1993–96, Save the Children Fund 1994–96; tstee: Runnymede Tst 1990–97, Imperial War Museum 1999–2006, Van Leer Gp Fndn and Van Leer Jerusalem Inst 2012–, Walter and Liesel Schwab Charitable Tst, Westheimer Tst, Rayne Fndn 2016–, Lyons Learning Project 2016–; regular broadcaster; Hon Dr: Univ of Humberside, Univ of Ulster, Univ of Stirling, City Univ, Oxford Brookes Univ, Univ of Teesside, Univ of Nottingham, Open Univ, Queen's Univ Belfast, Sheffield Hallam Univ, Univ of Aberdeen, Univ of Southampton, Univ of London 2006; Hon DD Univ of Cambridge 2015; hon fell Mansfield Coll Oxford 1997; Hon FCGI 1998, Hon FRCP 2004, Hon FRCGP 2006, Hon FRCPsych 2007, Hon FRCOG 2013; *Books* The Story of Judaism (for children, 1986), Caring for Dying People of Different Faiths (1987, 3 edn 2004), Days of Decision (ed, 1987), Whatever's Happening to Women (1991), A Necessary End (ed with John White, 1991), The Things That Matter (ed, 1993), Ethics and Healthcare: Research Ethics Ctees in the UK (1992), On Being Jewish (1995), Dying Well: A guide to enabling a good death (1999, 2 edn 2004), Hidden Assets: Values and decision-making in the NHS (ed with Bill New, 2002), The Moral State We're In (2005), Not Dead Yet: A manifesto for old age (2008), Is That All There Is? Leaving a Legacy (2011); *Style*— The Baroness Neuberger, DBE; ✉ House of Lords, London SW1A 0PW

NEUBERGER OF ABBOTSBURY, Baron (Life Peer UK 2007), of Abbotsbury in the County of Dorset; Sir David Edmond Neuberger; kt (1996), PC (2004); s of Prof Albert Neuberger, CBE, FRS (d 1996), and Lilian Ida, *née* Dreyfus; *b* 10 January 1948; *Educ* Westminster, ChCh Oxford; *m* Angela, da of late Brig Peter Holdsworth; 1 da (Jessica b 1977), 2 s (Nicholas b 1979, Max b 1981); *Career* N M Rothschild & Sons 1970–73, called to the Bar Lincoln's Inn 1974 (bencher 1993), QC 1987, recorder 1990–96, former jt head of Falcon chambers, judge of the High Court of Justice (Chancery Div) 1996–2004, Chancery supervising judge (Midlands, Wales & Chester, and Western Circuits) 2001–04, Lord Justice of Appeal 2004–07, judge i/c modernisation 2004–07, Lord of Appeal in Ordinary 2007–09, Master of the Rolls and head of civil justice 2009–12, pres Supreme Court of the UK 2012–; chm Advsy Ctee on Spoilation of Art during the Holocaust 1997–; chm of tstees Schizophrenia Tst 1997–2014, chm Advsy Cncl Nat Archives 2009–12, chm Magna Carta Tst 2009–12, tstee Mental Health Research UK 2014–; govr Univ of Arts London (formerly London Inst) 2000–10; Hon MRICS 2008; *Clubs* Garrick; *Style*— The Rt Hon the Lord Neuberger of Abbotsbury; ✉ Supreme Court of the United Kingdom, Parliament Square, London SW1P 3BD

NEUMAN, Per; *Career* md Estée Lauder Companies UK 1988–2011; *Style*— Per Neuman, Esq; ✉ Estée Lauder Companies, 73 Grosvenor Street, London W1K 3BQ

NEUMANN, Daniela; da of Isacco Aronne Neumann (d 1997), and Renate, *née* Fromm; *b* 11 November 1966, Hong Kong; *Educ* St Christopher Sch Letchworth, Nat Westminster Press Journalism Coll Hastings (NCTJ); *Children* 1 s (Jackson); *Career* early career as newspaper reporter and sub-ed, then TV researcher; controller ITV2 2002–06 (also ed Factual ITV1), head of factual entertainment and features Wall to Wall Prodns 2006–07, dir of progs Virgin Media TV 2007–11, controller of entertainment ITV 2011–12, vice-pres programming Viasat Broadcasting 2011–; memb BAFTA; *Television* prodr London Tonight (London News Network); assoc prodr: Michael Winner's True Crimes (and scriptwriter), Somalia Special, War Against the Mafia; prodr and dir: Special Operations 1994–95, Speakeasy does the Business 1995, Cops, Missing, Ibiza Uncovered 1997, The London Programme 1998, Airline 1998–99, Hello Mum 1999, Blagging Britain 2000–01; series prodr: Des Res 1987, Dinner Dates 1997, Friday Night Fever 1997–98; series ed: Crime Monthly 1995, Crime Net 1996; dir: Emmerdale 1999–2000, Brookside 2000, The Bill 2000; exec prodr Reps in Ibiza 2001; *Style*— Ms Daniela Neumann; ☎ 07710 214828

NEVILE, Christopher William Kenneth; s of Kenneth Nevile (d 1960), of Swinderby, Lincs, and Elizabeth Mary, *née* Brown; *b* 27 April 1957; *Educ* St Hugh's Wood Hall SPA, Rugby, Univ of Exeter (LLB); *m* Sept 1993, Charlotte Brodie (Charlie), da of Dr Jeremy Lee-Potter, *qv*, of Stoborough, Dorset, and Lynda Lee-Potter; 1 s (Kit Brodie Kenneth b 9 Oct 1995), 1 da (Mia Brodie Calypso b 20 Jan 1999); *Career* stockbroker; assoc dir Scrimgeour Vickers until 1987; dir Adams & Nevile Ltd 1987–95; md Granville Private Banking 1995–2000, dir Granville plc 1997–2000, md Nevile Merriam Investment Mgmnt 2000–03, dir Sanlam Private Investments (formerly Principal Investment Management) 2003–, dir Granville Bank, md Granville Pension Mgmnt; *Recreations* fishing, riding, music, cricket; *Clubs* Holmes Place (Barbican); *Style*— Christopher W K Nevile, Esq

NEVILL, Amanda Elizabeth; CBE (2015); *b* 21 March 1957; *Educ* Bar Convent York, British Inst France; *m* 3 May 1980 (m dis 1986), Dominic John Nevill, s of John Nevill, of Folkstone, Kent; 2 da; *Career* Rowan Gallery London 1978–79, Francis Kyle Gallery London 1979–80, Bath Int Festival Contemporary Art Fair 1980–84, sec Royal Photographic Soc Bath 1990–94 (admin 1985), head Nat Museum of Photography, Film & Television 1994–2003, dir BFI 2003–; Hon DLitt Univ of Bradford 2000, Hon Dr Univ of York 2015; Hon FRPS, FRSA 1996; *Style*— Ms Amanda Nevill, CBE; ✉ British Film Institute, 21 Stephen Street, London W1T 1LN

NEVILLE, Dan; s of Thomas Neville (d 1967), of Kiltannan Croagh, Co Limerick, and Esther, *née* Giltenane (d 2004); *b* Co Limerick Ireland; *Educ* Univ of Limerick, NUI Cork; *m* 1974, Goretti, *née* O'Callaghan (d 2009); 2 s (Thomas, Daniel), 2 da (Maria, Maeve); *Career* memb Seanad Eireann (Fine Gael) Lab Panel 1989–1997, TD (Fine Gael) Limerick West 1997–2016; chm Fine Gael Parliamentary 2014–16; memb Limerick CC 1985–2003; memb Mid-Western Health Bd 1992–99; pres Irish Assoc of Suicidology, dir Irish Palatine Assoc; Magill Campaigning Politician of the Year 2005; *Style*— Dan Neville, Esq; ✉ Kiltannen Croagh, Co Limerick, Ireland (☎ 00 353 61 396351, e-mail nevilledan8@gmail.com, www.danneville.ie)

NEVILLE, Dame Elizabeth Louise; DBE (2003), QPM (1996), DL (Wilts 2011); da of Dr Adam Neville, CBE, and Dr Mary Hallam, *née* Cousins; *b* 5 February 1953; *Educ* Univ of Oxford (MA), Univ of London (PhD); *m* 2015, Rory Angus Cameron Carter; 1 s (Matthew Edward Burbeck b 1983), 1 da (Katherine Mary Burbeck b 1985); *Career* joined Metropolitan Police 1973, transferred Thames Valley Police 1986, Asst Chief Constable Sussex Police 1991–94, Dep Chief Constable Northants Police 1994–97, Chief Constable Wilts Constabulary 1997–2004; non-exec dir Serious Fraud Office 2004–12, ind complaints assessor for agencies of the Dept for Transport 2004–10, Policy Authy memb Civil Nuclear Constabulary 2005–12, ind adjudicator Companies House 2007, memb Determinations Panel Pensions Regulator 2011, non-exec memb Bd Insolvency Service 2013, lay memb Ind Appeals Body PhonepayPlus 2013, ind adjudicator Regulator of Community Interest Companies 2013, memb Regulatory Decisions Ctee FCA 2013; dir E Neville Ltd 2008; tstee Wiltshire Bobby Van; patron Swindon Sanctuary; fell and memb Ct Univ of Northampton 2004–, hon fell St Hilda's Coll Oxford 2006; High Sheriff Wilts 2010–11; Hon LLD Southampton Solent Univ 2004; *Publications* British Horseracing Authority and Integrity in Horseracing: an Independent Review (2008); *Recreations* skiing, riding, opera; *Clubs* Reform; *Style*— Dame Elizabeth Neville, DBE, QPM, DL

NEVILLE, Gary; *b* 18 February 1975; *Educ* Elton HS Bury; *Career* football pundit, coach and former professional footballer; Manchester United: Sch of Excellence 1986, signed schoolboy forms 1989, trainee 1991, first team debut European Cup v Torpedo Moscow 1992, League debut v Coventry May 1994, 400 appearances, capt 2005–10, Premier League champions 1996, 1997, 1999, 2000, 2001, 2003, 2007 2008 and 2009, winners FA Cup 1996, 1999 and 2004 (runners up 1995 and 2005), winners European Champions League 1999, ret 2011; England: 85 full caps, debut v Japan 1995, memb squad European Championships 1996, 2000 and 2004, memb squad World Cup 1998 and 2006; football pundit Sky Sports 2011–, memb coaching staff England 2012–, mangr Valencia CF 2015–; *Recreations* golf; *Style*— Gary Neville

NEVILLE, Philip (Phil); *b* 21 January 1977; *Educ* Elton HS Bury; *Career* football coach and former player; clubs: Manchester United FC 1988–2005 (Sch of Excellence 1988, signed schoolboy forms 1990, trainee 1993, first team debut 1995, 263 appearances, Premier League champions 1996, 1997, 1999, 2000, 2001 and 2003, FA Cup winners 1996, 1999 and 2004 (finalists 1995 and 2005), winners European Champions League 1999), Everton FC 2005–13 (242 appearances); England: 59 caps, full debut v China 1996, memb squad European Championships 2000 and 2004; first team coach Manchester United 2013–14, asst coach Valencia 2015–; *Recreations* golf, cricket; *Style*— Phil Neville

NEVILLE-JONES, Baroness (Life Peer UK 2007), of Hutton Roof in the County of Cumbria; Dame (Lilian) Pauline Neville-Jones; DCMG (1996, CMG 1987), PC (2010); da of Roland Neville-Jones, RAMC (ka 1941), and Cecilia Emily Millicent Winn, *née* Rath, step da of Dr John Michael Winn; *b* 2 November 1939; *Educ* Leeds Girls' HS, Lady Margaret Hall Oxford (BA); *Career* HM Dip Serv 1963–96: joined FCO 1963, third sec Salisbury Rhodesia 1964–65, third sec (later second sec) Singapore 1965–68, FCO 1968–71 (dealing with Med), first sec Washington 1971–75, dep chef de cabinet (later chef de cabinet) to Christopher Tugendhat, Cmmn of Euro Communities Brussels 1977–82, sabbatical RIIA London and Institut Français des Relations Internationales Paris 1982–83, head of policy planning staff FCO 1983–87, min (econ) Bonn Embassy 1987–91 (min 1988–91), dep under sec for overseas and defence Cabinet Office 1991–94, chm Jt Intelligence Ctee 1993–94, political dir FCO 1994–96; sr advsr to Carl Bildt, High Rep for the Civilian Peace Implementation for Bosnia Feb-July 1996; head of global business strategy NatWest Markets 1996–98, chm NatWest Markets France 1996–98, vice-chm Hawkpoint Partners (memb of Natwest Gp) 1998–2000; chm Qinetiq Gp plc 2003–06; a govr BBC 1998–2004; chm Information Assurance Advsy Cncl 2003–07; head Cons Pty Nat and Int Security Policy Gp 2006–08, shadow security min and nat security advsr to Ldr of the Oppn 2007–10, min of state for security 2010–11, special govt rep to business on cyber security 2011–14, sr advsr Ridge-Schmidt Cyber 2015–; memb Jt Ctee on the Nat Security Strategy 2012–; memb: Cncl IISS 1996–2008, Cncl City Univ 1997–2003, Cncl Univ of Oxford 2003–06, Engrg and Physical Sciences Research Cncl 2013–, Cncl Lancaster Univ 2015–; Hon DUniv Open Univ 1998, Hon DSc (Econ) Univ of London 1999, Hon DSc City Univ 2007; Chevalier de le Légion d'Honneur 2009; *Recreations* cooking, gardening, antiques; *Style*— The Rt Hon the Baroness Neville-Jones, DCMG; ✉ House of Lords, London SW1A 0PW (e-mail nevillejonesp@parliament.uk)

NEVILLE-ROLFE, Baroness (Life Peer UK 2013), of Chilmark in the County of Wiltshire; Dame Lucy Jeanne Neville-Rolfe; DBE (2012), CMG (2005); Lady Packer; da of Edmund Neville-Rolfe, and late Margaret Neville-Rolfe; *b* 2 January 1953; *Educ* Somerville Coll Oxford (MA, hon fell 2003); *m* Sir Richard John Packer, KCB; 4 s; *Career* MAFF: joined 1973, private sec to Min of Agric, Fisheries and Food 1977–79, European Community Sheepmeat and Milk 1979–86, Land Use 1986–88, Food Safety Act Div 1988–90, head of personnel 1990–92; memb PM's Policy Unit 1992–94, under sec 1994, dir Deregulation Unit DTI then Better Regulation Unit Cabinet Office 1995–97; Tesco plc: gp dir of corp affrs 1997–2006, co sec 2004–06; non-exec dir: John Laing Construction 1991–92, ITV plc 2010–14; chm Dobbies Garden Centres plc 2007–11; memb Bd of Mgmnt Br Retail Consortium 1998–2012 (dep chm 2003–12), chm Confederation of Br Industry (memb Economics and European Ctees 1998–2013); vice-pres EuroCommerce 1998–2008, pres EuroCommerce 2012–14; non-exec dir: Bd of Mgmnt FCO 2000–05, Carbon Tst 2008; memb: UNICE Task Force on Enlargement 1999–2004, Dep PM's Local Govt Funding Ctee 2003–04, ESRC Panel on Cultures of Consumption 2003–07, Corporate Leaders Gp on Climate Change 2005–13, China-Britain Business Cncl 2005–13, Foresight Obesity Project 2006–07, UK India Business Cncl 2008–13, Efficiency Bd Cabinet Office 2010–14; Parly under-sec of state for business, innovation adn skills and minister for intellectual property 2014–, parly under-sec of state for culture, media and sport 2015–; memb Governing Body London Business Sch 2011–; FCIS 2010; *Recreations* cricket, racing, gardening, art, architecture, theatre; *Style—* The Baroness Neville-Rolfe, DBE, CMG; ✉ House of Lords, London SW1 0PW (☎ 020 7219 5353)

NEVIN, Charles William; s of John Francis Nevin (d 1991), of St Helens, Lancs, and Jean Emmie, *née* Davey (d 2013), of Chingford, Essex; *b* 27 March 1951; *Educ* Mount St Mary's Coll, UC Oxford; *m* 1988, Liv Barbara, da of William Bernard O'Hanlon and Inger Luise, *née* Bye; 2 s (Jack Cristian Diaz O'Hanlon b 1991, William Luis Arturo Gatica O'Hanlon b 1994); *Career* called to the Bar Gray's Inn 1975; Granada Television 1974–75, Liverpool Daily Post and Echo 1975–79, Daily and Sunday Telegraph 1979–88; freelance writer 1988–; *Publications* Lancashire, Where Women Die of Love (2004), The Book of Jacks (2008), So Long Our Home: Knowsley Road 1890–2010, Lost In The Wash With Other Things (2016); *Recreations* watching Rugby League agitatedly and musing at the foot of stairs; *Clubs* Berkshire Press, St Helens Bowling (country memb); *Style—* Charles Nevin; ✉ Wallbridge Mills, The Retreat, Frome, Somerset BA11 5JU (e-mail cnevin@nevinsltd.co.uk)

NEWALL, Christopher Stirling; s of late Peter Stirling Newall, and Rosemary, *née* Marriage; *b* 8 April 1951; *Educ* The Downs Sch, Abbotsholme Sch, Courtauld Inst London (BA); *m* 10 Oct 1985 (m dis 2009), Jenifer Hylda, da of late Sir Derek Ryan, 3 Bt; 2 s (Alfred Stirling b 8 Feb 1987, George Stirling b 20 Jan 1990); *Career* writer and art historian; conslt Dept of Victorian Paintings Sotheby's 1994–; research fell Univ of Northumbria 1996–98; assoc ed Oxford DNB 1997–2003; sec Ruskin Today (centenary events programme) 2000; Companion of Guild of St George 1995; *Books* Victorian Watercolours (1987), The Art of Lord Leighton (1990), The Grosvenor Gallery Exhibitions (1995); exhbn catalogues: George Price Boyce (Tate Gallery 1987), Victorian Landscape Watercolors (contrib, Yale Center for British Art 1992), Victorian Painting (contrib, Neue Pinakothek Munich and Prado Madrid 1993), John William Inchbold (Leeds City Art Gallery 1993), Frederic Leighton (contrib, Royal Acad of Arts 1996), The Age of Rossetti, Burne-Jones & Watts – Symbolism in Britain 1860–1910 (contrib, Tate Gallery 1997), La Era Victoriana (contrib, Museo Nacional de San Carlos Mexico City), The Victorian Imagination (Bunkamura Museum of Art Tokyo and touring 1998), Espejismos del Medio Oriente: Delacroix a Moreau (contrib, Museo Nacional de San Carlos Mexico City 1999–2000), Pre-Raphaelites Exhibition – from Manchester City Art Galleries and other Collections (MOMA Shiga and touring 2000), John Brett: a Pre-Raphaelite on the Shores of Wales (Nat Museum of Wales 2003), Pre-Raphaelite Vision: Truth to Nature (jtly, Tate Britain (co-curated with Allen Staley) 2004), The Poetry of Truth: Alfred William Hunt and the Art of Landscape (Ashmolean Museum Oxford and Yale Center for British Art New Haven 2004–05); *Style—* Christopher Newall, Esq; ✉ Old School House, North Street, Hundon, Sudbury, Suffolk CO10 8ED

NEWALL, 2 Baron (UK 1946); Francis Storer Eaton Newall; DL (London); s of Marshal of the RAF 1 Baron Newall, GCB, OM, GCMG, CBE, AM (d 1963, Chief of Air Staff during Battle of Britain); *b* 23 June 1930; *Educ* Eton, RMA Sandhurst; *m* 1956, Pamela, da of Hugh Rowcliffe, TD (d 1978), by his 1 w, Margaret (da of Sir Henry Farrington, 6 Bt); 2 s, 1 da; *Heir* s, Hon Richard Newall; *Career* took Cons whip House of Lords; Capt 11 Hussars, served Germany, Malaya, Singapore, NI; adj Royal Glos Hussars; conslt and company dir; Cons whip and oppn front bench spokesman House of Lords 1976–79, fndr memb House of Lords All-Pty Def Study Gp, delg WEU and Cncl of Europe 1983–98, responsible for Farriers Registration Acts and Betting and Gaming Amendment (Greyhound Racing) Acts; led Parly visits to Cyprus, Oman, Bahrain, Qatar, Morocco; fndr Turfed Out Peers Soc (TOPS); chm: New Muscovy Co 2002–08, Code Circus Ltd 2004–; chm Br Greyhound Racing Bd 1985–97, former pres Soc for Protection of Animals Abroad (SPANA), chm Br Moroccan Soc 2000–05; friend of Romania; Liveryman Worshipful Co of Farriers, memb Ct of Assts Worshipful Co of Merchant Taylors (Master 1985–86); *Books* Chance & Choice (2014); *Recreations* shooting, tennis, travel; *Clubs* Cavalry and Guards'; *Style—* The Rt Hon the Lord Newall, DL; ✉ Wotton Underwood, Aylesbury, Buckinghamshire (☎ 01844 238376, e-mail newall@mypostoffice.co.uk)

NEWARK, Archdeacon of; *see:* Peyton, Ven Nigel

NEWARK, Quentin; s of Derek Newark, and Jean, *née* Thornhill; *b* 24 September 1961; *Educ* Purley HS for Boys, Kingston Poly (fndn course), Brighton Poly (BA); *Career* book designer: Mitchell Beazley Publishers 1985, Faber and Faber Publishers 1985–86; Pentagram Design: sr designer 1986–91, clients incl Faber and Faber, Santa Barbara Museum of Art, Washington Museum of Art, Asea Brown Boveri, V&A Museum (identity and signage); Atelier Design (partnership with John Powner): formed 1991, projects incl Br Rail exhibition on the environment, The Encyclopaedia of the 21st Century for Mitchell Beazley, work for Philips, Wiggins Teape and Arthur Anderson; memb 02 int environmental design gp; memb Sign Design Inst; lectured at Pembroke Coll Oxford and Epsom Sch of Art and Design; *Style—* Quentin Newark, Esq; ✉ 37 Kenilworth Road, London E3 5RH (☎ 020 8981 6612); The Old Piano Factory, 5 Charlton Kings Road, London NW5 2SB

NEWBERRY, Patrick John (Pat); s of Thomas Newberry (d 2010), and Jean, *née* Knill (d 1997); *b* 14 October 1956, Glos; *Educ* Bristol Cathedral Sch, Univ of Southampton (BSc); *m* 19 July 1980, Elizabeth Jane, da of Peter Ware, of Church Knowle, Dorset, and Margaret Maud Lancelyn Green; 3 s (Nicholas Peter Knill b 10 April 1984, John Alfred Lancelyn b 26 May 1986, Edwin Gilbert Knill b 21 Nov 1989), 1 da (Nancy Harriet Lancelyn b 16 June 1995); *Career* chartered accountant 1980; Coopers & Lybrand: ptnr 1988–98, head Fin Servs Business Devpt Gp 1995–97; PricewaterhouseCoopers: ptnr 1998–2013, global ldr of insurance consulting 1998–2001, head of UK financial servs consulting and memb Mgmnt Consulting Bd 2001–03, UK financial servs advsy ldr 2003–08, memb Supervisory Bd 2003–13, head of private sector consulting 2008–09, commercial managing ptnr consulting 2010–12; chm FS Regulatory Practice 2009–12; pres Mgmnt Consultancies Assoc 2010–11, non-exec dir Unipart Expert Practices Ltd 2013–, non-exec dir and chm Audit Ctee Paragon Bank plc 2014–, non-exec dir Shepherd & Wedderburn 2015–; memb Cncl Cornish Buildings Gp 2014–; vice-chm Cornish Buildings Gp 2016–; author of numerous articles in financial press; govr Belmont Preparatory Sch 2012–15; highly commended Wolfson Economics Prize 2014–; FCA, FRSA; *Recreations* sailing, book collecting, Cornish history; *Clubs* Salcombe Yacht; *Style—* Pat Newberry, Esq, FCA, FRSA; ✉ Pendragon House, Stoke Climsland, Cornwall PL17 8NZ (☎ 01579 370119, e-mail patricknewberry3@gmail.com)

NEWBERY, Prof David Michael; CBE (2012); s of late Alan Newbery, of Gosport, Hants, and late Betty Newbery; *b* 1 June 1943; *Educ* Portsmouth GS, Trinity Coll Cambridge (scholar, MA, PhD), ScD; *m* 1975, Dr Terri Apter, da of Dr Nathaniel Apter; 2 da (Miranda b 1979, Julia b 1983); *Career* economist Treasy Tanzanian Govt 1965–66; Univ of Cambridge: asst lectr 1966–71, lectr 1971–86, reader in economics 1986–88, dir Dept of Applied Economics 1988–2003, prof of applied economics 1988–2010 (emeritus prof 2010–), professorial fell Churchill Coll 1988–2010 (teaching fell 1965–88, emeritus prof 2010–); res assoc Cowles Fndn Yale Univ 1969, assoc prof Stanford Univ 1976–77, visiting prof Princeton Univ 1985, visiting scholar IMF 1987, Ford visiting prof Univ of Calif Berkeley 1987–88, sr res fell Inst for Policy Reform 1990–95; div chief Public Economics Div World Bank 1981–83; memb Environmental Economics Academic Panel DEFRA (formerly DETR) 1992–2012, pres Euro Economic Assoc 1996, chair Lead Expert Gp Foresight Land Use Futures 2008–10, dep ind memb Single Electricity Market Ctee Island of Ireland 2012–17, pres Int Assoc for Energy Economics 2013; memb Panel: Ofgem Low Carbon Network Fund 2010–14, Gas Network Innovation Competition 2014–; Frisch medal Econometric Soc 1990, Harry Johnson prize Canadian Economics Assoc 1993; fell: Centre for Economic Policy Res 1984–, Econometric Soc 1989; FBA 1991; *Books* Project Appraisal in Practice (jtly, 1976), The Theory of Commodity Price Stabilization: a study in the economics of risk (with J E Stiglitz, 1981), The Theory of Taxation for Developing Countries (ed, 1987), Hungary, An Economy in Transition (ed, 1993), Tax and Benefit Reform in Central and Eastern Europe (ed, 1995), Privatization, Restructuring and Regulation of Network Utilities (2000); *Recreations* skiing; *Clubs* Oxford and Cambridge; *Style—* Prof David Newbery, CBE, FBA; ✉ Faculty of Economics, University of Cambridge, Sidgwick Avenue, Cambridge CB3 9DE (☎ 01223 335248, fax 01223 335299, e-mail dmgn@econ.cam.ac.uk)

NEWBIGGING, Sir David Kennedy; kt (2011), OBE (1982), DL (Wilts 1993); s of David Locke Newbigging, CBE, MC (and bar) (d 1948), and Lucy Margaret Newbigging (d 1970); *b* 19 January 1934, Tientsin, China; *Educ* Oundle; *m* 1968, Carolyn Susan, da of Geoffrey Band (d 1974); 1 s, 2 da; *Career* 2 Lt Nat Serv KOSB; Jardine Matheson & Co Ltd: joined 1954, dir 1967, md 1970, chm and sr md 1975–83; chm: Hongkong & Kowloon Wharf & Godown Co Ltd 1970–80, Hong Kong Land 1975–83 (also md), Hongkong Electric Holdings Ltd 1982–83 (dir 1975–83), Jardine Fleming Holdings Ltd 1975–83, Hong Kong Tourist Assoc 1977–82, Hong Kong General C of C 1980–82, Rentokil Gp plc 1987–94 (dir 1986–94), Redfearn plc 1988, NM UK Limited 1990–93, Ivory and Sime plc 1992–95 (dir 1987–91), Maritime Tport Services Ltd 1993–95, Faupel plc 1994–2005 (dir 1989–93), Equitas Holdings Limited 1995–98, Equitas Management Services Limited 1995–98, Equitas Reinsurance Limited 1995–98, Equitas Limited 1996–98, Friends Provident plc (formerly Friends Provident Life Office) 1998–2005 (dir 1993, dep chm 1996–98), Thistle Hotels plc 1999–2003, Talbot Holdings Ltd 2003–07, Synesis Life Ltd 2006–08; dep chm: Provincial Gp plc 1985–91 (dir 1984–91), Benchmark Gp plc 1996–2004; dir: Hongkong & Shanghai Banking Corp 1975–83, Hongkong Telephone Co Ltd 1975–83, Rennies Consolidated Holdings Ltd 1975–83, Provincial Insurance plc 1984–86, Provincial Life Assurance Co Ltd 1984–86, The British Coal Corp (formerly the National Coal Bd) 1984–87, CIN Management Ltd 1985–87, United Meridian Corp (USA) 1987–98, Wah Kwong Shipping Holdings Ltd (Hong Kong) 1992–99, Market Bd Corp of Lloyd's 1993–95, Merrill Lynch & Co Inc 1996–2007, Ocean Energy Inc (USA) 1998–2003, Paccar Inc (USA) 1999–2006, Wah Kwong Maritime Tport Hldgs Ltd (Hong Kong) 2008–, Academic Partnerships LLP Dallas USA 2012–15; memb: Int Cncl Morgan Guaranty Tst Co of NY 1977–85, Hongkong Legislative Cncl 1978–82, Hongkong Exec Cncl 1980–84; chm Cancer Research UK 2004–10 (dep chm Cncl of Tstees 2002–04); tstee UK Tst for Nature Conservation in Nepal (formerly King Mahendra UK Tst for Nature Conservation) 1988–; chm: Wilts Community Fndn 1991–97, Cncl The Mission to Seafarers 1993–2006 (vice-chm Cncl and chm Exec Ctee 1986–93), Academic Partnerships Int Ltd 2012–15; High Sheriff Wilts 2003–04; Liveryman Worshipful Co of Grocers; *Recreations* Chinese art, most outdoor sports; *Clubs* Boodle's, Hongkong (Hong Kong), Hong Kong Jockey, The Bohemian (San Francisco); *Style—* Sir David Newbigging, OBE, DL; ✉ 119 Old Church Street, London SW3 6EA (☎ and fax 020 7352 1558)

NEWBOLD, Prof Robert Frank; s of Francis James Newbold, of Oxon, and Aileen Mary, *née* Bird; *b* 5 February 1950; *Educ* Abingdon Sch, Aston Univ (BSc), Univ of London (PhD, DSc); *m* 1972, Ann, da of Thomas Hood; *Career* Inst of Cancer Research London 1973–87 (res fell 1973–84), scientific dir Ludwig Inst for Cancer Research Sydney Aust 1987–89; Brunel Univ: head Dept of Biology and Biochemistry 1991–2001, dean Faculty of Science 1996–99, dir Brunel Inst of Cancer Genetics and Pharmacogenomics 2000–, dean Faculty of Life Sciences 2001–04; memb: Govt ctees on mutagenicity and carcinogenicity of chemicals in food, consumer products and the environment 1991–2000, Advsy Bd UICC Fellowship Int Union Against Cancer (UICC-WHO) 2003–; co-ordinator multinational EU framework (FP) projects on molecular mechanisms of human cancer devpt for FP3 1992–95, FP4 1996–99, FP5 2000–04, FP6 2004–08 and FP7 2008–12; tstee Hillingdon Hosp Post Grad Centre 1996–2004; memb Bd of Eds Int Jl of Cancer 2005–12, author of over 100 scientific papers on cancer genetics and carcinogenesis in learned jls; CBiol, FRSB 1990, FRSM 1993, FRCPath 2001, FRSA 2002; *Recreations* jazz and blues guitar, motor sport, natural history, country pursuits; *Clubs* Middlesex CCC; *Style—* Prof Robert Newbold; ✉ College of Life and Health Sciences, Brunel University, Uxbridge, Middlesex UB8 3PH (☎ 01895 266290, fax 01895 269787, e-mail robert.newbold@brunel.ac.uk)

NEWBON, Gary; s of Jack Newbon (d 1982), and Preeva, *née* Cooklin (d 2009); *b* 15 March 1945; *Educ* Culford Sch Bury St Edmunds; *m* 26 Oct 1973, Katharine Janet, da of Bernard While (d 1982), of Birmingham; 1 da (Claire Rosalie b 5 June 1975), 2 s (Laurence Jon, Neil Christie (twins) b 16 Aug 1977); *Career* journalist Jeacock's News Agency Cambridge 1964–67; sports writer Hayter's Sports Agency, sports presenter Westward TV Plymouth 1968–71; ATV Network Ltd: sports presenter 1971–74, sports presenter and ed 1974–81; controller of sport Central TV and Carlton TV 1982–2004, presenter Sky Sports 2004–; ITV reporter: Olympic Games 1972, 1980 and 1988, World Cup Soccer 1974, 1982, 1986, 1990, 1994, 1998 and 2002; memb: Lord's Taverners, Variety Club of GB; nat patron Deafblind UK; Grand Order of Water Rats; Officer de l'Ordre des Coteaux de Champagne; *Books* Over the Sticks and Under Starters Orders (with late Michael Ayres, 1970 and 1971); *Recreations* jazz, blues, rock and roll, drinking champagne and wine; *Clubs* Garrick, Groucho; *Style—* Gary Newbon, Esq

NEWBOROUGH, 8 Baron (I 1776); Rt Hon Prof Robert Vaughan Wynn; 10 Bt (GB 1742); s of 7 Baron Newborough, DSC (d 1998), of Rhug, Corwen, N Wales, by his 1 w, Rosamund, da of late Maj Robert Barbour, of Bolesworth Castle, Tattenhall, Cheshire; *b* 11 August 1949; *Educ* Milton Abbey; *m* 1, 1981, Mrs Sheila Christine Wilson, da of William A Massey; 1 da (Hon Lucinda Rosamond b 1982); m 2, 16 April 1988, Mrs Susan E Hall, da of late Andrew Lloyd, of Malta; *Heir* cous, Antony Charles Vaughan Wynn; *Career* landowner and organic farmer; dir: Peplow Training and Recruitment Services Ltd, Legends Park Ltd, Rhug Ltd, Rhug Energy Ltd; hon fell and hon prof (for servs to the environment) Glynd?r Univ 2015; *Recreations* skiing, sailing, shooting; *Style—* The Rt Hon Prof the Lord Newborough, ARAgS; ✉ Rug Hall, Corwen, North Wales, LL21 0EH; Peplow Hall, Peplow, Market Drayton, Shropshire TF9 35P

NEWBY, Prof Sir Howard Joseph; kt (2000), CBE (1995); s of Alfred Joseph Newby, and Constance Annie, *née* Potts; *b* 10 December 1947; *Educ* John Port GS Etwall, Atlantic Coll Glamorgan, Univ of Essex (BA, PhD); *m* 1, 4 July 1970 (m dis 2003), Janet Elizabeth; 2 s (Stephen b 1980, Jake b 1983); m 2, May 2005, Sheila; *Career* Univ of Essex: lectr in sociology 1972–75, sr lectr 1975–79, reader 1979–83, prof of sociology 1983–88; dir ESRC Data Archive 1983–88, chm ESRC 1988–94, vice-chllr Univ of Southampton 1994–2001, chief exec HEFCE 2001–06, vice-chllr UWE 2006–08, vice-chllr Univ of Liverpool 2008–15; prof of sociology and rural sociology Univ of Wisconsin Madison USA 1980–83; visiting appts: Univ of NSW Sydney 1976, Univ of Newcastle upon Tyne 1983–84; chm Centre for Exploitation of Science and Technol 1995–99; pres UUK 1999–2001; *Books* incl: The Deferential Worker (1977), Green and Pleasant Land? (2 edn, 1985), Country Life (1987), The Countryside in Question (1988); jtly: Community Studies (1971), Property Paternalism and Power (1978), The Problem of Sociology (1983), Social Class in Modern Britain (1988); *Recreations* family life, gardening, Derby County, railways; *Style—* Sir

N

Howard Newby, CBE; ✉ The Foundation Building, 765 Brownlow Hill, Liverpool L69 7ZX (☎ 0151 794 2003, e-mail howard.newby@liv.ac.uk, website www.liv.ac.uk)

NEWBY, Baron (Life Peer UK 1997), of Rothwell in the County of West Yorkshire; Richard Mark (Dick) Newby; OBE (1990), PC (2014); s of Frank and Kathleen Newby, of Rothwell; *b* 14 February 1953; *Educ* Rothwell GS, St Catherine's Coll Oxford (MA); *m* 1978, Hon Ailsa Ballantyne Thomson, da of Baron Thomson of Monifieth, KT, PC; 2 s (Hon Mark George b 1985, Hon Roger James Swift b 1987); *Career* HM Customs and Excise: joined 1974, private sec to Perm Sec 1977–79, princ Planning Unit 1979–81; dir of corp affairs Rosehaugh plc 1988–92, dir Matrix Communications Consultancy Ltd 1992–99, chm Reform Publications Ltd 1993–2008, dir Flagship Gp 1999–2001, chm Live Consulting 2001–12, chm Live Sport CIC 2010–12; nat sec SDP 1981–88, dir of external communications Lib Dem Gen Election Team 1996–97, sits as Lib Dem peer in House of Lords, Treasy spokesman 1997–2010, COS to Rt Hon Charles Kennedy, MP, *qv* 1999–2006, co-chair Lib Dem Parly Treasy Policy Ctee 2010–12, Govt dep chief whip 2012–15, Lib Dem chief whip 2012–, Govt Treasy spokesman House of Lords 2012–15; Capt of the Queen's Bodyguard Yeoman of the Guard 2012–15; *Recreations* football, tennis, cricket, reading; *Clubs* MCC; *Style—* The Rt Hon the Lord Newby, OBE, PC; ✉ House of Lords, London SW1A 0PW (mobile 07802 887606, e-mail newbyr@parliament.uk)

NEWCOMBE, Barry; s of Ronald William Newcombe (d 1991), of Northampton, and Doris May, *née* Underwood (d 1991); *b* 21 December 1939; *Educ* Northampton GS; *m* 30 Dec 1967, Maureen, da of Douglas Brooks; 1 da (Kerry Margaret b 18 June 1968), 1 s (Andrew James b 1 Nov 1970); *Career* sports writer; trainee journalist then rugby corr Chronicle and Echo Northampton 1957–64, staff writer Hayters's Agency 1964–65; rugby and tennis corr: Evening Standard 1965–84, Sunday Express 1984–96; sports reporter Daily Express 1996–97, currently freelance journalist, chief exec Hayters's Agency 1999–2001; UK Olympic press attaché: Sydney 2000, Athens 2004, Beijing 2008, London 2012; pres Rugby Writers' Club, chm Sports Journalists' Assoc 2006–13, treas Lawn Tennis Writers' Assoc, former press offr Teddington Soc; memb Ctee Torch Trophy Tst; *Books* Carling's England (1991), Upfront with Jeff Probyn (1993), Lawrence Dallaglio – Diary of a Season (1997); *Recreations* woodland studies; *Style—* Barry Newcombe, Esq; ✉ Springwood, 9 Sands Road, The Sands, Farnham, Surrey GU10 1PX (☎ 07711 690760, e-mail barrynewcombe@gmail.com)

NEWCOME, Rt Rev James William Scobie; *see:* Bishop of Carlisle

NEWELL, Christopher William Paul; s of Lt-Col Nicolas Gambier Newell (d 1980), and Edith Alice, *née* Edgill (d 1984); *b* 30 November 1950; *Educ* Wellington, Univ of Southampton (LLB); *m* 1998, Teresa Mary; 1 da (Natalie Bridget Rosie b 2003); *Career* called to the Bar Middle Temple 1973, in private practice 1973–75, legal asst then sr legal asst Dept of DPP 1975–79, sr legal asst Law Offr's Dept 1979–83, sr legal asst Dept of DPP 1983–86, asst DPP 1986, branch crown prosecutor CPS 1986–87, asst legal sec Law Offr's Dept 1987–89; CPS: dir of HQ casework 1989–93, dir of casework 1993–96, dir of casework evaluation 1996–98, dir of casework 1998–2005, princ legal advsr to DPP 2005–09; vice-chair Centre for Accessible Environments 2004–08; sr vice-chair Criminal Law Ctee Int Bar Assoc 2002–06; tstee: Crime Reduction Initiatives 2001–11, Nat Deaf Children's Soc 2001–08, Centre for Accessible Environments 2001–08, Friends of W Byfleet Health Centre 2009– (chair 2012–); govr Pyrford C of E Primary Sch 2008–14, memb Wisley with Pyrford Parochial Church Cncl 2010– (vice-chair 2013–); *Recreations* sport, travel, family; *Style—* Christopher Newell, Esq

NEWELL, David Richard; s of late Dick Newell, and Davida, *née* Juleff; *b* 21 September 1951; *Educ* Shrewsbury, Univ of Birmingham (LLB), Univ of Southampton (MPhil); *m* 1978, Cora Sue, *née* Feingold; 1 da (Rebecca); *Career* admitted slr 1978 (articles Lawford & Co 1976–78); Univ of Leicester: lectr in law 1978–86, postgrad tutor 1979–84, dir employment law postgrad prog 1983–86; Newspaper Soc: head of govt and legal affrs 1984–96, dir 1997– (dep dir 1992–97); sec Parly and Legal Ctee Guild of Editors 1984–97; dir: ABC 1997–, Press Standards Bd of Fin 1997–2014, Advtg Standards Bd of Fin 1998–, Publishers NTO 2001–05, Newspaper Publishers Assoc 2007–14; ceo News Media Assoc 2014–; memb: Confedn of Communication and Info Industries 1984–, Ctee of Advtg Practice 1984–2005, Ctees Advtg Assoc 1984–, Employment and Media Ctees Law Soc 1990–97, Campaign for Freedom of Info 1990–2005 (Award for campaigning against official secrecy 1989), Advtg Law Gp 1995–2005, UK Assizes Gp 1995–2005, Bd Euro Newspapers Publishers' Assoc 1996– (chm Legal Framework Ctee 1995–98), CPU 1997–2005, Cncl World Assoc of Newspapers 1997–, Cncl CBI 1999–2005; Special Award UK Press Gazette 1988, Special Newspaper Industry Award 2010; hon legal advsr Leicester Legal Advice Centre 1979–84; *Publications* The New Employment Legislation: a guide to the Employment Acts 1980 and 1983 (1983), Understanding Recruitment Law (1984), How to Study Law (jtly, 1986, 6 edn 2010), Financial Advertising Law (jtly, 1989), Aspects of Employment Law (jtly, 1990), Law for Journalists (jtly, 1991), Tolleys Employment Law (jtly, 1994, 2 edn 2000), The Law of Journalism (jtly, 1995), Copinger on Copyright (contrib, 1998); res papers and articles on employment law, media and legal policy issues; *Recreations* country and seaside walks, sailing, tennis; *Style—* David Newell, Esq; ✉ News Media Association, 292 Vauxhall Bridge Road, London SW1V 1AE (☎ 020 7963 7480, e-mail ns@newspapersoc.org.uk)

NEWELL, Donald; s of Stephen Newell (d 1982), and Ida Laura, *née* Hatch (d 1992); *b* 31 August 1942, Turnford, Herts; *Educ* Cheshunt GS; *m* 22 June 1968, Rosemary, *née* Litler-Jones; 1 s (Simon b 12 July 1971), 2 da (Sarah b 3 Oct 1973, Alexandra b 18 Nov 1978); *Career* Hillier Parker May and Rowden: managing ptnr 1986–90, sr ptnr 1990–98; chm EMEA Div CBRichard Ellis Servs Inc 1998–2000; non-exec dir: London Merchant Securities plc 1998–2007, Derwent London plc 2007–11, ret; fndr memb British Cncl for Offices (pres 1992–93); Liveryman: Worshipful Co of Pattenmakers 1979 (Master 2004–05), Worshipful Co of Chartered Surveyors 1993; FRICS 1968; *Recreations* travel and sport; *Clubs* Bucks, MCC; *Style—* Donald Newell, Esq; ✉ e-mail newelldon@aol.com

NEWELL, Dame (Priscilla) Jane; DBE (2013, OBE 1997), JP (Liverpool 1993–94, Inner London 1995–2013); *née* Watts; da of late (Arthur Ronald) Michael Watts, and Sylvia Margaret Scarfe, *née* McNabb; *b* 13 April 1944, London; *Educ* Merrow Grange Convent Guildford, Guildford Tech Coll, Victoria Univ of Wellington NZ (BA, sr scholar, postgrad scholar); *m* 1, 22 Jan 1977, Prof Kenneth Wyatt Newell (d 1990); m 2, 12 April 2007, Lord Cuckney (d 2008); *Career* int civil servant WHO 1965–77, linguistics tutor Victoria Univ of Wellington and tutor to Chinese exchange students NZ Miny of Foreign Affrs 1982–83, school administrator and sec Voluntary Funds Ctee Liverpool Sch of Tropical Med 1984–92, non-service assessor Assessment and Consultancy Unit Home Office 1994–2006; tstee GlaxoSmithKline Pension Plan (formerly Glaxo-Wellcome Pension Plan) 1994–2004; chm: United Utilities Pension Scheme 1998–2005, Electricity Supply Pension Scheme (UU Gp) 1998–2005, Dixons Gp Retirement and Employee Security Scheme 2004–07, Royal Mail Pension Plan 2005–12, Royal Mail Defined Contribution Plan 2009–12, John Lewis Partnership Pensions Tst 2013–; vice-pres Pensions Archive Tst 2009–, govr Pensions Policy Inst 2009–; non-exec dir: United Utilities plc 1996–2006, Synesis Life Ltd 2007–08; fndr tstee Maxwell Pensioners Tst 1992 (chm 1995–97), tstee Common Purpose Charitable Tst 1995–2000, tstee Age UK 2009–15; non-exec dir Royal Liverpool Univ Hosp Tst 1992–95, dep chm Glaxo Tstee Companies 1994–96; vice-pres Liverpool Sch of Tropical Med 1997– (chm 1995–97), pro-chllr and chair Bd of Govrs London South Bank Univ 1999–2007, patron Hillcroft Coll 2012–; Hon LLD London South Bank Univ 2008; *Recreations* gardening, walking, music; *Clubs* Athenaeum; *Style—* Dame Jane Newell, DBE; ✉ John Lewis Partnership Pensions Trust, Partnership House, Carlisle Place, London SW1P 1BX

NEWELL, Michael Cormac (Mike); *b* 28 March 1942; *Educ* Univ of Cambridge (MA); *m*; 1 da, 1 s; *Career* television and film director; Granada TV 1963–69, subsequently freelance dir of TV dramas; dir Fifty Cannon Entertainment; *Television films* incl The Melancholy Hussar (TV film, BBC) 1973, Baa Baa Black Sheep (Granada) 1974, Gift of Friendship (YTV) 1974, Lost Your Tongue (Granada) 1974, Brassneck (Play for Today, BBC) 1975, Ready When You Are Mr McGill (Granada) 1975 (BAFTA nominee, ITC entry for Monte Carlo Festival), Of The Fields Lately (offical entry Prague Festival) 1975, Destiny (BBC) 1977, Mr & Mrs Bureaucrat (BBC) 1977, Tales Out of School – Birth of a Nation (CBC) 1982, Blood Feud (3 pt mini-series) 1982–83 (Emmy nomination), Common Ground (CBS) 1990; *Films* incl: The Man in the Iron Mask (ITC) 1976, The Awakening (Orion) 1977, Bad Blood 1980, Dance with a Stranger 1984 (Prix de la Jeunesse Directors Fortnight Cannes), The Good Father 1985 (Prix Italia), Amazing Grace and Chuck 1986, Soursweet 1987, Enchanted April 1991, Into the West 1992, Four Weddings and a Funeral 1994 (David Lean Award for Best Achievement in Dir and Best Film BAFTA Awards, Lloyd's Bank People's Vote Most Popular Film, Cesar for Best Foreign Film, London Film Critics' Circle Br Film of the Year & Br Dir of the Year, also Academy Award nominee for Best Film & DGA nominee for Best Dir of a Feature Film), An Awfully Big Adventure 1995 (official entry Directors Fortnight Cannes), Donnie Brasco 1997, Pushing Tin 1998, Mona Lisa Smile 2003, Harry Potter and the Goblet of Fire 2005, Love in the Time of Cholera 2007, Prince of Persia: The Sands of Time 2010, Great Expectations 2012; as exec prodr: Best Laid Plans 1999, High Fidelity 2000, Traffic 2000; *Style—* Mike Newell, Esq

NEWELL, Robert Fraser; CVO (2011, LVO 2000); *b* 3 May 1943; *Educ* Univ Coll Sch London; *m* 29 May 1969, Shahnaz, *née* Bakhtiar; 2 da (Catherine b 27 Oct 1971, Lillian b 28 March 1974); *Career* hotel mgmnt positions London, Iran and Kenya 1965–75, dir of admin Kenya Utalii Coll 1974–79, visiting lectr Ecole Hoteliere de Lausanne 1983–2000, DG Royal Over-Seas League until 2011 (vice-pres 2011–), ret; memb Ctee Kenya Soc 2000–, memb Advsy Bd Spirit of Rememberance 2011–; chm Assoc of London Clubs 1992–95; memb Cncl of Cwlth Socs 1991–2011; vol Chain of Hope 2001–, tstee Bridge of Hope 2013– (chair of tstees 2013–); *Recreations* grandchildren, music, tennis; *Clubs* Royal Over-Seas League; *Style—* Robert Newell, Esq, CVO; ✉ Pichlhofstrasse, 6, Top 8, Kaprun 5710, Austria

NEWEY, Adrian Martin; OBE (2012); s of Richard Martin Newey, of Stratford-on-Avon, Warks, and Joan Edwina, *née* Calvert; *b* 26 December 1958; *Educ* Repton, Leamington Coll of FE (OND), Univ of Southampton (BSc); *m* 1, 13 Aug 1983 (m dis 1991), Amanda, *née* Hitchens; 2 da (Charlotte Katie b 28 Aug 1986, Hannah Louise b 3 Feb 1989); m 2, 1 Aug 1992, Marigold Phillippa, da of Peter Proudfoot; 1 da (Imogen Victoria b 30 Aug 1993), 1 s (Harrison William Innes b 25 July 1998); *Career* race car designer; aerodynamicist Formula One project Fittipaldi 1980–82; March Engineering: race engr Formula 2 1982, designer American series sports racing car 1982–84 (won championship 1983 and 1984), designer and race engr Indycars USA 1984–87 (won Indianapolis 500 each year); tech dir Formula 1 March Racing 1987–90, chief designer Formula One Williams Grand Prix Engineering 1990–97 (won Drivers' Championship 1992, 1993, 1996 and 1997, Constructors' Championship 1992, 1993, 1994, 1996 and 1997), tech dir Formula 1 McLaren International Ltd 1997–2006 (won Drivers' Championship 1998 and 1999, and Constructors' Championship 1998), chief technical offr Red Bull Formula 1 team 2006– (won 8 Formula 1 World Championships 2010–13 (4 Drivers', 4 Constructors'), Segrave Trophy 2010, Bluebird Trophy 2012); Hon DTech Robert Gordon Univ, Hon DSc Univ of Southampton; *Recreations* skiing, waterskiing, tennis; *Clubs* BRDC, VSCC; *Style—* Adrian Newey, Esq, OBE

NEWEY, Hon Mr Justice; Sir Guy Richard Newey; kt (2010), QC (2001); s of His Hon John Newey, QC (d 1994), and Mollie Patricia, *née* Chalk (d 2008); *b* 21 January 1959; *Educ* Tonbridge, Queens' Coll Cambridge (MA, LLM), Cncl of Legal Educn; *m* 2 Aug 1986, Angela Clare, da of Hugh Ross Neilson; 1 s (Timothy Guy b 31 March 1989), 3 da (Emma Katherine, Natasha Clare (twins) b 18 Oct 1990, Elspeth Patricia Irene b 21 Sept 1994); *Career* in practice Chancery Bar 1983–2010; jr counsel to the Crown (Chancery/A Panel) 1990–2001, jr counsel to the charity commissioners 1991–2001, actg deemster IOM 2003–11, inspr into the affrs of MG Rover 2005–09, dep High Court judge 2006–10, High Court judge 2010–, Chancery supervising judge (Midland, Wales and Western Circuit) 2014–; govr New Beacon Sch Sevenoaks 2001–09; *Publications* Directors' Disqualification (contrib), Civil Court Service (contrib), Equity and Administration (contrib); *Style—* The Hon Mr Justice Newey; ✉ Royal Courts of Justice, Strand, London WC2A 2LL

NEWING, Prof Angela; JP; da of James Grainger (d 1964), and Mabel, *née* Steel (d 1975); *Educ* Univ of Bristol (BSc, MSc), Columbia Pacific Univ CA (PhD); *m* 1965, Peter Newing; *Career* basic grade physicist Royal Sussex County Hosp 1960–65, teacher of physics, mathematics and games Chipping Campden Comp Sch 1968, sr grade physicist Cheltenham Gen Hosp 1968–81 (princ grade 1981–89, top grade dir of med physics for Glos 1989–2000), first dir Glos Royal & Cranfield Univ Inst of Med Sciences 1994–96, visiting prof of med physics Cranfield Univ 1994–2009, supervisor of res students; papers published in numerous learned jls, ed HPA Bulletin 1980–93, lectr; memb bd Hosp Physicists' Assoc & Inst of Physics & Engrg in Med (IPEM) 1980–83, 1986–88 and 1991–94; IPEM: external assessor training scheme 1988–2001, memb Training and Assessment Bd 1986–95, registrar of training scheme 1986–88, memb Radiotherapy Physics Topic Gp 1988–91, memb Inst of Physics Benevolent Fund Ctee 1988–92 and 1995–2001, chm Jt Accreditation Panel for Post-Graduate Training Centres 1989–94, chm Training & Educn Ctee 1991–92, tstee IOP Mayneord Philips Bequest 1993–2003 (chm tstees 1995–97 and 2001–02), Dept of Health assessor for Sr NHS posts 1994–2001, sec Radiology History & Heritage Tst 1997–2000, non-exec dir Royal Nat Hosp for Rheumatic Diseases Bath Somerset 2000–06, chm SW branch Inst of Physics 2011– (treas 2010–11), memb Cncl Inst of Physics 2014–; chm N Glos Bench 2003–06, dep chm Glos Co Bench 2007–; dep chm Liquor Licensing and Betting Ctee 2001–06; mathematical puzzle setter for Sunday Times and Daily Telegraph, memb BBC Radio 4 panel for Puzzle Panel; fell Inst of Physics, fell IPEM; FRSM, FIEE, CPhys; *Recreations* maze designer, campanologist, collector of mechanical puzzles; *Style—* Prof Angela Newing; ✉ Gaudete, 1 Hambutts Mead, Painswick, Gloucestershire GL6 6RP (☎ 01452 814360, e-mail profnewing@btinternet.com)

NEWLAND, Prof Adrian Charles; CBE (2010); *b* 26 August 1949; *Educ* City of Norwich Sch, Downing Coll Cambridge (MA), London Hosp Med Coll (MB BCh); *m* 1973, Joanna Mary, da of Prof Thurstan Shaw, CBE, FSA, FBA; 1 da (Emily Ruth b 1978), 1 s (Thomas William Derek b 1980); *Career* prof of haematology Bart's and The Royal London Sch of Med and Dentistry 1992–, concurrently dir of pathology Bart's Health NHS Tst and chair NICE Diagnostic Advsy Ctee, dir of research Bart's and the London NHS Tst 1997–2001, dir of pathology Bart's and the London NHS Tst 2008–14; chm Jt Ctee of Higher Med Trg (Haematology) 1991–2001; memb: Policy Advsy Ctee UK Accreditation Service, Med Research Cncl Leukaemia Trials Ctee 1991–2010, Med and Scientific Panel Leukaemia Research Fund 1992–95, London Clinical Senate; chm Assoc of Profs in Haematology 1993–; pres Br Soc for Haematology 1998–99 (scientific sec 1989–95), pres RCPath 2005–08 (memb Cncl 1993–96 and 1999–2002, vice-pres 2002–05), pres-elect Int Soc of Haematology 2014–16; chm Intercollege Cmmn on Haematology, Trg and Educn Ctee of the Int Soc of Haematology, memb DH Commissioning Gp for Blood 2007–14, chm Nat Blood Transfusion Ctee 2009–14, memb Med Ctee and patron Thalassaemia

Soc, vice-chair Nat Chemotherapy Clinical Advsy Gp, chair Healthcare Forum, memb Policy Advsy Ctee UK Accreditation Service, new clinical advsr Transforming Cancer Support Team NHSE London 2013–, chair Healthcare Advsory Gp UKAS 2013–, vice-chair Chemotherapy Clinical Advsy Gp NHSE 2013–; med advsr: Leukaemia Care Soc, ITP Patient Support Assoc; Bhagwan Singh travelling fell 1993, Sir John Dacie lectr Royal Coll of Pathologists 2008, BSH Medal 2008; hon sec Acad of Medical Royal Colls 2007–11; FRCPath 1991, FRCP 1992; *Publications* author of numerous pubns in the field of haematology incl 16 books or chapters in books; *Recreations* fine wine, walking, foreign travel; *Clubs* Athenaeum, MCC; *Style*— Prof Adrian Newland, CBE; ✉ Flat 109, Waterdale Manor House, Harewood Avenue, London NW1 6JX (☎ 020 7563 7065); Department of Haematology, Royal London Hospital, Whitechapel, London E1 1BB (☎ 020 3246 0338, fax 020 3246 0351, e-mail a.c.newland@qmul.ac.uk)

NEWLAND, Prof David Edward; s of Robert William Newland (d 1979), of Knebworth, Herts, and Marion Amelia, *née* Dearman (d 1993); *b* 8 May 1936; *Educ* Alleyne's Sch Stevenage, Selwyn Coll Cambridge (MA, ScD), MIT (ScD); *m* 18 July 1959, Patricia Frances, da of Philip Mayne, of Marton, N Yorks; 2 s (Andrew David William b 1961, Richard David Philip b 1963); *Career* English Electric Co London 1957–61, instr and asst prof MIT 1961–64, lectr (later sr lectr) Imperial Coll London 1964–67, prof of mechanical engrg Univ of Sheffield 1967–76; Univ of Cambridge: prof of engrg (1875) 1976–2003, prof emeritus 2003–, fell Selwyn Coll 1976–, head Dept of Engrg 1996–2002, dep vice-chllr 1999–2003; dir Cambridge-MIT Inst 2000–02; memb Royal Cmmn on Environmental Pollution 1984–89, visitor Tport and Road Res Laboratory 1990–92, memb Engrg Cncl Working Party on Engrs and Risk Issues 1991–94, tech advsr London Millennium Bridge Tst 2000–01; consulting forensic engr; author; memb Cncl Royal Acad of Engrg 1985–88; govr St Paul's Schs 1978–93, churchwarden Ickleton 1979–87, pres Selwyn Coll Alumni Assoc 2013–14; Freeman City of London 2000, Liveryman Worshipful Co of Engrs 2001; Hon DEng Univ of Sheffield 1997; FREng 1982, FIMechE, FIET; *Books* An Introduction to Random Vibrations, Spectral and Wavelet Analysis (1975, 3 edn, 1993), Mechanical Vibration Analysis and Computation (1989), Discover Butterflies in Britain (2006), Britain's Butterflies (2 edn, 2010), Britain's Day-flying Moths (2013), Britain's Butterflies (3 edn, 2015); *Recreations* engineering, photography, entomology; *Clubs* Athenaeum; *Style*— Prof David Newland, FREng; ✉ Selwyn College, Cambridge CB3 9DQ (e-mail den1000@cam.ac.uk)

NEWLANDS, David Baxter; s of George Frederick Newlands (d 1981), and Helen Frederica Newlands; *b* 13 September 1946; *Educ* Edinburgh Acad; *m* 31 March 1973, Susan Helena, da of Ernest Ferguson Milne, OBE, of Walton on the Hill, Surrey; 2 da (Katharine b 11 Jan 1977, Jennifer b 17 Nov 1978), 2 s (Edward b 27 June 1981, Andrew b 27 Sept 1983); *Career* ptnr Touche Ross and Co 1977–86 (joined 1963), fin dir Saatchi and Saatchi plc 1986–89, fin dir GEC plc 1989–97; non-exec chm: Paypoint 1998–, Prospect Investment Mgmnt 1999–, Britax International plc 2000–01, Tomkins plc 2000–10, Kesa Electricals 2003–12, OBIO (formerly Open Business Exchange) 2004–09, HellermannTyton plc 2013–; chm Impress Coöperatieve UA 2007–; non-exec dir: Weir Gp 1997–2003, Global Software Services 1998–2004, London Regnl Transport 1999–2001, Standard Life Assurance Co 1999–2006; chm of tstees SeeAbility 2001–07; FCA 1969; *Recreations* golf, bridge; *Clubs* RAC, Walton Heath Golf (dir 2001–), Sutton and Epsom RFC, Caledonian Royal and Ancient Golf Club of St Andrews, Golf House (Elie); *Style*— David Newlands, Esq

NEWLANDS, Prof George McLeod; s of George Newlands (d 1973), of Perth, and Mary Newlands; *b* 12 July 1941, Perth, Scotland; *Educ* Perth Acad, Univ of Edinburgh (MA, BD, PhD), Univ of Heidelberg, Churchill Coll Cambridge (MA), Univ of Edinburgh (DLitt); *m* 1 Sept 1967, (Mary) Elizabeth, da of Rev Prof Ronald S Wallace, of Edinburgh; 3 s (Stewart b 1971, Murray b 1974, Craig b 1977); *Career* minister Church of Scotland, priest C of E; lectr in divinity Univ of Glasgow 1969–73, univ lectr in divinity Univ of Cambridge 1973–86, fell Wolfson Coll Cambridge 1975–82, fell and dean Trinity Hall Cambridge 1982–86, prof of divinity Univ of Glasgow 1986–2008 (dean Faculty of Divinity 1988–90, hon research prof 2008–), princ Trinity Coll 1991–97 and 2002–07; pres Soc for the Study of Theology 2013–14; hon fell Sch of Divinity Edinburgh 2010–; FRSA 2005, FRSE 2008; *Books* Hilary of Poitiers (1978), Theology of the Love of God (1980), The Church of God (1984), Making Christian Decisions (1985), God in Christian Perspective (1994), Generosity and the Christian Future (1997), Scottish Christianity in the Modern World (2000), John and Donald Baillie: Transatlantic Theology (2002), The Transformative Imagination (2004), Believing in the Text (jt ed, 2004), Fifty Key Christian Thinkers (jt ed, 2004), Traces of Liberality (2006), Christ and Human Rights (2006), The God of Love and Human Divinity: Essays for George Newlands (2007), Faith and Human Rights (jtly, 2008), Hospitable God (jtly, 2010), Spirit of Liberality (2014); *Recreations* walking, music; *Clubs* New (Edinburgh); *Style*— Prof George Newlands; ✉ 49 Highsett, Cambridge CB2 1NZ (☎ 07786 930941, e-mail newlands71@hotmail.com or g.newlands@arts.gla.ac.uk, website www.georgenewlands.com)

NEWLANDS OF LAURISTON, William Alexander; also Baron of Miltonhaven; s of Frank Newlands (d 1971), of Ballinluig, Perthshire, and Annie Shand-Henderson (d 1986); the family is descended from Jasper Newlands of that Ilk (in record 1469); Lauriston Castle first recorded 1243, Glenfiddich award 1992; matriculated as feudal Baron of Miltonhaven 2003; *b* 5 November 1934, Tibbermore, Perthshire; *Educ* Dollar Acad, Robert Gordon's Coll Aberdeen, Churchill fell 1968; *m* 1, 1960 (m dis 1976), Kathleen Cook; 2 da (Fiona b 1960, Riona b 1962), 1 s (Hamish Newlands of Lauriston Yr b 1965 d 2012); *m* 2, 1985, Dorothy Walker, *qv*; *Heir* gs, Duncan Harald Newlands of Lauriston; *Career* Far East Air Force 1953–55; formerly with: Game Conservancy, Int Union for Conservation of Nature (Morges, Switzerland); travel ed (as Willy Newlands) Daily Mail 1982–92; ed and presenter Scots Away (TV series) 1993; contrib to nat newspapers and magazines; Travel Writer of the Year 1983–84 and 1987–88; memb Convention of the Baronage of Scotland, memb Guild of Freemen of the City of London, Freeman City of Glasgow, memb Incorporation of Wrights in Glasgow; Churchill fell 1968 (wildlife mgmnt USA); FSA Scot; *Books* incl: Hobby Farm: Ideas for the New Countryside (2006); *Clubs* City Livery; *Style*— William Newlands of Lauriston; ✉ Lauriston Castle, St Cyrus, Kincardineshire (☎ 01674 850488, mobile 07807 201636, e-mail wnewlands@aol.com); Church Cottage, Church Street, Old Hatfield, Herts AL9 5AP

NEWLING, Caro; adopted da of Alfred John Newling, and Evelyn Fowler; *Educ* Brighton & Hove HS, Roedean, Univ of Warwick, Webber Douglas Academy of Dramatic Arts; *Partner* Gary Hamilton Powell; *Career* formerly with Almeida Theatre, Ballet Rambert and RSC, exec prodr Donmar Warehouse 1992–2002 (estab as producing house with Sam Mendes, CBE, *qv*), co-fndr/co-dir (with Sam Mendes, CBE and Pippa Harris, *qqv*) Neal Street Prodns 2003–; prodns incl: The Bridge Project, Shrek the Musical, Charlie and the Chocolate Factory; West End and Broadway prodns incl: This House, The Painkiller, Enron, Three Days of Rain, Mary Stuart, Hamlet, The Vertical Hour, Sunday in the Park with George, All About My Mother; currently pres Soc of London Theatre; chair: Paines Plough, Linbury Prize for Stage Design; memb Bd of Mgmnt Soc of London Theatre, tstee Nat Theatre 2003–10, former tstee Chichester Festival Theatre, former tstee Adventures in Motion Pictures; *Style*— Ms Caro Newling; ✉ Neal Street Productions, 26–28 Neal Street, London WC2H 9QQ (website www.nealstreetproductions.com)

NEWLYN, Prof Lucy Anne; da of Prof Walter T Newlyn (d 2002), and Doreen Harrington Newlyn; *b* 16 September 1956, Uganda; *Educ* Lawnswood HS Leeds, Lady Margaret Hall Oxford (open scholar, BA, DPhil); *m* 3 Jan 1991, Martin Slater; 1 da (Emma b 1995); *Career* Univ of Oxford: lectr Lincoln Coll, Lady Margaret Hall, Mansfield Coll and ChCh 1981–86, official fell and tutor in English St Edmund Hall 1986– (stipendiary lectr 1984–86), CUF lectr in English 1986–, prof of English language and lit 2004–; hon prof Dept of English Univ of Wales Aberystwyth; Rose Mary Crawshay Prize Br Acad 2001; *Books* incl: Coleridge, Wordsworth and the Language of Allusion (1986), Paradise Lost and the Romantic Reader (1993), Reading, Writing and Romanticism: The Anxiety of Reception (2000), Ginnel (2005); *Recreations* swimming, gardening; *Style*— Prof Lucy Newlyn; ✉ 53 Latimer Road, Oxford OX3 7PG (☎ 01865 435020); St Edmund Hall, Oxford OX1 4AR (☎ 01865 279081, e-mail lucy.newlyn@seh.ox.ac.uk)

NEWMAN, Rt Rev Adrian; *see:* Stepney, Bishop of

NEWMAN, Andrew William; s of Alistair John Newman, and Geraldine Elizabeth Maguire, *née* Long; *b* 4 November 1969; *Educ* St Paul's, UCL (BSc); *m* 31 Aug 2002, Terry Louise, *née* Burgess; 2 s (Frederick Ralph Stanley b 9 Dec 2000, William Robert Shrek b 22 May 2003); *Career* TV writer and prodr 1993–98 (shows incl The Word The Big Breakfast, Brass Eye, The Sunday Show The Eleven O'Clock Show and Ali G), commissioning ed entertainment Channel 4 1998–99, head of programmes E4 1999–2001, controller of entertainment Channel 5 2001–03; Channel 4: head of entertainment 2003–06, head of entertainment and comedy 2006–09; Objective Prodns: chief creative offr 2009–11, chief exec 2011–; *Recreations* collecting vintage fashion, obsessively watching television, magic; *Style*— Andrew Newman, Esq

NEWMAN, Catherine Mary; QC (1995); da of Dr Ernest Newman (d 1971), of London, and Josephine, *née* McLaughlin (d 1991); *b* 7 February 1954; *Educ* Convent of The Sacred Heart HS, UCL (LLB); *m* 1982 (m dis 2008), Ian Gouldsbrough; 1 s (Charles b 1987), 1 da (Mary Hope b 1991); *Career* called to the Bar Middle Temple 1979 (Harmsworth scholar), bencher 2002, recorder of the Crown Court, dep High Court judge; tstee CAFOD; *Recreations* lunching with friends, reading fiction; *Style*— Miss Catherine Newman, QC; ✉ Maitland Chambers, 7 Stone Buildings, Lincoln's Inn, London WC2A 3SZ (☎ 020 7406 1200, fax 020 7406 1300)

NEWMAN, Derek Anthony; s of Maurice John Newman, of Ashtead, Surrey, and Christine Newman, *née* Grieve; *b* 7 April 1944; *Educ* Chorlton GS Manchester, City Univ (MBA); *m* 1968, Patricia Ann Wynne; 3 c (Michelle b 15 March 1972, David b 14 Jan 1975, Lisa b 3 Nov 1977); *Career* audit mangr Touche Ross 1968–73 (articled clerk 1965–68), fin controller First National Finance Ltd 1973–75; Chemical Bank: fin controller 1975–76, vice-pres fin 1976–78, vice-pres and head of corp fin NY 1978–81, vice-pres fin insts 1981–85; Canadian Imperial Bank of Commerce: gen mangr UK and Ireland 1985–86, sr vice-pres Europe, Africa and ME 1987–90 (vice-pres 1986–87), head of Europe 1990–91, chief executive CIBC/Wood Gundy Group Europe 1990–91; chief operating offr Summit Group plc 1991–94; chief fin offr: Nomura Securities plc, IBJ-Nomura Financial Products plc; FCA; *Recreations* windsurfing, golf, swimming; *Clubs* RAC; *Style*— Derek Newman, Esq; ☎ 07803 628845

NEWMAN, Sir Geoffrey Robert; 6 Bt (UK 1836), of Mamhead, Devonshire; s of Sir Ralph Alured Newman, 5 Bt (d 1968), and Hon Ann Rosemary Hope Newman, *née* Hope-Morley (d 2009); *b* 2 June 1947; *Educ* Heatherdown Sch, Kelly Coll; *m* 1980, Mary Elizabeth, yr da of Col Sir Martin St John Valentine Gibbs, KCVO, CB, DSO, TD (d 1992); 3 da (Frances Joyce b 1983, Elsie Laura (Mrs Newman Curtis) b 1987, Louisa Bridget b 1990), 1 s (Robert Melvil b 1985); *Heir* s, Robert Newman; *Career* 1 Bn Grenadier Gds 1967–70, Lt T&AVR until 1979; Daniel Greenaway & Sons Ltd 1973–75; memb Transglobe Expedition 1977–79; dir Blackpool Sands (Devon) Utilities Co Ltd 1970–; prodn controller Wadlow Grosvenor International 1980–90 (corporate film and video prodn); chm Marine Conservation Soc 2001–10, tstee Britannia Museum BRNC 2007–; walk leader/guide The Wayfarers 1990–2005; vice-chm and dir Dartmouth & District Tourism Services Ltd 1992–2003, memb Devon Assoc of Tourist Attractions 1995–, chm Dartmouth Swimming Pool 1998–2013, pres Dartmouth and Kingswear Soc 2001–, memb Dartmoor Water Power Gp 2007–, chm Dartmouth and District Indoor Pool Tst 2008–; FRGS; *Style*— Sir Geoffrey Newman, Bt

N

NEWMAN, Iain Bernard; s of Rev David Newman, and Anne, *née* Taylor; *b* 5 January 1966, Yateley, Hants; *Educ* St Bees Sch Cumbria, Mansfield Coll Oxford (BA); *m* 30 July 1994, Victoria, *née* Chesworth; 1 da (Anna b 16 March 1998), 2 s (Peter b 5 Nov 2000, Mark b 9 Jan 2002); *Career* slr; Nabarro LLP (formerly Nabarro Nathanson): trainee 1988–90, assoc 1991–97, ptnr 1997–; memb Law Soc; *Recreations* children, cricket, rugby; *Style*— Iain Newman, Esq; ✉ Nabarro LLP, 125 London Wall, London EC2Y 5AL (☎ 020 7524 6423, fax 020 7868 3423, e-mail i.newman@nabarro.com)

NEWMAN, Kevin; *b* 1957; *Educ* Keele Univ (BA), Univ of Essex (MA); *m* Cathy; 2 s (Benjamin b 1989, Joshua b 1991), 1 da (Naomi b 1996); *Career* trainee programmer rising to sr project mangr Mars Group Services 1981–85; Woolworths plc: joined as info centre mangr 1985, then business systems mangr, dir of Mgmnt Info Systems (i/c all gp IT) until 1989; First Direct: i/c systems devpt prior to launch 1989, ops dir 1990–91, chief exec 1991–97; dir global distribution Citibank NY 1997–; *Recreations* squash, golf, running, gym workout, skiing, American football; *Style*— Kevin Newman, Esq; ✉ Citibank, NA Global Consumer Citibanking, One Court Square, 40th Floor, Long Island City, NY 11120, USA (☎ 718 248 4754, fax 718 248 5303)

NEWMAN, Lorraine; *Career* EastEnders (BBC1): joined as script sec, subsequently series prodr, acting exec prodr then exec prodr 2012–13; exec prod BBC Drama Prodn 2013–; *Style*— Ms Lorraine Newman

NEWMAN, Paul; s of Christopher William Newman (d 2002), and Nesta, *née* Morgan (d 1997); *b* 5 March 1958, Wales; *Educ* Clare Coll Cambridge (MA), City Univ London (Dip), Cncl of Legal Educn London; *m* 17 Oct 1987, Veronica, *née* Grant; 2 s (David b 18 Jan 1993, Jonathan b 25 Dec 2000); *Career* called to the Bar Gray's Inn 1982 (pupil master); barr specialising in construction law, property/chancery, mediation and arbitration; barr in private practice Manchester 1986–88, with slrs practice Cardiff 1990–2006, resumed practice as barr London and Bristol 2006–; memb: Assoc of Wales and Border Counties Mediators, Assoc of SW Mediators, Soc of Construction Law, Adjudication Soc; memb: Radnorshire Soc, Honourable Soc of Cymmrodorion; highly commended Hudson Prize for Construction Law 1997; accredited adjudicator and mediator, TECBAR listed arbitrator, mediator and adjudicator; FCIArb 1999 (sits as arbitrator, chm Wales Branch 2015–); author, co-author and contrib to numerous titles on construction law and dispute resolution; regular contrib: Slrs Jl, Legal Executive, Construction Law, Tottel's Construction Newsletter; *Recreations* outdoors, family, reading, theatre, travel, other languages: French, German and Spanish; *Style*— Paul Newman, Esq; ✉ 77 Roath Court Road, Cardiff CF24 3SF; 3 PB Barristers, 3 Paper Buildings, Temple, London EC4Y 7EU (☎ 020 7583 8055, e-mail paul.newman@3pb.co.uk); Pendragon Chambers, Suite 7, The J Shed, Kings Road, Swansea SA1 8PL (☎ 01792 411188)

NEWMAN, Paul Stephen; s of Gordon Patrick Newman, of Bexhill, E Sussex, and Maureen Winifred, *née* Lee; *b* 16 October 1954; *Educ* Caterham Sch, Univ of Southampton (BA); *m* 3 Sept 1983 (m dis 2006), Rosemary Jane; 1 da (Katy Mary b 8 Sept 1985); *Career* Mirror Gp Newspapers trg scheme 1977–79, sports ed Barnet Press 1979–80, sub ed Daily Mail 1980–81, various posts on sports desk culminating in asst sports ed The Times 1981–90; The Independent: dep sports ed 1990–91, sports ed 1991–2004, chief sports feature writer 2004–, tennis corr 2006–; former chm Crystal Palace Supporters' Tst and Crystal Palace Youth Tst; *Recreations* tennis, Crystal Palace FC, France; *Style*— Paul Newman, Esq; ✉ Sports Desk, The Independent, 2 Derry Street, London W8 5HF (e-mail p.newman@independent.co.uk)

NEWMAN TURNER, Roger Geoffrey; s of Frank Newman Turner (d 1964), of Letchworth, Herts, and Lorna Mary, *née* Clarke (d 1976); *b* 29 April 1940; *Educ* Sidcot Sch, Br Coll of Naturopathy and Osteopathy (Naturopathic Dip, Dip Osteopathy), Br Coll of Acupuncture (Licentiate Dip Acupuncture, BAc); *m* 1966, Birgid, da of Carl Rath, of Stuttgart; 1 da (Nicole b 1966), 1 s (Julian b 1968); *Career* naturopath, osteopath and acupuncturist in private practice 1963–2016; sec Res Soc for Natural Therapeutics 1966–75, ed Br Jl of Acupuncture 1982–93, pres Br Acupuncture Assoc 1990–92, chm Res Cncl for Complementary Med 1993–97 (tstee 1983–2010); memb Register of Naturopaths, memb Gen Osteopathic Cncl; fell Br Acupuncture Cncl, fell Br Naturopathic Assoc; *Books* incl: First Aid Nature's Way (1969), Diets to Help Hay Fever and Asthma (1970), Diets to Help Heart Disorders (1971), Diets to Help Control Cholesterol (1978), Naturopathic Medicine (1984, 2 edn 2000), Self Help for Angina (1987), Hay Fever Handbook (1988), Banish Back Pain (1989); *Recreations* acting, singing, theatre, opera, cricket; *Style*— Roger Newman Turner, Esq; ✉ 111 Norton Way South, Letchworth, Hertfordshire SG6 1NY (☎ 01462 684232, website www.naturomed.co.uk)

NEWRY AND MORNE, Viscount; Robert Francis John; s and h of 6 Earl of Kilmorey, PC, *qv*; *b* 30 May 1966; *Educ* Eton, Lady Margaret Hall Oxford, Imperial Coll London (MBA); *m* 13 April 1991, Laura Mary, o da of Michael Tregaskis, of Cosham, Hants; 1 da (Hon Julia Helen Mary b 11 March 1997), 1 s (Hon Thomas Francis Michael b 25 Sept 1998); *Career* prodn controller Bissell 1988–89, sales mangr Lewmar Marine 1990–92, business devpt mangr Inchcape Pacific 1994–97; dir Inchcape NRG 1997–99, dir ops Gilman Office Automation 1999–2001; dir: Morne Consultancy 2000–02, Network Programs Europe 2001–02, NewField IT Ltd 2003–13, md Arctic Shores Ltd 2013–; assoc dir Ricoh UK Ltd 2001–03, non-exec dir Purpose Software Ltd 2014–; Freeman City of London 2007, memb Worshipful Co of Info Technologists 2007; *Style*— Viscount Newry and Morne

NEWSON, Marc Andrew; CBE (2012); s of Paul Newson, and Carol Conomos, *née* Rolfe; *b* 20 October 1963, Sydney, Australia; *m* 5 July 2008, Charlotte, *née* Stockdale; 2 da (Imogen b 10 Aug 2007, Lucienne b 4 March 2011); *Career* designer; adjunct prof in design Hong Kong Poly Univ 2007, adjunct prof in design Sydney Coll of the Arts 2007; Design Miami Designer of the Year Award 2006, London Design Medal London Design Festival 2008, Raymond Loewy Fndn Lucky Strike Designer Award 2011; hon doctorate Sydney Coll of the Arts; RDI 2006; *Museum Collections* Art Gallery of South Australia Adelaide, Nat Gallery of Victoria Melbourne, (Powerhouse Museum Sydney, Fondation Cartier pour l'art contemporain Paris, Fond Nat d'Art Contemporain Puteaux, Musée des Arts Décoratifs Paris, Musée Nat d'Art Moderne Centre Pompidou Paris, Museum für Angewandte Kunst Museum of Applied Arts Frankfurt, MAKK Museum für Angewandte Kunst Museum of Applied Arts Cologne, Museum fur Kunst und Gewerb Hamburg, Vitra Design Museum Weil am Rhein, Israel Museum Jerusalem, Museum do Design e da Moda Lisbon, Museum für Gestaltung Zürich), Design Museum London, Manchester City Gallery, V&A Museum, Carnegie Museum Pittsburgh, Cooper-Hewitt Nat Design Museum NY, High Museum of Art Atlanta, Indianapolis Museum of Art, Museum of Modern Art NY, San Francisco Museum of Modern Art; *Solo Exhibitions* incl: Kelvin40 (Fondation Cartier pour l'art contemporain Paris) 2004, Groninger Museum Netherlands 2004, Design Museum London 2004–05, Gagosian Gallery NY 2004–05, 2008 and 2010, Philadelphia Museum of Art 2013–14; *Group Exhibitions* incl: Design en Stock: collection fonds national d'art contemporain (Palais de la Porte dorée Paris) 2004, Big Band: destruction et création dans l'art du XXème siècle (Centre Pompidou Paris) 2005, Collection of the Fondation Cartier pour l'art contemporain (Museum of Contemporary Art Tokyo) 2006, Depuis la Dernière Fois (Musée Art Moderne Saint-Etienne and Musée des Arts Décoratifs Paris) 2006, Déjà Vu (FRAC Nord-Pas de Calais Lens) 2007, Avant-Après la conscience du temps (Cité de l'artichecture et du patrimoine Paris) 2007, Design Contre Design 2 Siècles de Création (Galerie Nationale du Grand Palais Paris) 2007–08, La Galerie des Galeries Aujourd'hui plus qu'hier et moins de demain (Galeries Lafayette Paris) 2009, UFO Blurring the Boundaries between Art & Design (Dusseldorf) 2009, Studio Berg Milan 2009, Design Real (Serpentine Gallery) 2009; *Recreations* classic cars; *Clubs* George, Groucho; *Style*— Marc Newson, Esq, CBE; ✉ Marc Newson Ltd, 7 Howick Place, London SW1P 1BB (☎ 020 7932 0990, e-mail pod@marc-newson.com, website www.marc-newson.com)

NEWSON, Zoe; da of Ricky Newson, of East Bergholt, Suffolk, and Helen Anne, *née* Peck; *b* 24 March 1992, Ipswich, Suffolk; *Educ* East Bergholt High; *Career* Paralympic powerlifter; achievements incl: World Jr Champion 2010, Gold medal Powerlifting British Championships 2011 (jr European record), Bronze medal (-40kg) Paralympic Games 2012; *Style*— Miss Zoe Newson; ✉ Twitter @zoenewson92

NEWSON-SMITH, Sir Peter Frank Graham; 3 Bt (UK 1944), of Totteridge, Co Hertford; s of Sir John Kenneth Newson-Smith, 2 Bt (d 1997), and his 1 w, Vera Margaret Greenhouse Allt (d 2001); paternal gf was Lord Mayor of London; maternal gf was Dr Greenhouse Allt, CBE, princ of Trinity Coll of Music London; *b* 8 May 1947; *Educ* Dover Coll, Trinity Coll of Music; *m* 1974, Mary-Ann, da of Cyril C Collins, of Old Woodstock, Oxon, and formerly w of Anthony Owens; 1 s (Oliver Nicholas Peter b 1975), 1 da (Emma Jo b 1977); *Heir* s, Oliver Newson-Smith; *Career* dir of music Clayesmore Preparatory Sch until 2003; hon treas MMA 2002–06, chm Young Musicians of Muscat Adjudication Panel 2002–07; Freeman City of London 1969, Liveryman Worshipful Co of Musicians 1971; *Recreations* gardening, sailing; *Style*— Sir Peter Newson-Smith, Bt; ☎ 01258 820652, e-mail peternewson@gmail.com

NEWTH, Jonathan Gildon; s of Terence Conrad Newth (d 1994), of Appledore, Devon, and Winifred Gertrude Mary, *née* Lack (d 1991); *b* 6 March 1939; *Educ* Aldenham, Central Sch of Speech and Drama; *m* 1, 1964 (m dis 1978), Joanna, da of Dr S V Brookes; 2 s (Benjamin b 1965, Daniel b 1968); m 2, 1979, Gay, da of R A Wilde; 3 da (Rosalind b 1980, Eliza b 1982, Charlotte b 1988), 1 s (George b 1985); *Career* actor; *Theatre* Open Air Theatre Regents Park: Lysander in A Midsummer Night's Dream 1966, Camillo in A Winters Tale 1988, Quince in A Midsummer Night's Dream 1988; RSC: Bonaventure in 'Tis Pity She's a Whore 1991–92, Capulet in Romeo and Juliet 1991–92, Player King in Hamlet 1992–93, Duke Frederick and Duke Senior in As You Like It 2005–06; other roles incl: The School for Scandal (Theatre Royal Haymarket and USA) 1962–63, The Creeper (St Martins) 1965, Robert in Meeting At Night (Duke of York's) 1972, Richard in Rents (Lyric Hammersmith) 1982, Col Tallboys in Too True to be Good 1986, Fred in The Viewing (Greenwich) 1987, Bill Coles in Other Peoples Money (Lyric) 1990, Leonato in Much Ado About Nothing (Queens) 1993, Mr Bennet in Pride and Prejudice (nat tour) 1995, Vertigo (Theatre Royal Windsor) 1998, Brovik in The Master Builder (English touring theatre) 1999, Don Luis & Francisco in Don Juan (English touring theatre) 1999, Clive in The Circle (Oxford Stage Co) 2000, David Bliss in Hay Fever (Oxford Stage Co) 2001, Tiresias/Shepherd in King Oedipus (Paphos Int Theatre Festival) 2002, Sir Horace Broughton in Office Games (Pleasance Theatre) 2003, Prospero in The Tempest (Theatre Royal Bury St Edmunds and touring) 2004; The Expedition of Humphry Clinker (own adaptation, first performance Bath Literature Festival) 2003, Lord Burleigh in Mary Stuart (Nuffield Theatre) 2004, Duke of Venice in Othello (Shakespeare's Globe) 2007, Cyrus Miles in Swimming with Sharks (Vaudeville Theatre) 2007–08, Don Alejandro in Zorro (Garrick Theatre) 2008, Robert in Many Moons (Theatre 503), Chancellor in The Spire (Salisbury Playhouse) 2012; *Television* incl: Lord Rochford in The Six Wives of Henry VIII 1968, Capt Blamey in Poldark 1972, Brig Jefferson in Tenko 1984, Josh in Fainthearted Feminist 1984, Boustead in Voyage Around My Father 1984, Russell in After Henry 1987–92, Matthew Pocket in Great Expectations 1988, Dr Eliot in Casualty 1996, Geoffrey in The Lost Art of Christopher Jefferies 2014; *Radio* incl: Green Mansions and The Siege of Krishnapur (Book At Bedtime); *Film* incl: Far from the Madding Crowd, Yellow Dog, Pope John Paul II, North Sea Hi-Jack, Accounts, Judge in Incognito, A Secret Audience, The Affair of the Necklace; *Style*— Jonathan Newth, Esq; ✉ c/o Caroline Dawson Associates, 125 Gloucester Road, London SW7 4TE (☎ 020 7373 3323, fax 020 7373 1110)

NEWTON, Air Vice Marshal Barry Hamilton; CB (1988), CVO (2002), OBE (1975); s of Bernard Hamilton Newton, FCA, and Dorothy Mary, *née* Thomas; *b* 1 April 1932; *Educ* Highgate; *m* 1959, Lavinia, da of Col John James Aitken, CMG, DSO, OBE; 1 s (Charles), 1 da (Melanie); *Career* RAF Coll Cranwell 1951, No. 109 Sqdn (target marking) 1954, Flt Cdr No. 76 Sqdn (nuclear weapon trials) Australia and Christmas Island 1955–58, flying instructor Cranwell 1959, Sqdn Cdr No. 6 Flying Training School RAF Acklington 1961, PSO to C-in-C RAF Germany 1966–69, OC Ops Wing RAF Cottesmore 1969, Defence Policy Staff 1972, Directing Staff NDC 1974; Cabinet Office 1975, Defence Policy staff 1978, Air Cdre Flying Trg 1982, sr RAF memb RCDS 1983–86, Cmdt JSDC 1986–88, dir Staff (Forward Plans) RCDS 1988–89; ADC to HM The Queen 1982–83, Gentleman Usher to HM The Queen 1989–2002, Extra Gentleman Usher 2002–; vice-chm Cncl TAVRA 1989–99, Hon Air Cdre 606 (Chiltern) Sqdn RAuxAF 1997–2007, Hon Inspr-Gen RAuxAF 2000–09, pres UK Reserve Forces Assoc 2005–13; Freeman City of London 2002, Hon Freeman Worshipful Co of Lightmongers 2002, Liveryman Hon Co of Air Pilots 2007; *Publications* Monument to Courage (2012); *Recreations* country pursuits, military history; *Clubs* RAF; *Style*— Air Vice Marshal B H Newton, CB, CVO, OBE; ✉ c/o National Westminster Bank plc, 48 Blue Boar Row, Salisbury, Wiltshire SP1 1DF

NEWTON, Prof Ian; OBE (1999); s of Haydn Edwin Newton (d 1980), of Chesterfield, Derbys, and Nellie, *née* Stubbs (d 1986); *b* 17 January 1940, Chesterfield, Derbyshire; *Educ* Chesterfield Boys' GS, Univ of Bristol (BSc), Univ of Oxford (DPhil, DSc); *m* 21 July 1962, Halina Teresa, da of Edward Bialkowski; 2 s (Michael Peter b 1965, Robert Edward b 1967), 1 da (Diana Catherine b 1969); *Career* postdoctoral research Univ of Oxford 1964–67; Nature Conservancy Edinburgh: research on waterfowl populations 1967–71, research on birds of prey 1971–79; Inst of Terrestrial Ecology: head of Pollution Research Unit 1979–84, special merit post grade 5 1992– (grade 6 1984–92); visiting prof in ornithology Univ of Oxford 1994–; memb Bd Peregrine Fund US 1989– (chm Bd 2005–08), vice-pres RSPB 2009–, vice-pres Hawk & Owl Tst 2014–; Union Medal Br Ornithologists Union 1988, Gold Medal Br Ecological Soc 1989, Medal RSPB 1991, President's Award Raptor Research Fndn 1993, Marsh Award in Conservation Biology Zoological Soc 1995, Elliott Cowes Award American Ornithologists Union 1995, Godman-Salvin Medal Br Ornithologists Union 2010; Hon DSc Univ of Sheffield 2001; memb: Br Ecological Soc (pres 1994–95), Br Ornithologists' Union 1984 (vice-pres 1989–93, pres 1999–2003), Br Tst for Ornithology (chm Cncl 2008–13); hon fell American Ornithologists Union, memb RSPB (chm Conservation Ctee 1997–2003, chm Cncl 2003–08); hon memb: Br Ecological Soc 1999, Sociedad Española de Ornithogia 2004; FRS 1993, FRSE 1994; *Books* Finches (1972), Population Ecology of Raptors (1979), The Sparrowhawk (1986), Lifetime Reproduction in Birds (ed, 1989), Population Limitation in Birds (1998), The Speciation and Biogeography of Birds (2003), The Migration Ecology of Birds (2008), Bird Migration (2010), Bird Populations (2013, Marsh Award for Best Ecology Year Br Ecological Soc 2014); *Recreations* walking, travel, fruit growing; *Style*— Prof Ian Newton, OBE, FRS, FRSE; ✉ Centre for Ecology and Hydrology, MacLean Building, Benson Lane, Crownmarsh Gifford, Wallingford, Oxfordshire OX10 8BB (e-mail ine@ceh.ac.uk)

NEWTON, Mark Robert; s of Robert William Banner Newton (d 1982), and Cicely Kathleen, *née* Radmall (d 1989); *b* 2 June 1954, Northampton; *Educ* Eton, RAC Cirencester; *m* 12 May 1979, Diana Sarah, da of Maj Sir Robert David Black, 3 Bt, of Goring-on-Thames, Oxon; 2 s (William David Rupert b 7 Dec 1989, James Robert George b 3 Nov 1993); *Career* chartered surveyor; ptnr Fisher German 1985–; memb Langtons Ward Harborough DC 1995–2003; chm Midlands Branch Royal Forestry Soc 1994–95; chm Leics and Rutland Branch Art Fund 2000–; memb: Game Conservancy (chm Leics Branch Game Conservancy Tst 1995–97), CLA (chm Leics and Rutland Branch 2004–07), Historic House Assoc; tstee Henry Smiths Charity 1999–; High Sheriff Leics 2006–07; FRICS 1986; *Recreations* fishing, shooting, stalking; *Clubs* Old Etonian Angling (chm 2008–); *Style*— Mark Newton, Esq, FRICS; ✉ The Old Rectory, Church Langton, Leicestershire LE16 7SX (☎ 01858 545600); Fisher German, 40 High Street, Market Harborough, Leicestershire LE16 7NX (☎ 01858 411215, fax 01858 410207, mobile 07860 514474, e-mail mark.robert.newton@outlook.com, website www.fishergerman.co.uk)

NEWTON, (John) Nigel; s of Peter Leigh Newton, and Anne St Aubyn Newton; *b* 16 June 1955, San Francisco; *Educ* Deerfield Acad Mass, Selwyn Coll Cambridge (MA); *m* 1981, Joanna Elizabeth, *née* Hastings-Trew; 1 s, 2 da; *Career* asst sales dir Macmillan 1976–78, sales dir then dep md Sidgwick & Jackson 1978–86, fndr and chief exec Bloomsbury Publishing plc; chm Br Library Tst, pres BookAid Int, chm Charleston Tst, memb Man Booker Prize Advsy Ctee, past chair World Book Day 2006, past memb Publishers Assoc Cncl, memb Visting Ctee Cambridge Univ Library; tstee: Garrick Charitable Tst, Asham Tst, Int Inst for Strategic Studies; *Recreations* walking, travel, tennis; *Clubs* Hurlingham, Garrick; *Style*— Nigel Newton, Esq; ✉ Bloomsbury Publishing plc, 50 Bedford Square, London WC1B 3DP (☎ 020 7631 5600, e-mail nigel.newton@bloomsbury.com)

NEWTON, Dr Rodney Stephen; s of Amos Bernard Newton (d 1981), of Birmingham, and Winifred Nellie, *née* York (d 1999); *b* 31 July 1945, Birmingham; *Educ* King's Heath HS Birmingham, Lordwood Boys' Sch Birmingham, Birmingham Sch of Music, Univ of Salford (MA, PhD); *m* 19 Sept 1970 (m dis 1999), Jennifer Kathleen, da of Denis Williams, of Halesowen, Worcs; 2 s (Matthew b 15 Sept 1977, Christopher b 24 April 1980); *Career* orchestral timpanist, percussionist, composer, arranger, conductor, music publisher, lectr and writer 1967–; BBC trg orchestra 1967–70, ENO orchestra 1974–85, promotion mangr United Music Publishers 1979–82, music conslt London Film Sch 1988–2010, princ lectr in film music composition London Coll of Music 1997–2000 (lectr in composition and orchestration 1995–97), visiting lectr in film music Royal Acad of Music 1995–98; co-ordinator of light music Williams Fairey Band 1997–2004 (composer-in-residence 2004–05), music assoc Cory Band 2004–, arranger-in-residence Band of the Coldstream Gds 2006–12; features ed British Bandsman magazine 2001–10; gen ed Prima Vista Musikk 2006–; compositions in: 14 symphonies, 5 string quartets, flute concerto, euphonium concerto, tuba concerto, music for brass band, wind band, chamber and vocal works; film and TV scores incl: The Pyrates, The Watch House (BBC TV), Lucinda Lambton's A-Z of Britain (BBC TV), Theatre of Paint (BEU Prodns), Change at Clapham Junction (Thames TV); commercial recordings incl: Variations for Percussion, Four Spanish Impressions, Capriccio, Heroes and Warriors, Five Greek Sketches, Seascapes, Phantasm, Prince Bishops, The Defenders, Dick Turpin's Ride to York, The King of Elfland's Daughter, Echoes of the East, Twm Sion Cati; memb: Musicians' Union, Br Acad of Composers, Songwriters and Authors, Knights of St Columba, Concert Artistes' Assoc; hon memb Birmingham Conservatoire 1996, hon assoc London Film Sch 2010; FRSA 2008; *Recreations* reading, cinema, eating out, charity work; *Clubs* CAA; *Style*— Dr Rodney S Newton; ✉ 169 Shurland Avenue, East Barnet, Hertfordshire EN4 8DF (e-mail rs.newton007@btinternet.com); c/o London Film School, 24 Shelton Street, London WC2H 9HP (fax 020 7497 3718, e-mail film.school@lfs.org.uk)

NEWTON, Stewart Worth; *b* 31 October 1941; *m* Jannion (d 2006); 3 da (Catherine, Antonia, Lucy); *Career* investment mgmnt; formerly with: Touche Ross Chartered Accountants, W Greenwell stockbrokers, Ivory & Sime plc; fndr Newton Investment Management, ret

2002; chm The Real Return Holding Co Ltd 2003–; non-exec dir HSBC Holdings plc 2002–; memb: Investment Ctee Wellcome Tst, Advsy Bd East Asia Inst Univ of Cambridge, Cambridge Investment Bd 2006, Cncl Imperial Coll 2007–; advsr Royal Marsen Hosp 2008–; FCA; *Style*— Stewart Newton, Esq

NEWTON, Thandiwe (Thandie); da of Nick Newton, and Nyasha Newton; *b* 6 November 1972, London; *Educ* Downing Coll Cambridge; *m* 1998, Ol Parker; 2 da (Ripley b 2000, Nico b 2004), 1 s (Booker Jombe b 2014); *Career* actress; *Film* incl: Interview with the Vampire 1994, Beloved 1998, Mission: Impossible II 2000, The Chronicles of Riddick 2004, Crash 2004 (Best Actress in a Supporting Role BAFTA, Br Supporting Actress of the Year London Film Critics Circle Award), The Pursuit of Happyness 2006, Run Fatboy Run 2007, RocknRolla 2008, W 2008, 2012 2009, Huge 2010, Vanishing on 7th Street 2010, For Colored Girls 2010, Retreat 2011, The Prophet 2011, Good Deeds 2012; *Television* incl ER 2003–05 and 2009; *Style*— Ms Thandie Newton; ✉ c/o Independent Talent Group, 40 Whitfield Street, London W1T 2RH

NEWTON DUNN, William Francis (Bill); s of Lt-Col Owen Frank Newton Dunn, OBE (d 1995), and Barbara Mary, *née* Brooke (d 1995); *b* 3 October 1941; *Educ* Marlborough, Gonville & Caius Cambridge (MA), INSEAD Fontainebleau (MBA); *m* 17 Oct 1970, Anna Terez Arki; 1 s (Thomas b 1973), 1 da (Daisy b 1976); *Career* MEP: (Cons) Lincolnshire 1979–94, (Cons) E Midlands 1999–2000, (Lib Dem) E Midlands 2000–14; European Parliament Quaestor 2009–12; chm and jt ldr Cons MEPs 1993–94 (dep ldr 1991–93); memb: Devpt Ctee, Organised Crime Ctee; formerly with Fisons Fertilisers; *Books* Why The Public Shoud Be Worried By The EEC's Democratic Deficit (1986), Greater in Europe (1986), Big Wing (1992), The Man Who Was John Bull (1996), The Devil Knew Not (2000), Europe Needs an FBI (2004), Memories of the First European Parliament (2008), What Do MEPs Do? (2015); *Style*— Bill Newton Dunn, Esq; ☎ 07939 250473

NEYROUD, Peter William; CBE (2011), QPM (2004); s of John Arthur Lucien Neyroud, of Winchester, Hants, and Penelope Mary Anne, *née* Edwards; *b* 12 August 1959; *Educ* Winchester, Oriel Coll Oxford (MA), Univ of Portsmouth (MSc), Wolfson Coll Cambridge (Dip Applied Criminology); *m* 16 Aug 1986, Sarah, *née* Longman; 2 s, 2 da; *Career* Police Constable rising to Detective Supt then dir of intelligence Hampshire Constabulary 1980–97; West Mercia Constabulary: Asst Chief Constable (Support) 1998–2000, Asst Chief Constable (Territorial Policing) 2000, Dep Chief Constable 2000–02; Chief Constable Thames Valley Police 2002–05, chief exec Nat Policing Improvement Agency 2006–; visiting fell Nuffield Coll Oxford 2007–, Sir Leon Radzinowicz visiting fell in criminology Univ of Cambridge 2008; ACPO: memb 1998, portfolio holder Police Use of Firearms 2000–02, lead on Criminal Justice 2000–04, vice-pres 2004–06, former vice-chm Human Rights Ctee; memb: Cncl Justice 1997–2006, Sentencing Guideline Cncl 2004–10; ind reviewer Parole Bd 2006–; Home Office Police Research Award for Multi-Agency Approaches to Racial Harassment 1990, Gary P Hayes Award US Police Executive Research Forum 2004; FRSA 2000; *Publications* Policing, Ethics and Human Rights (2001), Public Participation in Policing (2001), Police Ethics for the 21st Century (in The Handbook of Policing, 2003), Dictionary of Policing (2008); *Recreations* running, writing, gardening and reading; *Style*— Peter Neyroud, Esq, CBE, QPM

NG, Dr Weng Cheong; s of Kam Sooi Ng, and Ng-Sung Ngan-Lui; *b* 18 September 1943; *Educ* Methodist Boys' Sch Penang, Univ of Singapore (MB BS), Royal Coll of Physicians and Surgeons (DPath), Univ of London (DCP), Univ of Mahidol (DTM&H); *m* 25 Sept 1971, Chew Pek Choo, da of Chew Poh Leang; 1 s (Paul b 4 Jan 1979); *Career* MO: Rural Health Trg Sch Jitra Malaysia 1970–71, Inst of Med Res Kuala Lumpur Malaysia 1971–75; registrar Gen Infirmary Salisbury 1978; sr registrar: Southampton and Poole Gen Hosps 1978–80, Pathology Dept Singapore 1981–83; conslt histopathologist Princess Margaret Hosp Swindon 1983–; memb: Assoc of Clinical Pathologists, Br Soc of Clinical Cytology, BMA; MRCPath 1979, FCAP 1982, FRCPath 1991; *Recreations* chess, music, swimming; *Style*— Dr Weng Cheong Ng; ✉ Pathology Department, Princess Margaret Hospital, Okus Road, Swindon, Wiltshire SN1 4JU (☎ 01793 426336)

NIBLETT, His Hon Judge Anthony Ian; s of Albert William Niblett (d 2001), and Jessie Alma, *née* McMickan (d 2016); *b* 11 June 1954; *Educ* Varndean GS Brighton, Univ of Birmingham (LLB), Coll of Law; *m* 12 Oct 1991, Valerie Ann, da of Robert Ranger; 1 da, 1 s; *Career* called to the Bar Inner Temple 1976, in practice SE Circuit 1977–2002, recorder 1998–2002 (asst recorder 1993–98), circuit judge (SE Circuit) 2002–; memb: SE Area Legal Aid Ctee 1988–2002, Professional Conduct Ctee Bar Cncl 1993–97, SE Circuit Ctee 1995–98 and 2000–02; jr Sussex Bar Mess 1986–95, govr Varndean Coll Brighton 1997–2003; *Recreations* travel, history, gardening; *Style*— His Hon Judge Niblett; ✉ The Law Courts, High Street, Lewes, East Sussex BN7 1YB

NIBLETT, Dr Robin; CMG; *Educ* New Coll Oxford (BA, MPhil, DPhil); *Career* Center for Strategic and International Studies (CSIS): research assoc Political-Military Studies Program Washington 1988–1992, European rep London 1992–97, dir then sr vice-pres Strategic Planning Washington 1997–2001, exec vice-pres Washington 2001–06, dir Europe Program and Initiative for a Renewed Transatlantic Partnership 2004–06; dir Chatham House 2007–; non-exec dir Fidelity European Values Investment Tst, chm Global Agenda Cncl on Europe World Economic Forum 2012–13, chair Br Acad Steering Ctee Languages for Security Project 2013, chm Experts Gp NATO Summit 2014, special advsr Foreign Affrs Ctee House of Commons 2015–; Bene Merito Medal Polish Govt 2012; *Publications* Rethinking European Order (contrib and co-ed, 2001), America and a Changed World: A Question of Leadership (contrib and ed, 2010), Britain, Europe and the World: Rethinking the UK's Circle of Influence (2015); *Style*— Dr Robin Niblett, CMG; ✉ The Royal Institute of International Affairs, Chatham House, 10 St James's Square, London SW1Y 4LE

NICE, Prof Sir Geoffrey; kt (2007), QC (1990); s of William Charles Nice (d 1992), and Mahala Anne, *née* Tarryer (d 1982); *b* 21 October 1945; *Educ* St Dunstan's Coll Catford, Keble Coll Oxford; *m* 1974, Philippa, da of Kemlo Abbot Cronin Gross, OBE; 3 da (Amelia b 1975, Tabitha b 1976, Mahalah b 1980); *Career* barr; recorder Crown Court 1987–; memb Criminal Injuries Compensation Bd 1995–2001; bencher Inner Temple 1996, sr trial attorney Int Criminal Tbnl for the former Yugoslavia 1998–2001, princ trial attorney Milosevic Trial 2002–06, ad hoc cmmr Royal Court of Jersey 2005–07; Gresham prof of law 2012–, professorial research fell Univ of Buckingham 2014–; memb: Bd Indict 2001–04, Advsy Bd Impunity Watch 2006–, Advsy Bd Inst of Strategic Dialogue Weidenfeld Scholars 2011–; dep chm Bar Standards Bd 2009–12; Parly candidate (SDP/Lib Alliance) Dover 1983 and 1987; tstee Keyboard Tst; Hon LLD Univ of Kent at Canterbury 2005; *Books* The United Nations Security Council in the Age of Human Rights (contrib, 2014); *Recreations* music, skiing, tennis; *Clubs* Reform; *Style*— Professor Sir Geoffrey Nice, QC; ✉ Gresham College, Barnard's Inn Hall, Holborn, London EC1N 2HH

NICHOL, David Brett; s of Philip George Nichol (d 1974), of Gullane, E Lothian, and Kathleen, *née* Brett (d 2000); *b* 20 April 1945; *Educ* Sedbergh; *m* 22 July 1977, Judith Mary, da of Godfrey Arthur Parker (d 1966), of Godalming, Surrey; 4 da (Alexandra b 1979, Tessa b 1981, Leonie b 1982, Flora b 1986); *Career* CA; Deloitte & Co 1962–68, County Bank London 1968–70, Martin Corpn Australia 1970–71, W I Carr Hong Kong 1971–72, dir Ivory & Sime plc 1972–92, md Ivory & Sime Asia Ltd 1989–91, ptnr Rossie House Investment Management 1992–2010; chm Pacific Assets Trust plc 2004–15 (non-exec dir 1985); tstee Royal Botanic Gdns Edinburgh 1986–89; FCA; *Recreations* shooting, golf, gardening; *Clubs* New (Edinburgh), R&A, Hon Co of Edinburgh Golfers, Shek-o (Hong Kong); *Style*— David Nichol, Esq; ✉ Rossie, Forgandenny, Perthshire PH2 9EH (☎ 01738 813314, e-mail davidnichol@rossiehouse.co.uk)

NICHOL, Sir Duncan Kirkbride; kt (1993), CBE (1989); s of James Nichol (d 1989), and Mabel Nichol (d 1984); *b* 30 May 1941; *Educ* Bradford GS, Univ of St Andrews (MA); *m* 18 March 1972, Elizabeth Elliott Mitchell, da of Herbert Wilkinson (d 1967), of Blackpool; 1 s (Andrew b 1973), 1 da (Rachael b 1977); *Career* hosp sec Manchester Royal Infirmary 1969–73, dep gp sec and acting gp sec Univ Hosp Mgmnt Ctee of S Manchester 1973–74, dist admin S Manchester Dist 1974–77, area admin Salford DHA 1977–81, regnl gen mangr Mersey RHA 1984–89 (regnl admin 1981–84), ceo NHS Mgmnt Exec 1989–94; prof and dir Health Servs Mgmnt Unit Victoria Univ of Manchester 1995–98; chm: Clinical Pathology Accreditation 2000–09, Primary Insurance Gp 2001–07, HM Courts Serv for England and Wales 2008–, Skills for Justice 2010–, Synergyhealth 2012–, Countess of Chester Hosp Fndn Tst 2012–; non-exec dir: BUPA 1994–2001, Correctional Services Strategy Bd 2000–06, Synergy Healthcare 2002–, Deltex Medical 2004–, Christie Hosp Fndn Tst 2008–12, UK Accreditation Service 2009–; cmmr for judicial appts 2001–06, chm Parole Bd for Eng and Wales 2004–08, chm QC Selection Panel 2005–08; memb Central Health Servs Cncl 1980–81, pres IMSM 1984–85, chm Kings Fund Educn Ctee 1991–94, govr Henley Mgmnt Coll 1993–98, chm Acad for Healthcare Science 2012–; Hon DLitt Univ of Salford 1991; CIMgt 1988, FHSM 1990; *Recreations* golf, walking; *Clubs* Athenaeum; *Style*— Sir Duncan Nichol, CBE; ✉ 1 Pipers Close, Heswell, Wirral, Merseyside CH60 9LJ (☎ 0151 342 2699)

NICHOL, Ian James; s of Thomas Nichol (d 1989), and Joan Lena May, *née* Lambourne (d 2005); *b* 20 December 1954, Kingston upon Thames, Surrey; *Educ* Tiffin Boys Sch Kingston upon Thames, Solihull Sch, Queens' Coll Cambridge (scholar, MA, Penny White prize); *m* 16 March 1996, Valerie Mary, *née* Piper; *Career* various accountancy and tax appts 1977–88, ptnr Touche Ross & Co 1988–92, ptnr and head of profit-related pay practice PricewaterhouseCoopers (formerly Coopers & Lybrand) 1992–2001, princ Ian Nichol Training 2001–; cmmr Criminal Cases Review Cmmn 2003–13, cmmr Press Complaints Cmmn 2006–12 (dep chm 2010–12); tstee and memb Cncl Assoc of Taxation Technicians 2002–04; govr Lawrence Sheriff Sch Rugby 2012–; memb: ICAEW 1980, Chartered Inst of Taxation 1981; *Publications* Employment Tax Essentials (contributing ed, 2001–03), Tax Planning for Family and Owner-Managed Companies (co-author, 2002); *Recreations* food, wine and spirits, keeping slightly fit, public speaking; *Style*— Ian Nichol, Esq; ✉ mobile 07971 862180, e-mail ijnichol@btinternet.com

NICHOLAS, HE Garvin Edward Timothy; s of Edward Nicholas, and Simona Nicholas; *b* 24 January 1967, Trinidad; *Educ* Trinity Coll Moka Maraval Trinidad, Oxford Brookes Univ (LLB), City Univ Inns of Court Sch of Law London (Postgrad Dip); *m* Dr Nicola Alcala; 1 s (Alexei b 30 Aug 1996); *Career* Trinidadian diplomat; local govt cncllr Diego Martin Regnl Corp 1992–96 (also chm Fin and Gen Purposes Ctee), legal counsel to Ldr of the Oppn Trinidad and Tobago 2003, temp senator Upper House of Parliament Trinidad and Tobago 2003–04, political ldr Movement for Nat Devpt 2007–10, press sec Office of the PM of the Repub of Trinidad and Tobago 2010, high cmmr to UK 2010–14 caretaker for the constituency of St Joseph Trinidad and Tobago 2014–15, AG Trinidad and Tobago 2015–; *Recreations* scuba diving, golf, travel, football; *Clubs* Rotary Club of Port of Spain West (past pres, Paul Harris fell); *Style*— Mr Garvin Nicholas; ✉ 13 Hillsdale, St Lucien Road, Petit Valley, Trinidad and Tobago (e-mail galnic@yahoo.com)

NICHOLL, Elizabeth (Liz); CBE (2015, OBE 2006, MBE 2000); *née* Daley; *b* 13 August 1952, Barry, S Wales; *m* 26 Jan 1980, Andrew Nicholl; 1 da (Lucy Elizabeth b 17 Nov 1982), 1 s (Simon Thomas b 15 May 1984); *Career* former international netball player, gen sec Women's Inter-University Athletic Bd 1977–79, chief exec England Netball 1980–82 and 1986–99; UK Sport: dir of elite sport until 1999–2009, chief operating offr 2009–10, chief exec 2010–; vice-chair Central Cncl of Physical Recreation (renamed Sport and Recreation Alliance) 1997–99, vice-chair Commonwealth Games England 1998–2004; *Books* Heathfield House HS Cardiff, Univ of Nottingham (BSc), Univ of Leicester (PGCE), Loughborough Univ (MSc); *Recreations* gardening, sailing, walking, running, sport in general; *Style*— Mrs Liz Nicholl, CBE; ✉ UK Sport, 21 Bloomsbury Street, London WC1B 3HF (☎ 020 7211 5101, e-mail liz.nicholl@uksport.gov.uk, website www.uksport.gov.uk)

N

NICHOLLS, Dr Christine Stephanie; da of Christopher James Metcalfe (d 1986), of Mombasa, Kenya, and Olive, *née* Kennedy (d 1982); *b* 23 January 1943; *Educ* Kenya HS, Lady Margaret Hall Oxford (MA), St Antony's Coll Oxford (DPhil); *m* 12 March 1966, Anthony James Nicholls, s of Ernest Alfred Nicholls (d 1981), of Carshalton, Surrey; 1 s (Alexander b 1970), 2 da (Caroline b 1972, Isabel b 1974); *Career* Henry Charles Chapman res fell Inst of Cwlth Studies Univ of London 1968–69, freelance writer BBC 1970–74, ed Dictionary of National Biography 1989–95 (asst ed 1977–89); monthly blog on historical topics for Old Africa magazine; *Books* The Swahili Coast (1971), Cataract (with Philip Awdry, 1985), Dictionary of National Biography 1961–70, 1971–80, 1981–85 and 1985–90, Power – A Political History of the Twentieth Century (1990), Missing Persons (1993), Hutchinson Encyclopaedia of Biography (ed, 1996), David Livingstone (1998), A History of St Antony's College Oxford 1950–2000 (2000), Elspeth Huxley (2002), Red Strangers: The White Tribe of Kenya (2005), A Kenya Childhood (2011); *Recreations* reading novels, playing the flute; *Style*— Dr Christine Nicholls; ✉ 27 Davenant Road, Oxford OX2 8BU (☎ 01865 511320, e-mail cs.nicholls@tiscali.co.uk, website www.csnicholls.co.uk)

NICHOLLS, Clive Victor; QC (1982); s of Alfred Charles Victor Nicholls, and Lilian Mary, *née* May; *b* 29 August 1932; *Educ* Brighton Coll, TCD (MA, LLB), Sidney Sussex Coll Cambridge (BA, LLM); *m* 23 July 1960, Alison Virginia, da of late Leonard Arthur Oliver; 3 s (Jeremy Oliver b 1962, James Colin Oliver b 1967, John Patrick Oliver b 1969), 3 da (Jacqueline Alison b 1963, Judi Victoria b 1965, Jill Caroline b 1965); *Career* called to the Bar Gray's Inn 1957 (bencher 1989); recorder of the Crown Court 1984–98, head of chambers 1994–2010; barr Supreme Court of the Australian Capital Territory 1991; tstee and former chm Bob Champion Cancer Tst; patron: Multiple Birth Assoc, Fair Trials Int; The Law of Extradition and Mutual Assistance (co-author, 2002, 3 edn 2013); *Recreations* sailing, fly fishing; *Clubs* Garrick, Royal Western Yacht Club of England; *Style*— Clive Nicholls, Esq, QC; ✉ 3 Raymond Buildings, Gray's Inn, London WC1R 5BH (☎ 020 7400 6400, fax 020 7400 6464)

NICHOLLS, Colin Alfred Arthur; QC (1981); s of Alfred Charles Victor Nicholls (d 1987), and Lilian Mary, *née* May (d 1990); *b* 29 August 1932; *Educ* Brighton Coll, Univ of Dublin (MA, LLB); *m* 23 Oct 1976, Clarissa Allison Spenlove, da of Clive Dixon (d 1976); 2 s (Benjamin Clive b 30 Aug 1977, Jonathan Charles b 6 Jan 1979); *Career* called to the Bar Gray's Inn (Albion Richardson Award) 1957 (bencher 1989); recorder of the Crown Ct 1983–99; Cwlth Lawyers' Assoc: vice-pres 1985–96, hon treas 1997–2003, hon sec 1999–2003, pres 2003–05, hon life pres 2007; chm: Cwlth Working Gp on Cybercrime 2012, Cwlth Working Gp on the Review of the Cwlth Computer and Computer Related Crime Model Law 2016; memb Cwlth Expert Gp on the Rule of Law 2011; tstee: Cwlth Human Rights Initiative 1998–2007, Cwlth Law Conf Fndn 2003–07; patron Multiple Births Fndn, govr Fedn of Br Artists 2001–07; hon memb Historical Soc TCD 1958– (auditor 1956); fell Soc of Advanced Legal Studies; *Publications* Corruption and the Misuse of Public Office (jtly, 2006, 3 edn 2016); *Recreations* painting (exhibitor RHA, ROI, NEAC); *Clubs* Garrick; *Style*— Colin Nicholls, Esq, QC; ✉ 3 Raymond Buildings, Gray's Inn, London WC1R 5BH (☎ 020 7400 6400, fax 020 7400 6464)

NICHOLLS, David Alan; *b* 30 November 1966, Eastleigh, Hants; *Educ* Toynbee Comp Sch, Barton Peveril Sixth Form Coll, Univ of Bristol (BA), American Musical and Dramatic Acad NY; *Partner* Hannah; 2 c; *Career* author and screenwriter; early career as actor (incl appearances at Battersea Arts Centre, W Yorks Playhouse, Birmingham Rep and RNT); *Television* Cold Feet 2000 (Br Acad Television Craft Award for Best New Writer (Fiction)), I Saw You 2000 and 2002, Rescue Me 2002, ShakespeaRe-Told: Much Ado About Nothing (BBC) 2005, Aftersun (BBC) 2006, Tess of the D'Urbervilles (BBC) 2008, The 7.39 (BBC) 2014; *Film* Simpatico 1999, Starter for Ten 2006, And When Did You Last See Your Father? 2007, One Day 2010, Great Expectations 2012, Far from the Madding Crowd 2015; *Theatre* Aftersun (Old Vic) 2005; *Books* Starter For Ten (2003), The Understudy (2005), One Day (2009, Popular Fiction Book of the Year Galaxy Nat Book Award 2010), Us (2014, longlisted Man Booker Prize, longlisted Carnegie Award, Nat Book Award of the Year 2015); *Style*— David Nicholls, Esq; ✉ c/o Jonny Geller, Curtis Brown Group Ltd , Haymarket House, 28–29 Haymarket, London SW1 4SP

NICHOLLS, David Alan; CB (1989), CMG (1984); s of Thomas Edward Nicholls (d 1971), and Beatrice Winifred Nicholls (d 1992); *Educ* Cheshunt GS, St John's Coll Cambridge (MA); *m* 1955, Margaret; 2 da (Amanda, Camilla); *Career* entered Home Civil Serv 1954; asst sec MOD 1969–75, Cabinet Office 1975–77, under sec MOD 1977–80, asst sec-gen NATO 1980–84, dep under sec MOD 1984–90; defence conslt; visiting fell Magdalene Coll Cambridge 1989–90, sr Pol-Mil assoc Inst for Foreign Policy Analysis 1990–; memb Visiting Ctee Royal Coll of Art 1991–93; hon sr lectr Univ of Birmingham 1992–2000; assoc fell RIIA 1990–92, memb Cncl London C of C and Indust 1994–2005; chm Soc for Italic Handwriting 1985–96; *Recreations* sketching; *Clubs* Nat Lib; *Style*— David Nicholls, Esq, CB, CMG; ✉ c/o HSBC Bank, Church Stretton, Shropshire SY6 6BT

NICHOLLS, David Andrew; s of Gordon Robert Nicholls (d 1973), of Deal, Kent, and Maureen Rachel, *née* Waddon (d 2004); *b* 15 January 1957, Deal, Kent; *Educ* Walmer Secdy Sch Deal, Thanet Tech Coll Broadstairs, Westminster Coll London (City and Guilds); *m* Claire; 4 s (Daniel Gordon Charles b March 1985, Dean Stephen Robert b Oct 1989, Dylan b 2008, Declan b 2011); *Career* chef de partie Waldorf Hotel London 1975–76, successively chef tournant, saucier then gardemanger Dorchester Hotel London 1976–79, chef saucier then sous chef Hotel Intercontinental London 1979–81, chef/dir The Old Lodge Restaurant Limpsfield Surrey 1981–83, head chef Waltons Restaurant London 1983–86; exec chef: Britannia Intercontinental Hotel London 1986–89, Royal Garden Hotel London 1989–92; exec head chef Ritz Hotel London 1992–98, exec chef and dir of food and beverage Mandarin Oriental Hyde Park Hotel 1998–2007, gp dir for food and beverage Mandarin Oriental Hotel Gp 2007–; Chef of the Year Catey Awards 2005; memb: British Div Toques Blance, Guild de Fromagers France; hon memb Chain de Rotisseurs; chm: Académie Culinaire de France Grande Bretagne (Affiliates), Exec Chefs Worldwide Soc (UK Div); chm and fndr Nicholls Spinal Injury Fndn 2005; *Publications* Off Duty (2006); *Recreations* golf, squash, gardening; *Style*— David Nicholls, Esq; ✉ Mandarin Oriental Hotel Group, Kings Court, 2–16 Goodge Street, London W1T 2QA (☎ 020 7908 7838, fax 020 7908 7880, e-mail dnicholl@mohg.com, website www.mandarinoriental.com)

NICHOLLS, Prof (Ralph) John; s of Clifton Wilson Nicholls (d 1991), and Muriel Morten, *née* Heathcote; *b* 20 May 1943, Wilby, Northants; *Educ* Felsted, Gonville & Caius Coll Cambridge (MA), London Hosp Med Sch (scholar), Univ of Cambridge (MB BChir, MChir); *m* 1966, Stella Mary; 4 c (b 1967, 1969, 1972 and 1977); *Career* The London Hosp: lectr in surgery Surgical Unit 1972, sr registrar 1974–76; clinical asst Chirurgische Universitatsklinik Heidelberg (Alexander von Humboldt fell) 1976–77, resident surgical offr St Mark's Hosp 1978, conslt surgn St Mark's Hosp and sr lectr (ICRF) St Bartholomew's Hosp 1978–82, conslt surgn St Thomas' Hosp 1982–93; currently: visiting prof of colorectal surgery Imperial Coll London, emeritus conslt surgn St Mark's Hosp, former civilian advsr in surgery RAF, conslt Policlinico di Monza Italy; past pres Section of Coloproctology RSM, past pres Assoc of Coloproctology of GB and I, pres Euro Assoc of Coloproctology, sec Euro Bd of Coloproctology; past memb Specialist Advsy Ctee in Gen Surgery; ed Colorectal Disease; memb Academie Nationale de Chirugie; hon memb: Br Soc of Gastroenterology, Swiss Soc for Gastroenterology, French Soc of Proctology, Chilean Soc of Surgery, Spanish Soc of Surgery, Assoc Française de Chirurgie, Br Soc of Gastroenterology; Medal Academie Nationale de Chirugie; hon fell: Brasilian Coll of Surgns, American Coll of Surgery, American Soc of Colon and Rectal Surgeons, Br Soc of Gastroenterology, Italian Soc of Colorectal Surgery, American Coll of Surgeons; Hon FRCSEd, Hon FRCSGlas, FRCS (Halett prize), fell Assoc of Polish Surgeons; *Books* Colorectal Disease: An Introduction for Surgeons and Physicians (jt ed, 1981), Coloproctology: Diagnosis and Outpatient Management (with R E Glass, 1985), Restorative Proctocolectomy (ed with N J McC Mortensen and D C C Bartolo, 1993), Colon and Rectal Surgery (ed with R R Dozois, 1997), Corman's Colon & Rectal Surgery 6th Edition (assoc ed, 2012); contrib various book chapters and author of numerous pubns in learned jls; *Recreations* history, languages, walking, music; *Clubs* Athenaeum, St Alban's; *Style*— Prof John Nicholls; ✉ 116 Harley Street, London W1G 7JL (☎ 020 7935 0924, e-mail j.nicholls@thelondonclinic.co.uk)

NICHOLLS, Jonathan Clive; s of David and Jill Nicholls; *b* 27 October 1957; *Educ* Uppingham, Univ of Manchester (BA Economics and Accountancy), Harvard Business Sch (PMD); *Career* auditor Peat Marwick Mitchell & Co 1979–83, chief accountant P S Refson & Co (merchant bank) 1983–85; Abbey National Building Society: mangr Fin Servs 1985–86, commercial mangr Business Devpt 1987–88; dir Corp Fin and Capital Markets Abbey National Treasury Services plc 1988–94, dir and dep chief exec Abbey National Treasury Services plc and dep treas Abbey National plc 1994–96, finance dir Hanson plc 1998–2006 (treas 1996–98), finance dir Old Mutual plc 2006–08; non-exec dir: Man Gp plc 2004–06, Great Portland Estates plc 2009–; ACA 1982, FCT 1989; *Recreations* sailing, skiing, cycling, travel, food and wine, opera; *Style*— Jonathan Nicholls, Esq

NICHOLLS, Mark Patrick; s of Patrick Nicholls, and Patricia, *née* Dickson; *b* 5 May 1949, Gloucester; *Educ* Oundle, Christ's Coll Cambridge; *m* 8 July 1978, Catherine, *née* Betts; 5 c; *Career* admitted slr 1974; Linklaters 1972–76, dir and head corp fin SG Warburg Gp plc 1976–96, chief exec private equity gp Royal Bank of Scotland 1996–2003, dep chm Venture Production plc 2004–09, chm EcoSecurities Gp plc 2005–09, chm West Bromwich Building Soc 2010–, chm Rathbone Bros plc 2010–; non-exec dir: City of London Investment Tst plc 1997–2007, Bovis Homes Gp plc 1997–2007, Portman Building Soc 2002–07, Alexander Forbes Ltd (South Africa) 2004–07, Evolution Gp plc 2006–09, Northern Investors Co plc 2006–, Nationwide Building Soc 2007–09; chm St Mary's Paddington Charitable Tst 2000–08, protector Nat Lottery Fair Share Fund 2003–14; *Recreations* golf, tennis; *Style*— Mark Nicholls, Esq

NICHOLLS, Dr (Jill) Nicola; LVO (2013); da of Alan Keep (d 2009), and Barbara, *née* Chapman (d 1996); *b* 13 February 1958, Epping, Essex; *Educ* Loughton County High, Univ of Bristol (BSc), Univ of Cambridge (PhD); *m* (m dis); 1 s (Henry b 1984), 1 da (Emily b 1987); *Career* research fell Gonville and Caius Coll Cambridge 1982–88, dir Charterhouse Devpt Capital (now Charterhouse Capital Ptnrs LLP) Charterhouse plc 1985–2012; dir BPP Univ Ltd 2008–14; chair Woodland Tst 2010–16; dir Buro Happold Engrs Ltd; *Style*— Dr Nicola Nicholls, LVO; ✉ Buro Happold Engineering Limited, 17 Newman Street, London W1T 1PD

NICHOLLS, Robert Michael (Bob); CBE (1995); s of Herbert Edgar Nicholls (d 1977), and Bennetta L'Estrange, *née* Burges (d 2002); *b* 28 July 1939; *Educ* Hampton Sch, UCW (BA, treas Students' Union, dep ldr expedition to Kurdistan), Univ of Manchester (DSA); *m* 9 Dec 1961, Dr Deirin Deirdre O'Sullivan, da of Dr Frank O'Sullivan (d 1955); 4 s (Kevin Paul b 1965, Clive Ranulf John b 1967, Liam Dougal b 1969, Alec Eoin b 1971); *Career* house govr St Stephen's Hosp Chelsea 1966–68, asst clerk of the govrs St Thomas' Hosp 1968–72, dep gp sec Southampton Univ Hosp Mgmnt Ctee 1972–74, dist admin Southampton and SW Hants Health Dist 1974–77, area admin Newcastle Area HA 1977–81, regnl admin S Western Regnl HA 1981–85, dist gen mangr Southmead Health Dist 1985–88, chief exec Oxford Regnl HA 1988–93, seconded as exec dir London Implementation Gp NHS Mgmnt Exec 1993–96, health mgmnt conslt 1996–2004, chm Nat Clinical Assessment Authy 2003–05, NHS regnl appts cmmr for London 2005–08; health assoc conslt Br Cncl 1997–2005; non-exec dir Nestor Healthcare 1997–2003 (sr non-exec dir 2001–03); fell Inst of Health Serv Mangrs (former memb Cncl, nat pres 1983–84); memb: King's Fund Educn Ctee 1974–79, Health Educn Cncl 1984–87, Calman Ctee on Med Trg 1993, GMC 1996–2005 (chair Preliminary Proceedings Ctee 1999–2003), Clinical Advsy Bd Oxford Univ Med Sch 2001–08, Oxford A Research Ethics Ctee 2015–; chair Gen Pharmaceutical Cncl 2009–14, chair Intensive Care Nat Audit & Research Centre (ICNARC) 2016–; assoc fell Templeton Coll Oxford 1996–2001, visiting prof Bucks New Univ 2014–; FHSM 1993 (AHSM 1965); *Books* Resources in Medicine (contrib, 1970), Working with People (contrib, 1983), Rationing of Health Care in Medicine (contrib, 1993), Doctors in Society (contrib, 2005); *Recreations* cricket, golf, walking, bird watching, opera, jazz; *Clubs* Lensbury, Studley Wood Golf; *Style*— Bob Nicholls, Esq, CBE; ✉ Maple Lodge, 62A Queens Road, Thame OX9 3NQ (☎ 01844 261748, e-mail rmnicholls@btinternet.com)

NICHOLLS, Simon James; s of James Derrick Nicholls (d 1981), and Marcia Ann, *née* Bacon (d 1996); *b* 25 November 1955, Shropshire; *Educ* Bridgnorth GS, Wolverhampton Poly, Coll of Law Chester; *m* 15 May 1982, Juliet, *née* Price; 2 da (Grace Edith b 16 July 1992, Isabelle Florence b 2 Oct 1995); *Career* slr specialising in criminal defence; asst slr then ptnr Overbury Steward and Eaton Solicitors 1980–96, fndr and ptnr Nicholls and Co 1996–99, ptnr Belmores (following merger) 1999– (currently dir); memb Law Society 1980; *Recreations* riding a customised Harley Davidson, running, skiing; *Clubs* Final Chapter Motorcycle Gang, Norwich City FC, First Night Riders; *Style*— Simon Nicholls, Esq; ✉ 164 Saint Clements Hill, Norwich NR3 4DG (☎ 01603 499995); Belmores Solicitors, 40 Crown Road, Norwich NR1 3DX (☎ 01603 499999, fax 01603 499998, e-mail simon@belmores.co.uk, website www.belmores.co.uk)

NICHOLLS, Susan Frances (Sue) (Hon Mrs Eden); da of Baron Harmar-Nicholls, JP (Life Peer and 1 Bt, d 2000); *b* 23 November 1943; *m* 6 July 1993, Mark Eden, the actor/writer; *Career* actress; trained RADA; early theatre work nationwide, appeared in London Assurance (RSC); numerous TV roles incl: Crossroads, The Fall and Rise of Reginald Perrin, Rent-a-Ghost, Up the Elephant and Round the Castle, Audrey Roberts in Coronation Street 1979–; *Style*— Sue Nicholls

NICHOLLS OF BIRKENHEAD, Baron (Life Peer UK 1994), of Stoke D'Abernon in the County of Surrey; Sir Donald James Nicholls; kt (1983), PC (1986); yr s of late William Greenhow Nicholls and late Eleanor Jane Nicholls; *b* 25 January 1933; *Educ* Birkenhead Sch, Univ of Liverpool (LLB), Trinity Hall Cambridge (MA, LLB); *m* 1960, Jennifer Mary, yr da of late W E C Thomas, MB, BCh, MRCOG, JP; 2 s (John Peter b 30 Nov 1963, Christopher William b 14 Feb 1971), 1 da (Gillian Mary b 26 Nov 1965); *Career* 2 Lt RAPC 1951–53; called to the Bar Middle Temple 1958 (bencher 1981, treas 1997), QC 1974, judge of the High Court of Justice (Chancery Div) 1983–86; Lord Justice of Appeal 1986–91; vice-chllr of the Supreme Court 1991–94; Lord of Appeal in Ordinary 1994–2007, Second Sr Lord of Appeal 2002–07; non-perm memb Hong Kong Court of Final Appeal 1998–2004; *Clubs* Athenaeum (tstee 1998–2011); *Style*— The Rt Hon the Lord Nicholls of Birkenhead, PC; ✉ House of Lords, London SW1A 0PW

NICHOLS, Dinah Alison; CB (1995); da of Sydney Hirst Nichols (d 1982), and Elsie Freda, *née* Pratt (d 2005); *b* 28 September 1943; *Educ* Wyggeston GS for Girls Leicester, Bedford Coll London (Reid arts scholar, BA); *Career* Miny of Tport: asst princ 1965–69, Winston Churchill Meml fellowship to study tport in Japan 1969, asst private sec to the Min of Tport 1969–70, princ Railways Policy 1970–74; princ Cabinet Office 1974–77, asst sec (Radioactive Waste) DOE 1977–80, asst sec (Ports) Dept of Tport 1980–81, asst sec (Inner Cities) DOE 1981–83, princ private sec to the Sec of State for Tport 1983–85; DOE (latterly DETR then DEFRA): dir Admin Resources 1985–88, under sec (Water) 1988–91, dep sec (Property and Construction) 1991–93, DG (Housing and Construction) 1994–96, DG Environment 1996–2002; non-exec dir: John Laing ETE 1987–90, Anglian Water plc 1992–95, Include 1995–2000, Shires Smaller Companies plc 1999–2012, Pennon Gp plc 2003–13; memb Commonwealth War Graves Cmmn 1993–96, cmmr Crown Estate 2003–13, chair National Forest Co 2005–11, dir The Land Tst 2010–; dir Toynbee Housing Assoc 1996–2007, chm Toynbee Partnership Housing Assoc 2002–07, chm Groundwork North London 2004–09, chair Keep Britain Tidy 2012–, ind memb Cncl Nat Tst 2013–, dir SW Lakes Tst 2014–; tstee: Travel Fndn 2003–10, Groundwork London 2009–10; Freeman City of London 2008, Liveryman Worshipful Co of Water Conservators 2008, memb Worshipful Co of Musicians 2016; hon fell Royal Holloway Coll 1997, FRSA; *Recreations* mountain and fell walking, choral singing, music, theatre, travel; *Clubs* Assoc of Br Membs of the Swiss Alpine Club, Goldsmiths Choral Union, Aldersgate Gp, Green Alliance; *Style*— Ms Dinah Nichols, CB

NICHOLS, (Peter) John; s of late Peter Nichols, of Bowdon, Cheshire, and Edith Nan, *née* Rhodes; *b* 24 December 1949; *Educ* Shrewsbury, Univ of Leicester (BSc); *m* 15 Sept 1973, late Elaine Mary, da of late William H W Chadwick; 2 s (James b 1979, Matthew b 1982), 1 da (Katharine b 1986); *Career* Nichols plc: joined 1970–, dir 1978–86, md 1986–99, chm 1999–; *Recreations* golf, sailing, skiing; *Clubs* Ringway Golf, Abersoch Golf, South Caernarvonshire Yacht, Bowdon Lawn Tennis; *Style*— John Nichols, Esq; ✉ Hatton Cottage, Hatton, Cheshire WA4 5NY; Nichols plc, Laurel House, Ashton Road, Newton Le Willows, Lancashire WA12 0HH (☎ 01925 222222, fax 01925 222233, mobile 07764 933194, e-mail john.nichols@nicholsplc.co.uk)

NICHOLS, Peter Richard; s of Richard George (d 1965), of Bristol, and Violet Annie Ladysmith Poole (d 1992); *b* 31 July 1927; *Educ* Bristol GS, Bristol Old Vic Theatre Sch; *m* 1960, Thelma, da of George Reginald Reed, of Bristol (d 1995); 1 s (Daniel), 3 da (Abigail d 1971, Louise, Catherine); *Career* actor, teacher, journalist, playwright and director; visiting writer Nat Inst of Educn Singapore 1994; FRSL; *Screen and Stage* plays incl: The Gorge (TV), A Day in the Death of Joe Egg (stage and screen), Forget-me-not Lane (stage), Privates on Parade (stage and screen), Passion Play (stage), Poppy (stage musical), Blue Murder (writer and dir, Show of Strength Co Bristol) 1995 (nat tour 1996), So Long Life (Show of Strength Co Bristol and nat tour) 2000, Lingua Franca (stage) 2010; *Awards* 4 Evening Standard Drama, 2 Oliviers, Critics' Circle, Tony, Ivor Novello Award for Best British Musical (for Poppy); *Publications* Feeling You're Behind (autobiography, 1984), Diary 1969–77; author of various papers; *Recreations* reading his own diary, complaining about cars and muzak; *Style*— Peter Nichols, Esq, FRSL

NICHOLS, Richard Stephen; s of Basil Nichols, and Jean Nichols; *b* 18 May 1965; *Educ* Royal GS Newcastle upon Tyne, St Catharine's Coll Cambridge (MA); *m* 3 June 1995, Deborah Rachel Cantrell; 1 s (Mark b 15 July 1998), 1 da (Louise b 30 Aug 2000); *Career* with Price Waterhouse (London) 1987–94, sr fin analyst British Gas plc 1994–96, dep gp fin dir Citigate Communications Gp Ltd 1996–97; Incepta Gp plc: dep gp fin dir 1997–98, gp fin dir 1998–2001, chief exec 2001–; ACA; *Recreations* golf, tennis, Newcastle United FC; *Clubs* Harpenden Golf, Woburn Golf and Country, Brocket Hall Golf, Harpenden Lawn Tennis; *Style*— Richard Nichols, Esq; ✉ Incepta Group plc, 3 London Wall Buildings, London Wall, London EC2M 5SY (☎ 020 7282 2800, fax 020 7256 7542)

NICHOLS, Roger David Edward; s of Edward Compton Lowther Nichols (d 1945), and Dorothy Norah, *née* West (d 1994); *b* 6 April 1939; *Educ* Harrow, Worcester Coll Oxford (open exhibitioner, MA); *m* 11 April 1964, Sarah, eld da of Antony Bydder Edwards; 2 s (Thomas Edward b 7 March 1965, Jeremy Owen b 22 Aug 1966), 1 da (Olwen Beatrice b 5 May 1969); *Career* asst master St Michael's Coll Tenbury 1966–73, lectr Open Univ 1974–80, lectr Univ of Birmingham 1974–80; freelance writer and broadcaster 1980–; FRCO 1964; Chevalier de la Légion d'honneur 2006; *Books* Debussy (1972), Messiaen (1975), Ravel (1977), Debussy Letters (ed and trans, 1987), Ravel Remembered (1987), Pelléas et Mélisande (with R Langham Smith, 1989), Debussy Remembered (1992), Conversations with Madeleine Milhaud (1996), Mendelssohn Remembered (1997), The Life of Debussy (1998), The Harlequin Years (2002), Camille Saint-Saëns on Music and Musicians (2008), Ravel (2011); *Recreations* playing chamber music, walking the Welsh hills; *Style—* Roger Nichols, Esq; ✉ The School House, The Square, Kington, Herefordshire HR5 3BA (☎ 01544 231742, e-mail roger@nicholsnet.org)

NICHOLS, Most Rev Vincent Gerard; *see:* Westminster, Archbishop (RC) of

NICHOLSON, Sir Bryan Hubert; kt (1987), GBE (2005); s of Reginald Hubert Nicholson (d 1977); *b* 6 June 1932; *Educ* Palmers Sch Grays, Oriel Coll Oxford; *m* 1956, Mary Elizabeth, da of Albert Cyril Harrison; 2 c; *Career* Nat Serv Lt; dir Sperry Rand (Australia) Pty Ltd 1966–69, dir Sperry Rand Ltd UK 1969–72; chm: Rank Xerox (UK) Ltd 1980–84 (dir 1972–84, dir Rank Xerox Ltd 1977–87), Manpower Services Cmmn 1984–87, The Post Office (also chief exec) 1987–92, BUPA 1992–2001, Varity Europe Ltd 1993–96, Cookson Gp plc 1998–2003, GOAL plc 2001–05, Financial Reporting Cncl 2001–05 (memb 1993–98 and 2001–05, dep chm 1993–96); non-exec dir: Evode Group plc 1981–84, Baker Perkins Holdings plc 1982–84, GKN plc 1991–2000, LucasVarity plc 1996–99, Equitas Holdings Ltd 1996–2005, Newsquest plc 1997–99, EDI plc 2005–12, Victoria plc 2012; CBI: chm Educn and Trg Affrs Ctee 1990–93, dep pres 1993–94, pres 1994–96; chm: Nationalised Industries Chairmen's Gp 1988–90, CNAA 1988–91, Nat Cncl for Vocational Qualifications 1990–93, The Industrial Soc 1990–93; memb: NEDC 1985–92; dir Accountancy Fndn 2000–04 (chm 2003–04), tstee Int Accoutning Standards Ctee Fndn 2006–12; pro-chllr and chm Cncl Open Univ 1996–2004, chllr Sheffield Hallam Univ 1992–2001; pres Nat Centre for Young Epilepsy 2005–11; Hon FCGI; *Recreations* tennis, bridge; *Clubs* Oxford and Cambridge (chm 1995–97); *Style—* Sir Bryan Nicholson, GBE; ✉ Point Piper, Lilley Drive, Kingswood, Surrey KT20 6JA

NICHOLSON, Clive Anthony Holme; s of Dennis Thomas Holme Nicholson, MBE (d 2009), and Eileen Blanche, *née* Fitkin (d 2005); *b* 24 February 1947; *Educ* Merchant Taylors'; *m* 1, 12 Dec 1970 (m dis 2003), Patricia Mary, da of Ernest Johnson (d 1979); 3 da (Amanda b 5 Dec 1972, Zoe b 27 May 1975, Gemma b 8 Aug 1981); m 2, 15 April 2006, Patricia Ann Lotery; *Career* CA; Deloitte & Co Lusaka Zambia 1970–72; Saffery Champness (formerly Safferys) 1972– (ptnr 1975–2013, managing ptnr 1990–2002, conslt 2013–); treas London Soc of Rugby Football Union Referees; Liveryman Worshipful Co of Merchant Taylors 1974; FCA 1979; *Recreations* golf; *Clubs* Roehampton; *Style—* Clive A H Nicholson, Esq; ✉ 30 Shrewsbury Avenue, East Sheen, London SW14 8JZ; Saffery Champness, Lion House, Red Lion Street, London WC1R 4GB (☎ 020 7841 4000, fax 020 7841 4100)

NICHOLSON, Graham Beattie; s of John Arthur Nicholson (d 1975), and Ena Patricia Nicholson; *b* 22 February 1949; *Educ* Bloxham Sch, Trinity Hall Cambridge; *Children* 1 da (Vanessa b 1978); *Career* slr; Freshfields Bruckhaus Deringer LLP: joined 1971, NY office 1979–80, ptnr 1980–2008, Singapore office 1980–83, managing ptnr Co Dept 1986–90, managing ptnr 1990–93; chief legal advsr and advsr to the Govr Bank of England 2009–; memb City of London Slrs' Co 1983; memb Law Soc; dir Barbican Centre Tst 2009–13; *Recreations* music, sailing, racquet sports; *Style—* Graham Nicholson, Esq; ✉ Bank of England, Threadneedle Street, London EC2R 8AH (☎ 020 7601 3919, e-mail graham.nicholson@bankofengland.co.uk)

NICHOLSON, James Frederick (Jim); MEP (UUP) N Ireland; s of Thomas Richard Nicholson (d 1987), of Ballyards, Armagh, and Matilda, *née* Morrow (d 1984); *b* 29 January 1945; *m* 30 Nov 1968, Elizabeth, *née* Gibson; 6 s, 1 da; *Career* elected: Armagh Dist Cncl 1975–97, NI Assembly 1982–86; MP 1983–85; MEP (UUP) N Ireland 1989–; farmer; *Recreations* walking, football; *Style—* Jim Nicholson, Esq, MEP; ✉ Strandtown Hall, 2–4 Belmont Road, Belfast BT4 2AN (☎ 028 9047 4634, e-mail jim.nicholson@uup.org, website www.jim-nicholson.eu)

NICHOLSON, Lindsay; da of Anthony Cuthbertson-Nicholson, and Sheila Rose, *née* Pigram; *Educ* UCL (BSc), NCTJ; *Career* journalist; trainee Mirror Gp Newspapers 1978–82, health and beauty ed Honey 1983–85, features ed Best 1987, asst ed Woman 1992–95, ed-in-chief Prima 1995, ed-in-chief Good Housekeeping 1999–, editorial dir National Magazine Co and Good Housekeeping 2006–; chairwoman: BSME 1997, PTC Ed Ctee 2002–04, Women in Journalism 2002–04; Press Complaints Cmmr 2007–14; UCL Cncl memb 2014–; PPA Ed of the Year (consumer magazines) 1999 and 2015, PPA Magazine of the Year 2006, PPA Media Brand of the Year 2015; tstee Home-Start 2000–08, patron The WAY (Widowed and Young) Fndn 2007–13; hon visiting prof City Univ 2007–; churchwarden St Brides' Fleet Street 2012–13; *Publications* Living on the Seabed (2005); *Recreations* dressage, ballet; *Clubs* Groucho; *Style—* Ms Lindsay Nicholson; ✉ Hearst Magazines UK, 72 Broadwick Street, London W1F 9EP (☎ 020 7439 5247, fax 020 7439 5591, e-mail lindsay.nicholson@hearst.co.uk); Good Housekeeping, 72 Broadwick Street, London W1F 9EP (☎ 020 7439 5247, fax 020 7439 5591)

NICHOLSON, Michael Thomas; OBE (1991); s of Maj Allan Alfred Nicholson, RE (d 1956), of Romford, and Doris Alice, *née* Reid (d 1963); *b* 9 January 1937; *Educ* Prince Rupert Wilhelmshaven Germany, Univ of Leicester (BA); *m* Diana; 2 s (Tom b 17 Jan 1972, William b 19 May 1973), 1 adopted da (Natasha b 7 Oct 1982); *Career* served RAF 1955–57; political writer DC Thompson 1962–63; ITN: foreign corr 1963–82 and 1985–, bureau corr Southern Africa 1976–81, newscaster 1982–85, Washington corr Channel 4 1989; currently: corr Tonight prog (ITV), contrib Radio 4; wars covered incl: Nigeria/Biafra 1968–69, Ulster 1968–75, Vietnam 1969–75, Cambodia (incl invasion of Laos) 1972–75, Jordan (incl Dawson's Field and Black September) 1970, Indo-Pakistan War 1971, Yom Kippur War 1973, Rhodesian War 1973–80, invasion of Cyprus 1974, Beirut Lebanon 1975, Angolan Civil War 1975–78, Falklands War (awarded Falklands medal) 1982, Gulf War (awarded Gulf medal) 1991; Hon MA Univ of Leicester; FRGS 1983, fell Royal Cwlth Soc 1983; *Awards* American Emmy nomination 1969, British Broadcasting Guild award 1974, RTS award 1974, Silver Nymph award (for Vietnam report) Monte Carlo Film Festival 1975, RTS Reporter of the Year (for Angola 1979, for Falklands 1983, for Yugoslavia 1992), BAFTA Richard Dimbleby award 1983, VALA award 1983, RTS Journalist of the Year 1991; *Books* Partridge Kite (1978), Red Joker (1979), December Ultimatum (1981), Across The Limpopo (1985), Pilgrims Rest (1987), A Measure of Danger (1991), Natasha's Story (1993, basis of film Welcome to Sarajevo), A State of War Exists: Reporters in the Line of Fire (2013); *Recreations* tennis, sailing; *Style—* Michael Nicholson, Esq, OBE; ✉ c/o PFD, 34 Russell Street, London WC2B 5HA (☎ 020 7344 1000)

NICHOLSON, Patricia Alexandra; *née* Young; da of Donald Young, of Gosforth, Newcastle upon Tyne, and Margaret, *née* Bailes; *b* 2 December 1955, Newcastle upon Tyne; *Educ* La Sagesse Convent Sch, Westminster Coll (HND), Garnet (CertEd); *m* 23 Sept 1978, David John Nicholson (d 2014); *Career* grad mgmnt trainee Grand Met Hotels 1977–78, trg exec Centre Hotels 1978–80, lectr S Warks Coll of FE 1981–87, jt prop Holbeck Ghyll Country House Hotel 1988–2010 (4 AA Red Stars, 3 AA Rosettes, Michelin Star 2000, Cumbria Tourist Bds Hotel of the Year 2000–01, Best Hotel Northern Hospitality Awards 2006, Cumbria Restaurant of the Year Good Food Guide Special Awards 2007, Taittinger Wine List of the Year Condé Nast Johansens Awards of Excellence 2007, The Good Food Guide Wine List of the Year 2009, ranked number 24 in the top 40 restaurants featured in The Good Food Guide 2009); vice-chm Kendal Coll Consultative Ctee, memb Ctee Cumbria Tourist Bd Devpt Workforce, memb Small Luxury Hotels of the World, memb Pride of Britain; MIH; *Recreations* golf, watching football, dining out, wine and food appreciation, cooking, skiing, fishing, walking the dog, fly fishing, bridge, fell walking; *Clubs* Windermere Golf; *Style—* Mrs Patricia Nicholson; ✉ website www.luxurywindermerecottages.com

NICHOLSON, Sir Paul Douglas; KCVO (2011), kt (1993); eld s of Frank Douglas Nicholson, TD, DL (d 1984), and Pauline (d 2010), yr da of Maj Sir Thomas Lawson-Tancred, 9 Bt; *b* 7 March 1938; *Educ* Harrow, Clare Coll Cambridge; *m* 1970, Sarah, 4 and yst da of Sir Edmund Bacon, 13 and 14 Bt, KG, KBE, TD (d 1982), of Raveningham Hall, Norfolk; 1 da (Lucy b 3 July 1972); *Career* Lt Coldstream Guards 1956–58; chartered accountant Price Waterhouse 1964; chm Vaux Group plc 1976–99 (exec 1965, dir 1967); non-exec dir: Tyne Tees TV plc 1981–1997, Northern Development Company 1987–99, Northern Electric plc 1990–1997, Yorkshire Tyne Tees TV Holdings plc 1992–1997, The Scottish Investment Trust plc 1998–2005, Steelite International 2000–02; chm: Northern Region CBI 1977–79, Northern Bd Nat Enterprise Bd 1979–84, Northern Investors Ltd 1984–89, Tyne & Wear Devpt Corp 1987–98, Brewers and Licensed Retailers' Assoc 1994–96; pres: North East C of C 1995–96, Co Durham Fndn 2002– (chm 1995–2002); High Sheriff Co Durham 1980–81, HM Lord-Lt Co Durham 1997–2013 (DL 1980–97); Liveryman Worshipful Co of Grocers; *Publications* Brewer at Bay (2003); *Recreations* shooting, deerstalking, driving horses (pres Coaching Club 1990–97); *Clubs* Boodle's, Pratt's, Northern Counties; *Style—* Sir Paul Nicholson, KCVO; ✉ Quarry Hill, Brancepeth, Durham DH7 8DW (☎ 0191 378 0275, office tel 0191 378 2455, fax 0191 378 3015, e-mail sirpdn@aol.com); 6 Campden House Close, London W8 7NU (☎ 020 7937 2332)

NICHOLSON, Peter Charles; CBE (2004); s of Charles Arthur Nicholson (d 1993), and Kathleen Mary, *née* Carr (d 1998); *b* 10 April 1934; *Educ* Cheltenham Coll; *m* 1, Tessa, *née* Clarke (d 1980); 1 da (Jane Elizabeth b 1961), 2 s (Charles Edward b 1963, David George b 1965); m 2, 1981, Lesley-Jane, *née* Wynne-Williams; *Career* naval architect Fleet Air Arm 1952–54; dir: Camper & Nicholsons Ltd 1965–88 (chm 1969–88), Crest Nicholson plc 1972–2002 (exec 1972–88, non-exec 1988–2002), Original 106 FM Ltd 2005–08; chm: Carisbrooke Shipping plc 1990–1999, RMG Wealth Mgmnt LLP 2011–; non-exec dir: Lloyds Bank plc 1990–95, MIF Ltd 1993–2001, TEN Ltd 2001–, Lloyds TSB Group plc 1995–2000, Solent Regional Radio Ltd 1996–2000 (chm); younger bro Trinity House, chm RNLI 2000–04, Br delg IYRU 1969–94, tstee Br Marine Industries Fedn 1988–; pres: Solent Cruising and Racing Assoc 2004–15, Solent Protection Soc 2005–14; *Recreations* yachting, skiing, golf; *Clubs* Royal Yacht Sqdn (Cdre 1996–2001), Royal Thames Yacht (Rear Cdre 1980–83), RORC, Royal Southern Yacht, Ski Club of GB, Stoneham Golf; *Style—* Peter Nicholson, Esq, CBE; ✉ Mere House, Hamble, Southampton SO31 4JB (☎ 023 8045 5019)

NICHOLSON, Robin Alaster; CBE (1999); s of Gerald Hugh Nicholson (d 1970), of Bayford, and Margaret Evelyn, *née* Hanbury (d 2000); *b* 27 July 1944; *Educ* Eton, Magdalene Coll Cambridge (MA), UCL (MSc), RIBA Sch (design prize); *m* 18 Dec 1969, Fiona Mary, *née* Bird; 3 s (Zachary Luke b 7 March 1971, Solomon Rufus Seb b 13 Sept 1974 d 2014, Caspian Ned b 5 June 1978); *Career* architect; YRM 1966–67, Evan Walker Associates Toronto 1967, James Stirling Chartered Architects London 1969–73, Boza Lührs and Muzard Santiago Chile 1973, UCL 1974–76, Poly of N London 1976–79, ptnr Edward Cullinan Architects 1979–2012, sr ptnr Cullinan Studio 2012–; visiting fell Univ of Wales 1984, hon prof Univ of Nottingham 2013–; memb Cncl RIBA 1991–97 (vice-pres 1992–94), chm Construction Industry Cncl 1998–2000 (vice-chm 1997–98 and 2000–01), cmmr Cmmn for Architecture and the Built Environment (CABE) 2002–10, non-exec memb Nat House Building Cncl (NHBC) 2007–14, chm Cambs Quality Panel 2010–; convenor The Edge; RIBA, FRSA, Hon FIStructE 2002, Hon FCIBSE 2013; *Publications* Understanding the Context (in Future City Architecture for Optimal Living); *Recreations* gardening, making, climate change; *Style—* Robin Nicholson, Esq, CBE; ✉ Cullinan Studio, 5 Baldwin Terrace, London N1 7RU (☎ 020 7704 1975, fax 020 7354 2739, e-mail robin.nicholson@cullinanstudio.com)

NICHOLSON, Sir Robin Buchanan; kt (1985); s of late Carroll Nicholson and Nancy Esther Nicholson (d 1993); *b* 12 August 1934; *Educ* Oundle, St Catharine's Coll Cambridge (PhD); *m* 1, 1958, Elizabeth Mary (d 1988), da of Sir Sydney Caffyn; 1 s, 2 da; m 2, Yvonne, *née* Appleby; *Career* Univ of Cambridge: demonstrator in metallurgy 1960, lectr in metallurgy 1964, fell Christ's Coll 1962–66 (hon fell 1984); prof of metallurgy Univ of Manchester 1966; md Inco Europe 1976–81 (dir 1975–81), chief sci advsr Cabinet Office 1981–85; exec dir Pilkington plc 1986–96; non-exec dir: Rolls Royce plc 1986–2005, BP plc 1987–2005; memb SRC 1978–81, Cncl Univ of Exeter 2005–; Liveryman Worshipful Co of Goldsmiths; FRS 1978, FREng 1980, FIM, MInstP; *Clubs* MCC; *Style—* Sir Robin Nicholson, FREng, FRS; ✉ Elds Gorse Cottage, Minn Bank, Willoughbridghe, Market Drayton, Shropshire, TF9 4EU

NICHOLSON, Vanessa-Mae Vanakorn; *b* 27 October 1978; *Educ* Francis Holland Sch for Girls, Central Conservatoire Beijing, Royal Coll of Music; *Career* violinist; live performances worldwide incl: Times Square NY, Kremlin Palace Moscow, Paralympics opening ceremony Salt Lake City 2002, Buckingham Palace, Soweto township SA, venues in USA, Middle East, China, SE Asia, Russia, Kazakstan, UK, Europe, Baltic States, Mexico and S America; actress: Arabian Nights (TV) 2000, Gangs of New York (film) 2002; model for Jean Paul Gaultier Paris Fashion Week; patron: Red Cross, RSPCA; *Albums* The Violin Player 1995, The Classical Album 1 1996 (Best-Selling Classical Artiste World Music Awards), Storm 1997, China Girl (The Classical Album 2) 1998, The Original Four Seasons 1998, The Classical Collection – Part 1 2000, Subject to Change 2001, The Best of Vanessa Mae 2002, Choreography 2004; *Style—* Miss Vanessa-Mae Nicholson

NICHOLSON, William; OBE (2015); *b* 12 January 1948; *Educ* Downside, Christ's Coll Cambridge; *m* 1988, Virginia; 3 c; *Career* screenwriter, playwright and novelist; early career as documentary film maker BBC; FRSL; *Plays* Shadowlands (Queen's Theatre) 1989 (Best Play Evening Standard Drama Award 1990), Map of the Heart (Globe) 1991, Katherine Howard (Chichester Festival) 1998, The Retreat From Moscow (Chichester Festival) 1999 and (Booth Theatre NY) 2003, Crash (West Yorkshire Playhouse) 2010; *Film* incl: Nell 1994, Shadowlands 1994, Firelight 1997, Gladiator 2000, Elizabeth: The Golden Age 2007, Les Misérables 2012, Mandela: Long Walk to Freedom 2013, Everest 2014; *Books* The Society of Others (2004), The Trial of True Love (2005), Wind On Fire trilogy (The Wind Singer (Smarties Gold Award 2000, Blue Peter Book of the Year 2001), Slaves of the Mastery, Firesong), Noble Warriors Trilogy (Seeker (2005), Jango (2006), Noman (2007)), The Secret Intensity of Everyday Life (2009), All the Hopeful Lovers (2011), Rich and Mad (2012), The Golden Hour (2012), Motherland (2013), Reckless (2014), The Lovers of Amherst (2015); *Style—* William Nicholson, Esq, OBE; ✉ c/o The Agency, 24 Pottery Lane, Holland Park, London W11 4LZ

NICHOLSON OF WINTERBOURNE, Baroness (Life Peer UK 1997), of Winterbourne in the Royal County of Berkshire; Emma Harriet Nicholson; 3 da of Sir Godfrey Nicholson, 1 and last Bt (d 1991), and Lady Katharine Constance, *née* Lindsay (d 1972), da of 27 Earl of Crawford and Balcarres; *b* 16 October 1941; *Educ* Portsdown Lodge Sch, St Mary's

Sch Wantage, Royal Acad of Music (LRAM, ARCM); *m* 9 May 1987, Sir Michael Harris Caine (d 1999), s of Sir Sydney Caine, KCMG; 2 step c (1 decd); *Career* computer software programmer and systems engr ITC (now ICL) 1962–66, computer conslt John Tyzack & Ptnrs 1967–69, computer and gen mgmnt conslt McLintock Mann and Whinney Murray 1969–74; dir of fundraising Save the Children Fund 1977–85 (joined 1974), fndr and memb Bd Stichting Redt de Kinderen (Netherlands) 1982–88, fndr and memb Comité d'Honneur Sauvez Les Enfants (France) 1983; conslt 1985–87: World Assoc of Girl Guides and Girl Scouts, The Duke of Edinburgh's Award Scheme, Foster Parents Plan UK, Westminster Children's Hosp; Parly candidate (Cons) Blyth Valley 1979, MP (Cons until Dec 1995, whereafter Lib Dem) Devon W and Torridge 1987–97; vice-chm Cons Party (with special responsibility for women) 1983–87, alternate memb UK Delgn to WEU and Cncl of Europe 1990–92, PPS to Michael Jack as min of state 1992–95 (successively at Home Office, MAFF and HM Treasy), Lib Dem spokesperson for overseas devpt and human rights 1996–97, front bench spokesperson on Data Protection House of Lords 1998; MEP (Lib Dem) SE England 1999–2009; fndr and exec chm Iraq Britain Business Cncl (IBBC) 2009–, non-exec dir and chm Supervisory Bd Jt Leasing Co 2013–; Euro Parl 1999–2004 term: vice-chm Foreign Affairs, Human Rights, Common Def and Security Policy Ctee, rapporteur for Iraq and Romania, memb Women's Rights and Equal Opportunities Ctee, memb Interparly Delgn to Mashreq Countries and the Gulf States, memb European Parliament Delgn to the Euro-Mediterranean Forum, memb Stability Pact for SE Europe Parly Gp, sub memb Agric and Rural Devpt Ctee and EP/Romania Jt Parly Ctee, sub-memb Parly Co-operation Ctee for Kazakhstan, Kyrgyzstan, Uzbekistan, Tajikistan, Turkmenistan and Mongolia; Euro Parl 2004–09 term: vice-pres Foreign Affrs Ctee (memb 2007–09), memb Human Rights Sub-Ctee, pres Perm Ad Hoc Delgn for Relations with Iraq, memb Delegn for Relations with Iran, sub-memb Ctee on Budgets, sub-memb Delgn for Relations with the Mashreq Countries, memb Euromed Parly Assembly (vice-pres Women's Rights Ctee), rapporteur for Kashmir, rapporteur for Romania until 2007, shadow rapporteur Iraq, EU-India Free Trade Agreement, A Special Place for Children in EU External Action; chief observer EU Election Observation Mission to Yemen 2006, memb EU Election Observation Missions to Palestine, Azerbaijan, Afghanistan 2005, Lebanon 2005 and 2009, Armenia 2007, Pakistan 2008, memb UN Election Observation Missions to Iraq 2005, memb EP Delgn OSCE Election Observation Mission to Moldova 2009 memb Cncl of Europe Delgn to OSCE Election Observation Mission to Kazakhstan 2011, memb UK Delgn to the Parly Assembly of the Cncl of Europe and the European Security and Defence Assembly 2010–, UK Trade Envoy to Iraq 2014–; WHO envoy for Health, Peace and Devpt (appointed 2002); All-Pty Parly Gps: chm Oman, Kuwait, UNA Advsy, former co dep chm Br Iranian, former vice chm Penal Affrs, former treas Romanian Children, former treas Positive European, treas Br Caribbean, former sec Syrian, Human Rights, fndr and former chm Euro Information Market, chm Foreign Affrs 2010–, vice-chm Human Trafficking 2010–, Georgia 2010, Jordan, European Reform, treas Islamic Finance, Br Iraq (former chm), Bulgaria, Moldova, Romania, Saudi Arabia (former treas), Transatlantic and International Security; memb Bd: MRC 1991–94, Fndn for Dialogue Among Civilizations 2007–13, Global Warming Policy Fndn 2009–, Architecture Devpt Agency 2014–; memb Cncl: UNICEF, Howard League for Penal Reform, Media Soc; memb: Euro Standing Ctee A, Standing Ctee on Statutory Instruments, Select Ctee on Employment 1990–91, Conservative Backbench Environment Ctee 1990–91 (sec and subsequently chm), Parly Panel RCN 1990–92, Lib Dem Foreign Affairs team in House of Lords, American Bar Assoc ME & N Africa Cncl, Durham Global Security Inst Strategic Advsy Bd 2011–, House of Lords Ad Hoc Select Ctee on Soft Power & the UKs Influence 2013–14; vice-chm European Movement; pres numerous charitable orgns in Devon; vice-pres: Assoc of Dist Cncls, Br Tinnitus Assoc, Nat Assoc for Maternal and Child Welfare, Small Farmers' Assoc, Br Leprosy Relief Assoc (LEPRA), The Little Fndn, The Child Psychotherapy Tst, The Missing Persons Hotline; patron numerous charitable and other orgns incl: Int Ctee for a Free Iraq, Ecaterina Iliescu Meml Lecture, Br Deaf Accord, Nat Deaf Blind and Rubella Assoc, AMANA (soc to promote understanding of Islam), Soc for the Freedom of the City of London Municipality, Freedom Cncl, Reading Industrial Therapy Orgn, Women into IT Fndn, Women's Engrg Soc, Women's Business Assoc, Federal Tst for Educn and Res, Devon Daycare Tst, Sense South West, Opera South West, PHAB South West, Deaf Educn through Listening and Talking (DELTA), Nat Music and Disability Information Service, Cities in Schools, The Manningford Tst, Relatives' Assoc (former memb Mgmnt Bd); vice-patron Blind In Business; fndr and chm AMAR Appeal (later AMAR Int Charitable Fndn) 1991–, fndr and pres Asociatia Children's High Level Gp (ACHLG) 2006–; chm: Iraqi Humanitarian Relief Ctee until 1996 (also vice-patron until 1996), Access for Disabled People to Arts Premises Today (ADAPT) until 1996 (currently tstee and vice-patron), Blind in Business 1993–95, Emily Trust Appeal Ctee (chm 1993–95), UNA Advsy Gp UNESCO (co-chm, chm 1998–), Int Year of the Disabled UNESCO; former co-chm High Level Gp for Romanian Children and High Level Gp for Moldovan Children; vice-pres Methodist Homes for the Elderly; formerly dir Shelter; tstee: Covent Garden Cancer Res Tst, Motor Neurone Disease Assoc, World Meml Fund for Disaster Relief, Africa '95; memb: Mgmnt Bd European Movement, Guild of Mgmnt Conslts, Forum UK, RIIA, Centre for Policy Studies, Inst of Economic Affrs, Cncl for Arab-Br Understanding, Prince of Wales Advsy Tst on Disability, Advsy Cncl Justis Legal Databases, Exeter Univ Devpt Ctee, Br Romanian Assoc, West Regnl Assoc for the Deaf, Editorial Panel 300 Group, Advsy Bd Women of Tomorrow Awards, London Business Women's Network, Appeal Ctee Royal Acad of Music, Advsy Cncl United World Fndn, Advsy Cncl Centre for Adoptive Identity Studies Univ of E London; fndr and pres Caine Prize for African Writing 1999–, chm Booker Prize for Russian Fiction 1999–, vice pres Booker Prize Fndn, memb Advsy Bd and judge Franklin D Roosevelt Int Disability Rights Award 2011–13; visiting fell St Antony's Coll Oxford 1995–96 (sr assoc memb 1997–98, 1998–99 and 2001–); Hon Dr: Univ of North London 1998, Victor Babes Univ Timosoara 2002, Univ of Birmingham 2004, Dimitrie Cantemir Christian Univ Bucharest 2006, Acad of Economic Studies Bucharest, Oklahoma City Univ 2010, Kingston Univ 2014; memb Ct: Univ of Reading, Univ of Southampton, Univ of Exeter, Univ of Sussex; Freeman Worshipful Co of Info Technologists; hon advsr to the Iraqi PM in the field of health 2008–14, high representative of the President of the Republic of Moldova 2007–10, high representative for Romanian Children 2009–; fell Industry and Parliament Tst, fell Federal Tst for Education and Res; FRSA 1990; *Books* Why Does the West Forget? (1993), Secret Society: Inside and Outside the Conservative Party (1996), The Southern Mesopotamian Marshlands: Reclaiming the Heritage of a Civilisation (ed, 2012); author of various articles and pamphlets; *Recreations* music (organ, piano, cello and singing), chess, walking, reading; *Clubs* Reform; *Style—* The Rt Hon Baroness Nicholson of Winterbourne; ✉ House of Lords, London SW1A 0PW

NICKELL, Prof Sir Stephen John; kt (2015), CBE (2007); s of John Edward Hilary Nickell (d 1962) and Phyllis, *née* Vicary (d 1975); *b* 25 April 1944; *Educ* Merchant Taylors', Pembroke Coll Cambridge (scholarship, BA), LSE (MSc, Ely Devons prize); *m* 25 June 1976, Susan Elizabeth, da of Peter Nicholas Pegden, of Bridlington, E Yorks; 1 da (Katherine Jane b 30 Sept 1979), 1 s (William Thomas b 16 Oct 1981); *Career* mathematics teacher Hendon Co Sch 1965–68; prof of economics: LSE 1979–84 (lectr 1970–77, reader 1977–79), (and dir) Inst of Economics and Statistics Univ of Oxford 1984–98; professorial fell Nuffield Coll Oxford 1984–98, school prof of economics LSE 1998–2005, warden Nuffield Coll Oxford 2006–12; memb Bank of England Monetary Policy Ctee 2000–06, memb UK Budget Responsibility Ctee 2010–; chm Research Grants Bd ESRC 1990–94 (also memb); pres: European Assoc of Labour Economists 1999–2002, Royal Economic Soc 2001–04 (memb Cncl 1984–94); IZA Prize in Labour Economics 2008; hon doctorate Univ of Warwick 2008; hon fell: Nuffield Coll Oxford 2003, Pembroke Coll Cambridge 2006; hon memb: American Economic Assoc 1997, American Acad of Arts and Sciences 2006; fell Econometric Soc 1980 (memb Cncl 1987–93), FBA 1993, fell Soc of Labor Economists 2007; *Books* The Investment Decisions of Firms (1978), The Rise in Unemployment (ed, 1987), Unemployment (1991), The Unemployment Crisis (1994), The Performance of Companies (1995); *Recreations* reading, cricket; *Style—* Prof Sir Stephen Nickell, CBE, FBA; ✉ e-mail steve.nickell@nuffield.ox.ac.uk

NICKLIN, Stephen Richard; s of Richard Patrick Nicklin (d 1982), and Elsie Joan, *née* Crisp (d 2012); *b* 20 April 1952; *Educ* Sloane GS; *m* 3 March 1979, Theresa, da of Vincent O'Shea (d 1995), and Kathleen, *née* Ward (d 2013), of Collooney, Co Sligo; 3 s (Edward b 1981, Anthony, Luke (twins) b 1988), 1 da (Emily b 1985); *Career* BBC 1970; unit mangr: Newsnight BBC 1984–87, American Elections BBC 1984, Election 87 BBC 1985–87; ITN: unit mangr Channel 4 News 1987–89, editorial mangr 1989–91, home news mangr 1991–93, input mangr 1993–94, gen mangr ITV Dept 1994–95, resource mangr 1996–97, head of commercial resources 1997–99, health & safety mangr 2000–10, health & safety conslt 2010–15 (ret); chartered memb Inst of Occupational Health and Safety (CMIOSH), memb Int Inst of Risk and Safety Mgmnt (MIIRSM); *Style—* Stephen Nicklin, Esq; ✉ e-mail stevenicklin@hotmail.co.uk

NICKOLLS, Malcolm Charles; s of Capt Charles Nickolls (d 1985), and Lillian Rose, *née* Taylor; *b* 20 March 1944; *Educ* Rickmansworth GS, Univ of London (LLB), Brighton Coll of Art (DipArch), Thames Poly (Dip Landscape Architecture); *m* 26 Aug 1967, Mary Delia Margaret, da of Ronald Edward Groves, CBE; 2 da (Joanna Helen b 8 Nov 1973, Deborah Sally b 31 Aug 1976); *Career* architect and landscape architect; currently in private practice; princ building J Paul Getty Jr Conservation Centre (Nat Film Archive); ARCUK (now ARB): memb Cncl 1979–, hon offr 1982–, chair Professional Purposes 1982–92, vice-chair Cncl 1992–94, chair Cncl 1994–97, memb Bd 2000; RIBA: memb Cncl 1989–96, chair Discipline Ctee 1992–94; external examiner: Univ of Brighton 1998–, Univ of Northumbria 2001–04; MCIArb 1976, MLI 1977, FRSA 1989; *Recreations* cycling, computers, technology, science, invention; *Clubs* Mensa; *Style—* Malcolm Nickolls, Esq; ✉ 27 Rickfords Hill, Aylesbury, Buckinghamshire HP20 2RT (☎ 01296 397272, e-mail malcolm@nickolls.com)

NICKSON, John Denis; s of Denis Bailey Nickson (d 1990), and Joan Margaret, *née* Ferguson (d 2006); *b* 10 April 1947, Lytham St Annes, Lancs; *Educ* Giggleswick Sch Yorks, UCL (BA); *m* Simon Rew (21 Dec 2005, Civil Partnership conversion); *Career* Br Cncl 1977–89 (head of press 1983–87, dir of info and business rels 1987–89), dir of devpt and public affrs ENO 1989–96, dir of devpt and Royal Acad Tst Royal Acad 1996–2005, dir Tate Fndn 2005–07 (dir emeritus 2008–11); memb Cncl RCM, tstee London Music Masters, tstee Opera Rara; *Books* Giving is Good For You (2013); *Recreations* weather, walking, music and the arts; *Style—* John Nickson, Esq; ✉ e-mail johndnickson@gmail.com

NICOL, Hon Mr Justice; Sir Andrew George Lindsay Nicol; kt (2009), QC (1995); s of Duncan Rennie Nicol (d 1991), and Margaret Nicol (d 1967); *b* 9 May 1951; *Educ* City of London Freemen's Sch, Selwyn Coll Cambridge (BA, LLB), Harvard Law Sch (LLM); *m* 2005; *Children* 2 s; *Career* special asst to dir Housing and Community Dept State of Calif 1975–76, asst Allen Allen & Hemsley Slrs Sydney 1976–77, lectr in law LSE 1977–87; called to the Bar Middle Temple 1978 (bencher 2004), asst recorder 1998–2000, recorder 2000–09, dep judge High Ct 2003–09, judge of the High Ct of Justice (Queen's Bench Div) 2009–, presiding judge SE Circuit 2011–14; chair Immigration Law Practitioners' Assoc 1997–2000; *Books* Subjects, Citizens, Aliens and Others (with Ann Dummett, 1990), Robertson and Nicol on Media Law (with G Robertson QC, 1992, 5 edn 2007), Media Law and Human Rights (with G Millar QC and Andrew Sharland, 2001, 2 edn 2009); *Recreations* family, walking, sailing; *Style—* Sir Andrew Nicol; ✉ Royal Courts of Justice, Strand, London WC2A 2LL

NICOL, Michael John; s of John Chalfont Nicol, of Barnet, Herts, and Jean Etta, *née* Crawley; *b* 8 May 1940; *Educ* Queen Elizabeth's Sch Barnet, Univ of London (LLB); *m* (m dis 1985), Carol Ann, *née* Howie; 3 da (Kate b 1969, Amanda b 1971, Lucy b 1975); *Career* admitted slr 1963; currently conslt Wedlake Bell; memb Law Soc 1963; *Recreations* bridge, badminton, croquet; *Clubs* MCC; *Style—* Michael Nicol, Esq

NICOL, Prof Richard Charles; s of George Richard Nicol, and Alice, *née* Ardley; *b* 14 July 1948; *Educ* UCL (BSc(Eng), PhD); *m*; 2 c; *Career* British Telecommunications plc: joined 1970, head of research 1998–2001; fndr and chief exec Fynntek Ltd 2001–15; chm: Suffolk New Coll Corporation 2010–13, Suffolk New Acad Tst 2013–14; CEng, FREng, FIET; *Recreations* sailing, DIY, football (watching Ipswich Town FC); *Clubs* Ipswich and Suffolk; *Style—* Dr Richard Nicol; ✉ e-mail fynntek@gmail.com

NICOL, Stuart Malcolm; s of James Nicol (d 2000), and Mavis Betty, *née* Gay; *b* 10 October 1957, Kano, Nigeria; *Educ* Hurst Community Sch Baughurst, Berkshire Coll of Art and Design, West Bromwich Poly (Cert); *m* 5 Nov 1983 (m dis 1996); partner, Arlene Melville; *Career* photographer: London Evening Standard 1978–86, Sunday Times 1986–88, Sunday Telegraph 1988–89; picture ed The European newspaper 1990–92, conslt ed colour reproduction The Times 1992, photographer Daily Mirror 1993–95, picture ed Daily Record 1995–2005, gp picture ed Press Assoc 2006–; memb Guild of Picture Eds; Br Young Photographer of the Year 1978, Br Photographer of the Year 1988; *Recreations* golf; *Clubs* Balmore Golf; *Style—* Stuart Nicol, Esq; ✉ PA Group Photos, 292 Vauxhall Bridge Road, London SW1V 1AE (☎ 020 7963 7155, fax 020 7963 7191, e-mail stuart.nicol@pressassociation.co.uk)

NICOLAIDES, Prof Kypros Herodotou; s of Dr Herodotos Nicolaides, of Paphos, Cyprus, and Antigoni, *née* Theodotos; *b* 9 April 1953; *Educ* The English Sch Nicosia, KCL (BSc), King's Coll Hosp Med Sch (MB BS); *Career* house offr in gen surgery Eastbourne Gen Hosp 1979, house offr in obstetrics and gynaecology KCH 1980 (house offr in gen med 1979–80), med offr Cyprus Nat Gd 1980; SHO in obstetrics and gynaecology: City Hosp Nottingham 1981–82, Queen's Univ Hosp Nottingham 1982; prof of fetal med (personal chair) and conslt in obstetrics KCH Sch of Med 1992– (res fell and hon registrar 1982–83, lectr and hon registrar 1983–86, sr lectr and hon sr registrar 1986–89, sr lectr and conslt 1989–92), dir Harris Birthright Res Centre for Fetal Med KCH Sch of Med 1989– (dep dir 1986–89); RCOG rep Working Pty on the Recognition and Mgmnt of Fetal Abnormalities 1988; memb: SE Thames Regnl Specialist Subctee in Genetics 1989–92, Euro Ctee on Doppler Technol in Perinatal Med 1989, Med Advsy Bd of the Toxoplasmosis Tst 1989–, Advsy Bd for Support After Termination for Abnormality 1991–, Euro Inst of Prenatal Diagnosis Dexeus Univ Inst 1991, Jt WHO and World Fedn of Haemophilia Study Gp on the Control of Haemophilia 1992, SELCA Diabetes Forum Gp 1992; memb Editorial Bds: Fetal Diagnosis and Therapy, Ultrasound in Obstetrics and Gynaecology, Israeli Jl of Obstetrics and Gynaecology, Turkish Jl of Obstetrics and Gynaecology, Progresos en Diagnostico Prenatal, Jl of Maternal-Fetal Med, References on Gynecologie Obstetrique, Ultrasound; pres Cyprus Assoc of Perinatology 1990; memb: Int Fetoscopy Gp 1982, Int Fetal Surgery and Med Soc 1984, Panhellenic Soc of Perinatology 1985, The Neonatal Soc 1988, Asociación Espanola de Diagnostico Prenatal 1989, Indian Soc for Prenatal Diagnosis and Therapy 1989, Soc for Research into Hydrocephalus and Spina Bifida 1989, Euro Soc of Paediatric Urology 1990, Int Soc of the Fetus as a Patient 1991, Devptal Pathology Soc 1992; MRCOG 1984; *Publications* author of invited papers and review articles, and ed of various chapters in med reference books; *Style*— Prof Kyprianos Nicolaides; ✉ Harris Birthright Research Centre for Foetal Medicine, King's College Hospital Medical School, Denmark Hill, London SE5 9RS (☎ 020 7346 3040, fax 020 7738 3740)

NICOLLS, Andrew Darsie; s of Simon Hugh Nicolls (d 1964), and Pat Pell, *née* Van Den Bergh; *b* 2 December 1962; *Educ* Radley, UC Cardiff; *Partner* E J O Wilson; *Career* with Barclays DeZoete Wedd 1985–92, dir Ludgate Communications 1995–98, founding ptnr Penrose Financial 1998–2010, md MHP 2010–13, vice-chm Hudson Sandler 2013–; patron Lighthouse, memb Ctee Terrence Higgins Tst; *Books* Tartanware (with Princess Ira von Furstenberg); *Recreations* interior design, fitness, travel; *Style*— Andrew Nicolls, Esq; ✉ Hudson Sandler, 29 Cloth Fair, London EC1A 7NN (☎ 020 3128 8100), e-mail anicolls2@gmail.com)

NICOLSON, Adam; *see:* Carnock, 5 Baron (UK 1916)

NICOLSON, Fiona; da of Edward James Hart, of Helensburgh, and late Margaret McLean, *née* Wilson; *b* 22 June 1954; *Educ* Glasgow HS for Girls, Jordanhill Coll of Educn Univ of Glasgow (MA, LLB, DipLP, teaching cert); *m* 2, 10 April 1996, Francis Hugh Binnie, s of late Dr H Binnie; 2 c from prev m (Alexander David Nicolson b 28 Sept 1976, Anna Fiona Jane Nicolson b 17 April 1978); *Career* partner and head Intellectual Property Gp Bird Semple Fyfe Ireland 1991–93 (slr and assoc 1986–91), partner and head Intellectual Property and Technology Department Maclay Murray & Spens 1994–2009, partner Bristows 2009–; hon vice-pres: St Andrews Clinics for Children, Law Society of Scotland (member 1986–, notary public), Law Society England & Wales (member 2011–); past pres and memb Cncl Licensing Executives Society Britain and Ireland; vice-chair Licensing Executives Society International; vice-pres and memb Bd Licensing Executives Society International, convener Accreditation Panel for Intellectual Property Law Society of Scotland; past chair Lexmundi Intellectual Property Practice Group; trustee and vice-chair: Med Research Scotland, member BIA Regenerative Medicine Industry Group; MInstD; *Publications* A Directory of Technology Transfer Services in Scotland (co-ed, 1992); *Recreations* yoga, boats, travel; *Style*— Ms Fiona Nicolson; ✉ Bristows, 100 Victoria Embankment, London EC4Y 0DH (☎ 020 7400 8000, fax 020 7400 8050, DX 269 Chancery Lane, e-mail fiona.nicolson@bristows.com)

NICOLSON, John; MP; s of John Nicolson, and Marion, *née* Stant; *b* Glasgow; *Educ* Univ of Glasgow (MA), Harvard Univ (Kennedy scholar, Harkness fell, English Speaking Union scholar); *Partner* Juliano Zini; *Career* speechwriter US Senate, political corr On The Record (BBC), reporter Newsnight; presenter: ITV, BBC News 24, BBC Breakfast; MP (SNP) E Dunbartonshire 2015–; SNP shadow min for culture, media and sport; memb Select Ctee DCMS; *Publications* contrib to numerous newspapers incl: The Times, The Sunday Times, Observer, Harvard Int Review; *Recreations* cinema, golf, music, opera, reading, travel, walking; *Style*— John Nicolson, Esq, MP; ✉ House of Commons, London SW1A 0AA (e-mail john.nicolson.mp@parliament.uk)

NICOLSON, Rebecca; da of Nigel Nicolson, OBE (d 2004), and Philippa, *née* Tennyson d'Eyncourt; *Educ* St Paul's Girls' Sch, St Hugh's Coll Oxford; *Career* features ed The Observer 1990–92, ed Observer Magazine 1992–93, features ed The Spectator 1993–95, dep ed (review) Sunday Telegraph 1995–98, dep ed Independent on Sunday 1998–99; currently publisher Short Books; *Books* published incl: The Good Granny Guide (by Jane Fearnley Whittingstall, 2005), Amo, Amas, Amat (by Harry Mount, 2006), It's All Greek to Me (by Charlotte Higgins, 2008), Social Social Animal (by David Brooks, 2011), How to Be a Bad Birdwatcher (by Simon Barnes, 2012), How to Be Danish (by Patrick Kingsley, 2013), A Commonplace Killing (by Sian Busby, 2014), The Fast Diet (by Mimi Spencer & Michael Mosley, 2014), The 8 Week Blood Sugar Diet (by Michael Mosley, 2015); *Recreations* horse racing, gardening; *Style*— Ms Rebecca Nicolson; ✉ Short Books, Screenworks, 22 Highbury Grove, London N5 2ER (☎ 020 7833 9429, mobile 07770 235117, e-mail rebecca@shortbooks.biz)

NICOLSON, Sanders Nairn; s of William Holmes Nicolson (d 1966), of Glasgow, and Eleanor Mary, *née* Dunlop; *b* 23 July 1944; *Educ* Glasgow HS for Boys, Gordonstoun, Regent St Poly London; *Children* 1 s (Jamie Nairn Nicolson-Gray b 13 May 1986), 1 da (Rosanna Cailin Nicolson-Gray b 14 Dec 1988); *Career* starving artist, gardener and dish washer 1966–68, self-taught fashion photographer Foto Partners 1968–71, freelance photographer 1971–; clients incl: Next, Barbour, Stella Artois, Goretex, Boots, Max Factor, De Beers; solo exhibitions incl: Waves (Pentax Gallery London) 1979, Maske (The Association Gallery London) 1989; judge: Assoc of Photographers Awards 1996, D&AD Awards 2002; recipient: Assoc of Photographers (formerly AFAEP) Awards 1984, 1986, 1989, 1993, 1997, 1998 and 2002, D&AD Awards; *Recreations* fly fishing, gardening, music, food and wine, painting, photography; *Style*— Sanders Nicolson, Esq; ✉ e-mail mail@sandersnicolson.com, website www.sandersnicolson.com

NICOLSON, Seamus; *b* 23 February 1971, London; *Educ* Kingston Univ (BA), RCA (MA); *Career* photographer; photographed Vivienne Westwood advtg campaign 2004; Individual Artist Award London Arts Bd 1998, finalist Mandarina Duck Prize 2000; *Solo Exhibitions* Galerie Peter Borchardt Hamburg 1998, The Agency Contemporary Art London 1998, 2000, 2001, 2003 and 2004, Galeria Alberto Peola Turin 2000 and 2002, Galeria Metropolitana Barcelona 2001, Van Ram Gallery Gent 2004, Street Theatre: New Photographic (Galerie Peter Borchardt Hamburg) 2005, Works 1996–2006 (Museum Van Bommel Van Dam Venlo) 2006; *Group Exhibitions* Becks New Contemporaries (Camden Art Centre London) 1997, Art Forum Berlin (The Agency Berlin) 1997, Modern Narrative (Arts Sway Gallery Lymington) 1997, Supa Store (Cornerhouse Manchester) 1997, Group Show (UP & CO Gallery NY) 1997, Three Out Of Camden (Galerie Dorothee de Pauw Brussels) 1998, Shoreditch Biennial London 1998, Photofest Arles 1998, The Agency Contemporary Art Basel 1998, Sorted (Ikon Gallery London) 1998, John Kobal Prize (Nat Portrait Gallery London) 1998, Remix (Musée des Beaux Arts Nantes) 1998, Silence (Galeria Alberto Peola Turin) 1999, Berlin Artforum 1999, Surveying the Landscape (Lombard Freid NY) 1999, Tales of The Cities (The Agency London) 1999, Art Cologne 1999 and 2000, Bologna Artfair 2000, I'm Really Really Sorry (Luciano Inga-Pin Milan) 2000, Psychosoma (Lombard Freid NY) 2000, Artissima 00 Turin 2000, ARCO Agency Gallery UK Pavilion Madrid 2001, Night on Earth (Kunsthalle Muenster) 2001, Neue Welt (Frankfurter Kunstverein Frankfurt) 2001, The Centenery Development (Tate Britain London) 2001, Air Guitar (Milton Keynes Gallery) 2002, Shopping (Schirn Kunsthalle Frankfurt) 2002, Tate Liverpool 2002–03, MOMA Sao Paolo 2004, Stranger then Fiction (Leeds) 2003, British Photography (Huis Marseilles Amsterdam) 2004, Art Cologne (Galerie Peter Borchardt Hamburg) 2004; *Work in Permanent Collections* incl: Tate Modern, Art Cncl, Br Govt Art Collection, Ferens Art Collection Hull, Contemporary Art Soc London, Deka Bank Kunstsammlung Frankfurt; *Style*— Seamus Nicolson, Esq

NIELSEN, Beverley; da of Dr Stanley Nielsen, of Leigh, and Ethel Mary, *née* Jenkins; *b* 25 January 1960; *Educ* Trinity Coll Dublin (BA), Michael Smurfit Grad Sch of Mgmnt UC Dublin; *m* 1992, J Robert Emmerson, s of Dr R Emmerson; 2 s (Niels Robert Stanley b 26 Sept 1994, Charles Christian William b 16 Dec 1997), 1 da (Amelia Catherine b 25 July 1999); *Career* CBI: policy advsr European Affrs Gp until 1982, dep mangr Brussels 1982–84; sales and mktg co-ordinator Liz Leveque Fashions Inc NY 1984–85, PR offr Flora Kung Inc NY 1985–86, fashion asst Vogue magazine NY 1985–86, mktg exec Visnews Ltd London 1986–87, institutional equity dealer National City Brokers Dublin 1987–89, broadcast sales exec CNN Int Sales Ltd London 1989–91; CBI: asst dir North West 1992–95, dir West Midlands 1995–2000, customer rels and mktg dir 2000–01; chief exec Heart of England Tourist Bd 2001–03; Aga Foodservice Gp plc: non-exec dir 2001–03, md Fired Earth 2003, retail dir Aga, special projects dir 2005; fndr dir Midlands Excellence Ltd 1996–97, dir West Midlands Enterprise Ltd 1997–99, vice-chm West Midlands IOD 2006; non-exec dir: 100.7 Heart FM 1996–, 102.2 Galaxy Radio 1999–, Chrysalis Radio, Unicorn Tourism Ltd 2001–; princ fell Warwick Manufacturing Gp Univ of Warwick 2000–; memb: Midlands Advsy Cncl on Arts and Business 1996–, Cncl Univ of Birmingham 1997–2000, Advsy Bd Aston Business Sch 1999–2000, Chllr's Forum Coventry Univ, Chllr's Forum Staffordshire Univ 1999–2001; govr UC Worcester 1999–2002; Businesswoman of the Year Variety Club Midlands 1998; Hon MA Coventry Univ 1999; *Style*— Ms Beverley Nielsen

NIELSEN, Kester Carl (Kes) (KOEFOED-); s of Christian Koefoed-Nielsen, of Herts, and Mary Hayward, *née* Wright; *b* 9 December 1972, Newcastle-upon-Tyne; *Educ* Brockenhurst Coll Hants, Manchester Metropolitan Univ (BA); *m* 18 Sept 1999, Gaynor, *née* Finlan; 2 da (Kate b 19 Nov 1999, Sylvie b 27 Aug 2002), 1 s (Rafferty b 4 Feb 2008); *Career* bookseller Waterstone's 1994–2000, non-fiction mktg mangr Waterstone's HQ 2000–01, fiction buyer WH Smith HQ 2001–04, dir of book buying Amazon.co.uk 2004–09, dir of clothing Amazon.co.uk 2009–; *Recreations* music, food, wine, walking; *Style*— Kes Nielsen, Esq; ✉ Amazon.co.uk, Patriot Court, 1–9 The Grove, Slough SL1 1QP (☎ 020 8636 9225, e-mail kes@amazon.co.uk)

NIENOW, Prof Alvin William; s of Alvin William Nienow (d 1969), and Mary May, *née* Hawthorn (d 1968); *b* 19 June 1937, London; *Educ* St Clement Dane's GS, UCL (BSc, PhD, DSc); *m* 29 Aug 1959, Helen Mary; 1 da (Fiona Mary b 1961), 2 s (Gary John b 1963, Peter William b 1965); *Career* chem engr various industries 1958–63, hon research fell UCL 1980– (lectr and sr lectr 1963–80); Univ of Birmingham: prof of chemical engrg 1980–89, prof of biochemical engrg 1989–2004, emeritus prof 2004–; memb Rhône Poulenc Conseil Technologique 1988–2000 (pres 1998–2000); sr visiting fellowship Japanese Soc for Promotion of Sci 1986, hon visiting prof Sichuan Union Univ China 1996, visiting prof of biochemical engrg Loughborough Univ 2010, visiting prof Aston Univ 2015–; author and co-author of over 400 papers in chem and biochem engrg jls and conf proceedings; ed (Euro and Africa) Jl of Chemical Engrg Japan 2001–05; memb Ed Bd: Canadian Jl of Chemical Engrg (int advsr) 1989–2005, Biotechnology and Bioengineering 2003–; SERC: chm Chem Engrg Sub Ctee 1981–83, memb Biotechnology Directorate Ctee 1990–93, memb Engrg Bd 1991–94; Inst of Chem Engrs: memb Cncl and hon librarian 1984–88, rep on Euro Fedn of Chem Engrs Sci Advsy Ctee 1987–94, memb Euro Fedn Biotechnology Bioreactor Performance Working Party 1988–; AFRC: memb Cncl, memb Food Res Ctee and chm Engrg Advsy Gp 1987–89, Food Res Grants Bd 1988–91; BBSRC: Planning and Resource Ctee, Engrg and Physical Sciences Ctee 1994–96; memb: Advsy Ctee Czech Triennial Int Chem Engrg Congress 1986–2002, DTI Mgmnt Gp LINK in Biochem Engrg 1988–2002, Standing Ctee for Engrg Royal Acad of Engrg 1996–99, Governing Body Silsoe Research Inst 1996–98, Peer Review Coll Danish Cncl for Strategic Research 2008–; speaker Inst Engrs Australia Chemical Coll Bd 1999; Moulton medallist IChemE 1984, Jan E Purkyne medal Czech Acad of Science 1993, Donald Medal Inst of Chem Engrs 2000, Lifetime Contribution Award European Fedn of Chemical Engrs Working Pty on Mixing 2003, Special Contribution Medal Szczecin Univ of Technol Poland 2008; Hon Dr West Pomeranian Univ of Technol Poland 2010, Hon Dr Loughborough Univ 2012; FIChemE 1980 (MIChemE 1964), FREng 1985, hon memb Czech Soc of Chemical Engrg 2008; *Books* Mixing in the Process Industries (1985, 2 edn 1993, paperback edn 1997); *Recreations* sport, travel, dancing, skiing (3 Vallees Escapade, 2012 and 2015); *Clubs* MCC, Edgbaston Priory, Reading Cricket and Hockey; *Style*— Prof Alvin W Nienow, FREng; ✉ Department of Chemical Engineering, The University of Birmingham, Birmingham B15 2TT (e-mail a.w.nienow@bham.ac.uk)

NIGHT, Rebecca; *Educ* Rose Bruford Drama Sch, Nat Youth Theatre; *m* Harry Hadden-Paton; 1 da (Martha Rose b 2013); *Career* actress; *Theatre* The Importance of Being Earnest (Theatre Royal Bath and Vaudeville Theatre), The Grapes of Wrath (Chichester Festival Theatre) 2009, A Flea in Her Ear (Old Vic) 2011; *Television* Fanny Hill (BBC) 2007, Wuthering Heights (ITV) 2008, Caught in a Trap (ITV) 2008, The Courageous Heart of Irene Sendler (Hallmark) 2009, Law and Order: Shaken (ITV) 2010, This September (ZDF) 2010, Starlings (Sky 1) 2012; *Film* Modern Life Is Rubbish 2009, Suspension of Disbelief 2012, Cold 2013, Dartmoor Killing 2014; *Style*— Ms Rebecca Night; ✉ c/o Independent Talent Group, 40 Whitfield Street, London W1T 2RH (☎ 020 7636 6565)

NIGHTINGALE, Annie; MBE (2001); da of Basil John Nightingale, and Celia, *née* Winter; *Educ* St Catherine's Convent Twickenham, Lady Eleanor Holles Sch, Univ of Westminster; *Career* broadcaster; presenter: BBC Radio 1 1970–, Old Grey Whistle Test (BBC TV) 1978–82; columnist: Daily Express, Sunday Mirror; feature writer: Cosmopolitan magazine, Punch magazine; reporter and feature writer Brighton Evening Argus; ambass Prince's Tst; BASCA Gold Award for Services to Music 1992, Women of the Year Lifetime Achievement Award 1998, Muzik Magazine Caner of the Year Award 2001, inducted into Radio Acad Hall of Fame 2004, Best Radio Show Int Breaks Poll Awards 2006, 2007, 2008 and 2009, Radio Acad John Peel Award for Outstanding Contribution to Music Radio 2008, Breaks Poll Outstanding Contribution ot Breaks 2009; *Publications* Chase the Fade (1982), Wicked Speed (2000); Annie on One (compilation CD 1995), Y4K Annie Nightingale Presents (compilation CD, 2007); *Clubs* Cobden, The End; *Style*— Ms Annie Nightingale, MBE; ✉ BBC, Yalding House, 152–156 Great Portland Street, London W1N 4DJ (☎ 020 7765 4762, e-mail annie.nightingale@bbc.co.uk, website www.myspace.com/djannienightingale and www.facebook.com/djannienightingale, Twitter @aanightingale)

NIGHTINGALE, Caroline Ann; *see:* Slocock, Caroline Ann

NIGHTINGALE, Mary; da of David Trewyn Nightingale (d 2013), and Jennifer Constance Mary, *née* Tetley (d 2012); *Educ* Bedford Coll London (BA); *m* 2000, Paul Fenwick; 1 da, 1 s; *Career* presenter ITV News; *Recreations* skiing, travel; *Style*— Ms Mary Nightingale; ✉ Noel Gay Artists, 19 Denmark Street, London WC2H 8WJ

NIGHTINGALE, Neil; *Educ* Collyer's GS Horsham, Wadham Coll Oxford (MA); *Career* BBC: joined as researcher 1983, prodr BBC Natural History Unit 1989–95 (credits incl: Natural World, Wildlife on One, Lost Worlds Vanished Lives, The Private Life of Plants (Emmy Award 1995)), ed The Natural World 1995–2001 (RTS Best Documentary Series), ed Wildlife Specials 2001–03 (winner BAFTA Awards), exec prodr Wild Africa, Wild Down Under, Congo and Wild Battlefields, head BBC Natural History Unit 2003–09, creative dir BBC Earth 2009–, exec prodr Great Barrier Reef 2012, dir Walking With Dinosaurs 3D 2013, dir and prodr Enchanted Kingdom 3D 2014, dir Prehistoric Planet 3D 2014, dir and prodr Wild Africa 3D 2015, exec prodr Earthflight 3D and Predators 3D 2016; *Publications* New Guinea, An Island Apart (1992), Wild Down Under (2003); *Recreations* sailing, scuba diving; *Style*— Neil Nightingale; ✉ BBC Earth, Whiteladies Road, Bristol BS8 2LR

NIGHTINGALE, Richard Mervyn; s of Edward Humphrey Nightingale, CMG (d 1996), of Nunjoro Farm, Naivasha, Kenya, and Evelyn Mary, *née* Ray; *b* 9 July 1954; *Educ* Rugby, Emmanuel Coll Cambridge (MA, DipArch); *Career* architect; with practices in Nairobi, London and Hong Kong 1977–81, Colin St John Wilson and Partners 1981–85, estab Cullum and Nightingale Architects 1985 (became Kilburn Nightingale Architects 2010); articles published in: Architects Journal, Building Design, International Architect, Interni, Baumeister, Building Magazine, Perspectives in Architecture, Architectural Review, Architecture Today; taught at Univs of Bath, Cambridge, East London, Lincoln and Sheffield; work exhibited at: Royal Acad, RIBA, Fitzwilliam Museum Cambridge,

Building Centre London, Br Cncl Nairobi; tstee Southwark Festival 1996–2002; RIBA; FRSA 1999; *Building work published* House in Hampstead (1988), New British High Commission Nairobi (1989 and 1997), New Teaching Space North Westminster Sch (1991), Extensions Central Sch of Speech and Drama (1994, 1998), Harley Davidson Showroom (2000), New Eden House Bequia (2003), Embassy Theatre London (2003), Guludo Eco-Resort Mozambique (2005), British High Commission Kampala (2006), Library Emmanuel Coll Cambridge (2011); *Recreations* tennis, travel, taking pictures; *Style*— Richard Nightingale, Esq; ✉ 30A Parkhill Road, London NW3 (☎ 020 7482 1213); Kilburn Nightingale Architects, 26 Harrison Street, London WC1H 8JW (☎ 020 7812 1102, e-mail r@richardnightingale.com)

NIGHTINGALE OF CROMARTY, John Bartholomew Wakelyn; Baron of Cromarty (feudal); er s Michael David Nightingale of Cromarty, OBE (d 1998); *b* 7 September 1960; *Educ* Winchester, Magdalen Coll Oxford (MA, DPhil); *m* 24 December 1996, Lucy Charlotte, da of Dr Patrick Drummond Fergusson (d 1997); 1 s (Thomas b 1999), 1 da (Alice b 2002); *Career* Harmsworth sr res scholar Merton Coll Oxford 1984–86; fell Magdalen Coll Oxford 1986– (tutor in modern history 1993–), fell Winchester Coll 2002–; chm: Black Isle Civic Tst 1993–, Cromarty Arts Tst 1998–; tstee: Cromarty Harbour Tst, Wye Rural Museum Tst 1999–; vice-pres Romney Marsh Historic Churches Tst 2005–; *Publications* Monasteries and Patrons in the Gorze Reform (2001); also articles on medieval history; *Recreations* woodland management, restoration of old buildings; *Clubs* Athenaeum; *Style*— John Nightingale; ✉ Cromarty House, Ross and Cromarty IV11 8XS; 25 West Square, London SE11 4SP

NIGHY, William Francis (Bill); s of Alfred Martin Nighy, and Catherine Josephine, *née* Whittaker; *b* 1949; *Educ* John Fisher GS Surrey, Guildford Sch of Acting; *Career* actor; *Theatre* RNT productions incl: Illuminatus!!!, A Map of the World, Skylight, Pravda, King Lear, The Seagull, Arcadia, Mean Tears, Blue/Orange; other productions incl: Rudy in The Milk Train Doesn't Stop Here Any More (professional debut, Watermill Theatre Newbury), Betrayal (Almeida), A Kind of Alaska (Donmar Warehouse), Landscape and Silence (Chester Gateway), Illuminations (Lyric Hammersmith), Speak Now (Traverse Theatre Edinburgh), The Warp (ICA), The Vertical Hour (Music Box Theatre NY); *Television* Soldiers Talking Cleanly, Deasey's Desperate, Dreams of Leaving, Easter 2016, The Last Place on Earth, Antonia and Jane, The Men's Room, Absolute Hell, The Maitlands, Longitude, People Like Us, Auf Wiedersehen Pet, The Lost Prince, Ready When You Are Mr McGill, State of Play, The Young Visiters, The Girl in the Cafe, Gideon's Daughter, Page Eight; *Radio* The Lord of the Rings, Bleak House, Little Dorrit, Strangers on a Train, The Mind Body Problem, Beaumarchais, Pravda, Skylight, Arcadia, Romeo and Juliet, The Libertine, The Information, People Like Us, No Commitments, Death of the Heart; *Film* Still Crazy, Blow Dry, Lucky Break, Fairy Tale, The Lawless Heart, Indian Summer, I Capture the Castle, Underworld, Love Actually, Enduring Love, Shaun of the Dead, Hitchhiker's Guide to the Galaxy, Notes on a Scandal, Pirates of the Caribbean: Dead Man's Chest, Pirates of the Caribbean: At World's End, Valkyrie,Underworld: Rise of the Lycans, The Boat That Rocked, G-Force, Glorious 39, Astro Boy, Wild Target, Harry Potter and the Deathly Hallows: Part I, Rango, Arthur Christmas; *Awards* Barclays Theatre Managers Award 1997, Peter Sellers Evening Standard Comedy Award 1999 and 2004, LA Critics Circle Best Suppporting Actor 2004, London Critics Circle Best Supporting Actor 2004, BAFTA Best Supporting Actor 2004, BAFTA Best Actor 2004 (for State of Play), Golden Globe Best Actor 2007 (for Gideon's Daughter); *Recreations* books, walks, rhythm and blues, air guitar; *Style*— Bill Nighy, Esq; ✉ c/o Markham & Froggatt Ltd, Julian House, 4 Windmill Street, London W1P 1HF (☎ 020 7636 4412)

NIMMO, Alison; CBE (2004); *Career* dir of design and regeneration 2007–12, chief exec Crown Estate 2012–; non-exec dir Berkeley Gp; tstee UK Green Building Cncl; memb Cncl Imperial Coll London; *Style*— Ms Alison Nimmo, CBE; ✉ The Crown Estate, 16 New Burlington Place, London W1S 2HX (website www.thecrownestate.co.uk, Twitter @TheCrownEstate)

NIMMO, Prof Walter Sneddon; CBE (2014); s of Thomas Russell Nimmo, and Margaret Sneddon (d 2004); *b* 2 April 1947, Whitburn, W Lothian; *Educ* Bathgate Acad, Univ of Edinburgh (BSc, MB ChB, MD); *m* 4 July 2004, Norma Kellet; 1 s (John b 21 Aug 1976), 1 da (Kathryn b 7 Nov 1980); *Career* Sir Stanley Davidson lectr in clinical pharmacology Univ of Edinburgh 1973–76, lectr in anaesthesia Univ of Edinburgh 1977–79, sr lectr in anaesthesia Univ of Glasgow 1979–84, prof of anaesthesia Univ of Sheffield 1984–88, chm and chief exec Inveresk Clinical Research 1988–96, chief exec Inveresk Research 1996–2004; non-exec dir Aberforth Smaller Companies Trust plc 2004–14; tstee Nat Museums of Scotland; Scottish Entrepreneur of the Year 2002; MD (hc) Univ of Edinburgh; FRCA 1977, FRCP 1984, FANZCA 1988, FRCPEd 1988, FRCPGlas 1988, FFPM 1993, FRSE 2000, FRCSEd; *Books* editor of 11 textbooks in anaesthesia, clinical measurement and drug absorption, author of over 100 papers in academic jls; *Recreations* songwriter, cabaret performer, music, reading, travel; *Clubs* New (Edinburgh); *Style*— Prof Walter Nimmo, CBE

NINKOV, Mladen; s of Stevan Ninkov (d 2013), and Smiljka Ninkov (d 2003); *b* 4 May 1961, Perth, Australia; *Educ* Univ of WA (Queen Elizabeth II Silver Jubilee scholar, BJuris, LLB), Trinity Hall Cambridge (LLM); *m* 3 Feb 1991, Peggy, *née* Collins; 2 da (Natasha b 15 Oct 1992, Tatiana b 16 Sept 1996), 1 s (Stevan b 5 Aug 1994); *Career* barr and slr Supreme Court of Western Aust 1985; barr and slr Freehill, Hollingdale and Page 1985–86, Skadden, Arps, Slate, Meagher and Flom 1986–87, vice-pres Prudential-Bache Securities Inc 1987–91, dir and head of int fin ANZ Grindlays plc 1991–93, subsequently md Maxwell Central and East European Ptnrs plc, currently princ Keynes Capital, chm Griffin Mining 2000– (formerly pres), currently chm Spitfire Oil, former chm Westgold Resources NL; former dir: Ramsgate Resources NL, Mt Monger Gold Project Pty Ltd, Castle Hill Resources NL, Matu Mining Pty Ltd; *Recreations* tennis, skiing, golf, Formula 1; *Clubs* Queen's, Royal Perth Golf; *Style*— Mladen Ninkov, Esq; ✉ Keynes Capital, Level 9, BGC Centre, 28 The Esplanade, Perth, WA 6000, Australia; Keynes Capital, 60 St James Street, 6th and 7th Floors, London SW1A 1LE (☎ 020 7629 7772, fax 020 7629 7773)

NISBET, Andrew; s of Peter Nisbet, and Mary, *née* Lalonde; *b* 21 August 1960, Weston-super-Mare, Somerset; *Educ* St Peter's Weston Super-Mare, Kings Coll Taunton; *m* 6 July 1985, Anne Marie, *née* West; 1 s (Joseph Peter b 2 March 1988), 1 da (Emily Rose b 8 Sept 1990); *Career* Peter Nisbet Ltd 1978–83, Nisbets plc 1983–; High Sheriff City and County of Bristol 2012–13; tstee Bristol Music Tst 2013–, govr Merchants' Acad 2015–; memb Soc of Merchant Venturers 2008–; *Style*— Andrew Nisbet, Esq

NISBET, Prof Hugh Barr; s of Thomas Nisbet (d 1977), of Edinburgh, and Lucy Mary, *née* Hainsworth; *b* 24 August 1940; *Educ* Dollar Acad, Univ of Edinburgh (MA, PhD), Univ of Cambridge (LittD); *m* 1, 26 Dec 1962 (m dis 1981), Monika Luise Ingeborg, da of Wilhelm Otto Uecker, of Guben, Germany; 2 s (Arnold b 1966, Marcus b 1968); m 2, 24 Nov 1995, Angela Maureen Parker, da of Cecil Chapman, of Great Yarmouth; *Career* reader Univ of Bristol 1972–73 (asst lectr 1965–67, lectr 1967–72), prof of German Univ of St Andrews 1974–81, prof of modern languages (German) Sidney Sussex Coll Cambridge 1982–2007 (life fell 2008–); memb: Ctee Modern Humanities Res Assoc 1972–84, Gen Teaching Cncl Scotland 1978–81, Bd of Govrs Dollar Acad 1978–81, Cncl English Goethe Soc 1978–, Ctee Goethe-Gesellschaft 1991–95, Nat Cncl for Modern Languages 1983–90; pres Br Soc Eighteenth Century Studies 1986–88 (vice-pres 1984–86), tstee Kurt Hahn Tst 1988–95, memb Cncl Lessing-Akademie 2008–, pres Modern Humanities Res Assoc 2010; *Books* Herder and the Philosophy and History of Science (1970), Goethe and the Scientific Tradition (1972), Lessing: Eine Biographie (2008, Hamann-Forschungspreis 2010, Einhard Prize for Biography 2011, revised edition in English (Gotthold Ephraim Lessing: His Life, Works, and Thought) 2013); *Recreations* music, art history; *Style*— Prof H B Nisbet; ✉ Sidney Sussex College, Cambridge CB2 3HU (☎ 01223 338877)

NISH, David Thomas; s of Thomas Nish, and Jean C M, *née* Scott; *Educ* Paisley GS, Univ of Glasgow; *m* Caroline M, *née* Smith; *Career* ptnr Price Waterhouse 1993–97; ScottishPower plc: dep fin dir 1997–99, fin dir 1999–2005, gp dir Infrastructure Divison 2005–06; Standard Life plc: gp fin dir 2006–09, ceo 2010–; dep chm ABI, former memb Urgent Issue Task Force of the Accounts Standards Bd (UITF); non-exec dir Green Investment Bank 2012–; former non-exec dir: Thus plc, Northern Foods plc, Royal Scottish Nat Orch; Scottish Fin Dir of the Year 2000 and 2009; MICAS 1984; *Recreations* cycling, travel, family; *Style*— David Nish, Esq; ✉ Standard Life plc, Standard Life House, 30 Lothian Road, Edinburgh EH1 2DH

NIVEN, Dr Alastair Neil Robertson; LVO (2012), OBE (2001); s of Harold Robertson Niven (d 1999), and Elizabeth Isobel Robertson, *née* Mair (d 1993); *b* 25 February 1944; *Educ* Dulwich Coll, Univ of Cambridge (MA), Univ of Ghana (MA), Univ of Leeds (PhD); *m* 22 Aug 1970, Helen Margaret, da of Claude William Trow (d 1983); 1 da (Isabella b 1981), 1 s (Alexander b 1985); *Career* lectr: Univ of Ghana 1968–69, Univ of Leeds 1969–70, Univ of Stirling 1970–78; dir gen Africa Centre London 1978–84, Chapman fell Inst of Cwlth Studies Univ of London 1984–85, special asst to Sec Gen Assoc of Cwlth Univs 1985–87, dir of literature Arts Cncl of GB 1987–97 (Arts Cncl of England since 1994), dir of literature Br Cncl 1997–2001, princ King George VI and Queen Elizabeth Fndn of St Catharine's Cumberland Lodge Windsor 2001–13, assoc dir Iraq Br Business Cncl 2013–; chm: Public Schs Debating Assoc England and Wales 1961–62, Literature Panel Gtr London Arts Assoc 1981–84, UK Cncl for Overseas Student Affrs 1987–92, Southern Africa Book Devpt Educnl Tst 1997–2003, Annual Register 2013–, Border Crossings 2013–; pres English PEN 2003–07, tstee Cncl for Educn in the Cwlth 2013–; judge of the Booker Prize 1994 and 2014, chm of jury Stakis Prize for Scottish Writer of the Year 1998, chm of jury English Speaking Union Marsh Prize for Biography 1999–2011; *Books* D H Lawrence: The Novels (1978), The Yoke of Pity: The Fictional Writings of Mulk Raj Anand (1978), D H Lawrence (1980), The Commonwealth of Univs (with Sir Hugh W Springer, 1987), Under Another Sky: The Commonwealth Poetry Prize Anthology (ed, 1987), Enigmas and Arrivals: An Anthology of Commonwealth Writing (co-ed with Michael Schmidt, 1997); *Recreations* theatre, travel, cat sitting; *Clubs* Athenaeum; *Style*— Dr Alastair Niven, LVO, OBE; ✉ 51 Hanover Gardens, London SE11 5TN (☎ 01784 432316, fax 01784 497799, e-mail alastairniven@gmail.com)

NIXON, David; OBE (2010); s of David Nixon, of London, and Alice, *née* Charvill; *b* Windsor, Ontario; *Educ* Nat Ballet Sch of Canada (Peter Dwyer scholarship, Canada Cncl grant); *m* 29 June 1985, Yoko Ichino; *Career* princ dancer: Nat Ballet of Canada, Deutsche Oper Berlin, Bayerisches Staatsballett Munich; guest artist: Hamburg Ballet, Staatsoper Ballet Berlin, Komische Oper Berlin, Birmingham Royal Ballet, Royal Winnipeg Ballet; guest choreographer: Royal Winnipeg Ballet, Cape Town City Ballet, Ballet du Rhin, Nat Ballet of Estonia, Alberta Ballet; dir: BalletMet Columbus OH 1995–2001, Northern Ballet Theatre 2001–; Best Male Dancer of the Year Munich, Dir of the Year Dance Europe 2004 and 2007; *Style*— David Nixon, Esq, OBE; ✉ Northern Ballet Theatre, Quarry Hill, Leeds LS2 7PA (☎ 0113 220 8000)

NIXON, Prof James Robert; OBE (2015), DL (Co Down); s of Dr Robert Samuel Nixon, of Bangor, Co Down, and Veda, *née* McKee; *b* 2 September 1943; *Educ* Bangor GS, Trinity Coll Dublin (MB BCh, BAO, MA), Univ of Liverpool (MChOrth); *m* 23 June 1967, Katherine, da of Ronald Stoddart Nesbitt, of Dublin; 1 da (Holly b 1968), 1 s (Alexander b 1972); *Career* formerly: conslt orthopaedic surgn Belfast City Hosp, med dir Green Park Healthcare Tst Belfast; currently: pt/t conslt orthopaedic surgn Musgrave Park Hosp, hon prof of orthopaedic surgery Queen's Univ Belfast; examiner: RCS Ireland, FRCS in Orthopaedics (FRCSOrth); pres Br Hip Soc 2002–03 (vice-pres 2000–02), pres NI Medico-Legal Soc 2001–02, sec Irish Orthopaedic Assoc; chm RYA NI 1983–86; FRCSI 1971, FRCS 1972; *Recreations* sailing, fishing, beekeeping; *Clubs* Royal Ulster Yacht, Irish Cruising, Royal Cruising; *Style*— Prof James Nixon, OBE, DL, FRCS; ✉ 48 Ballydorn Road, Killinchy, Co Down, Northern Ireland BT23 6QB (☎ 028 9754 3336, e-mail nixon-j@sky.com)

NIXON, John Edwin; s of late Edwin Nixon, and Dorothy, *née* Hall; *b* 5 December 1948; *Educ* Univ of Edinburgh Med Sch (MB ChB, ChM), Univ of Oxford (MA), FRCS; *m* Bridget Anne, da of late Dr S John Coulson, of Stratton-on-the-Fosse, Somerset; 1 s (David John b 1976), 2 da (Susannah Jane b 1980, Natasha Elizabeth b 1985); *Career* former clinical reader in orthopaedic surgery Univ of Oxford, hon conslt orthopaedic surgn Nuffield Orthopaedic Centre, former conslt orthopaedic surgn KCH; currently hon conslt orthopaedic surgn Charing Cross and Hammersmith Hosp, sr examiner Univ of London, external examiner Univ of Oxford, Univ of Nottingham and KCL, hon sr lectr Imperial Coll Sch of Med, chair London Clinic Orthopaedic Gp, past fell Green Coll Oxford, past organiser annual spinal surgery course Imperial Coll London; ed and pt author int reference work on Spinal Stenosis, also numerous pubns on joint replacement, arthroscopy, trauma, foot surgery and spinal surgery and spinal biomechanics; past pres W London Medicochirurgical Soc; tstee DISCS Charity, chm IDF Educn Tst; memb: BMA, memb SICOT; fell: Girdlestone Orthopaedic Soc, Br Assoc of Spinal Surgeons, Br Assoc of Children's Orthopaedic Surgery, Br Assoc of Surgns of the Knee, Br Hip Soc, Br Orthopaedic Spinal Sugeon, Chelsea Clinical Soc, Royal Instn, Br Orthopaedic Assoc; FRSM, fell Medical Soc of London, FRGS; *Publications* ed-in-chief reference work on Lumbar Spinal Stenosis, contrib to numerous other textbooks and author of numerous jl pubns on hip surgery, knee surgery, spinal surgery and medical educn; *Recreations* family, travel, sailing (yachtmaster ocean), skiing, theatre; *Clubs* Athenaeum, Royal Lymington Yacht, Royal Ocean Racing, Little Ship; *Style*— John E Nixon, FRCS; ✉ The London Clinic, 116 Harley Street, London W1G 7JL (☎ 020 7034 6160 (medicolegal PA) or 07860 267861 (direct))

NIXON, Prof John Forster; s of Edward Forster Nixon, MBE (d 1989), and Mary, *née* Lytton (d 1993); *b* 27 January 1937; *Educ* Whitehaven GS, Univ of Manchester (BSc, PhD, DSc), Univ of Cambridge, Univ of Southern Calif; *m* 19 Nov 1960, Kim, da of John Thomas Smith (d 1987); 1 da ((Susan) Joanna Forster b 16 July 1964), 1 s (Jonathan Forster b 23 March 1966); *Career* ICI research fell Cambridge 1962–64, lectr in chemistry Univ of St Andrews 1964–66; Univ of Sussex: lectr in chemistry 1966, reader 1975, prof 1986–2002, dean Sch of Chemistry 1989–92, research prof 2002–11, emeritus prof 2011–; Royal Soc Leverhulme sr research fell 1993–94, visiting fell Research Sch of Chemistry ANU Canberra 2004; visiting prof: Victoria Univ Canada 1971, Simon Fraser Univ Canada 1976, Indian Inst of Sci Bangalore 2001–02 and 2004–05, Indian Inst of Science Educn and Research Trivandrum India 2010; titular memb Inorganic Nomenclature Cmmn IUPAC 1986–88; memb: Inorganic Chemistry Panel SERC 1986–89, Editorial Bd Phosphorus, Sulphur, Silicon Jl 1989–2006, Dalton Cncl 1994–97, Scientific Advsy Bd Internet Jl of Chemistry 1997–2000, EPSRC 2001–, Bd of Dirs Main Gp Chemistry Ctee, Int Bd of Phosphorus Chemistry; FRS 1994; *Awards* Royal Soc of Chemistry: Corday-Morgan medal and prize 1973, Main Gp Element prize and medal 1985, Tilden lectureship and prize 1992, Alexander von Humboldt prize 2001–02 and 2009–11, Ludwig Mond lectr and medal winner RSC 2002–03, Geza Zemplen medal Budapest Inst of Technol 2003; *Publications* Phosphorus: The Carbon Copy (jly, 1998); 396 contribs to a variety of chemistry jls; *Recreations* walking, theatre, watching cricket, cycling; *Style*— Prof John Nixon, FRS; ✉ Department of Chemistry and Biochemistry, School of Life Sciences, University of Sussex, Brighton, East Sussex BN1 9RQ (☎ 01273 678536, fax 01273 876687); Juggs Barn, The Street, Kingston, Lewes, East Sussex (☎ 01273 483993)

NOAH, Prof Norman David; s of Jack David Noah (d 2002), of Wallington, Surrey, and Jane Rachel, *née* Samuel (d 1961); *b* 7 July 1939, Rangoon, Burma; *Educ* Burma, India and London, St Thomas' Hosp Med Sch London (MB BS); *m* 7 March 1971, Veronica Hilary, da of Bruno Kiwi; 2 s (Benedict Joel David b 16 April 1974, Joshua Luke Alexander b 2 July 1975), 1 da (Olivia Rachel Emma b 16 Feb 1979); *Career* house surgn Worthing Hosp 1964; St Thomas' Hosp: house physician 1964–65, SHO 1965–66, registrar 1966; SHO West End Hosp for Neurology and Neurosurgery 1967–68, research asst Dept of Experimental Pathology Cardiothoracic Inst The Brompton Hosp and registrar Paddington and Kensington Chest Clinic and St Charles' Hosp London 1968–70, sr epidemiologist Epidemiological Research Lab Central Public Health Lab London 1971–76, hon community physician Brent and Harrow AHA 1977–78, conslt epidemiologist Communicable Disease Surveillance Centre 1977–89, hon sr lectr Dept of Clinical Epidemiology and Social Med Royal Free Hosp Sch of Med 1979–89, hon conslt in control of infection Shenley Hosp 1983–89, prof and head Dept of Public Health and Epidemiology King's Coll Hosp Sch of Med and Dentistry 1989–98, dir of public health King's Healthcare 1989–98, prof of epidemiology and public health LSHTM 1998–; distinguished visitor Dept of Public Health and Primary Care Royal Free Hosp Sch of Med 1989–94, conslt in communicable disease Thames Region NRA Environment Agency 1989–2000, hon conslt Acupuncture Cncl of GB 1990–2004, hon conslt Communicable Disease Surveillance Centre 1993–98, conslt epidemiologist PHLS Communicable Disease Surveillance Centre Colindale 1998–2003, visiting prof Istituto di Igiene Univ of Rome 1996, 1998, 1999, 2000, 2001 and 2002; jt conslt to WHO/Int Epidemiological Assoc on epidemiology 1987, advsr to Aust Nat Univ Canberra on formation of CDSC/CDC type centre for surveillance of infectious diseases 1989, chm WHO meeting on acute respiratory infections Geneva 1990, advsr to WHO and Govt of China on the surveillance and control of infectious diseases March 1995, conslt Tesco Influenza Panel; sec and memb Exec Cncl Int Epidemiological Assoc 1993–96; external examiner: Univ of Manchester 1992–95, Royal London Hosp Sch of Med 1996–2000, Dept of Public Health Univ of Glasgow 1996–2002, Kuwait Nat Univ 1997, UCL 2004; memb: MRC Sub-Ctee on Respiratory Syncytial Virus 1980–94, Med Advsy Ctee Nat Meningitis Tst 1987–2002, RCP Working Pty on Prevention 1988–91, Specialist Advsy Ctee and Educn Ctee FPHM 1993–96, Med Advsy Ctee Br Liver Tst 1994–98; editorial rep and memb Cncl Section of Epidemiology and Community Med RSM 1981–96, sr ed and managing ed Epidemiology and Infection 2002–; author of various books and book chapters and numerous original and leading articles in learned jls; MFCM, FFPH, FRCP (MRCP); *Publications* Controlling Communicable Disease (2006); *Recreations* cricket, music, food and wine, travel, hoarding (magpie syndrome) and oniomania; *Clubs* MCC; *Style*— Prof Norman Noah; ✉ Orley Rise, Orley Farm Road, Harrow-on-the-Hill, Middlesex HA1 3PE (☎ 020 8422 2649); Department of Epidemiology and Public Health, London School of Hygiene and Tropical Medicine, Keppel Street, London WC1E 7HT (☎ 020 7299 4767, e-mail norman.n@noark.plus.com)

NOAKES, Michael; s of Basil Henry Noakes (d 1969), of Horley and then Reigate, Surrey, and Mary Josephine, *née* Gerard (d 1989); *b* 28 October 1933, Brighton, E Sussex; *Educ* Downside, Reigate Sch of Art, RA Schs London; *m* 9 July 1960, late Dr Vivien Noakes, FRSL, the writer, da of Marcus Langley (d 1977), of Reigate, Surrey; 1 da (Anya b 1961), 2 s (Jonathan b 1963, Benedict b 1965); *Career* Nat Serv 1954–56, Subaltern; portrait and landscape painter; numerous TV and radio appearances on art subjects; subject of: Portrait BBC 2 (with Eric Morley, 1977 and 1978), Changing Places BBC1 (with Jak, 1989); art corr Town & Around BBC 1964–68; ROI: elected memb 1964, vice-pres 1968–72, pres 1972–78, hon memb Cncl 1978–, fell 1996–; RP: elected memb 1967, memb Cncl 1969–72, 1972–74, 1978–80, 1993–95, 2004 and 2006–07; dir Fedn of Br Artists 1981–83 (govr 1972–81); hon memb: Nat Soc, United Soc; former chm Contemporary Portrait Soc, former pres Soc of Catholic Artists; judge Miss World Contest 1976; platinum disc award (for record sleeve Portrait of Sinatra, 1977); Freeman City of London; former FRSA; *Exhibitions* RA, ROI, RBA, RSMA, RP, Nat Soc, Young Contemporaries, Contemporary Portrait Soc, Grosvenor and Upper Grosvenor Galleries, Grafton Galleries (also New Grafton, Upper Grafton), Woodstock Galleries, RGI, Christie's, Tryon; *Represented in Collections of* HM The Queen, Royal Collection Windsor, Prince of Wales, Br Museum, Nat Portrait Gallery Perm Collection, numerous univs, House of Commons, Frank Sinatra, Guildhall London; *Portraits* incl: The Queen and most other members of the Royal Family, Pope Benedict XVI, President Clinton, Margaret Thatcher (when PM and after), and numerous other figures from service, academic, business and theatre life, as well as many sitters whose portraits were commissioned by their families; *Group Portraits* incl: Queen Elizabeth The Queen Mother opening Overlord Embroidery to public view (with The Duke of Norfolk, Princess Alice Countess of Athlone, Earl Mountbatten, and others), The Princess Royal being admitted to Livery of Worshipful Co of Woolmen, The Five Lords of Appeal in Ordinary for the Middle Temple (Lord Cross, Lord Diplock, Lord Salmon, Lord Wilberforce, Lord Simon), a commission for the Corporation of London to mark the Royal Silver Wedding featuring all senior members of the Royal Family at that time; designer of a £5 coin to mark the 50th birthday of The Prince of Wales 1998; *Books* A Professional Approach to Oil Painting (1968), contrib to various journals and books on art subjects; illustrator The Daily Life of the Queen: an Artist's Diary (by Vivien Noakes); *Recreations* idling; *Clubs* Garrick; *Style*— Michael Noakes; ✉ Eaton Heights, Eaton Road, Malvern WR14 4PE (☎ 01684 575530, website www.michael-noakes.co.uk)

NOAKES, Baroness (Life Peer UK 2000), of Goudhurst in the County of Kent; Dame Sheila Valerie Noakes; DBE (1996); da of Albert Frederick Masters, and Iris Sheila, *née* Ratcliffe; *b* 23 June 1949; *Educ* Eltham Hill GS, Univ of Bristol (LLB); *m* 3 Aug 1985, (Colin) Barry Noakes, s of Stuart Noakes, of Brenchley; *Career* KPMG: joined 1970, ptnr 1983–2000; seconded to: HM Treasy as accounting/commercial advsr 1979–81, Dept of Health as fin dir on NHS Mgmnt Exec 1988–91; sr non-exec dir Court of the Bank of England 1994–2001; memb: London Soc of CAs 1984–88, Cncl ICAEW 1987–2002 (pres 1999–2000); memb: Ctee of Enquiry MAFF 1988–2000, Mgmnt Bd of Inland Revenue 1992–99, NHS Policy Bd 1992–95, Private Fin Panel 1993–97, Bd of Companions Inst of Mgmnt 1997–2002, Public Services Productivity Panel 1998–2000, Cncl Inst of Business Ethics 1998–2003; memb Bd: ENO 2000–08, Carpetright plc 2001–14, Hanson plc 2001–07, SThree plc 2001–07, John Laing plc 2002–04, The Racing Tst 2002–04, Social Market Fndn 2002–05, ICI plc 2004–07, Severn Trent plc 2008–14, Royal Bank of Scotland Gp plc 2011–; dep chm Ofcom 2014–; cmmr of Public Works Loan Bd 1995–2001; Cons front bench spokesman House of Lords: work and pensions 2001–08, health 2001–03, treasy 2003–10; tstee Thomson Reuters Founder Share Co Ltd 1998–; govr London Business Sch 1998–2001; memb Cncl: Marlborough Coll 2000–02, Eastbourne Coll 2000–04; Hon DBA London Guildhall Univ, Hon LLD Univ of Bristol, Hon DSc Univ of Buckingham; FCA; *Books* Tolley's Stamp Duties (1980); *Recreations* skiing, horse racing, opera, early classical music; *Style*— Baroness Noakes, DBE; ✉ House of Lords, London SW1A 0PW (☎ 020 7219 5230, fax 020 7219 4215, e-mail noakess@parliament.uk)

NOBES, Prof Christopher William; s of Harold Alfred Nobes, and Beryl Muriel, *née* Ramsay; *b* 20 March 1950; *Educ* Portsmouth GS, Univ of Exeter (BA, PhD); *m* 27 March 1982 (m dis 1988); *Career* head internal audit Hambro Life Assurance 1973–75, lectr Univ of Exeter 1975–82; prof of accounting: Univ of Strathclyde 1982–86, Univ of Reading 1987–2007, Royal Holloway Univ of London 2007–; memb Accounting Standards Ctee UK and Ireland 1987–90, vice-chm Accounting Ctee Fédération des Experts Comptables Européens, UK rep on Bd of Int Accounting Standards Ctee 1993–2001; FCCA 1973; *Books* incl: Comparative International Accounting (1981, 9 edn 2006), Accountants' Liability in the 1980's (with E P Minnis 1985), Issues in Multinational Accounting (with R H Parker 1988), Interpreting European Financial Statements (1994), Pocket Accounting (2002); contribs incl: The Fourth Directive and the United Kingdom (1984), Imputation Systems of Corporation Tax within the EEC (1984, 1985); *Style*— Prof Christopher Nobes; ✉ Department of Management, Royal Holloway, University of London, Egham, Surrey TW20 0EX

NOBLE, Adrian Keith; s of William John Noble (d 1987), of Chichester, W Sussex, and Violet Ena, *née* Wells (d 2003); *b* 19 July 1950; *Educ* Chichester HS, Univ of Bristol (BA), Drama Centre London; *m* June 1991, Joanne, *née* Pearce; 1 s, 1 da; *Career* assoc dir Bristol Old Vic Co 1976–80; RSC: assoc dir 1981–89, artistic dir 1991–2003 (artistic dir elect 1990); guest dir Manchester Royal Exchange Theatre Co; visiting prof London Inst 2001, hon fell Guildhall Sch of Music and Drama; Hon DLitt: Univ of Birmingham 1994, Univ of Bristol 1996, Univ of Exeter 1999, Univ of Warwick 2001; hon bencher Middle Temple 2001; *Theatre* prodns Stratford incl: King Lear 1993, A Midsummer Night's Dream 1994, Romeo and Juliet 1995, The Cherry Orchard 1995, Cymbeline 1997, The Lion, the Witch and the Wardrobe 1998, The Seagull 1999, The Secret Garden 2000; Chitty Chitty Bang Bang (London Palladium) 2002, Brand 2003, Summer and Smoke 2006; *Opera* The Fairy Queen (Aix en Provence) 1989 (Grand Prix des Critiques), Il Retour d'Ulysses (Aix en Provence) 2000 (Grand Prix des Critiques), Magic Flute (Glyndebourne) 2004, Cosi fan Tutti (Opera de Lyon) 2006, Macbeth (Met Opera NY), Marriage of Figaro (Opera de Lyon) 2007, Carmen (Paris) 2009, Alcina (Staatsoper Vienna), Xerxes (Theatre an der Wien), Don Carlo (Bolshoi), Simon Boccanegra (Rome); *Films* A Midsummer Night's Dream 1996; *Awards* 12 nominations Olivier Awards, Best Director and Best Revival CRITICS Awards; *Books* How to Do Shakespeare 2010; *Style*— Adrian Noble, Esq; ✉ c/o Independent Talent Group, 40 Whitfield Street, London W1T 2RH (☎ 020 7636 6565)

NOBLE, Rt Rev Brian Michael; *see:* Shrewsbury, Bishop of (RC)

NOBLE, Prof Denis; CBE (1998); s of George Noble (Flt Lt RFC, d 1957), and Ethel, *née* Rutherford; *b* 16 November 1936, London; *Educ* Emanuel Sch London, UCL (BSc, PhD); *m* Jan 1965, Susan Jennifer (d 2015), da of Flt Lt Leslie H Barfield; 1 da (Penelope Jean b 27 Aug 1967), 1 adopted s (Julian Aidan b 29 Aug 1970); *Career* asst lectr in physiology UCL 1961–64, tutorial fell Balliol Coll Oxford 1963–84, praefectus of Holywell Manor 1971–89, Burdon Sanderson prof of cardiovascular physiology Univ of Oxford 1984–2004 (emeritus prof 2004–); fell UCL 1986; fndr dir: Oxsoft Ltd 1984–, Physiome Sciences Inc 1994–2003; numerous appearances on radio and TV, various articles published in nat press; foreign sec Physiological Soc 1986–92 (hon sec 1974–80), chm Int Congress of Physiological Sciences 1993, sec-gen Int Union of Physiological Sciences 1994–2001, memb Founding Gp Save British Science, pres Int Union of Physiological Sciences 2009–; Gold Medal Br Heart Fndn 1985, Pierre Rijlant Prize Royal Acad of Med Belgium 1991, Pavlov Medal Russian Acad of Sciences 2004, Mackenzie Medal Br Cardiac Soc 2005; correspondant étranger de l'Académie Royale de Medecine de Belgique; hon memb: American Physiological Soc 1996, Japanese Physiological Soc 1998; Hon DSc Univ of Sheffield 2004, Doctorat (hc) Université de Bordeaux 2005, Hon DSc Univ of Warwick 2008; FRS 1979, Hon FRCP 1994 (Hon MRCP 1988), FMedSci 1998; *Books* The Initiation of the Heart Beat (1975), Electric Current Flow in Excitable Cells (1975), Goals, No Goals and Own Goals (1989), Sodium-Calcium Exchange (1989), The Logic of Life (1993), Ethics of Life (1997), The Music of Life (2006), Journey in Physiology Toward Enlightenment (2012); *Recreations* foreign languages, guitar; *Style*— Prof Denis Noble, CBE, FRS; ✉ Department of Physiology, Anatomy and Genetics, Parks Road, Oxford OX1 3PT (☎ 01865 272533, fax 01865 272554, e-mail denis.noble@dpag.ox.ac.uk)

NOBLE, Prof Michael William John; CBE (2008, OBE); s of William John Noble (d 1987), and Violet, *née* Wells (d 2003); *b* 25 January 1948, Isleworth, Middlesex; *Educ* Magdalen Coll Oxford (BA, MSc), Coll of Law; *m* 1; 2 s (Stefan b 16 Dec 1980, David b 1 Oct 1984); m 2, 21 June 2004, Gemma, *née* Wright; *Career* admitted slr 1974; articled clerk, asst slr then ptnr Ferguson Bricknell & Co 1971–81, community welfare rights lawyer Barton Project Oxford 1981–83 and 1985–86; Univ of Oxford: student unit supervisor and researcher Dept of Social Policy and Social Intervention 1986–91, lectr then reader in social policy 1991–2004, prof of social policy 2004–13, emeritus prof Univ of Oxford, emeritus fell Green Templeton Coll Oxford, hon fell Human Sciences Research Cncl SA, hon prof Rhodes Univ SA; exec dir Southern African Social Policy Research Inst SA; memb: Law Soc, Social Policy Assoc, South African Statistical Soc; FRSS; *Publications* incl: Measuring Multiple Deprivation at the Small Area Level: The English indices of deprivation 2000, 2004, 2007 and 2010 (jtly, 2000, 2005, 2008 and 2011), The Northern Ireland Multiple Deprivation Measure (2001 and 2005), Growing Together or Growing Apart? Geographic Patterns of Change in IS and JSA-IB Claimants in England 1995–2000 (2002), Scottish Index of Deprivation (2003), Older People Count: The Help the Aged Income Index for older people in England and Wales 2003 (2003), The English Indices of Deprivation (2004), The Provincial Indices of Multiple Deprivation for South Africa 2001 (jtly, 2006), The South African Index of Multiple Deprivation for Children 2001 (jtly, 2007), The South African Index of Multiple Deprivation for Children 2007 at Municipality Level (jtly, 2009), Constituency-level Namibian Index of Multiple Deprivation 2001 (jtly, 2011), Using the National Income Dynamics Study as the base micro-dataset for a tax and transfer South African Microsimulation Model (jtly, 2011), Multiple Depravation and Income Poverty at Small Area Level in South Africa in 2011 (jtly, 2013), Income Poverty at Small Area Level in South Africa in 2011 (jtly, 2014); numerous chapters in learned jls; *Style*— Prof Michael Noble, CBE; ✉ e-mail michael.noble@saspri.org

NOBLE, Tim; s of David Noble, and Mary Noble; *b* 1966; *Educ* Cheltenham Art Coll, Nottingham Poly (BA), RCA (MA); *Career* artist; collaborator with Sue Webster, *qv*; residency Dean Clough Halifax 1989–92; *Two-Person Exhibitions* British Rubbish (Independent Art Space London) 1996, Home Chance (Rivington St London) 1997, Vague Us (Habitat London) 1998, WOW (Modern Art London) 1998, The New Barbarians (Chisenhale Gallery London) 1999, I Love You (Deitch Projects NY) 2000, British Wildlife (Modern Art London) 2000, Masters of the Universe (Deste Fndn Athens) 2000, Instant Gratification (Gagosian Gallery Beverly Hills) 2001, Ghastly Arrangements (Milton Keynes Gallery) 2002, Black Magic (MW Projects London) 2002, Real Life is Rubbish (Statements at Art Basel Miami) 2002, PS1/MOMA (Long Island City NY) 2003, Modern Art is Dead (Modern Art London) 2004, Noble & Webster (MFA Boston) 2004, The New Barbarians (CAC Málaga) 2005, The Joy of Sex (Kukje Gallery Seoul) 2005, The Glory Hole (Bortolami Dayan NY) 2005; *Group Exhibitions* incl: Lift (Brick Lane London) 1993, Hijack (NY London and Berlin) 1994, Fete Worse Than Death (Hoxton Square London) 1994, Absolut Art (RCA London) 1994, Self Storage (Artangel London) 1995, Hanging Picnic (Hoxton Sq London) 1995, Fools Rain (ICA London) 1996, Turning the Tables (Chisenhale Gallery London) 1997, Livestock Market (London) 1997, Sex and the British (Galerie Thaddaeus Ropac Salzburg and Paris) 2000, Man-Body in Art from 1950 to 2000 (ARKEN Copenhagen) 2000, Apocalypse (Royal Acad of Art London) 2000, Tattoo Show

N

(Modern Art London) 2001, Form Follows Fiction (Castello di Rivoli Turin) 2001, Casino 2001 (SMAK Ghent) 2002, 2001 A Space Oddity (A22 Projects London) 2001, Shortcuts (Nicosia Municipal Arts Centre Cyprus) 2001, Art Crazy Nation (Milton Keynes Gallery) 2002, State of Play (Serpentine Gallery London) 2004, New Blood (Saatchi Gallery London) 2004, Monument To Now (Dakis Joannou Collection Athens) 2004, Masquerade (MCA Sydney) 2006; *Clubs* Colony Room; *Style*— Tim Noble, Esq; ✉ c/o Modern Art, 10 Vyner Street, London E2 9DG (☎ 020 8980 7742, e-mail info@modernartinc.com)

NOBLE, Sir Timothy Peter; 4 Bt (UK 1923); yr s of Sir Andrew Napier Noble, 2 Bt, KCMG (d 1987); *b* 21 December 1943; *Educ* Eton, UC Oxford (MA), INSEAD Fontainebleau (MBA); *m* 1976, Elizabeth Mary, da of late Alexander Wallace Aitken; 1 da (Sasha Heidi Elizabeth b 1978), 2 s (Lorne Andrew Wallace b 1980, Andrew Iain Brunel b 1984); *Career* called to the Bar Gray's Inn 1969; exec dir Lyle Shipping plc Glasgow 1976–83; Noble Group Ltd Edinburgh: chief exec 1983–2000, chm 2000–07; chm: Darnaway Venture Capital plc, Spark Energy Ltd; *Publications* Noble Blood (2007); *Recreations* golf, skiing, tennis, bridge, astronomy, poetry; *Clubs* Bruntsfield, Summit; *Style*— Sir Timothy Noble, Bt; ✉ Ardnahane, Barnton Avenue, Edinburgh EH4 6JJ

NOBLE-ROGERS, James; s of Peter Rogers, and Joyce Dixon, *née* Bishop; *b* 8 March 1961, Amersham, Bucks; *Educ* Hatfield Poly (BA), Univ of Nottingham (MA), City Univ London (Dip); *m* Bea Noble-Rogers; *Career* civil servant DES/DfEE 1987–96, head of allocations Teacher Trg Agency 1996–2000, head of governance RNIB 2000–04, exec dir Univs Cncl for the Educn of Teachers (UCET) 2004–; hon fell Univ of Wolverhampton; Hon MEd Univ of Hertfordshire; *Recreations* cycling, current affairs; *Clubs* Newcastle Cricket; *Style*— Mr James Noble-Rogers; ✉ 24 Hartside Gardens, Newcastle upon Tyne NE2 2JR; UCET, 9–11 Endsleigh Gardens, London WC1H 0EH (☎ 020 7580 8000, fax 020 7232 0577, e-mail j.rogers@ucet.ac.uk, website www.ucet.ac.uk)

NOBLETT, Ven William Alexander; CBE (2012); s of Joseph Henry Noblett, and Hilda Florence Noblett; *b* Dublin; *Educ* HS Dublin, Salisbury and Wells Theol Coll, Univ of Southampton (BTh), Univ of Oxford (MTh); *m* Margaret; 1 s (Andrew); *Career* ordained: deacon 1978, priest 1979; curate Sholing Southampton 1978–80, rector Ardamine Union 1980–82, chaplain RAF 1982–84, vicar Middlesbrough St Thomas 1984–87; chaplain HMP: Wakefield 1987–93, Norwich 1993–97, Full Sutton 1997–2001; chaplain-gen and archdeacon to HM Prisons 2001–11, canon of York Minster 2001–12 (canon emeritus 2012–), chaplain to HM The Queen 2005–, hon canon Liverpool Cathedral 2009–12; *Books* Prayers for People in Prison (1998), Inside Faith: Praying for People in Prison (2009); *Recreations* reading, music; *Clubs* RSA; *Style*— The Ven William Noblett, CBE; ✉ e-mail williamnoblett@gmail.com

NOEL, Lady Celestria; *see:* Hales, Lady Celestria Magdalen Mary

NOEL, Hon Gerard Eyre; s of 4 Earl of Gainsborough, OBE (d 1927); *b* 1926; *Educ* Georgetown USA, Exeter Coll Oxford; *m* 1958, Adele Julie Patricia, da of late Maj V N B Were and Mrs M J Were, OBE; 2 s, 1 da; *Career* called to the Bar Inner Temple 1952; author, journalist and lectr; Catholic Herald: ed 1971–83, editorial dir 1983–; contested (Lib) Argyll 1959; vice-pres Cncl of Christians and Jews 2003 (hon treas 1974–79); sr research fell St Anne's Coll Oxford 1993–97; Freeman City of London, Liveryman Worshipful Co of Stationers and Newspapermakers; FRSL; *Publications* author of 30 books, incl: Paul VI, The Path from Rome, Goldwater, Harold Wilson, Princess Alice, The Great Lock-Out of 1926, The Anatomy of the Catholic Church, Ena, Spain's English Queen, Gold Staff Office, Coronation 1953; also various translations; *Clubs* Pratt's, Garrick, White's; *Style*— The Hon Gerard Noel, FRSL; ✉ Westington Mill, Chipping Campden, Gloucestershire GL55 6EB; Herald House, Lamb's Passage, London EC1Y 8TQ

NOEL, Hon Thomas; s of 5 Earl of Gainsborough; *b* 9 March 1958; *Educ* Ampleforth, RAC Cirencester (MRAC 1980); *Career* Savills 1981–83, Humberts 1983–84; dir: Bride Hall plc 1987– (joined 1984, now non-exec dir), Barnsdale Lodge Ltd 1989–, First City Air; chm and chief exec Metropolitan Realty Tst (UK) Ltd 1984–; memb: CLA, Royal Forestry Soc; FRICS 1982; *Recreations* shooting, skiing, flying fixed and rotary aircraft (vintage and modern); *Clubs* Pratt's, The Air Squadron; *Style*— The Hon Thomas Noel; ✉ Bride Hall plc, 49 Hays Mews, London W1 (☎ 020 7493 3996, fax 020 7499 4388)

NOEST, Peter J; s of Maj A J F Noest, of Dulwich (d 2011), and Maria Gerbrands-Noest (d 2016); *b* 12 June 1948; *Educ* St George's Coll Weybridge, RAC Cirencester; *m* 1, (m dis 1993), Lisabeth Penelope Moody; 1 s (Timothy Peter b 1974); m 2, 1993, Jocelyn Claire (d 2003), yr da of Alan Douglas Spencer (d 2000); 1 s (Thomas Andrew Spencer b 1995); *Career* chartered surveyor (land agency and general practice); Knight Frank & Rutley: ptnr Amsterdam 1972–77, ptnr London 1977–81, full equity ptnr 1981, resigned 1983; sr commercial ptnr Hampton & Son 1984–88, dir Lambert Smith Hampton 1988–92; md: Capital Consultancy Group 1993–2011, P H Gillingham (Investments) Ltd 1986–, Cotswold Land and Estates Ltd 2000–09, P H Gillingham Gp Ltd 2003–; FRICS; *Books* Estates Gazette (contrib, 1985); *Recreations* shooting, hunting, photography, France, farming, conservation, forestry, travel, food and wine; *Style*— Peter Noest, Esq; ✉ Bedwell House, Northleach, Cheltenham GL54 3LU

NOGUERA, Anthony; *b* 17 July 1969, Cheltenham, Glos; *Educ* Whitefriars Sch Cheltenham, Univ of Birmingham; *m* Lucy Anne, *née* Mallon; 1 s (Louis b 25 Oct 2001), 1 da (Madalena b 31 Jan 2004); *Career* fomer ed various music magazines, sr features writer Sky magazine 1998–99, ed FHM 1999–2001 (joined as features ed 1995), ed-in-chief FHM Int 1999–2001, ed-in-chief Arena 2001–05, ed-in-chief Emap East (men's div) Arena, Zoo, Arena Homme-Plus 2005–; ed largest selling single issue of a Br monthly magazine ever FHM July 2000 (1.2 million copies); Emap Ed of the Year 1999, Ed of the Year BSME 2000; *Recreations* Jeet Kune Do (brown belt); *Style*— Anthony Noguera, Esq; ✉ Emap, Mappin House, 4 Winsley Street, London W1W 8HF

NOKES, Caroline Fiona Ellen; MP; da of Roy Perry, and Veronica, *née* Haswell; *b* 26 June 1972; *Educ* Romsey Sch, Peter Symonds' Coll Winchester, Univ of Sussex; *Children* 1 da (Tabitha b 26 July 1998); *Career* MP (Cons) Romsey and Southampton N 2010–; *Style*— Ms Caroline Nokes, MP; ✉ House of Commons, London SW1A 0AA

NOLAN, Andrea Mary; OBE; *Educ* TCD (BVMS); *Career* Univ of Glasgow: prof of veterinary pharmacology 1998, head Div of Veterinary Pharmacology, dean Faculty of Veterinary Medicine 1999, vice-princ for learning and teaching 2004, sr vice-princ and dep vice-chllr 2009; princ and vice-chllr Edinburgh Napier Univ 2013–; FRSE; *Style*— Prof Andrea Nolan, OBE, FRSE

NOLAN, Benjamin; QC (1992); s of Benjamin Nolan (d 1951), and Jane, *née* Mercer (d 2001); *b* 19 July 1948; *Educ* St Joseph's Coll Blackpool, Newcastle upon Tyne Poly, Univ of London (LLB); *Children* 2 da (Georgina b 19 Aug 1978, Katharine b 29 Nov 1980); *Career* called to the Bar 1971; recorder 1989–, head of chambers 1998–2003 and 2009–, dep judge of the High Court 1998–; *Recreations* travel, cooking, swimming, walking; *Style*— Benjamin Nolan, Esq, QC; ✉ Dere Street Chambers, 33 Broad Chare, Newcastle upon Tyne NE1 3DQ (☎ 0191 232 0541, e-mail bnqc@aol.com)

NOLAN, Hon Michael Alfred Anthony; QC (2015); s of Baron Nolan, PC, DL (Life Peer) (d 2007), and Margaret, *née* Noyes; *b* 17 June 1955; *Educ* Ampleforth, St Benet's Hall Oxford (MA), City Univ (Dip Law); *m* 26 May 1984, Adeline Mei Choo, da of Henry S H Oh, of Singapore; 2 s (Hugh b 1986, Felix b 1992), 1 da (Sophia Min b 1989); *Career* called to the Bar Middle Temple 1981; contrib to Atkins Court Forms (Arbitration, Carriers, Commercial Court, Insurance); memb: Commercial Bar Assoc (exec 1998–2001), London Common Law and Commercial Bar Assoc; *Recreations* swimming, tennis, skiing, books, plays, films, opera; *Clubs* Oxford Union, Millennium, Hurlingham, MCC; *Style*— The Hon Michael Nolan, QC; ✉ Quadrant Chambers, Quadrant House, 10 Fleet Street, London EC4Y 1AU (☎ 020 7583 4444, fax 020 7583 4445, e-mail info@quadrantchambers.com)

NOLAN, Dr Philip Michael Gerard (Phil); s of Philip Nolan (d 1979), and Mary, *née* Corrigan; *b* 15 October 1953; *Educ* Queen's Univ Belfast (BSc, PhD), London Business Sch (MBA); *m* 27 May 1978, Josephine, da of Andrew Monaghan; 2 s (Andrew b 2 Oct 1991, Christopher b 23 June 1994); *Career* lectr in geology Univ of Ulster 1979–81; geologist BP 1981–87, commercial and planning roles Head Office BP Exploration 1987–93, magr acquisitions and disposals BP Exploration 1993–95, md (secondment from BP) Interconnector (UK) Ltd 1995, dir Transco E Area BG plc 1996, md Transco 1997, appointed BG Bd 1998; chief exec: Transco BG plc 1998–2000, Lattice Gp plc 2000–02, eircom Ltd 2002–06; chm: Infinis 2007–10, Sepura plc 2007–10, John Laing plc 2010–, Ulster Bank 2013–, Affinity Water 2013–; non-exec dir: De La Rue plc 2001–09, Providence Resources plc 2003–, Enquest plc 2013–; chm Irish Mgmnt Inst 2006; *Recreations* walking, golf, listening to music, reading, watching football; *Style*— Dr Phil Nolan

NOON, Baron (Life Peer UK 2011), of St John's Wood in the London Borough of Camden; Sir Gulam Kaderbhoy Noon; kt (2002), MBE (1994); *b* 24 January 1936, Mumbai; *Career* entrepreneur; fndr, chm and md Bombay Halwa Ltd 1972–, fndr Noon Products Ltd 1989 (sold to Kerry Foods Ltd 2005, continues as chm); non-exec dir: NeutraHealth plc 2004–15, Obento Ltd 2004–; ind dir Zee Telefilms Ltd 2006–, dir Zee Entertainment Studios Ltd 2008–; fndr and chm Asian Business Assoc 1995–2000, dir Covent Garden Market Authy 1995–2000, pres London Chamber of Commerce and Industry 2002–03, dir Britain in Europe 2004–07, memb Bd TfL 2004–08, memb Advsy Bd on Naturalisation and Integration Home Office 2004–08, fndr memb Advsy Bd Br Olympic Assoc 2007–; tstee and chm Bd Noon Fndn 1995, fndr memb Cancer Research UK 2002; memb: Advsy Cncl The Prince's Tst 1996, Ethnic Minority Business Forum 2000–03, Bd CARE Int UK 2002–06; tstee: Arpana Charitable Tst UK 1996–2006, Meml Gates Tst 1998, Br Food Tst 1999, Maimonides Fndn 2002–08; fndr and chief tstee Noon Hosp and Research Centre 2008–; Asian of the Year 1994, Carlton Television Multicultural Achievement Award for Outstanding Contrib to Br Business 2002, South of Britain Lifetime Achievement Award Asian Jewel Award 2003, Best Business Ldr Sage Business Award 2003, Asian Business Award 2004, Gold Medal Pravasi Bharatiya Samman Award 2006 (presented by the Pres of India), Watford & Northwest London Business Person of the Year Award 2006, Global Indian Rajiv Gandhi Award 2007, AAA Platinum Award for Life Time Achievement 2012; chllr Univ of E London 2013–; fell Birkbeck Univ 2012; Hon MUniv Surrey 1998; Hon DUniv: Central England 2002, Middlesex 2002, W London; Hon DBA: London Guildhall Univ 2001, Kingston Univ 2005, Univ of E London 2009; Hon LLD Univ of Warwick 2010, Hon DLitt De Montfort Univ 2011; *Books* Noon Book of Authentic Indian Cookery (2001), Noon, With a View (2008); *Recreations* Cricket; *Clubs* Surrey CCC (hon life vice-pres 2005–); *Style*— The Lord Noon, MBE; ✉ Noon Group, 25 Queen Anne's Gate, London SW1H 9BU (☎ 020 7654 1600, fax 020 7654 1601); House of Lords, London SW1A 0PW

NOON, Jamie Darren; s of Russ Noon, and Kath, *née* Wakefield; *b* 9 May 1979, Goole, E Yorks; *Educ* Northumbria Univ (BSc), Vocational Trg Charitable Tst (Dip); *m* 16 July 2004, Rachel, *née* Littlewood; 1 s (Lewis Benjamin b 18 Feb 2005), 1 da (Elodie Grace b 7 Oct 2006); *Career* rugby union player; with: Newcastle Falcons 1998–2009 (winners Tetley Bitter Cup 2001, Powergen Cup 2004), CA Brive 2009–; England: 38 caps, debut v Canada 2001, finalists World Cup France 2007; *Recreations* mountain biking, fly fishing, squash, football, reading; *Style*— Jamie Noon, Esq

NOON, Paul; OBE (2013); s of Thomas Noon, of Orpington, Kent, and Barbara, *née* Grocott; *b* 1 December 1952, Crewe, Cheshire; *m* 12 Feb 1977, Eileen, *née* Smith; 2 da (Helen b 7 Jan 1981, Alice b 2 Feb 1986); *Career* Prospect (formerly Inst of Professional Civil Servants, then Inst of Professional Mangrs and Specialists): negotiator 1974–99, gen sec 1999–2012; regnl dir (West Midlands) UKTI 2012–; chair Cncl of Civil Service Unions 2001–03 and 2009–, dir Trade Union Fund Mangrs 2002–; TUC Gen Cncl: memb 2001–, memb Exec Ctee 2002–; *Style*— Paul Noon, Esq, OBE; ✉ UKTI, 1 Victoria Street, London SW1H 0ET

NORBURY, Peter; s of Harold Norbury (d 1987), and Mabel Victoria, *née* Whittaker (d 1984); *b* 12 January 1953, Manchester; *Educ* Manchester Grammar, Univ of Sheffield (LLB), Coll of Law; *m* 11 April 1987, Elizabeth, *née* Standley; 2 s (Robert Edward b 21 May 1988, Michael Peter b 1 Oct 1990); *Career* admitted slr 1978; slr specialising in employment law; ptnr Eversheds 1984–; chm Wigan Warriors Rugby League Club 1998–99, chm Disciplinary Ctee Rugby Football League; memb: Law Soc 1978, Employment Lawyers Assoc, Industrial Soc; *Recreations* cricket, football, golf, rugby league; *Style*— Peter Norbury, Esq; ✉ Eversheds, Eversheds House, 70 Great Bridgewater Street, Manchester M1 5ES (☎ 0161 831 8000, fax 0161 831 8888, e-mail peternorbury@eversheds.com)

NORFOLK, Andrew Mark; *b* 8 January 1965, Canterbury; *Educ* Kent Coll Canterbury, Ashville Coll Harrogate, Durham Univ; *Career* Scarborough Evening News 1989–95, Yorkshire Post 1995–2000, The Times 2000– (currently chief investigative reporter); Paul Foot Award 2012, Orwell Prize for Journalism 2013, Journalist of the Year Br Journalism Awards 2014, News reporter of the Year & The Cudlipp Award Press Awards 2015; *Recreations* cricket, golf, tennis, football; *Style*— Andrew Norfolk, Esq; ✉ The Times, The News Building, 1 London Bridge Street, London SE1 9GF

NORFOLK, 18 Duke of (Premier E Dukedom 1483 with precedence 1397); Edward William Fitzalan Howard; DL (W Sussex) 2002; also Earl of Arundel (E 1139 if the claim by tenure, which was admitted by the Crown in 1433, is recognised; otherwise 1292; either way, the Premier E Earldom), Baron Beaumont (E 1309), Baron Maltravers (E 1330), Earl of Surrey (E 1483), Baron FitzAlan, Baron Clun, Baron Oswaldestre (all E 1627), Earl of Norfolk (E 1644), and Baron Howard of Glossop (UK 1869); Earl Marshal and Hereditary Marshal of England (1672); s of 17 Duke of Norfolk, KG, CB, CBE, MC, DL (d 2002); *b* 2 December 1956; *Educ* Ampleforth, Lincoln Coll Oxford; *m* 27 June 1987, Georgina Susan, yr da of John Temple Gore; 3 s (Henry Miles, Earl of Arundel and Surrey b 3 Dec 1987, Lord Thomas Jack b 14 March 1992, Lord Philip b 14 July 1996), 2 da (Lady Rachel Rose b 10 June 1989, Lady Isabel Serena b 7 Feb 1994); *Heir* s, Earl of Arundel and Surrey; *Career* chm: Sigas Ltd 1979–88, Parkwood Group Ltd 1989–2002; Dep Earl Marshal of England 2000–02, Earl Marshal of England 2002–; Liveryman Worshipful Co of Fishmongers; *Recreations* motor racing, skiing, shooting; *Clubs* British Racing Drivers (Silverstone); *Style*— His Grace the Duke of Norfolk; ✉ Arundel Castle, Arundel, West Sussex (☎ 01903 883400)

NORFOLK, Peter; OBE (2009, MBE 2005); *b* 13 December 1960; *Career* wheelchair tennis player; achievements incl: Gold medal quad singles Paralympics Athens 2004 and Beijing 2008, Silver medal quad doubles Paralympics Athens 2004, Bronze medal quad doubles Paralympics Beijing 2008, Silver medal quad doubles Paralympics London 2012; founding ptnr EPc; *Style*— Peter Norfolk, Esq, OBE; ✉ website www.epc-wheelchairs.co.uk

NORGROVE, Sir David; kt (2016); s of Douglas Norgrove, and Ann Norgrove; *b* 23 January 1948; *Educ* Christ's Hosp, Exeter Coll Oxford (BA), Emmanuel Coll Cambridge (DipEcon), LSE (MSc); *m* 1977, Jenny Stoker; 1 s, 2 da; *Career* HM Treasy 1972–85 (seconded to First Nat Bank of Chicago 1978–80), private sec to PM 1985–88, Marks & Spencer 1988–2004 (exec dir and chair Pensions Fund Tstees 2000–04), chair Pensions Regulator 2005–10, chair PensionsFirst 2011–; chair: Low Pay Cmmn 2009–, Finance Ctee Amnesty Int,

Govt Review of Family Justice System 2010–11, Family Justice Bd 2012–; non-exec dir Strategic Rail Authy 2002–04; tstee: Hanover Tst 1993–2000, Media Tst 1998–2003, Mencap 2000–03, Br Museum 2004–12 (dep chair 2010–12); *Style*— Sir David Norgrove

NORMAL, Henry; *Career* comedy writer; co-prop Baby Cow Prodns (with Steve Coogan); co-writer: Paul Calf Video Diary 1994, Three Fights, Two Weddings and a Funeral 1994, Coogan's Run 1995, The Tony Ferrino Phenomenon 1997, The Parole Officer 2002; co-writer and assoc prodr: The Mrs Merton Show 1996 and 1997, Mrs Merton and Malcolm 1997, The Royle Family 1998; co-creator and co-writer The Man Who Thinks He's It 1998; exec prodr: Marion and Geoff 2000, Combat Sheet 2001 (script ed), Human Remains 2001 (script ed), Dr Terrible's House of Horrible 2001 (co-writer), 24 Hour Party People 2002, The Sketch Show 2002 (script ed), The Private Life of Samuel Pepys 2003, Whine Gums 2003 (BANFF Rockie Award 2004), Posh and Becks' Big Impression 2003, Marion and Geoff 2 2003, Cruise of the Gods 2003, I Am Not An Animal 2004, The Keith Baret Show 2004, The Mighty Boosh 2004–06 (NME Award 2007 and 2009, RTS Award 2008), Nighty Night 2004–05 (Br Comedy Award 2004, RTS Award 2004, Rose d'Or Award 2005), Ideal series 1–7 2005–11, Sensitive Skin 2005 and 2007, Saxondale 2006–07, Snow Cake 2006, Gavin and Stacey 2007–09 (Br Comedy Award 2007 and 2008, Broadcast Award 2008 and 2009, South Bank Show Award 2008, BAFTA Award 2008, Televisual Bulldog Award 2008 and 2010, TV Choice Award 2010, Nat Television Award 2010), Gavin and Stacey Christmas Special 2008, The Last Word Monologues 2008, Steve Coogan: The Inside Story 2009, Home Time 2009, FHM Stand Up Hero 2009 and 2010, The Trip 2010, Chekhov: Comedy Shorts 2010, Gavin and Stacey – The Outtakes 2010, Lizzie and Sarah 2010, Mid Morning Matters with Alan Partridge 2010, Alan Partridge and Other Less Successful Characters 2010, The Shadow Line 2011, Totally Tom 2011, Starlings 2012, Moone Boy 2012, Hunderby 2012, Hebburn 2012, Uncle Wormsley's Christmas, Alan Partridge: Welcome to the Places of My Life 2012, Alan Partridge on Open Books with Martin Bryce 2012, Moone Boy 2013, Starlings 2013, Gifted 2013, Common Ground 2013, Philomena 2013 (film), Svengali 2013 (film), Northern Soul 2013 (film); prodr Alan Partridge: Alpha Papa 2013 (film); BAFTA Award 1994, 1996, 1997, 2002 and 2003, Br Comedy Award 1996 and 1998, Silver Rose of Montreux 1997, South Bank Award 1998, Banff Rockie Award 2001; *Style*— Henry Normal, Esq; ✉ Baby Cow Productions, 33 Foley Street, London W1W 7TL (☎ 020 7612 3370, fax 020 7612 3352, e-mail info@babycow.co.uk)

NORMAN, Archibald John (Archie); s of Dr Archibald Norman, MBE; *b* 1 May 1954; *Educ* Emmanuel Coll Cambridge (MA), Harvard Business Sch (MBA); *m* Vanessa Mary, *née* Peet; 1 da (Florence); *Career* formerly: with Citibank NA, ptnr McKinsey & Co Ltd (joined 1979); fin dir Kingfisher plc 1986–91, chm Chartwell Land plc until 1991, chief exec Asda plc 1991–96 (chm 1997–2000), chm Energis 2002–05, chm Aurigo Mgmnt 2006–09, chm HSS 2007–12, chm ITV plc 2010–; non-exec dir British Rail (now Railtrack) 1992–2000; dir: Coles Australia 2007–, Target Australia 2013–; sr advsr Lazard UK 2004–13 (chm 2013–), advsr Wesfarmers Australia 2007–; MP (Cons) Tunbridge Wells 1997–2005; chief exec and dep chm Cons Pty 1997–99; shadow min for Europe 1999–2000, shadow sec for environment, tport and the regions 2000–01; Retailer of the Year 2006, Inst for Turnaround Chairman's Award 2010, Mktg Soc Hall of Fame; hon degrees: Univ of York, Leeds Met Univ; *Style*— Archie Norman, Esq; ✉ ITV plc, The London Television Centre, Upper Ground, London SE1 9LT (☎ 020 7157 3070, e-mail barbara@itv.com)

NORMAN, Jeremy Gordon; yr s of Roland Frank Holdway Norman (d 1958), of London, and Muriel (Peggy) Harvard, *née* Johnson (later Mrs Sim, d 1997); *b* 18 May 1947; *Educ* St Andrew's Eastbourne, Harrow, Univ of Cambridge (MA); *Partner* since 1978 (civil partnership 21 Dec 2005), Derek Norton Frost, *qv*; *Career* chm and md Burke's Peerage Ltd 1974–83; started and owned night clubs: Embassy 1978–80, Heaven 1979–83, eMbargo 1989–91, Leopard Lounge 1997–98; chm and md Soho Gyms Group (Ovalhouse Ltd) 1994–; dir: Blakenhall & Co Ltd (t/a The Furniture Cave), Citychance Ltd (property); formerly dir: Pasta Pasta, La Reserve Wines; currently journalist and author; fndr tstee Nat Aids Tst (resigned 1989), fndr chm CRUSAID (resigned 1987), tstee Aidsark; *Publications* No Make-Up: Straight Tales from a Queer Life (autobiography, 2006); *Recreations* boats, gym, natural history, archaeology, history, politics; *Clubs* Mark's, Pitt (Cambridge, former tstee and hon treas); *Style*— Jeremy Norman, Esq; ✉ The Furniture & Arts Building, 533 King's Road, London SW10 0TZ (☎ 020 7828 1776, e-mail jeremy@sohogyms.com, website www.sohogyms.com); Aidsark (website www.aidsark.org)

NORMAN, (Dr) (Alexander) Jesse; MP; s of Sir Torquil Patrick Alexander Norman; *b* 23 June 1962, London; *Educ* Eton, Merton Coll Oxford (open exhibitioner, BA), UCL (MPhil, PhD); *m* 1992, Kate, da of Lord Bingham of Cornhill, KG, PC (Life Peer 1996, d 2010); 2 s, 1 da; *Career* Sabre Fndn: project dir 1989–91, mangr then asst dir 1991–97; dir BZW 1997, teaching fell and lectr UCL 1998–2003, lectr Birkbeck Coll London 2003, exec dir Policy Exchange 2005–06, hon res fell UCL 2005–10; MP (Cons) Hereford and Herefords S 2010–; memb Treasy Select Ctee 2010–; dir: Classical Opera Co 2004–, Roundhouse 2007–; tstee: Kindle Centre 2007–, Hay Festival 2008–; patron: Herefords Riding for Disabled 2009–, No 1 Ledbury Road 2010–, Music Pool 2010–, Herefords Mind 2011–; pres Hereford Hosp Radio 2011–; vice-pres: Ross Horticultural Soc 2011–, Herefords and Glos Canal Tst 2011–; The Achievement of Michael Oakeshott (1992), Breaking the Habits of a Lifetime: Poland's first steps to the market (1992), After Euclid: visual reasoning and the epistemology of diagrams (2006), Compassionate Conservatism (2006), Compassionate Economics (2008), Churchill's Legacy (2009), The Big Society (2010), Edmund Burke: Politician, Philosopher, Prophet (2013); also author of pamphlets, essays, journalism and academic articles; *Recreations* music (especially jazz and opera), hill walking, sports, cinema; *Clubs* Westfields Football; *Style*— Jesse Norman, MP; ✉ Suite 3, Penn House, Broad Street, Hereford HR4 9AP; House of Commons, London SW1A 0AA (e-mail jesse.norman.mp@parliament.uk)

NORMAN, Nigel James; 4 Bt (UK 1915), of Honeyhanger, Parish of Shottermill, Co Surrey; s of Sir Mark Annesley Norman, 3 Bt, DL (d 2013); *b* 5 February 1956; *m* 1, 1985 (m dis 1989), Joanna Rosemary Jane, da of Michael Montagu George Naylor-Leyland, MC, of Coates, Glos; m 2, 1994, Juliet Clare Louise, da of Richard Lloyd Baxendale, of Aston Rowant, Oxon; 3 s (Antony b 10 March 1995, Mark b 26 May 1996, Harry b 28 June 2002), 1 da (Sophie b 11 Sept 1997); *Career* 13/18 Royal Hussars (QMO), (dispatches 1979), Sultan of Oman's Armoured Regt, ret Maj 1983; with Morgan Grenfell Asset Management Ltd (dir Morgan Grenfell International Funds Management Ltd 1990–2000), md Deutsche Asset Management Ltd 2002–05, head Middle East and Africa Aberdeen Asset Management 2005–; *Clubs* White's, Annabel's, Pratt's; *Style*— Sir Nigel Norman, Bt; ✉ Holly Grove House, Wilcote, Chipping Norton, Oxfordshire OX7 3EA

NORMAN, Robert David (Rob); s of Malcolm Norman (d 1971), of London, and Angela Frances, *née* Cymbalist; *b* 30 March 1960; *Educ* UCS, Pinner VI Form Coll, Trent Poly (BA); *m* 1, 1986; m 2, 1996, Katherine Jane Helen, da of Stanley Marber; *Career* mgmnt trainee Texaco UK 1978–79, software mktg mangr Data Communications Corp 1983–84, media planner/buyer Colman RSCG 1985–86 (media trainee 1984), account dir CIA Group plc 1987 (sr media planner 1986), exec media dir WM Media Ltd (jt venture between CIA Group plc and Woollams Moira Gaskin O'Malley Ltd) 1990–94 (dir 1988–89), head of Euro Interactive Media Div CIA Group plc 1994–97 (conslt 1997–), sr vice-pres Prisma Sports and Media 1997–; currently: ceo Outrider Worldwide, ptnr CIA Worldwide, chm Mediaedge:cia UK; chm Sutton Jones Multimedia; MInstD 1989; *Recreations* bobsleighing (completed Cresta Run), collecting antiquarian cookery books, pop art, supporting Tottenham Hotspur FC, opera; *Style*— Rob Norman, Esq

NORMAN, Russell; s of Ernest Clifford Norman, of London, and Carole Julia Beadle, *née* Giddy; *b* 9 December 1965, London; *Educ* Sunderland Poly, Inst of Educn Univ of London; *m* March 2004, Jules McNally Norman; 1 s (Oliver Edward b 5 June 1991), 2 da (Martha Gwen b 3 Dec 2005, Mabel Maud b 12 March 2007); *Career* restaurateur, writer, broadcaster and teacher; head of drama Bentley Wood Sch Harrow 1994–97, mangr Joe Allen London 1997–99, gen mangr Circus London 1999–2002, gen mangr Zuma London 2002–06, operations dir Caprice Hldgs 2006–09; fndr and co-owner Polpo Ltd; presenter The Restaurant Man (BBC2) 2014, contributing ed and food columnist Esquire Magazine; Tatler Restaurateur of the Year 2012; *Books* Polpo – A Venetian Cookbook (of Sorts) (2012, Waterstones Book of the Year 2012), Spuntino – Comfort Food (New York Style) (2014); *Recreations* Scrabble, travel; *Clubs* Groucho; *Style*— Russell Norman, Esq; ✉ c/o Cathryn Summerhayes, William Morris Endeavor, 100 New Oxford Street, London WC1A 1HB (☎ 020 8929 8409, e-mail csummerhayes@wmeentertainment.com, website www.russellnorman.net)

NORMINGTON, David John; GCB (2011, KCB 2005, CB 2000); s of Ronald Normington (d 1976), and Kathleen Williams, *née* Towler; *b* 18 October 1951; *Educ* Bradford GS, CCC Oxford (MA); *m* 30 March 1985, Winifred Anne Charlotte, *née* Harris, CBE; *Career* Dept for Educn and Employment (formerly Dept of Employment): joined 1973, private sec to Permanent Sec 1976–77, head Employment Policy Div 1977–79, head Industrial Rels Div 1979–82, area magr Manpower Servs Cmmn 1982–83, princ private sec to Sec of State for Employment 1983–84, regnl dir employment service (London and S East) 1987–89, dir of strategy and employment policy 1989–92, dir personnel and development 1992–95, dir Personnel and Support Servs 1995–97, DG Strategy Int and Analytical Servs 1997–98, DG Schools 1998–2001; perm sec: DfES 2001–05, Home Office 2006–10, first Civil Service cmmr and cmmr for public appointments 2011–; *Recreations* cricket, tennis, watching ballet, gardening; *Style*— Sir David Normington, GCB

NORRIE, 2 Baron (UK 1957); George Willoughby Moke; s of 1 Baron Norrie, GCMG, GCVO, CB, DSO, MC (d 1977), and Jocelyn Helen (d 1938), da of Richard Henry Gosling, of Hawthorn Hill; *b* 27 April 1936; *Educ* Eton, RMA Sandhurst; *m* 1, 1964 (m dis 1997), Celia Marguerite, JP, da of Major John Pelham Mann, MC, of New Orleans, USA; 2 da (Hon Clare b 1966, Hon Julia b 1968), 1 s (Hon Mark Willoughby John b 1972); m 2, Mrs Pamela Ann (Annie) McCaffry, da of Sir Arthur Ralph Wilmot, 7 Bt (d 1942); *Heir* s, Mark Norrie; *Career* cmmnd 11 Hussars (PAO) 1956, ADC to C in C ME Cmd 1960–61, GSO3 (int) 4 Gds Bde 1967–69, ret 1970; dir: Fairfield Nurseries (Hermitage) Ltd 1976–89, Int Garden Centre (Br Gp) Ltd 1984–86, Conservation Practice Ltd 1988–91, Hilliers (Fairfield) Ltd 1989–97; non-exec dir Philip T English Int Financial Servs Ltd 2007–12; advsr: S Grundon (Waste) Ltd 1991–2001, CH2M Hill Ltd 1994–96; memb House of Lords EC Ctee (Environment) 1988–92; pres: Newbury Branch Royal Br Legion 1971–96, Conservation Volunteers (formerly Br Tst for Conservation Volunteers) 1987–2014, Int Cultural Exchange 1988–2000, Nat Kidney Fedn 1994–2001, The Salespeople's Charity (formerly Commercial Travellers Benevolent Inst) 1992–; vice-pres: Cncl for Nat Parks 1991–, Tree Cncl 1991–2001; patron: Age Resource 1991–2004, Faure-Alderson Romanian Appeal 1993–2001, Janki Fndn 1997–; UK patron Royal Life Saving Soc 1994– (memb Cwlth Cncl 1999–); memb Cncl: Winston Churchill Meml Tst 1993–2010, Royal Scottish Forestry Soc 2012–; govr Dunstan Park Sch Thatcham 1989–94; Green Ribbon Political Award for Services to the Environment House of Lords 1993; Freeman City of London 1999; memb Br Soc of Dowsers 1999–; *Clubs* MCC, Cavalry and Guards'; *Style*— The Rt Hon the Lord Norrie; ✉ Holehouse, Penpont, Thornhill, Dumfries DG3 4AP (☎ 01848 600243)

NORRINGTON, Ian Arthur; s of Charles Arthur Norrington (d 2001), and Georgina Marina, *née* Beardmore (d 1974); *b* 1 October 1936; *Educ* Downside; *m* 21 Sept 1968, Brigitte Maria, *née* Albrecht; 1 s (Christopher Charles b 1972), 1 da (Antonia Jane b 1974); *Career* Midshipman RNVR served Home and Med Fleets (Amphibious Warfare Squadron) 1955–57, Sub Lt RNVR 1957, Lt RNR 1958; De Beers Consolidated Mines Ltd (The Diamond Trading Co Ltd) 1957–71: ptnr W I Carr Sons and Co 1971–79, ptnr Grieveson Grant and Co 1979–86, dir Kleinwort Benson Securities Ltd 1986–90, conslt Fiduciary Trust International Ltd 1990–91, assoc Walker Crips Weddle Beck plc 1991–2009; vice-pres St Gregory's Soc (Downside Old Boys) 1996– (pres 1993–96); Liveryman Worshipful Co of Goldsmiths 1984; memb Stock Exchange 1974–92, MSI (Dip); *Recreations* fishing, philately; *Clubs* MCC, Naval, Downside Wanderers CC; *Style*— Ian Norrington, Esq; ✉ Flat 2, 18 Waterden Road, Guildford, Surrey GU1 2AY

NORRIS, Alan John; s of Jesse Oliver Norris (d 1980), of Newport, Gwent, and Queenie Iris Norris; *b* 7 June 1942; *Educ* St Julian's Newport, Newport and Monmouthshire Coll of Advanced Technol (HNC, Dip); *m* 1, 31 July 1965 (m dis 1969), Jane Margot Inkin, da of Vernon Dixon; m 2, 14 June 1975 (m dis 2001), Penelope Catherine, da of Lt-Col (William) Edwin Daniel (d 1974); 1 s (Oliver William Edwin b 28 June 1982); m 3, 7 Feb 2005, Juliet Quartermain; 1 da (Genevieve Louise b 11 Dec 1998), 1 s Elliot Jonathan b 11 July 2001); *Career* graduate trainee to orgn and method offr Alcan 1960–66, princ orgn and method offr Osram (GEC) 1966–67, latterly systems and programming mangr United Glass (formerly sr systems analyst, computer ops mangr) 1967–76, London branch mangr Computer People 1976–79, chm and chief exec Gatton Consltg Gp (formerly Computastaff Gp) 1979–98, chm Genorel Ltd and Genorel Soft Drinks Ltd 2007–13; owner Hotel Caprice Wengen; Freeman City of London, Liveryman Worshipful Co of Information Technologists; MInstM 1968; *Recreations* skiing, golf, travel, wine, meteorology, psychology; *Clubs* RAC; *Style*— Alan Norris, Esq; ✉ Woodlands House, Chestnut Close, Warren Drive, Kingswood, Surrey KT20 6QB (☎ 01737 833678, fax 01737 833550, e-mail ajnmail@aol.com); Hotel Caprice, Wengen, CH 3823, Switzerland (☎ 00 41 33 856 0606, fax 00 41 33 856 0607, website www.caprice-wengen.ch)

NORRIS, Hon Mr Justice; Sir Alastair Hubert Norris; kt (2007); s of Hubert John Norris, and Margaret Murray, *née* Savage (d 1992); *b* 17 December 1950; *Educ* Pate's GS Cheltenham, St John's Coll Cambridge; *m* 1982, Patricia Lesley Rachel, da of Leslie Mark White; 2 da (Frances b 12 June 1986, Meredith b 21 May 1990), 1 s (Edmund b 10 July 1992); *Career* called to the Bar Lincoln's Inn 1973, QC 1997, asst recorder 1998, recorder 2000, specialist circuit judge Chancery Court (Midland Circuit) 2001–07, judge of the High Court of Justice (Chancery Div) 2007–; chm Haven Green Housing Assoc; FCIArb 1991; *Recreations* sailing; *Clubs* Gloucestershire CCC, Teifi Boating (Cardigan); *Style*— The Hon Mr Justice Norris

NORRIS, Prof Christopher Charles; s of Charles Frederick Norris (d 1979), of Leigh-on-Sea, Essex, and Edith Eliza, *née* Ward (d 2008); *b* 6 November 1947; *Educ* East Ham GS, Univ of London (BA, PhD); *m* 17 April 1971, Alison, da of Thomas W Newton and Kathleen, *née* Davidson, of Fakenham, Norfolk; 2 da (Clare Tamasin b 1978, Jennifer Mary b 1983); *Career* lectr Univ of Duisburg W Germany 1974–76, asst ed Books and Bookmen 1976–77; Univ of Wales: lectr 1978–85, reader 1985–87, personal chair 1987–97, distinguished research prof 1997–; visiting prof: Univ of Calif Berkeley 1986, City Univ of NY 1988, Tulane Univ 1992, Dartmouth Coll New Hampshire 1994, Univ of Santiago de Compostela 1997–; assoc fell Dept of Philosophy Univ of Warwick 1990–; vice-pres British Soc of Aesthetics 1993–96, pres Welsh Inst for Philosophy 2003–; *Books* incl: William Empson and the Philosophy of Literary Criticism (1978), Deconstruction: Theory and Practice (1982), Shostakovich: the man and his music (ed, 1982), The Deconstructive Turn: Essays in the Rhetoric of Philosophy (1983), Inside the Myth:

N

George Orwell – views from the left (ed, 1984), The Contest of Faculties: Philosophy and Theory after Deconstruction (1985), Derrida (1987), Post-Structuralist Readings of English Poetry (ed, 1987), Paul de Man: Deconstruction and the Critique of Aesthetic Ideology (1988), What Is Deconstruction? (jtly, 1988), Deconstruction and the Interests of Theory (1989), Music and the Politics of Culture (ed, 1989), What's Wrong with Postmodernism (1990), Spinoza and the Origins of Modern Critical Theory (1991), Uncritical Theory: Postmodernism, Intellectuals and the Gulf War (1992), The Truth About Postmodernism (1993), William Empson: the critical achievement (ed, 1993), Truth and the Ethics of Criticism (1994), Reclaiming Truth: contribution to a critique of cultural relativism (1996), Resources of Realism: prospects for post analytic philosophy (1996), New Idols of the Cave: on the Limits of Anti-realism (1997), Against Relativism: Philosophy of Science, Deconstruction and Critical Theory (1997), Quantum Theory and the Flight from Realism: philosophical responses to quantum mechanics (2000), Minding the Gap: epistemology and philosophy of science in the two traditions (2000), Deconstruction and the Unfinished Project of Modernity (2000), The Cambridge History of Literary Criticism Vol 9: philosophical, psychological and historical approaches (ed, 2001), Truth Matters: realism, anti-realism and response-dependence (2002), Hilary Putnam: realism, reason, and the uses of uncertainty (2002), life.after.theory (jtly, 2003), Jacques Derrida (ed, 4 vols, 2003), Philosophy of Language and the Challenge to Scientific Realism (2004), Language, Logic and Epistemology (2004), Epistemology: Key concepts (2005), On Truth and Meaning (2006), Platonism, Music and the Listener's Share (2006), Fiction, Philosophy and Possible Worlds (2007), Badiou's Being and Event: a reader's guide (2009), Re-Thinking the Cogito: naturalism, rationalism and the venture of thought (2010), Derrida, Budiou and the Formal Imperative (2012), Philosophy Outside-In: a critique of academic reason (2013), The Cardinal's Dog and Other Poems (2013), Deconstruction After All: Reflections and Conversations (2015); Critics of the Twentieth Century (gen ed); *Recreations* music (memb Côr Cochion, Cardiff), cycling, model aircraft; *Clubs* S Bristol Model Aircraft; *Style—* Prof Christopher Norris; ✉ 3 Tyn-y-Wern Villas, Trethomas, Caerphilly CF83 8FQ (☎ 07891 911257); Philosophy Section, University of Cardiff, PO Box 94, Cardiff CF10 3EU (☎ 029 2087 5412, telex 498635, fax 029 2087 4618, e-mail norrisc@cardiff.ac.uk)

NORRIS, Prof David Owen; s of Albert Norris, of Long Buckby, Northants, and Margaret Amy, *née* Owen; *b* 16 June 1953; *Educ* Daventry GS, Royal Acad of Music, Keble Coll Oxford (MA); *Children* 2 s (Barnaby William b 1987, Josiah George b 1989); *Career* pianist; prof: Royal Acad of Music 1978–89, Royal Coll of Music 1999–; dir: Petworth Festival 1986–92, Cardiff Festival 1992–95; chm Steans Inst Chicago 1991–98, Gresham prof of music 1993–97; Univ of Southampton: AHRB fell in creative and performing arts 2000–, prof 2007–; visiting prof RCM 2007–, visiting prof RNCM 2010–; radio presenter; premiere recordings incl concertos, songs and piano music by Elgar, Quilter, Lambert, Dyson, Phillips, Hely-Hutchinson, Arnell and Schubert; compositions incl: radio-opera Die! Sober Flirter 1991, Think Only This (song-cycle) 2001, Prayerbook (oratorio) 2006, piano concerto 2008/14, Tomorrow Nor Yesterday (song-cycle) 2012, Symphony 2013, Turning Points (cantata) 2015, HengeMusic (for saxophones, organ and film) 2015; first Gilmore Artist 1991; hon fell Keble Coll Oxford; FRAM, FRCO, FSA 2015; *Recreations* detective fiction, the A303; *Style—* Prof David Owen Norris; ✉ Music Building 2, Highfield Campus, University of Southampton, Southampton SO17 1BJ (website www.davidowennorris.com)

NORRIS, Senator David Patrick Bernard Fitz-Patrick; s of John Bernard Norris (d 1950), and Aida Margaret, *née* Fitz-Patrick (d 1967); *b* 31 July 1944, Leopoldville, Belgian Congo (now Kinshasa, Democratic Republic of the Congo); *Educ* St Andrew's Coll the HS Dublin, Reade Pianoforte Sch, TCD; *Career* sr lectr in English and coll tutor TCD 1968–94; memb (senator) Seanad Éireann (Ind) Univ of Dublin 1987–, memb Jt Ctee on Foreign Affrs; memb: Irish Fedn of Univ Teachers, Royal Dublin Soc, Nat Union of Journalists, Amnesty Int, Irish Actors Equity, Royal Zoological Soc of Ireland; hon life memb: Univ Philosophy Soc, Coll Historical Soc; life memb: Friends of St Patrick's Cathedral (memb Bd), Dublin Univ Central Athletics Ctee, TCD Assoc; chm: Friends of the Library TCD, James Joyce Cultural Centre (also fndr), N G George's St Preservation Soc (also fndr); vice-pres Children of Ireland Peace Garden Tst; Gold and Silver Medals Univ Philosophical Soc, Gold Medal Brazilian Acad of Letters, Lord Mayor's Award Dublin 2009; broadcaster and author of articles on various literary, sociological and legal topics, speaker at int scholarly gatherings; Irish presidential candidate 2011, Father of the House; Hon Dr in Utroque Jure (Hon LLD) Trinity Coll Dublin 2015; James Joyce's Dublin (1982), Proceedings of the International James Joyce Symposium (1984), James Joyce for Beginners (1992), Joyce in the Hibernian Metropolis (co-ed, 1996), A Kick Against the Pricks (autobiography, 2012, nominated Bord Gáis Energy Irish Book of the Year Award, nominated Political Biography of the Year Political Book Award); *Recreations* swimming, marathon running, music, reading, travel; *Style—* Senator David Norris; ✉ Seanad Éireann, Leinster House, Kildare Street, Dublin 2, Ireland (☎ 00 353 1 618 3104, e-mail david.norris@oireaclitas.ie)

NORRIS, Rufus; *Educ* RADA; *Career* director; dir NT; *Theatre* incl: Afore Night Come (Young Vic) 2001 (Most Promising Newcomer Evening Standard Award), Festen (Almeida Theatre, West End and Broadway) 2004 (Best Dir Evening Standard Award and Best Dir Critics' Circle Award), Vernon God Little (Young Vic), Cabaret (West End), Les Liaisons Dangereuses (Broadway), Death and the King's Horseman (NT) 2009, London Road (NT) 2011 (Best Musical Critics' Circle Award), Amen Corner (NT) 2013, Table (NT) 2013, Behind the Beautiful Forevers (NT) 2014, Everyman (NT) 2015; *Opera* Dr Dee (ENO, with Damon Albarn, *qv*); *Film* Broken 2012, London Road 2015; *Style—* Rufus Norris, Esq; ✉ c/o Nick Marston, Curtis Brown, Haymarket House, 28–29 Haymarket, London SW1Y 4SP

NORRIS, Steven John; s of John Francis Birkett Norris, and Eileen Winifred, *née* Walsh; *b* 24 May 1945; *Educ* Liverpool Inst HS, Worcester Coll Oxford (MA); *m* 1, 23 Aug 1969 (m dis), Peta Veronica, da of Rear Adm Peter Cecil-Gibson, CB; 2 s; m 2, Emma Courtney; 1 s; *Career* MP (Cons): Oxford E 1983–87, Epping Forest 1988–97; memb Select Ctee on Social Servs 1985, PPS to Home Sec 1990–92, Parly under-sec of state Dept of Transport (min for transport, London local transport and road safety) 1992–96; mayoral candidate (Cons) London 2000 and 2004; chm Jarvis plc 2003–, AMT-Sybex 2005–; DG Road Haulage Assoc 1997–99; cncllr Berks CC 1977–85, memb Berks Area Health Authy 1979–82, vice-chm W Berks DHA 1982–85; patron: Transport 2000 from 1996, Sustrans 1996–; chm Nat Cycling Strategy Bd 2001–04; former fndr Alcohol and Drug Addiction Prevention and Treatment Tst; fndr and former chm: The Crime Concern Trust Ltd, The Grant Maintained Schs Tst; hon memb Cyclists' Touring Club 1996–; Freeman City of London; Liveryman: Worshipful Co of Coachmakers and Coach Harness Makers, Worshipful Co of Watermen and Lightermen of the River Thames; Companion Inst of Civil Engrs, FIHT, FIMI, FCIT; *Recreations* reading; *Clubs* Brooks's, RAC; *Style—* Steven Norris, Esq

NORRIS, William John; QC (1997); s of John Phillips Norris, QGM, of Salisbury, Wilts, and Joan Hattersley, *née* Barnes; *b* 3 October 1951; *Educ* Sherborne, New Coll Oxford (MA); *m* 3 Oct 1987, Lesley Jacqueline, da of Douglas Osborne, of Hythe, Kent; 2 da (Charlotte Louise b 15 Oct 1988, Emily Clare b 6 Oct 1990); *Career* called to the Bar Middle Temple 1974 (bencher); former amateur jockey, tstee Injured Jockeys Fund; *Books* Kemp and Kemp: The Quantum of Damages (gen ed), The Collected Letters of C W Catte (ed), Perhaps it will brighten up later (2004); *Recreations* racing, sailing, cricket; *Clubs* Royal Cruising, Royal Lym Yacht, Lobsters; *Style—* William Norris, Esq, QC; ✉ 39 Essex Street, London WC2R 3AT

NORRISS, Air Marshal Sir Peter Coulson; KBE (2000), CB (1996), AFC (1977); s of Arthur Kenworthy Norriss, and Marjorie Evelyn, *née* Coulson; *b* 22 April 1944; *Educ* Beverley GS, Magdalene Coll Cambridge (MA), Harvard Business Sch (AMP); *m* 7 August 1971, Lesley Jean, *née* McColl; 2 s (Mark Alastair b 6 Feb 1973, Angus John b 26 Aug 1974), 1 da (Katie Elizabeth b 15 Feb 1977); *Career* RAF; joined 1966, flying instr RAF Coll Cranwell 1969–71; Buccaneer: pilot 1972–74, chief flying instr 1974–76; personal air sec to Parly Under Sec 1977–79, Sqn Cdr Buccaneer XVI 1980–83, head RAF Presentation Team 1984, Tornado and Victor Station Cdr RAF Marham 1985–87, Dep Dir subsequently Dir Operational Requirements 1988–91, DG Air Procurement 1991–98, Dep Chief Defence Procurement 1998–2000, def conslt 2001–15; chm Microturbo Ltd 2002–07; non-exec dir: Chemring Gp plc 2004–13, Turbomeca UK Ltd 2008–09; patron Cambridge UAS, pres RAF Oxford and Cambridge Soc 2008–; FRAeS (pres 2003–04); *Recreations* golf, skiing, tennis; *Clubs* RAF; *Style—* Sir Peter Norriss, KBE, CB, AFC; ✉ e-mail peter.norriss@hedgeapple.co.uk

NORTH, Christopher; *Career* md Phaidon Press until 2006; Amazon.co.uk Ltd: joined as vice-pres books 2006, vice-pres for media products until 2010, md 2010–; *Style—* Christopher North, Esq; ✉ Amazon, 60 Holborn Viaduct, London EC1A 2FD

NORTH, Sir Peter Machin; kt (1998), CBE (1989), Hon QC (1993); s of Geoffrey Machin North (d 1974), and Freda Brunt, *née* Smith (d 1991); *b* 30 August 1936; *Educ* Oakham Sch, Keble Coll Oxford; *m* 1960, Stephanie Mary North, OBE, DL, eld da of Thomas L Chadwick (d 1963); 1 da (Jane Amanda b 1962), 2 s (Nicholas Machin b 1964, James William Thomas b 1971); *Career* Lt Royal Leics Regt Cyprus 1955–56; teaching asst Northwestern Univ Sch of Law Chicago 1960–61; lectr: UCW Aberystwyth 1961–63, Univ of Nottingham 1963–65; tutor in law Keble Coll Oxford 1965–76 (fell 1965–84), law cmmr for Eng and Wales 1976–84, princ Jesus Coll Oxford 1984–2005, vice-chllr Univ of Oxford 1993–97; chm: Road Traffic Law Review 1985–88, Ind Review of Parades and Marches in NI 1996–97, Ind Ctee for the Supervision of Standards of Telephone Information Services 1999–2006, Fin Ctee OUP 2005–08, Review of Drink and Drug Driving 2009–10; vice-chm Ashmolean Museum Oxford 2006–07 (visitor 2004–07); memb Sr Salaries Review Body 2004–12, chm Standing Advsy Ctee on Private Int Law 2006–09; hon fell: Jesus Coll Oxford, Keble Coll Oxford, Univ of Wales Bangor, Trinity Coll Carmarthen, Univ of Wales Aberystwyth; Hon LLD: Univ of Reading, Univ of Nottingham, Univ of Aberdeen, Univ of New Brunswick; Hon Dr of Humane Letters Univ of Arizona; hon bencher Inner Temple; FBA; *Recreations* gardening, cricket, grandchildren; *Style—* Sir Peter North, CBE, QC, FBA; ✉ Jesus College, Oxford OX1 3DW

NORTH WEST EUROPE, Archdeacon of; *see:* Allen, Ven Geoffrey Gordon

NORTHAM, Jeremy Philip; s of John Northam, and Rachel Northam; *b* 1 December 1961; *Educ* King's Coll Sch Cambridge, Bristol GS, Bedford Coll (BA); *Career* actor; *Theatre* incl: National Theatre 1989–91: The Voysey Inheritance, Hamlet, The Shaughraun, The School for Scandal; RSC 1992–94: Love Labour's Lost, The Country Wife, The Gift of the Gorgon; other credits incl: The Three Sisters 1991, The Way of the World 1992, Certain Young Men (Almeida) 1999, Old Times (Donmar) 2004; *Television* incl: Journey's End 1988, Piece of Cake 1988, A Fatal Inversion 1991, Poirot 1993, A Village Affair 1994, The Tribe 1997, Martin & Lewis 2002, The Tudors 2007–08, Miami Medical 2010, White Heat 2012; *Films* incl: Wuthering Heights 1992, Soft Top Hard Shoulder 1992, Voices 1994, Carrington 1995, The Net 1995, Emma 1996, Mimic 1997, Amistad 1997, The Misadventures of Margaret 1998, Gloria 1999, The Winslow Boy 1999, An Ideal Husband 1999, Happy Texas 1999, The Golden Bowl 2000, Possession 2001, Enigma 2001, Gosford Park 2001, The Singing Detective 2002, Cypher 2002, Stroke of Genius 2003, Guy X 2004, A Cock and Bull Story 2005, The Invasion 2007, Creation 2009, Glorious 39 2009; *Awards* incl: Olivier Award Most Promising Newcomer 1990, Evening Standard Film Actor 2000, Film Critic's Circle British Actor Award 2000; *Style—* Jeremy Northam, Esq

NORTHAMPTON, 7 Marquess of (UK 1812); Spencer Douglas David Compton; DL (Northants 1979); also Earl of Northampton (UK 1618), Earl Compton, and Baron Wilmington (both UK 1812); patron of 9 livings; s of 6 Marquess of Northampton, DSO (d 1978), and his 2 w, Virginia (d 1997), yst da of David Rimington Heaton, DSO, of Brookfield, Crownhill, S Devon; *b* 2 April 1946; *Educ* Eton; *m* 1, 1967 (m dis 1973), Henriette Luisa Maria, o da of late Baron Adolph William Carel Bentinck, sometime Netherlands ambass to France; 1 s, 1 da; m 2, 1974 (m dis 1977), Annette Marie, da of Charles Anthony Russell Smallwood; m 3, 1977 (m dis 1983), Rosemary Ashley Morritt, o da of P G M Hancock, of Truro, and formerly w of Hon Charles Dawson-Damer (bro of 7 Earl of Portarlington); 1 da; m 4, 1985 (m dis 1989), Hannelore Ellen (Fritzi), da of late Hermann Erhardt, of Landsberg-am-Lech, and formerly w of Hon Michael Pearson (now 4 Viscount Cowdray); 1 da; m 5, 1990 (m dis 2013), Mrs Pamela Kyprios; m 6, 2013, Tracy Caroline Goodman; *Heir* s, Earl Compton; *Career* landowner; proprietor of Compton Wynyates (built 1480–1520) and former proprietor of Castle Ashby (constructed 1574, with an Inigo Jones frontage of 1635, remains in the Compton family); Pro Grand Master United Grand Lodge of England 2001–09; *Recreations* Freemasonry; *Clubs* Turf; *Style—* The Most Hon the Marquess of Northampton, DL; ✉ Compton Wynyates, Tysoe, Warwick CV35 0UD

NORTHBROOK, 6 Baron (UK 1866), of Stratton, Co Hants; Sir Francis Thomas Baring; 8 Bt (GB 1793); o s of 5 Baron Northbrook (d 1990), and Rowena Margaret, da of Brig-Gen Sir William Henry Manning, GCMG, KBE, CB (d 1932); *b* 21 February 1954; *Educ* Winchester, Univ of Bristol; *m* 27 June 1987 (m dis 2006), Amelia Sarah Elizabeth, er da of Dr Reginald David Taylor, of Hursley, Hants; 3 da (Hon Arabella Constance Elizabeth b 1989, Hon Venetia Harriet Anne b 1991, Hon Cosima Evelyn Maud b 1994); m 2, 29 Aug 2013, Charlotte Lee, er da of Thomas W Pike; *Heir* (to Baronetcy only) kinsman, Peter Baring; *Career* trainee accountant Dixon Wilson Ltd 1976–80, Baring Brothers & Co Ltd 1981–89, investment mangr Taylor-Young Investment Management Ltd 1990–93, investment mangr Smith & Williamson 1993–95, dir Mars Asset Management Ltd 1996–2006; landowner; oppn whip 1999–2000, memb House of Lords Select Ctee on Equality Act 2010 and Disability 2015–16; tstee: Winchester Med Tst 1990–97, CLA (Hants Ctee) 1999–2000, Fortune Forum 2006–; *Recreations* cricket, tennis, skiing, shooting, fishing; *Clubs* White's, Pratt's, Beefsteak, Gunmakers; *Style—* The Rt Hon Lord Northbrook; ✉ House of Lords, London SW1A 0PW

NORTHCOTT, Alex; *b* 1968; *Educ* Univ of St Andrews (MA); *Career* Capt 7th Gurkha Rifles 1992; account mangr Ludgate Communications 1996, assoc in media rels team JPMorgan 1997, vice-pres Corp Communications Div Morgan Stanley 1999, ceo Gorkana 2003–; *Style—* Alex Northcott, Esq; ✉ Gorkana, 2nd Floor, 27a Floral Street, London WC2E 9EZ

NORTHCOTT, Montague Walter Desmond; s of Cdr W C Northcott, JP, DL, RNR (d 1965), and Irene Violet, *née* Lay (d 1972); *b* 25 April 1931; *Educ* Harrow; *m* 24 Aug 1966, Annie Margaret Durrance; 1 s (Richard Walter Montague b 1967), 1 da (Joanna Rosemary Marion b 1969); *Career* Royal Navy 1949–51; Cunard Steamship Co 1951–67, Hogg Robinson Travel 1968–96; underwriting member of Lloyd's 1977–95; tstee Northcott Fndn 1965–2011; govr: Haberdashers' Aske's Schs 1972–82, Jones GS Fndn 1985–88; chm St Andrews Church Little Berkhamsted Restoration Appeal 1987–91; Master: Worshipful Co of Haberdashers 1985, Worshipful Co of Painter-Stainers 1989; Liveryman Worshipful Co of Loriners; *Recreations* painting, geneology, swimming, gardening; *Clubs*

RAC; *Style*— Montague Northcott, Esq; ✉ 11 Watton House, Watton-at-Stone, Hertfordshire SG14 3NZ

NORTHEDGE, Richard; *b* 3 September 1950; *Career* journalist; Estates Times 1973–76, property ed Investors Chronicle 1976–78, property ed Evening Standard 1978–80; Daily Telegraph: columnist 1980–83, personal fin ed 1983–86, dep City ed 1986–98; dep ed Sunday Business 1998–2001, exec ed The Business 2001–02, freelance writer and columnist 2002–; contrib: The Times, Daily Telegraph, Wall Street Jl, The Spectator, Independent on Sunday; daily blog Dofonline; global research HSBC Investment Bank 2011–; Services Journalist of the Year 1999, Banking Journalist of the Year 2003; *Publications* Consumers' Guide to Personal Equity Plans; *Recreations* riding; *Style*— Richard Northedge, Esq; ☎ 020 7602 8277, e-mail richardnorthedge@yahoo.co.uk

NORTHESK, 15 Earl of (S 1647); Dr Patrick Charles Carnegy; also Lord Rosehill and Eglismauldie (S precedence 1639); s of Canon Patrick Charles Alexander Carnegy (d 1969), and Joyce Eleanor, *née* Townsley (d 1995); *b* 23 September 1940; *Educ* Trinity Hall Cambridge (MA, PhD); *m* 28 Nov 2010, Jill Gomez, *qv*, da of Albert Clyde Gomez (d 1973), and Denise Price Denham (d 2009); *Career* writer, lectr, broadcaster on music, theatre and lit; journalist TES 1964–69, asst ed TLS 1969–78, ed music books Faber and Faber Ltd 1978–88, dir Faber Music Ltd 1979–88, dramaturg Royal Opera House 1988–92, Leverhulme research fell 1994–96; broadcasting incl contribs to BBC Radio 4's arts magazine Kaleidoscope; documentaries on: Kafka, Thomas Mann, Wagner's Ring; Stratford theatre critic The Spectator 1998–2013; founding memb Bayreuth Int Arts Centre; memb: BBC Central Music Advsy Ctee 1986–89, BBC Gen Advsy Cncl 1990–96; *Books* Faust as Musician: A Study of Thomas Mann's novel 'Doctor Faustus' (1973), Christianity Revalued (ed, 1974), Wagner and the Art of the Theatre (2006, Royal Philharmonic Soc Music Award, Special Jury Prize George Freedley Memorial Award); *Recreations* mountains, model engineering, gardening; *Style*— The Earl of Northesk; ✉ patrick.carnegy@btopenworld.com

NORTHMORE-BALL, Martin Dacre; s of Dr Godfrey Dacre Jennings Ball (d 2001), of Warminster, Wilts, and Judith Marion, *née* Northmore (d 1979); *b* 14 February 1943; *Educ* Clifton, King's Coll Cambridge (MA), St Thomas' Hosp Med Sch (MB BChir); *m* 26 July 1969, Averina Constance Frances, da of Prof Sir Francis Gerald William Knowles, 6 Bt (d 1974), of Avebury Manor, Wilts; 2 s (Dacre b 1970 d 1975, Lawrence b 1986), 1 da (Laetitia b 1976); *Career* registrar Charing Cross and King's Coll Hosps 1973–76, sr registrar Addenbrooke's Hosp Cambridge 1979–81 (registrar 1975–78), clinical fell Univ of Toronto 1978–79, conslt orthopaedic surgn and dir Unit for Joint Reconstruction Robert Jones and Agnes Hunt Orthopaedic Hosp Oswestry 1981–2006, sr clinical lectr Keele Univ 1995–2001; co-ed-in-chief Hip International 1994–2001 (memb Editorial Bd 2001–07); memb Ind Monitoring Bd HM Young Offenders Inst Stoke Heath 2008–10, memb Ind Monitoring Bd HM Prison Erlestoke 2010–11; memb Steering Ctee Avebury World Heritage Site (UNESCO) 2012–; cncllr Fyfield and West Overton Parish Cncl 2011–15; memb: BMA, European Hip Soc; fndr memb Br Hip Soc; FRCS 1973, FBOA, CIMechE; *Books* Clinical Challenges in Orthopaedics: The Hip (sr co-author, 2002); *Recreations* study of antiquities, books, travel; *Style*— Martin Northmore-Ball, Esq; ✉ Yew Tree Cottage, West Overton, Marlborough, Wiltshire SN8 4ER (☎ 01672 861636)

NORTHOVER, James Walter Edward; s of Maurice Alexander Northover (d 1975), and Gladys Mary, *née* Frost (d 1981); *b* 19 November 1946; *Educ* Ardingly, Kingston Coll of Art, London Coll of Printing (DipAD, BA), Univ of the Arts London (MA); *m* 1975, Gillian Mary Denise, da of John Thomas Kinsman; 2 da (Sophie b 1979, Romy b 1982), 1 s (Maxim b 1984); *Career* sr designer Conran Design Group 1970–72, assoc dir Fitch & Co 1972–75, md Lloyd Northover (graphic design, corp identity and design mgmnt conslts) 1975–93, chm Lloyd Northover 1993–2012 (formerly Citigate Lloyd Northover); dir: Citigate Bass Yager (USA) 1997–2000, Citigate Asia 1997–2003; chm Incepta Middle East 2003–06, dir Jim Northover Ltd 2011–, chm Industry Partners 2012–; current and former clients incl: BAA, Barbican Centre, Barclays de Zoete Wedd, Bath Spa Univ, Belfast City Cncl, Br Cncl, BRS, BUPA, Centro, China Light & Power, Commercial Bank of Qatar, Courtaulds, Dept for Educn and Skills, Dubai International Financial Centre, Exxon, HMSO, Hong Kong Mass Transit Railway Corporation, John Lewis Partnership, Land Transport Authority of Singapore, Millennium Commission, National Savings and Investments, Tesco, Univ of the Arts London, De La Warr Pavilion; memb Advsy Bd: Univ of the Arts London Information Environments Res Unit, Brunel Univ Business Sch Brand Mgmnt Prog; Design Effectiveness Awards 1989 (Grand Prix), 1992, 1998, 2001 and 2005, Rebrand 100 Distinction Award 2014, Transform Gold Award 2014; lectr at business and design confs, author of various articles for business and design media; memb: D&AD Assoc; FCSD, FRSA, FISTD; *Style*— Jim Northover; ✉ 14–15 Newbury Street, London EC1A 7HU (☎ 020 7796 1165, e-mail jim@jimnorthover.com, website www.jimnorthover.com)

NORTHOVER, Baroness (Life Peer UK 2000), of Cissbury in the County of West Sussex; Lindsay Patricia Northover; PC; *née* Granshaw; da of (Maurice Colin) Charles Granshaw, of Worthing, W Sussex, and Patricia Winifred, *née* Jackson; *b* 21 August 1954; *Educ* Brighton and Hove HS, St Anne's Coll Oxford (MA), Bryn Mawr Coll and Univ of Pennsylvania (MA, PhD); *m* 1988 (sep), John Martin Alban Northover, s of (William) Joseph Northover; 2 s (Thomas Charles b 23 Jan 1989, Joseph Mark b 9 Nov 1990), 1 da (Louisa Alice Lindsay b 28 March 1993); *Career* research fell UCL and St Mark's Hosp London 1980–83, research fell St Thomas' Hosp Med Sch London 1983–84, lectr in history of modern med Wellcome Inst and UCL 1984–91; chair Women Lib Dems 1992–95; House of Lords: Lib Dem spokesperson on health 2000–02, Lib Dem spokesperson on int devpt 2002–10, Govt whip and spokesperson on health, int devpt, justice and women and equalities until 2012, Baroness-in-Waiting to HM the Queen 2010–15, lead Govt spokesperson on int devpt 2011–14, lead Govt spokesperson on women and equalities DEFRA and DCMS 2012–14, spokesperson for Dept for Educn 2013–, parly under-sec of state Dept for Int Devpt 2014–15, Lib Dems princ parly spokesperson on Int Devpt 2015–, PM's trade envoy to Angola 2016–; memb Select Ctee of Embryonic Stem Cell Research 2001–02, memb Select Ctee on the EU and Sub-Ctee on Foreign Affrs, Defence and Int Devpt 2003–04 and on Economic Affrs 2008–10; tstee Lib Dems 2009–11, pres Lib Dem Women 2014–; vice-chair Cwlth Parly Assoc of UK 2008–10; memb Cncl ODI 2005–10, tstee Tropical Health and Educn Tst 2007–10; memb Advsy Cncl Wilton Park 2016–; tstee Bryn Mawr Coll Assoc GB, tstee UNICEF UK 2009–10; hon assoc prof Inst of Global Health Imperial Coll London 2016–; FRSA 2013; *Publications* author and co-author of various academic books and articles; *Style*— The Rt Hon the Baroness Northover; ✉ House of Lords, London SW1A 0PW

NORTHRIDGE, Nigel; *b* 31 January 1956; *Educ* Sullivan Upper Sch, NI Poly; *m* Linda Elizabeth; 1 s (Richard b 3 March 1984), 2 da (Kate b 30 May 1986, Emma b 31 Aug 1991); *Career* Gallaher Ltd: joined as trainee mangr 1976, asst brand mangr 1981–84, mktg, mangr 1984–86, divnl dir Iberia 1986–89, gen mangr Europe 1989–90, bd dir Gallaher Int Ltd 1989–90, md Gallaher (Dublin) Ltd 1990–94, sales and mktg dir and memb Bd Gallaher Tobacco Ltd 1994, chief exec Gallaher Gp plc 2000–; non-exec dir: Aggreko plc, Paddy Power plc; *Style*— Nigel Northridge, Esq

NORTHROP, Antony Patrick Clinton; *Educ* King's Sch Canterbury, Univ of Oxford; *m* Hilary; 2 s (Augustus, Joshua), 1 da (Elektra); *Career* former md Lazard Brothers, fndr md Touchstone Securities Ltd until 2007, ptnr G P Bullhound 2007–14, co-fndr NOR Capital 2014; *Style*— Antony Northrop, Esq; ✉ e-mail northropant@icloud.com

NORTHUMBERLAND, 12 Duke of; Sir Ralph George Algernon Percy; 15 Bt (E 1660), DL (1997); also Baron Percy (GB 1723), Earl of Northumberland and Baron Warkworth (GB 1749), Earl Percy (GB 1776), Earl of Beverly (GB 1790), and Lord Lovaine, Baron of Alnwick (GB 1784); 2 s of 10 Duke of Northumberland, KG, GCVO, TD, PC (d 1988); suc bro 11 Duke of Northumberland (d 1995); *b* 16 November 1956; *Educ* Eton, ChCh Oxford; *m* 1979, (Isobel) Jane Miller, da of John Walter Maxwell Miller Richard, of Edinburgh; 2 da (Lady Catherine Sarah b 1982, Lady Melissa Jane b 1987), 2 s (George Dominic, Earl Percy b 1984, Lord Max Ralph b 1990); *Heir* s, Earl Percy; *Career* chartered surveyor, landowner; MRICS; *Recreations* shooting, fishing, painting, skiing, tennis, snooker; *Style*— His Grace the Duke of Northumberland, DL; ✉ Alnwick Castle, Northumberland NE66 1NG; Syon House, Brentford, Middlesex TW8 8JF

NORTON, Her Hon Judge Heather Sophia; *Career* called to the Bar 1988; recorder 2007, circuit judge (South Eastern Circuit) 2012–; tstee Safe Partnership; *Publications* Pace: A Practical Guide to the Police and Criminal Evidence Act 1984 (jtly, 2 edn 2010); *Style*— Her Hon Judge Norton; ✉ Canterbury Crown Court, The Law Courts, Chaucer Road, Canterbury CT1 1ZA

NORTON, Prof (Michael) James; s of Christopher Stephen Norton, of Birchington, Kent, and Lilian Ivy, *née* Buckley; *b* 15 December 1952; *Educ* Roan Sch for Boys Blackheath (exhibitioner), Univ of Sheffield (BEng, Mappin medal); *m* 29 May 1976, Barbara, da of Joseph Leslie Foster; 1 s (Stephen b 26 July 1979); *Career* Exec engr Computer Systems Div Post Office (Telecoms) 1974–81; British Telecom: head of gp Systems Evolution and Standards Dept 1981–83, seconded to IT Standards Unit DTI 1983, head of section SESD 1983–84, sr mangr Advanced Networks Mktg BT National Networks 1984–86, sr mangr Int Business Devpt BT International 1986–87; dir Vendor Consultancy Practice Butler Cox plc 1987–90, dir of mktg Cable & Wireless Europe 1990–93, chief exec Radiocommunications Agency DTI 1993–98, dir Electronic Commerce Team, Performance & Innovation Unit, Cabinet Office 1999, head of e-Business Policy IOD 1999–2001, chm Deutsche Telekom Ltd 2001–02, sr policy advsr e-Business and e-Government IOD 2004–08, chair Professionalism Bd and vice-pres BCS 2008–11 (pres 2011–12), tstee BCS 2014–15; non-exec dir: Securicor plc 2000–02, Telemetrix plc 2000–04, 3i European Technology Trust 2000–04, F&C Capital and Income Investment Tst 2001–14, Applegate Marketplace Ltd 2015–; sr independent dir Zetex plc 2004–08, tstee and dir BCS Learning & Devpt Ltd 2014–15; memb: Bd Parly Office of Sci and Technol 2001–, Strategic Stakeholder Gp Nat Hi-Tech Crime Unit 2005–06, Cncl Parly IT Ctee 2005–11, Ind Climate Change Email Review 2010, Engrg Policy Ctee and Fin Ctee Royal Acad of Engrg 2014–; chair UK Spectrum Policy Forum 2013–15; cmmr IPPR Cmmn on Nat Security in the 21st Century 2007–09; visiting prof of electrical engineering Univ of Sheffield 1998–; govr Univ of Coventry 2012– (dep chair Audit and Risk Ctee 2015–); chartered dir 2005; DEng Univ of Sheffield 2003, Hon LLD Univ of Bath 2012; FIEE 1997 (AMIEE 1974), FRSA 1995, FInstD 2001, FBCS 2005, FREng 2011; *Publications* The Challenges of Cyberspace: living and working in a digital society; *Recreations* reading, music, amateur radio; *Style*— Prof James Norton; ✉ 179b Kimbolton Road, Bedford MK41 8DR (☎ 01234 325844, e-mail jim@profjimnorton.com, website www.profjimnorton.com)

NORTON, John Charles; *b* 22 April 1937; *Educ* Dulwich Coll, UC Oxford (MA); *m* 1962, Dianne, *née* Lloyd; 2 s (James b 1963, Adam b 1968), 1 da (Emma b 1966); *Career* ptnr Arthur Andersen 1971–95 (joined 1961), dir Arab-Br C of C 1995–2008, dir SOCO International plc 1997–2016; former memb Oil Indust Accounting Ctee; govr Dulwich Coll 1998–2008; FCA 1974 (ACA 1964), FInstPet 1975; *Recreations* opera, rugby, golf, travel; *Clubs* Brooks's, Vincent's (Oxford); *Style*— John Norton, Esq

NORTON, John Lindsey; s of Frederick Raymond Norton (d 1981), and Doris Ann, *née* Jobson (d 1988); *b* 21 May 1935; *Educ* Winchester, Univ of Cambridge (MA); *m* 10 Oct 1959, Judith Ann, da of Brig Arthur Bird; 3 da (Bridget Ann b 6 Dec 1960, Claire Elizabeth b 25 May 1963, Sophie b 6 April 1965); *Career* Binder Hamlyn: joined 1963, ptnr (specialist in taxation, fin advice) 1966, nat managing ptnr 1981–87, chm BDO Binder (int firm) 1987–91, sr ptnr Binder Hamlyn 1992–96; chm Thames Valley Power Ltd 1995–, chm Barking Power Ltd 1995–97 and 1999– (dep chm 1997–99), dir H P Bulmer Holdings plc 1997–2003; chm NSPCC 1995–2001 (treas 1991–95); FCA; *Recreations* gardening, walking, music, theatre, a little golf; *Style*— John Norton, Esq; ✉ c/o Barking Power Ltd, Chequers Lane, Dagenham, Essex RM9 6PF (☎ 020 8984 5000, fax 020 8984 5001, e-mail johnnorton@clara.co.uk)

NORTON, Richard William Fisher; s of Richard Glover Norton (d 2003), and Philippa Margaret, *née* Fisher (d 1995); *b* 4 October 1959; *Educ* Summer Fields, Radley; *m* 1987, Caroline Nicola Amy, da of Col Charles Taylor, MC, and Diana Elizabeth, *née* Gott; 2 da (Victoria b 1992, Lucinda b 1994); *Career* slr Linklaters & Paines 1983–87, slr and ptnr Charles Russell Speechlys LLP 1987–; *Recreations* golf, shooting and dogs; *Clubs* MCC, Annabel's, Cavalry and Guards, St Enedoc Golf, Wychwood Golf; *Style*— Richard Norton, Esq; ✉ Shawswell Grange, Rendcomb, Gloucestershire GL7 7HD; Charles Russell Speechlys LLP, Compass House, Lypiatt Road, Cheltenham, Gloucestershire GL50 2QJ

NORTON, Robert; s of Ernest Robert Norton (d 1981), and Elsie Margaret, *née* Nix (d 1981); *b* 6 January 1941; *Educ* Downing Coll Cambridge, St Thomas' Hosp Med Sch (MA, MB BChir); *m* 29 July 1967, Ann Venetta Anderson, da of Romeo Alfredo Pazzi (d 1967); 2 s (Andrew b 20 Nov 1968, Christopher b 26 July 1970), 1 da (Colette b 23 Nov 1972); *Career* sr registrar in cardiothoracic surgery Edinburgh Royal Infirmary and City Hosps 1976–80; conslt cardiothoracic surgn West Midlands Regnl Health Authy 1980–, clinical tutor Univ of Warwick Med Sch 2006– (hon clinical teaching fell 2016), pt/t conslt surgn Univ Hosps of Coventry and Warwickshire 2006–; memb Soc of Cardiothoracic Surgns; Intercollegiate Bd examiner 1992–97; FRCS 1972; *Clubs* Daimler and Lanchester Owners; *Style*— Robert Norton, Esq; ✉ 6 Amherst Road, Kenilworth, Warwickshire CV8 1AH (e-mail 83robertnorton@gmail.com)

NORTON, Prof Trevor Alan; s of Alan Norton, and Agnes, *née* Walsh; *b* 28 July 1940; *Educ* Blyth GS, Univ of Liverpool (BSc, PhD); *m* 26 July 1968, Win Marian; 1 da (Rachel Jane b 1971), 1 s (Paul Martin b 1974); *Career* regius prof of marine biology Bergen 1981, titular prof of botany Univ of Glasgow 1982–83, prof of marine biology Univ of Liverpool 1983–2005 (emeritus prof 2005–), dir Port Erin Marine Laboratory 1983–2005; author of 200 research pubns; pres: Br Phycological Soc 1989–91, Int Phycological Soc 1991–93; chm Aquatic Life Sciences NERC 1988–90, memb Cncl Marine Biological Assoc UK; hon research fell Centre for Manx Studies 2007–; FRSE 1985, FBS 1987; *Books* The Zonation of Rocky Shores (in The Ecology of Rocky Coasts, 1985), Marine Ecology in Biology of the Red Algae (1990), The Exploitable Living Resources of the Irish Sea (1990), Stars Beneath the Sea (1999), Reflections on a Summer Sea (2001), Out of the Past (2003), Under Water to get out of the Rain (2005), Smoking Ears and Screaming Teeth (2010), Imagination and a Pile of Junk (2014); *Recreations* writing, gardening, watching movies, grandchildren; *Style*— Prof Emeritus Trevor Norton

NORTON OF LOUTH, Baron (Life Peer UK 1998), of Louth in the County of Lincolnshire; Prof Philip Norton; s of George Ernest Norton (d 1987), and Ena Dawson, *née* Ingham (d 2005); *b* 5 March 1951; *Educ* Univ of Sheffield (BA, PhD), Univ of Pennsylvania (MA); *Career* Univ of Hull: lectr in politics 1977–82, sr lectr in politics 1982–84, reader in politics 1984–86, prof of govt 1986– (youngest prof of politics in UK), dir Centre for Legislative Studies 1992–; chm: Cmmn to Strengthen Parliament 1999–2000, Cons Academic Gp 2000–, House of Lords Select Ctee on the Constitution 2001–04, All-Pty Gp on the

N

Constitution 2010–15; co-chair Parly Univ Gp 2010–, co-chair Higher Educn Cmmn 2013–; memb Exec Ctee: Study of Parl Gp 1981–93 and 2012–, Political Studies Assoc of UK 1983–89, Br Politics Gp in USA 1983–95 and 2009–11 (pres 1988–90), Res Ctee of Legislative Specialists Int Political Science Assoc 1991– (co-chair 1994–2003); pres Politics Assoc 1993–2008, memb Cncl Hansard Soc 1997–, vice-pres UK Political Studies Assoc 1999–, tstee History of Parliament 2000–; assoc ed Political Studies 1987–93, ed Jl of Legislative Studies 1995–; chm Standards Ctee Kingston upon Hull City Cncl 1999–2003; Freeman of the City of Kingston upon Hull 2016; Hon LLD Univ of Lincoln 2011; FRSA 1995, AcSS 2001; *Books* incl: The Commons in Perspective (1981), Conservatives and Conservatism (jtly, 1981), The Constitution in Flux (1982), The British Polity (1984, 5 edn 2010), Legislatures (ed, 1990), Back from Westminster (jtly, 1993), Does Parliament Matter? (1993), The Conservative Party (ed, 1996), Parliaments in Contemporary Western Europe (ed 3 vols, 1998–2002), Parliament in British Politics (2005, 2 edn 2013), A Century of Constitutional Change (ed, 2011), Eminent Parliaments (ed, 2012), Politics UK (jtly, 8 edn 2013), The Voice of the Backbenchers (2013); *Recreations* table tennis, walking; *Clubs* Royal Over-Seas League; *Style*— Prof the Rt Hon the Lord Norton of Louth; ✉ Department of Politics, University of Hull, Hull HU6 7RX (☎ 01482 465863, fax 01482 466208, e-mail p.norton@hull.ac.uk); House of Lords, London SW1A 0PW (e-mail nortonp@parliament.uk)

NORTON-TAYLOR, Richard Seymour; *b* 6 June 1944; *Educ* King's Sch Canterbury, Hertford Coll Oxford (BA), Coll of Europe Bruges; *Career* freelance journalist; positions 1969–73 incl: EEC corr Washington Post, writer The Economist, writer Financial Times, broadcaster BBC Brussels; The Guardian: corr Brussels 1973–75, corr Whitehall 1975–85, security and intelligence corr 1985–; writer on defence and security, contrib to various radio and TV progs on the intelligence services; memb: Advsy Cncl RUSI, Bd and Policy Cncl Liberty; life memb NFU; Freedom of Information Campaign Journalist of the Year 1986, Freedom of Information Campaign Special Award 1995; FRSA 2014; *Books* Whose Land Is It Anyway (1981), The Ponting Affair (1985), Blacklist (1988), In Defence Of The Realm? (1990), GCHQ: A Conflict of Loyalties 1984–1991, Truth is a Difficult Concept: Inside the Scott Inquiry (1995), Knee Deep in Dishonour: The Scott Report and its Aftermath (1996), Sleaze, The Corruption of Parliament (contrib, 1997), The Hutton Inquiry and its Impact (2004); *Plays* Half The Picture (1994, (based on Scott arms to Iraq inquiry)), Nuremberg (1996), The Colour of Justice (1999), Justifying War (2003), Bloody Sunday (2005, Olivier Award for Outstanding Theatre Production 2006), Called to Account (2007), Tactical Questioning (2011); *Recreations* cinema, gardening, tennis, travel, walking; *Style*— Richard Norton-Taylor, Esq; ✉ e-mail richardnortontaylor21@gmail.com, Twitter @NortonTaylor

NORWICH, 71 Bishop of (cr 1094) 1999–; Rt Rev Graham Richard James; s of late Lionel Dennis James, and late (Florence Edith) May, *née* James; *b* 19 January 1951; *Educ* Northampton GS, Lancaster Univ (BA), Univ of Oxford (DipTh), Cuddesdon Theol Coll (CertTheol); *m* 21 Jan 1978, Julie Anne, da of Stanley William Freemantle; 2 da (Rebecca Alice b 5 Oct 1980, Victoria Rachel b 1983 d 1984), 1 s (Dominic Richard b 12 April 1985); *Career* ordained: deacon 1975, priest 1976; asst curate Christ the Carpenter Peterborough 1975–78, priest-in-charge later team vicar Christ the King Digswell Welwyn Garden City 1979–83, selection sec/sec for continuing ministerial educn 1983–85, sr selection sec ACCM 1985–87, chaplain to the Archbishop of Canterbury 1987–93, bishop of St Germans 1993–99; chair: Rural Bishops' Panel 2001–06, Central Religious Advsy Ctee to BBC and Ofcom 2004–07, Miny Div C of E 2006–, Standing Conf on Religion and Belief BBC 2009–11; memb Archbishop's Cncl 2006–10, House of Lords Select Ctee on Communications 2011–; C of E lead spokesman on the media 2011–; memb Bd Countryside Agency 2001–06, pres Royal Norfolk Agric Assoc 2005–06; memb House of Lords 2004–; Hon DCL UEA 2015, Hon DCL Norwich Univ of the Arts 2016; *Books* Say One for Me (contrib, 1991), New Soundings (ed, 1997), A Fallible Church (contrib, 2008), The Lent Factor (2014); *Recreations* theatre, walking, secondhand bookshops; *Clubs* Athenaeum, Norfolk; *Style*— The Rt Rev the Lord Bishop of Norwich; ✉ Bishop's House, Norwich, Norfolk NR3 1SB (☎ 01603 629001, e-mail bishop@dioceseofnorwich.org)

NORWICH, 2 Viscount (UK 1952); John Julius Cooper; CVO (1993); s of 1 Viscount Norwich, GCMG, DSO, PC (Duff Cooper), sec of State for War 1935–37, First Lord of Admiralty 1937–38, min of Info 1940–41, and ambass to France 1944–47 (d 1954), and Lady Diana Cooper, *née* Manners (d 1986); *b* 15 September 1929; *Educ* Upper Canada Coll Toronto, Eton, Univ of Strasbourg, New Coll Oxford; *m* 1, 1952 (m dis 1985), Anne Frances May, da of Hon Sir Bede Clifford, GCMG, CB, MVO (yst s of 10 Baron Clifford of Chudleigh), and Alice, *née* Gundry, of Cleveland, Ohio; 1 s, 1 da; m 2, 1989, Mary (Mollie), da of 1 Baron Sherfield, GCB, GCMG, and former w of Hon Hugo John Laurence Philipps (later 3 Baron Milford); *Heir* s, Hon Jason Cooper; *Career* author, broadcaster (as 'John Julius Norwich'); with FO 1952–64; former chm Venice in Peril Fund, chm World Monuments Fund UK; maker of some thirty programmes (historical or art-historical) for television; FRSL, FRGS, FRSA; Ordine al Merito della Repubblica Italiana, Ordine della Solidarietà Italiana; *Books* two-volume history of Norman Sicily: The Normans in the South, The Kingdom in the Sun (published in one volume as The Normans in Sicily, 1992); two-volume history of Venice: The Rise to Empire, The Greatness and the Fall; Mount Athos, Sahara, The Architecture of Southern England, Fifty Years of Glyndebourne; three-volume History of Byzantium: The Early Centuries, The Apogee, The Decline and Fall; Shakespeare's Kings, Paradise of Cities, Christmas Crackers, More Christmas Crackers, Still More Christmas Crackers, The Middle Sea (History of the Mediterranean), Treasures of Britain (ed), Trying to Please (memoirs, 2008), The Popes: A History (2011), Darling Monster (ed, 2013), A History of Enland in 100 Places (2011); *Recreations* Venice, commonplace books, nightclub piano; *Clubs* Beefsteak; *Style*— The Rt Hon the Viscount Norwich, CVO; ✉ 24 Blomfield Road, London W9 1AD (☎ 020 7286 5050, e-mail jjnorwich@dial.pipex.com)

NOTLEY, Somerled MacDonald; s of Lt Col George Harry Norman Notley, of Kirkcaldy, Fife, and Catherine, *née* MacDonald; *b* 30 March 1954; *Educ* George Watson's Coll Edinburgh, Univ of Edinburgh (LLB); *Career* apprentice Menzies Dougal & Milligan 1977–79; slr: Church of Scotland 1979–80, Standard Life Assurance Co 1980–81; Brodies: legal asst 1981–87, assoc 1987–89, ptnr 1989–2007, conslt 2007–; memb: Law Soc, Soc of Writers to HM Signet 1993, Notary Public 2004; *Recreations* angling, skiing, music, reading, antiques; *Style*— Somerled Notley, Esq; ✉ Brodies WS, 15 Atholl Crescent, Edinburgh EH3 8HA (☎ 0131 228 3777, e-mail somerled.notley@brodies.co.uk)

NOTT, David Malcolm; OBE (2012); s of Malcolm George Nott (d 2004), and Yvonne Margaret, *née* Jones; *b* 6 July 1956, Carmarthen, Wales; *Educ* Hulme GS, St Andrews Univ (BSc), Univ of Manchester (MBChB, MD); *m* 31 Jan 2015, Eleanor, *née* Jupp; 1 da (Molly Violet Annie b 22 July 2015); *Career* conslt surgn Chelsea and Westminster Hosp 1992–; volunteer humanitarian surgn Medecins Sans Frontieres, Red Cross and Syria Relief 1993–; co-fndr David Nott Fndn 2015–; Robert Burns Humanitarian of the Year Award 2016; FRCS 1985; Hon DSc Univ of Salford 2015; OStJ 2011; *Publications* incl medical and surgical pubns; *Recreations* skiing, flying; *Style*— Mr David Nott, OBE; ✉ Twitter @NottFoundation

NOULTON, John David; s of John Noulton (d 1993), of London, and Kathleen, *née* Sheehan (d 2008); *b* 5 January 1939; *Educ* Clapham Coll; *m* 7 Oct 1961, Anne Elizabeth (d 2012), da of Edward Byrne (d 1985); 3 s (Mark John b 1963, Stephen Anthony b 1965, Simon Anthony b 1966), 1 da (Jane Antonina b 1968); *Career* asst princ Dept of Tport 1970–72, princ DOE 1972–76, private sec to Min of State Rt Hon Denis Howell, MP 1976–78, sec Property Servs Agency 1978–81, under sec Dept of Tport 1985–89 (asst sec 1981–85); dir British Channel Tunnel Co plc 1982–89, chm Channel Tunnel Intergovernmental Cmmn 1989, dir Marine and Ports 1989, admin dir Transmanche Link 1989–92, dir public affairs Eurotunnel plc 1992–2004, advsr to Chm London Olympic Devpt Authy 2005–06, conslt tport and public affrs 2007–; tstee Franco-British Cncl 2003–09 (treas 2007–09); MCIT 1986, companion memb ICE 1994; *Recreations* walking, Mediterranean gardening, boating, writing, music; *Clubs* Royal Motor Yacht; *Style*— John Noulton, Esq; ✉ 74 Garricks House, Wadbrook Street, Kingston-upon-Thames KT1 1HS (☎ 020 8546 3855, e-mail johnnoulton@aol.com); Penthouse, The Dunes, 135 Banks Road, Poole, Dorset BH13 7QQ (☎ 01202 706423)

NOURSE, Christopher Stuart; s of Rev John Nourse (d 2006), of Devon, and Helen Jane Macdonald, *née* Allison (d 1992); *b* 13 August 1946, Salisbury, Wilts; *Educ* Hurstpierpoint Coll, Univ of Edinburgh (LLB), Inns of Court Sch of Law, Middle Temple; *Partner* Charles Shu Ming Chan (civil partnership 18 July 2008); *Career* legal exec Life Offices Assoc 1970–72; various arts mgmnt positions: ROH, English Opera Gp, Royal Ballet New Gp 1972–76; gen mangr Sadler's Wells Royal Ballet 1976–86, admin dir Sadler's Wells Royal Ballet (later Birmingham Royal Ballet) 1986–91, asst to gen dir ROH 1991–96, admin dir ROH Tst 1996–97, project mangr A Statue for Oscar Wilde appeal launch Nat Portrait Gallery 1997, exec dir Rambert Dance Co 1997–2001, md English Nat Ballet 2001–03; arts and dance conslt 2005–: admin Nat Dance Awards 2005–10, exec dir Frederick Ashton Fndn 2011, project mangr Dance Proms 2011–14; tstee and non-exec dir and vice-chm London Dance Network 1998–2000, tstee Nat Youth Dance Tst 2002–06, tstee Youth Dance England 2004–16, dir Dancers Pension Scheme 2006–15 (chm 2010–15), chm Dame Margot Fonteyn Scholarship Fund 2007–, non-exec dir Candoco Dance Co 2008–14; govr The Royal Ballet (Royal Ballet/Birmingham Royal Ballet/Royal Ballet School) 2008–, tstee Cecchetti Soc Tst 2011–; FRSA 1998; *Publications* 'To Birmingham and beyond' in About the House (book, 1989), 'Parting Company' in Opera House (magazine, 1997); *Recreations* ballet, opera, theatre and visual arts, music, eating out, the Orient, the countryside, ballroom dancing; *Clubs* Travellers; *Style*— Christopher Nourse, Esq; ✉ 278 Earl's Court Road, London SW5 9AS

NOURSE, Edmund; QC (2015); *Career* called to the Bar 1994; *Style*— Edmund Nourse, Esq, QC; ✉ One Essex Court, Temple, London EC4Y 9AR

NOURSE, Rt Hon Sir Martin Charles; kt (1980), PC (1985); s of late Henry Edward Nourse, MD, MRCP, of Cambridge, and Ethel Millicent, da of Rt Hon Sir Charles Henry Sargant, Lord Justice of Appeal; *b* 3 April 1932; *Educ* Winchester, CCC Cambridge; *m* 1972, Lavinia, da of late Cdr David Malim; 1 da (Charlotte b 1975), 1 s (Harry b 1977); *Career* 2 Lt (Nat Service) Rifle Bde 1951–52, London Rifle Bde Rangers (TA) 1952–55, Lt 1953; called to the Bar Lincoln's Inn 1956 (bencher 1978, treas 2001); memb Gen Cncl of the Bar 1964–68, jr counsel to Bd of Trade in Chancery Matters 1967–70, QC 1970, attorney-gen Duchy of Lancaster 1976–80, judge of the Courts of Appeal of Jersey and Guernsey 1977–80, judge of the High Court of Justice (Chancery Div) 1980–85, a Lord Justice of Appeal 1985–2001, vice-pres Court of Appeal (Civil Div) 2000–01, acting Master of the Rolls June-Oct 2000; pres Cncl of Inns of Court 1992–95, dep chm Takeover Appeal Bd 2001–15; hon fell CCC Cambridge 1988, fell Winchester Coll 1993–2006; *Style*— The Rt Hon Sir Martin Nourse; ✉ Dullingham House, Dullingham, Newmarket, Cambridgeshire CB8 9UP

NOUSS, Hunada; *Career* former fin dir Diageo/Burger King; DG fin and corporate servs Dept for Communities and Local Govt 2007–10, DG finance Dept for Work and Pensions 2010–; FCA,CTA; *Style*— Ms Hunada Nouss; ✉ Department for Work and Pensions, Caxton House, Tothill Street, London SW1H 9DA

NOWELL, Jonathan Charles Peter; s of David Charles Nowell, and Joan Nowell; *Educ* Stamford Sch, Westfield Coll London (BA); *Career* publishing dir Pearl & Dean Gp 1987–91, publisher motoring titles EMAP 1991–95, publisher and gp md J Whitaker & Sons Ltd 1995–2001, pres Nielsen Book 2001–16, ceo Jonathan Nowell & Co Ltd 2016–; sr advsr Trillium Ptnrs 2016–; memb: Publishers Assoc, Booksellers Assoc, Book Soc, Book Industry Communication; *Recreations* ex-player and ardent rugby fan, fishing (coarse and game), wine, cricket; *Clubs* Groucho, Soho House; *Style*— Jonathan Nowell, Esq; ✉ 5 Midhurst Avenue, London N10 3EP (e-mail jcpnowell@yahoo.co.uk); 23 Berkeley Square, London W1J 6HE

NSEIR, Tarek Antoine; s of Tony Nseir, and Nahla Nseir; *b* 6 May 1981, Lebanon; *Educ* Rugby, Univ of Newcastle (BSc), MIT; *Career* support gp mangr Accenture 1999–2001, md Revelation Design 2001–03, fndr and md TH_NK (website desgn and digital strategy agency) 2003– (fourth fastest-growing agency UK technol co Deloitte Technol Fast 50 2007) ; Young Entrepreneur of the Year Entrepreneur's Forum 2006, David Goldman Award for Business Innovation Univ of Newcastle Business Sch 2006, Young Business Executive of the Year The Jl North East Business Awards 2006; *Recreations* travel, flying, skydiving; *Style*— Tarek Nseir, Esq; ✉ TH_NK, 55 Degrees North, Pilgrim Street, Newcastle Upon Tyne NE1 6BF (☎ 0191 241 7000, fax 0191 241 7002, e-mail tarek.nseir@think.eu, website www.think.com)

NUDD, Prof Graham Raymond; s of Raymond Charles Nudd (d 1966), and Eva May, *née* Ayling (d 1989); *b* 18 March 1940, Brockham, Surrey; *Educ* Collyers Sch Horsham, Univ of Southampton (BSc, PhD); *m* 1966, Laura Mary, *née* Brandram-Adams; 1 da (Alison Elizabeth b 1974); *Career* scientist for NASA Apollo Lunar Scientific Package flown on Apollo Mission 12 Ann Arbor USA 1966–68, head of computer architecture Hughes Res Laboratories Calif 1968–84; Univ of Warwick: Lucas prof of electronics and computer sci 1984–85, chm Computer Science Dept 1984–2006, prof of computer sci 1985–2008, emeritus prof 2008–; lectr: UCLA, Univ of Southern Calif, Calif Inst of Technol, CALTECH Pasadena; consIt for several organisations incl GEC and US Navy; fndr and dir of several high tech start-up companies; FIEEE, FIEE, FREng; *Publications* author of over 200 publications on computer and electronics systems; *Recreations* boating, rural preservation, living quietly in the Cotswolds; *Style*— Prof Graham Nudd, FREng; ✉ Department of Computer Science, University of Warwick, Coventry CV4 7AL (☎ 02476 523366, e-mail grn@dcs.warwick.ac.uk)

NUGEE, Hon Mr Justice; Sir Christopher George Nugee; kt (2013), QC (1998); s of Edward Nugee, Esq, TD, QC (d 2014), and Rachel *née* Makower (d 2015); *b* 23 January 1959; *Educ* Radley, CCC Oxford (BA), City Univ (Dip Law); *m* 1991, Emily Thornberry, MP, *qv*, da of Cedric and Sallie Thornberry; 2 s (Felix Henry b 10 Dec 1991, Patrick George b 8 July 1999), 1 da (Rose Elizabeth b 2 Oct 1993); *Career* called to the Bar Inner Temple 1983 (Queen Elizabeth scholarship, bencher 2003); in practice at Chancery Bar 1984–13, Eldon law scholar 1984, recorder 2002–13, dep judge of the High Court 2003–13, judge Courts of Appeal Jersey and Guernsey 2011–13, judge of the High Court of Justice (Chancery Div) 2013–; memb: Bar Cncl 1991–93 (Professional Conduct Ctee 1992–96), Assoc of Pension Lawyers Main Ctee 1998–2002; *Recreations* cycling, my family, tideway sculling; *Style*— The Hon Mr Justice Nugee; ✉ Rolls Building, Royal Courts of Justice, 7 Rolls Buildings, Fetter Lane, London EC4A 1NL

NUGENT, John; s of John Nugent (d 1985), and Margaret, *née* Reilly; *b* 16 April 1970, Dublin, Ireland; *Educ* Synge Street Christian Bros Dublin, Dublin Coll of Catering; *m* 14 June 1997 (sep); 1 s (Harry Charles b 29 Nov 2001); *Career* ceo Searcy until 2007 (launched restaurant, private dining, bar and events business at 30 St Mary Axe (the Gherkin) London, The Portrait Restaurant Nat Portrait Gall, 1802 Canary Wharf and The Champagne Bar St Pancras), previously md Richard Corrigan Restaurants Ltd (incl Lindsay House Restaurant London and Bentley's Seafood Restaurant London), chief exec Green Fortune 2007– (responsible for devpt of dining and bar facilities at Kings Place London and running of Kings Place Events); *Style—* John Nugent, Esq; ✉ Green & Fortune, c/o Kings Place, 90 York Way, London N1 9AG (☎ 020 7014 4119, e-mail john.nugent@kingsplace.co.uk or john.nugent@greenandfortune.co.uk, website www.greenandfortune.co.uk)

NUÑEZ, Marianela; da of Norberto Nuñez, and Elena Clarijo de Nuñez; *b* 23 March 1982, Buenos Aires, Argentina; *Educ* Teatro Colón Ballet Sch, Royal Ballet Sch; *Career* ballet dancer; princ Royal Ballet 2002– (joined 1999); *Performances* incl: Kitri, Swanilda, Sugar Plum Fairy, Gamzatti, Nikiya, Aurora, Lilac Fairy, Olga in Onegin, Myrtha, Mitzi Caspar, Princess Louise and Lescaut's Mistress in Mayerling, Polyhymnia, Lykanion, Raymonda Act III, Monotones I, Agon, The Vertiginous Thrill of Exactitude, This House Will Burn, The Leaves Are Fading, Sinfonietta, The Four Temperaments, Diana and Actaeon pas de deux, La Neige in Les Saisons, Acheron's Dream; *Style—* Miss Marianela Nuñez; ✉ c/o The Royal Ballet, Royal Opera House, Covent Garden, London WC2E 9DD

NUNN, Michael; OBE (2012); s of Reginald Edward Nunn, and Shirley Louise, *née* Morrison; *b* 1 July 1967; *Educ* Bush Davies Sch, Royal Ballet Sch; *m* Belinda Hatley; 1 s (George Jacob Nunn b 27 Sept 2003); *Career* dancer; with Royal Ballet 1987–99 (first soloist 1997–99), fndr memb K Ballet 1999, fndr (with William Trevitt , *qv*) George Piper Dances 2001; *Performances* Sir Kenneth MacMillan repertoire: cr The Friend in The Judas Tree, Romeo and Benvolio in Romeo and Juliet, Offertoire in Requiem, The Brother in My Brother, My Sisters, Des Grieux and The Gaoler in Manon, Bethena Waltz in Elite Syncopations, Crown Prince Rudolf in Mayerling, The Boy in The Invitation, one of the Four Officers and Anna's Husband in Anastasia, The King of the East in The Prince of the Pagodas, Kulygin in Winter Dreams, The Orange Boy in La Fin du Jour, second movement in Concerto; Sir Frederick Ashton repertoire: Beliaev in A Month in the Country, The Prince in Cinderella, white pas de deux in Les Patineurs, Dorkon in Daphnis and Chloe, pas de deux in Birthday Offering, Elgar in Enigma Variations, Thais pas de deux, Monotones II, Symphonic Variations; cr roles: lead in William Tuckett's Present Histories, role in Matthew Hart's Fanfare, Act II sextet in Twyla Tharp's Mr Worldly Wise, lead couple in Christopher Wheeldon's Souvenir, part II in Page's Two Part Invention, The Ringmaster in Sawdust and Tinsel, Glen Tetley's Amores; other roles incl: Albrecht in Giselle, Suitor, Prince Florimund and Gold variation in The Sleeping Beauty, Rag Mazurka Boy in Nijinska's Les Biches, Mazurka and pas de deux in Fokine's Les Sylphides, pas de trois in Balanchine's Agon, fourth movement in Symphony in C, pas de trois in David Bintley's Galanteries, Mars in The Planets, first princ man in Cheating, Lying, Stealing, The Man in Dream of Angels, first section in William Forsythe's In the Middle Somewhat Elevated, leading man in Steptext, William Tuckett's A Shropshire Lad (Dance Bites tour 1995), Ashley Page's Pursuit, Room of Cooks (Dance Bites tour 1997), Herman Schmerman, Twyla Tharp's Push Comes to Shove, Consort Lessons; television appearances with Royal Ballet: La Valse (Channel 4), 1997 Farewell Gala (Channel 4), The Judas Tree (Channel 4), The Ancient Mariner (BBC2), featured in The House (BBC2); perfs with George Piper Dances incl: Steptext, Sigue, Truly great thing, Critical Mass and Torsion, other mens wives, Approximate Sonata I, V, Mesmerics, restaged Halleloo, choreographed Moments of Plastic Jubilation; also with William Trevitt: co-filmed and co-directed Ballet Boyz and Ballet Boyz II – The Next Step (Channel 4), presented 4Dance (Channel 4) 2003 and 2004, created Critic's Choice ***** (featuring Matthew Bourne, *qv*, Michael Clark, Akram Khan, *qv*, Russell Maliphant, *qv* and Christopher Wheeldon) 2004, Broken Fall (commissioned by Russell Malipahnt, premiered ROH) 2004, dir and choreographer Naked (premiered at Sadler's Wells) 2005; *Awards* nominated South Bank Show Dance Award 2001 and 2003, nomination (for Memerics) Best New Dance Production Laurence Olivier Award 2004, winner (for Broken Fall) Best New Dance Production Laurence Olivier Award 2004; *Recreations* Film, Travel, Music, Literature; *Style—* Michael Nunn, Esq, OBE; ✉ George Piper Dances, Sadler's Wells, Rosebery Avenue, London EC1R 4TN (☎ 020 7863 8238, e-mail michael@gpdances.com)

NUNN, Sir Trevor Robert; kt (2002), CBE (1978); s of Robert Alexander Nunn, and Dorothy May, *née* Piper; *b* 14 January 1940; *Educ* Northgate GS Ipswich, Downing Coll Cambridge (BA), Univ of Newcastle upon Tyne (MA); *m* 1, 1969 (m dis 1986), Janet Suzman, *qv*; 1 s (Joshua b 1980); m 2, 1986 (m dis 1991), Sharon Lee, *née* Hill; 2 da (Laurie b 1986, Amy b 1989); m 3, 1994, Imogen Stubbs, *qv*; 1 da (Ellie b 1991), 1 s (Jesse b 1996); *Career* theatre and film director; RSC: assoc dir 1964–68, chief exec and artistic dir 1968–78, chief exec and jt artistic dir 1978–86; artistic dir RNT 1997–2003; memb Arts Council 1994–96; *Theatre and Film* Belgrade Theatre Coventry: The Caucasian Chalk Circle, Peer Gynt, Around the World in Eighty Days (musical); RSC: The Revenger's Tragedy, The Relapse, The Alchemist, Henry V, The Taming of the Shrew, King Lear, Much Ado About Nothing, The Winter's Tale, Henry VIII, Hamlet, Antony and Cleopatra (also for ATV, BAFTA Award for Best Single Play Prodn), Hedda Gabler (also as a film), Macbeth (also for Thames TV), Coriolanus, Julius Caesar, Titus Andronicus, Romeo and Juliet, The Comedy of Errors (also for ATV, musical version – Ivor Novello Award for Best British Musical, SWET Award for Best Musical), The Alchemist, As You Like It, Once in a Life-time (Plays and Players London Theatre Critics' Award – Best Production, New Standard Drama Awards – Sydney Edwards Award for Best Director), Three Sisters, Nicholas Nickleby (New Standard Drama Awards – Sydney Edwards for Best Director, SWET Award for Best Director, Drama Review London Theatre Critics' Award – Best Production, Tony Award – Best Director, special citation as Outstanding Broadway Production in All Categories, Emmy Award – Best Best TV Serial; shown on TV in London and NY, with John Caird), Juno and the Paycock (Drama Review London Theatre Critics' Award – Best Revival), Henry IV Parts I and II, All's Well That Ends Well, Peter Pan (with John Caird), Les Miserables (London and Worldwide, with John Caird), Fair Maid of the West, Othello (also for BBC TV), The Blue Angel (Stratford 1991, Globe 1992), Measure for Measure (Stratford) 1991 (Young Vic) 1992; freelance dir: Cats (worldwide, Tony Award – Best Director of a Musical) 1981, Idomeneo (Glyndebourne Opera) 1982, Starlight Express (London and NY) 1984, Lady Jane (film) 1985, Chess (London and NY) 1986, Porgy and Bess (Glyndebourne Opera 1986, Royal Opera House 1992), Aspects of Love (London and NY) 1989, The Baker's Wife 1989, Timon of Athens (Young Vic Theatre, Evening Standard Award for Best Dir) 1991, Cosi Fan Tutte (Glyndebourne Opera) 1991, Heartbreak House (Yvonne Arnaud Guildford and Haymarket) 1992, Arcadia (RNT 1993, Haymarket 1994, NY 1995), Sunset Boulevard (London and Los Angeles 1993, NY 1994), Twelfth Night (film) 1996, The Lady From the Sea 2003, Richard II (Old Vic) 2005; RNT: Enemy of the People 1997, Mutabilitie 1997, Not About Nightingales 1998, Oklahoma! 1998, Betrayal 1998, Troilus and Cressida 1999, Merchant of Venice 1999, Summerfolk 1999, Albert Speer 2000, The Cherry Orchard 2000, My Fair Lady 2001, South Pacific 2001, A Streetcar Named Desire 2002, Sophie's Choice 2002, Anything Goes 2002, Love's Labour's Lost 2003, Skellig 2003, Hamlet 2004, We Happy Few 2004; West End: The Woman In White 2004, Acorn Antiques: The Musical! 2005, Porgy and Bess 2006, The Seagull 2007, King Lear 2007, Gone with the Wind 2008, Inherit The Wind 2009, A Little Night Music 2009, Aspects of Love 2010, Birdsong 2010, Flare Path 2011, The Lion In Winter 2011; *Books* A; *Style—* Sir Trevor Nunn, CBE; ✉ 49B British Grove, London W4 2NL (☎ 020 8563 7273)

NUNNELEY, Sir Charles Kenneth Roylance; kt (2003); s of Robin Michael Charles Nunneley (d 2005), of Holt, Norfolk, and Patricia Mary, *née* Roylance (d 1999), of Harrietsham, Kent; *b* 3 April 1936; *Educ* Eton; *m* 1961, Catherine Elizabeth Armstrong, da of Sir Denys Burton Buckley, MBE (d 1998), of London; 1 s (Luke b 1963), 3 da (Alice b 1964, Clare b 1967, Frances b 1969); *Career* 2 Lt Scots Gds, served chiefly BAOR; merchant banker; Robert Fleming Holdings: dir 1968–96, dep chm 1986–96, former chm or dir of various other Fleming gp cos; chm: Save & Prosper Gp (Fleming subsid) 1989–96, Fleming Income & Capital Investment Tst 1992–2002, Nationwide Building Society 1996–2002 (dir 1994–2002), Monks Investment Tst 1996–2005 (dir 1977–2005), Nationwide Fndn 1997–2001, JP Morgan Income and Capital Investment Tst 2002–07, Edinburgh Fund Managers Gp 2003; dep chm Clerical Medical & General Life Assurance Society 1978–96 (dir 1974–96); dir: Macmillan Ltd 1982–95, HM Publishers Holdings 1995–96; memb Advsy Bd Aberdeen Charitable Funds 2011–; chm: Institutional Fund Mangrs' Assoc 1989–92, IMRO 1992–97 (dir 1986–97), Nat Tst 1996–2003 (chm Fin Ctee 1991–96, memb Cncl 1992–2003, memb Exec Ctee 1992–2003); chm Cncl N Wessex Downs Area of Outstanding Natural Beauty 2004–10; govr Oundle Sch 1975–99; memb Ct of Assts Worshipful Co of Grocers 1975– (Master 1982–83); CA 1961; *Recreations* walking, theatre, photography; *Clubs* Hurlingham; *Style—* Sir Charles Nunneley; ✉ 116 Rivermead Court, Ranelagh Gardens, London SW6 3SD (☎ 020 7731 0506)

NURNBERG, Andrew John; s of Walter Nurnberg, OBE (d 1991), and Rita, *née* Kern (d 2001); *b* 16 October 1947; *Educ* St Benedict's Sch Ealing, Univ of London (BA); *m* 22 Oct 1983, Harriet Goodman; 1 s (Alexander b 31 May 1985), 1 da (Lucy b 10 Sept 1987); *Career* literary agent Robert Harben Literary Agency 1973–77; fndr Andrew Nurnberg Assocs 1977 (offices in London, Moscow, Prague, Warsaw, Budapest, Sofia, Riga, Istanbul, Beijing and Taipei); Br Cncl scholarship Moscow State Univ 1968–69; vice-pres Assoc of Authors' Agents 1991; memb Finance Ctee: St Etheldreda's Church London 1982–87, St Patrick's Catholic Church London 1993–; *Publications* The Green Frog Service (with M Raeburn and L Voronikhina, 1995) author of various articles; *Recreations* mountain climbing, cooking, music, reading; *Clubs* Reform, Alpine; *Style—* Andrew Nurnberg, Esq; ✉ Andrew Nurnberg Associates Ltd, 20–23 Greville Street, London EC1N 8SS (☎ 020 3327 0400, fax 020 7430 0801)

NURSE, Sir Paul Maxime; kt (1999); *b* 25 January 1949; *Educ* Harrow County GS, Univ of Birmingham (BSc, John Humphrey's Meml Prize), UEA (PhD); *m*; 2 da; *Career* research fell: Dept of Zoology Univ of Edinburgh 1974–78, Sch of Biology Univ of Sussex 1980–84; head of Cell Cycle Control Laboratory ICRF London 1984–87, Iveagh prof of microbiology Univ of Oxford 1987–91, Napier research prof of the Royal Soc Univ of Oxford 1991–93, DG ICRF 1996–2002 (previously dir of lab research), ceo Cancer Research UK 2002–03, pres Rockefeller Univ NY 2003–11, dir and ceo Francis Crick Inst 2010–; pres Royal Soc 2010–15; visiting prof Univ of Copenhagen 1981; author of over 100 pubns in learned jls; speaker at over 200 seminars in research insts worldwide, speaker chm and organiser at over 30 int meetings and confs dealing with yeast molecular biology and genetics and cell cycle and growth control; pres UK Genetical Soc 1990–94, memb EMBO 1987; FRS 1989, memb Academia Europaea 1992, foreign assoc US Nat Acad of Sciences 1995; *Awards* Fleming lectr Soc of Gen Microbiology 1985, Florey lectr Royal Soc 1990, Marjory Stephenson lectr Soc of Gen Microbiology 1990, CIBA Medal UK Biochemical Soc 1991, Louis Jeantet Prize for Medicine Switzerland 1992, Gairdner Fndn Int Award 1992, Royal Soc Wellcome Medal 1993, Jimenez Diaz Meml Award Spain 1993, Rosenstiel Award and Medal USA 1993, Dunham lectr Harvard Univ 1994, Purkyne Medal Czech Republic 1994, Pezcoller Award for Oncology Research Italy 1995, Bradshaw lectr RCP London 1995, Royal Soc Royal Medal 1995, Dr Josef Steiner Prize Switzerland 1996, Dr H P Heineken Prize for Biochemistry and Biophysics The Netherlands 1996, General Motors Cancer Research Fndn Alfred P Sloan Jr Prize and Medal USA 1997, Albert Lasker Basic Med Research Award USA 1998, Nobel Prize in Physiology or Medicine 2001 (jtly with Leland H Hartwell and Sir Tim Hunt, FRS, *qv*), Romanes Lecture 2003, Royal Society Copley Medal 2005; fell American Acad of Arts and Sciences 2006; Legion d'Honneur 2003; *Style—* Sir Paul Nurse, FRS; ✉ The Francis Crick Institute, 1 Midland Road, London NW1 1AT

NUSSEY, Dr Ian David; OBE (1988); s of Dr Adolph Marcus Nussey (d 1993), and Susannah Rayner Nussey (d 1981); *b* 4 April 1936; *Educ* Bromsgrove Sch, Downing Coll Cambridge (MA, Engrg Assoc prize), Univ of Birmingham (PhD); *m* 1976, Gillian Patricia, da of Dr Thomas Russell and Enid Stanley Stevens; 2 da (Emma Frances Guest (step da) b 1966, Jessica Clare b 1977); *Career* Lucas Industries 1958–62, IBM United Kingdom Ltd 1963–2015 (chm Technical Consultancy Gp 1991–98, vice-pres IBM Acad of Technol 1998–99, Univ Relations 2000–15); contrib to various jls associated with mfrg and info technol; various public service appts; visiting prof: Loughborough Univ 1973–76, Univ of Newcastle upon Tyne 1976–2002, Univ of Salford 1983–94, Cardiff Univ 1986–; memb Cncl Univ of Warwick 1989–2002; vice-pres: Inst of Mfrg Engrs 1990–91, IEE 1995–98 (chm Mfrg Div 1991–92); memb: EPSRC Coll of Peers 1995–, Senate Engrg Cncl 1996–97, Cncl Royal Acad of Engrg 2005–13; Sargent Award Soc of Mfrg Engrs USA 1988, Viscount Nuffield Silver Medal IEE 2000, Chllr's Medal Univ of Warwick 2006, IET Mountbatten Medal 2013, President's Medal Royal Acad of Engrg 2016; hon fell Cardiff Univ 2007, Hon DEng Univ of Glasgow 2008; Freeman City of London, Liveryman Worshipful Co of Engrs 1983; FREng 1985, Hon FIET, FIMechE, FBCS, FSME, FRSA; *Recreations* gardening, theatre-going, hillside conservation, golf; *Clubs* Athenaeum; *Style—* Dr Ian Nussey, OBE, FREng; ✉ Cidermill House, Ardens Grafton, Alcester, Warwickshire B49 6DS (☎ 01789 773356)

NUTBEAM, Prof Don; *b* Newbury, Berks; *Educ* Univ of Southampton (PhD); *m* 26 May 1978, Sarah Anne, *née* Choules; 1 da (Aimee b 26 May 1983), 1 s (Benjamin b 6 May 1986); *Career* various roles in NHS and univs 1978–90; Univ of Sydney: prof and head Sch of Public Health 1990–2000, pro vice-chllr and head Coll of Health Sciences 2003–06, provost and dep vice-chllr 2006–09, prof of public health 2016–; head of public health Dept of Health 2000–03; vice-chllr Univ of Southampton 2009–15; FFPH; *Publications* author of numerous books and scientific pubns; *Recreations* watching sport, gardening; *Clubs* Athenaeum; *Style—* Prof Don Nutbeam; ✉ Sydney School of Public Health, University of Sydney, Camperdown, Sydney NSW 2006, Australia

NUTTALL, Christopher Guy; s of Derek Reginald Nuttall, of Northwich, Cheshire, and Doris Joan Bentley, *née* Johnson; *b* 16 August 1957; *Educ* Sir John Deane's GS Northwich, UCL (BA); *m* 1993, Nishanthri Wickramasinghe, of Colombo, Sri Lanka; 1 da (Constance Geneva b 16 Oct 1995), 1 s (Kesara Calvin b 2 March 1998); *Career* journalist; Warrington Guardian Series newspapers 1978–81; BBC: journalist 1982–99, foreign corr BBC World Serv 1988, Sri Lanka corr 1988–90, Washington corr BBC World Serv 1991–93, foreign affrs corr BBC World Serv 1994–95, Ankara corr BBC World Serv 1995–97, world ed BBC News Online 1997–98, internet corr BBC News 1998–99; internet ed Sunday Business 1999, sr writer Industry Standard Europe 2000, reporter FT 2001–, technol corr 2003–13, writer FastFT and #techFT 2013–16, news ed TMT 2016–; winner communications section Business Journalist of the Year Awards 2000; *Recreations* cycling, cinema, computers; *Style—* Christopher Nuttall, Esq; ✉ Financial Times, One Southwark Bridge, London SE1 9HL

NUTTALL, David John; MP; s of Roy Nuttall, of Rotherham, S Yorks, and Kathleen, *née* Hughes (d 1985); *b* 25 March 1962, Sheffield; *Educ* Aston Comp Sch Rotherham, Univ of London (external); *m* 19 Nov 2004, Susan, *née* Finn; *Career* admitted slr 1990, Notary Public 1998; MP (Cons) Bury N 2010–; *Style—* David Nuttall, Esq, MP; ✉ House of Commons, London SW1A 0AA (website www.davidnuttall.info)

NUTTING, David Anthony; DL (Essex 1988); yr s of Rt Hon Sir (Harold) Anthony Nutting, 3 Bt (d 1999); *b* 13 September 1944; *Educ* Eton, Trinity Coll Cambridge (MA); *m* 25 April

1974, Tessa Anne, o da of Sir Nigel John Mordaunt, 13 Bt, MBE (d 1979); 3 da (Belinda b 18 Aug 1975, Serena b 24 Nov 1977, Alexandra b 27 Dec 1978); *Career* chm: Select Sires Ltd 1982–89, Bridge Farm Dairies Ltd 1987–95, Strutt & Parker (Farms) Ltd 1987–2012; dir Lavenham Fen Farms Ltd; chm: Essex Agric Soc 1985–90, Br Cattle Breeders Club 1978–79; memb Advsy Bd Inst of Animal Physiology 1983–86; pres Holstein Friesian Soc 1990; tstee Cambridge Univ Veterinary Sch Tst 1994; Freeman Worshipful Co of Farmers 1975; *Recreations* fishing, shooting, racing; *Style*— David Nutting, Esq, DL; ✉ 1 Whitbreads Business Centre, Chatham Green, Chelmsford CM3 3FE (☎ 01245 363030)

NUTTING, Sir John Grenfell; 4 Bt (UK 1902), of St Helens, Booterstown, Co Dublin, QC (1995); s of Rt Hon Sir (Harold) Anthony Nutting, 3 Bt (d 1999); *b* 28 August 1942; *Educ* Eton, McGill Univ Montreal (BA); *m* 1973, Diane, da of Capt Duncan Kirk, and widow of 2 Earl Beatty; 1 da (Victoria Emily b 1975), 1 s (James Edward Sebastian b 1977), 1 step s, 1 step da; *Heir* s, James Nutting; *Career* called to the Bar Middle Temple 1968, bencher 1991; first sr treasy counsel 1993–95 (jr treasy counsel 1981, first jr treasy counsel 1987–88, sr treasy counsel 1988–93), recorder of the Crown Court 1986–2012, judge of the Cts of Appeal of Jersey and Guernsey 1995–2014, sr judge 2014, cmmr for Interception of Communications (Jersey and Guernsey) 1998–2005, dep judge of the High Court (Queen's Bench and Chancery Div) 1998–2012, cmmr for Regulation of Investigatory Powers (Jersey and Guernsey) 2004–14; memb Bar Cncl 1976–80 and 1986–87, chm Young Bar 1978–79, vice-chm Criminal Bar Assoc 1995–97; memb Lord Chllr's Advsy Ctee on Legal Educn and Conduct 1997–99, memb Lord Chllr's Review Cmmn on the Rehabilitation of Veterans in the Criminal Justice System 2014–; pres NE Milton Keynes Cons Assoc 1990–93; chm: Helmsdale River Bd 2001–, Helmsdale Dist Salmon Fishery Bd 2001–; memb Appointments Panel Ind Supervisory Authy for Hunting 2001–05, Burghley Horse Trials Ltd 2011–, memb Provost's Appeal Panel Eton Coll 2012–; patron Philharmonia Orch 2001–10, chm of the govrs Burghley House Preservation Tst 2009–, tstee Tst House Tst 2010–, chm Henry VI Soc Eton Coll 2014–; FRPSL 1970; *Publications* Report of the Inquiry into Former Armed Service Personnel in Prison (2011); *Clubs* White's, The Other; *Style*— Sir John Nutting, Bt, QC; ✉ K3, Albany, Piccadilly, London W1J 0AY

NYE, Robert Thomas; s of Oswald William Nye (d 1990), of Southend-on-Sea, Essex, and Frances Dorothy, *née* Weller (d 2000); *b* 15 March 1939, London; *Educ* Southend HS; *m* 1, 1959 (m dis 1967), Judith Pratt; 3 s (Jack, Taliesin, Malory); *m* 2, 1968, Aileen, da of Robert Campbell (d 1972), of Beith, Ayrshire; 1 da (Rebecca), 1 step s (Owen), 1 step da (Sharon); *Career* poet, novelist and critic; gen literary reviewer The Scotsman 1962–2000, reviewer of new fiction The Guardian 1966–92, poetry ed The Scotsman 1967–2000, poetry critic The Times 1971–96, gen literary reviewer The Times 1996–2003; FRSL 1977; *Awards* Eric Gregory award 1963, Scottish Arts Cncl bursary 1970 and 1973 and publication award 1970 and 1976, James Kennaway meml award 1970, Guardian Fiction prize 1976, Hawthornden prize 1977, Soc of Authors' travelling scholarship 1991, granted Civil List pension 2000, Authors' Fndn Award 2003 and 2007, Cholmondeley Award 2007; *Poems* Juvenilia 1 (1961), Juvenilia 2 (1963), Darker Ends (1969), Agnus Dei (1973), Two Prayers (1974), Five Dreams (1974), Divisions on a Ground (1976), A Collection of Poems 1955–88 (1989), 14 Poèmes (1994), Henry James and other Poems (1995), Collected Poems (1995), The Rain and the Glass: 99 Poems, New and Selected (2005), Sixteen Poems (2005), One or Two Swallows (2008), An Almost Dancer: Poems 2005–2011 (2012); *Novels* Doubtfire (1967), Falstaff (1976), Merlin (1978), Faust (1980), The Voyage of the Destiny (1982), The Memoirs of Lord Byron (1989), The Life and Death of My Lord Gilles de Rais (1990), Mrs Shakespeare: The Complete Works (1993), The Late Mr Shakespeare (1998); *Short Stories* Tales I Told My Mother (1969), The Facts of Life and Other Fictions (1983); *Editions* A Choice of Sir Walter Ralegh's Verse (1972), William Barnes of Dorset: A Selection of his Poems (1973), A Choice of Swinburne's Verse (1973), The Faber Book of Sonnets (1976), The English Sermon 1750–1850 (1976), PEN New Poetry 1 (1986), First Awakenings: The Early Poems of Laura Riding (with Elizabeth Friedmann and Alan J Clark, 1992), A Selection of the Poems of Laura Riding (1994), Some Poems by Ernest Dowson (2006), Some Poems by Thomas Chatterton (2008), Some Poems by Clere Parsons (2008), The Liquid Rhinoceros and Other Uncollected Poems by Martin Seymour-Smith (2009), Some Poems by James Reeves (2009); *Plays* Sawney Bean (with William Watson, 1970), The Seven Deadly Sins: A Mask (1974), Penthesilea, Fugue and Sisters (1975); *Stories for Children* March Has Horse's Ears (1966), Taliesin (1966), Beowulf (1968), Wishing Gold (1970), Poor Pumpkin (1971), Once Upon Three Times (1978), Out of the World and Back Again (1977), The Bird of the Golden Land (1980), Harry Pay the Pirate (1981), Three Tales (1983), Lord Fox and Other Spine-Chilling Tales (1997); *Recreations* gambling; *Style*— Robert Nye, Esq; ✉ c/o Vivienne Schuster, Curtis Brown, Haymarket House, 28–29 Haymarket, London SW1Y 4SP (☎ 020 7393 4400, fax 020 7393 4401/02, e-mail cb@curtisbrown.co.uk)

NYMAN, Bernard Martin; s of Raymond Nyman (d 2006), and Jean, *née* Geffner (d 1984); *b* 27 February 1954, London; *Educ* Royal Liberty Sch Gidea Park, Univ of Sheffield (BA); *m* July 1986, Carole Gloria, da of Harold Stern (d 2006); 2 da (Jessica b 29 Nov 1988, Ella b 9 June 1993); *Career* articled clerk Wedlake Bell London 1977–79, admitted slr 1979, slr Rubinstein Callingham 1979–83, ptnr Rubinstein Callingham 1983–94 (merged with Manches & Co), ptnr Manches & Co 1994–98 (specialising in intellectual property law and defamation with particular reference to print and electronic publishing industry), sole prop B M Nyman & Co 1999–; tstee: The Enid Blyton Tst for Children 2000–07, The Cleft Lip and Palate Assoc 2003–14; memb: Law Soc 1979; *Publications* The Encyclopaedia of Forms and Precedents (Copyright section Vol 21 (2), 1991, 4 edn 2015), Adams: Character Merchandising (contrib, 2 edn 1996), Copinger & Skone James on Copyright (contrib, 14 edn 1999, supplement 2002, 15 edn 2005, supplements 2006, 2007 and 2009, 16 edn 2010, supplement 2013), Entertainment Law Review (former regular contrib); *Recreations* jazz, films, theatre, family, cricket; *Style*— Bernard Nyman, Esq; ✉ B M Nyman & Co, 25 Limes Avenue, London N12 8QN (☎ 020 3601 4163, fax 020 8445 2852, e-mail bernie@bmnyman.co.uk, website www.bmnyman.co.uk and http://uk.linkedin.com/in/bernienyman, blog http://publishinglawguru1.wordpress.com, Twitter @ukpublishinglaw)

NYMAN, Michael; CBE (2008); *b* 23 March 1944, London; *Educ* Royal Acad of Music (BMus), KCL; *Career* composer and musician; fndr MN Records 2005; music critic The Listener, The New Statesman, The Spectator and Studio International 1968–78 (introduced the word 'minimalism' as a description of music); actor Subterrain 2001; composer in residence Badisches Stadtstheater Karlsruhe 2002–; subject of Homage to Michael Nyman RomaEuropa Festival Rome 2001; Flaiano Award for contribution to film 2001, Ivor Novello Classical Music Award 2011; *Film Scores* Keep It Up Downstairs 1976, 1–100 1977, A Walk through H 1977, Vertical Features Remake 1978, The Falls 1980, The Draughtsman's Contract 1982, Brimstone and Treacle 1982, Frozen Music 1983, Nelly's Version 1983, The Cold Room 1984, A Zed and Two Noughts 1985, Ballet Méchanique 1986, Drowning by Numbers 1987, Monsieur Hire 1989, The Cook, The Thief, His Wife & Her Lover 1989, Le Mari de la Coiffeuse (The Hairdresser's Husband) 1991, Les Enfants Volants 1991, Prospero's Books 1991, Songbook 1992, The Piano 1992, A La Folie (Six Days, Six Nights) 1994, Carrington 1994, The Diary of Anne Frank 1995, The Ogre (Der Unhold) 1996, Gattaca 1997, The End of the Affair 1999, Wonderland 1999, Ravenous (with Damon Albarn, *qv*) 1999, Acts Without Words 1 2000, The Claim 2000, That Sinking Feeling 2000, 24 Heures de la Vie d'une Femme 2002, The Actors 2002, Nathalie 2004, Detroit: Ruin of a City 2005, 9 Songs 2005, A Cock and Bull Story 2005, The Libertine 2005, Man on Wire 2008; *Other Recordings* Michael Nyman Band: Decay Music 1976, English Experimental Music 1977, Masterwork Samples 1979, From Brussels With Love 1980, Miniatures 1980, Michael Nyman 1981, Mozart 1981, The Kiss and Other Movements 1985, The Man who Mistook his Wife for a Hat 1987, And Do They Do/Zoo Caprices 1989, La Traversée de Paris 1989, Out of the Ruins 1989, The Nyman/Greenaway Soundtracks 1989, String Quartet Nos 1–3 1991, The Essential Michael Nyman Band 1992, Michael Nyman for Yohji Yamamoto 1993, Time will Pronounce 1993, Michael Nyman – Live 1994, Noises, Sounds and Sweet Airs 1994, Taking a Line for a Second Walk 1994, The Piano Concerto/MGV 1994, Plus que Tango 1995, The Piano Concerto/On the Fiddle/Prospero's Books 1995, The Piano Concerto and other Themes 1995, After Extra Time 1996, Century XXI UK N-Z 1996, Concertos 1997, Enemy Zero 1997, The Very Best of Michael Nyman 1997, An Eye for a Difference 1998, Federico Garcia Lorca – De Granada a la Luna 1998, Practical Magic 1998, Strong on Oaks, Strong on the Causes of Oaks 1998, The Piano Concerto/Where the Bee Dances 1998, The Suit and the Photograph 1998, Twentieth Century Blues – The Songs of Noel Coward 1998, Michael Nyman Band Live in Concert 1999, Nyman & Greenaway 1999, The Commissar Vanishes 1999, Miniatures 2 2000, The Very Best of Michael Nyman Film Music 1980–2001 2001, Facing Goya 2002, String Quartets Nos 2–4 2002, Sangam – Michael Nyman meets Indian Masters 2003, Mozart 252 2008, 8 Lust Songs: I Sonetti Lussuriosi; performed by other artists: The Fourth Wall 1981, Beyond Modernism 1991, Bow Out 1992, Piano Circus 1992, Saxophone Works 1992, Contini/Interzone 1993, The Contemporary Trumpet 1993, First & Foremost 1995, Saxophone Songbook 1995, Visions 1995, Meeting Point 1996, Cinema Emotion 1997, Pick it Up 1997, Duo Dilemme – Nouvelle Musique pour Saxophone & Piano 1998, The English Patient and other arthouse classics 1998, Art House Café 2 1999, The Golden Section/Wallace Collection 1999, Ahn Trio – Ahn-Plugged 2000, Overture to Orpheus/Elaine Funaro 2001, Ahn Trio – Groovebox 2002, The Piano Sings 2005, Man and Boy: Dada 2005, The Piano 2005, The Draughtsman's Contract 2005, Nyman/Greenway Revisited 2005, The Libertine 2005, Six Celan Songs/The Ballad of Kastriot Rexhepi 2006, Acts of Beauty/Exit No Exit 2006, Nyman Brass 2006, Love Counts 2007; *Publications* George Frederic Handel – Concerto Grosso, B Minor for String Orchestra, Op 6, No 12 (ed, 1968), Down by the Greenwood Side, A Dramatic Pastoral (author of libretto for work by Sir Harrison Birtwistle, CH, *qv*, 1971), Henry Purcell – Come Let Us Drink – Catches, Compleat, Pleasant and Divertive (ed, 1972), George Frederic Handel – 12 Grand Concertos, Opus 6 (ed, 1973), Bentham and Hooker (1973), Experimental Music – Cage and Beyond (1974, 2 edn with a foreword by Brian Eno, *qv* 1999), Henry Purcell – Complete Catches (ed, 1995), Sublime the photobook (2008); author of numerous articles; *Style*— Michael Nyman, Esq, CBE; ✉ Michael Nyman Ltd, 5 Milner Place, London N1 1TN (☎ 020 7226 3188, fax 020 7689 0824, website www.michaelnyman.com)

O

O'BRIEN, Barry John; s of John O'Brien, and Patricia, *née* Barry; *b* 27 October 1952; *Educ* St Illtyd's Coll Cardiff, UCL (LLB); *m* 29 Sept 1984, Susan Margaret; 2 s (William James, Thomas Barry), 1 da (Joanna Elizabeth); *Career* slr Slaughter and May 1978–83 (articled clerk 1976–78), ptnr Freshfields Bruckhaus Deringer (formerly Freshfields) 1986–2014(slr 1983–86), chm European M+A and Corp Finance JEffries Int 2014–; chair of govrs Arnold House Sch, chair of govrs Haggerston Community Sch, govr Rugby Sch; Liveryman Worshipful Co Slrs; memb Law Soc; fell UCL (2013); *Recreations* sport; *Clubs* Glamorgan CCC (chm), Athenaeum, MCC, Walbrook, Brocket Hall Golf, Hunstanton Golf, Loch Lomond Golf; *Style—* Barry J O'Brien, Esq; ✉ 9 Highbury Terrace, London N5 1UP

O'BRIEN, Prof Denis Patrick; s of Patrick Kevin O'Brien (d 1944), of Welwyn, Herts, and Dorothy Elizabeth, *née* Crisp (d 1985); *b* 24 May 1939; *Educ* Douai Sch, UCL (BSc Econ), Queen's Univ Belfast (PhD); *m* 1, 5 Aug 1961, Eileen Patricia (d 1985), da of Martin O'Brien (d 1987), of Bognor Regis, W Sussex; 1 s (Martin Michael), 2 da (Ann Elizabeth, Alison Mary); m 2, 11 Sept 1993, Julia, da of John Brian Stapleton, of Gosport, Hants; 1 da (Juliet Florence); *Career* reader in economics Queen's Univ Belfast 1970–72 (asst lectr 1963–65, lectr 1965–70), prof of economics Univ of Durham 1972–97 (emeritus prof 1998–); memb Cncl Royal Economic Soc 1978–83; distinguished fell History of Economics Soc 2003; FBA; *Books* J R McCulloch (1970), The Correspondence of Lord Overstone (3 vol, 1971), Competition in British Industry (jtly, 1974), The Classical Economists (1975), Competition Policy, Profitability and Growth (jtly, 1979), Pioneers of Modern Economics in Britain (jtly, 1981), Authorship Puzzles in The History of Economics: A Statistical Approach (jtly, 1982), Lionel Robbins (1988), Thomas Joplin and Classical Macroeconomics (1993), Methodology, Money and the Firm (2 vols, 1994), The Classical Economists Revisited (2004), History of Economic Thought as an Intellectual Discipline (2007), The Development of Monetary Economics (2007), Taxation and the Promotion of Human Happiness (ed with J Creedy, 2009), Darwin's Clever Neighbour: George Warde Norman and his Circle (ed with J Creedy, 2010); *Recreations* the violin; *Style—* Prof D P O'Brien, FBA; ✉ c/o Dr Julia Stapleton, School of Government, University of Durham, The Al Quasimi Building, Elvet Hill Road, Durham DH1 3TU

O'BRIEN, Dr (John) Michael; s of Peter O'Brien (d 1977), of Melton Mowbray, Leics, and Nellie, *née* Harrap (d 1975); *b* 30 December 1935, Stockport, Cheshire; *Educ* Stockport GS, Univ of Manchester Med Sch (MB ChB, pres Univ Boat Club, sec Univ Athletic Union), Univ of Liverpool (DPH, Trevor Lloyd Hughes gold medal and prize); *m* 1960, Constance Amy, da of Albert Edward Dalton (d 1955); 2 da (Sarah Jane b 1963, Rachel Elizabeth b 1964); *Career* house offr posts Manchester Royal Infirmary and St Mary's Hosp Manchester 1962, tutor in clinical surgery (hon registrar) Manchester Royal Infirmary 1963, princ in gen practice Kidsgrove 1964 and 1965, med inspr of aliens and Cwlth immigrants 1966–81, dep med offr of health and dep princ sch med offr Kingston upon Hull 1969 and 1970 (actg sr asst med offr 1968), dep port med offr Hull and Goole Port HA 1969–70, dep county med offr and dep princ sch med offr Durham CC 1970–74 (pt/t factory doctor 1971–73), area med offr Durham AHA 1974–81; Northern RHA: regional specialist in community med 1981–85, actg postgrad dean 1984–85; E Anglian RHA: regional dir of public health 1985–93, exec dir 1990–93; postgraduate advsr in public health med Northern and Yorkshire RHA 1994–97, chm Standing Clinical Advsy Gp Newcastle and N Tyneside HA 1994–96, memb Cncl Univ of Newcastle upon Tyne 1994–99 (hon sr research assoc Dept of Med 1994–98), chm Northumberland HA 1995–2002; pres: Faculty of Public Health Med 1992–95 (vice-pres 1989–92), Soc of Public Health 1995–96; memb various working parties for Govt depts incl Working Pty on Health of the Nation and the Med Profession 1995; sr memb Hughes Hall Cambridge 1987–93, assoc lectr MB and DPH Courses Univ of Cambridge Clinical Sch 1989–93; chm: Bd of Mgmnt Inst of Public Health Cambridge 1991–93, Public Health Med Consultative Ctee 1992–94, Northern Cancer Network Steering Gp 1996–98; vice-chm Conf of Colls 1993–95, memb Cncl Royal Inst of Public Health 1997–2004 (chm 1999–2002); author of numerous pubns in professional and academic jls; QHP 1990–93; Duncan Meml Medal Liverpool 1997; FFPHM RCP 1980, FRCP 1990 (memb Cncl 1992–95), FRCPath 1992, Hon FFOM 1993, FRCPE 1996, Hon FFPHMI 1997, Hon FRIPH 2003 (vice-pres 2003–09), Hon FRSPH 2009, Hon FFPH 2011; *Recreations* gardening; *Style—* Dr Michael O'Brien; ✉ Catbells, 2 Ullswater Drive, Great Warford, Alderley Edge, Cheshire SH9 7WB (☎ and fax 01565 872948, e-mail jm.obrien@btinternet.com)

O'BRIEN, Neil; OBE (2016); *Educ* ChCh Oxford; *Career* dir Policy Exchange 2008–13, special advsr to George Osborne, *qv*, 2012–; *Style—* Neil O'Brien, Esq, OBE; ✉ House of Commons, London SW1A 0AA

O'BRIEN, Prof Patrick Karl; s of William Patrick O'Brien, of Coggeshall, Essex, and Elizabeth, *née* Stockhausen; *b* 12 August 1932; *m* 15 April 1959, Cassy, da of Charles Cobham; 2 da (Karen b 18 Nov 1964, Helen b 18 Nov 1966), 1 s (Stephen b 23 March 1972); *Career* Univ of London: res fell 1960–63, lectr 1963–70, reader in economics and econ history 1967–70, univ reader in econ history and professorial fell St Antony's Coll Oxford 1984–90 (univ lectr in econ history and faculty fell 1970–84), prof of econ history and dir of the Inst of Historical Research (IHR) Univ of London 1990–98; centennial prof of econ history LSE 1999, prof of global economic history LSE 2009; convenor European Research Cncl Project on the Devpt and Diffusion of Useful and Reliable Knowledge in the East and the West 1368–1846; pres Econ History Soc 1998–2001; Hon DUniv: Carlos III Madrid 1999, Uppsala 2000; hon foreign fell American Historical Assoc 2014; FRHistS, FAE, FBA, FRSA; *Books* The Revolution in Egypt's Economic System (1966), The New Economic History of the Railways (1977), Economic Development in Britain and France 1780–1914: Two Paths to the Twentieth Century (jtly with C Keyder), Productivity in the Economics of Europe in the 19th and 20th Centuries (jt ed, 1983), Railways and the Economic Development of Western Europe 1914–1930 (ed, 1983), International Productivity Comparisons 1750–1939 (ed, 1986), The Economic Effects of the Civil War (1988), The Industrial Revolution and British Society (ed with R Quinalt, 1993), The Industrial Revolution in Europe (ed, 1994), The Costs and Benefits of European Imperialism (ed with L Prados de la Escosura, 1998), Industrialization, 4 Vols (ed, 1998), Atlas of World History (ed, 2000), Urban Achievement in Early Modern Europe (jt ed, 2001), The Hegemonies: Britain 1846–1914 and the United States 1941–1989 (ed with A Clesse, 2002), The Political Economy of British Historical Experience 1688–2002 (ed with D Winch, 2002), The Rise of the Fiscal States 1500–1914 (2012); contrib to numerous learned jls; *Recreations* art history, walking; *Style—* Prof Patrick O'Brien, FBA; ✉ 66 St Bernard Road's, Oxford OX2 6EJ; London School of Economics and Political Science, Houghton Street, Aldwych, London WC2A 2AE (☎ 020 7955 6586, e-mail p.o'brien@lse.ac.uk)

O'BRIEN, His Hon Patrick William; s of William Columba O'Brien, of Melksham, Wilts, and Ethel Minnie, *née* Austin; *b* 20 June 1945; *Educ* St Joseph's Acad Blackheath, Queens' Coll Cambridge (MA, LLM),; *m* 23 May 1970, Antoinette Magdeleine, da of Louis Wattebot; 1 s (Nicholas William Wattebot O'Brien b 11 Oct 1971), 2 da (Dr Charlotte Clementine Wattebot O'Brien b 11 Aug 1973, Juliet Gisela Magdeleine Wattebot O'Brien b 11 April 1975); *Career* called to the Bar Lincoln's Inn 1968 (Mansfield scholar, additional bencher 2003); in practice in chambers of Lord Havers 1970–91, recorder 1987–91 (asst recorder 1984–87), circuit judge (SE Circuit) 1991–2014, ret, dep circuit judge 2014–; *Publications* Great Oxford (contrib, 2004); *Recreations* music, cricket; *Clubs* MCC, Highgate CC, Great Canfield CC, Kent CCC, Norfolk; *Style—* His Hon Patrick O'Brien

O'BRIEN, Rebecca; *Career* ind film prodr; co-fndr (with Ken Loach, *qv*) Sixteen Films Ltd; memb Bd: SW Screen, Film Industry Trg Bd; *Films* prodn mangr: Crystal Gazing 1982, Sacred Hearts 1984; location mangr: My Beautiful Laundrette 1985, Sammy and Rosie Get Laid 1987; prodr: Friendship's Death 1987, Hidden Agenda 1990, Land and Freedom 1995, Bean 1997, My Name Is Joe 1998, Bread and Roses 1999, Princesa 2000, The Navigators 2001, Sweet Sixteen 2002, 11'09'01 2003, Ae Fond Kiss 2004 (FIPRESCI Award and UNESCO Award Venice Film Festival), Tickets 2005, The Wind That Shakes The Barley 2006 (Palme d'Or Cannes Film Festival 2006), It's A Free World 2008, Route Irish 2010; exec prodr: Unstrung 2007, Summer 2007, Jean Charles 2008, Oranges and Sunshine 2010; *Television* prodn mangr: Six of Hearts 1985, Up Line 1986, Dispatches – Arthur Scargill 1991; prodr: Echoes 1988, A Statement of Affairs 1992, Dispatches – The Doughty Street Papers 1993, The Flickering Flame 1996; *Style—* Ms Rebecca O'Brien; ✉ c/o Sixteen Films Ltd, 187 Wardour Street, London W1F 8ZB

O'BRIEN, Richard; s of Alec James Morley-Smith, of Tauranga, New Zealand, and Doreen Mary, *née* O'Brien; *m* 1, 1971 (m dis 1979), Kimi Wong; 1 s (Linus b 1 May 1972); m 2, 1982, Jane Elizabeth Moss; 1 s (Joshua b 22 June 1983), 1 da (Amelia b 9 Jan 1989); *Career* actor, presenter and writer 1967–; dir Druidcrest Music Publishing; memb: Equity, Publishing Rights Soc; *Theatre* incl: Robert and Elizabeth, Gulliver's Travels, Hair, Jesus Christ Superstar; four prodns at Royal Court Theatre (writer of two incl The Rocky Horror Show), Mephistopheles Smith in Disgracefully Yours, performed in Chitty Chitty Bang Bang (London Palladium) 2002; *Television* A Hymn for Jim (writer, BBC), The Crystal Maze (presenter, Channel 4) 1987–93, The Ink Thief (actor, Tyne Tees for ITV) 1993; *Film* The Rocky Horror Picture Show, Dark City, Spice World, Ever After, Dungeons and Dragons 1999, Mumbo Jumbo 2000, Night Train 2008; *Albums* Absolut O'Brien (jazz) 1999; *Awards* for Rocky Horror Show: Evening Standard Award for Best Musical of 1973, Plays and Players Award for Best Musical of 1973, Golden Scroll Award from The Academy of Science Fiction, Fantasy and Horror Films; *Recreations* work; *Clubs* The Chelsea Arts, The Gothic Soc, Groucho; *Style—* Richard O'Brien, Esq

O'BRIEN, Prof Sean Patrick; s of Patrick Francis O'Brien (d 1981), and Mary Irene, *née* Doonan (d 2007); *b* 19 December 1952, London; *Educ* Selwyn Coll Cambridge (BA), Univ of Birmingham (MA), Univ of Hull, Univ of Leeds (PGCE); *m* Gerry Wardle; *Career* poet, critic, playwright, short story writer, novelist, broadcaster and ed; fell in creative writing Univ of Dundee 1989–91, Northern Arts literary fell Univs of Durham and Newcastle 1992–94; teacher of English Beacon Community Coll Sussex 1981–89, teacher Sheffield Hallam Univ 1998–2006 (prof of poetry 2003); Newcastle Univ: visiting prof Sch of English Language Literature and Linguistics 2005–06, prof of creative writing 2006–; Br Cncl visiting writer: Univ of Odense 1996, Hokudai Univ Sapporo 1997; writer in residence: South Bank Centre Poetry Int 1998, Univ of Leeds 1999, Live Theatre Newcastle 2001–03; vice-pres Poetry Soc 2006–11; Gregory Award 1979, Somerset Maugham Award (for the Indoor Park) 1984, Cholmondeley Award 1988, E M Forster Award American Acad of Arts and Letters 1993, Forward Prize for Best Collection 1995 (for Ghost Train), 2001 (for Downriver) and 2007 (for The Drowned Book), Northern Writer of the Year Northern Arts 2001, Best Single Poem Forward Poetry Prize (for Fantasia on a Theme of James Wright) 2006, Northern Rock Fndn Writer's Award 2007, T S Eliot Prize (for The Drowned Book) 2007; Hon Dr: Univ of Northumbria 2003, Univ of Hull 2009; FRSL 2007; *Plays* Laughter When We're Dead, My Last Barmaid: A Dramatic Monologue in Verse, Downriver: A Jazz Musical, Enlightenment: A Verse Play, Hi De Heidegger, The Black Path, From the Underworld, The Birds, Keepers of The Flame, We, Headcase, To Encourage the Others, Doing the Inferno, The Ministry of Fear, Don Gil of the Green Breeches; *Poetry* collections: The Indoor Park (1983), The Frighteners (1987), HMS Glasshouse (1991), Ghost Train (1995), Penguin Modern Poets 5 (1995), Downriver (2001), Rivers (co-author, 2002), Cousin Coat: Selected Poems 1976–2001 (2002), The Drowned Book (2007), November (2011), Collected Poems (2012), The River Road (2014), The Beautiful Librarians (Roehampton Poetry Prize, shared with Carole Satyamurti, 2015), Hammersmith (poetry chapbook, 2016); The Firebox: Poetry in Britain and Ireland After 1945 (ed, 1998), Ten Hallam Poets (jt ed, 2005), Andrew Marvell: poems selected by Sean O'Brien (ed, 2010) Train Songs: Poetry of the Railway (jt ed, 2013); *Other Works* The Deregulated Muse (criticism, 1998) The Silence Room (short story collection, 2008), Afterlife (novel, 2009), Journey to the Interior: Ideas of England in Contemporary Poetry (lectures, 2014), Once again Assembled Here (novel, 2016), The Railwayman (graphic novel, jt author, 2016), Quartier Perdu (short story collection, 2017); also contrib to various anthologies, magazines and newspapers; *Recreations* reading, walking, watching films; *Clubs* Vujonistas (Newcastle); *Style—* Prof Sean O'Brien; ✉ School of English Literature, Language and Linguistics, Percy Building, Newcastle University, Newcastle-upon-Tyne NE1 7RU (e-mail sean.o'brien@newcastle.ac.uk, website www.ncl.ac.uk/ell/people/profile/sean.o'brien)

O'BRIEN, Prof (Patrick Michael) Shaughn; s of Patrick Michael O'Brien (d 1978), and Joan, *née* Edleston (d 1999); *b* 1 April 1948; *Educ* Pontypridd Boys' GS, Univ of Wales, Welsh Nat Sch of Med (MB BCh, MD), Keele Univ (DSc); *m* 10 Aug 1985, Sandra Louise, da of Edward Arthur Norman (d 1979), of Henley-on-Thames, Oxon; 1 s (James b 1986), 1 da (Louise b 1988); *Career* lectr and hon sr registrar Univ of Nottingham 1979–84, sr lectr and hon conslt in obstetrics and gynaecology Royal Free Hosp Sch of Med London 1984–89; Keele Univ: fndn prof of obstetrics and gynaecology 1989–, memb Senate 1996–99, memb Cncl 1996–99 and 2001–04, chm Educn Ctee Sch of Postgraduate Med 1996–;

N Staffs Hosps: conslt obstetrician and gynaecologist 1989–, postgraduate clinical tutor 1996–2000; RCOG: publications offr 1996–99, memb Scientific Advsy Ctee 1996–99, convenor of study groups 1996–99, chm Publications Editorial Ctee 1996–99, fndr ed-in-chief The Obstetrician and Gynaecologist 1998–2004, memb Cncl 1999–, memb Fin and Exec Gp 2001–02, vice-pres 2004–07, int fell Cncl 2008–; ed-in-chief Map of Medicine 2008–; computerised measurement of disorders of the menstrual cycle 2001; inventor of symptometrics, inventor Menstrual Pictogram, inventor Prementrics App (on App Store) for quantifying and diagonising Premenstrual Syndrome; chm: N Staffs Med Inst 2002–04 and 2015– (hon sec 2001–02), Int Soc for Premenstrual Disorders 2008–, Br Soc for Psychosomatic Obstetrics and Gynaecology and Andrology 2011–; pres Birmingham and Midlands Obstetric and Gynaecological Soc 2015–16; memb Bd of Tstees Shrewsbury Girls' HS, memb Cncl of Govrs Shrewsbury and Telford Fndn Tst; FRCOG 1991 (MRCOG 1979); *Books* Premenstrual Syndrome (1987), Problems of Early Pregnancy (1997), Evidence-based Fertility Treatment (1998), Gene Identification, Manipulation and Therapy (1998), Fetal Programming: Intrauterine Influences on Adult Disease (1999), Hormones and Cancer (1999), Introduction to Research Methodology for Specialists and Trainees (1999), Placenta: Basic Science and Clinical Practice (2000), Disorders of the Menstrual Cycle (2000), Psychological Disorders in Obstetrics and Gynaecology for the MRCOG and Beyond (2006), Introduction to Research Methods for Specialists and Trainees (forthcoming), Biopsychosocial Factors in Obstetrics and Gyanecology; RCOG Yearbook of Obstetrics and Gynaecology: vol 5 (1997), vol 6 (1998), vol 7 (1999), vol 8 Millennium Edition (2000); devised and published: The Menstrual Pictogram (2002), Menstrual Symptometrics (2002), The Premenstrual Disorders: PMS and PMDD (2007), Introduction to Research Methodology (2007); author of numerous papers in learned jls on premenstrual syndrome, menopause, fetal monitoring, pregnancy hypertension, labour, prostaglandins, disorders of the menstrual cyle, menorrhagia, renin angiotensin system, selective serotonin reuptake inhibitors; *Recreations* music, jazz, clarinet, saxophone, skiing, sailing, sculpture (exhibited at Nat Fine Arts Competition Weston Park 2013 and 2014); *Clubs* RSM; *Style*— Prof P M S O'Brien; ✉ Cardington House, Shrewsbury, SY1 1ES; Keele University, Academic Obstetrics & Gynaecology, Maternity Hospital, University Hospital of North Staffordshire, Stoke-on-Trent, Staffordshire ST4 6QG (☎ and fax 01782 552472, e-mail shaughn.obrien@uhns.nhs.uk)

O'BRIEN, Rt Hon Stephen; PC (2013); s of David O'Brien, and Rothy O'Brien; *b* 1 April 1957; *Educ* Sedbergh (music scholar), Emmanuel Coll Cambridge (MA), Coll of Law Chester; *m* 1986, Gemma, *née* Townshend; 2 s (James, Angus), 1 da (Clara); *Career* slr Freshfields 1981–88, dir and gp sec Redland plc 1988–98, int business conslt 1998–2015; MP (Cons) Eddisbury (by-election) 1999–2015; PPS to Rt Hon Earl of Ancram, DL, QC, MP 2000–01, oppn whip 2001–02, shadow min for the Treasy 2002–03, shadow sec of state for industry 2003–05, shadow min for skills and higher educn 2005, shadow min for health and social care 2005–10, Parly under-sec of state Dept for Int Devpt 2010–12, PM's envoy and UK special rep to the Sahel 2012–15, under-sec-gen for humanitarian affrs and emergency relief coordinator UN 2015–; memb: Educn Select Ctee 1999–2001, Environment, Food and Rural Affrs Select Ctee 2001; sec Cons Pty Backbench Ctee on Trade and Industry 1999–2001, sec Cons Pty Backbench Ctee on NI 1999–2001, actg dir Cons Pty Ldr's Office 2001; chm All Pty Parly Malaria and Neglected Tropical Diseases Gp; memb: Br-American Gp, Int Parly Union, Cwlth Parly Assoc; assoc memb Br-Irish Inter-Parly Body 2000–10; Parly advsr: ICSA 2000–10, Manufacturing Technols Assoc 2005–10; global advocate Roll Back Malaria Partnership UN/WHO; Cons Pty: special advsr (construction sector) Cons Business Liaison Unit 1998–2001, chm Chichester Cons Assoc 1998–99 (hon vice-chm 1999–), memb Nat Membership Ctee 1999–2001, Parly rep Westminster Candidates Assoc 2000–01 (memb Exec Ctee 1998–99); UK Building Materials Prodrs (BMP) 1995–99 (memb Ctee of Mgmnt, memb President's Strategy Ctee and chm Public and Parly Affrs Ctee), CBI 1995–98 (memb SE Regnl Cncl, memb Int Investment Panel); non-exec dir Univ of Cambridge Careers Serv Syndicate 1992–99; bd tstee Innovative Vector Control Consortium 2008–10 and 2015–; memb Cncl Scot Business in the Community 1995–98; dir City of London Sinfonia 2001–15; tstee Reigate Priory Museum 1992–98, bd tstee and vice-chm Liverpool Sch of Tropical Medicine 2006–10 and 2013–15, non-exec dir Small Business Research Tst 2006–08; vice patron Trade Aid 2005–, chm Malaria Consortium 2006–10, patron Malaria No More 2014–15; nominated Channel 4 Political Award for Campaigning Politician 2008, nominated ePolitix Int Politician of the Year 2008, e-Gov Unsung Hero of the Year Award 2009, Malaria No More Action on Malaria Champions Award 2014; memb Law Soc; FCIS 1997; *Recreations* music, fell-walking; *Clubs* Winsford Constitutional & Conservative, Cheshire Pitt; *Style*— The Rt Hon Stephen O'Brien

O'BRIEN, Sir (Robert) Stephen; kt (2012), CBE (1987); s of Robert Henry O'Brien (d 1969), and Clare Winifred, *née* Edwards (d 1975); *b* 14 August 1936; *Educ* Sherborne, Rose Bruford Coll (BA); *m* 1, 1958 (m dis 1989), Zoe O'Brien; 2 s (Dermot b 1962, Paul b 1969), 2 da (Rachel b 1965, Louise b 1966); m 2, 30 June 1989, Meriel, *née* Barclay; *Career* Charles Fulton and Co Ltd: joined 1956, dir 1964, chm 1970–82; chief exec: Business in the Community 1983–92 (vice-chm 1992–2005, vice-pres 2005–), London First 1992–2002 (jt pres 2005–07, vice-chm London First Centre); chm Int Health Ptnrs 2009–14, chm Barts Health NHS Tst 2012–15; dir UCL Partners 2011–15; chm Foreign Exchange & Currency Deposit Assoc 1968–72; pres Proshanti, vice-pres Business in the Community; chm: Christian Action 1976–88, Fullemploy Gp 1973–91, UK 2000 1988–91, Tower Hamlets PCT 2005–10; dep chm Water City Devpts 2004–15; ambass Teach First 2004– (founding chm 2004–10); tstee Prince's Youth Business Tst 1987–97, chm London Regnl Cncl Prince's Tst 1999–2006, dir Prince of Wales Int Business Ldrs' Forum, tstee Mayor's Fund for London, promoter Adab Tst (South Asian and Muslim mainstream employment), tstee Barts Charity, memb Advsy Cncl and former tstee Olive Tree Educnl Tst, memb Advsy Bd Community Security Tst, memb Pres's Ctee Young Epilepsy, tstee Centre for London 2011–15, tstee Fndn for Future London 2015–; dir Greenwich Theatre 1999–2005, tstee and vice-chm Church Urban Fund 1994–2002; memb Bd of Govrs Univ of East London 2005– (chm 1999–2005); ordained deacon 1971, hon curate St Lawrence Jewry 1973–82; Hon LLD Univ of Liverpool 1994, Hon DSc City Univ 2000; Hon DUniv: Middx 2001, East London 2005, Queen Mary Univ of London 2012; FRSA (memb Cncl 1987–91); *Recreations* gardening, cooking, opera, East London and its communities; *Style*— Sir Stephen O'Brien, CBE

O'BRIEN, Timothy Brian; s of Brian Palliser Tighe O'Brien (d 1966), and Elinor Laura, *née* Mackenzie (d 2002); *b* 8 March 1929, Shilong Assam, India; *Educ* Wellington, CCC Cambridge (MA), Yale Univ; *m* 22 Nov 1997, Jenny Jones; *Career* designer; BBC Design Dept 1954, Assoc Rediffusion 1955–56, head of design ABC TV 1956–65, theatrical designer (in partnership with Tazeena Firth 1974–79); prodns incl: Love's Labour's Lost (RSC) 1990, War and Peace (Kirov St Petersburg) 1991, Eugene Onegin (ROH) 1993, The Merry Wives of Windsor (RNT) 1995, Outis (La Scala Milan) 1996, Twelfth Night (Clwyd) 1999, Macbeth (Clwyd) 2000, Romeo and Juliet (Clwyd) 2002, Werther (Sao Carlos Lisbon) 2004, Ulysses Comes Home (Birmingham Opera Co) 2005, Das Rheingold (Sao Carlos Lisbon) 2006, Die Walküre (Sao Carlos Lisbon) 2007, Siegfried (Sao Carlos Lisbon) 2008, Götterdämmerzung (Sao Carlos Lisbon) 2009; chm Soc of Br Theatre Designers 1984–91; tstee Useful Simple Tst 2008–; Gold Medal for set design Prague Quadriennale 1975, jt winner Golden Triga for best national exhibit Prague Quadriennale 1991; Master Faculty of Royal Designers for Industry 1999–2001; RDI 1991; *Recreations* sailing; *Style*— Timothy O'Brien, Esq; ✉ The Level, Blackbridge Road, Freshwater Bay, Isle of Wight PO40 9QP (☎ 01983 759447, e-mail all@highwaterjones.com, website www.highwaterjones.com)

O'BRIEN, Tony; s of Padraig O'Brien (d 2002), and Sheila, *née* Crowe (d 2005); *b* 17 January 1951; *Educ* Univ of Cambridge (MA), Univ of Manchester (Dip Teaching English Overseas, PGCE), Inst of Educn Univ of London (MA); *m* 1975, Yolanda, *née* Lange; 3 da (Becci b 1978, Emily b 1980, Anna b 1984); *Career* VSO Aswan Egypt 1971–73, lectr Univ of Tabriz Iran 1975–77; Br Cncl: dir of studies Morocco 1978–82, conslt London 1982–86, dir English language centres Singapore and Hong Kong 1986–94, dir Morocco 1994–97, dir (ELT) and devpt dir knowledge and learning centres 1997–2002, dir Sri Lanka 2002–06, dir Poland 2006–11, dir Serbia 2011–12, dir Western Balkans 2012–15; author of numerous articles for professional pubns 1975–2002; tstee Int House London 1997–2001; chair Advsy Bd Creative Mentorship 2013–; founding fell Br Inst of ELT 1999; *Books* Nucleus: Medicine (1980), Teacher Development, Evaluation and Teacher Profiles in TESOL (1986); *Recreations* travel, walking, sports; *Style*— Tony O'Brien, Esq; ✉ 2 Seymour Grove, Warwick CV34 6LS (e-mail tonyob2@me.com)

O'CATHAIN, Baroness (Life Peer UK 1991), of The Barbican in the City of London; Detta Bishop; OBE (1983); da of Caoimhghin O'Cathain (d 1986), of Dublin, and Margaret, *née* Prior (d 1977); *b* 3 February 1938; *Educ* Laurel Hill Limerick, UC Dublin (BA); *m* 4 June 1968, William Ernest John Bishop (d 2001), s of William Bishop (d 1968), of Bristol; *Career* former md milk mktg Milk Mktg Board, md Barbican Centre 1990–95; dir Midland Bank plc 1984–93; non-exec dir: Tesco plc 1985–2000, Sears plc 1987–94, British Airways plc 1993–2004, BET plc 1994–96, BNP Paribas Holdings (UK) Ltd 1995–2005, Thistle Hotels plc 1996–2003, South East Water plc 1998–2008, William Baird plc 2000–02, Alders plc 2000–03; pres CIM 1998–2001 (vice-pres 1996–98), chm Chichester Cathedral Cncl 2010–; *Recreations* reading, walking, swimming, gardening, music; *Style*— The Baroness O'Cathain, OBE; ✉ House of Lords, London SW1A 0PW (☎ 020 7219 0662, e-mail ocathaind@parliament.uk)

O'CONNELL, Dr David Henry Anthony; s of late David Andrew O'Connell, and late Ellen Mary, *née* Paul; *b* 26 February 1955, Cork, Ireland; *Educ* Presentation Brothers Coll Cork, UC Cork (MB BCh, BAO, DRCOG, MICGP); *Career* family doctor, house physician and house surgn Royal Hosp Wolverhampton 1978–79, GP registrar St Bartholomew's and Hackney Hosp Vocational Trg Scheme 1979–82, private GP 1982–; chm dist jr exec City and Hackney Health Dist 1980–81, med advsr and memb Mgmnt Ctee St Wilfrid's Residential Home Chelsea 1984–2003, dir of various med cos 1990–, chief med offr Natural Biosciences 2014–; memb Exec Ctee, sec Audit Sub-Ctee and chm Insurance Sub-Ctee Independent Doctors' Forum, memb Cncl RSH 1994–97, co-fndr and chm London Irish Med Assoc (later Irish Medical Soc of GB) 2000–03, chm Cryprus Branch Conservatives Abroad 2006–09, pres Cyprus-Irish Soc 2006–08; Freeman City of London, Liveryman Worshipful Soc of Apothecaries 1995 (Yeoman 1985); memb BMA 1978–; fell: Med Soc of London 1985, Chelsea Clinic Soc 1985; FRSM 1982, FRSA 1989, FRIPHH 1993, FRSH 1994; Knight of Magistral Grace Sovereign Mil Order of Malta 1993 (Cross of Merit 1987, Bronze Medal 1994, Cross Grand Offr 2012), Offr Order of St Maurice and St Lazarus 2001, Knight Merit Sacred Military Constantinian Order of St George 2011; *Publications* Jetlag – How to Beat It (1998); *Recreations* learning, sleeping, travelling; *Clubs* RAC, Polish Hearth, Garrick; *Style*— Dr David H A O'Connell; ✉ 41 Elystan Place, Chelsea Green, London SW3 3JY (☎ 020 7584 9779, fax 020 7584 3779, e-mail info@drdavidoconnell.co.uk)

O'CONNELL, Sir Maurice James Donagh MacCarthy; 7 Bt (UK 1869), of Lakeview, Killarney, Co Kerry, and of Ballybeggan, Tralee, Co Kerry; er s of Sir Morgan Donal Conail O'Connell, 6 Bt (d 1989), and Elizabeth, *née* MacCarthy-O'Leary; *b* 10 June 1958; *Educ* Ampleforth; *m* 11 Sept 1993, Francesca Susan, o da of Clive Raleigh (d 2004), of Hong Kong; 1 s (Morgan Daniel Clive MacCarthy b 17 Nov 2003); *Heir* s, Morgan Daniel Clive MacCarthy O'Connell; *Style*— Sir Maurice O'Connell, Bt; ✉ Lakeview House, Killarney, County Kerry, Republic of Ireland

O'CONNELL, HE Ruairi; s of Frederick Michael O'Connell (d 1989), and Dora Ann, *née* Mahon (d 1998); *b* Southampton; *Educ* St Benet's Hall Oxford (BA), UCL (MA); *m* 4 June 2010, Elida Lawton, *née* Ramadani; *Career* diplomat; Eastern Adriatic Dept FCO 2001–02, second sec (Political) later dep head of mission Pritina 2004–08; FCO: advsr/head of unit for the Foreign Sec's Special Rep on Climate Change 2008–10, head of strategy and analysis Finance Directorate 2010–11, dep dir London 2012 and GREAT Campaign 2012–13, head Illegal Wildlife Trade Project 2013–14, dep dir Head of NATO Summit Unit Directorate for Defence and Int Security 2014–15, ambass to Repub of Kosovo 2015–; *Recreations* reading, rugby, Saracens RFC, Everton FC; *Style*— HE Mr Ruairi O'Connell; ✉ c/o FCO (Pristina), King Charles Street, London SW1A 2AH

O'CONNELL, Stephen (Steve); AM; s of Ronald O'Connell (d 1988), and Phyllis, *née* Gadd; *b* 9 September 1956, Dulwich, London; *Educ* Brockley GS; *m* 5 Nov 1999, Michele, *née* Cook; 2 s (Joseph b 10 Feb 1985, Benjamin b 20 Nov 1990); *Career* ind fin advsr and mortgage broker Barclays Bank 1976–2006; cncllr (Kenley Ward) London Borough of Croydon 2002– (cabinet memb for safety 2006–08, dep ldr 2006–08, cabinet memb for econ devpt 2008–09, cabinet memb for community safety 2009–11, cabinet memb for finance and performance 2011, shadow cabinet memb for safer communities 2014–), memb London Assembly (Cons) Croydon and Sutton 2008–; chair Police and Crime Ctee (PCC), chair RSPCA Caterham and Purley; memb: Friends of Kenley Airfield, Crystal Palace FC (season ticket holder), various residents assocs; tstee Crystal Palace FC Fndn, tstee PYPP; FRSA; *Recreations* dog walking, reading; *Style*— Steve O'Connell, Esq, AM; ✉ GLA, City Hall, The Queen's Walk, London SE1 2AA (☎ 020 7983 4405, fax 020 7983 4419, e-mail steve.o'connell@london.gov.uk, website www.steve.oconnell.org, Twitter @SteveO_Connell)

O'CONNOR, Bridget Anne (Biddie); da of John O'Connor (d 1994), of Manchester, and Joan Mears (d 1984); *b* 28 April 1958, Chesterfield, Derbys; *Educ* St Helena Sch Chesterfield, St Hugh's Coll Oxford (BA), Sidney Sussex Coll Cambridge (PGCE); *m* 8 Jan 1982, Simon Salem; 1 da (Harriet Clara b 30 Nov 1988); *Career* asst teacher (classics) Francis Holland Sch Clarence Gate 1981–83, teacher and head Classics Dept Old Palace Sch of John Whitgift Croydon 1983–90, head of dept, head of sixth form and dep head Haberdashers' Aske's Sch for Girls Elstree 1991–2002, headmistress Loughborough HS 2002–11, headmistress Haberdashers' Aske's 2011–; *Recreations* reading, cookery, walking, visiting galleries, art; *Style*— Miss Biddie O'Connor; ✉ Haberdashers' Aske's School for Girls, Alderham Road, Elstree WD6 3BT (☎ 020 8266 2300, fax 020 8266 2303, e-mail admin@habsgirls.org.uk)

O'CONNOR, HE Christopher Paul; OBE (2012); *m* Martha Dorothy Nelems; 2 da; *Career* diplomat; FCO: desk offr Greece/Turkey 1993–94, Int Orgns Research Gp 1994; 2 sec political Riyadh 1996–99, 1 sec political UK Delegation NATO 1999, seconded to Canadian Dept for Foreign Affrs 1999–2000, head Political Section Ottawa 2000–03, head ME Peace Process Team FCO 2003–05, dep head of mission Beirut 2006–08, ambass to Tunisia 2008–; *Style*— HE Mr Christopher O'Connor, OBE; ✉ British Embassy, Rue du Lac Windermere, Les Berges du Lac, Tunis 1053, Tunisia

O'CONNOR, David Andrew; s of John O'Connor, and Pauline, *née* Mathews; *b* 11 November 1977, Birkenhead, Wirral; *Educ* Pensby HS for Boys, Wirral; *m* 19 Sep 2000 Monika, *née* Michalczuk; 1 da (Matilda b 18 March 2008); *Career* former mangr: Chez Bruce, The Square, The Ledbury; currently prop (with Joe Mercer Nairne, *qv*) and mangr Medlar Restaurant (Michelin star 2013–); *Clubs* cinema, reading, football fanatic, chess; *Style*— David O'Connor, Esq; ✉ Medlar Restaurant, 438 Kings Road,

Chelsea, London SW10 0LJ (☎ 020 7349 1900, e-mail info@medlarrestaurant.co.uk, website www.medlarrestaurant.co.uk); 47b Leathwaite Road, London SW11 1XG (☎ 07790 901586)

O'CONNOR, Sir Denis Francis; kt (2010), CBE (2002), QPM (1996); s of Denis O'Connor (d 1978), and Ellen, *née* Walsh (d 1961); *b* 21 May 1949, Ireland; *Educ* Univ of Southampton (BEd), Cranfield Univ (MSc); *m* 3 April 1972, Louise, *née* Harvey; 2 da (Tanya b 1976, Annabel b 1983), 1 s (Denis b 1978); *Career* Met Police Serv 1968–70 and 1974–85, Supt Surrey Police 1985–88, Chief Supt Met Police Serv 1989–91, Asst Chief Constable Surrey Police 1991–93, Dep Chief Constable Kent Police 1993–97, Asst Cmmr Met Police Serv 1997–2000, Chief Constable Surrey Police 2000–04, HM Inspr of Constabulary Nat Team 2004–09, HM Chief Inspr of Constabulary 2009–12; *Recreations* walking, reading, trying to keep up with my children; *Style—* Sir Denis O'Connor, CBE, QPM

O'CONNOR, Des; CBE (2008); *b* 12 January 1932; *m* 16 Sept 2007, Jodie Brooke Wilson; 1 s (b 2004); 4 da by previous marriages; *Career* entertainer and chat-show host; former Butlin's Red Coat; Special Recognition Award Nat TV Awards 2001, Lifetime Achievement Special Recognition Award Nat TV Awards 2003; *Theatre* professional debut Palace Theatre Newcastle 1953, compere Sunday Night at the London Palladium, completed 1,000th performance at London Palladium in his own show, one-man show UK, Canada and Australia since 1980, pantomime Cinderella (London Palladium 1985), numerous Royal Show appearances (incl host Royal Variety Performance 1997), Dreamboats and Petticoats (Playhouse London) 2011–12, The Wizard of Oz (London Palladium 2012); Canada and USA: headlined three seasons London Palladium Show in Toronto and Ottawa, seasons at The Royal York Hotel and Royal Alexandra Theatre, two all-star galas at The MGM Grand Hotel Las Vegas; Australia: theatre and cabaret performances over many years, broke all box office records St George's League Club Sydney 1975, appeared at Sydney Opera House; *Television* host: Spot the Tune 1958, own series since 1963, two series screened US then worldwide 1975, Des O'Connor Tonight 1977–2002 (awarded Nat TV Awards Most Popular Talk Show 1995 and 1997), Des O'Connor Now 1985, TV Times Awards ceremony 1989–90 and 1990–91, Take Your Pick 1992, 1994 and 1996, Pot of Gold 1993 and 1995, An Audience with Des O'Connor 2001, Des O'Connor on Des O'Connor 2001, The Way They Were 2001, Fame in the Family 2000–, Today With Des And Mel 2002–06 (RTS Programme Award for Best Daytime Programme 2003), Des O'Connor Comedy Tonight 2003, host Countdown 2007–08, The One and Only Des O'Connor 2012; *Recordings* first record Careless Hands reached number one in charts and sold over one million copies 1967, numerous hit singles and albums released since, album Des O'Connor sold over 250,000 copies 1984, released Sky Boat Song with Roger Whittaker entering Top Twenty charts 1986, album Portrait for Columbia (Gold on release) 1992, Inspired 2008; *Books* Bananas Can't Fly (autobiography, 2001), Laughter Lines (comic verse, 2014); *Style—* Des O'Connor, Esq, CBE; ✉ c/o Lake-Smith Associates (☎ 020 7836 1040, e-mail pat@lakesmith.co.uk)

O'CONNOR, Joseph Victor; s of John Oliver Vincent O'Connor, of Dublin, and Joanna Marie, *née* O'Grady (d 1985); *b* 20 September 1963; *Educ* Blackrock Coll Dublin, UC Dublin (BA, MA), UC Oxford, Univ of Leeds (MA); *m* 1998, Anne-Marie *née* Casey, of London; 2 s (James Casey b 24 July 2000, Marcus Casey b 16 May 2004); *Career* writer; fndr memb Amnesty Educn Tst (Ireland); *Awards* Hennessy First Fiction Award 1989, New Irish Writer of the Year 1989, Travel Writing Award Time Out Magazine 1990, special Jury Prize (for A Stone of the Heart) Cork Int Film Festival 1992, shortlisted Whitbread Prize 1992, Macaulay fell Irish Arts Cncl 1993, shortlisted Sunday Independent Irish Novel of the Year Award 2002, New York Times Notable Book of the Year 2003, Prix Littéraire Européen Madeleine Zepter 2004, Premio Giuseppi Acerbi for New Literature 2004, Hennessy/Sunday Tribune Hall of Fame Literary Award 2004, nominated Dublin Int IMPAC Literary Award 2004, American Library Assoc Notable Book Award 2004, Neilsen-Bookscan Golden Book Award 2005, Premio Napoli 2005, fell Cullman Centre for Scholars and Writers New York Library 2005; *Fiction* Cowboys and Indians (1991), True Believers (short stories, 1991), Desperadoes (1994), The Salesman (1997), Inishowen (2000), The Comedian (novella, 2000), Star of the Sea (2002); *Filmscripts* A Stone of the Heart (1992), The Long Way Home (1993), Ailsa (1993); *Stage Plays* Red Roses and Petrol (1995), The Weeping of Angels (1997), True Believers (1999); *Other* Even the Olives Are Bleeding: the Life and Times of Charles Donnelly (1992), The Secret World of the Irish Male (1994), Sweet Liberty: Travels in Irish America (1996), The Irish Male at Home and Abroad (1996), The Last of the Irish Males (2001), Yeats is Dead: A Serial Novel by Fifteen Irish Writers for Amnesty International (ed, 2001); *Style—* Joseph O'Connor, Esq; ✉ c/o Blake Friedmann Literary Agency, 122 Arlington Road, London NW1 7HP (☎ 020 7284 0408, e-mail carole@blakefriedmann.co.uk)

O'CONNOR, Mike; CBE (2000); s of John O'Connor (d 1966), and Kathleen, *née* Golden (d 2012); *b* 15 December 1956, London; *Educ* Univ of Keele (BSc), Imperial Coll London (MSc, DIC); *Partner* Elizabeth Owen; *Career* civil servant Dept of Health, Treasury and Cabinet Office 1982–89, dir Coronary Prevention Gp 1989–92, dir Consumers International 1993–96, chief exec Millennium Cmmn 1996–2005, chief exec Olympic Lottery Distributor 2005–10, chief exec Consumer Futures 2010–13, chief exec Step Change Dept Charity 2014–; hon treas Mental Health Fndn 2001–09; founding memb Keele Univ Coll of Fellows; *Style—* Mike O'Connor, Esq, CBE; ✉ Step Change Dept Charity, Lynton House, 7–12 Tavistock Square, London WC1H 9LT (☎ 020 7391 4593, website www.stepchange.org)

O'CONNOR, Patrick Michael Joseph; QC (1993); *b* 7 August 1949; *Educ* St Francis Xavier's Sch Liverpool, UCL; *m* 1986; 2 da; *Career* called to the Bar Inner Temple 1970 (bencher 2008); author of articles in Criminal Law Review and other journals; *Books* Justice in Error (contrib, 1993), The Privy Council and the Prerogative (2009); *Style—* Patrick O'Connor, Esq, QC; ✉ 53–54 Doughty Street, London WC1N 2LS (☎ 020 7404 1313, fax 020 7404 2283/4, e-mail p.oconnor@doughtystreet.co.uk, website www.doughtystreet.co.uk)

O'CONOR DON, Desmond Roderic O'Conor; er son of Denis Armar, O'Conor Don, Prince of Connacht (d 2000), and Elizabeth, *née* Marris (Mrs Elizabeth Cameron, d 2009); *b* 22 September 1938; *Educ* Sherborne; *m* 23 May 1964, Virginia Anne, da of late Sir Michael Williams, KCMG, and Joy, *née* Holdswoth Hunt; 2 da (Emma Joy (Mrs Leveson-Gower) b 17 April 1965, Denise Sarah (Mrs Wheeler) b 8 Dec 1970), 1 s (Philip Hugh b 17 Feb 1967); *Heir* s, Philip O'Conor; *Career* Bank of London and Montreal Ltd Guatemala and Honduras 1960–64, J Henry Schroder Wagg & Co Ltd London 1964–79, dir Schroders Int Ltd London 1977–79; KleinwortBenson Ltd London: dir 1979–1998, gp dir 1989–98, sr conslt 1998–2002; sr advsr: Latin American Capital Partners IILC NY until 2004, Darby Latin American Mezzanine Fund LP Washington until 2004; UK ceo and head London Office Antofagasta plc and dir of subsids 2004–13, ret; non-exec dir: BlackRock Latin American Investment Tst plc 1998–2014, ret; chm: Int Fin Servs London Latin American Advsy Gp 2000–06, Br Chilean C of C 2003–09; chm Sailors and Soldiers Home Eastbourne 1987–2010; memb Standing Cncl of Irish Chiefs and Chieftans Dublin, vice-pres Irish Genealogical Soc; Knight Grand Cross of the Order of the Immaculate Conception of Vila Vicosa 1993, Knight Cdr Military and Hospitaller Order of St Lazarus of Jerusalem Grand Priory of Ireland 2002, Knight Cdr Order of Bernardo O'Higgins (Chile) 2006; *Recreations* tennis, walking, shooting; *Clubs* Kildare Street and Univ (Dublin), Cavalry and Guards'; *Style—* The O'Conor Don; ✉ Horsegrove House, Rotherfield, East Sussex TN6 3LU (☎ 01892 852667)

O'DAY, Prudence Anne (Prue); da of Dr Kevin John O'Day (d 1961), of Melbourne, and Bernadette Anne Hay (d 1983), of London; *b* 12 June 1946, Melbourne; *Educ* Mandeville Hall Melbourne, UCL, Westminster Coll; *m* 16 Jan 1971, Donald William Sievwright Anderson; 1 s (William Sievwright b 23 April 1975), 1 da (Amelia (Amy) b 11 Feb 1977); *Career* managed London Graphic Arts Gallery 1966–68, work with Ira Gale (Rembrandt expert) 1968–69, volunteer ICA Galleries 1968–69, researcher and buyer London Arts Gallery 1969–71, fndr (with husband) Anderson O'Day (formerly 20th Century Prints) 1971 (dir 1986–) and Anderson O'Day Gallery 1986–95; art advsr and curator 1971–; curator survey exhbn of British prints Brooklyn Museum NYC 1974; co-fndr and treas Portobello Galleries Assoc 1986–, co-fndr Portobello Contemporary Art Festival 1986, co-fndr and sec Portobello Arts trust 1988–; mentor to Glasgow Gallery of Modern Art Art Fund Int 2009–; memb: Steering Ctee Art Works for London Lighthouse 1993 1991, Selection Panel Cleveland Drawing Biennale 1991, Bd Landscape Fndn 1999; chair Bd The Showroom London 2006–13, memb Cncl ICA London 2014–; *Books* Prints & Drawings Fifteenth to Twentieth Century (1969), Ian Jones – Exhibition Catalogue (1991); *Recreations* politics, theatre, dance, contemporary art, literature and music, cinema, gardening, birdwatching, swimming, tennis and most sports as a spectator; *Style—* Ms Prue O'Day; ✉ Anderson O'Day Fine Art, 5 St Quintin Avenue, London W10 6NX (e-mail info@andersonoday.co.uk, website www.andersonoday.co.uk)

O'DONNELL, Baron (Life Peer UK 2012), of Clapham in the London Borough of Wandsworth; Sir Augustine Thomas (Gus) O'Donnell; GCB (2011, KCB 2005, CB 1994); s of James O'Donnell, and Helen, *née* McLean; *b* 1 October 1952; *Educ* Salesian Coll London, Univ of Warwick (BA), Nuffield Coll Oxford (MPhil, Soccer blue); *m* 1979, Melanie Joan Elizabeth, *née* Timmis; 1 da (Kirstin Elizabeth b 3 Nov 1990); *Career* lectr in political economy Univ of Glasgow 1975–79, economist HM Treasy 1979–85, first sec Br Embassy Washington DC 1985–88, sr econ advsr HM Treasy 1988–89, press sec to the Chllr 1989–90, press sec to the PM 1990–94, dep dir HM Treasy and UK rep EU Monetary Ctee 1994–97, min (econ) Br Embassy Washington and UK exec dir IMF and World Bank Gp 1997, dir of macroeconomic policy and prospect directorate/head UK Govt Economic Service 1997–2000, md macroeconomic policy and int fin HM Treasy 2000–02, Chllr's G7 dep 2000–02, perm sec HM Treasy 2002–05, sec to the Cabinet and head of the Home Civil Serv 2005–11; advsr TD Bank 2012–, chm Frontier Economics 2013–; non-exec dir Brookfield Asset Mgmnt 2013–, chair Public Interest Bd PwC 2016–; memb Economist Tst 2013–, chair of tstees Pro Bono Economics 2016–; pres Cncl Inst for Fiscal Studies 2016–; *Recreations* golf, tennis, soccer, cricket, bridge; *Clubs* All England Lawn Tennis; *Style—* The Lord O'Donnell, GCB; ✉ House of Lords, London SW1A 0PW

O'DONNELL, Hugh; s of John O'Donnell of Ireland, and Jean O'Donnell; *Educ* Camberwell Coll of Art, Falmouth Coll of Art (BA), Birmingham Coll of Art (HDip AD, prize Sir Whitworth Wallace Tst), RCA; *m* Tina Eden; 1 da (Kristie b 1983); *Career* artist; *Solo Exhibitions* incl: Works on Paper (Nishimura Gallery Tokyo) 1976, Air Gallery London 1977, Paintings and Drawings (Ikon Gallery Birmingham) 1979, Rahr-West Museum Wisconsin 1983, Marlborough Gallery (London 1985, NY 1986 and 1987), Works on Paper and Monoprints (Marlborough Gallery NY) 1984, Works on Paper (Marlborough Graphics London) 1984, Paintings (Marlborough Gallery NY) 1987, Paintings (Eva Cohen Gallery Chicago 1990, Hokin Gallery Palm Beach Florida 1989), Paintings and Works on Paper (Eva Cohen Gallery Chicago) 1990, Paintings (Marlborough Gallery NY) 1991, The Lake Series (Denise Cade Gallery NY 1992, Jan Abrams Gallery LA 1994, Freedman Gallery Pennsylvania 1995, Art Museum Univ of Memphis 1995), The Body Echo Project (Freedman Gallery Pennsylvania 1995, Art Museum Univ of Memphis 1995); *Group Exhibitions* incl: first exhibition 1972, Br Art Now (Guggenheim Museum NY) 1980, Decorative Arts Award 1988 (designs for jewels – collaboration with Ros Conway, Sotheby's London MOMA), Kyoto Japan, Arte & Alchimia (XLII Venice Biennale) 1986, The Question of Drawing (South Campus Gallery Miami, travelled) 1989, Works on Paper: Amenoff, Barth, O'Donnell (Tomoko Liguori Gallery NY) 1990, Marlborough en Pelaires (Centre Cultural Contemporani Pelaires Palma de Mallorca) 1990, Drawings Only (Denise Cade Gallery NY) 1992, Innovations in Collaborative Print Making: Kenneth Tyler 1963–92 (Yokohama Museum of Art and tour of Japan) 1992–93, Drawing in Black and White: Selections from the Permanent Collection (MOMA NY) 1993, First Thoughts: Working Drawings by Seven Artists (Bristol-Myers Squibb Co Princeton) 1993, Selection of Prints from Graphics Studio (Greenfield Gallery LA) 1993, Works on Paper (Margret Biederman Gallery Munich) 1994, The Computer in the Studio (DeCordova Museum and Sculpture Park Lincoln MA) 1994, Works Selected by Dore Ashton (Bill Maynes Gallery NY) 1994–95, An American Passion: The Kasen Summer Collection of Contemporary British Painting (McLellan Galleries Glasgow) 1994–95; selected public collections: Br Cncl UK, Solomon R Guggenheim Museum NY, London Contempory Arts Soc, Met MOMA NY, MOMA NY, V&A, Arts Cncl of GB, Virginia Museum of Fine Arts, Nat Gallery of Art Washington DC; Purchase award Arts Cncl of GB 1978 (Arts Cncl award 1978); set and costume designs for: Red Steps (London Contemporary Dance Theatre), Drawn Breath (Siobhan Davies Dance Company, 1989 Digit Dance award); numerous appearances on American television; *Style—* Hugh O'Donnell, Esq; ✉ 34 Shearer Road, Washington, CT 06793, USA (☎ 00 1 203 860 868 9770, fax 00 1 203 860 868 9717)

O'DONNELL, James Anthony; s of Dr James Joseph Gerard O'Donnell (d 1978), and Dr Gillian Anne O'Donnell; *b* 15 August 1961; *Educ* Westcliff HS, Royal Coll of Music, Jesus Coll Cambridge (organ scholar, open scholar in music, MA, hon fell 2011); *Career* master of music Westminster Cathedral 1988–99 (asst master 1982–88); organist and master of the chorists Westminster Abbey 2000–; Royal Acad of Music: lectr in church music studies 1990–, prof of organ 1997–2004, visiting prof 2004–, visiting prof of choral conducting 2012–; RCO Performer of the Year 1987, Gramophone Record of the Year and Best Choral Record 1998, Royal Philharmonic Soc Award (with the choir of Westminster Cathedral) 1998; pres RCO 2011–13 (memb Cncl 1989–2003); Hon DMus Univ of Aberdeen 2013; Hon RAM 2001, Hon FGCM 2001; FRCO 1983, FRSCM 2000, FRCM 2009; KCSG (Papal) 1999; *Recreations* opera, food and wine; *Clubs* Athenaeum; *Style—* James O'Donnell, Esq; ✉ The Chapter Office, Westminster Abbey, 20 Dean's Yard, London SW1P 3PA (☎ 020 7654 4854, fax 020 7654 4859, e-mail music@westminster-abbey.org)

O'DONNELL, Paul Simon; s of Brian Patrick O'Donnell, of Haywards Heath, W Sussex, and Maureen Shirley, *née* MacDonald; *b* 20 July 1962, Ramsgate, Kent; *Educ* Univ of Hull (BA), Inst of Direct Mktg (Dip), École des Hautes Études Commerciales Paris; *m* 3 May 2000, Ai Bee, *née* Lim; 1 da (Billie Ai-Lin b 17 Feb 2002); *Career* Ogilvy & Mather Direct: account mangr London 1985–87, planning dir London 1987–89, md Singapore 1990–93, md Hong Kong 1993–95; pres Asia/Pacific Ogilvy & Mather 1995–98, exec vice-pres network devpt Ogilvy & Mather London 1998–2000, chm OgilvyOne London 2002–04, chm OgilvyOne EMEA 2005–, vice-chm Ogilvy Gp EMEA 2007–; tstee Inst of Direct Mktg 2006–; MIPA; *Recreations* tennis, skiing, sailing; *Clubs* Hospital; *Style—* Paul O'Donnell, Esq; ✉ Ogilvy Group, 10 Cabot Square, Canary Wharf, London E14 4QB (☎ 020 7345 3148, e-mail paul.o'donnell@ogilvy.com)

O'DONOGHUE, (James) Bernard; s of Bartholomew James O'Donoghue (d 1962), of Cullen, Co Cork, and Mary Josephine, *née* McNulty (d 1979); *b* 14 December 1945; *Educ* Coláiste Pádraig Millstreet Co Cork, St Bede's Coll Manchester, Lincoln Coll Oxford (BA, BPhil); *m* 23 July 1977, Heather O'Donoghue, Vigfusson-Rausing reader in old Icelandic Univ of Oxford and fell of Linacre Coll Oxford, da of Roderick MacKinnon, and Sheila

O

MacKinnon; 2 da (Ellen Mary b 11 Sept 1978, Josephine Sheila b 26 Dec 1986), 1 s (Thomas Roderick b 4 Jan 1981); *Career* writer; trainee systems analyst IBM (UK) 1968–69; tutor in English language and Medieval literature Magdalen Coll Oxford 1971–95, fell in English Wadham Coll Oxford 1995–2011 (emeritus fell 2011–), adjunct prof of English UC Cork 2012; Cholmondeley Award for Literature 2009; Hon DA Univ of Sunderland 2006; memb AUT 1971–; fell English Assoc, FRSL 1999; *Books* The Courtly Love Tradition (1982), Seamus Heaney and the Language of Poetry (1994), Oxford Irish Quotations (ed, 1999), Sir Gawain and the Green Knight (trans, 2006), Cambridge Companion to Seamus Heaney (2009), Reading Chaucer's Poems (2015); *Poetry* Razorblades and Pencils (1984), Poaching Rights (1987), The Absent Signifier (1990), The Weakness (1991, Southern Arts Award), Gunpowder (1995, Whitbread Poetry Prize), Here Nor There (1999), Outliving (2003), Selected Poems (2008), Farmers Cross (2011), The Seasons of Cullen Church (2016); *Recreations* classical and Irish music, Manchester City FC, Cork Gaelic football team; *Style*— Bernard O'Donoghue, Esq; ⊠ 14 Hill Top Road, Oxford OX4 1PB (☎ 01865 243662); Wadham College, Oxford OX1 3PN

O'DONOGHUE, Denise; OBE (1999); da of late Micheal O'Donoghue, and late Maura O'Donoghue; *Educ* St Dominic's Girls' Sch, Univ of York (BA); *m* 1, 1987 (m dis 1997), Jimmy Mulville; *m* 2, 2006, Michael Holland; *Career* with Coopers & Lybrand 1979–81, dir IPPA 1981–83, with Holmes Assocs 1983–86, md Hat Trick Productions Ltd 1986–2006, md Hat Trick Films Ltd 1995–2006, pres of int television prodns NBC Universal 2009–10, md ITV Studios UK 2010–14, exec dir ITV Studios 2014–; numerous awards incl: RTS, BAFTA, Press Guild, Emmy; CCMI (CIMgt 1998), FRTS 1998; *Style*— Ms Denise O'Donoghue, OBE

O'DONOGHUE, Hugh Eugene (Hughie); s of Daniel O'Donoghue (d 1994), and Sabina Carey (d 1976); *b* 5 July 1953; *Educ* St Augustine's RC GS Manchester, Trinity and All Saints' Colls Leeds, Goldsmiths Coll London (MA, CertEd); *m* 18 May 1974, Clare, da of Thomas Patrick Reynolds (d 1987); 2 s (Matthew Thomas b 12 Nov 1974, Vincent John Domhnall b 26 July 1987), 1 da (Kathryn Sabina b 20 July 1985); *Career* artist; solo exhibitions incl: Air Gallery London 1984, Nat Gallery London 1985, Fabian Carlsson Gallery London 1986 and 1989, Galleria Carini Florence Italy 1987, Art Now Gallery Gothenburg Sweden 1987, Kilkenny Festival 1991, Gallery Helmut Pabst Frankfurt 1991, Thirteen Drawings from the Human Body (Jill George Gallery) 1993, A Painted Passion (Atlantis Upper Gallery London) 1993, Eigse Carlow 1995, Via Crucis (Haus der Kunst Munich) 1997, A Line of Retreat (Purdy Hicks Gallery London, Galerie Helmut Pabst Frankfurt) 1997, Carborundum Prints (Galerie Karl Pfeffere Munich, Cartwright Hall Bradford, Rubicon Gallery Dublin) 1997, Corp, Paintings and Drawings of the human body 1984–1998 (Irish MOMA Dublin, Whitworth Art Gallery Manchester) 1998–99, Episodes from the Passion (RHA Gallagher Gallery Dublin) 1999, Niobes Children (Galerie Karl Pfefferle Munich) 1999, Musik alter Zeiten (Ancient Music) (Galerie Helmut Pabst Frankfurt) 2000, Naming the Fields (Rubicon Gallery Dublin) 2001, Navigation (Mayo General Hosp) 2001, Richer Dust: Carborundum Prints and related paintings and drawings 1995–2000 (Fitzwilliam Museum Cambridge, Djanogly Art Gallery Nottingham, Abbot Hall Gallery Kendal, Victoria Art Gallery Bath) 2001–2002, Ten Years: Panting Memory and the human form (Model Arts and Niland Gallery Sligo) 2002, Course of the Diver (Galerie Karl Pfefferle Munich, Purdy Hicks Gallery London) 2002, Richer Dust (Gas Hall Gallery Birmingham) 2003, Painting Caserta Red (Imperial War Museum London, Imperial War Museum Manchester) 2003; gp exhibitions incl: Whitechapel Open (Whitechapel Art Gallery London) 1982, 1983, 1986, 1988 and 1992, 10 Years at Air (Air Gallery London) 1984, Works on Paper (Anthony Reynolds Gallery London and Galleria Carini Florence Italy) 1986, New Year New Work (Fabian Carlsson Gallery London) 1987, Nuovi Territori dell Arte: Europa/America (Francavilla al Mare Abruzzo) 1987, The Romantic Tradition in Contemporary British Painting (Sala de Exposiciones Murcia, Circulo de Bellas Artes Madrid, Ikon Gallery Birmingham) 1988, Landscape and Beyond (Cleveland Gallery Middlesbrough) 1988, Ways of Telling (Oriel Mostyn Llandudno) 1989, Drawing '89 Cleveland 9th Int Drawing Biennale (prizewinner), School of London 1989, Works on Paper (Odette Gilbert Gallery London) 1989, Roads to Abstraction (Whitworth Art Gallery Manchester) 1990, The Forces of Nature – Landscape as Metaphor (Manchester City Art Galleries) 1990, Drawing Show 11 (Jill George Gallery London) 1990, Ten Artists in Residence (National Gallery London) 1991, The Figure Laid Bare (Pomeroy Purdy Gallery London) 1992, The Man, the Form and the Spirit (Connaught Brown London) 1992, Whitechapel Open Exhibition Part One (invited artist) (Whitechapel Art Gallery London) 1992, Six British Artists (De Serpentini Gallery Rome) 1992, The Figure Laid Bare (Pomeroy Purdy Galley London) 1992, Paint Marks (Kettles Yard Cambridge, and tour) 1994, Credo (Purdy Hicks Gallery London) 1994, Famine (Claremorris County Mayo) 1995, Andata e Ritorno: British Artists in Italy 1980–96 (Royal Albert Memorial Museum Exeter) 1996, Natural Forms (Reeds Wharf Gallery London) 1996, Last Dreams of the Millenium: The re-emergence of British Romantic Painting (Univ Art Gallery Calif State Univ Stanislaus, Main Art Gallery Calif State Univ Fullerton, Univ of Hawaii Manoa) 1997–98, When Time began to Rant and Rage: Figurative Painting from 20th Century Ireland (Walker Art Gallery Liverpool, Berkley Art Museum Univ of Calif, Grey Art Gallery NY, Univ of Michigan Museum of Art Ann Arbour) 1999, Graphic! British Prints Now (Yale Center for British Art New Haven) 1999, Geschichte und Erinnerung in der Kunst der Gegenwart (History and Memory in Contemporary Art) (Schirn Kunsthalle Frankfurt) 2000, Five Centuries of Genius: European Master Printmaking (Art Gallery of S Aust Adelaide) 2000, The Times of Our Lives: Endings (Whitworth Art Gallery Manchester) 2000, An Artists Century: Master Works and Self Portraits of 20th Century Irish Artists (RHA Gallagher Gallery Dublin) 2000, Drawing Parallels (Waterhall Gallery of Modern Art Birmingham) 2002–03, The Journey (Whitworth Art Gallery Manchester) 2002–03, Contemporary Prints (Ashmolean Museum Oxford) 2003; work in numerous public collections incl: Arts Cncl of GB, Arts Cncl of NSW Adelaide, Ashmolean Museum Oxford, Birmingham Museums and Art Gallerys, British Museum London, Cartwright Hall Bradford, Cleveland County Museums Middlesbrough, Djanogly Art Gallery Univ of Nottingham, Ferens Art Gallery Hull, The Fitzwilliam Museum Cambridge, Huddersfield Art Gallery, Hugh Lane Gallery Dublin, Hunterian Art Gallery Glasgow, Imperial War Museum London, Irish MOMA Dublin, Nat Gallery London, Trinity Coll Dublin, Univ of Birmingham, Univ Coll Cork, Univ of Michigan Museum of Art Ann Arbour, Victoria Art Gallery Bath, Whitworth Art Gallery Manchester, Yale Center for Br Art; *Awards* Artist's awards Lincolnshire and Humberside Arts Assoc 1977, 1978 and 1979, Artist in Industry fellowship Yorkshire Arts Assoc 1983, artist in residence Nat Gallery London (Nat Gallery and Arts Cncl of GB) 1984, artist in residence St John's Coll Oxford 2000; *Publications* incl: Hughie O'Donoghue Paintings and Drawings 1983–86 (1986), Hughie O'Donoghue Opera 1986–87 (1987), Crow Paintings Hughie O'Donoghue (1989), Fires (1989), Thirteen Drawings from the Human Body (1993), Via Crucis (1997), A Line of Retreat (1997), Hughie O'Donoghue a catalogue 1979–97 (1998), Episodes from the Passion (1998), Niobes Children (1998), Music alter Zeiten (2000), Smoke Signals (2000), Richer Dust: Carborundum Prints and Related Paintings and Drawings 1995–2000 (Craig Hartley, 2003), Hughie O'Donoghue: Painting, Memory, Myth (James Hamilton, 2003); *Style*— Hughie O'Donoghue, Esq; ⊠ Kilfane Glebe, Thomastown, Co Kilkenny, Ireland; c/o Purdy Hicks Gallery, 65 Hopton Street, London SE1 9GZ (☎ 020 7401 9229)

O'DONOGHUE, Rt Rev Patrick; *see:* Lancaster, Bishop of (RC)

O'DONOGHUE, (Michael) Peter Desmond; s of Michael John O'Donoghue, of Sevenoaks, Kent, and Elizabeth Anne Hawkins, *née* Borley; *b* 5 October 1971, Sevenoaks, Kent; *Educ* Dulwich Coll, Gonville & Caius Coll Cambridge (MA); *m* 7 Sept 2002, Dr Catherine Ann Wolfe; 1 s (Thomas Michael Wolfe b 25 Nov 2004), 1 da (Madelaine Elizabeth Wolfe b 12 Dec 2007); *Career* ind genealogist, historian and researcher 1994–2003, research asst Coll of Arms 1994–2005, Bluemantle Pursuivant of Arms 2005–12, York Herald of Arms 2012–; jt ed The Coat of Arms (jl of Heraldry Soc); Freeman City of London, Liveryman Armourers' and Brasiers' Co; FSA 2015; *Publications* The Electrical Contractors' Association 1901–2001 (2001); articles in heraldic and genealogical journals and elsewhere; *Style*— Peter O'Donoghue, Esq, York Herald; ⊠ College of Arms, Queen Victoria Street, London EC4V 4BT (☎ 020 7332 0776, e-mail york@college-of-arms.gov.uk)

O'DONOGHUE, Rodney Charles (Rod); s of George Albert O'Donoghue (d 1988), and Doris Ada, *née* Matthews (d 2001); *b* 10 June 1938; *Educ* Merchant Taylors; *m* 17 Oct 1964, Kay Patricia, da of Clifford Montague Lewis; 2 s (Mark Christopher b 20 Feb 1970, Richard James b 24 Sept 1977), 1 da (Kerry Frances b 26 July 1974); *Career* articled clerk Singleton Fabian & Co CAs 1956–61, audit staff Monkhouse Stoneham & Co 1961–63, fin dir Kimberly-Clark Ltd 1965–72 (asst fin mangr 1963–65), gp controller Rank Xerox Group 1972–83, gp fin dir Pritchard Services Group 1983–86, exec dir Inchcape plc 1986–98 (gp fin dir 1986–97); historian, genealogist and writer 1998–; fndr Worldwide O'Donoghue Soc; FCA (ACA 1961); *Books* O'Donoghue – People and Places (1999), Heroic Landscapes: Irish Myth and Legend (2011); *Publications* contrib regular articles in O'Donoghue Soc jl; *Recreations* nature, golf, walking, music, history, genealogy, writing; *Clubs* Authors'; *Style*— Rod O'Donoghue, Esq; ⊠ 30 Canonbury Park South, London N1 2FN (e-mail rod@odonoghue.co.uk, website www.odonoghue.co.uk)

O'DONOVAN, Hugh; *b* 19 August 1952; *Educ* Univ of Oxford (BA); *Career* called to the Bar 1975; admitted slr 1988; barr in private practice 1975–85, barr Knapp-Fishers 1985–87, ptnr Richards Butler 1989–91 (barr 1987–88), ptnr Denton Wilde Sapte 1991–2004 (head of aviation regulatory and commercial law), barr Quadrant Chambers 2004–; *Publications* Halisbury's Laws of England (co-author of Aviation title, 2003); *Style*— Hugh O'Donovan, Esq; ⊠ Quadrant Chambers, Quadrant House, 10 Fleet Street, London EC4Y 1AU (☎ 020 7583 4444, fax 020 7583 4455, e-mail hugh.odonovan@quadrantchambers.com)

O'DONOVAN, Rev Prof Oliver Michael Timothy; s of Michael O'Donovan, and Joan Knape; *b* 28 June 1945, London; *m* 1978, Joan Lockwood; 2 s (Matthew Augustine b 1981, Paul Jeremiah b 1986); *Career* ordained: deacon 1972, priest 1973; tutor Wycliffe Hall Oxford 1972–77, hon asst curate St Helen's Abingdon 1972–76, prof of systematic theology Wycliffe Coll Toronto Sch of Theology 1972–82 (asst 1977–81, assoc 1981–82), memb Church of England Bd for Social Responsibility 1976–77 and 1982–85, examining chaplain to Bishop of Toronto and memb Candidates Ctee of Diocese of Toronto 1978–82; Univ of Oxford: regius prof of moral and pastoral theology and canon of ChCh 1982–2006 (emeritus canon 2012–), librarian ChCh 2002–06; prof of Christian ethics and practical theology Univ of Edinburgh 2006–12 (emeritus prof 2012–); McCarthy visiting prof Gregorian Univ Rome 2001, hon prof Sch of Divinity Univ of St Andrews 2013–; canon provincial and canon theologian York 2015–; pres Soc for Study of Christian Ethics 1997–2000; chm Bd Faculty of Theolgy Univ of Oxford 1990–92; memb: Canadian Anglican-Roman Catholic Dialogue 1979–82, Jt Orthodox-Anglican Doctrinal Discussions 1982–85, Archbishop of Canterbury's Gp on the Law of Affinity 1982–84, Working Pty on Human Fertilization and Embryology of the Church of England Bd for Social Responsibility 1982–85, Mgmnt Ctee Ian Ramsey Centre St Cross Coll Oxford 1983–89, Anglican Roman Catholic Int Cmmn 1985–90, Cncl Wycliffe Hall Oxford 1985–95, House of Bishops' Working Gp on Marriage in Church after Divorce 1996–98, Church of England Doctrine Cmmn 1996–97, Faith and Order Advsy Gp Archbishops' Cncl 2004–10, Gen Synod C of E 2005–06; Faith and Order Cncl 2011–15; Chevasse lectr Wycliffe Hall Oxford 1985, Church of Ireland Theological lectr Queen's Univ Belfast 1986 and 2006, pastoral theology lectr Univ of Durham 1987, select preacher Univ of Oxford 1982, 1987, 1988 and 1993, Assize preacher Birmingham Cathedral 1988, Hulsean preacher Univ of Cambridge 1989; visiting lectr St Patrick's Coll Maynooth Ireland 1989, Payton lectr Fuller Theological Seminary Passadena Calif 1989, Paddock lectr Gen Theological Seminary NY 1990–, Hulsean lectr Univ of Cambridge 1994, Hooker lectr McMaster Univ Ontario 1996, Cheung Siu Kwai lectr St John's Coll Hong Kong 2002, Bampton lectr Univ of Oxford 2003, Birks lectr McGill Univ Montreal 2009; FBA 2000, FRSE 2009; *Books* The Problem of Self-Love in Saint Augustine (1980), Begotten or Made? (1984), Resurrection and Moral Order (1986), On the Thirty Nine Articles: a Conversation with Tudor Christianity (1986), Peace and Certainty; a theological essay on deterrence (1989), The Desire of the Nations: rediscovering the roots of political theology (1996), From Irenaens to Grotius (with Joan Lockwood O'Donovan, 1999), Common Objects of Love: moral reflection and the shaping of community (2002), The Just War Revisited (2003), Bonds of Imperfection: Christian politics past and present (jtly, 2004), The Ways of Judgment (2005), A Conversation Waiting to Begin (2009), The Word in Small Boats (2010), Self, World and Time (2013), Finding and Seeking (2014); *Recreations* music, walking; *Style*— The Rev Prof Oliver O'Donovan; ⊠ 6a Comely Park, Dunfermline, Fife KY12 7HU (☎ 01383 740797, e-mail oliver.odonovan@ed.ac.uk)

O'DONOVAN, Timothy Charles Melville (Tim); s of John Conan Marshall Thornton O'Donovan (d 1964), of London, and Enid Muriel Liddell (d 1958); *b* 10 February 1932; *Educ* Marlborough; *m* 19 Sept 1958, Veronica Alacoque, da of Leslie White (d 1981), of Hawkley, Hants; 2 s (Michael b 1962, Richard b 1966); *Career* Nat Serv with Life Gds 1950–52; dir Common Cause Ltd 1964–95, chm Eckersley Hicks & Co Ltd Lloyd's Brokers 1979–84, dir of public affrs Bain Clarkson 1987–91; chm: A Princess for Wales Exhibition 1981, Pollution Abatement Technol Award Scheme 1983–87, Better Environment Awards for Industry 1987–92; hon sec Soc of the Friends of St George's and Descendants of the Knights of the Garter 1992–2002; capt of lay stewards St George's Chapel Windsor Castle 2010–14 (steward 1978, dep vice-capt 1983–93, vice-capt 1993–2010); tstee The Environment Fndn 1985–2010, div pres Windsor Div St John's Ambulance 2001–08; Berkshire rep NACF 2003–08; memb The Queen's Birthday Ctee 1986, memb Queen's Diamond Jubilee Ctee Windsor 2010–12; exhibitions organised: E-II-R – A Celebration 1986, Sixty Years a Queen (Windsor Castle) 1987, Ninety Memorable Years to Celebrate The Queen Mother's 90th birthday, The Queen is Crowned (Windsor Castle) 1993, Prince Philip His Life and Work 1996, The Queen at Windsor 2002, The Duke of Edinburgh's 90th Birthday (Windsor Castle) 2011, Our Diamond Queen (Windsor Castle) 2012, The Queen is Crowned 2013, The Longest Reign (Windsor Castle) 2015, Long to Reign Over Us. A 90th Birthday Tribute to HM The Queen (Windsor Castle) 2016; author of annual survey of Royal Family duties since 1979 in The Times and Illustrated London News; memb President's Club Thames Hospicecare Windsor; received Royal Maundy from The Queen at St George's Chapel 2016; FRSA 1984; *Books* Above The Law?; *Recreations* watching cricket, photography, collecting royal memorabilia, reading the Court Circular; *Style*— Tim O'Donovan, Esq, FRSA; ⊠ Mariners, 11 The Avenue, Datchet, Berkshire SL3 9DH

O'DOWD, Sir David Joseph; kt (1999), CBE (1995), QPM (1988), DL (Northants 2002); s of Michael Joseph O'Dowd (d 1972), and Helen, *née* Merrin (d 2010); *b* 20 February 1942, Blackburn, Lancs; *Educ* Gartree HS Oadby, Univ of Leicester (Dip Social Studies), Open Univ (BA), Aston Univ (MSc), FBI Nat Acad USA; *m* 7 Sept 1963, Carole Ann, da of

Charles Albert Watson, of Leicester; 1 da (Sharon Marie b 3 Dec 1964), 1 s (Andrew David b 29 Jan 1967); *Career* Sgt, Inspr and Chief Inspr CID Leicester City Police 1961, Supt W Midlands Police Coventry and Birmingham 1977; head of traffic policing, dir of complaints and discipline Investigation Bureau and head of strategic planning and policy Analysis Unit Metropolitan Police New Scotland Yard 1984; Chief Constable Northants Police 1986–93 (Asst Chief Constable head of operations 1982), HM Inspr of Constabulary 1993–96, HM Chief Inspr of Constabulary 1996–2001, law enforcement conslt 2001–11; dep chair British Transport Police Authy 2004–11; Cabinet Office Top Mgmnt Prog 1986, rep Br Chief Constables Nat Exec Inst FBI Acad Washington 1988; visiting teaching fell Mgmnt Centre Aston Univ Birmingham, visiting prof Bristol Business Sch UWE; Hon DSc Aston Univ; fell Univ of Northampton; High Sheriff Northants 2006–07; Freeman City of London 2007; CCMI (CIMgt) 1988; OStJ 1988; *Recreations* golf; *Clubs* Northampton Golf, Aphrodite Hills Golf (Paphos, Cyprus (Capt 2015)); *Style*— Sir David J O'Dowd, CBE, QPM, DL

O'DRISCOLL, Suzanne Elizabeth; da of William George O'Driscoll, of Blackthorn, Oxon, and Cynthia Anne, *née* Wright; *b* 7 June 1955; *Educ* St Joseph's Convent Reading, Berkshire Coll of Art, Central Sch of Art and Design London (BA), Slade Sch of Fine Art UCL (MND, Boise travelling scholarship to Mexico and Guatemala); *Career* artist; work in various collections; artist in residence: Bracknell Sch Berkshire 1987, Rhos y Gwalian Wales 1987, Maidenhead Teachers Centre 1988; featured in Assessment and Evaluation in the Arts 1987; Edwin Austin Meml Rome scholarship 1993/94; *Solo Exhibitions* incl: Air Gallery 1984, South Hill Park Art Centre Bracknell 1987, Anderson O'Day Gallery London 1987 and 1989, Solomon Gallery Dublin 1992, CCA Galleries Oxford 1993, Rostra Gallery Bath 2000, Forest Art Centre New Milton 2002; *Group Exhibitions* incl: Three Decades of Artists from Inner London Art Schs 1953–83 (Royal Acad London) 1983, St John's Smith Square 1985, Space Artists (B P London) 1985, Air Gallery Picture Fair 1986, Anderson O'Day Gallery London 1986, Open Studio Show Berry St London 1987, Heads (Anderson O'Day Gallery London) 1987, Contemporary Arts Soc Market London annually 1987–, Oxford Gallery 1988, Drawing Show (Thumb Gallery London) 1988, Fish Exhibition (South Hill Park Bracknell) 1988, Int Contemporary Art Fair London 1989 and 1990, Bath Contemporary Arts Fair 1989 and 2000, Painting of the Week (Channel 4 TV) 1989, Works on Paper (Thumb Gallery London) 1990, Encounters (Oxford Gallery) 1991, Art for a Fairer World OXFAM touring 1992, Archer Exhbn London 1992, Subtitles Mostra (Br Sch at Rome) 1994, Cairn Gallery 1999, (Equinox) Nailsworth (CCA Galleries) 1999, Rostra Gallery Bath 1999, 2000 and 2001, New Landscapes (CCA Galleries) 2000, Taurus Gallery Oxford 2000 and 2001; *Commissions* for: Southampton Gen Hosp 1985, Harold Wood Gen Hosp1986, Radcliffe Infirmary Oxford 1986, RA Baileys Dublin 1994, UDV UK 2000, flowerbed design Abingdon (Year of the Artist) 2001, Accenture 2001, J Sainsbury plc 2001, Pernod Richard (Abelour Distillery), Chivas Bros London 2003 and 2004; *Style*— Ms Suzanne O'Driscoll; ✉ The Studio, Ash Barn House, Blackthorn, Bicester, Oxfordshire OX25 1TG (☎ 01869 323992)

O'FARRELL, Maggie; *b* 1972, NI; *Career* writer; previously worked as journalist; *Books* After You'd Gone (2000, Betty Trask Award), My Lover's Lover (2002), The Distance Between Us (2004, Somerset Maugham Award), The Vanishing Act of Esme Lennox (2006); *Style*— Ms Maggie O'Farrell

O'FLYNN, Patrick James; s of Patrick J J O'Flynn, and Mary, *née* Stebbing; *b* 29 August 1965; *Educ* Parkside Community Coll Cambridge, Long Rd Sixth Form Coll Cambridge, King's Coll Cambridge (BA), City Univ (Dip Journalism); *m* 1997, Carole Ann, da of John Radbone; 1 da (Phoebe b 20 May 1997), 1 s (Raphael b 11 March 1999); *Career* journalist; reporter: Hull Daily Mail 1989–92, Birmingham Post 1992–93; political corr Birmingham Post 1993–96, dep political ed Sunday Express 1996–97, political ed Daily Express 2000–05 (chief political corr 1998–2000); MEP (UKIP) Eastern England 2014–; Yorkshire Journalist of the Year 1991–92; *Style*— Patrick O'Flynn, Esq

O'GRADY, Frances; *b* 9 November 1959, Oxford; *Family* 2 c; *Career* early career with TGWU; TUC: joined 1994, subsequently campaigns offr then dir New Unionism project, head Orgn and Servs Dept 1998–2003, dep gen sec 2003–12, gen sec 2013–; currently memb: IPPR Policy Advsy Gp, Apprenticeship Ambassadors Network, Low Pay Cmmn, Green Economy Cncl; fell City and Guilds; *Style*— Ms Frances O'Grady; ✉ Trades Union Congress, Congress House, Great Russell Street, London WC1B 3LS (☎ 020 7467 1249, fax 020 7467 1277, e-mail fogrady@tuc.org.uk)

O'GRADY, Paul James; MBE (2008); *b* 14 June 1955, Birkenhead, Wirral; *Children* 1 da (Sharyn); *Career* comedian and presenter; *Television* Paul O'Grady's Orient 2000, Paul O'Grady's America 2001, Outtake TV 2002, Eyes Down 2003, The Paul O'Grady Show (ITV then Channel 4) 2004–09 (Best TV Comedy Entertainment Personality Br Comedy Award 2005, Best Entertainment Performance BAFTA 2005), Paul O'Grady Live! (ITV) 2010–11, Paul O'Grady: For the Love of Dogs (ITV) 2012–14 (Factual Entertainment National Television Awards 2013 and 2014), Nellie and Melba (Sky Arts) 2012, Little Cracker – Boo! (Sky Arts), Paul O'Grady's Working Class (BBC1) 2013, Paul O'Grady's Animal Orphans (ITV) 2014 and 2015, The Paul O'Grady Show (ITV) 2013 and 2014; as Lily Savage: The Big Breakfast (Channel 4), Blankety Blank (BBC then ITV), Lily Live! (ITV) 2000; *Theatre* Prisoner Cell Block H – The Musical, Annie, Chitty Chitty Bang Bang; *Radio* Paul O'Grady (BBC Radio 2) 2009–; *Books* At My Mother's Knee...and Other Low Joints (autobiography, 2008), The Devil Rides Out (autobiography, 2010), Still Standing – The Lily Years (autobiography, 2012); *Style*— Paul O'Grady, Esq, MBE; ✉ c/o BM Creative Management Ltd, Second Floor, Aldwych House, 81 Aldwych, London WC2B 4HN (e-mail bmcreative@dircon.co.uk)

O'HAGAN, Simon Timothy Byard; s of Maj Alan Bernard O'Hagan, and Heather Mary Byard, *née* White; *b* 25 September 1957; *Educ* King's Sch Rochester, Univ of Birmingham (BA); *m* 6 May 1989, Lindsay Carol; 2 da (Isabel Clare b 23 Dec 1990, Eleanor Catherine b 8 Nov 1993); *Career* journalist: The Kent Messenger 1978–81, The Times 1982–89, The Independent on Sunday 1990–2006; asst ed The Independent 2006–; *Recreations* cycling; *Clubs* Black's; *Style*— Simon O'Hagan; ✉ The Independent, 2 Derry Street, London W8 5HF (e-mail s.ohagan@independent.co.uk)

O'HANLON, Ardal; s of Rory O' Hanlon, and Teresa, *née* Ward; *Career* stand-up comic; fndr memb Comedy Cellar Dublin; Hackney Empire New Act of the Year 1994, Top TV Comedy Newcomer Br Comedy Awards 1996, Best Comedy Actor BAFTA 1998; patron Aisling Return to Ireland Project, hon pres Edinburgh Univs and Heriot-Watt Celtic Supporters Club; *Television* Father Dougal in Father Ted (C4), George/Thermoman in My Hero (BBC 1), Eamonn in Big Bad World (ITV); presenter Stand-Up Show (BBC 1); *Theatre* The Weir (West End) 2013; *Books* Talk of the Town (1997); *Recreations* sleeping; *Style*— Ardal O'Hanlon, Esq; ✉ Dawn Sedgwick Management, 3 Goodwins Court, London WC2N 4LL (☎ 020 7240 0404, e-mail dawnsedgwick@compuserve.com)

O'HANLON, Redmond Douglas; s of Canon William Douglas O'Hanlon, of Swanage, Dorset, and Philippa Katherine O'Hanlon; *b* 5 June 1947; *Educ* Marlborough, Merton Coll Oxford (MA, MPhil, DPhil); *m* 6 April 1967, Belinda Margaret, da of Desmond Ingham Harty; 1 da (Puffin Annabelinda b 26 Feb 1985), 1 s (Galen Redmond b 2 Aug 1988); *Career* writer; St Antony's Coll Oxford: sr scholar 1971–72, Alistair Horne res fell 1972–73, sr visitor 1985–89, sr assoc memb 1989–95; ed natural history TLS 1981–95; memb: Literature Panel Arts Cncl 1971–74, Soc for the History of Natural History 1982, Br Ornithological Union 1986; Le Prix de L'Astrolabe 1989; FRGS 1984, FRSL 1993; *Books* Charles Darwin 1809–1882: A Centennial Commemorative (contrib, 1982), Joseph Conrad and Charles Darwin: The Influence of Scientific Thought on Conrad's Fiction (1984), Into the Heart of Borneo (1984), In Trouble Again, A Journey between the Orinoco and the Amazon (1988), Congo Journey (1996, Best Non-Fiction Book American Libraries Assoc 1997), Trawler, A Journey through the North Atlantic (2003); *Recreations* pond-watching by torchlight; *Clubs* Rainforest; *Style*— Redmond O'Hanlon, Esq, FRSL; ✉ c/o United Agents, 12–26 Lexington Street, London W1F 0LE (☎ 020 3214 0800, fax 020 3214 0801, website www.unitedagents.co.uk)

O'HARE, Kevin Patrick; s of Michael J O'Hare, and Anne Veronica, *née* O'Callaghan; bro of Michael O'Hare, *qv*; *b* 14 September 1965, Yorks; *Educ* White Lodge (Royal Ballet Lower Sch), The Royal Ballet Upper Sch, Royal Danish Ballet; *Career* former ballet dancer with Birmingham Royal Ballet (formerly Sadler's Wells Royal Ballet): first soloist 1989, principal dancer 1990; roles incl: Prince Sigfried in Swan Lake, Albrecht in Giselle, The Poet in Les Syphides, Colas in La Fille Mal Gardée, The Prince in Sleeping Beauty, Oberon in A Midsummer Night's Dream, Man in Two Pigeons, Edward in Edward II; dances principal roles in ballets by Ashton, Balanchine, Bintley and Macmillan, created roles in ballets by David Bintley, Graham Lustig and William Tukett, debut as Romeo in new prodn of Macmillan's Romeo and Juliet 1992, guest appearance with Royal Ballet Covent Garden 1992, and in Milan, Brussels, Hong Kong, China, Japan, Holland and Poland; ret from dancing 2000, trainee co mangr RSC 2000, co mangr Birmingham Royal Ballet 2001–04; Royal Ballet: joined as co dir 2004, dir 2012–; organised the international charity gala Stepping Heals at Birmingham Hippodrome 1997, organised an evening of new dance works Changing Stages MAC Birmingham 1998; govr Royal Ballet Sch 2000–; memb jury of many ballet awards incl Young Br Dancer of the Year and Prix de Lausanne; hon doctorate Univ of Hull 2014; *Style*— Kevin O'Hare, Esq; ✉ The Royal Ballet, Royal Opera House, Covent Garden, London WC2E 9DD

O'HARE, Michael James; s of Michael Joseph O'Hare, and Anne Veronica, *née* O'Callaghan; bro of Kevin O'Hare, *qv*; *b* 7 December 1960; *Educ* Marist Coll Hull, The Royal Ballet Sch; *m* 1996, Julie Ann, *née* Francis; 1 da (Georgia Mai b 28 April 1998); *Career* ballet dancer; The Birmingham Royal Ballet (formerly Sadler's Wells Royal Ballet): joined 1980, soloist 1984, princ 1987–2002, asst ballet master 2002–08 (teacher 2000–), ballet master 2008– (sr ballet master 2014–15); sometime teacher: Royal Ballet Sch 1997–, Yorkshire Ballet Assembly 1997–; performed a wide range of princ roles within repertoire (character, demi-character and classical) in ballets by: Ashton, MacMillan, Balanchine, De Valois, Cranko and others; the first dancer to perform all three male roles (Alain, Colas and Widow Simone) in Ashton's La Fille Mal Gardée; has danced numerous seasons at Sadler's Wells, the ROH Covent Garden and The Birmingham Hippodrome and has toured extensively worldwide; has worked with numerous younger choreographers; created role of Will Mossop in Hobson's Choice with choreographer David Bintley (first performance Royal Opera House 1989 and shown on BBC 2 1990); performances incl: Eros in Sylvia (David Bintley), Satan in Job (De Valois Ballet, at Coventry Cathedral), La Fille Mal Gardée and The Two Pigeons (at Teatro Regio Torino), The Prodigal Son (Balanchine), The Prince in The Sleeping Beauty, Carmina Burana and the role of Gabriel Oak in Far From the Madding Crowd (both David Bintley) 1996, Edward in Edward II (David Bintley), Mr O'Reilly in The Prospect Before Us (De Valois), Richard III in Shakespeare Suite (David Bintley), Arthur in Arthur Part I and Part II (David Bintley), Hoofer in Slaughter on 10th Avenue (Balanchine), Kostchei in The Firebird 2006, Lord Capulet in Romeo and Juliet 2006, The Red King in Checkmate (Sadler's Wells Theatre and Nat Theatre Munich), Drosselmeyer in The Nutcracker (Sir Peter Wright), Dr Coppelius in Coppélia (Sir Peter Wright), The Merchant in Beauty and the Beast (David Bintley) 2006; recent performances incl: Dr Coppelius in Coppelia (London Coliseum), The Grandfather in The Nutcracker (Sir Peter Wright), The Merchant in Beauty and the Beast, The Beggar in Miracle in Gorbals (Gillian Lynne revival), Widow Simone in La Fille Mal Gardée (Frederick Ashton, Birmingham Hippodrome and with the Mikhailovsky Ballet in St Petersburg) 2014, Yslaev in A Month in the Country (choreographed by Frederick Ashton, Birmingham Hippodrome) 2016; *Style*— Michael O'Hare, Esq; ✉ The Birmingham Royal Ballet, Birmingham Hippodrome, Thorp Street, Birmingham B5 4AU (☎ 0121 245 3500)

O'HORA, Prof Ronan; s of Desmond O'Hora, and Gertrude, *née* Maguire; *b* 9 January 1964; *Educ* St Bede's Coll Manchester, RNCM; *m* 5 Jan 1991, Hannah Alice, *née* Bell; *Career* concert pianist; London concerto debut with Philharmonia Barbican Hall 1989, London recital debut Wigmore Hall 1989, US debut with Florida Philharmonic Orch Miami 1990; played with orchs incl: Royal Philharmonic, London Philharmonic, BBC Symphony and Philharmonic Orchs, Acad of St Martin-in-the-Field's, Hallé Orch, Royal Liverpool Philharmonic, Tonhalle Orch of Zurich, Indianapolis Symphony Orch; played concertos and recitals in numerous countries incl: Germany, France, Switzerland, Holland, Italy, Scandinavia, Belgium, Austria, Yugoslavia, Poland, Ireland, Portugal, Canada, Czechoslovakia; sr tutor RNCM 1996–99; Guildhall Sch of Music and Drama: head of keyboard studies 1999–, fell 2004–, head of advanced performance studies 2008–; fell Royal Northern Coll of music 1999–; *Awards* Silver Medal Worshipful Co of Musicians 1984, Dayas Gold Medal 1984, Stefania Niekrasz Prize 1985; *Recordings* Britten Music for Two Pianos (with Stephen Hough), concertos by Grieg, Tchaikovsky and Mozart with the RPO, solo recordings of Chopin, Schubert and Debussy; numerous recordings for broadcasting cos incl: BBC TV and Radio, Netherlands TV and Radio, Polish TV, Czech TV; *Recreations* theatre; *Style*— Ronan O'Hora, Esq; ✉ c/o Guildhall School of Music and Drama, Silk Street, Barbican, London EC2Y 8DT (☎ 020 7628 2571)

O'KANE, Maggie; s of Peter O'Kane, of Skerries, Co Dublin, and Maura, *née* McNeil; *Educ* Assumption Convent Ballynahinch Co Down, Loreto Convent Balbriggan Co Dublin, Coll of Commerce Dublin, UC Dublin (BA), Inst de Journaliste en Europe Paris; *m* John Mullin; 2 c (Billy, Ruby); *Career* reporter Magill Magazine Ireland 1980–82, journalist Sunday Tribune Ireland 1982–84, TV reporter Irish television 1984–89, scholarship to Journalistes En Europe Fndn Paris 1989, covered E Europe for Irish Times and RTE 1989–90, Gulf War for The Irish Times, freelance 1991– (working for Mail on Sunday, The Guardian, The Economist and Sunday Times in Beirut, Kuwait, N Iraq, Croatia and Bosnia), currently special corr The Guardian and editorial dir Guardian Films; television progs incl: documentary on Haiti (BBC) 1995, documentary on anniversary of Gulf War (Channel 4) 1996, documentary on Third World debt; *Awards* Journalist of the Year What the Papers Say Awards 1992, Journalist of the Year and Foreign Corr (jt) British Press Awards 1992, Foreign Corr (jt) of the Year Amnesty Int 1993, Br TV Documentary Award (for Bloody Bosnia) Channel 4 1993, runner-up RTS Reporter of the Year 1993, James Cameron Award for int and domestic reporting 1996, runner-up Int Foreign Corr Amnesty Int 1998, shortlisted Foreign Corr of the Year 2000, European Journalist of the Year 2002; *Style*— Ms Maggie O'Kane; ✉ GuardianFilms, 90 York Way, London N1 9GU (☎ 020 7278 2332, fax 020 7239 9787)

O'KEEFFE, Bartholomew (Batt); TD; s of Daniel O'Keeffe (d 1979), of Cullen, Co Cork, and Ellen, *née* O'Connell (d 1989); *b* 2 April 1945, Co Cork; *Educ* St Brendan's Coll Killarney, UC Cork; *m* Oct 1970, Mary, *ée* Murphy; 1 s (Mark), 3 da (Elaine, Hilda, Patrice); *Career* formerly lectr in communications and gen studies; TD (Fianna Fáil) Cork South Central 1987–89, memb (senator) Seanad Éireann (Fianna Fáil) Lab panel 1989–92, TD (Fianna Fáil) Cork North West; min of state Dept of the Environment, Heritage and Local Govt 2004–07, min for housing, urban renewal and devpt areas Dept of the Environment, Heritage and Local Govt 2007–08, min for educn and science 2008–10, min for enterprise,

O

trade and innovation 2010–; *Style*— Batt O'Keeffe, Esq, TD; ✉ 8 Westcliffe, Ballincollig, Co Cork, Ireland (☎ 00 353 21 4871393, e-mail minister@entemp.ie)

O'LEARY, Dermot; s of Sean O'Leary, and Maria O'Leary; *Educ* St Benedict's RC Sch, Colchester Sixth Form Coll, Univ of Middlesex (BA); *m* 14 Sept 2012, Dee Koppang; *Career* runner and devpt researcher Barraclough Carey 1995–96; researcher 1996–97: Chapter One, Dove Prodns, Princess Prodns; TV presenter 1997– (progs incl T4, Barfly Sessions, Big Brother's Little Brother, Big Breakfast, Top of the Pops, TFI Friday, SAS – Are You Tough Enough?, X Factor and National Television Awards); presenter and assoc prodr: Recovered 2001–, Dermot's Sporting Buddies 2001–; radio presenter: Dermot's Saturday Club (BBC Radio 2) 2004–05, The Dermot O'Leary Show (BBC Radio 2) 2005– (Best Music Prog Sony Award 2013); owner Murfia Prodns 2001–; columnist Sky magazine 2000–; Best Newcomer Irish World 2000, TV Personality of the Year GQ 2001, Elle Style Award 2001; patron Everyman 2002–; worked with charities incl: NSPCC, Centrepoint, Terrence Higgins Tst, CAFOD, Cinemagic; *Recreations* diving and all things oceanic, learning to speak Italian, boxing, marathon running; *Style*— Dermot O'Leary, Esq

O'LEARY, Steve; OBE; *Career* dir of int servs Business Gp UK Trade and Investment; *Style*— Steve O'Leary, Esq, OBE; ✉ UK Trade and Investment, Kingsgate House, 66–74 Victoria Street, London SW1E 6SW

O'LOAN, Baroness (UK Life Peer 2009), of Kirkinriola in the Co of Antrim; Dame Nuala Patricia O'Loan; DBE (2008); *b* 20 December 1951, Bishop's Stortford, Herts; *Educ* Convent of the Holy Child Harrogate, KCL (LLB), Coll of Law London; *m* Declan O'Loan; 5 s; *Career* slr Supreme Court of Eng and Wales 1976–, lectr in law Ulster Poly 1976–80; Univ of Ulster: lectr in law 1984–92, Jean Monnet chair in European law 1992–99, sr lectr in law 1992–2000; Police Ombudsman for NI 2000–07; special cmmr: Cmmn for Racial Equality 2004–05, Equality and Human Rights Cmmn 2008–09, Review of Outsourcing Abuse UKBA 2009–10; chair: Daniel Morgan Ind Panel (appointed by the Home Sec) 2014–, Catholic Cncl Ind Inquiry into Child Sexual Abuse 2016–; chm NI Consumer Cncl for Electricity 1997–2000; memb: Energy and Tport Gp Gen Consumer Cncl for NI 1991–96 (convenor 1994–96), UK Domestic Coal Consumer Cncl 1992–95, Ministerial Working Gp on the Green Economy 1993–95, N Health and Social Servs Bd 1993–97 (convenor for complaints 1996–97), Police Authy for NI 1997–99, Int Gp for Dialogue and Peace 2007–; roving ambass and special envoy (for Ireland) for conflict resolution to Timor-Leste 2008–11, special envoy (Ireland) for UN Secruity Resolution 1325; expert memb European Cmmn Consumers Consultative Cncl 1994–95; lay visitor to RUC Stations 1991–97; chair Maynooth Univ 2010–; memb Royal Irish Acad 2013, memb Royal Dublin Soc; *Publications* author of more than 150 pubns on law, policing and other issues; *Recreations* reading, music; *Style*— The Baroness O'Loan, DBE; ✉ e-mail nualaoloan@googlemail.com

O'NEIL, William A; CMG (2004), CM (1995); *Educ* Univ of Toronto; *m*; 3 c; *Career* various engrg positions Federal Dept of Tport 1949–55, successively div engr, regnl dir and dir of construction St Lawrence Seaway Authy 1955–71, cmmr Canadian Coast Guard and dep admin Canadian Marine Transportation Admin (CMTA) Federal Dept of Tport 1975–80 (dep admin Marine Servs CMTA 1971–75); St Lawrence Seaway Authy 1980–90: pres and ceo, dir Canarctic Shipping Company, pres Seaway International Bridge Corporation, memb Bd Thousand Islands Bridge Authy; sec-gen International Maritime Organisation (IMO) 1990– (Canadian rep to Cncl 1972–90, chm Cncl 1980–90); Canadian delg Permanent International Assoc of Navigation Congresses 1984–90, chm Canadian Ctee Lloyd's Register of Shipping 1987–88, memb Bd Int Maritime Bureau 1991–, chm Governing Body Int Maritime Law Inst 1991–; Nat Union of Marine Aviation and Shipping Tport Offrs (NUMAST): hon memb 1995, NUMAST Award 1995; hon titular memb Comité Maritime International 2001; hon memb: Canadian Maritime Law Assoc 1989, Hon Co of Master Mariners 1990, Int Maritime Pilots' Assoc 1991, Soc of Naval Architects and Marine Engrs Singapore 1992, Int Fedn of Shipmasters Assocs 1993, Int Assoc of Lighthouse Authorities 1994, Soc of Naval Architects and Marine Engrs USA 1995, Co of Master Mariners India 1998; chllr World Maritime Univ 1991– (memb Bd of Govrs and Exec Ctee 1983–90); Hon Dip Canadian Coast Guard Coll 1990, Hon Cdre Canadian Coast Guard 1981; Distinguished Public Service Award US Govt 1980, Admiral's Medal Canada 1994, Commander Ordre National des Cèdres Lebanon 1995, SEATRADE Personality of the Year Award 1995, Gold Medal Professional Engrs Ontario 1995, memb Engrg Alumni Hall of Distinction Univ of Toronto 1996, Silver Bell Award Seamen's Church Inst NY 1997, Orden Vasco Nunez de Balboa en el Grado de Gran Cruz Panama 1998, Connecticut Maritime Assoc Cdre Award USA 1998, Dioscuri Prize Lega Navale Italiana Agrigento Italy 1998, Vice Adm 'Jerry' Land Medal of the Soc of Naval Architects and Marine Engrs USA 1999, Halert C Shepheard Award USA 2000, medal for distinguished services to the DG for maritime affrs Colombia 2001, Communications and IT in Shipping (CITIS) 2002 Lifetime Achievement Award 2002, Golden Jubilee Medal Canada 2002, 15 November 1817 Medal Uruguay 2002; Freeman (hc) Worshipful Co of Shipwrights 2002; Hon LLD: Univ of Malta 1993, Meml Univ of Newfoundland Canada 1996; Hon DSc Nottingham Trent Univ 1994; Dr jur (hc) Korea Maritime Univ 2002; memb: Assoc of Professional Engrs of Ontario (Engrg Medal for engrg achievement 1972), American Soc of Civil Engrs; hon memb Baltic Exchange 1999; foreign memb Royal Acad of Engrg 1994, hon fell Nautical Inst UK 1996, Hon FRIN 1999, FILT, FRSA, FREng 1994, Hon FRINA 1998; *Style*— William A O'Neil, Esq, CMG, CM, FREng; ✉ 4 Albert Embankment, London SE1 7SR (☎ 020 7587 3100, fax 020 7587 3210, e-mail secretary-general@imo.org)

O'NEILL, Dennis James; CBE (2000); s of Dr William Patrick O'Neill (d 1986), of Pontarddulais, S Wales, and Eva Ann, *née* Rees; *b* 25 February 1948; *Educ* Gowerton GS, studied singing privately with Frederick Cox in London and Campogalliani, Mantova, Ricci in Rome; *m* 1, 4 April 1970 (m dis 1987), Margaret Ruth, da of Rev Edward Collins, of Old Harlow, Essex; 1 da (Clare b 21 July 1977), 1 s (Sean b 22 Dec 1979); m 2, 11 Jan 1988, Ellen, da of Hans Einar Folkestad, of Tybakken, Norway; *Career* tenor and broadcaster; operatic debuts: Royal Opera House Covent Garden 1979 (annually thereafter), Metropolitan Opera NYC 1986, Vienna State Opera 1981, Hamburg State Opera 1981, San Francisco 1984, Chicago Lyric 1985, Paris Opera 1986, Deutche Oper Berlin 1989, Bayerische Staatsoper 1992 (annually thereafter); many recordings; presenter Dennis O'Neill BBC 2; pres Friends of WNO, fndr Dennis O'Neill Bursary; hon fell Univ of Wales; FTCL, ARCM, FWCMD; *Recreations* cookery; *Style*— Dennis O'Neill, Esq, CBE; ✉ c/o Ingpen & Williams Ltd, 7 St George's Court, 131 Putney Bridge Road, London SW15 2PA (☎ 020 8874 3222, fax 020 8877 3113)

O'NEILL, Derham Charles; s of Charles Daniel O'Neill (d 1984), and Phyllis, *née* Derham (d 1983); *b* 4 July 1943, Crosby, Lancs; *Educ* St Mary's Coll Crosby, Univ of Manchester (LLB), Manchester Business Sch (MBA); *m* 1, 5 Aug 1967, Patricia (d 2008), da of William Kay (d 1963); 1 da (Katharine Alexandra b 1975), 1 s (Derham Aidan b 1977); m 2, 12 June 2010, La Contessa Elisabeth Bonamy-O'Neill, da of late Philippe Bonamy; *Career* admitted slr 1968; md Brown Shipley Fund Mgmnt Ltd 1979–80, corp fin ptnr Clifford Turner (now Clifford Chance) 1981–97, investment banking, private equity and pension issues advsr 1997–; chm Schroder Asia Property Managers Ltd 2008–13; non-exec dir F&C Asset Mgmnt plc and other cos; memb AIM Appeals Ctee London Stock Exchange 1996–2003; *Books* Management Buyouts (contrib, 1988); *Recreations* writing poetry, short stories and novels, skiing, swimming, moral philosophy; *Clubs* East India; *Style*— Derham O'Neill, Esq; ✉ Clifford Chance, 10 Upper Bank Street, London E14 5JJ (☎ 020 7600 1000, fax 020 7600 5555, e-mail derham_oneill@msn.com)

O'NEILL, Eamonn Patrick; Dr; s of Edward O'Neill, of Co Offaly, Ireland, and Bridget, *née* O'Reilly; *b* 25 March 1967; *Educ* St Aidan's HS Wishaw, Univ of Strathclyde (BA, PhD); *m* 21 Sept 1991, Sarah, da of Prof David Kellam Sterling; 2 s (Lorcan Patrick, Cormac Patrick b 21 Nov 2008 (twins)); *Career* investigative journalist and writer; freelance journalist 1989–90, researcher rising to prodr and dir Scottish Television 1990–96, prodr network factual progs Scottish Television Enterprises 1996, contributing ed Esquire 1998; Univ of Strathclyde: lectr in journalism, prog dir MSc Investigative Journalism; prodr various documentaries Channel 4; contrib to newspapers and magazines incl The Herald 2003–; nominated BAFTA Documentary Award for The Truth of Christmas Island (Dispatches strand) 1991; runner-up: British Press Awards Feature Writer of the Year 2005, Paul Foot Award for Investigative Journalism 2005, Tom Renner Award Investigative Reporters and Eds Annual Awards USA 2008; memb NUJ; *Books* No Risk Involved (1991), Outlaws (1998), Matadors (1999); *Recreations* running, reading, writing, wife, family; *Clubs* Frontline; *Style*— Dr Eamonn O'Neill; ✉ home tel 01896 833510, mobile 07879 696764, e-mail eamonnoneill@aol.com, website www.eamonnoneill.com; work tel 0141 552 4400, e-mail eamonn.o-neill@strath.ac.uk

O'NEILL, Baron (Life Peer UK 2015) of Gatley in the County of Greater Manchester; (Dr) (Terence) James (Jim) O'Neill; s of Terence O'Neill (d 2004), and Kathleen, *née* Simpson (d 1997); *b* 17 March 1957, Manchester; *Educ* Univ of Sheffield (BA, MA), Univ of Surrey (PhD); *m* 18 June 1983, Caroline; 2 c; *Career* Bank of America 1982–83, Marine Midland Bank 1983–88, Swiss Bank Corporation 1988–95, Goldman Sachs 1995– (currently md and head of global economics research); non-exec dir Manchester United plc 2004–05; author of numerous articles on economic matters particularly on exchange rates; creator of BRICs acronym (standing for Brazil, Russia, India and China); chm Shine Tst; *Recreations* sport, travel, cinema; *Style*— The Lord O'Neill of Gatley; ✉ Goldman Sachs International, Peterborough Court, 133 Fleet Street, London EC4A 2BB (☎ 020 7774 2699, fax 020 7774 2643, e-mail jim.oneill@gs.com)

O'NEILL, John Joseph (Jonjo); s of Thomas O'Neill, and Margaret O'Neill; *b* 13 April 1952; *Educ* Castletownroche Nat Sch; *m* 1997, Jacqueline, *née* Bellamy; 3 s, 2 da; *Career* jockey and racehorse trainer; nat hunt jockey 1969–87, winner 901 races, champion jockey 1977–78 (winner record 149 races) and 1979–80; winner: Cheltenham Gold Cup 1979 and 1986, Champion Hurdle 1980 and 1984, Coral Welsh Nat 2002 (with Mini Sensation and Synchronised), Irish Grand Nat 2007 (with Butler's Cabin), English Grand Nat 2010 (with Don't Push It), Cheltenham Gold Cup 2012 (with Synchronised); trainer 1987–, trained over 1,750 winners incl Gipsy Fiddler (Windsor Castle Stakes Royal Ascot), Well Sharp (Ascot Stakes Royal Ascot), Tominator (Northumberland Plate) and winners at Cheltenham Nat Hunt Festival, Aintree Festival and Punchestown; trained 26 winners at Cheltenham Nat Hunt Festival incl: Danny Conners, Front Line, Master Tern, Rith Dubh, Inching Closer, Sudden Shock, Spectroscope, Creon, Native Emperor, Iris's Gift, Black Jack Ketchum, Butler's Cabin, Wichita Lineman, Drombeag, Albertas Run, Synchronised, Sunnyhillboy, Alfie Sherrin, Holywell, Tarquin du Seuill and More of That; trained 23 winners at Aintree Festival incl: Radiation, Sudden Shock, Quazar, Carbury Cross, Intersky Falcon, Master Tern, Clan Royal, Iris's Gift (twice), Classic Native, Rhinestone Cowboy, Black Jack Ketchum, Refinement, Exotic Dancer, Two Miles West, Albertas Run, Sunnyhillboy, Don't Push It, Eastlake; 31 Grade 1 winners, three winners at Punchestown: Quazar, Predator, Refinement; Ireland's People of the Year Award 1986; *Style*— Mr Jonjo O'Neill; ✉ Jackdaws Castle, Temple Guiting, Cheltenham, Gloucestershire GL54 5XU (☎ 01386 584209, fax 01386 584219, e-mail reception@jonjooneillracing.com, website www.jonjooneillracing.com)

O'NEILL, Prof Paul Anthony; s of Joseph O'Neill, and Jean, *née* Bradbury; *b* 14 March 1955; *Educ* St Thomas Aquinas GS Leeds, Univ of Manchester (BSc, MB ChB, MD); *m* 1978, Jo, *née* Beeston; 1 s (David b 5 Oct 1986), 1 da (Alice b 19 May 1990); *Career* house physician Univ Hosp of S Manchester 1979, house surgn Manchester Royal Infirmary 1980, SHO Univ Hosp of S Manchester 1981–82, res fell Manchester Royal Infirmary and ICI Pharmaceuticals 1982–84, registrar Bristol Royal Infirmary 1984–86, lectr Univ Dept of Geriatric Med Manchester 1986–89, hon conslt in geriatric med Univ of Manchester 1989–, sr lectr and hon conslt in geriatric med S Manchester Univ Hosps NHS Tst 1992–2000, prof of med educn Univ of Manchester 2000–06 (assoc dean of med undergrad studies 1998–2004, dir of educn 2004–06), head Manchester Med Sch 2006–; educn fell and memb Faculty Harvard Macy Prog 1999–, examiner RCP 1999–; subject reviewer Quality Assurance Agency 1998–2002, Quality Assurance of Basic Med Educn (QABME) visitor GMC 2004–; ldr Physicians as Educators prog RCP 1999; memb: Br Geriatrics Soc 1986–, Cncl Assoc for the Study of Med Educn (ASME) 1994–; govr UHSM Fndn NHS Tst 2007–; cncl and chair Professional Standards Ctee Acad Medical Educators 2009–; Norman Exton Smith Prize Br Geriatrics Soc 1990, Elizabeth Brown Prize Br Geriatrics Soc 1991, Dhole Bequest Br Geriatrics Soc 1991, Nat Teaching and Learning Fellowship 2001; FRCP 1994 (MRCP 1982); *Publications* Master of Medicine (jtly, 1997, 2 edn 2001), Clinical Skills and OSCE (jtly, 2000, 2 edn 2006), OSCEs in Surgery (jtly, 2007); author of numerous articles, papers and chapters in books; *Recreations* cooking, gardening, Bonsai trees, walking, windsurfing, sailing, skiing; *Style*— Prof Paul O'Neill; ✉ Faculty of Medical and Human Sciences, Stopford Building, University of Manchester, Oxford Road, Manchester M13 9PL (☎ 0161 275 7792, e-mail p.a.oneill@manchester.ac.uk)

O'NEILL, Peter; *Educ* Queen's Univ Belfast (BSc, MSocSci, LLM); *Career* former dir of student movement in NI, currently chief exec NI Human Rights Cmmn; *Style*— Peter O'Neill, Esq; ✉ Northern Ireland Human Rights Commission, Temple Court, 39 North Street, Belfast BT1 1NA

O'NEILL, 4 Baron (UK 1868); Sir Raymond Arthur Clanaboy O'Neill; KCVO (2009), TD (1970); s of 3 Baron O'Neill (ka Italy 1944); the O'Neills stem from the oldest traceable family in Europe; *b* 1 September 1933; *Educ* Eton, RAC Cirencester; *m* 11 June 1963, Georgina Mary, da of late Lord George Montagu Douglas Scott (3 s of 7 Duke of Buccleuch), of Weekley, Northants; 3 s (Hon Shane b 25 July 1965, Hon Tyrone b 24 June 1966, Hon Rory b 20 Dec 1968); *Heir* s, Hon Shane O'Neill; *Career* short service cmmn 11 Hussars Prince Albert's Own 1952–53, joined NI Horse (TA) 1954; Maj cmdg D (N Irish Horse) Sqdn The Royal Yeomanry Regt 1967–69, cmdg N Irish Horse Cadres 1969–71, RARO 1971; Hon Col: D Sqdn (RYR) 1986–91, 69 (N Irish Horse) Signals Sqdn (V) 1988–93; dir: Shanes Developments Ltd, Shanes Castle Estates Co; chm: Ulster Countryside Ctee 1971–75, NI Tourist Bd 1975–80; former dir Romney Hythe & Dymchurch Railway plc; tstee Ulster Folk and Tport Museum 1969–90 (vice-chm 1987–90); pres: The Railway Preservation Soc of Ireland 1964–, NI Assoc of Youth Clubs (Youth Action) 1968–2007, The Royal Ulster Agric Soc 1984–86 (chm Fin Ctee 1974–83); memb: NT Ctee for NI 1980–91 (chm 1981–91), Cncl for Nature Conservation and Countryside 1989–92; cmmr Museums and Galleries Cmmn 1987–94; chm: NI Museums Advsy Ctee 1989–91, NI Museums Cncl 1993–98; memb Bd Nat Gallery of Ireland 1993–97; HM Lord-Lt Co Antrim 1994–2008 (DL 1967); *Recreations* railways, vintage motoring, gardening, walking, swimming; *Clubs* Turf; *Style*— The Rt Hon the Lord O'Neill, KCVO, TD; ✉ Shanes Castle, Antrim BT41 4NE (☎ 028 94463264, fax 028 94468457); Conigre House, Calne, Wiltshire

O'NEILL, Sally Jane; QC (1997); da of Maj John O'Neill RA (ret) (d 1971), and Frances Agnes, *née* Riley (d 2006); *b* 30 September 1953; *Educ* St Joseph's Convent Stafford,

Alleyne's GS Uttoxeter; *m* 1986, David Bloss Kingsbury; *Career* called to the Bar Gray's Inn 1976 (bencher 2002); asst recorder 1997–2000, recorder 2000–; chm Criminal Bar Assoc 2007–08; *Recreations* gardening, tennis, skiing, sailing, bulldogs, P G Wodehouse; *Style*— Miss Sally O'Neill, QC; ✉ Furnival Chambers, 32 Furnival Street, London EC4A 1JQ (☎ 020 7405 3232)

O'NEILL, Terence Patrick (Terry); s of Leonard Victor O'Neill (d 1980), of Cork, Ireland, and Josephine Mary, *née* Gallagher (d 1978); *b* 30 July 1938; *Educ* Gunnersbury GS; *m* 1, Vera Day; 1 s (Keegan Alexander), 1 da (Sarah Jane); m 2, Faye Dunaway; 1 s (Liam Walker); m 3, Laraine Ashton; *Career* professional jazz drummer since 1952 in leading London clubs incl The Flamingo, The Florida and The Mapleton; Nat Serv PT instr; professional photographer: took first published pictures of The Beatles and The Rolling Stones, photographic biographer of emerging 60s personalities incl Jean Shrimpton, Terence Stamp and Michael Caine, became int celebrity photographer to politicians, royalty and rock and pop stars, work published in 52 countries (average 500 front covers per annum); *Books* Legends, Celebrity, Sinatra, Frank and Friendly, Eltonography; *Recreations* music, reading, cooking, all sport; *Style*— Terry O'Neill, Esq

O'NEILL OF BENGARVE, Baroness (Life Peer 1999), of the Valley of the Braid in the County of Antrim; Onora Sylvia; CH (2014), CBE (1995); da of Sir Con Douglas Walter O'Neill, KCMG (d 1988), and Rosemary Margaret, *née* Prichard, later Lady Garvey (d 2011); *b* 23 August 1941, Aughafatten, Co Antrim; *Educ* St Paul's Girls' Sch, Somerville Coll Oxford (scholar, MA), Harvard Univ (PhD); *m* 1963 (m dis 1974), Edward John Nell, s of Edward John Nell; 2 s (Hon Adam Edward O'Neill b 1967, Hon Jacob Rowan b 1969); *Career* asst then assoc prof Barnard Coll Columbia Univ NYC 1970–77, lectr then prof of philosophy Univ of Essex 1978–92, princ Newnham Coll Cambridge 1992–2006, pres British Acad 2005–09; visiting appts: Australian Nat Univ 1984, Univ of Santa Clara 1985, Wissenschaftskolleg Berlin 1989–90; pres Aristotelian Soc 1988–89; chm Nuffield Cncl on Bioethics 1996–98; Nuffield Fndn: tstee 1997–2010, chm 1998–2010; memb Human Genetics Advsy Cmmn 1996–99 (chm 1999); MRC 2012–, chair Equalities and Human Rights Cmmn 2012–16; foreign hon memb: American Acad of Arts & Sciences 1993, Austrian Acad of Scis 2002, Norwegian Acad 2006; foreign memb American Philosophical Soc 2003; FBA 1993 (former pres), FMedSci 2002, Hon MRIA 2003, Hon FRS 2007; Pour le Mérite (German order) 2015, Bundesverdienstkreuz 2016; *Books* Acting on Principle (1976, 2 edn 2014), Faces of Hunger (1986), Constructions of Reason (1989), Towards Justice and Virtue (1996), Bounds of Justice (2000), Autonomy and Trust in Bioethics (2002), A Question of Trust (2002), Rethinking Informed Consent in Bioethics (jtly, 2007), Constructing Authorities: Reason, Politics and Interpretation in Kant's Philosophy (2016), Justice Across Boundaries: Whose Obligations? (2016), Speech Rights, Speech Wrongs (2016); *Recreations* walking and talking; *Style*— The Rt Hon Baroness O'Neill of Bengarve, CH, CBE, PBA; ✉ 11a Stonefield Street, London N1 0HW; House of Lords, London SW1A 0PW

O'NEILL OF CLACKMANNAN, Baron (Life Peer UK 2005), of Clackmannan in Clackmannanshire; Martin John O'Neill; *b* 6 January 1945; *Educ* Trinity Acad Edinburgh, Heriot-Watt Univ, Moray House Educn Coll Edinburgh (pres Scottish Union of Students); *m* 1973, Elaine Samuel; 2 s; *Career* former insurance clerk, asst examiner Scottish Estate Duty Office, secondary schoolteacher, tutor Open Univ; MP (Lab): Stirlingshire E and Clackmannan 1979–83, Clackmannan 1983–97, Ochil 1997–2005; memb Select Ctee on Scottish Affrs 1979–80; oppn front bench spokesman on: Scottish Affrs 1980–84, defence and disarmament 1984–88; princ oppn spokesman on: defence 1988–92, energy 1992–95; chm Trade and Industry Select Ctee 1995–2005; pres Specialist Engrg Contractors' Gp; hon degree Heriot-Watt Univ 2011; *Style*— The Lord O'Neill of Clackmannan; ✉ House of Lords, London SW1A 0PW

O'NIONS, Prof Sir (Robert) Keith; kt (1999); *b* 26 September 1944; *Educ* Univ of Nottingham (BSc), Univ of Alberta (PhD); *m*; 3 da; *Career* postdoctoral fell Univ of Alberta 1969, Unger Verlesen fell Univ of Oslo 1970, lectr in geochemistry Univ of Oxford 1972–75 (demonstrator in petrology 1971–72), assoc prof then prof of geology Columbia Univ NY 1975–79, Royal Soc research prof Univ of Cambridge 1979–95, official fell Clare Hall Cambridge 1980–95, prof of the physics and chemistry of minerals Univ of Oxford 1995–2003 (head Dept of Earth Sciences 1995–99), professorial fell St Hugh's Coll Oxford 1995–2003 (hon fell 2004–), fell Wolfson Coll Oxford 2004–; memb Cncl of Science and Technol 1998–2000, chief scientific advsr MOD 2000–04, DG Research Cncls Office of Science and Technol/DTI 2004–08, dir Inst for Security Sci and Technol Imperial Coll London 2008–; Sherman Fairchild distinguished scholar Caltech 1988; author of numerous articles in learned jls and chapters in books; NERC: memb Earth Sciences Ctee 1985–90, memb Earth Sciences Technol Bd 1996–99, chm Br Geological Survey Audit 1998; gen sec Cncl European Union of Geosciences 1985–87, pres European Assoc of Geochemistry 1992–95, memb Cncl Royal Soc 1994–95, cncllr Geochemical Soc 1997–2000, memb Jury Institut Universitaire de France 1997–99; chm Bd of Tstees Natural History Museum 2003– (memb 1995–); J B Macelwane Award American Geophysical Union 1979, Bigsby Medal Geological Soc of London 1983, Hallimond lectr Mineralogical Soc 1985, UK-Canada Rutherford lectr Royal Soc 1986, William Smith lectr Geological Soc of London 1986, Ingerson lectr Geological Soc of America 1990, Arthur Holmes Medal European Union of Geosciences 1995, Lyell Medal Geological Soc of London 1995, Jaeger-Hales lectr ANU 1998, Urey Medal European Assoc of Geochemistry 2001, Bruce Preller prize lectr RSE 2004; MA (by incorporation): Univ of Cambridge 1980, Univ of Oxford 1995; hon fell Univ of Cardiff 2000; Hon DSc Heriot-Watt Univ 2004; fell American Geophysical Union 1980, memb Norwegian Acad of Science and Letters 1980, memb Academia Europaea 1990, hon fell Indian Acad of Sciences 1998, foreign fell Indian Nat Science Acad 2001; FRS 1983, Geochemistry fell 1997, FInstP 1999, Hon FREng 2005; *Style*— Prof Sir Keith O'Nions, FRS

O'PREY, Prof Paul; CBE (2016); s of Desmond O'Prey, and Ada, *née* Reid; *b* 2 April 1956, Southampton; *Educ* St George Sch Southampton, King Edward VI Sch Southampton, Keble Coll Oxford, Univ of Bristol (PhD); *m* Maria Pilar, *née* Garcia Navarro; 1 s (Llorenç b 8 Sept 1979), 1 da (Mireia b 1 March 1987); *Career* sec to Robert Graves 1977–81; Univ of Bristol: English tutor 1989–93, warden Goldney Hall 1989–2004, sr warden 1993–95, dep res devpt 1995–99, dir of res and enterprise 1999–2002, dir of academic affrs 2002–04; Univ of Roehampton: prof of modern lit 2004–, vice-chllr 2004–; memb Bd Univs UK, memb Cncl Imperial War Museum, memb Editorial Bd Despatches; Hon DLitt Univ of Bristol 2011, Hon Dr of Humane Letters Manhattenville Coll NY 2011; *Publications* In Broken Images: Selected Letters of Robert Graves 1914–46 (1982), Joseph Conrad, Heart of Darkness (ed,1983), Between Moon and Moon: Selected Letters of Robert Graves 1946–1972 (1989), Robert Graves: Selected Poems (ed, 1986), The Reader's Guide to Graham Greene (1988), The House of Ulloa (1990), Robert Graves: Collected Writings on Poetry (1995), First World War: Poems From the Front (ed, 2014), Mary Borden, Poems of Love and War (ed, 2015), Laurence Binyon, Poems of Two Wars (ed, 2016); various chapters in books and articles in jls; *Clubs* Athenaeum; *Style*— Prof Paul O'Prey, CBE; ✉ Vice-Chancellor's Office, Roehampton University, Roehampton Lane, London SW15 5PJ (☎ 020 8392 3101, e-mail paul.oprey@roehampton.ac.uk)

O'RAHILLY, Prof Sir Stephen; kt (2013); s of late Patrick O'Rahilly, and Theresa Emer O'Rahilly; *b* 1 April 1958, Dublin, Ireland; *Educ* Nat Univ of Ireland (scholar, MB BCh, BAO, MD, D K O'Donovan medal in med, Coleman Saunder's medal in paediatrics); *m* 7 Sept 1990, Suzy Oakes (d 2011); *Career* surgical house offr Mater Hosp Dublin 1982 (med house offr 1981–82); med SHO: Bart's 1982–83, Hammersmith Hosp 1983–84; research fell in endocrinology Univ of Oxford 1984–87, hon registrar and Br Diabetic Assoc Redcliffe-Maud fell Nuffield Dept of Clinical Med Radcliffe Infirmary 1986–87; clinical registrar in endocrinology: John Radcliffe Hosp Oxford 1987–88, Radcliffe Infirmary Oxford 1989–91; MRC travelling fell Harvard Med Sch Div of Endocriniology Beth Israel Hosp Boston Mass 1989–91, hon conslt physician Addenbrooke's Hosp Cambridge 1994–; Univ of Cambridge: Wellcome sr research fell in clinical sci 1991–95, prof of metabolic med Depts of Med and Clinical Biochemistry 1996–2002, prof of clinical biochemistry and med 2002–; SmithKline Beecham visiting prof SKB Philadelphia PA 1995, R D Lawrence lectr Br Diabetic Assoc 1996, visiting prof Univ of Witwatersrand Johannesburg SA 1996, Bayer lectr Bichemical Soc UC Dublin 1997, lectr Univ of Washington 1999, Clinical Endocrinology Tst lectr 1999; Rufus Cole lectr Rockefeller Univ 2000, McCallum lectr Univ Toronto 2000, Kroc lectr Univ of Massachusetts 2007; memb: Research Ctee Br Diabetic Assoc 1996–2001, Wellcome Tst Clinical Interest Gp 1996–2002 (chm 1999–); assoc ed Diabetologia 1995–98, scientific ed Jl of Endocrinology 1996–2004, memb Editorial Bd Clinical Endocrinology 1997–2000; scientific papers in the area of metabolic disease; chm MRC Translational Research Overview Gp 2008–11; invited lectures at regnl, nat and int meetings; memb: Br Diabetic Assoc, American Diabetes Assoc, Euro Assoc for the Study of Diabetes, Soc for Endocrinology (pres 2014–16), Endocrine Soc (USA), Biochemical Soc, Assoc of Physicians of GB, Royal Soc Sectional Ctee 10 2013–14 (chm 2015–16); hon memb American Assoc of Physicians 2004, fell Pembroke Coll Cambridge 2007–; Soc of Endocrinology Medallist 2000, Graham Bull Prize RCP, Heinrich Wieland Prize 2002, Carl Gottschalk Award Univ of Carolina 2003, Rolf Luft Award Karolinska Inst 2005, Solomon Benson Award Mt Sinai Med Sch NY 2007, Clinical Investigator Award Endocrine Soc USA 2007, Feldberg Prize 2007, Dale Medal Soc for Endocrinology 2010, InBev-Baillet Latour Health Prize 2010, Randall lectr Biochemical Soc 2012, Juhling Lectr 2012, Edward K Dunham lectureship for the promotion of medical sci Harvard Medical Sch 2015, European Soc of Endocrinology Hormone Medal Lecture; Ulysses Medal Univ Coll Dublin 2013, TOPS Research Achievement Award The Obesity Soc 2013, Distinguished Grad Award Univ Coll Dublin 2014, Zulch Prize 2014, Baly Medal 2014, Debrecen Prize for Molecular Medicine 2014, European Soc of Endocrinology Hormone Medal 2015, EASD/ Novo Nordisk Fndn Diabetes Prize for Excellence 2015; Hon DSc: UC Dublin 2008, Univ of Warwick 2009, Univ of Buckingham 2013; Hon LLD Univ of Dundee 2012; foreign assoc Nat Acad of Sciences USA 2011, hon memb German Soc for Internal Medicine 2011; FRCPI 1996 (MRCPI 983), FRCP 1996 (MRCP 1984), FMedSci 1999, FRCPath 2002, FRS 2003; *Recreations* tennis, reading, travel, music; *Style*— Prof Sir Stephen O'Rahilly; ✉ Institute of Metabolic Science, Addenbrooke's Hospital, Box 289, Cambridge CB2 0QQ (e-mail so104@medschl.cam.ac.uk)

O'REILLY, Sir John James; kt (2007); s of Patrick William O'Reilly (d 1969), of Bromsgrove, Worcs, and Dorothy Anne Lewis (d 1968); *b* 1 December 1946; *Educ* Sacred Heart Coll Droitwich, Brunel Univ (BTech, DSc), Univ of Essex (PhD); *m* Lesley, da of W Johnson; *Career* Ultra Electronics Ltd 1969–72, sr lectr Univ of Essex 1972–85, researcher PO Res Centre 1978–79, prof of electronic engrg and head of dept Univ of Wales at Bangor 1985–93, princ research fell BT Laboratories 1993–94, chair of telecommunications UCL 1994–2001, head Dept of Electronic and Electrical Engrg UCL 1997–2001, chief exec EPSRC 2001–06, vice-chllr Cranfield Univ 2006–13, DG knowledge and innovation Dept for Business, Innovation and Skills 2013–; chief exec/dep chm IDB Ltd 1985–94, chm Cast Ltd 2005–07; chm UK Network Interoperability Consultative Ctee 1996–2008, chm NICC Standards Ltd 2008–; memb Oftel Tech Experts Advsy Gp 1996–2003, chm SERC Communications and Distributed Systems Ctee, memb SERC/DTI Info Technol Advsy Bd 1991–94, memb OST ITEC Tecnol Foresight Panel 1994–99, memb Technol Strategy Bd DTI 2004–06; IEE: memb Cncl 1998–2007, chm Electronics and Communications Div 1999–2000 (dep chm 1998–99), memb Bd of Tstees 2001–05, vice-pres 2001–02, dep pres 2002–04, pres 2004–05; memb Cncl Royal Acad of Engrg 2000–03 and 2008–; dir ERA Fndn 2008–; hon fell: Univ of Wales Bangor, UCL 2008; Hon DUniv Essex; foreign memb: Acad Hassan II des Scis and Techniques, Acad das Crências de Lisboa 2008; CEng, Hon FIET 2011 (FIEE 1988, MIEE 1983), FREng 1993, Hon FIChemE 2004, FLSW 2011; *Books* Telecommunication Principles (1984, 2 edn 1989), Optimisation Methods in Electronics and Communications (1984), Problems of Randomness in Communications Engineering (1984); *Recreations* music, theatre, cooking; *Style*— Sir John O'Reilly, FREng, FLSW; ✉ Department for Business, Innovation and Skills, 1 Victoria Street, London SW1H 0ET (☎ 020 7215 1219, e-mail john.oreilly@brs.gsi.gov.uk)

O'REILLY, Most Rev Philip Leo; *see:* Kilmore, Bishop of (RC)

O'RIORDAN, Prof Timothy (Tim); OBE (2010), DL (Norfolk 1998); s of Kevin Denis O'Riordan (d 2000), and Norah Joyce, *née* Lucas (d 1996); *b* 21 February 1942; *Educ* George Heriot's Sch Edinburgh, Univ of Edinburgh (MA), Cornell Univ (MS), Univ of Cambridge (PhD); *m* 18 May 1968, Ann Morison, da of Elmsley Philip (d 1992); 2 da (Katharine Louise b 24 Jan 1977, Alice Janet b 31 May 1979); *Career* asst prof Dept of Geography Simon Fraser Univ Burnaby BC 1967–70 (assoc prof 1970–74); UEA: reader Sch of Environmental Scis 1974–80, prof 1980–2005, prof emeritus 2006–; assoc dir Centre for Social and Economic Research on the Global Environment 1991–2001; memb: Broads Authy (chm Environment Ctee 1989–98), ESRC (chm Environment Working Gp 1981–90), Dow Chemical Corporate Environmental Advsy Ctee 1992–98, Core Faculty HRH The Prince of Wales's Business and Environment Prog 1994–, Environmental Advsy Bd Eastern Gp plc 1996–, Lord Provost of Edinburgh's Cmmn on Sustainable Devpt 1998, UK Sustainable Devpt Cmmn 2000–08, Cncl Soil Assoc 2005–, Asda Corporate Responsibility Advsy Bd 2006–; advsr to HRH The Prince of Wales's Accounting for Sustainability Project 2007; pres Norfolk Branch CPRE 2003–; tstee Norfolk Citizenship Initiative 2012–15; Sheriff of Norwich 2009–10; Distinguished Friend of Oxford 2011; FBA 2000; *Books* Progress in Resource Management (1971), Environmentalism (1976, 1981), Sizewell B: An Anatomy of the Inquiry (1988), The Greening of the Machinery of Government (1990), Interpreting the Precautionary Principle (1994), Environmental Science for Environmental Management (1994), Politics of Climate Change: A European Perspective (1996), Ecotaxation (1997), The Transition to Sustainability: A European Perspective (1998), Environmental Science for Environmental Management (2 edn 1999), Globalism, Localism and Identity (2000), Reinterpreting the Precautionary Principle (2001), Biodiversity, Sustainability and Human Communities (2002), Addressing Tipping Points (2013); *Recreations* classical music (double bass playing), swimming, bird watching; *Style*— Prof Tim O'Riordan, OBE, DL, FBA; ✉ Wheatlands, Hethersett Lane, Colney, Norwich NR4 7TT (☎ 01603 810534)

O'SHEA, Colette; da of Bernard O'Shea (d 2009), and Teresa, *née* Riches; *b* 1 April 1968, Romford; *Educ* Chelmsford County HS, Univ of Reading (BSc), Polytechnic of East London (MSc), City Univ Business Sch (Dip), Cranfield Business Dirs Prog; *Career* Mercers' Co: asset mangr 1989–99, head of estates 1999–2003; Land Securities: various devpt and devpt mgmnt roles 2003–08, head of devpt London 2008–14, md London 2014–; FRICS 1992; *Recreations* reading, travel, walking, cycling; *Style*— Ms Colette O'Shea; ☎ 07802 801569; Land Securities Group plc, 5 Strand, London WC2N 5AF (☎ 020 7024 3823, e-mail colette.o'shea@landsecurities.com, website www.landsecurities.com)

O'SHEA, Prof Michael Roland; s of Capt Jack Arthur O'Shea, and Ellen, *née* Hughes; *b* 5 April 1947; *Educ* Forest Hill Sch London, Univ of Leicester (BSc), Univ of Southampton (PhD); *m* 1977 (m dis 1991), Barbara, *née* Moore; 1 da (Linda b 1978 d 1990); *Career*

Univ of Calif Berkeley: NATO fell 1971–73, NIH fell 1973–75; SRC fell Univ of Cambridge 1975–77, asst prof Univ of Southern Calif Los Angeles 1977–79, assoc prof Brain Research Inst Univ of Chicago 1979–85, prof of neurobiology Univ of Geneva 1985–88, prof of molecular cell biology Univ of London 1988–91; Univ of Sussex: dir Interdisciplinary Research Centre Sussex Centre for Neuroscience 1991–, dir Centre for Computational Neuroscience and Robotics 1996–; author of numerous papers on neuroscience in learned jls; memb: NSPCC, Soc for Neuroscience; *Recreations* classical music, mountaineering, modern poetry, the public understanding of science, triathlons, restoration of classic Lotus, gardens; *Clubs* Club Lotus; *Style*— Prof Michael O'Shea; ✉ 29 Eldred Avenue, Brighton, East Sussex BN1 5EB; School of Life Sciences, University of Sussex, Falmer, Brighton BN1 9QG

O'SHEA, Prof Sir Timothy; kt (2008); s of John Patrick O'Shea, and Elisabeth Hedwig Oberhof; *b* 1949, Hamburg, Germany; *Educ* Univ of Sussex, Univ of Leeds; *m* Prof Eileen Scanlon; 2 s, 2 da; *Career* fndr Computer Assisted Learning Research Gp Open Univ, research fell Dept of Artificial Intelligence Univ of Edinburgh 1974–78, master Birkbeck Coll London 1998–2001, pro-vice-chllr Univ of London 2001–02, princ Univ of Edinburgh 2002–; chair Scottish Inst for Enterprise; chair Bd of Dirs Edinburgh Festival Fringe, chair Newbattle Abbey Coll Tst; memb Governing Cncl Chinese Govt's Confucius Inst Headquarters, convenor Scottish Govt's Further & Higher Educn Sector Oversight Bd for Information & Communications Technol; memb: Fin Servs Advsy Bd Scottish Govt, Sponsor Bd Digital Public Servs, Advsy Bd Inst for Cultural Diplomacy; memb Univ Cncl All-Party Parliamentary Univ Gp, chair Coursera Univ Advsy Bd; FRSE 2004; Self-Improving Teaching Systems (1979), Learning and Teaching with Computers (jtly) 1983, Artificial Intelligence: Tools, Techniques and Applications (jtly) 1984, Advances in Artificial Intelligence (ed, 1985), Intelligent Knowledge-based Systems: An Introduction (co-ed, 1987), Educational Computing (co-ed, 1987), New Directions in Educational Tech (co-ed, 1992); over 100 jl articles; *Clubs* Oyster (Edinburgh), Caledonian; *Style*— Prof Sir Timothy O'Shea; ✉ The Principal's Office, The University of Edinburgh, Old College, South Bridge, Edinburgh EH8 9YL (e-mail principal@ed.ac.uk, website www.ed.ac.uk)

O'SULLIVAN, Bernard Gerard; s of Dr Jeremiah O'Sullivan (d 2000), and Margret Winifred, *née* O'Leary; *b* 3 December 1958, Manchester; *Educ* St Gregory's GS Manchester, Blackpool Coll of FE; *m* 31 March 2001, Clare Gillian, da of Clarence William Street; *Career* commercial photographer; Manchester Royal Eye Hosp 1982–83, Macclesfield Silk Heritage 1984–85, Mac of Manchester 1986–89, Photographic Images 1989–91, prop Inside-Out Photography 1991–; chm BIPP NW Region 2010–13; BIPP Nat Commercial Photographer of the Year 1997, BIPP NW Regn Architectural Award 1989, 1992, 1998, 1999, 2001 and 2004, BIPP NW Regn Photographer of the Year 2003, BIPP Presidential Award for services to the BIPP (National), BIPP NW Regn Industrial Photography Award 2003, BIPP NW Regn Peter Kaye Award for services to the BIPP; Cdre Fairfield Golf and Sailing Club 1994 and 1995; ABIPP 1991; *Recreations* walking, reading, cooking; *Style*— Bernard O'Sullivan, Esq; ✉ 14 Sibson Road, Chorlton-cum-Hardy, Manchester M21 9RH (☏ 0161 860 5769, mobile 07831 344722); Pen-Y-Ghent, Manchester Road, Tideswell, Derbyshire SK17 8LL; Inside-Out Photography, 14 Sibson Road, Chorlton-cum-Hardy, Manchester M21 9RH (☏ 0161 881 3385, e-mail info@insideoutphoto.co.uk, website www.insideoutphoto.co.uk)

O'SULLIVAN, Michael Joseph; CMG (2008); s of Patrick Joseph O'Sullivan, and Mary Elizabeth, *née* Herbert; *b* 21 December 1958; *Educ* St Philip's Coll Birmingham, BNC Oxford (BA), Wolfson Coll Cambridge (MPhil); *m* 17 July 1989, Moira, da of late James McDonald Boyd Grant; 2 da (Kira b 2 Oct 1990, Lara b 1 May 1992), 1 s (James b 23 June 1994); *Career* VSO English teacher Xiangtan China 1982–84; Br Cncl: asst dir Beijing 1987–90, UK corp planner 1991–93, dir S China 1993–95, head of corporate planning 1995–97, policy dir Asia Pacific 1997–2000, dir China 2000–; *Style*— Michael O'Sullivan, Esq, CMG

O'SULLIVAN, Patrick H P; *b* 15 April 1949; *Educ* TCD, LSE; *m* ; 3 c; *Career* audit sr and articled clerk Arthur Andersen & Co Dublin 1971–74; Bank of America NT & SA: vice-pres/section mangr Bank of America London 1975–82, vice-pres/mangr Bank America Int Miami 1982–83, chief fin offr US Wholesale Banking LA 1983–85, pres Bank America World Trade Corp San Francisco 1985, vice-pres Sales and Mktg Germany 1987; gen mangr BA Futures Inc 1987–88, exec dir and fin controller Goldman Sachs 1988–89 (chm New Products Ctee), int md Financial Guaranty Insurance Co 1990–93, head of int banking and structured fin Barclays/BZW 1994–96, chief operating offr BZW 1996–97, chief exec Eagle Star Insurance Co Ltd 1997–98; Zurich Gp: ceo gen insurance and banking 1998–2002, gp fin dir 2002–07, memb Gp Exec Ctee 2002–09, chief growth offr Zurich Financial Services 2007–09, vice-chm Gp Mgmnt Bd; non-exec dir Collins Stewart plc 2006–; memb IASB Working Gp on FRS Accounting, memb Pilgrims Soc; FCA 1985; *Style*— Patrick O'Sullivan, Esq

O'SULLIVAN, Ronnie; OBE (2016); *b* 5 December 1975, Chigwell, Essex; *Career* professional snooker player 1992–; ranked 1 in world 2002–05; scorer fastest professional 147 maximum break (5 minutes 20 seconds) 1997; tournament winner: UK Championship 1993, 1997, 2001 and 2007, British Open 1994, B&H Masters 1995 and 2005, Asian Classic 1996, German Open 1996, Regal Masters 1998, 2000 and 2002, Liverpool Victoria Charity Challenge 1998, Regal Scottish Open 1998, 2000 and 2002, China Open 1999 and 2000, TSN Champions Cup 2000, Embassy World Championship 2001 and 2004, Citywest Irish Masters 2001, 2003 and 2005, Matchroom Premier League 2001, 2002, 2004, 2005, 2006, 2007, 2008 and 2010, Welsh Open 2004 and 2005, Totesport Grand Prix 2004, Saga Insurance Masters 2007 and 2009, NI Trophy 2008, Shanghai Masters 2009; *Recreations* running, watching Arsenal FC; *Clubs* Grove Acad (Romford); *Style*— Ronnie O'Sullivan, Esq, OBE

O'SULLIVAN, Sally Angela; da of Albert James Lorraine (d 1995), of Jersey, Channel Islands, and Joan, *née* Crawley (d 1969); *b* 26 July 1949; *Educ* Ancaster House Sch Bexhill-on-Sea, Trinity Coll Dublin; *m* 2 Oct 1980, Charles Martin Wilson; 1 s (Luke b 18 Dec 1981), 1 da (Lily b 21 Aug 1985), 1 step da (Emma b 18 July 1970); *Career* freelance writer 1971–77, dep ed Women's World 1977–78, freelance writer NY 1978–80; women's ed: Daily Record 1980–81, Sunday Standard 1981–82; ed Options 1982–88, launch ed and originator Country Homes & Interiors 1986; ed: She 1989, Harpers & Queen 1989–91; ed-in-chief: Good Housekeeping 1991–95, Ideal Home, Woman & Home, Homes & Gardens, Country Homes & Interiors and Homes & Ideas 1995–98; launch ed: Living Etc, 25 Beautiful Homes; chief exec Cabal Communications 1998–2003, editorial dir Highbury House 2003–05, chair August Media 2005–; Magazine Ed of the Year 1986 and 1994; memb: Broadcasting Standards Cmmn 1994–2001, Foresight Retail and Consumer Services Panel 1999–2001; non-exec dir: London Transport 1995–2000, Anglia Water 1996–2000, Elizabeth Finn Homes Ltd 2015–; tstee Elizabeth Finn 2010–, dep chair Turn2Us 2014–, memb Ctee Edinburgh Tst 2015–; fell Univ of Central Lancs; *Books* Things My Mother Never Told Me, Looking Good; *Recreations* family, riding, farming; *Style*— Sally O'Sullivan; ✉ August Media, Zetland House, Scrutton Street, London EC2A 4HJ (website www.augustmedia.net)

O'SULLIVAN, Zoë; QC (2015); *Educ* Univ of Oxford (MA); *Career* called to the Bar 1993; *Style*— Ms Zoë O'Sullivan, QC; ✉ One Essex Court, Temple, London EC4Y 9AR

O'TOOLE, Dr Liam Bernard; s of Bernard O'Toole, and Anne, *née* Edwards; *b* 27 November 1960, Liverpool; *Educ* Tiffin Boys' Sch Kingston upon Thames, UC of N Wales Bangor (BSc), Univ of Sheffield (PhD); *m* 25 April 1992, Sarah, *née* Davidson; 2 s (Calum, Joseph), 1 da (Bridie); *Career* post-doctoral research asst Dept of Biology and Pre-clinical Medicine Univ of St Andrews 1987–89, Royal Soc/CNRS exchange fell Univ of Nice 1989, research info offr Br Diabetic Assoc 1990–92; MRC: research prog mangr Physiological Medicine Infections Bd 1992, prog mangr Int Section 1992–94, clinical trials mangr 1994–97, bd prog mangr Molecular and Cellular Medicine Bd 1997–2001; admin dir Nat Cancer Research Inst 2001–04, ceo UK Clinical Research Collaboration 2004–08, ceo Arthritis Research UK 2009–; head Office for Strategic Coordination of Health Research 2007–09; memb: Ctee Social Care (WORD) 2007–, User Panel Ctee EPSRC 2008–09, Exec Cncl Assoc of Medical Research Charities 2012–; author of articles in learned jls; *Recreations* family, rugby, scuba diving, tennis; *Style*— Dr Liam O'Toole; ✉ Arthritis Research UK, 41 Portland Place, London W1B 1QH

OAKENFOLD, Paul; s of Peter Oakenfold, and Sheila Nicholson Oakenfold; *b* 30 August 1967; *Educ* Westminster Tech Coll; *Career* DJ; head: A&R Polo Records, A&R Profile Records; UK rep Def Jam Records; fndr and owner Perfecto Records; club nights incl: Funhouse 1984, The Project 1987, Spectrum 1987, Future 1988, Land Of Oz 1990, Cream, Liverpool (residency) 1997–99, Home (London, residency) 1999; supported U2 on world tour, toured with Happy Mondays, Lenny Kravitz, Madonna and U2; also recorded as: Electra 1988–89, Movement 98 1990, B Real 1993, [State Of] Grace 1993–97, Rise 1994, Perfecto Allstarz 1995, Virus 1995–97, Planet Perfecto 1997–, Perfecto FC 2000, Bunker 2000, Element Four 2000; Biggest DJ in the World Guinness Book of World Records 1999; involved with Nat Literacy Tst, Cancer Research World DJ Day; prodr Madonna single Celebration; scored and contributed music to major Hollywood films incl Swordfish, Matrix Reloaded, Collateral, The Pink Panther, Nobel Son and Nothing Like The Holidays; *Albums* incl: Voyage Into Trance 1995 (re-released 2001), Fluoro 1996, Live In Oslo 1997, Global Underground: New York 1998, Tranceport 1998, Resident: Two Years of Oakenfold at Cream 1999, Perfecto Presents Another World 2000, Travelling 2000, Swordfish: The Album 2001, Perfecto Presents: Paul Oakenfold in Ibiza 2001, Bust A Groove 2002, Bunkka 2002, Perfecto Presents: Great Wall 2003, Creamfields 2004, A Lively Mind 2006, Paul Oakenfold: Greatest hits and remixes 2007, Greatest Remixes 2008, Pop Killer; *Awards* DJ of the Year Dance Acad Awards 2002, BAFTA Award 2002, Grammy Award 2002, Award for Swordfish BMI Film and Television Awards 2002, Int DJ of the Year Dance Acad Awards 2003, DJ of the Year Dance Music Festival 2003; Grammy nominations (Best Electronic Dance Album 2004 (for Creamfields) and 2006 (for A Lively Mind), Best Dance Recording 2009 (for Celebration (prodr)); *Recreations* football; *Style*— Paul Oakenfold, Esq

OAKES, Robin Geoffrey; s of Geoffrey Albert Oakes (d 1999), of Norwich, and Doris Florence, *née* Catton (d 2003); *b* 18 February 1946; *Educ* City of Norwich Sch, Univ of Birmingham (BCom); *m* 16 Aug 1969, Lorna Hazel, da of Albert O'Neill (d 2001); 3 da (Claire Lorna b 8 April 1972, Helen Esther b 1 July 1974, Juliet Elizabeth b 14 Aug 1980); *Career* articled clerk Coopers & Lybrand 1968–71 (later gp audit mangr); Mazars LLP (formerly Neville Russell then Mazars Neville Russell): joined as nat audit and accounts tech mangr 1981–83, sr mangr 1983–84, ptnr 1985–99, sr ptnr London regn 1999–2006, ret 2007; conslt and non-exec dir 2007–; seminar speaker and author of various articles; FCA 1979 (ACA 1971); *Books* An Industry and Accounting Guide: Insurance Brokers (1990, 4 edn 2006); *Recreations* charity trustee, church leadership, family, garden; *Style*— Robin Oakes, Esq; ✉ e-mail robin_oakes@hotmail.com

OAKESHOTT OF SEAGROVE BAY, Baron (Life Peer UK 2000), of Seagrove Bay in the County of Isle of Wight; Matthew Alan; s of Keith Robertson Oakeshott, CMG (d 1974), of Horsham, W Sussex, and Jill Oakeshott, *née* Clutterbuck (d 2013); *b* 10 January 1947; *Educ* Charterhouse, UC Oxford, Nuffield Coll Oxford (scholar, MA); *m* 1976, Prof Philippa Poulton, MD, da of Dr Christopher Poulton; 2 s (Joseph Andrew b 1979, Luke Christopher b 1985), 1 da (Rachel Jill b 1982); *Career* economist Kenya Miny of Fin and Econ Planning 1968–70, special advsr to Rt Hon Roy Jenkins, MP 1972–76, investment mangr then dir Warburg Investment Mgmnt Ltd 1976–81, investment mangr Courtaulds Pension Fund 1981–85, fndr and jt md OLIM Ltd 1986–2012, chm OLIM Property Ltd 2012–; jt investment dir Value & Income Tst plc 1986–; city cnclr (Lab) Oxford 1972–76; Parly candidate: (Lab) Horsham and Crawley Oct 1974, (SDP/Lib Alliance) Cambridge 1983; memb SDP Nat Ctee 1981–82; a Lib Dem Treasy spokesman House of Lords 2001–11, Lib Dem Pensions spokesman House of Lords 2002–10, chm Business Advsy Gp to Rt Hon Vince Cable, MP, *qv*, 2010–14 (resigned Lib Dems 2014); govr Nat Inst of Economic and Social Research, former tstee Overseas Devpt Inst,; *Books* By-Elections in British Politics (contrib, 1973); *Recreations* music, elections, supporting Arsenal; *Style*— The Rt Hon the Lord Oakeshott of Seagrove Bay; ✉ House of Lords, London SW1A 0PW (Twitter @oakeshottm)

OAKHAM, Archdeacon of; *see:* Painter, Ven David Scott

OAKLEY, Christopher John; CBE (1999); s of Ronald Oakley (d 1965), of Tunbridge Wells, Kent, and Joyce Barbara, *née* Tolhurst (d 1996); *b* 11 November 1941; *Educ* The Skinners Sch Tunbridge Wells; *m* 1 (m dis 1986), Linda Margaret, da of William John Edward Viney, of Tunbridge Wells, Kent; 1 s, 2 da; m 2 (m dis 2003), Moira Jean, da of H Martingale; 1 s, 2 step da; m 3, Lisa, da of J Hanson, of Ottery St Mary, Devon; 1 step da; *Career* dep ed Yorkshire Post 1976–81, ed Lancashire Evening Post 1981–83; dir: Lancashire Evening Post Ltd 1982–83, Liverpool Echo, Liverpool Daily Post and Echo Ltd 1983–89; ed-in-chief/md Birmingham Post and Mail Ltd 1989–91, gp chief exec Midland Independent Newspapers Ltd 1991–97, regnl md Mirror Gp Newspapers 1997–98, chief exec Regional Independent Media 1998–2002, chm and chief exec HRM Partnership Ltd 2002–04, chm and chief exec MEF Comm V (formerly Comm VA MEF), chm Newsco-Insider Ltd 2002–14, chm Chapter Eight Ltd 2009–14, chm Royal Armouries Trading and Enterprises Ltd 2011–12; pres: Guild of British Newspaper Editors 1990–91, Newspaper Soc 1997–98; patron Hollybank Tst 1999, tstee Royal Armouries 2002–10, tstee TV for the Environment 2010; fell Univ of Central Lancs 1998; *Publications* What do We Mean By Local? (contrib, 2012, 2 edn 2013); *Style*— Christopher Oakley, Esq, CBE; ✉ MEF Comm V, Dreve des Pins 40, B-1420 Braine-l'Alleud, Belgium (e-mail ochris829@aol.com)

OAKLEY, Eric; *Career* gp chief exec Haynes Publishing Gp plc; *Style*— Eric Oakley, Esq; ✉ Haynes Publishing Group plc, Sparkford, Yeovil, Somerset BA22 7JJ

OAKLEY, Geoffrey Michael Whittall; s of Harold Whittall Oakley, of St Martins, Guernsey, and Hazel Louise, *née* Peters; *b* 22 April 1953; *Educ* Oundle; *m* 3 April 1987, Joanna Helen, da of Fred Morgan Hodges, of Harborne, Birmingham; 2 da (Georgina Louise b 1987, Olivia Sarah Helen b 1990), 1 s (Nicholas Frederick James b 1989); *Career* ptnr Margetts & Addenbrooke 1977–86; dir: National Investment Group plc 1986–90, Capel-Cure Myers Capital Management 1990–98, Portway Investments Ltd (formerly J A Main) 1996; non-exec dir: Aero Needles Group plc 1976–84, Margetts Financial Services Ltd (now Margetts Hldgs Ltd) 1985; pres Br Jewellery and Giftware Fedn 2003–04; govr Birmingham Royal Inst for the Blind, tstee John Feeney Charitable Tst; CISI (memb Stock Exchange 1976), memb Int Stock Exchange 1986; *Recreations* theatre, local history, the arts; *Style*— Geoffrey Oakley, Esq; ✉ St Mary's Close, 10 St Mary's Road, Harborne, Birmingham B17 0HA (☏ 0121 427 7150); Portway Investments Ltd, Newland House, 137–139 Hagley Road, Edgbaston, Birmingham B16 8UA (☏ 0121 454 2066)

OAKLEY, Michael Dudley; s of Lt Cdr (George) Eric Oakley, RN (d 1996), of Clifton-on-Teme, Worcs, and Dr Margaret Dorothy Dudley, *née* Brown (d 1993); *b* 5 November 1944; *Educ* Oundle, Coll of Law; *m* 7 Oct 1967, Jennifer Catherine, da of Richard Percy Lazenby (d 1987), of Bulmer, York; 2 da (Catherine b 2 Nov 1969, Victoria b 6 Nov 1971), 1 s (William b 3 Oct 1973); *Career* slr; former ptnr Oakleys, former conslt Crombie

Wilkinson; HM sr coroner N Yorks E 1979–, NP 1985–, chm Appeals Tbnl 1992–2016, immigration judge 2001–16; pres Coroners Soc of Eng and Wales 2004–05; lay memb Gen Synod C of E representing Diocese of York 1980–95; memb: Working Party on Ordination of Women to the Priesthood, Cathedral Statutes Cmmn, various legislative revision ctees, panel of chm of Gen Synod; govr Queen Margaret's Sch (York) Ltd; pres Yorkshire Law Soc 1991–92; Master Merchant Taylors' Co of York 1998–99; *Recreations* tennis, golf, fishing, gardening; *Clubs* Army and Navy; *Style*— Michael Oakley, Esq; ✉ Rose Cottage, Oswaldkirk, York YO62 5XT (☎ 01439 788339, fax 01439 788037, mob 07860 789957, e-mail moakleyrosecott@aol.com)

OAKLEY, Robin Francis Leigh; OBE (2001); s of Joseph Henry Oakley, of East Molesey, Surrey, and Alice Barbara Oakley; *b* 20 August 1941; *Educ* Wellington, BNC Oxford (MA); *m* 4 June 1966, Carolyn Susan Germaine, da of late Leonard Rumball; 1 da (Annabel Louise Germaine b 19 July 1971), 1 s (Alexander Guy Leigh b 12 Aug 1973); *Career* political corr Liverpool Daily Post 1967–70 (feature writer then sub ed 1964–67), Crossbencher columnist then asst ed Sunday Express 1970–79, political ed and asst ed Now! magazine 1979–81, asst ed Daily Mail 1981–86, political ed The Times 1986–92, political ed BBC 1992–2000, European political ed CNN 2000–08, contrib CNN 2008–; racing columnist The Spectator 1995–, racing writer for various pubns incl FT; lectr and after dinner speaker; *Publications* Valley of the Racehorse (2000), Inside Track (2001), Frankincense and More – The Barry Hills Biography (2010), The Cheltenham Festival – A Centenary History (2011), Clive Brittain, the Smiling Pioneer (2012), Britain and Ireland's Top 100 Horses of All Time (2012), Tales From The Turf (2013); *Recreations* theatre, horse racing, swimming, bird watching; *Clubs* RAC; *Style*— Robin Oakley, Esq, OBE; ✉ 24 Bridge End, Dorchester-on-Thames, Wallingford, Oxfordshire OX10 7JP (☎ 01865 341441, e-mail robin.oakley278@gmail.com)

OATES, Baron (Life Peer UK 2015), of Denby Grange in the County of West Yorkshire Jonathan (Jonny); s of John Oates, and Sylvia Mary Harris; *b* 28 December 1969, London; *m* 24 June 2006, David Hill; *Career* dir Bell Pottinger 2004–07 and 2008–09, dir of policy and communications Lib Dems 2007–08, dir of election communications 2009–10, dep dir of communications 10 Downing Street 2010, COS to Rt Hon Nick Clegg, MP, *qv* 2010–15; *Recreations* cinema, reading, travel, walking, poetry; *Style*— The Lord Oates; ✉ House of Lords, London SW1A 0PW (Twitter oates_jonny)

OATES, Laurence Campbell; CB (2006); s of Stanley Oates (d 1995), and Norah, *née* Meek (d 1984); *b* 14 May 1946; *Educ* Beckenham and Penge GS, Univ of Bristol (LLB); *m* 26 Oct 1968, Brenda Lilian, da of John Trevor Hardwick, of Stourbridge, W Midlands; 1 da (Marianne Louise b 1972), 1 s (Adrian Laurence b 1974); *Career* called to the Bar Middle Temple 1968, in practice 1969–76; legal advsr Dept of Employment involved in industrial relations law reform 1977–80, legal sec Law Offrs' Dept advising on civil and constitutional law 1981–84, asst treasy slr Dept of Transport advising on civil aviation law 1984–88, under sec and head Legal and Law Reform Gp Lord Chllr's Dept 1989–92, circuit admin Midland & Oxford Circuit 1992–94, assoc head Policy Gp Lord Chllr's Dept 1995–96, dir Magistrates' Courts Gp Lord Chllr's Dept 1996–99, official slr to the Supreme Court 1999–2006 (public tstee 2001–06), lay advsr Royal Coll of Paediactrics and Child Health 2006–12; tstee Royal Hosp for Neuro-disability Grange Centre and Just Advocacy 2007–; govr Woking Coll 2007–, tstee Citizens Advice Woking and Citizens Advice Surrey 2014–, dir Healthwatch Surrey 2015–; *Publications* Court of Protection Practice (jtly, 2009, 2 edn 2010); *Recreations* music, golf; *Style*— Laurence Oates, Esq, CB; ✉ Cedar Waters, White Rose Lane, Woking, Surrey GU22 7JY

OATES, Roger Kendrew; s of William Oates (d 1987), and Mary Dorothy, *née* Mayne (d 1957); *b* 25 June 1946; *Educ* Thirsk Sch, York Sch of Art, Farnham Sch of Art (DipAD), Kidderminster Coll; *m* 31 July 1976, Fay Morgan Oates, *qv*, da of Phillip Hughes Morgan; 1 s (Daniel Morgan Oates b 25 Jan 1979); *Career* textile designer; set up own studio Ledbury Herefords 1971–75, dir and chm Craftsman's Mark Ltd 1971–75, lectr at numerous colls of art England and Aust 1971–75; Morgan Oates partnership at The House in the Yard Ledbury 1975–86, Morgan & Oates Co Ltd 1986–97 (designing for own label and clients incl Ralph Lauren, Christian Dior, Sonia Rykiel, Donna Karan and Laura Ashley); sr ptnr Roger Oates Design Associates partnership 1987–98, dir Roger Oates Design Co Ltd 1998–; work in exhibitions incl: The Craftsman's Art (V&A Museum) 1973, The House in the Yard – Textiles from the Workshop of Fay Morgan & Roger Oates (Welsh Arts Council Cardiff and tour) 1978, Tufted Rugs (Environment London) 1980, Texstyles (Crafts Council London and tour) 1984–85, Design Awards (Lloyd's Building London) 1988; awarded: USA ROSCOE Award 1984, British Design Award 1988, Duke of Edinburgh's certificate for services to design, Weavers Co Silver Medal 2011 (with Fay Morgan Oates); contrib various TV prodns; FRSA; *Style*— Roger Oates, Esq; ✉ Roger Oates Design Company Ltd, The Long Barn, Eastnor, Ledbury, Herefordshire HR8 1EL (☎ 01531 632718, fax 01531 631361, e-mail director@rogeroates.com, website www.rogeroates.com); Roger Oates Design Company Ltd, 1 Munro Terrace, Cheyne Walk, London SW10 0DL (☎ 020 7351 2288, fax 020 7351 6841)

OATES, Seamus; s of Tom Oates, and Jennifer, *née* Coles; *b* 7 July 1964, Bristol; *Educ* BSc, PGCE, NPQH, Nat Ldr of Educn (NLE); *m* 7 Dec 1992, Joanna, *née* Restall; 1 s (Tom b 21 Mar 1991), 1 da (Lucy b 29 Mar 1995); *Career* teacher 1986–95, dir Kingwood CLC 1999–2001, headteacher Bridge Academy 2001–10, exec headteacher and ceo Tri-Borough Alternative Provision (TBAP) Multi-Academy Tst 2010–; memb Youth Justice Bd, dir The Family Sch, chair DFE AP Reference Gp; ASCR; *Recreations* gardening, reading, travel, walking, kitesurfing; *Style*— Seamus Oates, Esq; ✉ TBAP Trust, The Bridge AP Academy, Finlay St, London SW6 6HB (☎ 020 7610 8340, e-mail head@tbap.org.uk, website www.tbap.org.uk, Twitter @headTBAP)

OATLEY, Joe; *Educ* Univ of Cambridge (MA); *m* Jane; 1 da (Sophie), 1 s (Patrick); *Career* Mercer Mgmnt Consultancy 1990–95, corporate devpt exec Spirent plc 1995–97, md Penny & Giles 1997–2003, md Weir Strachan & Henshaw 2004–07, chief exec Hamworthy plc 2007–; *Recreations* tennis, triathlon; *Style*— Joe Oatley, Esq; ✉ Hamworthy plc, Fleets Corner, Poole, Dorset BH17 0JT

OATLEY, Dr Neil Vernon; s of Ronald Stanley Oatley, of Istead Rise, Kent, and Audrey Helen, *née* Munday; *b* 12 June 1954; *Educ* Gravesend GS, Loughborough Univ (BTech, DTech); *m* 7 July 2001, Peta Geraldine Brown; *Career* race car designer (Formula One); engr Williams Grand Prix Engineering 1977–84, designer Formula One Race Car Engineering 1984–86; McLaren International: designer 1986–, chief designer 1989–2002, exec dir of engrg 2002–06, dir of design and devpt 2006–; *Recreations* music (rock and classical), motorcycling, reading; *Style*— Dr Neil Oatley; ✉ Culvers, Littleworth Road, Seale, Surrey GU10 1JN (☎ 01252 782210); McLaren Racing Ltd, McLaren Technology Centre, Chertsey Road, Woking, Surrey GU21 4YH (☎ 01483 261146, fax 01483 215572, e-mail neil.oatley@mclaren.com, website www.mclaren.com)

OBERTELLI, Ricci; *Educ* Hotel Mgmnt and Catering trg course Italy; *Career* hotelier; extensive experience in London including Claridge's, The Savoy and The Ritz, subsequently various mgmnt positions rising to sales and mktg dir Four Seasons Inn on the Park; The Dorchester: mangr rising to dir and gen mangr 1986–95 (responsible for complete refurbishment 1988–90), dir of operations Dorchester Gp 1997–, global devpt dir 2004–; dep nat delegate for GB Euro Hotel Mangrs Assoc; Master Innholder; memb: Chaîne des Rotisseurs, Réunion des Gastronomes, Ordre des Coteaux de Champagne, Acad of Food and Wine Serv, Inst of Dirs; FCIMA; *Style*— Ricci Obertelli, Esq; ✉ Dorchester Collection, 3 Tilney Street, London W1K 1JB (☎ 020 7629 4848, fax 020 7355 4649, e-mail robertelli@dorchestergrouphotels.com, website www.dorchestercollection.com)

OBHOLZER, Dr Anton Meinhard; s of Anton Max Karl Obholzer (d 1985), of Cape Town, South Africa, and Eva Maria Clarissa, *née* von Hartungen (d 1985); *b* 16 November 1938; *Educ* Christian Brothers' Coll Kimberley, Univ of Stellenbosch (BSc), Univ of Cape Town (MB ChB, DPM); *m* 16 Feb 1963, Annabel Harriet Barbara, da of Dr Christopher Jarvis Molteno; 1 da (Clarissa Judith b 9 Dec 1966), 2 s (Anton Manfred b 29 June 1968, Rupert John b 27 March 1970); *Career* conslt child psychiatrist Child Guidance Trg Centre 1975–80; conslt psychiatrist Tavistock Clinic 1980– (chm 1985–93), chief exec Tavistock and Portman NHS Tst 1993–; hon prof: Univ of Vienna 1994, Univ of Klagenfurt 1994, Univ of Innsbruck 1994; memb Br Psycho Analytical Soc, FRCPsych (memb Cncl 1991–97); *Books* with M Baraitser: Cape Country Furniture (1978), Town Furniture of the Cape (1985), The Cape House and its Interior (1987), Cape Antique Furniture (2004); The Unconscious at Work (ed with Vega Roberts, 1994); *Style*— Dr Anton Obholzer; ✉ Tavistock and Portman NHS Trust, 120 Belsize Lane, London NW3 5BA (☎ 020 7435 7111, fax 020 7447 3709)

OBOLENSKY, Prince Nikolai (Nick); Prince; s of Prince Michael Obolensky (d 1995), of Madrid, Spain, and Anne, *née* Helbronner (d 1980); descends from Rurik who conquered Russia in 860s; *b* 7 June 1956; *Educ* Harrow, RMA Sandhurst, Univ of Durham (BA), IMEDE Lausanne (MBA, valedictorian); *m* 1987, Charlotte Isabella, *née* Sharpe; 2 da (Isabella b 28 Oct 1993, Larissa b 7 Sept 1995), 1 s (Alexei b 24 Nov 1990); *Career* Maj 17/21 Lancers 1986– (cmmnd 1976, Lt 1978, Capt 1981), ret 1988; Ernst & Young CAs: conslt 1989, sr conslt 1990, managing conslt 1991; Gateway/Somerfield Foodmarkets: exec co-ordinator of change prog 1991, launch dir of new fascias 1992, devpt dir 1993; md Rurikof & Co 1993–98, ptnr Harding & Yorke 1994–96, UK ptnr The Vth Dimension Partnership 1996–; devpt dir The Centre for Tomorrow's Co 1995–97; ceo: Tomorrow's Co Enterprise Ltd 1997–2000, Tomorrow's Co Ltd 2000–01, Musikline Ltd 2001–05, W2 Green Energy (formerly C&C Green Energy) 2008– (chm 2009–10), Complex Adaptive Leadership Ltd 2012–; ceo and chm Your Release Ltd 2001–05; chm Project Ulysses Ltd 2009–13; ptnr Green Earth Partnership 2010–13; assoc prof of leadership Nyenrode Univ until 2006, Netherlands Business Sch 1999– (MBA Professor of the Year 2001–02 and 2002–03), visiting prof for Leadership INSEAD France 2002–05, visiting prof Erasmus Univ 2010–12, visiting prof CEDEP 2013–, visiting prof for leadership IMD Business Sch Switzerland 2015–; fell Centre for Mgmnt Devpt London Business Sch 2003–05; hon fell Centre for Leadership Studies Univ of Exeter; FCMC, FRGS, FRSA, MInstD; *Books* Practical Business Re-engineering: Tools and Techniques for Achieving Effective Change (1994), A Strategy for the Ecu (jtly 1990), Management Consultancy – a handbook for best practice (jtly, 1998), RSA: On Work and Leadership (jtly, 2001), Chaos Leadership & Polyarchy (2008), Complex Adaptive Leadership – Embracing Paradox and Uncertainty (2010, 2 edn 2014), Leading Complex Projects (2013); *Recreations* mountaineering, surfing, skiing, scuba diving; *Style*— Prince Nikolai Obolensky; ✉ c/o National Westminster Bank, 315 Station Road, Harrow, Middlesex HA1 2AD (fax 01225 430534, e-mail nick@obolensky.com)

OBORN, Peter Mill; s of Gerald Oborn, and Pauline, *née* Scott (d 2001); *b* 27 October 1955; *Educ* Melville Coll Edinburgh, Edinburgh Coll of Art/Heriot-Watt Univ (BArch, MArch); *Partner* Amanda Reekie; *Career* architect; Abbey Hanson Rowe: regnl mangr Manama Bahrain 1986–87, estab London office 1988, fixed share ptnr 1992–94, then equity ptnr; projects incl: major housing estate refurbishments incl Mozart and Wellington Estates Acton, numerous lottery sports projects, new HQ National Bank of Bahrain, Asprey refurbishment New Bond St; currently vice-pres int RIBA; memb Sports Cncl Panel of Expert Advisers for the Lottery Sports Fund; also involved with: Community Bldg in Britain, Permaculture Assoc; RIBA, ARIAS; *Recreations* horse riding; *Clubs* Arts; *Style*— Peter Oborn, Esq; ✉ RIBA, 66 Portland Place, London W1B 1AD

OCEAN, Humphrey; s of Capt Maurice Erdeswick Butler-Bowdon, OBE (d 1984), and Anne, *née* Darlington (d 1999); *b* 22 June 1951; *Educ* Ampleforth, Canterbury Coll of Art (BA); *m* 3 March 1982, Miranda, da of Dr Michael Argyle, of Oxford; 2 da (Ruby b 1982, Beatrice b 1986); *Career* artist; prof of perspective Royal Acad of Arts 2012–; presenter Life Class: Today's Nude (Artangel and Channel 4) 2009; Imperial Tobacco Portrait Award 1982, Wellcome Sci-Art Award 1998; hon fell Kent Inst of Art and Design (KIAD); Hon Dr Canterbury Christ Church Univ 2012, Hon Dr Univ of Kent 2015; RA 2004; *Solo Exhibitions* incl: Nat Portrait Gallery 1984, Ferens Art Gallery Hull 1986–87, Double-Portrait (Tate Gallery Liverpool) 1991–92, urbasuburba (Whitworth Art Gallery Manchester and tour) 1997–98, The Painter's Eye (Nat Portrait Gallery) 1999, how's my driving (Dulwich Picture Gallery) 2003, Sidney Cooper Gallery Univ of Christ Church Canterbury 2009, Jesus Coll Cambridge 2011, A handbook of modern life (Nat Portrait Gallery) 2013; *Work in Collections* British Council, Imperial War Museum, Scot Nat Portrait Gallery, Ferens Art Gallery, Southwark Collection, Nat Portrait Gallery, Wolverhampton Art Gallery, Royal Library, Nat Maritime Museum, Whitworth Art Gallery Manchester, Victoria & Albert Museum, Pallant House Gallery Chichester; *Books* The Ocean View (1982), Big Mouth: The Amazon Speaks (1990), Zeebrugge by Humphrey Ocean (2002), A handbook of modern life (2013); *Style*— Humphrey Ocean, Esq, RA; ✉ 22 Marmora Road, London SE22 0RX (☎ 020 8693 8387, studio ☎ 020 8761 7400, website www.humphreyocean.com)

ODAM, Prof George Neville; s of George Odam (d 1979), of Beccles, Suffolk, and Muriel, *née* Tawell (d 1964); *b* 30 September 1938; *Educ* Sir John Leman Sch, Univ of Manchester (BA), Univ of London (Music Teachers' Cert), Univ of Southampton (BMus, MPhil); *m* 15 April 1963, Penelope Anne Lloyd, da of Oliver Lloyd Smith (d 1979), of Beccles, Suffolk; 1 s (Timothy b 1964), 1 da (Joanna b 1966); *Career* composer; Totton GS Hants 1961–65, Bath Spa Univ (formerly Bath Coll of Higher Educn) 1966– (prof of music educn 1993–99); GSMD: research fell in teaching and learning 1999–, head of research and staff devpt 2003–07, ret 2007; compositions: Cantata for Christmas 1967, Angry Arrow 1969, St George and the Dragon 1970, Tutankhamun 1971, Inca 1975, Robin Hood 1978, Peredur (opera) 1979, Concerto for piano and timpani 1980, Baba Yaga 1984, Morning Service in G 2001, Evening Service in F 2002, Humira Mass 2011, In Love with God: anthem 2011, Light Invisible: Cantata 2015, Organ Sonata No. 1 The Four Elements 2015, Year Songs 2015, Granada Dreaming for solo guitar 2015; fndr and conductor Nat Scouts and Guides Symphony Orch, chm UK Cncl for Music Educn and Trg 1988–91, vice-chm SEAC Music Ctee, chm MusicSpace UK 2004–; memb: ISM (warden of MES 1986–87), SW Arts Bd 1994– (chm Educn Steering Gp Ctee 1988–94); chm Nat Music & Disability Info Serv 1991–94; Music Industries Assoc Award for Outstanding Servs to Music Educn 1994; FGSM 2007; *Books* Silver Burdett and Ginn Music Books 1–4 (1989), The Sounding Symbol (1995), The Sounds of Music Books 1–7 (1996), Seeking the Soul: The Music of Alfred Schnittke (ed, 2001), Britten: Voice and Piano (preface and ed, 2003), The Reflective Conservatoire (ed, 2005), Gustav Mahler: new insights into his life, times and work (ed, 2007), The Musician's Body: a maintenance manual for peak performance (jtly, 2007), Landscapes of the Mind: The Music of John McCabe (composter and ed, 2008); CD: The Airmen: songs of Martin Shaw; *Recreations* drawing and painting, computer graphics and DTP, poetry, travel; *Style*— Prof George Odam; ✉ e-mail georgeodam@mac.com, website www.george-odam.co.uk, Twitter @georgeodam

ODDIE, Bill; *b* 7 July 1941; *Educ* Halesowen GS, King Edward's Sch Birmingham, Pembroke Coll Cambridge; *m* 1, Jean Hart; 2 da (Kate b 1968, Bonnie b 1971); m 2, Laura Beaumont; 1 da (Rose b 1985); *Career* writer and performer; memb: cncl RSPB, Wildfowl and

Wetland's Tst, The Worldwide Fund for Nature; pres Northumberland Wildlife Tst; rep: Birdlife Int, Friends of The Earth, Plantlife, RSNC; *Theatre* as writer/performer incl: Cambridge Circus (transfered from Cambridge Footlights to London, NZ, USA), TW3 (touring co); as performer incl: Cousin Kevin in Tommy, Koko in Mikado (ENO), Childrens Variety Show (London Palladium); one pantomime as performer, one as writer; *Television* as writer/performer incl: TW3 (first appearances), The Braden Beat, BBC3, Twice A Fortnight (first series, co-writer Graeme Garden, *qv*, BBC), Then Broaden Your Mind (with Graeme Garden and Tim Brooke-Taylor, *qv*), The Goodies (co-writer Graeme Garden, eight series, 3 specials, twice winner Silver Rose of Montreux), From the Top (Central); with co-writer Laura Beaumont: The Bubblegum Brigade (HTV); as writer incl: scripts for That Was the Week That Was, numerous sketches for TW3, Ronnie Barker, Tommy Cooper etc; with Graeme Garden incl: Doctor In the House (50 episodes), At Large, The Astronauts (Central), Jim Henson's Animal Show (scripts and songs); as presenter incl: The Saturday Banana (Southern), Time for a Story (Granada), Fax (3 series, BBC), Ask Oddie (2 series, HTV), Festival (BBC), SpringWatch (BBC), AutumnWatch (BBC), various SpringWatch specials; as narrator incl: Tubby the Tuba, The Snowman, Peter and the Wolf; numerous voice overs for commercials and animations; Wildlife progs incl: Oddie in Paradise (Papua New Guinea), The Great Bird Race, The Bird Business, For the Birds (USA cable), Bird in the Nest (BBC), Birding with Bill Oddie (three series, 1997, 1998 and 2000), Bill Oddie Goes Wild (three series, BBC), Bill Oddie's How to Watch Wildlife (BBC), Springwatch with Bill Oddie (BBC); guest appearance The Detectives (with Jasper Carrott and Robert Powell); *Radio* I'm Sorry I'll Read That Again (co-writer Graeme Garden, over 100 shows, BBC); as presenter incl: Breakaway (BBC), numerous shows on Jazz FM and GLR; *Recordings* with The Goodies: 5 top ten singles incl The Funky Gibbon, The Inbetweenies (both silver), 3 albums (1 silver); From the Top; *Books* as writer, illustrator and photographer incl: Bill Oddie's Little Black Bird Book, Gone Birding, Follow that Bird, Gripping Yarns, Bird Watching with Bill Oddie, Bird Watching for Under Tens, Bill Oddie's Colouring Guides, Bill Oddie's How to Watch Wildlife; numerous articles for magazine and newspapers; numerous Goodies Books with Graeme Garden and Tim Brooke-Taylor; with Laura Beaumont The Toilet Book (UK and worldwide); One Flew into the Cuckoo's Egg (autobiography, 2008); *Recreations* sports, drums, percussion, saxophone, music; *Style—* Bill Oddie; ✉ c/o All Electric Productions, PO Box 1805, Andover, Hampshire SP10 3ZN (☎ 01264 771726, fax 01264 771725)

ODDIE, Christopher Peter; s of late Alfred Birtwistle Oddie, of Lancs, and late Elsie Mary, *née* Bateman; *b* 26 September 1948; *Educ* King Edward VII Sch Lytham; *m* 12 June 1971, Gail, da of late Maj Horace George Ablett; 2 s (Simon Christopher b 19 Sept 1975, Matthew David b 1 July 1979); *Career* CA 1978; articled clerk T & H P Bee Preston 1967–72; ptnr: Tyson Westall CAs Lancs 1973–76, Grant Thornton CAs 1976–86; sr ptnr Lonsdale and Partners CAs Lancaster and branches 1986–2005; chm Inspiration Marine Gp Ltd 2005–; FICA; *Recreations* sailing; *Clubs* Royal Southern Yacht Club; *Style—* Christopher Oddie, Esq; ✉ Inspiration Marine Group, Chandlery Building, Hamble Point Marina, Hamble, Southampton SO31 4NB (e-mail chris@inspirationmarine.co.uk)

ODDIE, Elaine Anne; OBE (2003); da of Brian John Cory, of Hartley, Kent, and Molly Cory; *b* 11 February 1955; *Educ* Gravesend Girls' Sch, King's Coll Cambridge (MA); *m* 3 July 1976 (m dis), Alan James Oddie; *Career* articled clerk Brebner Allen & Trapp 1976–79, fin accountant Yardley International Ltd 1979–82; ptnr Mason Charlesworth & Co 1982–89, ptnr Morison Stoneham 1989–2000, dir Tenon 2000–03, ptnr NSO Associates LLP 2003–; memb N Thames Gas Consumers' Cncl 1981–84, pres S Essex Soc of Chartered Accountants 1990–91, pres Chelmsford Chamber of Commerce 1997–99 and 2001–03, chair Essex Chambers of Commerce 2003–; memb Cncl ICAEW 1991–2001, chair Eastern England Industrial Devpt Bd 2000–04; tstee Helen Rollason HEAL Cancer Charity 2004–; govr Chelmsford Coll 2001–; memb Exec Ctee Squash Rackets Assoc 1994–2002, treas Road Runners Club 2003–; FCA 1989 (ACA 1979); *Recreations* squash, running; *Style—* Ms Elaine Oddie, OBE; ✉ 7 Bellway Court, Grosvenor Road, Westcliff-on-Sea, Essex SS0 8EP; NSO Associates LLP, 75 Springfield Road, Chelmsford, Essex CM2 6JB (☎ 01245 455400, fax 01245 494177, e-mail elaine.oddie@nso-associates.co.uk)

ODDY, Jason Matthew; s of Noel Carter Oddy, and Joy Oddy; *Educ* Marlborough, UCL (MA); *Children* 2 da (Vita b 1 Jan 2009, Madeleine b 9 July 2012), 1 s (Mac b 9 July 2012); *Career* photographer and writer: The Independent, Modern Painters, Art Review, The AA Files, The Observer, Aperture (US), Portfolio, Nest (US); *Solo Exhibitions* The Henry Peacock Gallery London 1999 and 2000, Architectural Assoc 2000, Yossi Milo Gallery NY 2000, The Photographers' Gallery London 2001, 2003 and 2006, Royal Pump Rooms Museum Leamington Spa 2002, Galerie Serieuze Zaken Amsterdam 2002, Frederieke Taylor Gallery NY 2002 and 2004, Gallerie Vassie Amsterdam 2005, Univ of Herts Galleries 2007, Catalyst Arts Belfast 2007, Camera 16 Milan 2011, James Hockey Gallery Farnham 2013, Smiths Row Bury St Edmunds 2014, Gallery 52 Brazilian Embassy London 2016; *Group Exhibitions* Paris Photo 2002, 2003 & 2005, Sperture Fndn NY 2007, Flowers East London 2007, Photo 50 London 2007, The Milan Triennale 2014, Tropenmusem Amsterdam 2015, MuCEM Marseilles 2016; *Publications* featured in: The Independent, Modern Painters, Art Review, The AA Files, The Observer, Portfolio, Aperture (US), Newsweek (US), Time Magazine (US), Vanity Fair (US), Nest (US), The NY Times Magazine (US), D la Repubblica (Italy), L'Espresso (Italy), Le Monde 2 (France), Citizen K (France), Vrij Nederland (The Netherlands), El Semenal (Spain); *Style—* Jason Oddy, Esq; ✉ Gallery Vassie, Langestraat 47, 1015 AK Amsertdam, The Netherlands (☎ 07903 089654, e-mail info@jasonoddy.com, website www.jasonoddy.com)

ODELL, Prof Peter Randon; s of Frank James Odell (d 1978), of Coalville, Leics, and Grace Edna, *née* Randon (d 1954); *b* 1 July 1930; *Educ* King Edward VII GS Coalville, Univ of Birmingham (BA, PhD, W A Cadbury Prize, univ grad scholarship), Fletcher Sch of Law and Diplomacy Tufts Univ (AM); *m* 17 Aug 1957, Jean Mary, da of Ewan John McKintosh (d 1991), of Isle of Man; 2 s (Nigel Peter b 1958, Mark John b 1965), 2 da (Deborah Grace b 1960, Susannah Mary b 1967); *Career* RAF Educn Offr 1954–57, Flying Offr 1954–56, Flt Lt 1956–57; economist Shell International Petroleum Company Ltd 1958–61, sr lectr in economic geography LSE 1966–68 (lectr 1961–66), prof of economic geography Netherlands Sch of Economics 1968–73; Erasmus Univ Rotterdam: prof of economic geography 1973–81, prof of int energy studies 1982–91, prof emeritus 1992–; visiting prof: Coll of Europe Bruges 1984–90, LSE 1985–2001, Univ of Plymouth 1997–2003; Killam visiting fell Univ of Calgary 1989, visiting scholar Univ of Cambridge 1996–2000; special advsr to Sec of State for Energy 1977–79, specialist advsr House of Commons Select Ctee 2001–02; Int Assoc for Energy Econs Prize for Outstanding Contrib to Energy Economics 1991, Royal Scottish Geographical Soc Centenary Medal 1993, OPEC Biennial Award for lifetime achievement as an energy analyst 2006; Euro Parly candidate (SLD) Suffolk and SE Cambs 1989; memb Int Assoc for Energy Economics, RIIA 1962; FRGS 1954, FEI 1973, FRSA 1977; *Books* An Economic Geography of Oil (1963), Natural Gas in Western Europe – A Case Study in the Economic Geography of Energy Resources (1969), Oil and World Power (1970, 8 edn 1986), Economies and Societies in Latin America – A Geographical Interpretation (with D A Preston, 1973, 2 edn 1978), The North Sea Oil Province: A Simulation of its Development 1969–2029 (with K E Rosing, 1975), The West European Energy Economy – The Case for Self-Sufficiency (1976), The Pressures of Oil – A Strategy for Economic Revival (with L Vallenilla, 1978), The Future of Oil (with K E Rosing, 1980, 2 edn 1983), The International Oil Industry (with J Rees, 1987), Global and Regional Energy Supplies (1991), Energy in Europe: Resources and Choices (1998), Fossil Fuel Resources in the 21st Century (1999), International Oil and Gas, Crises and Controversies 1961–2000 vol 1: Global Issues (2001) International Oil and Gas, Crises and Controversies 1961–2000 vol 2: Europe's Entanglement (2002), Why Carbon Fuels will Dominate the 21st Century's Energy Economy (2004), Energy Resources: a Long-term Production Scenario (2009), Managing the UK's Remaining Oil and Gas Resources: a Future Role for the State (2010), An Energetic Life: the Memoirs of Peter R Odell from 1930–2010 (2010), An Economic Geography of Oil (2013), Oil and World Power (2013); *Recreations* mountain walking, local history, performing and visual arts; *Style—* Prof Peter Odell; ✉ 7 Constitution Hill, Ipswich IP1 3RG (☎ 01473 253376, e-mail peterodell2@btinternet.com)

ODONE, Cristina; da of Augusto Odone, of Washington DC, and Ulla Sjöström Odone; *b* 11 November 1960; *Educ* Nat Cathedral Sch Washington, St Clare's Hall Oxford, Worcester Coll Oxford (BA); *m* Edward Lucas; 1 da (Isabella b 6 Aug 2003); *Career* freelance journalist 1982–83 (articles published in Cosmopolitan, Harper's & Queen, TES, Daily Telegraph, Company, The Independent); journalist: The Catholic Herald 1983–85, The Times Diary 1986; conslt Odone Assocs Washington DC (lobbyists at World Bank on behalf of euro cos) 1987–92, ed The Catholic Herald 1992–96, TV critic The Daily Telegraph 1996–98, dep ed New Statesman 1998–2004, presenter Dispatches: Women Bishops 2005, writer The Telegraph 2010; *Books* The Shrine (novel, 1996), A Perfect Wife (novel, 1997); *Recreations* reading, walking, travelling, entertaining; *Style—* Miss Cristina Odone

OF MAR; *see:* Mar

OFFER, Prof Avner; s of Ivriyah Offer, and Zvi Offer; *b* 15 May 1944, Gvat, Israel; *Educ* Hebrew Univ of Jerusalem (BA), St Antony's Coll Oxford, Univ of Oxford (DPhil); *m* 1966, Leah Koshet; 1 da, 1 s; *Career* jr research fell Merton Coll Oxford 1976–78; Univ of York: lectr in economic and social history 1979–90, reader in economic and social history 1990–91; sr fell Center for Historical Analysis Rutgers Univ USA 1991, professorial fell and reader in recent social and economic history Nuffield Coll Oxford 1992–2000, fell All Souls Coll Oxford 2000–, Chichele prof of economic history Univ of Oxford 2000–11 (sr research fell 2011–14); Hartley research fell Univ of Southampton 1981–82, visiting assoc Clare Hall Cambridge 1984, research fell Inst of Advanced Studies ANU 1985–88, sr visiting fell Remarque Inst NYU 1999; memb: Advsy Bd History of the London Co Cncl 1983–85, Editorial Bd Rural History 1989–94, Editorial Bd Jl of Mktg History; author of numerous articles in learned jls incl: The Public Historian, Modern Law Review, Economic History Review, Historical Jl, Past and Present, Jl of Contemporary History; numerous invited talks and lectures internationally; memb: ESRC Bd for Post-Grad Trg in Economics and Social History (also research training referee), ESRC Sociology History, Anthropology and Geography Research Coll, Economics and Economic History Section Ctee Br Acad, Comité Scientifique Centre de Recherch Historial de la Grande Guerre (France), Ctee Social History Soc 1992–99, Cncl and Exec Ctee Economic History Soc 2001–08; govr History of Advtg Tst 1996–98; FBA 2000, AcSS 2003; *Books* incl: Property and Politics 1870–1914: Landownership, Law, Ideology and Urban Development in England (1981), The First World War: An Agrarian Interpretation (1989, Trevor Reese Meml Prize for Imperial and Cwlth History 1992), In Pursuit of the Quality of Life (ed, 1996), Why is the Public Sector so Large in Market Societies? The Political Economy of Prudence in the UK, c1879–2000 (2003), The Challenge of Affluence: Self-control and Well-being in the United States and Britain since 1950 (2006), Insecurity, Inequality and Obesity in Affluent Societies (2012), Burn Mark: A Photographic Memoir of the Six Day War (2014), The Nobel Factor: The Prize in Economics, Social Democracy and the Market Turn (2016); *Recreations* literature, visual arts, classical music; *Style—* Prof Avner Offer; ✉ All Souls College, Oxford OX1 4AL (☎ 01865 279379, fax 01865 279299, e-mail avner.offer@all-souls.ox.ac.uk, website https://sites.google.com/site/avoffer/avneroffer)

OFFER, Ven Clifford Jocelyn; s of Rev Canon Clifford Jesse Offer (d 1964), of Ightham, Kent, and Jocelyn Mary, *née* Kerr; *b* 10 August 1943; *Educ* King's Sch Canterbury, St Peter's Coll Oxford (sent down), Univ of Exeter (BA), Westcott House Theol Coll; *m* 1980, Dr Catherine Mary Lloyd, da of Dr George Marner Lloyd; 2 da (Isabel Mary b 28 Sept 1981, Rebecca Catherine b 11 Oct 1985); *Career* curate of Bromley Parish Church 1969–74, team vicar Parish of Southampton (City Centre) 1974–83, team rector of Hitchin 1983–93, archdeacon of Norwich and canon librarian of Norwich Cathedral 1994–2008 (archdeacon emeritus 2008–), dir Norwich Diocesan Bd of Fin 1996–2008; chm: Norwich Advsy Bd of Mission and Miny 1994–98 and 2000–03, Norwich Course Mgmnt Ctee 1998–2003, Norwich Bd of Miny 2003–08; memb: Gen Synod C of E 1998–2005, Ctee Centre for East Anglian Studies 1999–2008; Warden of Readers 1994–2008, Bishop's advsr 1995–; Assoc Community of St Egidio; FRSA; *Books* King Offa in Hitchin (1992), In Search of Clofesho (2002); *Recreations* model making, medieval and saxon history, collecting Merchant Navy Livery Co buttons, walking; *Clubs* Norfolk; *Style—* The Ven Clifford Offer

OFFORD, Dr Matthew James; MP; s of Christopher Offord, and Hilda, *née* Pritchard; *b* 1969; *Educ* Amery Hill Sch Alton, Nottingham Trent Univ (BA), Univ of Lancaster (MA), KCL (PhD); *m* 12 June 2010, Claire, *née* Rowles; *Career* BBC 2001–10; MP (Cons) Hendon 2010–; FRGS; *Recreations* sailing, scuba diving, literature, wine, travel; *Style—* Dr Matthew Offord, MP; ✉ website www.matthewofford.co.uk; House of Commons, London SW1A 0AA

OFFORD, Prof Robin Ewart; s of Frank Etchelles Offord (d 1994), and Eileen Elisabeth, *née* Plunkett (d 2006); *b* 28 June 1940; *Educ* Owen's Sch, Peterhouse Cambridge (MA, PhD); *m* 3 July 1963, Valerie Edna, da of Ronald Wheatley (d 1971); 1 s (Alan b 1964), 2 da (Jane b 1967, Alice b 1973 d 2006); *Career* fell UC Oxford 1968–73 (univ lectr in molecular biophysics 1972–80), fell and tutor in biochemistry ChCh Oxford 1973–80; Université de Genève: prof and dir Département de Biochimie Médicale 1980–2004, founding dir Département de Biologie Structurale et Bioinformatique 2004–05, emeritus prof 2005–; pres Sch of Basic Med Geneva 1994–2001 (vice-pres 1992–94), jt fndr Swiss Inst Bioinformatics, founding pres and exec dir Mintaka Fndn for Medical Research 2005–; dir Geneva Bioinformatics SA 1998–2000, jt fndr, pres and exec vice-chm GeneProt Inc 2000–01; chm: Dutch Govt Panel on Proteomics 2002, Int Scientific Cncl Netherlands Proteomics Centre 2003–, Advsy Bd Eclosion (Geneva's incubator for life sciences start-ups) 2003–, Bd of Tstees Torrey Pines Inst for Molecular Studies (Calif and Florida) 2009– (tstee 2005–); ed Biochemical Journal 1972–79; memb: local ctees of Christian Aid 1970–80, editorial bds of various scientific jls 1972–, various ctees and bds of the UK MRC and UK Miny of Health 1976–80, Comité Scientifique de la Fondation Jeantet de Médecine 1985–88; jt sci fndr: Gryphon Sciences Corporation S San Francisco 1994, Ciphergen Inc; pres American Peptide Soc 2013– (memb Cncl 1999–, sec 2003–11, pres-elect 2011); shared L'agefi (fin jl) Man of the Year Switzerland award 2002, Makineni Prize Lectr American Peptide Soc 2005, shared Tribune de Genève Man of the Year – Culture Award 2008, shared Ashoka Switzerland Special Jury Prize 2014, shared Geneva University Innovation Prize 2014, successful finalist 5th Saving Lives at Birth competition Washington 2016; *Publications* A Guidebook to Biochemistry (with M D Yudkin, 1971, various new edns and foreign translations 1972–), Comprehensible Biochemistry (with M D Yudkin, 1973), Biochemistry (1975, Spanish translation 1976), Semisynthetic Peptides and Proteins (with C di Bello, 1977), Simple Macromolecules (1979), Macromolecular Complexes (1979), Semisynthetic Proteins (1980); almost 200 articles in scientific jls; *Recreations* linguistics, scuba diving (PADI master instructor), windsurfing; *Clubs* Royal Overseas League; *Style*— Prof Robin Offord; ✉ Fondation Mintaka pour la Recherche Medicale, 14 Chemin des Aulx, 1228 Plan-les-Ouates, Switzerland (☎ 00 41 79 293 5781, e-mail robin.offord@mintakafoundation.org)

OFILI, Christopher (Chris); *b* 1968; *Educ* Thameside Coll of Technol, Chelsea Sch of Art (Christopher Head drawing scholarship, BA), Hochschule der Kunst Berlin, RCA (MA), Br Cncl Travel Scholarship Zimbabwe; *Career* artist; tstee Tate Gallery 2003–05; hon fell Univ of the Arts London 2004; *Solo Exhibitions* Paintings and Drawings (Kepler Gallery London) 1991, Gavin Brown's Enterprise NY 1995, Afrodizzia (Victoria Miro Gallery London) 1996, Pimpin ain't easy but it sure is fun (Contemporary Fine Art Berlin) 1997, Southampton City Art Gallery 1998, Serpentine Gallery London 1998, Whitworth Art Gallery Manchester 1998–99, Afrobiotics (Gavin Brown's Enterprise NY) 1999, Chris Ofili Drawings (Victoria Miro Gallery London) 2000, Watercolours (Gallery Side 2 Tokyo) 2001, Freedom One Day (Victoria Miro Gallery London) 2002, Within Reach (50th Venice Biennale) 2003, Afro Muses (The Studio Museum Harlem NY) 2005, The Blue Rider (Contemporary Fine Arts Berlin) 2005, The Upper Room (Tate Britain London) 2005–07, The Blue Rider Extended Remix (kestnergesellschaft Hanover) 2006; *Group Exhibitions* incl: BP Portrait Award (National Portrait Gallery) 1990 and 1991, BT New Contemporaries (Cornherhouse Gallery Manchester and tour) 1993–94, About Vision: New British Painting in the 1990s (cmmnd by Absolut Vodka, MOMA Oxford and tour) 1995–96, Belladonna (ICA London) 1997, Pictura Britannica (Museum of Contemporary Art Sydney and tour) 1997–, Sensation: Young British Artists from the Saatchi Collection (Royal Acad London and tour) 1997–98, 20th John Moores Liverpool Exhibition of Contemporary Painting (Walker Art Gallery Liverpool) 1997, Carnegie International (Carnegie Museum of Art Pittsburgh) 1999–2000, 6th International Istanbul Biennial 1997, Trouble Spot Painting (Museum voor Hedendaagse Kunst Antwerp) 1999, Dimensions Variable (Br Cncl touring exhibition incl Helsinki City Art Museum, Stockholm Royal Acad of Free Arts and Prague Nat Gallery of Modern Art) 1997–2000, The Jerwood Fndn Painting Prize (Jerwood Gallery London) 1998, The Turner Prize (Tate Gallery London) 1998, Sydney Biennale 2000, Painting at the Edge of the World (Walker Arts Center Minneapolis) 2001–, Form Follows Fiction (Castello di Rivoli Turin) 2001–, Public Offerings (Museum of Contemporary Art LA) 2001–02, One Planet under a groove: Hip Hop and Contemporary Art (Bronx Museum of the Arts NY touring to Walker Arts Center Minneapolis and Spelman Museum of Fine Art Atlanta) 2001–02, Cavepainting (Santa Monica Museum of Art) 2002, drawing now: eight propositions (MOMA QNS NY) 2002–03, Paradise (National Gallery, Laing Art Gallery Newcastle upon Tyne and City Museum and Art Gallery Bristol) 2003, Fabulism (Joslyn Art Museum Omaha) 2004, Monument to Now (The Dakis Joannou Collection DESTE Fndn for Contemporary Art Athens) 2004, Artists & Prints (MOMA NY) 2005, Getting Emotional ICA Boston 2005, Translation (Palais de Tokyo Paris) 2005; *Awards* Christopher Head drawing scholarship 1989, Erasmus exchange to Berlin 1992, Br Cncl travel scholarship Zimbabwe 1992, second prizewinner Tokyo Print Biennale 1993, Wingate Young Artist Award 1996, Turner Prize 1998, South Bank Show Award – Visual Arts 2004; *Style*— Chris Ofili, Esq

OGDEN, Sir Peter James; kt (2005); s of James Platt Ogden (d 1994), and Frances Ogden (d 2015); *b* 26 May 1947; *Educ* Rochdale GS, Univ of Durham (BSc, PhD), Harvard Business Sch (MBA); *m* 22 Aug 1970, Catherine Rose, da of Harold Blincoe; 1 da (Tiffany b 1 Oct 1975), 2 s (Cameron b 9 Oct 1977, Edward b 18 Aug 1981); *Career* exec dir Merrill Lynch International Bank Ltd 1976–81; md: Merrill Lynch White Weld Capital Markets Group 1976–81, Morgan Stanley & Co 1981–87 (advsy dir 1987–95); chm: Computacenter Ltd 1981–98 (non-exec dir 1998–), Dealogic Ltd 1988–, Omnia Ltd 1996–2003; non-exec dir: Abbey National plc 1996–2004, Psion Ltd 1999–2005; visiting prof Dept of Physics Univ of Durham 2003; fndr, chm and tstee The Ogden Trust 1999– (projects funded incl The Ogden Centre for Fundamental Physics at Durham University); hon fell Hughes Hall Cambridge 1999; Hon MA Univ of Cambridge 2001, Hon DCL Univ of Durham 2002, Hon DSc Univ of Warwick 2009; Hon CPhys 2000, Hon FInstP 2010; *Style*— Sir Peter Ogden

OGILVIE, Dame Bridget Margaret; AC (2007), DBE (1996); da of late John Mylne Ogilvie, and Margaret Beryl, *née* McRae; *b* 24 March 1938; *Educ* New England Girls' Sch, Univ of New England (BRurSc), Univ of Cambridge (PhD, ScD); *Career* worked in Parasitology Div Nat Inst for Med Research 1963–81, Ian McMaster fell Animal Health Div CSIRO 1971–72; Wellcome Trust: co-ordinator Tropical Med Prog 1979–81, dep sec and asst dir 1981–84, dep dir Science 1984–89, dir Science Progs 1989–91, the dir 1991–98; visiting prof Dept of Biology Imperial Coll London 1985–92, visiting prof UCL 1998–; chm: AstraZeneca Science Teaching Tst 1998–2006, Assoc of Med Research Charities 2002–07, Governing Body Lister Inst 2002–; vice-chm Sense about Science 2003–, memb UK Cncl for Science and Technol 1993–2000, memb Advsy Ctee for Science, Technol and Business The British Library 1999–2002; tstee: Science Museum 1992–2003, Nat Endowment for Science, Technology and the Arts (NESTA) 1998–2002, Scottish Science Tst 1998–2002, Cancer Research UK (formerly Cancer Research Campaign) 2001–; chm Ctee of the Public Understanding of Science 1998–2002, chm Governing Body Inst of Animal Health 1998–2003, chm Medicines for Malaria Venture (MMV) 1999–2006; contrib to numerous scientific papers and jls; non-exec dir: Lloyds TSB Group plc 1995–2000, Zeneca Group plc 1997–99, Astra Zeneca 1999–2006, Manchester Technol Fund 1999–2004; High Steward Univ of Cambridge 2000–; Distinguished Alumni Award Univ of New England 1994, Lloyd of Kilgerran Prize 1994, Australian Soc of Med Research Medal 2000, Kilby Award 2003, Duncan Davies Meml Medal 2004, Ralph Doherty Meml Medal Qld Inst of Med Res 2006; Hon DSc: Univ of Nottingham 1994, Univ of Salford 1994, Univ of Westminster 1994, Univ of Glasgow 1995, Univ of Bristol 1995, Aust Nat Univ 1995, Univ of Buckingham 1996, Nat Univ of Ireland 1996, Oxford Brookes Univ 1996, Nottingham Trent Univ 1996, Univ of Greenwich 1997, Univ of Auckland 1998, Univ of Durham 1998, Univ of Kent 1998, Imperial Coll of Science, Technol and Med London 1999, Univ of Exeter 1999, Univ of Leicester 2000, Univ of Manchester 2001, Univ of St Andrews 2001, Univ of Wollongong 2005; Hon MD Univ of Newcastle upon Tyne 1996, Hon LLD Univ of Dublin 1996, Hon LLD Univ of Leicester 2000, Hon Dr Univ of Edinburgh 1997; hon fell: UCL 1993, Girton Coll Cambridge 1993, St Edmund's Coll Cambridge 1999; hon memb: Br Soc for Parasitology 1990, American Soc of Parasitologists 1992, Br Veterinary Assoc; hon assoc RCVS 1993; fndn hon fell RVC 1994, Hon FRCP 1996 (Hon MRCP 1992), Hon FIBiol 1998, Hon FRSM 1999; FIBiol 1985, FRCPath 1992, FMedSci 1998, FRS 2003, hon fell BAAS 2006 (hon memb 2005); *Style*— Dame Bridget Ogilvie, AC, DBE; ✉ University College London, Medical School Administration, Gower Street, London WC1E 6BT (☎ 020 7679 4602)

OGILVY, Sir Francis Gilbert Arthur; 14 Bt (NS 1626), of Inverquharity, Forfarshire; o s of Sir David John Wilfrid Ogilvy, 13 Bt (d 1992), and Penelope Mary Ursula, *née* Hills; *b* 22 April 1969; *Educ* Edinburgh Acad, Glenalmond, RAC Cirencester, Univ of Reading (BSc); *m* 12 Oct 1996, Dorothy Margaret, eldest da of Rev Jock Stein, and Rev Margaret Stein, of Kincardine, by Alloa; 3 s (Robert David b 8 July 1999, Calum John b 24 Sept 2001, Hamish Walter b 9 Aug 2003), 1 da (Elspeth Katherine b 16 Oct 2005); *Heir* s, Robert Ogilvy; *Career* chartered surveyor; MRICS; *Recreations* hill-walking with my son, the tonic of the outdoors, adrenalin from sport and the joy of music; *Style*— Sir Francis Ogilvy, Bt; ✉ Winton House, Pencaitland, East Lothian EH34 5AT (☎ 01875 340222, e-mail f.ogilvy@wintonhouse.co.uk)

Ogilvy, Lauren Louise; *b* 11 June 1984, Torquay, Devon; *Educ* Royal Ballet Sch (Lynn Seymour Award, Phyllis Bedells Award, Young British Dancer of the Year, Critics Circle Award, Woman of the Future); *Career* ballerina; Royal Ballet: joined 2002, soloist 2003–06, first soloist 2006–08, princ dancer 2008–; roles incl: Juliet, Manon, Princess Aurora, Nikiya, Sugar Plum Fairy, Odette/Odile, Cinderella, Giselle, Sylvia, Symphony in C, Serenade, Ballo della Regina, Scenes de Ballet, Alice in Wonderland, Chroma, Qualica & Infra; patron: London Children's Ballet, Nat Youth Ballet; *Recreations* cinema, music, theatre; *Clubs* Ivy, Hospital; *Style*— Miss Lauren Cuthbertson; ✉ Royal Ballet, Royal Opera House, Covent Garden, London WC2E 9DD (e-mail britishballerina@gmail.com, website laurencuthbertson.com, Twitter @londonballerina); c/o Storm Artists, London, SW3 3TD

OGNALL, Hon Sir Harry; kt (1986), DL (W Yorks 2000); s of late Leo Ognall, and Cecilia Ognall; *b* 9 January 1934; *Educ* Leeds GS, Lincoln Coll Oxford (MA), Univ of Virginia (LLM); *m* 1; 2 s, 1 da; m 2, 1977, Elizabeth Young; 2 step s; *Career* called to the Bar Gray's Inn 1958 (bencher 1983); joined NE Circuit, recorder of the Crown Court 1972–86, QC 1973, judge of the High Court of Justice (Queen's Bench Div) 1986–2000, memb Criminal Injuries Compensation Bd 1976, arbitrator Motor Insurers' Bureau Agreement 1979–85, memb Senate of Inns of Ct 1980–83 (memb Planning Ctee and Professional Conduct Ctee), chm Criminal Ctee Judicial Studies Bd 1986–89, memb Parole Bd England & Wales 1989–91 (vice-chm 1990–91), judicial memb Proscribed Orgns Appeal Cmmn 2001–; chm EWitness Ltd 2000–05; *Recreations* photography, bridge, grandchildren; *Clubs* Ilkley Bowling; *Style*— The Hon Sir Harry Ognall, DL

OGORKIEWICZ, Prof Richard Marian; s of Col Marian Anthony Ogorkiewicz (d 1962), of Poland, and Waldyna, *née* Pryfer (d 1986); *b* 2 May 1926; *Educ* SRW Sch Warsaw, Lycée de C Norwid Paris, George Heriot's Sch Edinburgh, Imperial Coll London (BSc, MSc); *m* 2005, Jocelyn Marie Bernier; *Career* devpt engr: Ford Motor Co 1952–55, Humber Ltd 1955–57; lectr in mech engrg Imperial Coll London 1957–85, conslt to various cos involved with armoured fighting vehicles 1972–; consulting ed Int Defense Review 1988–; visiting prof RMCS; memb various sci advsy ctees: Miny of Aviation 1964–70, Miny of Technol 1967–71, MOD 1972–2006; pres Friends of the Tank Museum Dorset 1987–93 (tstee 1993–); FIMechE 1970; *Books* Armour (1960), Design and Development of Fighting Vehicles (1968), Armoured Forces (1970), Technology of Tanks 2 vols (1991), Tanks: 100 Years of Evolution (2015); *Recreations* gardening, walking; *Style*— Prof Richard Ogorkiewicz; ✉ 18 Temple Sheen, East Sheen, London SW14 7RP (☎ 020 8876 5149)

OGSTON, Hamish MacGregor; CBE (2011); s of Robert Davidson Ogston, and Pauline Jeannette Ogston; *Educ* Cranleigh Sch, Univ of Manchester (BSc); *Career* co-fndr and chair Countdown plc 1970, co-fndr Supreme Awards 1977–79, co-fndr Guinness World of Records 1979–82, co-fndr and chm CPP Gp plc 1980–2010, investor in mktg rights to World Cup 1982, launched Sportsworld Gp plc 1982; Ernst & Young Entrepeneur of the Year Financial Services Award 2000; Outstanding Alumnus of the Year Award Univ of Manchester 2002; memb Ct of Benefactors of York Minster, vice-pres Georgian Theatre Royal Richmond N Yorks; FRSA, FRGS; *Recreations* travel, skiing, sailing, music, friends; *Style*— Hamish Ogston, Esq, CBE

OGUNDEHIN, Michelle; *b* 5 November 1967, Salford; *Educ* Bartlett Sch of Architecture UCL (DipArch); *m* 1994 (m dis) E Dunne; 1 s (b 13 April 2014); *Career* ed-in-chief Elle Decoration UK (Highly Commended Lifestyle Mag of the Year PPA Awards 2004, 2005 and 2006, Highly Commended Ed of the Year PPA Awards 2011, Specialist Consumer Mag of the Year PPA Awards 2011 and 2013); non-exec dir S Coast Design Forum 2008–13; *Television* co-presenter: Grand Designs RIBA House of the Year 2015, Inside Out Homes (Channel 4) 2016; tstee V&A Museum 2008–15, non-exec dir V&A Enterprises Bd 2009–15; ambass for diversity in public appts 2009–11; *Recreations* cinema, basset hounds; *Clubs* Soho House; *Style*— Ms Michelle Ogundehin; ✉ Elle Decoration, Hearst Magazines UK, 72 Broadwick Street, London W1F 9EP (e-mail editor@elledecoration.co.uk, Twitter @Mogundehin)

OGUS, Hugh Joseph; MBE (2012); s of Louis Ogus (d 1951), of London, and Anne, *née* Goldstein (d 1986); *b* 23 January 1934; *Educ* Central Fndn Sch London, QMC London (BA); *m* 14 Aug 1960, Mavis, da of Michael Mendel (d 1971), of London; 1 s (Simon b 1964), 1 da (Deborah b 1967); *Career* various jr mgmnt posts Philips Electrical Ltd 1957–67, commercial dir Salamandre Metalworks Ltd 1968–73, chm and md Poselco Ltd 1984–94 (md 1973–84), dir Cryselco Ltd 1992–93, chm Fusebox Ltd 1990–2000, dir Galaxy Consultancy Ltd 2000–10, non-exec chm DSG Asia (Hong Kong-based) 2000–10, dir Players Joys Ltd (The Players' Theatre) 2004–15, chm Construction Liveries Gp 2006–12; memb Cncl: Light Industry Fedn 1977–2000 (pres 1982–83), CIBSE 1986–89 and 1993–96 (chm Lighting Div 1993–94, vice-pres 1994–96); fndr chm Lighting Educn Tst 1995–2013 (non-exec chm of tstees 2013–); chm of govrs: Mill Hill Oral Sch for Deaf Children 1987–89 (treas 1977–87), Mary Hare GS for the Deaf 1992–2008 (vice-chm of govrs 1984–92, chm of fin 1980–94, vice-pres 2008–); vice-chm of govrs London Sch of Foreign Trade 1982–87; Freeman City of London 1983, Liveryman Worshipful Co of Lightmongers (Master 1994–95 and 2009–10); CEng, FCIBSE (Gold Medal 2014), FSLL, Hon FCGI 2014; *Recreations* music, travel, swimming, horology; *Style*— Hugh J Ogus, Esq, MBE; ✉ 9 Wellington House, Aymer Drive, Stanmore, Middlesex HA7 3ES (☎ 020 8954 0657, e-mail hughogus@btinternet.com); websites www.maryhare.org.uk and www.lighting-education-trust.org

O

OKEWALE, Tunde; MBE (2016); *b* 1 December 1983, Lagos, Nigeria; *Educ* London Met Univ, BPP Law Sch; *Career* called to the Bar 2007; barr Doughty Street Chambers 2011–; social entrepreneur Urban Lawyers 2010–, patron Hackney Community Law Centre 2013–; external conslt Amber and Greene 2012–; Young Barrister of the Year Lawyer Monthly Barrister Awards 2012, Ten Outstanding Young People Award JCI London 2013, 33 in GQ's Most Influential Men under 381/2 2014, Diversity Champion UK Diversity Legal Awards 2014, Chambers and Partners Bar Award for Outstanding Contribution to Diversity 2015; Freeman Worshipful Co of World Traders 2013–; *Recreations* cinema, fashion, motorsport, music, reading, travel; *Style*— Tunde Okewale, MBE; ✉ Doughty Street Chambers, 53–54 Doughty Street, London WC1N 2LS (☎ 020 7404 1313, e-mail t.okewale@doughtystreet.co.uk, website www.tundeokewale.com, Twitter @urbnlawyer)

OKRI, Ben; OBE (2001); s of Silver Okri, and Grace Okri; *b* 15 March 1959; *Educ* Univ of Essex; *Career* novelist, poet, essayist and short story writer; broadcaster and presenter BBC 1983–85, poetry ed W Africa 1983–86, fell commoner Trinity Coll Cambridge 1991–93, hon fell Mansfield Coll Oxford 2014; visiting prof Sch of English Univ of Leicester 2012; vice-pres Caine Prize for Africa 2012; one of 200 leaders of tomorrow World Economic Forum 1993; memb: Soc of Authors, PEN International, Cncl RSL 1999–2004, Bd RNT 1999–2006; Hon DLit: Univ of Westminster 1997, Univ of Essex 2002, Univ of Exeter 2004; Hon Dr of Utopia Univ van het Algemeen Belang Belgium 2009, Hon DLit Univ of London SOAS 2010, Hon Dr of Arts Univ of Beds 2010, Hon Dr of Literature Univ of Pretoria 2014; FRSL 1997, FRSA 2003; *Awards* Cwlth Prize for Africa 1987, Paris Review Prize for Fiction 1987, Booker Prize 1991, Premio Letterario Internazionale Chianti Ruffino-Antico Fattore 1993, Premio Grinzane Cavour 1994, Crystal Award 1995, Premio Palmi 2000, Grinzane Prize for Africa 2008, Int Literary Award of Novisad 2008; *Books* Flowers and Shadows (novel, 1980), The Landscapes Within (novel, 1982), Incidents at the Shrine (stories, 1986), Stars of the New Curfew (stories, 1988), The Famished Road (novel, 1991), An African Elegy (poems, 1992), Songs of Enchantment (novel, 1993), Astonishing the Gods (novel, 1995), Birds of Heaven (essays, 1996),

Dangerous Love (novel, 1996), A Way of Being Free (essays, 1997), Infinite Riches (novel, 1998), Mental Fight (poetry, 1999), In Arcadia (novel, 2002), Starbook (novel, 2007), Tales of Freedom (novella and stokus, 2009), A Time for New Dreams (poetic essays, 2011), WILD (poems, 2012), The Age of Magic (novel, 2014); *Recreations* cinema, music, opera, reading, travel, walking, silence; *Style*— Ben Okri, Esq, OBE, FRSL; ✉ c/o The Marsh Agency Limited, 50 Albemarle Street, London W1S 4BD (☎ 020 7493 4361, fax 020 7495 8961, website www.marsh-agency.co.uk)

OLDERSHAW, Dr Paul John; s of Harold Oldershaw (d 1981), and Irene, *née* Summerlin (d 1999); *b* 23 September 1947; *Educ* Henry Mellish GS Nottingham, Emmanuel Coll Cambridge (exhibitioner and scholar in natural scis, MB BChir, MA, MD, Colin McKenzie prize, Albert Hopkinson award, Peake prize), St Thomas' Hosp Med Sch; *Career* jr hosp appts St Thomas', St Peter's and Brompton Hosps 1973–75, rotating med registrar Worthing Gen Hosp (gen med) and St Thomas' Hosp (gen med and nephrology) 1975–77, Br Heart Fndn research fell St Thomas' Hosp Med Unit 1977–79, cardiac registrar Brompton Hosp 1979–81, sr registrar Cardiac Dept St George's Hosp 1981–82; Royal Brompton Nat Heart and Lung Hosp: conslt cardiologist 1982–, dir of cardiology 1992–; Br Cardiac Soc: memb Cncl 1986–90, sec 1988–92, chm Pubns Ctee 1990–93, memb Prog and Meetings Ctee 1991–95; Br Heart Fndn: memb Educn Ctee 1986–90, memb Factfile Ctee 1986–90; Euro Soc of Cardiology: memb Scientific Exec Ctee 1990–, memb Valvular Heart Disease Working Pty 1992–; memb Adult Congenital Heart Disease Working Pty Br Cardiac Soc 1993–; numerous post-graduate awards incl Br Heart Fndn Research Award (with Andrew Bishop) to study right ventricular function using impedance catheterisation 1993–; memb Editorial Bds: Br Heart Jl 1986–90, Int Jl of Cardiology 1986–92, Euro Heart Jl 1990–; referee: BMJ, Lancet; memb: Med Research Soc 1977, Br Cardiac Soc 1981; FRCP 1990 (MRCP 1975), FESC 1991 (MESC 1982), FACC 1991 (MACC 1982); *Books* A Practice of Cardiac Catheterisation (with D Mendel, 1986), Textbook of Adult and Paediatric Echocardiography and Doppler Echocardiography (with M St John Sutton, 1989), Cardiology Dictionary (with R A Anderson and J R Dawson, 1990), A Practical Guide to Congenital Heart Disease in Adults (with A Redington and D F Shore, 1994); author of numerous pubns in academic jls; *Recreations* opera, wine; *Style*— Dr Paul Oldershaw; ✉ 76 Carlton Hill, St John's Wood, London NW8 (☎ 020 7625 6829); Royal Brompton Hospital, Sydney Street, London SW3 6NP (☎ 020 7352 8121, fax 020 7351 8629)

OLDFIELD, Bruce; OBE (1990); *b* 14 July 1950; *Educ* Spennymoor GS Durham, Ripon GS, Sheffield Poly (DipEd), Ravensbourne Coll of Art, St Martin's Coll of Art; *Career* fashion designer; designed for Henri Bendel NY and other stores 1973–74, freelance cmmns incl film wardrobe for Charlotte Rampling 1974–75, first collection 1975, estab couture div 1978, opened London boutique and redeveloped ready-to-wear collection with couture collection 1984–, Br rep Aust Bicentennial Wool Collection Fashion Show Sydney Opera House 1988, opened second London boutique dedicated to weddings 2009; lectures: Fashion Inst NY 1977, LA County Mus 1983, Int Design Conference Aspen Colorado 1986; vice-pres Barnardos 1998–, memb Panel Whitbread Literary Awards 1987, organised Bruce Oldfield for Barnardos gala evenings attended by HRH The Princess of Wales 1985 and 1988, govr London Inst 1999–2002; Northern Personality of the Year Variety Club 1985, subject of TV documentary A Journey into Fashion (Tyne Tees TV) 1990, tstee Royal Acad of Arts 2000–02; hon fell: Sheffield Hallam Univ 1987, RCA 1990, Hatfield Coll Durham 1991; Hon DCL Univ of Northumbria at Newcastle 2001, DUniv UCE 2005, Hon DLitt Univ of Hull 2009; *Books* Bruce Oldfield's Season (contrib, 1987), Rootless (autobiography, 2004); *Recreations* reading, music, films, driving; *Style*— Bruce Oldfield, Esq, OBE; ✉ c/o Bruce Oldfield Ltd, 27 Beauchamp Place, London SW3 1NJ (☎ 020 7584 1363, fax 020 7761 0351, e-mail hq@bruceoldfield.com, website www.bruceoldfield.com)

OLDFIELD, Michael Gordon (Mike); s of Raymond Henry Oldfield, of Stuttgart, Germany, and Maureen Bernadine, *née* Liston (d 1976); *b* 15 May 1953; *Educ* Highlands Sch Reading, Hornchurch GS Essex, St Edward's Reading, Presentation Coll Reading; *Partner* 1; 2 s (Dougal b 17 Sept 1981, Luke b 11 April 1986), 1 da (Molly b 30 Nov 1979); ptnr 2; 1 s (Noah b 8 March 1990), 1 da (Greta b 28 April 1988); *Career* musician; first recording with sister Sally Oldfield 1969, 3 recordings with Kevin Ayres 1970–72; solo albums: Tubular Bells 1973, Hergest Ridge 1974, Ommadawn 1975, Incantations 1978, Platinum 1979, QE2 1980, Five Miles Out 1982, Crises 1983, The Killing Fields 1984, Discovery 1984, Islands 1987, Earth Moving 1989, Amarok 1990, Heaven's Open 1991, Tubular Bells II 1992, The Songs of Distant Earth 1994, Voyager 1996, Tubular Bells III 1998, Guitars 1999, The Millennium Bell 1999, Light and Shade; various major tours incl two world tours; 50 Gold and 15 Platinum discs worldwide, Grammy award, Golden Globe, Ivor Novello and BAFTA nominations; Freeman City of London; involved with Blue Peter Cambodian Appeal and hostage release work; *Recreations* skiing, cycling, squash; *Style*— Mike Oldfield, Esq

OLDFIELD, Richard John; DL; s of Christopher Oldfield (d 1981), and Bridget Ford, *née* Craigie; *b* 11 October 1955, London; *Educ* Eton, New Coll Oxford (BA); *m* 1, 1982, Hon Alexandra Davidson (d 1995); 1 da (Leonora b 21 Feb 1985), 2 s (Christopher b 8 Dec 1986, Henry b 25 Sept 1991); m 2, 1997, Amicia de Moubray; 1 s (Edward b 6 April 1998); *Career* S G Warburg and Mercury Asset Mgmnt Gp 1977–1996, chief exec Alta Advsrs Ltd 1997–2005, chief exec Oldfield Ptnrs LLP 2005–; chm Keystone Investment Tst plc 2001–10, chm Investment Ctee Univ of Oxford and Oxford Univ Endowment Mgmnt Ltd 2007–14, dir Witan Investment Tst 2011–, dir Shepherd Neame Ltd 2016–; pres Demelza House Children's Hospice 2005– (former chm and tstee); tstee: Leeds Castle Fndn 2001–11, Canterbury Cathedral Tst 2009–, Clore Duffield Fndn 2013–; High Sheriff Kent 2008–09, Vice Lord-Lt Kent 2011–, Seneschal Canterbury Cathedral 2014–; *Publications* Simple But Not Easy (2007); *Recreations* riding, writing, reading; *Clubs* White's, Beefsteak; *Style*— Richard Oldfield, Esq, DL; ✉ Doddington Place, nr Sittingbourne, Kent ME9 0BB (☎ 01795 886385, e-mail rjo@oldfieldpartners.com)

OLDHAM, Gavin David Redvers; s of David George Redvers Oldham, of Bucks, and Penelope Barbara, *née* Royle; *b* 5 May 1949; *Educ* Eton, Trinity Coll Cambridge (MA); *m* 17 May 1975, Virginia Russell, da of late Rodney Fryer Russell, of Dorset, and Elisabeth Jane, *née* Shettle; *Career* CSE Aircraft Services Ltd 1971–76, ptnr Wedd Durlacher Mordaunt & Co 1984–86 (joined 1976), secretariat Barclays de Zoete Wedd 1984–86, chm Barclayshare Ltd 1989–90 (chief exec 1986–89); chief exec The Share Centre Ltd 1990–2013 (chm 2014–), chief exec Share plc 2000–13 (chm 2014–), chm The Share Fndn 2005–, md Share Radio Ltd 2014–; dir West Highland Air Transport Ltd 1998–, tstee Personal Finance Educn Gp 2003–14, dir Buckinghamshire Business First Ltd 2011–12; memb Economic Research Cncl 1989–; church cmmr 1998–2013 and 2015– (dep chair Assets Ctee 2013–); memb: Gen Synod (House of Laity) for Dio of Oxford 1995–, Ethical Investment Advsy Gp (C of E) 1998–2013; MInstD, FSI; *Clubs* Leander, Royal Motor Yacht; *Style*— Gavin Oldham, Esq; ✉ Oxford House, Oxford Road, Aylesbury, Buckinghamshire HP21 8SZ (☎ 01296 439100, fax 01296 414410, e-mail gavin.oldham@share.co.uk)

OLDING, Prof Simon; s of Roy Edward Olding, of Dawlish, Devon, and Rita Frances, *née* Heard; *b* 9 March 1954, Exeter; *Educ* Hele's GS Exeter, Fitzwilliam Coll Cambridge (Leathersellers scholar, MA), Univ of Edinburgh (PhD); *m* July 1990, Isabel, da of Noel Hughes; 2 da (Mabel, Madeleine); *Career* asst keeper for ceramics Glasgow Museums and Art Galleries 1980–82 (grad trainee 1979–80), asst curator (art) Salisbury Museum 1982–85, London museums offr and asst dir for museum devpt Area Museums Serv for SE England 1985–89, head of arts and museums Bournemouth Borough Cncl 1989–98, dir of policy and research Heritage Lottery Fund 1998–2002, dir Crafts Study Centre Univ for the Creative Arts 2002–; pres Walford Mill Craft Centre; dep chair The Leach Pottery, patron Stroud Int Textiles; hon fell Arts Univ Bournemouth 2000; FMA 1991 (AMA 1982, Trevor Walden prize), FRSA 1994, FTS 2002; *Books* Michael Cullimore (1986), A Vision of Dartmoor (jtly, 1990), Exploring Museums – London (1991), Marcus Tate Photographs (1993), Russell-Cotes Commissions (1994), So Fair a House (1997), Martyn Brewster (1997), Emma Stibbon (1998), London Museums and Collections (co-ed, 1998), Essays for the Opening of the Crafts Study Centre (co-ed, 2004), Magdalene Odundo (jtly, 2004), John Hinchcliffe (2006), Peter Thursby (jtly, 2007), Rezia Wahid: Wovenair (2007), Martyn Brewster (jtly, 2007), Matthew Burt: idea to object (2008), Three by One: a selection from 3 public craft collections by Alison Britton (co-ed, 2009), The RJ Lloyd ceramics collection: the artist as collector (ed, 2010), The Etchings of Bernard Leach (2010), The Art of R J Lloyd (2012); *Recreations* the SW of England, modern craft, walking in Dorset, writing; *Style*— Prof Simon Olding; ✉ Crafts Study Centre, University for the Creative Arts, Falkner Road, Farnham, Surrey GU9 7DS (☎ 01252 891450)

OLDMAN, Gary; *b* 21 March 1958, New Cross, London; *Educ* Rose Bruford Drama Coll (BA); *m* 1, Lesley Manville, *qv*; 1 s (Alfie); m 2, Uma Thurman, the actress; m 3, Donya Fiorentino; 2 s (Gulliver Flynn b 20 Aug 1999, Charlie); m 4, 31 Dec 2008, Alexandra Edenborough; *Career* actor; performed in various plays Royal Court Theatre and RSC 1984–87; *Theatre* incl The Pope's Wedding (Royal Court) 1995; *Television* Mean Time 1981, The Firm 1988, Jesus 1999; *Films* incl: Sid and Nancy 1986, Prick Up Your Ears 1986, Tracks 29 1988, Criminal Law 1988, Rosencrantz and Guildenstern are Dead 1990, State of Grace 1990, JFK 1991, Dracula 1992, True Romance 1993, Romeo is Bleeding 1993, Immortal Beloved 1994, Leon 1994, Murder in the First 1994, Basquiat 1996, Fifth Element 1997, Air Force One 1997, Lost in Space 1998, The Contender 2000 (also exec prodr), Nobody's Baby 2001, Interstate 60 2001, Hannibal 2001, Tiptoes 2003, Sin 2003, Harry Potter and the Prisoner of Azkaban 2004, Batman Begins 2005, Harry Potter and the Goblet of Fire 2005, Harry Potter and the Order of the Pheonix 2007, The Dark Knight 2008, The Unborn 2009, Rain Fall 2009, A Christmas Carol 2009, Planet 51 2009, The Book of Eli 2010, Red Riding Hood 2011, Harry Potter and the Deathly Hallows: Part 2 2011, Tinker, Tailor, Soldier, Spy 2011, The Dark Knight Rises 2012; wrote, directed and co-produced Nil By Mouth 1997, produced Plunkett & Macleane 1999; *Awards* Time Out's Fringe Award for Best Newcomer 1985; BAFTA: Best Actor nomination for Prick Up Your Ears 1988, Best British Film, Best British Screenplay; Channel Four Director's Award at the 51st Edinburgh Festival; *Style*— Gary Oldman, Esq

OLDRIDGE, John Norman Leslie; *b* 26 January 1947; *Educ* Oundle, Oxford Sch of Architecture (DipArch); *Career* currently sr ptnr Chapman Taylor Partners (joined 1973, assoc 1977, ptnr 1987); RIBA 1977, memb Ordre des Architectes 1990; *Recreations* offshore sailing; *Clubs* Royal Yacht Squadron, Royal Southampton Yacht; *Style*— John Oldridge, Esq

OLDWORTH, Richard Anthony; s of Anthony Gilbert Frederick Oldworth, and Patricia, *née* Thompson; *b* 5 June 1957; *Educ* Radley, City of London Poly; *m*; 3 da; *Career* chartered accountant; Peat Marwick Mitchell 1976–80, corp finance exec County Bank 1980–83, Bisgood Bishop & Co 1983–84, chm Buchanan Communications 1984–; ACA 1980; *Recreations* flying, motorsport; *Clubs* City of London, Royal Solent Yacht, Helicopter Club of GB, Historic Sports Car; *Style*— Richard Oldworth, Esq; ✉ Buchanan Communications Ltd, 107 Cheapside, London EC2V 6DN (☎ 0207 466 5000, fax 0207 466 5001)

OLINS, Rufus; s of Wally Olins, *qv*, and Renate, *née* Steinert; *b* 24 February 1961; *Educ* UCS London, Univ of York (BA); *m* 30 Sept 1995, Sara, *née* Scott; 1 da (Eliza b 23 Nov 1996), 1 s (Clem b 15 Feb 1999); *Career* Campaign 1986–89, Sunday Times 1989–94, Eastern Express Hong Kong 1994–95, Sunday Times 1996–98; Management Today: ed 1998–99, ed-in-chief and publishing dir 1999–2000; Haymarket Management Publications Ltd: publishing dir 2001–02, md 2003–06; md Haymarket Brand Media until 2008, chief exec Warc (formerly World Advertising Research Center) 2008–11; memb: Advsy Cncl RSA, Devpt Bd Nat Portrait Gallery, Bd Almeida Theatre; vice-patron Working Families, govr Salusbury Sch; *Recreations* cinema, cooking, tennis, cycling; *Style*— Rufus Olins, Esq

OLISA, Kenneth Aphunezi (Ken); OBE; *b* 13 October 1951; *Educ* High Pavement GS Nottingham, Fitzwilliam Coll Cambridge (IBM scholar, MA); *m*; 2 da; *Career* systems engr rising to product mktg mangr IBM (UK) Ltd 1974–81, various sr mktg positions rising to vice-pres worldwide mktg then md Wang (UK) Ltd and latterly sr vice-pres and gen mangr EMEA Wang Laboratories Inc 1981–92; Interregnum plc: fndr chm and ceo 1992–2006, non-exec chm 2006–; chm: Metapraxis Ltd 1993–2004, DMA-TEK Ltd 1994–98; dir: BDO Stoy Hayward Consulting 1994–97, Voss Net plc 1994–97, ProMetrics Gp Ltd 1994–97, Thumb Candy Ltd 1994–97, Pro-Bel Ltd 1995–96, Lambeth Healthcare NHS Tst 1995–99, Geoconference Ltd 1996–2000, CallCentric Ltd 1997–2000, Open Text Corp 1998–, uDate.com Ltd 2000–03, Datapoint 2000–02, Adaptive Inc 2002–, Yospace Technologies Ltd 2003–, Biowisdom 2004–, Reuters plc 2004–; cmmr Postal Servs Cmmn 2000–04; chm Thames Reach Bondway 1994–, dir Fitzwilliam Society Tst Ltd 1994–, govr Peabody Tst 1998–; Br Venture Capital Assoc/Real Deals Private Equity Personality of the Year 2003; Freeman City of London, Liveryman Worshipful Co of Info Technologists; FRSA; *Style*— Ken Olisa, Esq

OLIVEIRA, Prof David Benjamin Graeme; s of Anthony Benjamin Oliveira (d 1983), and Pamela Avril, *née* Maitland-Heriot; *b* 11 September 1955, London; *Educ* CCC Cambridge (Smyth scholar, MB BChir, MA), Westminster Hosp Med Sch London, PhD (London); *m* 14 April 1984, Patricia Margaret, da of Gp Capt J E F Williams, CBE; 2 s (Benjamin b 30 April 1985, Samuel b 26 May 1987), 1 da (Amelia b 24 Nov 1988); *Career* house physician then house surgn Westminster Hosp London 1979–80; SHO: Hammersmith Hosp London 1980–81, Nat Hosp for Nervous Diseases Queen Square 1981, Brompton Hosp London 1981–82, Renal Unit Guy's Hosp London 1982; registrar rotation Ealing Hosp then Renal Unit Hammersmith Hosp 1982–84, MRC trg fell UCL 1984–87; Univ of Cambridge: Lister Inst research fell Sch of Clinical Med 1987–95, univ lectr 1995; Addenbrooke's Hosp Cambridge: sr registrar in nephrology 1990–91, hon conslt physician 1991–95; fndn prof of renal med St George's Hosp Med Sch 1995–; memb Lister Inst of Preventive Med; author of numerous articles in learned jls; FRCP; *Recreations* natural history (especially insects and orchids), computers; *Style*— Prof David Oliveira; ✉ Division of Renal Medicine St George's, University of London, Cranmer Terrace, Tooting, London SW17 0RE (☎ 020 8725 5035, e-mail doliveir@sgul.ac.uk)

OLIVER, Prof Alexander Duncan (Alex); s of Michael John Oliver, and Suzanne Nesta Newman; *b* 24 August 1966; *Educ* Bristol GS, Clare Coll Cambridge (MA), Yale Univ (MA, MPhil), Clare Coll Cambridge (PhD); *m* 1988, Catrin Hutton; 1 s, 1 da; *Career* Mellon Fell Yale Univ 1988–90, Univ of Cambridge: research fell Gonville and Caius Coll 1993–94, dir of studies in philosophy Sidney Sussex Coll 1993–97, temp asst lectr in philosophy 1994–95, fell Gonville and Caius Coll 1994–96 and 2004–, asst lectr 1995–97, dir of studies in philosophy Trinity Hall 1995–98, dir of studies in philosophy Queens' Coll 1996–2002, fell Queens' Coll 1996–2004, lectr 1998–2000, dir of graduate studies Faculty of Philosophy 1999 and 2000, sr lectr 2000–05, dir of studies in philosophy Gonville and

Caius Coll 2004–15, reader 2005–12, chm Faculty of Philosophy 2008–09, prof of philosophy 2012–; Leverhulme Tst Major Research Fellowship 2002–04, Pilkington Prize 2005, Mind Assoc Sr Research Fellowship 2012–13; LittD (Cambridge 2014); memb: Ctee Analysis Tst 1996– (sec 1996–2000), Knowledge Transfer Panel Arts and Humanities Research Cncl 2007–09; *Publications* Properties (with D H Mellor, 1997), The Force of Argument (with Jonathan Lear, 2010), Plural Logic (with Timothy Smiley, 2013); numerous articles in philosophical jls.; *Recreations* beer, Italy, labrador retrievers, reggae music; *Clubs* Athenaeum, Elizabethan (Yale); *Style*— Prof Alex Oliver; ✉ Gonville and Caius College, Cambridge CB2 1TA

OLIVER, Bill; *b* 26 June 1956, Sunderland; *Educ* Univ of Exeter (BSc); *Career* formerly with: Alfred McAlpine, Barratt; fin dir Dwyer Estates plc 1994–2000, St Modwen Properties plc: fin dir 2000–03, md 2003–04, chief exec 2004–; FCA; *Style*— Bill Oliver, Esq; ✉ St Modwen Properties plc, Park Point, 17 High Street, Longbridge, Birmingham B31 2UQ

OLIVER, Hon David Keightley Rideal; QC (1986); o s of Baron Oliver of Aylmerton, PC (Life Peer, d 2007), and his 1 w, Mary Chichester, *née* Rideal (d 1985); *b* 4 June 1949; *Educ* Westminster, Trinity Hall Cambridge (BA), Université Libre de Bruxelles (Lic Special en Droit Européen); *m* 1, 5 April 1972 (m dis 1987), Maria Luisa, da of Juan Mirasierras, of Avenida Reina Vitoria, Madrid, Spain; 2 s (Daniel b 1974, Thomas b 1976); m 2, 20 Feb 1988 (m dis 2004), Judith Britannia Caroline, da of David Henry John Griffiths Powell; 2 s (Rhodri b 1990, Alexander Rollo Tristram b 1993); *Career* called to the Bar Lincoln's Inn 1972 (bencher 1994); standing counsel to DG of Fair Trading 1980–86; *Recreations* gardening, bird watching, rough shooting, horse racing, tennis; *Style*— The Hon David Oliver, QC; ✉ Thirteen Old Square Chambers, 13–14 Old Square, Lincoln's Inn, London WC2A 3KE (☎ 020 7831 4445, e-mail dkrow@btinternet.com, website www.13oldsquare.com)

OLIVER, Prof (Ann) Dawn; Hon QC (2013); da of Ernest Gordon Borrett Taylor (d 1989), and Ann Zoë Mieke Taylor (d 1961); *b* 7 June 1942; *Educ* Notting Hill and Ealing HS, Newnham Coll Cambridge (MA, PhD, LLD); *m* 6 Jan 1967, Sir Stephen J L Oliver, *qv*, s of Capt P D Oliver, RN (d 1979); 2 da (Rebecca b 1969, Rosemary b 1972), 1 s (Adam b 1970); *Career* called to the Bar Middle Temple 1965 (bencher 1996, treas 2011); in practice 1965–69, conslt Legal Action Gp 1973–76, assoc memb Blackstone Chambers Temple 1994–2013; UCL: lectr in law 1976–88, sr lectr 1988–90, reader in public law 1990–93, prof of constitutional law 1993–2008 (emeritus 2008–), dean of the faculty and head of dept 1993–98 and 2007; memb: Inst of Public Policy Res working gp on a constitution for the UK 1990–91, Hansard Soc Cmmn on Election Campaigns 1990–91, Study of Parliament Gp 1992– (pres 2010–15), Justice Working Party on Interventions in Public Interest Cases 1994–95, Royal Cmmn on Reform of House of Lords 1999, Fabian Soc Cmmn on the Future of the Monarchy 2002–03, Animal Procedures Ctee 2003–11; chair Advtg Advsy Ctee ITC 1999–2003; tstee Br Inst of Int and Comparative Law 2011–; ed Public Law 1993–2001; assoc fell Newnham Coll Cambridge 1996–99; hon fell Soc of Advanced Legal Studies 1997, hon fell UCL 2001; FBA 2005; *Books* The Changing Constitution (ed with J L Jowell, 1985, 8 edn with J L Lowell and C O'Cinneide, 2015), Cohabitation – The Legal Implications (1987), New Directions in Judicial Review (ed with J L Jowell, 1988), Economical with the Truth – The Law and the Media in a Democracy (ed with D Kingsford Smith, 1989), Government in the United Kingdom: The Search for Accountability, Effectiveness and Citizenship (1991), The Foundations of Citizenship (with D Heater, 1994), Public Service Reforms (with G Drewry, 1996), Halsbury's Laws of England Constitutional Law (4 edn, ed with Lord Lester of Herne Hill, QC, 1996), The Law and Parliament (ed with G Drewry, 1998), Common Values and the Public – Private Divide (1999), Constitutional Reform in the UK (2003), Human Rights and the Private Sphere (ed with J Fedtke, 2007), Justice, Legality and the Rule of Law, Lessons from the Pitcairn Prosecutions (ed, 2009), The Regulatory State: Constitutional Implications (ed with T Prosser and R Rawlings, 2010), How Constitutions Change: A Comparative Study (ed with C Fusaro, 2011), Parliament and the Law (ed with A Horne and G Drewry, 2013), Constitutional Guardians: the House of Lords (2015); *Recreations* walking, Aldeburgh, travel, theatre and cinema, art history, family; *Style*— Professor Dawn Oliver; ✉ University College London, Laws Faculty, Bentham House, Endsleigh Gardens, London WC1H 0EG (☎ 020 7679 1409, e-mail d.oliver@ucl.ac.uk)

OLIVER, Dr Ian Thomas; QPM (1984); s of Thomas Oliver, GM (d 1967), and Mary Elizabeth, *née* Burton (d 2000); *b* 24 January 1940, Isleworth, Middx; *Educ* Hampton GS, Univ of Nottingham (LLB, MPhil), Univ of Strathclyde (PhD); *m* 22 Feb 1964, Elsie, *née* Chalmers; 1 da (Stephanie Katherine b 20 Dec 1965), 2 s (Guy Thomas b 29 Sept 1967, Craig Stewart b 15 May 1969); *Career* Offr RAF 1959–61; Constable rising to Supt Metropolitan Police 1961–77, awarded Cwlth Fndn bursary to Kenya 1972, asst Chief Constable Mgmnt Servs Northumbria Police 1978–79 (Chief Supt 1977–78), Chief Constable Central Scotland Police 1979–90, Chief Constable Grampian Police 1990–98; head of rule of law Civilian Military Mission Helmand (CMMH) Afghanistan 2009–; awarded Winston Churchill Travelling Fellowship to North America (drugs educn progs) 1986, visiting lectr Univ of Teeside 2001; drug trg conslt Aberdeen Coll of FE 2005–; memb: various ctees IACP 1982–98 (int vice-pres 1997–98), Editorial Bd Criminal Law Review 1989–98, Home Sec's Firearms Consultative Ctee 1989–98, Steering Gp for Royalty Protection Home Office 1990–98, Service Authy for Nat Criminal Intelligence Service 1997–98, Bd Int Scientific and Medical Forum on Drug Abuse 1999–, Inst on Global Drug Policy 2001–, Advsy Bd EURAD (Europe Against Drugs) 2007–; chm Crime Ctee ACPO Scotland 1997–98 (pres 1983–84 and 1993–94); conslt: UN Drug Control Programme, Police Reform Programme United Nations Office on Drugs and Crime (UNODC) Kenya 2014; columnist Aberdeen Press & Journal 2001–05, memb Editorial Bd Jl of Global Drug Policy and Practice 2005; memb: Int Criminal Justice Symposium SUNY 1982, L'Ordre de Bon Temps Nova Scotia 1985; chm Nat Police Lifeboat Appeal Ctee 1990–92; tstee: Mayor of Bulawayo's Children's Fund 2005, A to Z Tst (Aid to Zimbabwe) 2008–; Civilian Service Medal Afghanistan 2012; FRSA 1993; *Books* The Metropolitan Police Approach to the Prosecution of Juvenile Offenders (1977), Police, Government and Accountability (1987, 2 edn 1996), Drug Affliction: What you need to know (2006); *Clubs* RAF; *Style*— Dr Ian Oliver, QPM; ✉ e-mail snowbird@ifb.co.uk

OLIVER, Jamie Trevor; MBE (2003); s of Trevor Oliver, and Sally Oliver; *b* May 1975; *Educ* Westminster Catering Coll; *m* 2000, Jools; 3 da (Poppy Honey b 18 March 2002, Daisy Boo b 10 April 2003, Petal Blossom Rainbow b 3 April 2009), 1 s (Buddy Bear Maurice b 15 Sept 2010); *Career* formerly: chef in France, head pastry chef Neal Street Restaurant London, chef River Café London, conslt chef Monte's London; currently prop: Fifteen London (fndr 2002), Union Jacks, Jamie's Italian, Barbecoa, Jamie Oliver Diner; designer of small electrical kitchen equipment for Philips and cookware for Tefal; *Television* The Naked Chef (three series, BBC), Jamie's Kitchen (Channel 4) 2002, Jamie's School Dinners (Channel 4) 2005, Jamie's Chef (Channel 4) 2007, Jamie At Home (Food Network) 2007, Jamie's Ministry of Food (Channel 4) 2008, Jamie's American Road Trip (Channel 4) 2009, Jamie's Family Christmas (Channel 4) 2009, Jamie Oliver's Food Revolution (ABC) 2010, Jamie's Great Britain 2011, Jamie's 15 Minute Meals 2012, Jamie and Jimmy's Food Fight Club 2012, Jamie's Money Saving Meals 2013, Jamie & Jimmy's Friday Night Feast 2014; also Jamie's Food Tube www.youtube.com/jamieoliver; *Awards* incl: GQ Man of the Year 2000, GQ Best Chef Award in the USA, Most Stylish Male TV Personality award Elle Style Awards 2000, TV Quick Award for Best TV Cook 2000, BAFTA (for The Naked Chef) 2001, Tatler Best Restaurant Award (for Fifteen) 2003, Academy Award of Excellence Tio Pepe Carlton London Restaurant Awards 2003, Time Out Special Award for Outstanding Achievement 2003, Glenfiddich Food and Drink Awards 2003, Outstanding Reality Programme Emmy Award (for Jamie Oliver's Food Revolution) 2010, TED Award 2010; *Books* The Naked Chef (1999), The Return of The Naked Chef (2000, WH Smith Book Award 2001), Happy Days with The Naked Chef (2001), Jamie's Kitchen (2003, WH Smith Book Award), Jamie's Dinners (2004), Something for the Weekend (2005), Jamie's Italy (2005), Cook with Jamie: My Guide to Making You a Better Cook (2006), Jamie at Home: Cook Your Way to the Good Life (2007), Jamie's Ministry of Food: Anyone Can Learn to Cook in 24 Hours (2008), Jamie's America (2009), Jamie Does... (2010), Jamie's 30-Minute Meals (2010), Jamie's Great Britain (2011), Jamie's 15 Minute Meals (2012), Save with Jamie (2013); also writes for Jamie Magazine (available in UK, Germany, Holland, Russia, France and Estonia); *Style*— Jamie Oliver, Esq, MBE

OLIVER, Rt Rev John Keith; s of Walter Keith Oliver (d 1977), of Danehill, E Sussex, and Ivy, *née* Nightingale (d 1981); *b* 14 April 1935; *Educ* Westminster (fell 2003–), Gonville & Caius Coll Cambridge (MA, MLitt); *m* 16 Sept 1961, Meriel (d 2014), da of Sir Alan Moore, Bt (d 1959), of Battle, E Sussex; 2 s (Thomas b 1964, Henry b 1968), 1 da (Mary b 1971 d 2002); *Career* curate Hilborough Gp of Parishes Norfolk 1964–68, chaplain and asst master Eton Coll 1968–72; team rector: S Molton Gp 1973–82 (rural dean 1974–80), Central Exeter 1982–85; archdeacon of Sherborne, canon of Salisbury and priest-in-charge W Stafford 1985–90, bishop of Hereford 1990–2003, hon asst bishop Diocese of Swansea and Brecon 2004–; chaplain Royal Agric Benevolent Inst 2003–13 (tstee 2005–13); chm C of E's Advsy Bd of Min 1993–98; chm Rural Support Network (West Midlands) 2003–07, tstee Marches Energy Agency 2004–13, memb NI Office Cmmn of Inquiry into murder of Billy Wright 2004–10; memb House of Lords 1997–2003; pres: Nat farm Attractions Network 2009–13, Auto-cycle Union 2009–; Freeman of the City of Hereford 2002; FRAgS 2012 (ARAgS 2007); *Recreations* railways, music, architecture, walking, motorcycling; *Clubs* Oxford and Cambridge, Herefordshire CCC, Farmers'; *Style*— The Rt Rev John Oliver; ✉ The Old Vicarage, Glascwm, Powys LD1 5SE

OLIVER, Keith Edward; *b* 5 September 1956, London; *Career* slr specialising in commercial, regulatory and insolvency litigation; Peters & Peters: joined as trainee, ptnr 1983, sr ptnr 2005–, head of commercial litigation/commercial fraud; vice-pres d'honneur Assoc Internationale des Jeunes Avocats (AIJA), founding past pres AIJA Commercial Fraud Cmmn; memb: Int Bar Assoc, Br Italian Lawyers' Assoc; *Recreations* the arts, football (playing and spectating), wine appreciation; *Style*— Keith E Oliver, Esq; ✉ Peters & Peters, 15 Fetter Lane, London EC4A 1BW (☎ 020 7822 7722, mobile 07785 232122, fax 020 7822 7788, e-mail keoliver@petersandpeters.com)

OLIVER, Mark Leo; s of Rudolf Oliver, of London, and Anita, *née* Levinson; *b* 19 September 1963; *Educ* Orange Hill HS, Hertford Coll Oxford (BA); *m* (m dis), Victoria Rosalind, *née* Pugh; *Career* econ analyst National Economic Research Associates 1985–87 (work incl conslt to Peacock Ctee on funding of the BBC), conslt and media gp mangr Deloitte Haskins & Sells Consultancy 1987–89; BBC Policy and Planning Unit: business analyst 1989–90, business policy advsr to BBC Bd of Mgmnt (on corp strategy and operational efficiency and effectiveness) 1990–93, chief advsr (corp strategy) 1993–95; md Oliver & Ohlbaum Associates Ltd 1995–; *Style*— Mark Oliver, Esq; ✉ Oliver & Ohlbaum Associates Ltd, 5 Lambton Place, London W11 2SH (☎ 020 7313 5900, fax 020 7985 0645)

OLIVER, Sir (James) Michael Yorrick; kt (2003), DL (2004), JP (1987); s of Sqdn Ldr George Leonard Jack Oliver (d 1984), of Mallorca, and Patricia Rosamund, *née* Douglas; *b* 13 July 1940; *Educ* Brunswick Sch, Wellington; *m* 22 June 1963, Sally Elizabeth Honor, da of George Gerhard Exner (d 1965), of London W1; 2 da (Sophia Tugela Rosamund b 14 Oct 1969, Justine Umthandi Electra b 29 Dec 1971); *Career* asst mangr Rediffusion Ltd Leicester 1959–63, mangr Helios Ltd Johannesburg 1965–70; ptnr Kitcat & Aitken 1977–86 (joined 1970), dir Kitcat Aitken & Co 1986–90, md Carr Kitcat & Aitken 1990–93; dir Lloyds Investment Managers Ltd 1994–98; dir: Oliver's Wharf Management Co 1970–2003, Garbhaig Hydro Power Co 1988–2000, Highland Light & Power 1994–2001, Hill Samuel UK Emerging Companies Investment Tst 1995–2000, The Central & Eastern European Fund 1995– (chm), The Euro-Spain Fund 1996–2005, The Portugal Growth Fund Ltd 1996–2001, European Growth Fund 2001–08, Europa Oil & Gas (Hldgs) plc 2004–10 (chm), Zirax plc 2005–10 (chm), Hampden Capital plc 2005–10, Helios Underwriting (named Hampden Underwriting plcuntil 2014) 2007– (chm); tstee: UK Growth & Income Fund, The Income Plus Fund (chm), Zenex Fndn 1998–99; Alderman Ward of Bishopsgate 1987–2009 (memb Common Cncl 1980–87), Sheriff City of London 1997–98, Lord Mayor of London 2001–02; chllr City Univ 2001–02; govr: Bishopsgate Fndn, King Edward's Sch Witley, Christ's Hosp 1979–2006, Univ of East London 1999–2003, The Hon the Irish Soc 2007–09; chm: Cncl of Tstees The Museum in Docklands 1993–2002, City of London Centre St John Ambulance 1998–2006; memb Bd of Govrs Museum of London 2003–09; memb: City of London Archaeological Tst, Ctee City of London Historical Soc; memb Ct of Assts Worshipful Co of Ironmongers (Master 1991–92); Hon LLD, Hon DLitt; FSI; KStJ; *Recreations* archaeology, travel, photography; *Clubs* City of London, East India; *Style*— Sir Michael Oliver; ✉ Paradise Barns, Bucks Lane, Little Eversden, Cambridge CB23 1HL (☎ 01223 263303, e-mail olivers@petticoat.demon.co.uk)

OLIVER, Prof Raymond; s of Joseph Oliver (d 1995), and Ethel Margaret, *née* Anderson (d 1993); *b* 26 November 1951; *Educ* Beath HS, Heriot-Watt Univ (BSc, PhD); *m* 1974, Darina Maria, da of late Ondrej ?urilla; 1 da (Clara Cecilia b 1977), 1 s (Peter Duncan b 1983); *Career* ICI: process engr Runcorn 1974–81, sr process engr Billingham 1981–86, engrg assoc 1986–89, conslt ICI Explosives Canada 1987–97, co research assoc 1989–94, mangr Particle Process Engrg Gp 1990–94, ICI fell 1994–2004; Cenamps: non-exec dir 2003, dir science and innovation 2005–08; dir Arrow Science Consltg 2008; prof of interactive materials Sch of Design Northumbria Univ 2010; visiting prof: Univ of Nottingham 1996, Univ of Leeds 2003, Univ of Palermo 2004, Univ of Newcastle 2006; visiting prof of functional materials Royal Coll of Art 2010; memb: Royal Acad of Engrg/Royal Soc Working Gp on Nanoscience and Nanomanufacturing 2003–04, Royal Soc 'Science in Soc' Working Gp 2004, Bd Organic Electronics Assoc Europe 2006; assessor EU FW/7 Thematic Area NMP & ICT 2004; memb Industrial Advsy Bd Univ of Newcastle upon Tyne, memb Industrial Liaison Ctee UCL; Hon DEng Heriot-Watt Univ 2001; FIChemE 1995, CEng 1995, FREng 1998; *Publications* incl: Granulation (book, 1981), Jet Induced Emulsification (paper, 1991); over 100 refereed papers, lectures and talks in jls and int conferences; *Recreations* theatre, visual art, contemporary music, golf, travel; *Style*— Prof Raymond Oliver, FREng

OLIVER, Sir Stephen John Lindsay; kt (2007), QC (1980); s of Phillip Daniel Oliver (Capt RN, d 1979), of Carlton, and Audrey Mary Taylor (d 2001); *b* 14 November 1938, Dartmouth, Devon; *Educ* Rugby, Oriel Coll Oxford (MA); *m* 1967, Prof (Ann) Dawn Oliver, *qv*, da of Gordon Taylor (d 1989); 2 da (Rebecca Dawn (Mrs Holloway) b 20 April 1969, Rosemary Hope b 21 July 1972), 1 s (Adam James b 2 July 1970); *Career* RNVR (submariner) 1957–59; barr; bencher 1987, asst Parly boundary cmmr, recorder 1989–91, circuit judge SE Circuit 1991–92, presiding special cmmr 1992–2009; pres: VAT Tbnls 1992–94, VAT and Duties Tbnls 1994–2009, Financial Services and Markets Tbnl 2001–10, Pensions Regulator Tbnl 2005–10, First Tier Tax Chamber 2009–11; vice-pres Upper Tier Finance and Tax Chamber 2009–11; mediator 2012–; chm Blackheath Concert Halls 1986–92, memb Cncl London Sinfonietta 1993–2014; tstee: Britten-Pears Fndn 2001–09, TaxAid 2006–13; Hon FCInstT 1997; *Recreations* music, golf, film; *Style*— Sir Stephen Oliver, QC; ✉ 16 Bedford Row, London WC1R 4EF (☎ 020 7414 8080, e-mail stephen@oliver.net)

OLIVER, Timothy Patrick (CAMROUX-); s of Wing Cdr George Leonard, DFC, AFC (d 1984), and Patricia Rosamund, *née* Douglas; *b* 2 March 1944; *Educ* Christ's Hosp; *m* 18 July 1966, Susan Elizabeth, da of Maj Frederick Wilson Hanham, of Bucks; 2 s (James Richard b Sept 1967, Charles Guy b 1 April 1970), 1 da (Alexa Kate Louise b 25 Dec 1974); *Career* asst gen mangr IGI (SA) 1969–71; dir: Manson Byng Gp 1971–, Hampden Russell plc 1987–; chm: Hampden Insurance Holdings Ltd 1973–, Market Run-Off Services plc 1984–, Hampden plc 1993–, Hampden Gp BV 1998–, Hampden Legal plc 1998–, Hampden Capital plc 1998–; memb Economic Research Cncl; chm Historic Houses Assoc Thames and Chilterns 2001–04; Freeman City of London 1966, Master Worshipful Co of Ironmongers 2002; FRGS 1963, FInstD; *Recreations* shooting, fishing, skiing, tennis, dogs; *Clubs* Brook's, City of London, City Livery Yacht, City Livery, Lloyds, Chatham House, Oxford Business Alumni; *Style*— Tim Oliver, Esq; ✉ Hampden House, Great Hampden, Buckinghamshire HP16 9RD (☎ 01494 488888, fax 01494 488686); Hampden plc, 42 Crutched Friars, London EC3N 2AP (☎ 020 7863 6620, mobile 07775 501248, e-mail tim.oliver@hampden.co.uk); Hampden Capital plc, 40 Gracechurch Street, London EC3V 0AA

OLIVER, Vaughan William; s of Ernest Oliver, and Doreen, *née* Tindale; *b* 12 September 1957; *Educ* Ferryhill GS, Newcastle upon Tyne Poly (BA); *Career* graphic designer, art dir; packaging designer: Benchmark 1980, Michael Peters Gp 1981; record cover designer (under name 23 Envelope, with Nigel Grierson), 4AD (record co) 1983–88, freelance (under name v23, with Chris Bigg) 1988–98, ptnr v23 (with Chris Bigg) 1998–; record covers for gps incl: Cocteau Twins, Heidi Berry, His Name is Alive, Lush, Pixies, The Psychedelic Furs, This Mortal Coil, The Breeders, David Sylvian; gp exhibitions incl: British Design, New Traditions (Boymans Museum Rotterdam) 1989, Pictures of Rock (Denmark) 1990, British Design 1790–1990 (Calif) 1990, Best of British Design (Tokyo) 1990, The Art of Selling Songs 1690–1990 (V&A) 1991; solo exhibitions: Exhibition/Exposition (Nantes, St Brieuc 1990, Paris 1991), Expo 23 (Tokyo) 1991, Glove (Osaka) 1992 and (Tokyo) 1993, 13 Year Itch (ICA London) 1993, This Rimy River (LA and UK) 1994, Is Minty a Man? (Newcastle upon Tyne) 1996; other design work includes: book jackets (Serpents Tail, Picador), book design (Tokyo Salamander, Shinro Ohtake), freelance music projects (Virgin, RCA, East West), TV title sequences for BBC2 (Snub TV, Gimme 8), conf publicity (Kingston Poly, V&A Museum), fashion catalogue (John Galliano, Aspesi), TV station identity, design and direction (Documania, Canal Plus, Madrid), posters (Angelin Preljocaj, Paris and Young Vic London), TV advert (Microsoft); memb Assoc of Music Indust Designers (AMID); *Style*— Vaughan Oliver, Esq; ✉ v23, Crombie Mews, 11A Abercrombie Street, London SW11 2JB (☎ 020 7978 6636/4860, fax 020 7978 5552)

OLIVER-BELLASIS, Hugh Richard; s of Lt-Col John Oliver-Bellasis, DSO, JP, DL (d 1979), and Anne Mary, *née* Bates (d 2006); *b* 11 April 1945; *Educ* Winchester, RMA Sandhurst; *m* 7 Aug 1971, Daphne Phoebe, da of Christopher Parsons, of Hatchwood House, Odiham (d 1999); 2 da (Joanna (Mrs Andrew Runciman) b 8 April 1975, Nicola (Mrs Thomas Chapman) b 12 June 1978); *Career* 2 Lt Royal Fusiliers City of London Regt 1964, Welsh Gds 1970, Maj 1977 (ret); dir Manydown Co Ltd 1964–2007; Parish Cncl 1980–2001; pres Br Crop Prodn Cncl 2003–07; chm Br Deer Soc 1986–96, vice-chm Game Conservancy Tst 1999–; memb Grasshoppers' Assoc 1989, memb Force Strategy Ind Advsy Gp Hants Constabulary 2011 (chm 2012); Freeman City of London 1967; Liveryman: Worshipful Co of Merchant Taylors 1971 (memb Ct of Assts 1998, Master 2006–07), Worshipful Co of Gunmakers 1990; FRAgS 1992 (ARAgS 1990); *Recreations* field sports, wine, food, photography, woodturning; *Clubs* Army and Navy, Boodle's, MCC; *Style*— Hugh Oliver-Bellasis, Esq, FRAgS; ✉ Wootton House, Wootton St Lawrence, Basingstoke, Hampshire RG23 8PE (☎ 01256 780336, e-mail hugh@monkeyloader.com)

OLIVER-JONES, His Hon Stephen; QC (1996); s of Arthur William Jones (d 2002), of King's Stanley, Glos, and Kathleen, *née* Woodcock (d 1993); *b* 6 July 1947; *Educ* Marling Sch Stroud, Univ Coll Durham (BA); *m* 16 Dec 1972, Margaret Anne, da of Ronald Thomas Richardson (d 2014); 1 da (Claire Felicity b 22 March 1979), 1 s (Robin Stephen b 19 March 1982); *Career* lectr in law Durham Tech Coll 1968–70, called to the Bar Inner Temple 1970 (bencher 2010), recorder 1993 (asst recorder 1988), circuit judge (Midland & Oxford Circuit) 2000–15, designated civil judge Coventry and Walsall 2001–08, judge of the First-Tier Health, Educn and Social Care Chamber (Mental Health) 2008–; memb: Mental Health Review Tbnl 1997–2008, Civil Procedure Rule Ctee 2002–08; *Recreations* fly fishing, book-collecting; *Clubs* East India; *Style*— His Hon Stephen Oliver-Jones, QC; ✉ e-mail soliverjones@msn.com

OLIVIERI, René; s of Hal W Bowen (d 2000), and Dixie Ann Olivieri, *née* Mann (d 1995); *b* 1 May 1953, Everett, WA; *Educ* Univ of Oregon (BA), Univ of Stuttgart (scholar), Johns Hopkins Univ (MA); *m* 2004, Dr Anne Luetcke-Olivieri; 1 step s (Julius Luetcke b 15 July 1993), 1 step da (Katharina Luise Luetcke b 29 Nov 1994); *Career* ed MIT Press 1978–80; Blackwell Publishers: econs publisher 1980–83, editorial dir 1983–85, dep md 1985–88, md 1988–2000; ceo Blackwell Publishing Ltd 2000–07; chm: InfoSource Inc 1990–2000, Polity Press 1995–2000, Marston Book Distributors 1998–2000; memb Bd HE Funding Cncl for England 2007–; tstee Tubney Charitable Tst 2002– (chm 2007–); *Recreations* tennis, skiing, scuba diving, pilates, music, literature, theatre, horse riding; *Style*— René Olivieri, Esq; ✉ 18 Farndon Road, Oxford OX2 6RT (☎ 01865 315131, e-mail olivieri@nildram.co.uk)

OLLERENSHAW, Eric; OBE (1991); s of Eric Ollerenshaw, and Barbara Ripley; *Educ* Hyde Co GS, LSE (BSc), Garnet Coll of Educn; *Career* teacher 1973–99; GLA: memb London Assembly (Cons) London (list) 2000–04, ldr Cons Gp, dep chair Econ Devpt Ctee, memb Met Police Authy; MP (Cons) Lancaster and Fleetwood 2010–15; PPS to Rt Hon the Baroness Warsi, *qv*, 2010–; *Recreations* reading, history; *Style*— Eric Ollerenshaw, OBE; ✉ House of Commons, London SW1A 0AA

OLLERENSHAW, Stephen Christopher; s of Roy Ollerenshaw, of Padstow, Cornwall, and Kim, *née* Hartland (d 1991); *b* 9 April 1970, Birmingham; *Educ* Sollihull Sch, Univ of Essex (BA, MA), Coll of Law Guildford, Univ of Birmingham; *m* Lauren, *née* Steadman; *Career* slr specialising in IT law; slr: Osborne Clarke 1997–98 (trainee slr 1995–97), Wragge & Co 1998–2002; co-founding ptnr Technology Law Alliance Slrs 2003–; author of various pubns in legal and IT press, business mentor with various univs; memb Law Soc; *Recreations* motor cars, football, guitar, gardening, classic wooden boats, ornithology; *Clubs* Goodwood Road Racing (GRRC); *Style*— Stephen Ollerenshaw, Esq; ✉ Technology Law Alliance, 7 Stratford Place, London W1C 1AY (☎ 0845 351 9092, e-mail stephen.ollerenshaw@tlawa.co.uk)

OLLEY, Martin Burgess; s of Robert William Olley (d 1969), of Sheringham, Norfolk, and Dorothy Lillian Alexander, *née* Burgess (d 1941); *b* 11 August 1932; *Educ* Gresham's, Coll of Estate Mgmnt London; *m* 1 (m dis 1971), Averil Rosemary Phyllis, *née* Cann; 2 s (Clive Matthew Burgess b 1961, Edward Martin Burgess b 1967), 1 da (Lucy Ann Burgess b 1963); m 2, 1980, Moira Bernadette, da of Joseph Kelly (d 1968); *Career* RAF 1950–52; Norwich Union: London Estates mangr 1973–80, Norwich estates mangr 1980–82, chief estates mangr 1983–; memb Gen Cncl Br Property Fedn, former pres Norwich Wanderers CC; Freeman City of London 1974, Liveryman Worshipful Co of Woolmen 1978; FRICS; *Recreations* golf, boating, squash, tennis, walking; *Clubs* RAC, Norfolk Broads Yacht; *Style*— Martin Olley, Esq; ✉ 1 Marston Lane, Eaton, Norwich, Norfolk NR4 6LZ (☎ 01603 456495); 55 Netheravon Road, Chiswick, London W4 2NA (☎ 020 8994 1392); Norwich Union Real Estate Managers Ltd, Sentinel House, 37 Surrey Street, Norwich NR1 3PW (☎ 01603 682256, fax 01603 683950)

OLLIFF, Barry Martin; s of Clarence Martin William Olliff, and Patricia Joan, *née* Greenley; *b* 31 December 1944; *Educ* Hinchley Wood County Secdy Sch; *m* Margaret Ann, da of Francis Samuel Thomas Cleave; 1 s (Andrew James), 1 da (Samantha Claire); *Career* various appts in investment depts of: Rowe Swann & Co Stockbrokers 1962–63, Denny Bros/Pinchin Denny Stockjobbers 1963–79, Laing & Cruickshank Stockbrokers 1979–86 (dir 1983–86); md Olliff & Partners plc 1987–97; ceo: City of London Unit Trust Managers 1991–, City of London Investment Gp 1997–; MSI; *Recreations* cricket, skiing; *Style*— Barry Olliff, Esq; ✉ City of London Investment Group plc, 77 Gracechurch Street, London EC3V 0AS (☎ 020 7711 0771, fax 020 7711 0772)

OLSEN, John Richard; s of (Lawrence) Nigel Guy Olsen, and Rosemary Elizabeth, *née* Kies, of Saffron Walden, Essex; *b* 7 January 1964, Herts; *Educ* Charterhouse, Univ of Durham (BA Archaeology); *m* 9 May 1992, Juliet Mary; 2 da (Lucy b 15 Dec 1993, Samantha b 24 Jan 1998), 1 s (Jack b 30 Aug 1995); *Career* PR exec; Broad Street Associates PR 1986–89, Shandwick Consultants 1990–97 (latterly dir), fndr and managing dir Hogarth 1997–2010, md MHP Communications 2010–; chm Bd of Govrs Halstead Sch Woking 2009–; *Recreations* sailing, golf, hillwalking, fishing; *Style*— John Olsen, Esq; ✉ St Breward, Rickford, Worplesdon, Surrey GU3 3PH (☎ 01483 235188)

OLVER, Sir Richard; kt (2013); *b* 1947, Woodford Green, Essex; *Career* BP: joined 1973, vice-pres BP Pipelines Inc BP N America 1979, divnl mangr for new technology 1983, divnl mangr of corp planning 1985, gen mangr (gas) BP Exploration Europe 1988, head of corporate strategy and COS to the Chm 1990, chief exec BP Exploration USA 1992, dep chief exec BP Exploration 1995, dir of exploration and prodn BP 1998 and BP Amoco plc 1999–2002, dep gp chief exec BP plc 2003–04; non-exec chm BAE Systems plc 2004–14; non-exec dir: Reuters Gp plc 1997–2008 (sr ind dir 2004–08), Thomson Reuters 2008–09; advsr: Clayton Dubilier and Rice 2008–, HSBC; UK business ambass 2008–; chair Educn for Egrg 2009–, memb Trilateral Cmmn, memb UK PM's Business Advsy Gp 2010–; DSc (hc): City Univ 2004, Cranfield Univ 2006; CEng, FICE, FREng; *Recreations* sailing, skiing, ballet, fine arts; *Style*— Sir Richard Olver

OLYMPITIS, Emmanuel John; s of John Emmanuel Olympitis, and Argyro, *née* Theodorou; *b* 19 December 1948; *Educ* King's Sch Canterbury, UCL (LLB); *m* 1, 26 Oct 1979 (m dis 1983), Jan Cushing; 1 s (John); m 2, 1 Dec 1995, Emily Clare, da of Michael John Benjamin Todhunter, *qv*; 2 s (Michael, Alexander (twins)), 1 da (Olympia); *Career* chief exec and dir Aitken Hume International plc 1986–89; chm Johnson & Higgins Ltd 1993–96, gp md Johnson & Higgins Holdings Ltd 1992–96; chm: Pacific Media plc 1999–2004 (non-exec dir 2004–), Bella Media plc 2003–04, Lyra Investments Ltd 2004–; dir Norman 95 SpA; memb: GB Int Fencing Squad 1966–70, Kent County Fencing Team 1966–70 (foil and épée champion 1966); *Books* By Victories Undone (1988); *Recreations* writing, sailing; *Clubs* Turf, Special Forces; *Style*— Emmanuel Olympitis, Esq; ✉ Kalymnos, Dodecanese Islands, Greece

ONDAATJE, Sir (Philip) Christopher; kt (2003), OC (1993), CBE (2000); s of Philip Mervyn Ondaatje, of Sri Lanka, and Doris, *née* Gratiaen; bro of Michael Ondaatje, *qv*; *b* 1933, Kandy, Sri Lanka; *Educ* St Thomas' Coll Ceylon, Blundell's; *Career* Nat and Grindlays Bank London 1951–55, Burns Bros & Denton Toronto 1955–56, Montrealer Magazine and Canada Month Magazine 1956–57, Maclean-Hunter Publishing Co Ltd Montreal 1957–62, The Financial Post Toronto 1963–65, Pitfield Mackay Ross & Co Ltd Toronto 1965–69; fndr and former chm: The Pagurian Corp Ltd 1967–89, Loewen Ondaatje McCutcheon & Co Ltd 1970–88; former vice-chm Hees Int Bancorp Inc; fndr and chm: The Ondaatje Fndn, The Ondaatje Prize for Portraiture (in assoc with RSPP), RSL Ondaatje Prize; hon govr Art Gallery of Nova Scotia; life patron Bd Portrait Fund Nat Portrait Gall; memb Advsy Bd: RSPP, Lakefield Coll Sch Ontario; govr emeritus Blundell's Sch; memb Canadian Olympic Bob-Sled Team 1964; Royal Canadian Geographical Soc Gold Medal 2011; LLD (hc) Dalhousie Univ 1994, Hon DLitt Univ of Buckingham 2003, Hon DLitt Univ of Exeter 2003, Hon DLitt Macquarie Univ Australia 2011; FRSL, FRGS; *Books* The Prime Ministers of Canada 1867–1967, The Prime Ministers of Canada 1867–1985, Olympic Victory (1964), Leopard in the Afternoon (1989), The Man-Eater of Punanai (1992), Sindh Revisted (1996), Journey to the Source of the Nile (1998), Hemingway in Africa (2003), Woolf in Ceylon (2005), The Power of Paper (2007), The Glenthorne Cat (2008), The Last Colonial (2012), Love Duet (2013); *Clubs* Travellers, Somerset CCC (life memb), Lyford Cay (Bahamas), MCC; *Style*— Sir Christopher Ondaatje, Esq, OC, CBE

ONDAATJE, (Philip) Michael; s of Philip Mervyn Ondaatje, of Sri Lanka, and Doris, *née* Gratiaen; bro of Christopher Ondaatje, *qv*; *b* 12 September 1943; *Educ* St Thomas' Coll Sri Lanka, Dulwich Coll, Bishop's Univ Quebec, Univ of Toronto (BA), Queen's Univ Ontario (MA); *Career* prof English Dept Glendon Coll York Univ Toronto 1970–; ed Coach House Press 1970–94; Booker Prize for Fiction 1992; *Books* The Dainty Monsters (1967), The Man with Seven Toes (1969), The Collected Works of Billy The Kid (1970), The Broken Ark: A Book of Beasts (ed, 1971), Rat Jelly (1973), Coming Through Slaughter (1976), Personal Fictions: Stories by Munro, Wiebe, Thomas, and Blaise (ed, 1977), Elimination Dance (1978), There's a Trick with a Knife I'm Learning to Do (1979), The Long Poem Anthology (ed, 1979), Tin Roof (1982), Claude Glass (1982), Running in the Family (memoir, 1982), Secular Love (1984), In the Skin of a Lion (1987), From Ink Lake: Canadian Stories (ed, 1990), The Brick Reader (co-ed, 1991), The Cinnamon Peeler (poetry, 1991), The English Patient (1992, made into film 1996), Handwriting (1998), Lost Classics (co-ed, 2000), Anil's Ghost (2000), The Conversations: Walter Murch and the Art of Editing Film (2002), The Story (2005), Divisadero (2007); *Style*— Michael Ondaatje, Esq

ONIONS, Jeffery Peter; QC (1998); s of Derrick Onions (d 2005), and Violet, *née* Bond (d 1975); *b* 22 August 1957; *Educ* St Albans (Abbey) Sch, St John's Coll Cambridge (MA, LLM, Hockey blue); *m* 29 Aug 1987, Sally Louise, da of Roy Hine; 1 da (Grace b 8 Aug 1992); *Career* called to the Bar Middle Temple 1981 (Astbury scholar, bencher); elected memb Bar Cncl 1987–89; memb Audit Ctee Roehampton Univ 2010–15; *Recreations* cricket, wine, opera; *Clubs* MCC, Hawks' (Cambridge), Surrey CCC, Middlesex CCC, 1890; *Style*— Jeffery Onions, Esq, QC; ✉ 1 Essex Court, Temple, London EC4Y 9AR (☎ 020 7583 2000, fax 020 7583 0118)

ONIONS, His Hon Judge Robin William; s of late Ernest Onions, DFC, and late Edith Margaret Onions; *Educ* Priory GS Shrewsbury, LSE (LLB); *Career* admitted slr 1973, sr ptnr Lanyon Bowdler (formerly J C H Bowdler & Sons) 1993–2000 (ptnr 1977–2000), slr advocate 1995, asst recorder 1992, recorder 1995, circuit judge (Midland Circuit) 2000–; memb Law Soc; *Recreations* cricket, football, travel, walking, gardening, keeping fit; *Clubs* Shrewsbury Town FC, Cound Cricket (vice-pres); *Style*— His Hon Judge Onions; ✉ Wolverhampton Crown Court, Pipers Row, Wolverhampton WV1 3LQ (☎ 01902 481000, fax 01902 481001, mobile 07968 791012)

ONSLOW, Hon Richard; s of Rt Hon Lord Onslow of Woking, KCMG, PC (Life Peer, d 2001), and Lady June Hay (d 2002); *b* 27 June 1956; *Educ* Harrow, Univ of Oxford (MA), City Univ (DPL); *m* 27 July 1985, Phyllida (d 2000), da of Michael Moore, OBE, of Lindsey, Suffolk; 1 s (Thomas), 1 da (Isabella); *Career* called to the Bar Inner Temple 1982, recorder of the Crown Court; *Recreations* country pursuits, Tarrant Gunville Horse Show; *Clubs* MCC, Stragglers of Asia Cricket, Lords and Commons Cricket, Usk Valley Casting; *Style*— The Hon Richard Onslow; ✉ 3 Paper Buildings, 4 St Peter Street, Winchester, Hampshire (☎ 01962 868884)

ONSLOW-COLE, Julia Elizabeth; da of Michael Onslow-Cole (d 1986), and Joy Elizabeth Watson, OBE, JP, of Poole, Dorset; *b* 30 September 1959, London; *m* 12 April 1986, Neil Howard Thomas, FRCP, FRCPCH, DCH, s of Howard Donald Thomas; 4 da; *Career* ptnr

Pricewaterhouse Coopers Legal LLP (also legal markets leader and head of global immigration business practice); memb: Cncl Int Bar Assoc, Advsy Panel Office of the Immigration Services Cmmr; former memb Advsy Bd on Naturalisation and Integration to the Immigration Minister; chair Int Bar Assoc Charitable Tst and the Human Rights Inst Tst, vice-chair Int Bar Assoc Global Employment Inst; former dir Immigration Law Practitioners' Assoc; memb UK Assoc of European Law, memb COMPAS Advsy Bd, memb Advsy Bd Univ of Oxford, memb Migration Matters Tst, int assoc memb American Immigration Lawyers Assoc; chair of London Firsts's Immigration Working Gp; FSALS; *Publications* contributing co-ed: Butterworths Immigration Law Service, Sweet & Maxwell's Immigration Law and Practice, Macdonald's Immigration Law and Practice; Tottel's Immigration Law and Practice (gen ed, 4 edn 2009), Getting the Deal Through: Corporate Immigration 2015; *Style*— Ms Julia Onslow-Cole

ONWIN, Glen; *b* 1947, Edinburgh; *Educ* Edinburgh Coll of Art (DA), Moray House Coll of Educn; *Career* artist; art teacher Edinburgh 1972–79; Edinburgh Coll of Art Sch of Drawing and Painting: pt/t lectr 1979–87, lectr 1987–94, dir of postgrad studies 1992–2010, sr lectr 1994–2010, prof 2008–10, prof emeritus 2010–; visiting lectr: Glasgow Sch of Art 1979, Duncan of Jordanstone Coll of Art 1980, Grays Sch of Art Aberdeen 1983; worked Scottish Arts Cncl Studio Amsterdam 1979; memb Bd New 57 Gall 1974–84; exhbn selector Scottish Art Now 1982; Scottish Arts Cncl 1972; *Solo Exhibitions* Scottish Arts Cncl Gallery 1975, Serpentine Gallery London 1975, Arnolfini Gallery Bristol 1978, ICA London 1978, Third Eye Glasgow 1979, Fruit Market Gallery Edinburgh 1979, AIR Gallery London 1982, Crawford Arts Centre St Andrews 1989, Space-Ex Exeter 1989, John Hansard Gallery Southampton 1991, As Above so Below (Square Chapel Halifax, an installation with The Henry Moore Sculpture Trust), Flammable Solid Flammable Liquid (Tramway Glasgow, site specific installation) 1994, and others; *Group Exhibitions* Video Exhibition (Serpentine Gallery) 1975, Scottish Sculpture (Kelvingrove Museum Glasgow) 1975, Ulster Museum of Art Belfast 1976, Aspects of Landscape (British Cncl touring exhbn) 1976, Works on Paper (RA) 1977, Scottish Nat Gallery of Modern Art Edinburgh 1978, Invited Artists (RSA Festival Exhbn) 1979, Un Certain Art Anglais (ARC Musee d'Art Moderne Paris) 1979, JP2 Palais des Beaux Arts Brussels 1979, Demarcations (Demarco Gallery Edinburgh) 1984, City Arts Centre Edinburgh 1985, Sarajevo Winter Festival Sarajevo 1988, Scottish Art Since 1900 (Scottish Nat Gallery of Modern Art 1989 and Barbican 1990), Fruitmarket Open (Fruitmarket Gallery Edinburgh) 1990, From Art to Archaeology (S Bank Centre touring) 1991–92, A Quality of Light (St Ives Cornwall) 1997, Working Drafts (Envisioning the Human Genome Exhbn 2/10 Gallery London) 2002, An Turas (collaborative architecture/sculpture structure Isle of Tiree) 2003, Place of Origin (collaborative sculpture/landscape project Kemney Aberdeenshire) 2003–; *Public Collections* British Cncl, Contemporary Arts Soc, Scottish Arts Cncl, Scottish Nat Gallery of Modern Art, Univ of Salford, Arts Cncl of GB, Kelvingrove Museum, City Art Centre Edinburgh, Whitworth Art Gallery Manchester, Tate Gallery, Yorkshire Sculpture Park, Scottish Parliament, Royal Scottish Acad, Southampton City Art Gallery, Univ of Dundee; *Style*— Glen Onwin, Esq; ✉ 77 Duke Street, Leith, Edinburgh EH6 8HN (e-mail onwin@btopenworld.com, website www.onwin.co.uk)

ONWURAH, Chinyelu Susan (Chi); MP; *b* 12 April 1965; *Educ* Kenton Sch, Imperial Coll London (BEng), Manchester Business Sch (MBA); *Career* chartered engr 2003, worked in UK, France, US and Nigeria; former head of telecoms technol OFCOM; MP (Lab) Newcastle upon Tyne Central 2010–, shadow min of business, innovation and science 2010–13, shadow min Cabinet Office 2013–15, shadow min for culture and the digital economy 2015–; *Style*— Ms Chi Onwurah, MP; ✉ House of Commons, London SW1A 0AA (website www.chionwurahmp.com, Twitter @chionwurah)

OPENSHAW, David Kay; s of Frank Kay Openshaw, of Nelson, Lancs, and Florence Openshaw; *b* October 1946; *Educ* Nelson GS, Wadham Coll Oxford, Univ of Bradford Mgmnt Centre; *m* Jacqueline; 1 da (Jane), 1 s (Tom); *Career* ops dir Volvo UK 1980–85, md Lex Specialist Car Group 1986–90, vice-pres Lex Electronics USA 1990–91, md Motorway Tyres and Accessories Ltd 1992–97, mgmnt conslt 1997–; non-exec dir Thames Valley Enterprise 1996–97; croquet player: memb Harrow Oak Croquet Club 1971– (capt 1976–), memb GB team 1979–2002 (capt 1982–94 and 1999–2002); honours incl: Br Open champion 1979, 1981 and 1985, Br mens champion 1981, 1991 and 1995, US Open champion 1991, Canadian Open champion 1991, runner-up World Championship 1991, Br Mixed Doubles champion 2002 and 2003 (with Kathleen Priestley), Scottish Open champion 2006; GB rep: v Aust and NZ 1979, 1982, 1986, 1990, 1993 and 2000, v USA 1985, 1987, 1988, 1989, 1990, 1991, 1992, 1993, 1994, 1997, 1999, 2000 and 2002, v Ireland 2000; record for longest winning sequence of matches (39) May-Aug 1981; pres World Croquet Fedn 2003–09; chess: 4th Br Under 16 Chess Championship 1963, rep Lancs 1966–70, capt Oxford Univ 1968; int dir English Chess Fedn 2012–15; *Style*— David Openshaw, Esq

OPENSHAW, Hon Mr Justice; Sir (Charles) Peter Lawford Openshaw; kt (2005), DL (Lancs 2000); s of His Hon Judge William Harrison Openshaw, DL (d 1981), of Broughton, Lancs, and Elisabeth Joyce Emily, *née* Lawford; *b* 21 December 1947; *Educ* Harrow, St Catharine's Coll Cambridge (MA); *m* 15 Dec 1979, Caroline Jane Swift, QC (Hon Mrs Justice Swift), *qv*, da of Vincent Seymour Swift, of Brookhouse, Lancs; 1 da (Alexandra b 1984), 1 s (Henry b 1986); *Career* called to the Bar Inner Temple 1970 (bencher 2003); practised on Northern Circuit, junior 1973, asst recorder 1984–88, recorder 1988–99, QC 1991, sr circuit judge (Northern Circuit) 1999–2005, hon recorder Preston 1999–2005, judge of the High Court of Justice (Queen's Bench Div) 2005–, presiding judge North Eastern Circuit 2008–12; memb Criminal Procedure Rules Ctee 2005–; dir criminal judiciary Judicial Coll 2013–; hon canon Blackburn Cathedral 2008; *Recreations* fishing, gardening, country life; *Style*— The Hon Mr Justice Openshaw, DL; ✉ Royal Courts of Justice, Strand, London WC2A 2LL

OPIE, Alan John; OBE (2013); s of Jack Opie (d 1985), and Doris Winifred, *née* Bennetts; *b* 22 March 1945; *Educ* Truro Sch, Guildhall Sch of Music and Drama (AGSM), London Opera Centre (Cinzano scholar); *m* 18 April 1970, Kathleen Ann, da of Ernest Smales; 1 s (James Alexander b 1976), 1 da (Helen Louise b 1979); *Career* princ baritone ENO 1973–96; performed with: Royal Opera, Glyndebourne Festival Opera, Scottish Opera, Opera North, Eng Opera Gp, Chicago Lyric Opera, Bayreuth Festival, Paris Opera, Netherlands Opera, Brussels Opera, Hong Kong Festival, Buxton Festival, Stadtsoper Berlin, Bavarian State Opera, Wexford Festival, NY Met Opera, BBC Symphony Chorus and Orch (BBC Proms) 1996, La Scala Milan 1996, Gothenburg Symphony Orch (BBC Proms) 1997; concerts in: UK, Europe, USA and Australia; recordings with: CBS, EMI, Decca, Hyperion, Chandos; Grammy winner 1997 and 1998, Olivier Award nomination for outstanding achievement in opera for Falstaff 1998; *Recreations* golf; *Clubs* Leatherhead Golf; *Style*— Alan Opie, Esq, OBE

OPIE, Julian Gilbert; s of Roger G Opie, and Norma Opie; *b* 12 December 1958, London; *Educ* Magdalen Coll Sch Oxford, Chelsea Sch of Art, Goldsmiths Sch of Art London; *m* Aniela Opie; 3 da (Elena, Imogen, Padmini), 1 s (Paul); *Career* artist; solo exhbns: Lisson Gallery London 1983, 1996, 2000, 2001, 2004, 2008, 2011 and 2012, ICA London 1985, Kunsthalle Berlin 1991, Kohji Ogura Gallery Tokyo 1991, Wiener Secession Vienna 1992, Hayward Gall London 1993, Kunstverein Hanover 1994, Tramway Glasgow 1994, Barbara Thumm Gallery Berlin 1999, 2002 and 2004, Morrisson Judd London 1999, Meymac Centre d'Art Contemporain Abbaye St Andre France 2000, Alan Cristea London 2000, 2003, 2006, 2008 and 2011, Ikon Gallery Birmingham 2001, Patrick de Brock Gallery Knokke 2001 and 2004, Atelier Augarten Galerie Belvedere Vienna 2002, Barbara Krakow Gallery Boston MA 2002, 2007 and 2010, Mario Sequeira Gallery Braga 2002, 2005 and 2010, Rebecca Camhi Gallery Athens 2002, Galerie Bob Van Orsouw Zurich 2003, 2006 and 2011, Neues Museum Nuremberg 2003, Galerie Krobath Wimmer Vienna 2004, MCA Chicago 2004, Wetterling Gallery Stockholm 2004, Gallery Valentina Bonomo Rome 2005, Gallery MGM Oslo 2005, Scai the Bathouse Tokyo 2005, La Chocolateria Santiago de Compostela 2005, ICA Boston MA 2005–06, Museum of Indianapolis 2006, CAC Malaga 2006, Julian Opie in the 90s (King's Lynn Art Centre) 2007, San Diego Museum of Art 2007, Tokyo Met Museum of Photography 2008, Mie Prefecture Museum Japan 2008, Art Tower Mito Japan 2008, Krobath Wimmer Vienna 2008, MAK Vienna 2008, Patrick de Brock Knokke Belgium 2009, SCAI the Bathhouse Tokyo 2009, Sakshi Gallery Mumbai 2009, Kukje Gallery Seoul 2009, Dancing in Kivik (Kivik Art Centre Osterlen Sweden) 2009, Valentina Bonomo Rome 2009, Galerist Istanbul 2010, IVAM Valencia 2010, Krobath Berlin 2011; cmmns incl cover design for Blur: The Best of 2000 (winner Music Week CADS 2007); other projects and cmmns: Perimeter wall paintings HM Prison Wormwood Scrubs 1994, Imagine You Are Moving Heathrow Airport 1997, outdoor installation Public Art Fund City Hall Park NYC 2004, INFRA ROH 2009, Nat Portrait Gall 2011, Promenade Calgary Canada 2012; works in public collections: Aberdeen Art Gallery, Arts Cncl of GB, Banque Bruxelles Lambert, Carnegie Museum Pittsburgh, Collection Essl Vienna, Contemporary Art Soc, Daimler Chrysler Berlin, Dresdner Bank Berlin, Deutsche Bank Frankfurt, Daros Collection Zurich, Fonds Nat d'Art Contemporain France, Fundacion Caja de Pensiones Madrid, Gana Art Centre Seoul, Gjensidige Oslo, ICA Boston, Institut Valenciá d'Art Modern, Kunsthalle Bern, Kunsthaus Bregenz, Kunsthaus Zurich, Kresge Art Museum Michigan State Univ, Lenbachhaus Städtische Galerie Munich, Maison Europeene de la Photographie Paris, Museet for Samtidskunst Oslo, Museo d'Arte Contemporanea Prato, Museum of Fine Arts Boston, Museum of Modern Art NY, Neue Galerie Sammlung Ludwig, Neues Museum Nuremberg, Nat Gall of Victoria Melbourne, Nat Portrait Gallery London, Stedelijk Museum Amsterdam, Br Cncl, Br Museum, Calouste Gulbenkian Fndn Portugal, Govt Art Collection London, Israel Museum Jerusalem, Museum of Contemporary Art of Leon, Nat Museum of Art Osaka, Takamatsu City Museum of Art Japan, Tate Gallery London, V&A, Wadsworth Atheneum; Sargant fell British Sch Rome 1995–96, residency at Atelier Calder Sache France 1996; *Publications* Julian Opie: Portraits, Julian Opie; Art Tower Mito, Recent Works: MAK, Julian Opie: IVAM, Julian Opie: The Complete Editions 1984–2011; *Style*— Julian Opie, Esq; ✉ c/o Lisson Gallery, 52–54 Bell Street, London NW1 5DA (websites www.lisson.co.uk and www.julianopie.com)

OPPENHEIM-BARNES, Baroness (Life Peer UK 1989), of Gloucester in the County of Gloucestershire; Sally Oppenheim-Barnes; PC (1979); da of late Mark and Jeanette Viner, of Sheffield; *b* 26 July 1930; *Educ* Sheffield HS; *m* 1, 1949, Henry M Oppenheim (d 1980); 2 da (Hon Carolyn (Hon Mrs Selman) b 1951, Hon Rose Anne (Hon Mrs Mattick) b 1955), 1 s (Hon Phillip b 1956); m 2, 1984, John Barnes (d 2004); *Career* MP (Cons) Gloucester 1970–87 (when her s Philip was elected MP 1983, it was the first time that both a mother and son sat in the same Parl); formerly social worker with ILEA; chm Cons Parly Prices and Consumer Protection Ctee 1973–74 (vice-chm 1971–73), front bench oppn spokesman (seat in Shadow Cabinet) Prices and Consumer Protection 1974–79, min state (consumer affrs) Dept of Trade 1979–82, chm Ctee of Enquiry into Pedestrian Safety at Public Road Level Crossings 1982–; non-exec dir: Boots Co Main Bd 1982–93, Fleming High Income Investment Tst 1989–96, HFC Bank plc 1990–98; memb House of Commons Ctee of Privileges, pres Br Red Cross Soc Glos Dist; chm Nat Consumer Cncl 1987–89; Nat Waterway Museum Tst until 1990; *Recreations* bridge; *Clubs* Glos Cons; *Style*— The Baroness Oppenheim-Barnes, PC

OPPENHEIMER, Nicola Anne; da of Basil Vincent Brotherton (d 1961), and Joan Pamela, *née* Green (d 2003); *b* 30 September 1950; *Educ* St Margaret's Sch Bushey, QMC London (LLB); *m* 14 April 1973, His Hon Michael Oppenheimer; 1 da (Rebecca Anne Julia b 14 April 1978), 1 s (James Felix Vincent b 15 Oct 1980); *Career* called to the Bar Middle Temple 1972; Lord Chancellor's Dept: legal asst Criminal Appeal Office 1973–77, sr legal asst 1978–85, Judicial Appointments Div 1985–87, head Personnel Mgmnt Div 1987–91, head Legal Servs and Agencies Div 1991–93, princ estab and fin offr 1993–96; Cabinet Office: princ estab and fin offr 1996–2000, fell Knowledge Mgmnt Centre for Mgmnt and Policy Studies 2000–2001; ptnr Odgers Berndtson 2001–13 (advsr 2013–); chair Orchid Music Charitable Tst; tstee: The Early Opera Co, Spitalfields Music, Tenebrae, The English Concert; *Recreations* early music, theatre, walking; *Style*— Mrs Nicola Oppenheimer; ✉ 58 Airedale Avenue, London W4 2NN (e-mail naoppenheimer@gmail.com)

OPPERMAN, Guy Thomas; MP; *b* 18 May 1965; *Educ* Harrow Sch, Univ of Buckingham, Univ of Lille; *Career* former steeplechase jockey; former barr 3PB; cncllr Kennet DC 1995–99, MP (Cons) Hexham 2010–; *Style*— Guy Opperman, Esq, MP; ✉ House of Commons, London SW1A 0AA

OPPETIT, Bernard; s of Marcel Oppetit, of Paris, France, and Jacqueline, *née* Barail; *b* 5 August 1956, Algiers, Algeria; *Educ* Ecole Polytechnique Paris; *m* 26 Oct 1985, Anne, *née* Brisset, 3 s (Octave b 28 Sept 1986, Ernest b 10 Dec 1990, Gabriel b 21 Jan 1992), 1 da (Alice b 10 Nov 1987); *Career* Paribas: joined Paris 1979, vice-pres NY 1987–95, md London 1995–2000; chm and ceo Centaurus Capital 2000–; dir Natixis; memb Supervisory Bd HLD; *Recreations* music, sailing; *Clubs* Queen's, Arts; *Style*— Bernard Oppetit, Esq; ✉ Centaurus Capital, 33 Cavendish Square, London W1G 0PW (☎ 020 7852 3800, fax 020 7852 3850, e-mail bernard@centaurus-capital.com)

ORANGE, Jason Thomas; *b* 10 July 1970, Manchester; *Educ* South Manchester HS, South Trafford Coll; *Career* singer and songwriter; memb Take That 1990–96 and 2006–; *Albums* Take That and Party 1992, Everything Changes 1993, Nobody Else 1995, Greatest Hits 1996, Never Forget: The Ultimate Collection 2005, Beautiful World 2006, The Circus 2008; *Singles* Do What You Like 1991, Promises 1991, Once You've Tasted Love 1992, It Only Takes a Minute 1992, I Found Heaven 1992, A Million Love Songs 1992, Could It Be Magic 1992, Why Can't I Wake Up With You 1993, Pray 1993 (UK no 1), Relight My Fire 1993 (with Lulu, UK no 1), Babe 1993 (UK no 1), Everything Changes 1994 (UK no 1), Love Ain't Here Anymore 1994, Sure 1994 (UK no 1), Back For Good 1995 (UK no 1), Never Forget 1995 (UK no 1), How Deep Is Your Love 1996 (UK no 1), Patience 2006 (UK no 1), Shine 2007 (UK no 1), I'd Wait For Life 2007, Rule The World 2007, Greatest Day 2008 (UK no 1), Up All Night 2009, Said It All 2009, The Flood 2010, Kidz 2011; *Awards* BRIT Awards: Best Br Single 1993 (for Could It Be Magic), 1994 (for Pray), 1996 (for Back For Good), 2007 (for Patience) and 2008 (for Shine), Best Br Video 1994 (for Pray), Best Br Live Act 2008, Best Br Band 2011; MTV Europe Music Awards: Best Group 1994, Best Live Act 1995; Most Performed Work Ivor Novello Awards 2008 (for Shine), PRS For Music Outstanding Contribution to British Music Ivor Novello Award 2012; *Style*— Mr Jason Orange

ORCHARD, Dr Robin Theodore; s of George William Orchard (d 1991), of Bexley Heath, Kent, and Christobel Edith Orchard; *b* 4 October 1940; *Educ* Chislehurst and Sidcup GS, Charing Cross Hosp Med Sch Univ of London (MB BS); *m* 5 June 1965, Ann Seymour, da of Dr Thomas Seymour Jones (d 1986), of Wimborne, Dorset; 2 s (Timothy, Christopher), 2 da (Kathryn, Elizabeth); *Career* sr registrar Charing Cross Hosp WC2 and W6 1970–74, sr lectr in med Royal Dental Hosp 1976–82, post grad clinical tutor St Helier Hosp 1978–86; conslt physician 1974–: St Helier Hosp Carshalton, Sutton Hosp, St Anthony's Hosp N Cheam; hon sr lectr St George's Hosp Med Sch 1982–, Univ of

O

London examiner in medicine and dental surgery 1982–; churchwarden St John's Selsdon Sy 1982–87, memb Addington Deanery Synod 1988–; Univ memb Croydon D H A 1987–90, med dir St Helier Hosp Tst 1991–99, memb Cncl St George's Hosp Med Sch 1991–99; FRCP 1982, FRSM, MRCS; *Recreations* cricket, golf, C of E, Italian wine; *Style*— Dr Robin Orchard; ✉ St Helier Hospital, Wrythe Lane, Carshalton SM5 1AA (✆ 020 8644 4343)

ORCHARD-LISLE, Mervyn Christopher; s of Ulric Lock Orchard-Lisle (d 1955), and Thelma Julie Spelman, *née* Burdett (d 2000); *b* 6 June 1946; *Educ* Marlborough, Univ of Newcastle upon Tyne (BA, BArch); *m* 24 March 1979, Angela Jane, da of Edmund Louis Saunders (d 1996); 1 da (Lucy b 1983), 1 s (Alexander b 1985); *Career* chartered architect in private practice 1973–, sr ptnr Gotelee Orchard-Lisle 1984–; RIBA 1973; *Recreations* watercolours, books, past and present family life; *Style*— Mervyn Orchard-Lisle, Esq; ✉ The Old Rectory, Monksilver, Taunton, Somerset TA4 4HY (✆ 01984 656550); Gotelee Orchard-Lisle, 3 Cromwell Place, Northbrook Street, Newbury, Berkshire RG14 1AF (✆ 01635 36600, fax 01635 31421, e-mail mol@go-l.co.uk)

ORD-SMITH, HE Robin Jeremy; MVO; s of Derek Ord-Smith (d 2013), and Mary Ord-Smith (d 2005); *b* 8 October 1965, Ferndown, Dorset; *Educ* Univ of Surrey (BSc); *Children* 3 s; *Career* diplomat; asst desk offr Germany FCO 1989–90, Kuwait Emergency Unit Consular Unit FCO 1990–91, entry clearance offr Algiers 1991, vice-consul Bucharest 1991–94, third sec political and press Kuala Lumpur 1994–97, second sec Kuala Lumpur 1998, dep head Indonesia and E Timor Section FCO 1999–2000, mktg mangr Japan BAE Systems Tokyo 2000–01, first sec commercial Tokyo 2001–06, dir trade promotion Tokyo 2006–07, asst private sec to HRH The Duke of York, KG 2007–10, policy and communications strategist High Value Opportunities Prog UK Trade and Investment 2010–11, dir UK Trade and Investment Iraq 2011, ambass to Tajikistan 2012–15, ambass to the Kyrgyz Repub 2015–; *Recreations* golf, travel; *Clubs* R&A Golf St Andrews, Woking Golf, Maple Leaf Golf Kyrgyzstan, Lucifers Golfing Soc, Travellers; *Style*— HE Mr Robin Ord-Smith, MVO; ✉ c/o FCO (Bishkek), King Charles Street, London SW1A 2AH

ORDE; *see also:* Campbell-Orde

ORDE, Sir Hugh Stephen Roden; kt (2005), OBE (2001), QPM (2010); s of Thomas Henry Egil Orde, and Stella Mary Orde; *b* 27 August 1958; *Educ* Univ of Kent (BA); *m* 1, 1985 (m dis 2010), Kathleen Helen; 1 s (Jonathan b 12 April 1986); m 2, 2011, Denise Wooton; 2 da (Robyn b 2000, Anya b 2010), 1 s (Fabian b 2006); *Career* joined Met Police 1977, Sgt Brixton 1982, Police Staff Coll 1983, Inspr Greenwich 1984–90 (Bramshill Sch 1984–87), Staff Offr to Dep Asst Cmmr SW London (Chief Inspr) 1990, Chief Inspr Hounslow 1991–93, Supt Territorial Support Gp 1993–95, Detective Chief Supt Major Crimes SW Area 1995–98, Cdr Crime S London 1998, Dep Asst Cmmr (Cmmr's Command) 1999–2002, Chief Constable Police Serv NI 2002–09; pres ACPO 2009–; *Recreations* marathon running, wine, gardening; *Style*— Sir Hugh Orde, OBE, QPM; ✉ ACPO, 1st Floor, 10 Victoria Street, London SW1H 0NN

ORIVE, José; *Career* exec dir Int Sugar Org 2013–; *Style*— José Orive, Esq; ✉ International Sugar Organization, 1 Canada Square, London E14 5AA

ORKNEY, 9 Earl of (S 1696); (Oliver) Peter St John Fitz-Maurice; also Viscount Kirkwall and Lord Dechmont (both S 1696); s of Lt-Col Frederick Oliver St John, DSO, MC (d 1977), and gs of late Sir Frederick Robert St John, KCMG (yst s of late Hon Ferdinand St John, 2 s of 3 Viscount Bolingbroke and St John); through Sir Frederick's w, Isabella Fitz-Maurice (gda of 5 Earl of Orkney); suc kinsman, 8 Earl, 1998 (has not yet established his right to the peerages); *b* 27 February 1938; *Educ* Univ of Lausanne, Univ of British Columbia (BA, Int Student of the Year 1958), LSE (MA), Univ of London (PhD); *m* 1, 1963 (m dis 1985), Mary Juliet, da of W G Scott-Brown; 3 da (Lady Juliet Elizabeth b 1964, Lady Nicola Jane b 1966, Lady Lucy Margaret b 1972), 1 s (Oliver Robert, Viscount Kirkwall and Master of Orkney b 1969); m 2, 1985, Mary Barbara Huck, da of Dr D B Albertson; 1 step s (Anthony Cameron St John), 3 step da (Dawn Marie, Caroline Jane, Erin Katherine); *Heir* s, Viscount Kirkwall and Master of Orkney; *Career* lectr UCL 1963–64; Univ of Manitoba: lectr 1964–66, asst prof 1966–72, assoc prof 1972–98, prof of political scis 1998–; visiting prof: Carleton Univ 1981–82, Canadian Forces Base Lahr 1985, 1990 and 1991, Univ of Victoria 1987 and 2002; reg quarterly lectr USAF Special Ops Sch Revolutionary Warfare Course Hurlburt Field FL 1994–2003, regular lectr UND Law Sch N Dakota, keynote speaker N Dakota Aerospace Sch, annual lectures to MSSTA on ME and terrorism 1998–; numerous lectures, speeches, seminars, symposia and radio & TV commentaries on intelligence, terrorism, insurgency, foreign policy, air piracy, Algeria and the Middle East 1977–; ptnr Heartland Assocs Inc 1998–; conslt: Canadian Armed Forces, Air Canada, CBC Radio, USAF Special Ops Sch FL, Auditor Gen Dept Canada on Airport Security, US Govt Washington Counter-Insurgency in Iraq; memb Advsy Ctee on Acad Relations Dept of External Affairs Canada 1980–90, dir Counter Terror Study Centre 1985–94, pres Agassiz Inst for the Study of Conflict 1993–, chair Foreign Affairs Canadian Govt Scholarship Ctee 1998–2001; Social Scis and Humanities Res Cncl (SSHRC) Grant 1982, Univ of Manitoba Outreach Award 1996, Olive Beatrice Stanton Award for Teaching Excellence 1997; memb: RIIA 1962, Canadian Inst of Int Affrs 1964 (pres Winnipeg Branch 1971–73, chm Winnipeg Branch 1973–74 and 1996–99), UN Assoc of Canada 1980, Canadian Assoc for the Study of Intelligence & Security 1986 (Prairie rep 1996); memb Advsy Bd Winnipeg Cameron Highlanders 2000; patron: Orkney Homecoming 1999, Monarchist League Winnipeg; Robert S Maxwell SS Beaver Award 2009, St Andrews Soc Winnipeg Citizen of the Year 2010; first fell Royal Military Inst of Manitoba 2007; hon life memb: Manitoba Social Sci Teachers' assoc 2013–, Intrepid Soc of Manitoba 2014, Royal Commonwealth Soc 2015; *Books* Fireproof House to Third Option (1977), Mackenzie King to Philosopher King (1984), Air Piracy, Airport Security and International Terrorism: Winning the War Against Hijackers (1991), From the Great War to the Global Village (2003); *Recreations* tennis, squash, swimming, boating, cycling, heritage and photography; *Style*— The Rt Hon the Earl of Orkney; ✉ 597 Gertrude Avenue, Winnipeg, Manitoba, Canada, R3L 0M9 (✆ 00 1 204 284 1089, e-mail hrtland@mts.net)

ORLEBAR, Christopher John Dugmore; s of Col John H R Orlebar, OBE (d 1989), of St Helens, IOW, and Louise, *née* Crowe (d 1997); *b* 4 February 1945; *Educ* Rugby, Univ of Southampton, Coll of Air Trg Hamble; *m* 5 Feb 1972, Nicola Dorothy Mary, er da of Dr Leslie Ford (d 1987), of Sheringham, Norfolk; 1 s (Edward b 1977), 1 da (Caroline b 1979); *Career* Cadet Pilot Southampton Univ Air Sqdn 1964–66, trainee pilot Coll of Air Trg Hamble 1967–69, First Offr and Navigator VC10 (awarded basic Instr Trg Course), CAA course Stansted for examiner/instr 1973, Sr First Offr Concorde 1976–86, appointed examiner/instr to Concorde Fleet, chartered 2 Concordes for celebration of 50 anniversary of Schneider Trophy 1981; organised BBC documentary on Concorde in QED series 1983, writer and presenter BBC TV series Jet Trail 1984, initiator and conslt Faster than a Speeding Bullet (Channel 4 Equinox) 1989, tech conslt Channel 4 documentary on Air Traffic Control in Equinox series 1993; Capt Boeing 737: BA 1986–2000, trg capt 1994–2001, Maersk Air Ltd 2000–01; Freeman City of London 1975, Liveryman Guild of Air Pilots and Air Navigators; FRAeS 1999 (MRAeS 1984, chm Weybridge branch 2007); *Books* The Concorde Story (1986, 7 edn 2011, reprint 2005, 2006, 2007 and 2008, over 110,000 copies sold); *Recreations* family, photography, music, sailing, canoeing, tennis, gardening; *Clubs* Air League; *Style*— Captain Christopher Orlebar, FRAeS; ✉ Holt Cottage, Fairoak Lane, Oxshott, Surrey KT22 0TW (✆ 01372 842100, e-mail chris.orlebar@ntlworld.com)

ORMAN, Dr Stanley; s of Jack Orman (d 1974), and Ettie, *née* Steiner (d 1984); *b* 6 February 1935, London; *Educ* Hackney Downs GS, King's Coll London (BSc, PhD); *m* 1960, Helen, da of Joseph Hourman (d 1982); 1 s (David b 1961), 2 da (Ann b 1963, Lynn b 1969); *Career* Fulbright scholar, postdoctoral research Brandeis Univ, research in materials science 1961–74, chief weapon system engr Chevaline 1981–82, min and cnsllr Br Embassy Washington 1982–84, under sec MOD 1984, DG Strategic Def Initiative Participation Office 1986–90 (dep dir Awre Aldermaston 1984–86); chief exec GTS Inc Washington 1990–96, chief exec Orman Assoc Inc 1996–; Jelf medallist King's Coll London 1957; *Publications* Faith in G.O.D.S – Stability in the Nuclear Age (1991), An Uncivil Civil Servant (2013); author of over 300 pubns on materials science, defence and international issues; *Recreations* reading, designing bow ties, tennis, embroidery; *Style*— Dr Stanley Orman; ✉ 11420 Strand Drive #104, Rockville, Maryland 20852, USA (✆ 00 1 240 221 3689, e-mail stanley011@verizon.net)

ORME, Prof Michael Christopher L'Estrange; s of Christopher Robert L'Estrange Orme, TD (d 1979), of Poole, Dorset, and Muriel Evelyn Janet, *née* Thomson (d 2005); *b* 13 June 1940, Derby; *Educ* Sherborne, Univ of Cambridge (MA, MB BChir, MD); *m* 1, 15 April 1967, (Joan) Patricia (d 2013), da of Stanley Abbott, OBE (d 2004), of Coulsdon, Surrey; 1 s (Robert Martin b 10 July 1969); m 2, 24 Jan 2015, Hilary Margaret Day; *Career* Univ of Liverpool: sr lectr clinical pharmacology 1975–81, reader 1981–84, prof pharmacology and therapeutics 1984–2001 (ret), dean of Faculty of Med 1991–96; dir of educn and trg NW Regnl Office NHS Exec 1996–2001; hon conslt physician Liverpool HA; memb GMC 1994–96; sec: Clinical Pharmacology Section Br Pharmacological Soc 1982–88, Clinical Section Int Union of Pharmacology 1987–92; chm Euro Assoc of Clinical Pharmacology and Therapeutics 2003–07 (hon sec 1993–2003); govr Glos Hosps NHS Fndn Tst 2008–10 (dep chm of govrs 2009–10); govr Birkenhead School Ltd 1991–2005; Hon DSc Univ of Salford 2010, Hon MD Int Med Univ Malaysia 2004, Hon MD Karolinska Inst Stockholm 2013; FRCP 1980, FMedSci 1998, Hon FRCGP 1998, FFPHM 2000, hon fell Br Pharmacological Soc 2015; *Books* Medicines – The Self Help Guide (1988), Human Lactation (1989), Therapeutic Drugs (1991); *Recreations* sailing, astronomy; *Style*— Prof Michael Orme; ✉ 4 Bishton Drive, Pershore, Worcestershire WR10 3ED (✆ 01386 561713, e-mail michaelorme@larkhouse.co.uk)

ORME, Canon Prof Nicholas; s of Edward Howell Orme, and Kathleen, *née* Plowright (d 1971); *Educ* Bristol Cathedral Sch, Magdalen Coll Oxford (MA, DPhil, DLitt), DD; *m* 4 July 1981, Rona, da of James S Monro; 1 da (Verity b 1984); *Career* Univ of Exeter: lectr 1964–81, reader in history 1981–88, prof of history 1988–2007 (emeritus prof 2007–), Nuffield Fndn res fell 1991–92, Leverhulme Tst res fell 1993–94; visiting appointments: Merton Coll Oxford, St John's Coll Oxford, Univ of Arizona, Univ of Minneapolis, Univ of Victoria (BC); vice-pres Devon and Cornwall Record Soc; past pres: Devon History Soc, Bristol and Gloucestershire Archaeological Soc, Devonshire Assoc, Somerset Archaeological Soc; past chm Exeter Cathedral Fabric Advsy Ctee; lay canon Truro Cathedral 2005–11 (canon emeritus 2011–), reader C of E; corresponding fell Medieval Acad of America 2003; FRHistS 1979, FSA 1985; *Books* English Schools in the Middle Ages (1973), Education in the West of England (1976), The Minor Clergy of Exeter Cathedral (1980), Early British Swimming (1983), From Childhood to Chivalry (1984), Education and Society in Medieval and Renaissance England (1989), John Lydgate, Table Manners for Children (ed, 1989), Unity and Variety: A History of the Church in Devon and Cornwall (ed, 1991), Nicholas Roscarrock's Lives of the Saints (ed, 1992), The First English Hospitals 1070–1570 (with Margaret Webster, 1995), White Bird Flying (1995), English Church Dedications (1996), Education in Early Tudor England (1998), The Saints of Cornwall (2000), Medieval Children (2001), Death and Memory in Medieval Exeter (with David Lepine, 2003), The Survey of Cornwall by Richard Carew (2004), Medieval Schools (2006), Cornish Wills 1342–1540 (2007), The Cathedral Cat (2008), Exeter Cathedral: The First Thousand Years (2009), Victoria History of the County of Cornwall, Vol 2 (2010), Westbury-on-Tyrm: monastery, minster, college (with John Cannon, 2010), Fleas, Flies and Friars: Children's Poetry of the Middle Ages (2011), English School Exercises 1420–1530 (2013), The Church in Devon 400–1560 (2013), The Minor Clergy of Exeter Cathedral, Biographies: 1250–1548 (2013), The Churches of Medieval Exeter (2014); *Style*— Canon Prof Nicholas Orme; ✉ Department of History, University of Exeter, Amory Building, Rennes Drive, Exeter EX4 4RJ

ORMEROD, Ben; s of John Ormerod, and Paula Taylor; *b* 24 October 1958; *Educ* St Christopher's Sch Letchworth, Central Sch of Speech and Drama; *m* m, 2002 (sep 2008), Aïcha Kossoko; *Career* lighting designer; began career with Andrew Visnevski's Cherub Co; other cos incl: Kick Theatre, Buick of Sighs, ATC, Cheek by Jowl, 7:84 Scotland, Théâtre de Complicité, Major Road; designed lighting for The Calico Museum Ahmedabad; *Theatre* for RNT incl: Bent, Accidental Death of an Anarchist, The Winter's Tale, Uncle Vanya, Remembrance of Things Past; RSC incl: The Revenger's Tragedy, The Two Gentlemen of Verona, Henry V, Julius Caesar, A Dog in the Manger, Tamar's Revenge, The House of Desires, Pedro Urdemalas, Headcase, Macbeth; for Leicester Haymarket incl: Krapp's Last Tape (also Riverside Studios) 1990, Our Country's Good 1991; for West Yorkshire Playhouse incl: Life is a Dream 1992, Betrayal 1994; for English Touring Theatre incl: Hamlet (also Donmar Warehouse) 1993, No Man's Land 1994, A Doll's House 1994, Hedda Gabler (also Donmar Warehouse) 1996, The Seagull (also Donmar Warehouse) 1997, The Master Builder 1999, John Gabriel Borkmann 2003, Rosencrantz and Guildenstern are Dead 2005, The Old Country (also Trafalgar Studios) 2006, The Changeling 2007; other credits incl: Pal Joey (Bristol Old Vic) 1991, A View from the Bridge (Sheffield Crucible) 1991, Cyrano de Bergerac (Vembo Theatre, Athens) 1992, Coriolanus (Rennaissance, Chichester Festival) 1992, Macbeth (Tzeni Karezi, Athens) 1994, The Winslow Boy (Plymouth Theatre Royal, tour, The Globe) 1994, Casement (Moving Theatre at Riverside Studios) 1995, A Crocodile Looking at Birds (Lyric Hammersmith) 1995, The Government Inspector (Tzeni Karezi Theatre, Athens) 1995, Hamlet (OSC) 1996, The Beauty Queen of Leenane (Druid Theatre Co and Royal Court) 1996, Silence Silence Silence (Mladinsko Theatre, Ljubljana) 1996, Oedipus Tyrannus (Epidaurus) 1996, Passing Places (Edinburgh) 1997, Leenane Trilogy (Druid and Royal Court) 1997, Man with Connections (Porta Theatre Athens), The Wake and The Colleen Bawn (Abbey Theatre Dublin) 1998, The Beauty Queen of Leenane (Broadway) 1998, The Freedom of the City (Abbey Theatre Dublin and Lincoln Center, New York) 1999, The Country Boy (Druid Theatre Co) 1999, God's Plenty (Rambert) 1999, Measure for Measure (Library Theatre Manchester) 2000, Death of a Salesman (Birmingham Rep) 2000, The House (Abbey Dublin) 2000, Pera Palas (Gate Theatre London) 2000, Abandonment and Shetland Saga (Traverse Edinburgh) 2000, Andromache (Living Pictures) 2000, The Circle (Oxford Stage Co) 2000, Rose Rage (Newbury) 2001, The Father (Theatro Synchrono Athens) 2001, Made in China (Peacock Dublin), Macbeth (Ludlow Castle) 2001, A Streetcar Named Desire (Northern Ballet Theatre) 2001, Putting it Together (Chichester) 2001, The Caretaker (ETT) 2001, Murder (Gate Theatre London) 2001, The Nest (Living Pictures) 2001, Ibi l'ohun (Brest) 2001, Ghosts (ETT) 2002, Rose Rage (Theatre Royal Haymarket) 2002, Journey to the West (Tara Arts) 2002, The Constant Wife (Apollo and Lyric Theatres London) 2002, Enemy of the People (Theatr Clwyd) 2002, Babes in Arms (Guildhall Sch) 2002, The Circle (nat tour) 2002, Macbeth (Albery) 2002, The Hinge of the World (Guildford) 2003, Rose Rage (Chicago Shakespeare) 2003 and 2004, Bedroom Farce (Synchrono Theatro Athens) 2003, the Marquise (nat tour) 2003, Calico (Duke of York's London) 2003, A Midsummer Night's Dream (BAM NY) 2004, Double Cross (Windsor) 2004, A Winter's Tale (Propeller) 2005,

A Night at the Dogs (Soho Theatre) 2005, The Importance of Being Earnest (Abbey Dublin) 2005, Who Killed Mr Drum (Riverside Studios) 2005, The Rivals (nat tour) 2005, The Seagull (Bristol Old Vic) 2005, See How They Run (nat tour and Duchess West End) 2006, The Best of Friends (Hampstead Theatre) 2006, An Ideal Husband (Theatr Clywd) 2006, Dick Whittington (Barbican) 2006, Twelfth Night (Propeller at the Old Vic) 2006, Ghosts (Bristol Old Vic) 2007, Leaves (Druid/Royal Ct) 2007, Macbeth (Theatro Sychrono Athens) 2007, The Big House (Abbey Dublin) 2007, Last Easter (Birmingham Rep) 2007, Legal Fictions (nat tour and Savoy West End) 2007, The Dresser (Watford) 2008, The Merchant of Venice (Propeller) 2008, A Midsummer Night's Dream (Propeller) 2009, Two Men of Florence (Huntington, Boston) 2009, Dimetos (Donmar Warehouse) 2009, Serious MOney (Birmingham Rep) 2009, The Last Days of a Reluctant Tyrant (Abbey, Dublin) 2009; as dir: Dimetos (Gate Theatre) 2003, Four Tales from the Dakalog (also adaptation E15 drama sch) 2006, Mephisto (E15) 2007; *Opera and Musicals* credits incl: La Voix Humaine and Savitri (Aix-en-Provence) 1990, Punch and Judy (Aldeburgh Festival) 1991, The Turn of the Screw (Bath and Wessex Opera) 1993, The Wildman (Aldeburgh Festival) 1995, The Mask of Orpheus (QEH/BBCSO) 1996, Beatrice Cenci (Spitalfields Opera) 1998, The Coronation of Poppea (Purcell Quartet tour of Japan) 1998, Baa Baa Black Sheep (Opera North and BBC 2), La Traviata (ENO) 2006, Sweeney Todd (Royal Festival Hall) 2007, Zorro (nat tour and Garrick West End) 2008, Falstaff (Scottish Opera) 2008, Jeanne d'Arc (Santa Cecelia Rome) 2008; *Dance* See Blue Through (Ballet Gulbenkian Lisbon) 2001, (Phoenix Dance) 2005 and (Introdans Holland) 2006, I Remember Red (Cullberg Ballet Stockholm) 2002, Tender Hooks (Ballet Gulbenkian Lisbon) 2003 and (Skanes Dance) 2005, Outsight (Ballet Gulbenkian Lisbon) 2004, Essance (Walker Dance Park Music ROH2) 2005, Journey (Candoco) 2005, Askungen (Gotesborg Opera) 2007, Frame of View (Cedar Lake Dance NY) 2009, Zorro (Folies Bergere Paris) 2009; *Awards* TMA Best Design Award for Life is a Dream (jtly with Neil Warmington and Mic Pool); *Style—* Ben Ormerod, Esq; ✉ website www.benormerod.com

ORMEROD, Paul; s of John Ormerod, of Rochdale, Lancs, and Doris, *née* Parker (d 2000); *b* 20 March 1950; *Educ* Manchester Grammar, Christ's Coll Cambridge (MA), St Catherine's Coll Oxford (MPhil); *m* 1975, Pamela, da of Sidney Meadows; 1 s (Andrew Whitworth b 3 Sept 1982); *Career* economist and author; res offr NIESR 1973–80, dir of economics Henley Centre for Forecasting, currently dir Volterra Consulting; *Books* The Death of Economics (1994), Butterfly Economics (1998), Why Most Things Fail (2005); *Style—* Paul Ormerod, Esq

ORMOND, Prof Leonée; *née* Jasper; *b* 27 August 1940; *Educ* Ware GS for Girls, St Anne's Coll Oxford (BA), Univ of Birmingham (MA); *m* 11 May 1963, Richard Louis Ormond, CBE, *qv*, s of Conrad Ormond (d 1979); 2 s (Augustus b 1972, Marcus b 1974); *Career* KCL: asst lectr 1965–68, lectr 1968–85, sr lectr 1985–89, reader in English 1989–96, prof of Victorian studies 1996–2006 (prof emerita 2006–); chair Tennyson Res Pubns Bd, tstee G F Watts Gallery Compton Surrey, chair Cncl Kipling Soc 2011–14, tstee Museum of Music History; pres Dickens Fellowship 2007–09, fell English Assoc; FRSA, FKC 2008; *Books* George Du Maurier (1969), Lord Leighton (with Richard Ormond, 1975), J M Barrie (1987), Alfred Tennyson: a Literary Life (1993), Linley Sambourne: Illustrator and Punch Cartoonist (2010); *Recreations* mountain walking; *Clubs* Univ Women's, RSA; *Style—* Prof Leonée Ormond; ✉ English Department, King's College, Strand, London WC2R 2LS

ORMOND, Richard Louis; CBE (2001); s of Conrad Eric Ormond (d 1979), of Old Rectory, Cleggan, Co Galway, and Dorothea Charlotte (d 1987), da of Sir Alexander Gibbons, 7 Bt; *b* 16 January 1939; *Educ* Marlborough, Brown Univ RI, ChCh Oxford (MA); *m* 11 May 1963, Prof Leonée Ormond, *qv*; 2 s (Augustus b 1972, Marcus b 1974); *Career* dep dir Nat Portrait Gallery 1975–83 (asst keeper 1965–75), dir Nat Maritime Museum 1986–2000 (head of Picture Dept 1983–86), Kress prof Nat Gallery of Art Washington DC 2001–02, dir Sargent Catalogue Raisonné Project 2000–; dep chm Museums Training Inst 1994–97; chm of tstees Watts Gallery Compton, pres Friends of Leighton House, former tstee Mariners Museum Newport News VA; *Books* J S Sargent (1970), Early Victorian Portraits in the National Portrait Gallery (1973), Lord Leighton (with Leonée Ormond, 1975), Sir Edwin Landseer (1982), The Great Age of Sail (1986), F X Winterhalter and the Courts of Europe (1987), Frederic, Lord Leighton (jtly, 1996), Sargent Abroad (jtly, 1997), John Singer Sargent: The Early Portraits (with Elaine Kilmurray, 1998), John Singer Sargent (ed with Elaine Kilmurray, 1998), John Singer Sargent: Portraits of the 1890s (with Elaine Kilmurray, 2002), John Singer Sargent: The Later Portraits (with Elaine Kilmurray, 2003), John Singer Sargent: Figures and Landscapes, 1874–1882 (with Elaine Kilmurray, 2006), Sargent's Venice (jtly, 2006), Rule Britannia (with James Taylor, 2007), John Singer Sargent: Venetian Figures and Landscapes, 1898–1913 (with Elaine Kilmurray, 2009), Edwin Landseer: The Private Drawings (2009), Sargent and the Sea (with Sarah Cash and others, 2009), John Singer Sargent: Figures and Landscapes 1883–1899 (with Elaine Kilmurray, 2010), G F Watts: The Hall of Fame (with Leonée Ormond, 2012), John Singer Sargent: Figures and Landscapes 1900–1907 (with Elaine Kilmurray, 2012), John Singer Sargent: Figures and Landscapes 1908–1913 (with Elaine Kilmurray, 2014), Sargent: Portraits of Artists and Friends (jtly, 2015); *Recreations* cycling, opera, theatre; *Clubs* Garrick; *Style—* Richard Ormond, Esq, CBE; ✉ 8 Holly Terrace, London N6 6LX

ORR, Prof Christopher John (Chris); MBE; *b* 8 April 1943; *Educ* Beckenham & Penge GS, RCA (MA); *Career* artist 1967–; exhibited internationally; prof and head Printmaking Dept RCA 1998–2008 (prof emeritus 2008–); RA 1995 (elected treas 2014), FRCA; *Work in Collections* Arts Cncl of GB, Br Cncl, V&A, RA, Science Museum, Ulster Folk & Tport Museum, Govt Art Collection, British Museum, Queen's Collection; *Books* Chris Orr's John Ruskin (1976), Many Mansions (1990), The Small Titanic (1994), Happy Days (1999), Semi-antics (2001), The Disguise Factory (2003), City of Holy Dreams (2007), The Multitude Diaries (2008), Chris Orr: the Making of Things (2013); *Style—* Prof Chris Orr, MBE, RA

ORR, Deborah Jane; da of John Scott Orr, of Motherwell, and Winifred Meta, *née* Avis; *b* 23 September 1962; *Educ* Garrion Acad Wishaw, Univ of St Andrews (MA); *m* 1997, William Woodard (Will) Self, *qv*; 2 s (Ivan William Scott b Sept 1997, Luther James David b Aug 2001); *Career* dep ed City Limits magazine and contrib New Statesman until 1990, ed Guardian Weekend 1993–98 (joined The Guardian 1990), freelance journalist 1998–, currently columnist The Independent; *Style—* Ms Deborah Orr

ORR, Gordon Inglis; s of John Inglis Orr (d 1993), of Broughty Ferry, Scotland, and Doris May, *née* Hoyle (d 1959); *b* 13 December 1946; *Educ* Audely Park Sch, S Devon Coll of Art (RSA bursary), Kingston Coll of Art (BA); *m* 1981, Susan Mary, yst da of James Hervey Hall; 1 da (Jenny Susanah Inglis b 1982), 1 s (Jonathon Inglis b 1985); *Career* interior designer Conran Design Group 1970–73, creative dir (interior design) Shuttleworth Farmer Orr Design Consultants 1973–76 (projects incl creation of Virgin Records retail chain), md Shuttleworth Orr Design Consultants London and Maclaren Orr Design Consultants Edinburgh 1976–83, creative dir (interiors) DIA Interiors (Lopex Gp) 1984–86, jt md Sparkes Orr Design Consultants London 1986– (devpt of subsid companies Lighting Design House, Swain Communications and Rawcliffe & Associates since 1992), chm Robson Design Associates Bristol 1990–95; major design projects incl: Somerfield (new trading concept of Gateway) 1989–90 (winner Retail Environments category Design Week Awards 1991), Dales (new discount trading concept for Asda) 1992–93, Shoe Express (new discount trading concept for BSC) 1993; FRSA 1966, FInstD 1978; *Recreations* sailing, opera, Scottish country dance; *Style—* Gordon Orr, Esq

ORR EWING, Sir Archibald Donald; 6 Bt (UK 1886), of Ballikinrain, Stirlingshire, and Lennoxbank, Co Dumbarton; s of Sir Ronald Archibald Orr Ewing, 5 Bt (d 2002); *b* 20 December 1938; *Educ* Gordonstoun, Trinity Coll Dublin (BA); *m* 1, 1965 (m dis 1972), Venetia Elizabeth, da of Maj Richard Turner; m 2, 1972, Nicola Jean-Anne, da of Reginald Baron (Barry) Black (d 1996), of Fovant, Wilts, and (Eloise) Jean Horatia, *née* Innes-Ker (d 1996), niece of 8 Duke of Roxburghe; 1 s (Capt Alastair Frederick Archibald b 26 May 1982); *Heir* s, Capt Alastair Orr Ewing; *Career* landowner; memb Queen's Body Guard for Scotland (Royal Co of Archers); Grand Master Mason of Scotland 1999–2004 and 2005–08; *Recreations* shooting, fishing, opera, theatre; *Clubs* New (Edinburgh); *Style—* Sir Archibald Orr Ewing, Bt; ✉ Cardross, Port of Menteith, by Stirling FK8 3JY (☎ and fax 01877 385223, e-mail orrewing.archie@yahoo.co.uk)

ORTON, Rev Giles Anthony Christopher; s of late Dr Francis John Orton, of Sheffield, and Helen Davina Orton; *b* 18 August 1959, Nacton, Suffolk; *Educ* King Edward VII Sch Sheffield, The Queen's Coll Oxford (Hastings exhibitioner, MA), Chester Coll of Law, St Stephen's House Oxford; *m* 11 April 1987, (Kathryn) Jane, *née* Robinson; 3 s (Hugh b 16 Nov 1989, Ralph b 21 Oct 1991, Guy b 9 Nov 1996); *Career* slr DLA 1983–87 (trainee slr 1981–83); Eversheds: joined 1987, ptnr 1989–2016, head of litigation (East Midlands) 1994–2001, head of pensions 2001–06, head of pensions litigation 2006–16, conslt 2016–; chm Bridge Tstees Ltd 1992–, pres Assoc of Corporate Tstees 2012–15 (chm Pensions Ctee 2003–06); memb: Law Soc 1983–, Assoc of Pension Lawyers 1994– (chm Litigation Ctee 1998–2008); memb Derby City Cncl 1988–92; deacon and curate St Laurence Long Eaton 2016–; *Recreations* country pursuits, gardening, bridge; *Clubs* Carlton; *Style—* The Rev Giles Orton; ✉ Brun Meadows, Brun Lane, Kirk Langley, Ashbourne, Derbyshire DE6 4LU (☎ 01332 824233, e-mail gilesorton@fastmail.fm); Eversheds LLP, One Wood Street, London EC2V 7WS (☎ 0845 497 1094, e-mail gilesorton@eversheds.com)

OSBORN, Prof Marilyn Jean; *née* Hoggan; da of William Hoggan, of Meopham, Kent (d 2013), and Jean, *née* Bruce (d 1999); *b* 30 October 1943; *Educ* LSE (BSc), Univ of Bristol (PhD); *m* 25 July 1968, Dr Albert Osborn (d 1998), s of Albert Osborn, and Henrietta Osborn; 2 s (Steven James b 5 July 1971, Richard Paul b 16 Sept 1974); *Career* pt/t tutor in sociology of educn Open Univ 1972–79, research assoc Nat Inst of Adult Continuing Educn Leicester 1979–87, Canadian studies project offr Canadian High Cmmn London 1987–88, sr scientific offr ESRC 1988–89, currently emeritus prof of educn Grad Sch of Educn Univ of Bristol (previously reader, sr research fell, dir MPhil/PhD prog, co-dir Centre for Int and Comparative Studies and dir of research); examiner and reviewer: ESRC Studentship (ESRC), Social Sciences and Humanities Research Cncl (SSHRC), European Science Fndn (ESF); memb: Editorial Bd COMPARE, Scientific Ctee Politiques d'Education et de Formation (jl), Scientific Ctee Revue Internationale d'Education (jl), Adjudication Ctee Social Sciences and Humanities Research Cncl of Canada, Irish Research Cncl; memb: BERA, Br Assoc for Int and Comparative Educn (BAICE), Comparative Educn Soc in Europe (CESE); *Publications* Learning from Comparing, Vol 2: Policy, Professionals and Development (jt ed, 2000), What Pupils Say: Changing Policy and Practice in Primary Education (jtly, 2000), What Teachers Do: Changing Policy and Practice in Primary Education (jtly, 2000), Promoting Quality in Learning: A Comparative Study in England and France (jtly, 2001), A World of Difference? Comparing Learners Across Europe (jtly, 2003); also author of book chapters and jl articles; *Recreations* walking, theatre, cinema, reading fiction and biographies; *Style—* Prof Marilyn Osborn; ✉ Graduate School of Education, University of Bristol, 35 Berkeley Square, Bristol BS8 1JA (☎ 0117 331 4319, fax 0117 925 1537, e-mail marilyn.osborn@bristol.ac.uk)

OSBORN, Neil Frank; s of George James Osborn, of Hemel Hempstead, Herts, and Georgina Rose, *née* Nash; *b* 24 October 1949; *Educ* St Albans Sch, Worcester Coll Oxford (MA); *m* 15 April 1975, Holly Louise, da of Lt-Col George Francis Smith, of McLean, VA; *Career* reporter The Daily Progress Charlottesville VA 1972–74, freelance reporter Lloyd's List and Liverpool Daily Post 1975–77, sr ed Institutional Investor NY 1978–83, US ed Euromoney NY 1983–85, ed Euromoney London 1985–90, publisher Euromoney 1990–; dir: Euromoney Inc 1985–, Euromoney Institutional Investor plc (formerly Euromoney Publications) 1988–; non-exec dir RBC Information Systems Moscow 2002–14; memb Exec Bd Family Welfare Assoc 1994–2002; *Clubs* Carlton; *Style—* Neil Osborn, Esq; ✉ Flat 4, 16 Wetherby Gardens, London SW5 OJP; Euromoney Institutional Investor plc, 6–8 Bouverie Street, London ECY 8AX (☎ 020 7779 8888, fax 020 7779 8653, e-mail nosborn@euromoneyplc.com)

O

OSBORN, Sir Richard Henry Danvers; 9 Bt (E 1662), of Chicksands, Beds; s of Sir Danvers Lionel Rouse Osborn, 8 Bt (d 1983), and Constance Violette, *née* Rooke (d 1988); *b* 12 August 1958; *Educ* Eton; *m* 25 Feb 2006, Belinda Mary Elworthy; 1 da (Lara Constance Elizabeth b 20 June 2006); *Heir* kinsman, William Osborn; *Career* Christie's 1978–83, ind fine paintings conslt P & D Colnaghi Ltd 1984–87, dir Paul Mitchell Ltd (picture conservation and framing) 1991–2002, Richard Osborn Fine Art (fine art consultancy); *Recreations* real tennis, shooting, racing, golf; *Clubs* Turf, MCC, Queen's, Pratt's, NZ Golf, White's; *Style—* Sir Richard Osborn, Bt; ✉ 48 Lessar Avenue, London SW4 9HQ; Richard Osborn Fine Art, Ormond House, Ormond Yard, 3 Duke of York Street, St James's, London SW1Y 6JP

OSBORN, Shane Edward; s of Anthony Osborn (d 1985), and Patricia Osborn, of Perth, Aust; *b* Perth, Aust; *Educ* Willeton Sr HS Perth (HS Cert), Bently Tech Coll Perth (Dip Cookery); *Career* chef; sous chef rising to head chef Pied à Terre London 1998–2011 (8 out of 10 Good Food Guide 2001–11, 2 Michelin Stars 2003–11), head chef St Betty Hong Kong 2012–; *Publications* Starters (2004); *Recreations* cycling, diving, mountaineering, skydiving; *Style—* Shane Osborn, Esq

OSBORNE, Clive Maxwell Lawton; JP (Cheshire 2014); s of Raymond Peter Osborne (d 1997), of Newcastle-under-Lyme, and Eileen Mary Lawton (d 2014); *b* 20 July 1955; *Educ* Newcastle HS, ChCh Oxford (open exhibition, MA); *m* Oct 1985, Ursula Frances Amanda, da of Francis Eric Futcher; 1 da (Georgina Rosamund Lawton b 1988), 1 s (Thomas Francis Lawton b 1991); *Career* called to the Bar Gray's Inn (Holker sr scholar, bencher 2009), joined Home Office 1980, asst legal advsr Home Office 1991–97, legal dir DTI 1997–99, asst legal advsr NI Office 1999–2001, dep legal advsr Home Office and NI Office 2001–05, legal advsr Serious Organised Crime Agency 2005–12; hon steward Westminster Abbey 2014–15; Freeman City of London 2014, Liveryman Worshipful Co of Glaziers and Painters of Glass 2014 (Steward 2016–17); *Clubs* Travellers, Potters (Stoke-on-Trent), Old Newcastillian (pres 2014); *Style—* Clive Osborne, Esq, JP; ✉ e-mail cmlosborne21@gmail.com

OSBORNE, David Francis; s of William Henry Osborne (d 1969), of Surrey, and Beatrice Irene, *née* Hinge; *b* 24 October 1937; *Educ* Dulwich Coll, Jesus Coll Oxford (MA); *Children* 1 s (Martin b 1965), 2 da (Katharine b 1967, Juliet b 1968); *Career* Unilever Ltd 1960–66, PA International Management Consultants 1966–82, Hill Samuel & Co Ltd 1982–87, dir Electra Investment Tst plc 1981–96, dir Electra Fleming Ltd 1987–97; chm: Corporate Ventures Ltd 1996–99, Akhter Group 1997–99, Italian Private Equity Fund 1998–, Art Work Investment Ltd 2003–; dir B& S Equities (Lugano), dir Dinimia (Spain) 1997–2003; MIMgt, MICMA, MIMC; *Recreations* cricket, golf, gardening, reading, travel, languages, opera, bridge; *Clubs* MCC; *Style—* David Osborne, Esq; ✉ Mayflower Cottage, Lower Assendon, Oxfordshire RG9 6AH (☎ 01491 572004)

OSBORNE, Rt Hon George Gideon Oliver; CH (2016), PC (2010), MP; s and h of Sir Peter Osborne, 17 Bt, *qv*, and Lady Osborne, *née* Felicity Loxton-Peacock; *b* 23 May 1971, London; *Educ* St Paul's, Davidson Coll NC (Dean Rusk scholar), Magdalen Coll Oxford (scholar, MA, ed Isis); *m* 1998, Hon Frances Victoria, da of Baron Howell of Guildford,

PC (Life Peer), *qv*; 1s (Luke Benedict b 2001), 1 da (Liberty Kate b 2003); *Career* head of political section Cons Research Dept 1994–95, special advsr MAFF 1995–97, sec to the shadow cabinet and political sec to the Ldr of the Oppn 1997–2001, MP (Cons) Tatton 2001–; oppn whip 2003, oppn Treasy spokesman 2003–04, shadow chief sec of the Treasy 2004–05, shadow Chancellor of the Exchequer 2005–10, Chllr of the Exchequer 2010–16, first sec of state 2015–16; memb Public Accounts Ctee House of Commons 2001–03; vice-pres E Cheshire Hospice; *Recreations* walking in the Peak District, film, theatre; *Style*— The Rt Hon George Osborne, CH, MP; ✉ House of Commons, London SW1A 0AA (☎ 020 7219 8214)

OSBORNE, Georgiana Louise; *née* Moore; da of Richard Douglas Moore, and June Louise, *née* Peachey; *b* Invercargill, NZ; *Educ* Wellington Diocesan Sch for Girls (Nga Tawa) Marton NZ, Victoria Univ of Wellington (BA), Univ of Lausanne (Philips overseas scholar); *m* 1968, James Carnegy Osborne, 3 s, 1 da; *Career* HM Lord-Lt Angus 2001–; JP 2001–08; Br Red Cross: dep pres Angus Branch 1991–98, pres Tayside Branch 1999–2004 (patron 2004–), Badge of Hon for Outstanding Serv Br Red Cross Soc 2004 (Badge of Hon for Distinguished Serv 1996); pres Perth and Kinross branch SSAFA 2006–09, jt pres Dundee and Angus branch SSAFA 2010–, vice-pres Black Watch Assoc; patron Dorward House Montrose 2006–, hon vice-pres Tayside Symphony Orch, hon pres Strathmore Assoc 2013–, hon vice-pres Boys' Brigade Dundee and Angus Battalion 2012–, hon vice-pres Tayside Opera 2013–; tstee: Queen Mother's Meml Fund for Scotland 2003–08, Angus Coll Charitable Tst 2004–12; OStJ; *Recreations* music, the arts, tennis, golf; *Style*— Mrs Georgiana L Osborne; ✉ Balmadies, Guthrie, Forfar, Angus DD8 2SH (☎ and fax 01307 818242)

OSBORNE, Ven Hayward John; s of Ernest Osborne, and Francis Joy, *née* Perman; *Educ* Sevenoaks Sch, New Coll Oxford (MA), King's Coll Cambridge (PGCE), Wescott House Theol Coll Cambridge; *Career* curate Bromley Parish Church 1973–77, team vicar Halesowen 1977–83, team rector St Barnabas Worcester 1983–88, vicar St Mary Moseley 1988–2001, area dean Moseley 1994–2001, hon canon Birmingham Cathedral 2000, archdeacon of Birmingham 2001–; memb Gen Synod 1988–2015; *Style*— The Ven the Archdeacon of Birmingham; ✉ 23 Carisbrooke Road, Birmingham B17 8NN (e-mail archdeaconofbham@birmingham.anglican.org)

OSBORNE, Iain; *b* 15 February 1969, Manchester; *Educ* Queen's Coll Oxford (BA), Univ of Manchester (MA); *Career* DTI 1993–97, McKinsey & Co 1997–98, Global TeleSystems plc 1998–2001, Ofgem 2001–06, chief exec NI Authy for Utility Regulation; FEI 2007; *Recreations* books, gardens, concertina; *Style*— Iain Osborne, Esq; ✉ Northern Ireland Authority for Utility Regulation, Queens House, 14 Queens Street, Belfast BT1 6ER

OSBORNE, John Leslie; s of Frederick James Osborne, of Lampeter, Wales, and May Doris, *née* Brown; *b* 20 March 1942, London; *Educ* The London Hosp Med Coll (MB BS); *Family* 2 da (Clare b 1969, Julia b 1981), 2 s (Andrew b 1972, James b 1979); m Nov 2012, Ceri M, *née* Phillips; *Career* lectr in obstetrics and gynaecology Inst of Obstetrics and Gynaecology 1974–79; conslt obstetrician and gynaecologist UCHL; formerly conslt obstetrics and gynaecology Queen Charlotte's and Chelsea Hosps; hon sr lectr: Inst of Urology, Inst of Obstetrics and Gynaecology; Freeman Worshipful Soc Apothecaries; chm: Elizabeth Garrett Anderson Appeals Tst, TASK Women's Health; FRCOG 1985 (MRCOG 1973), memb RSM; *Recreations* music, photography, old cars (Bentley); *Clubs* Bentley Drivers'; *Style*— John Osborne, Esq; ✉ University College London Hospital, 2nd Floor North, 250 Euston Road, London NW1 2PG

OSBORNE, John Michael; s of Claudius Hase Osborne, and Irene Oliver, *née* Chaffé; *b* 30 October 1953; *Educ* Whitchurch GS, Univ of Sheffield (BSc); *m* 2 July 1983, Helen Elizabeth, da of Richard Derek Gommo; 1 da (Claire Hannah b 11 April 1986), 1 s (Nicholas John b 14 April 1988); *Career* Equity & Law: joined 1975, devpt mangr 1986, planning mangr 1986–88, mangr Equity & Law Home Loans 1988–92, mangr and dir Equity & Law Unit Trust 1990–98, actuary 1990–92, head of business devpt 1992–98, head of finance and operations AXA Assurance 1998–2000; fndr and md Hase Osborne Asset Mgmnt (ind fin advsrs, formerly Twigden Osborne Asset Mgmnt) 2000–; FIA 1981; *Recreations* golf, tennis; *Style*— John Osborne, Esq; ✉ Hase Osborne Asset Management, Chiltern Court, Back Street, Wendover, Buckinghamshire HP22 6EP (☎ 01296 620950)

OSBORNE, Sir Peter George; 17 Bt (I 1629), of Ballintaylor, Co Tipperary; s of Lt-Col Sir George Francis Osborne, 16 Bt, MC (d 1960), and Mary, *née* Horn (d 1987); Richard Osborne cr 1 Bt of Ireland 1629, and supported Parl against the crown; 2, 7, 8, 9 and 11 Bts were MPs (8 Bt, PC); *b* 29 June 1943; *Educ* Wellington, ChCh Oxford; *m* 1968, Felicity, da of late Grantley Loxton-Peacock; 4 s (George Gideon Oliver, b 1971, Benedict George b 1973, Adam Peter b 1976, Theo Grantley b 1985); *Heir* s, George Osborne, MP, *qv*; *Career* chm Osborne & Little plc; *Clubs* White's; *Style*— Sir Peter Osborne, Bt; ✉ 51 Lansdowne Road, London W11 2LG

OSBORNE, Richard Ellerker; s of William Harold Osborne (d 1984), and Georgina Mary, *née* Farrow (d 1997); *b* 22 February 1943; *Educ* Worksop Coll, Univ of Bristol (BA, MLitt); *m* 18 Jan 1986, Hailz-Emily, da of Michael Ewart Wrigley (d 2007), of Streetly, W Midlands; 1 s (Harry George Ellerker b 6 May 1992); *Career* asst master Bradfield Coll 1967–88; contrib: Records and Recording 1967–73, BBC Radio 3 1971–, Gramophone 1974–, Opera, The Spectator, Times Literary Supplement; music critic The Oldie 1992–; chm Music Section Critics' Circle 1984–87; *Books* Rossini (1986), Conversations with Karajan (1989), Karajan: a Life in Music (1998), Till I End My Song (2002), Rossini: His Life and Works (2007), Karajan: Mensch und Mythos (2008), Garsington Opera, a celebration (2011), Music and Musicians of Eton: 1440 to the present (2012), The Grange, Hampshire (2012), Ferdinand Hiller Conversations with Rossini (ed and trans, 2015); *Recreations* food and wine, cricket, fell walking; *Style*— Richard Osborne, Esq; ✉ 2 Vaughan Copse, Eton, Berkshire SL4 6HL

OSBORNE, Robert (Bob); s of Walter Richard Osborne and Maud Osborne; *b* 18 April 1948; *Educ* Sedgehill Sch London, Univ of Warwick (BSc), Imperial Coll London (MSc, DIC); *m* 1970, Madeline, *née* Chatterton; 2 da (Tamsin b 20 March 1978, Jessica b 22 July 1981); *Career* concert promoter and dir Moon Enterprises (concert promotions) 1970, maths teacher Leamington Spa 1970–71, maths and science publisher Penguin Education 1971–74, publishing dir then dep md Hutchinson Educational 1974–84, publishing dir then dep md Heinemann Educational Books 1984–88, md Harcourt UK Schools Publishing 1988–2004, strategic devpt dir Pearson Edexcel 2004–; educational publishing conslt 2006–; *Recreations* France, music, travel; *Style*— Bob Osborne; ✉ e-mail bobosborne100@gmail.com

OSBORNE, Sandra; *b* 23 February 1956; *Educ* Camphill Sr Secdy Sch, Univ of Strathclyde (MSc), Jordanhill Coll (Dip Community Educn); *Career* cncllr Kyle and Carrick DC 1990–95, cncllr S Ayrshire Cncl 1994–97, women's aid worker Kilmarnock (for 15 years) until 1997, convenor Housing and Social Work Community Services until 1997; MP (Lab): Ayr 1997–2005, Ayr, Carrick and Cumnock 2005–15; PPS to: Rt Hon Brian Wilson, *qv*, until 2001, Rt Hon George Foulkes, MP, *qv*, 2001–02, Rt Hon Helen Liddell, MP, *qv*, 2002–03; *Style*— Ms Sandra Osborne; ✉ Constituency Office, 139 Main Street, Ayr KA8 8BX (☎ 01292 262906)

OSGERBY, Jay; OBE (2013); s of Paul Osgerby, of Oxon, and Wendy, *née* Hickman; *b* 23 October 1969, Oxford; *Educ* Ravensbourne Coll London (BA), RCA (MA); *m* 27 May 2000, Helen Louise; 2 da (Eva Jasmine b 28 Oct 2002, Sophia Elizabeth b 1 Oct 2005), 1 s (Felix Theo William b 8 March 2008); *Career* designer; fndr BarberOsgerby 1996–, founding dir and co-owner Universal Design Studio Ltd 2001–, founding dir and co-owner MAP 2012; clients incl: Vitra, B&B Italia, Knoll, Louis Vuitton, Flos, Venini, Cappellini; commissioned to design furniture for De La Warr Pavilion Bexhill on Sea, RIBA, Portsmouth Cathedral; commissioned to design Olympic and Paralympic Torches for London Olympics 2012, commissioned to design £2 coin commemorating the London Underground's 150th anniversary; exhibited at: V&A, Haunch of Venison London, Sotheby's London, MOMA NY, Int Furniture Fair NY, Design Museum London, Crafts Cncl London, Design Miami/Basel; work in permanent collections: V&A London, Met Museum of Art NY, Design Museum London, Art Inst of Chicago, Indianapolis Museum of Art, Cooper-Hewitt Smithsonian Design Museum; external examiner Royal Coll of Art; Hon DA Oxford Brookes Univ 2012; fell Ravensbourne Coll; MCSD 2003, FRSA 2005, RDI 2007; *Awards* incl: Best New Designer ICFF NY 1998, shortlisted for Compasso d'Oro 2004, Jerwood Prize for Applied Arts 2004, Furniture Designer of the Year Blueprint Magazine 2005, Best Product Red Dot Award 2006, Designer of the Future (with Established & Sons) Basel 2006, Designers of the Year Elle Decoration 2007, Chicago Athenaeum Good Design Award 2011, D&AD Yellow Pencil 2012, Icon Magazine Design Studio of the Year 2012, World Technology Award for Design 2012, Design Museum Design of the Year and Product Design of the Year 2012, German Design Cncl German Design Award 2013, Maison & Objet Designers of the Year 2013, shortlisted for Compasso d'Oro 2013; *Publications* The Design Work of Edward Barber & Jay Osgerby (2011), Ascent (2011); *Style*— Jay Osgerby, Esq, OBE, RDI; ✉ 37–42 Charlotte Road, London EC2A 3PG (☎ 020 7033 3884, fax 020 7033 3882, website www.barberosgerby.com)

OSHO, Andi; *b* 27 January 1973, London; *Career* comedian and actress; *Stand up* incl: Afroblighty 2010, All the Single Ladies 2011; *Theatre* incl: Cigarettes, Coffee and Paranoia (King's Head Theatre) 2005, Yellowman (Liverpool Everyman) 2006, Eurydice (RSC) 2009; *Television* as actress incl: Life of Riley, Holby City, Psychoville; other appearances incl: Mock the Week, Michael McIntyre's Comedy Roadshow, Never Mind the Buzzcocks, Live at the Apollo, Edinburgh Comedy Festival Live, Stand Up for the Week; *Style*— Ms Andi Osho

OSMAN, David Antony; s of Colin Alfred Earnest Osman, of Cockfosters, Herts, and Grace Florence, *née* White; *b* 13 April 1953; *Educ* Minchenden GS, Univ of Nottingham (BA); *m* 4 Sept 1976, Helen, da of Randall Jones-Pugh, of Roch, Dyfed; 2 da (Caroline b 15 Nov 1984, Nicola b 23 Jan 1988); *Career* dir RP Publishing Co Ltd 1975–78 (non-exec dir 1978–95), non-exec dir RP Typesetters Co Ltd 1980–96; UK economist Joseph/Carr Sebag & Co 1978–82, UK and int economist Laing & Cruickshank 1982–84, int economist James Capel & Co 1984–91; stockbroker: Sassoon (Europe) Ltd 1991–92, Smith New Court Far East/Merrill Lynch 1992–99; dir Cojent Ltd 1999–2014, economist and stockbroker SCS (UK) Ltd 1999–2005, economist and stockbroker UOB Kay Hian (UK) Ltd 2005– (dir 2007–); fndr memb Enfield SDP 1981–87, SDP/Lib Alliance Pty candidate for Upminster 1983, vice-chm City SDP 1984–88 (fndr memb and sec), fndr and memb Enfield Lib Democrats 1988–2011; memb Soc of Business Economists; *Recreations* chess, cycling, golf, snooker, walking, poetry; *Clubs* Old Minchendenians Golf Soc; *Style*— David Osman, Esq; ✉ 10 Old Park Ridings, Winchmore Hill, London N21 2EU (☎ 020 8360 4343); UOB Kay Hian (UK) Limited, 14 Austin Friars, London EC2N 2HE (☎ 020 7972 0880, fax 020 7972 0882)

OSTERFIELD, Mark; s of J R Osterfield, Crowhurst, Surrey, and Patricia, *née* Tobin; *b* 14 October 1963, Hampshire; *Educ* Keble Coll Oxford (BA), Univ of Middx (BA); *Career* library mangr Swiss Cottage Central Library 1997–2004, project mangr Kilburn Library 2004–05, project dir Tate St Ives Phase Two 2005–07, exec dir Tate St Ives 2007–; currently: non-exec dir Borlase Smart John Wells Tst, non-exec tstee Kestle Barton Tst, non-exec dir Kestle Barton Arts Ltd, non-exec tstee Truro and Penwith Mutli-Acad Tst, non-exec tstee little Parc Owles Tst; *Style*— Mark Osterfield, Esq; ✉ Tate St Ives, Porthmeor Beach, St Ives, Cornwall TR26 1TG (☎ 01736 791103, e-mail mark.osterfield@tate.org.uk)

OSTLER, Catherine Emma; da of John Ramsdell Ostler (d 1998), and Patricia Ann, *née* Leonard; *Educ* Cheltenham Ladies Coll (scholar), St Hilda's Coll Oxford (scholar, MA); *m* 13 Sept 2003, Albert Nathaniel Read, s of Piers Paul Read, FRSL, *qv*; 2 da (Clementine Margaret b 14 March 2003, Angelica Albertine b 6 March 2007), 1 s (Nathaniel John Basil b 10 Dec 2004); *Career* features ed Tatler 1994, features writer Mail on Sunday 1994–96; ed: The Express Saturday Magazine 1996–99, The Times Weekend 1999–2000, peoplenews.com 2000–01, ES Magazine 2002–09, Tatler 2009–10; contributing ed Daily Mail 2011–, contributing ed Newsweek 2014–; *Style*— Ms Catherine Ostler; ✉ c/o Daily Mail, Northcliffe House, 2 Derry Street, London W8 5TT

OSTRIKER, Prof Jeremiah P; *b* 13 April 1937, New York; *Educ* Harvard Univ (AB), Univ of Chicago (PhD); *m* Dec 1959, Alicia, *née* Suskin; *Career* postdoctoral fell Univ of Cambridge 1964–65; Princeton Univ: research assoc and lectr 1965–66, asst prof 1966–68, assoc prof 1968–71, prof 1971–2012, chm Dept of Astrophysical Sciences and dir Princeton Univ Observatory 1979–95, Charles A Young prof of astronomy 1982–2002, provost 1995–2001; Plumian prof of astronomy and experimental philosophy Inst of Astronomy Univ of Cambridge 2001–04, prof of astronomy Columbia Univ 2012–; Regents fell Smithsonian Inst 1984–85 and 1987, visiting prof Harvard Univ 1984 and 1987, visiting Miller prof Univ of Calif Berkeley 1990; tstee and memb Editorial Bd Princeton Univ Press 1982–84 and 1986, tstee American Museum of Nat History 1997–2007; American Astronomical Soc: memb 1963–, memb Cncl 1978–80, chm Ctee on Astronomy and Public Policy 1988–89; IAU: memb 1966–, US rep 1978–81, pres Cmmn 48 High Energy 1991–94 (vice-pres 1988–91); Nat Acad of Sciences: memb Exec Ctee of Decennial Surveys 1969–73, 1978–83 and 1988–91, memb 1974–, astronomy rep Class Membership Ctee 1977, 1978, 1987, 1988 and 1993, memb Assembly of Mathematical and Physical Sciences 1977–80, memb Cmmn on Physical Sciences, Mathematics and Resources 1987–91, memb Ctee on Astronomy and Astrophysics 1992–95, memb Cncl 1992–95, memb Bd of Govrs 1993–95, memb Audit Ctee 1994–95; memb American Philosophical Soc 1994–, assoc memb RAS 1994–, foreign memb Royal Netherlands Acad of Arts and Sciences 1999–, treas and memb Governing Bd US Nat Acad of Sciences 2008–16; Helen B Warner Prize American Astronomical Soc 1972, Henry Norris Russell Prize American Astronomical Soc 1980, Vainu Bappu Meml Award Indian Nat Sci Acad 1993, Karl Schwarzschild Medal Astronomische Gesellschaft 1999, US Nat Medal of Sci 2000, Golden Plate Award American Acad of Achievement 2001, Gold Medal Royal Astronomical Soc 2004, Chinese Acad of Sci Einstein Professorship 2009, Catherine Wolf Bruce Gold Medal 2011, James Craig Watson Medal of NAS 2012, The White House Champions of Change 2013, Gruber Cosmology Prize 2015; Nat Sci Fndn Fellowship 1960–65, Alfred P Sloan Fellowship 1970–72, Sherman Fairchild Fellowship Californian Instn of Technology 1977, Regents Fellowship Smithsonian Inst 1984–87; Hon DSc Univ of Chicago 1992; fell AAAS 1992 (memb 1975), foreign memb Royal Soc 2007; *Books* Development of Large-Scale Structure in the Universe (1991), Unsolved Problems in Astrophysics (ed with J N Bachall, 1997), Dreams, Stars and Electrons: Selected Writings of Lyman Spitzer, Jr (ed with Lyman Spitzer Jr, 1997), Formation of Structure in the Universe (ed with A Dekel, 1999), Heart of Darkness: Unravelling the Mysteries of the Invisible Universe (with Simon Mitton, 2013); *Recreations* photography; *Style*— Prof Jeremiah Ostriker; ✉ Columbia University, Department of Astronomy, 550 West 120th Street, New York, NY 10027

OSWALD, Sir (William Richard) Michael; KCVO (1998, CVO 1988, LVO 1979); s of Lt-Col William Alexander Hugh Oswald, ERD (d 1974), of Weybridge, Surrey, and Rose-Marie, *née* Leahy (d 1985); *b* 21 April 1934; *Educ* Eton, King's Coll Cambridge (MA); *m* 21 April 1958, The Lady Angela Mary Rose, CVO, da of 6 Marquess of Exeter, KCMG (d 1981); 1 da (Katharine Davina Mary (Mrs Alexander Matheson) b 1959), 1 s (William Alexander Michael b 1962); *Career* 2 Lt 1 Bn King's Own Royal Regt 1953, BAOR and Korea, Lt 8 Bn Royal Fusiliers (TA) 1955, Capt 1958–61; mangr Lordship and Egerton Studs Newmarket 1962–69, dir The Royal Studs 1997–98 (mangr 1970–97), racing mangr for HM Queen Elizabeth The Queen Mother 1970–2002, Nat Hunt racing advsr to HM The Queen 2002–; pres The Thoroughbred Breeders Assoc 1997–2001 (memb Cncl 1964–2001); chm Bloodstock Industry Ctee Animal Health Tst 1986–2002; tstee Br Veterinary Assoc Tst 1998–2004; Liveryman Worshipful Co of Shipwrights; Hon DSc De Montfort Univ 1997; Hon Air Cdre 2620 Co of Norfolk Sqdn RAuxAF 2001–; *Recreations* painting, military history; *Clubs* Army and Navy, Jockey, RAF; *Style*— Sir Michael Oswald, KCVO; ✉ 6 St Olave's Court, St Petersburgh Place, London W2 4JY (☎ 020 7229 0773); The Old Rectory, Weasenham St Peter, King's Lynn, Norfolk PE32 2TB (☎ 01328 838311)

OTAKA, Tadaaki; Hon CBE (1997); s of Hisatada Otaka, conductor and composer, and Misaoko Otaka; *b* 8 November 1947; *Educ* Toho Gakuen Sch of Music (second prize Min-On Conducting Competition), Vienna Hochschule (Austrian State scholar); *m* 1978, Yukiko; *Career* conductor; began playing violin aged 5, studied conducting under Prof Hideo Saito and Prof Hans Swarowsky, student at NHK (Japanese Broadcasting Corp) Symphony Orch 1968–70; professional broadcasting debut 1971 with NHK Symphony Orch (asst conductor various int tours 1969–73), NY debut 1985 with American Symphony Orch; perm conductor Tokyo Philharmonic Orch 1971–91 (conductor laureate 1991–), conductor NHK New Year Opera Concert annually 1980–, chief conductor Sapporo Symphony Orch 1981–2014, princ conductor BBC Nat Orch of Wales 1987–95 (conductor laureate 1996–), chief conductor Yomiuri Nippon Symphony Orch 1992–, music advsr and princ conductor Kioi Sinfonietta Japan 1995–, dir Britten-Pears Orch 1998–2001, princ guest conductor Melbourne Symphony Orch 2010–12, prem conductor NHK Symphony Tokyo 2010–14, artistic dir New Nat Theatre Tokyo 2010–14; made various int tours incl: Vienna, Czechoslovakia, Germany, Russia, Indonesia, Australia, N America, Far East (BBC NOW); worked with other orchs incl: London Philharmonic, City of Birmingham Symphony, Royal Liverpool Philharmonic, Hallé, London Symphony, BBC Symphony, Brno State Philharmonic, Vancouver Symphony, Oregon Symphony, Helsinki Philharmonic, Turku Philharmonic, Orchestre National de Lille, Dresden Philharmonic, Polish Nat Radio Symphony, Hong Kong Philharmonic, Melbourne Symphony, Sydney Symphony, Rotterdam Philharmonic, Oslo Philharmonic, Bamberg Symphony, Strasbourg Philharmonic, Royal Philharmonic; opera: Salome (Welsh Nat Opera) 1991; various recordings with BBC Welsh Symphony Orch, Britten's Peter Grimes with Yomiuri Nippon Symphony Orch; Suntory Music Award 1992, Hon Doctorate Univ of Wales 1993; *Recreations* fishing, tennis, cooking; *Style*— Mr Tadaaki Otaka, CBE; ✉ c/o Askonas Holt, Lincoln House, 300 High Holborn, London WC1V 7JH (☎ 020 7400 1700, fax 020 7400 1799, e-mail info@askonasholt.co.uk, website www.askonasholt.co.uk)

OTOO-OYORTEY, Naana; MBE (2009); *b* Ghana; *Educ* Univ of Ghana, Univ of Sussex (MPhil); *Career* Commonwealth Secretariat 1994–96, Int Planned Parenthood Fedn 1996–2007, currently exec dir Fndn for Women's Health Research and Devpt (FORWARD); memb Bd ACORD, pres End FGM European Network; 1000 Most Influential People in London Evening Standard 2014; *Recreations* reading, travel; *Style*— Ms Naana Otoo-Oyortey, MBE; ✉ FORWARD, Suite 2.1 Chandelier Building, 2nd Floor, 8 Scrubs Lane, London NW10 6RB (☎ 020 8960 4000, website www.forwarduk.org.uk, Twitter @Naayosuwa)

OTTAWAY, Rt Hon Sir Richard Geoffrey James; kt (2014), PC (2013); s of Prof Christopher Wyndham Ottaway (d 1977), and Grace Ottaway; *b* 24 May 1945; *Educ* Backwell Sch, Univ of Bristol (LLB); *m* 1982, Nicola Evelyn, da of John Kisch, CMG; *Career* Lt RN, Lt Cdr RNR; admitted slr 1977, ptnr Wm A Crump Slrs 1981–87; MP (Cons): Nottingham N 1983–87, Croydon S 1992–2015; PPS to Baroness Young and Tim Renton, MP as Mins of State at FCO 1985–87, PPS to Michael Heseltine, MP as Pres of the Bd of Trade and then as Dep PM 1992–95, asst Govt whip 1995–96, a Lord Cmmr HM Treasy (Govt whip) 1996–97, oppn whip and spokesman for London 1997–98, shadow local govt min and shadow min for London 1998, oppn defence spokesman 1999, shadow Paymaster Gen 2000–01, shadow sec of state for the environment 2004–05; memb: Standards and Privileges Select Ctee 2001–04, Foreign Affrs Select Ctee 2003–04, Parly Intelligence and Security Ctee 2005–10; chm: All Pty Gp on Population and Devpt 1992–95, All Pty Singapore Gp 1997–2000, All Pty Malaysia Gp 1999–; dir Coastal Europe 1988–95; *Books* Road to Reform, Thoughts for a Third Term (jtly, 1987), Less People, Less Pollution (1990); *Recreations* yacht racing, jazz; *Clubs* Royal Corinthian Yacht, Island Sailing; *Style*— The Rt Hon Sir Richard Ottaway; ✉ House of Commons, London SW1A 0AA (☎ 020 7219 3000)

OTTER, Stephen; QPM (2009); s of Tony Otter, and Rosemary Otter; *b* 24 May 1962, Bethnal Green, London; *Educ* LSE (MSc), Univ of Cambridge (postgrad dip); *m* Sophie; 3 s, 1 da; *Career* Thames Valley Police 1982–85, Royal Hong Kong Police 1985–88, Met Police 1989–2001, Avon & Somerset Police 2001–07, chief constable Devon & Cornwall Constabulary 2007–; FRSA; *Recreations* reading, listening to music, gardening; *Style*— Stephen Otter, Esq, QPM; ✉ Police Headquarters, Middlemoor, Exeter, Devon EX2 7HQ (☎ 01392 452011, e-mail stephen.otter@devonandcornwall.pnn.police.uk)

OTTLEY, Robert Jeremy Mark Linn; *Career* ptnr W Greenwell & Co and dir Greenwell Montagu Stockbrokers 1968–92, sr investment dir HSBC Investment Management (formerly James Capel) 1992–2001; chm and dir various investment cos 1996–2015; *Style*— Robert Linn Ottley; ✉ e-mail rlo@ottley.co.uk

OTTOLENGHI, Yotam; *Career* restaurateur; previous roles incl: asst Pastry Dept The Capital restaurant, pastry chef Kensington Place Gp, head pastry chef Baker and Spice Chelsea; patron chef: Ottolenghi 2002–, NOPI 2011–; columnist Guardian Weekend magazine; *Books* Ottolenghi Cookbook (2008), Plenty (2010), Jerusalem (2012), Plenty More (2014), The NOPI Cookbook (2015); *Recreations* Pilates; *Style*— Yotam Ottolenghi, Esq; ✉ Ottolenghi, 63 Ledbury Road, London W11 2AD (e-mail contact@ottolenghi.co.uk)

OULTON, Claire; da of Prof Leslie Zisman, and Sally Zisman; *Educ* Lady Eleanor Holles Sch, Somerville Coll Oxford (MA), KCL (PGCE); *m*; 2 c; *Career* teacher Benenden Sch 1984–88, head of history Charterhouse 1988–94, headmistress St Catherine's Sch Bramley 1994–2000, headmistress Benenden Sch 2000–14; *Recreations* reading, gardening, cooking, walking; *Style*— Mrs Claire Oulton; ✉ Benenden School, Benenden, Cranbrook, Kent TN17 4AA (☎ 01580 240592, fax 01580 240280, e-mail cmo@benenden.kent.sch.uk)

OULTON, Therese; da of Robert Oulton, and Matilda, *née* Glover; *b* 20 April 1953; *Educ* St Martin's Sch of Art London, RCA London; *Career* artist; shortlisted Turner Prize; *Solo Exhibitions* incl: Peterborough City Museum and Art Gallery 1984, Fool's Gold: New Paintings (Gimpel Fils London) 1984, Recent Painting (MOMA Oxford) 1985, Marlborough Graphics London 1987, 1989, 1992, 1994 and 1998, Marlborough Fine Art London 1987, 1990, 1991, 1992, 1997, 2000 and 2003, New Paintings (Hirschl & Adler (Modern) NY) 1989, Marking Time (LA Louver Gallery) 1994, Recent Paintings (Marlborough Gallery NY) 1994, Illuminations (Oxford Gallery) 1999; *Public Collections* Arts Cncl of GB, British Cncl, British Museum, Fitzwilliam Museum Cambridge, Metropolitan Museum of Art NY, Museum of Fine Art Boston, National Gallery of Victoria Melbourne, Tate Britain, V&A, Yale Center for British Art; *Style*— Ms Therese Oulton

OUNSLEY, Margaret Mary; da of Laurence Kelly, and Maureen Reid; *b* 30 August 1958; *Educ* Cardinal Newman RC Comp Sch Luton, Luton VI Form Coll, Bulmershe Coll of HE (BEd); *m* 1980, Robert Ounsley; 2 s (Thomas b 8 Oct 1985, James 2 Oct 1987); *Career* teacher 1980–85, co-ordinator Southern Region Nat Local Govt Forum Against Poverty (NLGFAP) 1994–97, political offr Lab Gp Local Govt Assoc 1997–99, political advsr to Govt chief whip House of Lords 2000–06, head of public affrs WWF 2006–; memb Reading BC 1990–94; memb: Lab Pty, Child Poverty Action Gp, Greenpeace; FRSA 2008; *Publications* Talking of Coley (1989), The Politics of Poverty (jtly, 1995); *Recreations* badminton, walking, reading, talking; *Style*— Ms Margaret Ounsley

OUSELEY, Hon Mr Justice; Sir Duncan Brian Walter Ouseley; kt (2000); s of Maurice Henry Ouseley (d 1978), Margaret Helen Irene, *née* Vagts (d 1997); *b* 24 February 1950; *Educ* Trinity Sch Croydon, Fitzwilliam Coll Cambridge (MA, exhibitioner) UCL (LLM); *m* 27 April 1974, Suzannah Valerie, *née* Price; 3 s (Daniel b 18 Jan 1979, Jonathan b 24 May 1980, Robert b 2 March 1988); *Career* called to the Bar Gray's Inn 1973 (Atkin scholar 1972, bencher 2000); jr counsel to Crown Common Law 1986–92, QC 1992 (NI 1997), recorder 1994–2000 (asst recorder 1991–94), jt head of chambers 4–5 Gray's Inn Square 2000, dep judge of the High Court 2000, judge of the High Court of Justice (Queen's Bench Div) 2000–, lead judge Administrative Court 2010–15; pres Immigration Appeal Tribunal 2003–05, chm Special Immigration Appeal Cmmn 2003–06; chm examination in public of: Shropshire Structure Plan First Alterations 1985, Hampshire Structure Plan 1991; vice-chm Planning and Environmental Bar Assoc 2000; hon fell Fitzwilliam Coll Cambridge 2011; *Recreations* family, sport, music, wine; *Clubs* Garrick; *Style*— The Hon Mr Justice Ouseley; ✉ Royal Courts of Justice, Strand, London WC2A 2LL

OUSELEY, Baron (Life Peer UK 2001), of Peckham Rye in the London Borough of Southwark; Sir Herman George Ouseley; kt (1997); s of Johnny Ouseley, and Daphne Coggins, of Guyana; *b* 24 March 1945; *Educ* William Penn Sch Dulwich, Catford Coll; *Career* town planning mangr 1963–70, social care mangr for elderly 1970–73, community relations exec 1973–79, race relations policy advsr Lambeth BC 1979–81, dir Policy Unit GLC 1981–84, asst ceo London Borough of Lambeth 1984–86, chief exec ILEA 1988–90 (dir of educn 1986–88), chief exec London Borough of Lambeth 1990–93, chm Cmmn for Racial Equality 1993–2000, Different Realities Partnership Ltd 2000–06; non-exec dir: Focus Consultancy Ltd 2001–10, Brooknight Security Ltd; chm Policy Research Inst on Ageing and Ethnicity 1997–2010, memb Cncl Inst of Race Relations 1986–; pres Local Govt Assoc 2002–05; chm: Kick It Out 1993–, Preset Educn and Employment Charitable Tst 1997–; tstee Manchester United Fndn 2006–; patron: Presentation Housing Assoc 1990–2002, Daneford Tst 2001–, Nat Black Police Assoc 2007–; *Publications* The System (1981); various pamphlets and articles on aspects of equality and local government; *Style*— The Lord Ouseley

OUTLAW, Nathan Daniel; s of Clive Outlaw, of Maidstone, Kent, and Sharon, *née* Munn; *b* 7 March 1978, Maidstone, Kent; *Educ* Holmsdale Sch Snodland, Thanet Tech Coll; *m* 6 Oct 2001, Rachel, *née* Morris; 1 s (Jacob Anthony b 6 May 2003), 1 da (Jessica b 11 May 2005); *Career* chef: Hotel Intercontinental Hyde Park Corner London 1996–97, Chavot Restaurant Fulham London 1997–98; second chef: Seafood Restaurant Padstow Cornwall 1998–99, Lords of the Manor Glos 1999–2001; head chef The Vineyard at Stockcross Berks 2001–03, prop and chef Black Pig Rock Cornwall 2003–04 (Michelin Star 2004), head chef St Ervan Manor Padstow 2005–06 (Michelin Star 2006), head chef Restaurant Nathan Outlaw Marina Villa Hotel 2007–09 (Michelin Star 2008), prop Nathan Outlaw Seafood and Grill Rock 2009–, prop Outlaw's at St Enodoc Hotel Rock 2009–, head chef Restaurant Nathan Outlaw St Enodoc Hotel Rock 2010–14 (2 Michelin Stars), conslt chef Outlaw's at the Capital Knightsbridge 2012–, chef and prop Outlaw's Fish Kitchen Port Isaac 2013–, conslt chef The Mariners' Public House Rock 2014–; nat finalist Roux Scholarship 2001, second place Young Chef and Young Waiter of GB 2002; memb Royal Acad of Culinary Arts 2014; *Books* Nathan Outlaw's British Seafood (2012), Nathan Outlaw's Fish Kitchen (2014); *Recreations* collecting cookery books, Star Wars, music; *Style*— Nathan Outlaw, Esq; ✉ Nathan Outlaw Restaurants Ltd, St. Enodoc Hotel, Rock, Cornwall PL27 6LA (☎ 01208 862737, website www.nathan-outlaw.com, Twitter @Nathanoutlaw)

OUTRAM, Christopher David; s of Joseph Outram (d 1972), and Vera Anne, *née* Ogden (d 2014); *b* 4 April 1949; *Educ* King's GS, Atlantic Coll, Univ of Birmingham (BSc, BComm, Economics prize, Engineering prize), INSEAD Business Sch (MBA); *m* (m dis 2001), Anne Marie, da of Noel Leslie Costain; 2 da (Sophie Marie Elizabeth b 26 Sept 1981, Verity Clementine b 24 Nov 1983); *Career* Mobil Oil Company 1972–73, Air Products 1973–74, mktg mangr CCL Systems 1974–76, INSEAD Business Sch 1976–77, strategy conslt Boston Consulting Group 1977–79, strategic planning dir Van Gelder Papier 1979–81, strategy conslt/ptnr Booz Allen & Hamilton 1981–86 (vice-pres 1986), fndr and ptnr OC&C Strategy Consultants 1986– (chm 1986–); non-exec chm iPulse; chm: United World Schools, Beat (eating disorders assoc); *Books* Making Your Strategy Work (2013), Digital Stractics (2015); *Recreations* learning piano and golf and other leisure activities, reading, travelling; *Clubs* RAC, Beaconsfield Golf; *Style*— Christopher Outram, Esq; ✉ c/o Jo Falcon-Cross (PA), OC&C Strategy Consultants, 6 New Street Square, London EC4A 3AT (☎ 020 7010 8026)

OVENDEN, Reverend Canon John Anthony; LVO (2007); s of Edward Clifford Lewis Ovenden (d 1996), and Marjorie Mabel Ovenden (d 2006); *b* 26 May 1945; *Educ* chorister St Paul's Cathedral, Ardingly (music scholar), Borough Rd Coll of Educn, Salisbury & Wells Theol Coll, Open Univ (BA), King's Coll London (MA), Univ of Oxford (MA); *m* 27 July 1974, Christine, da of John Broadhurst; 2 s (Julian, Nicholas), 1 da (Anne-Clare); *Career* ordained: deacon 1974, priest 1975; curate: Handsworth (Sheffield) 1974–77, Isfield (Chichester) 1977–80, Uckfield 1977–80; priest i/c Stuntney (Ely) 1980–85, minor canon, precentor and sacrist Ely Cathedral 1980–85, vicar St Mary's Primrose Hill London 1985–98, canon of St George's Chapel Windsor Castle and chaplain in the Great Park 1998–2012, chaplain to HM The Queen 2002–15, fell and dean of chapel Harris Manchester Coll Oxford 2012–15, chaplain Mansfield Coll 2014–; fell Cumberland Lodge Windsor Great Park; Freeman City of London; *Publications* Christians and Muslims in the Commonwealth (contrib); contrib Affirming Catholicism Magazine; *Recreations* sport, theatre, walking; *Style*— The Reverend Canon John Ovenden, LVO; ✉ Little Croft, Great Rissington, Gloucestershire GL54 2LN (☎ 01451 8211533, mobile 07778 299829, e-mail johnovenden@btinternet.com); Mansfield College, Mansfield Road, Oxford OX1 3TF (☎ 01865 270967)

OVEREND, John Edward; s of John Magri Overend, and Valerie Angela, *née* Kingston; *b* 14 May 1963, Watford, Herts; *Educ* Merchant Taylors' Sch Northwood, Univ of North London (BA); *m* 8 June 2001, Paivi Sinikka, *née* Piironen; 1 s (Charles Lawrence b 19 Feb 2006), 1 da (Grace Valerie b 6 March 2009); *Career* mktg asst Mitsubishi Electric 1983–84, media mangr Dorland Advg 1986–88, buyin dir (print and TV) Zenith Media 1988–94, ind media conslt 1995–98, dir (broadcast and print) PHD Media 1998–2003, md Opera Media (Omincom Media Gp UK) 2004–; *Style*— John Overend, Esq; ✉ Chestnut House, 71 St Johns Road, Penn, Buckinghamshire HP10 8HU; Opera Media, Fitzroy House, 11 Chenies Street, London WC1E 7EY (☎ 07795 642486, e-mail john.overend@omnicommediagroup.com)

OVEREND, Sandra Glynis; MLA; da of Billy Armstrong, *qv*, and Glynis, née Vance; *b* 11 May 1973, Magherafelt; *Educ* Cookstown HS, Univ of Ulster (BA, DipHE); *m* 10 April

O

1997, Nigel Overend; 1 da (Courtney b 22 Jan 2001), 2 s (Joshua b 20 Oct 2002, Nathan b 30 July 2005); *Career* asst accountant 1996–98, office mangr for Billy Armstrong, MLA 1998–2011; MLA (UU) Mid-Ulster 2011–; chairperson Bellaghy Primary Sch Parents' Assoc, memb Select Vestry Ballyscullion Parish Church; *Recreations* cycling, reading; *Style*— Mrs Sandra Overend, MLA; ✉ Northern Ireland Assembly, Parliament Buildings, Belfast BT4 3XX (☎ 028 9052 0305, e-mail sandra.overend@mla.niassembly.gov.uk); Mid-Ulster Constituency, 1 High Street, Moneymore BT45 7PB (☎ 028 8674 8090, Twitter @over2sandra)

OVERY, Prof Richard James; s of James Herbert Overy, and Margaret Grace, *née* Sutherland; *b* 23 December 1947; *Educ* Sexey's Blackford GS, Gonville & Caius Cambridge (MA, PhD); *m* 1, 1969 (m dis 1976), Tessa, *née* Coles; 2 da (Emma Gabrielle b 14 Oct 1969, Rebecca Lucy b 28 Sept 1972), 1 s (Jonathan Frederick b 10 July 1974); m 2, 1979 (m dis 1992), Jane, *née*Ellwood; m 3, 1992 (m dis 2004), Kim, *née* Turner; 2 da (Alexandra Elizabeth b 7 July 1993, Clementine Jann b 31 March 1998); *Career* Univ of Cambridge: research fell Churchill Coll 1972–73, coll lectr Queens' Coll 1973–79, univ asst lectr 1976–79; KCL: lectr 1980–88, reader 1988–92, prof of modern history 1992–2004; prof of history Univ of Exeter 2004–; T S Ashton prize 1983, Cass prize 1987, Samuel Eliot Morison prize 2001, Wolfson prize 2005, Hessell-Tiltman Prize 2005, James Doolittle Award 2010, Cundill Award for Historical Literature 2014; tstee RAF Museum 1999–2003, chair RAF Museum Research Bd 2013–; hon fell Centre for Second World War Experience; FRHS 1997, FBA 2000, FKC 2003, FRSA 2006, memb European Acad for Sciences and Arts 2013; *Publications* The Air War 1939–1945 (1980), Goering (1984), The Road to War (1989), War and Economy in the Third Reich (1994), Why the Allies Won (1995), Russia's War (1998), The Times History of the 20th Century (1998), The Battle (2000), Interrogations (2001), The Dictators: Hitler's Germany, Stalin's Russia (2004), The Morbid Age: Britain Between the Wars (2009), 1939: Countdown to War (2009), The Third Reich: A Chronicle (2010), The Bombing War: Europe 1939–1945 (2013), Times History of the World (gen ed, 5, 6, 7, 8 and 9 edns), The History of the World in 100 Battles (2014); *Recreations* opera, twentieth century art; *Clubs* The Academy; *Style*— Prof Richard Overy; ✉ Department of History, University of Exeter, Amory Building, Rennes Drive, Exeter EX9 4RJ (☎ 020 8457 5795, e-mail r.overy@ex.ac.uk)

OWEN, Albert; MP; s of late William Owen, of Holyhead, and late Doreen, *née* Woods; *b* 10 August 1959; *Educ* Holyhead Comp Sch, Coleg Harlech (Dip Industrial Rels & Welsh Studies), Univ of York (BA); *m* Angela Margaret, da of John James Magee; 2 da (Rachel Lynne b 10 Jan 1985, Fiona Angela b 18 July 1986); *Career* merchant seafarer 1975–92, in fulltime educn 1992–97, mangr Centre for the Unwaged 1997–2001; MP (Lab) Ynys Môn 2001–, memb Welsh Affrs Select Ctee 2001–05, memb Accomodation and Works Ctee 2001–05, chair All Party Parly Gp for the UK Aluminium Industry; memb Holyhead Town Cncl 1997–99; chair Anglesey Regeneration Partnership 1999–, dir Ynys Môn Homeless Forum, chair Ctee Community Hall, memb Ctee Workers' Educnl Assoc (N Wales) until 2001; govr Coleg Harlech until 2001; *Recreations* cycling, hill walking, cooking, gardening; *Clubs* Holyhead Sailing (hon memb); *Style*— Albert Owen, Esq, MP; ✉ House of Commons, London SW1A 0AA; 18 Thomas Street, (Ty Cledwyn) Holyhead, Isle of Anglesey LL65 1RR (☎ 01407 765750, fax 01407 764336, e-mail owena@parliament.uk)

OWEN, (Alfred) David; OBE (1997); s of Sir Alfred George Beech Owen, CBE (d 1975), and Eileen Kathleen Genevieve, *née* McMullan (d 1995); *b* 26 September 1936; *Educ* Brocksford Hall, Oundle, Emmanuel Coll Cambridge (MA); *m* 1966, Ethne Margaret, da of Frank H Sowman, of Solihull; 2 s, 1 da; *Career* Nat Serv Lt RASC; conslt Rubery Owen Group (chm 1969–2010); dir: National Exhibition Centre Ltd 1982–2006, Severn Valley Railway (Holdings) plc 1984–; warden Birmingham Assay Office 1999–2005; memb BOTB 1979–83; pres: Birmingham C of C 1980–81, Comité de Liaison de la Construction d'Equipments et de Pièces d'Automobiles 1988–90, Commercial Trailer Assoc 1992–2004, Comité de Liaison de la Construction de Carrosseries et de Remorques 1998–99; vice-pres SMMT 1987–90 (hon treas 2001–); tstee Community Development Fndn 1978–97, memb Bd Br Library 1982–90, memb Advsy Cncl NCVO, dir Black Country Living Museum Tst 1975–2015, chm of tstees Charles Hayward Fndn 2004–09, memb Aston Univ Devpt Bd; Liveryman Worshipful Co of Coachmakers and Coach Harness Makers; Hon DSc Aston Univ 1988; Hon DUniv Central England 2000; *Recreations* industrial archaeology, ornithology, walking, photography, music; *Clubs* National; *Style*— A David Owen, Esq, OBE; ✉ Mill Dam House, Mill Lane, Aldridge, Walsall WS9 0NB; Rubery Owen Holdings Ltd, PO Box 10, Darlaston, Wednesbury, West Midlands WS10 8JD (☎ 0121 526 8189, e-mail david.owen@ruberyowen.com)

OWEN, Baron (Life Peer UK 1992), of the City of Plymouth; David Anthony Llewellyn Owen; CH (1994), PC (1976); s of Dr John William Morris Owen (d 1994), and Molly Owen (d 2001); *b* 2 July 1938; *Educ* Bradfield Coll, Sidney Sussex Coll Cambridge, St Thomas' Hosp London (BA, MB BChir, MA); *m* 1968, Deborah (Mrs Deborah Owen, literary agent), da of late Kyrill Schabert, of Long Island, NY; 2 s (Tristan Llewellyn b 1970, Gareth Schabert b 1972), 1 da (Lucy Mary b 1979); *Career* St Thomas' Hosp: house appts 1962–64, neurological and psychiatric registrar 1964–66, res fell med unit 1966–68; contested (Lab) Torrington 1964, MP (Lab) Plymouth Sutton 1966–74, MP (Lab until 1981, SDP 1981–92) Plymouth Devonport 1974–92; PPS to MOD (Admin) 1967, Parly under sec of state for def (RN) 1968–70, resigned over EEC 1972, Parly under sec of state DHSS 1974, min of state DHSS 1974–76 and FCO 1976–77, sec of state for foreign and Cwlth affairs 1977–79, oppn spokesman on energy 1979–81; fndr memb SDP 1981, chm SDP Parly Ctee 1981–82, dep leader SDP 1982–83, elected SDP Leader following resignation of Rt Hon Roy Jenkins after election 1983, resigned over merger with Liberals 1987, re-elected SDP leader 1988–90; memb: Palme Cmmn on Disarmament and Security Issues 1980–89, Ind Cmmn on Int Humanitarian Issues 1983–86, Carnegie Cmmn on Preventing Deadly Conflict 1994–99, Eminent Persons Gp on Curbing Illicit Trafficking of Small Arms and Light Weapons 2000–02; EU co-chm Steering Ctee Int Conf on Former Yugoslavia 1992–95; chm: Humanitas 1990–2001, New Europe 1999–2005, Europe-Steel 2000–, Yukos Int 2002–05; exec chm Global Natural Energy plc 1995–2006, dir Intelligent Energy 2003–05; non-exec dir: Coats Viyella plc 1994–2001, Abbott Laboratories 1995–2011, Europe Steel 2000–15, Hyperdynamics 2009–14; dir Centre of Int Health and Co-operation 1990–; co-fndr Social Market Fndn 1989–, fndr supporter Charter 2010; chllr Univ of Liverpool 1996–2009; sits as Ind Social Democrat Cross Bench Peer in House of Lords; pres River Thames Soc, patron Greenham Common Tst, chm Daedalus Tst 2011–; hon fell: Sidney Sussex Coll Cambridge 1977, King's Coll, St Thomas' Hosp; FRCP; *Books* A Unified Health Service (1968), The Politics of Defence (1972), In Sickness and in Health (1976), Human Rights (1978), Face The Future (1981), A Future That Will Work (1984), A United Kingdom (1986), Personally Speaking (to Kenneth Harris) (1987), Our NHS (1988), Time to Declare (autobiography, 1991), Seven Ages (an anthology of poetry, 1992), Balkan Odyssey (1995), Hubris Syndrome (2007, revised edn 2012), In Sickness and in Power: Illness in Heads of Government during the last 100 years (2008, revised edn 2016), Nuclear Papers (2009), Time to Declare: Second Innings (updated edited autobiography, 2009), Europe Restructured: The Eurozone Crisis and Its Aftermath (2012, revised edn Europe Restructured: Vote to Leave 2016), Bosnia-Herzegovina: The Vance/Owen Peace Plan (2013), The Hidden Perspective – The Military Conversations 1906–1914 (2014), The Health of the Nation: NHS in Peril (2014), Cabinet's Finest Hour: The Hidden Agenda of May 1940 (2016); *Recreations* sailing, reading; *Style*— The Rt Hon Lord Owen, CH, FRCP; ✉ 78 Narrow Street, Limehouse, London E14 8BP (☎ 020 7987 5441, e-mail davidowen@lorddavidowen.co.uk, website www.lorddavidowen.co.uk); House of Lords, London SW1A 0PW (fax 01442 876108); secretary Maggie Smart (☎ 01442 872617)

OWEN, Prof (David) Gareth; s of Oscar Vivian Owen (d 1988), and Mary Gwladys, *née* Davies (d 1961); *b* 6 November 1940; *Educ* Christ Coll Brecon, Downing Coll Cambridge (MA, PhD), Univ of London (BD); *m* 2 July 1966, Ann Valerie, da of Stanley Wilfred Owen Wright (d 1988); 2 da (Ceridwen b 1969, Rachel b 1971); *Career* graduate engr John Laing & Son 1966–67, sr engr Marconi Space and Defence Systems Portsmouth 1970–72; Heriot-Watt Univ: lectr Dept of Civil Engrg 1972–75, sr lectr Dept of Offshore Engrg 1977, head of dept 1981–91, prof of offshore engrg 1986–, seconded to Scottish Higher Educn Funding Cncl 1992–95, dir of quality 1995–96, dean of engrg 1996–99, asst princ 1997–99, vice-princ 1999–2001, head Sch of Textiles and Design 2002–; visiting assoc prof Univ of New Hampshire 1976; pres: Edinburgh and Leith Petroleum Club 1991–92, Scottish Oil Club 1999–2001; FICE, CEng, FRSA; *Recreations* music, travel, languages; *Style*— Prof D Gareth Owen; ✉ 7 Oak Lane, Edinburgh EH12 6XH (☎ 0131 339 1740, e-mail dgarethowen@blueyonder.co.uk)

OWEN, (John) Graham; s of (John) Hugh Owen, of Bridgend, and Mair Eluned, *née* Evans; *b* 30 August 1952; *Educ* Epsom Coll, Guy's Hosp (BDS, LDS, RCS); *m* Belle Steadman, da of Harry Mooney (d 1985), of Hounslow; 3 s (Robert b 28 Dec 1981, Jonathan b 27 June 1984, Martin b 17 Oct 1986), 1 da (Annabelle b 7 Feb 1983); *Career* Guy's Hosp: house offr 1977, SHO 1978, lectr in maxillofacial and oral surgery 1978–80 (pt/t 1980); hon sec Dental Soc of London 1990–97 (pres 1997–98); memb Wales in London Soc; FRSM 1996; *Recreations* golf, rugby, cricket; *Clubs* Athenaeum, MCC, Westerham Golf, Beckenham RFC, London Welsh RFC; *Style*— Graham Owen, Esq; ✉ High View, 339 Main Road, Westerham Hill, Kent TN16 2HP (☎ and fax 01959 573180)

OWEN, HE Jane; *b* Bilston, W Midlands; *Educ* Ellerslie Sch Malvern, Trinity Coll Cambridge (BA); *m* David Donnelly; 1 da (Phoebe), 1 s (James); *Career* diplomat; Latin American Dept FCO 1987–88, Japanese language trg FCO 1988–90, second sec (commercial) Tokyo 1990–93, head Exports to Japan Unit DTI 1993–96, EU Dept FCO 1996–98, dep head of mission Vietnam 1998–2001, dir of trade promotion Tokyo 2002–06, dir UK Trade and Investment India 2006–10, ambass to Norway 2010–; *Style*— HE Ms Jane Owen; ✉ British Embassy, Oslo, Norway

OWEN, John Aubrey; s of Douglas Aubrey Owen (d 1964), and Patricia Joan, *née* Griggs (d 1968); *b* 1 August 1945; *Educ* City of London Sch, St Catharine's Coll Cambridge (MA); *m* 8 May 1971, Julia Margaret, da of Thomas Gordon Jones (d 1993), of Shrewsbury, Salop; 1 s (Charles Aubrey b 1972), 1 da (Lucy Margaret b 1975); *Career* joined Miny of Tport 1969, asst private sec to Min for Tport Industries 1972, DOE 1972–75, Dept of Tport 1975–78, seconded to Cambs CC 1978–80; DOE: joined 1980, regnl dir Northern Regnl Office DOE and Dept of Tport 1987–91, dir of personnel mgmnt 1991–95, dir Skills, Enterprise and Regeneration Govt Office for London 1995–2001; sr ptnr Inside Advice 2001–; chm Mosaic Homes (formerly New Islington and Hackney Housing Assoc) 2002–06, dep chm Family Mosaic 2006–15; MInstD; *Recreations* gardening; *Clubs* Middx CCC; *Style*— John Owen, Esq; ✉ 33 Valley Road, Welwyn Garden City, Hertfordshire AL8 7DH (☎ 01707 321768, e-mail johna.owen@ntlworld.com)

OWEN, Prof John Wyn; CB (1994); s of Idwal Wyn Owen (d 1984), of Bangor, and Myfi, *née* Hughes; *b* 15 May 1942; *Educ* Friars Sch Bangor, St John's Coll Cambridge (BA, MA), King's Fund Hosp Admin Staff Coll (FHSM Dip HSM); *m* 1 April 1967, Elizabeth Ann, da of William MacFarlane (d 1980), of Bangor; 1 da (Sian b 1971), 1 s (Dafydd b 1974); *Career* hosp sec Glantawe HMC Swansea 1967–70, staff trg offr Welsh Hosp Bd Cardiff 1968–70, divnl admin Univ Hosp of Wales HMC Cardiff 1970–72, asst clerk St Thomas' Hosp London 1972–74, admin St Thomas' Health Dist 1974–79; exec dir United Medical Enterprises London 1979–85; dir: Allied Medical Group London 1979–85, Br Nursing Cooperations London 1979–85, Allied Med Gp Healthcare Canada 1982–85, Allied Shanning London 1983–85; chm Welsh Health Common Servs Authy 1985–94, dir Welsh NHS 1985–94, DG NSW Health Dept Sydney 1994–97, chm Australian Health Ministers' Advsy Cncl 1995–97, dep chm Strategic Planning and Evaluation Ctee Nat Health & Research Cncl 1995–97; chm CMG DOH London 1999; sec Nuffield Tst London 1997–2005, chm Univ of Wales Inst Cardiff 2005–11, persona chair Univ of Wales 2012; visiting fell LSE 1997–, sr assoc Judge Inst of Mgmnt Studies Univ of Cambridge 1997–, adjunct prof of public health Univ of Sydney Aust, hon prof Coll of Medicine Swansea Univ 2013–; memb: Personnel Standards Lead Body 1992–94, Cncl Univ of Wales Coll of Med 1997–, Canada-UK Cncl 2014–; dir Madariaga European Fndn Brussels 2005–15, non-exec dir UK Health Protection Agency 2006–13, chair Health Protection Committee Welsh Govt 2014–; sr global health advsr InterAction Cncl 2015–; chair Canada-UK Colloquium 2013–; tstee: Florence Nightingale Museum Tst 1983–90, Mgmnt Advsy Serv 1986–90; jt sec London branch Cambridge Soc 1999–2011 vice-pres Johnians St John's Coll Cambridge 2015–; organist United Free Church Cowbridge 1985; fell: Univ Coll of Wales Aberystwyth, Univ Coll of Wales Bangor, Australian Coll of Health Service Execs; memb Inst of Med (USA); hon memb Gorsedd of Bards; Hon DUniv Glamorgan 1999, Hon DSc City Univ 2004; FHSM, FRSM, Hon FFPM, Hon FRSA, FRCP, FLSW 2010 (treas 2012–), FRSPH 2013 (professorial fell 2012), Hon FRCP (Hon MRCP); *Books Publications* various health professional pubns; *Recreations* organ playing, opera, travel; *Clubs* Athenaeum, Cardiff and County; *Style*— Prof John Wyn Owen, CB, FRSPH, FLSW; ✉ Newton Farm, Cowbridge, South Glamorgan CF7 7RZ (☎ 01446 775113, e-mail johnwynowen@uwic.ac.uk and johnwyn@btinternet.com)

OWEN, Mark Anthony Patrick; s of Keith Owen, and Mary Owen; *b* 27 January 1972, Oldham; *Educ* St Augustine's Catholic Sch Oldham; *m* 2009, Emma Ferguson; 1 s (Elwood Jack b 19 Aug 2006), 2 da (Willow Rose b 25 Nov 2008, Fox India b 24 July 2012); *Career* singer and songwriter; memb Take That 1990–96 and 2006–, solo career 1996–2006; *Albums* with Take That: Take That and Party 1992, Everything Changes 1993, Nobody Else 1995, Greatest Hits 1996, Never Forget: The Ultimate Collection 2005, Beautiful World 2006, The Circus 2008, Progress 2010; solo: Green Man 1996, In Your Own Time 2003, How the Mighty Fall 2005; *Singles* with Take That: Do What You Like 1991, Promises 1991, Once You've Tasted Love 1992, It Only Takes a Minute 1992, I Found Heaven 1992, A Million Love Songs 1992, Could It Be Magic 1992, Why Can't I Wake Up With You 1993, Pray 1993 (UK no 1), Relight My Fire 1993 (with Lulu, UK no 1), Babe 1993 (UK no 1), Everything Changes 1994 (UK no 1), Love Ain't Here Anymore 1994, Sure 1994 (UK no 1), Back For Good 1995 (UK no 1), Never Forget 1995 (UK no 1), How Deep Is Your Love 1996 (UK no 1), Patience 2006 (UK no 1), Shine 2007 (UK no 1), I'd Wait For Life 2007, Rule The World 2007, Greatest Day 2008 (UK no 1), Up All Night 2009, Said It All 2009, The Flood 2010, Kidz 2011; solo: Child 1996, Clementine 1997, I Am What I Am 1997, Four Minute Warning 2003, Alone Without You 2003, Makin' Out 2004; *Awards* BRIT Awards: Best Br Single 1993 (for Could It Be Magic), 1994 (for Pray), 1996 (for Back For Good), 2007 (for Patience) and 2008 (for Shine), Best Br Video 1994 (for Pray), Best Br Live Act 2008, Best Br Band 2011; MTV Europe Music Awards: Best Group 1994, Best Live Act 1995; Most Performed Work Ivor Novello Awards 2008 (for Shine), PRS For Music Outstanding Contribution to British Music Ivor Novello Award 2012; *Style*— Mr Mark Owen

OWEN, Michael James; s of Colin Owen, of Church Village, Mid Glamorgan, and Susan Rosemary, *née* Hopkins; *b* 7 November 1980, Church Village, Mid Glamorgan; *Educ* Bryn Celynnog Comp Sch Pontypridd, Univ of Herts (BSc); *m* 4 July 2004, Lucy Jayne; 2 da

(Ellie Beth b 2 Aug 2002, Olivia Louise b 13 June 2005), 1 s (Sonny James b 24 Sept 2008); *Career* rugby union coach and former player; clubs: Pontypridd 1998–2003 (joined as youth player, winners Principality Cup and finalists Parker Pen Shield 2002), Newport Gwent Dragons 2004–08, Saracens 2008–10; Wales: 41 caps (6 as capt), debut v South Africa 2002, winners Grand Slam 2005; memb British and Irish Lions touring squad New Zealand 2005 (capt v Argentina), memb Barbarians squad 2008; coach Wales Under 18s 2011, head coach Hertford RFC 2011 (gained promotion and won Herts Presidents Cup 2011), head coach Herts County Seniors 2014– (coach 2011–, County Championship Finalists); qualified teacher (PE), dir of rugby Haileybury Coll 2013; commentator Rugby World Cup (ITV and Talksport) 2011, regular contrib to Talksport, Five Live and Radio Wales; Michael Owen Rugby Acad La Manga Club Spain; *Books* Michael Owen, My Story; *Style*— Mr Michael Owen; ✉ 3 Hailey Close, Hertford, Hertfordshire SG13 7NP

OWEN, Michael James; s of Terry Owen, and Janette Owen; *b* 14 December 1979; *m* 24 June 2005, Louise Bonsall; 1 da (Gemma Rose); *Career* professional footballer; clubs: Liverpool FC until 2004 (joined club aged 11, memb winning Youth Cup team 1995/96, scored on Premiership debut v Wimbledon 1997, Premiership Golden Boot 1997/98 (23 goals), Worthington Cup 2001, FA Cup 2001, UEFA Cup 2001, FA Charity Shield 2001, European Super Cup 2001), FC Real Madrid 2004–05, Newcastle United FC 2005–09, Manchester United FC 2009–12 (Premier League champions 2011), Stoke City 2012–13, ret; England: 89 full caps (40 goals), debut v Chile Feb 1998, memb squad World Cup 1998, 2002 and 2006, memb squad European Championships 2000 and 2004; Young Player of the Year PFA Awards 1998, BBC Sports Personality of the Year 1998, European Footballer of the Year 2001; *Recreations* golf (handicap of 8), snooker, table tennis, my Staffordshire Bull Terrier (Bomber); *Style*— Michael Owen, Esq

OWEN, Prof Sir Michael John (Mike); kt (2014); s of Dr John Robson Owen, of Emsworth, Hants, and Mary Gillian, *née* Dowsett; *b* 24 November 1955, Birmingham; *Educ* Sherborne, Univ of Birmingham (BSc, PhD, MB ChB, Marjorie Hutching's Prize in Psychiatry); *m* 28 Sept 1985, Dr Deborah Cohen; 1 da (Laura b 30 May 1987), 2 s (Joe b 13 July 1989, Rob b 13 Feb 1992); *Career* house physician Queen Alexandra Hosp Portsmouth 1983–84, house surgn Dept of Neurosurgery Queen Elizabeth Hosp Birmingham 1984, SHO Div of Psychiatry Northwick Park Hosp and Clinical Research Centre Harrow 1984–85, registrar then sr registrar Bethlem Royal and Maudsley Hosps London 1985–90, research worker Genetics Section Inst of Psychiatry London 1986–87, MRC trg fell St Mary's Hosp Med Sch London 1987–90, hon lectr Inst of Psychiatry London 1988–90; hon conslt psychiatrist: S Glamorgan HA 1987–90, Univ Hosp Wales 1990– (clinical dir of psychiatry 1994–99); Univ of Wales Coll of Med Cardiff: sr lectr Dept of Psychological Med and Inst of Med Genetics 1990–95, prof of neuropsychiatric genetics 1995–98, prof of psychological med 1998–, head Dept of Psychological Med 1998–, memb Mgmnt Bd and Mgmnt Bd Exec 1999–2004, pro-vice-chllr for research 2001–04, chair Div of Community Specialities 2002– (vice-chair 2000–02); examiner Univs of: London, Antwerp, Helsinki, Lille, Bristol, Birmingham, Southampton; memb Editorial Bd: Human Molecular Genetics, Molecular Psychiatry, Archives of Gen Psychiatry, Schizophrenia Research, International Jl of Neuropsychopharmacology, Annals of Med, Psychiatric Genetics; reviewer for jls incl: Nature, Nature Med, Nature Genetics, Human Molecular Genetics, Molecular Psychiatry, Br Jl of Psychiatry, Psychological Med; keynote lectures incl: distinguished guest lectr Trinity Coll Dublin 2001, distinguished visiting prof NYU Sch of Med 2002, Eli Lilly lectr RCPsych 2002; memb: Research Ctee Mental Health Fndn 1993–96, Neurosciences and Mental Health Grants Ctee MRC 1995–97, Links with Industry Grants Ctee MRC 1995–2001, Special Ctee on Univ Psychiatry 1996–2002, Med and Scientific Advsy Bd Alzheimer Disease Soc 1996–, Advsy Bd MRC 1997–2000, Working Pty on Ethics in Research RCPsych 1999, Neurosciences and Mental Health Bd MRC 2000–04, Cncl Acad of Med Sciences 2001–04, Ctee of Scientists Human Frontier Science Prog; pres Int Soc of Psychiatric Genetics 2000–05 (memb Bd of Dirs 1993–); Stromgren Medal 2010, Lieber Prize 2012, William K Warren Distinguished Investigator Award 2013; FRCPsych 1997 (MRCPsych 1987), FMedSci 1999; *Publications* Seminars in Psychiatric Genetics (jtly, 1994), Psychiaric Genetics and Genomics (jt ed, 2002); author of numerous contribs to academic jls; *Recreations* fishing; *Style*— Prof Sir Mike Owen; ✉ MRC Centre for Neuropsychiatric Genetics and Genomics, Neuroscience and Mental Health Research Institute, Cardiff University, Hadyn Ellis Building, Maindy Road, Cardiff CF24 4HQ (✆ 029 2068 6062, e-mail owenmj@cf.ac.uk)

OWEN, Nicholas David Arundel; s of Tom Owen (d 1981), and Diana Owen; *b* 10 February 1947; *m* Brenda; 1 da (Rebecca b 22 Dec 1969), 1 s (Anthony b 2 Oct 1976); 1 step da (Justine b 26 April 1972), 1 step s Daniel b 10 Oct 1974); *Career* journalist: Surrey Mirror 1964–68, London Evening Standard 1968–70, Daily Telegraph 1970–72, Financial Times 1972–79, Now! Magazine 1979–81; reporter and presenter BBC TV News 1981–84, presenter ITN 1984–2007, presenter BBC News 2007–, presenter Classic FM 2009–; *Books* History of the British Trolleybus (1972), Days Like This (2012); *Recreations* railways, reading, bridge, golf; *Style*— Nicholas Owen, Esq; ✉ BBC News (✆ 020 8743 8000, e-mail nicholas.owen@bbc.co.uk)

OWEN, Dr Richard Charles; s of Alfred Roy Warren Owen (d 1978), of Rottingdean, E Sussex, and Florence Mary, *née* Walker; *b* 14 July 1947; *Educ* Varndean GS, Univ of Nottingham (BA), LSE (MSc, PhD), Stanford Univ (Harkness scholarship); *m* 1 May 1982, Julia Anne, da of Clive Raymond Crosse; 2 da (Eleanor Owen b 2 May 1983, Isabel Owen b 2 May 1983), 1 s (Laurence b 22 Aug 1988); *Career* script writer and prodr BBC External Servs 1973–79, asst prodr BBC TV Current Affrs 1979–80; The Times: leader writer 1980–82, Moscow corr 1982–85, Brussels corr 1985–88, Jerusalem corr 1988–91, dep foreign ed 1991–92, foreign ed 1992–96, Rome corr 1996–2010; freelance writer 2010–; *Books* Letters from Moscow (1985), Crisis in the Kremlin (1986), The Times Guide to 1992, Britain in a Europe without Frontiers (1990), The Times Guide to World Organisations (1996), Lady Chatterley's Villa: DH Lawrence on the Italian Riviera (2014); *Style*— Mr Richard Owen; ✉ e-mail owen.roma@gmail.com

OWEN, His Hon Judge Robert Frank; QC (1996); s of Tudor Owen (d 1994), of Clwyd, and (Alice) Pat, *née* Ferris; *b* 31 May 1953; *Educ* St Asaph GS, Prestatyn HS, PCL (Univ of London external LLB); *m* 24 May 1980, Anna Elizabeth, da of Richard Shaw; 3 s (Jonathan Robert b 31 Jan 1982, William Tudor b 25 May 1985, Thomas Rufus b 7 March 1989); *Career* called to the Bar Gray's Inn 1977; asst recorder 1998, recorder 2000, circuit judge (Midland Circuit) 2009–; *Recreations* walking, gardening, sport; *Style*— His Hon Judge Robert Owen, QC; ✉ Birmingham Civil Justice Centre, Priory Courts, 33 Bull Street, Birmingham B4 6DS

OWEN, Robert John Vernon (Robbie); s of David Tudor Owen (d 1987), and Marjorie Eugenie, *née* Burgess; *b* 14 September 1965, Wolverhampton; *Educ* Malvern Coll, Queen Mary Coll Univ of London (BA), Guildford Coll of Law; *m* 26 May 1995, Laura Joanna, *née* Baxter; 2 s (Patrick David Vernon b 1 Dec 1996, (Oliver) Harry Royce b 15 July 1998), 1 da (Freya Laura b 15 May 2000); *Career* Bircham Dyson Bell LLP (formerly Bircham & Co): trainee slr 1987–89, asst slr 1989–91, ptnr 1991–2013; ptnr Pinsent Masons LLP 2013–; Roll A Parly agent 1991; memb: Law Soc 1989, Soc of Parly Agents 1991; FICE; *Recreations* skiing, sailing, rugby, running, cycling, gym, gardening; *Clubs* RAC; *Style*— Robbie Owen, Esq; ✉ 138 Rosendale Road, West Dulwich, London SE21 8LG (✆ 020 8761 9706); Pinsent Masons LLP, 30 Crown Place, Earl Street, London EC2A 4ES (✆ 020 7418 7000, fax 020 7418 7050, e-mail robbie.owen@pinsentmasons.com)

OWEN, Sir Robert Michael; kt (2001); s of Gwynne Llewellyn Owen (d 1986), of Fowey, Cornwall and Phoebe Constance Owen; *b* 19 September 1944; *Educ* Durham Sch, Univ of Exeter (LLBHyoro Performing Arts Centre Japan; *m* 9 Aug 1969, Sara Josephine, da of Sir Algernon Rumbold, KCMG, CIE; 2 s (Thomas b 10 Nov 1973, Huw b 4 Jan 1976); *Career* called to the Bar Inner Temple 1968 (bencher 1995); recorder 1987, QC 1988, dep judge of the High Court 1994, judge of the High Court of Justice (Queen's Bench Div) 2001–14 (ret), presiding judge Western Circuit 2005–08; chm Litvinenko Inquiry 2014–15; chm London Common Law and Commercial Bar Assoc 1993–95 (vice-chm 1991–93), chm Gen Cncl of the Bar 1997 (vice-chm 1996), govr Coll of Law 1998–2004, memb Bd Judicial Coll 2011–12; tstee Ind Parly Standards Authy (IPSA) 2016; chm VCJD Tst 2002–; chm Consultative Ctee Fowey Harbour Cmmn 2006–10, chm Br Int 6m Assoc 2015; tstee Pestalozzi Int Village Tst 2013; Hon LLD Univ of Exeter; assoc fell Inst of Advanced Legal Studies 1998, FRSA 1998; *Clubs* RYS, Travellers, MCC; *Style*— Sir Robert Owen

OWEN, Prof (David) Roger Jones; s of Evan William Owen (d 1952), of Llanelli, and Margaret, *née* Jones (d 1990); *b* 27 May 1942; *Educ* Llanelli Boys' GS, UC Swansea (BSc, MSc), Northwestern Univ USA (PhD), Univ of Wales (DSc); *m* 12 Feb 1964, Janet Mary, da of William James Pugh (d 1983), of Llanelli; 2 da (Kathryn b 1967, Lisa b 1970); *Career* prof Univ of Wales 1982, dir Inst for Numerical Methods in Engrg Univ of Wales Swansea 1987–98; chm Rockfield Software Ltd, dir Pineridge Press Ltd; author of numerous pubns; memb: Cncl Nat Assoc On Finite Element Methods and Standards, various EPSRC ctees; Hon Dr: Univ of Porto Portugal 1998, ENS Cachan France 2007, Polytechnic Univ of Catalunya Spain 2012, Univ of Split Croatia 2015; founding FLSW, FICE 1983, FREng 1996, FRS 2009, foreign memb US Nat Acad of Engrg (NAE) 2011, foreign memb Chinese Acad of Sciences 2011; *Books* with E Hinton: Finite Element Programming (1977), An Introduction to Finite Element Computations (1979), Finite Elements in Plasticity (1980), A Simple Guide to Finite Elements (1980), Engineering Fracture Mechanics: Numerical Methods and Applications (1983); Computational Methods for Placticity: Theory and Application (with E A de Souza Neto and D Peric, 2008); *Recreations* flying, golf, tennis; *Clubs* Langland Bay Golf, Swansea; *Style*— Prof Roger Owen, FRS, FREng; ✉ Civil and Computational Engineering Centre, University of Wales Swansea, Singleton Park, Swansea SA2 9PP (✆ 01792 295252, fax 01792 295676, e-mail d.r.j.owen@swansea.ac.uk)

OWEN, Susan Jane (Sue); CB (2010); *Educ* Newnham Coll Cambridge (MA), UC Cardiff (MSc); *m* 1987, Prof M C Albrow; 1 s (Tom Albrow-Owen b 1991); *Career* HM Treasy 1989–98, Foreign Office 1999–2002, HM Treasy 2002–06, DG corporate performance Dept for Int Devpt 2006–09, DG Strategy Gp Dept for Work and Pensions 2009–13, perm sec DCMS 2013–; *Style*— Ms Sue Owen, CB; ✉ Department for Culture, Media & Sport, 100 Parliament Street, London SW1A 2BQ

OWEN, Tudor Wyn; s of Abel Rhys Owen (d 1974), of Aberdare, Glamorgan, and Mair, *née* Jenkins (d 2004); *b* 16 May 1951; *Educ* Aberdare GS, KCL (LLB); *Career* called to the Bar Gray's Inn 1974; in practice SE Circuit, recorder of the Crown Court 1991; inspr DTI 1989; memb: Ctee Criminal Bar Assoc 1987–91 (treas 1988–91), Gen Cncl of the Bar 1988–94, Bar Professional Conduct Ctee 1989–91, Bar Public Affairs Ctee 1990–91, Bar Ctee 1990–92 (vice-chm 1991–92), Gen Mgmnt Ctee 1992–93, Professional Standards Ctee 1992–93, SE Circuit Ctee 1992–96; FRAeS 2002; *Recreations* motor racing, flying helicopters and WWII fighter aircraft, shooting, skiing, riding the Cresta Run, music; *Clubs* Garrick, St Moritz Tobogganing; *Style*— Tudor Owen, Esq; ✉ Chambers, 9–12 Bell Yard, London WC2A 2LF (✆ 020 7400 1800, fax 020 7404 1405, DX 390 Chancery Lane)

OWEN-JONES, His Hon Judge David Roderic; s of (John) Eryl Owen-Jones, CBE, JP, DL (d 2000), and Mabel Clara, *née* McIlvride (d 2000); *b* 16 March 1949; *Educ* Llandovery Coll, UCL (LLB, LLM); *Career* called to the Bar Inner Temple 1972, ad eundem Lincoln's Inn 1993; in practice SE Circuit; Wales & Chester circuit, recorder of the Crown and Co Court; memb Lord Chancellor's Advsy Ctee on the Appointments of JPs for Inner London 1986–91, actg Met stipendiary magistrate 1991–93, circuit judge (South Eastern Circuit) 2011–; Parly candidate: (Lib) Carmarthen Div Feb and Oct 1974, (Lib Alliance) Rugby and Kenilworth 1983 and 1987; govr Int Students Tst 1981–84 and 1992– (tstee 1981–), vice-chm Assoc of Lib Dem Lawyers; hon legal advsr to Hon Soc of Cymrodorion 2006; memb Worshipful Livery Co of Wales; FRSA 1984; *Books* The Prosecutorial Process in England and Wales (jtly); *Recreations* theatre, historical biography; *Clubs* Nat Lib (tstee, chm 1988–91), Reform; *Style*— His Hon Judge Owen-Jones; ✉ Basildon Crown Court, The Gore, Basildon, Essex SS14 2BU (✆ 01268 45800)

OWENS, Prof David Howard; s of Maurice Owens, of Derby, and Joan, *née* Browes; *b* 23 April 1948; *Educ* Dronfield Henry Fanshawe, Imperial Coll London (BSc, PhD); *m* 18 July 1969, Rosemary, da of John Cecil Frost, of Sheffield; 1 s (Benjamin David b 1976), 1 da (Penelope Rosemary Jane b 1979); *Career* scientific offr UKAEA Atomic Energy Estab Winfrith 1969–73, reader in control engrg Univ of Sheffield 1982 (lectr 1973, sr lectr 1981), prof of dynamics and control Univ of Strathclyde 1988–90 (prof of engrg mathematics 1985); Univ of Exeter: prof of systems and control engrg 1990–99, dir Sch of Engrg 1995–98, head Sch of Engrg and Computer Sci 1998–99; chm Exeter Enterprises Ltd 1998–99; Univ of Sheffield: prof of control and systems engrg 1999–2010 (emeritus prof 2010–), head dept Automatic Control and Systems Engrg 1999–2008, dean Faculty of Engrg 2002–06; dir Iter8 Control Systems Ltd 2007–10, dir Iterate Control Ltd 2010–14; sr prof of engrg Zhengzhou Univ China 2016–2021; ctee work and conference orgn: IEE, IMechE, IMA, Health and Safety Cmmn, UK Automatic Control Cncl (chm 1999–2002); govr Sheffield Teaching Hospitals NHS Fndn Tst 2012–15, govr Henry Fanshawe Fndn 2014–18; Freeman Co of Cutlers in Hallamshire 2007–; FIMA 1976–2009, FIEE 1996 (MIEE 1979), MIEEE 1990–2008, FIMechE 2001, FREng 2008; *Books* Feedback and Multivariable Systems (1978), Multivariable and Optimal Systems (1981), Analysis and Control of Multipass Processes (jtly, 1982), Stability Analysis of Linear Repetitive Processes (jtly, 1992), Control Systems Theory and Applications for Linear Repetitive Processes (jtly, 2007), Iterative Learning Control: an optimization paradigm (2015); *Recreations* sketching, reading, guitar; *Clubs* Sheffield Vulcan Rotary, Hallamshire 41; *Style*— Prof David Owens; ✉ Department of Automatic Control and Systems Engineering, University of Sheffield, Mappin Street, Sheffield S1 3JD

OWENS, Her Hon Judge Eleanor Jayne; da of Peter Michael Slaughter, and Veronica Audrey, *née* Head; *Educ* Univ of Cambridge (MA), LLB; *Career* admitted slr 1997; recorder 2009, circuit judge (South Eastern Circuit) 2014–; lead judge SE Region Court of Protection 2015–; *Recreations* cinema, gardening, opera, reading, walking, horse riding; *Style*— Her Hon Judge Owens; ✉ c/o Reading Family Court Hearing Centre, 160–163 Friar Street, Reading RG1 1HE

OWENS, Lynne; CBE (2015), QPM (2008); *Educ* MA; *Career* Met Police Service: Dep Asst Cmmr 2009–10, Asst Cmmr 2010–12; Chief Constable Surrey Police 2012–16; dir Gen Nat Crime Agency 2016–; *Style*— Ms Lynne Owens, CBE, QPM; ✉ National Crime Agency, Spring Gardens, Citadel Place, Tinworth Street, London SE11 5EF (Twitter @NCA_LynneOwens)

OWENS, Matthew; *b* 17 January 1971; *Educ* Chetham's Sch of Music Manchester, The Queen's Coll Oxford (John Betts organ scholar, MA, dir chapel choir), RNCM (MusM, PPRNCM), Sweelinck Conservatorium Amsterdam, Inst of Educn Univ of London; *m* 2004, Dr Alison Jane Darragh; 1 s (James Matthias Benjamin b 2012); *Career* organist, conductor and composer; tutor in organ studies and choral directing studies RNCM and tutor in organ and academic studies Chetham's Sch of Music Manchester 1994–2001, sub-organist Manchester Cathedral 1996–99, organist and master of the music St Mary's Episcopal Cathedral Edinburgh and tutor in organ studies St Mary's Music Sch Edinburgh 1999–2004, organist and master of the choristers Wells Cathedral 2005–, tutor in organ studies Wells Cathedral Sch 2006–13; musical dir, organist and singer Daily Service (BBC Radio 4) 1993–99, asst and assoc conductor Nat Youth Choir of GB 1993–2000, artistic dir and conductor Exon Singers 1997–2011, fndr and artistic dir Cathedral Cmmns 2005–; composer 2000–; dir and tutor of organ and choral workshops Edinburgh Organ Acad, Edinburgh Soc of Organists, Incorporated Assoc of Organists and Soc for the Promotion of New Music RSCM 1997–; pres Edinburgh Soc of Organists 2004, pres Cathedral Organists' Assoc 2010–13; numerous recordings as conductor and solo organist; broadcasts and recitals in UK and overseas; author of articles in Choir & Organ and Organists' Review 1996–2005, assoc ed Friends of Cathedral Music Magazine 2005–, compositions published by OUP and Novello; 13 prizes Royal Coll of Organists, Silver medal Worshipful Co of Musicians 1994; hon fell Guild of Church Musicians 2012; FRCO 1994 (ARCO 1994); *Recreations* walking, reading; *Style*— Matthew Owens, Esq; ✉ Wells Cathedral Music Office, Chain Gate, Cathedral Green, Wells, Somerset BA5 2UE (☎ 01749 674483)

OWUSU, Elsie Margaret Akua; OBE (2003); da of Paul Kofi Owusu (d 1971), and Joyce Ophelia, *née* Biney; *b* 9 December 1953; *Educ* AA Sch of Architecture, Chelsea Coll of Art; *Children* 1 da (Kesewa Hennessy b 13 Dec 1971); *Career* architect (special conservation); in private practice Elsie Owusu Architects 1986–, ptnr Feilden and Mawson LLP 2006–15; arts projects incl: International Centre for Performing Arts, Contemporary African Art Gallery Greenwich, Global Trade Centre Offices and gallery space; major projects incl: International Centre for Performing Arts, Contemporary African Art Gallery, Global Trade Centre, E London Black Women's Centre, Palatine Road Centre Hackney, Lagos Bus Rapid Transit System, Accra Bus Rapid Transit System, UK Supreme Ct (lead architect for interiors), Green Park Station (ptnr-in-charge), St Bernard's Hosp Ealing (ptnr-in-charge); numerous housing schemes incl: Ebony House Neasden, Lido Square Haringey, Rendlesham Road Hackney, John Kallis Court Oxford, Mulgrave Street Development Liverpool, Hughes House Oxford; community centres incl East London Black Women's Centre; current projects incl: House for ShonibareMBE Nigeria, Kumasi City Hall Ghana, eco-home in Sussex; lectr in architecture Poly of N London and of E London 1986–90; fndr memb and chair Soc of Black Architects 1990–92, chair Housing Corpn Race in Housing Gp 1991–92, fndn memb Black Int Construction Orgn 1996–, acting chair then chair Aduna 2006–09, ambass Creative Partnerships 2006–; memb: Architects' Team: Solon SE Housing Assoc 1981–85, Women's Design Serv 1985–86, Exec Ctee Fedn of Black Housing Orgns 1994–96 (sec 1987), Educnl Visiting Bd RIBA 1995–97, Creative Britain Panel Design Cncl 1997, Cncl Nat Tst 2001–04, Bd Arts Cncl England 2002–09, Enabling Panel Cmmn for Architecture and the Built Environment 2003–09, Bd Royal African Soc 2007– (currently tstee); vice-chair London Sch of Architecture 2014–; assessor: Civic Tst Awards 1997, Design Cncl Millennium Products Awards 1998–; vice-pres Women's Transportation Seminar 2005–08; cmmr Haringey Employment Cmmn 1996; sponsor Project Aurifex; govr: Middx Univ 1998, Coll of NE London 1998–2000; various TV appearances incl: presenter Who Pays the Piper (Channel 5 series on architecture) 1997, presenter and panel memb Zeitgeist (Channel 4) 1998; memb Cncl and tstee: RIBA 2015–, Architectural Assoc 2015–; memb Br Inst of Interor Design (BIID); FRSA 2015; *Publications* Accommodating Diversity (jtly, 1993), Building E=Quality (ed and jt author, 1996); *Recreations* walking, reading, drawing, dreaming; *Clubs* Athenaeum; *Style*— Ms Elsie Owusu, OBE

OXBURGH, Baron (Life Peer UK 1999), of Liverpool in the County of Merseyside; Sir (Ernest) Ronald Oxburgh; KBE (1992); *b* 2 November 1934; *Educ* Liverpool Inst, UC Oxford (BA), Princeton Univ (Sir John Dill fell, Class of 1897 fell, PhD); *m* 1958; 3 c; *Career* Univ of Oxford: demonstrator and lectr in geology 1960–78, official fell and tutor St Edmund Hall 1964–78 (admissions tutor 1965–77), vice-chm then chm Faculty of Physical Scis 1975–78; Univ of Cambridge: professorial fell Trinity Hall 1978–82, prof of mineralogy and petrology 1978–91, head Dept of Mineralogy and Petrology 1978–80, head Dept of Earth Sciences 1980–88, pres Queens' Coll 1982–89, hon prof Dept of Earth Scis Univ of Cambridge 2001–; chief scientific advsr MOD 1988–93 (chm inquiry into safety of UK nuclear weapons 1991), rector ICSTM 1993–2001; visiting prof: Caltech 1967–68, Cornell Univ 1967–68, 1973–74 and 1986, Stanford Univ 1973–74; Sherman Fairchild distinguished visiting scholar Caltech 1985–86, Allan Cox distinguished visiting prof Stanford Univ 1987; chm: Royal Soc Working Pty on Support of Geophysics 1984–85, Univ Grants Ctee Review of Earth Sciences 1986–87, UK Inter-agency Ctee on the Environment and Global Change 1994–97, Non-Exec Bd Centre for Defence Analysis 1995–97, Int Panel to review future of med educn Singapore 2000–01, SETNET 2002–05; assessor Advsy Bd for the Research Cncls 1988–90; memb: Cncl Royal Soc 1987–89, Advsy Cncl for Sci and Technol 1988–92, SERC 1988–93, NERC 1988–93, Univ and Polys Grants Ctee for Hong Kong 1989–2002, Conseil Scientifique pour l'Enseignement Superieur Paris 1992–94, Cmmn of Inquiry on the future of Oxford Univ 1994–97, EPSRC Users' Panel 1994–97, Cncl for Industry and HE 1994–2000, Cncl Parly Office on Sci and Technol 1995–, Nat Academies Policy Advsy Gp Working Pty on the future of the res base 1995–96, Nat Ctee of Inquiry into HE (Dearing Ctee) 1996–97, Cncl Fndn for Sci and Technol 1996–, Int Academic Advsy Panel Singapore 1997–2002, Conseil d'Administration Ecole Polytechnique France 1997–2002, Cncl Asian Univ of Sci and Technol 1997–2009, Conseil Nat de la Sci Miny of Educn, Research and Technol France 1998–2001, House of Lords Select Ctee on Sci and Technol 1999–2005 (chm 2001–05), Advsy Cncl for Science and Technol Singapore 2001–12, Research Innovation and Enterprise Cncl Singapore 2012–; sometime memb: Cncl Geological Soc, Editorial Bd Geological Soc, Editorial Bd Jl of Geophysical Research, Editorial Bd Sci and Public Affrs, Governing Body Northern House Sch Oxford, A C Irvine Fund Tstees, NERC Geological Scis Trg Awards Ctee (also chm), NERC Univ Affrs Ctee, Mgmnt Ctee Oxford Colls' Admissions Office, various ctees of Royal Soc and Univ of London; chm: D1Oils plc 2006–08, 2OC 2007–, Falck Renewables 2007–10, BlueNg 2008–11, GEO (Greener Energy Options) 2011; vice-pres GLOBE UK 2009; non-exec dir: Hammersmith Hosps NHS Tst 1994–97, UK Nirex Ltd 1996–97, Shell Transport & Trading Co plc 1996– (chm 2004–05); advsr: Climate Change Capital 2005–, Low Carbon Accelerator 2006–08; environment advsr: Deutsche Bank, McKinsey; tstee Nat History Museum 1993– (chm of tstees 1999–2002); memb: Cncl RCA 1993–2001, Cncl Winston Churchill Tst 1995–2009, Ct Univ of Leicester 1996–2000; foreign corr: Geologische Bundesanstalt Austria 1969, Geological Soc of Vienna 1972; Lyell Fund Award Geological Soc of London 1969, Bigsby Medal Geological Soc 1979, Sir Peter Kent lecture Geological Soc 1995, Thomson Medal Inst of Measurement & Control 2012, Melchett Award Energy Inst 2014; dr (hc): Univ of Paris VI-VII 1986, Univ of Leicester 1990, Loughborough Univ 1991, Univ of Edinburgh 1994, Univ of Birmingham 1996, Univ of Liverpool 1996, Univ of Southampton 2003, Lingnan Univ Hong Kong 2006, Liverpool John Moores Univ 2006, Univ of Newcastle 2007, Univ of Leeds 2009, Univ of Wyoming 2011, Univ of St Andrews 2013; hon fell: Trinity Hall Cambridge 1982, University Coll Oxford 1983, St Edmund Hall Oxford 1986, Queens' Coll Cambridge 1992, City & Guilds of London Inst 1996, Energy Inst 2006; pres: Euro Union of Geosciences 1985–87 (former chm Editorial Bd), Br Assoc for the Advancement of Sci 1995–96, Geological Soc of London 2000–02, Inst of Measurement & Control 2012–14; corresponding memb: Venezuelan Acad of Scis 1989, Australian Acad of Scis 1999; memb Deutsche Akademie der Naturforscher Leopoldina 1994; foreign assoc: US Acad of Sci 2001, American Philosophical Soc 2005; fell Geological Soc of America 1971, fell American Geophysical Union 1981, fndn memb Academia Europaea 1988; Hon FIMechE 1993, Hon FREng 2000; FRS 1978; Amigo de Venezuela 1995, Officier dans l'Ordre des Palmes Académiques 1995, Singapore Public Serv Medal 2008, hon citizen of Singapore 2012; *Publications* author of numerous articles and papers published in learned jls; *Recreations* mountaineering, orienteering, theatre, reading, repairing old cars; *Clubs* Atheaeum; *Style*— The Rt Hon the Lord Oxburgh, KBE; ✉ House of Lords, London SW1A 0PW (e-mail oxburghe@parliament.uk)

OXFORD AND ASQUITH, 3 Earl of (UK 1925) Raymond Benedict Bartholomew Michael Asquith; OBE; s of 2 Earl of Oxford and Asquith, KCMG (d 2011); *b* 24 August 1952; *Educ* Ampleforth, Balliol Coll Oxford; *m* 1978, Clare, da of Francis Pollen (d 1987), and Thérèse, da of His Hon Sir Joseph Sheridan, and gda of late Arthur Pollen (gn of Sir Richard Pollen, 3 Bt) by his w Hon Daphne Baring, da of 3 Baron Revelstoke; 1 s (Mark Julian (Viscount Asquith) b 13 May 1979), 4 da (Lady Magdalen Katharine b 1981, Lady Frances Sophia b 1984, Lady Celia Rose b 1989, Lady Isabel Anne b 1991); *Heir* s, Viscount Asquith; *Career* HM Dip Serv 1980–97: FCO 1980–83, first sec (Chancery) Moscow 1983–85, FCO 1985, on loan to Cabinet Office 1985–92, cnsllr (Political) Kiev 1992–97; dir Meteor Asset Mgmnt 2010, dir Hansa Tst 2013; *Style*— The Earl of Oxford and Asquith, OBE

OYELOWO, David; OBE (2016); *b* 1 April 1976, Oxford; *Educ* LAMDA; *m* Jessica; 3 s, 1 da; *Career* actor; *Theatre* Volpone (RSC) 1999, Antony and Cleopatra (RSC) 1999, Henry VI (RSC) 2001 (Ian Charleson Award), Prometheus Bound 2005; *Television* incl: Spooks 2002–04, As Time Goes By 2005, Five Days 2007, The No 1 Ladies' Detective Agency 2008, A Raisin in the Sun 2008, Sweet Nothing in My Ear 2008, Small Island 2009, Blood and Oil 2010; *Film* incl: As You Like It 2006, The Last King of Scotland 2006, Who Do You Love 2008, Rage 2009, Rise of the Planet of the Apes 2011, The Help 2011, 96 Minutes 2011, Middle of Nowhere 2012, Red Tails 2012, The Paperboy 2012, Lincoln 2012, Jack Reacher 2012, Complicit 2013, The Butler 2013, Nina 2014, Interstellar 2014, Selma 2015; *Style*— Mr David Oyelowo, OBE; ✉ c/o Christian Hodell, Hamilton Hodell, 20 Golden Square, London W1F 9JL

ÖZVEREN, Ali Evrenay; s of Hamdi Özveren (d 1992), of Ankara, Turkey, and Zehra, *née* Zincirci (d 1992); *b* 6 October 1945; *Educ* Ankara Coll, Dept of Architecture Middle East Tech Univ Ankara (BArch); *m* 13 Nov 1976, Susan Catherine, da of Arthur Frank William Gimbert; 1 s (Jan Emil b 28 Dec 1979); *Career* GMW Architects London: joined as architectural asst 1970, completed univ educn in Turkey, assoc 1979, ptnr 1984, a sr ptnr 1991, conslt 2005; md GMW Architects Istanbul 2005–; design conslt TAV Airport Operators 2008; built projects in London incl: Royal Mail (S London Postal Sorting Office Battersea), Wates City of London Properties (City Tower Basinghall St), Vestey Estates (34 Leadenhall St), Sun Alliance Group Properties (1 King William St), Land Securities (Regis House King William/Monument St), Gt Portland Estates (95 New Cavendish St); award-winning overseas projects incl: Wholesale Food Market Dubai, Retail Food Market Dubai, New Int Terminal Istanbul Atatürk Airport, New Domestic and Int Terminals Ankara Esenboga Airport and Mugla Dalaman Airport Turkey, Riga Int Airport Latvia, Scopje Int Airport Macedonia, Terminal 5 at Riyadh Airport Saudi Arabia; registered memb Chamber of Architects of Turkey 1971; FCSD 1992, FRSA 1995; *Recreations* modern art, travel, opera; *Style*— Ali Özveren, Esq; ✉ GMW MIMARLIK, 32 Holloway Drive, Virginia Water, Surrey GU25 4SY (☎ 07769 173484, e-mail ozveren@btinternet.com)

P

PACHACHI, Reema; da of Dr Adnan Pachachi, and Selwa Ali, *née* Jawdat; *b* 10 April 1951; *Educ* Brearley Sch NY, UN Sch NY, Central Sch of Art & Design (BA), RCA (MA, Anstruther award); *m* 14 Dec 1977, John William Dennis; 2 s (Said b 26 Jan 1981, Kareem b 23 May 1986), 1 da (Aisha b 23 Nov 1983); *Career* jewellery designer; visiting lectr Central St Martin's and Dundee Coll of Art; opened own shop 1994, sells collections internationally through major department stores and fashion boutiques, creates individual pieces for private customers; designer and creative dir De Beers 2002–04 *Exhibitions* Passing Out (Goldsmiths' Hall London) 1979, Arnolfini Gallery Bristol 1979, Ehrman Gallery London 1980, Artwear NY 1980, New Faces (Br Crafts Centre London) 1981, Jugend Gestaltet Munich 1981, Loot (Goldsmiths' Hall London) 1981, British Women Artists (House of Commons) 1981, Dazzle (NT) 1981–82, New Ashgate Gallery Farnham Surrey 1982, Byzantium Gallery NY 1982 (Christmas Exhbn) and 1993 (Spring/Christmas Exhbn), Nat Assoc of Decorative & Fine Art Socs' Clothes and Jewellery Show 1985, Precious Elements (Usher Gallery Lincoln) 1986, Sotheby's Decorative Arts Award Exhbn London 1988, History of Contemporary Jewellery Exhbn (Sheehan Gallery Washington) 1991; exhibits twice a year during London Fashion week; work in permanent collection of Crafts Cncl of GB (listed in their Index of Excellence); jewellery designs for Arabella Pollen and Geoffrey Beene; took part in a major 18ct gold project with Engelhard-Clal and World Gold Cncl; *Recreations* reading, dancing, swimming; *Style*— Ms Reema Pachachi

PACKARD, Richard Bruce Selig; s of John Jacob Packard (d 1992), of Delray Beach, Florida, and (Priscilla) Lilian, *née* Joseph (d 2013); *b* 20 February 1947; *Educ* Harrow, Middlesex Hosp Med Sch (MD, DO); *m* 1, 21 March 1974 (m dis 1986), Veronica Susan, da of Michael Bird, CBE (d 1991), of Esher, Surrey; 2 s (Rupert Alexander b 1978, Hugo Philip b 1980), 1 da (Elvira Rose b 1984); m 2, 24 April 1986, Fiona Catherine, da of Walter F Kinnear (d 1997), of Kilspindie, Perthshire; 1 s (Ian Charles b 1990), 1 da (Lucy Catherine b 1992); *Career* specialist trg in ophthalmology; house surgn in ophthalmology Middx Hosp 1970; held various jr med appointments 1971–75, res surgical offr Moorfields Eye Hosp 1975–78, sr registrar in ophthalmology Charing Cross Hosp Fulham 1978–82, conslt ophthalmic surgn and clinical dir Prince Charles Eye Unit King Edward VII Hosp Windsor 1982–2016; currently chm Cyclotron Tst for Cancer Treatment, dep chm Fedn of Ind Practitioner Orgns 2009; past chm Oxford RHA Ophthalmology Sub-Ctee, UK rep Int Med Panel for the Advance of Cataract Treatment 1992–; memb American Acad of Ophthalmology, memb Prog Ctee American Soc of Cataract and Refractive Surgery 2011, memb Bd Euro Soc of Cataract and Refractive Surgery, chm Assoc of Ophthalmologists 2007–14; International Intraocular Club Medal 2014, Binkhorst Medal European Soc of Cataract and Refractive Surgns 2015, Lifetime Achievement Award UK and Ireland Soc of Cataract and Refractive Surgns 2015; FRCS 1976, FRCOphth 1991; *Books* Cataract and Lens Implant Surgery (jtly, 1985), Emergency Surgery (jtly, 1986), Manual of Cataract and Lens Implant Surgery (jtly, 1991), Phacoemulsification (jtly, 1994), Phaco 2000 (jtly, 1997), Complicated Phaco (jtly, 2000), Principles of Practice (jtly, 2002), Mastering the Art of Bimanual Microincisional Phaco Emulsification (jtly, 2005), The Art of Microincisional Cataract Surgery (jtly, 2010), The Eye in History (jtly, 2013), Multifocal Intraocular Lenses (jtly, 2014), A Textbook of Ocular Coherence Tomography (jtly, 2014); *Recreations* fly fishing, wine, music; *Clubs* Garrick, MCC, IIIC; *Style*— Richard Packard, Esq; ✉ Arnott Eye Associates, 22A Harley Street, London W1G 9BP (☎ 020 7580 1074 and 020 7580 8792, fax 020 7255 1524, e-mail post@arnotteye.com, website www.arnotteye.com)

PACKER, Jane; da of Maurice Packer, of Chadwell St Mary, and Brenda Packer; *b* 22 September 1959, Chadwell St Mary; *m* 20 July 1990, Gary Wallis; 2 c (Rebby b 28 Aug 1991, Lola b 9 Sept 1993); *Career* florist; opened Jane Packer Flowers: James Street London 1981, St John's Wood London 1994, Marylebone London 1995, NY 2001, Seoul S Korea 2001 and 2002, Tokyo 2001 and 2002; opened Jane Packer Sch of Flowers: London 1989, Tokyo 1990; launched: branded products 1990, ceramics 1995 (winner Top Drawer exhbn award London 1995), fragrance, ceramics and glassware 2000, International Greetings stationary 2004; conslt M&S horticulture 1987–2000, part of Designers At Debenhams 2001–; lectr tours: Europe 1988–89, USA 1989 and 1995, Japan 1991–98, UK 1996–98, France 1998; Spring lectr Cultural Centre Tokyo 1993; keynote speaker: American Soc of Perfumers NY 2002, Walters Museum Baltimore 2004, Hortifair Amsterdam 2004; Jane Packer Tulip developed by Vandershoot Holland 1997; Prince Phillip Medal 2005; *Commissions* incl: bridal flowers for HRH the Duke and Duchess of York 1986, BBC TV 1992; Marks and Spencer at RHS Hampton Court Flower Show: stand 1991–92 (award winner 1991–92), garden 1993–98, (RHS Gold Medal winner 1993–97, RHS Silver Medal 1998); *Television* reg appearances on BBC, ITV, Carlton, GMTV, Thames and American television 1986–; reg appearance Good Morning (BBC) 1995; subject of documentary (BBC) 1996, presenter The Flower Show (BBC) 1998, Big in Japan (six part series, BBC Style) 1999; *Publications* Celebrating With Flowers (1986), Flowers For All Seasons: Spring, Summer, Autumn, Winter (four part work, 1989), New Flower Arranging (1993), A Complete Guide (1994), Living With Flowers (1995), Fast Flowers 1998, Flowers, Design, Philosophy (1999), World Flowers (2003), Colour (2007), Flower Course (2008); *Style*— Ms Jane Packer; ✉ 32–34 New Cavendish Street, London W1G 8UE (☎ 020 7935 0787, fax 020 7935 2135, e-mail office@janepacker.com)

PACKER, Rt Rev John Richard; s of late Rev Canon John William Packer, and late Hilda Muriel, *née* Hatch; *b* 10 October 1946; *Educ* Manchester Grammar, Keble Coll Oxford (BA Modern History, BA Theol, MA), Univ of York (Dip); *m* 30 Dec 1971, Barbara Priscilla Deborah, da of late Donald Fingland Jack, of Scarborough, N Yorks; 1 da (Catherine Ruth b 1976), 2 s (Richard James b 1978, Timothy Stephen b 1980); *Career* curate St Peter's St Helier Morden 1970–73, dir of pastoral studies Ripon Hall 1973–75, Ripon Coll Cuddesdon 1975–77, chaplain St Nicolas' Abingdon 1973–77, vicar Wath upon Dearne with Adwick upon Dearne 1977–86, rural dean Wath 1983–86, rector Sheffield Manor 1986–91, rural dean Attercliffe 1990–91, archdeacon of W Cumberland 1991–96, priest i/c Bridekirk 1995–96, bishop of Warrington 1996–2000, bishop of Ripon and Leeds 2000–14, hon asst bishop of Newcastle 2014–; memb Gen Synod C of E 1985–91, 1992–96 and 2000–14; House of Lords 2006–14; *Recreations* history, walking; *Style*— The Rt Rev John Packer; ✉ Devonshire House, Alma Place, Whitley Bay, Tyne and Wear NE26 2EQ (☎ 0191 253 4321, e-mail bppacker@googlemail.com)

PACKER, Philip Michael (Phil); MBE (2010); *b* 16 September 1972; *Educ* Eltham Coll, RMA Sandhurst; *Career* provost offr Royal Military Police 1997–2010; sustained spinal cord injury 2008; fundraiser through numerous physical challenges incl: Channel Row 2009, London Marathon in 14 days 2009, climbing El Capitan 2009, 3 peaks in 72 hours, London Marathon in 26 hours 2010, 2012 miles (310 marathon distances) in 331 days 2012, completed marathon in London 2014 (reducing marathon time from 14 days in 2009 to 14 hours); fndr and chief exec British Inspiration Tst (BRIT) 2010–; campaigner to reduce stigma attached to mental ilness, influencer and champion of young people suffering from trauma and adversity, inspirational and motivational speaker; ambass: Prince's Tst 2009–, Douglas Bader Fndn 2009–, Calvert Tst 2009–, UK Scouting Assoc 2012–; special ambass RYA Sailability 2009–; patron: Cardiac Risk in the Young (CRY) 2009–, NSPCC Team GO 2009–; vice-patron Helen Rollason Cancer Charity 2009–; envoy: Royal Navy and Royal Marines Children's Fund 2010–, Combat Stress 2010–; Hon MA(Ed) Univ of Chichester 2013, Hon MA Univ of Chester 2014; FRSA 2009; *Awards* BBC Sports Personality of the Year Helen Rollason Award 2009, Fundraiser of the Year Pride of Britain Award 2009; *Style*— Phil Packer, MBE, MA(Ed), MA, FRSA; ✉ website www.philpacker.com; c/o Trudy Baxter (e-mail Trudy@BritishInspirationTrust.org.uk, website www.BritishInspiratonTrust.org.uk)

PACKER, Robin John; s of Edwin James Packer, and Alma, *née* Lodge; *b* 6 May 1948; *Educ* Catford Sch; *m* 1 Aug 1970, Diane Irana, da of Kenneth Derek Jones; 2 da (Melanie b 28 Dec 1973, Natalie b 1 Aug 1977); *Career* de Zoete & Gordon 1964–66, Govett Sons 1966–74, Cazenove 1974–76; Wood MacKenzie & Co: joined 1976, ptnr 1984–87, dir 1986–87; joined UBS Phillips & Drew 1987, currently a md UK equities Warburg Dillon Read (formerly UBS Ltd); memb local Cons Assoc; MSI; *Recreations* golf, game fishing; *Style*— Robin Packer, Esq; ✉ Southfields, Telegraph Hill, Higham by Rochester, Kent ME3 7NW (☎ 01634 721420); Warburg Dillon Read, 100 Liverpool Street, London EC2 (direct ☎ 020 7901 1386)

PACKHAM, Jenny; da of Colin Packham, of Southampton, and Marion Rita, *née* Smith; *b* 11 March 1965; *Educ* Bitterne Park Sch Southampton, Southampton Art Coll (DA TEC) St Martin Sch of Art London (BA, RSA bursary award and fellowship); *Partner* Mathew John Anderson; 2 da (Georgia Packham Anderson b 8 Nov 1993, Isabella Packham Anderson b 3 Jan 1998); *Career* fashion designer specialising in evening wear, lingerie, accessories and bridal wear; creative dir Jenny Packham co; clients incl VIPs (HRH The Duchess of Cambridge, Kate Winslet, Angelina Jolie, Adele, Catherine Zeta Jones, Kate Hudson, Dita Von Teese, Keira Knightley, Beyonce, Sandra Bullock, Cameron Diaz and Jennifer Lopez) and boutiques on Mount St Mayfair, Elizabeth St Belgravia and rue du Faubourg Saint-Honoré Paris (also incl Harrods, Harvey Nichols, Neiman Marcus, Bergdoorf Goodman and Saks); nine Condé Nast Bride Awards, Designer of the Year 2007, Int Designer of the Year 2007, Br Bridal Designer of the Year 2008; FRSA; *Recreations* contemporary art, travelling; *Style*— Ms Jenny Packham; ✉ Zoomphase Ltd T/A Jenny Packham, Unit A Spectrum House, 32–34 Gordon House Road, London NW5 1LB (☎ 020 7267 1864)

PACKSHAW, Charles Max; s of Savile Packshaw (d 1969), and Muriel, *née* Newton; *b* 30 January 1952; *Educ* Westminster, Univ of Bristol (BSc), London Business Sch (MSc); *m* 9 July 1983, Helena Mary, da of Peter Youngman; 2 s (Harry b 1984, Edward b 1987), 1 da (Olivia b 1989); *Career* with Costain 1973–78, sr conslt Cresap 1980–84, md Lazard Bros Co Ltd (joined 1984) until 2002, head of UK advsy HSBC Bank plc 2002–; non-exec dir: City Centre Restaurants plc 1996–2001, Diagonal plc 2002–04, Diploma plc 2013–; CEng, MICE 1978; *Clubs* Brooks's, Hurlingham; *Style*— Charles Packshaw, Esq

PACKSHAW, Justin James; MBE (2016), DL (2016); s of Robin Packshaw, and Annie, *née* Warrack; *b* 13 March 1965, London; *Educ* Wolverstone Hall, Univ of Edinburgh (MBA); *m* 26 July 2002, Tamsin de Roemer; 1 da (Lula), 1 s (Blake); *Career* entrepreneur, philanthropist, speaker and adventurer; offr Br Army 1985–1994 (Outstanding Service Royal Dragoon Guards); expeditions incl: Whitbread Round the World Yacht Race 1989, riding horses across Mongolia 1996, motorbiking in Africa 1999, Magnetic N Pole 2005, Geographic N Pole 2008 and 2015, Mount Everest 2011, Geographic S Pole 2012, Shackleton Expedition 2014; co-fndr and ceo De Roemer 2007–; int speaker 2010–; thought ldr Paypal, memb Influencer Advsr Bd Hewlett Packard, fndn ambass Sage; fell Explorers Club; FRGS; *Books* Artic Enterprise – North Pole (2016); *Style*— Justin Packshaw, Esq, MBE, DL; ✉ 42 Casselden Road, London NW10 8QR (e-mail jp@deroemer.com, website www.justinpackshaw.com, Twitter @Justin_Packshaw); De Roemer, 14 Porchester Place, London W2 2BS

PADEL, Ruth Sophia; da of John Padel (d 1999), and Hilda, *née* Barlow; *b* 8 May 1946, London; *Educ* N London Collegiate Sch, Lady Margaret Hall Oxford (scholar, BA), Univ of Oxford (PhD); *m* 1984 (m dis 1999), Prof Myles Burnyeat; 1 da (Gwen b 1985); *Career* poet and writer; lectr CCC Oxford, Kings Coll Cambridge and Wadham Coll Oxford 1974–79; res fell Wolfson Coll Oxford, Bowra res fell Wadham Coll Oxford 1978–79, poetry fell KCL 2013–; resident poet Henry Wood Promenade Concerts, first resident writer Somerset House 2008, resident writer Christ's Coll Cambridge 2009, resident writer Environment Inst UCL 2010, first resident writer ROH Covent Garden 2014; winner Nat Poetry Competition 1997; memb: Poetry Soc (chair 2004–07), PEN, Bombay Natural History; FRSL 1999, FRZS (memb Cncl 2012); *Poetry* Alibi (1985), Summer Snow (1990), Angel (1993, Poetry Book Society Recommendation), Whom Gods Destroy (1995), Fusewire (1996), Rembrandt Would Have Loved You (1998, Poetry Book Society Choice), Voodoo Shop (2002, Poetry Book Society Recommendation), 52 Ways of Looking at a Poem (2004), The Soho Leopard (2004, Poetry Book Society Choice), The Poem and the Journey (2007), Darwin – A Life in Poems (2009), Silent Letters of the Alphabet (2010), The Mara Crossing (2012), Learning to Make an Oud in Nazareth (2014); *Non-Fiction* In and Out of the Mind: Greek Images of the Tragic Self (1992), Whom Gods Destroy: Elements of Greek and Tragic Madness (1995), I'm A Man: Sex, Gods and Rock 'n' Roll (2000), Tigers in Red Weather (2005); *Fiction* Where the Serpent Lives (2010); *Recreations* singing, travel; *Clubs* Academy; *Style*— Ms Ruth Padel; ✉ c/o R Kirby, United Agents (e-mail hthompson@unitedagents.co.uk)

PADGHAM, Hugh Charles; s of Charles Arthur Padgham, of Aylesbury, Bucks, and Ursula Mary, *née* Samuelson; *b* 15 February 1955, Chalfont St Giles, Bucks; *Educ* The Beacon Sch Chesham Bois, St Edward's Sch Oxford; *m* Cath Kidston, MBE, *qv*; *Career* asst Advision Studios 1974–75, engr/asst Lansdowne Studios 1975–77, engr Townhouse

P

Studios 1977–80, record prodr and engr 1980–; owner Sofa Sound Studio (recording studio); companion Liverpool Inst of Performing Arts (LIPA) 2015; produced and engineered: Split Enz' Conflicting Emotions (A&M 1980) and Time and Tide (A&M 1982), The Police's Ghost in The Machine (A&M 1981, Platinum disc) and Synchronicity (A&M 1983, Platinum disc), Phil Collins' Face Value (Virgin 1983, 6 Platinum discs), No Jacket Required (Virgin 1985, Platinum disc), Hello I Must Be Going (Virgin 1988, Platinum disc) and But Seriously (Virgin 1989, 8 Platinum discs), Genesis' Genesis (Virgin 1983, 2 Platinum discs) and Invisible Touch (Virgin 1986, 4 Platinum discs), XTC's English Settlement (Virgin 1983, Silver disc), Human League's Hysteria (Virgin 1984, Gold disc), David Bowie's Tonight (EMI 1985, Gold disc), Paul Young's Between Two Fires (CBS 1986, Platinum disc), Paul McCartney's Press To Play (Parlaphone 1988, Gold disc), tracks from Julia Fordham's Porcelain (Circa 1989, Silver disc) and Julia Fordham (Circa 1988, Gold disc), Sting's The Soul Cages (A&M 1991) and Ten Summoner's Tales (A&M 1993), Melissa Etheridge's Yes I Am (Island 1993, Grammy 1995), Billy Pilgrim's (debut album, Atlantic 1994), Melissa Etheridge's Your Little Secret (Island Records 1995), Phil Collins' Dance into the Light (Atlantic/EW 1996), Bee Gees' 3 Tracks (A&M 1996), Beth Hart Band's Immortal (Lava/143 Records 1996), Sting's Mercury Falling (A&M 1996), Clannad's Lore (BMG/Atlantic 1996), Miyazawa's Sixteenth Moon (EMI Japan 1997), Kami Lyle's Blue Cinderella (MCA USA 1997); engineered: XTC's Drums and Wires (Virgin 1979) and Black Sea (Virgin 1980), Genesis' Abacab (Virgin 1983, Gold disc), Peter Gabriel's The Third (Virgin 1986, Gold disc); mixed and produced McFly debut album 2003–04; mixed numerous singles/tracks incl: Hall and Oates' H2O (RCA 1982, Platinum disc), Sting's Nothing Like The Sun (A&M 1987, Platinum disc), Phil Collins' In The Air Tonight (Virgin 1988 remix, Gold disc), remix of Joan Armatrading's Love & Affection (A&M 1991), Trisha Yearwood's Walkaway Joe (MCA Int 1994), Self's Breakfast with Girls (Dreamworks/Spongebath 1998), McFly's Room on the Third Floor (debut album 2004, 2 Platinum discs), Islands in the Stream (Mercury 2009, Comic Relief single feat stars from Gavin and Stacy, Sir Tom Jones and Robin Gibb); worked with various other artists incl: Mansun, Sheryl Crow, Tin Machine, Psychedelic Furs, Robbie Nevil, Kim Richey, Mark Joseph, The Tragically Hip; *Awards* Best British Producer Music Week Awards 1985 and 1990, Producer of the Year and Album of the Year Grammy Awards 1985, Best Producer nomination BPI Awards 1985 and 1986, Brit Awards Best Single 1989, Record of the Year Grammy Award 1990, Best Engineer Grammy Awards 1994, Billboard Tribute 1997; *Recreations* motor racing, tennis, cricket, skiing; *Style*— Hugh Padgham, Esq; ✉ c/o Joe D'Ambrosio Management Inc, 1311 Mamaroneck Avenue, Suite 220, White Plains, NY 10605–5222, USA

PADMORE, Elaine Marguirite; OBE (2012); da of Alfred Padmore (d 1971), and Florence, *née* Stockman (d 2004); *b* 3 February 1947; *Educ* Newland HS Hull, Arnold Girls' Sch Blackpool, Univ of Birmingham (MA, BMus), Guildhall Sch of Music London; *Career* musician, singer, prodr, writer and broadcaster; ed Music Dept OUP 1970–71, lectr in opera Royal Acad of Music 1972–85, radio prodr Music Dept BBC 1971–76, chief prodr opera BBC Radio 1976–82, announcer BBC Radio 3 1982–90; artistic dir: Wexford Festival Opera 1982–94, Classical Productions (UK) Ltd 1990–92, London Opera Festival 1991, Opera Ireland (formerly Dublin Grand Opera Soc) 1991–93, Royal Danish Opera 1993–2000; dir of opera ROH 2000–11; Sunday Independent Award for servs to music in Ireland 1987; Hon DMus Univ of Birmingham; Hon FTCL, Hon ARAM, Hon FBC; Knight of the Order of the Dannebrog (Denmark) 1994; *Books* Wagner (Great Composers series), New Grove Dictionary of Music and Musicians (contrib); *Recreations* gardening, cats; *Style*— Miss Elaine Padmore, OBE; ✉ e-mail elainepadmore@gmail.com

PAGAN, Hugh Edmund; s of Francis Edmund Pagan (d 2002), of London, and Margaret Jocelyn, *née* Neel (d 1971); *b* 4 October 1944; *Educ* Westminster, ChCh Oxford (MA); *m* 15 Feb 1974, Jill, da of Robert William Charles Catling, of Manchester; 2 s (Robert Edmund b 1974, Thomas Helier b 1978); *Career* antiquarian bookseller; dir B Weinreb Architectural Books Ltd 1978–87, md Hugh Pagan Ltd 1987–; jt ed Br Numismatic Jl 1971–76; Br Numismatic Soc: memb Cncl 1969–76 and 1979–, pres 1984–88, vice-pres 1992–, John Sanford Saltus Gold medal 1989, hon memb 2016–; vice-chm Prep/Organising Ctee Int Numismatic Congress London 1986, memb Br Acad Ctee for Sylloge of Coinage of the Br Isles 1988–; fell Royal Numismatic Soc 1976 (memb Cncl 1981–84), FSA 1986; *Publications* vol on Anglo-Saxon coins in Grosvenor Museum Chester (SCBI vol 64, 2012), Royal Numismatic Soc 150th Anniversary publication (jtly, 1986), contrib to volumes on Anglo-Saxon coinage, contrib articles in British Numismatic Journal; *Recreations* British political history; *Clubs* Garrick; *Style*— Hugh Pagan, Esq, FSA

PAGAN, Jill Catling; da of Robert William Charles Catling (d 1967), of Manchester, and Edna Catling (d 1978); *Educ* Loreburn Coll, Inns of Court Sch of Law; *m* 15 Feb 1974, Hugh Edmund, s of Francis Edmund Pagan, of Albany, London; 2 s (Robert b 27 Dec 1974, Thomas b 17 Jan 1978); *Career* called to the Bar Inner Temple 1972; int tax conslt: Tansley Witt & Co 1975–79, Thomson McLintock KMG 1980–82; practised at Revenue Bar 1982–89, int tax conslt J F Chown & Co Ltd 1989–92, memb Panel of Experts IMF 1992–, conslt OECD 1993; dir Hugh Pagan Ltd 1987–; contrib ed International Tax Report 1982–95, founding ed Inner Temple Yearbook; author numerous articles on int fin, int and UK taxation; memb Bar Liaison Ctee Inner Temple 1985–90, memb Ctee UK Branch Int Fiscal Assoc 1985–98; *Books* Taxation Aspects of Currency Fluctuations (1983, 2 edn 1992), Transfer Pricing Strategy in a Global Economy (with J Scott Wilkie, 1993); *Recreations* family, tennis, travel; *Style*— Mrs Jill Pagan; ✉ 2 The Coppice, Brockenhurst, Hampshire SO42 7QZ (☎ 01590 623381, e-mail jill@hughpagan.com)

PAGE, Adrienne May; QC (1999); da of late Gwythian Lloyd Page, and Betty, *née* Spring; *b* 14 July 1952; *Educ* Godolphin Sch Salisbury, Univ of Kent at Canterbury (BA); *m* 1983 (m dis 2007), Anthony Crichton Waldeck, s of Ivor Waldeck; 1 step s, 1 step da; *Career* called to the Bar Middle Temple 1974 (Bencher 2003); practising barrister specialising in defamation and privacy, asst recorder/recorder (SE Circuit) 1995–2004, jt head of chambers 5RB 2003–11; *Recreations* gardening; *Clubs* Beaulieu River Sailing; *Style*— Miss Adrienne Page, QC; ✉ 5RB, 5 Gray's Inn Square, Gray's Inn, London WC1R 5AH (☎ 020 7242 2902, fax 020 7831 2686, website www.5RB.com)

PAGE, Prof Alan Chisholm; s of Samuel Chisholm Page, of Broughty Ferry, and Betsy Johnston, *née* Melville; *b* 7 April 1952; *Educ* Grove Acad Broughty Ferry, Univ of Edinburgh (LLB), City Univ (PhD); *m* 16 Aug 1975, Sheila Duffus, da of Ian Dunlop Melville, of Glasgow; 1 s (Michael b 1983), 1 da (Rebecca b 1986); *Career* lectr in law Univ of Cardiff 1975–80; Univ of Dundee: sr lectr in law 1980–85, head Dept of Public Law 1981–86, prof of public law 1985–, head Dept of Law 1985–95 and 2004–06, dean Faculty of Law 1986–89, dean Sch of Law 2006–, dep Principal (Research Governance) 2012–; memb Tax Law Review Ctee 1994–2004, lead assessor in law Scottish HE Funding Cncl 1995–96; *Books* Legislation (2 edn, 1990), Investor Protection (1992), The Executive in the Constitution (1999), Constitutional Law of Scotland (2015); *Recreations* mountaineering; *Style*— Prof Alan Page; ✉ Westlands, Westfield Road, Cupar, Fife (☎ 01334 655576); School of Law, University of Dundee, Dundee DD1 4HN (☎ 01382 384633, fax 01382 226905, e-mail a.c.page@dundee.ac.uk)

PAGE, HE Andrew John Walter; s of John Henry Page, and Carol Mary, *née* Macnutt; *b* 17 September 1965, Cuckfield, W Sussex; *Educ* Windlesham House Sch, Lancing Coll (scholarship), Jesus Coll Cambridge (classical scholarship, lawn tennis and real tennis blues); *Career* diplomat; investment analyst County Nat West 1987–90; asst desk offr Economic Relations Dept FCO 1990–91, 2 sec (political/economic/information) Kiev 1993–96, press offr News Dept FCO 1996–98, head South Africa Section FCO 1998–2000, secondment to Quai d'Orsay (Africa Directorate) Paris 2000–01, 1 sec (political) Paris 2001–04, dep head Russia, South Caucasus and Central Asia Directorate FCO 2004–08, ambass to Slovenia 2009–13, secondment to PwC as sr adviser European Banking 2014–16; *Recreations* real tennis, lawn tennis, squash, golf, crosswords, bridge, literature, music, theatre; *Clubs* Hawks, Jesters, Petworth House Tennis, Queen's, MCC, W Sussex Golf; *Style*— Mr Andrew Page; ✉ 95 Belgrave Road, Flat 3, London SW1V 2BQ (☎ 07502 959555, e-mail ajw.page@gmail.com)

PAGE, Ben; s of Charles Page, of Exeter, and late Elizabeth, *née* Barrett; *b* 9 January 1965, Exeter; *Educ* Exeter Coll, St John's Coll Oxford (BA); *m* 1994 (m dis 2012), Janet, *née* Pritchard; 1 s (Horace b 16 Aug 1995); *Career* MIL (later NOP) 1986–87; MORI: researcher and mangr 1987–95, dir/ptnr 1995–2000, chm Ipsos MORI Social Research Inst and md Ipsos MORI Public Affrs 2001–09, chief exec Ipsos MORI UK 2009–; cmmr CABE, cmmr 20/20 Public Services Tst; memb Advsy Gp: CBI, IPPR, Social Market Fndn, Kings Fund; contrib to The Guardian, MJ and LGC; prize for best research for business improvement Br Market Research Assoc 2001, Silver medal Market Research Soc 2005; memb Market Research Soc 2004–; FRSA 2003; *Books* Blair's Britain 1997–2007 (2007); *Recreations* Italy, art history, architecture, worrying, skateboarding, jazz; *Style*— Ben Page, Esq; ✉ Ipsos MORI, 3 Thomas More Square, London E1W 1WY (☎ PA (Monica Kowalczyk) 020 7347 3242, fax 020 7347 3804, e-mail ben.page@ipsos.com, website www.ipsos-mori.com, Twitter @BenAtIpsosMori)

PAGE, Prof Christopher Howard; s of Ewert Lacey Page, and Marie Victoria, *née* Graham; *b* 8 April 1952; *Educ* Sir George Monoux Sch, Univ of Oxford (MA), Univ of York (DPhil); *m* 1, 15 Sept 1975 (m dis 2003), Régine, *née* Fourcade; m 2, 18 Sept 2004, Anne, *née* Dunan; *Career* currently prof of medieval music and literature Univ of Cambridge, fell Sidney Sussex Coll Cambridge (formerly fell Jesus Coll Oxford); presenter Radio 3 series Spirit of the Age; ldr of the ensemble Gothic Voices and prodr of acclaimed records; Gramophone Early Music Records of the Year: Hildegard of Bingen 1983 (also Guardian Choral Record of the Year), The Service of Venus and Mars 1988, A Song for Francesca (1989); chm Nat Early Music Assoc, chm Plainsong and Medieval Music Soc, fell Fellowship of Makers and Restorers of Historical Instruments, FSA, FBA 2013; *Books* Voices and Instruments of the Middle Ages (1987), Sequences of Hildegard of Bingen (1986), The Owl and the Nightingale (1989), Summa Musice (1991), Discarding Images (1994), The Christian West and its Singers (2010); *Recreations* research and performance; *Style*— Prof Christopher Page; ✉ Sidney Sussex College, Cambridge CB2 3HU

PAGE, Christopher John (Chris); s of Albert Harold Page (d 1987), and Doris May, *née* Clarke (d 2005); *b* 28 May 1947; *Educ* Eton House Sch, London South Bank Univ (Grad DipArch); *m* 7 July 1979, Janice Anne, da of late Andrew John Sharman, of Wickford, Essex; 1 s (Richard b 1981), 1 da (Jacqueline b 1984); *Career* architect/program mangr and illustrator; sr ptnr Page Architects 1986–; chm Atlanta Signs, ptnr Animatic Media Gp, ptnr Flip-Time; *Recreations* sailing, sketching, pre-history in UK; *Clubs* Eton House Old Boys, Thorpe Bay Yacht; *Style*— Chris Page, Esq; ✉ The Barn, Poynters Lane, Southend-on-Sea, Essex SS3 9TS (☎ 01702 300647, e-mail chrispage@pagearchitecture.com, websites www.sportscars.tv and www.ipt-a.com); Studio Five, Crouchmans Yard, Poynters Lane, Southend-on-Sea, Essex SS3 9TS; 11 Calle Pinsa, Pollenca 07470, Mallorca, Spain

PAGE, David Norman; s of Bernard Page, of Edinburgh, and Catherine Page, *née* Adam; *b* 4 September 1957; *Educ* Bearsden Acad Strathclyde, Univ of Strathclyde (BSc, BArch); *Career* sr ptnr PagePark Architects 1981–; lectr Dept of Architecture and Building Science Univ of Strathclyde 1982–94; hon prof Edinburgh Coll of Art, Hon Dr Univ of Strathclyde 2004; RSA; *Style*— David N Page, Esq; ✉ PagePark Architects, The Italian Centre, 49 Cochrane Street, Glasgow (☎ 0141 552 0686)

PAGE, Dianne; da of William John Griffiths Bryce, of Walton, Warks, and Audrey Jean, *née* Smith; *b* 14 May 1946; *Educ* Regis Sch Tettenhall, Wolverhampton Poly (Dip); *Career* Sulzer Brothers Switzerland 1965–66, Alusuisse UK 1966–72, Tower Housewares 1972–80, md Barkers Public Relations 1980–2002, exec chm McCann-Erickson Public Relations 2002–; chm Inst of Consumer Sciences; FIPR; *Books* Pressure Cooking Explained (1979), Slow Cooking Explained (1982), Food Processors Explained (1984); *Recreations* painting, theatre, opera; *Style*— Mrs Dianne Page; ✉ McCann-Erickson Public Relations, McCann House, Highlands Road, Solihull B90 4WE (☎ 0121 713 3500)

PAGE, Prof Edward Charles; s of Edward Charles Page (d 1998), and Winifred Victoria Page; *b* 19 October 1953; *Educ* William Ellis GS, Kingston Poly (BA), Univ of Strathclyde (MSc, PhD); *m* Christine Mary, da of Henry Batty; 1 s (Martin Edward b 4 Oct 1979), 2 da (Miriam Victoria b 16 May 1984, Florence Carmel b 9 May 1987); *Career* lectr Univ of Strathclyde 1978–81, successively lectr, sr lectr, reader and prof of politics Univ of Hull 1981–2001, Sidney and Beatrice Webb prof of public policy LSE 2001–; visiting assoc prof Texas A&M Univ 1986–87; dir Future Governance Prog ESRC 1998–2004; FBA 2001; *Books* Political Authority and Bureaucratic Power: A Comparative Analysis (2 edn, 1992), Governing the New Europe (co-ed, 1995), People Who Run Europe (1997), Bureaucratic Elites in Western Europe (1999), Governing By Numbers: Delegated Legislation and Everyday Policy Making (2001), Policy Bureaucracy: Government with a Cast of Thousands (co-author, 2005); *Recreations* jazz; *Style*— Prof Edward Page; ✉ Department of Government, London School of Economics and Political Science, Houghton Street, London WC2A 2AE (☎ 020 7849 4269, fax 020 7831 1707, e-mail e.c.page@lse.ac.uk)

PAGE, Emma; *Educ* Univ of Oxford (MA); *Children* 2 s, 1 da; *Career* detective writer; *Books* Final Moments (1987), A Violent End (1988), Deadlock (1991), Mortal Remains (1992), In The Event of My Death (1994), Murder Comes Calling (1995), Hard Evidence (1996), Intent to Kill (1998), Say it with Murder (2000) and others; *Style*— Ms Emma Page; ✉ 55–56 Russell Square, London WC1B 4HP

PAGE, Gordon Francis de Courcy; CBE (2000), DL (Dorset 2006); s of Sir Frederick William Page, CBE (d 2005), and Lady Kathleen de Courcy Page (d 1993); *b* 17 November 1943; *Educ* Cheltenham Coll, St Catharine's Coll Cambridge (MA); *m* 29 March 1969, Judi, *née* Mays; 2 da (Rebecca b 28 March 1970, Fiona b 27 Sept 1973), 2 s (Damian b 30 Jan 1972, Christopher (twin) b 27 Sept 1973); *Career* with Rolls Royce plc 1962–89; Cobham plc: md flight refuelling 1990, gp dep chief exec 1991, gp chief exec 1992, chm 2001–08; dir Lockheed Martin UK Ltd 2005–10; non-exec chm: Air Tanker Hldgs plc 2000–, FKI plc 2004–08, Hamworthy plc 2004–12, PHWarr plc 2008–; pres SBAC 1997–98 and 2002–03, dir Industrial Advsy Bd DBERR 2000–04 (chm 2004–08); chm: Bournemouth, Dorset and Poole Economic Partnership 2000–09, Wessex Multi-area Partnership 2009–11, Dorset Local Enterprise Partnership 2012–; tstee Dorset Community Fndn 2008–15, dir Bournemouth Cncl Trading Co Ltd 2014–; govr Canford Sch 2003–11 (chm 2008–11), pro-chllr Cranfield Univ 2007–12; Hon DSc Cranfield Univ 2003, Hon DBA Bournemouth Univ 2009; FInstD 1990, FRAeS 1994 (pres 2006–07, Hon FRAeS 2009), CCMI 1996 (pres 2002–03), FRSA 1999; *Recreations* theatre, gardening, classic cars; *Style*— Gordon Page, Esq, CBE, DL; ✉ Avon Reach, The Close, Avon Castle, Ringwood, Hampshire BH24 2BJ (☎ 01425 475365, fax 01425 475680, mobile 07768 715501, e-mail gordonpage@outlook.com)

PAGE, Howard William Barrett; QC (1987); *b* 11 February 1943; *Educ* Radley, Trinity Hall Cambridge (MA, LLB); *m* Helen Joanna Page, CVO, *née* Shotter, 3 c; *Career* called to the Bar 1967, bencher Lincoln's Inn; dep pres Lloyd's Appeal Tbnl until 2010, cmmr Royal Court of Jersey; *Style*— Howard Page, QC; ✉ 6 New Square, Lincoln's Inn, London

WC2A 3QS (☎ 020 7242 6105, fax 020 7405 4004, e-mail clerks@serlecourt.co.uk, website www.serlecourt.co.uk)

PAGE, Roy Malcolm; s of Alec Page (d 1980), and Janet, *née* Hutton (d 2003); *b* 24 June 1950, Surbiton, Surrey; *Educ* Wymondham HS, Thetford GS, Univ of Portsmouth (BSc), Univ of Reading (PGCE), Nat Coll for Sch Leadership (NPQH, Nat Ldrs in Educn); *m* Aug 1973, Marilyn; 1 s (James Anthony b 2 April 1977), 1 da (Katie Louise (Mrs Oliver Clark) b 24 April 1980); *Career* Royal GS High Wycombe: teacher of mathematics 1972, housemaster 1982, dep headmaster 1989, sr dep headmaster 2001, headmaster 2006–15; memb: Nat Tst, RSPB, RHS; memb ASCL; *Recreations* hockey, cricket, golf, rugby, fitness, bird watching; *Clubs* Rotary (Princes Risborough), Lansdowne; *Style*— Roy Page, Esq; ✉ Elm End House, Henton, Nr Chinnor, Oxfordshire OX39 4AH (☎ 01844 351292, e-mail roympage@gmail.com)

PAGE, Stephen Alexander; s of James Cornish Page, and Frances, *née* Drake; *b* 17 February 1965, Birmingham; *Educ* Bromsgrove Sch, Univ of Bristol (BA); *m* 1993, Caroline Elizabeth Hird; 2 s (Frank, Ned); *Career* Fourth Estate Ltd: sales and mktg dir and dep md 1994–2000, md 2000; gp sales and mktg dir HarperCollins 2000–01, chief exec and publisher Faber & Faber 2001–; founding memb Reading Partners 2002; pres Publishers' Assoc 2006–07; non-exec memb Bd: Creative Skillset 2011, Bloomsbury Publishing plc 2013–; expert panellist DCMS Reviews of E-Lending and Public Libraries 2013–14; Vista Industry Achievement Award 2007, Most Inspiring Digital Publishing Person FutureBook Awards 2013; *Recreations* music (listening and playing drums in Lone Tree Quartet), reading, film, theatre, cooking; *Style*— Stephen Page; ✉ Faber & Faber Ltd, Bloomsbury House, 74–77 Great Russell Street, London WC1B 3DA (☎ 020 7927 3815, e-mail stephen.page@faber.co.uk, Twitter @stephenpub)

PAGE, Prof Trevor Francis; s of Cyril Francis Page (d 1980), of Lichfield, Staffs, and Gladys Mary, *née* Boston (d 2009); *b* 6 January 1946; *Educ* King Edward VI GS Lichfield, Jesus Coll Cambridge (MA, PhD, ScD); *m* 7 Aug 1971, Andrea Gail, da of Cyril James Jones, of Cambridge; 1 s (Matthew Nicholas James b 1976), 1 da (Victoria Sophie Louise b 1979); *Career* Univ of Cambridge: SRC res fell 1971–72, demonstrator in metallurgy and materials sci 1972–76, lectr 1976–86, fndn fell Robinson Coll 1976–86; Univ of Newcastle upon Tyne: Cookson Gp prof of engrg materials 1987–2008, head Material Div 1989–2000, pro-vice-chllr (research) 2000–04, pro-vice-chllr (external affrs and research liaison) 2004–08, sr research prof 2008–; non-exec dir Centre for Process Innovation; author of numerous scientific papers, reviews and encyclopaedia articles on materials sci, the applications of microscopy, the devpt of ceramic materials and surface engrg, tribology, nanotechnology and nano-mechanics; EPSRC: Structural Materials Coll 1995–2005; memb Materials Research Soc USA 1995–2006; chm Tyne & Wear Metallurgical Soc 1988–90; fell: Royal Microscopical Soc 1971, Inst of Metals 1984, Inst of Ceramics 1987; FIM 1991, CEng 1991, FInstP 2002, FREng 2007; *Recreations* family, classical music, opera, theatre, cinema, food and wine, photography, gardening; *Clubs* Athenaeum; *Style*— Prof Trevor Page; ✉ School of Chemical Engineering and Advanced Materials, Merz Court, Newcastle University, Newcastle upon Tyne NE1 7RU (☎ 0191 208 7516, fax 0191 208 8480, e-mail trevor.page@ncl.ac.uk)

PAGET, Henry James; s and h of Lt-Col Sir Julian Tolver Paget, 4 Bt, CVO, *qv*; *b* 2 February 1959; *Educ* Radley; *m* 8 Sept 1993, Mrs Margrete E Varvill, da of late Halfdan Lynner; 1 s (Bernard Halfdan b 4 July 1994), 1 da (Daphne Ampuria b 9 Sept 1996); *Career* Coldstream Guards; sr ptnr St James's Place; *Recreations* fishing, shooting and property renovation; *Style*— Henry Paget, Esq; ✉ Glenlivet House, by Ballindalloch, Banffshire AB37 9DJ (☎ 01807 590376)

PAGNAMENTA, Peter John; s of Charles Francis Pagnamenta (d 2010), and Daphne Isabel, *née* Kay (d 1990); *b* 12 April 1941; *Educ* Shrewsbury, Trinity Hall Cambridge; *m* 13 April 1966, Sybil, da of Frances Howard Healy, of NY; 1 da (Zoe b 1969), 1 s (Robin b 1973); *Career* writer and TV prodr; BBC: joined 1964, asst prodr Tonight 1965, prodr 24 Hours 1966, prodr New York office 1968, ed 24 Hours 1971, ed Midweek 1972, ed Panorama 1975; dir news and current affairs Thames Television 1977; BBC: prodr All Our Working Lives 1984, ed Real Lives series 1984, head Current Affairs Group 1985, prodr Nippon 1990, prodr People's Century (26 part series) 1995–96; fndr Pagnamenta Assocs 1997; *Books* All Our Working Lives (jtly, 1984), The Hidden Hall (ed, 2005), Sword and Blossom (jtly, 2006), Cambridge: An 800th anniversary portrait (ed, 2008), Prairie Fever (2012); *Style*— Peter Pagnamenta; ✉ 6 Hamilton House, Vicarage Gate, London W8 4HL

PAHOR, Dr Ahmes Labib; s of Prof Pahor Labib (d 1994), of Cairo; *b* Cairo; *Educ* Cairo Univ (MB BCh, DLO), Ain Shams Univ Cairo (DMScPath), RCS(Ed) (Cert of Higher Surgical Trg in ENT), ECFMG (Philadelphia), Inst of Higher Coptic Studies Cairo (MA), DHMSA (Soc of Apothecaries London), Cert of Specialist Trg (EU), Radboud Univ Nijmegan Holland (PhD); *Career* intern Cairo Univ Hosp 1964–65, SHO Miny of Health Cairo 1965–66, asst researcher (demonstrator) Pathology and Cytology Dept Nat Research Centre Miny of Scientific Research Cairo 1966–70, clinical attachment Surgical Dept Moyle Hosp Larne Co Antrim 1970, SHO ENT Dept Waveney Hosp Ballymena, SHO Birmingham and Midland ENT Hosp 1972, registrar Eye and Ear Clinic Royal Victoria Hosp Belfast and Belfast City Hosp 1972–74, sr registrar at various Midlands hosps 1974–78, conslt ENT surgeon City Hosp Dudley Rd (Sandwell and West Birmingham HA – teaching) 1978–2002 (hon conslt 2002–), conslt ENT surgn Priory Hosp Birmingham; hon sr clinical lectr Med Sch Univ of Birmingham; memb: Ethical Ctee Sandwell Dist Gen Hosp 1981–92, Regnl Aural Servs Ctee, Regnl ENT Registrars and Sr Registrars Ctee 1987–2002; co-fndr, co-organiser and tutor: Temporal Bone Surgery Course Birmingham 1980–89, Combined Univs Advanced Otology Course 1987–2002; lectr on operating Selly Oak Hosp Birmingham; examiner: Midland Inst of Otology Dip for Nurses 1979–89, fellowship examination (ENT) RCS(Ed), Occulus fellowship (Eye) Exams Birmingham Midland Eye Hosp; author of articles and papers in professional jls and pubns in English and Arabic; many lectures to professional bodies worldwide incl Inst d'Egypte Cairo 1981 and RSM London 1995; fndr sec British Soc for the History of ENT; memb: NY Acad of Scis, BMA, RSM, BAOL, Midland Inst of Otology (hon librarian 1996–2001), Br Paediatric Otolaryngology Soc, Otology Research Soc, Soc of Authors 1979–82, Medical Writers' Gp 1980, Irish Otolaryngology Soc, European Rhinologic Soc, Int Hist of Medicine Soc, Int Hippocratic Fndn of Kos Greece, Int Assoc of Coptic Studies, Birmingham History of Medicine Soc, Br Soc History of Medicine, Advsy Bd Otolaryngology RCS(Ed); fndr memb Imhotep Scientific Soc Cairo, fndr memb Coptic Culture Soc; memb: Sandwell Social Evening Ctee, Rotary Club Birmingham (memb Int Ctee); Freeman City of London, Liveryman Worshipful Soc of Apothecaries; MRCS, LRCP, FRCSEd, FICS; *Books* Oto-Rhino-Laryngology in Ancient Egypt, Dr Pahor Labib: Egyptologist (2009); *Recreations* travelling, reading, writing, golf, Tai Chi; *Clubs* Harborne Golf; *Style*— Dr Ahmes L Pahor; ✉ 34 Ingham Way, Harborne, Birmingham B17 8SN (e-mail ahmes2@hotmail.com, website www.pyramids3.netfirms.com)

PAICE, James Edward Thornton; s of late Edward Percival Paice, and late Winifred Mary, *née* Thornton; *b* 24 April 1949; *Educ* Framlingham Coll, Writtle Agric Coll (NDA); *m* 6 Jan 1973, Ava Barbara; 2 s (Gordon b 1976, James b 1977); *Career* gen mangr/exec dir Framlingham Mgmnt and Training Services Ltd 1985–87 (non-exec dir 1987–89), non-exec dir United Framlingham Farmers Ltd 1989–94; MP (Cons) Cambs SE 1987–2015; PPS to min for Agric, Fisheries and Food then sec of state for the Environment 1990–94; Parly under sec of state: Dept of Employment 1994–95, DfEE 1995–97; oppn frontbench spokesman on agric, fisheries and food 1997–2001, shadow min Home Office 2001–04, shadow agriculture min 2004–10, min of state for agriculture and food 2010–12; *Recreations* the countryside, shooting; *Style*— James Paice

PAIGE, Elaine; OBE (1995); da of Eric Bickerstaff (d 2005), and Irene Johnson (d 2001); *b* 5 March 1948, Barnet, Herts; *Educ* Southaw Girls Secdy Modern Barnet, Aida Foster Stage Sch Temple Fortune; *Career* actress and singer since 1964; pres Dan Maskell Tst; Hon DLitt 2012; *Theatre* musicals incl: created role of Eva Peron in Evita (London stage) 1978, created role of Grizabella in Cats 1981, created role of Florence in Chess 1986, Reno Sweeney in Anything Goes 1989, Edith Piaf in Piaf (West End and tour) 1993, Norma Desmond in Sunset Boulevard (London 1995, Broadway 1996–97), Celimène in The Misanthrope (Peter Hall Theatre Co) 1998, Anna in The King and I (London Palladium) 2000–01, Where There's a Will (Peter Hall Theatre Co UK tour) 2003, Mrs Lovett in Sweeney Todd (NYC Opera) 2004, title role in The Drowsy Chaperone (Novello Theatre) 2007, Elaine Paige 40th Anniversary World Concert Tour 2008, Carlotta Campion in Follies (Kennedy Center Washington DC) 2011, (Marquis Theater NY) 2011–12 and (Ahmanson Theater Los Angeles) 2012; *Television* incl: Love Story, The Lady Killers, Phyllis Dixey, View of Harry Clark, Unexplained Laughter, Boston Pops (PBS), Showstoppers: Performance at the White House 1988, South Bank Show – The Faces of Elaine Paige (ITV) 1996, Miss Marple: A Murder is Announced (ITV) 2004, Where The Heart Is (ITV) 2005, Beautiful People (BBC) 2009, Elaine Paige Celebrating 40 Years On Stage (PBS and Sky Arts) 2009, The Elaine Paige Show (Sky Arts) 2014, A Midsummer Night's Dream (BBC 1) 2016; *Films* incl: Oliver, Whatever Happened to What's His Name, A Closed Book 2009, I'm Still Here 2015; *Recordings* incl: Stages (triple platinum) 1983, Cinema (gold) 1984, Chess 1985, I Know Him So Well (duet with Barbara Dickson, No 1 Hit Single) 1985, Love Hurts (platinum) 1985, Christmas 1986, Memories (compilation album, platinum) 1987, The Queen Album (8th consecutive gold album) 1988, Love Can Do That 1991, Romance and the Stage 1993, Elaine Paige – Piaf 1994, Encore 1995, On Reflection 1998, A Collection 2003, Centre Stage 2004, Essential Musicals 2006, Elaine Paige Live Celebrating a Life on Stage 2008, Elaine Paige & Friends (gold album 2010, The Ultimate Collection 2014, I'm Still Here – Live at the Royal Albert Hall (CD) 2015; *Concerts* in: Australia, New Zealand, South Africa, Middle East, Far East, USA and Europe; UK concert tours 1985, 1987, 1991, 1993 1994, 2004, 2006, 2008, 2009 and 2011; Lincoln Theater NY 2012, 50th Anniversary Concert Tour 2014; *Radio* Elaine Paige On Sunday (BBC Radio 2) 2004–; *Awards* Show Business Personality of the Year Variety Club of GB Award (for Evita), Swet Award for Best Actress in a Musical (for Evita), Rear of the Year Award 1984, Recording Artiste of the Year Variety Club of GB (for album Christmas), Head of the Year Award! 1987, Br Academy of Songwriters, Composers and Authors Gold Badge of Merit 1993, Variety Club Award for Actress of the Year 1995, Olivier Award nomination for Outstanding Performance of the Year by an Actress in a Musical (for Chess and Anything Goes), Olivier Award nomination for Best Actress in a Musical (for Piaf and Sunset Boulevard), HMV Lifetime Achievement Award 1996, Nat Operatic & Dramatic Assoc Lifetime Achievement Award 1999, Drama Desk Award nomination for Outstanding Featured Actress in a Musical (for Sweeney Todd), Variety Club Award Special Presentation for 40 Years On Stage 2009, Drama Desk nomination for Outstanding Featured Actress in a Musical 2012 (for Follies), Best Featured Actress in a Musical (Touring) BroadwayWorld LA Award (for Follies) 2013, Best Musical Theater Album Grammy Award nomination (for Follies) 2013, Inspiration Award Women Supporting Breast Cancer Breakthrough 2014; *Books* Memories: Celebrating 40 Years in the Theatre (2008); *DVDs* Elaine Paige Celebrating 40 Years On Stage (2010), I'm Still Here – Live at the Royal Albert Hall (2015); *Recreations* clay pigeon shooting, tennis, painting; *Clubs* The Hospital Club, BAFTA, Queens Tennis; *Style*— Miss Elaine Paige, OBE; ✉ website www.elainepaige.com; UK drama agent: Jonathan Arun (e-mail jonathan@jonathanarun.com); USA drama agent: Josh Pultz/DGRW Inc (e-mail josh@dgrwinc.com)

PAIN, Jacqualyn Christina Mary; da of J K Pain, of Oxford, and J W Pain, *née* Underwood; *b* 31 August 1957; *Educ* Sch of St Helen and St Katharine Abingdon, Univ of Wales (BA, MA), Univ of London (MA, PGCE), Univ of Leicester (MBA); *Career* teacher: Tiffin Girls' Sch Kingston upon Thames 1981–83, Old Palace Sch Croydon 1983–84, James Allen's Girls' Sch London 1984–96; on secondment Inst of Educn Univ of London 1992–94, dep head Northwood Coll 1996–2000, head Henrietta Barnett Sch London 2000–05, head St Albans HS for Girls 2005–08, head Northwood Coll 2009–; MInstD; *Recreations* running, gym; *Clubs* Univ Women's; *Style*— Ms Jacqualyn Pain; ✉ Northwood College, Maxwell Road, Northwood, Middlesex HA5 2YE

PAINE, Sir Christopher Hammon; kt (1995); s of Maj John Hammon Paine (d 1987), of Great Coxwell, Oxon, and Hon Mrs J Shedden, MBE, *née* Vestey (d 1991); *b* 28 August 1935; *Educ* Eton, Merton Coll Oxford (MA, MSc, DM); *m* 3 Nov 1959, Susan, da of late D Martin, of Bridgwater, Somerset; 2 s (Edward b 1960, Simon b 1964), 2 da (Lucy b 1962, Alice b 1968); *Career* conslt in radiotherapy and oncology Oxford 1970–95 (hon conslt 1996–), dir clinical studies Univ of Oxford 1980–84, gen mangr Oxfordshire HA 1984–88; chm RSM Support Services Ltd 2005–15; memb Advsy Bd Weill Cornell Med Coll in Qatar 2002–14; pres: RCR 1992–95, RSM 1996–98, BMA 2000–01; med dir Advsy Ctee for Distinction Awards 1994–99; Liveryman Worshipful Soc of Apothecaries; FRCP, FRCR, Hon FRSCEd, hon fell Faculty of Radiologists Royal Coll of Surgns Ireland, hon fell Hong Kong Coll of Radiologists; *Recreations* gardening; *Clubs* Farmers'; *Style*— Sir Christopher Paine; ✉ The Avenue, Wotton Underwood, Aylesbury, Buckinghamshire HP18 0RP (☎ 01296 770742)

PAINE, Graham Ernest Harley; s of late Harley Joseph Paine, of Kingston on Thames, Surrey, and Ninette, *née* Sutch; *b* 2 September 1954; *Educ* Dulwich Coll, Univ of Bristol (LLB); *Career* admitted slr 1980; ptnr Wilde Sapte 1984–2000 (articled clerk 1978–80, asst slr 1980–84), ptnr Dentons UKMEA LLP (formerly Denton Wilde Sapte) 2000–; licensed insolvency practitioner; memb: Assoc of Business Recovery Professionals (R 3), Law Soc, Insolvency Lawyers Assoc; *Recreations* golf, skiing, theatre, swimming; *Style*— Graham Paine, Esq; ✉ Dentons UKMEA LLP, 1 Fleet Place, London EC4M 7WS (☎ 020 7246 7000, fax 020 7246 7777, e-mail graham.paine@dentons.com)

PAINE, Jack; *Career* dir (procurement) Dept for Transport; *Style*— Jack Paine, Esq; ✉ Department for Transport, Great Minster House, 33 Horseferry Road, London SW1P 4DR

PAINES, Alison Jane Sargent; *née* Roberts; da of Eric Sargent Roberts (d 1969), and Audrey Lilian May, *née* Rosevear (d 2011); *b* 27 July 1955, London; *Educ* Notting Hill & Ealing HS GDST, Girton Coll Cambridge (MA), Coll of Law Lancaster Gate; *m* 11 May 1985, Nicholas Paul Billot Paines, *qv*; 1 s (Rupert b 8 Sept 1986), 3 da (Emily b 10 June 1989, Katherine b 14 Aug 1992, Victoria b 7 June 1998); *Career* slr; articled clerk then asst slr Crossman Block & Keith 1979–88; Withers LLP: asst slr 1988–91, ptnr 1991–, head of charities practice 2000–; govr Godolphin & Latymer Sch 2002 (dep chair 2015); memb Exec Ctee Charity Law Assoc 1995–2007 and 2008–11 (dep chair 2004–07, chair 2008–11); *Publications* Practical Trust Precedents (contrib), Tolley's Charities Manual (contrib), Tolley's Revenue Law (contrib), Oxford University Press's International Charitable Giving (ed and contrib, 2012); *Style*— Mrs Alison Paines; ✉ Withers LLP, 16 Old Bailey, London EC4M 7EG (☎ 020 7597 6057, fax 020 7597 6543, e-mail alison.paines@withersworldwide.com)

PAINES, Nicholas Paul Billot; QC (1997); s of Anthony John Cooper Paines (d 2004), and Anne, *née* Billot; *b* 29 June 1955; *Educ* Downside, Univ of Oxford (MA), Université Libre

P

de Bruxelles (Licence Spéciale en Droit Européen); *m* 11 May 1985, Alison Jane, *qv*, da of Eric Sargent Roberts (d 1969); 1 s (Rupert b 1986), 3 da (Emily b 1989, Katherine b 1992, Victoria b 1998); *Career* called to the Bar: Gray's Inn 1978 (bencher 2016), NI 1996; practising barr 1980–2013, recorder 2003–, dep judge Upper Tbnl 2008– (assigned to First Tier Tax Tbnl 2009); dep social security cmmr 2000–08, dep High Court judge 2010–, law cmmr 2013–; memb Bar Cncl 1991–96, treas Bar European Gp 2001– (chm 1996–98); jt gen ed Common Market Law Reports 1996–2010; memb: Cncl St Christopher's Fellowship 1984–2002, Supplementary Panel of Counsel to the Crown (Common Law) 1993–97; *Books* Halsbury's Laws of England (contrib), Vaughan Law of the European Communities (contrib), Value Added Tax Commentary and Analysis (contrib); *Recreations* family life; *Style—* Nicholas Paines, Esq, QC; ✉ Law Commission, 1st Floor, Tower, 52 Queen Anne's Gate, London SW1H 9AG

PAISLEY OF ST GEORGE'S, Baroness (Life Peer 2006), of St George's in the County of Antrim; Eileen Emily Paisley; *née* Cassells; da of Thomas James Cassells (d 1980), and Emily Jane, *née* Stitt (d 1978); *b* 2 November 1931, Belfast; *Educ* Belfast Shorthand Inst and Business Trg Coll; *m* 13 Oct 1956, The Rt Hon Rev Ian Richard Kyle Paisley (d 2014); 3 da (Hon Sharon Kyle b 1957, Hon Rhonda Elaine Kyle b 1959, Hon Cherith Jane Kyle b 1965), 2 s (Hon Ian Richard Kyle Paisley, MP, *qv*, Hon Rev James Cassells Kyle b 1966 (twins)); *Career* cncllr St George's Ward Belfast Corp 1967–74, MLA 1973–74, memb NI Constitutional Convention 1975–76; *Books* Take a Break (series); *Recreations* family, grandchildren and great-grandchildren; *Style—* The Baroness Paisley of St George's; ✉ Director, Bannside Library Ltd, 135–139 Upper Newtownards Road, Belfast, BT4 3HX (✆ 028 90 671 676, e-mail paiselyeileen@yahoo.co.uk, website www.bannsidelibrary.com)

PAJARES, Ramon; OBE (2000); s of Juan Antonio Pajares Garcia (d 1954), of Jaen, Spain, and Rosario Salazar (d 1964); *b* 6 July 1935; *Educ* sr sch Jaen, Madrid Inst of Hotel and Tourism Studies; *m* 13 July 1963, Jean Kathleen, 2 da (Sofia Ramona b 14 June 1967, Maria del Rosario b 25 Aug 1969), 1 s (Roberto Javier b 17 March 1971); *Career* Nat Serv Spanish Navy 1955–57; Hotel Ritz Barcelona 1954–55, Hotel San Jorge Playa de Aro 1957, Hotel Parque Llavaneras 1957–59, Mansion Hotel Eastbourne 1959–61, Kleiner Reisen Koblenz 1961, Hotel Feldbergerhof Feldberg 1961–62, Le Vieux Manoir Morat 1962, Hotel Reina Isabel Las Palmas 1965–69, food and beverage dir Inn on the Park 1969–71, gen mangr San Antonio Lanzarote 1972–74, gen mangr Inn on the Park London (later renamed Four Seasons Park Lane London) 1975–82 (regnl vice-pres Europe 1982–94), md The Savoy Group 1994–99; memb: Académie Culinaire de France 1971–, Cookery and Food Assoc 1973, Confrèrie de la Chaîne des Rotisseurs 1978–, Confrèrie des Chevaliers du Sacavin 1979–, Caballeros del Vino 1987; Freeman City of London 1988; FHCIMA 1982, Master Innholder 1988; Officier de L'Ordre des Coteaux de Champagne, Chevalier du Tastevin 1982; *Awards* medal of Merito Civil awarded by HM King of Spain 1984, Hotelier of the Year award of Br Hotel and Catering Industry 1984, Personalité de l'An?ee for The Hotel Indust 1986, medal of Oficial de la Orden de Isabel la Católica awarded by HM King of Spain 1989, Caterer and Hotel Keeper Special Award 1997, European Hotel Design and Devpt Lifetime Achievement Award 1998, Hotels Magazine Hotelier of the World Award 1998, Waterford Wedgwood Hospitality Award 1999, British Travel Industry Hall of Fame Award 1999, Silver medal for services to tourism awarded by Spanish Govt 2000; *Style—* Ramon Pajares, Esq, OBE

PAKENHAM, Kate; *Educ* Univ of Cambridge; *Career* prodr Old Vic Theatre (joined 2001), exec prodr Donmar Warehouse 2012–; *Style—* Ms Kate Pakenham; ✉ Donmar Warehouse, 41 Earlham Street, London WC2H 9LX

PAKENHAM, Hon Kevin John Toussaint; yst s of 7 Earl of Longford, KG, PC (d 2001), and Elizabeth, Countess of Longford, CBE (d 2002); *b* 1 November 1947; *Educ* Ampleforth, New Coll Oxford (MA), St Antony's Coll Oxford (MPhil); *Career* Rothschild Intercontinental Bank 1972–75, American Express Bank 1975–83, md Foreign & Colonial Management 1983–88; chief exec: John Govett Ltd 1988–2000, AIB Asset Management Ltd 1997–2000; md Putnam Lovell NBF Securities Inc 2000–11, md Jefferies Int 2007–11, dir Pakenham Ptnrs 2011–; tstee Ireland Fund of GB 1989–2005, chm and tstee Lonford Tst 2002–, tstee Pilgrim Tst 2014–; *Books* The Gathering Bunker (1996), A Green Too Far (1998); *Clubs* MCC, Hurlingham, Rye Golf, Walton Heath Golf; *Style—* Kevin Pakenham

PAKENHAM, Thomas Frank Dermot; *see:* Longford, 8 Earl of

PAKENHAM, Tom; *Educ* Univ of Cambridge; *Career* admitted slr 2004; co-fndr (with Jonny Goldstone, *qv*) Green Tomato Cars 2006–; memb Law Soc; *Style—* Tom Pakenham, Esq; ✉ website www.greentomatocars.com

PALACHE, Robert; s of Ralph Palache, of London, and Rosalind, *née* Simons; *b* 11 November 1957; *Educ* JFS Sch, Magdalene Coll Cambridge (MA); *Family* 2 da (Abigail b 22 Aug 1984, Dora b 24 May 1987); *Career* slr Coward Chance 1982–87, ptnr Clifford Chance 1988–98 (slr 1987), dir and jt head Securitisation Div Nomura International plc 1998–2001, md and head of real estate, corporate securitization and infrastructure finance Barclays Capital 2001–06, md Global Capital Markets Div Morgan Stanley 2006–08, exec dir Dept for Business, Innovation and Skills 2008–; FRSA; *Recreations* reading, sports and theatre; *Clubs* City of London; *Style—* Robert Palache, Esq

PALASTANGA, Prof Nigel Peter; s of Joseph Peter Palastanga (d 2000), of Cwmbran, Wales, and Mildred Joan Palastanga (d 1988); *b* 10 May 1947; *Educ* Sladen Sch Kidderminster, RAMC Apprentices' Coll Ash Vale, Army Sch of Physiotherapy Woolwich, King's Coll Hosp Sch of Physiotherapy London, Open Univ (BA), NE London Poly (DMS), Univ of London (MA); *m* 1 April 1976, Dorothy Barbara; 1 da (Hazel b 24 Feb 1977), 1 s (Tom b 30 Jan 1981); *Career* physiotherapist (RAMC) Royal Herbert Hosp Woolwich 1969–71, student physiotherapy teacher KCH London 1971–73, teacher Army Sch of Physiotherapy Woolwich 1973–76, asst princ Sch of Physiotherapy Addenbrooke's Hosp Cambridge 1980–88 (physiotherapy teacher 1976–80), princ Cardiff Sch of Physiotherapy 1988–2005, dean Sch of Healthcare Studies Univ of Wales Coll of Med Cardiff 1995–2002, pro-vice-chllr Univ of Wales Coll of Med 1999–2005, pro-vice-chllr Cardiff Univ 2004–07, pro-vice-chllr Univ of Wales 2008–12; fell: Chartered Soc of Physiotherapy, Higher Educn Acad; *Books* Clayton's Electrotherapy (8 edn 1982, 9 edn 1986), Modern Manual Therapy (2 edn 1995), Anatomy and Human Movement (1989, 6 edn 2012), Anatomy and Human Movement Pocketbook (2008); *Recreations* sailing, walking, rugby; *Style—* Prof Nigel Palastanga

PALCA, Julia; *Educ* Durham Univ; *m* Nicolas Stevenson; 3 s; *Career* ptnr and conslt Olswang LLP until 2012; chm: Royal Free Charity 2009–, Macmillan Cancer Support 2010– (tstee 2001–); tstee: Koestler Tst until 2015, Nuffield Tst, Olswang Fndn; special advsr Prison Reform Tst; *Style—* Ms Julia Palca; ✉ Macmillan Cancer Support, 89 Albert Embankment, London SE1 7UQ

PALEY, Maureen; da of Alfred Paley, and Sylvia Paley; *b* 17 September 1959, NYC; *Educ* Sarah Lawrence Coll Bronxville NY, Brown Univ RI (Minnie Helen Hicks Prize, Pentax Prize, BA), RCA (MA); *Career* worked in photography and film 1980–84, freelance curator 1980–84; fndr and dir Maureen Paley (formerly Interim Art) 1984–; curator: Antidotes to Madness? (Riverside Studios London) 1986, Photography as Performance (Photographer's Gall London) 1986, Wall Works (The Cornerhouse Manchester) 1987, Symptoms of Interference, Conditions of Possibility: Ad Reinhardt, Joseph Kosuth, Felix Gonzalez-Torres (Camden Arts Centre London) 1994, Wall to Wall (Serpentine Gall, Southampton City Art Gall, Leeds City Art Gall) 1995, The Cauldron (Henry Morre Sculpture Tst Halifax); visiting lectr: RCA, Chelsea Coll of Art; other teaching positions incl: Bournemouth and Poole Coll of Art 1981–83, Architectural Assoc 1981–82; memb Frieze Art Fair Ctee 2003–13, patron and donor Tate, patron and donor ICA, fndr, donor and supporter Creative Industries Fedn, memb Patron Circle Michael Clark Co, memb Gallery Circle Nottingham Contemporary; contrib Open Sch East, individual friend Swiss Inst NYC, tstee Space London; benefactor: Serpentine Gallery, South London Gallery; patron: Whitechapel Gallery, Chisenhale Gallery, White Columns NYC, Artists Space NYC, The Showroom; donor: Camden Art Centre, RCA fund, Artangel Trust; supporter: Studio Voltaire, The Kitchen NYC, Peer London; memb Soc of London Art Dealers 2007; *Publications* Technique Anglaise (1991), Wall to Wall (1994), The Cauldron (1996), Gillian Wearing: Signs that say what you want them to say and not signs that say what someone else wants you to say (1997), Art London (1999, 2 edn 2000), Gillian Wearing: Family History (2007), Paul P. Peter Hujar (2008), Keith Arnatt works 1967–1996 in association with the Keith Arnatt Estate (2012); *Clubs* Annabel's, Groucho, Soho House, Shoreditch House, Dover Street Arts; *Style—* Miss Maureen Paley; ✉ 21 Herald Street, London E2 6JT (✆ 020 7729 4112, fax 020 7729 4113, e-mail info@maureenpaley.com, website www.maureenpaley.com)

PALIN, Michael Edward; CBE (2000); s of late Edward Palin, and late Mary Palin; *b* 5 May 1943; *Educ* Shrewsbury, BNC Oxford (BA); *m* 16 April 1966, Helen Margaret, *née* Gibbins; 2 s (Thomas Edward b 8 Oct 1968, William Michael b 19 Nov 1970), 1 da (Rachel Mary b 13 Jan 1975); *Career* actor and writer; winner Michael Balcon Award for Outstanding Contribution to Cinema (jtly with Monty Python team) 1987, BBC Personality of the Year TRIC Awards 1998, Lifetime Achievement Award Br Comedy Awards 2002, BAFTA: Special Award 2005, Fellowship 2013; pres: RGS 2009–12, Campaign for Better Transport; *Theatre* playwright The Weekend (Strand Theatre) 1994, Monty Python Live (mostly) (O2) 2014, Travelling to Work Live Tour 2014, Michael Palin Live on Stage (Australia) 2015, The Thirty Years Tour 2015; *Television* actor and writer: Monty Python's Flying Circus (BBC) 1969–74, Ripping Yarns (BBC) 1976–80; actor: Three Men in a Boat (BBC) 1975, GBH (Channel Four) 1991, Remember Me (BBC) 2014; presenter and writer of expedition series: Around the World in 80 Days (BBC) 1989, Pole to Pole (BBC) 1992, Full Circle With Michael Palin (BBC) 1997 (Most Popular Documentary Series Nat TV Awards), Michael Palin's Hemingway Adventure (BBC) 1999, Sahara with Michael Palin 2002, Himalaya 2004 (Best Presenter Award RTS); presenter: Palin's Column (Channel Four) 1994, Palin on Redpath (BBC) 1997, The Bright Side of Life (BBC) 2000, The Ladies Who Loved Matisse 2003, Michael Palin and the Mystery of Hammershoi 2005, Michael Palin's New Europe 2007, Timewatch: The Last Day of WWI (BBC) 2008, Brazil with Michael Palin (BBC) 2012, The Wipers Times (BBC2) 2013, Michael Palin in Wyeth's World (BBC) 2013, Clangers (Narration) 2015, Michael Palin's Quest for Artemisia (BBC) 2015; *Films* actor and writer: And Now for Something Completely Different 1970, Monty Python and The Holy Grail 1974, Monty Python's Life of Brian 1979, Time Bandits 1980, Monty Python's The Meaning of Life 1982, American Friends 1991; actor: Jabberwocky 1976, A Private Function 1984, Brazil 1985, A Fish Called Wanda 1988 (Best Supporting Actor BAFTA Awards); actor, writer and co-prodr The Missionary 1983, Fierce Creatures 1997; *Books* Monty Python's Big Red Book (jtly, 1970), Monty Python's Brand New Book (jtly, 1973), Dr Fegg's Encyclopedia of All World Knowledge (jtly, 1984), Limericks (1985), Around the World in 80 Days (1989), Pole to Pole (1992), The Weekend (1994), Hemingway's Chair (novel, 1995), Full Circle (1997), Full Circle – The Photographs (1997), Michael Palin's Hemingway Adventure (1999), Sahara (2002), The Pythons Autobiography by the Pythons (jtly, 2003), Himalaya (2004, TV & Film Book of the Year Br Book Awards), Michael Palin Diaries 1969–79: The Python Years (2006), New Europe (2007), Michael Palin Diaries 1980–88: Halfway to Hollywood (2009), Brazil (2012), The Truth (novel, 2012), Diaries: Travelling to Work 1988–1998 (2014); for children: Small Harry and the Toothache Pills (1981), The Mirrorstone (1986), The Cyril Stories (1986); co-writer Ripping Yarns (1978) and More Ripping Yarns (1980); *Clubs* Athenaeum; *Style—* Michael Palin, Esq, CBE; ✉ c/o Mayday Management PS Ltd, 34 Tavistock Street, London WC2E 7PB (✆ 020 7497 1100, e-mail paulbird@maydaymgt.co.uk)

PALING, Robert Roy; s of Reginald Roy Paling (d 1978), and Margery Emily, *née* Lyford (d 2004); *b* 10 June 1940; *Educ* Shrivenham Sch, Faringdon Sch, The Coll Swindon; *m* 20 Feb 1965, Judith Dow, da of Reginald Albert Sheppard (d 1985); 1 da (Portia Dow (Mrs Duncan Trow) b 1968); *Career* sr conveyancing exec Lemon & Co Slrs Swindon 1980–96 (conslt 1996–); ptnr Dow Sheppard Relocation 1996–2015; cmmr for oaths 1994–2004; compiled Mortgage Guide for CBI Employee Relocation Cncl 1988; sr Jt-Master Shrivenham Beagles 1969–2004; memb: Old Berks Hunt, Assoc of Masters of Harriers and Beagles 1970, Soc Licensed Conveyancers 1987–2004; assoc Inst of Legal Execs 1965–2004, tstee The Roman Research Tst 1991–98; *Recreations* hunting, riding, shooting, polo; *Clubs* Cavalry and Guards, Cirencester Park Polo, Edgeworth Polo; *Style—* Robert Paling, Esq; ✉ Orchard House, High Street, Shrivenham, Swindon, Wiltshire SN6 8AW (✆ 01793 782789)

PALLANT, John; s of Dennis Pallant, of Southsea, Hants, and Doreen, *née* Hirst; *b* 10 August 1955; *Educ* St John's Coll Southsea, Univ of Reading (BA); *Career* copywriter: Griffin & George Ltd 1977, Acroyd Westwood Associates 1977, Boase Massimi Pollitt 1978, Collett Dickenson Pearce 1980, Gold Greenless Trott 1982; copywriter and creative gp head Boase Massimi Pollitt 1983; Saatchi & Saatchi: copywriter 1988, gp head 1991, dep creative dir and Exec Bd dir 1995, creative dir 1996–97, jt exec creative dir 1997–98, dep exec creative dir 1999–2003, European creative dir 2003–; *Awards* D & AD awards (for TV, press, public service and poster campaigns): Gold 1985, Silver 1981 (two), 1985 (three), 1989 and 1992; Br TV awards: Silver 1981, Gold 1992; Cannes Int Advtg awards: Silver 1981, Bronze 1988, Gold 1992; Campaign Press awards: Gold 1985, Silver 1985 (two), 1989 and 1990; Campaign Poster awards: Gold 1985, Silver 1983, 1985 (two), 1990 (two); Independent Radio awards Silver 1990; NY One Show awards Gold and Best of Show award 1992 and Silver 1997; IMSA Int Advtg awards Grand Prix for cinema 1992; *Style—* John Pallant, Esq; ✉ Saatchi & Saatchi, 80 Charlotte Street, London W1A 1AQ (✆ 020 7636 5060 ext 3501, fax 020 7637 8489)

PALLETT, Julian Charles; s of Trevor William Pallett, and Hilary, *née* Williams; *b* 22 September 1958, Solihull; *Educ* Waverley GS Birmingham, Wadham Coll Oxford (MA); *Career* slr; Gowling WLG (UK) LLP (formerly Wragge & Co LLP): articled clerk 1981–83, asst slr/assoc 1983–90, ptnr (head of restructuring and corporate recovery) 1990–; memb: Law Soc 1983, Birmingham Law Soc 1983; memb Ironbridge Gorge Museum Tst, pro-chllr and chair of govrs Univ of Worcester 2008–15; Hon DLL Univ of Worcester; FRSA; *Recreations* music, history, architecture, running; *Style—* Julian Pallett, Esq; ✉ Gowling WLG (UK) LLP, 4 More London Riverside, London SE1 2AU (✆ 020 3636 7876, e-mail julian.pallett@gowlingwlg.com)

PALLEY, Eall Marcon (Marc); s of Dr Ahrn Palley (d 1993), of Zimbabwe, and Dr Claire Palley, *née* Swait; *b* 2 May 1954; *Educ* Clifton Coll, St John's Coll Oxford (MA); *m* 28 July 1979, Sabina Mary, da of Maj-Gen F W E Fursdon (d 2007); 3 s (Charles b 9 Dec 1982, Frederick b 6 June 1985, Harry b 15 May 1988); *Career* admitted slr 1978; Allen & Overy 1976–85, ptnr Berwin Leighton Paisner 1985–; *Style—* Marc Palley, Esq; ✉ Berwin Leighton Paisner LLP, Adelaide House, London Bridge, London EC4R 9HA (✆ 020 3400 1000, fax 020 3400 1111, e-mail marc.palley@blplaw.com)

PALLISER, Charles; *b* 11 December 1947; *Educ* Exeter Coll Oxford (BA), Wolfson Coll Oxford (BLitt); *Career* author; lectr: Dept of Eng Studies Univ of Strathclyde 1974–90, Univ of Rutgers (spring semester) 1986; *Publications* The Journal of Simon Owen (BBC radio play, 1982), The Quincunx (1989, Sue Kaufman prize for first fiction 1991), The Sensationist (1991), Obsessions – Writing (1991), Betrayals (1994), The Unburied (1999), Rustication (2013); also various scholarly articles published on George Eliot, Henry James and William Faulkner; *Style—* Charles Palliser, Esq; ✉ c/o Giles Gordon, Curtis Brown, 28/29 Haymarket, London SW1Y 4SP (0202 396 6600)

PALLISER, Prof David Michael; s of Herbert Leslie Palliser (d 1973), and Doris Violet, *née* Brown (d 1969); *b* 10 September 1939; *Educ* Bootham Sch York, Worcester Coll Oxford (MA, DPhil); *Career* asst princ Home Civil Serv 1961–64, res fell Keele Univ 1967–73, successively lectr, sr lectr and reader in economic history Univ of Birmingham 1974–85, G F Grant prof of history Univ of Hull 1985–94, prof of medieval history Univ of Leeds 1994–2004; hon visiting prof in history Univ of York; vice-pres Royal Historical Soc 2007–10, tstee Marc Fitch Fund 2012–; FRHistS 1974, FSA 1977; *Books* The Staffordshire Landscape (1976), Tudor York (1979), York (jtly, 1980), The Age of Elizabeth (1983, 2 edn 1992), The Cambridge Urban History of Britain, vol 1 (ed, 2000), The Diocesan Population Returns for 1563 and 1603 (jtly, 2005), Towns and Local Communities in Medieval and Early Modern England (2006), Medieval York 600–1540 (2014); *Style—* Prof D M Palliser, FSA; ✉ The Herb Garden, Great Street, Norton-Sub-Hamdon, Somerset TA14 6SJ (☎ 01935 881961)

PALMANO, Cindy; da of Roger Rennels Palmano, and Jean Frances Palmano; *b* 30 January 1963; *Educ* Enfield Chace Sch for Girls, Central Sch of Art; *Children* 1 s (Buster Luke Meeuwissen Palmano b 23 Dec 1987); *Career* photographer; work represented in the Nat Portrait Gallery and Nat Museum of Photography; magazine work incl: American, English Spanish and German Vogue, Tatler, Harpers & Queen, Face, Sunday Times, Vanity, Vanity Fair, Country Life; advtg work for clients incl: Fendi, Calugia & Giannelli, Jasper Conran, Georgina Godley, Fendissme, Shiseido International, Merloni, Tom Dixon, Kodak International, The Wool Board, Harvey Nichols, Debenham's, Pommery Champagne, Principals, Ignis, Kiss FM, Harrods; dir of music video for Tori Amos (four nominations MTV awards 1992), art dir 3 album campaigns for Tori Amos; *Exhibitions* 20th Century Aquisitions (Nat Portrait Gallery) 1986, First Int Photography Biennial (Nat Museum of Bradford) 1987, Fashion and Surrealism (NY Inst of Technol) 1988, The Photographers Gallery 1989, British Cncl 1989 and 1992, Arles 1991, Bliss (RCA) 1992, Positive View (Saatchi Gallery) 1994; *Style—* Miss Cindy Palmano; ✉ (☎ 020 7490 0630, fax 020 7490 3113)

PALMER, 4 Baron (UK 1933), of Reading, Co Berks; Sir Adrian Bailie Nottage Palmer; 4 Bt (UK 1916); s of Col the Hon Sir Gordon William Nottage Palmer, KCVO, OBE, TD (d 1989), and Lorna Eveline Hope Palmer, DL, *née* Bailie (d 2004); suc uncle, 3 Baron Palmer (d 1990); *b* 8 October 1951; *Educ* Eton, Univ of Edinburgh; *m* 1, 7 May 1977 (m dis 2004), Cornelia Dorothy Katharine, da of Rohan Nicholas Wadham, DFC, of Exning, Suffolk; 2 s (Hon Hugo Bailie Rohan b 1980, Hon George Gordon Nottage b 1985), 1 da (Hon Edwina Laura Marguerite (Hon Mrs Charlton) b 1982); m 2, Oct 2006 (m dis 2013), Loraine McMurrey; *Heir* s, Hon Hugo Palmer; *Career* mangr Assoc Biscuits Belgium 1974–77; farmer; sec Royal Caledonian Hunt 1989–2005, chm Historic Houses Assoc for Scotland 1994–99 (vice-chm 1993–94); memb Cncl: Historic Houses Assoc for Scotland 1980–99, Historic Houses Assoc 1981–99, Scottish Landowners Fedn 1987–93; Scottish rep European Landowning Orgn 1986–92, chm Country Sports Defence Tst 1994–; pres Br Assoc of Biofuels (BABFO) 2001–; memb Queen's Body Guard for Scotland (Royal Co of Archers) 1990–96; elected hereditary peer House of Lords 1999–, chm All Pty Gp on Energy Costs; sec Scottish Peers Assoc 2007–; *Recreations* gardening; *Clubs* New (Edinburgh), Pratt's; *Style—* The Rt Hon the Lord Palmer; ✉ Manderston, Duns, Berwickshire TD11 3PP (☎ 01361 883450, fax 01361 882010)

PALMER, Adrian Oliver; QC (1992); s of Richard Palmer, and Patricia, *née* Gambling; *b* 20 August 1950; *Educ* Clifton, St John's Coll Cambridge; *m* 1974, Rosemary, da of Mortimer Shaw; 1 da (Emily b 10 March 1978), 1 s (William b 8 Sept 1982); *Career* called to the Bar 1972, recorder (Western Circuit) 1992; dep High Ct Judge 1999, head of chambers; PNBA, PIBA; *Recreations* gardens, sheep, walking; *Style—* Adrian Palmer, Esq, QC; ✉ Guildhall Chambers, 22–26 Broad Street, Bristol BS1 2HG (☎ 0117 930 9000, fax 0117 930 3800, e-mail adrian.palmer@guildhallchambers.co.uk)

PALMER, Prof Andrew Clennel; s of Gerald Basil Coote Palmer (d 2004), and Muriel Gertrude, *née* Howes (d 1982); *b* 26 May 1938; *Educ* Royal Liberty Sch Romford, Univ of Cambridge (MA), Brown Univ USA (PhD); *m* 10 Aug 1963, Jane Rhiannon, da of George Ewart Evans; 1 da (Emily Abigail b 18 Sept 1971); *Career* lectr in mechanical engrg Univ of Liverpool 1965–67, lectr in engrg Univ of Cambridge 1967–75, chief engr R J Brown and Associates 1975–79, prof of civil engrg UMIST 1979–82, vice-pres engrg R J Brown and Associates 1982–85, md Andrew Palmer and Associates 1985–93, tech dir SAIC Ltd 1993–96; Jafar research prof of petroleum engrg Univ of Cambridge 1996–2005, Keppel prof Nat Univ of Singapore 2006–12; visiting prof Harvard Univ 2002–03; pres Pipeline Industries Guild 1998–2000; CEng, memb Soc of Petroleum Engrs, FICE 1986, FREng 1990, FRS 1994; *Books* Structural Mechanics (1976), Subsea Pipeline Engineering (with R A King, 2004), Dimensional Analysis and Intelligent Experimentation (2008), Arctic Offshore Engineering (with K R Croasdale, 2012), Introduction to Petroleum (2016); *Recreations* cooking, travel, languages, glassblowing; *Clubs* Athenaeum; *Style—* Prof Andrew Palmer, FRS, FREng; ✉ 200 Pasir Panjang Road, #02–15, Singapore 188571 (☎ 00 65 9836 1848, e-mail andrewpalmer241@gmail.com)

PALMER, Caroline Ann (Cally); CBE (2006); da of Christopher Palmer, of Calgary, Canada, and Ann, *née* Atkinson; *Educ* Woking Girls' GS, Univ of London (BA), London Business Sch (MSc); *m* 4 Oct 1986, Ian Julian Makowski, s of Julian Makowski; 2 s (Christopher b 24 Oct 1994, Julian b 6 June 1996), 1 da (Alexandra (twin) b 6 June 1996); *Career* Gen Mgmnt Trg Scheme SE Thames RHA 1980–83; SW Surrey RHA: hosp admin Haslemere & Dist Hosp March-Aug 1983, asst unit admin St Luke's Hosp 1983–85; Royal Free Hampstead NHS Tst (formerly Royal Free Hosp): dep gen mangr Acute Unit 1987–90 (assoc unit admin 1985–87), gen mangr Tst Implementation 1990–91, gen mangr Lawn Road Div 1991–94, dir of servs/dep chief exec 1994–98; chief exec Royal Marsden NHS Tst 1998–; sec to Tstees Royal Marsden Hosp Cancer Fund, dir RMH Cancer Fund Trading Co Ltd; memb: Cncl Inst of Cancer Research, London Business Sch Alumni Assoc; MHSM 1983; *Recreations* music, ballet, art; *Style—* Miss Cally Palmer, CBE; ✉ The Royal Marsden NHS Trust, Fulham Road, London SW3 6JJ (☎ 020 7352 8171, fax 020 7376 4809)

PALMER, Duncan Roderick; *b* 14 November 1958; *Educ* Leys Sch Cambridge, Westminster Coll (HND), Havard Business Sch (PMD); *Career* actg food and beverage mangr The Dubai International 1982–83 (asst food and beverage mangr 1981–82), res mangr Mandarin Oriental Macau 1984–86 (food and beverage mangr 1983–84), mangr Mandarin Oriental Manila 1986–88, res mangr The Oriental Bangkok 1988–89; gen mangr: Mandarin Oriental Jakarta 1989–95, The Savoy 1995–97, The Connaught 1997–2002, The Sukhothai Bangkok 2002–04; md The Langham Hotel London 2004–; Freeman City of London; Master Innholder, MHCIMA; *Style—* Duncan Palmer, Esq; ✉ Langham Hotel, 1c Portland Place, Regent Street, London W1B 1JA (☎ 020 7636 1000, fax 020 7436 1346)

PALMER, Dame Felicity Joan; DBE (2011, CBE 1993); *Educ* Erith GS, Guildhall Sch of Music and Drama (AGSM, FGSM), Hochschule für Musik Munich; *Career* mezzo-soprano; Kathleen Ferrier Meml Prize 1970; major appearances at concerts in: Britain, America, Belgium, France, Germany, Italy, Spain, Poland, Czechoslovakia, Russia; operatic appearances: London and throughout England, La Scala Milan, Paris, Bordeaux, Houston, Chicago, NY, San Francisco, Geneva, Amsterdam, Toronto, Leipzig, Madrid, Berne, Zürich, Frankfurt, Hanover, Vienna, Munich, Berlin, Tokyo; peformances incl: Last Night of the Proms 1987, First Night of the Proms 1999; recordings with maj record cos incl recital records and two Victorian ballad records; *Style—* Dame Felicity Palmer, DBE; ✉ c/o Intermusica, Chrystal Wharf, 36 Graham Street, London N1 8GJ (☎ 020 7608 9900)

PALMER, Geoffrey; OBE (2005); *b* 4 June 1927; *Educ* Highgate Sch; *Career* actor; *Theatre* incl: Difference of Opinion (Garrick), West of Suez (Royal Court), Savages (Royal Court), On Approval (Haymarket), Eden End (NT), Private Lives (Globe), St Joan (Old Vic), Tishoo (Wyndhams), Kafka's Dick (Royal Court), Piano (NT); *Television* incl: The Fall and Rise of Reginald Perrin, Butterflies, The Insurance Man, The Last Song, Absurd Person Singular, Fairly Secret Army, Seasons Greetings, A Question of Attribution, As Time Goes By, Alice Through the Looking Glass, Margaret Thatcher: The Long Walk to Finchley, Parade's End, Bert and Dickie, Henry IV Part II; *Films* incl: O Lucky Man, The Honorary Consul, Clockwise, A Zed and Two Noughts, A Fish Called Wanda, The Madness of George III, Her Majesty Mrs Brown, Tomorrow Never Dies, Anna and the King, Peter Pan, Piccadilly Jim, The Pink Panther 2, WE, Paddington Bear; *Recreations* fly fishing; *Clubs* Garrick; *Style—* Geoffrey Palmer, Esq, OBE

PALMER, Howard William Arthur; QC (1999); s of William Alexander Palmer, CBE, DL, of Bussock Wood, Newbury, and Cherry Anne, *née* Gibbs; *b* 24 June 1954; *Educ* Eton (scholarship, 1st Cricket XI), UC Oxford (MA), Coll of Law; *m* 1983, Catherine Margaret, da of late Brig T G H Jackson; 3 da (Laura b 11 March 1984, Emily b 25 Jan 1986, Harriet b 14 May 1991), 1 s (Thomas b 15 April 1988); *Career* called to the Bar 1977; lectr in law King's Coll London 1977–78, barrister-at-law 1978, recorder of the Crown Court 2006–; memb Cncl Univ of Reading 2008–; *Recreations* cricket, country sports, theatre, hedgelaying; *Clubs* MCC, Berkshire CCC; *Style—* Howard Palmer, Esq, QC; ✉ 2 Temple Gardens, Temple, London EC4Y 9AY (☎ 020 7822 1200, fax 020 7822 1300, e-mail hpalmer@2tg.co.uk)

PALMER, John; *Career* Euro ed The Guardian 1975–97; political dir European Policy Centre Brussels 1997–2006; secondments: dir Gtr London Enterprise Bd 1983–86, memb Bd London Tport 1985–86; author, experienced radio tv broadcaster; memb Advsy Cncl: European Policy Centre Brussels, Federal Tst; visiting fell European Inst Univ of Sussex; *Publications* European Without America (1989), Trading Place, the Future of the European Community (1990); *Style—* John Palmer, Esq; ✉ 74 Stretton Mansions, Glaisher Street, London SE8 3JP (☎ 020 8691 6551, e-mail john.anthony.palmer@gmail.com)

PALMER, Dr Keith Francis; OBE; s of Frank Palmer (d 1987), of Cardiff, and Gwenda Evelyn, *née* Merrick; *b* 26 July 1947; *Educ* Howardian HS Cardiff, Univ of Birmingham (BSc, PhD), Univ of Cambridge (Dip Devpt Econ); *m* 10 Aug 1974, Penelope Ann, *née* McDonagh; 4 da (Alexandra b 1977, Georgia b 1979, Katherine b 1981, Megan b 1982); *Career* NATO postdoctoral res fell Lamont Geophysical Observatory NY 1971–73, first asst sec (fin) Miny Fin Papua New Guinea 1974–78, with IMF/World Bank 1978–84, vice-chm investment banking N M Rothschild & Sons Ltd 1997–2002 (dir corp fin 1984–93, md corp fin 1993–97); chm Cambridge Economic Policy Associates Ltd, chm AgDevCo Ltd, chm Infra Co Hldgs Ltd; non-exec dir Monitor; tstee Kirkhouse Tst; *Recreations* geology, music, running; *Style—* Dr Keith Palmer, OBE; ✉ e-mail keith.palmer32@btinternet.com

PALMER, Martin Giles; s of Rev Derek George Palmer, and Celilie June, *née* Goddard; *b* 14 October 1953; *Educ* Hartcliff Comp Sch Bristol, Commonweal Comp Sch Swindon, Selwyn Coll Cambridge (MA); *m* 1, 27 Sept 1975 (m dis 2005), Sandra Ann, da of Rudi Fischer, of Aust; 1 s (James Richard b 25 June 1978), 1 da (Elizabeth Francis b 8 Dec 1981); m 2, 2 Sept 2006, Victoria Finlay; *Career* Church Missionary Soc vol Christian Children's Home Hong Kong 1972–73, nat pres Student Christian Movement while student of theol and religious studies Cambridge 1973–76, res work on Hong Kong for World Cncl of Churches Prog to Combat Racism and Hong Kong Res Project 1976–77, regnl organiser Christian Educn Movement Gtr Manchester 1977–79, fndr dir Centre for the Study of Religion and Educn in the Inner City Manchester 1977–83, dir Int Consultancy on Religion, Educn and Culture (clients incl WWF) 1983–, fndr dir Sacred Land Project 1997–; religious advsr to HRH Prince Philip (pres WWF Int) 1986–; fndr: Christian Stateman magazine 1978–, International Labour Reports magazine 1983–; co fndr: International Sacred Literature Tst 1990, Sacred Earth Drama 1991; sec gen Alliance of Religions and Conservation 1995–; co-chair UN/ARC Prog on Faiths and Climate Change and the Natural Environment; lectr worldwide, contrib to various magazines and papers and to radio and TV progs incl being religious corr for This Sunday (ITV) 1993; Sandford Award for Religious Radio 1996; fell Club of Rome 2012; *Books* incl: Faiths and Festivals (1984), Worlds of Difference (1985), Genesis or Nemesis (1988), Contemporary I Ching (1989), Taoism (1991), Dancing to Armageddon (1992), Living Christianity (1993), Tao Te Ching (1993), Chuang Tzu (1995), Sacred Britain (co-author, 1997), The Jesus Sutras (2001), Sacred History of Britain (2002), Faith and Conservation (co-author, 2003), The Times: Mapping History – World Religions (ed, 2004), Atlas of Religion (co-author, 2007), Sacred Land (2012), The Most Venerable Book – Shang Shu (2014); *Recreations* brass rubbing, numismatics, cooking, icons, anything Chinese; *Style—* Martin Palmer; ✉ ARC, 6 Gay Street, Bath BA1 2PH (e-mail martinp@arcworld.org)

PALMER, Prof Norman Ernest; CBE (2006), Hon QC (2010); s of Norman George Palmer, of Grays, Essex, and Muriel, *née* Walker; *b* 16 August 1948; *Educ* Palmer's Endowed Sch Grays, Magdalen Coll Oxford (Ford fndn scholar, exhibitioner, MA, Shepherd Prize, BCL); *m* 1, 1971 (m dis), Judith Ann Weeks; 1 da (Victoria Olivia b 1974); m 2, 1994, Ruth Redmond-Cooper; 1 da (Lilian Mary Rose b 1999); *Career* called to the Bar Gray's Inn 1973, in practice SE Circuit, head of chambers 2 Field Ct 1992–99; law reform cmmr Tasmania 1976–77; prof of law: Univ of Reading 1981–84 (head Dept of Law 1982–84), Univ of Essex 1984–90 (dean Faculty of Law 1985–88), Univ of Southampton 1990–91 (concurrently dep dean Faculty of Law); UCL: prof of commercial law 1991–2001, acad dir Inst for Philanthropy 2000–01, prof of the law of art and cultural property 2001–04 (emeritus prof 2004–), visiting prof of law KCL 2005–, adjunct prof of law Univ of Tasmania 2008–, visiting prof of law Univ of Notre Dame 2014–; E W Turner Meml lectr and visiting prof of law Univ of Tasmania 1999; Mallesons visiting fell Univ of Western Aust 1993, Ross Parsons visiting prof Univ of Sydney 1990 and 1991; sec and jt dir Int Cultural Property Soc 1990–95, princ academic advsr Inst of Art and Law 1995–, accredited mediator Centre for Dispute Resolution 1999–; chm: Ministerial Advsy Panel on Illicit Trade in Cultural Objects 2000–05, Treasure Valuation Ctee 2001–, Departmental Working Gp on Human Remains in Public Collections 2001–03, ArtResolve 2014–; pres Fndn for Int Cultural Diplomacy 2006–; memb: Treasure Trove Reviewing Ctee 1996–97, Standing Conference on Portable Antiquities and Portable Antiquities Working Gp 1996–, Treasure Valuation Ctee 1997–, Spoliation Advsy Panel 2000–; ed-in-chief: Int Jl of Cultural Property 1990–95, Art Antiquity and Law 1996–; DUniv (hc) Geneva 2005; FRSA 1999, Hon RICS 2004, FSA 2005; *Publications* Bailment (1979, 3 edn 2009), Halsbury's Laws of England (contrib, 1984–99), Emden's Construction Law (5 vols, jtly 1990), Product Liability in the Construction Industry (with E McKendrick, 1993), Interests in Goods (ed with E McKendrick and contrib, 1993, 2 edn 1998), Butterworth's Manual of Construction Law (with Ruth Redmond-Cooper and S Bickford-Smith, 1993), Encyclopaedia of Forms and Precedents (contrib, 1994, 2000 and 2004), Laws of Australia (contrib, 1995), Art Loans (1997), The Recovery of Stolen Art (with Ruth Redmond-Cooper, Prof A Hudson and Sir Anthony Mason, 1998), Cultural Property Statutes (1999,

2 edn 2004), Museums and the Holocaust: Law, Principles and Practice (2000), English Private Law (contrib, 2000 and 2004, 2 edn 2007), The Individual Liability of Museum Personnel (2011), Art Advocacy and Adventure (2015); also author of numerous papers in various learned journals and periodicals; *Recreations* literature, archaeology, biography, antique motor cars, memorial verse; *Style—* Prof Norman Palmer, CBE, QC, FSA; ✉ 3 Stone Buildings, Lincolns Inn, London WC2A 3XL (☎ 020 7242 4937, e-mail npalmer@3sb.law.co.uk)

PALMER, Prof Richard M; *Educ* Univ of London (BDS, PhD); *Career* lectr Royal Dental Hosp London 1978–85, currently prof and head of restorative dentistry GKT Dental Inst KCL; pres British Soc of Periodontology 2003–04; memb: Assoc of Dental Implantology, British Soc of Periodontology, European Assoc of Osseointegration, Int Assoc for Dental Research; Colgate Prize 1986, Colyer Prize RSM 1986; FDSRCS 1979, FDSRCSE 1997; *Style—* Prof Richard M Palmer; ✉ GKT Dental Institute, Guy's Tower, King's College London, Guy's Hospital, London SE1 9RT

PALMER, Prof Robert Leslie; s of Reginald John Freeman Palmer (d 1987), of Leamington Spa, and Marion May, *née* Sims (d 1988); *b* 15 March 1944; *Educ* Warwick Sch, St George's Med Sch Univ of London (MB BS); *m* 19 July 1969, Mary Violet, da of Frank Carter, of Stamford Hill, London; 1 da (Rebecca b 23 Oct 1971); *Career* res worker and hon lectr St George's Hosp Med Sch Univ of London 1971–73, lectr in psychiatry St Mary's Hosp Med Sch 1974–75; Univ of Leicester: sr lectr in psychiatry 1975–2005, conslt psychiatrist and hon prof of psychiatry 2005–; ed European Eating Disorders Review 1996–; author of papers on psychiatry and psychosomatic med especially clinical eating disorders; former examiner: for membership RCPsych, Univ of London final MB examination, Nat Univ of Singapore M Med Sci; MRCPsych 1972, FRCPsych 1984; *Books* Anorexia Nervosa: a guide for sufferers and their families (1980 and 1989), Helping People with Eating Disorders (2000); *Recreations* reading, jogging, birdwatching; *Style—* Prof Robert Palmer; ✉ University Department of Psychiatry, Brandon Mental Health Unit, Leicester General Hospital, Gwendolen Road, Leicester LE5 4PW (☎ 0116 225 6211, fax 0116 225 6235, e-mail rlp@le.ac.uk)

PALMER, Prof Stuart Beaumont; s of Frank Beaumont Palmer (d 1990), and Florence Beryl, *née* Wilkinson (d 1995); *b* 6 May 1943, Ilkeston, Derbys; *Educ* Ilkeston GS, Univ of Sheffield (BSc, PhD, DSc); *m* 1966, Susan Mary, da of Arthur Clay; 2 s (Richard Stuart b 30 May 1967, Anthony John b 7 May 1969), 1 da (Katherine Mary b 20 Dec 1973); *Career* reader in applied physics Univ of Hull 1967–87; Univ of Warwick: prof of experimental physics 1987–2010, chm Physics Dept 1989–2001, pro-vice-chllr 1995–2001, acting vice-chllr 2001, dep vice-chllr 2001–10, emeritus prof 2010–; visiting prof: Univ of Grenoble 1982–83, Queen's Univ Ontario 1986; adjunct prof Queensland Univ of Technology Brisbane Australia 2011–; sec gen Int Union of Pure and Applied Physics 2012–14; ed-in-chief Nondestructive Testing and Evaluation (jl); memb Cncl Cardiff Univ 2014– (chair 2016–); tstee Univs Superannuation Scheme 2016–; Hon DSc Univ of Warwick 2011; FInstP 1978 (hon sec 2009–), FInstNDT 1982, FIEE 1992, CEng 1992, FRSA 1999, FREng 2000; *Publications* Advanced University Physics (with M S Rogalski, 1995, 2 edn 2005), Quantum Physics (with M S Rogalski, 1999), Solid State Physics (with M S Rogalski, 2000), Encyclopaedia Britannica (ed Physics section, 1968–89); also author of over 270 research papers; *Recreations* tennis, sailing, music; *Clubs* Athenaeum, Hull Sailing, Coventry Flying, Warwick Tennis; *Style—* Prof Stuart Palmer; ✉ Max Gate, Forrest Road, Kenilworth, Warwickshire CV8 1LT; University of Warwick, International Manufacturing Centre, Coventry CV4 7AL (☎ 02476 574004)

PALMER, Sue; *b* 1948, Manchester; *Educ* Moray House Coll Edinburgh (CertEd), Open Univ (Dip), Univ of Manchester (MEd); *Career* primary teacher and head teacher 1974–83, educnl writer and speaker 1983–; gen ed Longman Book Project 1990–93, ind conslt various educnl publishers, BBC, Nat Literacy Strategy and other literacy orgns 1994–2006, contrib Times Educnl Supplement and nat press, columnist Child Education 1995–2007, researcher, writer and speaker on child devpt in the modern world 1998–; pres Montessori AMI UK 2009–; organiser: Balance Campaign 1990, Time To Teach Campaign 2006; chair: Scottish Play Cmmn 2009–13, Scottish Play Policy Forum 2009–13, Upstart Scotland Campaign 2015–; memb: UK Reading Assoc 1976–90, Advsy Gp Talk To Your Baby Nat Literacy Tst 2002–09, Educnl Writers' Gp Soc of Authors 2005–07; ambass Reading is Fundamental Nat Literacy Tst; tstee Play Scotland 2010–14; patron: Save Childhood Movement, English Speaking Bd, Children's Football Assoc, Carefree Kids, The Children's Wood; assoc Basic Skills Agency; FRSA 2001, fell English Assoc 2006 (tstee 1999–2006); *Publications* over 200 educnl books, TV programmes and software packages; Foundations of Literacy (2005, 4 edn 2014), Toxic Childhood: how the modern world is damaging our children and what we can do about it (2006, revised and updated 2015), Detoxing Childhood (2007), 21st Century Boys (2010), 21st Century Girls (2014), Upstart: the case for raising the school starting age and providing what the under-sevens really need (2016); *Recreations* books, films, campaigning for children's right to active, outdoor play; *Style—* Ms Sue Palmer; ✉ c/o LBA Literary Agency, 91 Great Russell Street, London WC1B 3PS (e-mail sue@suepalmer.co.uk, website www.suepalmer.co.uk)

PALMER, Prof Timothy Noel (Tim); CBE (2015); s of Alfred Henry Palmer (d 1987), of Oxshott, Surrey, and Anne Josephine, *née* Hayes (d 2001); *b* 31 December 1952, Kingston upon Thames, Surrey; *Educ* Wimbledon Coll, Univ of Bristol (BSc), Wolfson Coll Oxford (DPhil, DSc); *m* 21 Oct 1978, Gillian, da of Philip Dyer; 3 s (Samuel James b 27 Jan 1985, Gregory Thomas b 19 Nov 1988, Brendan George b 13 Sept 1993); *Career* visiting scientist Univ of Washington 1981–82, PSO Meteorological Office 1978–86, div head European Centre for Medium-Range Weather Forecasts 1986–; co-ordinator EU Provost and Demeter Climate Projects, co-chair UN/World Meteorological Orgn (WMO) Clivar Scientific Steering Gp; Royal Soc 2010 anniversary research prof 2010–, professorial fell Jesus Coll Oxford 2010–; memb External Advsy Bd: Earth Inst Columbia Univ, Hadley Centre; lead author Third Assessment Report Intergovernmental Panel on Climate Change, also author of over 160 peer-reviewed pubns and two books; pres Royal Meteorological Soc 2010–; Royal Soc Esso Energy Award, Royal Meteorological Soc Buchan Award, American Meteorological Soc Charney Award, American Meteorological Soc Carl Gustav Rossby Medal 2010, Inst of Physics Dirac Gold Medal for theoretical physics 2014; fell American Meteorological Soc, FRMetS 1978, FRS 2003, memb Academia Europaea 2004, foreign memb American Philosophical Soc 2015; *Recreations* golf, cycling, skiing, playing guitar; *Clubs* W Berks Golf; *Style—* Prof Tim Palmer, CBE; ✉ Atmospheric, Oceanic and Planetary Physics, University of Oxford, Parks Road, Oxford OX1 3PU (☎ 01865 272897, fax 01865 272923, e-mail t.n.palmer@atm.ox.ac.uk)

PALMER, (Ann) Veronica Margaret; OBE (1993, MBE 1977); da of late Luke Murray, of Trim, Co Meath, Ireland, and Mary, *née* Neville; *b* 20 March 1940; *Educ* Convent of Mercy Trim; *m* Barrie Palmer, s of Arthur Alfred Palmer, and Dorothy Palmer; 3 da (Judith, Susan, Linda); *Career* student teacher 1958–61; RAF 1961–78, ret as Sqdn Ldr 1978; Parly sec Brewers' Soc 1981–88, DG Confedn of Passenger Transport UK 1989–2001, chm NI Transport Holding Co 2005–11 (dir 2002–); non-exec dir Arriva plc 2001–09; memb Cmmn for Integrated Transport 1999–2002, memb Bd BTA 2000–03; Freeman City of London, Liveryman Worshipful Co of Carmen 1997; *Recreations* hill walking, reading, theatre and horse racing; *Clubs* RAF; *Style—* Mrs Veronica Palmer, OBE; ✉ Tully House, Beachamwell Road, Cockley Cley, Norfolk PE37 8AR (☎ 01760 725496)

PALMER OF CHILDS HILL, Baron (Life Peer UK 2011), of Childs Hill in the London Borough of Barnet; Monroe Edward Palmer; OBE (1981); s of William Polikoff (d 1994), of Westcliff, Essex, and Sybil, *née* Gladstein (d 1980); *b* 30 November 1938; *Educ* Orange Hill GS; *m* 21 Jan 1962, Susette Sandra, da of Jeanne Hall, of London; 2 s (John b 1963, Andrew b 1965), 1 da (Fiona b 1981); *Career* former ptnr Silver Altman; treas Lib Pty 1977–83, cllr London Borough of Barnet 1986–2014, Parly candidate (Lib Dem) Hastings & Rye 1992 and 1997; FCA; *Recreations* politics, riding, fishing, reading; *Clubs* Nat Lib; *Style—* The Lord Palmer of Childs Hill, OBE; ✉ House of Lords, London SW1A 0PW

PALOMBA, Louise J; *née* Pritchard; *b* 9 July 1964, S Wales; *Educ* Leicester Poly, Univ of Cambridge; *m*; 2 c; *Career* architect; Leonard Manasseh Partnership 1985–86, Panter Hudspith Architects 1989–91, Rogers Stirk Harbour & Partners (formerly Richard Rogers Partnership) 1990–; *Projects* incl: Channel 4 TV HQ London, Strasbourg Ct of Human Rights, Bordeaux Law Cts, Thames Valley Univ Learning Resource Centre Slough, Lloyds Register of Shipping London, Heathrow Airport Terminal 5, Madrid Airport, Mossbourne Community Acad Hackney, Berkeley Hotel London; competitions: Euston Station, Oslo Airport, Tadawul HQ, Skywalk Project, Deptford Project; *Style—* Ms Louise Palomba; ✉ Rogers Stirk Harbour & Partners, Thames Wharf, Rainville Road, London W6 9HA

PALUMBO, Baron (Life Peer UK 1991), of Walbrook in the City of London; Peter Garth Palumbo; s of late Rudolph Palumbo, and Elsie Palumbo; *b* 20 July 1935; *Educ* Eton, Worcester Coll Oxford (MA); *m* 1, 1959, Denia (d 1986), da of late Maj Lionel Wigram; 1 s, 2 da; m 2, 1986, Hayat, er da of late Kamel Morowa; 2 da (Hon Petra Louise (The Lady Lovat) b 1989, Hon Lana Rose b 1991), 1 s (Hon Philip Rudolph b 1992); *Career* chm: Tate Gallery Fndn 1986–87, Painshill Park Tst Appeal 1986–96, Arts Cncl of GB 1989–94, Serpentine Gallery 1994–2014 (chm emeritus 2014–); tstee: Mies van der Rohe Archive 1977–, Tate Gallery 1978–85, Whitechapel Art Gallery Fndn 1981–87, Natural History Museum 1994–2004, Design Museum 1995–2005; memb Cncl Royal Albert Hall 1995–99, chm jury Pritzker Architecture Prize 2004–16; tstee and hon treas Writers' and Scholars' Educnl Tst 1984–99, dir and memb Bd Andy Warhol Fndn for the Visual Arts 1994–97; chllr Univ of Portsmouth 1992–2000; govr: LSE 1976–94, Royal Shakespeare Theatre 1995–2000, Whitgift Sch 2002–10 (advsr emeritus Bd of Govrs 2010–); Patronage of the Arts Award Cranbrook Acad of Arts Detroit 2002; Liveryman Worshipful Co of Salters; Hon DLitt Univ of Portsmouth 1993; Hon FRIBA, Hon FFB 1994, Hon FIStructE 1994; Nat Order of the Southern Cross (Federal Repub of Brazil) 1993; *Recreations* music, travel, gardening, reading; *Clubs* White's, Pratt's, Athenaeum, Garrick, Knickerbocker; *Style—* The Lord Palumbo; ✉ 2 Astell Street, London SW3 3RU (☎ 020 7351 7371)

PANAYI, Prof Gabriel Stavros; s of Stavros Panayi, of Cyprus, and Maria, *née* Tarsides; *b* 9 November 1940; *Educ* Royal GS Lancaster, Gonville & Caius Coll Cambridge (Sir Lionel Whitby Medal), St Mary's Hosp Med Sch London (ScD, MD, Max-Bonn Pathology Medal); *m* 11 March 1973, Alexandra, da of Alexander Jourrou; 2 s (Stavros b 5 July 1977, Alexander b 8 Feb 1982); *Career* house physician Queen Elizabeth Hosp Welwyn Garden City 1965–66, house surgn St Mary's Hosp London 1966, SHO in medicine Gen Hosp Nottingham 1966, SHO in pathology Central Middx Hosp London 1967, jr res fell MRC St Mary's and Kennedy Inst of Rheumatology London 1967–69, clinical res fell Northern Gen Hosp Edinburgh 1970–73; GKT (formerly UMDS): Arthritis and Rheumatism Cncl (ARC) lectr 1973–76, ARC sr lectr 1976–80, ARC prof of rheumatology 1980–; RSM: former sec Exec Ctee Section for Medicine, Experimental Medicine and Therapeutics, pres Section for Clinical Immunology and Allergy; former memb Exec Ctee Heberden Soc; BSR: pres 2000–02, memb Exec Ctee, Heberden orator; Kave Berglund lectr Univ of Lund, Nana Svartz Lectr Swedish Acad of Med; memb: BSI, AASI, American Coll of Rheumatology; FRCP; *Books* Annual Research Review of Rheumatoid Arthritis (1977–81), Immunopathogenesis of Rheumatoid Arthritis (1979), Essential Rheumatology for Nurses and Therapists (1980), Scientific Basis of Rheumatology (1982), Seronegative Spondyloarthropathies Clinics in Rheumatic Diseases (1985), Immunogenetics (1985); *Recreations* photography, painting, reading; *Style—* Prof Gabriel Panayi; ✉ Nuffield House, Guy's Hospital, London SE1 9RT (☎ 020 7188 5880, fax 020 7188 5883, e-mail gabriel.panayi@kcl.ac.uk)

PANAYIOTOU, Panos; *b* 1953; *m* 1, 1973 (m dis), Svanhvit Olafsdottir; 1 da (Astria Lydia b 1985); m 2, 2007, Antonia Poiitaridou; *Career* architect; Scott Brownrigg & Turner Ltd: joined 1982, dir 1990–2013, memb Bd of Dirs 1993–2013, design dir until 2013; work incl: Lulu Leisure Island Abu Dhabi, designs and implementation for refurbishment of Berkeley Square House London 1981, design and implementation 7 Dials residential devpt Fairfield Court Covent Garden 1988, designs for Digital's Southern Logistics Centre Reading 1988, design and implementation for offices and residential devpt Orange Street London 1989, design and implementation Jardin House Crutched Friars City of London, design and implementation BP Engineering HQ Uxbridge, concept design BBC HQ White City, masterplanning and design concept Camden Goods Yard, design proposals and implementation of office devpt Denison House Victoria London 1990, masterplan major office and retail park Athens 1994, Mythos Park (theme park) Athens 1995, leisure and sports resort Mallorca 1997, design and implementation for Elysium Resort Hotel Paphos, Napa Plaza Hotel Ayia Napa, Amathus Vacation Resort Cyprus; fndr Panos Panayiotou + Assocs Designs; work incl: redevelopment for the Larnaca Marina, award-winning projects of Pearl of Limassol and Duma designs; RIBA 1981, ARCUK 1981; *Publications* High Rise Buildings (for Russian Architectural Magazine); *Recreations* gliding; *Style—* Panos Panayiotou; ✉ Panos Panayiotou + Associates, Leontiou A 254, Maximos Court Office 17, 3020 Limassol Cyprus (☎ 00 35 725 333 394, fax 00 35 725 333 394, e-mail panos@ppa-architects.com, website www.ppa-architects.com)

PANCHENKO, Oxana; da of Vladimir Borisovitch Panchenko (d 1988), of Ukraine, and Valentina Timofeyerna, *née* Nychoroshkova; *b* 28 November 1970, Kiev, Ukraine; *Educ* Kiev Ballet Sch; *m* 7 April 1995, Jeremy Seth Gilbert, s of Terry Gilbert; *Career* dancer; Kiev Opera House 1988–90, sr soloist with English Nat Ballet 1990–93, Munich Ballet 1993–95, modelling work 1995–97, City Ballet of London 1997 and 2000, Wayne Sleep's Aspects of Dance 1999, K Ballet 2001, George Piper Dances 2001–, Adventures in Motion Pictures 2003–04; featured in The Rough Guide to Choreography (Channel 4) 2004, asst Strictly Bolshoi documentary (Ballet Boyz Prodns) 2007; *Performances* with Kiev Opera House: Two Friends of Kitri in Don Quixote, Swan Lake, Ophelia in Hamlet, Juliet in Romeo and Juliet, Effirn in La Sylphide, roles in La Bayadere; with English Nat Ballet: Olga in Onegin, Bianca in The Taming of the Shrew, Zivia in Romeo and Juliet by Ashton, Act III Pas de Trois in La Bayadere, Peasant Pas de Deux and Myrtha in Giselle, Big Swans and Pas de Trois in Swan Lake, Apollo by Balanchine, Snow Queen, Mirlitons and Arabian Dance in The Nutcracker, the Waltz in Les Sylphides, Zobeide in Sherherazade, White Girls in Etudes, Pas de Quatre in Raymonda, Autumn Fairy in Cinderella; with Munich Ballet: princ roles in Sinfonietta and Svadebka by Kylian, Brief Fling by Twyla Tharp, Symphony in C by Balanchine, Complete Consort by Bintley, Swan Lake, Giselle, The Nutcracker, Don Quixote, A Midsummer Night's Dream; with City Ballet of London: princ role in The Sleeping Beauty, princ role in Sinfonietta Giocosa, Five Tangos by Hans Van Manen, Entre Dos Aguas by Robert North, solo in TBA by Christopher Hampson, *qv*, Ghost of Christmas Past in Christmas Carol by Christopher Hampson; with Wayne Sleep's Aspects of Dance: Dineresade by Christopher Hampson, solo in Dragon Fly, Pas de Deux in Sleeping Beauty, Canciones by Christopher Hampson; with K Ballet: Rhapsody by Ashton, Six Faces by Adam Cooper; with George Piper Dances: Steptext by William Forsythe, Sigue by Paul Lightfoot, Moments of Plastic Jubilation by Michael Nunn, *qv*, and William Trevitt, *qv*, Truly Great Thing by Charles Linehan, Lady Barnard in Other Mens Wives by Matthew Hart, *qv*, Mesmerics by

Christopher Wheeldon, Trio by Russell Maliphant, *qv*, Ophelia in Non Exuent by Cathy Marston, Approximate Sonata I, V by William Forsythe, Broken Fall by Russell Maliphant, Follow By William Trevitt; The Queen in Swan Lake (with Adventures in Motion Pictures) 2003–04; other performances incl: Amox 2007, Riapertura 2007 (both Ballet Boyz Gala Royal Festival Hall), Mesmerics 2007, Propeller 2007 (both with Morphoses), Greatest Hits (Sadler's Wells Theatre); *Awards* Outstanding Performance Time Out Award 2001 (for Steptext), Outstanding Female Classical Artist Critics Circle National Dance Award 2003; *Recreations* travel, music, reading, yoga, films, dogs; *Style—* Mrs Oxana Panchenko; ✉ George Piper Dances, Sadler's Wells Theatre, Rosebery Avenue, London EC1R 4TN (☏ 020 7278 5508)

PANDE, Dr Shiv Kumar; MBE (1989), JP (Liverpool 1982), DL (Merseyside 2002); *b* Jawad, India; *Educ* HS Bombay, Inter-Sci Jai Hind Coll Bombay, Vikram Univ Ujjian (MB BS), Univ of Indore (MS); *Career* hosp appts Indore, Gwalior and Bombay 1963–70 (lectr in surgery Med Coll Jabalpur 1968–71), SHO A&E Dept Royal Albert Edward Infirmary Wigan 1971; registrar in cardiothoracic surgery: London Chest Hosp 1972, Royal Liverpool Children's, Broadgreen and Fazakerley Hosps Liverpool 1972–74; A&E med asst various Liverpool hosps 1974, clinical med offr Child Health and Family Planning St Helens and Knowsley HA 1974–95, princ in gen practice Liverpool 1976– (trainee 1974–75, locum/ptnr 1975–76); chm int seminars Delhi (Family Planning in India) 1990 and Cairo (Recent Advances in Treatment of AIDS) 1992; memb GMC 1994– (treas 1999–), assoc memb Fitness to Pracice Panel GMC 2003–; Overseas Doctors Assoc: nat vice-chm 1987–93, chm Merseyside and Cheshire Div 1994–96, nat gen sec 1996–; sec (N region) Indo-Br Assoc 1982–; advsr and presenter This is your Right? (Granada TV) 1980–92; memb Advsy Panel: Radio Merseyside 1982–87, BBC North TV 1983–88; interviewed variously for local, nat and int press, radio and TV; fndr memb Inter Faith Merseyside; memb (N Region) BAFTA, memb Med Journalists Assoc/Assoc of Broadcasting; Lloyds TSB Asian Jewel Award 2004; FRIPHH 1988, MFCH 1990, FRCGP 2003 (MRCGP 1996); *Recreations* cricket (doctor on duty at One Day Internationals and Test Matches at Lancs CCC since 1984), fundraising for charity; *Style—* Dr Shiv Pande, MBE; ✉ e-mail shiv.pande@talk21.com.uk and shivpande@yahoo.com, website www.merseyworld.com/iba/

PANDOR, Dr Shabir Ahmed Gulam; s of Gulam Mahomed Pandor, of Lusaka, Zambia, and Khadija Badat; *b* 1 January 1955; *Educ* Epsom Coll, UCL (LDS RCS, BDS), MFGDP(UK), MFHom (Dip Homotox); *m* 17 Dec 1985 (m dis), (Maria) Suzy, da of Burghart Ferenc (d 1991), of Budapest, Hungary; 1 da (Aneesa b 21 Jan 1988); *Career* assoc dentist in practice: Chatham Kent 1980–81, Kingsway London 1979–80 and 1981–85; in own surgery Harley St 1985–; fndr and ceo I-Leap Fndn; memb: BDA 1979, Faculty of Gen Dental Practioners (UK), British Endodontic Soc, British Homeopathic Dental Assoc, Br Med Acupuncture Soc, Int Assoc of Oral Med and Toxicology (IAOMT), Biological Dentistry, European Soc for Oral Laser Applications (ESOLA); *Recreations* golf, complementary med, charity work with i-leap; *Style—* Dr Shabir Pandor; ✉ 44 Harley Street, London W1G 9PS (☏ 020 7580 1076, fax 020 7580 8702, e-mail sapandor@aol.com)

PANESAR, Mudhsuden Singh (Monty); *b* 25 April 1982, Luton; *Educ* Stopsley HS Bedford, Loughborough Univ; *Career* cricketer; with Northants CCC (first team debut 2001); England: 20 Test caps, 25 one day int appearances, one Twenty20 appearance, Test debut v India 2006, memb touring squad Australia 2006–07, memb squad World Cup 2007, ranked 6th best test match bowler in the world 2007; *Style—* Monty Panesar, Esq

PANFORD, Frank; QC (1999); s of Frank Essansoh Martin Panford (d 1993), and Susanna, *née* Holdbrook-Smith (d 1996); *b* 23 January 1949; *Educ* Holborn Coll of Law (LLB), Univ of Cambridge (LLB), Hague Acad of Int Law (Diplôme de Droit Privé); *m* 1, 1979 (m dis 1985), Hilary Anne Luper; m 2, 1994, Najma Khanzada, da of Kabir Khan; 3 da (Lisa Esi b 1983, Safi-Ullah Kwame b 1998, Nur Ato Kwamena 1999); *Career* called to the Bar Middle Temple 1972, lectr in law Univ of Westminster 1974–94, legal advsr/film examiner Br Bd of Film Classification 1984–90, practising barrister 1992–; *Recreations* african politics, music, cooking, travel; *Style—* Frank Panford, Esq, QC

PANJA, Dr Ayan; s of Dr S K Panja, and Dr M Panja; *b* 24 June 1973, Rochford, Essex; *Educ* Brighton Coll, Imperial Coll Sch of Medicine (MB BS); *Career* pre-registration house offr posts Stoke Mandeville Hosp Bucks and Royal Surrey County Hosp 1999–2000, sr house offr posts John Hampden Unit Aylesbury, Thame Community Hosp, Stoke Mandeville Hosp Bucks and Bucks Health Authy 2000–02, sr registrar and GP Aston Clinton Surgery 2002–04, sr ptnr princ GP Greens Medical Practice Haringey 2004–11, GP Medici Practice Luton 2004–, ptnr princ GP Maltings Surgery St Albans 2011–; presenter/expert Street Doctor (BBC 1) 2006–08, expert/judge Knowitalls (BBC 2) 2009, commentator The Noughties (BBC 3) 2009, medical expert Celebrity Quitters (Five) 2009–10, resident doctor 3@3 (ITV 1) 2010, presenter The Health Show (BBC World News) 2011–12, presenter Healthcheck, resident doctor BBC World News 2013–, presenter Health Freaks (Channel 4) 2013; contrib for expert comment to various magazines, websites and pubns incl Mens Health, The Guardian and FQ, editorial advsr NHS Choices; health campaigner; memb: GMC, Medical and Dental Defence Union of Scotland, BMA, Soc of Authors, Assoc of Broadcasting Doctors; DRCOG 2000, DFFP 2001, MRCGP 2003, FRSA; *Books* An Essential Medical Miscellany (2005), Medical Word SuDocu (2005); *Recreations* family life, the arts, singing, travelling, popular culture, playing the piano and tennis, health PR work, writing and editing; *Clubs* House of St Barnabas; *Style—* Dr Ayan Panja; ✉ website www.drayan.co.uk, Twitter @dr_ayan; The Maltings Surgery, 8–10 Victoria Street, St Albans AL1 3JB (website www.maltingssurgery.co.uk); c/o Jon Fowler, Peters Fraser Dunlop, Drury House, 34–43 Russell Street, London WC2B 5HA (☏ 020 7344 1000, e-mail jfowler@pfd.co.uk)

PANK, Edward Charles; s of Charles Clifford Pank (d 1974), of Norwich, and Marjorie Eira, *née* Bringloe (d 1988); *b* 5 June 1945; *Educ* Framlingham Coll, Trinity Hall Cambridge (MA), St Thomas' Hosp Univ of London (MB BS); *m* 17 Sept 1983, (Judith) Clare, da of Anthony Pethick Sommerville (d 1988), of Minchinhampton; *Career* admitted slr 1969; early career as merchant banker (incl dir Slater Walker Ltd 1974–76), subsequently medical dr St Thomas's Hosp London and Queen Elizabeth Hosp King's Lynn, co slr and sec ICAP plc (formerly Exco International plc) 1987–2003; non-exec dir: Bestpark Int Ltd 2004–, West Norfolk NHS Primary Care Tst 2004–; Liveryman Worshipful Soc of Apothecaries 1986; MRCS, LRCP; *Style—* Edward Pank, Esq

PANNICK, Baron (Life Peer UK 2008), of Radlett in the County of Herts; David Philip Pannick; QC (1992); s of Maurice Arthur Pannick (d 2000), and Rita Lois, *née* Cushcat (d 2011); *b* 7 March 1956; *Educ* Bancroft's Sch, Hertford Coll Oxford (MA, BCL); *m* 1, Denise (d 1999), da of Maurice Sloam; 2 s (Samuel b 1983, Joel b 1985), 1 da (Shula b 1988); m 2, Nathalie, da of David Trager-Lewis; 2 da (Katie b 2005, Sophie b 2008), 1 s (James b 2007); *Career* called to the Bar Gray's Inn 1978, jr counsel to the Crown Common Law 1988–92; fell All Souls Coll Oxford 1978–, hon fell Hertford Coll Oxford 2004–; *Books* Judges (1987), Advocates (1992), Human Rights Law and Practice (with Lord Lester of Herne Hill, 1999, 2004 and 2009), I Have to Move my Car (2008); *Recreations* theatre, watching television, supporting Arsenal FC; *Style—* The Lord Pannick, QC; ✉ Blackstone Chambers, Blackstone House, Temple, London EC4Y 9BW (☏ 020 7583 1770, fax 020 7822 7222)

PANNONE, Rodger John; DL; s of Cyril John Alfred Pannone (d 1982), and Violet Maud, *née* Weekes (d 1987); *b* 20 April 1943; *Educ* St Brendan's Coll Bristol, Manchester Coll of Law, London Coll of Law; *m* 13 Aug 1966, Patricia Jane, da of William Todd; 2 s (Mark b 24 Oct 1969, Richard b 7 Oct 1971), 1 da (Elizabeth b 19 July 1979); *Career* admitted slr 1969; conslt and former sr ptnr Pannone & Partners; Law Soc of Eng and Wales: memb Cncl 1978–96, dep vice-pres 1991–92, vice-pres 1992–93, pres 1993–94; chm Coll of Law 1999–2005; memb Lord Chllr's Advsy Ctee on Civil Justice 1985–88, former memb Supreme Court Rule Ctee; chm Renovo plc 2006–, non-exec dir Cooperative Legal Services Ltd 2006–; chm Manchester Concert Hall Ltd 1994–2007, chm Cncl Univ of Manchester 2000–04; vice-pres: Acad of Experts 1992–, Manchester Community Tst 1992–; hon fell: Manchester Met Univ 1994, Univ of Birmingham; Hon DLitt Univ of Salford 1993, LLD (hc) Nottingham Trent Univ 1993, Hon LittD Univ of Manchester 2004, Hon LLD Coll of Law; hon life memb Canadian Bar; FRSA 1993; *Recreations* fell walking, wine and food, travelling; *Clubs* St James's (Manchester), Wyresdale Anglers; *Style—* Rodger Pannone, Esq, DL; ✉ website www.pannone.com/people-profiles/rodger.pannone@pannone.co.uk

PANTER, Sir Howard Hugh; kt (2013); *b* 25 May 1949; *Educ* Clayesmore Sch Dorset, LAMDA; *m* 1994, Rosemary Squire, OBE, *qv*; 1 da (Kate b 2002); *Career* md and prodr Turnstyle Gp Ltd 1987–92, co-fndr Ambassador Theatre Gp 1992– (jt chief exec and creative dir 2000–16); chm Rambert Dance Co 2009–, dir Rocky Horror Co Ltd; memb Devpt Bd LAMDA; *Style—* Sir Howard Panter; ✉ Ambassador Theatre Group, 2nd Floor, Alexander House, Church Path, Woking, Surrey GU21 6EJ (website www.atgtickets.com)

PANTLING, Nigel Antony; s of Anthony Pantling, and Brenda, *née* Chambers; *b* 17 July 1950, Bedford; *Educ* Cedars GS Leighton Buzzard, Univ of Durham (BSc); *m* 1, 19 April 1973 (m dis), Jennifer, *née* English; 1 da (Katy Alexandra b 30 Aug 1981), 1 s (James Edward b 16 Jan 1984); m 2, 19 Dec 1991 (m dis), Mary Allen; m 3, 13 Nov 2010, Jean Sprackland, *née* Lockley; *Career* Capt RA 1968–76; Home Office 1976–85, corp fin dir Schroders 1985–94, head of corp fin Hambros Bank 1994–97, strategy advsr to chief execs 1997–; non-exec dir: Camden and Islington NHS Tst 1992–98, One Housing Gp 2010–13; tstee: Dulwich Picture Gall 1994–2005, City Parochial Fndn 1997–2010 (chair 2007–10), Almeida Theatre 2000–09, Arvon Fndn 2005–14 (chair 2005–14), Fight for Sight 2011– (chair 2014–), Park Theatre 2015– (also chair); govr James Allen's Girls Sch 1996–2001; Chartered Fell CISI, FRSA; *Books* Belfast Finds Log (poetry, 2014); *Recreations* singing, collecting contemporary art, poetry; *Style—* Nigel Pantling, Esq; ✉ e-mail nigel@nigelpantling.com

PANTON, David Renault; OBE (2014); *b* 1948, Beds; *Educ* Univ of Surrey (MPhil); *Career* co-fndr, chm and dir of artists' charity Acme Studios 1972–; *Style—* David Panton, Esq, OBE; ✉ Acme Studios, 44 Copperfield Road, Bow, London E3 4RR

PANTON, Janice; MBE (1999); *née* White; da of Peter White (d 1963), of NY, and Ellen Lynch, *née* Peters (d 2000); *b* 22 January 1948; *Educ* Univ of Westminster (MA); *m* 30 July 1977, Roger Huntley, s of Albert Kenneth Panton; 2 s (Stuart Roger b 28 Sept 1978, Kevin Huntley b 31 May 1980); *Career* pt/t teacher 1981–85, legal sec 1989–98, UK rep Govt of Montserrat and head Montserrat Govt UK Office 1998–; tstee: Montserrat Aid Ctee 1989–, Montserrat Fndn, Refuge; *Publications* Waiting on the Volcano (1996); *Recreations* music, gardening, reading; *Style—* Mrs Janice Panton, MBE; ✉ 13 Hyde Park Gardens, Winchmore Hill, London N21 2PN (☏ 020 8360 2392, e-mail janice.panton@gmail.com); Monserrat Government UK Office, 180–186 Kings Cross Road, London WC1X 9DE (☏ 020 7520 2622, fax 020 7520 2624, e-mail j.panton@montserrat-gov.org)

PANTON-LEWIS, Catherine Rita; da of John Panton, MBE, of Larbert, Stirlingshire, and Elizabeth Renwick, *née* Seaton; *b* 14 June 1955; *Educ* Larbert HS, Univ of Edinburgh (MA), Thames Valley Univ (Postgrad Dip Hospitality Mgmnt); *m* 11 April 1991, Philip Lewis, of Llandybie, Dyfed; *Career* golfer; Scot girls champion 1969, Br amateur champion 1976, Scot Sportswoman of the Year 1976, E of Scot women's champion 1976; memb Br World Cup Amateur Team 1976, Vagliano Team 1977, played on USLPGA Tour 1983–85, qualified to play on US Women Sr Golf Tour 2004, capt Rest of the World team vs USA Honda Cup 2008, 2009 and 2010; winner: 1979 Women's Professional Golf Tour Order of Merit, 14 tournaments on the Ladies European Tour incl Portugese Open in 1986 and 1987 and Scot Women's Open in 1988, United Insurance section Ladies' Barbados Open 1993, Southern England Student Sports Assoc Championships 1994, English Ladies' Senior Int Open 2010, 2011, 2014 and 2015; Glenmuir WPGA Club Professionals' Champion 2007; exec dir McDonald's WPGA Championship of Europe 1996–99, events mangr Ronald McDonald House Charities Grand Banquet and Golf Cup 2000–02, staff professional The Berkshire Golf Club 2002–07, sec Sunningdale Ladies Golf Club 2007–08, asst sec The Berkshire Golf Club 2008–; memb: PGA (advanced fell), LET 1978, US Legends' Tour (formerly US Women Srs' Golf Assoc); inductee into Univ of Edinburgh Sports Hall of Fame 2011; *Recreations* reading, current affairs, stock market, cinema, horse racing, golf, su doku; *Clubs* Glenbervie Golf, Pitlochry Golf, Silloth Golf, The Berkshire, Sunningdale Ladies' Golf, Blair Atholl Golf; *Style—* Mrs Catherine Panton-Lewis

PAPADOPOULOS, Dr Marios; MBE (2014); *b* 20 December 1954; *Educ* City Univ (DMA); *m* Anthi Papadopoulos; 1 s, 1 da; *Career* pianist and conductor; fndr and music dir Oxford Philharmonic Orchestra (formerly Philomusica) 1998–; fell by special selection Keble Coll Oxford 2004, hon fell Worshipful Co of Musicians 2010; *Clubs* Oxford & Cambridge; *Style—* Dr Marios Papadopoulos, MBE; ✉ 29 Teignmouth Road, London NW2 4EB (e-mail marios@oxfordphil.com)

PAPHITI, Brig Anthony Steven; s of Serghios Anthony Paphiti, of Melton Mowbray, Leics, and Dorothy Lilian, *née* Wilson; *b* 12 May 1952; *Educ* King Edward VII GS Melton Mowbray, Univ of Leeds (LLB), Cncl of Legal Educn; *m* 1978, Ingrid, *née* Timm; 2 da (Anja Maria b 7 Feb 1980, Sophie Louise b 17 April 1982); *Career* called to the Bar Inner Temple 1975; pupillage at 9 & 10 King's Bench Walk 1976–77, in private practice 1977–81; Army Legal Servs: joined 1981, legal offr HQ BAOR 1981–83, legal offr HQ 4 Div 1983–86, legal offr HQ 3 Div 1986–87, OIC Criminal Injuries Compensation Cell 1987–89, Cdr Legal HQ 4 Div 1989–92, first legal advsr to NATO HQ ARRC 1992–95, memb MOU Negotiating Team, legal advsr to Cdr for Support Croatia and author Tech Arrangements between NATO and Croatia 1995–96, Cdr Legal HQ 1 (UK) Armd Div 1996–97, Col Prosecutions Germany 1997–2000, Brig Advsy 2001–02 and 2005–06, Brig Prosecutions 2002–06, currently military law conslt; mentioned in despatches 1990; co-vice chm Employed Barrs' Ctee Bar Cncl 2006; memb: Int Soc for Mil Law and the Law of War, Inter-Agency Judicial Appts Working Gp 2002; lay memb Leicester Univ Hospitals Tsts Ethics Ctee; *Books* Military Justice Handbook for Court Martial Practitioners (2013); *Recreations* cycling, walking, gardening, music; *Style—* Brig Anthony Paphiti; ✉ c/o Directorate of Army Legal Services, 426 Ramillies Building, Marlborough Lines Monxton Road, Andover SP11 8HJ (☏ 07802 416935, e-mail anthony@aspals.com)

PAPPANO, Sir Antonio; kt (2012); s of Pasquale Pappano (d 2004), and Carmela Maria Scinto; *b* 30 December 1959, Epping, Essex; *Educ* Pimlico Sch, Central HS Bridgeport CT; *m* 27 Feb 1995, Pamela Bullock; *Career* conductor; early career: rehearsal pianist NYC Opera, repetiteur and asst conductor numerous theatres incl NY City Opera, Gran Teatro del Liceu (Barcelona), Frankfurt Opera, Lyric Opera of Chicago and Bayreuth Festival; music dir: Norske Opera Oslo 1990–92, Théâtre Royal de la Monnaie Belgium 1992–2002, ROH 2002–, Accademia Nazionale di Santa Cecilia Rome 2005–; principal guest conductor Israel Philharmonic Orchestra 1997–2000; conductor of orchs worldwide incl: Boston Symphony Orch, Chicago Symphony Orch, Cleveland Orch, LA

P

Philharmonic Orch, NY Philharmonic Orch, Berlin Philharmonic Orch, Concergebouw Orch, LSO, Orchestre de Paris, Munich Philharmonic Orch, Vienna Philharmonic Orch; conducted prodns at Theatre Royal de la Monnaie incl: Salome, Un ballo in maschera, Die Meistersinger von Nürnberg, Carmen, Otello (Verdi), Peter Grimes, La traviata, Tristan und Isolde, Le nozze di Figaro, Der Rosenkavalier, Il trittico, Erwartung/Verklärte Nacht, Pelléas et Mélisande, Don Carlos, Aida; conducted prodns at ROH incl: Ariadne auf Naxos, Wozzeck, Falstaff, Madama Butterfly, I pagliacci, Don Giovanni, Aida, Lady Macbeth of Mtsensk, Faust (Gounod), Peter Grimes, La Gioconda, Werther, Der Ring des Nibelungen, La fanciulla del West, Carmen, Fidelio, Don Carlo and Sir Harrison Birtwistle's The Minotaur (world première), Mark-Anthony Turnage's Anna Nicole (world premiere), Les Troyens; Artist of the Year Gramophone Magazine 2000, Conductor of the Year Royal Philharmonic Soc 2005; Cavaliere di Gran Croce dell'Ordine al Merito della Repubblica Italiana 2012; *Recordings* Don Carlos, La bohème, La rondine (Best Recording of the Year Gramophone Magazine), Il trittico, Werther, Manon, Tosca, Il trovatore, Wintermärchen, The Turn of the Screw, Tristan & Isolde; with Accademia Nazionale di Santa Cecilia: Madama Butterfly, Guillaume Tell, Aida, Verdi Requiem, Rossini Stabat Mater, Respighi Roman Trilogy, Rachmaninov Symphony No 2, Britten War Requiem, Mahler Symphony No 6; with soloists incl: Plácido Domingo, Han-Na Chang, Maxim Vengerov, Janine Janson, Leif Ove Andsnes, Ian Bostridge, Natalie Dessay, Nina Stemme; *Clubs* Garrick; *Style*— Sir Antonio Pappano; ✉ c/o IMG Artists, 111 Power Road, London W4 5PY (☎ 020 7957 5800, e-mail nmathias@imgartists.com)

PARASKEVA, Rt Hon Dame Janet; DBE (2010), PC (2010); da of Antonis Paraskeva, and Doris Amanda, *née* Fowler (d 1986); *b* 28 May 1946; *Educ* Worcester Coll, Open Univ (BA); *m* (m dis 1988), Alan Richard Derek Hunt; 2 da (Amanda Joanne b 10 Feb 1970, Suzanna Maria b 19 Nov 1971); *Career* science teacher Shenley Court Comp Sch 1967–69, mathematics teacher St Thomas Aquinas GS 1969–71, pt/t Bromsgrove Club for the Mentally Handicapped 1969–71, dir Friday Toys 1970–73, sr youth worker Fillongley Youth Centre 1972–74, pt/t lectr N Warks Inst of Educn 1973–74, field work co-ordinator Warks Assoc of Youth Clubs 1973–74, projects offr NAYC (now Youth UK) 1974–78, head Youth Work Unit Nat Youth Bureau 1978–81, dist inspr (Youth and Adult) ILEA 1981–83, HMI (Youth and Community) DES 1983–88; dir: Nat Youth Bureau 1988–90, Nat Youth Agency 1990–95, Nat Lottery Charities Bd for England 1995–2000; chief exec Law Soc 2000–06, first civil serv cmmr 2005–10; chair: Olympic Lottery Distributor 2006–13, Child Maintenance and Enforcement Cmmn 2007–12, Child Exploitation and Online Protection Centre 2008–10, Plan (Int) UK 2009, Jersey Appts Cmmn 2014–, Cncl for Licensed Conveyances 2015–; memb Youth Justice Bd for England and Wales 1998–2000, ind memb Consumer Cncl for Water 2005–08, non-exec dir Serious Organised Crime Agency 2005–10, non-exec dir Assets Recovery Agency 2007–08, memb Cncl Competition Cmmn 2012–14; JP 1993–2000; non-exec dir Fosse Community Health Tst 1992–99; memb Cncl Univ of Leicester 1998–; Robert Schuman Silver Medal for European Unity 1978; various contribs to TES, educnl and legal pubns; Hon LLD Univ of Brighton 2006, Hon MLitt Univ of Worcester 2009, Hon LLD Univ of Leicester; *Style*— The Rt Hon Dame Janet Paraskeva, DBE; ✉ Plan International UK, Finsgate, 5–7 Cranwood Street, London EC1V 9LH

PARAVICINI, Nicolas Vincent Somerset; DL (Powys 2006); s of Col Vincent Rudolph Paravicini, TD, Croix de Guerre (d 1989), and Elizabeth Mary (Liza) Maugham (Baroness Glendevon, da of author W Somerset Maugham, d 1998); *b* 19 October 1937; *Educ* Eton, RMA Sandhurst; *m* 1, 4 April 1966 (m dis 1986), Mary Ann Parker Bowles; 2 s (Charles b 1968, Derek b 1979), 1 da (Elizabeth Ann (Mrs Robert Hall) b 1970); m 2, 18 Dec 1986 (Susan Rose) Sukie, da of Lt Alan Phipps, RN (ka 1943), and Hon Lady Maclean; *Career* The Life Gds 1957–69, served Aden, Oman, Cyprus and Malaysia, Adj 1963–65, ADC to C-in-C Far East 1965–66, ret Maj; dir Joseph Sebag & Co 1972–79, chm A Sarasin & Co Ltd 1980–89, md Sarasin (UK) Ltd 1983–89, chm and chief exec Sarasin Investment Management Ltd 1983–90, conslt Bank Sarasin & Co 1990–, chief exec MacIntyre Investments Ltd 1990–92, chief exec Ely Place Investments Ltd 1992–98; memb London Stock Exchange 1972–80; pres: Brecknockshire Agric Soc 1998–99, SSAFA Powys 2002–12; dir Christ Coll Fndn 2002–10, dep chm Investment Ctee Rep Body Church in Wales 2006–12 (memb 2001–12); tstee Nat Heart & Lung Inst 2004–08; Freeman City of London 1984; *Recreations* country pursuits, watching cricket; *Clubs* White's, Pratt's, Corviglia Ski; *Style*— Nicolas Paravicini, Esq, DL; ✉ Wishford Farmhouse, Great Wishford, Salisbury, Wiltshire SP2 0NN (☎ 01722 790905)

PARBHOO, Santilal Parag; s of Parag Parbhoo (d 1964), of Cape Town, South Africa, and Jasoda Pemi, *née* Ramjee (d 1961); *b* 16 January 1937; *Educ* Livingstone HS Cape Town, Univ of Cape Town (MB ChB), Queen's Univ Belfast (PhD); *m* 8 Jan 1969, (Constance) Ann, da of William Joseph Cedric Craig, of Belfast, NI; 2 s (Mark b 20 July 1970, Alan b 18 Feb 1977), 1 da (Kathryn b 1 Feb 1974); *Career* house surgn New Somerset Hosp Cape Town 1961, sr house surgn Edendale Hosp Pietermaritzburg 1961–62, tutor and registrar Royal Victoria Hosp Belfast 1964–65 (clinical asst 1962–64); surgical registrar: NI Hosp 1965–68, Frenchay Hosp Bristol 1973–74; conslt and sr lectr Royal Free Hosp and Sch London 1974–91 (research fell and lectr 1968–72); conslt: Royal Medical Services Jordan 1980–87, Bristol Myers Oncology UK 1984–86, Hosp of St John and St Elizabeth London 1991–2009; Royal Free Hosp London: fndr Breast Unit 1978, chm Div of Surgery 1987–89, conslt surgn (gen and breast) 1991–2001, chm Breast Cancer Tst 2000–09, hon conslt surgn 2001–09; chm Surgical Bd of Studies Royal Free Hosp Sch of Med 1984–91; fndr Cancerkin 1986 (dir Cancerkin 1987–2009, medical dir Cancerkin Lymphoedema Clinic 1990–2009, pres 2009–16); past memb Int Soc of Lymphology, fndr memb Ludwig Int Breast Cancer Study Gp 1978; memb: Gujerati Arya Assoc London, Sci Advsy Ctee UK Breast Cancer Forum 2002–; past memb Med Advsy Ctee Women's Nationwide Cancer Control Campaign; Br Cncl research fell 1962–64, Br Cncl younger workers interchange fell 1971, Winnifred Ladds Scholar 1971, NATO int research travelling fell 1991–92; patron Maggie's @ Cancerkin Centre 2016–; visiting prof: Univ of Milan, Amman Univ, Univ of Cape Town, Cairo Univ, Tanta Univ; hon memb Argentinian Coll of Vascular and Lymphatic Surgery 2002–; hon fell: Hong Kong Soc of Surgns, Egyptian Soc of Hepatology 1989 (medal received 1989); fell: Br Assoc for Surgical Oncology, Assoc of Surgns of GB and I; FRCS (Eng) 1967; *Books* contrib: 8th Symposium on Advanced Medicine (1972), Symposium on Organ Preservation (1973), Scientific Foundations of Surgery (1974), Management of Portal Hypertension (1979), Metastases – Clinical & Experimental Aspects (1980), Systemic Control of Breast Cancer (1981), Necrosis in Cancer Tissue (1982), Prolonged Arrest of Breast Cancer (1982), Cancer Treatment: End Point Evaluation (1983), Bone Metastasis: Monitoring and Treatment (with B A Stoll, 1983), Pointers to Cancer Prognosis (1986), Breast Conservation Surgery (1993), Scintimammography: A Guide to Good Practice (with J Buscombe and J Hill, 1998), Progress in Lymphology XVI (1998), Law, Medicine & Ethics (2007); *Recreations* walking, gardening, philately; *Clubs* Retired Consultant Staff (RFH); *Style*— Santilal Parbhoo, Esq; ✉ Cancerkin Centre, Royal Free Hospital, Pond Street, London NW3 2QG (☎ 020 7830 2323, e-mail spparbhoo@gmail.com, website www.cancerkin.org.uk)

PAREKH, Baron (Life Peer UK 2000), of Kingston upon Hull in the East Riding of Yorkshire; Prof Bhikhu Chhotalal; s of Chhotalal Ranchhoddas Parekh, of Washington DC, USA, and Gajaraben Parekh; *b* 4 January 1935; *Educ* HDS HS India, Univ of Bombay (BA, MA), Univ of London (PhD); *m* 14 April 1959, Pramila, da of Kanaiyalal Keshavlal Dalal, of Baroda, India; 3 s (Raj, Nitin, Anant); *Career* tutor LSE 1962–63, lectr Univ of Glasgow 1963–64; Univ of Hull: successively lectr, sr lectr then reader 1964–82, prof of politics 1982–2000, emeritus prof 2000–; centennial prof LSE 2001–03, prof of political philosophy Univ of Westminster 2001–09; vice-chllr Univ of Baroda 1981–84 (lectr 1957–59); visiting prof: Univ of Br Columbia 1967–68, Concordia Univ Montreal 1974–75, McGill Univ Montreal 1976–77, Harvard Univ 1996, Univ of Pompeau Fabra Barcelona 1997, Univ of Pennsylvania 1998, Ecole des Hautes Etudes en Sciences Sociales Paris 2000; guest prof Inst of Advanced Studies Vienna 1997; distinguished visiting prof Univ of Maine 2007, distinguished professorial fell Centre for the Study of Developing Socs Delhi India 2008–; chm: Nat Survey of the Ethnic Minorities in Britain Advsy Ctee 1993–97, Cmmn on the Future of Multi-Ethnic Britain 1998–2000; dep chm Cmmn for Racial Equality 1985–90, memb Nat Cmmn on Equal Opportunities CVCP 1994–99; tstee: Runnymede Tst 1986–2003, Inst for Public Policy Research 1988–96, Gandhi Fndn 1988– (pres 2013), Inst of Cwlth Studies 1991–97; Asian of the Year 1991, BBC Special Lifetime Achievement Award for Asians 1999, Sir Isiah Berlin Prize for Lifetime Contribution to Political Studies 2003, Distinguished Global Thinker Award 2005, Pride of India Award 2006; pres: Acad of Learned Socs for the Social Sciences 2004–08, Br Assoc of South Asian Studies 2004–07; fell Asiatic Soc Bombay 2004; hon prof Univ of Wales Aberystwyth; recipient of hon doctorates from 16 univs; FRSA 1990, FBA 2003; Pravasi Bharatiya Samman (India) 2005, Padma Bhushan (India) 2007; *Books* incl: Hannah Arendt (1981), Karl Marx's Theory of Ideology (1982), Contemporary Political Thinkers (1982), Gandhi's Political Philosophy (1989), Colonialism, Tradition and Reform (1989), Critical Assessments of Jeremy Bentham (4 vols, 1993), Decolonisation of Imagination (1996), Crisis and Change in Contemporary India (1996), Gandhi (1997), Rethinking Multiculturalism (2000), A New Politics of Identity (2008), Talking Politics (2011), Debating India (2016); *Recreations* reading, walking, music; *Style*— The Rt Hon The Lord Parekh; ✉ 211 Victoria Avenue, Hull HU5 3EF (☎ 01482 345530, e-mail profparekh@gmail.com); House of Lords, London SW1A 0PW (☎ 020 7219 5353)

PARFITT, Andrew (Andy); *b* 24 September 1958; *Educ* Bristol Old Vic Theatre Sch; *m* Laura; 2 da (Lucy Sarah b 11 July 1998, Eva Kathryn b 5 April 2001); *Career* studio mangr BBC then prodr/presenter BFBS; BBC: rejoined as educn prodr, successively features prodr Radio 4, asst ed Radio 5, chief asst to controller of Radio 1, ed commissioning and planning Radio 1, managing ed Radio 1 1994–96, dep controller Radio 1 1996–98; controller: Radio 1 1998–2011, 1 Xtra until 2011, Asian Network until 2011 BBC Switch; grad Wharton Advanced Mgmnt Prog 2000; winner Sony Creative Award; fell Radio Acad; *Style*— Andy Parfitt, Esq

PARFITT, David John; s of late William Arnold Parfitt, and late Maureen, *née* Collinson; *b* 8 July 1958, Caversham, Berks; *Educ* Bede GS Sunderland, Barbara Speake Stage Sch London; *m* 1, 1988 (m dis 1993), Susan Coates; 1 s (William Michael b 6 Sept 1990); m 2, 1996, Elizabeth Ann Barron; 2 s (Thomas Richard b 23 Aug 1998, Max Christopher b 18 May 2001); *Career* prodr 1985– (actor 1970–88); co-fndr: Renaissance Theatre Co 1987–, Renaissance Films 1988–92, Trademark Films 2000–, Trademark Theatre Co 2000–; BAFTA: memb Bd of Tstees 2000–11, chair of film 2004–07, chm 2008–10; chm Film London 2011–; tstee Chicken Shed Theatre Co 1997–2011, patron Royalty Theatre Sunderland 1999–; Hon Dr of Arts Univ of Sunderland 1999, Hon Dr Drama RSAMD 2001; *Theatre* as prodr for Renaissance Theatre Co: Tell Me Honestly (Not the RSC Stratford and London) 1985, John Sessions at the Eleventh Hour 1986, Romeo & Juliet 1986, Public Enemy 1987, Napoleon 1987, Renaissance Nights 1987, Twelfth Night 1988, Much Ado About Nothing, Hamlet and As You Like It (West End and nat tour) 1988, Look Back in Anger (West End and nat tour) 1989, Napoleon, The American Story (West End and nat tour) 1989, Scenes from a Marriage (West End) 1990, A Midsummer Night's Dream and King Lear (West End, nat tour and world tour) 1990, Travelling Tales (West End and nat tour) 1991, Uncle Vanya (West End and nat tour) 1991, Coriolanus (Chichester Festival) 1992, Les Liaisons Dangereuses (West End) 2004, Elling (Bush Theatre and West End) 2007, Backbeat (Glasgow Citz) 2010, A Bunch of Amateurs (Watermill Theatre Newbury) 2014; *Television* assoc prodr: Twelfth Night (Thames Television/Renaissance Theatre Co) 1988, Look Back in Anger (First Choice/Renaissance Theatre Co) 1989; prodr Parade's End (Mammoth Screen/Trademark Films) 2011–12, Glyndebourne: The Untold History (Trademark Films/BBC4) 2014, Danielle de Niese: Birth of an Opera (Trademark Films for BBC4) 2016; *Film* Henry V 1988 (assc prodr), Peter's Friends 1992 (line prodr), Swan Song 1992 (nomination Best Live Action Short American Acad Awards) , Much Ado About Nothing 1993, Frankenstein 1994 (co-prodr), The Madness of King George 1995 (Best Br Film BAFTA Awards), Twelfth Night 1996, The Wings of the Dove 1997, Shakespeare in Love 1999 (7 American Acad Awards incl Best Picture, 4 BAFTA Awards incl Best Film), Gangs of New York 2001 (prodn conslt), I Capture the Castle 2002, Chasing Liberty 2004, A Bunch of Amateurs 2008, Dean Spanley 2008 (exec prodr), My Week with Marilyn 2011, The Wipers Times 2013, Loving Vincent 2016; *Style*— David Parfitt, Esq; ✉ Trademark Films, 14a Goodwin's Court, London WC2N 4LL (☎ 020 3322 8900, e-mail mail@trademarkfilms.co.uk, website www.trademarkfilms.co.uk)

PARFITT, Judy Catherine Clare; da of Laurence Hamilton Parfitt (d 1973), and Catherine Coulton; *Educ* Notre Dame Convent, RADA; *m* 25 Aug 1963, Anthony Francis Steedman, s of Baron Anthony Ward; 1 s (David Lawrence b 29 Sept 1964); *Career* actress; *Theatre* incl: D H Lawrence trilogy (Royal Court), Annie in A Hotel in Amsterdam 1968, Queen Mary in Vivat! Vivat! Regina! (Piccadilly) 1970, Family Dance (Criterion), Cleopatra (Young Vic), Duchess of Malfi (Royal Court), Ranyevskya in The Cherry Orchard (Riverside Studios) 1978, Eleanor in Passion Play (Wyndham's) 1980, A Dream of People (RSC), Molière's The Sisterhood and Valentine's Day, Mrs Birling in An Inspector Calls (RNT prodn at Aldwych) 1993, Night Must Fall (Lyceum Theatre Broadway) 1999, Therese Raquin (RNT), Really Old, Like 45 (Royal Nat Theatre); *Television* numerous prodns incl: Villette, E Nesbit in The Edwardians 1973, Lady Constance Lytton in Shoulder to Shoulder, Malice Aforethought 1979, Pride and Prejudice, Death of a Princess, You Never Can Tell, Alice Through The Looking Glass, Post Mortem, Angel Pavement, Secret Orchards, Jewel in the Crown 1984 (BAFTA Best Actress nomination), The Charmer 1987, The Charmings (USA series), Hilda Spearpoint in The Gravy Train 1989 and The Gravy Train Goes East 1992, The Borrowers (BBC), Lifeboat (BBC), Inspector Alleyn (BBC), September (mini-series), Harriet Collard in The Blackheath Poisonings (TV film), Loving (Screen Two), Heavy Weather (BBC), The Final Act (Granada), Element of Doubt, Holding the Baby, Berkley Square, ER, The Hunt, Murder in Mind, Hearts of Gold, Death on the Nile (ITV), The Long Firm (BBC), Funland (BBC 3), Heartland, Midsomer Murders, Mrs Clenham in Little Dorrit (BBC), Jonathan Creek (Christmas special), Just William, Sister Monica Joan in Call the Midwife (BBC), Vera (ITV), The Game (BBC), Up The Women (BBC); *Film* incl: Gertrude in Hamlet, Madam Sarti in Galileo, Getting it Right, Diamond Skulls, Maurice 1986, Vera Donovan in Dolores Claiborne, Lady Mount-Temple in Wilde, The Ruby Ring, Queen Marie in Ever After, The Bourne Identity, Maria Thinns in The Girl with a Pearl Earring (BAFTA Best Supporting Film Actress nomination), Asylum, My Talks with Dean Spanley, WE; *Recreations* needlepoint, gardening, antiques, talking; *Style*— Miss Judy Parfitt

PARFORD, Simon William; s of Lt-Cdr John Littleton Parford, RN (ret), MBE, of Plymouth, and Barbara Daphne, *née* Hawton; *b* 12 November 1958, Singapore; *Educ* Plymouth Coll, Birmingham Poly, Guildford Law Coll; *m* 5 Sept 1987, Karen, *née* Jones; 1 s (Alexander John b 25 March 1991), 1 da (Chloe Jillian b 5 March 1995); *Career* admitted slr 1983; Wolferstans: articled clerk 1981–83, slr 1983, ptnr 1988–, head Clinical Negligence Dept 1991–2016; tstee Headway Plymouth 1992–, tstee Chestnut Appeal 2010–; memb: Law

Soc 1983, Plymouth Law Soc 1983, Assoc of Personal Injury Lawyers (APIL) 1993; *Recreations* watching rugby, drinking wine, playing tennis; *Clubs* OPM (Old Plymothians and Mannameadians), Plymouth Albion RFC; *Style—* Simon Parford, Esq; ✉ Wolferstans, 60–66 North Hill, Plymouth PL4 8EP (☎ 01752 292217, e-mail sparford@wolferstans.com)

PARHAM, HE Philip John; CMG; s of John Carey Parham, of Sunninghill, and Christian Mary, *née* Fitzherbert; *b* 14 August 1960, Nairobi, Kenya; *Educ* Eton (King's scholar), ChCh Oxford (MA); *m* 7 Sept 1985, Kasia, *née* Giedroyc; 2 da (Mary 16 June 1986, Elizabeth 28 Sept 1994), 5 s (Joseph 19 Feb 1988, Francis-Christian 17 June 1989, Anthony 27 Oct 1990, Charles 16 April 1992, John 22 Jan 1996); *Career* Morgan Grenfell 1983–89, Barclays de Zoete Wedd 1989–93 (dir 1992–93), S Asia Dept FCO 1993–94, private sec to Parly Under Sec of State FCO 1995, policy planning staff FCO 1995–96, first sec Br Embassy Washington 1996–2000, dir trade and investment Br Embassy Riyadh 2000–03, head Iraq Ops Unit FCO 2003–04, head Counter-Terrorism Policy Dept FCO 2004–06, high cmmr Dar es Salaam 2006–09, ambass and dep perm rep to UN NY 2009–13, ambass to UAE 2014–; hon fell Harris Manchester Coll Oxford; Liveryman Worshipful Co of Skinners; *Recreations* family, gardening, theology, genealogy, the parentage of Mary Anne Smythe; *Style—* HE Mr Philip Parham, CMG; ✉ British Embassy, PO Box 248, Abu Dhabi, United Arab Emirates (☎ 00 9 712 610 1100, e-mail philip.parham@fco.gov.uk)

PARIS, Andrew Martin Ingledew; s of Vernon Patrick Paris (d 1999), of Sussex, and Heather Constance Ingledew, *née* Dear (d 2008); *b* 27 November 1940; *Educ* London Hosp Med Coll (MB BS); *Family* 1 da (Claire Elizabeth Ingledew); m Susan Philippa, da of Perys Goodwin Jenkins (d 1969), of London; *Career* conslt urological surgn The Royal London Hosp 1976–2005, conslt urological surgn St Bartholomew's Hosp 1994–2005, emeritus consulting urological surgn The Royal London and St Bartolomew's Hosps 2005–, clinical dir of surgery Barts and the London NHS Tst 1979–2002; hon conslt surgn The Italian Hosp 1979–90; hon surgn St John Ambulance Air Wing (fndr memb); author of papers on transplantation and urology; chm Marie Celeste Samaritan Soc 2006–, tstee Longship Museum 2004–; Freeman City of London 1984, Master Worshipful Soc of Apothecaries 2007 (memb Ct of Assts); FRCS 1971, FRSM (vice-pres Section of Urology 1988 and 1989); OStJ 1985; *Recreations* sailing, skiing, croquet, beekeeping; *Clubs* Athenaeum, Aldeburgh Yacht, Thorpeness Croquet; *Style—* Andrew Paris, Esq; ✉ The Old Vicarage, Aldringham Cum Thorpe, Suffolk IP16 4QF (e-mail andrewparis@tiscali.co.uk)

PARISH, Michael Robert (Mike); s of Francis (Checker) Parish (d 2006), and Betty, *née* Bryant; *b* 19 May 1959, London; *Educ* St Marylebone GS, Battersea GS, Univ of Leicester (BA, dep pres Students' Union); *m* 26 July 1986, Karen, *née* Britton; 1 da (Kate b 16 Dec 1987), 2 s (George b 27 Nov 1989, Charles b 13 July 1992); *Career* mgmnt trainee Nat Freight Corporation 1981, md Tradeteam 1995–97, dvnl chief exec Exel 1997–2001, chief exec Care UK plc 2001–; tstee and non-exec dir NHS Confederation 2010–15; *Publications* Going with change: Allowing new models of healthcare to be provided for NHS patients (with Paul Corrigan, CBE); *Recreations* running, cycling, football (West Ham United supporter), pinball; *Style—* Mike Parish, Esq

PARISH, Neil Quentin Gordon; MP; s of Reginald and Kathleen Parish; *b* 26 May 1956; *Educ* Brymore Sch; *m* 1981, Susan Gail; 1 s (Jonathan), 1 da (Harriet); *Career* farmer; cncllr Pawlett PC 1980–95, cncllr Sedgemoor DC 1983–95 (dep ldr 1989), cncllr Somerset CC 1989–93, Parly candidate (Cons) Torfaen (Pontypool and Cwmbran) 1997; MEP (Cons) SW England 1999–2009, MP (Cons) Tiverton and Honiton 2010–; memb: EU Agric Ctee, Fisheries Ctee, Environment Ctee; chair Environment, Food and Rural Affairs Select Ctee 2015–; Cons agric and fisheries spokesman 2001; chm Aust and NZ EU Delegation 2004–; memb Pawlett Parish Cncl 1980–99; *Recreations* swimming, walking; *Style—* Neil Parish, Esq, MP; ✉ House of Commons, London SW1A 0AA

PARISH, Prof Richard; CBE (2014); s of Leslie Thomas Parish, FCCA, and Winifred Alice Parish; *b* 11 October 1951; *Educ* Univ of London (BSc external), South Bank Poly (Dip Health Educn), Huddersfield Univ (MEd); *m* 1976, Joan Margaret, *née* Shepherd; 1 s, 1 da; *Career* dir of health promotion Stockport HA 1980–85, head of progs Heartbeat Wales and sr lectr WNSM 1985–87, dir of ops Health Promotion Authy for Wales 1987–90, princ and chief exec Humberside Coll of Health 1990–96, prof of public health and dir health and community studies Sheffield Hallam Univ 1996–97, prof and head of health studies Univ of York 1997–99, regnl dir (educn and trg) NHS Eastern Region 1999, chief exec Health Devpt Agency, chief exec Royal Soc for the Promotion of Health until 2013; currently chair Pharmacy and Public Health Forum; FRSH 1988, CBiol 1989, MIBiol 1989, MIPR 1989, MHSM 1991, Hon MFPHM 2001; *Publications* author of pubns on health promotion and health policy; *Recreations* photography, rambling, cycling; *Style—* Prof Richard Parish, CBE

PARISH, Prof Richard John; s of late John Alfred Parish, and late Dorothy Evelyn, *née* Turner; *Educ* Cranbrook Sch, Univ of Newcastle upon Tyne (BA), Keble Coll Oxford (DPhil, MA); *Career* lectr Univ of Liverpool 1973–76; Univ of Oxford: lectr in French 1976–95, prof of French 1996–2015, chm Sub-Faculty of French 1997–2000, pro-proctor 1998–99, Bampton lectr 2009; St Catherine's Coll Oxford: fell and tutor 1976–2015, sr tutor 1991–95, vice-master 1997–2000, dean of degrees 2015–; memb Exec Ctee Soc for French Studies 2003–07; external assessor Govt of Ireland HE Authy 1998–2002; govr St Mary's Sch Ascot 2010–; Commandeur dans l'Ordre des Palmes Académiques (France) 2012 (Officier 2001); *Books* Pascal's Letters Provinciales: A Study in Polemic (1989), Racine: The Limits of Tragedy (1993), Scarron: Le Roman Comique (1991), Catholic Particularity in Seventeenth-Century French Writing (2011); editor of various editions, author of articles and reviews; *Recreations* music, Pevsnering, wine; *Clubs* Athenaeum; *Style—* Prof Richard Parish; ✉ St Catherine's College, Oxford OX1 3UJ (☎ 01865 271700, fax 01865 271768, e-mail richard.parish@stcatz.ox.ac.uk)

PARISH, Sarah; da of William Parish, of Yeovil, Somerset, and Thelma, *née* Cromarty; *b* 7 June 1968, Yeovil, Somerset; *m* 15 Dec 2007, James Murray; 2 da (Ella-Jayne Thelma b 3 May 2008 d 2009, Nell 21 Nov 2009); *Career* actress; Best Actress RTS 1998; *Theatre* Nine (Donmar Warehouse) 1998, Popcorn 1999, Way Upstream (Chichester Fest Theatre) 2015; *Television* incl: Peak Practice 1997–99, Smoke 2001, Hearts and Bones 2001, Impact 2002, Sirens 2002, Cutting It 2002–05, Unconditional Love 2003, Reversals 2003, Our Hidden Lives 2005, ShakespeaRe-Told: Much Ado About Nothing 2005, If I Had You 2006, Aftersun 2006, Doctor Who 2006, Recovery 2007, Sex, the City and Me 2007, Baby Boom 2007 (as dir), Mistresses 2008–10, The Pillars of the Earth 2009, Monroe 2011, Harfields and McCoys 201, Monroe 2 2012, Atlantis 2013/14, Breathless 2013, WIA 2014–15, Trollied 2015; *Film* incl: The Wedding Date 2004, The Holiday 2006; *Style—* Ms Sarah Parish; ✉ c/o Sue Lattimer, A R G, 4 Great Portland Street, London W1W 8PA (☎ 020 7436 6400, Twitter @drsarahparish)

PARK, (James) Graham; CBE; s of James Park, OBE, JP (d 1959), of Salford, and Joan Clay, *née* Sharp (d 1987); *b* 27 April 1941; *Educ* Malvern Coll, Univ of Manchester (LLB); *m* 28 June 1969, Susan, da of Dr Charles Sydney Douglas Don (d 1973), of Manchester; 1 s (James b 1973); *Career* slr, former ptnr H L F Berry & Co 1969–2003 (conslt 2004–07); Parly candidate (Cons) 1974 and 1979, chm Altrincham Sale Constituency Cons Assoc 1983–87, chm NW Area Cons 1992–95, nat vice-pres 1995–98, pres Nat Convention Cons Pty 1998–99, chm Cons Pty Conference 1998, Cons Pty Compliance Offr, chm Cons Pty Constitutional Ctee 2000–06; memb: Ct Univ of Salford 1987–97, Parole Bd 1996–2002 and 2003–10, Criminal Injuries Compensation Appeal Panel 2000–11, Mental Health Review Tbnl 2003–12; fitness to practice chair Nursing and Midwifery Cncl 2012–; tbnl judge 2007–12; *Recreations* cricket, motor racing; *Style—* Graham Park, Esq, CBE; ✉ HLF Berry & Co, 758 Oldham Road, Failsworth, Manchester M35 9XB (☎ 0161 681 4005)

PARK, John William; MSP; s of George Park (d 1997), of Dunfermline, Fife, and Elizabeth, *née* Morris; *b* 14 September 1973, Dunfermline, Fife; *Educ* Woomill HS Dunfermline, Adam Smith Coll Kirkcaldy, Lauder Coll Dunfermline; *m* Lisa; *Career* electrical fitter Rosyth Dockyard 1989–98, trade union convenor Rosyth Dockyard 1998–2001, cmmns offr AEEU 2001–03, head of employee rels Babcock Naval Servs 2003–04, asst gen sec Scot TUC 2004–07, MSP (Lab) Mid Scot and Fife 2007–; memb Lab Party 1996–; *Recreations* football, walking, cinema; *Style—* John Park, Esq, MSP; ✉ The Scottish Parliament, Edinburgh EH99 1SP (☎ 0131 348 6753, fax 0131 348 6755, e-mail john.park.msp@scottish.parliament.uk)

PARK, Nicholas Wulstan (Nick); CBE (1997); *b* 1958; *Educ* Sheffield Sch of Art, Nat Film and TV Sch; *Career* producer/director of animated films; dir Aardman Animations (joined 1985); work incl: A Grand Day Out (BBC2) 1989 (BAFTA Best Animated Short 1990, Academy Award nomination 1990), Creature Comforts (Channel 4) 1990 (winner Academy Award for Best Animated Short 1990) and subsequent adaptation for series of 13 Heat Electric commercials (winners of various D&AD and other advtg industry awards), The Wrong Trousers (BBC2) 1993 (winner Academy Award for Best Animated Short and BAFTA Award for Best Short Animated Film 1994), A Close Shave 1995 (BAFTA for Best Animated Film 1995, Emmy for Best Popular Arts Programme 1996, four British Animation Awards 1996, Academy Award 1996), Chicken Run (with Pete Lord) 2000 (winner of many awards), Wallace & Gromit: The Curse of the Were-Rabbit 2005 (Academy Award 2006, Best Feature Film Children's BAFTA Awards 2006), Shaun the Sheep (series) 2007–09, Wallace and Gromit in A Matter of Loaf and Death 2008; *Style—* Nick Park, Esq, CBE

PARK, Richard; *b* 10 March 1948; *Career* Capital Radio 1987–2001; fndr and dir: Wildstar Records 1996–2001, Park Mgmnt 2001–, Park Records 2003–; gp exec dir and dir of broadcasting Global Radio 2007–; headmaster Fame Academy and Comic Relief Does Fame Academy (both BBC) 2002–07; fell Radio Acad; *Style—* Richard Park, Esq; ✉ Global Radio, 30 Leicester Square, London WC2H 7LA

PARKER, Alan; s of Frederick Parker, and Edith, *née* Cavell; *b* 26 August 1944; *Educ* Royal Acad of Music; *m* Stephanie, *née* Moore; 1 da (Jessica b 6 May 1979), 1 s (Josh b 25 Nov 1980); *Career* composer; worked with many leading performers incl: Dusty Springfield, Neil Diamond, John Denver, David Bowie, John Lennon, Paul McCartney; fndr memb: Blue Mink, The Congregation; writing extensively for 9 Lives Music Worldwide; involved with Lady Taverners (charity); FRSA; *Television and Documentaries*; over 80 prodns incl: Underwater Coast (BBC), The Way We Used To Live (YTV), The Outsiders (Channel 4), River Journeys (BBC), De-Beers Diamond Day, BMW (promo film), Esso (promo film), Horses in Our Blood (YTV), Westland Helicopters, Westland Aerospace, Men on Violence (LWT), Van der Valk (Thames), Jupiter Moon (BSkyB), Minder (Thames), Red Fox (LWT), Man & Animal (Carlton), Catherine Cookson's The Round Tower, Catherine Cookson's Colour Blind, Bomber (ITV), Tough Love (ITV), Victoria and Albert (BBC), The Swap (ITV), The Cry (ITV), Walking With Cavemen (BBC), The Crooked Man (ITV), D-Day (BBC), Marian Again (ITV), Fallen Angel (ITV), Coast (BBC); *Films* over 20 features incl: Jaws 3D (Universal, nominated Oscar 1985), Frankenstein (HBO), Mixed Doubles, American Gothic (Brent Walker), Philby Burgess & McClean (Granada), Nolan (Granada), The Glory Boys (YTV), Mirage (Granada), Sea of Serpents (Brent Walker), Out of Time (Alexandra), Voice of the Heart (Portman), To Be the Best (Gemmy), The Ice Man (MGM), Wild Justice (Berlusconi), What's Eating Gilbert Grape (Paramount), The Phoenix and the Magic Carpet (Miramax), Rhodes (Zenith/BBC, nominated Ivor Novello 1997), Hostile Waters (HBO/BBC), Up on the Roof (Granada Films/Rank), Oktober (Carnival), The Unknown Soldier (Carlton), Nancherrow (LWT), Diana Queen of Hearts (NBC), Victoria and Albert (BBC), The Swap (ITV), The Cry (ITV), Stormbreaker; *Jingles* 28 jingles and campaigns incl: Kellogg's Branflakes, Wrangler Jeans, Levis Jeans, Volkswagen Jetta & Polo, Heinz, Citröen, Ford Fiesta & Ford Cars (Germany), Tuborg Lager, Tango, Partners Against Crime (dir Mike Newell, ITV), Kronung Coffee; *Recreations* shooting, tennis, antiques; *Style—* Alan Parker, Esq, FRSA; ✉ c/o SMA Talent, The Cottage, Church Street, Fressingfield, Suffolk IP21 5PA (☎ 01379 586734)

PARKER, Sir Alan; kt (2014); s of Sir Peter Parker, KBE, LVO (d 2002), and Gillian, *née* Rowe-Dutton (d 2010); *b* 1956; *m* 1, 22 March 1977 (m dis), Caroline Louise, da of Thaddeus Gordon, of Yates; 1 s (Samuel b 1 Oct 1982), 3 da (Jessica Alexandra b 18 Aug 1984, Natasha Rose b 11 Dec 1987, Flora Liberty b 28 Feb 1991); m 2, 9 March 2007, Jane Hermione, da of Blaise Hardman, and Caroline Hardman; 3 s (William Peter Blaise b 27 June 2005, Peter Alan Jack b 15 Aug 2007, Adam Inigo Tom b 27 July 2009), 1 da (Isla Catherine b 20 Sept 2012); *Career* dep md Broad Street Associates 1982–87, sr ptnr then chm Brunswick Group 1987–; chm: Save the Children UK 2008–16, UK Now 2011–, Save the Children Int 2016–; chm HRH Duke of Edinburgh Cwlth Study Conf 2011–; UK business ambass 2010–, global ambass SOAS 2011–; memb: Temenos Acad, Bd FilmClub, Advsy Bd Videre; tstee: Business Commitment to the Environment (BCE) Environmental Leadership Awards Scheme, House of Illustration, Queen Elizabeth Diamond Jubilee Tst 2012–; *Recreations* friends; *Style—* Sir Alan Parker; ✉ Brunswick Group LLP, 16 Lincoln's Inn Fields, London WC2A 3ED (☎ 020 7396 5332, fax 020 7396 7456)

PARKER, His Hon Judge Alan Philip; adopted s of Harold Frederick Parker, and Irene Florence, *née* Gibbons; *b* 9 March 1953, Birmingham; *Educ* King Edward VI GS Aston, Univ of Manchester, Coll of Law Chester; 28 May 2012, Brendan Handley (civil partnership converted 2 June 2015); *Career* admitted slr 1978, called to the Bar 1995; articled to J H Duncombe, Esq, Messrs Wragge & Co 1976–78, asst slr Dudley MBC 1979–80, asst slr Office of the Chief Crown Prosecutor W Midlands 1980–82, recorder 2005, fee-paid judge First-tier Tbnl (Health, Educn and Social Care Chamber) 2011, circuit judge (Midland Circuit) 2012–; memb Restricted Patients Panel 2011; *Recreations* music (Californian folk rock), contemporary art (abstract expressionism), classic cars, Welsh Springer Spaniels, Sussex Spaniels; *Style—* His Hon Judge Alan Parker; ✉ Warwickshire Justice Centre, Newbold Terrace, Leamington Spa, Warwickshire CV32 4EL (e-mail HHJudgeAlan.Parker@judiciary.gsi.gov.uk)

PARKER, Sir Alan William; kt (2002), CBE (1995); s of William and Elsie Parker; *b* 14 February 1944, London; *Educ* Dame Alice Owen's School Islington; *m* 1 (m dis), Annie Inglis; 4 c; m 2, Lisa Moran; 1 c; *Career* filmmaker; early career as advtg copywriter with Collett Dickinson Pearce; chm UK Film Cncl 1999–2004, former chm Bd of Govrs BFI, founding memb Directors Guild of GB; Michael Balcon Award BAFTA 1985; fell BAFTA 2013; *Films* incl: The Evacuees 1975 (Best Dir BAFTA), Bugsy Malone 1976 (Best Screenplay BAFTA), Midnight Express 1978 (Best Dir BAFTA, Oscar and Golden Globe nominations for Best Dir), Fame 1980, Shoot the Moon 1982, Birdy 1984 (Grand Prix Special du Jury Cannes Film Festival), Angel Heart 1987, Mississippi Burning 1988 (Oscar, BAFTA and Golden Globe nominations for Best Dir), Come See the Paradise 1990, The Commitments 1990 (Best Dir BAFTA), The Road to Wellville 1994, Evita 1996 (BAFTA nomination Best Adapted Screenplay, Golden Globe nomination Best Dir), Angela's Ashes 1999, The Life of David Gale 2003; music videos incl The Wall by Pink Floyd 1982; *Books Non-Fiction* Evita, the Making of a Movie; *Novels* Bugsy Malone, Puddles in the Lane, The Sucker's Kiss; *Compendiums of Cartoons* Hares in the Gate,

P

Making Movies, Will Write and Direct for Food; *Recreations* Arsenal FC, painting; *Clubs* Chelsea Arts; *Style*— Sir Alan Parker, CBE; ✉ website www.alanparker.com

PARKER, Andrew; *Educ* Univ of Cambridge; *Career* MI5: joined 1983, dir for NI terrorism, protective security and serious crim 2002–05, dir of int terrorism 2005–07,dep DG 2007–13, DG 2013–; *Style*— Andrew Parker, Esq; ✉ PO Box 3255, London SW1P 1AE

PARKER, Prof Andrew; s of John Humphrey Parker, and Doreen May, *née* Jones; *b* 4 January 1954, Burnley; *Educ* Clare Coll Cambridge (BA, PhD, ScD); *Career* Univ of Oxford: Beit meml fell Physiology Dept 1979–80, Rudolph and Ann Rork Light res fell St Catherine's Coll and Physiology Dept 1980–83, official fell St Catherine's Coll 1985–90, official fell and tutor in physiology St John's Coll 1990–, prof of physiology 1996– (univ lectr 1985–96), memb Sci Ctee MRC Res Centre in Brain and Behaviour 1991–93, memb Sci Ctee McDonnell-Pew Centre for Cognitive Neuroscience 1994– (actg dir 1995–96), course dir grad prog in neuroscience 2000–; visiting scientist MIT Artificial Intelligence Lab USA 1984, visiting scientist Schlumberger Palo Alto Res Calif 1985; memb: Neuroscience Grants Panel The Wellcome Tst 1992–97, Advsy Bd MRC 1997–, Jl Ethics Panel Physiological Soc 2000–, Editorial Bd Vision Research 2000–, Organising Ctee Euro Conf on Visual Perception 1998; acted as referee for papers in numerous jls; visiting scholar Getty Res Inst LA 2002, Royal Soc Leverhulme sr research fell 2004–05; 21st Century Scientist Award James S McDonnell Fndn 2000, Royal Soc Wolfson Reserach Merit Award 2005–10; FSB; *Publications* more than 65 papers in various leading jls incl Nature, Annual Review of Neuroscience and Jl of Neuroscience; *Style*— Prof Andrew Parker; ✉ Department of Physiology, Anatomy and Genetics, Sherrington Building, Parks Road, Oxford OX1 3PT (☎ 01865 272504 (department), tel 01865 277321 (college), fax 01865 272543, e-mail andrew.parker@dpag.ox.ac.uk)

PARKER, Andrew John Cunningham; s of John Bertram Parker, of Suffolk, and Sally Elizabeth, *née* Warnes; *b* 13 February 1959, Bedford; *Educ* King Edward VI Sch Norwich, CCC Cambridge (MA); *Career* admitted slr 1983; slr: Daynes Chittock & Back 1983–90, Pengilly & Ridge 1990–91; slr then ptnr Keeble Hawson 1991–94, ptnr Irwin Mitchell 1994–97, ptnr Wansbroughs Willey Hargrave (subsequently Beachcroft Wansbroughs, now Beachcroft LLP) 1997– (currently head of strategic litigation); assessor Lord Justice Jackson's Review of Civil Costs 2009–; pres Forum of Insurance Lawyers 2000–01; memb: Civil Procedure Rule Ctee 2003–, Court of Appeal Civil Users Gp, Costs Practitioners Gp, Ctee London Slrs Litigation Assoc; *Recreations* travel, family, cricket; *Style*— Andrew Parker, Esq; ✉ Beachcroft LLP, 100 Fetter Lane, London EC4A 1BN (☎ 020 7242 1011, fax 020 7894 6240, e-mail aparker@beachcroft.com)

PARKER, Barrie Charles; s of Stanley Charles Digby Parker, of Southampton, Hants, and Betty Doreen, *née* Calverley; *b* 2 October 1940, London; *Educ* City of London Sch, Charing Cross Med Sch, Univ of London (MB BS); *m* 1, 27 April 1967, Ann Teressa (d 2009), da of William Rae Ferguson; m 2, 13 Aug 2010, Narasri Vatsandatatha, da of Wasan N Ying; *Career* sr registrar Charing Cross and Royal Nat Orthopaedic Hosps 1973–76; conslt orthopaedic surgn: Kingston Hosp 1976–2003, SW London Elective Orthopaedic Centre Epsom 2004–05; med dir: Kingston Hosp NHS Tst 1994–2001, SW London Elective Orthopaedic Centre 2003–05; former regnl advsr RCS England; hon treas Br Orthopaedic Assoc 1998–2003 (memb Cncl 1995–97); FRCS 1970, FRSM 1974, FBOA 1976, LRPS 2013; *Recreations* photography, travel; *Clubs* London Irish RFC, Kingston Med, Bookham Camera; *Style*— Barrie Parker, Esq; ✉ 2 The Laurells, Fetcham, Surrey KT22 9GZ (01372 450300, e-mail b.parker605@btinternet.com)

PARKER, Bruce Rodney Wingate; s of Robert Parker (d 1988), and Doris Maud, *née* Wingate (d 1995); *b* 20 July 1941; *Educ* Elizabeth Coll Guernsey, Univ of Wales (BA), Univ of Reading (DipEd); *m* 1, 1967 (m dis 1985), Anne Dorey; 2 s (James b 9 Aug 1968, Charles b 4 Aug 1974 d 2009), 1 da (Sarah (m Huw Thomas, *qv*, b 28 Dec 1969); m 2, 2002, Suzanne Stevens; 1 step s (Rupert); *Career* house master Elizabeth Coll Guernsey 1964–67, BBC News and Current Affrs reporter, presenter and prodr 1967–; progs incl: Nationwide, Antiques Roadshow, Mainstream, Badger Watch, Songs of Praise, South Today; political corr BBC South 1991–98, political ed 1998–2003, presenter BBC South of Westminster 1992–2003, frequent contribs to numerous radio and TV progs, helped devise and first presenter of Antiques Roadshow (BBC 1); RTS Reporter of the Year 1982, RTS Industry Achievement Award 1997, BBC DG's Special Award 2002; former memb Educn Advsy Ctee Hampshire CC, former chm of govrs Harestock Sch Winchester; chm Elizabeth Coll (Guernsey) Fndn 2008–, chm Gibson Fleming Tst, chm of tstees Winchester Cathedral Friends, tstee Winchester Cathedral Tst; chm Appleshaw Parish Cncl 2011–16; *Books* Everybody's Soapbox (with Nigel Farrell, 1983), History of Elizabeth College Guernsey (2011); *Recreations* travel, gardening, rifle-shooting, writing; *Clubs* Cwlth Rifle, N London Rifle, Dead Donkey (Guernsey); *Style*— Bruce Parker, Esq; ✉ Bridge Cottage, Appleshaw, Hampshire SP11 9BH (☎ 01264 772251, e-mail brwparker@gmail.com)

PARKER, Cameron Holdsworth; CVO (2007), OBE (1993); s of George Cameron Parker, MBE (d 1967), of Monifieth, Angus, and Mary Stevenson, *née* Houston (d 1985); *b* 14 April 1932; *Educ* Morrisons Acad Crieff, Univ of Glasgow (BSc); *m* 1, 20 July 1957, Elizabeth Margaret (d 1985), da of Andrew Sydney Grey Thomson (d 1957), of Dundee; 3 s (David b 1958, Michael b 1960, John b 1964 d 2010); m 2, 23 May 1986, Marlyne (d 2009), da of William Honeyman (d 1966), of Glasgow; *Career* chm John G Kincaid & Co Ltd 1976–80 (md 1967–80), chm and chief exec Scott Lithgow Ltd 1980–83, bd memb Br Shipbuilders Ltd 1977–80 and 1981–83, vice-chm Lithgows Ltd 1991–97 (md 1984–92); dir: Campbeltown Shipyard Ltd 1984–94, J Fleming Engineering Ltd 1984–94, Lithgow Electronics Ltd 1984–94, Malak Off & Wm Moore Ltd 1984–94, McKinlay & Blair Ltd 1984–94, Prosper Engineering Ltd 1984–94, A Kenneth & Sons Ltd 1985–94, Landcatch Ltd 1985–94, Glasgow Iron and Steel Co Ltd 1985–94, Argyll and Clyde Health Bd 1991–95, Scottish Homes 1992–96, Clyde Shaw Ltd 1992–94; memb Cncl CBI Scotland 1986–92; HM Lord-Lt Renfrewshire 1998–2007 (DL 1993–98); pres SSAFA Forces Help Renfrewshire 1998–2007, hon pres Accord Hospice Paisley 1998–2007; Freeman City of London, Liveryman Worshipful Co of Shipwrights 1981; Hon DUniv Paisley 2003; FIMarEST 1965; *Recreations* golf, gardening; *Style*— Cameron Parker, Esq, CVO, OBE; ✉ The Heath House, Rowantreehill Road, Kilmacolm, Renfrewshire PA13 4PE (☎ 01505 873197)

PARKER, His Hon Judge Christopher James Francis; QC (2006); *Career* called to the Bar 1986; asst recorder 1999, recorder 2000, circuit judge (South Eastern Circuit) 2012–; *Style*— His Hon Judge Christopher Parker, QC

PARKER, Cornelia; OBE (2010); da of Frank Parker, and Irmgarde Clothilde Maria Diesch; *b* 14 July 1956, Cheshire; *Educ* Gloucestershire Coll of Art and Design, Wolverhampton Poly (BA), Univ of Reading (MFA); *m Children* 1 da (b 2001); *Career* sculptor; numerous awards, commissions, projects and residencies including residency at ArtPace Foundation for Contemporary Art San Antonio Texas (solo exhibition) 1997; curator Govt Art Collection Exhbn Whitechapel 2011; subject of What Do Artists Do All Day? Cornelia Parker (BBC 4) 2013; Hon DUniv Wolverhampton 2000; RA 2009; *Solo Exhibitions* incl: Chisenhale Gallery London 1991, Deitch Projects New York 1998, Serpentine Gallery London 1998, ICA Boston 2000, Chicago Arts Club 2000, Aspen Museum of Art Colorado 2000, Philadelphia ICA 2000, Galleria Civica d'Arte Moderna Italy 2001, D'Amelio Terras NY 2003, Guy Bartschi Geneva 2003, Yerba Buena Center for the Arts San Francisco 2005, Brontë Parsonage Museum W Yorks 2006, IKON Birmingham 2007, Museo De Arte de Lima Peru 2008, Two Rooms Auckland 2010, Baltic Gateshead 2010, York St Mary's (in assoc with Tate) 2011, Whitechapel Gallery 2011, Galeria Carles Tache Barcelona 2013, Frith St Gallery 2013, Galeria Guy Bartschi Geneva 2014, Ikon Icons – 1980s (Ikon Gallery Birmingham) 2014, Whitworth Art Gallery Manchester 2015; *Group Exhibitions* incl: The British Art Show (Mclellan Galleries Glasgow, Leeds City Art Gallery, Hayward Gallery) 1990, São Paulo Bienal Brazil 1994, The Maybe – collaboration with Tilda Swinton (Serpentine Gallery) 1995, Turner Prize (Tate Gallery) 1997, Material Culture (Hayward Gallery) 1997, New Art from Britain (Kunstraum Innsbruck) 1998, 1st Melbourne Int Biennial 1999, Postmark: An Abstract Effect (Site Santa Fe) 1999, Violent Incident (Tate Gallery Liverpool) 1999, Interventions (Milkwaukee Art Museum) 2000, Between Cinema and a Hard Place (Tate Modern) 2000, Anteprima Bovisa Milano Europa 2000, New Collections Displays 1900 to the Present (Tate Britain) 2001–02, New Collection Displays: Truths and Fictions (Tate Liverpool) 2002, Days Like These (Tate Triennial Tate Britain) 2003, Speaking with Hands (Guggenheim Museum NY) 2004, Water, Air, Earth, Ice: At the origins of life between Art and Science (Museum of Modern Art Villa Croce Genoa) 2005, Projektion (Museum of Art Luzern) 2006, Thread (Ingleby Gallery Edinburgh) 2006, Resonance (Frith Street Gallery) 2006, Living in the Material World (Nat Art Centre Tokyo) 2007, Collective One (Galerie Guy Bartschi) 2007, Conversations (Kettle's Yard Cambridge) 2008, Revolutions – Forms that Turn (16th Biennale of Sydney) 2008, Selection (D'Amelio Terras NY) 2009, Medals of Dishonour (Br Museum) 2009, On Line: Drawing Through the Twentieth Century (MoMA NY) 2010, The Future Demands Your Participation (Minsheng Art Museum Shanghai) 2010, Summer Exhibition (Royal Acad of Arts) 2011, A Million Miles From Home (Folkestone Triennial) 2011, Travelling Light: Government Art Collection selected by Simon Schama (Whitechapel Gallery) 2011, Positions (Galerie Eigen+Art Leipzig) 2012, Encounter (Royal Acad in Asia Inst of Contemporary Arts Singapore) 2012, The Unseen (Fourth Guangzhou Triennial) 2012, White Light/White Heat (Instituto Veneto di Scienze Lettere ed Arti Venice Biennale) 2013, Where ar we Standing? Earth, Memory and Resurrection (Aichi Triennale Nogoya Japan) 2013, Nuage (Musée Réattu Arles) 2013, Homelands (touring Delhi, Kolkata, Mumba, Bengaluru India) 2013, Mortality: Death and the Imagination (Holden Gallery Manchester Sch of Art) 2013, Exploding Utopia (Laure Genniard Gallery) 2013, Drawn Together: Artist as Selector (Jerwood Gallery Hastings) 2014, Summer Exhibition (RA London, curated Black and White room) 2014, El Hotel Eléctrico (MHKA Museum of Contemporary Art Antwerp) 2014, Edwin Carels (as curator) Yoko Ono (as curator, Guggenheim Bilbao Museum), Dries Van Noten (as curator, Fashion Galleries Les Arts Décoratifs Paris), Keywords: Art, Culture and Society in 1980s Britain (as curator, Tate Liverpool), Gwangju Biennale (Gwangju S Korea) 2014, Unsettled (Shenzen Sculpture Beinnial China) 2014; *Collections* incl: Tate Gallery, MoMA NY, Musee d'Art Modern Centre Pompidou France, Arts Cncl, Govt Art Collection, Br Museum, Museum of Contemporary Art San Diego and various private and public collections in Europe and the USA; *Commissions* V&A 2001, BBC Radio 3 2003, Kunsthalle Dusseldorf and Von der Heydt Museum Wuppertal 2006, Jupiter Artland Edinburgh 2010; *Publications* Cornelia Parker (with B Ferguson and J Morgan, 2000), Cornelia Parker (by Iwona Blazwick, 2013), The Twenty-First Century Art Book (by David Trigg, Eliza Williams and Jonathan Griffin, 2014), Cornelia Parker (by Mary Griffiths, 2015); *Style*— Ms Cornelia Parker, OBE; ✉ Frith Street Gallery, 17–18 Golden Square, London W1F 9JJ (☎ 020 7494 1550, fax 020 7287 3733, e-mail info@frithstreetgallery.com)

PARKER, David; s of George Telford Parker, of Innerliethen, Scottish Borders, and Shirley Anne, *née* Burns; *b* 28 January 1974, Manchester; *Educ* Heriot Watt Univ (BSc, Storage UK Award); *m* 30 Aug 1997, Ruth, *née* Widdowson; 1 s (Angus Edward James b 3 March 2009); *Career* freelance IT conslt 1995–98, special needs technol advsr Heriot Watt Univ 1998–2002; cncllr Scottish Borders Cncl 1995– (dep ldr 2002–03, ldr 2003–); ldr ind membs Convention of Scottish Local Authorities 2007–; *Recreations* walking, cycling, cooking, wine appreciation; *Style*— Councillor David Parker; ✉ 6 Shielswood Court, Tweedbank, Galashiels TD1 3RH (☎ 01896 750344); Scottish Borders Council, Council Headquarters, Newtown St Boswells, Melrose TD6 0SA (☎ 01835 826571, fax 01835 825142, e-mail dparker@scotborders.gov.uk)

PARKER, Prof David; *b* 28 September 1949; *Educ* Univ of Hull (BSc), Univ of Salford (MSc), Cranfield Sch of Mgmnt (PhD); *Career* sr lectr Univ of Birmingham Business Sch 1993–97; prof of business economics and strategy: Aston Univ Business Sch 1997–2003, Sch of Mgmnt Cranfield Univ 2003–09 (now emeritus prof); visiting prof and dir of regulation research prog Centre for Research on Regulation and Competition Victoria Univ of Manchester (now Univ of Manchester) 2000–07; memb Competition Cmmn (formerly Monopolies and Mergers Cmmn) 1999–2007, memb UK Govt's Regluation Policy Ctee 2009–; official historian of privatisation UK Govt; assoc Public Administration International 2001–; numerous advsy and trg appts around the world incl economic advsr Office of Utilities Regulation Jamaica 2002–06; FRSA 1998, FBAM 2001, AcSS 2003; *Publications* incl: The Impact of Privatisation: Ownership and Corporate Performance in the UK (jtly, 1997), Privatisation and Supply Chain Management (jtly, 1999), Privatisation and Corporate Performance (ed, 2000), Globalisation and the Sustainability of Development in Latin America: Perspectives on the New Economic Order (jt ed, 2002), International Handbook on Privatisation (jt ed, 2003), Leading Issues in Competition, Regulation and Development (jtly, 2003), International Handbook of Economic Regulation (jtly, 2005), Official History of Privatisation Vol 1 (2009); *Style*— Prof David Parker; ✉ Cranfield School of Management, Cranfield, Bedford MK43 0AL (☎ 01234 751122, fax 01234 751806, e-mail david.parker@cranfield.ac.uk)

PARKER, Prof David; s of Joseph William Parker (d 2008), and Mary, *née* Hill (d 1988); *b* 30 July 1956, Leadgate, Co Durham; *Educ* Durham Johnston Secdy Sch, King Edward VI GS Stafford, ChCh Oxford (open exhibitioner, MA, Clifford Smith Prize), Hertford Coll Oxford (Carreras sr studentship, DPhil); *m* 27 July 1979, Fiona Mary, *née* MacEwan; 2 da (Eleanor Francoise b 4 Jan 1983, Julia Rose b 4 Aug 1984), 1 s (Philip James b 13 March 1988); *Career* Univ of Durham: lectr in chemistry 1982–89, sr lectr 1989–92, prof of chemistry 1992–, head Dept of Chemistry 1995–98 and 2003–06; visiting prof Université Louis Pasteur Strasbourg 1993, visiting prof Monash Univ 1998; chm RSC UK Supramolecular and Macrocycles Gp 1996–2000, chm Perkin 2 Scientific Editorial Bd 1996–2000, chm Chemical Soc Reviews Editorial Bd 2002–07; memb: Perkin Cncl RSC 1990–93 and 1996–99, RSC-FCMG/BCMG Ctee 1993–96, NECRC Scientific Ctee 1994–98; Coll Lectureship Hertford Coll Oxford 1979, NATO Fellowship 1980–81, Hickinbottom Fellowship RSC 1988–89, Royal Soc Leverhulme Tst Sr Research Fellowship 1998–99, Tilden Lectureship and Silver Medal RSC 2003–04; Corday-Morgan Medal and Prize RSC 1987, ICI Prize in Organic Chemistry 1991, Inderdisciplinary Award RSC 1995, Inaugural IBC Award in Supramolecular Science and Technol 2000, Inaugural RSC Award in Supramolecular Chemistry 2002, Ludwig Mond Award in Inorganic Chemistry RSC 2011, Lecoq de Boisbaudran Award in Rare Eath Science 2012; memb American Chemical Soc 1980–; ESPRC RISE Fell 2014; CChem 1978, FRSC 1988, FRS 2002; *Recreations* cricket, golf; *Clubs* Durham City Cricket, Brancepeth Castle Golf; *Style*— Prof David Parker; ✉ Department of Chemistry, University of Durham, South Road, Durham DH1 3LE (☎ 0191 334 2033, fax 0191 384 4737, e-mail david.parker@dur.ac.uk)

PARKER, Diana; da of Howard Parker (d 1967), and Avis Parker (d 1991); *b* 30 October 1957, Gosforth, Newcastle upon Tyne; *Educ* Univ of Cambridge (MA, MPhil); *m* 16 March 1991, Dr John Landers; *Career* admitted slr; specialises in family law; chm Withers LLP 1999–2007; memb: Law Soc, Int Acad of Matrimonial Lawyers; tstee: Inst for

Philanthropy, Common Purpose; *Recreations* allotments; *Style*— Ms Diana Parker; ✉ Withers LLP, 16 Old Bailey, London EC4M 7EG (☎ 020 7597 6198, fax 020 7597 6543, e-mail diana.parker@withersworldwide.com)

PARKER, Edward Barnwell; s of Herbert Blake Parker, and Diana Katharine, *née* Barnwell; *b* 13 October 1965; *Educ* Winchester Coll, RMA Sandhurst; *m* 31 Dec 1992, Harriet Marry, *née* Douglas-Bate; 1 s (Jack Andrew Barnwell b 19 March 1997), 2 da (Kitty Mary Barnwell b 22 March 1999, Olivia Voilet Barnwell b 21 March 2002); *Career* Br Army (serving in Royal Green Jackets) 1984–92; Cazenove & Co 1992–95, md Salomon Brothers/Citigroup 1995–2003, md Edward Parker Wines 2003–12; co-fndr Walking with the Wounded 2010–; dir Kett Country Cottages, ambass Skillforce; *Recreations* walking, theatre, reading, sailing, Norwich City FC, keeping fit, expeditions and adventure; *Style*— Edward Parker, Esq; ✉ Walking with the Wounded, Stody Hall Barns, Stody, Melton Constable, Norfolk NR24 2ED (☎ 01263 863900, e-mail edward@wwtw.org.uk)

PARKER, Prof (Noel) Geoffrey; s of late Derek Geoffrey Parker, and Kathleen Betsy, *née* Symon; *b* 25 December 1943, Nottingham; *Educ* Nottingham HS, Christ's Coll Cambridge (MA, PhD, LittD); *Children* 3 s, 1 da; *Career* fell Christ's Coll Cambridge 1968–72; Univ of St Andrews: reader in modern history 1978–82 (lectr 1972–78), prof of early modern history 1982–86; visiting prof: Vrije Universiteit Brussels 1975, Univ of British Columbia Vancouver 1979–80, Keio Univ Tokyo 1984; Lees Knowles lectr in mil history Univ of Cambridge 1984, Charles E Nowell distinguished prof of history Univ of Illinois at Urbana-Champaign 1986–93 (chm of dept 1989–91), Robert A Lovett prof of mil and naval history Yale Univ 1993–96, Andreas Dorpalen prof of European history and assoc Mershon Center for Int Security 1997– (distinguished univ prof 2007–); British Acad Exchange fell Newberry Library Chicago 1981, corresponding fell Spanish Royal Acad of History 1988–, J S Guggenheim Fndn fell 2001–02, H F Guggenheim sr fell 2002–03, Carnegie Centennial Prof St Andrews Univ 2016; Hon Doctorate in history and letters Vrije Universiteit Brussels 1990, Hon Dr Katholieke Universiteit Brussels 2005, Hon Dr Universidad de Burgos 2010; foreign memb: Academia Hispano-Americana Cadiz 2004, Koninklijke Akademie voor Wetenschappen Amsterdam 2005; FBA 1984, corresponding fell RSE 2016; Encomienda Order of Isabel the Catholic (Spain) 1988, Caballero Gran Cruz Order of Isabel the Catholic (Spain) 1992, Caballero Gran Cruz Order of Alfonso the Wise (Spain) 1996; *Awards* American Military Inst Best Book of the Year award for The Military Revolution (*see* Books) 1989, Dexter Prize for the best book published 1987–90 on the hist of technol for The Military Revolution 1990, Samuel Eliot Morrison Prize for teaching and publishing in the field of military history 1999, Alumni Assoc Distinguished Teaching Award Ohio State Univ 2006, A H Heikenen Fndn Prize for History Royal Netherlands Acad of Sciences 2012; *Books* The Army of Flanders and The Spanish Road 1567–1659 (1972, 2 edn 2004), The Dutch Revolt (1977, 3 edn 1985), Philip II (1978, 4 edn 2001), Europe in Crisis 1598–1648 (1979, 3 edn 2001), Spain and the Netherlands 1559–1659 (1979, 2 edn 1990), The Thirty Years' War (1984, 3 edn 1997), The World – An Illustrated History (ed 1986, 4 edn 1995), The Military Revolution – Military Innovation and the Rise of the West 1500–1800 (1988, 4 edn 2000), The Spanish Armada (with Colin Martin 1988, 4 edn 1999, revised Spanish edn 2011), The Cambridge Illustrated History of Warfare (ed, 1995, 3 edn 2008), The Times Compact History of the World (ed, 1995, 5 edn 2008), Spain, Europe and the Atlantic World – Essays in Honour of John H Elliott (ed, 1995), The Reader's Companion to Military History (ed, 1996), The Grand Strategy of Philip II (1998, 2 edn 1999), Success is Never Final. Empire, War and Faith in Early Modern Europe (2002), Felipe II: la biografía definitiva (2010), Global Crisis: war, climate change and catastrophe in the Seventeenth Century (2013, Society for Military History best book of the year award 2014, Br Acad Medal for landmark academic achievement 2014), Imprudent King. A new biography of Philip II (2014); author of numerous articles and reviews and ed numerous other books; numerous books translated into Chinese, Czech, Dutch, French, German, Japanese, Polish, Spanish, Turkish; *Recreations* travel, archaeology; *Style*— Prof Geoffrey Parker; ✉ The Ohio State University, 106 Dulles Hall, 230 Annie and John Glenn Avenue, Columbus, Ohio 43210-1367, USA (☎ 00 1 614 292 2674, fax 00 1 614 292 2282)

PARKER, Emeritus Prof Geoffrey Alan; s of Alan Parker (d 1989), and Gertrude Ethel, *née* Hill (d 1992); *b* 24 May 1944; *Educ* Lymm GS Cheshire, Univ of Bristol (BSc, Rose Bracher prize for biology, PhD), King's Coll Cambridge (MA); *m* 29 July 1967, Susan Mary (d 1994), da of Harold Alfred William Wallis; 1 da ((Nicola) Claire b 27 Aug 1973), 1 s (Alan Leslie b 4 April 1977); m 2, 25 Oct 1997, Carol Elizabeth, da of Harold Emmett; 1 step da (Maxine Sylvia b 18 July 1983); *Career* Univ of Liverpool: asst lectr in zoology 1968–69, lectr 1969–76, sr lectr 1976–80, reader 1980–89, prof Dept of Environmental and Evolutionary Biology 1989–96, prof Inst of Integrative Biology (formerly Sch of Biological Scis) 1996–2009 (emeritus prof 2009–); sr research fell King's Coll Research Centre Cambridge 1978–79, Nuffield Science research fell Univ of Liverpool 1982–83, SERC sr research fell Univ of Liverpool 1990–95; memb Editorial Bd: Heredity 1983–88, Ethology, Ecology and Evolution 1989–95, American Naturalist 1991–92, Journal of Evolutionary Biology 1991–96, Proceedings of the Royal Society of London, Series B 1991–97; consulting ed Animal Behaviour 1977–78 and 1980–82; memb Cncl: Assoc for Study of Animal Behaviour 1979–82 (memb 1976–), Int Soc for Behavioural Ecology 1986–88 (memb 1986–); memb: Br Ecological Soc 1965–2009, American Soc of Naturalists 1978–92, European Soc for Evolutionary Biology 1991–; Niko Tinbergen lectr Assoc for the Study of Animal Behaviour 1995, medal of Assoc for the Study of Animal Behaviour 2002, Animal Behaviour Soc Distinguished Animal Behaviourist Award 2003, Spallanzani medal Biology of Spermatozoa conf 2005, Frink medal Zoological Soc of London 2005, W D Hamilton lectr Int Soc for Behavioural Ecology 2006, Darwin Medal Royal Soc 2008; Hon DSc Univ of Bristol 2011; FRS 1989, Hon FRES 2012; *Books* Evolution of Sibling Rivalry (co-author, 1997); also author of over 200 scientific articles in learned jls; *Recreations* breeding, showing and judging exhibition bantams (Supreme Champion, Nat Poultry Club GB show 1997), playing jazz clarinet and tenor saxophone (mainly Dixieland) in local bands; *Clubs* Partridge & Pencilled Wyandotte (hon sec and treas 1987–94, pres 2003–), Poultry Club of GB (memb Cncl 1986–90 and 2004–08, pres 2003–06), Plymouth Rock (vice-pres 2002–10); *Style*— Emeritus Prof Geoffrey Parker, FRS; ✉ Institute of Integrative Biology, Biosciences Building, University of Liverpool, Liverpool L69 7ZB (e-mail gap@liv.ac.uk)

PARKER, Guy; *Educ* Univ of Kent; *Career* Advertising Standards Authy: joined 1992, dep DG and dir of complaints and investigations 2008–09, chief exec 2009–; chm European Advertising Standards Alliance 2013–16 (memb Exec Ctee 2007–), memb Cosmetic Interventions Advsy Bd UK Govt 2013–, memb Fundraising Regulators Standards Ctee 2016–, memb Consumer Protection Partnership Strategic Gp BIS 2016–; *Style*— Guy Parker, Esq; ✉ Advertising Standards Authority, Mid City Place, 71 High Holborn, London WC1V 6QT

PARKER, James Mavin (Jim); s of James Robertson Parker (d 1983), of Hartlepool, Cleveland, and Margaret, *née* Mavin; *b* 18 December 1934; *Educ* Guildhall Sch of Music and Drama; *m* 1; 1 da (Louise b 1964); m 2, 2 Aug 1969, Pauline Ann, da of John George, of Reading, Berks; 2 da (Claire b 1974, Amy b 1976); *Career* musician 4/7 Dragoon Gds; composer and conductor, joined Barrow Poets 1963; composed music for: Banana Blush (John Betjeman), Captain Beaky (Jeremy Lloyd); printed music: Follow the Star (Wally K Daly), Ground Force and other pieces (brass band), The Golden Section (brass quintet), All Jazzed Up (various instruments and piano), The Music of Jim Parker (various instruments and piano); childrens musicals: five Childrens Musicals (Tom Stanier), English Towns (flute and piano), A Londoner in New York (suite for brass), All Jazzed Up (oboe and piano), Mississippi Five (woodwind quintet); clarinet concerto, Light Fantastic (suite for brass), Mexican Wildlife (for brass quintet), Boulevard (for woodwind quintet), Bonjour M Grappelli (for string quartet), A Journey to South America (for recorder and harpsichord), Hoofers (for oboe and piano); film and TV music: Mapp and Lucia, Wynne and Penkovsky, Good Behaviour, The Making of Modern London, Girl Shy (Harold Lloyd), The Blot, Wish Me Luck, Anything More Would be Greedy, Parnell and the Englishwoman, Soldier Soldier, The House of Eliott, Body and Soul, Goggle Eyes, House of Cards, To Play The King (BAFTA Award for Best TV Music 1993), The Final Cut, Moll Flanders (BAFTA Award for Best TV Music 1996), Tom Jones (BAFTA Award for Best TV Music 1997), A Rather English Marriage (BAFTA Award for Best TV Music 1998), Lost For Words, The Midsomer Murders, Foyle's War, Born and Bred; Hon GSM 1985; GSM (Silver medal) 1959, LRAM 1959; *Recreations* twentieth century art, literature; *Style*— Jim Parker, Esq; ✉ 16 Laurel Road, London SW13 0EE (☎ and fax 020 8876 8442, e-mail jimparker322@gmail.com)

PARKER, Sir (Thomas) John; GBE (2012), kt (2001); s of Robert Parker (d 1957), and Margaret Elizabeth, *née* Bell; *b* 8 April 1942; *Educ* Belfast Coll of Technol, Queen's Univ Belfast; *m* July 1967, Emma Elizabeth, da of Alexander Blair, of Ballymena, NI; 1 s (Graham b 31 July 1970), 1 da (Fiona b 1 June 1972); *Career* shipbuilder and engr; Harland & Wolff Ltd: memb Ship Design Team 1963–69, ship prodn mangr 1969–71, prodn drawing office mangr 1971–72, gen mangr Sales and Projects Dept 1972–74; md Austin & Pickersgill (shipbuilders) Sunderland 1974–78, dep chief exec British Shipbuilders Corp 1980–83 (bd memb for shipbuilding mktg and ops 1978–80), chm and chief exec Harland & Wolff plc 1983–93 (non-exec dir 1993–96); chm: Babcock Int Gp plc 1994–2000 (dep chm and chief exec 1993–94), Lattice Gp plc (following demerger from BG Gp) 2000–02 (non-exec dir BG Gp plc 1997–2000), Firth Rixon 2001–03 (dep chm 1999–2001), RMC Gp 2002–04 (dep chm 2001–02), National Grid Transco plc (following Lattice's merger with National Grid) 2002–11, Peninsular and Oriental Steam Navigation Co (P&O) 2005–07 (dep chm Feb-May 2005), Anglo American plc 2009–, Mondi plc (jt chm); dep chm DP World Dubai 2007–15; dir: QUBIS Ltd Belfast 1984–93, British Coal Corp 1986–93, Fred. Olsen Norway 1989–93, GKN plc 1993–2003, P&O Princess Cruises 2000–03, Brambles Industries plc 2001–03, Carnival Corp and Carnival plc (formerly P&O Princess Cruises) 2003–, EADS/Airbus Gp 2007–; memb Ct of Dirs Bank of England 2004–09 (sr non-exec dir and chm); vice-pres Engrg Employers Fedn; memb: Cncl RINA 1978–80 and 1982– (vice-pres 1985, pres 1996–99), Int Ctee Bureau Veritas Paris 1981–97, Gen Ctee Lloyd's Register of Shipping 1983– (chm Technical Ctee 1996–2001), Industry Devpt Bd NI 1983–87, Br Ctee Det Norske Veritas Oslo 1984–94, Ctee of Mgmnt RNLI 1998–, Smeatonian Soc of Civil Engrgs; chllr Univ of Southampton 2006–11; Worshipful Co of Shipwrights (Liveryman 1978, prime warden 2000–01); Hon DSc: Queen's Univ of Belfast 1985, Univ of Ulster 1992, Univ of Abertay 1997, Univ of Surrey 2001, Univ of Southampton 2006, Plymouth Univ 2012, Univ of Aston 2012, Imperial Coll 2013; Hon ScD TCD 1986; FRINA 1978, FIMarE 1979, FREng 1982 (pres 2011–14); *Recreations* sailing, reading, music, the countryside; *Clubs* Royal Ulster Yacht, Royal Thames Yacht, Royal Yacht Sqdn; *Style*— Sir John Parker, GBE, FREng

PARKER, John Robert; s of John Thomas Parker, and Jennie, *née* Hardman (d 1997); *b* 30 April 1953; *Educ* Lancaster Royal GS, Hertford Coll Oxford (MA); *m* 1975, Fiona Jayne, *née* Rae; 1 s (Philip b 1979), 1 da (Claire b 1981); *Career* accountant Price Waterhouse 1975–79; Building Design Partnership: mgmnt accountant 1979–85, chief accountant 1985–89, equity ptnr (fin and admin ptnr) 1989–97, fin dir 1997–; dir Wren Insurance Assoc Ltd; FCA 1979; *Recreations* church work (memb UK Christians in Sci Assoc), reading (incl interest in sci devpts), walking; *Clubs* RAC; *Style*— John Parker, Esq; ✉ Building Design Partnership Ltd, 11 Ducie Street, PO Box 85, Manchester M60 3JA (☎ 0161 828 2200, e-mail john.parker@dbp.com)

PARKER, The Hon Mrs Justice; Dame Judith Mary Frances; DBE (2008), QC (1991); *Educ* Somerville Coll Oxford (BA); *Career* called to the Bar Middle Temple 1973; practising barr specialising in family law; dep High Ct judge Family Div 1997, recorder 2000 (asst recorder 1998–2000), judge of the High Court of Justice (Family Div) 2008–; regular lectr on all aspects of family law; fell Int Acad of Matrimonal Lawyers; Encyclopaedia of Financial Provision in Family Matters (contrib), Essential Family Practice (consltg ed); *Style*— The Hon Mrs Justice Parker; ✉ The Royal Courts of Justice, Strand, London WC2A 2LL

PARKER, Rt Hon Sir Kenneth Blades; kt (2009), PC; *Career* called to the Bar 1975; QC 1992; High Court judge 2009–16, ret; *Style*— The Rt Hon Sir Kenneth Parker; ✉ The Royal Courts of Justice, Strand, London WC2A 2LL

PARKER, Malcolm Peter (Mal); s of William Harvey Parker (d 1999), and Mary Jean, *née* Spinks (d 2009); *b* 4 June 1946; *Educ* Kings Sch Grantham, Oxford Sch of Architecture; *m* 21 June 1975, Linda Diane, da of Emmanuel Theodore, of London; 2 da (Charlotte b 1982, Georgina b 1984); *Career* architect; Tom Hancock Assocs 1972–73, John Winter Assocs 1973–74, Pentagram 1974–76, Richard Ellis 1976–78, founding ptnr Dunthorne Parker Architects 1978–; projects incl: offices for BUPA, Brooke-Bond, Capital Radio and Swiss Life, office investments for Rolls Royce, Rank Xerox, Windsor Life, General Motors Pension Funds and Sackville Property Ltd, industrial parks, Royal Bank of Scotland branches, historic shopping schemes in Oxford, Colchester, High Wycombe and Bury St Edmunds, retail stores for Pramerica, J Sainsbury, Local Authy Mutual Investment Tst, Henderson Global, Kier Property, hotels in Central London, recording studios for Nat Broadcasting Sch and Chrysalis Records, hostel for High Cmmr for Malaysia, restoration of Grade I listed bldgs Golden Cross in Oxford and Red Lion in Colchester and Grade II offices in Clifton, residential schemes in Whitehall and City of London for Royal Bank of Scotland; awards incl: Office Agents Soc Building of the Year 1999, Robertson Award, Ideas in Architecture Award, Oxford Preservation Tst Award, Royal Tunbridge Wells Civic Soc Conservation Award, Civic Tst Award; RIBA 1973, MCSD 1985; *Recreations* golf, cycling, skiing, sailing, walking, philately, theatre, opera, concerts, reading, etymology; *Clubs* Reform; *Style*— Mal Parker, Esq; ✉ Dunthorne Parker Architects, Unit 22, The Artworks Elephant, Elephant Road, London SE17 1AY (☎ 020 7258 0411, e-mail mal.parker@dunthorneparker.co.uk, website www.dunthorneparkerarchitects.co.uk)

PARKER, Martin; s of Leonard Parker, of Newcastle upon Tyne, and Winifred, *née* Callighan; *b* 20 June 1959, Newcastle upon Tyne; *Educ* Gosforth HS Newcastle upon Tyne, Univ of Leicester (LLB), Guildford Coll of Law; *m* 17 Dec 2005, Faye Louise, *née* Barker; 1 da (Alice Mathilda b 15 Feb 2007), 1 s (Theodore Samuel b 30 March 2009); *Career* admitted slr 1983; slr: Harbottle & Lewis 1983–87, Northern Engineering Industries plc 1987–89; Northumbrian Water Group Ltd: joined 1990, head of gp legal services 1998–2003, co sec and gen counsel 2003–; *Recreations* tennis, theatre, Newcastle United FC; *Style*— Martin Parker; ✉ Northumbrian Water Group Ltd, Boldon House, Wheatlands Way, Pity Me, Durham DH1 5FA (☎ 0191 301 6746, fax 0191 301 6705, e-mail martin.parker@nwl.co.uk)

PARKER, Michael Antonio; CBE (2011); *Educ* Brunel Univ (BSc), Birkbeck Coll London (MSc), Univ of Lancaster (Cert); *Career* sr ptnr Parkers 1997–2007; non-exec dir: Guy's and St Thomas's Hosp NHS Tst 1997–2002 (vice-chm and chair Audit Ctee 2000–02), Food Standards Agency 2006–; chair King's Coll Hosp NHS Fndn Tst 2002–; lectr: Univ of E London Business Sch 1997–2000, Queen Mary and Westfield Coll Univ of London 1998–2000; visiting lectr: INSEAD Business Sch 2006, SAID Business Sch 2008–11; dir

P

KCH Commercial Services Ltd; coordinator (ceo) Caribbean Teachers' Assoc 1983–85, memb Fndn Tst Finance Facility 2004–05, tstee Tropical Health and Educn Tst 2005–09, chair Bd of Govrs Royal Coll of Nursing Inst 2006–08 (external advsr Audit Ctee 2006–), external advsr Pension Ctee Royal Coll of Nursing 2009–11, patron Big Issue Malawi 2009–, pres Sickle Cell Soc 2009–, treas Mary Seacole Meml Statute Appeal; FCCA 2000 (memb 1995, memb Health Panel 2005–, chm Corporate Governance and Risk Management Ctee 2010–), FRSA 2010; *Style—* Michael Parker, Esq, CBE; ✉ King's College Hospital, Denmark Hill, London SE5 9RS

PARKER, Maj Sir Michael John; KCVO (2000, CVO 1991), CBE (1996, MBE (Mil) 1968); s of Capt S J Wilkins, and V S M Wilkins, *née* Parker; assumed his mother's maiden name in lieu of his father's patronymic by Deed Poll 1959; *b* 21 September 1941; *Educ* Dulwich Coll, Hereford Cathedral Sch, RMA Sandhurst; *m* February 2005, Emma Mary Bagwell Purefoy, *née* Gilroy; *Career* Capt The Queen's Own Hussars 1961–71, Maj TA Special List attached The Queen's Own Hussars 1972–; deviser and prodr of large-scale civilian and mil events; antique dealer; vice-pres: Morriston Orpheus Choir, Queen Elizabeth The Queen Mother's Meml Fund, Support for Africa, CIB; tstee ABF The Soldiers Charity 2003–13; patron: Chicken Shed Theatre Co, Brooklands SLD Sch; KStJ 1985 (OStJ 1982), Grand Offr Order of al Istiqlal (Jordan) 1987; *Main Productions* Becket 1963, Richard III (Berlin TV) 1964, Berlin Tattoo 1965, 1967, 1971, 1973, 1975, 1977, 1979, 1981, 1983, 1986, 1988 and 1992, British Week Brussels 1967, The Royal Tournament 1974–99, The Edinburgh Military Tattoo 1992–94, The Aldershot Army Display 1974, 1975, 1977, 1979, 1981 and 1983, Wembley Musical Pageant 1979, 1981 and 1985, over 70 other events around the world; *National Events* HM The Queen's Silver Jubilee Celebrations 1977, The Great Children's Party (Int Year of the Child) 1979, Carols for the Queen 1979, The Royal Fireworks 1981, The Great Children's Party Hyde Park 1985, HM Queen Elizabeth The Queen Mother's 90th Birthday Celebrations 1990, Economic Summit Spectacular (G7) Buckingham Palace 1991, HM The Queen's 40th Anniversary Celebration 1992, British National Day Expo'92 Seville Spain, 50th Anniversary VE Day Celebrations Hyde Park and Buckingham Palace 1995, 50th Anniversary VJ Day Celebrations Horseguards and Buckingham Palace 1995, HM Queen Elizabeth The Queen Mother's 100th Birthday Celebrations 2000, All the Queen's Horses Windsor 2002, The London Golden Jubilee Weekend Festival 2002 (incl National Beacon and Fireworks); *Other Events* Son et Lumière on Horse Guards Parade 1983 and 1985, Americas Cup Newport 1983, King Hussein of Jordan's 50th Birthday Celebrations 1985, Royal Weddings 1987 and 1993 and Coronation Celebration 1988 and 1993, Joy to the World (Christmas celebration Royal Albert Hall) 1988–97, International Horse Shows Olympia (finales), Wembley and Birmingham (variously), World Equestrian Games Stockholm, National Day Celebrations Oman (Royal Equestrian Day) 1990, Fortress Fantasia Gibraltar 1990, P&O 150th Anniversary Celebration Greenwich 1992 (further 18 shows in Hong Kong, Cyprus, Jordan, USA, Canada, Germany and UK), Wedding of Prince Abdullah Bin Al Hussein of Jordan (now King of Jordan), Memphis in May International Festival Tattoo USA 1993 and 1994, Opening of The Queen Elizabeth Gate Hyde Park London 1993, Firework Display to mark opening of The Channel Tunnel Folkestone 1994, The Spirit of Normandy (Royal Albert Hall) 1994, Multi-media Show for Normandy 50th Celebration Portsmouth 1994, The Army Benevolent Fund Drumhead Serv 1994, Pavarotti International Horse Show (finales) Modena Italy 1993 and 1994, P&O ship naming Shekou China 1994, P&O ship namings Portsmouth and USA 1995, Jersey Liberation Fireworks 1995, Oriana Gala Sydney 1996, naming of Dawn Princess Fort Lauderdale 1997, The Countryside Rally Hyde Park 1997, Gala for naming of Grand Princess NY 1998, Unveiling Ceremony for the Albert Meml London 1998, Centenary Celebrations for King Abdul Aziz Riyadh Saudi Arabia 1999, Royal Military Tattoo Horse Guards 2000, Reaching Out For Africa Royal Albert Hall 2002 and 2007, Opening of Meml Gates Constitution Hill 2002, Opening of Memphis Symphony Orchestra Concert Hall 2003, Ship naming of Minerva II Port of London 2003, Not Forgotten Assoc Christmas Show St James's Palace 2003–10, Music on Fire! RMA Sandhurst 2004, 2006 and 2008, Centenary Cavalcade Royal Welsh Agricultural Show 2004, Liberation Day Son et Lumière Jersey 2005, Royal Yacht Sqdn Cowes Trafalgar Celebration 2005, Glory of Wales Denbigh 2005, Not Forgotten Assoc Veterans Day Concert Tower of London 2006 and 2008 and Painted Hall Greenwich 2007, NFA 90th Anniversary ballroom of Buckingham Palace 2010; *Awards* Evening Standard Ambass for London 1995, Walpole Gold Medal for Excellence 2002, Walpole Award for Best Cultural Achievement 2002, CIB Communicator of the Year 2002, SPAM Lifetime Achievement Award 2002, RTS Derek Harper Technical Award; *Publications* The Awful Troop Leader's Gunnery Crib (1969), It's All Going Terribly Wrong (2012); *Recreations* antiques, painting, giving parties; *Clubs* Cavalry and Guards; *Style—* Maj Sir Michael Parker, KCVO, CBE

PARKER, Mike Howard; s of Michael Harding Parker, and Margaret Elfrida, *née* Armstrong; *b* 24 April 1956; *Educ* Chelmer Valley HS Chelmsford; *m* 31 May 1980, Teresa Marie, *née* Soler (d 1990); 1 da (Laura Michelle b 4 Dec 1980); partner, Anna Marie Treacher; *Career* reporter Essex Chronicle 1973–77, freelance reporter 1977–82, reporter and feature writer News of the World 1982–87; Daily Star: reporter Jan-Sept 1987, night news ed 1987–88, dep news ed 1988–89, features ed 1989–94, asst ed 1994–; assignments covered in N and S America, W Indies, Africa, Middle East, Russia and throughout Europe; Nat Newspaper Consumer Journalist of the Year 1988; *Books* The World's Most Fantastic Freaks (1982); *Recreations* tennis, theatre, travel; *Style—* Mike Parker, Esq

PARKER, Gen Sir Nicholas Ralph (Nick); KCB (2009), CBE (2001); s of Captain Blake Parker, RN (d 2015), and Diana Katherine, *née* Barnwell; *b* 13 October 1954, Winchester; *Educ* Sherborne, RMA Sandhurst, Royal Coll of Defence Studies; *m* 1979, Rebecca Clare, *née* Wellings; 2 s (Timothy b 1980, Harry b 1983); *Career* served Br Army 1973–2013; Cdr: 2 Bn Royal Green Jackets 1993–95, 20 Armoured Bde (Bosnia) 1996–99; Cdr Jt Task Force Sierra Leone and advsr to Pres 2001, Dep Cdr Multinational Corps Iraq 2005–06, GOC NI 2006–07, Dep Cdr Int Security Assistance Force Afghanistan 2009–10, C-in-C Land Forces 2010–12; dir The Military Mutual 2014–, chm Coote Capital 2014–; chm Step up to Serve 2014–, dir Invictus Games 2014, tstee Team Rubicon 2015–, cmmr Citizens UK Cmmn on Islam Participation and Public Life 2015, chm Salute My Job 2015–; sr assoc fell RUSI 2013–; *Recreations* gardening, fishing, Coronation Street; *Clubs* Army and Navy; *Style—* General Sir Nick Parker, KCB, CBE

PARKER, Oliver Tom; s of Sir Peter Parker (d 2002), and Lady Jill Parker, *née* Rowe-Dutton; *b* 6 September 1960; *Educ* St Paul's; *Partner* Cassia Kidron; 1 da (Bel b 19 Aug 1996), 1 s (Otis Saxon b 12 Oct 2001), 1 step s (Cato Sandford b 25 May 1989); *Career* film dir, screenplay writer and actor; writer and dir: Othello 1996, An Ideal Husband 1999 (BAFTA nomination for Best Adapted Screenplay 1999), The Importance of Being Earnest 2002, Fade to Black 2006; dir I Really Hate My Job 2006, co-dir and co-prodr St Trinian's 2007, dir Dorian Gray 2009, dir and co-prodr St Trinians II 2009, dir Johnny English Reborn 2011, dir Dad's Army 2016; short films: A Little Loving 1994, The Short Cut 1994, Unsigned 1994; for TV: Billingsgate Alfie 1996, Copper Clive 1996, The Private Life of Samuel Peypes 2003; extensive stage, television and film acting roles; patron Big Arts Week; *Recreations* tennis, football; *Clubs* Groucho, Electric; *Style—* Oliver Parker, Esq; ✉ c/o Sue Rodgers, ICM, Oxford House, 76 Oxford Street, London W1D 1BS (☎ 020 7636 6565)

PARKER, Sir (William) Peter Brian; 5 Bt (UK 1844), of Shenstone Lodge, Staffordshire; o s of Sir (William) Alan Parker, 4 Bt (d 1990), and Sheelagh Mary, *née* Stevenson; *b* 30 November 1950; *Educ* Eton; *m* 1976, Patricia Ann, da of late R and late Mrs D E Filtness, of Lea Cottage, Beckingham, Lincoln; 1 da (Lucy Emma b 1977), 1 s (John Malcolm b 1980 d 2003); *Heir* kinsman, Timothy John Parker; *Career* FCA; sr ptnr Stephenson Nuttall & Co Newark Notts; *Style—* Sir Peter Parker, Bt; ✉ Apricot Hall, Sutton-cum-Beckingham, Lincoln LN5 ORE

PARKER, Peter Robert Nevill; s of Edward Parker, and Patricia, *née* Sturridge; *b* 2 June 1954, Hereford; *Educ* Canford Sch, UCL (BA); *Career* freelance literary journalist 1978–, author 1987–, columnist and diarist Hortus (gardening jl) 1990–2002, assoc ed Oxford DNB 1996–2004 (advsy ed 2006–); memb Exec Ctee PEN 1993–97, tstee PEN Literary Fndn 1993–2009 (chair 1999–2000); memb Editorial Bd: London Library Magazine 2008–, A Magazine (RIBA Friends of Architecture) 2014–; memb: Ctee London Library 1999–2002 (chm Books Sub-Ctee 1999–2002 and 2004–07, tstee 2004–07), Cncl RSL 2004–14 (vice-chair 2008–14), Linley Library Advsy Ctee RHS 2008–13 (chm 2009–13); FRSL 1997; *Books* The Old Lie: The Great War and the Public-School Ethos (1987), Ackerley: A Life of J R Ackerley (1989), The Reader's Companion to the Twentieth-Century Novel (ed, 1994), The Reader's Companion to Twentieth-Century Writers (ed, 1995), Isherwood: A Life (2004), The Last Veteran: Harry Patch and the Legacy of War (2009), Housman Country: Into the Heart of England (2016); *Recreations* gardening, cinema; *Style—* Peter Parker, Esq, FRSL; ✉ c/o Rogers, Coleridge & White, 20 Powis Mews, London W11 1JN (☎ 020 7221 3717, fax 020 7229 9084)

PARKER, Peter William; TD (1966); s of William Nichol Parker (d 1978), of Burnley, and Muriel, *née* Constantine (d 1965); *b* 13 June 1933; *Educ* Winchester, New Coll Oxford (MA); *m* 5 Oct 1963, Janet Pusey (d 1998), da of Tom Rymer Till (d 1982), of Caerleon; 1 da (Lucy (Mrs Leverett) b 1966), 2 s (Tom b 1968 d 2009, Daniel b 1971); *Career* Nat Serv; 2 Lt E Lancashire Regt 1952 (actg capt 1953), TA 4 E Lancashire Regt 1953–67 (Maj 1965); Phillips & Drew 1956–85: ptnr 1962, dep sr ptnr 1983; chm Phillips & Drew International Ltd 1980–85; memb: Cncl Inst of Actuaries 1977–82 and 1986–92 (vice-pres 1988–91), Cncl CGLI 1991–2007, Royal Patriotic Fund Corp 1991–2011, Ctee RUKBA 1996–2006, Investigation Ctee ICAEW 1999–2003; memb Archbishops' Review of Bishops' Needs and Resources 1999–2002, memb Pensions Bd C of E 2003–11, church cmmr 2003–11; tstee Tower of London Choral Fndn 1983–2015, govr Sidney Perry Fndn 1983– (chm 2004–), treas Egypt Exploration Soc 1988–2003, govr Music Therapy Charity 1989–, tstee Tower of London Chapels Royal Fndn 2015–; Liveryman Worshipful Co of Actuaries (Master 1989–90); Hon FCGI, FIA 1963, FCSI; SBStJ; *Recreations* music, gardening, travel, typography; *Clubs* City of London, Naval and Military; *Style—* Peter Parker, Esq, TD; ✉ 1 Turner Drive, London NW11 6TX (☎ 020 8458 2646, fax 020 8455 8498)

PARKER, His Hon Judge Philip Laurence; QC (2000); *Career* called to the Bar 1976; asst recorder 1994, recorder 1999, circuit judge (Midland Circuit) 2008–; *Style—* His Hon Judge Parker, QC; ✉ Birmingham Crown Court, Queen Elizabeth II Law Courts, 1 Newton Street, Birmingham B4 7NA

PARKER, Sir Richard William; *see:* Hyde Parker, Sir Richard William

PARKER, Prof Robert Henry (Bob); s of Henry William Parker (d 1978), of London, and Gladys Mary, *née* Bunkell (d 1939); *b* 21 September 1932; *Educ* Paston Sch North Walsham, UCL (BScEcon); *m* 5 Oct 1955, (Marie) Agnelle Hilda, da of Antoine Yves Laval (d 1962), of Mauritius; 1 s (Michael b 1956), 1 da (Theresa b 1959); *Career* accountant Cassleton Elliott and Co Lagos Nigeria 1958–59, lectr in commerce Univ of Adelaide 1960–61, sr lectr in commerce Univ of W Aust 1962–66, P D Leake res fell LSE 1966, reader in mgmnt accounting Manchester Business Sch 1966–68, assoc prof of finance INSEAD Fontainebleau 1968–70; prof of accountancy: Univ of Dundee 1970–76, Univ of Exeter 1976–97 (prof emeritus 1997–); professorial fell Inst of CAs of Scotland 1991–96, ed Accounting and Business Research 1975–93; FCA 1968 (ACA 1958); *Books* Topics in Business Finance and Accounting (jtly, 1964), Readings in Concept and Measurement of Income (jtly, 1969, 2 edn 1986), Management Accounting – An Historical Perspective (1969), Understanding Company Financial Statements (1972, 6 edn 2007), Accounting in Scotland – A Historical Bibliography (jtly, 1974, 2 edn 1976), The Evolution of Corporate Financial Reporting (jtly, 1979), British Accountants – A Biographical Sourcebook (1980), Accounting Thought and Education (jtly, 1980), Bibliographies for Accounting Historians (1980), Comparative International Accounting (jtly, 1981, 12 edn 2012), Macmillan Dictionary of Accounting (1984, 2 edn 1992), Papers on Accounting History (1984), The Development of the Accountancy Profession in Britain to the Early Twentieth Century (1986), Issues in Multinational Accounting (jtly, 1988), A Dictionary of Business Quotations (jtly, 1990), Accounting in Australia – Historical Essays (1990), Consolidation Accounting (jtly, 1991), Collins Dictionary of Business Quotations (jtly, 1991), Accounting History – Some British Contributions (jtly, 1994), Financial Reporting in the West Pacific Rim (jtly, 1994), An International View of True and Fair Accounting (jtly, 1994), Accounting History from the Renaissance to the Present (jtly, 1996), Milestones in the British Accounting Literature (jtly, 1996), Readings in True and Fair (jtly, 1996), Accounting in France/ La comptabilité en France: Historical Essays/ Etudes historiques (jtly, 1996), Professional Accounting and Audit in Australia 1880–1900 (jtly, 1999), Major Contributors to the British Accountancy Profession (jtly, 2012); *Recreations* local history, genealogy; *Style—* Prof Bob Parker; ✉ St Catherines, New North Road, Exeter EX4 4AG (☎ 01392 255154); University of Exeter Business School, Streatham Court, Exeter EX4 4PU (☎ 01392 723201, fax 01392 723210, e-mail r.h.parker@exeter.ac.uk)

PARKER, Robert John; s of Eric Robert Parker (d 1984), and Joan Marjorie Parker (d 1991); *b* 22 February 1952; *Educ* Whitgift Sch, St John's Coll Cambridge (MA); *m* 28 Aug 1982, Claudia Jane, da of Col Alexander Akerman; 3 s (Felix Alexander b 12 Feb 1987, Toby, Benjamin (twins) b 14 Oct 1991); *Career* asst dir NM Rothschild & Sons Ltd 1976–82, exec dir investment Credit Suisse First Boston Group 1982–94; Credit Suisse Asset Management Ltd: chief exec 1995–98, global head institutional business devpt 1997–2002, vice-chm 1998–, memb Chm's Bd and Investment Ctee; dir: Central European Growth Fund plc 1994–2000, Credit Suisse Asset Management Deutschland GmbH 1995–2001, Credit Suisse Asset Management France SA 1997–2001; Freeman City of London, Liveryman Worshipful Co of Farriers; *Style—* Robert Parker, Esq; ✉ Credit Suisse, One Cabot Square, London E14 4QJ

PARKER, His Hon Judge Steven Nigel; s of Brian Parker, and Sylvia Parker; *b* Newent, Glos; *m* 1988, Jane *née* Ridgway; *Career* called to the Bar 1987; dep district judge 2000, recorder 2008, circuit judge (Northern Circuit) 2013–; *Recreations* sailing, theatre, sport; *Style—* His Hon Judge Steven Parker; ✉ Liverpool Civil and Family Court, 35 Vernon Street, Liverpool L2 2BX

PARKER, Timothy Charles (Tim); s of Clifford Parker (d 1999), and Eileen, *née* Jupp; *b* 19 June 1955, Aldershot, Hants; *Educ* Pembroke Coll Oxford (MA), London Business Sch (MSc); *m* 4 Aug 1984, Therese, *née* Moralis; 2 da (Louise b 14 Oct 1985, Josephine b 9 Dec 1997), 2 s (Antony b 7 March 1990, George b 21 Sept 1991); *Career* chief exec: Kenwood Appliances 1989–96, Clarks Shoes 1996–2002, Kwik-Fit 2002–04 (non-exec dep chm 2004–06), The AA 2004–07; 1 dep mayor London and chief exec GLA Gp 2008; chm: Emerging Africa Infrastructure Fund 2005–08, Nine Entertainment Gp Australia 2008–11, Autobar Gp 2012–14, Samsonite Corp, British Pathé, National Trust 2014–; advsr CVC Capital Ptnrs 2008–, chm and ceo Samsonite Int SA 2009–; non-exec dir: Legal & General Gp 2001–04, Alliance Boots plc (formerly Boots Gp plc), Compass Gp plc 2007–09; tstee Royal Acad of Music; memb Bd Audit Cmmn; FRSA; *Recreations* music, running, reading; *Clubs* Travellers, Garrick; *Style*— Tim Parker, Esq

PARKES, Timothy Charles; TD (1988); s of Frank Leonard Parkes (d 1955), of Leamington Spa, Warks, and Marie Joan Parkes, *née* Morris (d 1999); b 13 August 1954; *Educ* Royal Masonic Sch, Wadham Coll Oxford (MA); m 31 Aug 1985, Wendy Patricia, da of Maj Vincent Reginald Hook, of Ufford, Suffolk; 1 s (Charles Alexander Frederick b 1988), 2 da (Laura Claire Venetia b 1990, Eleanor Juliet Lucy b 1992); *Career* TACSC 1989 (Maj TA Royal Yeomanry 1984–90); admitted slr 1980; ptnr Herbert Smith Freehills LLP 19897–2015; chm: Law Soc Far East Ctee 1997–99, Regulatory Decisions Ctee Financial Conduct Authy 2016–, Enforcement Decisions Ctee Payment Systems Regulator 2016–; memb: Judicial Studies Bd Hong Kong 1990–95, Civil Court Users' Ctee Hong Kong 1993–95, Cncl Law Soc of Hong Kong 1993–95 and 2002–05; chm: Wadham Coll Oxford Law Soc 2010–15, Oxford Univ Law Devpt Ctee 2013–15, Wadham Coll Oxford Devpt Cncl; memb Law Soc of England and Wales; chm Kent and Sharpshooters Yeomanry Museum Tst 1997–2001; tstee Army Museums Ogilby Trust; hon legal advsr Matilda Int Hosp Hong Kong 2002–05; Freeman Worshipful Co of Slrs 1982; FCIArb; *Publications* The Civil Procedure Rules Ten Years On (2009); *Recreations* tennis, painting, reading; *Clubs* Cavalry and Guards', Hong Kong, Royal Hong Kong Jockey; *Style*— Timothy Parkes, Esq, TD; ✉ Berghersh Place, Witnesham, Ipswich, Suffolk IP6 9EZ (☎ 01473 785504, fax 01473 785159)

PARKIN, Catherine Elizabeth (Kate); da of Ian Stuart Parkin, of Alderton, Glos, and Elizabeth, *née* Downey; b 9 April 1959; *Educ* Tewkesbury Comp, Cheltenham GS, St Catherine's Coll Oxford (MA), Goldsmith's Coll London (MA); m 29 Aug 1983, William John Urwick Hamilton, s of Mark Hamilton; 2 da (Susannah Elizabeth Rose b 18 April 1989, Mary Isabel Angelica b 19 April 1993); *Career* grad trainee Thomson Publishing 1980–81, editorial controller Macmillan London Ltd 1981–85; Transworld Publishers Ltd: ed 1985–86, sr ed 1986–87 editorial dir 1987–89; editorial dir Collins Publishers 1989–91; Random House UK: publishing dir Century 1991–93, publisher Century Arrow 1993–2000, md Century Hutchinson William Heinemann and Arrow 2000; with John Murray Publishers 2005–; coach Way Ahead Gp; *Recreations* reading, cooking, gardening, music; *Style*— Ms Kate Parkin

PARKIN, Ian Michael; s of George Harold Parkin (d 1996), of Worthing, W Sussex, and Ethel Mary, *née* Fullerton (d 2002); b 15 October 1946; *Educ* Dorking Co GS, Open Univ (BA); m 30 April 1977, Patricia Helen, da of Maj Frederick James Fowles, MC (d 1982); 2 s (Andrew b 1978, Richard b 1984), 1 da (Jennifer b 1981); *Career* CA; formerly: sr ptnr Pannell Kerr Forster CI 1979–90, sr ptnr Brownes CAs Jersey, dir Citadel Trust Ltd Jersey 1990–93, ptnr Moores Rowland Jersey 1993–95; dir: Compass Trust Company Ltd Jersey, Cater Allen Trust Company (Jersey) Ltd 1994–99, Chatsworth Property Services Ltd 1999–; FCA 1979; *Recreations* golf, reading; *Style*— Ian Parkin, Esq; ✉ Le Petit Jardin, La Rue a la Pendue, Millais, St Ouen, Jersey (☎ 01534 483218, fax 01534 486092, e-mail ian@chatsworthjersey.com)

PARKIN, Sara Lamb; OBE (2000); *née* McEwan; da of Dr George Lamb McEwan (d 1996), of Isle of Islay, Argyll, and Marie Munro, *née* Rankin (d 2013); b 9 April 1946; *Educ* Barr's Hill GS Coventry, Bromsgrove Coll, Edinburgh Royal Infirmary (RGN), Univ of Michigan, Leeds Poly; m 30 June 1969, Donald Maxwell Parkin, s of Donald Harry Parkin (d 2001), of Lincolnshire, and Lesley Mary, *née* Tyson (d 2002); 2 s (Colin McEwan b 28 March 1974, Douglas Maxwell b 12 Sept 1975); *Career* staff nurse and ward sister Edinburgh Royal Infirmary 1970–74, nursing res asst and undergraduate tutor Univ of Edinburgh 1972–73, memb Cncl Brook Advsy Serv 1974–76, Leeds AHA 1976–80, self employed writer and speaker on green issues 1981–; princ assoc Sustainability Literacy Project 2016–; Green Pty: memb Cncl 1980–81, int liaison sec 1983–90, chair Exec 1992; co-sec Euro Greens 1985–90 (ed Newsletter 1986–89); dir Forum For The Future 1995–; memb: Bd Environment Agency of England and Wales 2000–06, Cncl NERC 2003–09, Bd Leadership Fndn for HE 2003–09, Bd European Trg Fndn 2009–15, Bd HE Acad 2014–, Bd Carnegie Tst for the Univs of Scotland 2016–; chair Richard Sandbrook Tst 2010–; assoc Engrg Cncl; hon fell Soc for the Environment, Companion ICE, hon fell Inst of Energy; *Publications* incl: Green Parties: An International Guide (1989), Green Light on Europe (ed, 1991), Green Futures (1991), The Life and Death of Petra Kelly (1994), The Positive Deviant: Sustainability Leadership in a Perverse World (2010); also author of various nat and Euro Green Election manifestos; *Recreations* walking, gardening, theatre, opera; *Style*— Sara Parkin; ✉ The Sustainability Literacy Project, 173 Hoxton Street, London N1 6PJ (☎ 020 7739 5263, mobile 07801 827878, e-mail slp@saraparkin.org, website www.saraparkin.org)

PARKINS, Graham Charles; QC (1990); *Educ* Univ of London (LLB); *Career* called to the Bar Inner Temple 1972, recorder of the Crown Court 1989–; memb Criminal Bar Association; *Style*— Graham Parkins, Esq, QC; ✉ 18 Red Lion Court, London EC4A 3EB

PARKINSON, Charles Nigel Kennedy; s of Prof C Northcote Parkinson (d 1993), and Ann, *née* Fry (d 1982); b 1 March 1954, Singapore; *Educ* Rugby, Emmanuel Coll Cambridge (MA); m 21 July 1983, Clare, *née* Haynes; 3 da (Sophia b 9 June 1989, Emma b 18 Jan 1991, Zoe b 25 July 1994), 1 s (Edward b 25 Feb 1996); *Career* CA 1978, called to the Bar 1981; KPMG 1975–78 and 1981–83, Morgan Grenfell 1979–80, Pannell Kerr Forster 1983–2004, Rothschild Asset Mgmnt (CI) Ltd 1989–2001, min Treasy and Resources Dept States of Guernsey 2004–; chm Eastern European Property Fund Ltd; non-exec dir: Mapeley Ltd, Dexion Equity Alternative Ltd, Burford Capital Ltd, Bailiwick Investments Ltd; FCA 1978; *Publications* Taxation in France (2004); *Recreations* sailing, boating, skiing, golf; *Clubs* Guernsey Yacht; *Style*— Charles Parkinson, Esq; ✉ Treasury and Resources Department, States of Guernsey, Sir Charles Frossard House, St Peter Port, Guernsey GY1 1FH (☎ 01481 717000, fax 01481 713787)

PARKINSON, Malcolm Ross; MBE (2012); s of F C D Parkinson (d 1983), and Alexa St Clair, *née* Ross (d 1999); b 20 April 1948; *Educ* Sutton Valence; m 1972, Beatrice Maria, da of Prof C Schwaller; 1 da (Charlotte b 1978), 1 s (Alexander b 1981); *Career* trainee navigation offr Cunard then actg 4th offr T & J Brocklebank Ltd 1964–69, trainee account exec BBD&O Ltd 1969–72, account dir Leo Burnett Inc 1972–74, jt md DWK Ltd 1974–76, dir B & Q Ltd 1976–84, chief exec F W Woolworth Ltd and dir Woolworth Holdings plc 1984–87, md Retail Corporation plc 1989–92, md Siegel & Gale Ltd (UK and EMEA) 1993–96, gp chief exec Landmark Retail plc 1997–2000; chm: Imatronic Ltd 1989–93, James Latham plc (dir 1992–2008); dir: Malross Management Ltd 1983–2008, Latham Timber Centres Ltd 1992–97, Powerbreaker plc 1992–97, Applied Chemicals Ltd 1992–97, Cardionetics plc 1996–2001, Allen Int Consulting Gp Ltd 2009–; chm Capel Manor Coll 2008–14; memb Worshipful Co of Gardeners; fell Mktg Soc; *Recreations* sailing, shooting; *Clubs* Royal Thames Yacht; *Style*— Malcolm Parkinson, Esq, MBE; ✉ Holly Bank, Church Lane, Sway, Hampshire SO41 6BA (☎ 01590 683899)

PARKINSON, Sir Michael; kt (2008), CBE (2000); b 28 March 1935, Yorkshire; *Educ* Barnsley GS; m 22 August 1959, Mary Heneghan; 3 s (Andrew, Nicholas, Michael); *Career* TV and radio presenter, journalist and writer; prodr/interviewer Granada TV 1963–66 (Granada's Scene, Granada in the North, World in Action, What The Papers Say), exec prodr and presenter LWT 1968–69; presenter: 24 Hours (BBC) 1966–67, Cinema (Granada TV) 1969–70, Tea Break and Where in the World (Thames TV) 1971; host: Parkinson (BBC) 1972–82 and 1998–2004 (Channel 10 and ABC Australia 1979–85), Parkinson (ITV) 2004–07; co-fndr and presenter TV-AM 1983–84; presenter: Give Us A Clue (Thames TV) 1984–92, Desert Island Discs (BBC Radio 4) 1986–88; host: Parkinson One to One (Yorkshire TV) 1987–88, Parky (Thames TV) 1989, The Michael Parkinson Show (LBC) 1990–92; presenter: Help Squad (TVS) 1991–92, Ghostwatch (BBC) 1992, Parkinson on Sport (BBC Radio 5) 1994–97, Parkinson's Sunday Supplement (BBC Radio 2) 1996–2007, My Favourite Things (BBC Radio 2) 2012–; host: Going For a Song (BBC) 1995–99, Parkinson: Masterclass (Sky Arts) 2012–; fndr Pavilion Books 1980; sometime columnist and feature writer: Sunday Times, Guardian, Daily Express, The People, The Listener, Daily Mirror, New Statesman, Mail on Sunday; sometime columnist Radio Times; Sports Feature Writer of the Year (British Sports Journalism Awards) 1995, Sports Writer of the Year British Press Awards 1998, Variety Club's Media Personality of the Year 1998, Sony Radio Award for Parkinson's Sunday Supplement 1998, Comic Heritage Gold Award for Special Contribution to the World of Entertainment 1998, Yorkshire Man of The Year 1998, BASCA Gold Award 1998, National Television Awards Most Popular Talk Show for Parkinson 1998, 1999, 2000 and 2001, Broadcasting Press Guild Award for Best Performance in Non-Acting Role 1999, Best Light Entertainment Performance BAFTA 1999, Media Soc Award for Distinguished Contribution to the Media 2000, Bernard Delfont Award for Outstanding Contibution to Showbusiness Variety Club of GB 2007; chllr Nottingham Trent Univ 2008–14; Hon DUniv Humberside 1999, Hon DLitt Univ of Huddersfield 2008; fell BFI 2000; *Books* Football Daft (1968), Cricket Mad (1969), Pictorial History of Westerns (with Clyde Jeavons, 1969), Sporting Fever (1974), Best – An Intimate Biography (1975), A-Z of Soccer (with Willis Hall, 1975), Bats in the Pavilion (1977), The Woofits (1980), Parkinson's Lore (1981), The Best of Parkinson (1982), Sporting Lives (1992), Sporting Profiles (1995), Michael Parkinson on Golf 1999, Michael Parkinson on Football (2001), Michael Parkinson on Cricket (2002), Parky – My Autobiography (2008), Parky's People (2010); *Recreations* sport (particularly cricket and golf); *Style*— Sir Michael Parkinson, CBE; ✉ Parkinson Productions, Braywick House West, Windsor Road, Maidenhead, Berkshire SL6 1DN (☎ 01628 628711)

PARKS, Timothy Harold (Tim); s of Harold James Parks (d 1980), and Joan Elizabeth, *née* MacDowell; b 19 December 1954; *Educ* Westminster City Sch London, Downing Coll Cambridge (BA), Harvard Univ (MA); m 15 Dec 1979, Rita Maria, *née* Baldassarre; 1 s (Michele Roberto b 3 June 1985), 1 da (Stefania Angela b 20 Jan 1988); *Career* writer; marketing exec Tek Translation & International Print London 1979–80, freelance teacher and translator Verona 1981–85, lettore Univ of Verona 1985–, visiting lectr Istituto Universitario di lingue Moderne Milan 1992–; memb Soc of Authors 1986–; *Fiction* Tongues of Flame (1985, Somerset Maugham award, Betty Trask award), Loving Roger (1986, John Llewellyn Rhys award), Home Thoughts (1987), Family Planning (1989), Cara Massimina (as John MacDowell, 1990), Goodness (1991), Shear (1993), Mimi's Ghost (1995), Europa (1997, shortlisted for Booker Prize), Destiny (1999), Judge Savage (2003), Rapids (2005), Talking About It (short stories, 2005), Cleaver (2006); numerous short stories; series of trans from Italian incl work by Calvino, Moravia, Tabucchi and Calasso; *Non-Fiction* Italian Neighbours (1992), An Italian Education (non-fiction, 1997), Translating Style: English Modernists and their Italian Translations (1997), Adultery and Other Diversions (essays, 1998), Hell and Back (essays, 2001), A Season with Verona (2002), Medici Money, Banking, Metaphysics and Art in Fifteenth Century Florence, a work of history (2005); numerous academic pubns; *Recreations* cycling, squash; *Style*— Tim Parks; ✉ website www.timparks.com

PARMINTER, Baroness (UK Life Peer 2010), of Godalming in the County of Surrey; Kathryn (Kate) Parminter; da of James Parminter, and June Parminter; b 24 June 1964; *Educ* Millais Sch Horsham, Collyer's Sixth Form Coll, LMH Oxford (MA); m 9 July 1994, Neil Sherlock; 2 da (Rose Sherlock b 26 July 2000, Grace Sherlock b 16 Aug 2003); *Career* grad mktg trainee The Nestlé Co Ltd 1986–88, Parly researcher for Simon Hughes MP 1988–89, sr account exec Juliette Hellman PR 1989–90; RSPCA: PR offr 1990–92, head of campaigns and events 1992–95, head of public affrs 1996–98, chm Campaign for the Protection of Hunted Animals 1997–98; dir CPRE 1998–2004; tstee IPPR 2007–; cncllr Horsham DC 1987–95; memb House of Lords Select Ctee on the EU 2013–15, memb Select Ctee on Nat Policy for the Built Environment 2015–16; memb and tstee Lib Dems (elected to nat Federal Exec 2008–10), dep ldr Lib Dem Gp House of Lords 2015–; memb National Trust, vice-pres RSPCA 2010–13, patron Meath Epilepsy Tst 2010–; *Publications* Working For and Against Government in Pressure Group Politics in Modern Britain (1996), A Third Sector as well as a Third Way (jtly, 2001); *Recreations* Pre-Raphaelite paintings, walking; *Clubs* National Liberal; *Style*— The Baroness Parminter; ✉ House of Lords, London SW1A 0PW

PARMOOR, 5 Baron (UK 1914); His Hon (Michael Leonard) Seddon Cripps; s of (Matthew) Anthony Leonard Cripps, CBE, DSO, TD, QC, and Dorothea Margaret Cripps; b 18 June 1942, Ashby-de-la-Zouch, Leics; *Educ* Eton; m 1971, Elizabeth Anne, da of Maj Millward-Shennan, of Moorside, Caldy-in-Wirral; 1 da (Hon Stephanie Margaret Julia b 1974), 1 s (Hon Henry William Anthony b 2 Sept 1976); *Heir* s, Henry Cripps; *Career* called to the Bar: Middle Temple 1965, Lincoln's Inn 1969, Inner Temple 1975; circuit judge (South Eastern Circuit) 1998–2012; pres Immigration Servs Tbnl 2000–10, judge First Tier Tbnl 2010–12, judge Upper Tbnl 2010–12; *Style*— His Hon The Lord Parmoor; ✉ Bessemers, Moor Wood, Lane End, High Wycombe, Buckinghamshire HP14 3HZ

PARR, Martin; s of Donald Parr (d 1999), and Joyce, *née* Watts; b 23 May 1952; *Educ* Surbiton GS, Manchester Poly (Dip Creative Photography); m 1980, Susie, da of Douglas Mitchell; 1 da (Ellen b 18 April 1986); *Career* photographer; visiting lectr: Nat Coll of Art and Design Dublin and Chelsea Sch of Art 1975–82, Sch of Documentary Photography Newport 1982–1984, W Surrey Coll of Art and Design 1983–90; visiting prof of photography Univ of Industrial Arts Helsinki 1990–92; memb Magnum Photo Agency 1994–; Arts Cncl of GB Photography Award 1975 and 1979; *Solo Exhibitions* incl: Home Sweet Home (Impressions Gallery York and Arnolfini Gallery Bristol) 1974, Beauty Spots (Impressions Gallery York and tour) 1976, Photographers' Gallery London 1977, Fotomania Gallery Barcelona 1978, The Non-Conformists (Camerawork London) 1981, Rural Irish Photographers (Neikrug Gallery NY) 1982, Bad Weather (Photographers' Gallery London and tour) 1982, International Photography Festival Malmo 1983, British Photographic Art (Geology Museum Beixing) 1984, A Fair Day (Orchard Gallery Derry and tour) 1984, George Eastman House Rochester 1985, Point of Sale (Salford City Art Gallery) 1986, The Last Resort (Serpentine Gallery London) 1986, Museum Folkwang Essen 1986, Arles Festival 1986, Fotograficentrum Stockholm 1986, Amsterdam Manifestation 1986, ICP Midtown NY 1987, Spending Time (Nat Centre of Photography Paris) 1987, Kodak Gallery Tokyo and Osaka 1988, The Cost of Living (RPS Bath and tour) 1989, Janet Borden NY 1991 and 1996, Gallery Jacques Gordat Paris 1991, Signs of the Times (Janet Borden NY) 1992, Kiek in de Kok Gallery Tallinn 1992, A Year in the Life of Chew Stoke (Chew Stoke Village Hall) 1993, Bored Couples (Gallery du Jour Paris and tour) 1993, Home and Abroad (Watershead Gallery Bristol and int tour) 1993, From A to B (27 Welcome Break service stations across UK) 1994, Curitiba Photo Festival 1994, Small World (Photographers' Gallery London) 1995, Small World and From A to B (Nat Centre of Photography Paris) 1995, Gallery du Jour Paris 1995 and 2000, West Bay (Rocket Gallery London) 1997, Ooh La La (Nat Museum of Photography Bradford) 1998, Japonais Endormis (Gallery du Jour Paris) 1998, Gallery Riis Oslo 1999, Common Sense (43 locations worldwide) 1999, Benidorm (Sprengel Museum Hanover) 1999, 20/21 Gallery Essen 2000, Autoportrait (Tom Blau Gallery London) 2000, Japonais Endormis (Kunsthalle Rotterdam) 2000, Kulturbeutel (Old Post Office Mitte Berlin) 2000, Think of England (Rocket Gallery London) 2001, Martin Parr: Photographic Works 1971–2000 (Barbican Art Gallery London) 2002, Parrworld (Haus de Kunst Munich) 2008; *Group Exhibitions* incl: Butlins by the Sea (Impressions Gallery York) 1972, Personal Views 1860–1977 (Br Cncl touring show) 1978, Art for Society (Whitechapel Art Gallery London) 1978, Three Perspectives on Photography (Hayward Gallery London) 1979, New Work in Britain (Photographers' Gallery London) 1981, Strategies – recent developments in British photography (John Hansard Gallery Southampton) 1982, Quelques Anglais (Centre Nationale de la Photographie Paris) 1985, British Contemporary Photography (Houston Foto Festival) 1986, New Documents (Museum of Contemporary Photography Chicago) 1986, Attitudes to Ireland (Orchard Gallery Derry) 1987, Mysterious Coincidences (Photographers' Gallery London) 1987, Inscriptions and Inventions (Br Cncl touring exhbn) 1987, A British View (Museum für Gestalturg Zurich) 1988, Through the Looking Glass, British Photography 1945–1989 (Barbican Centre London) 1989, The Art of Photography (Royal Acad London) 1989, Foto Biennale (Enschede) 1989, The Past and Present of Photography (MOMA Tokyo) 1990, British Photography from the Thatcher Years (MOMA NY) 1991, Voir la Suisse Autrement (Fribourg) 1991, Imagina (World Fair Seville) 1992, Photographs from the Real World (Lillehammer Art Museum) 1993, Sobre Santiago, Tres de Magnum (Santiago) 1993, European Photography Award 1985–1994 (Kultur Zentrum Bad Hamburg) 1994, Internationale Foto-Triennale (Esslingen) 1995, Zurich (Kunsthaus Zurich) 1997, Trois Grands Egyptiennes (Musée de la Photographie Charleroi) 1997, No Sex Please, we're British (Shisheido Dept Store Tokyo) 1998, Our Turning World: Magnum Photographers 1989–1999 (Barbican Art Gallery London) 1999, Cruel & Tender (Tate Modern London) 2003; *Work in Public Collections* incl: Arts Cncl of GB, Union Bank of Finland Helsinki, Museum for Fotokunst Odense, V&A, George Eastman House Rochester, Bibliotheque Nationale Paris, MOMA NY, Philadelphia Museum of Art, MOMA Tokyo, Calderdale Cncl Halifax, Getty Museum Malibu, Walker Art Gallery Liverpool, Kodak France, Museum Folkwang Essen, Seagrams Collection NY, MOMA Tempere, Br Cncl London, Irish Arts Cncl, Australian Nat Gallery, Paris Audiovisual, Sprengel Museum Hannover, Yokohama Museum of Art, Tokyo Metropolitan Museum of Photography, San Francisco MOMA, Stedelijk Museum Amsterdam, Tate Modern London; *Books* Bad Weather (1982), A Fair Day (1984), The Last Resort (1986, 2 edn 1998), The Actual Boot – the Photographic Postcard 1900–1920 (1986), The Cost of Living (1989), Signs of the Times (1992), Home and Abroad (1993), From A to B (1994), Small World (1995), West Bay (1997), Flowers (1999), Common Sense (1999), Boring Postcards (1999), Autoportrait (2000), Think of England (2000), Boring Postcards USA (2000), Langweilige Postkarten (2001), Phone Book (2002), 7 Communist Still Lives (2003), Fashion Magazine (2005), Mexico (2006), Parking Spaces (2007), Parrworld (2008), Playas (2009), Luxury (2010), Up and Down Peachtree (2012), No Worries (2012), Life is a Beach (2012), The Non-Conformists (2013), We Love Britain (2014), Black Country Stories (2014), Hong Kong (2014), Autoportrait (2015), Cakes & Balls (2016), Real Food (2016); subject of book Martin Parr by Val Williams (2002); *Clubs* Clifton Poker Sch; *Style*— Martin Parr, Esq; ✉ Magnum Photos, 63 Gee Street, London EC1V 3RS (☎ 020 7490 1771)

PARR, Simon; QPM (2014); *Career* former head Operations Dept Sussex Police, Dep Chief Constable Herts Police 2006–10 (joined 2004), Chief Constable Cambs Police 2010–; *Style*— Simon Parr, Esq, QPM; ✉ Cambridgeshire Constabulary Headquarters, Hinchingbrooke Park, Huntingdon, Cambridgeshire PE29 6NP

PARRATT, Prof James Roy; s of James John Parratt, and Eunice Elizabeth Parratt; *b* 19 August 1933; *Educ* St Clement Danes Holborn Estate GS, Univ of London (BPharm, MSc, PhD, DSc (Med)), Univ of Strathclyde (DSc), Univ of Cambridge (DipTh); *m* 7 Sept 1957, Pamela Joan Lyndon, da of Stanley Charles Marels; 2 s (Stephen John Lyndon b 14 March 1960, Jonathan Mark b 21 March 1969), 1 da (Deborah Joy b 3 Sept 1965); *Career* sr lectr Dept of Physiology Univ of Ibadan Nigeria 1958–66; Univ of Strathclyde: sr lectr then reader Dept of Pharmacology 1966–74, personal chair in pharmacology 1975, newly established chair in cardiovascular pharmacology 1983–, chm and head Dept of Physiology and Pharmacology 1986–90, emeritus prof 1998–, res prof 2001–; prof Dept of Pharmacology Albert Szent-Györgyi Med Univ Szeged Hungary 1996– (Hon MD 1989), emeritus fell Leverhulme Tst 2001–03, Albert Szent-Györgyi Res Fellowship Hungarian State Govt 2003; former chm Br Soc Cardiovascular Res; hon memb: Pharmacological Soc Hungary 1976, Slovak Medical and Cardiological Socs 1997, Czech Cardiological Soc 1998; Polish Physiological Soc Medal 1989, J Purkinje Gold Medal Acad of Scis of the Czech Republic 1995, Lifetime Achievement Award Int Acad of Cardiovascular Scis 2014; memb Br Cardiac Soc, FRSE 1986, FIBiol, FRCPath, FRPharmS, FESC, fell Int Soc for Heart Res (FISHR), hon fell Br Pharmacological Soc; *Books* Early Arrhythmias Resulting From Myocardial Ischaemia; Mechanisms and Prevention by Drugs (1982), Calcium Movement and its Manipulation by Drugs (1984), Myocardial Response to Acute Injury (1992), Ischaemic Preconditioning (1996); *Recreations* music, jam-making, Scottish islands, Christian ministry (Scottish Baptists Lay Preachers Assoc); *Style*— Prof James Parratt, FRSE; ✉ 10 St Germains, Bearsden, Glasgow G61 2RS (☎ 0141 942 7164); Department of Physiology and Pharmacology, University of Strathclyde, Strathclyde Institute for Biomedical Sciences, 27 Taylor Street, Glasgow G4 0NR (☎ 0141 548 2858, fax 0141 552 2562, telex 77472, e-mail pimjam.parratt@btinternet.com); Department of Pharmacology, Szent-Györgyi Albert Medical University, Dóm tér 12, Szeged, Hungary (☎ 36 62 54 56 73, e-mail jr.parratt@phcol.szote.u-szeged.hu)

PARRIS, Matthew Francis; s of late Leslie Francis Parris, and Theresa Eunice, *née* Littler; *b* 7 August 1949; *Educ* Waterford Sch Swaziland, Clare Coll Cambridge, Yale Univ USA; *Partner* Julian Glover (civil partnership 2006); *Career* author, journalist and broadcaster; FO 1974–76, Cons Research Dept 1976–79, MP (Cons) West Derbyshire 1979–86, presenter Weekend World LWT 1986–88, currently freelance broadcaster and columnist The Times and other jls; Political Journalist of the Year 2014 and various other journalistic awards; *Publications* author of books on politics, humour and travel incl: Chance Witness: An Outsider's Life in Politics (2002), Castle in Spain: A mountain ruin and an impossible dream (2005), Parting Shots – Undiplomatic diplomats (2010), The Spanish Ambassador's Suitcase – and other stories (2012); *Recreations* travelling; *Style*— Mr Matthew Parris; ✉ c/o The Times, 1 London Bridge Street, London SE1 9GF

PARRITT, Clive Anthony; s of Allan Edward Parritt, MBE (d 1998), and Peta, *née* Lloyd; *b* 11 April 1943; *Educ* privately; *m* 1, 28 Sept 1968 (m dis 1984); 2 s (James b 1977, Daniel b 1980); m 2, 5 Oct 1985, Deborah, da of Kenneth Jones (d 2009); 2 s (Matthew b 1987, Thomas b 1989); *Career* CA; successively ptnr 1973–82: Fuller Jenks Beecroft, Mann Judd, Touche Ross & Co; Baker Tilly: ptnr 1982–2001, managing ptnr 1987–96, chm 1996–2001; chief exec The Business Exchange plc 2001–03 (dir 2001–2004); chm: Baronsmead Investment Trust plc 1994–98, Baronsmead VCT2 plc 1998–2016, BG Training Ltd 2004–; dir: Herald Investment Trust plc 1994–2005, Harvard Managed Offices Ltd 2003–, London & Associated Properties plc 2006–, Baronsmed AIM VCT plc 2006–10, Jupiter US Smaller Cos 2006–, Industrial Pipefreezing Services Ltd 2007–, DiGiCo Global Ltd 2007–16, Audiotonix Ltd 2014–16; memb Advsy Panel Enterprise and Deregulation Unit DTI 1986–88; memb: Nat Assoc of CA Students Soc 1965–67 (chm London Branch 1965–66), Cncl ICAEW 1983–2014 (vice-pres 2009–10, dep pres 2010–11, pres 2011–12); chm London Soc of CAs 1982–83 (treas 1980–82); chm Redhill and Reigate Round Table 1976–77; treas Br Theatre Assoc 1984–87; govr Arnold House Sch 2003–10; Liveryman Worshipful Co of Chartered Accountants; FCA 1966, CF, FIIA, FRSA; *Recreations* theatre, entertaining, gardening; *Style*— Clive Parritt, Esq; ✉ 34 Eton Avenue, London NW3 3HL (☎ 020 7794 2443 (home), 07713 621274 (office), e-mail clive@parritt.com)

PARROTT, Andrew Haden; s of Reginald Charles Parrott, BEM (d 1979), of Walsall, and Edith Dora Parrott (d 2012); *b* 10 March 1947; *Educ* Queen Mary's GS Walsall, Merton Coll Oxford (open postmastership, BA); *m* 1 (m dis); m 2, 23 June 1986, Emily, da of William Payne Van Evera, of Duluth, MN; 1 da (Kate b 3 Aug 1995); *Career* conductor; fndr and artistic dir Taverner Choir, Consort and Players 1973–; music dir: London Mozart Players 2000–06, NY Collegium 2002–08; guest conductor: Europe, Scandinavia, USA, Canada, Israel and others; appeared at festivals incl: BBC Proms, Edinburgh, Lucerne, Salzburg, Tanglewood; sr hon research fell Univ of Birmingham; memb Royal Musical Assoc; *Recordings* over 60 incl works by: Machaut, Josquin, Taverner, Tallis, Gabrieli, Monteverdi, Purcell, Vivaldi, Bach, Handel, Mozart, Beethoven and twentieth-century composers; *Publications* New Oxford Book of Carols (jt ed), The Essential Bach Choir, Composers' Intentions?, various articles; *Style*— Andrew Parrott, Esq; ✉ c/o Rayfield Allied, Black Prince Road, London SE1 7SJ (☎ 020 3176 5500, fax 0700 602 4143, e-mail info@rayfieldallied.com)

PARROTT, Graham Joseph; *b* 17 August 1949; *Career* memb Bd Granada Gp (merged to form ITV plc 2004) 1992–2004 (joined 1973), dir ITN 1997–2004, dir GMTV Ltd 1999–2004, gp commercial dir and co sec ITV plc, chm ITV Pension Scheme 1990–2012; chm: The Local Radio Co plc 2004–07, Cancer Research Campaign Pension Scheme 2007–, Rexam Pension Plan 2012–; memb Assoc of Professional Pension Tstees; dir: Elecrent Insurance Ltd 1989–2004, Christmas Prepayment Assoc 2007–10; FCIS; *Style*— Graham Parrott, Esq; ☎ 07787 288764, e-mail gparrott@btconnect.com

PARROY, Michael Picton; QC (1991); s of Leopold Gerald May Parroy (d 1982), and Elizabeth Mary, *née* Picton-Bayton (d 1979); *b* 22 October 1946; *Educ* Malvern Coll, BNC Oxford (MA); *m* 18 Nov 1978, Susan Patricia Blades Winter; *Career* called to the Bar Middle Temple 1969 (Winston Churchill exhibitioner, bencher 2001), recorder 1990– (asst recorder 1986), head of chambers 1995–2004; *Books* Halsbury's Law of England (co-author, 4 edn vol 40); *Recreations* stone carving, gardening; *Style*— Michael Parroy, Esq, QC; ✉ 3 Paper Buildings, Temple, London EC4Y 7EU (☎ 020 7583 8055, fax 020 7353 6271)

PARRY, Bryn; OBE; *m* Emma Parry, OBE, *qv*; 1 s (Tom), 2 da (Sophie, Louisa); *Career* served with Royal Green Jackets; cartoonist Bryn Parry Studios until 2009, co-fndr (with wife Emma Parry, OBE) Help for Heroes 2007; *Style*— Bryn Parry, Esq, OBE; ✉ Help for Heroes, 14 Parker's Close, Downton Business Centre, Salisbury, Wiltshire SP5 3RB

PARRY, His Hon David Johnston; s of Kenneth Johnston Parry (d 1942), and Joyce Isobel Cooper (d 2008); *b* 26 August 1941; *Educ* Merchant Taylors' Northwood, St Catharine's Coll Cambridge (MA), Higher Cts (Criminal Proceedings) Advocacy qualification 1994; *m* 20 April 1968, Mary, da of George Percy Harmer; 1 s (Andrew Kenneth b 4 Feb 1970), 3 da (Susanna b 25 Feb 1971, Annette b 26 Nov 1973, Marita b 12 July 1976); *Career* articled clerk Turberville Smith & Co Uxbridge, admitted slr 1968, ptnr (then co sr ptnr) Dixon Ward Slrs 1969–95; recorder 1991–95 (asst recorder 1986–91), circuit judge (SE Circuit) 1995–2002 (dep circuit judge 2003–07); pt/t chm Ind Tbnl Serv 1993–96, admin Richmond and Twickenham Duty Slr Scheme 1990–95, patron Richmond Legal Advice Serv 1995– (co-chm 1969–95), pt/t chm Lord Chancellor's Advsy Ctee for South West London 2007–11; Freeman City of London, Liveryman Worshipful Co of Merchant Taylors; memb: Law Soc, London Criminal Courts Slrs' Assoc; *Recreations* music, literature, theatre, travel, DIY; *Clubs* Old Merchant Taylors', Nothing, Roehampton; *Style*— His Hon David Parry

PARRY, Sir Eldryd Hugh Owen; KCMG (2011), OBE (1982); s of Owen Brynog Parry (d 1954), of Cardiff, and Constance Lilian, *née* Griffiths (d 1974); *b* 28 November 1930; *Educ* Shrewsbury, Emmanuel Coll Cambridge (MA, MD), WNSM; *m* 26 Aug 1960, Helen Madeline, da of (Arthur) Humphry House (late Maj RAC WWII, d 1955), of Wadham Coll, Oxford; 1 s (David b 1962), 3 da (Julia b 1964, Anna b 1965, Victoria b 1968); *Career* jr appts Cardiff Royal Infirmary, Nat Heart Hosp and Hammersmith Hosp 1956–65; assoc prof of med: Haile Sellassie I Univ Addis Ababa 1966–69, Ahmadu Bello Univ Zaria Nigeria 1969–77; fndn dean Faculty of Health Sciences Univ of Ilorin Nigeria 1977–80, dean Sch of Med Sciences Univ of Science and Technol Kumasi Ghana 1980–85, dir Wellcome Tropical Inst 1985–90, sr res fell LSHTM 1990–95 (hon prof 1995–), special prof Sch of Med and Surg Sciences Univ of Nottingham 1997–; chm Tropical Health and Educn Tst (THET) 1989–2007, memb Med and Dental Cncl Ghana 1980–85, memb Cncl All Nations Christian Coll 1986–99, founding memb Amoud Univ Faculty of Medicine and Surgery Somaliland 2006; Albert Cook meml lectr Kampala 1974; Frederick Murgatroyd Prize RCP 1974, Donald Mackay Medal 1998, Centennial Lifetime Achievement Medal RSTMH 2007; hon fell: LSHTM 1997, Univ of Wales Coll of Med 2004, Emmanuel Coll Cambridge 2007; Hon DSc Univ of Kumasi 2003; fell W African Coll of Physicians 1976, fndn fell Ghana Coll of Physicians and Surgns 2003; FRCP 1970, Hon FRSTM&H 1993, Hon FRCS 2008; *Books* Principles of Medicine in Africa (4 edn, 2013); *Recreations* allotment, Ceredigion, violin; *Style*— Sir Eldryd Parry, KCMG, OBE; ✉ 21 Edenhurst Avenue, London SW6 3PD (e-mail eldryd@thet.org)

PARRY, Emma; OBE; *née* Ponsonby; da of Myles Ponsonby, CBE (d 1999), and Anne, *née* Maynard; *b* 29 October 1959; *Educ* New Hall Sch Essex; *m* 1 Aug 1981, Bryn Parry, OBE, *qv*; 1 s (Tom), 2 da (Sophie, Louisa); *Career* co-fndr (with husband Bryn Parry, OBE) Help for Heroes 2007–; *Books* Home on the Range (with Bryn Parry, 2002); *Recreations* cycling, ballet, baking, walking; *Clubs* Special Forces Club; *Style*— Mrs Emma Parry, OBE; ✉ Help for Heroes, 14 Parker's Close, Downton Business Centre, Salisbury, Wiltshire SP5 3RB

PARRY, Eric Owen; s of Eric Parry, CBE (d 1995), and Marion, *née* Baird; *b* 24 March 1952; *Educ* Shrewsbury, Univ of Newcastle upon Tyne (BA), Royal Coll of Art (MA), Architectural Assoc (AADipl); *m* 5 Sept 1981, Jane, *née* Sanders; 1 da (Anna Aurelia b 19 Aug 1986); *Career* fndr princ Eric Parry Architects Ltd 1983–; princ bldgs and architectural projects incl: W3 Stockley Park Heathrow 1991, Foundress Court (new court containing 90 student rooms and Master's Lodge) Pembroke Coll Cambridge 1995–97, new masterplan for Granta Park S Cambs 1996–97, head conslt for restoration of Mandarin Oriental Hyde Park Hotel London 1996–97, condominium of 30 luxury appartments Kuala Lumpur Malaysia 1996–97, 30 Finsbury Square 2000–02, 10 Paternoster Square The London Stock Exchange 2001–03, Royex House London Wall 2001–, St Martin-in-the-Fields 2002–, numerous private and smaller cmmns; lectr Univ of Cambridge 1983–97; visiting appts: Grad Sch of Design Harvard, Univ of Houston, Tokyo Inst of Technol; examiner at several schs of arch; chair RIBA Awards Gp 2002–04; memb: Cncl Architectural Assoc, Kettles Yard Ctee Cambridge, Arts Cncl of England Advsy Panels for Visual Arts, Exhbns and Architecture; RIBA 1983; author/subject of Eric Parry Architects Vol I (2002) and various articles in professional jls; *Style*— Eric Parry, Esq

PARRY, Jann; da of John Hywel Parry (d 1992), and Evelyn Florence, *née* Upton (d 2012); *Educ* Kingsmead Coll Johannesburg, Univ of Cape Town (BA), Girton Coll Cambridge (BA, Cwlth scholar); *m* 15 April 1994, Richard Ruegg Kershaw (d 2014); *Career* prodr BBC Radio World Service 1970–89; dance critic: The Listener 1981, The Spectator 1982 and 1995–96, The Observer 1983–2006, dancetabs.com 2006–; memb: Dance Panel Arts Cncl 1988–90, Exec Ctee Dance UK 1991–2000, Critics' Circle; *Publications* Different Drummer: the life of Kenneth MacMillan (2009, Theatre Book Prize, De Valois Award for Outstanding Achievement); *Style*— Ms Jann Parry; ✉ 82 Prince of Wales Mansions, Prince of Wales Drive, London SW11 4BL (☎ 020 7738 8732, e-mail jdance@

waitrose.com); c/o Georgina Capel, Capel and Land, 29 Wardour Street, London W1V 3HB

PARRY, John Kelsall; s of Edward Parry (d 1983), of Birmingham, and Kathleen Mary, *née* Allen; *b* 28 August 1936; *Educ* Loughborough GS, London Sch of Journalism (Dip); *m* 18 Dec 1960, Judy Valerie Cornwell, *qv*, da of late Darcy Nigel Barry Cornwell, of Gympie, Aust; 1 s (Edward Dylan Parry b 20 June 1965); *Career* reporter Evening Argus Brighton 1960–62, feature writer then William Hickey diarist Daily Express London 1962–67, reporter Tomorrow's World BBC TV 1967–70; BBC Radio News and Current Affrs: reporter and presenter World at One, PM and The World This Weekend 1971–82, arts corr 1982–95; writer for The Times, columnist The Spectator 1996–, ed Sculpture 1997–99; *Publications* Not for Wimps: Men and the Ageing Game (2008); *Recreations* theatre, travel, reading, cooking; *Clubs* Garrick; *Style—* John Parry, Esq

PARRY, Kevin Allen Huw; s of H L Parry (d 1983), and F E Parry, *née* Jones; *b* 29 January 1962; *Educ* Olchfa Swansea, Robinson Coll Cambridge (MA); *m* 1, 28 May 2000, J C Parry, *née* Phillips (d 2008); 1 da (Charlotte Elizabeth b 6 April 2001), 1 s (James David Hugh b 20 Sept 2002); m 2, 14 Dec 2013, Catherine Jane Parry, *née* Brock; 1 da (Alicia Victoria Emma b 8 Oct 2014); *Career* KPMG: joined 1983, qualified CA 1986, ptnr 1994, managing ptnr 1998–99, memb UK Mgmnt Team London Bd 1998–99; chief exec Management Consulting Gp plc 2000–08, chief fin offr Schroders plc 2009–13; non-exec dir: Schroders plc 2003–08 (chm Audit Ctee), Knight Frank 2004–08, Daily Mail and General Tst plc 2014– (chm Audit Ctee), Homes and Communities Agency 2014–, Standard Life plc 2014– (chm Audit Ctee); chm Intermediate Capital Gp plc 2016– (non-exec dir 2009–), dep chm Royal Nat Children's Fndn; memb Ct Worshipful Co of Chartered Accountants in England and Wales; memb ICAEW 1986, FCA; *Recreations* watching cricket and rugby, shooting; *Clubs* Oxford and Cambridge, Walbrook; *Style—* K A H Parry, Esq; ✉ e-mail kevin@kevinparry.com

PARRY, (George) Mervyn; s of late George Alwyn Parry, and late Aileen Maude, *née* Long; *b* 16 March 1951; *Educ* KCS Wimbledon, Downing Coll Cambridge (Squire scholar, BA, 3 Badminton half blue); *m* 1 Aug 1987, Jill Patricia, da of William Odiam; 2 da (Imogen Sophie b 21 June 1989, Annabel Rose b 1 Sept 1992); *Career* Allen & Overy: articled clerk 1973–75, asst slr 1975–85, ptnr 1985–; memb Law Soc 1973; *Recreations* photography, mountain walking, wine, opera, family, sport; *Style—* Mervyn Parry, Esq; ✉ Allen & Overy, One New Change, London EC4M 9QQ (☎ 020 7330 3000, fax 020 7330 9999, e-mail mervyn.parry@allenovery.com)

PARRY, Roger George; CBE (2014); *b* 4 June 1953; *Educ* Sutton GS, Univ of Bristol (BSc), Jesus Coll Oxford (MLitt); *m* 1990, Johanna; 1 s (Benjamin b 1993); *Career* broadcaster BBC and ITV 1977–85, conslt McKinsey & Co 1985–88; devpt dir: WCRS Group 1988–90, Aegis Group 1990–94; pres Carat North America 1994–95; ceo: More Gp plc 1995–98, Clear Channel International 1998–2006; exec chm Media Square plc 2007–11; chm: Johnston Press plc 2001–09, Future plc 2001–11, Mobile Streams plc 2005–, You Gov plc 2007–, MSQ Partners 2011–, Aves Enterprises 2013–; co-fndr Chrysalis Vision 2013–; chm Shakespeare's Globe Tst 2005–13; visiting fell Univ of Oxford; *Books* People Businesses (1991), Enterprise (2003), Making Cities Work (2004), The Ascent of Media (2011), Delivering the Neural Nudge (2013); *Recreations* tennis, squash, croquet, skiing; *Clubs* MCC, Garrick; *Style—* Roger Parry, Esq, CBE; ✉ MSQ Partners, 10 Rathbone Place, London W1T 1HP (☎ 020 3026 6601, e-mail roger@rogerparry.com)

PARRY, Stephen (Steve); s of David Harold Parry, and Pauline Parry; *b* 2 March 1977; *Educ* Liverpool Blue Coat Sch, Florida State Univ (BSc), Dip Mgmnt Devpt; *Career* swimmer; achievements in 200m butterfly incl: 15 nat titles, NCAA champion 1997, Bronze medal European Championships 1997 and 2000, Bronze medal Commonwealth Games 1998, sixth place Olympic Games Sydney 2000, ranked number one in world 2000, Br and Cwlth record holder (1 min 56.3 secs); Bronze medal 4x50m relay European Championships 2000, winner World Cup Melbourne and Shanghai 2002, European champion 2002, Bronze medal Olympic Games Athens 2004; tstee Liverpool Sports Partnership; *Recreations* golf, tennis, books; *Clubs* City of Manchester Aquatics, Stockport Metro; *Style—* Steve Parry, Esq

PARRY-JONES, Dr Richard; CBE (2005); *b* 15 September 1951, Wales; *Educ* Univ of Salford; *Career* engr; Ford Motor Co: joined 1969, mangr Small Car Programs 1982, exec engr Technological Research in Europe 1985, responsible for Vehicle Concepts 1986, dir Vehicle Concepts Engrg USA 1988, i/c Mfrg Ops Cologne Germany 1990, chief engr Vehicle Engrg 1991, vice-pres Small and Medium Car Vehicle Centre Europe 1994–97, vice-pres Global Product Devpt 1998–2007, chief technical offr 2001–07; technol, environment and transport conslt 2007–; non-exec dir GKN plc 2008–; visiting prof Dept of Aeronautical and Automative Engrg Loughborough Univ 2001; memb: Engineering Technology Board (ETB), Advsy Bd Warwick Business Sch, Int Advsy Cncl Int Mgmnt Bd (IMB); Man of the Year Autocar 1994, Man of the Year Automobile USA 1997, Golden Gear Award Washington Automotive Press Assoc 2001, Marketing Statesman of the Year Sales and Marketing Execs of Detroit 2001; Hon Dr Loughborough Univ 1995; FREng 1997, FIMechE; *Style—* Dr Richard Parry-Jones, CBE, FREng

PARSONS, Charles Andrew (Charlie); s of Anthony Maxse Parsons (d 1999), and Rosamund, *née* Hurst; *b* 7 August 1958; *Educ* Tonbridge, Pembroke Coll Oxford (MA, pres JCR); *Career* reporter Ealing Gazette 1980–82, researcher London Weekend Television 1982–87, series ed Network 7 (Channel Four) 1988 (prodr 1987), series ed Club X (Channel Four) 1989; exec prodr for Planet 24 Productions Ltd (formerly 24 Hour Productions Ltd): The Word 1990, Handel's Messiah at The Point Dublin 1991, The Big Breakfast 1992–2002, Gaytime TV 1995–, Desire 1996–99; jt md Planet 24 Ltd 1992–99, ceo Castaway Television Ltd 2001–; prodr In the Heights (King's Cross Theatre) 2015– (winner 3 Olivier Awards 2016), prodr Guys and Dolls (Savoy Theatre and Phoenix Theatre) 2016 (nominated for 6 Olivier Awards 2016); chm: Runaway Entertainment Ltd, Charlie Parsons Creative, CPC Connect; exec prodr Keenen Ivory Wayans Show, exec prodr Survivor (UBS and ITV) 2001–; prodr: Never Forget 2007, In the Heights (Southwark Playhouse), Water Babies (Curve Leicester); media conslt 1999–; patron London Film Sch; Freeman: City of London, Worshipful Co of Haberdashers; memb: RTS, BAFTA, IOD; *Awards* Royal Instn of Chartered Surveyors Best News Award for The London Programme 1985–86, BAFTA Originality Award 1987 and Gold Hugo Chicago Film Festival 1988 for Network 7, Silver Medal NY Int Film Festival for The Word 1991, RTS Best Team Award for The Big Breakfast 1992, Emmys for Survivor 2001 and 2002, Special Class Outstanding Non-Fiction Programme Acad of Television Arts and Science USA; *Style—* Charlie Parsons, Esq; ✉ Castaway Television, 2nd Floor, Aldwych House, London WC2E 4HN (e-mail charlie@castawaytelevision.com)

PARSONS, Sir John Christopher; KCVO (2002, CVO 1998, LVO 1992); s of late Arthur Christopher Parsons, of Odiham, Hants, and Veronica Rosetta de Courcy, *née* Glover; *b* 21 May 1946; *Educ* Harrow, Trinity Coll Cambridge (MA); *m* 20 Feb 1982, Hon Anne Constance Manningham-Buller, da of 1 Viscount Dilhorne, PC; 2 s (Michael b 1983, David b 1985), 1 da (Lilah b 1988); *Career* chartered accountant; Dowty Gp Ltd 1968–72, Peat Marwick Mitchell & Co 1972–85; asst treas to HM The Queen 1985–87, dep keeper of the Privy Purse and dep treas to HM The Queen 1988–2002, extra equerry to HM The Queen 2002–; dep dir (fin) Royal Collection 1992–93; lay memb Chapter Peterborough Cathedral 2011–14 (treas 2004–14, lay canon 2014–); govr Elstree Sch 1987–2014 (vice-chm of govrs 2002–09, chm 2009–14); tstee and treas Music in Country Churches 2006–, tstee Country Houses Fndn 2006–, memb Cncl and treas Int Dendrology Soc 2009–; FCA, FIC; *Clubs* Brooks's, Pratt's; *Style—* Sir John Parsons, KCVO; ✉ The Old Rectory, Eydon, Daventry, Northamptonshire NN11 3QE

PARSONS, Kathryn; da of James Parsons, and Marie Parsons; *Educ* Channing Sch for Girls London, Downing Coll Cambridge; *Career* channel planner Ogilvy 2000–03, co-fndr The Scarlett Mark 2008–10, co-fndr and co-ceo Decoded 2011– (technol educn business demystifying code, data and hacking for business globally); campaigner for mandatory code on the nat curriculum 2014; chairwoman Panel for a £20m Nat Inst of Coding in the Chllr's Budget 2016; *Recreations* incl hiking, hacking; *Style—* Ms Kathryn Parsons; ✉ Decoded, 25a Underwood Row, London N1 7LQ (☎ 020 3583 0972, e-mail ask@decoded.com)

PARSONS, Nicholas; CBE (2014, OBE 2004); s of Dr Paul Frederick Nigel Parsons (d 1981), of Hampstead, London, and Nell Louise, *née* Maggs (d 1980); *b* 10 October 1923; *Educ* St Paul's, Univ of Glasgow; *m* 1, 1954 (m dis 1989), Denise Pauline Rosalie, da of Claud Bryer; 1 da (Suzy Zuleika (Mrs James Buchanan) b 13 June 1958), 1 s (Justin Hugh Bryer b 24 Dec 1960); m 2, 1995, Ann Reynolds; *Career* actor, presenter, comedy performer; Variety Club Radio Personality of the Year 1967, entered in the Guinness Book of Records for longest after dinner humorous speech 1978, Lifetime Achievement Sony Radio Award 2011; involved with children's charities incl The Lord's Taverners (past pres) and NSPCC (govr), Barker of The Variety Club of GB; ambass Childline and Silverline; tstee: Aspire, Br Dyslexia Assoc, Br Stammering Assoc; rector Univ of St Andrews 1988–91, Hon LLD Univ of St Andrews, Hon DA Univ of Lincoln, Hon DL Univ of Leicester; *Theatre* The Hasty Heart (London), Jack in Charley's Aunt (Palace Theatre) 1947, Arsenic and Old Lace (tour) 1948, in repertory Bromley 1949–51, in cabaret 1951–65 (Quaglinos, Colony, Cafe de Paris, Blue Angel, Pigalle, Society), as comedian (Windmill Theatre) 1953, revues (London fringe theatres and Lyric Revue) 1953, 1st and 2nd Edition (Watergate Theatre) 1954, Swing Along with Arthur Haynes (Palladium) 1963, starred in Boeing Boeing (Duchess Theatre) 1967–68, Say Who You Are (Vaudeville Theatre) 1968, Uproar in the House (Whitehall Theatre) 1968, Darling I'm Home (tour) 1978, Stage Struck (tour) 1980, Keeping Down with the Joneses (tour) 1981, Charlie Girl (Victoria Palace and nat tour) 1987–88, the Narrator in Into the Woods (Stephen Sondheim musical, Phoenix Theatre) 1990–91, Rocky Horror Show (Duke of York's Theatre) 1994 and 1995 (tour 1996, 1998–99 and 2000), numerous pantomimes and 3 one-man shows (Edward Lear Show performed at Edinburgh Festival 1990, BBC Radio 1996, tour on cruise ships ongoing), Nicholas Parsons A Laugh a Minute (tour and cruise ships, ongoing), Nicholas Parsons Happy Hour (Edinburgh Fringe The Pleasance, annually) 2000–; *Television* comedy work in partnership with Eric Barker 1952–55, comedy partnership with Arthur Haynes 1956–66, Last Train to Surbiton (comedy series, BBC) 1966, Benny Hill Show 1969–70, host of Sale of the Century (Anglia TV) 1971–84 and The All New Alphabet Game (LWT Night Network) 1988, Mr Jolly Lives Next Door (for Comic Strip) 1988, The Curse of Fenric (Dr Who story, BBC) 1989, host of Laughlines (BSB) 1990, Just a Minute (Carlton TV) 1994 and 1995, Just a Minute (BBC) 1999 and 2012; *Radio* since 1952 incl: various prodns for BBC Drama Repertory Company 1953, host Just a Minute 1967– (over 900 shows), Listen to This Space (first radio satire show) 1967–92, How Pleasant to Know Mr Lear (solo show) 1995–96; *Film* Brothers-in-Law, Carlton Browne of the FO, Happy is the Bride, Don't Raise the Bridge Lower the River, Spy Story, Simon and Laura, Upstairs Downstairs, Too Many Crooks, Eyewitness, Carry On Regardless, Murder Ahoy; writer and dir of 5 comedy documentaries for cinema and TV for own production co; *Books* Egg on the Face (1985), The Straight Man – My Life in Comedy (autobiography, 1994), Nicholas Parsons, with just a touch of hesitation, repetition and deviation – a life in comedy (memoires, 2012), Welcome to Just A Minute – a history of the show by its chairman for over 40 years (2014); *Recreations* gardening, photography; *Clubs* Garrick; *Style—* Nicholas Parsons, CBE; ✉ e-mail nicholas_parsons@btinternet.com; c/o Jean Diamond, Diamond Management, 31 Percy Street, London W1T 2DA (☎ 020 7631 0400, fax 020 7631 0500, e-mail jd@diman.co.uk)

PARSONS, Robin Edward; s of Anthony Maxse Parsons (d 1999), and Rosamund, *née* Hurst (d 2009); *b* 30 December 1948; *Educ* Uppingham, UCL (LLB); *m* 27 May 1972, Elizabeth Hamilton Floyd; 2 da (Sonia Katharine Elizabeth, Alexandra Geraldine); *Career* asst slr Coward Chance (now Clifford Chance) 1973–75 (articled clerk 1971–73); Cameron Markby Hewitt (now CMS Cameron McKenna): asst slr 1975–77, ptnr 1977–99, estab Paris Office 1980; ptnr Eversheds 1999–2000, ptnr Sidley Austin LLP 2000–10 (of counsel 2010–16); visiting lectr KCL 2010–13, lectr at numerous legal conferences and seminars; ed Butterworth's Jl of Int Banking and Financial Law 2012–, author of articles for legal jls; Freeman Worshipful Co of Haberdashers, Freeman Worshipful Co of Slrs; memb City of London Finance Law Ctee 1998–2011; *Publications* Yeowart and Parsons on the Law of Financial Collateral (jtly, 2016); *Recreations* tennis, squash, skiing, French; *Style—* Robin Parsons, Esq; ✉ 6 Calverley Park Gardens, Tunbridge Wells, Kent TN1 2JN (☎ 01892 535913)

PARSONS, Sandra Kay; da of John Kenneth Parsons, of London, and Kathleen, *née* Stirling; *b* 8 September 1961; *Educ* Archbishop Tennison's GS Croydon; *m* 22 Jan 1994, Dr Serge Nikolic, s of Ljubisa Nikolic; 1 da (Isabella b 1 Sept 1995), 1 s (Luke b 26 April 2001); *Career* journalist; reporter Luton News 1982–85, Wolverhampton Express and Star 1985–87, Today 1987–90, Daily Mail 1990–95, asst ed The Times 1995–2008, literary ed Daily Mail 2008–; *Recreations* reading, my children; *Style—* Ms Sandra Parsons; ✉ The Daily Mail, 2 Derry Street, London W8 5TT (☎ 020 7938 6000)

PARSONS, Susie; da of Alfred Parsons, of East Grinstead, West Sussex, and late Dorothy, *née* Barratt; *b* 29 April 1950, Cuckfield, West Sussex; *Educ* East Grinstead Co GS, Lancaster Univ (BA), KCL (PGCE); *Partner* Dave Perry; 1 s (Ben b 1976); *Career* educn offr then community educn dir Shelter 1974–77, housing projects offr N Kensington Law Centre 1977–81, chief offr Paddington and N Kensington Community Health Cncl 1981–84, gen mangr London Energy and Employment Network 1984–87, head of press, publicity and info London Borough of Hackney 1987–94, exec dir then chief exec London Lighthouse 1994–98, chief exec Cmmn for Racial Equality 1999–2001, ind mgmnt conslt 2001–02, chief exec Campaign for Learning 2002–05, md Susie Parsons Mgmnt Solutions Ltd 2005–, jt md Lasting Transformation Ltd 2011; author of articles and pubns on health, social care, equality and lifelong learning; former memb Bd Kensington & Chelsea Tenant Mgmnt Orgn; former memb Bd: ACEVO, Quality Standards Task Gp NCVO, Cncl Inst for Employment Studies; chair Bd Golborne Forum; FRSA 1996; *Publications* School and Community in the Inner City (jtly, 1977), Workout (jtly, 1979), London Energy Action Plan (1986), Good Practice Guide to District Heating (1988), Taking the Lead (1992), The Right Side of the Law (1993), 50/50: Equality for Women Managers by the Year 2000 (jtly, 1995), Learning to Learn in Schools (jtly, 2003 and 2005), Give Your Child a Better Chance (2003), Promoting Diversity in the Workplace (contrib, 2004), QCA Futures Programme (contrib, 2005), Learning to Learn for Life (jtly, 2005), Reinventing Education (contrib, 2005), Board Training (jt ed, 2005); *Style—* Ms Susie Parsons; ✉ 171 Oxford Gardens, London W10 6NE (☎ 07968 801948, e-mail susie@spms.org.uk)

PARTINGTON, Prof (Thomas) Martin; CBE, Hon QC; s of Thomas Paullet Partington (d 1980), and Alice Emily Mary, *née* Jelly (d 1970); *b* 5 March 1944, Maidstone, Kent; *Educ* King's Sch Canterbury, Univ of Cambridge (BA, LLB); *m* 1, 15 Aug 1969 (m dis 1973), Marcia Carol, *née* Leavey; 1 s (Daniel b 1971); m 2, 21 Oct 1978, Daphne Isobel, *née* Scharenguivel; 1 s (Adam b 1979), 1 da (Hannah b 1980); *Career* lectr: Univ of Warwick 1969–73, LSE 1973–80; Brunel Univ: prof of law 1980–87, dean Faculty of Social Sciences

P

1985–87; Univ of Bristol: asst lectr 1966–69, prof of law 1987–2005, dean Faculty of Law 1988–92, pro-vice-chllr 1995–99, emeritus prof 2006–; called to the Bar Middle Temple 1984 (bencher 2006), in practice Arden Chambers London 1993–2000 and 2006–10, Law Cmmr 2001–05; memb: Lord Chllr's Advsy Ctee on Legal Aid 1988–91, Law Soc Trg Ctee 1989–93, Judicial Studies Bd 1992–94, Cncl on Tbnls 1994–2000, Civil Justice Cncl 1998–2005, Public Legal Educn Taskforce 2006; special conslt Law Cmmn 2006–07, academic advsr Coll of Law (now Univ of Law) 2006–14; conslt: Public Admin Select Ctee 2012, Qatar Financial Authy 2012–13; expert consultee: Leggatt Review of Tbnls 2000–01, Employment Tribunals Task Force 2002; chm: Ctee Heads of Univ Law Schs 1990–92, Socio-Legal Studies Assoc 1993–95, Social Security Appeal Tbnls 1990–94 (pt/t), Med Appeal Tbnls and Disability Appeal Tbnls 1992–94 (pt/t), Cncl Dispute Service 2008–10, Bd Dispute Service 2010–; non-exec dir United Bristol Hosp NHS Tst 1998–2000; FRSA 1999; *Books* Landlord and Tenant (1975), Housing Law: Cases, Materials and Commentary (with Jonathan Hill, 1991), Claim in Time (1994), Housing Law (with Andrew Arden and Caroline Hunter, 1994), Administrative Justice in the 21st Century (with Michael Harris, 1999), Introduction to the English Legal System (2000, 11 edn 2016), Law's Reality (2008), Social Security Law: UK (4 edn 2012), Halsbury's Laws of England Vol 65 (conslt ed, 2015); *Recreations* music, walking, cooking, foreign travel; *Style—* Prof Martin Partington, CBE, QC; ✉ 8 Clifton Hill, Bristol BS8 1BN (☎ 0117 973 6294)

PARTINGTON, Robin Courtland; s of Dr James Ernest Partington (d 1967), of Bolton, and June, *née* Whittenbury; *b* 5 August 1960; *Educ* Bolton Sch Bolton, Univ of Liverpool Sch of Architecture (BA, BArch); *m* 22 Sept 1990 (m dis 2015), Sally Maurice, da of Maurice Owen Jones; 2 s (Oliver Courtland b 7 July 1997, Teilo Courtland b 24 Jan 2001); *Career* training (year out) Scott Brownrigg and Turner Guildford 1981–82; Foster & Partners (formerly Sir Norman Foster & Partners): joined 1984, assoc 1987, project dir 1988, dir 1992–2001; dir Hamiltons 2001–09, fndr Robin Partington Architects 2009–; RIBA 1985, ARCUK 1985, RIAS 1996; *Recreations* sailing, shooting, reading, skiing, travel, walking; *Style—* Robin Partington, Esq; ✉ Robin Partington Architects, Castlewood, 85 New Oxford Street, London WC1A 1DG

PARTON, Geoffrey Paul; s of Walter St John Parton (d 1962), and Betty Mary, *née* Herring; *b* 25 April 1947; *Educ* Belfairs HS; *m* 1973, Patrika Anne, da of John McClemont; 1 s (John Vivian Henry b 1981), 2 da (Hannah Mary b 1978, Frances Anne b 1980); *Career* dir Marlborough Fine Art London (joined 1969); numerous exhibitions organised incl those of R B Kitaj and Frank Auerbach; memb Exec Ctee Soc of London Art Dealers 1991–; *Style—* Geoffrey Parton, Esq; ✉ Marlborough Fine Art, 6 Albemarle Street, London W1S 4BY

PARTON, Nicholas George; s of Maj Michael Henry Parton, and Jean Mary, *née* Saxby; *b* 1 June 1954; *Educ* Haileybury, Grenoble Univ, Liverpool Poly (BA); *m* 12 Sept 1981, (Elizabeth) Querida, da of late John Wilfred da Cunha, of Churchill, Avon, and Janet, *née* Savatard; 3 da (Amy b 1983, Phoebe b 1986, Felicity b 1988), 2 s (Sam b 1984, John (Jack) b 1996); *Career* admitted slr 1979; articled clerk Bremmer Sons & Corlett 1977, Holman Fenwick & Willan 1980, Middleton Potts 1983; ptnr: Taylor Garrett 1985–89, Taylor Joynson Garrett 1989–92, Jackson Parton 1992–; memb Law Soc 1979; *Recreations* skiing and sailing; *Clubs* Trearddur Bay Sailing; *Style—* Nicholas Parton, Esq; ✉ 31 Ambleside Avenue, London SW16 1QE (☎ 020 3091 3814, e-mail nickparton@aol.com); Pant y Llin, Ravenspoint Road, Trearddur Bay, Anglesey LL65 2YU (☎ 01407 860376); Le Mazuet, Bellentre, Aime, Savoie, France; Jackson Parton, 4th Floor, 1 Alie Street, London E1 8DE (☎ 020 7702 0085, fax 020 7702 0858, e-mail mail@jacksonparton.com or n.parton@jacksonparton.com)

PARTRIDGE, Prof Derek; *b* 24 October 1945; *Educ* UCL (BSc), Imperial Coll London (DIC, PhD); *m* 27 Aug 1971, Mehrazar; 2 da (Mischa b 1974, Morgan b 1976); *Career* lectr in computer sci Univ of Nairobi Kenya 1972–74, asst prof, assoc prof then full prof Dept Computer Sci New Mexico State Univ USA 1975–86, prof of computer sci Univ of Exeter 1987– (head of dept 1989–94); visiting fell Univ of Essex 1981–82, visiting lectr Univ of Queensland 1983–84; involved with Nat Youth Theatre 1966–68; FRSA, AAAI, AISB; *Books* incl: Artificial Intelligence: Applications in the Future of Software Engineering (1986), Computers for Society (contrib, 1986), The Encyclopaedia of Microcomputers (contrib, 1988), Machine Learning (contrib, 1989), The Foundations of Artificial Intelligence: A Source Book (contrib, 1989); *Recreations* reading, writing, natural history, football; *Style—* Prof Derek Partridge

PARTRIDGE, Prof Dame Linda; DBE (2009, CBE 2003); da of George Albert Partridge, of Bath, and Ida, *née* Tucker; *b* 18 March 1950; *Educ* Convent of the Sacred Heart, Univ of Oxford (Christopher Welch scholar, BA, DPhil); *m* 1, 1983 (m dis 1990), V French; m 2, 1996, M J Morgan; *Career* NERC postdoctoral fell Univ of York 1974–76; Univ of Edinburgh: demonstrator 1976–78, lectr 1978–87, reader 1987–92, prof of evolutionary biology and Darwin research fell 1992–93; Weldon prof of biometry UCL 1994–, NERC research prof 1997–2002, BBSRC professorial fell 2002–07; dir Inst of Healthy Ageing UCL 2007–, dir Max Planck Inst of the Biology of Ageing Cologne 2008–; pres: Int Soc for Behavioural Ecology 1990–92, Assoc for the Study of Animal Behaviour 1995–97, Genetical Soc 2000–03; Frink Medal Zoological Soc of London 2000, Sewall Wright Prize American Soc of Naturalists 2002, Fndn IPSEN Longevity Prize 2004, Lord Cohen Medal British Soc for Research on Ageing 2004, Medal of Assoc for the Study of Animal Behaviour 2005, Living Legend Help the Aged 2006, Thomassen a Thuessink Medal 2008, Darwin-Wallace Medal 2009, Women of Outstanding Achievement Award for Science Discovery UKRC for Women 2009, Royal Soc Croonian Prize lecture 2009; Hon DSc Univ of St Andrews 2004, Hon DSc Univ of Oxford 2011, Hon DSc Univ of Bath 2011, Hon DSc Univ of Brighton 2012; memb EMBO 2005; FRSE 1992, FRS 1996, FMedSci 2004; *Recreations* gardening, sailing, tennis, bird watching; *Style—* Prof Dame Linda Partridge, DBE, FRS, FRSE, FMedSic

PARTRIDGE, Prof Martyn Richard; s of Maj Raymond John Bruce Partridge, RA (d 2004), and Grace, *née* Darch (d 2012); *b* 19 May 1948; *Educ* Pocklington Sch, Univ of Manchester (MB ChB, MD); *m* 23 June 1973, Rosemary Jane Emily, da of Lt (John) Dennis Radford, of Hove, E Sussex; 2 da (Judith Stephanie Louise b 10 June 1977, Philippa Rachel Jane b 26 Feb 1981), 1 s (Richard John Oliver b 15 Feb 1979); *Career* resident med offr Nat Heart Hosp London 1975–76, med registrar Royal Post Grad Med Sch London 1976–78, sr Jules Thorne res fell Middx Hosp 1978–80; sr med registrar: London Chest Hosp 1980–81, UCH 1981–82; conslt physician Whipps Cross Hosp London 1982–2001, prof of respiratory med Imperial Coll London Nat Heart and Lung Inst (NHLI) 2002–; sr vice dean Lee Kong Chian Sch of Medicine Singapore 2010–13; author of various pubns of respiratory med and terminal care; past pres British Thoracic Soc, former chief med advsr Nat Asthma Campaign; FRCP, FRSM; *Recreations* travel, railways, music, church and family; *Style—* Prof Martyn Partridge; ✉ Imperial College London SW3 6LY (e-mail m.partridge@imperial.ac.uk)

PASCO, Adam Gerhold; s of Cecil Filmer Pasco (d 1974), and Sheila Mary, *née* Gerhold; *b* 11 January 1957; *Educ* George Abbot Sch Guildford, NE Surrey Coll of Technology (Higher Nat Dip Applied Biology), Univ of Nottingham (BSc); *m* 8 August 1992, Jayne Petra, *née* Fisher; 1 da (Danielle Jean b 16 September 1994), 1 s (Luke Peter Graham b 10 October 1996); *Career* Garden Answers: tech ed 1982–84, ed 1984–88; ed Garden News 1988–90, ed (and launched) BBC Gardeners' World Magazine 1991–2012, gardening corr Daily Telegraph 1995–98, editorial dir BBC Easy Gardening Magazine 2003–06 (ed (and launched) 2002–03), content creator World Radio Gardening, ed Waitrose Garden Magazine 2016–; md Adam Pasco Media 2013–; memb Garden Media Guild (formerly Garden Writers' Guild) 1992–; memb: Garden Organic, Woodland Tst, RHS; *Publications* The Garden Manager (CD-ROM, 1998), The Collins Complete Garden Manual (1998), The Greenfingers Book (1999), Collins Gardeners' Calendar (2000); *Recreations* gardening, electric guitar, writing, walking, photography, cooking, travel, family life, ukulele; *Style—* Adam Pasco, Esq; ✉ Adam Pasco Media, 43 Latham Avenue, Orton Longueville, Peterborough PE2 7AD (mobile 07816 662390, e-mail adam@adampascomedia.com, website www.adampascomedia.com)

PASCOE, (Gerald) John; s of Rick Pascoe, and Roma Pascoe; *b* 19 January 1949; *Educ* St Brendan's Coll Bristol, Wimbledon Sch of Art (BA); *Career* asst designer Derby Playhouse and resident designer Bristol Old Vic and Sheffield Crucible 1971–74, artistic dir Il Licinium (Italy's only Shakespeare theatre) 2012; teacher/lectr Prior Park Coll Bath and Univ of Bath 1974–79; designer/director for opera; credits for set design incl: Giulio Cesare (ENO, TV and video) 1979, Lucrezia Borgia (ROH and Teatro dell'Opera Rome) 1980, Alcina (also costumes, Sydney Opera House) 1980, Tosca (WNO) 1980, Giulio Cesare (San Francisco Opera and Grand Théatre De Genève Switzerland) 1981, Anna Bolena (Canadian Opera) 1984, Cosi fan tutte (Dallas Opera) 1984, Giulio Cesare (Metropolitan Opera) 1988, Orlando (Lyric Opera of Chicago and San Francisco Opera) 1985, Norma (also costumes, Santiago) 1986, Amahl (also costumes, ROH) 1986, Apollo et Hyacinthus (Cannes) 1990, Maria Golovin (Spoleto Festival) 1991, Tosca (Opera Nice) 1991, Anna Bolena (Washington Opera) 1993, Anna Bolena (San Francisco Opera) 1995, The Telephone/The Medium (Spoleto Festival) 2002, Don Pasquale (Michigan Opera Theater) 2002, Turandot (L'Opera de Quebec) 2003, Manon Lescaut (Washington Nat Opera) 2004, Democracy (Washington Nat Opera) 2005; credits as dir and/or design incl: La Bohème (Northern Ireland Opera) 1983 and 1992, Solomon (Göttingen Händel Festival) 1985, Platée (Spoleto Festival) 1987, Anna Bolena (ROH) 1987, Platée (Brooklyn Acad of Music) 1988, Norma (Michigan Opera Theatre and Opera Pacific) 1989, Maria Padilla (Opera Omaha) 1989, Don Giovanni (Michigan Opera and Opera Pacific) 1990, Dido and Aeneas 1991, La Boheme 1992, La Traviata 1993, Rigoletto 1994, Don Giovanni (Miami) 1997, Pretty Baby (world premier, New Orleans) 1997, Hänsel und Gretel (Chicago Opera Theater) 1998, Giulio Cesare (Metropolitan Opera) 1999, Lucia di Lammermoor (Connecticut Grand Opera) 1999, The Barber of Seville (Chicago Opera Theatre) 1999, Rigoletto (Connecticut Grand Opera) 1999, Giulio Cesare (Washington Opera) 2000, Don Pasquale (Virginia Opera) 2001, Il Barbieri di Siviglio (Virginia Opera) 2001, Don Giovanni (Washington Opera and Michigan Opera Theater) 2003, The Medium (Monte Carlo Opera) 2005, Ercole sul Termodonte (Spoleto Italy, also on DVD) 2006 (DVD of the Year Award 2007), Don Giovanni (Washington Nat Opera) 2007, Ariodante (Spoleto, also on DVD) 2007, Lucrezia Borgia (Washington Nat Opera) 2008 and (San Francisco) 2011, Carmen (Palm Beach) 2010, Flora (Spoleto Festival USA) 2010, Don Giovanni (season opening of Dallas Lyric Opera) 2010, (Miami) 2011 and (Washington Nat Opera) 2012–13, Cyrano (Miami) 2011, The Medium (centenary of birth of composer GC Menotti, Spoleto Festival USA) 2011, Manon Lescaut (Washington Nat Opera) 2012–13, Antonio and Cleopatra (Il Licinium) 2012, Dodicesima Motte (Il Licinium) 2013; portraits: Lise Lindstrom 2010, Marsia Holzer 2010, Dimitri Horostovsky 2010; designed concert gowns for Renée Fleming (also costumes for La Traviata Metropolitan Opera House 2003) and gown for Joan Sutherland (featured in meml exhbn at ROH 2011); fndr The Bath & Wessex Opera (UK); interior decorating and murals for private clients incl: Renée Fleming, Michael Bolton; work featured in: Vogue, House & Gardens, Art & Antiques 1994, PBS (TV programme) 1996; keynote speaker V&A Museum Festival of Scene Design 2009; *Recreations* listening to opera, rock climbing; *Style—* John Pascoe, Esq; ✉ c/o Robert Lombardo Associates, 61 West 62nd Street, Suite 6F, New York, NY 10023, USA (☎ 00 1 212 586 4453, website www.johnpascoe.com)

PASCOE, Nigel Spencer Knight; QC (1988); s of Ernest Sydney Pascoe (d 1970), and Cynthia, *née* Holtom (d 1992); *b* 18 August 1940; *Educ* Epsom; *m* 1964, Elizabeth Anne, da of Bryan Walter; 4 da (Gillie, Jemma, Dimity, Miranda (decd)), 2 s (Hallam, Tristan); *Career* called to the Bar Inner Temple 1966 (bencher 1998); in practice Western Circuit (ldr 1995–98), recorder of the Crown Court 1979–; chm Bar Public Affrs Ctee 1997–98, pres Mental Health Review Tbnl 2001–; chm Editorial Bd Counsel 1999–2006; fndr ed All England Quarterly Law Cassettes; memb Hampshire CC 1979–83; *Plays* performances: The Trial of Penn and Mead (one man show, Edinburgh Fringe Festival) 1994, Merely Players (Shakespearean one man show) 2004, Christmas Carol (with Elizabeth Pascoe, 2014), Sweet Reason (2014); publications: The Nearly Man (1993), The Trial of Penn and Mead (1994), Pro Patria (1996), Who Killed William Rufus? (2000), Without Consent (2005), To Encourage the Others (2006), Last Call to San Giorgio (2014), Sleeping Dogs (2015), From Portsmouth to Pickwick (2016), My Country Right or Wrong (2016); *Recreations* acting, cricket, theatre, writing, presenting legal anthologies with Elizabeth Pascoe, after dinner speaking; *Clubs* Garrick; *Style—* Nigel Pascoe, Esq, QC; ✉ 3 Pump Court, Upper Ground, Temple, London EC4Y 7AJ (☎ 020 7353 0711)

PASSI, Nitin; *Career* fndr and ceo Missguided 2009–; *Style—* Nitin Passi, Esq; ✉ Missguided, 75 Trafford Wharf Road, Manchester M17 1ES

PASSMORE, George; *see:* George

PASSMORE, Jeremy Cedric; s of John Passmore, and Pamela, *née* Dunkels; *b* 30 March 1952, Kent; *Educ* Cranleigh Sch, Trinity Coll Cambridge (open exhibitioner, MA); *m* 3 Sept 1977, Diana, *née* Willmott; 3 da (Sophia Katharine b 13 Sept 1981, Jennifer Melissa, Felicity Diana (twins) b 17 May 1985); *Career* slr; Frere Cholmeley: articled clerk 1975–77, slr 1977–79; Thomson Snell & Passmore: slr 1979–81, ptnr 1981–, head Private Client Dept 2003–14; memb: Charity Law Assoc, Law Soc, Soc of Estates and Trust Practitioners; *Recreations* the arts, gardening; *Style—* Jeremy Passmore, Esq; ✉ 1 The Old Riding School, Leyswood, Groombridge, Tunbridge Wells, Kent TN3 9PH (☎ 01892 861015); Thomson Snell & Passmore, 3 Lonsdale Gardens, Tunbridge Wells, Kent TN1 1NX (☎ 01892 701344, fax 01892 701122, e-mail jeremy.passmore@ts-p.co.uk)

PATE, Malcolm Gregory; s of Orran Pate, of Albrighton, Salops, and Kathlene Pate (d 2004); *b* 10 July 1943, Walsall, W Midlands; *Educ* Wednesbury Tech Coll; *m* 7 April 1969, Susan Jenifer, *née* Nicholas; 1 da (Dr Lorna Wendy (Mrs Harries) b 6 April 1970); *Career* dir F C Wilkins Ltd 1970–73; md: Precolor Sales Ltd 1970–2000, Cabinmill Ltd 1984–2000, Clipperlight Ltd 2004–; ldr Salops CC 1999–2001 and 2005–09 (chm 2009–); memb: W Midlands Regnl Assembly, Bridgnorth DC (past chm), Albrighton Parish Cncl (past chm); chm Salops Unitary Implementation Exec, chm Salops Pension Fund, past chm Salops Assoc of Parish and Town Cncls, custodian tstee Albrighton Village Halls Tst, chm W Mercia Police Authy (chm Audit Ctee), vice-patron Dissabled Sailors Assoc; *Recreations* sailing, gardening, antiques, music; *Clubs* Royal Channel Island Yacht, St Hellier Yacht; *Style—* Councillor Malcolm Pate; ✉ Peel Cottage, Holyhead Road, Albrighton, West Midlands WV7 3BT (☎ 01902 373217, fax 01902 375317, e-mail mdoone@aol.com); Shropshire County Council, Shirehall, Abbey Foregate, Shrewsbury, Shropshire SY2 6ND

PATEL, Bhikhu C; *b* Kenya; *Educ* BA, DipArch; *Career* co-fndr (with bro, Vijay Patel, *qv*) and memb Bd: Waymade plc, Atnahs Pharma (UK) Ltd; Hon LLD Univ of Bristol, Hon DSc Anglia Ruskin Univ; RIBA 1978, CCMI; *Style—* Bhikhu Patel, Esq; ✉ Waymade plc, Sovereign House, Miles Gray Road, Basildon SS14 3FR (☎ 01268 535200, fax 01236 535299)

PATEL, Dr Chaitanya; CBE (1999); s of Bhupendra Patel (d 1997), and Ashru Patel (d 2004); *b* 14 September 1954; *Educ* Univ of Southampton; *m* Katharine Anne; 2 da (Meera Jade b 7 Oct 1987, Hannah Anjuli b 5 March 1990); *Career* physician 1979–85, investment banker 1985–88; MRC research fell Pembroke Coll Oxford 1985; fndr chm Ct Cavendish 1988–96, chief exec Care First 1996–97; chief exec Westminster Health Care plc 1999–2002, ceo Priory Group 2002–07; chm: HC-One, Court Cavendish, Elysian Capital; dep chm Care Mgmnt Gp; memb Better Regulation Task Force 1997–2002; appeal chm Combat Stress Appeal The Enemy Within, memb Inst for Public Policy Research (IPPR), tstee Windsor Leadership Tst, patron Br Olympics Team 2012 Appeal; fndr Bright Future Tst; Care Personality of the Year (Caring Times) 1999, Social Entrepreneur of the Year Asian Business Award 2011, Care Personality of the Year Nat Care Award 2012, Outstanding Contrib by an Individual Health Investor Award 2013; Hon DUniv Open Univ; FRSA, FRCP 1999 (MRCP); *Publications* Better Regulation Task Force reports: Long Term Care 1998, Early Education and Daycare 1998, Red Tape Affecting Head Teachers 2000; *Recreations* golf, music, painting, films; *Clubs* RAC, Queenwood Golf, Mark's, Soho House, Arts, Harry's; *Style—* Dr Chaitanya Patel, CBE; ✉ Court Cavendish, Robin Hill, Warren Lane, Oxshott KT22 0ST

PATEL, Kishore; *m* Fiona Cairns, *qv*; *Career* co-fndr Fiona Cairns Ltd 1986, clients incl Harrods, Selfridges, Waitrose, Fortnum and Mason, The Conran Shop, Eat Your Hearts Out, and the wedding cake for the marriage of HRH Prince William of Wales to Catherine Middleton; *Style—* Kishore Patel, Esq; ✉ Fiona Cairns Ltd, 8 Churchill Way, Fleckney, Leicestershire LE8 8UD

PATEL, Prof Minoo Homi; s of Homi Edalji Patel, of Hounslow, Middlesex, and Doly Homi Patel; *b* 28 July 1949; *Educ* Univ of London (BSc, PhD); *m* Irene Veronica, da of Harry Kay, of Basildon, Essex; 2 s (Zubin Homi b 1973, Darren Lindsay b 1975); *Career* res engr Queen Mary Coll London 1973–76, UCL 1976–2002 (successively lectr, reader 1987–89, Kennedy prof of mechanical engrg 1989–2002, latterly head of dept), currently prof and head Sch of Engrg Cranfield Univ; dir: BPP Ocean Technology Ltd 1983–, Pamec Technology Ltd 1986–, BPP Technical Services Ltd 1989–, UCLi Ltd 1990–1995; FREng, FRINA, FIMechE, CEng; *Books* Dynamics of Offshore Structures (1989), Compliant Offshore Structures (1990); *Recreations* gliding, jogging; *Style—* Prof Minoo Patel, FREng; ✉ School of Engineering, Cranfield University, Cranfield, Bedfordshire MK43 0AL

PATEL, Baron (Life Peer UK 1999), of Dunkeld in Perth and Kinross; Prof Sir Narendra Babubhai (Naren); KT (2010), kt (1997); s of Babubhai Patel, of London, and Lalita Patel (d 1992); *b* 11 May 1938; *Educ* Univ of St Andrews (MB ChB); *m* 25 Sept 1970, Helen, da of Wilfred Dally; 1 da (Hon Susan b 29 Nov 1971), 2 s (Hon Mark, Hon Neil (twins) b 18 May 1975); *Career* conslt obstetrician and hon prof Ninewells Hosp Univ of Dundee 1974–2003; author of pubns in areas of fetal growth, preterm labour, clinical audit and quality healthcare; MD (hc) Univ of Stellenbosch; former chm: Acad of Med Royal Colls, NHS Quality Improvement Scotland, Advsy Ctee Scientific Advances and Genetics; chm Steering Ctee Stem Cell MRC UK; chair Nat Patient Safety Agency 2005, vice-pres RSE 2006, chair UK Stem Cell Network; memb Science and Technol Ctee House of Lords 1999, memb Armed Forces Diversity Panel 1999; memb Cncl Stroke Assoc; Hon DSc: Napier Univ Edinburgh, Univ of Aberdeen, Univ of St Andrews; Hon LLD Univ of Dundee, Hon Dr Univ of Athens; FRCOG 1987 (MRCOG 1970), FMedSci, FRSE; Hon FRCPEd, Hon FRCPGlas, Hon FRCSEd, Hon FRCS(Eng), Hon FRCA, Hon FRCPI, Hon FRCGP, Hon FRCPsych, Hon FFPHM; hon fell: Royal Aust and NZ Coll of Obsetriticians and Gynaecologists, German, Canadian, Finnish, Argentine, Italian, Chilean and Thai Socs of Obstetrics and Gynaecology, Indian, Sri Lankan, American, Canadian, South African and Thai Colls of Obstetrics and Gynaecology; *Style—* The Rt Hon Lord Patel, KT; ✉ Birkenbrae, Spoutwells, Dunkeld PH8 0AZ (☎ 01350 727366, e-mail patel_naren@hotmail.com)

PATEL, Pankaj; MBE (2006); *b* Tanzania; *Educ* South Bank Univ (BA), RIBA (DipArch); *Career* architect; MacCormac Jamieson Pritchard, ptnr Patel Taylor Architects 1989–; prof Welsh Sch of Architecture Cardiff, sr lectr South Bank Univ, external examiner Oxford Brookes Univ, examiner Univ of Sheffield, advsr Government Off for London, memb CABE Design Review Ctee; *Competitions* incl: Sainsbury's supermarket 1987, sheltered accommodation Clywd Wales 1989, the city and the river Antwerp Belgium 1990, Choral and Music Centre Rhondda Heritage Park Wales 1990, Europan II Châteauroux France 1991, Peckham London 1991, Ayr Citadel 1993, Europan III Pierre-Bénite France 1994, Thames Barrier Park London 1995, Footbridge Balmaha Scotland 1996, Portland College Nottinghamshire 1998; *Awards* Royal Acad Summer Exhibition Non-members Award 1988, RIBA Architecture Award (for Arts Centre Wales) 1992, Geoffrey Gribble Conservation Award (for PACE Counselling Centre London) 1995, Glass and Glazing Award (for PACE Counselling Centre London) 1995, Saltire Geddes Planning Award (for Ayr Citadel Scotland) 1995, 4 RIBA Architecture Awards 2001 (for Thames Barrier, Benslow Music Sch, Peace Park Pavilion, Apartment, Battersea), Civic Tst Landscape Award 2002 (for Thames Barrier Park); *Style—* Pankaj Patel, Esq, MBE; ✉ Patel Taylor Architects, 53 Rawstorne Street, London EC1V 7NQ (☎ 020 7278 2323, fax 020 7278 6242, e-mail pta@pateltaylor.co.uk)

PATEL, Rt Hon Priti; PC (2016), MP; *b* 29 March 1972, London; *Educ* Keele Univ, Univ of Essex; *m* 2004, Alex Sawyer; 1 s (Freddie b 2008); *Career* dep press sec to Rt Hon William Hague, MP 1998–2000, assoc dir Weber Shandwick Worldwide 2000–03, corporate affrs mangr Diageo plc 2003–07, dir corporate communications Weber Shandwick Worldwide 2007–10; MP (Cons) Witham 2010–14; exchequer sec to the treasy 2014–15, min of state for employment 2015–16, sec of state for int devpt 2016–; *Style—* The Rt Hon Priti Patel, MP; ✉ House of Commons, London SW1A 0AA

PATEL, Dr Vijay C; s of late Chhotabhai Patel, and Shantaben Patel; *b* 10 November 1949, Kenya; *Educ* De Montfort Univ (BSc); *Career* pharmacist; co-fndr (with bro, Bhikhu Patel, *qv*) and memb Bd: Waymade Healthcare plc, Atnahs Pharma (UK) Ltd; hon doctorate Anglian Ruskin Univ, Hon DSc De Montfort Univ; Melvin Jones fell Lions Club Int; memb Gen Pharmaceutical Cncl; MRPharmS, CCMI, FRSA; *Recreations* collecting watches, sports cars, hill walking; *Style—* Dr Vijay Patel; ✉ Waymade plc, Sovereign House, Miles Gray Road, Basildon SS14 3FR (☎ 01268 535200, fax 01236 535299)

PATEL OF BLACKBURN, Baron (Life Peer UK 2000), of Langho in the County of Lancashire; Adam Hafejee; s of Hafejee Ismail Patel (d 1996), and Aman Hafejee Patel; *b* 7 June 1940, Gujarat, India; *Educ* Univ of Baroda India (BCom); *m* 10 May 1964, Aysha; 4 s, 4 da; *Career* accountant Ivan Jacques Chartered Accountants Blackburn and accountant S & RD Thornton Chartered Accountants Preston 1967–74; chief internal auditor Zamtan Lusaka Zambia; md Comet Cash and Carry Co Ltd 1977–97; chm Blackburn and District Cwlth Friendship Soc 1966–67; fndr and gen sec Blackburn Indian Workers Assoc 1967–74 (pres 1977–); magistrate Divisional Petty Sessions of Blackburn 1984–95; fndr memb Blackburn Community Relations Cncl (now Blackburn with Darwen Racial Equality Cncl) subsequent treas, vice-chm and chm, currently hon vice-pres under presidency of Rt Hon Jack Straw, MP; chm UK Hagg Ctee, chm Br Hajj Delegation FCO 2001–; fndr chm and former pres Lancashire Cncl of Mosques 1989–; fndr dir Lancashire TEC until 1996, fndr dir Blackburn Partnership; non-exec dir Lancashire Enterprises plc (now Enterprises plc); exec memb Blackburn City Challenge and its Forward Strategy Gp 1993–98; memb: Labour Pty 1966–, NW Conciliation Ctee Race Relations Bd until 1974, Lancashire CC Standing Adsvy Cncl on Religious Educn, Ethnic Minority Panel of Blackburn, Hyndburn and Ribble Valley Health Tst, Home Secretary's Race Relations Advsy Forum, Christian/Muslim Inter-Faith Forum (jt chm); memb and tstee E Lancashire Racial Harrassment Partnership; chm and tstee W Brookhouse Community Centre Blackburn; one of five nat counsellors of Muslim Cncl of Br; special interests: educn, trg and re-training for life skills, all aspects of race and community relations, the economy, ethnic minority health concerns and religious understanding; pres E Lancashire Co Scout Cncl; govr Bolton Inst; *Recreations* community and social work, gardening, football, cricket; *Style—* The Rt Hon the Lord Patel of Blackburn; ✉ Snodworth Hall, Snodworth Road, Langho, Lancashire BB6 8DS (☎ 01254 240346, fax 01254 249584, e-mail lordadampatel@hotmail.com)

PATERSON, Bill; *b* 3 June 1945; *m* Nov 1984, Hildegard Maria Bechtler, *qv*; 1 s (Jack b 10 April 1985), 1 da (Anna b 28 Sept 1989); *Career* actor; fell Royal Conservatoire of Scotland; *Theatre* for 7:84 Theatre Co Scotland: incl: Willie Rough (Royal Lyceum), Great Northern Welly Boat Show (Edinburgh Festival), The Game's a Bogey, Little Red Hen and The Cheviot, The Stag and The Black Black Oil, Mongrel's Heart (Edinburgh Lyceum) 1994; London prodns incl: Treetops (Riverside), Writer's Cramp (Hampstead/Bush), Ella (ICA), Whose Life Is It Anyway? (Savoy), And Me Wi' A Bad Leg Tae (Royal Court), A Man With Connections (Royal Court/Traverse), Crime and Punishment (Lyric Hammersmith), Guys and Dolls (NT), title role in Schweyk In The Second World War (NT), Good Person of Sezuan (NT), Death and the Maiden (Royal Court/Duke of York's), Misery (Criterion) 1992–93, Ivanov (Almeida) 1997, Marriage Play (NT) 2001, Earthquakes in London (NT) 2010, An No More Shall We Part (Hampstead Theatre and Traverse Theatre) 2012; *Television* for BBC: The Cheviot, The Stag and The Black Black Oil, Licking Hitler, The Vanishing Army, The Lost Tribe, United Kingdom, The Cherry Orchard, Smiley's People, Stan's Last Game, One of Ourselves, Lily My Love, The Singing Detective, The Interrogation of John, Yellowbacks, Tell Tale Hearts, Wall of Silence, Oliver's Travels, Ghostbusters of East Finchley, The Writing on the Wall; other credits incl: Aufwiedersehen Pet (Central), Traffik (Channel Four) 1993, Shrinks (Euston Films), God On The Rocks (Channel Four), The Crow Road 1996, Melissa 1997, Mr White Goes To Westminster 1997, Wives and Daughters 1999, Rebel Heart 2000, The Whistleblower 2001, Dr Zhivago 2002, Danielle Cable Eye Witness 2003, Sea of Souls 2003–06, Tell Me Lies 2004, Criminal Justice (BBC) 2008, Little Dorrit (BBC) 2008, Law and Order UK, Spanish Flu: The Fogotten Fallen; *Radio* incl: Byline, A Man With Connections, Flowers in the Sky, Hiroshima The Movie, A Good Man in Africa, Hedda Gabler, The Caucasian Chalk Circle, Tales From the Backgreen (wrote and read); *Film* incl: The Ploughman's Lunch, The Killing Fields, Comfort and Joy, A Private Function, Defence of the Realm, Friendships Death, The Witches, Baron Munchausen, Truly Madly Deeply, Victory, Richard III, Hilary and Jackie 1998, Sunshine 1998, Crush 2001, Bright Young Things 2004, Ragtale 2005, Miss Potter 2006, Amazing Grace 2007, How to Lose Friends and Alienate People 2008, Creation; *Publications* Tales from the Back Green (2008); *Style—* Bill Paterson, Esq; ✉ c/o Gordon and French, 12–13 Poland Street, London W1V 3DE (☎ 020 7734 4818, fax 020 7734 4832)

PATERSON, Christopher Douglas (Chris); s of David D Paterson, and Lynn S Paterson; *b* 30 March 1978, Edinburgh; *Educ* Galashiels Acad, Moray House Inst of Educn (Dip PE Teaching); *m* June 2008, Claire, *née* Elliott; *Career* rugby union player; clubs: Gala RFC 1996–99 (as amateur, winners Melrose Sevens 1999, winners Scottish Cup 1999, Second Div champions), Edinburgh Rugby (formerly Edinburgh Reivers) 1999–2007 and 2008–, Gloucester 2007–08; int: Scotland Schs 1996, Scotland U19 1997, Scotland U21 1998–99, Scotland A 1999, Scotland Sevens 1999, Scotland 1999– (debut v Spain, capt Six Nations Championship 2004); most capped Scottish player of all time (100 caps), highest Scottish points scorer of all time (over 730 points), third highest try scorer of all time (22 tries), first Scottish player to make 50 European appearances; Scotland Player of the Year 2003, Scotland Player of the World Cup 2003, World Try of the Year v South Africa 2003; *Style—* Chris Paterson, Esq; ✉ c/o Scottish Rugby Union, Murrayfield, Edinburgh EH12 5PJ

PATERSON, Christopher John; s of John Paterson (d 2008), and Mary Kathleen, *née* Body; *b* 9 January 1947; *Educ* Peterhouse S Rhodesia, Univ of Exeter (BA), Stanford Exec Prog, Univ of Oxford (PGCert); *m* 15 Dec 1973, Gillian Diana, da of Geoffrey Piper, of Christchurch, Dorset; 1 da (Sarah b 1978), 1 s (Timothy b 1981); *Career* Nat Serv Royal Rhodesia Regt 1965–66; Macmillan: joined 1970, publisher Nature 1980–81, md College Press Zimbabwe 1983–85, chm Macmillan Southern Africa 1983–2008, md Macmillan Press 1985–91, dir Macmillan Publishers Ltd 1989–2008, chm Macmillan Education 1999–2008, int publishing conslt 2008–; memb Singapore Br Bus Cncl 1999–2004, chm Int Bd and memb Cncl Publishers Assoc 2000–06, chm Southern Africa Bus Assoc 2002–05, chm Cwlth Orgns Ctee on Zimbabwe 2010–12; memb Chllr's Advsy Ctee Univ of Exeter 1994–2000, sec Exeter Cathedral Fabric Advsy Ctee 2010–; govr Peterhouse Zimbabwe 2000–; *Recreations* gardening, running; *Clubs* Harare, Henley RFC; *Style—* Christopher Paterson, Esq

PATERSON, Don; OBE (2008); s of Russell Leslie Paterson, of Dundee, and Jean Louise, *née* Cougan; *b* 30 October 1963; *Educ* Kirkton HS; *Career* poet and musician; writer in residence Univ of Dundee 1993, poetry ed Picador, lectr Sch of English Univ of St Andrews; Eric Gregory Award 1990, winner Arvon/Observer Poetry competition 1994, Queen's Gold Medal for Poetry 2010; memb Jazz band Lammas; FRSL; *Recordings* Talisker 1987, Lammas 1992, Lammas: This Morning 1994, Lammas: The Broken Road 1995, Lammas: Sourcebook 1997, Sea Changes 1999; *Books Publications* Nil Nil (1993, Forward prize for Best First Collection, Scottish Arts Cncl Book Award), God's Gift to Women (1997, T S Eliot Award, Geoffrey Faber Memorial Prize, SAC Book Award), The Eyes (1999, SAC Book Award), Landing Light (2003, Whitbread Poetry Prize Prize, T S Eliot Award), Book of Shadows (2004), Orpheus (2006), The Blind Eye (2007), Best Thought, Worst Thought (2008), Rain (2009, Forward Poetry Prize), Reading Shakespeare's Sonnets: A New Commentary (2010), Smith: A Reader's Guide to the Poetry of Michael Donaghy (2014); *Style—* Don Paterson, Esq, OBE; ✉ c/o Faber & Faber Ltd, Bloomsbury House, 74–77 Great Russell Street, London WC1B 3DA

PATERSON, Douglas Gordon James; s of Gordon Mellish Paterson, of Moor Park, Herts, and Anne Barbara Bolam, *née* Mason; *b* 24 October 1943; *Educ* George Watson's Coll Edinburgh, Univ Coll Sch, Univ of St Andrews (MA); *m* 29 May 1972, Pamela Jane, da of William Taylor Rollo (d 1984); 2 s (Christopher Douglas Mark b 18 Oct 1973, Nicholas Gordon William b 13 May 1975), 1 da (Alice Elspeth Jane b 21 March 1977); *Career* PricewaterhouseCoopers (formerly Coopers & Lybrand before merger): qualified CA 1968, Cologne office 1970–71, London office 1972–76, ptnr Switzerland 1977–80, ptnr UK 1979–2001; non-exec dir: Goldman Sachs Int Bank 2002–, Close Brothers Gp 2004–12, ImmuPharma plc 2006–07, The Derivatives Consulting Gp Ltd 2007–08, Rothesay Life Ltd 2007–15, Montague Place Custody Service 2009–, Butterfield UK Ltd 2014–, JDX Base 60 Ltd 2015–; non-exec offr Generation Investment Mgmnt LLP 2005–; FCA 1968, ATII 1968; *Recreations* tennis, photography, walking, reading; *Clubs* Caledonian; *Style—* Douglas Paterson, Esq

PATERSON, Ewan Gill; s of Patrick Paterson (d 2010), and Pamela Paterson (d 1997); *b* 1 February 1963; *Educ* various schs in Africa and UK, Univ of Manchester (BSc, first XI football), Imperial Coll London (Britoil scholarship, MSc, first XI football); *m* 25 Aug 2001, Tricia Leslie, *née* Black; 1 da (Olivia Pamela b 2003), 1 s (James Gardiner b 2003); *Career* exploration geologist (North Sea) Exlog Inc 1984–86, advtg account handler McCann-Erickson Advertising 1987–88, advtg copywriter Yellowhammer Advertising 1988–90, copywriter Young & Rubican (incl campaigns for Pirelli and Colgate) 1990–95; BMP DDB (now DDB London): copywriter (campaigns incl London Transport, Volkswagen and The Guardian) 1995–2002, jt creative dir 2002–04; creative dir Bartle Bogle Hegarty 2004–06 (incl global Vodafone campaign Make the Most of Now), exec

P

creative dir CHI & Ptnrs (formerly Clemmow Hornby Inge) 2006–10 (incl Britvic Drench campaign Brains Perform Best When Hydrated), chief creative offr DDB Chicago 2010–14 (incl Get to a Better State campaign for State Farm Insurance, Taste the Rainbow for Mars Skittles and various campaigns for McDonalds N America and Pepsi Beverages), creative ptnr BBHSport London 2014– (incl campaigns for Adidas and BA, Samsung, Rugby World Cup 2015); judge: D&AD 1997, 2002, 2004, 2006 and 2009, CLIO Awards 2003, Cannes Advtg Festival 2009; memb Lab Pty; *Awards* Br Television Awards Commercial of the Year (for Pirelli) 1996 and Gold Award (for Britvic) 2009, Cannes Advtg Festival over 40 Lions (for Volkswagen, Sony, Pirelli, London Transport, Britvic, The Guardian, Unilever, TalkTalk, The Times, State Farm and AdCouncil) 1997–2012, Silver Pencil D&AD (for London Transport) 1998, (for Vodafone) 2006 (for Prince's Tst) 2007, (for Big Yellow Storage) 2008 and (for Sunday Times) 2011, runner-up Agency of the Year Cannes Advtg Festival (DDB London) 2004; *Clubs* Manchester City FC, Royal Mid-Surrey Golf, Olympic Barnes; *Style*— Ewan Paterson, Esq; ✉ BBHSport, 60 Kingly Street, London W1 (e-mail ewangillpaterson@gmail.com)

PATERSON, Gil; MSP; *Career* cncllr Strathclyde Regnl Cncl, exec vice-convenor Local Govt, exec vice-convenor Administration; MSP (SNP): Scotland Central 1999–2003, W of Scotland 2007–11, Clydebank & Milngavie 2011–; *Style*— Gil Paterson, Esq, MSP

PATERSON, Graham Julian; s of Peter James Paterson, *qv*, and Beryl, *née* Johnson; *b* 7 June 1955; *Educ* Dulwich Coll, Magdalen Coll Oxford (BA); *Career* journalist Daily Telegraph 1977–86, ed 7 Days Section Sunday Telegraph 1988–89 (assoc ed 1987–88, home ed 1986–87); The Times: asst ed 1989–, chief asst to the ed and features ed 1993–95, foreign ed 1995–99, exec ed 1999–2001, home ed 2001–03, ed tabloid edn 2003–04; dep foreign ed Sunday Times 2005–; *Clubs* Travellers; *Style*— Graham Paterson, Esq; ✉ The Sunday Times, 3 Thomas More Square, London E98 1ST

PATERSON, Prof Ian; s of Angus Paterson (d 1986), and Violet Paterson (d 1978); *b* 4 May 1954, Dundee; *Educ* Kirkton HS Dundee, Univ of St Andrews (BSc), Univ of Cambridge (PhD); *m* 18 June 1977, Nina, *née* Kuan; *Career* research fell Christ's Coll Cambridge 1978–79, NATO/SERC postdoctoral research fell Columbia Univ NY 1979–80, lectr in chemistry UCL 1980–83; Univ of Cambridge: univ lectr Dept of Chemistry 1983–97, reader in organic chemistry 1997–2000, prof of organic chemistry 2001–; Jesus Coll Cambridge: teaching fell 1983–2001, dir of studies in chemistry 1991–97, professorial fell 2002–; visiting prof Univ of Rennes I France 1993; various consultancies with pharmaceutical cos; Hickinbottom fell RSC 1989–91, Wilsmore fell Univ of Melbourne 2010; FRS 2005, FRSE 2010, FRSC 2015 (MRSC); *Awards* Meldola Medal and Prize RSC 1983, Pfizer Award in Chemistry (UK) 1990 and 1993, ICI (AstraZeneca) Award in Organic Chemistry (UK) 1990, Organic Reactions Lectr (USA) 1992, Bader Prize RSC 1996, RSC Award in Synthetic Organic Chemistry 2001, Robert Robinson Lectureship Award RSC 2004, Tilden Prize RSC 2009, Natural Product Chemistry Award RSC 2014; *Publications* extensive pubns in jls incl Angewandte Chemie, Organic Letters and Jl of the American Chemical Soc; *Recreations* walking, gardening, travel; *Style*— Prof Ian Paterson; ✉ Department of Chemistry, University of Cambridge, Lensfield Road, Cambridge CB2 1EW (☎ 01223 336407, fax 01223 336362, e-mail ip100@cam.ac.uk)

PATERSON, Jan; MBE; *Career* formerly dep dir of communications BOA, currently ceo Br Olympic Fndn and dir Olympic Relations BOA; dep chef de mission Sport London 2012, chef de mission Glasgow Commonwealth Games 2014; *Style*— Ms Jan Paterson, MBE; ✉ British Olympic Association, 60 Charlotte Street, London W1T 2NU

PATERSON, Mark; *Educ* SAE Inst (BA); *Career* sound mixer; Goldcrest Films 2003–; *Film* incl: Alien Autopsy 2006, Children of Men 2006, Hot Fuzz 2007, Starburst 2007, Love in the Time of Cholera 2007, Happy-Go-Lucky 2008, The Boy in the Striped Pyjamas 2008, The Imaginarium of Doctor Parnassus 2009, Paul 2011, Attack the Block 2011, The Pirates! In an Adventure with Scientists! 2012, Les Misérables 2012 (Best Sound Editing and Mixing Satellite Award 2013, Best Sound BAFTA 2013, Best Sound Mixing Acad Award 2013), The World's End 2013; *Style*— Mark Paterson, Esq; ✉ Todd AO, 3000 Olympic Boulevard, Santa Monica, CA 90404, USA

PATERSON, Rt Hon Owen William; PC (2010), MP; s of late Alfred Dobell Paterson, and late Cynthia Paterson; *b* 24 June 1956; *Educ* Radley, CCC Cambridge (MA), Nat Leathersellers Coll Northampton; *m* 1980, Hon Rose Ridley, da of 4 Viscount Ridley, KG, GCVO, TD (d 2012); 2 s (Felix b 1986, Ned b 1988), 1 da (Evie b 1992); *Career* md British Leather Co Ltd 1993–99; MP (Cons) Shropshire N 1997– (Parly candidate Wrexham 1992); PPS to Rt Hon Iain Duncan Smith, MP, *qv*, 2001–03; shadow min for agric 2003–05, shadow min of state for tport 2005–07, shadow sec of state for NI 2007–10, sec of state for NI 2010–12, sec of state for environment, food and rural affrs 2012–14; co-chm Parly Manufacturing Industry Gp 1997–98; memb: Welsh Grand Ctee 1997–2000, Welsh Affrs Select Ctee 1997–2001, Inter-Parly Union 1997, Parly Waterways Gp 1997–, Cons Friends of Israel, Franco-Br Parly Relations Ctee 1997–, All-Pty Racing Gp, Cons Way Forward Gp, Euro Scrutiny Select Ctee 1999–2001, Agric Select Ctee 2000–01; pres COTANCE (Confedn of European Tanners) 1996–98; vice-chm All-Pty BBC Gp; dep chm Ellesmere Community Care Centre Tst 1991–97, memb Cncl Inst of Orthopaedics 1992–; Liveryman Worshipful Co of Leathersellers; *Style*— The Rt Hon Owen Paterson, MP; ✉ House of Commons, London SW1A 0AA (☎ 020 7219 5185, fax 020 7219 3955, e-mail patersono@parliament.uk)

PATERSON, Rt Rev Robert Mar Erskine; *see:* Sodor and Man, Bishop of

PATERSON, Steven; MP; *b* 25 April 1975, Stirling; *Educ* Stirling HS, Univ of Stirling (BA); *Career* media and communications mangr for Bruce Crawford, MSP 2006–15, MP (SNP) Stirling 2015–; cncllr Stirling E Ward 2007–15; *Style*— Steven Paterson, Esq, MP; ✉ Springfield House, Laurehill Business Park, Stirling FK7 9JQ (☎ 01786 406375, e-mail steven.paterson.mp@parliament.uk, website www.stevenforstirling.com)

PATERSON, Prof William Edgar; OBE (1999); s of William Edgar Paterson (d 1978), of Comrie, Perthshire, and Williamina, *née* McIntyre (d 2003); *b* 26 September 1941; *Educ* Morrison's Acad, Univ of St Andrews (MA, class medallist), LSE (S H Bailey scholar, MSc, PhD); *m* 1, 1964, Jacqueline, *née* Cramb (d 1974); 2 s (William b 1970, John b 1973); m 2, 1979, Phyllis MacDowell; 1 da (Alison b 1980), 1 step s (Colin b 1970), 1 step da (Catherine b 1975); *Career* lectr in int relations Univ of Aberdeen 1967–70; Univ of Warwick: Volkswagen lectr in German politics 1970–75, sr lectr 1975–82, reader 1982–89, prof and chm of dept 1989–90; Salvesen prof of European Insts and dir Europa Inst Univ of Edinburgh 1990–94, prof of German politics and fndn dir Inst for German Studies Univ of Birmingham 1994–2009, hon prof in german politics Univ of Aston 2009–; dir Königswinter Conf; chm: Assoc for the Study of German Politics 1974–76, Univ Assoc for Contemporary European Studies 1989–94, One Europe or Several Prog 1994–95, German-British Forum 2006–13; memb: ESRC Research Priorities Bd 1994–99 (chm 2005–13), Kuratorium Allianz Kultur Stiftung 2001–05, Advsy Bd Centre for Br Studies Humboldt-Univ Berlin; founding ed German Politics 1991–2001, co-ed Jl of Common Market Studies 2003–08, memb Editorial Bd Int Affairs; hon vice-pres Assoc for the Study of German Politics 2000; Lifetime Award Assoc for the Study of German Politics 2004, Lifetime Achievement Award in European Studies Univ Assoc for Contemporary European Studies 2007, Special Recognition Award for Excellence in the Study of German Politics, UK-German Relations and European Integration Political Studies Assoc 2012; assoc fell RIIA 1994; FRSE 1994, FRSA 1998, FAcSS 2000; Officer's Cross of the Federal Republic of Germany 1999; *Publications* incl: Federal Republic of Germany and the European Community (jtly, 1987), Government and the Chemical Industry (jtly, 1988), The Kohl Chancellorship (co-eds, 1998), Germany's European Diplomacy (jtly, 2000), The Future of the German Economy (co-ed, 2000), Developments in German Politics III (jtly, 2003), Governance in Contemporary Germany (co-ed, 2005), The Gathering Crisis: Germany and the 2005 Election (jtly, 2008), Research Agendas in European Union Studies, Stalking the Elephant (co-ed, 2009), Developments in German Politics 4 (co-ed, 2014), The European Union in Crisis (co-ed, 2016); author of numerous articles in learned jls; *Recreations* walking; *Clubs* Reform; *Style*— Prof William Paterson, OBE, AcSS, FRSE, FRSA; ☎ 01926 492492, e-mail w.paterson@aston.ac.uk

PATIENCE, His Hon Andrew; QC (1990); s of William Edmund John Patience (d 1960), and Louise Mary (d 1998); *b* 28 April 1941; *Educ* Whitgift Sch Croydon, St John's Coll Oxford (MA); *m* 1975, (Jean) Adèle, *née* Williams (Her Hon Judge Williams), *qv*; 1 da (Louise b 1981), 1 s (David b 1984); *Career* called to the Bar Gray's Inn 1966; recorder of the Crown Court 1986–99, circuit judge (SE Circuit) 1999–2011, resident judge Maidstone Crown Court 2000–10, hon recorder of Dover 2001–, Kent Ambassador 2011–; patron Chatham Dockyard Historical Soc 2012–, ambassador Chatham Historical Dockyard Tst 2015–; pres Br Red Cross Kent 2012–; *Recreations* mimicry, complaining, horse racing; *Clubs* Oxford and Cambridge; *Style*— His Hon Andrew Patience, QC; ✉ e-mail drongoes@gmail.com

PATON, Andrew John; s of John William Davies Paton, of Birmingham, and Peggy Irene Lois Paton; *b* 15 March 1957, Birmingham; *Educ* Bishop Vesey's GS Sutton Coldfield, Univ of Exeter (LLB); *m* 18 Sept 1982, Catherine, *née* Andrews; 1 da (Hannah b 1987), 2 s (Tom b 1994, Rory b 1997); *Career* admitted slr 1981; ptnr Pinsent Masons 1986– (slr 1981–86); accredited mediator 1990, jt fndr Panel of Ind Mediators (PIM), chm Assoc of Midlands Mediators; author of numerous articles on mediation; dir ADR Net Ltd 1991–; memb Law Soc 1981, MCIArb 2003; *Recreations* sailing, tennis, golf; *Clubs* Edgbaston Priory Tennis, Barnt Green Sailing; *Style*— Andrew Paton, Esq; ✉ Pinsent Masons, 3 Colmore Circus, Birmingham B4 6BH (☎ 0121 200 1050, fax 0121 626 1040, e-mail andrew.paton@pinsents.com)

PATON, Maureen Virginia; da of William Harney, and Blanche, *née* Adams (later Mrs Paton); *Educ* Watford Tech HS, Univ of Leicester (BA); *m* 21 May 1977, Liam Michael Maguire (d 2006), s of William Maguire; *Career* journalist and author; trainee with British Printing Corporation on various pubns, subsequently with IPC Business Press, The Express 1979–98; freelance feature writer on subjects incl arts, showbusiness and women's issues 1998–; contrib to pubns incl: The Independent, The Guardian, You magazine, Daily Mail, The Times, Daily Telegraph, Sunday Telegraph, Sunday Express, The Stage, Saga Magazine, The Lady; memb: NUJ, Broadcasting Press Guild, Women In Journalism, Press Club; *Books* Alan Rickman: The Unauthorised Biography, The Best of Women: The History of The Women of the Year; *Recreations* jazz, rock and blues, vintage fashion, yoga, pilates; *Style*— Maureen Paton; ✉ mobile 07775 888491, e-mail maurpaton@btinternet.com, website www.maureenpaton.co.uk

PATON WALSH, Gillian (Jill); CBE (1996); da of John Llewellyn Bliss (d 1979), and Patricia, *née* Dubern (d 1977); *b* 29 April 1937; *Educ* St Michael's Convent Sch N Finchley, St Anne's Coll Oxford (MA, DipEd); *m* 1 1961, Antony Edmund Paton Walsh (d 2003); 1 s (Edmund Alexander b 1963), 2 da (Margaret Anne b 1965, Helen Clare b 1966); m 2 2004, John Rowe Townsend (d 2014); *Career* teacher Enfield Girls GS 1959–62, Arts Cncl Creative Writing Fellowship 1976–78, perm visiting faculty memb Centre for Children's Literature Simmons Coll Boston Mass 1978–86, Gertrude Clarke Whittall lectr Library of Congress 1978, judge Whitbread prize 1984, chm Cambridge Book Assoc 1987–89, ptnr Green Bay Pubns; memb: Ctee Children's Writers Gp, Mgmnt Ctee Soc of Authors; adjunct Br Bd memb Children's Literature New England, memb cncl Soc of Authors 1999; pres Dorothy L Sayers Soc 2015; FRSL 1996; *Books* Hengest's Tale (1966), The Dolphin Crossing (1967), Wordhoard (1969), Fireweed (1970), Farewell, Great King (1972), Goldengrove (1972), Toolmaker (1973), The Dawnstone (1973), The Emperor's Winding Sheet (1974), The Butty Boy (1975), The Island Sunrise: Prehistoric Britain (1975), Unleaving (1976), Crossing to Salamis, The Walls of Athens, Persian Gold (1977–78), A Chance Child (1978), The Green Book (1981), Babylon (1982), Lost & Found (1984), A Parcel of Patterns (1984), Gaffer Samson's Luck (1985), Five Tides (1986), Lapsing (1986), Torch (1987), A School for Lovers (1989), Birdy and The Ghosties (1989), Can I Play? (1990), Grace (1991), When Grandma Came (1992), Matthew and The Seasingers (1992), The Wyndham Case (1993), Knowledge of Angels (1994, Booker Prize nominee), Pepi and the Secret Names (1994), A Piece of Justice (1995), Connie Came to Play (1995), Thomas and the Tinners (1995), The Serpentine Cave (1997), Thrones, Dominions (completion of Dorothy L Sayers novel, 1998), A Desert in Bohemia (2000), A Presumption of Death (based on notes by Dorothy L Sayers, 2002), Debts of Dishonour (2006), The Bad Quarto (2007), The Attenbury Emeralds, based on the characters of Dorothy Sayers (2010), The Late Scholar, based on the characters of Dorothy Sayers (2013); *Recreations* reading, walking, sewing, photography; *Clubs* Athenaeum; *Style*— Mrs Jill Paton Walsh, CBE, FRSL; ✉ c/o Veronique Baxter, David Higham Associates, 7th Floor Waverley House, 7–12 Noel Street, London W1F 8GQ

PATRICK, HE Andrew; *Career* diplomat; desk offr Security Policy Dept FCO 1989–91, third then second sec Nicosia 1991–95, first sec UK Delgn NATO Brussels 1995–96, head Serbia, Kosovo, Albania and Macedonia Section FCO 1996–98, private sec to Foreign Sec FCO 1998–2000, head of knowledge prog FCO 2000–01, head of newsroom FCO 2001–04, dep head of mission Pretoria 2004–07, dep head of mission Kabul 2007–09, additional dir S Asia FCO 2009–13, ambass to Burma 2013–; *Style*— HE Mr Andrew Patrick; ✉ c/o FCO (Rangoon), King Charles Street, London SW1A 2AH

PATRICK, Andrew Graham McIntosh; s of Dr James McIntosh Patrick, OBE, RSA, ARE, ROI, LLD (d 1998), and Janet, *née* Watterston (d 1983); *b* 12 June 1934; *Educ* Harris Acad Dundee; *Career* The Fine Art Soc: joined 1954, dir 1966, md 1976–2003, dep chm 2003–; ret to create garden in Morocco; presenter of hundreds of exhbns, mostly of Br artists but covering all aspects of the visual arts; memb: Exec Ctee Soc of London Art Dealers (chm 1983–86), Cncl The Br Antique Dealers' Assoc 1986–93, Curatorial Ctee Nat Tst for Scot 1986–89, Art in Lieu Panel 2001–13; chm Decorative Arts Soc 2005–08; *Recreations* collecting: pictures, Japanese prints, camels, etc; *Clubs* Garrick; *Style*— Andrew McIntosh Patrick, Esq; ✉ Flat 6, 55 Great Cumberland Place, London W1H 7LJ (☎ 020 7258 3322)

PATRICK, Bruce Robertson; s of Francis Wheatly Patrick, of Edinburgh, and Isabel, *née* Spencer; *b* 26 November 1945; *Educ* Glasgow Acad, Edinburgh Acad, Exeter Coll Oxford (BA), Univ of Edinburgh (LLB, Green Prize for criminal law, Millar Prize for Scots law); *m* 9 Feb 1980, Hilary Jane, eld da of Richard Alan Sutton; 2 da (Ruth b 5 Nov 1980, Catherine b 4 July 1982), 1 s (Robert James b 9 July 1984); *Career* apprentice Mitchells Johnston Solicitors Glasgow 1971–73; asst: Maclay Murray & Spens Glasgow 1973–75, Coward Chance Solicitors London 1975–76; Maclay Murray & Spens: ptnr Company Dept 1976–2003 (Glasgow office 1976–77, Edinburgh office 1978–2003), managing ptnr 1991–94, sr ptnr 2000–03, conslt 2003–06; pt/t tutor in law Univ of Edinburgh 1980–84; completed Glasgow marathon 1985; non-exec dir Dunedin Enterprises Investment Tst plc 2003–; memb: Law Soc of Scotland 1973 (vice-convenor Company Law Ctee), Royal Faculty of Procurators Glasgow 1976, Soc of WS 1980; *Books* IBA Handbook on Maritime Law (contrib Scottish section, 1983); *Recreations* sailing, golf, hill walking, rugby (now spectator), occasional gardening; *Clubs* Luffness Golf, Prestwick Golf, Clyde Cruising; *Style*— Bruce Patrick, Esq

PATRICK, (Katherine) Emily (Mrs Michael Perry); da of William Pitt Patrick, of Folkestone, Kent, and Rosemary Martha, *née* Pulvertaft; *b* 4 October 1959; *Educ* Folkestone GS,

Architectural Assoc, Univ of Cambridge (MA); *m* 16 Oct 1986, Michael Luke Perry, s of David Edward Perry, of Hitchin, Herts; 2 da (Beatrice Lillian b 9 Sept 1987, Isabel Eliza b 5 March 1990), 1 s (Alfred Oberon Patrick b 4 April 1994); *Career* artist; exhibited at: King St Gallery, Wraxall Gallery, Long & Ryle Int, Maine Gallery, Mall Galleries, Lefevre Gallery, Nat Portrait Gallery, Napier Gallery; one man shows at: Agnew's 1986, 1989, 1992 and 1995, 27 Cork Street London 1997, 2000 and 2013, Hanover Sq Gallery NY 1997, 32 Dover St London 2002, 2005, 2007 and 2010, 8 Duke Street St James's 2015; painted Lord Cottesloe 1983, painted HRH The Princess of Wales, portrait for Royal Hants Regt 1987, painted Sir Konrad Schiemann, portrait for European Court of Justice 2014; first winner of Royal Soc of Portrait Painters' Caroll Prize 1988; *Style—* Emily Patrick; ✉ e-mail mail@emilypatrick.com

PATRICK, Keith Ian; s of Hubert Eric Patrick (d 1983), and Edna May, *née* Hart (d 2010); *b* 23 February 1952; *Educ* Watford Boys' GS, Watford Sch of Art, Hockerill Coll, Camberwell Sch of Art (BA); *m* 1989, Maria Teresa Lorés Bergua (Maite Lorés); 1 step s (Fabian Hutchinson b 25 July 1973), 1 step da (Anna Nuria Smythe b 4 May 1981); *Career* worked and exhibited as practising artist 1974–83, art critic 1983–; works published in numerous art jls at home and abroad, guest ed Studio International 1984, ed Art Line Magazine 1990–96, ed Contemporary Visual Arts Magazine 1996–2001, ed Contemporary Magazine 2001–03; curator of exhibitions incl: The Romantic Tradition in Contemporary British Painting (Spain and England touring) 1988, Romantic Visions (Camden Arts Centre) 1988, From Bacon to Now – The Outsider in British Figuration (Palazzo Vecchio Florence) 1991–92, Contemporary Br Sculpture – Henry Moore to the 90s (Spain and Portugal touring) 1995, Jaume Plensa: Close Up (Ljubljana) 2001, Video London (Madrid, Barcelona) 2005, 2006 and 2007, Fràgil (Barcelona) 2008; Int Assoc of Art Critics: assoc 1984, sec Br Section 1986–89, pres Br Section 1991–94, vice-pres Int Section 1993–96; conslt ed working with various museums in Europe 2005–; *Publications* Oil on Canvas (1997), Jaume Plensa: The Crown Fountain (2008); *Style—* Keith Patrick, Esq; ✉ e-mail keith@keithpatrick.net

PATRICK, Peter Laurence; s of Anthony Frederick Herbert Patrick, of St Peters, Broadstairs, Kent, and Joyce Stanley, *née* Sowerby; *b* 11 July 1946; *Educ* Alleyne's Sch Stevenage, UC Durham (BA); *m* 22 April 1972, Teresa Mary Patrick, da of William Roland Mills, MBE, of Billericay, Essex; 1 s (Edward William b 4 Nov 1973), 1 da (Frances Elizabeth b 10 July 1975); *Career* CA 1972; Price Waterhouse & Co: Newcastle 1967–70, London 1970–73, Paris 1973–76; computer audit mangr Howard Tilly & Co 1976–78, head of inspection Hambros Bank Ltd 1978–86, co sec Hambros plc and Hambros Bank Ltd 1986–98; ct sec HAC 1999–2011; cncllr: Billericay E Basildon DC 1984–96 and 1998–2002, Polestead PC Suffolk, Babergh DC Suffolk (Berners Ward); chm Fin Ctee Basildon DC 1992–95, dep chm (Finance) S Suffolk Cons Assoc 2006–09; chm Towngate Theatre Co Basildon 1988–89, tstee Adventure Unlimited (Chelmsford Dio Youth Charity) 1978–2012, tstee Essex Young Musicians' Tst until 2015; churchwarden 2005–16 and memb choir St Mary's Boxford; *Recreations* singing, gardening, politics, history, architecture; *Style—* Peter Patrick, Esq; ✉ Amberley, Whitestreet Green, Boxford, Suffolk CO10 5JN (☎ 01787 210346, e-mail ppat@btinternet.com)

PATTEN, Brian; *b* 7 February 1946; *Career* poet and author; Freeman City of Liverpool 2001; hon fell Liverpool John Moores Univ 2002; Hon DLitt Univ of Liverpool 2006, Hon DUniv Open Univ 2013; FRSL 2003; poetry: Little Johnny's Confessions (1967), The Mersey Sound (with Adrian Henri and Roger McGough, 1967), Penguin Modern Poets (1967), Notes to the Hurrying Man (1969), The Irrelevant Song (1971), The Unreliable Nightingale (1973), Vanishing Trick (1976), The Shabby Angel (1978), Grave Gossip (1979), Love Poems (1981), Clares Countryside (1978), New Volume (1983), Storm Damage (1988), Grinning Jack (Selected Poems, 1990), Armada (1997), New Collected Love Poems (2007), Penguin Selected Poems (2007); novels: Mr Moon's Last Case (1975), The Story Giant (2001); plays: The Pig and the Junkle (1975), The Mouth Trap (with Roger McGough, 1982), Blind Love (1983), Gargling with Jelly – The Play! (1989); for younger readers: The Elephant and the Flower (1969), Jumping Mouse (1971), Emma's Doll (1976), The Sly Cormorant and the Fish (1977), Gangsters Ghosts and Dragonflies (ed, 1981), Gargling with Jelly (1985), Jimmy Tag-along (1988), Thawing Frozen Frogs (1990), The Puffin Book of Twentieth Century Children's Verse (ed, 1991), Grizzelda Frizzle (1992), The Magic Bicycle (1993), Impossible Parents (1994), The Utter Nutters (1994), The Puffin Book of Utterly Brilliant Verse (ed, 1998), Beowulf: a Retelling (1999), The Blue and Green Ark (1999), Little Hotchpotch (2000), Juggling with Gerbils (2000), Ben's Magic Telescope (2002), The Story Giant (2002), The Monsters' Guide to Choosing a Pet (with Roger McGough, 2004), Collected Love Poems (2007), Mersey Sound (2007), View from the Boathouse Window (2010), The Big Snuggle-up (2011), Can I Come Too? (2013), Monster Slayer (2016); *Recreations* river cruising; *Clubs* Chelsea Arts; *Style—* Brian Patten, Esq; ✉ c/o Rogers, Coleridge and White, 20 Powis Mews, London W11 1JN (☎ 020 7221 3717, fax 020 7229 9084, website www.brianpatten.co.uk)

PATTEN, Baron (Life Peer UK 1997), of Wincanton in the County of Somerset; John Haggitt Charles Patten; PC (1990); s of late Jack Patten, and late Maria Olga, *née* Sikora; *b* 17 July 1945; *Educ* Wimbledon Coll, Sidney Sussex Coll Cambridge (MA, PhD), Univ of Oxford (MA); *m* 1978, Louise Alexandra Virginia Patten, *qv*, da of late John Rowe; 1 da (Hon Mary-Claire b 10 June 1986); *Career* MP (Cons): Oxford 1979–83, Oxford W and Abingdon 1983–97 (ret); PPS to mins of state at the Home Office 1980–81; Parly under sec of state: NI Office 1981–83, DHSS 1983–85; min of state: for housing, urban affrs and construction 1985–87, Home Office 1987–92; sec of state for education 1992–94; non-exec dep chm CCF Charterhouse plc 2000–1, sr advsr Charterhouse Devpt Capital 2001–; advsr Lockheed Martin Overseas Corp 1997–, non-exec dir Lockheed Martin UK Holdings Ltd 1999–; memb Advsy Bd Thomas Goode & Co Ltd 1997–; fell Hertford Coll Oxford 1972–94, hon fell Harris Manchester Coll Oxford 1996; Liveryman Worshipful Co of Drapers; *Books* The Conservative Opportunity (with Lord Blake), Things to Come: The Tories in the 21st Century, Not Quite the Diplomat, and four other books; *Recreations* talking with my wife and daughter; *Style—* The Rt Hon the Lord Patten, PC; ✉ House of Lords, London SW1A 0PW

PATTEN, Lady; Louise Alexandra Patten; *b* 2 February 1954; *Educ* St Paul's Girls' Sch, St Hugh's Coll Oxford (MA); *m* 1978, Baron Patten, PC (Life Peer), *qv*; 1 da; *Career* with: Citibank NA 1977–81, Wells Fargo Bank NA 1981–85, PA Consulting Gp 1985–93; memb UK Advsy Bd Bain & Co 1997– (ptnr 1993–97); non-exec dir: Hilton Gp 1993–, Harveys Furnishings plc 1996–2000, Great Universal Stores 1997–, Somerfield plc 1998– (actg chm 1999–2000), Brixton plc 2001– (chm 2003–), Bradford & Bingley plc 2003–, Marks and Spencer Group plc 2006–; *Style—* The Lady Patten; ✉ c/o Bain & Co, 40 Strand, London WC2N 5HZ

PATTEN, Rt Hon Lord Justice; Rt Hon Sir Nicholas John Patten; kt (2000), PC (2009); *b* 7 August 1950; *Career* called to the Bar Lincoln's Inn 1974 (bencher 1997); QC 1987, dep judge of the High Court 1998–2000, judge of the High Court (Chancery Div) 2000–09, vice-chllr Co Palatine of Lancaster 2005–08, Lord Justice of Appeal 2009–; chm Chancery Bar Assoc 1997–99; *Style—* The Rt Hon Lord Justice Patten; ✉ Royal Courts of Justice, Strand, London WC2A 2LL

PATTEN OF BARNES, Baron (Life Peer UK 2005), of Barnes in the London Borough of Richmond; Christopher Francis (Chris) Patten; CH (1998), PC (1989); s of late Francis Joseph Patten; *b* 12 May 1944; *Educ* St Benedict's Ealing, Balliol Coll Oxford; *m* 1971, (Mary) Lavender St Leger, da of late Maj John Thornton, by his late wife Joan Coulton, *née* Walker-Smith, sister of 1 Baron Broxbourne; 3 da (Hon Kate, Hon Laura, Hon Alice); *Career* CRD 1966–70, dir 1974–79; worked in Cabinet Office 1970–72, Home Office 1972, PA to Chm Cons Party 1972–74, MP (Cons) Bath 1979–92; PPS to: Norman St John-Stevas as Chllr Duchy of Lancaster and Ldr House of Commons 1979–81, Patrick Jenkin as Sec of State for Social Servs 1981; jt vice-chm Cons Fin Ctee 1981–83, under sec of state NI Office 1983–85; min of state DES 1985–86, min of state for overseas devpt 1986–89, sec of state for the environment 1989–90, chm Cons Pty and Chancellor of the Duchy of Lancaster 1990–92, govr and C-in-C of Hong Kong 1992–97; chm Independent Cmmn on Policing for NI 1998–99; EU cmmr for external affairs 1999–2004; chllr Univ of Oxford 2003–; chm BBC Tst 2011–14; awarded several honorary degrees; distinguished hon fell Massey Coll Univ of Toronto 2005, hon fell Balliol Coll Oxford, hon fell St Anthony's Coll Oxford; Hon FRCPE 1994; *Books* East and West (1998), Not Quite The Diplomat (2005), What Next? Surviving the 21st Century (2008); *Recreations* reading, tennis; *Clubs* Beefsteak, RAC, Oxford and Cambridge, Athenaeaum; *Style—* The Rt Hon the Lord Patten of Barnes, CH, PC

PATTENDEN, Prof Gerald; s of Albert James Pattenden, and Violet Eugenia, *née* Smith; *b* 4 March 1940; *Educ* Brunel Univ (BSc), Queen Mary Univ of London (PhD, DSc); *m* 3 Aug 1969, Christine Frances, da of Charles Leo Doherty; 3 da (Caroline Sarah b 1971, Rebecca Jane b 1974, Katherine Rachael b 1977); *Career* lectr UC Cardiff 1966; Univ of Nottingham: lectr 1972, reader 1975, prof 1980, Sir Jesse Boot prof of organic chemistry 1988–2005, pro-vice-chllr 1997–2003, research prof 2005–09, emeritus prof 2010–; chem conslt; pres Perkin Div Royal Soc of Chemistry 1995–97; scientific ed J Chem Soc, Perkin Trans I 1995–98; also author of 485 res pubns and editor of over 20 books; memb Cncl Royal Soc; RSC honours incl: Corday-Morgan Medallist 1975, Simonsen Medal 1987, Tilden Medal 1991, Award for Synthetic Organic Chemistry 1992, Award for Heterocyclic Chemistry 1994, Pedler Medal 1995, Award in Natural Product Chemistry 1997, Hugo Müller lectr 2000, Robert Robinson lectr 2007, Merck Award Lecture and Medal 2009; hon fell Queen Mary Coll London; LLD (hons) (Univ of Nottingham, 2015); FRSC, CChem, FRS; over 490 pubs in sci lit and ed of several books; *Recreations* sport, DIY, gardening; *Style—* Prof Gerald Pattenden, FRS; ✉ School of Chemistry, University of Nottingham, Nottingham NG7 2RD (☎ 0115 951 3530, e-mail gp@nottingham.ac.uk)

PATTENDEN, Stephanie Jane; da of John Anthony Pattenden, and Patricia Marguerite Sadlier, *née* Harrison; *Educ* St Anne's Coll Sanderstead, St Aidan's Coll Durham (BSc), KCL (PGCE); *Career* maths teacher Harrow Co Girls' GS (latterly Lowlands Sixth Form Coll) 1973–75, maths teacher and second mistress St Paul's Girls' Sch 1975–85, head Maths Dept and Sixth Form The Lady Eleanor Holles Sch 1985–92, dep head S Hampstead HS 1992–97, headmistress Francis Holland Sch 1997–2012; memb Mathematical Assoc; *Recreations* music, hill walking, bell ringing; *Style—* Miss Stephanie Pattenden; ✉ c/o Francis Holland School, 39 Graham Terrace, London SW1W 8JF (☎ 020 7730 2971, fax 020 7823 4066, e-mail office@fhs-sw1.org.uk)

PATTERSON, Aaron Joseph; s of William Patterson (d 1998), and Elizabeth, *née* Leach (d 1979); *b* 10 June 1969; *m* 10 Oct 1992, Clare Anna, da of William George Parker; 2 s (William Aaron b 8 Nov 1998, George Joseph b 16 Aug 2001); *Career* chef; successively apprentice chef, commis chef, chef de partie, sr chef de partie then pastry chef Hambleton Hall Hotel Leics 1985–90, successively commis chef, demi chef de partie, chef de partie then sr chef de partie Le Manoir Aux Quat' Saisons Oxon 1990–92 (employee of the year 1991); staigiare 1985–90: Le Crocodile Strasbourg, La Tante Claire London, The Belfry London; head chef Hambleton Hall Hotel 1992– (4/5 Good Food Guide 2000 and 2001, 8 out of 10 Good Food Guide 2001); presenter Wild About Food (TV prog); *Books* Wild About Food; *Recreations* reading, sport, travelling; *Style—* Aaron Patterson, Esq; ✉ Hambleton Hall Hotel, Hambleton Village, nr Oakham, Rutland LE15 8TH (☎ 01572 756991, fax 01572 724721)

PATTERSON, (George) Benjamin (Ben); s of Prof Eric James Patterson (d 1972), of Alphington Cross, Devon, and Dr Ethel Patterson, *née* Simkins (d 1993); *b* 21 April 1939; *Educ* Westminster, Trinity Coll Cambridge (MA), LSE; *m* 5 Dec 1970, Felicity Barbara Anne, da of Gordon W Raybould, of Sundridge, Kent; 1 s (Alexander b 6 Dec 1974), 1 da (Olivia b 15 April 1977); *Career* tutor Swinton Coll Masham 1961–65, ed CPC Monthly Report 1965–73, dep head European Parly London Office 1973–79, dir Wiltenbridge Ltd 1980–93; MEP (EDG until 1992, then EPP) Kent West 1979–94, spokesman on economic monetary and industrial policy 1984–89, bureau memb EDG/EPP 1989–94, vice-pres European Parl Econ, Monetary and Industrial Ctee 1992–94, Secretariat European Parliament 1994–2004; hon MEP 1994; dir CJA Consultants Ltd 2005–; cncllr London Borough of Hammersmith 1968–71; MInstD; *Books* The Character of Conservatism (1973), Direct Elections to the European Parliament (1974), Vredeling and All That (1984), VAT: The Zero Rate Issue (1988), European Monetary Union (1991), A European Currency (1994), Options for a Definitive VAT System (1995), The Co-ordination of National Fiscal Policies (1996), The Consequences of Abolishing Duty Free (1997), Adjusting to Asymmetric Shocks (1998), The Feasibility of a 'Tobin Tax' (1999), Exchange Rates and Monetary Policy (2000), Tax Co-ordination in the EU (2002), Background to the Euro (2003), The Euro: Success or Failure (2006), Understanding the EU Budget (2012), The Conservative Party and Europe (2012), An Exercise in Causality (as George Anthony, 2014); *Recreations* walking; *Clubs* Bow Group, IoD; *Style—* Ben Patterson, Esq; ✉ Brambles, Hurst Lane, Sedlescombe, East Sussex TN33 0PE (e-mail gb.patterson@btinternet.com); 38 Le Village, Montségur 09300, Ariège, France (☎ 00 33 5 61 64 01 19); 33 Brunswick House, Fulham Reach, London W6 9LH

P

PATTERSON, Christina Mary; da of John Allan Patterson, and Anne Marie Patterson; *Educ* Guildford Co Sch, Univ of Durham (BA), UEA (MA); *Career* press officer A & C Black Ltd then press officer Faber and Faber 1988–90, programmer and presenter Lit Prog RFH 1990–98; The Poetry Soc: ran Poetry Places Scheme 1998–2000, dir 2000–03; The Independent: dep literary ed 2004–07, assoc ed (comment) 2007, writer and columnist 2008–13, now freelance writer, broadcaster, journalist and campaigner; freelance journalist for pubns incl The Sunday Times and The Guardian (formerly freelance journalist for The Observer, The Independent, Time, The Spectator and New Statesman); regular commentator and press reviewer Sky News, blogger Huffington Post; chair of judges: Geoffrey Faber Memorial Prize 2000, Forward Poetry Prize 2001; *Publications* contrib to The Cambridge Guide to Women's Writing in English (1999), ed The Forward Book of Poetry (2002); *Recreations* following politics, current affairs, reading, cinema, music, travel, theatre, the visual arts; *Style—* Ms Christina Patterson; ✉ e-mail me@christinapatterson.co.uk

PATTERSON, Hon Mrs Justice; Dame Frances Silvia Patterson; DBE (2013), QC (1998); *Educ* Queen's Sch Chester, Univ of Leicester; *m* 1980, Dr Graham Nicholson; 3 c; *Career* called to the Bar Middle Temple 1977 (bencher 2005); memb Kings Chambers (formerly 40 King Street) Manchester 1979–2010 (head 2004–10), recorder 2000– (asst recorder 1997–2000), dep judge of the High Court of Justice 2008, judge of the High Court of Justice (Queen's Bench Div) 2013–; public law cmmr Law Cmmn 2010–13; memb Law Reform Working Party on Planning and Environmental Law, Planning and Environment Bar Assoc, Administrative Law Bar Assoc; *Publications* contrib Journal of Planning Law, Judicial Review: Law and Practice – Second Edition 2015; *Style—* The Hon Mrs Justice Patterson; ✉ Royal Courts of Justice, Strand, London WC2A 2LL

PATTERSON, Gavin; *Educ* Univ of Cambridge; *Career* Procter & Gamble 1992–99, Telewest 2000–04; BT Gp plc: md Consumer Div 2004–08, chief exec BT Retail 2008–13, chief exec 2013–; non-exec dir Br Airways 2011–; pres Advertising Assoc 2011–14; memb Advsy Bd Cambridge Judge Business Sch 2010–13; tstee Br Museum 2012–; *Style—*

Gavin Patterson, Esq; ✉ BT Group plc, BT Centre, 81 Newgate Street, London EC1A 7AJ

PATTERSON, Glenn; s of Phares Patterson, and Agnes Alexandra (Nessie), née Murphy; b 9 August 1961; Educ Methodist Coll Belfast, UEA (BA, MA), Queen's Univ Belfast (DLitt); Partner Ali Fitzgibbon; Career writer; artist in the community Arts Cncl of NI 1989–91, creative writing fell UEA 1992, writer in residence UC Cork 1993–94, writer in residence Queen's Univ Belfast 1994–97, lectr Seamus Heaney Centre for Poetry Queen's Univ Belfast 2005–; memb: Arts Cncl NI 1996–99, Aosdána 2006–; Rooney Prize for Irish Literature 1988, secdy Betty Trask Award 1988, Lannan Literary Fellowship 2008–09; Books Burning Your Own (1988), Fat Lad (1992), Black Night at Big Thunder Mountain (1995), The International (1999), Number 5 (2003), That Which Was (2004), Lapsed Protestant (2006), The Third Party (2007), Open Upon a Hill (2008), The Mill for Grinding Old People Young (2012), The Rest Just Follows (2013), Here's Me Here (2015); Film co-writer Good Vibrations 2013; Style— Glenn Patterson; ✉ c/o Antony Harwood Ltd, 103 Walton Street, Oxford OX2 6EB (☎ 01865 559615)

PATTERSON, Dr Linda Joyce; OBE (2000); da of Thomas William Matthew Patterson (d 1981), of Liverpool, and Mary Frances, née Ollerhead; b 12 April 1951; Educ Liverpool Inst HS for Girls, Middx Hosp Med Sch London (MB BS, MRCP); Partner Christopher Stephen Green; Career pre-registration house offr Stoke-on-Trent and Gloucester 1975–76, SHO/registrar in pathology Charing Cross Hosp 1976–77, SHO in gen med Manchester Royal Infirmary 1978–80, tutor in med Univ of Manchester 1980–82, sr registrar in gen and geriatric med Withington Hosp Manchester and Bolton 1982–84, asst prof of geriatric med Univ of Saskatchewan Canada 1985, conslt physician in geriatric med Burnley Gen Hosp 1986–2008, conslt physician East Lancs PCT 2008–11; clinical dir of med for the elderly Burnley Gen Hosp 1992–95, med dir Burnley Health Care NHS Tst 1995–2000, med dir Cmmn for Health Improvement 2000–04; clinical vice pres RCP 2010–13; non-exec dir Nat Patient Safety Agency 2006–12; King's Fund travelling scholar; memb: Standing Ctee of Membs RCP 1986–89, Geriatric Med Speciality Ctee RCP 1987–90 and 1994–2002, Audit Ctee Br Geriatrics Soc 1990–, NW Region Speciality Trg Ctee in Geriatric Med 1992–, Exec Ctee Manchester Med Soc 1993–, GMC 1994–99; non-exec dir Calderdale and Huddersfield NHS Fndn Tst 2013–; FRCPE 1991, FRCP 1993; Recreations member of Labour Party, Medical Practitioners Union, playing the piano and enjoying opera; Style— Dr Linda Patterson, OBE; ✉ Knott Hall, Charlestown, Hebden Bridge, West Yorkshire HX7 6PE (☎ 01422 845390)

PATTERSON, Dr Mark Jonathan David Damian Lister; s of Alfred Patterson (d 1972), and Frederica Georgina Mary Hammersley, née Lister Nicholson; b 2 March 1934; m 25 Oct 1958, Jane Teresa Mary Scott, da of David Dominic Scott Stokes, of London; 1 s (Damian b 1967), 2 da (Rebecca b 1972, Victoria b 1977); Career NHS, Univ of London and MRC 1959–67, conslt haematologist NHS and sr lectr Univ of London 1967–84; conslt haematologist: Bradford Royal Infirmary 1990–94, Royal Cornwall Hosps 1994–96, Leighton District Gen Hosp 1996–; hon conslt haematologist Manchester Royal Infirmary 1997–; Parly candidate (Cons) Ealing N 1974, memb GLC 1969–73 and 1977–81; memb Worshipful Soc of Apothecaries 1965; MB BS, MRCS, LRCP, MRCP; Recreations historic restoration of ancient buildings, organising musical events; Style— Dr Mark Patterson; ✉ Wolverton Manor, Shorwell, Newport, Isle of Wight PO30 3JS (☎ 01983 740609, fax 01983 740977, e-mail markpatterson@wolvertonmanor.co.uk)

PATTERSON, Neil Michael; s of Robin Shanks Patterson (d 1964), and Nancy Mearns, née Milne (d 1997); b 22 March 1951; Educ Trinity Coll Glenalmond, Watford Art Sch; m 23 July 1983, Doris Karen, da of Ceferino William Boll, of Saguier, Argentina; 1 s (Robin William); Career sr writer: Hall Advertising Edinburgh 1972, Saatchi & Saatchi 1973; exec creative dir: TBWA 1983–85, Young & Rubicam 1985–90; creative ptnr Mitchell Patterson Grime Mitchell (formerly Mitchell Patterson Aldred Mitchell) 1990–2004, freelance writer, dir Little Writing Monkey Ltd 2004–; river columnist: Trout & Salmon, Trout Fisherman, Fly-Fishing & Fly-Tying; Television The Take (Sky Sports); Awards 1 D&AD Gold Pencil, 5 D&AD Silver Pencils, 5 Silver Campaign Press Awards, 2 Silver Campaign Poster Awards, 3 Silver Br Television Advertising Awards, 2 Silver and 4 Bronze Creative Circle Awards, 2 Gold Clios, Angling Writers Assoc Best Angling Writer of the Year 2004, Angling Writers Assoc Best Angling Travel Writer of the Year 2004, nomination Columnist of the Year Scottish Magazine Award 2009; Books Chalkstream Chronicle, Distant Waters, The Complete Fly Fisher, The Art of the Trout Fly, The One That Got Away; Recreations fly fishing, guitar, cooking; Clubs Flyfishers, D & AD; Style— Neil Patterson, Esq; ✉ 18 Colet Gardens, London W14 9DH (☎ 020 8563 7110); Wilderness Lodge, Elcot, Newbury, Berkshire RG20 8NH

PATTERSON, Noel Anthony; s of Arthur Patterson (d 1975), and Doreen Violet, née Smith; b 29 December 1952; Educ Penarth GS, Univ of Wales Coll of Cardiff (BScEcon), LSE (MSc), Queens' Coll Cambridge (MPhil, coach Univ Amateur Boxing Club); m Janet Susan, da of Leonard George Frederick Boyle (d 2005); 3 s (Frederick James b 12 June 1990, Arthur Henri b 4 July 1994, Edmund Louis b 20 July 1997); Career furniture remover Lyon France 1974–75, exec offr PO Telecommunications London 1977–78, industrial rels offr Alcan Aluminium (UK) Ltd Rogerstone Gwent 1978–80; Mobil Oil Co Ltd: employee rels advsr London 1980–85, terminals mangr Midlands and West 1985–86, gen mangr Gatwick Refuelling Servs Gatwick 1986–87, industrial rels mangr Coryton Refinery 1987–88; employee rels mangr Watney Truman Ltd London 1988–89, human resources mangr Grand Metropolitan Brewing Ltd London 1989–91, employee rels mangr Courage Ltd London 1991–92, dir Patterson James Management Consulting 1993–95, assoc Harold Whitehead & Partners Ltd 1994–95; Matthew Clark plc: dir of personnel 1995–99, sales dir 1999–2000, regnl md 2000–01; HR dir Red Bull UK Ltd 2001–07, head of HR Tradex Insurance Co Ltd 2007–08, head of industrial rels and diversity Metronetrail Ltd 2008–09, dir Patterson James Mgmnt Consulting 2009–13, head of HR and IR Kier Gp plc 2013–; assoc PTP Assocs 2011–13; memb Nat Examining Bd for Supervision and Mgmnt (steering ctee) 1994–98, lectr in mgmnt Richmond upon Thames Coll 1994; memb UK Warehousing Assoc (steering ctee) 1999; regular contrib to: Modern Management, Professional Manager, Progress and numerous other mgmnt jls; assoc Inst of Occupational Safety and Health (AIOSH) 2004, MCIM (dip) 1993, FInstD 1990, FCIPD 1990, FCMI 1990, FRSA 2004; Recreations reading, writing, sports and fatherhood; Clubs Oxford and Cambridge, Richmond Golf, Glamorganshire Golf, London Welsh RFC, Glamorgan CCC; Style— Noel Patterson, Esq; ✉ 16 St Pauls Road, Richmond, Surrey TW9 2HH (☎ 020 8948 2045, e-mail n.patterson@blueyonder.co.uk)

PATTERSON, Prof Paul Leslie; s of Leslie Patterson, of Exeter, and Lilian Anne, née Braund; b 15 June 1947; Educ RAM; m 12 Dec 1981, Hazel Rosemary, da of Dr Alexander Wilson, of Winchester; 1 da (Philippa b 1983), 1 s (Alastair b 1986); Career composer; dir twentieth century music Univ of Warwick 1976–81; Royal Acad of Music: prof of composition 1972–, head of composition 1985–97, Manson prof of composition 1997–2015; artistic dir: Exeter Festival 1991–97, PLG Young Composers' Forum 1998–; external examiner: London Coll of Music 1998–2002, RM Sch of Music 1998–2002, Royal Northern Coll of Music 2002–, Colchester Inst 2002–05; music advsr N Devon Festival 1999–2000; visiting prof of composition Christchurch Univ Canterbury 2000–; composer of large-scale choral music incl: Mass of the Sea, Stabat Mater, Te Deum, Requiem, Voices of Sleep, Little Red Riding Hood, Three Little Pigs, Orchestra on Parade, Magnificat Violin Concerto, Millennium Mass, Cello Concerto; other compositions incl: orchestral music, symphony, concertos, chamber music, organ music, film and TV music; performances world-wide by leading musicians; featured composer at festivals incl: Llandaff 1985,

Greenwich 1985, PLG 1987, Cheltenham 1988, Three Choirs 1988, Patterson South Bank 1988, Peterborough 1989, Southwark 1989–91, Cheltenham 1990, Exeter 1991, World Harp Congress Hong Kong 2017; BBC Radio 3 Composer of the Week June 1997; composer in residence: Eng Sinfonia Nottingham 1969–70, SE Arts Canterbury 1981–83, Truro Festival 1992–94, Nat Youth Orch 1997–2010, Presteigne Festival 2001; cmmns incl: BBC, RPO, LPO, Polish Chamber Orch, Kings Singers, Eng Chamber Orch, London Sinfonietta, Bach Choir, Acad of Saint Martins in the Field, Birmingham Symphony Orch, Nash Ensemble, LMP, OSJ, Residente Orch Holland/Zurich Chamber Orch, Basle Symphony Orch; recordings for: EMI, Hyperion, ASV, Priory, Pearl, Phillips; memb: Arts Cncl Recordings Ctee, BBC Reading Panel, RPS Award Panel; pres RAM Club 1992–94, pres and patron numerous choral socs and choirs; Leslie Boosey Award PRS/RPS 1996; memb BASCA Ctee 2009; FRAM 1982 (ARAM 1978), FRSA 1989, Hon FLCM 1998, FRNCM 2007; Medal of Honour Miny of Culture Poland 1987, Gold Medal Poland 2009; Publications Fantasia for Harp and Orchestra (2014), Volcano for Organ (2015), Hastings Toccata for Piano (2016); Recreations sailing, swimming, supporting Arsenal FC, computers; Clubs Brixham Yacht; Style— Prof Paul Patterson; ✉ 31 Cromwell Avenue, Highgate, London N6 5HN (☎ 020 8348 3711, mobile 07792 809825, e-mail musicpp@ hotmail.com)

PATTERSON, Simon; Educ King's Coll Cambridge (MA), Stanford Univ Grad Sch of Business (MBA); Career formerly: md BMC, sr vice-pres Asia Pacific and product devpt dir GF-X; currently md Silver Lake (joined 2005), tstee Nat History Museum 2015–; Style— Simon Patterson, Esq; ✉ Silver Lake Europe LLP, Broadbent House, 65 Grosvenor Street, London W1K 3JH

PATTISON, Prof George Linsley; s of George William Pattison (d 1981), and Jean, née Allan; b 25 May 1950; Educ Perse Sch Cambridge, Univ of Edinburgh (MA, BD), Univ of Durham (PhD, DD); m 25 Feb 1971, Hilary Christine, da of Robert Gilchrist Cochrane; 2 da (Charlotte Ann b 14 April 1972, Elisabeth Linsley b 20 Feb 1980), 1 s (Neil John Robert b 15 Aug 1976); Career ordained: deacon 1977, priest 1978; curate St James Newcastle upon Tyne 1977–80, priest-in-charge St Philip and St James Kimblesworth Co Durham 1980–83, rector Badwell Ash Great Ashfield Hunston and Stowlangtoft with Langham 1983–91, dean of chapel King's Coll Cambridge 1991–2001; assoc prof Univ of Århus 2002–03, Lady Margaret prof Univ of Oxford 2004–13, canon Christ Church Cathedral Oxford 2004–13, 1640 prof Univ of Glasgow 2013–; ed Modern Believing 1994–98; visiting research prof Univ of Copenhagen 1997 and 2000, visiting prof Univ of Århus 2005–12, visiting prof Univ of Copenhagen 2012–; memb Advsy Bd Søren Kierkegaard Research Centre Copenhagen 2000–; vice-pres Modern Church People's Union 1998–2008; Montgomery fell Dartmouth Coll 2013; Books Art, Modernity and Faith (1991, 2 edn 1997), Kierkegaard: The Aesthetic and the Religious (1992, 2 edn 1999), Kierkegaard on Art and Communication (ed, 1993), Pains of Glass (with Wendy Beckett, 1995), Spirit and Tradition (with Stephen Platten, 1996), Agnosis: Theology in the Void (1996), Kierkegaard and the Crisis of Faith (1997), The End of Theology and the Task of Thinking about God (1998), 'Poor Paris!' Kirkegaard's Critique of the Spectacular City (1998), Kierkegaard: The Self in Society (ed with S Shakespeare, 1998), Anxious Angels (1999), the Later Heidegger (2000), A Short Course in the Philosophy of Religion (2001), Dostoevsky and the Christian Tradition (ed with D Thompson, 2001), Kierkegaard: Religion and the Nineteenth Century Crisis of Culture (2002), Kierkegaard's Upbuilding Discourses (2002), A Short Course in Christian Doctrine (2005), The Philosophy of Kierkegaard (2005), Thinking about God in an Age of Technology (2005), God and Being (2011), Kierkegaard's Pastoral Dialogues (with Hell Møller Jensen, 2012), Kierkegaard and the Theology of the Nineteenth Century (2012), Kierkegaard and the Quest for Unambiguous Life (2013), The Oxford Handbook of Kierkegaard (ed with John Lippitt, 2013), The Oxford Handbook of Theology and Modern European Thought (ed with Nicholas Adams and Graham Ward, 2013), Heidegger on Death (2013), The Heart Could Never Speak (2013), Eternal God/Saving Time (2015), Paul Tillich's Philosophical Theology (2015); Recreations walking, art, theatre, cities; Style— Prof George Pattison

PATTISON, Lindsay; da of Desmond James (d 2010), and Christine, née Houlton, of Oxfordshire; b 17 April 1973, Chipping Norton; Educ Univ of Stirling (BA); m 28 April 2011, David; Career media mangr Team Y&R 1998–2001, brand mangr Sony Ericsson 1998–2001, managing ptnr PHD 2003–09, UK ceo and global chief strategy offr Maxus 2009–14, ceo Maxus Global 2014–; pres WACL 2014–15, vice-chair World Economic Forum Global Agenda Cncl Future of Media, chair Media 360 Conference 2014, Cannes Lions judge 2015; 100 Women to Watch Cranfield FTSE Bd 2014, 2015 and 2016, Women to Watch Ad Age 2015, Debrett's 500 2015; Publications articles and blog posts in pubns and for orgns incl: Huffington Post, Ad Age, Guardian, Ad News Aus, Campaign & Campaign Live, Media Week, Daily Telegraph, The Drum, WEF Agenda, Campaign US, Marketing Acad; Recreations modern art, fashion, travel, sport, food!; Style— Mrs Lindsay Pattison; ✉ Maxus UK, 11–33 St John Street, London EC1M 4AA (☎ 020 7025 3934, e-mail lindsay.pattison@maxusglobal.com, website www.maxusglobal.com, Twitter @lindsaymaxus)

PATTISON, Vivienne Louise; b 30 April 1969; Educ Univ of Wales (BA); m 1994, Rev Paul White; 1 da, 1 s; Career publicity asst Hodder & Stoughton 1992–94, press offr Health Educn Authy 1994–95, press offr Penguin Books 1995–97, account dir Midas PR 1998–2009, dir Mediawatch UK 2009–; Recreations reading, the arts, my children; Style— Miss Vivienne Pattison; ✉ Mediawatch UK, 3 Willow House, Kennington Road, Ashford, Kent TN24 0NR (☎ 01233 633936, fax 01233 633836, e-mail vivienne@mediawatchuk.org)

PATTMAN, Dr Richard Stewart; MBE; s of Robert Pearson Pattman, VRD (d 1998), and Joyce Mary, née Long (d 1989); b 19 April 1950; Educ Glasgow Acad, Sedbergh, Univ of Glasgow (MB ChB); m 27 April 1976, (Mary) Geraldine, da of John Purcell (d 1983), of Glasgow; 1 s (Stewart John b 1979); Career house offr and registrar in gen med Western Infirmary Gartnavel Glasgow 1976, sr registrar in genito-urinary med Royal Infirmary Glasgow 1976–79, conslt in genito-urinary med and clinical lectr to Univ of Newcastle upon Tyne 1979–2010, ret; ed Oxford Handbook of GUM, HIV and AIDS; FRCPG 1986, FRCP 1991 (MRCP 1976), FFFP 2007 (MFFP 1995); Recreations gardening, fishing; Style— Dr Richard S Pattman, MBE

PATTON, Prof Michael Alexander; s of Henry Alexander Patton, of Donaghadee, and Margaret Murray, née Drennan; b 15 April 1950; Educ Campbell Coll Belfast, Pembroke Coll Cambridge (MA), Univ of Edinburgh (MB ChB, MSc); m 4 June 1977, Jaqueline Heidi, da of John Pickin, OBE, of Wyck Rissington, Glos; 1 s (Alistair b 10 April 1979), 1 da (Rebecca b 21 Sept 1983); Career dir Regnl Genetics Serv SW Thames RHA; St George's Hosp Med Sch: conslt 1986–2013, sr lectr 1986–92, reader 1992–98, prof 1998–; med advsr to various parent gps for inherited disease, med dir Scientific Ctee Birth Defects Fndn (New Life); examiner: Univ of London, RCPath, Univ of Sheffield, Univ of Manchester, Univ of Wales; inspr Human Fertilisation and Embryology Authy 1991–96; chm Ethics Ctee RCPCH 2001–04 (memb 1996–2004), pres Medical Genetics Section RSM 2004–06; med dir TDL Pathology, conslt clinical geneticist Portland Hosp London, med dir HSL Pathology 2015–; dean of enterprise and innovation St Georges Univ 2009–12; memb Editorial Bd: Irish Medical Jl, Chinese Jl Gen Practice; memb: Exec Ctee London Genetic Knowledge Park 2002–07, Advsy Bd IKON Warwick Business Sch, Ctee Genetic Interest Gp, Ctee Clinical Genetic Soc; fndr memb Expert Witnesses Inst; hon visiting fell Green Coll Oxford, visiting prof Univ of Exeter, hon prof UCL; MInstD, FRCP 1993 (MRCP 1979), FRCPCH 1997; Books Contact a Family Directory (1992 and subsequent edns); numerous scientific and medical peer-reviewed pubns; *Recreations* skiing, sailing, watercolour painting; *Style—* Prof Michael Patton; ✉ 126 Woodlands Road, Little Bookham, Surrey KT23 4HJ (☎ 01372 456327, fax 01372 453151); St George's University of London, Cranmer Terrace, London SW17 0RE (e-mail mpatton@sgul.ac.uk); website www.geneticconsultant.co.uk

PAUL, Dr (Peter) Michael; s of Thomas James Paul, of Woore, Salop, and Nora, *née* Wilcox; *b* 26 September 1947; *Educ* Queen Elizabeth GS Wakefield, St Andrews Univ (BSc), Univ of Manchester (MB ChB); *m* 22 June 1974, Susan Margaret, da of Frank Pickles; *Career* house offr Wythenshaw Hosp Manchester 1973–74, SHO Casualty Dept Westminster Hosp London 1974, vocational trg scheme Aylesbury 1974–77, ptnr in practice White Bungalow Surgery Sunninghill 1977–86, private GP and med dir Gen Med Clinics plc London 1986–2003, private GP and sr ptnr MSA & Co 2003–; med offr Ascot Priory Convent 1977–86, memb Ctee and hon treas Thames Valley Faculty RCGP 1980–86, fndr and hon sec Independent Doctors Forum 1989–96, gen practice trainer, pt/t lectr Red Cross; memb Ctee Ascot Volunteer Bureau 1981–86; DObstRCOG, FPA Cert, MRCGP, memb BMA, FRSM; *Recreations* theatre, reading, walking; *Clubs* RAC, ROSL; *Style—* Dr Michael Paul; ✉ Wood End House, High Lane, Barnoldswick BB18 5SN; OurNHS LLP, Wood End House, High Lane, Barnoldswick BB18 5SN (☎ 0845 644 6672, e-mail michael.paul@ournhs.co.uk)

PAUL, Nancy Catherine Trask; da of Frank Stone Trask (d 1983), of Deer Lodge, Montana, USA, and Cora Nichols (d 1964); *b* 1 June 1936; *Educ* Powell County HS, DL Montana, Univ of Montana USA (BA, MA); *m* 1, 17 Sept 1960 (m dis 1982), William J Paul, Jr; 2 s (William James Paul, III b 19 Nov 1962, Michael Justin Paul b 18 June 1971), 1 da (Elisa Anne Paul b 7 Sept 1969); m 2, 11 April 1992, David A Tyrell; *Career* lectr in psychology Univ of Montana 1958–60, assoc mgmnt prof Brunel Univ 1979–; dir: Paul Mgmnt Ltd 1979–89, Excel International Ltd 1989–; author of pubns on: the effects of divorce on men and women, orgns and work in the UK and USA; maker of numerous award winning videos; fndr memb Inst of Transactional Analysis, hon memb Int Inst of Transactional Analysis Assoc; memb: American Acad of Mgmnt, Int OD Network; *Books* The Right to Be You (1985), The Principles of Project Management (1991), Meetings, Your Guide to Making Them Work (1991); *Recreations* mountaineering, classical music; *Style—* Mrs Nancy Paul; ✉ Excel International, 2810 Contour Road, Missoula, Montana 59802, USA (☎ and fax 00 1 406 549 4021)

PAUL, Richard; *Educ* Bartlett Sch of Architecture and Planning (BSc, Dipl Arch); *Career* architect; Foster Associates: joined 1982, project dir 1985, main bd of dir 1988; Richard Rogers Partnership: joined 1991, assoc dir 1996; *Projects* incl: Hongkong and Shanghai Bank HQ, Century Tower, Stokley Park B3 bldg, King's Cross Masterplan, King's Cross rail terminal, ITN HQ, St Sebastian Convention and Congress Hall Spain, Hanseem Housing S Korea, Potsdamer Platz Masterplan Berlin Germany, Spandau Masterplan Berlin Germany, Treptow Germany, B4/B6 offices Berlin Germany, Saitama Arena, Seol Broadcasting System HQ South Korea, Nippon TV HQ Tokyo Japan, Baby Dome Greenwich, Rome Congress Hall Italy, Chiswick Park Masterplan London; *Style—* Richard Paul, Esq; ✉ Richard Rogers Partnership, Thames Wharf, Rainville Road, London W6 9HA

PAUL, Baron (Life Peer UK 1996), of Marylebone in the City of Westminster; Rt Hon Swraj Paul; PC (2009); s of Payare Paul (d 1944), of Jalandhar, India, and Mongwati, *née* Lal; *b* 18 February 1931; *Educ* Univ of Punjab (BSc), MIT (BSc, MSc); *m* 1 Dec 1956, Aruna, da of Ramnath Vij, of Calcutta; 3 s (Hon Ambar, Hon Akash (twins) b 20 Dec 1957, Hon Angad b 6 June 1970 d 2015), 2 da (Hon Anjli b 12 Nov 1959, Ambika b 1963 d 1968); *Career* dir family owned Apeejay-Surrendra Gp India 1952–66, came to England 1966, estab Natural Gas Tubes Ltd 1968; chm: Caparo Group Ltd 1978–, Caparo Industries plc 1980–2015, Caparo Inc USA 1988–2008; pro-chllr Thames Valley Univ 1998–2000, chllr Univ of Wolverhampton 1999–, chllr Univ of Westminster 2006–14; memb Bd London Devpt Agency 2000–07; Hon PhD American Coll of Switzerland 1986, Hon DSc Univ of Hull 1992, Hon DHL Chapman Univ California 1996, Hon Dr Univ of Bradford 1997, Hon DLit Univ of Westminster 1997, Hon DrUniv of Central England 1999, Hon DSc Univ of Birmingham 1999, Hon PhD Thames Valley Univ 2000, Hon DCS Univ of Hartford USA 2002, Hon Dr State Univ of Mgmnt Moscow 2002, Hon Dr Punjab Tech Univ Jalandhar 2005, Hon PhD Ambedkar Nat Inst of Technol India 2006; Order of Padma Bhushan India 1983; *Books* Indira Gandhi (1985), Beyond Boundaries (1998); *Clubs* MCC; India: Royal Calcutta Turf, Royal Calcutta Golf, Cricket of India (Bombay); *Style—* The Rt Hon Lord Paul; ✉ Caparo Group Ltd, Caparo House, 103 Baker Street, London W1U 6LN (☎ 020 7486 1417)

PAULSON, Prof Lawrence C; s of Michael S Paulson, and Mae K Paulson; *b* 20 September 1955, Philadelphia, PA; *Educ* Caltech (BS, Motorola Project Award), Stanford Univ (PhD); *m* Elena Tchougounova-Paulson; 2 c; *Career* research asst Univ of Edinburgh 1982–83; Univ of Cambridge: asst dir of research 1983–93, lectr 1993–, reader in computational logic 1998–2002, prof of computational logic 2002–; fell Clare Coll Cambridge 1987– (memb Computer Ctee, dir of studies in computer science); delivered numerous lectures worldwide; *Publications* Logic and Computation: Interactive proof with Cambridge LCF (1987), ML for the Working Programmer (1991, 2 edn 1996), Isabelle: A Generic Theorem Prover (1994), Isabelle/HOL: A Proof Assistant for Higher-Order Logic (with Tobias Nipkow and Markus Wenzel, 2002); also numerous refereed articles in learned jls and conf proceedings; *Recreations* gardening, cycling, ballroom dancing; *Style—* Prof Lawrence C Paulson; ✉ University of Cambridge Computer Laboratory, William Gates Building, Cambridge CB3 0FD (☎ 01223 334623, fax 01223 334678, e-mail lp15@cam.ac.uk)

PAULSON-ELLIS, Jeremy David; s of Christian William Geoffrey Paulson-Ellis (d 1982), and Vivien Joan Paulson-Ellis (d 1966); *b* 21 September 1943; *Educ* Sherborne; *m* 27 April 1973, Jennifer Jill, da of Angus Harkness (d 1991); 1 da (Vivien b 1974), 2 s (Nicholas b 1976, Matthew b 1984); *Career* Citicorp Scrimgeour Vickers International Ltd (formerly Vickers da Costa & Co): joined 1964, ptnr 1970, dir 1974, chm 1985–88; chm: Genesis Investment Management LLP 1989–2009, JP Morgan Japan Investment Tst plc 1996–2014, Mekong Enterprise Fund II Ltd; dir: MCB Capital Markets Ltd, Genesis Emerging Markets Fund Ltd 1989–2009, Genesis Chile Fund Ltd 1989–2005, Genesis Malaysia Maju Fund Ltd 1990–2006, Korea Asia Fund Ltd 1991–96, Genesis Condor Fund Ltd 1991–2008, Second India Investment Fund Ltd 1992–2000, Vietnam Fund Ltd 1996–2004, Redgate Asset Management; memb Investment Advsy Cncl: Korea International Trust 1982–87, Seoul International Trust (chm) 1985–87, Thailand Fund 1986–88; ind memb Heathrow Airport Consultative Ctee 1984–88; MSI 1970; AMSIA; *Recreations* tennis, travel; *Style—* Jeremy Paulson-Ellis, Esq; ✉ WFS Investments Ltd, A4, Speldhurst Business Park, Langton Road, Speldhurst, Kent TN3 0AQ (☎ 020 7201 7200, e-mail jeremypaulsonellis@wfsil.co.uk)

PAVORD, Anna; da of Arthur Vincent Pavord (d 1989), of Abergavenny, Monmouthshire, and Christabel Frances, *née* Lewis (d 1978); *b* 20 September 1940; *Educ* Abergavenny HS for Girls, Univ of Leicester (BA); *m* Trevor David Oliver Ware, s of John Ronald Ware; 3 da (Oenone b 15 Dec 1967, Vanessa b 7 June 1970, Tilly b 8 Dec 1974); *Career* copywriter Lintas Advertising Agency 1962–63, Line-Up BBC TV 1963–70 (prodn asst rising to dir), contrib Observer 1970–92, gardening corr The Independent 1986–2016, assoc ed Gardens Illustrated 1993–2008; writer and presenter Flowering Passions (10-part series, Channel 4); Gold Veitch Meml Medal RHS 1991; memb: Gardens Panel Nat Tst 1996–2006 (chm 2002–06), English Heritage Parks and Gardens Panel 2001–10; Hon DLitt Univ of Leicester 2005; *Books* Foliage (1990), The Flowering Year (1991), Gardening Companion (1992), The Border Book (1994), The New Kitchen Garden (1996), The Tulip (1999), Plant Partners (2001), The Naming of Names (2005), Bulb (2009), The Curious Gardener (2010), Landskipping (2016); *Recreations* gardening, sailing, walking in Sikkim, collecting string, black and white films; *Style—* Ms Anna Pavord; ✉ Caradoc King, United Agents, 12–26 Lexington Street, London W1F 0LE

PAWLAK, His Hon Judge Witold Expedyt; s of Felicjan Pawlak, and Jolanta Pawlak; *b* March 1947; *Educ* St Joseph's Coll Beulah Hill, Trinity Coll Cambridge (MA); *m* 1971, Susan, *née* Dimsdale; 1 da (Lucy b 28 Feb 1980), 1 s (Nicholas b 1 Jan 1984); *Career* called to the Bar Inner Temple 1970; circuit judge 2004–; *Style—* His Hon Judge Pawlak; ✉ Wood Green Crown Court, Woodall House, Lordship Lane, Wood Green, London N22 5LF (☎ 020 8826 4100)

PAWLOWSKI, Prof Mark; s of Kazimierz Pawlowski, of London, and Maria Zwienislawa, *née* Konkol; *b* 15 September 1953; *Educ* St Benedict's Sch Ealing, Univ of Warwick (LLB), Wadham Coll Oxford (BCL); *m* 19 April 1986 (m dis 2006), Lidia Maria, da of Capt Jerzy de Barbaro (of the Barbaro family, Venice); m 2, 9 Dec 2006, Chrisoulla Atkinson, da of Charalambos Georghiou, of Cyprus; 2 step-da (Evangeline Atkinson, Sophia Atkinson); *Career* called to the Bar Middle Temple 1978; in practice at Chancery Bar 1980–91; Univ of Greenwich (formerly Thames Poly): pt/t lectr 1980–83, lectr 1983–84, sr lectr 1984–95, reader in property law 1995–99, prof of property law 1999–; visiting prof UCL 1990–, memb convocation Wadham Coll Oxford 1983; ed: Jl of Rent Review and Lease Renewal, Landlord and Tenant Review; author of numerous articles in learned jls on property, equity and trusts, landlord and tenant law 1984–; Sweet & Maxwell Law prizewinner 1974; sr fell HE Acad 2013; memb: Middle Temple, Soc of Legal Scholars, Assoc of Law Teachers; ACIArb 1990; *Books* Casebook on Rent Review and Lease Renewal (with Diana Brahams, 1986), The Forfeiture of Leases (1993), Casebook on Landlord and Tenant Law (with James Brown, 1995), Law Q & A, Landlord and Tenant (with James Brown, 1995, 3 edn, 2005), The Doctrine of Proprietary Estoppel (1996), Leasing Commercial Premises (1999), Undue Influence and the Family Home (with James Brown, 2002), Kenilworth – Portrait of a Town & Castle (with John H Drew, 2003); *Recreations* tennis, gardening, foreign travel, film; *Style—* Prof Mark Pawlowski; ✉ School of Law, University of Greenwich, Queen Mary Court, Greenwich Maritime Campus, 30 Park Row, London SE10 9LS (☎ 020 8331 9463, fax 020 8331 8473, e-mail m.pawlowski@gre.ac.uk)

PAWSEY, John; s of Albert Pawsey, and Doris Pawsey; *b* 11 December 1940, London; *Educ* Brentwood Sch (head of house, capt of cricket, Essex Co youth cricketer); *Children* 2 da (Helen b 4 Sept 1975, Hannah b 1 Aug 1977); *Career* managing ed Leslie Frewin Publishers 1965–69, assoc ed Reader's Digest 1969–71, dir Elm Tree Books Hamish Hamilton 1971–73, dir Mitchell Beazley Marketing Ltd 1973–76, prop John Pawsey Literary Agency 1981–; *Recreations* reading, writing, watching cricket; *Style—* John Pawsey, Esq; ✉ e-mail john.pawsey@virgin.net

PAWSEY, Mark Julian Francis; MP; s of James Pawsey; *Educ* Lawrence Sheriff Sch Rugby, Univ of Reading (BSc); *Career* fndr and md Central Catering Supplies Ltd 1982–2008; MP (Cons) Rugby 2010–; *Style—* Mark Pawsey, Esq, MP; ✉ House of Commons, London SW1A 0AA (☎ 020 7219 7136, e-mail mark.pawsey.mp@parliament.uk)

PAWSON, Anthony John Dalby; s of Donald Pawson, and Kathleen, *née* Goodwin; *b* 14 October 1946; *Educ* Kent Coll Canterbury, City Univ (BSc); *m* 1969, Kathleen, *née* Chisholm (d 2004); 1 s, 1 da; *Career* MOD: joined 1967, private sec to Chief of Air Staff 1978–80, first sec UK Delgn to NATO 1981–83, private sec to Sec of State for NI 1990–92, RCDS 1992, asst under sec of state (fleet support) 1993–95; under sec (overseas and defence) Cabinet Office 1995–97, DG mktg MOD 1997–98, DG defence export services MOD 1998–2003, DG of corporate communication 2003–04, dep chief of def intelligence 2004–07, DG security review MOD 2008–; *Recreations* cricket, rugby; *Clubs* Tunbridge Wells Rugby, Borderers' Cricket; *Style—* Anthony Pawson, Esq

PAWSON, John; s of Jim Pawson (d 1990) and Winifred, *née* Ward (d 1991); *b* 6 May 1949; *Educ* Eton, AA Sch of Architecture; *m* 20 Sept 1989, Catherine, da of Frederick Berning; 2 s (Caius b 1986, Benedict b 1990), 1 step-da (Phoebe Greenwood b 1978); *Career* architectural designer, estab office 1981; projects incl: Calvin Klein flagship store, Cathay Pacific lounges Hong Kong, Novy Dvur Monastery Czech Repub, Sackler Crossing, Royal Botanic Gardens Kew, Chroma set design ROH, Martyrs Pavilion St Edward's Sch Oxford, Casa delle Bottere Treviso Italy, Moritzkirche interior renovation Augsburg Germany, new Design Museum London; *Publications* subject of: John Pawson (1992, updated 1998), Critic vol 3 (1996), John Pawson Works (2000), Themes and Projects (2002), El Croquis 127 (2005), Leçons du Thoronet (2006), Plain Space (2010), El Croquis 158 (2011), Katalog (2012); author of: Minimum (1996, mini edn 1998), Living and Eating (with Annie Bell, 2001), A Visual Inventory (2012); *Style—* John Pawson, Esq; ✉ Unit B, 70–78 York Way, London N1 9AG (☎ 020 7837 2929, fax 020 7837 4949, e-mail email@johnpawson.com)

PAXMAN, HE (Timothy) Giles; CMG (2013), LVO (1989); s of Arthur Keith Paxman, and Joan McKay, *née* Dickson; bro of Jeremy Paxman, *qv*; *b* 15 November 1951; *Educ* Malvern Coll Oxford, New Coll Oxford; *m* 1980, Segolene Claude Marie; 3 da; *Career* diplomat; with DOE 1974–78, Ecole Nationale d'Administration Paris 1978–79, with Dept of Tport 1979–80, first sec UKREP Brussels 1980–84, EC Dept (External) FCO 1980–84, Southern European Dept FCO 1986–88, head of Chancery Singapore 1988–91, dep head Assessments Staff Cabinet Office 1991–93, cnsllr (economic and commercial affrs) Rome 1994–98, cnsllr (political and institutional affrs) UKREP Brussels 1999–2002, min and dep head of mission Paris 2002–05, ambass to Mexico 2005–09, ambass to Spain 2009–13; *Recreations* sailing, golf, travel; *Style—* Mr Giles Paxman, CMG, LVO; ✉ e-mail gilespaxman@gmail.com; c/o Foreign & Commonwealth Office, King Charles Street, London SW1A 2AH

PAXMAN, Jeremy Dickson; s of Arthur Keith Paxman, formerly of Yorks, and Joan McKay, *née* Dickson, of Yorks; bro of Giles Paxman, LVO, *qv*; *b* 11 May 1950; *Educ* Malvern Coll, St Catharine's Coll Cambridge (exhibitioner); *Career* journalist Northern Ireland 1974–77, BBC Tonight 1977–79, Panorama (BBC1) 1979–84; presenter: Six O'Clock News (BBC1) 1985–86, Breakfast Time (BBC1) 1986–89, Newsnight (BBC2) 1989–2014, Did You See? (BBC2) 1991–93, University Challenge (BBC2) 1994–, You Decide – with Paxman (BBC1) 1995–96, Start the Week (Radio 4) 1998–2002; numerous contribs to radio, newspapers and magazines; RTS Int Current Affairs Award 1984, Richard Dimbleby Award BAFTA 1996 and 2000, RTS Interviewer of the Year 1997, 1998 and 2008, Variety Club Media Personality of the Year 1999, RTS Journalism Presenter of the Year 2002; Hon PhD: Univ of Leeds 1999, Univ of Bradford 1999, Open Univ; hon fell: St Catharine's Coll Cambridge, St Edmund Hall Oxford; *Books* A Higher Form of Killing (jtly, 1982), Through the Volcanoes (1985), Friends in High Places (1990), Fish, Fishing and the Meaning of Life (1994), The English: A Portrait of a People (1998), The Political Animal: An Anatomy (2002), On Royalty (2006), The Victorious: Britain Through the Paintings of the Age; *Recreations* fly fishing, mountains; *Style—* Jeremy Paxman, Esq; ✉ c/o Capel & Land Ltd, 29 Wardour Street, London W1D 6PS

PAY, Antony Charles; s of Arthur Morris Pay, of London, and Charlotte Pay; *b* 21 February 1945; *Educ* Leyton Co HS, Corpus Christi Coll Cambridge (MA), LRAM 1962; *m* 14 April 1980, Suki, da of Louis Towb, of Newcastle; 2 s (Sam b 24 April 1981, Mungo b 20 Aug 1984); *Career* principal clarinet and fndr memb London Sinfonietta 1968–83; principal clarinet: Royal Philharmonic Orch 1968–78, Acad of St Martin-in-the-Fields 1979–84; prof of Clarinet Guildhall Sch of Music and Drama 1982–90; memb: Nash Ensemble 1968–83, Tuckwell Wind Quintet 1973–77; soloist with many orchestras incl: RPO, LPO, Philharmonia, Berlin Radio Orch, San Francisco Symphony, RAI Torino, Acad of St Martin-in-the-Fields, London Sinfonietta; conducted: London Sinfonietta, Acad of St Martin-in-the-Fields, Philharmonia, Royal Philharmonic, San Diego Symphony, Stockholm Philharmonic, music teacher at: Accademia Perosi Biella Italy, Accademia Chigiana Siena Italy; numerous recordings of clarinet concerti and various chamber music discs; Hon RAM 1986; *Recreations* reading, computers; *Style*— Antony Pay, Esq; ✉ c/o Rayfield Allied, Southbank House, Black Prince Road, London SE1 7SJ

PAYKEL, Prof Eugene Stern; s of Joshua Paykel (d 1962), and Eva Paykel (d 1991); *b* 9 September 1934; *Educ* Auckland GS NZ, Univ of Otago (MB ChB, MD), Univ of Cambridge (MD), Univ of London (DPM); *m* 7 July 1969, Margaret, da of John Melrose (d 1966); 2 s (Nicholas b 1971, Jonathan b 1973); *Career* registrar then sr registrar Maudsley Hosp London 1962–65, asst prof of psychiatry and co-dir (later dir) Depression Res Unit Yale Univ 1966–71, prof of psychiatry St George's Hosp Med Sch Univ of London 1977–85 (conslt and sr lectr 1971–75, reader 1975–77), prof of psychiatry Univ of Cambridge and fell Gonville & Caius Coll 1985–2001 (emeritus prof and emeritus fell 2001–); ed Psychological Med 1994–2006; pres Collegium Internationale Neuropsychopharmacologicum 2000–02; pres: Br Assoc for Psychopharmacology 1982–84 (hon sec 1979–82), Marcé Soc 1992–94; chief scientist advsr Mental Illness Res Liaison Gp DHSS 1984–88, memb Neuro Sciences Bd MRC 1981–85 and 1995–99, tstee Mental Health Fndn 1988–95, chm Jt Ctee on Higher Psychiatric Trg 1991–95 (hon sec 1988–90), chm Pharmacopsychiatry Section and regnl rep World Psychiatric Assoc 1992–99; ed Jl of Affective Disorders 1979–93; formerly examiner: Univ of Edinburgh, Univ of Nottingham, Univ of Manchester, Univ of London, Chinese Univ of Hong Kong; vice-pres RCPsych 1994–96 (examiner, chm Social and Community Psychiatry Section 1984–88, memb Cncl, memb Exec and Fin Ctee and various other ctees); Foundations Fund Prize for Res in Psychiatry 1978, second prize Anna Monika Stiftung 1985, ECNP-Lilly Clinical Neuroscience Award 2001; Maudsley lectr RCPsych 1988; FRCP 1977 (MRCP 1961), FRCPEd 1978 (MRCPEd 1960), fndr FMedSci 1998, Hon FRCPsych 2001 (MRCPsych 1971, FRCPsych 1977); *Books* The Depressed Woman (1971), Psychopharmacology of Affective Disorders (1979), Monoamine Oxidase Inhibitors – the State of the Art (1981), Handbook of Affective Disorders (1982, 2 edn 1992), Community Psychiatric Nursing for Neurotic Patients (1983), Depression – an Integrated Approach (1989), Prevention in Psychiatry (1994); *Recreations* opera, music, theatre; *Style*— Prof Eugene Paykel; ✉ Department of Psychiatry, University of Cambridge, Douglas House, 18B Trumpington Road, Cambridge CB2 8AH

PAYNE, Anthony Edward; s of Edward Alexander Payne (d 1958), and Muriel Margaret Elsie, *née* Stroud (d 1991); *b* 2 August 1936; *Educ* Dulwich Coll, Univ of Durham (BA); *m* 24 Sept 1966, Jane Marian, da of Gerald Manning (d 1987); *Career* composer; visiting Milhaud prof of music Mills Coll Oakland California 1983, teacher in composition NSW Conservatorium Sydney Aust 1986 and Univ of West Australia 1996, visiting professorial fell in composition Univ of E Anglia 2012; memb: Soc for the Promotion of New Music (chm 1969–71), Macnaghten Concerts Soc (chm 1965–67), Boise Mendelssohn Fndn, Br Acad of Composers and Songwriters, RSM, RVW Tst; hon memb Royal Philharmonic Soc 2000; Hon DMus: Univ of Birmingham 2001, Kingston Univ 2003, Univ of Durham 2007; FRCM 2005; *Works* incl: Phoenix Mass 1968–72, Paraphrases and Cadenzas (for 3 players) 1969, Sonatas & Ricercars (for wind quintet) 1970, Paean (for solo piano) 1971, Concerto for Orchestra 1974, Fire on Whaleness (for brass band) 1975, The World's Winter (for soprano and 8 players) 1976, String Quartet 1978, The Stones and Lonely Places Sing (for 7 players) 1979, The Song of the Clouds (for oboe and orchestra) 1980, A Day in the Life of a Mayfly (for 6 players) 1981, Evening Land (for soprano and piano) 1981, Spring's Shining Wake (for chamber orchestra) 1981, Songs and Seascapes (for strings) 1984, The Spirit's Harvest (for orchestra) 1985, The Song Streams in the Firmament (for 6 players) 1986, Half Heard in the Stillness (for orchestra) 1987, Consort Music for String Quintet 1987, Sea Change (for 7 players) 1988, Time's Arrow (for orchestra) 1990, Symphonies of Wind and Rain (for chamber orchestra) 1991, A Hidden Music (for chamber orchestra) 1992, The Seeds Long Hidden..... Orchestral Variations 1994, Empty Landscape – Heart's Ease (for 6 players) 1995, completion of Elgar's Third Symphony 1994–97, Piano Trio 1998, Scenes from The Woodlanders (for soprano and 4 players) 1999, Of Knots and Skeins (for violin and piano) 2000, Twixt Heaven and Charing Cross (for unaccompanied choir) 2001, Visions and Journeys (for orchestra) 2002, Poems of Edward Thomas (for soprano and 4 players) 2003, Storm Chorale (for solo violin) 2003, Horn Trio 2005, completion of Elgar's Sixth Pomp and Circumstance 2005, Windows on Eternity (for chamber orchestra) 2006, Piano Quintet 2007, Out of the Depths Comes Song (for cello and piano) 2008, From a Mouthful of Air (for 5 players) 2009, The Period of Cosmography (for orchestra) 2009, String Quartet No 2 2010, arrangement of Bruckner's Second Symphony (for chamber orchestra) 2011, The Undiscovered Country (for 8 players) 2012, orchestration of Vaughan Williams 4 Last Songs 2013, orchestrations of Vaughan Williams' 2 Nocturnes (2014), Of Land and Sea and of the Sky (for chorus and orchestra, 2014–15); *Books* Schoenberg (1968), Frank Bridge Radical and Conservative (1984), Elgar's Third Symphony, The Story of the Reconstruction (1998); *Recreations* films, British countryside; *Style*— Anthony Payne, Esq; ✉ 2 Wilton Square, London N1 3DL (☎ 020 7359 1593, e-mail paynecomp@gmail.com)

PAYNE, Prof Anthony Philip; s of Philip Charles Payne, and Pamela Burgoyne, *née* Daniels (d 1982); *b* 9 July 1947; *Educ* Eastbourne GS, Univ of Reading (BSc), Univ of Birmingham (PhD); *m* 28 July 1970, Ruth Mary, da of Donald Jack Beake; 2 s (Christopher Jeremy b 7 Nov 1977, Alexander Richard b 24 Jan 1980); *Career* MRC jr res fell Dept of Anatomy Univ of Birmingham 1971–73; Dept of Anatomy Univ of Glasgow: temp lectr 1973–76, lectr 1976–84, sr lectr 1984–94, head 1993– (acting head 1990–92), prof 1994–; memb Editorial Bd Jl of Anatomy 1993–; memb: The Anatomical Soc (memb Cncl 1993–), Euro Neuroscience Assoc, Soc for Endocrinology, Soc for the Study of Fertility; *Books* Social Behaviour in Vertebrates (1976), Animal Behaviour (consulting ed, 1976 and 1980); *Recreations* reading, ornithology; *Style*— Prof Anthony Payne; ✉ Neuroscience and Biomedical Systems, Institute of Biomedical and Life Sciences, Thomson Building, University of Glasgow, Glasgow G12 8QQ

PAYNE, Prof Sir David Neil; kt (2013), CBE (2004); *Career* dir Optoelectronics Res Centre and Zepler Inst Univ of Southampton; co-fndr and dir York Technology and the York Gp; co-fndr, dir and chm Southampton Photonics Inc (now SPI Lasers plc); res interests in optical communications 1969–; frequently invited speaker to major int confs especially in USA and Japan; holder of 40 patents; published over 650 papers; hon prof: Beijing Univ of Post and Telecommunications 2008, Beijing Jao Tong Univ Beijing 2009, Nanjing Univ 2010; memb Royal Norwegian Soc of Sciences and Letters 2003, memb Russian Acad of Scis 2007; FRS 1992, FRSA, fell Optical Soc of America 1996, FREng 2005, FIEE 2005, FREng 2005; *Awards* Electronics Divisional Bd Premium of IEE (5 times), Gyr and Landis Commemorative Prize (twice), best paper Euro Conf on Optical Communications, Academic Enterprise Award 1982, Queens Award for Industry 1986, Tobie Award, John Tyndall Award (USA) 1991, Rank Prize Fund 1991, Japanese Computers and Communications Prize 1993, Benjamin Franklin Medal (USA) 1998, ISI Certificate for one of world's most cited authors 2000, Basic Research Award Eduard Rhein Fndn (Germany) 2001, Mountbatten Medal IEE 2001, Kelvin Medal of the Eight

UK Engineering Institutions 2004, finalist MacRobert Award Royal Acad of Engrg 2005, IEEE Photonics Award for outstanding achievements in photonics 2006, Marconi Prize and Fellowship 2007, Millennium Prize Laureate 2008, ICT Hall of Fame 2008, AILU Award 2010, SPIE Laser Luminaries 1 of 24 for the 50th anniversary of the laser 2010, Wolfson James Clerk Maxwell Award IEEE/RSE 2014, Engineering and Physical Sciences RISE Fellowship 2015, Debrett's 500 Most Influential People 2015 and 2016; *Style*— Prof Sir David Payne, CBE, FRS, FREng; ✉ Optoelectrics Research Centre, Building 46, University of Southampton, Southampton SO17 1BJ (☎ 023 8059 4521, fax 023 8059 3142, e-mail dnp@orc.soton.ac.uk)

PAYNE, Ian Philip Milner; s of Philip Stuart Payne (d 1977), of Nottingham, and Joyce Marion Milner (1964); *b* 4 October 1944, Nottingham; *Educ* Oundle; *m* 22 July 1967, Julia Elizabeth, *née* Raven; 1 s (Myles Philip Milner), 2 da (Nicola Elizabeth, Sara Louise); *Career* admitted slr 1968; Freeth Cartwright & Sketchley (now Freeths LLP): ptnr 1972–, sr ptnr 1992–, currently advsr to props of owner-managed businesses on wealth mgmnt; memb Law Soc; *Recreations* skiing, golf, tennis, music, shooting; *Clubs* RAC; *Style*— Ian Payne, Esq; ✉ Freeths LLP, Cumberland Court, 80 Mount Street, Nottingham NG1 6HH (☎ 0115 936 9369, fax 0115 859 9642, e-mail ian.payne@freeths.co.uk)

PAYNE, (Geoffrey John) Nicholas; s of John Laurence Payne (d 1961), and Dorothy Gwendoline, *née* Attenborough; *b* 4 January 1945; *Educ* Eton, Trinity Coll Cambridge (BA); *m* 6 Jan 1986, Linda Jane, da of Donald Wallace Adamson (d 1992), of Bristol; 2 s (Ralph John Anthony b 1986, Oliver Nicholas Pearsall b 1988); *Career* fin asst Royal Opera House 1968–70, subsid offr Arts Cncl of GB 1970–76, fin controller WNO 1976–82, gen admin Opera North 1982–93, artistic co-ordinator Leeds Festival 1990, dir Royal Opera 1993–98, gen dir ENO 1998–2002, dir Opera Europa 2003–; hon memb Guildhall Sch of Music and Drama, hon memb Royal Northern Coll of Music, Hon Dr Leeds Metropolitan Univ; *Style*— Nicholas Payne, Esq; ☎ 020 7713 9055, e-mail nicholas.payne@opera-europa.org

PAYTON, Michael; Hon QC (2012); s of Geoffrey Payton (d 1983), and Pamela Carey, *née* Miller-Kerr; *b* 8 June 1944, Llandrindod, Wells; *Educ* Felsted Sch (exhibitioner); *m* 25 Aug 1977, Sally; 2 da (Anna b 1 Feb 1978, Lucy b 17 Dec 1980); *Career* admitted slr 1966; sr ptnr Clyde & Co 1984–2013 (ptnr 1971–, chm 2013–); chm Slrs' Indemnity Mutual Insurance Assoc 1984–2009, chm Exec Ctee Br Maritime Law Assoc 1986–, chm Int Dispute Resolution Centre 2011–; memb Law Soc 1967–; Sr Ptnr of the Year Legal Business Awards 2004, Sr Ptnr of the Year Legal Week 2011; *Recreations* France, horse racing; *Clubs* Garrick, MCC; *Style*— Michael Payton, Esq, QC; ✉ Clyde & Co, St Botolph Building, 138 Houndsditch, London EC3A 7AR (☎ 020 7876 5000, fax 020 7876 5111, e-mail michael.payton@clydeco.com)

PEACE, David Neil; s of Basil Dunford Peace, of Ossett, W Yorks, and Felicity Wilkinson, MBE; *b* 9 April 1967; *Educ* Batley GS, Wakefield Dist Coll, Manchester Poly (BA); *m* 1996, Izumi, *née* Goto; 1 s (George Basil b 1997), 1 da (Emi b 2000); *Career* writer; *Awards* Cognac Prix du Roman Noir 2002, Granta Best of Young British Novelists list 2003, James Tait Black Award 2004, Deutscher Krimi Preis 2006, QC Writer of the Year 2007; *Books* Nineteen Seventy-Four (1999), Nineteen Seventy-Seven (2000), Nineteen Eighty (2001), Nineteen Eighty-Three (2002), GB84 (2004), The Damned Utd (2006), Tokyo Year Zero (2007); *Style*— David Peace, Esq; ✉ c/o Mr William Miller, English Agency (Japan) Ltd, Tokyo, Japan; c/o Faber & Faber Ltd, 3 Queen Square, London WC1N 3AU

PEACE, Elizabeth; CBE (2008); *b* 5 December 1952; *m* Nigel David Peace; 2 s (Alexander b 11 Jan 1985, Edward b 18 Jan 1988); *Career* dir of corporate affrs DERA (subsequently Qinetiq plc) 1990–2001, ceo Br Property Fedn 2002–; non-exec dir: Turley Assocs, Morgan Sindall plc; memb Bd Peabody, tstee LandAid; Liveryman Worshipful Co of Chartered Surveyors 2007; hon doctorate Univ of Westminster; hon fell RIBA; *Style*— Mrs Elizabeth Peace, CBE; ✉ British Property Federation, St Albans House, 5th Floor, 57059 Haymarket, London SW1Y 4QX (e-mail lpeace@bpf.org.uk)

PEACE, Sir John Wilfred; kt (2011); *Educ* RMA Sandhurst; *Career* joined Great Universal Stores plc 1970, co-fndr CCN Ltd 1980–96 (chief exec 1991–96), ceo Experian Ltd 1996–2000, memb Bd Great Universal Stores plc 1997–2006, gp chief exec GUS plc (formerly Great Universal Stores plc) 2000–06, chm Burberry 2002–, chm Experian (following demerger from GUS) 2006–14, chm Standard Chartered plc 2009–; memb Pres's Ctee CBI; Lord-Ltd of Notts 2012–; CCMI, FRSA; *Recreations* riding, golf; *Style*— Sir John Peace; ✉ Standard Chartered plc, 1 Basinghall Avenue, London EC2V 5DD

PEACH, Emeritus Prof (Guthlac) Ceri Klaus; s of Wystan Adams Peach (d 1990), and Charlotte Marianne, *née* Klaus (d 1998); *b* 26 October 1939; *Educ* Howardian HS Cardiff, Merton Coll Oxford (MA, DPhil); *m* 5 Sept 1964, Susan Lesley, *née* Godfrey; 2 s (Huw Richard Wystan b 3 Nov 1966, Guy Morgan Klaus b 18 June 1968), 1 da (Katelin Lydia (Mrs Thomas) b 19 April 1972); *Career* Univ of Oxford: demonstrator 1964–66, faculty lectr in geography 1966–92, prof of social geography 1992–2007, head of dept Sch of Geography 1995–98, emeritus prof 2007; fell and tutor St Catherine's Coll Oxford 1969–2007 (sometime dean, sr tutor and finance bursar, pro-master 1993–94, emeritus fell 2007–); prof of social geography Inst for Social Change Univ of Manchester 2007–11; visiting fell Dept of Demography ANU 1973; visiting prof: Dept of Sociology Yale Univ 1977, Dept of Geography Univ of Br Columbia 1998, Dept of Sociology Harvard Univ 1998, Office of Population Research Princeton Univ 2006; Fulbright visiting prof Dept of Geography Univ of Calif Berkeley 1985; distinguished social geography scholar Assoc of American Geographers 2008, distinguished scholar of ethnic geography Assoc of American Geographers 2008; memb Univ of Oxford Hebdomadal Cncl 1996–2000; memb: Inst of Br Geographers 1960, Assoc of American Geographers 1974; FRGS 1963; *Books* West Indian Migration to Britain: a social geography (1968), Urban Social Segregation (ed, 1975), Ethnic Segregation in Cities (co-ed, 1981), South Asians Overseas (co-ed, 1990), The Ethnic Minority Populations of Great Britain (1996), Islam in Europe (co-ed, 1997), Global Japan (co-ed, 2003); *Recreations* travelling, reading, opera, rowing; *Clubs* Leander; *Style*— Emeritus Prof Ceri Peach; ✉ St Catherine's College, Oxford OX1 3UJ (☎ 01865 271700)

PEACOCK, Christopher Arden (Chris); s of Ralph Warren Peacock (d 1987), and Phyllis Emily Alice, *née* Hardwicke (d 1999); *b* 9 April 1945; *Educ* Wellington; *m* 1, 1968 (m dis); 2 da (Julie b 1971, Susannah b 1973); *m* 2, 1979; 3 c (Samantha b 1980, Charles b 1982, Thomas b 1986); *Career* Kemsley Whiteley Ferris 1963–66, Daniel Smith Briant & Done 1966–72; Jones Lang Wootton: joined 1972, ptnr 1974, chm and head Ptnr Agency 1988, managing ptnr Continent of Europe 1992–96, chief exec Jones Lang Wootton Europe 1996–97 (int chief exec 1997–99), pres and ceo Jones Lang LaSalle 2002–04 (pres, dep chief exec and chief operating offr 1999–2002); non-exec dir: Slough Estates 2004–, Land Locator Co 2005–, Howard de Walden Estates 2006–; Freeman City of London, memb Ct of Assts Worshipful Co of Pewterers; FRICS 1982 (ARICS 1970); *Recreations* golf, sailing, tennis, travel, shooting; *Clubs* Walton Heath Golf; *Style*— Chris Peacock, Esq

PEACOCK, Geraldine; CBE (2001); *b* 26 January 1948; *Educ* Redland HS for Girls Bristol, Univ of Durham (BA), Univ of Calif (Rotary Int fell), Univ of Newcastle upon Tyne (CQSW, Dip Applied Social Work Studies); *Career* 1969–1989: sr social work practitioner, lectr in social policy and social work theory and practice, trg conslt to govt depts and local authorities, dep dir London Trg for Care; chief exec: Nat Autistic Soc 1989–97, Guide Dogs for the Blind Association 1997–2003; chair Charity Cmmn 2004–06 (non-exec cmmr 2003–06), interim chair Futurebuilders 2004–; civil serv cmmr 2001–; chm ACEVO 1996–2000 (vice-chm 1995–96, memb Exec Ctee), vice-chm The Int Fedn of

Guide Dog Schs for the Blind 2001–; memb: Residential Homes Tbnl 1995–98, Cncl Industrial Soc 1996–2002, Social Investment Task Force 2000, Project Advsy Gp Performance and Innovation Unit (PIU) Voluntary Sector 2001, Advsy Ctee Active Community Unit Home Office; chm Voluntary Sector Women Leaders Network (Groundbreakers); tstee: NCVO 1999–2003, Inge Wakehurst Tst; voted Britain's most admired charity chief exec 2003; *Publications* Social Work and Received Ideas (with C Rojek and S Collins, 1989), The Haunt of Misery (with C Rojek and S Collins, 1990); author of numerous articles and conference papers; *Style—* Ms Geraldine Peacock, CBE

PEACOCK, Ian Douglas; OBE (1998); s of Andrew Inglis Peacock (d 1981), of Sevenoaks, Kent, and Minnie Maria, *née* King (d 1978); *b* 9 April 1934; *Educ* Sevenoaks Sch; *m* 1, 21 July 1962 (m dis), Joanna Hepburn, da of George Milne MacGregor (d 1993), of Strathaven, Lanarkshire; 1 s (Colin Michael b 8 Sept 1963), 1 da (Susan Jean b 2 May 1965); m 2, 12 Oct 2008, Philippa Katharine, da of Eric Arthur Bland, DSO (d 2003); *Career* PO RAF 1953–54, Flying Offr RAuxAF 1955–58; md: Slazenger Ltd 1976–83 (mktg dir 1973–76), Sports Mktg Surveys Ltd 1983–85; chief exec LTA 1986–96; vice-pres Golf Fndn 2003– (dir and memb Cncl 1984–, chm 1996–2003); chm: Golf Ball 1975–96, Torch Trophy Tst 1998–2006 (vice-pres 2006–); pres Br Sports and Allied Industries Fedn 1983–85, pres UK Tennis Industry Assoc 2008–; dir: Br Tennis Fndn 1997–2007, The Tennis Fndn 2007–; dir Wembley National Stadium Ltd (formerly English National Stadium Development Co) 1998–2002, tstee Wembley National Stadium Tst 1998–2009; *Recreations* golf, painting; *Clubs* All England Lawn Tennis, RAF, Royal Ashdown Forest Golf, Queen's; *Style—* Ian Peacock, Esq, OBE; ✉ 135 More Close, St Paul's Court, West Kensington, London W14 9BW

PEACOCK, Ian Rex; s of late Mervyn George Peacock, and late Evelyn Joyce, *née* Gay; *b* 5 July 1947, Bristol; *Educ* Kingswood GS Bristol, Trinity Coll Cambridge (MA), Open Univ; *m* 31 March 1973, Alyanee, da of Lt-Gen Amnuay Chya-Rochana; 1 s (Christopher George Insree b 5 May 1982); *Career* mangr Economics and Statistics Dept Unilever 1968–73, economist Cripps Warburg Ltd 1973–75; Kleinwort Benson Gp: int loan admin 1975–76, asst mangr syndication 1976–78, mangr Banking Dept Hong Kong 1978–81, asst dir domestic banking 1981–85, dir North American banking NY 1985–87, dir LBO Unit and head of loan syndications 1987–1990, jt head of financing and gp dir 1990–94; BZW Ltd: co-head merchant banking NY 1994–96, chief operating offr Investment Banking Div 1996–97; special advsr Bank of England 1998–2000, dep chm Lombard Risk Mgmnt 2000–10, non-exec chm MFI Furniture Gp plc 2000–06, chm Mothercare plc 2002–11; sr advsr Close Brothers Corporate Finance 2005–08, conslt Bd C Hoare and Co 2008–10 (dir 2010–); non-exec dir: Norwich and Peterborough Building Soc 1997–2005, i-documentsystems Gp plc 2000–04; chm Finance Advsy Ctee Westminster Abbey 2003–; tstee: WRVS 2001–07, Chiswick House and Gardens; chm Family Mosaic Housing Assoc 2007–13, chm Housing Finance Corp 2013–; city fell Hughes Hall Cambridge 2009–12, Quondam fell Hughes Hall Cambridge 2012–; *Clubs* Athenaeum; *Style—* Ian Peacock, Esq; ✉ e-mail ianrpeacock@hotmail.com

PEACOCK, Jonathan Mark; s of John Keith Peacock, of Stoke-on-Trent, and Gloria Theresa, *née* Martin; *b* 16 December 1961, Stoke-on-Trent; *Educ* St Joseph's Coll Trent Vale, Univ of Hull (LLB), UCL (LLM); *m* 14 Feb 2008, Julie Ann Lewis, *née* Miller; 1 s (Jacob b 14 July 1993), 1 da (Asha b 30 Oct 1999); *Career* admitted slr 1993; slr specialising in medical law and patients' rights; Shoosmiths & Harrison Solicitors 1989–95, Irwin Mitchell Solicitors 1996– (ptnr 1999); chair Grafton Manor Research and Ethics Ctee 2004–; dir Tindal St Press; tstee: Headway UK, Birmingham Citizens Advocacy (dep chair), Linota; memb Law Soc 1993; *Recreations* literary fiction, cinema, tennis, running; *Style—* Jonathan Peacock, Esq; ✉ Irwin Mitchell Solicitors, Imperial House, 31 Temple Street, Birmingham B2 5DB (✆ 0121 214 5217, e-mail jonathan.peacock@irwinmitchell.com)

PEACOCK, Lynne Margaret; da of George Beare (d 1986), of London, and Elsie, *née* Humphries; *b* 26 December 1953; *Career* Woolwich (Building Soc) plc: mktg devpt mangr 1983–87, mktg mangr 1987–91, head of mktg 1991–94, gen mangr 1994–96, ops dir 1996–2000, chief-exec 2000–03; chief exec Clydesdale Bank 2003–11; non-exec dir: Scottish Water 2009–, Nationwide Building Soc 2011–, Standard Life 2012–; *Style—* Ms Lynne Peacock

PEACOCKE, Prof Christopher Arthur Bruce; s of Arthur Robert Peacocke, and Rosemary Winifred Mann; *b* 22 May 1950; *Educ* Magdalen Coll Sch Oxford, Exeter Coll Oxford (MA, BPhil, DPhil); *m* 3 Jan 1980, Teresa Anne, *née* Rosen; 1 s, 1 da; *Career* jr research fell The Queen's Coll Oxford 1973–75, prize fell All Souls Coll Oxford 1975–79, fell and tutor and CUF lectr in philosophy New Coll Oxford 1979–85, Susan Stebbing prof of philosophy KCL 1985–88; visiting prof: Univ of Calif Berkeley 1975, Univ of Michigan Ann Arbor 1978, UCLA 1981, Univ of Maryland 1987, NYU 1996–99; visiting fell ANU 1981, fell Centre for Advanced Study in the Behavioral Sciences Stanford 1983–84, Waynflete prof of metaphysical philosophy Univ of Oxford 1989–2000, fell Magdalen Coll Oxford 1989–2000, Leverhulme personal res prof 1996–2000, prof of philosophy NYU 2000–04, prof of philosophy Columbia Univ 2004–, Wollheim prof of philosophy UCL 2007–, Johnsonian prof of philosophy Columbia Univ 2013– (chair Philosophy Dept 2013–); Whitehead Lectures Harvard Univ 2001, Kant Lectures Stanford Univ 2003, Context and Content Lectures Instut Jean Nicod Ecole Normale Superieure Paris 2010, Kohut Lectures Univ of Chicago 2011; Euro Soc for Philosophy and Psychology: memb Steering Ctee 1991–95, memb Advsy Bd 1995–99, memb Bd 1999–; papers on philosophy of mind, language and logic and metaphysics; pres Mind Assoc 1986; FBA 1990, fell American Acad of Arts and Sciences 2010; *Books* Holistic Explanation: Action, Space, Interpretation (1979), Sense and Content (1983), Thoughts: an Essay on Content (1986), A Study of Concepts (1992), Being Known (1999), The Realm of Reason (2004), Truly Understood (2008), The Mirror of the Wolrd: Subjects, Consciousness and Self-Consciousness (2014); *Recreations* music, visual arts; *Style—* Prof Christopher Peacocke, FBA; ✉ Department of Philosophy, 708 Philosophy Hall, Columbia University, 1150 Amsterdam Avenue, MC4971, New York NY 10027

PEAFORD, Alan James; MBE; s of James William Thomas Peaford (d 1986), and Iris Maud, *née* Tustain; *b* 31 October 1952; *Educ* Ockendon Court, Harlow Coll, Cranfield (Mktg Mgmnt Dip); *m* 17 Dec 1978, Jane Elizabeth, da of John Donald Saxton; 2 da (Sara Jane b 20 Aug 1980, Victoria Lesley b 28 March 1985), 1 s (Thomas James Charles b 16 Feb 1982); *Career* journalist; Express Newspapers 1971–74, Westminster Press 1975–76, Times Newspapers 1977–, night ed Arab Times 1977–78, dep ed Gulf Daily News 1978–79, PR and communications mangr British Petroleum 1980–88, md Charles Barker 1988–90, chm Trident Communications 1990–2004, chm Aerocomm Ltd 2004–; awards: Foreign Corr of the Year 1977, Safety Writer of the Year 1982, Aerospace Journalist of the Year (Airshows) 2001, 2005 and 2007; nat chm BAIE 1989–90 (memb 1981, fell 1986), memb Cncl Nat Youth Theatre 1999–; chm Treetops 2002–, pres Cornelia de Lange Syndrome Fndn 2011– (chm 1990–2011); pres Fedn of European Editors 1995–2000, pres BACB 2000–11, pres Inst of Internal Communications 2011–12; FRSA; *Books* Pocket Guide to Business Aircraft (2008), Facing Challenges; *Recreations* flying, golf, tennis, watching West Ham; *Clubs* Aviation, RIBI; *Style—* Alan Peaford, Esq

PEAKER, Prof Malcolm; s of late Ronald Smith Peaker, of Stapleford, Nottingham, and Marian, *née* Tomasin; *b* 21 August 1943; *Educ* Henry Mellish GS Nottingham, Univ of Sheffield (BSc, DSc), Univ of Hong Kong (PhD); *m* 23 Oct 1965, Stephanie Jane, da of late Lt Cdr J G Large, DSC; 3 s (Christopher James Gordon, Alexander John, Nicholas Edward); *Career* ARC Inst of Animal Physiology 1968–78, head Dept of Physiology Hannah Res Inst 1978–81, dir and Hannah prof Univ of Glasgow 1981–2003; Hon DSc Univ of Hong Kong; FZS 1969, FIBiol 1979, FRSE 1983, FRS 1996; *Books* Salt Glands in Birds and Reptiles (1975), Avian Physiology (ed, 1975), Comparative Aspects of Lactation (ed, 1977), Physiological Strategies in Lactation (ed, 1984), Intercellular Signalling in the Mammary Gland (ed, 1995), Biological Signalling and the Mammary Gland (ed, 1997); *Recreations* zoology, natural history, golf; *Clubs* Royal Troon Golf; *Style—* Prof Malcolm Peaker, FRSE, FRS; ✉ 13 Upper Crofts, Alloway, Ayr KA7 4QX

PEARCE, Caroline Jill; *née* Mitchell; da of late Charles Martin Mitchell, and Audrey Joan, *née* Noyes; *b* 17 April 1973, Epsom, Surrey; *Educ* Parsons Mead Sch Ashtead, Epsom Coll, Univ of Cardiff (BSc Econ), Journalism Training Centre Mitcham; *m* 31 Aug 2001, Timothy Joseph John Pearce; 1 da (Gabriella Grace Anne b 9 Oct 2003), 1 s (Jake Alexander Kenneth b 24 May 2006); *Career* editorial asst The Lawyer Magazine Centaur Communications 1994; EMAP plc: sub ed Screen International 1994, prodn ed Screen International 1996; Global Professional Media Ltd: prodn ed Legal Week 1998, managing ed Legal Week 1999, gp managing ed 2000; gp managing ed Alternative Assets Div and Mortgage Div Incisive Media 2007; freelance conslt and ed 2009; PPA Int Magazine of the Year (for Screen Int) 1997/8, PPA Weekly Business Magazine of the Year (for Legal Week) 2001/2 (shortlisted 2005), Incisive Media Awards Editorial Team of the Year (for Legal Week) 2006; *Recreations* swimming, theatre, film, cooking, tennis; *Style—* Mrs Caroline Pearce

PEARCE, Prof Eur Ing Christopher Michael; *Educ* Newent Sch, Univ of Bath (prizewinner, BSc); *Career* Dowty Group plc: apprentice 1970–74, designer and ldr Dowty Rotol Ltd 1974–79, propeller project engr Dowty Rotol Ltd 1979–84, gp trg mangr Dowty Gp plc 1984–86, chief engr Dowty Fuel Systems Ltd 1986–87, dir of engineering Dowty Fuel Systems Ltd 1987–89, dir of ops Dowty Fuel Systems Ltd 1989–90, dir and gen mangr Dowty Aerospace Hydraulics 1990–93, dir of Dowty Aerospace 1993–94; tech dir Ricardo Aerospace Ltd, Ricardo Hitec Ltd and Geschäftsfuhrer Ricardo Technology GmbH (Ricardo Group plc) 1994–97, tech and quality dir INBIS Gp Ltd and INBIS Ltd 1997–2006, tech dir Assystem SA 2006–12, tech and quality dir Assystem UK Ltd 2006–12, conslt 2013–14, ret 2015; visiting prof Xi'an Jiaotong Univ (People's Republic of China), former Royal Acad of Engrg visiting prof Univ of Salford; Sir George Dowty prizewinner, Sir Roy Fedden prizewinner; CEng 1981, FREng 1993, MRAeS 1981, FIMechE 1991, FIET 2001; *Recreations* active church memb, fell walking, table tennis (former rep Univ of Bath); *Style—* Prof Eur Ing Christopher Pearce, FREng; ✉ e-mail chrismpearce@yahoo.co.uk

PEARCE, Dave; s of Donald Pearce, and Edith Pearce; *b* 14 June 1963; *Educ* Esher Coll Surrey; *m* Fiona; *Career* UK and int club DJ and music prodr 1985–; presenter and prodr BBC Radio London/GLR 1983–90, Breakfast and Drivetime presenter Kiss 100 1990–95, presenter BBC Radio 1 1995–2008, presenter BBC 6Music and BBC Radio 2 2008–; presenter and music conslt Behind The Beat (BBC) 1988, presenter The Dance Years (ITV) 2001, corr DJ Int TV 2013–; A&R dir: Polydor Records 1988–89, BMG Records 2001–04; columnist: The Sun 1998–2000, Daily Star 2002–04; music conslt film SW9 2001 (winner Best Film Soundtrack Br Independent Film Awards 2001); *Recordings* Dave Pearce Dance Anthems vols 1–5, various Euphoria dance mix albums, Dave Pearce Trance Anthems 2008, 2009 and 2010; *Recreations* reading political biographies, walking, cinema; *Style—* Dave Pearce, Esq; ✉ c/o Wise Buddah Ltd, 74 Great Titchfield Street, London W1W 7QP (✆ 020 7307 1607, fax 020 7307 1608)

PEARCE, Gareth David; s of late Howard Spencer Pearce, and Enid Norma, *née* Richards; *b* 13 August 1953; *Educ* Abingdon Sch, Balliol Coll Oxford (MA); *m* Virginia Louise, da of late Desmond Campbell Miller; 4 da (Caroline, Emma, Davina, Leonora); *Career* CA: Peat Marwick Mitchell & Co 1975–81, Electra Investment Tst plc 1982–86, Smith & Williamson 1986–2013 (gp md 1995–2000, exec chm 2000–13); dir National Mutual Life Assurance Soc 1997–2002; FCA 1997 (ACA 1979); *Clubs* Hurlingham; *Style—* Gareth Pearce, Esq; ✉ Bewley Court, Lacock, Wiltshire SN15 2PG (✆ 01249 730573)

PEARCE, Howard John Stredder; CVO (1993); s of Ernest Victor Pearce, and Ida, *née* Booth; *Educ* City of London Sch, Pembroke Coll Cambridge (MA, LLB); *Career* joined FCO 1972, third sec Buenos Aires 1975–78, FCO 1978–83, first sec and head of Chancery Nairobi 1983–87, asst later dep head of personnel ops FCO 1987–90, dep head of mission Budapest 1991–94, fell Center for Int Affairs Harvard Univ 1994–95, head Central European Dept FCO 1996–99, high cmmr to Malta 1999–2002, govr of Falkland Islands and Cmmr for S Georgia and the S Sandwich Islands 2002–06; sr assoc memb St Antony's Coll Oxford; memb Exec Ctee VSO 1988–90; *Recreations* classical music, opera, reading, hill walking, travel; *Clubs* Oxford and Cambridge; *Style—* Howard Pearce, Esq, CVO

P

PEARCE, Prof John Barber; s of Arnold Porteous Pearce (d 1979), and Ruth, *née* Parry; *b* 27 October 1940; *Educ* Michael Hall (Rudolph Steiner Sch), UCL, UCH (MB BS, DCH, MPhil); *m* 1965, (Jean) Mary, da of Derek Wynne Bogle; 3 da (Rachel Christina b 1 Dec 1966, Clare Judith b 10 Oct 1968, Anna Jane b 19 March 1971); *Career* postgrad: Bart's 1967–71, Maudsley Hosp 1971–75; conslt child and adolescent psychiatrist Guy's Hosp London 1975–87, sr lectr in child and adolescent psychiatry Univ of Leicester 1987–91, prof of child and adolescent psychiatry Univ of Nottingham 1991–99 (emeritus prof 1999–); conslt child and adolescent psychiatrist Cornwall Partnership Tst 2005–; formerly examiner (MSc in Human Communication) Univ of London, examiner (DCH) RCP 1989–99; RCPsych: formerly sec Child and Adolescent Psychiatry Speciality Advsy Ctee, formerly examiner membership exam, sec Child and Adolescent Section 1993–95 (formerly academic sec), memb Jt Ctee for Higher Psychiatric Trg 1993–99; regnl advsr Med Cncl on Alcoholism 1992–99; expert on childhood problems for nat and local radio and TV and for nat newspapers and mags; memb: BMA, Assoc of Psychologists and Psychiatrists; FRCPCH, FRCP, FRCPsych; *Books* The 'Kids Work Out' Guide for Parents (1987), Worries and Fears (1989), Bad Behaviour (1989), Tantrums and Tempers (1989), Fighting, Teasing and Bullying (1989), Food: Too Faddy Too Fat (1991), Family and Friends (1991), Bad Behaviour, Tantrums and Tempers (1993), Good Habits – Bad Habits (1994), Growth and Development – Too Fast Too Slow (1994), Baby and Toddler Sleep Programme (1997); also author of book chapters and scientific papers concerning childhood depression and suicide, the psychiatric consequences of physical illness, bullying and general child psychiatric topics; *Recreations* narrowboating and sailing, playing the cello occasionally, restoring anything, travelling with my wife; *Clubs* Wadebridge Boat, Hillingdon Canal; *Style—* Prof John Pearce; ✉ Child and Adolescent Mental Health Service, Trengweath Cottage, Penny Street, Redruth TR15 2SP

PEARCE, Jonathan; *b* 23 December 1959; *Educ* Univ of Birmingham (BA), National Broadcasting Sch; *m* Amanda; 2 3 (Sam b 1999, William b 2001, Elizabeth b 2003); *Career* freelance football reporter BBC Radio Bristol 1980–83; sports ed: Radio West Bristol 1983–84, Southern Sound Radio 1984, Radio West/GWR Bristol 1984–86, BBC Radio 2 Local Radio Network London 1986–87; sports ed and commentator Capital Radio 1987–2002, freelance reporter, commentator and presenter Sky TV 1991–97, football commentator Channel 5 TV 1997–2004, football commentator BBC Radio Five Live 2002–05; presenter: The Footballers Football Show (Sky TV) 1991–93, Sports Talk (Granada Talk TV) 1996–97, Up for the Cup (LWT) 1997, Robot Wars (BBC) 1997–2005, Jonathan Pearce's Football Night (Channel 5) 2000–04, BC Radio Five 6-0-6 2002–03, BBC Radio Five Mid-week Sport on Five 2003–05; commentator Match of the Day 2004–; several voice-overs for various video prodns, radio and TV ads; *Awards* New York Radio Festival Gold Medal 1990, 1992 and 1999 (Silver Medal 1991, Bronze Medal 1993), Best Sports Prog of the Year Sony Radio Awards 1990 and 1992, Best Sports Commentator

Sony Radio Awards 1996, Variety Club Independent Radio Personality of the Year 1996; *Recreations* all sport (trained with Bristol City FC as a teenager); *Style—* Jonathan Pearce, Esq

PEARCE, Nicholas; s of Peter Pearce (d 1988), and Lynda, *née* Price; *b* 24 May 1968, London; *Educ* Univ of Manchester (BA), Univ of Oxford (MPhil); *m* 1 Sept 2000, Rebecca Asher; 1 s (Henry), 1 da (Erica); *Career* special advsr Dept for Educn and Employment 1999–2001, special advsr Home Office 2001–03, dir Inst for Public Policy Research 2003–07, head of policy PM's Office until 2010, dir Inst for Public Policy Research 2010–; memb UK-India Round Table; non-exec dir RIBA Tst 2008–; hon FRIBA 2013; Social Justice (jt ed, 2005), Freedom's Orphans (jt ed, 2006), Politics For A New Generation (jt ed, 2007); *Style—* Nicholas Pearce, Esq; ✉ Institute for Public Policy Research, 4th Floor, 13–14 Buckingham Street, London WC2N 6DF

PEARCE, Reynold (Ren); *Educ* Trent Poly Nottingham (BA Fashion), Central St Martin's Sch of Art London (MA); *Career* fashion designer; former asst to designers incl John Galliano and Roland Klein, fndr ptnr own label Pearce Fionda (with Andrew Fionda, *qv*) 1994–; New Generation Designers of the Year (Br Fashion Awards) 1995, Newcomers Award for Export (Br Knitting and Clothing Export Cncl/Fashion Weekly) 1995, World Young Designers Award (Int Apparel Fedn Istanbul) 1996, Glamour Category Award (Br Fashion Awards) 1997; worldwide stockists incl: Liberty, Harrods, Harvey Nichols and Selfridges (UK), Saks 5th Avenue and Bergdorf Goodman (USA), Lidia Shopping (Italy), CRC (Thailand), Brown Thomas (Ireland); gp exhbns incl: Design of the Times (RCA) 1996, The Cutting Edge of British Fashion 1947–1997 (V&A) 1997; *Style—* Ren Pearce

PEARCE, His Hon Judge Richard William; s of Raymond Pearce, and Muriel, *née* Riley; *b* 21 January 1963, Brereton, Cheshire; *Educ* Abbot Byrne Sch Burton-On-Trent, Trinity Coll Cambridge; *m* 12 July 1986, Dr Teresa Regan; 1 da (Lucy), 2 s (Ben, Joel); *Career* called to the Bar 1985; recorder 2008–15, circuit judge (Northern Circuit) 2015–; govr Broad Oak Primary Sch, memb Parrs Wood HS Multi-Acad Tst; *Recreations* cinema, gardening, music, reading, skiing, travel, walking; *Style—* His Hon Judge Pearce; ✉ Chester Civil and Family Justice Centre, Trident House, Little St John Street, Chester, Cheshire CH1 1SN

PEARCE, Prof Dame Shirley Anne; DBE (2014, CBE 2005); da of Derek Pearce, of Norfolk, and Nancy, *née* Ferris; *b* 19 February 1954, Cirencester; *Educ* Norwich HS for Girls, St Anne's Coll Oxford (BA), Inst of Psychiatry Univ of London (MPhil), Univ of London (PhD); *m* Aug 1980, Robert Pugh; 2 s (Jonathan Robert b 31 March 1988, Thomas George b 22 Sept 1985); *Career* clinical psychologist St Mary's Hosp London 1977–81, lectr then sr lectr in psychology UCL 1981–94, prof of health psychology UEA 1994–2006, pro-vice-chllr Health and Professional Schs UEA 2000–06, vice-chllr Loughborough Univ 2006–; cmmr Healthcare Cmmn 2004–07; memb: Health Ctee Univs UK 2005–07, Equality Challenge Unit 2006–08 (also dir), HEFCE Bd Strategic Advsy Ctee for Business and Community 2006–08, E Midlands Regnl Sports Bd Sport England 2006–08, FE-HE 2012 Steering Gp Univs UK 2006–07, Cncl for Industry and HE, Bd of Tstees Youth Sport Tst 2007–, Bd Univs and Colls Employers Assoc 2007–, HEFCE Bd Strategic Advsy Ctee for Enterprise and Skills 2008–, HEFC Matched Funding Scheme for Voluntary Giving Advsy Gp 2008–, UKRIO Bd Panel for Research Integrity in Health and Biomedical Sciences 2008–; The Practice of Behavioural Medicine (co-ed, 1989), Psychological Factors in Measurement of Pain (contrib, 2000); numerous articles in learned jls; *Recreations* running, gardening; *Style—* Prof Dame Shirley Pearce, DBE; ✉ Loughborough University, Ashby Road, Loughborough LE11 3TU (☎ 01509 222002, fax 01509 223900, e-mail s.pearce@lboro.ac.uk)

PEARCE, Prof Susan Mary; *b* 20 March 1942; *Educ* Wycombe HS for Girls, Somerville Coll Oxford (MA), Univ Southampton (PhD); *m*; *Career* curatorial asst Dept of Archaeology Nat Museums of Merseyside 1965; Exeter City Museum: curator of antiquities 1965–78, sr curator (dep dir post) 1978–84; tutor Univ of Exeter 1972–84; Dept of Museum Studies Univ of Leicester: sr lectr 1984–89, dir and head of dept 1989–96, dean of arts 1996–, personal professorship in museum studies 1992–; tutor and examiner dip of Museum Assoc 1976–79; visiting lectr: Dept of Rhetoric Univ of Calif Berkeley 1982, Dept of Museum Studies Univ of Brno Czechoslovakia 1988; memb: Area Archaeological Advsy Ctee 1976–81, Archaeology Advsy Ctee Exmoor Nat Park 1979–84, Nat Trust Archaeological Advsy Ctee 1979–84, Govt Ctee for Reviewing Works of Art for Export 1990–92, Scholarship Assessment Panel Cwlth Inst 1991–; sec, chm and pres Devon Archaeological Soc 1973–79, exec sec Devon Ctee for Rescue Archaeology 1978–83, chm Leicester Univ Press Ctee 1991–, treas and chm Museums Ethnographers Gp 1976–83; Museums Assoc: Cncl memb 1989–, vice-chair Educnl Bd 1989–, professional vice-pres 1990–92, pres 1992–; Winston Churchill Travelling Fellowship (to visit Central Arctic) 1975, Catherine and Leonard Woolley Fellship grant Somerville Coll Oxford (res Balearic Isles) 1984; FSA 1979, FMA 1980 (AMA 1973); *Books* The Kingdom of Dumnonia – Studies in History and Tradition in SW Britain AD 350–1150 (1978), The Archaeology of SW Britain (1981), The Early Church in W Britain and Ireland (ed, 1982), The Bronze Age Metalwork of SW Britain (pts 1 and 2, 1983), Museum Studies in Material Culture (ed, 1989), Archaeological Curatorship (1990), Objects of Knowledge (ed, 1990), Museum Economics and the Community (ed, 1991), Museum Studies Bibliography (ed, 1991), Museums and Europe (ed, 1992), Museums, Objects and Collections – A Cultural Study (1992), Museums and the Appropriation of Culture (ed, 1993), Art in Museums (ed, 1994), Collecting in the European Tradition (1995), Collecting in Contemporary Practice (1998); author of numerous papers for confs and jls; *Style—* Prof Susan M Pearce, FSA; ✉ Department of Museum Studies, University of Leicester, 105 Princess Road East, Leicester LE1 7LG (☎ 0116 252 3963)

PEARCE, Teresa; MP; *née* Farrington; da of Arthur Farrington (d 2009), and Josephine, *née* Van Holsbeke (d 2013); *b* 1 February 1955, Southport, Lancs; *Educ* St Thomas More Sch Eltham; *Children* 2 da (Sarah Louise b 7 Oct 1973, Gemma Elizabeth b 25 Dec 1979); *Career* former sr mangr PricewaterhouseCoopers; MP (Lab) Erith and Thamesmead 2010–; *Recreations* cinema, reading, 1980s soul music; *Clubs* Erith Slopes Book; *Style—* Ms Teresa Pearce, MP; ✉ House of Commons, London SW1A 0AA (website www.teresapearce.co.uk)

PEARCE-HIGGINS, His Hon Judge Daniel John; QC (1998); *b* 26 December 1949; *Educ* St Paul's, Univ of Bristol (BSocSci), Inns of Court Sch of Law; *Career* called to the Bar Middle Temple 1973 (bencher 2009); recorder 1999–2004 (asst recorder 1995–99), circuit judge (Midland Circuit) 2004–, designated civil judge Hereford and Worcester; memb Mental Health Tbnl 2000–; memb Prog Advsy Ctee Cumberland Lodge 2008–; CEDR accredited mediator 1999–2004, FCIArb 1999–2004; *Style—* His Hon Judge Pearce-Higgins, QC; ✉ Worcester Combined Court Centre, Shirehall, Forgate Street, Worcester WR1 1EQ

PEARCEY, Leonard Charles; s of Leonard Arthur Pearcey (d 1992), of Dorset, and Jessie Sinclair, *née* Millar (d 1965); *b* 6 June 1938; *Educ* Christ's Hosp, CCC Cambridge (MA); *Career* PA to md Hargreaves Group 1957–59, dir of studies Rapid Results Correspondence Coll 1962–63, teacher Wimbledon 1964–65, arts admin Harold Holt Ltd 1965–66, music dir Guildhall Sch of Music and Drama 1966–70; competition sec Int Violin Competition 1966–70, dir Merton Festival 1972–76; involved in numerous major arts and religious radio and TV programmes incl BBC Radio 2 Young Musician competition, Book at Bedtime, Music Now, The Arts This Week, Seeing and Believing, Meeting Place and Songs of Praise; own series as singer and guitarist (Gold disc 1990), composer of numerous songs and arrangements; dedicatee Peter Wishart Five Psalms 1968; film commentary Robert Graves House Deia 2006–; prodr and presenter: P&O cruise-ship naming ceremonies (incl NY with Sophia Loren and Olivia de Havilland), various other major presentations, conferences and award ceremonies incl 9 Ivor Novello Awards, numerous voice-overs; admin BBC Radio Times Drama Awards and Comedy Awards 1972–90, stage co-ordinator and compere World Travel Market 1980–2006, dir Music at Leisure Series 1988–2015; ed Music Teacher Magazine 1980–85, feature columnist Classical Music Magazine 1979–85; Mayoress (sic) London Borough of Merton 1973–74; pres Bath Choral Soc 2011–15; memb Bd Theatre Royal Bath 2009– (chair Creative Fund 2015–); memb: Actors Equity, National Tst; life memb/assoc: Bath Preservation Tst, K&A Canal Tst, Victoria Art Gallery, Holburne Museum, RNLI, Mediterranean Garden Soc; patron Cavell Nurses' Tst 2013–15, ambass Quartet Fndn, tstee Bath Theatre Tst 2016–; *Books* The Musician's Survival Kit (1979); *Recreations* travel; *Style—* Leonard Pearcey, Esq; ✉ Apartment 22, The Tramshed, Beehive Yard, Bath BA1 5BB

PEAREY, David Dacre; *b* 15 July 1948; *m* 1996, Susan Anne, *née* Knowles; 1 da; *Career* diplomat; first sec FCO 1983, dep high cmmr Kampala 1987, first sec then cnsllr FCO 1990, cnsllr (commercial and economic) Lagos 1995, dep high cmmr Karachi 2000, high cmmr to Malawi 2005–06, govr British Virgin Islands 2006–; *Style—* David Pearey, Esq; ✉ c/o Foreign & Commonwealth Office, King Charles Street, London SW1A 2AH

PEARL, David Alan (aka David Pearlman); s of Harry Pearlman (d 1974), and Blanche, *née* Tafel; *b* 25 October 1945, London; *Educ* state schs Tottenham; *m* 19 Jan 1982, Susan Jayne, *née* Kaye; 1 s (Howard b 4 Dec 1975), 2 da (Laura b 16 Nov 1982, Gabriella b 25 July 1987); *Career* entrepreneur; co-fndr Pearl & Coutts Ltd, fndr Structadene Ltd; charter fndr memb Duke of Edinburgh Award, supporter Nat Youth Theatre; *Recreations* buying property, occasionally watching Spurs (vice-pres); *Style—* David Pearl, Esq; ✉ Structadene Limited, 3rd Floor, 9 White Lion Street, London N1 9PD (☎ 020 7843 3775, fax 020 7843 3799, e-mail david.p@pearl-coutts.co.uk)

PEARL, David Brian; s of Leonard Pearl (d 1983), past Lord Mayor of Westminster, and Rivka Chenevix-Trench (d 2011); *b* 6 August 1944, Newton Abbot, Devon; *Educ* Wellington Coll; *m* 1972, Rosamond Mary Katharine, da of Lt Cdr C G de L'isle Bush (d 2003), of Frampton-upon-Severn, Glos; 2 s, 1 da; *Career* articled clerk Cooper Brothers (qualified CA); md: Meru Group Ltd 1972–76, Promotions House plc 1976–84; chm: London Securities plc 1984–94, Premier Asset Management plc 1995–97; chm Sovereign Mines of Africa plc 2008–16, currently chm Pearl Capital Partners Ltd; dir Roadmender Ltd; non-exec dir Stanley Leisure plc 1995–2001; underwriting memb Lloyds of London 1977–90; vice-chm Medway Ports Authy (Dept of Tport appointment) 1987–93, chm The Crown Suppliers (Dept of Environment appointment) 1989–90; cncllr Westminster City Cncl 1974–82 (local sch govr, London Tourist Bd rep, dep Lord Mayor, chief whip); past chm: St Marylebone Cons Assoc, London Central Euro Cons Assoc, Cons Party Property Advsy Ctee SE Region; *Recreations* greyhound breeding, golf; *Clubs* White's, Reform, MCC, Royal St George's, Tralee Golf, Sunningdale Golf; *Style—* David B Pearl, Esq, FCA; ✉ Ballyneale House, Ballingarry, County Limerick, Ireland

PEARL, His Hon David Stephen; s of late Chaim Pearl, and late Anita, *née* Newman; *b* 11 August 1944, Southport, Lancs; *Educ* George Dixon's Sch Birmingham, Westminster City Sch, Univ of Birmingham (LLB), Queens' Coll Cambridge (LLM, MA, PhD); *m* 1, 7 April 1967 (m dis 1983), Susan, da of late Joseph Roer, of Croydon, Surrey; 3 s (Julian Kim b 1969, Daniel Benjamin Meir b 1971, Marcus Alexander Jethro b 1974); m 2, 4 Oct 1985, Gillian, da of late Ryszard Maciejewski, of Melbourn, Herts; 1 step s (Benjamin), 1 step da (Sarah); *Career* called to the Bar Gray's Inn 1968 (bencher 2002); fell and dir studies in law Fitzwilliam Coll Cambridge 1969–89 (life fell 1989), lectr Univ of Cambridge 1972–89, prof of law and dean Sch of Law UEA 1989–94 (hon prof 1995–), recorder of the Crown Court 1992–94 (asst recorder 1985–92), circuit judge 1994–2012, dep judge of the High Ct 2008–12, judge Upper Tbnl 2009–12; pt/t adjudicator Immigration Act 1980–92, pt/t chm Immigration Appeal Tbnl 1992–94, chief adjudicator Immigration Appeals 1994–97, pres Immigration Appeal Tbnl 1997–99; nat chair Medical Practitioner Tbnl Service 2012–; Judicial Studies Bd: memb Civil and Family Ctee 1994–96, memb Tbnls Ctee 1996–99 and 2004–12, dir of studies 1999–2001; pres Care Standards Tbnl 2001–08, cmmr Judicial Appts Cmmn 2006–12, legal chair Restricted Patients Panel 2009–15; Int Soc on Family Law: gen sec 1985–91, vice-pres 1991–97; asst dep coroner Cambridge 1978–89; city cncllr Cambridge 1972–74, co cncllr Cambs 1974–77, ind person Standards Ctee Uttlesford District Cncl 2015–; *Books* A Textbook on Muslim Personal Law (1979, jtly, 3 edn 1998), Social Welfare Law (jtly, 1981), Interpersonal Conflict of Laws (1981), Family Law and Society (jtly, 1983, 6 edn 2008), Family Law and Immigrant Communities (1986), Blood Testing, Aids and DNA Profiling (jtly, 1990), Frontiers of Family Law (jt ed, 1993), Clarke, Hall and Morrison on Children (jt ed 2002–14); *Recreations* amateur dramatics; *Style—* His Hon David Pearl; ✉ Medical Practitioners Tribunal Service, 7th Floor, St James's Buildings, 79 Oxford Street, Manchester M1 6FQ

PEARLMAN, Joseph Joshua (Jerry); MBE; s of Samuel Myer Pearlman, MM (d 1981), and Sarah Rachael Pearlman (d 1983); *b* 26 April 1933; *Educ* Keighley Boys GS, King James VI GS Bishop Auckland, Univ of London (LLB); *m* 18 June 1962, Bernice; 2 da (Kate, Debbie); *Career* Nat Serv Lt RASC; admitted slr 1956; fndr Pearlman Grazin & Co 1958–95, conslt Zermansky & Ptnrs 2004–; advsr to Omukama of Bunyoro-Katara Uganda 1960–61 and 2000–; hon slr: Sikh Temple Leeds 1965–2005, Etz Chaim Synagogue Leeds 1997–2000, Hindu Temple Leeds 1998–2006; pres: Leeds and W Riding Medico Legal Soc 1975–76, Leeds Law Soc 1985–86; ministerial appointed memb Yorkshire Dales Nat Park Ctee 1983–92 and 1998–2007 (dep chm 2001–07, dep chm Planning Ctee 2000–02), memb Adjudication Ctee Slrs' Complaints Bureau 1986–88, chm Open Spaces Soc 1988, vice-chm Yorkshire Dales Millennium Tst 1996–98 (tstee 1996–), memb Nat Countryside Access Forum 1999–2006, memb Alwoodley Parish Cncl Leeds (chm Planning Ctee), memb Yorks Dales Local Access Forum 2009–, memb Leeds Local Access Forum 2009– (vice-chm 2011–), chm Yorks and Humber Regnl Access Forum 2012–, memb Alwoodley Neighbourhood Planning Gp; vice-pres Ramblers' Assoc 2004– (pres W Riding area, hon slr 1988–2008); Yorks Rural Lifetime Achievement Award 2009; Liveryman Patternmakers' Guild; *Recreations* rambling, eating, drinking; *Clubs* Royal Overseas League; *Style—* Jerry Pearlman, Esq, MBE; ✉ 10 Lakeland Crescent, Leeds LS17 7PR (☎ 0113 267 1114); Zermansky & Partners, 27 Park Square, Leeds LS1 5JS (☎ 01132 459766, fax 01132 467465, e-mail jjp@pearlman.co.uk)

PEARMAN, Hugh Geoffrey; s of late Douglas Pearman, and late Tegwyn, *née* Jones; *b* 29 May 1955; *Educ* Skinners' Sch Tunbridge Wells, Durham Univ (BA); *m* Kate Hobson; 2 s, 2 da; *Career* Building Design newspaper 1978–82 (latterly news ed), joined as gp ed BDP 1982, architecture and design critic Sunday Times 1986–, ed RIBA Jl 2006–; contrib: NY Times, Wall St Jl, The Scotsman, Architectural Record, Art Quarterly, World of Interiors, Royal Acad Magazine; co-fndr RIBA Stirling Prize 1996 (judge 1996–98); memb Cncl Architectural Assoc 2012 (hon vice-pres 2014–); visiting prof in architecture RCA 2015–; hon fell RIBA 2001; *Books* incl: Contemporary World Architecture, Airports: a century of architecture; *Recreations* reading (especially Victorian and Edwardian novels), walking, industrial archaeology; *Clubs* The Architecture, Critic's Circle, RSA; *Style—* Hugh Pearman, Esq; ✉ e-mail hughpearman@blueyonder.co.uk, website www.hughpearman.com, Twitter @hughpearman, Facebook /hugh.pearman.7

PEARMAN, Ian; *b* 1974; *Career* currently ceo AMV BBDO; young global ldr WEF; chm Nat Advertising Benevolent Soc (NABS), tstee The Media Tst; memb Mktg Gp of GB, fell Marketing Soc; *Style—* Ian Pearman, Esq

PEARS, David; *b* 24 April 1968; *Educ* City of London Sch; *Career* landowner; with The William Pears Group; *Style—* David Pears, Esq

PEARS, Trevor Steven; CMG (2011); *b* 1964; *Career* dir William Pears Gp; exec chm Pears Fndn; *Style—* Trevor Pears, Esq, CMG; ✉ Pears Foundation, Clive House, Old Brewery Mews, Hampstead, London NW3 1PZ

PEARSALL, Dr Fiona Jean Burns; da of Dr Ian Stewart Pearsall (d 1982), and Jean Dawson, *née* Burns; *b* 5 May 1963; *Educ* Craigholme Sch for Girls Glasgow, Hutchesons' GS Glasgow, Univ of Glasgow (MB ChB, MSc), FRCA (Dip), postgrad dip law; *Career* house offr (med and surgery) Western Infirmary Glasgow 1986–87, registrar (anaesthesia) Victoria Infirmary Glasgow 1988–91 (SHO (anaesthesia) 1987–88), research asst Univ of Glasgow 1991–93, SHO (anaesthesia) Western Infirmary Glasgow 1993; Glasgow Royal Infirmary: registrar (anaesthesia) 1993–94, sr registrar 1994–96, conslt anaesthetist 1996–; clinical dir Anaesthetics, ITU and Theatres N Glasgow Univ NHS Div 2004–; memb: GMC 1994–2003, Professional Conduct Ctee, BMA; medical screener; *Recreations* drawing and watercolour painting, music, ornithology; *Clubs* RSM; *Style—* Dr Fiona Pearsall; ✉ Directorate of Anaesthesia, Glasgow Royal Infirmary, Castle Street, Glasgow (☎ 0141 211 4620/1, fax 0141 211 4622)

PEARSE, Dr Barbara Mary (Mrs M S Bretscher); *b* Wraysbury, Bucks; *Educ* UCL (BSc, PhD, Jack Drummond Prize for Biochemistry); *m* M S Bretscher; 1 da (Nicola b 15 Aug 1978), 1 s (Andrew Jonathan b 15 Sept 1981); *Career* MRC Lab of Molecular Biology: jr research fell 1972–74, jr Beit meml fell 1974–77, SRC advanced fell 1977–82, memb scientific staff 1982–; appointed to MRC 1981–82, visiting prof Dept of Cell Biology Stanford Med Centre USA 1984–85; fell UCL 1995, fell commoner Lucy Cavendish Coll Cambridge 1997; K M Stott Prize for scientific research Newnham Coll Cambridge 1979, EMBO Gold Medal and Prize 1987; memb EMBO 1982, FRS 1988; *Publications* author of numerous articles, chapters and contribs to books and jls; *Recreations* wild flowers, planting trees, fresh landscapes; *Style—* Dr Barbara Pearse; ✉ MRC Laboratory of Molecular Biology, Francis Crick Avenue, Cambridge Biomedical Campus, Cambridge CB2 0QH (e-mail bulbeck@mrc-lmb.cam.ac.uk)

PEARSE, Lesley Margaret; da of Geoffrey Arthur Sargent, and Marie, *née* Glynn; *Educ* Northbrook C of E Sch London; *Children* 3 da (Lucy, Samantha, Joanne); *Career* writer; previously various dead-end jobs; memb: Romantic Writers Assoc, W Country Writers; pres (Bath and Wilts) NSPCC, patron Nat Parents' Assoc; *Books* Georgia (1993), Tara (1994), Charity (1995), Ellie (1996), Camellia (1997), Rosie (1998), Charlie (1999), Never Look Back (2000), Trust Me (2001), Father Unknown (2002), Till We Meet Again (2002), Remember Me (2003), Secrets (2004); *Recreations* gardening, reading, DIY; *Style—* Ms Lesley Pearse; ✉ c/o Darley Anderson, Estelle House, 11 Eustace Road, London SW6 1JB (☎ 020 7385 6652)

PEARSE WHEATLEY, Robin John; s of John Edward Clive Wheatley, MC, JP (d 1998), and Rosemarie Joy, *née* Malet-Veale; *b* 23 May 1949; *Educ* Leys Sch Cambridge, Inns of Court Sch of Law; *m* 1, 1979 (m dis 2003), Victoria Perez de Ascanio; 2 da (Victoria-Eugenia Amabel b 16 Dec 1983, Rafaela Eleanor b 11 Jan 1986), 1 s (Edward Victor Francisco de Borga b 23 Dec 1988); m 2, 4 May 2006, Hilary Bonnie Heald, da of Paul Nelson Heald and June MacKay Heald, of CA; *Career* called to the Bar Inner Temple 1971, recorder of the Crown Court 1992– (asst recorder 1987–92); councillor RBK and C 1974–78; chm London Area Nat Fedn Self Employed and Small Business 1989–92; Cons Parly candidate Lewisham Deptford 1983, Cons Euro candidate London South Inner 1989; Knight of Grace Constantine Order of St George; *Recreations* swimming, tennis, skiing; *Clubs* Hurlingham; *Style—* Robin Pearse Wheatley, Esq; ✉ Chalet St Hilaire, Préplan 163, 1911 Ovronnaz, Switzerland (☎ 00 41 273 064072)

PEARSON, David; s of Michael Pearson, of Cleethorpes, Lincs, and Joan, *née* Armstrong; *b* 2 September 1978, Cleethorpes, Lincs; *Educ* Lindsey Sch Cleethorpes, Franklin Coll Grimsby, Grimsby Art Coll (GNVQ), Leeds Coll of Art & Design (HND), Central St Martins Coll (BA); *Career* book designer Penguin Books Ltd 2002–07, dir Type As Image 2007–; RDI 2015; *Exhibitions* curator: Hans Schmoller: the Penguin Years (St Bride Library London) 2005, Designing Modern Life (Design Museum London) 2005, 70 Years of Penguin Design (V&A London) 2005, Type As Image (Kemistry Gallery London) 2014; exhibitor: The Book Corner (Br Library London) 2002, Designer of the Year (Design Museum London) 2005, The European Design Show (Design Museum London) 2005, Love & Money: the Best of British Design Now (Br Cncl London) 2006, X Exhibition (Shenzhen China) 2007; *Awards* winner: D&AD Yellow Pencil for Book Design 2005, Creative Review's Best in Book category 2005, Creative Review's Creative Futures for Typography 2005, D&D Yellow Pencil for Book Design 2014, Creative Review's Best In Category 2014, ABCD Awards 2014; nominee: Design Museum Designer of the Year 2005, D&AD Yellow Pencil for Book Design 2006, D&AD Yellow Pencil for Typography 2006; in-book selection for the D&AD Awards for Branding 2007, incl in The Guardian Britain's Top 50 Designers 2007, two in-book selections for the D&AD Awards for Book Design 2008, D&AD Yellow Pencil for Book Design 2009, two in-book selections for the D&AD Awards for Book Design and Typography 2011; *Clubs* Alliance Graphique Internationale (AGI) 2014; *Style—* David Pearson, Esq; ✉ Studio 1, 1 Back Hill, London EC1R 5HT (☎ 020 7837 6654, e-mail david@typeasimage.com, website www.typeasimage.com)

PEARSON, David Charles; s of Eric Charles Pearson (d 2010), and Joan Esdaile, *née* Wyatt (d 1997); *b* 14 June 1950; *Educ* Manchester Grammar, Blake Sch Minnesota USA (American Field Service Scholar), New Coll Oxford (MA); *m* 17 Dec 1982, Carmen Libera, da of Sidney Chellew; 1 s (Andrew b 16 April 1976), 1 da (Michelle Valentina b 25 April 1984); *Career* unit sales mangr Procter & Gamble Ltd 1971–75; Mars Inc: area sales mangr Pedigree Petfoods 1976–78, product gp mangr Pedigree Petfoods 1978–80, int mktg mangr Kal Kan LA USA 1980–81, gen mangr Effem Chile 1981–83; ptnr and mktg dir Crombie Eustace Ltd 1983–84, dir and gen mangr Pillsbury UK Ltd 1984–88; Sony UK Ltd: md Consumer Products 1988–98, dep md and chm European Consumer Mktg 1992–93, regnl dir Consumer Sales North 1993–95, md UK Sales Co 1995–98, memb Mgmnt Bd Consumer Gp Europe 1996–98, md 1997–98; md International Brands Pentland Gp plc 1998–2000, ceo NXT plc 2000–05, gp ceo QM Gp Ltd 2006–07; dir JPMorgan Japanese Investment Tst plc 2003–13, chm Vividas Gp plc 2007–09, chm innovITS Ltd 2007–13, bd mentor Criticaleye 2007–, chm TSB ITSS Steering Gp 2008–11; dir Simple Audio Ltd 2012–13; lectr at various mktg conferences 1989–; pres AFS International Scholarships UK 1971–74; winner Hall of Fame ITV Award for Mktg 1995; chm Mktg Soc Consumer Electrical/Electronics Sector 1993–98, chm Digital Engineering and Test Centre 2016–; memb: Mktg Soc 1978–80 and 1985–, CBI Mktg Strategy Gp 1988–93, Editorial Bd Jl of Brand Mgmnt 1993–2011, CBI Nat Cncl 1997–98; Duchy of Cornwall Market Advsy Gp 1991–96; LEA govr St Albans Girls' Sch 2002–06 (vice-chm 2003–06, chm 2006, hon govr 2007–), govr Univ of Beds 2006–12 (hon fell 2012); Liveryman Worshipful Co of Marketors 2004– (Ct Asst 2011–13, Warden 2013–16, Master 2016–17); fell Mktg Soc 1995, FRSA 1995, FCIM 2010; *Publications* regular contrib to Marketing Magazine; The 20 Ps of Marketing (2013); *Recreations* opera, walking, Manchester United FC; *Clubs* English Speaking Union, Cofradia del Vino Chileno, Cripplegate Ward, City Livery; *Style—* David Pearson, Esq; ✉ 9 The Warren, Harpenden, Herts AL5 2NH (☎ 01582 4762748, e-mail david@davidcpearson.co.uk, website www.davidcpearson.co.uk)

PEARSON, Dr Donald William Macintyre; s of William Clark Gilmour Pearson (d 1982), of New Cumnock, Ayshire, and Morag Macrae, *née* Macintyre (d 1961); *b* 5 September 1950; *Educ* Cumnock Acad Cumnock Ayrshire, Univ of Glasgow (BSc, MB ChB, MRCP); *m* 26 Aug 1972, Margaret Jessie Kennedy, da of James Harris, of Auchenleck, Ayrshire; 2 s (Andrew b 1979, Donald b 1984), 1 da (Gillian b 1977); *Career* registrar Univ Dept of Med Glasgow Royal Infirmary 1979–81, sr registrar in med diabetes and endocrinology Grampian Health Authy 1982–84, hon sr lectr Univ of Aberdeen 1984– (lectr in med 1981–82), conslt physician Aberdeen Royal Hosps NHS Tst 1984–; memb: Br Diabetic Assoc, Scottish Soc for Experimental Med, Aberdeen Medico-Chirurgical Soc, Scottish Soc of Physicians, BMA; MRCP 1979, FRCPGlas 1988, FRCPEd 1990; *Books* Carbohydrate Metabolism in Pregnancy and the New Born (ed with Sutherland and Stowers, 1989); *Recreations* golf; *Style—* Dr Donald Pearson; ✉ Diabetic Clinic, Woolman Hill, Aberdeen Royal Infirmary, Aberdeen (☎ 01224 681818)

PEARSON, Dr Graham Scott; CB (1990); s of Ernest Reginald Pearson (d 1996), and Alice, *née* Maclachlan (d 1987); *b* 20 July 1935; *Educ* Woodhouse Grove Sch Bradford, Univ of St Andrews (BSc, PhD); *m* 10 Sept 1960, Susan Elizabeth Meriton, da of Dr John Meriton Benn, CB (d 1992); 2 s (Gavin b 1963, Douglas b 1965); *Career* Univ of Rochester NY 1960–62, princ scientific offr Rocket Propulsion Estab 1967–69 (sr sci offr Westcott 1962–67), explosives and propellants liaison offr Br Embassy Washington DC 1969–72, asst dir Naval Ordnance Servs Bath 1973–76, tech advsr explosives and safety Chevaline 1976–79, princ superintendent Perme Westcott 1979–80, dep dir 1 and 2 Rarde Fort Halstead 1980–83, DG R&D Royal Ordnance Factories 1983–84, dir Chemical Def Estab Porton Down 1984–91, DG and chief exec Chemical and Biological Def Estab MOD Porton Down 1991–95, asst chief scientific advsr (non-proliferation) MOD 1995; Univ of Bradford: hon sr visiting research fell in peace studies 1996–97, hon visiting prof in int security 1997–; archivist Hidcote 2002–; CChem, FRSC 1985; *Books* The UNSCOM Saga: Chemical and Biological Weapons Non-Proliferation (1999), The Search for Iraq's Weapons of Mass Destruction: Inspection, Verification and Non-Proliferation (2005), Hidcote: The Garden and Lawrence Johnston (2007, 3 edn 2013), Lawrence Johnston The Creator of Hidcote (2010, 3 edn 2015); contrib: Advances in Inorganic and Radiochemistry Vol 8 (1966), Advances in Photochemistry Vol 3 (1964), Oxidation and Combustion Reviews Vol 3 and 4 (2 edn, 1969), Biological Weapons: Weapons of the Future (1993), Non-Conventional Weapons Proliferation in the Middle East (1993), US Security in an Uncertain Era (1993), Control of Dual Threat Agents: The Vaccines for Peace Programme (1994), Weapons Proliferation in the 1990s (1995), Strengthening The Biological Weapons Convention: Key Points for the Fourth Review Conference (1996), The Transfer of Sensitive Technologies and the Future of Control Regimes (1997), Dismantlement and Destruction of Chemical, Nuclear and Conventional Weapons (1997), Conversion of Former BTW Facilities (1988), Biological Weapons: Limiting the Threat (1999), Biological Warfare: Modern Offense and Defense (2000), Verification of the Biological and Toxin Weapons Convention (2000), Nuclear Disarmament: Obstacles to Banishing the Bomb (2000), Strengthening the Biological Weapons Convention: Key Points for the Fifth Review Conference (2001), Scientific and Technical Means of Distinguishing Between Natural and Other Outbreaks of Disease (2001), The Role of Biotechnology in Countering BTW Agents (2001), Maximising the Security and Development Benefits from the Biological and Toxin Weapons Convention (2002), The Implementation of Legally Binding Measures to Strengthen the Biological and Toxin Weapons Convention (2004), Public Health Response to Biological and Chemical Weapons (WHO Guidance) (2004), Encyclopedia of Bioterrorism Defense (2005, 2 edn 2011), Deadly Cultures: Biological Weapons since 1945 (2006), Strengthening the Biological Weapons Convention: Key Points for the Sixth Review Conference (2006), Chemical Warfare Agents: Toxicology and Treatment (2007), Terrorism, War or Disease? Unraveling the Use of Biological Weapons (2008), Strengthening the Biological Weapons Convention: Key Points for the Seventh Review Conference (2011), Turning International Obligations into Effective National Action: The 2007–2010 Intersessional Process of the Biological Weapons Convention (2011), The BTWC Seventh Review Conference: A Modest Outcome (2012), Moving Towards Enhanced Assurance of Compliance with the Biological and Toxin Weapons Convention (2013), Moving Towards Consensus (2014), Reviving the Intersessional Process: Achieving Effective Action (2015), Preventing Biological Threats: What You Can Do (2015), Strengthening the Biological Weapons Convention: Key Points for the Eighth Review Conference (2016); *Recreations* reading, archival research, walking, photography, foreign travel; *Style—* Dr Graham S Pearson, CB; ✉ Division of Peace Studies, University of Bradford, Bradford, West Yorkshire BD7 1DP (☎ 01274 234186, fax 01274 235240)

PEARSON, Hugh John Hampden; *Educ* Charterhouse, King's Coll London (LLB); *m*; 2 da, 1s; *Career* retired slr; treas South African Townships Health Fund 1989–2002, memb Cncl The Pensions Policy Inst 2002–07, chm Maltings Arts Dorchester 2007–, chm Roehampton Club Tst 2011–; *Recreations* reading, hill walking, croquet, bridge, opera; *Clubs* MCC, Roehampton; *Style—* John Pearson, Esq

PEARSON, Josie; MBE (2013); *b* 3 January 1986, Bristol; *Career* Paralympic athlete; achievements incl Gold medal (discus) Paralympic Games 2012; *Style—* Ms Josie Pearson, MBE; ✉ Twitter @josie_pearson

PEARSON, Sir Keith Samuel; kt (2010), JP, DL (Cambs 2011); *b* 6 April 1947, Fulwood, Lancs; *m* 22 June 1968, Christine Annette, *née* Pearce; 1 s (Julian Keith); *Career* BUPA UK Gen Mgmnt 1976–89, ceo BUPA Hong Kong 1989–93, ceo AON Thailand and Singapore 1993–97, ceo Summerlands Consultants Ltd 1997–2004; chair: NHS South Somerset PCG and PCT 1998–2004, NHS Norfolk Suffolk and Cambs Strategic Health Authy 2004–06, NHS East of England Strategic Health Authy 2006–10, NHS Confederation 2010–12, Health Educn England 2012–; chair Medical Revalidation Prog Bd GMC 2009–, chair Nat Advsy Gp on Health in Criminal Justice 2009–; magistrate 1999–; *Books* Children In Her Shadow (novel, 2011); *Clubs* Tanglin (Singapore), Royal Over-Seas League; *Style—* Sir Keith Pearson, JP, DL

PEARSON, (David) Lee; CBE (2009, OBE 2004, MBE 2000); *b* 4 February 1974; *Career* Paralympic equestrian; achievements incl: 3 Gold medals (individual dressage, freestyle dressage and team dressage) Paralympic Games 2000, 3 Gold medals (individual dressage, freestyle dressage and team dressage) Paralympic Games 2004, Nat Br Dressage Elementary Restricted Champion (able-bodied) 2004, 3 Gold medals (individual dressage, freestyle dressage and team dressage) Paralympic Games 2008, Gold medal (team dressage), Silver medal (individual dressage) and Bronze medal (freestyle dressage) Paralympic Games 2012; hon doctorate Univ of Staffs 2005; *Style—* Lee Pearson, Esq, CBE

PEARSON, Luke Neil; s of Raymond Pearson, and Sheila, *née* Bevan; *b* 15 December 1967, Portsmouth; *Educ* Central St Martins Sch of Art London (BA), RCA (MA); *Partner* Ana Saenz Castellano; 1 da (Marta Ana); *Career* early career as sr designer Studio X (with Ross Lovegrove, *qv*); co-fndr (with Tom Lloyd, *qv*) PearsonLloyd 1997–; projects incl: first class seat for Virgin Atlantic Airways, Artemide, Knoll International, Magis, Walter Knoll; visiting lectr Royal Coll of Art (running Platform 6 with Michael Marriott); *Awards* incl: FX Designers of the Year 2002, Industrial Product Design Award Design Week Awards 2004; *Style—* Luke Pearson, Esq; ✉ Pearson Lloyd, 117 Drysdale Street, London N1 6ND (☎ 020 7033 4440)

PEARSON, Maxwell John (Max); *b* 30 July 1959; *Educ* King's Sch Canterbury, Keele Univ; *m* 2 s; *Career* journalist and broadcaster; BBC radio: local radio 1982–84, prodr Today Prog (Radio 4) 1984–85; English language output ed UAE govt Dubai 1985–87, freelance corr NBC (USA) radio 1985–87, reporter (travelled by bicycle in Indian sub-continent

P

with tape recorder) BBC World Serv, CBC Canada and ABC Aust 1987–88; presenter BBC radio 1988–; progs incl: Newshour (World Serv), The World Tonight (Radio Four), The World Today (World Serv), live hosting of World Serv output from various locations worldwide incl elections and interviews with world ldrs; Sony Radio Acad Gold Award News Presenter of the Year 1997, Foreign Press Assoc Silver Award Radio Story of hte Year 2008, Sony Radio Acad Gold Award News and Current Affrs Prog of the Year 2009; *Recreations* golf, tennis; *Clubs* Royal Ashdown Forest Golf, Artisans Section (Cantelupe); *Style—* Max Pearson, Esq; ✉ BBC World Service, BBC Broadcasting House, Portland Place, London W1A 1AA

PEARSON, Nicholas; *m* Daisy Garnett; *Career* publishing dir 4th Estate; *Style—* Nicholas Pearson, Esq; ✉ 4th Estate, 1 London Bridge Street, London SE1 9GF

PEARSON, Nicholas (Nick); *b* 24 March 1951; *Educ* King Edward Sch Birmingham, Lincoln Coll Oxford (BA); *m* 1982, Chooi Yong Fong; 1 s (Oliver b 1985), 1 da (Sarah b 1989); *Career* Herbert Smith & Co 1974–79; Baker & McKenzie: based Hong Kong 1979–88, ptnr 1982–2006, based London 1988–2006, head Global Dispute Resolution Dept and Civil Fraud Gp until 2006; insolvency practitioner 1990–; memb Law Soc; *Recreations* tennis, cricket, walking; *Clubs* MCC; *Style—* Nick Pearson, Esq

PEARSON, Dr Richard Martin; s of late Leonard Louis Pearson, of Bournemouth, and late Anne, *née* Tobias; *b* Kilwinning, N Ayrshire; *Educ* Royal GS High Wycombe, Gonville & Caius Coll Cambridge, St Mary's Hosp London; *Career* house surgn Addenbrooke's Hosp Cambridge 1967, house physician St Mary's Hosp London 1968, res fell and registrar Hammersmith Hosp 1971–73, sr registrar Royal Free Hosp 1977–80; conslt physician: Victoria and Kilton Hosps Bassetlaw 1980–81, Queen's Hosp Romford and St Bartholomew's Hosps 1981–2011; FRCP; *Recreations* opera, fitness, dance; *Clubs* Savile; *Style—* Dr Richard Pearson; ✉ London Medical Centre, 144 Harley Street, London W1G 7LD (☎ 020 7935 0023, fax 020 7354 1501)

PEARSON, Sara Ann; da of John Vernon Henry Franklin, of Robertsbridge, E Sussex, and Jeanette Marguerite, *née* Webster; *b* 1 August 1953; *Educ* Rosary Priory Convent; *m* 4 Oct 1974 (m dis 1999); 2 da (Chloe Ann b 15 March 1978, Clementine Sara b 29 Nov 1985), 1 s (Charlie Jon Eric b 29 Oct 1979); *Career* Sunday Telegraph, fndr The SPA Way Ltd and Cogn8; *Recreations* travel, running, building bonfires; *Style—* Mrs Sara Pearson

PEARSON LUND, Peter Graham; s of Douglas Pearson Lund, CBE (d 1974), and Honor Winifred (d 1996); *b* 9 September 1947; *Educ* Shiplake Coll Henley, Guildford Sch of Art; *m* 16 Nov 1968, Isabelle McLachlan; 2 s (Piers b 19 Oct 1969, Oliver b 10 Dec 1971); *Career* Tilney & Co 1969–70, Cazenove and Co 1970–73, Antony Gibbs 1973–75; md Henderson Unit Trust Management (dir Henderson Administration Ltd) 1975–85, Gartmore Fund Managers Ltd (dir Gartmore plc) 1985–96; principal Gartmore Fund Managers Ltd 1996–99; chief exec Rathbone Unit Trust Management Ltd 1999–, memb Bd Rathbone Bros plc 2005–; *Recreations* tennis, skiing, sailing; *Style—* Peter Pearson Lund, Esq; ✉ Rathbone Unit Trust Management Limited, 159 New Bond Street, London W1S 2UD

PEARSON OF RANNOCH, Baron (Life Peer UK 1990), of Bridge of Gaur in the District of Perth and Kinross; Malcolm Everard MacLaren Pearson; s of late Col John MacLaren Pearson; *b* 20 July 1942; *Educ* Eton; *m* 1, 1965 (m dis 1970), Francesca Frua, da of Giuseppe Frua de Angeli; 1 da (Hon Silvia Maria Francesca (Hon Mrs Le Marchant) b 1966); m 2, 1977 (m dis 1995), Hon (Francesca) Mary Charteris, o da of late Baron Charteris of Amisfield, GCB, GCVO, QSO, OBE, PC; 2 da (Hon Marina b 1980, Hon Zara Alexandra Mary b 1984); m 3, 1997, Caroline, da of Maj Hugh Launcelot St Vincent Rose; *Career* chm PWS Holdings plc; hon treas CNAA 1983–93; memb House of Lords Select Ctee on the European Communities 1991–96; hon pres of RESCARE (nat soc for people with learning disabilities and their families) 1994–; patron The Register of Chinese Herbal Medicine 1998–; Hon LLD from CNAA; *Clubs* White's, Swinley Forest Golf; *Style—* The Lord Pearson of Rannoch; ✉ House of Lords, London SW1A 0PW

PEART, Susan Rhona; *Educ* Felixstowe Coll; *Career* Cosmopolitan magazine 1979–84, Daily Express 1984–87; ed: Sunday Express Magazine 1989–91 (dep ed 1987–89), Weekend Times 1992–93, YOU magazine 2000– (dep ed 1993–2000); Supplement of the Year Br Press Awards 2008, 2009 and 2010, runner up Catherine Pakenham Award 1981; chairwoman BSME 2004 (memb 1987); *Recreations* entertaining, theatre, films; *Style—* Ms Susan Peart; ✉ e-mail sue.peart@mailonsunday.co.uk

PEASE, William Simon; *see:* Wardington, 3 Baron

PEASNELL, Prof Kenneth Vincent (Ken); *b* 2 February 1945; *Educ* Univ of Sheffield (Postgrad Dip Business Studies), LSE (MSc), Lancaster Univ (PhD); *m*; 2 c; *Career* trainee accountant Melman Pryke & Co London 1961–67, fin analyst IBM (UK) Ltd 1968–69; Lancaster Univ: P D Leake res fell Dept of Accounting and Fin 1970–72, research fell ICRA 1972–75, lectr in accounting and fin 1976–77, Wolfson prof of accounting and fin 1977–87 and 1998–, head Dept of Accounting and Fin 1978–83, assoc dean Mgmnt Sch 1987–91 and 1994–97, research prof of accounting and dir ICRA 1987–97; memb Lancaster Univ: Fin Ctee 1980–83 and 1990–91, Academic Promotions Ctee 1986–87, Ctee for Research 1986–97, Ctee for Colleges 1991, Budgeting and Monitoring Ctee 1994–97, Senate 1978–83, 1990–91 and 1998–, Univ Cncl 1987–91; visiting prof: Dept of Accounting Univ of Sydney 1983–84, Graduate Sch of Business Stanford Univ April-July 1984; memb Editorial Bd: Accounting Review 1977–82 and 1989–93, Accounting and Business Res 1980–81, Journal of Business Fin and Accounting 1980–84; ed Accounting and Business Research 1993–, Issues in Accounting 1995–, Br Accounting Review 1998–2001; external examiner: Univ of Birmingham 1979–80, Univ of Bristol 1979–82, Univs of Manchester and Warwick 1981–83, Manchester Business Sch 1987–90, LSE 1993–; external assessor for professorial or readership appointments at numerous univs; memb Exec Ctee Cncl of Depts of Accounting Studies 1979–84, chm Assoc of Univ Teachers of Accounting 1981–82; ICAEW: memb Res Sub-Ctee of Tech and Res Ctee 1979–82, memb Tech Ctee 1985–87, memb Educn and Training Advsy Gp 1987–90; memb Academic Accountants' Panel Accounting Standards Bd 1990– (Accounting Standards Ctee 1987–90), academic advsr to Accounting Standards Ctee on Off-Balance Sheet Financing 1988–90, memb Business and Mgmnt Studies Sub-Ctee of Univ Grants Ctee 1984–89; Univs Funding Cncl: chm Accountancy Panel 1989, Accountancy Subject advsr 1989–91; dir and hon treas Dukes Playhouse Ltd 1988–93; Distinguished Academic of the Year Award Chartered Assoc of Cert Accountants and Br Accounting Assoc 1996; FCA 1975 (ACA 1967); *Publications* author of numerous articles in academic, professional and miscellaneous publications and contribs to books; British Financial Markets and Institutions (with C W R Ward, 1985, 2 edn with J Piesse and C W R Ward, 1995), Off-Balance Sheet Financing (with R A Yaansah, 1988), Discounting in Corporate Financial Reporting (with C J Lovejoy, M Y Talukdar and P A Taylor, 1989); *Style—* Prof Ken Peasnell; ✉ Management School, Lancaster University, Lancaster LA1 4YX (☎ 01524 593977, fax 01524 594334, e-mail k.peasnell@lancaster.ac.uk)

PEAT, Adam Erskine; OBE (2009); s of late Raymond B B Peat, and late Cynthia Elisabeth Peat; *b* 30 November 1948; *Educ* Stowmarket County GS, Pembroke Coll Oxford (open exhbn, MA); *m* 1973, Christine Janet, da of late James Huzzard Champion; 1 s (Andrew James b July 1979), 1 da (Joanna Jane b Nov 1982); *Career* Welsh Office: joined 1972, princ 1977, private sec to Sec of State 1982–83, asst sec 1984; acting dir CADW 1984–85, head Housing Div Welsh Office 1985–89, chief exec Housing for Wales 1989–98, dir Housing Dept Welsh Office 1998–99, dir Local Govt, Communities and Culture Gp Nat Assembly for Wales 1999–2003, ombudsman Public Services Wales 2003–; *Style—* Adam Peat, Esq, OBE; ✉ The Public Services Ombudsman for Wales, 1 Ffordd yr Hen Gae, Pencoed CF35 5LJ (☎ 01656 641150, fax 01656 641199)

PEAT, Prof Jeremy Alastair; OBE (2012); s of J S G Peat, and Pamela Peat; *b* 20 March 1945, Haywards Heath, W Sussex; *Educ* St Paul's Sch, Univ of Bristol, UCL; *m*; 2 da; *Career* econ advsr: Br Embassy Bangkok 1972–74, Govt of Botswana 1980–84, HM Treasy 1984–85, Scotland Office 1985–93, gp chief economist Royal Bank of Scotland 1993–2005; memb Bd of Govrs and nat govr for Scotland BBC 2005–06 (chm Audit Ctee 2005–06), memb BBC Tst and nat tstee for Scotland 2006–11, chair BBC Pension Tst 2005–12; dir David Hume Inst 2005–14; memb: Competition Cmmn 2005–14, Bd Royal Zoological Soc of Scotland 2010– (chair Bd of Tstees 2012–), Bd Sottish Enterprise 2011–, Competition and Markets Authy 2014–; former memb Cncl Scottish Econ Soc, vice-chair Scottish HE Funding Cncl 2001–06; columnist Herald Newspaper 2005–; former visiting prof Univ of Edinburgh Sch of Mgmnt, hon prof Heriot Watt Univ, visiting prof Univ of Strathclyde Int Public Policy Inst 2014–; Hon LLD Univ of Aberdeen, Hon DLitt Heriot Watt Univ; FCIBS, FRSE, FRSA, FRCPE; *Books* An Illustrated Guide to the Scottish Economy (with Stephen Boyle, 1999), Scotland in a Global Economy; the 2020 Vision (jt ed, 2002); *Recreations* golf, walking dogs, reading; *Style—* Prof Jeremy Peat, OBE; ☎ 07770 544914, e-mail jeremy.a.peat@gmail.com

PECKHAM, Prof (Lady) Catherine Stevenson; CBE (1998); da of Dr Alexander King, CBE, CMG, of Paris, and Sarah Maskell, *née* Thompson; *b* 7 March 1937; *Educ* St Paul's Girls' Sch, Univ of London (MB BS, MD); *m* 7 Oct 1958, Prof Sir Michael John Peckham, *qv*, s of William Stuart Peckham (d 1981); 3 s (Alexander b 1962, Daniel Gavin b 1964, Robert Shannan b 1965); *Career* reader in community med Charing Cross Hosp Med Sch 1977–85, prof of paediatric epidemiology Inst of Child Health and hon conslt Hosp for Sick Children Great Ormond St 1985– (sr lectr and hon conslt 1975–77), hon conslt Public Health Laboratory 1985–; memb: US Fulbright Cmmn 1987–95, Med Advsy Ctee Br Cncl 1992–95, Advtg Standards Authy 1993–99, New Millennium Experience Co Bd 1998–99, Nuffield Cncl on Bioethics 1999–, Cncl Inst of Educn 1999–; FFPHM 1980, FRCP 1988, FRCPath 1992, FRCOG 1994, FMedSci 1998 (founding fell); *Recreations* flute; *Style—* Prof Catherine Peckham, CBE; ✉ Institute of Child Health, Guilford Street, London WC1

PECKHAM, Prof Sir Michael John; kt (1995); s of William Stuart Peckham (d 1981), and Gladys Mary, *née* Harris (d 1998); *b* 2 August 1935; *Educ* William Jones W Monmouthshire Sch, St Catharine's Coll Cambridge (MA, MD), UCH Med Sch; *m* 7 Oct 1958, Prof Catherine Stevenson Peckham, CBE, *qv*, da of Dr Alexander King, CMG, CBE, of London; 3 s (Alexander b 1962, Daniel Gavin b 1964, Robert Shannan b 1965); *Career* Capt RAMC 1960–62; clinical res cncl scholar MRC Paris 1965–67, dean Inst of Cancer Res London 1984–86 (sr lectr 1972–74, prof 1974–86), civilian conslt to RN 1975–86, dir Br Postgrad Med Fedn 1986–90, dir of res and devpt Dept of Health 1991–95, dir Sch of Public Policy UCL 1996–; chm Nat Educn Res Forum 1999–; special tstee Guy's Hosp & St Thomas' Hosp Bd of Special Tstees 1996–2000; pres: Euro Soc of Therapeutic Radiology and Oncology 1984–85, Br Oncology Assoc 1986–88, Fedn of Euro Cancer Socs 1989–91; ed-in-chief European Journal of Cancer 1990–95, fndr Bob Champion Cancer Tst; memb New Millennium Experience Co Bd 1998–99; former memb special health authy: Hosps for Sick Children Gt Ormond St, Brompton and Nat Heart Hosp, Hammersmith Hosp, Imperial Cancer Res Fund (vice-chm Cncl); artist: solo exhbns Oxford, London and Edinburgh 1965–; Hon DSc Loughborough Univ of Technol 1992; Dr (hc): Université de Franche-Compté Besançon 1991, Katholieke Universiteit Leuven 1993; hon fell St Catharine's Coll Cambridge 1998; foreign assoc memb Nat Acad of Sciences Inst of Med Washington 1994; FRCP, FRCR, FRCPath, FRCPG, FRCS; *Recreations* painting; *Style—* Prof Sir Michael Peckham

PECORELLI, Giuseppe; s of Leopoldo Pecorelli, of Rivello, Italy, and Maria, *née* Sersale; *b* 30 April 1939, Rivello, Italy; *Educ* Giorgio Vasari Coll of Accountancy Arezzo Italy; *m* 28 Nov 1964, Penelope Ann, *née* Birch; 3 s (Daniel Leopoldo Enrico, Nicholas Luigi Paolo (twins) b 24 July 1966, Giuseppe Patrick 6 Jan 1970), 1 da (Marie-Louise Elizabetta b 13 June 1968); *Career* md Trusthouse Forte Hotels and main bd dir Forte plc 1965–85 (also sometime pres Travel Lodge USA), chief exec Ciga Hotels (owned by the Aga Khan) 1985–87, dir Sun Int 1987–90, fndr and chm Exclusive Hotels 1988–; FHCIMA; *Recreations* golf, oil painting; *Clubs* North Hants Golf; *Style—* Giuseppe Pecorelli, Esq; ✉ Exclusive Hotels, Pennyhill Park Hotel & Spa, London Road, Bagshot, Surrey GU19 5EU (☎ 01276 478428, e-mail barbara@exclusive.co.uk)

PEDDIE, Hon Ian James Crofton; QC (1992); s of Lord Peddie, MBE, JP (Life Peer; d 1978), and Lady Hilda Peddie (d 1985); *b* 1945; *Educ* Gordonstoun, UCL (LLB); *m* 1976, Susan Renée, da of Edmund John Brampton Howes; 2 s (James, Thomas), 2 da (Kate, Nichola); *Career* called to the Bar Inner Temple 1971; recorder 1997– (asst recorder 1993–97); *Style—* The Hon Ian Peddie, QC; ✉ Garden Court Chambers, 57–60 Lincoln's Inn Fields, London WC2A 3LS (☎ 020 7993 7600)

PEDLER, Garth; s of Thomas Wakeham Pedler (d 1984), of Exeter, and Ruby, *née* Cornish (d 1996); *b* 21 February 1946; *Educ* King's Coll Taunton; *Career* with Touche Ross & Co 1969–73, independent taxation conslt; contributor on fiscal matters: Sunday Telegraph 1991–96, Sunday Times 1993–97; developed BR's first fully funded annual omphalotic national rail timetable, centred on Totnes 1996–2003; memb Old Boys' Ctee King's Coll Taunton 1972–; FCA, ATII (1969–2014); *Books* The 9.5mm Vintage Film Encyclopaedia (ed and jt author), A Prep School in Somerset: King's College Taunton Junior School to 1982, Rail Operations Viewed from South Devon, Biography of Joan Morgan, My Career in Accountancy; contributor to Classic Images USA 1982–93; *Recreations* rambling, swimming and collection of hardback books; *Style—* Garth Pedler, Esq; ✉ Hay Hill, Totnes, Devon TQ9 5LH

PEDLEY, Prof Timothy John; s of Richard Rodman Pedley (d 1973), and Jean Mary Mudie Pedley, *née* Evans (d 2002); *b* 23 March 1942, Leicester; *Educ* Rugby, Trinity Coll Cambridge (Wrangler, Mayhew Prize, MA, PhD, ScD); *m* 1965, Avril Jennifer Martin Uden, da of B G Grant-Uden (d 1990); 2 s (Jonathan Richard b 1968, Simon Grant b 1969); *Career* post-doctoral fell Mechanics Dept Johns Hopkins Univ 1966–68, lectr Physiological Flow Studies Unit and Dept of Mathematics Imperial Coll London 1968–73; Dept of Applied Mathematics and Theoretical Physics (DAMTP) Univ of Cambridge: successively asst dir of research, lectr then reader in biological fluid dynamics 1973–89, G I Taylor prof of fluid mechanics 1996–2009, head 2000–05, emeritus prof of fluid mechanics 2009–; prof of applied mathematics Univ of Leeds 1990–96 (head Dept of Applied Mathematics 1991–94); Gonville & Caius Coll Cambridge: fell and dir of applied mathematics 1973–89, professorial fell 1996–2009, life fell 2009–; pres: World Cncl for Biomechanics 2002–06, Inst of Maths and its Applications 2004–05, Cambridge Philosophical Soc 2006–07, Int Union of Theoretical and Applied Mechanics 2008–12; ed Jl of Fluid Mechanics 2000–06; lectures: GI Taylor (Cambridge) 1998, Clifford (Tulane Univ) 2002, Rutherford (Royal Soc and RSNZ) 2003, Talbot (Univ of Illinois) 2004, Prandtl Meml 2007, Ascher H Shapiro (MIT) 2010; memb: American Soc of Mechanical Engrs 1990, Soc for Experimental Biology 1993, European Mechanics Soc 1994 (memb Cncl 1995–2000), Soc of Mathematical Biology 1990, London Mathematical Soc 1997, American Physical Soc 2001, Cncl EPSRC 2009–13, Cncl Royal Soc 2012–13; sometime govr: Perse Sch Cambridge, Batley GS; Adams Prize Univ of Cambridge 1977, Gold medal Inst of Maths and its Applications 2008; Hon DSc Imperial Coll London 2013; foreign assoc US Nat Acad of Engrg 1999, foreign fell Acad Sci-India 2007, C V Raman chair Indian Acad of Scis 2016; sr fell EPSRC 1995–2000; FIMA 1981, FRS 1995; fell American Inst of Med and Biological Engrg 2001, fell American Physical Soc 2005, memb

Academia Europaea 2011; *Books* Scale effects in animal locomotion (ed, 1977), The mechanics of the circulation (jtly, 1978), The fluid mechanics of large blood vessels (1980), Biological fluid dynamics (co-ed, 1995); *Recreations* bird watching, reading, crosswords; *Style—* Prof Timothy Pedley; ✉ Department of Applied Mathematics & Theoretical Physics, University of Cambridge, Centre for Mathematical Sciences, Wilberforce Road, Cambridge CB3 0WA (✆ 01223 339842, fax 01223 760497, e-mail tjp3@damtp.cam.ac.uk)

PEDRICK, Susan (Sue); da of Wilf Rolph, and Maureen, *née* Cooper; *b* 15 May 1978; *Educ* Walbottle Sch, Newcastle Coll; *m* 26 Sept 2015, Wayne Pedrick; 1 da (Ellie b 29 May 2008); *Career* swimmer; 50m freestyle: personal best 25.57 secs 1998, Silver medal European Short Course Championships 1996, Gold medal Cwlth Games 1998, Bronze medal European Short Course Championships (Cwlth record) 1998; 100m freestyle: personal best 55.17 secs 1998, Bronze medal (relay) European Championships 1995, Gold medal Cwlth Games (Games record) 1998, Gold medal (relay) Cwlth Games 1994, Silver medal (relay) Cwlth Games 1998, Gold medal European Short Course (Cwlth record) 1998, Gold medal European Championships Istanbul 1999; personal best 100m butterfly 59.95 secs (first British woman to swim inside one minute); 100m individual medley: Gold medal European Short Course Championships 1996 (Bronze medal 1998); Bronze medal (relay) 100m medley Cwlth Games 1998; 200m individual medley: personal best 2 mins 15.39 secs 1998, Gold Medal European Shortcourse Championships 1996, Bronze medal World Short Course Championships 1998, Bronze medal Cwlth Games (British record) 1998, Bronze medal European Short Course Championships 1998; memb Olympic squad 1996 and 2000; centre mangr Riverside Community Resource Tst Kent; memb Millennium Youth Games Project; hon ambass of Newcastle 1998; *Awards* Newcastle sports personality of the year 1998; *Recreations* spending a lot of time with my family; *Clubs* City of Newcastle Swimming; *Style—* Mrs Sue Pedrick

PEEBLES, Robert Andrew (Andy); s of Robert Peebles (d 1961), and Mary Jean, *née* Simmonds (d 1992); *b* 13 December 1948; *Educ* Bishop's Stortford Coll, Bournemouth Coll of Tech; *Career* radio presenter: BBC Radio Manchester 1973, Piccadilly Radio Manchester 1974–78, BBC World Serv 1978–88, BBC Radio One 1978–92, BBC Schools Radio 1983–87, BBC Radio Sport 1983–2005, BBC Radio Lancashire 1992–99, BBC Radio Two 1997–2002, BBC Radio North 1999–2005, Jazz FM 2003–05, Smooth Radio 2004–13, Gold Radio 2013–14; *Books* The Lennon Tapes (1981), The Elton John Tapes (1981); *Recreations* sport, cinema, photography; *Clubs* Lancashire CCC; *Style—* Andy Peebles, Esq; ✉ c/o Jo Parsons, e-mail info@musicmajors.co.uk

PEEL, Fiona Natalie; OBE (2001), DL; *Educ* St Thomas' Hosp London (SRN), Univ of Exeter (BA), Univ of Wales Cardiff (LLM); *m* 1973 (m dis 2006), Hon Robert Michael Arthur Peel; 3 da (Kathryn b 1978, Hermione b 1979, Eleanor b 1981); *Career* chair: Gwent Community Health NHS Tst 1993–98, Cancer Servs Coordinating Gp Wales 1997–2010, Gwent HA 1998–2003, Cardiff Local Health Bd 2006–09; memb Gen Optical Cncl 2009–; memb: Cncl UWCM 1996–2003, Cncl Univ of Wales Cardiff 2000–03, Cncl Cardiff Univ 2004–, Cncl GMC 2004–08; chm Welsh Wound Innovation Initiative 2014–; involved with Tenovus Cancer Support; *Clubs* Cardiff and County; *Style—* Mrs Fiona Peel, OBE, DL

PEEL, Jane Elizabeth; da of William Richard Peel (d 1994), and Josephine Irene, *née* Stewart (d 1995); *b* 4 October 1960; *Educ* Highbury Hill HS London, Harlow Tech Coll (NCTJ Cert), Fletcher Sch of Law and Diplomacy Medford MA; *Career* reporter Barnet Press/ Enfield Gazette 1981–84, sr reporter Lincolnshire Echo 1984–85; BBC: reporter BBC Radio Lincolnshire 1985–86, news prodr BBC Essex 1986–87, news ed BBC Essex 1987–89, reporter BBC national radio 1989–90, home and legal affrs corr 1990–2001, news corr 2001–; *Recreations* running, waterskiing, snow skiing; *Style—* Ms Jane Peel; ✉ BBC News, New Broadcasting House, B1D, Portland Place, London W1A 1AA (✆ 020 3614 3666, e-mail jane.peel@bbc.co.uk)

PEEL, Prof John David Yeadon; s of Prof Edwin Arthur Peel (d 1992), of Birmingham, and Nora Kathleen, *née* Yeadon (d 1988); *b* 13 November 1941; *Educ* King Edward's Sch Birmingham, Balliol Coll Oxford (MA), LSE (PhD), Univ of London (DLit); *m* 4 Sept 1969 (m dis 2000), Jennifer Christine Ferial, da of Maj Kenneth Nathaniel Pare; 3 s (David Nathaniel Yeadon b 16 March 1972, Timothy James Olatokunbo b 27 Jan 1974, Francis Edwin b 30 March 1977); m 2, 8 April 2014, Anne Ogbigbo; *Career* asst lectr and lectr in sociology Univ of Nottingham 1966–70, lectr in sociology LSE 1970–73, visiting reader in sociology and anthropology Univ of Ife Nigeria 1973–75, Charles Booth prof of sociology Univ of Liverpool 1975–89 (dean of Faculty of Social and Environmental Studies 1985–88), visiting prof of anthropology and sociology Univ of Chicago 1982–83, prof of anthropology and sociology with reference to Africa SOAS Univ of London 1989–2007 (dean of undergraduate studies 1990–94, emeritus prof 2007–), Birkbeck lectr in ecclesiastical history Univ of Cambridge 2009, Winchester lectr in world religions Univ of Oxford 2011; ed Africa (jl of Int African Inst) 1979–86, gen ed Int African Library 1985–; writer of numerous scholarly articles in Africanist, anthropological and sociological jls; Amaury Talbot Prize for African Anthropology 1983 and 2000, Herskovits Award for African Studies (USA) 1984 and 2001; memb Assoc of Social Anthropologists 1979, pres African Studies Assoc of UK 1996–98; Hon DLitt Univ of Birmingham 2012; FBA 1991 (vice-pres 1999–2000); *Books* Aladura: A Religious Movement among the Yoruba (1968), Herbert Spencer: The Evolution of a Sociologist (1971), Ijeshas and Nigerians: The Incorporation of a Yoruba Kingdom (1983), Religious Encounter and the Making of the Yoruba (2000), Christianity and Social Change in Africa: Essays in Honor of J D Y Peel (festschrift, 2005), Christianity, Islam and Orisha-religion: Three Traditions in Comparison and Interaction (2015); *Recreations* gardening, fell walking, French great churches; *Style—* Prof J D Y Peel, FBA; ✉ Department of Anthropology and Sociology, School of Oriental and African Studies (University of London), Thornhaugh Street, London WC1H 0XG (✆ 020 7898 4407, e-mail jdy.peel@btinternet.com)

PEEL, Richard Martin; s of Robert Horace Peel, of Boston, Lincs and Joan Ella, *née* Martin; *b* 23 April 1952; *Educ* Boston GS, Lanchester Poly (BA); *m* 26 May 1984, Diane Joan, da of Laurie Almond, of Perth, Ontario, Canada; 1 da (Charlotte Emma b 1976); *Career* cricket corr Northampton Chronicle and Echo 1976–79 (journalist 1973–79), press offr Milton Keynes Devpt Corp 1979–83; BBC: press offr 1983, sr press offr 1983–85, chief press offr 1985–87, chief asst info 1987–88, head of publicity and PR BBC News and Current Affrs 1988–93, head of communications and info BBC News and Current Affrs 1993–96, controller of communication and info BBC News 1996–97, controller of mktg and communication BBC News 1997–98; dir corp affrs England and Wales Cricket Bd 1998–2000, dir of public affairs, nations and regions ITC 2000–03, communications advsr Ofcom 2003; md, Communications and Public Reporting The Audit Cmmn 2004–06, dir RPPR; sr ptnr HPL 2006–08; dir corporate affrs Camelot 2008–10, md RPPR 2011; dir and tstee Youth Music, pres Media Soc; memb: BAFTA, RTS, London Business Sch Alumni; MCIM; *Recreations* walking, reading, music; *Clubs* Reform, Lord's Taverners, Cricket Writers; *Style—* Richard Peel, Esq; ✉ Lower Farm, Buckland, Buckinghamshire HP22 5HY (mobile 07805 083595, e-mail rppr@hotmail.co.uk, website www.rppr.biz)

PEEL, 3 Earl (UK 1929); Sir William James Robert Peel; 8 Bt (GB 1800), GCVO (2006), PC (2006), DL (N Yorks 1998); Viscount Peel (UK 1895) and Viscount Clanfield (UK 1929); s of 2 Earl Peel (d 1969, himself gs of 1 Viscount, who was in turn 5 s of Sir Robert Peel, 2 Bt, the distinguished statesman); *b* 3 October 1947; *Educ* Ampleforth, Tours Univ, RAC Cirencester; *m* 1, 1973, Veronica Naomi Livingston, da of Alastair Timpson; 1 s (Ashton Robert Gerard, Viscount Clanfield), 1 da (Lady Iona Joy Julia b 1978); m 2, 1989, Hon Charlotte Clementine, *née* Soames, da of Baron Soames, GCMG, GCVO, CH, CBE, PC (Life Peer, d 1987), and formerly w of (Alexander) Richard Hambro, *qv*; 1 da (Lady Antonia Mary Catherine b 14 Dec 1991); *Heir* s, Viscount Clanfield; *Career* vice-pres Game and Wildlife Conservation Tst 2008– (formerly chm, pres until 2008), chm The Standing Conference for Countryside Sports, former pres Yorkshire Wildlife Tst; memb: Prince's Cncl 1993–, Exec Ctee The Moorland Assoc, Cncl for English Nature, Bd The Countryside Movement, Bd Countryside Alliance; former memb Yorkshire Dales National Park Ctee, former pres Gun Trade Assoc; Lord Warden of the Stannaries and Keeper of the Privy Seal of the Duke of Cornwall 1994–2006, Lord Chamberlain to HM's Household 2006–, chllr Royal Victorian Order 2006–; *Style—* The Earl Peel, GCVO, DL; ✉ Eelmire, Masham, Ripon, North Yorkshire HG4 4PF

PEGDEN, His Hon Judge Jeffrey Vincent; QC (1996); s of George Vincent Pegden (d 1994), and Stella Blanche Katherine, *née* Maxted (d 2008); *b* 24 June 1950; *Educ* Wallington County GS, Univ of Hull (LLB, pres Univ Law Soc); *m* 5 Sept 1981, Delia Mary, da of Paul and Lucy Coonan; 1 s (Oliver Roderick William b 30 May 1982), 1 da (Antonia Catherine Lucy b 15 Aug 1985); *Career* called to the Bar Inner Temple 1973 (bencher 2002); recorder 1996–2007, circuit judge (South Eastern Circuit) 2007–; Bar Cncl of England and Wales rep Criminal Bar Assoc 1993–95; judicial memb SE Circuit; course dir ciminal seminars Judicial Coll 2010–; Liveryman Worshipful Co of Clockmakers 2002; FRSA; *Recreations* music, reading, walking, gardening, sailing; *Style—* His Hon Judge Pegden, QC

PEGG, Jonathan; s of Mr and Mrs B T Pegg; *b* 21 April 1973, Senegal; *Educ* Cheam Sch, Eton, Univ of East Anglia; *m*; *Career* literary agent Curtis Brown 1997–2008, fndr Jonathan Pegg Literary Agency 2008–; *Clubs* Century; *Style—* Jonathan Pegg, Esq; ✉ Jonathan Pegg Literary Agency, 32 Batoum Gardens, London W6 7QD (✆ 020 7603 6830, website www.jonathanpegg.com)

PEGG, Dr Michael Stuart; s of Gilbert Seaton Pegg, of Reigate, Surrey and Waldy Greta, *née* Jonsson; *b* 15 June 1948; *Educ* The GS Reigate, UCL, Westminster Med Sch (BSc, MB BS), Cardiff Law Sch (LLM); *m* 17 Jan 1983, Kaija Kaarina, da of Niilo Sarolehto, of Espoo, Finland; 1 da (Antonia Alexandra b 9 Aug 1984), 1 s (Justin William b 12 June 1986); *Career* conslt anaesthetist Royal Free Hosp 1981–, hon sr lectr Royal Free Hosp Med Sch 1981–; memb: BMA, Assoc of Anaesthetists; FRCA; *Style—* Dr Michael Pegg; ✉ Newstead, 3 Canons Close, Radlett, Hertfordshire WD7 7ER (✆ 01923 856640, fax 01923 858430, e-mail m.pegg@btinternet.com); Department of Anaesthetics, Royal Free Hospital, Pond Street, London NW3 2QG

PEGG, Simon; *b* 14 February 1970, Glos; *Educ* Univ of Bristol; *Career* actor, writer, comedy performer; *Television* as actor incl: Faith in the Future 1995, Big Train (also writer) 1998, Spaced (also writer) 1999–2000, Hippies 1999, Band of Brothers 2001; *Film* as actor incl: Shaun of the Dead (also co-writer) 2004, Mission Impossible III 2006, The Big Nothing 2006, The Good Night 2006, Hot Fuzz (also writer) 2007, Run Fat Boy Run 2007, How to Lose Friends and Alienate People 2008, Star Trek 2009, Ice Age: Dawn of the Dinosaurs 2009, Burke and Hare 2010, The Chronicles of Narnia: The Voyage of the Dawn Treader 2010, Paul 2011 (also writer (with Nick Frost, *qv*)), The Adventures of Tintin 2011, Mission Impossible 4: Ghost Protocol 2011; *Style—* Simon Pegg, Esq; ✉ c/o Dawn Sedgwick Management, 3 Goodwins Court, Covent Garden, London WC2N 4LL (✆ 020 7240 0404, fax 020 7240 0415)

PEIRSON, Richard; s of Geoffrey Peirson (d 1986), of Purley, Surrey, and Beryl Joyce, *née* Walder (d 1999); *b* 5 March 1949; *Educ* Purley GS, Univ of Liverpool (BSc); *m* 1, 31 May 1975 (m dis), Jennifer Margaret, da of late F E Fernie; 1 s (James Richard b 1978), 1 da (Caroline Jane b 1980); m 2, 16 Feb 1991, Victoria, da of R P Steiner; 2 s (Charles Hamilton b 1993, George Alexander b 1996); *Career* Arthur Andersen & Co 1970–72, Colegrave & Co 1972–73, J & A Scrimgeour Ltd 1973–75, Carr Sebag & Co (formerly W I Carr Sons & Co) 1975–82, Grieveson Grant & Co 1982–86, Kleinwort Benson Investment Management Ltd 1986–94, Framlington Investment Management Ltd 1994–; Liveryman Worshipful Co of Glaziers and Painters of Glass; FCSI; *Recreations* tennis, interior design, reading, collecting watercolours; *Clubs* City of London; *Style—* Richard Peirson, Esq; ✉ 2 Old Place, The Green, Richmond, Surrey TW9 1NQ (✆ 020 8940 2013); Axa Framlington Investment Management Ltd, 7 Newgate Street, London EC2A 7NX (✆ 020 7330 6552, fax 020 7330 6570, e-mail richard.peirson@axa-im.com)

PEISER, Graham Allan; s of Eric George Peiser (d 1991), of Bucks, and Honor, *née* Greenwood (d 1988); *b* 26 March 1940; *Educ* Aldenham, Coll of Estate Mgmnt; *m* 26 Sept 1970, Jennifer Ann, da of Dr John Richard Cooper; 2 da (Georgina b 1972, Lucy b 1976); *Career* chartered surveyor and arboriculturist; ptnr: Fuller Peiser 1970–91, Graham Peiser Properties 1991–, Hyrons Trees 1992–; Liveryman Worshipful Co of Glass Sellers; FRICS; *Style—* Graham A Peiser, Esq; ✉ Boxwood, Dimmocks Lane, Sarratt, Rickmansworth, Hertfordshire WD3 6AP (✆ 01923 269136)

PELHAM, Clare Elizabeth; *b* 11 May 1959; *Educ* LSE (BScEcon); *Career* dir of corporate affrs HM Prison Service 1998–2001, dir Cabinet Office 2001–02, dir Coca-Cola GB and I 2002–03, dir Dept of Constitutional Affrs 2004–06; chief exec: Judicial Appointments Cmmn 2006–10, Leonard Cheshire Disability 2010–; *Style—* Ms Clare Pelham; ✉ Leonard Cheshire Disability, 66 South Lambeth Road, London SW8 1RL (✆ 020 3242 0202, e-mail chief.executive@leonardcheshire.org, website www.leonardcheshire.org, Twitter @clarepelham)

PELHAM, Sir Hugh Reginald Brentnall; kt (2011); s of Reginald Arthur Pelham, (d 1981), and Pauline Mary, *née* Brentnall (d 2006); *b* 26 August 1954; *Educ* Marlborough, Christ's Coll Cambridge (MA, PhD); *m* 25 May 1996, Dr Mariann Bienz, *qv*; 1 s, 1 da; *Career* res fell Christ's Coll Cambridge 1978–84, postdoctoral fell Dept of Embryology Carnegie Inst of Washington Baltimore MD 1979–81; MRC Laboratory of Molecular Biology Cambridge: staff memb 1981–, head Cell Biology Div, dep dir 1996–2006, dir 2006–; visitor Univ of Zürich 1987–88; awards: Colworth medal Biochemical Soc 1988, EMBO medal 1989, Louis Jeantet prize for med 1991, King Faisal int prize for science 1996; memb: EMBO 1985, Academia Europaea 1990; FRS 1988, FMedSci 1998; *Style—* Sir Hugh Pelham, FRS; ✉ MRC Laboratory of Molecular Biology, Francis Crick Avenue, Cambridge Biomedical Campus, Cambridge CB2 0QH (✆ 01223 267000, fax 01223 268300, e-mail hp@mrc-lmb.cam.ac.uk)

PELHAM BURN, Angus Maitland; JP, DL (1978); s of Brig-Gen Henry Pelham Burn, CMG, DSO (d 1958), and Katherine Eileen, *née* Staveley-Hill (d 1989); *b* 13 December 1931, London; *Educ* Harrow, N of Scotland Coll of Agric; *m* 19 Dec 1959, Anne Rosdew, da of Sir Ian Algernon Forbes-Leith, 2 Bt, KT, MBE (d 1973); 4 da (Amanda b 1961, Lucy b 1963, Emily b 1964, Kate b 1966); *Career* Hudson's Bay Co 1951–58, wolf bounty offr Ontario 1956–58; chm and dir MacRobert Farms (Douneside) Ltd 1970–87, chm Pelett Administration Ltd 1973–95; dir: Aberdeen and Northern Marts Ltd 1970–86 (chm 1974–86), Aberdeen Meat Marketing Co Ltd 1973–86 (chm 1974–86), Bank of Scotland 1977–2000 (dir Aberdeen and North Local Bd chm 1973–2000), Prime Space Design Ltd 1981–87, Taw Meat Co 1984–86, Status Timber Systems 1986–90, Skeendale Ltd 1987–88, Abtrust Scotland Investment Co plc 1989–96, Dana Petroleum plc 1999–2008; chm: Aberdeen Asset Management plc (and predecessor firms) 1993–2000 (dir 1985–98), Scottish Provident Institution 1995–98 (dir 1975–, chm 1991–95), Global Philanthropic International Ltd 2002–11, Oilcats Ltd 2005–06; memb: Kincardine CC 1967–75 (vice-convener 1973–75), Grampian Regnl Cncl 1974–94, Aberdeen Assoc for the Prevention of Cruelty to Animals 1975–96 (dir 1984–94, chm 1984–89), Accounts Cmmn 1980–94 (dep chm 1987–94), Cncl Winston Churchill Meml Tst 1984–93, Exec Cncl Scottish

P

Veterans' Residences until 2002; chm: Aberdeen Airport Consultative Ctee 1986–2006, Order Ctee Order of St John (Aberdeen) Ltd 1992–97 (memb 1987–); tstee The Gordon Highlanders Regimental Tst until 2001, memb Gordon Highlanders Museum Mgmnt Ctee 1994–2009; memb Queen's Body Guard for Scotland (Royal Co of Archers) 1968–2010; general cmmr of income tax Kincardine Div 1997–2001; dir Lathallan Sch 2001–04; patron Knockando Woolmill Tst 2011–; JP Kincardine and Deeside 1984–2004; Vice Lord-Lt Kincardineshire 1978–99; Liveryman Worshipful Co of Farmers until 1988; Hon LLD Robert Gordon Univ Aberdeen 1996; CStJ; *Recreations* vegetable gardening, photography; *Clubs* Royal Northern & Univ (Aberdeen); *Style—* Angus Pelham Burn, Esq, JP, DL, LLD; ✉ Kennels Cottage, Dess, Aboyne, Aberdeenshire AB34 5AY (☎ 01339 884445, e-mail snow.bunting2@gmail.com)

PELLEW, Robin Anthony; OBE (2006); s of Cdr Anthony Pellew RN, (d 1992), and Margaret Critchley, *née* Cookson (d 2009); *b* 27 September 1945; *Educ* Marlborough, Univ of Edinburgh (BSc), UCL (MSc), Univ of London (PhD); *m* 1974, Pamela, da of Dr Desmond MacLellan; 1 da (Sophie Harriet b 1979), 1 s (Toby James Pownoll b 1982); *Career* chief research scientist Serengeti Research Inst Tanzania 1972–78, research fell Physiology Lab Univ of Cambridge 1978–82, dir Biological Sciences Cambridge University Press 1985–87 (science ed Biological Sciences 1985–87), dir World Conservation Monitoring Centre Cambridge 1987–94, DG WWF-World Wide Fund for Nature (UK) 1994–98, chief exec Animal Health Tst Newmarket 1999–2001, chief exec Nat Tst for Scotland 2001–06, chm Cambridge Past, Present and Future 2007–; chm Cambridge Preservation Soc 2007–; non-exec dir Nat Forest Co 2007–14; memb Cncl: RGS 1993–96, Conservation Science Ctee Zoological Soc of London 1996–2001, Round Table on Sustainable Development UK 1994–99; memb Partnership Bd Gtr Cambridge Partnership 2008–12; Busk Medal for Conservation RGS 1992; fell British Ecological Society 1982, FZS 1992, FRSA 1992; *Publications* author of numerous scientific papers and conservation articles in academic journals, magazines and newspapers; *Recreations* travel, wildlife; *Style—* Robin Pellew, Esq, OBE; ✉ 32 Selwyn Gardens, Cambridge CB3 9AY (☎ 01223 327321)

PELLING, Prof Christopher Brendan Reginald; s of Reginald Pelling (d 1990), of Cardiff, and Brenda, *née* Sadler (d 2000); *b* 14 December 1947, Newport, Gwent; *Educ* Cardiff HS, Balliol Coll Oxford (MA), ChCh Oxford; *m* 1973, Margaret Ann, *née* Giddy; 1 s (Charles b 1978), 1 da (Sally b 1983); *Career* research fell Peterhouse Cambridge 1972–74, McConnell Laing fell and praelector in classics UC Oxford 1975–2003 (lectr 1974–75), regius prof of Greek Univ of Oxford 2003–; FBA 2009, FLSW 2011; *Books* Plutarch: Life of Antony (1988), Literary Texts and the Greek Historian (2000), Plutarch and History (2002), Plutarch: Life of Caesar (2011); *Recreations* cricket, golf, music (especially Broadway), conviviality; *Clubs* MCC; *Style—* Prof Christopher Pelling; ✉ Christ Church, Oxford OX1 1DP

PELLING, Rowan Dorothy; da of Ronald Alfred Pelling, and Hazel, *née* Underwood (d 2003); *Educ* Walthamstow Hall Sevenoaks, St Hugh's Coll Oxford; *Career* editorial asst Private Eye then GQ, ed The Erotic Review 1997–, dir The Erotic Print Soc, dir Dedalus Ltd; columnist GQ, Independent on Sunday and Daily Telegraph; *Books* The Erotic Review Bedside Companion (ed, 2000), The Decadent Handbook (ed, 2006); *Recreations* reading, buying shoes, growing broad beans, Formula 1, flirting; *Clubs* The Academy, Blacks; *Style—* Ms Rowan Pelling; ✉ e-mail editrice@eroticreview.org

PELLY, Frances Elsie; da of Russell Steele Pelly (d 1993), and Agnes Mysie, *née* MacPherson (d 2003); *b* 21 July 1947; *Educ* Morrison's Acad, Duncan of Jordanstone Coll of Art; *Career* sculptor; *Recreations* riding, gardening, studying wildlife, travelling; *Style—* Frances Pelly, RSA; ✉ Quoyblackie, Rendall, Orkney KW17 2HA (☎ 01856 751464)

PELLY, Sir Richard John; 7 Bt (UK 1840), of Upton, Essex; s of Richard Heywood Pelly (d 1988), and Mary Elizabeth, *née* Luscombe; *b* 10 April 1951; *Educ* Wellington, Wadham Coll Oxford (BA); *m* 1983, Clare Gemma, da of late Harry Wilfred Dove, of Winchester, Hants; 3 s (Anthony Alwyne b 1984, James Richard b 1986, Harry Philip b 1988); *Heir* s, Anthony Pelly; *Career* with: Price Waterhouse & Co 1974–79, Birds Eye Walls Ltd 1979–81, New Century Software Ltd 1981–98; farmer 1991–; *Style—* Sir Richard Pelly, Bt; ✉ The Manor House, Preshaw, Upham, Southampton SO32 1HP

PEMBERTON, Antony Francis; DL (2001); s of Sir Francis William Wingate Pemberton (d 2011), and Diana Patricia Pemberton (d 1999); *b* 24 February 1942; *Educ* Eton, Trinity Coll Cambridge (MA); *m* 7 Jan 1967, Victoria Anne, da of Maj Antony Gibbs (d 2000); 2 s (Richard Francis Antony b 9 July 1970, Charles Jeremy b 23 June 1972); *Career* farmer and estate mangr; Liveryman Worshipful Co of Farmers; High Sheriff Cambs 2000–01; FRAgS 1998; *Recreations* sailing, shooting, fishing; *Style—* Antony Pemberton, Esq, DL; ✉ Trumpington Hall, Cambridge CB2 9LH (☎ 01223 841101)

PEMBERTON, Dr James; s of Tom Winstanley Pemberton, of Sheffield, and Marjorie, *née* Chesney; *b* 21 December 1940; *Educ* King Edward VII Sch Sheffield, St Bartholomew's Hosp Med Sch (MB BS, MRCP, BSc scholarship, Hayward prize); *m* Sylvia Ann, *née* Finnigan; 4 c (Philippa Louise b 12 Sept 1968, Tom Winstanley b 12 Oct 1969, James Wentworth b 25 June 1971, Sam b 28 April 1981); *Career* St Bartholomew's Hosp: house physician 1968, house surgn 1969, registrar Pathology Dept 1970, registrar in med 1970–71, registrar in diagnostic radiology 1971–73; sr registrar in diagnostic radiology King's Coll Hosp 1973–74, conslt radiologist St Thomas' Hosp 1974–2001; admin head Radiology Dept Lambeth and S Western Hosps 1975–77; organiser Scientific Exhibition Jl Annual Congress of the Combined Royal Colls of UK, Netherlands and BIR 1978 and 1979; chm: Radiology Sub Ctee St Thomas' Hosp 1978–80 and 1984–86, Dist Working Pty on Jr Hosp Med and Dental Staff Hours of Work 1988; St Thomas' Hosp: chm Dist Working Pty on Junior Doctors' Rotas (Safety Nets), memb Dist Manpower Ctee 1986–92, chm Med and Surgical Offrs Ctee 1993–95, pres Sch of Radiography; memb: Regnl Manpower Ctee 1986–90, Regnl Radiology Specialists Sub-Ctee 1984–90; former pres Symposium Mammo Graphicum; memb BIR: Prog Ctee 1976–79, Med Ctee 1977–79 and 1990–92, Cncl 1990–93, Radiation Protection Ctee 1990–92; med lectr for: RCR, Br Cncl, FRCS Course and FRCR Course in Radiotherapy St Thomas' Hosp; author of numerous pubns in learned jls; MRCS 1967, LRCP 1967, DMRD 1972, FFR 1974, FRCR 1976; *Recreations* watching Arsenal FC, horseracing; *Style—* Dr James Pemberton; ✉ 18 Village Way, Dulwich, London SE21 7AN (☎ 020 7737 2220)

PEMBERTON, Her Hon Judge Jessica Louise Chantall; *Career* admitted slr 1994, called to the Bar 2007; recorder 2012, circuit judge (North Eastern Circuit) 2014–; *Style—* Her Hon Judge Pemberton; ✉ c/o Hull Combined Court Centre, Lowgate, Hull, North Humberside HU1 2EZ

PEMBERTON, Melody MacDonald; *née* Wilson-MacDonald; da of Gp Capt Duncan Stuart Wilson-MacDonald, DSO, DFC, RAF, and Rosemary; *Educ* St Georges Sch Montreux Switzerland, Heathfield Sch Ascot Berks, Villa Curonia Florence Italy; *m* 1991, Nigel Digby Pemberton; 1 s (Christie Digby MacDonald Pemberton b 14 Aug 1992); *Career* fashion model 1968–78, house model Fortnum & Mason Ltd 1976, Rolls Royce and Bentley chauffeuse Jack Barclay Ltd 1978–82, interior designer 1986–; actively involved in campaigning against animal abuse, in particular factory farming and vivisection, and live exports of animals; *Books* Caught in the Act (1994); *Recreations* horse riding, swimming, gardening; *Clubs* Special Forces; *Style—* Mrs Melody Pemberton; ✉ Lyne Place Manor, Virginia Water, Surrey GU25 4ED (e-mail melodypemberton@mac.com); Bamboo Pen, Box 274, Montego Bay, Jamaica, West Indies

PEMBERTON, Steve James; s of Derek James Pemberton (d 1998), and Margaret, *née* Catterall; *b* 1 September 1967, Blackburn, Lancs; *Educ* Bretton Hall Coll (BA); *Partner* Alison Rowles; 2 s (Lucas James b 13 May 2000, Adam Elliot b 14 Jan 2006), 1 da (Madeleine Ann b 15 Feb 2003); *Career* actor and writer; Hon DLitt Univ of Huddersfield; *Theatre* The League of Gentlemen Are Behind You (Hammersmith Apollo and tour), A Local Show for Local People (Theatre Royal Drury Lane and tour) 2000–01, Marc in Art (Whitehall Theatre) 2002, The Exonerated 2006, The Drowsy Chaperone 2007, The Rocky Horror Show 2007 and 2009, The 25th Annual Putnam County Spelling Bee (Donmar Warehouse) 2011, She Stoops to Conquer (National Theatre) 2012; *Television* The League of Gentlemen 1999, 2000 and 2002 (awards include BAFTA Best Comedy Series, RTS Award for Best Entertainment and Golden Rose of Montreux), The League of Gentlemen Christmas Special 2000, Gormenghast 2000, Shameless 2003, Poirot: Death on the Nile 2004, Blackpool 2004, The Last Detective 2005, Under the Greenwood Tree 2005, Hotel Babylon 2005, Benidorm 2007, The Bad Mother's Handbook 2007, Kingdom 2007, The Old Curiosity Shop 2007, Marple 2008, Dr Who 2008, Whitechapel 2009, Going Postal 2010, Psychoville 2010, Happy Valley 2014, Mapp and Lucia 2014, Inside No. 9 2014; *Radio* On The Town With The League of Gentlemen 1997 (Sony Silver for Best Radio Comedy); *Film* Birthday Girl 2002, Churchill – The Hollywood Years 2003, The Life and Death of Peter Sellers 2003, The Hitchhiker's Guide to the Galaxy 2005, Match Point 2005, The League of Gentlemen's Apocalypse 2005, Lassie 2006, Free Jimmy 2006, I Could Never Be Your Woman 2006, Mr Bean's Holiday 2007; *Publications* A Local Book For Local People (2000), The League of Gentlemen: Scripts and That; *Style—* Steve Pemberton, Esq; ✉ c/o Caroline Chignell, PBJ Management Ltd, 25 Roathbone Street, London W1T 1LG (☎ 020 7287 1112); c/o Nicki van Gelder, Conway van Gelder Grant, 8–12 Broadwick Street, London W1F 8HW (☎ 020 7287 0077)

PEMBROKE, Dr Andrew Charles; s of Geoffrey Vernon Worth Pembroke (d 1983), of Bexhill-on-Sea, E Sussex, and Mary Constance, *née* Purkis (d 1978); *b* 1 June 1947; *Educ* Winchester (scholar), King's Coll Cambridge (scholar and sr scholar, MA, MB BChir), Bart's Med Coll; *m* 1977, Jacqueline Beatrice, da of Percival Henry Gage Hall; 3 s (Thomas Peter Ignatius b 1980, Charles Dominic b 1985, Theodore Philip Gervase b 1987), 2 da (Beatrice Mary b 1978, Olivia Constance b 1982); *Career* med registrar Hackney Hosp 1974–75, sr registrar in dermatology London Hosp 1975–78; conslt dermatologist: King's Coll Hosp 1981–94 (sr registrar in dermatology 1978–81), Bromley Hosps NHS Tst 1994–; hon treas: Br Assoc of Dermatologists 1987–92, Br Skin Fndn 1996–; chm SE Thames Regnl Specialty Sub-Ctee for Dermatology 1987–91; FRCP 1988; *Style—* Dr A C Pembroke; ✉ 28 Dartford Road, Sevenoaks, Kent TN13 3TQ (☎ 01732 450197)

PEMSEL, David; *b* 31 March 1968; *m* Kate Stanners; 1 s (Otto b 10 April 2003); *Career* managing ptnr St Luke's 1996–2000, ptnr Shine 2000–02, mktg dir ITV 2005–10, gp mktg dir, chief mktg offr, chief communications offr then dep chief exec Guardian News and Media 2010–15, ceo Guardian Media Gp 2015–; non-exec dir: British Fashion Cncl 2016–, Ascential plc 2016–; memb: IPA, BAFTA, Mktg Soc, Mktg Gp of GB; *Recreations* cinema, cycling, reading, tennis, travel; *Clubs* Ivy, Soho House; *Style—* David Pemsel, Esq; ✉ Guardian News and Media, 90 York Way, London N1 9GU (☎ 020 3353 3969, e-mail david.pemsel@theguardian.com, website www.theguardian.com, Twitter @davidpemsel)

PENDLETON, Victoria; CBE (2013, MBE 2009); da of Max Pendleton, of Stotfold, Beds, and Pauline Pendleton; *b* 24 September 1980; *Educ* Fearnhill Sch Letchworth, Northumbria Univ; *Career* track cyclist; achievements in int competition incl: Gold medal (individual sprint) World Championships 2005, Gold medal (individual sprint) and Silver medal (500m time trial) Cwlth Games 2006, Silver medal (individual sprint) World Championships 2006, 3 Gold medals (individual sprint, team sprint and keirin) World Championships 2007, 2 Gold medals (individual sprint and team sprint) and Silver medal (keirin) World Championships 2008, Gold medal (individual sprint) Olympic Games 2008, Gold medal (sprint), Silver medal (team sprint) and Bronze medal (500m time trial) World Championships 2009, Silver medal (team sprint) European Championships 2010, Gold medal (sprint) and Silver medal (keirin) World Championships 2010, 2 Gold medals (team sprint and keirin) European Championships 2011, Silver medal (team sprint) and Bronze medal (sprint) World Championships 2011, Gold medal (sprint) World Championships 2012, Gold medal (keirin) and Silver medal (sprint) Olympic Games 2012, several Gold medals and podium finishes in World Cup series races; Sunday Times Sportswoman of the Year 2007, Sportswoman of the Year Sports Journalists' Assoc of GB 2007; *Style—* Ms Victoria Pendleton, CBE; ✉ website www.victoriapendleton.co.uk; c/o Three60 Sports Management, Chapel Close, Ashley House, Clifton, Banbury OX15 0PF

PENDRY, Prof Sir John Brian; kt (2004); s of Frank Johnson Pendry (d 1978), and Kathleen, *née* Shaw (d 2001); *b* 4 July 1943; *Educ* Ashton-under-Lyne GS, Downing Coll Cambridge (MA, PhD); *m* 15 Jan 1977, Patricia, da of Frederick Gard, of London; *Career* res fell in physics Downing Coll Cambridge 1969–75, memb tech staff Bell Laboratories USA 1972–73, sr asst in res Cavendish Laboratory Cambridge 1973–75 (postdoctoral fell 1969–72), SPSO and head Theory Gp SERC Daresbury Laboratory 1975–81; Imperial Coll London: prof of theoretical solid state physics 1981–, assoc head Dept of Physics 1981–92, head Dept of Physics 1998–2001; dean Royal Coll of Sci 1993–96; chm Inst of Physics Publishing 2007–11; chm Physics Sub-Panel RAE 2008 2005–08, chm Bd Cockcroft Inst 2010–12; memb: Physics Ctee SERC (chm Panel Y) 1985–88, Sci Bd SERC 1992–93, Cncl Royal Soc 1992–94, Cncl PPARC 1998–2002; Cwlth scholarships cmmr 1998–2000; Inst of Physics Dirac Medal and Prize 1996, Royal Soc Bakerian lecture 2005, EU Descartes Prize for extending electromagnetism through Novel Artificial Materials 2005, Royal Medal 2006, Centenary Kelvin lecture Inst of Engrg and Technol 2009, UNESCO-Niels Bohr Gold Medal 2009, W E Lamb Medal for Laser Science and Quantum Optics 2010, Newton Medal Inst of Physics 2013, Kavil Prize for Nanotechnology 2014, EPS Quantum Electronics and Optics for Fundamental Aspects 2015, Dan David Prize for Nanotechnology 2016; hon fell Downing Coll Cambridge 2005; FRS 1984, FInstP 1984 (memb Cncl 2007–11), fell Optical Soc of America 2005, fell American Acad of Arts and Sciences 2012, foreign assoc US Nat Acad of Sciences 2013, foreign memb Norwegian Acad of Sciences 2014; *Recreations* music, piano playing, gardening, photography; *Clubs* Athenaeum, Oxford and Cambridge; *Style—* Prof Sir John Pendry, FRS; ✉ Metchley, Knipp Hill, Cobham, Surrey KT11 2PE (☎ 01932 864306); The Blackett Laboratory, Imperial College, London SW7 2AZ (☎ 020 7594 7606)

PENDRY, Baron (Life Peer UK 2001), of Stalybridge in the County of Greater Manchester; Thomas (Tom) Pendry; PC (2000); s of L E Pendry, of Broadstairs, Kent; *b* 10 June 1934; *Educ* St Augustine's Ramsgate, Univ of Oxford; *m* 1966 (sep 1983), Moira Anne, da of A E Smith, of Derby; 1 s, 1 da; *Career* electrical engr; Nat Serv RAF 1955–57; joined Lab Pty 1950, NUPE official 1960–70, memb Paddington Cncl 1962–65, chm Derby Lab Pty 1966; MP (Lab) Stalybridge and Hyde 1970–2001, oppn whip 1971–74, a Lord Cmmr of the Treasy (Govt whip) 1974–77 (resigned), Parly under sec of state NI Office 1978–79; oppn spokesman: on NI 1979–81, on overseas devpt 1981–82, on devolution and regnl affrs 1982, on Sport 1992; shadow min for sport and tourism 1992–97; chm: All-Pty Football Gp 1975–92, PLP Sports Gp 1984–2013, All-Pty Tourism Gp 1997–2013; co-chm All-Pty Jazz Appreciation Gp; pres Football Fndn 2003–, chm Football Tst 1998–2003, steward Br Boxing Bd of Control 1987–2003; RAF Far East boxing champion 1956, colonial middleweight boxing champion Hong Kong 1957, boxed for Univ of Oxford 1958–59; Freeman Borough of Tameside 1975, Lordship of Mottram in Longdendale 1975 (granted by Tameside Borough Cncl to commemorate services as an MP for 25 years); *Books* Taking it on the Chin: Memoirs of a Parliamentary Bruiser (2016); *Recreations* sports of all kinds; *Clubs* Stalybridge Labour (hon pres), Vincent's (Oxford), Lord's

Taverners, MCC, Garrick; *Style*— The Rt Hon the Lord Pendry, PC; ✉ Alice House, Old Road, Stalybridge, Cheshire SK15 2RG

PENFOLD, Adrian Philip; OBE (2015); s of Albert Penfold (d 1958), and Dorothy Jane, *née* Milner (d 1989); *b* 9 March 1952, Buckinghamshire; *Educ* Bedford Modern Sch, Univ of Essex (BA), Kingston Poly (Dip); *m* July 1976, Elspeth Anne, *née* Hemery; 3 s (Daniel Liam b 1978, James Geoffrey b 1981, Michael Leonard b 1984); *Career* planning asst Beds CC 1973, career grade planner then memb then ldr devpt control team London Borough of Hammersmith and Fulham 1976–88, planning exec then head central enterprise zone team London Docklands Devpt Corp 1988–90, asst devpt servs mangr then head of planning and design Dartford BC 1990–96; British Land Co plc: chief planner 1996–2001, head planning and environment 2001–10, head of planning and corporate responsibility 2010–, memb Bd British Land Corporation Ltd; led Penfold Review of Non-Planning Consents 2010; MRTPI 1978, FRSA, FRICS; *Recreations* sport, walking, travel; *Clubs* Reform, Architecture; *Style*— Adrian Penfold, Esq, OBE; ✉ 11 Cliveden Road, Wimbledon, London SW19 3RD (☎ 020 8715 7739, e-mail apenfold52@gmail.com); The British Land Company plc, York House, Seymour Street, London W1H 7LX (☎ 020 7467 3481, e-mail adrian.penfold@britishland.com)

PENFOLD, Derek John; s of Joseph Penfold, of Tiverton, Devon, and Catherine, *née* O'Sullivan; *b* 17 July 1948, Tunbridge Wells, Kent; *Educ* Clapham Coll, City of Westminster Coll, NW London Poly (LLB); *Partner* Louisa Denman; 1 da (Rose b 25 Jan 2000); *Career* features ed Estates Times 1975–78, dep ed Estates Gazette 1980–86 (news ed 1978–80), property analyst Alexanders Laing & Cruickshank 1986–87; dir: Streets Communications 1987–89, Phillips Communications 1990–91, Derek Penfold Associates 1991–94; ed Estates Times 1994–96; dir: Publishing Business Ltd 1996–97, CMT International 1998–2001; communications dir HOK International Ltd 2005–; chm Greenwich Theatre 1976–87 (dir 1975–90), dir Greenwich Young People's Theatre 1980–88, former chm Greenwich Festival; London Borough of Greenwich cncllr 1971–78, (chm Leisure Ctee, chief whip); memb Advsy Panel on town centre planning London Borough of Hammersmith and Fulham; chm The Story of Christmas Charity Appeal, tstee LandAid Charitable Tst, ambass Museum of London Archaeology; Freeman City of London; fell Land Inst; *Publications* extensive journalism; *Recreations* theatre, architecture, gardens and gardening, London post-medieval archaeology, London history; *Clubs* Globe Rowing, Walbrook and Broad Street Wards, Architecture, Tyburn Anglers, Volestranglers, Max Wall Soc; *Style*— Derek Penfold, Esq; ✉ 89A Edith Road, London W14 0TJ (☎ 020 7603 6495, e-mail derekjpenfold@aol.com)

PENKETT, Prof Stuart Arthur; s of Arthur Penkett (d 1963), of Leeds, and Ilene Maud, *née* Henshaw (d 1988); *b* 3 January 1939, Eccles; *Educ* Eccles GS, Univ of Leeds (BSc, PhD); *m* 2 June 1962, Marigold, *née* Gibbens; 2 da (Fiona Sally b 24 Feb 1968, Rebecca Gayle b 26 July 1973), 2 s (Clive Stuart b 11 June 1969, Christopher John b 18 Feb 1972); *Career* postdoctoral research fell Univ of Southern Calif 1963–65, Unilever Research Labs Welwyn 1965–68, Atomic Energy Research Estab Harwell 1968–85, Nat Center for Atmospheric Research Boulder 1985; UEA: NERC reader in atmospheric chemistry 1985–90, prof of atmospheric chemistry 1990–2004, emeritus prof 2004–; affiliate scientist Nat Center for Atmospheric Research Boulder 1997–2000 (reviewer 1997), reviewer Aeronomy Lab Nat Oceanic and Atmospheric Administration (NOAA) 1998; vice-chm EUREKA Scientific Steering Ctee Environmental Project EUROTRAC 1986–96; chm: IGBP IGAC Symposium Fuyi Yoshida 1994, NERC ACSOE Community Pro 1995–2000, Ctee of the CEC European IGAC Project Office (EIPO) 1996–2002, Scientific Advsy Gp for Reactive Gases World Meteorological Orgn Global Atmospheric Watch (WMO GAW) 2005–13; European convenor Int Global Atmospheric Chemistry/ North Atlantic Regnl Experiment (IGAC/NARE) 1990–2005; memb: Dept of Environment review gps on Stratospheric Ozone and Photochemical Oxidants, UK Meteorological Office Hadley Centre Scientific Advsy Gp, NERC Atmospheric Science Ctee, EU Jt Environment Centre Ispra, UN Environment Prog Assessment of Stratospheric Ozone; memb: US Nat Acad of Sciences, World Meteorological Orgn, European Science Fndn, European Research Cncl, Royal Soc; author of over 200 pubns since 1965, also many citations; Royal Meteorological Soc Gaskell Medal 1987, Elsevier Science Haagen-Smit Award 2003, Leverhulme emeritus fell 2005–06; memb Academia Europaea 1988, foreign memb Max Planck Soc 1987; FRMetS; *Recreations* walking, American geography and history, European history, railways; *Style*— Prof Stuart Penkett; ✉ University of East Anglia, School of Environmental Sciences, Norwich NR4 7TJ (☎ 01603 501051, e-mail m.penkett@uea.ac.uk)

PENMAN, John; s of John Penman, of Cumbernauld, and Sarah, *née* Welsh; *b* 10 January 1962; *Educ* St Gregory's Secdy Sch Glasgow, Greenfaulds HS Cumbernauld, Napier Coll Edinburgh; *m* 24 Oct 2003, Lucy Jane Patton; 1 da (Daisy b 15 Sept 1999); *Career* chief reporter Carlisle Evening News and Star 1987–91, asst new ed The Northern Echo 1991–94, dep news ed The Scotsman 1994–98 (political ed 1996–98), asst ed Daily Record 1998, new business dir Daily Record and Sunday Mail 1998–2000, ed-in-chief/md Business a.m. 2000–02, Business and Fin ed Scottish Daily Record 2003–05, ed-in-chief Scottish Business Insider 2003–05, business ed Scotland The Sunday Times 2005–09, dir of corp communications for Scotland Lloyds Banking Gp 2011–; highly commended Campaigning Journalist of the Year Award 1992, Scottish Daily Newspaper of the Year 2000, runner-up UK Daily Newspaper of the Year 2000, Best Designed Newspaper Newspaper Awards 2001, UK Regnl Business and Fin Newspaper of the Year 2002, runner-up Business Journalist of the Year Scottish Press Awards 2006; memb SO Ctee on Media Regulation Scot Parl 1998; *Recreations* watching Partick Thistle FC, walking, cycling, running; *Style*— John Penman, Esq; ✉ Lloyds Banking Group, 69 Morrison Street, Port Hamilton, Edinburgh EH3 8YF (☎ 0131 655 5483)

PENN, David John; s of late Surgn Capt Eric Arthur Penn, DSC, of W Mersea, Essex, and late Catherine Penn; *Educ* Dulwich Coll, St Catherine's Coll Oxford (MA); *m* 1993, Catherine Janet Davidson; 1 s (Alexander Eric Davidson b 12 Jan 1995), 1 da (Flora Catherine Davidson b 25 Jan 1999); *Career* keeper Imperial War Museum: Dept of Info Retrieval 1970–77, Dept of Firearms 1973–76, Dept of Exhibits and Firearms 1976–2005; memb: Home Office Firearms Consultative Ctee 1989–2004 (chm 2000–04), National Historic Ships Ctee 1995–99; pres Arms and Armour Soc; vice-pres: Muzzle-Loaders Assoc of GB, Hist Breechloading Smallarms Assoc, BASC; sec Br Shooting Sports Cncl, conslt Fndn for European Socs of Arms Collectors; Freeman City of London 1982, Liveryman Worshipful Co of Gunmakers 1982; FSA 1989; *Books* Imperial War Museum Film Cataloguing Rules (with R B N Smither, 1976); *Recreations* shooting; *Clubs* Army & Navy; *Style*— David Penn, Esq, FSA; ✉ PO Box 53608, London SE24 9YN

PENNANT-REA, Rupert Lascelles; s of late Peter Athelwold Pennant-Rea, MBE, of Burford, Oxon, and late Pauline Elizabeth, *née* Creasy; *b* 23 January 1948; *Educ* Peterhouse Zimbabwe, TCD (BA), Univ of Manchester (MA); *m* 24 Dec 2011, Cinzia, *née* De Santis; *Children* from a previous relationship: 1 da (Emily b 1982), 2 s (Rory b 1983, Edward b 1986); *Career* with Confedn of Irish Industry 1970–71, Gen & Municipal Workers Union 1972–73, Bank of England 1973–77; The Economist: economics corr 1977–81, economics ed 1981–85, ed 1986–93; dep govr Bank of England 1993–95; chm: The Stationery Office 1996–2005, PGI plc 1997–, Security Printing and Systems 1999–2006, Acuity Growth VCT plc 2001–11, Henderson Gp plc 2005–13, The Economist Gp Ltd 2009–; non-exec dir: Sherritt Int 1995–2007, British American Tobacco plc 1995–2007, First Quantum Minerals 2001–11, Gold Fields 2002–13, Go-Ahead Gp plc 2002–13, Times Newspapers 2003–, Financial News Gp 2003–07, Specialist Waste Recycling 2008–, Hochschild plc 2011–13; chm: The Shakespeare Schs Festival 2001–15, Royal London Gp 2012–; tstee Speakers Tst 2015–; *Books* Gold Foil (1978), Who Runs The Economy? (jtly, 1979), The Pocket Economist (jtly, 1982), The Economist Economics (jtly, 1986), Public Choice Analysis of Economic Policy (jt ed, 2000); *Recreations* music, tennis, fishing, family, golf; *Clubs* MCC, Reform, Harare; *Style*— Rupert Pennant-Rea, Esq; ✉ c/o Royal London Group, 55 Gracechurch Street, London EC3V 0RL

PENNING, Rt Hon Michael; PC (2014), MP; *b* 1957, London; *Educ* King Edmund Comp; *m* 2 c; *Career* Grenadier Guards (served NI, Kenya and Germany); fireman; former political advsr Cons Shadow Cabinet under William Hague, former dep head of media Cons Pty; MP (Cons) Hemel Hempstead 2005– (Parly candidate (Cons) Thurrock 2001), Parly under-sec of state for tport 2010–12, min of state for NI 2012–13, min of state Dept for Work and Pensions 2013–14, min of state for police 2014–16, min of state for armed forces 2016–; *Style*— The Rt Hon Michael Penning, MP; ✉ House of Commons, London SW1A 0AA

PENNINGTON, Prof (Thomas) Hugh; CBE (2013); s of Thomas Wearing Pennington (d 1993), and Dorothy Pennington (d 1989); *b* 19 April 1938; *Educ* Lancaster Royal GS, St Thomas' Hosp Med Sch (MB BS, Clutton Medal, Bristowe Medal, Beaney Prize, Foord Caiger Prize, PhD); *m* 1965, Carolyn Ingram, da of George Beattie; 2 da; *Career* asst lectr med microbiology St Thomas' Hosp Medical Sch 1963–67, postdoctoral fell Univ of Wisconsin Madison 1967–68, lectr and sr lectr MRC Virology Unit and Dept of Virology Univ of Glasgow 1969–79, prof of bacteriology Univ of Aberdeen 1979–2003 (dean Faculty of Med 1987–92, emeritus prof 2003–); external examiner at several Br univs; chm: Expert Gp on the 1996 E.coli Outbreak in Central Scotland, Public Inquiry into 2005 E.coli Outbreak in S Wales 2006–09; govr Rowett Research Inst 1980–88 and 1995–2004; memb: BBC Broadcasting Cncl for Scotland 2000–05 (vice-chair), Scottish Food Advsy Ctee Food Standards Agency 2000–05, BBC Rural Affairs Advsy Ctee 2005–09, World Food Prog Tech Advsy Gp 2002–07; pres Soc for Gen Microbiology 2003–06; Caroline Walker Tst Consumer Advocate Award 1997, RIPHH and Soc of Public Health John Kershaw Meml Prize 1998, Soc of Food Hygiene Technol 25th Anniversary Award 2004, Soc of Chemical Industry Joseph Lister Medal 2009, Royal Environmental Health Inst of Scotland Award for Meritorious Endeavours in Environmental Health 2010; Hon DSc: Lancaster Univ, Univ of Strathclyde, Univ of Aberdeen, Univ of Hull, Harper Adams Univ; FRCPath, FRCPEd, FMedSci, FRSE, FRSA; *Publications* Molecular Virology (with D A Ritchie, 1975), When Food Kills (2003), Have Bacteria Won? (2016); numerous papers on molecular virology, molecular epidemiology, the systematics of pathogenic bacteria, food safety and E.coli 0157, contrib London Review of Books; *Recreations* collecting books, dipterology; *Style*— Prof Hugh Pennington, CBE, FRSE; ✉ 13 Carlton Place, Aberdeen AB15 4BR (☎ 01224 645136, e-mail mmb036@abdn.ac.uk)

PENNINGTON, Michael Vivian Fyfe; s of Vivian Maynard Cecil Pennington (d 1984), and Euphemia Willock Fyfe (d 1987); *b* 7 June 1943; *Educ* Marlborough, Trinity Coll Cambridge (BA); *m* 10 Oct 1964 (m dis 1967), Katharine, da of Peter Barker; 1 s (Mark Dominic Fyfe b 12 Aug 1966); *Career* actor; memb RSC 1964–66; freelance, West End and TV plays 1966–73: The Judge, Hamlet, A Woman of No Importance, Savages; leading memb RSC 1974–81: Angelo in Measure for Measure, Mercutio in Romeo and Juliet, Edgar in King Lear, Berowne in Love's Labour's Lost, Mirabell in Way of the World, title role in Hippolytus, title role in Hamlet, Donal Davoren in Shadow of a Gunman; NT 1984: title role in Strider, Jaffier in Venice Preserved, solo performance of Anton Chekhov; subsequent credits: The Real Thing (West End) 1985, Oedipus The King (BBC) 1985; artistic dir English Shakespeare Co until 1993 (fndr and leading actor 1986–92, participated in four round the world tours); roles incl: Richard II, Henry V, Coriolanus, Leontes in The Winter's Tale, Macbeth; other credits: Summer's Lease (BBC) 1989, Playing with Trains (RSC Barbican) 1989, Vershinin in Three Sisters (Gate Theatre Dublin) 1990, Edward Damson in The Gift of the Gorgon (RSC Barbican and Wyndham's) 1993, Old Times and One for the Road (Dublin Pinter Festival), Claudius and the Ghost in Hamlet (Peter Hall Co) 1994, Taking Sides (Chichester Festival, Criterion) 1995, Archie Rice in The Entertainer (Hampstead) 1996; Old Vic 1997 incl: Waste, The Seagull, The Provoked Wife, Anton Chekhov; also Alceste in The Misanthrope and Domenico in Filumena (Piccadilly Theatre) 1998, Oscar Wilde in Gross Indecency (Gielgud Theatre) 1999, Timon in Timon of Athens (RSC Stratford and Barbican), Nandor in The Guardsman (Albery Theatre) 2000, Prentice in What the Butler Saw 2001, John in The Shawl 2001, Walter Burns in The Front Page (Chichester Theatre) 2002, title role in John Gabriel Borkman (English Touring Theatre) 2003, Dr Dorn in The Seagull (Edinburgh Festival) 2003, George III in The Madness of King George (W Yorks Playhouse) 2003, Cecil in When the Night Begins (Hampstead Theatre) 2004, Nathan in Nathan the Wise (Hampstead Theatre) 2005, Sydney Cocherell in The Best of Friends (nat tour) 2006, Robert Maxwell in The Bargain (nat tour) 2007, Charles Dickens in Little Nell (Peter Hall Co) 2007, Richard Strauss in Collaboration (Chichester) 2008, Sweet William (solo Shakespeare show, nat and int tour, West End and DVD) 2008–13, Wilhelm Furtwangler in Taking Sides (Duchess Theatre) 2009, Love is My Sin (int tour) 2009–10, The Master Builder 2010, Fabio in The Syndicate (Chichester) 2011, Rubek in When We Dead Awaken (Print Room) 2012, Antony in Antony and Cleopatra (Chichester) 2012, Captain Edgar in The Dance of Death (Gate Theatre) 2013, John of Gaunt in Richard II (RSC) 2013, title role in King Lear (Theatre for a New Audience, NY) 2014, Anthony Blunt in Single Spies (Rose Theatre) 2014, Euripides in Macedonia (BBC Radio) 2015, Antigonus in The Winter's Tale (Kenneth Branagh Theatre Co) 2015 (nominated Olivier Award), title role in King Lear (nat tour) 2016; dir: Twelfth Night (English Shakespeare Co 1991, Haiyuza Co Tokyo 1993, Shakespeare Repertory Co Chicago 1996), A Midsummer Night's Dream (Regents Park Open Air Theatre) 2003; film Michael Foot in The Iron Lady 2011; *Books* Rossya: A Journey Through Siberia (1977), English Shakespeare Company: The Story of the Wars of The Roses (1990), Hamlet: A User's Guide (1995), Twelfth Night: A User's Guide (1999), Are You There, Crocodile – Inventing Anton Chekhov (2002), A Midsummer Night's Dream: A User's Guide (2004), Sweet William – Twenty Thousand Hours with Shakespeare (2012, nominated Sheridan Morley Prize), Let Me Play the Lion Too – How To Be An Actor (2015, nominated Sheridan Morley Prize), King Lear in Brooklyn (2016); *Recreations* reading, music; *Clubs* Garrick; *Style*— Michael Pennington, Esq; ✉ c/o Diamond Management, 31 Percy Street, London W1T 2DD

PENNY, Martin Richard; s of Jack Penny (d 1990), of Yeadon, W Yorks, and Edith, *née* Emsley (d 2006); *b* 13 February 1953, Leeds, W Yorks; *Educ* Aireborough GS, Univ of Leeds (BSc); *m* 12 May 1979, Diana, *née* Birkinshaw; 2 s (Alexander Martin b 20 Aug 1984, James Richard b 7 Dec 1985); *Career* md and chm OHS Ltd Environmental Conslts 1981–; ceo Jemella Gp Ltd 2001–; Ernst & Young Nat Consumer Products Entrepreneur of the Year 2005, NE Regnl Entrepreneur of the Year 2005; *Recreations* tennis, squash, walking, skiing, reading; *Clubs* Ilkley Tennis (chm 1998–2000); *Style*— Martin Penny, Esq; ✉ Jemella Ltd, Unit 12 Ryefield Way, Silsden, West Yorkshire BD20 0EF (☎ 01535 651 500)

PENNY, Sir Nicholas Beaver; kt (2015); s of Joseph Noel Bailey Penny, QC (d 1998), and Agnes Celia, *née* Roberts (d 1969); *b* 21 December 1949; *Educ* Shrewsbury, St Catharine's Coll Cambridge (MA), Courtauld Inst London (MA, PhD); *m* 1, 1971 (m dis), Anne Philomel, *née* Udy; 2 da (Caroline Emily, Elizabeth Joan (twins) b 26 Jan 1977); m 2, 1994, Mary Crettier; *Career* Leverhulme fell Clare Coll Cambridge, lectr Dept of History of Art Univ of Manchester 1975–82, Slade prof of fine art Univ of Oxford 1980–81, sr

P

res fell King's Coll Cambridge 1982–84, keeper of Western art Ashmolean Museum and professorial fell Balliol Coll Oxford 1984–89, Clore curator of Renaissance painting National Gallery London 1990–2002 (keeper 1998–2002); National Gallery of Art Washington DC: Andrew W Mellon prof Center for Advanced Studies in the Visual Arts 2000–02, sr curator of sculpture and decorative arts 2002–08; dir Nat Gall London 2008–15; fell American Acad of Arts and Sciences 2007, FBA 2010; Cavaliere dell'Ordine al merito della Repubblica Italiana 1990; *Books* Church Monuments in Romantic England (1977), Piranesi (1978), Taste and the Antique (with Francis Haskell, 1981), Mourning (1981), The Arrogant Connoisseur (ed with Michael Clarke, 1982), Raphael (with Roger Jones, 1983), Reynolds (ed, 1986), Alfred and Winifred Turner (1988), Lucian Freud, Works on Paper (with Robert Flynn Johnson, 1988), Ruskin's Drawings (1988), From Giotto to Dürer (with Jill Dunkernon et al, 1991), European Sculpture in the Ashmoleam Museum: 1540 to the Present Day (1992), The Materials of Sculpture (1993), Frames (1997), From Dürer to Veronese (with Jill Dunkerton et al, 1999), Art of the Renaissance Bronze (with Anthony Radcliffe, 2004), The Sixteenth Century Paintings in the National Gallery London: Paintings from Bergamo, Brescia and Cremona (2004), The Sixteenth Century Paintings in the National Gallery London: Paintings from Venice 1540–1600 (2008), Director's Choice (2011), The Sansovino Frame (with Peter Schade and Harriet O'Neill, 2015); *Style*— Sir Nicholas Penny

PENNY, Hon Peter George Worsley; s and h of 3 Viscount Marchwood, *qv*; *b* 8 October 1965; *Educ* Winchester; *m* 1995, Annabel C, yr da of Rex Cooper, of E Bergholt, Suffolk; 1 da (India Rose b 21 March 1997), 1 s (Kit b 8 Sept 1999); *Career* assoc dir The HMG Group plc 1990–92, md The Staveley Gp Ltd 1996–; *Recreations* racing, tennis, cricket, shooting; *Style*— The Hon Peter Penny

PENRHYN, 7 Baron (UK 1866); Simon Douglas-Pennant; s of Maj the Hon Nigel Douglas Pennant (d 2000), and Margaret, *née* Kirkham (d 1939); suc unc, 6 Baron Penrhyn, 2003; *b* 28 June 1938, Glasgow; *Educ* Eton, Clare Coll Cambridge (BA, Cricket blue); *m* 5 Oct 1963, Josephine, *née* Upcott; 2 da (Hon Sophie Margaret (Mrs Michael Trotter) b 11 Dec 1964, Hon Harriet Josephine (Mrs Claus Garbers) b 25 May 1972), 2 s (Hon Edward Sholto b 6 June 1966, Hon Hugo Charles b 21 April 1969); *Heir* s, Hon Edward Douglas-Pennant; *Career* main bd dir Brintons Ltd; *Recreations* travel, golf, gardening, music; *Clubs* MCC; *Style*— The Rt Hon the Lord Penrhyn

PENROSE, Ian; *Career* chief exec Arena Leisure plc until 2005, chief exec Sportech plc 2005–; tstee Nat Football Museum; *Recreations* Preston North End FC; *Style*— Ian Penrose, Esq; ✉ Sportech plc, 101 Wigmore Street, London W1U 1QU

PENROSE, John; MP; *b* 22 June 1964; *Educ* Ipswich Sch, Univ of Cambridge, Columbia Univ; *m* Dido Harding; *Career* risk mangr J P Morgan 1986–90, mgmnt conslt McKinsey and Co 1992–94, commercial dir Thomson Publishing 1995–96, md schs publishing Pearson plc 1996–2000, chm Logotron Ltd 2000–08; Parly candidate (Cons): Ealing Southall 1997, Weston-super-Mare 2001; MP (Cons) Weston-super-Mare 2005–; Parly under-sec of state for tourism 2010–12, Govt whip and Lord Cmmr 2013–; *Style*— John Penrose, Esq, MP; ✉ House of Commons, London SW1A 0AA (e-mail penrosej@parliament.uk, website www.johnpenrose.org)

PENROSE, Dr Richard James Jackson; s of Walter James Pace (d 1944), and Gertrude May, *née* Penrose (d 1981); name changed by deed poll 1968; *b* 12 October 1941; *Educ* Haberdashers' Aske's, Charing Cross Hosp Med Sch London (MB BS), DPM 1970; *m* 1 May 1976, Lynda Elisabeth, da of Dr Reginald John Alcock, of Kemble; 2 s (James b 1977, William b 1980); *Career* Charing Cross Hosp: house surgn in ENT 1966, house physician in gen med and neurology 1967, SHO in psychiatry 1968; sr registrar in psychiatry St George's Hosp London 1971–75 (SHO and registrar 1968–71); conslt psychiatrist: St George's Hosp 1975–89, West Park Hosp Epsom 1975–81, Springfield Hosp 1981–89, Epsom Gen Hosp 1989–97, The Priory Hosp Roehampton 1997–; visiting lectr Univ of Surrey 1999–; fndr memb Br Assoc for Psychopharmacology; LRCP, MRCS, FRCPsych (MRCPsych 1973); *Books* various articles in jls on life events, brain haemorrhage, depression and drug treatment; *Recreations* music, gardening, reading; *Style*— Dr Richard Penrose; ✉ The Priory Hospital, Priory Lane, London SW15 5JJ (☎ 020 8876 8261)

PENROSE, Prof Sir Roger; OM (2000), kt (1994); s of Prof Lionel S Penrose FRS (d 1972), and Dr Margaret, *née* Leathes (d 1989); *b* 8 August 1931; *Educ* UCL (BSc), St John's Coll Cambridge (PhD); *m* 1, 1958 (m dis 1980), Joan Isabel Wedge; 3 s (Christopher Shaun b 1963, Toby Nicholas b 1964, Eric Alexander b 1966); m 2, 1988, Vanessa Dee Thomas; 1 s (Maxwell Sebastian b 26 May 2000); *Career* conslt National Research Development Corporation London 1956–57, asst lectr in mathematics Bedford Coll London 1956–57, res fell St John's Coll Cambridge 1957–60; concurrently res fell 1959–61: Princeton Univ (NATO res fell), Syracuse Univ and Cornell Univ; res assoc Dept of Mathematics King's Coll London 1961–63, prof of applied mathematics Birkbeck Coll London 1967–73 (reader 1964–66), Rouse Ball prof of mathematics Wadham Coll Oxford 1973–98 (prof emeritus 1998–); prof of mathematics (pt/t) Rice Univ 1982–87, prof of physics and mathematics (pt/t) Syracuse Univ 1987–93, prof of physics and mathematics at Penn State Univ 1993–, Gresham prof of geometry Gresham Coll London 1998–; visiting assoc prof of mathematics and physics Univ of Texas 1963–64; visiting appts: Yeshiva Univ, Princeton Univ, Cornel Univ, Univ of Chicago, lectr at Battelle Inst Seattle; Adams Prize 1966, Dannie Heineman Prize 1971, Eddington Medal 1975, Gravity Research Fndn 1975, Royal Medal 1985, Wolf Prize (for physics) 1988, Dirac Medal and Prize 1989, Albert Einstein Medal 1990, Science Book Prize 1990, Naylor Prize 1991, Forder lectr 1992–93; hon degrees: Univ of New Brunswick 1992, Univ of Surrey 1993, Univ of Bath 1994, Univ of London 1995, Univ of Glasgow 1996, Univ of Essex 1996, Univ of St Andrews 1997, Univ of Santiniketan India 1998, Open Univ 1998, Univ of Southampton 2002; memb Cncl: Royal Society 1980–82, London Mathematical Society 1983–87, Inst of Mathematics and Its Applications 1982–85 and 1990–93; pres Int Soc for Gen Relativity and Gravitation 1992–95; memb Polish Acad Sciences 1996, US Nat Acad of Sciences; fell: Wadham Coll Oxford 1973–98 (emeritus fell 1998–), UCL 1975, Univ of Calif 1978, Birkbeck Coll London 1996; hon fell St John's Coll Cambridge 1987, hon fell Inst of Physics 1999; FRS 1972; *Books* Techniques of Different Topology in Relativity (1972), Spinors and Space Time (with W Rindler, vol 1, 1984, vol 2, 1986), The Emperor's New Mind (1989), Shadows of the Mind (1994), The Nature of Space and Time (with Stephen Hawking, 1996), The Large, the Small and the Human Mind (1997); also co-edited numerous learned books and many scientific articles in academic jls; *Style*— Prof Sir Roger Penrose, OM; ✉ Mathematical Institute, 24–29 St Giles, Oxford OX1 3LB (☎ 01865 273546, fax 01865 273583, e-mail rouse@maths.ox.ac.uk)

PENROSE, Roger Ian; s of Edward Charles Penrose, of Plymouth, and Grace Feltis, *née* Bond; *b* 15 September 1953; *Educ* Plymouth Coll, Univ of Bath (BSc, BArch); *m* 7 Aug 1976, Janet Elaine, da of Richard Alan Harvey, RN; 2 s (Richard Merrick b 1984, Simon Tristan b 1987), 1 da (Laura Jane b 1989); *Career* princ Ian Penrose and Associates (chartered architects), md Ian Penrose Architects Ltd 1987–; *Recreations* motorcycling, sailing, cycle, swimming; *Clubs* OPM, IMTC, Royal Western Yatch Club of England; *Style*— R I Penrose, Esq; ✉ Redlands, Mount Tavy Road, Tavistock, Devon, PL19 9JL

PENSON, Alan Anthony; *b* 30 January 1952; *Educ* Dulwich Coll, St Catharine's Coll Cambridge (MA); *m* 1976, Jane; 1 s (Alexander b 1983), 1 da (Mary b 1985); *Career* Price Waterhouse 1974–85, gp chief exec Clarke Hooper plc 1992 (fin dir 1986–92), gen mangr Interwood Marketing (UK) plc 1993, gp fin dir Grey Communications Group Ltd 1994–95, princ Penson Associates 1996–; FCA; *Style*— Alan Penson, Esq; ✉ Penson Associates, Fairfield House, Dodds Lane, Chalfont St Giles, Buckinghamshire HP8 4EL (☎ 01494 778946, fax 0870 134 7896, e-mail alan@penson.co.uk)

PENTREATH, Prof (Richard) John; s of John Alistair Dudley Pentreath (ka Burma 1945), and Mary Lena, *née* Gendall; *b* 28 December 1943; *Educ* Sir Humphry Davy GS, Univ of London (BSc, DSc), Univ of Auckland (Commonwealth scholar, PhD); *m* Elisabeth Amanda, *née* Leach; 2 da (Tamsin Sarah b 22 Feb 1971, Lamorna Kate b 7 Nov 1974); *Career* MAFF: Science Res Cncl fell 1969 and memb scientific staff 1969–89, head Radiobiological Res 1985–87, head Aquatic Environment Protection Div and Res Support Gp and dep dir Fisheries Res 1988–89; chief scientist and dir of water quality Nat Rivers Authy 1989–95, chief scientist and dir of environmental strategy Environment Agency 1995–2000, res prof Environmental Systems Science Centre Univ of Reading 2000–07, prof emeritus Univ of Reading 2007–, research fell Plymouth Marine Lab 2009–; hon prof UEA 1996–2008, visiting prof Imperial Coll London 1997–2003; non-exec dir Research Sites Restoration Ltd 2009–; memb: Nat Environment Res Cncl 1992–98, Advsy Bd Centre for Social and Economic Res on the Global Environment 1994–2005, HE Funding Cncl Res Assessment Panel 1995–96 and 1999–2001, Cncl Marine Biological Assoc UK 1997–2000, Cncl Assoc for Schs Science Engrg and Technol (ASSET) 1998–99, Int Cmmn on Radiological Protection (ICRP) 2003–13 (emeritus memb 2014–); chm ICRP Ctee on Environmental Protection 2005–13; tstee Sir Alister Hardy Fndn for Ocean Science 2001–; ind memb Jt Nature Conservation Ctee 2000–06; pres: Cornwall Wildlife Tst 2003–, Cornwall Sustainable Building Tst 2005–11; Hon DSc: Univ of Hertfordshire 1998, UWE 1999, Univ of Plymouth 2002; CBiol, FSB, FSRP, CRadP; *Publications* Nuclear Power, Man and the Environment (1980); numerous papers and reports; *Recreations* visual arts, Cornish history, tall ship sailing; *Style*— Prof John Pentreath; ✉ Environmental Systems Science Centre, University of Reading, Whiteknights, PO Box 238, Reading RG6 6AL (☎ 0118 931 8741)

PENTY, Prof Richard Vincent; s of Peter Penty (d 1991), and (Patricia) Janet, *née* Shelbourne (d 1987); *b* 9 September 1964, Nottingham; *Educ* Repton, Sidney Sussex Coll Cambridge; *m* 1 Aug 1992, Victoria, *née* Eve; 2 s (George b 29 May 1994, Edward b 22 June 1998), 1 da (Katherine b 19 June 1996); *Career* lectr Sch of Physics Univ of Bath 1990–95, lectr rising to prof Dept of Electrical and Electronic Engrg Univ of Bristol 1995–2001, prof Univ of Cambridge 2001–, fell Sidney Sussex Coll Cambridge 2002– (dep vice master 2008, vice master 2011–12, acting master 2012–13, master 2013–); dir PervasID Ltd 2012–; FIET, SMIEEE, FREng 2013; *Recreations* reading, running; *Clubs* Oxford & Cambridge; *Style*— Prof Richard Penty; ✉ Sidney Sussex College, Sidney Street, Cambridge CB2 3HU (☎ 01223 338800)

PEPINSTER, Catherine; da of Michel Joseph Pepinster (d 1974), and Winifred, *née* Jones; *b* 7 July 1959, London; *Educ* Univ of Manchester (BA), City Univ London (Dip), Heythrop Coll London (MA); *m* 2003, Kevin Charles Morley; *Career* local newspaper reporter Manchester and London 1981–85, property corr Sheffield Morning Telegraph 1985–86, chief reporter Estate Times 1986, news ed Building 1987–89, reporter The Observer 1989–90, news ed Time Out 1990–94; asst news ed The Independent 1994–95, news ed Independent on Sunday 1997–98 (dep news ed 1995–97), features ed The Independent 1998, exec ed The Independent of Sunday 2002–04 (asst ed 1999–2002), ed The Tablet 2004–; *Recreations* walking, reading, architecture, Belgian culture; *Clubs* Reform; *Style*— Ms Catherine Pepinster; ✉ The Tablet, 1 King Street Cloisters, Clifton Walk, London W6 0QZ (☎ 020 8748 8484, fax 020 8748 1550, e-mail cpepinster@thetablet.co.uk)

PEPLOE, Guy; s of Denis Frederick Neil Peploe, RSA, and Elizabeth Marion, *née* Barr; *b* 25 January 1960; *Educ* The Edinburgh Acad, Univ of Aberdeen (MA); *Career* exhibition offr Royal Scottish Acad 1983, res asst Scottish Nat Gallery of Modern Art 1983–85, md The Scottish Gallery 1991– (dir 1984–); *Publications* SJ Peploe 1871–1935 (2000), Pat Douthwaite (2016); *Recreations* golf, mycology; *Style*— Guy Peploe, Esq; ✉ The Scottish Gallery, 16 Dundas Street, Edinburgh EH3 6HZ (☎ 0131 558 1200, fax 0131 558 3900)

PEPPER, Prof Gordon Terry; CBE; s of Harold Terry Pepper (d 1973), and Jean Margaret Gordon, *née* Furness (d 1963); *b* 2 June 1934; *Educ* Repton, Trinity Coll Cambridge (MA); *m* 30 Aug 1958, Gillian Clare, da of Lt-Col William Helier Huelin (d 1978); 3 s (Alasdair b 1960, Harry b 1967, Mark b 1969), 1 da (Linda (Ninna) b 1961); *Career* Nat Serv cmmnd RCS 1952–54; Equity and Law Life Assurance Soc 1957–60; W Greenwell & Co: joined 1960, ptnr 1962, jt sr ptnr 1980; chm Greenwell Montagu & Co 1986–87, dir and sr advsr Midland Montagu (Holdings) Ltd 1987–90, chm Payton Pepper & Sons Ltd 1987–97 (dir 1986–97); City Univ Business Sch: dir Centre For Financial Markets 1988–98, prof 1991–98 (hon visiting prof 1987–90 and 1998–2011); dir Lombard Street Research Ltd 1998–2015 (chm 2000–09); memb: Ctee on Industry and Fin Nat Econ Devpt Cncl 1988–90, Econ and Social Res Cncl 1989–93; FIA 1961, FSIP; *Publications* Money, Credit and Inflation (1990), Money, Credit and Asset Prices (1994), Inside Thatcher's Monetarist Revolution (1998), Monetarism Under Thatcher: Lessons for the Future (with M Oliver, 2001), The Liquidity Theory of Asset Prices (with M Oliver, 2006), articles in various econ and fin jls; *Recreations* sailing, walking, family; *Clubs* Reform, Royal Ocean Racing, Royal Channel Islands Yacht; *Style*— Prof Gordon Pepper, CBE; ✉ Durnsford Mill, Mildenhall, Marlborough, Wiltshire SN8 2NG (☎ 01672 511073, e-mail gordonpepper@btopenworld.com)

PEPPER, Prof Sir Michael; kt (2006); s of Morris Pepper (d 1982), and Ruby, *née* Bloom (d 2006); *b* 10 August 1942, London; *Educ* St Marylebone GS, Univ of Reading (BSc, PhD); *m* Oct 1973, Dr Jeannette Denise, da of Albert Josse, of London; 2 da (Judith Leah, Ruth Jennifer); *Career* res physicist The Plessey Co Ltd 1969–82, res Cavendish Lab 1973–, princ res fell GEC plc 1982–87, prof of physics Univ of Cambridge 1987–2009, Pender prof of nanoelectronics UCL 2009–; hon prof of pharmaceutical science Univ of Otago NZ 2005–11, hon prof of physics UCL 2009–, visiting prof in physical sciences and engrg Univ of Oxford 2010–; Warren res fell Royal Soc 1978–86, fell Trinity Coll Cambridge 1982–; jt md Toshiba Research Europe Ltd 1990–2007, jt fndr and dir TeraView Ltd 2001–; Guthrie Prize and Medal Inst of Physics 1985, Hewlett-Packard Europhysics Prize 1985, Hughes Medal of Royal Soc 1987, Mott Prize and Medal Inst of Physics 2000, Royal Medal Royal Soc 2005, Gold Medal for Business and Innovation Inst of Physics 2010; various named lectures incl: Mountbatten Meml Lecture IEE 2003, Bakerian lectr Royal Soc 2004, Saha Meml Lecture Kolkata 2008, Cherwell-Simon Meml Lecture Oxford 2010, CV Raman Meml Lecture Indian Inst of Science Bangalore 2010, Cockroft-Walton Lecture Inst of Physics 2013, Faraday Medal Inst of Engrg and Technol 2013, Dirac Lecture Univ of NSW 2013, Dirac Prize and Medal Australia Inst of Physics Univ of NSW 2013, Kelvin Lecture Inst of Engrg and Technol 2015; ScD Univ of Cambridge 1989; FRS 1983, FREng 2009, Hon FInstP 2012, memb Academia Europea 2012; *Publications* incl pubns on physics of semiconductors and quantum processes in nanostructures; *Recreations* travel, music, walking, whisky tasting; *Clubs* Arsenal FC, Athenaeum; *Style*— Prof Sir Michael Pepper, FRS, FREng; ✉ London Centre for Nanotechnology, 17–19, Gordon Street, London WC1H 0AH (e-mail michael.pepper@ucl.ac.uk and mp10000@cam.ac.uk)

PEPPER, Simon Richard; OBE (2000); s of Dr Richard Pepper (d 1992), and Patricia, *née* Mackenzie (d 2009); *b* 27 September 1947, Worthing, W Sussex; *Educ* Univ of Aberdeen (BSc), UCL (MSc), Univ of St Andrews (LLD); *m* 1973, Morag; 1 da (Jessica b 1975), 1 s (Duncan b 1978); *Career* dir WWF Scotland 1985–2005, memb Deer Cmmn Scotland 2005–10, memb Bd Scottish Natural Heritage 2010–; memb Nat Ctee Forestry Cmmn Scotland 2003–09, external memb Cabinet Sub-Ctee on Sustainable Scotland 2004–07, memb Scottish Ctee Heritage Lottery Fund 2011–; rector Univ of St Andrews 2005–08; *Recreations* enjoying the wild; *Style—* Mr Simon Pepper, OBE

PEPPERCORN, David James Creagh; s of James Kenneth Peppercorn (d 1991), and Ida Alice Knight (d 1985); *b* 25 August 1931; *Educ* Beaumont Coll, Trinity Coll Cambridge (MA); *m* 1, 11 April 1959, Susan Mary Sweeney; 3 da (Caroline b 1961, Sarah b 1963, Frances b 1964); m 2, 10 June 1977, Serena Sutcliffe, *qv*; *Career* int wine conslt; dir: Morgan Furze & Co Ltd 1958–74, Peter Dominic 1964–74, Gilbey Vintners 1969–74, Wine Standards Bd of the Vintners' Co 1987–93, French Wine Farmers Ltd 1993–99; memb Inst of Masters of Wine 1962 (chm 1968–70); judge at Premier Concours Mondial (Budapest 1972); André Simon Meml Prize 1983, Lifetime Achievement Award Bacchus Soc of America 2006; Liveryman Worshipful Co of Vintners 1952, memb Worshipful Co of Watermen and Lightermen of the River Thames; Chevalier dans l'Ordre des Arts et des Lettres (France) 1988; *Books* Drinking Wine (with Bryan Cooper, 1979), Bordeaux (1982, 2 edn 1991), Pocket Guide to the Wines of Bordeaux (1986, 2000, 2002 and 2004, translated into German 1986, 2000 and 2002, French 1987 and 1993, Danish 1987, Swedish 1988, Japanese 1990 and 1999, also American edn 1987), Wine Report (Bordeaux Section, 2008); *Recreations* music, walking, travelling; *Clubs* Garrick, MCC, Saintsbury; *Style—* David Peppercorn, Esq, MW; ✉ 2 Bryanston Place, London W1H 2DE

PEPPIATT, Dr Michael Henry; s of Edward George Peppiatt (d 1983), of Stocking Pelham, Herts, and Elsa Eugénie Peppiatt (d 1997); *b* 9 October 1941; *Educ* Brentwood Sch, Göttingen Univ, Trinity Hall Cambridge (MA, PhD); *m* 1989, Dr Jill Patricia Lloyd, *qv*, da of Peter Brown; 1 da (Clio Patricia b 16 Feb 1991), 1 s (Alexander Michael b 23 April 1994); *Career* art critic The Observer 1964, arts ed Réalités Paris 1966–68, art and literary ed Le Monde 1969–71; Paris arts corr: New York Times, Financial Times, Art International 1973–86; ed and publisher Art International 1987–; exhibition organiser: Sch of London (Louisiana Museum Humlebaek) 1987, Francis Bacon retrospective (Museo d'Arte Moderna Lugano) 1993, Ecole de Londres (Musée Maillol Paris) 1998, (Kunsthaus Vienna) 1999, Zoran Music Retrospective (Sainsbury Centre Norwich) 2000, Raymond Mason Retrospective (Musée Maillol Paris) 2000, Alberto Giacometti Retrospective (Sainsbury Centre Norwich) 2001, Fondation de l'Hermitage Lausanne 2002, Aristide Maillol Retrospective (IVAM Valencia) 2002, Christian Schad Retrospective (with Jill Lloyd, Musée Maillol Paris) 2002, (Neue Galerie New York) 2003, Francis Bacon Retrospective (IVAM Valencia) 2003, Musée Maillol Paris 2004, Antoni Tàpies (Centro Cultural Banco do Brasil São Paulo) 2005, Caravaggio/Bacon (Galleria Borghese Rome) 2009, Dado: Sculptures (Venice Biennale) 2009, Maillol (Caixa Catalunya Barcelona) 2010, Giacometti: An Intimate Portrait (Eykyn-Maclean NY) 2010, Giacometti: L'anima del Novecento (Maga Gallarate) 2011, Giacometti (Kunstforum, Hamburg) 2013, Miró (Kunst Forum Hamburg and Kunstsammlung Düsseldorf) 2015; memb: Soc of Authors, Royal Soc of Lit; *Publications* Imagination's Chamber – Artists and Their Studios (1983), School of London (1987), Francis Bacon: Anatomy of an Enigma (1996), Entretiens avec Francis Bacon (1998), Entretiens avec Zoran Music (1999), Francis Bacon à l'atelier (2000), Alberto Giacometti in Postwar Paris (2001), L'Atelier d'Alberto Giacometti (2003), Francis Bacon: The Sacred and the Profane (2003), Les dilemmes de Jean Dubuffet (2006), Francis Bacon in the 1950s (2006), Van Gogh and Expressionism (ed with Jill Lloyd, 2007), Francis Bacon: Studies for a Portrait (2008), Lucian Freud (2010), In Giacometti's Studio (2010), Interviews with Artists 1966–2012 (2012), Nicolas de Staël (2013), Voices of Contemporary Art (2014), Henri Cartier-Bresson (2014), Francis Bacon In Your Blood (2015); *Recreations* squash, real tennis, lawn tennis; *Clubs* Jeu de Paume (Paris), RAC, Oxford & Cambridge; *Style—* Dr Michael Peppiatt; ✉ 16 Rue Michel le Comte, 75003 Paris (e-mail m.peppiatt@zen.co.uk or michael@michaelpeppiatt.com, website www.michaelpeppiatt.com)

PERAHIA, Murray; *b* New York; *Educ* Mannes Coll; *Career* pianist and conductor; studied with Mieczyslaw Horszowski; winner Leeds Int Piano Competition 1972; co-dir Aldeburgh Festival 1981–89 (first concert appearance 1973); Hon FRCM, Hon RAM; princ guest conductor Acad of St Martin in the Fields; recitals in NY, London, Berlin, Zurich, Vienna; orchs played with incl: Berlin Phiharmonic, Philharmonia Orch, Acad of St Martin in the Fields, Israel Philharmonic, Chicago Symphony, Met Orch (Carnegie Hall); *Recordings* exclusive Sony recording artist; complete Mozart piano concertos (directing English Chamber Orch), complete Beethoven concertos (with Concertgebouw Orch under Bernard Haitink), Mendelssohn and Chopin concertos, Schubert's Winterreise (with Peter Pears and Dietrich Fischer-Dieskau), Bartok's Sonata for Two Pianos and Percussion (with Sir Georg Solti, winner 1989 Grammy Award), Brahms' G minor Quartet (with Amadeus Quartet), Chopin's Études (winner Grammy Award 2002); *Style—* Murray Perahia, Esq; ✉ c/o Askonas Holt, Lincoln House, 300 High Holborn, London WC1V 7JH (e-mail info@askonasholt.co.uk)

PERCIVAL, Catherine (Kate); da of Peter Greenwood Owen, and Barbara, *née* Sarvis; *b* 30 June 1959, UK; *Educ* Univ of Monaco (MSc, Thesis Prize); *m* Christopher O'Donoghue; 2 da (Sophie Rogerson (*née* Percival) b 14 Sept 1981, Olivia Percival b 24 July 1987); *Career* formerly worked in property, chm Creative and Marketing Servs Div Chime Communications plc 1997–2001, co-fndr and ceo Grace Belgravia 2012–; *Recreations* cinema, opera, reading, sailing, skiing, travel, walking; *Clubs* Arts, 5 Hertford Street, 67 Pall Mall; *Style—* Ms Kate Percival; ✉ Grace Belgravia,11c West Halkin Street, London SW1X 8JL (website www.gracebelgravia.com, Twitter @gracebelgravia.com)

PERCY, Humphrey Richard; s of Adrian John Percy, of Tunbridge Wells, Kent, and Maisie, *née* Gardner; *b* 2 October 1956; *Educ* Winchester; *m* 27 April 1985, Suzanne Patricia Spencer, da of Maj Bruce Holford-Walker, of London; 2 s (Luke, Christopher), 2 da (Daisy, Emma); *Career* J Henry Schroder Wagg & Co Ltd 1974–80, dir Barclays Merchant Bank Ltd 1985–86 (joined 1980); Barclays de Zoete Wedd Ltd: dir 1986–94, dep treas 1986–89, md and head Swaps and Options Gp Europe 1989–92, md and global head of foreign exchange Barclays Bank plc 1992–94, divnl md Barclays Bank plc 1992–94; exec dir Strategic Asset Management Ltd Bermuda 1994–95; Westdeutsche Landesbank Girozentrale (WestLB): gen mangr London 1995–2002, md and head of European treasury 1995–96, md and global head of treasury 1997–2000, chief exec and head of global financial markets 2000–02, dir of various WestLB cos; chm and fndr SGM-Foreign Exchange Ltd 2002–, global head of futures ICAP plc 2004–05, chief exec Bank of London and The Middle East plc 2006–; dir: Core 12 LLC, Sloane LLC, Moorgate LLC, Trophy LV Fund, Trophy LV Master Fund; memb Int Advsy Ctee Thomas Cook 1996–97; MCIB; *Recreations* walking, skiing, reading, travel, wine, history; *Clubs* Capital, Knole; *Style—* Humphrey Percy, Esq; ✉ Bank of London and The Middle East plc, Sherborne House, Cannon Street, London EC4N 5AT

PERCY, Prof John Pitkeathly (Ian); CBE (1997); s of John Percy (d 1984), of Edinburgh, and Helen Glass, *née* Pitkeathly (d 1988); *b* 16 January 1942; *Educ* Edinburgh Acad, Univ of Edinburgh; *m* 26 June 1965, Sheila Isobel, da of Roy Toshack Horn (d 1957), of Edinburgh; 2 da (Jill Sheila b 12 April 1969, Sally Charlotte b 24 Dec 1972); *Career* chartered accountant; asst Graham Smart & Annan 1960–68, ptnr Martin Currie & Scott 1969–71; Grant Thornton: ptnr 1971–95, London managing ptnr 1981–88, Scottish sr ptnr 1991–95; chm: Kiln plc 2002–05, Companies House 2002–06 (memb Steering Bd 1995–2001); dep chm: Scottish Provident Institution 1993–2001, The Weir Group plc 2005– (non-exec dir 1996–), Ricardo plc 2000–; non-exec dir: Deutsche (Scotland) Ltd 1992–2001, William Wilson Holdings Ltd 1993–2005, Cala Group Ltd 2001–; chm: Accounts Cmmn for Scotland 1992–2001, ICMG Corporate Governance Cmmn until 2001; vice-chm UK Auditing Practices Bd 1991–2001, UK memb Int Audit Practices Cmmn 1995–2000, memb Scottish Legal Aid Bd 2000–06; pres ICAS 1990–91; hon prof of accountancy Univ of Aberdeen; chm of govrs The Edinburgh Acad 1992–2000; chm Queen Margaret Univ Edinburgh 2004–; elder St Cuthbert's Church of Scotland 1966; Freeman: City of London 1982, Worshipful Co of Painter-Stainers 1982; Hon LLD Univ of Aberdeen 1999; CA 1967, MAE 1989, FRSA 1989, CIMgt 2001; *Recreations* golf, trout fishing; *Clubs* Hon Co of Edinburgh Golfers, R&A, RAC, New (Edinburgh), Caledonian; *Style—* Prof Ian Percy, CBE

PERCY, Keith Edward; s of Cyril Edward Percy, of London, and Joyce Rose Percy; *b* 22 January 1945; *Educ* Wanstead Co HS, Univ of Manchester (BA); *m* 14 Feb 1970, (Rosemary) Pamela, da of Thomas William Drake, of London; 1 da (Elizabeth b 1974), 1 s (Nicholas b 1977); *Career* head research Phillips & Drew 1976–83 (joined 1967), exec chm Phillips & Drew Fund Management 1983–90; chief exec: UBS Asset Management (UK) Ltd 1989–90, Morgan Grenfell Asset Management Ltd 1990–96; exec chm SG Asset Management 1999–2009, advsr GLG Ptnrs 2009–; dir: Standard Life Equity Income Tst 1991–, Brunner Investment Tst plc 2004–16 (chm 2005–16), JP Morgan Japanese Investment Tst 2004–, Henderson Smaller Cos Investment Tst plc 2006–; chm RAW Communications Ltd 1998–2003; non-exec dir: Smiths Industries Med Systems 1977–2000, IMRO 1987–95, The Children's Mutual 2009–13, F&C Asset Mgmnt 2011–14; memb Cncl Soc of Investment Analysts 1976–87, chm FTSE Actuaries Share Indices Steering Ctee, dir FTSE Int 1995–96; *Recreations* tennis, rugby, music, theatre, travel; *Clubs* The City; *Style—* Keith E Percy, Esq

PERCY-DAVIS, Sarah Anne; da of Guy Harvey, of Bromsgrove, Worcs, and Jane, *née* Taylor; *b* 2 October 1971; *Educ* The Alice Ottley Sch Worcester, Br Inst Florence, Oxford Brookes Univ (BA), Christie's Education (RSA Dip Fine and Decorative Art); *m* 18 Sept 2004, Nicholas Percy-Davis; *Career* Phillips Fine Art Auctioneers: ceramics porter 1994, saleroom mangr Picture Dept 1994–95, head of Picture Dept 1997–98; picture specialist and jt head Regular Auction Dept Sotheby's 1998–2000; prodr Brando Quilici Prodns Rome 2000–03; produced documentaries for Discovery Channel incl: Ultimate Guide: Iceman, Ultimate Guide: Volcano, Iceman the Sequel, John Paul II: His Life and Legacy; prodr Atlantic Prodns London 2003–04; produced documentaries for Discovery Channel, Channel 5, BBC Worldwide, La 7 and Spiegel incl: Mysterious Death of Cleopatra, Mystery of the Tibetan Mummy; chief exec LAPADA 2004–; *Style—* Mrs Sarah Percy-Davis; ✉ LAPADA, 535 Kings Road, Chelsea, London SW10 0SZ (☎ 020 7823 3511, fax 020 7823 3522, mobile 07970 870703, e-mail spercy-davis@lapada.org)

PERCY-ROBB, Prof Iain Walter; s of Capt Ian Ernest Percy-Robb (d 1967), and Margaret Drysdale Carrick, *née* Galbraith (d 1991); *b* 8 December 1935; *Educ* George Watson's Coll Edinburgh, Univ of Edinburgh (MB ChB, PhD); *m* 22 May 1961, Margaret Elizabeth, da of Dr Ronald Leslie Cormie (d 1997), of Glasgow; 2 s (Michael Iain b 1964, Stephen Leslie b 1966), 2 da (Jane Elizabeth b 1962, Claire Margaret b 1971); *Career* MRC int travelling res fell Cornell Univ 1972–73; Univ of Edinburgh: res scholar 1963–65, lectr 1965–68, sr lectr 1968–76, reader 1976–84; prof of pathological biochemistry Univ of Glasgow 1984– (assoc dean of educn Faculty of Med); chm Informed Software Ltd 1987–97; memb Scot Swimming Team Empire and Cwlth Games Cardiff 1958; FRCPE, FRCPath; *Books* Lecture Notes on Clinical Chemistry (jtly, 1984), Diseases of the Gastrointestinal Tract and Liver (jtly, 1989), Muir's Textbook of Pathology (jtly, 1992); *Recreations* golf; *Clubs* Royal Burgess Golfing Soc (Edinburgh), The Glasgow GC; *Style—* Prof Iain Percy-Robb

PEREIRA, Dr (Raul) Scott; s of Dr Helio Gelli Pereira, FRS (d 1994), and Dr Marguerite Pereira, *née* Scott (d 1988); *b* 14 April 1948; *Educ* Mill Hill Sch, Trinity Coll Cambridge, Univ of Oxford Med Sch; *m* 14 April 1972, Hilary Glen, da of Prof Vernon Rycroft Pickles, of Oxford; 1 s (Thomas b 1979), 1 da (Penelope b 1977); *Career* pathology trainee Northwick Park Hosp Harrow 1973–76, res sr registrar Westminster Hosp and Med Sch 1976–79, clinical scientist MRC Clinical Res Centre Harrow 1979–83, res fell West Middlesex Univ Hosp 1983–86; conslt and sr lectr in immunology: St Helier Hosp, Carshalton and St George's Hosp Med Sch Tooting 1986–96; sr lectr and conslt immunologist Chelsea & Westminster Hosp (Imperial Coll Sch of Med) 1996–2000; dir of clinical audit and effectiveness Royal Coll of Pathologists 2000–; vice-pres Residential Boat Owners' Assoc; *Recreations* offshore cruising, boating; *Style—* Dr Scott Pereira

PEREIRA GRAY, Prof Sir Denis John; kt (1999), OBE (1981); s of Dr Sydney Joseph Pereira Gray (d 1975), of Exeter, and Alice Evelyn, *née* Cole (d 1999); *b* 2 October 1935; *Educ* Exeter Sch, St John's Coll Cambridge (MA, MB BChir), Bart's Med Sch; *m* 28 April 1962, Jill Margaret, da of Frank Carruthers Hoyte (d 1976), of Exeter; 1 s (Peter b 1963), 3 da (Penelope b 1965, Elizabeth b 1968, Jennifer b 1970); *Career* in gen med practice 1962–2000, prof of gen practice Univ of Exeter 1986–2001 (sr lectr 1973–86), regnl advsr in gen practice Univ of Bristol 1975–96, conslt advsr in gen practice to CMO DHSS 1984–87, dir Postgrad Med Sch Exeter 1987–97, assoc med postgrad dean Univ of Bristol 1992–96, dir of postgrad gen practice educn (SW Region) 1996–2000; elected memb: Cncl RCGP 1971–2000 (chm 1987–90, pres 1997–2000), GMC 1994–2003; pres: Soc of Med Illustrators 1997–2000, Soc for the Social History of Med 1999; chm: Acad of Med Royal Colls 2000–02 (vice-chm 1998–2000), Nuffield Tst 2003–06 (governing tstee 1994–2006); ed Med Annual 1983–87, hon ed RCGP journal 1972–80 and pubns 1976–2000; chm Jt Ctee on Postgrad Trg for Gen Practice 1994–97, patron Nat Assoc for Patient Participation, pres What About the Children? 2008, vice-chm Ethics and Confidentiality Ctee Nat Info Governance Bd 2009–11; Hunterian Soc Gold Medal 1966 and 1969, Sir Charles Hastings Prize 1967 and 1970, James Mackenzie Lecture 1977, George Abercrombie Award 1978, Gale Memorial Lecture 1979, RCGP Fndn Cncl Award 1980, Sir Harry Platt Prize 1981, Haliburton Hume Memorial Lecture 1988, McConaghey Memorial Lecture 1988, Northcott Memorial Lecture 1988, Harvard Davis Lecture 1988, Murray Scott Lecture 1990, Harben Lecture 1994, Sally Irvine Lecture 1995, annual address Royal Soc of Health 1997, Albert Wander Lecture RSM 1998, Andrew Smith Memorial Lecture 1998, Reading Oration 1998, Sir David Bruce Lecture 1999, Tom Stewart Lecture 2000, Purves Oration 2000, Frans Huygen Lecture (The Netherlands) 2001, Long Fox Lecture 2002, Deakin Lecture (Aust) 2005, Goodman Lecture 2013, Starfield Lecture 2015; hon fell Queen Mary Univ of London, hon prof Peninsula Coll of Medicine and Dentistry 2010–12, hon prof Univ of Exeter Medical Sch 2013; Hon DSc De Montfort Univ, Hon DM Univ of Nottingham 2003, Hon DSc Univ of Exeter 2009; hon memb Cuban Family Practitioners Assoc 2000, hon memb Polish Coll of GPs 2000, foreign memb Inst of Med USA 2000; FRCGP 1973 (MRCGP 1967), FRSA 1989, Hon FRSH 1997, FRCP 1999, Hon FFPH 2000, Hon FIHSM 2000, Hon FRCPI 2001; Running a Practice (jtly, 1978), Training for General Practice (1981), Forty Years On: The Story of the First 40 Years of the Royal College of General Practitioners (ed, 1992); author of articles in The Lancet, BMJ, British Journal of General Practice, Medical Education; *Recreations* reading, walking; *Clubs* RSM, Royal Over-Seas League; *Style—* Prof Sir Denis Pereira Gray, OBE; ✉ Alford House, 9 Marlborough Road, Exeter, Devon EX2 4TJ (☎ 01392 218080); University of Exeter, Smeall Building, Exeter Medical School, St Luke's Campus, Exeter EX1 2LU

PERERA, Prof Katharine Mary; da of Arnold Lacey, of Wallasey, and Eileen, *née* Haylock; *b* 12 December 1943; *Educ* Wallasey HS for Girls, Bedford Coll London (BA), Univ of Manchester (MA, PhD); *m* 1967, Suria Perera; *Career* VSO Malaysia 1965–66, teacher Merseyside 1967–72, lectr Padgate Coll of HE 1973–76; Univ of Manchester: lectr 1977–91, prof 1991–, sr pro-vice-chllr 2000– (pro-vice-chllr 1994–); non-exec dir Salford Royal Hosps NHS Tst 1999–, chair of govrs Withington Girls' Sch 1998–, govr NE Wales Inst of HE 2001–, memb bd Leadership Fndn for HE 2003–; *Books* Children's Writing and

P

Reading (1984), Understanding Language (1987), Growing Points in Child Language (1994); *Recreations* walking, reading, music (memb Hallé Concerts Soc); *Style*— Prof Katharine Perera; ✉ School of English and Linguistics, University of Manchester, Oxford Road, Manchester M13 9PL (☎ 0161 275 3190, fax 0161 275 3187, e-mail k.perera@man.ac.uk)

PERETZ, George; QC (2015); *Educ* William Ellis Sch London, Exeter Coll Oxford (BA); *m* 1995, Mandy, *née* Brown; 1 da (Eleanor b 1998); *Career* called to the Bar 1990; legal advsr OFT 1992–97, barr Monckton Chambers 1998–; judge First-Tier Tbnl (Social Entitlement Chamber); jt convener UK State Aid Law Assoc; *Recreations* music, opera, reading, travel, walking, clarinet, piano; *Style*— George Peretz, Esq, QC; ✉ Monckton Chambers, 1 & 2 Raymond Buildings, Gray's Inn, London WC1R 5NR

PERGANT, Jean-Jacques; s of Jean Pergant (d 1974), and Anne-Marie, *née* François; *b* 24 February 1949; *Educ* Coll Episcopal St Etienne Strasbourg, Lycée Technique Hotelier de Strasbourg, McGill Univ Mgmnt Inst Montreal (Sr Mgmnt Prog), Exec TV Workshop NY (media trg), Nottingham Trent Univ (Cert Enterprise Mgmnt); *m*; 2 c; *Career* hotelier; served French Forces 1969–70; various jr managerial positions in hotel business London, Paris and Canary Islands 1968–74, various mgmnt positions within Four Seasons Hotels and Resorts Gp 1974–91 (latterly gen mangr Four Seasons Hotel Ottawa 1986–91), gen mangr Hanbury Manor Hotel, Golf & Country Club 1991–94, gen mangr The Berkeley Hotel (Savoy Gp) London 1994–2002, sr vice-pres and md Savoy Gp 2002–04, pres Boca Raton Resort & Club FL 2004–05, pres LXR Luxury Resorts 2005–; chm West One Hotel Managers Gp London 2000; memb: London Divnl Ctee Br Hospitality Assoc, HCIMA; Officier/Maitre de Table La Chaîne des Rotisseurs, Grand Officier L'Ordre Illustre des Chevaliers de Meduse, Cdr La Commanderie de Bordeaux, Chev Chancellerie Franco-Britannique; *Recreations* triathlons, photography, watercolours, interior design; *Style*— Jean-Jacques Pergant, Esq; ✉ LXR Luxury Resorts, WHM LLC, 501 East Camino Real, Boca Raton, Florida 33432, USA

PERHAM, Rt Rev Michael Francis; s of Raymond Maxwell Perham (d 1992), of Dorchester, and Marcelle Winifred, *née* Barton; *b* 8 November 1947; *Educ* Hardye's Sch Dorchester, Keble Coll Oxford (open exhbn, MA), Cuddesdon Theol Coll; *m* Dr Alison Jane Grove, da of Douglas Grove; 4 da (Rachel b 1984, Anna b 1986, Sarah b 1987, Mary b 1990); *Career* curate St Mary Addington Croydon 1976–81, chaplain to the Bishop of Winchester 1981–84, team rector Oakdale Team Miny Poole 1984–92, canon residentiary and precentor Norwich Cathedral 1991–98, vice-dean of Norwich 1995–98, provost of Derby 1998–2000, dean of Derby 2000–04, bishop of Gloucester 2004–14, hon asst bishop Dios of Bath and Wells, Carlisle, Portsmouth and Salisbury 2016–; sec C of E Doctrine Cmmn 1979–84; memb: C of E Liturgical Cmmn 1986–2001, Archbishops' Cmmn on Church Music 1998–92, Gen Synod C of E 1989–92 and 1993–, Cathedrals Fabric Cmmn for England 1996–2001; memb House of Lords 2009–14; chm: Praxis 1990–97, Cathedrals' Liturgy Gp 1993–2001, Archbishops' Cncl 1999–2004, Church Heritage Forum 1999–2001, Business Ctee Gen Synod 2001–04, Governing Body SPCK 2006–12 (memb 2002–12), C of E Hosp Chaplaincies Cncl 2007–10; vice-chair C of E Mission and Public Affrs Cncl 2007–10; pres Retired Clergy Assoc 2007–14, pres Affirming Catholicism 2010–14; bishop protector Soc of St Francis 2005–14; pres Alcuin Club 2005–; pro-chllr Cncl Univ of Glos (vice-chair 2013) 2004–15, chair and govr Ripon Coll Cuddesdon 2009–15 (hon fell 2014), chair Bd of Govrs Univ of St Mark and St John Plymouth 2016–; visiting scholar Sarum Coll 2015–; vice-pres WATCH 2011–; Freeman City of Gloucester 2014; Hon DPhil Univ of Glos; fell Woodard Corp 2000–04; FRSCM 2002; *Publications* The Eucharist (1978), The Communion of Saints (1980), Liturgy Pastoral and Parochial (1984), Waiting for the Risen Christ (with Kenneth Stevenson, 1986), Towards Liturgy 2000 (ed, 1989), Liturgy for a New Century (ed, 1991), Welcoming the Light of Christ (with Kenneth Stevenson, 1991), Lively Sacrifice (1992), The Renewal of Common Prayer (1993), Model of Inspiration (ed, 1993), Celebrate the Christian Story (1997), The Sorrowful Way (1998), A New Handbook of Pastoral Liturgy (2000), Signs of Your Kingdom (2002), Glory in our Midst (2005), To Tell Afresh (2010), The Hospitality of God (with Mary Gray-Reeves, 2011), Jesus and Peter: Growing in Friendship with God (2012), Echoing the Word (with Paula Gooder, 2013); *Recreations* reading, writing, creating liturgical texts, walking in the Yorkshire dales; *Style*— The Rt Rev Michael Perham; ✉ The Old Mill, Bleadney, Wells, Somerset BA5 1PF (☎ 07837 815605, landline 01749 670239, e-mail michaelperham47@gmail.com)

PERKIN, (George) David; s of Alan Spencer Perkin (d 1996), of Leeds, and Vera Perkin (d 1958); *Educ* Leeds Modern Sch, Pembroke Coll Cambridge (BA, MB BChir), KCH; *m* 11 July 1964, Louise Ann, da of Sqdn Ldr John Boston, of Sevenoaks; 2 s (Michael b 1968, Matthew b 1971), 1 da (Emma b 1969); *Career* conslt neurologist Hillingdon Hosp 1977–2001, conslt neurologist Charing Cross Hosp 1977–2006; co-chm RCP Speciality Question Group 1998–2002, memb RCP Part II Examining Bd 1994–2003; FRCP 1985 (MRCP 1969); *Books* Optic Neuritis and its Differential Diagnosis (1978), Basic Neurology (1986), Atlas of Clinical Neurology (1986, 3 edn 2011), Diagnostic Tests in Neurology (1988), Pocket Guide to Clinical Examination (1993, 4 edn 2009), Color Atlas and Text of Neurology (1998, 3 edn 2011), Clinical Examination (1992, 4 edn 2008); *Recreations* reading, music, bridge; *Style*— Dr David Perkin; ✉ Charing Cross Hospital, Fulham Palace Road, London W6 8RF (☎ 020 8846 1153, fax 020 8846 7487, mobile 07967 975138, e-mail gdperkin@gmail.com)

PERKINS; *see also:* Steele-Perkins

PERKINS, Alice Elizabeth; CB (2002); da of Derrick Leslie John Perkins (d 1965), and Elsa Rose, *née* Rink (d 1986); *b* 24 May 1949; *Educ* North London Collegiate Sch, St Anne's Coll Oxford (BA); *m* 10 Nov 1978, Rt Hon Jack Straw, MP, *qv*; 1 s (William David John Straw b 21 Sept 1980), 1 da (Charlotte Alice b 18 Aug 1982); *Career* DSS (formerly DHSS): joined as admin trainee 1971, private sec to Min of State 1974–75, princ 1975, asst to Chm of Supp Benefits Cmmn 1975–77, asst sec 1984–90, under sec and dir of personnel 1990–93; HM Treasy: head Def and Material Gp 1993–95, dep dir of public spending 1995–98; dir of corp mgmnt Dept of Health 1998–2000; head Corp Devpt Gp Cabinet Office 2001–05; chm Post Office Ltd 2011–; non-exec dir: Littlewoods Organisation plc 1997–2000, Taylor Nelson Sofres plc 2005–, BAA plc 2006, BBC Exec Bd; business coach JCA Gp Ltd 2006–; external memb Cncl Univ of Oxford 2006–14; hon fell St Anne's Coll Oxford 2007; *Recreations* gardening, looking at pictures; *Style*— Ms Alice Perkins, CB

PERKINS, David Charles Langrigge; s of Charles Samuel Perkins, OBE (d 1987), of Newcastle upon Tyne, and Victoria Alexandra Ryan (d 1991); *b* 31 May 1943; *Educ* Uppingham, Univ of Newcastle upon Tyne (LLB); *m* 1, 1971 (m dis 2000), Sandra Margaret, da of Frank Gerard Buck; 4 s (Benedict William Charles Heritage b 21 June 1972, Rory Philip Francis b 12 Oct 1979, Guy Ranulf David Westbury b 27 Jan 1983, Rupert Alexander David Langrigge b 19 Nov 1973 d 1981), 1 da (Davina Helen Alexandra b 20 May 1978); m 2, 29 Nov 2003, Marie-Ann Strömbäck; *Career* admitted slr 1969; Theodore Goddard & Co 1967–72, Clifford-Turner 1972–87, ptnr Clifford Chance 1987–2003, ptnr Milbank, Tweed, Hadley & McCloy 2003–09, ptnr Arnold and Porter 2010–13; arbitrator and mediator: WIPO, Hong Kong Int Arbitration Centre, JAMS Int, Kuala Lumpur Regional Centre for Arbitration (KLRCA), Singapore Int Arbitration and Mediation Centres (SIAC/SIMC), Ind Film and TV Alliance (IFTA), Nat Arbitration Assoc, American Arbitration Assoc/Int Centre for Dispute Resolution (AAA/ICDR), Pacific Int Arbitration Centre (PIAC), IP Panel Shenzen Centre for Int Arbitration (SCIA); chm: ICC Dispute Resolution Bd London Court of Int Arbitration (LCIA); memb Advsy Bd Munich Intellectual Property Dispute Resolution (IPDR) Forum; Exec Cmmn Union of Euro Practitioners in Industrial Property (Union-IP); author of over 50 pubns in jls and books, numerous lectures at international conferences; memb Law Soc; CIArb; *Recreations* golf, tennis; *Clubs* Northumberland Golf, Hurlingham; *Style*— David Perkins, Esq; ✉ The Old Vicarage, Sevenhampton, Cheltenham, Gloucestershire GL54 5SW (☎ 01242 821246, fax 01242 821113, e-mail davidclperkins@gmail.com, dperkins@jamsinternational.com)

PERKINS, Douglas; *b* 1943, Llanelli, Dyfed; *Educ* Llanelli Boys' GS, Cardiff Univ; *m* 25 March 1967, Dame Mary Perkins, DBE, *qv*; 2 da (Cathryn Llywella b 14 Oct 1967, Juliette Mary b 16 Oct 1968), 1 s (John Douglas b 4 Aug 1972); *Career* owner and optometrist Bebbington and Perkins 1966–80 (sold 23 stores 1980), co-fndr Specsavers Optical Gp 1984 (currently chm); Liveryman Worshipful Co of Spectacle Makers, Freeman City of London; hon fell: Cardiff Univ 2005, Swansea Univ 2006; Hon DUniv Anglia Ruskin Univ 2006, hon doctorate Plymouth Univ 2012; FCOptom 1967; *Recreations* tennis, walking, rugby, yoga; *Style*— Douglas Perkins, Esq; ✉ Specsavers Optical Group Ltd, La Villiaze, St Andrews, Guernsey GY6 8YP

PERKINS, Dr Ed; *Educ* Christ's Coll Cambridge (MA, PhD); *Career* prodr BBC Six O'Clock News 2002–05, asst prog ed ITN 2005–07, dep press sec to HM The Queen and head of news The Royal Household 2007–12, press sec to TRH The Duke and Duchess of Cambridge and Prince Harry 2012–; *Style*— Dr Ed Perkins; ✉ Kensington Palace, London W8 4PU

PERKINS, Ian Richard Brice; s of Francis Layton Perkins, CBE, DSC (d 1994), of London, and Josephine Louise, *née* Brice (d 1999); *b* 15 November 1949; *Educ* Charterhouse; *m* 5 April 1975, Melissa Anne, da of Sir John Milne; 2 da (Lisa Elizabeth b 5 Feb 1980, Tania Catherine Brice 29 Jan 1982), 1 s (Roderick John Bloomfield b 2 Oct 1984); *Career* W I Carr 1968–70 and 1971–72, Fergusson Bros Johannesburg 1970–71, Greenshields Inc 1972–79; James Capel and Co: joined 1979, pres James Capel Inc NY 1986–88, dir 1988–91; ceo King & Shaxson Holdings plc 1994–97 (dir 1991–97), dir Gerrard Group plc 1997–2000; chm: Gerrard & King Ltd 1997–99, GNI Ltd 2001–03 (ceo 1999–2001), King & Shaxson Ltd 2003–10, ILEX Asset Mgmnt 2005–10, Cambria Africa plc 2012–; dir: King & Shaxson Bond Brokers 1996–2003, Lombard Street Research 1998–2003; Freeman City of London 1973, memb Ct of Assts Worshipful Co of Skinners (Freeman 1975); *Recreations* golf, tennis, skiing; *Clubs* Boodle's, Honourable Co of Edinburgh Golfers (Muirfield), Swinley Forest, Leopard Creek, Morfontaine; *Style*— Ian Perkins, Esq; ✉ Moth House, Brown Candover, Alresford, Hampshire SO24 9TT (☎ 01256 389260, mobile 07831 674585, e-mail ian@mothhouse.net)

PERKINS, Prof John Douglas; CBE (2007); s of Douglas Herbert Perkins (d 1997), of Kent, and Isobel Mary Perkins; *b* 18 March 1950, Yeovil, Somerset; *Educ* Royal GS Guildford, Univ of London (BSc, MA, PhD, FCGI, DIC, Dip TCDHE, Hinchley Meml Medal); *m* 1, 11 June 1975 (m dis 1992), Chantal Marie, da of Claude Paul Ernest Lestavel; 1 s (Matthew John b 1987); m 2, 14 April 2009, Jennifer Anne, da of Peter Chambers (d 1996); *Career* univ demonstrator in chemical engrg Univ of Cambridge 1973–77, seconded to ICI Agric Div as res engr 1975–76, sr lectr in chemical engrg Imperial Coll London 1983–85 (lectr 1977–83), ICI prof of process systems engrg Univ of Sydney 1985–88; Imperial Coll London: prof of chemical engrg 1988–99, dir Centre for Process Systems Engrg 1992–98, head Dept of Chemical Engrg 1996–2001, Courtaulds prof of chemical engrg 2000–04, princ Faculty of Engrg 2001–04, visiting prof 2012–; vice-pres and dean of engrg and physical sciences Univ of Manchester 2004–09 (hon prof 2009–), provost MASDAR Inst of Sci and Technol 2009–10, chief scientific advsr Dept of Business, Innovation and Skills 2012–15; memb Foresight Manufacturing Panel Office of Science and Technol 1994–99, memb Cncl EPSRC 2012–15, UK delegate EU Jt Research Centre Bd 2012–15; dir JP2 Consulting Ltd 2015–; CEng, CSci, CMath; fell Inst of Mathematics and its Applications 1992 (assoc fell 1976, memb Cncl 2015–), FIChemE 1986 (memb Cncl 1997–2002, dep pres 1999–2000, pres 2000–01), FREng 1993 (memb Cncl 2004–10, vice-pres 2007–10), FCGI 1996, FRSA 2004, FIET 2015; *Publications* Professor John Perkins' Review of Engineering Skills (Dept of Business, Innovation and Skills 2013); *Recreations* gastronomy, cinema, theatre; *Style*— Prof John Perkins, CBE, FREng; ✉ 52 Mercury Buildings, 15 Aytoun Street, Manchester M1 3BL (e-mail johnperkins50@btinternet.com)

PERKINS, Dame Mary Lesley; DBE (2007); *née* Bebbington; da of (George) Leslie Bebbington (d 1985), and Eileen Hilda Constance, *née* Mawditt (d 2005); *b* 14 February 1944, Bristol; *Educ* Fairfield GS Bristol, Cardiff Univ; *m* 25 March 1967, Douglas John David Perkins, *qv*; 2 da (Cathryn Llywella b 14 Oct 1967, Juliette Mary b 16 Oct 1968), 1 s (John Douglas b 4 Aug 1972); *Career* owner and optometrist Bebbington and Perkins 1966–80 (sold 23 stores 1980), fndr Specsavers 1984 (jt owner with husband), fndr Specsavers HearCare; memb Gen Optical Cncl 1966; pres Age Concern Guernsey, govr Ladies' Coll Guernsey; patron: Kidscape, Hearing Dogs, Everywoman, British Citizen Awards 2015; Liveryman Worshipful Co of Spectacle Makers, Freeman City of London; Community and Vocational Service Award Rotary Intl 2005; hon graduate Assoc of Dispensing Opticians 2014; hon fell Cardiff Univ 2005, hon doctorate Plymouth Univ 2012, hon doctorate Stirling Univ 2014, hon doctorate Univ of Bradford 2015; hon chartered dir IOD; FBOA 1967; OStJ 2015; *Recreations* choir, walking, yoga, seven grandchildren, tai chi; *Style*— Dame Mary Perkins, DBE; ✉ Specsavers Optical Group Ltd, La Villiaze, St Andrews, Guernsey GY6 8YP (☎ 01481 234811, fax 01481 233714, e-mail mary.perkins@specsavers.com)

PERKINS, Michael John; s of Phillip John Broad Perkins, OBE, DL (d 1982), of Lymington, Hants, and Jane Mary, *née* Hope (d 2006); *b* 31 January 1942; *Educ* Eton, RNC Dartmouth; *m* 9 Nov 1968, Nicola Margaret, da of Air Cdre William Vernon Anthony Denney, of Amersham, Bucks; 1 s (Robert b 1971), 1 da (Caroline b 1973); *Career* RN 1961–66, Sub Lt 1963, Lt 1965; sr ptnr Westlake Clark & Co Chartered Accountants 1996–99 (ptnr 1981–99), dir NEWSCOM plc 1981–2000, dir New Milton Property 2002–11; treas: New Forest Assoc 1997–2010, New Forest Agric Show Soc 2001–07, Romsey Decorative Fine Arts Soc 2012–; Freeman City of London 1964, Liveryman Worshipful Co of Haberdashers 1964; CA (Canada) 1973, FCIS 1982; *Recreations* sailing, skiing, shooting, fly fishing; *Clubs* Royal Lymington Yacht, Royal Naval Sailing Assoc; *Style*— Michael Perkins, Esq; ✉ Critchells Farmhouse, Lockerley, Romsey, Hampshire SO51 0JD (☎ 01794 340281, e-mail perkins.lockerley@yahoo.co.uk)

PERKINS, (Matthew) Toby; MP; *b* 12 August 1970; *m* 30 Aug 1996, Suzie, *née* Francis; 1 s (Lewis), 1 da (Chloe); *Career* MP (Lab) Chesterfield 2010–, shadow min for small business 2011–15, shadow min for the Armed Forces 2015–; *Recreations* tennis, cricket; *Style*— Toby Perkins, Esq, MP; ✉ House of Commons, London SW1A 0AA

PERN, Andrew; *Career* prop and head chef The Star Inn Yorks 1996– (Michelin Star 2002–); *Books* Black Pudding & Foie Gras (2008), Loose Birds and Game (2010); *Style*— Andrew Pern, Esq; ✉ The Star Inn, Harome, Near Helmsley, North Yorkshire YO62 5JE

PEROLLS, Graham Keith; CMG (2014), OBE; s of Norman Grahame Perolls (d 1980), and Ellen Clara, *née* Eames (d 1984); *b* 21 September 1950, Dartford, Kent; *Educ* Dartford GS, Lund Univ; *m* 19 Feb 1982, Carolyn Angela Perolls; 4 da (Sharon b 1984, Esther b 1986, Deborah b 1989, Anna b 1991), 1 s (Cornel b 1988); *Career* dir KT Coachworks Ltd 1969–2008, fndr and exec dir Hospices of Hope 2005–; AIL; *Style*— Graham Perolls, Esq, CMG, OBE; ✉ Hospices of Hope, 11 High Street, Otford, Kent TN14 5PG

PEROWNE, Adm Sir James Francis; KBE (Mil) (2000, OBE (Mil) 1983); s of Lt Cdr John Herbert Francis Perowne (d 1999), and (Mary) Joy, *née* Dibb (d 2006); *b* 29 July 1947; *Educ* Sherborne, BRNC Dartmouth; *m* 1, 22 May 1971 (m dis 1990), Susan Anne, da of Cdr Peter John Holloway, of Western Australia; 4 s (Julian b 1972, Samuel b 1975, Roger b 1977, Timothy b 1977); m 2, 15 Feb 1992, Caroline Nicola, da of Dr T Grimson (d 2008); *Career* CO: HMS Opportune 1976–77, HMS Superb 1981–83, HMS Boxer 1986–88, asst dir Underwater Warfare MOD 1988–90, Second Submarine Sqdn 1990–92, HMS Norfolk and 6 Frigate Sqdn 1992–94; Sr Naval Memb RCDS 1995–96, Flag Offr Submarines, Cdr Submarines Eastern Atlantic and North West Europe and COS (Ops) to C-in-C Fleet 1996–98, Dep Supreme Allied Cdr Atlantic 1998–2002; pres: Submariners' Assoc 2002–16, Assoc of Royal Navy Offrs and Royal Navy Benevolent Soc for Offrs 2003–14; chm: Central Region Ctee Watervoice 2002–05, Consumer Cncl for Water Midlands Region 2005–07, Consumer Cncl for Water Central and Eastern Region 2007–10; memb: Judiciary Review Bd Min of Justice 2006–12, Fitness to Practice Panels GMC 2006–14; non-exec dir S Staffs Water plc 2011–; tstee Br Forces Fndn 2002–, chm Cncl Queen Mother Meml Fund 2003–06, chm James Caird Soc 2006–, chm Leics and Rutland Branch SSAFA 2011–14, constable and govr Windsor Castle 2014–; *Recreations* golf, gardening; *Clubs* RN; *Style—* Adm Sir James Perowne, KBE; ✉ c/o ARNO, 70 Porchester Terrace, Bayswater, London W2 3TP (e-mail jamesperowne@aol.com)

PEROWNE, Julia; da of Robert Perowne, and Lehr, *née* Matsell; *b* 3 August 1981, Norfolk; *Educ* Oundle, Univ of Edinburgh (MA); *Career* Ann Scott Assocs 2004–06, int client dir The Massey Partnership 2006–10, dir travel and consumer Lewis PR 2010–11, co-fndr (with Paul Charles) and md Perowne Charles Communications (PCC) 2011–16, fndr and ceo Perowne International 2016–; *Recreations* horse riding, skiing, tennis, travel; *Style—* Ms Julia Perowne; ✉ 6A Campden Hill Gardens London, W8 7AY (☎ 07785 990115); PCC, 9 Ledbury Mews North, London W11 2AF (☎ 020 7792 8884, e-mail jp@verypcc.com, website www.verypcc.com)

PERRETT, Amanda Jill; da of Guy Harwood, the racehorse trainer, and Gillian, *née* Lawson; *b* 31 December 1969, London; *m* 2 July 1995, Mark Edward Perrett, the former jockey; 1 s (Ryan Phillip b 4 March 2006), 1 da (Emma Gill b 4 Nov 2007); *Career* racehorse trainer; former jockey, more than 100 winners in flat and Nat Hunt races, first female jockey to ride in Champion Hurdle (Cheltenham Festival); trainer (succeeding f, Guy) Coombelands Stables 1996–, trained more than 300 winners, horses incl Indian Lodge, Tungsten Strike, Tillerman and Carnival Dancer; *Style—* Mrs Amanda Perrett; ✉ Coombelands Racing Stables, Pulborough, West Sussex RH20 1BP (☎ 01798 873011, fax 01798 875163, e-mail aperrett@coombelands-stables.com, website www.amandaperrett.com)

PERRIAM, Wendy Angela; da of Edward Francis Leopold Brech, of Esher, Surrey, and Irene Ella, *née* Thompson; *b* 23 February 1940; *Educ* Combe Bank Convent, St Anne's Coll Oxford (MA), LSE; *m* 1, 22 Aug 1964, Christopher Hugh Tyack, s of Dr Norman Tyack; 1 da (Pauline Maria b 31 Dec 1965); m 2, 29 July 1974, John Alan Perriam, s of John Perriam; *Career* author and creative writing tutor; formerly copywriter: Colman Prentis & Varley, Notley & Pritchard Wood; articles and stories published in magazines and newspapers incl: She, Cosmopolitan, For Women, Woman's Jl, The Lady, Image, Penthouse, Esquire, Sunday Times, Daily Telegraph, Daily Mail, Evening Standard, Independent, Daily Express; essays, poems and stories included in: Arts Cncl Anthology, SE Arts anthologies, Seven Deadly Sins, Best Short Stories, The Picador Book of Erotic Prose, The Literary Companion to Sex, The Second Penguin Book of Modern Women's Short Stories, The Death of a Child, Standpoint; memb: Soc of Authors, PEN, Br Actors Equity; hon doctorate Kingston Univ 2013; *Books* Absinthe for Elevenses (1980, reissued 1991), Cuckoo (1981, reissued 1992), After Purple (1982, reissued 1993), Born of Woman (1983, reissued 1993), The Stillness The Dancing (1985, reissued 1994), Sin City (1987, reissued 1994), Devils, for a Change (1989), Fifty-Minute Hour (1990), Bird Inside (1992), Michael, Michael (1993), Breaking and Entering (1994), Coupling (1996), Second Skin (1998), Lying (2000), Dreams, Demons and Desire (2001), Tread Softly (2002), Virgin in the Gym and Other Stories (2004), Laughter Class and Other Stories (2006), The Biggest Female in the World and Other Stories (2007), Little Marvel and Other Stories (2008), The Queen's Margarine and Other Stories (2009), Broken Places (2010), I'm on the Train! and Other Stories (2012), An Enormous Yes (2013), Bad Mothers, Brilliant Lovers (2015); *Recreations* cinema, reading; *Style—* Wendy Perriam; ✉ c/o Jonathan Lloyd, Curtis Brown, 4th Floor, Haymarket House, 28–29 Haymarket, London SW1Y 4SP (☎ 020 7396 6600, website www.wendyperriam.com)

PERRING, Sir John Raymond; 2 Bt (UK 1963), of Frensham Manor, Surrey; TD (1965); s of Sir Ralph Edgar Perring, 1 Bt (d 1998), by his late w Ethel Mary, da of Henry Theophilus Johnson, of Putney; *b* 7 July 1931; *Educ* Stowe; *m* 1961, Ella Christine, da of late Maj Anthony George Pelham; 2 s (John Simon Pelham b 1962, Mark Ralph Pelham b 1965), 2 da (Emma (Mrs Christian Heyman) b 1963, Anna (Mrs Edward Standish) b 1968); *Heir* s, John Perring; *Career* chm: Perring Furnishings Ltd 1981–88, Perrings Finance Ltd 1986–2007, Ranyard Nursing Home 1992–2001; cncl memb Retail Consortium 1972–91 (hon treas 1973–78); Master: Worshipful Co of Furniture Makers 1978–79, Merchant Taylors' Co 1988–89 and 1994–95; one of HM Lieutenants of the City of London 1963–, Sheriff City of London 1991–92; chm Wimbledon Decorative and Fine Arts Soc 1999–2002, pres Old Stoic Soc 2002–03, pres Bishopsgate Ward Club 1997–98, govr Bishopsgate Fndn 1992–2002; OStJ; *Style—* Sir John Perring, Bt, TD

PERRINS, Robert Charles Grenville (Rob); *b* 5 April 1965; *Educ* Marlborough, Aston Univ; *m* Vanessa, *née* Gullis; 2 s (Ralph b 26 April 2000, Humphrey b 23 Nov 2001); *Career* CA 1992; Ernst & Young 1987–91, Shanks 1991–94; Berkeley Gp: joined 1994, md Berkeley Homes plc 2001–02, gp fin dir 2002–; *Style—* Rob Perrins, Esq; ✉ The Berkeley Group plc, Berkeley House, 19 Portsmouth Road, Cobham, Surrey KT11 1JG (☎ 01932 868555, fax 01932 860403, e-mail rob.perrins@berkeleygroup.co.uk)

PERROTT, Prof Ronald Henry; *b* 27 December 1942; *Educ* Queen's Univ Belfast (BSc, PhD); *m* 4 April 1974, Valerie Mary Perrott; 1 s (Simon b 2 March 1976); *Career* prof of software engrg: Univ of Wisconsin 1968–69, NASA Res Centre Calif 1977–78, CERN Geneva 1984–85, Queen's Univ Belfast 1985–; visiting prof Univ of Oxford; memb: EC Working Gp on High Performance Computing, IT Advsy Bd to DTI and SERC, EU IST Monitoring Panel, OST Informatics Ctee; ed Jl of Scientific Programming; NI BCS IT Professional of the Year 1993, ACM Distinguished Service Award; fell US Assoc for Computing Machinery 1997; FBCS, FRSA, FIEEE 2004; *Books* Operating Systems Techniques (1972), Software Engineering (1978), Pascal for Fortran Programmers (1983), Parallel Programming (1987), Software for Parallel Computers (1991); *Recreations* skiing, squash, tennis; *Style—* Prof Ronald Perrott; ✉ e-mail r.perrott@gmail.com; Oxford e-Research Centre, 7 Keble Road, University of Oxford, Oxford OX1 3QG (☎ 028 9066 7893, e-mail ron.perrott@oerc.ox.ac.uk)

PERRY, Adam; *b* 14 October 1958; *Career* broadcasting prodn; Yorkshire TV 1978–86, Central TV 1986–94, Carlton Productions 1994–96, head of regnl productions and special events Channel 5 1996–2001, creative dir World of Wonder 2001–06; Media Trust: head of progs and campaigns Community Channel 2007–08, gen mangr prodn and digital media 2008–09, outreach mangr Community Channel 2009–11, community voices devpt mangr 2011–; dir Birmingham Int Film and TV Festival 1994–98; memb RTS; *Style—* Adam Perry, Esq

PERRY, Hon Alan Malcolm; s of Baron Perry of Walton (Life Peer, d 2003), and Anne Elizabeth, *née* Grant; *b* 6 February 1950; *Educ* George Heriot's Sch Edinburgh, Trinity Coll Oxford (MA); *m* 1976, Naomi Melanie, da of Dr Abraham Freedman, MD, FRCP, of London; 3 s (Daniel b 1980, Guy b 1982, Edmund b 1986); *Career* Harmsworth scholar, admitted slr 1982, currently ptnr D J Freeman; *Recreations* painting, making music, gardening; *Style—* The Hon Alan Perry; ✉ 43 Meadway, London NW11 7AX; D J Freeman, 43 Fetter Lane, London EC4A 1NA (☎ 020 7583 4055, telex 894579)

PERRY, Claire Louise; MP; *b* 3 April 1964; *Educ* Brasenose Coll Oxford, Harvard Univ (MBA); *Children* 2 da, 1 s; *Career* MP (Cons) Devizes 2010–; PPS to Philip Hammond, *qv*, 2012–13, govt whip 2013–14, Parly under-sec of state for tport 2014–; *Style—* Mrs Claire Perry, MP; ✉ House of Commons, London SWA1 0AA

PERRY, David Gordon; s of Elliott Gordon Perry (d 1994), of Kemble, Glos, and Lois Evelyn, *née* Allen; *b* 26 December 1937; *Educ* Clifton, Christ's Coll Cambridge (Rugby blue); *m* 16 Sept 1961, Dorne Mary, da of Edwin Timson Busby (d 1980), of Braybrooke, Leics; 4 da (Belinda b 1963, Philippa b 1964, Rebecca b 1967, Joanna b 1970); *Career* Nat Serv 2 Lt Parachute Regt 1956–58; Br Printing Corp (BPC) Ltd: md Fell & Briant Ltd (subsid) 1966–78, chief exec Packaging and Paper Products Div 1978–81, dir 1981; John Waddington plc: md 1981–88, chief exec 1988–92, chm 1993–97; chm Anglian Gp plc 1996–2001; non-exec dir: Dewhirst Group plc 1992–2001, National and Provincial Building Soc 1993–96, Kelda Gp plc 1996–2000, Euler Hermes UK plc 1998–2008, Bellway plc 1999–2010, Minorplanet Systems plc (chm 2005–07); fifteen caps England Rugby XV 1963–66 (capt 1965); CIMgt 1986, FIP; *Recreations* golf, music; *Style—* David Perry, Esq; ✉ 2 Oyster Mews, Bosham Lane, Bosham, West Sussex PO18 8HG

PERRY, George Cox; s of George Cox Perry (d 1962), of Berkhamsted, Herts, and Hortense Irene Emily Sadler (d 1983); *b* 7 January 1935, London; *Educ* Tiffin Sch, Trinity Coll Cambridge (MA, ed Varsity); *m* 1 (m dis 1976), Susanne Puddefoot (d 2010); m 2, 1976, Frances Nicola, da of Sidney Murray Scott (d 1987); 1 s (Matthew Richard Scott b 1977); *Career* advtg (creative) T Eaton Co Montreal 1957, sub ed The Sphere 1957–58, copywriter J Walter Thompson 1958–62; Sunday Times: sub ed 1962–63, asst to the ed (magazine) 1963–65, projects ed 1965–69, asst ed 1967–77, sr ed 1977–85, films ed 1985–98; chief exec: Cameo Editions 1998–2000, Boulevard Classics 2000–05; chm Forever Ealing 2000–02, exec dir Nevada Int Film Festival 2011–14, dir Agostini Hldgs 2016–, dir Bellflower Prodns 2016–; managing ed Crossbow 1965–70, organiser The Great British (photographs by Arnold Newman, Nat Portrait Gallery) 1979; external examiner London Coll of Printing 1984–90; dir Cinema City 1970; film critic: The Illustrated London News 1982–88 and 1992–99, Jazz-FM 1990–92; presenter Radio 2 Arts 1990–97; chm (film) The Critics' Circle 1991–94 (vice-chm 1987–91), pres The Critics' Circle 1998–2000 (vice-pres 1996–98); juror Carl Foreman Award BAFTA 1998–2005; comitato Borgo di Colleoli Palaia Italy 2011–; *Books* incl: The Films of Alfred Hitchcock (1965), The Penguin Book of Comics (1967), Rule Britannia the Victorian World (with Nicholas Mason, 1974), The Great British Picture Show (1974), Movies from the Mansion (1976), Forever Ealing (1981), Life of Python (1983), Rupert – A Bear's Life (1985), Bluebell (adapted as BBC drama serial, 1986), The Complete Phantom of the Opera (1987), Sunset Boulevard: from Movie to Musical (1993), The Life of Python (1994), Director's Cuts: Steven Spielberg (1998), Magic Movie Moments (2000), London in the Sixties (2001), Paris in the Sixties (2001), New York in the Sixties (2001), San Francisco in the Sixties (2001), Héros d'Hollywood (with Matthew Perry, 2002), Films Cultes (with Matthew Perry, 2002), James Dean (2005), Bogie (with Richard Schickel, 2006), You Must Remember This (with Richard Schickel, 2008), Bette Davis: Larger Than Life (with Richard Schickel, 2009), Jack Robinson On Show: Portraits 1958–72 (2011); *Recreations* walking, talking, watching movies, travelling, taking pictures; *Style—* George Perry, Esq; ✉ 7 Roehampton Lane, London SW15 5LS (☎ 020 8878 1187, e-mail georgeperry2001@aol.com)

PERRY, Grayson; CBE (2013); *b* 24 March 1960; *Career* artist; winner Turner Prize 2003; RA 2011; *Solo Exhibitions* James Birch Gallery London 1984 and 1985, The Minories Colchester 1986, Birch & Conran London 1986, 1987, 1988 and 1990, Garth Clark Gallery NY 1991, David Gill Gallery London 1991–92, Clara Scremini Gallery Paris 1994, Anthony d'Offay Gallery London 1994 and 1996–97, Laurent Delaye Gallery London 2000, fig-1 London 2000, Stedelijk Museum Amsterdam 2002, Guerrillla Tactics (Stedelijk Museum Amsterdam) 2002, Guerrilla Tactics (Barbican Art Centre) 2002; *Group Exhibitions* Young Contemporaries (ICA London) 1982, Ian Birkstead Gallery London 1983, Essex Artists (Epping Forest Museum and The Minories Colchester) 1985, Curious Christian Art (James Birch Gallery London) 1985, Gallozi e La Placa NY 1985, Mandelzoon Rome 1986, Read Stremmel Gallery San Antonio Texas 1988, Words and Volume (Garth Clark Gallery NY and Nishi Azabu Wall Tokyo) 1989, Essex Ware (Chelmsford and tour) 1991–92, Fine Cannibals (Oldham Art Gallery and tour) 1992, The Raw and the Cooked (Barbican Art Gallery London and tour) 1993–95, Indigo Gallery Boca Raton Florida 1995, Whitechapel Open (Whitechapel Gallery London) 1995, Philippe Rizzo Gallery Paris 1995, Hot Off the Press (Tullie House Glasgow, Norwich, Croydon Clock Tower and Crafts Cncl London) 1996–97, Objects of our Time (Crafts Cncl London, Edinburgh, Manchester, Belfast, Cardiff and American Crafts Museum NY) 1997–98, Craft (Richard Salmon Gallery London and Kettle's Yard Cambridge) 1997–98, Glazed Expressions (Orleans House London) 1998, Over the Top (Ikon Gallery Birmingham and tour) 1998, 250 Vases, Plates and Services (Stedelijk Museum Amsterdam) 1999, Decadence (Crafts Cncl London) 1999, Narrative (Garth Clark Gallery NY) 1999, A Sense of Occasion, mac (Birmingham and tour) 2000 and 2001, Protest and Survive (Whitechapel Art Gallery London) 2000, British Art Show 5 (tour) 2000–01, East Wing Collection No 5: Looking With/Out (Courtald Inst of Art London) 2001 and 2002, Carts and Rafts! (Camberwell Coll of Arts London) 2001, Invitation á...Laurent Delaye Gallery invitée par la galerie Anton Weller (Galerie Anton Weller Paris) 2001, New Labour (Saatchi Gallery London) 2001, The Other Britannia (Tecla Sala Barcelona and tour) 2001, Self Portrayal (Laurent Delaye Gallery London) 2001, The Galleries Show (Royal Acad) 2002, Liverpool Biennial 2002; *Work in Public Collections* Br Cncl, Crafts Cncl of Eng, Stedelijk Museum Amsterdam, Shigarake Ceramic Cultural Park Japan, Syracuse Museum NY State, Hydra Fndn Greece, Pottery Museum Stoke-on-Trent, MOMA Glasgow, Fondation Musée d'Art Moderne Grand-Duc Jean Luxembourg, Saatchi Collection London; *Style—* Grayson Perry, Esq, CBE; ✉ c/o Victoria Miro Gallery, 16 Wharf Road, London N1 7RW (☎ 020 7336 8106, e-mail info@victoria-miro.com)

PERRY, Dr Ian Charles; s of Capt Sidney Charles Perry (d 1984), of Bush Hill Park, Middx, and Marjorie Ellen, *née* Elliott; *b* 18 April 1939; *Educ* Highgate Sch, Guy's Hosp London (MB BS), RAF Inst of Aviation Med (Dip Aviation Med); *m* 27 July 1963, Janet Patricia (d 2010), da of Maj Albert Edward Watson, of Burton Bradstock, Dorset; 2 da (Johanna Elizabeth b 18 Oct 1964, Helen b 7 July 1967); m 2, 9 May 2015, Marion Elizabeth Verschoyle; *Career* Lt RAMC 1963, Capt 2 i/c 24 Field Ambulance Aden 1965 and 1967 (SMO Aden Bde 1966), SMO (specialist in aviation med) Army Air Corps Centre 1967–68, 200 Army Pilots Course 1968–69, Maj SMO Conslt Aviation Med Army Air Corps Centre 1969, chm NATO (AG ARD) Aircrew Fatigue Panel 1969–72, ret 1973, RARO 1973–, TA (AAC) 1989–94; princ aviation and occupational med practice 1973–; conslt: IAOPA, Br Helicopter Advsy Bd, European Aviation Safety Authy (EASA) Med Expert Gp; memb: Int Acad of Aviation and Space Med, US/AOPA Bd of Aviation Med Advsrs; former chm: Br Assoc of Aviation Conslts, Grateley PC, Grateley PTA; past chm Int Acad of Aviation and Space Med Scholarship Ctee; tstee Preservation of Rural Eng; sec Nurdling Assoc of England; Freeman City of London 1973, Liveryman Worshipful Co of Gunmakers, Master Worshipful Co of Air Pilots 1996; MAE, MFOM, FRAeS, FAMA, FCMI (FIMgt 1998), CFIOSH 1988; *Publications* Aviation Medicine and The Royal Flying

P

Corps, Cross and Cockade International 39/2 2008; author of papers on aviation med; *Recreations* orchids, golf, shooting, Royal Flying Corps history; *Clubs* Cavalry and Guards', Tidworth Golf; *Style*— Dr Ian Perry; ✉ The Old Rectory, St John's Hill, Shaftesbury SP7 8HG (☎ 01747 852982, mobile 07836 664670, e-mail ian@ianperry.com, websites www.ianperry.com)

PERRY, Dr J David; *b* 21 April 1946; *Educ* Bristol GS, Middx Hosp Med Sch (MB), Univ of London (BSc, MB BS); *Career* house physician Oldchurch Hosp Romford then house surgn Middx Hosp 1971, casualty MO Middx Hosp and SHO in gen and chest med The London Hosp 1972–74, registrar in gen and chest med The London Hosp 1975–76 (SHO and registrar Dept of Rheumatology 1974–75), sr registrar in rheumatology The London Hosp and Prince of Wales Hosp Tottenham 1976–77, sr registrar in rheumatology Colchester and The London Hosp 1977–79, conslt rheumatologist The London Hosp (now Royal Hosps Tst) 1979–, clinical dir Musculoskeletal Directorate Royal Hosps Tst; univ teacher Univ of London; hon sr lectr Bart's London Hosp Med Coll and Queen Mary Westfield Coll, MO BAAB, med dir Crystal Palace Nat Sports Centre, co-organiser and treas Therapy Pool Appeal The London Hosp (pool opened by HRH The Princess Royal), memb Hispanic Soc Goldsmiths' Coll, former sec NE Thames Regnl Advsy Sub-ctee on Rheumatology and Rehabilitation, sec RSM Sports Med Section, hon sec Jt Med Cncl Royal Hosps NHS Tst, regnl advsr NE Thames RCP 2003; FRCP 1986; *Books* Hutchison's Clinical Methods (contrib chapter The Locomotor System, 18 edn, 1984 and 1995), Rheumatology Examination and Injection Techniques (jtly, 1992, 2 edn 1999); chapters in: Sports Medicine (ed J B King, 1992), Rheumatology (eds Klippel & Dieppe, 1994, 2 edn 1998); *Style*— Dr J David Perry; ✉ The Royal London Hospital, Mile End, London E1 1BB (☎ 020 7377 7859, fax 020 7377 7807); London Independent Hospital (☎ and fax 020 7791 1688)

PERRY, Jane; da of Evan Morgan Perry (d 1989), of Brighton, E Sussex, of Hilda Ellen, *née* Webb; *b* 28 September 1948; *Educ* Brighton and Hove HS for Girls GPDST, Univ of Exeter (BA); *m* 4 Nov 1972 (sep 1983), Derek John Brandon; 2 s (James Martin b 24 Dec 1977, Thomas Henry b 21 April 1980); *Career* advtg exec; research exec BMRB 1969–71, research assoc J Walter Thompson NY 1971–72, research mangr Manchester Evening News 1972–77, UK mangr IMS London 1977–82, media research mangr Davidson Pearce (now BMP) 1982–87: Young & Rubicam: media research mangr 1987–89, Euro media research dir 1989–2000; res dir The Media Edge EMEA 2000, chm EAAA Media Res Gp 1996–2000, media ed of Admap 2000–; FIPA 1995; *Books* European Marketing and Media Pocket-Book (annually 1991–2001), European Media Cost Comparison (1991, 1993, 1995–97), European Media Overspill (1992), Global Media Cost Comparison (1998, 2000–01), Asia-Pacific Marketing & Media pocket-book (2000), Americas Marketing & Media pocket-book (2000); *Style*— Ms Jane Perry, FSA, FIPA; ✉ Admap, World Advertising Research Centre, Farm Road, Henley-on-Thames, Oxfordshire RG9 1EJ (☎ 01491 411000, fax 01491 418600, e-mail jane2perry@hotmail.com)

PERRY, Prof John Grenville; s of Frederick Perry (d 1974), of Stoke-on-Trent, and Elsie, *née* Till (d 1998); *b* 21 May 1945; *Educ* Longton HS Stoke-on-Trent, Univ of Liverpool (BEng, MEng), Univ of Manchester (PhD); *m* 20 April 1968, Ruth Katharine, da of Eric Stanley Forrester (d 1989), of Fulford, Staffs; 2 s (Jonathan b 17 Nov 1970, Timothy b 10 June 1972); *Career* engr Costain Ltd 1967–70, project engr ICI Ltd 1970–74, sr lectr UMIST 1984–88 (lectr 1974–84); Univ of Birmingham: Beale prof 1988–2006, head Sch of Civil Engrg 1988–2000, dep dean Faculty of Engrg 1995–97, emeritus prof 2006–; former chm local branch Lib Pty; non-exec dir Heartlands and Solihull NHS Tst 1998–2008; govr Bromsgrove Sch 1998–; MAPM 1988, FICE 1993 (MICE 1975); *Publications* co-author of the New Engineering Contract; author of over 70 pubns; *Recreations* ornithology, swimming, fell walking; *Style*— Prof John Perry; ✉ School of Civil Engineering, The University of Birmingham, Edgbaston, Birmingham B15 2TT (☎ 0121 4145048)

PERRY, Sir Michael Sydney; GBE (2002, CBE 1990, OBE 1973), kt (1994); s of Lt Cdr Sydney Albert Perry, RNVR (d 1979), of Douglas, IOM, and Jessie Kate, *née* Brooker; *b* 26 February 1934; *Educ* King William's Coll IOM, St John's Coll Oxford (MA); *m* 18 Oct 1958, Joan Mary, da of Francis William Stallard (d 1948), of Worcester; 2 da (Carolyn b 1962, Deborah b 1963), 1 s (Andrew b 1967); *Career* Nat Serv RN 1952–54; Unilever plc: joined 1957, dir 1985–96, vice-chm 1991–92, chm and chief exec 1992–96; chm Centrica plc 1997–2004 (sometime dep chm predecessor companies, joined Bd as non-exec dir 1994), dep chm Bass plc 1996–2001; non-exec chm Dunlop Slazenger Group Ltd 1996–2002; non-exec dir: Br Gas 1994–97, Marks and Spencer plc 1996–2001; chm Chairmen's Counsel Ltd 2006–12; vice-pres Liverpool Sch of Tropical Med; pres The Mktg Cncl 2000–04, vice-pres Chartered Inst of Mktg; chm: Shakespeare Globe Tst 1993–96, Leverhulme Tst 2008–13 (tstee 1992–); dir Three Choirs Festival Assoc 2006–; tstee: Glyndebourne Arts Tst 1998–2005, Dyson Perrins Museum Tst 2000–, Daiwa Fndn 2008–; *Recreations* music (choral), golf; *Clubs* Oriental; *Style*— Sir Michael Perry, GBE; ✉ Bridges Stone Mill, Alfrick, Worcestershire WR6 5HR (☎ 01886 833290)

PERRY, Dr Nicholas Mark; s of (Sidney) Arthur Perry, of London, and Constance Frances, *née* Sheere; *b* 23 October 1950; *Educ* Westminster, Bart's Med Sch (MB BS); *m* 12 May 1979, Angela Judith, da of Anthony Hillier Poil; 1 s (Alexander William Mark b 10 Oct 1983), 1 da (Francesca Elizabeth Sarah b 21 Feb 1987); *Career* house surgn Bart's 1975, house physician St Leonard's Hosp Hoxton 1976, SHO A/E Bart's 1976–78, SHO Hackney Hosp 1978–79, SHO in urology Bart's 1979–80; registrar in diagnostic radiology: St Thomas' Hosp 1980–82, Bart's 1982–83; sr registrar Bart's, Chase Farm Hosp and N Middx Hosp 1983–85, sr registrar Bart's, Great Ormond Street, Hackney and Homerton Hosps 1985–88; conslt radiologist: Bart's 1988–2010, King Edward VII Hosp Sister Agnes, Princess Grace Hosp; conslt in breast screening Europe Against Cancer Euro Cmmn 1991–2000; quality assurance dir London Region Breast Screening Prog 1988–2002, clinical dir Central and E London Breast Screening Serv 1990–2008, dir London Breast Inst; Nat Breast Screening Prog: chm: Advsy Ctee Euro Network of Reference Assessment Centres (EUREF) 1996–, Detection and Diagnosis Section Euro Soc of Mastology (EUSOMA), Quality Assurance Mangrs Gp 1989–98, Equipment Ctee 1989–95; memb: European Gp for Breast Cancer Screening, BMA, British Assoc of Surgical Oncology, Euro Soc of Mastology; FRCS 1980, FRCR 1984; *Books* Radiological Casebook (1988), European Guidelines for Quality Assurance in Mammography Screening (2001), European Guidelines for Quality Assurance in Breast Cancer Screening and Diagnosis (2006); *Recreations* antiquarian books, lawn tennis (capt English Public Schs 1967, British Univs' Doubles champion 1974, vice-pres United Hosps Lawn Tennis Club, pres Bart's and Royal London Hosps Lawn Tennis Club 2000–05), lawn tennis memorabilia; *Clubs* Hurlingham, All England Lawn Tennis, Ocean Reef (Key Largo), Cooden Beach Golf; *Style*— Dr Nicholas Perry; ✉ 67 Newstead Way, London SW19 5HR

PERRY, Nick; *b* 1961; *Educ* Univ of Hull, Nat Film and TV Sch; *Career* playwright; TV dramas and stage plays incl: Arrivederci Millwall 1985 (prod, jt winner of Samuel Beckett Award 1986), Smallholdings (Kings Head) 1986, Rockliffe's Babies (contrib to BBC series), Tales of Sherwood Forest (for Central TV), Clubland (BBC), The Vinegar Fly (Lyric Theatre Belfast) 1994, Near Cricket St Thomas, 1919 (McCarthy Theatre Scarborough) 1997, Steal Away (Sky films) 1999, The Escapist (Sky films) 2001, Superbomb (BBC) 2006, An Illustrated Talk (Newtown Theatre Sydney) 2008; radio plays incl: The Loop (BBC Radio 4) 2009 (Sony Bronze Award), Referee (BBC Radio 4) 2011, London Bridge (BBC Radio 4) 2013, November Dead List (BBC Radio 4) 2014, The Transfer (BBC Radio 4) 2015; *Style*— Nick Perry, Esq; ✉ c/o Rochelle Stevens & Co, 2 Terretts Place, Upper Street, London N1 1QZ (☎ 020 7359 3900, fax 020 7354 5729, e-mail rochelle@rochellestevens.com)

PERRY, Dr Robert Henry; s of Frank Perry (d 1992), of Sileby, Loughborough, Leics, and Lois Ellen, *née* Harriman (d 2004); *b* 20 August 1944; *Educ* Loughborough GS, Univ of St Andrews (MB ChB), Univ of Newcastle upon Tyne (DSc); *m* 5 June 1971, Elaine King, da of James Cyril King Miller, WS (d 1979), of Colinton, Edinburgh; 1 s (Jonathan b 1972), 1 da (Nicolette b 1973); *Career* Newcastle Gen Hosp: sr registrar in neuropathology 1975–79, clinical scientist MRC Neuroendocrinology Unit, conslt neuropathologist 1980–; Univ of Newcastle: sr lectr in neuropathology 1986–91, reader in neurochemical pathology 1991–99, prof in neuropathology 1999–; author of res pubns on neuropathological correlations of dementia, dementia with Lewy bodies, Alzheimer's disease, Parkinson's disease and related topics; memb Br Neuropathological Soc; FRCP, FRCPath; *Recreations* sailing, skiing, salads, croquet; *Style*— Dr Robert Perry; ✉ Dilston Mill House, Corbridge, Northumberland NE45 5QZ (☎ 01434 632308); Neuropatholgy Department, Newcastle General Hospital, Westgate Road, Newcastle upon Tyne NE4 6BE (☎ 0191 256 3688, fax 0191 250 3196, e-mail robert.perry@ncl.ac.uk)

PERRY, Rupert; CBE (1997); s of Graham Perry (d 1968), and Ms Leece (d 1984); *b* 14 January 1948; *Educ* Gresham's; *Children* 1 da (Perignon b 3 Nov 1974), 1 s (Manhattan Graham b 22 Nov 1979); *Career* Campbell Connelly Music Publishers 1967–69, professional mangr Radio Luxembourg Music Publishers 1969–71, PA to gp dir Records EMI Ltd 1971–72; Capitol Records LA: dir Int Artists' Repertoire 1972–76, vice-pres A&R 1976–82; pres EMI America Records LA 1982–84, exec asst to chm of EMI Music Worldwide LA 1984–85, md EMI Australia 1985–86, pres and ceo Records UK & Eire 1986–95, pres and ceo Europe 1995–99, chm Records Group UK & Eire 1995–99; chm BPI 1993–95 (vice-chm 1990–93); sr vice-pres EMI Recorded Music 1999–2002; Int Fedn of the Phonographic Industry: chm European Regional Bd 1998–2002 (memb 1994–2002), memb Main Bd 1998–2002; visiting prof Syracuse Univ 2011, 2012 and 2013; memb: Music Sound Fndn, Nat Acad of Recording Arts & Sciences Inc (NARAS); *Publications* Northern Songs (with Brian Southall); *Recreations* the countryside, wine, music, soccer; *Clubs* Reform, Groucho, Bibury Tennis, Home House; *Style*— Rupert Perry, Esq, CBE; ✉ 6217 Rockcliff Drive, Los Angeles, CA 90068, USA (☎ 001 323 465 2285, mobile 07747 665976, e-mail rupertperry@hotmail.com)

PERRY, Stephen Lawrence Andrew; s of Jack Perry (d 1996), of London, and Doris-Kate Perry (d 1985); *b* 12 September 1948; *Educ* UCL (LLB); *m* 24 Dec 1980 (m dis 1998), Wendy, da of Joseph Bond (d 1957), and Lillian Bond; 1 da (Jodie b 1981), 1 s (Jack b 1984); partner, Sarah Ann Marie Webb; 1 s (Samuel Jack b 4 Sept 2004), 1 da (Rosie Kate Elizabeth b 22 Feb 2006); *Career* md London Export Corporation Ltd; chm 48 Group Club, chm Icebreakers UK Ltd; dir Somerstown Community Sports Centre; fell UCL; *Recreations* football; *Clubs* RAC, Oriental; *Style*— Stephen Perry, Esq; ✉ 30 Aberdare Gardens, London NW6 3QA

PERRY OF SOUTHWARK, Baroness (Life Peer UK 1991), of Charlbury in the County of Oxfordshire; Pauline Perry; *née* Welch; da of John George Embleton Welch (d 1963), and Elizabeth, *née* Cowan (d 1982); *b* 15 October 1931; *Educ* Wolverhampton Girls' HS, Girton Coll Cambridge (MA); *m* 26 July 1952, George Walter Perry (d 2008), s of Percy Walter Perry (d 1939); 3 s (Hon Christopher b 1953, Hon Timothy b 1962, Hon Simon b 1966), 1 da (Hon Hilary (Hon Mrs Winstone) b 1955); *Career* lectr in philosophy: Univ of Manitoba 1956–59, Univ of Massachusetts 1961–62; pt/t lectr in educn: Univ of Exeter 1963–66, Univ of Oxford 1966–70; access course tutor 1966–70, HM Chief Inspr of Schs 1981–86 (inspr 1970–74, staff inspr 1975–81), vice-chllr South Bank Univ (formerly South Bank Poly) 1987–93, pres Lucy Cavendish Coll Cambridge 1994–2001, pro-chllr Univ of Surrey 2001–06; chair Cncl Roehampton Univ 2001–05; freelance journalist and broadcaster; author of various books, chapters in books and numerous published articles, various radio and TV appearances; memb Prime Minister's Advsy Panel for the Citizen's Charter 1993–97; memb: House of Lords Select Ctee on the Scrutiny of Delegated Powers 1994–98, House of Lords Select Ctee on Stem-Cell Research, House of Lords Select Ctee on Science and Technol, Jt Select Ctee on Human Rights; Cons Pty whip House of Lords 2011–16; jt chm All-Pty Parly Univs Gp 1996–2009; chm: South Bank Univ Enterprise Ltd 1988–93, DTI Export Gp for Educn and Training Sector 1993–98, Friends of Southwark Cathedral 1996–2002, Judges Panel for Chartermark Award 1997–2002, Archbishop's Review of the Crown Appointments Cmmn 1999–2001, Nuffield Cncl on Bio-Ethics Inquiry into the Use of Animals in Sci Research 2003–05, CGLI Ctee on Quality and Standards 2005–10; non-exec dir Addenbrooke's NHS Tst 1998–2001; memb: Governing Body Inst of Devpt Studies 1987–95, British Cncl's Ctee on Int Co-operation in HE 1987–96, ESRC 1988–91, Cncl Fndn for Educn Business Partnerships 1990–91, Bd South Bank Centre 1992–95, Ct Univ of Bath 1992–98, Bd of Patrons of the Royal Soc 1996–2001, Bd ESU 1998–2003, QCA Advsy Ctee on Standards 2004–08; rector's warden Southwark Cathedral 1990–94; patron: British Youth Opera 1993–, Alzheimer's Research Tst 1993–, British Friends of Neve-Shalom Wahat-al-Salaam 2003–; pres: Ctee for Independent Further Education (CIFE) 2001–13, Fndn for HE 2002–06, City & Westminster Branch CMI; vice-pres: Soc for Res in HE 1993–99, CGLI 1994–99; govr Greshams Sch 2000–06; Freeman City of London 1992, Liveryman Worshipful Co of Bakers 1992, Hon Freeman Fishmongers Co 2006; hon fell Sunderland Poly 1990, hon fell Girton Coll Cambridge 1995, hon fell Lucy Cavendish Coll Cambridge 2001, hon fell Roehampton Univ 2005; Hon LLD: Univ of Bath 1991, Univ of Aberdeen 1994, South Bank Univ 1994; Hon DLitt Univ of Sussex 1992, Hon DEd Univ of Wolverhampton 1994, Hon DUniv Surrey 1995, Hon DLitt City Univ 2000, Hon Dr of Humanities Mercy Coll NY 2014; Hon FCP 1987, Hon FRSA 1988, CCMI (CIMgt) 1993, hon fell C&G 2000; Numerous articles in professional journals and national presss. 4 books and contributions (chapters) to 12 books; *Recreations* music, walking; *Clubs* IOD; *Style*— The Rt Hon Baroness Perry of Southwark; ✉ House of Lords, London SW1A 0PW (e-mail pp204@supanet.com)

PERSAUD, Prof the Hon Bishnodat; s of Dhwarka Persaud, and Dukhni, *née* Surujbali; *b* 22 September 1933, Cumberland Village, Guyana; *Educ* Univ of Reading (Postgrad Dip Agric Econs, PhD), Queen's Univ Belfast (BScEcon); *m* Aug 1962, Lakshmi; 3 c (Rajendra, Avinash, Sharda); *Career* res fell Inst of Social and Econ Res Univ of the WI 1965–74; Cwlth Secretariat: chief econs offr Commodities Div 1974–76, asst dir Econ Affrs Div 1976–81, dir and head Economic Affrs Div 1981–92; Univ of the WI Jamaica: prof of sustainable devpt 1992–96, hon prof 1996–; co-leader IDB Team on Socio-Economic Reform in Guyana 1994, chief tech co-ordinator Int Negotiations Caribbean Community 1996, sr assoc Caribbean Regnl Negotiating Machinery 2002–10, advsr to Cwlth Secretariat and World Bank on small states 2005–06; memb: Bd of Dirs Central Bank Barbados 1973–74, Bd Cwlth Equity Fund 1989–93, Univ of Guyana Review Cmmn 1991 and 1996, Bd of Tstees Guyana Rainforest Programme 1992–2002, UN Ctee for Devpt Policy 1995–2000, Cmmn on Cwlth Studies 1995–96, Jamaica Conservation Tst 1995–99, Worldaware (UK) 1996–2006, Cwlth Partnership for Technol Mgmnt (UK) 1997–2001, Bd of Tstees Ramphal Centre 2009–12; served on many cmmns of enquiry and on int expert gps; numerous speeches and lectures incl address to Euro Foreign and Security Policies Conf of the Euro Movement 1991, numerous radio broadcasts and TV appearances in Cwlth countries; memb Chatham House; FRSA; CHB 2014; *Books* Developing with Foreign Investment (jtly, 1987), Economic Policy and the Environment (jtly, 1995); contrib chapters to many books, and articles and book reviews to professional and learned jls; *Clubs* RAC; *Style*— Prof the Hon Bishnodat Persaud

PERSEY, Lionel Edward; QC (1997); s of Dr Paul Ronald Persey (d 1996), of London, and Irene, *née* Levinson (d 2007); *b* 19 January 1958; *Educ* Haberdashers' Aske's, Univ of Birmingham (Holdsworth Prize, LLB), Université de Limoges, Inns of Court Sch of Law; *m* 1984, Lynn, da of Gordon Mear; 1 s (b 1999); *Career* called to the Bar Gray's Inn 1981 (Lord Justice Holker sr Award, Band Commercial Prize); in commercial and maritime practice 1982–, recorder 2002–; dep judge High Court 2010; memb: Supplementary Panel of Treasury Counsel 1992–97, Commercial Bar Assoc, London Common Law and Commercial Bar Assoc; *Recreations* classical music, opera, reading, gardening; *Clubs* Reform; *Style—* Lionel Persey, QC; ✉ Quadrant Chambers, Quadrant House, 10 Fleet Street, London EC4Y 1AU (☎ 020 7583 4444, fax 020 7583 4455, e-mail lionel.persey@quadrantchambers.com)

PERT, Prof Geoffrey James (Geoff); s of Norman James Pert (d 1984), and Grace Winifred, *née* Barnes (d 2008); *b* 15 August 1941; *Educ* Norwich Sch, Imperial Coll London (BSc, PhD, Rowing purple); *m* 16 Sept 1967, Janice Ann, *née* Alexander; 1 da (Erin Mary b 3 Dec 1968); *Career* asst prof Univ of Alberta 1967–70, successively lectr, sr lectr, reader and prof Univ of Hull 1970–87, prof of physics Univ of York 1987–2007 (emeritus prof of physics 2007–); FInstP 1978, FRS 1995; *Publications* Introductory Fluid Mechanics (2013); numerous scientific pubns; *Recreations* hill walking, gardening; *Clubs* Arctic; *Style—* Prof Geoff Pert; ✉ York Plasma Institute, Department of Physics, University of York, Heslington, York YO10 5DD (☎ 01904 324910, fax 01904 432214, e-mail gjp1@york.ac.uk)

PERT, His Hon Judge Michael; QC (1992); s of Lt Henry McKay Pert, RN (ret), and Noreen Margaret Mary, *née* Murphy; *b* 17 May 1947; *Educ* St Boniface's Coll Plymouth, Univ of Manchester (LLB); *m* 29 July 1971, Vivienne Victoria, da of Ernest George Braithwaite; 2 da (Lucy Claire b 27 Aug 1975, Katherine Olivia b 10 Feb 1979), 1 s (Benjamin McKay b 4 March 1977); *Career* called to the Bar Gray's Inn 1970; recorder 1988–2004 (asst recorder 1984–88), circuit judge (Midland Circuit) 2004–; *Recreations* bee keeping, sailing; *Style—* His Hon Judge Pert, QC

PERTWEE, Christopher Ferens; DL (Essex 1996); s of Norman Pertwee, and Eileen Pertwee; *b* 25 November 1936; *Educ* Tonbridge; *m* 1960, Carole, da of A G Drayson, of Sutton Valence, Kent; 3 s (Mark, Julian, Nicholas); *Career* chm Pertwee Holdings Ltd 1970–; pres UK Agric Supply Trade Assoc 1982–83; pro-chllr Univ of Essex 1998–2006 (memb Cncl 1990–98); pres: Essex Agric Soc 2003–04, Colchester Catalyst Charity (chm 1993–2004); dir Essex Community Fndn 1996–2000; chm St Helena Hospice 2008–13; hon fell Univ of Essex 1996; High Sheriff Essex 1995–96; Master Worshipful Co of Farmers 1998–99; *Recreations* sport, gardening, antiques; *Style—* Christopher Pertwee, DL; ✉ Tye House, High Street, Hadleigh, Suffolk, IP7 5EJ

PERTWEE, Richard James Charles Drury; s of Capt James Waddon Martyn Pertwee, CBE (d 2000), of Winchester, Hants, and Margaret Alison, *née* Elliott; *b* 2 May 1955; *Educ* Sherborne, Worcester Coll Oxford (BA); *m* 15 Aug 1981, Gail, da of Wilfred McBrien Swain, OBE (d 1983); 2 da (Laetitia b 1984, Sophie b 1987); *Career* joined RNR 1978, Sub Lt 1980, res 1982; Richards Butler & Co: articled clerk 1978–80, slr 1980–82; asst then ptnr: Trevor Robinson & Co 1982–85, Joynson-Hicks 1985–89; ptnr Taylor Wessing (formerly Taylor Joynson Garrett) 1989–2006 (managing ptnr 1993–95, conslt 2006–13); dir: Mentor UK Ltd 2008–09, Cranstoun Drug Services 2010–, Bowel Disease Research Fndn 2015–; magistrate SE Hants 2006–14; govr Prince's Mead Sch Winchester 2008–15; *Recreations* tennis, cricket; *Clubs* Sherborne Pilgrims, Vincent's (Oxford), MCC; *Style—* Richard Pertwee, Esq; ✉ 4 St James Lane, Winchester, Hampshire SO22 4NX (☎ 01962 863881, e-mail richard.pertwee@btinternet.com)

PESARAN, Prof (Mohammad) Hashem; s of Jamal Pesaran (d 1973), and Effat Pesaran (d 2009); *b* 30 March 1946; *Educ* Univ of Salford (BSc, Athletics colours), Harvard Univ, Univ of Cambridge (PhD, Basketball half-blue); *m* 1969, Marian Fay, *née* Swainston; 3 s (Bijan b 12 Oct 1973, Jamal b 5 Jan 1975, Hassan Ali b 30 Dec 1992), 2 da (Eva-Leila b 24 Sept 1978, Natasha Guiti b 19 March 1990); *Career* 1 Lt Farahabad Barracks Tehran 1976; jr res offr Dept of Applied Economics Univ of Cambridge and lektor Trinity Coll Cambridge 1971–73, head Econ Res Dept Central Bank of Iran 1974–76 (asst to Vice-Govr 1973–74), under sec Miny of Educn Iran 1977–78; Univ of Cambridge: teaching fell and dir of studies in economics Trinity Coll 1979–88, lectr in economics 1979–85, reader in economics 1985–88, prof of economics and professorial fell Trinity Coll 1988–; prof of economics and dir Prog in Applied Econometrics UCLA 1989–93, res fell Inst for Study of Labor (IZA) Bonn 1999–, res fell CESifo Research Network Munich 2000–, John Elliott chair in economics and prof of economics Univ of Southern Calif 2005– (John Elliott distinguished chair in economics 2013), dir USC Dornsife Centre for Applied Financial Economics 2012–, founding dir Int Assoc for Applied Econometrics 2013–, dir USC Dornsife Inst for New Economic Thinking 2014–; visiting lectr Harvard 1982, visiting fell ANU 1984 and 1988; visiting prof: Univ of Rome 1986, UCLA 1987–88, Inst of Advanced Studies Vienna 1991, Univ of Pennsylvania 1993, Univ of Southern Calif 1995, 1997 and 1999; fell Judge Business Sch Cambridge 2009–10 and 2010–11, hon fell Grad Sch of Business and Economics Maastricht Univ 2013–; dir: Camfit Data Ltd 1986–, Acorn Investment Trust 1987–89 and 1991–93, Cambridge Econometrics 1985, 1988–89 and 1992–96 (hon pres 1996–); non-exec dir Chiltern Gp 1999–; pres Int Iranian Economic Assoc 2013; memb: HM Treasy Academic Panel 1993–, Advsy Ctee UK Meteorological Office 1994–97, Bd of Tstees Economic Research Forum of Arab Countries, Iran and Turkey 1996–2001, Cncl of Advsrs for the MENA region World Bank 1996–2000, Bd of Tstees Br Iranian Tst 1997–, Academic Econometric Panel Office for Nat Statistics 1997–2000, Cncl Royal Economic Soc 2007–10; charter memb Oliver Wyman Inst 1997–2000; memb Editorial Bd: Cambridge Jl of Economics 1981–89, Econometric Theory 1984–87, Cyprus Jl of Economics 1990–, Hellenic Review 1993–96, Net Exposure: The Electronic Jl of Fin Risk 1996–2001, Review of Middle East Economics and Finance 2007–, Int Review of Economics and Finance 2010–14, Iranian Jl of Economic Studies 2010–; assoc ed: Econometrica 1984–85, Jl of Economic Dynamics and Control 1995–2011; fndr ed Jl of Applied Econometrics 1986–2014, advsy ed Korea and the World Economy 2001–; memb Advsy Bd Jl of Economic Surveys 1995–; George Sell Prize Inst of Petroleum 1990, Royal Econ Soc Prize for 1990–91 1992, Best Paper Award Econometric Reviews 2002–04, Best Paper 2004–05 Award Int Jl of Forecasting 2007, Multa Scripsit Award in recognition of cumulative contibs to the Jl of Econometric Theory and to the sci of econometrics 2008, Reuters Citation Laureate in Economics 2013, Reuters 'World's Most Influential Scientific Minds' 2014, Isaac Kerstenetsky Scholarly Achievement Award 2014; Hon DLitt Salford 1993, hon doctorate Univ of Goethe Frankfurt 2008, hon doctorate Maastricht Univ 2013; fell: Econometric Soc 1989, Jl of Econometrics 1990; FBA 1998; *Books* World Economic Prospects and the Iranian Economy – a Short Term View (1974), Dynamic Regression – Theory and Algorithms (jtly, 1980), Keynes' Economics – Methodological Issues (jt ed, 1985), The Limits to Rational Expectations (1987), Data-FIT – an Interactive Software Econometric Package (jtly, 1987), Disaggregation in Economic Modelling (jt ed, 1990), Microfit 3.0 – an Interactive Software Econometric Package (jtly, 1991), Non-Linear Dynamics, Chaos and Econometrics (jt ed, 1993), Handbook of Applied Econometrics Vol 1 (jt ed, 1995), Working with Microfit 4.0 – Interactive Econometric Analysis (jtly, 1997), Handbook of Applied Econometrics Vol II (jt ed, 1997), Energy Demand in Asian Developing Economies (jtly, 1998), Analysis of Panels and Limited Dependent Variables (jt ed, 1999), Global and National Macroeconometric Modelling: A Long-Run Structural Approach (jtly, 2006), Explaining Growth in the Middle East (jt ed, 2007), Time Series Econometrics using Microfit 5 (jtly, 2009), The GVAR Handbook: Structure and Applications of a Macro Model of the Global Economy for Policy Analysis (jtly, 2013); *Recreations* basketball, swimming, squash, jogging; *Style—* Prof Hashem Pesaran, FBA; ✉ Trinity College, Cambridge CB2 1TQ (☎ 01223 338403, fax 01223 335471, e-mail hashem.pesaran@econ.cam.ac.uk, website www.econ.cam.ac.uk/faculty/pesaran); Department of Economics, University of Southern California, 3620 South Vermont Avenue, KAP 300, Los Angeles, CA 90089, USA (☎ 001 213 740 3510, e-mail pesaran@usc.edu)

PESCHARDT, Michael Mogens; s of Mogens Jan Hagbarth Peschardt, and Betty Joyce, *née* Foster; *b* 17 November 1957; *Educ* Merchant Taylors', Univ of Sussex; *m* 9 July 1977, Sarah Louise, da of Tom James Vaughan; 3 s (Joseph Mogens b 1980, Jack Oliver b 1982, Samuel Thaddeus b 1984), 1 da (Lily Mae b 1993); *Career* news prodr BBC Radio Manchester 1980–82, chief parly journalist BBC Regnl Broadcasting until 1986, sports reporter BBC TV News, currently Australia corr BBC TV, presenter BBC World (progs incl Peschardt's People and Australia Direct); *Recreations* surfing, football; *Style—* Michael Peschardt, Esq

PESCOD, District Judge Peter Richard; s of Philip Pescod (d 1965), of Darlington, Co Durham, and Elsie, *née* Parnaby; *b* 29 June 1951; *Educ* Queen Elizabeth GS Darlington, Univ of Newcastle upon Tyne (LLB); *m* 15 April 1978, Barbara Jane, da of John Magoveny King, of Morpeth, Northumberland; 1 da (Jennifer b 21 May 1981), 1 s (Henry b 12 April 1983); *Career* admitted slr 1975; ptnr Hay and Kilner 1976–2002; dist judge (NE Circuit) 2002–; memb Northumberland CC 1989–93; Parly candidate (Cons) Blaydon 1987 and 1992; vice-pres Forum of Insurance Lawyers 1993–95; memb: Northumberland FPC 1985–90 (chm Med Serv Ctee 1988–96), Family Health Services Appeal Authy 1996–2002, Nat Tst, Eng Heritage, Law Soc; chm of govrs Ovingham Middle Sch 1993–96, chm Ovington Parish Cncl 2007–; *Recreations* drama, auction sales, building, landscape gardening, architecture; *Clubs* Royal Thames Yacht, Newcastle upon Tyne Lit and Phil; *Style—* District Judge Pescod; ✉ The Law Courts, Quayside, Newcastle upon Tyne NE13 1LA (☎ 0191 201 2000, fax 0191 201 2001)

PESKIN, Richard Martin; s of Leslie Peskin (d 1980), and Hazel Pauline Peskin (d 1980); *b* 21 May 1944; *Educ* Charterhouse, Queens' Coll Cambridge (MA, LLM); *m* 6 Feb 1979, Penelope Ann Elizabeth Howard, *née* Triebner; 1 s (Michael b 1966), 2 da (Elizabeth b 1969, Virginia b 1979); *Career* Great Portland Estates plc: dir 1968–2009, dep md 1972–85, md 1985–2000, chm 1986–2009; memb London Bd Royal & Sun Alliance Gp 1990–2009; chm Internos Global Investors LLP 2009–, chm Cuts Ice Ltd 2012–; FRSA 1989, CIMgt 1989, FRICS 2010; *Recreations* crosswords, fine wine, golf; *Clubs* MCC (memb Estates Ctee 1999–2005), RAC, Mark's, Annabel's; *Style—* Richard Peskin, Esq; ✉ 41 Circus Road, London NW8 9JH (☎ 020 7289 0492)

PESTON, (Hon) Juliet Clare Elaine; da of Baron Peston (Life Peer), *qv*, and Helen, *née* Conen; sis of Robert Peston, *qv*; *b* 5 August 1961; *Educ* Highgate Wood Comp, Creighton Comp, Trinity Coll Cambridge; *Career* chef: Alastair Little 1985–96, Lola's 1996–99; exec chef: The Cow 1999–2000, Alastair Little Restaurants 2002–09, Coach & Horses London EC1 2003–04, Lola's 2004–05; Chef of the Year The Independent 1995, Best New Restaurant Time Out 1997, Best Brunch Time Out 1998, Best Gastropub Time Out 2004, Remy Martin Award 2004; *Clubs* Groucho, Colony, Jerry's; *Style—* Miss Juliet Peston; ✉ 24 Westminster Gardens, Marsham Street, London SW1P 4JD (☎ 020 7828 3141)

PESTON, Robert James Kenneth; (Hon); s of Baron Peston (Life Peer), *qv*, and Helen, *née* Cohen; bro of Juliet Peston, *qv*; *b* 25 April 1960, London; *Educ* Highgate Wood Comp Sch, Balliol Coll Oxford (MA); *m* 9 May 1998, Sian Elizabeth Busby (d 2012); 1 s (Maximilian b 8 March 1997), 1 step s (Simon Ryninks b 1 Nov 1985); *Career* journalist; city corr The Independent 1986–89, dep city ed Sunday Correspondent 1989–90, city ed Independent on Sunday 1990–91; FT: banking ed 1991–93, head of investigations 1993–95, political ed 1995–2000, fin ed 2000; editorial dir Collins Stewart Quest 2001–02, columnist Daily Telegraph 2001, assoc ed The Spectator 2001, business columnist New Statesman and Sunday Times 2002, city ed and asst ed Sunday Telegraph 2002–06, business ed BBC News 2006–, economics ed BBC 2014–; presenter and writer Super Rich: The Greed Game 2008 (documentary), presenter and writer Britain's Banks: too big to save? 2011 (documentary), presenter and writer The Party's Over – How the West Went Bust Parts 1 and 2 2011 (documenary series), presenter and writer The Great Euro Crash with Robert Peston 2012 (documentary), presenter Robert Peston Goes Shopping (documentary series) 2013, presenter and writer How China Fooled the World, with Robert Peston 2014, presenter and writer Quelle Catastrophe – France, with Robert Peston (documentary) 2015, presenter Robert Peston Interview Show (Radio 4 interview series, with Eddie Mair) 2015; patron Pro Bono Economics, fndr Speakers for Schools, tstee Educn and Employers Taskforce; official honoree Webby Awards 2010; hon fell Aberystwyth Univ 2011; Hon DLitt Heriot-Watt Univ 2010; *Awards* What Papers Say Investigative Journalist of the Year 1994, Wincott Sr Fin Journalist of the Year 2005, London Press Club Scoop of the Year 2007, Wincott Prog of the Year 2007, Business Journalism Awards Journalist of the Year 2007/08, Scoop of the Year RTS TV Journalism Awards 2007, Television Journalist of the Year, Specialist Journalist of the Year and Scoop of the Year RTS TV Journalism Awards 2008, Broadcaster of the Year and Online Media Award Harold Wincott Awards 2008, Best Performer in a Non-acting Role Broadcasting Press Guild Awards 2009, Business Journalist of the Year London Press Club Awards 2009, Political Journalist of the Year Political Studies Assoc 2009, Business Journalist of the Year Press Gazette 2009, Mainstream Blogger of the Year EI Comment Award 2011, Financial/Economic Story of the Year Foreign Press Assoc Award 2012, Lung Cancer Journalist of the Year Global Lung Cancer Coalition 2014; Brown's Britain (2005), Who Runs Britain? (2008), How Do We Fix This Mess (2012); *Recreations* Arsenal, ballet, rock, food; *Clubs* Groucho; *Style—* Robert Peston, Esq; ✉ W1 NBH 02C, BBC Broadcasting House, Portland Place, London W1A 1AA (☎ 020 3614 0823, e-mail robert.peston@bbc.co.uk); website www.speakers4schools.org

PETCH, Howard Wesley; CBE (2003, OBE 1997); s of Herbert Petch (d 1966), and Annie, *née* Hall (d 1972); *b* 14 December 1943, Guisborough, N Yorks; *Educ* Guisborough GS, Askham Bryan Coll, Lancs Coll of Agric (NDA); *m* 16 Aug 1973, Shirley Joyce, *née* Riding (d 2014); 2 s (Craig Stuart b 1976, Gavin Roy b 1980), 1 da (Tracey Dawn b 1977); *Career* farming in family business 1960–65, VSO Zambia 1966–67, sr lectr/sr warden Myerscough Coll 1969–79, vice-princ Warwickshire Coll of Agric 1979–85, princ Bishop Burton Coll 1985–97, exec dir Napaeo (Assoc of Land Based Colleges) 1997–2006, chief exec Landex 2006–09; memb: LSC, Bd Countryside Agency 2005–, Bd Cmmn for Rural Communities 2006–12; chair Bd of Tstees Arthur Rank Centre 2014–; former JP; FRASE 2001; *Recreations* sport, gardening, walking; *Style—* Howard Petch, Esq, CBE; ✉ e-mail howardpetch@btinternet.com

PETCH, Dr Michael Charles; OBE (2001); s of Dr Charles Plowright Petch (d 1987), of Wolferton, Norfolk, and Edna Margaret, *née* Stirling; *b* 15 July 1941, Woking, Surrey; *Educ* Gresham's, St John's Coll Cambridge, St Thomas' Hosp (MA, MD, MB BChir); *m* 19 April 1965, Fiona Jean Shepheard, da of Cdr David George Fraser Bird, of Nyewood, W Sussex; 2 s (Tom b 1966, Simon b 1968), 1 da (Amanda b 1971); *Career* sr registrar Nat Heart Hosp 1971–77; conslt cardiologist: Addenbrooke's Hosp 1977–2003 (emeritus conslt cardiologist 2003–), Papworth Hosp 1977–2008; pt/t conslt cardiologist Queen Elizabeth Hosp Kings Lynn 2008–; former assoc lectr Univ of Cambridge; memb Cncl Br Cardiac Soc 1985–89; MRCP 1967, FRCP 1980, fell American Coll of Cardiology 1980, fell Euro Soc of Cardiology 1995 (emeritus fell 2009); *Publications* Heart Disease (1989); contrib: British Med Jl, Lancet, Heart; author of over 100 papers; *Recreations* natural

P

history, sailing, opera, beagling; *Clubs* United Oxford and Cambridge; *Style*— Dr Michael Petch, OBE; ✉ Manor Farmhouse, Wolferton, Kings Lynn, Norfolk PE31 6HA (☎ 01485 540651, mobile 07887 650735, fax 01485 545810, e-mail mc.petch@btinternet.com)

PETER, John Anthony; s of Dr András Péter (d 1944), and Veronika, *née* Nagy (d 1977); *b* 24 August 1938; *Educ* various state schs in Hungary, Campion Hall Oxford (MA), Lincoln Coll Oxford (BLitt); *m* 1, 1978, Linette Katharine (d 2012), da of Rai Bahadur Amar Nath Purbi and Lilian Roberts; m 2, 2013, Judith Leonore Burnley; *Career* reporter and editorial asst Times Educational Supplement 1964–67; The Sunday Times: editorial staff 1967–79, dep arts ed 1979–84, chief drama critic 1984–2003, contributing drama critic 2003–10; fndr and dir Ian Charleson Award 1991–; hon doctorate De Montford Univ Leicester 1996; *Books* Vladimir's Carrot: Modern Drama and the Modern Imagination (1987); *Style*— John Peter, Esq; ✉ The Sunday Times, 3 Thomas More Square, London E98 1XY (☎ 020 7782 5000, e-mail jp@aloss.eu)

PETERBOROUGH, Lord Bishop of 2010–; Rt Rev Donald Allister; *Educ* Birkenhead Sch, Peterhouse Cambridge (BA, MA), Trinity Coll Bristol, Univ of Chester (DTh); *m* 17 July 1976, Dr Janice Allister, *née* Reynolds; 1 s (b 1977), 2 da (b 1980, 1984); *Career* ordained 1976, curate St George's Church Hyde 1976–79, curate St Nicholas's Church Sevenoaks 1979–83, vicar Christ Church Birkenhead 1983–89, rector St Mary's Church Cheadle 1989–2002, (dean Cheadle deanery 1999–2002), archdeacon of Chester 2002–10; memb: Gen Synod 2005–, House of Lords 2014–; memb Cncl for Christian Unity 2006– (chm 2013–); *Recreations* walking, science fiction, medical ethics; *Clubs* Farmers; *Style*— The Rt Rev the Lord Bishop of Peterborough; ✉ The Bishops Office, The Palace, Peterborough PE1 1YA

PETERKEN, Dr George Frederick; OBE (1994); s of Stanley Peterken (d 1982), and Norah, *née* Broomfield (d 1989); *b* 21 October 1940; *Educ* Haberdashers' Aske's Hampstead, KCL (BSc, AKC), UCL (PhD), Univ of London (DSc); *m* 1964, Susan, da of Alec Walker; 2 s (Andrew b 1967, Michael b 1969); *Career* res demonstrator Botany Dept UCW Aberystwyth 1964–65, scientific co-ordinator Nature Conservancy 1965–67; woodland ecologist 1969–92 with: Nature Conservancy, Nature Conservancy Cncl, Jt Nature Conservation Ctee; Bullard fell in forest res Harvard Univ 1989–90, Leverhulme res fell 1990; ind ecology conslt 1993–; past pres Gwent Wildlife Tst, memb Jt Advsy Ctee Lower Wye Valley AONB, memb Br Ecological Soc 1962–; *Publications* Woodland Conservation and Management (1981), Natural Woodland: Ecology and Conservation in Northern Temperate Regions (1996), Wye Valley (2008), Meadows (2013); also author of numerous book chapters, articles in specialist jls, book reviews, popular articles, and conference proceedings; *Recreations* bowling, golf, estate mgmnt, hill walking; *Style*— Dr George Peterken, OBE; ✉ Beechwood House, St Briavels Common, Lydney, Gloucestershire GL15 6SL (☎ 01594 530452)

PETERS, Andi; *b* 29 July 1970; *Educ* Emanuel Sch; *Career* television presenter, prodr and dir, first LWT music exec prodr, commissioning ed for children and young people Channel Four Television Corp 1998–2002, exec ed of popular music BBC 2003–; *Television* presented for BBC: But First This (BFT) 1989, CBBC 2 1989, The Broom Cupboard 1990–92, Smash Hits Awards 1993, 1994 and 1995, Children In Need 1993 and 1994, The Ozone (also prodr/dir) 1993–96, Live and Kicking 1993–96, The Travel Quiz 1994, Take Two 1995, EEK 1995, Good Fortune 1995, Short Change 1996, City Hospital 2006; for ITV as presenter: Free Time 1988, The Noise 1996–97, The Weekend Show 1997, Celebrity 2000, Dancing on Ice Extra 2006 (and tour 2007, 2008 and 2009), Sunday Feast 2006; regular presenter Andi Meets (Channel Four) 1999–; as prodr: Train 2 Win, The Ozone 1993–96, An Audience with The Spice Girls 1997; presenter for Channel Four: Miami Spice 1998, Masterchef 2008; presenter Golden Globes (Sky One) 2009, voiceover The Big Reunion (ITV 2) 2013–; *Radio* Hit Music Sunday (Capital FM) 2002–03, Heat Radio 2008–; *Awards* twice winner Top Personality on TV (voted by Newsround), three times winner Smash Hits Poll for Best TV Presenter; *Style*— Andi Peters, Esq; ✉ c/o George Ashton, James Grant Media Ltd, 94 Strand on the Green, London W4 3NN (☎ 020 8742 1950, fax 020 8742 4951, e-mail enquiries@jamesgrant.co.uk)

PETERS, Prof Andrew Raymond (Andy); s of Raymond Barlow Peters, of Shepshed, Leics, and Dorothy Ellen, *née* Sparrow; *b* 10 December 1949; *Educ* Ashby de la Zouch Boys' GS, RVC (BVetMed, MRCVS), Open Univ (BA), Univ of Nottingham (PhD), Univ of London (DVetMed, DSc); *m* Jean Elizabeth, *née* Pallett; 3 s (Daniel Joseph b 13 July 1980, Thomas Michael b 13 June 1982, Robert James b 1 Jan 1987); *Career* practising vet surgn 1972–74, demonstrator in animal physiology Univ of Nottingham 1974–79, sr vet offr Meat and Livestock Cmmn 1979–87, sr exec (pharmaceuticals) British Technology Group 1987–88, regulatory mangr Hoechst Animal Health 1989–93, prof of animal health and prodn RVC Univ of London 1993–98, sr dir (vaccine devpt) VMRD Pfizer Ltd 1998–2006; fndr Arpexas Ltd 2006–; conslt Genecom 2006–; memb RZS: Animal Welfare Ctee, UK Vet Products Ctee, UK Advsy Gp on Vet Residues; UK rep Standing Ctee Int Congress on Animal Reproduction; memb: Assoc of Vet Teachers and Research Workers, Br Soc of Animal Science, BVA, Br Cattle Vet Assoc, Pig Vet Soc; FRCVS 1982, FIBiol 1983; *Books* Reproduction in Cattle (1986), Vaccines for Veterinary Applications (1993); also author of approx 140 published papers in animal/vet science journals, reg contrib to scientific and industry confs; *Recreations* hill walking, running, swimming, DIY building; *Style*— Prof Andy Peters

PETERS, Her Hon Judge Emma Kate; *Career* called to the Bar 1991; asst judge advocate general 2010, recorder 2012, circuit judge (SE Circuit) 2016–; *Style*— Her Hon Judge Emma Peters

PETERS, Frank David; s of Alfred George Charles Peters (d 1985), and Georgina, *née* Robins; *b* 7 January 1952; *Educ* Kings Heath Boys' Tech Sch, Birmingham Coll of Art & Design, Lanchester Poly (Cert in Design Visual Communication (3 Dimensions)); *Partner* Carmen Martinez-Lopez; 1 da (Christina Onesireosan-Martinez b 15 Aug 1976); *Career* exhbn designer 1975–77, proprietor own co 1977–80 (sold to Badger Graphics), freelance designer 1980–84; fndr: Creative Facility Associates (gp mktg, PR & translation servs) 1984–, Sherborne Group (interior design & build contractors and exhbn contractors) 1994–, Mera Properties (residential and commercial property developers); currently involved in design mgmnt and mktg in leisure, entertainment and educn sectors (work incl Euro motor show stands for Land Rover/Rover motor show stand Geneva, etc); memb Policy Ctee Birmingham Design Initiative; co-creator Birmingham Contemporary Music Gp (under artistic direction of Sir Simon Rattle); exec dir CSD; memb Steering Ctee: West Midlands Creative Industries Forum, Centre Product Design Information; FRSA, MCSD; *Recreations* cooking, film, classical music; *Clubs* Edgbaston Priory; *Style*— Frank Peters, Esq; ✉ Creative Facility Associates Ltd, Number One, of Sherborne Gate, Sherborne Street Wharf, Birmingham B16 8DE (☎ 0121 608 6000, fax 0121 608 2223)

PETERS, James; s of Joseph Peters (d 1997), and Mary, *née* Hunt (d 2009); *b* 30 March 1958, Farnham, Surrey; *m* 29 July 1993, Penny, *née* Lennard; 1 s (Christopher b 3 Feb 1986), 1 da (Sarah b 13 July 1989); *Career* dir Powerline Electronics Ltd 1980–88, dep chm XP Power plc 1988–; *Style*— James Peters, Esq; ✉ XP Power plc, Horseshoe Park, Pangbourne, Berkshire RG8 7JW (☎ 0118 976 5080, e-mail jpeters@xppower.com)

PETERS, Prof (Adrien) Michael; s of Adrien John Peters, and Barbara Muriel Peters; *b* 17 May 1945, Lancaster; *Educ* Middlesbrough HS, Liverpool Inst HS, St Mary's Hosp Med Sch London (BSc), Univ of Liverpool (MB ChB, MD), Univ of London (MSc); *m* 1; 1 s; m 2, 1980, Rosemary Cox; 2 s, 1 da; *Career* house offr Victoria Central Hosp Wallasey 1970–71, house offr Queen Elizabeth Hosp Gateshead 1971–72, lectr in physiology Univ of Liverpool 1972–74, GP NSW 1974–78, GP Liverpool 1978–79, res fell Dept of Diagnostic Radiology Royal Postgrad Med Sch London and hon sr registrar Dept of Diagnostic Radiology Hammersmith Hosp 1979–82, res physician Glaxo Gp Res Ltd 1982–84 (concurrently hon pt/t conslt in med imaging Dept of Diagnostic Radiology Hammersmith Hosp), sr lectr in diagnostic radiology (nuclear med) Royal Postgrad Med Sch London 1984–89 (reader in nuclear med 1989–95), hon sr lectr in nephrology Inst of Child Health Univ of London 1984–93, hon conslt in diagnostic radiology Hammersmith Hosp 1984–99 (conslt-in-charge (nuclear med) Dept of Diagnostic Radiology 1991–99), hon conslt in paediatric radiology Hosp for Sick Children Gt Ormond St London 1988–94 and 1996–2001 (conslt 1984–88), prof of diagnostic radiology Royal Postgrad Med Sch London 1995–97 (memb Higher Degrees Ctee 1996–97), prof of diagnostic radiology Imperial Coll Sch of Med London 1997–99 (departmental rep Higher Degrees Ctee 1997–99, memb Safety Ctee 1996–98, chm Radiation Safety Ctee 1996–98), hon conslt in nuclear med Hammersmith Hosp 1999–2000, prof of nuclear med Univ of Cambridge and hon conslt in nuclear med Addenbrooke's Hosp Cambridge 1999–2004, professorial fell New Hall Cambridge 1999–2004, prof of applied physiology Brighton and Sussex Medical Sch 2004–; visiting fell Div of Nuclear Med Dept of Radiology Hosp for Sick Children Toronto 1985; regnl advsr in nuclear med E Anglia; memb: Panel on Radiolabelled Platelet Survival Studies Int Ctee for Standardisation in Haematology Radionuclide Panel 1988, Advsy Gp – Pharmacology Working Pty MRC Cyclotron Unit Hammersmith Hosp 1995, Standards of Care Ctee Br Thoracic Soc 1995, Advsy Gp – Radiochemistry Working Pty MRC Cyclotron Unit Hammersmith Hosp 1996, Int Consensus Ctee Quality Assurance of Quantitative Measurements of Renal Function from the Renogram 1996, Radiation Safety Ctee Hammersmith Hosps Tst 1997–98; memb Editorial Bd: Br Jl of Radiology 1989–95, Euro Jl of Nuclear Med 1990–, Nuclear Medicine Communications 1997–; memb: Br Nuclear Med Soc 1987– (memb Cncl 1989–92), BIR 1989– (memb Nuclear Med Sub-Ctee 1989–92), Soc of Nuclear Med 1992–; FRCR 1995, FRCPath 1996 (MRCPath 1984), FRCP 1997 (MRCP 1993), FMedSci 2002; *Publications* Physiological Measurements with Radionuclides in Clinical Practice (jtly, 1998), Nuclear Medicine in Radiological Diagnosis (ed, 2003); author of articles in learned jls; *Recreations* soccer, jazz, dogs, walking; *Style*— Prof Michael Peters

PETERS, Prof Nicholas Simon; s of Lawrence Peters, of London, and Valerie, *née* Benjamin; *b* 18 February 1960; *Educ* Latymer Upper Sch, Royal Free Hosp Sch of Med London (MB BS), Univ of London (MD); *m* 18 June 1992 (m dis), Charlotte, da of Geoffrey Darke; 2 s; *Career* postgrad med trg Bart's and St Thomas' Hosp 1986–88, cardiology trg Nat Heart and Royal Brompton Hosps 1988–91, Br Heart Fndn jr res fell 1991–93, sr registrar (cardiology) Hammersmith Hosp 1993–95, sr lectr and conslt St Mary's Hosp Paddington 1995–98, prof of cardiology and conslt St Mary's Hosp Imperial Coll London 1998–; prof of pharmacology Coll of Physicians and Surgns Columbia Univ NY 1997–, dir of electrophysiology research American Cardiovascular Research Inst 2001–, Med Ctee ARA 1999–; ed European Heart Jl 1996–; FRCP 1998 (MRCP 1987), fell American Coll of Cardiology 2003; *Publications* more than 150 scientific papers, book chapters and reviews on cardiology and heart rhythm disturbances; *Recreations* rowing (several times nat champion 1976–78, represented England 1978), running, art, classic cars; *Clubs* Leander; *Style*— Prof Nicholas Peters; ✉ 4th Floor, Imperial Centre for Translational and Experimental Medicine, Hammersmith Campus, Du Cane Road, London W12 0NN (☎ 020 7594 1880, e-mail n.peters@imperial.ac.uk)

PETERS, Prof Timothy John; s of Stanley Frederick Peters (d 1993), of Uley, Dursley, Gloucester, and Paula, *née* March (d 1973); *b* 10 May 1939, Manchester; *Educ* King's Sch Macclesfield Cheshire, Univ of St Andrews (MB ChB, MSc, DSc), Univ of London (PhD), The Rockefeller Univ NY, Univ of Birmingham (MA); *m* 21 Sept 1965, Judith Mary, da of Dr William Basil Bacon (d 1983), of Manchester; 2 da (Carolyne b 1967, Sarah b 1969), 1 s (Christopher b 1983); *Career* successively lectr, sr lectr then reader Royal Postgrad Med Sch Univ of London 1972–79, head Div of Clinical Cell Biology Medical Res Cncl Harrow 1979–88, head Dept of Clinical Biochemistry GKT 1988–2004, dir of pathology King's Healthcare 1992–2000, sub-dean for research and higher degrees King's Coll Sch of Med and Dentistry 1992–2000, assoc dean (flexible trg) Thames Postgraduate Med and Educn Dept Univ of London 2000–04; Raine visiting prof Univ of Madison USA 1994, Br Cncl visiting prof Dept of Biochemistry Univ of Western Australia 1995, hon sr research fell Inst of Archaeology and Antiquity Univ of Birmingham 2006–15; ed Alcohol and Alcoholism 1991–94, ed-in-chief Addiction Biology 1995–2000; tstee and memb Cncl Sir Richard Stapley Educational Tst 1992–2008, tstee and chair Areca Concern 2001–15, memb Academic and Curatorial Ctee Ironbridge Inst Coalbrookdale Salops 2009–, memb Curatorial Ctee Nat Waterways Museum Ellesmere Port 2007–10; FRCP 1974, FRCPE 1981, FRCPath 1984, FRSA 1996; *Publications* International Handbook of Alcohol Dependence and Problems (ed jtly, 2001), Biochemistry and Molecular Biology in the Post-genomic Era (in Biochemistry Illustrated jtly, 5 edn 2005), medical history research papers incl History of Psychiatry 2010–13 (in Jl of the Royal Coll of Physicians of Edinburgh 2010–13), industrial archaeology research papers incl Jl of the Railway and Canal Soc 2010, ICE Engineering History and Heritage 2013 and 2015; *Recreations* medical history, industrial archaeology; *Style*— Prof Timothy J Peters; ✉ e-mail timothy@ironlock.f2s.com

PETERSON, Alan Edward; s of Edward Peterson, MBE (d 2005), of Cardiff, and Nell, *née* James (d 2011); *b* 22 October 1947; *Educ* Loughborough Univ (BTech); *m* 5 June 1971, Margaret Diane; 1 s (Hywel Rhys b 8 Feb 1978); *Career* gen mgmnt Alcan (UK) 1973–81, chm West & Welsh Holdings 1982–89, md ACI Rockware Gp 1990–95, chief exec Meyer International plc 1996–2000; chm: The Peterson Consultancy Ltd 2000–13, Rubicon Retail Ltd 2001–05, Paperpak Holdings Ltd 2002–07, Refresco Holdings BV 2003–06, HSS Hire Service Holdings Ltd 2004–07, Azelis Holdings SA 2008–12, Enterprise Gp Holdings 2011–13, HSS Hire Gp 2012–, Peterson Consultancy Services Ltd 2013–, Pattonair Hldgs Ltd 2015–, BBI Diagnostics Gp 2015–; chm Appeal Bd Wales NSPCC 2016–; Hon Col Army Cadets Wales 2016–; CCMI; *Recreations* opera, cricket, rugby, Nat Hunt race horse owner; *Clubs* Ivy, Cardiff RFC, Cardiff and County, Glamorgan CCC; *Style*— Alan Peterson, Esq; ✉ e-mail aep@alanepeterson.com

PETERSON, Gilles; MBE (2004); s of Armin Moehrle (d 2002), of Switzerland, and Michelle Fouquet; *b* 28 September 1964, Caen, France; *m* 22 Dec 1999, Atsuko Hirai; 2 s (Olivier b 9 Oct 1997, Luc b 21 Sept 2001); *Career* DJ, prodr and head Brownswood Recordings; early DJ residencies incl: Electric Ballroom, Special Branch at The Royal Oak, Dingwalls Camden 1986–92, Heaven, That's How it Is; fndr (with James Lavelle) That's How It Is (nightclub) 1993, currently plays regularly worldwide incl Worldwide Festival France and Leysin Swiss Alps; fndr: Acid Jazz (record label), Talkin' Loud Records (Phonogram) 1989 (releases incl Roni Size's New Forms (winner Mercury Music Prize 1997)); DJ on pirate radio stations incl: Invicta, KJazz, Solar Radio, On Horizon; presenter: BBC Radio London, Jazz FM, Kiss FM 1990–98, Worldwide on BBC Radio 1 1998– (Best Specialist Radio Show Sony Awards 2000), BBC 6Music; Outstanding Contribution to Dance Music 2011, Indie Champion AIM Ind Music Awards 2013; hon MA Univ of Nottingham; *Albums* incl: Jazz Juice, compiled EMI Blue Note artists series, Gilles Peterson in Africa, Gilles Peterson in Brazil, Gilles Peterson: Worldwide, Vol 2, and Vol 3, Gilles Peterson: Worldwide/Programme 4, Desert Island Mix: Journeys By DJs, Impressed with Gilles Peterson Vol 1 and Vol 2, Brownswood Bubblers series, Gilles Peterson Presents series; *Style*— Gilles Peterson, Esq, MBE; ✉ c/o John Slade, Elastic Artist Agency, Flat 5, 3 Newhams Row, London SE1 3UZ (☎ 020 7367 6224, fax 020 7367 6206, e-mail john@elasticartists.net)

PETFORD, Prof Nick; *b* 27 May 1961, London; *Educ* Goldsmiths Coll (BSc), Univ of Liverpool (PhD), Univ of Cambridge (MA), Univ of Liverpool (DSc), Harvard Business Sch (Gen Mgmnt Prog); *Career* Royal Soc research fell Churchill Coll Cambridge 1991–94, prof of earth and planetary sciences Kingston Univ 1995–2006, with BP 2001, pro-vice-chllr Bournemouth Univ 2006–10, vice-chllr and CEO Univ of Northampton; presenter The Volcano That Stopped Britain (Channel 4) 2010; memb Bd UnLtd 2015–; Murchison Fund Geological Soc 1999; FGS 1986, FRSA 2012; *Books* Field Description of Igneous Rocks (2011); *Recreations* football; *Clubs* Athenaeum; *Style*— Prof Nick Petford; ✉ The University of Northampton, Avenue Campus, St George's Avenue, Northampton NN2 6JD

PETHERICK, Simon; *Educ* Merton Coll Oxford; *Career* advertising and publicity Robert Hale Publishers 1982–86, mktg dir Central Office of Information 1986–93, md Royal Parks Enterprises 1996–2001, md Hardy Amies London 2001–03, md Animate Communications Ltd 2003–06, md Beautiful Books 2005–11, md The House of Britannia 2013–; dir The Word Machine Community Interest Co 2011–; *Style*— Simon Petherick, Esq

PETHICK, Jan Stephen; s of Maj Thomas Francis Henry Pethick (d 1981), of Ventnor, IOW, and Denise Joyce, *née* Clark (d 1994); *b* 16 September 1947; *Educ* Clifton Coll, Jesus Coll Oxford; *m* 20 Dec 1974, Belinda Patricia, da of Douglas Collins, of Hare Hatch, Berks; 2 da (Emily b 26 May 1975, Nancy b 15 April 1977), 1 s (Benjamin b 18 May 1981); *Career* stock jobber/trader Pinchin Denny & Co 1969–74, Midland Doherty Eurobond Trading 1975–77, exec dir Bonds Lehman Bros Kuhn Loeb 1977–84, md Shearson Lehman Hutton International Inc 1986–90, dir Luthy Baillie Dowsett Pethick & Co Ltd 1990–96 (also co-fndr), head of global debt origination Dresdner Kleinwort Benson 1996–2000; md and chm of debt capital markets Europe Merrill Lynch International 2000–; memb Bd London Sch of Hygiene and Tropical Medicine 2006; chm of tstees Childhood First; High Sheriff Gtr London 2007–08; *Recreations* golf, tennis; *Clubs* New Zealand Golf, Queen's Tennis, Turf, Swinley Forest Golf, Royal St George's Golf, Portland Bridge; *Style*— Jan Pethick, Esq; ✉ 71 Kew Green, Kew, Richmond, Surrey TW9 3AH (☎ 020 8940 2426); Merrill Lynch International, 2 King Edward Street, London EC1A 1HQ (☎ 020 7995 2638)

PETHIG, Prof Ronald (Ron); s of Charles Edward Pethig (d 1997), of Sanderstead, Surrey, and Edith Jane, *née* Jones; *b* 10 May 1942; *Educ* Purley GS, Univ of Southampton (BSc, PhD, DSc), Univ of Nottingham (PhD); *m* 10 Aug 1968, Angela Jane, da of John Stephen Sampson, of Tibshelf, Derbys (d 1973); 1 s (Richard John b 16 June 1971), 1 da (Helen Jane b 17 Jan 1976); *Career* ICI fell Univ of Nottingham 1968–71, corpn memb Marine Biological Laboratory Woods Hole USA 1982–, adjunct prof of physiology Med Univ S Carolina USA 1984–90; Univ of Wales: reader 1982–86, personal chair 1986–, dir Inst of Molecular and Biomolecular Electronics 1986–1998, dean Faculty of Sci 1991–93; prof of bioelectronics Sch of Engrg Univ of Edinburgh 2008–; dir P & B (Sciences) Ltd 1989–2000; vice-pres for research then pres and ceo Aura Biosystems Systems Inc 2000–03 (currently memb Bd); Marine Biological Lab Woods Hole: corporation memb 1982, adjunct sr scientist 2005–, Eugene and Millicent Bell endowed fell in tissue engrg 2006–: memb: SERC Molecular Electronics Ctee 1991–94, Int Evaluation Ctee of Swedish Nat Bd for Industrial and Tech Devpt 1991–92, Exec Ctee Snowdonia National Park Soc 1991–94, Industry and Engrg Ctee Royal Cmmn for the Exhibition of 1851 2013–; Innovation Prize IEE/IMechE/Br Design Cncl 1988, Innovation Award Inst of Physical Sciences in Medicine 1994, Innovation Award Biological Engrg Soc 1994, first recipient of Herman P Schwan Award Oslo 2001; CEng 1975, FIEE 1986; *Books* Dielectric and Electronic Properties of Biological Materials (1979), Introductory Bioelectronics: For Engineers and Physical Scientists (jtly, 2012); *Recreations* mountain walking, restoring old scientific instruments, bird watching; *Style*— Prof Ron Pethig; ✉ School of Engineering, University of Edinburgh, The King's Buildings, West Mains Road, Edinburgh EH9 3JF (☎ 0131 650 5650, e-mail ron.pethig@ed.ac.uk)

PETIT, Sir Dinshaw Manockjee; 5 Bt (UK 1890), of Petit Hall, Island of Bombay; né Jehangir Petit but obliged, under a trust created by Sir Dinshaw Manockjee Petit, 1 Bt, to adopt the name of the first Bt; s of Sir Dinshaw Manockjee Petit, 4 Bt (d 1998); *b* 21 January 1965; *Educ* Pierrepont Sch, New Hampshire Coll; *m* 1994, Laila, da of Homi F Commissariat; 1 s (Rehan b 4 May 1995), 1 da (Aisha b 30 Jan 1998); *Heir* s, Rehan Petit; *Career* pres: N M Petit Charities, Sir D M Petit Charities, F D Petit Sanatorium, Persian Zoroastrian Amelioration Fund, Petit Girls' Orphanage, D M Petit Gymnasium, J N Petit Inst, Bombay Native Dispensary, Bai Avabai F Petit Residuary Estate Tst, N.M. Petit Charitable Inst, Two Account Tst 1998; memb Mgmnt Ctee: B D Petit Parsi Gen Hosp, Garib Zarthostiona Rehethan Fund; tstee: Bai Sakarbai Dinshaw Petit Hosp for Animals, Concern India Fndn, J B Petit Sch for Girls 2007; memb Bd of Govrs Veermata Jijabai Tech Inst 1998–2015, memb Governing Body The K R Cama Oriental Inst 2008–; fndr memb Nat Centre for the Performing Arts (NCPA India) 2008–; Chevalier de l'ordre National du Merite 2005; *Style*— Sir Dinshaw Petit, Bt; ✉ Petit Hall, 66 Nepean Sea Road, Bombay 400 006, India (☎ 00 91 22 2363 7333, fax 00 91 22 2264 4680, e-mail jehpetit@gmail.com)

PETIT, Pascale; da of Michel Petit, and Muriel, *née* McCarthy; *b* 20 December 1953, Paris, France; *Educ* Glos Coll of Art and Design (BA), RCA (MA); *m* Brian Fraser; *Career* poet; poetry ed Poetry London 1989–2005 (tstee 2007–12), tutor The Poetry Sch 1997–2000, 2007–08 and 2013–15, tutor Tate Modern 2006–15, Royal Literary Fund fell Middx Univ 2007–09, core course tutor for MSt creative writing Univ of Oxford 2007–; translations of poems by Yang Lian, Zhai Yongming, Xi Chuan, Zhou Zan, Wang Xiaoni (all from Chinese) and Amir Or (from Hebrew) published in Poetry Review, Poetry London, Modern Poetry in Translation, The Wolf and Guardian Online; shortlisted Forward Prize for Best Single Poem 2000, selected as a Next Generation Poet Arts Cncl/Poetry Book Soc 2004, Arts Cncl England Grant for the Arts Award 2005, 2007, 2013 and 2016, Soc of Authors grant 2007 and 2011; Royal Literary Fund fell Courtauld Inst of Art 2011–12; FZS; *Books* Heart of a Deer (1998), Tying the Song (co-ed, 2000), The Zoo Father (2001, Arts Cncl of England Writers' Award 2001, New London Writers' Award 2001, Poetry Book Soc recommendation, shortlisted T S Eliot Prize 2002), El Padre Zoológico /The Zoo Father (2004, bilingual edn Mexico), The Huntress (2005, shortlisted T S Eliot Prize 2006), The Wounded Deer: Fourteen Poems after Frida Kahlo (2005), The Treekeeper's Tale (2008), What the Water Gave Me – Poems after Frida Kahlo (2010, shortlisted T S Eliot Prize 2010, shortlisted Wales Book of the Year 2011), Fauverie (2014, shortlisted T S Eliot Prize 2014); *Recreations* travel in the Venezuelan Amazon, Mexico, China, Nepal, Kazakhstan and Israel, going to contemporary art exhibitions; *Style*— Pascale Petit; ✉ website www.pascalepetit.co.uk, blog http://pascalepetit.blogspot.com; Seren, 57 Nolton Street, Bridgend CF31 3AE (☎ 01656 663018, fax 01656 649226, e-mail general@serenbooks.com, website www.serenbooks.com); c/o Neil Astley (editor), Bloodaxe Books, Eastburn, South Park, Hexham, Northumberland NE46 1BS (☎ 01434 611581, e-mail editor@bloodaxebooks.com)

PETO, Sir Henry Christopher Morton Bampfylde; 5 Bt (UK 1927); s of Sir Michael Henry Basil Peto, 4 Bt (d 2008), and Sarah Susan Worthington, da of Maj Sir Dennis Frederick Stucley, 5 Bt (d 1983); *b* 8 April 1967, London; *Educ* Eton, Oxford Brookes Univ (BSc); *m* 1998, Louise Imogen, da of late Christopher Balck-Foote; 2 da (Atlanta Daisy b 28 Nov 2001, Rosa Dandelion b 12 April 2006), 1 s (Jake Christopher Bampfylde b 11 Oct 2004); *Heir* s, Jake Peto; *Career* chartered surveyor; MRICS; *Recreations* tennis, football, politics; *Style*— Sir Henry Peto, Bt

PETO, Sir Richard; kt (1999); *b* 14 May 1943; *Educ* Univ of Cambridge (MA), Univ of London (MSc); *Career* research offr MRC Statistical Research Unit 1967–69; Dept of the Regius Prof of Med Univ of Oxford: research offr 1969–72, lectr 1972–75, reader 1975–79; Nuffield Dept of Clinical Med Univ of Oxford: univ reader in cancer studies 1979–92, prof of med statistics and epidemiology 1992–, co-dir (with Prof Rory Collins, *qv*) Clinical Trial Service Unit and Epidemiological Studies Unit (CTSU); fndn fell Green Coll Oxford 1979–; General Motors visiting prof Int Agency for Research on Cancer (IARC) Lyon 1992; hon prof Chinese Acad of Preventive Med 1989–, adjunct prof Cornell Univ 1990–, hon prof Peking Union Med Coll 1995–; Caradog Jones lectr RSS 1992, Rickman Godlee lectr UCL 1999; MA (by incorporation) Univ of Oxford 1974, Hon Dr Univ of Tampere 1992, Hon DSc Univ of London 1999, Hon DSc Univ of Southampton 2003; hon memb Swedish Soc of Internal Med 1988, academician Acad of Finland 2001, membre étranger Associé de l'Académie des Sciences France 2002; FRS 1989, Hon FFPHM 1992, fndr fell Acad of Med Sciences 1998, Hon FRCP 1999 (Hon MRCP 1987); Offr Cross of the Order of Merit (Poland) 2002; *Awards* Guy Silver Medal RSS 1986, Helmut Horten Fndn Award (jtly) 1989, Gairdner Fndn Award Canada 1992, Frohlich Award NY Acad of Sciences 1993, Donald Reid Medal London Sch of Hygiene 1993, Polish Cardiac Soc Medal of Merit 1993, La Médaille de la Ville de Paris (Échelon Vermeil) 1994, European Award for Excellence in Stroke Research (jtly) 1995, Oettlé Meml Medal SA 1996, Prix Raymond Bourgine for Achievement in Cancer Research (jtly) 1996, Gold Award Polish Health Promotion Fndn 1997, Prix Louis Jeantet for Med 1997, 10th World Conf on Tobacco or Health Award 1997, Fothergill Medal Med Soc of London (jtly) 1998, Leverhulme Prize Liverpool Sch of Tropical Med (jtly), 1998, Polish Presidential Public Health Award 2000, Int Aspirin Sr Award (jtly) 2000, Prince Mahidol Award for Public Health (jtly) Thailand 2000, Lynn Sage Distinguished Award in Breast Cancer Research 2001, King Olav V Prize Norwegian Cancer Soc (jtly) 2002, Mott Prize General Motors Cancer Research Fndn 2002, Royal Medal Royal Soc 2002; *Style*— Sir Richard Peto, FRS; ✉ Clinical Trial Service Unit and Epidemiological Studies Unit, Richard Doll Building, Old Road Campus, Oxford OX3 7LF

PETRE, 18 Baron (E 1603); John Patrick Lionel Petre; KCVO (2016); o s of 17 Baron Petre (d 1989), and Marguerite Eileen, *née* Hamilton; *b* 4 August 1942; *Educ* Eton, Trinity Coll Oxford (MA); *m* 16 Sept 1965, Marcia Gwendolyn, o da of Alfred Plumpton, of Portsmouth; 2 s (Hon Dominic William b 1966, Hon Mark Julian b 1969), 1 da (Hon Clare Helen b 1973); *Heir* s, Hon Dominic Petre; *Career* chm: Essex St John Ambulance 1992–2002, Essex Land and Business Assoc 1998–2001, Brentwood Theatre Tst 1998–2002; HM Lord-Lt Essex 2002– (DL 1991); *Style*— The Rt Hon the Lord Petre, KCVO; ✉ Writtle Park, Highwood, Chelmsford, Essex

PETRIE, Sir Peter Charles; CMG (1980); 5 Bt (UK 1918); s of Sir Charles Petrie, 3 Bt (d 1977), and of Cecilia, Lady Petrie (d 1987); suc his half-bro, Sir Richard Petrie, 4 Bt 1988; *b* 7 March 1932; *Educ* Westminster, ChCh Oxford (MA); *m* 1958, Countess Lydwine Maria Fortunata, da of Count Charles Alphonse von Oberndorff, of The Hague and Paris; 2 s, 1 da; *Heir* s, Charles Petrie; *Career* 2 sec UK Delegation NATO Paris 1958–61, first sec New Delhi 1961–64, chargé d'affaires Katmandu 1963, Cabinet Office 1965–67, UK Mission to UN (NY) 1969–73, cnsllr (head of Chancery) Bonn 1973–76, head of Euro Integration Dept (Int) FCO 1976–79, min Paris 1979–85; ambass to Belgium 1985–89; advsr to govr Bank of England on Euro and Parly affairs 1989–2003; memb: Institut de l'Euro Lyon Conseil d'Administration 1995–99, Franco-British Cncl 1995–2003 (chm 1997–2002); corresponding memb Académie de Comptabilité Paris 1996–, memb Cncl City Univ 1997–2002; *Clubs* Brooks's, Jockey (Paris); *Style*— Sir Peter Petrie, Bt, CMG; ✉ 16A Cambridge Street, London SW1V 4QH; 40 Rue Lauriston, 75116 Paris, France; 4 Hameau du Jardin, 50310 Lestre, France (e-mail lydwinepo@aol.fr)

PETROPOULOS, Denis Andreas; s of John Petropoulos (d 2003); *b* 30 November 1956, London; *Educ* Westminster, Univ of Surrey; *m* 1984; *Career* jt md Braemar Seascope Ltd (exec dir Braemar Shipping Servs plc 2007–); *Style*— Denis Petropoulos, Esq; ✉ Braemar Shipping Services plc, 35 Cosway Street, London NW1 5BT

PETT, David John; *Educ* Wanstead HS, Lincoln Coll Oxford (exhibitioner, MA), Coll of Law Guildford; *m* 1993, Ksymena; 2 s (Daniel b 1997, Alex b 1999); *Career* articled clerk Bond Pearce Plymouth 1978–80, asst slr (tax) Clifford-Turner 1980–83; Pinsent & Co (later Pinsent Curtis Biddle then Pinsent Masons): slr 1983, ptnr 1985–2009, nat head of tax and pensions 1995–2001, non-exec memb Bd 2001–08; Pett, Franklin & Co LLP 2009–; memb Share Plan Lawyers Gp, memb Inland Revenue Advsy Gp on Employee Share Schemes 1999–2000, public memb Network Rail 2002–11; tstee Thinktank (Birmingham Museum of Science and Industry) 2002–12, tstee CBSO Endowment Fund 2009– (chm 2014–), tstee CBSO Devpt Fund 2012–; ranked leading individual employee share schemes lawyer (Chambers and Legal 500) 2014 and 2015; *Books* A Practical Guide to Employee Share Schemes (1989), ESOPs – The Use of Trusts with Employee Share Schemes (1991), Employee Share Schemes Handbook (1993), The New Employee Share Incentives: AESOPs and EMI (with David Cohen, 2001); Employee Share Schemes (2 vols, looseleaf, 1996–); *Recreations* orchestral timpanist; *Style*— David Pett, Esq; ✉ Pett, Franklin & Co LLP, Victoria House, 116 Colmore Row, Birmingham B3 3BD (☎ 0121 348 7878, mobile 07836 657658, e-mail david.pett@pettfranklin.com, website www.pettfranklin.com)

P

PETTER, Hugh David Michael; s of Michael Gordon Petter (d 2010), and Evelyn Mary, *née* Leakey (d 1997); *b* 5 September 1966; *Educ* Sheredes Sch Hoddesdon, Portsmouth Poly (BA, DipArch); *m* 20 May 1995, Chloë Susannah, da of Rory Forrester, and Antonia Forrester (d 1997); 1 s (Harry Alexander James b 9 July 1999), 1 da (Charlotte Antonia Evelyn b 19 Dec 2000); *Career* architect; dir ADAM Architecture 1997– (assoc 1993–97); sr tutor Prince of Wales's Inst of Architecture 1992–98 (estab fndn course); memb: Traditional Architects Gp, Building Sub-Ctee Br Sch at Rome 1999–2004, Int Bilding Study Gp 2000–07, Exec Ctee The Georgian Gp 2003–, Educn Working Gp The Georgian Gp 2004–11, Devpt Advsy Gp Br Sch at Rome 2004–07, London Branch Ctee Country Land and Business Assoc 2006–10, Cncl of Advsrs Inst of Classical Architecture and Classical America 2007–, Estates Ctee Twyford Sch 2009–11; external examiner: Coll of Estate Mgmnt Prog in Conservation of the Historic Environment Univ of Reading 2011–, RIBA Planning Gp 2012–; govr Building Crafts Coll 2010–12; bro Art Workers' Guild 2002– (chm 2006–09); memb: Int Network for Traditional Building, Architecture and Urbanism (INTBAU), RIBA, ARB, Inst of Classical Architecture NY, Europa Nostra 2002–, Arts and Crafts Movement in Surrey; FRSA, academician Acad of Urbanism; *Awards* Palladio Award (for Millennium Gate Atlanta) 2006, winner RIBA competition to renovate and extend Grad II Listed house 2006, Georgian Gp Giles Worsley Award for a New Building in a Georgian Context 2007, commended Cheltenham Civic Tst Award 2008 (all for new villa Cheltenham), McGraw-Hill Southeast Construction's Best Public Building Award 2008 (for Millennium Gate Atlanta), Best Luxury Home Daily Mail UK Property Award 2008, Best Luxury Home Herald Property Award 2009 and Highly Commended 2011, Best Luxury Home UK Property Award 2011 (all for new Arts & Crafts house Avenel Scotland); *Publications* Lutyens in Italy: the Building of the British School at Rome (1992); contrib: Annali Accademici Canadesi Vol VIII (1992), The Golden City: Essays on the Architecture and Imagination of Beresford Pite (1993), The Classicist Vol II (1995), Ancient Rome: the Archaeology of the Eternal City (2000), The British School at Rome: One Hundred Years (2001), The Classicist: A Decade of Art and Architecture (2002), New Classicism (2004), New Palladians: Modernity and Sustainability for 21st Century Architecture (2010), 21st Century Houses – 150 of the

World's Best Homes (2010), Robert Adam: The Search for a Modern Classicism (2010), The Art of Classical Details: Theory, Design and Craftsmanship (2013); *Recreations* fly fishing, shooting, English watercolours and prints, architectural history, gardens, photography, Italy, my family; *Clubs* Black's; *Style—* Hugh Petter, Esq; ✉ ADAM Architecture, Old Hyde House, 75 Hyde Street, Winchester, Hampshire SO23 7DW (e-mail hugh.petter@adamarchitecture.com)

PETTIFER, Brian Warren Bowers; s of Fred Tyler Pettifer (d 1965), of Grimsby, Lincs, and Chrystine, *née* Thompson (d 2010); *b* 10 October 1935; *Educ* Oundle, Univ of Hull (BA), Open Univ (BSc); *m* 2 Oct 1965, Veronica Mary, da of Dr Georg Tugendhat (d 1973), of Essex; 3 s (Crispin b 1967, Adam b 1969, Daniel b 1970), 1 da (Teresa b 1974); *Career* served HAC 1963–66; admitted slr 1963; in own practice 1966–92, ptnr Rollit Farrell & Bladon 1992–98; underwriter Lloyd's 1977–98; pt/t lectr Univ of Hull 1994–; pres Cleethorpes Cons Assoc 1998–2001; cncllr: Lindsey CC 1970–74, Humberside CC 1974–77; chief whip Cons Pty and shadow chm for planning 1974–77; chm: Humberside Youth Assoc 1974–75, Barton-on-Humber Youth Centre Mgmnt Ctee 1974–88, Humberside European Conservative Cncl 1983–86; capt Law Soc Golf Club 1985–86, hon steward Wimbledon Tennis tournament 1989–; Liveryman Worshipful Co of Makers of Playing Cards 1991; NP, FCIArb, FHEA 2001; *Recreations* skiing, golf, tennis; *Clubs* Oriental, Ski Club of GB; *Style—* Brian Pettifer, Esq; ✉ Cob Hall, Priestgate, Barton-on-Humber, North Lincolnshire DN18 5ET (☎ 01652 632248)

PETTIGREW, James (Jim); *Educ* Univ of Aberdeen (LLB), Univ of Glasgow (Dip); *Career* CA; formerly gp treas Sedgewick Gp plc, chief fin offr ICAP plc 1999–2006, chief operating offr Ashmore Gp plc 2006–07, ceo CMC Markets plc 2007–09; non-exec dir: Edinburgh Investment Tst plc, Pacific Investments; MCT; *Style—* Jim Pettigrew, Esq

PETTIT, Rosemary; da of late G H N Pettit, and Ruby, *née* Garner; *b* 22 May 1944; *Educ* Bury St Edmunds GS, Bedford Coll London (BSc), Inst of Educn Univ of London (PGCE); *Career* primary sch teacher 1966–68, copy ed Penguin Books 1971–73, researcher LWT 1973–74, section ed Marshall Cavendish 1974–75, jt ed Traditional Acupuncture Jl 1982–90, jt ed Clarion (jl of Gladstone Club) 1982–86, prop Blenheim Books 1992–; sec: Ind Publishers' Guild 1979–89, Book Packagers' Assoc 1985–98, Directory & Database Publishers Assoc (DPA) 1989–2005; dir Paddington Industrial Association Ltd 1984–86, memb Mgmnt Ctee Paddington Law Centre 1984–86, traditional crafts organiser Art in Action 1984–89, dir Publishing Nat Trg Orgn 1990–2003; judge DPA Awards 1993–2004, dir Digital Content Forum 1999–2005; journalist travel, gardening and obituaries 2000–; memb: Publishing Assessment Section Nat Cncl for Vol Qualifications 1989, Books-across-the-Sea Ctee ESU 1989–2005, Cncl Advtg Standards Bd of Fin 1991–2005, Bd Liberal Democrat News 1993–96, PPA Parly and Legal Consultative Gp 1994–2005, Business Information Forum 1997–2005; memb Liberal Party 1979, Westminster N Lib Democrat Assoc (sec, membership sec, vice-chm, chm) 1979–90; Social and Liberal Democrat candidate for By Election 1989 (Cncl elections 1982), chm Kensington Liberal Democrat Assoc 1993–95; membership sec Brackenbury Residents Assoc 2000–12, memb Ctee Hammersmith Soc 2010– (chm 2012–15, membership sec 2015–), memb Fulham Palace Community Forum 2012–15, chm Hammersmith and Fulham Cmmn on Air Quality 2015–, memb Hammersmith Residents Working Pty 2015–; *Books* The Craft Business (1975), Occupation Self Employed (2 edn, 1981), Five Go To Parliament (1992); *Style—* Ms Rosemary Pettit; ✉ 45 Bradmore Road, London W6 0DT (☎ 020 8846 9707, e-mail rosemary@rosemarypettit.plus.com)

PETTITT, Adam Sven; s of Robin Garth Pettitt (d 1992), and Elizabeth Margaret, *née* Jenkins (d 1970); *b* 5 February 1966, Wimbledon; *Educ* Halisham Sch, Eastbourne Sixth Form Coll, New Coll Oxford (MA); *m* 2 August 1997, Barbara, *née* Sauron; 2 s (Louis b 20 Dec 2001, Felix b 18 April 2007), 1 da (Emilie b 5 May 2003); *Career* asst master Eton Coll 1988–92, head of German Oundle Sch Cambs 1992–94, head of modern languages Abingdon Sch Oxon 1994–98, second master Norwich Sch 1998–2006, headmaster Highgate Sch 2006–; govr: Brighton Coll, The Hall Sch Hampstead, London Acad of Excellence; memb HMC 2006; *Recreations* reading, cross-country running, old buildings; *Clubs* Athenaeum; *Style—* Adam Pettitt, Esq; ✉ Highgate School, North Road, London N6 4AY (☎ 020 8347 3576, e-mail hmoffice@highgateschool.org.uk)

PETTMAN, Prof Barrie Owen; Baron of Bombie (1999); s of Matthew Mark Pettman (d 1967), and Ivy, *née* Warcup (d 2001); *b* 22 February 1944; *Educ* Hull GS, Hull Tech Coll (BSc), City Univ Business Sch (MSc, MBA, PhD), International Mgmnt Centres (DLitt, DBA); *m* 1, 1970 (m dis 1986), Heather Richardson; m 2, 1987, Norma (d 1991); m 3, 1992, Maureen, da of George Crowther (d 1944); *Career* lectr Dept of Social Admin Univ of Hull 1970–82, dir Manpower Unit Univ of Rhodesia 1978–79, registrar Int Mgmnt Centres 1983–; dir: MCB Univ Press 1970–2004, Int Inst of Social Econ 1972–; ed: International Journal of Social Economics 1973–79, International Journal of Manpower 1980–84, Management Research News 1981–2005, Equal Opportunities International 1981–2005 (asst ed 1982–), International Journal of Manpower 1980–84, International Journal of Sociology & Social Policy 1984–2005, International Journal of New Ideas 1992–98; jt ed Managerial Law 1975–2005; asst ed: Employee Relations 1978–82, Archives of Economic History 1983–; visiting prof Canadian Sch of Mgmnt 1983–2003, Home Sec's rep Humberside Police Authy 1994–2000; hon vice-pres Br Soc of Commerce 1975–; chm: Inst of Sci Business 1972–79, Inst of Trg and Devpt Humberside Branch 1990–2000; pres Burke's Peerage & Gentry (UK) Ltd 2003–; memb: Manpower Soc 1977–91, Int Inst of Social Econs; FCI, FRGS, FRSA, FIMfgE, FIMS, FCIPD, FCMI; *Books* Training and Retraining (1973), Labour Turnover and Retention (1975), Equal Pay (1975), Manpower Planning Workbook (1976, 1984), Industrial Democracy (1984), Discrimination in the Labour Market (1980), Management: A Selected Bibliography (1983), The New World Order (1996), Social Economies in Transition (1996), Self Development (1997), The Internationalisation of Franchising (1998), The Ultimate Wealth Book (1998), What Self-Made Millionniares Really Think, Know and Do (2002); *Recreations* golf, shooting; *Clubs* The Reform, Royal Over-Seas League; *Style—* Prof Barrie Pettman, Baron of Bombie; ✉ Enholmes Hall, Patrington, Hull HU12 0PR (☎ 01964 630033, fax 01964 631716, e-mail bopmpettman@btinternet.com)

PETTS, Prof Geoffrey E; s of late Horace Charles Petts, and Eva Maud Petts; *b* 28 March 1953, Folkestone, Kent; *Educ* Ashford GS (now Norton Knatchbull Sch) Kent, Univ of Liverpool (BSc), Univ of Southampton (PhD); *m* 1977, Judith, *née* Armitt; *Career* Univ of Loughborough: lectr in geography 1979–86, sr lectr in geography 1986–89, prof of physical geography 1989–94, head Dept of Geography 1991–94; Univ of Birmingham: prof of physical geography 1994–, dir of environmental sci and mgmnt 1994–97, dir Centre for Enviromental Res and Trg 1997–2007, head Sch of Geography and Environmental Sci 1998–2001, pro-vice-chllr 2001–07; vice-chllr and pres Univ of Westminster 2007–; hon prof Beijing Normal Univ 2011; dir Int Water Res Assoc 1992–94; UNESCO: memb Scientific Advsy Panel Man and Biosphere Prog 1989–97, memb Scientific Advsy Ctee IHP Eco-Hydrology Prog 1998–2000; memb: Scientific Advsy Bd US Dept of the Interior, Fish and Wildlife Serv 1989–99, Scientific Ctee on Water Res Int Cncl for Sci (ICSU) 1996–2003; life memb Freshwater Biological Assoc, pres Int Soc for River Science 2011–13, pres Br Hydrological Soc 2015–17; chair Podium (UK HE and FE for London 2012), chair London Higher 2014–18; Busk Medal of the Royal Geographical Soc 2007, Lifetime Achievement Award Int Soc for River Science 2009; FRSA, FRGS; *Books* Rivers (1983), Impounded Rivers: Perspectives for Ecological Management (1984), Rivers and Landscape (jtly, 1985), Regulated Rivers in the UK (jt ed, 1988), Alternatives in River Regulation (jt ed, 1989), Water, Engineering and Landscape (jt ed, 1990), Lowland Floodplain Rivers: Geomorphological Perspectives (jt ed, 1992), River Conservation and Management (jt ed, 1992), Rivers Handbook Vol 1 (jt ed, 1992) and Vol 2 (jt ed, 1994), Hydrosystemes Fluviaux (jt ed, 1993), Changing River Channels (jt ed, 1995), Man's Influence on Freshwater Ecosystems and Water Use (ed, 1995), Fluvial Hydrosystems (jt ed, 1996), River Restoration (jt ed, 1996), River Flows and Channel Forms (jt ed, 1996), River Biota (jt ed, 1996), Global Perspectives on River Conservation (jt ed, 2000), Urban Rivers: Our Inheritance and Future (jtly, 2002), Braided Rivers (jt ed, 2006); *Recreations* The Artic, antiquarian books on all aspects of water, rivers and artic exploration, watercolour painting, golf, hockey, cricket, fishing; *Clubs* East India, Tenterden Cricket (life vice pres, pres 2012–), The Forty; *Style—* Prof Geoffrey Petts; ✉ The University of Westminster, 309 Regent Street, London W1B 2HW (☎ 020 7911 5115, e-mail g.petts@westminster.ac.uk)

PETTS, Prof Judith Irene; CBE (2012); *née* Armitt; *b* 7 January 1954, Ramsgate, Kent; *Educ* Northern Grammar Girls' Sch Portsmouth, Univ of Exeter; *m* 1977, Geoffrey Petts; *Career* pro-vice-chllr research and knowledge transfer Univ of Birmingham 2007–10, dean Faculty of Social and Human Sciences Univ of Southampton 2010–13, pro-vice-chllr research and enterprise Univ of Southampton 2014–16, vice-chllr Univ of Plymouth 2016–; memb: Cncl NERC 2000–06, NERC Innovation Advsy Panel, Advsy Bd Veolia Environmental plc 2000–14, Royal Cmmn on Environmental Pollution 2005–11, Science Advsy Cncl Defra 2011–16, Sciencewise Expert Resource Centre Steering Gp, Cncl BBSRC 2014–; FASS, FRGS, FRSA; *Recreations* Arctic travel; *Style—* Prof Judith Petts, CBE; ✉ Office of the Vice-Chancellor, University of Plymouth, 18 Portland Villas, Drake's Circus, Plymouth PL4 8AA

PEYTON, Kathleen Wendy; MBE (2014); da of William Joseph Herald, and Ivy Kathleen, *née* Weston; *b* 2 August 1929; *Educ* Wimbledon HS, Manchester Sch of Art (ATD); *m* Sept 1950, Michael Peyton; 2 da (Hilary b 1956, Veronica b 1958); *Career* author; art teacher Northampton HS 1953–55; memb Soc of Authors; *Publications* incl: as Kathleen Herald: Sabre the Horse from the Sea (1947), The Mandrake (1949), Crab the Roan (1953); as K M Peyton: Flambards (1967, Guardian award, televised 1977), The Edge of the Cloud (1969, Carnegie medal), Flambards in Summer (1969), Pennington's Seventeenth Summer (1970), A Pattern of Roses (1972), Prove Yourself a Hero (1977), A Midsummer Night's Death (1978), Flambards Divided (1981), Dear Fred (1981), Who, Sir? Me, Sir? (1983), The Sound of Distant Cheering (1985), Darkling (1989), No Roses Round the Door (1990), Late to Smile (1992), The Wild Boy and Queen Moon (1993), Snowfall (1994), The Swallow Tale (1996), Swallow Summer (1997), Unquiet Spirits (1997), Firehead (1998), Blind Beauty (1999), Stealaway (2001), Small Gains (2003), Greater Gains (2005), Blue Skies and Gunfire (2006), Minna's Quest (2007), No Turning Back (2008), Far from Home (2009), Paradise House (2012), Wild Lily (2016); *Recreations* walking, gardening, sailing; *Style—* Mrs Kathleen Peyton, MBE; ✉ Rookery Cottage, North Fambridge, Chelmsford, Essex CM3 6LP (☎ 01621 828 545)

PEYTON, Rt Rev Dr Nigel; *see:* Brechin, Bishop of

PEYTON-JONES, Dame Julia; DBE (2016, OBE 2003); da of Jeremy Norman Peyton-Jones (d 1985), and Rhona Gertrude Jean, *née* Wood (d 2005); *b* 18 February 1952; *Educ* Byam Shaw Sch of Drawing and Painting (London Weekend TV/Byam Shaw bursary 1973–75, dip, LCAD Distinct), RCA (MA, John Minton travelling scholar); *m* 1975 (m dis 1985), Prosper Riley-Smith; *Career* painter 1974–87; fndr cataloguer 20 Century Pictures Dept Phillips Auctioneers London 1974–75, lectr in painting and humanities Edinburgh Sch of Art 1978–79, curator Atlantis Gallery 1980–81, exhbn organiser Wapping Artists Open Studios Exhbn 1981–82, exhbn organiser Tolly Cobbold Eastern Arts 4th Nat Exhbn 1982–84, exhbn organiser Raoul Dufy 1877–1953 (Hayward Gallery) 1983–84, exhbns sponsorship offr Arts Cncl and S Bank Bd 1984–87, exhbn organiser Linbury Prize for Stage Design 1986–87, curator Hayward Gallery 1988–91, dir Serpentine Gallery 1991–2016; Arts Cncl: purchaser Arts Cncl Collection 1989–90, Visual Arts Projects Ctee 1991–93, Visual Arts, Photography and Architecture Panel 1994–96, Film and TV Panel 1996–97; tstee: PADT 1987–88, Chisenhale Tst 1987–89, New Contemporaries 1988–90, The Place 2002–03; memb Exec Ctee Linbury Prize for Stage Design 1988–96; judge: Citibank Private Banking Photography Prize 1997, BP Portrait Award Nat Portrait Gallery 1997, 1998 and 1999, Tate Gallery Turner Prize 2000; memb Ct of Govrs London Inst 1998–2002; Hon FRCA 1997, Hon FRIBA 2003; *Recreations* opera, theatre, cinema; *Style—* Dame Julia Peyton-Jones, DBE; ✉ Serpentine Gallery, Kensington Gardens, London W2 3XA (☎ 020 7402 6075, fax 020 7402 4103)

PFEFFER, Dr Jeremy Michael; s of Maurice Leslie Pfeffer, of Manchester, and Hannah, *née* Posen; *b* 23 September 1946; *Educ* Manchester Grammar, UCH London (MB BS, BSc); *m* 5 Sept 1972, Vivian Barbara, da of Dr Eric Norman, of Liverpool; 2 s (James b 1978, Paul b 1979), 1 da (Kate b 1992); *Career* house surgn Professorial Surgical Unit UCH London 1972, house physician Newmarket Gen Hosp 1972–73, sr house offr and registrar chest med Papworth Hosp Cambridge 1973–74, sr house offr psychiatry Fulbourn Hosp Cambridge 1974–75, sr house offr and registrar psychiatry Bethlem Royal and Maudsley Hosp 1975–78, sr registrar psychiatry The London and Bethlem Royal and Maudsley Hosps 1978–80; conslt psychiatrist: The Royal London Hosp 1980–96, Royal Brompton Hosp 1994–; former hon sr lectr London Hosp Med Coll, hon sr lectr Nat Heart and Lung Inst ICSTM 1996–; former examiner RCPsych, variously offr and memb psychiatric ctees at local regnl and nat level; memb RSM, FRCPsych 1988 (MRCPsych 1977), FRCP 1990 (MRCP 1974); *Books* Medicine and Psychiatry: A Practical Approach (ed with Francis Creed, 1982), Psychiatric Differential Diagnosis (with Gillian Waldron, 1987); *Recreations* music, reading, food, football; *Style—* Dr Jeremy M Pfeffer; ✉ Pinero House, 115A Harley Street, London W1G 6AR (☎ 020 7935 3878)

PHAM, Prof Duc-Truong; OBE (2003); *Educ* Univ of Canterbury NZ (BEng, PhD, DEng); *m* Paulette; 1 da (Kim); *Career* lectr Univ of Birmingham 1979–88, prof of computer-controlled manufacture Cardiff Univ 1988–2011, head Sch of Mechanical Engrg Univ of Birmingham 2011–15, Chance prof of engrg Univ of Birmingham 2011–; FREng, FLSW, FSME, CEng, FIET, FIMechE; *Books* Robot Grippers (ed with WB Heginbotham, 1986), Expert Systems in Engineering (ed, 1988), Artificial Intelligence in Design (ed, 1990), Neural Networks for Identification, Prediction and Control (with X Liu, 1995), Intelligent Quality Systems (with E Oztemel, 1996); *Style—* Prof Duc-Truong Pham, OBE; ✉ School of Mechanical Engineering, University of Birmingham, Edgbaston, Birmingham B15 2TT

PHARAOH, Paul Grenville; s of late Morton Grenville Pharaoh, of Salt, Staffs, and late Kathleen Jean, *née* Bishop; *b* 16 April 1947, Chesterfield, Derbys; *Educ* Chesterfield GS, Bishop Vesey's GS, Univ of Manchester (LLB), Liverpool Coll of Commerce; *m* 27 Oct 1969, Lynn Margaret, da of Alan Edward Francis; 1 da (Claire Rachael b 9 Oct 1973), 1 s (Richard Paul b 13 Jan 1976); *Career* admitted slr 1971; ptnr Bettinsons 1973–90, ptnr Shakespeares 1990–96; ptnr Martineau 1996–2010, ret; memb Cncl Birmingham Law Soc 1981–93, memb Cncl Law Soc of England and Wales 1990–2002; hon sec W Midland Assoc of Law Socs 1988–90; memb: Investigations Ctee CIPFA 2003–12, Conduct and Competence Ctee Nursing and Midwifery Cncl 2009–, Investigating Ctee Taxation Disciplinary Bd 2009–, Disciplinary Panel Inst for Learning 2009–12, Cncl Aston Univ 2009–15, Audit Ctee Univ of Cumbria 2010–, Conduct Ctee CIMA 2011–, Fitness to Practise Panel Health Care Professions Cncl 2011–; hon sec Birmingham Settlement 1986–90, chm Advsy Ctee Ind Inquiry into W Midlands Police Serious Crime Squad 1989–91; memb: Ct Univ of Birmingham 1980–90, Cncl Birmingham Medico-Legal Soc 1989–91, Irton PCC 2002–; memb Corp of Lakes Coll W Cumbria 1999–2012; tstee:

Eskdale Mill and Heritage Tst 2007–, Santon Bridge Inst 2008–; memb Law Soc 1971; *Recreations* theatre, reading, hill walking; *Style*— Paul Pharaoh, Esq; ✉ 45 Pilkington Avenue, Sutton Coldfield, West Midlands B72 1LA (☎ 0121 354 4099)

PHARO-TOMLIN, Col John Axel; s of Axel Christian Pharo-Tomlin (d 1965), of Dane Court, St Peter's-in-Thanet, Kent, and Edith Madelaine Quayle, *née* Tomlin (d 1974); *b* 8 April 1934; *Educ* Radley, RMA Sandhurst; *m* 1, 19 Dec 1964, Joanna Marguerite Kate (d 1991), da of Lt-Col John Boileau Pemberton (d 1974), of Axminster, Devon; 1 s (Edward b 1968), 2 da (Sally (Mrs Thomas Gandon) b 1965, Alice (Mrs Stephen Reid) b 1975); m 2, 22 June 2002, Dr Christine Elizabeth Keown, da of Donald Keown, of Eastbourne, E Sussex; *Career* cmmnd 14/20 King's Hussars 1954, Adj 1961, instr RMA Sandhurst 1963, RNSC 1966, Sqdn Ldr 14/20 King's Hussars 1967, GSO 2 Singapore Dist 1968, Second-in-Cmd Duke of Lancaster's Own Yeo 1971, Bde Major 11 Armoured Bde 1972, GSO 1 Operational Requirements MOD 1975, CO 14/20 King's Hussars 1977 (despatches 1979), Col AG 16/17/18 MOD 1980, Col M1 (A) MOD 1984, ret 1986; mangr Banque Paribas London 1986–92; memb Mole Valley DC 1992–99; pres Leigh and District Cottage Garden Soc 1999–2015; Freeman City of London 1987; FIMgt 1984–99; *Books* The Ramnuggur Boys (2002); *Recreations* country pursuits, politics, music; *Clubs* Cavalry and Guards'; *Style*— Col John Pharo-Tomlin; ✉ Peverel, Leigh, Reigate, Surrey RH2 8NX (☎ 01306 611247, e-mail japt75@gmail.com)

PHELPS, Prof Alan David Reginald; s of (Joseph John) Reginald Phelps (d 1984); *b* 2 June 1944; *Educ* King's Coll Cambridge (MA), UC Oxford (DPhil, MA); *m* 1970, Susan Helen, *née* Marshall; 1 da (Katherine Lucy Helen b 1988); *Career* postgrad asst CERN Geneva 1966, postgrad research Univ of Oxford 1966–69, research assoc UKAEA Culham 1969; postdoctoral research fell: Univ of Oxford 1970, Imperial Coll London 1970–72; Nat Acad of Scis research assoc AFCRL USA 1972–73, research offr Univ of Oxford 1973–78; Univ of Strathclyde: lectr in physics 1978–89, sr lectr 1989–92, reader 1993, prof of plasma physics 1993–2011, head Dept of Physics and Applied Physics 1998–2001 (dep head 1993–98 and 2004–08), prof 2011–; memb Physics Coll EPSRC 1995–2009, MIEEE, fell American Physical Soc, CPhys, FInstP (chm Plasma Physics Gp 1995–97), FRSE 1997; *Publications* author of over 350 research papers in jls, conference proceedings and reports 1966–; *Recreations* country pursuits, hill-walking; *Style*— Prof Alan Phelps, FRSE; ✉ Department of Physics, University of Strathclyde, John Anderson Building, Glasgow G4 0NG (☎ 0141 548 3166, fax 0141 552 2891, e-mail a.d.r.phelps@strath.ac.uk)

PHELPS, Annamarie; CBE (2016); da of Vincent Stapleton, and Ethna, *née*Morrissey; *b* 24 May 1966, Kingsbury, Brent; *Educ* Loreto Coll St Albans, St John's Coll Cambridge (MA); *m* 1997, Richard Charles Phelps; 2 s (Thomas, James), 1 da (Cecilia); *Career* former rower; major championships: Silver medal (lightweight coxless four) World Championships 1991, Silver medal (lightweight coxless four) World Championships 1992, Gold medal (lightweight coxless four) World Championships 1993, Bronze medal Commonwealth Regatta (lightweight coxless four) 1994, Silver medal (lightweight coxless four) World Chamionships 1994, 1st place and world's best time Olympic Qualifying Regatta Lucerne W8+ 1996, competed at Olympic Games Atlanta 1996; Br Rowing: lead safeguarding offr, dep chm 2002–13, chm and dir 2013–; vice-chm and tstee Br Paralympic Assoc 2013–, memb Bd BOA 2015–; steward Henley Royal Regatta; memb Safeguarding Adults Steering Gp Sports & Recreation Alliance 2010–; govr (safeguarding lead govr Eudcnl and Pastoral Ctee) Latymer Upper Sch 2015–; The Fine Art Society plc 1994–: exec dir 1996–2002, non-exec dir 2002–; Liveryman Worshipful Co of Goldsmiths, Freeman and Ct Asst Co of Watermen & Lightermen; *Recreations* reading, art, cooking; *Clubs* Thames Rowing (hon vice-pres); *Style*— Mrs Annamarie Phelps, CBE; ✉ British Rowing, 6 Lower Mall, Hammersmith, London W6 9DJ (☎ 020 8237 6703, Twitter @PhelpsAnnamarie)

PHELPS, John Christopher; s of Anthony John Phelps, CB (d 2014), and Sheila Nan, *née* Rait (d 1967); *b* 25 May 1954; *Educ* Whitgift Sch S Croydon, Univ of Liverpool (LLB); *m* 1, 13 April 1985 (m dis 1997), Isabelle Michele Jeanine, da of Maurice Albert Haumesser (d 1987), of Nancy, France; 1 s (Christopher b 1988), 1 da (Jessica b 1991); m 2, 5 April 2002 (m dis 2007), Sarah Katharine, da of Charles Reginald Pressley, of Goring-by-Sea, West Sussex; 1 da (Hannah Lily b 23 Aug 2003); m 3, 25 Oct 2009, Christine, da of John Herbert Simmons, of Eastbourne, E Sussex; *Career* admitted slr 1978; ptnr DAC Beachcroft LLP 1986–2016; Freeman City of Oxford; *Books* VAT for Solicitors (with Julian Gizzi, 1993, 3 edn 2002); *Recreations* football, rugby and cricket spectator, reading; *Clubs* MCC; *Style*— John Phelps, Esq; ✉ e-mail mr.flipflop@me.com

PHELPS, Maurice; s of Harry Thomas Phelps (d 1973), and Lilian Carter; *b* 17 May 1935; *Educ* Wandsworth Sch, CCC Oxford (BA); *m* 1960, Elizabeth Anne Hurley; 2 s, 1 da; *Career* personnel dir Heavy Vehicle Div Leyland Vehicles 1977–80, Bd memb personnel British Shipbuilders 1980–87, Br Ferries Ltd 1987–89, managing ptnr Emslie Phelps Associates and Value Through People Ltd, chm EP-Saratoga (Europe) Ltd; Freeman City of London, Freeman Worshipful Co of Watermen and Lightermen; *Publications* The People Policies Audit (1999), Measuring the People Contribution (2000), Human Resources Benchmarking (2002), A Thameside Family (2007), The Adventures of Mr Golly (2007); *Recreations* surfing, sailing, squash; *Style*— Maurice Phelps, Esq; ✉ Abbotsfield, Goring Heath, Oxfordshire RG8 7SA (☎ 01491 681916); Maurice Phelps Associates (e-mail mail@mauricephelps.com)

PHILIP, Rt Hon Lord; Alexander Morrison Philip; PC (2005); s of Alexander Philip, OBE (d 1979), and Isobel Thomson Morrison; *b* 3 August 1942; *Educ* HS of Glasgow, Univ of St Andrews (MA), Univ of Glasgow (LLB); *m* 9 Oct 1971 (m dis 2013), Shona Mary, da of Kenneth Macrae, of St Andrews; 3 s (Jamie b 24 Oct 1977, Colin b 8 June 1979, Tom b 25 June 1983); *Career* slr 1967–72, admitted Faculty of Advocates 1973, QC (Scot) 1984, advocate depute 1982–85, chm Med Appeal Tbnls 1987–92, chm Scottish Land Court and pres Lands Tbnl for Scotland 1993–96, Senator Coll of Justice in Scotland (Lord of Session) 1996–2007; chm Mull of Kintyre Review 2010–11; contrib Oxford DNB; *Recreations* piping, golf; *Clubs* Royal Scottish Pipers' Soc (Edinburgh) (hon Pipe Major 2011–13), Hon Co of Edinburgh Golfers, Prestwick Golf, New (Edinburgh); *Style*— The Rt Hon Lord Philip; ✉ Parliament House, Edinburgh EH1 1RQ (☎ 0131 225 2595)

PHILIP, Prof George David Edge; s of David Philip (d 1957), and Elsie, *née* Edge (d 1995); *b* 29 October 1951, London; *Educ* Christ's Hosp, Oriel Coll Oxford (BA), Nuffield Coll Oxford (DPhil); *m* 14 Aug 1974, Carol, *née* Egan; *Career* research fell Inst of Latin American Studies London 1975–76, LSE: lectr in Latin American politics 1976–86, reader in comparative and Latin American politics 1986–2001, prof of comparative and Latin American politics 2001–, head Dept of Govt 2004–07, vice-chair Appointments Ctee 2007–10; chm Third World Politics Gp European Consortium for Political Research 1999–2003; editorial advsr Political Economy in Latin America series 2000–02; The Rise and Fall of the Peruvian Miltary Radicals 1968–76 (1978), Oil and Politics in Latin America: Nationalist Movements and State Companies (1982), The Military in South American Politics (1985), Politics in Mexico (ed, 1985), Political Dilemmas of Military Regimes (co-ed, 1986), The Mexican Economy (ed, 1988), The Presidency in Mexican Politics (1992), The Political Economy of International Oil (1994), Democracy in Latin America: Surviving conflict and crisis? (2003), The Triumph of Politics: the return of the Left in Venezuela, Bolivia and Ecuador (jtly, 2011); author of jl articles and chapters; *Recreations* following political events and occasionally writing about them; *Clubs* Oxford and Cambridge; *Style*— Prof George Philip; ✉ London School of Economics, Houghton Street, London WC2A 2AE (☎ 020 7955 7191, e-mail g.philip@lse.ac.uk)

PHILIPPS, Hon Roland Alexander; s of 3 Baron Milford (d 1999), of Llanstephan, Powys, and Viscountess Norwich, *née* Mary Makins, of London; *b* 20 September 1962; *Educ* Eton, Trinity Coll Cambridge (MA); *m* 1991, Felicity Kate Rubinstein, *qv*, da of Hilary Rubinstein, *qv*; 1 s (Nathaniel Alexander b 19 Dec 1996); *Career* publishing dir: Macmillan London 1989–94, Hodder and Stoughton 1994–2002; md John Murray (Publishers) 2002–, dir Hodder Headline Ltd 2003–04; *Recreations* reading, food, conversation; *Style*— The Hon Roland Philipps; ✉ 231 Westbourne Park Road, London W11 1EB

PHILIPSBORN, Chris; s of John David Philipsborn (d 2011), and Edwige, *née* Auffret; *b* 29 March 1965, Washington DC; *Educ* Marlborough, LSE (BA); *m* (m dis); 3 s (Jack David b 3 Oct 1995, Sam Edwin b 28 Dec 1997, Benjamin Brazil b 28 June 1999); *Career* research asst Sir Fergus Montgomery MP 1985–88, London ed North-West Evening Mail 1989–91, La Paz corr BBC, FT and Economist 1992–94, campaigns offr Help the Aged 1994–95, head Parly Unit The Law Soc of England and Wales 1995–98, sr UK public affrs advsr BT 1998–2000, head European Corporate Affrs BT 2000–05, dir for Europe Salzburg Global Seminar 2006–07, dir of communications and public affrs Sellafield Ltd 2007–09, dir of communications and mktg Age Ltd 2010–13, ptnr Kreab Worldwide 2013–; memb European Business Govt Relations Cncl 2000–; non-exec dir Nuclear Industries Assoc 2008–09; *Publications* Fodor's South America (co-author, 1994–98); numerous articles in the FT, Economist and New Statesman 1992–94; *Recreations* music, sailing, skiing, travel, walking; *Clubs* Buck's, Travellers, Hurlingham; *Style*— Chris Philipsborn, Esq; ✉ Kreab Worldwide, Sixth Floor, 90 Long Acre, London WC2E 9RA (☎ 020 7074 1800, e-mail cphilipsborn@kreab.com, website www.kreab.com, Twitter @ChristopherR)

PHILLIMORE, 5 Baron (UK 1918); Sir Francis Stephen Phillimore; 6 Bt (UK 1881); o s of 4 Baron Phillimore (d 1994), and Anne Elizabeth, *née* Smith Dorrien Smith (d 1995); *b* 25 November 1944, Isles of Scilly; *Educ* Eton, Trinity Coll Cambridge; *m* 1971, Nathalie, da of late Michel Antony Pequin, of Paris, France; 1 da (Hon Arabella Maroussia b 22 Feb 1975), 2 s (Hon Tristan Anthony Stephen b 18 Aug 1977, Hon Julian Michel Claud b 3 Nov 1981); *Heir* s, Hon Tristan Phillimore; *Career* called to the Bar Middle Temple 1972; ret 2002; steward Hurlingham Polo Assoc, pres Binfield Heath Polo Club; vice-pres: Henley Soc, Henley and Dist Agricultural Assoc; Liveryman Worshipful Co of Fishmongers (memb Ct of Assts); Commendatore del'Ordine della Stella della Solidarieta Italiana; *Recreations* travel, the arts, polo, real tennis, sailing, shooting, Venetian rowing; *Clubs* Royal Yacht Sqdn, Brooks's, Pratt's, City Barge; *Style*— The Rt Hon the Lord Phillimore; ✉ 23 Phillimore Gardens, London W8 7QG

PHILLIPS, Adrian Alexander Christian; CBE (1998); s of Eric Lawrance Phillips, CMG (d 2010), and Phyllis Mary, *née* Bray (d 1991); *b* 11 January 1940; *Educ* The Hall Sch, Westminster, ChCh Oxford (MA), UCL (DipTP); *m* 16 Feb 1963, Cassandra Frances Elais, da of late David Francis Hubback, CB, of London; 2 s (Oliver b 1965, Barnaby b 1968); *Career* Planning Serv Miny of Housing 1962–68, sr res offr then asst dir Countryside Cmmn 1968–74, asst to Exec Dir then head of Programme Co-ordination Unit UN Environment Programme Nairobi 1974–78, programme dir Int Union for Conservation of Nature & Natural Resources Switzerland 1978–81, dir gen Countryside Cmmn 1981–92, prof of countryside and environmental planning Univ of Wales Cardiff 1992–2001; chm: World Cmmn on Protected Areas 1994–2000, Wales Ctee RSPB 1992–98, Policy Ctee CPRE 2001–06, Glos Environmental Tst 2001–09, Glos Native Partnership 2015–; advsr Heritage Lottery Fund 1995–; tstee: WWF/UK 1997–2003, Woodland Tst 2004–08, National Tst 2005–12; numerous articles on landscape, environment, protected areas and countryside; hon fell Landscape Inst; MRTPI 1966, FRGS 1983; *Recreations* walking, stroking the cat; *Style*— Adrian Phillips, Esq, CBE; ✉ e-mail adrian.phillips@gmx.com

PHILLIPS, Alice; *née* Alban; da of David Alban, of Sedbergh, Cumbria, and Lesley Alban; *b* 1 August 1960; *Educ* Kendal HS for Girls, Newnham Coll Cambridge (MA); *m* 9 Aug 1986, Simon Phillips; 1 da (Joanna Ruth b 22 April 1999); *Career* teacher of English rising to head of English Royal Masonic Sch Rickmansworth 1983–93, dep head Tormead Sch Guildford 1993–99, head St Catherine's Sch Bramley 2000–; memb GSA 2000– (pres 2014), memb Bd Independent Schs Cncl 2016– (vice-chm 2016); govr Yehudi Menuhin Sch; memb Guildford Chamber Choir; MInstD; *Recreations* choral singing, gardening, cookery, drum playing; *Clubs* Univ Women's, Landsdowne; *Style*— Mrs Alice Phillips; ✉ St Catherine's School, Station Road, Bramley, Guildford, Surrey GU5 0DF (☎ 01483 899605, e-mail headmistress@stcatherines.info)

PHILLIPS, Ben; *b* 10 October 1992, Bridgend, Wales; *Career* social influencer (8 million Facebook followers, 1.1 million Instagram followers, 1.1 million YouTube subscribers); *Style*— Ben Phillips, Esq; ✉ Twitter @BenPhillipsUK

PHILLIPS, (William) Bernard; s of Stanley George Phillips (d 1968), of Sutton Coldfield, and Enid Effie, *née* Eades (d 1998); *b* 26 April 1944; *Educ* Bishop Vesey GS Sutton Coldfield, Hertford Coll Oxford (MA); *m* 1, 13 May 1967 (m dis 1986), Christine Elizabeth, da of Arthur Charles Wilkinson, of Maidstone; 3 s (Andrew b 1968, Simon b 1972, William b 1974); m 2, 1 Aug 1987 (m dis 2013), Deborah Grace, da of Ellis Green (d 1975); *Career* schoolmaster 1966–67, lectr 1967–70; called to the Bar Inner Temple 1970, in practice NE Circuit 1970–2014, recorder 1989– (asst recorder 1984–89); legal assessor: GMC 2002–, General Pharmaceutical Cncl 2006–; memb Inner Temple 1964; *Recreations* cookery, gardening, collecting books; *Style*— Bernard Phillips, Esq

PHILLIPS, Caryl; *b* 13 March 1958; *Educ* The Queen's Coll Oxford (BA); *Career* author and stage/screen writer; author of articles in various jls; writing instructor Arvon Fndn 1983–; writer in residence: The Factory Arts Centre 1980–82, Literary Criterion Centre Univ of Mysore 1987, Univ of Stockholm 1989, Amherst Coll MA 1992–98 (also co-dir Creative Writing Center, visiting writer 1990–92, prof of English 1994–98, Hon AM 1995), Nat Inst of Educn Singapore 1994; Barnard Coll Columbia Univ NY: prof of English and Henry R Luce prof of migration and social order 1998–2005, dir Barnard Forum on Migration 1998–2005, dir of initiatives in the humanities 2003–05; prof of English Yale Univ, visiting prof of English Dartmouth Coll 2008; visiting lectr: Univ of Ghana 1990, Univ of Poznan 1991; visiting prof of English NYU 1993, visiting prof in Humanities Univ of West Indies 1999; visiting writer Humber Coll Toronto 1992 and 1993; conslt ed Faber Inc 1992–94, contrib ed Bomb Magazine 1993, series ed Faber & Faber 1996–2000, co-prodr The Final Passage (Channel 4) 1996; memb: Drama Panel Arts Cncl 1982–85, Prodn Bd BFI 1985–88, Bd Bush Theatre 1985–89, Bd The Caribbean Writer 1989; hon sr memb Univ of Kent 1988, Hon DUniv Leeds Metropolitan 1997, Hon DLitt Univ of the W Indies 2010; Br Cncl Fiftieth Anniversary fell 1984, Guggenheim Fndn fell 1992, hon fell Queen's Coll Oxford 2006; FRSL 2000; *Awards* Arts Cncl Bursary in Drama 1984, BBC Giles Cooper Award (for The Wasted Years) 1984, Malcolm X Prize for Literature (for The Final Passage) 1985, Martin Luther King Meml Prize (for The European Tribe) 1987, Sunday Times Young Writer of the Year (for Cambridge) 1992, Rockefeller Fndn Bellagio Residency 1994, James Tait Black Meml Prize (for Crossing the River) 1994, Lannan Literary Award 1994, Nat Book Critics Circle finalist in fiction (for A Distant Shore) 2004, Cwlth Writers Prize Best Book (for A Distant Shore) 2004; *Television and Radio Dramas* Lost in Music (BBC) 1984, The Hope and the Glory (BBC) 1984, The Record (Channel 4) 1985, The Wasted Years (radio play) 1985, The Prince of Africa (radio play) 1987, Crossing the River (Radio 3) 1987, Writing Fiction (Radio 4) 1991, The Final Passage (Channel 4) 1996, A Kind of Home: James Baldwin in Paris (Radio 4) 2004, Hotel Cristobel (Radio 3) 2005, A Long Way From Home (Radio 3) 2008;

Television and Radio Documentaries Welcome to Birmingham USA (Central) 1983, Black on Black (LWT) 1983, St Kitts Independence (Radio 4) 1983, Bookmark (BBC) 1984, Sport and the Black Community (Radio 4) 1984, No Complaints – James Baldwin at 60 (Radio 4) 1985, Darker Than Blue: Curtis Mayfield (BBC) 1995, The Spirit of America (Radio 4) 1995, These Islands Now: Transformations in British Culture (Radio 3) 1995, Extravagant Strangers (Radio 3) 1997, Fifty Years of West Indian Migration (Radio 4) 1998, Martin Luther King: 'I Have a Dream' Speech (Radio 4) 2003, I Too Am America: Slavery in New York City (Radio 4) 2004; *Film* Playing Away 1987, The Mystic Masseur 2001; *Fiction* The Final Passage (1985), A State of Independence (1986), Higher Ground (1989), Cambridge (1991), Crossing the River (1993), The Nature of Blood (1997), A Distant Shore (2003), Dancing in the Dark (2005), In the Falling Snow (2009); *Non-Fiction* The European Tribe (1987), Extravagant Strangers: A Literature of Belonging (ed, 1997), The Right Set: An Anthology of Tennis Writing (ed, 1999), The Atlantic Sound (2000), A New World Order (2001), Foreigners (2007), Colour Me English (2011); *Plays* Strange Fruit (1980), Where There is Darkness (1982), The Shelter (1983), Rough Crossings (2007); *Recreations* running, golf; *Style—* Caryl Phillips, Esq; ✉ c/o Georgia Garrett, A P Watt, 20 John Street, London WC1N 2DR (☎ 020 7282 3106, fax 020 7282 3142)

PHILLIPS, Dr Celia Mary; er da of Percival Edmund Phillips (d 1989), and Marjorie, *née* Hughes (d 2004); *b* 16 December 1942, Longton, Staffs; *Educ* Dunfermline HS, Windsor Sch Hamm, High Wycombe HS, LSE (BSc, PhD); *m* 23 June 1973, Rev Preb Ronald Frederick Swan, *qv*, o s of Frederick William Swan (d 1975), of Southampton; 1 da (Elly b Dec 1974), 1 s (Toby b May 1978); *Career* LSE: lectr 1967–99, dean of undergraduate studies 1986–89, sr tutor Interdisciplinary Inst of Mgmnt 1994–99, sr fell in social statistics 1999–, assoc dean (gen course) 2004–; memb Educn Ctee ILEA 1975–78, tstee St Catherine's Cumberland Lodge Windsor 1987–2007; govr: Sir John Cass's Fndn and Red Coat C of E Secdy Sch 1997– (chm of govrs 2000–05), London Met Univ 2002–06, Brockenhurst Coll 2008–; bishops' selector 2003–; hon citizen Tralee 1991; FRSS; memb Order of St Lazarus; *Books* Changes in Subject Choice at School and University (1969), Statistical Sources in Civil Aviation (1979), The Risks in Going to Work (with J Stockdale, 1989), Violence at Work (with J Stockdale, 1991), The Management of a Local and an International Shopping Centre (in Cases in Marketing, ed Hanne Hartvig Larsen, 1997), Understanding Marketing: A European Casebook (ed jtly, 2000); *Recreations* choral singing (Chelsea Opera Group and others), boating, walking, reading; *Clubs* Lymington Town Sailing, Royal Lymington Yacht, Royal Over-seas League; *Style—* Dr Celia Phillips; ✉ Statistics Department, London School of Economics and Political Science, Houghton Street, London WC2A 2AE (☎ 020 7955 7644, fax 020 7790 2518, e-mail c.phillips@lse.ac.uk)

PHILLIPS, Prof David; CBE (2012, OBE 1999); s of Stanley Phillips (d 1979), of South Shields, Tyne & Wear, and Daphne Ivy, *née* Harris (d 2004); *b* 3 December 1939; *Educ* South Shields Grammar Tech Sch, Univ of Birmingham (BSc, PhD); *m* 21 Dec 1970, (Lucy) Caroline, da of Clifford John Scoble, of Plymouth, Devon; 1 da (Sarah Elizabeth b 1975); *Career* Fulbright fell Univ of Texas Austin USA 1964–66, exchange fell Royal Soc/Acad of Sciences USSR 1966–67; Univ of Southampton: lectr 1967–73, sr lectr 1973–76, reader 1976–80; The Royal Inst of GB: Wolfson prof of natural philosophy 1980–89, dep dir 1986–89; Imperial Coll London: prof of physical chemistry 1989–2006, head of dept 1992–2002, Hofmann prof of chemistry 1999–2006, dean Faculties of Life Sciences and Physical Sciences 2002–05, sr dean 2005–06, professor emeritus 2006–, fell 2008; res scientist in applications of lasers in chemistry biology and med, author of 602 scientific papers reviews and books in this field, various appearances on BBC TV and Radio incl Royal Inst Christmas Lectures for Young People with JM Thomas 1987; chair UK Chemical Stakeholder Forum DEFRA 2013–; vice-pres and gen sec Br Assoc for the Advancement of Science 1988–89; RSC Nyholm lectr 1994, Michael Faraday Award Royal Soc 1997, Porter Medal 2010; Hon DSc: Univ of Birmingham 2011, Univ of Southampton 2012, Univ of Durham 2013, Univ of Leicester 2014, Univ of Westminster 2014; Hon LLD Univ of Bath 2013; FRSC 1976 (pres 2010–12), FCGI 2005, FRS 2015; *Books* Time-correlated Single-photon Counting (with D V O'Connor), Time-resolved Vibrational Spectroscopy (with G H Atkinson), Jet-Spectroscopy and Molecular Dynamics (with J M Hollas), Life and Scientific Legacy of George Porter (with J Barber); *Recreations* music, theatre, popularisation of science, tennis; *Clubs* Athenaeum; *Style—* Prof David Phillips, CBE, FRS; ✉ 195 Barnett Wood Lane, Ashtead, Surrey KT21 2LP (☎ 01372 274385); Department of Chemistry, Imperial College London, Exhibition Road, London SW7 2AZ (☎ 020 7594 5716, e-mail d.phillips@imperial.ac.uk)

PHILLIPS, Sir (John) David; kt (2000), QPM (1994); s of late Percy Phillips, and Alfreda, *née* Crane; *b* 1944; *Educ* Univ of Manchester (BA); *m* Nancy Wynn, da of late Eric Rothwell; 1 s (John M b 1977); *Career* Asst Chief Constable Gtr Manchester Police 1983–88, Dep Chief Constable Devon and Cornwall Constabulary 1988–93, Chief Constable Kent Constabulary 1993–2003, dir Nat Centre for Policing Excellence 2003–; pres ACPO 2002–03; hon fell Christchurch Coll Canterbury; Hon LLD Univ of Coventry 2010; CCMI; *Recreations* golf, cricket, walking, reading; *Style—* Sir David Phillips, QPM

PHILLIPS, David Anthony; OBE (1994); s of Garfield Phillips (d 1981), and Elvira, *née* Roberts (d 1981); *b* 27 April 1943; *Educ* Cardiff HS, Univ of Bristol Dental Sch (BDS, Paediatric Dentistry prize, Prosthetics prize, American Soc of Paedodontics award); *m* 1968, Anne, *née* Llewellyn Evans; 1 da (Rachel b 1971); *Career* house offr (oral surgery) Bristol Royal Infirmary 1965–66, dental practitioner 1966–81; Med Protection Soc: dental sec 1981–85, dep sec Dental Div 1985–89, sec Bd of Dental Protection 1989–98, dental dir Dental Protection 1989–98; int conslt Dental Protection Ltd 1998–99; non-exec dir Herts NHS Tst 1994–95, chm Wellhouse NHS Tst 1995–99; chm: DenCare Ltd 1999–2003 (non-exec dir 1997–99), Denplan Ltd 2000– (memb Advsy Bd 1988–), Two-Ten Health Ltd 2000–, Oasis Dental Care Ltd 2003–; dir W E H Oakley Ltd 1996–2003; non-exec dir Oasis Healthcare plc 2004–; specialist advsr House of Commons Select Ctee on Health 1992–94; pres Metropolitan Branch BDA 1991–92; lay memb General Osteopathic Cncl 1997–2003 (chm Professional Conduct Ctee 1998–2003, treas 2001–03); memb Advsy Bd Nat Soc of Dental Practitioners USA 1988–, supporting memb FDI, fndr memb Cwlth Dental Assoc; dir George Warman Pubns 1991–; chm: CandoCo Dance Co 2000–, Cordent Tst 2002– (memb Bd 1989–); memb Bd and tstee Different Strokes Charity 2000–; elected memb GDC 2002; FRSM, fell Int Coll of Dentists, FDSRCS 2001; *Recreations* golf, gardening, oil painting, sculpture; *Clubs* East India; *Style—* David Phillips, Esq, OBE; ✉ Eaglewood, Sheethanger Lane, Felden, Hertfordshire HD3 0BG (☎ 01442 252348, fax 01442 404197, mobile 07980 037272, e-mail david.aphillips@mac.com)

PHILLIPS, Prof David George; s of George Phillips, and Doris Phillips; *b* 15 December 1944, London; *Educ* Sir Walter St John's Sch London, St Edmund Hall Oxford (DipEd, MA, DPhil); *m* 6 April 1968, Valerie Mary, *née* Bache; 2 da (Rebecca Jane b 19 May 1970, Janet Catherine b 13 May 1972); *Career* teacher: Huntingdon GS 1967–69, Chipping Norton Sch 1969–75; Univ of Oxford: tutor then lectr in educnl studies 1975–96, reader in comparative educn 1996–2000, prof of comparative educn 2000–12 (emeritus prof 2012–); fell St Edmund Hall Oxford 1984–2012 (emeritus fell 2012–), emeritus research fell Leverhulme Tst 2012–14; ed: Oxford Review of Educn 1984–2003, Research in Comparative and Int Educn 2006–16; series ed Oxford Studies in Comparative Educn 1992–, chm Editorial Bd Comparative Educn 2009–15 (ed 2015–); memb: Teacher Educn Cmmn Wissenschaftsrat 1990–91, Cncl German Inst for Int Educnl Research 1992–94 (memb Scientific Ctee 1992–98), Educnl Science Cmmn Miny of Science, Research and the Arts Germany 2003–04; chm Br Assoc for Int and Comparative Educn 1998–2000; FRSA 1987, FAcSS 2002, FRHistS 2002; incl: Zur Universitätsreform in der Britischen Besatzungszone 1945–1948 (1983), The Second Foreign Language: Past Development, Current Trends and Future Prospects (jtly, 1983), Diversification in Modern Language Teaching: Choice and the National Curriculum (jtly, 1993), Pragmatismus und Idealismus: Das 'Blaue Gutachten' und die Britische Hochschulpolitik in Deutschland 1948 (1995), Education in Germany: Tradition and Reform in Historical Context (ed, 1995), Education in Eastern Germany Since Unification (ed, 2000), Implementing European Union Education and Training Policy: A Comparative Study of Issues in Four Member States (jt ed, 2003), Educational Policy Borrowing: Historical Perspectives (jt ed, 2004), Comparative and International Education: An Introduction to Theory, Method and Practice (jtly, 2006), The German Example: English Interest in Educational Provision in Germany Since 1800 (2011), Investigating Education in Germany: Studies From a British Perspective (2015); subject of Cross-national Attraction in Education: Accounts from England and Germany – A Festschrift for David Phillips (2006); author of numerous jl articles; *Recreations* travel, walking, art history, old books; *Style—* Prof David Phillips; ✉ St Edmund Hall, Oxford OX1 4AR; Department of Education, 15 Norham Gardens, Oxford OX2 6PY (☎ 01865 274024, fax 01865 274027)

PHILLIPS, David John; QC (1997); s of Sir Raymond Phillips (d 1982), of Teddington, and Lady Phillips, *née* Evans; *b* 4 May 1953; *Educ* Rugby, Univ of Aix-en-Provence, Balliol Coll Oxford (MA); *m* Ann Nicola, da of Ronald Beckett (d 1971); 1 da (Meredith Rose b 1990), 1 s (Edward Raymond b 1993); *Career* called to the Bar Gray's Inn 1976, Wales & Chester Circuit 1977 (Arden, Atkin, Mould & Reid Prize 1977), recorder of the Crown Court 1998– (asst recorder 1994–98), head of chambers 199 Strand London 2000–06, dep High Court judge 2002–; dir Disability Law Service; legal chm FAPL Tbnl, legal chm Sports Dispute Resolution Panel, judicial chm Nat Greyhound Racing Club Appeal Tbnl; admitted to the Bar of Gibraltar 2004, memb of the Bar of the Eastern Carribean 2005; memb Ctee Barristers' Benevolent Assoc 1993– (jt hon treas 1999–); *Recreations* hill walking, cinema; *Style—* David Phillips, QC; ✉ Wilberforce Chambers, 8 New Square, Lincoln's Inn, London WC2A 3QP (☎ 020 7306 0102, fax 020 7306 0095, e-mail dphillips@wilberforce.co.uk)

PHILLIPS, Graham D; *Educ* Univ of Liverpool (BArch); *Career* architect; Arup Associates 1971–75; Foster & Partners: joined 1975, resident dir Hong Kong 1979–86, md Hong Kong 1985–86, ptnr 1991–, md 1993–; memb HKIA, RIBA; *Projects* incl: offices for IBM at Greenford, HongKong Bank, Sainsbury building Univ of East Anglia, Chek Lap Kok Airport Hong Kong; *Style—* Graham D Phillips, Esq; ✉ Foster & Partners, Riverside 3, 22 Hester Road, London SW11 4AN

PHILLIPS, Dr Helen Mary; s James Phillips, Anne, *née* Duggan; *b* 29 May 1966, Dublin; *Educ* Univ Coll Dublin (BSc, PhD); *m* 2009, Adrian Belton; *Career* Environment Agency: joined 1996, area mangr Thames Region 1998–2001, head of strategic devpt 2001, dir Wales 2002–06; Natural England: chief exec 2006–12, memb Bd, accounting offr; Kelda Gp: dir of customer service and networks Yorkshire Water 2012–14, chm Loop Customer Mgmnt Ltd 2012–14; chm Chesterfield Royal Hosp NHS Fndn Tst 2015–; lead accounting offr Jt Nature Conservation Ctee 2006–11, memb Advsy Bd Sheffield Business Sch 2012–, lay memb Legal Servs Bd 2015–; FSB; *Recreations* opera, skiing, walking; *Clubs* Farmers; *Style—* Dr Helen Phillips; ✉ Chesterfield Royal Hospital, NHS Foundation Trust, Chesterfield Road, Calow, Chesterfield S44 5BL

PHILLIPS, Sir Jonathan; KCB (2009); s of Gilbert Reginald Phillips, of Wednesbury, W Midlands, and Ruby May, *née* Hughes; *b* 21 May 1952; *Educ* Queen Mary's GS Walsall, St John's Coll Cambridge (MA, PhD), Inst of Educn Univ of London (PGCE); *m* 31 Aug 1974, Amanda Rosemary, da of Ivor William Broomhead; 2 s (Ian Benjamin b 25 Oct 1980, Alexander Thomas b 22 May 1982); *Career* DTI: joined 1977, seconded to Economics Directorate CBI 1982–83, seconded as sec to Ctee of Inquiry into Regulatory Arrangements at Lloyd's 1986–87, asst sec DTI 1987–93; under sec and head Exec Agencies Directorate Dept of Transport 1993–96, dir of investigations and enforcement DTI 1996–98, dir of fin and resource mgmnt DTI 1998–2000, DG resources and services DTI 2000–02, seconded as operating strategy dir Sea Systems BAE Systems 2002, political dir NI Office 2002–05, perm sec NI Office 2005–10; warden Keble Coll Oxford 2010–; memb Bd Cooperation Ireland 2010–, tstee Esmee Fairbairn Fndn 2011–, memb Bd Charlie Goldsmith Assocs 2011–, pres Friends of the Oxford Bach Choir 2012–, chair Tstees of Schola Cantorum 2013–; *Clubs* Athenaeum, Oxford and Cambridge; *Style—* Sir Jonathan Phillips, KCB; ✉ Keble College, University of Oxford, Oxford OX1 3PG (☎ 01865 272727, e-mail jonathan.phillips@keble.ox.ac.uk)

PHILLIPS, Leslie Samuel; CBE (2008, OBE 1998); s of Frederick Arthur Phillips (d 1934), and Cecelia Margaret, *née* Newlove (d 1984); *b* 20 April 1924; *Educ* Chingford Sch, Italia Conti; *m* 1 (m dis), Penelope Noel, da of Richard Thorpe Bartley (d 1963); 2 da (Caroline Elizabeth b 30 Oct 1949, Claudia Mary b 4 Oct 1951), 2 s (Andrew Richard Bartley b 21 Nov 1954, Roger Quention b 16 Nov 1959); m 2, Angela Margaret (d 2011), da of Lt-Col Alexander Scoular (d 1978); 1 step s (Daniel Alexander Scoular b 6 Sept 1970); *Career* actor, director and producer; Mil Serv DLI; vice-pres Royal Theatrical Fund, fndr memb Theatre of Comedy; began acting 1935, numerous comedy and serious roles; vice-pres Disabled Living Fndn 2002–; Evening Standard Special Award for life-long contribution to British cinema 1997, Dilys Powell Award for lifetime achievement London Critics Circle 2007; Comic Icon Loaded Magazine Awards 2003, Greatest Living Engllishman Loaded Magazine Awards 2006, Best Trouper Oldie Magazine Awards 2007; *Theatre* incl: Dear Octopus, On Monday Next, For Better For Worse, The Man Most Likely To..., Chapter 17, Pride and Prejudice, The Merry Wives of Windsor, Camino Real, Love for Love, The Cherry Orchard, Passion Play, Painting Churches, August, Woof, RSC 1996–98, On the Whole its Been Jolly Good, Naked Justice; *Television* incl: Our Man At St Mark's, Summer's Lease, Chancer, Life After Life, Who Bombed Birmingham?, Rumpole, Mr Palfrey, Thacker, The Oz Trial, Lovejoy, The Changeling, Bermuda Grace, Royal Celebration, Vanity Dies Hard, Love on a Branch Line, Honey for Tea, 2 Golden Balls, The Pale Horse, The Canterville Ghost, Edgar Wallace (series, Germany), Tales of the Crypt, L for Liverpool, Dalziel and Pascoe, One Foot in the Past, The Best of British, The Sword of Honour, Take A Girl Like You, It's Only TV But I Like It, Legends, Into The Void, Holby City, Jonathan Ross Show, Midsomer Murders, Where The Heart Is, Revolver, Unto the Wicked 2002, The Last Detective 2007, Harley St; *Radio* incl: The Navy Lark, Round the World in 80 Days, Wind in the Willows, Philip and Rowena, England Their England, Great Pleasure, Maclean – The Memorex Years, Coward Centenary, Me and Little Boots, Cousin Bette, Bristow (Coward Centenary), Queen Mother 100th Birthday, Backbencher, Les Misérables, Democracy and Language, Tales from the Backbench, Professor Branestorm, Queen Mother Memoriam, Ghosts of Albion, Cads, Dr Who, The Hitch Hiker's Guide to the the Galaxy, Princess Seraphina; *Film* over 100 films incl: Ferdinando, Les Girls, Carry On Nurse, Doctor in Love, The Longest Day, Out Of Africa, Empire of the Sun, Scandal, King Ralph, August, Day of the Jackal, Saving Grace, Cinderella, Harry Potter and the Philosopher's Stone, Tomb Raider, Thunderpants, Three Guesses, Harry Potter and the Chamber of Secrets, Carry on Columbus, Churchill – The Hollywood Years, Colour Me Kubrick, Millions, Venus (Best Supporting Actor Br Ind Film Awards 2006, nominated Best Supporting Actor BAFTA Awards 2007), Is There Anyone There?; *Books* Hello (autobiography, 2006); *Style—* Leslie Phillips, Esq, CBE; ✉ c/o Independent Talent Group, 76 Oxford Street, London W1D 1BS (☎ 020 7636 6565); c/o Curtis Brown, 29 Haymarket, London SW1Y 4SP

PHILLIPS, Capt Mark Anthony Peter; CVO (1974), ADC(P); s of Maj Peter William Garside Phillips, MC (d 1998), late 1 King's Dragoon Gds, and Anne Patricia, *née* Tiarks (d 1988); *b* 22 September 1948; *Educ* Marlborough, RMA Sandhurst; *m* 1, 1973 (m dis 1992), HRH The Princess Royal (*see* Royal Family section); 1 s (Peter b 15 Nov 1977), 1 da (Zara b 15 May 1981); m 2, 1997, Sandy, da of James Pflueger, and Nancy Pflueger, of Honolulu, Hawaii, and former w of Stephen Clarke; 1 da (Stephanie Noelani Sanford 2 Oct 1997); *Career* 1 The Queen's Dragoon Gds 1969, Regtl Duty 1969–74, co instr RMA Sandhurst 1974–77, Army Trg Directorate MOD 1977–78, ret; student RAC Cirencester 1978–79; personal ADC to HM The Queen 1974–; memb GB three day event teams: World Championships 1970, European Championships 1971, Olympic Games Munich 1972 (team Gold medal), Olympic Games Mexico 1968 (reserve), Olympic Games Montreal 1976 (reserve), Olympic Games Seoul 1988 (team Silver medal); winner Badminton Horse Trials 1971, 1972, 1974 and 1981 (second person ever to win event four times); dir: Gleneagles Mark Phillips Equestrian Centre 1988–92, Gloucestershire TEC 1991–97, Equiland Ltd; govr Hartpury Coll until 2000; memb Royal Caledonian Hunt; patron Young Glos; int trainer and course designer; chm British Equestrian Olympic Fund 1989–96, tstee Br Equestrian Fedn Fund 1997–; chef d'équipe and coach: Spanish Equestrian Team 1992, US Equestrian Team 1993–; farmer; Liveryman Worshipful Cos of: Farriers, Saddlers, Loriners; Hon Liveryman Worshipful Co of Farmers; Freeman: Worshipful Co of Carmen, City of London; hon fell Br Horse Soc 2005; *Clubs* Buck's (hon memb); *Style*— Captain Mark Phillips, CVO, ADC(P); ✉ Aston Farm, Cherington, Tetbury, Gloucestershire GL8 8SW

PHILLIPS, Mark Daniel; *b* 3 April 1961, Manchester; *Educ* Manchester Grammar, University Coll London (LLB), Coll of Law; *Career* admitted slr 1986; slr specialising in new media, video and computer games, interactive entertainment and publishing; Clifford Turner (latterly Clifford Chance) 1984–88, (also Van Dourne & Sjollema Amsterdam 1985), Harbottle and Lewis 1988– (ptnr 1990–, jt head eCommerce and Technol Gp); tstee and dir Performing Arts Labs Ltd, memb Exec Ctee Edinburgh Interactive Entertainment Festival; memb: Law Soc 1986, Soc for Computers and Law; *Recreations* family, sport, the arts; *Style*— Mark Phillips, Esq

PHILLIPS, Mark Paul; QC (1999); s of Norman John Phillips, and Wendy Sharron, *née* Cashman; *b* 28 December 1959; *Educ* The John Hampden Sch High Wycombe, Univ of Bristol (LLB, LLM); *m* 1, 11 Aug 1984, Deborah Elizabeth, *née* Fisher (d 2010); 2 da (Kathryn Mary b 22 Oct 1990, Sarah Olivia Enid b 4 Aug 1993), 1 s (Jack Nathan Robert b 7 April 1996); m 2, 9 July 2011, Samantha Jayne, *née* Wilding; 1 s (Max Paolo Cohen b 22 Feb 2013), 2 step-da (Adriana Sophia Rohde b 13 Feb 1992, Ava Rosa Lock-Phillips b 26 Feb 2007); *Career* called to the Bar Inner Temple 1984; practising commercial law and specialising in insolvency, city and sport work at the 3–4 South Square chambers 1986–, recorder 2000–07 (asst recorder 1998–2000); memb Cncl: Insolvency Lawyers Assoc 1999–2005 (vice-pres 2001–02, pres 2002–03), Assoc of Business Recovery Professionals 2004– (fell 2004); memb Int Insolvency Inst 2007–; memb: Nat Youth Theatre of GB 1977–82, Br Debating Team to USA Speaking Union 1983; *Books* Byles on Bills of Exchange (contrib, 1988), Paget's Law of Banking (contrib, 1989, 1996, 2003 and 2007), Butterworth's Insolvency Law Handbook (co-ed, 1990–2013); *Recreations* football, motorsport, theatre, dating my wife; *Style*— Mark Phillips, Esq, QC; ✉ 3/4 South Square, Gray's Inn, London WC1R 5HP (✆ 020 7696 9900, fax 020 7696 9911, e-mail markphillips@southsquare.com or markphillipsqc@btinternet.com)

PHILLIPS, Mike; OBE (2007); s of George Milton Phillips (d 1972), and Marjorie Phillips, of New York; *Educ* Highbury Sch London, Univ of London (BA), Univ of Essex (MA), Goldsmiths Coll London (PGCE); *partner* Dr J Owen; 2 s (Akwesi George b 17 Oct 1974, Ivan Akojo Romario b 12 July 1994); *Career* writer; teacher and community worker, ed Westindian World, educn offr BBC 1977–79, tv prodr Diverse Productions, sr lectr in media studies Univ of Westminster 1983–93, writer in residence Royal Festival Hall South Bank Centre 1996–97; freelance journalist and broadcaster BBC World Service, Radio Four, Guardian, Sunday Times, Observer; winner Silver Dagger The Crime Writers Assoc 1990, Arts Fndn Thriller Writing Fellowship 1997–98; govr Middlesex Univ 2002–; tstee Nat Heritage Meml Fund 2002–; Hon DUniv Middlesex 2001; FRSA, FRSL; *Books* Community Work and Racism (1982), Smell of the Coast (short stories, 1987), Blood Rights (1989), The Late Candidate (1990), Boyz N The Hood (1991), Notting Hill in the Sixties (1991), Whose Cities? (contrib, 1991), Shelter Anniversary Book (contrib, 1991), Point of Darkness (1994), An Image to Die For (1995), The Dancing Face (1997); as Joe Canzius: Fast Road To Nowhere (1996), A Shadow of Myself (2000), London Crossings (2001); screenplays: Bloodrights (BBC Television, 1990), The Late Candidate, Yardie (BBC), Expendable Man; *Recreations* gardening, reading, contemporary music; *Style*— Dr Mike Phillips, OBE, FRSL; ✉ c/o Harper Collins UK, 77–85 Fulham Palace Road, London W6 8JB (✆ 020 8741 7070)

PHILLIPS, (David) Nicholas; s of (David) Cecil Phillips (d 1988), of Sandwich, Kent, and Megan, *née* Davey (d 2000); *b* 13 January 1953; *Educ* Dover Coll; *m* 13 Sept 1980 (m dis 2000), Anne Rosemary, da of Ernest Frank Robert Cross (d 1980), of Salfords, Surrey; 1 s (Oliver Nicholas b 1984), 2 da (Lucy Vanessa b 1987, Amelia Fleur b 1991); m 2, 9 April 2002, Angelica Anatolyevna Osipova, da of Anatoly Osipov (d 2003); 1 s (Lucius Nicholas Anatole b 2010), 1 da (Olivia Angelica Sophia b 2012); *Career* admitted slr 1977; ptnr: Stephenson Harwood 1987–2003, Hill Dickinson 2003–; memb Law Soc 1977; Freeman Worshipful Co of Slrs 1980; Liveryman Worshipful Co of Shipwrights 2000; *Recreations* sailing, scuba diving, shooting; *Style*— Nicholas Phillips, Esq; ✉ 303 Cardamom Building, 31 Shad Thames, London SE1 2YR (✆ 020 7407 0914); Hill Dickinson LLP, The Broadgate Tower, 20 Primrose Street, London EC2A 2EW (✆ 020 7280 9102, fax 020 7283 1144)

PHILLIPS, Patricia Ruth; *Career* Miny of Agriculture, Fisheries and Food 1984–91, secondment to EU Cncl Secretariat Brussels 1988, Civil Serv Fulbright Fellowship Univ of Minnesota 1991–92, 1 sec (agriculture and trade policy) Washington 1992–97; FCO: policy planning staff 1997–98, private sec to Min for Africa 1998–2000, dep head Near East and North Africa Dept 2000–02; cnsllr (economic, trade and investment) The Hague 2002–04, dep head of mission Amman 2004–07, ambass to Angola 2007–09, counsellor FCO 2009–14; *Style*— Ms Patricia Phillips

PHILLIPS, (Jeremy) Patrick Manfred; QC (1980); s of Manfred Henry Phillips (d 1963), and Irene Margaret, *née* Symondson (d 1970); *b* 27 February 1941; *Educ* Charterhouse; *m* 1970, Virginia Gwendolyn Dwyer; 2 s (Rufus b 1969, d 1989, Marcus b 1970); m 2, 1976, Judith Gaskell Hetherington; 2 s (Tobias b 1982, Seamus b 1985), 2 da (Rebekah b 1979, Natasha b 1980); *Career* articled clerk Thomson McLintock & Co CAs 1958–61; called to the Bar Gray's Inn 1964, pracisting barr 1964–2003; head of chambers: 2 Temple Gardens 1991–98, New Court Chambers 2000–03; DTI inspr into affairs of Queens Moat House plc 1993; landowner (900 acres); owner and dir of ops of Kentwell Hall 1971–, deviser and originator of Kentwell Hall's annual re-creation of Tudor domestic life 1978–; sometime contrib to successive ed of Cooper's Manual of Auditing and Cooper's Students' Manual of Auditing; dir Care International UK 1986–98; *Books* author of various articles and pamphlets on Kentwell Hall, Tudor domestic life and heritage educn; *Recreations* Kentwell Hall, Tudor buildings, Tudor domestic life; *Style*— Patrick Phillips, Esq, QC

PHILLIPS, Peter; *b* 15 October 1953, Southampton; *Educ* Winchester, St John's Coll Oxford (organ scholar); *m* 1997, Caroline; 1 s (Edmund b April 1997); *Career* fndr dir The Tallis Scholars (choral gp specialising in Renaissance sacred music, around 80 concerts a year, 99 in 2013, 40th anniversary of the group) 1973–, co-fndr and dir Gimell Records Ltd 1980– (affiliated to Philips Classics 1996–2000), dir of music Merton Coll Oxford 2008–16 (Bodley fell 2010); co fndr and artistic dir Tallis Scholars Summer Schs: Oakham/Uppingham 2000–14, Seattle 2005–13, Sydney 2007–12; music columnist The Spectator 1983– (cricket corr 1989); contrib: Musical Times (proprietor 1995–), Early Music, New Republic, Guardian, Times Literary Supplement, Music and Letters, Sunday Telegraph, The Listener, RA Magazine, The Times, Evening Standard, BBC Music Magazine; numerous TV and radio broadcasts on progs incl Music Weekly (BBC Radio 3 and World Service) and Kaleidoscope and Today (Radio 4), Tallis Scholars and Gimell Records subject of South Bank Show documentary (LWT) 1990 and cover feature Gramophone magazine 1994; live broadcasts from BBC Proms 1988, 2001, 2003, 2007, 2008, 2011, 2013 and (television and radio) 2014, Edinburgh Festival 1995, 2007, 2010, 2014 and 2015, Aldeburgh 2016, Bath and Cheltenham Festivals, regular tours of Europe, US and Far East, broadcast from Sistine Chapel featured on Japanese and Italian TV to mark cleaning of Michelangelo's Last Judgement, collaboration with BBC 4 on Life and Music of William Byrd 2003; conducted: Dutch Chamber Choir, Collegium Vocale Gent, BBC Singers, Finnish Radio Choir, Taipei Chamber Singers, Musica Reservata Barcelona, El Leon de Oro Oviedo, Markell's Voices Novosibirsk, Tudor Choir Seattle, Intrada Moscow; Gramophone Magazine Hall of Fame 2013; Chevalier de l'Ordre des Arts et des Lettres (France) 2005; *Recordings* incl: Josquin: Pange lingua (Gramophone Magazine Record of the Year 1987), Victoria: Requiem (Ritmo Early Music Award Spain, 1988), Lassus: Missa Osculetur me (Priz Diapason d'Or 1989), Josquin's L'Homme armé Masses (Prix Diapason d'Or 1989, International Record Critics' Award 1990), Palestrina's Missa Assumpta est Maria (Gramophone Early Music Award 1991), de Rore: Missa Praeter rerum seriem (Gramophone Early Music Award and Classic FM People's Choice 1994), John Browne: Music for the Eton Choirbook (Gramophone Early Music Award 2005), Josquin: Missa Sine Nomine (Prix Diapason d'Or 2008), Josquin: Missa Malheur me bat (Grammy nomination 2011), De beata virgine (Prix Diapason d'Or de l'Année 2012), Jean Mouton: Missa Dictes moy toutes voz pensées (Prix Diapason d'Or 2013), Arvo Pärt – Tintinnabuli (2015), Taverner: Missa Corona Spinea (2015); *Books* English Sacred Music 1549–1649 (1991), Companion to Medieval and Renaissance Music (contrib, 1992), What We Really Do (2003, revised edn 2013); *Recreations* cooking, black and white photography, cricket, Arabia; *Clubs* Chelsea Arts, MCC; *Style*— Peter Phillips, Esq; ✉ 22 Gibson Square, London N1 0RD (✆ 020 7354 0627, e-mail gibsonsq@gmail.com); 48 rue des Francs-Bourgeois, 75003 Paris, France; Merton College, Oxford OX1 4JD

PHILLIPS, Richard A R; s of Sir Raymond Phillips, and Hazel, *née* Evans; *b* 26 April 1955, Teddington, Middx; *Educ* Rugby, Balliol Coll Oxford (BA, Elton Shakespeare prize); *Family* 1 s (Alexander b 1991), 3 da (Meriel b 1997, Branwen b 1997, Anna b 2004); *Career* slr specialising in railways, privatisations, public/private partnerships and project finance; ptnr Freshfields Bruckhaus Deringer 1989–; memb Law Soc; FRSA; *Style*— Richard Phillips, Esq; ✉ Freshfields Bruckhaus Deringer, 65 Fleet Street, London EC4Y 1HS (✆ 020 7832 7136, e-mail richard.phillips@freshfields.com)

PHILLIPS, Richard Charles Jonathan; QC (1990); s of Air Cdre M N Phillips (d 1986), and Dorothy Ellen, *née* Green (d 1987); *b* 8 August 1947; *Educ* King's Sch Ely (King's scholar), Sidney Sussex Coll Cambridge (exhibitioner); *m* 9 Sept 1978, Alison, OBE, DL, da of David Arthur Francis; 1 da (Ella Rose b 31 March 1995); *Career* called to the Bar 1970, specialises in town and country planning and local govt; asst Parly boundary cmmr for England; govr King's Sch Ely; *Recreations* natural history, travel, photography; *Style*— Richard Phillips, Esq, QC; ✉ Francis Taylor Building, Temple, London EC4Y 7BY (e-mail clerks@ftb.eu.com)

PHILLIPS, Rear Adm Richard Thomas Ryder; CB (1998); s of Brig T H Phillips (d 1979), and Arabella Phillips (d 1989); *b* 1 February 1947; *Educ* Wrekin Coll, BRNC Dartmouth, RNC Greenwich, Jt Defence Coll Canberra, Univ of Oxford Business Sch, Astridge Business Sch; *m* 1, Sue Elizabeth, *née* Groves (d 1996); 1 da (Sara Arabella); m 2, Belinda, *née* Round Turner; 1 step s (Richard), 1 step da (Emma); *Career* joined RN 1965; served in: HMS Penelope, HMS Glamorgan; CO HMS Scimitar 1974–76; warfare offr HMS Naiad 1976–78, Lt Cdr (CO) HMS Hubberston 1978–80, exec offr HMS Apollo 1980, Cdr 1981, Aust Def Coll 1981, Cdr (Training) HMS Raleigh 1982, Directorate of Naval Plans MOD 1982–85; CO: HMS Charybdis 1985, HMS Scylla 1986; Capt 1986, asst dir of defence operational requirements MOD 1987, CO HMS Cornwall 1988–90, Top Mgmnt Prog Cabinet Office 1990–91, Capt Royal Naval Presentation Team 1991–92, Cmdr 1992, COS Surface Flotilla 1993, CO HMS Illustrious 1993, ADC to HM The Queen 1993–95, Rear Adm 1996, Asst Chief of the Defence Staff (Operational Requirements) MOD 1996–99, ret; dir Future Systems Marconi Naval System 1999–2000, dir BAE Systems Ops Gp 2000–02, dir BAE Sea Systems 2002–04, ceo/clerk Worshipful Co of Haberdashers 2004–13, dir Renaissance Capital Oil and Gas 2010–11, dir SMG Defence 2011–13, vice-chm JMW Energy Ventures (Bahrain) 2013–; Younger Bro Trinity House 1984–; Freeman: City of London, New Orleans, Fort Lauderdale; FNI 1998; *Recreations* sailing, shooting, skiing; *Clubs* Royal Yacht Squadron; *Style*— Rear Adm Richard Phillips, CB, FNI

PHILLIPS, Robert Sneddon (Robbie); s of William James Phillips (d 1982), and Mary Jane Sneddon (d 1983); *b* 15 September 1932; *Educ* George Heriot's Sch Edinburgh, Univ of Edinburgh (MB ChB); *m* 2 Oct 1957, Isabella Newlands (Ella), da of George Forrest (d 1969); 1 da (Gillian Moir b 16 March 1961), 1 s (Graeme Robert b 2 Nov 1964); *Career* Surgn Lt RNVR 1957–59; conslt orthopaedic surgn 1967–; contrib to numerous pubns on orthopaedic matters; memb Methodist Church; public speaker on works of Robert Burns; FBOA, FRCSEd, FRCS; *Recreations* golf (pres Cheshire Union of Golf Clubs 2005–06); *Clubs* Stockport Cricket, Hazel Grove Golf, Forty, MCC, Rotary; *Style*— Robbie Phillips, Esq; ✉ 7 Rookwood Hill, Bramhall, Stockport, Cheshire SK7 3EH (✆ 0161 440 8037)

PHILLIPS, Prof Robin Kenneth Stewart; s of John Fleetwood Stewart Phillips, and Mary Gordon, *née* Shaw; *b* 18 November 1952, Barnstaple, Devon; *Educ* Royal Free Hosp (MB BS), St Mary's Hosp London (MS); *m* 14 June 1975, Janina, da of Jan and Elizabeth Nowak; 1 da (Eva b 1982), 1 s (Henry b 1984); *Career* conslt surgn St Mark's Hosp 1987– (clinical dir 2006–), sr lectr Bart's 1987–90, conslt surgn Homerton Hosp 1990–93, dean St Mark's Academic Inst 1997–2002, prof of colorectal surgery Imperial Coll 2000–; pres Br Colostomy Assoc 2000–05, vice-pres Section of Coloproctology RSM 2000 (pres 2006–07), dir Polyposis Registry Cancer Research UK (CRUK)1993–2013, hon admin dir INSIGHT (Int Soc for the Investigation of Gastrointestinal Hereditary Tumours) 2009–11; FRCS 1979, FRCSEd (ad eundem) 2002, FRCPSGlas 2003; *Publications* author of over 200 reviewed pubns on colorectal disorders; *Recreations* fly fishing, being walked by the dog, wine, family; *Style*— Prof Robin Phillips; ✉ e-mail robin@rksphillips.go-plus.net; St Mark's Academic Institute, St Mark's Hospital, Harrow, Middlesex HA1 3UJ (✆ 020 8235 4251, fax 020 8235 4277, e-mail bharti.huda@nhs.net)

PHILLIPS, Dame Siân; DBE (2016, CBE 2000); da of David Phillips (d 1961), and Sally, *née* Thomas (d 1985); *Educ* Pontardawe GS, Cardiff Coll Univ of Wales (BA), RADA (Meggie Albanesi scholarship, Bancroft Gold medal); *m* 1, 1956 (m dis 1959), Dr D Roy; m 2, 1959 (m dis 1979), Peter O'Toole (d 2013); 2 da (Kate b 1961, Pat b 1964); m 3, 1979 (m dis 1992), Robin David Sachs, s of Leonard Sachs (d 1990); *Career* actress; former BBC News reader/announcer Wales; dir Film Wales, vice-pres Royal Welsh Coll of Music and Drama, vice-pres and tstee Actors Benevolent Fund, patron RAFT; memb: Gorsedd of Bards 1960, Drama Ctee Arts Cncl 1970–75, Arts Cncl Touring Co Wales; govr Welsh Coll of Music and Drama, former govr St David's Theatre Tst; fell Welsh Coll of Music and Drama 1991; delivered RTE annual (Huw Wheldon) lecture on BBC TV 1993; Special

Award BAFTA Wales 2000; Hon DLitt Univ of Wales 1983; hon fell: Cardiff Coll Univ of Wales 1980, Polytechnic of Wales 1988, Trinity Coll Carmarthen 1998, Swansea Coll Univ of Wales 1998; FRSA 2002; *Theatre* prodns incl: Hedda Gabler 1959, Ondine, Duchess of Malfi 1961, Lizard on the Rock 1961, Gentle Jack 1963, Maxibules 1964, Night of the Iguana 1964 (best actress nomination), Ride a Cock Horse 1965, Man and Superman (best actress nomination), Man of Destiny 1966, The Burglar 1967, Epitaph for George Dillon 1972, A Nightingale in Bloomsbury Square 1973, The Gay Lord Quex 1975, Spinechiller 1978, You Never Can Tell 1979, Pal Joey 1979–81 (best actress in a musical nomination), Dear Liar 1982, Major Barbara (NT) 1983, Peg 1984, Gigi 1985, Thursday's Ladies 1987, Brel 1988, Paris Match 1989, Vanilla 1990, The Manchurian Candidate 1991, Painting Churches (Playhouse), Ghosts 1993 (nomination Artist of the Year, Wales), Marlene (RNT Studio) 1994, An Inspector Calls (Royale Broadway) 1995, A Little Night Music (RNT, Olivier Award nomination for Best Supporting Performance in a Musical 1996) 1995–96, Marlene (nat tour, nomination Olivier Best Actress in a Musical Award) 1996, Marlene (int tour) 1998, Marlene (Broadway, DramaDesk and Tony nominations for Best Actress in a Musical) 1999, Lettice and Lovage (UK tour) 2001, My Old Lady (Dolittle, LA) 2001–02, My Old Lady (NY) 2002, The Old Ladies 2003, The Dark (Donmar) 2004, The Unexpected Man (UK tour) 2005, Quartet Theatre on the Bay (NY) 2005, Regrets Only (Manhattan Theatre Club) 2006, Great Expectations (RSC) 2007, Liaisons Dangeureuses (NY) 2007–08, Calendar Girls (UK tour and Noel Coward Theatre) 2008–09, Cabaret (UK tour and Pizza on the Park London) 2009, Juliet and her Romeo (Bristol Old Vic) 2010, A Little Night Music (St Louis Opera) 2010, Bitter Sweet (US) 2011, Lovesong (London and UK tour) 2011, Little Dogs (Nat Theatre of Wales) 2012, Cabaret (Savoy Theatre West End) 2012 (Olivier Award nomination), This Is My Family (Sheffield Crucible) 2013 (Best Supporting Performance UK Theatre Award), People (NT) 2013, The Importance of Being Earnest (Shakespeare Theatre, Washington DC, and Harold Pinter Theatre West End) 2014, Les Blancs (NT) 2016; *Television* drama series incl: Shoulder to Shoulder, How Green was my Valley (BAFTA Best Actress Award), Crime and Punishment, Tinker Tailor Soldier Spy, Barriers, The Oresteia of Aeschylus, I Claudius (BAFTA Best Actress Award and Best Performance Royal TV Soc), Vanity Fair, Shadow of the Noose, Snow Spider (BAFTA nomination), Emlyns Moon (1990, BAFTA Best Actress nomination), Perfect Scoundrels 1991, The Chestnut Soldier 1991 (BAFTA nomination), The Borrowers 1992, host BAFTA Wales Award Ceremony, Scolds Bridle, The Aristocrats 1999, The Magician's House (2 series) 1999 and 2000, Nikita 1999, The Last Detective, Murder Room, Midsomer Murders 2005 and 2009, Poirot 2007, Missing 2010, New Tricks 2010, Lewis 2010, Under Milk Wood (BBC) 2014; *Film* incl: Becket 1963, Goodbye Mr Chips 1968 (Best Supporting Actress awards), Murphy's War 1970, Under Milk Wood 1971, Dune (dir David Lynch) 1984, Valmont (dir Milos Forman) 1989, Dark River, A Painful Case (RTE), Age of Innocence (dir Martin Scorsese) 1992, Heidi (Disney), House of America (dir Marc Evans) 1997, Alice Through the Looking Glass 1998, Coming and Going 2000; *Radio* incl: Bequest to a Nation, Antony and Cleopatra, Henry VIII, All's Well That Ends Well, Oedipus, Phaedra, The Maids, A Leopard in Autumn; *Records* Pal Joey, Gigi, Peg, Bewitched Bothered and Bewildered (single), I Remember Mama, A Little Night Music, Desirée 1900, Mme Armfeldt 1996, Marlene 1997, And So It Goes (solo) 2002; *Other* Falling in Love Again (concert tour Israel and UK, cabaret engagement Fire Bird Cafe NYC) 1999 and 2000, Almost like being in Love (cabaret, RNT) 2001, Falling in Love Again (cabaret season) 2001, Divas at the Donmar 2001, Falling in Love Again (cabaret tour) 2003, Siân Phillips Crossing Borders (Wiltons Music Hall) 2011; *Books* Siân Phillips' Needlepoint (1987), Private Faces (autobiography, 1999), Public Places (autobiography vol II, 2001), Public Places (2003); *Recreations* gardening, drawing, needlepoint; *Style*— Dame Siân Phillips, DBE

PHILLIPS, His Hon Judge Simon Benjamin; QC; *Educ* Harrow, Univ of Sussex (BA), Trinity Hall Cambridge (LLM); *Career* called to the Bar 1985; recorder 2002, fee-paid immigration judge Asylum and Immigration Tbnl 2006–15, circuit judge (NE Circuit) 2015–; memb Gen Cncl of the Bar 2014–; *Recreations* golf, tennis, squash; *Style*— His Hon Judge Simon Phillips, QC

PHILLIPS, Hon Mr Justice; Sir Stephen Edmund Phillips; kt (2013), QC (2002); *Career* called to the Bar (Gray's Inn) 1984; recorder 2000, judge of the High Court of Justice (Queen's Bench Div) 2013–; *Style*— The Hon Mr Justice Phillips; ✉ Royal Courts of Justice, Strand, London WC2A 2LL

PHILLIPS, Stephen James; QC (2009), MP; *Educ* Oriel Coll Oxford (BA, BCL); *m* (m dis 2013) Fiona; 3 c; *Career* called to the Bar Lincoln's Inn 1993; MP (Cons) Sleaford and Hykeham N 2010–; *Style*— Stephen Phillips, Esq, QC, MP; ✉ House of Commons, London SW1A 0AA

PHILLIPS, Stephen Paul; s of Alfred Phillips, and Flora, *née* Kelvin; *b* 26 November 1959, Glasgow; *Educ* Hutchesons' GS Glasgow, Univ of Glasgow (LLB); *m* 1 May 1987, Rona Cameron; 2 da (Catriona b 17 Feb 1994, Lucy b 8 March 1997); *Career* admitted slr 1982; slr specialising the public and wider not-for-profit sector; ptnr: Alexander Stone & Co 1987, Burness LLP (following merger) 1998–; dir Four Acres Charitable Tst; memb Law Soc of Scotland 1982; incl SCVO Guide to Constitutions and Charitable Status (2006); *Recreations* skiing, hill walking, DIY, photography, piano; *Style*— Stephen Phillips, Esq; ✉ e-mail stephillips1@btinternet.com

PHILLIPS, (Mark) Trevor; OBE (1999); s of George Milton Phillips (d 1972), of Georgetown, Guyana, and Marjorie Eileen, *née* Canzius; *b* 31 December 1953, London; *Educ* Wood Green Sch, Queen's Coll Georgetown, Imperial Coll London (BSc); *m* 25 July 1981 (m dis), Asha Aline Francine, da of Padmashree Jehangir Bhownagary, of Bombay and Paris; 2 da (Sushila b 11 July 1984, Holly b 7 Jan 1988); *m* 2, 21 Sept 2013, Helen Veale; *Career* pres NUS 1978–80; LWT: researcher (Skin, The London Programme) 1980–82, prodr (Black on Black, Club Mix, The Making of Britain, Devil's Advocate) 1982–86; reporter This Week Thames TV 1986–87; LWT: ed and presenter The London Programme 1987–99, presenter Nation 1992–93, head of current affairs 1993–94, exec prodr factual progs 1995–98; md Pepper Productions 1994–2000; memb London Assembly (Lab) London 2000–03, chair London Assembly 2000–03; chm: Cmmn for Racial Equality 2003–06, Cmmn for Equality and Human Rights 2006–12; dir: Equate Organisation 2007–08, Diversity Analytics 2013–, Webber Phillips Ltd 2014–; chm: London Arts Bd, Runnymede Tst 1993–98, Hampstead Theatre 1994–98, London Tourist Bd 2001, Cncl RTS 2001–, Cncl Liberty 2002–; memb Arts Cncl of England 1997–98; presenter: The Midnight Hour (BBC) 1994–97, In Living Colour (BBC) 1996–98, Crosstalk (LNN) 1996–99, The Material World 1998–99; US Prized Pieces Winner (public affrs/news) 1985, RICS Journalist and Broadcasters Award 1988, Royal Television Soc Awards 1988, 1993 and 1998; Hon MA; Hon DLitt: Westminster Univ, South Bank Univ, City Univ; memb RTS 1990; ARCS, FRSA; Chevalier de la Légion d'Honneur 2007; *Books* Partners In One Nation (1986), Windrush: The Irresistible Rise of Multicultural Britain (co-author), Britain's Slave Trade (introduction); *Recreations* music, crosswords, America, running; *Clubs* The Groucho, Home House; *Style*— Trevor Phillips, Esq, OBE

PHILLIPS, Trevor Thomas (Tom); CBE; s of David John Phillips, and Margaret Agnes, *née* Arnold; *b* 24 May 1937; *Educ* Henry Thornton GS, St Catherine's Coll Oxford (MA), Camberwell Sch of Arts and Crafts (NDD); *m* 1, 12 Aug 1961 (m dis 1988), Jill Purdy; 1 da ((Eleanor) Ruth b 21 Jan 1964), 1 s (Conrad Leofric (Leo) b 26 Jan 1965); *m* 2, 26 Oct 1995, Fiona Maddocks, qv; *Career* artist; visiting artist and Josep Lluis Sert practitioner in the arts Carpenter Center Harvard 1993; composer of the opera IRMA (recorded twice by Obscure Records 1977 and Matchless Recordings 1988, performed at Bordeaux

Festival, Istanbul Festival and ICA); librettist Heart of Darkness chamber opera (premier Linbury Theatre ROH 2011); writer and critic for TLS and RA Magazine; translated, illustrated, printed and published Dante's Inferno 1983, TV dir of A TV Dante for Channel 4 with Peter Greenaway (first prize Montreal Festival 1990, Prix Italia 1991); chm Royal Acad Library 1989–94, chm of exhbns Royal Acad until 2007; visitor Inst for Advanced Study Princeton 2005–11, Slade Prof of Art History Univ of Oxford 2005–06; vice-chm copyright Cncls 1984–88, hon pres S London Art Soc 1988–, pres Heatherley's Sch of Art 2004; tstee: Nat Portrait Gallery 1998, Br Museum 1999; pres Cncl John Lewis Partnership 2015–; fell London Inst 1999; hon fell: St Catherine's Coll Oxford 1992, Bretton Hall Univ of Leeds 1994; hon memb RSPP 1999; RE 1987, RA 1989 (ARA 1984) *Work in Collections* Tate Gallery, V&A, Br Museum, Nat Portrait Gallery, Br Cncl, MOMA NY, Philadelphia Museum, Library of Congress, Bibliothèque Nationale Paris, Aust Nat Gallery Canberra, Museum of Fine Arts Budapest; *Exhibitions* worldwide since 1969 incl: retrospective exhibition (Kunsthalle Basel, Germeente Museum The Hague, Serpentine Gallery London) 1974–75, portrait retrospective (Nat Portrait Gallery) 1989, N Carolina Museum 1990, retrospective (Royal Academy) 1992, new works (V&A) 1992, retrospective (Yale Center for British Art) 1993, Univ of Penn 1993, South London Gallery 1997, Dulwich Picture Gallery 1997, Modern Art Museum Fort Worth 2001, Flowers Gallery London 2012, MassMoCa 2013, Flowers Gallery London 2013, dedicated room Summer Exhbn RA 2015; curator: Africa – The Art of a Continent (Royal Acad) 1993–95, We Are The People National Portrait Gallery 2004, Flowers Gallery London 2004, Flowers Gallery NY 2005, Ashmolean Museum Oxford 2006, Keillor Library Nat Gallery of Scotland 2007, Williamson Museum and Art Gallery Birkenhead 2008, Oxfordshire Museum 2009; *Designed Tapestries* St Catherine's Coll Oxford, HQ Channel 4, Morgan Grenfell Office; *Other Work* incl paintings, sculpture and glass screen The Ivy Restaurant, designer The Winter's Tale (Globe Theatre) 1997, translator and designer Otello (ENO, 1998), designer The Entertainer (Derby Playhouse) 2003, designer The Magic Flute (Holland Park Opera) 2008, Royal Mint London Silver Kilo Coin 2012, Royal Mint Benjamin Britten Centenary Coin; *Books* Trailer (1971), Works and Texts to 1974 (1975), A Humument (1980, revised edns 1987, 1997, 2005, 2012 and 2016), Heart of a Humument (1985), Where Are They Now – The Class of '47 (1990), Works and Texts Vol II (1992), A Humument – Variants and Variations (1992, revised 2012), Merely Connect (with Salman Rushdie, 1994), Aspects of Art (1997), Music in Art (1997), The Postcard Century (2000), Waiting For Godot (2000), We Are The People (2004), Merry Meetings (2005), Goldweights: Miniature Sculptures from Ghana 1400–1900 (2009), Vintage People of Photo Postcards (series, incl Women and Hats 2010, Readers 2010, Bicycles 2011, Weddings 2011, Menswear 2012 and Fantasy Transport 2012), The Sound in my Life (2015), Irma: An Opera (2015); *Recreations* watching cricket, collecting postcards, playing ping pong; *Clubs* Chelsea Arts, Groucho, SCCC; *Style*— Tom Phillips, Esq, CBE, RA; ✉ 57 Talfourd Road, London SE15 (✆ 020 7701 3978, fax 020 7703 2800, e-mail tom@tomphillips.co.uk, websites www.humument.com, www.tomphillips.co.uk and www.webberphillips.com)

PHILLIPS OF SUDBURY, Baron (Life Peer UK 1998), of Sudbury in the County of Suffolk; Andrew Wyndham Phillips; OBE (1996); *b* 15 March 1939; *Educ* Uppingham, Trinity Hall Cambridge (BA); *m* 1968, Penelope Ann, *née* Bennett; 2 da (Hon Caitlin, Hon Alice), 1 s (Hon Oliver); *Career* admitted slr 1964, fndr Bates, Wells & Braithwaite London 1970; co-fndr Parlex Group (trans Euro lawyers' gp) 1971; non-exec dir of various companies 1970–; fndr chm Legal Action Gp 1971, fndr and chm Citizenship Fndn 1989– (currently pres); fndr Lawyers in the Community 1987, co-fndr Solicitors Pro Bono Gp – Law Works (currently pres), fndr Phillips Fund; freelance journalist and broadcaster, inter alia 'legal eagle' on BBC Radio 2 Jimmy Young Show 1975–2001, presenter The London Programme (LWT) 1980–81; fndr memb Nat Lotteries Bd 1994–96; memb Cncl Charter 88 until 1994; memb Scott Tst (Guardian/Observer owners) 1994–2004; chllr Univ of Essex 2002–13; vice-pres Gainsborough's House; patron of several charities; resigned House of Lords 2015; Privacy Int Winston Parliamentarian of the Year 2001, Third Sector Luke Fitzherbert Lifetime Achievement Award 2009, first PILnet European Pro Bono Award 2010; *Publications* The Living Law, Charitable Status – A Practical Handbook (1980, many edns); *Recreations* local history, architecture and the Arts, theatre, assorted sports, books, walking; *Style*— The Lord Phillips of Sudbury, OBE; ✉ River House, The Croft, Sudbury, Suffolk CO10 1HW (✆ 01787 882151, e-mail andrew_w_phillips@yahoo.com)

PHILLIPS OF WORTH MATRAVERS, Baron (Life Peer UK 1999), of Belsize Park in the London Borough of Camden; Sir Nicholas Addison Phillips; KG (2011), kt (1987), PC (1995); *b* 21 January 1938; *Educ* Bryanston, King's Coll Cambridge; *m* 1972, Christylle Marie-Thérèse Rouffiac, *née* Doreau; 2 da, 1 step s, 1 step da; *Career* RNVR 1956–58; called to the Bar Middle Temple 1962; jr counsel to MOD and to Treasy in Admty matters 1973–78, QC 1978, recorder of the Crown Court 1982, judge of the High Court of Justice (Queen's Bench Div) 1987–95, a Lord Justice of Appeal 1995–99, a Lord of Appeal in Ordinary 1999–2000, Master of the Rolls 2000–05, Lord Chief Justice 2005–08, Sr Lord of Appeal in Ordinary 2008–09, pres Supreme Court 2009–12, pres Qatar Int Court 2012–, non-resident judge Court of Final Appeal Hong Kong 2012–; arbitrator 2012–; chm: BSE Inquiry 1998–2000, Lord Chllrs' Advsy Ctee on Public Records 2000–; pres: Br Maritime Law Assoc 2005 (vice-pres 1993–2005), European Maritime Law Assoc 2012–, Br Inst of Int and Comparative Law 2016–; chm: Law Advsy Ctee Br Cncl 1991–97, Cncl of Legal Educn 1992–97; memb: Advsy Cncl Inst of European and Comparative Law 1999–, Cncl of Mgmnt Br Inst of Int and Comparative Law 1999–, Advsy Cncl Inst of Global Law 2000–; visitor: Nuffield Coll Oxford 2000–05, UCL 2000–05, Darwin Coll 2005–08; visiting prof KCL 2012–; govr Bryanston Sch 1975– (chm of govrs 1981–2008); hon fell: King's Coll Cambridge 2003, Univ of London 2006, Hughes Hall 2010; Hon LLD Univ of Exeter 1998, Hon DCL City Univ 2003, Hon LLD Univ of Birmingham 2003, Hon DCL Washington and Lee Univ 2009, Hon DCL Wake Forest Univ 2010, Hon LLD BPP Univ 2014; hon fell Soc for Advanced Legal Studies 1999; *Clubs* Brooks's, Garrick; *Style*— The Rt Hon Lord Phillips of Worth Matravers, KG, PC

PHILLIPSON, HE Antony John; *Educ* Malborough Coll, Keble Coll Oxford (BA); *m* Julie; 3 s; *Career* diplomat; DTI: desk offr Technol Progs and Servs Div 1993–94, desk offr Competition Policy Div 1994–95, desk offr N American Trade Policy Unit 1995–96, private sec to Sec of State for Trade and Industry 1996–98, princ private sec to Sec of State for Trade and Industry 1998–2000; first sec trade policy Washington 2000–02, counsellor trade/tport then counsellor global issues Washington 2002–04, PM's private sec for foreign affrs No 10 Downing St 2004–07, Iran co-ordinator ME and N Africa Directorate FCO 2007–10, high cmmr to Singapore 2011–; *Style*— HE Mr Antony Phillipson; ✉ British High Commission, 100 Tanglin Road, Singapore 247919

PHILLIPSON, Brian; s of Robert Phillipson (d 2011), and Elizabeth, *née* Conway; *b* 18 April 1953, Tynemouth, Tyne & Wear; *Educ* CCC Cambridge (MA), Open Univ (Cert); *m* 5 April 1975, Denise; 1 da (Janet Margaret b 1978), 3 s (Andrew Christian b 1979, Jonathan Joseph b 1988, James Richard Alexander b 1990); *Career* apprentice then various posts in technical depts BAC Warton 1971–81, posts in prodn control and manufacturing systems rising to head of dept British Aircraft Corp Preston 1981–87, head of project then project dir European Fighter Aircraft BAe Warton 1987–90, dir of projects BAe Military Aircraft Div Warton 1990–93, RCDS 1994, dir of strategy and planning British Aerospace plc 1995–96, md Eurofighter GmbH 1997–99; BAE Systems plc: md Type 45 Destroyer 2000–01, gp md Sea Systems 2002–03, gp md Major Prog Assurance 2003–

04; Eurofighter GmbH: prog mgmnt dir 2004–07, chief operating offr 2007–09; dir engrg Marshall Aerospace 2009–13, md Engrg Solutions Marshall Aerospace Defence Gp 2014–15, ceo Baycamb Ltd 2015–; non-exec dir Gooch & Housego plc 2015–, conslt Marshall ADG 2015–; memb Cncl RINA 2002–04; N E Rowe Medal RAeS 1975, BAC Portal Gold Award 1976, Katie Wingfield Award ABARC/RAeS 1979; Liveryman Worshipful Co of Engrs 2002, Freeman City of London 2002; CEng, FRAeS 1994, FRINA 2002, FREng 2004; *Recreations* garden, skiing, hiking, theatre, music; *Style—* Brian Phillipson, Esq; ✉ Marshall Aerospace, The Airport, Cambridge CB5 8RX (☎ 01223 373737, fax 01223 321032, e-mail baycambltd@gmail.com)

PHILLIPSON, Bridget Maeve; MP; *b* 19 December 1983, Gateshead, Tyne and Wear; *Educ* St Robert of Newminster Sch Washington, Hertford Coll Oxford (BA); *m* 2009, Lawrence Dimery; 1 da (b Oct 2011), 1 s (b Nov 2015); *Career* MP (Lab) Houghton & Sunderland S 2010–; *Style—* Ms Bridget Phillipson, MP; ✉ House of Commons, London SW1A 0AA (☎ 020 7219 7087, e-mail bridget.phillipson.mp@parliament.uk)

PHILLIPSON, Prof David Walter; s of Herbert Phillipson (d 1992), of Castle Bytham, Lincs, and Mildred, *née* Atkinson (d 1995); *b* 17 October 1942; *Educ* Merchant Taylors', Gonville & Caius Coll Cambridge (MA, PhD, LittD); *m* 1967, Laurel, *née* Lofgren; 1 s (Arthur Veric b 1970), 1 da (Tacye Elizabeth b 1978); *Career* sec/inspr Nat Monuments Cmmn Northern Rhodesia and Zambia 1964–73, asst dir Br Inst in Eastern Africa 1973–78 (pres 1994–2005), keeper of archaeology, ethnography and history Glasgow Museums 1979–81; Univ of Cambridge: dir Univ Museum of Archaeology and Anthropology 1981–2006, fell Gonville & Caius Coll 1988–2006 (emeritus fell 2006–), reader in African prehistory 1991–2001, prof of African archaeology 2001–2006; ed African Archaeological Review 1987–94; Reckitt Archaeological Lecture Br Acad 2000; assoc fell Ethiopian Acad of Sciences 2014; FSA 1979 (treas 1987–93), FBA 2002; *Books* Mosi-oa-Tunya: a handbook to the Victoria Falls Region (ed, 1975), Prehistory of Eastern Zambia (1976), Later Prehistory of Eastern and Southern Africa (1977), African Archaeology (1985, 3 edn 2005), The Monuments of Aksum (1997), Ancient Ethiopia (1998), Archaeology at Aksum, Ethiopia, 1993–7 (2000), Ancient Churches of Ethiopia (2009), Foundations of an African Civilisation (2012); numerous contribs to edited vols and learned jls; *Clubs* Oxford and Cambridge; *Style—* Prof David Phillipson; ✉ 11 Brooklyn Terrace, Threshfield, Skipton BD23 5ER

PHILLIPSON, Peter; OBE (2010); *b* 6 March 1954; *Educ* Newcastle Poly; *Career* Gillette Co: salesman/area sales mangr UK 1978–1983, brand mangr deodorants UK 1983–85, brand supervisor UK 1985–86, mktg mangr Europe 1986–88, new business devpt dir North Atlantic 1988–89, mktg dir Europe 1989–90; United Distillers (Guinness plc): mktg dir UK 1990–92, mktg dir Int 1992–94; md First Choice Holidays and exec dir First Choice Holidays and Flights plc 1994–96, Diageo plc 1996–99 (md United Distillers UK, memb bd United Distillers Ltd, memb bd Dillon's Ireland); chief exec: Eldridge Pope & Co plc 1999–2001, Tussauds Gp 2001–07; Merlin Entertainment Gp 2007–; non-exec dir Saga Gp Ltd; *Style—* Peter Phillipson, Esq, OBE

PHILP, Chris; MP; *m* Elizabeth; 2 c; *Career* MP (Cons) Croydon S 2015–; *Style—* Chris Philp, Esq, MP; ✉ House of Commons, London SW1A 0AA

PHILP, Prof Ian; CBE (2008); s of Thomas Philp (d 1995), of Edinburgh, and Agnes, *née* Yule; *b* 14 November 1958; *Educ* George Watson's Coll, Univ of Edinburgh; *m* 1984, Anne, *née* Boyd; 2 da (Hannah Louise b 24 July 1985, Emily Kathryn b 18 Jan 1987), 1 s (Alexander Thomas b 6 April 1992); *Career* postgrad trg in geriatric med, internal med, gen practice, rehabilitation med and public health in England, Scotland and USA 1981–90; hon conslt geriatric med Univ of Southampton 1990–94, hon conslt and prof of geriatric med Univ of Sheffield 1994–2009, hon prof Univs of Sheffield and Warwick 2009–; nat dir for older people Dept of Health 2000–08, chief medical offr Hull and E Yorks Hosps, dep medical dir Heart of England NHS Fndn Tst 2015–; creator EASYCare Project for preventive care for older people 1989–; Nuffield fell Br Geriatrics Soc 1989; presenter How to Live Longer (BBC 1) 2006; David Wallace Medal Aust Gerontological Soc 1991, UK Hosp Dr Team of the Year (Care of the Elderly) 1998, Queen's Anniversary Prize for HE 2002; FRCPEd 1993, FRCP 1995, FFPH 2007; *Publications* Assessing Elderly People (ed, 1994), Outcomes Assessment in Elderly People (ed, 1997), Family Care of Older People in Europe (ed, 2001); *Recreations* international cinema, independent travel; *Style—* Prof Ian Philp, CBE; ☎ 07867 443644, e-mail ian.philp@heartofengland.nhs.uk

PHILP, Prof Mark François Edward; s of Albert Frederic Philp, of Cumbria, and Myriam, *née* Coulon; *b* 17 May 1952, Liverpool; *Educ* Chislehurst and Sidcup GS, Univ of Bradford (BA, CQSW), Univ of Leeds (MSc), Univ of Oxford (MPhil, DPhil); *m* 9 Feb 2004, Sarah Catherine Turvey, da of Charles Robert Turvey; 1 s (Joseph b 31 July 1985), 2 da (Ruth b 5 Dec 1988, Hannah b 3 June 1993); *Career* jr research fell Jesus Coll Oxford 1980–83, fell and tutor Oriel Coll Oxford 1983–2013 (vice-provost 2008–11), head Dept of Politics and Int Relations Univ of Oxford 2000–05, prof of history and politics Dept of History Univ of Warwick 2013–; dir European History Research Centre 2014–; memb Advsy Bd Ctee on Standards on Public Life 2002–; memb: Political Studies Assoc 1983, American Political Science Assoc 2001; FRHistS 1998; Officier des palmes académiques (France) 2009; *Books* Godwin's Political Justice (1986), Paine (1989), The French Revolution and British Popular Politics (ed, 1991), Political and Philosophical Writings of William Godwin (7 vols, ed, 1992), Napoleon and the Invasion of Britain (with A Franklin, 2003), Resisting Napoleon (2006), Political Conduct (2007), Thomas Paine (2007), Reimagining Democracy in the Age of Revolutions (ed with J Innes, 2013), Reforming Ideas in Britain (2013); *Recreations* music, swimming, literature; *Style—* Prof Mark Philp; ✉ Department of History, University of Warwick, Warwick CV4 7AN (e-mail mark.philp@warwick.ac.uk)

PHILPOT, Dr Elizabeth; *née* Devereux-Massey; da of William Edmund Devereux Massey, CBE (d 1991), of Dorking, Surrey, and Ingrid, *née* Glad-Block (d 2003); *b* 8 April 1943; *Educ* Heathfield Sch Ascot, Courtauld Inst Univ of London (BA), Univ of Glasgow (MLitt), Univ of Gothenburg (PhD), Johann Wolfgang Goethe-Universität Frankfurt am Main (Dip); *m* 10 Sept 1977, Timothy Stephen Burnett Philpot, s of Christopher Burnett Philpot (d 1971), of Pickering, N Yorks; *Career* asst keeper of the muniments Westminster Abbey 1968–69, admin asst Bedford Coll London 1969–70; HM Dip Serv 1970–82: third sec Brasilia Embassy, info attaché Paris Embassy; freelance lectr and art historian 1982–, lectr in history of art Univ of Surrey 1990–2003, tutor in history of art Workers' Educational Assoc 1992–2002 and 2010–13, lectr Assoc for Cultural Exchange Study Tours Cambridge 1993–94, artistic dir Musée de Faykod France 1999–; memb Low Countries Sculpture Soc 2002; chm Reigate Branch Nat Cncl of Women of GB 1990–93, memb Nat Cncl of Women of GB Health Ctee 1988–94, pres Inner Wheel Club of Dorking 2011–12, vice-pres Assoc L'Art de Maria de Faykod 2013, vice-pres Assoc Chemin de Croix à Lourdes de Maria de Faykod 2014, first vice-chm District 25 Assoc of Inner Wheel Clubs of GB and I 2014; Freeman City of London 1975, Liveryman Worshipful Co of Clockmakers 1983 (Steward 1989); Dame Chanoinesse de l'Ordre Hospitalier, Curieux et Courtois, des Chevaliers de Saint-Bacchus 2014; *Publications* Judith and Holofernes: Changing Images in the History of Art (essay included in Translating Religious Texts, 1993), Mary Magdalene – Saint or Sinner? The Visual Image, and also The Triumph of Judith – Power and Display in Art (two papers in Talking it Over: Perspectives on Women and Religion 1993–95, ed jtly), The Fourth-Century Mosaics of the Roman Villa at Lullingstone in Kent (essay in KAIROS Studies in Art History and Lit in honour of Prof Gunilla Åkerström-Hougen, 1998), Susanna: Indecent Attraction/Fatal Exposure (essay in Believing in the Text, 2004), Film and Apocryphal Imitation of the Feminine: Judith of Bethulia (essay in Theology and Literature: Rethinking Reader Responsibility, ed jtly, 2006), Old Testament Apocryphal Images in European Art 2009; *Recreations* art history, travel, photography, horology, theatre, music, swimming; *Clubs* Penn; *Style—* Dr Elizabeth Philpot; ✉ Ivinghoe, 9 Croft Avenue, Dorking, Surrey RH4 1LN (☎ and fax 01306 882739, e-mail elizabethphilpot@aol.com)

PHILPOTT, HE Hugh Stanley; s of Gordon Cecil Haig Philpott, and Janet Downer, *née*; *b* 24 January 1961, Wiltshire; *Educ* BA; *m* 16 June 1984, Janine Frederica; 1 da (Clarissa Helena Mabel b 5 July 1998); *Career* diplomat; asst desk offr Security Dept FCO 1980–82, pro-consul Oslo 1982–84, language training 1984–85, vice-consul Budapest 1985–87, third sec Iraq 1988–90, asst desk offr for Israel and Lebanon FCO 1990–91, desk offr Bermuda, Turks and Caicos Islands and Anguilla and Cayman Islands FCO 1991–93, second sec (Political) Washington DC 1993–97, prog mangr Russia E Europe and Central Asia Dept DFID 1997–99, head Bermuda and Caribbean Section Overseas Territories Directorate FCO 1999–2001, dep head of mission Muscat 2001–04, dep head Overseas Territories Dept FCO 2005–07, dep cmmr Br Indian Ocean Territory 2005–07, dep head Science and Innovation Gp FCO 2007–08, head Science and Innovation Network and dep head Int Science and Innovation Unit FCO and BIS 2008–12, language training 2012–13, temporary assignments Kyiv and Astana 2014–15, ambass to Tajikistan 2015–; *Recreations* music, opera, travel, language learning; *Style—* HE Mr Hugh Philpott; ✉ c/o FCO (Dushanbe), King Charles Street, London SW1A 2AH (e-mail hugh.philpott@fco.gov.uk, website www.fco.gov.uk)

PHIN, Dr Nicholas Fulton (Nick); *b* 5 May 1958; *Educ* Kilmarnock Acad, Univ of Glasgow (MB ChB), Univ of Wales Cardiff (LLB (Legal Aspects of Med)); *Career* dir of public health: Grimsby HA 1991–92, Scunthorpe and Grimsby 1992–96, Dyfed Powys HA 1996, Telford and Wrekin Primary Care Tst, Shropshire Co; currently head Legionnaires Dept Health Protection Agency; FFPHM 1998 (MFPHM 1991); *Style—* Dr Nick Phin

PHIPPARD, Sonia Clare; CBE (2015); da of Brig Roy Gordon Phippard, and Gillian Anne, *née* Menzies; *Educ* Wadhurst Coll, Somerville Coll Oxford; *m* 2001, Michael Hartley; *Career* joined civil service 1981; Cabinet Office (MPO) 1981–87, Dept of Educn and Science 1987–89, princ private sec to Cabinet Sec 1989–92, project dir Next Steps 1992–94, seconded Coopers & Lybrand 1995–97, dir Central Secretariat Cabinet Office 2000–01 (dep dir 1997–99), dir of sustainable agriculture and livestock products DEFRA 2001–06, dir food and farming (EU and analysis) DEFRA 2006–10, dir water and flood risk mgmnt DEFRA 2010–15, DG Environment and Rural DEFRA 2015–; *Recreations* amateur dramatics, food, time with friends; *Style—* Miss Sonia Phippard, CBE; ✉ c/o Nobel House, 17 Smith Square, London SW1P 3JR

PHIPPEN, Peter S; s of Dennis Phippen, of Worthing, W Sussex, and Margaret, *née* Sangster; *b* 9 February 1960; *Educ* Reading Sch, Churston GS, Fitzwilliam Coll Cambridge (MA); *m* 1983, Liz, *née* Walden; 4 c (Ben b 1988, Jessie b 1991, Harriet b 1993, Sam b 2000); *Career* IPC Magazines: grad trainee 1982–83, asst publisher 1983–84, assoc publisher 1984–86, mktg mangr 1986–87; BBC Magazines: mktg mangr 1987–88, mktg dir 1988–90, publishing dir (Radio Times and others) 1990–93, md 1993–97; md BBC Worldwide (UK) 1997–98; chief exec BBC Worldwide Americas 1998–2001, md BBC Magazines 2001–11; chm: Frontline Ltd, BBC Haymarket Exhibitions Ltd, Galleon Ltd, Origin Publishing Ltd, Sift 2012–; *Recreations* squash, triathlons, history, playing jazz piano, walking; *Clubs* Soho House; *Style—* Peter Phippen, Esq

PHIPPS, Matthew Llewelyn; s of Michael Phipps, of Bridgend, S Wales, and Sian, *née* Morgan; *b* 9 October 1966, Cardiff; *Educ* Cheltenham Coll, Univ of Reading, Univ of Westminster, Inns of Court Sch of Law; *m* 3 April 1999, Caroline, *née* Evans; 1 da (Caitlin b 17 May 2001), 1 s (Iolo b 31 Dec 2002); *Career* admitted slr 1999; slr specialising in liquor entertainment licensing; Eversheds 1995–2001, assoc Osborne Clark 2001–04, ptnr TLT Slrs 2004–; memb Law Soc 1999; *Recreations* rugby, wine, cooking; *Clubs* Cardiff and County, Newport Boat; *Style—* Matthew Phipps, Esq; ✉ TLT Solicitors, One Redcliff Street, Bristol BS1 6TP (☎ 0117 917 8020, e-mail mphipps@tltsolicitors.com)

PHOENIX, Prof David Andrew (Dave); OBE (2010), DL (Greater London 2015); s of Derek Phoenix, of Bolton, Lancs, and Edna, *née* Tate; *b* 26 February 1966, Daveyhulme, Gtr Manchester; *Educ* Univ of Liverpool (BSc, PhD, DSc), Open Univ (BA, MA, MBA); *m* 6 Aug 1994, Stephanie, *née* Bailey; 1 s (Adam b 11 April 1996), 2 da (Lauren b 18 Dec 1998, Rebecca b 13 June 2003); *Career* Univ of Central Lancs: inaugural head of forensic science 2000–03, prof of biochemistry 2000–, dean of science 2003–08, dep vice-chllr 2008–, chm UCLan Biotechnology Ltd (Shenzhen) 2010–13, founding chair UCLan Biomedical Technology Ltd (Shenzhen) 2011, founding chair and academic lead UCLan Cyprus 2011–13; vice-chllr and ceo London South Bank Univ 2014–; dir: Nat Centre for Univs and Business 2015–, Univs UK 2015–; chm Millionplus 2015; visiting conslt biochemistry Royal Preston Hosp 1996–2014, hon conslt in clinical biochemistry Lancs Teaching Hosps Fndn Tst 2014–; former UK rep European Ctee Biological Assocs; former visiting prof Moscow Inst of Physical Engrg, visiting prof Sichuan Univ China 2013–, visiting prof KCL 2014–; DCMS tstee Museum of Science and Industry Manchester; tstee: Darwin Acad, Kirkham GS, Science Museum Gp (PM's appt) 2015–; Individual Excellence Award from Vice Premier China Liu Yandong 2014; Hon DUniv Bolton 2013; Freeman Worshipful Co of Bakers 2016; CBiol 1991, CChem 1991, CMath 1999, FSB, FRSC, FIMA, fell Royal Soc of Medicine, sr fell HE Acad 2008, AcSS 2012, FRCPEd 2013, FRSA; Br Empire Silver Cross MOSI 2010; *Publications* Introductory Mathematics for Life Scientists (1997), Protein Targeting and Translocation (1998), Antimicrobial Peptides (2013), Novel Antimicrobial Agents and Strategies (2014); over 250 academic pubns; *Recreations* science, theatre, music; *Style—* Prof Dave Phoenix, OBE, DL; ✉ Office of the Vice Chancellor, London South Bank University, 103 Borough Road, London SE1 0AA (☎ 020 7215 6001, e-mail phoenixd@lsbu.ac.uk)

PIA, Paul Dominic; WS (1971); s of Joseph Pia (d 2001), and Louise, *née* Lombardi (d 1979); *b* 29 March 1947, Edinburgh; *Educ* Holy Cross Acad Edinburgh, Univ of Edinburgh (LLB), Univ of Perugia (Dip); *m* 9 July 1977, Anne Christine, *née* Argent; 3 da (Camilla Francis b 16 Sept 1980, Roberta Anne b 19 July 1985, Sophie-Louise b 24 April 1988); *Career* slr; trainee Lindsays WS 1968–70; ptnr Burness LLP (previously W & J Burness WS) 1974– (joined 1970); memb Scottish Cons and Unionist Assoc 1969–74, chm Edinburgh S Young Cons 1969–71; dir: Imaginate (Scottish int children's festival) 1989–94, Dewar Arts Awards 2002–07; memb Bd Japan Soc of Scotland 1990– (chm 1996–2000), tstee Big Issue Fndn Scotland 1998– (chm 2003–07), fndr memb Scottish N American Business Cncl (dir 2000–04), tstee Baxters Fndn/Gordon & Ena Baxter Fndn 2002–, memb Corp Governance Unit IOD 2003–04, ind memb Nominations Ctee Scottish Enterprise Edinburgh & Lothian 2005–07, assoc memb Scottish Fedn of Housing Assocs; chm project to create Edinburgh-Kyoto Friendship Garden at Lauriston Castle Edinburgh 2000; memb Law Soc of Scotland 1971, NP 1971; FInstD 1980; Care, Diligence and Skill: a corporate governance handbook for arts organisations (co-author, 1990, 5 edn 2002); *Recreations* hill walking, travel, languages, oriental culture; *Style—* Paul Pia, Esq, WS; ✉ 67 Woodfield Park, Edinburgh EH13 0RA (☎ 0131 441 7057); Burness Paull, 50 Lothian Road, Festival Square, Edinburgh EH3 9WJ (☎ 0131 473 6106, fax 0131 473 6006, e-mail paul@paulpia.com)

PIATKUS, Judith (Judy); da of Raphael Emmanuel Assersohn (d 1988), and Estelle Freda, *née* Richenberg (d 1993); *b* 16 October 1949; *Educ* South Hampstead HS, Regent Coll London (Dip), Regent Univ (MA); *m* 1, 5 Dec 1971 (m dis 1985), Brian John Piatkus; 1 s, 2 da; m 2, 30 Dec 1990, Cyril Bernard Ashberg; 1 step da; *Career* fndr and md Piatkus Books 1979–2007, fndr Conscious Café 2011, angel investor, strategic advsr to SMEs,

P

keynote speaker; Women in Publishing Pandora Award 2005, RNA Lifetime Achievement Award 2009, 100 Women of Spirit Award 2016; Little Book of Women's Wisdom by Judy Ashberg (2001), Lovers Wisdom (2004); *Recreations* enjoying conversations about consciousness; *Style—* Ms Judy Piatkus; ✉ e-mail info@judypiatkus.com, websites www.judypiatkus.com and www.consciouscafe.org, Twitter @judypiatkus

PIATT, Andrew; s of Kenneth Piatt, and Edna, *née* Williams; *b* 6 June 1964, Culcheth, Cheshire; *Educ* Culcheth HS, Univ of Southampton (LLB); *m* 17 April 1993, Keren, *née* Williams; 2 s (Adam b 25 March 1996, Gareth b 13 Feb 2000); *Career* called to the Bar 1987, admitted slr 1997; non-practising barr: South Ribble BC 1987–88, St Helens BC 1988–96; ptnr DLA Slrs 1996–2003, ptnr, head Nat Real Estate Gp and head of planning law Halliwells Slrs LLP 2003–10, ptnr and head of planning law Gateley plc Slrs 2010–; author of articles on planning law in Estates Gazette, Jl of Planning and Environmental Law and Local Government News; *Recreations* gardening, gym, skiing; *Style—* Andrew Piatt, Esq; ✉ Gateley plc Solicitors, Ship Canal House, 98 King Street, Manchester M2 4WU (☎ 0161 836 7724, fax 0161 836 7701)

PICARDA, Hubert Alistair Paul; QC (1992); s of Pierre Adrien Picarda (d 1985), and Winifred Laura, *née* Kemp (d 1988); *b* 4 March 1936; *Educ* Westminster, Magdalen Coll Oxford (MA, BCL, open exhibitioner), UCL (Bunnell Lewis prize for Latin verse); *m* 1, 4 March 1976 (m dis 1995), Ann Hulse, da of Stanley Stone; 1 s (Dominic Nicholas Piers b 7 March 1977), 1 da (Claudia Caroline Holly b 19 Feb 1979); m 2, 26 April 2000, Sarah Elizabeth, da of His Hon Judge Goss (d 1963); *Career* called to the Bar Inner Temple 1962, Profumo scholar 1963, admitted ad eundem Lincoln's Inn and Gray's Inn 1965, night lawyer with Daily Express and Sunday Express (Beaverbrook Newspapers) 1964–72, in practice Chancery Bar 1964–; memb Senate of Inns of Ct and Bar Cncl 1978–81; managing ed: Charity Law and Practice Review 1992–, Receivers Administrators and Liquidators Quarterly 1993–; memb Editorial Bd: Butterworths Jl of Int Banking and Fin Law, Tst Law Int, Jl of Business Law; visiting lectr in receivership law Malaysian Bar Cncl, Sabah Law Assoc and Law Socs of Singapore and Hong Kong 1994, visiting lectr in banking and derivative trading law Malaysian Bar Cncl and Advocates Assoc of Sarawak 1995 and Law Soc of Singapore and Malaysian Bar Cncl 1996, visiting lectr Singapore Legal Acad 2000–01, visiting lectr Univ of Melbourne 2012, visiting lectr Université de Montréal 2015; W A Lee Equity Lecture Queensland Univ of Technol Aust 2001; hon pres Charity Law Assoc 1992–; memb: Insolvency Lawyers' Assoc, Chancery Bar Assoc, Inst of Conveyancers (pres 2000); *Books* Picarda Law and Practice Relating to Charities (1977, 4 edn 2010), Picarda Law Relating to Receivers Managers and Administrators (1984, 4 edn 2006, supplement 2014); *Recreations* Andalusian baroque, Latin, Spain in WWII, Early Romantic music, conversation; *Clubs* Turf, Beefsteak, Pratt's, White's; *Style—* Hubert Picarda, Esq, QC

PICARDIE, Justine; *m* Hon Philip Astor; *Career* ed Harper's Bazaar 2012–; *Books* If the Spirit Moves You: Life and Love After Death (2002), Truth or Dare: A Book of Secrets Shared (2004), Wish I May (2004), My Mother's Wedding Dress: The Life and Afterlife of Clothes (2006), Daphne: A Novel (2008), Coco Chanel: The Legend and the Life (2010), Dior by Avedon (2015); *Style—* Ms Justine Picardie; ✉ Harper's Bazaar, Hearst, 72 Broadwick Street, London W1F 9EP

PICK, Prof John Morley; s of John Mawson Pick, of Ripon, N Yorks, and Edith Mary, *née* Morley; *b* 12 October 1936; *Educ* King Edward VI Sch Retford, Univ of Leeds (BA, PGCE), Univ of Birmingham (MA), City Univ (PhD); *m* 19 April 1960, Ann Clodagh, da of Sydney Simmons Johnson (d 1983), of Eastbourne, E Sussex; 1 s (Martyn b 1963), 1 da (Catherine b 1965); *Career* dir Dillington House Coll of Adult Educn and Arts Centre 1973–76, head of arts policy and mgmnt studies City Univ 1976–90, Gresham prof of rhetoric Gresham Coll 1983–88, prof of arts mgmnt City Univ 1985–91 (prof emeritus 1991–); visiting prof in arts mgmnt South Bank Univ 1997–2001, distinguished visiting scholar Univ at Buffalo NY 2006–; *Books* Arts Administration (1980), The State of The Arts (1981), The West End: Mismanagement And Snobbery (1983), The Theatre Industry (1984), The Modern Newspeak (1985), Managing The Arts? (1987), Arts in a State (1988), Vile Jelly (1991), Arts Administration: Politics, Bureaucracy and Management in the Arts (1995), Building Jerusalem: The Arts, Industry and the British Millennium (1999), Managing Britannia (2002), Mr Phipps' Theatre (2006), The Aesthetic Contract (2009), Ebb Tide; A Memoir (2016); *Recreations* theatre, writing, comedy; *Style—* Prof John Pick; ✉ 97A South Street, Eastbourne, East Sussex BN21 4LR

PICKARD, David Keith; s of Roger Willows Pickard (d 2007), and June Mary, *née* Golby (d 2010); *b* 8 April 1960; *Educ* King's Sch Ely, St Albans Sch, Corpus Christi Coll Cambridge (choral scholar, MA); *m* Elizabeth, *née* Finney; 2 s (Adam b 16 Feb 1994, Oliver b 22 Feb 1996); *Career* co mangr ROH 1984–87, administrator New Shakespeare Co 1987–89, md Kent Opera 1989–90, asst dir Japan Festival 1991 1990–92, artistic administrator European Arts Festival 1992–93, chief exec Orchestra of the Age of Enlightenment 1993–2001, gen dir Glyndebourne Festival Opera 2001–15, dir BBC Proms 2015–; tstee Shakespeare Globe Tst 2005–14; *Recreations* playing piano duets, cooking; *Style—* David Pickard, Esq; ✉ BBC Proms, Broadcasting House, London W1A 1AA

PICKARD, J Nigel; s of Ralph Pickard, and Jane, *née* Potts; *b* 10 March 1952, Worthing, West Sussex; *Educ* Truro Sch, Gregg Sch Southampton, Southampton Coll of Art (Dip); *m* 9 March 1974, Hazel; 2 s (Daniel b 5 Jan 1980, Matthew (twin) b 5 May 1982), 1 da (Rebecca (twin) b 5 May 1982); *Career* film ed 1972–77, floor mangr and asst dir 1977–79, prog dir 1979–83, exec prodr 1983–85, controller of children's progs TVS 1986–89, controller entertainment and drama features Scottish TV 1989–91, dir of progs Family Channel 1992–96, vice-pres prodns Flextech and gen mangr Challenge TV and Maidstone Studios 1997–98, controller CITV 1998–2000, controller CBBC 2000–02, dir of progs ITV 2002–06, gp ceo MEAA, UK Kids and family Zodiak Media 2006–14, ceo Spindrift Media 2014–, dir Dial Square 86 2014–, pres TRX 2015–, dir Nevision 2015–, non-exec dir Beano Studios 2016–; Special Award Children's BAFTA Awards 2006; memb BAFTA, FRTS; *Recreations* golf, walking, sailing, shooting; *Style—* Nigel Pickard, Esq; ✉ Spindrift Media, Peasridge Farmhouse, Frittenden, Kent TN17 2BD (e-mail nigel.spindrift@gmail.com); Dial Square 86, Somerset House, Strand, London WC2R 1LA (☎ 020 7257 9546, e-mail nigel.pickard@dialsquare86.com, nigel.pickard@trx.tv, n.pickard@nevision.com)

PICKARD, Prof John; *b* 11 September 1963; *Educ* Univ of Wales at Bangor (BMus, PhD), Royal Conservatory The Hague (Dutch govt scholarship); *Career* composer; studied with William Mathias then Louis Andriessen; lectr Univ of Wales Bangor 1989–93, prof of composition and applied musicology Univ of Bristol 2009– (sr lectr 1993–2009); compositions incl: 5 symphonies (No 3 cmmnd by BBC 1996), Piano Sonata, The Flight of Icarus (cmmnd by BBC 1991, London première BBC Proms 1996), Channel Firing (premièred BBC Nat Orch of Wales) 1993, String Quartets Nos 1 and 3 (cmmnd by Britten Quartet), String Quartet No 2 (cmmnd by Allegri Quartet), String Quartet No 4 (cmmnd by Sorrel Quartet), String Quartet No 5 (cmmnd by The Carr-Gregory Tst), Piano Concerto (cmmnd by Dresdner Sinfoniker) 2000, Agamemonon's Tomb (cmmnd by Huddersfield Choral Soc) 2008, Sixteen Sunrises (cmmnd by Nagoya Philharmonic Orchestra) 2014, various orchestral, choral brass band and chamber works; gen ed Elgar Complete Edition 2003–; *Recordings* Piano Sonata/ A Starlit Dome, String Quartets Nos 2–4, String Quartets Nos 1&5, Violin Sonata/ Piano Trio/ Valedictions/ Insomnia/ Snowbound, Gaia Symphony (symphony no 4), The Flight of Icarus/ The Spindle of Necessity/ Channel Firing, Sea-Change/ Piano Concerto/ Tenebrae; *Recreations* astronomy, gardening, swimming; *Style—* Prof John Pickard; ✉ c/o Bardic Edition, 2 George Street, Huntly, Aberdeenshire, Scotland AB54 8BT (☎ and fax 01296 428609, website www.johnpickard.co.uk); sales agent Schott Music Ltd, 48 Great Marlborough Street, London W1F 7BB (☎ 020 7534 0710)

PICKARD, Paul; *Career* portrait photographer, sittings incl: Queen Elizabeth II, Malala Yousafzai, Vivienne Westwood; *Style—* Paul Pickard; ✉ website www.paulpickard.com

PICKEN, Andrew; OBE (2006); s of Ian Picken, of Highgate, London, and Jo, *née* Powell (d 2000); *b* 27 March 1952, London; *Educ* Univ of Cambridge (MA), Univ of Sussex (MPhil), Open Univ (MSc); *m* 22 April 1978, Janet, *née* Mullins; 1 da (Judith b 19 Dec 1980), 1 s (Robert b 20 Dec 1983); *Career* prog devpt and trg offr President's Award Scheme VSO Kenya 1973–75, asst plant breeder Twyford Seeds Ltd 1975–77, Scientific Office Glasshouse Crops Res Inst 1977–85; Br Cncl: science offr Belgrade 1986–88, first sec (educn and science) Madras 1988–91, first sec (sci and technol) Ankara 1991–95, contract dir Manchester 1995–98, sr business mangr Manchester 1998–2002, dir Islamabad and acting dir Pakistan 2002–05, sr advsr Health Projects Manchester 2005–06, dep dir social devpt Indonesia 2006, dir Philippines 2006–09, sr govt advsr London 2010–12, dir Social Enterprise Europe 2013–; author of many and various glasshouse crop physiology pubns; former pres Littlehampton Rotaract Club; tstee: Gen Initiative, Village Water, Herts Action on Disability; *Publications* many and various glasshouse crop physiology; *Recreations* reading, history; *Clubs* Hatfield Rotary; *Style—* Andrew Picken, Esq, OBE; ✉ 32 Sherrardspark Road, Welwyn Garden City, Hertfordshire AL8 6JS

PICKEN, Ralph Alistair; yr s of late Dr David Kennedy Watt Picken, TD, JP, DL, of Cardiff, and late Liselotte Lore Inge, *née* Regensteiner; *b* 23 May 1955; *Educ* Shrewsbury, Univ of Birmingham (LLB); m Harold Bush-Howard, PhD (civil partnership converted 4 Feb 2006), yst s of Willie Bush Archbold, and Alice Howard Hoy, of Old Providence Island, Colombia; *Career* admitted slr 1980; conslt Trowers & Hamlins LLP, 2012–: joined 1981, resident Muscat 1981–86, ptnr 1984–2012, managing ptnr 1996–99; memb: Law Soc, Anglo-Omani Soc, City of London Solicitors Co; Freeman of the City of London; *Recreations* theatre, opera, travel, wine; *Clubs* MCC, Chatham Dining; *Style—* Ralph Picken, Esq; ✉ 15 Jeffreys Street, London NW1 9PS (☎ 07802 387717, e-mail jstreet@btinternet.com)

PICKERING, Alan Michael; CBE (2004); s of Frank Pickering, and Betty Pickering; *b* 4 December 1948, York; *Educ* Exhall Grange Sch Coventry, Univ of Newcastle upon Tyne (BA); *Career* clerical offr British Railways 1967–69, head of membership servs EETPU 1972–92, ptnr Watson Wyatt 1992–2008, chm BesTrustees plc 2009–; chm: Nat Assoc of Pension Funds 1999–2001, European Fedn for Retirement Provision 2001–04, Plumbing Industry Pension Scheme 2001–, Life Acad 2006–13, Royal Mail Statutory Pension Scheme 2012–; memb Occupational Pensions Bd 1992–97 (vice-chm 1995), non-exec dir Pensions Regulator 2005–13; memb Rules Ctee Br Horseracing Authy 2009–, memb Cncl Racehorse Owners Assoc 2011–, vice-pres Racehorse Owners Assoc 2015–; frequent contrib to numerous periodicals; assoc Pension Mgmnt Inst 1982; A Simpler Way to Better Pensions (2002); *Recreations* long-distance running as a participant, horse racing as an owner, travelling at home and abroad; *Clubs* Blackheath Harriers (pres 1992–93); *Style—* Alan Pickering, Esq, CBE; ✉ BesTrustees plc, Five Kings House, 1 Queen Street Place, London EC4R 1QS (☎ 020 7332 4100, fax 020 7332 4108, e-mail alan.pickering@bestrustees.co.uk)

PICKERING, John; s of Leslie Pickering (d 1982), and Audrey Margaret, *née* Green; *b* 23 July 1955, Rotherham, S Yorks; *Educ* Oakwood Comp Sch Rotherham, Thomas Rotherham Sixth Form Coll Rotherham, Univ of Manchester (LLB), Coll of Law Chester; *m* 20 Nov 1981, Julie; 1 da (Lauren Sarah b 26 Aug 1984), 1 s (Joseph John b 2 Feb 1989); *Career* admitted slr 1979; currently gp chief exec Irwin Mitchell (joined as articled clerk, ptnr 1980, nat head of personal injury 1984–2009); slr rep CMO's Advsy Gp on reform of the law on clinical negligence; pres Pan European Orgn of Personal Injury Lawyers (PEOPIL) 2004–09, sr fell Assoc of Personal Injury Lawyers (formerly Coll of Personal Injury Law), tstee Neurocare, tstee and vice-chair Child Brain Injury Tst 1995–2004; memb: Aust Lawyers Alliance, SA Assoc of Personal Injury Lawyers, American Assoc for Justice (memb Bd Govrs 1995–2009), Civil Justice Cncl 2013–; author of various articles for legal jls, co-ed Jordans Civil Court Service; memb: Law Soc (memb and assessor for Personal Injury Panel, memb Clinical Negligence Panel), Action against Medical Accidents (AvMA, memb Clinical Negligence Panel); *Recreations* theatre, music, tennis, motor sports, golf; *Clubs* Hallamshire Tennis and Squash, Abbeydale Golf; *Style—* John Pickering, Esq; ✉ Irwin Mitchell, Riverside East, 2 Millsands, Sheffield S3 8DT (☎ 0870 1500 100, e-mail john.pickering@irwinmitchell.com)

PICKERING, Prof John Frederick; s of William Frederick Pickering (d 1973), of Slough, Berks, and Jean Mary, *née* Clarke (d 2005); *b* 26 December 1939; *Educ* Slough GS, UCL (BSc, PhD, DSc); *m* 25 March 1967, Jane Rosamund, da of Victor William George Day (d 1993), of Bristol; 2 da (Rachel b 1970, Catherine b 1974); *Career* industrial market research exec 1961–62; lectr: Univ of Durham 1964–66, Univ of Sussex 1966–73; sr directing staff Admin Staff Coll Henley 1974–75; UMIST: prof of industrial economics 1975–88, vice-princ 1983–85, dean 1985–87; Univ of Portsmouth (formerly Portsmouth Poly): vice-pres 1988–90, actg pres 1990–91, dep pres 1991–92, dep vice-chllr 1992–94; conslt economist 1994–; prof of business strategy Univ of Bath 1997–2000; visiting prof: Univ of Durham Business Sch 1995–98, Univ of Southampton Sch of Mgmnt 2001–04; memb: Retail Prices Index Advsy Ctee 1974–95, MMC 1990–99, Competition Cmmn Appeal Tbnl 2000–03, Competition Appeal Tbnl 2003–11, Strategic Advsy Bd for Intellectual Property Policy 2008–10; memb Gen Synod C of E 1980–90, church cmmr 1983–90; pres BCMS-Crosslinks 1986–92; non-exec dir Staniland Hall Ltd 1987–94; tstee and chm VTCT 2004–06; memb and chm Rowlands Castle Parish Cncl 2011–16; memb Royal Economic Soc 1973, MInstD; FIMgt 1987, FRSA 1998; *Books* Resale Price Maintenance in Practice (1967), The Small Firm in the Hotel and Catering Industry (jtly, 1971), Industrial Structure and Market Conduct (1974), The Acquisition of Consumer Durables (1977), The Economic Management of the Firm (jt ed, 1984); *Recreations* cricket, classical music, theatre; *Clubs* IOD, Sussex CCC; *Style—* Prof J F Pickering; ✉ 1 The Fairway, Rowlands Castle, Hampshire PO9 6AQ (☎ 023 9241 2007)

PICKERING, Paul Granville; s of Arthur Samuel Pickering (d 1962), of Rotherham, S Yorks, and Lorna Cynthia, *née* Groocock; *b* 9 May 1952; *Educ* Royal Masonic Schs Bushey, Univ of Leicester (BA, Sports colours); *m* 11 Dec 1983, Alison, da of Albert Leslie Beckett; 1 da (Persephone Alyce b 1 Feb 1993); *Career* Thomson Graduate Trg Scheme, Latin America corr Now! magazine, columnist The Times, Sunday Times and Punch 1981–84, novelist 1984–; Br Cncl reading tour of France 1995; included in Best of Young British Novelists (WH Smith Top 10) 1989; memb Soc of Authors; FRGS; *Novels* Wild About Harry (1985), Perfect English (1986), The Blue Gate of Babylon (1989, New York Times Notable Book of the Year), Charlie Peace (1991), The Leopard's Wife (2010), Over The Rainbow (2012); *Anthologies* Winter's Tales (short story, 1989), Hakakawa Japan (short story, 1993) Oldie Magazine (short stories, 1999); *Plays* After Hamlet (New Grove Theatre, 1994), Beach (1998), Walk Her Home (Louvre Paris, 1999); *Film Script* Gypsy Wedding (2012); *Recreations* scuba diving, bird-watching; *Clubs* Holland Park Lawn Tennis, Chelsea Arts; *Style—* Paul Pickering, Esq; ✉ c/o Andrew Kidd, Aitken Alexander Associates Ltd, 18–21 Cavaye Place, London SW10 9PT (☎ 020 7373 8672, e-mail andrew@aitkenalexander.co.uk)

PICKERING OF KINTRADWELL, Ralph Bernard; s of George Cecil Pickering (d 2007), of Lockerbie, Dumfriesshire, and Janet, *née* McEachern; *b* 21 February 1958; *Educ* Dumfries Acad, Napier Univ (BA); *m* 26 April 1986 (m dis 2006), Fiona Margaret, da of Dr John Richard Campion Stubbs, of Sleaford, Lincolnshire; 1 s (Lewis John Fitzyork b 28 Oct 1990), 1 da (Ellen Mary Elizabeth b 5 May 1993); *Career* land manager and accountant; 5th laird of Kintradwell 1986–; land mangr Smiths Gore 1979–85, sr ptnr Pickering Gordon & Co 1985–91, with Norwich Union 1991–93, with Sony IT Europe 2001–08, Brussels Accountants 2008–14, with Fitzyork & Ptnrs 2015–; prop Fitzyork Estates 1986–, Decor 8 Interior Design Belgium 2003–05; chm Fitzyork Estates Ltd 2011–15, chm Hayman Commissioning Services SPRL 2011–14, ptnr Fitzyork Genealogists & Probate Researchers 2011–14, ceo Master Quality Healthcare Servs Ltd 2015–, chief economist Egudi Oil & Gas Exploration and Research 2016–; dir: Nith Tyne Developments Ltd 1988–91, Galpi Consulting Ltd 2007–11, Global Alliance SPRL 2010–; chm Pickering Mensah (Ghana) Ltd 2007–; elder Kirkbean Church 1990– (memb Congregational Bd 1987–2001, property convenor 1995–2001), elder St Andrews Church Brussels 2001– (property convenor 2003–05); treas: Kirkbean Sch Bd 1996–2000, African Enterprise Belgium 2009–11; chm Kirkbean Hall and Amenity Ctee 1993–97 and 1999–2000, chm Dumfries and Galloway Branch Architectural Heritage Soc of Scotland 2000–02 (memb Ctee 1998–), chm Global Finance Conslt Ltd Ghana 2015; cnslt Gold Plus Micro Finance Ltd Ghana 2015–; memb: Dumfries and Lockerbie Agric Soc 1978–2000, Scottish Landowners' Fedn 1987–2001, Kirkbean Community Cncl 1988–2000, Huddersfield and Dist Family History Soc 1989–; life memb Nat Tst for Scotland 1988–; Belgian coordinator Orphans' Future (Ukraine) 2006–; author of various articles on architecture; *Recreations* painting, fishing, gardening, domestic architecture, travel, antiques; *Clubs* Royal Over-Seas League; *Style*— Ralph Pickering of Kintradwell; ✉ Hillside, Lockerbie, Dumfriesshire DG11 2RJ (☎ 01576 203929, e-mail ralph_pickering@hotmail.com); Kintradwell, Brora, Sutherland; Monrovia Estate, Korforidua, Ghana

PICKETT, Prof John Anthony; CBE (2004); s of Samuel Victor Pickett (d 1983), of Glenfield, Leicester, and Lilian Frances, *née* Hoar; *b* 21 April 1945, Leicester; *Educ* King Edward VII GS, Univ of Surrey (BSc, PhD); *m* 11 July 1970, Ulla Birgitta, da of John Skålén; 1 da (Hilda Amelia b 14 Nov 1975), 1 s (Erik Jarl b 30 Jan 1981); *Career* postdoctoral fell UMIST 1970–72, sr scientist Chem Dept Brewing Res Fndn 1972–76, princ scientific offr Dept of Insecticides and Fungicides Rothamsted Experimental Station 1976–83, head Biological and Ecological Chem Dept Rothamsted Research 1984–2010, scientific dir Rothamsted Centre for Sustainable Pest and Disease Mgmnt 2007–10, scientific ldr of chemical ecology Rothamsted Research 2010–14; hon prof Univ of Nottingham 1991–, Michael Elliott distinguished research fell Rothamsted Research 2010–; chm Advsy Ctee Sch of Applied Chem Univ of N London 1993–95, hon memb Academic Staff Univ of Reading 1995–, external examiner Imperial Coll London and Univ of Sussex, cncllr Int Soc of Chemical Ecology 1991–2000 (vice-pres 1994, pres 1995), scientific advsr Int Fndn for Sci Stockholm 1996–, expert advsr Nat Strategy on Climate Change and Low Carbon Devpt Govt of Rwanda 2010–14, presenter of expert evidence Parly Office of Science and Technol (POST) to HoL on genetically modified insects and disease control 2015; chm: Working Gp on the Future of Sites of Special Sci Interest (SSSIs) Royal Soc 2000–01, Copus Grants Panel Royal Soc 2002–04, External Scientific Advsy Gp on Pesticides Gates Fndn 2005–, Royal Soc Pfizer Award Seminar 2011 and 2012, Panel Royal Soc DFID Capacity Building Intiative 2013–16 (memb Panel since 2012); memb: Visiting Gp IPO-DLO Netherlands 1993, Conference Grants Ctee Royal Soc 1997–99, Sectional Ctee Royal Soc 1997–2000 and 2007–09, Deutsche Akademie der Naturforscher Leopoldina 2001, Scientific Advsy Bd Max-Planck-Gesellschaft Inst of Chemical Ecology Jena Germany 2003– (chm 2007–), Governing Cncl Int Centre of Insect Physiology and Ecology (ICIPE) Nairobi 2005–06 and 2014 (chm 2007–13), Dorothy Hodgkin Fellowship Selection Panel Royal Soc 2006–08, Final Award Ctee Leverhulme-Royal Soc Africa Award 2008, Defence Scientific Advsy Cncl Ind Scientific and Technical Advice Register 2008–, Royal Soc Review Gp Royal Soc Policy Study on Biological Approaches to Enhance Food-Crop Prodn 2008, Medals and Awards Ctee Royal Soc 2009–11, Bd of Tstees Int Inst of Tropical Agriculture 2010–16, Scientific Advsy Bd Vector-Based Control of Transmission: Discovery Research (Bill and Melinda Gates Fndn Grand Challenges in Global Health supported prog under the auspices of the Fndn of the Nat Insts of Health USA) 2010–, Informal Research Advsy Gp (iRAG) on Research Policy Dept for Int Devpt 2010–13, HEFCE REF 2014 Sub-Panel 5 Biological Sciences 2010–14, Inst for Life Sciences External Advsy Ctee Univ of Southampton 2011, Review Panel for Sustainable Crop Prodn Research Int Devpt Prog 2011–14, Advsy Bd Integrated Striga Mgmnt in Africa 2012–, BBSRC Pool of Experts Responsive Mode Grants 2012–, Review Panel for grant proposals submitted to Global Innovation Initiative Br Cncl USA 2013–, Panel Research Excellence Framework 2014, Scientific Bd Agroscope Swtizerland 2014–, GM Science Update Panel Cncl for Science and Technol 2014 and 2015; assessor Grants for R&D Technology Strategy Bd 2011–, reviewer of the retrospective study of the Rockerfeller Prog on rice biotechnology research Bill and Melinda Gates Fndn 2013; chm Royal Soc Working Gp on Devpt for Biofuels 2006–07, Summer Science Exhbn Ctee (formerly Soiree Ctee) Royal Soc 2008– (chm 2010–12), ex-officio memb Hooke Ctee Royal Soc 2010–12, chair External Advsy Bd Sch of Chemistry Cardiff Univ 2015–, chair Technical Ctee on push-pull technology IBCARP Steering Ctee icipe 2015–; guest ed The Biochemist 1998; memb Editorial Bd: Jl of Chemical Ecology 1991–, Int Jl of Tropical Insect Sci 2006–, Phytochemistry Letters 2007–, Phytochemistry 2008–; ed in chief Philosophical Transactions B 2016–; memb BCPC Editorial Advsy Bd The Pesticide Manual 2011–; patron Butterfly World 2008–, tstee Br Crop Prodn Cncl (BCPC) 2014–; memb Ctee SAABMiller Award 2015–; memb Governing Body (as pres for Royal Soc) Uppingham Sch 2007–; Royal Soc Croonian Prize lectr 2008; The Rank Prize Nutrition and Crop Husbandry 1995, Int Soc of Chemical Ecology Silver Medal 2002, Wolf Fndn Prize in Agriculture 2008, Millennium Award ASSOCHAM's 9th Knowledge Millennium Summit New Delhi (and Millennium Address speaker) 2011, Int Congress of Entomology Cert of Distinction 2012; Hon DSc Univ of Nottingham, Hon BSc Univ of Surrey 2011; hon life memb Assoc of Applied Biologists (AAB) 2004, foreign memb Royal Swedish Acad of Agric and Forestry 2005, foreign assoc Nat Acad of Sciences 2014; CChem 1975; FRSC 1982, FRES, MACS 1993, FRS 1996 (memb Cncl 2000–02), MRI 1997, Hon FRES 2010 (pres 2014–16), hon memb Chemical Soc of Ethiopia 2010, memb Soc for Experimental Biology (SEB) 2015; *Publications* over 515 plus patents; *Recreations* jazz trumpet playing; *Style*— Prof John Pickett, CBE, FRS; ✉ Department of Biological Chemistry and Crop Protection, Rothamsted Research, Harpenden, Hertfordshire AL5 2JQ (☎ 01582 938321, fax 01582 762595, mobile 07720 430117, e-mail john.pickett@rothamsted.ac.uk)

PICKLES, Rt Hon Sir Eric; kt (2015), PC (2010), MP; *b* 20 April 1952; *Educ* Greenhead GS, Leeds Poly; *m* Sept 1976, Irene; *Career* cncllr Bradford Met DC 1979–91 (chm Social Servs Ctee 1982–84, chm Educn Ctee 1984–86, ldr Cons Gp 1987–91, ldr of the Cncl 1988–90), MP (Cons) Brentwood and Ongar 1992–; PPS to Min for Industry DTI 1993, vice-chm Cons Pty 1993–97, opposition frontbench spokesman on social security 1998–2001, shadow min for tport and for London 2001–02, shadow sec of state for local govt 2002–07, dep chm Cons Pty 2005–09, shadow sec of state for communities and local govt 2007–10, chm Cons Pty 2009–10, sec of state for communities and local govt 2010–15; memb Select Ctee: Environment 1992–93, Tport 1996–97, Environment, Tport and Regions 1997–; chm All Pty Film Industry Gp 1997–2002; memb Cons Pty Nat Union Exec Ctee 1975–91, nat chm Young Conservatives 1980–81; dep ldr Cons Gp on the Assoc of Met Authorities 1989–91, chm Cons Pty Nat Local Govt Advsy Ctee 1992– (memb 1985–); memb Cncl of Europe 1997–98; local govt ed Conservative Newsline 1990–; memb Yorks RHA 1982–90; *Recreations* films, opera, golf, bird watching; *Style*— The Rt Hon Sir Eric Pickles, MP; ✉ House of Commons, London SW1A 0AA

Pickstock, Samuel Frank (Sam); CBE (1989); s of Francis John Pickstock (d 1981), of Stafford, and Hilda Jane, *née* Billington (d 2012); *b* 10 August 1934; *Educ* King Edward VI GS Stafford; *m* 1957, Edith, da of Joseph Lawton (d 1980), of Hanley; *Career* dir: John McLean & Sons Ltd and its subsids 1976–94, Tarmac Properties Ltd and its subsids 1977–91, Tarmac plc 1984–94, Tarmac Atlantic Wharf Developments Ltd 1985–94; chief exec John McLean & Sons Ltd (chm subsids) 1981–94; dir: Countryside Properties plc 1994–2003, Eco Energy Controls Ltd 1995–, Stonepine Management Services Ltd 1996–; CCMI, FInstLEx, FInstD; *Recreations* as interested as ever in the politics of housing from 1918 to the present day and enthusiastically telling people about the Kli-mat Intelligent control for 'wet' central heating systems; *Style*— Sam Pickstock, Esq, CBE; ✉ The Crows Nest Holding, Coton End, Gnosall, Stafford (☎ 01785 822755); The Lodge at Crows Nest, Coton End, Gnosall, Stafford (☎ 01785 823173)

PICKTHORN, Sir James Francis; 3 Bt (UK 1959), of Orford, Co Suffolk; s of Sir Charles William Richards Pickthorn, 2 Bt (d 1995), and Helen Antonia, *née* Mann; *b* 18 February 1955; *Educ* Eton; *m* 17 Jan 1998, Clare, da of Brian Craig-McFeely; 2 s (William Edward Craig b 1998, George Arthur Henry b 2001); *Heir* s, William Pickthorn; *Career* chartered surveyor; ptnr Kinney & Green 1991–94, fndr Pickthorn estate agent and chartered surveyor 1994–; memb HAC; Liveryman Worshipful Co of Bowyers; *Recreations* sailing; *Style*— Sir James Pickthorn, Bt; ✉ 45 Ringmer Avenue, London SW6 5LP; Pickthorn (☎ 020 7621 1380, e-mail james.pickthorn@pickthorn.co.uk)

PICKUP, David Francis William; CB (2002); s of late Joseph Pickup, and Muriel, *née* Clark; *b* 28 May 1953; *Educ* Poole GS, Central London Poly, Inns of Court Sch of Law; *m* 1975, Anne Elizabeth Round; *Career* called to the bar 1976, called to the bar Gibraltar 1988; HM Treasy Slrs Dept: legal asst Litigation Div 1978–81, sr legal asst Energy Dept 1981–87, head Judicial Review Section Litigation Div 1987–88, princ establishment fin and security offr 1988–90, head Chancery Litigation Div 1990–91, head MOD Advsy Div 1991–95; the slr HM Customs & Excise 1995–2005, DG HM Revenue and Customs 2006–07, Attorney-Gen of the Falkland Islands 2007–11; *Recreations* golf, skiing, music, food and wine, travel; *Clubs* Kington Golf; *Style*— David Pickup, Esq, CB; ✉ Post House, Marston, Pembridge, Leominster, Herefordshire HR6 9JA (☎ 01544 388264, e-mail dfwp.aep@icloud.com)

PICKUP, Ronald Alfred; s of Eric Pickup (d 1981), of Chester, and Daisy, *née* Williams; *b* 7 July 1940; *Educ* King's Sch Chester, Univ of Leeds (BA), RADA; *m* 9 Aug 1964, Lans Talbot, da of Claude Traverse, of Encino, CA, USA; 1 s (Simon b 1971), 1 da (Rachel b 1973); *Career* actor; in rep Leicester 1964, first title role Shelley (Royal Court) 1965, Nat Theatre Co 1966–72; memb Global Co-operative for a Better World; Hon DLitt Univ of Chester 2010; *Theatre* roles incl: Rosalind in all-male As You Like It (NT), Long Day's Journey Into Night (NT), Richard II (NT), The Cherry Orchard (West End), Amy's View (RNT) 1997 and (Broadway) 1999 (nominated Olivier Award 1998), Romeo and Juliet (NT) 2001, Peer Gynt (NT) 2001, Proof (Donmar Warehouse) 2002, Look Back in Anger 2006, Uncle Vanya (Rose Theatre) 2008, Waiting For Godot (West End) 2011–12; *Television* incl: Verdi in Life of G Verdi 1979, Einstein in Life of Einstein (both European co-prodns), Jennie, Orwell (nominated BAFTA 1984), Fortunes of War, Behaving Badly 1988, Not with a Bang 1988, Time to Dance 1991, The Riff-Raff Element (BBC) 1992–93, The Rector's Wife (film for TV) 1993, The Cold Light of Day (Screen 2, BBC) 1994, Message for Posterity (BBC revival of Dennis Potter's work), Ruth Rendell's Case of Coincidence 1994, The Dying Day 1995, title role in Henry IV (adapted by John Caird for BBC) 1995, Hornblower 1998, Hetty Wainthropp Investigates, Casualty, Ivanhoe (6 part series), Dalziell & Pascoe (BBC), The Bill (ITV), Inspector Lynley Mysteries (BBC), Waking the Dead (BBC), Midsomer Murders (ITV) 2007, The Last Detective (ITV), Featherboy (BBC), Cambridge Spies (BBC), Worst Week of My Life 2005–07, Holby 2007, The Jury 2011, Pramface 2012, Atlantis (BBC) 2014, The Crown (Netflix) 2016; *Films* incl: Day of the Jackal, The Thirty Nine Steps, Never Say Never Again, The Mission, The Fourth Protocol, Eleni, My Friend Walter, Bring Me The Head of Mavis Davis, Breathtaking, The Secret Passage, Tulse Luper Suitcase, Evilenko, Greyfriars Bobby 2007, Prince of Persia 2008, The Best Exotic Marigold Hotel 2012, The Second Best Exotic Marigold Hotel 2014; *Recreations* walking, reading, listening to music, opera; *Style*— Ronald Pickup, Esq

PICKWOAD, Michael Mervyn; s of William Mervyn Pickwoad (d 1976), of Windsor and Ludham, and Anne Margaret, *née* Payne Cook (d 1992); *b* 11 July 1945; *Educ* St George's Sch Windsor Castle, Charterhouse, Univ of Southampton (BSc Eng); *m* 27 Oct 1973, Vanessa Rosemary, da of Leslie William Orriss, of Cookham, Berks; 3 da (Zoë b 1975, Katharine b 1977, Amy b 1979); *Career* film production designer; architectural models for Nat Tst 1972, series of four architectural drawings for Hugh Evelyn Prints 1973, exhibition design Treasures of the Mind (TCD Quatercentenary Exhibition) 1992, exhibitor Directors Eye (MOMA Oxford) 1996, gallery design for eastern art collection Ashmolean Museum Oxford 1997, exhbn design for 26 Characters (The Story Museum Oxford) 2014; memb: Georgian Gp, BAFTA, GBFD; *Television* incl: Ex 1991, Murder Most Horrid 1991, Running Late 1992, Class Act 1993, The Dying of the Light (YTV) 1994, Cruel Train (Screen 2) 1994, Witness Against Hitler (Screen 2) 1995, Kavanagh QC 1995, Element of Doubt (Carlton) 1996, Kavanagh QC 1997, Cider With Rosie (Carlton) 1998, A Rather English Marriage (Screen 2) 1998, David Copperfield (TNT Network) 1998, The Last of the Blonde Bombshells (BBC) 1999, The Sleeper (TV Film, BBC) 2000, Hans Christian Andersen, My Life as a Fairytale (Hallmark) 2001, Wild West (BBC) 2002, Death in Holy Orders (BBC) 2002, The Deal (Channel 4) 2003, Sad Cypress (LWT) 2003, The Hollow (LWT) 2003, Death on the Nile (LWT) 2003, Frances Tuesday (ITV Network) 2004, Archangel (BBC) 2004, The Queen's Sister (Channel 4) 2005, Sweeney Todd (BBC) 2005, Longford (Channel 4) 2006 (nomination BAFTA Awards), Towards Zero (ITV) 2006, Nemesis (ITV) 2006, Bertrams Hotel (ITV) 2006, Ordeal by Innocence (ITV) 2007, The Old Curiosity Shop (ITV) 2007, Lost in Austen (ITV) 2007, The Prisoner (AMC/ITV) 2008 (nominated ADG Award), Kidnap & Ransom (ITV) 2010, Doctor Who (BBC) 2010–16 (design for new Tardis interior 2011), Doctor Who 50th anniversary special The Day of the Doctor 2013, Class 2016; *Film* incl: Comrades 1985, Withnail and I 1986, The Lonely Passion of Judith Hearne 1987, How to Get Ahead in Advertising 1988, The Krays 1989, Let Him Have It 1990, Century 1992, Food of Love 1996, Honest 1999, High Heels, Low Lifes 2000; *Music Videos* incl: I'll Save the World (Eurythmics) 1999, 17 Again (Eurythmics) 1999; Architectural Models for National Trust (1972), series of four architectural drawings for Hugh Evelyn Prints (1973, change of section) model of St George's Chapel, Windsor, for quincentenary (1975), model of Lundy Island Lighthouse for The Landmark Tst (1975); *Recreations* architectural history, drawing, photography, sailing, history of transport; *Style*— Michael Pickwoad, Esq; ✉ 22 Beech Croft Road, Oxford OX2 7AZ (☎ 01865 511106, e-mail mandvpickwoad@hotmail.com); Casarotto Marsh Ltd, Waverley House, 7–12 Noel Street, London W1F 8GQ (☎ 020 7287 4450)

PICOT, Derek A; s of Leslie Picot (d 2002), and Dorothy, *née* Johnson (d 2010); *b* 11 March 1952, Jersey; *Educ* Queen's Coll Taunton, Ealing Hotel Sch (Dip); *m* 11 Dec 1981, Joanna,

P

née Boursin; 1 da (Dominique b 30 April 1984), 1 s (Stefan b 18 Feb 1986); *Career* Savoy Hotel Gp 1972–80, exec asst mangr Hilton Int 1980–84, resident mangr Mandarin Oriental 1984–86, gen mangr Sheraton London 1986–95, regnl dir Meridien Canada 1995–98, vice-pres Meridien London 1999–2001, regnl dir Meridien Aust 2002, regnl gen mangr Jumeirah London 2003–08, regnl vice-pres Europe and North Africa Jumeirah Int 2008–15, dir MRP Hotels 2016–; non-exec dir Wesley Hotel Gp; conslt Derek Picot Consultancy 2015–; tstee Sidney Lawton Music Tst; Master Innholder (tstee Master Innholders Charitable Tst); Freeman City of London; Hon DSc Univ of W London; fell Inst of Hospitality, hon fell Acad of Food and Wine 2010; *Publications* Hotel Reservations (1994); *Recreations* tennis, cycling, boating, skiing; *Style*— Derek Picot, Esq, FHI, MI; ✉ e-mail derek.picot@mrp-hotels.com

PICTON-TURBERVILL, Geoffrey; s of Wilfrid Picton-Turbervill (d 2002), and Shirley, *née* Masser; *b* 11 May 1959; *Educ* Marlborough, ChCh Oxford (MA), Guildford Coll of Law; *m* 27 June 1987, Mary Teresa, da of David Mowbray Balme; 2 s (Harry David b 23 Oct 1990, Thomas Joshua b 11 Nov 1995), 2 da (Lucy Charlotte b 19 Sept 1992, Isabel Cara b 27 April 1997); *Career* trainee slr Farrer & Co 1983–85; Ashurst 1986–: asst slr 1986–90, assoc ptnr 1990–94, ptnr 1994– (head of global energy specialising in oil and gas transactions and other energy projects and related fin transactions 2004–14), resident ptnr New Delhi Office 1994–95; memb: Law Soc, Int Bar Assoc, Energy Inst, Assoc of Int Petroleum Negotiators, RIIA; Int Energy Lawyer of the Year England 2014; *Publications* Oil & Gas: A Practical Handbook (2009 and 2015), Global Legal Insights – Energy (2013); *Recreations* family, music, sport; *Clubs* MCC, Vincent's (Oxford); *Style*— Geoffrey Picton-Turbervill, Esq

PIDD, Prof Michael; s of Ernest Pidd, of Sheffield, and Marion, *née* Clark; *b* 3 August 1948, Sheffield, S Yorks; *Educ* High Storrs GS Sheffield, Brunel Univ (BTech), Univ of Birmingham (MSc), Univ of Lancaster (PhD); *m* 2 Jan 1971, Sally Anne, da of Eric Victor Nutt, of London; 2 da (Karen b 18 Aug 1977, Helen b 22 Jan 1981); *Career* team leader operational res Cadbury Schweppes Ltd 1971–75, lectr in operational res Aston Univ 1975–79; Lancaster Univ: lectr then sr lectr in operational res 1979–92, prof of mgmnt studies 1992–96, prof of mgmnt science 1996–, head of Dept of Mgmnt Science 1997–2000, assoc dean (research) Mgmnt Sch 2002–06; pres Operational Res Soc 2000–01, chair Business and Mgmnt Study Panel (i36) RAE 2008, chair Business and Mgmnt Study Panel (C19) REF 2014; winner President's medal OR Soc; memb: INFORMS, Operational Res Soc, Acad of Mgmnt, Br Acad of Mgmnt; companion of operational research; FBAM, AcSS; *Publications* Computer Simulation in Management Science (1984, 1988, 1992, 1997 and 2004), Computer Modelling for Discrete Simulation (1989), Tools for Thinking: Modelling in Management Science (1996, 2003 and 2009), System Modelling: Theory and Practice (2004), Measuring the Performance of Public Services: Theory and Practice; numerous jl papers; *Recreations* fell-walking, church activities; *Style*— Prof Michael Pidd; ✉ Department of Management Science, The Management School, Lancaster University, Bailrigg, Lancaster LA1 4YX (☎ 01524 593870, fax 01524 844885, e-mail m.pidd@lancaster.ac.uk)

PIDGEON, Caroline Valerie; MBE (2013), AM; da of Eric Pidgeon, and Valerie Pidgeon; *b* 29 September 1972, Eastleigh, Hants; *Educ* Univ of Wales Aberystwyth (BScEcon); *m* 22 July 2006, Paul Miles; 1 s (Henry b 25 July 2013); *Career* previously with: Guy's and St Thomas's NHS Fndn Tst, Croydon HA, Brent Cncl; cncllr Southwark BC 1998–2010, memb London Assembly (Lib Dem) London (list) 2008–; tstee Centre for Literacy in Primary Educn; *Recreations* cinema, modern art; *Style*— Ms Caroline Pidgeon, MBE, AM; ✉ GLA, City Hall, The Queen's Walk, London SE1 2AA (☎ 020 7983 4362, e-mail caroline.pidgeon@london.gov.uk, website www.carolinepidgeon.org, Twitter @CarolinePidgeon)

PIDGLEY, Anthony William; CBE (2013); s of William Pidgley (d 1967), of Hersham, Surrey, and Florence, *née* Smith (d 1990); *b* 6 August 1947; *Educ* Ambleside Sch, Hersham Surrey; *m* 1, 7 May 1966, Ruby Theresa, da of Walter John Williams, of East Molesey, Surrey; 1 s (Tony b 17 Sept 1968), 1 da (Tania b 12 June 1966); m 2, 21 Feb 1999, Sarah Jane, *née* Hill; 2 da (Annabella b 18 Nov 2004, Jessica b 6 March 2007); *Career* fndr P & J Plant Hire 1963 (sold business 1968), dir Crest Nicholson plc (formerly Crest Homes) 1968–75, jt fndr The Berkeley Group plc 1976–; pres London Chamber of Commerce; tstee: The Berkeley Fndn, Princess Alice Hospice, Sir Simon Milton Fndn, Open City; vice-pres Wildfowl and Wetland Tst; SBStJ 1987; *Recreations* shooting; *Clubs* Ritz, Peak Carlton Towers, Tramps; *Style*— Anthony Pidgley, Esq, CBE; ✉ The Berkeley Group plc, Berkeley House, 19 Portsmouth Road, Cobham, Surrey KT11 1JG (☎ 01932 868555, fax 01932 868667)

PIERCE, David Glyn; s of Gwilym John Pierce, of London, and Hilda Alice Pierce; *b* 1942; *Educ* Stationers' Co Sch London, Univ of Exeter (BA); *m* 1, 1963, Anne Valerie Sherwood; 1 s (Adam b 1967), 1 da (Rebecca b 1970); m 2, 9 Feb 1991, Victoria Isobel, da of Samuel Seymour, of Seattle, Washington, USA; 1 da (Alexandra b 1988), 1 s (Marcus b 1992); *Career* TV time buyer Garland Compton 1964–68 (media trainee 1963), head of Media Gp Foote Cone & Belding 1968–77, head of TV buying Everetts 1977–82; Media Campaign Services: joined 1982, assoc dir responsible for planning and research 1987–; MCAM 1981; *Recreations* competitive cycling, memb Velo Club des Londres; *Style*— David Pierce, Esq; ✉ Media Campaign Limited, 20 Orange Street, London WC2H 7ED (☎ 020 7389 0800, fax 020 7839 6997)

PIERCY, Prof Nigel Francis; s of Gilbert Piercy (d 1984), of Cambridge, and Helena Gladys, *née* Sargent (d 2001); *Educ* Cambridge GS for Boys, Heriot-Watt Univ (BA, DLitt), Univ of Durham (MA), Univ of Wales (PhD); *m* 1 (m dis), (Patricia) Jean; 1 s (Niall Christopher b 1979); m 2, Stephanie Monica, da of Eric James Oscar Burges (d 1991); m 3, Nikala; *Career* planner Amersham International 1974–77; sr lectr Newcastle Poly 1977–81 (lectr 1972–74); Univ of Wales: lectr 1981–83, sr lectr 1983–86, reader 1986–88, prof of mktg and strategy Cardiff Business Sch 1988–96, Sir Julian Hodge chair in mktg and strategy Cardiff Business Sch 1996–2001, prof of strategic mktg and dir strategic sales res consortium Cranfield Univ 2002–03 (head Mktg Gp 2003); Univ of Warwick prof of mktg 2003–, chair of Sales and Account Mgmnt Research Unit, chair of Sales and Strategic Customer Mgmnt Network, assoc dean Warwick Business Sch 2009–13; dean Sch of Mgmnt Univ of Swansea 2013–15; visiting prof: Neeley Sch of Business Texas Christian Univ 1993–94, Haas Sch of Business Univ of Calif Berkeley 1994, Fuqua Sch of Business Duke Univ NC 1999, Univ of Vienna 2003; Author of the Year UK Inst of Mktg 1980–82; FCIM 1988; *Books* Export Strategy (1982), Managing Marketing Information (with M Evans, 1983), The Management Implications of New Information Technology (ed, 1984), Marketing Organisation (1985), Management Information Systems (ed, 1986), Marketing Budgeting (1986), Preparing Marketing for the New Millenium (ed, 1991), Market-Led Strategic Change (1991, 4 edn 2009), Marketing Stategy and Competitive Positioning (jt author, 1998, 5 edn 2011), Strategic Management: Strategizing Your Way to the Future (1999), Tales From the Marketplace: Stories of Revolution, Reinvention and Renewal (1999), Strategic Marketing (with D Cravens, 10 edn 2012), Total Integrated Marketing (jt author, 2003), Strategic Customer Management: Strategising the Sales Organisation (jt author, 2009), Principles of Marketing (jtly, European edn, 6 edn 2012); *Style*— Prof Nigel Piercy; ✉ 11 Johnsons Field, Olney, Buckinghamshire MK46 5JF (mobile 07786 390004, e-mail nigelpiercy@aol.com)

PIERRE, Antony David (Tony); s of Jean Pierre, of Chislehurst, Kent, and Sara Fajga, *née* Libchaber; *b* 25 February 1956; *Educ* Alleyn's Sch Dulwich, Cass Business Sch (BSc); *m* 27 May 1990, Michelle Linda, da of late Bernard Langdon; 1 da (Klara Sophie b 2 Aug 1991), 1 s (Magnus George b 11 May 1995); *Career* CA 1981, currently ptnr Baker Tilly Corp Finance; FCA 1992 (ACA 1982); FRSA; *Recreations* skiing, squash, tennis, theatre, opera; *Clubs* RAC; *Style*— Tony Pierre, Esq; ✉ Baker Tilly, 2 Bloomsbury Street, London WC1B 3ST (☎ 020 7413 5100, fax 020 7413 5101, e-mail tony.pierre@bakertilly.co.uk)

PIERS, Sir James Desmond; 11 Bt (I 1661); s of Sir Charles Robert Fitzmaurice Piers, 10 Bt (d 1996); *b* 24 July 1947; *m* 1975, Sandra Mae Dixon; 1 da (Christine Sarah b 1976), 1 s (Stephen James b 1979); *Heir* s, Stephen Piers; *Career* barr and slr; ptnr Fasken, Martineau & DuMoulin; *Style*— Sir James Piers, Bt; ✉ Fasken, Martineau & DuMoulin, 2100–1075 West Georgia Street, Vancouver, BC, Canada V6E 3G2 (☎ 00 1 604 631 4769, fax 00 1 604 631 3232, e-mail jpiers@van.fasken.com)

PIERS, Martin James; s of Karl Piers, of Ewell, Surrey, and Meryl Menzies; *b* 12 September 1954; *Educ* Hertford GS, Univ of Southampton (LLB); *m* 26 Feb 1993, Ana Maria, da of Raphael Ortega, of Malaga, Spain; *Career* admitted slr 1979; ptnr Gouldens (latterly Jones Day) 1983–2007 (head Europe Employment Law Gp), global head of legal recruitment Hudson 2007–; lectr on dir personal liability and employment law; contrib business law section FT; memb: Employment Lawyers Assoc, European Employment Lawyers Assoc; *Books* Guide to Directors and Officers Liability and Loss Prevention (1989); *Recreations* theatre, tennis, walking; *Clubs* RAC; *Style*— Martin Piers, Esq; ✉ website www.hudson.com

PIETERSEN, Kevin Peter; MBE (2006); s of Jannie Pietersen, and Penny Pietersen; *b* 27 June 1980, Pietermaritzburg, South Africa; *Educ* Maritzburg Coll, Univ of South Africa; *m* 2007, Jessica Taylor; 1 s (Dylan b 2010); *Career* cricketer; clubs: KwaZulu-Natal 1998–2000, Nottinghamshire CCC 2001–04, Hampshire CCC 2005–10, Surrey CCC 2010–; England: 104 Test caps, 136 one day appearances, 31 Twenty20 appearances, capt 2008–09, one day debut v Zimbabwe 2004, Test debut v Australia 2005 (memb Ashes winning team), memb squad World Cup WI 2007, memb squad Twenty20 World Cup 2007; Emerging Player of the Year and One-Day Player of the Year Int Cricket Cncl Awards 2005; *Publications* Crossing the Boundary (2006); *Style*— Mr Kevin Pietersen, MBE; ✉ website www.kevinpietersen.com

PIGGOT, James A (Jay); *Educ* Univ of Cardiff (BA), Pembroke Coll Cambridge (PGCE), Univ of Liverpool (MA); *m* Poppy; 3 c; *Career* English teacher Millfield Sch Somerset then Eton until 2006; headmaster: Campbell Coll Belfast 2006–12, Epsom Coll 2012–; *Style*— Jay Piggot, Esq; ✉ The Headmaster's House, Epsom College, Epsom, Surrey KT17 4JQ (☎ 01372 821004, fax 01372 821005, e-mail headmaster@epsomcollege.org.uk, website www.epsomcollege.org.uk)

PIGOT, Sir George Hugh; 8 Bt (GB 1764), of Patshull, Staffs; s of Maj-Gen Sir Robert Anthony Pigot, 7 Bt, CB, OBE (d 1986), and his 1 w, Honor, *née* Gibbon (d 1964); *b* 28 November 1946; *Educ* Stowe; *m* 1, 2 Dec 1967 (m dis 1973), Judith Sandeman, er da of late Maj John Hele Sandeman Allen, RA; 1 da (Melanie Barbara b 4 Dec 1969); m 2, 2 Feb 1980 (m dis 1993), Lucinda Jane, yr da of Donald Charles Spandler; 2 s ((George) Douglas Hugh b 17 Sept 1982, (Robert) Edward Richard b 26 Sept 1984); m 3, 5 April 2006 (m dis 2008), Odette Kruger, yr da of Walter Stanley, of Port Elizabeth, South Africa; *Heir* s, Douglas Pigot; *Career* with Coutts & Co 1965–67, Hogg Robinson & Gardner Mountain 1967–69; freelance photographer 1970–77, founded Padworth Fisheries (trout farm) 1977, chm and md Padworth Fisheries Ltd 1981–95, mgmnt conslt Positive Response 1995–; dir Southern Trout Ltd 1993–95 (md 1994–95), md Custom Metalcraft Ltd 1998–, dir Integrated Fire Protection Ltd 2008–; memb Cncl British Trout Assoc 1986–93 (hon treas 1990–92); sec-gen Residential Sprinkler Assoc 1998–2003 (administrator 2007–), chief exec Fire Sprinkler Assoc 2003–2007; *Recreations* trout, classic cars, golf; *Style*— Sir George Pigot, Bt; ✉ Mill House, Mill Lane, Padworth, Berkshire RG7 4JX (☎ 0118 971 2322, fax 0118 971 3015)

PIGOTT-SMITH, Timothy Peter (Tim); s of Harry Thomas Pigott-Smith (d 2005), and Margaret Muriel, *née* Goodman (d 2006); *b* 13 May 1946; *Educ* Wyggeston Boys GS Leicester, King Edward VI GS Stratford-upon-Avon, Univ of Bristol (BA), Bristol Old Vic Theatre Sch; *m* 1972, Pamela, da of Alfred Miles; 1 s (Tom Edward b 1976); *Career* actor, director and writer; govr Bd RSC 2005, govr Bd Hampstead Theatre 2010; Hon DLitt: Univ of Leicester, Univ of Bristol; *Theatre* numerous tours and rep incl: Birmingham, Cambridge, Nottingham and Bristol; Bristol Old Vic 1969 (incl: Major Barbara, As You Like It), Prospect Theatre 1970–71 (incl: Much Ado About Nothing, Boswell's Johnson, Hamlet (tour and West End)), RSC 1972–75 (incl: Roman Plays, Cymbeline, Dr Watson in Sherlock Holmes (London and Broadway), RNT 1987–88 (incl: Coming into Land, Octavius Caesar in Antony & Cleopatra, Henry Moule in Entertaining Strangers, Winter's Tale, Cymbeline, Tempest); other credits incl: Traps (Royal Court) 1977, Benefactors (Vaudeville) 1984, Bengal Lancer (Leicester Haymarket and Lyric Hammersmith) 1985, Old Times 1993, Mr Rochester in Jane Eyre (Playhouse) 1993–94, Robert Ross in The Picture of Dorian Gray (Lyric Hammersmith) 1994, Retreat (Orange Tree) 1995, The Letter (Lyric Hammersmith) 1995, The Alchemist, Mary Stuart (RNT) 1996, Heritage (Hampstead Theatre Club) 1997, The Iceman Cometh (Almeida, Old Vic and Broadway) 1998–99, Five Kinds of Silence (Lyric Hammersmith) 2000, Julius Caesar (Barbican) 2002, Christmas Carol (Lyric Hammersmith) 2002, Mourning Becomes Electra (RNT) 2003, Hecuba (Donmar Warehouse) 2004, Women Beware Women (RSC) 2006, See How They Run (Duchess) 2006, Pygmalion (Theatre Royal Bath and nat tour) 2007 and 2008 and (Old Vic) 2008, Little Nell (Theatre Royal, Bath) 2007, Enron (Noel Coward Theatre) 2010 (nomination Best Supporting Actor Olivier Award 2010), Educating Rita (Trafalgar Studios) 2010, A Delicate Balance (Almeida) 2011, King Lear (W Yorks Playhouse) 2011, Prospero in The Tempest (Theatre Royal Bath) 2012, Stroke of Luck (Park Theatre Finsbury Park) 2014, Who's Afraid of Virginia Woolf (Bath Theatre Roya) 2014, Charles III (Almeida and Wyndhams Theatre) 2014; Compass Theatre (artistic dir 1989–92) incl: Julius Caesar, Amadeus, Royal Hunt of the Sun (dir) 1989, Playing the Wife (dir); also dir Company by Samuel Beckett (Edinburgh, Fringe First Award) 1987, Hamlet (Regent's Park) 1994, The Real Thing (nat tour); *Television* incl: The Glittering Prizes, Wings, Eustace and Hilda, The Lost Boys, Henry IV (part 1), Measure for Measure, Fame is the Spur, School Play, Francis Crick in Life Story, The True Adventures of Christopher Columbus, The Bullion Boys, The Shadowy Third, No Mama No, I Remember Nelson, The Traitor, Struggle, Wilderness Years, Ronald Merrick in Jewel in the Crown (BAFTA, TV Times, Broadcasting Press Guild Best Actor Awards), The Chief, Calcutta Chronicles (documentary), Innocents, The Vice, Pompeii, Eroica, North and South, Taken at the Flood, Holby Blue, Midsomer Murders, Foyle's War 2009, On Expenses 2009, Money 2009, The Little House 2010, The Hour 2011, Strike Back 2012, Downton Abbey 2012, Wodehouse in Exile (BBC 4) 2012, Suspicions of Mr Whicher, Great Train Robbery 2013, Bletchley Circle 2013, 37 Days 2013; *Film* incl: Aces High, Joseph Andrews, Sweet William, The Hunchback of Notre Dame, The Day Christ Died, Richard's Things, Clash of the Titans, Escape to Victory, State of Emergency, Remains of the Day, Bloody Sunday, Laissez Passer, Gangs of New York, The Four Feathers, Alexander, Entente Cordiale, V for Vendetta, Fly Boys, Quantum of Solace, Alice in Wonderland, Red 2 2012, Jupiter Ascending; *Books* Out of India (anthology, 1986), Baker Street Mysteries (series incl The Dragon Tattoo (2007), Rose of Africa (2009) and The Shadow of Evil (2009)); *Recreations* music, reading; *Clubs* 2 Brydges Place, BAFTA, MCC; *Style*— Tim Pigott-Smith

PIKE, Malcolm J; *Career* admitted slr 1984; slr specialising in employment law; ptnr Addleshaw Goddard 1992– (divnl managing ptnr Commercial Services Div, head

Manchester Office); chm Rugby Football League Contract Disputes Panel; memb: Int Bar Assoc, Employment Lawyers Assoc, Bd European Employment Lawyers Assoc; Butterworth's Encyclopaedia of Forms and Precedents (advsy ed and contrib), Essential Facts Employment (legal ed), The Lawyers Factbook (ed and contrib), Jordan's Employment Law (contrib); *Style*— Malcolm Pike, Esq; ✉ Addleshaw Goddard, 100 Barbirolli Square, Manchester M2 3AB (☎ 0161 934 6443, e-mail malcolm.pike@addleshawgoddard.com)

PIKE, Rosamund; *Career* actress; judge Costa Book Award 2008; *Theatre* Hitchcock Blonde (Royal Court and Lyric Theatre), Summer & Smoke (Nottingham Playhouse, Apollo Theatre London), Gaslight (Old Vic Theatre); *Television* Wives and Daughters, Trial & Retribution IV, Love in a Cold Climate, Foyle's War; *Film* A Rather English Marriage, Die Another Day, Promised Land Hotel, The Libertine (Best Supporting Actress Br Ind Film Awards 2005), Pride and Prejudice, Doom, Devil You Know, Fracture, Fugitive Pieces, In Education, Surrogates, An Education, Gone Girl; *Style*— Ms Rosamund Pike; ✉ c/o United Agents Ltd, 12–26 Lexington Street, London W1F 0LE (☎ 020 3214 0800, fax 020 3214 0801, website www.unitedagents.co.uk)

PILCHER, Dr Rosamunde; OBE (2002); *Career* writer; Hon LLD Univ of Dundee 2010; *Books* incl: A Secret to Tell (1955), April (1957), The Day of the Storm (1960), On my Own (1965), Sleeping Tiger (1967), Another View (1969), The End of Summer (1971), Snow in April (1972), The Empty House (1973), Under Gemini (1977), Wild Mountain Thyme (1980), The Carousel (1983), Voices in Summer (1985), The Shell Seekers (1988), The Blue Bedroom and Other Stories (1990), September (1990), Another View (1990), Flowers in the Rain and Other Stories (1991), Coming Home (1995), The Key (1996), Winter Solstice (2000); *Style*— Dr Rosamunde Pilcher, OBE

PILGER, John Richard; s of Claude Harold Pilger (d 1989), and Elsie, *née* Marheine (d 1989), of Sydney; *b* Sydney; *Educ* Sydney HS; *Children* 1 s (Sam b 1973), 1 da (Zoe b 1984); *Career* journalist, film-maker and author; trained with Sydney Daily Telegraph and Sunday Telegraph; formerly with: Reuter London, Daily Mirror, World in Action (Granada TV), ATV/Central TV; has written for: Daily Mirror, New Statesman, New York Times, Los Angeles Times, The Nation, Guardian, Independent, The Age, Aftonbladet, Il Manifesto; war corr: Vietnam, Cambodia, Indo-Pakistan, Biafra, Middle East; has made 60 documentary TV films, many with late David Munro, notably Year Zero – The Silent Death of Cambodia (1979), Death of a Nation, the Timor Conspiracy (1994), Inside Burma: Land of Fear (1996), The War on Democracy (2007), The War You Don't See (2010) and Utopia (2013–14), The Coming War on China (2016); Edward Wilson fell Deakin Univ Aust 1995, visiting prof Cornell Univ NY; awards incl: Descriptive Writer of the Year 1966, Reporter of the Year 1967, Journalist of the Year 1967, International Reporter of the Year 1970, News Reporter of the Year 1974, Campaigning Journalist of the Year 1977, Journalist of the Year 1979, Reporter Sans Frontières 1980, UN Media Peace prize 1980, UN Media Gold Medal 1981, George Foster Peabody Award (US) 1990, Richard Dimbleby Award (BAFTA) 1991, American Acad Award (Emmy) 1991, Sophie Prize for Human Rights (Norway) 2003, RTS Award 2005, Sydney Peace Prize 2009, Grierson Tstees Award for Documentary Film-making 2011; Hon DLitt: Staffordshire Univ 1994, Kingston Univ 1999, Rhodes Univ SA 2008; Hon DPhil Dublin City Univ 1995, Hon Dr Arts Oxford Brookes Univ 1997, Hon DLaws Univ of St Andrews 1999, Hon DUniv Open Univ 2001, Hon DPhil Rhodes Univ South Africa, Hon DLitt Lincoln Univ; memb NUJ; *Books* The Last Day (1975), Aftermath: the Struggle of Cambodia and Vietnam (1983), The Outsiders (1984), Heroes (1986), A Secret Country (1989), Distant Voices (1992), Hidden Agendas (1998), The New Rulers of the World (2002), Tell Me No Lies: Investigative Journalism and its Triumphs (ed, 2004), Freedom Next Time (2006–07); *Recreations* swimming, sunning, mulling, reading; *Style*— John Pilger, Esq; ✉ 57 Hambalt Road, London SW4 9EQ (☎ 020 8673 2848, e-mail jpilger2003@yahoo.co.uk, website www.johnpilger.com)

PILGRIM, Martin George; s of George Pilgrim (d 1997), of Gillingham, Kent, and Audrey, *née* Dowden (d 2006); *b* 10 February 1950, London; *Educ* Gillingham GS, Univ of Kent at Canterbury (MA); *m* 1974, Angela, *née* Staples; 2 da (Eleanor b 1981, Ruth b 1984); *Career* various finance posts Kent CC 1968–81, under sec (finance) Assoc of Met Authorities 1981–96, dep sec Assoc of Met Authorities 1996–97, chief exec London Cncls (formerly Assoc of London Govt) 1997–2007; chair London Sustainability Exchange 2007–15; memb Bd Film London 2005–11; hon treas: Daycare Tst 2007–13, Family Rights Gp 2011–, Family and Childcare Tst 2013–; Prince's Tst: tstee 2009–10, chm England Cncl 2009–13, memb Nat Advsy Bd 2010–13; tstee Young Women's Tst (formerly Platform 51) 2013–, tstee Diana Award 2013, dir Swanswell 2014; author of articles in academic jls and local govt press; CIPFA 1973; *Recreations* keeping fit, hill walking, moderate skiing, France and French; *Style*— Martin Pilgrim, Esq; ✉ 73 Hamelin Road, Gillingham, Kent ME7 3ER (☎ 01634 574852, e-mail mpilgrim@easynet.co.uk)

PILKINGTON, Lionel Alexander (Leo); s of Maj Arthur Henry Lionel Alexander Pilkington, and Pauline Eva, *née* Cox; *b* 5 August 1947; *Educ* Stowe, Keele Univ (BA); *Partner* Prof Alison Clarke; *Career* called to the Bar Inner Temple 1974; in practice 1974–80, ed Euro Law Centre 1980–85, info offr Clifford Chance 1985–90, sr crown prosecutor 1990–2001 and 2004–05, Crown Advocate 2005–16; memb Police Complaints Authy 2001–04; *Recreations* squash, opera, other (classical) music, photography, reading; *Clubs* RAC; *Style*— Leo Pilkington, Esq; ✉ 37 Albert Square, London SW8 1BY (☎ 020 7582 3196, fax 020 7273 6401, mobile 07720 061894, e-mail leopilkington@gmail.com)

PILKINGTON, Stephen Charles (Steve); CBE (2005), QPM (1998); s of Charles Leonard Pilkington, of Hampshire, and Joan, *née* Herd; *Educ* Andover GS, Queen Elizabeth Coll London (BSc, PhD); *m* Anne; 3 s; *Career* Met Police: joined 1972, sergeant 1976–78, inspr 1978–82, i/c unit HQ East Dulwich 1982–84, promoted to chief inspr 1984–87, (seconded to Police Exec Research Forum Washington DC 1984), superintendent 1987–89, divnl superintendent then chief superintendent 1989–94, cdr 1994–96, dep to asst cmmr for central London 1996–98; chief constable Avon and Somerset Constabulary 1998–; *Recreations* walking, canoeing, gardening, ornithology; *Style*— Steve Pilkington, Esq, CBE, QPM; ✉ Avon and Somerset Constabulary, Police Headquarters, PO Box 37, Valley Road, Portishead, Bristol BS20 8QJ (☎ 01275 816000, e-mail chief.constable@avsom.police.uk)

PILLAY, Prof Gerald John; DL (Merseyside 2009); s of Jimmy M Pillay (d 1991), of Durban, SA, and Thena G, *née* Kodi; *b* 22 December 1953, Natal, SA; *Educ* Univ of Durban-Westville (BA, BD, DTheol), Rhodes Univ (PhD); *m* 3 Dec 1983, Nirmala; 2 s (Kirubin M b 15 April 1992, Sudershan J b 17 Aug 1994); *Career* lectr then sr lectr in church history Univ of Durban-Westville 1979–87, prof of modern church history Univ of SA 1988–96, fndn prof of theology Otago Univ NZ 1997–2003 (dean of liberal arts 1998–2003), vice-chllr and rector Liverpool Hope Univ 2003–; tstee Hope Coll Michigan 2013; DLitt (hc) Hope Coll Michigan 2013, hon fell Harris Manchester Coll Oxford 2015; FRSA 2005; *Publications* Religion at the Limits? Pentecostalism among Indian South Africans (1994), A History of Christianity in South Africa (co-ed, 1994); contrib chapters in books and author of articles in learned jls; *Recreations* music, gardening; *Style*— Prof Gerald Pillay, DL; ✉ Liverpool Hope University, Hope Park, Liverpool L16 9JD (☎ 0151 291 3403, fax 0151 291 3100, e-mail pillayg@hope.ac.uk, website www.hope.ac.uk)

PILLING, John R; s of Arthur Maurice Pilling (d 1986), and Hope Elizabeth Clarke Pilling, *née* Brinton (d 1992); *b* 11 October 1944, London; *Educ* Shrewsbury, Bromsgrove and Worcester Coll of FE (ONC, HNC); *m* July 1970, Clare Patricia, *née* North; 2 da (Serena Hope (Mrs White) b 12 Oct 1972, Victoria Blanche (Mrs Williams) b 14 Feb 1975); *Career* Brintons Ltd carpet mfrs: apprentice and mgmnt trainee 1963–67, asst prodn engr 1967–70, prodn engr 1970–80, engrg divnl mangr 1980–88, engrg dir (main bd) 1988–92, mfrg dir (main Bd) 1992–98, gp mfrg dir 1998–2002, gp md 2002–04, exec vice-chm 2004; dir Moghul Interiors 2004–; supporter No Euro campaign; Freeman City of London, Liveryman Worshipful Co of Weavers (memb Ct of Assts and Upper Bailiff 2010–11); CEng, FREng 2003, FIMechE (MIMechE 1971); *Recreations* travelling and understanding cultural diversity, the Peninsular Wars and historical perspective around the Duke of Wellington, gardening (especially trees and shrubs), shooting, dogs and dog handling, trout fishing, tennis, garden, estate and home improvements, golf; *Style*— John R Pilling, Esq; ✉ e-mail johnrpilling@gmail.com

PILLOW, Nathan; QC (2015); *Educ* Magdalen Coll Oxford (BA); *Career* called to the Bar (Gray's Inn) 1997 (Prince of Wales Scholarship); *Style*— Nathan Pillow, Esq, QC; ✉ Essex Court Chambers, 24 Lincoln's Inn Fields, London WC2A 3EG (e-mail npillow@essexcourt.com)

PILSWORTH, Michael John (Mick); s of Alwyne Pilsworth, of Retford, Notts, and Catherine, *née* Silverwood; *b* 1 April 1951; *Educ* King Edward VI GS Retford, Univ of Manchester (BA, MA), Univ of Bournemouth (MA); *m* 7 Oct 1972 (m dis 2004), Stella Frances, da of Donald Lionel Hore, of Bristol; 1 da (Rosa Grace b 8 March 1977), 1 s (Thomas James b 18 Dec 1984); m 2, 22 Aug 2004, Deborah Anne-Marie, da of Sylvester Martin, of Dublin; *Career* research asst Inst of Advanced Studies Manchester Poly 1972–73, lectr in adult educn Univ of Manchester 1976–78 (research fell 1973–75), research assoc Centre for TV Research Univ of Leeds 1979, prog devpt exec London Weekend TV 1983–84 (researcher 1979–82), gp devpt controller TVS Entertainment plc 1987–88 (head of prog planning and devpt 1985–86), chief exec MGMM Communications Ltd 1988–89, md Alomo Productions Ltd 1990–93, md SelecTV plc 1993 (dir 1990–93), chief exec Chrysalis TV Gp and dir Chrysalis plc 1993–2002, md Martini Media Ltd 2002–, chm Motive TV 2005–16, ceo Chrysalis Vision Ltd 2014–; memb RTS; *Books* Broadcasting in The Third World (1977); *Recreations* swimming, tennis, cinema, reading; *Clubs* Groucho; *Style*— Mick Pilsworth, Esq; ✉ 16 Castleknock Green, Castleknock, Dublin 15, Ireland (☎ 00 353 822 3248)

PIMBLEY, Stephen John; s of John Pimbley, of Cardiff, S Glamorgan, and Marjorie, *née* James; *b* 18 January 1959; *Educ* Stanwell Sch Penarth S Glamorgan, Middx Poly (BA), Royal Coll of Art (MA); *m* 30 April 1994, Katherine, da of Dennis Lannon; 1 s (Sydney b 16 Jan 1996); *Career* successively: architect Richard Rogers Partnership, architect/dir Troughton McAslan Ltd; architect/dir SMC Alsop (formerly Alsop & Störmer, Alsop Architects then Alsop and Ptnrs) until 2008, currently owner and dir SPARK; ARCUK 1987, RIBA 1988; *Style*— Stephen Pimbley, Esq

PIMLOTT, Graham; CBE (2010); *Career* admitted slr 1976, later ptnr Lovell White Durrant slrs, sec Takeover Panel 1981–83, corp fin dir Kleinwort Benson 1986–89, head of corp fin then chief exec Merchant Banking Div Barclays de Zoete Wedd 1989–96, dir of planning, ops and technol Barclays plc 1997–99; chm: Tilney Gp Holdings Ltd, Tesco Personal Finance Ltd 2008–, Grosvenor Ltd 2009–; non-exec dir: Tesco plc 1993–2005, Hammerson plc 1993–2005 (dep chm), Provident Financial plc 2003–07, Tesco Personal Finance Ltd 2008–, Inchcape plc 2008–10; chm Export Credit Guarantee Dept 2004–10, memb Auditing Practices Bd 2002–10; *Style*— Graham Pimlott, Esq, CBE

PINCHER, Christopher John; MP; s of John Pincher, of Wombourne, Staffs, and Sandra, *née* Mills; *b* 24 September 1969, Walsall, W Midlands; *Educ* Ounsdale Sch Wombourne, LSE (BSc); *Career* Accenture 1993–2010; MP (Cons) Tamworth 2010–; *Recreations* horse racing, motor sports, history; *Clubs* Travellers'; *Style*— Christopher Pincher, Esq, MP; ✉ House of Commons, London SW1A 0AA (☎ 020 7219 7169, e-mail christopher.pincher.mp@parliament.uk, website www.christopherpincher.com, Twitter @chrispincher)

PINCHES, Stuart John Allison; s of George Arthur Pinches (d 1993), and Marjorie Allison; *b* 2 April 1947; *Educ* Friern Barnet GS, Poly of Central London (Dip Photography & Film); *m* 18 Dec 1970 (m dis 1991), (Brigid) Imelda, da of Patrick Behan (d 1969), of Edenderry, Co Offaly, Eire; m 2, 21 June 1994 (sep 2003), Sandie, da of Stanley Montague, of London; *Career* gen mgmnt exec United Artists Corporation Ltd 1968–70, project mangr Organon International BV Holland 1971–73, md Viscom Ireland Ltd Dublin 1974–77, assoc dir Purchasepoint Group London 1978–79, divnl md Viscom Group London 1979–81, head of Programme Servs TVS plc 1981–85, md AKA Ltd London 1986–87, jt md Roach and Partners Ltd 1989–93, fndr SP Management Consulting (UK) 1993, pres and ceo Pinches Management Consulting USA Inc 1995–2000; exec mgmnt and consulting assignments for: MTV Networks Europe, Village Roadshow/Austereo/Optus, Pittard Sullivan, Emap plc, Pacific Investments, Media Advisors Int, Capital Media Gp plc, Sportsworld Media Gp plc, Ascent Media Gp Inc, BBC Broadcast Ltd; *Recreations* personal development and fitness, collecting music, motor sport, photography; *Clubs* Goodwood Road Racing; *Style*— Stuart Pinches, Esq; ✉ 53 Pier House, Cheyne Walk, London SW3 5HG (☎ 020 7349 0391, mobile 07711 203046, e-mail stuart@wise-ones.co.uk)

P

PINCKNEY, David Charles; s of Dr Charles Percy Pinckney (d 1982), of Ascot, Berks, and Norah Manisty, *née* Boucher (d 1988); *b* 13 September 1940; *Educ* Winchester, New Coll Oxford (MA); *m* 25 May 1974, Susan Audrey, da of Col Austin Richards (d 1974), of Writtle, Essex; 2 da (Katherine b 1974, Caroline b 1976), 1 s (Charles b 1977); *Career* sr audit ptnr Peat Marwick Mitchell CAs France 1977–83 (London 1963–67, Paris and Lyons 1968–83), md Wrightson Wood Financial Services Ltd 1984–86, gp fin dir Thornton and Co Ltd 1987–97, vice-chm AXA Investment Managers 1998–2003; chm: Ventus VCT plc 2005–, Syndicate Asset Mgmnt plc 2005–10, Rutley European Property Ltd 2005–10; dir East Hampshire Housing Assoc 1995–99; govr Br Sch Paris 1981–83; memb Ctee of Mgmnt Inst of Child Health 1992–96; FCA (ACA 1966); *Recreations* skiing, international travel, classic cars; *Clubs* Brooks's (chm 1999–2002), Hurlingham, Vincent's (Oxford); *Style*— David Pinckney, Esq; ✉ Southcot House, Chapmanslade, Westbury, Wiltshire BA13 4AU (☎ 01373 832568)

PINCUS, George Bernard; MBE (2013); s of Dr Joseph Victor Pincus (d 1947), and Ruth, *née* Burns (d 2003); *b* 13 November 1942; *Educ* Epsom Coll; *m* 1, 21 May 1965 (m dis); 2 s (Benjamin b 1969, Damian b 1970); m 2, 20 Dec 1986, Carolyn, *née* Shaljean; *Career* md: PVAF 1974–84, BBDO Ltd 1984–90, Interpartners 1990–93; dir Retail Marketing Partnership 1990–93, chm The Works London Ltd 1998–2004; chm Cncl Epsom Coll 2003–09 (memb 1965–, vice-chm 1995–2003); govr Bishop David Brown Acad Woking 2015–; *Recreations* visual arts, theatre, history, travel; *Style*— George B Pincus, Esq, MBE; ✉ Briars Hatch, Guildford Road, East Horsley, Surrey KT24 5RY; office ☎ 01483 281938

PINDER, Dr Jennifer Marion; da of John Raymond Pinder (d 1988), of Doncaster, S Yorks, and Elizabeth Ross, *née* Ward (d 1991); *b* 15 December 1947; *Educ* Queen Ethelburga's Sch Harrogate, Doncaster Tech Coll, Univ of Sheffield (BDS), RCS England (MGDS), Birkbeck Coll London (BSc), Dip; *m* 15 Dec 2011, Ross Henderson; *Career* in gen dental practice in various locations incl City of London 1971–75, Sunnybrook Hosp Univ of Toronto 1976–78, assoc in gen dental practice City of London 1978–88, in own practice 1988–2002, assoc gen dentis Bupa Dental Centre City of London 2002–; chm and pres Gen Dental Practitioners Assoc 1983–87, fndr chm Women in Dentistry 1985–87 (hon pres 1997–2000), pres Metropolitan Branch BDA 1990–91 (sec 1987–94); memb: GDC 1984–2001, Standing Dental Advsy Ctee 1990–93, Standing Ctee on Dental and Surgical Materials 1992–94, Bd Faculty of Gen Dental Practitioners 1992–98 (vice-dean 1995–96),

Stakeholder Bd Southern Trains 2006; fndr JMP Coaching (private coaching business) 2009–, coach and mentor London Postgrad Deanery 2009– (ILM Level 7 Certificate in Leadership and Mentoring 2015); professional genealogist, family story researcher 2015–; govr Eastman Dental Hosp 1986–91; graduate memb Br Psychological Soc; memb: AGRA, Assoc for Coaching, Inst of Leadership and Mgmnt; FFGDP (UK) RCS 2006, RSM; *Recreations* Burmese cats, genealogy, embroidery, gardening; *Style*— Dr Jennifer Pinder; ✉ 16 Chelsfield Gardens, London SE26 4DJ (☎ 020 8291 0063, e-mail jenniferpinder1@btinternet.com, Twitter @jenniferpinder); BUPA Dental Centre, 77 Cornhill, London EC3V 3QQ (☎ 020 7200 5800, website www.dentistforphobics.co.uk)

PINE, Courtney; CBE (2009, OBE 2000); *b* 18 March 1964; *Career* jazz musician (saxophonist, also plays clarinet, flute and keyboards); fndr memb: Jazz Warriors 1985, The Abiba Jazz Arts 1985; presenter: Millennium Jazz (BBC Radio 2) 1999, Global Jazz Tour (BBC World Service) 2000–01, Courtney Pine's Jazz Crusade (BBC Radio 2) 2001–, UK Black (BBC Radio 2) 2003, Jazz Makers (BBC Radio 2) 2004; musical dir BBC Windrush Gala Concert; MOBO Award for Best Jazz Act 1996 and 1997 (nominated 2001), Best Live Band BBC Jazz Awards 2002, Gold Badge Award Br Acad of Composers and Songwriters; fell Leeds Coll of Music 2002, Hon DMus Univ of Westminster; *Albums* Journey To The Urge Within 1986 (Silver Award), Out Of Many One People (with Jazz Warriors) 1987, Destiny's Song & The Image Of Pursuance 1988, The Vision's Tale 1989, Closer To Home 1990, Within the Realm of Our Dreams 1991, To the Eyes of Creation 1993, Modern Day Jazz Stories 1996 (nominated Mercury Music Prize 1996), Underground 1997, Another Story (remixes) 1998, Back in the Day 2000, Devotion 2003; *Soundtracks* History is Made at Night 1999, It Was an Accident 2000 (nominated Best Ind Film Score Award), Mandela: A Living Legend (BBC 1) 2002; *Style*— Courtney Pine, Esq, CBE

PINHORN, Margaret (Maggie) (Mrs Martin Dyke-Coomes); da of George Herbert Pinhorn (d 1996), and Mary Elizabeth Suther (d 1963); *b* 1 November 1943; *Educ* Walthamstow Hall Sch for Girls Sevenoaks, Central Sch of Art and Design London; *m* 24 June 1978, Martin Dyke-Coomes, *qv*, s of Ernest Thomas Dyke-Coomes, of Crawley, W Sussex; 1 s (Ned Alexander b 1981), 1 da (Amy Elizabeth b 1983), 2 adopted s (Anthony b 1967, Claude b 1973); *Career* artist, dir, designer, prodr; fndr of Alternative Arts 1971– and dir: Covent Garden St Theatre 1975–88, Soho Street Theatre 1988–93; started career in films in 1965 at Pinewood Studios in Art Dept of James Bond movie; worked on Br feature films incl: Chitty Chitty Bang Bang, Otley, Till Death Us Do Part; ind film maker, made Dynamo (1970), and Tunde's Film (1973); started Basement Community Arts Workshop in Cable Street 1972; made one of the first 'Open Door' progs for BBC TV and went on to res and present the first BBC TV series 'Grapevine' for Community Programmes Unit; nat co-ordinator of the Assoc of Community Artists 1974–79; vice-chm Tower Hamlets Arts Ctee 1975–79; memb: Arts Cncl Community Art Ctee 1975–79, Gtr London Arts Community Arts Ctee 1979–81; dir: Circus UK 1985–2010, Alternative Art Galleries 1991–95, Spitalfields Arts Devpt Prog 1993–2010, Alternative Fashion Week 1993–, Cityside Regeneration Raising the Profile prog 1998–2002, Photomonth E London Photography Festival 2001–, Photo-Space Gallery 2009–10, Alternative Arts Consultancy 2010–; FRSA; *Recreations* being with my children, creative cooking, collecting wines, travel, philosophy, the arts; *Style*— Ms Maggie Pinhorn; ✉ Alternative Arts, Montefiore Centre, Hanbury Street, London E1 5HZ (☎ 020 8800 6665, e-mail info@alternativearts.co.uk, website www.alternativearts.co.uk)

PINKER, Prof Robert Arthur; CBE (2005); s of Joseph Pinker (d 1976), and Dora Elizabeth, *née* Winyard (d 1987); *b* 27 May 1931; *Educ* Holloway Co Sch, LSE (Cert Soc Sc), Univ of London (BSc, MSc); *m* 24 June 1955, Jennifer Farrington (1994), da of Fred Boulton (d 1941); 2 da (Catherine b 1963, Lucy b 1965); *Career* Nat Serv, 2 Lt Royal Ulster Rifles 1951–52; TA, Lt London Irish Rifles 1952–54; head of Sociology Dept Goldsmiths Coll London 1964–72, Lewisham prof of social admin Goldsmiths and Bedford Colls London 1972–74, prof of social studies Chelsea Coll London 1974–78; LSE: prof of social work studies 1978–93, prof of social admin 1993–96 (prof emeritus 1996–), pro-dir 1985–88; pro-vice-chllr for social sci Univ of London 1988–90; chm: Social Admin Assoc 1974–77, Advsy Cncl Centre for Policy on Ageing 1971–81 (chm of govrs 1981–94), Jl of Social Policy 1981–86 (ed 1977–81), Editorial Bd Ageing and Soc 1981–91; scientific advsr Nursing Res DHSS 1974–79 and 1980–82; memb: Social Sci Res Cncl 1972–76, Working Pty on Role and Tasks of Social Workers Barclay Ctee 1981–82, Cncl Advertising Standards Authy 1988–96, Cncl Direct Mail Accreditation and Recognition Centre 1995–96; govr Goldsmiths Coll London 2001–07; Press Complaints Cmmn: memb 1991–2003, actg chm 2002–03, int conslt 2003–12, ind reviewer 2012–14; chm Deptford Challenge Tst 2006–14; hon fell Goldsmiths Coll London 1999; LLD (hc) Ulster Univ 2016; fell Soc of Eds 2004; Social Theory and Social Policy (1971), The Idea of Welfare (1979), Social Work in an Enterprise Society (1990), Privacy and Personality Rights (jtly, 2010); *Recreations* reading, writing, travel, unskilled gardening; *Style*— Prof Robert Pinker, CBE; ✉ 76 Coleraine Road, Blackheath, London SE3 7PE (☎ 020 8858 5320, e-mail rpinker@freenetname.co.uk)

PINNELL, Raoul Michael; s of late David Andrew Pinnell, OBE, and Madeleine Laura, *née* Farrell; *b* 13 June 1951; *Educ* Bradfield Coll, Ealing Sch of Mgmnt (HND Business Studies), PCL (Dip Mktg), Imede Switzerland (PED); *m* 31 Aug 1976, Judith Jane, da of John Goslett, MBE; 2 s (Henry b 19 May 1983, Philip b 8 July 1985); *Career* H J Heinz 1971–72, Findus 1972–75, Table Top South Africa 1975–77; Nestlé 1979–89, mktg dir Prudential Assurance Co Ltd:1989–94, dir of mktg National Westminster Bank plc 1994–96, vice-pres Shell International Petroleum Co Ltd 1996–2003, chm Shell Brands Int AG 2004–07; chm: Strategic Investment Partners 2009–10, Careers Devpt Gp 2009–12, Bromley Healthcare 2011–; non-exec dir: Leonard Cheshire Disability 2007–13, History of Advtg Tst 2007–10, Coast Ltd 2008–10, Queen Elizabeth Hosp NHS Tst 2008–09, Bexley Care NHS Tst 2009–10; FCIM; *Clubs* IOD; *Style*— Raoul Pinnell, Esq

PINNINGTON, Christopher John; s of William Pinnington, of Cheshire, and Dorothy Pinnington (d 1970); *b* 22 July 1956; *Educ* Stonyhurst, Univ of Bristol (BSc); *m* 1986, Fiona, da of D N A McLure; 2 s (James b 1989, Benjamin b 1995), 1 da (Harriet b 1991); *Career* graduate trainee rising to assoc dir D'Arcy Masius Benton & Bowles 1978–82, dir Wight Collins Rutherford Scott 1982–88, managing ptnr Ball WCRS Sydney 1988–90, managing ptnr FCO Ltd 1990–93, ceo Euro RSCG Wnek Gosper 1993–2004, chief exec Euro RSCG Worldwide UK 2004–06, chief operating offr Euro RSCG Worldwide 2006–09, chief operating offr Havas Worldwide Gp 2009–14, global advsr Havas Worldwide 2014–; non-exec dir Futerra, non-exec dir Heals; MIPA; *Recreations* sailing, tennis, advertising; *Clubs* Hurlingham, RAC; *Style*— Christopher Pinnington, Esq; ✉ Havas Worldwide, Cupola House, 15 Alfred Place, London WC1 (☎ 020 7240 4111)

PINNOCK, Trevor David; CBE (1992); s of Kenneth Alfred Thomas Pinnock, of Canterbury, Kent, and Joyce Edith, *née* Muggleton; *b* 16 December 1946; *Educ* Canterbury Cathedral Choir Sch, Simon Langton GS Canterbury, Royal Coll of Music (winner maj performance prizes organ and harpsichord); *Career* harpsichordist and conductor; London debut with Galliard Harpsichord Trio (jt fndr) 1966, solo debut Purcell Room London 1968, NY debut Metropolitan Opera conducting Giulio Cesare 1988; formed The English Concert 1972 (dir 1973–2002), London debut of the English Concert English Bach Festival 1973; artistic dir and princ conductor Nat Arts Centre Orchestra Ottawa 1991–96; conductor The English Concert BBC Proms; tours of Europe, USA, Canada, Japan, South America (solo, with The English Concert, and as orchestral conductor); memb European Brandenburg Ensemble (tours of UK and Far East) 2006–; Baroque Instrumental Section Gramophone Award 2001 (for recording of Bach Partitas); Hon Dr Univ of Kent, Hon PhD Univ of Ottawa 1993; Hon RAM; Officier de l'Ordre des Arts et des Lettres (France) 1998; *Recordings* extensive discography incl solo, concerto and chamber work; *Style*— Trevor Pinnock, Esq, CBE; ✉ c/o Askonas Holt, Lincoln House, 300 High Holborn, London WC1V 7JH (☎ 020 7400 1751, fax 020 7400 1799, e-mail info@askonasholt.co.uk)

PINSENT, Sir Matthew Clive; kt (2005), CBE (2001, MBE 1993); s of Rev Ewen Macpherson Pinsent, of Child Okeford, Dorset, and Jean Grizel, *née* McMicking; *b* 10 October 1970; *Educ* Eton, St Catherine's Coll Oxford (BA); *m* 19 Oct 2002, Demetra, *née* Koutsoukos; 2 s (Jonah, Lucas b 26 June 2006 (twins)), 1 da (Eve b 17 March 2008); *Career* amateur rower; memb Leander Club 1989–, sr int debut 1989 (jr debut 1987), ret from int competition 2004; honours incl: Gold medal coxless pairs World Jr Championships 1988, Bronze medal coxed fours World Championships 1989, Gold medal coxless pairs World Championships 1991 (new world record 6 mins 21 secs), 1993, 1994 (new world record 6 mins 18 secs), 1995, 2001 and 2002 (new world record 6 mins 14 secs), Gold medal coxless pairs Olympic Games Barcelona 1992 (new Olympic record 6 mins 27 secs), Gold medal coxless pairs Olympic Games Atlanta 1996, Gold medal coxless fours World Championships 1997, 1998 and 1999, Gold medal coxless fours Olympic Games Sydney 2000, Gold medal coxed pairs World Championships 2001, Gold medal coxless fours Olympic Games Athens 2004; flagbearer Olympic Games Sydney 2000; memb IOC 2002–04; pres OUBC 1992–93 (twice univ boat race winner); winner Team of the Year BBC Sports Personality of the Year Awards 1996 (with Steve Redgrave) and 2004 (with James Cracknell, Ed Coode and Steve Williams), Thomas Keller medal FISA 2005; currently sports broadcaster BBC; *Recreations* golf; *Style*— Sir Matthew Pinsent, CBE; ✉ c/o Leander Club, Henley-on-Thames, Oxfordshire RG9 2LP (☎ 01491 575782)

PINTUS, Matthew; s of Ronald Pintus, of Surrey, and Carmel, *née* Corcoran; *b* 14 September 1956; *Educ* Ampleforth, Univ of Warwick, Guildford Coll of Law; *Career* Russell Cooke Potter and Chapman 1981–85, Macfarlanes 1985– (currently ptnr i/c of probate); memb Soc of Tst and Estate Practitioners; *Publications* Butterworths Wills Probate and Administration (ed Contentious Matters section), Butterworths Encyclopaedia of Forms and Precedents (ed Insolvent Estates section); *Recreations* bridge, opera, sailing; *Clubs* 5 Hertford St, Garrick; *Style*— Matthew Pintus, Esq; ✉ Macfarlanes, 10 Norwich Street, London EC4A 1BD (☎ 020 7831 9222, fax 020 7831 5607)

PIPER, Geoffrey Steuart Fairfax; DL (Merseyside 1993); s of Sqdn Ldr Donald Steuart Piper (d 1972), of Bakewell, Derbys, and Nancy Fairfax, *née* Robson (d 1990); *b* 8 June 1943; *Educ* Repton, Pembroke Coll Cambridge (MA); *m* 29 July 1967, Susan Elizabeth, da of Roswell Douglas Arnold; 3 da (Jennifer (Mrs Simms) b 1968, Angela (Mrs Golton) b 1970, Caroline (Mrs Hugh Strickland) b 1973), 1 s (Charles b 1980); *Career* ptnr i/c Deloitte Haskins & Sells: CI 1980–86, Liverpool 1986–90; chm Coral Products plc 2006–11 (dir 1995–2011); pres: Jersey Soc of Chartered and Certified Accountants 1983–85, Liverpool Soc of CAs 1999–2000; chm Business Opportunities on Merseyside 1987–93, chief exec NW Business Leadership Team 1990–, dir Mersey Partnership 1993–2007, memb NW Regnl Assembly 1998–2008, dep chm LSC Gtr Merseyside 2001–03, chm NW Regnl Review Bd 2003–08, chm London 2012 NW Business Forum; FCA 1973; *Recreations* sport, poetry, painting; *Clubs* Royal & Ancient, MCC, Lincoln City FC; *Style*— Geoffrey Piper, Esq, DL; ✉ Leighton Hall, Parkgate, Cheshire CH64 3TQ; North West Business Leadership Team, Daresbury Laboratories, Keckwick Lane, Daresbury, Warrington, Cheshire WA4 4AD (☎ 01925 212078, e-mail geoffrey.piper@nwblt.co.uk)

PIPER, Kate Elizabeth (Katie); *b* 12 October 1983; *Career* campaigner, author and television presenter; estab Katie Piper Fndn 2009; television: Katie: My Beautiful Face (Channel 4) 2009, Katie: My Beautiful Friends (Channel 4) 2010, Katie: The Science of Seeing Again (Channel 4) 2012, Bodyshockers (Channel 4) 2014; *Books* Beautiful (autobiography, 2011), Things Get Better (2012), Start Your Day With Katie (2012), Beautiful Ever After (2015); *Style*— Ms Katie Piper; ✉ Katie Piper Foundation, Building 3, Chiswick Park, 566 Chiswick High Road, Chiswick, London W4 5YA; c/o Fresh Partners Talent Management, 1 Hardwick's Square, Wandsworth, London SW18 4AW

PIRIE, David Alan Tarbat; s of Maj Halyburton Berkeley Pirie, MC, TD, DM (d 1984), and Joyce Elaine, *née* Tarbat; *Educ* Trinity Coll Glenalmond, Univ of York (BA); *m* 21 June 1983, Judith Leslie, da of Maj William Leslie Harris (d 1985); 1 da (Alice b 1984), 1 s (Jack b 1987); *Career* writer, film and TV critic; Time Out: TV critic 1970–74, film critic 1974–80, film ed 1981–84; film critic 1976–: Kaleidoscope (BBC Radio 4), BBC World Service, Capital Radio; contrib 1976–: The Times, Sunday Times, The Media Show, Did You See?, The South Bank Show, Sight and Sound, Movie Magazine; film columnist Options Magazine 1981–92, literary ed Event Magazine 1980–81; film and TV screenwriter 1984–; works incl: Rainy Day Women 1984 (winner Drama Prize NY Film and TV Festival), Total Eclipse of the Heart (screenplay), Mystery Story (screenplay from own novel), Wild Things (BBC TV film) 1989, Never Come Back (winner Best Mini-series prize Chicago Film Festival) 1990, Ashenden (TV series) 1991, Natural Lies (TV series) 1992, Black Easter (winner Best TV Feature Prize Chicago Film Festival), The Element of Doubt (TV film) 1996, Breaking the Waves (collaboration on Lars von Trier's award-winning feature film), The Woman in White (BAFTA nominated TV serial, winner Drama Prize Houston Int TV & Film Festival 1998), Murder Rooms: The Dark Beginnings of Sherlock Holmes (Edgar nominated TV series), The Wyvern Mystery (TV film) 1999, The Safe House (TV series), Murder Rooms (TV series) 2001 (winner Best TV Detective Series Crimescene/Sherlock Holmes Magazine/NFT Awards 2002), Night Gallery (US TV) 2002, Sad Cypress (TV film) 2003, The Strange Case of Arthur Conan Doyle (TV film) 2004, Murderland (TV serial) 2009; sr tutor Br Film and TV Prodrs Assoc Advanced Screenwriting Course 1990–; *Books* Heritage of Horror (1973), Mystery Story (1980), Anatomy of the Movies (1981), The Patient's Eyes (2001), The Night Calls (2002), The Dark Water (2004), A New Heritage of Horror (2007), Gothic: The Dark Heart of Film (contrib, 2013); *Recreations* running; *Clubs* Soho House; *Style*— David Pirie, Esq; ✉ c/o Stephen Durbridge, The Agency (London) Ltd, 24 Pottery Lane, London W11 4LZ (☎ 020 7727 1346, fax 020 7727 9037, e-mail info@theagency.co.uk)

PIRIE, Dr (Duncan) Madsen; s of Douglas Gordon Pirie, and Eva, *née* Madsen; *b* 24 August 1940; *Educ* Univ of Edinburgh (MA), Univ of St Andrews (PhD), Univ of Cambridge (MPhil); *Career* prof of philosophy and logic Hillsdale Michigan USA 1975–78, pres Adam Smith Institute 1978–, memb PM's Citizen's Charter Panel 1991–95; sr visiting fell Dept of Land Economy Univ of Cambridge 2010–; *Books* Trial and Error & The Idea of Progress (1978), Test Your IQ (with Eamonn Butler, 1983), Micropolitics (1988), Privatization (1988), Boost Your IQ (with Eamonn Butler, 1991), The Sherlock Holmes IQ Book (with Eamonn Butler, 1995), How to Win Every Argument (2006), Children of the Night (2007), Dark Visitor (2007), The Waters of Andros (2007), Freedom 101 (2008), 101 Great Philosophers (2009), The Emerald Warriors (2011), Tree Boy (2011), Economics Made Simple (2012), Think Tank (2012), Silver Dawn (2013), Team Games (2013); *Recreations* films; *Style*— Dr Madsen Pirie; ✉ Adam Smith Institute, 23 Great Smith Street, London SW1P 3BL (☎ 020 7222 4995, fax 020 7222 7544)

PIRRET, David John; s of George Riddle Pirret, of Edinburgh, and Marion, *née* Taylor Maxwell; *b* 29 December 1952; *Educ* Eastwood HS Glasgow, Univ of Strathclyde (BA); *m* 1 March 1980, Patricia Zoe Frances, da of Maj Patrick Dennis Warren; 1 da (Heather Marion Joy b 30 Nov 1981), 2 s (Andrew George Nigel, James Patrick Gordon (twins) b 5 Jan 1985); *Career* divnl mangr Shell Chemicals UK Ltd 1987–89, lubricants dir Shell UK Ltd 1989–92, retail dir Shell UK Ltd 1992–96, head of mktg Shell Int Petroleum Co

Ltd 1996–97, pres and co chm Shell Brasil SA 1997–2001, exec vice-pres global businesses Shell Int Petroleum Co Ltd 2001–02, ceo and pres Pennzoil Quaker State Co USA 2002–03, ceo Shell Lubricants 2003–, dir Shell Int Petroleum Co Ltd 2006–; *Recreations* golf, sailing; *Clubs* RAC; *Style*— David Pirret, Esq

PISSARIDES, Prof Sir Christopher Antoniou; kt (2013); s of Antonios Pissarides, of Cyprus, and Eudokia, *née* Georgiades; *b* 20 February 1948; *Educ* Pancyprian Gymnasium Nicosia, Univ of Essex (BA, MA), LSE (PhD); *m* 1, 24 July 1986 (m dis 2009), Francesca Michela, da of Antonio Cassano, of Rome; 1 s (Antony b 1987), 1 da (Miranda b 1988); m 2, 8 Oct 2011, Le Wa (Rachel) Ngai; 1 s (Nicolas b 2012); *Career* LSE: lectr 1976–82, reader 1982–86, prof 1986–, convener Economics Dept 1996–99, dir Macroeconomics Research Prog 1990–2007, dir Int Summer Sch in Economics 1993–96 and 2001–03, chm Centre for Macroeconomics 2012–, Regius prof of economics 2013–; prof of European studies Univ of Cyprus 2011–; research fell: Centre for Economic Policy Research 1994–, Inst for the Study of Labor (IZA) Bonn 2001–; visiting prof: Harvard Univ 1979–80, Princeton Univ 1984, European Univ Inst 1989, Univ of Calif Berkeley 1989–90; IAS Helmut & Anna Pao Sohmen prof-at-large Hong Kong Univ of Science and Technol 2012–, head Growth Lab St Petersburg State Univ; hon prof: Univ of the Aegean, KI Kazakh Economic Univ 2012; Houblon-Norman fell Bank of England 1994; memb Bd Review of Economic Studies 1983–92, chm Cncl of Nat Economy Cyprus 2013–; bd chm Economica 2007–12 (ed 1980–83, assoc ed 1996–), assoc ed Economic Jl 2000–05; conslt: World Bank, EU, OECD; expert Treasy Ctee House of Commons 2001–05, memb Cyprus Monetary Policy Ctee 2000–07, non-national sr assoc Forum for Economic Research in the Arab Countries, Iran and Turkey 2002–, memb Employment Taskforce EC 2003–04; memb Interim Governing Bd Univ of Cyprus 1989–95; jt winner IZA Prize in Labor Economics 2005, jt winner Nobel Prize in Economics 2010; hon doctorate: Univ of Cyprus 2009, Athens Univ of Economics and Business, Univ of Essex, Azerbaijan Univ of Economics; memb: Royal Economic Soc (memb Cncl 1996–2001), European Economic Assoc (memb Cncl 2005–11, vice-pres 2009, pres elect 2010, pres 2011); fell Econometric Soc (memb Cncl 2005–10), FBA 2002, fell Soc of Labor Economists 2008, fell Economic Theory 2012, foreign fell Acad of Athens 2011, fell European Economic Assoc 2011, fell Academia Europea 2011, hon lifetime memb American Economic Assoc 2011; Repub of Cyprus Aristeion for the Arts, Literature and Sciences 2008; *Books* Labour Market Adjustment (1976), Equilibrium Unemployment Theory (1990, 2 edn 2000), Job Matching, Wage Dispersion and Unemployment (with Dale T Mortensen, ed by Konstantinos Tatsiramos and Klaus F Zimmermann, 2011), After the Crisis: The Way Ahead (with Jean-Paul Fitoussi and others, 2010); also author of articles in professional jls; *Recreations* gardening, cooking; *Style*— Prof Sir Christopher Pissarides; ✉ London School of Economics and Political Science, Houghton Street, London WC2A 2AE (☎ 020 7955 7513, fax 020 7831 1840, e-mail c.pissarides@lse.ac.uk)

PISTORIUS, Professor Carl WI (Calie); s of Carl WI Pistorius, and Iolanthé, *née* Tancred; *b* 9 August 1958, Pretoria, SA; *Educ* Univ of Pretoria (BSc, BEng), Ohio State Univ (MS, PhD), MIT (SM), Harvard Business Sch (AMP); *m* Michèle Emily Olivier; *Career* Univ of Pretoria: head Electrical and Electronic Engrg 1989–94, dir Inst for Technological Innovation 1994–98, dir IT 1998–99, dean Faculty of Engrg, the Built Environment and IT 2000–01, vice-chllr and princ 2001–09; vice-chllr Univ of Hull 2009–; CEng 2010, FIET 2010; *Publications* Introduction to the Uniform Geometrical Theory of Diffraction (jtly, 1990); articles in IEEE Transactions on antennas and propagation research policy, technological forecasting and social change; *Style*— Professor Calie Pistorius; ✉ University of Hull, Cottingham Road, Hull HU6 7RX (☎ 01482 465131, e-mail calie.pistorius@hull.ac.uk, website www.hull.ac.uk)

PITCHER, Sir Desmond Henry; kt (1992); s of George Charles Pitcher (d 1968), of Liverpool, and Alice Marion, *née* Osborne (d 1985); *b* 23 March 1935; *Educ* Liverpool Coll of Technol; *m* 1, 1961 (m dis 1973), Patricia, *née* Ainsworth; 2 da (Stephanie, Samantha (twins) b 18 May 1965); m 2, 1978 (m dis 1984), Carol Ann, *née* Rose; 2 s (George b 1 Oct 1978, Andrew b 1 March 1981); m 3, 1991, Norma Barbara, *née* Niven; *Career* devpt engr A V Roe & Co 1957–58, systems engr Automatic Telephone & Electrical Co 1958–60, nat mangr engrg Sperry Univac Ltd 1961–69; md: MDS (Data Processing) Ltd 1969–71, Sperry Univac Ltd 1971–73; dep chm Sperry Rand Ltd 1973–76 (dir 1971–73), vice-pres Int Div Sperry Univac Corp 1973–76, dir Br Layland Motor Corp 1976–78; md: Truck and Bus Div BL Ltd 1976–78, Plessey Telecommunications and Office Systems 1978–83; dir Plessey Co 1979–83, non-exec vice-chm The Littlewoods Organisation 1993–95 (chief exec 1983–93), chm and dir Sign Brick 1999–2012; dir: United Utilities plc (formerly North West Water Gp plc) 1990–98 (dep chm 1991–93, chm 1993–98), Steeltower 2001–12, Knowledgebutton Ltd 2002–05; non-exec dir: NatWest Bank (Northern Advsy Bd) 1989–92, National Westminster Bank plc 1994–98; dep chm Everton FC Ltd 1990–98 (dir 1987–98), chm Merseyside Devpt Corp 1991–98, chm Westminster Green Mgmnt Co Ltd 2010–14; memb Twickenham Advsy Panel Regeneration London Borough of Richmond upon Thames 2011; chm and tstee: Rocking Horse Appeal, Royal Liverpool Childrens Hosp 1997–2003 (vice-pres 2004–); tstee Outward Bound; Faraday lectr 1973–74; Faraday Lectures Instn of Electrical Engrs 1974–75 ('The Social Computer', delivered in 14 cities on 32 occasions to students and gen public, one of the first to indicate international data communication), visiting prof of business policy Univ of Manchester 1993–98, hon fell Liverpool John Moores Univ 1993, various lectures on social implications of computers and micro-electronics; DL Merseyside 1993–99; Freeman: City of London 1987, Worshipful Co of Info Technologists 1987; CEng, FIEE 1968, FBCS 1975, Hon FIDE 1977, CIMgt 1985, FRSA 1987; *Publications* Water Under the Bridge – 30 Years of Industrial Management (2003); *Recreations* football, opera, golf; *Clubs* Brooks's, Royal Birkdale Golf, Carlton, RAC, Royal Liverpool Golf, Lancashire CC; *Style*— Sir Desmond Pitcher; ☎ 01264 735257, e-mail desmondpitcher@aol.com

PITCHFORD, Rt Hon the Lord Justice; Sir Christopher John Pitchford; kt (2001), PC (2010); *b* 28 March 1947; *Educ* Dyffryn Comp Newport, Queen's Coll Taunton, QMC (LLB); *Career* called to the Bar Middle Temple 1969; recorder 1987, QC 1987, dep judge of the High Court 1995–2000, leader Wales & Chester Circuit 1999–2000, judge of the High Court (Queen's Bench Div) 2000–10, a presiding judge of the Wales & Chester Circuit 2002–, a Lord Justice of the Court of Appeal 2010–; arbitrator Motor Insurers' Bureau 1994–2000; *Style*— The Rt Hon the Lord Justice Pitchford

PITFIELD, Michael; s of Edward George Pitfield (d 1976), and Robina Heslop (d 1996); *b* 22 May 1945; *Educ* Univ of London (BSc), Univ of Reading (MA), Henley Business Sch (PGCert); *m* 1972 (m dis 2004), Angela May, da of Albert Victor McCallin (d 1969); 2 s (Alexander b 1975, Alastair b 1982), 1 da (Anna b 1979); *Career* asst dir Inst of Personnel Mgmnt 1978–89 (special advsr 1989–2010), dir Thames Valley Business Sch 1989–90, dir of int business Henley Business Sch 1990–2006 (visiting exec fell 2006–), business devpt advsr and exec coach 2006–, UK mgmnt devpt advsr European Fndn for Mgmnt Devpt 2006–10 (hon memb 2006–), workplace initiative advsr Stonewall 2006–10, MBA advsr Royal Holloway London 2007–11, business devpt advsr Windsor Leadership Tst 2013–, mentor The FSE Gp 2014–, chm and non-exec dir Entrusted Consulting Ltd 2015–, business advsr The Late Payment Directory 2016–; regular contrib to newspapers, magazines and journals, frequent speaker at int conferences and seminars; memb: European Business Govt Rels Cncl 1993–2000, Bd of Tstees IPRF 1995, Bd Henley-Nederland, Bd Henley in Denmark, Bd Club 7 Pinewood Studios 2002–11 (chm 2008–11), Bd Endless Perception Ltd 2006–10, Thames Valley Chamber of Commerce 2015–, Fedn of Small Businesses 2015–; chm Advsy Bd: Cygnus Devpt Inc (USA) 2000–06, Eisenburg Ltd 2015–; emeritus memb Bd UNICON (USA) 1994– (chm 1997); St George's Chapel Windsor Castle: memb Guild of Stewards 2006, gp visits co-ordinator 2014–; Freeman City of London 2016; chartered marketer 1999; Chartered FCIPD1980, FRSA 1992, MIPRA 1994, FCIM 1998, memb IOD 2015; *Books* How To Take Exams (1980), Developing International Managers (1996), IPD Guide to International Management Development (1997); *Recreations* writing, genealogy, history, cinema, travel; *Style*— Michael Pitfield, Esq; ✉ 65 Fountain Gardens, Windsor SL4 3SY

PITHER, Dr Charles Edward Pither; s of late David E Pither, and June, *née* Cadisch; *b* 21 July 1953; *Educ* Aldenham, St Thomas' Hosp Med Sch London (MB BS); *m* 22 Sept 1979 (m dis 2008), Jane Patricia Anne, da of Cdr David Roberts, MBE, RN; 3 da (Claire Elizabeth Wensley b 12 July 1982, Kate Victoria b 14 Nov 1984, Stephanie Jane Eleanor b 22 Dec 1986); *Career* instr in anaesthesia Univ of Cincinnati Med Center Ohio 1984 (fell in pain control and regnl anaesthesia 1983–84); St Thomas' Hosp: lectr and hon sr registrar 1984–85, conslt pain specialist 1986–2004, med dir INPUT Pain Mgmnt Unit 1989–2004, formerly med dir (pain servs) Powys Health Care Tst, former med dir The Realhealth Inst, dir Lex Medica Ltd; past pres Soc for Back Pain Research, past tstee Backcare; winner Sci art 2001; co-winner: King's Fund maj grant 1987, Evian Health Award 1993; FRCA 1982; *Recreations* gardening, country sports, vintage motor cars, travel; *Style*— Dr Charles Pither; ✉ Muswell Hill Farm, Brill, Buckinghamshire HP18 9XD (☎ 01844 238923)

PITKEATHLEY, Baroness (Life Peer UK 1997), of Caversham in the Royal County of Berkshire; Jill Elizabeth Pitkeathley; OBE (1993); *née* Bisson; da of Roland Wilfred Bisson (d 1980), of St Sampson's, Guernsey, and Edith May *née* Muston (d 2001); *b* 4 January 1940, Guernsey, CI; *Educ* Ladies' Coll Guernsey, Univ of Bristol (BA); *m* 1, 1961 (m dis 1978), William Pitkeathley, s of Joseph Pitkeathley; 1 s (Hon Simon William b 9 May 1964), 1 da (Hon Rachel b 2 Aug 1966); m 2, 2008, David Emerson; *Career* social worker Manchester and Essex 1961–67, voluntary servs co-ordinator NHS 1970–82, Nat Consumer Cncl 1983–86, chief exec Carers UK (formerly Nat Cncl for Carers) 1986–98; chair: New Opportunities Fund 1998–2004, Children and Families Ct Advsy and Support Service (CAFCASS) 2003–08, Cncl for Professional Standards Authy (formerly Healthcare Regulatory Excellence (CHRE)) 2009–15 Big Society Tst 2015–; pres: Community Cncl for Berks, Volunteering England; chair: Future Builders Advsy Panel 2005–, Third Sector Advsy Body 2008–; Hon Dr: Univ of Bristol, London Met Univ; *Books* It's My Duty Isn't It? (1989), Only Child: How to Survive Being One (1994), Cassandra and Jane (2004, US 2008), Dearest Cousin Jane (2010); *Recreations* walking, theatre, grandchildren, gardening; *Style*— The Rt Hon the Lady Pitkeathley, OBE; ✉ House of Lords, London SW1A 0PW (☎ 020 7219 0358, e-mail brittans@parliament.uk (assistant Stephanie Brittan))

PITMAN, Jennifer Susan (Jenny); OBE (1998); *née* Harvey; da of George Harvey, and Mary Harvey; *b* 11 June 1946; *Educ* Sarson Secdy Girls' Sch; *m* 1, 1965 (m dis), Richard Pitman; 2 s (Paul Richard, Mark Andrew Pitman, *qv*); m 2, 1997, D Stait; *Career* national hunt racehorse trainer 1975–99; dir Jenny Pitman Racing Ltd 1975–; author; major races won incl: Midlands National 1977 (Watafella), Massey Ferguson Gold Cup 1980 (Bueche Giorod), Welsh National 1982 (Corbiere), 1983 (Burrough Hill Lad) and 1986 (Stears By), Grand National 1983 (Corbiere) and 1995 (Royal Athlete), King George VI Gold Cup 1984 (Burrough Hill Lad), Hennessy Gold Cup 1984 (Burrough Hill Lad), Cheltenham Gold Cup 1984 (Burrough Hill Lad) and 1991 (Garrison Savannah), Whitbread Trophy 1985 (Smith's Man), Ritz Club National Hunt Handicap 1987 (Gainsay), Sporting Life Weekend Chase 1987 (Gainsay), Philip Cornes Saddle of Gold Final 1988 (Crumpet Delite), Welsh Champion Hurdle 1991 (Wonderman) and 1992 (Don Valentino), Scottish Grand National 1995 (Willsford), Sun Alliance Chase 1996 (Nathen Lad), Supreme Novice Hurdle 1996 (Indefence), Ladbroke Hurdle Leopardstown 1997 (Master Tribe), Racing Post Chase Kempton 1997 (Mudahim), Irish National Fairyhouse 1997 (Mudahim), Stayers Hurdle Cheltenham (Princeful) 1998; first woman to train Grand National and Gold Cup winners, trainer of Esha Ness (winner of the aborted Grand National 1993); awards incl: Golden Spurs Racing Personality of the Year 1983, Cwlth Sports Awards 1983 and 1984, Piper Heidsieck Trainer of the Year 1983–84 and 1989–90, Variety Club of GB Sportswoman of the Year 1984, Golden Spurs Best National Hunt Trainer 1984; *Books* Glorious Uncertainty (autobiography, 1984), Jenny Pitman The Autobiography (1998); novels: On the Edge (2002), Double Deal (2002), The Dilemma (2003), The Vendetta (2004), The Inheritance (2005); *Style*— Mrs Jenny Pitman, OBE; ✉ Owls Barn, Kintbury, Hungerford, Berkshire RG17 9SX (☎ 01488 669191, fax 01488 668774, e-mail jenny.pitman@btconnect.com)

PITMAN, Mark Andrew; s of Richard Thomas Pitman, and Jennifer Susan (Jenny) Pitman, OBE, *qv*; *b* 1 August 1966; *Educ* Wycliffe Coll; *m* 1995, Natasha Susan Cowen; 2 da (Darcy Rose b 11 Oct 1996, Tahlia b 6 Jan 2001); *Career* national hunt jockey; debut 1983, professional 1984; trainer 1997–; second yst jockey to complete the National Course 1984, second place Conditional Jockey Championship 1986–87; asst trainer to Mrs Jenny Pitman 1993– (retained jockey 1988–93); career best of 57 winners in a season 1989–90 (incl second place in Cheltenham Gold Cup and won Ritz Club Jockey of the Meeting Aintree), second in Grand National Aintree 1991; maj races won incl: Tote Cheltenham Gold Cup 1991, Welsh Champion Hurdle 1991, The Martell Cup Steeple Chase, The Mumm Club Novices Steeple Chase, The Larchlap Chase, The Midlands Grand National, The EBF Hurdle Final, The Charterhouse Mercantile Chase, The Swish Hurdle, The John Bull Chase, The Sporting Life Weekender HCP Chase, The Old Road Securities Novice Chase, The Souter of Stirling Novices Chase; trainer 1997–2006; trained winners incl: Royal & Sun Alliance Novice Hurdle, Weatherbys Champion Bumper, Hennessy Gold Cup, Charisma Gold Cup, Tolwirth Hurdle, 2nd in Martell Grand National; bloodstock agent 2006–; television and radio presenter 2006–; *Style*— Mark Pitman, Esq; ✉ Owl's Barn, Kintbury, Hungerford, Berkshire RG17 9SX (☎ 07836 792771, e-mail mark@markpitmanracing.co.uk, website www.markpitmanracing.co.uk)

PITT, Nicholas John; s of George Stanhope Pitt (d 1983), of E Horsley, Surrey, and Lesley Henrietta, *née* Bayley; *b* 21 October 1950; *Educ* Aldenham, Lancaster Univ; *m* 18 June 2008, Alison Jane Lang; 1 s (Oscar Theodore b 3 April 2009); *Career* sub ed Stratford Express 1977–79, sports writer The Sunday Times 1979–87, chief sports writer London Daily News 1987; The Sunday Times: dep sports ed 1988–94, sports ed 1994–96, sports writer 1996–; ed Close Up magazine 2006–; special award Br Sports Journalism Awards 1985; *Books* The Paddy and The Prince (1998); *Recreations* golf, tennis; *Clubs* Sheen Tennis and Squash, Priory Park Tennis; *Style*— Nicholas Pitt, Esq; ✉ The Sunday Times, 1 Pennington Street, London E1 9XW (☎ 020 7782 5714, fax 020 7782 5720, e-mail pittnj@globalnet.co.uk)

PITT, Ruth Angela; da of Graham James Tyrrell Pitt, of Bristol, and Jean, *née* Patterson; *b* 14 August 1952; *Educ* Chew Valley Sch, Weston-super-Mare Tech Coll, Univ of York (BA); *Partner* Ali Rashid; 1 da (Rebecca), 2 s (Josef, Thomas); *Career* trainee feature writer and sub ed IPC Magazines 1977–80; freelance writer and broadcaster for various women's magazines, newspapers, Radio Tees and BBC Radio 4 1973–80, creative writing teacher Ryedale Evening Inst 1973–80, reporter and prodr Radio Tees and Radio Aire 1980–82, sr reporter and presenter Yorkshire TV 1982–88, fndr and md Real Life Productions 1988–96, guest presenter Woman's Hour (BBC Radio 4) 1993–96, head of documentaries, religion and schools Granada TV 1996–99, ed Everyman series (BBC 1) April 1999–2000, subsequently creative dir documentaries BBC, exec dir Screen England 2009–; advsy chair Guardian Edinburgh International TV Festival 1998, judge Sony Radio Awards 2004; formerly: memb and advsr Yorks and Humberside Arts Bd, memb

P

North British Housing Assoc; memb: RTS 1993, BAFTA 1996; *Awards* Best Regnl Current Affrs Series RTS 1993, runner-up Options Business Woman of the Year 1995, NW Best Documentary Prize RTS 1998, Brian Redhead Special Award RTS 1998, Best Documentary Broadcast Production Awards 1998, Int Emmy 1998, NY Festival World Medal 1998, Sandford St Martin Premier Award 2003; *Recreations* running, walking, skiing, cooking, yoga, reading, family life; *Style*— Ms Ruth Pitt

PITT-KETHLEY, (Helen) Fiona; da of Rupert Singleton Pitt-Kethley (d 1975), and Olive, *née* Banfield; *b* 21 November 1954; *Educ* Haberdashers' Aske's Girls' Sch, Chelsea Sch of Art (BA, Biddulph painting prize); *m* 1995, James Plaskett; 1 s (Alexander Michael b 15 Sept 1996); *Career* poet, travel writer, novelist and journalist; *Books* poetry collections: Sky Ray Lolly (1986), Private Parts (1987), The Perfect Man (1989), Dogs (1993), Double Act (1996), Memo from a Muse (1997), Selected Poems (2008); others: Journeys to the Underworld (travel book, 1988), The Misfortunes of Nigel (novel, 1991), The Literary Companion to Sex (anthology, 1992), The Maiden's Progress (novella, 1992), Too Hot to Handle (essays and letters, 1992), The Pan Principle (travel book, 1993), The Literary Companion to Low Life (anthology, 1995), Red Light Districts of the World (essays, 2000), Baker's Dozen (novel, 2000), My Schooling (autobiography, 2000); *Recreations* Kyokushin karate, rock-hunting, snorkelling, adopting feral cats, fishing, swimming, hill-walking; *Style*— Ms Fiona Pitt-Kethley; ✉ e-mail livinginspain@hotmail.com, website www.fionapitt-kethley.com

PITTAWAY, David Michael; QC (2000); s of Michael Pittaway, JP, MRCVS, of Coventry, and Heather Yvette, *née* Scott; *b* 29 June 1955; *Educ* Uppingham, Sidney Sussex Coll Cambridge (exhibitioner, MA); *m* 26 March 1983, Jill Suzanne, da of Dr Ian Douglas Bertie Newsam, MRCVS, of Cambridge; 2 s (James Frederick Henry b 9 July 1986, Charles Edward Benet b 22 July 1989); *Career* called to the Bar Inner Temple 1977 (bencher 1998, reader 2016); recorder Midland & Oxford Circuit 2000– (asst recorder 1998–2000), dep judge of the High Court 2008; acting chllr Dio of Birmingham 2003–05, chllr Dio of Peterborough 2006–; legal memb Mental Health Tbnl 2002–16, legal assessor GMC 2002–04, legal assessor RCVS 2004–; chm: Professional Negligence Bar Assoc 2005–07, Educn Ctee Inner Temple 2005–09, Educn Ctee Bar Cncl 2008–11, Neuberger Working Gp Bar Cncl 2010–11; memb: Exec Ctee Inner Temple 1994–98, 2004–09 and 2012–, Bar Cncl 1999–2005 and 2008–11 (memb Mgmnt Ctee 2008–11), Cncl Inns of Court 2008–11 (tstee 2013–); govr Compton Verney House Tst 2010–12 (chm Devpt Bd 2010–12), tstee Nat Educn Tst 2011–14, memb Cncl Cheltenham Ladies Coll 2011–; FCIArb 1986; Pittaway & Hammerton Professional Negligence Cases (1998), Atkin's Court Forms (vols 8, 28 and 29 (2)); *Recreations* gardening, music, travel; *Clubs* Garrick, RAC, Redclyffe Yacht, Wareham; *Style*— David Pittaway, Esq, QC; ✉ Hailsham Chambers, 4 Paper Buildings, Temple, London EC4Y 7EX (☎ 020 7643 5000, e-mail david.pittaway@hailshamchambers.com)

PITTOCK, Prof Murray; s of Dr Malcolm Pittock, and Dr Joan, *née* Mould; *b* 5 January 1962; *Educ* Aberdeen GS, Univ of Glasgow (Bradley Medal, Buchanan Prize, Fotheringham Bursary, MA), Balliol Coll Oxford (Snell exhibitioner, ESU scholar, Nat Speech Communication Assoc of America visiting scholar, DPhil), Univ of Glasgow (DLitt); *m* 15 April 1989, Dr Anne Pittock; 2 da (Alexandra b 31 Jan 1990, Davidona b 7 June 1994); *Career* formerly: head College of Arts and vice-princ Univ of Glasgow, prof of Scottish and Romantic Literature Univ of Manchester, prof of literature Univ of Strathclyde, reader Univ of Edinburgh; pro vice-princ and Bradley prof of English Literature Univ of Glasgow 2015–; sr Warnock fell Yale Univ 1998 and 2000–01, visiting fell in advanced Welsh and Celtic studies Univ of Wales 2002; visiting prof: Trinity Coll Dublin 2008, Charles Univ Prague 2010, Notre Dame 2014, New York Univ 2015; assoc ed Oxford DNB 1998–, jt founding ed Scottish Studies Review 2000–07; pres Scottish Ctee of Profs of English 2001–03; memb: Fellowship Ctee Lit, Language and History and Creative Industries RSE, Humanities Research Ctee RSE 2006–10, AHRC English Postgraduate Panel 2006–08, Advsy Gp Scottish Govt 2009, Int Ctee RSE 2016–; convenor Nat Champions' Gp Scottish Studies 2011–13; BP Humanities Research Prize 1992–93, Chatterton lectr in poetry Br Acad 2002, nominated, called or shortlisted for various prizes incl Orwell, James Russell Lowell, Saltire and Wolfson prizes; various invited lectureships; pres: Boswell Soc 2001–02, Edmund Burke Soc; tstee: Jacobite Studies Tst 2003–, Ossian Monument Tst 2012; hon advsr Nat Tst for Scotland, hon advsr Nat Galleries of Scotland 2015–; FRHistS 1992, FSA Scot 1995, fell English Assoc (FEA) 2001, FRSA 2002, FRSE 2004, FHEA, hon fell Assoc for Scottish Literary Studies 2015; *Books* The Invention of Scotland (1991, 2 edn 2014), Spectrum of Decadence: The Literature of the 1890s (1993, 2 edn 2014), Poetry and Jacobite Politics in Eighteenth-Century Britain and Ireland (1994, paperback edn 2006), The Myth of the Jacobite Clans (1995, 2 edn 2009), Inventing and Resisting Britain (1997), Jacobitism (1998), Celtic Identity and the British Image (1999), Scottish Nationality (2001), A New History of Scotland (2003), The Edinburgh History of Scottish Literature (co-ed, 2006), The Reception of Sir Walter Scott in Europe (ed, 2007, 2 edn 2014), James Boswell (2007), Scottish and Irish Romanticism (2008, paperback edn 2011), The Road to Independence? (2008, 2 edn 2014), Loyalty and Identity (co-ed, 2010), Edinburgh Companion to Scottish Romanticism (ed, 2011), Robert Burns in Global Culture (ed, 2011), Material Culture and Sedition (2013), The Reception of Robert Burns in Europe (ed, 2014), Culloden (2016); *Recreations* walking, debating (memb Br Isles debating team 1984, former Oxford Union debating champion, convenor of debates and dep speaker for life Glasgow Univ Union), chess; *Clubs* Adam Smith, Oxford & Cambridge; *Style*— Prof Murray Pittock, FRSE; ✉ 7 University Gardens, Glasgow G12 8QH

PITTS, His Hon Judge Anthony Brian; s of Sir Cyril Pitts, and Barbara, *née* Sell; *b* 18 May 1946; *Educ* Cranleigh Sch, Pembroke Coll Oxford; *m* 21 June 1980, Sally-Jane, *née* Spencer; 1 s, 1 da; *Career* called to the Bar 1975; recorder of the Crown Court 1997, circuit judge (SE Circuit) 2002–; *Style*— His Hon Judge Pitts

PIZZEY, Erin Patria Margaret; *née* Carney; da of Cyril Carney, MBE (d 1980), and Ruth Patricia Last; *b* 19 February 1939, Tsingtao, China; *Educ* Leweston Manor Sherborne; *m* 1, 1961 (m dis 1979), John Leo Pizzey; 1 s (Amos b 1967), 1 da (Cleo b 1961); *Career* author, journalist and social reformer; fndr of the Int Shelter Movement for Battered Men, Women and Children; advsr on child advocacy and safe houses Slovenia; memb: Royal Soc of Literature, Soc of Authors; Int Order of Volunteers for Peace Diploma of Honour 1981, Nancy Astor Award for Journalism 1983, Distinguished Leadership Award (World Congress of Victimology) 1987, Valentino Palm d'Oro Award for Literature 1994; hon citizen of San Ginani D'Asso Italy 1993; patron: Care and Comfort Romania 1998, Mankind 2004, Derwent Domestic Violence Forum 2005, Compassion in Care 2006; opened refuge for victims of domestic violence Bahrain (the first in the Arab world) 2007; has contributed to many leading newspapers and journals; author of articles: Choosing a Non-Violent Relationship, Sexual Abuse Within the Family; TV documentaries incl: Scream Quietly 1975, Chiswick Women's Aid 1977, That Awful Woman 1987, Cutting Edge: Sanctuary 1991, Who's Failing the Family 1999; *Non-Fiction* Scream Quietly or the Neighbours Will Hear (1974), Infernal Child (1978), The Sluts Cookbook (1981), Erin Pizzey Collects (1983), Prone To Violence (1982), All In The Name of Love, Wild Child (autobiography, 1995), Grandmothers of the Revolution (2000), Women on Men – Who are the Victims (2000), This Way to the Revolution (autobiography, 2011); *Fiction* The Watershed, In the Shadow of the Castle, The Pleasure Palace, First Lady, The Consul General's Daughter (1988), The Snow Leopard of Shanghai (1989), Other Lovers (1991), Morningstar (1992), Swimming With Dolphins (1993), For the Love of a Stranger (1994), Kisses (1995), The Wicked World of Women (1996), The Fame Game (2000); *Short Stories* The Man in the Blue Van, The Frangipani Tree, Addiction, Dancing; *Recreations* reading, cooking, antiques, violin, wine, travel; *Style*— Erin Pizzey; ✉ Flat 5, 29 Lebanon Park, Twickenham TW1 3DH (☎ 020 8241 6541, e-mail pizzey@blueyonder.co.uk, website www.erinpizzey.com)

PLANER, Nigel George; s of George Victor Planer, and (Margaret) Lesley, *née* Weeden (d 2000); *b* 22 February 1953; *Educ* Westminster, Univ of Sussex, LAMDA; *m* 1, 19 Aug 1989 (m dis 1994), Anna, da of Michael Lea; 1 s (Stanley b 5 Sept 1988); m 2, 3 April 1999 (m dis 2003), Frankie, da of Gerald Park; 1 s (Harvey b 3 Aug 1999); *Career* actor and writer; Hon DArt Edinburgh Napier Univ 2011; memb: Equity 1977, Writers' Guild 1987; *Theatre* incl: Leeds Playhouse, Young Vic, Oxford Playhouse, Hampstead Theatre, Regent's Park; memb original cast Evita, Man of the Moment, Angry Old Men, Chicago, Feel Good, High Life, We Will Rock You, Wicked, Hairspray, Charlie and the Chocolate Factory; *Television* leading roles incl: Shine on Harvey Moon, Rollover Beethoven, King and Castle, The Young Ones, Filthy Rich and Catflap, Number Twenty Seven, Blackeyes, Frankenstein's Baby, The Comic Strip Presents, The Bill, The Naked Actor, Bonjour La Classe, Wake Up With, The Magic Roundabout, Cuts, The Grimleys, The Flood, Hogfather, Miss Marple, Hacks, Hunt for Tony Blair; *Films* incl: The Supergrass, Brazil, Yellowbeard, More Bad News, The Strike, Land Girls, Bright Young Things, Virgin Territory, The List, I Give it a Year; *Scripts* incl: Radio 4 sketches, Not the Nine O'Clock News, Funseekers (Channel 4 film), King and Castle (Thames); plays incl: On the Ceiling (Birmingham Rep, Garrick Theatre London and BBC Radio 4), Death of Long Pig (Finborough Theatre) 2009, The Magnificent Andrea (BBC Radio 4) 2011; *Live appearances* incl: fndr memb Comic Strip, Comedy Store, Edinburgh Festival, MTV NY, Adelaide Festival (Aust), Hammersmith Odeon; *Awards* winner BPI Award Best Comedy Record 1984; *Books* Neil's Book of the Dead (1983), I, An Actor (1987), A Good Enough Dad (1992), Let's Get Divorced (1994), Therapy and How to Avoid It (1996), Unlike the Buddha (1997), The Right Man (1998), Faking It (2001), On the Ceiling (2005), Death of Long Pig (2008), Journal of Stevenson Studies (2013); *Style*— Nigel Planer, Esq; ✉ c/o United Agents Ltd, 12–26 Lexington Street, London W1F 0LE (☎ 020 3214 0800, fax 020 3214 0801)

PLANT, Charles William; CBE (2015); s of James Plant (d 2008), and Nancy, *née* Webb (d 2003); *b* 28 October 1944, Neyland, Pembrokeshire; *Educ* Newcastle-under-Lyme HS, St John's Coll Cambridge (McMahon law scholar, MA), Coll of Law; *m* 28 Sept 1968, Anne, *née* Jacobsen; 1 s (Nicholas), 2 da (Justine, Georgina); *Career* admitted slr 1969; Herbert Smith LLP: articled clerk 1967–69, asst Litigation Dept 1967–76, ptnr 1976–2005, conslt 2005–; ed-in-chief Blackstone's Civil Practice; chm of govrs Coll of Law 2007–09; memb: Lord Chllr's Advsy Ctee on Legal Educn and Conduct 1994–2000, Legal Servs Consultative Panel 2000–03, Law Soc; chair Slrs Regulation Authy 2010–14; Hon LLD Univ of Law; *Recreations* golf, art, French Riviera; *Clubs* Athenaeum; *Style*— Charles Plant, Esq, CBE; ✉ e-mail charlesplant@btinternet.com

PLANT, Dr Gordon Terence; s of Thomas Edmund Plant (d 1998), and Sheila May, *née* Atkinson; *b* 4 July 1952; *Educ* Woking Co GS for Boys, Downing Coll Cambridge (scholar, MA, MD), St Thomas' Hosp Med Sch London (exhibitioner, MB BChir); *m* 29 April 1978, Dr Marilyn Jane Plant, *née* Dirkin; 3 da (Eleanor Margaret, Emma Louise, Katharine Elizabeth); *Career* house physician St Thomas' Hosp London 1977–78, SHO Westminster Hosp 1978–80, registrar Addenbrooke's Hosp Cambridge 1980–82, Wellcome Tst research assoc Physiological Lab Univ of Cambridge 1982–86, registrar and sr registrar Nat Hosp for Neurology and Neurosurgery London 1986–89, research fell Smith-Kettlewell Research Inst Univ of Calif San Francisco 1989–90, conslt neurologist Nat Hosp for Neurology and Neurosurgery London, Moorfields Eye Hosp and Med Eye Unit St Thomas' Hosp London 1991–, service dir neuro-ophthalmology Moorfields Eye Hosp 1994–, hon conslt St Luke's Hosp for the Clergy; hon sr lectr: UCL 1991–, GKT (formerly UMDS) 1991–; visiting prof City Univ 2006–, visiting prof Wills Eye Inst 2011; assoc ed Opthalmologica 2001–12, ed-in-chief Neuro-opthalmology 2008– (memb Editorial Bd 2003–); RSM: vice-pres Section of Ophthalmology 2001–04, pres Section of Clinical Neurosciences 2011–12; memb: BMA, Assoc for Research in Vision and Opthalmology 1986, European Brain and Behaviour Soc 1990, Br Isles Neuro-ophthalmology Club 1991, American Acad of Sciences 1993, European Neuro-ophthalmology Soc 1994, Ophthalmic Club 1994; fndr UK Neuro-Ophthalmology Special Interest Gp 2005; MRC Travelling Fellowship 1989–90; FRSM 1993, FRCP 1994, FRCOphth 2005; *Publications* Optic Neuritis (ed, 1986); numerous pubns concerning neurology, neuro-ophthalmology and visual science in academic jls; *Recreations* music, painting; *Style*— Dr Gordon T Plant; ✉ The National Hospital for Neurology and Neurosurgery, Queen Square, London WC1N 3BG (☎ 020 7391 8956, fax 020 7391 8994, e-mail gordon.plant@uclh.nhs.uk)

PLANT OF HIGHFIELD, Baron (Life Peer UK 1992), of Weelsby in the County of Humberside; Prof Raymond Plant; s of Stanley Plant (d 1983), and Marjorie Plant; *b* 19 March 1945; *Educ* Havelock Sch Grimsby, King's Coll London (BA), Univ of Hull (PhD); *m* 27 July 1967, Katherine Sylvia, da of Jack Dixon (d 1989); 3 s (Hon Nicholas b 1969, Hon Matthew b 1971, Hon Richard b 1976); *Career* sr lectr in philosophy Univ of Manchester 1967–69, prof of politics Univ of Southampton 1979–94, master St Catherine's Coll Oxford 1994–99; Univ of Southampton: pro-chllr 1996–99, prof of European political thought 2000–; prof of jurisprudence and political philosophy KCL 2002–; Sciences Po Paris: Vincent Wright prof 2008, Gresham prof 2012–15; visiting prof Univ of Winchester 2008, visiting prof Univ of Tallinn Estonia; lectures: Stevenson (Univ of Glasgow) 1981, Agnes Cumming (UC Dublin) 1988, Stanton (Univ of Cambridge) 1989–90 and 1990–91, Sarum (Univ of Oxford) 1991, Ferguson (Univ of Manchester) 1995, Gore (Westminster Abbey) 1996, Scott Holland (Manchester Cathedral) 1996, J P MacIntosh Meml (Univ of Edinburgh) 1996, Eleanor Rathbone (Univ of Bristol) 1997, G Ganz Univ of Southampton 2005, Boutwood Univ of Cambridge 2006, Bampton Univ of Oxford 2007; chm: Lab Pty Cmmn on Electoral Systems 1991–93, Fabian Soc Cmmn on Citizenship and Taxation 1998–2000; author and contrib to New Statesman and Society, The Independent, The Times, etc; pres Acad of Learned Societies in the Social Sciences 1999–2001, pres NCVO; lay canon Winchester Cathedral; Isiah Berlin Prize 2011; memb: Fabian Soc, Political Studies Assoc UK; fell Univ of Cardiff 1999; hon fell: St Catherines's Coll Oxford 2000, Harris Manchester Coll Oxford 2000; Hon DLitt: Univ of Hull, London Guildhall Univ; Hon DUniv: York 2007, Winchester 2008, Tallinn 2012; Hon LLD Univ of Southampton 2012; FRSA 1992; *Books* Social and Moral Theory in Social Work (1970), Hegel: An Introduction (1973), Community and Ideology (1974), Political Philosophy And Social Welfare (1981), Philosophy Politics and Citizenship (1984), Equality Markets And the State (1984), Conservative Capitalism in Britain And The United States: A Critical Appraisal (1988), Citizenship Rights and Socialism (1989), Modern Political Thought (1991), Hegel on Philosophy and Religion (1997), Politics, Theology and History (2001), The Neo-Liberal State (2009); *Recreations* ornithology, opera, Bach, Mozart; *Style*— Prof the Rt Hon Lord Plant of Highfield; ✉ 6 Woodview Close, Bassett, Southampton SO2 3P2 (☎ 023 8076 9529, e-mail raymond.plant@kcl.ac.uk)

PLANTE, Prof David; *b* 4 March 1940; *Educ* l'Université de Louvain Belgium, Boston Coll (BA); *Career* instr of English English Sch Rome 1961–62, instr of English Boston Sch of Modern Languages MA 1964–65, instr of French St John's Prep Sch Devon MA 1965–66, writing workshop City Literary Inst London 1970–74, bursary Arts Cncl 1977; writer in residence: UEA 1977–78 (Henfield fell 1977), Tulsa Univ OK 1980–82, King's Coll Cambridge 1985–86, Adelphi Univ Garden City NY 1988, Université du Québec Montréal

1990; Guggenheim fell 1982; lectr Gorky Inst of Literature Moscow 1990; Columbia Univ NY: prof of writing 1998–, dir Fiction Concentration Writing Div 2000–, memb Ctee on Instruction Sch of the Arts; sr memb King's Coll Cambridge 1997; fell NY Inst for the Humanities NYU; FRSL 2002; *Awards* Pushcart Prize (for profile Jean Rhys: A Remembrance) 1982, O Henry Prize (for short story Work) 1983, Prize for Artistic Merit American Acad and Inst of Arts and Letters 1983, Award of Excellence Boston Coll 2000, Pushcart Prize (for essay Returning to Providence) 2001; *Publications* novels: The Ghost of Henry James (1970), Slides (1971), Relatives (1972), The Darkness of the Body (1974), Figures in Bright Air (1976), The Family (1978, nominated US Nat Book Award 1978), The Country (1981, reissued 1983), The Woods (1982), The Francoeur Novels: The Family, The Woods, The Country (1984), The Foreigner (1984), The Catholic (1986, reissued 1987), The Native (1991), The Accident (1991), Annunciation (1994), The Age of Terror (1999, reissued 2000); other work: Difficult Women: Portraits of Jean Rhys, Sonia Orwell, Germaine Greer (non-fiction, 1983, reissued 1986), The Mystery of Our Suffering (play, 2000), American Ghosts, a Memoir (2005), ABC (2007); author of numerous short stories, profiles, essays, articles and reviews; *Style*— Prof David Plante

PLANTEROSE, Rowan Michael; s of Anthony Ernest Charles Planterose, of Lewes, E Sussex, and Jean D'Arcy, *née* Palmer (d 2008); *b* 19 February 1954; *Educ* Eastbourne Coll, Downing Coll Cambridge (MA, LLB); *m* 23 Oct 1999, Elizabeth Zoe Claire, *née* Dawson; 1 da (Abigail d'Arcy b 24 Feb 2001); *Career* called to the Bar 1978; chartered arbitrator 2002; slr, ptnr Davies Arnold Cooper 2004–11 (managing ptnr 2007–08), ptnr DAC Beachcroft LLP 2011–15 (conslt 2015–); FCIArb 1989 (memb Cncl 1991–2000); *Publications* Bernstein: Dispute Resolution Handbook (co-author, 4 edn 2003), The Arbitration Act 1996: A Commentary (5 edn, 2014); *Recreations* squash, skiing, gliding; *Style*— Rowan Planterose, Esq; ✉ DAC Beachcroft LLP, 1 Minster Court, Mincing Lane, London EC3R 7AA (☎ 020 7894 6320, e-mail rplanterose@dacbeachcroft.com, website www.dacbeachcroft.com)

PLASCHKES, Sarah Georgina; QC (2011); *Career* called to the Bar 1988; recorder 2004, circuit judge (SE Circuit) 2015–; *Style*— Her Hon Judge Plaschkes, QC

PLASCOW, Ronald; s of Oscar Plascow, and Liese Plascow (d 2004); *b* 22 October 1956, London; *Educ* Latymer Upper Sch, Univ of Bordeaux, Univ of Sheffield (LLB); *m* June 1984, Joanna Plascow; 2 da (Clare b 2 May 1986, Harriet b 16 Jan 1989); *Career* admitted slr 1981; Franks Charlesly & Co: articled clerk 1979–81, asst slr 1981–82; slr and divnl legal advsr Trafalgar House plc 1982–84, sr slr Lovell White Durrant 1984–89; Mills & Reeve: slr 1989–91, ptnr 1991–2016, head Construction and Engrg Team until 2016, conslt Projects Construction and Engrg Team 2016–; memb: Law Soc 1981, Soc of Construction Law, Technol and Construction Slrs' Assoc; Tolley's Guide to Construction Contracts (1999); *Recreations* reading, walking dogs, films, music (jazz), theatre, art; *Style*— Ronald Plascow, Esq; ✉ Mills & Reeve, Bontanic House, 100 Hills Road, Cambridge CB2 1PH (☎ 01223 222261, fax 01223 222221, e-mail ron.plascow@mills-reeve.com)

PLASKETT, Maj-Gen Frederick Joseph; CB (1980), MBE (1966); s of Frederick Joseph Plaskett (d 1982), and Grace Mary Plaskett (d 1988); *b* 23 October 1926; *Educ* Wallasey GS, Chelsea Poly; *m* 1, 9 Sept 1950, Heather (d 1982), da of Maurice William Kington (d 1976), of Salisbury, Wilts; 4 da (Helen b 1951, Wendy b 1954, Kate b 1960 d 2010, Lucy b 1965); m 2, 1984, Mrs Patricia Joan Healy, da of Richard Upton, of Wimborne, Dorset; *Career* RN (Fleet Air Arm) 1944–45, Army 1945–81 (cmmnd India 1945); regtl and staff appts: India, Korea, Japan, Malaya, W Africa, Germany, UK; ret as Maj-Gen; dir gen Tport and Movements (Army) 1981; Col Cmdt RCT 1981–91; cmmr Royal Hosp Chelsea 1985–88; dir gen Road Haulage Assoc Ltd 1981–88; dir: Paccar UK (Foden Trucks) 1981–97, Road Haulage Insurance Services 1983–88, Br Road Fedn 1982–88, BR London Midland Regn 1986–92 (chm 1989–92); Freeman City of London 1979, Liveryman Worshipful Co of Carmen 1979; FCILT; *Publications* Shoot Like a Gentleman (memoir, 2005); numerous articles and reviews in military, transport and leisure jls; *Recreations* sailing, fishing, gardening; *Style*— Maj-Gen Frederick Plaskett, CB, MBE; ✉ c/o National Westminster Bank plc, The Commons, Shaftesbury, Dorset SP7 8JY

PLATA, Rick; *b* 12 May 1958; *Educ* Haliford GS, Kingston Coll Surrey; *m* 20 Sept 1987, Robin Beth, da of Joseph Moskowitz, of NY; 1 s (Matthew b 14 June 1992), 1 da (Alexandra b 25 March 1995); *Career* sr planner/buyer Foote Cone and Belding 1980–82 (asst media planner/media planner 1979–80), media mangr The Leagas Delaney Partnership 1982–84; Laing Henry Advertising: dir of media planning 1984–86, media/bd dir (concurrently md Communique Media ind media co within agency) 1986–89; sr vice-pres/dir of business devpt Hill Holliday Connors Cosmopolus Advertising Inc NY 1992–93 (sr vice-pres/media dir 1989–92), media dir/Euro media co-ordinator Burkitt Weinreich Bryant Clients and Co Ltd 1993–95; head of sales NBC Europe 1996–98 (head of strategic planning NBC Super Channel 1995–96), dir of advertising and sales Fox Kids Europe 1998–2004, commercial dir Corbis 2005, sales dir Getty Images 2006–07, ceo Imagine Fashion 2008–11, int commercial dir FMG 2011–12, conslt/non-exec dir ComFederation 2012–13, commercial dir Bloomberg TV Africa 2013–15 (head of mktg 2014–15); sometime memb: Educn Ctee IPA, Media Ctee American Assoc of Advtg Agencies, Editorial Bd Agency Magazine; recipient: Media Week award, recognition and distinction for work performed on behalf of NYC (given by Mayor David Dinkins) 1991; memb: NY Advtg Club, Soc of Advtg Media Professionals, D&AD, IAA 1999, Internet Advtg Bureau (IAB) 2002; *Recreations* tennis, golf, theatre, music; *Clubs* Groucho, Blue Bird, RAC; *Style*— Rick Plata, Esq

PLATELL, Amanda Jane; da of Francis Ernest Platell, and Norma June, *née* Malland; *b* 12 November 1957; *Educ* Penrhos Methodist Ladies Coll, Univ of Western Aust (BA); *Career* reporter Perth Daily News 1978–81, Sydney Bureau chief Perth Daily News 1983; sub ed: Sydney Sun 1984, Harpers Bazaar 1985, Today Newspaper 1986; metro dep ed London Daily News 1987, dep ed Today 1987–92 (features prodn ed 1987), gp managing ed Mirror Group Newspapers 1993, also dir of marketing MGN 1993, mktg dir Independent 1993–95, md Independent and Independent on Sunday 1995–96, ed Sunday Mirror 1996–97, ed Sunday Express 1998–99, head of media Conservative Party 1999–2001; columnist New Statesman, writer and columnist Daily Mail 2001; presenter Morgan and Platell (Channel 4) 2004–; *Books* Scandal (1999); *Recreations* cars, eating out, travelling, cooking, gardening, drawing; *Style*— Miss Amanda Platell

PLATFORD, Richard John; s of Eric Roy Platford, of Great Warley, Essex, and Joan Mary, *née* Willis; *b* 20 January 1945; *Educ* Felsted, Trinity Hall Cambridge (MA), London Business Sch (MBA), Birkbeck Coll Univ of London (Cert of HE); *m* 1, 29 Dec 1973 (m dis), Marie Renee, da of Rene Louis de Peyrecave; 4 s (James Alexander b 11 July 1976, Giles Richard b 26 April 1978, Edward William, Thomas Henry (twins) b 14 April 1983); m 2, 10 May 2008, Laure Leroch, da of Victor Le Roch; 1 s (Matisse b 28 Oct 2003); *Career* mgmnt trainee Rolls Royce Aero Engines 1963–64, systems implementation offr Rolls Royce 1967–69, trainee Paris then prodn controller/materials mangr Milan Otis Elevator 1971–75, dir of materials Clark Equipment 1976–78; PricewaterhouseCoopers (formerly Coopers & Lybrand before merger): conslt 1978–79, ptnr Manufacturing Europe 1983–87 (mangr 1979–83), ptnr Manufacturing UK 1987–91, chm Int Pharmaceutical Sector Programme 1991–98, global ldr Pharmaceutical Gp 1998–2000, ptnr Pharmaceutical Gp 2000–02; ptnr IBM Business Consulting Services 2002–05, co-fndr and ceo CellVir 2006–08, ceo Mellitech 2008–13, co-fndr Theranexus 2013–; Freeman City of London, Liveryman Worshipful Co of Needlemakers; CEng, MIEE 1978, fell British Prodn and Inventory Control Soc 1978, MIMgt 1979, MIMC 1985; *Recreations* golf, tennis, skiing, opera, music, history of art 1400–1700; *Style*— Richard Platford, Esq; ✉ Zuidstraat 86 B1.1, 8630 Veurne, Belgium

PLATT, Adrian; s of Clifford Lowe Platt, OBE (d 1982), of Chislehurst, Kent, and Katharine Eileen, *née* Everington (d 1975); *b* 28 November 1935; *Educ* Marlborough, Univ of Lyons; *m* 24 Sept 1960, Valerie, da of Richard Bois (d 1956); 2 da (Emma (Mrs Stephen Howard) b 1965, Katie (Mrs Giles Lawton) b 1967); *Career* Nat Serv 4 RHA 1954–56, TA HAC 1956–62; dir Sedgwick Collins Ltd 1964–; chm: Sedgwick Forbes Marine Ltd 1968–69, Sedgwick Forbes Bland Payne Marine Ltd 1969–; dir: Sedgwick Group plc 1981–93 (md special projects 1991–93), Sedgwick Group Development Ltd 1993–99; chm: Sedgwick Marine and Aviation Group 1986–88, Sedgwick Ltd Development Group 1988–93, Sedgwick James Overseas Cos Ltd 1990–91; chm Marine Exec Ctee Lloyds Insurance Brokers 1969, dep chm Ctee Lloyds Insurance Brokers 1970; memb East European Trade Cncl 1990–95; chm Exec Ctee Court of Mary Rose 1980–90, tstee Mary Rose Tst 1983–2004, dir Cncl for Music in Hosps; govr Corp of the Sons of the Clergy; Past Master Worshipful Co of Vintners (Liveryman 1956), Freeman Worshipful Co of Shipwrights 1988; FInstD; *Recreations* golf, music, walking, reading; *Clubs* HAC, Sloane, Effingham Golf, St Enodoc Golf, Clovelly Golf (S Africa); *Style*— Adrian Platt, Esq; ✉ Hatchfield Cottage, Butlers Hill, West Horsley, Surrey KT24 6AZ (☎ 014865 4729, e-mail adrianplatt@btinternet.com)

PLATT, David Wallace; QC (2011); s of Christopher Platt, of Knock, Ulster, and Susan Harriette La Nauze, *née* Wallace; *b* 1964, NI; *Educ* Campbell Coll, Trinity Hall Cambridge (MA); *m* 2007, Jessica Emily Darya Perks; 1 s (Harry Wallace b 31 Dec 2013), 1 da (Emily Susan b 27 Dec 2015); *Career* called to the Bar Middle Temple 1987; TV presenter BBC NI, freelance broadcaster and media trainer; Parly candidate (Cons) Cambridge 1997; chm Cambridge Univ Cons Assoc 1986, formerly political research asst and aide House of Commons and Cons Central Office; former London memb Exec CPRE; former govr Churchill Gardens Primary Sch, former govr Pimlico Sch, former tstee Borealis Theatre Gp; *Books* Educating Our Future (1986), Blue Tomorrow (2001); *Recreations* politics, theatre, opera, conservation, Greek history, J R R Tolkien, Dorset; *Clubs* Brooks's, Annabel's; *Style*— David Platt, Esq, QC; ✉ Crown Office Chambers, 2 Crown Office Row, Temple, London EC4Y 7HJ (☎ 020 7797 8100, e-mail platt@crownofficechambers.com)

PLATT, Dame Denise; DBE (2004, CBE 1996); da of Victor Platt (d 1980), of Cheshire, and May, *née* Keeling (d 1996); *b* 21 February 1945; *Educ* Congleton GS for Girls, UC Cardiff (BSc(Econ)); *Career* social worker Middx Hosp 1968–73, sr social worker Guy's Hosp 1973–76, gp ldr Southwark Social Servs 1976–78, princ social worker Hammersmith Hosp 1978–83, dir of Social Serv London Borough Hammersmith and Fulham 1986–94 (asst dir 1983–86), under sec social servs Assoc of Metropolitan Authorities (AMA) 1994–97, head of social servs Local Government Assoc 1997–98, chief inspr Soc Servs Inspectorate Dept of Health 1998–2004, chair Cmmn for Social Care Inspection 2004–09; chair Local Innovation Awards Scheme 2009–10; pres Assoc of Dirs of Social Servs 1993–94, vice-chair Nat Cncl for Domiciliary Care Servs until 1995, chair Nat Inst for Social Work 1997–98; memb: Ministerial Action Gp on AIDS 1991–93, Advsy Gp Policy Studies Inst until 1994, Academic Cncl Royal Postgrad Med Sch until 1994, Dept of Health Steering Gp Community Care Devpt Prog (formerly Dept of Health Caring for People Advsy Group), Cncl Central Cncl for Educn and Trg in Social Work (CCETSW), Home Sec's Task Force on Youth Justice 1997–98, Disability Rights Task Force 1997–98, Ind Reference Gp on Mental Health 1997–98, Strategic Review of London's Health Servs 1997–98, Ind Review Bd Cheshire Fire & Rescue Serv 2007–, Ctee on Standards in Public Life 2008–; cmmr Audit Cmmn 2007–10; tstee and dir Family Planning Assoc 2005–10, chair Nat AIDS Tst 2006– (tstee and vice-chm until 1998), tstee NSPCC 2006–, tstee Adventure Capital Fund 2008–12, tstee Lloyds TSB Fndn for England and Wales 2011–; govr Univ of Bedfordshire 2006–12; Hon DSocSci Brunel Univ 1998, Hon LLD Univ of Brighton 2008; AIMSW 1968, FRSA 2002; *Recreations* music, watercolours, walking; *Clubs* Reform; *Style*— Dame Denise Platt, DBE; ✉ e-mail damedenise@btinternet.com

PLATT, Eleanor Frances; QC (1982); er da of Dr Maurice Leon Platt (d 1966), of Sussex, and Sara, *née* Stein (d 1983); *b* 6 May 1938; *Educ* Univ of London (LLB); *m* 1963, Frederick Malcolm Lind; 1 da (Amanda b 1965), 1 s (Jonathan b 1969); *Career* called to the Bar Gray's Inn 1960; jt head of specialist family law chambers 1990–2007, recorder SE circuit 1982–2004, dep judge (Family Div) High Court of Justice 1987–2004; memb: Matrimonial Causes Rule Ctee 1986–90, Gene Therapy Advsy Ctee 1993–98; treas Family Law Bar Assoc 1990–95 (acting chm 1995), dep chm NHS Tbnl 1995–2002, legal assessor: GDC 1995 and 2008–15, GMC 1995–; vice-pres Bd of Deputies of British Jews 2003–06 (chm Law Parly and General Purposes Ctee 1988–94); chm New London Synagogue 1994–99; pres Jewish Family Mediation Register 1998; pres Medico-Legal Soc 2002–04; memb Family Mediators Assoc 1997; FRSM; *Recreations* the arts, travel, family; *Style*— Miss Eleanor Platt, QC; ✉ One Garden Court, Temple, London EC4Y 9BJ (☎ 020 7797 7900, fax 020 7797 7929, e-mail platt@1gc.com)

PLATT, Jane Christine; CBE (2013); da of George Platt, of Gayton, Wirral, and Miriam Platt; *b* 8 January 1957, Liverpool; *Educ* St Catherine's Coll Oxford (MA); *m* 1980, David Bill; *Career* chief exec Barclays Stockbrokers and Barclays Bank Tst Co 1996–2001, pres asset mgmnt Reuters 2001–03, chief operating offr Reuters Business Divs 2003–04, chief exec NS&I 2006–; dir: Edinburgh UK Tracker Tst plc 2004–06, Witan plc 2005; non-exec dir Financial Conduct Authy 2013–; tstee Reuters Pension Fund 2004; chartered fell Securities Inst 1996; hon doc in laws Univ of Warwick 2015; past Master Worshipful Company of Int Bankers; *Recreations* theatre, opera; *Clubs* Cornhill; *Style*— Ms Jane Platt, CBE; ✉ 1 Drummond Gate, London SW1V 2QX

PLATT, Richard Andrew; *b* 1947; *Educ* Samuel Pepys Secdy Modern Sch Brockley; *m* Jocelyn; 3 s (Stephen b 1977, James b 1981, Nicholas b 1983), 2 da (Rebecca b 1988, Georgina b 1994); *Career* media buyer Masius Wynne Williams 1970–76, dep md Tape Consultancy 1976–82, asst programmer Network 10 Sydney 1982–84, head of programming Sky Channel 1984–88, dir of progs Maxwell Entertainment 1988–89, controller of progs Scansat 1989–91; dir of broadcasting: Meridian Television 1995– (controller of programming 1991–95), MAI Media 1995–, United Broadcasting and Entertainment 1997–; dir of broadcasting and channel devpt United Broadcasting and Entertainment 1998–2000; dir: Rap Consultancy 1991–2014, ITFC Ltd 1995–2000, United Interactive 1998–99, Rapture 1998–2000, TSMSI 1998–2000, Wapbeats International Ltd 2001–02, the24 Ltd 2003–09, iNXMediaUK Ltd 2008–09; *Recreations* soccer, photography, cinema, theatre; *Style*— Richard Platt; ☎ 07710 013908, e-mail richard@ppafactor.co.uk

PLATT, Stephen; s of Kenneth Norman Platt, of Stoke-on-Trent, and Joyce, *née* Pritchard; *b* 29 September 1954; *Educ* Longton HS Stoke-on-Trent, Wade Deacon Sch Widnes, LSE (BSc); *Children* 1 da (Rachel Louise b 22 Sept 1977); *Career* teacher Moss Brook Special Sch 1972–73, dir Self Help Housing Resource Library 1977–79, co-ordinator Islington Community Housing 1979–83, ed Roof 1986, news ed New Society 1986–87 (actg ed 1987–88); ed: Midweek 1988–89, Enjoying the Countryside 1989–90, New Statesman 1990–96; currently journalist and writer incl editorial conslt Channel 4 1996–2014; website and conrib ed Time Team 1999–2014, website ed Dispatches 1999–2005, contrib Red Pepper 2005–; co-ordinator Maasai Culture and History Project 2003–05; conslt HouseMark 2009–; *Recreations* archaeology, amphibians, bears (real and fictional), countryside, football, growing things, mountains, music, running; *Clubs* Red Rose, Port Vale; *Style*— Stephen Platt, Esq; ✉ 46 Tufnell Park Road, London N7 0DT (☎ 020 7263 4185, e-mail mail@steveplatt.net)

PLATTEN, Guy; *Career* deck offr Royal Fleet Auxiliary Serv 1982–93, inspector of lifeboats RNLI 1993–98, salvage MOD 1998–2001, dir of marine operations Northern Lighthouse Bd 2001–07, md Caledonian Maritime Assets Ltd 2007–, ceo UK Chamber of Shipping 2014–; memb Royal Inst of Navigation 2001; *Style*— Guy Platten, Esq; ✉ e-mail gplatten@ukchamberofshipping.com

PLATTEN, Rt Rev Dr Stephen George; s of Capt George Henry Platten, RM (d 1969), of Enfield, Middx, and Marjory Agnes, *née* Sheward (d 2000); *b* 17 May 1947; *Educ* Stationers' Co's Sch, Univ of London (BEd), Trinity Coll Oxford (DipTh, BD), Cuddesdon Theol Coll; *m* 1 April 1972, Rosslie, da of David Robert Thompson, of Newbury, Berks; 2 s (Aidan Stephen George b 1976, Gregory Austin David b 1978); *Career* with Shell International Petroleum Co Ltd 1966–68; ordained: deacon 1975, priest 1976; asst curate St Andrew Headington Oxford 1975–78, chaplain and tutor Lincoln Theol Coll 1978–82, diocesan dir of ordinands and canon residentiary Portsmouth Cathedral 1983–89, dir of post-ordination trg and continuing ministerial educn Dio of Portsmouth 1984–89, hon canon Canterbury Cathedral 1990–95, Archbishop of Canterbury's sec for ecumenical affairs 1990–95, anglican sec Anglican-RC International Cmmn (II) 1990–95, dean of Norwich 1995–2003, bishop of Wakefield 2003–14, rector St Michael Cornhill City of London 2014–; asst bishop Dios of London, Newcastle and Southwark 2014–; min provincial Euro Province 3 Order Soc of St Francis 1991–96; memb Faith & Order Advsy Gp of C of E 2000–10, chm C of E Liturgical Cmmn 2005–, memb Cathedrals Fabric Cmmn of England 2005–, chm Faith and Order Cmmn 2010– (memb 2010–12); chm Soc for Study of Christian Ethics 1983–88, guestmaster Nikaean Club 1990–95, dir SCM Press 1990–2004, chm SCM-Canterbury Press 2001–; memb Cncl Hymns Ancient and Modern 1998– (chm 2014–), memb Order of St John Chapter to South and West Yorks Priory 2003–14, memb Cncl Royal Sch of Church Music 2014–; memb House of Lords 2009–14; tstee Media Standards Tst; memb Exec Georgian Gp 2014–; Cheney lecture Yale 1998, Warburton lecture Lincolns Inn 2004; Liveryman Worshipful Co of Stationers and Newspapermakers 2004– (memb Ct 2011–); Hon DLitt UEA 2003, Hon DUniv Univ of Huddersfield 2012; *Books* Deacons in the Ministry of the Church (contrib, 1987), Ethics – Our Choices (sr ed, 1989), Spirituality and Psychology (contrib, 1990), Say One for Me (contrib, ed A W Carr, 1992), Pilgrims (1996), Spirit and Tradition: An Essay on Change (with George Pattison, 1996), Augustine's Legacy: Authority and Leadership in Anglicanism (1997), New Soundings (ed with Graham James and Andrew Chandler, 1997), Flagships of the Spirit (ed with Christopher Lewis, 1998), Seeing Ourselves (ed and contrib, 1998), The Pilgrim Guide to Norwich (1998), Cathedrals and Abbeys of England (1999), The Retreat of the State (ed and contrib, 1999), Ink and Spirit (ed and contrib, 2000), Runcie: On Reflection (2002), A New Dictionary of Liturgy and Worship (contrib, 2002), Jesus in History, Thought and Culture (contrib, 2003), Open Government (ed, 2003), Anglicanism and the Western Christian Tradition (ed and contrib, 2003), In Search of Humanity and Deity: A Celebration of John Macquarrie's Theology (contrib, 2006), Dreaming Spires: Cathedrals and a New Age (ed and contrib), Rebuilding Jerusalem (2007), Vocation: Singing the Lord's Song (2007), Reinhold Niebuhr and Contemporary Politics (ed with Richard Harries and contrib, 2010), Comfortable Words: Polity, Piety and the Book of Common Prayer (ed and contrib, 2012), Unity in Process: Reflections on Ecumenical Activity (contrib, 2012); author of contribs to theol and educnl jls; *Recreations* reading, music, walking, Northumberland, Land Rovers; *Clubs* Athenaeum, City Univ; *Style*— The Rt Rev Dr Stephen Platten; ✉ St Michael's Rectory, St Michael's Alley, London EC3V 9DS (☎ 020 7283 3121, e-mail stephen.platten@icloud.com)

PLATTS-MILLS, Jonathan Lewis (Jo); s of John Faithful Fortescue Platts-Mills (d 2001), and Janet Katherine, *née* Cree (d 1992); bro of Mark Platts-Mills, QC, *qv*; *b* 11 March 1939; *Educ* Bryanston (capt rowing 1st eight), Balliol Coll Oxford (MA, head of Torpids); *m* 1, 1966 (m dis 1998); 1 s (Thomas Tiberius b 17 March 1968), 1 da (Ioana Patricia b 19 Nov 1970); m 2, 1999, Else, *née* Trad; *Career* grad apprentice Davy United Sheffield 1960–62, plate mill project engr Romania 1965–67, cold rolling mill project mangr Algeria 1969–73, project mangr Humphreys and Glasgow London 1973–76; Lonrho plc gp: various appts incl sr exec project mangr Volkswagen UK HQ, sugar mills in Benin, re-estab Lonrho ops in Tanzania, started Lonrho business in USSR 1989, assoc dir 1990–91, main bd dir i/c new projects CIS, Zaïre, Angola and Belgium 1991–97; currently working for the expansion of fish and other marine resources worldwide; Yeoman Worshipful Co of Ironmongers; FIMechE 1992; *Recreations* hill walking, occasional rowing and sailing; *Clubs* Athenaeum, Leander; *Style*— Jo Platts-Mills, Esq; ✉ Notre Dame des Auges, 04700 Lurs, France (☎ 00 33 4 92 79 01 02, mobile 00336 7682 5031, e-mail jo.platts-mills@wanadoo.fr)

PLATTS-MILLS, Mark Fortescue; QC (1995); s of John Faithful Fortescue Platts-Mills (d 2001), and Janet Katherine, *née* Cree (d 1992); bro of Jonathan (Jo) Platts-Mills, *qv*; *b* 17 January 1951; *Educ* Bryanston, Balliol Coll Oxford (BA); *m* 1982, Dr Juliet Anne Britton; 1 s (John b 1988); *Career* called to the Bar Inner Temple 1974; memb Inner Temple and Lincoln's Inn; *Recreations* sailing, hockey, gardening; *Style*— Mark Platts-Mills, Esq, QC; ✉ 8 New Square, Lincoln's Inn, London WC2A 3QP (☎ 020 7405 4321)

PLAUT, (Eur Ing) Rudolf (Rudi); CBE (1998, OBE 1993); s of Dr H C Plaut (d 1979), and Ilse Plaut (d 1994); *b* 19 February 1932; *Educ* Whitgift Sch, City Univ (BSc, pres Students' Union); *m* 1960, Margaret Gray; 1 s, 2 da; *Career* Nat Serv 1956–58; asst departmental mangr Steel Co of Wales Ltd 1958–61, dir Moplant Ltd 1961–72; chm: Northmace & Hendon Ltd 1973–2013 pres 2013–; chm Techniquest Enterprises Ltd 1986–2002, NCF Asset Finance Ltd 1992–2002, Greyfriars Capital Ltd 2003–; chm Advsy Bd Xenos Wales Business Angels Network 1996–2001; founding chm Techniquest (Science Centre) 1986–2002; CBI: chm SE Wales Area 1987–91, chm Wales Economic Trends Panel 1998–2012, memb Wales Regnl Cncl 1990–97 and 1998–2012, memb Educn and Trg Affrs Ctee (UK) 1996–2006; chm and pro-chllr Univ of Glamorgan 1991–96, chm HE Engrg Panel Welsh Jt Educn Ctee 1985–88, chm Qualifications, Curriculum and Assessment Authy for Wales 1993–98; memb: Wales Advsy Bd for Local Authy HE 1987–90, Gen Teaching Cncl for England 2000–01 (chm Registration Ctee), Br Cncl Ctee for Wales 2000–06, Wales and W Regnl Ctee RSA 2002–04 and 2009–10; assessor for public appts Wales and NI, tstee Darwin Centre for Biology and Med 1993–2003; hon treas South Wales Baptist Coll 1980–2000, tstee S Wales Baptist Assoc 2003–08 (moderator 2005–07); vice-pres Mid Glamorgan Scout Assoc (formerly co cmmr) 1978–, pres Scouts Wales 2012–; Liveryman Welsh Livery Guild 1993; Hon Dr Univ of Glamorgan 1997, hon fell Cardiff Met Univ 2014; Wales Region Team RSA 2012–; CEng, CCMI, Eur Ing, FRSA, FIMechE; author of several articles in various learned jls and various appearances on TV news and current affrs progs; *Recreations* walking, swimming, family; *Style*— Rudi Plaut, Esq, CBE; ✉ Northmace & Hendon Ltd, Northmace House, Taffs Well, Cardiff CF15 9XF (☎ 029 2081 5204, fax 029 2081 3959, e-mail rudi.plaut@northmace.com)

PLAZAS, Mary; da of Francisco Plazas, and Albertina, *née* de Oliveira; *b* 9 September 1966; *Educ* Didcot Girls' Sch, RNCM (Dip Professional Performance, GMus, Alexander Young Award, Curtis Gold Medal, Claire Croiza Prize for French Song), Nat Opera Studio (Peter Moores Fndn Award); *Career* soprano; studied with Ava June RNCM, Eric Tappy Geneva 1994; operatic debut ENO 1992; co princ ENO 1995–98; pres Bicester Choral and Operatic Soc, pres Wallingfor Chameleon Arts, patron Opera Anywhere; *Performances* solo recitals incl: Wigmore Hall, Purcell Room, Birmingham Town Hall, The Royal Exchange Theatre Manchester, Herbert von Karajan Centre Vienna; festivals incl: Cheltenham Festival, Aldeburgh Festival, Chester Festival 1995, Bath Festival, Bregenz Festival; roles incl: The Voice from Heaven in Verdi's Don Carlos (ENO 1992, Royal Opera BBC Proms 1996), title role in The Cunning Little Vixen (ENO), Susanna in Le Nozze di Figaro (Opera North), Elisetta in Il Matrimonio Segreto (Opera North), Adina (English Touring Opera), Anne Truelove (Opera Factory, London and Lisbon 1994, New Israeli Opera 1999), Poulenc's La Voix Humaine (Aix-en-Provence, RNCM), Madame Silvaklang in Die Schauspieldirektor (Garsington Opera), Marzelline in Fidelio (ENO), Mimi in La Bohème (ENO, Opera North and Royal Albert Hall), Leila in The Pearl Fishers (ENO), Frasquita and Michaela in Carmen (ENO), Oscar (ENO), Nanetta in Falstaff (ENO), Adina (ENO), Dorabella (ENO), Fiordiligi (ENO), Elvira (ENO, Glyndebourne Touring Opera and Valladolid), Salud La Vida Breve (Opera North), second angel in Pfitzner's Palestrina (Royal Opera House and New York), Tina in Flight by Jonathan Dove – World Premiere (Glyndebourne Touring Opera & Festival), Duchess in Powder Her Face (Thomas Adès, Aldeburgh, Almeida) 1999 and (LSO) 2006, Mimi in La Bohème (Bregenz Festival) 2001 and 2002 and (Western Aust Opera) 2007, Mum in Greek (London Sinfonietta) 2003, Mrs Coyle in Owen Wingrave (Concertgebouw Amsterdam) 2003, Anne Truelove (Bavarian State Opera Munich) 2003, Blue Fairy in Pinocchio (world premiere, Opera North) 2007, Elizabeth in Roberto Devereux (Buxton Festival) 2007, Nedda in Pagliacci (ENO) 2008, Lady Sarashina by Eotvos (Opera Comique Paris) 2009, Lucrezia Borgia (Buxby Festival) 2009; concerts incl: Haydn's Creation (conducted by Sir David Willcocks, Royal Albert Hall), Tippett's A Child of our Time (Royal Festival Hall and St Petersburg), Mahler 8 (conducted by Sinopoli, Royal Albert Hall), Brahms Requiem (with CBSO, Sakari Oramo), Shostakovich 14 (with Irish Chamber Orch), Karin in world premiere of Gerald Barry's The Bitter Tears of Petra Van Kant (with Dublin Symphony Orch), Carl Davis and Paul McCartney's Liverpool Oratorio (Liverpool Cathedral) 2007; performances with: LSO, BBC National Orch of Wales and Hallé Orch under Kent Nagano and Mark Elder, BBC Philharmonic under Giannandrea Noseda; *Television* First Enchantress in Dido and Aeneas (conducted by Richard Hickox, BBC Television, also recorded for Chandos) Powder Her Face (Channel 4), Flight (Glyndebourne, Channel 4); *Recordings* Mercadante's Emma d'Antiocchia (A Hundred Years of Italian Opera/Opera Rara), Pacini's Maria d'Ingilterra (Opera Rara with Philharmonia under David Parry), L'Enfant et Les Sortilèges (LSO under Previn), Marguerite in Faust (Chandos/Parry/Philharmonia), Adina in L'Elisir (Chandos/Parry/Philharmonia), Micaela in Carmen (Chandos/Parry/Philharmonia), Liu in Turandot (Chandos/Parry/Philharmonia), Zerlina in Don Giovanni (Chandos/Parry/Philharmonia), Fauré's La Naissance de Vénus (BBC Philharmonic under Yan Pascal Tortelier); *Awards* winner Nat Fedn Music Socs/Esso Award for Young Singers 1989, Isobel Baille Performance Award 1990, Kathleen Ferrier Memorial Scholarship 1991; *Recreations* cinema, tap dancing, cross stitch, listening to the radio, meeting friends, godchildren; *Style*— Ms Mary Plazas; ✉ c/o Owen/White Management, 59 Lansdowne Place, Hove, East Sussex BN3 1FL (☎ 01273 727127, fax 01273 328128, e-mail owenwhite@compuserve.com)

PLEMING, Nigel Peter; QC (1992); s of Rev Percy Francis Pleming (d 1978), of Lincs, and Cynthia Myra, *née* Cope, later Mrs Tuxworth (d 2001); *b* 13 March 1946; *Educ* Tupton Hall GS Derby, King Edward VI GS Spilsby, Liverpool Coll of Commerce, Kingston Poly (LLB), UCL (LLM); *m* 22 Sept 1979, Evelyn Carol Joan, *née* Hoffmann; 2 da (Joanna b 10 April 1985, Katherine b 11 Jan 1989), 1 s (William b 29 Oct 1986); *Career* lectr in law 1969–73; called to the Bar Inner Temple 1971, in practice 1973–; bencher Inner Temple, judge of the Courts of Appeal of Guernsey and Jersey; Hon LLD Kingston Univ 1999; *Recreations* sport, music; *Clubs* RAC, Garrick; *Style*— Nigel Pleming, Esq, QC; ✉ 39 Essex Chambers, 81 Chancery Lane, London WC2A 1DD (☎ 020 7832 1111, fax 020 7353 3978)

PLENDER, (William) John Turner; s of William Plender (d 1977), of Wiltshire, and Averil Maud, *née* Turnbull; m, 2, Stephanie, *née* Harris; 2 s; *b* 9 May 1945; *Educ* Downside, Oriel Coll Oxford; *m* (m dis 1989), Sophia Mary, *née* Crombie; 1 s, 2 da; m 2, Stephanie, *née* Harris; 2 s; *Career* CA and writer; Deloitte Plender Griffiths & Co 1967–70, Investors' Chronicle 1970–71, The Times 1972–74, fin ed The Economist 1974–79, FCO 1980–81, freelance journalist, publisher and broadcaster 1982–, currently contrib ed FT; chm Pensions Investment Research Consultants Ltd (PIRC) 1992–2002, dir Quintain plc 2002–10 (chm 2007–09), tstee Pearson Gp Pension Fund 2010–; chm Advsy Cncl Centre for the Study of Financial Innovation 1997–; memb: London Stock Exchange Quality of Markets Advsy Ctee 1992–95, DTI Co Law Review Steering Gp 1998–2001, Advsy Bd Assoc of Corp Treasurers 2002–, World Bank OECD Private Sector Advsy Gp on Corp Governance 2002–; dir Official Monetary and Fin Insts Forum 2012– (chm 2014–); Senior Wincott Award for excellence in financial journalism 1994; FCA 1970; *Books* That's The Way The Money Goes (1981), The Square Mile (with Paul Wallace, 1985), A Stake In The Future (1997), Going Off the Rails (2003), Ethics and Finance (jtly, 2007), Capitalism: Money, Morals and Markets (2015); *Recreations* piano, the arts, walking, wine; *Clubs* Travellers; *Style*— John Plender, Esq; ✉ Financial Times, 1 Southwark Bridge, London SE1 9HL (☎ 020 7873 3000, fax 020 7873 3748, e-mail john.plender@ft.com)

PLENDERLEITH, Ian; CBE (2002); s of Raymond William Plenderleith, and Louise Helen, *née* Martin; *b* 27 September 1943; *Educ* King Edward's Sch Birmingham, ChCh Oxford (MA), Columbia Business Sch NY (MBA, Beta Gamma Sigma medal); *m* 1, 1 April 1967 (m dis 2007), Kristina Mary, da of John Hardy Bentley, OBE (d 1980); 2 da (Melanie b 1969, Cressida b 1976), 1 s (Giles b 1972); m 2, 31 Aug 2007, Elizabeth Ann Campbell Barrell; *Career* Bank of England 1965–2002: seconded as tech asst to UK Exec Dir International Monetary Fund Washington DC 1972–74, private sec to Govr 1976–79, alternate dir Euro Investment Bank 1980–86, head Gilt Edged Div 1982–90, govt broker 1989–2002, assoc dir i/c market operations 1990–94, exec dir i/c fin market ops 1994–2002, alternate dir Bank for International Settlements Basel 1994–2002, dir Bank of England Nominees Ltd 1994–2002, memb Monetary Policy Ctee 1997–2002; dep govr and memb Monetary Policy Ctee South African Reserve Bank 2003–05; dir London Stock Exchange 1989–2001 (dep chm 1996); non-exec dir: Sanlam Ltd 2006–13, BMCE Bank Int plc (formerly Medicapital Bank plc) 2006–16, Bond Exchange of S Africa 2007–09, Europe Arab Bank plc 2009–12, Sanlam UK Ltd 2010– (also chm), Morgan Stanley Int Ltd 2011– (also chm), Sanlam Private Investments (UK) Hldgs Ltd 2013–; chm B H Macro Ltd 2007–; int conslt Invoice Clearing Bureau (S Africa) 2006–, sr advsr Anthem Corporate Finance 2009–12; chm: Stock Borrowing and Lending Ctee 1990–95, G-10 Governors Gold and Foreign Exchange Ctee 1995–2001, Sterling Money Markets Liaison Gp 1999–2002, Co-op for Public Deposits 2003–, South African Money Markets Liasion Gp 2004–; co-chm Government Borrowers Forum 1991–94; memb: Editorial Bd OECD Study on Debt Mgmnt 1990–93, G-10 Ctee on Global Financial System 1994–2002, Sr Advsy Cncl Int Capital Markets Assoc 2006–, Advsy Bd Central Banking Pubns 2006–, Advsy Bd Assoc of Corporate Treasurers 2007–; hon sec Tillington CC 1983–2003; memb: Advsy Bd Inst of Archaeology Devpt Tst UCL 1987–96, Bd of Overseers Columbia Business Sch 1991–2009, Legal Risk Review Ctee 1991–92, Fin Law Panel 1992–94, Fundraising Planning Gp St Bartholomew's Hosp 1992–94, Cncl Br Museum Friends 1993–99, 2000–03 and 2005–11, Bd of City Arts Tst 1997–2003, Fundraising Planning Ctee Bart's and London Hosps 1998–2003, External Advsy Panel Oxford Mathematical Inst 2000–03, Advsy Bd Oxford Business Alumni 2002–03, Br Museum Townley Steering Gp 2002–03, Christ Church Devpt Bd 2002– (memb Fin Ctee 1998–2003), Advsy Bd Global Borrowers and Investors Forum 2003–05, Assoc of Black Securities and Investment Professionals 2005–06, Advsy Bd Witwatersrad Business Sch 2007–12; vice-pres London Old Edwardians

Assoc Ctee 2004– (memb 1996–); memb: Advsy Bd The Actors Centre 2002–, Cncl Shakespeare's Globe 2002–; chm of govrs Reed's Sch 2008– (chm Reed's Sch Fndn Appeal 2006–07); FSI 1991; Liveryman Worshipful Co of Innholders 1977 (memb Investment Ctee 2007–), Liveryman Worshipful Co of Bankers 2010; FACT 1989; *Recreations* archaeology, theatre, cricket, travel; *Clubs* Tillington CC, MCC, London Capital (memb Advsy Bd 2002–), Athenaeum (chm Investment Ctee 2008–14); *Style—* Ian Plenderleith, Esq, CBE; ✉ Goldneys, River, Petworth, West Sussex GU28 9AU (☎ 01798 861250, mobile 07702 833231, e-mail ianplenderleith@yahoo.co.uk)

PLEYDELL-BOUVERIE, Hon Peter John; DL (Wilts 2009); 2 s of 8 Earl of Radnor, *qv*, of Longford Castle, Salisbury, and his 1 w Anne, *née* Seth-Smith; *b* 14 January 1958, London; *Educ* Harrow, Trinity Coll Cambridge; *m* 14 June 1986, Hon Jane Victoria, da of Baron Gilmour of Craigmillar, PC (Life Peer), *qv*; 2 s (Timothy b 12 June 1987, Jamie b 23 July 1989), 2 da (Lara b 20 Dec 1993, Clare (twin) b 20 Dec 1993); *Career* assoc dir Kleinwort Grieveson Investment Mgmnt Co and fund mangr Grieveson Grant & Co 1980–86, investment dir Fidelity Int and Fidelity Investment Services Ltd 1986–96; currently dir: Ebble Devpts, Longford Farms Ltd, Fidelity China Special Situations plc 2010–; chm Avon and Stour Rivers Assoc, patron Downton Heritage Trail, govr Wilts Historic Buildings Tst Ltd 2010–, tstee Salisbury Museum; High Sheriff Wilts 2007–08 (Under-Sheriff 2005–06); *Recreations* fishing, countryside, opera, ballet; *Style—* The Hon Peter Pleydell-Bouverie, DL; ✉ Newcourt, Downton, Salisbury, Wiltshire SP5 3JF (☎ 01722 410495, e-mail peter.pb@virgin.net)

PLOTKIN, Prof Henry Charles; s of Bernard Solomon Plotkin (d 1985), of Johannesburg, South Africa, and Edythe, *née* Poplak (d 1987); *b* 11 December 1940; *Educ* Highlands North HS Johannesburg, Univ of the Witwatersrand (BSc), Univ of London (PhD); *m* 1975, Victoria Mary, *née* Welch; 1 da (Jessica b 12 Dec 1976), 1 s (Jocelin b 29 Jan 1980); *Career* MRC scientist 1965–72 (MRC travelling fell 1970–72, postdoctoral fell Stanford Univ 1971–72); UCL: lectr 1972–88, reader 1988–93, prof 1993–, head Dept of Psychology 1993–98; memb: Experimental Psychology Soc 1968, Assoc for Study of Animal Behaviour 1972; *Books* The Nature of Knowledge (1994), Evolution in Mind (1997), The Imagined World Made Real (2002), Evolutionary Thought in Psychology: A Brief History (2004), Necessary Knowledge (2007), Evolutionary Worlds Without End (2010); also 3 edited and co-edited anthologies, approximately 100 scientific papers; *Recreations* music, house in France, family, Spurs supporter, books; *Style—* Emeritus Prof Henry Plotkin; ✉ Department of Psychology, University College London, Gower Street, London WC1E 6BT (☎ 020 7679 7573, fax 020 7436 4276, e-mail h.plotkin@ucl.ac.uk or vicky.plotkin@btopenworld.com)

PLOWMAN, Jon; OBE (2013); s of C Plowman, and F J Plowman; *Educ* Stanborough Sch Welwyn Garden City, UC Oxford; *Career* former asst dir Royal Court Theatre, then freelance theatre dir and prodr Granada TV; currently head of comedy entertainment BBC; work incl: French and Saunders (BAFTA Award), Murder Most Horrid, Absolutely Fabulous (3 series, Int Emmy for Best Popular Arts Prog 1993 and 1994, and 2 BAFTA Awards), A Bit of Fry & Laurie (4th series), Smith & Jones (2 series), The Vicar of Dibley, Ted & Alice, The Office (2 Golden Globe Awards); exec prodr: Shooting Stars, Gimme, Gimme, Gimme, In The Red, Comedy Nation, Goodness Gracious Me, League of Gentlemen, Comic Relief, Little Britain; 3 BAFTA nominations, 1 Int Emmy; FRTS, FRSA; *Clubs* National Liberal; *Style—* Jon Plowman, Esq, OBE; ✉ c/o BBC TV Entertainment Group, Television Centre, Wood Lane, London W12 7RJ (☎ 020 8743 8000)

PLOWRIGHT, Joan Ann; (Lady Olivier), DBE (2004, CBE 1970); da of William Ernest Plowright; *b* 28 October 1929; *Educ* Scunthorpe GS, Laban Art of Movement Studio, Old Vic Theatre Sch; *m* 1, 1953 (m dis), Roger Gage; m 2, 1961, Sir Laurence Olivier, later Baron Olivier (Life Peer, d 1989); 1 s, 2 da; *Career* leading actress stage, film and television; memb Cncl RADA, vice-pres English Stage Co; Int Award 18th Annual Crystal Awards Women in Film USA 1994; DLitt Univ of Hull 2001; *Theatre* first stage appearance If Four Walls Told (Croydon Rep Theatre) 1948, with Bristol Old Vic and Old Vic Co South Africa Tour 1952, first London stage appearance in The Duenna (Westminster) 1954, Moby Dick (Duke of York's) 1955, with Nottingham Playhouse 1955–56, with English Stage Co (Royal Court) 1956, The Crucible, Don Juan, The Death of Satan, Cards of Identity, The Good Woman of Setzuan, The Country Wife (transferred to Adelphi 1957), The Chairs, The Making of Moo (Royal Court) 1957, The Entertainer (Palace) 1957, The Chairs, The Lesson (Phoenix NY) 1958, The Entertainer (Royale NY) 1958, The Chairs, The Lesson, Major Barbara (Royal Court) 1958, Hook Line and Sinker (Piccadilly) 1958, Roots (Royal Court and Duke of York's) 1959, Rhinoceros (Royal Court) 1960, A Taste of Honey (Lyceum NY) 1960 (Tony Award for Best Actress); leading actress with NT 1963–74; opening season 1963: St Joan, Uncle Vanya, Hobson's Choice; The Master Builder 1964, Much Ado About Nothing 1967 and 1968, Three Sisters 1967 and 1968, The Advertisement 1968, Love's Labour's Lost 1968, The Merchant of Venice 1979, A Woman Killed With Kindness 1971, The Rules of the Game 1971, Eden End 1974; Rosmersholm (Greenwich) 1973, Saturday, Sunday, Monday (Queen's) 1974–75, The Sea Gull (Lyric) 1975, The Bed Before Yesterday (Lyric) 1975 (Variety Club of GB Award 1977), Filumena (Lyric) 1977 (SWET Award 1978), Enjoy (Vaudeville) 1980, The Cherry Orchard (Haymarket) 1983, The House of Bernarda Alba (Globe) 1986; Chichester Festival: Uncle Vanya, The Chances 1962, St Joan (Evening Standard Award for Best Actress), Uncle Vanya 1963, The Doctor's Dilemma, The Taming of the Shrew 1972, Cavell 1982, The Way of the World 1984, If we are Women (Greenwich Theatre) 1995, Absolutely! (perhaps) (Wyndhams Theatre) 2003; directed: A Prayer for Wings 1985, Married Love 1988, Time and The Conways 1990/91; *Films* The Entertainer 1960, Equus, Britannia Hospital 1962, Three Sisters 1970, Wagner, Revolution 1985, Drowning by Numbers 1988, The Dressmaker 1988, I Love You to Death 1989, Avalon 1989, Denis, Last Action Hero 1992, Driving Miss Daisy 1992, A Place for Annie 1993, Widows Peak 1993, A Pin for the Butterfly 1993, On Promised Land 1994, Hotel Sorrento 1994, A Pyromaniacs Love Story 1994, The Scarlet Letter 1994, Jane Eyre 1995, Mr Wrong 1995, 101 Dalmatians 1996, The Assistant 1997, Dance With Me, Tea With Mussolini, Tom's Midnight Garden, Dinosaur (voice), Callas Forever, George and the Dragon, Bringing Down the House, I am David, Mrs Palfrey at the Claremont 2007–08, The Spiderwick Chronicles 2007; films for TV incl: The Merchant of Venice, Brimstone and Treacle, A Dedicated Man, House of Bernada Alba (1991), Stalin (Best Supporting TV actress Golden Globe 1993), Enchanted April (BBC Screen Two, Best Supporting Film Actress Golden Globe 1993, Best Supporting Film Actress Oscar Nomination 1993) 1992, Clothes in The Wardrobe 1992, Return of the Native 1994; *Books* And That's Not All (autobiography, 2001); *Recreations* reading, music, entertaining; *Style—* Dame Joan Plowright, DBE; ✉ c/o Independent Talent Group Ltd, Oxford House, 76 Oxford Street, London W1N 0AX (☎ 020 7636 6565, fax 020 7323 0101)

PLOWRIGHT, Rosalind Anne; da of Robert Arthur Plowright, and Celia Adelaide Plowright; *b* 21 May 1949; *Educ* Notre Dame HS Wigan, Royal Northern Coll of Music Manchester; *m* 1984, James Anthony Kaye; 1 s (Daniel Robert), 1 da (Katherine Anne); *Career* soprano; London Opera Centre 1974–75, debut as Agathe in Der Freischütz (Glyndebourne Chorus and Touring Co) 1975, with ENO, WNO and Kent Opera 1975–78, Miss Jessel in Turn of the Screw (ENO) 1979, Ortlinde in Die Walküre (Royal Opera House debut) 1980; 1980–81: Bern Opera (Adriadne, Alceste), Frankfurt Opera (Ariadne, Aida, Il Trovatore), Munich Opera (Ariadne); debuts: USA, Paris, Madrid and Hamburg 1982, La Scala, Milan, Edinburgh Festival, San Francisco and Carnegie Hall NY 1983, Berlin, Houston, Pittsburgh, San Diego and Verona 1985, Rome, Florence and Holland 1986, Tulsa, NY Philharmonic, Buenos Aires, Santiago, Chile, Israel, Paris Opera and Bonn 1987, Lausanne, Geneva, Oviedo and Bilbao 1988, Zurich, Copenhagen and Lisbon 1989, Vienna, Torre del Lago and Bregenz 1990, Athens 1995, Scotland 1999; *Roles* principal roles incl: Amelia in Un Ballo in Maschera, Amneris in Aida, Desdemona in Otello, Elisabetta in Don Carlos, title role in Norma, Leonora in La Forza del Destino, title role in Tosca, title role in Medea, Lady Macbeth in Macbeth, title role in Ariadne auf Naxos, Abigaille in Nabucco, Giorgetta in Il Tabarro, title role in La Giaconda (Opera North) 1993; *Recordings* for EMI: Mary Stuart, Otello, Les Côntes d'Hoffman; for Deutsche Grammophon: Il Trovatore, La Forza del Destino, Mahler Resurrection Symphony; La Vestale for Orfeo Records, Elijah for Chandos Records; *Awards* incl: First Prize Int Competition for Opera Singers (Sofia 1979), Prix Fndn Fanny Heldy (Nat Acad du Disque Lyrique 1985); *Recreations* fell walking; *Style—* Miss Rosalind Plowright; ✉ c/o Victoria Smith Management, 2 Police Cottages, North End Lane, Droxford, Hampshire S032 3QN (☎ 01489 878787)

PLUMB, Baron (Life Peer UK 1987), of Coleshill in the County of Warwickshire; (Charles) Henry Plumb; kt (1973), DL (Warks 1977); s of Charles Plumb, of Ansley, Warks, and Louise, *née* Fisher; *b* 27 March 1925; *Educ* King Edward VI Sch Nuneaton; *m* 1947, Marjorie Dorothy, da of Thomas Victor Dunn, of Bentley, Warks; 1 s (Hon John Henry), 2 da (Hon Mrs Holman (d 2008), Hon Mrs Mayo); *Career* MEP (Cons) The Cotswolds 1979–99, chm Agric Ctee Euro Parl 1979–82, ldr (Cons) EDG Euro Parl 1982–87, pres Euro Parl 1987–89; non-exec dir: Fisons 1979–85, Lloyds Bank 1979–89, United Biscuits 1979–89; pres NFU 1970–79 (dep pres 1966–69, vice-pres 1964–66, memb Cncl 1959–), chm Br Agric Cncl 1975–79; pres Warks County Fedn of Young Farmers' Clubs 1974–, pres Nat Fedn 1976–86; memb Cncl: CBI, Animal Health Tst; pres: COPA 1975–77, RASE 1977 (dep pres 1978), Int Fedn of Agric Prodrs 1979–, Royal Agricultural Benevolent Inst 1989–2011, National Sheep Assoc 2001–11; chllr Coventry Univ 1995–; hon pres Ayrshire Cattle Soc; chm Int Policy Cncl on Agric, Food and Trade; pres: Conservative Countryside Forum 1998, Campden and Chorleywood Food Research Assoc 1998; govr City Technol Coll Kingshurst 1988–2002; fndr Henry Plumb Fndn Charitable Tst 2013; Bledisloe Medal RASE 1978, Judges Award Farm Business 2012, Lifetime Achievement Award Farmers Weekly 2013, British Farming Award Farmer Guardian 2014; Hon Liveryman Worshipful Co of Fruiterers 1991, memb Ct of Assts Worshipful Co of Farmers (Master 2006–); hon fell Wye Coll London, hon fell Duchy Coll, hon fell Royal Agricultural Coll Cirencester (govr 1990–98); Hon DSc Cranfield 1983, hon dr of public serv Columbia Univ 2010; FRSA 1970, FRAgS 1974; Order of Merit (Fed Repub of Germany) 1976, Grand Cross Order of Merit (Portugal) 1987, Order of Merit (Luxembourg) 1988, Grand Cross Order of Civil Merit (Spain) 1989, Knight Cdr Cross of the Order of Merit (Fed Repub of Germany) 1990; *Publications* The Plumb Line – A Journey Through Agriculture and Politics (2001), Modern Agriculture in Africa; *Clubs* Farmers'; *Style—* The Lord Plumb, DL; ✉ Maxstoke, Coleshill, Warwickshire B46 2QJ (☎ and fax 01675 464156); House of Lords, London SW1A 0PW (fax 020 7219 1649, e-mail plumbh@parliament.uk)

PLUNKETT, His Hon Judge Andrew Christopher; *Career* called to the Bar Gray's Inn 1983; recorder 2002–05, circuit judge (Midland Circuit) 2005–; *Style—* His Hon Judge Plunkett; ✉ c/o Worcester Combined Court, Shirehall, Foregate Street, Worcester WR1 1EQ

PLYMOUTH, Bishop of 2015–; Rt Rev Nicholas Howard Paul McKinnel; s of Hugh Robert McKinnel (d 1985), and Hazel, *née* Howard (d 1993); *b* 19 August 1954, Liverpool; *Educ* Marlborough, Queens' Coll Cambridge (MA), Wycliffe Hall Oxford (MA); *m* 1981, Jacqueline Anne, *née* Shipley; 3 da (Gemma b 1984, Charlotte b 1988, Clare b 1991), 1 s (James b 1985); *Career* curate St Mary's West Kensington 1980–83, Anglican chaplain Univ of Liverpool 1983–87, rector Hatherleigh, Meeth, Exbourne and Jacobstowe 1987–94, rector St Andrews Plymouth and St Pauls Stonehouse 1994–2012, prebendary Exeter Cathedral 2002, bishop of Crediton 2012–15; Hon DD Plymouth Univ 2013; ✉ 108 Molesworth Road, Plymouth, PL3 4AQ (☎ 01752 500059, e-mail bishop.of.plymouth@exeter.anglican.org)

POBERESKIN, Louis Howard; *b* 16 August 1948; *Educ* Case Western Reserv Univ (BS, MD); *m* 1, 28 Nov 1980; 2 da (Sarah b 1983, Lisa b 1983); m 2, 21 April 2005, Caroline; *Career* sr registrar in neurosurgery Addenbrooke's Hosp Cambridge 1981–85, conslt neurosurgeon Derriford Hosp 1985–; FRCSEd 1987; *Style—* Louis Pobereskin, Esq; ✉ Department of Neurosurgery, Derriford Hospital, Plymouth (☎ 01752 437681, fax 01752 763395, e-mail lpobereskin@nhs.net)

POCOCK, Sir Andrew John; KCMG (2015, CMG 2008); s of John Francis Pocock, of Maraval, Trinidad, and Vida Erica, *née* Duruty; *b* 23 August 1955, Port of Spain, Trinidad; *Educ* St Mary's Coll Port of Spain (Island schol), Queen Mary Coll Univ of London (BA, MA), Peterhouse Cambridge (PhD); *m* 4 Nov 1995, Julie, *née* Mason; *Career* joined UN Dept FCO 1981, second then first sec Br High Cmmn Lagos 1983–86, first sec: Southern African Dept FCO 1986–88, Br Embassy Washington USA 1988–92, Personnel Mgmnt Dept FCO 1992–94; asst head S Asia Dept FCO 1994–96, cnsllr seconded to RCDS 1996, dep high cmmr Canberra 1997–2001, head Southern African Dept FCO 2001–03, high cmmr to Tanzania 2003–06, ambass to Zimbabwe 2006–09, dir Africa FCO 2010, high cmmr to Canada 2011–12, high cmmr to Nigeria 2012–15, ret; *Recreations* reading, walking, tennis, cricket; *Style—* Sir Andrew Pocock, KCMG

PODGER, Geoffrey John Freeman; CB (2003); s of late Leonard Podger, and late Beryl Enid, *née* Freeman; *b* 3 August 1952; *Educ* Worthing HS for Boys, Pembroke Coll Oxford (open scholar, MA); *Career* MOD: admin trainee 1974–77, seconded to Int Staff NATO HQ Brussels 1977–79, princ 1979–82; DHSS 1982–88, on loan as sec to Port Stanley Hosp Fire Inquiry Falkland Islands 1985; Dept of Health: private sec to Chm NHS Management Bd 1985–87, asst sec 1987, princ private sec to sec of state for Social Servs 1987–88, project mangr NHS Review 1988–92, head International Relations Unit 1992–93, under-sec for Health Promotion 1993–96; under-sec (Food Safety and Science Group) MAFF 1996–97, under-sec (Jt Food Safety and Standards Gp) Dept of Health and MAFF 1997–99, chief exec Food Standards Agency 2000–03, exec dir European Food Safety Authy (EFSA) 2003–05, chief exec HSE 2005–; *Clubs* Athenaeum; *Style—* Geoffrey Podger, Esq, CB; ✉ 5N.3 Redgrave Court, Merton Road, Bootle, Merseyside L20 7HS

POET, Bruno; s of Robert Poet, of Wolverhampton, and Margarete Poet; *b* 2 July 1972; *Educ* Oundle, Mansfield Coll Oxford (BA); *m* Annabel; 1 da (Emilia); *Career* lighting designer; theatre credits incl: Every Good Boy Deserves Favour, From Morning to Midnight, Timon of Athens, London Road, Frankenstein (Knight of Illumination Award 2011, winner Best Lighting Design Olivier Award 2012), Season's Greetings, Treasure Island, Travelling Light, Light Shining in Buckinghamshire (all NT), Romeo and Juliet (RSC), Midnight's Children (RSC, Barbican, New York and tour), All About My Mother, Cause Célèbre, Sweet Bird of Youth, Fortune's Fool (all The Old Vic), Phaedra (Donmar Warehouse), A Prayer for my Daughter (Young Vic), Dumb Show (Royal Ct), Volpone (Royal Exchange Manchester), From Here to Eternity (West End), Carousel (Opera North, Barbican and Théâtre du Chatelet Paris), King Lear (English Touring Theatre and The Old Vic), Coram Boy (Bristol Old Vic), Being Shakespeare (West End, Brooklyn Acad of Music and Chicago Shakespeare), The Birthday Party (Sheffield Crucible), Miss Saigon (West End), Two Gentlemen of Verona (RSC); for Opera North: Manon, Dido and Aeneas/Les Noces, A Midsummer Night's Dream, Roméo et Juliette, From the House of the Dead, The Makropulos Case, Macbeth; opera credits incl: Carmen (ENO and Den Norske Opera), Don Giovanni, La Donna del Lago, Rise and Fall of the City of Mahagonny, Quartett (ROH), Il Due Foscari (Los Angeles Opera, Palau de les Arts Valencia and ROH), Cunning

P

Little Vixen (Royal Danish Opera), Rinaldo (Lyric Opera Chicago), Rusalka (Sydney Opera House, Victorian Green Room Award, nomination Helpmann Award), Al Gran Sole Carico d'Amore (Salzberg Festival and Staatsoper Berlin), Cavalleria Rusticana and Pagliacci (Royal Danish Theatre and Den Norske Opera), Partenope (Royal Danish Opera), Pelleas et Melissande (Buenos Aires), L'Arbore di Diana (Barcelona, Madrid and Montpellier), I Puritani (Amsterdam, Geneva and Athens), La Bohème (Washington National Opera), La Clemenza di Tito and L'Arbore di Diana (Liceo Barcelona), Hansel und Gretel (Garsington Opera) 2014 (16th consecutive season); lighting design for Sigur Ross world tour (Knight of Illumination Award 2013); memb Assoc of Lighting Designers 1996–; *Recreations* sailing, skiing, travel; *Style*— Bruno Poet, Esq; ✉ Dodbrook Cottage, Dodbrook, Milbrook, Cornwall PL10 1AN (☎ 01752 822983, mobile 07973 600987, e-mail bruno@brunopoet.co.uk, website www.brunopoet.co.uk); c/o Clare Vidal Hall, 57 Carthew Road, London W6 0DU (☎ 020 8741 7647, fax 020 8741 9459)

POGGE von STRANDMANN, Prof Hartmut Johann Otto; s of Dr Johann Leopold Pogge (d 1945), and Erica, *née* von Strandmann (d 1995); *Educ* J H Voss-Gymnasium Eutin, Bonn Univ, Berlin Univ, Hamburg Univ, Univ of Oxford (DPhil); *m* 1970, Hilary M Bennett; 1 da, 1 s; *Career* sr scholar St Antony's Coll Oxford 1962–66, research fell and jr dean Balliol Coll Oxford 1966–70, lectr in modern European history Univ of Sussex 1970–77, official fell and praelector in modern history UC Oxford and univ lectr Univ of Oxford 1977–2005 (emeritus fell 2005–), curator UC Oxford 1985–2006, prof of modern history Univ of Oxford 1996–, dir Modern European History Research Centre Univ of Oxford 1998–2002; visiting prof: S Carolina, Rostock Univ, Washington and Lee Univ VA, Windhoek Namibia, Research Centre for Social Sciences Berlin 2006–07; lectured widely in Britain, Germany, USA, Australia and Russia; Studienstiftung des Deutschen Volkes 1964–66, Akademiestipendium 1974–76, Br Acad Res Readership 1986–88; Arbeitskreis Deutscher England Forschung 1984–, Freundes Kreis des German Historical Insts London 1985–95, memb Deutscher Historiker Verband; sec and chm Hanseatic Scholarship Scheme Univ of Oxford 1970–2016, univ chm Gibbs Tst Fund 2001–06; memb Nat Tst, friend of the Ashmolean Museum; FRHistS 1985; *Books* Die Erforderlichkeit des Unmoeglichen (1965), Unternehmens Politik und Unternehmens Fuehrung (1978), Walther Rathenau: Industrialist, Banker, Intellectual and Politician. Notes and Diaries (1985), The Coming of the First World War (1988), The Revolutions in Europe 1848–1849: From Reform to Reaction (2000), Ins tiefste Afrika: Paul Pogge und seine präkolonialen Reisen ins südliche Kongobecken (2004), Imperialismus am Grünen Tisch: Dentsche Kolonialpolitik zwischen wirtschaftlicher Ausbeutung und zivilisatorischen Bemühungen (2009); *Recreations* tennis, walking, swimming, music, theatre, art, reading; *Style*— Prof Hartmut Pogge von Strandmann; ✉ University College, Oxford OX1 4BH (☎ 01865 276602)

POLAK, Prof Dame Julia Margaret; DBE (2003); da of Carlos Polak, and Rebeca, *née* Mactas; *b* 29 June 1939; *Educ* Univ of Buenos Aires (MD, Dip Histopathology), Univ of London (DSc); *m* 1961, Daniel Catovsky, s of Felix Catovsky; 1 da (Marina b 1963), 2 s (Elliot Sebastian b 1973, Michael David b 1976); *Career* Buenos Aires: demonstrator 1961–62, SHO in surgery and med 1962, registrar and sr registrar 1963–67; Royal Postgrad Med Sch (Imperial Coll Sch of Med at Hammersmith Hosp following merger 1997): res asst Dept of Histochemistry 1968–69, asst lectr 1970–73, lectr 1973–79, sr lectr 1979–82, reader 1982–84; Dept of Histopathology Hammersmith Hosp: hon conslt 1979–, prof of endocrine pathology 1984–, dep dir 1988–91, head Dept of Histochemistry 1991–; ed of numerous med jls and organiser of int and nat med meetings; external ctees incl: chm Immunocytochemistry Club, chm Br Endocrine Pathologists Club, memb Exec Ctee Cncl Circulation of American Heart Assoc, memb Cncl Histochemical Soc of GB 1984–86, memb Bd of Studies on Pathology; memb learned socs incl: American Thoracic Soc, Br Cardiac Soc, Br Neuroendocrine Gp, Cwlth Assoc for Devpt, IBRO, NY Acad of Sciences; memb: BMA, RSM, American Assoc of Pathologists; FRCPath 1986 (memb 1974); Benito de Udaondo Cardiology prize 1967; *Books* incl: Gut Hormones (with S R Bloom, 1981), Basic Science in Gastroenterology, Vol I: Structure of the Gut (jtly, 1982), The Systematic Role of Regulatory Peptides (with S R Bloom and E Lindenlaub, 1983), Immunolabelling for Electron Microscopy (with I M Varndell, 1984), Endocrine Tumours – The Pathobiology of Regulatory Peptide-producing Tumours (with S R Bloom, 1985), Regulatory Peptides (1989), In Situ Hybridization: Principles and Practice (with J O D McGee, 1990), Electron Microscopic Immunocytochemistry: Principles and Practice (with J V Priestley, 1992), Diagnostic Histopathology of Neuroendocrine Tumours (1993), Clinical Gene Analysis and Manipulation – Tools, Techniques and Troubleshooting (with J A Z Jankowski and Sir David Weatherall, 1996), Future Strategies for Tissue and Organ Replacement (with Larry L Hench and P Kemp, 2002); *Style*— Prof Dame Julia Polak, DBE; ✉ Honorary Principal Research Fellow, Department of Chemical Engineering, Room 144, Roderic Hill Building, Imperial College, South Kensington Campus, London SW7 2AZ (e-mail julia.polak@imperial.ac.uk)

POLE; *see also:* Carew Pole

POLGLASE, Timothy; s of Frank Polglase, of Fowey, Cornwall, and Betty, *née* Skinner (d 2002); *b* 15 January 1962, Newton Abbot, Devon; *Educ* Fowey Sch, St Austell Sixth Form Coll, St John's Coll Oxford (MA), Coll of Law Guildford; *m* 9 Aug 1991, Laura Elizabeth, *née* Duncan; 2 da (Katherine Isobel b 22 Jan 1994, Amy Elizabeth b 14 Oct 1996); *Career* Norton Rose: articled 1984–86, slr 1986–94 (secondments to Milbank, Tweed, Hadley & McCloy NY 1988–89 and Bank of England 1990–91), ptnr 1994–2002; ptnr Allen & Overy LLP 2002–; author of articles in professional pubns; memb City of London Slrs Co 1994; *Recreations* sailing, skiing; *Clubs* Royal Ocean Racing, Royal Fowey Yacht, Hayling Island Sailing; *Style*— Timothy Polglase, Esq; ✉ Allen & Overy LLP, One Bishops Square, London E1 6AD (☎ 020 3088 0000, fax 020 3088 0088, e-mail tim.polglase@allenovery.com)

POLIAKOFF, Stephen; CBE (2007); s of Alexander Poliakoff (d 1996), and Ina, *née* Montagu (d 1992); *b* 1 December 1952; *Educ* Westminster, Univ of Cambridge; *m* 5 Oct 1983, Sandy Welch; 1 da (Laura b 4 March 1985), 1 s (Alexander b 22 Jan 1991); *Career* playwright and screenwriter; FRSL; *Theatre* Clever Soldiers (Hampstead Theatre) 1974, The Carnation Gang (Bush Theatre) 1974, Hitting Town (Bush Theare) 1975, City Sugar (Comedy Theatre) 1975 (Evening Standard Award for Most Promising Playwright), Heroes (Royal Court Theatre) 1975, Strawberry Fields (NT) 1977, Shout Across the River (RSC) 1978, American Days (ICA) 1979, Summer Party (Crucible Theatre Sheffield) 1980, Favourite Nights (Lyric Theatre Hammersmith) 1981, Breaking The Silence (RSC) 1984, Coming in to Land (Nat Theatre) 1987, Playing with Trains (RSC) 1989, Sienna Red (Peter Hall Co) 1992, Sweet Panic (Hampstead Theatre) 1996, Blinded By The Sun (NT) 1996 (Critics Circle Award for Best Play), Talk of the City (RSC) 1998, Remember This (NT) 1999, My City (Almeida Theatre) 2011; *Television* Stronger Than The Sun (BBC) 1977, Caught on a Train (BBC) 1980 (BAFTA Award for Best Single Play), Soft Targets (BBC) 1982, She's Been Away (BBC) 1989 (Venice Film Festival Award), The Tribe (BBC) 1997, Shooting the Past (BBC) 1999 (RTS Award for Best Drama, Prix Italia), Perfect Strangers (BBC) 2001 (RTS Awards for Best Writer and Best Drama, BAFTA Dennis Potter Award 2002, Peabody Award), The Lost Prince (BBC) 2003 (3 Emmy Awards), Friends and Crocodiles (BBC) 2006, Gideon's Daughter (BBC) 2006 (2 Golden Globe Awards, Peabody Award), Joe's Palace (BBC) 2007, Capturing Mary (BBC) 2007, A Real Summer (BBC) 2007, Dancing on the Edge (BBC) 2013; *Film* Bloody Kids 1980, Runners 1983, Hidden City 1988, Close My Eyes 1991 (Evening Standard Award for Best British Film 1992), Century 1994, Food of Love 1998, 1939 (working title) 2009, Glorious 39 2009;

Publications Stephen Poliakoff Plays: One (Clever Soldiers, Hitting Town, City Sugar, Shout Across the River, American Days, Strawberry Fields), Two (Breaking the Silence, Playing with Trains, She's Been Away, Century), Three (Caught on a Train, Coming in to Land, Close My Eyes); Perfect Strangers (screenplay), Remember This, Shooting the Past (screenplay), Sienna Red, Sweet Panic/Blinded by the Sun, Talk of the City, The Lost Prince (screenplay), Friends & Crocodiles/Gideon's Daughter (screenplays), Joe's Palace/Capturing Mary (screenplays), My City (play text), Dancing on the Edge (screenplay); *Recreations* cinema, cricket, conservation; *Style*— Stephen Poliakoff, Esq, CBE, FRSL

POLIN, Mark Andrew; QPM (2010); *Educ* Open Univ (MBA); *Career* joined City of London Police 1983 (rising to chief inspector); Gwent Police: supt 1998–99, chief supt and divisional cdr Caerphilly Div 1999, head Professional and Ethical Standards Dept 2002; dep chief constable Glos Police 2007–09 (formerly asst chief constable), chief constable North Wales Police 2009–; *Style*— Mark Polin, Esq, QPM; ✉ North Wales Police Headquarters, Glan-y-Don, Abergele Road, Colwyn Bay LL29 8AW

POLIZZI DI SORRENTINO, (Hon) Olga; CBE (1990); eldest da of Baron Forte (Life Peer) (d 2007); *b* 1947; *Educ* St Mary's Sch Ascot; *m* 1, Sept 1966, Marchese Alessandro Polizzi di Sorrentino (decd), s of Gen Polizzi di Sorrentino (d 1980); 2 da (Alexandra b 28 Aug 1971, Charlotte b 9 April 1974); *m* 2, Oct 1993, (Hon) William Hartley Hume Shawcross, *qv*, s of Baron Shawcross, GBE, PC, QC (Life Peer, d 2003); *Career* exec dir Forte plc until 1996; dep chm Rocco Forte Hotels Ltd; dir: Hotel Tresanton Ltd, Hotel Endsleigh Ltd, Millers Bespoke Bakery; elected to Westminster City Cncl 1989–94; tstee: St Mary's Sch Ascot, Italian Medical Charity, King Edward VII & St Agnes Hosp, Lord Forte Fndn; chm Trusthouse Charitable Fndn; govr Landau Forte Coll; Ordine della stella della solidarieta Italiana; *Style*— Mrs Olga Polizzi, CBE; ✉ Rocco Forte Hotels, 70 Jermyn Street, London SW1Y 6NY (☎ 020 7321 2626, fax 020 7321 2424, e-mail opolizzi@roccofortehotels.com)

POLKINGHORNE, Rev Dr John Charlton; KBE (1997); s of George Baulkwill Polkinghorne (d 1981), and Dorothy Evelyn, *née* Charlton (d 1983); *b* 16 October 1930; *Educ* Elmhurst GS Street, Perse Sch Cambridge, Trinity Coll Cambridge (BA, PhD, MA, ScD), Westcott House Cambridge; *m* 26 March 1955, Ruth Isobel (d 2006), da of Hedley Gifford Martin (d 1979); 2 s (Peter b 1957, Michael b 1963), 1 da (Isobel Morland b 1959); *Career* Nat Serv RAEC 1948–49; fell Trinity Coll Cambridge 1954–86 (hon fell 2015); lectr: Univ of Edinburgh 1956–58, Univ of Cambridge 1958–65 (reader 1965–68, prof of mathematical physics 1968–79); ordained: deacon 1981, priest 1982; curate: Cambridge 1981–82, Bristol 1982–84; vicar Blean Kent 1984–86, fell, dean and chaplain Trinity Hall Cambridge 1986–89 (hon fell 1989), pres Queens' Coll Cambridge 1989–96 (fell 1996–, hon fell 1996), Proctor in Convocation 1990–2000, hon fell St Edmund's Coll Cambridge 2002; chm: Ctee on Use of Foetal Material 1988–89, Nuclear Physics Bd 1978–79, Task Force to Review Servs for Drug Misusers 1994–96, Advsy Ctee on Genetic Testing 1996–99; memb: SRC 1975–79, Doctrine Cmmn 1989–96, Human Genetics Advsy Cmmn 1996–99, Human Genetics Cmmn 2000–02; chm govrs Perse Sch 1972–81; Templeton Prize 2002, Gen Theological Seminary NY; Hon DD: Univ of Kent 1994, Univ of Durham 1999, en Theological Seminary 2010, Wycliffe Coll Toronto 2011; Hon DSc: Univ of Exeter 1994, Univ of Leicester 1995, Marquette Univ 2003; Hon DHum Hong Kong Baptist Univ 2006; FRS 1974; *Books* The Analytic S-Matrix (1966), The Particle Play (1979), Models of High Energy Processes (1980), The Way the World Is (1983), The Quantum World (1984), One World (1986), Science and Creation (1988), Science and Providence (1989), Rochester Roundabout (1989), Reason and Reality (1991), Science and Christian Belief (1994), Serious Talk (1995), Scientists as Theologians (1996), Beyond Science (1996), Searching for Truth (1996), Belief in God on an Age of Science (1998), Science and Theology (1998), Faith, Science and Understanding (2000), Faith in the Living God (2001), The God of Hope and the End of the World (2002), Quantum Theory (2002), Living with Hope (2003), Science and the Trinity (2004), Exploring Reality (2005), Quantum Physics and Theology (2007), From Physicist to Priest (2007), Theology in the Context of Science (2008), Questions of Truth (2009), Encountering Scripture (2010), Science and Religion in Quest of Truth (2011); *Recreations* gardening; *Style*— The Rev Dr John Polkinghorne, KBE, FRS; ✉ Queen's College, Cambridge CB3 9ET

POLL, Prof (David) Ian Alistair; OBE (2002); s of Ralph Angus Poll (d 2006), and Mary, *née* Hall (d 2012); *b* 1 October 1950, Mirfield, W Yorks; *Educ* Heckmondwike GS, Imperial Coll London (BSc), Cranfield Inst of Technol (PhD); *m* 31 May 1975, Elizabeth Mary, da of Ewart John Read (d 1968), of Painswick, Glos; 2 s (Edward b 1977, Robert b 1980), 1 da (Helen b 1984); *Career* Future Projects Dept Hawker Siddeley Aviation 1972–75, sr lectr in aerodynamics Cranfield Inst of Tech 1985–87 (res asst 1975–78, lectr 1978–85); Univ of Manchester: prof of aeronautical engrg and dir Goldstein Laboratory 1987–95, head Engrg Dept 1991–94, head Aerospace Div 1994–95; fndr and md Flow Science Ltd 1990–95; Cranfield Univ: head Coll of Aeronautics 1995–2000, prof of aerospace engrg 1995–2012, dir Coll of Aeronautics 2001–04, emeritus 2012–; Cranfield Aerospace Ltd: fndr and md 1996–99, tech dir 1999–2004, business devpt and tech dir 2004–, non-exec dir 2012; fndr and chief exec Poll AeroSciences 2012; chm Defence Scientific Advsy Cncl MoD 2011–13; visiting scientist: DFVLR Göttingen W Germany 1983, NASA Langley Res Centre VA 1983, 1989 and 1990, NASA Ames Research Centre CA 1995 and 1998, Stanford Univ 1998; memb: Fluid Dynamics Panel NATO Advsy Gp for Aerospace R&D 1991–97, Aerospace Ctee DTI 1999–2004, Aerospace Technol Steering Gp 2004–, CAA Uninhabited Air Vehicle Steering Ctee 2006–; RAeS: memb Cncl 1996–2010, vice-pres 1998–2000, pres 2001, chm Learned Soc Bd 1997–2000, chm Cranfield Univ Branch 1997–2012 (pres 2012–), chm Strategic Review Bd 2000, chair Uninhabited Air Vehicle Ctee 2005–, Hodgson Prize 2001, Wilbur and Orville Wright lectr 2002, Lanchester lectr 2008; Int Cncl of the Aeronautical Scis (ICAS): memb Gen Assembly 1997–2012, chair Prog Ctee 2006–08 (memb 1997–), pres Int Cncl 2008–10, hon fell 2013; memb Cncl Air League 1997–2012, memb Cncl UK Aerodynamics Centre 2012–; vice-pres (technical progs) Confedn of Euro Aerospace Socs (CEAS) 2003–04, sr vice-pres City and Guilds Coll Assoc 2004–06; memb Cncl Royal Acad of Engrg 2004–07; memb Home Office Scientific Advsy Cncl (HOSAC) 2012–13, memb Nat Environment Research Cncl Dept for Business Innovation and Skills 2014–, memb Audit and Risk Ctee Natural Environment Research Cncl (NERC) 2015–; author of over 100 papers on aerodynamics, aeronautics and aviation; memb Br Flying Assoc (A certificate 2015); AIAA Dryden lectureship in research 2010, Von Karman Lecture Royal Aeronautical Soc 2016; Liveryman Worshipful Co of Coachmakers and Coach Harness Makers; ACGI 1972; memb RUSI 2005–; CEng 1978, FRAeS 1987, FREng 1996, HonFAIAA 2013 (FAIAA 2000), FCGI 2004; *Recreations* golf, political debate; *Clubs* Athenaeum, RAF; *Style*— Prof Ian Poll, OBE, FREng; ✉ Cranfield University, Cranfield, Bedfordshire MK43 0AL (☎ 01234 754743, fax 01234 751181, e-mail d.i.a.poll@cranfield.ac.uk)

POLLACK, Anita Jean; da of John Samuel Pollack (decd), of Sydney, Aust, and Kathleen, *née* Emerson (decd); *b* 3 June 1946; *Educ* Sydney Tech Coll (Dip Advertising), City of London Poly (BA), Birkbeck Coll London (MSc); *m* Philip Stephen Bradbury; 1 da (Katherine Louise Pollack Bradbury b 4 Sept 1986); *Career* former advtg copywriter Aust, book ed London 1970–74, res asst to late Rt Hon Barbara Castle 1981–89, MEP (Lab) London SW 1989–99, head of European policy English Heritage 2000–2006, European conslt 2006–16; *Publications* Wreckers or Builders? A History of Labour Members of the European Parliament 1979–99 (2009), New Labour in Europe: leadership and lost opportunities (2016); *Recreations* family; *Style*— Ms Anita Pollack; ✉ 139 Windsor Road, London E7 0RA (☎ 020 8471 1637, website www.anitapollack.eu)

POLLARD, Sir Charles; kt (2001), QPM (1990); s of Humphrey Charles Pollard (d 1990), and Margaret Isobel, *née* Philpott (d 1986); *b* 4 February 1945; *Educ* Oundle, Univ of Bristol (LLB); *m* 13 July 1972, Erica Jane Allison, da of Gordon Daniel Jack; 2 s (Jonathan, Christopher), 1 da (Rosemary); *Career* Met Police 1964–66, travelled abroad 1967, Met Police 1968–80 (latterly Chief Inspr); Sussex Police: Supt Eastbourne Sub-Div 1980–84, Chief Supt Operational Support Dept HQ Lewes 1984–85; asst Chief Constable Thames Valley Police 1985–88, dep asst cmmr i/c Plus Programme and later SW Area Met Police 1988–91, Chief Constable Thames Valley Police 1991–2002; chm Justice Research Consortium 2002–06, reader in criminology Univ of Pennsylvania 2002–06; chm Oxford Common Purpose 1996–98, vice-chm Thames Valley Partnership 1991–2002, chm Restorative Solutions cic 2006–, vice-chair Why Me – Victims for Restorative Justice 2008–16; visiting fell Nuffield Coll Oxford 1993–2001; bd memb Youth Justice Bd for England and Wales 1998–2004 (acting chm 2003–04), memb Bd Centre for Mgmnt and Policy Studies 2000–02; memb ACPO (chm Quality Serv Ctee 1991–94, chm No 5 (S East) Region 1996–99); contributes to nat media and learned journals on policing, criminal justice and restorative justice; Dr of Laws (hc): Univ of Buckingham 2001, Univ of Bristol 2003; *Recreations* walking, bridge, tennis, family pursuits; *Clubs* Royal Over-Seas League; *Style*— Sir Charles Pollard, QPM, LLB

POLLARD, David Nigel; s of John Stuart Pollard (d 2001), and Ruth, *née* Rath; *b* 30 August 1956, Leeds, Yorks; *Educ* Cranbrook Sch, St John's Coll Cambridge, Coll of Law Chester; *m* 15 June 1991, Louise Elizabeth, *née* O'Hara; 2 da (Jessica, Elizabeth), 1 s (Andrew); *Career* admitted slr: Eng and Wales 1980, Hong Kong 1986; slr specialising in pensions and employment law; articled clerk then slr Lewis Lewis & Co 1978–82; Freshfields: slr London and Singapore offices 1982–90, ptnr 1990–2015; co-ed Trust Law Int jl; Wallace Medal Assoc of Pension Lawyers 1998; chm Assoc of Pension Lawyers 2001–03, former vice-chair Industrial Law Soc, memb Law Soc; *Publications* Guide to the Pensions Act 1995 (ed, 1995), Corporate Insolvency: Employment and Pension Rights (5 edn 2013), The Law of Pension Trusts (2013), Freshfields on Corporate Pensions Law (ed, 4 edn 2015); *Recreations* Cwlth pensions cases; *Clubs* Singapore Cricket; *Style*— David Pollard, Esq; ✉ 55 Colebrooke Row, Islington, London N1 8AF (☎ 020 7359 4215, e-mail teampollard@yahoo.co.uk); Freshfields Bruckhaus Deringer, 65 Fleet Street, London EC4Y 1HS (☎ 020 7832 7060, fax 020 7832 7001, e-mail david.pollard@freshfields.com)

POLLARD, Eve (Lady Lloyd); OBE (2008); da of Ivor Pollard, and Mimi Pollard; *m* 1, 8 Dec 1968 (m dis), Barry Winkleman; 1 da (Claudia b 15 Jan 1972); m 2, 23 May 1979, Sir Nicholas Lloyd, *qv*; 1 s (Oliver b 6 Aug 1980); *Career* fashion ed: Honey 1967–68, Daily Mirror Magazine 1968–69; reporter Daily Mirror 1969–70; women's ed: Observer Magazine 1970–71, Sunday Mirror 1971–81; asst ed Sunday People 1981–83, features ed and presenter TV-am 1983–85; ed: Elle (launch, USA) 1985–86, Sunday Magazine (News of the World) 1986, You Magazine (Mail on Sunday) 1986–87, Sunday Mirror and Sunday Mirror Magazine 1988–91, Sunday Express and Sunday Express magazine 1991–94; devised two series Frocks on the Box for ITV 1985; chm Eve Pollard Fashion Designs; hon pres Women in Journalism 1999– (chair 1995–99), Editor of the Year Newspaper Focus Awards 1990; memb: English Tourist Bd 1993–2000, Newspaper Panel Competition Cmmn 1999–2007; chair UK Advsy Bd Reporters Without Borders (RSF) 2016–; visiting fell Bournemouth Univ; vice-chm Wellbeing charity; *Books* Jackie (1971), Splash (jtly Val Corbett and Joyce Hopkirk, 1995), Best of Enemies (1996), Double Trouble (1997), Unfinished Business (1998), Jack's Widow (2006); *Style*— Miss Eve Pollard, OBE; ✉ c/o Jackie Gill Management Ltd, 3 Warren Mews, London W1T 6AN (☎ 020 7383 5550, e-mail jackie@jackiegill.co.uk); Eve Pollard Designs (e-mail info@donnaeveningwear.co.uk)

POLLARD, Ian Douglas; s of Douglas Pollard, DFC (ka 1945), and Peggy, *née* Murfitt (d 1989); *b* 9 June 1945; *Educ* Perse Sch Cambridge; *m* 25 July 1964, Dianna, da of Prof Alexander Deer, of Cambridge; 3 da (Juliette b 1964, Samantha b 1966, Arushka b 1987), 2 s (Rufus b 1992, Kian b 1995); *Career* chm and md Flaxyard plc 1972–; architectural designer of: Marcopolo (Observers Bldg) 1987, Sainsbury's Homebase Kensington 1988, Martin Ryan Inst for Marine Scis Galway 1991; designer and creator of gardens at Hazelbury Manor Wilts and Abbey House Gardens Malmesbury Wilts; featured as 'naked gardener' in Going to Work Naked (ITV) 2005; ARICS; *Recreations* gardening, cycling, diving; *Style*— Ian Pollard, Esq; ✉ The Abbey House, Market Cross, Malmesbury, Wiltshire SN16 9AS (☎ 01666 827650, fax 01666 822782, e-mail info@abbeyhousegardens.co.uk)

POLLARD, John Stanley; s of Prof Arthur Pollard (d 2002), of North Cave, Humberside, and Ursula Ann Egerton, *née* Jackson (d 1970); *b* 4 January 1952; *Educ* King's Sch Macclesfield, Hymers Coll Hull, Univ of Leeds (LLB); *m* 14 Sept 1974, Clare Judith, da of Arnold Walter George Boulton (d 1992), of Cookham Dean, Berks; 3 s (Samuel John b 1979, Joseph William b 1981, Edward George b 1984); *Career* admitted slr 1977; HM asst coroner Cheshire, HM coroner Manchester S District, HM asst coroner Manchester W District; memb Congleton Town Cncl 1983–2007; Parly candidate (SDP) Crewe and Nantwich 1983; chm LRC (4 x 4) Ltd 1999–2012, chm Dane Housing Ltd 1999–2008, dir Dane Housing Ltd 1999–2008, chm and dir Plus-Dane Housing Gp 2008–10; memb: Law Soc, Coroners Soc of England and Wales (memb Nat Cncl, pres 2012–13); FRSM 2007; *Recreations* football, sport, gardening, politics; *Style*— John Pollard, Esq; ✉ HM Coroner, Mount Tabor, Mottram Street, Stockport SK1 3PA (☎ 0161 474 3993, fax 0161 474 3994, e-mail john.pollard@stockport.gov.uk)

POLLARD, Prof (Alan) Mark; s of Alan Pollard (d 1985), and Elizabeth Pollard (d 1998); *b* 5 July 1954, Auckland, NZ; *Educ* Heckmondwyke GS, Sowerby Bridge GS, Univ of York (BA, DPhil); *m* 1992, Dr Rebecca Nicholson; 2 da (Sarah Elizabeth b 8 May 1993, Louise Etta b 22 April 1997); *Career* analytical research offr Research Lab for Archaeology Univ of Oxford 1978–84, lectr in inorganic chemistry UC Cardiff 1984–90, prof of archaeological sciences Univ of Bradford 1990–2004 (head of dept 1990–99, pro-vice-chllr (research) 2001–04), Edward Hall prof of archaeological science Univ of Oxford 2004–; nat co-ordinator for science-based archaeology 1987–90; MRSC 1990, FSA 1993; *Publications* author of more than 200 pubns incl: Archaeological Chemistry (jtly, 1996, 2 edn 2008), Handbook of Archaeological Science (jt ed, 2001); *Recreations* cycling, morris dancing and playing, stamps; *Style*— Prof Mark Pollard; ✉ Research Laboratory for Archaeology and the History of Art, University of Oxford, Dyson Perrins Building, South Parks Road, Oxford OX1 2QY (☎ 01865 285228)

POLLINS, Martin; s of Harry Pollins (d 1969), of London, and Hetty Pollins (d 1991); *b* 11 December 1938, London; *Educ* Brighton Tech Sch; MBA 1999; *m* 1, March 1963 (m dis 1980); m 2, Dec 1980, Susan Elizabeth, da of Arthur Edwin Hines, of Brighton; 4 s (Andrew, Richard, Nicholas, Matthew), 1 da (Anna); *Career* chartered accountant; ptnr PRB Martin Pollins 1968–2005; chm: Professional Enterprise Gp plc 1986–97, Britton Price Ltd 1996–2009, Bizezia Ltd 2001–; dir: Network Technology plc 1995–2006, Movision Entertainment Ltd 2002–; memb Cncl ICAEW 1987–96; FCA 1964, ATII 1964; *Recreations* spectator of sport; *Style*— Martin Pollins, Esq; ✉ Fletchings, North Common Road, Wivelsfield Green, Haywards Heath, East Sussex RH17 7RJ; Bizezia Limited, Kingfisher House, Hurstwood Grange, Hurstwood Lane, Haywards Heath, West Sussex RH17 7QX (☎ 01444 8842212, e-mail mpollins@bizezia.com)

POLLITT, Prof Christopher John; s of Almora John Pollitt, and Freda Hebbert, *née* Ashcroft; *b* 7 February 1946; *Educ* Oriel Coll Oxford (MA), LSE (PhD); *Partner* Hilkka Helena Summa; 2 s from prev m (Thomas John b 22 April 1971, Jack Christopher b 12 Aug 1972); *Career* asst princ then princ Home Civil Serv (MOD, Miny of Technol, DTI), lectr then sr lectr in govt Open Univ 1975–90; Brunel Univ: prof of govt and co-dir Centre for the Evaluation of Public Policy and Practice 1990–98, dean Faculty of Social Scis 1994–97, prof of public mgmnt Erasmus Univ Rotterdam 1999–2006, prof of public mgmnt Univ of Leuven 2006–; hon jt ed Public Admin 1980–88, non-exec dir Hillingdon Hosp Tst 1995–97; numerous research grants and consultancies with public and govt bodies incl: ESRC, EC, HM Treasy, OECD, World Bank; memb Cncl RIPA 1990–92, pres Euro Evaluation Soc 1996–98; Hon PhD Univ of Vaasa Finland; *Books* incl: Managerialism and the Public Services (1990, 2 edn 1993), The Essential Public Manager (2003), Public Management Reform: a Comparative Analysis (with Geert Bouckaert, 2004), Time, Policy, Management (2008); *Recreations* squash, walking, owl-watching; *Style*— Prof Christopher Pollitt; ✉ Instituut voor de Overheid, Parkstraat 45, BE-3000 Leuven, Belgium (e-mail christopher.pollitt@soc.kuleuven.be)

POLLOCK; *see also:* Montagu-Pollock

POLLOCK, Sheriff Alexander; s of late Robert Faulds Pollock, OBE, and late Margaret Findlay Pollock, *née* Aitken; *b* 21 July 1944; *Educ* Rutherglen Acad, Glasgow Acad, BNC Oxford (Domus exhibitioner, MA), Univ of Edinburgh (LLB), Perugia Univ (for foreigners); *m* 1975, Verena Francesca Gertraud Alice Ursula, da of late J Reginald Critchley, of Ware, Herts; 1 da (Francesca b 1976), 1 s (Andrew b 1979); *Career* slr 1970–73, advocate Scottish Bar 1973–91; MP (Cons): Moray and Nairn 1979–83, Moray 1983–87; memb Commons Select Ctee on Scottish Affrs 1979–82; PPS to George Younger: as Sec of State for Scotland 1982–86, as Sec of State for Def 1986–87; sec Br Austrian Parly Gp 1979–87, Advocate Depute 1990–91; Floating Sheriff of Tayside, Central and Fife at Stirling 1991–93, Sheriff of Grampian, Highland and Islands at Aberdeen and Stonehaven 1993–2001, at Inverness and Portree 2001–05, at Inverness 2005–09; memb Queen's Body Guard for Scotland (Royal Co of Archers) 1984–; *Clubs* New (Edinburgh), Highland (Inverness); *Style*— Sheriff Alexander Pollock; ✉ Drumdarrach, Forres, Moray IV36 1DW

POLLOCK, David Raymond John; s of Eric John Frank Pollock (d 1992), of Dulwich, and Beryl Olive, *née* Newens (d 1982); *b* 22 October 1949, London; *Educ* Dulwich Coll, Keele Univ (BA), Univ of Oxford (PGCert); *m* 30 July 1975, Barbara Ann (d 2005), da of Henry Chambré, MBE, of Hendon; 1 da (Sarah Charlotte Chambré b 23 Aug 1980), 1 s (Thomas Hugo John b 19 March 1984); m 2, 22 Dec 2015, Judith Alison (Sally) Simpson, da of David Brown, of Kirkham, Lancs; *Career* MOD: admin trainee 1972, higher exec offr 1975 (private sec to Chief Sci Advsr), princ 1978; asst dir Primary Markets Div Int Stock Exchange 1989–91 (head of Industry Policy Unit 1986, head of Business Devpt Primary Mkts Div 1988), dir Newspaper Publishers Assoc 1992–97 (dir designate 1991), dir Electrical Contractors' Assoc 1997–2010 (gp chief exec 2007–10, gen sec European affrs 2010–13); chm Oxon Artweeks Festival 2011–; memb: Cncl until 1998 and Fin Ctee until 2011 Royal Instn of GB, Asia House (lectured on Lao textiles 2004 and 2009), Soc of Archer Antiquaries, S American Explorers' Club Lima Peru, Vernacular Architecture Gp, Oxon Buildings Record; Liveryman Worshipful Company of Stationers and Newspaper Makers, Freeman Worshipful Co of Constructors; FRSA; *Recreations* architecture, country pursuits, travel, tribal textiles, drawing and painting, books, conviviality; *Style*— David Pollock, Esq; ✉ The Lawn, Market Street, Charlbury OX7 3PJ

POLLOCK, David (Charles) Treherne; BEM (2013); s of Brian Treherne Pollock (d 1994), and Helen Evelyn (d 1995), da of Brig-Gen Sir Eric Holt-Wilson, CMG, DSO; *b* 7 April 1938; *Educ* St Andrew's Pangbourne, Nowton Court, The Hill Sch, St Lawrence Coll; *m* 1961, Lisbeth Jane, *née* Scratchley; 2 s (Piers, Blair), 1 da (Sophie-Jane (Mrs Richard Johnson)); *Career* cmmnd The Gordon Highlanders 1956–59; The Economist 1961–68; dir: Mathers & Streets Ltd 1968–69, Charles Barker (City) Ltd 1969–70, Dewe Rogerson Ltd 1970–88, Dewe Rogerson Group Ltd 1975–88, Maxwell Stamp plc 1988–2002; tstee Restoration of Appearance and Function Tst (RAFT) 1994– (chm 2000–08); *Clubs* City of London; *Style*— David Treherne Pollock, Esq, BEM; ✉ 9 The Chase, London SW4 0NP (☎ 020 7622 1535, e-mail d@trehernepollock.com); Chateau de Jasses, 64190 Jasses, Pyrenees Atlantiques, France (☎ 00 33 55 96 61 408)

POLLOCK, Prof Griselda Frances Sinclair; da of Alan Winton Seton Pollock (d 1986), and Kathleen Alexandra, *née* Sinclair (d 1964); *b* 11 March 1949; *Educ* Queen's Coll London, Lady Margaret Hall Oxford (MA), Courtauld Inst of Art (MA, PhD); *m* 30 Oct 1981, Prof Antony Bryant, s of Paul and Leonie Bryant, of London; 1 s (Benjamin b 22 March 1983), 1 da (Hester b 7 Feb 1986); *Career* lectr in art history Univ of Manchester 1974–77; Univ of Leeds: lectr in art history and film 1977–85, sr lectr 1985–90, prof of social and critical histories of art 1990–, dir Centre for Cultural Studies 1987–2000, exec Centre for Jewish Studies 1995–, dir Centre for Cultural, Analysis Theory and History 2001–; Slade prof of fine art Univ of Cambridge 2007–08; author of numerous articles in jls; Tate Gallery Liverpool Advsy Bd 1988–94; FRSA 1996; *Books* Millet (1977), Vincent Van Gogh (1978), Mary Cassatt (1980), Old Mistresses Women Art and Ideology (1981), The Journals of Marie Bashkirtseff (1985), Framing Feminism: Art and the Women's Movement (1987), Vision and Difference: Feminism, Femininity and the Histories of Art (1988), Dealing with Degas (co-ed with R Kendall, 1992), Avant-Garde Gambits 1888–1893: Gender and the Colour of Art History (1992, Walter Neurath Meml Lecture), Generations and Geographies in the Visual Arts (1996), Avant-Gardes and Partisans Reviewed (with Fred Orton, 1996), Mary Cassatt (1998), Differencing The Canon (1999), Looking Back to the Future (2000), Encountering Eva Hesse (with Vanessa Corby, 2006), Psychoanalysis and the Image (2006), Museums after Modernism (2007), Encounters in the Virtual Feminist Museum (2007), Conceptual Odysseys (2007), The Sacred and the Feminine (with Victoria Turvey Sauron, 2008), Bluebeard's Legacy: Death and Secrets from Barfok to Hitchcock (with Victoria Anderson, 2008), Digital and Other Virtualities: Renegotiating the Image (with Antony Bryant, 2010), Bracha L Ettinger: Art as Compassion (with Catherine de Zegher, 2011), Concentrationary Cinema: Aesthetic Resistance in Alain Resnais's Night and Fog 1955 (with Max Silverman, 2011, Krazsna-Krausz Prize for Best Book on the Moving Image 2011), After-Affects/After-Images: Trauma and Aesthetic Transformation (2013), Visual Politics of Psychoanalysis: Art and the Image in Post-Traumatic Cultures (2013); *Recreations* running, cinema, opera; *Style*— Prof Griselda Pollock; ✉ CentreCATH, Old Mining Building, University of Leeds, Leeds LS2 9JT (e-mail g.f.s.pollock@leeds.ac.uk, website www.leeds.ac.uk/cath)

POLLOCK, John; *Educ* Hutchesons' GS Glasgow, Univ of Strathclyde (BSc); *Career* Legal & General Gp plc: IT 1980–89, ops 1990–94, sales dir 1994–96, md Legal & General Asia 1996–98, ops dir 1998–2003, memb Bd 2003–; memb The Children's Tst; FRGS 2005; *Style*— John Pollock, Esq; ✉ Legal & General Group plc, 1 Coleman Street, London EC2R 5AA (☎ 01737 370370, e-mail john.pollock@landg.com)

POLLOCK, Peter Glen; s of Jack Campbell Pollock (d 1953), and Rebecca Shields Marshall, *née* Clarke (d 1985); *b* 6 September 1946, London; *Educ* Nautical Coll Pangbourne, Univ of St Andrews (MA); *m* 3 Sept 1977, Nicola Sara, da of Derek William Bernard Clements, of Cirencester, Glos; 2 s (Jonathan William Campbell b 1982, Matthew Charles Simon b 1984), 1 da (Antonia Rebecca b 1991); *Career* fin dir: Hawker Siddeley Power Transformers Ltd 1978–83, Fisher Controls Ltd 1983–85; gp chief exec ML Holdings plc 1985–92, mgmnt conslt Peter Pollock & Co 1992–94; dir: Faversham Oyster Fishery Co 1993–94, Menvier Swain Group plc 1993–97, Mentmore Abbey plc (formerly Platignum plc) 1994–99, Ferrabyrne Ltd 2009–; chm: Valetmatic Holdings Ltd 1994–97, Second Phase Industries Ltd 1994–, Lionheart plc 1997–2004 (dir 1996–2004), Ferrabyrne 2012–;

P

chief exec LPA Group plc 1997–; memb: Ctee RUKBA 1985–98, Cncl SBAC 1989–92; Railway Industry Assoc: memb Fin Ctee 2000–, memb Cncl 2011–, chm Fin Ctee 2012–; Liveryman Worshipful Co of Coachmakers and Harnessmakers; FCA 1973; *Recreations* music, tennis, skiing, golf; *Clubs* Naval, Knole, Wildernesse; *Style*— Peter Pollock, Esq; ✉ Platt Common House, St Mary's Platt, Sevenoaks, Kent TN15 8JX (mobile 07881 626123, e-mail ppollock@lpa-group.com)

POLLOCK-HILL, Stephen David; s of Malcolm William Lyttleton Pollock-Hill (d 1995), of Malaga, Spain, and Jeanne, *née* Beale (d 2005); *b* 22 March 1948, London; *Educ* Harrow, Sorbonne, Univ de Madrid, Univ de Vienna, Hatfield Poly (HND); *m* 18 June 1983, Samantha Ann Maria Russell, da of Sir (William) Russell Lawrence, QC (d 1976); 1 s (Robert b 1977), 1 da (Talitha Louise b 1985); *Career* documentalist Mead Carney France (mgmnt conslts) 1970–71; Nazeing Glass Works: sales liaison offr 1972, sales rep 1973, sales mangr 1975, export mangr 1976, sales dir 1980–91, jt md 1990–98, chm 1992–; chm and md Nazeing Glass Investments 1990–, chm Globe Trotter Suitcase Co Ltd 2003–05; memb Euro Domestic Glass Ctee 1978–90, chm Sci Museum Glass Gallery Ctee 1978–90, memb Cncl Glass Mfrs' Cncl 1980–88, chm GMF Domestic and Handmade Glass Ctee 1980–88, chm Br Glass Educnl Tst 2000–, Euro domestic glass advsr EEC-CPIV Ctee Brussels 1985–90, memb Cncl Br Glass 2007–10, pres Br Glass 2010 (memb Bd, vice-pres 2011), vice-chm Br Glass Fndn 2010–11 (tstee), curator Museum of 20th Century Br Domestic Glass, vice-chm Glass Fndn 2009–10; inventor and patent holder World First Non Toxis Crystal; chm: CPRE Herts 1993–96 (vice-pres 1998–), Herts Business Link Lea Valley Branch 1998–2002, IOD Herts Branch 2000–03; dir Bd Herts Business Link 2000–03; memb Fin and Gen Purposes Ctee Tree Cncl 1989–95; memb Advsy Ctee European Business Sch London 1994–98 (memb Academic Bd 1998–2005), memb Devpt Ctee Univ of Hertfordshire 1995–99; co-fndr CASE (Campaign Against Stevenage Expansion), ctee memb and vice-chm The Friends of Forster Country 2005–; memb E of Eng Sustainable Devpt Round Table 2003–08; life memb: Nat Tst, Int Wine & Food Soc; memb: Glass Circle, Glass Assoc; Freeman City of London, Liveryman Worshipful Co of Glass Sellers; *Publications* The Portland Vase: Could the Portland Vase have been made for Caesar Augustus? (2008); *Recreations* conservation, lawn tennis, real tennis, gardening, trees, fine wine, writing, glass; *Clubs* Hatfield House Real Tennis; *Style*— Stephen Pollock-Hill, Esq; ✉ Nazeing Glass Investments Ltd, Broxbourne, Hertfordshire EN10 6SU (☎ 01992 464485, fax 01992 450966, e-mail s.pollock-hill@nazeing-glass.com)

POLTIMORE, 7 Baron (UK 1831); Sir Mark Coplestone Bampfylde; 12 Bt (E 1641); s of Capt the Hon Anthony Gerard Hugh Bampfylde (d 1969), and Brita Yvonne (now Mrs Guy Elmes), *née* Baroness Cederström; suc gf, 6 Baron, 1978; *b* 8 June 1957; *Educ* Radley; *m* 12 June 1982, Sally Anne, da of Dr Norman Miles (d 2013); 2 s (Hon Henry Anthony Warwick b 3 June 1985, Hon Oliver Hugh Coplestone b 15 April 1987), 1 da (Hon Lara Fiona Brita b 14 May 1990); *Heir* s, Hon Henry Bampfylde; *Career* Christie's: assoc dir Picture Dept 1984, dir and head of 19th Century Picture Dept 1987–97, chm Christie's Australia plc 1997–2000, dep chm Christie's Europe 1998–2000; md e-auction room 2000–02; Sotheby's: sr dir 2002, chm 19th and 20th century pictures 2004–06, chm Sotheby's UK 2006–08, chm Sotheby's Russia and dep chm Sotheby's Europe 2008–; former chm UK Friends of Bundanon; *Books* Popular 19th Century Painting, A Dictionary of European Genre Painters (with Philip Hook, 1986); *Clubs* White's; *Style*— The Rt Hon the Lord Poltimore; ✉ North Hidden Farm, Hungerford, Berkshire RG17 0PY

POMEROY, Sir Brian Walter; kt (2012), CBE (2006); *b* 26 June 1944; *Educ* The King's Sch Canterbury, Magdalene Coll Cambridge (MA); *m* 7 Aug 1974, Hilary Susan; 2 da (Gabriela b 1975, Alisa b 1977); *Career* ptnr Touche Ross mgmnt conslts (now Deloitte Consulting): ptnr 1975, seconded as under sec in DTI 1981–83, sr ptnr Deloitte Consulting 1995–99 (md 1987–95); non-exec dir: Rover Gp plc 1985–88, FSA 2009–13, Financial Conduct Authy 2013–16; memb Ctee of Enquiry into Regulatory Arrangements at Lloyd's 1986, ind memb Cncl Lloyd's 1996–2004, dep chm Lloyd's Regulatory Bd 1996–2002; chm QBE Insurance Europe Ltd 2013–14, non-exec dir QBE Insurance Gp Ltd 2014–; chm: AIDS Awareness Tst 1993–96, Centrepoint 1993–2001, European Public Health Fndn 1997–2004, The King's Consort 2000–05, Homeless Link 2001–05, Raleigh Int 2005–07, Financial Inclusion Taskforce HM Treasy 2005–11, Payments Cncl 2007–09, Gambling Cmmn 2007–11, Photographers' Gallery 2007–13, Ind Cmmn on Equitable Life Payments 2010–11, Responsible Gambling Strategy Bd 2012–13; memb: Cncl Mgmnt Conslts Assoc 1996–99, Disability Rights Task Force 1997–99, Cmmn on Citizenship and Taxation 1998–2000, Nat Lottery Cmmn 1999–2008 (chm 1999–2000 and 2002–03), Bd Social Market Fndn 2000–, Pensions Protection and Investments Accreditation Bd 2000–05, Audit Cmmn 2003–09, Ind Inquiry into Drug Testing at Work 2003–04, Financial Reporting Review Panel 2004–13; tstee: Money Advice Tst 1999–2009 (ambass 2010–), Space Studios 2004–05, Children's Express 2004–07, Lloyd's Charitable Tst 2004–10, Photographers' Gallery 2006–14, Photography Oxford 2016–; chair Action Gp on Cross-Border Remittances 2014–, pres Financial Inclusion Cmmn 2014–; chair Kraszna-Krausz Fndn 2016–, memb Awards Ctee Royal Photographic Soc 2016–; Master Co of Mgmnt Conslts 2000–01; FCA 1978, FRSA 1994, ARPS 2004; *Publications* articles on public finance, regulation and public-private partnership; *Recreations* photography, cinema, cycling, music; *Style*— Sir Brian Pomeroy, CBE; ✉ 7 Ferncroft Avenue, London NW3 7PG (☎ 07785 304368, e-mail pomeroybw@aol.com)

POMFRET, Christopher Charles (Chris); s of Jack Gregson Pomfret (d 1987), and Eileen Norah Pomfret (d 2007); *b* 15 November 1949, Liverpool; *Educ* Simon Langton GS for Boys Canterbury, Univ of Southampton (BSc); *m* 1975, Jacqueline Ruth; 2 da (Helen Victoria b 1976, Suzanne Mary b 1979), 1 s (David Charles b 1982); *Career* Unilever: trainee Van den Berg and Jurgens Ltd 1971–73, public affrs mangr Unilever Ltd 1973–76, sales rep rising to sr brand mangr Walls Ice Cream 1976–80, mktg controller Gelato Brazil 1980–82, gen mktg mangr Birds Eye Walls 1983–90, mtkg dir Cogesal Paris 1990–92, sr mktg memb global ice cream strategy Rotterdam 1992–94, sr vice-pres European ice cream strategy Rotterdam 1994–97, business dir frozen foods Birds Eye Walls Ltd 1997–2003, mktg and sustainability co-ordinator Unilever plc 2003–04; dir Mktg and Sustainability Consultancy Ltd 2005–; memb: Cncl ISBA until 2003 (also dir), Bd Food Standards Agency 2005–10 (actg chm Welsh Advsy Ctee 2006), Govt Round Table on Sustainable Consumption until 2006, Customer Ctee on Life and Pensions ABI 2005–11, Expert Panel on Cabinet Office Food Policy 2007–08, Sea Fish Industry Bd 2010–12; chair Cornwall and Isles of Scilly Local Enterprise Bd 2011–; memb Corporate Advsy Bd and sr assoc Prog for Sustainability Leadership Univ of Cambridge 2003–12, memb Advsy Bd European Centre for Environment and Human Health Univ of Exeter, memb Cncl Univ of Exeter 2013–15, chair Bd of Govrs Falmouth Univ 2015–; tstee: CHASE 2004–09, Cornwall Air Ambulance Tst 2013, Hall for Cornwall 2016;; *Publications* Can Sustainability Sell? (2002), I Will If You Will (co-author, 2006); *Recreations* music, golf, travel, gardening, sailing, cooking; *Clubs* St Enodoc Golf, Rock Sailing, Farmer's; *Style*— Chris Pomfret, Esq

POMMIER, Pascal; s of Jean-Jacques Marcel Pommier, of Paray-le-Monial, France, and Yvette Renee Monique, *née* Gonnin; *b* 15 December 1964; *Educ* Ces Cours Jean Jeaures (DEFO Dip), CFA Mercurey Coll (CAP); *m* 24 Sept 1999, Joanna Moussa; 2 da (Marina Georgia b 14 Oct 2006, Georgia Maria b 1 Oct 2007), 1 s (Theodore Luca b 9 March 2009); *Career* chef; apprenticeship Hotel Moderne Charolles France 1980–82, Hotel Belvedere du Pelvoux Pelvoux France 1982–83, Mil Serv Macon France 1983–84, Restaurant Alain Raye Albertville France 1985–86, The Mill House Hotel Kingham Oxon 1986–88, The Normandie Hotel Bury Lancs 1988–96 (Lancashire Life Restaurant of the Year 1988, Ackerman Clover Award annually 1989–96, 3 AA Rosettes annually 1990–96, County Restaurant of the Year Good Food Guide 1993 and 1994, Egon Ronay Star annually 1990–96, Michelin Star 1995 and 1996), The Captain's Table Woodbridge Suffolk 1998– (2 AA Rosettes annually 1999–2002 and 2006– (1 AA Rosette annually 2003–05), Michelin Bib Gourmand annually 1999–, Good Food Guide annually 1999–, 1 Star Harden Guide 2007); *Recreations* rugby, football, travel; *Style*— Pascal Pommier, Esq; ☎ 01394 383145, website www.captainstable.co.uk

POND, Christopher Richard (Chris); s of late Charles Richard Pond (d 1986), and late Doris Violet, *née* Cox (d 1998); *b* 25 September 1952; *Educ* Minchenden Sch Southgate, Univ of Sussex (BA); *m* 1, 28 Dec 1990 (m dis 1999), Carole Tongue, *qv*, da of Archer Tongue; 1 da; m 2, 21 March 2003, Lorraine, da of Roualeyn Melvin; 1 da; *Career* research asst Birkbeck Coll London 1974–75, research offr Low Pay Unit 1975–79, lectr in econs Civil Serv Coll 1979–80, dir Low Pay Unit 1980–97 (chair 1997–99); MP (Lab) Gravesham 1997–2005, memb Select Ctee on Social Security 1997–99, PPS to Rt Hon Dawn Primarolo, MP (as Paymaster Gen) 1999–2003, Parly under sec of State Dept of Work and Pensions 2003–05; chief exec Nat Cncl for One Parent Families 2005–07; FSA: dir of financial capability 2007–10, sr advsr 2010–11, head of consumer affrs 2011–; chair Capacity Builders UK Ltd 2005–09, vice-chair End Child Poverty 2007; memb: FSA Working Gp on Families 2005, FSA Steering Gp on Financial Capability 2006, Cncl Inst of Fiscal Studies 2006–, Thoresen Review Reference Gp 2007; ind advsr HMRC Ctee on Ethics and Responsibility 2010–; former memb Mgmnt Ctees of Unemployment Unit and Child Poverty Action Gp; non-exec dir Cape Claims Servs 2006–; conslt on social policy to EC 1995–96; visiting lectr in econs Univ of Kent 1981–82, visiting prof/research fell Univ of Surrey 1984–86, conslt Open Univ 1987–88 and 1991–92, hon visiting prof Middx Univ 1996–; tstee Family and Parenting Inst 2009–; memb: TGWU, Royal Acad; *Books* Inflation and Low Incomes (1975), Trade Unions and Taxation (1976),To Him Who Hath (1977), The Povery Trap: a study in statistical sources (1978), Taxing Wealth Inequalities (1980) Taxation and Social Policy (1981), Low Pay: Labour's Response (1983), The Changing Distribution of Income, Wealth and Poverty, in Restructuring Britain (1989), A New Social Policy For The Active Society (chapter in Old and New Poverty, 1995), Beyond 2002 – Long Term Policies for Labour (jtly, 1999); *Recreations* running, reading; *Clubs* Gravesend Road Runners and Athletics (18 marathons completed); *Style*— Chris Pond, Esq

PONDER, Prof Sir Bruce Anthony John; kt (2008); s of late Anthony West Ponder, and Dorothy Mary, *née* Peachey (d 2008); *b* 25 April 1944; *Educ* Charterhouse, Jesus Coll Cambridge (open scholar, MA), St Thomas' Hosp Med Sch (open scholar, MB BChir), UCL (PhD); *m* 2 Aug 1969, Margaret Ann, da of John Eliot Hickinbotham; 3 da (Jane b 2 March 1971, Katherine b 20 March 1973, Rosamund b 10 Sept 1975), 1 s (William b 5 June 1976); *Career* house physician St Thomas' Hosp 1968, house surgn Kent and Canterbury Hosp 1969, house physician Brompton Hosp 1969, SHO Lambeth and St Thomas' Hosp 1969, med registrar St Thomas' and Worthing Hosps 1970–73, clinical res fell ICRF 1973–77, Hamilton Fairley fell Cancer Research Campaign (CRC) Harvard Med Sch 1977–78, clinical scientific offr ICRF Bart's 1978–80, CRC fell and sr lectr in med Inst of Cancer Research and Royal Marsden Hosp 1980–86, head of human cancer genetics Inst of Cancer Research 1987–89, reader in cancer genetics and hon conslt physician Royal Marsden, St George's and Guy's Hosps 1987–89, hon conslt physician Addenbrooke's and Royal Marsden Hosps 1989–2013; Univ of Cambridge: dir CRC Human Cancer Genetics Group 1989–2008, CRC prof of human cancer genetics 1992–96, prof of clinical oncology 1996–2006, Li Ka Shing prof of oncology 2006–11; co-dir: Strangeways Research Laboratories Cambridge 1996–2008, Hutchison/MRC Research Centre 2000–15; dir Cancer Research UK Cambridge Research Inst 2005–13, dir Cambridge Cancer Centre 2006–15, chm Scientific Cncl of WHO Int Agency for Cancer Research Lyon 2006–08; Gibb fell CRC 1990, fell Jesus Coll Cambridge 1992; Croonian lectr RCP 1997; treas Br Assoc for Cancer Research 1983–86 (pres 2010–14), memb Bd of Dir American Assoc for Cancer Research 2008–13, fndr memb Acad of the American Assoc for Cancer Research 2013–, tstee Cancer Research UK 2016–; Int Public Service Award Nat Neurofibromatosis Fndn 1991, Merck Prize European Thyroid Assoc 1996, Hamilton-Fairley Award European Soc for Medical Oncology 2004, Bertner Award M D Anderson Hosp 2007, Alfred G Knudsen Award Nat Cancer Inst USA 2008, Ambuj Nath Bose Prize RCP 2008, Donald Ware Waddell Award Univ of Arizona 2010, Lifetime Achievement Award Cancer Research UK 2013; FRCP 1988 (MRCP 1970), FMedSci 1998, FRCPath 2001, FRS 2001; *Books* Cancer Biology and Medicine (series ed with M J Waring, 1989–96); author of more than 500 pubns in scientific jls; *Recreations* gardening, golf, travel, wine, photography; *Clubs* Royal West Norfolk Golf; *Style*— Prof Sir Bruce Ponder

PONSONBY, Thomas Charles George; s of George Thomas Ponsonby (d 1984), of Thurles, Co Tipperary, and Elizabeth Penelope Melville, *née* Wills; *b* 23 August 1950; *Educ* Eton, Trinity Coll of Music, Eurocentre Neuchâtel, Br Inst Florence; *m* 1980 (m dis 1985), Elisabeth Marie Philippine, da of Jean Masurel, of Paris; 1 s (Sebastian Jean b 1983); *Career* asst Foreign Tours Dept Ibbs & Tillett 1974–78, asst to Victor Hochhauser 1978–81, tour mangr Euro Community Youth Orch and Chamber Orch of Europe 1982–83, Music Dept Br Cncl 1983–89, exec dir Br Assoc of Concert Agents 1989–94, Business Relations Dept British Cncl 1995–96, project asst IMG Artists 1997, mangr public relations Van Walsum Management Ltd 1997–2000, administrative dir Jerwood Charitable Fndn 2000–11; memb: King Edward VII British-German Fndn, Stefan Zweig Ctee Br Library; tstee Colin Keer Tst; *Recreations* mountains, food, architecture; *Style*— Thomas Ponsonby, Esq; ✉ 28 Brook Green, London W6 7BL

PONSONBY OF SHULBREDE, 4 Baron (UK 1930), of Shulbrede, Sussex; Frederick Matthew Thomas Ponsonby; JP (Westminster Bench 2005–11, Inner London Youth Panel 2008–11, Central London Bench 2012–, Central London Youth Panel 2012–, Greater London Family Panel 2012–); also Baron Ponsonby of Roehampton (Life Peer UK 2000), of Shulbrede in the County of West Sussex; sits as Baron Ponsonby of Roehampton; o s of 3 Baron Ponsonby of Shulbrede (d 1990), and his 1 w, Ursula Mary, *née* Fox-Pitt; *b* 27 October 1958; *Educ* Holland Park Comprehensive Sch, UC Cardiff, Imperial Coll London; *m* 7 July 1995, Sarah Catriona, *née* Jackson; 1 da (Eve Elizabeth b 3 April 1991), 1 s (Cameron John Jackson b 4 Aug 1995); *Heir* s, Cameron Ponsonby; *Career* cncllr London Borough of Wandsworth 1990–94; Lab Pty educn spokesman House of Lords 1992–97, memb European Sub-Ctee C 1997–98, memb Science and Technol Select Ctee 1998–99, memb Constitution Select Ctee 2000–01; delg to: Cncl of Europe 1997–2001 (chm UK 50th Anniversary Ctee), WEU 1997–2001, OSCE 2001–10; FIMMM (FIMM 1996); *Style*— The Rt Hon Lord Ponsonby of Shulbrede, JP; ✉ House of Lords, London SW1A 0PW

PONTER, Prof Alan Robert Sage; s of Arthur Tennyson Ponter (d 1964), of Bath, and Margaret Agatha Ponter (d 1974); *b* 13 February 1940; *Educ* King Henry VIII GS Abergavenny, Imperial Coll London (BSc, ARCS, PhD), Univ of Cambridge (MA); *m* 1, 12 Sept 1962, Sonia (d 1999), da of Robert Hutchinson Valentine (d 1997), of Workington, Cumbria; 1 s (David Robert Arthur b 1964 d 1986), 3 da (Ruth Virginia b 1964, Kathryn Emma b 1968, Alexandra Margaret Valentine b 1980); m 2, 15 April 2006, Rosemary Fiona, da of Rhys Albert Davies (d 1980), of Llansadwrn, Carmarthenshire; *Career* visiting lectr Iowa Univ 1964, res fell Brown Univ RI 1964–65, lectr Univ of Glasgow 1965–66, sr asst researcher Engrg Dept Univ of Cambridge 1966–69, fell Pembroke Coll Cambridge 1967–69, prof of engrg Brown Univ USA 1976–78; Univ of Leicester: lectr

1969–74, reader 1974–76, prof of engrg 1978–, pro-vice-chllr 1987–91 and 1993–96; visiting prof Univ of Calif Santa Barbara 1991–92, conslt prof Univ of Chongqinq People's Repub of China 1991–; memb several SERC and EPSRC ctees and working parties on mechanical engrg, conslt to EEC and others on structural integrity of structures particularly at high temperatures; *Publications* Creep of Structures (1982), about 150 articles in applied mathematics and engrg literature; *Recreations* reading, music and walking; *Style—* Prof Alan Ponter; ✉ Flat 4, 20 Great Pulteney Street, Bath BA2 4BT (☎ 01225 334301); University of Leicester, University Road, Leicester LE1 7RH (☎ 01225 334301, fax 0116 252 2525, e-mail asp@le.ac.uk)

PONTIUS, His Hon Judge Timothy Gordon; s of Gordon Stuart Malzard Pontius (d 1993), and Elizabeth Mary, *née* Donaldson (d 1996); *b* 5 September 1948; *Educ* Boroughmuir Sr Secdy Sch Edinburgh, Univ of London (LLB, external); *Career* called to the Bar Middle Temple 1972, in practice at Criminal Bar 1972–88, judge advocate 1988, asst judge-advocate gen HM Forces 1991, recorder 1993–95, circuit judge (SE Circuit) 1995–2016, ret; *Recreations* music, swimming, travel, playing the piano; *Style—* His Hon Judge Pontius; ✉ The Central Criminal Court, Old Bailey, London EC4M 7EH (☎ 020 7248 3277)

PONTON, Prof John Wylie (Jack); s of late John Ronald Ponton, of Berwickshire, and late Nancy, *née* Wylie; *b* 2 May 1943; *Educ* Melville Coll Edinburgh, Univ of Edinburgh (BSc, PhD); *m* 1973, Katherine Jane Victoria, da of Jack Eachus; *Career* Univ of Edinburgh 1967– (successively lectr, sr lectr, ICI prof of chemical engrg), res fell McMaster Univ Canada 1969–70, NATO fell and assoc prof Case Western Reserve Univ 1975, process engr ICI Mond Div 1979; contribs to jls of chemical, mech, electrical and info engrg; foreign fell Russian Acad of Technological Scis 1992; FIChemE, FREng 1991, FRSA 1993; *Recreations* music, gardening, cycling, amateur radio (GM0RWU); *Style—* Prof Jack Ponton, FREng; ✉ Legerwood, Earlston, Berwickshire TD4 6AS; Department of Chemical Engineering, University of Edinburgh, King's Buildings, Edinburgh EH9 3JL (☎ 0131 650 4858, fax 0131 650 6551, e-mail jack@ecosse.org)

POOLE, Anthony; s of Gregory Bordinal Poole, of Stamford, and Anne, *née* Beveridge (d 1974); *b* 14 February 1960; *Educ* Ermysted's GS Skipton, Univ of Leeds (BSc), Leeds Sch of Architecture (BA Arch, DipArch); *m* Margaret, *née* McManus; 1 da (Hannah Isabel 12 June 1996), 1 s (Matthew Alexander 3 Jan 2000); *Career* architect; Jack Whittle & Partners Chester 1984–85, McCormick Associates Chester 1985, Martin Joyce & Associates Leeds 1987–88; Sheppard Robson (architects, planners and interior designers) London: joined 1988, assoc 1996–98, ptnr 1998–; Wellcome Tst Genome Campus Cambridge 1993–96, Edward Jenner Inst for Vaccine Research Compton 1996–98, Dept of Epidemiology Univ of Oxford 1996–98, Imperial Coll-Royal Sch of Mines 1999, Dept of Biomedical Sci Univ of Manchester 1999, Chemistry Dept Queen Mary & Westfield Coll London 2000, Napp Pharmaceuticals 2001, Dept of Biological Anthropology Univ of Cambridge 2001, Dept of Experimental Physics Queen's Univ Belfast 2001; RIBA; *Recreations* cricket, sailing, skiing; *Style—* Anthony Poole, Esq; ✉ Sheppard Robson, 77 Parkway, London NW1 7PU (☎ 020 7504 1700, fax 020 7504 1701, e-mail tony.poole@sheppardrobson.com)

POOLE, (Richard) Bruce; s of David Poole, and Iris Poole; *Educ* Charterhouse, Univ of Exeter, Westminster Coll; *Career* chef; trainee mangr Stakis Hotel plc, commis chef Bibendum 1990–92, chef de partie The Square 1992–93, head chef Chez Max 1993–94, head chef/proprietor Chez Bruce 1994– (one Michelin Star 1999, Carlton London Best Br Restaurant 1999, 3 AA Rosettes, 6/10 Good Food Guide), proprietor La Trompette (one Michelin Star), proprietor The Glasshouse (one Michelin Star); active participant Leuka 2000 (charity dinners, guest appearances and cookery demonstrations); *Recreations* cycling, football, wine; *Style—* Bruce Poole, Esq; ✉ Chez Bruce, 2 Bellevue Road, Wandsworth Common, London SW17 7EG (☎ 020 8672 0114, fax 020 8767 6648)

POOLE, 2 Baron (UK 1958); David Charles Poole; s of 1 Baron Poole, PC, CBE, TD (d 1993), and his 1 w, Betty Margaret, *née* Gilkison (d 1988); *b* 6 January 1945, Welshpoole, Montgomershire; *Educ* Dragon Sch, Gordonstoun, ChCh Oxford, INSEAD Fontainebleau; *m* 2004, Kate Watts; *Heir* s, Hon Oliver Poole; *Career* Samuel Montagu & Co 1967–74, Bland Payne & Co 1974–78, Capel-Cure Myers 1978–87, Bonomi Gp 1987–90, James Capel 1990–94 (chm James Capel Corporate Finance Ltd, exec dir James Capel & Co Ltd), seconded as memb Policy Unit Prime Minister's Office 1992–94, ceo Ockham Holdings plc 1994–2002, md Aldgate & Co Ltd 2002–; non-exec dir RGA (UK) Ltd 2002–; *Recreations* sailing; *Clubs* Brooks's; *Style—* The Lord Poole

POOLE, David James; s of Thomas Herbert Poole (d 1978), and Catherine, *née* Lord (d 1980); *b* 5 June 1931; *Educ* RCA; *m* 5 April 1958, Iris Mary, da of Francis Thomas Toomer (d 1968); 3 s (Edward b 1959, Vincent b 1960, Bruce b 1964); *Career* served RE 1949–51; sr lectr in painting and drawing Wimbledon Sch of Art 1961–77; featured in series Portrait (BBC TV) 1976, featured in magazine Frankfurter Allgemeine 1986; pres Royal Soc of Portrait Painters 1983–91; ARCA 1954, RP 1968; cmmnd by the City of London Corp to paint the official portrait group of the Royal Family to commemorate HM Queen Elizabeth II Silver Jubilee Luncheon; *Portraits* incl: HM The Queen, HRH Prince Philip, HM Queen Elizabeth the Queen Mother, HRH The Princess Royal, HRH The Prince of Wales, HRH The Duke of York, HRH Prince Edward, Earl Mountbatten, distinguished membs of govt, HM Forces, industry, commerce, medical, the academic and legal professions, Sir Alan Lascelles, Lord Charteris, Sir Michael Adeane, Sir Philip Moore, Sir William Heseltine, Sir Robert Fellowes, Sir Robin Janvrin, private secs to HM The Queen; *Solo Exhibitions* London 1978 and 2008, Zürich 1980; *Work in Private Collections* HM The Queen, Australia, Bermuda, Canada, France, Germany, Italy, South Africa, Saudia Arabia, Switzerland, USA; *Recreations* travel, being in the country; *Style—* David J Poole, Esq, PPRP, ARCA; ✉ Trinity Flint Barn, Weston Lane, Weston, Petersfield, Hampshire GU32 3NN (01730 265075)

POOLE, (Francis) Henry Michael; s of Charles Frederick John Kaitting Poole (d 1976), of Lanteglos-by-Fowey, Cornwall, and Stella Mary Grant, *née* Morris; *b* 23 September 1949; *Educ* Eton, Trinity Hall Cambridge; *m* 20 Sept 1975, Diana Mary Olga, da of Eric Arthur Parker (d 1983), of Headcorn, Kent; 2 da (Angelica Lucy Daphne b 1978, Stella Antonia Felicity b 1980), 1 s (Frederick Henry Eric b 1983); *Career* Credit Lyonnais Securities (formerly Laing and Cruickshank Institutional Equities): joined 1971, ptnr 1979, dir 1985–, conslt 2001–04; estab Henry Poole Consulting 2004–; non-exec dir Rockware Gp 1986–87; FSI (memb London Stock Exchange 1979); *Books* European Paper Directory (1988), Knowing When to Stop (2001); *Recreations* bridge, history, riding, mountain walking; *Style—* Henry Poole, Esq; ✉ 74 Hornton Street, London W8 4NU; Gibbet Oast, Leigh Green, Tenterden, Kent TN30 7DH (e-mail henry@henrypooleconsulting.co.uk)

POOLE, Sheriff Isobel Anne; OBE (2013); da of John Cecil Findlay Poole (d 1985), and Constance Mary, *née* Gilkes (d 1992); *b* 9 December 1941; *Educ* Oxford HS for Girls, Univ of Edinburgh (LLB); *Career* advocate 1964, former standing jr counsel to the Registrar Gen for Scot; Sheriff of: Lothian and Borders 1979–, Edinburgh 1986–2007 (pt/t sheriff 2007–13); external examiner Comparative Criminal Procedure Univ of Edinburgh 2001–02; chair Sir Walter Scott Club Edinburgh 2004–07; memb: Sheriffs' Cncl 1980–85, Scot Lawyers' Euro Gp; *Publications* contrib Dictionary of National Biography; *Recreations* country, the arts, houses, gardens, friends; *Clubs* Scottish Arts, New (Edinburgh); *Style—* Sheriff Isobel Anne Poole, OBE; ✉ Sheriffs' Chambers, Sheriff Court House, 27 Chambers Street, Edinburgh EH1 1LB

POOLE, James; *Educ* Univ of Cambridge (BA); *m* Jenny, *née* White; 2 c; *Career* journalist and ed (10 yrs at Sunday Times and dep city ed and foreign ed Business News and ed Multinational Business), subsequently head of corp affrs Barclays, vice-chm Shandwick Consultants Ltd until 1999, investor rels and corp communications dir Old Mutual plc 1999–; advsr to: Dept of Tport (on privatisation of BR), British Gas (on demerger plans), Marks & Spencer and Shell (on critical issues); judge Financial Journal's Fin Journalist and Young Fin Journalist of the Year 1993, 1994 and 1995; memb: Euro Public Affrs Forum, Spokesman Gp IIMR; MIPR; *Style—* James Poole, Esq

POOLE, (Jeremy) Quentin Simon; s of Graham Poole, of Kingswear, S Devon, and Dr Jill Poole, *née* Prichards; *b* 7 January 1955; *Educ* Epsom Coll, Univ of Warwick (LLB); *Career* admitted slr 1981; sr ptnr Wragge & Co 2003– (ptnr 1985–, managing ptnr 1995–2003); memb: Birmingham Law Soc 1981, Law Soc 1981; *Recreations* cricket; *Style—* Quentin Poole, Esq; ✉ Wragge & Co, 55 Colmore Row, Birmingham B3 2AS (☎ 0121 233 1000, fax 0121 214 1099, telex 338728 WRAGGE G)

POOLER, Amanda Elizabeth (Mandy); da of Kenneth Hindley Pooler, of Bolton, Lancs, and Adrianne, *née* Sherlock; *b* 23 May 1959; *Educ* Bolton Sch, Jesus Coll Oxford (MA); *m* Paul Andrew Eden; 2 c (Max, Eleanor (twins) b 18 June 1990); *Career* grad recruit (mktg) Thomson Organisation 1980–82; Ogilvy & Mather advtg agency: joined 1982, bd dir 1989, media dir 1990–98; UK md then chief exec MindShare 1998–2001; WPP: ceo The Channel 2002–06, dir Kantar UK 2006–; chair AGB Nielsen Media Research UK; Advertising Woman of the Year (Adwomen) 1994; memb Mktg Soc; FIPA; *Style—* Ms Mandy Pooler; ✉ Kantar Group, 6 More London Place, Tooley Street, London SE1 2QY

POOLES, Michael Philip Holmes; QC (1999); s of Dennis John Pooles (d 1999), and Joan Ellen, *née* Holmes; *b* 14 December 1955, Burgh Apton, Norfolk; *Educ* Perse Sch Cambridge, QMC London (LLB); *m* 17 April 1982, Fiona, *née* Chalmers; 2 s (Alexander David Grant b 21 Oct 1985, Guy Philip Grant b 16 June 1988); *Career* called to the Bar Inner Temple 1978 (Scarman scholar, Treas's prize); practising barr Hailsham Chambers 1980– (head of chambers 2004–09), recorder Crown Ct 2000–12; memb: Professional Conduct and Complaints Ctee Bar Cncl 1997–2000, Legal Servs Ctee Bar Cncl 2000–05, Bar Standards Bd 2006–10; govr Perse Sch Cambridge; *Recreations* reading, gardening; *Clubs* RAC; *Style—* Michael Pooles, Esq, QC; ✉ Hailsham Chambers, 4 Paper Buildings, Temple, London EC4Y 7EX (☎ 020 7643 5000, e-mail michael.pooles@hailshamchambers.com)

POOLEY, Dr Derek; CBE (1995); s of Richard Pike Pooley (d 1988), of Port Isaac, Cornwall, and Evelyn, *née* Lee (d 1985); *b* 28 October 1937; *Educ* Sir James Smith's Sch Camelford, Univ of Birmingham (BSc, PhD); *m* 1961, Jennifer Mary, da of William Arthur Charles Davey (d 1980), of Birmingham; 2 s (Michael Bruce b 1967, Benjamin John b 1969), 1 da (Miriam Jane b 1973); *Career* head Materials Devpt Div Harwell 1976–81, dir energy research Harwell 1981–83, chief scientist Dept of Energy 1983–86, dir Winfrith Technology Centre 1989–90, md AEA Nuclear Business Gp 1991–94, chief exec UKAEA 1996–98, ind conslt 1998–, chm Waste Mgmnt Technology Ltd 2006–08; *Recreations* travel, walking, history, gardening; *Style—* Dr Derek Pooley, CBE; ✉ 11 Halls Close, Drayton, Abingdon, Oxfordshire OX14 4LU (☎ 01235 559454)

POOLEY, Prof Frederick David; s of Frederick Pooley (d 1964), and Ellen, *née* Dix (d 1996); *b* 3 February 1939; *Educ* Univ of Wales Coll of Cardiff (BSc, MSc, PhD); *m* 18 Aug 1962, Patricia Mary, da of John Boyt Williams (d 1992), of Abergavenny, Gwent; 2 s (Anthony John b 1964, Andrew David b 1966), 1 da (Susan Elizabeth b 1968); *Career* res fell MRC 1966–69; Univ of Wales Coll of Cardiff: lectr in minerals engrg Dept of Mineral Exploitation 1969–76, sr lectr 1976–77, reader 1977–87, prof Sch of Engrg 1987–2006; research prof Cardiff Medical Sch 2006–; author of numerous papers and articles on dust disease, res and biological treatment of minerals; fell Minerals Engrg Soc 1986; CEng 1977, FIMMM 1994; *Recreations* sailing; *Clubs* PH Yacht; *Style—* Prof Frederick Pooley; ✉ Medical Microscopy Sciences Medical School, Cardiff University, Heath Park, Cardiff CF14 4XN (☎ 029 2077 7963)

POOLEY, Graham Howard John; s of John Henry William Pooley (d 2004), and Joan Margaret, *née* Price (d 1983); *b* 11 March 1949; *Educ* Brentwood Sch, Oriel Coll Oxford (MA); *m* 8 May 1971 (m dis 1993); 1 s (Oliver Edward b 1973), 1 da (Laura Kathleen May b 1976); *Career* dir Barclays de Zoete Wedd Ltd 1986–89, md Chase Investment Bank 1989–92, in own consultancy co 1993–; Chelmsford borough cncllr 1995–2003; memb Lib Dem Pty; *Recreations* music, bridge, Essex past and present, family friends and good conversation; *Style—* Graham Pooley; ✉ 49 Lockside Marina, Hill Road South, Chelmsford, Essex CM2 6HF (☎ 01245 351633)

POOLEY, Joseph; s of Arthur Edward Pooley, of Richmond, N Yorks, and Marjorie, *née* Lister; *b* 8 December 1946; *Educ* Barnard Castle Sch, Univ of Newcastle upon Tyne (MB BS, MD); *m* 2 July 1977, Jane Elizabeth, da of Ronald George Mills; 1 s (Nicholas James b 21 Sept 1985), 1 da (Victoria Jane b 15 Aug 1988); *Career* house surgn and house physician Royal Victoria Infirmary Newcastle upon Tyne 1971–72, demonstrator in anatomy Med Sch Univ of Newcastle 1972–73, sr surgical house offr Royal Victoria Infirmary 1973–74, registrar in surgery Newcastle Surgical Rotation 1974–77, orthopaedic surgical registrar Royal Victoria Infirmary 1978, res assoc Dept of Surgical Science Univ of Newcastle 1978–80, sr registrar in orthopaedic surgery Northern Region 1980–83, sr lectr in orthopaedics Univ of Newcastle 1985–97 (lectr 1983–85); conslt orthopaedic surgn: Royal Victoria Infirmary and Freeman Hosp 1985–97, Queen Elizabeth Hosp Gateshead 1997–; British Orthopaedic Research Soc: President's medal 1978–80, travelling fell 1983; British Orthopaedic Assoc: Robert Jones Gold medal and prize 1983, Euro travelling scholar 1984; memb: BMA 1972, British Orthopaedic Research Soc 1980, British Orthopaedic Oncology Soc 1988; FRCS (MRCS 1977); *Recreations* tennis, walking, music; *Style—* Joseph Pooley, Esq; ✉ Department of Orthopaedic Surgery, Queen Elizabeth Hospital, Gateshead, Tyne & Wear NE9 6SX (☎ 0191 487 8989)

P

POOLEY, Moira Helen; da of Roger Francis Lewis (d 1978), of Chadwell Heath, Essex, and Kathleen, *née* Kingseller; *b* 17 June 1950; *Educ* Ursuline Convent Brentwood, QMC London (LLB); *m* 1, May 1971 (m dis); 1 s (Oliver Edward b 24 March 1973), 1 da (Laura Kathleen May b 10 Nov 1976); m 2, 16 April 1993, Anthony Goldstaub, QC; 1 da (Harriet Helena b 8 May 1996); *Career* called to the Bar Middle Temple 1974; memb local govt and planning bar assocs; vice-chm: Little Baddow Parish Cncl 1981–84, Barnston Parish Cncl 1988–92; chm: Social Security Appeal Tbnl 1986–, Nat Insurance Tbnl 1986–; *Recreations* poultry keeping, archaeology, cookery; *Style—* Mrs Moira Pooley; ✉ 4 King's Bench Walk, Temple, London EC4Y 9DL (☎ 020 7353 3581)

POON, Prof Wilson Che Kei; s of C P Poon, and K Y Poon; *b* 1962; *Educ* St Paul's Co-Educnl Sch Hong Kong, Rugby, Peterhouse Cambridge, St John's Coll Cambridge (PhD); *m* 1988, Heidi; 1 da (Rebecca b 1998), 1 s (Aidan b 2000); *Career* research fell St Edmund's Coll Cambridge 1987–88, lectr Portsmouth Poly 1989; Sch of Physics Univ of Edinburgh: lectr 1990–97, sr lectr 1997–99, prof (ad hominem) 1999–2016, prof of natural philosophy 2016–; author of more than 180 papers in learned jls; FInstP, FRSE 2004; *Recreations* piano, drawing; *Clubs* New Club Edinburgh; *Style—* Prof Wilson Poon; ✉ School of Physics and Astronomy, The University of Edinburgh, James Clerk Maxwell Building, Peter Guthrie Tait Road, Edinburgh EH9 3FD (☎ 0131 650 5297, e-mail w.poon@ed.ac.uk)

POOTS, Edwin; MLA; *b* 27 May 1965; *Career* memb NI Forum 1996–98, MLA (DUP) Lagan Valley 1998–, min for culture, arts and leisure 2007–, min of environment 2009–11, min of health, social services & public safety 2011–14; cncllr Lisburn City Cncl 1997– (dep mayor 2008–); *Style—* Alderman Edwin Poots, MLA; ✉ DUP Constituency Office, 29 Castle Street, Lisburn BT27 4DH (☎ 028 92 603003, e-mail edwin@edwinpoots.co.uk)

POPAT, Baron (Life Peer UK 2010), of Harrow in the London Borough of Harrow; Dolar Popat; s of Amarshibhai Haridas Popat, and Parvatiben Amarshibhai Popat; *b* 1953, Tororo, Uganda; *m* 1980, Sandhya; 3 s (Hon Rupeen *b* 1983, Hon Paavan *b* 1985, Hon Shivaan *b* 1989); *Career* business and corp fin specialist; whip Cons Pty 2012–13, memb House of Lords SME Exports Ctee 2012–13, whip House of Lords 2013–; founding chm Conservative Friends of India, pres Harrow E Cons Assoc 2010–13, chair One Nation Forum, sec Anglo-Asian Cons Assoc; founding dir St Luke's Hospice; affiliated memb CIMA 1977; *Style—* The Lord Popat; ✉ House of Lords, London SW1A 0PW (📞 020 7219 0295)

POPAT, Surendra (Andrew); CBE (1997); s of Dhirajlal Kurji Popat (d 1989), of Putney, London, and Kashiben, *née* Chitalia (d 1963); *b* 31 December 1943; *Educ* Govt Secdy Sch Dar Es Salaam Tanzania, Univ of London (LLB), Univ of Calif (LLM); *m* 4 Feb 1995, Suzanne Joy, da of Edward James Wayman (d 1976); 1 s (Chetan Andrew *b* 10 May 1999); *Career* called to the Bar Lincoln's Inn 1969, apptd list of the dir of public prosecutions by the then attorney gen Sir Michael Havers 1984, admitted memb Inner Temple 1985, recorder of the Crown Ct 1998– (asst recorder 1992–98); legal memb Criminal Injuries Compensation Appeals Panel 2000–; contested (Cons) Palewell Ward E Sheen 1978, Parly candidate (Cons) Durham NE gen election 1983, Parly candidate (Cons) Bradford S 1992 gen election, treas Surbition Cons Assoc 1985, dir John Patten's election campaign 1987, contested (Cons) European Parliament Election London Regn 1999; chm Disraeli Club (Cons Pty orgn to promote intellectual dialogue) 1993–; memb Professional Conduct Ctee GMC 2000–; memb Professional Performance Ctee GMC 2002–; tstee Brooke Hosp for Animals 1998–2000; Freeman City of London 1987, Liveryman Worshipful Co of Plaisterers 1987 (memb Ct of Assts 2001–); *Recreations* travel, theatre, cricket, tennis, reading historical biographies; *Clubs* Carlton, MCC; *Style—* Andrew Popat, Esq, CBE

POPE, Cathryn Mary; *b* 6 July 1957; *Educ* RCM, Nat Opera Studio; *Career* soprano; debut Sophie in Werther (ENO) 1982, int debut Gretel in Hänsel and Gretel (Netherlands Opera Amsterdam); *Roles* with ENO incl: Gretel in Hänsel and Gretel 1987 and 1990, Despina in Cosi fan Tutte 1988, Oksana in Christmas Eve 1988, Leila in The Pearl Fishers 1988, Mélisande in Pelléas and Mélisande 1990, Pamina in The Magic Flute 1990, Donna Elvira in Don Giovanni 1991, Susanna in The Marriage of Figaro 1991 and 1993, Goosegirl in Königskinder 1992, Tatyana in Eugene Onegin 1994; other performances incl: Marguerite in Faust (New Sussex Opera) 1989, Nedda in Pagliacci, Emma in Khovanshchina, Micaela in Carmen, Giorgetta in Il Tabarro; *Recordings* incl Anne Truelove in The Rake's Progress (Decca); *Style—* Miss Cathryn Pope; 📞 and fax 01932 248518

POPE, Jeff; *Career* television and film prodr and screenwriter; head of factual drama ITV; *Television* prodr and writer: Fool's Gold 1992 (also writer), The Magician 1993 (also writer), Open Fire 1994, The One That Got Away 1996, Expert Witness 1996 and 2001, The Bob Mills Show 1997, The Place of the Dead 1997 (also writer), The Murder of Stephen Lawrence 1999, This is Personal: The Hunt for the Yorkshire Ripper 2000, Essex Boys 2000 (also writer), Bob Martin 2000 (also writer), My Beautiful Son 2001, Hot Money 2001, Stan the Man 2002 (also writer), Danielle Cable: Eyewitness 2003, Wall of Silence 2004, Dirty Filthy Love 2004 (also writer), Christmas Lights 2004 (also writer), Pierrepoint 2005 (also writer), Planespotting 2005, See No Evil: The Moors Murders 2006 (Best Drama Serial BAFTA 2007), Murder in the Outback 2007, Northern Lights 2007 (also writer), Clash of the Santas 2008 (also writer), The Fattest Man in Britain 2009 (also writer), Come Rain Come Shine 2010 (also writer), Mo 2010, Appropriate Adult 2011, Mrs Biggs 2012 (also writer), The Security Men 2013 (also writer), Lucan 2013 (also writer); *Film* writer Philomena 2013 (Best Screenplay Award Venice Film Festival 2013, Best Adapted Screenplay BAFTA 2014), prodr and writer Cilla 2014 (Alan Clarke special award BAFTA 2015); *Style—* Jeff Pope, Esq; ✉ c/o Natasha Galloway, United Agents, 12–26 Lexington Street, London W1F 0LE

POPE, Jeremy James Richard; OBE (1985), DL; s of Philip William Rolph Pope (d 1996), of Dorchester, Dorset, and Joyce Winifred Harcourt, *née* Slade; *b* 15 July 1943; *Educ* Charterhouse, Trinity Coll Cambridge (MA); *m* 1969, Hon Jacqueline Dorothy Mametz Best, da of Lt-Col 8 Baron Wynford, MBE, DL, of Dorchester, Dorset (d 2002); 3 s (Rory *b* 1970, Rupert *b* 1973, Toby *b* 1977); *Career* admitted slr 1969; dir: Eldridge Pope & Co plc 1969–99 (md 1988, dep chm 1987–99), Winterbourne Hosp plc 1981–89 (fndr chm), JB Reynier Ltd 1984–99; chm: Realstream Ltd 1987–92, Highcliff Hotel (Bournemouth) Ltd 1988–99, EP Fine Wines Ltd 1999–2001, Chilworth Science Park Ltd 2001–04, Milk Link Ltd 2001–05, Exeter Investment Gp plc 2002 (dir 1999–2004), Chilworth Manor Ltd; fndr chm English Farming & Food Partnerships 2003–08, fndr chm Elite Event Properties Ltd 2008–12; dir EXPIA CIC Ltd 2013–14; chm Smaller Firms' Cncl CBI 1981–84; memb: Dept of Trade Advsy Panel on Co Law 1980–81, NEDC 1981–85, Royal Cmmn on Environmental Pollution 1984–92, Exec Ctee Food and Drinks Fedn (dep pres 1987–90), Top Salary Review Body 1986–93, Bd SW England RDA 1998–2004 (dep chm 1999–2004); chm: Wessex Medical Tst 1992–98 (tstee 1991–97), Mgmnt Ctee Devonshire and Dorset Regimental Museum 1995–2000, Dorset Area Economic Partnership, Bournemouth, Dorset and Poole Economic Partnership 1998–2000, SW Chamber of Rural Enterprise (CORE) 2001–03; dep chm Dorset Olympic Bd 2010–13; dir Dorset TEC 1998–2000, memb Bd Bournemouth, Dorset and Poole LSC 2000–03, memb Wessex Regnl Ctee Nat Tst 2007–11; tstee: Devonshire and Dorset Regiment's Regimental Charities 1995–2000, Tank Museum 2000–, Jurassic Coast Tst (formerly World Heritage Coast Tst) 2004–, Springboard 2009–11, Dorset Shrieval Charitable Tst 2012–14, Safewise 2013–; dir Weymouth and Portland Nat Sailing Acad 2004–13 (vice-chm 2008), chm Spirit of the Sea Festival Weymouth 2009–13; memb Exec Ctee Brewers' Soc 1977–88; govr Forres Sch Swanage 1983–92; High Sheriff of Dorset 2012–13; memb Law Soc; Liveryman: Worshipful Co of Innholders (Renter Warden 2005, Upper Warden 2007, Master 2008), Worshipful Co of Gunmakers; Hon DLitt Bournemouth Univ; FRSA 1989, FRAgS 2008 (ARAgS 2003); *Recreations* gardening, field sports, cooking, beekeeping; *Style—* Jeremy Pope, Esq, OBE, DL; ✉ Field Cottage, West Compton, Dorchester, Dorset DT2 0EY (📞 and fax 01300 321104, e-mail jeremy.pope@btconnect.com)

POPE, Martin John; s of Anthony Peter Pope, and Patricia, *née* Servant; *b* 8 August 1963; *Educ* Dame Alice Owen Sch Potters Bar, Barnet Art Coll, Stradbroke Coll Sheffield (NCTJ); *Children* 1 da (Isabella *b* 25 Aug 2003); *Career* chief photographer: The Hendon Times 1987–90, Katz Pictures 1990–2006, K2 @ Katz Pictures 2002–06, syndication @ Camera Press 2005–; features photographer Daily Telegraph 1995–; assignments incl: Romania 1990 and 1991, Albanian elections 1992, Somalia famine 1992, Iraqi Kurdistan 1993, gold panning/AIDS Zimbabwe 1993, South Africa in transition 1993–94, life after the Zapatista rebellion Chiapas Mexico 1995, rural Uganda 1999, rebuilding communities Rwanda 1999, living with Islam Beirut, Damascus and Cairo 2002, America's War on Terrorism Djibouti 2004; work included in World Press Exhbn 1994; Fuji Feature Award 1992, Canon Press Photo of the Year 1992, Kodak Portfolio Award 1993; *Style—* Martin Pope, Esq; 📞 07850 656962, e-mail martin@martinpopephotographer.com, website www.martinpopephotographer.com

POPESCU, Mark Cannan; s of Julian John Hunter Popescu, of Mellis, Suffolk, and Christine Pullein-Thompson (d 2005); *b* 9 September 1960; *Educ* King James Coll Henley, Univ of Exeter (BA); *Partner*, Lesley Pauline Tring; 2 s (Oliver Jack *b* 2 April 1989, Daniel Edward *b* 3 Jan 1991), 1 da (Anna Helen *b* 9 July 1997); *Career* reporter Devonair Radio Exeter 1983–84, news ed GWR Radio Swindon 1984–86, prodr BBC Radio News London 1986–87; ITN: prodr News at One 1987–88, home news ed 1988–89, ed Forward Planning

1989–91, political news ed Westminster 1991–94, ed The Lunchtime News 1994–96, ed News at Ten and head of Special Progs ITN for ITV 1996–98; ed BBC Six O'Clock News 1999–2001, ed BBC Ten O'Clock News 2001–03, editorial dir BBC News 24 2004– (sr ed 1998); maj assignments incl: Romanian Revolution 1990 (sr prodr), Kuwait City 1991 (sr prodr), General Election 1992 (campaign news ed), Party Confs 1991, 1992 and 1993 (ed); *Recreations* kite flying, cooking and oneirology; *Style—* Mark Popescu, Esq

POPHAM, Phil; *b* Redditch, Worcs; *Educ* Univ of Aston (BSc); *Career* Jaguar Land Rover: joined as grad trainee 1988, mktg dir 1995–97, vice-pres of mktg Land Rover N America 1998–99; head of operations Volkswagen Commercial Vehicles 1999–2001; Jaguar Land Rover: UK sales dir 2001–03, md Jaguar and Land Rover (UK) 2003–06, md Land Rover 2006–10, gp sales dir 2010–13, gp mktg dir 2013–14; ceo Sunseeker Int Ltd 2014–; *Style—* Phil Popham, Esq

POPHAM, Stuart Godfrey; Hon QC (2011); s of George Popham (d 1986), and Ena, *née* Davison (d 1999); *b* 20 July 1954; *Educ* Reed's Sch Cobham, Univ of Southampton (LLB); *m* 1978, Carolyn, da of John Dawe; 2 da (Laura *b* 1983, Emma *b* 1990), 1 s (Ben *b* 1984); *Career* admitted slr 1978; sr ptnr Clifford Chance 2003–10 (joined 1976, ptnr 1984); vice-chm of banking for EMEA Citigroup 2011–; non-exec dir Legal and General Gp plc 2011–; chair CBI London Cncl 2008–09 (vice-chair 2010), chair The City UK 2009–14; chair Cncl RIIA 2012–; memb Cncl RNLI 2011– (tstee 2013–, vice-chm 2015–); govr Birkbeck Coll London 2012–; memb Law Soc 1978; *Recreations* sailing, water sports, theatre, ballet; *Clubs* Hayling Island Sailing, Royal Thames Yacht; *Style—* Stuart Popham, Esq; ✉ Citi, Citigroup Centre, 33 Canada Square, Canary Wharf, London E14 5LB (e-mail stuart.popham@citi.com)

POPLE, Andrew Howard; *Educ* BA, MPhil, MBA; *Career* with Bank of England 1983–88; Abbey National plc: regnl dir 1992–94, dir Life Assurance Div and chief exec subsid Scottish Mutual 1994–96, md Retail Banking 1996–2002; ceo and vice-chm Kessler Financial Services International 2003–12, princ AHP Ptnrs LLP 2012–; *Style—* Andrew Pople, Esq; ✉ AHP Partners LLP, 11 Waterloo Place, London SW1Y 4AU

POPPLEWELL, Hon Mr Justice; Sir Andrew John Popplewell; kt (2011), QC (1997); s of Sir Oliver Popplewell, and Catherine Margaret, *née* Storey; *b* 14 January 1959; *Educ* Radley, Downing Coll Cambridge (MA); *Career* called to the Bar Inner Temple 1981; recorder 2002, judge of the High Court of Justice (Queens Bench Div) 2011–; *Clubs* Hawks' (Cambridge); *Style—* The Hon Mr Justice Popplewell; ✉ Royal Courts of Justice, Strand, London WC2A 2LL

PORRITT, (Hon Sir) Jonathon Espie; 2 Bt (UK 1963), of Hampstead, Co London; does not use title; er s of Baron Porritt, GCMG, GCVO, CBE (Life Peer and 1 Bt; d 1994), and his 2 w, Kathleen Mary, *née* Peck (d 1998); *b* 6 July 1950; *Educ* Eton, Magdalen Coll Oxford; *m* 1986, Sarah, da of Malcolm Staniforth, of Malvern, Worcs; 2 da (Eleanor Mary *b* 1988, Rebecca Elizabeth *b* 1991); *Heir* bro, Hon Jeremy Porritt; *Career* chm Green Pty 1978–82, dir Friends of the Earth 1984–90; dir Forum for the Future, co fndr Real World, co-dir Prince of Wales's Business and Environment Prog; chm UK Sustainable Devpt Cmmn 2000–09, pres Conservation Volunteers 2014–; chllr Keele Univ 2012–; author and broadcaster; writer and presenter: Where On Earth Are We Going? (BBC) 1991, How To Save The World (Channel 4) 1992; *Books* Seeing Green: the Politics of Ecology Explained, The Friends of the Earth Handbook, The Coming of the Greens, Where On Earth Are We Going?, Save the Earth, Captain Eco, Playing Safe: Science and the Environment, Capitalism as if the World Matters, The World We Made; *Style—* Jonathon Porritt; ✉ 9 Lypiatt Terrace, Cheltenham, Gloucestershire GL50 2SX

PORTAL, Sir Jonathan Francis; 6 Bt (UK 1901), of Malshanger, Church Oakley, Co Southampton; s of Sir Francis Spencer Portal, 5 Bt (d 1984), and his 2 w, Jane Mary, da of late Albert Henry Williams, OBE; *b* 13 January 1953; *Educ* Marlborough, Univ of Edinburgh (BCom); *m* 9 Oct 1982, Louisa Caroline, er da of Sir John Hervey-Bathurst, Bt, *qv*; 3 s (William Jonathan Francis *b* 1987, Robert Jonathan *b* 1989, John Arthur Jonathan *b* 1993); *Heir* s, William Portal; *Career* chartered accountant; chief accountant Seymour Int Press Distributors 1986–89, gp fin controller Henderson Admin Gp plc 1989–91, fin dir Grosvenor Venture Managers Ltd 1992–93, mangr int 3i Group plc 1995–97, self employed fin dir 1993–; Liveryman Clothworkers' Co; FCA 1977; *Recreations* travel, music, country sports; *Style—* Sir Jonathan Portal, Bt; ✉ Burley Wood Ashe, Basingstoke, Hampshire RG25 3AG (📞 01256 770269, e-mail jonathanp@jpdirectors.com)

PORTAS, Mary; da of Samuel Edward Newton (d 1980), of Watford, Herts, and Mary Theresa, *née* Flynn (d 1977); *b* 28 May 1960; *Educ* Watford Coll of Art (HND in visual merchandising); *m* 5 Sept 1987 (m dis), Graham Charles Portas; 1 s (Mylo *b* 19 Jan 1994), 1 da (Verity *b* 23 Nov 1995); partner, Melanie Jane Rickey (civil partnership 3 May 2010); *Career* leading retail marketer and broadcaster; visual merchandiser Harrods dept store until 1984, visual mangr Top Shop (150 stores) 1984–91; Harvey Nichols: head of marketing 1989–91, mktg dir 1991–97 (most notable window designs for Harvey Nichols incl Financial Times newspaper sculptures and empty charity Christmas windows); fndr Yellow Door consultancy 1997–; television shows: Mary Queen of Shops (BBC) 2007–10, Mary Queen of Charity Shops (BBC) 2009, Mary Portas: Secret Shopper (Channel 4) 2011, Mary Queen of Frocks (Channel 4) 2011, Mary's Bottom Line (Channel 4) 2012; columnist Saturday Telegraph Magazine; retail ventures incl Mary & House of Frasier 2011 and opened Mary's Living and Giving Shops for Save The Children; appointed by PM to lead review into the future of Britain's high streets 2011; global retail ambass for Save The Children 2009; recipient various awards for best window design, int lectr on the art of visual mktg; MInstD 1994; memb: RSA 1994, Mktg Gp of GB 1995; *Books* Windows: The Art of Retail Display (2000); *Recreations* art, wine, gardening; *Style—* Ms Mary Portas; ✉ Portas Agency, 11–15 Emerald Street, London WC1N 3QL (website www.portasagency.com)

PORTEN, Anthony Ralph; QC (1988); s of Ralph Charles Porten (d 1976), and Joan, *née* Edden (d 2013); *b* 1 March 1947; *Educ* Epsom Coll, Emmanuel Coll Cambridge (BA); *m* 17 Oct 1970, Kathryn Mary, da of John Rees Edwards, JP (d 1988); 2 da (Lucinda *b* 1973, Deborah *b* 1976); *Career* called to the Bar Inner Temple 1969 (bencher 2002); recorder of the Crown Court 1993–2001, head of chambers 2–3 Gray's Inn Square 2001–06; asst cmmr Boundary Cmmn for England; fell Soc for Advanced Legal Studies; *Recreations* walking, reading, golf; *Clubs* Hawks, Claremont Park Golf, Blacknest Golf; *Style—* Anthony Porten, Esq, QC; ✉ Claremont Cottage, The Reeds Road, Frensham, Surrey GU10 3DQ (e-mail arporten@gmail.com)

PORTER; *see also:* Horsbrugh-Porter

PORTER, Dr Angus; *b* 9 June 1957; *Educ* Univ of Cambridge (MA, PhD); *m*; 3 c; *Career* formerly with Mars Confectionery (sometime UK sales dir and UK mktg dir), md Consumer Div BT plc 2000–03 (previously UK consumer mktg dir), customer dir and memb Bd Abbey National plc 2003–05, chief exec Added Value until 2008, gp strategy dir Thomas Cook Gp plc 2008–09 (non-exec dir 2007–08), ceo Professional Cricketers' Assoc 2010–; non-exec dir: MyTravel Gp plc 2002–07, Alliance & Leicester 2008, co-chm Direct Wines Ltd 2013– (non-exec dir 2009–), TDC (Denmark) 2010–, Punch Taverns plc 2012–; *Clubs* MCC; *Style—* Dr Angus Porter

PORTER, Rt Rev Anthony; *see:* Sherwood, Bishop of

PORTER, Colin Grant; s of William Graham Porter (d 1973), and Edna May, *née* Wilson; *b* 18 March 1951; *Educ* Syon Sch Isleworth, Harrow Sch of Art, Wolverhampton Sch of Art (BA); *m* 15 July 1972, Janice Ann, da of Albert Edward Manning; 4 s (Joel Edward William *b* 26 Oct 1976, James Henry *b* 30 Aug 1978, William Alexander *b* 11 Feb 1982,

Theo Hugh b 2 April 1989); *Career* jr graphic designer Fitch & Company 1977, graphic designer Murdoch Design Associates 1973–74, assoc dir Fitch & Company 1978–79 (sr designer 1974–79), founding ptnr Coley Porter Bell 1979–99 (chm 1994–99), co-fndr and chm Corpbrand Identity 1999–2005; regular tutor and speaker on design and design management for various orgns incl Design Cncl and Market Res Soc; awarded: 3 Clios (US) 1989, 1 Clio (US) 1990, 3 Clios (US) 1991, Design Business Assoc Design Effectiveness Award 1990, various D & AD Awards; one-man painting exhibition (Smith's Gallery Covent Garden) 1991; fndr memb and bd dir Design Business Assoc (chm 1997–99); memb: D & AD 1975, FCSD 1986; *Recreations* painting, collecting paintings and ephemera; *Style*— Colin Porter, Esq

PORTER, Henry Christopher Mansel; s of Maj Harry Robert Mansel Porter, MBE, of Pershore, Worcs, and Anne Victoria, *née* Seymour; *b* 23 March 1953; *Educ* Wellington, Univ of Manchester (BA), Perugia Univ Italy; *m* Elizabeth Mary Elliot; 2 da (Miranda Victoria Elliot b 30 Oct 1985, Charlotte Mary Clementine Elliot b 22 Oct 1988); *Career* journalist; Evening Standard 1979–81, feature writer Sunday Times 1981–83 (columnist 1983–87); ed: Illustrated London News 1987–89, Sunday Correspondent Magazine 1989–90; exec ed Independent on Sunday 1990–91, columnist The Observer 2000–, also currently London ed Vanity Fair; *Books* Lies, Damned Lies and Some Exclusives (1984), Remembrance Day (1999), A Spy's Life (2001), Empire State (2003), Brandenberg (2005), The Dying Light (2009); *Recreations* walking, painting, art galleries, reading; *Style*— Henry Porter, Esq; ✉ Vanity Fair, Condé Nast Publications Ltd, 1 Hanover Square, London W1R 1JU (☎ 020 7499 9080)

PORTER, Prof Sir Keith Macdonald; kt (2010); s of Albert Porter, and Hilda, *née* Bird; *b* Swindon, Wilts; *Educ* St Thomas's Hosp Medical Sch; *m* 12 Jan 2008, Shamim, *née* Donnelly; 2 s (Matthew b 17 May 1986, James b 20 Feb 1987), 2 da (Sarah b 30 Oct 1989, Lucy b 14 Jun 2009); *Career* qualified 1974, higher surgical training West Midlands Surgical Training Prog, conslt Birmingham Accident Hosp (now moved to Queen Elizabeth Hosp Birmingham) 1986–, clinical lead for receiving injured soldiers from Iraq and Afghanistan; pres Trauma Care, immediate past pres Facility of Pre-Hosp Care RCS(Ed), immediate past pres Intercollegiate Bd for Training in Emergency Pre Hosp Medicine; hon fell RSM, hon fell Br Assoc, FRCS, FRCSEd, fell in immediate care RCSEd (FIMCRCS(Ed)), fell Faculty of Sport and Exercise Medicine, FCEM, FRSA 2006; OStJ 2012; *Publications* over 100 peer review publications and major contribution and editorship of 10 books; *Recreations* walking; *Style*— Prof Sir Keith Porter; ✉ Queen Elizabeth Hospital, Mindelsohn Way, Edgbaston, Birmingham B15 2WB (☎ 0121 371 4955, e-mail keith.porter@uhb.nhs.uk, website www.uhb.nhs.uk)

PORTER, Marguerite Ann (Mrs Henson); MBE (2015); da of William Albert Porter, and Mary Maughan; *b* 30 November 1948; *m* 1, 1970 (m dis 1978), Carl Myers; m 2, 1 Aug 1986, Nicholas Victor Leslie Henson, *qv*, s of Leslie Henson; 1 s (Keaton Leslie b 24 March 1988); *Career* Royal Ballet Co: joined 1966, soloist 1973, princ 1978–85, guest artist 1985–, currently govr; danced The Queen in Matthew Bourne's Swan Lake (Broadway) 1998; choreographer: Dancing at Lughnasa (Royal Lyceum Edinburgh), Private Lives (RNT); dir Yorkshire Ballet Seminars; *Publications* Ballerina – A Dancer's Life (1989); Marguerite Porter's Balletcise (video, 1992); *Recreations* motherhood, reading, friends, theatre, choreography; *Style*— Ms Marguerite Porter, MBE

PORTER, Mark Edward; s of Robert George Porter, of Oxted, Surrey, and Sybil Elizabeth, *née* Brebner (d 1998); *b* 15 March 1960, Aberdeen; *Educ* Trinity Sch of John Whitgift Surrey, Trinity Coll Oxford (MA); *m* June 2001, Elizabeth, *née* Hubbard; 2 s (Alexander George b 2003, Finlay John b 2007); *Career* art dir several magazines 1986–93, freelance art dir and design conslt 1993–95; The Guardian: assoc art dir 1995–98, art dir 1998–2000, creative dir 2000–10; design conslt and princ Mark Porter Assocs 2010–; contrib to many books and jls on magazine and newspaper design; memb Alliance Graphique Internationale 2004; Gold medal D&AD 2006 (Silver medal 1996, 2004 and 2006), Gold and Silver medals Soc of Pubn Designers NY 2003; *Recreations* family, food and cooking, hispanophilia; *Style*— Mark Porter, Esq; ✉ Mark Porter Associates, 9 Liberia Road, London N5 1JP (e-mail info@markporter.com)

PORTER, Richard Bruce; s of Maynard Eustace Prettyman Porter (d 1984), and Irene Marjorie, *née* Turner (d 1994); *b* 20 January 1942; *Educ* St Joseph's Coll Ipswich, City of London Coll (BSc Econ); *m* 1965, Susan Mary, da of Philip Early; 2 da (Anna Lucie b 10 Feb 1970, Kitty b 10 Jan 1972); *Career* market researcher: A C Nielsen 1965–70, Brooke Bond Oxo 1970–75; mgmnt conslt Peat Marwick 1975–81 (incl postings as project dir and devpt economist India and SE Asia), environmental conslt Africa and Far East Environmental Resources Ltd 1981–84, ptnr Strategy Consltg Unit KPMG 1984–94, exec dir Sight Savers (charity) 1994–2005, dep dir Int Agency for the Prevention of Blindness (IAPB) 2005–08, chm Fred Hollows Fndn (UK) 2009–; *Books* jt author: Energy from Waste, Science Parks and the Growth of High Technology Firms; *Recreations* cinema, theatre, tennis, reading, bridge; *Style*— Richard Porter, Esq; ✉ 15 Park Road, Burgess Hill, West Sussex RH15 8EU (☎ 01444 232602, e-mail richard.porter@sky.com)

PORTER, Richard James; s of Capt James Graham Porter, of Conwy, Gwynedd, and Ann, *née* Wharry; *b* 28 November 1951; *Educ* Eton, UC Oxford (MA, MSc, BM BCh); *m* 26 July 1974, Diana Isabel, da of Douglas James Roper Austin (d 1979); 2 da (Charlotte b 1977, Alice b 1980); *Career* sr registrar in obstetrics and gynaecology St Mary's Hosp London and Addenbrooke's Hosp Cambridge 1984–88, conslt in obstetrics and gynaecology Bath Royal United Hospital NHS Tst 1989–, dir Maternity Services Wilts Health Care 1992–, obstetric advsr WHO (Europe, Central Asia and Russia) 1995–; chm Assoc for Community Based Maternity Care 2000–; FRCOG 1998 (memb 1982); *Recreations* wine, theatre; *Style*— Richard Porter, Esq; ✉ Weston Lea, Weston Park, Bath BA1 4AL (☎ 01225 425618); Bath Clinic, Claverton Down Road, Bath BA2 7BR (☎ 01225 835555)

PORTER, Richard William; s of Dr W A Porter, of Hove, E Sussex, and Phyllis May, *née* Richardson; *b* 25 March 1946; *Educ* Brighton Coll; *m* 1 Oct 1988, Tracy Jane Vallis-Porter, da of Stanley Vallis; 1 da (Emily Louise b 17 Jan 1994); *Career* insurance broker: Halford Shead Lloyd's Broker 1965–71, G P Turner 1971–73; Alexander and Alexander Ltd (formerly Alexander Stenhouse UK Ltd): joined 1973, mangr Reading Branch 1974–78, unit dir City Branch 1978–81, exec dir mktg London and Lloyd's 1981–82, devpt dir City Branch 1983–86, divnl dir Central Insurance 1987–88, exec dir 1989–94, ceo Alexander and Alexander Europe Ltd 1995–98; dir EMANI 2000–; dir Rosehill Sports Ltd 2012–; memb: RIIA, Inst of Risk Mgmnt 1997; FCII 1971, MIMgt 1984; *Recreations* squash, rugby; *Style*— Richard Porter, Esq; ✉ Holmgarth, Betchworth Avenue, Earley, Berkshire RG6 7RJ (☎ 0118 926 5637, e-mail rporter@theporters100.com)

PORTER, Ronald Frank; yst s of Frank Porter, and Mary, *née* MacRae (of the Clan MacRae, of Eilean Donan Castle); *b* 25 September 1949, London; *Educ* Sir Thomas Abney's, KCL (LLB); *Career* freelance journalist 1971–; memb: Br Assoc of Journalists 1992–, Good Food Spy 1994–, Royal Soc of St George (City of London branch), Victorian Soc, Cons Policy Forum, Cons Foreign and Cwlth Assoc, 1912 Club, Irish Peers Assoc; memb HM Treasy's Approved Investors Gp 2003–: Br Govt Stocks 2003–; patron Nat Art Collections Fund; cncllr Sevenoaks (Dunton Green) 1986–90, sch govr 1986–92; patron Leighton House 2007–, benefactor Wallace Collection 2012–, conslt Arts Int and Gallery 5 2012–, patron Friends of the Castle of Mey; memb Hon Soc of Gray's Inn 1970 (formerly a Gerald Moody scholar); Brother Justicia Lodge; Freeman of City of London 1995; FLS 2012; Knight Cdr of the Order of Stanislas 1997, Chevalier Knight Templars 1996; *Publications* contrib to various jls and magazines mainly on food, wine and politics for magazines such as What's On, Aspire and New World; book reviewer Political Quarterly 1980–; Obituaries contrib mainly to The Independent, The Times and Daily Telegraph; contrib Conservative History Journal; *Recreations* wining and dining, reading political biographies, having a good time in general; *Clubs* Nat Liberal (non-political memb), Farmers', Ritz Casino, Naval, Royal Cwlth, ESU, Club for Acts and Actors; *Style*— Ronald Porter; ✉ c/o 1 Fleet Street, London EC4Y 1BD (e-mail ronald-porter@hotmail.co.uk)

PORTES, Prof Richard David; CBE (2003); s of Herbert Portes; *b* 10 December 1941; *Educ* Yale Univ, Balliol Coll and Nuffield Coll Oxford (Rhodes scholar); *m* 1, 1963 (m dis), Barbara Frank; 1s (Jonathan b 1966), 1 da (Alison b 1968); m 2, 2006, Hélène Rey; 1 da (Ana b 2006); *Career* fell Balliol Coll Oxford 1965–69; prof of economics: Princeton Univ 1969–72, Univ of London 1972–94, London Business Sch 1995–; dir d'études EHESS Paris 1978–2011, pres Centre for Econ Policy Research 1983–, sec-gen Royal Economic Soc 1992–2008; vice-chair Advsy Scientific Ctee and co-chair Jt Expert Gp on Shadow Banking European Systemic Risk Bd 2015–; Tommaso Padoa-Schioppa prof (part-time) European Univ Inst 2014–; memb Cncl on Foreign Relations; hon fell Balliol Coll Oxford 2014–; fell Econometric Soc 1983, FBA 2004; *Books* Planning and Market Relations (1971), Deficits and Detente (1983), Threats to International Financial Stability (1987), Global Macroeconomics (1987), Blueprints for Exchange Rate Management (1989), External Constraints on Macroeconomic Policy (1991), Economic Transformation of Central Europe (1993), European Union Trade with Eastern Europe (1995), Crisis? What Crisis? Orderly Workouts for Sovereign Debtors (1995), Crises de la Dette (2003), International Financial Stability (2007), Macroeconomic Stability and Financial Regulation (2009), The Social Value of the Financial Sector (2013); *Recreations* swimming, music and opera, living beyond my means; *Clubs* 67 Pall Mall; *Style*— Prof Richard Portes, CBE, FBA; ✉ Department of Economics, London Business School, Regent's Park, London NW1 4SA (☎ 020 7000 8424, fax 020 7000 8401, e-mail rportes@london.edu, website http://faculty.london.edu/rportes)

PORTILLO, Rt Hon Michael Denzil Xavier; PC (1992); yst s of Luis Gabriel Portillo (d 1993), and Cora Waldegrave, *née* Blyth; *b* 26 May 1953; *Educ* Harrow Co Sch for Boys, Peterhouse Cambridge (MA); *m* 12 Feb 1982, Carolyn Claire, da of Alastair G Eadie; *Career* Ocean Transport and Trading Co 1975–76, Cons Res Dept 1976–79, special advsr to Sec of State for Energy 1979–81, Kerr McGee Oil (UK) Ltd 1981–83, special advsr to sec of state for Trade and Industry 1983, special advsr to Chllr of the Exchequer 1983–84; MP (Cons): Enfield Southgate 1984–97, Kensington and Chelsea 1999–2005 (Parly candidate Birmingham Perry Barr 1983); asst Govt whip 1986–87, Parly under sec of state for Social Security 1987–88, min of state for Tport 1988–90, min for Local Govt and Inner Cities 1990–92, chief sec to the Treasy 1992–94, sec of state for Employment 1994–95, sec of state for Defence 1995–97; shadow Chllr of the Exchequer 2000–01; memb Int Cmmn on Missing Persons in the former Yugoslavia; non-exec dir BAE Systems 2002–06; television credits: Portillo's Progress (Channel 4) 1998, Great Railway Journeys: Granada to Salamanca (BBC TV) 1999, Art that Shook the World: Richard Wagner's Ring (BBC TV) 2002, Portillo in Euroland (BBC TV) 2002, Elizabeth I (BBC TV) 2002, When Michael Portillo became a Single Mum (BBC TV) 2003, Dinner with Portillo (several series, BBC 4), panellist This Week (BBC 1); radio credits: The Things We Forgot to Remember (BBC Radio 4), panellist The Moral Maze (BBC Radio 4); columnist Sunday Times 2004–; *Clubs* Chelsea Arts; *Style*— The Rt Hon Michael Portillo; ✉ Suite 99, 34 Buckingham Palace Road, London SW1W 0RH

PORTLAND, 12 Earl of (GB 1689); Timothy Charles Robert Noel Bentinck; also Viscount Woodstock, Baron Cirencester (both GB 1689), and Count Bentinck (Holy Roman Empire); o s of 11 Earl of Portland (d 1997), and his 1 w, Pauline (d 1967), da of late Frederick William Mellowes; *b* 1 June 1953; *Educ* Harrow, UEA (BA), Bristol Old Vic Theatre Sch; *m* 1979, Judith Ann, da of John Robert Emerson, of Cheadle, Staffs; 2 s (William Jack Henry, Viscount Woodstock b 19 May 1984, Hon Jasper James Mellowes b 12 June 1988); *Heir* s, Viscount Woodstock; *Career* film, TV, radio and theatre actor as Timothy Bentinck; voice artist; David Archer in The Archers (BBC Radio 4); winner Celebrity Mastermind 2012; *Publications* Avant Garde a Clue (e-book), Colin the Campervan (2015), Oh Lord! (e-book translation from the French novel by Laure Elisac), Avant Garde a Clue (e-book); travel articles Mail on Sunday; *Recreations* house renovation, songwriting, scuba diving; *Clubs* BAFTA, Century; *Style*— The Earl of Portland; ✉ website www.bentinck.net, Twitter @timbentinckagent; agent Cassie Mayer, e-mail info@cassiemayerltd.co.uk; voice agent Hobson's International, e-mail voices@hobsons-international.com

PORTMAN, 10 Viscount (UK 1873); Christopher Edward Berkeley Portman; s of 9 Viscount Portman (d 1999); *b* 30 July 1958; *m* 1, 30 July 1983, Caroline, da of Terence Ivan Steenson, of Caversham, Berks; 1 s (Hon Luke Oliver Berkeley b 31 Aug 1984); m 2, 7 Dec 1987, Patricia Martins, da of Bernardino Pim, of Rio de Janeiro, Brazil; 2 s (Hon Matthew Bernardo Berkeley b 24 Sept 1990, Hon Daniel Edward Berkeley b 27 July 1995); *Heir* s, Hon Luke Portman; *Career* chm Portman Settled Estates Ltd; former chm Natural BioSciences SA; dir: Brickleton Integrated Technologies, Bioquiddity LLC, Agua Via (UK) Ltd; *Recreations* computer science, molecular nanotechnology (8th colleague of The Foresight Inst for Molecular Nanotechnology Palo Alto CA); *Style*— The Viscount Portman; ✉ The Portman Estate, Ground Floor, 40 Portman Square, London W1H 6LT (☎ 020 7563 1400, fax 020 7563 1402, e-mail info@portmanestate.co.uk, website www.portmanestate.co.uk)

PORTMAN, Rachel Mary Berkeley; OBE (2010); da of Berkeley Charles Portman, and Penelope, *née* Mowat; *b* 11 December 1960; *Educ* Charterhouse, Worcester Coll Oxford (exhibitioner); *m* 25 Feb 1995, Count Uberto Pasolini Dall'Onda; 3 da (Anna Gwendolen b 27 Sept 1995, Giulia Ginevra b 20 March 1998, Niky Joan Pasolini b 19 Aug 1999); *Career* composer; BMI Richard Kirk Award 2010; *Film* Experience Preferred but not Essential (Channel 4), Reflections (Court House Films), Sharma and Beyond (Enigma/Goldcrest), Antonia and Jane (BBC Films), Rebecca's Daughters, Life is Sweet (Thin Man Films), Where Angels Fear to Tread (Stagescreen), Used People (20th Century Fox), Benny and Joon (MGM), Friends (Working Title), Great Moments in Aviation (Miramax), The Joy Luck Club (Disney), Sirens (Miramax), War of the Buttons (Warner Bros), The Road to Wellville (Columbia), Only You (Tri-Star/Columbia), Smoke (Miramax), A Pyromaniac's Love Story (Hollywood), To Wong Foo (Universal), Palookaville (Samuel Goldwyn Co), Adventures of Pinocchio (New Line/Savoy Pictures), Emma (Miramax), Marvin's Room (Miramax), Addicted to Love (Warner Bros), Beauty and the Beast II (Disney), Home Fries (Warner Bros), Beloved (Disney), The Other Sister (Disney), Ratcatcher (Pathe Films), The Cider House Rules (Miramax) 1999, The Closer you Get (Fox Searchlight Pictures) 1999, The Legend of Bagger Vance (DreamWorks), Chocolat (Miramax) 2000, The Emperor's New Clothes 2001, Hart's Ward 2001, The Truth About Charlie 2002, Nicholas Nickleby 2002, Human Stain 2002, Mona Lisa Smile 2003, Because of Winn-Dixie 2004, Manchurian Candidate 2004, Oliver Twist 2005, Infamous 2006, The Lake House 2006, Miss Potter 2006, The Duchess 2008, Grey Gardens 2008, Never Let Me Go 2010; *Television* incl: Last Day of Summer (Moving Picture Co), Reflections (Channel 4), Four Days in July (BBC TV), Good as Gold (BBC TV), The Little Princess (LWT), 1914 All Out (Yorkshire TV), Falklands War: Untold Story (Yorkshire TV), Short and Curlies (Portman/British Screen/Channel 4), 90 Degrees South (John Gau Prodns), Cariani and The Courtesans (BBC TV), Storyteller (Henson Orgn), Loving Hazel (BBC TV), Sometime in August (BBC TV), Charlie the Kid (Thames TV), Living with

P

Dinosaurs (Henson Orgn), Oranges Are Not the Only Fruit (BBC TV), Nice Work (BBC TV), The Woman in Black (Central Films), Widowmaker (Central Films), Shoot to Kill (Zenith/Yorkshire TV), Mr Wakefield's Crusade (BBC Wales), Think of England (BBC TV), Twice Through the Heart (BBC TV), The Cloning of Joanna May (Granada TV), Flea Bites (BBC TV), Elizabeth R (BBC TV); *Other* trailer for Mike Leigh (London Film Festival), Ourselves Alone (Royal Court Theatre), Fantasy for Cello and Piano (Salisbury Festival), The Little Princess Opera 2003, The Water Diviner's Tale (BBC Prom) 2007, Much Ado About Nothing (Nat Theatre) 2007, Little House on the Prairie 2008; *Awards* BFI Young Composer of the Year 1988, Tric Celebrity Awards Schneider Trophy for Theme Music of the Year (for Precious Bane) 1989, Bafta Award Nominations for Best Score (for Oranges Are Not the Only Fruit 1989 and The Woman in Black), Women in Film/Rank Films Laboratories Award for Creative Originality 1996, Academy Award for Best Original Musical or Comedy Score (for Emma) 1996, Int Prize for Film and Media Music 1997, Academy Award nomination for Best Original Score (for The Cider House Rules) 1999, Flanders International Film Festival Award (Ratcatcher) 1999, Academy Award nomination for Best Original Score (for Chocolat) 2000, Grammy nomination for Best Score Soundtrack (for The Cider House Rules) 2000, Muse Award New York Women in Film and Television 2000, Women in Music Touchstone Award 2001; *Style—* Ms Rachel Portman, OBE

PORTMANN, Prof Bernard Claude; s of late Henry Paul Portmann, and Emilie Emma, *née* Jaques; *b* 6 February 1940, Ste Croix, Switzerland; *Educ* Calvin Coll Geneva, Geneva Univ (MB, Swiss Med Dip, MD); *m* 1, 1963 (m dis 1969); 1 c (Sandra b 7 Aug 1964); m 2, 1970, Hermine Elisabeth, da of Leo Bertholdt Neumann; 2 c (Barbara b 8 Feb 1971, Jan b 26 Oct 1972); *Career* lectr in pathology Univ Hosp Geneva 1968–72 (house offr 1966–67); KCH London: research fell Liver Unit 1973–75, res histopathologist 1975–78, conslt 1978–2009, prof of hepatopathology 1997–2009; prof emeritus Univ of London 2010–; hon sr lectr Univ of London 1978–97; assoc ed Jl of Hepatology 1995–99, special section ed Liver Transplant 2002–04; travelling fellowship: Swiss Acad of Medicine King's Coll Hosp London 1972–73, Mount Sinai Med Center NY 1982; memb: Br Soc Gastroenterology, European Soc Pathology, Int Acad of Pathology, European Assoc for the Study of the Liver, American Assoc for the Study of Liver Diseases; former memb Ctee Br Assoc for Study of the Liver; FRCPath 1989 (MRCPath 1977); *Books* Pathology of the Liver (jtly, 1994, 6 edn 2012), The Practice of Liver Transplantation (jtly, 1995); *Recreations* DIY, reading, art exhibitions, travelling; *Style—* Prof Bernard Portmann; ✉ 20 Ewelme Road, Forest Hill, London SE23 3BH (☎ 020 8699 6717, e-mail bernardportmann32@gmail.com)

PORTO, Sue; da of Colin Iliffe, of Weymouth, Dorset, and Sylvia Iliffe; *b* 8 November 1969, Weymouth, Dorset; *Educ* Weymouth GS, Open Univ (Cert); *Children* 1 da (Laura b 14 April 1995), 2 s (Harry b 27 Sept 1997, Archie b 1 Jan 2006); *Career* sr mangr and head of nat trg and clinical support and sr investigating offr HM Prison Service 1992–2007, regnl dir SW of England Prince's Tst 2007–10, ceo Beanstalk (formerly Volunteer Reading Help) 2010–15, ceo St John's Hosp Bath 2015–; memb: Ella Leadership Fndn, NCVO; listed in Evening Standard's London's 1000 Most Influential People 2011; *Recreations* running, horse riding; *Style—* Ms Sue Porto; ✉ Volunteer Reading Help, Charity House, 14–15 Perseverance Works, 38 Kingsland Road, London E2 8DD (☎ 020 7749 7963, e-mail sue.porto@vrh.org.uk, website www.vrh.org.uk, Twitter @sueportovrh)

PORTSDOWN, Archdeacon of; *see:* Lowson, Ven Christopher

PORTSMOUTH, Bishop of 2010–; Rt Rev Christopher Richard James Foster; s of Joseph James Frederick Foster, and Elizabeth, *née* Gibbs; *b* 1953, Wednesbury, Staffs; *Educ* UC Durham (BA), Univ of Manchester (MA(Econ)), Trinity Hall Cambridge (MA), Westcott House Cambridge; *m* 1, 1982, Julia Marie, *née* Jones (d 2001); 1 s (Richard Edward Joseph b 1983), 1 da (Miriam Laura Elizabeth b 1985); m 2, 2006, Sally Elizabeth, *née* Davenport; *Career* lectr in economics Univ of Durham 1976–77; ordained: deacon 1980, priest 1981; asst curate Tettenhall Regis Team Miny Wolverhampton 1980–82, chaplain Wadham Coll Oxford 1982–86, asst priest Univ Church of St Mary the Virgin with St Cross and St Peter in the East Oxford 1982–86, vicar Christ Church Southgate 1986–94, Continuing Ministerial Educn (CME) dir Edmonton Episcopal Area 1988–94, sub dean and residentiary canon Cathedral and Abbey Church of St Alban 1994–2001, bishop of Hertford 2001–10; memb Cncl Westcott House Cambridge 2004–12, chair of dirs and convener Enabling Gp Churches Together in England 2012–16 (dir 2012–), memb Church Cmmrs Pastoral Ctee 2013–14, memb Dioceses Cmmn 2014–, introduced as Lord Spiritual House of Lords 2014–; Univ of Herts: govr 2002–10, chm Finance and Gen Purposes Ctee 2007–10; memb Cncl Ripon Coll Cuddesdon 2014– (chm 2015–), govr Univ of Portsmouth 2014–; Hon DLitt Univ of Herts 2011; *Style—* The Rt Rev the Lord Bishop of Portsmouth; ✉ Bishopsgrove, 26 Osborn Road, Fareham, Hampshire PO16 7DQ (☎ 01329 280247, e-mail bishop@portsmouth.anglican.org)

PORTSMOUTH, Bishop of (RC) 2012–; Rt Rev Philip Anthony Egan; *b* 14 November 1955; *Educ* KCL; *Career* assistant priest St Anthony's Woodehouse Park Manchester 1984–88, asst chaplain Univ of Cambridge 1988–91, chaplain Arrowe Park Hosp Wirral 1991–94, prof of fundamental theology and dean of studies Oscott Coll Birmingham 1995–2007, parish priest Our Lady and St Christopher's Stockport 2008–10, vicar gen Diocese of Shrewsbury 2010–12; *Style—* The Rt Rev the Bishop of Portsmouth; ✉ Bishops House, Edinburgh Road, Portsmouth PO1 3HG

PORTSMOUTH, 10 Earl of (GB 1743); Quentin Gerard Carew Wallop; DL (Hants 2004); also Baron Wallop (GB 1720), Viscount Lymington (GB 1720); Hereditary Bailiff of Burley in the New Forest; s of Viscount Lymington (d 1984) and his 2 w Ruth Violet, née Sladen (d 1978); suc gf 9 Earl (d 1984); *b* 25 July 1954; *Educ* Eton, Millfield; *m* 1, 1981 (m dis 1985), Candia Frances Juliet, only da of Colin McWilliam, and Margaret, *née* Henderson; 1 s (Oliver Henry Rufus, Viscount Lymington b 22 Dec 1981), 1 da (Lady Clementine Violet Rohais b 20 Nov 1983); m 2, 1990, Annabel, eldest da of Dr Ian Fergusson, and Rosemary, *née* Howard; 1 da (Lady Rose Hermione Annabel b 23 Oct 1990); *Heir* s, Viscount Lymington; *Career* non-exec dir Grainger Trust plc 1987–2002; pres Basingstoke Cons Assoc; pres Hampshire Branch Br Red Cross 2010–, churchwarden St Andrew's Church Farleigh Wallop, chm Hants branch Game Conservancy Tst 2001–05; Liveryman Worshipful Co of Fishmongers (memb Ct of Assts 2006); *Recreations* shooting, travel, wine, food, promoting access to justice, hunting; *Clubs* Buck's, White's, Int Assoc of Cape Horners, Hampshire Hunt; *Style—* The Rt Hon the Earl of Portsmouth, DL; ✉ Farleigh House, Farleigh Wallop, Basingstoke, Hampshire RG25 2HT (☎ 01256 321026)

PORTWIN, Guy Lyster; s of Edwin Thomas Portwin, of Herts, and Elizabeth Emily Louise, *née* Gadd; *b* 28 December 1949; *Educ* Merchant Taylors'; *Family* 4 c (Liza, Emma, Guy, John); m 2001, Polly Jane, *née* Hance; *Career* dir: Comprint Ltd 1972–86, Wheatland Journals Ltd 1973–90, Turret Press (Holdings) Ltd 1979–84; md Turret-Wheatland Ltd 1984–88; chm: Turret Group plc 1988–90, Hill Media Ltd 1991–, Trophex Ltd 1991–, Hill Communications Ltd 1992–, Toy News Ltd 1992–95; dir: European Toy Fair Ltd, Millhouse Publishing International Ltd 1992–94, Association Publishing Ltd 1995–; MFH: Jt Master Bicester Hunt with Whaddon Chase 1996–99, Jt Master Vale of Aylesbury Hunt 2000–02, Jt Master Vale of Aylesbury with Garth and S Berks Hunt 2003–05 (dep chm 2007–10, sr jt master 2008–10), sr jt master Kimblewick Hunt 2010–13, dir and SE region chm Countryside Alliance 2013–; FInstD 1985; *Recreations* riding, reading; *Style—* Guy Portwin, Esq; ✉ Round Hill, Kimblewick, Aylesbury, Buckinghamshire HP17 8TB (e-mail guyportwin@hotmail.com); Hill Media Ltd, Marash House, 2/5 Brook Street, Tring, Hertfordshire HP23 5ED (☎ 01442 826826, fax 01442 823400)

PORTWOOD, Nigel; *Educ* Univ of Cambridge, INSEAD (MBA); *Career* Pearson plc: joined Strategy and Devpt Gp 1995, dir of strategy 1997–99, ceo Pearson Educn EMEA 1999–2002; exec vice-pres global operations Penguin Gp 2003–08, chief exec OUP 2009–; *Style—* Nigel Portwood, Esq; ✉ Oxford University Press, Great Clarendon Street, Oxford OX2 6DP

POSNANSKY, Jeremy Ross Leon; QC (1994); s of late Anthony Victor Posnansky, and late Evelyn Davis, JP, *née* Leon (previously Posnansky); *b* 8 March 1951; *Educ* St Paul's, Coll of Law London; *m* 31 Dec 1974, Julia Mary, da of Richard Sadler, MBE (d 1967), of Bournemouth; 2 da (Charlotte b 1976, Zoë b 1979); *Career* called to the Bar Gray's Inn 1972 (bencher 2003), admitted to the Bar of Antigua and Barbuda; in ind practice at the Bar 1972–2007, asst recorder 1995–98, recorder 1998–2002, dep judge of the High Court (Family Div); admitted slr 2007, ptnr Farrer & Co LLP 2007–16 (conslt 2016–); memb Inner London Family Courts Servs and Business Ctees 1991–94; memb Hon Soc of Gray's Inn; *Recreations* scuba diving, travel, photography, gardening; *Style—* Jeremy Posnansky, Esq, QC; ✉ Farrer & Co, 66 Lincoln's Inn Fields, London WC2A 3LH (☎ 020 3375 7000)

POSNER, Lindsay Steven; s of Dennis Posner, and Pauline Posner; *b* 6 June 1959; *Educ* Latymer GS, Univ of Exeter (BA), RADA; *Partner* Megan Wheldon; 2 da (Merle, Maud), 1 s (Nat); *Career* assoc dir Royal Court Theatre 1986–92; plays directed: The Treatment, Death and the Maiden (Best Play Olivier Awards), American Bagpipes, Colquhoun and MacBryde, Blood, Downfall, Ambulance, Ficky Stingers, The Doctor of Honour, Cheek By Jowl (Sheffield), Leonce and Lena, American Buffalo (Young Vic), The Misanthrope (Young Vic), The Provok'd Wife (Old Vic), Handel's Giulo Cesare (Royal Opera), After Darwin (Hampstead), Volpone (RSC Swan), Taming of the Shrew (RSC tour), The Rivals (RSC Swan), Twelfth Night (Royal Shakespeare Theatre), A Life in the Theatre (Apollo), The Hypochondriac (Almeida), Power (RNT), Oleana (Garrick), The Birthday Party (Duchess), Fool for Love (Apollo), Sexual Perversity in Chicago (Comedy), Tartuffe (RNT), Guilo Cesare (ROH), Love Counts (Almeida), Tom & Viv (Almeida); dir of The Maitlands (BBC), dir of Jenufa; *Style—* Lindsay Posner

POSNER, Prof Rebecca; da of William Reynolds (d 1958), and Rebecca, *née* Stephenson (d 1988); *b* 17 August 1929; *Educ* Nuneaton HS for Girls, Somerville Coll Oxford (BA, DPhil); *m* 5 Aug 1953, Michael Vivian Posner, CBE (d 2006), s of Jack Posner (d 1978); 1 s (Christopher Nicholas b 14 Sept 1965), 1 da (Barbara Virginia b 7 July 1968); *Career* res fell Girton Coll Cambridge 1960–63, prof of French studies and head of Dept of Modern Languages Univ of Ghana 1963–65, reader in linguistics Univ of York 1965–78, professorial fell St Hugh's Coll Oxford 1978–96 (hon fell 1996–), prof of the romance languages Univ of Oxford 1978–96 (emeritus prof 1996–), research assoc Oxford Univ Centre for Linguistics & Philology 1996–, Leverhulme emeritus fell 1997; pres Philological Soc 1996–2000 (vice-pres 2000–); memb: Linguistic Soc of America, Société de Linguistique Romane, Linguistics Assoc of GB, Modern Humanities Res Assoc, Soc for French Studies, Assoc for French Language Studies; *Books* Consonantal Dissimilation in the Romance Languages (1960), The Romance Languages (1966), Introduction to Romance Linguistics (1970), Trends in Romance Linguistics and Philology (with J N Green, 1980–93), The Romance Languages (Cambridge Language Survey, 1996), Linguistic Change in French (1997), Las Lenguas romances (1998); *Recreations* gardening, walking, music; *Style—* Prof Rebecca Posner; ✉ Rushwood, Jack Straw's Lane, Oxford (☎ 01865 763578, e-mail rebecca.posner@st-hughs.ox.ac.uk)

POST, Martin Richard; s of Kenneth Richard Post (d 1973), and Barbara Ruby, *née* Arnell; *b* 3 September 1958; *Educ* Watford GS for Boys (head prefect), Univ of York (BA), Darwin Coll Cambridge (PGCE), Open Univ (MA); *m* 23 Dec 1999, Kathryn Jane, da of William Watts; 1 s (Benjamin Richard b 27 Jan 2003); *Career* teacher: Kings Sch Rochester 1982–84, Mill Hill Co HS 1985–89, Richard Hale Sch Hertford 1989–95; headmaster Watford GS for Boys 2000– (dep head 1995–2000); pres Old Fullerians Assoc; *Recreations* sports of all types, reading, my family; *Style—* Martin Post, Esq; ✉ Watford Grammar School for Boys, Rickmansworth Road, Watford, Hertfordshire WD18 7JF (☎ 01923 208900, fax 01923 208901, e-mail head@watfordboys.herts.sch.uk)

POSTE, Dr George H; CBE (1999); *Educ* Univ of Bristol (BVSc, PhD); *Career* SmithKline Beecham plc: joined Smith Kline & French Laboratories 1980, various sr R&D appts, chm research and devpt 1992–97, main bd dir 1992–, chief science and technol offr 1997–99; ceo Health Technology Networks 1999–; chm: diaDexus, Structural GenomiX; memb Bd: AdvancePCS, Monsanto; Pitt fell Pembroke Coll Cambridge 1996–, pres Arizona Biodesign Inst Arizona State Univ 2003–; co-ed Cancer and Metastasis Reviews, co-ed Advanced Drug Delivery Reviews, former chm Editorial Bd Bio/Technology, memb editorial bds of various other jls; memb UK Human Genetics Advsy Ctee, memb US Defense Science Bd Dept of Defense, memb Cncl on Foreign Rels; former memb US Govt Ctees on: Nat Insts of Health, NASA, Office of Technol Assessment, State Dept, Commerce Dept, Defense Dept; former chm: R&D Steering Ctee Pharmaceutical Mfrs' Assoc Washington DC, Scientific Ctee Assoc of the British Pharmaceutical Industry; sometime memb governing body: Gordon Research Confs, Nat Fndn for Biomedical Research, Life Sciences Research Fndn, Center for Molecular Genetics and Med Stanford Univ, Philadelphia Coll of Pharmacy and Science, Alliance for Ageing, Keystone Center, Royal Soc of Med Fndn, US Nat Center for Genome Resources; Hon DSc: Univ of Bristol 1987, Univ of Sussex 2000; Hon LLD: Univ of Bristol 1995, Univ of Dundee 1998; distinguished fell Hoover Inst Stanford Univ; FRCVS 1987, FRCPath 1989, Hon FRCP 1993, FRS 1997, FMedSci 1997; *Recreations* military history, photography, motor racing; *Style—* Dr George Poste, CBE, FRS; ✉ Health Technology Networks, PO Box 647, Gilbertsville, PA 19525, USA (☎ 610 705 0828, fax 610 705 0810, e-mail gposte@healthtechnetwork.com)

POSTGATE, Prof (John) Nicholas; s of Ormond Oliver Postgate (d 1989), of Winchester, Hants, and Patricia Mary, *née* Peet; *b* 5 November 1945; *Educ* Winchester, Trinity Coll Cambridge (BA); *m* 1, 1968 (m dis 1999), Carolyn June, da of Dr Donald Arthur Prater; 1 s (Richard Laurence b 30 March 1973), 1 da (Elizabeth Anne b 14 July 1975); m 2, Sarah Helen, da of Ronald Blakeney; 1 s (Louis Alexander Ormond b 13 Dec 2000), 2 da (Jessica Laura b 28 March 2002, Florence Maude Elif b 4 July 2010); *Career* asst lectr in Akkadian SOAS Univ of London 1967–71; fell Trinity Coll Cambridge 1970–74; dir British Sch of Archaeology in Iraq 1975–81 (asst dir 1972–75); Univ of Cambridge: lectr in history and archaeology of the ancient Near East 1982–85, reader in Mesopotamian studies 1985–94, prof of Assyriology 1994–2013; dir of excavations: Abu Salabikh Iraq 1975–89, Kilise Tepe Turkey 1994–98 and 2007–12; FBA 1993; *Books* Taxation and Conscription in the Assyrian Empire (1974), Fifty Neo-Assyrian Legal Documents (1976), The First Empires (1977), Early Mesopotamia: Society and Economy at the Dawn of History (1992), A Concise Dictionary of Akkadian (jtly, 1999), Languages of Iraq, Ancient and Modern (ed, 2007), Bronze Age Bureaucracy (2013); edns of cuneiform texts and articles in learned jls; *Recreations* Squash; *Style—* Prof Nicholas Postgate, FBA

POTTER; *see also:* Lee-Potter

POTTER, Christopher John; s of Frank Potter (d 1995), and Catherine, *née* Kerr; *b* 1 April 1959; *Educ* King's Coll London (BSc, AKC, MSc), London Coll of Music (ALCM); *Career* writer, former publisher Fourth Estate, ed-in-chief Harper Press 2003–; titles commissioned incl: The Stone Diaries by Carol Shields (winner Pulitzer Prize 1994), The Shipping News by E Annie Proulx (winner Pulitzer Prize 1995), Longitude by Dava

Sobel (Book of the Year 1996), Fermat's Last Theorem by Simon Singh (1997), The Hours by Michael Cunningham (winner Pulitzer Prize 1999), The Amazing Adventures of Kavalier and Clay by Michael Chabon (winner Pulitzer Prize 2001), Bel Canto by Ann Patchett (winner Orange Prize 2002); Ed of the Year (NIBBIES) 1994; *Books* You Are Here: A Portable History of the Universe (2009), How to Make a Human Being: A Body of Evidence (2014); *Recreations* piano; *Clubs* Soho House; *Style*— Christopher Potter, Esq; ✉ 30 Rhondda Grove, London E3 5AP (☎ and fax 020 8980 7301)

POTTER, David Roger William; s of late William Edward Potter, and late Joan Louise, *née* Frost; *b* 27 July 1944; *Educ* Bryanston, UC Oxford (MA); *m* 1, 1966 (m dis 1984), Joanna Trollope, *qv*; 2 da (Louise (Mrs Paul Ansdell) b 1969, Antonia (Mrs Jon Prentice) b 1971); m 3, 1991, Jill, da of James Benson; 1 da (Harriet b 1993); *Career* National Discount Co 1964–69; md: Credit Suisse First Boston 1969–81, Samuel Montagu and various subsidiaries 1981–87, Midland Montagu Corporate Banking 1987–89, David Potter Consultants 1989–90; chm and chief exec Guinness Mahon & Co Ltd 1990–98, gp chief exec Guinness Mahon Holdings 1990–98; dep chm Investec Bank UK 1998–99; chm Camco Int 2006–10; dir: Thomas Cook Group 1989–91, The Rose Partnership 2000, Noble Gp 2000–10, WMC Communications 2001–03, Spark Ventures 2002– (chm 2010), Numerica Gp plc 2003–05, Solar Integrated Technologies 2004–09, Deltron Electronics 2005–06, Ortus VCT Tst 2005– (chm 2011–13), Quercus plc 2006–14 (chm 2009–14), Vycon Inc 2007–09 (chm 2008–09); non-exec dir: Maven Income and Growth VCT 4 2013–15, Illustrated London News 2013–; non-exec dir Fundsmith Emerging Equity T\st 2014–, memb Advsy Bd Alva Capital; former chm Bd London Film Cmmn; memb: Bd of Advsrs The Capital Club of London, Cncl Centre for the Study of Financial Innovation; former govr and hon treas KCL, former govr Godolphin and Latymer Sch, chm Nat Film & TV Sch Fndn, former govr Bryanston Sch, chm Bryanston Fndn; tstee: Worldwide Volunteering, Nelson Mandela Childrens Fndn; memb Worshipful Co of Int Bankers; FKC 2005; *Recreations* shooting, golf, gardening; *Clubs* Vincent's (Oxford), London Capital, Garrick, Swinley Forest Golf; *Style*— David R W Potter, Esq; ✉ Brook House, Donnington, Newbury, Berkshire RG14 2JT (e-mail david@davidpotter.org)

POTTER, Edward; s of Flt Lt Edward Josef Data (d 1974), of Krakow, Poland, and Eleanor, *née* Bolton (d 1976); *b* 15 September 1941; *Educ* Bolton Tech Sch, Manchester Regnl Coll of Art, Oxford Sch of Architecture (DiplArch); *Career* architect; ptnr Edward Potter Assocs (chartered architects in gen practice and specialists in restoration of historic buildings); chm: S London Soc of Architects 1993–95, Wandsworth Soc Open Spaces Ctee 1993–2005; dir Sculpture House Kingston upon Thames 1995–2002, tstee Phoenix Members Bar Club 2014–; RIBA rep Wandsworth Conservation Advsy Ctee 1995–; RIBA Thesis Prize 1968; RIBA, FIAS, FCIOB; *Recreations* railways; *Clubs* Chelsea Arts; *Style*— Edward Potter, Esq; ✉ 59 Westover Road, London SW18 2RF (☎ 020 8870 7595)

POTTER, Jon Nicholas; s of Robert Edward Potter, and June, *née* Rosemayer; *b* 19 November 1963; *Educ* Burnham GS, Univ of Southampton (BA), Aston Business Sch (MBA); *m* Tracy Clare, *née* Holland; 2 s (Max Frederick b 4 April 1997, Hugo Nicholas b 24 March 1999), 2 da (Sophie Ann, Lucy Thérèse (twins) b 31 May 2002); *Career* hockey player; memb Hounslow Hockey Club (capt Nat League winners 1990 and 1992); Bronze medal Olympic Games LA 1984, Silver medal World Cup London 1986, Silver medal Euro Cup Moscow 1987, Gold medal Olympic Games Seoul 1988, Gold medal Euro Cup Winners Cup 1990, Bronze medal Euro Cup 1991, 6th Olympic Games Barcelona 1992; 234 int caps; England capt World Cup 1994; most capped male GB player; Hockey Player of the Year 1987–88; mktg mangr: KP Foods 1988–92, Nestlé Rowntree 1992–95; mktg dir ?okoládovny (Nestle Prague) 1995–97; Guinness Ltd: Euro mktg dir 1997–99, global brands dir 2000; global brand dir Guinness Diageo 2000–04, gen mangr Diageo venture Africa 2005–07, pres Diageo vodka and rum mktg portfolio 2007–08, chief mktg offr Diageo N America 2008–10, sr ptnr Mckinney Rogers 2010–12, chief mktg offr and exec vice-pres Moet Hennessy USA 2012–15, md Chandon California 2016–; *Recreations* fitness, yoga, travel, food and wine, music; *Style*— Jon Potter, Esq; ✉ 250 Putnam Road, New Canaan, CT 06840, USA (e-mail jpotter6@mac.com)

POTTER, Rt Hon Sir Mark Howard; PC (1996), kt (1988); s of Prof Harold Potter (d 1951), and Beatrice Spencer, *née* Crowder (d 1978); *b* 27 August 1937; *Educ* Perse Sch Cambridge, Gonville & Caius Coll Cambridge (MA); *m* 1962, Undine Amanda Fay, da of Maj James Eric Miller (Rajputana Rifles); 2 s (Nicholas b 6 Sept 1969, Charles b 27 Dec 1978); *Career* cmmnd 15 Medium Regt RA 1958, 289 Light Para Regt RHA (TA) 1960–65; asst supervisor legal studies Univ of Cambridge (Gonville & Caius, Queen's, Sydney Sussex, Girton) 1961–68; called to the Bar Gray's Inn 1961 (bencher 1987), practised Fountain Court, QC 1980, judge of the High Court of Justice (Queen's Bench Div) 1988–96, presiding judge Northern Circuit 1991–94, judge in charge Commercial Ct 1994–95, a Lord Justice of Appeal 1996–2010, pres Family Div and head of family justice 2005–10, pres Court of Protection 2007–10; chm: Bar Public Affrs Ctee 1987, Lord Chancellor's Advsy Ctee on Legal Educn and Conduct 1998–99, Legal Services Consultancy Panel 2000–05; vice-chm: Cncl of Legal Educn 1989–91, Advsy Ctee Lord Chllr's Civil Justice Review 1985–88; hon fell: Gonville & Caius Coll Cambridge 1998–, KCL 2005–; tstee: Somerset House Tst, Gt Ormond Street Hosp Charity; pres Personal Support Unit; *Recreations* family, sporting; *Clubs* Garrick, Saintsbury, St Enedoc and Denham Golf; *Style*— The Rt Hon Sir Mark Potter; ✉ Fountain Court Chambers, London EC4Y 9DH (e-mail mhp@fountaincourt.co.uk)

POTTERTON, Homan; s of Thomas Edward Potterton (d 1960), and Eileen, *née* Tong (d 1990); *b* 9 May 1946; *Educ* Kilkenny Coll, Trinity Coll Dublin (BA, MA), Univ of Edinburgh (Dip History of Art); *Career* cataloguer Nat Gallery of Ireland 1971–73, asst keeper Nat Gallery London 1974–80, dir Nat Gallery of Ireland 1980–88, ed Irish Arts Review 1993–2001 (publisher 2000–01); contrib: Burlington Magazine, Apollo, Connoisseur, Country Life, Financial Times; FSA, HRHA; *Books* Irish Church Monuments 1570–1880 (1975), A Guide to the National Gallery (1976), The National Gallery, London (1977), Reynolds and Gainsborough – Themes and Painters in the National Gallery (1976), Pageant and Panorama – The Elegant World of Canaletto (1978), Irish Art and Architecture (with Peter Harbison and Jeanne Sheehy, 1978, reissued 1993), Venetian Seventeenth Century Painting (1979), Dutch Seventeenth and Eighteenth Century Paintings in the National Gallery of Ireland – a complete catalogue (1986) The Golden Age of Dutch Paintings from the National Gallery of Ireland (exhibition catalogue, 1986), Rathcormick: A Childhood Recalled (2001), Potterton People and Places: Three Centuries of an Irish Family (2006); *Clubs* St Stephens's Green (Dublin); *Style*— Homan Potterton, Esq; ✉ e-mail hpotterton@orange.fr; Colombel Bas, 81140 Castelnau-de-Montmiral, France (☎ and fax 00 33 5 63 40 53 52, website www.potterton.ie)

POTTS, David Tom; CBE (2013); s of Tom Potts (d 1989), and Enid Elizabeth, *née* Carter (d 1964); *b* 18 March 1957, Manchester; *Educ* Hartshead Co Sch Ashton-under-Lyne; *Children* 2 s (Daniel Edward Tom b 20 May 1986, George David b 4 July 1989); *Partner* Jane Elizabeth Holt, *née* Searle; *Career* Tesco plc: joined as gen asst Manchester 1973, store mangr Ryde IOW 1981, dir London 1989, ceo NI and I 1994, plc bd dir 1998–2012, dir i/c UK ops 2000–10, ceo Asia 2010–12; fndr Pug Retail Ltd 2014; chief exec Morrisons 2015–; *Recreations* golf, football, cinema, travel, walking; *Clubs* Manchester City FC; *Style*— David Potts, Esq, CBE

POTTS, Michael Stuart; DL (Merseyside 2000); s of late Thomas Edmund Potts, ERD, of Bray on Thames, Berks, and late Phyllis Margaret, *née* Gebbie; *b* 2 September 1938, Sheffield; *Educ* Hilton Coll South Africa, Repton; *m* 23 May 1964, Virginia May Lindsay, da of late Gp Capt Hugh Whittall Marlow, OBE, AFC, of Cape Town, South Africa; 3 s (Andrew b 1966, Alexander b 1968, Rupert b 1970); *Career* chartered accountant; ptnr Coopers & Lybrand: Ireland 1968–70, UK 1970–92 (sr ptnr Liverpool Office 1971–92); dir: H J Uren & Sons Ltd 1993–2003, W O & J Wilson Ltd 1994–2008; pres North West Cancer Research 2002– (chm 1993–2002 and 2013–15); dir: Mersey Regnl Ambulance Service (NHS Tst) 1993–99, Grosvenor Grain & Feed Co Ltd 1999–2004, Universities Superannuation Scheme Ltd 1999–2007; pres Liverpool Soc of Chartered Accountants 1982–83; memb Cncl: Merseyside C of C and Industry 1974–92 (hon treas 1974–82), Univ of Liverpool 1979–89 and 1993–2006 (dep treas 1986–89, hon treas 1993–99, pres 1999–2004, pro-chllr 2004–06), ICAEW 1988–92; High Sheriff of Merseyside 2006; Liveryman: Worshipful Co of Clockmakers, Worshipful Co of Chartered Accountants, Hon LLD Univ of Liverpool 2007; FRSA 2001, FCA; Potts of Leeds: Five Generations of Clockmakers (2006); *Recreations* sailing, golf, motoring, horology; *Clubs* Dee Sailing (Cdre 1979–80), Royal Liverpool Golf (treas 1992–96), Aston Martin Owners', Antiquarian Horological Soc; *Style*— Michael Potts, Esq, DL; ✉ Prospect House, The Parade, Parkgate, South Wirral, Cheshire CH64 6SA (☎ 0151 336 1795, e-mail mspotts@pottsclocks.co.uk)

POTTS, Prof Paul John; CBE (2009); s of Michael Henry Potts (d 1960), of Sheffield, and Sylvia Brenda Potts; *b* 21 January 1950, Sheffield; *Educ* Worksop Coll; *m* 1, 1976 (m dis 1994), Gabrielle Jane Fagan; 1 s, 2 da; m 2, 1994, Judith Anne Fielding; *Career* gen reporter Sheffield Star 1968–74, lobby corr Yorkshire Post 1974–78; gen reporter: Daily Telegraph 1978–81, Mail on Sunday 1981–82; political ed News of the World 1982–86, dep ed The Express 1988–95 (political then asst ed 1986–88); Press Association: ed-in-chief 1995–, gp chief exec 2000–10; chm Bd of Dirs Canada Newswire 2003–10; non-exec dir Channel 4 2012–; visiting prof of journalism Univ of Sheffield 2010–; Hon DLitt Univ of Sheffield 2002; *Recreations* all sports, horse racing, history; *Clubs* Garrick; *Style*— Prof Paul Potts, CBE; ✉ e-mail pauljpotts@googlemail.com

POULTER, Dr Daniel Leonard James; MP; *Educ* Univ of Bristol, Guy's, King's and St Thomas' Sch of Medicine; *Career* medical doctor; dep ldr Reigate and Banstead Cncl 2008–10, MP (Cons) Suffolk Central & Ipswich N 2010–; *Style*— Dr Daniel Poulter, MP; ✉ 19 The Business Centre, Earl Soham, Suffolk IP13 7SA; House of Commons, London SW1A 0AA

POULTER, John; *Educ* Berkhamsted Sch, Queen's Coll Oxford (open scholar, MA); *Career* sales mangr Telsec Instruments 1965–67, sales mangr Cambridge Instruments 1967–72, industrial exec Wm Brandts 1972–73, mktg and sales dir Cambridge Instruments 1973–77, gen mangr Robinsons 1977–81, md Vokes Ltd 1981–88; Spectris plc (formerly Fairey Gp plc): chief exec 1988–2001, non-exec chm 2001–; non-exec chm: Kymata Ltd 1998–2001, Wyko Gp Ltd 2001–04, Snell and Wilcox Ltd 2002–, Filtronic plc 2006–; non-exec dir: Crest Packaging plc 1993–96, BTP plc 1996–2000, Lloyds Smaller Companies Investment Tst plc 1992–2002, Kidde plc 2000–05 (chair Remuneration Ctee), Smaller Companies Value Tst plc 2002–, RAC plc 2002–05 (chair Remuneration Ctee), London Metal Exchange Ltd 2002–05, Macquarie European Infrastructure plc 2003–05, Suffolk Life plc 2006–; *Style*— John Poulter, Esq; ✉ Spectris plc, Station Road, Egham, Surrey TW20 9NP

POUND, Stephen Pelham; MP; s of Pelham Pound, and Dominica, *née* James; *b* 3 July 1948; *Educ* Hertford GS, LSE (Dip Industrial Relations, BSc, pres Union); *m* 1976, Maggie, da of Lyndon Griffiths; 1 da (Emily Frances b 1988), 1 s (Pelham Joseph b 1990); *Career* seaman 1965–66, bus conductor 1966–68, bookseller's clerk 1969–70, hospital porter 1971–79, student LSE 1979–84, housing offr 1984–97; MP (Lab) Ealing N 1997–; cncllr Ealing 1982–, mayor of Ealing 1995–96; *Recreations* watching football, playing cricket, collecting comics and listening to jazz; *Clubs* St Joseph's Catholic Social, Fulham FC Supporters'; *Style*— Stephen Pound, Esq, MP; ✉ House of Commons, London SW1A 0AA (☎ 020 7219 1140, fax 020 7219 5982, e-mail stevepoundmp@parliament.uk)

POUNDER, Prof Derrick John; s of Wilfred Pounder, of Pen-y-coedcae, Mid Glamorgan, and Lilian, *née* Jones; *b* 25 February 1949; *Educ* Pontypridd Boys GS, Univ of Birmingham (MB, ChB); *m* 28 Nov 1975, Georgina, da of Patrick Kelly, of Tullamore, Co Offaly; 2 da (Sibéal b 30 March 1985, Sinéad b 9 Sept 1991), 1 s (Emlyn b 18 May 1989); *Career* lectr then sr lectr in forensic pathology Univ of Adelaide, dep chief med examiner Edmonton Alberta and assoc prof Univs of Alberta and Calgary 1985–87, prof of forensic med Univ of Dundee 1987–2014; consltg expert to UN, OSCE, Cncl of Europe and Int Criminal Court; past chm Physicians for Human Rights, past memb Bd of Govrs UN Vol Fund for Victims of Torture; clerk Llantrisant Town Tst 2014–; Freeman Llantrisant; FRCPA, FFPathRCPI; *Recreations* photography, medieval architecture, almost-lost causes; *Style*— Prof Derrick Pounder; ✉ The Barn, Edwinsford, Talley, Llandeilo SA19 7BX (☎ 01558 685125, e-mail derrickpounder@yahoo.co.uk)

POUNDER, Prof Robert Edward (Roy); *b* 31 May 1944, Nottingham; *Educ* Eltham Coll, Peterhouse Cambridge (state scholar, exhibitioner, sr scholar, MA, Prize in Natural Sciences (twice), Prize in Med (twice)), Guy's Hosp Med Sch London (clinical entrance scholar), Univ of Cambridge (BChir, MB, MD), Univ of London (DSc); *m* Prof Christine A Lee, *qv*; 2 s (Jeremy, Tom); *Career* house physician Guy's Hosp London 1969–70, house surgn Addenbrooke's Hosp Cambridge 1970, SHO (med) Hammersmith Hosp London 1971, SHO (cardiology) Brompton Hosp London 1971–72, registrar then sr registrar (gen med, gastroenterology and diabetes) Central Middx Hosp 1972–76, sr registrar (gen med) St Thomas' Hosp London 1976–80 (locum conslt physician 1977–78), hon conslt physician Royal Free Hosp London 1980–2005; Royal Free Hosp Sch of Med (later Royal Free and UC Med Sch UCL): sr lectr in med 1980–85, reader in med 1985–92, clinical sub-dean 1986–88, prof of med 1992–2005, dir Centre for Gastroenterology (jtly with Dept of Med UCL Med Sch) 1994–2002, vice-head Dept of Med 1995–2005, pres SCR 1996–2002; assoc med dir Gray's Inn Div Royal Free Hampstead NHS Tst 1992–96, memb Exec Ctee Royal Free Hampstead NHS Tst 1994–96, non-exec memb Bd Camden and Islington HA 1996–2002; scientific sec VIII European Helicobacter pylori Study Gp Meeting Edinburgh 1993–95; delivered numerous invited and plenary lectures in UK and overseas; clinical vice-pres RCP 2002–04 (memb Cncl 1987–89 and 1997–2000, assoc int dir for Australasia and Far East 2004–08), chm of tstees Alimentary Pharmacology and Therapeutics Tst 1988–99; memb Cncl Br Digestive Fndn 1987–98 (chm Bd of Tstees 1997–98); founding ed Alimentary Pharmacology and Therapeutics 1987–, founding ed-in-chief GastroHep.com 2000–, co-fndr and chm RotaGeek.com 2009–; memb: Friends of Peterhouse (sometime chm Cncl), 1942 Club, Wilks XV, Sir Arthur Hurst Dining Club; govr St Paul's Sch 2001–10 (dep chm 2007–09); fell American Coll of Gastroenterology (memb Int Ctee); memb: Br Soc of Gastroenterology (hon sec 1982–86, memb Cncl 1996–99), American Gastroenterological Assoc; FRCP 1984 (MRCP 1971), Hon FRACP 2008, Hon FRCPI 2010; *Books* Long Cases in General Medicine (ed, 1983, 2 edn 1988), Doctor, There's Something Wrong with my Guts (ed, 1983), Recent Advances in Gastroenterology (ed vols 6–10, 1986–94, biennial), Diseases of the Gut and Pancreas (jt ed, 1987, 2 edn 1994), Advanced Medicine 23 (jt ed, 1987), The British Society of Gastroenterology 1937–1987: A Collection of Scientific Papers (ed, 1987), Classic Papers in Peptic Ulcer (conslt ed, 1988), A Colour Atlas of the Digestive System (jtly, 1989), Landmark Papers: The Histamine H2-Receptor Antagonists (ed, 1990), European Word Book of Gastroenterology (jt ed, 1994), Bockus Gastroenterology (section ed, 1994), Current Diagnosis and Treatment (jt ed, 1996), Inflammatory Bowel Disease (jtly, 1998); *Clubs* Garrick; *Style*— Prof Roy Pounder; ✉ High Tun Cottages, Itlay, Daglingworth, Gloucestershire GL7 7JA

P

POUNDS, Prof Kenneth Alwyne (Ken); CBE (1984); s of Harry Pounds (d 1976), and Dorothy Louise, *née* Hunt (d 1981); *b* 17 November 1934; *Educ* Salt Sch Shipley, UCL (BSc, PhD); *m* 1, 29 Dec 1961, Margaret Mary (d 1976), da of Patrick O'Connell (d 1969); 2 s (David Edwin b 12 May 1963, John Michael b 13 April 1966), 1 da (Jillian Barbara b 12 June 1964); m 2, 10 Dec 1982, Joan Mary, da of Samuel Millit (d 1983); 1 s (Michael Andrew b 5 Aug 1983), 1 da (Jennifer Anne b 22 Feb 1987); *Career* Univ of Leicester: asst lectr 1960, lectr 1962, dir X-Ray Astronomy Gp 1969–94, reader in physics 1971, prof of space physics 1973–, head of physics 1986–93 and 1998–2002; chief exec Particle Physics and Astronomy Res Cncl 1994–98; author of over 300 publications worldwide; fndr memb BNSC Mgmnt Bd; memb Cncl: SERC (chm Astronomy, Space and Radio Bd 1980–84), Royal Soc 1986–87; pres Royal Astronomical Soc 1990–92; Hon DUniv York 1984; Hon DSc: Loughborough Univ 1992, Sheffield Hallam Univ 1997, Univ of Warwick 2001, Univ of Leicester 2005; fell UCL 1993, distinguished hon fell Univ of Leicester 2013; FRS 1981; *Recreations* cricket, football, music; *Style*— Prof Ken Pounds, CBE, FRS; ✉ 12 Swale Close, Oadby, Leicestershire (☎ 0116 271 9370); University of Leicester, Leicester LE1 7RH (☎ 0116 252 3509, fax 0116 252 3311, e-mail kap@le.ac.uk)

POUNTNEY, David Willoughby; CBE (1994); s of Edward Willoughby Pountney (d 1997), and Dorothy Lucy, *née* Byrt (d 1984); *b* 10 September 1947; *Educ* St John's Coll Choir Sch Cambridge, Radley, St John's Coll Cambridge (MA); *m* 1, 23 Feb 1980, Jane Rosemary, da of Maj James Emrys Williams (d 1978); 1 da (Emilia b 1981), 1 s (James b 1984); m 2, 14 Sept 2007, Nicola Raab; *Career* dir of productions: Scottish Opera 1976–80, ENO 1983–93; dir of operas in: Ireland, Holland, Germany, Italy, Aust and USA, all maj Br cos; princ productions incl: Janácek cycle (Scot Opera, WNO), Bussoni's Dr Faust (ENO, Deutsche Oper), The Lady Macbeth of Mtensk (ENO), Hänsel and Gretel (ENO, Evening Standard Award), Wozzeck, Pelleas et Mélisande, world première of Philip Glass' The Voyage (Met Opera NY) 1992, Die Soldaten (Ruhr Triennale) 2006, Kommilitonen (RAM London) 2011, Lulu (WNO) 2013, Die Zauberflöte (Bregenz Lake stage) 2013–14, Guillaume Tell (WNO) 2014, Pelléas et Mélisande (WNO) 2015, Figaro Gets a Divorce (WNO) 2016, In Parenthesis (WNO) 2016; translated numerous operas from Czech, Russian, German and Italian and original libretti for Steven Oliver, Sir Peter Maxwell Davies and John Harle; dir for Nottingham Playhouse: Twelfth Night, As You Like It; Intendant Bregenzer Festspiele 2003–14; artistic dir and ceo WNO 2011–; Chevalier de l'Ordre des Arts et des Lettres (France), Cavalier's Cross of the Order of Merit of the Republic of Poland 2013, Ehrenkreuz des Bundes Österreich; *Books* Der Fliegende Engländer, Die Bregenzer Festspiele und ihr Intendant David Pountney von 2004 bis 2014; *Recreations* croquet, cooking, gardening; *Clubs* Garrick; *Style*— David Pountney, Esq, CBE

POVEY, Sir Keith; kt (2001), QPM (1991); s of Trevor Roberts Povey (d 1983), and Dorothy, *née* Parsonnage (d 1965); *b* 30 April 1943; *Educ* Abbeydale GS Sheffield, Univ of Sheffield (Bramshill scholar, BA); *m* 1964, Carol Ann, da of late Albert Harvey; 2 da (Allyson Patricia b 11 Sept 1965, Louise Ann b 23 Feb 1970); *Career* Sheffield City Police 1961–84; posts incl: cadet 1961, constable 1962, chief inspr HM Inspector of Constabulary NE Region 1981–82 (memb Secretariat Home Office Enquiry into Yorkshire Ripper case), FBI Academy USA 1982, supt and sub-divnl cdr Sheffield City Centre 1982–84 (ground cdr for policing during miners' dispute at Orgreave Coking Plant); staff offr HM Chief Inspector of Constabulary Home Office 1984–86 (reported on Zimbabwe Republic Police 1984), asst chief constable Humberside 1986–90, deputy chief constable Northants 1990–93, chief constable Leicestershire Constabulary 1993–97, HM Inspector of Constabulary 1997–2001, HM Chief Inspector of Constabulary 2002–05; ACPO: chm General Purposes Ctee, chm Crime Prevention Sub-Ctee, head Working Gp on Police Patrol, rep Home Office Working Party on Special Constabulary; *Recreations* jogging, flying; *Style*— Sir Keith Povey, QPM

POW, Rebecca; MP; da of Michael Pow, and Norah, *née* Crees; *b* 10 October 1960, Bath; *Educ* La Sainte Union Convent Grammar Bath, Wye Coll Univ of London (BSc); *m* 14 Sept 1989, Charles Clark; 2 da (Verity b 29 Feb 1992, Victoria b 15 May 1994), 1 s (James b 9 Nov 1998); *Career* BBC prodn training, Radio West 1983–84, NFU Taunton 1984–86, presenter/ prodr Farming Today BBC Radio 4 1986–88, presenter West Country Farming and environment corr (first on TV) HTV 1988–2005, prodr-dir eco/ rural progs and presenter Garden Club Channel 4 2003–15, owner Pow Prodns 2015–; MP (Cons) Taunton Deane 2015–; parish cncllr Stoke St Mary, school govr, tstee Somerset Wildlife Tst 2003–15, memb Cncl Royal Bath and West show 2013–; memb: Guild of Architectural Journalists, Garden Media Guild; *Publications* All Gardens Great and Small (1994); columns: Amateur Garden Magazine, Kitchen Garden, Western Daily Press, Somerset Life; *Recreations* cricket, gardening, tennis, nature, wildlife, vegetable growing; *Style*— Ms Rebecca Pow, MP; ✉ Tuckers Farmhouse, Stoke St Mary, Taunton TA3 5BY (☎ 07900 685303); House of Commons, London SW1A 0AA (☎ 020 7219 4831, e-mail rebecca.pow.mp@parliament.uk, website www.rebeccapow.org.uk, Twitter @Pow_Rebecca)

POWELL, Anthony; s of Arthur Lawrence Powell (d 1939), of Manchester, and Alice, *née* Woodhead; *b* 2 June 1935; *Educ* William Hulmes GS Manchester, St Andrew's Coll Dublin, Central Sch of Arts and Crafts London; *Career* costume and set designer for theatre and film; served Royal Corps of Signals (Br Army occupation of the Rhine) 1953–55; asst to Sir Cecil Beaton and Oliver Messel; lectr in theatre design Central Sch of Art and Design 1958–71, RSA scholar 1958, freelance design conslt Sabre Sportwear and Jantzen Swimwear 1960–69, Br Colour Cncl 1965–67, numerous building interior designs incl Sutton Place 1981–83; art dir photographic shoots (Snowdon) for Issey Miyake London, Tokyo 1988–89; Agatha Christie and Archeology Exhbn (Essen, Vienna, Basle, Berlin and Br Museum London) 2001–02; RDI 1999; Hon FRCA 1997, Hon Fell Univ of the Arts London 2002; Hon DDes Univ of Greenwich 2003; *Theatre* Women Beware Women (RSC) 1961, School for Scandal (Haymarket and NY) 1961, Comedy of Errors (RSC and world tour) 1963, The Rivals (Haymarket) 1966, Fish Out of Water (London) 1971, Private Lives (London, NY, USA tour) 1972, The Confederacy and Tonight We Improvise (Chichester Festival Theatre) 1974, Ring Round the Moon (Ahmanson Theatre LA) 1975, Amadeus (Paris) 1981, Lettice and Lovage (costumes for Maggie Smith, NY) 1990, Hay Fever (London and provincial tour) 1992, Trelawny of the Wells (RNT) 1992, Sunset Boulevard (London/LA 1993, Broadway 1994, Frankfurt/Toronto 1995, Aust and US tour 1996), Tom Sawyer (musical, Broadway) 2001, Cole Porter's Anything Goes (RNT and Theatre Royal) 2002–03, Hedda Gabler (Théâtre Marigny Paris) 2003, My Fair Lady (Théâtre du Châtelet Paris) 2010, (Mariinsky Theatre St Petersburg) 2011–12 and 2013 and (Chicago Lyric Opera) 2017, Singin' in the Rain (Théâtre du Châtelet Paris) 2015 and 2016, and (NY) 2017; *Opera* Rinaldo (Sadlers Wells Opera and Komische Oper Berlin) 1960, La Belle Hélène (Sadlers Wells Opera) 1962, Il Seraglio (Sadlers Wells Opera) 1962, Capriccio (Glyndebourne Festival Opera) 1965, Martins Lie (for US TV) 1965, Capriccio (Paris Opera) 2004; *Films* Royal Hunt of the Sun 1968, Joe Egg 1969, A Town Called Bastard 1970, Nicholas and Alexandra 1971, Travels with my Aunt 1972, Papillon 1973, That Lucky Touch 1974, Buffalo Bill and the Indians 1975, Sorcerer 1976, Death on the Nile 1977, Tess 1978–79, Priest of Love 1980, Evil Under the Sun 1981, Indiana Jones and the Temple of Doom 1983, Pirates 1984–85, Ishtar 1985–86, David Lean's Nostromo (preparation) 1986–87 and 1989, Frantic 1987, Indiana Jones and the Last Crusade 1988, Hook 1990–91, Walt Disney's 101 Dalmatians (costumes for Glenn Close) 1996, The Avengers 1997, The Ninth Gate 1998, Walt Disney's 102 Dalmations 1999, Miss Potter 2006; *Awards* for Best Costume Design incl: Tony Award for School for Scandal 1963, US Academy Award for Travels with my Aunt 1973, LA Drama Critics' Circle Awards (sets and costumes) for Ring Around the Moon 1975, Br and US Academy Awards for Death on the Nile 1979, US Academy Award for Tess 1981, César Award (France) for Pirates 1987, Drama-logue Critics Award and LA Drama Critics' Circle Award for Sunset Boulevard 1993; US Academy Award nominations for: Pirates 1987, Hook 1992, 102 Dalmations 2001; Career Achievement Award (Costume Designers' Guild Hollywood) 2000, Irene Sharaff Lifetime Achievement Award (Theatre Devpt Fund NY) 2004, Tirelli Lifetime Achievement Award (Italy) 2007; *Publications* numerous books written about him and his work, incl Costume Designers (2004) and Hollywood Sketchbook, a Century of Costume Illustration (2012); *Recreations* music, gardening, collecting, laughing; *Style*— Anthony Powell, RDI; ✉ c/o Michael McCoy, Independent Talent Group Ltd, 40 Whitfield Street, London W1T 2RH (☎ 020 7636 6565, mobile 07771 613696, e-mail michaelmccoy@independenttalent.com)

POWELL, Ashley Craig; s of Anthony and Sandra Powell; *b* 13 February 1962; *Educ* Whitefield Comp; *m* 15 June 1997 Marcia Estelle, da of Gerald Altman (d 1999); *Career* professional toastmaster; sr dep pres Guild of Int Professional Toastmasters 1990–2009; chm Br Professional Toastmasters Authy, chm Toastmasters for Royal Occasions; sr dep princ: Ivor Spencer Sch for Professional Toastmasters, Ivor Spencer Int Sch for Butler Administrators/Personal Assistants 1997–2009; sr consIt Guild of Professional After Dinner Speakers; assoc Guild of Int Butler Administrators/Personal Assistants, assoc LAMDA; memb Guild of Int Professional Toastmasters 1990– (Toastmaster of Year 2001); *Recreations* after dinner speaking, organising special events; *Style*— Ashley Powell, Esq; ✉ 9 Lancaster House, Park Lane, Stanmore, Middlesex HA7 3HD (☎ 020 8385 7644, mobile 07956 214631)

POWELL, Sir (John) Christopher; kt (2009); s of Air Vice-Marshal John Frederick Powell, OBE, AE, and Geraldine Ysolda, *née* Moylan; bro of Baron Powell of Bayswater, KCMG (Life Peer), and Jonathan Nicholas Powell, *qqv*; *b* 4 October 1943; *Educ* Canterbury Cathedral Choir Sch, St Peter's Sch York, LSE (BSc); *m* 1973, Rosemary Jeanne, da of Ralph Symmons; 2 s (Ben b 1974, Jamie b 1977), 1 da (Lucy b 1980); *Career* account mgmnt trainee Hobson Bates 1965–67, account mangr Wasey's 1967–69; BMP DDB: joined as ptnr and shareholder 1969, jt md 1975–86, chief exec 1986–98, chm 1999–2003; non-exec dir: Riverside Studios 1989– (chm 2011–), United News and Media plc 1995–2006, Britain in Europe 2005–15, Dr Foster LLP 2006–15 (chm 2009–14); memb Advsy Bd PricewaterhouseCoopers 2005–16; pres IPA 1993–95; chm: IPPR 2001–08 (tstee 1999–), NESTA 2003–09, Parcel Poke Ltd 2009–15, Advertising Standards Bd of Finance 2010–, Royal Mail Advertising Advsy Bd 2013–; dep chm Public Diplomacy Bd 2006–09; dep chm Riverside Community NHS Tst 1994–2000, chm Ealing and Hounslow HA 2000–02, tstee Alzheimer's Soc 2012–; *Recreations* riding, tennis, gardening, theatre; *Style*— Sir Christopher Powell

POWELL, David (Dick); s of Arthur Barrington Powell, CMG, of Pwllmeyni, Gwent, and Jane, *née* Weir; *Educ* Ampleforth, Manchester Poly (DipAD), RCA (MDesRCA, Burton award 1975 and 1976); *m* (Jennifer) Lucy, da of Peter Talbot Willcox; 1 da (Jemma b 25 July 1980), 3 s (Oscar b 1 Sept 1983, Freddie b 24 Feb 1985, Gus b 5 Dec 1992); *Career* product designer; co-fndr CAPA Partnership 1976–79, freelance designer 1980–83, fndr (with Prof Richard Seymour, *qv*) Seymour-Powell 1984– (clients incl Unilever, Panasonic, Tefal, LG, Nestle and Diageo), global design advsr Samsung Electronics 2005–08, gp creative dir Loewy 2009–; memb: Design Cncl 1996–2000, Design Business Assoc, D&AD Exec, Int Advsy Panel Design for Singapore 2009–; pres D&AD 2005–06, chm D&AD 2010; Hon Dr of Fine Arts Center of Creative Studies Detroit 2002; *Television* BBC Design Classics, Designs on Britain and LWT Design Education series 1986, subject of Channel 4 Designs on Your... series 1998, Better By Design (six part Channel 4 series) 2000, BBC Innovation Nation 2000, contrib BBC Genius of Design (five part series for BBC 2) 2010; *Awards* Best Overall Design and Product Design (for Norton F1 motorcycle) Design Week Awards 1990, D&AD Silver Award (for Technophone Cellular Telephone) 1991, ID Award and D&AD Silver Award (for MuZ Skorpian motorcycle) 1993, winner Product Design category BBC Design Awards 1994, CSD Minerva Award (for MuZ Skorpian) 1994, ID Award (for Sun Voyager) 1994, D&AD President's Award (for outstanding contribution to design) 1995, DBA Design Effectiveness Award 1995, 2002, 2003, 2004 and 2005, Special Commendation Prince Philip Designers' Prize 1997 and 2008 (shortlisted 2003), Janus France 1998, Starpack Award 2003, corp film for Samsung European Premium Design 2003, Gerald Frewer Meml Trophy Inst of Engrg Designers 2003, Best Consumer Product (for ENV motorbike) Design Week Awards 2006, Gold Medal (for ENV motorbike) IDEA/Business Week Awards (USA) 2006, Gold Award (for Dove Petal Actuator) Starpack Awards 2007, Gold winner (for Thermastone) EID (Excellence in Design) Awards (USA) 2007, Best Re-packaging of a brand (for Axe/Lynx – project Neutron) UK Packaging Awards 2007, winner (for Thermastone) Chicago Athenaeum Good Design Awards 2007, winner (for LG70 Television for LG) iF Awards (Germany) 2008, winner in product design category (for Huntleigh Healthcare Bed) Red Dot Awards (Germany) 2008, D&AD Silver (for AMS Quantum Saddle) 2009, Best Project in Aviation (for Aircruise concept) Condé Nast Traveller Marriot Design & Innovation Awards 2010; *Books* Presentation Techniques (1985, revised edn 1988, translations in Dutch and Spanish); *Recreations* motorcycles; *Style*— Dick Powell, Esq; ✉ Seymour Powell, The Factory, 265 Merton Road, London SW18 5JS (☎ 020 7381 6433, e-mail design@seymourpowell.com, website www.seymourpowell.com)

POWELL, Gregory; *b* 21 January 1948, Edgware, Middx; *Educ* Birkbeck Coll London (BSc), LSE (LLB); *Career* admitted slr; trainee slr W H Thompson, investigating offr Local Govt Ombudsman, founding ptnr Powell Spencer & Ptnrs Slrs; pres London Criminal Courts Slrs Assoc; Criminal Legal Aid Lawyer of the Year 2004–05; *Style*— Gregory Powell, Esq; ✉ Powell Spencer & Partners, 290 Kilburn High Road, London NW6 2DD (e-mail gregpowell@psplaw.co.uk)

POWELL, Ian; *Career* PricewaterhouseCoopers LLP: joined as grad trainee 1977, ptnr 1991–, memb Exec Bd 2006–, chm and sr ptnr 2008–; *Recreations* motorsports, theatre; *Style*— Ian Powell, Esq; ✉ PricewaterhouseCoopers LLP, 1 Embankment Place, London WC2N 6RH

POWELL, Jeffrey Richard (Jeff); s of late Alfred William John Powell, and late Dorothy Faith, *née* Parkin; *b* 21 February 1942; *Educ* Buckhurst Hill Co HS, Regent St Poly; *m* 1 (m dis); 2 da (Natalie Jane b 22 May 1972, Natasha Dawn b 14 April 1974); m 2, 20 Feb 1987, Maria del Consuelo Ortiz de Powell, da of late Gen Jose Ortiz Avila; 1 s (Jeffrey Jose b 17 March 1988); *Career* Walthamstow Guardian 1959–66 (jr reporter, sports ed); Daily Mail: sports sub ed 1966–69, football reporter 1969–71, chief soccer corr 1971–89, chief sports feature writer 1989–; British Sports Reporter of the Year 1978, 1983 and 1985, British Sports Journalist of the Year 1985, British Sports Feature Writer of the Year 1995, Sports Reporter of the Year British Press Awards 2005, Variety Club Award for Lifetime Achievement in Sports Journalism 2005, SJA Award for Lifetime Achievement In Sports Journalism 2014; memb: Football Writers' Assoc 1969 (chm 1982–83 and 1989–90), Sportswriters' Assoc 1969, Boxing Writers' Club 1999; *Books* Bobby Moore, The Authorised Biography; *Recreations* golf, tennis, theatre, opera, chess, squash; *Clubs* RAC, Tramp, Harris Golf; *Style*— Jeff Powell, Esq; ✉ Daily Mail, Northcliffe House, 2 Derry Street, Kensington, London W8 5TT (☎ 020 3615 1219, mobile 07711 898832, e-mail jeff.powell@dailymail.co.uk or jeffreyrpowell@aol.com, Twitter @jeffpowell_mail)

POWELL, John Lewis; QC (1990); s of Gwyn Powell (d 1981), of Ammanford, Carmarthenshire, and Lilian Mary, *née* Griffiths; *b* 14 September 1950; *Educ* Christ Coll Brecon, Amman Valley GS, Trinity Hall Cambridge (MA, LLB); *m* 1 Sept 1973, Eva Zofia Lomnicka, *qv*; 3 c (Sophie Anna b 14 Feb 1980, Catrin Eva (Katie) b 3 Jan 1982, David John b 3 Feb 1985); *Career* called to the Bar Middle Temple (Harmsworth scholar) 1974, bencher 1998; head of chambers 1997–2000; recorder and dep high ct judge; currently memb chambers 4 New Square 2000–; Parly candidate (Lab) Cardigan 1979; pres Soc of Construction Law 1991–93, chm Law Reform Ctee General Cncl of the Bar 1997–98; memb Chancery Bar Assoc; PNBA; *Books* Encyclopedia of Financial Services Law (with Prof Eva Lomnicka), Professional Negligence (with R Jackson), Palmer's Company Law (jt ed, 25 edn 1991), Issues and Offers of Company Securities: The New Regimes; *Recreations* travel, sheep farming, walking, international politics; *Style—* John L Powell, Esq, QC

POWELL, Jonathan Leslie; s of James Dawson Powell, and Phyllis Nora, *née* Sylvester; *b* 25 April 1947; *Educ* Sherborne, UEA; *m* 29 Dec 1990, Sally Brampton; *Career* script ed then prodr Granada TV 1969–77; BBC TV: prodr 1977–84 (prodr of classic serials incl The Mayor of Casterbridge, Tinker Tailor Soldier Spy, Testament of Youth, The Barchester Chronicles and The Old Men at the Zoo), head of drama series and serials 1984–87, head Drama Group 1987, controller of BBC1 1988–92; dir of drama and international devpt Carlton Television 1993–; prof Media Dept Royal Holloway London; memb Cncl BAFTA 1998–2000; *Recreations* fishing; *Style—* Jonathan Powell, Esq

POWELL, Jonathan Nicholas; s of Air Vice-Marshal John Frederick Powell, OBE, AE, and Geraldine Ysolda, *née* Moylan; bro of Baron Powell of Bayswater, KCMG (Life Peer), and Sir (John) Christopher Powell, *qqv*; *b* 14 August 1956; *Educ* Univ Coll Oxford (MA), Univ of Pennsylvania (MA); *m* 1, (m dis 1997), Karen Drayne; 2 s (John b 10 Sept 1982, Charles b 14 Aug 1985); m 2, 2007, Sarah Helm; 2 da (Jessica Sophie b 25 Oct 1997, Rosamund Ysolda b 31 March 1999); *Career* with: BBC 1978, Granada TV Manchester 1978–79; FCO 1979–81, second sec Br Embassy Lisbon 1981–83; first sec: FCO London 1983–85, CDE Stockholm 1985, CSCE Vienna 1985–89; FCO London 1989–91, first sec Br Embassy Washington 1991–95; COS to Rt Hon Tony Blair, MP: as Ldr of Oppn 1995–97, as PM 1997–2007; md Morgan Stanley 2008–09 (sr advsr 2008–13); conslt Centre for Humanitarian Dialogue 2008–13; advsr Save The Children 2008–, estab and ceo Inter Mediate 2011–; *Publications* Great Hatred Little Room: Making Peace in Northern Ireland (2008), The New Machiavelli: How to Wield Power in the Modern World (2010), Talking to Terrorists: How to End Armed Conflicts (2014); *Style—* Jonathan Powell, Esq; ✉ Inter Mediate, 3 Dean Trench Street, London SW1P 3HB (e-mail lornamccaig@inter-mediate.org)

POWELL, (Geoffrey) Mark; s of Francis Turner Powell, MBE (d 2009), and Joan Audrey, *née* Bartlett (d 2003); *b* 14 January 1946; *Educ* Tonbridge, St Chad's Coll Durham (BA); *m* 1, 1971 (m dis 2010), Veronica Joan, da of Paul Frank Rowland of Clymping, Sussex; 2 da (Jessica (Mrs James Cobb) b 1973, Catriona (Mrs Sebastien Cavanagh) b 1976); m 2, 2011, Margaret Elizabeth Victoria (Alva) Patton, *née* Smyth; *Career* L Powell Sons & Co 1968–72, ptnr Powell Popham Dawes & Co 1972–77, dir Laing & Cruickshank 1977–86; chief exec: CL-Alexanders Laing & Cruickshank Holdings Ltd 1987–89 (dir 1986–89), Laurence Keen 1989–95; chm: Rathbone Brothers plc 2003–11 (gp md 1995–2003), SVM UK Active Fund plc 2006–11 (dir 2004–11); dir HG Capital Tst plc 2010–; dir Assoc of Private Client Investment Managers and Stockbrokers 1994–2007 (chm 2000–06), memb Takeover Panel 2001–07; memb Cncl REACH 1996–2001, tstee Fight for Sight 1999–2014, memb Investment Ctee C of E Pensions Bd 2007–15, memb Finance Advsy Ctee Westminster Abbey 2012– (chm 2015–), chm Restoration and Devpt Tst Chichester Cathedral 2015–; Freeman City of London 1967, memb Ct of Assts Worshipful Co of Haberdashers 1989– (Master 2008–09 and 2012–13); FCSI (memb London Stock Exchange 1971), FRSA; *Recreations* national hunt racing, golf, theatre, opera, wine (Maitre Emérité La Commanderie du Vin de Bordeaux a Londres); *Clubs* MCC, City of London, Boodle's, West Sussex Golf, Trevose Golf; *Style—* Mark Powell, Esq; ✉ Rumbolds Farmhouse, Plaistow, West Sussex RH14 0PZ (☎ 01403 871514, mobile 07774 842329)

POWELL, Mark Anthony Richard; s of Lesley David Powell (d 1983), and Eileen, *née* Cavanagh; *b* 13 November 1960, London; *Educ* Neave Comp Sch Essex (capt of sch football, winners Havering Cup 1973–76); *m* Oct 1982, Maxine, *née* Farey; 2 da (Danielle b 2 June 1989, Ava b 28 Feb 1997), 1 s (Maxwell b 14 March 1993); *Career* tailor; shop mangr Robot Covent Garden 1983–85, shop owner Powell & Co Soho 1985–88, mangr Violet's nightclub Soho 1988–89; bespoke tailor: D'Arblay St London 1991–95, Newburgh St London 1995–98, Brewer St London 1998–; licensing deal in Japan 1995–2000; fashion shows: DTI Vienna 1997, Cafe de Paris London 1998, DTI Vietnam and Boston 1999, Sartoria Savile Row 2001 and 2002, Moda Moscow 2003; launched ready to wear clothing range Mark Powell London 2006, collaboration with Marks and Spencer for Autograph range 2007–; featured in exhbns incl: Cutting Edge (V&A) 1997, 21st Century Dandy (Br Fashion Cncl 2003, London Cut (Florence) 2007; *Recreations* travel, clothes, musical theatre, football, golf; *Clubs* Soho House, Union, Groucho; *Style—* Mark Powell, Esq; ✉ 2 Marshall Street, London W1F 9BA (☎ 020 7287 5498, e-mail mark@markpowellbespoke.co.uk)

POWELL, Michael Peter; s of Arthur Owen Powell (d 1967), of Oxford, and Jane, *née* Mustard; *b* 24 July 1950; *Educ* Wellington, New Coll Oxford (MA), Middx Hosp Med Sch (MB BS); *m* 13 Jan 1979, Dr Jennifer Shields, da of (Leslie) Stuart Shields, QC; 3 da (Ruth b 29 May 1981, Alice b 27 Sept 1983, Penny b 13 Sept 1986); *Career* registrar and research registrar Neurosurgery Dept Frenchay Hosp Bristol 1980–83; former neurosurgn: The Nat Hosp for Neurology and Neurosurgery (sr registrar 1983–85), UCH, RNOH London; ret 2012; hon conslt: Whittingdon Hosp, St Thomas' Hosp, St Luke's Hosp for the Clergy, King Edward VII Hosp for Offrs; civilian advsr in neurosurgery to the RAF; FRCS; *Style—* Michael Powell, Esq; ✉ The National Hospital, Queen Square, London WC1N 3BG (☎ 020 3448 4714)

POWELL, Neil Ashton; s of Ian Otho James Powell (d 1994), and Dulcie Delia, *née* Lloyd (d 2008); *b* 11 February 1948; *Educ* Sevenoaks Sch, Univ of Warwick (BA, MPhil); *Career* ed Tracks 1967–70, English teacher Kimbolton Sch Huntingdon 1971–74, head of English St Christopher Sch Letchworth 1978–86 (English teacher 1974–78), owner The Baldock Bookshop 1986–90; writer in residence Samuel Whitbread Sch Shefford 1988, resident tutor Arvon Fndn Totleigh Barton 1989, tutor Bd of Extra Mural Studies Univ of Cambridge 1991, tutor WEA Eastern Region 1994–2008, visiting tutor Norwich Sch of Art 1995–97; contrib poetry, fiction, essays and reviews to: Critical Quarterly, Encounter, The Guardian, The Independent, The Listener, London Magazine, New Statesman, PN Review, Poetry Review, The Spectator, Sunday Telegraph, Times Literary Supplement, various anthologies, BBC Radio 3 and Radio 4; Soc of Authors Gregory Award 1969; memb Soc of Authors 1974; *Books* Suffolk Poems (1975), At the Edge (1977), Carpenters of Light (1979), Out of Time (1979), A Season of Calm Weather (1982), Selected Poems of Fulke Greville (ed, 1990), True Colours: New and Selected Poems (1991), Unreal City (1992), The Stones on Thorpeness Beach (1994), Roy Fuller: Writer and Society (1995), Gay Love Poetry (ed, 1997), The Language of Jazz (1997), Selected Poems (1998), Collected Poems of Donald Davie (ed and introduced, 2002), Collected Poems of Adam Johnson (ed and introduced, 2003), George Crabbe: An English Life (2004), A Halfway House (2004), Amis and Son: Two Literary Generations (2008), Proof of Identity (2012), Benjamin Britten: A Life for Music (2013), Was and Is: Collected Poems (2017); *Style—* Neil Powell, Esq; ✉ c/o United Agents, 12–26 Lexington Street, London W1F 0LE

POWELL, Peter James Barnard; s of James Powell, and Margaret Powell; *b* 24 March 1951, Stourbridge, W Midlands; *Educ* Uppingham; *m* 1990 (m dis); *Career* radio DJ: BBC Radio Birmingham 1970, BBC Radio 1 1972 and 1977–88 (presented all primetime shows on network and recognised as having discovered numerous hit band incl Duran Duran, Spandau Ballet and Culture Club), Radio Luxembourg 1972–77; TV presenter Top of the Pops (BBC), annual coverage of Montreaux Rock Festival, Saturday Night Seaside Special and The Oxford Roadshow 1977–88; fndr and exec chm James Grant Mgmnt Ltd 1984, vice-chm James Grant Gp 2009–12 (non-exec group vice-chm 2012–); mangr of some of the biggest names in the media and entertainment industry incl: Phillip Schofield 1985–, Ant and Dec 1999–, Holly Willoughby, Piers Morgan, Davina McCall, Leigh Francis; dir Bd Formation plc 2008–09; *Recreations* sailing, world travel, politics, music; *Clubs* RORC, RYA, RAC; *Style—* Peter Powell, Esq; ✉ James Grant Group, 94 Strand on the Green, Chiswick, London W4 3NN (☎ 020 8742 4950, fax 020 8742 4951, e-mail peter@jamesgrant.co.uk)

POWELL, Philip B; s of Frank James Powell (d 1987), and Elizabeth Anne, *née* Hamel (d 1977); *b* 3 November 1951, Islington, London; *Educ* Highbury Co GS, LSE, UEA (BA); *m* 1, 10 March 1978 (m dis 1998), Jacqueline Anne, da of Frank Lloyd; 2 s (Matthew Frank b 16 Jan 1982, Christopher James b 22 May 1984), 1 da (Joanne Alice b 4 Jan 1988); m 2, 7 Sept 2007, Catherine Harding, da of John Mayes; *Career* successive positions with Bird's Eye Walls, Iglo Ola (Netherlands) and Lever Brothers (all part of Unilever plc) 1975–83, mktg mangr Colmans of Norwich Reckitt & Colman plc 1983–86, fndr The Marketing House Norwich 1986–88, dir of mktg Goodman Fielder Wattie NZ 1989–91, business devpt mangr Cow & Gate Nutricia 1991–93, mktg dir Office for National Statistics 1994–99, account dir TSO Ltd 2000–03, mktg controller Iceland Foods plc 2003–04, dir Heawood Research Ltd 2004–06, Danone Baby Nutrition 2006–11, managing conlst and interim mangr Marketing Solutions Ltd 1999–; fndr chm Canned Food Info Serv NZ 1990–91; memb: Infant & Diabetic Food Assoc 1991–92, Dissemination Ctee Govt Statistical Serv, EC Statistical Dissemination Working Pty; led EU mission on collaborative dissemination to Ottowa Canada 1996; MCIM; *Publications* Effective Presentation via User Consultation ISI Istanbul 1997, The Dynamics of the Information Market ISI Helsinki 1999; *Recreations* carpentry, history, books, squash, cinema, travelling, cooking, puzzles, quizzes; *Style—* Philip B Powell, Esq; ✉ 297 Southdown Road, Bath BA2 1HR (☎ 01225 344369, mobile 07785 957768, e-mail philip.powell@blueyonder.co.uk or philip@powell.im)

POWELL, Polly Augusta Marchant (Mrs Vaughan Grylls); da of Geoffry Powell (d 1999), and Philippa, *née* Cooper; *b* 1 August 1959; *Educ* Francis Holland Sch London, Univ of Manchester (BA); *m* 1994, Prof Vaughan Grylls, *qv*; 1 da (Hattie b 13 Aug 1992), 1 s (George 2 Oct 1994); *Career* founding publishing dir HarperCollins Illustrated 1998; publishing dir: Cassell Illustrated 2002, Chrysalis Books 2004; dir Anova Books Gp Ltd 2005– (ceo 2009), publisher and owner Pavilion Books 2013–; FRSA; *Recreations* tennis; *Clubs* Quo Vadis; *Style—* Ms Polly Powell; ✉ Pavilion Books Company Ltd, 1 Gower Street, London WC1E 6HD (☎ 020 7605 1400)

POWELL, Robert; *b* 1 June 1944; *Career* actor; *Theatre* incl: repertory Stoke-on-Trent 1964–65, Hamlet (Leeds) 1971, Travesties (RSC) 1975, Terra Nova (Watford) 1982, Private Dick 1982–83, Tovarich (Chichester Festival Theatre, nat tour then Piccadilly Theatre) 1991, Sherlock Holmes – The Musical (Bristol Old Vic and nat tour) 1993, Kind Hearts and Coronets (nat tour) 1998, Single Spies (nat tour) 2002, The Picture of Dorian Gray (nat tour) 2003; *Television* incl: Doomwatch 1969–70, title role in Shelley (BBC film) 1971, Jude the Obscure (BBC series) 1971, Mrs Warren's Profession 1972, Mr Rolls and Mr Royce 1972, Looking for Clancy (serial) 1975, title role in Zeffirelli's Jesus of Nazareth 1976 (Best Actor TV Times and Italian TV Times Awards, Int Arts Prize Fiuggi Film Festival, Grand Prize St Vincent Film Festival Italy), You Never Can Tell (BBC) 1977, The Four Feathers (NBC) 1978, Pygmalion 1981, The Hunchback of Notre Dame (CBS) 1982, Frankenstein (Yorkshire) 1984, Shaka Zulu (series) 1985, Richard Hannay in Hannay (Thames, 2 series) 1987–88, Ambrosius in Merlin and the Crystal Cave (Noel Gay/BBC) 1991, Cortez in The Golden Years (Brook/Channel Four) 1992, DC Dave Briggs in 5 series of The Detectives (BBC series) 1992–97, Mark Williams in Holby City (BBC series); *Films* incl: Secrets 1971, Running Scared 1972, The Asphyx 1972, Asylum 1972, title role in Ken Russell's Mahler 1974, Capt Walker in Ken Russell's Tommy 1975, Beyond Good and Evil 1977, The Thirty-Nine Steps 1978, Harlequin 1980 (Best Actor Paris Film Festival), Jane Austen in Manhattan 1980, The Survivor 1980, Imperative 1981 (Best Actor Venice Film Festival 1982), The Jigsaw Man 1982, What Waits Below 1983, D'Annunzio and I 1986, Down There in the Jungle (Venezuela) 1987, The Sign of Command 1989, The Long Conversation with a Bird 1990, The First Circle 1990, Once on Chunuk Bair 1991, The Mystery of Edwin Drood 1992, Colour Me Kubrick 2004; *Style—* Robert Powell, Esq; ✉ c/o Diamond Management, 31 Percy Street, London W1T 2DD (☎ 020 7631 0400, fax 020 7631 0500)

POWELL, Stephen Joseph; s of Joseph Thomas Powell (d 1958), of Goffs Oak, Herts, and Dorothy May, *née* Welch (d 2000); *b* 26 May 1943; *Educ* Cheshunt GS, The Royal Dental Hosp of London Sch of Dental Surgery (BDS, FDS RCS, MOrth RCS); *m* 6 July 1968, Yvonne Heather, da of Sydney Frederick Williams, of Pucklechurch, Avon; 2 da (Rebecca b 1986, Charlotte b 1991); *Career* sr registrar in orthodontics Hosp for Sick Children Gt Ormond St and The Royal Dental Hosp London 1972–74; conslt in orthodontics: St George's Hosp London 1975–2011, King's Coll Hosp GKT Sch of Med and Dentistry London 1986–; dir: SP Orthodontics Ltd, SCI Powell France; memb: Cncl Soc of St Augustine of Canterbury, BDA, Br Orthodontic Soc, European Orthodontic Soc, American Assoc of Orthodontists, RSM; *Publications* 3 Dimensional Facial Imaging at the Clinical Interface (1999); numerous other papers on therapeutic facial change and measurement; *Recreations* tennis, swimming, music, theatre, French culture; *Clubs* Athenaeum, RSM; *Style—* Stephen Powell, Esq; ✉ 5 Hood Road, Wimbledon, London SW20 0SR (☎ 020 8946 3401); Villa Rodica, 2 Avenue Fernand Martin, 06230 Ville Franche-sur-Mer, France (☎ 00 33 4 93 01 41 93); 2A Barham Road, Wimbledon, London SW20 0EU (☎ 020 8946 3064, mobile 07747 865563, e-mail stephenjpowelll@msn.com); Kings College Hospital Dental Institute, Bessemer Road, London SE5 9RS

POWELL, Timothy Martin (Minnow); s of Arthur Barrington Powell CMG, and Jane, *née* Weir; *b* 17 September 1954; *Educ* Ampleforth, Jesus Coll Oxford (BA); *m* Victoria Elizabeth, da of Peter Geoffrey Holmes; 2 s (Alexander James Barrington b 26 June 1987, Toby Peter Johnathan b 3 Aug 1990); *Career* Touche Ross (now Deloitte & Touche): joined 1976, CA 1979, ptnr 1985–2011; non-exec dir TUI Travel plc 2011–, non-exec dir Supergroup plc 2012–; FCA; *Recreations* golf; *Clubs* Royal Porthcawl Golf, Rye Golf, Royal St Georges Golf, R&A, Royal West Norfolk; *Style—* Minnow Powell, Esq

POWELL OF BAYSWATER, Baron (Life Peer UK 2000), of Canterbury in the County of Kent; Sir Charles David; KCMG (1990); s of Air Vice-Marshal John Frederick Powell, OBE, RAF, and Geraldine Ysolda, *née* Moylan; bro of Jonathan Nicholas Powell, and Sir (John) Christopher Powell, *qqv*; *b* 6 July 1941, Hayward's Heath, Sussex; *Educ* King's Sch Canterbury, New Coll Oxford (BA); *m* 24 Oct 1964, Carla, da of Domingo Bonardi, of Italy; 2 s (Hugh b 1967, Nicholas b 1968); *Career* memb HM Dip Serv, Helsinki, Washington, Bonn and EEC Brussels 1963–83, private sec and advsr on foreign affrs and defence to PM 1983–91 (under-sec 1987); memb House of Lords Select Ctee on the Constitution 2010–15; chm: Sagitta Asset Mgmnt 2001–05, Capital Generation Ptnrs

P

2006–12, Magna Holdgs Int 2006–13; dep chm: Trafalgar House 1994–96, Said Hldgs 1994–2000, Br Mediterranean Airways 1997–2007; dir: Hong Kong Land Hldgs 1991–2000 and 2008–, Matheson & Co 1991–, Mandarin Oriental Hotel Gp 1991–, Louis Vuitton Moet Hennessey SA 1994– (chm LVMH UK 1994–), Caterpillar Inc 2001–13, Textron Inc 2001–, Northern Tst Global Services 2006–14, Northern Tst Corp 2015–; former dir: Jardine Matheson 1991–2000, Nat Westminster Bank 1991–2000 (also chm Int Advsy Bd), Arjo Wiggins Appleton 1992–2000, J Rothschild Name Co 1999–2002; advsr BAe Systems 2006–; chm: Int Advsy Bd Rolls-Royce 2006–, GEMS General & Oriental 2005–13, Bowmark 2008–; memb Int Advsy Bd: Barrick Gold, ACE Insurance, Thales UK, Diligence, US Cncl on Foreign Relations 2012–; pres: Singapore-British Business Cncl 1995–2002, China-Britain Business Cncl 1997–2007, Asia Task Force 2007–14; business ambass 2011–; chm of tstees Oxford Business Sch 1999–; tstee: Aspen Int USA 1994–, Br Museum 1999–2010, Margaret Thatcher Archive Tst 2005–, Int Inst of Strategic Studies 2009–; tstee and chm Br Museum Tst 2011–; hon fell Ashmolean Museum, foundation fell Somerville Coll Oxford; Singapore Public Service Medal 1998; *Recreations* walking; *Clubs* Turf; *Style*— The Rt Hon the Lord Powell of Bayswater, KCMG; ✉ LVMH House, 15 St George Street, London W1S 1FH

POWELL-SMITH, Christopher Brian; s of Edgar Powell-Smith (d 1970), and Theodora Kirkham Baker (d 1984); *b* 3 October 1936; *Educ* City of London Sch, Law Soc's Sch of Law (Travers-Smith scholar, Clements Inn Prize); *m* 1964, Jenny, da of Douglas Goslett; 2 da (Amanda b 1968, Emily b 1972), 2 s (Giles b 1970, Edward b 1975); *Career* Cameron McKenna (formerly McKenna & Co): ptnr 1964–98, managing ptnr 1984–88, head Corp Dept 1988–92, sr ptnr 1992–97; non-exec chm Black & Decker Group Inc 1988– (non-exec dir 1970–), KBC Advanced Technology plc 2004– (non-exec dir 1997–); non-exec dir: Carlsberg Brewery Ltd 1987–92, Martins Printing Gp Ltd 1998–; memb Ctee of Mgmnt Thames Valley Housing Assoc 1995–; TA: cmdg offr HAC 1976–78, regtl Col and master gunner HM Tower of London 1978–80; tstee Richmond Parish Lands Charity 1997–; memb: Law Soc 1959, Int Bar Assoc 1975, City of London Slrs' Co 1987; *Recreations* golf, choral singing, walking; *Clubs* City of London, Brooks's, Royal Mid-Surrey Golf; *Style*— Christopher Powell-Smith, Esq, TD

POWELL-TUCK, Prof Jeremy; s of late Dr Geoffrey Alan Powell-Tuck, and Catherine Gwendoline, *née* Kirby, of Cleeve Hill, Glos; *b* 20 May 1948; *Educ* Epsom Coll, Univ of Birmingham (MB ChB, MD); *m* Fiona Caroline, da of Charles William Sandison Crabbe (d 1969); 1 s (Thomas b 1984), 2 da (Amy b 1987, Rosie b 1988); *Career* research fell St Mark's Hosp 1974–80, research fell Dept of Nutrition London Sch of Hygiene and Tropical Med 1980–81, sr registrar of med and gastroenterology Charing Cross, W Middx and Westminster Hosps 1981–88, head Human Nutrition Unit St Bartholomew's and the Royal London Hosp Sch of Medicine and Dentistry 1988–, conslt physician Bart's and The Royal London Hosp 1988–2008; lead English Nat Intestinal Failure Strategic Framework; emeritus prof of clinical nutrition; contrib chapters on nutritional therapy and gastro-intestinal disease; past memb Cncl Br Assoc for Parenteral and Enteral Nutrition (BAPEN), past chair BAPEN Medical, past chair Br Intestinal Failure Alliance; FRSM 1976, FRCP 1992 (MRCP 1973); *Recreations* choral music, tennis, sailing; *Style*— Prof Jeremy Powell-Tuck; ✉ 9 Horbury Crescent, London W11 3NF (☎ 020 7727 2528)

POWER, Prof Anne; CBE (2000, MBE); *Career* Martin Luther King Southern Christian Leadership Conference 1966, warden Africa Centre London 1966–67, co-ordinator Friends Neighbourhood House 1967–72, co-ordinator North Islington Housing Rights Project 1972–79, nat conslt DOE Priority Estates Project 1979–87, advsr Welsh Office and Rhondda BC 1989–93; LSE: successively academic visitor, visiting research assoc Dept of Social Policy 1981–88, currently professor in social policy; fndr dir Nat Tenants Resource Centre; dep dir Centre for Analysis of Social Exclusion; advsy memb panel of experts to EC on urban problems and social segregation in cities, memb Urban Task Force, cmmr Sustainable Devpt Cmmn, memb Govt Urban and Housing Sounding Bds; *Publications* Property Before People: The Management of Twentieth Century Council Housing (1987), Housing Management – A Guide to Quality and Creativity (1991), Hovels to High-rise – State Housing in Europe since 1850 (1993), Swimming Against the Tide: Polarisation or Progress on 20 Unpopular Council Estates 1980–95 (jtly, 1995), Dangerous Disorder: Riots and Violent Disturbances in Thirteen Areas of Britain 1991–92 (jtly, 1997), Estates on the Edge – The Social Consequences of Mass Housing in Northern Europe (1997), The Slow Death of Great Cities? Urban abandonment or urban renaissance (jtly, 1999), Cities for a Small Country (jtly, 2000), Boom or Abandonment (jtly, 2003), East Enders: Family and community in East London (jtly, 2003), Sustainable Communities and Sustainable Development: A Review of the Sustainable Communities Plan (2004), Jigsaw Cities: Big Places, Small Spaces (jtly, 2007), City Survivors: Bringing up children in disadvantaged areas (2007); also author of numerous governmental reports and articles in the press on social policy and housing issues incl One Size Doesn't Fit All (chair of ind cmmn of inquiry into the future of cncl housing in Birmingham); *Style*— Prof Anne Power, CBE; ✉ Department of Social Policy, London School of Economics and Political Science, Houghton Street, London WC2A 2AE (☎ 020 7955 6330, fax 020 7955 6571, e-mail anne.power@lse.ac.uk)

POWER, Jonathan Richard Adrian; s of Patrick Power (d 1994), of Boars Hill, Oxford, and Dorothy Power (d 1984); *b* 4 June 1941; *Educ* Liverpool Inst HS, Univ of Manchester (BA), Univ of Wisconsin (MA); *m* 1 (m dis 1988), Anne Elizabeth, da of Dennis Hayward, of Southampton; 3 da (Carmen b 18 Jan 1966, Miriam b 23 May 1968, Lucy b 24 Nov 1978); m 2, Jean-Christine, da of Arvid Eklund, of Gothenburg, Sweden; 1 da (Jenny b 25 June 1990); *Career* foreign affrs columnist International Herald Tribune 1974–91, independent foreign affrs columnist 1991– (column syndicated to 16 princ US, Canadian and European papers and 31 African, Asian, Latin American and Australasian papers), commentator on foreign affrs Int Herald Tribune 2003–08; frequent contrib Encounter and Prospect magazines; guest columnist: New York Times, Washington Post, LA Times; interviewer of over 60 world leaders for full-page publication; memb Int Inst for Strategic Studies 1980–2005, memb Common Room Queen Elizabeth House Univ of Oxford 1996–; lectr: Univ of Oxford, Univ of Cape Town, Univ of Lahore, Lund Univ; many TV documentaries for BBC, Granada, Thames and PBS, radio documentaries and talks for BBC Third Programme (Radio 3) and Radio 4; *Film* It's Ours Whatever They Say (Silver Medal Venice Film Festival 1972); *Books* Development Economics, World of Hunger, The New Proletariat, Against Oblivion, Vision of Hope – 50 Years of the United Nations, Like Water on Stone (2001), Conundrums of Humanity – The Big Foreign Policy Questions of Our Age (2013), Conundrums of Humanity – The Big Foreign Policy Questions of Our Day (2013), Ending War Crimes, Chasing the War Criminals (2016); *Recreations* walking, cycling, opera; *Style*— Jonathan Power, Esq; ✉ Adelgatan 6, Lund, Sweden (☎ 00 46 706 510879, e-mail jonatpower@aol.com)

POWERS, Anthony Jonathan William; s of Michael Powers (d 1994), and Frances, *née* Wilson; *b* 13 March 1953; *Educ* Marlborough, The Queen's Coll Oxford (BA), Univ of York (DPhil), private study with Nadia Boulanger; *m* 1984, Helen Frances, da of late Dr C Priday; 1 s (Richard b 1991), 1 da (Camilla b 1993); *Career* lectr in music Dartington Coll of Arts 1978–80, composer in res Southern Arts 1980–82, tutor in composition Univ of Exeter and Dartington Coll of Arts 1983–86, composer in res Univ of Wales Cardiff 1989–; chm Assoc of Professional Composers 1995–97 (memb 1985); *Compositions* incl: Stone, Water, Stars (BBC Symphony Orch) 1987, Horn Concerto (Royal Liverpool Philharmonic Orch) 1990, Cello Concerto (Kings Lynn Festival) 1990, Terrain (BBC Nat Orch of Wales) 1993, Symphony (BBC Nat Orch of Wales, premièred BBC Proms) 1996, Symphony No 2 (BBC Symphony Orch) 1999, A Picture of the World (BBC Singers) 2001, Air and Angels (Three Choirs Festival) 2003; *Style*— Mr Anthony Powers

POWERS, Dr Michael John; QC (1995); s of late Reginald Frederick Powers, of Parkstone, Dorset, and late Kathleen Ruby, *née* Whitmarsh; *b* 9 February 1947, Warwick; *Educ* Poole GS, Middx Hosp Med Sch London (BSc, MB BS, DA), Poly of Central London (Dip Law); *m* 1, 16 Nov 1968 (sep 1989), Meryl Julia, da of late Frank Edward Hall, of Bournemouth, Dorset; 1 da (Julia b 1972), 1 s (Andrew b 1982); m 2, 22 June 2001, Pamela Jean, da of late Ronald Barnes, of Manchester; *Career* registered med practitioner 1972–, house surgn Middx Hosp 1972–73, house physician Royal S Hants Hosp 1973–74, SHO Royal United Hosp Bath 1974–75, registrar (anaesthetics) Northwick Park Hosp Harrow 1975–77; called to the Bar Lincoln's Inn 1979 (bencher 1998), called to the Bar of Trinidad and Tobago 2012; practising at Common Law Bar specialising in med and pharmaceutical law, HM asst dep coroner Westminster 1981–87; pres SE England Coroners Soc 1987–88; students' cnsllr to Hon Soc of Lincoln's Inn 1983–90; Hon LLD Univ of Plymouth 2010; memb: Soc of Doctors in Law, Medico-Legal Soc; fell Faculty of Forensic and Legal Medicine 2007; *Books* The Law and Practice on Coroners (with Paul Knapman 1985), Casebook on Coroners (with Paul Knapman, 1989), Clinical Negligence (with Nigel Harris, 1990, 1994, 2000 and 2008), Sources of Coroners' Law (with Paul Knapman, 1999), Clinical Negligence (5 edn with Anthony Barton, 2015); *Recreations* helicopter pilot, music, photography; *Clubs* RSM (fell); *Style*— Dr Michael Powers, QC; ✉ 2nd Floor, 19 Old Buildings, Lincoln's Inn, London WC2A 3UP (☎ 020 7405 6965); Clerksroom, Equity House, Blackbrook Park Avenue, Taunton TA1 2PX (☎ 0845 083 3000, fax 0845 083 3001, e-mail powersqc@medneg.co.uk, website www.medneg.co.uk)

POWERS-FREELING, Laurel Claire; da of Lloyd Marion Powers, of Bloomfield Hills, Michigan, and Catharine Joyce, *née* Berry (d 1992); *b* 16 May 1957; *Educ* Bloomfield Andover HS Michigan, Barnard Coll Columbia Univ NY (AB), Alfred P Sloan Sch MIT (MS), Universite de Reims (Dip); *m* 28 Jan 1989, Dr Anthony Nigel Stanley Freeling, s of Prof Paul Freeling, OBE; 1 s (Matthew Charles Powers-Freeling b 26 Dec 1991), 1 da (Catharine Grace Powers-Freeling b 1 March 1994); *Career* sr conslt Price Waterhouse Boston and NY 1983–85 (conslt 1980–85), mangr McKinsey & Co Inc London and NY 1987–89 (conslt 1985–87), corp fin offr Morgan Stanley International London 1989–91; Prudential Corporation plc: dir of corp strategy 1991–93, dir of private financial planning servs 1993–94; gp fin dir Lloyds Abbey Life plc 1994–96, md Savings & Investments Lloyds TSB Gp plc 1997–98, dir retail devpt and fin UK Retail Bank Lloyds TSB Gp plc 1998–99, md Wealth Mgmnt Div Lloyds TSB Gp plc 2000–01, chief exec Marks and Spencer Money 2001–05 (bd memb Marks and Spencer plc 2001–04), sr vice-pres and UK country mangr American Express 2005–07, gp ceo Dubai First Int 2007–09; non-exec dir: Bank of England 2002–05, Environmental Resources Mgmnt Ltd 2005–09, Bank of Ireland UK, Findel plc until 2014, ACE European Gp Ltd, Premium Credit Limit; dir C Hoare & Co 2011–, memb Bd Call Credit Data System 2014–; govr Royal Acad of Music; *Recreations* classical music, needlework, cookery, wine; *Style*— Mrs Laurel Powers-Freeling

POWLES, Prof Raymond Leonard; CBE (2003); s of Leonard William David Powles (d 1989), and Florence Irene, *née* Conolly; *b* 9 March 1938; *Educ* Eltham Coll, Bart's Med Sch London (BSc, MB BS, MD); *m* 1980, Louise Jane, da of Roy Frederick Richmond; 3 s (Sam Tristan Richmond, Luke Alexander Richmond (twins) b 2 Feb 1982, Max Ashley Richmond b 30 May 1989), 1 da (Gabriella Louise b 12 April 1985); *Career* house physician Bart's London 1965–66, resident med offr Royal Marsden Hosp London 1967–68, Leukaemia Fund fell to Prof George Mathe Ville Juif Paris 1968, Tata Meml Fund leukaemia fell Royal Marsden Hosp and Inst of Cancer Res Sutton Surrey 1969–72, ICRF sr scientific offr Bart's 1972–74, conslt and head Leukaemia and Myeloma Units Royal Marsden Hosp 1974–2003; recognised teacher Univ of London 1977–, clinical tutor RCP 1990–, currently head Leukaemia and Myeloma Unit Parkside Cancer Clinic Wimbledon and Univ of London emeritus prof of haematological oncology ICR; invited lectures throughout world on leukaemia res and treatment, author of over 1200 scientific papers and book chapters on leukaemia; lifetime achievement award CPAA, India; chm Nuclear Accident Sub-Ctee EBMT, chm Scientific Ctee on Haemoportic Growth Factors American Soc of Haematology; dir: Biopartners GmbH, Myogenic Biotech Ltd; variously memb: Cancer Patient Aid Assoc, Royal Marsden Special HA, MRC Working Pty on Leukaemia, UK Cancer Co-Ordinating Sub-Ctee on Leukaemia and Bone Marrow Transplantation (UKCCCR), Dept of Health Standing Med Advsy Sub-Ctee on Cancer, Br Assoc for Cancer Res, American Cancer Soc Sci Writers' Alumni, Euro Bone Marrow Transplantation Soc Working Pty for Leukaemia, Int Bone Marrow Transplant Registry Advsy Ctee, WHO Ctee Int Prog of Leukaemia Effects of the Chernobyl Accident, EORTC Anti-Fungal Ctee, SW Thames Regional Negotiating Team (Drugs and Supplies), London Bone Marrow Transplant Gp, Bd New Health Network (also tstee), Dept of Health Ind Reconfiguration Panel, Dept of Health Perceptions of the NHS Panel (also co-ordinator), Healthcare Inspections Advsy Team Cabinet Office Public Sector Team; sometime hon conslt CEGB; med advsr: The Bud Flanagan Leukaemia Fund, Leukaemia Soc of Ireland; specialist leukaemia advsr to BACUP; variously memb Editorial Bd: Leukaemia Research, Bone Marrow Transplantation, Indian Jl of Cancer Chemotherapy, Indian Jl of Med and Paediatric Oncology, Experimental Haematology; memb Int Advsy Panel: for virus infections Wellcome Ltd, on fungus infections Pfizer Ltd, on leukaemia Pharmitalia Carlo Erba Ltd; memb: Bd Euro Soc for Med Oncology, Euro Bone Marrow Transplantation Soc, Int Soc for Experimental Haematology, Int Transplantation Soc, American Soc of Haematology, Int Immunocompromised Host Soc, Euro Haematology Assoc, Br Soc of Haematology, Br Transplantation Soc, Assoc of Cancer Physicians, Br Soc of Pharmaceutical Med, Br Acad of Forensic Scis, BMA; FRCP 1980, FRCPath 1993; *Recreations* sport, cinema, cooking; *Style*— Prof Raymond Powles, CBE; ✉ Little Garratts, 19 Garratts Lane, Banstead, Surrey SM7 2EA (☎ 01737 353632); Parkside Cancer Clinic, 49 Parkside, Wimbledon SW19 5NB (☎ 020 8944 7979, fax 020 8605 9103, e-mail myeloma@clara.co.uk)

POWLES, His Hon Stephen Robert; QC (1995); s of Andrew Frederick Arthur Powles, and Nora, *née* Bristol; *b* 7 June 1948; *Educ* Westminster, UC Oxford (MA); *m* 12 April 1975, Geraldine Patricia Hilda, da of Dr Campbell Millar Taggart Adamson; 1 s (Henry b 1979), 1 da (Olivia b 1981); *Career* called to the Bar: Middle Temple 1972 (Harmsworth maj exhibitioner, Astbury law scholar), Lincoln's Inn 1976; recorder of the Crown Court 1994–2005, circuit judge (SE Circuit) 2005–2014, ret; memb Panel of Tbnl Membs Accountancy Investigation and Discipline Bd 2004–; registered mediator CEDR, ACI, ADR Chambers (alternative dispute resolution gp), Railway Industry Dispute Resolution (RIDR), ResoLex; CIMechE; *Recreations* sailing, hill walking, joinery, my border terrier; *Clubs* Royal Solent Yacht; *Style*— His Hon Stephen Powles, QC; ✉ Henderson Chambers, 2 Harcourt Buildings, Middle Temple Lane, Temple, London EC4Y 9DB (☎ 020 7583 9020, fax 020 7583 2686, e-mail spowles@hendersonchambers.co.uk)

POWLES, Prof Trevor James; CBE (2003); s of Leonard William David Powles (d 1989), and Florence Irene, *née* Conolly; *b* 8 March 1938; *Educ* Eltham Coll, Bart's Med Coll (BSc, MB BS, PhD); *m* Penelope Margaret, da of Walter and Doreen Meyers, of Durban, South Africa; 2 s (James Watson b 19 Dec 1969, Thomas Bartholomew b 10 April 1971), 1 da (Lucy Alexandra b 31 Jan 1975); *Career* house physician and registrar Royal Postgrad Med Sch Hammersmith Hosp 1967–68, med registrar Bart's 1969–70, MRC clinical res fell Inst of Cancer Res London 1971–73; Royal Marsden Hosp London and Sutton: sr registrar and lectr 1974, sr lectr 1974–78, conslt physician 1978–2003, head

Breast Cancer Unit 1994–2003, med dir Common Tumours Div 2000–03; prof of breast oncolgy Inst of Cancer Research London 1998–2003 (emertitus prof 2003–); conslt med oncologist (breast cancer): Parkside Hosp Wimbledon 2003–, Lister Hosp London 2003–, St Anthony's Hosp Cheam 2003–, Harley St Clinic London 2005–07; medical dir Cancer Centre London at Parkside 2010–; visiting prof: MD Anderson Cancer Centre Houston USA 1993, Dana Faber Cancer Center Harvard 1996, Tom Baker Cancer Centre Calgary Canada 1998; memb Scientific Advsy Bd Breakthrough Breast Cancer until 2015; invited lectures throughout world on various aspects of breast cancer biology, diagnosis and treatment; McGuire Lectureship An Antonio 2000, All Parties Parly Award for Outstanding Achievement in Breast Cancer 2003, Brinker Award Susan Komen Fndn 2005; tstee Breast Cancer Res Tst, tstee Breakthrough Breast Cancer until 2015, vice-chm Breast Cancer Now 2015–; patron Breast Cancer Care; memb: Br Breast Gp, Assoc of Cancer Physicians, Int Soc for Cancer Prevention (vice-pres 1996–2009), Euro Soc for Med Oncology, American Soc of Clinical Oncology, Br Assoc of Cancer Research; FRCP 1983; *Books* Breast Cancer Management (jtly, 1981), Prostaglandins and Cancer (jtly, 1982), Medical Management of Breast Cancer (jtly, 1991); 365 peer-reviewed pubns in scientific jls; *Recreations* golf, fishing, skiing, reading, horse riding; *Clubs* RAC; *Style*— Prof Trevor Powles, CBE; ✉ Cancer Centre London, 49 Parkside, Wimbledon, London SW19 5NB (☎ 020 8247 3384)

POWNALL, David; *b* Liverpool; *Educ* Keele Univ; *Career* playwright and novelist; worked in motor industry and Zambian copper mining industry; former dramatist in residence: Century Theatre, Duke's Playhouse Lancaster; co-fndr Paines Plough Theatre Co; Hon DLitt Keele Univ 2000; FRSL 1976; *Awards* incl: John Whiting Prize (for Beef), Best Foreign Play on Broadway New York Theatre Yearbook, LS Directors' Award (for Livingstone and Sechele), nomination Best Play Plays and Players 1984, LA Drama Desk Awards 1988 (for Master Class), Giles Cooper Award for Radio Drama (twice), Sony Award (gold award, two silver awards), Best Radio Play Writers' Guild Award 2013; *Stage Plays* incl: Richard III, Motocar, Music to Murder By, An Audience Called Edouard, Beef, Livingstone and Sechele, Master Class, Elgar's Rondo, Getting the Picture, Death of a Faun; *Radio Plays* incl: Butterfingers, Flos, Pound on Mr Greenhill, Elgar's Third; *Publications* The Composer Plays: Master Class, Elgar's Rondo, Elgar's Third, Music to Murder By (collection, 1996), Plays One and Two and Seven Other Titles (collection), Writing Master Class (2013); author of 13 novels and a collection of short stories; *Style*— David Pownall, Esq, FRSL

POWNER, Prof Edwin Thomas (Eddie); s of Thomas Powner (d 1989), of Stoke on Trent, and Evelyn, *née* King; *b* 22 April 1938; *Educ* Univ of Durham (BSc), Univ of Manchester (MSc, PhD); *m* 8 Sept 1962, Barbara, da of William Henry Turner (d 1963), of Stoke on Trent; 2 s (Stephen John b 25 Dec 1966 d 13 March 1987, Peter David b 30 May 1972), 1 da (Suzanne b 18 March 1969); *Career* UMIST: electronics engr 1960–63, lectr 1963–74, sr lectr 1974–79, reader 1979–80, prof of electronic engrg 1980–92, vice-princ and pro-vice-chllr 1986–88, dean of technol 1989–92; Univ of Sussex: prof of electronic engrg 1992–, dean of engrg 1996–99, head of electronics, communication and electrical engrg; author of numerous tech pubns; Inst of Nat Electrical Engrs: past memb Cncl, chm Library Ctee, memb Professional Bd, memb Qualifications Bd, memb Accreditation Bd, local chm NW Centre 1988–89, memb Scholarships and Prizes Ctee; memb PHEE (Profs and Heads of Electrical Engrg Sectoral Gp Engrg Cncl); CEng, FIEE 1987 (MIEE 1965); *Books* Digital Simulation (jtly), Digital Signal Processing (jtly); *Recreations* photography, mechanisms and clocks, railways; *Style*— Prof Eddie Powner; ✉ School of Engineering and Design, University of Sussex, Falmer, Brighton BN1 9QT (☎ 01273 678586, fax 01273 678399, e-mail e.t.powner@sussex.ac.uk)

POWNER, John; s of John Reginald Powner, of Kensington, London, and Jean, *née* McLeish; *b* 18 May 1962; *Educ* The Campion GS Hornchurch, Southend Coll, Univ of Brighton (BA); *Career* graphic designer; designer Mitchell Beazley Publishing 1984–85, sr designer Pentagram Design 1986–91; fndr Atelier Works Design Consultancy 1991–2013, clients incl: Waterstone's, Waitrose, Orange, Polaroid, City of Sheffield, DCMS, English Heritage, Somerset House; ind design conslt 2013–; awards incl: Golden Grammia (packaging), LAOS Award (typography), D&AD Best of the Year, Design Week Awards commendation; *Publications* Works (1995), Howdah (2001); *Recreations* vintage motorcycles; *Clubs* D&AD, VMCC, Brough Superior; *Style*— John Powner, Esq; ✉ e-mail pownerjohn@gmail.com, website www.aterlierworks.co.uk

POYNTER, Kieran Charles; s of Kenneth Reginald Poynter (d 2009), and Catherine Elizabeth, *née* Reilley; *b* 20 August 1950, London; *Educ* Salesian Coll, Imperial Coll London (BSc, ARCS); *m* 20 Aug 1977, Marylyn, da of Cmdt Thomas Melvin (d 1969), of Athlone, Ireland; 3 s (Dominic b 1979, Benedict b 1980, Andrew b 1983), 1 da (Louise b 1981); *Career* CA 1974; PricewaterhouseCoopers LLP (formerly Price Waterhouse before merger): joined 1971, ptnr 1982, responsible for servs to insurance sector in UK 1983–94 and in Europe 1989–94, sr client ptnr 1993–98, memb Price Waterhouse World Firm Insurance Group 1986–94, memb Euro Supervisory Bd 1993–98, memb Exec 1994–98, managing ptnr 1996–2000, memb Global Bd 1997–98, memb UK Mgmnt Bd 1998–2008, chm and sr ptnr 2000–08; dir: DigitalTheatre.tv Ltd 2009–12, F&C Asset Mgmnt plc 2009– (chm 2013–), Nomura International plc 2009–15 (chm 2011–15), Br American Tobacco plc 2010–, Int Airlines Gp SA 2010–; memb: Insurance Ctee ICAEW 1983–95, Standing Inter-Professional Liaison Gp Accounting and Actuarial Professions 1987–97, Accounting and Auditing Standards Ctee Lloyd's of London 1988–90, Life Insurance Accounting Ctee ABI 1992–94, HM Govt Task Force on Deregulation of Fin Servs Sector 1993–94, Solvency and Reporting Ctee at Lloyd's 1994–96, Disputes Resolution Panel at Lloyd's 1996–98, Cncl for Industry and HE 1998–2008, PricewaterhouseCoopers Global Supervisory Bd 1998–2000, PricewaterhouseCoopers Global Leadership Team 2000–08, Steering Ctee Heart of the City 2000–14, President's Ctee CBI 2001–08, Cncl Prince of Wales Int Business Leaders Forum 2001–13, Transatlantic Cncl British American Business Inc 2001–08, Cncl NIESR 2004–13, IPPR Task Force on Ethnic Diversity in the Private Sector 2004, President's Ctee London First 2006–08, Pres's Gp Employers' Forum on Disability 2006, Chancellor's Financial Services Global Competitiveness Gp 2008–09; chm Gooda Walker Loss Review Ctee at Lloyd's 1991–92, chm Syndicate 387 Loss Review at Lloyd's 1992–93; dir Royal Automobile Club Ltd 2007–13; tstee: Industry in Educn 1999–2008, Royal Anniversary Tst 2007–16 (chm 2010–16); FCA 1979, FRSA 1994, KHS 1999; *Recreations* golf, shooting, watching sport; *Clubs* RAC, Brooks's; *Style*— Kieran Poynter, Esq; ✉ 15 Montpelier Mews , London SW7 1HB (☎ 020 7581 5812, mobile 07715 376784, e-mail kieranp@aol.com)

POYNTON, Malcolm; s of Norman Albert Pointon, and Jocelyn Margaret, *née* MacDonald; *b* 25 December 1966, NZ; *Educ* Auckland Univ; *m* 6 May 1998, Lisa, *née* Harriden; 1 da (Eden Odile b 1 Sept 2003); *Career* jr creative: Gurney Nagle Advtg Auckland 1985, HKM Advtg Auckland 1986, BBDO London 1989; writer HKM/Rialto Auckland 1989, art dir Omon Sydney 1990, founding ptnr and creative dir Green Girl Publishing Sydney 1993, sr creative The Campaign Palace Sydney, Melbourne and Auckland 1993, dep creative dir M&C Saatchi London 1995, exec creative dir Saatchi & Saatchi Sydney 2000, exec creative dir Ogilvy London 2003; more than 40 int advtg awards incl Gold award Cannes 1999, 2000, 2001, 2005, 2007, 2010, 2012, 2013, 2014 and 2016 (Silver 2000, 2001, 2005, 2006, 2007, 2013, 2015 and 2016, Bronze 1991, 1998, 2000, 2001, 2004, 2005, 2006, 2007, 2008, 2010, 2011, 2012, 2013, 2014, 2015 and 2016); memb D&AD, academy memb IADAS (Int Acad of Digital Awards and Sciences), patron RA; keynote speaker and jury pres London Int Awards, Clio Awards and Cannes Festival of Creativity; patron CALM (Campaign Against Living Miserably) UK; memb NZ yachting team 1984–85, memb Aust yachting team 1991, hon coach NZ Yachting Fedn; *Recreations* yachting, snowboarding, flyfishing, outdoor pursuits; *Clubs* Soho House, Union; *Style*— Malcolm Poynton, Esq; ✉ Cheil Worldwide, The Crane Building, 22 Lavington Street, London SE1 0NZ (☎ 020 7593 9300, e-mail malc@cheil.com)

POYSER, Dr Norman Leslie; s of George Clifford Poyser (d 1987), and Marjorie Ellis, *née* Knight (d 1982); *b* 9 August 1947; *Educ* High Pavement GS Nottingham, Sch of Pharmacy Univ of London (BPharm), Univ of Edinburgh (PhD, DSc, Sandoz prize); *m* 1, 1976, Valerie Lesley (d 1985), da of Dr James Rennie Whitehead; 1 s (Timothy James), 1 da (Natalie Claire); m 2, 1990, Moira Anderson Scott; 2 step da (Carolyn Scott, Beverley Begley); *Career* Univ of Edinburgh: ICI research fell 1971–73, MRC research fell 1973–75, lectr 1975–87, sr lectr 1987–, head Dept of Pharmacology 1995–98; memb: Soc for Endocrinology 1972, Br Pharmacological Soc 1974, Soc for Reproduction and Fertility 1975; *Publications* Prostaglandins in Reproduction (1981); numerous pubns incl original articles, contribs to books and review articles; *Recreations* tennis, bridge, golf, theatre-going, concert-going, watching sport on TV; *Clubs* Colinton Lawn Tennis (Edinburgh), Merchants of Edinburgh Golf, Dunbar Golf; *Style*— Dr Norman Poyser; ✉ University of Edinburgh, Hugh Robson Building, George Square, Edinburgh EH8 9XD (☎ 0131 651 1692, fax 0131 650 3711, mobile 07726 889885, e-mail norman.poyser@ed.ac.uk)

PRAG, Prof (Andrew) John Nicholas Warburg; s of Adolf Prag (d 2004), and Dr Frede Charlotte Prag, *née* Warburg (d 2004); *b* 28 August 1941, Oxford; *Educ* Westminster, BNC Oxford (Domus exhibitioner, hon scholar, MA, Dip Classical Archaeology, sr Hulme scholar, DPhil); *m* 5 July 1969, Dr Kay Prag, da of Douglas James Wright (d 1979), of Sydney, NSW; 1 s (Jonathan Ralph Warburg b 1975), 1 da (Kate Susannah b 1977); *Career* temp asst keeper Dept of Antiquities Ashmolean Museum Oxford 1966–67; Univ of Manchester: keeper of archaeology Manchester Museum 1969–2004, sr lectr 1977, hon lectr Dept of History 1977–83, hon lectr in archaeology 1984–2005, hon res fell Sch of History and Classics 2002–05, reader in classics and ancient history 2002–04, prof of archaeological studies 2004–05, prof emeritus of classics 2005–; hon prof Manchester Museum 2005–; visiting prof Dept of Classics McMaster Univ Hamilton Ontario 1978; memb Advsy Cncl Inst of Classical Studies Univ of London 2009–15; ed Archaeological Reports 1975–87, visiting fell British Sch at Athens 1994; family rep Advsy Bd Warburg Inst Univ of London; FSA 1977; *Books* The Oresteia: Iconographic & Narrative Tradition (1985), Making Faces Using Forensic and Archaeological Evidence (with Richard Neave, 1997, 2 edn 1999), Periplous: Papers on Classical Art and Archaeology Presented to Sir John Boardman (ed with G R Tsetskhladze and A M Snodgrass, 2000), Seianti Hanunia Tlesnasa: The Story of an Etruscan Noblewoman (with J Swaddling, 2002), The Archaeology of Alderley Edge (with Simon Timberlake, 2005), The Story of Alderley: Living with the Edge (ed and contrib, 2016); *Recreations* music, cooking, travel; *Style*— Prof A J N W Prag, FSA; ✉ The Manchester Museum, The University of Manchester, Manchester M13 9PL (e-mail john.prag@manchester.ac.uk)

PRAG, Thomas Gregory Andrew; s of Adolf Prag, of Frankfurt, and Frede Charlotte, *née* Warburg; *b* 2 January 1947; *Educ* Westminster, BNC Oxford (MA); *m* 4 April 1971, Angela Mary, da of late Leslie Hughes; 3 s (Benjamin David b 18 Nov 1972, Henry John b 17 Feb 1975, Nicholas Timothy b 18 Nov 1977); *Career* studio mangr BBC Radio Bush House 1968–70, BBC Radio Oxford 1970–78, prog organiser BBC Highland Inverness 1978–81, md and prog controller Moray Firth Radio 1981–2001 (chm 2000–01), memb for Scot Radio Authy 2001–03, chm Media Support Solutions 2001–; memb Highland Cncl 2007– (chm planning devpt and infrastructure 2012–), former pres Inverness C of C, former chm Highland Festival, fndr and sec Moray Firth Radio Charity Tst 1983–2008, former memb Bd of Govrs UHI Millennium Inst, former memb Bd Inverness Harbour Tst, memb Bd Inverness Airport Business Park, memb Bd of Govrs Eden Court Theatre 2007–; FIMgt, fell Radio Academy 1998; *Recreations* home and family, elderly Daimler convertible, novice golfer, gardening to feed marauding deer, rusty tenor in the choral society and back seat fiddler with the Truly Terrible Orchestra; *Clubs* Inverness Rotary, Royal Overseas League; *Style*— Thomas Prag, Esq; ✉ Windrush, Easter Muckovie, Inverness IV2 5BN (☎ 01463 791697, e-mail thomas@prags.co.uk)

PRAGNELL, Michael; s of George Pragnell, and Margaret, *née* Lowry; *b* 1946; *Educ* Douai Sch, St John's Coll Oxford (MA), INSEAD Fontainebleau (MBA); *m* 1983, Susan Williams; 2 s; *Career* Courtaulds Ltd 1968–72, Courtaulds N America Inc 1972–74, First National Bank of Chicago 1974–75; Courtaulds plc 1975–95: ceo Coatings 1986–92, dir 1990–95, chief fin offr 1992–94; ceo Zeneca Agrochemicals 1995–2000, dir Zeneca Group plc (later AstraZeneca plc) 1997–2000, fndr ceo and dir Syngenta AG Switzerland 2000–07; memb Supervisory Bd Advanta BV 1996–2000; non-exec dir: D S Smith plc 1996–2000, Vinci SA Paris 2009–; pres Crop Life International 2002–05; memb Swiss-American Bd Chamber of Commerce 2005–07; memb Bd INSEAD 2009–; chm of tstees Cancer Research UK 2010–; *Recreations* skiing, walking, shooting, theatre, opera, music, modern art, travel; *Style*— Michael Pragnell, Esq; ☎ 07789 986109, e-mail michael@pragnell.org

PRANCE, Prof Sir Ghillean (Iain) Tolmie; kt (1995); s of Basil Camden Prance, CIE, OBE (d 1947), and Margaret Hope, *née* Tolmie (d 1970); *b* 13 July 1937; *Educ* Malvern Coll, Univ of Oxford (MA, DPhil); *m* 13 July 1961, Anne Elizabeth, da of Rev Archibald MacAlister Hay (d 1980); 2 da (Rachel b 1963, Sarah b 1966); *Career* NY Botanical Gardens: res asst 1963–68, BA Krukoff curator Amazonian Botany 1968–75, dir res 1975–81, vice-pres 1977–81, sr vice-pres 1981–88, dir Inst Econ Botany 1981–88; adjunct prof City Univ NY 1968–99; ldr Amazonian Exploration Prog 1965–88; dir Royal Botanic Gardens Kew 1988–99, dir of science The Eden Project 1998–2012; visiting prof: tropical studies Yale Univ 1983–88, Univ of Reading 1988–; McBryde prof US Nat Tropical Botanical Garden Hawaii 2000–02 (sr fell 2003–); author of numerous papers and books; memb Bd of Dirs: Margaret Mee Amazon Tst 1988–98, Lovaine Tst 1989–99, Royal Botanic Gardens Kew Fndn 1990–99; exec dir Orgn Flora Neotropica (UNESCO) 1975–88, memb Mayor's Cmmn on Cable TV White Plains NY 1981–88, chm Advsy Ctee Sustainable Forestry Mgmnt Ltd 2006–09, chm A Rocha Int 2008–14; pres: Int Tree Fndn 2005–, Nature in Art 2010–; chm Mass Extinction Meml Observatory (MEMO) 2009–; tstee: Au Sable Inst of Environmental Studies 1984–2006, WWF 1989–93, Horniman Museum 1990–99, World Humanities Action Tst 1994–99, New Island Tst 1995–2009, Global Diversity Fndn 1999–2010 (chm), Brazilian Atlantic Rainforest Tst (chm), Exbury Garden Tst 2001–, Eden Tst 2009–; patron: Bioregional Devpt Gp 1995–, Sheffield Botanic Gardens Tst 1997–, Serra do Mar Reserva Ecologica (now Reserva Ecologica Guapi-açú) Brazil 1997–, Soc of Botanical Artists 1997–; International Cosmos prize 1993, Patrons Medal RGS 1994, Asa Gray Award American Soc of Plant Taxonomists 1998, Lifetime of Discovery Award RGS 1999, Fairchild Medal for Plant Exploration 2000, Distinguished Economic Botanist Award of Soc Econ Botany 2002, Allerton Award US Nat Tropical Botanical Garden 2005, Gold Medal NY Botanical Garden 2008; Dr (hc) Göteborgs Univ 1983; DSc (hc): Univ of Kent 1994, Portsmouth Univ 1994, Kingston Univ 1994, Univ of St Andrews 1995, Bergen Univ Norway 1996, Sheffield Univ 1997, Florida Int Univ 1997, Lehman Coll City Univ NY 1998, Univ of Liverpool 1998, Glasgow Univ 1999, Univ of Plymouth 1999, Keele Univ 2000, Univ of Exeter 2000, Univ of Glos 2009; hon fell Royal Botanic Garden Edinburgh 1995, hon research fell Royal Botanic Gardens Kew 1999, hon fell Assoc of Tropical Biology and Conservation 2007; FLS 1963, FRGS 1989, FRS 1993; fell AAAS 1990, assoc fell Third World Acad of Science 1993, fell Perak Acad of Science 2006; VMH, RHS 1999; foreign memb Royal Danish Acad Scis and Letters 1988, corr memb Brazilian Acad of Scis 1976, foreign memb Royal Swedish Acad Sci 1989;

P

Comendador Ordem Nacional do Cruzeiro do Sul (Brazil) 2000, Order of the Rising Sun Gold Rays with Neck Ribbon (Japan) 2012; *Books* Arvores De Manaus (1975), Extinction Is Forever (1977), Biological Diversification in the Tropics (1981), Leaves (1986), Amazonia (1985), Wild Flowers for all Seasons (1988), White Gold (1989), Out of the Amazon (1992), Bark (1993), The Earth Under Threat (1996), Rainforests of the World (1998), Rainforest: Light and Spirit (2008), Go to the Ant (2013), That Glorious Forest (2014); *Recreations* music; *Clubs* Explorers' (fell 1978); *Style*— Prof Sir Ghillean Prance, FRS; ✉ The Old Vicarage, Silver Street, Lyme Regis, Dorset DT7 3HS (☎ 01297 444991, e-mail siriain01@yahoo.co.uk)

PRASAD, Alfred Patrick; s of Dr Sreenivasan Rama Prasad, and Vincenza Prasad; *b* 4 December 1972, Wardha, India; *Educ* Inst of Hotel Mgmnt Madras; *m* 26 Oct 2007, Sunita Panjabi; *Career* chef; advanced chef training Maurya Sheraton Delhi, trained at Bukhara Delhi and Dum-Pukht Delhi, chef Dakshin ITC Sheraton Hotel Madras 1996–99, sous chef Veeraswamy London 1999–2001, exec chef Tamarind London 2002–12 (joined 2001, Michelin Star 2001–09 and 2011 14), dir of cuisine and exec chef Tamarind Collection 2013–14 (Tamarind Mayfair, Imli St Soho, Zaika, Kensington, Tamarind of London Newport Beach Calif); conducts regular masterclass and demonstrations at Divertimenti Cookery Sch and several food and community festivals in Switzerland, Bahrain, Mauritius, Sri Lanka and Italy, currently working on first ind restaurant and first book; founding memb Jeunes Restaurateurs Europe (JRE) UK, memb Slow Food UK, campaigner for food-based charities incl Action Against Hunger UK, Food Cycle and Akshaya Patra UK; *Recreations* travel, photography, tennis, badminton, guitar, basketball; *Style*— Alfred Patrick Prasad, Esq; ✉ 59 Wood Lane, Isleworth, London TW7 5EG (☎ 020 3605 1050, mobile 07787 542827, e-mail alfred@alfredprasad.com, website www.alfredprasad.com)

PRASAD, Dr Sunand; s of Devi Prasad, and Janaki Prasad; *b* 22 May 1950, Dehra Dun, India; *Educ* Univ of Cambridge, AA, RCA (PhD); *Career* architect; ptnr Edward Cullinan Architects 1978–84, co-fndr and sr ptnr Penoyre & Prasad 1988–; cmmr for architecture and the built environment 1996–2006, built environment expert Design Cncl 2012–; memb Mayor of London's Fourth Plinth Commissioning Gp 2004–10, pres RIBA 2007–09 (cncllr 2004–07), memb Mayor's Design Advsy Panel for London 2012–; chm Article 25, pres Architects' Benevolent Soc 2011–15; tstee: Centre for Cities 2010–14, Cape Farewell 2011–15, UK Green Building Cncl 2016–; hon doctor of art Univ of East London 2009; hon fell RAIS 2008, hon memb RTPI 2009, hon fell RAIC 2010, hon memb AIA; FCARM Presidential Medal Fedn of Mexican Architects 2009; *Publications* essay in Le Corbusier: Architect of the Century (1987), entry in Encyclopaedia of Vernacular Architecture (1997), entries in Macmillan Dictionary of Art (1997), Accommodating Diversity – a guide to the design of housing for minority ethnic, religious and cultural groups (1998), A Tale of Two Cities in Paradigms of Indian Architecture (ed GHR Tillotson, 1998), Inclusive Maps – Designing Better Buildings (ed Sebastian Macmillan, 2004), Transformations (2007), Changing Hospital Architecture (ed, 2008), Retrofit for Purpose (2014); *Recreations* cinema, music, reading, cycling, travel, walking, photography; *Style*— Dr Sunand Prasad; ✉ Penoyre & Prasad Architects, 28–42 Banner Street, London EC1Y 8QE

PRASHAR, Baroness (Life Peer UK 1999), of Runnymede in the County of Surrey; Usha Prashar; CBE (1995), PC (2009); *b* 29 June 1948; *Educ* Wakefield Girls' HS, Univ of Leeds (BA), Univ of Glasgow (Dip Social Admin); *m* 21 July 1973, Vijay Sharma; *Career* conciliation offr Race Rels Bd 1971–76, dir Runnymede Tst 1976–84, research fell Policy Studies Inst 1984–86, dir Nat Cncl for Voluntary Orgn 1986–91, chm The Parole Bd 1997–2000, First Civil Serv Cmmr 2000–05 (pt/t Civil Serv cmmr 1990–96), chair Judicial Appts Cmmn 2005–10; non-exec dir: Channel Four Television Corporation 1992–99, Unite Gp plc 2001–04, ITV plc 2005–10; visiting prof Univ of Exeter; memb: Arts Cncl of GB 1979–81 and 1994–97, Study Cmmn on the Family 1980–83, Social Security Advsy Ctee 1980–83, Exec Ctee Child Poverty Action Gp 1984–85, Gtr London Arts Assoc 1984–86, London Food Cmmn 1984–90, BBC Educnl Broadcasting Cncl 1987–88, Advsy Cncl Open Coll 1987–88, Elfrida Rathbone Soc 1988–91, Slrs' Complaints Bureau 1989–91, Lord Chllr's Advsy Ctee on Legal Educn 1991–97, Royal Cmmn on Criminal Justice 1991–93, Bd Energy Saving Tst 1992–97, Ealing Hounslow and Hammersmith HA 1993–96, Bd Salzburg Seminar 2000–04, House of Lords and House of Commons Jt Ctee on Human Rights 2001–04 and 2008–09, Iraq Inquiry 2009–; vice-pres Cncl for Overseas Student Affrs 1986–91, vice-chm Br Refugee Cncl 1987–90, chm English Advsy Ctee Nat AIDS Tst 1988–89, vice-pres Patients' Assoc 1990–91, pres Community Fndns Network, pres UK's Cncl for Int Student Affrs, pres Nat Literacy Tst 2011– (dep chm 1992–2000, chm 2000–05), dep chair Br Cncl 2012–; patron: Tara Arts, Runnymede Tst; tstee: Thames Help Tst 1984–86, Charities Aid Fndn 1986–91, Independent Broadcasting Telethon Tst 1987–93, Camelot Fndn 1996–2001, BBC World Service Tst 2001–05, Miriam Rothschild and John Foster 2007–10, Cumberland Lodge 2007, Runnymede Tst 2008; govr Ditchley Fndn 2003; memb Cncl Royal Holloway Coll London 1992–97, chllr De Montfort Univ 2000–06 (govr 1996–2006); hon fell Goldsmiths Coll London 1992; Hon LLD: De Montfort Univ, South Bank Univ, Univ of Greenwich 1998, Leeds Metropolitan Univ 1999, Univ of Exeter, Univ of Leeds, Aston Univ; FRSA 1989; *Books* contrib to: Britain's Black Population (1980), The System – A Study of Lambeth Borough Council's Race Relations Unit (1981), Scarman and After (1984), Sickle Cell Anaemia Who Cares? A Survey of Screening Counselling Training and Educational Facilities in England (1985), Routes or Road Blocks – A Study of Consultation Arrangements Between Local Authorities and Local Communities (1985), Acheson and After – Primary Health Care in the Inner City (1986); *Recreations* country walks, golf, music, reading, the arts; *Clubs* Royal Cwlth Soc; *Style*— The Rt Hon the Baroness Prashar, CBE; ✉ House of Lords, London SW1A 0PW

PRATLEY, David Illingworth; s of Arthur George Pratley, of Dorset, and Olive Constance, *née* Illingworth; *b* 24 December 1948; *Educ* Westminster, Univ of Bristol (LLB); *m* 1, 1996, Caryn Lois Faure Walker (d 2004); m 2, Diane Linda Fredericks; *Career* PR offr Thorndike Theatre Leatherhead 1970–71, press and publicity offr Queen's Univ Belfast 1971–72, dep dir Merseyside Arts Assoc 1972–76, dir Gtr London Arts Assoc 1976–81, regnl dir Arts Cncl of GB 1981–86, chm Dance Umbrella Ltd 1986–92, chief exec Royal Liverpool Philharmonic Soc 1987–88, md Trinity Coll of Music 1988–91, chm Nat Campaign for the Arts 1988–92, dir of leisure, tourism and economic devpt Bath City Cncl 1992–96, lottery policy advsr Arts Cncl of England 1996–; ptnr David Pratley Associates 1996–2015; chm: Lighthouse Poole 2009–16, Wilts Music Centre 2009–2015; *Recreations* arts, travel, gardens, countryside; *Style*— David Pratley, Esq; ✉ 55 Vanbrugh Court, Wincott Street, London SE11 4NR (☎ 020 7582 9265, e-mail dpratley@davidpratley.co.uk); 5 Little Burn, Sway, Hampshire SO41 6DZ (☎ 01590 683137)

PRATT, (Edmund) John; s of Edmund Addison Pratt (d 1970), and Ruth Marie Erneste, *née* Wilkinson; *b* 14 October 1944; *Educ* Warwick Sch, Imperial Coll London (BSc(Eng) Civil Engrg, MSc(Eng) Tport); *m* 21 Dec 1968, Jennifer Grace, *née* Reynolds (d 2009); 2 da (Polly Louise b 22 Nov 1972, Sophie Alice b 2 May 1974); *Career* engr Sir William Halcrow & Partners 1966–70, civil engr The Costain Group 1970–73, conslt P-E Consulting Group 1973–76, dir and gen mangr George Longden Construction Ltd (subsid of Whitecroft plc) 1976–79, northern UK gen mangr Damp Proofing Div Rentokil plc 1979–81, sales and mktg dir Steetley Brick Ltd 1981–85, gp mktg dir David Webster Ltd 1986–88, chm Leading Edge Management Consultancy Ltd 1994– (sr ptnr 1988–94); dir: CIM Holdings Ltd 1996–2002, CAM Fndn Ltd 2000–02, Marketing Developments Ltd 2000–; non-exec dir First Whitehall Properties Ltd 1998–2008; chm CIM 2000–01, non-exec dir Marketing Cncl 2000–02; Liveryman Worshipful Co of Marketors 2001–; FCIM, MIMC, MICE, CEng, CMC; *Recreations* classic cars, family history, cycling; *Style*— John Pratt, Esq; ✉ Leading Edge Management Consultancy Ltd, Cyber House, Molly Millars Lane, Wokingham, Berkshire RG41 2PX (☎ 01189 797800, fax 01189 797799, e-mail john.pratt@lead-edge.co.uk)

PRATT, Roger James Edward; s of Francis William Pratt, and Phillis May, *née* Swift; *Educ* Loughborough GS, Univ of Durham (BA), London Film Sch (Dip); *Career* cinematographer; memb: BAFTA 1993–, AMPAS 1995–, BSC; Tech Achievement Award RTS; *Films* asst cameraman Bleak Moments, second asst Monty Python and the Holy Grail; dir of photography: Brazil 1985, Mona Lisa 1986, Scoop 1987 (TV movie), Consuming Passions 1988, Batman 1989, The Fisher King 1991, Shadowlands 1993, The Line, the Cross and the Curve 1993, Frankenstein 1994 (nomination Best Cinematography BSC), Twelve Monkeys 1995, In Love and War 1996, The Avengers 1998, Grey Owl 1999, The End of the Affair 1999 (nomination Best Cinematography: BAFTA Awards, Oscars), 102 Dalmatians 2000, Chocolat 2000 (nomination Best Cinematography BAFTA Awards), Iris 2001, Harry Potter and the Chamber of Secrets 2002, Troy 2004, Harry Potter and the Goblet of Fire 2005, Closing the Ring 2007, Inkheart 2008, Dorian Gray 2009, The Karate Kid 2010; *Recreations* opera; *Clubs* Groucho; *Style*— Roger Pratt, Esq

PREBBLE, Lucy; *Educ* Univ of Sheffield; *Career* writer; Most Promising Playwright Critics' Circle Award 2004; *Television* Secret Diary of a Call Girl (ITV) 2007–08, untitled television pilot with Sarah Silverman (HBO) 2015; head scene writer for Destiny (video game) 2014; *Plays* The Sugar Syndrome (2003, George Devine Award 2004, Best New Play TMA Award 2004), ENRON (2009, Best New Play TMA Award 2009), The Effect (2012, Best New Play Critics Circle Award); *Style*— Ms Lucy Prebble; ✉ c/o Knight Hall Agency Limited, Lower Ground Floor, 7 Mallow Street, London EC1Y 8RQ

PREBBLE, Stuart Colin; s of Dennis Stanley (d 2000), and Jean Margaret, *née* McIntosh (d 1981); *b* 15 April 1951; *Educ* Beckenham & Penge GS, Univ of Newcastle upon Tyne (BA); *m* 25 Aug 1978, Marilyn Anne, da of George Charlton, of Newcastle upon Tyne; 2 da (Alexandra Juliette b 1979, Claire Samantha b 1982 d 1996); *Career* reporter BBC TV 1973–79; Granada TV: ed World in Action 1986–89 (prodr 1981–86), head of regnl progs 1989–92; controller of network factual programmes ITV Network Centre 1992–96, chief exec Granada Sky Broadcasting 1996–98; Granada Media Gp: dir of channels 1998–, md channels and interactive media 1999–; ceo ONdigital 1999–2001, chief exec ITV 2001–03, md Liberty Bell Productions 2003–; fndr Campaign for Quality TV; *Books* A Power in the Land (1988), The Lazarus File (1989), The Grumpy Old Men Handbook (2004), Grumpy Old Men: The Secret Diary (2005), Grumpy Old Christmas (2006), Grumpy Old Workers (2007), Grumpy Old Drivers (2008); *Recreations* music, writing, travel; *Style*— Stuart Prebble, Esq; ✉ Liberty Bell Productions, 4A Exmoor Street, London W10 6BD

PREBENSEN, Preben; *Educ* Magdalene Coll Cambridge; *m* Annie; 4 c; *Career* co-head European Investment Bank and chm London Mgmnt Ctee JP Morgan 1978–2001, chief exec Wellington Underwriting plc 2004–06, chief investment offr Catlin Gp plc 2006–09, chief exec Close Brothers Gp plc 2009–; *Style*— Preben Prebensen, Esq; ✉ Close Brothers Group plc, 10 Crown Place, London EC2A 4FT

PREDDY, Clifford Stanley Frank (Cliff); s of Stanley Preddy (d 1988), and Kathleen, *née* Turner; *b* 30 April 1947, Croydon; *Educ* John Newnham Sch Croydon, John Ruskin GS Croydon, Univ of Bristol (BSc, MSc); *m* 11 Aug 1970, Jill Mary; 1 da (Heloise b 1972), 1 s (Daniel b 1974); *Career* Logica: joined as mathematician/programmer 1969, conslt and project mangr 1972–79, various line mangr roles 1979–87, exec dir Logica plc 1987–96, md Logica UK 1990–96; fndr and md Charteris 1996–2000, non-exec dir Charteris plc 2000–13; chm CODASciSys plc (formerly Science Systems plc) 1997–2003 (non-exec dir 2003–06), non-exec dir CODA plc 2006–07; non-exec dir Computacenter plc 2002–10; FBCS 1995; *Style*— Cliff Preddy, Esq; ✉ e-mail cliffordpreddy@btinternet.com

PREECE, Ralph Stephen; s of John Raymond Preece, of 1 Ashgrove, Dinas Powis, South Glamorgan, and Doris, *née* Derrick; *b* 14 May 1946; *Educ* KCS, Cathays HS Cardiff; *m* 27 Dec 1969, Marilyn Preece, JP, da of Edwin Ralph Gardener Thomas; 2 da (Justine Claire b 28 Sept 1973, Natalie Jane b 27 Feb 1976); *Career* articled clerk Richard Davies & Co Cardiff 1965–70, qualified chartered accountant 1970, Coopers & Lybrand 1970–76 (Johannesburg, London, Cardiff), insolvency specialist Mann Judd Cardiff 1976–79; Deloitte & Touche (formerly Touche Ross): moved to Birmingham Office 1979, ptnr 1983, moved to Leeds Office, ptnr i/c Corp Special Servs (now Corp Recovery) 1983–, ptnr i/c London Office 1994–; memb Transvaal Soc of CAs 1972, FCA 1979 (ACA 1970), MICM 1986, MIPA 1988 (memb Cncl 1997–), memb Assoc Européene des Practiciens des Procedures Collectives 1988, MSPI 1990 (memb Cncl 1996–); *Recreations* gardening, golf; *Clubs* Leeds; *Style*— Ralph Preece, Esq; ✉ Deloitte & Touche, PO Box 810, Stonecutter Court, 1 Stonecutter Street, London EC4A 4TR (☎ 020 7936 3000, fax 020 7583 1198)

PREISKEL, Prof Harold Wilfred; s of David Preiskel (d 1983), of London, and Lili, *née* Wick; *b* 1 June 1939; *Educ* St Paul's, Guy's Med and Dental Sch (LDSRCS, BDS, FDSRCS, MDS), Ohio State Univ (MSc); *m* 22 Aug 1962, Nira, da of Joshua Orenstein (d 1977), of Tel Aviv; 3 s (Daniel b 1965, Ronald b 1969, Alon b 1976), 1 da (Daphne b 1979); *Career* house surgn 1962, lectr in restorative dentistry Royal Dental Hosp Sch of Surgery 1966–69, hon conslt Guy's Hosp 1971, chm London Dental Study Club 1971, examiner in dental prosthetics RCS 1972, staff examiner in prosthetic dentistry Univ of London 1974 (examiner 1969), pt/t conslt in prosthetic dentistry Guy's Hosp Dental Sch 1974 (sr lectr 1969, lectr 1962–66); prof KCL; estab an enviable reputation on the int lecture circuit and is active in research, teaching and practice; Thomas Hinman award Atlanta Georgia 1975, Int Circuit Course award of the American Coll of Prosthodontists 1988, Alumnus of the Year King's Coll Dental Inst 2007, Gtr NY Acad of Prosthodontic Distinguished 2008, Webb-Johnson Medal RCS 2008, Prosthodontic Hall of Fame Ohio State Univ 2014; pres Int Coll of Prosthodontists 1987–91 (first pres), past pres American Dental Soc of London, past pres BDA metropolitan branch 1981–82, vice-pres American Prosthodontic Assoc, past chm London Dental Soc Club, chm Int Prosthodontic Symposium 1982, first non-American pres American Prosthodontic Soc 2007; chm Editorial Bd of Int Jl of Prosthodontists 1988 (a founding ed), chm of tstees Alpha Omega Charitable Tst; fell: Int Coll of Dentists, Br Soc for Restorative Dentistry, Br Soc for Study of Prosthetic Dentistry, European Prosthodontic Assoc, European Dental Soc, American Dental Soc of London, American Dental Soc of Europe, Carl O Boucher Prosthodontic Soc, American Acad Esthetic Dentistry (fndr), American Equilibration Soc, Fédération Dentaire Internationale, Int Coll of Prosthodontists (fndr); active fell (only UK fell) Acad of Prosthodontics 2010; hon citizen of New Orleans 1978; *Books* author of textbooks that have become standard works throughout the world incl: Precision Attachments in Prosthodontics Vol 1 and 2 (trans in six languages), Overdentures Made Easy (published in German, Spanish, Japanese, Italian, Korean and Arabic); Wings of Youth (2013); also some 100 scientific pubns; *Recreations* classical music, aviation; *Style*— Prof Harold Preiskel; ✉ 25 Upper Wimpole Street, London W1G 6NF (☎ 020 7935 4525, fax 020 7486 8337, e-mail harold.preiskel@lineone.net)

PRENDERGAST, Sir (Walter) Kieran; KCVO (1991), CMG (1990); s of Lt Cdr Joseph Henry Prendergast (d 1989), and Mai, *née* Hennessy (d 1988); *b* 2 July 1942; *Educ* St Patrick's Coll Sydney, Salesian Coll Chertsey, St Edmund Hall Oxford; *m* 10 June 1967, Joan, da of Patrick Reynolds (d 1974); 2 s (Damian b 1968, Daniel b 1976), 2 da (Siobhain b 1971, Brigid b 1973); *Career* HM Dip Serv (ret); int civil servant: Istanbul 1964, Ankara 1965, FO 1967, Nicosia 1969, FCO 1972, The Hague 1973, asst private sec to two foreign secs (Rt Hon Anthony Crosland and Rt Hon Dr David Owen) 1976, UK Mission to UN New

York 1979, Tel Aviv 1982, head of Southern African Dept FCO 1986–89; high cmmr: Zimbabwe 1989–92, Kenya 1992–95; ambass to Turkey 1995–97, under sec-gen Political Affrs UN NY 1997–2005; dir: Albany Associates, The Ind Diplomat; sr advsr Centre for Humanitarian Dialogue; counsellor Dragoman Global, chm Anglo-Turkish Soc, tstee Beit Tst; *Recreations* family, walking, reading, wine; *Clubs* Beefsteak, Garrick; *Style*— Sir Kieran Prendergast, KCVO, CMG; ✉ Swallow Brook Barn, Pembridge, Herefordshire HR6 9JE; 333 Milkwood Road, London SE24 0HA; Bonneval, La Chapelle-aux-Saints, 19120, France

PRENTER, Patrick Robert; CBE (1995); s of Robert Gibson Prenter, OBE (d 1991), of Loanhead, Midlothian, and Katherine Emily, *née* Scott; *b* 9 September 1939, Edinburgh; *Educ* Loretto Sch Musselburgh, Trinity Hall Cambridge (MA); *m* 8 Dec 1962, Susan, *née* Patrick; 2 s (Richard Gibson Scott b 7 July 1963, Michael Hugh Patrick b 18 March 1970), 2 da (Lucinda Emily b 6 April 1967, Melinda Louise b 13 Oct 1978); *Career* md MacTaggart Scott 1967–99; Castle Rock Housing Assoc: memb Bd 1975–2005, chm 1995–2000; dir Forth Ports Authy 1984–91, pres Scot Engrg Employers' Assoc 1985–86, tax cmmr 1988–2003; dir Scot Chamber Orch 1995–2009; govr Loretto Sch 1982–89; JP 1980–2007; Lord-Lt Midlothian 2003–; *Recreations* music, opera, reading, gardening, golf, tennis, skiing; *Clubs* RAC, New (Edinburgh), Free Foresters, Hon Co of Edinburgh Golfers; *Style*— Patrick Prenter, Esq, CBE

PRENTICE, HE Christopher Norman Russell; CMG (2009); s of Ronald Prentice (d 1984), and Sonia, *née* Bowring; *b* 5 September 1954, London; *Educ* Shrewsbury, ChCh Oxford (BA); *m* 24 June 1978, Nina, *née* King; 2 s (Andrew b 26 Jan 1981, Robert b 27 Sept 1988), 2 da (Helen b 14 July 1982, Alessandra (Muffie) b 27 Nov 1985); *Career* diplomat; entered HM Dip Serv 1977, desk offr Near East and North Africa Dept FCO 1977–78, trg MECAS (Middle Eastern Centre of Arabic Studies) Lebanon and London 1978–79, third then second sec Kuwait 1980–83, Middle East analyst Assessments Staff Cabinet Office 1983–85, first sec (Near East and South Asia) Washington DC 1985–89, asst head European Community Dept (External) FCO 1989–90, asst private sec to Foreign Sec 1990–93, dep head of mission Budapest 1994–98, head Near East and North Africa Dept FCO 1998–2002, ambass to Jordan 2002–06, ambass to Iraq 2007–09, ambass to Italy 2011–16; *Recreations* photography, walking, cricket, mountains, golf; *Clubs* Athenaeum, MCC and other cricket clubs; *Style*— HE Mr Christopher Prentice, CMG; ✉ c/o Foreign & Commonwealth Office (Rome), King Charles Street, London SW1A 2AH

PRENTICE, Gordon; s of late William Prentice, and Esther Prentice; *b* 28 January 1951; *Educ* George Heriot's Sch Edinburgh, Univ of Glasgow (MA); *m* 20 Dec 1975, Bridget Prentice, *qv*, MP for Lewisham East, da of late James Corr; *Career* with Lab Pty Policy Directorate 1982–92, Lab Pty local govt offr 1985–92, MP (Lab) Pendle 1992–2010; London Borough of Hammersmith and Fulham: cncllr 1982–90, ldr Lab Gp 1984–88 (dep ldr 1982–84), ldr of Cncl 1986–88; *Style*— Gordon Prentice, Esq

PRENTICE, Nicholas John (Nick); s of late Norman Frank Prentice; *b* 14 February 1956; *Educ* Mount Grace Sch Potters Bar, Queens' Coll Cambridge (MA); *m* 28 Dec 1978, Jane Patricia; 2 da (Philippa Mary b 3 Dec 1981, Kate Victoria b 22 June 1983); *Career* Arthur Andersen: joined 1978, CA 1981, ptnr 1988–2002; ptnr Ernst & Young 2002–14; treas Birdlife International; Freeman City of London 1999; FCA 1981, ATII 1981; *Recreations* bird-watching, bridge, theatre, travel, genealogy; *Style*— Nick Prentice, Esq; ✉ e-mail njp@cantab.net

PRENTIS, Dave; *b* 29 May 1951, Leeds; *Educ* LSE (BA), Univ of Warwick (MA); *m* Elizabeth Snape; 2 da (Emma b 21 June 1989, Lauren b 14 Nov 1995); *Career* UNISON: dep gen sec 1993–2001, gen sec 2001–; Court of Dirs Bank of Eng 2012–; pres Public Services Int, non-exec dir UK Cmmn on Employment and Skills (UKCES); visiting fell Nuffield Coll Oxford; *Style*— Dave Prentis, Esq; ✉ UNISON, 130 Euston Road, London NW1 2AY (website www.unison.org.uk)

PRENTIS, Hon Victoria Mary Boswell; MP; da of The Lord Boswell of Aynho, *qv*, and Lady Boswell, *née* Rees; *b* 24 March 1971, Banbury, Oxon; *Educ* London Univ (ba), Downing Coll Cambridge (MA); *m* 1996, Sebastian Hugh Runton Prentis; 1 s (Boris b 2000 d 2000), 2 da (Matilda Yseult b 2001, Cressida Valentine b 2003); *Career* called to the Bar 1995; employed in govt legal service latterly as sr civil serv, MP (Cons) Banbury 2015–; *Recreations* the countryside, detective fiction, cider-making, fundraising; *Clubs* Carlton, Farmers'; *Style*— The Hon Victoria Prentis, MP; ✉ House of Commons, London SW1A 0AA (☏ 020 7219 8756, e-mail victoria.prentis.mp@parliament.uk, website www.victoriaprentis.com, Twitter @VictoriaPrentis)

PRESCOTT, Prof John Herbert Dudley; s of Herbert Prescott (d 1959), of Barrow-on-Humber, Lincs, and Edith Vera, *née* Crowder (d 1993); *b* 21 February 1937; *Educ* Haileybury, Univ of Nottingham (BSc, PhD); *m* 23 July 1960, Diana Margaret, da of Frank Mullock, of Poulton Hall, Chester; 2 s (Ian b 26 May 1961, Tony b 22 Aug 1962), 2 da (Joanna b 8 July 1965, Sarah-Vivien b 24 April 1968); *Career* dir H Prescott (Goxhill) Ltd 1959–78 (chm 1970–78), demonstrator in agric Univ of Nottingham 1960–63, lectr in animal prodn Univ of Newcastle upon Tyne 1963–74, animal prodn offr FAO UN (Argentina) 1972–74, head of animal prodn and devpt East of Scotland Coll of Agric 1974–78, prof of animal prodn Univ of Edinburgh 1978–84, dir Grassland Res Inst Hurley 1984–86, dir Animal and Grassland Res Inst 1986, dir of res Grassland and Animal Prodn 1986–88, princ Wye Coll London 1988–2000; dir Natural Resources Int Ltd 1997–2000 (chm and acting chief exec 1996); Meat and Livestock Cmmn: memb Beef Improvement Ctee 1984–90, memb Res Ctee 1988–90, memb Beef R&D Ctee 1990–94; chair: Tech Ctee on Response to Nutrients AFRC 1988–94, Nat Resources Int Fndn 1998–2004; pres: Br Soc of Animal Prodn 1988, Agric and Forestry Section BAAS 1994–95, chair Conf of Agric Profs 1989; memb: Cncl Br Grassland Soc 1984–87, Nat Agric Awards Ctee Nuffield and RASE 1997–2003; tstee East Malling Tst for Horticultural Res 1998–2010; Br Cncl: memb Ctee for Int Co-operation in HE (S America 1989–94, Southern Africa 1994–2000, Slovakia (mission) 1997, Southern Africa (mission) 1999), memb Agric and Vet Advsy Ctee 1988–96, chair Natural Resources Advsy Ctee 1997, vice-chair Sci Engrg and Environment Advsy Ctee 1997–2001, UK chair Treaty of Windsor with Portuguese Univs 1998–2010; Macaulay Land Use Res Inst: Sci Advsy Ctee 1990–92, Governing Body 1992–97; memb: Governing Body and Corp Hadlow Coll 1988–98, Cncl RVC 1988–98 and 2001–04, Cncl Univ of Kent at Canterbury 1988–2000; chm Sir George Stapledon Meml Tst 1992–2004; Liveryman Worshipful Co of Farmers 2000–; hon fell: Inst for Grassland and Environmental Res 1989, Wye Coll London 2000, ICSTM London 2001; FIBiol 1983, FRAgS 1986, FRSA 1999; *Recreations* walking, wildlife, country pursuits; *Clubs* Farmers'; *Style*— Prof John Prescott

PRESCOTT, Baron (Life Peer UK 2010), of Kingston upon Hull in the County of East Yorkshire; Rt Hon John Leslie Prescott; PC (1994); s of late John Herbert Prescott, JP, of Chester, and late Phyllis Prescott; *b* 31 May 1938; *Educ* Ellesmere Port Secdy Modern Sch, Ruskin Coll Oxford, Univ of Hull (BSc); *m* 1961, Pauline, da of Ernest Tilston, of Chester; 2 s; *Career* joined Lab Pty 1956; former trainee chef & merchant seaman (NUS official 1968–70); Parly candidate (Lab) Southport 1966, MP (Lab) Kingston upon Hull E 1970–2010, ldr Cncl of Europe 1973–75, PPS to sec of state for Trade 1974–76, ldr Lab Pty Delegn European Parl 1976–79 (memb 1975–79); oppn spokesman on: Tport 1979–81, Regnl Affrs 1981-Nov 1983; memb Shadow Cabinet 1983–97; oppn front bench spokesman on: Tport Nov 1983–84 and 1988–93, Employment 1984–87, Energy 1987–88, Employment 1993–94; dep ldr Lab Pty 1994–2007 (candidate Lab Pty dep leadership election 1988 and 1992, candidate leadership election 1994); dep PM 1997–2007, sec of state for the Environment, Tport and the Regions 1997–2001, First Sec of State 2001–07 (with responsibility for Local Govt and the Regions 2002–06); European lead negotiator Kyoto Climate Change Conference, ldr Cncl of Europe Delegation on Climate Change 2010–, appointed official advsr on climate change by the Rt Hon Ed Miliband, MP; *Publications* Alternative Regional Strategy: A Framework for Discussion (1982), Planning for Full Employment (1985), Real Needs – Local Jobs (1987), Moving Britain into the 1990s (1989), Moving Britain into Europe (1991), Full Steam Ahead (1993), Financing Infrastructure Investment (1993), Jobs and Social Justice (1993), Prezza: Pulling No Punches (2008); *Style*— The Rt Hon the Lord Prescott; ✉ House of Lords, London SW1A 0PW

PRESCOTT, Sir Mark; 3 Bt (UK 1938), of Godmanchester, Co Huntingdon; s of Maj (William Robert) Stanley Prescott (d 1962, yr s of Col Sir William Prescott, 1 Bt), by his 1 w (Hylda) Gwendolen, *née* Aldridge (d 1992), and n of Sir Richard Stanley Prescott, 2 Bt (d 1965); *b* 3 March 1948; *Educ* Harrow; *Heir* none; *Career* racehorse trainer; *Style*— Sir Mark Prescott, Bt; ✉ Heath House, Moulton Road, Newmarket, Suffolk CB8 8DU (☏ 01638 662117, fax 01638 666572, e-mail mark_prescott@btconnect.com)

PRESCOTT, Michael; s of Wilfred Prasad (d 1984), of London, and Gretel, *née* Kün, of London; *b* 21 November 1961; *Educ* Christ's Coll Finchley, St Catherine's Coll Oxford (BA), UC Cardiff (Dip Journalism); *m* 1990, Rachel, *née* Storm; 2 s, 1 da; *Career* reporter Coventry Evening Telegraph 1984–86, political corr Press Assoc 1986–89, political corr Sunday Correspondent 1989–90, political corr BBC Radio 1990–92; Sunday Times: political corr 1992–93, chief political corr 1993–99, political ed 1999–2001; head corp communications and vice-chm Public Affrs Weber Shandwick 2001–10, gp dir of corporate affrs BT 2010–; *Style*— Michael Prescott, Esq

PRESCOTT, Peter Richard Kyle; QC (1990); s of Capt Richard Stanley Prescott (d 1987), of Cordoba, Argentina, and Sarah Aitchison, *née* Shand; *b* 23 January 1943; *Educ* St George's Coll Argentina, Dulwich Coll, UCL (BSc), QMC (MSc); *m* 1, 23 Sept 1967, Frances Rosemary, da of Wing Cdr Eric Henry Bland (d 1980), of Tonge Corner, Sittingbourne; 1 da (Miranda Katherine b 1971), 2 s (Richard Julyan Kyle b 1973, Thomas Alexander Kyle b 1975); m 2, 5 July 2014, Gillian Luciana Leddy, da of Ernest Lees (d 2006); *Career* called to the Bar Lincoln's Inn 1970 (bencher 2001), dep judge of the High Court of Justice 1999–; *Books* The Modern Law of Copyright (with Hugh Laddie and Mary Vitoria, *qv*, 1980, 3 edn 2000); *Recreations* music, cooking, Latin American history, flying; *Style*— Peter Prescott, Esq, QC; ✉ 8 New Square, Lincoln's Inn, London WC2A 3QP (☏ 020 7405 4321, fax 020 7405 9955)

PRESCOTT, Richard; *b* 15 March 1962; *Educ* Calthorpe Park Comp Sch Fleet, W London Inst of HE (BA); *m*; 1 c; *Career* PR dept Sealink Br Ferries 1985–88, Attenborough Assocs PR 1988–90, PR mangr Mercury Communications 1990–93 (memb team which launched Mercury Music Prize 1992), corp PR mangr Whitbread plc 1993–97, dir of communications RFU 1997– (England media mangr during Rugby World Cup 2003); sometime freelance broadcaster, contrib BBC Radio Five Live 1992–94, sports commentator BBC GLR 1994–97; *Style*— Richard Prescott, Esq; ✉ Rugby Football Union, Rugby House, Rugby Road, Twickenham, Middlesex TW1 1DS

PRESCOTT THOMAS, Dr John Desmond; RD* (1977, clasp 1987), DL (Co and City of Bristol 2005); s of William Prescott Thomas (d 1973), and Beatrice Isobel, *née* Jones (d 2000); *b* 28 May 1942, Prestatyn, Flintshire; *Educ* Rhyl GS, Whitchurch GS, Jesus Coll Oxford (MA); *m* 1, 7 Oct 1967 (m dis 1993), Bridget Margaret, da of Rev Canon Adrian Denys Somerset-Ward (d 1976); 2 da (Viveka Ruth b 1969, Bronwen Jane b 1971); m 2, 14 Oct 1994, Dr Heather Elizabeth Graham; *Career* BBC: grad trainee 1963–65, asst prodr sch TV 1965–68, prodr 1968–76, sr prodr modern languages and European studies 1976–81, head of schs broadcasting TV 1981–84, head Bristol network prodn centre 1984–86, head of broadcasting South and West 1986–91; md Westcountry Television Ltd 1991–95; md JPT Media Assocs Ltd 1995–2009; wrote and produced: radiovision prog on Stanley Spencer's Burghclere paintings (Japan Prize nomination 1965), TV adaptation of Peter Carter's The Black Lamp, 12 Euro documentary and language series, two interactive trg resources, 28 int media consultancy projects; three BAFTA/RTS award nominations; visiting prof Faculty of Art Media and Design UWE (dep chm Bd of Govrs); Bolland Lecture Bristol Poly 1984, Arts Lecture Univ of Bath 2000, Keynote Lecture Koice Television Festival 2000; articles in pubns incl: TES, Br Language Teaching Jl, Le Français dans le Monde; former: chm SW Arts, dep chm The Harbourside Centre, vice-chm Channel West, dir SW Media Devpt Agency, dir Exeter and Devon Arts Centre, dir Watershed Arts Tst, memb Euro Bd CIRCOM Regional, dir @t Bristol; former tstee: Bath Int Festival, TV Tst for the Environment, The Exploratory, Bristol Cathedral Tst, St George's Music Tst; RNR: cmmnd 1963, qualified ocean cmd 1974, Cdr 1978, exec offr London Div 1983–84, Severn Div 1984–92; Dr of Arts (hc) UWE 2002; FRTS 1995; commandeur Commanderie de Bordeaux 1999; *Books* Two EFL stories for children, Encounter: France (1980), Dès le Début, Dicho y Hecho, Alles Klar (1983), The Media in Governance (co-author, 1998), The UNESCO Media Management Manual (2009); *Recreations* languages, travel, sailing, photography, playing the alto saxophone; *Clubs* Royal Naval Sailing Assoc; *Style*— Dr John Prescott Thomas, RD*, DL; ✉ Kensington Cottage, Kensington Place, Clifton, Bristol BS8 3AH (☏ 0117 973 9195, e-mail jptmedia@blueyonder.co.uk)

PRESLAND, Frank George; *b* 27 February 1944; *Educ* Univ of London (Fairbridge Cwlth scholar, BSc), Univ Coll of Rhodesia and Nyasaland; *Career* admitted slr 1973; Frere Cholmeley Bischoff: joined 1973, ptnr 1976–98, chm 1992–98; jt chm Eversheds (following merger) 1998–99; co-fndr and chief exec Twenty-First Artists (co-prop until 2005), chief exec Sanctuary Gp plc 2006–08; chm Rocket Music Entertainment Gp 2010–; dir Edge VCT 2005–; tstee: Elton John AIDS Fndn (UK and USA), The Elstree UTC; *Recreations* yachting; *Style*— Frank Presland, Esq

PRESLEY, Prof Emeritus John Ralph; s of Ralph Presley, of Dinnington, S Yorks, and Doris, *née* Edson; *b* 17 September 1945; *Educ* Woodhouse GS Sheffield, Lancaster Univ (BA), Loughborough Univ (PhD); *m* 15 July 1967, Barbara, da of Kenneth Mallinson, of Kegworth, Derby; 2 da (Joanne Marie b 29 July 1968, Catherine Jane b 2 Sept 1972), 1 s (John Robert Ralph b 9 June 1981); *Career* Loughborough Univ: lectr 1969–76, sr lectr 1976–81, reader 1981–84, prof of economics 1984–, dir Banking Centre 1985–89, head Dept of Economics 1991–96; sr economic advsr Miny of Planning Saudi Arabia 1979–80, chief economic advsr Saudi Br Bank 1979–2006, visiting scholar Harvard Univ 1982, visiting professorial fell Univ of Nottingham 1989–90; DTI: memb Ctee for ME Trade 1992–2000, chm Area Action Ctee for Gulf Cooperation Cncl Countries and Yemen 1993–98; assoc dir Maxwell Stamp plc 1981–; memb Exec Ctee Saudi-British Soc, memb Omani-British Friendship Assoc, chm Forward Planning Ctee Arab Gulf 1994–98; Islamic Devpt Bank Prize for Islamic Banking and Fin 2002; *Books* European Monetary Integration (with P Coffey, 1971), Currency Areas: Theory and Practice (with G E J Dennis, 1976), Robertsonian Economics (1978), Pioneers of Modern Economics Vol 1 (ed with D O'Brien , 1983), Directory of Islamic Financial Institutions (1988), Pioneers of Modern Economics Vol 2 (ed with D Greenaway, 1989), A Guide to the Saudi Arabian Economy (with A J Westaway, 1983, 2 edn 1989), Banking in the Arab Gulf (with R Wilson, 1991), Essays on Robertsonian Economics (ed, 1992), Robertson on Economic Policy (ed with S R Dennison, 1992), Islamic Finance (with P Mills, 1999); *Recreations* gardening, reading, music, travel, conservation; *Style*— Prof Emeritus John Presley; ✉ Station Farm, Station Road, Melbourne, Derbyshire DE73 8BQ (☏ 01332 865380, e-mail stationfarm2@yahoo.co.uk)

PRESS, Prof Malcolm; *Educ* Kingsbury HS, Univ of London (BSc), Univ of Manchester (PhD); *Career* res assoc UCL 1985–89, lectr then sr lectr Univ of Manchester 1989–94; Univ of Sheffield: reader 1994–98, prof 1998–2008, dir Res in the Environment 2001–08, head Animal and Plant Scis 2002–08; Univ of Birmingham: pro vice-chllr and head College of Life and Environmental Sciences 2008–13, pro-vice-chllr (Research and Knowledge Transfer) 2013–15; vice-chllr Manchester Met Univ 2015–; tstee: Royal Botanical Gardens (Kew), WWF (UK); *Style*— Prof Malcolm Press; ✉ Manchester Metropolitan University, All Saints Building, All Saints, Manchester M15 6BH (✆ 0161 247 1560, e-mail malcolm.press@mmu.ac.uk)

PRESS, Dr (Christopher) Martin; s of Gp Capt Charles Henry Press, of Great Gormellick, Cornwall, and Christina, *née* Hindshaw; *b* 24 January 1944; *Educ* Bedales, King's Coll Cambridge (BA), UCH (MB BChir, MA), Chelsea Coll London (MSc); *m* 10 June 1967, Angela Margaret, da of Charles Douglas Lewis, of Dibden, Hants; 5 s (Matthew b 1970, Joseph b 1972, Samuel b 1974, Benjamin b 1980, Daniel b 1984); *Career* med registrar Royal Post Grad Med Sch Hammersmith Hosp 1971–73, MRC research fell Univ of Calif 1973–75, asst prof of med and paediatrics Yale Univ Sch of Med 1981–87, ret conslt physician and hon sr lectr Royal Free Hosp Med Sch and dir Pancreatic Islet Transplantation Unit Royal Free Hosp; hon sec Transplantation Section RSM; memb: BMA, Br Diabetic Assoc, American Diabetic Assoc; *Recreations* orienteering, bell ringing, canal cruising; *Style*— Dr Martin Press; ✉ 99 Highfield Lane, Southampton SO17 1NN (✆ 023 8055 1617); Department of Endocrinology, Royal Free Hospital, London NW3 3QG (✆ 020 7830 2171)

PRESS, Michael Warner; s of Albert Edward Press, and Irene Mary Press; *b* 26 March 1947, Salt Lake City, UT, USA; *Educ* Colorado Coll (BS), Columbia Univ (MS); *m* 4 June 1969, Sean S, *née* Stevens; *Career* ceo KBC Advanced Technols; sr exec BP, exec vice-pres Amerada Hess; sr ind non-exec dir: Petrofac Ltd, Chart Industries Inc; *Style*— Michael Press, Esq; ✉ 2040 County Line Road, PO Box 327, Gates Mills, OH 44040, USA (e-mail mwpress13@msn.com); Petrofac Ltd, 4th Floor, 117 Jermyn Street, London SW1Y 6HH (✆ 020 7811 4900, fax 020 7811 4901)

PREST, Nicholas Martin; CBE (2001); s of Prof Alan Richmond Prest (d 1984), of Wimbledon, and Pauline Chasey, *née* Noble; *b* 3 April 1953; *Educ* Manchester Grammar, ChCh Oxford (MA); *m* 1985, Anthea Joy Elisabeth, da of Stuart John Guthrie Neal, of Wales; 2 da (Clementine Joy Chasey b 1987, Tabitha Rose Florence b 1992), 1 s (Frederick George Alan b 1989); *Career* entered civil serv MOD 1974 admin trainee, princ offr 1979; joined United Scientific Hldgs plc (later Alvis plc) 1982; Alvis plc: dir 1985–2004, chief exec 1989–2004, chm and chief exec 1996–2004; chm: Aveva Gp plc 2006–12, Cohort plc 2006–, Shephard Gp 2007–; chm Defence Manufacturers Assoc 2001–04, vice-chm Defence Industries Cncl 2004; *Recreations* walking, music, shooting; *Clubs* MCC, Cavalry and Guards; *Style*— Nicholas Prest, Esq, CBE; ✉ Pilstone House, Llandogo, Monmouth NP25 4TH (✆ 020 7792 4821)

PRESTON, John Anthony Russell; s of late Dennis Anthony Gurney Preston, and Margaretta Constance, *née* Higson; *b* 9 September 1953; *Educ* Marlborough; *m* 23 Nov 1991, Maria, *née* Djurkovic; *Career* stage mangr Open Space Theatre 1973, asst film ed 1974–78, freelance journalist 1981–83, TV ed Time Out 1983–86, ed Arts Section Evening Standard 1986–90, arts ed The Sunday Telegraph 1990–99, television critic, book critic and feature writer The Sunday Telegraph 1997–; *Books* Touching the Moon (1990), Kings of the Roundhouse (1994), Ghosting (1996), Ink (1999), The Dig (2007); *Style*— John Preston, Esq; ✉ c/o United Agents, 12–26 Lexington Street, London W1F 0LE (✆ 020 3214 0800, fax 020 3214 0801, website www.unitedagents.co.uk)

PRESTON, Michael David; s of Richard Preston, and Yetta, *née* Young (d 1958); *b* 12 December 1945; *Educ* St Paul's, Exeter Coll Oxford (sr open scholar, MA); *m* 1, 13 April 1969 (m dis 1994), Stephanie Ann, *née* Levy; 2 s (Matthew b 1972, Robert b 1975); m 2, 10 Jan 1998, Sherri Remmell, *née* Becker; 1 da (Hanna b 2000), 1 s (Samuel b 2002); *Career* articled clerk Price Waterhouse London; fndr shareholder and dir Sterling Publishing Group plc until 1995 (dep chm 1990–94), former dir Debrett's Peerage Ltd, ptnr Capidem LLP, chm Br American Auctions; FCA 1971; *Recreations* music, painting, wine; *Clubs* MCC; *Style*— Michael Preston, Esq; ✉ Capidem LLP, 6 Grosvenor Street, London W1K 4PZ (✆ 020 7647 9900, fax 020 7647 9911, e-mail mike@baauctions.net)

PRESTON, (Christopher) Miles Cary; s of Alan Tomlinson Preston, TD (d 2004), and Audrey Anne Flint, *née* Wood (d 2010); *b* 12 April 1950; *Educ* Shrewsbury; *m* 5 June 1974, Jane Mowbray, da of Norman Seddon Harrison (d 1988), and Jeanne, *née* Peirce (d 2007), of Blackheath, London; 2 da (Caroline Mowbray b 28 Dec 1978, Georgina Clare b 20 Nov 1986); *Career* admitted slr 1974; ptnr Radcliffes & Co 1980–94, sr ptnr Miles Preston & Co 1994–2016 (conslt 2016–); served on Sir Gervais Sheldon's Family Law Liaison Ctee 1982; Slrs' Family Law Assoc: fndr memb 1982, memb Main Ctee 1982–88, chm Working Pty on Procedure 1982–88; Int Acad of Matrimonial Lawyers: fndr memb 1986, govr 1986–92, pres English Chapter 1989, pres Euro Chapter 1989–92, parliamentarian to Main Ctee 1989–92, pres Main Acad 1994–96 (pres-elect 1992), counsel to Acad 2000–02; chm: Old Salopian Ctee 1992–94, Osteopathic Educnl Fndn 1994–; memb The President's Int Family Law Ctee 1994–; *Recreations* food, travel, rowing, classic cars; *Clubs* Turf, Leander, Sabrina (pres 2015–), Rolls Royce Enthusiasts, Bentley Drivers; *Style*— Miles Preston, Esq; ✉ Miles Preston & Co, 10 Bolt Court, London EC4A 3DQ (✆ 020 7583 0583, fax 020 7583 0128, e-mail miles.preston@milespreston.co.uk)

PRESTON, Prof Paul; CBE (2000); s of Charles Ronald Preston (d 1973), and Alice, *née* Hoskisson (d 1956); *b* 21 July 1946; *Educ* St Edward's Coll Liverpool, Oriel Coll of Oxford (BA, DPhil), Univ of Reading (MA); *m* 24 March 1983, Gabrielle, da of William Anthony Ashford-Hodges; 2 s (James Mark William b 20 Jan 1987, Christopher Charles Thomas b 2 April 1989); *Career* lectr in history Univ of Reading 1974–75; Queen Mary Coll: lectr 1975–79, reader 1979–85, prof 1985–91; LSE: prof of international history 1991–94, Principe de Asturias prof 1994–2011, emeritus prof 2011–; Marcel Proust chair European Acad of Yuste 2006; Comendador de la Orden de Mérito Civil 1987; Ramon Llull Int Prize 2005; FRHistS 1982, FBA 1994; Gran Cruz de la Órden de Isabel la Católica 2006; *Books* The Coming of the Spanish Civil War (1978), The Triumph of Democracy in Spain (1986), The Spanish Civil War (1986), The Politics of Revenge (1990), Franco: A Biography (Yorkshire Post Book of the Year, 1993), Comrades: Portraits from the Spanish Civil War (1999), Doves of War: Four Women of Spain (2002), Juan Carlos: A People's King (2004), We Saw Spain Die: Foreign Correspondents in the Spanish Civil War (2008), The Spanish Holocaust (2011), The Last Stalinist (2014); *Recreations* opera, classical music, modern fiction, wine, supporting Everton FC; *Style*— Prof Paul Preston, CBE, FBA; ✉ Department of International History, London School of Economics and Political Science, Houghton Street, London WC2A 2AE (✆ 020 7955 7107, fax 020 7955 6757, e-mail p.preston@lse.ac.uk)

PRESTRIDGE, Jeffrey John; s of Stanley Prestridge, of Sutton Coldfield, W Midlands, and Helen Joyce, *née* Carpenter; *b* 8 April 1959; *Educ* Bishop Vesey GS, Loughborough Univ (BSc); *m* 10 Sept 1983, Susan, *née* Dove; 3 s (Matthew Stanley George b 25 March 1991, Mark Christopher Jeffrey b 21 Sept 1992, James David Luke b 11 Feb 1994); *Career* articled clerk Price Waterhouse Chartered Accountants 1980–82, res asst Debenham Tewson Chinnocks 1982–84, self-employed 1984–86, dep ed World Investor 1986–87, economist Bristol & West Building Society 1987, dep ed Money Management Magazine 1987–90; family fin ed: The Sunday Telegraph 1990–94, The Mail on Sunday 1994–; winner of numerous awards for personal fin journalism; Financial Planning Certificate 2000; *Books* Jeff's Lunchbox (1992), Complete Personal Finance Guide (2001); *Recreations* swimming, running, photography, squash, fell walking, WBA FC, art galleries, cinema; *Clubs* Serpentine Running; *Style*— Jeffrey Prestridge, Esq; ✉ 41 Papermill Wharf, 50 Narrow Street, London E14 8BZ (✆ 07711 495140, e-mail jeff.prestridge@hotmail.co.uk); The Mail on Sunday, Northcliffe House, 2 Derry Street, London W8 5TS (✆ 020 3615 3201, e-mail jeff.prestridge@mailonsunday.co.uk)

PRESTWICH, Prof Michael Charles; OBE (2010); s of John Oswald Prestwich (d 2003), of Oxford, and Menna, *née* Roberts (d 1990); *b* 30 January 1943; *Educ* Charterhouse, Magdalen Coll Oxford, ChCh Oxford (MA, DPhil); *m* 11 May 1973, Margaret Joan, da of Herbert Daniel (d 1980), of Glossop; 2 s (Robin b 1974, Christopher b 1976), 1 da (Kate b 1980); *Career* res lectr ChCh Oxford 1965–69, lectr in medieval history Univ of St Andrews 1969–79; Univ of Durham: reader in medieval history 1979–86, prof of history 1986–2008, pro-vice-chllr 1992–99; FRHistS 1972, FSA 1980; *Books* War, Politics and Finance under Edward I (1972), The Three Edwards: War and State in England 1272–1377 (1980), Documents Illustrating the Crisis of 1297–8 in England (1980), Edward I (1988), English Politics in the Thirteenth Century (1990), Armies and Warfare in the Middle Ages: The English Experience (1996), Plantagenet England (2005), Knight (2010), Medieval People (2014); *Recreations* skiing; *Style*— Prof Michael Prestwich, OBE, FSA; ✉ Langdale, Hillrise Lane, Longframlington, Morpeth NE65 8BN (e-mail m.c.prestwich@durham.ac.uk)

PRETTY, Dr Katharine Bridget (Kate); CBE (2009); da of Maurice Walter Hughes (d 1975), of Birmingham, and Bridget Elizabeth Whibley, *née* Marples (d 2016); *b* 18 October 1945; *Educ* King Edward VI HS for Girls Birmingham, New Hall Cambridge (scholar, MA, PhD); m 1, 1967 (m dis), Graeme Lloyd Pretty; m 2, 1988, Prof Tjeerd Hendrik van Andel (d 2010); *Career* Univ of Cambridge: fell and lectr in archaeology New Hall 1972, admissions tutor New Hall 1979–82, sr tutor New Hall 1985–91 (emeritus fell 1995–), princ Homerton Coll 1991–2013 (hon fell 2013–), memb Univ Fin Bd 1986–96, chm Faculty Bd of Archaeology and Anthropology 1991–2004, memb Univ Gen Bd 1997, chm Cncl Sch of Humanities and Social Sciences 1997–2003, pro-vice-chllr 2004–10, dep vice-chllr 2010–13, chm Faculty Bd of Human, Social and Political Science 2011–13, sr fell McDonald Inst for Archaeological Research 2013–; sec Cambs Archaeological Ctee 1974–79; chm: RESCUE Br Archaeological Tst 1978–83, OCR (Oxford, Cambridge and RSA Examinations Bd) 1998–2004; vice-pres RSA 1998–2004, tstee Prince's Teaching Inst 2007–15, pres Cncl for Br Archaeology 2008–13 (hon vice-pres 2015–), memb Cncl Society of Antiquaries of London 2012–15; hon fell Harris Manchester Coll Oxford 2011–, lay memb Cncl Durham Univ 2014–; FSA 2000, FSA Scot 2013; *Recreations* archaeology in the Arctic, botany and gardening; *Clubs* University Women's; *Style*— Dr Kate Pretty, CBE; ✉ e-mail kp10002@cam.ac.uk

PREVETT, Geoffrey James (Geoff); s of James William Prevett, of Ewell, Surrey, and Helen Lillian, *née* Luckett; *b* 30 November 1944; *Educ* Westminster; *m* 25 June 1966, Joan, da of Thomas Bevan, of Maesteg, S Wales; 1 da (Melanie b 6 Feb 1973), 1 s (Christopher b 31 Jan 1980); *Career* admitted slr 1978; Travers Smith Braithwaite 1963–79, Lewis Lewis and Co 1979–82 (ptnr 1981), ptnr Eversheds (Jaques and Lewis before merger) 1982–; memb Law Soc; chartered arbitrator 2000; DipICArb, FCIArb; *Recreations* music, theatre, reading, cricket; *Style*— Geoff Prevett, Esq; ✉ 22 Northcliffe Close, Worcester Park, Surrey KT4 7DS (✆ 020 8337 3377); Eversheds, Senator House, 85 Queen Victoria Street, London EC4V 4JL (✆ 020 7919 4500, fax 020 7919 4919)

PREVEZER, Susan; (QC); da of Prof Sydney Prevezer (d 1997), and Enid Margaret, *née* Austin; *b* 25 March 1959; *m* 26 June 1994, Benjamin Matthew Freedman, s of Bill Freedman; 2 da (Edie b 30 April 1996, Toby b 5 Jan 1998); *Career* called to the Bar 1983; memb: Commercial Bar Assoc, Chancery Bar Assoc; *Style*— Ms Susan Prevezer, QC; ✉ Essex Court Chambers, 24 Lincoln's Inn Fields, London WC2A 3ED

PRICE, Charles Beaufort; s of Mervyn Beaufort Price, and Jessie Price; *b* 7 November 1945; *Educ* King's Coll Taunton, QMC (BA); *m* 29 May 1971, Patricia Ann; 1 s (Gareth Charles b 29 March 1978), 1 da (Isabelle Louise b 8 Sept 1981); *Career* md N M Rothschild & Sons (Singapore) Limited 1976–79, dir N M Rothschild & Sons Limited 1985–96 (chm Wales 1992–96); head of banking and treasury Singer & Friedlander Ltd 1997–; AIB; *Recreations* gardening, rugby, opera; *Style*— Charles Price, Esq; ✉ Singer & Friedlander Ltd, 21 New Street, Bishopsgate, London EC2M 4HR

PRICE, Prof Christopher Philip; s of Philip Bright Price (d 1955), and Frances Gwendoline Price (d 1986); *b* 28 February 1945; *Educ* Univ of London (BSc), Univ of Birmingham (PhD), Univ of Cambridge (MA); *m* 1968, Elizabeth Ann, da of late Frederick Dix, and Mary Dix; 2 da (Carolyn Sarah b 2 Jan 1974, Emma Jane b 21 Nov 1975); *Career* biochemist; basic grade biochemist Coventry & Warwick Hosp 1967–72, sr grade then princ grade biochemist E Birmingham Hosp 1972–76; conslt biochemist: Southampton Gen Hosp 1976–80, Addenbrooke's Hosp Cambridge 1980–88; prof of clinical biochemistry St Bartholomew's & The Royal London Sch of Med & Dentistry (formerly London Hosp Med Coll) 1988–2001; Barts and the London NHS Tst: clinical dir for biochemistry 1988–98, clinical dir for pathology 1998–2001; vice-pres of outcomes research Diagnostics Div Bayer Health Care 2002–05; visiting prof in clinical biochemistry Univ of Oxford 2006–; memb: Assoc for Clinical Biochemistry (chm 1991–94, pres 2003–06), American Assoc for Clinical Chemistry (memb Bd of Dirs 2000–03), Int Soc for Clinical Enzymology; Hon DSc De Montfort Univ 1998, Hon DSc Univ of Coventry 2011; CChem, CSci, FRSC, FRCPath (memb Cncl 1996–99), FACB; *Publications* ed 12 books incl Principles & Practice of Immunoassay (2 edn), Point of Care Testing (3 edn), Evidence-Based Laboratory Medicine (2 edn); over 400 research papers and reviews; *Recreations* walking, gardening, reading; *Style*— Prof Christopher Price

PRICE, Clair Jennifer (Jennie); da of Cliff Price, of Newport, Salop, and Beryl, *née* Agates; *b* 7 February 1960; *Educ* KCL (LLB); *m* 1, 7 Oct 1988 (m dis); m 2, 17 April 2010, David Teasdale; *Career* legal advsr Heating and Ventilation Contractors Assoc 1983–88, litigation lawyer Bristows 1989–90, head of legal and public affrs Building Employers Confedn 1990–96, dir Major Contractors Gp 1996–99, chief exec Construction Confedn 1999–2000, chief exec Waste and Resources Action Prog (WRAP) 2000–07, chief exec Sport England 2007–; chair Youth United Fndn 2015–; visiting fell Cranfield Sch of Mgmnt 2004; fndr memb Construction Industry Bd DETR, memb Environment Innovations Advsy Gp DTI; Hon MRICS 2000, FRSA 2002; *Style*— Ms Jennie Price; ✉ Sport England, 1st Floor, 21 Bloomsbury Street, London WC1B 3HF (✆ 020 7273 1601, e-mail jennie.price@sportengland.org, website www.sportengland.org)

PRICE, Prof Sir Curtis Alexander; KBE (2006 (honorary award made substantive on taking British citizenship), Hon KBE 2005); s of Dalias Price, and Lillian, *née* Alexander; *b* 7 September 1945; *Educ* Univ of Southern Illinois (BMus), Harvard Univ (AM, PhD); *m* 1981, Rhian, *née* Samuel; 1 step s; *Career* prof of music Washington Univ St Louis USA 1974–81; KCL: lectr in music 1981–84, reader in music 1984–88, King Edward prof 1988–95; principal RAM 1995–2008, warden New Coll Oxford 2009–16; pres Royal Musical Assoc; sec Purcell Soc; tstee: Handel Inst, Assoc Bd Royal School of Music, Amadeus Fndn, London String Quartet Competition, Mendelssohn Scholarship Fund, Purcell Sch; Knox travelling fell 1970, Guggenheim fell 1981; hon memb RAM 1993, FKC 1995, FRNCM 2001, FRCM 2002; *Awards*: Rockefeller Award 1973, Alfred Einstein Award American Musicological Soc 1977, Dent Medal Royal Musical Assoc 1985; *Books* Henry Purcell and the London Stage (1984), Music in the Early Baroque Era (1994), Italian Opera in Late Eighteenth Century London (1995); *Style*— Prof Sir Curtis Price, KBE

PRICE, David William James; s of Richard J E Price (d 1983), of Quinta da Romeira, Bucelas, Portugal, and Miriam Joan, *née* Dunsford; *b* 11 June 1947; *Educ* Ampleforth, CCC Oxford

(MA); *m* 1971, Shervie Ann Lander, da of Sir James Whitaker, 3 Bt (d 1999); 1 da (Hesther b 1971), 1 s (William b 1973); *Career* farmer and merchant banker; dir: Warburg Investment Management Ltd 1978, S G Warburg & Co Ltd 1982–87; chm Mercury Asset Management plc 1983–97, dep chm Mercury Asset Management Group plc 1987–97; chm: Aberdeen All Asia Tst 1997–2010, F & C Management 1999–2004; dir: Heritage Lincs 1997–2011, Scottish American Investment Co 1997–2012, Big Food Gp 2000–04, Melchior Japan Investment Tst 2006–11, Orders of St John Care Tst; cncllr London Borough of Lambeth 1979–82; *Clubs* Brooks's, Lincolnshire; *Style*— David Price, Esq; ✉ Eastgate Manor, 137 Eastgate, Louth, Lincs LN11 9QE

PRICE, Eric Hardiman Mockford; s of Frederick Hardiman Price, and Florence Nellie Hannah; *b* 14 November 1931; *Educ* St Marylebone GS, Christ's Coll Cambridge (BA, MA); *m* 3 Feb 1963, Diana Teresa Anne Mary Stanley, da of Stanley Joseph Leckie Robinson (d 1962), of Harbury Hall, Warwicks; 3 da (Caroline b 29 Jan 1964, Nichola b 28 March 1966, Ashling b 6 July 1970), 1 s (Julian b 27 Feb 1969); *Career* Nat Serv Army 1950–52, HAC 1952–57; economist: Central Electricity Authy Electricity Cncl 1957–58, Br Iron and Steel Fedn 1958–62; chief economist Port of London Authy 1962–67; Miny of Tport: sr econ advsr 1966–69, chief econ advsr 1969–71, dir of econs 1971–75; DOE: under sec econs 1972–76, dir of econs and statistics 1975–76; under sec econs and statistics: Depts of Trade Indust and Consumer Protection 1977–80; under sec and chief economic advsr: Dept of Energy 1980–92, DTI 1992–93; special conslt National Economic Research Associates 1993–2000; dir Robinson Bros (Ryders Green) Ltd 1985–; prop The Energy Economics Consultancy 1995–2000, ptnr in farm and stud enterprise 2000–; Br Inst of Energy Econs: memb Cncl 1980–2006, vice-chm 1981–82 and 1988–89, chm 1982–85, hon memb 2006–; FREconS, FRSS, FInstD, MInstPet; *Recreations* tennis, history, horseracing; *Clubs* Moor Park Golf (hon memb), Batchworth Park Golf, Riverside, Health & Leisure; *Style*— Eric Price, Esq; ✉ Batchworth House, Batchworth Heath Farm, London Road, Rickmansworth, Hertfordshire WD3 1QB (☎ 01923 824471, fax 01923 828895, e-mail erichmprice@tiscali.co.uk)

PRICE, Sir Francis Caradoc Rose; 7 Bt (UK 1815), QC (1992); s of Sir Rose Francis Price, 6 Bt (d 1979), and Kathleen June, yr da of Norman William Hutchinson, of Melbourne, Aust; *b* 9 September 1950; *Educ* Eton, Trinity Coll Univ of Melbourne, Univ of Alberta; *m* 1975, (Hon Madam Justice) Marguerite Jean, da of Roy Samuel Trussler, of Victoria, BC; 3 da (Adrienne Calantha Rose b 1976, Megan Kathleen Rose b 1977, Glynis Nicola Rose b 1982); *Heir* bro, Norman Price; *Career* barr and slr Canada, ptnr Reynolds Mirth Richards & Farmer; chartered arbitrator; *Books* Pipelines in Western Canada (1975), Mortgage Actions in Alberta (1985), Conducting a Foreclosure Action (1996); *Recreations* cricket, theatre, opera; *Clubs* Faculty; *Style*— Sir Francis Price, Bt, QC; ✉ 9626 95 Avenue, Edmonton, Alberta T6C 2A4, Canada (☎ home 00 1 780 469 9555, work 00 1 780 497 3388, fax 00 1 780 429 3044, e-mail fprice@rmrf.com)

PRICE, Frank Christopher (Chris); OBE (2008); s of Geoffrey Arthur Price, of Wilmslow, Cheshire, and Celia Price; *b* 1946; *Educ* Uppingham, Univ of Nottingham (industry scholar, BSc), Leicester Poly (DMS); *m* 1, 1970 (m dis 1992), Catherine; 1 s (Geoffrey Michael b 19 Sept 1974), 1 da (Anne Elisabeth b 17 Dec 1976); m 2, 1995, Sylvia; *Career* British Shoe Machinery Ltd: grad apprentice, mangr Machinery R&D Dept, memb Bd of Mgmnt 1981–85; engrg dir Rearsby Automotive Ltd Leicester 1985–87; USM TEXON Ltd (formerly United Machinery Gp Ltd): dir R&D 1987–93, dir Product and Process Devpt 1993–96; Rolls-Royce plc: engrg and technol dir Energy Businesses 1997–2001, engrg and technol dir Operations 2001–03, exec vice pres Engrg and Techol – Purchasing 2004–08; chm UPS2 Integrated Knowledge Centre 2008–13, chm Loxham Precision Ltd 2013–; named inventor on 20 patents; hon sr industry fell and hon visiting prof de Montfort Univ 1992–, special prof Univ of Nottingham 1996–; IMechE: chm E Midlands Branch 1986–88, vice-pres 1991–93, dep pres 1993–94, pres 1995–96; memb Senate Engrg Cncl, memb Smeatonian Soc of Civil Engrs (hon treas 2014–); Freeman City of London 1995, memb Ct of Assts Worshipful Co of Engrs 2002 (Liveryman 1995, Master Engr 2009); FIMechE 1985 (MIMechE 1976), FREng 1993 (hon treas 2003–09); *Recreations* skiing, theatre, walking, gardening, golf; *Clubs* Athenaeum; *Style*— Chris Price, Esq, OBE, FREng; ☎ 07852 495846, e-mail chris_price@talk21.com

PRICE, James Richard Kenrick; QC (1995); s of Lt-Col Kenrick Jack Price, DSO, MC (d 1982), and Juliet Hermione, *née* Slessor (now Mrs de Laszlo, wid of John de Laszlo); *b* 14 September 1948; *Educ* Eton, St Edmund Hall Oxford (BA); *m* 1983, Hon Virginia Yvonne, da of 5 Baron Mostyn, MC (d 2000); *Career* called to the Bar Inner Temple 1974; *Recreations* gardening, skiing, hill walking, fine and decorative arts, dogs; *Clubs* Brooks's, Beefsteak; *Style*— James Price, Esq, QC; ✉ Pettifers, Lower Wardington, Banbury, Oxfordshire OX17 1RU (☎ 01295 750232); 5 Gray's Inn Square, London WC1R 5AH (☎ 020 7242 2902, e-mail jamesprice@5rb.com)

PRICE, John Philip; s of late Eifion Wyn Price, of Rhayader, Powys, and Kathleen, *née* Woodfield; *b* 11 December 1949; *Educ* Monmouth, CCC Oxford (MA, BPhil); *Partner* Diana Elizabeth Chrouch; 1 da (Natasha Maya Celine); *Career* called to the Bar Inner Temple 1974; DG Dairy Industry Fedn (formerly Dairy Trade Fedn) 1986–98, co sec Express Dairies plc 1998–2003, dir of corporate affrs Arla Foods UK plc 2003–07, dir Competition Law Process Mgmnt Ltd 2008–14, co sec TestMatchExtra.com Ltd 2011–13; chm Review Bd for Government Contracts 2009–15; dir Express Tstees Ltd 2009–15; tstee Dairy UK Pension Scheme 2011–; *Books* The English Legal System (1979); *Clubs* Farmers; *Style*— John Price, Esq; ✉ 20 Rossmore Court, Park Road, London NW1 6XX (☎ 020 7723 9485)

PRICE, Lionel Dennis Dixon; s of Harold Price (d 1988), of Birkenhead, and Florence Mitchley, *née* Thompson (d 1996); *b* 2 February 1946; *Educ* Bolton Sch, CCC Cambridge (MA); *m* 19 Oct 1968, Sara Angela, da of Ronald William Holt (d 1991), of Gerrards Cross; 3 s (Matthew b 1972, Edward b and d 1974, James b 1975); *Career* Bank of England 1967–79, alternate exec dir IMF 1979–81; Bank of England: head Info Div 1981–84, head Int Div 1985–90, head Economics Div 1990–94, dir of Central Banking Studies 1994–97; md sovereign ratings Fitch IBCA Ltd 1997–2001, chief economist Fitch Ratings 2001–06; dir Rocol Ltd 1991–93; treas Policy Studies Inst 1993–97; tstee Bank of England Pension Fund 2009–, advsr Treasy Select Ctee 2011–13; *Recreations* genealogy, walking, constructing theatrical scenery; *Style*— Lionel Price, Esq; ✉ 102 Clarence Road, St Albans, Hertfordshire AL1 4NQ

PRICE, His Hon Nicholas Peter Lees; QC (1992); s of Frank Henry Edmund Price, MBE (Mil) (d 1991), and Agnes Lees, *née* Brittlebank (d 2010); *b* 29 September 1944, Broadstairs, Kent; *Educ* Prince of Wales Sch Nairobi, Univ of Edinburgh; *m* 4 Jan 1969, Wilma Ann Alison, *née* Steel; 1 s (James Alexander Lees b 9 March 1971), 1 da (Nicola Catherine Lees b 3 Nov 1973); *Career* called to the Bar Gray's Inn 1968 (bencher 2000), ad eundem memb Middle Temple; asst recorder 1983, recorder 1987–2006, circuit judge (SE Circuit) 2006–14, sr circuit judge and resident judge Crown Court Kingston Upon Thames 2011–14, ret, sr bencher 2015–; Bar Cncl: memb 1993–95, vice-chm Legal Servs Ctee 1993, vice-chm Public Affrs Ctee 1995, vice-chm Professional Conduct and Complaints Ctee 2005; memb: Continuing Educn Ctee Gray's Inn 1998–2002 (chm 2001–02), Inns Advocacy Trg Ctee (IATC) 2001, Bar Professional Standards Ctee 2002–04; *Style*— His Hon Nicholas Price, QC; ✉ The Crown Court at Kingston upon Thames, 6–8 Penrhyn Road, Kingston upon Thames, Surrey KT1 2BB (☎ 020 8240 2500)

PRICE, Prof Patricia M; da of Michael Hogan, of Coventry, Warks, and Jane, *née* Quill; *b* 13 August 1957; *Educ* Newnham Coll Cambridge (MA), King's Coll Hosp Med Sch (MB BChir, MRCP), Univ of Cambridge (MD, Lionel Whitby medal); *m* 1, 1984 (m dis), Dr C G A Price; 2 s (Oliver b 8 Oct 1986, Rory b 24 Sept 1988); m 2, 1994, Prof Terry Jones; 1 step da (Julia), 2 step s (Evan, Gareth); *Career* oncology training Radiotherapy and Oncology Unit Royal Marsden Hosp 1984–89, CRC clinical scientist Inst of Cancer Research 1988–89, conslt clinical oncologist Hammersmith, St Mary's and Ealing Hosps 1989–2000, reader in clinical oncology Imperial Coll Sch of Med 1997–2000, head Section of Cancer Therapeutics Imperial Coll Sch of Medicine until 2000, Ralston Paterson prof of radiation oncology Christie Hosp Univ of Manchester 2000–09, founding dir Univ of Manchester Wolfson Molecular Imaging Centre 2000–06, princ clinical scientist Univ of Manchester Wolfson Molecular Imaging Centre 2006–09; visiting prof Imperial Coll London 2010–, hon conslt oncologist Imperial Coll HCT 2010–; chair UK Academic Clinical Oncology and Radiobiology Research Network 2005–09; dir PET Research Advsy Co 2010–; memb various UK, European and American oncology advsy ctees and editorial bds, expert witness in oncology medico-legal cases 1990–; dir Price-Jones Ltd 2009–; chair of tstees Action Radiotherapy UK 2010–; raised over £20m in research grant funding; various prizes and awards incl: Varian Clinical Research Award Euro Soc for Therapeutic Radiology and Oncology 1985, Sterling Oncology Award 1989, Silver Award for Excellence in the NHS 2007; former sec and pres Br Oncological Assoc; FRCR 1987, FRCP 1995; *Publications* Treatment of Cancer (6 edn, 2014); over 300 pubns in the field of oncology; *Recreations* running, music, theatre, walking in Wales, family; *Clubs* RSM; *Style*— Prof Pat Price; ✉ Department of Surgery & Oncology, Imperial College London, Hammersmith Hospital, Du Cane Road, London W12 0NN (e-mail p.price@imperial.ac.uk)

PRICE, Dr Paul Anthony; s of Wolf Price, of London, and Dinah, *née* Shafar; *b* 15 May 1949; *Educ* Christ's Coll GS Finchley, UCL (BSc), UCH Med Sch (MB BS); *m* 15 March 1985, Sandra Margaret, *née* Miller; *Career* sr house offr physician: Brompton Hosp, Enfield Dist Gen Hosp 1973–75; hon registrar and Parkinson's Disease Soc res fell KCH 1977–78, registrar UCH 1978–79, hon sr registrar Bart's 1979–83, sr registrar St George's Hosp Gp London 1983–85, conslt physician and endocrinologist Great Western Hospital Swindon 1985–; cncl memb Section of Endocrinology RSM, memb Assoc of Br Clinical Diabetologists (ABCD), memb Soc for Endocrinology (SFE); FRCP, FRSM, memb BMA; *Books* chapters in books on neurology and endocrinology; *Recreations* music, playing the bassoon, walking, speaking Italian, travelling; *Clubs* European Doctors' Orchestra; *Style*— Dr Paul Price; ✉ 33 Gloucester Street, Cirencester GL7 2DJ (☎ 01285 654524, e-mail cirendoc@gmail.com); Ridgeway Hospital, Wroughton, Swindon SN4 8DD (☎ 01793 816061)

PRICE, Rt Rev Dr Peter Bryan; s of Rev Capt Alec H Price (d 1983), late RA, and Phyllis E M, *née* Bryan (d 1983); *b* 17 May 1944; *Educ* Glastonbury Sch Morden, Redland Coll Bristol (CertEd), Oak Hill Theol Coll London (Dip Patoral Studies), Heythrop Coll London (Research Studies); *m* Edith Margaret, MBE, da of Samuel Munro Burns; 4 s (David b 6 Aug 1968, Patrick b 26 Feb 1970, Neil b 5 Nov 1971, John-Daniel b 13 Sept 1982); *Career* asst teacher Ashton Park Sch 1966–70, sr tutor Lindley Lodge Young People's Centre 1970, head of religious studies Cordeaux Sch Louth 1970–72, student Oakhill Coll 1972–74, community chaplain Crookhorn and curate Christchurch Portsdown 1974–78, chaplain Scargill Community 1978–80, vicar of St Mary Magdalene Addiscombe 1980–88, chair Diocese of Southwark Bd of Mission 1987–92 (Bishop's advsr on church devpt 1980–86), chllr and residentiary canon Southwark Cathedral 1988–91, gen sec United Soc for the Propagation of the Gospel 1992–97, bishop of Kingston 1997–2001, bishop of Bath and Wells 2001–13; chair Southwark Diocesan Bd of Educn 1998–2004, chair Conciliation Resources 2013, memb Bd Inst of Policy Research Univ of Bath 2014–16; chair Manna Soc 1998–2002 (hon pres 2002–); patron: Action by Christians Against Torture 2002–13, St Margaret's Hospice 2002–13, Somerset Community Fndn 2002–13; memb SPCK Governing Body 1996–99, core memb New Way of Being Church 1998–2008; memb House of Lords 2008–13; visitor Wadham Coll Oxford 2002–13, chair Palace Tstees Wells 2002–13, pres Royal Bath & West Soc 2012–13 (vice-pres 2013–), co-fndr and tstee Burns Price Fndn 2015–; Hon LLD Univ of Bath 2013; *Books* Church as Kingdom (1987), Seeds of the Word (1996), Living Faith in the World (1998), Interactive Learning for Churches (1998), To Each Their Place (1998), Mark (2000), Jesus Manifesto (2000), Undersong (2002), Playing the Blue Note (2002), Changing Communities (2003), Value of Dialogue in Times of Hostility and Insecurity (2016); *Recreations* painting, walking, gardening, reading, conversation; *Clubs* Farmers; *Style*— The Rt Rev Dr Peter B Price; ✉ 4 Longways, Shaftesbury Road, Gillingham, Dorset SP8 4ED

PRICE, Richard Lloyd Duffield; s of David Henderson Price, and Janet Helen, *née* Duffield; *b* 13 April 1949; *Educ* Royal GS Newcastle upon Tyne, Magdalen Coll Oxford (BA), Univ of London (Postgrad Dip Applied Social Studies); *m* 1981, Joanna Mary, da of William Murray; 2 s (Gregory Richard Murray b 10 Sept 1982, Alastair Joseph Murray b 4 Oct 1985); *Career* probation offr Inner London Probation Serv 1973–77, info offr Personal Social Serv Cncl 1977–78, dep dir Int Year of the Child (UK) 1978–80, communications mangr Nexos Office Systems Ltd 1980–83, md The EuroPR Gp Ltd 1984–2009, md Interpret Int Ltd 2010–16; chm Prisoners Abroad, tstee The Sixteen, tstee Merton Homelessness Project; *Recreations* singing, cricket, family activities; *Clubs* Oxford and Cambridge; *Style*— Richard Price, Esq; ✉ Interpret International Ltd, 5 Wilton Crescent, Wimbledon, London SW19 3QY (e-mail richardldprice@hotmail.com)

PRICE, Richard Mervyn; OBE (1995), QC (1996); s of William James Price (d 1987), of S Yorks, and Josephine May, *née* Preston (d 2000); *b* 15 May 1948; *Educ* King Edward VII Sch Sheffield, King's Coll London (LLB); *m* 1971 (m dis 2007), Caroline Sarah, da of Geoffrey Ball, and Mary Ball, of Surrey; 1 s (Timothy George b 13 Jan 1975), 2 da (Kathryn Sara b 3 Dec 1977, Emma Charlotte Louisa b 28 July 1983); *Career* called to the Bar Gray's Inn 1969 (bencher 2002); standing counsel on election law Cons Central Office 1986–, recorder 2004–; chm Conduct Ctee Bar Cncl, memb Bar Standards Bd 2006–07, legal assessor Disciplinary Ctee RCVS 2007–, legal assessor to the Fitness to Practise Panels of the GMC/ Medical Practitioners Tbnl Service 2011–; *Recreations* politics, theatre, films, music, walking, cycling; *Clubs* RAC, Garrick; *Style*— Richard Price, Esq, OBE, QC; ✉ Littleton Chambers, 3 King's Bench Walk North, Temple, London EC4Y 7HR (☎ 020 7797 8600, fax 020 7797 8699)

PRICE, His Hon Richard Neville Meredith; s of Christopher Price (d 1980), and Valerie Ruby, *née* Greenham (d 1992); *b* 30 May 1945; *Educ* Marsh Court Stockbridge, Sutton Valence, Coll of Law Guildford; *m* Oct 1971, Avril Judith, da of Edward Purser Lancaster (d 1954), and Dorothy Margaret, *née* Collins; 3 s (Andrew b 10 Nov 1974, Simon b 24 Sept 1979, David b 10 June 1986); *Career* slr 1970–90, called to the Bar Middle Temple 1990, recorder 1990–96 (asst recorder 1986–90), circuit judge 1996–2014, ret, resident judge Isle of Wight 2002–11, resident judge Portsmouth 2004–11, hon recorder City of Portsmouth 2006–11; *Recreations* choral singing, sailing, reading, listening to music, appreciating Dr Who; *Clubs* Seaview Yacht; *Style*— His Hon Richard Price; ✉ Portsmouth Combined Court Centre, Courts of Justice, Winston Churchill Avenue, Portsmouth, Hampshire

PRICE, Richard Shirvell; MBE; s of Eric Shirvell Price, and Lucy; *b* 1933, Swansea; *Educ* Milton Acad Mass, Leeds GS, Liverpool Inst Sch, Univ of Leeds; *m* 1963, Joan, *née* Silk; 1 s, 1 da; *Career* served RNVR and RNR 1951–64; Nat Serv Supply Offr RN 1955–57; PRO Benger Laboratories Ltd 1957–59, freelance journalist 1957–59, sr PRO PIDA (Agricultural Authy) 1959, PRO, orgn mangr then sales controller Bayer (UK) 1960–62, fndr and ed PULSE (the GP newspaper, now published by Morgan Grampian) 1960–62, md Pharmacia (UK) Ltd 1962–65, sales dir Granada Television (Overseas) Ltd 1965–67,

P

former chm Primetime plc gp (included Primetime Television largest ind UK prog distributor) founded 1968; chm RPTA Ltd, former chm Watermill Theatre Newbury; chm The Performance Co; BAFTA: memb Cncl 1982–97, hon treas 1984–91, chm and tstee 1991–93, dep chm 1993–95; local cncllr Paddington 1963–65, Parly candidate (Cons) N Paddington 1969 and 1970; chm CPC study gps on Traffic and Broadcasting 1965–68; chm local MENCAP Soc 1980–86; govr: Parkwood Hall Sch 1986–2000 (chm of govrs 1990–94), Home Farm Tst for Learning Difficulties 1993– (chm 2000–04); chm LSE Media Advsy Gp 1995–97, memb Fulbright Advsy Ctee 1995–2001, former chm Charities Tax Gp 2003–; FRTS 1985 (memb Cncl 1975–83); *Recreations* antique maps, good wine; *Clubs* Savile (chm of tstees); *Style*— Mr Richard Price, MBE, FRTS; ✉ Beech Knoll, Aldbourne, Wiltshire SN8 2EJ (e-mail richardprice@rtpa.co.uk, website www.rpta.co.uk)

PRICE, Richard Stephen; s of Dr David Brian Price, OBE, of Bridgend, Mid Glamorgan, and Menna Myles, *née* Jones (d 1988); *b* 27 May 1953; *Educ* Cowbridge GS, Univ of Leeds; *m* 3 May 1980, Nicola Mary, da of Philip Griffin, of Henstridge, Somerset; 2 da (Roseanna b 4 Dec 1986, Susannah Kate Rhiannon b 1 Feb 1993), 1 s (Nicholas b 13 Sept 1988); *Career* admitted slr 1977, sr ptnr CMS Cameron McKenna (formerly McKenna & Co) 1984– (i/c ME practice 1984–88); memb City of London Slrs' Co, memb Law Soc; *Recreations* golf; *Style*— Richard Price, Esq; ✉ CMS Cameron McKenna, Mitre House, 160 Aldersgate Street, London EC1A 4DD (☎ 020 7367 3000, fax 020 7367 2000)

PRICE, Robin Mark Dodgson; s of Wilfred Barrie Price, of Knowle, West Midlands, and Jocelyn Mary, *née* Berry; *b* 30 April 1956; *Educ* The Leys Sch Cambridge, Univ of Bristol (LLB); *m* 27 Sept 1986, Jane, da of Vyvian Hugh Reginald Rawson; 1 s (Joe Gulliver b 19 Nov 1990), 1 da (Eleanor Alice b 22 Sept 1992); *Career* chartered accountant Arthur Young McClelland Moores 1978–82, md Frontline Video Ltd 1983–87, ptnr HHCL and Partners 1987–97, dir Chime Communications plc 1997–2002, chief operating offr McCann Erickson UK and Ireland and vice-pres operations McCann Erickson EMEA 2003–09, global commercial dir and chief financial offr What If! Hldgs Ltd 2009–13, gp finance dir Be Heard Gp 2015–; treas Nat Advertising Benevolent Soc 2010–; chair Dance Umbrella 2014–; FCA, FIPA; *Recreations* tennis, golf, cricket, ballet and modern dance; *Clubs* Roehampton; *Style*— Robin Price, Esq; ✉ Be Heard Group Plc, 53 Frith Street, London W1D 4SN (☎ 07770 382356, email robinprice@f2s.com)

PRICE, Roland John Stuart; s of Philip Stuart Price, of Tamworth, and Rowena Mary, *née* Jones; *b* 29 July 1961; *Educ* Sydney GS Aust, Royal Ballet Sch London; *Career* ballet dancer (ret); Gold Medal Adeline Genée Award 1978; princ dancer: Sadler's Wells Royal Ballet (now Birmingham Royal Ballet) 1984–95 (joined 1979), Boston Ballet USA 1990–94; princ roles incl: The Two Pigeons, La Fille Mal Gardée, Coppélia, Giselle, Romeo and Juliet, Swan Lake, The Sleeping Beauty, The Snow Queen, Abdallah, The Nutcracker, Études, many one act ballets incl creations by Macmillan and Bintley; Lawrence Olivier Award nominee 1980 and 1985; freelance dance teacher and coach 1999–, guest teacher Royal Ballet; *Recreations* opera; *Style*— Roland Price, Esq

PRICE, Stuart David; *b* 9 September 1977, Stockton on Tees; *Career* musician, songwriter and record prodr; albums as musician, songwriter and prodr: Liberation (Les Rythmes Digitales) 1996, Darkdancer (Les Rythmes Digitales) 1999, Blueprint (Jacques Lu Cont) 2000, Living in a Magazine (Zoot Woman) 2001, FabricLive.09 (Jacques Lu Cont) 2003, Zoot Woman (Zoot Woman) 2003, Things Are What They Used To Be (Zoot Woman) 2009, Palindrome (Ambient Album, Jacques Lu Cont) 2013, Tracques Vol. 1 EP (Tracques) 2013, Star Climbing 2014; albums as prodr: Random Order (Juliet) 2005, System (Seal, *qv*) 2007 (also co-writer of several tracks), Confessions on a Dancefloor (Madonna) 2008, Day and Age (The Killers) 2008, Complete Me (Frank Musik) 2009, Night Work (Scissor Sisters) 2010, Aphrodite (Kylie Minogue) 2010, Flamingo (Brandon Flowers) 2010, Progress (Take That) 2010, Progress EP (Take That) 2011, Electric (Pet Shop Boys) 2013, III (Take That) 2014, Helios (The Fray) 2014, Get to Heaven (Everything Everything) 2015; also prodr of various tracks on albums by The Killers, Keane, P Diddy, New Order, InnerPartySystem, Duffy, Hard-Fi, Example, Steve Angello; remixes for Madonna incl: Hung Up (as Man with Guitar), Sorry (as Man with Guitar), Get Together (as Paper Faces), Jump (as Paper Faces), I Love New York (as Paper Faces), Let It Will Be (as Paper Faces), Hollywood, Miles Away; remixes for The Killers incl: Mr Brightside, Human (as Thin White Duke); other remixes incl: It's My Life (No Doubt), Talk (Coldplay), Wrong (Depeche Mode) 2009 (as Thin White Duke), Jumping In The Pool (Friendly Fire), This Must Be It (Röyksopp), Undisclosed Desires (Muse); musical dir of Madonna's Drowned World Tour 2001, Re-Invenstion World Tour 2004 and Confessions Tour 2006, produced Pet Shop Boys medley at the Brit Awards 2009, in charge of 'sonic branding' and wrote theme tune 'Languages' London Olympics 2012; Grammy Award 2004 (for remix of It's My Life (No Doubt)), 2006 (for remix of Talk (Coldplay)) and 2007 (for Confessions on a Dancefloor (Madonna)), Int Hit of the Year Ivor Novello Award 2007 (for Sorry (Madonna)), Music Week Prodr of the Year 2011 (for Progress (Take That)), BBC Radio 1 Pete Tong's Hall of Fame 2015; *Style*— Stuart Price, Esq; ✉ c/o Becker Brown, Alma Studios, 32 Stratford Road, Kensington, London W8 6QF (☎ 020 7286 0332, e-mail info@beckerbrown.com)

PRICHARD, David; s of late Richard Evan Prichard, of Exmouth, Devon, and late Phyllis, *née* Hiscock; *b* 23 September 1948; *Educ* Kingston GS, Bartlett Sch of Architecture (BSc, DipArch, Sir Andrew Taylor Prize); *m* 23 Sept 1988, Catherine Jamison, da of Ian McCarter; 1 da (Isobel b 13 Nov 1984), 2 s (Charlie b 28 Feb 1986, George b 16 Dec 1988); *Career* architect; ptnr MacCormac Jamieson Prichard Architects 1979–2005, co-fndr (with Neil Deely) Metropolitan Workshop LLP 2005; buildings and masterplans at: Milton Keynes Devpt Corp, Warrington Devpt Corp, Queen Mary Univ of London, Spitalfields Market, LDDC, offices in Havant Hants CC, Bow HAT, Cable and Wireless Coll Coventry 1990–94 (Building of the Year Award 1994), Imperial Coll London, Gala Theatre Durham, Durham Clayport Library, Ballymun Regeneration Dublin, Meadowbank Club, Jersey Archive, City of Durham, Poplar, Adamstown Dist Centre, Dublin Docks, Oslo City Cncl, Dead Sea Regnl Plan; visiting lectr: Univ of Brighton, Univ of Cambridge; RIBA external examiner 1981–2003: Univ of Kent, UCL, Univ of North London, Edinburgh Coll of Art; Civic Tst: regnl and nat assessor 1990–2003, chm Nat Awards Panel 2004–, tstee 2004–; academician Acad of Urbanism; several RIBA Awards and Civic Tst Awards, RTPI of Ireland Planning Achievement Award 1999; RIBA 1974, FRSA, FICPD; *Recreations* family, walking, gardening; *Style*— David Prichard, Esq; ✉ Wilmot Cottage, Mote Road, Ivy Hatch, Sevenoaks, Kent TN15 0NT (☎ 01732 810063); Metropolitan Workshop LLP, 14–16 Cowcross Street, Farringdon, London EC1M 6DG (☎ 020 7566 0450, e-mail david.prichard@metwork.co.uk, website www.metwork.co.uk)

PRICHARD, Desmond George Michael (Des); OBE (2012), QFSM (2006); s of Aubrey Veron Prichard, of Milton Keynes, Bucks, and Ellen, *née* Grosse; *b* 9 December 1953, London; *Educ* Bletchley GS, Putteridgebury Coll (Dip), Henley Mgmnt Coll (MBA); *m* 25 July 1987, Ruth Ann, *née* Stanton; 1 s (Benjamin Thomas Stanton b 17 Jan 1991); *Career* joined Fire and Rescue Serv 1976; served in Beds and Bucks, lectr in command leadership and mgmnt Fire and Rescue Serv Coll 1991–94; E Sussex Fire Serv: asst chief fire offr 1995–96, dep chief fire offr 1996–2001; chief exec and chief fire offr E Sussex and Brighton & Hove 2001–15; dir Des Prichard Consulting Ltd 2015–; dir Cross Sector Leadership Exchange 2015–; chm Assoc of Princ Fire Offrs, bd dir for HR Chief Fire Offrs Assoc, bd dir Fire Sevice Nat Pensions Bd; Long Service and Conduct Medal 1996; memb Inst of Fire Engrs 1984, MCIPD 1994, chartered dir IOD 2007; *Recreations* rugby, skiing, theatre, watching Chelsea FC; *Clubs* Bletchley RUFC (vice-pres); *Style*— Des Prichard, Esq, OBE, QFSM; ✉ East Sussex Fire & Rescue Service Headquarters, 20 Upperton Road, Eastbourne, East Sussex BN21 1EU (☎ 01323 462060, e-mail des.prichard@esfrs.org)

PRICHARD, Mathew Caradoc Thomas; CBE (1992), DL (1994); s of Maj Hubert de Burgh Prichard, of Pwllywrach, Cowbridge (ka 1944), and Rosalind Margaret Clarissa Hicks, *née* Christie; *b* 21 September 1943; *Educ* Eton, New Coll Oxford (BA); *m* 1, 20 May 1967, Angela Caroline (d 2004), *née* Maples; 2 da (Alexandra b 1968, Joanna b 1972), 1 s (James b 1970); m 2, 10 Feb 2007, Lucinda Mary, *née* Oliver; *Career* chm Agatha Christie Ltd 1977–; chm Welsh Arts Cncl 1986–94, memb Arts Cncl GB 1983–94, pres Nat Museum of Wales 1997–2002 (vice-pres 1992–96), memb Bd WNO Ltd; High Sheriff Co of Glam 1973–74; *Recreations* golf, cricket, bridge; *Clubs* Boodle's, Cardiff and County, R&A, Royal Porthcawl Golf, MCC; *Style*— Mathew Prichard, Esq, CBE, DL

PRICHARD JONES, Kenneth Victor (Ken); s of John Victor Jones, MBE (d 1981), and Eunice Aldwyn Marie, *née* Prichard (d 1976); *b* 12 September 1946; *Educ* Clifton, Univ of Kent at Canterbury (BA); *m* 26 Sept 1967, Dagmar Eva, da of Col Pavel Svoboda (d 1993), of Putney, London; 3 s (Sebastian b 1973, Piers b 1975, Christian b 1980), 1 da (Lucy b 1978); *Career* admitted slr 1972; dir Collegiate Securities Ltd; memb Law Soc; friend of Keats-Shelley Meml Assoc; Medal of Honour for Conservation Europa Nostra 1994; breeder Dreadnought herd of White Park cattle; *Books* F is for Franchising (2 edn, 1983), Encyclopaedia of Forms and Precedents (Agency Documents vol, 1984, revised edn 1992), Merchandising (contrib, 1987), Commercial Hiring and Leasing (contrib, 1989), Encyclopaedia of Forms and Precedents (Food vol, 1995), The Law and Practice of Franchising (with Prof John Adams, 5 edn 2006); *Recreations* swimming, motor racing; *Clubs* Brooklands, Bluecoats, Veteran Car, Vintage Sports Car, Silverstone Classic, Goodwood Road Racing; *Style*— Ken Prichard Jones; ✉ Field Place, Warnham, West Sussex RH12 3PB (☎ 01403 269166, mobile 07836 768596, e-mail westwind@whiteparks.com)

PRIDAY, Charles Nicholas Bruton; s of Christopher Bruton Priday, QC (d 1992), and Jill Holroyd, *née* Sergeant; *b* 17 July 1959; *Educ* Radley, UC Oxford, City Univ London; *m* 17 July 1982, Helen Elizabeth, da of M M Jones; 2 da (Elizabeth b 1987, Emma b 1989); *Career* called to the Bar Middle Temple 1982; *Recreations* escaping to the Cotswolds, golf, tennis; *Clubs* Oxford Unicorns Real Tennis, Moreton Morrell Real Tennis; *Style*— Charles Priday, Esq; ✉ 7 King's Bench Walk, Temple, London EC4Y 7DS (☎ 020 7583 0404, fax 020 7583 0950, telex 887491 KBLAW)

PRIDAY, Helen Elizabeth; da of Michael Montague Jones (d 1995), of Radley, Oxon, and Alison Priscilla, *née* Shepherd (d 1993); *Educ* Dragon Sch Oxford, Radley; *m* 17 July 1982, Charles Nicholas Bruton Priday, *qv*, s of Christopher Bruton Priday, QC (d 1992), of London; 2 da (Elizabeth b 1987, Emma b 1989); *Career* publicity and promotions mangr W H Freeman & Co Oxford 1978–82, ed Pitkin Pictorials London 1982–83, mktg and publicity dir Times Books Angus and Robertson London 1983–, promotions dir The Times Supplements 1990–97 (The Times Literary Supplement, The Times Educational Supplement, The Times Higher Education Supplement), fndr: HP:M (Helen Priday Marketing) 1997–, Thinking Books 2008, Private Home Network 2008; dir Equus Event Ltd 2001–03; conslt: Daily Telegraph/House & Garden Fair 1999–, The Spirit of Christmas 2001–; memb Advsy Bd Maia Press; tstee Plantlife 2012–; MIDM, FRSA; *Recreations* walking in the Cotswolds, tennis, golf, good food and wine, travelling in France, Ile de Ré, gardening, theatre, opera; *Clubs* St Enodoc Golf, Great Rissington, Vauban Societé; *Style*— Mrs Helen Priday; ✉ websites www.thinkingbooks.net and www.privatehomenetwork.com

PRIDEAUX, Julian Humphrey; OBE (1995); s of Sir Humphrey Povah Treverbian Prideaux, OBE, DL (d 2014), and Cynthia, *née* Birch-Reynardson (d 2008); *b* 19 June 1942; *Educ* St Aubyn's Rottingdean, Eton, RAC Cirencester (Dip); *m* 5 Aug 1967, Rosamund Jill, da of Richard Patrick Roney-Dougal (d 1993), of Bridgnorth, Shropshire; 2 s (Adam b 1968, Nigel b 1971); *Career* land agent; Burd and Evans Chartered Surveyors Shrewsbury 1964–67; Col the Hon GC Cubitt and Others 1967–69; The National Trust: land agent Cornwall Region 1969–77, dir Thames and Chilterns Region 1978–86, chief agent 1987–97, dep DG and sec 1997–2002; tstee: Rural Housing Tst 2001–14, Nat Gardens Scheme 2003–05 (memb Cncl 1987–2005), Goldsmiths Centre 2007–11; memb Cncl Chelsea Physic Garden 2003–12 (chm Exec Ctee); FRICS 1974; *Recreations* walking; *Clubs* Farmers'; *Style*— Mr Julian Prideaux, OBE; ✉ Cromwell Lodge, 39 East Street, Coggeshall, Essex CO6 1SJ (☎ 01376 564437)

PRIEST, Christopher McKenzie; s of Walter Mackenzie Priest, and Millicent Alice, *née* Haslock; *b* 14 July 1943, Cheadle, Cheshire; *Educ* Cheadle Hulme Sch; *Children* 2 c (Simon Walter, Elizabeth Millicent (twins) b 23 Oct 1989); *Career* writer; tstee Hastings and Rother CAB 2000–07, memb Soc of Authors (Mgmnt Ctee); JP East Sussex 1996–2013; *Awards* James Tait Black Memorial Prize for Fiction 1995, World Fantasy Award 1996, Prix Utopia 2001, Grand Prix de l'Imaginaire 2001, Arthur C Clarke Award 2002; *Books* Indoctrinaire (1970), Real-Time World (short stories, 1974), Fugue for a Darkening Island (1972), Inverted World (1974), The Space Machine (1976), A Dream of Wessex (1977), An Infinite Summer (short stories, 1979), The Affirmation (1981), The Glamour (1984), The Quiet Woman (1990), The Book on the Edge of Forever (non-fiction, 1994), The Prestige (1995), The Extremes (1998), The Dream Archipelago (short stories, 1999), The Separation (2002), The Magic – The Story of a Film (non-fiction, 2008), Ersatz Wines (2008), It Came from Outer Space (non-fiction, 2008), The Islanders (2011), The Adjacent (2013), The Gradual (2016); *Style*— Christopher Priest; ✉ c/o United Agents Ltd, 12–26 Lexington Street, London W1F 0LE (☎ 020 3214 0800, fax 020 3214 0801, website www.unitedagents.co.uk)

PRIEST, Prof Eric Ronald; s of Ronald Priest, of Halesowen, Worcs, and Olive Vera, *née* Dolan; *b* 7 November 1943; *Educ* King Edward VI Birmingham, Univ of Nottingham (BSc), Univ of Leeds (MSc, PhD); *m* 25 July 1970, Clare Margaret, da of Rev William Henry Wilson, of St Andrews, Fife; 3 s (Andrew Nicholas b 1973, David Mark b 1978, Matthew Aidan b 1978), 1 da (Naomi Clare b 1982); *Career* Univ of St Andrews: prof of theoretical solar physics 1983, lectr in applied mathematics 1969, reader 1977, James Gregory prof of mathematics 1997, Wardlaw prof of mathematics 2002–; Hale Prize American Astronomy Soc 2002, Gold medal RAS 2009, Payne-Gaposchkin Medal Inst of Physics 2009; hon DSc Univ of St Andrews 2013; memb Norwegian Acad of Scis and Letters 1994; FRSE 1985, FRS 2002; *Books* Solar Flare Magnetohydrodynamics (1981), Solar Magnetohydrodynamics (1982), Solar System Magnetic Fields (1985), Dynamics and Structure of Solar Prominences (1989), Magnetic Flux Ropes (1990), Basic Plasma Processes on the Sun (1990), Advances in Solar System MHD (1991), Mechanisms of Chromospheric and Coronal Heating (1991), Dynamics of Solar Flares (1991), Magnetic Reconnection (2000), Magnetohydrodynamics of the Sun (2014); *Recreations* bridge, singing, hill walking, aerobics, children; *Style*— Prof Eric Priest, FRSE, FRS; ☎ 01334 474975; Mathematical Institute, University of St Andrews University, St Andrews, Fife KY16 9SS (☎ 01334 463709, fax 01334 463748, e-mail eric.r.priest@gmail.com)

PRIEST, Ian Michael; s of David Edward Priest, of Hartley, Kent, and Wendy Jean Margaret, *née* Hamley (d 2000); *b* 7 August 1963, Epsom, Surrey; *Educ* Whitgift Sch Croydon, Kingston Univ (BA); *m* 20 May 2000, Virginia Leigh, *née* Addicott; 2 da (Lily Margaret b 26 May 2001, Edie Grace b 6 Sept 2004), 1 s (Fynn Hamley b 10 March 2003); *Career* account exec rising to bd dir Int Mktg and Promotions 1986–93, ptnr rising to md Howell Henry Chaldecott Lury 1993–2001, founding ptnr Vallance Carruthers Coleman Priest 2002–, fndr Chime Ventures 2010, chief operating offr CSM Sport and Entertainment

2013–15, global ceo Grace Blue 2015–; exec bd memb Chime plc; memb: Mktg Soc 2003, Cncl IPA 2006 (pres 2013–15); *Clubs* Walton Heath Golf, Old Whitgiftian Rugby Football; *Style*— Ian Priest, Esq; ✉ Grace Blue, 4th Floor, Holborn Town Hall, 193–197 High Holborn, London WC1V 7BD (☎ 020 3206 9364, e-mail ian.priest@graceblue.com)

PRIEST, Keith; s of William John Priest, of Sunderland, and Christina, *née* Black; *b* 26 April 1950; *Educ* Bede Sch Sunderland, AA Sch of Architecture (AADipl); *m* 2 Aug 1979, Ann, *née* Buckley; 1 da (Lucy Eleanor); *Career* architect; Sir Denys Lasdun & Partners, design dir Wolff Olins design consits 1975–79, fndr ptnr Fletcher Priest Architects (London, Koln and Riga) 1979–; princ projects: Vodafone World HQ, IBM UK Labs, St Anne's Coll Oxford, Watermark Place/Angel Lane, Stratford City, Lothbury, London Planetarium, Sony Pictures, Peoplebuilding, Tornakalns Riga, Piccadilly Circus, Silvertown, St John's Coll Oxford, First Street, Angel Court; pres AA 2011–13; memb: Cncl AA 2002, Urban Gp Br Cncl of Offices; memb D&AD, tstee AA, tstee Fletcher Priest Tst; RIBA, FRSA; *Recreations* family and friends, reading, Italian tractors; *Clubs* Chelsea Arts, Architecture; *Style*— Keith Priest, Esq; ✉ Fletcher Priest Architects, 34/42 Cleveland Street, London W1T 4JE (☎ 020 7034 2200, fax 020 7637 5347, e-mail k.priest@fletcherpriest.com, website www.fletcherpriest.com); Fletcher Priest Bösl, Marsilusstrasse 20 50937, Köln, Germany (☎ 00 49 221 941 050, fax 00 49 221 941 0510, e-mail koeln@fletcherpriest.com); Fletcher Priest Architects, K.Barona iela 3–4, Riga LV1050, Latvia (☎ 00 371 67 217043, fax 00 371 67 217045, e-mail riga@fletcherpriest.com)

PRIEST, Margaret Diane (Mrs Tony Scherman); da of Arthur Edmund Priest (d 1995), and Gertrude, *née* Tommason (d 2007); *b* 15 February 1944, Tyringham, Bucks; *Educ* Dagenham Co HS Essex, SW Essex Tech Coll and Sch of Art Walthamstow, Maidstone Coll of Art (DipAD), RCA (John Minton scholar, MA, Silver medallist); *m* 1 Sept 1972, Tony Scherman, s of Paul Scherman (d 1996); 1 s (Leo b 2 April 1975), 2 da (Georgia Donna b 13 Jan 1978, Claudia Eve b 3 April 1980); *Career* artist; educator: Harrow Sch of Art 1970–74, St Martin's Sch of Art London 1972–76, Univ of Toronto Sch of Architecture 1983–95; prof of fine art Univ of Guelph Ontario 1983–2000 (prof emeritus 2000–), visiting critic to schs of art and architecture UK, USA and Canada; work in numerous public and private collections; public art projects incl: The Monument to Construction Workers (Cloud Gardens Park Toronto) 1993; memb Bd Ontario Coll of Art and Design 2005–11; *Exhibitions* major solo exhibitions incl: Arnolfini Gallery Bristol 1970 and 1974, Garage Art Limited London 1974, Felicity Samuel Gallery London 1976, Theo Waddington Gallery London, Toronto, New York and Montreal 1980–83, Marianne Friedland Gallery Toronto 1985 and 1987, Albemarle Gallery London 1989, To View from Here Gallery Hamilton and Macdonald Stewart Art Centre Guelph 1996, Kelowna Art Gallery Br Colombia 2000, Georgia Scherman Projects 2011; numerous gp exhibitions since 1969 in Eng, Scot, Yugoslavia, Switzerland, Belgium, Canada, USA, Australia, Germany and Italy; *Awards* Arts Cncl of GB 1969, Internationale Jugendtriennale Drawing Award 1979, Ontario Arts Cncl Drawing Award 1981, Governor Gen's Award for Architecture 1994, Ontario Confederation of Univ Faculty Assocs Teaching Award 1996; DFA (hc) OCAD Univ Ontario 2015; *Style*— Ms Margaret Priest; ✉ 1 Clarendon Avenue, Suite 200, Toronto, Ontario M4V 1H8, Canada (☎ 00 1 416 922 9699, e-mail info@margaretpriest.com)

PRIESTLEY, Hugh Michael; s of James Frederick Priestley, MC (d 2008), and Honor Purefoy, *née* Pollock (d 2012); *b* 22 August 1942; *Educ* Winchester, Worcester Coll Oxford (MA); *m* 9 July 1968, Caroline Clarissa Duncan, da of Brig John Hume Prendergast, DSO, MC (d 2007); 2 da (Alexandra b 1971, Susannah b 1974); *Career* The Times Newspaper 1964–66, Henderson Administration 1972–93, dir Rathbone Investment Mgmnt (formerly Laurence Keen) 1993–2005; chm Jupiter European Opportunities Tst; memb Investment Ctee Independent Age (formerly RUKBA); treas Nat Gardens Scheme Berks; govr Reed's Sch (pres Fndn Appeal 2010–11); hon fell UCL (treas 1981–98); *Recreations* children and grandchildren, shooting, watching share prices go up and down; *Clubs* City of London, Boodle's, MCC; *Style*— Hugh Priestley, Esq; ✉ 52 Chelsea Gate Apartments, 93 Ebury Bridge Road, London SW1W 8RB

PRIESTLY, Paul Graham; *b* 30 March 1958, Belfast; *Educ* Grosvenor GS, Belfast Coll of Business Studies, Queen's Univ of Belfast (BA); *Career* dir of resources NI Office 2003–07, dir of econ policy and regeneration Office of the First Min and Dep First Min 2007, perm sec Dept for Regnl Devpt 2007–; *Style*— Paul Priestly, Esq; ✉ Department for Regional Development, Clarence Court, 10–18 Adelaide Street, Belfast BT2 8GB

PRIESTMAN, Dr Jane; OBE (1991); da of Reuben Stanley Herbert (d 1986), and Mary Elizabeth, *née* Ramply (d 1957); *b* 7 April 1930; *Educ* Northwood Coll, Liverpool Coll of Art (NDD, ATD); *m* 1954 (m dis), Arthur Martin Priestman; 2 s (Matthew Temple b March 1958, Paul Dominic b June 1961); *Career* designer; design practice 1954–75, design mangr BAA 1975–86, dir of architecture and design British Railways Board 1986–91, design mgmnt conslt 1991–; visiting prof in int design De Montfort Univ; memb Design Cncl 1996–99, enabler CABE, chm RIBA Awards Gp, memb Home Office Design Review Panel; memb NHS Design Brief Working Gp; dir London Open City; govr: Cwlth Inst, Kingston Univ; Hon DDes: De Montfort Univ 1994, Sheffield Hallam Univ 1998; Hon FRIBA, FCSD; *Recreations* opera, city architecture, textiles, travel; *Clubs* Architecture; *Style*— Dr Jane Priestman, OBE; ✉ 30 Duncan Terrace, London N1 8BS (☎ 020 7837 4525, fax 020 7837 4525, e-mail janepriestman30@gmail.com)

PRIESTMAN, Paul Dominic; s of Martin Priestman (d 2003), of Bourne, Cambs, and Jane, *née* Herbert; *b* 8 June 1961; *Educ* St Christopher's Sch Letchworth, Central St Martin's (BA, RSA Student Design Award), RCA (MDes, RSA Student Design Award, DIA Mellchet Meml Award); *m* 18 Aug 1990, Hon Tessa Mitford, da of 5 Baron Redesdale (d 1991); *Career* designer; fndr Priestman Associates (now Priestman Goode Ltd) 1987; exhbns incl: Making Their Mark London 1987, Design Advantage (Design Cncl London) 1992, Best of British Design Hong Kong 1993, Design of the Times London 1995, Product of Desire Glasgow 1996, Design Cncl's 20 Designers Paris 1997, perm display Philadelphia MOMA 1998, Industry of One (Craft Cncl) 2001, Lateral Design (Glynn Vivian Art Gallery) 2001, Communicating Change Design Museum 2001, Joined Up Design for Schools (V&A) 2005, Designs of the Year Design Museum 2008, Design Museum Designs of the Year 2013, Life on Foot Design Museum 2015, The Origins of Tomorrow 2015; lectures incl: RSA, Design Cncl, Br Cncl, DTI, Bangkok, Johannesburg, New Delhi, São Paulo, ICA London, Tokyo, Aust, China, UK Southeast Asia Innovation Forum, Design Museum Annual Puma Sustainability Lecture, Int Rail Business Forum 1520, Product Design + Innovation Conference, Beijing Design Week, GREAT Festival, Metro Rail London, Middle East Rail, Economist Infrastructure Summit, keynote speech RSA Student Design Awards 2015, Design Cncl Design Summit 2015, Designs for Asia 2015, China UK Design Forum 2015, DBA Innovation Conf 2015; chair Design Business Assoc 2001–03; chair Design Sector Skills Panel 2005–06, memb Design Cncl 2005–06, memb Exec D&AD 2005–08, memb Cncl RCA 2007–; FRSA; *Awards* Second Int Design Comp Japan 1986, Best Foreign Product Award Japan 1989, Design Cncl Opportunity Ulster Award 1990, G Mark Award Japan 1991, Design Week Award Best Product 1991, 1993 and 2003 (highly commended 1994), Mother and Baby Award for Excellence 1994, ID Annual Design Review 1996, 1997 and 2000, finalist BBC Design Awards 1996, IF German Industrial Design Award 1998, Millennium Product Award 1999 (three) and 2000, Gold IDEA US Industrial Design Excellence Awards 2000 and 2001, Int Design Effectiveness Award 2002, winner of German IF Award for Priestman Goode website 2003, Design Week Awards for Best Consumer Product and Best Hospitality Environment 2005, Best Wine Bar (Vinoteca) Time Out Eating and Drinking Awards 2006, Food and Supermarket Design of the Year (M&S Deli) Retail Interiors Awards 2006, BDI Design Effectiveness Award (BT Homehub) 2007, Innovation Award (Water Watch) Future Friendly Awards 2008, Communication and Technol Award (Post a Phone) Condé Nast Traveller Innovation and Design Awards 2008, European Hotel Design Award 2008, Crystal Cabin Award 2008, Best Large Hotel (for Motel 6) and Best Transportation (for Swiss Airlines first class suite) Traveland Leisure Awards 2010, Best Transportation (for Norwegian Cruise Lines) Travel and Leisure Award 2011, Best Transport Condé Nast Traveller and Innovation and Design Award, Bronze IDEA Award 2012 (for Moving Platforms), Design Museum Designs of the Year 2013 (shortlist, Air Access), Best Cabin Interior Int Yacht and Aviation Award (TAM Airlines First Class), Silver IDEA Award 2013 (Air Access), Best Product (for New Tube for London) London Design Awards, Best Studio London Design Awards, Queen's Award for Enterprise in Int Trade, IDEA Award 2014 (for World View Experience), Best Transport Travel+ Leisure Award (for TAM Airlines First Class), Crystal Cabin Award Industrial Design and Visionary Concepts (for Embraer E2 Jets) 2015, IDEA Award (for New Tube for London) 2015, The Evening Standard London Progress 1000 2015, Design Week Hall of Fame 2015, The Drum Designerati 2015, Debrett's Britain's 500 Most Influential 2016; *Recreations* sailing, skiing, drawing; *Style*— Paul Priestman, Esq; ✉ c/o Anna Meyer, Priestman Goode, 150 Great Portland Street, London W1W 6QD (☎ 020 7580 3444)

PRIESTMAN, Dr Terrence James (Terry); s of Francis Dennis Priestman (d 1980), of Bournemouth, and Vera Mercy, *née* Jackman (d 1962); *b* 1 January 1945; *Educ* King Henry VIII Sch Coventry, King's Coll London, Westminster Med Sch London (MB BS, Frederick Bird prize); *Career* house offr: in radiotherapy and oncology Westminster Hosp London 1968, in gen surgery Bolingbroke Hosp London 1968–69; SHO: in gen med Willesden Gen Hosp 1969–70, in cardiology London Chest Hosp 1970, in radiotherapy and oncology Westminster Hosp 1970–71; sr registrar Christie Hosp and Holt Radium Inst Manchester 1973–74, conslt in radiotherapy and oncology Velindre Hosp Cardiff 1974–77, med advsr in oncology Wellcome Research Labs and hon conslt in radiotherapy and oncology Westminster Hosp 1977–81, conslt Queen Elizabeth and Dudley Road Hosps Birmingham 1981–89 (chm Div of Radiotherapy and conslt in administrative charge Dept of Radiotherapy and Oncology Queen Elizabeth Hosp 1982–87), conslt clinical oncologist Royal Hosp Wolverhampton 1989–2012, clinical dir of oncology and haematology New Cross Hosp Wolverhampton 2005–07; memb Med Exec Ctee Central Birmingham HA 1984–87; W Midlands RHA: memb Regnl Scientific Ctee 1986–91, chm Regnl Advsy Ctee on Radiotherapy and Oncology 1990–94; Royal Coll of Radiologists: memb Faculty Bd (Radiotherapy and Oncology) 1984–87 (elected) and 1987– (ex-officio), memb Cncl 1987–89, rep Br Assoc for Radiation Protection 1989–93 (chm 1990–91), rep Standing Intercollegiate Ctee on Nuclear Med 1989–94, registrar Faculty of Clinical Oncology 1994–96, dean Faculty of Clinical Oncology 1996–98, vice-pres 1997–98, chair The X-Appeal 2003–06; author of various book chapters and numerous original articles; ed Clinical Oncology 1989–94 (dep ed 1987–89), series ed CancerBACKUP pubns 1999–2002 (medical reviewer 2004–08), medical ed Macmillan Cancer Support 2008–; medical memb: Cncl Section of Oncology RSM 1986–87, Nat Ctee Br Assoc of Surgical Oncology 1981–84; Twining Medal for Research Royal Coll of Radiologists; MRCP 1971, DMRT 1972, FRCR (FFR) 1973, MD 1981, FRCP 1984; *Books* Cancer Chemotherapy: an introduction (3 edn, 1989), Coping With Chemotherapy (2005), Coping With Breast Cancer (2006), Coping with Radiotherapy (2007), Cancer Chemotherapy in Clincial Practice (2007, 2 edn 2012), Reducing Your Risk of Cancer (2008), The Cancer Survivor's Handbook (2009); *Recreations* watercolour painting; *Style*— Dr Terry Priestman; ✉ 86 Lichfield Road, Bow, London E3 5AL (e-mail terryp.doc@btopenworld.com)

PRIMAROLO, Baroness (Life Peer UK 2015), of Windmill Hill in the City of Bristol; Rt Hon Dame Dawn Primarolo; DBE (2014), PC (2002); *b* 2 May 1954; *Educ* Thomas Bennett Comp Sch Crawley, Bristol Poly (BA), Univ of Bristol; *m* 7 Oct 1972 (m dis), Michael Primarolo; 1 s (b 1978); m 2, 1990, Ian Ducat; *Career* former legal sec and advice worker 1972–75; cncllr Avon CC 1985–87; MP (Lab) Bristol S 1987–2015, memb Select Ctee on Members' Interests 1990–92, shadow min for health 1992–94, shadow spokesperson for treasy 1994–97, fin sec to the Treasy 1997–99, paymaster gen 1999–2007, min of state for public health 2007–09, min of state for children, young people and families 2009–10, dep speaker 2010–; *Style*— The Rt Hon the Baroness Primarolo, DBE; ✉ PO Box 1002, Bristol BS99 1WH (☎ 0117 909 0063); House of Commons, London SW1A 0AA (☎ 020 7219 3000, e-mail dawn.primarolo.mp@parliament.uk)

PRINCE, Dr John Anthony; s of Flt Lt Allan Leslie Prince (ka 1944), and Mary Pamela, *née* Paul; *b* 5 November 1941; *Educ* Giggleswick Sch, ChCh Oxford (MA, BM BCh, DIH, MRCGP, MFOM); *Career* conslt occupational physician: Occidental Oil Inc 1977–83, Tower Hamlets HA London Hosp 1983, London Borough of Tower Hamlets 1983–, News International 1985–86; memb Tower Hamlets DHA, former sr ptnr Tower Med Centre, special advsr on disablement to DSS, med offr Army Offr Selection Bd 2007–; memb: BMA, Soc of Occupational Med; FRSM; *Recreations* literature, history, antiquarianism, natural history, walking; *Style*— Dr John Prince; ✉ The Old Rectory, Sutton Mandeville, Salisbury, Wiltshire SP3 5NA

PRINGLE, Alexandra Jane Reina; da of Alexander James Sommerville Pringle, and Natalie May, *née* Afriat; sis of John Richard Pringle, *qv*; *b* 13 March 1953; *Educ* Kensington HS, Putney HS, Cambs Coll of Arts & Technol (BA), UCL (post grad res); *m* Rick Stroud; 1 s (Daniel Hilton b 30 April 1986); *Career* editorial asst Art Monthly 1976–78; editorial dir: Virago Press 1978–90 (dir 1984–), Hamish Hamilton 1990–94; dir Toby Eady Associates (literary agency) 1994–99, ed-in-chief Bloomsbury Publishing 1999–; patron Index on Censorship; Hon DLitt: Anglia Ruskin Univ, Univ of Warwick 2014; *Clubs* Chelsea Arts, Groucho; *Style*— Ms Alexandra Pringle; ✉ Bloomsbury Publishing, 50 Bedford Square, London WC1B 3DP (☎ 020 7631 5600, Twitter @AlexandraPring)

PRINGLE, Dame Anne Fyfe; DCMG (2010, CMG 2004); da of George Grant Pringle, of Glasgow, and Margaret Fyfe, *née* Cameron; *b* 13 January 1955; *Educ* Glasgow HS for Girls, Univ of St Andrews (MA); *m* 20 April 1987, Bleddyn Glynne Leyshon Phillips; *Career* joined FCO 1977, third sec Moscow 1980–83, vice-consul (commercial) San Francisco 1983–85, UK rep Brussels 1986–87, first sec FCO 1987–91, UK rep Brussels 1991–94 (on loan to European Political Co-operation Secretariat); FCO: African (Equatorial), Security Co-ordination Dept 1994–96, head Common Foreign and Security Policy Dept 1996–98, head Eastern Dept 1998–2001; ambass Czech Repub 2001–04, dir strategy and info FCO 2004–07, ambass Russian Fedn 2008–11, public appointments assessor 2012–16, UK special rep on deportation with assurances 2013–15; non-exec dir Ashmore plc 2013–; sr govr St Andrews Univ 2016–, non-exec dir Shakespeare's Globe Theatre 2016–; memb Bd VSO 1996–97; FRSA 2001; *Recreations* walking, skiing, music; *Clubs* Roehampton; *Style*— Dame Anne Pringle, DCMG; ✉ c/o Roehampton Club, Roehampton Lane, London SW15 5LR

PRINGLE, Hamish Patrick; s of Robert Henry Pringle (d 1990), of Nassau, Bahamas, and Pamela Ann, *née* Molloy; *b* 17 July 1951; *Educ* Trinity Coll Glenalmond, Trinity Coll Oxford (BA); *m* 24 July 1977, Vivienne Elizabeth, da of Dr H Michael Lloyd (d 1976), of Ripley, Surrey; 3 s (Sebastian b 1983, Benedict b 1985, Tristan b 1989), 1 da (Arabella Elizabeth Lloyd b 1993); *Career* grad trainee Ogilvy & Mather advtg 1973–74, account exec McCormick Richards 1974–75, account dir Boase Massimi Pollitt 1975–79, new business dir Publicis 1979–82, dir Abbott Mead Vickers/SMS 1982–86, md Madell Wilmot Pringle 1986–90, dir Leagas Delaney Partnership 1990–92; K Advertising

P

(formerly KHBB): new business dir 1992–93, gp account dir 1993, jt md 1993–97, chm and ceo 1994–97; vice-chm and mktg dir Saatchi & Saatchi 1997–99, Brand Beliefs Ltd 1999–; IPA: memb Cncl 1985–86 and 1992–, chm Advertising Effectiveness Awards Ctee 1994–96; chm NABS Gen Mgmnt Ctee 1996–98; MIPA 1985; *Recreations* sport, gardening, property development, art, family; *Style—* Hamish Pringle, Esq

PRINGLE, Jack Brown; s of John Pringle, of Nottingham, and Grace Mason, *née* Cowler; *b* 13 March 1952; *Educ* Nottingham HS for Boys, Univ of Bristol (BA, DipArch, professors' prize, travelling scholarship for architecture); *m* 1, 1992 (m dis 2002), Claire; 2 da (Maxine, Francesca); m 2, 2011, Holly Anne Porter; 1 da (Ava Grace); *Career* architect; Powell Moya and Partners 1973 and 1975–82; ptnr: Jack Pringle Architects 1982–85, Pringle Brandon Architects 1985–; RIBA: memb Cncl 1981–87 and 2002–, vice-pres 1982–83 and 2002–04, pres 2005–07, rep Br Cncl visit to Romania 1982, memb Educn Visiting Bd to Schs of Arch 1985–2005, memb visiting gp to China 1992 and 1993, chm Visiting Bd Sri Lanka Sch of Architects 1995, chair Professional Services Bd 2003–; memb CNAA Architecture Bd 1986–87; chair Article 25 devpt and disaster relief charity 2007–14, chair CIC 2012–14; RIBA 1975, FRSA 1981; Commandeur des Arts et Lettres; *Recreations* flying, sailing; *Clubs* Royal Ocean Racing, Chelsea Arts, Shoreditch House, Dover Street Arts; *Style—* Jack Pringle, Esq; ✉ Pringle Brandon Architects, 10 Bonhill Street, London EC2A 4QJ (☎ 020 7466 1000, e-mail j.pringle@pringlebrandon.com)

PRINGLE, John Richard; s of Alexander James Sommerville Pringle, of London, and Natalie May, *née* Afriat; bro of Alexandra Pringle, *qv*; gs of W M R Pringle, MP; *b* 30 May 1951; *Educ* Shrewsbury, AA Sch of Architecture (AADipl); *m* 1975, Penny Richards, *qv*, da of Denis George Richards, OBE; 1 s (Patrick b 1982), 1 da (Georgina b 1984); *Career* architect; Mario Pérez De Arce L Santiago de Chile 1972–73, Pascall & Watson London 1976–77, Scott Brownrigg & Turner Guildford 1977–78, ptnr Michael Hopkins & Partners 1981–96 (joined 1978), fndr ptnr Pringle Richards Sharratt 1996–; work incl: Sheffield Gallery and Winter Garden 1996–2002, Shrewsbury Music Sch 1999–2001, Oldham Cultural Quarter 1999–2001, Herbert Art Gallery & Museum Coventry 2002–, Hull History Centre 2005–10, West Ham Bus Garage 2006–10, William Morris Gallery Walthamstow 2009–12 (Museum of the Year 2013); lectr: Europe 1987–, N America 1995–; RIBA external examiner Univ of N London 1991–94, external examiner Univ of Nottingham 2003–06; AA: memb 1969, memb Cncl 1987–97, hon treas 1991–93, pres 1993–95; memb Project Enabling Panel CABE 2000–11, memb ARB/RIBA Validation Panel; tstee Michael Ventris Meml Fund 2003–; memb Bd Architectural Educn ARCUK 1986–93, chair Sheffield Urban Design Review Panel 2006–10, RIBA 1983 (memb Cncl 2002–06, hon treas 2002–05), memb English Heritage Urban Panel 2010–; *Recreations* travel, Italian, pinball machines; *Clubs* Chelsea Arts; *Style—* Mr John Pringle; ✉ Pringle Richards Sharratt, Studio 2.01, Canterbury Court, Kennington Park, 1 Brixton Road, London SW9 6DE (☎ 020 7793 2828, e-mail john.pringle@prsarchitects.com)

PRIOR, Frank; s of Francis Prior (d 1978), and Mary, *née* Ward (d 2013); *b* 20 January 1969; *m* 5 July 1997, Helen, *née* Isaacs; 1 da (Charlotte b 19 April 2001), 1 s (Oliver b 27 June 2003); *Career* slr: Cox Tredrea 1993–97, Williams Thompson 1998–2001, Paris Smith LLP 2001– (ptnr and head Family Team); memb Resolution 1998–; *Recreations* cinema, fashion, motorsport, music, walking; *Style—* Frank Prior, Esq; ✉ Paris Smith LLP, Number One London Road, Southampton SO15 2AE (☎ 07799 323445, e-mail frank.prior@parissmith.co.uk, website www.parissmith.co.uk)

PRIOR, James Edward Cairns (Jim); s of Robert Prior, and Kay Crossby, *née* Foster, of New Bradwell; *b* 13 June 1965, Leighton Buzzard; *Educ* UEA (BSc); *m* Céline Lynch; 1 da (Maisie Louisa Prior b 13 Aug 2000), 1 s (Rory Joseph Prior b 22 July 2005); *Career* formerly: dir of product and mktg EMEA Converse Inc 1997–2001, head of merchandise Levi Strauss UK 1994–97; ceo: The Partners 2001–, Lambie-Nairn, B to D Partnership (WPP); Gold Award D&AD; *Books* Preserved Thoughts (2013); *Recreations* tennis; *Clubs* Soho House; *Style—* Jim Prior, Esq; ✉ The Partners, Albion Courtyard, Greenhill Rents, Smithfield, London EC1M 6PQ (☎ 020 7608 0051, e-mail jim@the-partners.com, website www.the-partners.com, Twitter @Jim_Prior)

PRIOR, Baron (Life Peer UK 1987), of Brampton in the County of Suffolk; James Michael Leathes Prior; PC (1970); 2 s of Charles Bolingbroke Leathes Prior (d 1964), of Norwich; *b* 11 October 1927; *Educ* Charterhouse, Pembroke Coll Cambridge; *m* 30 Jan 1954, Jane Primrose Gifford, 2 da of Air Vice-Marshal Oswin Gifford Lywood, CB, CBE (d 1957); 3 s (Hon David, Hon Simon, Hon Jeremy), 1 da (Hon Mrs Roper); *Career* farmer and land agent in Norfolk and Suffolk; MP (Cons): Lowestoft 1959–83, Waveney 1983–87; PPS to: pres of BOT 1963, min of Power 1963–64, Rt Hon Edward Heath (leader of the oppn) 1965–70; min of Agric Fisheries and Food 1970–72, a dep chm Cons Pty 1972–74 (vice-chm 1965), lord pres of Cncl and ldr of House of Commons 1972–74, oppn front bench spokesman on employment 1974–79; sec of state: Employment 1979–81, NI 1981–84; chm: Industry and Parl Tst 1990–93, Rural Housing Tst, Great Ormond Street Hosp Special Tstees until 1994, Royal Vet Coll until 1994–98; memb: Tenneco Euro Advsy Cncl until 1997, American Int Gp Advsy Bd 1988–2006; non-exec chm Allders Ltd until 1994; chm: GEC plc 1984–98, African Cargo Handling Ltd 1998–2001, Ascot Underwriting 2001–06; dep chm Celtel (formerly MSI Cellular Investment BV) 2000–05; non-exec dir: United Biscuits (Holdings) plc until 1994, J Sainsbury 1984–96, Barclays plc 1984–88; chllr Anglia Poly Univ 1994–99; chm Arab-British C of C 1996–2003; *Books* A Balance of Power; *Recreations* cricket, gardening, philately, field sports, golf; *Style—* The Rt Hon Lord Prior, PC; ✉ House of Lords, London SW1A 0PW

PRIOR-PALMER, Simon Erroll; s of Maj-Gen George Erroll Prior-Palmer, CB, DSO (d 1977), by his 2 w, Lady Doreen, *née* Hope (d 1998), da of 3 Marquess of Linlithgow; bro of Lucinda Green, MBE, *qv*; *b* 5 February 1951, London; *Educ* Eton, ChCh Oxford (MA); *m* 1984, Lady Julia Lloyd George, da of 3 Earl Lloyd George of Dwyfor, DL, *qv*; 3 s (George b 1988, Arthur b 1991, Harold b 1998), 1 da (Lara b 1994); *Career* J P Morgan London and NY 1973–82; Credit Suisse First Boston: dir Investment Banking 1982, co-head Canadian Investment Banking 1982–84, md 1986, head UK Investment Banking 1987–98, sr advsr 2004–05; cmmr Postal Servs Cmmn (Postcomm) 2006–10, sr advsr FSA 2010–11; chm DJI Hldgs plc 2013–; dir: Gabriel Resources Ltd 2006–12, Burani Designer Hldgs NV 2007–09; tstee Macmillan Cancer Support 2000–13; FRSA 1989 (memb Cncl 2006); *Recreations* tennis, golf, skiing; *Clubs* White's; *Style—* Simon Prior-Palmer

PRISK, Mark; MP; *b* 12 June 1962; *Educ* Truro Sch, Univ of Reading; *m* 1989, Lesley; *Career* chartered surveyor; self-employed businessman and dir 1991–2001, writer for property and business media, regular speaker at business confs; Parly candidate (Cons): Newham NW 1992, Wansdyke 1997; MP (Cons) Hertford and Stortford 2001–, shadow fin sec to the Treasy, shadow paymaster gen 2002–04, opposition whip 2004–05, shadow min Business and Enterprise 2005–07, shadow min for Cornwall 2007–10, min of state Dept for Business, Innovation and Skills 2010–12, min of state for housing and local govt 2012–13, PM's envoy Nordic and Baltic Nations 2014–; memb Welsh Affrs Select Ctee 2001–05, chm Parliamentary Choir 2015–; *Recreations* Saracens RFC, playing the piano; *Style—* Mark Prisk, Esq, MP; ✉ House of Commons, London SW1A 0AA (☎ 020 7219 6358, website www.markprisk.com)

PRITCHARD, (Iorwerth) Gwynn; s of Rev Robert Islwyn Pritchard (d 1988), and Megan Mair, *née* Lloyd (d 2001); *b* 1 February 1946; *Educ* schs in England and Wales, King's Coll Cambridge (MA); *m* 1, 17 Oct 1970, Marilyn, née Bartholomew (d 1994); 2 s (Matthew Osian b 1975, Dafydd Islwyn b 1989), 1 da (Nia Siân b 1977); m 2, 18 Dec 1998, Althea Sharp; *Career* prodr and dir BBC OU Productions 1970–77; prodr: BBC Wales 1977–82, HTV Wales 1982–85; Channel 4 TV: commissioning ed 1985–88, sr commissioning ed educn 1989–92; BBC Wales: head of progs 1992–97, head of Welsh broadcasting 1997–2001; sec gen INPUT 2001–05, ind prodr 2001–; tstee: Welsh Writers Trust 1990–, Coleg Harlech 1992–2000; chair Cardiff Unitarians 2011–; memb Exec Ctee of Gen Assembly of Unitarian and Free Christian Churches 2015–; memb Bd Welsh Int Film Festival 1994–98; Winston Churchill Meml Fellowship 1973, Sir Huw Weldon Broadcasting Fellowship 1990; Chevalier de l'Ordre des Arts et des Lettres (France) 1990; *Publications* Dal Pen Rheswm (contrib ed, 1999); *Recreations* reading, swimming, walking; *Style—* Gwynn Pritchard, Esq; ✉ 25 Westbourne Road, Penarth, Vale of Glamorgan CF64 3HA (☎ 029 2070 3608, e-mail gwynnpritchard@hotmail.com)

PRITCHARD, Jane Mary; *née* Clarke; *b* 2 August 1959, Kent; *Educ* Holy Trinity Convent Bromley; *m* 1, 16 July 1988 (m dis 2008), Andrew Sizer; 1 da (Mary Natasha b 28 Feb 1991), 1 s (William James b 5 Feb 1996); m 2, 9 April 2009, Adam Pritchard; *Career* tax asst Smith & Williamson LLP 1977–80, advertisement asst Daily Mail 1981–82, sr account exec (sponsorship) Charles Barker Lyons 1982–87, account gp head Karen Earl Ltd 1987–90, client servs dir Strategic Sponsorship Ltd 1990–94, devpt dir Chartered Soc of Designers 1994–97, md Allies Ltd (sponsorship consits) 1997–2005, dir Business in the Community 2005–; *Recreations* running, travel, gardening, design and innovation, comedy; *Clubs* Bedford Harriers; *Style—* Mrs Jane Pritchard; ✉ Business in the Community, 137 Shepherdess Walk, London N1 7RG (☎ 020 7566 8718, e-mail jane.pritchard@bitc.org.uk)

PRITCHARD, Rt Rev John Lawrence; s of Neil Lawrence Pritchard (d 1999), of Lyndhurst, Hants, and Winifred Mary Coverdale, *née* Savill (d 1991); *b* 22 April 1948; *Educ* Arnold Sch Blackpool, St Peter's Coll Oxford (MA, DipTh), Ridley Hall Cambridge (Cert Pastoral Theol), St John's Coll Durham (MLitt); *m* 1972, Susan Wendy, da of George Edward Claridge; 2 da (Amanda Kate b 27 May 1976, Nicola Clare b 3 Nov 1977); *Career* asst curate St Martin's in the Bull Ring Birmingham 1972–76, diocesan youth chaplain and asst dir of religious educn Bath and Wells Dio 1976–79, vicar Wilton Parish Taunton 1980–88, warden Cranmer Hall St John's Coll Durham 1993–96 (dir of pastoral studies 1989–93), archdeacon of Canterbury 1996–2001, bishop of Jarrow 2002–07, bishop of Oxford 2007–14, ret; pres St John's Coll Durham 2006–11; chair Archbishops' Cncl Educn Div 2011–14; memb: Gen Synod C of E 1999–2001 and 2007–, Bd Church Army 2005–11, Miny Cncl 2008–11, House of Lords 2011–; pres Guild of Health 2005–14; tstee SPCK 2009– (chair 2011–); hon fell St Peter's Coll Oxford 2007, hon fell St John's Durham 2012–; *Books* Practical Theology in Action (1996), The Intercessions Handbook (1997), Beginning Again (2000), Living the Gospel Stories Today (2001), How to Pray (2002), The Second Intercessions Handbook (2004), Living Easter Through the Year (2005), How to Explain your Faith (2006), The Life and Work of a Priest (2007), Going to Church: A User's Guide (2009), Living Jesus (2010), God Lost and Found (2011), Living Faithfully (2013), Ten (2014), The Journey (2014), Something More (2016); *Recreations* fell walking, photography, music, travel, reading, writing, cricket; *Clubs* Nobody's Friends; *Style—* The Rt Rev John Pritchard; ✉ 42 Bolton Avenue, Richmond, North Yorkshire DL10 4BA (e-mail johnlpritchard@btinternet.com)

PRITCHARD, Mark Andrew; MP; s of Frank Pritchard (d 1983), and Romona, *née* Davies; *b* 22 November 1966, Manchester; *Educ* London Guildhall Univ (MA), CIM (DipM), Elim Coll (Cert), Univ of Buckingham (MA); *m* 20 May 1997 (m dis 2014), Sondra Janae; *Career* chief researcher Into the Voids (book on homelessness) 1992, asst ed Return Ticket (book on long-term unemployment) 1994, fndr own mktg communications co, co dir 1998–; MP (Cons) The Wrekin 2005– (Parly candidate (Cons) Warley 2001); memb: Environmental Select Ctee 2005–, EAC Select Ctee 2005–07, DWP Select Ctee 2006–08, Welsh Affrs Select Ctee 2008–, Transport Select Ctee 2008–, Jt Nat Security Strategy Ctee 2010–, NATO Parly Assembly 2010–14, Speaker's Panel 2013–, Br-Irish Parly Assembly 2013–; exec memb Br-American Parly Gp 2010–; vice-chm APPG on Social Care 2005–, vice-chm APPG on Argentina 2005–, sec Cons Parly Def Ctee, sec Cons Foreign Affrs Gp, chm APPG Russia 2007–09, chm APPG Philippines 2007–, dep chm Cons Pty Int Office 2010–12, sec 1922 Ctee, dep chm Cons Pty Int Dept 2010–13, chm Parly Gp for the ASEAN Region; memb Steering Gp to establish Habitat for Humanity 1994; MCIM, MCIPR, MCIJ, assoc memb Market Research Soc; *Recreations* skiing, writing, tennis; *Clubs* Carlton; *Style—* Mark Pritchard, Esq, MP; ✉ House of Commons, London SW1A 0AA (☎ 020 7219 8494, e-mail pritchardm@parliament.uk); Constituency Office, 25 Church Street, Wellington, Shropshire TF1 1DG (☎ 01952 256080)

PRITCHETT, Matthew (Matt); MBE (2002); s of Oliver Pritchett, feature writer, and Joan, *née* Hill, of London; gs of Sir Victor Sawdon Pritchett, CH, CBE (d 1997); *b* 14 July 1964; *Educ* Addey & Stanhope GS, St Martin's Sch of Art (graphics degree); *m* 12 Dec 1992, Pascale Charlotte Marie Smets; 3 da (Edith b 13 April 1994, Mary b 29 Jan 1996, Dorothy b 8 Oct 2001), 1 s (Henry b 26 Nov 1997); *Career* freelance cartoonist for New Statesman, Punch, Daily Telegraph and Spectator, front page cartoonist Daily Telegraph 1989–; Cartoonist of the Year What the Papers Say 1992, 2004 and 2006, Cartoon Arts Tst Award 1995, 1996, 1999, 2005 and 2006, Cartoonist of the Year UK Press Awards 1996, 1998, 2000, 2008 and 2009; *Books* Best of Matt (annually, 1991–); *Style—* Matt Pritchett, Esq, MBE

PROBY, Sir William Henry; 3 Bt (UK 1952) of Elton Hall, Peterborough, Cambs; CBE (2009), DL (Cambs 1995); s of Sir Peter Proby, 2 Bt (d 2002), and Blanche Cripps (d 2008), da of Col Henry Harrison Cripps; *b* 13 June 1949, Elton, Cambs; *Educ* Eton, Lincoln Coll Oxford (MA), Brooksby Coll of Agric; *m* 1974, Meredyth Anne, da of Timothy David Brentnall, of Preston, Rutland; 4 da (Alexandra (The Hon Mrs Rory Aitken) b 1980, Alice (Mrs Fergus Eckersley) b 1982, Frances Rose b 1986, Isabella b 1991); *Career* asst dir Morgan Grenfell 1980–82; dir: M M & K Ltd 1986–98, Ellis & Everard plc 1988–99, Booker Countryside Ltd 1994–96; chair MGM Life Assurance Soc 2008– (dir 2006–); pres Historic Houses Assoc 1993–98, memb Cncl Tate Britain 1999–2010, chair Nat Tst 2003–08, tstee Nat Portrait Gall 2009– (chm of tstees 2012); High Sheriff Cambs 2001–02; Liveryman The Grocers' Co; FCA 1975; *Recreations* shooting, music; *Clubs* Brooks's, Boodle's, Roxburghe, Dilittanti Soc; *Style—* Sir William Proby, Bt, CBE, DL; ✉ Elton Hall, Peterborough PE8 6SH (☎ 01832 280223, fax 01832 280584)

PROCHASKA, Dr Alice Marjorie Sheila; *née* Barwell; da of John Harold Barwell (d 1983), of Cambridge, and Hon Sheila Margaret Ramsay, *née* McNair (d 2000); *b* 12 July 1947; *Educ* Perse Sch for Girls Cambridge, Somerville Coll Oxford (MA, DPhil); *m* 25 June 1971, Franklyn Kimmel Prochaska, s of Franklin Anton Prochaska (d 1952), of Cleveland, USA; 1 da (Elizabeth b 1980), 1 s (William b 1982); *Career* asst keeper: London Museum 1971–73, Nat Archives 1975–84; sec and librarian Inst of Historical Res Univ of London 1984–92, dir of special collections British Library 1992–2001; univ librarian Yale Univ 2001–10, princ Somerville Coll Oxford 2010–; cmmr Royal Cmmn on Historical Manuscripts 1998–2001; author of numerous articles on archives and various aspects of Br history ca 1800 to present; organiser of special expos incl: London in the Thirties 1973, Young Writers of the Thirties 1976; memb: Nat Cncl on Archives (chm 1991–95), Steering Gp History at the Univs Def Gp 1987–92, Nat Curriculum History Working Gp Dept of Educn and Sci 1989–90, Heritage Educn Tst, Bd of Govrs London Guildhall Univ 1995–2001, Sir Winston Churchill Archive Tst 1995–2001 (chm 2010–), Steering Gp Digital Library Fedn 2001–, Assoc of Res Libraries 2001– (chair Ctee on Access and Collections 2003–05, chair Special Collections Working Gp 2007–09), Center for Research Libraries Bd 2003– (vice-chair 2005–07, chair 2007–09), Advsy Cncl Yale Center for British Art 2002–10, Section on Rare Books and Manuscripts Int Fedn of Library Assocs (chair 1999–2003), Main Panel D HEFCE Research Excellence Framework 2011–14; chm

Lewis Walpole Library Tstees 2001–09; pro vice-chllr Univ of Oxford 2015–; hon fell: Inst of Historical Res 2001, Royal Holloway Univ of London 2002; hon degree Univ of Aberdeen 2013; FRHistS 1987 (memb Cncl 1991–95, vice-pres 1995–99); *Books* London in the Thirties (1973), History of the General Federation of Trade Unions, 1899–1980 (1982), Irish History from 1700 – A Guide to Sources in the Public Record Office (1986), Margaretta Acworth's Georgian Cookery Book (ed with Frank Prochaska, 1987), Annual Reports of the Yale University Librarian 2002–10; *Recreations* family life, travel, reading, walking; *Clubs* Oxford and Cambridge; *Style*— Dr Alice Prochaska; ✉ Somerville College, Woodstock Road, Oxford OX2 6HD (e-mail alice.prochaska@some.ox.ac.uk)

PROCTOR, Prof Michael Richard Edward; s of Edward Francis Proctor, and Stella Mary Major Proctor, *née* Jones; *b* 19 September 1950, Bournemouth, Dorset; *Educ* Shrewsbury (entrance scholar), Trinity Coll Cambridge (scholar, MA, MMath, PhD, ScD); *m* 1, 1973 (m dis 1998), Linda Irene Powell; 2 s, 1 da; m 2, 1999, Elizabeth Julia Colgate, *née* Nuttall; 2 step s; *Career* Univ of Cambridge: res fell Trinity Coll 1974–77, asst lectr 1977–82, lectr 1982–93, reader 1993–2000, prof of astrophysical fluid dynamics 2000–, vice-master Trinity Coll 2006–12, provost King's Coll 2013–; instr and asst prof MIT 1975–77; tstee Gladstone Memorial Tst, Cambridge Trusts; govr: King's Sch Ely, Shrewsbury Sch; FRAS 1977, memb IAU 2000; FRS 2006, FIMA 2007; Magnetoconvestion (with N. O. Weiss, 2014), *Publications* over 180 publications in scientific jls; *Recreations* gardening, travelling; *Clubs* Oxford & Cambridge; *Style*— Prof Michael Proctor, FRS; ✉ King's College, Cambridge CB2 1ST (☎ 01223 331100, e-mail provost.email@kings.cam.ac.uk)

PROCTOR, Nigel Colin; s of Norman Henry Proctor, of Plymouth, Devon, and Edith Joyce, *née* Webb; *b* 20 May 1956, Gloucester; *Educ* Plymstock Sch Plymouth, Univ of Southampton (BSc), Coll of Law London; *m* 22 Aug 1981, Susan, *née* Lampard; 2 s (Nicholas James b 28 Nov 1988, Matthew Ross b 8 Aug 1992); *Career* admitted slr 1990; civil engr: D Balfour & Sons 1977–81, C H Dobbie & Ptnrs 1981–84; slr McKenna & Co 1984–95 (incl period as engrg asst and articled clerk); ptnr: Davies Arnold Cooper 1997–99 (slr 1995–97), Hammonds 1999–2005, Addleshaw Goddard 2005–12, Eversheds 2012–; memb Law Soc; CEng 1983, MICE 1983 (chm Manchester branch 2003–04), FCIArb 2000; *Style*— Nigel Proctor, Esq; ✉ Eversheds, 1 Wood Street, London EC2V 7WS

PROCTOR, Timothy D (Tim); *Educ* Univ of Wisconsin Madison, Univ of Chicago (JD, MBA); *Career* called to the Bar: NY, NJ, PA; attorney Union Carbide Corporation 1975–80; Merck & Co Inc: sr attorney 1980–83, sec New Products Ctee 1984–85, European counsel 1985–88, US div counsel 1988–91, vice-pres and assoc gen counsel 1991–92; gen counsel and sec Glaxo Wellcome Inc 1992–98 (vice-pres 1992–94, sr vice-pres 1994–96, sr vice-pres HR 1996–98), dir worldwide HR GlaxoSmithKline plc 1998–99, gen counsel and memb Exec Ctee Diageo plc 2000–; former memb Bd: Northwestern Mutual Life Insurance Co, CARE USA, Duke Univ Law Sch; memb Bd Wachovia Corp 2006–; memb: American Bar Assoc, Assoc of Corporate Counsel (former memb Bd), Int Bar Assoc; *Style*— Mr Timothy D Proctor; ✉ Diageo plc, 8 Henrietta Place, London W1G 0NB (☎ 020 7927 4902, fax 020 7927 5099)

PROESCH, Gilbert; *see:* Gilbert

PROFFITT, Stuart Graham; s of Geoffrey Arnold Proffitt, and Sheila Patricia, *née* Whitehurst; *Educ* Uppingham, Worcester Coll Oxford; *Career* editorial asst rising to non-fiction publishing dir Collins Publishers 1983–92, publisher HarperCollins Trade Div 1992–98, publishing dir Penguin Press 1998–; chm Samuel Johnson Prize for non-fiction 1998–; London Library Life in Literature Prize 2014; *Recreations* walking, reading, music; *Clubs* Brooks's; *Style*— Stuart Proffitt, Esq; ✉ Penguin Books, 80 Strand, London WC2 (☎ 020 7010 3000, fax 020 7010 6703)

PROFUMO, David John; s of John Dennis Profumo, CBE (d 2006), of London, and Valerie Babette Louise, *née* Hobson (d 1997); *b* 30 October 1955, London; *Educ* Eton (scholar), Magdalen Coll Oxford (Demy, MA); *m* 22 March 1980, Helen Ann, *née* Fraser; 2 s (Alexander James b 25 Sept 1983, Thomas David b 6 June 1986), 1 da (Laura Ann Louise b 24 Feb 1992); *Career* asst master Eton Coll 1978, asst master Shrewsbury Sch 1979, researcher English Dept KCL 1979–81, dep ed The Fiction Magazine 1982, columnist Daily Telegraph 1987–95; judge Booker Prize 1989; Geoffrey Faber Meml Prize 1989; memb Soc of Authors; FRSL 1997; *Publications* The Magic Wheel (co-ed with Graham Swift, *qv*, 1985), Sea Music (1988), In Praise of Trout (1989), The Weather in Iceland (1993), Bringing the House Down (2006); *Recreations* fishing, shooting, shopping; *Clubs* Flyfishers', Bundha; *Style*— David Profumo, Esq; ✉ c/o Gillon Aitken Associates Ltd, 18–21 Cavaye Place, London SW10 9PT (☎ 020 7373 8672, fax 020 7373 6002)

PROSSER, Sir David John; kt (2005); s of Ronald Thomas Prosser, and Dorothy Prosser; *b* 26 March 1944; *Educ* Ogmore GS, UCW Aberystwyth; *m* Nov 1971, Rosemary Margaret, da of Alan Snuggs; 2 da; *Career* Sun Alliance Group 1965–69, Hoare Govett 1969–73, CIN Management 1973–88; Legal & General Group plc: investment dir 1988–91, chief exec 1991–2006; chm RAC Ltd 2007–12; memb Bd: ABI 1995–2004, Intercontinental Hotel Gp plc 2003–08, Investec 2006–14; FIA 1971; *Recreations* golf, horses, family activities; *Clubs* RAC; *Style*— Sir David Prosser

PROSSER, Sir Ian Maurice Gray; kt (1995); s of Maurice Clifford Prosser (d 1992), and Freda Prosser (d 2008); *b* 5 July 1943; *Educ* King Edward's Sch Bath, Watford GS, Univ of Birmingham (BComm); *m* 1964 (m dis 2003), Elizabeth Herman; 2 da (Sarah, Joanna); m 2, 2003, Hilary Prewer; *Career* Coopers and Lybrand (accountants) 1964–69; InterContinental Hotel Gp plc (formerly Bass plc): joined Bass Charrington Ltd 1969, memb Main Bd 1978, vice-chm 1982–87, gp md 1984–87, chm and chief exec 1987–2000, chm 2000–03; chm: BP Pension Tstees 2010–, Aviva Staff Pension Tstee 2013–, CAMCare 2015–; non-exec dir: Brewers & Licensed Retailers Assoc (formerly Brewers' Soc) 1983–2000 (chm 1992–94), The Boots Co plc 1984–96, Lloyds TSB Group plc 1988–99, BP plc 1997–2010 (dep chm 1999–2010), Glaxo Smithkline (formerly Smithkline Beecham) 1999–2009 (sr ind non-exec dir), Hillshire Brands Co (formerly Sara Lee Corp) 2004–14; chm World Travel & Tourism Cncl 2000–03, chm Navy Army Airforce Insts 2008–; Hon DUniv Birmingham; Liveryman Worshipful Co of Brewers; FCA; *Recreations* golf, gardening; *Clubs* Leander; *Style*— Sir Ian Prosser

PROSSER, Prof James Anthony William (Tony); s of James Allan Prosser (d 1968), and Flora Gertrude, *née* Evans (d 2015); *b* 3 May 1954; *Educ* Ludlow GS, Univ of Liverpool (LLB); *m* 1998, Charlotte Louise, *née* Villiers; 1 da (Amelia Marisa Villiers b 2001), 1 s (Laurence Edward Villiers b 2002); *Career* res asst in law Univ of Southampton 1974–76; lectr in law: Univ of Hull 1976–79, Univ of Sheffield 1980–89; sr lectr in law Univ of Sheffield 1989–92, John Millar prof of law Univ of Glasgow 1992–2002, prof of public law Univ of Bristol 2002–; visiting prof: European Univ Inst 1990 (Jean Monnet fell 1987–88), Univ of Rome 1992, 1996 and 2003, Coll of Europe Bruges 2009–; memb: Soc of Public Teachers of Law 1976, Socio-Legal Studies Assoc 1990; FBA 2014; *Books* Test Cases for the Poor (1983), Nationalised Industries and Public Control (1986), Waiving the Rules (with C Graham, 1988), Privatizing Public Enterprises (with C Graham, 1991), Privatisation and Regulatory Change in Europe (with M Moran, 1994), Law and the Regulators (1997), Regulating the Changing Media (jtly, 1998), Regulation and Markets Beyond 2000 (jtly, 2000), The Limits of Competition Law (2005), The Regulatory Enterprise (2010), The Regulatory State-Constitutional Implications (with D Oliver and R Rawlings, 2010), The Economic Constitution (2014); *Recreations* walking, listening to jazz, travel; *Style*— Prof Tony Prosser; ✉ Department of Law, Wills Memorial Building, The University of Bristol, Queens Road, Bristol BS8 1RJ

PROSSER, Baroness (Life Peer UK 2004), of Battersea in the London Borough of Wandsworth; Margaret Theresa Prosser; OBE (1997); da of Frederick James (d 1973), of London, and Lilian Mary, *née* Barry (d 1983); *b* 22 August 1937; *Educ* St Philomena's Convent Carshalton, NE London Poly; *m* 15 Feb 1957 (m dis); 1 s (Hon Jeffrey Jonathan b 1958), 2 da (Hon Carol Ann b 1960, Hon Stella Jane b 1963); *Career* advice centre organiser Home Office Funded Community Devpt Project 1974–77, law centre advsr 1977–83; TGWU: dist organiser 1983–84, nat women's sec 1984–92, nat organiser 1992–98, dep gen sec 1998–2002; pres TUC 1995–96 (memb Gen Cncl 1985–96), treas Lab Pty 1996–2001; chair Women's Nat Cmmn 2002–07, dep chair Equality and Human Rights Cmmn (EHRC) 2006–12, tstee and vice-chair Industry and Parliament Tst 2012–; memb: Employment Appeal Tbnl 1995–2007, Central Arbitration Ctee 2000–02, Low Pay Cmmn 2000–05; non-exec dir Royal Mail 2004–10; assoc memb Inst of Legal Execs 1981–83; *Recreations* walking, cooking; *Style*— The Rt Hon the Lady Prosser, OBE; ✉ 281 Limpsfield Road, Warlingham, Surrey, CR6 9RL (e-mail prosserm@parliament.uk)

PROUD, Rt Rev Andrew John; *see:* Reading, Bishop of

PROUDMAN, Hon Mrs Justice; Dame Sonia Rosemary Susan Proudman; DBE (2008), QC (1994); da of Kenneth Oliphant Proudman, of London, and Sati, *née* Hekimian; *b* 30 July 1949; *Educ* St Paul's Girls' Sch, Lady Margaret Hall Oxford (MA); *m* 19 Dec 1987, David Crispian Himley Cartwright, s of Himley Cartwright, of Henley-on-Thames; 1 da; *Career* called to the Bar Lincoln's Inn 1972 (bencher 1996), in practice at the Chancery Bar 1972–2008, asst recorder 1997–2000, recorder 2000–08; dep judge of the High Ct 2001–08, judge of the High Ct of Justice (Chancery Div) 2008–; memb Univ of Oxford Law Faculty Advsy Bd 2000, memb QC Selection Panel 2005; hon fell Lady Margaret Hall Oxford 2009; *Clubs* Hurlingham, CWIL; *Style*— The Hon Mrs Justice Proudman, DBE

PROWSE, Dr Keith; s of Valentine Prowse (d 2002), of Rugby, Warks, and Irene Ellen, *née* Rogers (d 1989); *b* 23 December 1937; *Educ* Lawrence Sheriff GS Rugby, Univ of Birmingham (BSc, MB ChB, MD); *m* 22 Sept 1962, Hilary Ann, da of Reginald Varley (d 1971), of Sutton Coldfield, W Midlands; 1 da (Carolyn b 1972), 1 s (Robert b 1975); *Career* lectr in med Univ of Birmingham 1968–71, Inserm res fell unité 14 Centre Hospitalier Universitaire Nancy 1971–72, conslt physician N Staffs Hosp 1972–2002, sr clinical lectr in respiratory med Dept of Postgrad Med Keele Univ 1986–2002, med dir N Staffs Hosp NHS Tst 1993–2001; pres Br Thoracic Soc 1996–97 (chm 1992–96), vice-pres Br Lung Fndn 2009– (fndr memb Cncl, chm 2005–09), UK rep and hon sec Euro Bd Pneumology 1992–97 (pres 1997–2002); Hans Sloane fell and dir Int Office RCP 1999–2004; FRCP 1977; *Recreations* castles, owls, walking, music, travel; *Clubs* Y; *Style*— Dr Keith Prowse; ✉ Kyriole, Pinewood Road, Ashley Heath, Shropshire TF9 4PP (☎ 01630 672879); 540 Etruria Road, Basford, Newcastle, Staffordshire ST5 0SX (☎ 01782 630270)

PRYCE, Jonathan; CBE (2009); s of Isaac Price (d 1976), of N Wales, and Margaret Ellen, *née* Williams (d 1986); *b* 1 June 1947; *Educ* Holywell GS, Sch of Art Kelsterton, Edge Hill Coll of Educn, RADA; *Career* actor; patron: Friendship Works (formerly Friends United Network), Saving Faces; hon patron Northern Lights Symphony Orch; fell Welsh Coll of Music and Drama; Hon Dr Univ of Liverpool 2006; *Theatre* Everyman Theatre Liverpool 1972, Nottingham Playhouse 1974, RSC 1979 and 1986, Royal Court 1980, NT 1981, Lyric Hammersmith, Queens Theatre, Vaudeville Theatre, Drury Lane Theatre Royal 1989–90, Music Box and Belasco NY, Broadway Theatre NY; roles incl: Richard III, Hamlet, Macbeth, Petruchio, Angelo, Octavius Caesar, Mick in the Caretaker, Gethin Price in Comedians, Tallys Folly, Trigorin, Astrov, Engineer in Miss Saigon, Fagin in Oliver! (London Palladium) 1994–95, Prof Higgins in My Fair Lady (Nat Theatre and Theatre Royal) 2001; other credits incl: A Reckoning (Soho Theatre), The Goat or Who is Sylvia? (Almeida and Apollo) 2004, Dirty Rotten Scoundrels (NY) 2006, Glengarry Glen Ross (Apollo) 2007–08, Dimetos (Donmar Warehouse) 2009, The Caretaker (Liverpool Everyman) 2009, (Trafalgar Studios) 2010 and (world tour) 2012, King Lear (Almeida) 2012, My Fair Lady in Concert (Washington and Santa Barbara) 2013, Merchant of Venice (Globe Theatre) 2015 and (world tour) 2016; *Television* incl: Daft as a Brush, Playthings, Glad Day, Roger Doesn't Live Here Anymore, The Caretaker, Comedians, Timon of Athens, Martin Luther Heretic, Praying Mantis, Two Weeks in Winter, The Man from the Pru, Selling Hitler, Mr Wroe's Virgins, Thicker than Water, David, HR 2007, The Baker Street Irregulars 2007, Clone (BBC) 2008, Cranford II (BBC) 2009, Wolf Hall 2014, Game of Thrones 2015, Taboo 2016, To Walk Invisible 2016; *Film* incl: Voyage of the Damned, Breaking Glass, Loophole, Ploughmans Lunch, Something Wicked This Way Comes, Brazil, Man on Fire, Jumpin' Jack Flash, Doctor and the Devils, Haunted Honeymoon, Consuming Passions, The Adventures of Baron Munchausen, The Rachel Papers, Glengarry Glen Ross, The Age of Innocence, Barbarians at the Gate, Great Moments in Aviation, A Business Affair, Deadly Advice, Shopping, Carrington, Evita, Regeneration, Tomorrow Never Dies, Ronin, Stigmata, Very Annie Mary, What a Girl Wants, Pirates of the Caribbean: The Curse of the Black Pearl 2003, Just One of Those Things, Brothers Grimm, Pirates of the Caribbean: Dead Man's Chest 2006, Pirates of the Caribbean: At World's End 2007, Leatherheads 2007, My Zinc Bed 2008, Bedtime Stories 2008, GI Joe: The Rise of the Cobra 2009, Hysteria 2011, Borgriki 2011, Dreck 2012, GI Joe: Retaliation 2012, Dough 2014, The Salvation 2014, Listen Up, Philip 2014, Narcopolis 2014, Under Milk Wood 2014, The Ghost & The Whale 2015, Woman in Gold 2015, The White King 2016, One Last Dance 2016, The Healer 2016; *Awards* Tony Award and Theatre World Award (for Comedians) 1977, SWET/Olivier Award (for Hamlet) 1980, Olivier Award (for Miss Saigon) 1990, Variety Club of GB Stage Actor of 1990, Tony Award for Best Actor in a Musical 1991, Drama Desk Award, Cannes Film Festival Award for Best Actor (for Carrington) 1995, Evening Standard Award for Best Actor (for Carrington) 1995, Special Award BAFTA Cymru 2001; *Style*—Jonathan Pryce, Esq, CBE; ✉ c/o Julian Belfrage Associates, 3rd Floor, 9 Argyll Street, London W1F 7TG (☎ 020 7287 8544, fax 020 7287 8832); c/o Vanessa Green (PA, e-mail vgreen@dsl.pipex.com)

PRYCE, (George) Terry; CBE (1994); s of Edwin Pryce (d 1951), and Hilda, *née* Price (d 2004); *b* 26 March 1934; *Educ* Welshpool GS, Nat Coll of Food Technol; *m* 1957, Thurza Elizabeth, da of Arthur Denis Tatham (d 1942); 2 s (Simon Charles Conrad b 1961, Timothy John Robert b 1965), 1 da (Sarah Jane b 1970); *Career* Dalgety plc: dir 1972, md 1978–81, chief exec 1981–89; chm: Solway Foods Ltd 1990–94, Jas Bowman & Sons Ltd 1991–2015, York House Gp Ltd 1996–2003; dir HP Bulmer Holdings plc 1984–94; former chm Bd for Food Sci and Technol Univ of Reading, chm Horticultural Research Int 1991–1997; memb: Cncl AFRC 1986–94, Advsy Bd Inst of Food Research 1988–94; MFC, CCMI, FIFST; *Recreations* sport (golf), reading; *Clubs* Athenaeum, MCC; *Style*— G Terry Pryce, Esq, CBE

PRYCE-JONES, David Eugene Henry; s of Alan Pryce-Jones (d 2001), of Newport, RI, and Thérèse Fould-Springer (d 1953); *b* 15 February 1936, Vienna; *Educ* Eton, Magdalen Coll Oxford (MA); *m* 29 July 1959, Clarissa, *née* Caccia; 2 da (Jessica b 1961, Candida b 1963), 1 s (Adam b 1973); *Career* literary ed Spectator 1963–64, visiting lectr Univ of Iowa 1964–65, special corr Daily Telegraph 1966–82, visiting prof California State Coll Hayward 1968 and 1970, visiting prof California State Univ Berkeley 1972, sr ed National Review NY 1999; HH Wingate Prize 1986, Sunlight Fndn Prize 1989, Sternberg Award 2010; FRSL 1975; *Publications* fiction: Owls and Satyrs (1961), The Sands of Summer (1963), Quondam (1965), The Stranger's View (1967), Running Away (1971), The England Commune (1975), Shirley's Guild (1979), The Afternoon Sun (1986), Inheritance (1992), Safe Houses (2007); non-fiction: Graham Greene (1963), Next Generation: Travels in Israel (1965), The Hungarian Revolution (1969), The Face of Defeat (1972), Evelyn Waugh and his World (ed, 1973), Unity Mitford (1976), Vienna (1978), Paris in the Third Reich (1981), Cyril Connolly: Journal and Memoir (1983), The Closed Circle (1989), You Can't Be Too

Careful (1992), The War That Never Was (1995), Betrayal: France, The Arabs and The Jews (2006), Treason of the Heart (2011); *Recreations* travel, music; *Clubs* Beefsteak, Garrick; *Style*— David Pryce-Jones, Esq; ✉ c/o Christopher Sinclair-Stevenson, 3 South Terrace, London SW7 2TB (☎ 020 7581 2550)

PRYDE, Roderick Stokes; OBE (1999); s of William Gerard Pryde (d 1955), and Patricia Mary, *née* Stokes (d 1959); *b* 26 January 1953; *Educ* George Watson's Coll Edinburgh, Univ of Sussex (BA), UCNW (PGCE, TEFL); *m* 1, 16 July 1976 (m dis), Dominique, *née* Cavalier; 1 da (Claire Patricia b 12 Sept 1979); m 2, 25 March 1989, Susanne Mona Graham, da of George Hamilton; 2 da (Beatrice Grace Hamilton b 14 Oct 1989, Madeleine Eve Hamilton b 20 July 1993), 1 s (Frederick William Hamilton b 1 June 1991); *Career* lectr Univ of Dijon 1975–76, mgmnt trainee and English language co-ordinator Societé Française des Pneumatiques Michelin 1977–81; British Council: asst regnl language offr 1981–83, dir of studies Milan 1983–87, regnl dir Seville 1987–88, regnl dir Bilbao 1988–89, Japanese language trg SOAS 1989–90, dir Kyoto 1990–92, dir Western Japan 1992–94, dir English Language Centre Hong Kong 1994–98, dir Portugal 1998–2000, dir Educnl Enterprises 2000–02, asst DG 2002–05, regnl dir India and Sri Lanka 2005–09, currently dir Spain; *Recreations* reading, walking, swimming; *Clubs* Watsonian (Edinburgh), Commonwealth; *Style*— Roderick Pryde, Esq, OBE

PRYNNE, Andrew Geoffrey Lockyer; QC (1995); s of Maj-Gen Michael Whitworth Prynne, CB, CBE (d 1977), and Jean Violet, *née* Stewart (d 1977); *b* 28 May 1953; *Educ* Marlborough, Univ of Southampton (LLB); *m* 30 July 1977, Catriona Mary, da of Maj Henry Gordon Brougham (d 1958); 3 da (Jessica Jean, Miranda Wendy, Natasha Sally); *Career* called to the Bar Middle Temple 1975; CEDR accredited mediator 2000; *Recreations* sailing, shooting, music; *Clubs* Royal Yacht Sqdn, Royal Solent Yacht, Royal Southampton Yacht; *Style*— Andrew Prynne, Esq, QC; ✉ Temple Garden Chambers, 1 Harcourt Buildings Chambers, Temple, London EC4Y 9DA

PRYOR, Dr Arthur John; CB (1997); s of late Quinton Arthur Pryor, of Budleigh Salterton, Devon, and late Elsie Margaret, *née* Luscombe; *b* 7 March 1939; *Educ* Harrow Co GS, Downing Coll Cambridge (MA, PhD); *m* 1964, Marilyn Kay, da of late Sidney Petley; 1 da (Clare Marianne b 1969), 1 s (Mark John b 1973); *Career* asst lectr then lectr in Spanish and Portuguese UC Cardiff 1963–66, asst princ then princ DTI 1966–73, first sec Civil Aviation and Shipping British Embassy Washington DC 1973–75; DTI: princ Commercial Rels and Exports Div 1975–77, asst sec (Shipping Policy, Air Div, Int Trade Policy) 1977–85, regnl dir W Midlands 1985–88; DG Br Nat Space Centre 1988–93, under sec Competition Policy Div DTI 1993–96; competition conslt 1996–; memb: Inter-Agency Ctee on Global Environmental Change 1990–93, Reporting Panel of Competition Cmmn 1998–2003, Competition Appeal Tbnl (formerly Appeal Panel of Competition Cmmn) 2000–11; contrib to modern languages and space pubns; *Recreations* tennis, golf, book collecting; *Style*— Dr Arthur Pryor, CB; ✉ c/o Competition Appeal Tribunal, Victoria House, Bloomsbury Place, London WC1A 2EB

PRYOR, Nicholas David; s of (Richard) Vivian Pryo (d 2010), and Ruth Gibson, *née* Budd (d 2012); *b* 13 October 1946, London; *Educ* Whitgift Sch Croydon (Victoria Schol, Lewis Prizeman), Univ of Bristol (LLB), Coll of Law, LSE (Dip, MSc); *m* 1, (m dis); m 2, 13 Oct 2004, Lesley, *née* Stockwell; *Career* called to the Bar Middle Temple 1970 (Blackstone scholar, Churchill Prize), admitted slr 1981; asst litigation slr Rowe & Maw 1981–83, sr asst litigation slr Coward Chance (later Clifford Chance) 1983–90, litigation ptnr Manches & Co 1990–95, co slr and head UK Legal Dept Kwelm Insurance Services Ltd 1995–97, ind commercial mediator and conslt 1997–; non-exec dir CEDR 1995–98 (fndr memb Trg Faculty 1991); memb Mediation Panel: Ct of Appeal, London Ct of Int Arbitration, CIArb; fndr memb: Panel of Ind Mediators, Lamport Hall Gp; memb Lloyd's/Int Underwriting Assoc Mediation Steering Gp, fndr memb Ind Mediators 2006; accredited mediator: CEDR 1992, ADR; MCIArb 2001, memb CPR Inst of Dispute Resolution NY, distinguished fell Int Acad of Mediators 2009; *Publications* Mediators on Mediation (contrib, 2005), How to Master Commercial Meditation (contrib, 2014); *Recreations* opera, walking, historic motorsport, theatre; *Style*— Nicholas Pryor, Esq; ✉ c/o Nicky Doble, Independent Mediators Ltd (☎ 020 7127 9223, e-mail admin@independentmediators.co.uk)

PRZYBYLSKI, Steve; CBE (2010); s of Jerzy Przybylski (d 1962), and Mary Elisabeth, *née* Godfrey (d 2003); *b* 31 March 1950; *Educ* Lawrence Sheriff Sch Rugby, Weymouth GS; *m* 15 June 1981, Ellen, *née* Parkin; 2 da (Sarah Ellen b 18 June 1982, Rebecca Jane b 16 Jan 1986); *Career* DHSS 1970–79, Lord Chllr's Dept 1979–86; with CPS 1986–, head of resources and performance 1999–; govr Chelmsford County HS for Girls until 2008; *Recreations* sailing, rugby; *Clubs* Blackwater Sailing, Gateshead Fell RFC; *Style*— Steve Przybylski, Esq, CBE; ✉ Crown Prosecution Service, 50 Ludgate Hill, London EC4M 7EX (☎ 020 7796 8072, fax 020 7796 8368, e-mail steve.przybylski@cps.gsi.gov.uk)

PUCKRIN, Arthur William; s of Thomas William Puckrin (d 1977), of Middlesbrough, and Eleanor Mary, *née* Cumiskey; *b* 5 May 1938; *Educ* Middlesbrough HS, Univ of London (LLB, BL); Outward Bound Mountain Sch Ullswater; *m* 2 April 1966 (m dis 1994), Patricia Ann, da of Charles Henry Dixon (d 1972), of Middlesbrough; 2 s (Geoffrey Arthur b 1984, James William b 1986); m 2, 22 May 2013, Mary Miller, da of Joseph Vincent Miller, of Billingham; *Career* called to the Bar 1966; legal advsr Dorman Long Steel Ltd 1966–71, Parly advsr to City of London Corp 1971; memb Bar Assoc for Commerce Fin and Industry 1967–; athlete, long distance runner and long distance swimmer; record holder for: Pennine Way 250 miles, Southern Highlands of Scotland 170 miles, Welsh 14 Peaks over 3000 feet, N Yorks Moors 80 miles, Lyke Walk N Yorks Moors 120 miles; defeated 50 horses over 44 miles at Wolsingham Horse Trials, record holder for 110 mile walk Middlesbrough to York and back in 23 hours 40 mins; Ironman Triathlete 1997, Br Ironman (Age Gp) champion 1998, 1999, 2000, 2001, 2002, 2004, 2005 and 2006, Scottish Ironman Triathlon Champion 2000; represented GB World Triathlon Championships Nice 1997, Sweden 1999 (finished fifth place) and Ibiza 2003 (3 mile swim, 75 mile cycle and 20 mile run); bronze medallist Euro Sprint Quadrathon Championship 1998, Euro Quadrathon Champion Cyprus 1999, GB Quadrathon Champion 1999 (1.5 mile swim, 6 mile canoe, 40 mile cycle, and 6 mile run); bronze medallist World Quadrathon Championships Czech Republic 2000, World Quadrathlon Champion Montreal 2001; Double Ironman (5 mile swim, 224 mile cycle and 52 mile run): Age Gp Champion Canada 2001, 2002, 2003 and 2004, World Champion Mexico 2001, S American Champion Ecuador 2002, World Champion Quebec 2002; second place USA Triple Ironman Championships VA 2002 and fifth place 2004 (8 mile swim, 336 mile cycle and 80 mile run, oldest person ever to complete this distance); World Deca-Biathlon Champion Mexico 2002 (1,120 mile cycle and 262 mile run, first ever Br winner, world record time), competed World Deca-Triathlon Championship Hawaii 2004 (24 mile swim, 1,120 mile cycle and 262 mile run, world record time), South American 24 Hour Cycling Champion Mexico 2005 (world record distance), Deca-Triathlon Championship France 2006 (world record), World Cup Triple Ironman Championship Virginia 2006 (world record), Deca World Challenge Mexico 2006 (world record), Deca Ironman World Challenge Mexico 2007 (4th place), World Cup Triple Ironman USA 2007 (world record), World 12 hour Swimming Championship Zurich 2008 (world record) and 2009 (improved world record), World Championship Quintuple Ironman Mexico 2008 (3rd place), World Quadruple Ironman Champion Mexico 2009 (10 mile swim, 448 mile bike and 105 mile run, world record time), Scottish Masters 800m swimming champion Glasgow 2009, 2010, 2011, 2014 and 2015, 24 Hour Br Cycling Champion 2010 (world record distance, improved world record distance 2011), World Double Deca Biathlon Champion (48 mile swim, 2,240 mile cycle) Mexico 2010 (world record time), 12 Hour Br Cycling Champion 2011, Scottish Masters 400m swimming champion 2012, 2014 and 2015, Scottish Masters backstroke swimming champion (200m, 100m and 50m) 2014, Scottish Masters 200m swimming champion 2015, Scottish Masters freestyle swimming champion (100m, 200m, 400m and 800m) 2016, Scottish Masters backstroke swimming champion (100m and 200m) 2016; represented GB playing bridge on 8 occasions (with Patricia Ann Puckrin) incl 2 World Championships and four Euro Championships; life memb: Fell Runners' Assoc, Darlington HF Walking Club, Br Long Distance Swimming Assoc; life master English Bridge Union; Queen's Scout; FCIS 1977, MIMgt 1980; *Books* Racing Through Life; *Clubs* Hartlepool Bridge, Middlesbrough and Cleveland Harriers, Lyke Wake, Cleveland Triathlon, Road Runners, Cleveland Wheelers, Long Distance Walkers Assoc; *Style*— Arthur W Puckrin, Esq; ✉ 3 Romanby Gardens, Middlesborough TS5 8BW (☎ 01642 534841)

PUDDEPHATT, Andrew Charles; OBE (2003); s of Andrew Ross Puddephatt, and Margaret, *née* Deboo; *b* 2 April 1950; *Educ* Kingsbury Sch Dunstable, Sidney Sussex Coll Cambridge (BA), Architectural Assoc (dip); *Children* 2 da (Leni Joanne Wild, Kelly Wild); *Career* teacher ILEA 1979, computer programmer CAP/CPP 1979–81, researcher Jt Action Docklands Gp 1985–89, gen sec Liberty/The Nat Cncl for Civil Liberties 1989–95, dir Charter 88 1995–99, dir Article XIX 1999–2004; currently dir Global Ptnrs & Associates Ltd; chair Audit Ctee Parly Ombudsman; chair Coordinated Action Against Domestic Abuse (CAADA); *Recreations* music, literature; *Style*— Andrew Puddephatt, OBE

PUGH, Prof Alan; s of Albert Pugh (d 1989), and Stella, *née* Gough (d 1991); *b* 7 March 1936; *Educ* Whitchurch GS, UC of S Wales and Monmouthshire (BSc, Page Prize in Engrg), Univ of Nottingham (PhD); *m* Alison Jean (d 1995), da of Robert Lindsay; 1 da (Judith Caroline (Mrs Watson) b 30 Oct 1961), 1 s (Simon David b 7 Nov 1962); m 2, 1997, Dr Elizabeth Anne, da of Paul Bowler (d 2003); *Career* postgrad apprenticeship BBC 1957–59, design engr on Br nuclear submarine prog Rolls Royce 1959–61, lectr then sr lectr in electrical engrg Univ of Nottingham 1961–78 (J Langham-Thompson Premium 1968); Univ of Hull: prof of electronic engrg 1978–96, head of dept 1978–90, dean 1987–90, pro-vice-chllr 1990–93, emeritus prof 1996–; vice-pres IEE 1997–2000; memb NATO Collaborative Research Grant Ctee 1995–98, chm Permanent Steering Ctee European Standing Observatory on the Engrg Profession and Educn (ESOEPE) 2002–06, memb Int Advsy Panel Engrg Cncl 2002–, chm Accreditation of European Engrg Progs and Grads (EUR-ACE) Project Bd 2004–05, memb Admin Cncl European Network for Accreditation of Engrg Educn (ENAEE) 2006–09; FIEE 1979 (MIEE 1964), FRSA 1982, FREng 1992; *Books* Robot Vision (1983), Robot Sensors (Vol 1 – Vision, Vol 2 – Tactile and Non-Vision, 1986), Machine Intelligence and Knowledge Engineering for Robotic Applications (with A K C Wong, 1987); *Recreations* hill walking, flying, pottering around the house and garden; *Style*— Prof Alan Pugh, FREng; ✉ 33 Academy Drive, Dringhouses, York YO24 1UJ

PUGH, Alun John; s of Maurice Thomas Pugh, and Violet Jane Pugh; *b* 9 June 1955; *Educ* Tonypandy GS, Polytechnic of Wales, Univ Coll Cardiff; *m* 1978 (m dis 2002), Janet; 1 s, 1 da; *Career* lectr Brigend Coll 1983, sr lectr Newcastle Coll 1987, head of sch Llandrillo Coll 1992, asst princ West Cheshire Coll 1996; memb Nat Assembly for Wales (Lab) Clwyd West 1999–2007; currently min for culture, Welsh language and sport; *Recreations* mountaineering; *Clubs* Oesterreichische Alpenverein (Innsbruck), Colwyn Bay British Legion; *Style*— Mr Alun Pugh, Esq

PUGH, Dr John; MP; s of James Pugh, of Nottingham, and Patricia, *née* Caig; *b* 28 June 1948, Liverpool; *Educ* Univ of Durham (BA), Univ of Liverpool (MA), Victoria Univ of Manchester (PhD); *m* 24 Aug 1971, Annette, *née* Sangar; 1 s (David b 21 Oct 1977), 3 da (Nicola b 12 Nov 1979, Christina b 31 March 1981, Sarah b 5 Oct 1982); *Career* head of philosophy and religious studies Merchant Taylors' Sch Crosby 1985–2001; MP (Lib Dem) Southport 2001–; memb Tport, Local Govt and Regions Select Ctee 2001–05, Lib Dem spokesperson for educn 2002–05, Lib Dem spokesperson for tport 2005–, vice-chair All Pty Gp on Burma; cncllr Sefton MBC 1987–2002 (ldr Lib Dem Gp 1992–2001, cncl ldr 2000–01); former memb Merseyside Police Authy; memb CAMRA Campaign for Real Ale; *Publications* Christian Understanding of God; *Recreations* weightlifting, cycling; *Style*— Dr John Pugh, MP; ✉ 27 The Walk, Birkdale, Southport, Merseyside PR8 4BG (☎ 01704 569025); 35 Shakespeare Street, Southport, Merseyside PR8 5AB (☎ 01704 533555, fax 01704 884160); House of Commons, London SW1A 0AA

PUGH, Jonathan Mervyn Sebastian; s of late John Mervyn Cullwick Pugh, of Upton upon Severn, Worcs, and Kay Sanderson, *née* Fitzmaurice; *b* 17 February 1962; *Educ* Downside, Oxford Poly (BA); *m* 15 May 1992, Anna, *née* Forsyth; 1 s (Thomas b 3 May 1995), 1 da (Phoebe b 23 March 1998); *Career* freelance cartoonist and illustrator; regular contrib: Punch 1989–92, The Independent 1992–94; The Times: Diary cartoonist 1995, main pocket cartoonist 1996–2009; pocket cartoonist Daily Mail 2010–; Cartoon Art Tst Pocket Cartoonist of the Year 1998, 2000, 2001, 2007 and 2010, Press Gazette Cartoonist of the Year 2001 (finalist 1999, 2000, 2003 and 2014); *Clubs* Chelsea Arts; *Style*— Jonathan Pugh, Esq; ✉ The Daily Mail, Northcliffe House, 2 Derry Street, Kensington, London W8 5TT

PUGH, Richard Henry Crommelin; DL (Hereford and Worcester 1991); s of John James Edgar Pugh (d 1944), of Buxton, Derbys, and Charlotte Winifred Crommelin, *née* Sadler (d 1977); *b* 9 September 1927; *Educ* Buxton Coll, Univ of London (LLB); *m* 15 Aug 1953, Ann, da of Roy Waddington Swales (d 1979), of Fernilee, Derbys; 1 da (Helen b 1956), 1 s (Stephen b 1958); *Career* Nat Serv RAF 1947–49; qualified CA; Grattan Warehouses Ltd 1951–56; chm Kay & Co Ltd (Home Shopping Div of Great Universal Stores) 1968–96, dep chm The Great Universal Stores plc 1990–96; chm Whiteaway Laidlaw Bank 1990–96; chm: Worcester Cathedral Appeal and Tstees 1982–2002, Worcester Royal Infirmary NI Tst 1993–95; tstee Charles Hasting Educn Centre 1999–2003; Freeman City of London 1984, Liveryman Worshipful Co of Chartered Secretaries 1984 (memb Ct of Assts 1994); fell Worcester Coll of Further Educn; FCA 1951, FCIS 1995 (ACIS 1951), ACMA 1959, FRGS; OStJ (co-chm Order of St John 1994–98, memb Chapter Gen Order of St John 1996–98, memb Cncl Worcester Order of St John); *Recreations* travel, swimming, genealogy; *Style*— Richard Pugh, Esq, DL; ✉ 6 Swinton House, 85 Gloucester Terrace, London W2 3HB (☎ 020 7262 4252, e-mail rpugh2@hotmail.com)

PUGHSLEY, Alan; QPM (2015); *Career* Kent Police: joined as Asst Chief Constable 2009, subsequently head Kent and Essex Serious Crime Directorate, Dep Chief Constable 2011–14, Chief Constable 2014–; *Style*— Alan Pughsley, Esq, QPM; ✉ Kent Police Headquarters, Sutton Road, Maidstone, Kent ME15 9BZ

PUGSLEY, His Hon David Philip; s of Rev Clement Harry Howell Pugsley (d 1967), and Edith Alsop, *née* Schofield (d 1956); *b* 11 December 1944; *Educ* Shebbear Coll, St Catharine's Coll Cambridge (MA), Univ of Birmingham (MPhil 1995); *m* 31 Dec 1966, Judith Mary, da of John S Mappin, 2 da (Joanna Hazel b 28 March 1972, Alison Jane b 12 Feb 1974); *Career* called to the Bar Middle Temple 1968; chm Birmingham Region Industrial Tbnls 1985–92, recorder Midland & Oxford Circuit 1991–92 (practised until 1985), circuit judge (Midland & Oxford Circuit) 1992–2014, ret; memb Parole Bd 1998–2004 and 2010–12, ret; Freeman City of London 2006; *Books* Industrial Tribunals – Compensation for Loss of Pension Rights (jtly, 1990), Contract of Employment (jtly, 1997), Butterworth Employment Compensation Calculator (jtly, 1999); ed panel The Civil Court Practice (The Green Book); *Recreations* fishing, walking; *Clubs* Lansdowne; *Style*— His Hon David Pugsley; ✉ Combined Court Centre, Morledge, Derby DE1 2XE

PULFORD, John; MBE; s of George Pulford, of Manchester (d 1980), and Mary Beatrice, *née* Beigel (d 2004); *b* 3 July 1943, Macclesfield; *Educ* Cranfield Sch of Mgmnt (MBA); *m* 8 July 1972, Ann, *née* Baker; 2 s (Thomas George b 2 Jan 1979, Jonathan Henry b 17 Aug 1985), 1 da (Louise Elisabeth b 5 June 1983); *Career* mgmnt conslt Arthur Andersen 1969–82, dir Nesco Investments plc 1982–84, chief exec Colmore Investments Ltd 1984–92, mgmnt conslt 1992–96, chief exec Direct Image Systems and Communications 1996–2004, chief exec HenDi Gp Ltd 2004–09, dir Engage-Community 2009–; chm Govt and Industry Ctee BPIF; chm: Community Serv Vols, ACT (Arts Centre Tst) Cornwall, Ex Cathedra; memb Worshipful Co of Mgmnt Conslts 2003; *Recreations* voluntary sector, music; *Style*— John Pulford, Esq, MBE; ✉ Scawswater Mill, Idless, Truro, Cornwall TR4 9QR (☎ 01872 273734, mobile 07771 905300, e-mail john.pulford@hotmail.co.uk); Community Service Volunteers, 237 Pentonville Road, London N1 9NJ (e-mail jpulford@csv.org.uk)

PULIS, Anthony Richard (Tony); *b* 16 January 1958, Newport, Wales; *Career* football mangr and former player; player: Bristol Rovers 1975–81, Happy Valley 1981–82, Bristol Rovers 1982–84, Newport County 1986–89, Bournemouth 1986–89, Gillingham 1989–90, Bournemouth 1990–92; mangr: Bournemouth 1992–94, Gillingham 1995–99, Bristol City 1999–2000, Portsmouth 2000, Stoke City 2002–05, Plymouth Argyle 2005–06, Stoke City 2006–13, Crystal Palace 2013–; *Style*— Tony Pulis, Esq; ✉ Crystal Palace Football Club, Selhurst Park Stadium, Whitehorse Lane, London, SE25 6PU ST4 4EG

PULLEN, Dr Roderick Allen (Rod); *b* 11 April 1949; *m* 1971, Karen Lesley, *née* Sketchley; 4 s, 1 da; *Career* diplomat; with MOD 1975, second sec Brussels 1978, MOD 1980, first sec Madrid 1981, dep high cmmr Suva 1984–88, first sec FCO 1988–90, cnsllr (technol) Paris 1990–94, dep high cmmr Nairobi 1994–97, dep high cmmr Lagos 1997–2000, high cmmr to Ghana 2000–04, ambass to Zimbabwe 2004–06, UK special rep to the Sudan/Darfur Peace Process 2006, fell Trinity Coll Cambridge 2006–; *Style*— Dr Rod Pullen; ✉ Trinity College, Cambridge CB2 1TQ

PULLINGER, Anthony Giles Broadbent; s of Sir Alan Pullinger, CBE (d 2002), of Herts, and his 1 w, Felicity Charmian Gotch, *née* Hobson (d 1964); *b* 24 May 1955; *Educ* Marlborough, Balliol Coll Oxford; *m* 2 Oct 1982, Henrietta Mary Conyngham, da of Maj Richard Conyngham Corfield (d 1997), of Warks; 1 s (Jack b 1985), 2 da (Rosanna b 1988, Isla b 1992); *Career* stockbroker Laing & Cruickshank 1978–90, seconded to Panel on Takeovers and Mergers 1982–84, ptnr Laing & Cruickshank 1984–87, dir Alexanders Laing & Cruickshank 1985–89, dep DG Panel on Takeovers and Mergers 1990–; Freeman: City of London 1986, Worshipful Co of Grocers 1986; *Recreations* fishing, riding, mountaineering, music, travel, natural history; *Clubs* Naval; *Style*— Anthony Pullinger, Esq; ✉ The Panel on Takeovers and Mergers, 10 Paternoster Square, London EC4M 7DY (☎ 020 7382 9026, mobile 07738 563704, fax 020 7638 1554, e-mail tonypullinger@aol.com)

PULLMAN, Bruce John; s of Bernard John Pullman, of Brockenhurst, Hants, and Dorothy Jean, *née* Hayes; *b* 4 April 1957; *Educ* Canford Sch, Merton Coll Oxford (BA); *m* 14 July 1979, Joanna Alexis Hamilton, da of John Edward Hamilton Davies, of Whitby, N Yorks; 2 da (Rebecca b 1984, Abigail b 1985), 1 s (Joshua b 1989); *Career* NM Rothschild & Sons Ltd 1979–81, dir County NatWest Investment Management 1987–93 (joined 1981, responsible for quantitative investment research and product devpt), md Hill Samuel Investment Management 1993, dir QUANTEC Ltd (investment consultancy) 1993–94, head of fin engrg Smith New Court 1995, head of asset mgmnt consulting Merrill Lynch 1995–96, head of strategy Gartmore Investment Management 1997–98, md Astute Computers 1999–2001; exec dir: Choice Matching Ltd 2001–04, Harrier Music Ltd 2004–06, Osprey Music Ltd 2004–06, Prime Ribs Ltd 2006–07, Colour Envelopes Ltd 2007–10; dir Big Cat Electric Bikes 2010–11; chair Sch Ctee US Business Sch in Prague 2005–10; govr Eastleigh Coll 2008–10; MSI 1993; *Books* Portfolio Insurance (contrib, ed Donald L Luskin, 1988); *Recreations* Evangelical church, humanitarian aid and disaster relief to Eastern Europe, the former Soviet Union, the Philippines and Malawi, ministry to gypsies, rigid inflatable boats (RIBs); *Style*— Bruce Pullman, Esq; ✉ e-mail bp@pobox.com

PULLMAN, Philip; CBE (2004); s of Alfred Pullman (d 1953), and Audrey, *née* Merrifield (d 1990); *b* 19 October 1946; *Educ* Ysgol Ardudwy Harlech, Univ of Oxford (MA), Weymouth Coll of Educn (PGCE); *m* 1970, Judith; 2 s (James b 1971, Thomas b 1981); *Career* author; teacher middle sch Oxford 1972–86, pt/t sr lectr Westminster Coll Oxford 1986–96; Astrid Lindgren Memorial Award for Literature 2005; pres Soc of Authors 2013; patron Centre for the Children's Book Newcastle upon Tyne; hon fell: Westminster Coll Oxford 1999, Univ of Wales Bangor 2003; Hon DLitt: Oxford Brookes Univ 2002, UEA 2003, Univ of Oxford 2009; Hon DUniv: Surrey 2003, UCE 2003, Open 2008; Hon LLD Univ of Dundee 2007; Freeman City of Oxford 2007; FRSL 2001; *Publications* incl: Galatea (novel, 1978); children's books: The Ruby in the Smoke (1985, Int Reading Assoc Children's Book Award 1988), The Firework-Maker's Daughter (1995, Smarties Gold Award 1996), Clockwork, or All Wound Up (1996, shortlisted for Whitbread Children's Book of the Year 1997, shortlisted for Carnegie Medal 1997); novels for teenagers: The White Mercedes (1992), Northern Lights (1995, Guardian Children's Fiction Award 1996, Carnegie Medal 1996, Br Book Awards Children's Book of theYear 1996), The Subtle Knife (1997), Mossycoat (1998), I Was a Rat! (1999), Puss in Boots (2000), The Amber Spyglass (2000, Br Book Awards Children's Book of the Year 2001, Whitbread Book of the Year 2001, His Dark Materials trilogy adapted for stage 2003), Lyra's Oxford (2003), The Scarecrow and his Servant (2004), Once Upon a Time in the North (2008), The Good Man Jesus and the Scoundrel Christ (2010), Grimm Tales for Young and Old (2012); plays: Frankenstein (1992), Puss in Boots (produced 1997); author various short stories and articles; *Recreations* drawing; *Style*— Philip Pullman, Esq, CBE, FRSL; ✉ c/o A P Watt, United Agents LLP, 12–26 Lexington Street, London W1F 0LE

PUNTER, Prof David Godfrey; s of Douglas Herbert Punter (d 1958), of London, and Hilda Mary, *née* Manning (d 1996); *b* 19 November 1949; *Educ* Fitzwilliam Coll Cambridge (MA, PhD); *m* 1 (m dis 1988), Jenny Jane, *née* Roberts; 1 s (Joshua Anthony Kemble b 22 June 1982), 1 da (Miranda Catherine Amani b 30 Dec 1982); m 2, Caroline Mary, *née* Case; 1 da (Isobel Maeve b 16 Dec 1988); *Career* lectr UEA 1973–84 (sr lectr 1984–86), prof and head of dept Chinese Univ of Hong Kong 1986–88, prof of English studies Univ of Stirling 1988–2000 (head of dept 1988–94 and 1996), prof of poetry Univ of Bristol; visiting prof Fudan Univ Shanghai 1983; dep dir ILEA courses on sixth-form practical criticism teaching 1978 and 1980, dir Devpt of Univ English Teaching Project (DUET) 1985–86, judge Br Cncl Creative Writing Award in English Hong Kong 1987, memb Bd of Advsy Eds Text and Context 1987–93; conslt: Sch of Humanities and Arts Hampshire Coll MA 1983, curriculum devpt Univ of Hamburg 1989; co-organiser American Vision, Visions of America: New Directions in Culture and Literature conf Hong Kong, memb Bd of Dirs Edinburgh Book Festival 1992–98, pres Br Assoc for Romantic Studies 1993–95, specialist subject assessor Quality Assessment Exercise HEFCE 1994–95, advsr Romanticism Section ESSE Conf Glasgow 1995, co-organiser Second Conf Int Gothic Assoc Glasgow 1995, vice-chm Scottish Ctee of Professors of English 1995–2000, specialist subject assessor and team ldr Quality Assessment Exercise SHEFC 1996–98; co-fndr eco-thinktank Q500 2015; sec: Cncl for Univ English 1993–95, Cncl for Coll and Univ English 1994–95 (chm 1995–97); chm: Editorial Advsy Bd Gothic Studies 1995–, Exec Ctee Int Gothic Assoc 1995–; memb Editorial Bd: Stirling Edition of James Hogg 1991–94, Romanticism in Context 1995–, La Questione Romantica 1997–; memb of numerous academic ctees; fell Centre for European Romanticism Univ of Glasgow 1998–; DLitt Univ of Stirling 2000; FRSA 1998 (chair West Region 2012–), FSA Scot 1999; *Books* The Literature of Terror: A History of Gothic Fictions from 1765 to the Present Day (1980, trans Italian 1985), Romanticism and Ideology: Studies in English Writing 1765–1830 (with David Aers and Jonathan Cook, 1981), Blake, Hegel and Dialectic (1982), The Hidden Script: Writing and Unconscious (1985), Introduction to Contemporary Cultural Studies (1986), William Blake: Selected Poetry and Prose (1988), The Romantic Unconscious: A Study in Narcissism and Patriarchy (1989), Notes on Selected Poems of Philip Larkin (1991, reprinted 1995), The Gothic Tradition: Vol I of The Literature of Terror (new edn, 1996), The Modern Gothic: Vol II of The Literature of Terror (new edn, 1996), William Blake: The New Casebook (ed, 1996), Romanticism: Vol 36 of Annotated Bibliography of English Studies (ed, 1997), Notes on William Blake's 'Songs of Innocence and Experience' (1998), Gothic Pathologies: The Text, the Body and the Law (1998), Spectral Readings (ed, 1999), Companion to the Gothic (ed, 1999), Writing the Passions (2000), Postcolonial Imaginings (2000), The Gothis (with Glennis Byron, 2004), Writing in the 21st Century (2005), Metaphor (2007), Modernity (2007), Rapture: Literature, Addiction, Secrecy (2009), A New Companion to the Gothic (ed, 2012), The Encyclopaedia of the Gothic (ed, with William Hughes and Andrew Smith, 2013), The Literature of Pity (2014), The Gothic Condition: Terror, History and the Psyche (2016); also author of 40 jl articles and 53 book chapters; *Poetry* China and Glass, Lost in the Supermarket, Asleep at the Wheel, Selected Short Stories, Foreign Ministry; *Recreations* walking, throwing parties, travel; *Clubs* Oxford and Cambridge, Arts, Authors; *Style*— Prof David Punter; ✉ Department of English, University of Bristol, Bristol BS8 1TB (e-mail david.punter@bristol.ac.uk)

PURCELL, Michael Thomas; s of Thomas Bernard Purcell, and Edna Shelia, *née* Bache; *b* 26 November 1948, Birmingham; *Educ* Halesown Coll, Univ of Birmingham (LLB), Guildford Coll of Law; *m* 22 Sept 1979, Deborah Claire, *née* Lawrence; 2 s (Matthew John b 21 Aug 1982, Edward Thomas b 6 Feb 1986), 1 da (Claire Eleanor b 1 March 1990); *Career* admitted slr 1975, slr-advocate (Higher Courts) 2006; research asst to Dr John Pitcher New Coll Oxford 1973, asst slr Wallace Robinson & Morgan 1975, head Criminal Dept Derek T Prescott & Co 1978, fndr Purcell Parker & Co (formerly Michael T Purcell) 1979; memb: Birmingham Duty Slr Ctee 1990 (chm 1995), Appeals Ctee Legal Servs Cmmn 1998 (also memb Billing Appeals Ctee), Criminal Ctee Birmingham Law Soc 1999, Law Soc; church warden Hampton Arden Church 1985–95; friend: Royal Shakespeare Theatre, Birmingham Royal Ballet, Barber Inst of Fine Art Birmingham; *Recreations* collection of medieval manuscripts and bi-folum, chess, motor sport, theatre; *Style*— Michael Purcell, Esq; ✉ Hampton House, Bellemere Road, Hampton in Arden, Solihull, West Midlands B92 (☎ 0121 236 9781, e-mail allistrue@btinternet.com); Purcell Parker, 204–206 Corporation Street, Birmingham B4 6QB

PURCELL, Prof Wendy; da of late Michael Purcell, and late Joanne Howlin; *b* 21 June 1961; *Educ* Univ of Plymouth (BSc), Univ of Herts, UCL (PhD), Harvard Univ (Exec Educn); *m* 1987, Geoffrey Paul Hendron; *Career* Roehampton Inst 1990–92; Univ of Herts: sr lectr in physiology and pharmacology 1992–93, head Div of Physiology, Pharmacology and Toxicology 1993–97; Univ of the West of England: assoc dean and head Dept of Biological and Biomedical Sciences 1997–2000, exec dean Faculty of Applied Sciences 2000–05, pro-vice-chllr (research) 2003–05; dep vice-chllr Univ of Herts 2005–07; Plymouth Univ: vice-chllr and chief exec 2007–15, pres 2015–, emeritus prof in biomedicine 2016–; non-exec dir and chair Nominations Ctee Department of Business, Innovation and Skills UK Govt 2013–, memb Cabinet Office Talent Advsy Gp UK Govt 2015–; visiting scientist Harvard Univ 2016–; chair Cncl for Healthcare Science in HE 2011–; dir and tstee: Nat Maritime Aquarium 2010–, Environmental Assoc of Univs and Colls 2013–; FRSA; *Publications* Approaches to High Throughput Toxicity Screening (with C K Atterwill and P Goldfarb, 1999), Disruption and Distinctiveness in Higher Education (2014), Ten Reasons to Build Resilience into the Future of Your University – A Business Guide for University Governors (with I Paton, 2015), Differentiation of English Universities: The Impact of Policy Reforms in Driving a More Diverse Higher Education Landscape (with J Beer and R Southern, 2016), Direct Measurements of Oxygen Gradients in Spheroid Culture System Using Electron Paramagnetic Resonance Oximetry (with L M Langan, N J F Dodd, S F Owen, S K Jackson and A N Jha, 2016); numerous articles and reviews in jls and chapters in books; *Recreations* swimming, theatre, contemporary art; *Clubs* Farmers; *Style*— Prof Wendy Purcell; ✉ e-mail wendypurcell2001@yahoo.com

PURCHAS, Christopher Patrick Brooks; QC (1990); s of late The Rt Hon Sir Francis Purchas, and late Patricia Mona Kathleen, *née* Milburn; bro of Robin Purchas, QC, *qv*; *b* 20 June 1943; *Educ* Marlborough, Trinity Coll Cambridge; *m* 1, 7 Dec 1974 (m dis 1995), Bronwen Victoria Mary; 2 da (Léonie Melissa b 2 Aug 1978, Domino Octavia b 5 April 1983); m 2, 27 May 1998, Diana Hatrick, wid of Dr Ian Hatrick; *Career* called to the Bar Inner Temple 1966 (bencher 1995); recorder of the Crown Court 1986–, dep High Court judge 1999–; accredited ADR mediator 2004–; *Recreations* golf, tennis, shooting; *Clubs* W Sussex Golf, Boodles; *Style*— Christopher Purchas, Esq, QC; ✉ Crown Office Chambers, Temple, London EC4Y 7HJ (☎ 020 7797 8100, fax 020 7797 8101, e-mail purchas@crownofficechambers.com)

PURCHAS, Robin Michael; QC (1987); s of late Rt Hon Sir Francis Purchas, and Patricia Mona Kathleen, *née* Milburn; bro of Christopher Purchas, QC, *qv*; *b* 12 June 1946; *Educ* Marlborough, Trinity Coll Cambridge (MA); *m* 3 Sept 1970, (Denise) Anne Kerr, da of Capt David Finlay, RN; 1 s (James Alexander Francis b 27 Sept 1973), 1 da (Charlotte Robin b 3 Nov 1975); *Career* called to the Bar Inner Temple 1968 (bencher 1996); recorder of the Crown Court 1989–, dep High Court judge 1994–; memb Bar Cncl 2000–02; *Recreations* tennis, golf, fishing, skiing, opera, theatre; *Clubs* Queen's, Boodle's; *Style*— Robin Purchas, Esq, QC; ✉ Francis Taylor Building, Temple, London EC4Y 7BY (☎ 020 7353 8415, fax 020 7353 7622)

PURCHASE-HILL, Zac; MBE (2009); s of Nick Purchase, and Sara Plumb, *née* Holyer; *b* 2 May 1986, Cheltenham; *Educ* King's Sch Worcester; *m* Felicity Purchase-Hill, *née* Hill; *Career* rower; achievements incl: Gold medal lightweight single scull World Rowing U23 Championships 2005, Gold medal and world record lightweight single scull World Rowing Championships 2006 (Silver medal 2005), Bronze medal lightweight double scull World Rowing Championships 2007, Gold medal and Olympic record lightweight double scull Olympic Games Beijing 2008, Gold medal lightweight double scull World Championships 2010 and 2011, Silver medal lightweight double scull Olympic Games London 2012, multiple Gold medals and podium finishes World Cup races; *Clubs* Marlow Rowing; *Style*— Zac Purchase-Hill, Esq, MBE; ✉ e-mail contact:zacpurchase.com, website www.zacpurchase.com, Twitter @zacpurchase; c/o Chris Hughes, Sine Qua Non International, Chiltern House, Henley on Thames, Oxfordshire RG9 1AT (☎ 01491 845420)

PURDIE, Prof David Wilkie; s of Robert Wilkie Purdie (d 1990), and Jean Wilson Purdie (d 2000); *b* 13 August 1946; *Educ* Ayr Acad, Univ of Glasgow (MB ChB); *m* 24 June 1983 (m dis 2010), Dr Katharine Ann, da of Maj Thomas Arklay Guthrie; 1 s (Arklay Robert Wilkie b 1984), 2 da (Catriona Jean Chalmers b 1986, Mhairi-Rose Wilson b 1988); *Career* ship's surgn SS Canberra P&O Lines Ltd London 1970–71, SHO Western Infirmary and Queen Mother's Hosp Glasgow, MRC res registrar Univ of Glasgow 1973–75, registrar Queen Mother's Hosp and Western Infirmary Glasgow 1975–78, lectr Univ of Dundee 1978–83, sr lectr Univ of Leeds 1983–89, prof and dir of postgrad med educn Univ of Hull 1989–94, hon conslt gynaecologist Royal Hull Hosps Tst 1989–2003, fndn dean Postgrad Med Sch Univ of Hull 1994–95, head of clinical res Centre for Metabolic Bone

Disease Hull Royal Infirmary/Univ of Hull 1995–2003, conslt Edinburgh Osteoporosis Centre 2003–06; hon fell Sch of Clincal Sciences Univ of Edinburgh 2004–12, hon fell Inst for Advanced Studies in the Humanities Univ of Edinburgh 2012–; chm Br Menopause Soc 1997–99, memb Scientific Advsy Gp Nat Osteoporosis Soc; ed-in-chief The Burns Encyclopaedia, author of scientific articles on osteoporosis, oestrogen, oestrogen receptor modulation, and related subjects; author and freelance journalist, articles in The Scotsman, Sunday Times and Daily Telegraph, columnist Golf Int, speechwriter and speech ed for MPs, sports personalities and public figures; chm Sir Walter Scott Club 2007–13, past pres James Boswell Soc, mangr New Club (Edinburgh); patron: Nat Galleries of Scotland, Nat Library of Scotland; contributor JP Morgan Library NY; chm Edinburgh Burns Club; MD (commendation) 1990; FSA Scot 1981, FRCOG 1988, FRCPEd 1997, FRSSA 2009; *Books* The Greatest Game – The Ancyent & Healthfulle Exercyse of the Golff (2010), Ivanhoe: a Redaction of Sir Walter Scott's Novel (2012), The Burns Encyclopaedia (4 edn 2012), An Unpublished Letter and Draft MS of a poem of Robert Burns (2012), The Heart of Midlothian: a Redaction of Sir Walter Scott's novel (2013), Thring on Legislation (ed with M Mackenzie, 3 edn 2015); *Recreations* classical rhetoric, golf, Scottish Enlightenment studies, life and works of Sir Walter Scott, David Hume and Robert Burns; *Clubs* New (Edinburgh), Scottish Arts, Lord's Taverners, Sunningdale Golf, Pine Valley Golf (USA); *Style—* Prof David W Purdie, MD, FRCPEd; ✉ Duncan's Land, 4 India Place, Edinburgh EH3 6EH (☎ 0131 225 1199, mobile 07793 201039, e-mail dwpurdie@ednet.co.uk, website www.davidpurdie.co.uk); agent: Peter C Brown (e-mail pcbrown8@hotmail.com, mobile 07831 417432)

PURDY, District Judge (Magistrates' Courts); Quentin Alexander Purdy; s of Gordon Purdy, OBE, FRCS (d 1976), and Margaret Dorothy Annie, *née* Stokes; *b* 23 August 1960; *Educ* Gresham's, Leicester Poly (BA), UCL (LLM), Inns of Court Sch of Law (Bar exams); *m* 3 Sept 1988, Elizabeth Audrey, da of William Alfred Hazelwood (d 2004), of Paddock Wood, Kent; 2 da (Anna Elizabeth b 10 Oct 1992, Helen Sophie b 4 Oct 1994); *Career* called to the Bar Gray's Inn 1983 (A Band Tst Award); practising in Common Law Chambers London and on SE Circuit, cmmr for oaths; actg metropolitan stipendary magistrate 1998–2000, dep dist judge 2000–03, dist judge (Magistrates' Courts) 2003–; memb Cwlth Magistrates' and Judges' Assoc; deacon Dormansland Baptist Church 2001–08; *Publications* Archbold Magistrates' Court Criminal Practice (contrib ed, 2012–17); *Recreations* reading, foreign travel, walking, sailing, dog walking, cycling; *Style—* District Judge (Magistrates' Courts) Purdy; ✉ Westminster Magistrates' Court, 181 Marylebone Road, London NW1 5BR

PURI, Om; s of Tek Chand Puri (d 1990), and Tara Devi Puri (d 1967); *b* 18 October 1950; *Educ* Khalsa Coll Patiala India, Nat Sch of Drama Delhi (Dip), Film and TV Inst Pune India (Dip); *m* 1 May 1993, Nandita Chaudhuri; 1 s (Ishaan b 2 July 1997); *Career* actor; teacher of movement and speech Actor's Studio Mumbai 1977; *Television* incl: Sadgati (Deliverance) 1982, White Teeth 2002, Second Generation 2003, The Sea Captain's Tale (for the BBC's adaptation of Chaucer's Canterbury Tales) 2003; *Films* incl: City of Joy 1991, Wolf 1993, My Son the Fanatic 1997, East is East 1998, The Parole Officer 2000, Dev 2004, Lakshya 2004, Kyun...! Ho Gaya Na 2004, The King of Bollywood 2004, AK 47 2004, Stop! 2004, Kisna: The Warrior Poet 2005, Mumbai Express 2005, The Rising: Ballad of Mangal Pandey 2005, Kyon Ki... 2005, Deewane Huye Paagal 2005, The Hangman 2005, Rang De Basanti 2006, Baghi 2006, Malamaal Weekly 2006, Chup Chup Ke 2006, Don 2006, Baabul 2006, Is Pyaar Ko Kya Naam Doon 2007, Delhii Heights 2007, Khallas: The Beginning of End 2007, Fool N Final 2007, Buddha Mar Gaya 2007, Victoria No. 203: Diamonds Are Forever 2007, Dhol 2007, Charlie Wilson's War 2007, Shoot on Sight 2007, Welcome 2007, Lovesongs: Yesterday, Today & Tomorrow 2008, Yaariyan 2008, Mere Baap Pehle Aap 2008, Kismat Konnection 2008, Money Hai Toh Honey Hai 2008, Singh Is Kinng 2008, Mukhbiir 2008, Maharathi 2008, Chal Chala Chal 2009, Billu 2009, Delhi-6 2009, Road to Sangam 2009, Baabarr 2009, Wanted 2009, Life Goes On 2009, London Dreams 2009, Kurbaan 2009, Bolo Raam 2009, West Is West 2010; *Awards* Nat Award India 1982 and 1984, Soviet Land Nehru Award USSR 1987, Padmashree India 1990; *Recreations* gardening, travel, reading; *Style—* Om Puri, Esq

PURKIS, Dr Andrew James; OBE (2002); s of Clifford Henry Purkis, OBE (d 1994), of Trevone, N Cornwall, and Mildred Jeannie, *née* Crane (d 1993); *b* 24 January 1949; *Educ* Highgate Sch, CCC Oxford (BA), St Antonys Coll Oxford (DPhil); *m* 18 July 1980, Jennifer Harwood, da of Francis Harwood Smith, of Willaston, Cheshire; 1 da (Joanna b 1980), 1 s (Henry b 1982); *Career* princ NI Office 1977–80 (admin trainee 1973–76, private sec 1976– 1977), asst dir Nat Cncl for Voluntary Orgns 1986–87 (head of policy analysis 1980–84, head of policy planning 1984–86); dir Cncl for the Protection of Rural England 1987–91, public affrs sec to the Archbishop of Canterbury 1992–98, chief exec Diana Princess of Wales Memorial Fund 1998–2005, chief exec Tropical Health and Educn Tst 2005–09; chair Empty Homes Agency 2004–07; memb: Bd Charity Cmmn 2007–10, Parole Bd 2010–13, Bd Office of Adjudicator for HE 2010–; chm Pedestrians Assoc, chm Green Alliance, chair ActionAid UK 2009–15; FRSA 1989; *Books* Housing and Community Care (jtly, 1982), Health in the Round (jtly, 1984), Housing Associations in England and the Future of Voluntary Organisations (2010); *Recreations* walking, birdwatching, surf riding, travel, theatre, music; *Style—* Dr Andrew Purkis, OBE; ✉ 38 Endlesham Road, Balham, London SW12 8JL (☎ 020 8675 2439)

PURLE, His Hon Judge Charles Lambert; QC (1989); s of Robert Herbert Purle (d 1982), and Doreen Florence, *née* Button; *b* 9 February 1947, Leigh-on-Sea, Essex; *Educ* King Edward VI GS Retford, Univ of Nottingham (LLB), Worcester Coll Oxford (BCL); *m* 1, 1969 (m dis 1990), Lorna Barbara, da of Roy Sinclair Brown; 1 da (Sally b 12 Sept 1972), 1 s (William b 5 March 1977); m 2, 1991, Virginia Dabney Hopkins, da of Charles Peter Rylatt; 2 s (Charles Carter Lee b 19 June 1992, Harry George Hopkins b 13 Sept 1993), 2 da (Nancy Elizabeth Lambert b 5 Oct 1995, Helena Mary Rose b 22 Sept 1997); *Career* called to the Bar Gray's Inn 1970, in practice 1974–2007, specialist chancery circuit judge Birmingham Civil Justice Centre 2007–; *Recreations* opera, music, my children, horse racing; *Style—* His Hon Judge Purle, QC; ✉ Birmingham Civil Justice Centre, 33 Bull Street, Birmingham B4 6DS

PURNELL, Glynn; *b* Chelmsley Wood, Birmingham; *Career* chef de partie Simpsons Kenilworth 1996–2002, sous chef Hibiscus Ludlow 2002, head chef Jessica's Edgbaston 2003–07 (AA Restaurant of the Year 2004, Michelin Star 2005), head chef and prop Purnell's Birmingham 2007– (Michelin Star 2009–, AA Restaurant of the Year 2009), chef patron and prop The Asquith Edgbaston 2010–; *Style—* Glynn Purnell, Esq; ✉ Purnell's Restaurant, 55 Cornwall Street, Birmingham B3 2DH (☎ 0121 212 9799)

PURNELL, James; PC (2007); s of John Purnell, and Janet Purnell; *b* 2 March 1970, London; *Educ* Balliol Coll Oxford (BA); *m* 2015, Alexis Kirschbaum; 1 da (Percy b 2015); *Career* researcher to Rt Hon Tony Blair, *qv*, 1989–92, strategy conslt Hydra Assocs 1992–94, research fell IPPR 1994–95, head of corp planning BBC 1995–97, special advsr to Rt Hon Tony Blair 1997–2001, MP (Lab) Stalybridge and Hyde 2001–10, PPS to Ruth Kelly, MP, *qv*, as fin sec to HM Treasy; memb Work and Pensions Select Ctee House of Commons 2001–03, min for broadcasting and tourism 2005–06, min of state Dept for Work and Pensions 2006–07, sec of state for culture, media and sport 2007–08, sec of state for work and pensions 2008–09; film prodr Boston Consulting Gp 2012–13, dir strategy and digital BBC 2012–; former cncllr London Borough of Islington (chair Early Years Ctee, chair Housing Ctee); *Recreations* football, films, theatre, music; *Style—* James Purnell, Esq

PURNELL, Nicholas Robert; QC (1985); *b* 29 January 1944; *Educ* Oratory Sch, King's Coll Cambridge (open exhibitioner, MA); *m* 23 Jan 1970, Melanie, *née* Stanway; 4 s (Oliver b 22 Dec 1971, Edward b 29 May 1974, James b 11 Aug 1977, Sebastian b 29 Nov 1983); *Career* called to the Bar Middle Temple 1968 (bencher 1990); practising barr specialising in commercial fraud cases, currently head Cloth Fair Chambers; recorder 1986–2010; jr counsel to Inland Revenue 1977–79, jr Treasy counsel 1979–85; memb: Gen Bar Cncl 1974–92, Lord Chllr's Advsy Ctee on Legal Educn and Conduct 1991–97, Criminal Ctee Judicial Studies Bd; chm Criminal Bar Assoc 1990–91; govr Oratory Sch; fell Soc of Advanced Legal Studies, FICPD; *Style—* Nicholas Purnell, Esq, QC; ✉ Cloth Fair Chambers, 39–40 Cloth Fair, London EC1A 7NR

PURSLOW, Christopher George (Chris); s of George Ellis Purslow (d 1985), and Lillian Rose, *née* Embrey (d 2013); *b* 27 March 1946; *Educ* The High Sch Newcastle under Lyme, Univ of Bristol (BA, BArch); *m* 12 Aug 1970 (m dis 1977), (Sally) Louise, da of Dr Carl Basch, of South Orange, New Jersey; *Career* architect; Courtaulds Ltd Coventry 1967–68, Tarmac Ltd Wolverhampton 1968–69, Philip Johnson (Architect) NY 1969–72, Rice/Roberts (Architects) London 1972–74, London Borough of Islington 1974–88 (borough architect 1983–88), dir of architecture Glasgow 1988–96, chm Glasgow Print Studio, former dir Architects in Housing; RIBA, RIAS; *Recreations* theatre, music, architecture, skiing and making waves; *Style—* Chris Purslow, Esq; ✉ Rosslyn House, 1a Victoria Circus, Glasgow G12 9LH (☎ 0141 334 8162); Kilmory Ross, Tayvallich, Argyll PA31 8PQ (e-mail chris_purslow@btinternet.com)

PURVES, Elizabeth Mary (Libby); OBE (1999); da of James Grant Purves, CMG (d 1984), of Suffolk, and Mary, *née* Tinsley; *b* 2 February 1950; *Educ* Sacred Heart Tunbridge Wells, St Anne's Coll Oxford; *m* 1980, Paul Heiney, the broadcaster, s of Norbert Wisniewski (d 1970), of Sheffield; 1 s (Nicholas b 1982 d 2006), 1 da (Rose b 1984); *Career* journalist and broadcaster; presenter: Radio 4 Today, Midweek, The Learning Curve; radio documentaries incl: Street Gospel, Holy Bones, Mysterious Ways and others; chief theatre critic The Times 2010–13, ind theatre critic and fndr www.theatrecat.com 2013–; tstee Nat Maritime Museum 1996–2004; Columnist of the Year 1999; *Books* Britain at Play (1982), Adventures Under Sail (1982), Sailing Weekend Book (with Paul Heiney, 1985), How Not To Be A Perfect Mother (1986), One Summer's Grace (1989), How Not to Raise a Perfect Child (1991), How Not To Be The Perfect Family (1994), Holy Smoke (1998), Radio (2002); Novels: Casting Off (1995), A Long Walk in Wintertime (1996), Home Leave (1997), More Lives Than One (1998), Regatta (1999), Passing Go (2000), A Free Woman (2001), Mother Country (2002), Radio: A True Love Story (2002), Continental Drift (2003), Acting Up (2004), Love Songs and Lies (2006), Shadow Child (2009); *Recreations* theatre, yachting, walking, writing; *Clubs* Ocean Cruising, Royal Cruising; *Style—* Ms Libby Purves, OBE; ✉ website www.theatrecat.com; c/o The Times, News UK & Ireland Ltd, 1 London Bridge Street, London SE1 9GF

PURVES, Canon Dr (Andrew) Geoffrey; s of Maj Andrew Purves (d 1967), and Blanche, *née* Lawson (d 2012); *b* 12 June 1944; *Educ* Heaton GS, Univ of Durham (BA), Univ of Newcastle upon Tyne (BArch), Newcastle Univ (PhD); *m* 12 Oct 1968, (Elizabeth) Ann, da of James Campbell Finlay, of Newcastle upon Tyne; *Career* chartered architect; sr ptnr Geoffrey Purves Partnership (multi-disciplinary practice: architecture, planning, project mgmnt, econ and devpt consultancy, planning supervision) 1977–2003, chm Purves Ash LLP 2003–10, dir Purves Ash Mgmnt Services Ltd 2004–10; dir: Newcastle Arch Workshop Ltd 1985–98, RIBA Enterprises Ltd 1996–2002, Saunders and Purves Ltd, Purves Ltd, Clayton Development Ltd 1990–2010, Br Architectural Library Property Tst 1995–97; chm Northern Architecture Centre 1995–98; lectr (pt/t design tutor) Dept of Architecture Univ of Newcastle upon Tyne 1983–84, visiting research fell Centre for Arts and Humanities in Health and Med Univ of Durham 2001; RIBA: chm Northumbria Branch 1981–83, chm Northern Region 1988–89, memb Nat Cncl 1991–97, hon treas 1995–97; memb: English Partnership Northern Regnl Design Panel 1994–98, Architects Registration Bd Investigation Panel; memb Cncl ARCUK 1991–97; tstee Br Architectural Library Tst 1995–97; Architects' Benevolent Soc: memb Cncl 2000, hon treas 2002–, chm 2015; memb Ctee CIArb (Northumbria Branch) 2000–04; professional advsr Millennium Cmmn 1997–2002; chm Newcastle Diocesan Advsy Ctee 2000–16, chm Northumberland and Newcastle Soc 2008–, govr Heaton Manor Sch 2001–03, lay canon Cathedral Church of St Nicholas Newcastle upon Tyne 2010; Freeman City of London 1992, memb Worshipful Co of Chartered Architects 1992 (memb Ct of Assts 1999, Master 2014–15); RIBA, FRIAS, FRSA, MCIArb, FInstD; *Publications* Healthy Living Centres (2002), Churches of Newcastle and Northumberland (2006), Primary Care Centres: A Guide to Health Care Design (2009), Metric Handbook (contrib, 2012); author of various articles in professional and tech jls; *Recreations* sailing; *Clubs* Athenaeum, Clyde Cruising, Royal Northumberland Yacht, Northern Counties; *Style—* Canon Dr Geoffrey Purves; ✉ Purves Limited, Hawthorn House, Kirkwhelpington, Northumberland NE19 2RT (☎ 01830 540376, e-mail a.g.purves@btinternet.com)

PURVES, Peter John; s of (John) Kenneth Purves (d 1987), of Preston, Lancs, and Florence, *née* Patton (d 1976); *b* 10 February 1939; *Educ* Arnold Sch Blackpool, Alsager Teachers Training Coll (DipEd); *m* 1, 29 Sept 1962 (m dis 1981), Gillian Diane Emmett; 1 s (Matthew b 1963), 1 adopted da (Lisa b 1963); m 2, 5 Feb 1982, Kathryn Lesley Evans; *Career* producer, writer, director, actor and presenter; began in repertory theatre Barrow in Furness 1961–63, London Theatre and TV 1963–65; md Purves Wickes Video Projects Ltd 1984–; specialist presenters trainer BBC Elstree 1993–, princ tutor London Acad of Radio, Film and TV 2004; cruise ship speaker for Saga, Thomson, P&O and Cunard 2011–; official commentator: The Royal Show Stoneleigh 1993–2005, The Royal Bath and West of England Show Shepton Mallet 1997–2005, The Great Yorkshire Show Harrogate 2000, All About Dogs Brentwood 2001–06, Discover Dogs 2004–06 and 2008, The Wag and Bone Show 2005–06 and 2008, Guide Dogs Gala Day 2005–06 and 2008, Notcutts All About Dogs 2006–08; host and presenter: Tails of Achievement 2006–08, Guide Dog of the Year 2007–08, The Cold Wet Nose Show 2008; princ commentator: Suffolk Dog Day 2010, The Royal Anniversary Tst Guildhall London 2010, 2012 and 2014, Dunwich Heath Nat Tst Fun Day 2014–; pres: Rugby Animal Tst, Radio Nene Valley 1996, Canine Supporters Charity 1997–; memb bd New Wolsey Theatre Company Ipswich 2000–, princ Expertise (speaker/presentation consult), vice-patron Dog for the Disabled; *Theatre* incl: various pantomimes 1978– (incl dir: Jack and the Beanstalk (Theatre Royal Plymouth) 2005–06, Snow White (Orchard Theatre Dartford) 2007–08), Once in a Lifetime (Blackpool) 1981, prodr Bobby Davro's Not in Front of the Children 1993, Dick Whittington (Harpenden) 2012; *Television* BBC incl: Dr Who 1965–66, Blue Peter 1967–78, Special Assignments 1976–79, Crufts Dog Show 1976– (princ presenter and commentator 2005–, also presenter for Animal Planet TV USA 2005–), We're Going Places 1978–80, Stopwatch 1978–81, Kickstart 1978–92, darts presenter 1979–84, Ten Glorious Years 1989, Superdogs 1990–93, Crimewatch Midlands 1989–91, Blue Peter Theme Night 1998, The Office 2001, Fun at the Funeral Parlour 2001, Children in Need 2001, This is Dom Jolly 2003, The Way We Travelled 2003, Britain on the Box 2003, Inside Out 2003, The Underdog Show 2007, Blue Peter Quiz 2008, Doctor Who 50th anniversary programmes 2013 and ongoing, Celebrity Antiques Road Trip 2013, Celebrity Pointless 2013; other credits incl: Makers (HTV) 1983–84, Work Out (HTV) 1985, Babble (Channel 4) 1985–87, Pets Go Public (Channel 5) 1998–, Breed All About It (Discovery Channel) 1998–, Wild At Heart (Anglia) 2002, Kitchen Confidential (Anglia) 2002, The All New Harry Hill Show (ITV) 2003, RI:SE (C4) 2003, Pet Rescue (C4) 2003, The Doctor Who Story (BBC) 2004, TV's Greatest Moments (Five) 2004, The Evel Knievel

Story (Five) 2004, Retire Abroad (Overseas Property TV) 2006, Destination Lunch (Overseas Property TV) 2006, presenter CLA Game Fair (Horse and Country TV) 2008, Discovery Dogs (Horse and Country TV), Crufts Dog Show Live Webcast (Sunset and Vine TV); *Radio* presenter BBC Radio Northampton 1995–97, presenter Predictions for 2000 – The Tomorrow People (BBC Radio documentary) 2005, presenter Peter Purves' Advice Line Jack FM 2014; narrator BBC audio CD: Dr Who – The Massacre, Dr Who – The Myth Makers, Dr Who – The Celestrial Toymaker, Dr Who – The Dalek Masterplan, Dr Who – The Savages; narrator Big Finish Dr Who Companion Chronicles: Mother Russia (with Tony Millan, 2007), The Suffering (with Maureen O'Brien, 2010), The Perpetual Bond, The Cold Equations and The First Wave (trilogy with Tom Allen, 2011), Tales from the Vault 2011, The 5 Companions (with Jean Marsh and Peter Davison) 2011, The Anachronauts (with Jean Marsh) 2012, The Return of the Rocket Men (with Tim Treloar) 2012, Upstairs (with Maureen O'Brien) 2013, The War to End All Wars (2013), The Light at the End (with five doctors, 2014), The Bounty of Ceres (2014), An Ordinary Life (with Jean Marsh, 2014); *Publications* Tess, The Story of a Guide Dog (1980); ed Peter Purves' Mad About Dogs (monthly, 1997–99), Here's One I Wrote Earlier (autobiography, 2009); *Recreations* theatre, cinema, dog shows; *Clubs* Kennel; *Style*— Peter Purves, Esq; ✉ c/o Wendy Downes, Downes Presenters, 55 Montgomery Road, South Darenth, Kent DA4 9BH; personal e-mail (peter.purves@btinternet.com)

PURVES, Sir William; kt (1993), CBE (1988), DSO (1951); s of Andrew Purves (d 1945), and Ida Purves (d 1996); *b* 27 December 1931, Kelso, Scotland; *Educ* Kelso HS; *m* 1958 (m dis 1988), Diana Troutbeck, da of Nicholas Gosselin Pepp Richardson (d 1944); 2 s, 2 da; m 2, 9 Feb 1989, Rebecca Jane, *née* Lewellen; *Career* served Cwlth Division Korea; formerly with National Bank of Scotland (now Royal Bank of Scotland); Hongkong and Shanghai Bank: early appts Japan (mangr) and Hong Kong (chief accountant), gen mangr international 1979–82, exec dir Banking 1982–84, dep chm 1984–86, dep chm and chief exec 1986, chm The Hongkong and Shanghai Banking Corporation Ltd 1986–92, chm HSBC Holdings plc 1990–98 (concurrently chief exec 1990–92), chm Midland Bank plc 1993–98 (dir 1987–93); chm The British Bank of the Middle East 1979–98, dir Marine Midland Bank 1979–98; chm Hakluyt & Co Ltd 1999–2008; dep chm: Alstom SA 1998–2003, Aquarius Platinum 2004–12; non-exec dir: Shell Transport and Trading Co plc 1993–2002, East Asiatic Company Ltd A/S 1995–99, Reuters Founders Share Company Ltd 1998–2009, Trident Safeguards 1999–2003, Scottish Medicine 1999–2003, B W Gp Ltd 2003–12; memb: Int Cncl Textron Inc 1998–2002, Hong Kong Chief Exec's Cncl of Int Advsrs 1998–2002; pres Int Monetary Conf Toronto 1992; memb Gen Ctee Scottish Rugby Union 1997–99; Master Guild of Int Bankers 2004–05; Hon DUniv: Stirling, Sheffield, Strathclyde, Nottingham, Napier, Hong Kong; Dr (hc): Hong Kong Open, UMIST; FCIB, FCIB (Scotland); Grand Bauhina Medal (Hong Kong) 2001; *Clubs* Hong Kong, Hong Kong Jockey (hon steward), Hong Kong Golf, Caledonian (London), RAC; *Style*— Sir William Purves, CBE, DSO; ✉ Flat 1, Ebury House, 39 Elizabeth Street, London SW1W 9RP (☎ 020 7823 6775)

PURVIS, Christopher Thomas Bremner; CBE (2002); s of Dr Victor Bremner Purvis (d 1995), and Joanna Isabel, *née* Gibbs (d 1995); *b* 15 April 1951; *Educ* Bradfield Coll, Keble Coll Oxford (MA); *m* 21 June 1986, Phillida Anne, *née* Seaward; 3 da (Kerensa Toura Isabel b 26 March 1988, Xenobe Eva Wendela b 8 March 1990, Eila Blanche Honor b 27 Aug 1993), 1 s (Lucian Annesley Bremner b 31 May 1992); *Career* S G Warburg & Co Ltd (and successor firms): joined 1974, dir Warburg Investment Management International Ltd 1980, dir S G Warburg & Co Ltd 1983, mangr Tokyo office 1982–87 and 1989–92, md SBC Warburg 1995–97, advsr SBC Warburg (now UBS Investment Bank) 1997–2009; dir: F&C Pacific Investment Tst plc (now Witan Pacific Investment Tst plc) 1997–2006 (chm 2000–06), Fleming Japanese Smaller Companies Investment Tst plc 2000–03, Martin Currie Japan Investment Tst plc 2001–05, Aberdeen UK Tracker Tst plc (previously Tribune Tst plc) 2004–14; chief exec Japan 2001 Ltd 1999–2003; memb Ctee Tokyo Stock Exchange Membership 1990–92; pres: Acad of Ancient Music 2000–, Handel House Tst Ltd 2007– (chm and project dir 1997–2007, chm 2000–13); chm: Japan Arena 2004–, Barbican Centre Tst 2009–14; vice-pres Japan Soc (chm 2006–12); treas: ClementJames Centre 2003–14, IntoUniversity 2006–14; tstee: Sir Siegmund Warburg's Vol Sett 1997–, J Paul Getty Jr Charitable Tst 2004–, Winston Churchill Meml Tst 2007–11; govr Royal Acad of Music 2004–07; Order of the Rising Sun Gold and Silver Star (Japan) 2012; *Recreations* music, wine, reading; *Style*— Christopher Purvis, Esq, CBE; ✉ 4 Queensborough Studios, London W2 3SQ (☎ 020 7262 1470, e-mail christopher@purvis.co.uk)

PURVIS, John Robert; CBE (1990); s of Lt-Col Robert William Berry Purvis, MC; *b* 6 July 1938; *Educ* Cargilfield Edinburgh, Glenalmond Coll, St Salvator's Coll, Univ of St Andrews; *m* 1962, Louise S Durham; 1 s, 2 da; *Career* First Nat City Bank of NY 1962–69, Noble Grossart 1969–73, md Gilmerton Mgmnt Servs Ltd 1973–92, managing ptnr Purvis & Co 1986–; dir: James River (UK) Holdings Ltd 1988–95, Edgar Astaire & Co Ltd 1993–94, Jamont NV 1994–95, European Utilities Trust plc 1994–2007, Crown Vantage Ltd 1995–2001, Curtis Fine Papers Ltd 1995–2001; chm: Kingdom FM Radio Ltd 1997–2008 (dir 1997–2013), Belgrave Capital Mgmnt Ltd 1999–; MEP (EDG) Mid Scotland and Fife 1979–84, MEP (EPP/ED Cons) Scotland 1999–2009; chm Financial Future Forum 2009–15 (hon pres 2015–); vice-chm Economic and Monetary Affairs Ctee 2002–09; memb: Scottish Landowners' Fedn Taxation Ctee 1978–99, IBA London (chm for Scotland) 1985–89, Scottish Advsy Ctee on Telecommunications 1990–97; chm SCUA Econ Ctee 1986–97, vice-pres Scottish Cons & Unionist Assoc 1987–89; FInstD; *Recreations* gardening, travel, walking; *Clubs* Cavalry and Guards', Farmers', New (Edinburgh), Royal and Ancient (St Andrews); *Style*— John Purvis, Esq, CBE; ✉ PO Box 29222, St Andrews, Fife KY16 8WL (☎ 01334 475830, fax 01334 477754, e-mail purvisco@jpurvis.co.uk)

PURVIS, (Prof) Stewart Peter; CBE (1999); s of Peter Purvis (d 1998), and Lydia, *née* Stewart (d 1997); *b* 28 October 1947; *Educ* Dulwich Coll, Univ of Exeter (BA); *m* 2 Sept 1972 (m dis 1993), Mary, da of Arthur Presnail; 1 da (Helen b 1974); partner, Jacqui Marson; 2 s (Tom b 1994, Jess b 1999); *Career* formerly presenter Harlech TV, news trainee BBC 1969; ITN: journalist 1972, prog ed News at Ten 1980–83, ed Channel Four News 1983, dep ed 1983–89, ed 1989–91, ed-in-chief 1991–95, chief exec 1995–2003; prof of TV journalism City Univ London 2003–, visiting prof of broadcast media Univ of Oxford 2003; former pres EuroNews, former dir Royal Marsden NHS Tst, former dep chm Kings Cross Partnership; ptnr for content and standards Ofcom 2007–10; chair UK Govt Media Literacy Working Gp 2010, specialist advsr to House of Lords Select Ctee on Communications 2011, memb DCMS Selection Panel for Chm of BBC Tst 2011, non-exec dir Channel 4 Corp 2013–, tstee SSVC 2013–, vice-pres RTS 2013–; RTS awards for: The Pope in Poland 1979, Return of the Canberra 1982; Broadcasting Press Guild Award for Best News or Current Events Prog (Channel Four News) 1984, BAFTA award for Best News or Outside Broadcast (Channel Four News) 1987 and 1988, RTS Gold Medal for outstanding contrib to television 2009; Hon LLD Univ of Exeter 2005; FRTS; *Style*— Stewart Purvis, Esq, CBE

PURVIS OF TWEED, Baron (Life Peer UK 2013), of East March in the Scottish Borders; Jeremy Purvis; s of George Purvis, of Berwick-upon-Tweed, and Eileen Purvis; *b* 15 January 1974, Berwick-upon-Tweed; *Educ* Berwick-upon-Tweed HS, Brunel Univ (BSc); *Career* research asst to Rt Hon Sir David Steel, KBE, PC, DL (now Baron Steel of Aikwood (Life Peer)), *qv* 1993, Parly asst Liberal Int 1994, Parly asst ELDR (European Lib Dem and Reform Pty) Gp European Parliament 1995, PA to Rt Hon Lord Steel of Aikwood, KBE, PC, DL 1996–98, with GJW Scotland (Parly affrs co) 1998–2001, dir McEwan Purvis (strategic communications consultancy) 2001–03, MSP (Lib Dem) Tweeddale, Ettrick and Lauderdale 2003–11; Lib Dem finance spokesman 2003–05 and 2007–11, Lib Dem justice and home affrs spokesman 2005–07, Lib Dem energy and climate change spokesman 2015–; memb: UK Branch Cwlth Parly Assoc 2015–, UK Branch Inter Parliamentary Union 2016, House of Lords Int Relations Ctee 2016–; dir of campaigns Keep Scotland Beautiful; *Style*— The Lord Purvis of Tweed

PUTROV, Ivan; s of Oleksandr Ivanovich Putrov, of Kyiv, Ukraine, and Natalia Vasilievna Berezina; *b* 8 March 1980, Kyiv, Ukraine; *Educ* Kyiv State Choreographic Inst 1990–97, Royal Ballet Sch 1997–98; *Career* ballet dancer; Royal Ballet: joined 1998, princ dancer 2002– (currently Royal Ballet's youngest male princ); memb jury Serge Lifar Int Ballet Competition 2004; collaborated with many artists incl Jay Joplin, *qv*, Mario Testino, The Pet Shop Boys, Johnnie Shand Kydd, Mary Macartney Donald and Sam Taylor-Wood, *qv* (incl Strings); *Performances* with Royal Ballet incl: Albrecht in Giselle, Basilio in Don Quixote, Solor in La Bayadère, Boy with Matted Hair in Shadowplay, Prince Siegfried in Swan Lake, Jean de Brienne in Raymonda, Lensky in Onegin, Prince Desire in Sleeping Beauty, Franz in Coppélia, Prince and Hans-Peter in The Nutcracker (televised BBC), Le Spectre de la Rose, lead in Symphony in C, lead in The Four Temperaments, title role in The Prodigal Son, lead in Scènes de ballet, Beliaev in A Month in the Country, Prince Florimund in Awakening pas de deux (performed for 101st birthday of HRH the late Queen Elizabeth the Queen Mother); lead roles with ballet cos of nat theatres of Hungary and Ukraine incl: La Sylphide (broadcast to 85 countries on World Service), Le Spectre de la rose, Giselle, Carmen, Onegin; *Awards* Premier Prix Prix de Lausanne 1996, Gold Medal Serge Lifar Int Ballet Competition 1996, Gold Medal Nijinsky Festival 2001, Outstanding Young Male Dancer Critics' Circle Dance Awards 2002, Medal for Work and Achievement (awarded by pres of Ukraine) 2004; *Style*— Ivan Putrov, Esq; ✉ The Royal Ballet, Royal Opera House, Covent Garden, London WC2E 9DD (☎ 020 7212 9165, e-mail janine.limberg@roh.org.uk)

PUTTERGILL, Graham Fraser; s of Henry William Puttergill (d 1984), of Gonubie, South Africa, and Elizabeth Blanche, *née* McClelland (d 1991); *b* 20 March 1949; *Educ* St Patrick's Coll Port Elizabeth; *m* 7 Aug 1976, Susan Jennifer, da of Victor James Wilkinson, of Dorchester, Dorset; 2 s (Miles b 1982, David b 1987), 2 da (Robyn b 1985, Lucy b 1989); *Career* 1 Lt Cape Town Highlanders 1967–68; chm HSBC Benefit Consultants Ltd 1982–2000 (md 1977–82), exec chm HSBC Insurance Brokers Ltd 1985–2000, dep chm HSBC Insurance Holdings Ltd 1993–2000; vice-chm and ceo Premium Credit Ltd 2004–05 (chm 2000–04); chm of govrs Caldicott Sch 2004–15 (govr 2000–15); ACII 1973, FPMI 1983; *Recreations* family, golf, tennis, long distance cycling; *Clubs* Beaconsfield Golf (capt 2014), Pearl Valley; *Style*— Graham Puttergill, Esq; ✉ The Redwood, Long Grove, Seer Green, Buckinghamshire HP9 2QH (e-mail gputtergill@aol.com)

PUTTNAM, Baron (Life Peer UK 1997), of Queensgate in the Royal Borough of Kensington and Chelsea; Sir David Terence Puttnam; kt (1995), CBE (1983); s of Capt Leonard Arthur Puttnam, RA (d 1981), of Winchmore Hill, and Marie Beatrice, *née* Goldman; *b* 25 February 1941; *Educ* Minchenden GS London; *m* 22 Sept 1961, Patricia Mary, da of Maj John Frederick Jones, of Folkestone, Kent; 1 s (Hon Alexander David b 5 April 1966), 1 da (Hon Deborah Jane b 25 Jan 1962); *Career* film prodr; chm Enigma Productions Ltd 1978–, chm and ceo Columbia Pictures 1986–88; chm: Nat Film & TV Sch Ltd 1988–96, Nat Museum of Photography Film and Television 1994–2003, Nat Endowment for Science, Technology and the Arts (NESTA) 1998–2003, General Teaching Cncl 2000–02, Futurelab 2006–11, Atticus Educn 2012–; dep chm: Channel 4 2006–12, Profero 2010–14; dir: Anglia TV Group plc 1982–98, Chrysalis Group until 1996; non-exec dir: Promethean World plc, Huntsworth plc 2007–12; pres Cncl for Protection of Rural England 1985–92, pres Film Distributors' Assoc 2009–; advsr Dept of Educn and Skills 1997–2009; memb Educn Standards Task Force 1997–2001; co-fndr European Media Business Sch Madrid 1991; chm Ateliers du cinema Européen 1991–94, chm Nat Meml Arboretum 1993–2003, chm North Music Tst (The Sage Gateshead) 2007–12, vice chm Advsy Cncl Hansard Soc 2007; chair of tstees Nat Teaching Awards 1998–2009; chllr Open Univ 2006–; pres UNICEF UK 2002–09, chair Advsy Bd TSL Educn 2010–; tstee: Tate Gallery 1985–92, Science Museum 1996–2004, Royal Acad of Arts 2000–03, IPPR 2000–10, Sunderland AFC Fndn 2001–03, Thomson Fndn 2003–, Eden Project 2009–13, Transformation Tst 2009–11; vice-pres BAFTA 1994–2004; lay canon Durham Cathedral 2002–08; govr LSE 1997–2002; chllr Univ of Sunderland 1997–2007, chllr Open Univ 2007–14; Hon LLD Bristol 1983, Hon LittD Leeds 1992; Hon DLitt: Leicester 1986, Sunderland 1992, Univ of Bradford 1993, Humberside 1996, Univ of Westminster 1997, Univ of Kent at Canterbury 1998, City Univ 2000, Univ of Nottingham 2000, Queens Univ Belfast 2001, N London Univ 2001, Heriot Watt Univ 2001, Keele Univ 2002, Univ of Southampton 2002, Univ of Birmingham 2002, Abertay Dundee Univ 2003; Hon DMus RSAMD 1998; hon doctorate: Univ of Navarra Spain 1999, Sheffield Hallam Univ 2000, Univ of London 2001, King Alfred's Coll Winchester 2002, Herzen St Petersburg 2003, Univ of Surrey 2003, Thames Valley Univ 2004, Queen Margaret UC 2004, Brunel Univ 2004, Univ of Middx 2004, Greenwich Univ 2005, Open Univ 2007, Inst of Educn 2007, Nottingham Trent Univ 2008, Griffiths Unv Brisbane 2010; Hon Dr of Arts American Int Univ London 2000, Hon DEd Univ of Sunderland 2007, Hon DSc Nottingham Trent Univ 2008; hon fell: Manchester Poly, Chartered Soc of Designers 1990, Landscape Inst 1995, Cheltenham and Gloucester Coll of HE 1998, London Guildhall Univ 1999, Imperial Coll London 1999, Br Inst of Professional Photographers 2001; visiting prof Film Dept Univ of Bristol 1985–98; memb BFI, charter fell Coll of Teachers 2002, fell BAFTA 2006, fell New Media Consortium 2012; Freedom City of Sunderland 2007, Freeman Guild of Educators; FRGS, FRSA, FRPS, FCGI 1999, FRTS 2003; Cdr de l'Ordre des Arts et des Lettres (France) 2006 (Chevalier 1985, Officier 1992); *Awards* Special Jury Prize (Cannes) for The Duellists 1977, two Academy Awards and four Br Academy Awards for Midnight Express 1978, four Academy Awards (incl Best Film) and three Br Academy Awards (incl Best Film) for Chariots of Fire 1981, Michael Balcon Award for outstanding contrib to the Br film industry Br Academy Awards 1982 three Academy Awards and eight Br Academy Awards (incl Best Film) for The Killing Fields 1985, Palme D'Or for The Mission 1986, Lifetime Achievement Award Cannes Film Festival 1992, Benjamin Franklin Medal RSA 1997, Crystal Award World Economic Forum 1997, President's medal RPS 2003, Bicentenary Medal RSA 2007, Akiro Kurasawa Award Japan 2007; *Books* The Third Age of Broadcasting (co-author, 1982), Rural England (co-author, 1988), The Undeclared War: The Struggle for Control of the World's Film Industry (1997), Members Only: Parliament in the Public Eye (2005); *Recreations* reading; *Clubs* Athenaeum, MCC, Chelsea Arts; *Style*— The Rt Hon Lord Puttnam, CBE; ✉ c/o House of Lords, Westminster, London SW1A 0PW

PUXLEY, James Henry Lavallin; DL (Berks 2005); s of John Philip Lavallin Puxley, of Wickham Heath, Newbury, and Aline Carlos *née* Wilson; *b* 23 October 1948; *Educ* Eton, Univ of Bristol (BA), RAC Cirencester (Dip Rural Estate Mgmnt); *m* 26 April 1991, Deborah Anne, da of Col Iain Ferguson; 1 da (Felicia Margaret Lavallin b 19 January 1996); *Career* self employed mangr family estate; High Sheriff Berks 2000–2001, Lord-Lt Berks 2015 (Vice Lord-Lt 2011); ARICS 1976, MRAC 1974; *Recreations* country sports, travel; *Clubs* Traveller's; *Style*— James Puxley, Esq, DL; ✉ Welford Park, Welford,

P

Newbury, Berkshire RG20 8HU (☎ 01488 608691, fax 01488 657896, e-mail jpuxley@welfordpark.co.uk)

PYANT, Paul; s of Leonard Vincent Pyant (d 1976), of Croydon, Surrey, and Jean Pheobe, *née* Frampton; *b* 22 July 1953; *Educ* Haling Manor Croydon, RADA (1973 Charles Killick Award); *Career* lighting designer; prodn electrics and asst lighting mangr Glyndebourne Opera 1974–87, freelance 1988–; memb: Labour Party, CND, Nat Tst, Woodland Tst, Assoc of Lighting Designers, United Artists 829 (USA) 1994; *Theatre* NT (dir Nicholas Hytner, *qv*) incl: Wind in the Willows 1990, The Madness of George III 1991, Carousel 1992, Major Barbara 2008; NT (dir Trevor Nunn, *qv*): Arcadia 1993, Troilus & Cressida 1999, Candide 1999, The Relapse 2001, A Streetcar Named Desire 2003; NT (dir Sam Mendes, *qv*) incl: The Sea 1991, Othello 1997, King Lear 2014; Donmar Warehouse (dir Sam Mendes) incl: Assassins 1992, Cabaret 1993, Company 1993; Donmar Warehouse (dir David Leveaux, *qv*) Nine 1997, Electra 1998; other credits incl: Orpheus Descending (dir Sir Peter Hall, *qv*, London and New York (Broadway debut)) 1988, Single Spies (dir Alan Bennett, *qv*) 1988, The Tempest (RSC) 1993, Talking Heads (dir Alan Bennett) 1997, Long Day's Journey into Night 2000, Humble Boy (dir John Caird, *qv*, NT and West End) 2003, All's Well that Ends Well (RSC) 2003–04, The Woman in White (London and Broadway) 2004/05, The Home Place (Gate Dublin) 2005, Hay Fever 2006, Enjoy 2006, Lord of the Rings (Toronto and London) 2006/07, The Glass Menagerie 2007, Speed the Plow (Old Vic) 2008, Waiting for Godot 2009, The Bridge Project (with Sam Mendes, The Winter's Tale 2009, The Cherry Orchard 2009, The Tempest and As You Like It 2010, Richard III 2011), Grief (dir Mike Leigh, *qv*) 2011, Ecstasy (dir Mike Leigh) 2011, Hysteria 2012, Charlie and the Chocolate Factory (Theatre Royal Drury Lane) 2013, Oh What A Lovely War 2014, Versailles 2014; *Opera* incl: King Priam (Kent Opera) 1984, Xerxes (ENO) 1985, Lady Macbeth of Mtsensk (ENO) 1987, New Year (American opera debut) 1989, Death in Venice (Glyndebourne) 1990, Le Nozze Di Figaro (Wien Festival) 1991, Gawain (ROH Covent Garden debut) 1991, Fedora (Wien Staatsoper debut) 1994, Stiffelio (La Scala debut) 1995, Pique Dame (Metropolitan Opera debut) 1995, Don Giovanni (Kirov Opera debut) 2000, Boulevard Solitude (ROH) 2001, Vanessa (Opera de Monte Carlo debut) 2001, Peter Grimes (Salzburg debut) 2005, A Midsummer Night's Dream (Glyndebourne) 2006, The Minotaur (ROH) 2008, Brief Encounter (Houston) 2009, Der Rosenkavalier (Bolshoi Opera debut) 2012, Parsifal (ROH) 2012; *Ballet* for English Nat Ballet incl: Sleeping Beauty 1993, Giselle 1994, Cinderella 1997, Snow Queen 2007; for Northern Ballet Theatre incl: Romeo and Juliet 1991, Christmas Carol 1992, Swan Lake 1992, Cinderella 1993, Dracula 1996, Hunchback of Notre Dame 1998; *Awards* winner New York Critics' Award for Carousel 1994, Dora Mavor Award for best lighting of a musical (for Lord of the Rings) 2006, Knight of Illumination Award (for The Minotaur at ROH) 2008, 6 Best Lighting Award nominations Olivier Awards, winner Best Lighting Design Olivier Award 2014 (for Charlie and the Chocolate Factory), 2 Tony nominations, 3 Drama Desk nominations; *Recreations* steam locomotives, gardening, art galleries; *Style—* Paul Pyant, Esq; ✉ c/o Jeffrey Cambell Management (☎ 01323 730526, e-mail cambell@theatricaldesigners.co.uk)

PYE, Brig Hugh William Kellow; OBE (2003); s of Brig Randall Thomas Kellow Pye, DSO, OBE (d 2002), of Lindfield, W Sussex, and Peggy Muriel, *née* Sagar-Musgrave-Brooksbank (d 1999); *b* 23 May 1938, Haywards Heath; *Educ* Wellington, RMA Sandhurst; *m* 8 June 1968, Mary Ann, da of Cdr the Hon David Edwardes, DSC, RN (d 1983), of Wincanton, Somerset; 1 s (Robert Alec Kellow b 1970), 1 da (Victoria Ann (Mrs Colin Elwell) b 1973); *Career* cmmnd 12 Royal Lancers (POW) 1958, Cdr Berlin Armd Sqdn 1968, Staff Coll Camberley 1971, GSO2 INT JSIS Hong Kong 1972, Armed Forces Staff Coll Norfolk Virginia USA 1976, cmdg 9/12 Royal Lancers (POW) 1977–79 (despatches), AMS MS 4 1979–82, dep Chief of Staff (DCOS) and Cdr Br Contingent UNFICYP 1982–84, Col Co-ordination Staff Coll Camberley 1984–85, project mangr, Dep Cdr and advsr Oman Cmd and Staff Coll 1986–89, Dep Cdr SW Dist and Cdr Br Element AMF (L) 1990–92, ret; Hon Col: Leics and Derbys Yeo (PAO) TA 1992–2003, 9/12 Royal Lancers (POW) 1995–2003, City and Co of Bristol ACF 2000–04; treas Soc of Merchant Venturers Bristol 1992–2003; govr: Colston's Collegiate Sch 1992–2003 (chm 1994–2003), Colston's Girls' Sch 1992–2003; tstee: Gtr Bristol Fndn 1993–99, Cancer and Leukaemia in Childhood (CLIC) 1996–2004 (chm 1996–2004), Southwest Fndn 2000–08 (vice-chm 2001–03, chm 2003–08), CLIC Sargent 2005–06 (jt chm 2005–06), Bristol Cathedral Tst 2005–13 (vice-chm 2005–07, chm 2007–13, chm Cathedral Appeal 2005–13), Somerset Community Fndn 2007–09 (vice-pres 2009–); patron: Bristol Foyer 2000–03, Fast Track 2000–03; Hon LLD Univ of Bristol 2003; FRSA 2001; Sultan of Oman's Commendation Medal 1989; *Recreations* shooting, fishing, gardening; *Clubs* Cavalry and Guards'; *Style—* Brigadier Hugh Pye, OBE; ✉ Tuxwell Farm, Spaxton, Bridgwater, Somerset TA5 1DF (☎ 01278 671833, e-mail hughpye@btopenworld.com)

PYE, Tom; *Educ* Lincoln Coll of Art (BTEC Dip), Wimbledon Sch of Art (BA); *Career* theatre, set and costume designer; *Theatre* prodns incl: The Angel Project (13 Spaces/towerblocks accross the city, dir Deborah Warner, *qv*, Perth Int Arts Festival Aust), The Euston Project (dir Deborah Warner, The Euston Tower (LIFT), Diary of One Who Vanished (dir Deborah Warner, ENO/NT tour, London, Paris, Dublin, Amsterdam, NY and Munich), Turn of the Screw (dir Deborah Warner, ROH, Barbican and Bobigny Paris), Don Giovanni (Aix-en-Provence Festival and world tour), Jeanne D'Arc au Bucher (dir Deborah Warner, BBC Proms Royal Albert Hall), Fiddler on the Roof (Broadway), The Rape of Lucreita (Bayerische Opera), St John Passion (dir Deborah Warner, ENO), Medea (dir Deborah Warner, Queen's Theatre London and Abbey Theatre Dublin), The Power Book (NT), The Diary of One Who Vanished (ENO, RNT), Near Life Experience, The Magic Flute (Opera North); *Television* art director Just William (series II, Talisman Films/BBC); prodn designer: Medea, King Lear and Measure for Measure (BBC Open Univ, dir Fiona Shaw, *qv*), Twelfth Night (Channel 4), Helen West (ITV), The Late Michael Clark (BBC), Movie Talk and Preview (SKY TV), ITV Sports Awards (live from Wembley), pop promotions incl New Order, commercials incl Persil, Ford Fiesta, Zoom; scenic artist Comic Strip Presents (two series); *Films* prodn designer: Helen West (3 films for TV, Deep Sleep, Shadow Play, A Clear Conscience), Gloriana (dir Phyllida Lloyd, *qv*, film for TV), Maua King and Emperor (feature film), The Late Michael Clark (film for TV); art dir: Christie Malry's Own Double Entry (feature film), Richard II (dir Deborah Warner, film for TV), A Feast at Midnight (feature film); wardrobe asst Robin Hood Prince of Thieves (feature film); other prodn design incl: studio shows, award ceremonies and live specials for MTV Europe and VH1; *Clubs* Century; *Style—* Tom Pye, Esq; ✉ c/o Douglas & Kopelman Artists Inc, 393 West 49th Street, Suite 5G, New York NY 10019

PYE, William Burns; s of Sir David Pye, CB, FRS (d 1959), of Elstead, Surrey, and Virginia Frances, *née* Kennedy; *b* 16 July 1938; *Educ* Charterhouse, Wimbledon Sch of Art, Sch of Sculpture RCA; *m* 1963, Susan Marsh; 1 s (Tristram b 18 March 1966), 2 da (Rebecca Jane b 2 June 1968, Alexandra Virginia b 4 Aug 1973); *Career* sculptor; visiting prof Calif State Univ 1975–76; made films Reflections 1971, From Scrap to Sculpture 1971; elected pres Hampshire Sculpture Tst 2002; FRBS, Hon FRIBA, *Commissions and Sculptures on Public Sites* Zemran (South Bank London), King's Cross House Cmmn (Pentonville Rd London), water sculpture (Aston Univ Campus), mural at Vauxhall railway stn, Slipstream and Jetstream water sculptures (Gatwick North Terminal), Curlicue (Greenland Dock London Docklands), Chalice (Fountain Square, 123 Buckingham Palace Rd), Orchid (The Peacocks Woking), Aventino (Mercury House London), Cristos (St Christopher's Place London), Flyover (M25 Clacket Lane Service Station), Downpour (Br Embassy Muskat Oman), Derby Cascade (Market Square Derby), Cader Idris (Cardiff), Aquarena (Millennium Square Bristol), Wilton House (Wilts), Nat Botanic Garden of Wales, Jubilee Fountain (Lincoln's Inn London), eight features for water gardens Alnwick Castle, Colisée Pyramid (Le Colisée St Ouen Paris), Jefferson (Louisville Kentucky), Mesa (Phoenix Arizona), Eastgate (Cincinnati Ohio), Regency (Racine Wisconsin), San-Mateo (California), Kagoshima City (Japan), Hong Kong Int Airport, font for Salisbury Cathedral, UBC Botanic Gardens (Vancouver), Vannpaviljong (Drammen Norway), Caribdis Vortex (Campinas Brazil), Vortex (Ruwi Oman); *Work in Public Collections* incl: Arts Cncl of GB, MOMA NY, Contemporary Art Soc, Royal Albert Museum Exeter, Birmingham City Art Gallery, Szepmuveszeti Museum Budapest, Graves Art Gallery Sheffield, National Museum of Wales, Utsukushi-ga-hara Open Air Museum Japan, Nat Portrait Gallery; *Solo Exhibitions* incl: Redfern Gallery London 1966, 1969, 1973 and 1975, Bertha Schaefer Gallery NY 1970, Bear Lane Gallery Oxford 1972, Ikon Gallery Birmingham 1975, Morgan Thomas Gallery LA 1976, Yorkshire Sculpture Park 1978, Winchester Great Hall 1979, Welsh Touring Exhbn 1980, London Business Sch 1986, The Rotunda One Exchange Square Hong Kong 1987, New Art Centre Roche Ct 2004, England Gallery 2008; *Group Exhibitions* incl: Towards Art II (Arts Cncl Gallery), Internationale der Zeichnung (Darmstadt), Middleheim 10th Biennale of Sculpture (Antwerp), British Sculptors '72 (RA), British Painting and Sculpture Today (Indianapolis Museum of Art), Royal Jubilee Exhbn of Contemporary British Sculpture (London), Budapest Int Exhbn of Small Sculpture (Prix de Sculpture), British Sculpture in the 20th Century (Whitechapel Art Gallery), Welsh Sculpture Tst Inaugural Exhbn (Margam Park, Port Talbot), 6th Henry Moore Grand Prize Exhbn (Br nomination, Utsukushi-ga-hara Museum Japan), Chelsea Harbour Sculpture '93, sculpture at Schönthal Switzerland, Tate Britain 2004; *Awards* Prix de Sculpture Budapest In Sculpture Exhbn 1981, Vauxhall Mural Competition 1983, Peace Sculpture Competition (for Ackers Park Small Heath Birmingham) 1984, Art at Work Award Wapping Arts Tst (for Sculpture at Gatwick Airport) 1988, Assoc of Business Sponsorship of the Arts Award 1988, Royal UENO Award Japan 1989; *Books* William Pye: his work and his words; *Recreations* playing the flute; *Style—* William Pye; ✉ 43 Hambalt Road, Clapham, London SW4 9EQ (☎ 020 8673 2318, office ☎ 020 8682 2727, office fax 020 8682 3218, website www.williampye.com)

PYLKKANEN, Jussi; *Educ* King's Coll Sch Wimbledon, Lady Margaret Hall Oxford; *Career* Christie's: joined 1986, chm Impressionist and Modern Paintings Dept, memb Bd 2008–, pres Christie's Europe, ME and Russia 2010–15, global pres 2015–; tstee Dulwich Picture Gall London; *Style—* Jussi Pylkkanen, Esq; ✉ Christie's, 8 King Street, St. James's, London SW1Y 6QT

PYM, Hugh; *Educ* Marlborough, ChCh Oxford, UC Falmouth (postgrad dip); *Career* local radio Wilts Radio and Viking Radio Hull 1983–86, radio journalist BBC 1986–87, prod Business Daily (Channel 4) 1987–88, corr ITN 1988–98, freelance broadcaster Sky Television 1999–2000; BBC News: business corr 2001–06, economics corr 2006–09, chief economics corr 2009–; *Books* The Guinness Affair: Anatomy of a Scandal (jtly, 1987), Unit and Investment Trusts (1988), Gordon Brown: The First Year in Power (jtly, 1998); *Style—* Hugh Pym, Esq; ✉ BBC News, Wood Lane, London W12 7RJ

PYMAN, Avril; *see:* Sokolov, Dr Avril

PYMONT, Christopher Howard; QC (1996); s of late John Pymont, and late Joan, *née* Marmoy; *b* 16 March 1956; *Educ* Marlborough (scholar), Christ Church Oxford (scholar, MA); *m* 1996, Meriel Rosalind, da of Roger Lester and late Ann Lester of Pinner Hill; 1 da (Harriet Ann Eloise b 5 Feb 1998), 2 s (Nicholas John Frederick b 28 April 2000, Benedict Anthony Edmund b 26 Feb 2003); *Career* called to the Bar Gray's Inn 1979; specialist in chancery and commercial law, recorder 2004–, dep judge of the High Court 2008–, head Maitland Chambers 2012–; *Style—* Christopher Pymont, Esq, QC; ✉ Maitland Chambers, 7 Stone Buildings, Lincoln's Inn, London WC2A 3SZ

PYPER, Susan Elizabeth; *née* Harrison; *b* 12 December 1951, London; *Educ* Prendergast GS, Univ of Durham (BSc), Univ of London (postgrad dip); *m* 1987, Jonathan Pyper; 1 s (Anthony b 27 March 1988), 1 da (Elisabeth b 26 May 1989); *Career* forensic scientist Met Police 1973–76, offr RAF 1976–87, Milupa (UK) Ltd 1990–92, chm NHS tsts in London and W Sussex 1992–2005; lay memb Preliminary Investigation Ctee Royal Coll of Veterinary Surgeons 1999–2006, chm Royal W Sussex NHS Tst 2005–09; pres Sussex Community Fndn, chm Rgnl Environment Protection Advsy Ctee 2002–11, memb Rgnl Flood Defence Ctee 2002–11; HM Lord-Lt W Sussex 2008–; DStJ; *Recreations* skiing, fell walking, music, natural history, family, travel; *Clubs* RAF; *Style—* Mrs Susan Pyper, HM Lord-Lieutenant of West Sussex; ✉ Lieutenancy Office, County Hall, Chichester, West Sussex PO19 1RQ (☎ 01243 777951, e-mail john.williams@westsussex.gov.uk)

PYTEL, Walenty; s of Wladislaw Pytel, of Bath, and Jadwiga Pytel; *b* 10 February 1941; *Educ* Leominster Minster Sch, Hereford Coll of Art (NDD); *m* 7 Oct 1963, Janet Mary, da of William Sidney Spencer (d 1973), of Westington Court; 1 s (Jeremy Walenty Spencer b 1964), 1 da (Victoria Catharine Mary b 1968); *Career* artist, sculptor in bronze; works incl: mural Lord Montague Beaulieu 1972, Chanel Perfume Paris 1975, fountain sculpture cmmnd by MPs to commemorate Queen's Silver Jubilee New Palace Yard Westminster 1977, unicorn from HRH Princess Anne to Portuguese Govt 1979, Cwlth beasts for Sir Edward du Cann MP, Sir John Hall MP and Patrick Cooke, The Fosser in the grounds of JCB factory Uttoxeter, Take Off Birmingham Int Airport 1985, unicorn representing coat of arms for Lord and Lady Leigh Stoneleigh Abbey 1989, 5 vikings for Anders Wilhelmsen & Co 1996,17 ft war meml in bronze cmmnd by Ludlow Branch Royal Br Legion 2000, 3 25ft riverside sculptures cmmd by S Herefords DC 2000, 25ft dragonfly and butterfly cmmd by S Glos Cncl 2000, 10 Millennium Planet Walk sculptures cmmd by Tamworth BC 2000, 2 15ft cranes for Mazak Europe Machine Tools, Colin Grazier war meml Tamworth, Futuristic Runner for Royal Nat Coll fo the Blind to celebrate the 2012 Olympic Games, The Buzzaros Have Landed cmmd by Malvern Hills District Cncl 2013, Core of the Community mural (Fownhope Medical Centre) 2013; exhibitions: Marbella 1985, New Jersey 1987, San Diego 1987, Mitukoshi Gallery Tokyo 1987, Soc of Wildlife Artists Mall Galleries 1988 (award winner), Essen Germany 1989, Couvert de Recollets Cognac France 1992, Belvoir Castle 2002, Artparks 2003, Nature in Art Twigworth 2003, Santa YNez Valley Classic Art Show USA, Cornes Japan, Art & Gems, Dubai; work in various private collections; Coventry Design Award 2001 (for Wings over Water conservation area bridge); memb Soc of Br Sculptors; ambass for Herefords; ARBS; *Recreations* salmon fishing, game shooting, sailing; *Style—* Walenty Pytel, Esq; ✉ Hartleton, Bromsash, Ross-on-Wye HR9 7SB (☎ 01989 780536); Wyebridge Interiors, 26 High Street, Ledbury HR8 1DS (☎ 01531 634102, e-mail info@wyebridge.com, website www.wyebridge.com and www.presentsr4u.com)

Q

QASIM, Prof Waseem; *Educ* Univ of Newcastle (BMedSci, MB BS), UCL (PhD); *Career* conslt in paediatric immunology Great Ormond Street Hosp for Children NHS Tst 2007–; prof of cell and gene therapy Inst of Child Health UCL 2015–; NIHR Chair 2015; MRCP 1996, MRCPCH 1997; *Style*— Prof Waseem Qasim

QUAH, Prof Danny; s of Chong-eng Quah, of Penang, Malaysia, and Phaik-im, *née* Goh; *b* 26 July 1958, Penang, Malaysia; *Educ* Princeton Univ (AB), Harvard Univ (PhD); *m* Ai-Leen Lim; 2 s (Carter Tyson b 13 Aug 1994, Mason Tyson b 8 Nov 1996); *Career* asst prof of econs MIT 1986–91; LSE: lectr then reader in econs 1991–96, exec dir Nat Econ Performance Prog Centre for Econ Performance 1994–99, prof of econs 1996–, dir Andrew Mellon Prog for the Study of IT and the Weightless Economy 1998–2002, head Dept of Econs 2006–09, co-dir LSE Global Governance 2010–11, Kuwait prof of economics and int devpt 2012–, prof of int devpt 2013–, dir SE Asia Centre 20114–; visiting asst prof Harvard Univ 1990, Tan Chin Tuan visiting prof of economics Nat Univ of Singapore 2010–, Li Ka Shing prof of economics Lee Kuan Yew Sch of Public Policy Nat Univ of Singapore 2016–; conslt: Bank of Eng, World Bank, Monetary Authy of Singapore; memb Prog Ctee: Econometric Soc 1991, 1997, 1999, 2000 and 2003, European Econ Assoc 1995–96, Royal Econ Soc 1997–98; memb Nat Economic Advsy Cncl Malaysia 2009–11; prog chair European Econ Assoc 2000; assoc ed Jl of Econ Growth 1996–, res reader Br Acad 1996–98; one of ten ESRC Heroes of Dissemination 2001; govr NIESR 2002–16; *Publications* The Global Economy's Shifting Centre of Gravity (2011); *Recreations* taekwon-do (black belt, England Patterns Champion and sparring runner-up 2005, Britain sparring runner-up 2005); *Style*— Prof Danny Quah; ✉ Department of Economics, LSE, Houghton Street, London WC2A 2AE (☎ 020 7955 7535, e-mail d.quah@lse.ac.uk, website http://dannyquah.com)

QUANT, Dame Mary (Mrs A Plunket Greene); DBE (2015, OBE 1966); da of Jack Quant, and Mildred Quant; *b* 11 February 1934; *Educ* Goldsmiths' Coll of Art London; *m* 1957, Alexander Plunket Greene; 1 s (Orlando Plunket Greene); *Career* fashion designer; estab Mary Quant Gp of Cos 1955, Mary Quant cosmetics launched 1966, fndr Mary Quant Ltd (co-chm until 2000); non-exec dir House of Fraser plc 1997–; memb: Design Cncl 1971, Br and USA Bicentennial Liaison Ctee 1973, Advsy Cncl V&A 1976–78; winner: Maison Blanche Rex Award 1964, Sunday Times Int Award 1964, Piavola d'Oro Award 1966, Annual Design Medal Inst of Industrial Artists and Designers 1966, Hall of Fame Award Br Fashion Cncl 1990; sr fell RCA 1991, hon fell RSA 1993; hon fell Goldsmiths Coll London 1993; Hon BA Winchester Sch of Art 2000, Hon DUniv Wales 2001; FSIA 1967, RDI 1969, FRSA 1995; *Publications* Quant by Quant, Colour by Quant, Quant on Make-Up, Mary Quant Classic Make-Up & Beauty Book; *Style*— Dame Mary Quant, DBE; ✉ 39 Dalby Road, London SW18 1AW

QUARMBY, Dr David Anthony; CBE (2003); s of Frank Reginald Quarmby (d 1983); *b* 22 July 1941, Halifax, W Yorks; *Educ* Shrewsbury, King's Coll Cambridge (MA), Univ of Leeds (PhD, Dip Industrial Mgmnt); *m* 1968, Hilmary, da of Denis Hilton Hunter; 4 da; *Career* md London Tport Exec Buses 1978–84 (memb 1975–84), jt md J Sainsbury plc 1988–96 (dir 1984–96); chm: British Tourist Authy 1996–2003, English Tourist Bd 1996–99, Docklands Light Railway 1999–2001 (dir 1998), SeaBritain 2005 2003–05, Strategic Rail Authy (SRA) 2004–06 (shadow SRA 1999–2001, memb 2001–06, dep chm 2002–04), Transport Research Inst Edinburgh Napier Univ 2006–11, Ind Transport Cmmn 2007–09, English Tourism Intelligence Partnership 2007–11, RAC Fndn 2009–13, Freight Advsy Gp Canal and River Tst 2012–; memb Expert Panel Airport Cmmn 2013–15, pres Commercial Boat Operators' Assoc 2015–; dir: Colin Buchanan & Ptnrs 2007–08, NedRailways (now Abellio) 2007–11; conslt in transport planning, economics and policy 2006–; dep chm S London Econ Devpt Alliance 1999–2003, dep chm and sometime chm New Millennium Experience Co 1997–2001; non-exec dir: Bd DETR 1996–98, Greenwich Millennium Tst 1998–2000, London First 1998–2002; memb Transport for London 2000–04, memb Bd and tstee Elderhostel Inc 2006–09; pres Inst of Logistics 1996–99; chm: Retail Action Gp for Crime Prevention 1995–96, James Allen's Girls' Sch Dulwich 1995–98 (govr 1987–98, dep chm 1992–95), S London Business Leadership 1996–99; dir Blackheath Concert Halls 1990–94, pres Blackheath Soc 2002–16, tstee St Paul's Cathedral Fndn 2005–08; memb: Sch Curriculum and Assessment Authy 1993–95, Crime Prevention Agency Bd 1995–97, Panel 2000; memb Ct Univ of Greenwich 1999–2008; tstee Nat Maritime Museum 2005–13; Hon DSc Univ of Huddersfield 1999, Hon DEng Edinburgh Napier Univ 2008; FCILT, FTS, CORS, FCIHT, FRSA; *Recreations* music, singing, photography, walking, family life; *Clubs* Royal Automobile; *Style*— Dr David Quarmby, CBE, FRSA; ✉ 13 Shooters Hill Road, Blackheath, London SE3 7AR (☎ 020 8858 3962, e-mail david@quarmby.org.uk)

QUAST, Philip; s of Colin Philip Quast, and late Lorraine, *née* Elphick; *b* 30 July 1957; *Educ* Nat Inst of Dramatic Art Sydney (BA); *m* 3 Jan 1981, Carol, *née* Tart; 3 s (Edwin b 28 March 1990, Harrison b 1 Dec 1991, Toby b 18 May 1995); *Career* actor and singer; musical theatre performed with RSC, RNT, Sydney Theatre Co, Melbourne Theatre Co; tutor/teacher of musical theatre: Sydney, Melbourne, London, NY; acting and singing workshops at various insts; artist-in-res Nat Inst of Dramatic Art (NIDA) Sydney 2013; *Theatre* Aust theatre credits incl: Javert in Les Misérables (original Aust prodn, Sydney Critics Award, Mo Award 1987), Adam in The Mystery Plays of Wakefield, The Narrator in The Threepenny Opera, Jack in A Hard God, Orlando in As You Like It, Gower in Pericles, Flysche in Song of the Selchies, Henry/Laertes in The Marriage/Hamlet, Aufidius in Coriolanus, Wolf/Cinderella's Prince in Into The Woods, Dr Neville Craven in The Secret Garden (Sydney Critics Award, 2 Mo Awards), Captain Hook in Pan, Francisco in The White Devil, On the Wallaby, No End of Blame, A Month in the Country, Candide, Shark Infested Waters, Carmen – Another Perspective, Martin in The Goat or Who is Sylvia? (MTC) 2003, Willy Brandt in Democracy (STC) 2005, Lopakhin in The Cherry Orchard (STC) 2006, George Banks in Mary Poppins (Melbourne) 2010–11, Sir Humphrey Appleby in Yes, Prime Minister (Australian nat tour) 2012, Walter Burns in His Girl Friday (Melbourne Theatre Co) 2012, Pozzo in Waiting For Godot (Sydney Theatre Co) 2013, Pastor Manders in Ghosts (Melbourne Theatre Co) 2014; London credits incl: Javert in Les Misérables, George in Sunday in the Park with George (NT, Laurence Olivier Award 1991), The Hunting of the Snark, Saint Joan, The Fix (musical, Laurence Olivier Award 1998), Emile DeBeque in South Pacific (NT, Laurence Olivier Award 2002), Evita (West End, nominated Laurence Olivier Award 2007), Georges in La Cage aux Folles (West End) 2009, Judge Turpin in Sweeney Todd (ENO) 2015, Pozzo in Waiting for Godot (Beckett Festival Barbican) 2015; RSC: Fred/Chorus in A Christmas Carol, King of Navarre in Love's Labour's Lost, Lodovico in The White Devil, Banquo in Macbeth, Achilles in Troilus and Cressida, Archibald Craven in The Secret Garden, Antonio in The Merchant of Venice, Trigorin in The Seagull, Miles Glorious in A Funny Thing Happened on the Way to the Forum (NT), George Tenet in Stuff Happens (NT), Peron in Evita (West End, Olivier Award nomination 2007) 2006–07, Georges in La Cage aux Folles 2007–08; *Concerts* Javert in Les Misérables: 10th Anniversary Concert (Royal Albert Hall) 1995, Hey, Mr Producer! 1998 (concert in honour of Sir Cameron Mackintosh); The Stars Come Out, Night of 1000 Voices (Royal Albert Hall), Domar Diva (season) 2002, A Little Night Music (Comedy Theatre London) 2006, Follies Concert (London) 2007, Sweeney Todd (Royal Festival Hall) 2007, premier of Tsunami (Barbican) 2008, Australia Day Gala (Australia House London) 2010, Night of 1000 Voices (Royal Albert Hall) 2010, Judge Turpin in NY Philharmonic Orchestra's concert of Sweeney Todd 2014; *Television* General Cornelius in Cleopatra (US mini-series), The Minister in The Damnation of Harvey McHugh, Once in a Blue Moon, Playschool, Colour in the Creek, Flight into Hell, Cassidy, Fields of Fire, Brides of Christ, Police Rescue, Patrol Boat, All Good Friends, The Governor (series two), Ultraviolet, Corridors of Power, Bed of Roses (ABC), Silent Witness; *Films* Emoh Ruo, Around the World in 80 Ways, To Market, To Market, Napoleon; TV films: Army Wives, The First Kangaroos, Me & Mrs Jones, The Caterpillar Wish 2006, Clubland 2006, Saddam Husein in The Devils Double 2010, Ben Barnes in Truth 2015; *Recordings* South Pacific, The Secret Garden (RSC cast recording and Australian highlights CD), The Fix, Les Misérables (complete symphonic recording and 10th anniversary concert CD), Paris, Great Moments in Australian Musical Theatre, Once in a Blue Moon, Lift Off Live!, Play School, Napoleon, Philip Quast Live at the Donmar, Evita (London cast) 2006, Mary Poppins (Australian cast recording), Sweeney Todd (New York Philharmonic DVD, PBS Live from the Lincoln Center); *Style*— Philip Quast, Esq; ✉ website www.allthingsquast.info; c/o Conway van Gelder Ltd, 18–21 Jermyn Street, London SW1Y 6HP (☎ 020 7287 0077, fax 020 7287 1940); e-mail darukaproductions@gmail.com

QUASTEL, Dr Anthony Stephen; s of Gerald Quastel, of London, and late Rita Joy Leonora Quastel; *b* 14 November 1955; *Educ* St Dunstan's Coll Catford, Middx Hosp Med Sch Univ of London (MB BS); *Partner* Roger Colyer (civil partnership 9 Feb 2006); *Career* princ in gen practice 1984; res appts in med and surgery 1980–81, SHO in psychiatry Middx Hosp 1982, currently princ in gen practice; memb Obesity Mgmnt Assoc (chair Ethics Ctee); memb Cons Pty; FRSM; *Recreations* gardening, politics, talking; *Style*— Dr Anthony Quastel; ✉ Rome Cottage, 3 Rome Road, New Romney, Kent TN28 8DN (☎ 01797 362493); 17 South Street, Bromley, Kent (☎ 020 8464 4599, fax 020 8464 3471); 25 Rue de L'Abbaye, St Georges, 62770, France (☎ 00 33 3 21 03 71 87); 4/10 Ulica Trynitarska, Krakow, Poland (☎ 0048 124 210162); 5/166 Calle Wagner, San Miguel de Salinas, Spain (☎ 00 34 966 194 182)

QUAYLE, John Bryant; s of late George Quayle, and Christina, *née* Lonsdale (d 1994); *b* 13 October 1945; *Educ* Llandovery Coll, Fitzwilliam Coll Cambridge (MA, MB BChir), St George's Hosp Med Sch London (MChir); *m* 4 March 1972, Prudence Margaret, da of (John) Denis Smith; 3 da (Tamsin Elinor b 4 Jan 1975, Ruth Elizabeth b 26 Oct 1976, Anna Margaret 27 March 1979); *Career* sr surgical registrar (rotation) St George's Hosp London 1978–82 (house physician 1970), conslt surgn Royal Shrewsbury Hosp and Princess Royal Hosp Telford 1982–; memb Cncl Surgical Section RSM 1980–, memb Assoc for Coloproctology of GB and Ireland; memb Worshipful Soc of Apothecaries 1974; FRCS 1974; *Recreations* riding, sailing, music, walking; *Clubs* RSM; *Style*— John Quayle, Esq; ✉ Shropshire Nuffield Hospital (☎ 01743 282500); Royal Shrewsbury Hospital, Shrewsbury; Princess Royal Hospital, Telford

QUAYLE, Robert Brisco MacGregor; s of John Pattinson Quayle (d 2007), and Doreen Helen MacGregor, *née* MacMullen; *b* 6 April 1950; *Educ* Monkton Combe Sch, Selwyn Coll Cambridge (MA); *m* 30 Sept 1972, (Deborah) Clare, da of Sir (Francis) Alan Pullinger, CBE (d 2002); 2 da (Hannah b 1976, Eily b 1978), 3 s (Jonathan b 1981, William b 1985, Thomas b 1988); *Career* admitted slr 1974; Linklaters & Paines 1974–76, clerk of Tynwald and sec House of Keys 1976–87, ptnr Travers Smith Braithwaite 1987–90 (conslt 1990–98); chm: Ellan Vannin Fuels Ltd, Communicator Insurance Co Ltd, WH Ireland (Isle of Man) Ltd; Isle of Man Steam Packet Co; Q3 Acad; author of various articles on Parly affrs and history of IOM; *Recreations* family, church (licensed lay reader), music, pre-1960 cars; *Clubs* New (Edinburgh); *Style*— Robert Quayle, Esq; ✉ Mullen Beg, Patrick, Isle of Man (☎ 01624 842912, e-mail rqmann@manx.net)

QUEEN, Michael; *b* 27 September 1961; *Educ* Waltham Toll Bar Comp Sch Grimsby, Univ of Nottingham (BA); *m* ; 2 c; *Career* 3i: joined as investment exec 1987, dir 1990, seconded to HM Treasy 1994–96, dir 3i plc 1996, gp financial controller 1996–97, finance dir 1997–2005, dir 3i Gp plc, dir 3i Hldgs plc and Ship Mortgage Finance Co plc 1997, dir 3i Investments plc 2000, dir 3i Int Hldgs 2003, head of growth capital and dir Gardens Pension Tstees Ltd 2005, managing ptnr 3i Infrastructure until 2012; chm Br Venture Capital Assoc 2002–03, dir Northern Rock 2005, memb Financial Services Cncl CBI, non-exec dir PA Consulting 2012–; FCA 1997 (ACA 1986); *Style*— Michael Queen, Esq

QUEENSBERRY, 12 Marquess of (S 1682); Sir David Harrington Angus Douglas; 11 Bt (S 1668); also Viscount Drumlanrig, Lord Douglas of Hawick and Tibbers (both S 1628), and Earl of Queensberry (S 1633); s of 11 Marquess (d 1954), by his 2 w Cathleen, *née* Mann (d 1959); *b* 19 December 1929; *Educ* Eton; *m* 1, 1956 (m dis 1969), Ann, da of Maurice Sinnett Jones and formerly w of George Arthur Radford; 2 da (Lady Emma Cathleen b 1956, Lady Alice (Lady Alice Melia) b 1965); 1 s (Ambrose Carey b 1961, with Anne Carey); m 2, 1969 (m dis 1986), Alexandra Mary Clare Wyndham, da of Guy Wyndham Sich; 3 s (Sholto Francis Guy, Viscount Drumlanrig b 1967, Lord Milo Douglas b 1975, Lord Torquil Douglas b 1978), 1 da (Lady Kate Douglas b 1969); m 3, 3 July 2000, Hsueh-Chun Liao; 1 da (Beth Shan Ling b 1999); *Heir* s, Viscount Drumlanrig; *Career* late 2 Lt RHG; prof of ceramics RCA 1959–83; pres Design and Industries Assoc 1976–78; ptnr Queensberry Hunt design group; dir Highland Stoneware; tstee Paolozzi Fndn; sr fell RCA, Hon Dr Staffordshire Univ; *Style*— The Most Hon the Marquess of Queensberry; ✉ e-mail partners@queensberryhunt.com

QUELCH, Prof John Anthony; s of Norman Quelch (d 2006), of Stratford St Mary, Suffolk, and Laura Sally, *née* Jones (d 1997); *b* 8 August 1951; *Educ* King Edward VI Sch Norwich,

Exeter Coll Oxford (BA), Univ of Pennsylvania (MBA), Harvard Univ (MS, DBA); *m* 17 June 1978, Joyce Ann, da of Harold Loring Huntley; *Career* asst prof Univ of Western Ontario 1977–79; Harvard Business Sch: asst prof 1979–84, assoc prof 1984–88, prof of business admin 1988–93, Sebastian S Kresge prof of mktg 1993–98, sr assoc dean 2001–08, Lincoln Filene prof of business admin 2001–11; dean London Business Sch 1998–2001, dean and vice-pres China-Europe Int Business Sch 2011–; La Caixa visiting prof of int mgmnt and chm Academic Advsy Cncl China-Europe Int Business Sch 2009–; dir: Reebok Int Ltd 1984–96, WPP Group plc 1985–, US Office Products Co 1994–97, Cncl of Better Business Bureaux 1996–98, Pentland Group plc 1997–99, Graduate Mgmnt Admission Cncl 1998–2001, Blue Circle Industries plc 2000–01, easyJet plc 2000–03, Accion Int 2002–06, Alere Inc (formerly Inverness Medical Innovations Inc) 2003–, Pepsi Bottling Group 2004–10, Gentiva Health Services 2005–09, ViTrue 2006–08, Epiphany Biosciences 2007–10, BBC Worldwide Americas 2008–10; chm Massachusetts Port Authy 2002–11; hon consul-gen Kingdom of Morocco 2004–; *Books* Advertising and Promotion Management (1987), Multinational Marketing Management (1988), Sales Promotion Management (1989), How to Market to Consumers (1989), The Marketing Challenge of Europe 1992 (1991), Ethics in Marketing (1992), Marketing Management (1993), Cases in European Marketing Management (1994), Cases in Product Management (1995), Cases in Marketing Management and Strategy: An Asia Pacific Perspective (1996), Global Marketing Management (1999), Cases in Strategic Marketing Management: Business Strategies in Latin America (2001), Cases in Strategic Marketing Management: Business Strategies in Muslim Countries (2001), Problems and Cases in Health Care Marketing (2004), Marketing Management (2004), The Global Market (2004), The New Global Brands (2005), Business Solutions for the Global Poor (2007), Readings in Modern Marketing (2007), Greater Good: How Good Marketing Makes For Better Democracy (2008), How to Manage Marketing (2009); *Recreations* tennis, squash; *Clubs* Harvard (Boston), Brooks's; *Style*— Prof John Quelch; ✉ Office of the Dean, China Europe International Business School, 699 Hongfeng Road, Pudong, Shanghai, China 201206 (☎ 0086 21 2890 5890, fax 0086 21 2890 5678, e-mail jquelch@ceibs.edu, website www.ceibs.edu)

QUENBY, John Richard; s of Richard Quenby (d 1942), of Bedford, and Margaret, *née* Wyse (d 1991); *b* 30 October 1941; *Educ* Bedford Modern Sch, Open Univ (BA); *m* 1, (m dis 1997), Sandra, da of Col Noel Frederick Charles King (d 1974), of Sydney, Aust; 2 da (Georgia Margaret b 1970, Fiona Elizabeth b 1971); m 2, Frances, da of late Harvey Maynard (d 1997); *Career* dir Granada Computer Servs Ltd 1983–85, md Granada Overseas Hldgs Ltd 1985–89, dir and chm of various subsidiaries and assoc companies; chm CBQC Ltd 2002–04, non-exec dir Beds and Shires Health and Care NHS Tst 1992–97 (chm 1994–97); chief exec and dir RAC Motor Sports Assoc 1990–2001; dir: Trireme Tst 1994–97 and 2006– (chm 1995–97), Auto Cycle Union 1995–98, Speedway Control Bd 1995–2002 (chm 1998–2002), Motorcycle Circuit Racing Control Bd 1995–2000 (chm 1995–2000), branch chm Royal Br Legion 2005–06 and 2007–08, pres Old Bedford Modernians Club 2011–12, chm Friends of the Intelligence Corps Museum (Tst) 2011–15, hon archivist Bedford Modern Sch 2016–; *Recreations* cricket, historic motor racing; *Clubs* Bedford Rowing, MCC, RAC; *Style*— John Quenby, Esq; ✉ Royal Automobile Club, Pall Mall, London SW1Y 5HS

QUENTIN, Caroline; *b* 1961; *Career* actress; *Theatre* Roots (RNT), Our Country's Good (Garrick), Low Level Panic (Royal Court), Sugar and Spice (Royal Court), Les Miserables (Palace Theatre), Mirandolina (Lyric Hammersmith), The Live Bed Show (Garrick), The London Cuckolds (RNT); *Television* appearances incl: All or Nothing at All, Men Behaving Badly (six series and Christmas special) 1992–99, An Evening with Gary Lineker 1994, Jonathan Creek 1996–99 (three series), Kiss Me Kate 1998–2000 (three series), The Innocent (Granada) 2000, Hot Money (Granada) 2001, Goodbye Mr Steadman (Alibi) 2001, Blood Strangers (Granada) 2002, Blue Murder (Granada) 2003, Life Begins 2002–06, Von Trapped 2004, Blue Murder II 2004, Life of Riley 2009, Marple: The Mirror Crack'd from Side to Side 2010; Best Comedy Actress Comedy Awards 1995; *Style*— Ms Caroline Quentin

QUIGLY, Isabel Madeleine; da of Richard Quigly (d 1971), and Clarice, *née* Ford (d 1977); *b* 17 September 1926, Ontaneola, Santander, Spain; *Educ* Godolphin Sch Salisbury, Newnham Coll Cambridge (5 scholarships, BA); *m* 1953, R A Salimbeni; 1 s (Crispin Salimbeni b 1956); *Career* editorial asst Penguin Books 1949–52, freelance writer 1952–, tri-lingual job at League of Red Cross Societies Geneva 1954, lit ed The Tablet 1985–97, pt/t archivist RSL 1997–99; film critic The Spectator 1956–66; sometime lectr City Literary Inst and other freelance lecturing; translator of more than 100 books from Italian, Spanish and French; contrib numerous jls and newspapers; judge: Booker Prize, Guardian Children's Books Prize, Heinemann Award, Betty Trask Award, Winifred Holtby Prize, Valle Inclán Prize, Wingate Awards, Somerset Maugham Award, Margaret Rhondda Award, Time Life Award; appeared on television and radio progs incl: Kaleidoscope (BBC Radio 4), Woman's Hour (BBC Radio 4), numerous World Service broadcasts; memb Cncl Soc of Authors; past memb: Cncl RSL, Mgmnt Ctee Soc of Authors, Lit Panel Arts Cncl, Lit Panel SE Arts, Ctee of Mgmnt PEN; memb Ctee Translators Assoc; tstee: PEN Lit Fndn (until 2003), Pension Fund Ctee Soc of Authors; involved with: local charities, work for prisoners, children in hosp; memb: Soc of Authors 1955, PEN 1955; FRSL 1989; *Awards* John Florio Prize (for best trans from Italian with Silvano Ceccherini's The Transfer) 1966, runner-up for trans of Giorgio Bassani's The Garden of the Finzi-Continis; *Books* The Eye of Heaven (1955), Charlie Chaplin, Early Comedies (1968), The Heirs of Tom Brown: the English School Story (1982, 2nd edn 1982); ed: Shelley (1956), Stalky & Co (1987), The Royal Society of Literature, a portrait (2000); *Recreations* reading; *Style*— Isabel Quigly, FRSL; ✉ c/o RSL, Somerset House, Strand, London WC2R 1LA

QUIN, Jeremy Mark; MP; s of Rev David Quin, and Elizabeth, *née* Dennis (d 2012); *b* 24 September 1968, Aylesbury, Bucks; *Educ* St Albans Sch, Hertford Coll Oxford (BA); *m* 2003, Joanna, *née* Healey; *Career* Natwest Wood Mackenzie & Co 1990–99, BT Alex Brown 1999–2000, md Deutsche Bank 2000–15; MP (Cons) Horsham 2015–; *Style*— Jeremy Quin, Esq, MP; ✉ House of Commons, London SW1A 0AA

QUIN, Baroness (Life Peer UK 2006), of Gateshead in the County of Tyne and Wear; Joyce Gwendolen Quin; PC (1998); da of Basil Godfrey Quin, MC, and Ida, *née* Ritson; *b* 1944, Tynemouth; *Educ* Newcastle Univ (BA), LSE (MSc); *m* Francis Guy MacMullen; *Career* lectr and tutor in French and politics Univ of Bath and Durham Univ 1972–79; MEP (Lab) Tyne & Wear 1979–89; MP (Lab): Gateshead E 1987–97, Gateshead E and Washington W 1997–2005; memb Select Ctee on Treasy and the Civil Serv 1987–89; oppn spokesperson: on trade and indust 1989–92, on employment 1992–97, on Europe 1993–97; min of state: Home Office 1997–98, FCO 1998–99, MAFF 1999–2001; memb Cncl RCVS 1992–96; vice-pres Franco-British Soc 2013; visiting prof Centre for Urban and Regnl Devpt Studies Univ of Newcastle 2003; hon pres Northumberland Nat Park Fndn 2015; hon fell: Univ of Sunderland 1986, St Mary's Coll Durham 1993; Hon Freeman Borough of Gateshead 2006; Officier de la Légion d'Honneur 2010; *Books* The British Constitution – Continuity and Change (2010); *Recreations* Newcastle upon Tyne City Guide, Northumbrian pipes, walking, reading; *Style*— The Rt Hon the Lady Quin, PC

QUINLAN, Chris Charles; s of Edward Charles Quinlan, of Betchworth, Surrey, and June, *née* Richiardi; *b* 21 December 1954; *Educ* Alleyn's Sch Dulwich, Univ of Sheffield (LLB); *m* 4 April 1987 (m dis 1994); *Career* slr Wilkinson Kimbers 1981–83, advtg control offr IBA 1983–84, asst sec Beecham Gp plc 1984–85, controller of advtg The Cable Authy 1985–90, mktg dir Carlton Cabletime Ltd (subsid of Carlton Communications plc) 1990–92, dir Media Matrix Ltd 1992–; memb: Jt Industry Ctee for Cable Audience Res, Cable TV Assoc Mktg Gp, Bd of Mgmnt Gp 64 Theatre London; memb: Law Soc 1981, Mktg Soc 1992; chm Kingston and Surbiton Cons Assoc 2006; *Books* Making Sense of Computers in General Practice (jtly, 1995); *Recreations* ballooning, directing plays, inventing games; *Style*— Chris Quinlan, Esq; ✉ Media Matrix LLP, Old Boundary House, London Road, Ascot, Berkshire SL5 0DJ (☎ 01344 887888, e-mail chris.quinlan@media-matrix.org)

QUINN, (James Steven) Brian; s of James Joseph Quinn (d 1977), of Lancs, and Elizabeth, *née* Thomas; *b* 16 June 1936, Aintree, Liverpool; *Educ* Waterpark Coll S Ireland, UCD, King's Inn Dublin (LLB, BCL), Trinity Coll Dublin; *m* 1, 1963 (m dis 1998), Blanche Cecilia, da of Richard Francis James (d 1986), of Spain; 2 s (James b 1963, Alexander b 1969), 1 da (Susannah b 1965); m 2, 2004, Catherine; *Career* called to the Bar 2009; head Industrial Activities Prices and Incomes Bd 1969–71, dir M L H Conslts 1971–79, corporate devpt advsr Midland Bank Int 1977–80, chief industrial advsr Price Cmmn 1977–78; chm: Brightstar Communications 1983–85, BAJ Holdings 1985–87, Harmer Holbrook 1987–88; chm and chief exec Digital Computer Services 1989–96 (dir 1985–96), chm Loan Line 1998–2000, dir QM Security Ltd 2002–05, DG IIC 2003–08 (tstee 1982–97, chm Exec Ctee 1984–87, pres 1988–91, life tstee), dep chm IP Solutions Int Ltd Bahamas 2009–11; memb Exec Ctee Inst of Euro Trade and Technol 1983–98, chm Gtr London Regnl Cncl Inst of Mgmnt (formerly BIM) 1990–93, tstee Int Communications Centre San Diego State Univ 1990–2006, chm Editorial Bd The Professional Manager 1991–98; hon Irish consul for The Bahamas 2011–15; *Recreations* golf, reading, poetry, veteran vehicles; *Clubs* Athenaeum, Lansdowne, Royal Nassau Sailing; *Style*— Brian Quinn, Esq; ✉ Hicks Grove House, Weston, Hertfordshire SG4 7DX

QUINN, HE (James) Gregory (Greg); s of James Eric Quinn, and Gwendoline Audrey, *née* Coulter, of Portadown, NI; *b* 16 June 1971, Lurgan, NI; *Educ* Univ of Wales Aberystwyth (BSc), Open Univ (MA); *m* Aug 1995, Wendy Ann, *née* Dackombe; *Career* diplomat; research asst Library and Records Dept FCO 1995–98, desk offr for Estonia, Latvia and Lithuania Central European Dept FCO 1998–2000, dep head of mission (temporary duty) Tallinn 2000, political, press and public affrs offr Accra 2000–03, dep head of mission Minsk 2004–07, Iraq/ME liaison offr Washington/US State Dept 2007–09, head UN Political Team Int Orgns Dept FCO 2009–12, dep head of mission Astana 2012–14, high cmmr to Repub of Guyana and non-resident ambass to Suriname 2015–; *Recreations* golf, rugby, football, travel, history; *Style*— HE Mr Greg Quinn

QUINN, James Stephen Christopher (Jim); s of James Quinn (d 1988), of Stourbridge, W Midlands, and Kathleen, *née* Kearns (d 1989); *b* 11 July 1939, Wolverhampton; *Educ* Cotton Coll, Univ of Birmingham (LLB); *m* 5 Sept 1964, Patricia Anne, *née* George; 2 s (Adrian James b 3 July 1969, Simon Paul b 23 March 1971), 1 da (Anna Kathryn b 25 May 1973); *Career* admitted slr 1964; ptnr MFG Slrs (formerly Morton Fisher) 1965–2010 (conslt 2010–); dep registrar Co Court Midlands Circuit 1969–81; memb Lord Chllr's Advsy Panel 1990–99; memb: Law Soc, Common Law Bar Assoc, Inst for Continuing Educn; dir: Holy Trinity Convent Sch Ltd 1986–91, Wolverley NHS Tst 1991–95; chm Father Hudson's Soc 2003–13, dir Catenian Assoc 1993–2013, tstee Maryvale Inst, chm Friends of the Holy Land; Order of the Holy Sepulchre of Jerusalem; *Recreations* golf, caravanning, singing; *Style*— Jim Quinn, Esq; ✉ MFG Solicitors LLP, 20–21 The Tything, Worcester WR1 1HD (☎ 01905 610410, fax 01905 610191, e-mail jim.quinn@mfgsolicitors.com)

QUINN, Jane; OBE (2014); *Educ* Sacred Heart Convent Kent, Queen's Coll London; *m* Martin Duignan; *Career* co-fndr (with Erica Bolton, OBE) Bolton & Quinn Ltd 1981–; *Style*— Ms Jane Quinn, OBE; ✉ Bolton & Quinn Limited, 6 Addison Avenue, London W11 4QR

QUINN, Marc; *b* 1964, London; *Educ* Millfield, Univ of Cambridge; *Career* artist; *Selected Solo Exhibitions* Bronze Sculpture (Jay Jopling/Otis Gallery London) 1988, Bread Sculpture (Galerie Marquardt and Middendorf Gallery Washington, DC) 1990, Out of Time (Jay Jopling/Grob Gallery London) 1991, Marc Quinn (Galerie Jean Bernier Athens) 1993, Marc Quinn (Jay Jopling/Art Hotel Amsterdam) 1994, The Blind Leading the Blind (Jay Jopling/White Cube London) 1995, Art Now. Emotional Detox: The Seven Deadly Sins (Tate Gallery London) 1995, Marc Quinn (South London Gallery London) 1998, Still Life (White Cube London) 2000, A Genomic Portrait. John Sulston by Marc Quinn (Nat Portrait Gallery London) 2001, Tate Liverpool 2002, Behind the Mask: Portraits (Hatton Gallery Newcastle) 2002, The Overwhelming World of Desire (Paphiopedilum Winston Churchill Hybrid) (Goodwood Sculpture Park W Sussex) 2003, The Incredible World of Desire (IBM Building NY) 2004, Meat Sculptures (Mary Boone Gallery NY) 2005, Chemical Life Support (White Cube London) 2005, Recent Sculptures (Groninger Museum) 2006, MACRO Rome 2006, Mary Boone Gallery NY 2007, Marc Quinn (Scolacium Archaeological Park Catanzaro Italy) 2007, Marc Quinn (DHC/ART Foundation for Contemporary Art Montreal) 2007, Alison Lapper Pregnant (The Forum Rome) 2008, Evolution (White Cube London) 2008, Before, Now and After (Galerie Hopkins-Custot Paris) 2008, Marc Quinn (Gana Art Gallery Seoul) 2008, Iris (Mary Boone Gallery NY) 2009, Marc Quinn (Goss-Michael Foundation Dallas) 2009, Marc Quinn: Selfs (Beyeler Foundation Basel) 2009, Materialise, Dematerialise (Galerie Thaddaeus Ropac Salzburg) 2009, Carbon Cycle (Galerie Daniel Blau Munich) 2009, Il Mito (Casa Giuleta Verona) 2009, Marc Quinn (Patricia Low Contemporary Gstaad Switzerland) 2010, 33°5313N35°3017E (LAB Art, The Platinum Tower Beirut) 2010, Allanah, Buck, Catman, Chelsea, Michael, Pamela and Thomas (White Cube London) 2010, All of Nature Flows Through Us (Kistefos Museum Jevnaker Norway) 2011, Breath (centre sculpture in the London 2012 Paralympics Opening Ceremony) 2012, Marc Quinn (Musée Océanographique de Monaco) 2012, Marc Quinn (Galerie Thaddaeus Ropac Salzburg) 2012, Big Wheel Keeps on Turning (Multimedia Art Museum Moscow) 2012, Held by Desire (White Cube Hong Kong) 2013, Marc Quinn (Fondazione Giorgio Cini San Giorgio Venice) 2013, The Rush of Nature (Chelsea Flower Show London) 2013, All the Time in the World (Mary Boone Gallery NY) 2013, Planet (Gardens by the Bay Singapore) 2013, Violence and Serenity (Centro de Arte Contemporáneo Málaga) 2014, The Sleep of Reason (ARTER Space for Art Istanbul) 2014; *Selected Group Exhibitions* Young British Artists II (Saatchi Collection London) 1993, Time Machine (British Museum London) 1994, Life is too Much (Galerie des Archives Paris) 1994, Ripple Across the Water (Minato Prefecture and Shibuya Prefecture Tokyo) 1995, Contemporary British Art in Print (Scottish Museum of Modern Art Edinburgh) 1995, Faith, Hope, Charity (Kunsthalle Vienna) 1995, Time Machine (Musée Egizio Turin) 1995, Happy End (Kunsthalle Dusseldorf) 1996, Works on Paper (Irish Museum of Modern Art Dublin) 1996, Feed and Greed (MAK Vienna) 1996, Hybrid (De Appel Foundation Amsterdam) 1996, Thinking Print. Books to Billboards 1980–95 (Museum of Modern Art New York) 1996, A Ilha do Tesouro (Funda ao Calouste Gulbenkian Lisbon) 1997, The Body (Art Gallery of New South Wales Australia) 1997, Sensation (Royal Academy of Arts London) 1997, Follow Me (Kunstverein Kehdingen Freiburg) 1997, The Quick and the Dead: Artists and Anatomy (Royal College of Art London) 1997, Inner Self (Mitchell-Innes & Nash New York (1998), The Colony Room 50th Anniversary Art Exhibition (A22 Projects London) 1998, Group Exhibition (Galleri Faurschou Copenhagen (1998), A Portrait of Our Times: An Introduction to the Logan Collection (San Francisco Museum of Modern Art San Francisco) 1998, Physical Evidence (Kettle's Yard Cambridge) 1998, Presence (Tate Gallery Liverpool) 1999, Now it's my Turn to Scream (Haines Gallery San Francisco)

1999, Officina Europa (Galleria d'Arte Moderna di Bologna) 1999, Something Warm and Fuzzy (Demoines Art Centre) 1999, Out There (White Cube 2 London) 2000, Psycho (Anne Faggionato London) 2000, Conversation (Milton Keynes Gallery) 2000, Wellcome Wing (The Science Museum London) 2000, Heads and Hands (Decatur House Museum Washington) 2001, In the Freud Museum (Freud Museum London) 2002, Thinking Big: Concepts for 21st Century British Sculpture (Peggy Guggenheim Collection Venice) 2002, Rapture: Art's Seduction by Fashion Since 1970 (Barbican Gallery London) 2002, Statements 7 (50th Venice Biennale) 2003, FRESH: Contemporary British Artists in Print (Edinburgh Printmakers) 2003, Fourth Plinth Proposal (Nat Gallery London) 2003, Garden of Eden (Helsinki City Art Museum) 2004, The Body: Art & Science (Nat Museum Stockholm) 2005, Summer Exhibition (Royal Acad of Art London) 2005, Art Out of Place (Norwich Castle and Museum Art Gallery) 2005, Egomania (Museum of Contemporary Art Modena) 2006, Aftershock: Contemporary British Art 1990–2006 (Guangdong Museum of Art and Capital Museum Beijing) 2006–07, La Triennale di Milano 2007, A Matter of Life and Death (Holburne Museum Bath) 2007, Genesis (Centraal Museum Utrecht) 2007, Love (National Gallery London) 2008, Out of Shape Stylistic Distortions of the Human Form in Art (The Frances Lehman Loeb Art Center Poughkeepsie NY) 2008, Genesis Die Kunst der Schopfung (Zentrum Paul Klee Bern Switzerland) 2008, Statuephilia Contemporary Sculptors at the British Museum (British Museum) 2008, Beyond Limits (Chatsworth House) 2008, Nothing But Sculpture 8th International Sculpture Biennale (Carrara Italy) 2008, Open XI International Exhibition of Sculptures and Installations (Venice Lido and San Servolo Italy) 2008, Sphinxx (Stuart Shave/Modern Art London) 2008, Beyond Limits (Chatsworth House) 2008, The World in the Body (Mori Art Museum Tokyo) 2009, A Tribute to Ron Warren (Mary Boone Gallery NY) 2009, Messiah (Modem Centre for Modern and Contemporary Arts Debrecen Hungary) 2009, No Visible Means of Escape (Norwich Castle Museum) 2009, Assembling Bodies Art, Science and Imagination (Museum of Archaeology and Anthropology Univ of Cambridge) 2009, Fuentes Non-European In?uences on Contemporary Artists (Galerie Thaddaeus Ropac Paris) 2009, Innovations in the Third Dimension Sculpture of Our Time (Bruce Museum Greenwich CT) 2009, The Visceral Body (Vancouver Art Gallery) 2010, Crucible (Gloucester Cathedral UK) 2010, Cream (Kiasma, Museum of Contemporary Art Finland) 2010, The Foundation of Art, Scultpure and its Base since Auguste Rodin (Arp Museum Germany) 2010, Beyond Limits (Chatsworth House) 2010, Realismus: Das Abenteuer der Wirklichkeit (Realism: The Adventure of Reality) (Kunsthalle Emden, Kuntshalle Rotterdam & Kunsthalle Hypo-Kulturstiftung München) 2010, Surreal versus Surrealism in Contemporary Art (IVAM Valencia) 2011, Nothing in the World but Youth (Turner Contemporary, Kent) 2011, Penelopes Labour Weaving words and Images (Venice) 2011, Beyond Limits (Chatsworth House) 2011 and 2013, FIAC 2012 (Jardin des Tuilleries Paris) 2012, Marc Quinn & Darren Almond (Patricia Low Contemporary St Moritz) 2012, Louis Vuitton Timeless Muses (Tokyo Station Hotel Japan) 2013, Art Everywhere (30,000 public sites across the UK) 2014, Bad Thoughts (Stedelijk Museum Amsterdam) 2014, Selected Works from the YAGEO Foundation Collection (Nat Museum of Modern Art Tokyo) 2014, Leaping the Fence (Hestercombe House) 2014, East Wing Bienniale Exhibition (Courtauld Inst) 2014; work in private collections incl: British Museum London, Deutsche Bank London, Saatchi Collection London, Stedlijk Museum Amsterdam, Tate Gallery London, Museum of Modern Art New York; *Awards* Charles Wollaston Award 2001 RA, Fourth Plinth Commission for Trafalgar Square 2004; *Style*— Marc Quinn, Esq

QUINN, Prof Niall; s of Dr Brian Quinn (d 1997), and Mrs Mary Quinn (d 1998); *b* 24 August 1948; *Educ* Downside, Gonville & Caius Coll Cambridge (BChir, MA, MD), London Hosp Medical Sch; *m* 1, 23 March 1974, Sherazade Tafazzoli; m 2, 28 June 1985, Julie Brandler; *Career* méd res étranger Hôpital de la Salpêtrière Paris 1978–79, SHO Nat Hosp London 1979–80, research fell, hon lectr and lectr Maudsley and King's Coll Hosps and Inst of Psychiatry and KCH Med Sch 1980–88; Inst of Neurology UCL: lectr rising to reader 1988–97, clinical sub dean 1995–2004, prof 1997–2007, emeritus prof 2007–; hon conslt neurologist Nat Hosp for Neurology and Neurosurgery 1990–; visiting professorships incl Mayo Clinic Rochester USA and Int Movement Disorder Soc, visiting prof to Tbilisi, Delhi, Yerevan, Tallinn; named lectures incl: Cohen Meml Lecture (Johns Hopkins Baltimore), Cotzias (Spanish Soc of Neurology), John Penney Meml Lecture (Mass Gen Hosp Boston), David Marsden Lecture (Movement Disorder Soc Congress Istanbul); memb Editorial Bd: Jl of Neurology, Neurosurgery and Psychiatry 1990–94, Movement Disorders 1991–94, Lancet Neurology 2002–10, Jl of Parkinson's Disease 2011–, Movement Disorders Clinical Practice 2014–15, Parkinsonism and Related Disorders 2015–; memb Assoc of Br Neurologists, sr fell American Acad of Neurology, corresponding fell American Neurological Assoc, hon foreign memb Société Française de Neurologie; Int Parkinson and Movement Disorder Soc (MDS): sec 2001–02, chair European section 2005–06, hon life memb 2006; FRCP 1994; *Books* Disorders of Movement: Clinical, pharmacological and physiological aspects (jtly, 1989), Parkinsonism (jtly, 1997), Parkinson's disease and other movement disorders (jtly, 2008); author of over 400 original papers on movement disorders in peer review jls; *Recreations* Argentine tango, photography; *Clubs* Athenaeum, Hawks' (Cambridge); *Style*— Prof Niall Quinn; ✉ e-mail niallquinn@blueyonder.co.uk; Box 147, National Hospital for Neurology and Neurosurgery, Queen Square, London WC1N 3BG (☎ 020 3448 3782, e-mail cgardner@qsprivatehealthcare.com, website www.parkinsonsexpert.co.uk)

QUINT, (Joan) Francesca Rae; da of Dr George Gomez (d 2004), and Dr Joan Gomez (d 2012); *b* 1 October 1947; *Educ* St Paul's Girls' Sch, KCL (LLB, AKC, Leathes Prize); *m* 1, 14 June 1980, Dr Lancelot Lionel Ware, OBE (d 2000); m 2, 17 Sept 2006, (Charles) Edward Hoskins; *Career* called to the Bar Gray's Inn 1970 (Francis Bacon scholar 1969), ad eundem Lincoln's Inn 1980 (bencher 2008), called to the Bar of NI 2013; with Charity Cmmn 1972–89 (asst cmmr 1974, dep cmmr 1984); ind practice: Castle Chambers Exeter 1990–96, 11 Old Sq (East) 1990–2001, 11 Old Sq (West) 2001–06, Radcliffe Chambers 2006–; memb Bd Aspire Law LLP 2014–; memb Exec Ctee Charity Law Assoc 1995–2009, tstee Statute Law Soc 1987–2009, memb Chancery Bar Assoc 1990–; memb Exec Ctee Assoc of Charitable Fndns 1990–94, memb Advsy Bd Almshouse Assoc 1990–, memb Bd COIF Charity Funds 1995–2009; tstee: Bishopsgate Fndn 1991–94, St Peter's Convent Woking 1994–2004, Elizabeth Finn Care 1994–2012; dir Elizabeth Finn Homes Ltd 2005–12 (chm 2009–12); govr Dulwich Coll 2004–09, memb Mensa 1974– (co-pres Br Mensa 2015–), tstee ASPIRE 2013–15, external tstee Tilford Bach Soc 2014–; *Books* Butterworth's Encyclopaedia of Forms and Precedents (contrib Charities, 1987, 1996, 2002 and 2013), Running a Charity (1993, 2 edn 1997), Charity Law Association Model Governing Instruments (1996, 3 edn 2010), Charities: The law and practice (looseleaf, jtly); *Recreations* walking, classical music, theatre, art; *Style*— Ms Francesca Quint; ✉ Radcliffe Chambers, 11 New Square, Lincoln's Inn, London WC2A 3TS (☎ 020 7692 2064, fax 020 7405 2560, e-mail fquint@radcliffechambers.com, website www.radcliffechambers.com)

QUIRICI, Daniel; s of Ernest Quirici, of Paris, and Candide, *née* Postai; *b* 8 June 1948; *Educ* Ecole des Hautes Etudes Commerciales Paris (MBA), Stanford Univ (PhD); *m* 1 Sept 1972, Margaret, da of Donald Wright Mann, of NY; 2 s (Alexandre b 15 Aug 1973, Francois b 23 May 1979), 1 da (Florence b 14 Feb 1978); *Career* assoc prof HEC 1970–76, assoc Arthur D Little 1976–82, sr vice-pres Credit Commercial de France (CCF) Paris 1983–91, md CCF Holdings Ltd 1986–91, chief exec Deloitte & Touche (D & T) Corporate Finance Europe Ltd 1991–97, md Citigroup 1997–2003, ptnr Echo Capital Ltd 2003–; *Recreations* tennis, golf; *Clubs* RAC, Hurlingham; *Style*— Daniel Quirici, Esq; ✉ 8 Montpelier Square, London SW7 1JU (work e-mail daniel.quirici@echo-capital.com)

QUIRK, Hon Eric Randolph; s of Baron Quirk, CBE, FBA (Life Peer), *qv*, and Jean, *née* Williams (d 1995); *b* 30 December 1951; *Educ* Highgate Sch, UCL (LLB); *m* 1, 30 July 1977 (m dis 1995), Patricia Anne, da of Stanley Lawrence Hemsworth; 2 da (Catharine b 25 May 1979, Sara b 14 Nov 1980), 1 s (Richard b 2 April 1983); m 2, 17 June 2006, Sheila Basford, da of Gerald and Eileen Mann; *Career* admitted slr 1975; asst slr: Slaughter & May 1973–77, Alexander Tatham & Co 1978–81; ptnr: Alsop Wilkinson Manchester (formerly Lee Lane-Smith) 1981–93 (trg ptnr 1982–92), Laytons 1993–98, Fox Brooks Marshall (latterly Cobbetts) 1998–2006, Glaisyers 2006–; memb: Legal Resources Gp Educn Ctee 1988–93, UCL Alumnus Soc, Law Soc; chm Middlewich Concert Orch, friend Opera North; *Recreations* violin, string quartets, rugby and cricket spectator (season ticket holder Sale Sharks RUFC), language, fell walking, opera, 20th century theatre, gardening, architecture, political banter, finding humour in life; *Clubs* Lymm RUFC; *Style*— The Hon Eric Quirk; ✉ The Elms, Trouthall Lane, Plumley, Knutsford, Cheshire WA16 9RY (☎ 0161 833 5690, e-mail erq@glaisyers.com)

QUIRKE, Pauline; *b* 8 July 1959; *m* Steve; 1 s (Charlie), 1 da (Emily); *Career* actress; trained at Anna Scher Theatre; *Theatre* A Tale of Two Cities (Royal Court) 1979, Dick Whittington (Hackney Empire) 1990–91 *Television* incl: Dixon of Dock Green 1968, Eleanor 1973, Pauline's Quirkes 1975, Angels 1976, Pauline's People 1977, Shine on Harvey Moon 1982, Girls on Top 1985, Rockliffe's Babies 1987, Casualty 1986, Birds of a Feather 1989–94 and 2014, Jobs for the Girls 1993, The Sculptress 1995, First Sign of Madness 1996, Double Nougat 1996, Deadly Summer 1997, Real Women 1997–99, Maisie Raine 1998–99, David Copperfield 1999, Office Gossip 2000, Down to Earth 2000–02 (three series), Randall & Hopkirk 2001, Murder in Mind 2001, Being April 2002, Carrie's War 2003, Missing 2009, Emmerdale 2010–11, Broadchurch 2013; *Film* Little Dorrit 1986, The Elephant Man 1987, Getting it Right 1988, The Return of the Soldiers 1988, Still Lives-Distant Voices 1989, Our Boy (BBC Screen One) 1997, The Canterville Ghost (Carlton film) 1997, Check-Out Girl 1998, Arthur's Dyke 2000, Redemption RD 2001, Waiting for Giro 2003; *Awards* Best Comedy Newcomer 1991, British Comedy Actress Award 1993, Variety Club of GB BBC TV Personality of the Year 1994, TV Quick Awards Best Drama Actress 1998; nominated: BAFTA Best Actress Award 1997, Royal Television Soc Best Actress Award 1997, Nat Television Awards Most Popular Comedy Performer 1997; *Style*— Ms Pauline Quirke

QURESHI, Ashar; s of Azhar Naseem Qureshi (d 2001), and Faiza, *née* Feroze (d 1999); *b* 21 January 1965, Lahore, Pakistan; *Educ* Harvard Coll (BA), Harvard Univ (JD); *m* 15 Jan 1995, Mahreen, *née* Malik; 2 da (Raniyah b 11 Oct 1995, Aidah b 9 May 2001), 1 s (Ahad Abbas b 24 March 1999); *Career* admitted NY Bar 1990; slr specialising in int corporate finance and M&A; ptnr Cleary Gottlieb Steen & Hamilton LLP 1999–2010 (joined 1990), exec vice-chm Renaissance Gp 2010–11, ptnr Naya Capital Mgmnt 2012–; dir Hanson Asset Mgmnt 2012–; memb Advsy Bd Practising Law Inst; author of numerous pubns; vice-chm Luminaire Films 2012–; *Recreations* riding, polo, theatre; *Style*— Ashar Qureshi, Esq; ✉ Cleary Gottlieb Steen & Hamilton LLP, City Place House, 55 Basinghall Street, London EC2V 5EH (☎ 020 7614 2226)

QURESHI, Murad; AM; s of late Mushtaq Qureshi, and Khalida Qureshi; *b* 27 May 1965; *Educ* UEA (BA), UCL (MSc); *Career* worked in housing, devpt and regeneration until 2004; cnclr Church St ward City of Westminster 1998–2006; GLA: memb London Assembly (Lab) London (list) 2004–, memb Budget, Environment, Standards and Tport Ctees and London Fire and Emergency Planning Authy, chair London Waterways Cmmn; memb: Socialist Environment and Resources Assoc (SERA), Bd BRAC UK; *Recreations* cricket, football; *Clubs* MCC; *Style*— Murad Qureshi, Esq, AM; ✉ Greater London Authority, City Hall, The Queen's Walk, London SE1 2AA (☎ 020 7983 4400, fax 020 7983 5679, e-mail murad.qureshi@london.gov.uk)

QURESHI, Prof Shakeel Ahmed; s of Mohammed Aslam Qureshi, of Luton, Beds, and Sara Begum Qureshi; *b* 20 March 1952; *Educ* Thomas Rotherham Coll, Rotherham GS, Univ of Manchester Med Sch (MB ChB); *m* Azra Siddique, da of Mohammed Siddique Qureshi, of Rawalpindi, Pakistan; 1 da (Noreen b 14 April 1971), 3 s (Sajid Shakeel b 21 May 1977, Abid Shakeel b 14 Feb 1980, Imran Shakeel b 29 July 1982); *Career* house physician Luton and Dunstable Hosp Luton 1976–77, house surgn Manchester Royal Infirmary 1977, sr house physician Joyce Green Hosp Dartford 1977–79, med registrar Barnet Gen Hosp 1979–80, cardiology res registrar Harefield Hosp 1980–83; conslt paediatric cardiologist: Rawalpindi Pakistan 1983–85, Royal Liverpool Children's Hosp 1987–88 (sr registrar paediatric cardiology 1986), Guy's Hosp 1988–; prof of paediatric cardiology Guy's and St Thomas Hosp 2010–; assoc ed (Mentorship) Cardiology in the Young 2014–; memb: BMA 1976, Br Cardiac Soc, Br Paediatric Cardiac Assoc, Assoc of European Paediatric Cardiologists; pres Br Congenital Cardiac Assoc (BCCA) 2009–12, pres Assoc for European Paediatric and Congenital Cardiology (AEPC) 2010–13; FRCP 1994 (MRCP 1979); *Books* Percutaneous Interventions for Congenital Heart Disease (jt ed); *Recreations* cricket, golf; *Style*— Prof Shakeel A Qureshi; ✉ Department of Paediatric Cardiology, Evelina Children's Hospital, Guy's and St Thomas's Trust, Westminster Bridge Road, London SE1 7EH (☎ 020 7188 4547, fax 020 7188 4556)

Q

R

RAAB, Dominic Rennie; MP; *b* 25 February 1974; *Educ* Dr Challoners GS Amersham, Lady Margaret Hall Oxford, Jesus Coll Cambridge; *m* Erika; *Career* Linklaters 1998–2000, FCO 2000–06, COS to Rt Hon David Davis, *qv*, 2006–08, COS to Rt Hon Dominic Grieve, QC, MP, *qv*, 2008–10; MP (Cons) Esher & Walton 2010–, min for human rights and parly under-sec of state Min of Justice 2015–; *Books* The Assault on Liberty – What Went Wrong with Rights (2009), Britannia Unchained (2012); *Style—* Dominic Raab, Esq, MP; ✉ House of Commons, London SW1A 0AA (☎ 020 7219 7069)

RABAN, Jonathan; s of Rev Peter J C P Raban, and Monica, *née* Sandison; *b* 14 June 1942; *Educ* Univ of Hull (BA); *m* 1985 (m dis 1992), Caroline Cuthbert; m 2, 1992, Jean Lenihan; 1 da (b 1992); *Career* lectr in Eng and American Lit UCW 1965–67, UEA 1967–69, professional writer 1969–; Hon DLitt Univ of Hull; FRSL; *Books* The Technique of Modern Fiction (1969), Mark Twain: Huckleberry Finn (1969), The Society of the Poem (1971), Soft City (1973), Arabia Through The Looking Glass (1979), Old Glory (1981, Heinemann award RSL 1982, Thomas Cook award 1982), Foreign Land (1985), Coasting (1986), For Love and Money (1987), God, Man and Mrs Thatcher (1989), Hunting Mister Heartbreak (1990, Thomas Cook Award 1991), The Oxford Book of the Sea (ed, 1992), Bad Land: An American Romance (1996, Nat Book Critics' Circle Award 1997), Passage to Juneau: A Sea and its Meanings (1999), Waxwings (2003), Surveillance (2006), My Holy War (2006), Driving Home (2010, US edn 2011); *Recreations* sailing; *Clubs* Groucho, Rainier; *Style—* Jonathan Raban, Esq, FRSL

RABINOWITZ, Harry; MBE (1978); s of Israel Rabinowitz (d 1960), and Eva, *née* Kirkel (d 1971); *b* 26 March 1916, Johannesburg, SA; *Educ* Athlone HS, Univ of the Witwatersrand, London Guildhall Sch of Music; *m* 1, 15 Dec 1944 (m dis 2000), Lorna Thurlow, da of Cecil Redvers Anderson (d 1970); 2 da (Karen Lesley b 1947, Lisa Gabrielle b 1960), 1 s (Simon Oliver b 1951); m 2, 18 March 2001, Mary C Scott; *Career* Corpl SA Forces 1942–43; conductor BBC Radio 1953–60; head of music: BBC TV Light Entertainment 1960–68, LWT 1968–77; currently freelance conductor/composer; conductor: Hollywood Bowl 1983–84, Boston Pops 1985–92, London Symphony Orchestra, Royal Philharmonic Orchestra, Carnegie Hall 1996, Merchant Ivory 35th Anniversary Celebration; conductor for films: Chariots of Fire, Manhattan Project, Heat & Dust, The Bostonians, Maurice, Time Bandits, Return to Oz, L'Argent, Camille Claudel, Ballad of the Sad Cafe, J'Embrasse Pas, La Voix, Pour Sacha, Les Carnassiers, Howard's End, The Ark and the Flood, Tractions, The Remains of the Day, Shirley Valentine, Business Affair, Grosse Fatigue, Le Petit Garçon, The Flemish Board, Mantegna et Fils, La Fille de d'Artagnan, Death and the Maiden, Jefferson in Paris, Nelly and Mr Arnold, The Secret Agent, The Stupids, The Proprietor, Star Command, La Belle Verte, Surviving Picasso, The English Patient, Tonka, Amour Sorcier, My Story So Far, City of Angels, Place Vendôme, A Soldier's Daughter Never Cries, Message in a Bottle, Cotton Mary, The Talented Mr Ripley, The Golden Bowl, Possession, The Music Box, Le Divorce, Bon Voyage, Cold Mountain, Donkey Xote, This Is Elvis; TV: New Faces 1987–88, Paul Nicholas Special 1987–88, Julia MacKenzie Special 1986, Nicholas Nickleby, Drummonds, The Insurance Man, Absent Friends, Simon Wiesenthal Story, Marti Caine Special, Alien Empire, Battle of the Sexes; composer TV: Agatha Christie Hour, Reilly Ace of Spies, The Great Depression, Memento Mori; conductor theatre: World Premieres of 'Cats' and 'Song and Dance'; Discs: Michael Crawford, Sarah Brightman, The Music of Duke Ellington (with Johnny Mathis), The Music of George Gershwin (with Jack Jones), Radio City Christmas Album, 11 Japanese song hits (with RPO), Phil Woods: I Remember; awards: Br Acad of Songwriters, Composers and Authors (BASCA) Gold award 1986, Radio and TV Industries award 1984, Allmusic Lifetime Contrib Gold award 1990, Freeman City of London 1996; *Recreations* wine tasting, gathering edible fungi, listening to others making music; *Style—* Harry Rabinowitz, Esq, MBE; ✉ Yellow Cottage, Walking Bottom, Peaslake, Surrey GU5 9RR (☎ 01306 730674, e-mail mitziscott@aol.com)

RABINOWITZ, Laurence; QC (2002); s of Joseph Rabinowitz (d 1992), of SA, and Mary, *née* Alexander; *b* 3 May 1960; *m* 16 July 1989, Suzanne Jacqueline, da of Dr Alan Benster; 2 s (Samuel, Jacob), 1 da (Josephine); *Career* barr; jr counsel for the Crown (Chancery) 1995; bencher Middle Temple 2008; govr N London Collegiate Sch 2008; *Style—* Laurence Rabinowitz, Esq, QC; ✉ 1 Essex Court, Temple, London EC4Y 9AR (e-mail lrabinowitz@oeclaw.co.uk)

RACE, Russell John; JP, DL; s of Russell Edgar Race (d 1982), and Winifred Olive, *née* Clissold (d 1996); *b* 28 May 1946; *Educ* Sir Joseph Williamson's Mathematical Sch Rochester, Univ of Liverpool (BA); *Career* economist White Fish Authy 1967–70, dir ABN AMRO Hoare Govett 1985–97 (investment analyst 1970–76, corp fin 1976–97); dir: Goldshield Group plc 1998–2004, T Clarke plc 1998–, Neutec Pharma plc 2002–06; chm Chatham Maritime Tst, memb Ct of Assts Rochester Bridge Tst; memb Ct of Assts Worshipful Co of Glaziers & Painters of Glass; FRSA; *Recreations* music, sport, freemasonry; *Clubs* Naval and Military, London Capital, Castle (Rochester); *Style—* Russell Race, Esq, JP, DL; ✉ 3 Copse Close, Pattens Lane, Rochester, Kent ME1 2RS (☎ 01634 406347)

RADCLIFFE, David; *Career* Hogg Robinson Gp: joined 1978, memb Bd 1989–, chief exec 1997–; CIMgt, FInstSMM, FIoD; *Style—* David Radcliffe, Esq; ✉ Hogg Robinson Group, Global House, Victoria Street, Basingstoke, Hampshire RG21 3BT

RADCLIFFE, John Peter; s of John Maurice Radcliffe (d 1949), of Bristol, and Margery Bloomfield Lumsden (d 1974); *b* 9 January 1935; *Educ* Cheltenham Coll (open scholar), Clare Coll Cambridge (exhibitioner, MA); *m* 1, 5 Sept 1959, Bridget Jane, da of Dr William Leslie Cuthbert (d 1999), of Stirling; 2 da (Virginia Frances b 10 Oct 1961, Polly Clare b 10 Dec 1965), 1 s (Jonathan James b 31 July 1963); m 2, 21 May 2001, Sheila Mary, da of Patrick Butler, of Hatfield; *Career* asst to commercial mangr (economics) UKAEA Industrial Group 1960–61; BBC: prodr World Service Current Affairs 1961–64, prodr responsible for history BBC Schools Television 1965–70, sr prodr responsible for social sciences BBC Open Univ Prodns 1970–72, exec prodr BBC Continuing Educn Television 1972–84, exec prodr BBC Computer Literacy Project 1980–83, head of BBC Open Univ Prodn Centre 1984–89, md BBC Subscription Television 1990–93; exec prodr The MultiMedia Corp 1994–97, md Fast Media 1997–; *Recreations* hill walking, photography, literature, computing, conversation; *Style—* John Radcliffe, Esq; ✉ 106 Richmond Avenue, Islington, London N1 0LS (☎ 020 7837 5039, e-mail johnradcliffe@blueyonder.co.uk)

RADCLIFFE, Julian Guy Yonge; OBE (2000), QVRM (2004), TD; s of Maj Guy Lushington Yonge Radcliffe, MBE, and Anne Marigold, *née* Leyland; *b* 29 August 1948; *Educ* Eton, New Coll Oxford; *m* Frances Harriet Thompson; 2 s, 1 da; *Career* Lloyd's broker and underwriting memb of Lloyd's; md: Investment Insurance Int 1973–81, Control Risks Ltd 1976–81; dir: Credit Insurance Assoc Ltd 1975–83, Hogg Group plc 1986–94, Aon Risk Services (UK) Ltd (formerly Bain Hogg International) 1994–99, Loss Management Group 1994–2010; chm International Art and Antique Loss Register Ltd 1991–; cmmnd Royal Yeo 1971 (Lt-Col 1993), cmmnd Dorset Yeo 1997–99, Col MOD 2000; Upper Bailiff Worshipful Co of Weavers 1995–96; *Recreations* farming, shooting, military and strategic studies; *Clubs* City of London, Cavalry and Guards'; *Style—* Julian Radcliffe, Esq, OBE, QVRM, TD; ✉ 32 Brynmaer Road, London SW11 4EW; Art Loss Register, 63–66 Hatton Garden, London EC1N 8LE (e-mail julian.radcliffe@artloss.com)

RADCLIFFE, Mark; s of Philip Radcliffe, and Doreen, *née* Goad; *Educ* Bolton Sch, Univ of Manchester (BA); *Career* Piccadilly Radio 1979–83, prodr Radio 1 1983–85, head of music Piccadilly Radio 1985–86, prodr rising to sr prodr BBC Manchester 1986–, presenter (with Marc Riley, *qv*) BBC Radio 1 1991–2004, presenter Radio 2 (also sometime presenter Radio 4 and 5 Live, BBC TV), presenter Radio 2 Folk Show 2013–, currently presenter of afternoon show BBC 6 Music; dir M And TV prodns; co-fndr Halon Music Prize 2002; Sony Gold Awards 1992, 1998, 1999, 2001, 2007, 2008 (Best Music Prog) and 2009 (Best Music Presenter), NME Best DJ in the World Today 1997 and 1998; *Records* The Worst Album in the World (1999), Songs of the Back Bar (1999), Our Kid Eh (2001), On The Razzle (2002), Mahone Brew (2006), What Remains of the Day (2011); *Books* Show Business: Diary of a Rock & Roll Nobody (1999), Northern Sky (2005), Thank You for the Days (2008), Reeling in the Years (2011); *Recreations* just music and kids and Manchester City FC; *Style—* Mark Radcliffe, Esq; ✉ c/o PBJ Management, 7 Soho Street, London W1D 3DQ (☎ 020 7287 1112)

RADCLIFFE, Mark Hugh Joseph; OBE (2008), DL (Hants 1997); s of Hugh John Reginald Joseph Radcliffe, MBE (d 1993), and Marie-Thérèse (Mariquita), *née* Pereira; *Educ* Downside; *m* 20 Feb 1963, Anne, da of Maj-Gen Arthur Evers Brocklehurst, CB, DSO; 3 da (Lucinda b 1964, Emily Marie Louise (Mrs Alex Rogers) b 1968, Camilla Mary (Mrs James Forbes) b 1971); *Career* 2 Lt Coldstream Gds 1956–58; mktg mangr Cape Asbestos Ltd 1958–68, chief exec Lancer Boss Group Ltd 1968–74, md Triang Pedigree Ltd 1974–78, dir TI Group plc 1978–92, chm Upton Management Services Ltd 1992–2006; CBI: dep DG 1991–93, estab National Manufacturing Cncl 1991, advsr on industrial affrs 1991–94; non-exec chm: Metsec plc 1993–98, IE Gp plc 1997–2000; non-exec dir: London Stock Exchange 1993–98, William Jacks plc 1994–99, Reliance Security Group plc 1995–2005; ind dir Securities and Futures Authy Ltd 1993–2001; patron Meridian Tst 1996–2005, chm Hants Youth Options 1997–2007; High Sheriff Hants 1996–97, vice-pres Countess of Brecknock Hospice 1998–, govr Southampton Inst 1999–2000; FInstD; *Recreations* shooting, golf, tennis, fishing, gardening; *Clubs* Cavalry and Guards', Pratt's, MCC; *Style—* Mark Radcliffe, Esq, OBE, DL; ✉ The Malt House, Upton, Andover, Hampshire SP11 0JS (☎ 01264 736266)

RADCLIFFE, Paula Jane; MBE (2002); da of Peter Radcliffe, and Patricia Radcliffe, of Beds; *b* 17 December 1973; *Educ* Loughborough Univ (BA); *m* Gary Lough; 1 da (Isla Olivia b 17 Jan 2007); *Career* athlete; World Junior Cross Country champion 1992, Br champion 5000m 1995, 1996 and 1997, winner European Cross Country Championship 1998 and 2003, Silver medal 10000m World Championships 1999, winner Great North Run 2000 and 2003, World Half Marathon champion 2000, 2001 and 2003, fourth place 10000m Olympic Games 2000 (fifth place 5000m 1996), winner (long course) World Cross Country Championships 2001 and 2002 (second place 1997 and 1998, third place 1999, second place (short course) 2001), winner London Marathon 2002, 2003 (women's world record, 2 hours 15 mins 25 secs) and 2005 (women only world record 2 hours 17 mins and 42 seconds), Gold medal 5000m Cwlth Games 2002, Gold medal 10000m European Championships 2002, winner Chicago Marathon 2002, winner NY Marathon 2004, 2007 and 2008, Gold medal marathon World Championships 2005; twice winner NYC Road Mile, world best over 5 miles, 8 km and 10 km; UK and Cwlth record holder: 3000m (8 mins 22.20 secs), 5000m (14 mins 29.11 secs); UK and Cwlth record holder 10000m (30 mins 1.09 secs); European best over half marathon 66 mins 47 secs; Br Athletics Team Womens Capt 1998, 1999, 2000, 2001 and 2002; Junior Athlete of the Year 1992, Br Athletic Fedn Athlete of the Year 1997, Br Sports Writers Reebok Trophy 1997, Sunday Times Sportswoman of the Year 1999, Br Athletic Fedn and Sports Writers Female Athlete of the Year 1999 and 2001, Women of the Year Outstanding Achievement Award 2002, Int Assoc of Athletics Fedns World Female Athlete of the Year 2002, BBC Sports Personality of the Year 2002, Br Athletics Writers' Assoc Female Athlete of the Year 2002, 2003 and 2005, Walpole Sporting Award 2003; *Recreations* athletics, most sports, reading, relaxing; *Clubs* Bedford & County Athletics, British Milers, Loughborough Students Athletic; *Style—* Ms Paula Radcliffe, MBE; ✉ c/o Abigail Tordoff, Octagon, 81/83 Fulham High Street, London SW6 3TW (☎ 020 7862 0039, e-mail abigail.tordoff@octagon.com)

RADCLYFFE, Sarah; da of Capt Charles Raymond Radclyffe, of Lew, Oxon, and Helen Viola Egerton, *née* Cotton; *b* 14 November 1950; *Educ* Heathfield Sch Ascot; *m* 29 June 1996, William Penton Godfrey; 2 s (Sam Charles Radclyffe b 30 March 1989, Callum Penton Radclyffe Godfrey b 7 Feb 1995); *Career* film prodr 1978–; films incl: The Tempest 1979, My Beautiful Laundrette 1985, Caravaggio 1985, Wish You Were Here 1986, Sammy and Rosie Get Laid 1987, A World Apart 1988, Paperhouse 1989, Fools of Fortune 1990, Edward II 1991, Robin Hood 1991, Dakota Road 1992, Sirens 1993, Second Best 1993, Bent 1996, Cousin Bette 1997, Les Miserables 1998, The War Zone 1999, Ratcatcher 1999, There's Only One Jimmy Grimble 2000, Love's Brother 2003, Tara Road 2004, Free Jimmy 2006, How About You 2007, The Edge of Love 2008, Cirque du Freak: The Vampire's Assistant 2009, South Solitary 2010, Good Morning Karachi 2013; dir: Channel 4 1995–99, Film Cncl 1999–2004; govr BFI 1996–99; *Style—* Miss Sarah Radclyffe; ✉ Sarah Radclyffe Productions Ltd, 10–11 St George's Mews, London NW1 8XE (☎ 020 7483 3556, fax 020 7586 8063, e-mail sarah@srpltd.co.uk)

RADFORD, His Hon Judge David Wyn; s of late Robert Edwin Radford, CB, and late Eleanor Margaret, *née* Jones; *b* 3 January 1947; *Educ* Cranleigh Sch, Selwyn Coll Cambridge (MA, LLM); *m* 23 Sept 1972, Nadine, da of Joseph Poggioli, of London; 2 da (Carina b 1975, Lauren b 1986), 2 s (Simon b 1982, Peter b 1983); *Career* called to the

Bar Gray's Inn 1969 (bencher 2008); recorder 1993–96 (asst recorder 1988–93), circuit judge (SE Circuit) 1996–2002, sr circuit judge 2002–; hon recorder Redbridge 2009; Lib Parly candidate Hampstead 1975–83; *Recreations* spending time with family, visiting areas and places of natural and historical heritage, following soccer, reading widely; *Style—* His Hon Judge Radford; ✉ Snaresbrook Crown Court, Hollybush Hill, Snaresbrook, London E11 1QW

RADFORD, Jonathan Vaughan; s of Patrick Vaughan Radford, CBE, MC, TD, DL, of Langford Hall, Newark, Notts, and Evelyn, *née* Wilkinson; *b* 11 June 1959; *Educ* Eton, Univ of Bristol (BA); *m* 10 Dec 1999, Caroline, née Higgins; 1 da (Freya Chiara b 6 Jan 2002), 1 s (Enzo Vaughan b 8 Feb 2005); *Career* accountant; Peat Marwick Mitchell and Co London 1981–86, fin dir Stag Furniture Holdings plc 1992–95 (various mgmnt positions 1986–92), chief exec Elit Group Ltd 1996–2001; chm and non-exec dir various private cos; Freeman City of London 1987, Liveryman Worshipful Co of Furniture Makers 1987; ACIS 1990, FCA 1994 (ACA 1984); *Recreations* Venice and art; *Clubs* Annabel's; *Style—* Jonathan Radford, Esq; ✉ 20 St George's Square, Stamford, Lincolnshire PE9 2BN (☎ 01780 762770, e-mail jonathan@oasbyhouse.co.uk)

RADFORD, Matthew; *b* 1953; *Educ* Camberwell Sch of Art (BA); *Career* artist; teacher: Camberwell Sch of Art 1981–84, Drawing Center NY 1985–86, NY Studio Sch 1989–93; visiting lectr Slade Sch of Art 2000; *Solo Exhibitions* Letchworth Museum and Art Gallery 1980, Kettle's Yard 1984, Chuck Levitan NY 1985, Donald Wren Gallery NY 1987, Frank Bernarducci Gallery NY 1988 and 1990, CVII NY 1989, Tatistcheff Gallery Los Angeles 1993 (NY 1991), Grace Borgenicht Gallery NY 1993 and 1994, Houldsworth Fine Art London 1994 and 1997–2004 (annually), Newsreel: new etchings (Alan Cristea Gallery) 2003, Works on Paper (Advanced Graphics London) 2005, Paintings and Prints (Glasgow Print Studio) 2005, Farbe + Figur (Städtische Galerie Villingen-Schwenningen) 2005, The Space Between: New Paintings (SW1 Galleries London) 2006, Milton Gallery (St. Paul's School London) 2006, Random Empires (Chelsea Art Gallery Silicon Valley) 2006; *Group Exhibitions* Royal Festival Hall 1980, 1981 and 1983, RA Diploma Galleries 1980, Stock Exchange Gallery 1981, British Drawing (Hayward Gallery) 1982, The Drawing Center 1985 and 1993, Donald Wren Gallery 1987, New York Observed (Frank Bernarducci Gallery) 1988, Downtown Perspectives (Adelphi Univ NY) 1988, New York Art Now (Helander Gallery Palm Beach) 1989, Visions and Visionaries (Tavelli Gallery Aspen) 1989, Quest (NY Studio Sch) 1989, Social Studies (Lintas Worldwide NY) 1989, Art and Law (Minnesota Museum of Art and tour) 1990, New York at Night (Helander Gallery) 1990, Four Artists (Houldsworth Fine Art) 1990, New Faces, New Work (Tatistcheff & Co NY) 1991, On the Move (Champion Gallery Stamford) 1991, ICAF91, Houldsworth Fine Art 1991, 1992, 1993 and 1994, City (Martin County Cncl of the Arts Florida) 1992, Mall Galleries 1992, People (Gallery Three Zero NY) 1992, Art92, Isolation (Tatistcheff Gallery) 1992, Art93, Mostyn Open Exhibition 1993, Art94, Lew Allen Horwich Gallery Santa Fe 1994 and 1995, Grace Borgenicht Gallery 1994 and 1995, East Wing Exhibition Contemporary Art at the Courtauld 1996, A Selection of Post-War International Painting and Sculpture (Martin Browne Fine Art Sydney) 1997, Etchings from Hope Sufferance Press (Marlborough Fine Art London) 1998, Art Auction for Children of the Sudan (Bernard Jacobsen Gallery London) 1998, Artaid 98 (City Art Centre Edinburgh) 1998, New Showing (Houldsworth Fine Art London) 1999, Free Lemonade (Robert Miller Gallery NY) 2002, Advanced Graphics London 2003, Face Value (Chelsea Art Gallery Silicon Valley) 2005; *Work in Collections* incl: British Land Co, Champion Int Corporate, Credit Suisse, Deutsche Bank AG, Fidelity Insurance Co, Hiscox Holdings Ltd, McDonald's Corporation, Met Museum of Art NY, NY Public Library, Reader's Digest Collection, Yale Center for British Art; *Awards* Jeffrey Archer Prize 1981, GLC Award 1982, Eastern Arts Major Award 1983, Honarium-Drawing Center 1985, ED Fndn 1989, Platinum Disc five times (for Beautiful South's Carry On Up The Charts); *Recreations* cricket, literature and old films; *Style—* Matthew Radford, Esq

RADFORD, (Oswald) Michael James; s of Oswald Charles Radford, of Haslemere, Surrey, and Ruth, *née* Presser; *b* 24 February 1946; *Educ* Bedford Sch, Worcester Coll Oxford (BA), Nat Film and TV Sch; *m* 4 Aug 1990 (m dis 1997), Iseult Joanna, *née* St Aubin de Teran; 1 s (Felix Louis b 6 March 1991), 1 da (Amaryllis James b 23 Feb 2005); *Career* director; freelance film dir 1979–; govr Nat Film and TV Sch 1982–90; memb: DGA, American Acad; *Television* documentary films for BBC incl: The Madonna and The Volcano (Grand Prix Nyon Documentary Film Festival 1979), The Last Stronghold of the Pure Gospel, La Belle Isobel, The White Bird Passes (Scot Acad Award 1980); *Films* Another Time, Another Place 1983 (Best Film Award Cannes Film Festival, Special Jury Prize Celtic Film Festival, George Sadoul Prize Paris for Best Foreign Film), Nineteen Eighty Four 1984 (Standard Best Film of the Year Award), White Mischief 1988, Il Postino 1994 (David Lean Award for Best Direction, nominated for 5 Oscars incl Best Director and Best Screenwriter), B Monkey 1997, Dancing at the Blue Iguana 2000, The Letters 2002, The Merchant of Venice 2004, Flawless 2006, The Mule 2011, King Lear 2012; *Recreations* fishing, skiing, snooker; *Clubs* Groucho; *Style—* Michael Radford, Esq

RADICE, Baron (Life Peer UK 2001), of Chester-le-Street in the County of Durham; Giles Heneage Radice; PC (1999); s of Lawrence Wallace Radice (d 1996; himself s of Evasio Radice) and Patricia, eldest da of Sir Arthur Pelham Heneage, DSO, JP, DL, sometime MP for Louth; *b* 4 October 1936; *Educ* Winchester, Magdalen Coll Oxford; *m* 1, 1959 (m dis 1969), Penelope, er da of late Robert Angus, JP, DL, of Ladykirk, Ayrshire, by his w (subsequently Lady Moore); 2 da (Adele b 1961, Sophia b 1964); m 2, 1971, Lisanne, *née* Koch; *Career* former head Res Dept GMWU; MP (Lab): Chester-le-Street 1973–83, Durham N 1983–2001; chm Manifesto Gp in Labour Party 1980–83, oppn front bench spokesman on employment 1981–83, shadow educn sec 1983–87, memb Select Ctee on Treasy (chm 1997–2001), chm Select Ctee on Public Service 1996–97, chm European Econ Sub-Ctee House of Lords 2002–06, memb European External Affrs Sub Ctee House of Lords 2012–15; memb Cncl Policy Studies Institute 1978–82, chm European Movement 1995–2001, chm Br Assoc for Central and Eastern Europe 1997–2004, chm French-Br Cncl 2003–07, chm Policy Network 2007–09; *Style—* The Lord Radice, PC

RADLEY, Gordon Charles; s of late Ronald Neterfield Radley, and late Diana, *née* Nairn; *b* 26 March 1953; *Educ* Bromley GS, Stockwell Coll of Educn, Highbury Coll; *m* 4 May 1985, Joan Elizabeth, da of late Keith Smith, of Polegate, E Sussex; *Career* promotion prodr HTV 1974–76, promotion prodr Anglia TV 1977–78; presenter: Grampian TV 1979, Points West BBC TV West 1979–81, TVS 1981–85; presenter and reporter South Today BBC TV South, presenter, newsreader and reporter Anglia News Anglia TV 1988–90, anchor and interviewer Sky News 1995–; freelance presenter, reporter, prodr and dir satellite TV, BBC and ITV; media and PR conslt; dir Radley Corporation Ltd; *Recreations* country pursuits, cycling, keeping fit; *Style—* Gordon Radley, Esq; ✉ Wellington House, Tilford, Surrey GU10 2EH (☎ and fax 01252 794642)

RADLEY, Simon Harrison; *b* 21 May 1965; *Educ* Tring Comp Tring Herts, Westcroft Tutorial Coll Tring, S Cheshire Coll of FE Crewe Cheshire (City and Guilds), Oriental Cooking Sch Bangkok; *Career* chef; waiter Relais Beaujolais Maconnais Macon France June-Sept 1983, commis chef rising to chef de partie The Belfry Hotel Wilmslow Cheshire 1983–86, chef to partie rising to jr sous chef The Chester Grosvenor Hotel Chester 1986–87, chef de partie The Inigo Jones French Restaurant 1987–88, sr sous chef rising to head chef The Arkle Restaurant Chester Grosvenor Hotel Chester 1988–94 (1 Michelin star, 4 AA rosettes, 1 Egon Ronay star, Hotel of the Year Egon Ronay Cellnet Guide 1993), head chef New Hall County House Hotel Royal Sutton Coldfield 1994–98, exec chef Simon Radley at The Chester Grosvenor (previously The Arkle) 1998– (Michelin star 2009–); *Recreations* squash, mountain biking; *Style—* Simon Radley, Esq; ✉ Simon Radley at The Chester Grosvenor, Eastgate, Chester CH1 1LT

RAE, Barbara Davis; CBE (1999); da of James Rae, Provost (d 1982), of Crieff, Perthshire, and Mary, *née* Young; *Educ* Morrisons Acad Crieff, Edinburgh Coll of Art, Moray House Coll of Educn; *Career* artist; art teacher: Ainslie Park Comp Edinburgh 1968–69, Portobello Secdy Sch Edinburgh 1969–72; ectr in drawing painting and printmaking Aberdeen Coll of Educn 1972–74, lectr in drawing and painting Glasgow Sch of Art 1975–96, exchange teacher Fine Art Dept Univ of Maryland 1984; memb: Art Panel CNAA 1986–, Cncl RSW 1986–90 (vice-pres for East 1992–), Royal Fine Art Cmmn for Scotland 1995–2000; pres Soc of Scottish Artists 1982–84; tstee Arts Educn Tst 1986–90; chair of alumni Edinburgh Coll of Art 2008–; memb: RSA, RSW, RGI; DLitt Univ of Aberdeen 2003; Hon Dr of Art Napier Univ 1999, Hon DLitt Univ of Aberdeen 2003, Hon DLitt St Andrews Univ 2008; Hon Royal Etcher 2013; RA 1996, FRCA 2003, FRSE 2011; *Exhibitions* many solo exhbns in cities incl Edinburgh, London, Chichester, Belfast, Dublin, Oslo, New York, Chicago and Santa Fe, multiple solo exhbns during Edinburgh Int Arts Festival and at RA London; artworks translated into tapestries, ceramics and book covers; *Collections* work in numerous int private and public collections incl: Bank of England, HRH Prince Philip, Br Museum, Royal Bank of Scotland, Nat Gall of Modern Art Edinburgh; tapestry cmmn for Edinburgh Festival Theatre 1994, carpet cmmn for the Bute Room in the Royal Museum of Scotland; *Awards* Arts Cncl Award 1968, maj Arts Cncl Award 1975–81, Guthrie Medal RSA 1977, May Marshall Brown Award (RSW Centenary Exhibition) 1979, RSA Sir William Gillies Prize 1983, Calouste Gulbenkian Printmaking Award 1983, Alexander Graham Munro Award RSW 1989, Hunting Gp Prize 1990, Scottish PO Bd Award RSA 1990, Scottish Amicable Award RGI 1990, W J Burness Award RSA 1990; *Publications* Monograph (2008), Barbara Rae (2008), Barbara Rae – Prints (2010), Barbara Rae – Sketchbooks (2011); *Recreations* travel; *Style—* Dr Barbara Rae, CBE, RA

RAE, Fiona; *b* 10 October 1963, Hong Kong; *Educ* Croydon Coll of Art (Fndn Course), Goldsmiths' Coll of Art London (BA); *Career* artist; shortlisted Turner Prize 1991, shortlisted Eliette Von Karajan Prize for Young Painters (Austria) 1993; tstee Tate Gallery 2005–; *Solo Exhibitions* Third Eye Centre Glasgow 1990, Pierre Bernard Gallery Nice 1990, Waddington Galleries London 1991, Kunsthalle Basel 1992, ICA London 1993–94, John Good Gallery NY 1994, Galerie Nathalie Obadia Paris 1994, Waddington Galleries London 1995, Contemporary Fine Arts Berlin 1996, Saatchi Gallery London (with Gary Hume) 1997, The British School at Rome 1997, Luhring Augustine NY 1997, Kotyi Ogura Gallery Nagoya 1999, Luhring Augustine New York 1999; *Group Exhibitions* incl: Freeze (Surrey Docks London) 1988, Anderson O'Day Gallery London 1989, Promises promises (Serpentine Gallery London and École de Nîmes) 1989, Br Art Show (McLellan Galleries Glasgow, Leeds City Art Gallery, Hayward Gallery London) 1990, Aperto (Venice Biennale) 1990, Witte de With Center for Contemporary Art Rotterdam 1990, Anthony Reynolds Gallery London 1990, Who Framed Modern Art or The Quantitative Life of Roger Rabbit (Sidney Janis Gallery NY) 1991, Br Art from 1930 (Waddington Galleries London) 1991, A View of London (Salzburger Kunstverein) 1991, John Moores Liverpool Exhbn XVII (Walker Art Gallery) 1991, La Metafisica della Luce (John Good Gallery NY) 1991, Abstraction (Waddington Galleries) 1991, Turner Prize Exhbn (Tate Gallery London) 1991, The Contemporary Art Society: 80 Years of Collecting (Hayward Gallery and UK tour) 1991–92, Play between Fear and Desire (Germans van Eck Gallery NY) 1992, New Voices: Recent Paintings from the British Council Collection (Euro tour) 1992–95, A Decade of Collecting: Patrons of New Art Gifts 1983–93 (Tate Gallery) 1993–94, Moving into View: Recent British Painting (Arts Cncl Collection, Royal Festival Hall and UK tour) 1993–95, Unbound: Possibilities in Painting (Hayward Gallery) 1994, Chance, Choice and Irony (Todd Gallery London and John Hansard Gallery Univ of Southampton) 1994, Here and Now (Serpentine Gallery) 1994, Repicturing Abstraction (Marsh Art Gallery Univ of Virginia Richmond Va) 1995, From Here (Waddington Galleries and Karsten Schubert London) 1995, Malerei: Sechs Bilder, Sechs Positionen (Galerie Bugdahn und Kaimer Düsseldorf) 1995, Des limites du tableau: les possibles de la peinture (Musée Départemental de Rochechouart Haute-Vienne) 1995, Nuevas Abstracciones (Museo Nacional Centro de Arte Reina Sofia Madrid and also touring) 1996, About Vision: New British Painting in the 1990s (MOMA Oxford and UK tour) 1996–98, Treasure Island (Calouste Gulbenkian Fndn Lisbon) 1997, Ian Davenport, Michael Craig-Martin, Zebedee Jones, Michael Landy and Fiona Rae (Waddington Galleries London) 1997, Paintings and Sculpture (Luhring Augustine NY) 1997, Sensation: Young British Artists from The Saatchi Collection (Royal Acad) 1997, ACE! 1998, Axis 1998, UK Maximum Diversity 1998, Sensation: Young British artists from the Saatchi Collection (Museum für Gegenwart Berlin) 1998–99; *Collections* work in public collections incl: Arts Cncl of GB, Br Cncl, Contemporary Art Soc, Fonds National d'Art Contemporain (FNAC) Paris, Fonds Régional d'Art Contemporain d'Ile de France, Hamburger Bahnhof – Museum für Gegenwart Berlin SMPK Marx Collection, Musée Départemental de Rochechouart Haute-Vienne, Sintra MOMA Portugal – Berardo Collection, Tate Gallery, Walker Art Gallery Liverpool, Astrup Fearnley MOMA Oslo, Calouste Gulbenkian Foundation Lisbon, Fundación 'la Caixa' Barcelona, Government Art Collection, Southampton City Art Gallery; *Style—* Ms Fiona Rae; ✉ c/o Timothy Taylor Gallery, 15 Carlos Place, London W1K 2EX

RAE, Hon Lady Rita Emilia Anna; QC (Scot 1992); da of Alexander Smith Cowie Rae (d 1993), and Bianca Angela Carmela Ermanna, *née* Bruno; *b* 20 June 1950; *Educ* St Patrick's HS Coatbridge, Univ of Edinburgh (LLB); *Career* apprentice Biggart Lumsden & Co Glasgow (slrs) 1972–74, asst slr Biggart Baillie & Gifford Glasgow 1974–76, asst then ptnr Ross Harper & Murphy Glasgow 1976–81, admitted to Faculty of Advocates 1982, temp sheriff 1988–97, sheriff of Glasgow and Strathkelvin 1997–; temp Judge of the High Ct 2004–14, Senator of the College of Justice 2014; memb: Scottish Cncl on Human Bioethics 1995–97, Parole Bd for Scotland 2001– (vice-chair 2005–07), Sentencing Cmmn for Scotland 2004–07, Nat Strategic Advsy Bd on Violence Reduction 2010–; sec Glasgow Bar Assoc until 1981, tutor in advocacy and pleading Univ of Strathclyde until 1982; memb: Scot Assoc for Study of Offending (branch chair Glasgow 2003–14), SACRO, Univ of Glasgow Legal 40 2010–; dir Conforti Inst 2010–; *Recreations* walking, music, opera, theatre, reading, travelling to Italy, gardening, piano; *Style—* The Hon Lady Rae, QC; ✉ Parliament House, Edinburgh EH1 1RQ (☎ 0131 2252595)

RAE, Ronald; *b* 27 September 1946; *Educ* Ayr GS, Edinburgh Coll of Art; *Partner* Pauline MacDonald; *Career* sculptor, granite carver, painter and graphic artist; projects incl: granite sculptures – The Tragic Sacrifice of Christ 1978, Abraham 1981, Return of the Prodigal 1983, O Wert Thou in the Cauld Blast 1984, Man of Sorrows, John the Baptist, Famine, Cutty Stool 1985, The Good Samaritan 1997, St Kilda Wake 1989, Wounded Elephant 1990, Mother and Child 1991, Widow Woman, Insect and Celtic Cross 1992, Sacred Cow, Boy with Calf 1993, Elephant and Rhino, Flight into Egypt, Lazarus 1995, Fallen Christ, Christ the Healer, War Veteran 1997, Dung Beetle, Animals in War Meml, Bear 1998, Elephant and Calf, Tyger Tyger 1999, Wild Boar, Vulture and Carcass, Fish, Bison 2000, Pisces, Ox 2001, Baby Elephant with a Broken Trunk, The Lion of Scotland 2003 (on loan to St Andrew Square Edinburgh 2010–15), Heavy Horse and Foal 2007, Three Elephants 2008, St Francis 2009, Book Illustrations 2009–10, Carving Gorilla granite sculpture 2013–14; FRBS 1998 (memb RBS 1996); *Selected Exhibitions* Maclaurin Art Gall Ayr 1977, Compass Gall Glasgow and 369 Gall Edinburgh 1980, City Art Centre Edinburgh 1982, Open Eye Gall 1986, Glasgow Garden Festival 1988, St John's Church

Edinburgh 1989, Nunnery Square Sheffield 1994, Milton Keynes 1995–99, Royal Museum of Scotland 1996, Regent's Park London 1999–2002, The Jerwood Sculpture Park Witley Court 2000–, The Natural History Museum 2001, Sculpture Exhibition Yorkshire Sculpture Park 2002–06, Compass Gall 2004, Scottish Churches House 2004–05, The Balmaha Bibles 2004–08, Jerwood Sculpture Park Ragley Hall 2005, Sculpture Exhibition Holyrood Park 2006–08, Horse and Highland Cow (Isle of Eriska) 2008–, Sculpture Exhibition The Falkirk Wheel 2008–16, War Veteran (on loan to Campbell Park Milton Keynes 2015) and Animals in War Memorial sculptures (donated to Milton Keynes in memory of Edna Read 2015) 2008, Fallen Christ sculpture (donated to Isle of Iona) 2008, Fish sculpture (Waterfront at Cramond Edinburgh) 2009, Baby Boar sculpture (Aberdeen Airport), Baby Elephant sculpture 2011 (exhibited on the plaza at Edinburgh Airport 2015), Bible Illustrations 2011, Anti-war Poems 2011, Political Cartoons and Illustrated Books 2012–13, St Francis granite sculpture (on loan to Nat Tst for Scotland Threave Gardens) 2012–15 (purchased 2015), Heavy Horse and Foal sculpture (on loan to Scottish Canals on exhibition at Crinan Canal) 2012–15, Ronald Rae Exhibition of Illustrated Bibles and Books (Compass Gallery Glasgow) 2013, Gorilla Family and Baby Elephant (Edinburgh Airport Plaza) 2015, Baby Elephant (West End Edinburgh) 2016; *Books* Ronald Rae Sculpture (1994 and 2002), Ronald Rae Yorkshire Sculpture Park (2002), Ronald Rae at Holyrood Park (2007); *Recreations* writing poetry and philosophy, listening to classical music (guest speaker on BBC Radio 3), playing piano and guitar; *Style—* Ronald Rae, Esq, FRBS; ✉ mobile 07773 482336, e-mail pauline@ronaldrae.co.uk, website www.ronaldrae.co.uk

RAEBURN, James Blair (Jim); OBE (2008); s of James Raeburn (d 2002), of Jedburgh, and Martha, *née* Blair (d 1988); *b* 18 March 1947; *Educ* Hawick HS; *m* 22 June 1974, Rosemary, da of late Robert Bisset; 2 da (Nicola b 3 March 1976, Jill b 12 Nov 1977); *Career* dir: Scot Print Employers Fedn 1984–2007, Scot Newspaper Publishers Assoc 1984–2007, Press Standards Bd of Finance Ltd 1990–2013, Nat Cncl for the Trg of Journalists Ltd 1993–2006, Scot Daily Newspaper Soc 1996–2010, Publishing Nat Trg Orgn 2000–02, Scot Newspaper Soc 2010–12; moderator Soc of High Constables of Edinburgh 2015 and 2016; FCIS; *Clubs* Gullane Golf, Rotary of Portobello (Edinburgh); *Style—* Jim Raeburn, Esq, OBE; ✉ 44 Duddingston Road West, Edinburgh EH15 3PS

RAEBURN, Sheriff Susan Adiel Ogilvie; QC (Scot 1991); da of George Ferguson Raeburn (d 1993), of Aberdeenshire, and Rose Anne Bainbridge, *née* Morison (d 2006); *b* 23 April 1954; *Educ* St Margaret's Sch for Girls Aberdeen, Univ of Edinburgh (LLB); *Career* apprentice Messrs Fyfe Ireland 1974–76, admitted Faculty of Advocates 1977, sheriff of Glasgow and Strathkelvin 1993–2011 (temp sheriff 1988–93), sheriff of Grampian, Highland and Islands 2011–; pt/t chm: Social Security Appeal Tbnls 1985–92, Medical Appeal Tbnls 1992–93; *Recreations* the arts, travel; *Style—* Sheriff S A O Raeburn, QC; ✉ Sheriffs Chambers, Sheriff Court House, Elgin IV30 1BU (☎ 01343 542505)

RAFFAELLI, Surgn Vice Adm Philip Iain; CB (2012); s of Nello Raffaelli (d 1984), and Margaret, *née* Anderson (d 1995); *b* 24 November 1955, Kirkcaldy, Fife; *Educ* Univ of Edinburgh (BSc, MB ChB), LSHTM Univ of London (MSc), JSDC, RCDS; *m* 18 Nov 2006, Fiona Ivy Edwards; 1 s (Paul b 29 June 1978), 2 da (Jenny b 21 Jan 1980, Victoria b 4 Oct 1985); *Career* prof of naval occupational medicine Faculty of Occupational Medicine/ Royal Naval Medical Serv 1997–99, dir of health RN 1999–2002, medical OIC Inst for Naval Medicine 2003–04, chief exec Def Medical Educn and Trg Agency 2004–06; MOD: DG Medical Operational Capability 2006–, Medical DG (Naval) 2007–, Surgeon Gen 2009–12; co-dir Philip Raffaelli Assocs Ltd; memb Advsy Bd Tickets for Troops 2013–; chm AFOM Mgmnt Bd 1999–2002, chief examiner Faculty of Occupational Medicine 2002–05; Hon Physician to HM The Queen 2006; memb Ct of Govrs London Sch of Hygiene and Tropical Medicine 2007, memb Bd of Govrs Univ Hosp of Birmingham Fndn Tst 2010–12; offr Gosport Cons Assoc, borough cncllr Anglesey Ward Gosport 2016–; Eroll-Eldridge Prize 1990, Order of Military Medical Meri US Army 2011; hon fell Assoc of Surgeons of GB and Ireland 2011; MRCGP 1984, FFOM 1997 (MFOM 1989), FRCP 2009; Cdr Order of St John 2012 (Bro 2009); *Recreations* tennis, golf, guitar; *Clubs* RSM; *Style—* Surgn Vice Adm Philip Raffaelli, CB; ✉ Chadwick House, 14 St Mark's Road, Alverstoke, Gosport, Hampshire PO12 2DA

RAFFAN, Mark Thomas; s of Albert Smith Raffan, of Langley, Kent, and Joan, *née* Martin; *b* 18 May 1963; *Educ* Knoll Sch for Boys Hove, Brighton Tech Coll (City & Guilds); *m* 1993, Paula Georgia, da of George Kyriacou, of Limassol, Cyprus; 1 da (Georgia Naomi b 1993), 3 s (Charlie Laithe b 1995, Harry Thomas b 1997, Archie b 2004); *Career* trainee The Eaton Restaurant Hove 1978–81, chef de partie Gravetye Manor Hotel & Country Club 1984–85 (commis chef 1981–83), chef tournant Walper Terrace Hotel Kitchener Ontario Feb-June 1985, chef tournant Le Gavroche London 1985–86, chef Gravetye Manor Hotel 1988–91 (jr sous chef 1986–87, sous chef 1987–88), exec chef The Royal Palaces of HM King Hussein of Jordan 1991–95, head chef and co-prop Gravetye Manor Hotel 1999– (head chef 1995–); memb Acorn Club 1995–96; *Awards* Cookery and Food Assoc Gold Medal, Acorn Award 1990, Egon Ronay 1 star, Michelin star 1998; *Recreations* shooting, the countryside; *Style—* Mark Raffan, Esq; ✉ Gravetye Manor Hotel, Vowels Lane, East Grinstead, West Sussex RH19 4LJ (☎ 01342 810567, fax 01342 810080)

RAFFERTY, Rt Hon Lady Justice; Dame Anne Judith Rafferty; DBE (2000), PC (2011); da of John Rafferty (d 1953), of Lancashire, and Helena, *née* Marchant (d 1987), of Lancashire; *Educ* Wolverhampton Girls' HS, Univ of Sheffield (LLB), Inns of Court Sch of Law; *m* 1977, His Hon Brian Barker, CBE, QC), *qv*, eld s of William Barker; 4 da (Anne Camilla Frances b 11 April 1980, Helen Davina Gillow b 31 Aug 1981 d 5 July 1983, Edwina Mary Gillian b 6 Oct 1983, Felicity Abigail Clare b 5 June 1985); *Career* called to the Bar Gray's Inn 1973, pupillage with late Simon Evans (His Hon Judge Evans) at 4 Brick Court 1974, QC 1990, recorder SE Circuit 1991–, dep High Court judge 1996–, head of chambers 4 Brick Court (now 9 Bedford Row) 1993–2000, judge of the High Court of Justice (Queen's Bench Div) 2000–11, presiding judge SE Circuit 2003–06, a Lord Justice of Appeal 2011–; chm Bd Judicial Coll 2014–; Criminal Bar Assoc: sec 1989–91, vice-chm 1993–95, chm 1995–97; vice-chm Criminal Procedure Rule Ctee 2013–; memb: Pigot Ctee 1988–89, Royal Cmmn on Criminal Justice 1991–93, Sentencing Cncl 2010–12; govr Expert Witness Inst 1996–98; govr St Andrews Prep Sch Eastbourne 1990–2006 (chm 2001–03), memb Cncl Eastbourne Coll 1994–2006, memb Appeal Ct Univ of Oxford 2003–; chllr Univ of Sheffield 2015–; *Recreations* sea swimming; *Clubs* NOBS (E Sussex); *Style—* The Rt Hon the Lady Justice Rafferty, DBE; ✉ Royal Courts of Justice, Strand, London WC2A 2LL (☎ 020 7947 6761, fax 020 7947 6632, e-mail ladyjustice.rafferty@ejudiciary.net)

RAFFERTY, John Campbell; *b* 30 June 1951; *Educ* Edinburgh Acad, Univ of Edinburgh (LLB); *Career* Burness Solicitors (formerly W & J Burness): trainee slr 1973–75, asst slr 1975–77, ptnr 1977–; tutor in taxation Univ of Edinburgh 1973–77; dir F&C Private Equity Tst plc; FSI 1994, MInstD; hon consul for Canada; *Recreations* hill walking, skiing, gardening; *Clubs* New (Edinburgh); *Style—* John Rafferty, Esq; ✉ Burness Solicitors, 50 Lothian Road, Festival Square, Edinburgh EH3 9WJ (☎ 0131 473 6000, fax 0131 473 6006, mobile 07770 236 430)

RAFTERY, Andrew Thomas; s of Andrew Raftery (d 1987), of York, and Nora Maria, *née* Kelly; *b* 29 June 1943; *Educ* St Michael's Jesuit Coll, Univ of Leeds Sch of Med (BSc, MB ChB, MD); *m* 6 Aug 1980, Anne Christine, da of Norman Turnock, of Buxton, Derbys; 1 da (Catherine b 1981), 2 s (Andrew b 1985, Dominic b 1989); *Career* lectr in anatomy Univ of Leeds 1970–73, surgical registrar Yorkshire HA 1974–75, lectr in surgery Univ of Manchester 1976–80, lectr in surgery and hon conslt Univ of Cambridge 1980–83, conslt surgn (gen surgery and transplantation) Sheffield HA 1983–2008; hon teaching fell Hull York Medical Sch 2011–13; external examiner in surgery Univ of Cambridge 1983–2004; examiner Primary FRCS: England 1985–91, Glasgow 1989–; memb Ct of Examiners RCS 1991– (chm Ct of Examiners 1994–97), pres Br Assoc of Clinical Anatomists 1996–2000; RCS: invited memb Cncl 1994–97, memb Cncl 2001–07, chm Med Students Liaison Ctee 2004–07, vice-chm Patient Liaison Gp 2004–07; S Yorks Medico-Legal Soc: memb Ctee 2011–, vice-pres 2013–15, pres 2015–16; pres Sheffield Medico-Chirurgical Soc 2009–10; numerous contribs to books and jls; actor 2008–; stage roles: Confessions of a City, Enemy of the People, Alice, Lives in Art, Twenty Tiny Plays About Sheffield; several short films with Sheffield Hallam Univ; FRCS; A Pocketbook of Surgery (2006), Basic Science for the MRCS (2006), Applied Basic Science for Basic Surgical training (2008), A Pocketbook of Differential Diagnosis; *Recreations* horse racing, theatre, watercolour painting, after-dinner speaking; *Style—* Andrew Raftery, Esq; ✉ Carnbrea, 280 Ecclesall Road South, Sheffield S11 9PS

RAGGATT, Timothy Walter Harold; QC (1993); s of Walter George Raggatt (d 1976), and Norah Margaret Raggatt (d 1987), of Redditch, Hereford and Worcester; *b* 13 April 1950; *Educ* Redditch Co HS, King's Coll London (LLB); *m* 1991, Carol Marion, da of Wilfred Carl Overton; *Career* called to the Bar Inner Temple 1972 (bencher 1999); tutor Inns of Court Sch of Law 1972–73, pupillage 3 Fountain Court Birmingham 1973–74, recorder of the Crown Court 1994– (asst recorder 1991); memb Midland & Oxford Circuit 1974–; *Recreations* golf, bridge, scuba diving; *Clubs* Athenaeum, RAC, Blackwell Golf; *Style—* Timothy Raggatt, Esq, QC; ✉ 4 King's Bench Walk, Temple, London EC4Y 7DL (☎ 020 7353 3581, fax 020 7583 2257)

RAI, Dr Gurcharan Singh; s of Gurdev Singh Rai, of London, and Kartar Kaur Rai; *b* 30 July 1947; *Educ* Tollington GS London, Univ of Newcastle upon Tyne (MB BS, MD), Univ of London (MSc); *m* 8 Nov 1977, Harsha, da of Shri Lal Bhatia (d 1980), of India; 2 s (Sandeep b 30 Sept 1978, Gurdeep b 18 Nov 1981); *Career* house offr Nottingham Gen Hosp 1971–72, registrar in med Newcastle Univ Hosp 1974–76 (SHO 1972–73), sr res assoc Univ of Newcastle upon Tyne 1976–78, sr registrar in geriatric med Chesterton Hosp Cambridge 1978–80; conslt physician: Whittington Hosp 1980–, Royal Northern Hosp 1980–; sr lectr UC Med Sch 1980–; prof in geriatric med Univ of Nijmegen The Netherlands 1991–92; chm Regnl Advsy Cmmn Geriatric Med NE Thames Region; fell American Geriatrics Soc, memb Br Geriatrics Soc; FRSM (pres Section of Geriatrics and Gerontology 2006), FRCP 1988; *Books* Databook on Geriatrics (1980), Case Presentations in Clinical Geriatric Medicine (1987), Manual of Geriatric Medicine (1991), Multimedia Postgraduate Medicine (1998, 2 edn 2000), Medical Ethics and the Elderly (1999, 4 edn 2014), Elderly Care Medicine (2000), Elderly Medicine – A Training Guide (2002, 2nd edn 2007), Revision for MRCP Part 2: Clinical Long Cases (2003), Revision for MRCP Part 2: Data Interpretation (2003), Managing Cardiovascular Disease in the Elderly (2003), Essential Facts in Geriatric Medicine (2005, 2 edn 2010), Shared Care of Older People (2006), The Biology of Ageing and its Clinical Implications (2013); *Recreations* chess, stamp collecting; *Style—* Dr Gurcharan Rai; ✉ Care of Older People, Whittington Hospital, Magdala Avenue, London N19 5NF (☎ 020 7288 5326)

RAILTON, David; QC (1996); s of Andrew Scott Railton, and Margaret Elizabeth, *née* Armit; *b* 5 June 1957; *Educ* Balliol Coll Oxford; *m* 1996, Sinéad Major; 1 s (b 12 Nov 1998), 1 da (b 24 Jan 2002); *Career* called to the Bar Gray's Inn 1979 (bencher 2005), recorder 2000, dep judge of the High Ct of Justice 2013–; *Recreations* cricket, golf; *Style—* David Railton, Esq, QC; ✉ Fountain Court Chambers, Temple, London EC4Y 9DH (☎ 020 7583 3335)

RAINE, Craig Anthony; s of Norman Edward Raine, and Olive Marie Raine, *née* Cheesbrough; *b* 3 December 1944; *Educ* Barnard Castle Sch, Exeter Coll Oxford; *m* 1972, Elisabeth Ann Isabel, da of Dr Eliot Slater, OBE (d 1982); 1 da (Nina b 1975), 3 s (Isaac b 1979, Moses b 1984, Vaska b 1987); *Career* poet; emeritus fell New Coll Oxford 2010–, ed Areté magazine; FRSL 1984; *Publications* The Onion Memory (1978), A Martian Sends A Postcard Home (1979), Rich (1984), The Electrification of the Soviet Union (1986), A Choice of Kipling's Prose (ed, 1987), '1953' (1990, staged at Citizens' Theatre Glasgow 1992 and Almeida Theatre 1996), Haydn and the Valve Trumpet (1990), Rudyard Kipling: Selected Poetry (ed, 1992), History: The Home Movie (1994), Clay. Whereabouts Unknown (1996), A la recherche du temps perdu (2000), In Defence of T S Eliot (2000), Collected Poems 1978–1999 (2000), T S Eliot (2006), Heartbreak (novel, 2010), How Snow Falls (poems, 2010), The Divine Comedy (novel, 2012), More Dynamite (essays, 2013), My Grandmother's Glass Eye: A Look at Poetry (2016); *Recreations* music, skiing; *Style—* Craig Raine, Esq, FRSL; ✉ New College, Oxford OX1 3BN

RAINE, George Edward Thompson; s of Dr Reginald Thompson Raine, MC (and bar) (d 1960), of Stocksfield, Northumberland, and Mary Dorothy Raine; *b* 1 August 1934; *Educ* Rugby, Emmanuel Coll Cambridge (MA), St Thomas' Hosp Med Sch (MB BChir); *m* 11 June 1960, Ena Josephine, da of Joseph Noble; 1 da (Meriel b 1965); *Career* sr conslt orthopaedic surgn W Middlesex Univ Hosp 1974–96; orthopaedic surgn Royal Masonic Hosp London 1987–97, orthopaedic surgn to Brunel Univ Coll Sports and Dance Injuries Clinic; orthopaedic surgn to: Brentford FC 1987–97, Crystal Palace FC, various sporting bodies; formerly sr orthopaedic registrar: St George's Hosp London, Rowley Bristow Orthopaedic Hosp Pyrford Surrey, Centre for Hip Surgery Wrightington; former govr The Lady Eleanor Holles' Sch Hampton; vice-pres BackCare (formerly the Nat Back Pain Assoc); former examiner Chartered Soc of Physiotherapy; memb: Br Orthopaedic Sports Trauma Assoc, Expert Witness Inst; Freeman City of London 1987; fell British Orthopaedic Assoc, FRCS; *Recreations* English Lake District, foreign travel; *Clubs* Whitefriars, Athenaeum; *Style—* George E T Raine, Esq; ✉ Pelham's View, 32 Pelhams Walk, Esher, Surrey KT10 8QD (☎ 01372 466656, e-mail georgeraine32@gmail.com)

RAINE, Dr June Munro; CBE (2009); da of David Harris, of Saffron Walden, Essex, and Isobel *née* Munro; *b* 20 June 1952; *Educ* Herts and Essex HS Bishop's Stortford (Ashdown scholarship), Somerville Coll Oxford (Alice Horsman travelling fellowship, BA, MSc), Univ of Oxford Medical Sch (MRC postgraduate scholarship, BM BCh); *m* 18 Oct 1975, Anthony Evan Gerald (d 1995), s of John Wellesley Evan Raine, OBE; 1 s (Charles b 1984), 1 da (Juliet b 1986); *Career* sr med offr Medicines Div Dept of Health 1985–89; gp mngr Medicines Control Agency 1989–98; formerly dir Post-Licensing Div Medicines Control Agency, currently dir of vigilance and risk mgmnt of medicines Medicines and Healthcare Products Regulatory Agency (MHRA); princ assessor Medicines Cmmn 1992–; memb DTI Foresight Healthcare Task Force (Public and Patients) 1999–2000, memb various working gps of EC on aspects of pharmaceutical regulation; author various publications on pharmacology, adverse drug effects and regulation of medicines; FRSM, FRCPEd 1995, MRCP, MRCGP, MFPHM; *Recreations* music, opera, travel, skiing; *Style—* Dr June Raine, CBE; ✉ MHRA, 1 Buckingham Palace Road, London SW1W 9SZ

RAINES, Dr Catherine Lindsay; da of Kenneth William John Raines, of Leics, and Hilary Wynne, *née* Smith (d 1980); *b* 11 March 1963, Lichfield, Staffs; *Educ* Univ of London (BPharm, PhD); *Children* 2 s (Angus William Kirkby b 9 Feb 1996, Calum Patrick Kirkby b 6 Dec 1998); *Career* 25 years in international pharma, most recently: global head of supply chain and vice pres Corp Devpt (China) AstraZeneca, dep chief exec and dir of place Staffs CC until 2013, min and DG UK Trade and Investment China 2013–15, chief exec UK Trade and Investment 2015–; memb Royal Pharmaceutical Soc; FRSA; *Recreations* opera, reading, theatre and the visual arts; *Style—* Dr Catherine Raines; ✉ c/o Carl Ridgers (assistant), UKTI, 1 Victoria Street, London SW1H 0ET (e-mail chiefexecutive@ukti.gsi.gov.uk)

RAINGOLD, Gerald Barry; s of Henry Raingold (d 1979), of London, and Frances Raingold (d 1992); *b* 25 March 1943; *Educ* St Paul's, Inst of Chartered Accountants, London Grad Sch of Business Studies (MBA); *m* 12 July 1978, Aviva, da of Henry Petrie (d 1962), of London; 2 da (Nina b 2 Aug 1979, Karen b 23 July 1983), 1 s (Andrew b 18 Sept 1981); *Career* articled clerk then chartered accountant Cole Dickin & Hills 1963–68, Cooper Bros 1968–72 (mangr 1972), sr mangr corporate fin Wallace Brothers Bank 1972–76, sr conslt Midland Montagu Gp 1976–78, dep md Banque Paribas London 1978–95 (formerly mangr, sr mangr, asst gen mangr), chm Dawnay Day Corporate Finance Ltd 1995–, dep chm Dawnay Day Investment Bank 2008; non-exec dir: Pinnacle Insurance Gp plc, Simmons Bedding Gp plc, I Point Media plc, Hartfield Securities plc; memb: London Business Sch Alumni, City Ctee Inst of Mgmnt 1980–83, IOD City Branch, RIIA, Bus Graduates Assoc; Sloan fell MSc Prog London Business Sch; Freeman City of London 1987; FCA 1968, FInstD 1987, FRSA 1993; *Recreations* opera, ballet, tennis, reading; *Clubs* MCC, Naval; *Style—* Gerald Raingold, Esq; ✉ 12 Marston Close, London NW6 4EU (☎ 020 7328 5800, fax 020 7328 0286); Dawnay Day & Co Ltd, 10 Grosvenor Gardens, London SW1W 0DH (☎ 020 7630 4140, fax 020 7630 4141, mobile 07798 915511, e-mail gerald.raingold@dawnayday.com)

RAJA RAYAN, Raj Kumar; OBE (1999); s of Ramanathan Chelvarayan Raja Rayan, of Ceylon, and Lingamani, da of Prof C Suntharalingam; *b* 6 April 1953; *Educ* Harrow, Guy's Hosp Dental Sch (BDS), Eastman Dental Hosp (MSc); *m* Ahila, da of Sanmugam Arumugam, of Ceylon; 1 da (Dipa Lakshmi b 3 Nov 1980), 2 s (Darshan Kumar b 3 Aug 1982, Ravi Kumar b 11 Dec 1987); *Career* currently: dean Faculty of Gen Dental Practitioners UK, dean Royal Coll of Surgeons of England, practice Harley St, dir of primary dental care Eastman Dental Inst of Oral Health Scis (former dir Bd of Mgmnt); former assoc advsr Br Postgrad Med Fndn, accredited teacher Univ of London; emeritus examiner RCS for memb in Gen Dental Surgery; former examiner RCS for Diploma in Gen Dental Practice, fellowship examiner Examining Bd for Dental Surgery Assts; past pres Br Soc for General Dental Surgery; former chm Inst of Transcultural Oral Health, former chm of examinations Faculty of Gen Dental Practitioners UK (also former vice-dean); elected memb Gen Dental Cncl; former memb Conf of UK Advsrs NW Thames, past pres Anglo Asian Odontological Gp, fndr Central London MGDS Study Gp; Cottrell Award 1990, Ahmed Oration Indian Dental Assoc 1991, various nat and int lectures; life memb: Nat Autistic Soc, Music Acad of India, Int Inst of Tamil Studies, Judicial Appointments Ctee, Exec Ctee of Dentists Provident Soc (Friendly Soc); hon life memb: General Dental Practitioners Assoc, Anglo-Asian Odontological Gp, Indian Dental Assoc, Sri Lanka Dental Assoc; former memb: Lord Chllr's Advsy Ctee on JPs, Standing Advsy Ctee to Sec of State for Health; hon fell: Int Coll of Dentists, Pierre Fanchard Acad (former UK chm), FFGDP (UK), FDS RCS, LDS RCS, MGDS RCS, MRD RCS, RCPS, DRD RCS; *Books* Self Assessment Manual and Standards (manual of clinical standards in dental practice, contrib 1991), Path Ways in Practice (distance learning manual in dental practice, contrib 1993), Dentists Patients & Minorities – Towards the new Millennium (co-ed); Selection Criteria for Dental Radiography (RCS publication), Practical Dentistry – Dentistry Jl (ed-in-chief), MGDS Compendium; contributions to numerous learned jls (specialist in Restorative Dentistry); *Recreations* cricket, chess, bridge, golf; *Clubs* MCC, Magpies Cricket; *Style—* Raj K Raja Rayan, Esq, OBE; ✉ 46 Harley Street, London W1N 1AD (☎ and fax 020 7631 5213)

RAJAGOPAL, Dr Krishnamurthy (Raj); *Educ* IIT Madras (BTech), UMIST (MSc), Univ of Manchester (PhD); *m*; 2 c; *Career* BOC Group plc: various ops positions Edwards 1981–93, md Edwards Vacuum Equipment 1993–95, md Vacuum Technology Div 1995–97, chief exec BOC Edwards 1997–2006, exec dir BOC Group plc 2000–06; non-exec dir: FSI Int, Dyson Gp plc, WS Atkins plc 2008–; memb Cncl of Sci and Technol; IEE Gold Medal 2003; CEng, FIMechE, FIEE, FCMI, FREng; *Recreations* squash, golf; *Style—* Dr K Rajagopal

RAJAN, Amol; *b* 4 July 1983, Calcutta, India; *Educ* Graveney Sch London, Downing Coll Cambridge; *Career* ed The Independent 2013– (joined 2007); *Style—* Amol Rajan, Esq; ✉ The Independent, Northcliffe House, 2 Derry Street, London W8 5HF

RAJANI, Shashi Haridas; s of Haridas Savji Rajani (d 1989), and Gomtiben, *née* Suchak; *b* 24 May 1934; *Educ* HR Meml Central Sch Tabora Tanzania, Govt Secdy Sch Dar es Salaam Tanzania; *m* Chandrika (Sandra), da of Gordhandas Tulshidas Modi; 3 da (Rita b 24 June 1961, Priya b 13 March 1967, Nina Karen b 18 April 1973); *Career* called to the Bar Lincoln's Inn 1955, admitted slr 1975; advocate Tanzania 1956–70: in private practice 1956–64, asst then sr asst administrator-gen (incl official receiver in bankruptcies and company liquidations and several other statutory positions) Govt of Tanzania 1964–70, public prosecutor for bankruptcy offences 1964–70, public prosecutor for company law offences 1965–70, state attorney (criminal prosecutions and appeals) 1967–70, legal conslt Nat Bank of Commerce 1968–70; mangr Insolvency Dept Coopers & Lybrand CAs London 1970–76, sr asst slr Linklaters & Paines London 1977–88, sr asst slr Cameron Markby London 1988, ptnr Cameron Markby Hewitt 1989–93, ptnr and head Corp Rescue and Insolvency Gp Nicholson Graham & Jones 1994–2002, ptnr and head Business Recovery Gp Davies Arnold Cooper 2002–04, ptnr Moon Beever 2005–06, conslt Africa Legal Network 2007–10, conslt PKP French Slrs 2007–10, princ S H Rajani & Co 2008–10; licensed insolvency practitioner 1986; memb: Tanzania Law Soc 1956–70 (memb Cncl 1963–64), Law Soc 1976–2010 (chief insolvency assessor 2000–05, insolvency assessor 2006–10), City of London Law Soc 1984–2006 (memb Insolvency Law Sub-Ctee 1991–2006, dep chm 1995–98), INSOL Europe (formerly Euro Assoc of Insolvency Practitioners) 1980–2006, Insol Int 1980–, Insolvency Lawyers' Assoc 1990–99 (memb Cncl 1992–97), Soc of Practitioners in Insolvency (now Assoc of Business Recovery Professionals R3) 1991–2010 (memb Membership Ctee 1997–2003, memb Panel of Assessors 2003–10), Soc of English and American Lawyers 1992–95, Candlewick Ward Club 1998–2002, Admission, Licensing and Disciplinary and Appeal Ctees Assoc of Chartered Certified Accountants 2000–02 (memb Panel of Assessors 2003–), Soc of Asian Lawyers 2002–10 (chm Advsy Bd 2004–06); visiting prof London Guildhall Univ 1992–2010; pres of Hindu community in Dar es Salaam 1964–68; Freeman City of London 1984; Freeman City of London Solicitors' Co 1984–2007; *Publications* Tolley's Corporate Insolvency Handbook (1991), Tolley's Company Law (contrib insolvency and other chapters, 1983–), Insolvency Law & Practice (jl, chief ed 1989–), Tolley's Corporate Insolvency (1994), Tolley's Insolvency Law (looseleaf jt conslt ed 1996–), Tolley's Insolvency Costs & Fees (compiler, 1996–); *Recreations* tennis, table tennis, badminton, chess, music (electronic organ), snooker; *Style—* Shashi Rajani, Esq; ✉ Tudor Heights, Mill Lane, Broxborough, Hertfordshire EN10 7AZ (☎ 01992 466806, fax 01992 460707, mobile 07890 607577, e-mail shashirajani@hotmail.com)

RAKE, Sir Michael Derek Vaughan; kt (2007); s of Derek Shannon Vaughan Rake, and Rosamund, *née* Barrett; *b* 17 January 1948; *Educ* Wellington Coll; *m* 1 (m dis), Julia, *née* Cook; 3 s (Matthew b 5 Dec 1972, Jamie b 12 March 1974, Piers b 19 Dec 1976); m 2, Caroline, *née* Thomas; 1 s (Ashley b 1 July 1985); *Career* Turquands Barton Mayhew London and Brussels 1968–74; KPMG: joined Brussels 1974, ptnr 1979, ptnr i/c audit Belgium and Luxembourg 1983–86, resident sr ptnr Middle East 1986–89, ptnr London 1989–2007, memb UK Bd 1991–2006 (chm 1998–2006), sr ptnr KPMG UK 1998–2006, chm KPMG Europe 1999–2002, chm KPMG Int 2002–07; chm: BT Gp plc 2007–, easyjet 2010–13, Worldpay 2015–; memb Bd Barclays Gp plc 2008–16 (dep chm 2012–), memb Bd McGraw Hill Inc 2007–; chm BitC (Business in the Community) 2004–07, chair UK Cmmn for Employment and Skills 2007–10, chm Int Chamber of Commerce UK 2015–; memb: Bd Prince of Wales Int Business Leaders Forum 1999–2007, Bd Transatlantic Business Dialogue 2004–, Bd Business for New Europe 2006–, Int Business Cncl of World Economic Forum 2008–13, DTI Task Force on US/UK Regulation 2006–09, Oxford Univ Global Advsy Bd 2007–, BVCA Guidelines Monitoring Gp 2008–13; dir Financial Reporting Cncl 2008–11; sr advsr Chatham House 2008–, pres CBI 2013–; vice-pres RNIB 2003–, tstee Prince's Charities Fndn 2011–16; chair of govrs Wellington Coll 2007–16; William Pitt fell Pembroke Coll Cambridge 2010–, fell City & Guilds 2012; ICAEW, FCA 1970; *Recreations* tennis, skiing; *Style—* Sir Michael Rake

RALLS, His Hon Judge Peter John Henry; QC (1997); s of Ivan Jack Douglas Ralls, and Sybil Gladys White, *née* Child; *b* 18 July 1947; *Educ* Royal Russell Sch Surrey, UCL; *m* 1, 1978 (m dis), Anne Elizabeth, *née* Marriott; m 2, 1997, Tonia Anne, *née* Clarke; 1 da (Emily Catherine Louise b 1997), 2 s (Jonathan Jack Edward b 1998, Thomas William Randolph b 2001); *Career* VSO Swaziland 1965; called to the Bar Middle Temple 1972, former head of chambers 29 Bedford Row, asst recorder 1998–2000, recorder 2000–08, circuit judge (Western Circuit) 2008–; *Recreations* yacht racing, cricket (chm Cowes Combined Clubs); *Clubs* MCC, Royal London Yacht (Cowes, Cdre 1998), Royal Yacht Sqdn, Brooks's; *Style—* His Hon Judge Ralls, QC

RALPH, Prof Brian; s of Reginald James (d 1960), and Gwenthellian Anne, *née* Thomas (d 1990); *b* 4 August 1939; *Educ* City of Norwich Sch, Jesus Coll Cambridge (BA, MA, PhD, ScD); *m* 22 June 1961, Anne Mary, da of Leslie Ernest Perry, of Bath; 1 da (Zoanna); *Career* lectr Dept of Metallurgy and Material Sci Univ of Cambridge 1966–83 (demonstrator 1964–66, fell and tutor Jesus Coll 1964–83); prof and head Dept of Metallurgy and Material Sci Univ Coll Cardiff 1984–87, prof and head Dept of Materials Technol Brunel Univ 1987–93 (dean of technol 1991–96); hon prof Warsaw Univ of Technol 1994; co-ed over forty res monographs in the field of microscopy and physical metallurgy; Hon DEng Hanyang Univ S Korea 2006; FIM, FInstP, Hon FRMS, CEng, CSci, CPhys, Eur Ing; *Recreations* sailing, woodwork, music; *Clubs* Cardiff and County; *Style—* Prof Brian Ralph; ✉ Ty Carrog, St Brides-Super-Ely, Cardiff CF5 6EY (☎ 01446 760469); School of Engineering and Design, Brunel, The University of West London, Uxbridge, Middlesex UB8 3HP (☎ 01895 274000, fax 01985 203205, e-mail brian.ralph@brunel.ac.uk)

RALSTON, Dr Stuart Hamilton; *b* 24 October 1955; *Educ* Allan Glen's Sch Glasgow, Univ of Glasgow (MB ChB, MD); *Career* jr house offr Glasgow Royal Infirmary 1978–79, SHO Falkirk and Dist Royal Infirmary 1979–80, SHO Aberdeen Teaching Hosps 1980–81, registrar in gen med Glasgow Royal Infirmary 1981–84 (sr registrar 1984–86), sr registrar in gen med and rheumatology Southern Gen Hosp 1986–87, sr registrar in rheumatology Centre for Rheumatic Disease Glasgow Royal Infirmary 1987–89, locum conslt physician Stobhill Hosp Glasgow 1989, Wellcome sr research fell in clinical science and hon conslt physician Molecular Immunology Gp Rheumatic Diseases Unit Northern Gen Hosp Edinburgh then transferred to Univ Dept of Orthopaedic Surgery Western Infirmary Glasgow 1989–91, currently dir Inst of Med Sciences Univ of Aberdeen, prof of med and bone metabolism Dept of Med and Therapeutics Univ of Aberdeen Med Sch and hon conslt physician Aberdeen Royal Hosps NHS Tst (sr lectr and hon conslt physician 1991–94, reader 1994–); sec Area Ctee of Physicians Aberdeen Hosps 1997–99 (asst sec 1995–97), memb Med Receiving Unit Planning Gp Aberdeen Royal Hosps NHS Tst 1997–99; memb: Hip Fracture Working Pty RCPEd 1990–91, Oliver Bird Ctee for Research into Rheumatism Nuffield Fndn 1992–97, Research Sub-Ctee Arthritis Research Campaign 1995–99 and 2003–, Heberden Ctee Br Soc of Rheumatology 1997–2001, Older People's Research Grants Ctee PPP Healthcare Med Tst 1999–2002, Bd Int Bone and Mineral Soc 2001–, Ctee for Safety of Meds 2002– (memb Biologicals Sub-Ctee 1998–2002), Physiology and Pharmacology Panel Wellcome Tst 2002–, MRC: memb Molecular and Cellular Med Bd Grants Ctee A 1995–97, memb Molecular and Cellular Med Bd 1998–99, memb Physiological Med and Infections Bd 1999–2002; scientific advsr: Nat Assoc for Relief of Paget's Disease 1997–, Nat Osteoporosis Soc 1997–; examiner RCPEd 1996–; chm of organising ctees of various int confs and symposia; ed-in-chief Calcified Tissue Int 2000–, section ed European Jl of Endocrinology 1998–; Prix Osteofluor European 1986, Fitzgerald-Peel Prize Scottish Soc of Physicians 1986, Alexander Fletcher Prize and lectr RCPGlas 1987, Michael Mason Prize Br Soc of Rheumatology 1997, Paget Fndn Research Award 1999, Boy Frame Meml lectr Henry Ford Hosp Detroit 2002, Goodall Meml lectr RCPGlas 2002; pres: European Calcified Tissues Soc 1997–, UK Bone and Tooth Soc 1998–99 (memb Ctee 1992–94); memb: Royal Medico-Chirurgical Soc of Glasgow 1979–, Scottish Soc for Experimental Med 1982–, Br Soc for Rheumatology 1989–, Scottish Soc of Physicians 1990–, Soc for Endocrinology 1994–, Assoc of Physicians 1996–; MRCP 1980, FRCPGlas 1991, FRCPEd 1994, FMedSci 1999, FRSE 2005; *Style—* Dr Stuart Ralston; ✉ Molecular Medicine Centre, University of Edinburgh, Western General Hospital, Edinburgh EH4 2XU (☎ 0131 651 1037, fax 0131 651 1085)

RAMIREZ, Dr Janina; *Educ* St Anne's Coll Oxford, Univ of York (PhD); *Career* art historian; course dir Dept for Continuing Educn Univ of Oxford 2012–; television presenter: Treasures of the Anglo-Saxons (BBC 4) 2010, The Viking Sagas (BBC 4) 2011, Britain's Most Fragile Treasure (BBC 4) 2011, Illuminations: The Private Lives of Medieval Kings (BBC 4) 2012, Chivalry and Betrayal: The Hundred Years' War (BBC 4) 2013, Art of the Viking (BBC 4) 2013; *Style—* Dr Janina Ramirez; ✉ website www.janinaramirez.co.uk, Twitter @drjaninaramirez; c/o United Agents, 12–26 Lexington Street, London W1F 0LE

R

RAMPLING, Charlotte Tessa; OBE (2001); *b* 5 February 1946, Sturmer; *Career* actress; Hon Cesar for Career 2001; Chevalier de l'Ordre des Arts et des Lettres (France) 1990, Chevalier de la Legion d'Honneur 2002; *Films* incl: Rotten to the Core 1965, Georgy Girl 1966, The Long Duel 1967, The Damned 1969, Three 1969, How to Make it 1969, Tis Pity She's a Whore 1971, The Ski Bum 1971, Corky 1972, Asylum 1972, Henry VIII and his Six Wives 1973, Giordano Bruno 1973, Caravan to Vaccares 1974, Zardoz 1974, The Night Porter 1974, Flesh And The Orchard 1974, Yuppi Du 1975, Foxtrot 1975, Farewell my Lovely 1975, Sherlock Holmes in New York 1976, Orca the Killer Whale 1977, The Purple Taxi 1977, Stardust Memories 1980, The Verdict 1982, Infidelities 1983, Viva La Vie! 1984, He Died with his Eyes Open 1985, Sadness and Beauty 1985, Max my Love 1986, Mascara 1987, Angel Heart 1987, DOA 1988, Paris By Night 1988, Frames From the Edge 1989, Rebus 1989, Hammers Over the Anvil 1991, La Femme Abandonnée 1992, The Radetsky March 1993, Time is Money 1994, Murder in Mind 1994, Samson Le Magnifique 1995, Asphalt Tango 1996, Invasion of Privacy 1996, La Denière Fete 1996, The Wings of the Dove 1997, Great Expectations 1999, The Cherry Orchard 1999, Signs and Wonders 2000, Aberdeen 2000, Under the Sand 2000, The Fourth Angel 2001, Superstition 2001, Spy Game 2001, Summer Things 2003, I'll Sleep When I'm Dead 2003, Swimming Pool 2003, The Statement 2003, Immortal (Ad Vitam) 2004, Jerusalemski sindrom 2004, Le Chiavi di casa 2004, Vers le sud 2004, Basic Instict 2 2006, Babylon AD 2008, The Duchess 2008, Boogie Woogie 2009, Never Let Me Go 2010, 45 Years 2015; *Style—* Ms Charlotte Rampling, OBE

RAMPTON, (Anthony) James Matthew; s of John Richard Anthony Rampton, QC, of London, and Carolyn Mary, *née* Clarke; *b* 22 May 1964; *Educ* St Paul's, Davidson Coll NC (scholar), Exeter Coll Oxford (BA); *m* 1992, Mary Anne Howlett Jones; 3 da (Helen Catherine, Emma Sarah, Catherine Rachel); *Career* dep film ed (listings) The Independent 1988–89, TV writer The Independent on Sunday 1990–93, contributing features ed The Independent 1993–95, freelance feature writer 1995–; *Recreations* rugby, cricket; *Style—* James Rampton, Esq; ✉ c/o The Independent (☎ 020 7005 2000)

RAMROOP, Andrew Madan; OBE; s of Shunnin Ramroop (d 1995), and Baby Ramkissoon (d 2015); *b* 10 November 1952, Tunapuna, Trinidad, W Indies; *Educ* London Coll of Fashion; *Children* 1 s (David A Ramroop b 1 Feb 1975), 1 da (Mrs Marsha O'Sullivan b 16 May 1976); *Career* tailor; md Maurice Sedwell; princ Savile Row Acad; Mayor of London Trailblazer Award, Excellence Award London Development Agency, Nat Training Award 2007, Prof for Distinction in the Field of Tailoring Univ of the Arts London; *Recreations* cricket, fashion, walking, bicycle riding; *Style*— Andrew Ramroop, Esq, OBE; ✉ Maurice Sedwell, 19 Savile Row, London W1S 3PP (☎ 020 7734 0824, e-mail mauricesedwell@btclick.com, website www.savilerowtailor.com)

RAMSAY, Andrew Charles Bruce; CB (2007); s of Norman Bruce Ramsay (d 1952), and Marysha Octavia, *née* Skrynska (d 1960); *b* 30 May 1951; *Educ* Winchester, Univ of London (BA); *m* 9 July 1983, Katharine Celia, da of David Marsh; 2 da (Isobel Daisy b 22 Dec 1985, Octavia Beatrice b 5 July 1988); *Career* HM Civil Service: joined DOE and Dept of Tport 1974, private sec to jr min for Tport 1978–80, princ DOE and Dept of Tport 1980–85, asst sec DOE 1986–93, under sec and head Arts, Sport and Lottery Gp Dept of National Heritage 1993–96, head Corporate Services Gp 1996–2000, DG Creative Industries Broadcasting, Gambling and Lottery Gp DCMS (formerly Dept of National Heritage) 2000–06, DG Culture, Creativity and Economy Gp DCMS 2006–08, latterly DG Partnerships and Progs Gp DCMS; *Recreations* gardening, opera, birds; *Style*— Andrew Ramsay, Esq, CB

RAMSAY, Maj-Gen Charles Alexander; CB (1989), OBE (1979); s of Adm Sir Bertram Home Ramsay, KCB, KBE, MVO (Allied Naval C in C Invasion of Europe 1944, kas 1945), and Helen Margaret Menzies (d 1993); descended from Sir Alexander Ramsay, 2 Bt of Balmain, Kincardineshire; *b* 12 October 1936; *Educ* Eton, Sandhurst; *m* 1967, Hon Mary, da of 1 Baron MacAndrew, TD, PC (d 1979); 2 s, 2 da; *Career* cmmnd Royal Scots Greys 1956, Staff Coll, Canada 1967–68, cmd Royal Scots Dragoon Gds 1977–79, Cdr 12 Armd Bde and Osnabruck Garrison 1980–82, dep DMO MOD 1983–84, GOC Eastern Dist 1984–87; dir gen TA and Army Orgn 1987–89, resigned from Army 1989; chm: Eagle Enterprises Ltd (Bermuda) 1990–95, The Wine Co (Scotland) Ltd 1991–93, Cockburns of Leith Ltd 1993–2004; dir: John Menzies plc 1990–2004, Potomac Holdings Inc (USA) 1990–2005, Edinburgh Military Tattoo Ltd 1991–2007, Grey Horse Properties Ltd 1991–2012, Morningside Management llc (USA) 1993–2004; Col The Royal Scots Dragoon Gds 1992–98; memb Queen's Body Guard for Scotland (Royal Co of Archers); *Recreations* field sports, horse racing, country affrs, travel; *Clubs* Boodle's, Cavalry and Guards', New (Edinburgh), Pratt's; *Style*— Maj-Gen C A Ramsay, CB, OBE; ✉ Pittlesheugh, Greenlaw, Berwickshire TD10 6UL

RAMSAY, Gordon James; OBE (2006); *b* 8 November 1966, Glasgow; *Educ* Oxford Tech Coll; *m* Cayetana Elizabeth (Tana), da of Chris Hutcheson; 4 c (Megan, Jack (twin), Holly (twin), Matilda); *Career* apprentice footballer Glasgow Rangers FC until 1983; hotel and catering mgmnt course Oxford Tech Coll 1983–85; chef: Mayfair Intercontinental Hotel (under Michael Coker) 1985, Harvey's Restaurant London (under Marco Pierre White) 1985–87, Le Gavroche Restaurant London 1987–89, Hotel Diva Isola 2000 South of France (under Albert Roux) 1989–91, kitchens of Guy Savoy Paris 1991–93, Le Jamin Restaurant Paris (under Joel Robuchon) 1993, chef/proprietor Aubergine Restaurant Chelsea 1993–98 (1 Michelin star 1995 rising to 2 Michelin stars 1997–2009), chef and jt prop Gordon Ramsay Holdings Ltd 1997– (restaurants incl: Gordon Ramsay 1998– (2 Michelin stars 1999, 3 Michelin stars 2001), Pêtrus 1999– (1 Michelin star 1999, 2 Michelin stars 2007), Gordon Ramsay at Claridge's 2001– (1 Michelin star 2003–09), Verre at Hilton Dubai Creek 2001–, Angela Hartnett at the Connaught 2002–07 (1 Michelin star 2004), The Savoy Grill 2003– (1 Michelin star 2004), Boxwood Café 2004–, Maze 2005– (1 Michelin star 2006), Gordon Ramsay at The Conrad Tokyo 2005– (1 Michelin star 2008), La Noisette 2006–08 (1 Michelin star 2007), Gordon Ramsay at The London NY 2006–, The Narrow 2007–, The Devonshire 2007–10, The Warrington 2008–, Maze Grill 2008–, Murano 2008– (1 Michelin star 2009), York & Albany 2008–, Gordon Ramsay au Trianon 2008– (2 Michelin stars 2009), Gordon Ramsay at the London West Hollywood 2008– (1 Michelin star 2009)); Chef of the Year Catey Awards 2000 and 2006 (Newcomer of the Year 1995), numerous other awards, restaurants awarded top ratings in pubns incl Zagat, Harden's Guide and Good Food Guide; *Television* Ramsay's Kitchen Nightmares (Channel 4) 2004– (BAFTA Award), Hell's Kitchen (ITV) 2004 and (Fox US) 2005–, The F-Word (Channel 4) 2005–08, Cookalong Live (Channel 4) 2008; *Books* Passion for Flavour (1996), Passion for Seafood (1999), A Chef for all Seasons (2000), Just Desserts (2001), Secrets (2003), Gordon Ramsay Kitchen Heaven (2004), Gordon Ramsay Makes it Easy (2005), Gordon Ramsay's Sunday Lunch and Other Recipes from the F-Word (2006), Humble Pie (autobiography, 2006), Gordon Ramsay's Fast Food (2007), Gordon Ramsay's Playing with Fire (2007), Gordon Ramsay 3 Star Chef (2007), Gordon Ramsay's Healthy Appetite (2008), Gordon Ramsay Cooking for Friends (2008), Gordon Ramsay's Great British Pub Food (2009); *Style*— Gordon Ramsay, Esq, OBE; ✉ Gordon Ramsay, 1 Catherine Place, London SW1E 6DX (☎ 020 7592 1370)

RAMSAY, Prof Lawrence Eccles; s of William Ramsay (d 1970), of Ayrshire, Scotland, and Margaret Cables, *née* Eccles (d 1989); *b* 11 June 1943; *Educ* Cumnock Acad, Univ of Glasgow (MB ChB); *m* 17 Sept 1965, Mary Helen, da of Harry Hynd (d 1971), of Lanark, Scotland; 1 da (Helen b 1970), 3 s (William b 1972, Alan b 1974, Iain b 1983); *Career* Surgn Lt RN 1968–73, HMS Osprey 1968–69, HMS Jufair 1969–70, Admty Med Bd 1970–71, RNH Haslar 1971–73; lectr in medicine Univ of Glasgow 1977–78, conslt physician Royal Hallamshire Hosp 1978–, prof of clinical pharmacology and therapeutics Univ of Sheffield 1991– (reader in clinical pharmacology 1985–91); ed British Journal of Clinical Pharmacology 1988–94; visiting memb to Australasia for Br Pharmacological Soc 1989; memb: Cncl World Hypertension League 1989, Br Pharmacopoeia Cmmn 1980–98, Ctee on Review of Medicines 1982–91, Sub Ctee on Pharmacovigilance CSM 1992–98, Assoc of Physicians 1987; pres Br Hypertension Soc 1997–99 (sec 1985–89, vice-pres 1995–97); FRCP 1985 (memb 1970); *Recreations* soccer, golf, travel; *Style*— Prof Lawrence Ramsay; ✉ 85 Redmires Road, Lodge Moor, Sheffield S10 4LB (☎ 0114 276 6222)

RAMSAY, Louise; MBE (2000); da of Andrew Ramsay, and Jennifer, née Symons; *b* 9 August 1968; *Educ* Queen Anne's Sch Caversham; *Family* Patrick Rogers; 1 da (Isabel); *Career* dir of games services BOA 1991–2000 (attended 5 Olympic and Olympic Winter Games, dep chef de mission Sydney 2000), team mangr England rugby team 2001–04 (winners Six Nations Championship 2001 and 2003 (Grand Slam 2003), ranked no 1 in world for first time 2003, winners World Cup Aust 2003), team mangr Br and Irish Lions tour to NZ 2005, operations mangr Br and Irish Lions tour to South Africa 2009; *Recreations* travel, photography; *Style*— Ms Louise Ramsay, MBE

RAMSAY, Nick; AM; *b* 10 June 1975; *Educ* Croesyceiliog Comp Sch, Durham Univ, Cardiff Univ; *Career* memb Nat Assembly for Wales (Cons) Monmouth 2007–, shadow minister for local govt and public servs 2007–08, shadow min for finance and public delivery, chief whip and business mangr Welsh Cons Gp Nat Assembly for Wales 2008–, shadow min for enterprise, business and science 2011–14, shadow min for finance and Europe 2014–16, shadow min for finance 2016–; chair Public Accounts Ctee 2016–; *Recreations* tennis, rugby, keen supporter of local charities; *Style*— Nick Ramsay, Esq, AM; ✉ National Assembly for Wales, Cardiff Bay, Cardiff CF99 1NA (☎ 029 2089 8735)

RAMSAY, Richard Alexander McGregor; s of Alexander John McGregor Ramsay (d 1986), and Beatrice Kent, *née* Lanauze (d 2008); *b* 27 December 1949; *Educ* Trinity Coll Glenalmond, Univ of Aberdeen (MA); *m* 19 July 1975, Elizabeth Catherine Margaret, da of Robert Cecil Blackwood (d 1969); 1 da (Catherine Anne Blackwood b 1 Feb 1981), 1 s (Alistair Robert Blackwood b 19 Feb 1983); *Career* chartered accountant; articled clerk Price Waterhouse 1972–75, Grindlay Brandts Ltd 1975–78, Hill Samuel and Co Ltd 1979–88 (dir 1984–88, seconded as dir Industrial Devpt Unit DTI 1984–86), dir Barclays de Zoete Wedd Ltd 1988–93 (md Corp Fin Div 1990–93), dir Ivory & Sime Investment Management 1993–96, fin dir Aberdeen FC 1997–2000, md Regulation and Fin Affrs Ofgem 2001–03, dir Intelli Corp Fin Ltd 2003–09 (vice-chm 2003–05), dir Shareholder Exec 2007–11; non-exec dir: Artemis AiM VCT plc 2001–09 (chm 2001–03), Xploite plc 2007–10, Wolsey Gp Ltd 2008– (chm), Castleton Technology (formerly Redstone plc) 2010–14 (chm 2011–13), Northcourt Ltd 2011– (chm), Castle Tst plc 2011– (chm 2015), URICA Finance Ltd 2012– (chm 2012–15), Redcentric plc 2013–14 (chm), Seneca Global Income and Growth Tst plc (chm 2013–), John Laing Environmental Assets Gp Ltd 2013–; conslt Armstrong Bonham Carter 2007–; FCA; *Recreations* skiing, mountain walking, gardening, historic and classic cars; *Clubs* City of London; *Style*— Richard Ramsay, Esq; ✉ The Little Priory, Sandy Lane, South Nutfield, Surrey RH1 4EJ (☎ 01737 822329)

RAMSBOTHAM, Baron (Life Peer UK 2005), of Kensington in the Royal Borough of Kensington and Chelsea; Gen Sir David John Ramsbotham; GCB (1993, KCB 1987), CBE (1980, OBE 1974); s of Rt Rev Bishop John Alexander Ramsbotham (d 1989), of Hexham, Northumberland, and Eirian Morgan, *née* Morgan Owen (d 1988); *b* 6 November 1934; *Educ* Haileybury, CCC Cambridge (MA); *m* 26 Sept 1958, Susan Caroline, da of Robert Joicey Dickinson, of Corbridge, Northumberland (d 1980); 2 s (Hon James David Alexander b 30 Aug 1959, Hon Richard Henry b 8 June 1962); *Career* cmmnd Rifle Bde 1958, Royal Green Jackets CO 2 RGJ 1974–76, Cdr 39 Inf Bde 1978–80, RCDS 1981, dir PR (Army) 1982–84; Cdr: 3 Armd Div 1984–87, UK Field Army 1987–90; inspr gen TA 1987–90, Adj Gen 1990–93, ADC Gen 1990–93; HM Chief Inspr of Prisons for England and Wales 1995–2001; memb Cncl IISS 1996–2002; hon bencher Gray's Inn 2001; hon fell CCC Cambridge 2001, hon fell Royal Coll of Speech and Language Therapists 2012; Hon DCL 1999; CIMgt 1993; FRSA 1999, FCGI 1999; *Recreations* sailing, art and art history, penal reform; *Clubs* Beefsteak; *Style*— Gen the Lord Ramsbotham, GCB, CBE; ✉ House of Lords, London SW1A 0PW

RAMSBOTTOM, Paul Benjamin; s of Benjamin Ashworth Ramsbottom, of Luton, Beds, and Jean Margaret, *née* Kelsall; *b* 27 May 1976, Luton, Beds; *Educ* St Albans Sch (head boy), CCC Oxford (BA, MSt, DLitt); *m* 1 Nov 2002, Karen Rachel, *née* Taylor; 4 da (Lily Grace b 10 April 2005, Ella Rose b 9 Dec 2007, Phoebe Rachel b 29 Dec 2009, Annabel Mae b 4 Feb 2013); *Career* various roles Wolfson Fndn 1998–2007, chief exec Wolfson Fndn and Wolfson Family Charitable Tst 2007–; chm Savannah Educn Tst 2004–, chm Foundations Forum 2013–, tstee Mercy Ships UK 2015–; CCB fell Univ of Oxford 2009, Hon DLitt Univ of Bedfordshire 2013; FRSM 2007; *Recreations* exotic travel and food, theology, various sports; *Style*— Paul Ramsbottom, Esq; ✉ The Wolfson Foundation, 8 Queen Anne Street, London W1G 9LD (☎ 020 7323 3124, e-mail sue.hall@wolfson.org.uk, website www.wolfson.org.uk)

RAMSDALE, Dr David; s of William Ramsdale (d 1985), and Winifred, *née* Horne (d 2002); *b* 3 December 1950; *Educ* St Mary's Coll Blackburn, Univ of Manchester Med Sch (BSc, MB ChB, MD); *m* 6 March 1976, Bernadette; 2 s (Christopher b 17 Feb 1978, Mark b 10 June 1980), 1 da (Kathryn b 30 March 1982); *Career* research fell Dept of Cardiology Wythenshawe Hosp 1979–81, sr registrar in cardiology Sefton Gen Hosp, Broadgreen Hosp and Regnl Cardiothoracic Centre Liverpool 1981–87, conslt cardiologist The Cardiothoracic Centre Liverpool 1987–; memb: Br Pacing and EP Gp 1981, Br Cardiac Soc 1983, Br Cardiovascular Intervention Soc (former memb Cncl); chm Cardiothoracic Centre Heart Appeal; FRCP 1992 (MRCP 1978); *Publications* Practical Interventional Cardiology 1 (1997), and 2 (2001), Illustrated Coronary Intervention (2001), Color Atlas of Infective Endocarditis (2005), 100 Challenges in Clinical Medicine (2009), 100 Challenges in Cardiology (2010), Cardiac Pacing and Device Therapy (2012); numerous book chapters and more than 150 pubns on a wide variety of cardiovascular topics; *Recreations* golf, photography; *Clubs* Formby Golf; *Style*— Dr David Ramsdale; ✉ Liverpool Heart and Chest Hospital NHS Trust, Thomas Drive, Liverpool L14 3PE (☎ 0151 228 1616, fax 0151 220 8573, e-mail david.ramsdale@ctc.nhs.uk)

RAMSDALE, Prof Peter Alan; *Educ* UMIST (BSc), Univ of Birmingham (PhD); *Career* engr Plessey West Leigh, lectr in electronics Lanchester Poly Coventry 1970–74, sr lectr then princ lectr RMCS Shrivenham 1974–83, mangr Radio Lab rising to chief res fell and mangr Radio Dept STC Technology Ltd (STL) 1983–90, tech dir Unitel 1990–92, chief engr One2One (formerly Mercury Personal Communications and Unitel) 1992–2001 (also head Technol and Architecture Dept), prop Peter Ramsdale Ltd 2001–, fndr Spectrum Trading Associates 2004, dir Safe Haven Technologies Ltd 2004–06; responsible for major devpts in cellular radio and personal communications; memb: DTI/SERC/Industry LINK Personal Communications Mgmnt Ctee 1988–1991, EPSRC Communications Coll 1994–, Technology Foresight Prog Communications Panel Office of Sci and Technol 1994–98, Radiocoms Agency Radio Res Advsy Ctee 2000–2004; visiting prof: Centre for Satellite Engrg Res Univ of Surrey 1993–96, Centre for Communications Systems Engrg Res Univ of Surrey 1996–2004, Centre for Telecoms Res KCL 2004–; visiting lectr UCL 1996–2001 (memb Postgrad Courses Mgmnt Ctee); memb Cncl ERA Technology Ltd 1994–2000; IET (formerly IEE): chm Professional Gp E8 (Radiocommunication Systems) Ctee 1992–98, chm Communication Networks and Services TPN Exec Team 2004–(memb 2000–03), memb Electronics Divnl Bd; sometime memb Bd of Graduateship Examiners Inst of Physics; author of over 50 papers and nine patents, co-author of four books; CEng, FIET, FREng 1999; *Style*— Prof Peter Ramsdale; ✉ Peter Ramsdale Ltd, Bishops Cottage, Widdington, Saffron Walden, Essex CB11 3SQ (☎ 01799 540412, e-mail peter.ramsdale@btinternet.com)

RAMSDEN, Prof Richard Thomas; MBE (2015); s of late Thomas William Ramsden, of Balmerino, Fife, and late Elaine Napier, *née* Meikle; *b* 30 December 1944, Dundee; *Educ* Madras Coll St Andrews, Univ of St Andrews (MB ChB); *m* 1, 1968 (m dis 1984), Wendy Margaret, *née* Johnson; 2 da (Helen b 1972, Fiona b 1977), 1 s (Alistair b 1974); m 2, 1985, (Eileen) Gillian, da of late Clifford Whitehurst, and late Anne Whitehurst; 2 step s (Oliver Richardson b 1972, Giles Richardson b 1974); *Career* registrar and sr registrar otolaryngology Royal Nat Throat Nose and Ear Hosp London and London Hosp 1972–77; conslt otolaryngologist (now ret) and hon prof in otolaryngology Manchester Royal Infirmary and Salford Royal NHS Tst; hon lectr: Dept of Surgery Univ of Manchester, Dept of Audiology Speech Pathology and Educn of the Deaf Univ of Manchester 1977–2009; author of over 300 pubns in medical jls, mostly peer-reviewed; asst ed Jl of Laryngology and Otology; memb Editorial Bd: Otology and Neurology, Revue de Laryngologie Otologie Rhinologie, ENT Jl; memb Nat Ctee of Enquiry into Perioperative Deaths; memb Cncl Section of Otology RSM 1990–95 (sec, treas, vice-pres, pres 1994–95), co-fndr Euro Acad for Otology and Neuro-otology, examiner and memb Bd Intercollegiate Bd in Otolaryngology 1992–99, memb Ct of Examiners RCPSGlas 1987–2003, memb SAC in Otolaryngology 1998–2004; chm Br Cochlear Implant Gp 1989–96, memb Collegium Oto-Rhino-Laryngologicum Amicitiae Sacrum, memb UK Cncl on Deafness, corresponding memb Deutsche Gesellschaft für Hals-Nase-und Ohrenheilkunde; hon memb: Danish ENT Soc, Irish ENT Soc, American Otological Soc, Slovac Soc, German Skull Base Soc, Scottish ENT Soc; pres North of Eng Otolaryngological Soc 2000–01, past pres Br Skull Base Soc, pres Br Assoc of Otolaryngology 2006–09, pres ENT UK 2006–09; master Br Academic Conference in Otolaryngology 2010; patron Nat Assoc for Deafened People, tstee Dowager Eleanor Peel

Tst, tstee William Alwyn Fndn; med advsr Neurofibromatosis Assoc, advsr on otolaryngology Nat Inst for Clinical Excellence; Leon Goldmann prof lectr Univ of Cape Town 1998, Yearsley lectr 2001, Hunterian Oration Hunterian Soc 2008; winner Dalby Prize Royal Soc of Med 1992, Wilde Medal 1994, VS Subramaniam lectr and Gold Medal 1995, winner WJ Harrison Prize for Otology 1999, Jobson Horne Prize BMA 2001, Smyth Lecture and Medal Br Assoc of Otolaryngologists – Head and Neck Surgeons 2003, Brinkmann lectr and medal Univ of Nijmegen 2013, Toynbee lectr RSM 2013; memb BMA 1977, FRCS 1973 (memb Cncl 2006–09), FRCSEd (ad hominem) 2000; *Recreations* golf, otology, music (particularly woodwind); *Clubs* St Andrews New, RSM; *Style*— Prof Richard Ramsden, MBE; ✉ Church House, 28 High Street, Thame, Oxfordshire OX9 2AA (e-mail rramsden@quikmail.co.uk)

RAMSEY, Sir Vivian Arthur; kt (2005); s of Rt Rev Ian Thomas Ramsey (d 1972 former Bishop of Durham), and Margaret (Margretta), *née* McKay (d 1997); *b* 24 May 1950, Cambridge; *Educ* Abingdon Sch, Harley Sch Rochester NY USA, Oriel Coll Oxford (MA), City Univ (Dip Law); *m* 14 Aug 1974, Barbara, da of Lt-Col Gerard Majella Walker, of Hitchin, Herts; 2 da (Helen b 1980, Katharine b 1984), 2 s (Nicholas b 1981, James b 1986); *Career* grad engr Ove Arup & Ptnrs 1972–77, called to the Bar Middle Temple 1979 (bencher 2002); practising barr 1981–2005, arbitrator (incl ICC arbitration) 1988–2005 (mediator 1991–2005), QC 1992, asst recorder 1998–2000, recorder 2000–05, head of chambers Keating Chambers 2002–05, judge of the High Court of Justice (Queen's Bench Div) 2005–14, judge in charge Technol and Construction Court 2007–10; special prof Dept of Civil Engrg Univ of Nottingham 1990–, visiting prof Centre of Construction Law KCL 2007–; ctee official referee Bar Assoc 1986–91; treas: St Swithuns Hither Green 1977–84, Swanley Village Sports and Social Club 1986–2005 (chm 1990–98); chm Swanley Action Gp 1990–2005; memb American Coll of Construction Lawyers 2005– (co-chair Int Ctee 2008–11); President's Medal Soc of Construction Law 2010, Clare Edwards Award Technol and Construction Slrs' Assoc 2010; Liveryman Worshipful Co of Constructors 2009 (Freeman 1995, Hon Freeman 2011); MICE 1977; *Publications* Keating on Construction Contracts (7 edn, 2000, supplement 2004, 8 edn 2006, supplement 2008); also ed Construction Law Jl 1984–2005 (conslt ed 2005–); *Recreations* building renovation, vineyards; *Style*— Sir Vivian Ramsey; ✉ Royal Courts of Justice, Strand, London WC2A 2LL

RAMSHAW, Wendy Anne Jopling; CBE (2003, OBE 1993); da of Angus Ramshaw (d 1989), and Flora, *née* Hollingshead (d 1982); *b* 26 May 1939; *Educ* Sunderland Girls HS, Saint Mary's Convent Berwick-upon-Tweed, Coll of Art and Industrial Design Newcastle upon Tyne (NDD), Univ of Reading (ATD), Central Sch London; *m* David John Watkins, s of Jack Watkins; 1 da (Miranda Abigail Watkins b 22 April 1967), 1 s (Richard Mark Watkins b 11 July 1974); *Career* artist and designer; artist in residence Western Inst Aust (now Curtin Univ Aust) 1978–79, visiting artist in collaboration Wedgwood 1981–82, visiting artist Glass Dept RCA 1985, artist in residence Printmakers Workshop Inverness 1996, artists in residence (with Miranda Watkins) Pallant House Chichester 1999, artist in residence St John's Coll Oxford 2005, artist in residence Pilchuck Glass Sch Seattle 2006, artist in residence Somerset House 2010–12; visiting prof: San Diego State Univ 1984, Bezalel Acad Jerusalem 1984, RCA London 1998–2001; patron: Contemporary Applied Arts London, Bristol Cancer Help Centre; Lady Liveryman Worshipful Co of Goldsmiths 1986; hon fell London Inst (now Univ of the Arts London) 1999 (govr 2000–06); sr fell RCA London 2006; FCSD 1972, FRSA 1972–2011; RDI 1999; *Exhibitions* incl: Wendy Ramshaw – David Watkins (Goldsmiths Hall London) 1973, Nat Gallery of Victoria Aust 1978, V&A 1982, Bristol City Museum and Art Gallery (retrospective) 1983, Wendy Ramshaw/David Watkins (Schmuckmuseum Pforzheim) 1987, Jewellery Strategies/Jewellery Variations (Mikimoto Tokyo) 1993, Picasso's Ladies (V&A, American Craft Museum NY and Inst Mathildenhöhne Darmstadt) 1998–2001, Millennium Exhibition (Contemporary Applied Arts London) 2000, Room of Dreams (Scottish Gallery Edinburgh) 2002, Prospero's Table (Sofa Chicago) 2004, Wendy Ramshaw – Jewellery (Blackwell The Arts and Crafts House) 2004, COLLECT (V&A) 2005, Journey Through Glass (Scottish Gallery Edinburgh) 2007, Drawings in Gold (Bluecoat Liverpool and Lesley Craze Gallery London) 2008, Honey Bee & the Hive (Contemporary Applied Arts) 2010 (curator), Inspired (Electrum Gallery) 2012, Rooms of Dreams (Somerset House, Ruthin Craft Centre, Harley Gallery, Dovecot Studios and MIMA) 2012–14, The Inventor (Scottish Gallery) 2013, Pop Art Design (Barbican London) 2013, Black & White (Lesley Craze Gallery) 2014; *Selected Large-Scale Commissions* Garden Gate Fellows' Garden St John's Coll Oxford 1993, Double Screen EH9681 V&A 1996, Gate Mowbray Park Sunderland 1998–2001, Millennium Medal for HM The Queen 1999–2000, The Prince of Wales Medal (for Classic Design Awards) 2000, glass panels and bronze door handles Millennium Building Southwark Cathedral 2000, circular gates Sculpture at Goodwood 2001, Priors Court Sch Entrance Gate (collaboration with Richard Watkins) 2002, Garden Gate Clare Coll Cambridge 2009, New Edinburgh Gate Hyde Park London 2010, Kendrew Gates St John's Coll Oxford 2010, Portcullis Gates Davies Street Mayfair London 2014; *Work in Public Collections* incl: Br Museum, Musée des Arts Décoratifs Paris, MOMA Kyoto, Philadelphia Museum of Art, Schmuckmuseum Pforzheim, Stedelijk Museum Amsterdam, Cooper-Hewitt Museum Smithsonian Inst NY, V&A, Aust Nat Gallery Canberra, Kunstindustrimuseet Oslo, Royal Museum of Scotland Edinburgh, Science Museum London, Powerhouse Sydney, Museum of Fine Arts Boston, Museum of Fine Arts Houston, Met Museum of Art NY; *Awards* Cncl of Industrial Design Award 1972, De Beers Diamond Int Award 1975, Art in Architecture RSA 1993; *Publications* Wendy Ramshaw and Wedgwood (exhbn catalogue), From Paper to Gold (exhbn catalogue), Wendy Ramshaw and David Watkins, Jewel Drawings and Projects, Picasso's Ladies – Jewellery by Wendy Ramshaw, Wendy Ramshaw – The Big Works, Wendy Ramshaw – Jewellery (exhbn catalogue), Wendy Ramshaw – Drawings in Gold, subject of David Watkins Wendy Ramshaw – A Life's Partnership (by Graham Hughes), Wendy Ramshaw – Rooms of Dreams (exhbn catelogue); *Recreations* visiting museums and art galleries, travelling, reading; *Style*— Miss Wendy Ramshaw, CBE, RDI; ✉ c/o The Scottish Gallery, 16 Dundas Street, Edinburgh EH3 6HZ (website www.ramshaw-watkins.com)

RANA, Baron (Life Peer UK 2004), of Malone in the County of Antrim; Dijit Singh Rana; MBE (1996), JP (1986); s of late Paras Ram Rana; *b* 20 September 1938, India; *Educ* Punjab Univ; *m* 1966, Uma (d 2002), da of Kishore Lal Passi, of Phillaur, India; 2 c (Hon Rajesh b 1968, Hon Ramesh b 1970); *Career* pres: Belfast Chamber of Trade and Commerce 1991–92, NI C of C and Industry 2004–05; fndr: India Business Forum 1985, Rana Charitable Tst 1996; chm Thanksgiving Sq 2002–, pres GOPIO 2009– (exec vice-pres 2004–09); govr Lagan Coll 1990–94; hon consul for India in NI 2004–; Hon Dr: Univ of Ulster 1999, Queen's Univ Belfast 2004, Bengal Engrg and Science Univ W Bengal 2008; Pravasi Bharatiya Samman Award (India) 2007; *Style*— The Rt Hon the Lord Rana, MBE

RANDALL, Helen; da of Dennis Randall, of Oxon, and Monica, *née* Wilson; *b* May 1962, London; *Educ* Tunbridge Wells GS for Girls, Kent Coll for Girls, RSA (TEFL), Univ of Manchester (BA), City Univ London (DipLaw), Coll of Law London; *m* 2013, Maria Azucena Tejada-Randall; *Career* admitted slr 1991; articled clerk then slr Lovells 1988–95, slr London Borough of Camden 1995–97, ptnr Nabarro Nathanson 2001–04 (slr 1997–2001), ptnr Trowers & Hamlins LLP 2004–; chm New Local Govt Network (NGLN) 2004–08 (dir 2001–11); memb: Sir Ian Byatt's Procurement Task Force, Guardian Public Leaders Network; visiting prof Univ of Law 2015–18; *Publications* Butterworth's Local Government Act (1999), Tottel's Local Government Contracts and Procurement (2006), PFI Encyclopaedia (contrib); author of numerous NLGN pubns; *Recreations* herding cats and nailing jellies to walls; *Style*— Ms Helen Randall; ✉ Trowers & Hamlins LLP, 3 Bunhill Row, London EC1Y 8YZ (☎ 020 7423 8436, fax 020 7423 8001, e-mail hrandall@trowers.com)

RANDALL, Jeff William; s of Jeffrey Charles Randall (d 2012), and Grace Annie, *née* Hawkridge (d 2008); *b* 3 October 1954, London; *Educ* Royal Liberty GS Romford, Univ of Nottingham (BA), Univ of Florida; *m* 8 Feb 1986, Susan Diane, da of H W Fidler; 1 da (Lucy Susan b 10 Jan 1989); *Career* research economist Wolverhampton Poly 1980–82, Hawkins Publishers 1982–85, asst ed Financial Weekly 1985–86, city corr Sunday Telegraph 1986–88, city ed Sunday Times 1989–95 (joined 1988), dir Times Newspapers 1994–95, jt dep chm Financial Dynamics 1995–96, asst ed Sunday Times 1996, sports ed Sunday Times 1996–97, ed Sunday Business 1997–2001, business ed BBC 2001–05, ed-at-large Daily Telegraph 2005–13, presenter Jeff Randall Live (Sky News) 2007–14; columnist Sunday Telegraph 2001–04; presenter BBC Radio Five Live 2004–07; visiting fell Oxford Univ Business Sch 2007–, hon prof Univ of Nottingham Business Sch 2011–, memb Cncl Univ of Nottingham 2013–; dir Babcock Int 2014, dir Sandown Racecourse 2014–; FT Analysis Financial Journalist of the Year 1991, London Press Club Business Journalist of the Year 2001, Best Broadcast and Decade of Excellence Prizes Business Journalism Awards 2003, PR Week Communicator of the Year 2004, Harold Wincott Award for Best Business Broadcaster 2004, Best Business Broadcast Feature Business Journalism Awards 2007; Hon Dr: Anglia Ruskin Univ 2001, Univ of Nottingham 2006, BPP UC 2011; *Books* The Day That Shook the World (contrib, 2001); *Recreations* golf, horse racing; *Clubs* Brooks's, Thorndon Park Golf; *Style*— Jeff Randall, Esq

RANDALL, Rt Hon Sir (Alexander) John; kt (2013), PC (2010); s of Alec Randall (d 1996), and Joyce, *née* Gore (d 2012); *b* 5 August 1955; *Educ* Merchant Taylors' Northwood, SSEES Univ of London (BA); *m* 1986, Katherine, da of John Gray; 2 s (Peter b Oct 1989, David b Nov 1993), 1 da (Elizabeth b Dec 1995); *Career* md Randalls of Uxbridge Ltd 1986–97; MP (Cons) Uxbridge (by-election) 1997–2015; oppn whip 2000–05, Cons asst chief whip 2005–10, treas of HM Household and dep chief whip 2010–13; chm Uxbridge Cons Assoc 1994–97; tour ldr: Birdquest Holidays 1988–94, Limosa Holidays 1994–97; *Recreations* ornithology, opera, travel, rugby, cricket; *Clubs* Uxbridge Conservative, Saracens RFC, Middlesex CCC; *Style*— The Rt Hon Sir John Randall; ✉ House of Commons, London SW1A 0AA (☎ 020 7219 6885)

RANDALL, John Yeoman; QC (1995); s of Dr Richard Francis Yeoman Randall, of Market Harborough, and Jean Evelyn, *née* Child; *b* 26 April 1956; *Educ* Rugby, Loomis Inst Connecticut, Jesus Coll Cambridge (MA); *m* 1982 (sep), Christine, da of late (Gordon) Keith Robinson, and late Shirley Grace, *née* Temple, of Sydney, Aust; 1 s (Oliver Yeoman b 1985), 1 da (Sally Jenine b 1988); *Career* called to the Bar Lincoln's Inn 1978 (bencher 2003), called to the Bar NSW 1979; asst recorder of the Crown Court 1995–99, recorder of the Crown Court 1999–, dep judge of the High Court 2000–16; head of chambers 2001–04 (dep head 1998–2001), barr and slr WA 2001; chm Midland Chancery and Commercial Bar Assoc 1996–99, memb Legal Services Consultative Panel 2000–09; adjunct prof Univ of NSW 2013– (visiting fell 2004–13), sr fell Univ of Melbourne 2014–; *Books* The Tort of Conversion (jtly, 2009); *Recreations* travel, sports, music; *Style*— John Randall, Esq, QC; ✉ St Philip's Chambers, 55 Temple Row, Birmingham B2 5LS (☎ 0121 246 7000, fax 0121 246 7001, e-mail civil@st-philips.com)

RANDALL, Nicholas Justin Lee (Nik); s of William Randall, of Sevenoaks, and May; *b* 24 November 1958; *Educ* Sevenoaks Sch, Univ of Liverpool Sch of Architecture (Reilly Medal); *Partner* Susan Mary Corio; 1 s (Louis Homer Corio); *Career* architect; ptnr Alan Brookes Associates 1988 (became Brookes Stacey Randall Fursdon 1993 and Brookes Stacey Randall 1997); winners of 15 major design awards for projects incl: RIBA Awards 1992, 1995 and 1997, Civic Tst Awards 1993 and 1996, Royal Fine Art Cmmn, Sunday Times Building of the Year, Jeux d'Esprit Award 1995, Int Interchange of the Year 2003; work in permanent collection of the V&A Museum London; projects incl: East Croydon Station, The Lowe Flat and The Lowe House London, Thames Water Tower, The Churchill Centre Rotterdam, Transport Interchange Enschede, bridges at Cardiff Bay, The Art House London, The Boating Pavilion Streatley, Wembley Park 2000 (phase one), de Maere Textile Inst Enschede, Pet Shop Boys studio London; founding dir and chm Space Craft Architects 2003–14; projects incl: Harrietsham CEP Sch, Longlands for Urban Splash, O Central London (Best New Affordable Homes New Homes Design Awards 2008), Ebbsfleet Valley for Land Securities, Hinguar Sch (LABC Building Excellence Awards), The Table Restaurant, Golden Lane, The Bridge Master's House for City of London Corp; founding dir and chm reForm Architects 2014–; projects incl: Avondale Square for City of London Corp, Trinity Road for Dio of Southwark, Rotherhithe Bridge (commended AR Mipim Future Projects Awards, winner New London Architecture People's Choice Award 2016); co-chair Southwark Design Review Panel; *Recreations* design, painting, writing, family, friends, football, skiing, travelling; *Style*— Mr Nik Randall, RIBA; ✉ reForm Architects, 48a Union Street, London SE1 1TD (☎ 020 3696 5700, e-mail enquiries@reform-architects.london)

RANDALL, Paul Nicholas; s of late Jack Sidney Randall, and Grace Ruth, *née* Fletcher; *b* 26 January 1960, London; *Educ* City of London Sch, KCL (LLB, AKC), Coll of Law; *m* 27 April 1985, Anamaria Dans Randall, da of William Enrique Dans Coath; 2 s (James William Alexander b 6 Oct 1987, William Henry Charles b 7 Nov 1990); *Career* Wedlake Bell 1982–87, Ashurst 1987–; dir West of England Tst Ltd 2000–; *Style*— Paul Randall, Esq; ✉ Ashurst, Broadwalk House, 5 Appold Street, London EC2A 2HA (☎ 020 7638 1111)

RANDALL, Theo; *Career* restaurateur; former head chef River Café, estab Theo Randall at The InterContinental 2006 (Italian Restaurant of the Year London Restaurant Awards 2008); *Style*— Theo Randall, Esq; ✉ Theo Randall at The InterContinental, 1 Hamilton Place, Park Lane, London W1J 7QY (website www.theorandall.co.uk)

RANDALL-PAGE, Peter; s of Charles Randall-Page, and Joan Mary, *née* Teale; *b* 2 July 1954; *Educ* Eastbourne Coll, Bath Acad of Art (BA); *m* 10 March 1984, Charlotte Eve, da of Philip Harry Hartley; 1 s (Thomas Charles b 16 Sept 1984), 1 da (Florence Ruth b 7 Aug 1987); *Career* sculptor; solo exhibitions incl: Sculpture & Drawings 1980–1992 (Leeds City Art Galleries, Yorkshire Sculpture Park, Royal Botanic Garden Edinburgh and Arnolfini Gallery Bristol, organised by Henry Moore Centre Leeds), Boulders and Banners (Wenlock Priory, Shropshire and Reed's Wharf Gallery London) 1994, In Mind of Botany (Royal Botanic Gardens Kew) 1996, Whistling in the Dark (Ljubljana Slovenia, and Gouda The Netherlands) 1998, Nature of the Beast (Djanogly Gallery Nottingham, Graves Gallery Sheffield and Towner Gallery Eastbourne) 2001, Sculpture and Drawings (Natural History Museum London) 2003, Lyveden New Bield (sculpture) with accompanying works on paper (Fermynwoods Contemporary Art Northants) 2006, Sculpture in the Park (Uster Park Bradford) 2008, Stones Sunlight and Shadows: New Work in the Woods (New Art Centre) 2008, Rock Music Rock Art (Pangolin London) 2008, Yorks Sculpture Park 2009–10, New Drawings and Sculpture (Jerwood Space London) 2010, Clay Works (Purdy Hicks Gallery London) 2010, Showing His Hand (Drumcroon Gallery Wigan) 2011, Drawings (Southampton City Art Gallery) 2011, Recent Works (salon and forecourt Royal British Soc of Sculptors London) Drawings, Print & Sculpture on a Domestic Scale (Thelmal Hulbert Gallery Honiton) 2014, New Sculpture and Works on Paper (Peninsula Arts Plymouth Univ and Plymouth City Museum and Art Gallery) 2014, Upside Down and Inside Out (Pangolin

R

London) 2014, Peter Randall-Page: New Sculpture and Works on Paper, a partnership exhibition between Peninsula Arts, Plymouth Univ and Plymouth City Museum and Art Gall 2014, Peter Randall-Page at Arte Sella (Italy) 2015, Art in Nature/Act III: Peter Randall-Page at Villa Panza (Italy) 2015, Between Melting and Freezing (Millennium Gallery St Ives Cornwall) 2015, Mind Over Matter (Galerie Scheffel Bad Homburg Germany) 2015, Theme and Variation: The Making of the Bramall Frieze (Univ of Birmingham) 2015, On the Particular Experience of Being Alive, Peter Randall-Page at Antares Art Centre (Sippola Finland) 2016, Caught in the Act (Gibberd Gallery Harlow) 2016; group exhbns incl: Making It: Sculpture in Britain 1977–86 Yorkshire Sculpture Park 2015, Peter Randall-Page and Kate McGwire (Royal West of England Acad Bristol) 2015, Contemporary and Modern British Sculpture (Hignell Gallery London) 2016, Force of Nature (Galerie Valerie Bach Brussels) 2016, Sculpture on Display (Tremenheere Sculpture Gardens Cornwall) 2016, On Form-Sculpture in Stone (Asthall Manor Oxfordshire) 2016; commissions incl: National Trust Derwentwater 1995, LDDC Butlers Wharf London 1996, Manchester City Cncl St Ann's Square 1996, Lothian Regional Cncl and others Hunters Square Edinburgh 1996, BUPA House London 1996, Nuffield Coll Oxford 1999, Royal Botanic Gardens Kew, Millennium Seed Bank Wakehurst Place Sussex 2000, Sculpture at Goodwood 2000 and 2003, Univ of Cardiff 2006, Southward Cathedral 2006, Eden Project Cornwall 2007, Fisher SQ Cambridge 2007, Jerwood Sculpture Park 2009, Dulwich Picture Gallery 2010, Univ of Iowa 2011, Dartington Hall Tst 2011, Karlsruhe Univ 2013, Southmead Hosp Bristol 2014, Bramhall Music Building Univ of Birmingham 2014, Pearson Square (Fitzroy Place development) London 2015, The Laboratory at Dulwich College 2015; work in collections incl: Tate Gallery and British Museum, V&A Museum; res fell visual and performance arts Dartington Coll of Arts 1999–2000 and 2002–05; memb Design Team Educn Resource Centre (ERC) Eden Project 2002–05; invited artist Gwangju Biennale South Korea 2004; Marsh Award for Public Sculpture 2006; Hon DArts Univ of Plymouth 1999, Hon DLitt York St John Univ 2009, Hon DLitt Univ of Exeter 2010, Hon DLitt Bath Spa Univ 2013; FRSA, memb RBS, memb RWA, RA 2015; *Publications* Sculpture and Drawings: 1977–1992 (1992), In Conversation with Tess Jackson (1992), Boulders & Banners (1994), In Mind of Botany (1996), Whistling in the Dark (1998), Granite Song (1999), Nature of the Beast (2001), New Sculpture & Drawing (2006), Rock Music Rock Art (2008), Peter Randall-Page at the Yorkshire Sculpture Park (2009), Peter Randall-Page: Drawings (2014), Upside Down & Inside Out (2014), On the Particular Experience of Being Alive: Peter Randal-Page at the Art Gallery Antares, Finland (2016); *Clubs* Chelsea Arts; *Style—* Peter Randall-Page; ✉ Veet Mill Farm, Crockernwell, Exeter, Devon EX6 6NL (☎ 01647 281270, e-mail contact@peterrandall-page.com, website www.peterrandall-page.com and www.theoneandthemany.co.uk, Twitter @PRPsculpture)

RANDERSON, Baroness (Life Peer UK 2011), of Roath Park in the City of Cardiff; Jennifer Elizabeth (Jenny) Randerson; JP (1982); *née* Sinclair; *b* 26 May 1948; *Educ* Wimbledon HS, Bedford Coll London (BA), Inst of Educn Univ of London (PGCE); *m* 1970, Dr Peter Frederick Randerson; 1 s (James b 1976), 1 da (Eleri b 1979); *Career* teacher: Sydenham HS 1970–72, Spalding HS 1972–74, Llanishen HS 1974–76; lectr Coleg Glan Hafren Cardiff 1976–99; cncllr: Cardiff City Cncl 1983–96, Cardiff City and County Cncl 1995–2000 (ldr of the oppn 1995–99); memb Nat Assembly for Wales (Lib Dem) Cardiff Central 1999–2011, min for culture, sport and the Welsh language 2000–03, actg dep first min for Wales 2001–02, spokesperson on health and social servs and finance 2003–08, spokesperson on local govt 2007–08, Welsh Lib Dem shadow min for educn, economy and tport 2008–11, chm Assembly Business Ctee 2003–07, memb Equal Opportunities Ctee 2003–07, Parly under-sec of state for Wales 2012–15, Lib Dem spokesperson on transport 2015–, memb House of Lords EU Sub Ctee B 2015–; memb Lib Dem Pty 1979– (chair Welsh Exec 1988–90, Parly candidate Gen Election 1987, 1992 and 1997); memb: Reservoir Action Gp, Nat Tst, Friends of Nant Fawr; patron: Cardiff County and Vale of Glamorgan Youth Wind Band, Wales Cncl for Deaf People; govr Cardiff Met Univ 2011–12 and 2015–; hon fell Cardiff Univ 2011; *Recreations* travel, theatre and concert-going, gardening; *Clubs* Nat Lib; *Style—* The Baroness Randerson; ✉ House of Lords, London SW1A 0PW (☎ 020 7219 2538, e-mail randersonj@parliament.uk)

RANDLE, Prof James Neville; s of James Randle (d 1989), and Florence, *née* Wilkins (d 1980); *b* 24 April 1938; *Educ* Waverley GS Birmingham, Aston Tech Coll Birmingham; *m* 1963, Jean Violet (d 2006), da of Alfred Robert Allen; 1 s (Steven James b 1966), 1 da (Sally Joanne b 1968); *Career* Rover Co Ltd: apprentice 1954–61, tech asst 1961–63, project engr 1963–65; Jaguar Cars Ltd: project engr 1965–72, chief vehicle res engr 1972–78, dir of vehicle engrg 1978–80, dir of product engrg 1980–90, dir of vehicle and concept engrg 1990–91, leader of team that produced Jaguar XJ40 (winner Top Car award 1986) and Jaguar XJ220 (winner Turin and Horner prize 1988); ind engrg conslt 1991–; chm and chief exec Randle Engineering and Design 1994–, ceo Lea Francis Ltd 2000–, tech dir Gibbs Technologies 2003–05; dir: Automotive Engineering Centre Univ of Birmingham 1992–2006, Lea Francis Ltd 1997–; hon prof of automobile engrg Univ of Birmingham 1992–2006, visiting prof of engrg design Royal Acad of Engrg, visiting prof of mfrg engrg De Montfort Univ; non-exec dir United Turbine UK Ltd 1992–97, chm Coventry Autoplane Club 2007–; former memb Cncl IMechE (chm Automobile Div 1987–88), fndr memb Autotech, memb Prince Philip Design Award Ctee 1992–2002; Crompton Lanchester Medal 1986, James Clayton Prize 1986, Sir William Lyons International Award 1987, Prince Philip Design Awards Ctee 1992–2002; FREng 1988, FIMechE, FInstD, FRSA, RDI 1994, Hon FCSD 2000; *Recreations* flying, sailing, skiing, hill walking; *Style—* James Randle, RDI, FREng; ✉ Pear Tree House, High Street, Welford-on-Avon, Warwickshire CV37 8EF (e-mail j.n.randle@btinternet.com); Company ☎ 01789 751139, fax 01789 751140

RANDLE, Thomas John; s of Norvell Lee Randle (d 1989), and Mary Sylvia O'Connell (d 1999); *b* 21 December 1958; *Educ* Orange Coast Coll, Chapman Coll, Univ of Southern Calif; *Children* 1 da (Bella Sidney Randle Racklin b 14 July 1992); *Career* tenor; solo concert debut Bach Weinachtsoratorium (Leipzig Rundfunksinfonie) 1987, operatic debut as Tamino in The Magic Flute (ENO) 1988, Molgui in The Death of Klinghoffer (feature film, Channel 4); *Performances* incl: Tippett Songs for Dov (LA Philharmonic) 1985, Rossini Stabat Mater (London Philharmonic) 1988, Tamino in the Magic Flute (ENO 1988, 1989 and 1990, Glyndebourne Opera 1991), Handel Messiah (Royal Philharmonic) 1989, 1990 and 1991, Borodin La Mer (LSO) 1989, Haydn Die Jahreszeiten (Boston Symphony Orch) 1989, Beethoven Ninth Symphony (Scottish Chamber Orch 1989, Bergen Philharmonic Orch 1991, Prague Spring Festival 1996), Pelleas in Pelleas et Melisande (ENO) 1989, title role in Oedipus Rex (Madrid Opera) 1989, title role in L'Orfeo (Valencia 1989, Oviedo Opera Festival 1990), Haydn Die Schöpfung (Tivoli Festival Copenhagen 1990), Liszt Faust Symphony (BBC Scottish Symphony Orch (1990), Tippett The Ice Break (London Sinfonietta) Proms 1990, Ferrando in Cosi fan Tutte (Scottish Opera and Brussels Opera 1990, Geneva Opera 1992), Purcell Fairy Queen (Aix-en-Provence) 1989, Mozart Requiem (Acad of London) 1991, Paul McCartney Liverpool Oratorio 1992 (Ravinia Festival Chicago Aug, Helsinki Festival Finland Sept, Munich Symphony Orch Oct), Ferrando in Cosi fan Tutte (Geneva Opera) 1992, Pelleas in Pelleas et Melisande (with Peter Brook) Theatre Les Bouffes du Nord Paris (and Euro tour) 1992/93, Mozart Die Zauberflöte (Schleswig-Holstein Festival Hamburg 1993/94, Deutsche Oper Berlin 1996), Magic Flute (Auckland Opera NZ) 1993/94, Britten Gloriana, Earl of Essex (Opera North and Royal Opera House Covent Garden) 1993/94, Peter Schat World Premiere Opera Symposion (Netherlands Opera) 1993/94, Haydn L'Incontro Improviso (Garsington Opera Festival) 1993/94, Taverners' Apocalypse (world premiere, London Proms) 1993/94, Mozart Don Giovanni (Los Angeles Music Center Opera 1993/94, Munich Staatsoper 1995), Achilles in King Priam (ENO) 1995, Tippett The Mask of Time (LSO under Sir Colin Davis) 1995, Mendelssohn Elijah (Radio Orch France under Richard Hickox) 1995, Don Ramiro in La Cenerentola (Garsington Opera) 1995, Britten War Requiem (with BBC Scottish Symphony under Martyn Brabbins) 1995, title role in Handel Samson (with The Sixteen under Harry Christophers, Spanish tour) 1995, Mozart Requiem and Nono Canti di Vita e d'amore (concert tour with Bundesjugendorchester for Int Physicians for the Prevention of Nuclear War on 50th anniversary of Hiroshima bombing) 1995, Requiem der Versöhnung/Requiem of Reconciliation (world premiere with Israel Philharmonic under Helmuth Rilling) 1995, Mahler Das Klagende Lied (BBC Symphony under Alexander Lazarev, BBC Proms) 1995, Oberon in The Fairy Queen (ENO new prodn) 1995/96, Paris in La Belle Hélène (ENO new prodn) 1995/96, Gerald in Lakmé (Victoria State Opera Australia) 1996, title role in Idomeneo (Scottish Opera) 1996, The Country of the Blind (by Mark-Anthony Turnage, ENO/Aldeburgh Festival) 1997, Paul Bunyan (by Britten, Royal Opera House debut) 1997, title role in Solimano (by Hasse, Innstruck Festival and Deutsche Oper Berlin) 1997, Poisoned Kiss and A Cotswold Romance (concerts with LSO, under Richard Hickox, by R Vaughan-Williams) 1997, Tom Rakewell in The Rake's Progress (by Stravinsky, Netherlands Opera and Lausanne Opera) 1998–99, Gloriana (by Britten, BBC TV and Opera North) 1999, title role in Lucio Silla (Garsington Opera) 1998, Gawain (by Harrison Birtwhistle, ROH) 2000, The Last Supper (by Harrison Birtwhistle, world premiere, Statsoper Berlin with Daniel Barenboim) 2000, Tom Rakewell in Rake's Progress (Theâtre Champs Elysées) 2000/01, Loge in Das Rheingold (ENO) 2002, Benedict in Beatrice et Benedict (WNO) 2002, Bajazet in Tamerlano (Paris, London and Halle) 2002, Der Maler in Lulu (Netherlands Opera) 2002, Das Lied von der Erde (with Royal Opera Orch Covent Garden) 2002; *Recordings* incl: set of a cappella choral settings of sacred texts (Pater Noster, Stabat Mater, Vinea Mea, Electa, Benediction Amen, Ave Maria, Ave Verum Corpus) 1981–83, Purcell Fairy Queen (with Les Arts Florrissante under William Christie, from the Aix-en-Provence Festival) 1989, Tippett The Ice Break (with London Sinfonietta under David Atherton) 1990, complete Handel Messiah (with RPO under Owain Arwel Hughes), Handel Esther (with The Sixteen under Harry Christophers) 1995, Britten War Requiem (with BBC Scottish Symphony under Martyn Brabbins) 1995, Non Canti di Vita e d'amore (with Bamberg Symphony under Ingo Metzmacher) 1995, Handel Samson (with Harry Christopher and The Sixteen), A Cotswold Romance (with LSO, under Richard Hickox) 1997, Handel Tamerlano (with Trevor Pinnock and the English Concert) 2001; *Compositions* The Sculptor (opera), Los Nacimientos (song cycle for soprano and piano), Epitaph (song cycle for baritone and chamber orch); *Film* Molqi in The Death of Klinghoffer 2003, The Magic Flute 2006; *Recreations* motorsports (especially Formula One); *Style—* Thomas Randle, Esq; ✉ c/o IMG Artists, The Light Box, 111 Power Road, London W4 5PY (☎ 020 7957 5800, fax 020 7957 5801)

RANDOLPH, Prof Sarah Elizabeth; da of John Hervey Randolph (d 1975), of Sherborne, Dorset, and Dorothy Elizabeth, *née* Eyre; *b* Sherborne, Dorset; *Educ* St Anne's Coll Oxford (BA), KCL (PhD); *m* 27 March 1976, David John Rogers; 2 da (Emily Sarah b 9 July 1979, Thea Jane b 12 May 1982), 1 s (Jack David b 20 July 1984); *Career* Jubilee postdoctoral research fell Royal Holloway Univ of London 1973–74; Univ of Oxford: departmental demonstrator in vertebrate zoology Dept of Zoology 1974–80, lectr in zoology St Anne's Coll 1977–78, lectr in zoology New Coll 1979–80, Leverhulme Tst research fell Dept of Zoology 1980–85, Royal Soc univ research fell Dept of Zoology 1985–95, lectr in zoology Pembroke Coll 1988–91, extraordinary lectr in zoology New Coll 1991–95, Isobel Laing tutorial fell in med biology Oriel Coll 1994–99, Wellcome Tst sr research fell in basic biomedical sci Dept of Zoology 1995–2000, univ research lectr 1996–99, reader in parasite ecology 1999–2002, supernumerary fell Oriel Coll 1999–2001, NERC sr research fell Dept of Zoology 2000–05, prof of parasite ecology 2002–12, tutorial fell in biological sciences ChCh 2002–12, sr research fell EU Framework 6 EDEN project Dept of Zoology 2005–10, prof research fell Dept of Zoology 2010–12; Remote Sensing and Geographical Information Systems in Epidemiology (ed with S I Hay and D J Rogers, 2000); numerous jl articles, conf papers and book contribs; *Recreations* gardening, tennis, cycling, textiles; *Style—* Prof Sarah Randolph; ✉ Department of Zoology, University of Oxford, South Parks Road, Oxford OX1 3PS (☎ 01865 271241, fax 01865 271240, e-mail sarah.randolph@zoo.ox.ac.uk)

RANE, Prof Abhay; OBE (2014); *Educ* MS; *Career* conslt urological surgeon and clinical lead for urology Surrey and Sussex NHS Tst; adjunct prof of urology Univ of Southern Calif 2012–; FRCS; *Style—* Prof Abhay Rane, OBE; ✉ Surrey and Sussex Healthcare NHS Trust, East Surrey Hospital, Canada Avenue, Redhill RH1 5RH

RANG, Dr Humphrey Peter; *b* 13 June 1936; *Educ* Univ Coll Sch Hampstead, UCL (BSc, MSc), UCH Med Sch (MB BS), Balliol Coll Oxford (DPhil, MA); *Career* Univ of Oxford: J H Burn research fell Dept of Pharmacology 1961–64, research asst Dept of Pharmacology 1964–65, lectr 1965–72, fell and tutor in physiology Lincoln Coll 1967–72; prof of Pharmacology Univ of Southampton 1972–74; prof and head Dept of Pharmacology: St George's Hosp Med Sch London 1974–79, UCL 1979–83; dir Novartis Inst for Med Sciences (formerly Sandoz Inst for Med Research) 1983–97, head Scientific Advsy Bd Biofrontera AG 1997–2004; prof of pharmacology UCL 1995–2001, prof emeritus 2001–; visiting research assoc Dept of Pharmacology Albert Einstein Coll of Med NY USA 1966–67; organizing sec Symposia on Drug Action Biological Cncl 1979–84; conslt Sandoz Ltd Basle 1981–83; ed-in-chief Br Jl of Pharmacology 2005–08 (memb Editorial Bd 1968–74); memb Editorial Advsy Bd: Molecular Pharmacology 1975–90, Archives of Pharmacology 1977–95; memb: Neurosciences Bd MRC 1974–77, Ctee Br Pharmacological Soc 1977–80, Govt Grant Bd Royal Soc 1980–83, Exec Ctee Int Congress of Pharmacology 1981–84, Senate Univ of London 1981–83, Wellcome Tst Neurosciences Panel 1988–90, pres Br Pharmacological Soc 2014–15; Poulsson Medal Norwegian Pharmacological Soc 1994, Gaddum Medal Br Pharmacological Soc 1972, Vane Medal Br Pharmacological Soc 2009; memb Academia Europaea 1991, hon memb Hungarian Pharmacological Soc 2006; FRS 1980, FMedSci 1997; *Style—* Dr Humphrey Rang, FRS

RANGER, Kulveer Singh; *Educ* Latymer Upper Sch Hammersmith, Bartlett Sch of Architecture UCL (BSc), Kingston Business Sch (DMS); *Career* sr mgmnt conslt Nichols Gp 2000–08, dir of transport policy GLA 2008–; vice-chm (cities) Cons Pty 2007–08; memb Bd Transport for London; MAPM; *Style—* Kulveer Ranger, Esq; ✉ Greater London Authority, City Hall, The Queenâs Walk, More London, London SE1 2AA

RANK, John Rowland; s of Capt Rowland Rank, RFA (d 1939), of Aldwick Place, W Sussex, and Margaret, *née* McArthur (d 1988); n of late J Arthur Rank (Baron Rank, d 1972), fndr of Rank Orgn, and gs of late Joseph Rank, fndr of Rank Flour Milling; *b* 13 January 1930; *Educ* Stowe; *Career* property owner; Lord of the Manor of Saham Toney Norfolk; Rank Ltd 1948–50; patron Cancer Wise (formerly Wessex Cancer Help Centre); tstee Chichester Oxmarket Centre of Arts (former chm), patron Chichester Festival of Music Dance and Speech (affiliated to Int Fedn of Music Dance and Speech); former tstee: Stansted Park Fndn, Ian Askew Charitable Tst; former vice-chm Pallant House Chichester; hon patron Chichester Festival Theatre; former memb Cncl: Sussex Diocese, Friends of Chichester Cathedral, Funtington Parish; sometime memb Ct of Corp of Sons of Clergy; memb and hon sec Sennicotts Church Advsy Cncl; former memb Pagham PCC; vice-pres Chichester Fencing Club, pres Murray Club Chichester; Civic Award

Chichester City Cncl 2015; Freeman City of London 1989; *Recreations* theatre, architectural, gardening, travelling, art exhibitions; *Clubs* Georgian Gp, Regency Soc of Brighton and Hove, Sloane; *Style*— John Rank, Esq; ✉ Riverside, Old Bosham, Chichester, West Sussex PO18 8HP

RANKIN, Alastair John; s of William Brian Rankin (d 1976), and Margaret Christine, *née* Crawford (d 1983); *b* 5 September 1951, Belfast; *Educ* Royal Belfast Academical Instn, TCD (BA); *m* 26 Oct 1979, Gillian Elizabeth Susanne, *née* Dorrity; 2 s (Maurice John b 6 Aug 1982, Timothy Brian b 18 July 1985); *Career* Cleaver Fulton Rankin: apprentice slr 1974–77, asst slr 1977–80, ptnr 1980–2011, managing ptnr 2003–05, sr ptnr 2005–11, chm 2011–14, conslt 2014–15; pt/t chm Pension Appeals Tbnl 1998–, pt/t judge First Tier Tbnl (Tax Chamber) 2009–; slr General Assembly Presbyterian Church in Ireland 1993–2015, Law Soc of NI: memb 1977, memb Cncl 1985–, treas 1992–95, jr vice-pres 1995–96, pres 1996–97, sr vice-pres 1997–98; memb UK Delgn CCBE 1999–2014 (head 2005–06); hon sec Ulster Architectural Heritage Soc 1985–95; memb: Law Soc of Ireland 1997, Soc of Tst and Estate Practitioners (chm NI Branch 2007–09), Judicial Appts Cmmn NI 2011–; *Recreations* choral singing; *Clubs* Ulster Reform, Bushfoot Golf; *Style*— Alastair J Rankin, Esq; ✉ Cleaver Fulton Rankin, 50 Bedford Street, Belfast BT2 7FW (☎ 028 9024 3141, fax 028 9024 9096, e-mail a.rankin@cfrlaw.co.uk)

RANKIN, Ian James; OBE (2002); s of James Rankin (d 1990), and Isobel, *née* Vickers (d 1979); *b* 28 April 1960; *Educ* Univ of Edinburgh (MA); *m* 5 July 1986, Miranda, *née* Harvey; 2 s (Jack b 18 Feb 1992, Kit b 15 July 1994); *Career* writer and radio dramatist; presenter Ian Rankin's Evil Thoughts (Channel 4), reviewer Newsnight Review (BBC); books trans into 23 languages; memb: Crime Writers Assoc 1987– (pres 1999–2000), Soc of Authors; Gold Dagger Award 1997, Grand Prix du Roman Noir 2003; Hon Degrees: Univ of Abertay Dundee, Univ of St Andrews, Univ of Edinburgh; *Books* Inspector Rebus novels incl: Knots and Crosses, Hide and Seek, Tooth and Nail, A Good Hanging and Other Stories, Strip Jack, The Black Book, Mortal Causes, Let It Bleed, Black and Blue, The Hanging Garden, Dead Souls, Set In Darkness, The Falls, Resurrection Men, A Question of Blood, Fleshmarket Close (Crime Thriller of the Year Br Book Awards 2005), The Naming of the Dead, Exit Music; Jack Harvey novels incl: Blood Hunt, Bleeding Hearts, Witch Hunt; other pubns incl: Beggars Banquet (short stories), Watchman (novel); *Recreations* Times crossword, rock music, seedy bars; *Style*— Ian Rankin, Esq, OBE; ✉ c/o Curtis Brown Ltd, Haymarket House, 28–29 Haymarket, London SW1Y 4SP

RANKIN, Sir Ian Niall; 4 Bt (UK 1898), of Bryngwyn, Much Dewchurch, Co Hereford; s of late Lt-Col (Arthur) Niall Talbot Rankin, yr s of 2 Bt; s unc, Sir Hugh Rankin, 3 Bt 1988; *b* 19 December 1932; *Educ* Eton, ChCh Oxford (MA); *m* 1, 1959 (m dis 1967), Alexandra, da of Adm Sir Laurence George Durlacher, KCB, OBE, DSC; 1 da (Zara Sophia (Hon Mrs Humphrey Drummond) b 1960), 1 s (Gavin Niall b 1962); m 2, 1980 (m dis 1998), June, er da of late Capt Thomas Marsham-Townshend; 1 s (Lachlan John b 1980); m3, 2013, Mrs Prudence Mary Lane Fox; *Heir* s, Gavin Rankin; *Career* Lt Scots Gds (Res); dir of industrial cos: New Arcadia Explorations Ltd, Slumberfleece Ltd, I N Rankin Oil Ltd; patron The Samaritans, govr Moorfields Eye Hosp; FRGS; *Books* This Erratic Planet – What Happens When the Earth Changes Its Axis of Rotation (2010), A New Look at the Solar System (2015); *Recreations* shooting, yachting; *Clubs* Royal Yacht Sqdn, Pratt's, White's; *Style*— Sir Ian Rankin, Bt; ✉ 97 Elgin Avenue, London W9 2DA (☎ office 020 7286 0251, home 020 7286 5117)

RANKIN, John; CMG; s of late James Rankin, CBE, and Agnes Rankin; *b* 12 March 1957; *Educ* Univ of Glasgow, McGill Univ Montreal; *Career* diplomat; FCO: joined as asst legal advsr 1988, HM consul gen Boston 2003–07, dir Americas 2008–11, high cmmr to Sri Lanka and non-resident high cmmr to Maldives 2011–15, chargé d'affaires to Nepal 2015–; *Publications* incl articles on Scots law and international law; *Style*— Mr John Rankin, CMG; ✉ FCO, King Charles Street, London SW1A 2AH

RANKIN, (Christopher) Paul; s of Hugh Rankin, of Bangor, Co Down, and Iris, *née* Gracey; *b* 1 October 1959; *Educ* Royal Belfast Academical Instn, Hutchesons' GS Glasgow, Queen's Univ Belfast; *m* 22 March 1984, Jeanne Marie, da of Prof Richard Allen Lebrun, of Winnipeg, Canada; 2 da (Claire Nasya b 19 Aug 1986, Emily Paige b 25 March 1989); *Career* worked as waiter while travelling world 1981–83; chef: Le Gavroche 1984–86, Club 19 Saskatchewan 1986, (tournant) Four Seasons Hotel Vancouver 1987, Mount View Hotel Calistoga Napa Valley CA 1988; chef/prop Roscoff restaurant Belfast 1989–99; prop: Cafe Paul Rankin 1995–, Cayenne 1999–, Rain City 2002–, Roscoff Brasserie 2004–; awards for Roscoff: Michelin star 1991, Caterer and Hotelkeeper Newcomer of the Year 1991, included in Gault Milau 300 best restaurants in Europe, Britain's Best Restaurant Courvoisier's Book of the Best 1994, and Great British Chefs II 1995, 4/5 Good Food Guide 1996 and 1997; TV appearances on Hot Chefs 1991 and Gourmet Ireland (BBC) 1993, Ready Steady Cook (BBC) 1994–95; memb Académie Culinaire de Grande Bretagne; *Books* Hot Chefs (1991), Gourmet Ireland (1993), Hot Food, Cool Jazz (1994), Goumet Ireland II (1995), Ideal Home Cooking (1998), New Irish Cookery (2003); *Recreations* yoga, cycling, playing with the kids; *Style*— Paul Rankin, Esq

RANKIN, Yvonne; da of Ernest Ashton (d 1980), and Alva, *née* Brocklehurst; *b* 6 March 1962, Lancs; *Career* gen mangr Travel Gp United Norwest 1990–96, md Travelcare Gp 1996–98; Co-Operative Gp: chief gen mangr Specialist Retail 1998–2001, chief exec Specialist Retail Businesses 2001–05; chief exec Central and Southern Europe A S Watson 2005–07, chief exec Thresher Gp 2007–; non-exec dir Liverpool Women's Hosp; CIMgt 2000; *Recreations* travelling, theatre going; *Style*— Ms Yvonne Rankin; ✉ The Maples, Holmes Chapel Road, Over Peover, Cheshire WA16 9RD (fax 01565 572 3706, e-mail yvonne.rankin@hotmail.co.uk)

RANKIN-HUNT, Maj David; CVO (2014, LVO 2005, MVO 1993), MBE (2000), TD (1990); s of James Rankin-Hunt, of Wales, and Edwina Anne, *née* Blakeman; *b* 1956; *Educ* Christ Coll Brecon, St Martin's Sch; *Career* Lt Scots Gds, Maj The London Scottish Regt (51 Highland Vol) 1989– (a regimental tstee), Regtl Col The London Scottish Regt 2007–14; Dep Hon Col The London Regt 2007–14; Lord Chamberlain's Office 1981–: registrar 1987–89, employed in The Royal Collection 1989– (administrator 1993–2014); Norfolk Herald of Arms Extraordinary 1994–, dep inspr of Regtl Colours 1995–, dep inspr of RAF Badges 1996–; pres Berks, Bucks and Oxon branch Scots Guards Assoc 2007–10; county pres Berks St John Ambulance 1994–99, dir of ceremonies Priory for Wales Order of St John 1995–2004; lay steward St George's Chapel Windsor Castle 1987–; curatorial advsr Berkshire Yeomanry Museum, tstee Guards' Museum 2003–13; special advsr (hons) Govt of Grenada; hon consul Equatorial Guinea; tstee West India Ctee 2014–; KStJ; genealogist Antigua and Barbuda Orders of Chivalry 2005–14, Grand Cross Order of Merit and Knight Commander Order of the Nation Antigua and Barbuda, Grand Offr Mil Order of St George Tonga, Hon ADC to Govr-Gen of Antigua and Barbuda 2015–; *Recreations* military history, conservation issues, dogs, music, books; *Clubs* Army and Navy; *Style*— Maj David Rankin-Hunt, CVO, MBE, KCN, TD; ✉ 7 Cumberland Lodge Mews, The Great Park, Windsor, Berkshire SL4 2JD (☎ 01784 437269, e-mail hunt365@btinternet.com)

RANSLEY, Philip Goddard; *b* 17 August 1942; *Educ* Northgate GS Ipswich, Gonville & Caius Coll Cambridge (MA, annual prize), Guy's Hosp Med Sch London (MB BChir, Treas's medal and prize in clinical surgery); *Career* conslt urological surgn: Gt Ormond St Hosp for Sick Children 1977–2005, Guy's Hosp 1998–2005, The St Peter's Hosps 1977–98; sr lectr in paediatric urology Inst of Child Health and hon sr lectr in paediatric urology Inst of Urology London 1977–2007; pres Euro Soc for Paediatric Urology 1994–99; FRCS 1971; *Awards* Registrar's Prize NE Metropolitan Region Surgical Soc 1972, Simpla Prize for Research Br Assoc of Urological Surgns 1975, John Latimer Lecture American Urological Assoc 1982, Inaugural Nils Ericsson Meml Lecture 1984, Dantec Prize Br Assoc of Urological Surgns 1985, distinguished overseas guest Section of Surgery and hon fell American Acad of Pediatrics 1989, Dantec Prize Br Assoc of Urological Surgns 1991, St Peter's Medal Br Assoc of Urological Surgns 1999, Paediatric Urology Medal American Acad of Paediatrics 2001; Sitara-i-Imtaz (Pakistan) 2009; *Publications* author of numerous pubns in learned jls; *Style*— Philip Ransley, Esq; ☎ 020 7390 8323, fax 020 7390 8324, e-mail pgr2@doctors.org.uk

RANSLEY, Thomas (Tom); *b* 6 September 1985, Ashford, Kent; *Educ* Univ of York, Univ of Cambridge; *Career* rower; achievements incl: Silver medal (eights) World Championships 2010 and 2011, Bronze medal (eights) Olympic Games 2012, Gold medal (eights) Olympic Games 2016; *Clubs* York City Rowing; *Style*— Tom Ransley, Esq

RANSON, Lee; *m* Alexis Ranson; 2 da (Annabelle, Alana), 1 s (Owen); *Career* Eversheds LLP: joined as commercial litigator 1990, head Real Estate and Real Estate Litigation Gp 2006–09, managing ptnr 2009–; *Style*— Lee Ranson, Esq; ✉ Eversheds LLP, 1 Wood Street, London EC2V 7WS

RANSON, Dr Rosalind; *b* 15 January 1965; *Educ* King Edward VII Upper Sch Melton Mowbray, St George's Univ of London (MB BS), KCL (MA); *Career* GP London 1993–, deanery tutor London Deanery 2002–06, cmmr and GP expert on commission on human medicines 2007–; memb GMC 1999–2008 (chair Working Gp for the Devpt of Guidance 'Children and Young People: Doctors' Roles and Responsibilities' 2006–07, memb Standards and Ethics Ctee); author of contribs to learned jls; memb Medico-Legal Soc; MRCGP 1994; *Recreations* violin (quartet playing), skiing, sailing; *Style*— Dr Rosalind Ranson; ✉ website www.rosalindranson.com

RANTZEN, Dame Esther Louise (Mrs Desmond Wilcox); DBE (2015, CBE 2006, OBE 1991); da of Henry Barnato (Harry) Rantzen (d 1992), of London, and Katherine, *née* Leverson (d 2005); *b* 22 June 1940; *Educ* N London Collegiate Sch, Somerville Coll Oxford (MA); *m* 22 Dec 1977, Desmond Wilcox (d 2000); 2 da (Emily b 1978, Rebecca b 1980), 1 s (Joshua b 1981); *Career* television prodr and presenter; studio mangr BBC Radio 1963; BBC TV: researcher 1965, dir 1967, researcher and reporter Braden's Week 1968, presenter and prodr That's Life 1973–94, prodr documentary series The Big Time 1976; presenter: That's Family Life, Hearts of Gold 1988–94, Drugwatch, Childwatch, Esther 1994–2002, That's Esther; fndr and pres ChildLine; pres: Meet-a-Mum Assoc, Assoc of Youth with ME (AYME), anti-Bullying Alliance; vice-pres ASBAH, chm Commission4Children 2009, chair Silver Line Helpline 2012, tstee NSPCC 2006 (hon memb 1989); memb: Consumer Cncl 1981–90, Health Educn Authy 1989–95, patron: Hillingdon Manor Sch for Autistic Children, Princess Diana's Sch, The New Sch at West Heath; tstee Ben Hardwick Meml Fund; fell Liverpool John Moores Univ, hon fell Somerville Coll Oxford; Hon DLitt: South Bank Univ 2000, Southampton Inst, Univ of Portsmouth 2003, Univ of Staffs 2009, Univ of Wolverhampton 2009; *Awards* Special Judges' Award RTS 1974, BBC Personality of 1975 Variety Club of GB, Euro Soc for Organ Transplant Award 1985, Special Judges' Award for Journalism RTS 1986, Richard Dimbleby Award BAFTA 1988, RTS Hall of Fame 1997, Lifetime Achievement Award Women in Film and TV; *Books* Kill the Chocolate Biscuit (with Desmond Wilcox, 1981), Baby Love (with Desmond Wilcox, 1985), Ben – The Story of Ben Hardwick (with Shaun Woodward, 1985), Esther – The Autobiography (2001), A Secret Life (2003), If Not Now, When? (2008), Running Out of Tears (2011); *Recreations* growing old disgracefully; *Clubs* Hamsters; *Style*— Dame Esther Rantzen, DBE; ✉ ChildLine, London E1 6GL; c/o Billy Marsh Associates, 76a Grove End Road, London NW8 9ND (☎ 020 7383 9979)

RAPHAEL, Adam Eliot Geoffrey; s of Geoffrey George Raphael (d 1969), of London, and Nancy May, *née* Rose; *b* 22 April 1938; *Educ* Charterhouse, Oriel Coll Oxford (MA); *m* 16 May 1970, Caroline Rayner, da of George Ellis (d 1954), of Cape Town, South Africa; 1 s (Thomas Geoffrey b 1971), 1 da (Anna Nancy b 1974); *Career* 2 Lt RA 1956–58; political corr The Guardian 1974–76 (foreign corr Washington 1969–73 and South Africa 1973), exec ed The Observer 1988–93 (political corr 1976–81, political ed 1981–87), presenter Newsnight BBC TV 1987–88, writer on home affairs The Economist 1994–2004, ed The Good Hotel Guide 2004–; Investigative Reporter of the Year Granada 1973, Journalist of the Year British Press Awards 1973; *Books* My Learned Friends (1990), Grotesque Libels (1993), Ultimate Risk (1994); *Recreations* tennis, skiing, reading, golf; *Clubs* Garrick, RAC, Hurlingham; *Style*— Adam Raphael; ✉ 50 Addison Avenue, London W11 4QP (☎ 020 7603 9133)

RAPHAEL, Frederic Michael; s of Cedric Michael Raphael, TD (d 1979), and Irene Rose, *née* Mauser (d 2011); *b* 14 August 1931; *Educ* Charterhouse, St John's Coll Cambridge (maj scholar, MA); *m* 17 Jan 1955, Sylvia Betty, da of Hyman Glatt; 2 s (Paul b 1958, Stephen b 1967), 1 da (Sarah b 1960 d 2001); *Career* author; FRSL 1964; *Books* Obbligato (1956), The Earlsdon Way (1958), The Limits of Love (1960), A Wild Surmise (1961), The Graduate Wife (1962), The Trouble with England (1962), Lindmann (1963), Darling (1966), Orchestra and Beginners (1967), Like Men Betrayed (1970), Who Were You With Last Night? (1971), April, June and November (1972), Richard's Things (1973, screenplay 1981), California Time (1975), The Glittering Prizes (1976, TV plays 1976, Writer of the Year Award), Heaven and Earth (1985), After The War (1988), The Hidden I (1990), Of Gods and Men (1992), A Double Life (1993), Old Scores (1995), Coast to Coast (1998), Final Demands (2010, The Glittering Prizes III), Private Views (2015); short stories: Sleeps Six (1979), Oxbridge Blues (1980, TV plays 1984), Think of England (1986), The Latin Lover (1994), All His Sons (1999), Fame and Fortune (The Glittering Prizes II) (2007), Final Demands (2010); notebooks: Personal Terms (2001), Rough Copy (2004), Cuts and Bruises (2006), Ticks and Crosses (2008), Ifs and Buts (2011), There and Then (2013); screenplays: Nothing but the Best (1964), Darling (Acad Award, 1965), Two for the Road (1967), Far From the Madding Crowd (1967), A Severed Head (1972), Daisy Miller (1974), Rogue Male (1976), Something's Wrong (dir, 1978), School Play (1979), The Best of Friends (1979), Richard's Things (1980), Oxbridge Blues (1984), After the War (1989), The Man In The Brooks Brothers Shirt (dir 1990, ACE Award), Armed Response (1995), Eyes Wide Shut (1999), Coast to Coast (2002); biography: Somerset Maugham and his World (1977), Byron (1982) A Jew Among The Romans, Flavius Jusephus and His Legacy (2013), Correspondence: A Distant Intimacy (with Joseph Epstein); essays: Bookmarks (ed, 1975), Cracks in the Ice (1979), The Necessity of Anti-Semitism (1997), The Great Philosophers (ed with Ray Monk, 2000), The Benefits of Doubt (2003), How Odd of God (2015); autobiography: A Spoilt Boy (2003), Going Up (2015); From the Greek (play, 1979), Karl Popper: Historicism and Its Poverty (1998), Eyes Wide Open (1999), The Benefits of Doubt (2001), Some Talk of Alexander (2006); Petronius' Satyrica (solo trans, 2003); translations (with Kenneth McLeish): Poems of Catullus (1976), The Oresteia (1978, televised as The Serpent Son BBC 1979), Complete plays of Aeschylus (1991), Euripides' Medea (1994), Euripides' Hippolytos (1997); Sophokles' Aias (1998); *Recreations* tennis, bridge; *Style*— Frederic Raphael, Esq, FRSL; ✉ c/o Ed Victor Ltd, 6 Bayley Street, London WC1B

RAPLEY, Prof Christopher Graham (Chris); CBE (2003); s of Ronald Rapley, of Bath, and Barbara Helen, *née* Stubbs; *b* 8 April 1947; *Educ* King Edward's Sch Bath, Jesus Coll Oxford (MA), Victoria Univ of Manchester Jodrell Bank (MSc), Univ of London Mullard Space Sci Lab (PhD); *m* 13 June 1970, Norma, da of Y Khan, of Georgetown, Guyana; 2 da (Emma Jane, Charlotte Anne (twins) b 1971); *Career* UCL Dept of Space and Climate Physics: lectr 1981–87, reader 1988–91, prof of remote sensing science 1991–97; head Remote Sensing Gp MSSL 1982–94, exec dir Int Cncl of Scientific Unions Int Geosphere-

Biosphere Prog Royal Swedish Acad of Sciences Stockholm 1994–97, dir Br Antarctic Survey 1998–2007, dir Science Museum London 2007–10; fell St Edmund's Coll Cambridge 1999–, sr visiting scientist NASA Jet Propulsion Lab 2006–, prof of climate science UCL 2009–, visiting prof Imperial Coll London 2010; pres Scientific Ctee on Antarctic Research 2006–08 (hon fell 2008–); chair Int Polar Year 2007–2008 Planning Gp Int Cncl of Science 2003–04, memb Int Polar Year 2007–2008 Jt Ctee 2005–10, chair UCL Policy Cmmn on Communicating Climate Science 2012–, chair London Climate Change Partnership 2013–, chair European Space Agency DG's High Level Science Advsy Ctee 2014–16; author of over 150 research pubns on space astronomy and earth observation; Edinburgh Medal 2008; commissioned to write (with Duncan Macmillan) and perform play 2071 Royal Court 2014; hon prof UEA 1998–, fell UCL 2008– (hon prof 1998–); Hon DSc Univ of Bristol 2008, Hon DSc UEA 2010; memb American Geophysical Union, memb Academia Europaea 2010–; *Books* 2071 – The World We'll Leave Our Grandchildren (2015); *Recreations* digital photography; *Style*— Prof Chris Rapley, CBE; ✉ University College London, Department of Earth Sciences, Gower Street, London WC1E 6BT (☎ 020 7679 3560, e-mail christopher.rapley@ucl.ac.uk, Twitter @chrisrapley3131)

RAPLEY, Prof Jane Margaret; OBE (2001); da of John Edward Robert Rapley (d 2007), and Ella Mary, *née* Jones (d 1970); *b* 10 July 1946; *Educ* Ickenham HS, Ealing Sch of Art, Nottingham Coll of Art (DipAD), RCA (MA); *m* Feb 2009, Peter David Towse; 1 da ((Crystal) Bella Towse b 31 Oct 1984); *Career* design mangr (men's knitwear) Sabre International Textiles 1971–76, design and design mgmnt conslt Chateau Stores of Canada 1977–78, dir (men's casualwear) J R Associates 1977–81, retail dir South Molton Clothing Depot 1981–83, dir (men's retail and design collections) Burrows & Hare 1984–87, dir Peter Towse Design Servs 1983–; lectr on design history, design mgmnt, knitwear and menswear 1970–80: Middlesex, Brighton, Kingston, Trent and Lancashire Polys, Textile Inst, Costume Soc; lectr on: knitwear Central Sch of Art & Design 1977–81, menswear RCA 1981–84; Central Saint Martins Coll of Art & Design: head Textile Dept 1987–89, dean Sch of Fashion & Textiles 1989–2005, head 2006–12; pro vice-chllr UAL 2012; conslt HE Art, Design & Fashion/Fashion Business; memb Cncl Textprint 2002– (tstee 2015–); govr Cleveland Coll 2015; hon fell Musashino Univ Japan 2009, hon fell Falmouth Univ 2013; ACSD 1977–; FRSA 2002; *Books* The Art of Knitting, Shimi Jimi; *Recreations* reading the early works of Sergei Kaplovitch, reading about flora, fauna and food, collecting junk; *Style*— Prof Jane Rapley, OBE, ☎ 07515 686559, e-mail janerapley@ntlworld.com

RAPPORT, Prof Nigel Julian; s of Anthony David Rapport, of Cardiff, and Anita, *née* Bloom; *b* 8 November 1956, Cardiff; *Educ* Clifton, Gonville & Caius Coll Cambridge (scholar, MA), Univ of Manchester (PhD); *m* 3 May 1996, Elizabeth, da of Kenneth Munro; 1 s (Callum b 13 Sept 1987), 1 da (Emilie b 3 Jan 1999); *Career* Univ of St Andrews: chair of anthropological and philosophical studies 1996–, head Sch of Philosophical, Anthropological and Film Studies 2014–, sr Canada research chair in globalization, citizenship and justice Concordia Univ Montreal 2005; visiting prof: Univ of Copenhagen 2000 and 2013, Melbourne Univ 2004, Aarhus University 2011; external prof Norwegian Univ of Science and Technol Trondheim 2002–; Hd of Sch of Philosophy Social Anthropology and Film Univ of St Andrews 2014–; pres Anthropology and Archaeology Section BAAS 2001, sec Assoc of Social Anthropologists of the Cwlth 1994–98; Curl Essay Prize Royal Anthropological Inst 1996, BP Prize Lectureship RSE 1996, Henrietta Harvey Prize Lectureship Memorial Univ 2007, Rivers Medal Royal Anthropological Inst 2012; founding fell Inst of Contemporary Scotland 2000, FRSA 2002, FRSE 2003; *Books* incl: Talking Violence (1987), Diverse World Views in an English Village (1993), The Prose and the Passion (1994), Transcendent Individual (1997), Key Concepts in Social and Cultural Anthropology (2000), The Trouble with Community (2002), I am Dynamite: An Alternative Anthropology of Power (2003), Of Orderlies and Men: Hospital Porters Achieving Wellness at Work (2008), Anyone, the Cosmopolitan Subject of Anthropology (2012), Community, Cosmopolitanism and the Problem of Human Commonality (2012), Distortion and Love: An Anthropological Reading of the Art and Life of Stanley Spencer (2016); *Recreations* appreciating art and literature, travel, sport, music, reading, walking; *Style*— Prof Nigel Rapport

RAPSON, Sarah; *b* London; *Educ* London Business Sch (MBA); *Career* Identity and Passport Service: exec dir of service planning and delivery until 2010, chief exec 2010–13; registrar gen for England and Wales 2010–14, DG UK Visas and Immigration Home Office 2013–; *Style*— Ms Sarah Rapson; ✉ UK Visas and Immigration, Home Office, 2 Marsham Street, London SW1P 4DF

RASCH, Sir Simon Anthony Carne; 4 Bt (UK 1903), of Woodhill, Danbury, Essex; s of Sir Richard Guy Carne Rasch, 3 Bt (d 1996), and his 1 w, Anne Mary, *née* Dent-Brocklehurst (d 1989); *b* 26 February 1948; *Educ* Eton, RAC Cirencester; *m* 31 Oct 1987, Julia, er da of Maj Michael Godwin Plantagenet Stourton and Lady Joanna Stourton, *née* Lambart, da of Field Marshal 10 Earl of Cavan; 1 da (Molly Clare Anne b 10 Sept 1990), 1 s (Toby Richard Carne b 28 Sept 1994); *Heir* s, Toby Rasch; *Career* page of honour to HM 1962–64; chartered surveyor; Liveryman Worshipful Co of Grocers; *Clubs* Pratt's; *Style*— Sir Simon Rasch, Bt

RASHID, Prof Aly; *b* 14 October 1958; *Educ* Burnage HS Manchester, Univ of Manchester (MB ChB, DRCOG, MD); *m* Claire; 2 da (Eleanor, Rosalind), 1 s (Theo); *Career* house dr positions N Manchester Gen Hosp and Royal Preston Hosp 1982–83, vocational trg scheme in gen practice Hope Hosp Salford 1983, SHO 1984–85, trainee GP Swinton 1985–86; princ in gen practice: St Matthews Med Centre Leicester 1986–92, Countesthorpe Health Centre Leicester 1992–; formerly RCGP research fell in gen practice Dept of Community Health and clinical tutor in gen practice Med Sch Univ of Leicester; prof of primary health care De Montfort Univ 1998– (currently head Div of Primary Care); med dir Leics County and Rutland PCT; RCGP: memb Faculty Bd 1987–, memb Nat Cncl 1991–, memb Exec Ctee 1993–, nat chm of educn 1993–, RCGP observer Assoc of Univ Depts of Gen Practice 1993–, dir Nat Leadership Prog 2002–; performance assessor GMC 2000–; memb: Conf of Postgrad Advsrs in Gen Practice Univs of the UK 1993–, Jt Ctee on Postgrad Trg for Gen Practice (JCPTGP) 1996–, Advsy Gp on Med Educn and Trg in Gen Practice Dept of Health 1996–, Med Audit Advsy Gp (MAAG) 1996–; med writer Leicester Mercury 1989–92, also author of numerous pubns in academic jls; FRCGP 1991 (MRCGP 1986); *Recreations* tennis, cricket (former rep Manchester and Lancashire Colleges and capt Manchester Med Sch Cricket Team, currently player for village team Willoughby Waterleys); *Clubs* Carisbrooke Lawn Tennis (Leicester); *Style*— Prof Aly Rashid

RASHLEIGH, Jonathan Michael Vernon; s of Nicholas Vernon Rashleigh, of Norton Lindsey, Warks, and Rosalie Mary, *née* Matthews; *b* 29 September 1950; *Educ* Bryanston; *m* 5 April 1975, Sarah, da of John Norwood, of Knowle, W Midlands; 3 s (Charles b 1979, Hugh b 1986, Philip b 1988), 1 da (Julia b 1982); *Career* Ernst and Whinney 1968–76, 3i Group 1976–90 (dir 3i plc 1986–90); dir: Legal & General Investment Management Ltd 1991–93, National Australia Group 1993–95, Henderson Crosthwaite Ltd 1995–99, Investec UK Ltd 1999–2000; Freeman City of London, Liveryman Worshipful Co of Tobacco Pipe Makers and Tobacco Blenders 1972; MSI 1993; FCA 1979 (ACA 1974), FRSA 1995; *Recreations* chess, theatre, cricket, golf; *Style*— Jonathan Rashleigh, Esq; ✉ Longeaves, Norton Lindsey, Warwickshire CV35 8JL (☎ 01926 842523, e-mail jonathan@jrashleigh.freeserve.co.uk)

RATCLIFF, Rev Canon David William; s of George and Dorothy Ratcliff, of Canterbury, Kent; *b* 3 November 1937, Canterbury, Kent; *Educ* Canterbury Cathedral Choir Sch, St Michael's Sch Ingoldisthorpe, KCL, Edinburgh Theol Coll, London Univ; *m* 1963, Gillian Mary, da of Frederick and Dorothy Price; 3 s (Andrew b 1964, James b 1966, Timothy b 1970); *Career* asst curate Croydon 1962–69, vicar St Mary's Sittingbourne 1969–75, advsr in adult educn Dio of Canterbury 1975–91, chaplain-rector Anglican (Ecusa) Church Frankfurt-am-Main 1991–98, archdeacon of Germany and Northern Europe 1996–2005, canon of Gibraltar Cathedral 1996–2005, chaplain Anglican Church Stockholm 1998–2002; hon minor canon Canterbury Cathedral 1975–91 and 2003–13, hon chaplain Br Embassy Stockholm 1998–2002; hon pres Euro Assoc for Ecumenical Adult Educn 1982–88; founding memb Cncl of Anglican-Episcopal Churches in Germany, Br rep German EV Kirchentag Ecumenical Ctee 1978–97, previous memb European Movement of Christian Assoc for Europe; asst dir Telephone Samaritans 1966–75; chm Elham Environment Gp 2008; *Recreations* music, singing; *Style*— The Rev Canon David W Ratcliff; ✉ 9 The Orchards, Elham, Canterbury, Kent CT4 6TR (☎ 01303 840624, website www.elhamchurches.com)

RATCLIFFE, Anne Kirkpatrick; da of Dr John Kirkpatrick Ratcliffe (d 1997), and Alice Margaret, *née* Vaughan-Jones; *b* 19 April 1956; *Educ* Cheltenham Ladies' Coll, Univ of Southampton (BSc), City Univ (Dip Law); *Career* called to the Bar Inner Temple 1981; in practice SE Circuit 1981–; memb Family Law Bar Assoc, memb Soc of Cons Lawyers; *Recreations* collecting modern art, gardening; *Style*— Miss Anne Ratcliffe; ✉ 5 Pump Court, Temple, London EC4Y 7AP (☎ 020 7353 2532, fax 020 7353 5321)

RATCLIFFE, Prof (Richard) George; s of Dr Frederick William Ratcliffe, and Joyce Ratcliffe; *b* 3 April 1953; *Educ* Royal GS Newcastle upon Tyne, Manchester Grammar, Merton Coll Oxford (MA, DPhil); *m* 17 April 1982, Susan Margaret Hazelden; 1 s (James b 1983), 1 da (Aurelia b 1985); *Career* jr res fell Merton Coll Oxford 1978–81, higher scientific offr ARC Food Res Inst 1982–84; Univ of Oxford: lectr 1984–96, sr res fell New Coll 1984–89, fell and tutor in biological sci New Coll 1989–97 fell and tutor in biochemistry New Coll 1997–, reader 1996–2000, prof of plant scis 2000–; memb Advsy Bd Jl of Experimental Botany 1994–2012, ed (emerging technologies) Planta 2011– (memb Editorial Bd 2008–11), memb Advsy Bd Jl of Plant Physiology 2015–; memb Int Advsy Ctee Wageningen NMR Centre 1994–2009; visiting prof Université de Picardie Amiens 2001–04; tstee Harpur Tst 2015–, govr Bedford Girls' Sch 2016–; *Publications* Regulation of Primary Metabolic Pathways in Plants (ed with N J Kruger and S A Hill, 1999), Principles and Problems in Physical Chemistry for Biochemists (with N C Price, R A Dwek and M R Wormald, 2001); author of papers in scientific jls; *Recreations* book collecting, gardening, hill walking; *Style*— Prof R G Ratcliffe; ✉ New College, Oxford OX1 3BN; Department of Plant Sciences, University of Oxford, South Parks Road, Oxford OX1 3RB (☎ 01865 275000, e-mail george.ratcliffe@plants.ox.ac.uk)

RATCLIFFE, Prof Sir Peter John; kt (2014); *b* 14 May 1954, Lancs; *Educ* Lancaster Royal GS, Gonville and Caius Coll Cambridge (MB, ChB, MD); *m* Dr Fiona Ratcliffe; 2 da, 2 s; *Career* Nuffield prof of clinical medicine and head Nuffield Dept of Clinical Medicine Univ of Oxford 2003–16; dir Target Discovery Inst Univ of Oxford 2016–, clinical dir Francis Crick Inst 2016–; memb Ludwig Inst for Cancer Research, memb EMBO 2006; fell Magdalen Coll Oxford, hon fell Gonville and Caius Coll Cambridge; fell Acad of Med Sciences 2002, foreign hon memb American Acad of Arts and Sciences 2007; FRCP 1996 FRS 2002; *Recreations* gardening (when pressed), skiing; *Style*— Prof Sir Peter Ratcliffe, FRS; ✉ Target Discovery Institute, Nuffield Department of Medicine, University of Oxford, NDM Research Building, Old Road Campus, Oxford OX3 7FZ (e-mail peter.ratcliffe@ndm.ox.ac.uk, website www.ndm.ox.ac.uk/principal-investigators/researcher/peter-ratcliffe)

RATCLIFFE, (James) Terence; MBE (1987), JP (1972); s of John Ratcliffe (d 1995), of Bury, and Alice, *née* Bennet (d 1981); *Educ* Bury HS, Univ of Manchester (DipArch); *m* 8 Sept 1956, Mary Grundy (Molly), da of Reginald Victor Adlem (d 1990), of Bury; 3 s (Mark b 1961, Jonathon b 1964, Nicholas b 1965), 1 da (Elisabeth (twin) b 1965); *Career* architect, chm R G Partnership Ltd; ARIBA; *Recreations* athletics, YMCA; *Style*— Terence Ratcliffe, Esq, MBE; ✉ Ivy House, Bolton Road, West, Holcombe Brook, Bury, Lancashire; Ratcliffe Groves Partnership, 105 Manchester Road, Bury, Lancashire (☎ 0161 797 6000); Ratcliffe Groves Partnership, Brewers Hall, Aldermanbury Square, London (☎ 020 7600 6666)

RATHACAVAN, 3 Baron (UK 1953); Hugh Detmar Torrens O'Neill; 3 Bt (UK 1929); o s of 2 Baron Rathcavan, PC (d 1994), and his 1 w, Clare Désirée, *née* Blow (d 1956); *b* 14 June 1939; *Educ* Eton; *m* 28 March 1983, Sylvie Marie-Thérèse, da of late Georges Wichard du Perron, of Provence, France; 1 s (Hon François Hugh Nial b 26 June 1984); *Heir* s, Hon François O'Neill; *Career* Capt Irish Gds; journalist: Irish Times, Observer, Financial Times; chm: St Quentin Restaurants 1980–89, Brasserie St Quentin 2002–08; dir: Savoy Hotel Management and Savoy Restaurants 1989–94, Northern Bank Ltd 1990–97, The Old Bushmills Distillery Co Ltd 1990–99, The Brompton Bar and Grill Ltd 2008–14; chm: NI Airports 1986–92, NI Tourist Bd 1988–96; memb Br Tourist Authy 1988–96; memb: House of Lords Euro Select Ctee D, Br-Irish Interparliamentary Body 1994–99; *Recreations* food, travel, gardening; *Clubs* Beefsteak; *Style*— The Lord Rathcavan; ✉ 14 Thurloe Place, London SW7 2RZ (☎ 020 7584 5293, mobile 07860 746233, fax 020 7823 8846); Cleggan Lodge, Ballymena, Co Antrim BT43 7JW (☎ 028 2568 4209, fax 028 2568 4552, e-mail lordrathcavan@btopenworld.com)

RATHBONE, Jenny; AM; *b* Liverpool; *Educ* Univ of Essex (BA), Universidad Nacional Autonomade Mexico; *Partner* John Uden; 1 da (Eleanor b 1986), 1 s (Tomas b 1989); *Career* reporter-researcher World In Action (Granada TV) 1979–87, prodr A Matter of Life and Debt (Channel 4) 1987–88, prodr The Money Programme (BBC) 1989–96, cncllr London Borough of Islington 1998–2002, prog mangr Sure Start Hillmarton Islington 2002–07, memb Nat Assembly for Wales (Lab) Cardiff Central 2011–; chair Wales European Prog Monitoring Ctee, memb Public Accounts Ctee, memb Communications, Equalities and Local Govt Ctee; chair: Ind Review Panels of Complaints NHS London 1996–2003, Camden & Islington Health Action Zone Partnership 2000–01 (memb 1999–2002); lay memb Professional Exec Ctee Islington PCT 2002–06; memb Exec Ctee Fabian Soc 2010–12, memb Exec Ctee Welsh Lab 2012–; tstee Eleanor Rathbone Charitable Tst 1984–; govr: Llanedeyrn HS, Ysgol Pen y Groes; *Recreations* swimming, cycling, films, sustainable food markets; *Style*— Jenny Rathbone, AM; ✉ 165 Albany Road, Cardiff CF24 3NT (☎ 02920 256255); National Assembly for Wales (Cardiff Bay), Cardiff CF99 1NA (☎ 02920 898286, e-mail jenny.rathbone@wales.gov.uk)

RATHBONE, William; OBE (2012); s of William Rathbone (d 1992), of Charlbury, Oxon, and Margaret Hester (Peggie), *née* Lubbock (d 1986); *b* 5 June 1936; *Educ* Radley, ChCh Oxford (MA), IMEDE Lausanne (Dip Business Studies); *m* 1, 1960, Sarah Kynaston (d 2006), da of Brig Hugh S K Mainwaring, CB, CBE, DSO, TD (d 1976); 1 da (Lucy Elena b 17 April 1970), 1 s (William b 19 July 1974); *m* 2, 2010, Carolyn Wendy Dorothy Lloyd-Jacob, da of Eugene Henry Constantine Howard; *Career* Nat Serv cmmnd 2 Lt Royal Artillery 1954–56 (served Malaya 1955–56); The Ocean Group plc 1959–88: Elder Dempster Lines 1959–69 (based Nigeria and Ghana for 4 years), started up tanker and bulk carrier div 1969–71, IMEDE Lausanne 1972, dir Wm Cory & Sons Ltd 1973–74, gen mangr Ocean Inchcape Ltd 1974–79, exec dir Gastranco Ltd 1979–88; dir and chief exec Royal United Kingdom Beneficent Assoc and Universal Beneficent Soc 1988–2001; non-exec dir Rathbone Brothers plc (fund mgmnt and banking gp) 1994–2003; tstee: Queen's Nursing Inst, North Waltham Village Tst, Eleanor Rathbone Charitable Tst,

Hadfield Tst; memb Ct New England Co; memb Devpt Bd ChCh Oxford; vice-pres Christ Church (Oxford) United Clubs; Freeman City of London, Liveryman Worshipful Co of Skinners; *Recreations* the arts, opera, theatre, fishing, shooting, rowing, friends; *Clubs* Brooks's, Leander; *Style—* William Rathbone, Esq, OBE; ✉ 7 Brynmaer Road, London SW11 4EN (☎ 020 7978 1935)

RATLEDGE, Prof Colin; s of Fred Ratledge (d 1975), of Preston, Lancs, and Freda Smith Proudlock (d 1986); *b* 9 October 1936; *Educ* Bury HS, Univ of Manchester (BSc, PhD); *m* 25 March 1961, Janet Vivien, da of Albert Cyril Bottomley (d 1977), of Preston, Lancs; 3 da (Alison b 7 July 1964, Katherine b 15 March 1968 d 1968, Jane b 15 July 1971), 1 s (Stuart (twin) b 15 March 1968); *Career* research fellowship MRC Ireland 1960–64, research scientist Unilever plc 1964–67; Univ of Hull: lectr 1967–73, sr lectr 1973–77, reader 1977–83, personal chair 1983, head Dept of Biochemistry 1986–88, prof of microbial biochemistry 1988–2004 (emeritus prof 2004–); memb Euro Fedn of Biotechnol (Sci Advsy Ctee 1984–90), vice-pres Soc of Chem Industry 1993–96; chm: Biotech Ctee Soc of Chem Industry 1989–91, Br Co-ordinating Ctee for Biotechnol 1989–91, Food Research Grant Bd and memb Food Research Ctee AFRC 1989–92, Inst of Biology Biotechnol Gp 1989–2001, Inst of Biology Industrial Biology Ctee 1993–96; memb: Int Union of Biochemistry Biotechnol Ctee 1984–96, Int Cncl of Scientific Unions Press Ctee 1994–97; sec Int Ctee of Environmental and Applied Microbiology 1990–94; Kathleen Barton-Wright Meml lectr (Soc for Gen Microbiology and Inst of Biology) 1994, Australian Soc of Microbiology visiting lectr 1986, NZ Soc of Microbiology visiting lectr 1986, distinguished visitor Ben Gurian Univ of the Negev Israel 2008, visiting prof Univ of Malaysia 2008, visiting prof Univ of Jiangnan China 2010–13; ed-in-chief World Journal of Microbiology and Biotechnology 1986–2005, ed-in-chief Biotechnology Letters 1996–; hon dir Colin Ratledge Center for Microbial Lipids Shandong Univ of Technol China 2015–; Stephen S Chang Award American Oil Chemists Soc 2011; memb: Soc for Gen Microbiology, Biochemical Soc, American Oil Chemists Soc; FRSC 1970, FIBiol (now FRSB) 1983; *Books* The Mycobacteria (1977), Microbial Technology: Current State, Future Prospects (1979), The Biology of the Mycobacteria (vol 1 1982, vol 2 1983, vol 3 1989), Biotechnology for the Oils and Fats Industry (1984), Microbial Technology in the Developing World (1987), Microbial Lipids (vol 1 1988, vol 2 1989), Microbial Physiology and Manufacturing Industry (1988), Biotechnology: Economic and Social Aspects (1992), Industrial Applications of Single Cell Oils (1992), Biochemistry of Microbial Degradation (1993), Mycobacteria: Molecular Biology and Virulence (1999), Basic Biotechnology (2001, 3 edn 2006), Single Cell Oils (2005, 2 edn 2010); *Recreations* indulging our grandchildren, hill walking, bonsai gardening, bridge; *Style—* Prof Colin Ratledge; ✉ 49 Church Drive, Leven, Beverley, East Yorkshire HU17 5LH (☎ 01964 542690); Department of Biological Sciences, University of Hull, Hull HU6 7RX (☎ 01482 465243, e-mail c.ratledge@hull.ac.uk)

RATLIFF, John Harrison; s of Anthony Hugh Cyril Ratliff, and Jean, *née* Harrison; *b* 13 January 1957; *Educ* Clifton, UC Oxford (BA), Univ of Amsterdam (DIEI); *m* 27 July 1985, Pascale, da of Pierre Bourgeon; *Career* called to the Bar Middle Temple 1980; winner of Hon Sir Peter Bristow Award 1981, young lawyers prog Germany 1981–82, J C Goldsmith and Assoc Paris 1983–84, ptnr Stanbrook and Hooper Brussels 1987–99, ptnr Wilmer Cutler Pickering Hale and Dorr LLP 1999–; memb Int Bar Assoc; *Recreations* music, travel, sport; *Clubs* Reform; *Style—* John Ratliff, Esq; ✉ Wilmer Cutler Pickering Hale and Dorr LLP, Bastion Tower, Place du Champ de Mars / Marsveldplein 5, BE 1050, Brussels, Belgium

RATTER, Drew; *Career* convenor Crofters Cmmn; *Style—* Drew Ratter, Esq; ✉ Shetland College, University of the Highlands and Islands, Gremista, Lerwick, Shetland ZE1 0PX

RATTLE, Sir Simon Denis; OM (2014), kt (1994), CBE (1987); *b* 19 January 1955, Liverpool; *Educ* Royal Acad of Music; *m* 1, Elise Ross; 2 s; m 2, Candace Allen; m 3, Magdalena Kozena; 2 s, 1 da; *Career* conductor; played percussion with the Royal Liverpool Philharmonic Orch aged 15, asst conductor Bournemouth Symphony Orch and Sinfonietta 1974–76, assoc conductor Royal Liverpool Philharmonic and BBC Scottish Symphony Orchs 1977–80; City of Birmingham Symphony Orch: princ conductor and artistic advsr 1980–98, music dir 1990–98; chief conductor and artistic dir Berlin Philharmonic Orch 2002–18, music dir London Symphony Orch 2017–; currently recording for Berlin Philharmonic Media (Berliner Philarmoniker's in-house label), releases incl Bach's St Matthew and St John's Passions, the Schumann Symphonies and the Sibelius Symphonies; princ guest conductor LA Philharmonic 1979–94; princ guest conductor: Rotterdam Philharmonic 1981–84, Orch of the Age of Enlightenment 1992–; artistic advsr Birmingham Contemporary Music Gp 1992–; artistic dir South Bank Summer Music Festival 1981–83; worked with various other major orchs incl: London Sinfonietta, The Philharmonia, London Philharmonic, Berlin Philharmonic, Rotterdam Philharmonic, Stockholm Philharmonic, Philadelphia Orch, Chicago, San Francisco, Toronto, Cleveland and Boston Symphony Orchs; Festival Hall debut 1976, Glyndebourne debut 1977, US debut 1979, NY debut 1985, Concertgebouw Amsterdam debut 1986, US operatic debut 1988, Royal Opera House Covent Garden debut 1990, Vienna Philharmonic debut 1993; Hon DMus: Univ of Birmingham, Univ of Leeds, Univ of Liverpool, Univ of Oxford, Birmingham Conservatoire; Hon Senator Hanns Eisler Acad for Music Berlin 2005; Officier de l'Ordre des Arts et des Lettres (France) 1995; *Operas* conducted incl: The Cunning Little Vixen (Glyndebourne 1977 and Covent Garden 1990), Ariadne auf Naxos (Glyndebourne, 1981), Der Rosenkavalier (Glyndebourne, 1982, Deutsche Staatsoper Berlin, 2012 and Baden Baden Festival 2015), The Love for Three Oranges (Glyndebourne, 1983), Idomeneo (Glyndebourne, 1985), Katya Kabanova (ENO, 1985), Porgy and Bess (Glyndebourne, 1986), L'heure escagnole and L'enfant et les sortilèges (Glyndebourne, 1987), The Marriage of Figaro (Glyndebourne, 1989), Cosi fan Tutte (Glyndebourne, 1991), Pelléas et Mélisande (Netherlands Opera, 1993 and Salzburg Easter Festival, 2006), Don Giovanni (Glyndebourne, 1994), Parsifal (Netherlands Opera, 1997 and ROH, 2001), Britten's Peter Grimes (Salzburg Easter Festival, 2005), Wagner's Das Rheingold (Salzburg Easter Festival, 2007), Wagner's Die Walkuere (Salzburg Easter Festival, 2008), Wagner's Siegfried (Salzburg Easter Festival, 2009), Wagner's Götterdämmerung (Salzburg Easter Festival, 2010), R Strauss's Salome (Salzburg Easter Festival, 2011), Bizet's Carmen (Salzburg Easter Festival, 2012), Mozart's Magic Flute (Baden Baden Festival, 2013), Wagner's Ring Cycle (Deutsche Oper Berlin, 2013 and Wiener Staatsoper, 2015), Puccini's Manon Lescaut (Baden Baden Festival, 2014), Janacek's From the House of the Dead (Deutsche Staatsoper Berlin, 2014), Janacek's Katja Kabanova (Deutsche Staatsoper Berlin, 2014), Poulenc's Les Dialogues des Carmelites (Royal Opera House, 2014), Wagner's Tristan and Isolde (Baden Baden Festival and Metropolitan Opera, NY, 2016); *Recordings* over 70 for EMI incl: Mahler's 2nd (with CBSO, 1987, Gramophone Record of the Year and Best Orchestral Recording 1988), Turanglila Symphony (with CBSO, 1987, winner Grand Prix du Disque and Grand Prix Caecilia 1988), Porgy and Bess (with London Philharmonic, 1988, winner Gramophone Opera Award 1989, Int Record Critics' Award 1990, Grand Prix in Honorem de l'Académie Charles Cros 1990, Prix Caecilia, Br Phonographic Industry Classical Award, Edison Award), Szymanowski Litany for the Virgin Mary (Germany's Echo Award for best symphonic recording 1994), Schoenberg Chamber Symphony No 1 and Variations and Erwartung (with Birmingham Contemporary Music Gp and CBSO, Gramophone Best Orchestral Recording Award 1995), Szymanowski Stabat Mater (with City of Birmingham Symphony Chorus and CBSO, Gramophone Best Choral Award and Best Engrg Award 1995), Szymanowski Violin Concertos Nos 1 and 2 (with CBSO, Gramophone Best Concerto Award 1997); *Awards* Choc d'Anné for Brahms Piano Concerto Op 15 1990, Gramophone Artist of the Year 1993, Mountblanc de la Culture Award (for private vision) 1993, Toepfer Fndn of Hamburg Shakespeare Prize 1996, BBC Music Magazine Outstanding Achievement Award 1997, RSA Albert Medal 1997, Outstanding Achievement Award South Bank Show Awards 1999 (in honour of 18 years work with Birmingham Symphony Orch), Diapson Recording of the Year Award for Beethoven Piano Concertos 1999, Gramophone Best Opera Recording (for Szymanowski King Roger with CBSO) 2000; for recording of Mahler 10 with Berlin Philharmonic: Gramophone Best Orchestral Recording 2000, Gramophone Record of the Year 2000, Grammy Award for Best Orchestral Performance 2001; *Style—* Sir Simon Rattle, CBE; ✉ c/o Askonas Holt, Lincoln House, 300 High Holborn, London WC1V 7JH

RATTUE, Andrew; s of Maurice Rattue (d 1985), and Elenar, *née* Goodfellow (d 1997); *b* 10 December 1960, Salisbury, Wilts; *Educ* Bishop Wordsworth's Sch Salisbury, BNC Oxford (BA), Birkbeck Coll London (MA), KCL (PGCE); *m* 22 Oct 1988, Jacqueline, *née* Roynon; 1 da (Polly b 24 July 1993), 3 s (Ben b 30 March 1995, Joe b 26 Dec 1997, Sam b 19 June 2001); *Career* Mill Hill Sch 1985–88, Haberdashers' Aske's Sch Elstree 1988–93, Fulbright teaching exchange Greenhill Sch Dallas TX 1990–91, head of English Highgate Sch 1993–96, dep head Royal GS Guildford 1996–2005, headmaster RGS Worcester 2005–14, headmaster King's Coll Br Sch of Madrid 2014–; memb: Assoc of Sch and Coll Leaders 1996, HMC 2005; *Recreations* drama, American culture, the Victorians, sport, cooking; *Clubs* East India, Lansdowne; *Style—* Andrew Rattue, Esq; ✉ King's College, Paseo de los Andes 35, Soto de Viñuelas, Madrid, Spain (e-mail andrew.rattue@kingsgroup.org)

RAUSING, Kirsten; da of Gad Rausing (d 2000), and Birgit, *née* Mayne; *b* 6 June 1952, Lund, Sweden; *Career* moved to UK 1980; non-exec dir Tetra Pak International (now Tetra Laval Gp) 1983–; prop: Lanwades and St Simon Studs (both Newmarket), Staffordstown Stud (Co Meath); chm Thoroughbred Breeders' Assoc 2008–12 (vice-chm 1985–89 and 1991–95), dir British Bloodstock Agency plc 1994–2001, dir Jockey Club Estates 1994–2009, dir National Stud 1998–2003, dir British Bloodstock Agency Ltd 2010–, tstee Racing Fndn 2012–; fndr and tstee ALBORADA Tst 2001–; memb: Bd Fedn Europeenne des Assocs d'Eleveurs de Pur Sang Anglais 1994–2005 (chm 2002–05), Selbourne Ctee of Enquiry into Veterinary Research 1996–97, Faculty of Veterinary Science External Advsy Gp Univ of Liverpool 2007–; hon fell Wolfson Coll Cambridge 2009, hon assoc Royal Coll of Veterinary Surgeons 2013; Hon DUniv East Anglia 2008; *Publications* Statistical Overview of the Thoroughbred Breeding Industry in Europe (2004); *Clubs* Jockey; *Style—* Ms Kirsten Rausing; ✉ Tetra Laval Group, PO Box 430, CH-1009 Pully, Switzerland

RAUSING, Lisbet; da of Hans Anders Rausing, and Märit Margareta Elisabet, *née* Norrby; sis of Sigrid Rausing, *qv*; *b* 9 June 1960, Lund; *Educ* UC Berkeley (BA), Harvard Univ (PhD); *m* 1, 1988 (m dis 2002); 1 s, 1 da; m 2, 2002, Prof Peter Baldwin; *Career* sr research fell Centre for the History of Science, Technol and Medicine Imperial Coll London 2002–11; donor and memb Donor Bd Arcadia 2001–; memb Bd of Overseers Harvard Univ 2005–11, co-chair Harvard Campaign Planning Ctee 2012–; memb Advsy Bd Cambridge Conservation Initiative 2012–, memb Agricultural Forum 2015–; tstee Yad Hanadiv Advsy Ctee 2001–11; hon doctorate: Uppsala Univ 2007, Imperial Coll London 2007, SOAS 2004; fell Royal Swedish Acad of Agriculture and Forestry (KSLA); fell Linnean Soc, fell Br Acad, FRHistS, Hon FRSB; *Books* Linnaeus: Nature and Nation (1999), Corrour, A History of a Sporting Estate (with Brian Dick, 1998, 2 edn 2010); *Clubs* Athenaeum, Reform, Farmers; *Style—* Dr Lisbet Rausing; ✉ Nyland, Sixth Floor, 5 Young Street, London W8 5EH (e-mail celia.hamer@nyland.org.uk)

RAUSING, (Dr) Sigrid Maria Elisabet; da of Hans Anders Rausing, and Märit Margareta Elisabet, *née* Norrby; sis of Dr Lisbet Rausing, *qv*; *b* 29 January 1962, Lund, Sweden; *Educ* Univ of York (BA), UCL (MSc, PhD); *m* 1, 12 Dec 1996, Dennis Hotz; 1 s (Daniel b 21 Oct 1997); m 2, 14 Feb 2003, Eric Abraham; 1 step s (Alexis b 28 Feb 1981), 1 step da (Natalia b 16 Nov 1988); *Career* chair Sigrid Rausing Tst 1995–; publisher: Granta 2006–, Portobello Books 2006–; emeritus memb Bd Human Rights Watch NYC, memb Bd Coalition of the Int Criminal Court 2010–; hon fell: Anthropology Dept UCL 1997–98, LSE 2010–, St Antony's Coll Oxford 2014; Morrell Fellowship Univ of York 2012; Int Service Human Rights Award (Global Human Rights Defender, jtly) 2004, Beacon Special Award for Philanthropy 2005, Changing Face of Philanthropy Award Women's Funding Network 2006; hon doctorate Univ of York 2014, hon degree Univ of Kent 2016, hon degree Open Univ 2016; *Publications* History, Memory and Identity in Post-Soviet Estonia: The end of a collective farm (2004), Everything is Wonderful – Memories of a collective farm in Estonia (2014); author of articles in jls and chapters in books; *Recreations* riding, walking, conservation; *Clubs* Campden Hill Tennis, Groucho, Athenaeum; *Style—* Ms Sigrid Rausing; ✉ Sigrid Rausing Trust, 12 Penzance Place, London W11 4PA (☎ 020 7313 7720)

RAVEN, Hugh Jonathan Earle; s of John Earle Raven (d 1980), of Cambridge, and Constance Faith Alethea, *née* Hugh Smith; *b* 20 April 1961, London; *Educ* King's Coll Choir Sch, Marlborough Coll, Friend's Sch Saffron Walden, Cambridge Coll of Arts & Technol, Harper Adams Agricultural Coll, Univ of Kent at Canterbury; *m* 18 July 1992, Jane Stuart-Smith; 2 da (Kitty Sarah Faith b 8 Aug 1995, Madeline Emma Beatrix b 2 June 1997); *Career* cncllr (Lab) Royal Borough of Kensington and Chelsea 1990–94 (chair and dep ldr of oppn 1992–94), Parly candidate (Lab) Argyll and Bute 1999, 2001 and 2003, expert advsr Lab Party Environmental Policy Cmmn 1992–97, chair SERA (Lab Party environmental affiliate) 1997–99; memb: Rural and Agricultural Affrs Advsy Ctee BBC 1994–97, Bd Scottish Natural Heritage 2004–07, UK Sustainable Devpt Cmmn 2004–10; dir Morvern Community Devpt Co 2005–07, non-exec dir Ardtornish Estate Co 2015–; memb UK Exec Ctee Br American Project 1996–98; tstee: Soil Assoc 1991–99, Lochaber and Dist Fisheries Tst 1995–2006 (chm 1995–2002), RSPB 1997–2002, John Ellerman Fndn 2010–; chm: W Highland Coastal Tst 2011–, Marine Conservation Soc 2015–, Open Seas Tst 2015–, Environmental Funders' Network 2015–; *Publications* Off our Trolleys: Food retailing and the hypermarket economy (co-author, 1994), Modernising UK Food Policy: the case for reforming MAFF (co-author, 1996), Essential Scotland (contrib, 1998), Town and Country (contrib, 1998), Environment Scotland: Prospects for Sustainabaility (contrib, 1999), The Meat Business (contrib, 1999), Community and Environment (contrib, 1999); *Recreations* reading, theatre, sailing, walking, fishing; *Clubs* Soho House, Farmers'; *Style—* Hugh Raven; ✉ Kinlochaline, Morvern, by Oban, Argyll PA80 5UZ (☎ 01967 421394, e-mail hugh@ardtornish.co.uk); Ardtornish Estate Co Ltd, Argyll Ardtornish, by Oban PA80 5UZ

RAVEN, James (Jim); s of Patrick Raven, and Irene, *née* Cosson; *b* 23 June 1953; *Educ* William Penn Secdy Sch London; *m* 15 June 1975, Wendy Margaret; 3 da (Lyanne b 21 Sept 1976, Ellie b 17 Aug 1979, Jodie b 1 Nov 1985); *Career* trainee reporter Press Association 1969–70; reporter: SE London Mercury 1970–73, freelance 1973–75, Fleet St News Agency 1975, The Sun and freelance 1975–77, Sevenoaks Chronicle 1977–78, Kent Evening Post 1978–81; TVS Television: joined as scriptwriter 1981, later prodr, ed Coast to Coast (regnl news magazine prog) 1989–92 (formerly dep ed); Meridian Broadcasting: controller of news, sport and current affrs 1992–96, dir of news, sport and current affrs 1996–97, dir of news and sport 1997–98; dir of news strategy United Broadcasting and Entertainment 1997–99, md United Sport 1999–2000, md Granada Sport 2000–04, co-fndr and dir BigEasy Productions Ltd 2004–; London Young Journalist of the Year 1972; *Books* Pinnacle of Ice, The Triad Consignment, When Strangers Came, The Venice Ultimatum; *Recreations* painting, travelling, reading, writing; *Style—* Jim Raven, Esq;

R

✉ BigEasy Productions Ltd, 56 Atlantic Close, Ocean Village, Southampton SO14 3TB (website www.bigeasyproductions.co.uk)

RAVENS, Jan; *b* 14 May 1958, Clatterbridge; *Educ* Homerton Coll Cambridge (pres Footlights); *m* Max Hole, *qv*; 1 s (Louis); 2 s from prev m (Alfie, Lenny); *Career* actress and comedienne; *Theatre* incl: The Sloane Ranger Revue (Duchess Theatre), The End of the World Show (Chichester Studio), Loitering Within Tent (Chichester Studio), Ha Bloody Ha (Gate Theatre and Edinburgh), The Relapse (Chichester), Tom Jones (Watford), Twelfth Night (Birmingham Rep), After Easter (RSC), Pentecost (RSC, Best Play Evening Standard Awards 1995), The Children's Hours (Manchester Royal Exchange) 2008; *Television* appearances incl: Carrott's Lib (BBC), Spitting Image (Central), Luv (BBC), Alexei Sayle's Stuff (BBC), No Frills (BBC), An Actors Life For Me (BBC), Harry Enfield and Chums (BBC), One Foot In The Grave (BBC), The Final Frame (Channel 4), Duck Patrol (LWT), The Grimleys (series 1–3, Granada), Kiss Me Kate (BBC), Doctors (BBC), 2DTV (2 series, ITV), Bremner, Bird and Fortune (Channel 4), Alistair McGowan's Big Impression (3 series, BBC 1), Dead Ringers (7 series, BBC), Alter Ego (Ronin Entertainment), Midsomer Murders (ITV), The Truth About Food (BBC), Strictly Come Dancing (BBC), Skins (Channel 4), Celebrity Mastermind (BBC), Love Soup (BBC); *Radio* incl: Brunch (Capital), Hanna, I'll Find You (BBC Radio 4), The Treacle Well (BBC Radio 4), Life, Death and Sex With Mike and Sue (BBC Radio 4), Dead Ringers (10 series, BBC Radio 4), Revolting People (BBC Radio 4), Oxygen (BBC World Service); *Film* La Passione (Heathtour Films); *Style*— Ms Jan Ravens; ✉ c/o Amanda Howard Associates, 21 Berwick Street, London W1F 0PZ (☎ 020 7287 9277, fax 020 7287 7785, e-mail mail@amandahowardassociates.co.uk)

RAWCLIFFE, Roger Capron; s of Brig James Maudsley Rawcliffe, OBE, MC, TD (d 1965), and Margaret Duff Capron (d 1982); *b* 2 August 1934; *Educ* Rossall Sch (scholar), Trinity Coll Cambridge (open exhibitioner, Henry Arthur Thomas travelling scholarship, MA); *m* 1960, Mary Elizabeth White, da of Maurice White; 1 s (James Maurice b 1966); *Career* Nat Serv (Egypt) 1952 Grenadier Gds and E Lancs Regt, 2 Lt 1953, Lt 1954, Capt Stowe CCF 1963, Maj 1964, OC 1966, Hon Col IOM ACF 1987 (Gen Serv Medal, Cadet Forces Medal and Bar); articled to Sir Thomas Robson at Price Waterhouse; Stowe Sch: asst master 1960–80, head of dept 1967, housemaster 1969; lectr School of Extension Studies Univ of Liverpool 1981–2011; lectr Centre for Manx Studies 1997–2000; guest lectr Swan Hellenic Cruises 1967–2004; ptnr Pannell Kerr Forster 1982–91; dir: Rothschild Asset Management (Isle of Man) 1987–91, Isle of Man Breweries Ltd (now Heron and Brearley Ltd) 1992–2008, Singer & Friedlander (Isle of Man) 1992–2005; chm IOM Soc of Chartered Accountants 1993–94; govr Rossall Sch 1980–2001; tstee: King William's Coll 1987–94, Manx National Heritage 1991–2005; pres Br Heart Fndn (Isle of Man) 1990–, vice-chm Army Benevolent Fund (Isle of Man) 2008–; memb: HAC 1960, Soc of Tst and Estate Practitioners 1990; FCA 1970 (ACA 1960); *Books* A Time of Manx Cheer: A History of the Licensed Trade in the Isle of Man (co-author, 2002), No Man Is an Island: Fifty Years of Finance in the Isle of Man (2009); *Recreations* bridge; *Clubs* Sloane; *Style*— Roger Rawcliffe, Esq; ✉ The Malt House, Bridge Street, Castletown, Isle of Man IM9 1ET (☎ 01624 825667)

RAWKINS, His Hon Judge Jeremy John Bruce; *Career* admitted slr 1974; Northern Circuit: dep district judge 1988, district judge 1994, recorder 2001, circuit judge 2008–, designated family judge for Lancashire 2011; *Style*— His Hon Judge Rawkins; ✉ Designated Family Centre, Sessions House, Lancaster Road, Preston PR1 2PD

RAWLINGS, His Hon Judge Brian Kenneth; *Career* admitted slr 1986; recorder 2008, circuit judge (Midland Circuit) 2015–; *Style*— His Hon Judge Rawlings

RAWLINGS, Dr Hugh Fenton; CB (2011); s of William Rawlings, of Llandaff, Cardiff, and Marion, *née* Hughes; *b* 24 November 1950, Cardiff; *Educ* Cardiff HS, Worcester Coll Oxford (BA), LSE (PhD); *m* 6 Sept 1981, Gillian, *née* Douglas; 1 da (Isobel Angharad b 11 June 1985), 1 s (Duncan Geraint b 6 Oct 1988); *Career* lectr in law Univ of Bristol 1976–88, civil servant Welsh Office and Welsh Govt 1988– (currently dir constitutional affrs and inter-governmental relations); hon visiting prof Wales Governance Centre Univ of Cardiff; *Publications* Law and the Electoral Process (1988); *Recreations* reading, music, theatre, Welsh rugby; *Style*— Dr Hugh Rawlings, CB; ✉ 62 Adventurers Quay, Cardiff Bay, Cardiff CF10 4NQ (☎ 029 2048 3096); Welsh Government, Crown Buildings, Cathays Park, Cardiff CF10 3NQ (☎ 029 2082 6532, e-mail hugh.rawlings@wales.gsi.gov.uk)

RAWLINGS, Menna Frances; CMG (2014); *Educ* LSE (BSc), Open Univ (MBA); *m* Mark; 3 c; *Career* diplomat; European Community Dept (Internal) FCO 1989–90, stagiaire European Cmmn Brussels 1990–91, third later second sec (Institutions) UKRep Brussels 1991–93, second sec (Political/Economic) Nairobi 1993–96, press offr FCO 1996–98, head Political Section Tel Aviv 1998–2002, private sec to permanent under sec FCO 2002–04, Africa Directorate (G8/Africa) FCO 2005, cnsllr (Corp Services USA) and HM consul gen Washington 2008–11, dir HR FCO 2011–14, high cmmr to Australia 2015–; FCIPD 2012; *Style*— HE Mrs Menna Rawlings, CMG; ✉ Twitter @mennarawlings; c/o FCO (Canberra), King Charles Street, London SW1A 2AH

RAWLINGS, Baroness (Life Peer UK 1994), of Burnham Westgate in the County of Norfolk; Patricia Elizabeth Rawlings; da of late Louis Rawlings, and Mary, *née* Boas de Winter; *b* 27 January 1939; *Educ* Oak Hall Surrey, Le Manoir Lausanne, Univ of Florence, UCL (BA), LSE (Dip Int Rels); *m* 1962 (m dis 1967), David Wolfson (later Baron Wolfson of Sunningdale, *qv*); *Career* Parly candidate (Cons): Sheffield 1983, Doncaster 1987; special advsr to Min on Inner Cities DOE 1987–88; MEP (Cons) Essex SW 1989–94; memb Euro Parl Ctee on: Youth, Educn, Culture, Media, Sport, Foreign Affrs; vice-chm Euro Parl's Delgn to Romania, Bulgaria, and Albania; House of Lords: oppn whip 1997–98, oppn min for Foreign Affrs 1997–2010, oppn min for Int Devpt 1998–2010, Govt whip Dept for Culture Media and Sport and Scotland Office 2010–12; Baroness in waiting 2010–; chm Cncl KCL 1998–2007; BRCS: memb 1964–, chm Appeals London Branch 1964–88, Nat Badge of Hon 1981, hon vice-pres 1988–, patron London Branch 1997; pres: NCVO 2002–07, BADA 2005–12, Friends of Bada 2013–; memb: Children's Care Ctee LCC 1959–61, WMHNR Nursing Westminster Hosp to 1968, Br Bd of Video Classification, Cncl Peace Through NATO, IISS, Euro Union Women, Bd Br Assoc for Central & Eastern Europe 1994–2001, RIIA 1996–, Br Cncl 1997–2000, European Acad of Sciences and Arts 2010–; vice-pres EU Youth Orch 1992–, dir Eng Chamber Orchestra and Music Soc; tstee Chevening Estate 2002–; chm of govrs English Coll Prague 2008–; Hon DLitt Univ of Buckingham; hon fell: KCL 2003, UCL 2005; Bulgarian Order of the Rose Silver Class 1991, Grand Official Order of the Southern Cross Brazil 1997, Hon Plaquette Nat Assembly of the Repub of Bulgaria 2007; *Recreations* music, art, architecture, golf, travel, gardening; *Clubs* Grillions, Royal West Norfolk; *Style*— The Baroness Rawlings

RAWLINGS, Simon; *Career* creative dir David Collins Studio 1998–; *Style*— Simon Rawlings, Esq; ✉ David Collins Studio, 74 Farm Lane, London SW6 1QA

RAWLINS, Prof Sir Michael David; kt (1999); s of Rev Jack Rawlins (d 1946), of Kingswinford, Staffs, and Evelyn Daphne, *née* Douglas-Hamilton; *b* 28 March 1941; *Educ* Hawtreys, Uppingham, St Thomas' Hosp Med Sch London (BSc, MB BS, MD); *m* 3 Aug 1963 (m dis 2005), Elizabeth Cadbury Rawlins, JP, da of Edmund Hambly (d 1985), of Seer Green, Bucks; 3 da (Vicky b 1964, Lucy b 1965, Suzannah b 1972); *Career* lectr in med St Thomas' Hosp Med Sch London 1968–71, sr registrar Hammersmith Hosp London 1971–73, MRC visiting res fell Karolinska Inst Stockholm 1972–73, Ruth and Lionel Jacobson prof of clinical pharmacology Univ of Newcastle upon Tyne 1973–2006 (public orator 1990–93, emeritus prof 2006–); visiting prof Royal Perth Hosp WA 1980, Ruitinga van Sweiten prof Academic Med Centre Amsterdam 1998, hon prof London Sch of Hygiene and Tropical Medicine 2006–; author of papers on clinical pharmacology and therapeutics; pres RSM 2012–14; chm UK Biobank 2012–, chm Eastern Academic Health Service Network 2013–14, chair Medicines and Healthcare Products Regulatory Agency (MHRA) 2014–; memb: Nat Ctee Pharmacology 1977–83, Cncl St Oswalds Hospice 1977–98 (vice-pres 1998–), Ctee on Toxicity of Chemicals in Food Consumer Prods and Environment 1989–92; chm: Sub-Ctee Safety Efficacy and Adverse Reactions 1987–92, Ctee Safety of Meds 1993–98 (memb 1980–98), Advsy Cncl on the Misuse of Drugs 1998–2008, Nat Inst for Clinical Excellence 1999–2013; vice-chm Northern Regnl HA 1990–94, pres NE Cncl on Addictions 1990–2000; Bradshaw lectr RCP London 1987, William Withering lectr RCP London 1994, Wellcome lectr and medallist Soc of Apothecaries 1996, Sidney Watson Smith lectr RCPEd 1999, Wallace Hemingway lectr Univ of Bradford 2000, Nye Bevan lectr Br Oncology Assoc 2000, Bradlow Oration RCS 2002, Harveian Oration RCP 2008, Stevens lectr RSM 2010, Stanley Davidson lectr RCPEd 2010, Crookshank lectr RCR 2010, Fear meml lecture Dalhousie Univ, Jephcott lecture RSM 2015; Dixon Medal Ulster Med Soc 1994, Hutchinson Medal RSM 2003, Galen Medal Soc of Apothecaries 2010, Prince Mahidol Award for Medicine 2012; DL Tyne and Wear 1999–2008; Hon DUniv York 2007, Hon DCL Univ of Newcastle 2008, Hon DSc Univ of the Sciences Philadelphia 2010, Hon MD Univ of Sheffield 2012, Hon DSc Georgtown Univ 2013, Hon DSc Univ of Cambridge 2015; FRCP 1977 (MRCP 1968), FRCPE 1987, FFPM 1989, FRSM (pres 2012–14), FMedSci, Hon FRCA 2000, hon fell Br Pharmacological Soc 2007, Hon FRSS 2009, Hon FRCSEng 2012, Hon FRCGP 2013, FKC 2013, Hon FRCR 2014, Hon FFPM 2015; *Books* Variability in Human Drug Response (with S E Smith, 1973), Therapeutics, Evidence and Decision-making (2011); *Recreations* music; *Style*— Prof Sir Michael Rawlins

RAWLINS, Prof (John) Nicholas Pepys; s of Surgn Vice Adm Sir John Rawlins, KBE; *b* 31 May 1949, Floriana, Malta; *Educ* Winchester (rowing: winner Coxed Pairs Nat Youth Championships 1967, fourth place Coxed Pairs World Youth Championships 1967), UC Oxford (BA, DPhil, rowed Isis III 1969); *m* Prof Susan Hurley (d 2007); 2 s (Alasdair b 24 Oct 1989, Merryn b 1 June 1994); *Career* University Coll Oxford: Weir jr res fell 1978–80, sr res fell 1982, tutorial fell 1983–2005, professorial fell 2005–07, emeritus fell 2008–; Fogarty res fell Johns Hopkins Univ 1979–80, Royal Soc Henry Head res fell in neurology 1981–83; Univ of Oxford: lectr 1983, prof of behavioural neuroscience 1998–2005, Watts prof of psychology 2005–11, prof of behavioural neuroscience and pro-vice-chllr (devpt and external affrs) 2011–; professorial fell Wolfson Coll Oxford 2008–; author of over 200 professional articles published since 1976; co-chm Wellcome Tst Neuroscience Panel 2004–07 (memb 1996–2000, chm Cognitive and Higher Systems Sub-panel); memb: Nuffield Fndn Bioethics Panel, Wellcome Tst Basic Science Interest Gp 2000–04, Wellcome Tst Neuroscience Strategy Ctee 2004–07; tstee Schizophrenia Tst; memb Experimental Psychology Soc; FMedSci 2006, FBPsS 2011; *Recreations* walking, wine, snorkelling, skiing, period architecture, wildlife, food, gardens, my children; *Style*— Prof Nicholas Rawlins; ✉ University Offices, Wellington Square, Oxford OX1 2JD (☎ 01865 280520)

RAWLINSON, David Ian (Iain); s of (James) Keith McClure Rawlinson, and Griselda Maxwell, *née* Carlisle; *b* 18 September 1958, Liverpool; *Educ* Birkenhead Sch, Jesus Coll Cambridge (MA), Inns of Court Sch of Law; *m* 1, 1991 (m dis 1995); m 2, 1997 (m dis 2013); 1 s (Thomas Carlisle b 21 April 1999), 1 da (Kitty May Ogilvie b 24 Jan 2003); *Career* called to the Bar Lincoln's Inn 1981; corporate fin roles: Lazard Bros & Co Ltd 1986–94, Robert Fleming London 1994–95, Robert Fleming Johannesburg 1995–2000; head of corporate fin Robert Fleming South Africa (later Fleming Martin) 1997–2000, dir South Africa Holding Bd RF Holdings SA Ltd 2000, chief operating offr Fleming Family & Partners Ltd (FF&P) 2000–02, chief exec FF&P Advsy Ltd 2000–04, sr advsr FF&P 2004–05, chief exec The Highland Star Gp 2004–05; non-exec dir: Dana Petroleum plc 2004–10, Sindicatum Carbon Capital Ltd 2007–10, Global Philanthorpic Ltd (dep chm), Edgo Energy Ltd 2007–09; chm: Lithic Metals and Energy Ltd 2007–09, Online Radio Broadcasting Ltd 2009, Monarch Airlines Ltd 2009–11, Monarch Gp 2009–14, Asymmetric Return Capital 2015–; dir Rawlinson Partners Ltd, non-exec dir Parkmead Gp plc 2010–, ptnr Renegade Inc 2014–; chm: Tusk Tst 2005–13 (vice-pres and chm Devpt Bd 2013–), Online Radio Broadcasting Fndn, Rainmaker Fndn 2013–15; fell Centre for Social Innovation Cambridge Judge Business Sch 2016–; *Recreations* sailing, mountaineering, writing, military history, flying, music, Africa, Scotland; *Clubs* Royal Southampton Yacht Club, Beaulieu River Sailing; *Style*— Iain Rawlinson, Esq; ☎ 07799 882382, e-mail iain@rawlinsonpartners.com

RAWLINSON, Dr John Robert; s of Douglas Robert Rawlinson, of Radley, Oxon, and June Frances, *née* Vincent; *b* 26 November 1953, Brighton; *Educ* Henley GS, Abingdon Sch, ChCh Oxford (MA, BM, BCh); *m* 17 Nov 1979, Mary Helen, *née* Norwood; 1 da (Nichola Jane b 26 July 1982), 2 s (Peter John b 18 Sept 1983, James Edward b 19 Feb 1986); *Career* house offr in surgery Churchill Hosp Oxford 1979–80, house offr in med then SHO in A&E Gloucester Royal Hosp 1980–81, gen practice trg scheme Cirencester 1981–84, SHO in obstetrics and gynaecology Swindon 1984, princ GP Ascot 1984–; memb Cncl BMA 2004–06, memb Gen Practitioners Ctee 2008, memb Shadow Bd Clinical Commissioning Gp (CCG), memb Bd Health Educn England Thames Valley 2013–; memb Synod All Saints Church Wokingham Deanery 1996–99; FRCGP 2016 (MRCGP 2007); PCG Development Guide (chapter on Implications for Primary Care, 1999); *Recreations* photography, gardening, swimming, reading; *Style*— Dr John Rawlinson; ✉ Radnor House Surgery, 25 London Road, Ascot, Berkshire SL5 7EN (☎ 01344 874011, fax 01344 628868)

RAWNSLEY, Andrew Nicholas James; s of Eric Rawnsley, of Leeds, Yorks, and Barbara, *née* Butler; *b* 5 January 1962, Leeds, Yorks; *Educ* Lawrence Sheriff Sch, Rugby, Sidney Sussex Coll Cambridge (scholar, MA); *Career* writer and broadcaster; BBC 1983–85, The Guardian 1985–93 (political columnist 1987–93), assoc ed and chief political commentator The Observer 1993–; ed-in-chief politicshome.com 2008–09; presenter: A Week in Politics (Channel 4) 1989–97, The Agenda (ITV) 1996, Bye Bye Blues (Channel 4) 1997, Blair's Year (Channel 4) 1998, Westminster Hour (Radio 4) 1998–2006, The Unauthorised Biography of the United Kingdom (Radio 4) 1999, What the Papers Say (BBC) 2002–07 (incl Review of the Year), The Sunday Edition (ITV) 2006–08, The Rise and Fall of Tony Blair (Channel 4) 2007, Beyond Westminster (Radio 4) 2008–11, Gordon Brown: Where Did It All Go Wrong? (Channel 4) 2008, Crash Gordon: the inside story of the financial crisis (Channel 4) 2009, Cameron Uncovered (Channel 4) 2010, Roses and Thorns: The Inside Story of the Coalition (Channel 4) 2011, Leader Conference (Radio 4) 2011–; Student Journalist of the Year 1983, Young Journalist of the Year 1987, What the Papers Say Columnist of the Year 2000, Channel 4/House Magazine Political Awards Book of the Year 2001, Channel 4 Political Awards Journalist of the Year 2003, Public Affairs Award Political Journalist of the Year 2006, House Magazine Awards Commentator of the Year 2008; FRSA; *Publications* Servants of the People: The Inside Story of New Labour (2000, revised edn 2001), The End of the Party: The Rise and Fall of New Labour (2010); *Recreations* books, movies, wine, Mah Jong, scuba diving, skiing; *Style*— Andrew Rawnsley, Esq; ✉ The Guardian, Kings Place, 90 York Way, London N1 9GU (☎ 020 7278 2332, fax 020 7837 2114)

RAWORTH, Sophie Jane; *b* 15 May 1968, Surrey; *Educ* Putney HS, St Paul's Girls' Sch Hammersmith, Univ of Manchester, City Univ; *m* 2003, Richard Winter; 2 da, 1 s; *Career* BBC: news reporter Gtr Manchester Radio 1992–94, BBC Regions corr Brussels 1994–95, jt presenter Look North 1995–97, presenter Breakfast News 1997–2000, presenter

BBC Breakfast 2000–03, presenter Six O'Clock News 2003–05, presenter News at One 2006–, presenter of special broadcasts incl coverage of the Queen's Golden Jubilee and the Queen's 80th birthday; *Style—* Ms Sophie Raworth; ✉ BBC News, Wood Lane, London W12 7RJ

RAWSON, Prof Dame Jessica Mary; DBE (2002, CBE 1994); *née* Quirk; da of Roger Nathaniel Quirk, CB (d 1964), and Paula, *née* Weber (d 2005); *b* 1 January 1943, London; *Educ* St Paul's Girls' Sch, New Hall Cambridge (MA, LittD), SOAS Univ of London (BA); *m* May 1968, John Graham Rawson, s of Graham Stanhope Rawson (d 1953); 1 da (Josephine b 1972); *Career* asst princ Miny of Health 1965–67; Dept of Oriental Antiquities Br Museum: asst keeper II 1967–71, asst keeper I 1971–76, dep keeper 1976–87, keeper 1987–94; Univ of Oxford: warden Merton Coll 1994–2010, prof of Chinese art and archaeology 2002–, pro-vice-chllr 2005–10; guest prof Heidelberg Univ Kunst Historiches Institut 1989, visiting prof Dept of Art Univ of Chicago 1994 and 2011, guest prof Heidelberg Univ 2011; vice-chm GB China Centre 1985–87, chm Oriental Ceramic Soc 1993–97, govr SOAS Univ of London 1998–2003 (vice-chm 1999–2003); memb: Br Library Bd 1999–2003, Nuffield Languages Enquiry 1998–99; advsr: Centre of Ancient Civilisation, Inst of Archaeology, Chinese Acad of Social Sciences 2002–, Honours State Ctee 2005–08, Scholars Cncl Library of Congress 2005–11; vice-chm Crompton Verney Museum Tst 2010–; conslt Research Dept Palace Museum Beijing 2014–; govr: Latimer and Godolphin Sch 2004–08, St Paul's Girls' Sch 2010–14; Barlow Lecture Univ of Sussex 1979 and 1994, Levintritt Meml Lecture Harvard Univ 1989, Albert Reckitt Archaeological Lecture Br Acad 1989, A J Pope Meml Lecture Smithsonian Inst Washington 1991, Harvey Buchanan Lecture Cleveland Museum of Art 1993, Peter Murray Meml Lecture Birkbeck 1998, Spring Lecture Pratt Inst USA 1998, Sammy Yu-Kuen Lee Lecture Centre for Pacific Rim Studies UCLA Getty Museum 1998, KSLo Memorial Lecture Hong Kong 1998, Beatrice Blackwood Lecture Oxford 1999, Creighton Lecture Univ of London 2000, Zeitlyn Lecture Br Acad 2001, Clark Lecture Percival David Fndn SOAS Univ of London 2004, Woolf Lecture Oriental Ceramic Soc 2008, Fu Ssu-nian Lecture Inst of History and Philology Taiwan 2009, Heinz-Goetze Lecture Heiselberg Univ 2011, Frederick Mote Lecture Princeton Univ 2011, Celebration of 60 Years of the Dept of Museology and Archaeology Peking Univ 2012, William Cohn Lecture Ashmolean Museum 2014, Leon Levy Meml Lecture Inst for the Study of the Ancient World NY 2014, Sir Percival David Lecture London Univ 2016; Hon DLitt: Royal Holloway Coll London 1998, Univ of Sussex 1998, Univ of Newcastle upon Tyne 1999; hon prof: Xi'an Jiaotong Univ 2007, Univ of Sci and Technol Beijing 2008; Slade prof of Fine Art Univ of Cambridge 2013–14, fell St John's Coll Cambridge 2013–14; corresponding memb German Archaeological Inst 2007–, conslt to Research Dept Palace Museum Beijing 2014; FBA 1990, hon fell American Acad of Arts and Sciences 2012, academician China Acad of Arts 2013, memb Shanghai Archaeological Forum 2013, hon research assoc Shaanxi Provincial Inst of Archaeology 2013 (ambass 2014–); *Books* Animals in Art (1977), Ancient China, Art and Archaeology (1980), Chinese Ornament, the Lotus and the Dragon (1984), Chinese Bronzes, Art and Ritual (1987), Ancient Chinese Bronzes in the Collection of Bella and PP Chiu (1988), Western Zhou Bronzes from the Arthur M Sackler Collections (1990), Ancient Chinese and Ordos Bronzes (with Emma Bunker, 1990), British Museum Book of Chinese Art (ed, 1992), Chinese Jade from the Neolithic to the Qing (1995), Mysteries of Ancient China: New Discoveries from the Early Dynasties (1996), China: The Three Emperors (ed with Evelyn Rawski, 2005), Treasures from Shanghai: Ancient Chinese Bronzes and Jades (2009), China's Terracotta Army Stockholm (jt ed, 2010), Ancestors and Enternity, Essays on Chinese Archaeology and Art (2011); *Recreations* gardening; *Style—* Prof Dame Jessica Rawson, DBE, FBA; ✉ Merton College, Oxford OX1 4JD (☎ 01865 276351, fax 01865 276282, e-mail jessica.rawson@merton.ox.ac.uk)

RAWSTHORN, Alice; OBE (2014); da of Peter Rawsthorn, and Joan, *née* Schofield; *b* 15 November 1958; *Educ* Shevington Comp Wigan, Ramsey Comp Halstead, Clare Coll Cambridge (MA); *Career* grad trainee journalist International Thomson Orgn 1980–82, media ed Campaign magazine 1983–85, FT 1985–2001 (foreign corr, industry corr, design critic), dir Design Museum 2001–06; chair Design Advsy Gp Br Cncl 2003–06; columnist NY Times 2006–, design critic Int Herald Tribune 2006–13, columnist Frieze 2014–; memb: BBC Charter Review Panel 2004–06, World Economic Forum Global Agenda Cncl on Design 2008–, Bank of England Banknote Character Advsy Ctee 2015–16; tstee: Whitechapel Art Gallery 1994– (chair 2014–15), Arts Cncl of England 2007–13 (chair Turning Point Review of Contemporary Visual Arts 2001–07, lead advsr 2004–07), Michael Clark Dance Co 2013– (chair 2015–); chair Chisenhale Gallery 2012–; hon sr fell Royal Coll of Art 2003–, hon doctorate Univ of the Arts 2014–; *Books* Yves Saint Laurent (1996), Marc Newson (1999), Frieze Projects: Artists Commissions and Talks (2006), Fashion Theory: A Reader (2007), Don't Buy It If You Don't Need It (2007), AC/DC: Contemporary Art, Contemporary Design (2009), Rises in the East: A Gallery in Whitechapel (2009), Articulado: Art and Design (2010), C Virus Monobloc: The Infamous Chair (contrib, 2010), Designing Media (contrib, 2010), Hella Jongerius: Misfit (contrib, 2011), Ronan and Erwan Bouroullec: Works (2012) Ronan and Erwan Bouroullec: Bivouac (contrib, 2012), Hello World: Where Design Meets Life (2013), Richard Hamilton (contrib, 2014), Formafantasma (contrib, 2014), Martino Gamper: Design is a State of Mind (contrib, 2014), How Social Design Changes Our World (2014), Designing Everyday Life (2014), Design and Violence (2015), Michael Craig-Martin: Transience (2015); *Recreations* art, architecture, design, fashion, film, literature, cycling, hiking, Manchester United; *Style—* Ms Alice Rawsthorn, OBE; ✉ website www.alicerawsthorn.com

RAWSTHORNE, Anthony Robert; s of Frederic Leslie Rawsthorne (d 1991), and Nora, *née* Yates (d 2008), of Blundellsands, nr Liverpool; *b* 25 January 1943; *Educ* Ampleforth, Wadham Coll Oxford (MA); *m* 18 Dec 1967, Beverley Jean, da of Richard Osborne, and Jean; 1 s (Richard Anthony b 1968), 2 da (Josephine Alice b 1969, Mary-Anne b 1969); *Career* Home Office 1966–97: various positions incl Prison Dept, Race Relations Div, Criminal Dept 1966–77, head Crime Policy Planning Unit 1977–79, head Personnel Div 1979–82, sec Falkland Islands Review Ctee 1982, princ private sec to Home Sec 1983, head of div Immigration and Nationality Dept 1983–86, head Establishment Dept 1986–91, head Equal Opportunities and General Dept 1991, under sec/dep DG Policy and Nationality Immigration and Nationality Dept 1991–97, dir Customs Policy HM Customs & Excise 1997–2000, sr clerk House of Lords 2001–05, memb Professional Conduct Ctee and Fitness to Practise Panel GMC 2001–12; *Recreations* bridge, squash, art exhibitions; *Style—* Anthony Rawsthorne, Esq

RAY, Dr Christopher; s of Harold Ray (d 1977), and Margaret, *née* Noble; *b* 10 December 1951, Rochdale, Lancs; *Educ* Rochdale GS, UCL (BA), Churchill Coll Cambridge (PhD), Balliol Coll Oxford; *m* 20 March 1976, Carol Elizabeth, *née* Morrison; *Career* Bank of England 1976–78, Oxford Univ Press 1984–88, Nat Univ of Singapore 1988–89, Portland State Univ 1989–91, KCS Wimbledon 1996–2001, John Lyon Sch Harrow 2001–04, high master Manchester GS 2004–13; reporting inspector Ind Schs Inspectorate 2014–; HMC: chm 2012–13, vice-chm 2013–14; UK Int Educn Cncl 2013–15; MInstP 1996, FRSA 2004; *Books* The Evolution of Relativity (1987), Time, Space and Philosophy (1991), A Companion to the Philosophy of Science (contrib, 2000), The Head Speaks: Challenges and Visions in Education (contrib, 2008); *Recreations* chess, opera, fell walking, crime fiction; *Clubs* East India; *Style—* Dr Christopher Ray; ✉ East India Club, St James's Square, London SW1Y 4LH

RAY, Prof John David; s of Albert Ray (d 1961), and Edith, *née* Millward (d 2012); *b* 22 December 1945, London; *Educ* Latymer Upper Sch, Trinity Hall Cambridge (MA, Thomas Young Medal); *m* 1997, Sonia Falaschi-Ray; *Career* research asst British Museum 1970, lectr in Egyptology Univ of Birmingham 1970–77; Univ of Cambridge: reader 1977–2005, fell Selwyn Coll 1979–, Herbert Thompson prof of Egyptology 2005–13 (currently emeritus); memb Ctee Egypt Exploration Soc 1976–99; assessor Parly Review Ctee on Export of Works of Art 2004–; reviewer: The Times, TLS, Times Higher Educn Supplement; FSA 2000, FBA 2004; *Books* The Archive of Hor (1976), Reflections of Osiris: Lives from Ancient Egypt (2001), Demotic Papyri and Ostraca from Qasr Ibrim (2005), The Rosetta Stone and the Rebirth of Ancient Egypt (2007), Inscriptions from the Sacred Animal Necropolis at North Saqqara (2011), Demotic Ostraca from the Sacred Animal Necropolis at North Saqqara (2013); *Recreations* listening to Beethoven, being walked by a golden retriever; *Style—* Prof John Ray; ✉ Selwyn College, Cambridge CB3 9DQ (☎ 01223 335854, fax 01223 335837, e-mail jdr1000@cam.ac.uk)

RAY, Peggy Ruth; da of Robert Sayers Ray, of North Carolina, USA, and Marguerite, *née* McEachern; *b* 13 May 1954, Lima, Peru; *Educ* Int Sch of Geneva, Univ of Sussex (BA, LLB); *Career* admitted slr 1980; town planning offr Lincolnshire CC 1974–76; Donne Mileham & Haddock Slrs Brighton: trainee slr 1977–80, asst slr 1980–81; asst slr Wiseman Lee Slrs London 1981–85, co-fndr and ptnr Goodman Ray 1985–; recorder (South Eastern Circuit) 2007–; estab: www.carelaw.org.uk, Slrs Family Law Assoc Guide to Good Practice for Slrs Representing Children; memb: Resolution (formerly Slrs Family Law Assoc) 1985– (past roles incl memb Nat Ctee and chair Children's Ctee), Assoc of Lawyers for Children, Legal Aid Funding Review Panel; Unicef Child Rights Lawyer of the Year 2001, Legal Aid Lawyer (Family) of the Year 2005, Cornwell Award for Outstanding Contribution to Family Law 2014; memb Law Soc 1980 (past memb Family Law Ctee and Children Sub-Ctee); incl: Know-How for Family Lawyers (1993), Grandparents and the Law (2001); *Recreations* travel, walking, reading; *Style—* Ms Peggy Ray; ✉ Goodman Ray, 5 Cranwood Street, London EC1V 9EE (☎ 020 7608 1227, fax 020 7250 1786, e-mail peggyray@goodmanray.com)

RAY, Robert John; *Educ* Hatfield Poly; *Career* SCC & B Lintas 1983–86, Davidson Pearce 1986–87, DMB & B then The Media Centre 1987–97, fndr memb and jt md MediaVest 1997–2000, md Starcom Worldwide (P&G GBU EMEA) 2000–03, Robert Ray Associates 2003–05, mktg dir Newspaper Soc 2005–; memb Mktg Soc 2000; *Recreations* snowboarding, mountain boarding, motorcycle trials riding, cross-country running; *Style—* Robert Ray, Esq; ✉ Newspaper Society, St Andrew's House, 18–20 St Andrew's Street, London EC4A 3AY

RAYBAN, Chloë; *see:* Bear, Carolyn Ann

RAYLEIGH, 6 Baron (UK 1821) John Gerald Strutt; s of Hon Charles Richard Strutt (d 1981; s of 4 Baron Rayleigh), and Hon Mrs (Jean Elizabeth) Strutt, *née* Davidson, da of 1 Viscount Davidson; suc uncle 5 Baron Rayleigh 1988; *b* 4 June 1960; *Educ* Eton, RAC Cirencester; *m* 2 May 1991, Annabel Kate, yst da of Maj William Garry Patterson (d 2010), Life Guards, and Hon Sandra Debonnaire, *née* Monson, da of 10 Baron Monson; 4 s (Hon John Frederick b 29 March 1993, Hon William Hedley Charles b 11 Nov 1994, Hon Hugo Richard b 12 Feb 1998, Hon Theodore James b 16 Sept 2000); *Heir* s, Hon John Strutt; *Career* Lt Welsh Guards (ret); chm: Lord Rayleigh's Farms Ltd; Liveryman: Worshipful Co of Grocers, Worshipful Co of Farmers; *Style—* The Rt Hon the Lord Rayleigh

RAYMOND, Peter James; s of George Arthur Raymond (d 1986), of Tunbridge Wells, Kent, and Joyce, *née* Goodwin (d 1999); *b* 16 February 1947; *Educ* Tonbridge; *m* 1, (m dis); 1 s (Tom b 26 June 1974), 1 da (Anna b 16 Feb 1978); m 2, 11 April 1998, Lesley, *née* Keen; 1 step-da (Joanna b 13 June 1990); *Career* Cripps Harries Hall: joined 1967, admitted slr 1969, ptnr 1972–2010, head Private Client Dept 1990–96; notary public 1974–; Law Soc: memb Cncl 1996–2000, chm Probate Section 1997–99, memb Exec Probate Section 1999–2008; pres Tunbridge Wells Tonbridge and Dist Law Soc 1989 (former sec), hon slr Crowborough Citizens' Advice Bureau 1983–2003; vice-pres League of Friends Pembury Hosp (former chm), memb Cncl South of England Agric Soc 1971–86, memb Tunbridge Wells AHA 1987–89; *Style—* Peter Raymond; ✉ Sussex Barn, Robertsbridge, East Sussex TN32 5PA (☎ 01580 881600, e-mail peter_raymond@hotmail.com)

RAYNE, Hon Robert Anthony; s of Baron Rayne (Life Peer, d 2003), by his 1 w, Margaret (decd); *b* 1949; *m* Jane, da of late Robert Blackburn, the aviation pioneer; 1 s; *Career* London Merchant Securities plc: joined 1968, investment dir 1983, jt md 1998, ceo 2001–07; ceo LMS Capital plc 2007–10 (chm 2010–12, non-exec dir 2012–), non-exec chm Derwent London plc 2007–; dir: Weatherford Int Inc 1987, Westpool Investment Trust plc 1984–, Chyron Corp 2008–15; chm and tstee The Rayne Fndn, chm and tstee The Rayne Tst, tstee The Place to Be, tstee emeritus Nat Theatre Fndn; *Recreations* art, cycling; *Style—* The Hon Robert A Rayne; ✉ LMS Capital plc, 100 George Street, London W1U 8NU

RAYNER, Patrick Brear; s of Wing Cdr M O Rayner, OBE (d 2000), of Skipton, N Yorks, and Kathleen, *née* Brear (d 1998); *b* 11 November 1951; *Educ* Woolverstone Hall, Univ of St Andrews (Harkness scholar, MA); *m* 1, 29 Dec 1976 (m dis 1986), Susan Mary, *née* Gill; m 2, 30 April 1987, Stella Joanna, *née* Forge; 2 s (Edward b 24 April 1988, Frederick b 29 June 1992), 1 da (Margot b 30 Jan 1990); *Career* research asst BBC Scot 1975–76, research fell Univ of St Andrews 1976–77, freelance presenter and reporter 1977–78; BBC Scotland: features prodr 1978–82, radio drama prodr 1982–95, ed radio drama 1995–98, head of radio drama 1998–2010; *Awards* Pye Award for Best Prodn 1981, Sony Gold Awards 1986, 1993 and 1998, Sony Silver Awards 1987 and 1988, Sony Bronze 1994; *Publications* Handlist for the Study of Crime in Early Modern Scotland (1982); *Recreations* golf, cabinet-making; *Clubs* MCC, North Berwick Golf; *Style—* Patrick Rayner, Esq

RAYNER, Prof Steve; s of Lt-Col Harry Rayner (d 1991), and Esmé Rayner (d 2011); *b* 22 May 1953, Bristol; *Educ* Dorking Co GS, Univ of Kent at Canterbury (BA), UCL (PhD); *m* 1994, Heather Katz; 1 da (Jessica); *Career* lectr in social anthropology Extra-Mural Studies Dept Univ of London 1977–78; research assoc: Centre for Occupational and Community Research London 1979–83, Russell Sage Fndn NY 1980–81, Dept of Computer Sci Columbia Univ 1982–83 (visiting scholar 1981 and 1982); research assoc rising to sr research staff Energy Div Oak Ridge Nat Lab Tennessee 1983–91 (dep dir Center for Global Environmental Studies 1990–91), chief scientist Pacific Northwest Nat Lab 1996–99 (sr prog mangr Global Environmental Mgmnt Studies and mangr Global Change Gp 1991–96), chief social scientist Int Research Inst for Climate Prediction 1999–2002, prof of environmental and public affrs Sch of Int and Public Affrs Columbia Univ 1999–2002, dir Oxford Inst for Science, Innovation and Soc (formerly James Martin Inst) and James Martin prof of sci and civilization Univ of Oxford 2002–, professorial fell Keble Coll Oxford 2002–; visiting scholar Boston Univ Sch of Public Health 1982, adjunct asst prof of sociology Univ of Tennessee 1986, adjunct faculty US Govt Exec Seminar Center Oak Ridge Tennessee 1988–91, visiting assoc prof Prog in Science, Technol and Soc Cornell Univ 1990, adjunct assoc prof Science, Technol and Soc Grad Prog Virginia Poly Inst 1997–98, hon prof of climate change and soc Univ of Copenhagen 2008–13; former memb Editorial Bd: Environment, Integrated Assessment, Global Environmental Change, Population and Environment; memb Editorial Bd: Earthscan Science in Society book series (ed in chief), Environmental Science and Policy, City Culture and Society; former memb: Bd Fndn for Law Justice and Soc, Royal Cmmn on Environmental Pollution, Advsy Ctee UK Climate Impacts Prog, Bd of Advsrs Nanotechnology Policy Fndn, Sciencewise Steering Gp and Review Panel OST, Advsy Bd ESRC Genomics

R

Survey, Oxford Cmmn on Sustainable Consumption, Int Advsy Bd Encyclopedia of Global Environmental Change; past pres Sociology and Social Policy Section BAAS, lead author Working Gp III Intergovernmental Panel on Climate Change; Martin-Marietta Energy Systems Significant Event Award 1988 and 1989, Dir's Award for Scientific and Engrg Excellence Pacific Northwest Lab 1993, Homer M Calver Award Environment Section American Public Health Assoc 1994; memb: Assoc of Social Anthropologists of the Cwlth 1980, Soc for Risk Analysis 1984, Sigma Xi 1989, BAAS 2002, European Assoc for the Study of Sci and Technol 2002, Soc for the Social Study of Sci 2002; FRAI 1976, fell Soc for Applied Anthropology 1984, FRSA 2004, fell AAAS 2004; Measuring Culture: A Paradigm for the Analysis of Social Organization (jtly, 1985), Rules, Decisions and Inequality in Egalitarian Societies (jt ed, 1988), Making Markets: An Interdisciplinary Perspective on Economic Exchange (jtly, 1992), Human Choice and Climate Change: An International Assessment (4 vols, jt ed, 1998), Markets, Distribution, and Exchange after Societal Cataclysm (jtly, 2000), Unnatural Selection: The Challenges of Engineering Tomorrow's People (jt ed, 2008); author of over 100 articles in books and jls; *Recreations* building, gardening, boating; *Style*— Prof Steve Rayner; ✉ Institute for Science, Innovation and Society, 64 Banbury Road, Oxford OX2 5PN (☎ 01865 288938, e-mail steve.rayner@ox.ac.uk)

RAYNER, Timothy Michael; s of Peter Michael Rayner, of Norwich, and Valerie, *née* Bostock; *b* 4 August 1960, Blackpool; *Educ* Rossall Sch Fleetwood, KCL (LLB), College of Law Chester; *m* 5 Oct 2000, Elizabeth Ann, *née* Blease; *Career* admitted slr 1985; trainee slr Eversheds 1983–85, Addleshaw Sons & Latham 1986–95 (ptnr 1993–95); United Utilities plc: gp legal mangr 1995–98, gen counsel and co sec 1998–2007; gen counsel and co sec Rolls-Royce plc 2007–; memb Law Soc 1985; *Recreations* spectating motor sport, riding own showhunter; *Style*— Timothy Rayner, Esq; ✉ Rolls-Royce plc, 65 Buckingham Gate, London SW1E 6AT

RAYNER JAMES, Jonathan Elwyn; QC (1988); s of Basil James, and Moira Holding, *née* Rayner; *b* 26 July 1950; *Educ* KCS Wimbledon, Christ's Coll Cambridge (MA, LLM), Univ of Brussels (grad course Licencié Spécial en Droit Européen); *m* 3 Jan 1981, Anne, da of Henry McRae (d 1984); 1 s (Daniel Charles Rayner b 23 Dec 1981); *Career* called to the Bar Lincoln's Inn 1971 (Hardwick entrance scholar, Eastham (Maj) scholar, bencher 1994); in practice specialising in intellectual property Chancery Bar 1975–, recorder of the Crown Court 1998–2004 (asst recorder 1994–98); memb Editorial Bd Entertainment Law Review 1990–; memb: Chancery Bar Assoc 1975, Patent Bar Assoc; *Books* EEC Anti-Trust Law (co-author, 1975), Executors and Administrators, Halsbury Laws (co-ed 4 edn vol 17, 1976), Copinger and Skone James on Copyright (co-ed 12 edn, 1980 and 13 edn, 1991, 14 edn, 1998), The Encyclopaedia of Forms and Precedents (jt consltg ed for Intellectual Property matters vol 15, 1989); *Recreations* France; *Clubs* RAC; *Style*— Jonathan Rayner James, Esq, QC; ✉ Hogarth Chambers, 5 New Square, Lincoln's Inn, London WC2A 3RJ (☎ 020 7404 0404)

RAYNOR, His Hon Judge Philip; QC (1994); s of Wilfred Raynor, and Sheila Raynor, of Leeds; *b* 20 January 1950; *Educ* Roundhay Sch Leeds, Christ's Coll Cambridge (scholar, MA); *m* 20 Oct 1974, Judith; 1 da (Michelle b 10 Jan 1979), 1 s (Jonathan b 12 Jan 1984); *Career* lectr in law Univ of Manchester 1971–74, called to the Bar Inner Temple 1973, in practice Northern Circuit, recorder of the Crown Court 1993– (asst recorder 1988–93), head of chambers 40 King Street 1996–2001, dep judge of the High Court 2000–, circuit judge 2001–, specialist circuit judge Technol and Construction Court 2006–; *Recreations* travel, music, dining out; *Style*— His Hon Judge Raynor, QC; ✉ Manchester Civil Justice Centre, 1 Bridge Street West, Manchester M60 9DJ (☎ 0161 240 5000)

RAYNSFORD, Rt Hon Wyvill Richard Nicolls (Nick); PC (2001); s of Wyvill John Macdonald Raynsford (Capt Northants Yeo, ka 1944), and Patricia Howell, *née* Dunn (d 1956); *b* 28 January 1945; *Educ* Repton, Sidney Sussex Coll Cambridge (MA), Chelsea Sch of Art (Dip Art and Design); *m* 1, 30 Aug 1968 (m dis 2011), Anne Elizabeth, da of late Col Marcus Jelley, of Northampton; 3 da; m 2, 5 Oct 2012, Alison Seabeck, MP, *qv*; *Career* market res A C Neilsen Co Ltd 1966–68, Student Co-operative Dwellings 1972–73, SHAC (London Housing Aid Centre) 1973–86 (dir 1976–86), dir Raynsford Dallison Associates Ltd (housing conslts) 1987–93; cncllr London Borough of Hammersmith and Fulham 1971–75; MP (Lab): Fulham 1986–87, Greenwich 1992–97, Greenwich and Woolwich 1997–2015; front bench spokesman for London 1993–94, shadow housing and construction min and spokesman for London 1994–97, Parly under-sec of state for London and construction 1997–99, min of state for housing, planning and London Jul-Oct 1999, min of state for housing and planning 1999–2001, min of state for local govt and the regions 2001–05; chm: Fire Protection Assoc Cncl 2005, Construction Industry Cncl 2006–08, NHBC Fndn 2006, Centre for Public Scrutiny 2007–15, Strategic Forum for Construction 2008–10, Triathlon Homes 2011, Tideway Report Gp 2016–, Iceni Sustainability Cmmn 2016–; pres: NHIC 2008–15, Constructionarium 2008, Youthbuild 2008–15, Town and Country Planning Assoc 2015–; Hon DBA Univ of Greenwich 2015; Hon FICE 2003, Hon FRTPI 2005, Hon FRIBA 2007, Hon FIStructE 2007, Hon MRICS 2008, Hon MCIH 2009 (MIH 1978); *Books* A Guide to Housing Benefit (1982); *Style*— The Rt Hon Nick Raynsford

RAZ, Prof Joseph; s of Shmuel and Sonya Zaltsman; *b* 21 March 1939; *Educ* Hebrew Univ of Jerusalem (MJuris), Univ of Oxford (DPhil); *m* 8 Sept 1963 (m dis 1979), Yael; 1 s (Noam b 1969); *Career* lectr then sr lectr in Hebrew Univ of Jerusalem 1967–72; Balliol Coll Oxford: fell and tutor in jurisprudence 1972–85, prof of philosophy of law 1985–2006; research prof Univ of Oxford 2006–09; prof Columbia Univ NY 2002– (visiting prof 1995–2002), pt/t research prof KCL 2011–; hon foreign memb American Acad of Arts and Sciences 1992; Hon Dr: Catholic Univ Brussels 1993, KCL 2009, Hebrew Univ Jerusalem 2014; FBA 1987; *Books* The Concept of a Legal System (1970, 2 edn 1980), Practical Reason and Norms (1975, 2 edn 1990), The Authority of Law (1979), The Morality of Freedom (1986), Ethics in the Public Domain (1994), Engaging Reason (2000), Value, Respect and Attachment (2001), The Practice of Value (2003), Between Authority and Interpretation (2009), From Normativity to Responsibility (2011); *Style*— Prof Joseph Raz, FBA; ✉ Columbia Law School, 435 W116th Street, New York, NY 10027, USA (☎ 001 212 854 7467, fax 001 212 854 9646, e-mail jr159@columbia.edu, website http://josephnraz.googlepages.com/home)

RAZZALL, Baron (Life Peer UK 1997), of Mortlake in the London Borough of Richmond upon Thames; (Edward) Timothy Razzall; CBE (1993); s of Leonard Humphrey Razzall, of Barnes, London, a Master of the Supreme Court 1954–81, and Muriel, *née* Knowles (d 1968); *b* 12 June 1943; *Educ* St Paul's, Worcester Coll Oxford (BA); *m* 1 (m dis); 1 da (Hon Katharine Mary b 31 Oct 1970), 1 s (Hon James Timothy b 8 Nov 1972); m 2 (m dis), Deirdre Bourke, da of Duncan Taylor-Smith; *Career* admitted slr 1969; ptnr Frere Cholmeley Bischoff 1973–95; ptnr Argonaut Associates 1995–; London Borough of Richmond upon Thames: cncllr 1974–98, chm Policy and Resources Ctee and dep ldr 1983–96; treas: Lib Pty 1987–88, Lib Dems 1988–2000; DBIS spokesman for Lib Dems in House of Lords 1998–2014, chm Lib Dems Gen Election Campaign 1999–2006, Treasy spokesman for Lib Dems in House of Lords 2014–15, Cabinet Office spokesman for Lib Dems in House of Lords 2015–; *Recreations* all sports; *Clubs* Nat Lib, MCC, Soho House; *Style*— The Rt Hon Lord Razzall, CBE

REA, Rev Ernest; s of Ernest Rea (d 1975), of Belfast, and Mary Wylie, *née* Blue (d 1973); *b* 6 September 1945; *Educ* Methodist Coll Belfast, Queen's Univ Belfast (BA, BD), Union Theol Coll Belfast; *m* 1, 13 Sept 1973 (m dis 1994), Kathleen (Kay), da of Robert Kilpatrick (d 1987), of Belfast; 2 s (Stephen Ernest b 28 April 1975, Jonathan Robert b 17 April 1978); m 2, 1 July 1995, Gaynor Vaughan, da of David and Leah Jones, of Tamworth, Staffs; *Career* asst minister Woodvale Park Presbyterian Church Belfast 1971–74, minister Bannside Presbyterian Church Banbridge Co Down 1974–79; prodr religious progs BBC NI 1979–84, sr prodr religious progs BBC South and West 1984–88, editor Network Radio 1988–89, head of religious broadcasting BBC 1989–2001; presenter Beyond Belief (BBC Radio 4); *Recreations* theatre, reading, playing tennis and golf, music, good company; *Style*— The Rev Ernest Rea

REA, 3 Baron (UK 1937); Sir (John) Nicolas Rea; 3 Bt (UK 1935); s of Hon James Rea (d 1954; 2 s of 1 Baron Rea), by his 1 w, Betty, *née* Bevan (d 1965); suc unc, 2 Baron, 1981; *b* 6 June 1928; *Educ* Dartington Hall, Belmont Hall Sch Massachusetts, Dauntsey's Sch West Lavington, Christ's Coll Cambridge (MA, MD), UCH Med Sch London; *m* 1, 1951 (m dis 1991), Elizabeth Anne, da of William Hensman Robinson (d 1944), of Woking, Surrey; 4 s (Hon Matthew, Hon Daniel, Hon Quentin, Hon Nathaniel); m 2, 1991, Judith Mary, da of Norman Powell (d 1989), of Lytham St Annes, Lancs; 2 da (Bess b 1975, Rosy b 1978) from other relationships; *Heir* s, Hon Matthew Rea; *Career* Nat Serv Actg Sergeant Suffolk Regt; sits as Labour peer in House of Lords, dep spokesman on health and overseas devpt 1992–97; med practitioner in NHS general practice Kentish Town Health Centre 1957–62 and 1968–1993, ret; research fell Paediatrics Ibadan Univ Nigeria 1962–65, lectr in social med St Thomas' Hosp Med Sch London 1966–68; vice-chm Nat Heart Forum 1985–95 (pres 2013–); chm All-Pty Food and Health Forum 1992–2013; memb Cncl Outward Bound Tst 1988–95; DPH, DCH, DObst; FRSM (pres Section of Gen Practice 1985–86); FRCGP; *Recreations* music (bassoon), gardening; *Style*— The Rt Hon the Lord Rea; ✉ House of Lords, London SW1A 0PW (☎ 020 7607 0546, fax 020 7219 5969, e-mail reajn@parliament.uk)

REA, Stephen; *b* 31 October 1946, Belfast; *Educ* Belfast HS, Queen's Univ Belfast; *Career* actor; *Television* incl: K is for Killing 1974, I Didn't Know you Cared 1975, Professional Foul 1977, Four Days in July 1984, Nobody Here But Us Chickens 1989, Not With a Bang 1990, Hedda Gabler 1993, Citizen X 1995, Shadow of a Gunman 1995, Crime of the Century 1996, Snow in August 2001, Armadillo 2001, Horrible Histories 2001–02, Copenhagen 2002, Father and Son 2009, Single-Handed 2010, The Shadow Line 2011, Roadkill 2011; *Films* incl: Cry of the Banshee 1970, Angel 1982, Loose Connections 1983, The Company of Wolves 1984, The Doctor and the Devils 1985, Life is Sweet 1990, The Crying Game 1992, Bad Behaviour 1993, Interview with the Vampire 1994, Princess Caraboo 1994, Pret-á-Porter 1994, Angie 1994, Between the Devil and the Deep Blue Sea 1995, All Men are Mortal 1995, Lumiere and Company 1995, Michael Collins 1996, Trojan Eddie 1996, Last of the High Kings 1996, A Further Gesture 1996, Fever Pitch 1997, The Butcher Boy 1997, Double Ta 1997, Hacks 1997, This is my Father 1998, Still Crazy 1998, In Dreams 1998, Guinevere 1999, The Life Before This 1999, The End of the Affair 1999, The Musketeer 2001, On the Edge 2001, Evelyn 2002, Bloom 2003, The Halo Effect 2004, The I Inside 2004, The Good Shepherd 2004, Proud 2004, Control 2004, Tara Road 2005, Breakfast on Pluto 2005, River Queen 2005, V for Vendetta 2005, Sisters 2006, Sixty Six 2006, Until Death 2007, The Reaping 2007, Stuck 2007, The Devil's Mercy 2008, Child of the Dead End 2009, Nothing Personal 2009, Ondine 2009, The Heavy 2010, Blackthorn 2011, Stella Days 2011, Underworld: Awakening 2012; *Style*— Mr Stephen Rea; ✉ c/o Independent Talent Group, 40 Whitfield Street, London W1T 2RH

READ, Prof Andrew Fraser; s of Ronald Read, of Cambridge, NZ, and Sophie, *née* Carruthers; *b* 12 September 1962, Hawera, NZ; *Educ* Univ of Otago (BSc), Univ of Oxford (Cwlth scholar, DPhil); *m* 19 June 1992, Dr Victoria Braithwaite, da of Alan Braithwaite; 2 s (James Alan b 8 April 1995, Matthew Ronald b 9 June 1997); *Career* jr research fell ChCh Oxford 1988–92, lectr in zoology St Catherine's Coll Oxford 1989–90, Lloyds of London tercentenary fell Univ of Oxford 1991–92; Univ of Edinburgh: BBSRC advanced research fell 1993–97 (granted second fellowship 1998 but resigned), prof of natural history 1998–; adjunct prof Univ of Tromsø Norway 1992–97; Thomas Henry Huxley Award Zoological Soc of London 1991, Young Investigator Award American Soc of Naturalists 1991, Scientific Medal Zoological Soc of London 1999; FRSE 2003; *Books* The Evolutionary Biology of Parasitism (ed with A E Keymer, 1990), Parasite Variation: Ecological and Immunological Consequences (ed with M E Viney, 2002); *Recreations* barbeques; *Style*— Prof Andrew Read; ✉ University of Edinburgh, School of Biological Sciences, King's Buildings, Ashworth Laboratories, West Mains Road, Edinburgh EH9 3JT (☎ 0131 650 5506, fax 0131 650 5456, e-mail a.read@ed.ac.uk)

READ, Carly; *see*: Hesketh-Read, Carly

READ, Prof Frank Henry; s of Frank Charles Read (d 1976), and Florence Louisa, *née* Wright (d 1996); *b* 6 October 1934; *Educ* Haberdashers' Aske's, Univ of London (ARCS, BSc), Univ of Manchester (PhD, DSc); *m* 16 Dec 1961, Anne Stuart, da of Neil Stuart Wallace; 2 da (Kirsten Victoria b 17 Oct 1962, Nichola Anne b 12 Feb 1964), 2 s (Jonathon Hugh Tobias b 16 June 1965, Sebastian Timothy James b 18 Aug 1970); *Career* Univ of Manchester: lectr 1959–68, sr lectr 1968–74, reader 1974–75, prof of physics 1975–98, res dean of Faculty of Science 1993–95, Langworthy chair of physics 1998–2002, emeritus prof 2002–; vice-pres Inst of Physics 1984–89; conslt in charged particle optics 1976–; memb: Cncl of Royal Soc 1987–89, Sci Bd SERC 1987–90; FRS 1984, FInstP 1973, FIEE 1998; *Books* Electrostatic Lenses (1976), Electromagnetic Radiation (1980); *Recreations* landscaping, walking, travelling; *Style*— Prof Frank Read, FRS; ✉ Deakins Cottage, Orleton, Ludlow SY8 4HN (☎ 01568 780955); School of Physics and Astronomy, University of Manchester, Manchester M13 9PL (e-mail frank.read@physics.org)

READ, Dr Graham; *b* 16 January 1947; *Educ* Queen Elizabeth's GS Barnet, Fitzwilliam Coll Cambridge (open exhibitioner in natural scis, MA, MB BChir, coll prize, MRCP), Univ of Manchester Med Sch (surgical prize); *m* 13 April 1974, Joan Elizabeth, *née* Hughes; 2 s (Philip Alexander b 17 March 1976, Stuart Noel b 17 April 1979), 1 da (Helena Magdalen b 1 Aug 1977); *Career* jr posts in med Manchester Royal Infirmary and Crumpsall Hosp Manchester, registrar then sr registrar in radiotherapy Christie Hosp Manchester; currently: conslt in radiotherapy and oncology Christie Hosp Manchester and hon assoc lectr in radiotherapy Univ of Manchester, dir of cancer servs Royal Preston Hosp; head clinician Lancs and S Cumbria Cancer Network; memb: MRC Working Pty on Testicular Tumours 1979–, Cancer Statistics Gp Cancer Research Campaign 1982, MRC Working Pty on Advanced Bladder Cancer 1983–, NW Regnl Med Ctee 1988–92, Clinical Oncology Casemix Gps Devpt Project, Integrated Clinical Workstation Project, Cncl RCR (memb Faculty Bd of Clinical Oncology 1988–94); chm Clinical Oncology Speciality Working Gp NHSME Clinical Terms Project; memb: Br Assoc for Cancer Research, Br Inst of Radiology, Br Oncological Assoc, American Soc of Clinical Oncology; FRCR 1978, FRCP 2001; *Publications* author of numerous articles in the fields of testicular and bladder cancer and gen oncology, also author of book chapers; *Style*— Dr Graham Read; ✉ Director of Cancer Services, Royal Preston Hospital, Sharoe Green Lane North, Fulwood, Preston PR2 9HT (☎ 01772 716565, fax 01772 710089)

READ, Martin; s of Charles Enderby Read (d 1993), of Ulceby, Lincs, and Lillian Clara, *née* Chambers (d 1999); *b* 24 July 1938; *Educ* Queen Elizabeth's GS Alford, Wadham Coll Oxford (MA); *m* 27 April 1963, Laurette, da of J T Goldsmith (d 1960), of Hendon, London; 2 da (Robyn Lisa b 7 Sept 1966, Abigail Kim b 14 May 1970); *Career* articled clerk Hammond Suddards Bradford 1959–62; Slaughter and May: asst slr 1963–70, ptnr 1971–95, conslt 1995–99; past vice-chm Law Soc Standing Ctee on Company Law, past chm Company Law Sub-Ctee City of London Law Soc; memb Law Soc 1963; *Recreations* theatre, opera, literature, golf, cricket; *Clubs* MCC; *Style*— Martin Read, Esq;

✉ Michaelmas House, Bois Avenue, Chesham Bois, Amersham, Buckinghamshire HP6 5NS (☎ 01494 725121)

READ, Dr Martin Peter; CBE (2011); s of late Peter Denis Read, and late Dorothy Ruby Read; *b* 16 February 1950; *Educ* Queen Mary's GS Basingstoke, Peterhouse Cambridge (BA), Merton Coll Oxford (DPhil); *m* 1974, Marian Eleanor, *née* Gilbart; 1 s (Laurence), 1 da (Eleanor); *Career* various posts in sales, mktg, fin, ops, systems devpt Overseas Containers Ltd 1974–81, joined International Paint (Courtaulds) 1981, corp commercial dir Marine Coatings 1981–84 and gen mangr Europe 1984–85; joined GEC Marconi 1985, gen mangr Marconi Secure Radio 1986–87, dir Marconi Defence Systems Ltd 1987–89, md Marconi Command and Control Systems 1989–91, gp md Marconi Radar and Control Systems Gp 1991–93; gp chief exec Logica plc 1993–2007; non-exec dir: Asda plc 1996–99, The Boots Gp plc 1999–2006, Southampton Innovations Ltd 1999–2003, British Airways plc 2000–09, Siemens Hldgs plc 2008–09, Invensys plc 2009–14, Aegis Gp plc 2009–13, Lloyd's 2009–; sr advsr HCL 2008–12, sr advsr Candover Ptnrs 2008–09, sr advsr Actis 2011–13, sr advsr Zensar Technologies 2013–; chm: Remuneration Consultants Gp 2010–, Laird plc 2014–, Low Carbon Contracts Co 2014–, Electricity Settlements Co 2014–; tstee Nat Centre for Universities and Business (formerly Cncl for Industry and HE) 2007–14 (memb 2000–07); memb: President's Ctee CBI 2004–07, DTI Strategy Bd 2005–06, Int Advsy Bd CBI 2007–10; non-exec dir UK Govt Efficiency and Reform Bd 2010–15, chm UK Govt Sr Salaries Review Body 2015–; led govt review on improving the efficiency of back office systems and IT across the public sector 2008–09 and on mgmnt info 2012; tstee Winchester Science Centre (formerly Hampshire Technol Centre) 1990–, tstee Southern Focus (formerly Portsmouth Housing) Tst 1992–2000, dir Portsmouth Housing Assoc 1993–2007, govr Highbury Coll Portsmouth 1989–99, memb Cncl Univ of Southampton 1999–2015 (vice-chair 2008–15), tstee Shelter 2004–10 (memb Fin Ctee 2000–04), memb Cncl Shakespeare's Globe 2010–, chm Advsy Ctee Univ of Cambridge Library 2015– (memb 2007–); hon fell Merton Coll Oxford 2006–; Hon DTech Loughborough Univ 2000; CDipAF 1976, MInstD 1991, CIMgt 1994 (Gold Medal 2007), fell IET 2005; *Publications* article in Jl of Applied Physics; *Recreations* French and German novels, drama, military history, travel, gardening; *Style*— Dr Martin Read, CBE; ✉ c/o Company Secretary, Laird plc, 100 Pall Mall, London SW1Y 5NQ (☎ 020 7468 4040)

READ, Prof Nicholas Wallace (Nick); s of Wallace Frederick Read, of Blagdon Hill, Somerset, and Doris Vera, *née* Scriven; *b* 7 July 1945; *Educ* Taunton Sch, Gonville and Caius Coll Cambridge, London Hosp Medical Sch; *m* (m dis); 4 da (Esther b 1973, Katherine b 1978, Emily b 1982, Diane b 1986), 1 s (Alexander b 1980); *Career* conslt physician Northern General Hospital Sheffield 1981–2002, conslt physician and psychotherapist Claremont Hosp Sheffield 2001–10; prof of gastrointestinal physiology and nutrition Univ of Sheffield 1988–98 (prof of integrated med 1998–2002); dir Centre for Human Nutrition 1988–98; psychoanalytical psychotherapist 1997–; chair of tstees and medical advsr The IBS Network 2009–; memb: Br Soc of Gastroenterology 1974, Nutrition Soc 1986, UK Cncl for Psychotherapy 1998; FRCP 1987; *Books* Irritable Bowel Syndrome (1984, 2 edn 1990), BDS Textbook of Physiology (1988), Gastrointestinal Motility, Which Test (1989), Food and Nutritional Supplements (2001), Sick and Tired: Healing the Diseases Doctors Cannot Cure (2005), Irritable Bowel Syndrome Self-Management Programme (website, 2006), IBS Self Care Plan (website, 2013, revised 2016), Cooking for the Sensitive Gut (2016); *Recreations* hill walking, fell running, wild swimming, birdwatching, writing; *Style*— Prof Nick Read; ✉ Guides Cottage, Edensor, Bakewell DE45 1PH (e-mail nickwread@btinternet.com, website www.nickread.co.uk, www.mindbodydoc.wordpress.com, www.theibsnetwork.org and www.thesensitivegut.com)

READ, Prof Peter Leonard; s of Leonard Frederick Read, of Dunstable, Beds, and Dorothy Helen, *née* Moore; *b* 18 October 1953, Hampstead, London; *Educ* Univ of Birmingham (BSc), Univ of Cambridge (PhD); *m* 28 July 1979, Janette Dorothy Ann, *née* Kenny; 1 da (Elizabeth Helen Mary b 14 July 1985), 1 s (Nicholas Peter Robert b 23 April 1987); *Career* Met Office 1979–91; Univ of Oxford: fell by special election St Cross Coll 1989–91, MA (by incorporation) 1990, fell and tutor in physics Trinity Coll 1991–, lectr 1991–, titular reader 1999–2002, titular prof of physics 2002–, head Geophysical and Planetary Fluid Dynamics Research Gp Atmospheric, Oceanic and Planetary Physics Sub-Dept, head Atmospheric, Oceanic and Planetary Physics Sub-Dept 2008–; visiting prof: Université d'Aix-Marseille 2003, École Normale Superieure 2007; co-investigator: Composite Infrared Spectrometer Team NASA/European Space Agency Cassini Orbiter Mission (launched 1997), Pressure Modulator Infrared Radiometer Team NASA Mars Climate Orbiter Mission (launched 1998), Mars Climate Sounder Team NASA Mars Reconnaissance Orbiter Mission (launched 2005); memb Editorial Bd: Physics and Chemistry of the Earth 1996–2000, Surveys in Geophysics 1996–2006, Quarterly Jl RMS 2000–; memb Royal College of Organists; memb European Geophysical Soc 1980– (Golden Badge Award 2000, chair Nonlinear Processes in Geophysics Working Gp); FRAS 1979, FRMetS 1980 (memb Cncl 2000–02, Adrian Gill Award 2008); *Books* The Martian Climate Revisited: Atmosphere and Environment of a Desert Planet (with S R Lewis, 2004); *Recreations* singing, organist, walking, cycling; *Style*— Prof Peter Read; ✉ Atmospheric, Oceanic and Planetary Physics, Clarendon Laboratory, Parks Road, Oxford OX1 3PU (☎ 01865 272082, fax 01865 272923, e-mail p.read1@physics.ox.ac.uk)

READ, Dr Peter Robert; CBE (2000); s of Frederick John Read (d 1966), and Winifred Harriet, *née* Gregory; *b* 18 January 1939; *Educ* Purley Co GS, Charing Cross Hosp Med Sch; *m* 11 Oct 1965, Norma, *née* Rowlands; 1 da (Josephine Lisa b 24 April 1970), 1 s (Simon Jonathan b 10 June 1971),; *Career* Hoechst Gp of Companies 1971–99 (ret as chm); former sr non-exec dir SSL Int plc; non-exec dir: Vernalis plc, Innogenetics, Celltech Gp plc; past pres Assoc of Br Pharmaceutical Assoc, past chm Centre for Medicines Research, past chm Research Defence Soc; former memb Bd SE of England Devpt Agency (SEEDA); Freeman City of London, Liveryman Worshipful Soc of Apothecaries; Hon DSc De Montfort Univ; FFPM 1989, FRCP 1996; *Recreations* music, opera, garden, rugby; *Style*— Dr Peter Read, CBE; ✉ PCC, Marlow Road, Henley on Thames, Oxfordshire RG9 2HT

READ, Piers Paul; s of Sir Herbert Edward Read, DSO, MC (d 1968), and Margaret, *née* Ludwig (d 1996); *b* 7 March 1941; *Educ* Ampleforth, St John's Coll Cambridge (BA, MA); *m* 29 July 1967, Emily Albertine, da of (Evelyn) Basil Boothby, CMG, of London; 2 s (Albert b 1970, William b 1978), 2 da (Martha b 1972, Beatrice b 1981); *Career* author; artist in residence Ford Fndn Berlin 1963–64, sub ed Times Literary Supplement London 1965, Harkness fell Cwlth Fund NY 1967–68, adjunct prof of writing Univ of Columbia 1980; memb: Ctee of Mgmnt Soc of Authors 1973–76, Literature Panel Arts Cncl London 1975–77, Cncl RSL 2002–07; chm Catholic Writers' Guild 1992–97, govr Cardinal Manning Boys' Sch London 1985–90, bd memb Aid to the Church in Need 1988–2012, tstee Catholic Nat Library 1997–2010; FRSL 1972; *Books* Game in Heaven with Tussy Marx (1966), The Junkers (1968), Monk Dawson (1969), The Professor's Daughter (1971), The Upstart (1973), Alive: the story of the Andes Survivors (1974), Polonaise (1976), The Train Robbers (1978), A Married Man (1979), The Villa Golitsyn (1981), The Free Frenchman (1986), A Season in The West (1988), On the Third Day (1990), Quo Vadis The Subversion of the Catholic Church (1991), Ablaze, The Story of Chernobyl (1993), A Patriot in Berlin (1995), Knights of the Cross (1997), The Templars (1999), Alice in Exile (2001), Alec Guinness: The Authorised Biography (2003), Hell and Other Destinations (2006), The Death of a Pope (2009), The Misogynist (2010), The Dreyfus Affair (2012), Scarpia (2015); *Style*— Piers Paul Read, Esq, FRSL; ✉ 23 Ashchurch Park Villas, London W12 9SP (☎ 020 8740 9148, e-mail pierspaulread@gmail.com)

READ, Richard Michael Hodgson; s of Lt Richard Hodgson Read (d 1936), of Eastbrook Hall, Dinas Powis, and Dorothy Jessie, *née* Penwarden (d 1985); *b* 24 December 1936; *Educ* Clifton, St James' Sch Maryland, Univ of London (BSc); *m* 1, 21 July 1964 (m dis 1969), Jennifer Diane, da of Marcus Leaver (d 1966), of Mill Hill; m 2, 29 Oct 1993 (m dis 2005), Susan Anne Icke; *Career* CA; R H March Son & Co and Mann Judd & Co 1962–79, ptnr Touche Ross & Co 1979–81, dir various cos affiliated to Lloyd's 1981–90; chm: D G Durham Group plc 1988–93, Culver Holdings plc 1991–; underwriting memb Lloyd's; memb CBI: Smaller Firms Cncl 1973–79, Cncl 1978–79, Welsh Cncl; FCA; *Recreations* skiing, golf, swimming, gardening; *Clubs* Cardiff & County, Royal Porthcawl Golf; *Style*— Richard Read, Esq; ✉ Llanmaes, St Fagans, Cardiff CF5 6DU (☎ 029 2067 5100)

READE, Rt Rev Nicholas Stewart; s of Sqdn Ldr Charles Sturrock Reade (d 2000), of Staffs, and Eileen Vandermere, *née* Fleming (d 1994); *b* 9 December 1946; *Educ* Elizabeth Coll Guernsey, Univ of Leeds (BA, DipTh), Coll of the Resurrection Mirfield; *m* 17 July 1971, Christine, da of Very Rev R C D Jasper, CBE (d 1990); 1 da (Claire b 4 Jan 1978); *Career* ordained: deacon 1973, priest 1974; curate: St Chad Coseley 1973–75, St Nicholas Codsall and priest i/c Holy Cross Bilbrook 1975–78, vicar St Peter Upper Gornal and chaplain Burton Road Hosp Dudley 1978–82, vicar St Dunstan Mayfield and rural dean of Dallington 1982–88, vicar and rural dean of Eastbourne 1988–97, canon and preb of Chichester Cathedral 1990–97, archdeacon of Lewes and Hastings 1997–2004, bishop of Blackburn 2004–12, ret; hon asst bishop Dio in Europe 2013–, hon asst bishop Dio of Chichester 2013–, hon asst priest All Saints' Sidley 2013–, actg priest-in-charge St Barnabas' Bexhill-on-Sea 2014–; chm Chichester Diocesan Liturgical Ctee 1989–97, chair Archbishop's Cncl for the Deaf and Disabled 2008–12; memb: Bishop's Cncl and Standing Ctee of Chichester 1989–2004, Gen Synod C of E 1995–2000 and 2003–12, Sr Appointments Gp (Episcopal) 2008–12, Urban Bishops' Panel 2010–12; memb House of Lords 2009–12; pres: Eastbourne and Dist Police Court Mission 1994–, Crowhurst Healing Centre 2000–13; vice-pres Disabled Living 2005–12; tstee: St Wilfrid's Hospice Eastbourne 1995–98, UC Chichester (formerly Bishop Otter Coll) 1997–2004; patron: Sussex Heritage Tst 1998–2013, Rosemere Cancer Fndn 2004–12, Helping Hand 2005–12, Derian House Children's Hospice 2006–12, Skipton and E Lancs Rail Action Partnership 2006–, Stonyhurst Christian Heritage Tst 2010–, Caring and Sharing 2012–; govr: Bishop Bell C of E Aided Secdy Sch 1988–97 (chm 1988–92), St Mary's Hall Girls' Sch Brighton 2002–04; Warden Guild of Wt Raphael 2009–13; FRSA 2009; Companion of the Order of the Star of Ethiopia 2012; *Recreations* reading, particularly ecclesiastical and modern political biographies, cycling and walking; *Style*— The Rt Rev Nicholas Reade; ✉ 5 Warnham Gardens, Cooden, Bexhill-on-Sea TN39 3SP (☎ 01424 842673, e-mail nicholas.reade@btinternet.com)

READER, David George; s of Stanley Reader (d 2000), and Annie Reader; *b* 1 October 1947, Barrow-in-Furness, Cumbria; *Educ* Barrow GS; *m* 1969, Elaine, da of John Oswald McKnight; 1 s (Andrew b 1975), 1 da (Clare b 1980); *Career* joined FO 1964, high cmmr to Swaziland 2001–04, ambass to Cambodia 2005–08, special rep of Sec of State for Foreign Affrs 2009–; *Recreations* music, bird watching, hill walking; *Clubs* Royal Over-Seas League; *Style*— Mr David Reader

READING, Bishop of 2011–; Rt Rev Andrew John Proud; *b* 27 March 1954; *Educ* KCL, Lincoln Theological Coll, SOAS London; *m* Hon Janice, da of 2 Lord Brain, *qv*; 2 c; *Career* ordained: deacon 1980, priest 1981; curate Stansted Mountfitchet 1980–83, team vicar Borehamwood 1983–90, asst priest Hatfield 1990–92, rector St Mary's East Barnet 1992–2001, chaplain St Matthew's Church Addis Ababa 2002–07 (also canon honoris causa), canon All Saints' Cathedral Cairo 2005–07, bishop for the Horn of Africa 2007–11; *Style*— The Rt Rev the Bishop of Reading; ✉ Bishop's House, Tidmarsh Lane, Tidmarsh, Reading RG8 8HA

READING, Neil; *Career* fndr Neil Reading PR 1992–; clients incl: Christian and Nick Candy, John Bishop, John Cleese, Paul McKenna, Sir Lenny Henry, CBE, *qqv*, and Dawn French; *Clubs* Groucho, The Ivy; *Style*— Neil Reading, Esq; ✉ Neil Reading PR, 12 New Burlington Street, London W1S 3BF (☎ 020 7287 7711)

READING, Dr Peter Richard; s of Dr Harold Garnar Reading, and Barbara Mary, *née* Hancock (who d 2014); *b* 1 May 1956; *Educ* St Edward's Sch Oxford, Gonville & Caius Coll Cambridge (entrance and sr exhibitioner, MA), Moscow State Univ (Br Cncl research scholar), Univ of Birmingham (PhD); *m* Dr Catherine Austin, *née* Fountain; 1 s, 2 da, 2 step da; *Career* various appts as Health Serv mangr 1984–94; chief exec: Lewisham and Guy's Mental Health NHS Tst 1994–98, UCL Hosps NHS Tst 1998–2000, Univ Hosps of Leicester NHS Tst 2000–07; dir Peter Reading Strategic Cnsltg Ltd 2007–, interim chief exec Doncaster & Bassetlaw Hosps NHS Fndn Tst 2010–11, interim chief exec Peterborough & Stamford Hosps NHS Fndn Tst 2012–14; assoc dir PWC 2014–; CCMI 2006; *Recreations* history, film, 1960s and 1970s popular music; *Style*— Dr Peter Reading; ✉ e-mail info@peterreading.co.uk

READING, 4 Marquess of (UK 1926); Simon Charles Henry Rufus Isaacs; also Baron Reading (UK 1914), Viscount Reading (UK 1916), Earl of Reading and Viscount Erleigh (both UK 1917); s of 3 Marquess of Reading, MBE, MC (d 1980); *b* 18 May 1942; *Educ* Eton, Univ of Tours; *m* 1979, Melinda, yr da of Richard Dewar; 2 da (Lady Sybilla b 3 Nov 1980, Lady Natasha b 24 April 1983), 1 s (Julian Michael Rufus, Viscount Erleigh b 26 May 1986); *Heir* s, Viscount Erleigh; *Career* Lt 1st Queen's Dragoon Gds 1961–64; stockbroker 1964–74, memb London Stock Exchange 1970–74; mktg dir: Brahmaco Int 1975–80, Ralph Lauren Cosmetics 1979–83, Abbey Lubbock 1984–92, Abbey Sports and Events 1984–92; chm Lands End and John O'Groats 1992–96; dir: Flying Hosp Inc 1996–2000, Cure Int (UK) 2004–, Mertens House (St Petersburg) 2008–; pres Dean Close Sch 1990–2000; memb Cncl: The Garden Tomb in Jerusalem 2002–08, Anglo-Israel Assoc; patron Barnabas Fund 1998–, patron Nelson Recovery Tst; *Clubs* Cavalry and Guards', MCC, All England Lawn Tennis, Stoke Park (pres 2005–07); *Style*— The Most Hon the Marquess of Reading; ✉ Cecily Hill, Cirencester GL7 2EF

READY, Nigel Peter; s of Colin Peter Ready (d 1986), and Monica Isabel Elms, *née* Tapper (d 2007); *b* 13 July 1952, Dar es Salaam; *Educ* Wycliffe Coll, Jesus Coll Cambridge (MA); *m* 29 Dec 1973, Marisa, da of Germano Brignolo, of Asti, Italy; 1 da (Natasha Isabella b 1975), 2 s (Oliver James b 1976, Thomas Nigel b 1985); *Career* Notary Public 1980; Cheeswrights: ptnr 1981–2000, managing ptnr 1990–2009, sr ptnr 2000–12, hon chm 2012–; hon sec Soc of Public Notaries of London 1988–2000, vice-pres Fédération des Associations de Notaires Européens 1991–, chm Soc of Scrivener Notaries of London 2000–03, delegate European Affrs Cmmn Int Union of Notaries (UINL) 2011–, memb European Notarial Acad 2011–; dep cmmr of maritime affrs Republic of Vanuatu 1995–; Freeman City of London, memb Ct of Assts Worshipful Co of Scriveners (chm Notarial Ctee 1997–2009, Renter Warden 2000–01, Upper Warden 2001–02, Master 2002–03), Liveryman Worshipful Co of Shipwrights; ARPS; *Books* The Greek Code of Private Maritime Law (jtly, 1982), Brooke's Notary (10 edn 1988, Supplement 1991, 13 edn 2013, 14 edn 2013), Ship Registration (1991, 3 edn 1998), Ship Registration Law and Practice (consulting ed, 2002), T S Eliot's Four Quartets: A Photographic Exploration (2014), IMLI Manual on International Maritime Law (contrib, 2016); *Recreations* wine, opera, photography, travel; *Style*— Nigel Ready, Esq; ✉ Cheeswrights, 107 Leadenhall Street, London EC3A 4AF (☎ 020 7623 9477, e-mail nigel.ready@cheeswrights.co.uk, website www.nigelready.com)

REAMSBOTTOM, Barry Arthur; s of Agnes Mulholland; *b* 4 April 1949; *Educ* St Peter's RC Secdy Sch Aberdeen, Aberdeen Acad; *Career* trade union leader; scientific asst Isaac Spencer & Co Aberdeen 1966–69, social security offr DHSS Aberdeen 1969–76, area offr NUPE Edinburgh 1976–79; Civil and Public Servs Assoc: head of Educn Dept 1979–87, ed Red Tape (CPSA official jl) and press offr 1987–92, gen sec 1992–98; gen sec Public and Commercial Services Union 2001–02 (jt gen sec 1998–2001), exec sec to Speaker of House of Commons 2002–09; memb NUJ 1987–; fell Centre for American Studies Salzburg; *Recreations* golf, books, music, art appreciation, laughter and the love of friends; *Style—* Barry Reamsbottom, Esq; ✉ 156 Bedford Hill, London SW12 9HW (☎ 020 8675 4894, e-mail reamsy156@gmx.co.uk)

REARDON, Kate; *m* Charles Gordon-Watson; 1 s (Arthur Charles Edward Gordon-Watson b 27 Feb 2015 (twin)), 1 da (Katherine Thalia Peverly Gordon-Watson b 27 Feb 2015 (twin)); *Career* US Vogue 1988–90, Tatler 1990–97, Vanity Fair 1999–2011, fndr TopTips.com 2007, ed Tatler 2011–; memb Cancer Research UK 2007–; *Style—* Miss Kate Reardon; ✉ Tatler Magazine, Vogue House, 1 Hanover Square, London W1S 1JU (Twitter @katereardon)

REARDON SMITH, Sir (William) Antony John; 4 Bt (UK 1920), of Appledore, Co Devon; s of Sir William Reardon Reardon Smith, 3 Bt (d 1995), and his 1 w, Nesta, *née* Phillips (d 1959); *b* 20 June 1937; *Educ* Wycliffe Coll; *m* 1962, Susan Wight, da of Henry Wight Gibson, of Cardiff; 3 s ((William) Nicolas Henry b 1963, Giles Antony James b 1968, Harry Alexander b 1979), 1 da (Henrietta Nesta b 1965); *Heir* s, Nicolas Reardon Smith; *Career* dir Reardon Smith Line plc 1959–85, dir World Trade Centre 1986–87; chm GEM Containers 2012; tstee and chm Joseph Strong Frazer Trust; tstee Royal Merchant Navy Sch Fndn until 2004, govr Bearwood Coll until 2004; memb Milford Haven Port Authy to 1999, dir Milford Dock Co and Marine and Port Services to 1999; Liveryman Worshipful Co of Shipwrights, Liveryman Worshipful Co of World Traders, Liveryman Worshipful Co of Poulters, Liveryman Worshipful Co of Fuellers (Clerk 2002–14), memb Honourable Co of Master Mariners; Knight Grand Cross of the Military and Hospitaler Order of St Lazarus of Jerusalem (Bailiff 2002–08); *Recreations* golf, shooting, walking; *Style—* Sir Antony Reardon Smith, Bt; ✉ 26 Merrick Square, London SE1 4JB (☎ 020 7403 5723)

REAVILLE, Richard Maxwell; s of late Jack Reaville, and late Pauline Elizabeth, *née* Sharp; *b* 4 June 1954; *Educ* Claremont Sch Nottingham, Clarendon Coll of FE, RNCM, LTCL; *m* 1998, Cécile *née* Burel; *Career* opera singer (tenor); business career 1975–82, studied at RNCM with John Cameron 1982–86; professional debut as Don Jose in Carmen (WNO) 1985, solo debut in L'Incoronazione di Poppea (Glyndebourne) 1986, Glyndebourne Festival 2011 and 2016; currently working with WNO and future engagements incl work with Opera North, Grange Park Opera; Licentiate Trinity Coll London; *Performances* operas incl: Billy Budd (ENO), Tamino in The Magic Flute (London Chamber Opera), Ferrando in Cosi fan Tutte (Holland Park Festival), Lord Puff in The English Cat (Henze Biennial Festival Gütersloh and Berlin) 1989, Ernesto in Don Pasquale (tour), Simon Boccanegra (concert performance at Tivoli Festival Copenhagen) 1992, Eisenstein in Die Fledermaus (Mid Wales Opera) 1992, Hoffmann in Les Côntes d'Hoffman (Bristol) 1993, Don José in Carmen (European Chamber Opera) 1996; concert and recital performances incl: Mendelssohn Paulus (Staatskapelle Weimar), Verdi Requiem (with Orchestre Philharmonique de Loraine), Beethoven Ninth Symphony (with Odense Symphony Orch Denmark 1990, also Brussels, Namur and Dinant 1992, Brugge, Antwerp and Ninove with Belgium Nat Orch 1995), Mozart Requiem and Bach Johannes Passion (with Åarhus Chamber Orch Denmark, Randers Byorkester) Messiah, Dvorák Stabat Mater and Johannspassion (with Esbjerg Chamber Orch in tour of Denmark), Ligeti Grand Macabre (Odense Symphony Orch Denmark), J S Mayr Requiem (UK première at St John's Smith Square) 1992, Verdi Requiem (Köln, Düsseldorf and St Malo) 1993, Mozart Requiem (with Orchestre de Chambre de Wallonie at Knokke-Heist), Concert Rossini Petite Messe Solonelle (with Copenhagen Boys' Choir), Bach St John Passion arias (with Sönerjuland Orch Denmark under Nicholas Cleobury) 1995, Rossini Stabat Mater (Finland) 1995, Bach St Matthew Passion (with Jyvaskyla Orch Finland) 1996, Mahler Das Lieb Von Der Erde (with Örebro Chamber Orch Sweden and Randers Byorkester) 1997, The Last Temptations (Nilsia Festival Finland) 1999; various other concert engagements with orchs incl BBC Philharmonic and English String Orch; solo contract with Scot Opera in Param Vir's Broken Strings, concert engagements in Finland, France, Belgium and UK incl the world premiere of Anthony Gerard's Le Rêve est Notre Espor with l'Ensemble Orchestral de Paris; radio broadcast with Norwegian Radio of Britten's Serenade for Tenor, Horn and Strings 2001; *Recordings* incl: Billy Budd (ENO), The Love for Three Oranges (with Lyon Opera Orch, finest classical music recording award 1989), Puccini's Messe di Gloria (with Ostrava Choir and Orch of Czech Republic) 1995; *Recreations* politics, golf; *Style—* Richard Reaville, Esq; ✉ e-mail rcreaville@hotmail.com, website www.daviesmusic.org.uk and www.richardreavilletenor.com

REBUCK, Baroness (Life Peer UK 2014), of Bloomsbury in the London Borough of Camden; Dame Gail Ruth Rebuck; DBE (2009, CBE 2000); da of Gordon Woolfe Rebuck, and Mavis, *née* Joseph; *b* 10 February 1952; *Educ* Lycée Français de Londres, Univ of Sussex (BA); *m* 1 April 1985, Philip Gould (Baron Gould of Brookwood (Life Peer), d 2011); 2 da (Hon Georgia Anne Rebuck Gould 18 May 1986, Hon Grace Atalanta Rebuck Gould b 6 June 1989); *Career* prodn asst Grisewood & Dempsey 1975, ed then publisher Robert Nicholson Pubns 1976–79, publisher Hamlyn Paperbacks 1979–82, fndr ptnr and publishing dir non-fiction Century Publishing Co Ltd 1982–85, publisher Century Hutchinson 1985–89, chm Random House Div Random Century (Century Hutchinson bought by Random House Inc) 1989–91, chm and chief exec Random House Gp Ltd 1999–2013 (publisher of over 40 imprints incl: Jonathan Cape, Chatto & Windus, Century, William Heinemann, Hutchinson, Ebury, Bantam, Doubleday, Vintage, Arrow, Corgi, Black Swan, Harvill Secker, BBC Books and Virgin Books), chair Penguin Random House UK 2013–; non-exec dir: The Work Fndn 2001–08, BSkyB 2002–12, Koovs plc 2014–, Belmond Ltd 2015–, Guardian Media Gp 2016–; tstee: IPPR 1993–2003, Nat Literacy Tst 2007–14; memb Creative Industries Task Force 1997–2000; memb Cncl RCA 1999–2015, chair RCA 2015–; chair Quick Reads Adult Literacy Initiative 2006–, chair Cheltenham Lit Festival 2013–; FRSA 1989; *Recreations* reading, travel; *Style—* The Baroness Rebuck, DBE; ✉ Penguin Random House Group Ltd, 20 Vauxhall Bridge Road, London SW1V 2SA (☎ 020 7840 8882, fax 020 7233 6120)

RECORD, Norman John Ronald; s of George Ronald Record (d 1967), of Newton Abbot, Devon, and Dorothy Millie Rowland (d 1996); *b* 19 May 1934; *Educ* Wembley Co GS, UCL (BSc); *m* 1 April 1961, Susan Mary, da of Ernest Samuel Weatherhead (d 1969), of Paignton, Devon; 2 s (Guy b 1964, Justin b 1966); *Career* 2 Lt RAOC 1955–57; economist; formerly held planning and mktg posts in C & J Clark Ltd from 1964, and Perkins Engines Ltd 1957–64, corp planning dir C & J Clark Ltd 1980–91, business economics conslt 1991–; memb Cncl CBI 1982–93; memb Fabian Soc; author of papers on Macro-Economics; originator of The Theory of The Output Gap in the Control of The Economy; fell Soc Business Economists, FIMgt; *Recreations* current affrs, theatre, local history, swimming; *Clubs* Royal Over-Seas League; *Style—* Norman Record, Esq; ✉ 30 St Medard Road, Wedmore, Somerset BS28 4AY (☎ 01934 712 326, e-mail n.record@talk21.com)

REDDAWAY, Sir David Norman; KCMG (2013, CMG 1993), MBE (1980); s of late (George Frank) Norman Reddaway, CBE (d 1999), and Jean Muriel, *née* Brett, OBE; *b* 26 April 1953, Ottawa, Canada; *Educ* King's Coll Sch Cambridge, Oundle, Fitzwilliam Coll Cambridge (exhibitioner, MA); *m* 1981 (sep), Roshan Taliyeh, da of late Narcy Mirza Firouz, and late Louise Laylin Firouz; 2 s (Alexander Bahram b 1983, Milo Firouz b 1996), 1 da (Touran b 1987); *Career* volunteer teacher Ethiopia 1972, joined FCO 1975, language trg SOAS 1976, language trg Iran 1977, third then second sec (commercial) Tehran 1978–79, second then first sec (Chancery) Tehran 1979–80, first sec Madrid 1980–84, first sec FCO 1985–86, private sec to Min of State FCO 1986–88, first sec (external political) New Delhi 1988–90, chargé d'affaires Tehran 1990–93 (cnsllr 1991), minister Buenos Aires 1993–97, head of Southern European Dept FCO 1997–99, dir Public Services FCO 1999–2001, UK special rep for Afghanistan (with personal rank of ambass) 2002, visiting fell Harvard Univ 2002–03, high cmmr to Canada 2003–06, ambass to Ireland 2006–09, ambass to Turkey 2009–14; advsr then non-exec dir Beko plc 2014–; memb Int Advsy Bd Sch of Mgmnt Univ of Bath 2014–; memb Cncl of Experts Democratic Progress Inst 2015–; Clerk Goldsmiths' Co 2016; *Recreations* Persian carpets and art, skiing, tennis, watching rugby, kayaking; *Clubs* Hawks' (Cambridge), Royal Overseas League, Leander (Henley); *Style—* Sir David Reddaway, KCMG, MBE; ✉ Goldsmiths' Hall, Foster Lane, London EC2V 6BN

REDDIHOUGH, His Hon Judge John Hargreaves; s of Frank Hargreaves Reddihough, of Manchester, and Mabel Grace, *née* Warner; *b* 6 December 1947; *Educ* Manchester Grammar, Univ of Birmingham (LLB); *m* 26 June 1981, Sally Margaret, da of Bert Fryer, of Crawley, 1 da (Gayle b 1981), 1 s (Alex b 1984); *Career* called to the Bar Gray's Inn 1969; recorder 1994; circuit judge: Midland & Oxford Circuit 2000–01, NE Circuit 2001–09, SE Circuit 2009–; resident judge Grimsby Combined Court 2001–09; *Recreations* skiing, travel, gardening, music, reading; *Style—* His Hon Judge John Reddihough; ✉ Reading Crown Court, Old Shire Hall, The Forbury, Reading, Berkshire RG1 3EH (☎ 0118 967 4400)

REDDISH, John Wilson; s of Frank Reddish, of Middleton, Gtr Manchester (d 2015), and Elizabeth, *née* Hall (d 2014); *b* 19 January 1950; *Educ* Manchester Grammar, Lincoln Coll Oxford (MA); *m* 20 May 1978, Dawn Marian, da of Edward Henry John McKenzie Russell (d 1963); 1 da (Helena b 1987); *Career* teaching assoc Northwestern Sch of Law Chicago 1971–72, called to the Bar Middle Temple 1973, in practice 1974–2012; pt/t chm Special Educnl Needs Tbnl 1994–2008, pt/t chm Protection of Children Act Tbnl 2000–02 (temp pres 2001), pt/t chm Care Standards Tbnl 2002–08, pt/t tribunal judge Health, Educn and Social Care Chamber 2008–, pt/t tribunal judge Social Entitlement Chamber 2011–, memb Specialist Arbitration Panel at Sports Resolutions 2012–15; *Recreations* cricket, croquet; *Clubs* Dulwich Sports, Norwich Croquet; *Style—* John Reddish, Esq; ✉ e-mail jreddish@btinternet.com

REDDISH, Tim; OBE (2009, MBE 2001); s of Peter Reddish (d 1991), and Pauline, *née* Brown; *b* 12 April 1957, Nottingham; *m* Valerie, *née* Jones; 2 s (Paul b 29 June 1981, Christopher b 26 Dec 1982); *Career* former Paralympic swimmer (competed in 3 Paralympic Games, 3 World Championships and 5 European Championships, winner of a total of 22 Gold, 11 Silver and 10 Bronze medals, ret 2002); Br Disability Swimming: caretaker performance dir 2002, nat performance dir 2003–10, exec dir 2010–; swimming chairperson Int Paralympic Ctee 2006–08, chm/pres Br Paralympic Assoc 2008–, memb Bd LOCOG 2009–; launched enterprise consultancy timreddish.com, project mgmnt, people devpt, motivational and keynote presentations 2013; hon vice-pres Notts ASA 1997–; LLD (hc) Univ of Nottingham 2014; Hon Freeman City of Nottingham 2005; *Recreations* skiing, cycling, triathlon; *Style—* Tim Reddish, Esq, OBE; ✉ 24 Nuthall Gardens, Nottingham NG8 5GQ (☎ 07801 746701, e-mail tim@timreddish.com, Twitter @reddish_tim)

REDDY, Thomas; s of Thomas Reddy (d 1973), of Poulton-le-Fylde, and Charlotte Winifred Teresa, *née* Hickey (d 1987); *b* 6 December 1941; *Educ* Baines's Sch Poulton; *m* 30 Aug 1969, Phyllis Wendy, da of Stanley Smith (d 1969), of Manchester and Lytham St Anne's; 1 da (Verity b 1971), 1 s (Christian b 1973); *Career* journalist 1968–70, dir and exec creative dir Royds McCann 1970–87, chief exec Tom Reddy Advertising 1987–; broadcaster on advertising TV and radio;; *Recreations* book collecting; *Clubs* Manchester Tennis and Racquets; *Style—* Thomas Reddy, Esq; ✉ Tom Reddy Advertising (☎ 07802 444307, e-mail tomreddy1@mac.com)

REDESDALE, 6 Baron (UK 1902), of Redesdale, Co Northumberland, also cr Baron Mitford, of Redesdale in the County of Northumberland (Life Baron) 2000, and sits as such in the House of Lords; Rupert Bertram Mitford; o s of 5 Baron Redesdale (d 1991), and Sarah Georgina Cranstoun, *née* Todd; *b* 18 July 1967; *Educ* Milton Abbey, Highgate Sch, Univ of Newcastle upon Tyne (BA); *m* 1998, Helen, da of D H Shipsey; 1 s (Hon Bertram David b 2000), 2 da (Clementine Ann b 2001, Amelia Sarah b 2003); *Heir* s, Hon Bertram Mitford; *Career* overseas devpt spokesman for Liberal Democrats 1993–; memb Cncl Inst Advanced Motorists; *Style—* The Rt Hon Lord Redesdale; ✉ The School House, Rochester, Newcastle upon Tyne NE19 1RH; 2 St Mark's Square, London NW1 7TP

REDFARN, Stephen Charles; s of Dr Cyril Aubrey Redfarn (d 1988), of London, and Isabel Mary, *née* Williams (d 1987); *b* 7 May 1943; *Educ* Westminster, King's Coll London (BSc), Univ of Westminster (DBA); *m* 1990, Frances Yin Hong; 1 s (James Yin Aubrey b 26 Oct 1995); *Career* with Hill Samuel & Co Ltd 1966–68, dir Dawnay Day & Co Ltd investment bankers 1968–78, head of corp fin Henry Ansbacher & Co 1978–83, conslt Touche Ross 1983–87, head of capital markets AIB London 1987–90, chief exec Westcountry Television Ltd 1990–97; currently chm Media Equity Associates Ltd; external examiner in accounting CNAA 1986; chm Business Graduates Assoc 1981, vice-chm Plymouth Area Business Cncl; Freeman City of London, Liveryman Worshipful Co of Tallow Chandlers; *Recreations* fly fishing, collecting 18th century glass, exploring China; *Clubs* Reform, Royal Anglo Belgian, City of London; *Style—* Stephen Redfarn, Esq

REDFERN, Rt Rev Alastair Llewellyn John; *see:* Derby, Bishop of

REDFERN, (Margaret) June; da of John Towers Redfern, of West Ferry, Dundee, and Margaret, *née* Campbell (d 1979); *b* 16 June 1951; *Educ* Edinburgh Coll of Art; *Career* artist; pt/t tutor (fine art) Preston Poly 1982–83, jr fell (fine art) Cardiff Coll of Art 1983, artist in residence Nat Gallery London 1985; guest artist: Univ of Minnesota 1986, Kunstacademie I Trondheim 1992; Andrew Grant scholarship 1972–73, First Prize Scottish Young Contemporaries 1972, Scottish Arts Cncl Award 1982; patron Child Pyschotherapy Tst Scotland 1992–; *Solo Exhibitions* Scottish Arts Cncl Edinburgh 1976, Third Eye Centre Glasgow 1977, Leeds Educn Authy 1977, Women's Arts Alliance London 1978, Henderson Gallery Edinburgh 1978 (drawings 1980), 369 Gallery Edinburgh 1981, Air Gallery London 1984, Third Eye Centre Glasgow 1985, Marianne Deson Gallery Chicago 1985, Nat Gallery London 1986, Mercury Gallery Edinburgh 1987, Bradford Art Galleries and Museums 1987, Aberdeen Art Galleries and Museums 1988, Towner Art Gallery Eastbourne 1988, Mercury Gallery London 1988, Trinity Gallery London 1990, Compass Gallery Glasgow 1991, Bohun Gallery Henley 1992, 1994 and 1997, Wrexham Arts Centre 1992, Maclaurin Art Gallery Ayr 1992, Wrexham Library Arts Centre 1992 (touring Maclaurin Art Gallery and Museum Ayr 1992), MAC Birmingham 1993, Portal Gallery Bremen 1994, Scottish Gallery 1996, 1999 and 2001, Boundary Gallery London 1996, 1999 and 2001, Bohun Gallery 1998, Oilon Canvas Boundary Gallery 1998, Open Eye Gallery Edinburgh 2003, Caledonian Girls (Nicholas Hagen Fine Art London) 2004–05, Thompsons Gallery London 2004–08, Fosse Gallery 2007, Boaun Gallery 2008; *Invited Artist* Eiese Carlow Festival Exhibition Fosse Gallery 2010; *Public Collections* incl: Nat Gallery London, BBC TV, Robert Fleming plc, Hiscox Holdings, Charlotte Englehart Fndn Boston, Texaco, Albertina Museum Vienna, Procter & Gamble, Glasgow Art Galleries and Museums, Lillie Art Gallery Glasgow, Lithoprint

UK, 3i, Scottish Equitable Standard Life, New Hall Cambridge, DOC TV Canada, British Trade Commission NY, Scottish Life, and also paintings in various hospitals; *Television* incl: The Bigger Picture (BBC 2) 1994, Edinburgh Nights (The Late Show, BBC 2) 1994, Weathering the Storm (BBC Scotland and BBC 2), Oil on Canvas (BBC 2), Bonnard Omnibus (BBC2); *Style*— Ms June Redfern; ✉ 12 Lawley Street, London E5 0RJ (☎ 020 8985 1426, website www.juneredfern.com)

REDFERN, Simon; *Career* conslt rising to dir Connect 2001–06, assoc dir Fishburn Hedges 2006–11, ptnr Pagefield 2011–13; Starbucks: dir of UK corp affrs 2013–14, dir of EMEA corp affrs 2014–16, vice-pres of public affrs EMEA 2016–; *Style*— Simon Redfern, Esq; ✉ Starbucks Coffee Company, Building 4 Chiswick Park, 566 Chiswick High Road, London W4 5YE

REDGRAVE, Adrian Robert Frank; QC (1992); s of late Cecil Frank Redgrave, and Doris Edith Redgrave; *b* 1 September 1944; *Educ* Abingdon Sch, Univ of Exeter (LLB); *m* 7 Oct 1967, Ann, da of late Jack Bryan Cooper; 2 s (William Alexander Frank b 6 April 1971, Matthew Robert Charles b 23 May 1977), 1 da (Lucy Rebecca Jane b 28 Sept 1972); *Career* called to the Bar Inner Temple 1968, recorder 1985–; *Recreations* tennis, wine, garden, France, Bangalore Phall; *Style*— Adrian Redgrave, Esq, QC; ✉ 13 King's Bench Walk, London EC4Y 7EN (☎ 020 7353 7204)

REDGRAVE, Sir Steven Geoffrey (Steve); kt (2001), CBE (1997, MBE 1986); s of Geoffrey Edward Redgrave, of Marlow Bottom, Bucks, and Sheila Marion, *née* Stevenson; *b* 23 March 1962; *Educ* Marlow C of E First Sch, Holy Trinity Sch Marlow, Burford Sch Marlow Bottom, Great Marlow Sch; *m* 12 March 1988, (Elizabeth) Ann, da of Brian John Callaway, of Cyprus; 2 da (Natalie b 1991, Sophie b 1994), 1 s (Zak b 16 Feb 1998); *Career* sports conslt and former rower; notable achievements incl: runner-up double sculls World Jr Championships 1980, 20 wins Henley Royal Regatta 1981–2001, Gold medal coxed fours Olympic Games Los Angeles 1984, Wingfield Sculls champion 1985–89, Gold medal coxless pairs World Championships 1986 and 1987 (Silver medal coxed pairs 1987), 3 Gold medals Cwlth Games 1986 (single sculls, coxed fours, coxless pairs), Gold medal coxless pairs Olympic Games Seoul 1988 (Bronze medal coxed pairs), indoor world rowing champion 1991, world champion coxless pairs 1991, Gold medal coxless pairs Olympic Games Barcelona 1992, world champion coxless pairs 1993, 1994 and 1995, world record holder coxless pairs 1994, Gold medal coxless pairs Olympic Games Atlanta 1996, world champion coxless fours 1997, 1998 and 1999, Gold medal coxless fours Olympic Games Sydney 2000; flagbearer Olympic Games 1992 and 1996; winner Team of the Year (with M Pinsent) BBC Sports Personality of the Year Awards 1992 and 1996, BBC Sports Personality of the Year 2000, Golden Personality BBC Sports Personality of the Year Awards 2003; pres Amateur Rowing Assoc (ARA), dir Five Gold (www.fivegold.co.uk), hon vice-pres Diabetes UK; Hon DTech Loughborough Univ 2001; Hon DUniv: Buckingham, Nottingham, Durham, Hull, Buckinghamshire Chilterns UC, Reading, Heriot-Watt, Open Univ, Oxford Brookes, Aberdeen Univ; *Publications* A Golden Age (autobiography, with Nick Townsend), Steve Redgrave's Complete Book of Rowing, You Can Win at Life (with Nick Townsend); *Clubs* Marlow Rowing, Leander; *Style*— Sir Steve Redgrave, CBE; ✉ c/o PO Box 3400, Marlow, Buckinghamshire SL7 3WX (☎ 01627 483021, e-mail melanie@casitas.tv, website www.ssrct.co.uk and www.steveredgrave.com)

REDGRAVE, Vanessa; CBE (1967); da of Sir Michael Redgrave (d 1985), and Lady Redgrave (Rachel Kempson); sis of Lynn Redgrave, *qv*; *b* 30 January 1937; *Educ* Queensgate Sch, Ballet Rambert, Central Sch of Speech and Drama; *m* 1962 (m dis 1967), Tony Richardson (d 1991), s of Clarence Albert Richardson (d 1969); 2 da (Natasha Richardson (d 2009), Joely Richardson, the actresses); *Career* actress, numerous stage and film performances; fell BAFTA 2010; *Theatre* Touch of the Sun (Saville) 1958, A Midsummer Night's Dream (Stratford) 1959, Look on Tempests 1960, The Tiger and the Horse 1960, Lady from the Sea 1960; with Royal Shakespeare Theatre Co: As You Like It 1961, Taming of the Shrew 1961, Cymbeline 1962; The Seagull 1964, The Prime of Miss Jean Brodie (Wyndham's) 1966, Daniel Deronda 1969, Cato Street 1971, The Threepenny Opera (Prince of Wales) 1972, Twelfth Night (Shaw Theatre) 1972, Antony and Cleopatra (Bankside Globe) 1973, Design for Living (Phoenix) 1973, Macbeth (LA) 1974, Lady from the Sea (NY) 1976, Roundhouse 1979, The Aspern Papers (Haymarket) 1984, The Seagull (Queen's) 1985, Chekov's Women (Lyric) 1985, The Taming of the Shrew and Antony and Cleopatra (Haymarket) 1986, Ghosts (Young Vic, transferred to Wyndham's) 1986, Touch of the Poet (Young Vic, transferred to Comedy) 1988, Orpheus Descending (Haymarket) 1988 and (NY) 1989, A Madhouse in Goa (Lyric Hammersmith) 1989, When She Danced (Globe, Best Actress Evening Standard Drama Awards) 1991, Heartbreak House (Yvonne Arnaud Guildford and Haymarket) 1992, Maybe (Royal Exchange) 1993, John Gabriel Borkman (RNT) 1996, Lady Windermere's Fan (Haymarket) 2002, The Hollow Crown (Princess of Wales Theatre Toronto) 2004; theatrical debut as director: Antony and Cleopatra (Riverside Studios) 1995; *Films* A Suitable Case for Treatment 1966 (Cannes Festival Best Actress Award 1966), The Sailor from Gibraltar 1967, Blow-Up 1967, Camelot 1967, Red White and Zero 1967, Charge of the Light Brigade 1968, Isadora 1968, A Quiet Place in the Country 1968, The Seagull 1969, Drop-Out 1970, La Vacanza 1970, The Trojan Women 1971, The Devils 1971, Mary Queen of Scots 1972, Murder on the Orient Express 1974, Out of Season 1975, Seven Per Cent Solution 1975, Julia 1976 (Academy Award 1977, Golden Globe Award), Agatha 1978, Yanks 1978, Bear Island 1978, Playing for Time 1980, My Body My Child 1981, Wagner 1983, The Bostonians 1984, Wetherby 1985, Steaming 1985, Comrades 1987, Prick Up Yours Ears 1987, Consuming Passions 1988, A Man for All Seasons 1988, Orpheus Descending 1990, Young Catherine 1990, Howards End 1992 (best supporting actress Oscar nomination 1993), The Wall 1992, Great Moments in Aviation 1993, Mother's Boy 1993, The House of the Spirits 1993, Crime & Punishment 1993, They 1993, Little Odessa 1994, A Month by the Lake 1996, Déjà Vu 1996, Wilde 1997, Smilla's Feeling for Snow 1997, Mrs Dalloway 1997, Deep Impact 1997, Cradle Will Rock 1998, Mirka 1998, Uninvited 1998, Girl Interrupted 1999, A Rumour of Angels 2000, Crime and Punishment 2000, If These Walls Could Talk II 2000 (best actress Screen Actors Guild Awards 2001), The Fever 2002, The Keeper 2003, Venus 2006, The Riddle 2007, How About You 2007, Evening 2007, Atonement 2007, Eva 2009, Letters to Juliet 2010, Miral 2010, Coriolanus 2011 (Best Supporting Actress Br Ind Film Award 2011), Cars 2 2011, Anonymous 2011, Song for Marion 2012; *Television* incl: Nip/Tuck 2004–09, The Shell Seekers 2006, The Day of the Triffids 2009; *Publications* Pussies and Tigers (1963), Vanessa – An Autobiography (1992); *Style*— Miss Vanessa Redgrave, CBE

REDMAN, Prof Christopher Willard George; s of Prof Roderick Oliver Redman (d 1975), and (Annie) Kathleen Redman (d 1996); *b* 30 November 1941; *Educ* Perse Sch Cambridge, Univ of Cambridge (MA, MB BChir); *m* 8 Aug 1964, Corinna Susan, da of Prof Sir Denys Lionel Page, KBE (d 1978); 4 s (Paul b 1967, Andrew b 1969, George b 1972, Oliver b 1982), 1 da (Sophie b 1972); *Career* intern and resident dept of pathology Johns Hopkins Hosp Baltimore USA 1967, house offr Children's Hosp Sheffield 1969, sr house offr Jessop Hosp Sheffield 1969, lectr regius Dept of Med Radcliffe Infirmary Oxford 1970 (house offr 1968), prof Nuffield Dept of Obstetrics John Radcliffe Hosp Oxford 1993– (univ lectr 1976, clinical reader 1988, clinical prof 1992); FRCP 1982, FRCOG as eundum 1993; *Recreations* walking; *Style*— Prof Christopher Redman; ✉ Nuffield Department of Obstetrics and Gynaecology, John Radcliffe Hospital, Oxford OX3 9DU (☎ 01865 221009)

REDMAN-BROWN, Geoffrey Michael; s of Arthur Henry Brown (d 1999), of Newport, Gwent, and Marjorie Frances Joan, *née* Redman (d 1969); assumed by Deed Poll the additional surname of Redman before his patronymic 1960; *b* 30 March 1937; *Educ* Newport HS, Balliol Coll Oxford (MA); *m* 23 Feb 1988, Mrs Jean Wadlow; *Career* Nat Serv RAF 1956–58; Phillips & Drew (subsequently UBS Ltd): joined 1961, ptnr 1970–86, dir 1986–90, ret 1990; dir Jean Wadlow Associates Ltd 1991–2010 (chm 1994–2010); endowment fund tstee Balliol Coll Oxford 1988–2015, chm Balliol Coll Old Membs' Ctee 1991–2001; Prov Grand Master for Oxfordshire: United Grand Lodge of England 1985–2001, Grand Lodge of Mark Master Masons 1994–2004; Prov Grand Master for London and Metropolitan Counties Royal Order of Scotland 1996–2008; tstee New Masonic Samaritan Fund 1991–2001; chm The League of Remembrance 2005–15 (hon treas 1990–05); Freeman City of London, Liveryman Worshipful Co of Broderers 1977, Distinguished Friend of Oxford 2013; MSI (memb Stock Exchange 1967), AIIMR (AMSIA 1972); *Recreations* swimming, gardening, travel, opera and the arts; *Clubs* Garrick, City of London, RAC; *Style*— Geoffrey Redman-Brown, Esq; ✉ 5 Three Kings Yard, Davies Street, Mayfair, London W1K 4JR (☎ 07866 425 675, e-mail gmredmanbrown@btinternet.com)

REDMAYNE, Charlie; s of Richard Redmayne; half-bro of Eddie Redmayne, *qv*; *Career* exec vice-pres and chief digital offr HarperCollins until 2011, ceo Pottermore 2011–13, ceo HarperCollins UK 2013–; *Style*— Charlie Redmayne, Esq; ✉ HarperCollins, The News Building, 1 London Bridge Street, London SE1 9GF

REDMAYNE, Edward John David (Eddie); OBE (2015); s of Richard Redmayne, of London, and Patricia, *née* Burke; *b* 6 January 1982, London; *Educ* Colet Court (music scholar), Eton (music scholar), Trinity Coll Cambridge (choral scholar, BA); *m* 15 Dec 2014, Hannah Bagshawe; *Career* actor; *Theatre* Twelfth Night (Middle Temple Hall), The Goat or Who is Sylvia? (Almeida, Outstanding Newcomer Evening Standard Theatre Awards 2004 and Critic's Circle Theatre Awards 2005), Hecuba (Donmar Warehouse), Now or Later (Royal Court), Red (Donmar Warehouse and Broadway, Olivier Award, Tony Award), Richard II (Donmar Warehouse, Critic's Circle Award); *Film* Like Minds, The Good Shepherd, Elizabeth – The Golden Age, Savage Grace, The Other Boleyn Girl, Yellow Handkerchief, Powder Blue, Glorious 39, Black Death, My Week With Marilyn, Les Misérables, Jupiter Ascending, The Theory of Everything (Best Actor Golden Globes 2015, Best Actor Acad Award 2015), The Danish Girl 2015; *Television* Tess of the d'Urbervilles (BBC), The Pillars of the Earth, Birdsong; *Style*— Eddie Redmayne, Esq, OBE; ✉ Dallas Smith, United Agents, 12–26 Lexington Street, London W1F 0LE (e-mail kwhelan-foran@unitedagents.co.uk)

REDMOND, Prof Anthony Damien; OBE (1994); s of Gerard Redmond (d 1976), and Kathleen, *née* Bates (d 1997); *b* 18 November 1951, Failsworth, Manchester; *Educ* Cardinal Langley Sch, Univ of Manchester (MB ChB, MD); *m* 22 Dec 1972, Caroline Ann, da of Dr John Arthur Howarth, of Devon; 3 da (Katherine Mary b 12 Dec 1978, Sarah Michelle b 15 Sept 1980, Helen Margaret b 24 April 1982); *Career* dir S Manchester Accident Rescue Team 1987–92 (attended Armenian Earthquake 1988, Lockerbie Air Crash 1988, Iranian Earthquake 1990, Kurdish refugees 1991, Ex-Yugoslavia 1992), conslt in emergency med N Staffs Trauma Centre 1991–99, prof of emergency med Keele Univ 1995–99 (sr lectr 1992–95, now emeritus prof); chief exec UK-Med 1993–; WHO conslt Ex-Yugoslavia 1992–93, conslt Humanitarian Affairs Dept for Int Devpt 2000–; dir Operation Phoenix Sarajevo 1994–96 (ldr ODA med team Sarajevo 1993), memb UN Disaster Assessment and Co-ordination Team, med advsr Staffs Ambulance Service 1999–2000, med dir Univ Clinical Centre Pristina Kosovo 1999–2000, ldr Br Medical Team Earthquake in Sichuan China 2008, medical coordinator MERLIN surgical team Earthquake in Haiti 2010, UK-Med team ldr to Typhoon Haiyan Phlippines 2013, coordinator NHS deployment to ebola crisis Sierra Leone 2014–15; fndr ed Archives of Emergency Med 1984–93; Univ of Manchester: dean Hope Hosp 2006–12, prof of int emergency medicine 2007–, dir Humanitarian and Conflict Response Inst 2009–, pres-elect World Assoc for Disaster and Emergency Med 2015–, head WHO Collaborating Centre for Emergency Medical Teams and Emergency Capacity Building 2016–; assoc med dir BUPA 2001–06, sr memb Med Appeals Tbnl 2001–, non-exec dir Casualty Plus 2004–08, chm Manchester Medicolegal Services Ltd 1997–, pres Casualties Union 1998–2006; memb: Resuscitation Cncl UK, Fontmell Gp for Disaster Relief; hon memb 48 Group 2008, hon col 207 (Manchester) Field Ambulance 2014–; Soviet Order for Personal Courage 1989 (for work in Armenian Earthquake); Mancunian of the Year 1992, Humanitarian Award Int Fedn for Emergency Medicine 2010, World Assoc for Disaster and Emergency Medicine (WADEM) Humanitarian Award for Excellence in Disaster Mgmnt 2011; DMCC (Dip Med Care of Catastrophes Soc of Apothecaries of London) 2003; Hon DSc Univ of Glamorgan 2011; FRSM, MRCP UK 1981, FRCSEd 1982, MIMgt 1985, FFAEM 1995, FRCPGlas 1991, FFIMC, RCSEd 2002, FCMI 2008, fell Royal Coll of Emergency Medicine 2015, Hon MFPH 2016; *Publications* Lecture Notes on Accident and Emergency Medicine (1984), Accident and Emergency Medicine (jtly 1989), The Management of Major Trauma (1991), The ABC of Conflict and Disaster (2005), A Qualitative and Quantitative Study of the Surgical and Rehabilitation Response to the Earthquake in Haiti 2010 (jtly, 2011); *Recreations* music; *Style*— Prof Anthony D Redmond, OBE; ✉ e-mail tony.redmond@manchester.ac.uk

REDMOND, Sir Anthony Gerard (Tony); kt (2011); s of Alfonso Redmond (d 2002), of Liverpool, and Margaret Florence, *née* Judge (d 1984); *b* 18 May 1945; *Educ* St Mary's Coll Crosby; *m* 24 May 1973, Lady Christine Mary, da of Edmund Pinnington; 2 s (Dominic b 10 Aug 1976, Mark b 12 May 1980), 2 da (Emily b 9 July 1978, Sarah-Kate b 14 Aug 1984); *Career* chief accountant Liverpool City Cncl 1975–78, dep fin dir Wigan MBC 1978–82, treas and dep chief exec Knowsley MBC 1982–87, treas Merseyside Police Authy 1986–87, chief exec and fin dir London Borough of Harrow 1987–2001, chm and chief exec Cmmn for Local Admin and Local Govt Ombudsman 2001–10, vice-chair and cmmr Local Govt Boundary Cmmn 2011–; vice-chair Consumer Cncl for Water and chair London and SE Region; treas Unicef UK; friend Royal Acad, friend ROH; Freeman City of London; memb CIPFA 1969 (pres 2012–13), FRSA 1996, fell Inst of Revenues, Rating and Valuation 2011, FCPA 2012; *Recreations* sport in general, theatre, cinema, interest in ballet, fine wine; *Clubs* Waterloo, Wasps and Lancashire Rugby, MCC; *Style*— Sir Anthony Redmond; ✉ The Local Government Boundary Commission, Millbank Tower, Millbank, London SW1P 4QP

REDMOND, Imelda; CBE (2010); *Career* chief exec Carers UK until 2011; non-exec dir Homerton Univ Tst; *Style*— Ms Imelda Redmond, CBE

REDMOND, John Vincent; s of Maj Robert Spencer Redmond, TD, of Knutsford, Cheshire, and Marjorie Helen, *née* Heyes; *b* 10 April 1952; *Educ* Wrekin Coll, Western Reserve Acad Ohio, Univ of Kent at Canterbury (BA); *m* 21 May 1977, Tryphena Lloyd (Nina), da of Jenkin John Lloyd Powell, of Carmarthen, Dyfed; 2 s (William b 1981, Samuel b 1985); *Career* admitted slr 1976; Cobbetts Manchester 1974–75, Clyde & Co Guildford and London 1975–78, Laytons Bristol and London 1978–2000, Osborne Clarke 2000–10 (ptnr and head of construction law, conslt 2010–), ind arbitrator and construction adjudicator 2010–; chm Soc of Construction Law 1996–98; chartered arbitrator and adjudicator; memb Soc of Construction Arbitrators; memb Law Soc 1976, FCIArb; *Publications* Civil Engineering Claims, Adjudication in Construction Contracts; *Recreations* mountains, sailing, real tennis; *Style*— John Redmond, Esq; ✉ Hafod, Scot Lane, Chew Stoke, Bristol BS40 8UW (☎ 01275 331509, mobile 07788 584337, e-mail jvr@johnredmond.co.uk, website www.johnredmond.co.uk)

REDMOND, Stephen John; s of late Thomas Redmond, and late Mary Redmond; *b* 15 November 1955; *Educ* MCIPD (grad); *m* 1, 1978, Hazel (d 2004); 1 s (Matthew b 28 Oct

R

1982), 1 da (Hayley b 9 Feb 1985); m 2, 2006, Estelle (d 2012); *Career* HR conslt; British Coal plc: asst head of industry trg Western Area 1983–86, dep head of staff admin NE Area 1986–88; dir Personnel N Devon HA 1988–90, dir Personnel and Support Services Weston Area Health Tst 1990–95, dir HR Plymouth Hosp NHS Tst 1995–97, head of personnel Dept of Health 1997–99, nat dir HR NHS Wales Nat Assembly for Wales 1999–2006; non-exec dir: Revenue and Customs Prosecutions Office 2007–09, Crown Prosecution Service, The Coal Authy; assoc Mott McDonald Ltd; ind chair Doctors and Dentists Disciplinary Appeal Panels, ind panel chair Judicial Appointments Cmmn, chair Fitness to Practise Nursing and Midwifery Cncl, memb Judicial Conduct and Investigation Office, chair of appts Bar Standards Bd 2016–; CIPD; *Recreations* collector of antique and old cuff links (2500 pairs in the collection); *Style*— Stephen Redmond, Esq; ✉ e-mail stephen.redmond2@gmail.com

REDSHAW, Tina Susan; da of Trevor Redshaw (d 2004), and Doreen Cooper, *née* Langley; *b* 25 January 1961, Eastbourne, E Sussex; *Educ* Univ of York (BA), Open Univ (MSc); *m* Phongphun Khogapun; 1 da (Alisha Eve Redshaw b 25 Oct 2001); *Career* diplomat; dir Soc for Anglo-Chinese Understanding 1985–89; VSO: country prog dir China and Mongolia 1990–94, regnl prog dir SE Asia 1994–98, regnl funding mangr SE Asia (based Bangkok) 1998–99; entered HM Dip Serv 1999, first sec (political) Beijing 2000, ambass to East Timor 2003–07, head Energy, Environment, Infrastructure UKTI British Embassy Beijing 2007–; *Recreations* swimming, watching performing arts, listening to jazz, walking; *Style*— Ms Tina Redshaw; ✉ c/o Foreign & Commonwealth Office (Beijing), King Charles Street, London SW1A 2AH

REDWOOD, Dr David Robert; s of Edward James Redwood (d 1967), and Florence Maude Elizabeth, *née* Harper; *b* 4 November 1935; *Educ* King's Sch Worcester, Jesus Coll Cambridge (MA, MB BChir); *m* 1, 1960, Mehranguise (d 1980); 3 s (Michael b 1961, Simon b 1963, David b 1970); m 2, 1 May 1982, Janet Elizabeth (d 2000), da of George Young, CBE; 1 da (Katherine b 1984), 1 s (Jamie b 1987); *Career* head of cardiovascular diagnosis Nat Inst of Health Bethesda Maryland USA 1973–76 (visiting scientist 1968–76), head of cardiology Cedars of Lebanon Hosp Miami Florida USA 1976–77; conslt cardiologist: St George's Hosp London 1977–96, St Anthony's Hosp Cheam Surrey 1977–; author of chapters in cardiology textbooks and numerous papers in scientific jls; FRCP; *Recreations* sailing, walking, photography, golf; *Style*— Dr David Redwood; ✉ St Anthony's Hospital, London Road, Cheam, Surrey SM3 9DW (☎ 020 8337 6691)

REDWOOD, Rt Hon John Alan; PC (1993), MP; s of William Charles Redwood, of Kent, and Amy Emma, *née* Champion; *b* 15 June 1951; *Educ* Kent Coll Canterbury, Magdalen Coll Oxford (BA), St Antony's Coll Oxford (DPhil, MA), Level 6 CISI Investment Qualification; *m* 1974 (m dis 2004), Gail Felicity, da of Robert Stanley Chippington; 1 da (Catherine b 1978), 1 s (Richard b 1982); *Career* fell All Souls Coll Oxford 1972–86 and 2003–; investment analyst Robert Fleming & Co 1974–77, clerk, mangr then dir NM Rothschild Asset Mgmnt 1977–83, advsr to Treasy and Civil Service Select Ctee 1981, head Prime Minister's Policy Unit 1983–85, dir (Overseas Corporate Finance) NM Rothschilds 1986–87; non-exec dir: Norcros plc 1986–89 (chm 1987–89), BNB Resources plc 2000–07; chm and non-exec dir: Hare Hatch Hldgs 1999–2008, Concentric plc 2003–08, Pan Asset Capital Mgmnt 2007–10; MP (Cons) Wokingham 1987–; Parly under sec of state for corporate affrs DTI 1989–90, min of state for corporate affairs, fin servs and telecommunications 1990–92, min of state for local govt and inner cities DOE 1992–93, sec of state for Wales 1993–95 (resigned to contest Cons leadership), shadow trade and industry sec 1997–99, shadow sec for environment, tport and the regions 1999–2000, shadow deregulation sec 2004–05, chm Cons Party Economic Policy Review 2005–10, chm Cons Economic Affrs Ctee 2010–; Cons Pty leadership candidate 1995 and 1997; cncllr Oxfordshire CC 1973–77; assoc prof Middx Univ Business Sch 2000–; *Books* Reason, Ridicule and Religion: The Age of Enlightenment in England 1660–1750 (first published 1976, reissued 1996), Popular Capitalism (1987), The Global Marketplace (1994), Our Currency, Our Country (1997), The Death of Britain? (1999), Stars and Strife (2001), Just Say No (2001), Third Way Which Way (2002), Singing the Blues (2005), Superpower Struggles (2005), I Want to Make a Difference (2006), After the Credit Crunch (2009), The Future of the Euro (2012); *Recreations* village cricket, water sports; *Style*— The Rt Hon John Redwood, MP; ✉ House of Commons, London SW1A 0AA (☎ 020 7219 4205, website www.johnredwood.com)

REECE, Damian John; s of Malcolm Reece, of Mapperley Hall, Notts, and Sheila, *née* Moore; *b* 15 October 1966, Yalding, Kent; *Educ* St Joseph's Sch Horwich, Thornleigh Salesian Coll Bolton, Univ of Manchester (BA); *m* 15 July 1995, Page, *née* Shepherd; 1 da (Emily b 14 Sept 1998), 1 s (Findlay b 28 Feb 2000); *Career* staff writer Investors Chronicle 1993–94, dep personal fin ed Sunday Telegraph 1994–97, consumer industries corr Sunday Business 1997–99, asst city ed Sunday Telegraph 1999–2003, city ed The Independent 2003–05, dep city ed Daily Telegraph 2005–06, city ed Daily Telegraph 2006–07, head of business Telegraph Media Gp 2007–13, managing ptnr Instinctif Ptnrs 2013–; Personal Finance Journalist of the Year 1995, Consumer Industries Journalist of the Year 2000; A-Z Guide to Family Finance; *Recreations* arts, music, the great outdoors, sport, clocks; *Clubs* Ivy; *Style*— Damian Reece, Esq; ✉ Instinctif Partners, 65 Gresham Street, London EC2V 7NQ (☎ 020 7457 2020, mobile 07931 598593, e-mail damian.reece@instinctif.com)

REED, Sir Alec Edward; kt (2011), CBE (1994); s of Leonard Reed (d 1953), of London, and Annie, *née* Underwood (d 1983); *b* 16 February 1934; *Educ* Drayton Manor Grammar; *m* 16 Sept 1961, Adrianne Mary, da of Harry Eyre (d 1943); 2 s (James b 12 April 1963, Richard b 27 March 1965), 1 da (Alexandra b 22 Jan 1971); *Career* fndr chm: Reed Executive plc 1960–2000, Inter-Co Comparisons Ltd 1969–70, Reed Business Sch 1971, Medicare Ltd 1975–86; hon chm and chief exec Andrews and Ptnrs Ltd 1985–89; pres: Inst of Employment Conslts 1974–78, Int Confedn of Private Employment Agencies Assoc 1978–81; chm Employment Think Tank 1979; memb: Helpage Exec Ctee 1983–88, Oxfam Fundraising Ctee 1989–92, Cncl CIMA 1991–95; fndr: Womankind Worldwide 1988, Ethiopiaid 1989–, TheBigGive.org.uk 2007–; prof of enterprise and innovation Royal Holloway Univ of London 1993–2003, visiting prof London Guildhall Univ 1999–2006; hon fell Royal Holloway 1988, Hon PhD London Guildhall Univ, hon prof Univ of Warwick 2003, Hon DUniv Open Univ 2012; FCMA; *Books* Returning to Work (1989), Reed My Lips (1990), Innovation in Human Resource Management (2001), Capitalism is Dead: Peoplism Rules (2003), I Love Mondays (autobiography, 2012); *Recreations* portrait painting, family, theatre, cinema, tennis, riding, ballet, bridge; *Style*— Sir Alec Reed, CBE

REED, Crispin Grant John; s of Michael Reed, and Shelagh, *née* Jameson; *b* 30 July 1962; *Educ* Buckhurst Hill Co HS, Univ of Dundee (BA), CIM (DipM), C&G (Photography); *m* Jacqueline, *née* McMenemy; 2 s (Cameron John Adam b 28 Nov 2002, Fraser George Jameson b 15 Nov 2006); *Career* advtg exec: grad trainee Struthers Glasgow 1984–85; account exec Chetwynd Haddons 1985–86; Leo Burnett London: account mangr to account dir 1986–92; regnl account dir Leo Burnett Singapore 1992–95; bd dir and head account mgmnt Leo Burnett London 1995–99; dir in charge Collett Dickenson Pearce 1999–2000, former md Springer & Jacoby International (UK) and gp md Springer & Jacoby Gp UK, dir of brand communications Cradle 2003–05, sr vice-pres Europe Sterling Brands 2005–07, md Brandhouse 2007–12, md Europe Fusion Learning 2012–15, md JDO Ltd 2015–; memb Advsy Bd Branded Content Mktg Assoc, memb Superbrands Cncl, memb Advsy Bd Global Mktg Network; assoc memb D&AD, assoc Ashridge Mgmnt Coll; FRSA; *Publications* The 7 Myths of Middle Age (jtly, 2012); *Recreations* photography, golf, football, skiing; *Style*— Crispin Reed, Esq; ✉ Rowberry House, 8 Shadyhanger, Godalming, Surrey GU7 2HR (e-mail crispin_reed@hotmail.com or crispin@jdouk.com, website www.jdouk.com)

REED, Jamie; MP; *b* 4 August 1973; *Educ* Whitehaven Sch, Manchester Met Univ, Univ of Leicester; *Career* MP (Lab) Copeland 2005–; *Style*— Jamie Reed, MP; ✉ House of Commons, London SW1A 0AA

REED, Jane Barbara; CBE (2000); da of William Charles Reed, and Gwendoline Laura Reed; *b* 31 March 1940; *Educ* Royal Masonic Sch for Girls; *Career* ed Woman's Own 1969–79, publisher Quality Monthly Gp IPC 1979–81, ed-in-chief Woman 1981–83, md Holborn Publishing Gp IPC 1983–85, managing ed News UK Ltd 1986–89, dir of corp affrs News International 1989–2000 (conslt 2000–09), dir Times Newspapers Holdings Ltd 2002–; dir Nat Acad of Writing 2001–09; non-exec dir The Media Tst 2000–15; memb Cncl Nat Literacy Tst; govr Lady Margaret Acad 2012–; *Books* Girl about Town (1964), Kitchen Sink or Swim (with Deirdre Saunders, 1981); *Recreations* family, painting, writing, music, community; *Clubs* Groucho, Chelsea Arts; *Style*— Ms Jane Reed, CBE

REED, Ven John Peter Cyril; s of Cyril Gordon Reed (d 1992), and Madeleine Joan, *née* Stenning (d 1990); *b* 21 May 1951; *Educ* Monkton Combe Sch, KCL (BD), Ripon Coll Oxford (CertTheol); *m* 21 July 1979, Gillian Mary, da of Kenneth Frederick Coles (d 2001); 1 da (Jennie Elizabeth Antoinette b 21 July 1985), 1 s (Simon John Gordon b 7 Oct 1987); *Career* prod gp devpt Imperial Gp 1969–73, ops mangr Res & Mktg Wales Ltd 1973–75; curate Croydon Parish Church 1979–82, precentor Cathedral & Abbey Church of St Alban 1982–86, rector Timsbury and Priston Parishes 1986–93, team rector Ilminster & Dist Team Miny 1993–99, archdeacon of Taunton 1999–; *Recreations* cricket, fly fishing, real ale, surfing, gardening, music; *Clubs* Bath & Wells Clergy CC; *Style*— The Ven the Archdeacon of Taunton; ✉ 2 Monkton Heights, West Monkton, Taunton TA2 8LU (☎ 01823 413315, e-mail adtaunton@bathwells.anglican.org)

REED, Malcolm; CBE; *Career* chief exec Transport Scotland; *Style*— Malcolm Reed, Esq, CBE; ✉ Transport Scotland, Buchanan House, 58 Port Dundas Road, Glasgow G4 0HF

REED, Matthew; *b* 29 August 1968; *Educ* Univ of Nottingham (BEng), Univ of Oxford (MA), Univ of Surrey (MSc); *m* Dr Jennifer Candy; *Career* former mktg and supporter care dir Christian Aid, chief exec Cystic Fibrosis Tst 2010–12, chief exec Children's Soc 2012– (tstee 2010–12); MCMI, FRSA; *Style*— Matthew Reed, Esq; ✉ The Children's Society, Edward Rudolf House, Margery Street, London WC1X 0JL (e-mail matthew.reed@childrenssociety.org.uk)

REED, Lt Peter Kirby; MBE (2009); s of Leo Reed, of Nailsworth, Glos, and Susan, *née* Hollingsworth; *b* 27 July 1981, Seattle, USA; *Educ* Cirencester Deer Park Comp and Coll, Britannia RNC, UWE (BEng), Univ of Oxford (two Rowing blues); *Career* rower; offr rising to Sub Lt RN 1999–2001, appointed actg higher rank of Lt 2007, promoted to Lt 2008; memb: OUBC (incl varsity boat races 2004 and 2005 (winner)), Leander Club; winner: Stewards Cup Henley Royal Regatta 2005 and 2007, Nat Trials 2005, 2006, 2007, 2008, 2009, 2010, 2011 and 2012, Silver Goblets and Nichols Challenge Cup Henley Royal Regatta 2011 (course record); champion coxless fours World Cup 2005, 2006, 2008 and 2012, Gold medal coxless fours World Championships 2005 and 2006, Gold medal coxless fours Olympic Games Beijing 2008, champion coxless pair World Cup 2009, Gold medal coxless fours Olympic Games 2012, champion eights World Cup 2013, Gold medal men's eight World Championships 2013, Gold medal men's eight Olympic Games 2016; coxless four world best time Lucerne 2012; memb Henley Royal Regatta Stewards; Combined Servs Sportsman of the Year 2005 and 2008; largest recorded lung capacity in the world (11.68 litres); *Recreations* playing guitar and piano, hiking, music, travelling, cinema, photography; *Clubs* Vincent's (Oxford); *Style*— Lieutenant Pete Reed, MBE, RN; ✉ e-mail pete@petereed.com, website www.petereed.com, Twitter @petereed; c/o Sophie Callender, James Grant, 94 Strand on the Green, London W4 3NN (☎ 020 8742 4950, e-mail sophie@jamesgrantsports.com)

REED, Richard; CBE (2016); *Educ* St John's Coll Cambridge; *Career* co-fndr (with Adam Balon and Jon Wright) Innocent Drinks 1999 (sold to Coca-Cola 2013), currently co-fndr Jam Jar Investments; *Style*— Richard Reed, Esq, CBE

REED, Rt Hon Lord; Robert John Reed; PC (2008); *b* 7 September 1956; *Educ* George Watson's Coll, Univ of Edinburgh (LLB), Balliol Coll Oxford (DPhil); *m* 1988, Jane, *née* Mylne; 2 da; *Career* admitted Faculty of Advocates 1983, called to the Bar Inner Temple 1991 (bencher 2012); standing jr counsel: Scottish Educn Dept 1988–1989, Scottish Office Home and Health Dept 1989–1995, QC 1995, advocate depute 1996–98, a senator Coll of Justice 1998–2012, ad hoc judge European Court of Human Rights 1999–, a Justice of the Supreme Court 2012–; memb Advsy Bd Br Inst of Int and Comparative Law 2001–06 (tstee 2015–); expert advsr EC/Cncl of Europe Jt Initiative on Turkey 2002–04, chm Franco-Br Judicial Ctee 2005–12, pres EU Forum of Judges for the Environment 2006–08; convenor Children in Scotland 2006–12; hon prof Glasgow Univ 2006–; chm Centre for Commercial Law Univ of Edinburgh 2008–12, visitor Balliol Coll Oxford 2011–; Hon LLD Univ of Glasgow 2013; FRSE 2015; *Publications* Human Rights in Scotland (with J L Murdoch, 2001, 3 edn 2011); contrib to various books on constitutional and European law; *Style*— The Rt Hon Lord Reed; ✉ The Supreme Court of the United Kingdom, Parliament Square, London SW1P 3BD (☎ 020 7960 1960, fax 020 7960 1961)

REED, Ruth Madeline; da of Roger Green, and Pamela, *née* Bolas; *b* 28 September 1956, Winchester; *Educ* Univ of Sheffield (MA); *Children* 2 da; *Career* Hadfield Cawkwell Davidson 1984, sr architect South Yorks Housing Assoc, fndr Reed Architects 1992, pt/t ptnr Green Planning Solutions 2007, dir Green Planning Studio Ltd 2013–; visiting tutor Welsh Sch 1993; examiner: Welsh Sch of Architecture, Univ of Plymouth, Univ of Bath; course dir Postgrad Dip in Architectural Practice and prof of architectural practice Birmingham Sch of Architecture 2006–13; dir Associated Self-Build Architects; memb Cncl RIBA 2002–07 (vice-pres of membership 2005–07, chair CPD Sub-Ctee, pres elect 2008–09, pres 2009–11), pres Royal Soc of Architects in Wales 2003–05; RIBA Plan of Work 2013 Guide Town Planning (2014); *Recreations* walking, gardening, listening to music; *Style*— Ms Ruth Reed; ✉ Royal Institution of British Architects, 66 Portland Place, London W1B 1AD

REED HENDERSON, Annie; da of Albert Edwin Reed (d 1982), and Florence Dora, *née* Vinall (d 1990); *b* 20 March 1945, Blackburn, Lancs; *Educ* Swanley Secdy Modern Kent, Ravensbourne Coll of Art Bromley; *m* May 1970 (m dis 2002); 1 da (Johanna Alexis b Aug 1976), 1 s (James Edward b June 1978); *Career* fashion/photographic studios 1963–70, psychotherapist Priory Hosp 1990–2003, Lister Hosp 1990–91, cnsllr Dept of Psychological Medicine Cromwell Hosp 1991–94, session cnsllr Dept of Psychology Medicine Wellington Hosp 1995–99, session cnsllr Princess Grace Hosp 1999–; private practice (specialising in unexplained infertility) 1995–; full accredited memb Fedn of Drug and Alcohol Professionals (chair 1995–97), assoc memb EATA, memb Br Assoc for Counselling and Psychotherapy, assoc memb RSM 2008, assoc memb UKRCP 2010; *Publications* Therapy Today (contrib, 2008); *Recreations* music, art, ballet, gardening; *Clubs* Lunar; *Style*— Ms Annie Reed Henderson; ✉ 39 Winsham Grove, London SW11 6NB (☎ 020 7228 9880, mobile 07958 203256, website www.anniereedhenderson.com)

REEDIE, Sir Craig Collins; kt (2006), CBE (1999); s of Robert Lindsay Reedie (d 1993), of Stirling, Scotland, and Anne, *née* Smith (d 1993); *b* 6 May 1941, Stirling, Scotland; *Educ* HS of Stirling, Univ of Glasgow (MA, LLB); *m* 9 Sept 1967, Rosemary Jane, *née* Biggart; 1 s (Colin John b 13 Sept 1968), 1 da (Catriona Jane b 16 May 1972); *Career* Scottish Badminton Union: sec 1964–71, treas 1965–74, vice-pres 1974–77, pres 1977–79; Int

Badminton Fedn: memb Cncl 1970–77, vice-pres 1977–81, chm Cncl 1979–84, pres 1981–84, chm Business Ctee 1984–92, tech delg Olympic Games Barcelona 1992; chm BOA 1992–2005, dep chm UK Sport 1998–2002 (memb Cncl 1996–2002), memb Cncl Gen Assoc of Int Sports Fedns 1984–92 (treas 1988–92); IOC: appointed 1994, memb Marketing Cmmn 1995–2014, memb IOC Cmmn 2000, co-ordination Athens 2004, evaluation Bejing 2008, co-ordination Beijing 2008, memb Prog Cmmn 2006–14, Ethics Cmmn 2007–14, memb Exec Bd 2009–, vice-pres 2012–, evaluation Rio de Janeiro 2016, chair evaluation 2020; dir: Manchester Cwlth Games Ltd, Manchester 2002 Ltd; dir: London 2012 Ltd 2003–05, LOCOG 2005–13 (memb Audit and Renumeration Ctees); World Anti-Doping Agency: memb Exec Ctee Fndn Bd 2000–, chair Fin and Admin Ctee 2000–13, pres 2014–; memb Cncl European Olympic Ctees 2001–08, memb Exec Cncl Assoc of Nat Olympic Ctees 2002–08; Messrs Tindal, Oatts & Rodger Slrs 1964–66, DL Bloomer & Ptnrs Fin Advsrs 1966–2002 (sr ptnr 1985–2002); Univ of Glasgow: memb Ct 2000–08, chm Pension Scheme Tstees 2000–08, chm Investment Ctee 2000–08; memb NHS in Scotland Resource Allocation Steering Gp 1998–99; Hon DUniv Glasgow 2002, Hon LLD Univ of St Andrews 2005, Hon LLD Brunel Univ 2009, Hon DBA Univ of Lincoln 2010, Hon LLD Univ of W of Scotland 2012, Hon DSc Glasgow Caledonian Univ 2013, Hon D Univ of Stirling 2014; *Clubs* Ranfurly Castle Golf (capt 1989), Western Gailes Golf, Royal and Ancient, East India; *Style—* Sir Craig Reedie, CBE; ✉ Senara, Hazelwood Road, Bridge of Weir, Renfrewshire PA11 3DB (☎ 01505 613434, fax 01505 615295, mobile 07768 502971)

REEKIE, Jonathan; CBE (2013); s of Dr Andrew Reekie, of Marlborough, Wilts, and Virginia, *née* Cadbury; *b* 2 September 1964; *Educ* Marlborough, Bristol Business Sch; *m* 18 June 1993 (m dis 2007), Caroline, *née* Gibbs; 2 da (Honor b 25 May 1994, Rose b 17 Sept 1995); *Career* co mangr Musica Nel Chiostro Batignano Italy 1984–88 (dir 1989–2008), co co-ordinator Glyndebourne Festival Opera 1987–91, gen mangr Almeida Theatre 1991–97, chief exec Aldeburgh Music 1997–2014, dir Somerset House 2014–; dir Almeida Opera 1991–2002; arts advsr Paul Hamlyn Fndn, tstee Arts Fndn; Hon DMus Univ of E Anglia 2010; hon FRAM 2010; *Style—* Jonathan Reekie, Esq, CBE; ✉ Somerset House, Strand, London WC2R 1LA

REEN, Rob; s of William John Reen, of Swansea, and Olwen Beryl, *née* Kimmings; *b* 31 July 1951; *Educ* Penlan Sch Swansea, Cheltenham Coll of HE (BA), Univ of Wales Cardiff (PGCE); *m* Joan, da of Bob Kerfoot; 1 step s (Christopher), 1 step da (Kirsty); *Career* hotelier and painter; teacher in art and design Mayfield GS 1974–76, head Art and Design Sir Henry Floyd GS 1976–89; proprietor Ynyshir Hall 1989–; numerous exhbns and one-man shows, work in int collections; memb Welsh Rarebits consortium; *Awards* Welsh Tourist Bd 5 Star 2001, RAC Gold Ribbon Award 1993–96, AA Courtesy and Care Award 1994, AA 3 Red Star Status 1995–96; *Recreations* golf; *Clubs* Aberdovey Golf; *Style—* Rob Reen, Esq; ✉ Ynyshir Hall, Eglwysfach, Machynlleth, Powys SY20 8TA (☎ 01654 781209, fax 01654 781366)

REES, Brian Idris; OBE (2000); s of Sidney Rees, and Mary, *née* Thomas; *Educ* Neath GS for Boys, Christ's Coll Cambridge (MA, MB BChir, capt Cambridge Univ RFC 1966), St Bartholomew's Hosp London; *m* Sara Elizabeth, *née* Kipling; 2 da (Rachel Sara, Bethan Charlotte); *Career* sr registrar Univ Hosp Wales and Royal Gwent Hosp Newport, Gt Ormond St Hosp, conslt Univ Hosp Wales 1980–; memb Cncl RCS 2005–10; past pres Cardiff Medical Soc, pres Welsh Surgical Soc 2002; High Sheriff S Glamorgan 2008–09; FRCS (MRCS), LRCP; *Recreations* reading, poetry, rugby football (played for Wales 1967); *Clubs* Hawks' (Cambridge); *Style—* Brian Rees, Esq, OBE; ✉ St David's, 7 The Avenue, Llandaff, Cardiff CF5 2LP (☎ 029 2056 3109, e-mail brian.rees8@btinternet.com)

REES, Christopher Wyn; *b* 1955, Wales; *Educ* Christ's Coll Cambridge (MA); *Career* slr specialising in IT law; ptnr Herbert Smith LLP; Herbert Ruse Prizeman 1978; Database Law (1998); *Recreations* tennis, skiing, singing; *Clubs* Hurlingham, MCC; *Style—* Christopher Rees, Esq; ✉ Herbert Smith LLP, Exchange House, Primrose Street, London EC2A 2HS (☎ 020 7374 8000)

REES, Sir David Allan (Dai); kt (1993); *b* 28 April 1936, Silloth, Cumbria; *Educ* UCNW Bangor (BSc, PhD), Univ of Edinburgh (DSc), Sloan Sch of Industrial Mgmnt (Sr Execs Prog); *m* 1959, Myfanwy Margaret, *née* Parry Owen; 2 s, 1 da; *Career* lectr in chemistry Univ of Edinburgh 1960–70, visiting prof of biochemistry Univ of Wales Cardiff 1972–77, various positions rising to princ scientist and sci policy exec Unilever Research Colworth Lab Sharnbrook Bedford 1970–82, pt/t dir MRC Cell Biophysics Unit KCL 1980–82, dir Nat Inst for Med Res 1982–87, chief exec MRC 1987–96 (memb Cncl 1983–96, fndr dir MRC Collaborative Centre Mill Hill 1983–86); memb: LINK Steering Gp 1987–89, Advsy Bd for Res Cncls 1987–93, Ctee for the Euro Devpt of Sci and Technol (CODEST) 1991–94, Advsy Bd Forensic Scis Serv Agency 1992–, Euro Sci and Technol Assembly (ESTA) and Bureau 1994–; chm Euro Med Res Cncls 1990–94, vice-pres Fondation Louis Jeantet de Medicine 1991–1996, pres Euro Sci Fndn 1994–1999; Carbohydrate Chemistry Award Chemical Soc 1970, Colworth Medal Biochemical Soc 1970; Hon DSc: Edinburgh 1989, Wales 1991, Stirling Univ 1995, Leicester 1997; Hon DUniv York 2007; FRSC 1975, FRS 1981 (Philips lecture 1984, memb Cncl 1985–87), FIBiol 1983; Hon FRCP 1986, hon fell UCNW 1988, FKC 1989, FRCPEd 1998; *Publications* numerous res pubns in learned jls on biochemistry and biophysics, and on sci policy; *Style—* Sir Dai Rees, FRS; ✉ Ford Cottage, 1 High Street, Denford, Kettering, Northamptonshire NN14 4EQ (☎ 01832 733502, e-mail daireesl@btinternet.com)

REES, Edward Parry; QC (1998); s of Edward Howell Rees (d 1962), and Margaret Rees Rees, *née* Parry; *b* 18 June 1949; *Educ* Howardian HS Cardiff, Cowbridge GS, UCW Aberystwyth (LLB); *m* Kathleen, da of Stanley Wiltshire; 2 c; *Career* called to the Bar 1973; fndr memb Lawyers for Liberty, fndr memb and co-sec Lawyers for Nuclear Disarmament, memb Gen Cncl of the Bar (representative of the Criminal Bar Assoc) 1997–2000; hon fell in Criminal Process Sch of Law Kent Univ; *Publications* Blackstone's Guide to the Proceeds of Crime Act (2002, 5 edn 2014), The Law of Public Order and Protest (2010); *Recreations* family and garden; *Style—* Edward Rees, Esq, QC; ✉ Doughty Street Chambers, 53/54 Doughty Street, London WC1N 2LS (☎ 020 7404 1313, fax 020 7404 2283)

REES, Her Hon Judge Eleri Mair; da of Ieuan Morgan (d 1990), and Sarah Alice, *née* James; *b* 7 July 1953; *Educ* Ardwyn GS Aberystwyth, Univ of Liverpool (LLB); *m* 9 Aug 1975, Dr Alan Rees; *Career* called to the Bar Gray's Inn 1975; clerk to the Justices Bexley Magistrates' Court 1983–94, metropolitan stipendary magistrate (subsequently dist judge (Magistrates' Court)) 1994–2002, recorder 1997–2002, circuit judge (Wales & Chester Circuit) 2002– (sr circuit judge 2012–); liason judge for the Welsh language; ed Family Court Reporter 1992–94; memb Cncl Univ of Wales Cardiff 2002–09; hon recorder of Cardiff; *Recreations* travel, cookery, skiing; *Style—* Her Hon Judge Rees; ✉ c/o Cardiff Crown Court, The Law Courts, Cathays Park, Cardiff CF10 3PG

REES, Gareth Mervyn; s of Joseph Rees (d 1981), of Llangadog, Wales, and Gwen Rees (d 1988); *b* 30 September 1935; *Educ* Llandovery HS, St Mary's Hosp Univ of London (MB BS, MS); *m* 1, 1962 (m dis 1968), Anne Frisby Richards; 1 s (Philip b 1964); m 2, 1969, Prof Dame Lesley Rees, DBE, *qv*, da of Howard Leslie Davis (d 1942); *Career* house surgn and house physician St Mary's Hosp 1960, int res fell Dept of Heart Surgery Univ of Oregon Portland 1970; St Bartholomew's Hosp London: conslt heart surgn 1973–2000, conslt i/c Dept of Cardio-thoracic Surgery 1984–2000, sr surgeon St Bartholomew's Hosp 1996–2000, emeritus cardio-thoracic surgeon 2000–; conslt cardiac surgeon Harley Street Clinic; memb: Cardiac Soc, Int Coll of Surgns, Assoc of Thoracic Surgns UK; author of numerous scientific papers on subjects related to heart and lung surgery in specialist jls; FRCS 1966, FRCP 1983; *Recreations* fishing, skiing, rugby football; *Clubs* Garrick, Llandovery RFC; *Style—* Gareth Rees, Esq; ✉ 23 Church Row, Hampstead, London NW3 6UP; Loc Ceppatelli, Via Ceppatelli 51, Orbicciano, Camaiore 55041, Lucca, Italy; 2 Impasse du Petit St Martin 17630, La Flotte en Ré, Ile de Ré, France

REES, Geoffrey; CBE (2003); s of Sidney Rees (d 1996), of Neath, W Glamorgan, and Mary, *née* Thomas (d 1981); *b* 28 February 1946; *Educ* Neath Boys' GS, St Luke's Coll Univ of Exeter (RFC, Devon RFC, Neath RFC), Emmanuel Coll Cambridge (Rugby blue, capt CURUFC, London Welsh RFC, Middx RFC); *m* June 1974, Diana Jane, da of Peter Wride; 1 da (Rebecca Jane b Aug 1976), 1 s (Gareth Thomas b Jan 1978); *Career* asst history master Shene Boys' Sch Richmond 1969–71, history master and house tutor Eastbourne Coll 1974–76, head of humanities and head of sixth form Billericay Sch 1976–79, dir of studies Coombe Dean Sch Plymouth 1979–82, dep princ Bideford Community Coll 1982–85, headmaster Burrington Sch Plymouth 1985–87, princ Ivybridge Sports and Community Coll (formerly Ivybridge Community Coll) 1987–; chm Devon Science and Technol Regnl Orgn 1988–90; educn liaison offr IOD 1991–97; chm Devon Assoc of Secdy Heads 1992–94, vice-chm Devon Educn Business Partnership Cncl 1992–93; memb: Devon and Cornwall TEC Strategic Educn Forum 1993–95, SW Regl Cncl FEFC 1998–2000, Bd of Devon and Cornwall LSC 2001–; govr: Coll of St Mark and St John Plymouth 1998–2006, Univ of Plymouth 1999–2006; memb NAHT 1988–; FRSA 1994; *Recreations* rugby, sailing, surfing, theatre, travel; *Clubs* Welsh Academicals RFC, London Welsh RFC, Hawks' (Cambridge); *Style—* Geoffrey Rees, Esq, CBE; ✉ Ivybridge Sports and Community College, Harford Road, Ivybridge, Devon PL21 0JA (☎ 01752 691000/896662, fax 01752 691247, e-mail grees@ivybridge.devon.sch.uk)

REES, Dr Helene Ceredwyn; da of Delwyn Garland Rees, of South Yarra, Victoria, Aust, and Jean Helene, *née* Höette; *b* 8 April 1948; *Educ* Presbyterian Ladies Coll Melbourne Aust, Univ of Melbourne (MB BS), LLB 1996; *m* 1, 17 Dec 1971 (m dis 1984), David Alan McDonald, s of Alan McDonald; 2 s (Lachlan James b 11 March 1974, Alexander Rhys b 25 April 1980), 1 da (Kate Helene b 17 July 1975); m 2, 4 May 1991, Dr Christopher Daking Macfarlane Drew, s of late Sir Robert Drew, KCB, CBE; *Career* annual appts in gen med and surgery in maj teaching hosps in Melbourne 1972–73, in trg in pathology Melbourne Aust 1973–81 (The Royal Children's Hosp, Fairfield Infectious Diseases Hosp, Alfred Hosp, Prince Henry's Hosp), sr registrar in histopathology Hammersmith Hosp 1984–86 (registrar 1981–84), sr lectr and hon conslt in histopathology St Bartholomew's Hosp Med Coll 1986–94, pathologist Farrer-Brown Histopathology 1994–99, conslt histopathologist Hammersmith Hosps NHS Tst 1999–2003, conslt anatomical pathologist Royal Hobart Hosp 2004–; memb: Kew Soc, Hunterian Soc 1984, Graduate Union of Univ of Melbourne 1980, Soc of Doctors in Law 1993; vice-pres Med Soc of London 1990–91 (fell 1984); Freeman City of London 1986, Liveryman Worshipful Soc of Apothecaries 1989 (Yeoman 1985); FRCPA (Aust) 1980, FRCPath 1996 (MRCPath 1984); *Recreations* gymnastics, golf, classical music; *Clubs* Hogarth, Overstone Golf; *Style—* Dr Helene Rees; ✉ c/o Department of Anatomical Pathology, Royal Hobart Hospital, Liverpool Street, Hobart 7001, Tasmania

REES, John Charles; QC (1991); s of Ronald Leslie Rees (d 1985), of Cardiff, and Martha Terese, *née* Poole; *b* 22 May 1949; *Educ* St Joseph's Sch Cardiff, St Illtyd's Coll Cardiff, Jesus Coll Cambridge (McNair Scholar, MA, LLM, Russell Vick prize, Boxing blue); *m* 30 July 1970, Dianne Elizabeth, da of William Kirby, of Cardiff; 3 s (Christopher Lloyd b 26 Nov 1973, Jonathan Elystan b 27 Feb 1977, William Ronald b 7 Nov 1987), 1 da (Felicity Ann Rose b 21 Aug 1980); *Career* called to the Bar Lincoln's Inn 1972; chm Br Boxing Bd of Control (former chair Welsh Area Cncl); tstee and govr St John's Coll Cardiff 1987–2010 and 2016–; *Recreations* reading, music, sport (especially football and boxing); *Clubs* Hawks' (Cambridge); *Style—* John Rees, Esq, QC; ✉ Marleigh Lodge, Druidstone Road, Old St Mellons, Cardiff, South Glamorgan CF3 9XD (☎ 029 2079 4918); Sophia House, 28 Cathedral Road, Cardiff CF11 9LJ (☎ 029 2027 3313)

REES, Canon (Vivian) John Howard; s of Herbert John Rees, and Beryl, *née* Thomas; *b* 21 April 1951, Eastbourne, Sussex; *Educ* Skinners' Sch Tunbridge Wells, Univ of Southampton (LLB), Coll of Law London, Wycliffe Hall Oxford (MA), Univ of Leeds (MPhil); *m* 17 May 1980, Dianne Elizabeth, *née* Hamilton; 2 da (Katherine Elizabeth b 20 May 1987, Rebecca Frances Anne b 29 Oct 1989); *Career* admitted slr 1975; Cooke Matheson & Co 1975–76; ordained deacon Ripon Dio 1979, priest 1980; curate Moor Allerton Team Miny 1979–82, chaplain and tutor Sierra Leone Theological Hall Freetown 1983–85; slr and ptnr Winckworth Sherwood 1986–; registrar: Oxford Dio 1998–, Province of Canterbury 2000–, Clergy Discipline Tbnl 2006–; treas Ecclesiastical Law Soc 1995–2015 (chair 2015–), legal advsr Anglican Consultative Cncl 1998–, vice-chair Legal Advsy Cmmn C of E 2001–; provincial canon Canterbury Cathedral 2001–; chaplain to HM Queen 2014–; memb Law Soc 1975; *Recreations* walking, second-hand bookshops; *Clubs* Athenaeum, Nobody's Friends; *Style—* Canon John Rees; ✉ 36 Cumnor Hill, Oxford OX2 9HB (☎ 01865 865875, e-mail vjhrees@btinternet.com); Winckworth Sherwood, 16 Beaumont Street, Oxford OX1 2LZ (☎ 01865 297214, fax 01865 726274, e-mail jrees@wslaw.co.uk)

REES, Jonathan Nigel; s of Arthur Ernest Rees (d 1990), and Thelma Maureen, *née* Scott; *b* 29 September 1955; *Educ* Jesus Coll Oxford (MA); *m* 1 Sept 1996, Kathryn Jayne, da of Wilfred Taylor; 1 da (Elizabeth Margaret b 2000), 1 s (Nicholas John b 2002); *Career* with DTI 1977–81, private sec to min for Trade 1981–84, with EC 1984–86, with DTI 1986–89, industry cnsllr UK rep to the EU 1989–94, with DTI 1994, memb PM's Policy Unit 1994–97, dir Citizen's Charter Unit Cabinet Office 1997–2000, dir consumer and competition policy DTI 2000–04, dep ceo (policy) HSE 2004–08, DG Govt Equalities Office 2008–13; tstee/dir Citizens Advice Employers Network on Equality and Inclusion, dir Ombudsman Services, dir Lending Standards Bd, dir Personal Finance Soc; *Recreations* sport, travel, theatre; *Clubs* MCC; *Style—* Jonathan Rees, Esq; ✉ e-mail jandkrees@btinternet.com

REES, Laurence Mark; s of Alan Rees (d 1973), and Julia, *née* Mark (d 1977); *b* 19 January 1957; *Educ* Solihull Sch, Worcester Coll Oxford (BA); *m* 1987, Helena, *née* Brewer; 3 c; *Career* BBC TV: research trainee 1978–79, researcher 1979–81, dir and prodr 1982–92, ed Timewatch 1992–2003 (winner of 3 Emmy Awards as exec prodr for various historical documentaries 1993–95), creative dir BBC TV History progs 2000–; researcher Man Alive and That's Life 1979–81, dir Holiday 1982, writer and prodr 40 Minutes 1984–88, prodr and dir Clive James 1988–90, writer and prodr A British Betrayal 1990, writer and prodr History of Propaganda – We Have Ways of Making You Think 1992, exec prodr Remember Season on Anniversary Liberation of Auschwitz 1995, writer, dir and prodr The Nazis – A Warning From History 1997 (Broadcast Critics Award 1997, Broadcast Magazine Award 1997, George Foster Peabody Award 1997, Best Factual Series BAFTA 1997), writer and prodr War of the Century 1999, writer and prodr Horror in the East 2000, writer and prodr Auschwitz: the Nazis and the Final Solution 2005; Hon DLitt Univ of Sheffield 2005; *Books* Electric Beach (1990), Selling Politics (1992), The Nazis – A Warning From History (1997), War of the Century (1999), Horror in the East (2001), Auschwitz: The Nazis and the Final Solution (2005, History Book of the Year Br Book Awards), The Nazis: A Warning from History (2006), Their Darkest Hour (2007); *Recreations* my three children; *Style—* Laurence Rees, Esq

REES, Prof Dame Lesley Howard; DBE (2001); da of Howard Leslie Davis (d 1942), and Charlotte Patricia Siegrid, *née* Young (d 1960); *b* 17 November 1942; *Educ* Pate's Girls' GS Cheltenham, Malvern Girls' Coll, Bart's Med Coll (MB BS, MD, DSc); *m* 21 Dec 1969, Gareth Mervyn Rees, *qv*, s of Joseph Rees; *Career* ed Clinical Endocrinology 1979–84,

R

public orator Univ of London 1984–86, sub dean Bart's Med Coll 1983–87, chm Soc for Endocrinology 1984–87, sec gen Int Soc for Endocrinology 1984–2005, prof of chem endocrinology Bart's Med Coll, dean Bart's Med Coll 1989–95; dir Int Office and dir of educn Royal Coll of Physicians (London) 1997–2001; Hon DSc: Univ of Ulster, City Univ; FRCP 1979, FRCPath 1988, FMedSci; *Books* author numerous papers on endocrinology; *Recreations* poetry, music, art, cooking; *Clubs* RAF; *Style*— Prof Dame Lesley Rees, DBE; ✉ 23 Church Row, Hampstead, London NW3 6UP (☎ 020 7794 4936, e-mail lesleyrees@waitrose.com); 2 Impasse du Petit St Martin, La Flotte en Ré, Ile de Ré, France 17630 (☎ 00 33 5 4609 6287)

REES, Prof Michael Ralph; s of William Morris Rees, and Herta Klara Rees; *b* 19 April 1950; *Educ* Shene GS, UEA (BSc), Univ of Sheffield (MB ChB, Herbert Price Prize (jtly)), DMRD, Bangor Univ (Cert Ed), PGCert; *m* Ann; 2 da (Joanna, Jennifer); *Career* jr hosp appts Royal Infirmary and Royal Hallamshire and Northern Gen Hosps Sheffield 1976–79, sr registrar in radiology Sheffield Area and Trent Regnl Trg Scheme 1981–83 (registrar 1979–81), sr registrar in cardiac radiology Northern Gen Hosp Sheffield 1983–84, conslt cardiac radiologist Killingbeck Regnl Cario-thoracic Unit and St James Univ Hosp Leeds 1984–93, prof of radiological science Keele Univ Sch of Postgrad Med and conslt in cardiovascular intervention N Staffordshire Hosp Stoke-on-Trent 1993–95, prof of clinical radiology Univ of Bristol 1995–2005, prof of vascular studies Bangor Univ 2005–, head Sch of Medical Sciences Bangor Univ 2007–12, univ dir of medical devpt Bangor Univ 2012; res fell/assoc Dept of Radiology and Cardiology Univ of Iowa 1984–85, res assoc in cardiac imaging Deborah Heart & Lung Centre NJ 1985, prof of radiology and med (cardiology) Stanford Univ 1992–93; visiting prof Univ of Ioannina 1996–; chm: Nat Hosp Jr Staff Ctee 1979–84, Jr Membs Forum BMA 1982–83, Non Trust Hosps Gp Med Ctee 1991–93; co-chair Nat Academic Stakeholder Forum 2010, memb Advsy Bd Wales Nat Inst for Social Care and Health Research (NISCHR) 2011; elected memb GMC 1984–89; BMA: memb 1976, memb Cncl 1979–84 and 2003–, memb Leeds Exec Ctee 1986–88, memb Med Academic Staff Ctee 1995–2013 (also chm, then co-chair 2012–14), memb Central Conslts Staff Ctee 1996–2013, memb Negotiating Sub-Ctee 1996–, co-chair Med Academic Staff Ctee 2005–13, elected memb Cncl 2008–, memb Welsh BMA Cncl 2008–15, Wales ambass 2011; memb: American Med Assoc 1985–86, Radiological Soc of N America 1985, Br Cardiac Soc 1986–2013, Br Cardiovascular Intervention Soc 1987 (memb Cncl 1992–), Br Interventional Radiology Soc 1988, Cardiovascular Cncl American Heart Assoc 1988, Br Med Laser Assoc 1989 (memb Cncl 1990–), Cardiovascular and Interventional Radiology Soc of Europe 1990 (memb Membership Ctee 1993–99), European Med Laser Assoc 1992, Int Soc of Endovascular Surgery 1993, RSM 1993, Forum on Angiology 1993, BMA Bd of Science 1999–2003, Jt Conslts Ctee 2003–06, Nat Inst for Health Faculty Implementation Gp 2006, UK Healthcare Educn Advsy Ctee (representing Welsh Assembly) 2009–11, European Bd of Cardiac Radiology, HENSE (Health Educn Nat Strategic Exchange, representing BMA) 2009–, Bd of Science BMA 2011–14, Welsh BMA Cncl 2014–15, Scientific Priorities Ctee Nat Inst for Social Care, Health and Research (NISCHR) 2014–15; pres European Soc Cardiac Radiology 2008–11 (sec 1999–2005, vice-pres 2005–08), chm Cardiac Ctee European Soc of Radiology 2007, fndr memb Acad of Medical Educators 2009–; Betsi Cadwalladr Univ: assoc med dir Health Bd 2012, chair Health Professions Forum, memb Health Bd, dir of med devpt 2014–15, assoc med dir 2014–15, co-chair Med Academic Staff Ctee 2014–, currently med dir for workforce and professionalism; winner Assoc Medal BMA 2008; PhD (hc) Univ of Ioannina (Greece) 2006; fell: Int Coll of Angiology 1988, American Coll of Angiology 1992, HE Acad 2008–; medical leadership fell Academi Wales 2014–15; FRCPEd, FRCR, fell Acad of Medical Educators (FAcadMEd) 2015; *Publications* Every Doctor a Scientist and a Scholar (2015); over 100 peer-reviewed pubns and book chapters; *Recreations* gym exercise, walking; *Style*— Prof Michael Rees; ✉ Room 184, Brigantia Building, Clinical School, Penrallt Road, Bangor, Gwynedd LL57 2AS (e-mail m.rees@bangor.ac.uk)

REES, Morgan Alexander; s of Richard Rees, and Guity Saadat; *b* 8 November 1974, Southampton, Hants; *Educ* Cleeve Sch Cheltenham, Cardiff Univ; *Career* magazine ed; editorial asst Loaded 1994–97, commissioning ed GQ 1997–2000, assoc ed Jack 2000–01, dep ed Maxim 2001–03, ed/ed-in-chief Men's Health 2003–; New Ed of the Year BSME 2004, Ed of the Year Rodale Pubns 2005 and 2006, Men's Magazine's Ed of the Year BSME 2006, Ed of the Year PPA 2007, Rodale Pubns Edition of the Year 2007; memb BSME; *Recreations* surfing, kickboxing, Asain cinema, contemporary US literary fiction, architecture; *Style*— Morgan Rees, Esq; ✉ The National Magazine Company, 33 Broadwick Street, London W1F 0DQ (☎ 020 7339 4400, e-mail morgan.rees@natmag-rodale.co.uk)

REES, Nigel Thomas; s of (John Cedric) Stewart Rees (d 1989), and Frances Adeline, *née* Gleave (d 1982); *b* 5 June 1944; *Educ* Merchant Taylors' Crosby, New Coll Oxford (Trevelyan scholar, MA); *m* 6 May 1978, Susan Mary, da of Jack Bates (d 1962); *Career* radio and TV presenter, author, actor, guest speaker, lectr; BBC Radio 4: Today 1976–78, The Burkiss Way 1976–80, Quote...Unquote 1976–, Stop Press 1984–86; ITV: Amoebas to Zebras 1985–87, Challenge of the South 1987–88; ed The Quote...Unquote Newsletter 1992–; pres Johnson Soc 2006–07, judge Costa Novel Award 2007, patron PG Wodehouse Soc (UK) 2008–; *Books* Quote...Unquote (3 vols 1978–83), Graffiti (5 vols 1978–86), Why do We Say...? (1987), The Newsmakers (1987), Talent (1988), A Family Matter (1989), Dictionary of Popular Phrases (1990), Dictionary of Phrase and Allusion (1991), Best Behaviour (1992), Politically Correct Phrasebook (1993), Epitaphs (1993), As We Say In Our House (1994), Phrases and Sayings (1995), Cassell Dictionary of Clichés (1996), Dictionary of Slogans (1997), Cassell Companion to Quotations (1997), Cassell Dictionary of Anecdotes (1999), Cassell's Movie Quotations (2000), Cassell's Humorous Quotations (2001), A Word in Your Shell-like (2004), Cassell's Dictionary of Catchphrases (2005), Brewer's Famous Quotations (2006), A Man About a Dog (2006), All Gong and No Dinner (2007), More Tea, Vicar? (2009), Don't You Know There's a War On? (2011), my radio times (2012); *Recreations* listening to music, swimming; *Style*— Nigel Rees, Esq; ✉ 7 Hillgate Place, London W8 7SL (e-mail nigel.rees@btinternet.com)

REES, Paul; s of David Rees, of Wombourne, W Midlands, and Pauline, *née* Young; *b* 14 November 1967, West Bromwich; *Educ* Ounsdale HS Wombourne, Crewe and Alsager Coll (BA); *m* 14 Dec 2002, Denise Jeffrey; 2 s (Tom b 4 Jan 2005, Charlie b 22 April 2008); *Career* journalist; Brumbeat 1991–92, Raw 1992–94, ed Kerrang! 1999–2002 (joined 1995), ed-in-chief Q 2002–12, music critic 2012–; tstee You You Mentoring; Specialist Consumer Magazine of the Year PPA Awards 2001; *Style*— Paul Rees, Esq; ✉ Twitter @paulreesq

REES, Peter Wynne; CBE (2015); s of Gwynne Rees, of Virginia Water, Surrey, and Elizabeth Rodda, *née* Hynam (d 1990); *b* 26 September 1948, Swansea; *Educ* Pontardawe GS, Whitchurch GS, Bartlett Sch of Architecture, UCL (BSc), Welsh Sch of Architecture, Univ of Wales (BArch), Poly of the South Bank (BTP); *Career* architectural asst Historic Buildings Div GLC 1971–72, asst to Gordon Cullen CBE 1973–75, architect Historic Areas Conservation Div DOE 1975–79, asst chief planning offr Borough of Lambeth 1979–85; Corp of London: controller of planning 1985–87, city planning offr 1987–2014; prof of places and city planning UCL 2014–; tstee Bldg Conservation Tst 1987–91, fndr memb and dir Br Cncl for Offices; life memb: SPAB, Nat Tst; President's Award Br Cncl for Offices 2003, Barbara Miller Award Faculty of Building 2004, Offices Award for Outstanding Contribution 2010, Estates Gazette Award for Outstanding Contribution to Property 2013, College of Estate Management Property Award 2014; Hon Dr London South Bank Univ 2014; Freeman City of London 1985; FRTPI 1982, FRSA 1988, FRIBA 2011 (RIBA 1975), hon memb Architectural Assoc 2014; *Publications* City of London Unitary Development Plan; author of various technical planning pubns and contribs to professional jls; *Recreations* swimming, chamber music, tidying; *Style*— Peter Wynne Rees, Esq, CBE; ✉ UCL Faculty of the Built Environment, Central House (6.17), 14 Upper Woburn Place, London WC1H 0NN (☎ 020 3108 9572, e-mail peter.rees@ucl.ac.uk, website www.bartlett.ucl.ac.uk)

REES, Prof Philip Howell; CBE (2004); s of Foster Rees (d 2004), and Mona, *née* Howell (d 1995); *b* 17 September 1944; *Educ* King Edward's Sch Birmingham, St Catharine's Coll Cambridge (MA), Univ of Chicago (MA, PhD); *m* 1968, Laura, da of Edward C Campbell; 1 s (Gareth David b 19 June 1971), 1 da (Chloe b 16 March 1974); *Career* Univ of Leeds: lectr 1970–80, reader 1980–90, prof 1990–; Hofstee visiting fell NIDI The Hague 1995, distinguished visiting fell Univ of Adelaide 1996; co-ordinator ESRC/JISC Census Prog 1992–97 and 1998–2002; Gill Meml Award RGS 1996, Victoria Medal RGS 2009; FRGS 1970; FBA 1998; *Books* Spatial Population Analysis (1977), Residential Patterns in American Cities (1979), Population Structures and Models (1985), Migration Processes & Patterns (vol 2, 1992), Population Migration in the European Union (1996), The Determinants of Migration Flows in England (1998), Internal Migration and Regional Population Dynamics in Europe (1999), The Census Data System (2002), E-Learning for Geographers (2008); *Recreations* walking; *Style*— Prof Philip Rees, CBE, FBA; ✉ 3 Mavis Lane, Cookridge, Leeds LS16 7LL (☎ 0113 267 6968); School of Geography, University of Leeds, Leeds LS2 9JT (☎ 0113 343 3286, e-mail p.h.rees@leeds.ac.uk)

REES, Robert (Rob); MBE (2006), DL; s of Stephen Rees, and Gillian, *née* Chambers; *b* 28 June 1968, Ilford, Essex; *Educ* Forest Sch, Westminster Coll (Dip Catering); *m* 6 Dec 2002, Renata, *née* Petruv; 1 s (Jack William b 9 Dec 2005), 1 da (Madeleine Rose b 30 April 2007); *Career* chef; various positions 1987–: Le Gavroche, Bath Spa Hotel, Royal Crescent Hotel, Hyatt Grand Cayman, Circus, Splinter; dir: Country Elephant Ltd 1994–2007, Taste of West 2004–06, Rob Rees Ltd, The Cotswold Chef Ltd, Foodworks Australia Pty Ltd 2014–; chief exec Wiggly Worm Ltd; dir Stroud Mid Glos Educn Business Partnership, gen govr British Nutrition Fndn 2002–, chm Kraft Cares Health 4 Schools 2004–, chm Children's Food Tst 2011–15, pres Nutrition Australia 2016; food conslt and ambass Glos Food Vision, dir Glos Clinical Commissioning Gp 2011–14; creator Project Kitchen Impossible (with Michel Roux Jr, Channel 4); memb Bd: Food Standards Agency 2000–04, Meat Hygiene Ctee 2000–04, Sch Food Tst 2005–, England Mktng Advsy Bd; memb: Cotswold Area of Outstanding Natural Beauty (AONB) Conservation Bd 2004–06; freelance journalist for pubns incl: Cotswold Life, Citizen, BBC Gloucestershire; tstee Glos Co Assoc Blind 2004–06; supporter Sense; *Awards* Egon Ronay Star 1989, 2 AA Rosettes 1995–99, Michelin Bibendum 1999; *Books* A Year in Recipes and Landscapes – The Cotswold Chef; *Recreations* watching Arsenal FC, music, travel, food, watching Geelong AFL; *Clubs* Melbourne City FC; *Style*— Rob Rees, Esq, MBE, DL; ✉ 6 Guest Close, Kew, Melbourne, Victoria, Australia 3101 (☎ 00 614 1552 1724, e-mail cotswoldchef@googlemail.com, website www.robrees.com.au)

REES, Simon John; s of Dan Rees, of Epsom, Surrey, and Margaret May Rose, *née* Stephenson; *b* 7 July 1960; *Educ* Kingston GS; *m* 18 Aug 1984, Gillian Gaye, da of Kenneth Horne; 1 s (Jonathan Charles b 24 Nov 1987), 1 da (Charlotte Emma b 2 Oct 1989); *Career* media asst rising to TV buyer D'Arcy McManus & Masius 1978–81, sr planner/buyer Colman and Partners 1982–86 (TV buyer 1981–82); TMD Carat Advertising: sr TV buyer 1986–88, TV mangr then assoc dir 1988, broadcast dir and memb Bd 1989, head of Carat TV (UK) 1990–98, dep md 1995–98; MindShare (WPP jt media op of O&M and J Walter Thompson): UK md 1998–2001, ceo 2001–02; ceo Simon Rees Consultancy Ltd 2003–, ceo FiftyLessons 2004, ptnr ReInventive LLP, fndr dir Digital Planet Ltd 2006, ceo Avanti Screenmedia plc, advsr Oil Studios Ltd 2009 (chm 2009–), ceo Digital Cinema Media 2011–15, ptnr Cinevents Ltd 2016–; tstee Basic Needs 2006 (chair of tstees 2009–); fell: Acad of Chief Execs, Leaders Quest India and South Africa; MIPA, FRGS, FRSA; *Sporting Achievements* schoolboy hockey int (England) 1976–78, 96 full int caps hockey (indoor and field) Wales 1979–90; *Recreations* running, cycling, swimming, mountaineering, walking, golf, hockey (also hockey coach); *Clubs* Southgate Hockey (various League and Cup Winner medals), Berkshire Triathlon Squad; *Style*— Simon Rees, Esq

REES OF LUDLOW, Baron (Life Peer UK 2005), of Ludlow in the County of Shropshire; Prof Sir Martin John Rees; OM (2007), kt (1992); s of Reginald Jackson Rees (d 1994), and (Harriette) Joan, *née* Bett (d 1985); *b* 23 June 1942; *Educ* Shrewsbury, Trinity Coll Cambridge (MA, PhD); *m* 1986, Prof Dame Caroline Humphrey, DBE, *née* Waddington; *Career* prof Univ of Sussex 1972–73, Plumian prof of astronomy and experimental philosophy Univ of Cambridge 1973–91, dir Cambridge Inst of Astronomy 1977–91, Royal Soc research prof 1992–2003, master Trinity Coll Cambridge 2004–12; Astronomer Royal 1995–; pres: Royal Astronomical Soc 1992–94, BAAS 1994–95, Royal Soc 2005–10; Regents fell Smithsonian Inst Washington 1984–88, visiting prof Harvard Univ, visiting prof Univ of Leicester 2001–; tstee: British Museum 1996–2002, Nat Endowment for Science, Technology and the Arts (NESTA) 1998–2001, Inst for Advanced Study Princeton 1998–, Kennedy Meml Tst 1999–2004, IPPR 2001–, Nat Museums for Science and Industry 2003–12; foreign hon memb American Acad of Arts and Scis, memb Pontifical Acad of Scis, memb Academia Europaea; foreign memb: Royal Swedish Acad of Science, Accademia Lincei (Rome), Norwegian Acad of Sciences, Netherlands Acad of Arts & Sciences, Finnish Acad of Arts and Sciences 2003–; Balzan International Prize 1989, Bower Prize for Science Franklin Institute 1998, Gruber Cosmology Prize 2001, Einstein Award for Science 2003, Crafoord Prize Royal Swedish Acad of Science 2005, Templeton Prize 2011, Newton Prize 2012, Dirac Prize 2013; Hon Freeman Worshipful Co of Clockmakers; Hon DSc: Univ of Sussex, Univ of Uppsala, Keele Univ, Univ of Leicester, Univ of Newcastle, Univ of Copenhagen, Univ of Toronto, Univ of Durham, Univ of Oxford, Yale Univ, Open Univ, Univ of Liverpool, UEA, Univ of Melbourne, Univ of Cambridge, Univ of Bath, Univ of Greenwich; hon memb: American Philosophical Soc, Russian Acad of Science, US Nat Acad of Scis; fell King's Coll Cambridge 1969–2003, hon prof Imperial Coll London 2001–; hon fell: Indian Acad of Scis 1990–, Trinity Coll Cambridge 1995–, Jesus Coll Cambridge 1996–, King's Coll Cambridge 2007–; FRS, Hon FInstP, Hon FRAEng, Hon FBA, hon FMedSci, foreign memb Russian Acad of Sciences; Officier de l'Ordre des Arts et des Lettres (France) 1991, Order of the Rising Sun Gold and Silver Star (Japan) 2015; *Publications* Gravity's Fatal Attraction (1996), Before the Beginning (1997), Just Six Numbers (1999), New Perspectives in Astrophysical Cosmology (2000), Our Cosmic Habitat (2001), Our Final Century (2003), From Here to Infinity (2011); author of many scientific and general articles; *Recreations* rural pursuits; *Clubs* Athenaeum, Oxford and Cambridge; *Style*— The Rt Hon the Lord Rees, OM, FRS; ✉ c/o Trinity College, Cambridge CB2 1TQ

REES-MOGG, Hon Jacob William; MP; s of The Lord Rees-Mogg (d 2012); *b* 24 May 1969; *Educ* Eton, Trinity Coll Oxford; *m* 2007, Helena Anne Beatrix Wentworth Fitzwilliam, da of late Capt Somerset Struben de Chair; 4 s (Peter Theodore Alphege b 2007, Thomas Wentworth Somerset Dunstan b 2010, Anselm Charles Fitzwilliam b 2013, Alfred Wulfric Leyson Pius b 2016), 1 da (Mary Anne Charlotte Emma b 2008); *Career* fndr Somerset Capital Mgmnt 2007; MP (Cons) Somerset NE 2010–; *Style*— The Hon Jacob Rees-Mogg, MP; ✉ House of Commons, London SW1A 0AA

REEVE, John; s of Clifford Alfred Reeve, and Irene Mary Turnidge Osborne; *b* 13 July 1944; *Educ* Westcliff HS Essex; *m* 2, 21 Dec 1974, Sally Diane, da of Eric Welton; 1 da (Emily Virginia Welton b 27 Jan 1979); *Career* Corporation of Lloyd's 1960–62, Selby Smith &

Earle 1962–67, Peat Marwick Mitchell & Co 1967–68, Roneo Vickers Office Equipment Group 1968–76, Wilkinson Match Ltd 1976–77, Amalgamated Metal Corporation Ltd 1977–80, dir of fin British Aluminium Co plc 1980–83, dir of fin Mercantile House Holdings plc 1983–87; Sun Life Corporation plc: joined as dep gp md Sun Life Assurance Society plc 1988, gp md 1989–95, non-exec dir 1995–96; exec chm Willis Group Ltd 1995–2000; currently chm Temple Bar Investment Trust plc (dir 1992–), chm ALEA Gp Holdings (Bermuda) Ltd 2003–07, chm Coverzones Ltd 2007–10; The English Concert 1987– (chm 1993–2006); non-exec dir: HMC Group plc 1988–94, Lamarsh Services Ltd, Autologus Transfusion Ltd, Premium Credit Ltd 2012–; govr Research into Ageing 1991–96; pres Inst of Business Ethics 1997–2000 (dep pres 1991–96); chm: East London Partnership 1996–2000 (memb Bd 1991–2000), East London Business Alliance 2000–02; memb: Cncl Business in the Community 1995–2000, Life Insurance Cncl 1991–94, Bd Assoc of Br Insurers 1993–95, Exec Ctee Int Insurance Soc 1996–2001 (memb Bd 1993–2001), Int Advsy Bd British American Business Cncl 2000–01; dir London First 1998–2002; govr NIESR 1995–2000; FCA 1977 (ACA 1967), CCMI 1990, FRSA 1999; *Recreations* yachting, music, theatre; *Clubs* Athenaeum, Essex Yacht; *Style—* John Reeve, Esq

REEVE, Michael Arthur Ferard; MBE (2009); s of Maj Wilfrid Norman Reeve, OBE, MC (d 1976), of London, and Agnes Bourdon, *née* Ferard; *b* 7 January 1937; *Educ* Eton, UC Oxford (MA); *m* 30 Dec 1970, Charmian Gay (d 2014), da of David Royden Rooper, of London; 2 s (Hugo b 10 Dec 1973, Luke b 15 Sept 1977); *Career* dir: Elliott Group of Peterborough 1969–83, Charterhouse Bank 1965–74, Copleys Bank 1974–80, Rea Bros 1977–80, Greyhound Bank 1981–87, Collins Collins & Rawlence (Hamptons estate agents) 1982–85, The Tregeare Company Ltd 1981–2015, Finsbury Growth Income Trust plc 1991–2008 (chm), Nettleton & Co Ltd 2001–11; chm: Octopus AIM VCT plc 1998–2016, Saddleback Corp Ltd 2005–11, Longhorn Mining Ltd 2010–11; dir Silk Road Oil and Gas Ltd 2006–07; dir BSES Expeditions Ltd 2003–09; chm Airborne Forces Charities 2005–10, dir Parachute Regt Charity 2010–12; memb: RIIA, The Pilgrims; FCA 1964; *Recreations* gardening, reading; *Clubs* Boodle's; *Style—* Michael Reeve, Esq, MBE; ✉ 138 Oakwood Court, London W14 8JS (☎ 020 7602 2624)

REEVE, Prof Michael David; s of Arthur Reeve (d 1973), and Edith Mary, *née* Barrett (d 2001); *b* 11 January 1943; *Educ* King Edward's Sch Birmingham, Balliol Coll Oxford (Domus Scholar, Craven Scholar, Hertford Scholar, Ireland Scholar, Gaisford Prize for Greek Verse, Derby Scholar, MA); *m* 4 July 1970 (m dis 1999), Elizabeth Klingaman; 2 s (William Frederick b 23 Sept 1972, Edward Arthur b 19 Jan 1979), 1 da (Hilda Katharine (Mrs K Whiting) b 9 Feb 1976); *Career* Harmsworth sr scholar Merton Coll Oxford 1964–65, Woodhouse research fell St John's Coll Oxford 1965–66, gasthörer Free Univ Berlin 1965–66, fell and lectr in classics Exeter Coll Oxford and CUF lectr in classics Univ of Oxford 1966–84, emeritus fell Exeter Coll Oxford 1984–, Kennedy prof of Latin Univ of Cambridge 1984–2006 (dir of research 2006–07), fell Pembroke Coll Cambridge 1984–; gastprofessor Univ of Hamburg 1976, visiting lectr McMaster Univ 1979, visiting prof Univ of Toronto 1982–83; memb Editorial Bd: Materiali e Discussioni 1992–, Revue d'Histoire des Textes 1994–; chm Advsy Cncl Warburg Inst 2008–13; Premio Capitolino Rome 1991; corresponding memb Akademie der Wissenschaften Göttingen 1990–, foreign memb Istituto Lombardo Milan 1993–, accademico Ambrosiana Milan 2014–; FBA 1984; *Publications* Classical Quarterly (jt ed, 1981–86), Cambridge Classical Texts and Commentaries (ed, 1984–), Cambridge Classical Studies (jt ed, 1984–2007), Pembroke College Gazette (ed, 1992–97); Daphnis & Chloe (ed, 1982), Pro Quinctio (ed, 1992), Vegetius (ed, 2004), Geoffrey of Monmouth (ed, 2007), Manuscripts and Methods (2011); *Style—* Prof M D Reeve, FBA; ✉ Pembroke College, Cambridge CB2 1RF

REEVE, Roy Stephen; CMG (1998); s of Ernest Arthur Reeve, of London, and Joan, *née* Thomas; *b* 20 August 1941; *Educ* Dulwich Coll, LSE (BScEcon, MScEcon), Chartered Inst of Secs (postgrad scholar); *m* 6 June 1964, Gill, da of Leslie Lee (d 1993); 2 da (Kirsti Jane b 3 March 1969, Sally Elizabeth b 1 Aug 1971); *Career* HM Customs and Excise 1961–62; HM Dip Serv: joined FCO 1966, third sec Moscow 1968–71, first sec FCO 1973–78, first sec (commercial) Moscow 1978–80, FCO 1980–83, cnsllr on loan to Home Civil Serv 1983–85, dep consul-gen Johannesburg 1985–88, head of Commercial Mgmnt and Export Dept FCO 1988–91, consul-gen Sydney 1991–95, HM ambass Ukraine 1995–1999, ret; head of Mission to Armenia OSCE 1999–2003, ambass and head of OSCE Mission to Georgia 2003–, dep head EULEX Kosovo; hon sr res fell Centre for Russian and East European Studies Univ of Birmingham; *Recreations* motorcycling, scuba diving; *Clubs* Union (Sydney); *Style—* Mr Roy Reeve, CMG

REEVELL, Simon Justin; *b* 2 March 1966; *Educ* Manchester Poly, PCL, Inns of Court Sch of Law; *m* Louise; *Career* called to the Bar Lincoln's Inn 1990; MOD (Army) scholarship and cadetship Prince of Wales's Own Regt of Yorks; MP (Cons) Dewsbury 2010–15; *Style—* Simon Reevell, Esq; ✉ House of Commons, London SW1A 0AA

REEVES, Anthony Alan; s of Allen Joseph Reeves, MBE (d 1976), and Alice Turner, *née* Pointon (d 1966); *b* 5 March 1943; *Educ* Hanley HS, Coll of Law; *m* 19 Aug 1967 (m dis 2003), Jane, da of William Thowless (d 1942); 2 da (Rachel b 1969, Ruth b 1974), 1 s (Max b 1972); *Career* admitted slr 1965, sr ptnr KJD (formerly Kent Jones and Done Slrs) 1978–; chm: The Byatt Gp Ltd 1974–79, The CAS Group plc 1985–90, Gresley Brownhills Ltd (formerly Daniel Platt Ltd) 1992–2008, Domain Dynamics (Holdings) Ltd 2001–03, Epichem Gp Ltd 2005–07 (non-exec); non-exec dir: Steelite International plc 1983–2002, Stoke City FC 1984–85, Bullers plc 1984–86, Butler Woodhouse Ltd 1987–94, John Charcol Holdings Ltd 2006–10; dir and conslt: David Lean Films Ltd 1997–, Freeths LLP 2010–; sec Waterford Wedgwood Holdings plc 1986; chm of tstees: The Beth Johnson Endowment1973–, The David Lean Fndn 1997–; chm: Law Soc Sub-Ctee on Coal Mining Subsidence 1985–2005 (memb Law Soc), Keele Univ Devpt Tst 1993–2004; hon legal advsr Br Ceramic Confedn 2000–10; dir Directors UK Ltd; memb: Nat Exec Cncl Age Concern 1976–78, N Staffs Med Inst Cncl 1979–82, Cncl Keele Univ 1999–2003; hon life memb BAFTA 2002–; *Recreations* art, field sports, ballet, opera, gardening; *Style—* Anthony A Reeves, Esq; ✉ The Bradshaws, Codsall, Staffordshire WV8 2HU

REEVES, Anthony Henry; s of Herbert Henry Reeves (d 1999), and Kathleen Norah Reeves (d 1963); *b* 8 September 1940; *Educ* Sir Walter St Johns; *m* 1972, Jacqueline, da of Herbert Mitchell Newton-Clare, of Edgeworth, Glos; 4 s, 2 da; *Career* former dir Alfred Marks Bureau Ltd, chm and chief exec Lifetime Corp USA (acquired HCC 1986) 1986–93, chm Medic International 1993–96; chief exec Delphi Group Ltd (formerly Computer People Group plc) 1994–2001; chm and ceo: The Hot Gp plc 2001–05, Spur Lodge Ltd 2006–; chm Paystream Accounting Services Ltd 2006–15, exec chm Kellan Gp plc 2007–15, chm Cloudtag Inc 2013–; *Recreations* golf, running, cycling; *Clubs* RAC, Royal Wimbledon Golf, Reform, Royal Mid-Surrey Golf; *Style—* Anthony H Reeves, Esq; ✉ Spur Lodge, 142 Upper Richmond Road West, London SW14 8DS (☎ 020 8878 4738, e-mail tony.reeves@spurlodgelimited.com)

REEVES, Colin Leslie; CBE (1999); s of Leslie Reeves, of Warks, and Isabelle; *b* 4 April 1949; *Educ* Birkenhead Sch, Clare Coll Cambridge (MA), Univ of Wales Bangor (MSc, PhD), Liverpool John Moores Univ (CPFA), Cornell Univ (DipBA); *m* Christine, *née* Lloyd; 2 da (Helen Madeleine b 12 Aug 1981, Caroline Georgina b 11 Jan 1984); *Career* lectr Univ of Wales Bangor 1971–73, accountancy and audit asst Warrington Co Borough 1973–75, asst treas Ellesmere Port and Neston Borough Cncl 1975–80, dep dir of fin Stratford-upon-Avon DC 1980–84, dep dir of fin NW Thames RHA 1984–85, dir of fin Paddington and N Kensington DHA 1985–86, regnl dir of fin NW Thames RHA 1986–94, national dir of fin and performance NHS Exec 1994–2001, dir Accountancy Fndn Review Bd 2001–2003, self-employed healthcare conslt 2003–; memb: Advsy Ctee on Mentally Disordered Offenders Dept of Health/Home Office 1993–94, Nat Steering Gp on Capitation 1993–94, Nat Steering Gp on Capital 1993–94, Culyer Ctee on R&D 1993–94, Chllr of Exchequer's Private Finance Panel 1994–95, Butler Ctee on the Review of the Audit Cmmn 1995, Chief Medical Offr's Nat Screening Ctee 1996–2001, Review of the Office of Nat Statistics reporting to HM Treasy 1999, Bd Accountancy Nat Trg Orgn 1999–2001, Co-ordinating Gp on Audit and Accounting Issues DTI/HM Treasy 2002, Consultative Ctee on Review of the Listing Regime FSA 2002; chm Audit Ctee and vice-chm Oxford Radcliffe Hosps NHS Tst 2005–09; hon treas Headway 2002–, memb Finance and Audit Ctee Oxfam Int 2009–10, hon treas Florence Nightingale Fndn 2011–, hon treas Goring and Streatley Festival 2014–; memb: Nat Tst, RSPB, Woodland Tst; *Publications* The Applicability of the Monetary Base Hypothesis to the UK, the USA, France and West Germany (1974), Feasibility Study into the Implementation of a Capital Charges System in Chile (ODA, 1997); regular contrib to various professional jls; *Recreations* sport (especially cricket and golf), history of test match cricket, former regnl int and county hockey player; *Clubs* MCC, RAC, Goring and Streatley Golf, Henley Hawks Rugby Football, Flying Ferrets Golf Soc; *Style—* Dr Colin L Reeves, CBE; ✉ Battle Hill, Elvendon Road, Goring on Thames, Oxfordshire RG8 0DT; La Loma, Las Lomas, 29500 Alora, Malaga, Spain

REEVES, Prof Nigel Barrie Reginald; OBE (1987); s of Capt Reginald Arthur Reeves (d 1994), of Battle, E Sussex, and Marjorie Joyce, *née* Pettifer (d 1993); *b* 9 November 1939; *Educ* Merchant Taylors', Worcester Coll Oxford (BA), St John's Coll Oxford (DPhil); *m* 8 April 1982, Minou, da of Sadegh Samimi (d 1978); *Career* lectr in English Univ of Lund 1964–66, lectr in German Univ of Reading 1968–74, Alexander von Humboldt fell Univ of Tübingen 1974–75, Univ of Hamburg 1986; Univ of Surrey: prof of German 1975–90, head Linguistic and Int Studies Dept 1979–89, dean Faculty of Human Studies 1986–90, dir Surrey Euro Mgmnt Sch 1989–90; Aston Univ: prof of German and head of Languages and Euro Studies Dept 1990–96, pro-vice-chllr 1996–2007, prof emeritus 2007–; visiting prof and memb Cncl Euro Business Sch London 1983–90; chm Inst of Linguists 1985–88 (vice-pres 1989–2009); pres: Nat Assoc of Language Advsrs 1986–90, Assoc of Teachers of German 1987–89; vice-pres Conference of Univ Teachers of German 1995–97 (exec vice-pres 1988–91), chm Nat Congress on Languages in Educn 1986–90; memb: Governing Bd Inst of Germanic Studies Univ of London 1989–94, Academic Advsy Cncl Linguaphone Inst 1989–2005, Steering Ctee Centre for Modern Languages Open Univ 1991–95, Academic Advsy Cncl Univ of Buckingham 1991–2002, Educn Ctee London C of C and Industry Examinations Bd 1993–2006, Bd of British Training International 1998–2000, Advsy Cncl Scot Higher Educn Funding Cncl (SHEFC) Scotlang Project 2000–02, Irish Research Cncl for the Humanities and Social Sciences 2001, Univ Cncl for Modern Languages 2002–07; chm Academic Advsy Bd Br Inst of Traffic Educn Res 2001–02; tstee London C of C Industry Educn Tst 2001–08; chm of govrs: Matthew Boulton Higher and Further Educn Corp Birmingham 1999–2002 (govr 2002–07), Quality Assurance Agency Benchmarking Steering Ctee 2003–07, Languages Ladder Working Gp DfES 2004–06; medal Euro Fndn for Quality Mgmnt 1996; hon fell Hong Kong Translation Soc 2006, FIL 1981, FRSA 1986, CIEX 1986; Goethe Medaille (Goethe Inst Munich) 1989, Officer's Cross of the Order of Merit (Germany) 1999; *Books* Heinrich Heine, Poetry and Politics (1974, 2 edn 1994), Friedrich Schiller, Medicine, Psychology and Literature (with K Dewhurst, 1978), The Marquise of O and Other Short Stories by Heinr Kleist (with F D Luke, 1978), Business Studies, Languages and Overseas Trade (with D Liston, 1985), The Invisible Economy, A Profile of Britain's Invisible Exports (with D Liston, 1988), Making Your Mark, Effective Business Communication in Germany (with D Liston, M Howarth and M Woodhall, 1988), Franc Exchange, Effective Business Communication in France (with C Sanders, Y Gladkow and C Gordon, 1991), Spanish Venture. Basic Business Communication in Spanish (with B Gould, L Nogueira-Pache and K Bruton, 1992), Linguistic Auditing: A Guide to Identifying Foreign Language Communication Needs in Corporations (with C Wright, 1996), The European Business Environment: Germany (ed with Helen Kelly-Holmes, 1997), Pathways to Proficiency: The Alignment of Language Proficiency Scales for Assessing Competence in English Language (with Richard West, 2003); *Recreations* gardening, walking; *Style—* Prof Nigel Reeves, OBE; ✉ c/o Pro-Vice-Chancellor's Office, Aston University, Birmingham B4 7ET (☎ 0121 359 3611 ext 4214, fax 0121 359 2792)

REEVES, Philip Thomas Langford; s of Herbert John Reeves (d 1983), of Cheltenham, Glos, and Lilian, *née* Langford (d 1963); *b* 7 July 1931; *Educ* Naunton Park Secdy, Cheltenham Sch of Art, RCA; *m* 1961, Christina Donaldina, *née* MacLaren (d 1994); 1 da; *Career* artist; head of printmaking Glasgow Sch of Art 1972–91 (lectr in graphic design 1954–70); fndr memb: Edinburgh Printmaker's Workshop 1963, Glasgow Print Studio 1972; winner Glasgow Herald Art Exhbn 1980; memb: SSA 1965, Royal Glasgow Inst of the Fine Arts 1981; fell Royal Soc of Painter Etchers 1963; RSW 1959 (pres 1998), RSA 1976 (ARSA 1972); *Exhibitions* Compass Gall 1974, 1977 and 1990, Edinburgh Printmaker's Workshop (retrospective) 1981, New 57 Gall (retrospective) 1982, Mercury Gall 1987, Cyril Gerber Fine Art 1993, Paintings and Prints 1983–93 (Lillie Art Gall) 1993, Fine Art Soc 1994, Dick Inst 1994; *Recreations* table tennis, snooker; *Style—* Philip Reeves, Esq, RSA

REEVES, Rachel Jane; MP; *b* 13 February 1979; *Educ* New Coll Oxford (BA), LSE (MSc); *Career* economist Bank of England and Br Embassy Washington DC 2000–06, analyst Halifax Bank of Scotland 2006–09; MP (Lab) Leeds W 2010–, shadow chief sec to the Treasy 2011–13, shadow sec for the DWP 2013–15; *Style—* Ms Rachel Reeves, MP; ✉ House of Commons, London SW1A 0AA

REEVES, Vic; *né* (Roderick) James (Jim) Moir; *b* 24 January 1959; *Career* comedian, part of comedy duo with Bob Mortimer, *qv*; *Television* incl: Vic Reeves Big Night Out (Channel 4) 1990 & 1991, Weekenders (Channel 4) 1992, The Smell of Reeves and Mortimer (3 series, BBC) 1993, 1995 and 1998, A Night in with Vic and Bob (Boxing Day special) 1993, A Nose Through Nature (BBC) 1995, Shooting Stars (BBC) 1995, 1996, 1998, 2002 and 2003, It's Ulrika (BBC) 1997, Families at War (BBC) 1998–99, Bang Bang, It's Reeves and Mortimer (BBC) 1999, Randall and Hopkirk (Deceased) (2 series, BBC) 2000–02, On Set With Randall and Hopkirk (Deceased) (BBC) 2000, We Know Where You Live (Channel 4) 2001, contestant Celebrity Mastermind (BBC) 2002, Eluard in Surrealissimo – The Trial of Dalí (BBC) 2002, Catterick (BBC 3) 2004, All Star Comedy Show (ITV) 2004, Final Chance to Save (Sky One) 2005, Brainiac (series 5 and 6, Sky One) 2007–08, Pirate Ship Live (five) 2007; *Radio* Vic Reeves Big Night Out (Virgin Radio) 2005, Vic Reeves House Arrest (BBC Radio 2) 2007; *Film* Churchill: The Hollywood Years 2003; *Tours* Vic Reeves Big Night Out 1990 and 1991, The Smell of Reeves and Mortimer 1994 and The Weathercock Tour 1995, Shooting Stars (nat tour) 1996, Shooting Stars/Fast Show Live (Labatt's Apollo) 1998; *Video* incl: Shooting Stars – Unviewed & Nude 1996, Shooting Stars – Unpicked and Plucked 1997; *Recordings* Dizzy (single, UK no 1), I Will Cure You (album), I'm A Believer (EMF) 1995; *Exhibitions* Sunboiled Onions (Percy Miller Gallery London) 2000; *Awards* BAFTA Award for Originality 1991, Best Live Performance British Comedy Awards 1992, Best Comedy Series British Comedy Awards 1993, BAFTA Award for Best Light Entertainment 1997; *Books* Big Night In (1991), Smell of Reeves and Mortimer (1993), Shooting Stars (1996), Sunboiled Onions (1999), Me: Moir: Volume One, 0–20 (2006); *Style—* Vic Reeves; ✉ c/o PBJ and JBJ Management, 22 Rathbone Street, London W1T 1LA (☎ 020 7287 1112, fax 020 7287 1191, e-mail general@pbjmgt.co.uk, website www.pbjmgt.co.uk)

REGAN, Carolyn; *Educ* Lycée Français de Londres, Somerville Coll Oxford (BA); *Career* early career as European tour guide American Inst for Foreign Studies and PR offr New Shakespeare Theatre Co London; nat admin trainee NHS 1981–83, asst admin Middx Hosp London 1983–85, dir Services for People with Learning Disabilities Riverside HA 1985–89; Ealing HA: co-ordinator Services for Elderly People 1989–90, dir of purchasing 1990–92, acting chief exec 1992–93; dir of acute commissioning Ealing, Hammersmith & Hounslow Health Agency 1993–1996; chief exec: W Herts HA 1996–1999, E London & The City HA 1999–2002, NE London Strategic HA 2002–06, Legal Servs Cmmn 2006–10; interim chief exec Children's Legal Centre 2010–11, interim md Coram Children's Legal Centre 2011, interim md W London Clinical Commissioning Consortium 2011–; memb Cncl City Univ 2006–; tstee Action Space Ltd 2003–; *Recreations* aerobics, swimming, cooking, writing poetry, gardening, theatre; *Style*— Ms Carolyn Regan

REGAN, Prof Lesley; da of John Regan, of London, and Dorothy, *née* Thorne; *b* 8 March 1956, London; *Educ* Lady Eleanor Holles Sch, Royal Free Hosp Sch of Med (MB BS, MD); *m* 1990, Prof John Summerfield, s of Sir John Crampton Summerfield, CBE, QC (d 1997); 2 da (Jenny, Clare (twins) b 11 Dec 1992); 2 step da (Nuala, Jessica), 2 step s (Oliver, James); *Career* sr registrar in obstetrics and gynaecology Addenbrooke's Hosp Cambridge 1986–90; Univ of Cambridge: sr research assoc MRC Embryo and Genetic Research Gp 1986–88, dir of med studies Girton Coll 1986–90; sr lectr and conslt in obstetrics and gynaecology St Mary's Hosp London 1990–96, dir Subspecialty Trg Prog (RCOG) in Reproductive Med Imperial Coll Sch of Med Hammersmith and St Mary's Hosps London 1995–, prof and head Dept of Obstetrics and Gynaecology Imperial Coll at St Mary's Campus London 1996–, dep head Division Surgery, Oncology, Reproduction and Anaesthesia Imperial Coll 2006–; Aleck Bourne lectr 1990, Rosenfelder lectr 1999, Wim Shelleken lectr 2000, Alexander Gordon lectr 2003, Lettsomian lectr 2004, Green Armytage lectr (RCOG) 2006, Victor Bonney lectr 2007, Imperial Coll Centenary lectr 2008; visiting prof Harvard Center of Excellence for Women's Health 2000, visiting prof and examiner University of Hong Kong 2003, visiting prof in obstetrics and gynaecology to South Africa 2004; recipient research grant awards from: MRC 1992, 2000 and 2008, Arthritis and Rheumatism Cncl 1993, Wellbeing 1996, 2005, 2006, 2008 and 2009, Br Heart Fndn 1997, Save the Baby Charity 1990, 1996, 1998, 2001, 2003–06 (annually), Wellcome Tst 1999 and 2001, Royal Soc 2001, Health, Technology and Assessment UK 2003; tstee Inst of Obstetrics and Gynacology, tstee Save the Baby Charity, tstee CHARM, tstee Nat Confidential Inquiry into Patient Outcome and Death, professional advsr to Miscarriage Assoc, pres UK Assoc of Early Pregnancy Units 2005–, memb Cncl RCOG (elected memb for Int Representation 2006, chair Advocacy Ctee 2009–), tstee Wellbeing of Women; memb: Cncl Br Fertility Soc 1992–95, Euro Soc of Human and Reproduction and Embryology 1986, Fedn of Gynaecologists and Obstetricians 1997 (expert advsr in reproductive med and UK rep Women's Reproductive and Sexual Rights Ctee, chair Women's Sexual and Reprodutive Rights Ctee 2009–), Human Fertilisation and Embryology Authy 2008–; memb Editorial Bd: Human Fertility, Jl of Reproductive Immunology; contrib to TV documentaries: Staying Alive (Channel 4), Horizon – Waiting For A Heartbeat (BBC2) 2006, Horizon – Professor Regan's Beauty Parlour (BBC2) 2007, Horizon – Supermarket Trolley (BBC2) 2008, Horizon – Medicine Cabinet (BBC2) 2009, Horizon – Diet Clinics (BBC2) 2009, Horizon – Nursery (BBC2) 2009, Horizon – Health Spa (BBC2) 2009; Woman of Achievement Award 2005 (for services to med, particularly recurrent miscarriage and infertility); FRCOG 1998 (MRCOG 1985, memb Cncl, memb Int Exec Bd, memb Finance and Exec Ctee); *Publications* Miscarriage – What Every Woman Needs to Know (1997, republished 2001), Your Pregnancy Week By Week (2005); also author of articles on reproductive med incl the causes and treatment of infertility and recurrent miscarriage, also on minimally invasive treatment for uterine fibroids; *Recreations* writing and broadcasting for lay public on medical health issues, walking, music; *Style*— Prof Lesley Regan; ☎ 020 3312 1731; Department of Obstetrics and Gynaecology, Imperial College at St Mary's, Mint Wing, South Wharf Road, London W2 1NY (☎ 020 7886 1798, fax 020 7886 6054, e-mail l.regan@imperial.ac.uk)

REGAN, Michael Denis; s of Denis Charles Regan (d 1965), of Westcliff-on-Sea, Essex, and Selina, *née* Webb (d 2007); *b* 4 October 1955; *Educ* Westcliff HS for Boys, Pembroke Coll Oxford (MA); *m* 20 Feb 1987, Henrietta, da of Henry George Richard Falconar (d 1981), of Horsham, W Sussex; 1 s (George b 1987), 1 da (Grace b 1990); *Career* admitted slr 1980; Rowe and Maw (now Mayer Brown Int LLP): articled clerk 1978–80, asst slr 1980–85, ptnr 1985–, ptnr i/c Lloyd's office 1988–92; ACIArb 1984; *Books* JCT Management Contract (jtly); *Recreations* watching cricket; *Style*— Michael Regan, Esq; ✉ Mayer Brown International LLP, 201 Bishopsgate, London EC2M 3AF

REGESTER, Michael; s of Hugh Adair Regester (d 1994), of Royston, Herts, and Monique, *née* Levrey; *b* 8 April 1947; *Educ* St Peter's Sch Guildford Surrey, Newport GS Newport Essex; *m* 1 (m dis 1993), Christine Mary, da of Denis Harrison; 2 da (Lucinda Jane b 12 April 1971, Alice Mary b 8 Aug 1975); m 2, Leanne Tara, da of Margaret Moscardi; 1 s (Daniel b 13 Feb 1995), 1 da (Kimberley (twin) b 13 Feb 1995); *Career* mangr of public affrs (Euro, W Africa, ME) Gulf Oil Corporation 1975–80, jt md Traverse-Healy & Regester Ltd 1980–87, dir Charles Barker Public Relations 1987–90, md Regester plc 1990–94, ptnr Regester Larkin Ltd 1994–; memb Bd Int PR Assoc 1988, FIPR 1990, MInstPet 1990; *Books* Crisis Management (1987), Investor Relations (with Neil Ryder, 1990), Risk Issues and Crisis Management (with Judy Larkin, 2008); *Recreations* sailing, opera, cooking; *Style*— Michael Regester, Esq; ✉ Regester Larkin Limited, 6th Floor, 16 St Martins Le Grand, London EC1A 4EN (☎ 020 7029 3980, fax 020 7236 0471, e-mail mregester@regesterlarkin.com)

REGO, Dame Paula; DBE (2010); da of José Fernandes Figueiroa Rego (d 1966), of Portugal, and Maria De São José Paiva; *b* 26 January 1935; *Educ* St Julian's Sch Carcavelos Portugal, Slade Sch of Fine Art; *m* 1959, Victor Willing, s of George Willing; 2 da (Caroline b 1956, Victoria Camilla b 1959), 1 s (Nicholas Juvenal b 1961); *Career* artist; pt/t lectr Slade Sch of Fine Art 1983–90, assoc artist Nat Gallery London 1990, Gulbenkian Fndn bursary 1962–63; Hon Dr RCA; subject of book Paula Rego (by John McEwen, 1992); Premio Penagos Fundacion Mapre 2010; Hon DUniv: St Andrews 1999, UEA 1999; Hon Dr: Rhode Island Sch of Design 2000, The London Institute 2002, UCL 2004, Univ of Roehampton 2005; Hon DLitt Univ of Oxford 2005, hon fell Murray Edwards Coll Cambridge 2013, Hon LittD Univ of Cambridge 2015; *Solo Exhibitions* SNBA Lisbon 1965, Galeria S Mamede Lisbon 1971, Galeria da Emenda Lisbon 1974, Galeria Modulo Oporto 1977, Galeria III Lisbon 1978, Air Gallery London 1981, Edward Totah Gallery London 1982, 1984, 1985 and 1987, Arnolfini Bristol 1983, Gallery Espace Amsterdam 1983, Midland Group 1984, The Art Palace NY 1985, Travelling Show 1987, Retrospective Exhibition (Gulbenkian Fndn Lisbon and Serpentine Gallery London) 1988, Nursery Rhymes (Marlborough Graphics, travelling exhbn Plymouth, Manchester and elsewhere, Nat Gallery 1991, South Bank Centre) 1991–96, Peter Pan and Other Stories (Marlborough Fine Art) 1992, Peter Scott Gallery Lancaster Univ 1993, Dog Woman (Marlborough Fine Art) 1994, Marlborough Fine Art NY 1996, retrospective exhibition (Tate Gallery Liverpool and Centro Cultural de Belem Lisbon Portugal) 1997, Dulwich Picture Gallery 1998, Marlborough Fine Art Madrid 1999, Gulbenkian Fndn Lisbon 1999, Abbot Hall Kendal 2001, Yale Center for Br Art 2002, Museu Serralves Porto 2004–05, Tate Britain 2005, print retrospective touring exhbn (Talbot Rice Gallery Edinburgh, Brighton Museum and others) 2005–07, Marlborough Fine Art 2006, MNCA Reina Sofia Madrid 2007, Nat Museum of Women in the Arts Washington DC 2008, Marlborough NY 2008, Marco Monterrey 2010, Pinacoteca do Estado de Sao Paulo 2011, Gulbenkian Fndn Paris 2012; *Group Exhibitions* incl: S Paulo Biennale 1969 and 1985, Br Art Show 1985, Cries and Whispers (Br Cncl) 1988, Br Art (Japan) 1990, Innocence and Experience (Manchester City Art Gallery and touring) 1992, British Figurative Art in the 20th Century (British Arts Cncl and the Israel Museum Jerusalem) 1993, Unbound (Hayward Gallery) 1994, Saatchi Gallery 1994, Spellbound: Art and Film (Hayward Gallery) 1996, British Art Show (Hayward Gallery) 2000, Encounters (Nat Gallery) 2000, Darger-ism (American Folk Art Museum NY) 2008, At the Foundling (Foundling Museum London) 2010; *Books* Peter Pan, Nursery Rhymes, Pendle Witches, The Children's Crusade; subject of: Paula Rego by John McEwen (1992, 1997 and 2006), Paula Rego by Fiona Bradley (2002), Complete Graphic Work by Tom Rosenthal (2003, 2 edn 2012), Paula Rego's Map of Memory (by Dr Maria Manuel Lisboa); *Style*— Dame Paula Rego, DBE; ✉ Marlborough Fine Art, 6 Albemarle Street, London W1S 4BY (☎ 020 7629 5161, fax 020 7629 6338)

REICHMANN, Paul; s of Samuel Reichmann, and Renee Reichmann; *b* 1930, Vienna; *Career* co-fndr Olympia & York Developments Ltd; projects incl: First Canadian Place Toronto (offices) 1975, World Financial Center NY 1986, concept and realisation Canary Wharf project London 1987; exec chm Canary Wharf Group plc until 2003, chief exec Reichmann Group of Companies (incl International Property Corp); tstee and jt unitholder: Retirement Residences Real Estate Investment Tst, CPL Long Term Care Real Estate Investment Tst, IPC US Income Commercial Real Estate Investment Tst; *Style*— Paul Reichmann, Esq

REID, Alan; *b* 7 August 1954; *Educ* Ayr Acad, Univ of Strathclyde; *Career* cncllr (Lib Dem) Renfrew DC 1988–96; Parly candidate (Lib Dem): Paisley 1992, Dunbarton 1997; MP (Lib Dem) Argyll and Bute 2001–15; jr Lib Dem whip 2001–05, memb Broadcasting Select Ctee 2001–05, spokesperson on NI and Scotland 2008–; memb Scottish Lib Dem Pty Exec until 2003, spokesperson Scottish Lib Dem Common Fisheries Policy Reform 2001–05; memb AUT; *Style*— Alan Reid, Esq; ✉ House of Commons, London SW1A 0AA

REID, Sir (Philip) Alan; GCVO (2012, KCVO 2007); s of Philip Reid (d 1981), of Glasgow, and Margaret, *née* McKerracher (d 1976); *b* 18 January 1947; *Educ* Fettes, Univ of St Andrews (LLB); *m* 14 July 1971, Maureen Anne Reid, da of Alexander Petrie, of Cupar, Fife, Scotland; 1 da (Caroline b 1981), 1 s (Richard b 1984); *Career* exec chm KPMG Mgmnt Consultancy Europe, head UK Mgmnt Consultancy KPMG 1994–98 and int chm KPMG Mgmnt Consulting 1996–98; chief fin offr: KPMG UK 1998–2001, KPMG Europe 1999–2001, KPMG Int 1999–2001; chief operating offr KPMG 2001–02; Keeper of the Privy Purse and Treas to HM The Queen 2002–, Receiver Gen to Duchy of Lancaster 2002–; pres Management Consultancies Assoc 1997, pres King George V Fund for Actors and Actresses 2011–; tstee: Royal Collection Tst 2002–, Historic Royal Palaces Tst 2002–15 (dep chm 2007–15); vice-pres RNLI (tstee 2009–14, treas 2011–14); govr Edward VII Hospital (Sister Agnes) 2004–12; CA 1973, FTII 1981, FRSA 1993; *Recreations* family, Arsenal FC, films, golf, skiing; *Clubs* MCC; *Style*— Sir Alan Reid, GCVO; ✉ Buckingham Palace, London SW1A 1AA (☎ 020 7930 4832)

REID, Sir Alexander James; 3 Bt (UK 1897), of Ellon, Aberdeenshire; JP (Cambs and Isle of Ely 1971), DL (1973); s of Sir Edward James Reid, 2 Bt, KBE (d 1972), and Tatiana (Tania), *née* Fenoult (d 1992); *b* 6 December 1932; *Educ* Eton, Magdalene Coll Cambridge; *m* 1955, Michaela Ann, da of late Olaf Kier, CBE, of Royston, Herts; 1 s (Charles Edward James b 1956), 3 da (Christina b 1958, Jennifer) b 1959, Alexandra Catherine (Mrs Charles Lloyd) b 1965); *Heir* s, Charles Reid; *Career* 2 Lt 1 Bn Gordon Highlanders 1951, served Malaya; Capt 3 Bn Gordon Highlanders TA, ret 1964; chm: Ellon Castle Estates Co Ltd 1965–96, Cristina Securities Ltd 1970–, Cytozyme (UK) Ltd 1985–92; hon pres Clan Donnachaidh Soc (chm 1994–2003), govr Heath Mount Prep Sch 1970–92 (chm 1976–92); High Sheriff Cambridge 1987–88; Liveryman Worshipful Co of Farmers; *Clubs* Caledonian; *Style*— Sir Alexander Reid, Bt, DL; ✉ Lanton Tower, Jedburgh, Roxburghshire TD8 6SU (☎ 01835 863443)

REID, Dr Allan William; s of William Reid, and Abigail Simpson Reid; *Educ* Glasgow Acad, Univ of Glasgow (MB ChB); *Career* Glasgow Royal Infirmary: conslt radiologist 1989–, clinical dir (imaging) 1996–2000, head Dept of Radiology 2000–; conslt radiologist Ross Hall Hosp 1991–; memb Editorial Bd Jl of Endovascular Therapy; William Hunter Medal 1979; memb Int Soc for Endovascular Specialists 1996; FRCR 1986 (MRCR 1983), FRCP 2002; *Recreations* photography, travel, golf, swimming; *Clubs* Royal Scottish Automobile, Glasgow Golf; *Style*— Dr Allan Reid; ✉ Glasgow Royal Infirmary, Glasgow G31 2ER (☎ 0141 211 4783, fax 0141 211 4781, e-mail allan.reid@nhs.net); Ross Hall Hospital, Glasgow G52 3NQ

REID, Derek D; *Educ* Inverurie Acad, Univ of Aberdeen, Robert Gordon Univ; *m*; 2 c; *Career* Cadbury-Schweppes: joined 1968, variously dir foods business then tea business until 1986; involved with MBO of Cadbury-Schweppes to form Premier Brands plc 1986, left following takeover by Hillsdown Holdings plc 1990; dir various small cos; chief exec Scottish Tourist Bd 1994–96; chm Harris Tweed Textiles Ltd; visiting prof of tourism Univ of Abertay Dundee; Hon DBA Robert Gordon Univ 1995; *Recreations* Scottish contemporary art, classical music, cricket, golf, fishing; *Style*— Derek Reid, Esq; ✉ Broom Hill, Kinclaven, Stanley, Perthshire PH1 4QL (☎ and fax 01250 883209, e-mail dd.reid30@btinternet.com)

REID, (John) Dominic; OBE (2002); s of John Reid, OBE, RIBA, DL (d 1992), and Sylvia Mary, *née* Payne; *b* 24 September 1961; *Educ* Oundle (music scholar), Downing Coll Cambridge (MA), UCL (DipArch); *m* 18 May 1991, Suzanne Antoinette, *née* Schultz; 1 da; *Career* 2 Lt RA 1981; architect: Doshi-Raje India 1984–85, Austin-Smith: Lord 1986–89, Richard Horden Assoc Ltd 1989–90; ptnr John & Sylvia Reid 1990–92, md Reid & Reid 1992–, dir Designers Collaborative Ltd 1996–2000, chief exec London Film Cmmn 1999–2000; memb Cultural Strategy Partnership for London 1999–2000; pageantmaster Lord Mayor's Show 1992–, prodr Tribute & Promise Parade (VJ Day) 1995, conslt Flora London Marathon 1996–2000, prodr Reopening Canada House by HM The Queen 1998, prodr Reserve Forces Experience 1998, exec dir Oxford and Cambridge Boat Race 2000–04; pageantmaster The Queen's Golden Jubilee 2002: consl t: Olympic Parade of Heroes 2004, Virgin Atlantic Nassau and Cuba Inaugural Flight 2005; prodr San Carlos Falklands 25 2007, dir 2010 Anniversary Prog Royal Soc 2007–10; dir Holkham Country Fair 2012–, dir Chatsworth Country Fair 2013, dir of events Invictus Games 2014; md Invictus Games Fndn 2015–; govr Museum of London 2013–; Trooper rising to Capt TA 1990–2000; HM Lt City of London 2009–, Sgt-at-Mace Royal Soc 2010–, Hon Col City of London and NE Sector ACF 2015–; Liveryman Worshipful Co of Grocers; OStJ; *Books* Lord Mayor's Show: 800 Years 1215–2015 (2015); *Recreations* telemarking, sailing, cycling; *Clubs* HAC, Leander; *Style*— Dominic Reid, Esq, OBE; ✉ e-mail dominic@reidandreid.com

REID, Gavin Donald; s of Donald Reid (d 2006), and Elizabeth, *née* Pittilo; *b* 9 June 1966, Edinburgh; *Educ* Daniel Stewart's and Melville Coll Edinburgh, Napier Coll Edinburgh, RNCM (GMus, PPRNCM, Hiles Medal), Guildhall Sch of Music and Drama; *Partner* Lucy Rimmer; 2 s (James b 5 Aug 2004, Jack b 19 June 2006); *Career* freelance musician (trumpet), teacher and administrator 1989–2001, educn co-ordinator Bridgewater Hall Manchester 2001–02, gen mangr Manchester Camerata 2003–06 (educn co-ordinator 1996–2003), dir BBC Scottish Symphony Orch 2006–; fell Clore Leadership Prog 2004–05; *Recreations* family; *Style*— Gavin Reid, Esq; ✉ BBC Scottish Symphony Orchestra, City Hall, Candleriggs, Glasgow G1 1NQ (☎ 0141 338 2142, e-mail gavin.reid@bbc.co.uk)

REID, (James) Gordon; QC (Scot 1993); s of James Rae Reid (d 1977), of Edinburgh, and Constance May, *née* Lawrie (d 2005); *b* 24 July 1952; *Educ* Melville Coll Edinburgh, Univ of Edinburgh (LLB); *m* 12 Sept 1984, Hannah Hogg, da of William Hopkins; 3 s (William Lawrie b 21 July 1987 d 2006, James Hogg (twin), Jonathon Rae b 10 Dec 1989), 1 da (Joanna Margaret Grant b 26 Oct 1991); *Career* slr in Scot 1976–80 (apprentice slr 1974–76), admitted Faculty of Advocates 1980, standing jr counsel to Scot Office Environment Dept 1986–93, temp judge Court of Session 2002–, judge of the First-tier Tbnl and dep judge of the Upper Tbnl (Tax Chamber) 2009–; called to the Bar Inner Temple 1991; pt/t VAT chm 1997–2009, special cmmnr for income tax 1997–2009, chm Faculty of Advocates Dispute Resolution Service 2013–; arbiter under MIB Scheme; FCIArb 1994; *Recreations* tennis, general fitness, guitar; *Style*— J Gordon Reid, Esq, QC; ✉ Blebo House, By St Andrews, Fife KY15 5TZ; Terra Firma Chambers, Advocates' Library, Parliament House, Edinburgh EH1 1RF (clerk ☎ 0131 260 5830); Atkin Chambers, 1 Atkin Building, Gray's Inn, London WC1R 5BQ (☎ 020 7404 0102)

REID, Prof Gordon McGregor; *b* 9 February 1948, Glasgow; *Educ* Univ of Glasgow (Tech Cert Lab Sci), Univ of Wales Cardiff (BSc), Queen Elizabeth Coll London/British Museum of Natural History (PhD); *m*; 1 c; *Career* animal research technician Zoological Dept Univ of Glasgow 1966–68; VSO field biologist: Botswana 1968–69, Nigeria 1969–70; pt/t demonstrator in zoology Univ of London Colls and Examinations Lab 1974–78, lectr in biology Univ of Sokoto Nigeria 1979–81, conservation offr (natural history) Liverpool Museum 1982–84, keeper of natural history (conservation) Nat Museums on Merseyside Liverpool 1984–85, keeper of natural history Horniman Museum London 1985–91; North of England Zoological Soc at Chester Zoo: curator-in-chief 1992–95, dir and chief exec 1995–2010, dir emeritus 2010–; visiting research fell/guest lectr Nat Museum of Natural History Smithsonian Instn Washington and Nat Zoological Soc of Mexico, visiting prof Univ of Liverpool Dept of Veterinary Clinical Sci and Animal Husbandry 1999–, hon prof Univ of Beds 2010; an inspector of zoos (Govt appt) and conslt biologist to various WWF projects, Br Exec Serv Overseas inspr of Hungarian zoos 1998; memb: Cncl World Assoc of Zoos and Aquariums (chm Aquarium Ctee 2002–06), Cncl European Assoc of Zoos and Aquariums 2001–07 (co-chm Research Ctee), Cncl Assoc of Leading Visitor Attractions, Editorial Advsy Bd Int Zoo Yearbook 2000–, WWF Progs Ctee 2003–07; pres Linnean Soc of London 2003–06; memb: World Conservation Union (IUCN) (memb Strategy Advsy Bd Conservation Breeding Specialist 2007–), cultural consortium englandsnorthwest (chair Gardens Strategy 1999–2006); tstee Nat Museums Liverpool 2001–06 (memb HR Ctee and Human Remains Working Gp), global chair IUCN/Species Survival Cmmn (SSC)/Wetlands Int (WI) Freshwater Fish Specialist Gp, served on South African Agency for Science and Technology Advancement (SAASTA) strategic and operational review panel, pres World Assoc of Zoos and Aquariums (WAZA) 2007–09, chair Global Amphibian ARK Project until 2009; three new species of fish Labeo reidi, Nannocharax reidi and Doumea reidi named in honour 2010; hon fell Liverpool John Moore's Univ 2006, Hon Dr of Science Univ of Chester 2006, Hon Dr of Science Manchester Met Univ 2008; CBiol 1994, FIBiol 1994; Huesped de Honor of Bolivia 2004; *Publications* author of over 200 published works incl books, peer reviewed scientific papers and popular articles; *Style*— Prof Gordon McGregor Reid; ✉ North of England Zoological Society, Cedar House, Caughall Road, Upton, Cheshire CH2 1LH (☎ 01244 650201, fax 01244 380405, e-mail g.reid@chesterzoo.org)

REID, Harry William; s of William Reid (d 1989), and Catherine Robertson Craighead, *née* MacLean; *b* 23 September 1947; *Educ* Aberdeen GS, Fettes, Worcester Coll Oxford (BA); *m* 24 May 1980, Julie Wilson, da of late Henry Davidson; 1 da (Catherine MacGregor b 22 October 1983); *Career* The Scotsman: sometime sportswriter and feature writer, leader writer 1970–73, educn corr 1973–77, features ed 1977–81; sport and leisure ed Sunday Standard 1981–82; The Herald: exec ed 1982–83, dep ed 1983–97, ed 1997–2000, columnist 2004–; special advsr to SMG plc 2000–01, commissioning conslt St Andrew Press 2002–; visiting fell New Coll Univ of Edinburgh 2001; cmmnd by Church of Scotland to write special report on its situation, structure and prospects 2001, memb Church and Soc Cncl Church of Scotland 2005–06; govr Fettes Coll 2002–12; Oliver Brown Award 2008; Hon DUniv Glasgow 2001, Dr (hc) Univ of Edinburgh 2001; *Publications* Dear Country: A Quest for England (1992), Outside Verdict: An Old Kirk in a New Scotland (2002), The Final Whistle? Scottish Football: The Best and Worst of Times (2005), Deadline: The Story of the Scottish Press (2006), Reformation: The Dangerous Birth of the Modern World (2009); *Recreations* exploring Scotland and European cities, hill walking, supporting Aberdeen FC; *Style*— Harry Reid, Esq; ✉ 12 Comely Bank, Edinburgh EH4 1AN (☎ 0131 332 6690)

REID, Hubert Valentine; s of Robert Valentine Reid (d 1949), of Hove, E Sussex, and Doris, *née* Marchant (d 1997); *b* 24 November 1940; *Educ* Harrow; *m* 9 May 1964, Margaret; 3 s (Robert b 1966, Simon b 1968, Oliver b 1974); *Career* exec dir Hugh Baird & Sons Ltd 1971–77; Boddingtons Gp plc: exec dir 1977, asst md 1980, md 1984, chief exec 1985, chm 1995; chm: Enterprise Inns plc 1997–2012, Ibstock plc 1998–99 (non-exec dir 1995–99), Royal London Mutual Insurance Soc Ltd 1999–2005 (non-exec dir 1996–2005), Midas Income and Growth Tst plc (formerly Taverners Tst plc) 2004–13 (non-exec dir 1996–); dep chm Majedie Investments plc 2000–13 (dir 1999–); non-exec dir: Bryants Gp plc 1993– (chm 2000–01), Greenalls Gp plc 1996–97, Michael Page Int plc 2003–12; govr Harrow Sch 1993–2001, tstee John Lyons Charity 1993–2001; FInstD; *Recreations* golf, tennis; *Clubs* Naval and Military; *Style*— Hubert Reid, Esq

REID, Sir Robert Paul (Bob); kt (1990); *b* 1 May 1934, Cupar, Fife; *Educ* Univ of St Andrews (MA); *m* 1958, Joan Mary; 3 s (Douglas, William, Robert); *Career* Shell International Petroleum Co Ltd: joined 1956, posted overseas (Brunei, Nigeria, Thailand and Australia), dir 1984–90; chm and chief exec Shell UK Ltd 1985–90; chm: British Rail 1990–95, London Electricity plc 1994–97, Sears plc 1995–99, British Borneo Oil & Gas plc 1995–2000, ICE Futures Europe 1999–; dep govr Bank of Scotland 1997–2004; non-exec dir: Merchants Trust 1995–2008, Sun Life Financial Services of Canada 1997–2004, Avis Europe plc 1997–2004 (chm 2002–04), Siemens 1998–2006, Intercontinental Exchange Inc 2001–, HBOS plc 2001–04, CHC Helicopter Corporation 2004–08, Benalla Ltd 2004–, Diligenta Ltd 2005–, Jubilant Energy NV 2007–, EEA Helicopter Operations 2008–; chm: Fndn for Young Musicians 1994–, Learning Through Landscapes 2000–, Conservatoire for Dance and Drama 2001–11, Edinburgh Business Sch 2001–; memb Cncl for Industry and HE; tstee: Sci Museum 1987–92, Fndn for Young Musicians, Civic Tst, IPE Charitable Tst, ICE Futures Europe Charitable Tst 1999–; chllr Robert Gordon Univ 1993–2004; govr St Edwar's Sch 1987–; Hon LLD: Univ of St Andrews 1987, Univ of Aberdeen 1988; Hon DSc Univ of Salford 1990; Hon Dr: South Bank Univ 1995, Sheffield Hallam Univ 1995; Hon FCGI, FRSE, CIMgt; *Recreations* golf, opera; *Clubs* MCC, R&A, Royal Melbourne (Melbourne), Royal Mid-Surrey, Frilford Heath Golf; *Style*— Sir Bob Reid; ✉ 24 Ashley Gardens, London SW1P 1QD (☎ 020 7233 6349, e-mail bob.reid@theice.com)

REID, Dame Seona Elizabeth; DBE (2014, CBE 2008); da of George Robert Hall Reid (d 1981), of Glasgow, and Isobel Margaret, *née* Sewell; *b* 21 January 1950; *Educ* Park Sch Glasgow, Univ of Strathclyde (BA), Univ of Liverpool (DBA); *m* Cordelia Kate Elaine Ditton; *Career* business mangr Theatre Royal Lincoln 1972–73, PR offr Northern Dance Theatre 1973–76, PR offr Ballet Rambert 1976–79, freelance 1979–80, dir Shape London 1980–87, asst dir Strategy and Regnl Devpt Gtr London Arts 1987–90, dir Scottish Arts Cncl 1990–99, dir Glasgow Sch of Art 1999–2013; chair Nat Theatre of Scotland, Scottish cmmr UK-US Fulbright Cmmn, chair Bd Cove Park, dep chair Nat Heritage Meml Fund Heritage Lottery Fund, memb Bd Tate Gallery; tstee Edinburgh Int Cultural Summit Fndn; hon prof Univ of Glasgow; Hon DArts Robert Gordon Univ, Hon DLitt Univ of Glasgow, Hon DLitt Glasgow Caledonian Univ, Hon DLitt Univ of Strathclyde; FRSA, FRSE; *Recreations* walking, food, the Arts, travel; *Style*— Dame Seona Reid, DBE; ✉ e-mail seona@seonareid.co.uk

REID, Prof Stephen Robert; s of Stephen Robert Reid (d 1978), of Manchester, and Mary, *née* Beresford (d 1976); *b* 13 May 1945; *Educ* Chorlton GS Manchester, Victoria Univ of Manchester (BSc, PhD), Univ of Cambridge (MA, ScD); *m* 30 Aug 1969, Susan, da of Geoffrey Bottomley; 3 s (Andrew b 25 June 1971, David b 24 April 1974, Alistair 10 Oct 1980); *Career* research offr CEGB 1969–70; lectr: Dept of Engrg UMIST 1970–76, Dept of Engrg Univ of Cambridge 1976–80; Jackson prof of engrg sci Univ of Aberdeen 1980–84, Conoco prof of mech engrg UMIST (now Univ of Manchester) 1985–2004 (pro-vice-chllr for academic devpt 1992–95, pro-vice-chllr for research 2001–04, emeritus prof 2005–), 6th century research prof of dynamic structural mechanics Univ of Aberdeen 2006–13; ed-in-chief Int Jl of Mechanical Sciences 1987–2012; pres IMA 2000–01; author of over 200 tech papers; Safety Award in Mech Engrg IMechE; fell Clare Coll Cambridge 1977–80; FIMA 1982, FIMechE 1984, FASME 1992, FREng 1993, FRSE 2011; *Style*— Prof Stephen Reid, FREng, FRSE; ✉ 2 Waters Reach, Poynton, Stockport, Cheshire SK12 1XT (☎ 01625 872842, e-mail steve.reid@abdn.ac.uk or steve.reid@manchester.ac.uk)

REID, Susanna; da of Barry Reid, and Susan Smith, *née* Perring; *b* 10 December 1970, Croydon, Surrey; *Educ* Croydon HS, St Paul's Girls' Sch London, Univ of Bristol, Cardiff Sch of Journalism; *m* Dominic Cotton; *Children* 3 s; *Career* BBC Breakfast: weekend presenter 2004–12, weekday presenter 2012–14; Sunday Morning Live (BBC 1) 2011–12; presenter Good Morning Britain (ITV) 2014–; *Style*— Ms Susanna Reid; ✉ ITV, 200 Gray's Inn Road, London WC1X 8XZ (Twitter @susannareid100)

REID BANKS, Lynne; da of Dr James Reid-Banks (d 1953), and Muriel Alexandra Marsh (d 1982, actress, stage name Muriel Alexander); *b* 31 July 1929; *Educ* various schs in England and Canada, Italia Conti Stage Sch, RADA; *m* Chaim Stephenson, sculptor; 3 s (Adiel b 1965, Gillon b 1967, Omri b 1968); *Career* actress 1949–54, reporter ITN 1955–62, teacher of English Israel 1963–71; full time writer and lectr 1971–; visiting teacher and lectr to international schs: Tanzania 1988, Israel (Arab Sector) 1989, Nepal 1990, US (incl Navajo Reservation) 1991, India 1991 and 1997, Germany 1996, Canary Islands 1999, Bulgaria 1999, Paris 2000 and 2002, Trieste 2000, Budapest 2000, Geneva 2001 and 2004, Zimbabwe 2001, Australia 2001, South Africa 2004, Tobago 2005, Palestine 2005–14, Japan 2006; involved in video conferencing worldwide through Polycom/AT&T; author of several plays for stage, TV and radio, numerous articles in The Observer, The Guardian, TES, The Times, The Telegraph, Sunday Telegraph, The Independent and various magazines; J M Barrie Award 2013; memb: Soc of Authors, Equity, PEN; *Plays* It Never Rains (BBC TV, 1954), Already It's Tomorrow (BBC TV, 1955), All in a Row (1956), The Killer Dies Twice (1956), The Gift (1962), The Stowaway (BBC Radio, 1970), The Eye of the Beholder (1975), A Question of Principle (Radio 4, 1987), Travels of Yoshi and the Tea-Kettle (for children, Polka Theatre 1991–92, Fringe Award); *Fiction* The L-Shaped Room (1960, film 1962, 10 translations, several radio versions), An End to Running (1962), Children at the Gate (1968), The Backward Shadow (1970, serialised BBC Radio 4 2005), Two is Lonely (1974), Defy the Wilderness (1981), The Warning Bell (1984), Casualties (1987), Fair Exchange (1998); *Biographical novels* Dark Quartet – the story of the Brontës (1976, Yorks Arts Literary Award), Path to the Silent Country (sequel, 1977); *For young adults* One More River (1973, rewritten and reissued 1992), Sarah and After (1975), My Darling Villain (1977), The Writing on the Wall (1981), Melusine – a Mystery (1988), Broken Bridge (sequel to One More River, 1995); *Children's* The Adventures of King Midas (1977, rewritten and reissued 1993), The Farthest-Away Mountain (1977), I, Houdini (1978), The Indian in the Cupboard (1980, also film, Pacific NW Choice Award 1984, Calif Young Readers' Medal 1984, Virginia Children's Choice 1988, Massachusetts Children's Choice 1988, Rebecca Caudill Award 1988, Arizona Children's Choice 1989 and others), Maura's Angel (1984), The Fairy Rebel (1985), Return of the Indian (1986, Indian Paintbrush Award Wyoming 1989), Secret of the Indian (1989, Great Stone Face Children's Book Award Vermont 1991), The Magic Hare (1991), The Mystery of the Cupboard (1993, West Virginia Children's Book Award, 1995), Harry the Poisonous Centipede (1996, Smarties Silver Medal 1997, Nevada Children's Choice Award 2001), Angela and Diabola (1997), The Key to the Indian (1998), Moses in Egypt (1998), Alice-by-Accident (2000), Harry the Poisonous Centipede's Big Adventure (2000), The Dungeon (2002), Stealing Stacey (2004), Tiger, Tiger (2004), Harry the Poisonous Centipede Goes to Sea (2005), Bad Cat, Good Cat (2011), Uprooted – A Canadian War Story (2014); *History* Letters to My Israeli Sons (1979), Torn Country: An Oral History of Israel's War of Independence (1982); *Recreations* theatre, emailing and web-surfing, gardening, talking; *Clubs* The 55 Club (ITN ALumni); *Style*— Ms Lynne Reid Banks; ✉ c/o James Wills, Watson Little Ltd, Suite 315, Screenworks, 22 Highbury Grove, N5 2ER (website www.lynnereidbanks.com)

REID OF CARDOWAN, Baron (Life Peer UK 2010), of Cardowan Stepps in Lanarkshire; Rt Hon Dr John Reid; PC (1998); s of late Thomas Reid, and late Mary, *née* Murray; *b* 8 May 1947, Bellshill, N Lanarkshire; *Educ* St Patrick HS Coatbridge, Univ of Stirling (BA, PhD); *m* 1, Cathie (d 1998); 2 s (Kevin, Mark); m 2, 2002, Carine Adler; *Career* res Lab Pty in Scot 1979–83, advsr to Rt Hon Neil Kinnock MP 1983–85, Scot organiser Trade Unionists for Labour 1986–87; MP (Lab): Motherwell N 1987–97, Hamilton N and Bellshill 1997–2005, Airdrie and Shotts 2005–10; oppn front bench dep spokesman on children 1988–89, oppn front bench spokesman on Armed Forces 1990–97, min of state (armed forces) MOD 1997–98, min for tport 1998–99, sec of state for Scotland 1999–2001, sec of state for NI 2001–02, min without portfolio and chm Lab Pty 2002–03, ldr House of Commons and pres Cncl 2003, sec of state for health 2003–05, sec of state for defence 2005–06, sec of state Home Office 2006–07; memb Int Relations Ctee House of Lords 2016–; memb Lab Pty NEC 2001–03; chm Inst for Security and Resilience Studies and hon prof UCL 2008–, sr advsr Chertoff Gp; chm Celtic FC 2007–11; fell Armed Forces Parly Scheme; *Publications* Cyber Doctrine: Towards a Framework for Learning Resilience (jtly, 2011); *Recreations* crosswords, watching football, reading history; *Style*— The Rt Hon the Lord Reid of Cardowan; ☎ 020 7219 3000, e-mail reidja@parliament.uk; c/o Mary McKenna (☎ 07721 399181, e-mail mckennama@parliament.uk)

REID SCOTT, David Alexander Carroll; s of Maj Alexander Reid Scott, MC (d 1960), and Ann, *née* Mitchell (d 1953); *b* 5 June 1947; *Educ* Eton, Lincoln Coll Oxford (MA); *m* 1, 23 April 1972, Anne (d 1988), da of Phillipe Clouet des Pesruches (d 1977); 3 da (Iona b 1975, Camilla b 1976, Serena b 1979); m 2, 7 July 1990 (m dis 1997), Elizabeth, da of John Latshaw; m 3, 25 Sept 1997, Clare, da of Maj Ivan Straker; 1 s (Nico b 2001); *Career* 1 vice-pres White Weld & Co 1969–77, seconded sr advsr Saudi Arabian Monetary Agency 1978–83, md Merrill Lynch & Co 1983–84, md DLJ Phoenix Securities Ltd 1984–98, vice-chm Donaldson Lufkin & Jenrette 1998–2000, vice-chm CSFB 2000–01, chm Hawkpoint Ptnrs 2001–09, memb Advsy Div Stonehage Ptnrs 2010–14; chm Jack and Jill Children's Fndn; fell Eton Coll; *Recreations* Irish country life, field sports, arts, antiques; *Clubs* Turf, Kildare St, Whites; *Style*— David A C Reid Scott, Esq; ✉ Ballynure, Grange Con, Co Wicklow, W91 A2K3 Ireland (☎ 00 353 45 403162, e-mail david@reidscott.co.uk)

R

REID-ENTWISTLE, Dr Ian; s of John Morton Entwistle, and Mary, *née* Reid; *b* 29 September 1931; *Educ* Rivington and Blackrod Sch, Univ of Liverpool Med Sch (MB ChB, FRCGP, FFOM (I), FFOM, DFFP, Cert GAM); *m* 15 May 1969, Anthea Margaret (d 1979), da of Kenneth Evans, of West Kirby, Wirral; 2 s (John b 1972, Alexander b 1973); *Career* Surgn Lt HMS Eaglet RNR 1962–65; specialist (EU accredited) in occupational med RCP; princ med offr RMS Queen Mary, Queen Elizabeth and Queen Elizabeth II 1961–96; casualty offr David Lewis Northern Hosp Liverpool 1957, house physician to prof of child health Royal Liverpool Children's Hosp 1957, princ in private and NHS practice 1958–2001, med supt Cunard plc 1966–96, med conslt Br Eagle Int Airlines 1966–68, sr gp med conslt United Gas Industries 1971–80, conslt in occupational med to Nuffield Hosps 1993–95, med dir Berkeley St Travel Clinic 1996–2002, conslt occupational physician Previa UK Ltd 1996–2003, National Medical 1998–2003, BMI 1998–2007, med examiner Linpac Plastics Ltd 1998–2007; sr med conslt until 2001: BHS plc, Mothercare; ptnr Lawwise Medico-legal Consultants; pt/t med conslt: American Colloid Co 1989–95, Bass Taverns 1966–95, Spillers Foods Ltd 1966–97; pt/t authorised assessor and examiner: Civil Aviation Authy 1966–2007, Maritime and Coastguard Agency 1966–2007; examiner to Med Servs DWP 1995–2004; accredited specialist in occupational medicine; appointed selected medical practitioner in compliance with Home Office police pension regulations 2003–; conslt Pre-Retirement Assoc; chm Brewing Industry Med Advsrs 1987–97; treas and sec Merseyside and N Wales RCGP 1973–80 (bd memb 1963–89), jt treas and sec Soc of Occupational Med (Merseyside) 1961–67, memb Cncl Birkenhead Med Soc 1995– (pres 1998–99); memb: Aerospace Physiology and Med Working Pty Cncl of Europe 1974–, NASA 1969–; med advsr West Kirby Swimming Club for Disabled; underwriting memb Lloyd's 1978–2001; memb Soc of Occupational Med 1963, FRSM 1971, FRAeS, assoc fell Aerospace Med Assoc USA 1973, fndr memb RCP Faculty of Occupational Med 1978 (fell 1995), fndr memb Faculty of Occupational Medicine Royal Coll of Physicians of Ireland 1980 (fell 1986), FRCGP 1980 (MRCGP 1962), FCIM 1988, FRSA 2012; *Books* Exacta Mecanix (5 edn 1988), Exacta Paediatrica (3 edn 2003), Exacta Medica (4 edn 2003); *Recreations* motor racing, horticulture, horology, photography, railway modelling; *Clubs* Cheshire Pitt, Manchester Naval Offrs Assoc; *Style*— Dr Ian Reid-Entwistle; ✉ Knollwood, 42 Well Lane, Gayton, Wirral CH60 8NG (☎ 0151 342 2332, mobile 07795 096270); consultation suite: 42 Well Lane, Gayton, Wirral CH60 8NG (☎ 07050 261 980, e-mail entwistle@gmx.com)

REIDY, Dr John Francis; s of Frederick Cyril Reidy (d 1957), and Marie Isobel, *née* Smith (d 2002); *b* 25 August 1944; *Educ* Stonyhurst, St George's Hosp Med Sch and King's Coll London (MB BS, MRCS); *m* 25 Nov 1978, Dianne Patricia, da of Gerald Eugene Murphy, of Launceston, Tasmania; 1 s (Thomas Edward b 19 Nov 1980), 1 da (Laura Eugenie b 1 June 1982); *Career* conslt radiologist Guy's and St Thomas' Hosp 1980–2013, hon conslt radiologist Gt Ormond St Children's Hosp 1997–2007; Liveryman Worshipful Soc of Apothecaries; fell Cardiovascular and Interventional Soc of Europe, FRCR 1975, FRCP 1988 (MRCP 1970); *Books* numerous pubns on cardiovascular and interventional radiology; *Recreations* travel, gardening; *Clubs* MCC; *Style*— Dr John Reidy; ✉ 19 Cumberland Street, London SW1V 4LS (☎ 020 7834 3021, mobile 07974 694904, e-mail jeidy@doctors.net.uk)

REIF, Prof Stefan Clive; s of Peter Reif (d 1989), and Annie, *née* Rapstoff (d 2002); *b* 21 January 1944; *Educ* Boroughmuir Sch Edinburgh, Univ of London (BA, William Lincoln Shelley studentship, PhD), Univ of Cambridge (MA, LittD); *m* 1967, Shulamit (d 2010), da of Edmund (d 1995) and Ella Stekel (d 1992); 1 da (Tanya b 25 Dec 1968), 1 s (Aryeh b 30 Jan 1970); *Career* lectr in Hebrew and Semitic languages Univ of Glasgow 1968–72, asst prof of Hebrew language and literature Dropsie Coll Philadelphia 1972–73; Univ of Cambridge: dir Genizah Res Unit 1973–2006, head Oriental Div Univ Library 1983–2006, prof of medieval Hebrew studies 1998–2006, fell St John's Coll 1998–; chair Genizah Research Univ of Haifa 2013–; visiting prof: Hebrew Univ of Jerusalem 1989 and 1996–97, Univ of Pennsylvania 2001; memb Int Advsy Panel Int Soc for the Study of Deuterocanonical and Cognate Literature; memb: Br Assoc for Jewish Studies (pres 1992), Jewish Historical Soc of England (pres 1991–92), Cambridge Theological Soc (pres 2002–04); hon PhD Haifa Univ 2014; hon fell Mekize Nirdamim Soc Jerusalem; FRAS 1980; *Books* Shabbethai Sofer and his Prayer-Book (1979), Interpreting the Hebrew Bible (1982), Published Material from the Cambridge Genizah Collections (1988), Genizah Research After Ninety Years (1992), Judaism and Hebrew Prayer (1993), Hebrew Manuscripts at Cambridge University Library (1997), A Jewish Archive from Old Cairo (2000), Why Medieval Hebrew Studies? (2001), The Cambridge Genizah Collections: Their Contents and Significance (2002), Problems with Prayers (2006), Charles Taylor and the Genizah Collection (2009), Ha-Tefillah Ha-Yehudit (2010), The History and Religious Heritage of Old Cairo (2013), Death in Jewish Life (2014), Religious Identity Markers (2015), Ancient Jewish Prayers and Emotions (2015), Jewish Prayer Texts from the Cairo Genizah (2016); *Recreations* opera, cricket, football; *Style*— Prof Stefan Reif; ✉ St John's College, St John's Street, Cambridge CB2 1TP (☎ 01223 766370, fax 01223 333160, e-mail scr3@cam.ac.uk)

REILLY, Mary Margaret; da of John Patrick Reilly (d 1987), and Helena; *b* 22 May 1953; *Educ* Notre Dame, UCL (BA); *m* 17 March 1979, Mark Richard Charles Corby, s of Peter John Siddons Corby; 1 da (b 1981), 1 s (b 1986); *Career* ptnr Deloitte & Touche (now Deloitte LLP) 1987–2013; chm: London Devpt Agency 2004–08, London regnl cncl CBI 2004–06; non-exec dir: Crown Agents 2013–, Travelzoo Inc 2013–, Department of Transport 2013–, Woodford Investment Mgmnt LLP 2014–, Ferrexpo plc 2015–; tstee: Invictus Games Fndn, Inst of Imagination; fell UCL 2010; FCA 1989 (ACA 1978), FRSA 1989; *Recreations* country pursuits, opera, theatre; *Clubs* Reform; *Style*— Ms Mary Reilly; ✉ e-mail maryreilly38@gmail.com

REILLY, (David) Nicholas (Nick); CBE; s of John Reilly (d 1981), of Anglesey, and Mona, *née* Glynne Jones; *b* 17 December 1949; *Educ* Harrow, St Catharine's Coll Cambridge (MA); *m* Susan, *née* Haig; 2 da (Natasha b 1978, Jessica b 1981), 1 s (George b 1979); *Career* investment analyst 1971–74; General Motors: joined 1974, finance dir Moto Diesel Mexicana Mexico 1980–83, supply dir Vauxhall Motors 1984–87, vice-pres IBC 1987–90, mfrg dir Vauxhall Ellesmere Port 1990–94, vice-pres Quality General Motors Europe 1994–96, chm and md Vauxhall Motors 1996–2002, chm IBC Vehicles 1996–2002, memb Bd Saab GB 1996–2002, vice-pres General Motors Corp 1997–2006, gp vice-pres General Motors Corp 2006–, pres Asia Pacific ops General Motors 2006–, chm GM Daewoo 2006– (pres and ceo 2001–06), pres GM Europe 2009–; chm: Trg Standards Cncl 1997–2001, CBI Econ Affairs Ctee 1999–2001, Chester, Ellesmere, Wirral TEC (CEWTEC) 1990–94, Oundle Sch Fndn 1997–2001, Adult Learning Inspectorate (ALI) 2000–02; memb Cmmn for Integrated Tport 1998–2001; FIMI 1990 (vice-pres 1996); *Publications* Passion (Korean language, 2007); *Recreations* tennis, swimming, sailing, golf, skiing, watching rugby and other sports, music, opera, theatre; *Clubs* RAC, Oundle Rugby (founding memb), Luton Rugby, Leicester Rugby; *Style*— Nick Reilly, Esq, CBE

REINTON, Sigurd E; CBE (2008); s of Dr Lars Reinton (d 1987), and Ingrid, *née* Evang (d 1984); *b* 9 November 1941; *Educ* Univ of Oslo, Univ of Lund (MBA); *m* 19 Nov 1966, Arlette, da of Roger Dufresne; 2 da (Sandra b 27 Oct 1967, Karine 15 May 1971); *Career* Nat Serv 1960–61; co-fndr Audio Nike Lund 1964–66, account planner then account supr Young & Rubicam Stockholm/Copenhagen 1966–68; McKinsey & Co London: joined 1968, ptnr 1976–81, dir 1981–88; chm Express Aviation Services London 1988–91; dir: Aubin Holdings 1988–98, Freewheel Film Finance Ltd 2000–03, NATS Holdings Ltd 2007–13, Monitor 2012–16, NHS Improvement 2016–; chm Mayday Healthcare NHS Tst 1997–99, chm London Ambulance Service NHS Tst 1999–2009; memb Nat Cncl NHS Confedn 1998–2007; Ambulance Servs Assoc: memb Nat Cncl 2001–08, dir 2005–08; memb Advsy Bd The Foundation 2005–10, memb Bd Ambulance Service Network 2008–09; author of various articles on corp strategy (FT, McKinsey Quarterly); *Publications* articles on corp strategy in the FT and McKinsey Quarterly; *Recreations* political and economic history, theatre, flying (PPL/IR); *Clubs* RAC; *Style*— Mr Sigurd E Reinton, CBE; ✉ 8 Wickham Way, Beckenham, Kent BR3 3AA (☎ 020 8663 0221)

REISS, David; *Career* fndr Reiss 1971–; *Style*— David Reiss, Esq; ✉ Reiss, Reiss Building, 12 Picton Place, London W1N 1BA

REITER, Nick; *Educ* Lycee Francais de Londres, LSE; *m* ; 2 c; *Career* head of policy Highland Cncl 1996–98, chief exec Shetland Islands Cncl 1998–99, dir Deer Cmmn for Scotland 1999–2006, chief exec Crofters Cmmn 2006–; *Style*— Nick Reiter, Esq; ✉ Crofting Commission, Great Glen House, Leachkin Road, Inverness IV3 8NW

REITH, Gen Sir John George; KCB (2003, CB 2000), CBE (1991, OBE 1989); s of John Archibald Frederick Reith, and Jean Hope, *née* Cameron; *Educ* Eliots Green Sch, RMA Sandhurst, Army Staff Coll; *Career* MA to GOC Northern Ireland 1984–86 (mentioned in despatches 1985, 1986); CO 1 Bn Parachute Regt 1986–88, COS 1 Armed Div Germany 1988–90, COS 1 (UK) Div Gulf 1990–91, cmd 4 Armed Bde Germany 1992–93, cmd UN Sector SW Bosnia 1994, dir Int Organisations MOD 1994–95, dir Mil Ops MOD 1995–97, cmd Ace Mobile Force (Land) NATO 1997–99, cmd Albania Force NATO 1999, Asst Chief of Defence Staff (Policy) MOD 2000–01, Chief of Jt Ops 2001–04, DSACEUR NATO 2004–07, ret 2008; NATO lead sr mentor 2008–14; govr Millfield Sch (chair of govrs 2010–); GSM 1962 (with NI Bar 1971), Queen's Jubilee Medal 1977, Gulf Medal with Rosette (combat zone) 1991, Liberation Medal (Class 2, Kuwait) 1991, Victory Medal 1991 (Saudi Arabia), Queen's Commendation for Valuable Service 1994, UNPROFOR Medal 1994, Kosovo Medal 1999, Queen's Golden Jubilee Medal 2002; Freeman City of London; Cross of Merit (Class 2, Czech Republic) 1999, Order of the Golden Eagle (Albania) 1999; *Recreations* walking, gardening, cooking; *Clubs* Army and Navy; *Style*— Gen Sir John Reith, KCB, CBE

REITH, Dr William (Bill); s of Andrew Christie Millar Reith, of North Berwick, and Catherine Mathieson, *née* Wishart; *b* 17 August 1950; *Educ* North Berwick HS, Univ of Edinburgh (BSc, MB ChB, Judo blue); *m* Gillian (d 2009), da of John Brown; 2 da (Jane Susan b 27 March 1980, Sally Fiona b 7 May 1982); *Partner* Kari Millar; *Career* trainee Aberdeen Vocational Trg Scheme for General Practice 1975–78, princ in general practice Westburn Medical Gp Foresterhill Health Centre Aberdeen 1978–; regnl advsr in general practice Grampian Health Bd 1986–96 (assoc advsr 1983–86), special advsr in primary care Scottish Cncl for Postgrad Med and Dental Educn 1997–98; RCGP: chm NE Scotland Faculty Bd 1986–89, memb UK Cncl 1990–2003, chm UK Educn Network 1993–94, hon sec UK Cncl 1994–99, chm Scottish Cncl 2000–03, chm Postgrad Training Ctee 2005–11, chm Heritage Ctee 2011–; memb: Jt Ctee on Postgrad Trg for General Practice 1992–99, Clinical Res and Audit Gp Health Dept Scottish Office 1993–98, Scottish Acad of Med Royal Colls and Faculties 2000–07, Advsy Panel NHS Scotland Review of Mgmnt 2002–03; hon sr lectr Dept of General Practice Univ of Aberdeen 1993–98 (hon clinical lectr 1983–93); FRCGP 1991 (MRCGP 1978), FRCPEd 1994, FRSA 1998; *Recreations* food and wine, hill walking; *Style*— Dr Bill Reith; ✉ 54 Gray Street, Aberdeen AB10 6JE (☎ 01224 326380, mobile 07710 318485, e-mail bill.reith@btinternet.com)

RELPH, Simon George Michael; CBE (2004); s of Michael George Leighton Relph (d 2004), the film writer, director and producer, and Doris, *née* Ringwood (d 1978); *b* 13 April 1940, London; *Educ* Bryanston, King's Coll Cambridge (MA); *m* 14 Dec 1963, Amanda Jane, da of Col Anthony Grinling, MC (d 1981), of Dyrham Park, Wilts; 1 s (Alexander James b 16 June 1967), 1 da (Arabella Kate b 17 Sept 1975); *Career* film producer; asst dir feature films 1961–73, prodn admin Nat Theatre 1974–78, prodn supervisor Yanks 1978, exec prodr Reds 1979–80, prodr and co-prodr 1981–85 (The Return of the Soldier, Privates on Parade, The Ploughman's Lunch, Secret Places, Wetherby, Comrades), chief exec Br Screen Finance Ltd 1986–90, exec prodr Enchanted April 1991, co-prodr Damage 1992; prodr: Secret Rapture 1992, Camilla 1993, Look me in the Eye 1994, Blue Juice 1994, Slab Boys 1996, Land Girls 1997; exec prodr: Hideous Kinky 1998–99, Bugs (Imax 3D film); chm Children's Film and TV Fndn 1999–2005, chm BAFTA 2000–02, dir Bristol Old Vic 2000–06, dir South West Screen 2001–08; chm Screenwriters Festival 2006–08; non-exec dir: Arts Alliance Media 2006–16, Ritzy Cinema, Exeter Picturehouse 2006–12; memb Cncl RCA 1989–99, govr BFI 1991–97, govr Nat Film and TV Sch 2002–14; Hon DLitt Bath Spa Univ 2010; Hon FRCA; Chevalier de l'Ordre des Arts et des Lettres (France); *Publications* The View from Downing Street (with Jane Headland, 1991), The Relph Report (2002); *Recreations* golf, photography, fishing; *Style*— Simon Relph, Esq, CBE

REMFRY, David Rupert; MBE (2001) RA (2006); s of Geoffrey Rupert Remfry, of Worthing, W Sussex, and Barbara, *née* Ede; *b* 30 July 1942; *Educ* Hull Coll of Art; *Children* 3 s (Jacob Rupert b 1967, Samuel b 1968, Gideon Jethro b 1970), 1 step s (Joe b 1966); *Career* artist; Hugh Casson Drawing Prize Royal Academy of Arts Summer Exhibition 2010; hon doctorate Univ of Lincoln 2007; RWS 1987, RA 2006; *Solo Exhibitions* incl: Ferens Gallery Hull 1975 and 2005, Folkestone Art Gallery 1976, Middlesbrough Art Gallery 1981, Nat Portrait Gallery 1992, Boca Raton Museum of Art 1999 and 2002, Neuhoff Gallery NY 1999, 2001 and 2004, MoMA PSI 2001–02, V&A London 2003, Butler Inst of American Art OH 2004, Fitzwilliam Museum Cambridge 2005; *Work in Collections* Boca Raton Museum of Art, Royal Collection, Nat Portrait Gallery, V&A Museum, Middlesbrough Art Gallery, Swathmore Coll Pa, Museo Rayo Columbia, Minnesota Museum of American Art, Butler Inst of Art OH USA, Br Museum London, Fitzwilliam Museum Cambridge, Orlando Museum of Art FL, New Orleans Museum of Art USA, Bass Museum of Art Miami USA, Contemporary Art Soc London; *Books* David Remfry Drawings for Stella McCartney (2003), David Remfry: Dancers (2006), We Think the World of You: People and Dogs DrawnTogether (2015); *Recreations* opera and music generally, theatre, reading, dancing; *Clubs* Chelsea, Groucho, Soho House NY, Arts; *Style*— David Remfry, Esq, MBE, RA; ✉ c/o Royal Academy of Art, Piccadilly, London W1J 0BD (website www.davidremfry.com)

REMINGTON, Stephen; s of Douglas Gordon Remington (d 1983), and Marjorie, *née* Steel (d 1983); *b* 19 March 1947; *Educ* Wellington, Trinity Coll Dublin (BA); *Career* theatre mangr Nottingham Playhouse 1971–72, drama offr Eastern Arts Association 1972–74, dir The Playhouse Harlow 1974–79, chief exec Sadler's Wells London 1979–94 (joined as dir), chief exec Action for Blind People 1994–; chair Vision 2020 UK 2002–08; Princ/Dir of the Year UK Charity Awards 2000; Liveryman Worshipful Co of Spectacle Makers 2007; Chevalier de l'Ordre des Arts et des Lettres (France) 1991; *Recreations* gym, walking; *Clubs* Garrick; *Style*— Stephen Remington; ✉ Action for Blind People, 14–16 Verney Road, London SE16 3DZ (☎ 020 7635 4800, fax 020 7635 4900, e-mail stephen.remington@actionforblindpeople.org.uk)

REMNANT, Hon Philip John; CBE (2011); s and h of 3 Baron Remnant, CVO; *b* 20 December 1954; *Educ* Eton, New Coll Oxford (MA); *m* 1977, Caroline, da of Capt Godfrey Cavendish; 1 s (Edward b 1981), 2 da (Eleanor b 1983, Sophie b 1986); *Career* Peat Marwick Mitchell and Co 1976–82, Kleinwort Benson Limited 1982–90 (dir 1988–90); Barclays de Zoete Wedd Ltd: dir 1990, md corp fin 1992, jt head UK corp fin 1993–94, head UK corp fin 1994–95, dep chief exec corp fin 1995–97, co-head M&A (advsy) 1997; dep head UK investment banking Credit Suisse First Boston 1998–2001, DG The Takeover Panel 2001–03 and 2010, vice-chm and head UK investment banking Credit Suisse First Boston

2003–05, sr advsr Credit Suisse 2006–13; chm Shareholder Exec 2007–12, dir Northern Rock 2008–10, dir UK Financial Investments 2009–, chm City of London Investment Tst 2011–, sr ind dir Prudential plc 2013–, dir Severn Trent plc 2014–, chm M&G Gp 2016–; dep chm Takeover Panel 2012–; Alderman Ward of Bassishaw 2010–13; hon bencher Inner Temple 2014–; FCA, MSI; *Style*— The Hon Philip Remnant, CBE; ✉ Prudential plc, Laurence Pountney Hill, London EC4R 0HH

RENDEL, Christopher; s of Peter Leland Fitzgerald Rendel, of Hourne Farm, Crowborough, E Sussex, and Mona Catherine, *née* Milligan, of Hammersmith, London; *b* 1 February 1955; *Educ* Bryanston, Univ of Bristol; *m* Patricia Mary; 2 s (George Oliver b 1983, Charles William b 1988); *Career* advtg exec; account mangr Mathers & Bensons 1974–80, account dir Abbott Mead Vickers 1981–87, dir FCO 1987–90, gp dir Ogilvy & Mather 1990–95, md Foote Cone & Belding 1995–98, Windmill Partnership 1999–; dir Ambache Chamber Orch 1994–; MIPA; *Recreations* music, antiques, classic cars, tennis and (watching) football; *Style*— Christopher Rendel, Esq

RENDER, Phillip Stanley; s of Stanley Render, of Bransholme, Hull, and Bessie, *née* Bestwick; *b* 15 January 1944; *Educ* Malet Lambet HS Hull; *m* 21 Oct 1967, Patricia Mary, da of Alfred Bernard Rooms, of Hull; 2 s (Adrian b 1973, Andrew b 1978), 1 da (Suzanne b 1982); *Career* chartered surveyor in sole practice 1982–2016, dir Beverley Building Society 1986–2013; surveyor to Tstees Beverley Consolidated Charity 1973–2006; memb Exec Ctee E Yorks Branch Salmon and Trout Assoc; FRICS 1968; *Recreations* salmon and trout fishing, badminton; *Clubs* S Hunsley Fly Fishing; *Style*— Phillip Render, Esq; ✉ Virginia House, 245 Northgate, Cottingham, North Humberside (☎ 01482 848327)

RENFREW OF KAIMSTHORN, Baron (Life Peer UK 1991), of Hurlet in the District of Renfrew; (Andrew) Colin Renfrew; s of Archibald Renfrew (d 1978), of Giffnock, Glasgow, and Helena Douglas, *née* Savage (d 1994); *b* 25 July 1937; *Educ* St Albans Sch, St John's Coll Cambridge (BA, PhD, ScD); *m* 21 April 1965, Jane Margaret, da of Ven Walter Frederick Ewbank, Archdeacon Emeritus and Canon Emeritus of Carlisle Cathedral; 1 da (Hon Helena (Hon Mrs Renfrew-Knight) b 23 Feb 1968), 2 s (Hon Alban b 24 June 1970, Hon Magnus b 5 Nov 1975); *Career* Nat Serv Flying Offr (Signals) RAF 1956–58; reader in prehistory and archaeology Univ of Sheffield 1965–72 (formerly lectr and sr lectr), res fell St John's Coll Cambridge 1965–68, Bulgarian Govt scholarship 1966, visiting lectr UCLA 1967, prof of archaeology and head of dept Univ of Southampton 1972–81, Disney prof of archaeology Univ of Cambridge 1981–2004 (head of dept 1981–92), dir McDonald Inst for Archaeological Res 1992–2004 (sr fell 2004–); fell St John's Coll Cambridge 1981–86, master Jesus Coll Cambridge 1986–97 (fell 1986–); memb: Royal Cmmn for Historic Monuments of England 1977–87, Ancient Monuments Advsy Bd 1983–2002, Historic Bldgs and Monuments Cmmn 1984–86 (chm Sci Panel 1983–89); chm Nat Curriculum Art Working Gp 1990–91; tstee Br Museum 1990–2000; European Science Fndn Latsis Prize 2003, Balzan Prize 2004; Freeman City of London, Hon Citizen Deme of Sitagroi (Greece) 2000; Hon DLitt: Univ of Sheffield 1987, Univ of Southampton 1995, Univ of Liverpool 2004, Univ of Edinburgh 2004, Univ of St Andrews 2006, Univ of Kent at Canterbury 2007, Univ of London 2008; Dr (hc) Athens Univ 1991; hon prof Univ of Science and Technol Beijing 2005; hon fell: Jesus Coll Cambridge 1997, St John's Coll Cambridge 2005; FSA 1968, FSA Scot 1970, FBA 1980, Hon FRSE 2001; *Books* The Emergence of Civilisation (1972), The Explanation of Culture Change: Models in Prehistory (ed, 1973), British Prehistory, a New Outline (ed, 1977), Problems in European Prehistory (1979), Approaches to Social Archaeology (1984), The Archaeology of Cult: The Sanctuary at Phylakopi (1985), Archaeology and Language: The Puzzle of Indo-European Origins (1987), The Cycladic Spirit (1991), Loot Legitimacy and Ownership: the Ethical Crisis in Archaeology (2000), Figuring It Out (2003), Prehistory: The Making of the Human Mind (2007); *Recreations* modern art, travel; *Clubs* Athenaeum, Oxford and Cambridge; *Style*— Lord Renfrew of Kaimsthorn, FBA, FSA; ✉ McDonald Institute for Archaeological Research, Downing Street, Cambridge CB2 3ER (☎ 01223 333521); University of Cambridge, Department of Archaeology, Downing Street, Cambridge CB2 3DZ (☎ 01223 333521, fax 01223 333506)

RENNARD, Baron (Life Peer UK 1999), of Wavertree in the County of Merseyside; Christopher John Rennard; MBE; s of late Cecil Rennard, and Jean Rennard; *b* 8 July 1960, Liverpool; *Educ* Liverpool Blue Coat Sch, Univ of Liverpool (BA); *m* 1989, Ann, *née* McTegart; *Career* E Midlands regnl agent Lib Pty 1984–88 (election agent Mossley Hill Liverpool 1982–84), election co-ordinator Social and Lib Dems 1988–89, dir of campaigns and elections Lib Dems 1989–2003, chief exec Lib Dems 2003–09, dir of communications Br Healthcare Trades Assoc; *Style*— The Rt Hon the Lord Rennard, MBE; ✉ House of Lords, London SW1A 0PW (☎ 020 7219 6717)

RENNERT, Jonathan; s of Sidney Rennert, of London, and Patricia, *née* Clack; *b* 17 March 1952; *Educ* St Paul's, Royal Coll of Music (fndn scholar), St John's Coll Cambridge (organ scholar, MA); *m* 10 April 1992, Sheralyn, *née* Ivil; 1 da (Imogen b 7 Jan 1996); *Career* organ recitalist, conductor and writer; dir of music: St Jude's Church London SW5 1975–76, St Matthew's Ottawa 1976–78, St Michael's Cornhill City of London 1979–, St Mary-at-Hill City of London 1996–2008, musical dir St Cecilia Chorus 2009–; conductor: Cambridge Opera 1972–74, St Michael's Singers 1979–, The Elizabethan Singers 1983–88, St Mary-at-Hill Baroque Chamber Orch & Soloists 1996–2008; musical dir London Motet and Madrigal Club 1994–, master of choristers St Mary's Reigate Boys' Choir 1997–2000; many concert and recital tours on four continents; CD and LP recordings, radio and TV broadcasts as conductor, solo organist, organ accompanist, harpsichord continuo player; musician-in-residence Grace Cathedral San Francisco 1982; fndr and dir Cornhill Festival of Br Music; moderating and trg examiner Assoc Bd of the Royal Schs of Music, examiner Royal Coll of Organists, visiting examiner Univ of Chichester; course dir and past chm Central London District Ctee Royal Sch of Church Music; hon sec to the tstees Sir George Thalben-Ball Meml Tst, tstee Organists Charitable Tst; past pres The Organ Club, past memb Cncl Royal Coll of Organists; hon fell Royal Canadian Coll of Organists 1987; author of many articles in musical publications, and entries in The New Grove Dictionary of Music and Musicians and in Die Musik in Geschichte und Gegenwart; Master Worshipful Co of Musicians 2003–04, Warden Performers' and Composers' Section Incorporated Soc of Musicians 2002–03; ARCM 1970, LRAM 1970, FRCO 1970, Hon RSCM 2016; *Books* William Crotch 1775–1847 Composer Artist Teacher (1975), George Thalben-Ball (1979), Music, Musicians and Organs of St Michael's Cornhill (2010); *Style*— Jonathan Rennert, Esq; ✉ Station House, Station Approach West, Earlswood, Surrey RH1 6HP (☎ 07799 641699, e-mail jonathanrennert@hotmail.com)

RENNIE, Allan; *b* 5 July 1960, Stirling; *Educ* Kilsyth Acad; *Career* sub ed The Sun 1987, chief sub ed Sunday Scot 1990, asst features ed Evening News 1991, successively asst features ed, dep sports ed, features ed and asst ed Daily Record 1993, ed Sunday Mail 2000–08, currently md Media Scotland (publishers of the Daily Record and Sunday Mail); former chm: Scottish Daily Newspaper Soc, Newspaper Press Fund Glasgow; *Recreations* golf, running; *Clubs* 29; *Style*— Allan Rennie, Esq; ✉ Daily Record, One Central Quay, Glasgow G3 8DA (☎ 0141 309 3143, e-mail allan.rennie@trinitymirror.com)

RENNIE, Prof Ian George; s of Peter Bruce Rennie (d 2014), and Vera Margaret, *née* Haworth (d 2003); *b* 10 November 1952, Liverpool; *Educ* Prescot GS, Univ of Sheffield (MB ChB); *m* 1, 28 Aug 1976 (m dis 1986), Janet Mary Rennie; m 2, 19 July 1986, Sharon, da of Stanley Herbert Markland, of Waterloo, Liverpool; 1 s (James Peter b 1987), 1 da (Rachel Anne b 1988); *Career* lectr Dept of Ophthalmology Univ of Liverpool 1982–85, prof Dept of Ophthalmology and Orthoptics Univ of Sheffield 1995–2013 (sr lectr 1985–95), conslt ophthalmic surgn Royal Hallamshire Hosp 2013– (hon conslt ophthalmic surgn 1985–2013); non-exec dir Central Sheffield Univ Hosps Tst 1991–97; ed Eye 1995–2007, exec ed American Jl of Opthalmology; master Oxford Congress 2006–08; Ashton Medal 1995, Duke Elder Medal 2001, Percival J Hay Medal 2004, Owen Aves Medal 2004, Doyne Medal 2010; dip opthalmology European Cncl of Opthalmology 2003; memb RSM; FRCSEd 1981, FRCOphth 1989 (memb Cncl 1995–99, vice-pres 1999–2000, sr vice-pres 2000–03); FRCSGlas 2010; *Recreations* astronomy, flyfishing; *Style*— Prof Ian Rennie; ✉ Church Lane House, Litton, Buxton, Derbyshire SK17 8QU (☎ 01298 871586, fax 01298 872941, e-mail i.g.rennie@btinternet.com); Department of Ophthalmology, Royal Hallamshire Hospital, Sheffield (☎ 0114 271 1900)

RENNIE, Dr Janet Mary; da of Arthur Ball (d 1965), of Liverpool, and Marjorie Kennerley, *née* Jones; *b* 2 December 1954; *Educ* Belvedere Sch GPDST Liverpool, Univ of Sheffield (MB ChB, MD), Univ of London (DCH); *m* 1, 28 Aug 1976 (m dis 1986), Ian George Rennie, s of Peter Bruce Rennie; m 2, 28 Aug 1992, Ian Roscoe Watts, s of William Watts; *Career* jr hosp posts 1978–85, sr res asst Univ of Liverpool 1983–85, lectr in paediatrics Univ of Cambridge 1985–88, conslt neonatal med Rosie Maternity Hosp Cambridge 1988–95, conslt and sr lectr in neonatal med KCH London 1995–2004, conslt and sr lectr in neonatal med UCL Hosps 2004–; dir of med studies Girton Coll Cambridge 1991–95; assoc ed Archives of Disease in Childhood 1992–2001; memb: Ctee Neonatal Soc 1991–95, Ctee Br Assoc of Perinatal Medicine 1991–2001, Specialist Advsy Ctee Training Neonatal Med RCPCH 1998–2005 (chair 2001–05), Academic Bd RCPCH 1998–2001; chair NICE Clinical Guidelines in Devpt (GDG) on neonatal jaundice 2008–10; Hon MA Univ of Cambridge; memb: RSM, Neonatal Soc, Expert Witness Inst, Acad of Experts; FRCP, FRCPCH, FRCOG ad eundem 2008; *Books* Neonatal Cerebral Investigation, Neonatal Cranial Ultrasound, Textbook of Neonatology, Manual of Neonatal Intensive Care; numerous chapters in books on neonatal medicine; *Recreations* gym, piano, cooking; *Style*— Dr Janet Rennie; ✉ Elizabeth Garrett Anderson Obstetric Wing, University College London Hospitals, Neonatal Service, 2 North, 250 Euston Road, London NW1 2PQ (☎ 0845 155 5000 ext 8692 or 8094, e-mail jmr@janetrennie.com)

RENNIE, Rev Dr John Aubery; s of James Rennie (d 1987), and Ethel May, *née* Byford; *b* 19 January 1947; *Educ* KCS Wimbledon, Bart's Med Sch London; *m* 12 Aug 1972, Sheelagh Ruth, da of John Robert Winter, of White Cottage, Harmans Cross, Dorset; 3 da (Natasha Louise b 1973, Sara Rosalind b 1976, Rachel Suzannah b 1979), 1 s (Alexander John b 1982); *Career* lectr in surgery Charing Cross Hosp London, resident surgical offr St Mark's Hosp London, sr lectr and conslt King's Coll Hosp London (formerly sr registrar); fndr memb Bureau of Overseas Med Servs; ordained decon 2006, priest Salisbury Cathedral 2007, assoc priest Sherborne Abbey Benefice 2010–; memb Melbury Benefice Team W Dorset 2006–10; FRSM, FRCS; *Style*— The Rev Dr John Rennie; ✉ Rectory House, 2 Fore Street, Evershot, Dorset DT2 0JW (☎ 01935 83003); Department of Surgery, King's College Hospital, London SE5 (☎ 020 7346 3017, fax 020 7346 3438)

RENNIE, William Cowan (Willie); MSP; *b* 27 September 1967, Fife; *Educ* Paisley Coll of Technol; *m* Janet; 2 s; *Career* MP (Lib Dem) Dunfermline and West Fife 2006–10; MSP (Lib Dem): Mid Scotland and Fife 2011–16, NE Fife 2016–; *Recreations* running; *Clubs* Carnegie Harriers; *Style*— Willie Rennie, Esq, MSP; ✉ The Scottish Parliament, Edinburgh EH99 1SP

RENOU, Janet (Jan); da of Eric Jones (d 2002), and Norma, *née* Lynas; *b* 16 January 1956; *Educ* Cleveland GS for Girls, Loughborough Coll of Arts Design (BA), Leicester Poly (PGCE), Teacher Trg Agency (NPQH); *Children* 2 da (Amy Ellen b 13 Dec 1982, Sophie Elizabeth b 12 April 1988); *Career* teacher Rawlins Community Coll Loughborough 1979–89 (pastoral head years 10 and 11), post 16 co-ordinator and head of art and design Djanogly City Technol Coll Nottingham 1989–91, dir of studies rising to vice-princ Landau Forte Coll Derby 1991–2002, headteacher Skipton Girls' HS 2002–; memb SHA 1991–, tstee Craven Mechanics Inst; *Recreations* hill walking, drawing and painting, swimming, travel, theatre, reading, music; *Style*— Mrs Jan Renou; ✉ Skipton Girls' High School, Gargrave Road, Skipton, North Yorkshire BD23 1QL (☎ 01756 707600, fax 01756 701068, e-mail renouj@sghs.org.uk)

RENSHAW, Peter Bernard Appleton; s of Bernard Artoune Renshaw (d 1991), of Sale, Cheshire, and Elsie Renshaw, *née* Appleton (d 1954); *b* 23 July 1954; *Educ* Charterhouse, Selwyn Coll Cambridge; *m* 16 Oct 1982, Patricia Ann, da of Robert Vernon Caffrey, of Sale, Cheshire; 1 s (Thomas Peter b 1987); *Career* ptnr: Slater Heelis Slrs Manchester 1982–98 (articled clerk 1977–79, slr 1979–82), Addleshaw Booth & Co 1998–2002; chm Boutinot Ltd 2002–13, non-exec dir W R Swann & Co Ltd 1998–2009; NP 1988; memb Law Soc; FRSA 2007; *Recreations* walking, gardening, skiing; *Style*— Peter Renshaw, Esq; ✉ e-mail pbarenshaw@btinternet.com

RENTON, Dr Andrew; s of Michael Paul Renton, of London, and Yvonne Renee, *née* Labaton; *b* 8 February 1963; *Educ* Manchester Grammar, Univ of Nottingham (BA), Univ of Reading (PhD); *Career* fndr and artistic dir Quiet Theatre 1985–88, fndr memb Thin Men Performance Ensemble 1985–89, art critic Blitz magazine 1988–91, Br corr Flash Art magazine 1989–95, dir Cleveland (project space and imprint) London 1996–97, curator The Cranford Collection London 1999–, Slade curator Slade Sch of Fine Art London 2001–02 (lectr in theoretical studies 1997–2001), art columnist Evening Standard 2002–, dir of curating Goldsmiths Coll London 2003–; exhibitions curated: The Times London's Young Artists (Olympia London) 1991, Show Hide Show (Anderson O'Day London) 1991, Confrontaciones (Palacio di Velázquez Madrid) 1991–92, Molteplici Culture (Museo del Folklore Rome) 1992, Barcelona Abroad (Euro Visual Arts Centre Ipswich) 1992, Nothing is Hidden (London) 1992, Walter Benjamin's Briefcase (Oporto) 1993, Manifesta I (Rotterdam) 1996, Browser (Vancouver) 1997, Bankside Browser (Tate Modern) 1999, Total Object Complete with Missing Pots (Tramway Glasgow) 2001, Shumakom (Artists House Jerusalem) 2002; *Books* Technique Anglaise: current trends in British art (ed jtly, 1991); *Recreations* sleep; *Style*— Dr Andrew Renton; ✉ 5A Plympton Street, London NW8 8AB (☎ 020 7724 2988, fax 020 7724 2989, e-mail ar@ar001.co.uk)

R

RENTON OF MOUNT HARRY, Baron (Life Peer UK 1997), of Offham in the County of East Sussex; Ronald Timothy (Tim) Renton; PC (1989), DL (E Sussex 2004); yr s of Ronald Kenneth Duncan Renton, CBE (d 1980), by his 2 w Eileen, MBE, yst da of Herbert James Torr, of Morton Hall, Lincs, and gda of John Torr, MP for Liverpool 1873–80; *b* 28 May 1932; *Educ* Eton, Magdalen Coll Oxford (MA); *m* 1960, Alice Blanche Helen, da of Sir James Fergusson of Kilkerran, 8 Bt (d 1973); 2 s (Hon Alexander James Torre b 1961, Hon Daniel Charles Antony (twin) b 1965), 3 da (Hon Christian Louise b 1963, Hon (Katherine) Chelsea Renton, MBE (twin) b 1965, Hon Penelope Sally Rosita b 1970 d 2010); *Career* dir: Silvermines Ltd 1967–84, ANZ Banking Gp 1968–75; former md Tennant Trading; Parly candidate (Cons) Sheffield Park 1970, MP (Cons) Sussex Mid 1974–97, chm Cons Employment Ctee, PPS to John Biffen (as chief sec to Treasy) 1979–81, pres Cons Trade Unionists 1980–84 (vice-pres 1978–80), PPS to Sir Geoffrey Howe (as chllr and foreign sec) 1983–84, Parly under sec FCO 1984, min of state FCO 1984–87, min of state Home Office 1987–89, govt chief whip 1989–90, min for the Arts 1990–92, memb Select Ctee on Nat Heritage 1995–97, chm Sub-Ctee House of Lords Select Ctee on Europe 2002–06 (memb 1997–2001), chm House of Lords Info Ctee 2007–11; chm Br Hong Kong Parly Gp 1992–97, memb Advsy Bd Know-How Fund for Central and Eastern Europe FCO (assistance to Russia, Central and Eastern Europe) 1992–2000, vice-chm Br Cncl 1992–98; Parly conslt to Robert Fleming & Co 1992–97, chm Fleming Continental Euro Investment Trust plc 1999–2003 (dir 1992–99); fndr pres (with Mick

Jagger) Nat Music Day 1992; memb: Advsy Cncl BBC 1982–84, Governing Cncl Roedean Sch 1982–97 (pres 1998–2005), Devpt Cncl Parnham Tst 1992–2000, Criterion Theatre Tst 1992–2001, Advsy Cncl Br Conslts Bureau 1997–2002, Cncl Univ of Sussex 2000–05; pres Cncl Brighton Coll 2007–12; chm Cons Foreign and Cwlth Cncl 1983–84; tstee Mental Health Fndn 1985–89; chm Sussex Downs Conservation Bd 1997–2005, chm South Downs Jt Ctee 2005–09; *Publications* The Dangerous Edge (1994), Hostage to Fortune (1997), Chief Whip (2004); *Recreations* writing, cultivating a vineyard, opera; *Style*— The Rt Hon Lord Renton of Mount Harry, PC, DL; ✉ House of Lords, London SW1A 0PW

RENTOUL, (James) Alexander (Alex); s of Francis Rentoul, of Chiswick, London, and Sylvia Christian Rentoul; *b* 23 June 1952; *Educ* Westminster, Worcester Coll Oxford (MA); *m* 25 June 1983, Tessa Caroline Anna, da of Jeremy Stuart Latham; 3 da (Rebecca Katherine b 20 March 1990, Olivia Caroline Anna b 7 Dec 1991, Hannah Clementine Poppy b 6 March 1995); *Career* chartered accountant: KPMG Peat Marwick London 1975–79, Arthur D Little Inc London 1980–84, assoc dir corp devpt Martin Bierbaum plc 1984–85; sr planning mangr Imperial Group plc 1985, princ Fin Servs & Strategy Practice Booz Allen & Hamilton Inc London 1985–87, dir Sandler Rentoul Associates Ltd 1987–93, gp commercial dir Nurdin & Peacock plc 1993–96, sr conslt Garner International 1998, chief exec Upton & Southern Holdings plc 1998–99 (following acquisition of Garner International); md House Schools Gp 2002–; govr: Bassett House Sch, Orchard House Sch, Prospect House Sch; tstee Deborah Hutton Campaign 2008; ACA 1979; *Style*— J A Rentoul, Esq; ✉ 42 Hartington Road, London W4 3TX (☎ 020 8987 9777, fax 020 8987 9747, e-mail alex@rentoul.com); ☎ 020 8580 9626, e-mail alex.rentoul@houseschools.com

RENWICK, David; *Career* comedy screenwriter; Writers' Guild Award for Best Comedy Writer 1992, Writer's Award Broadcasting Press Guild 1997, BAFTA Dennis Potter Award 1999; *Work* with Andrew Marshall, *qv*, for LWT: End of Part One (Harlequin Award), Whoops Apocalypse (NY International Film and TV Festival Award, RTS Award 1981), Hot Metal (Emmy nomination); for BBC TV: Alexei Sayle's Stuff 1989–91 (International Emmy, BPG Award, RTS Award), If You See God, Tell Him 1993; others incl: The Burkiss Way (BBC Radio 4), The Steam Video Company (Thames), Whoops Apocalypse (film, ITC), Wilt (film, Rank/LWT); as solo writer: One Foot in the Grave (BBC 1) 1989–2000 (Br Comedy Award 1991, 1992, 1993, 1995, 1996, 1997 and 2001, RTS Awards 1992, 1993 and 1994, Br Academy Award 1992, TV and Radio Club Industries Award 1995), four episodes of Agatha Christie's Poirot (LWT) 1990–91, Angry Old Men (stage play and Radio 4) 1996, Jonathan Creek (BBC) 1997 (Br Academy Award 1997, RTS Award, Nat Television Award 1998, Broadcast Productions Award 1999); *Style*— David Renwick, Esq

RENWICK, 2 Baron (UK 1964), of Coombe, Co Surrey; Sir Harry Andrew Renwick; 3 Bt (UK 1927); s of 1 Baron Renwick, KBE (d 1973), by his 1 w, Dorothy, *née* Parkes; *b* 10 October 1935; *Educ* Eton; *m* 1, 1965 (m dis 1989), Susan, da of Capt Kenneth Lucking (decd), and Mrs M Stormonth Darling (decd); 2 s (Hon Robert b 19 Aug 1966, Hon Michael b 26 July 1968); m 2, 1989, Mrs Homayoun Mazandi, da of late Col Mahmoud Yasdanparst (Pakzad); *Heir* s, Hon Robert Renwick; *Career* dir Gen Technology Systems 1975–93; ptnr W Greenwell and Co 1963–80; pres EURIM (European Informatics Market) 2000– (chm 1993–2000); memb Cncl Nat Cncl of Educnl Technol 1994–97; memb House of Lords Select Ctee: on the Euro Communities 1988–92 and of Sub-Ctee B (energy tport and technol) 1987–92, on Sci and Technol 1992–96; vice-pres Parly IT Ctee 2006– (hon sec 1992–2000), hon sec Parly Space Ctee 1997–2000; vice-pres Br Dyslexia Assoc 1982– (chm 1977–82), chm Dyslexia Educnl Tst 1986–2002; *Clubs* White's, Turf, Carlton; *Style*— The Rt Hon Lord Renwick; ✉ 38 Cadogan Square, London SW1X 0JL (☎ 020 7584 9777, fax 020 7581 9777, e-mail renwickha@postmaster.co.uk)

RENWICK, Iain William; *b* 29 August 1958, s of Robert Coates Renwick (d 1987), and Ann Buchanan, *née* Dodds; *Educ* Univ of Glasgow; *m* 5 May 2006 (civil partnership), Christopher James O'Hare; *Career* ceo Liberty plc 2003–07; chm Crusaid; FRSA 2005; *Recreations* gardening, keep-fit, golf, tennis, diving; *Clubs* Soho House; *Style*— Iain Renwick, Esq

RENWICK OF CLIFTON, Baron (Life Peer UK 1997), of Chelsea in the Royal Borough of Kensington and Chelsea; Sir Robin William Renwick; KCMG (1989, CMG 1980); s of late Richard Renwick, of Edinburgh, and late Clarice, *née* Henderson; *b* 13 December 1937; *Educ* St Paul's, Jesus Coll Cambridge, Univ of Paris (Sorbonne); *m* Annie; 1 s (Alexander), 1 da (Marie-France); *Career* Nat Serv Army 1956–58; entered Foreign Service 1963, Dakar 1963–64, FO 1964–66, New Delhi 1966–69, private sec to Min of State FCO 1970–72, first sec Paris 1972–76, cnsllr Cabinet Office 1976–78, head Rhodesia Dept FCO 1978–80, political advsr to Lord Soames as Govr of Rhodesia 1980, visiting fellow Center for Int Affairs Harvard Univ 1980–81, head of Chancery Washington 1981–84, asst under sec of state FCO 1984–87; HM ambass: to South Africa 1987–91, to Washington 1991–95, ret; chm Fluor Ltd (UK) 1996–2011; dep chm: Robert Fleming (Holdings) Ltd 1999–2000, Fleming Family and Ptnrs 2000–15, dir Stonehage Fleming 2015–; vice-chm: Investment Banking JP Morgan (Europe) 2001–14, JP Morgan Cazenove 2005–14; dir: Richemont 1995–, British Airways 1996–2005, Fluor Corporation 1997–2008, Canal Plus 1997–99, BHP Billiton 1997–2005, SABMiller (formerly South African Breweries) 1999–2008, Gem Diamonds Ltd 2007–09, Vallar plc 2010–12, Excelsior Mining 2014–; sr advsr Appian Capital 2014–; tstee The Economist 1996–2010; Hon LLD Univ of the Witwatersrand, Hon DLitt Coll of William and Mary Williamsburg VA; hon fell Jesus Coll Cambridge 1992; FRSA; *Books* Economic Sanctions (1981), Fighting with Allies (1996), Unconventional Diplomacy (1997), A Journey with Margaret Thatcher (2013), Helen Suzman (2014), Hilary Clinton (2014), The End of Apartheid (2015); *Recreations* tennis, fly fishing; *Clubs* Hurlingham, Queen's, Brooks's, Pilgrims; *Style*— The Rt Hon Lord Renwick of Clifton, KCMG; ✉ 9 South Street, London W1K 2XA

REPIN, Vadim Victorovich; s of Victor Repin, of Novosibirsk, Russia, and Galina Karpova Repin; *b* 31 August 1971; *Educ* Novosibirsk Conservatory, Hochschule für Musik Lübeck; *Career* violinist; first prize Wieniawski Int Competition (aged eleven), winner Reine Elisabeth Concours; artistic dir Transsiberian Arts Festival 2014–; hon prof: Beijing Central Conservatory of Music 2014, Shanghai Conservatory 2015; Chevalier de l'Ordre des Arts et des Lettres 2010, Victoire D'Honneur 2010; appeared with numerous orchs incl: Concertgebouw Orch, Berlin Symphony, NHK of Japan, Kirov Orch, San Francisco Symphony Orch, RPO, Chicago Symphony Orch, Montreal Symphony Orch, Orchestre de la Suisse Romande, Detroit Symphony, Tonhalle Zürich Orch, New York Philharmonic, Los Angeles Philharmonic, Orchestre National de France; recitals incl: La Scala, Carnegie Hall, Vienna Musikverein, Suntory Hall, Tokyo; *Recordings* on Erato Disques: Shostakovich Violin Concerto Op 99 No 1 and Prokofiev Violin Concerto Op 63 No 2 (with Hallé Orch under Kent Nagano) 1995, Prokofiev Violin Sonata Op 80 No 1 and Op 94 No 2 (with pianist Boris Beresovsky) 1995, Tchaikovsky Violin Concerto and Sibelius Violin Concerto (with LSO under Emmanuel Krivine) 1996, Ravel Sonata & Medtner Sonata (with pianist Boris Beresovsky) 1997, Mozart Violin Concerti 2, 3 and 5 (with Vienna Chamber Orchestra under Yehudi Menuhin), Tutta Bravura 1999, Live at the Louvre 1999, Strauss Sonata, Stravinsky Divertimento, Bartok Rumanian Folkdances (with Boris Beresovsky) 2001; on Philips: Tchaikovsky & Miaskovsky Violin Concerti (with Mariinsky Orch under Valery Gergiev) 2003; on Deutsche Grammophon: Tanyev Piano Quintet and Trio (with Lynn Harrell on cello, Mikhail Pletnev on piano, Ilya Gringolts on violin and Nobuko Imai on viola) 2005, Beethoven: Violin Concerto op 61 (with Vienna Philharmonic Orchestra under Riccardo Muti) and Sonata No 9 'Kreutzer' (with Martha Argerich on piano) 2007, Brahms: Violin Concerto and Double Concerto (with Gewandhaus Leipzig under Riccardo Chailly and Truls Mørk on cello) 2008, Tchaikovsky and Rachmaninov: Piano Trios (with Lang Lang on piano and Mischa Maisky on cello) 2009, Violin Sonatas of Leo Janá?ek, Edvard Grieg, César Franck (with Nikolai Lugansky on piano) 2010; *DVDs* A Night of Encores (with Berlin Philharmonic Orchestra under Mariss Jansons) 2002, Bruch Violin Concerto No 1 (with Berlin Philharmonic Orchestra under Sir Simon Rattle) 2008, Vadim Repin – A Magician of Sound (documentary by Claudia Willke) 2010, Chausson Poème (with Israel Philharmonic Orchestra under Zubin Mehta) 2011; *Recreations* motoring; *Style*— Vadim Repin, Esq; ✉ c/o Eleanor Hope, Schönburgstrasse 4, A-1040 Vienna, Austria (☎ 00 43 1 585 3980, fax 00 43 1 585 398089)

REPTON, Bishop of 2007–; Rt Rev Humphrey Ivo John Southern; s of Guy Hugo Southern (d 1994), and Rosamund Antonia, *née* McAndrew; *b* 17 September 1960, London; *Educ* Harrow, ChCh Oxford (MA), Ripon Coll Cuddesdon Oxford (BA); *m* 8 June 1996, Emma Jane, *née* Lush; 2 da (Laura Caroline b 30 Dec 1997, Katharine Rachel (Kate) b 7 May 1999); *Career* ordained: deacon 1986, priest 1987; asst curate: St Margarets Rainham Kent 1986–89, Walton-on-the-Hill Liverpool 1989–92; vicar and team rector Hale with Badshot Lea Farnham Surrey 1992–99 (also ecumenical offr Guildford Dio), team rector Tisbury and Nadder Valley Wilts 1999–2007, rural dean Chalke Deanery Wilts 2000–07, chm House of Clergy Dio of Salisbury 2004–07, non-res canon and prebendary Salisbury Cathedral 2006–07; sch govr: Walton St Mary C of E Primary 1990–92, Hale Co Primary and Middle Schs 1992–99 (chm 1993–99), Farnham Heath End Comp Sch 1992–99, Nadder Valley Middle Sch 1999–2004 (chm 2000–04), Chilmark C of E Primary Sch 1999–2006, St John C of E Primary Sch 2004–07 (chm 2005–07); memb: Walton CAB Mgmnt Ctee 1989–92, Farnham Police and Community Partnership 1993–99; contrib author: Theology 2006 and 2008, Church Times 2006 and 2012, Church of England Newspaper 2008; *Recreations* conversation, cooking, horse racing, bonfires, English bull terriers, reading widely and walking gently; *Clubs* Brook's; *Style*— The Rt Rev the Bishop of Repton; ✉ Repton House, Lea, Matlock, Derbyshire DE4 5JP (☎ 01629 534 644, fax 01629 534 003, e-mail bishop@repton.free-online.co.uk)

RETALLACK, James Keith; s of Charles Keith Retallack (d 1975), of Birmingham, and Betty Margery, *née* Heaps (d 1978); *b* 8 July 1957; *Educ* Malvern, Univ of Manchester (LLB); *Career* articled clerk Lee Crowder & Co 1979–81, admitted slr 1981; Edge & Ellison: asst slr 1981–84, assoc 1984–88, ptnr 1988–, head Employment Unit 1990–, sr ptnr 1998–2000; Hammond Suddards Edge: ptnr 2000–01, head of Birmingham office 2000–01; gp resources dir Aggregate Industries plc 2001–05, legal and compliance dir Aggregate Industries Ltd 2005–11; chm Lone Star Land Ltd 2011–, chm Chase Commercial Ltd 2013–, dir Nexus Professional Network Ltd 2011–; govr Univ Coll Birmingham 2013–; *Recreations* music, reading, gardening, skiing, travel, shooting, fishing; *Style*— James Retallack, Esq; ✉ (☎ 07831 574568, e-mail jretallack@aol.com)

REUBEN, David; s of David Sassoon Reuben (d 1961), and Nancy, *née* Nissan-Jiddah; bro of Simon David Reuben, *qv*; *b* 14 September 1938; *Educ* Sir Jacob Sassoon HS Bombay, Sir John Cass Coll London; *m* 1976, Debra; 1 da (Jordana), 2 s (David, Jamie); *Career* dir Mount Star Metals until 1972, dir Metal Traders Gp 1974–77, chm Transworld Metal Group 1977–2000, jt ceo Reuben Brothers Ltd 1988–, co-fndr and tstee Reuben Brothers Fndn 2002–; Entrepreneur of the Year Variety Club Annual Property Awards 2005; *Recreations* painting, writing, golf, other sports; *Clubs* Coombe Hill Golf, Annabel's, Hurlingham, Wentworth; *Style*— David Reuben, Esq; ✉ Motcomb Estates Limited, Millbank Tower, 21–24 Millbank, London SW1P 4QP (☎ 020 7802 5000, fax 020 7802 5001)

REUBEN, Simon David; s of David Sassoon Reuben (d 1961), and Nancy, *née* Nissan-Jiddah; bro of David Reuben, *qv*; *Educ* Sir Jacob Sassoon HS Bombay, Sir John Cass Coll London; *m* Aug 1973, Joyce, *née* Nounou; 1 da (Lisa-Dana-Renee b 20 Jan 1978); *Career* md J Holdsworth & Co Ltd 1965–77, md Devereux Gp of Cos 1970–77, dir and jt princ Trans World Metals Gp 1977–2000, jt ceo Reuben Brothers Ltd 1988–, co-fndr and tstee Reuben Fndn 2002–; Entrepreneur of the Year Variety Club Annual Property Awards 2005; *Recreations* film, history, politics, avoiding cocktail parties; *Clubs* Yacht Club de Monaco, Monte Carlo Tennis, Hurlingham; *Style*— Simon Reuben, Esq; ✉ Reuben Brothers SA, 9 Place du Molard, 1204 Geneva, Switzerland (☎ 0041 22 787 5020, fax 0041 22 787 5029, e-mail rb@reubros.com or sreuben@libello.com)

REUPKE, Michael; s of Dr Willm Reupke (d 1968), and Frances Graham, *née* Kinnear (d 2005); *b* 20 November 1936; *Educ* Latymer Upper Sch, Jesus Coll Cambridge (MA), Coll of Europe Bruges (Dip Euro Studies); *m* (Helen) Elizabeth, da of Edward Restrick (d 1988); 1 s (Peter b 1965), 2 da (Alison b 1968, Rachel b 1971); *Career* Reuters 1962–89: trainee journalist 1962, journalist (Geneva, London, Conakry, Paris, Bonn) 1962–69, Euro mgmnt 1970–73, chief rep W Germany 1973–74, mangr Latin America 1975–77, ed-in-chief 1978–89, gen mangr 1989; conslt 1990–; dir: Visnews Ltd 1985–89, Compex Ltd 1992–2008, Radio Authy 1994–99 (degustateur officiel concours des grands vins de France 1997–2013); tstee Reuter Fndn 1984–89; memb Int Press Inst; FRSA; *Recreations* cooking, wine; *Clubs* Leander, RAC, Stroke Survivors; *Style*— Michael Reupke; ✉ 27A Upper High Street, Thame, Oxfordshire OX9 3EX

REVELL, Stephen Michael; s of Alfred Vincent Revell (d 2000), and Doris, *née* Peaty (d 1985); *b* 20 December 1956; *Educ* St Mary Coll Blackburn, Christ's Coll Cambridge (MA); *m* 10 Nov 1979, Anne Marie, da of Brian Higgins; *Career* ptnr Freshfields (now Freshfields Bruckhaus Deringer) 1987– (asst slr 1979–87, US managing ptnr 1998–2002, currently corp head Asia and managing ptnr Singapore); memb: Int Bar Assoc, American Bar Assoc, Law Soc; Freeman: Worshipful Co of Slrs 1988, City of London 1995; *Recreations* skiing, fell walking, travelling; *Style*— Stephen Revell, Esq; ✉ Freshfields Bruckhaus Deringer, 10 Collyer Quay #42-01, Ocean finance Centre, Singapore 049315 (☎ 020 7936 4000, fax 020 7832 7001, e-mail stephen.revell@freshfields.com)

REWSE-DAVIES, Jeremy Vyvyan; *b* 24 November 1939; *m* 1, 1961 (m dis) Teri Donn; 1 s (Jason Saul b 1968), 1 da (Jessica Lucy b 1968); m 2, 1975 (m dis), Kezia de Winne; m 3, 1983, Iga Przedrzymirska; 1 s (Alexander Henry Thomas b 1985); *Career* prodn designer BBC TV 1964–74 (jtly designed Dr Who Daleks), freelance interior and TV designer 1974–76; Office Planning Consultants: sr designer 1976–79, design dir 1979–81, md 1981–86; design dir and dep chm Business Design Group 1986–88, dir of design London Transport 1988–99; dir: 4IV Design Consultants 1999–2003, Rewse Davies Assoc 1999–2005, The Arts Club (London) Ltd 2001–04; pres Chartered Soc of Designers 1992–93; pres Partageart (Tarn et Garonne) 2007–10; FCSD 1978 (MCSD 1964), FRSA 1980; *Books* Designed for London (jtly, 1995), Modern Britain 1932–39 (jtly); *Recreations* birdwatching, drawing and trips to Africa; *Clubs* The Arts, The Authors; *Style*— Jeremy Rewse-Davies, Esq; ✉ 22 West Kensington Mansions, Beaumont Crescent, London W14 9PE (e-mail jrewsedavies@hotmail.com)

REYNARD, Dr Adrian John; s of Gordon Reynard, of W Sussex, and Daphne, *née* Rogers; *b* 23 March 1951; *Educ* Alleynes GS, Oxford Poly (HND Mech Eng, fndr pres Oxford Poly Automobile Club); *m* Gill; 4 c; *Career* project engr Br Leyland 1974–75, chief designer Hawke Racing Cars 1976–77, ceo Sabre Automotive Ltd/Reynard Racing Cars Ltd 1977–89, fndr chm and ceo Reynard Composites Ltd 1989, fndr chm and ceo Reynard Special Vehicle Projects and Reynard Aviation Ltd 1996; visiting prof of engrg and applied sci Cranfield Univ, visiting prof in motorsport design Oxford Brookes Univ 2000; Design Cncl Award 1990, Queen's Award for Export 1990 and 1996, Sir Henry Royce

Gold Medal for Excellence 1992, Castrol Inst of Motor Industry Gold Medal for contributions to the motor industry 1995, Crompton Lanchester Medal IMechE 2001, MIA Outstanding Contribution Award 2001; numerous motor racing trophies and championships; Hon DEng Oxford Brookes Univ 1994; FRSA 1991, FIMechE 1993, CRAeS 1997, FREng 1999; *Recreations* flying (private pilots licence), power boating, water skiing, scuba diving, clay pigeon shooting, model aircraft radio control flying, occasional karting; *Style—* Dr Adrian Reynard; ✉ website www.adrianreynard.com

REYNOLDS, Prof Alan James; s of Russell Hogarth Reynolds (d 1972), of Toronto, Canada, and Edith Emily, *née* Brownlow; *b* 8 September 1934; *Educ* Univ of Toronto (BASc), Univ of London (PhD); *m* 31 July 1962, Caroline Mary, da of Albert William Edwin Bury (d 1985), of Billericay, Essex; 2 s (Andrew Hogarth b 1963, James Haldane b 1967); *Career* research fell Cavendish Laboratory Univ of Cambridge 1960–62, assoc prof Dept of Civil Engrg and Applied Mechanics McGill Univ Montreal 1962–66; Brunel Univ: reader 1966–82, prof 1982–97, head Dept of Mechanical Engrg 1983–94, pro-vice-chllr 1991–96, prof emeritus 1997–; dir of research Buckinghamshire Coll 1995–99 (visiting prof 1999–2006), visiting prof London Inst 2000–04; memb CVCP Academic Audit Unit 1992–96, memb Cncl IMechE (chm Gtr London Branch) 1990–92 and 2001–05; MASCE 1963, FIMechE 1980, FRSA 1983; *Books* Thermofluid Dynamics (1970), Turbulent Flows in Engineering (1974, Russian edn 1976, Romanian edn 1980), The Finances of Engineering Companies (1992); *Style—* Prof Alan Reynolds; ✉ 30 Boileau Road, London W5 3AH (☎ 020 8248 7641); Higher Nanterrow Farm, Nanterrow Lane, Connor Downs, Hayle, Cornwall TR27 5BP (☎ 01209 715433)

REYNOLDS, Antony James (Tony); s of C V Reynolds, of Hertford, Herts, and Mildred Vera Reynolds; *b* 21 April 1936; *Educ* Westminster; *m* 14 June 1955, Grace; 2 da (Kim Laura b 1959, Briony Jane b 1963), 1 s (Kevin Antony b 1961); *Career* Procter & Gamble 1960–65, vice-pres sales and mktg Tenco Div Coca Cola Foods 1965–83, fndr own business (UB Group) 1983–95; currently chm: Boston Foods Ltd, Reynolds Management Services, Lasting Impressions Ltd; lectr on franchising; FCIM; *Recreations* water skiing, windsurfing, swimming; *Clubs* Rotary; *Style—* Tony Reynolds, Esq; ✉ Reynolds Management Services, Shardeloes House, The Thatchway, Angmering,West Sussex BN16 4HY (☎ 01903 784030, fax 01903 859237)

REYNOLDS, Prof David James; s of Leslie Reynolds (decd), and Marian, *née* Kay; *b* 17 February 1952; *Educ* Dulwich Coll, Gonville & Caius Coll Cambridge (MA, PhD); *m* 1977, Margaret Philpott Ray; 1 s; *Career* Harvard Univ: Choate fell 1973–74, Warren fell 1980–81; Univ of Cambridge: res fell Gonville & Caius Coll 1978–80 and 1981–83, asst history lectr 1984–88, lectr 1988–97, reader in int history 1997–2002, prof of int history 2002–, chair Faculty of History 2013–; writer/presenter for BBC TV: Churchill's Forgotten Years 2005, The Improbable Mr Attlee 2005, Armistice 2008, Summits (three-part series) 2008, Nixon in the Den 2010, World War Two: 1941 and the Man of Steel 2011, World War Two: 1942 and Hitler's Soft Underbelly 2012, Long Shadow (three-part series) 2014, World War Two: 1945 and the Wheelchair President 2015; writer/presenter America, Empire of Liberty (90-part history series, BBC Radio 4) 2008–09 (Voice of the Listener & Viewer Award Best New Radio Prog 2008, nomination Sony Radio Acad Award, shortlist Orwell Prize); FBA 2005; *Books* The Creation of the Anglo-American Alliance 1937–41 (1981, Bernath Prize Soc for Historians of American Foreign Relations 1982), An Ocean Apart: The Relationship between Britain and America in the 20th Century (jtly, 1988), Britannia Overruled: British policy and World Power in the 20th Century (1991), Allies at War: The Soviet, American, and British Experience 1939–45 (jt ed, 1994), The Origins of the Cold War in Europe (ed, 1994), Rich Relations: The American Occupation of Britain 1942–45 (1995, Soc for Military History Distinguished Book Award 1996), One World Divisible: A Global History since 1945 (2000), From Munich to Pearl Harbor: Roosevelt's America and the origins of the Second World War (2001), In Command of History: Churchill Fighting and Writing the Second World War (2004, Wolfson History Prize 2004), From World War to Cold War: Churchill, Roosevelt and the International History of the 1940s (2006), Summits: Six Meetings that Shaped the Twentieth Century (2007), FDR's World: War, Peace, and Legacies (jt ed, 2008), America, Empire of Liberty: A New History (2009), The Long Shadow: The Great War and the Twentieth Century (2013, Hessell-Tiltman Prize 2014); *Style—* Prof David Reynolds; ✉ Christ's College, Cambridge CB2 3BU (☎ 01223 334900)

REYNOLDS, Emma Elizabeth; MP; *Educ* Codsall HS, Wadham Coll Oxford (MA); *m* 16 April 2016, Richard Stevens; *Career* MP (Lab) Wolverhampton NE 2010–; *Style—* Ms Emma Reynolds, MP; ✉ 492A Stafford Road, Wolverhampton WV10 6AN (website www.emmareynolds.org.uk); House of Commons, London SW1A 0AA (e-mail emma.reynolds.mp@parliament.uk)

REYNOLDS, Dame Fiona Claire; DBE (2008, CBE 1998); da of Dr Jeffrey Alan Reynolds, and Margaret Mary, *née* Watson; *b* 29 March 1958; *Educ* Rugby HS for Girls, Newnham Coll Cambridge (MA, MPhil); *m* 23 May 1981, Robert William Tinsley Merrill; 3 da (Alice Kezia b 12 Nov 1990, Margaret Rose b 28 March 1992, Olivia Jane b 13 June 1995); *Career* sec Council for National Parks 1980–87; dir: Council for the Protection of Rural England 1992–98 (asst dir (policy) 1987–92), Women's Unit Cabinet Office 1998–2000; DG National Trust 2001–12, master Emmanuel Coll Cambridge 2013–; Global 500 UN Environment Prog Award 1990; *Recreations* walking, cycling, reading, classical music; *Style—* Dame Fiona Reynolds, DBE; ✉ Emmanuel College, Cambridge CB2 3AP

REYNOLDS, Prof Francis Martin Baillie; Hon QC (1993); s of Eustace Baillie Reynolds (d 1948), and Emma Margaret Hanby, *née* Holmes (d 1933); *b* 11 November 1932; *Educ* Winchester, Worcester Coll Oxford (scholar, MA, DCL); *m* 1965, Susan Claire, da of Hugh William Shillito; 2 s (Barnabas William Baillie b 1967, Martin Alexander Baillie b 1969), 1 da (Sophie Francesca b 1973); *Career* Bigelow teaching fell Univ of Chicago 1957–58, fell Worcester Coll Oxford 1960–2000 (emeritus fell 2001); called to the Bar Inner Temple 1961, hon bencher 1979; prof of law Univ of Oxford 1992–2000, emeritus prof 2001– (reader 1977–92); visiting lectr Univ of Auckland 1971 and 1977; Arthur Robinson & Hedderwicks visiting fell: Univ of Melbourne, Monash Univ 1989; Ebsworth & Ebsworth visiting prof Univ of Sydney 1993, Simpson Grierson visiting prof Univ of Auckland 1995, Koo & Partners visiting prof Univ of Hong Kong 2002, McWilliam visiting prof of commercial law Univ of Sydney 2012; visiting prof Nat Univ of Singapore 1984, 1986, 1988, 1990–92, 1994, 1996, 1997 (David Marshall visiting prof) and 2000–01, 2003, 2005, 2007 and 2009; visiting prof: UCL 1986–89, Univ of Otago 1993, Int Maritime Law Inst IMO Malta 1996–2016, Univ of Hong Kong 2008 and 2010–16; ed: Lloyd's Maritime and Commercial Law Quarterly 1983–87, The Law Quarterly Review 1987–2014; FBA 1988; *Books* Bowstead and Reynolds On Agency (co-ed 13, 14, 19 and 20 edns, ed 15, 16, 17 and 18 edns), Chitty On Contract (co-ed 24–32 edns), Benjamin's Sale of Goods (co-ed 1–9 edns), English Private Law (co-ed, 1–3 edns), Carver on Bills of Lading (with Sir Guenter Treitel, 2001, 3 edn 2011); *Recreations* music, walking, travel; *Style—* Prof Francis Reynolds, QC, FBA; ✉ 61 Charlbury Road, Oxford OX2 6UX (☎ 01865 559323, e-mail francis.reynolds@law.ox.ac.uk)

REYNOLDS, Gillian; MBE (1999); da of Charles Beresford Morton (d 1970), of Liverpool, and Ada Kelly (d 1962); *b* 15 November 1935, Liverpool; *Educ* Liverpool Inst HS for Girls, St Anne's Coll Oxford (MA), Mount Holyoke Coll; *m* 23 Sept 1958 (m dis 1983), Stanley Ambrose Reynolds, s of Ambrose Harrington Reynolds (d 1970), of Holyoke, USA; 3 s (Ambrose Kelly b 12 June 1960, Alexander Charles b 3 Jan 1970, Abel Stanley b 5 Sept 1971); *Career* TV and radio broadcaster 1964–; radio critic: The Guardian 1967–74, The Daily Telegraph 1975–; prog controller Radio City Liverpool 1974–75; Media Soc Gold Award for Distinguished Journalism 1999, Radio Acad Gold Award 2014, Arqiva Lifetime Achievement Award 2016; pres Assoc of Sr Members St Anne's Coll Oxford 1994–97 (hon fell); memb: Mount Holyoke Coll Alumnae Assoc, Cncl Soc of Authors 2000; tstee: Nat Museums and Galleries Merseyside 2001–08, Nat Media Museum 2008–; visiting fell Bournemouth Univ 2003; hon fell Liverpool John Moores Univ 2004; Hon DLitt Univ of Lancaster 2012; first fell Radio Acad 1990, FRTS; *Recreations* listening to the radio, the company of friends; *Style—* Mrs Gillian Reynolds, MBE; ✉ Flat 3, 1 Linden Gardens, London W2 4HA (☎ 020 7229 1893, e-mail avyx83@dsl.pipex.com)

REYNOLDS, Jane Caroline Margaret; JP (1991); da of Maj Thomas Reynolds, MC (d 1981), of Richmond, N Yorks, and Cynthia Myrtle Margaret, *née* Eden (later Mrs Witt, d 1982); *b* 4 March 1953; *Educ* Winchester Co HS for Girls, Brighton Poly, Lincoln Meml Clinic for Psychotherapy; *Career* student teacher St Mary's Wrestwood Educnl Tst Ltd 1970–72, offr i/c Gary Richard Homes Ltd 1972–76, matron Alison House (St John's Wood) Ltd 1976–81, dir The Westminster Soc for Mentally Handicapped Children and Adults 1983–87 (devpt offr 1981–83), hosp mangr Leavesden Hosp 1987–91, chief exec Royal Masonic Benevolent Instn 1991–2000, sec The Masonic Fndn for the Aged and the Sick 1992–2000; NHS Gen Mgmnt Training Scheme III, Cabinet Office Top Mgmnt Prog 1999; chair Continuing Healthcare Review Panel: NE London SHA 2003–06, SE London SHA 2004–06, NHS London 2008–13, NHS SE Coast 2009–10, NHS England (London Region) 2013–; memb: Registered Homes Act (1984) Tbnl Panel 1990–98, HM's Courts and Tbnls Service – Criminal Injuries Compensation (formerly Criminal Injuries Compensation Appeals Panel) 2000–, Gtr London Magistrates' Courts' Authy 2003–05, Postgrad Med Educn and Trg Bd 2003–10, Fitness to Practise Panel Gen Dental Cncl 2015–; chm Life Opportunities Tst 1989–2015 (pres 2015–), chm City of London Justice Rooms Charitable Tst 2008–, chm NHS Sussex (formerly NHS E Sussex Downs and Weald and NHS Hastings and Rother) Continuing Care Panel 2010–13, NHS E Sussex Clinical Commissioning Groups Continuing Healthcare Panel 2013–14; Freeman City of London 1993, Liveryman Worshipful Co of Glass-sellers 1994; FIMgt 1988 (MBIM 1977); *Recreations* travelling, the arts, seizing opportunities; *Style—* Miss Jane Reynolds, DMS, FCMI; ✉ 33 Carlton Mansions, Randolph Avenue, London W9 1NP

REYNOLDS, Jon; *Educ* Univ of Cambridge; *Career* co-fndr and ceo Swiftkey Ltd 2008–; *Style—* Jon Reynolds, Esq; ✉ SwiftKey Ltd, 91–95 Southwark Bridge Road, Southwark, London SE1 0AX

REYNOLDS, Jonathan Neil; MP; *Educ* Univ of Manchester, BPP Law Sch Manchester; *m* Claire; *Career* cncllr Tameside Met Borough Cncl 2007–11, MP (Lab) Stalybridge and Hyde 2010–; *Style—* Jonathan Reynolds, Esq, MP; ✉ The Constituency Office, Hyde Town Hall, Market Street, Hyde SK14 1AL; House of Commons, London SW1A 0AA

REYNOLDS, (James) Kirk; QC (1993); s of late Hon Mr Justice James Reynolds, of Helen's Bay, Co Down, and late Alexandra Mary Erskine, *née* Strain; *b* 24 March 1951; *Educ* Campbell Coll Belfast, Peterhouse Cambridge (MA); *Partner* Holger Andreas Baehr (civil partnership 2007); *Career* called to the Bar Middle Temple 1974 (bencher 2000); Hon LLD Univ of Beds 2009; Hon RICS 1997; *Books* Handbook of Rent Review (looseleaf, 1981, 58 updates to 2013), Dilapidations: the Modern Law and Practice (1994, 5 edn 2013), Essentials of Rent Review (1995), Renewal of Business Tenancies (1997, 4 edn 2012); *Style—* Kirk Reynolds, Esq, QC; ✉ Falcon Chambers, Falcon Court, London EC4Y 1AA (☎ 020 7353 2484, website www.falcon-chambers.com)

REYNOLDS, Michael Arthur; s of William Arthur Reynolds (d 1981), of Hakin, Dyfed, and Violet Elsie, *née* Giddings (d 1978); *b* 28 August 1943; *Educ* Milford Haven GS, Cardiff Coll of Art (DipAD); *m* 1 (m dis 1971), Patricia; 1 s (Joseph Michael b 1970); m 2 (m dis 1974), Judith; m 3 (m dis 1995), Jill Caroline; m 4, 22 Feb 2003, Gill Patricia; 2 s (Joseph Louis b 1987, Oliver James b 1992); *Career* creative dir KPS Ltd Nairobi 1968, copywriter J Walter Thompson 1971, gp head Benton & Bowles 1973; creative dir: ABM 1975, McCann Erickson 1979, Interlink 1981, MWK (and shareholder) 1983, Pearson Partnership 1987; film dir Good Film Co 1991–; gp creative dir Osprey Communications plc; dir and creative dir The Beeholm Partnership/Commune 2002–; writer and dir Dancing Aardvarks; MIPA; *Recreations* gardening, rare books, classic motorcars; *Clubs* Chelsea Arts; *Style—* Michael Reynolds, Esq; ✉ The Kennels, Exton Park, Cottesmore Road, Exton LE15 8AN (e-mail crazed@mikebeeholm.demon.co.uk); 14 Rue Porte Beraud, 87600, Rochechouart, France

REYNOLDS, Michael John; s of William James Reynolds (d 1981), and Audrey, *née* Turpitt; *b* 8 October 1950; *Educ* Felsted, Keele Univ, Strasbourg Univ (Droit Comparé); *Career* Allen & Overy: articled clerk 1974–76, asst slr 1976–81, seconded to EC 1978, ptnr and head EC Law Dept 1981–; visiting prof of Euro competition law Univ of Durham; chm Anti Trust Ctee Int Bar Assoc; memb Euro Ctee British Invisibles, Cncl Int Bar Assoc; *Recreations* boats, learning languages, travel; *Clubs* Travellers, Cercle Gaulois (Brussels), Warande (Brussels); *Style—* Michael Reynolds, Esq; ✉ Allen & Overy, One New Change, London EC4 (☎ 020 7330 3000, fax 020 7330 9999)

REYNOLDS, Dr Paul Joseph; s of Patrick Reynolds, and Catherine, *née* Miller; *b* 5 March 1957; *Educ* Univ of Strathclyde (BA), Univ of London (PhD, RSGS Scot Univs Medal); *m* 1984, Karen Solveig, *née* Eide; 1 s, 2 da; *Career* BT: joined 1983, various mgmnt roles 1983–89, sr mangr Int Voice Products 1989–91, dir Office of the Chm 1991–93, prog dir Info Communication and Entertainment 1993–94, gen mangr Scot 1994–97, dir Strategy 1997–98, dir networkBT 1998–99, md Networks and Info Services 1999–2000, former chief exec BT Wholesale, exec dir BT plc 2001–07, ceo and dir Telecom Corp of New Zealand Ltd 2007–; *Recreations* walking, skiing, guitar, photography; *Style—* Dr Paul Reynolds; ✉ Telecom New Zealand Limited, PO Box 1473, Christchurch, New Zealand

REYNOLDS, Roger; s of Arthur Wesley Reynolds, and Bernice Eileen Marcia, *née* Newman; *b* 25 January 1950, Romsey, Hants; *Educ* Romsey Secdy Modern; *m* 22 July 1972, Rosemary Eva; 1 da (Catherine Marie b 22 Dec 1976), 1 s (Paul Robert b 16 Sept 1979); *Career* Met Police: joined 1967, cadet corp 1967–69, constable 1969–76, sergeant 1976–99, ops head Traffic Cameras Unit 1992–99; RPS: memb 1984–, memb Cncl 1993–, pres 2003–05; memb Surrey Photographic Assoc 1989–, chm London Salon 2006–08, hon pres Gtr China Photographic Soc 2009–; Meritorious Service Award Photographic Alliance of GB (PAGB) 1996, Fenton Medal RPS 2002; fell British Photographic Exhbns, FRPS 1996 and 2000 (Hon FRPS 2003), fell British Professional Photographers' Assoc 2004; *Publications* Royal Photographic Society Portfolio One (ed, 2007), Royal Photographic Society Portfolio Two (ed, 2010), Royal Photographic Society Portfolio 3 (ed, 2013); *Recreations* travel, photography; *Style—* Roger Reynolds, Esq; ✉ The Royal Photographic Society, Fenton House, 122 Wells Road, Bath BA2 3AH (☎ 01225 462841)

REYNOLDS, Simon Anthony; s of Maj James Reynolds (d 1982), of Leighton Hall, Carnforth, Lancs, and Helen Reynolds (d 1977); *b* 20 January 1939; *Educ* Ampleforth, Heidelberg Univ; *m* 1970, Beata Cornelia, da of late Baron Siegfried von Heyl zu Herrnsheim (d 1982), of Schlosschen, Worms, Germany; 2 s, 2 da; *Career* dealer in fine art; co-curator Kingdom of the soul exhbn on German Symbolism (Birmingham Museum & Art Gallery) 2000; tour ldr European tours in co-operation with the Victorian Soc; *Books* The Vision of Simeon Solomon (1984), Hymns to Night...and the Poets of Pessimism (1994), Sir William Blake Richmond RA (biography, 1995); *Recreations* writing, collecting fine art, travelling; *Style—* Simon Reynolds, Esq; ✉ 64 Lonsdale Road, Barnes, London SW13 9JS (☎ 020 8748 3506, fax 020 8741 5923)

RHIND, Prof David William; CBE (2001); s of William Rhind (d 1976), and Christina, *née* Abercombie; *b* 29 November 1943, Berwick upon Tweed, Northumberland; *Educ* Berwick GS, Univ of Bristol (BSc), Univ of Edinburgh (PhD), Univ of London (DSc); *m* 27 Aug

1966, Christine, da of William Frank Young, of Berwick-upon-Tweed; 1 s (Jonathan b 1969), 2 da (Samantha b 1972, Zoe b 1979); *Career* res offr Univ of Edinburgh 1968–69, res fell RCA 1969–73, reader (former lectr) Univ of Durham 1973–81, prof of geography Birkbeck Coll London 1982–91, DG and chief exec Ordnance Survey 1992–98; vice-chllr City Univ 1998–2007; visiting fell: Int Trg Centre Netherlands 1975, ANU 1979; author of over 100 tech papers; chm: Cmmn on the Social Sciences of the Acad of Learned Socs for the Social Sciences 2000–03, London HE Consortium 2000–03, HE Staff Devpt Agency 2002–04, Statistics Cmmn 2003–08 (memb 2000–03), Islington Improvement Bd 2003–04, Business and Industry Strategy Gp Univs UK 2005–07, Mgmnt Bd London Science Hub 2006–08, Govt Advsy Panel on Public Sector Info 2008–15, Royal Soc Working Gp on role of STEM in innovation in the services sector 2008–09, Portsmouth Hosps NHS Tst 2009–12; ind chm Socio-Economic Ctee Nuclear Decommissioning Authy 2006–08; memb Cncl ESRC 1996–2000, chm ESRC CLOSER Governing Bd 2013–; non-exec dir Bank of England 2006–09 (chm Pension Tstee 2009–12); advsr House of Lords Select Ctee Sci of Technol 1984–85, memb Govt Ctee of Enquiry on Handling of Geographic Info 1985–87; hon sec RGS 1988–91, vice-pres Int Cartographic Assoc 1984–91, memb RSA Cmmn on Risk 2007–09, memb UK Statistical Authy Bd 2008–15 (dep chm 2012–15), memb Public Sector Transparency Bd 2013–15; pres Br Exploring Soc 2010–; tstee Nuffield Fndn 2008– (chm 2010–); govr: Bournemouth Univ 1995–98, Ashridge Mgmnt Coll 1999–2004; winner UK Assoc for Geographic Information Decadel Award 1997; Hon DSc: Univ of Bristol 1993, Loughborough Univ 1996, Univ of Southampton 1998, Kingston Univ 1999, Univ of Durham 2001, London Metropolitan Univ 2003, Royal Holloway Univ of London 2004, St Petersburg State Poly Univ 2007, Univ of Edinburgh 2009, City Univ London 2011, Univ of Aberdeen 2015; hon fell: Birkbeck Coll London 2000, Queen Mary Univ of London 2007; FRGS 1970 (Patron's Medal 1997), FRICS 1991, CIMgt 1998, FRS 2002, Hon FBA 2002, FRSS 2003; *Books* Land Use (with R Hudson, 1980), A Census User's Handbook (1983), An Atlas of EEC Affairs (with R Hudson and H Mounsey, 1984), Geographical Information Systems (ed, with D Maguire and M Goodchild, 1991, 2 edn with P Longley, M Goodchild and D Maguire, 1999), The New Geography (with J Raper and J Shepherd, 1992), Framework for the World (1997), Geographical Information Science and Systems (with P Longley, M Goodchild and D Maguire 2001, 4 edn 2015); *Recreations* rough gardening, grandchildren; *Clubs* Geographical; *Style—* Prof David Rhind, CBE, FRS; ✉ e-mail dwrhind@gmail.com

RHODES, Anthony John David; s of John Percy Rhodes (d 1985), of Leigh-on-Sea, Essex, and Eileen Daisy, *née* Frith (d 1984); *b* 22 February 1948; *Educ* Westcliff GS, CCC Cambridge (MA); *m* 14 Dec 1974, Elisabeth Marie Agnes Raymonde, da of Lt-Col Pierre Fronteau (d 2006), of Lisieux, France; 1 s (Christophe b 1978), 1 da (Sophie b 1984); *Career* Shell International Petroleum Co 1969–73, Ocean Transport & Trading Ltd 1975–80, Bank of America International Ltd 1980–95, Credit Suisse 1995–97, conslt in fin services 1997–98, HSBC 1998–2004, ind conslt 2004–; Liveryman Worshipful Co of Int Bankers; *Books* Syndicated Lending – Practice and Documentation (author and gen ed, 5 edn 2009), Euromoney Encyclopaedia of Debt Finance (gen ed, 2006, 2 edn 2011); *Recreations* opera, classical music, golf, printmaking, oil painting, travel; *Style—* Anthony Rhodes, Esq; ☎ 020 7359 0067, e-mail ajdrhodes@hotmail.com

RHODES, Prof (John) David; CBE (2000, OBE 1992); son of Jack Rhodes, and Florence Rhodes; *b* 9 October 1943; *Educ* Univ of Leeds (BSc, PhD, DSc), Univ of Bradford (DEng); *m* 1965, Barbara Margaret Pearce; 1 s, 1 da; *Career* research fell Univ of Leeds 1966–67 (research asst 1964–66), sr research engr Microwave Devpt Labs USA 1967–69; Dept of Electrical and Electronic Engrg Univ of Leeds: lectr 1969–72, reader 1972–75, prof 1975–81, industrial prof 1981–; fndr, chm and tech dir Filtronic Components Ltd 1977–2006, chm Filtronic plc (formerly Filtronic Comtek plc) 1994-Jan 2006 (ceo Jan-Sept 2006, conslt Sept 2006–); awards incl: Microwave Prize (USA) 1969, Browder J Thompson Award (USA) 1970, Queen's Award for Technological Achievement 1985, Queen's Award for Export Achievement 1988, Price Phillip Medal Royal Acad of Engrg 2003; Hon DEng Univ of Bradford 1988, Hon DSc Napier Univ 1995; FIEEE 1980, FIET (FIEE 1984), FREng (FEng 1987), FRS 1993; *Publications* Theory of Electrical Filters (1976), author of numerous technical papers; *Style—* Prof J David Rhodes, CBE, FREng; ✉ Department of Electrical and Electronic Engineering, University of Leeds, Leeds LS2 9JT; Filtronic plc, The Waterfront, Salts Mill Road, Shipley, West Yorkshire BD18 3TT

RHODES, Gary; OBE (2006); step s of John Smellie, of London, and Jean, *née* Ferris; *b* 22 April 1960; *Educ* Howard Sch Gillingham, Thanet Tech Coll (City and Guilds, Chef of the Year, Student of the Year); *m* 7 January 1989, Yolanda Jennifer, da of Harvey Charles Adkins; 2 s (Samuel James b 24 Sept 1988, George Adam b 17 May 1990); *Career* Amsterdam Hilton Hotel 1979–81 (commis de cuisine, chef de partie), sous chef Reform Club Pall Mall 1982–83, head chef Winstons Eating House Feb-Oct 1983, sr sous chef Capital Hotel Knightsbridge 1983–85; head chef: Whitehall Restaurant Essex 1985–86, Castle Hotel Taunton 1986–90 (Michelin star 1986), Greenhouse Restaurant Mayfair 1990–96 (Michelin star 1996); city rhodes 1997–2003 (Michelin star 1997), Rhodes in the Square 1998–2003 (Michelin star 2000), Rhodes & Co Edinburgh 1999–2002 (Bib Gourmand award 2001), Rhodes & Co Manchester 1999–2003 (Bib Gourmand award 2002), Rhodes & Co W Sussex 2001–2002, Rhodes Twenty Four London 2003– (Michelin star 2005), Rhodes at the Calabash Hotel Grenada W Indies 2003–, Rhodes W1 Brasserie at the Cumberland Hotel 2005–, Arcadian Rhodes (with P&O cruises) 2005–11, Rhodes D7 Dublin 2006–09, Oriana Rhodes (with P&O cruises) 2006–11, Rhodes Mezzanine Dubai 2007–, Rhodes W1 Restaurant at the Cumberland Hotel 2007– (Michelin star 2008), King's Rhodes Dorset 2008–09, Rhodes South Dorset 2008–10, Rhodes Twenty10 2010–; TV series (with accompanying books): Rhodes Around Britain (BBC) 1994, More Rhodes Around Britain (BBC) 1995, Open Rhodes Around Britain (BBC) 1996, Fabulous Food (BBC) 1997, New British Classics 1999, At the Table (BBC) 2000–01, Spring into Summer (BBC) 2002, Autumn into Winter (BBC) 2002, Hell's Kitchen 2005; other TV series: Rhodes Across India (UKTV Food) 2007, Local Food Heroes (UKTV Food) 2007 and 2008, Rhodes Across China (UKTV Food) 2008, Rhodes Across the Caribbean (UKTV Food) 2009, Rhodes Across Italy (Good Food) 2009; Special Catey Award 1996; culinary ambass of Grenada 2000; hon prof Thames Valley Univ 2003, hon fell Canterbury Christchurch Univ 2006, hon apprenticeship Apprenticeship Ambassadors Network 2007; FCGI 2005; *Books* Short Cut Rhodes (1997), Sweet Dreams (1998), The Cook Pack (2000), Gary Rhodes Step by Step Cooking (2001), The Complete Rhodes Around Britain (2001), Gary Rhodes Great Fast Food (2001), Food with Friends (2002), The Complete Cookery Year (2003), Keeping It Simple (2005), Time to Eat (2007), Gary Rhodes 365 (2008); *Style—* Gary Rhodes, Esq, OBE; ✉ website www.garyrhodes.com

RHODES, John Guy; s of Canon Cecil Rhodes, of Bury St Edmunds, and Gladys, *née* Farlie; *b* 16 February 1945; *Educ* King Edward VI Birmingham, Jesus Coll Cambridge (MA); *m* 11 June 1977, Christine Joan, da of Peter Dorrington Batt, MC, of Bury St Edmunds; 2 s (Alexander Luke b 1979, Nicholas Hugh b 1981); *Career* articled clerk Macfarlanes 1968; admitted slr 1970, slr specialising in trusts and tax for UK and int private clients, ptnr Macfarlanes 1975–2006 (sr advsr 2006–08), ind tstee and conslt Stonehage Financial Servs Ltd 2008–10, dir Stonehage Law Ltd 2010–, dir Stonehage Fleming Family and Ptnrs Ltd 2015–; *Recreations* woodlands, tennis, skiing, bee keeping; *Style—* John Rhodes, Esq

RHODES, Prof Peter John; s of George Thomas Rhodes (d 1969), and Elsie Leonora, *née* Pugh (d 1998); *b* 10 August 1940; *Educ* Queen Elizabeth's GS Barnet, Wadham Coll Oxford (minor scholar, MA), Merton Coll Oxford (Harmsworth sr scholar, Craven fell, DPhil); *m* 1971, (m dis 2001) Jan Teresa, da of John Mervyn Adamson; *Career* Univ of Durham: lectr in classics and ancient history 1965–77, sr lectr 1977–83, prof of ancient history 1983–2005, hon prof 2005–; jr fell Center for Hellenic Studies Washington DC 1978–79, visiting fell Wolfson Coll Oxford 1984, visiting research fell Univ of New England NSW Australia 1988, memb Inst for Advanced Study Princeton NJ 1988–89, visiting fell Corpus Christi Coll Oxford 1993, Leverhulme research fell 1994–95, visiting fell All Souls Coll Oxford 1998, Langford Family eminent scholar Florida State Univ 2002, Sackler lectr Tel Aviv Univ 2013; pres Classical Assoc 2014–15; Chancellor's Medal Univ of Durham 2015; FBA 1987, foreign memb Royal Danish Acad 2005, fell Fondazione Lorenzo Valla 2010; *Books* The Athenian Boule (1972), Commentary on the Aristotelian Athenaion Politeia (1981), Aristotle: The Athenian Constitution (1984), The Greek City States (1986, 2 edn 2007), Thucydides II (1988), Thucydides III (1994), The Development of the Polis in Archaic Greece (ed with L G Mitchell, 1997), The Decrees of the Greek States (with D M Lewis, 1997), Thucydides IV.1-V.24 (1999), Ancient Democracy and Modern Ideology (2003), Greek Historical Inscriptions 404–323 BC (with R G Osborne, 2003), Athenian Democracy (ed, 2004), A History of the Classical Greek World 478–323 BC (2005, 2 edn 2010), The Old Oligarch (with J L Marr, 2008), Thucydides, The Peloponnesian War (introduction and notes, 2009), Law and Drama in Ancient Greece (ed with E M Harris and D F Leão, 2010), Alcibiades (2011), A Short History of Ancient Greece (2014), Thucydides I (2014), Atthis: The Ancient Histories of Athens (2014), The laws of Solon: A New Edition with Introduction, Translation and Commentary (with D F Leão, 2015), Thucydides (2015), Ktema Es Aiei (A Possession for All Time) (Presidential address, Classical Association, 2015), Deformations and Crises of Ancient Civil Communities (ed, with V Gouchin, 2015); also author of various articles and reviews in learned jls; *Recreations* music, travel, typography; *Style—* Prof P J Rhodes; ✉ Department of Classics, University of Durham, 38 North Bailey, Durham DH1 3EU (☎ 0191 334 1670, fax 0191 334 1671)

RHODES, Robert Elliott; QC (1989); s of Gilbert Gedalia Rhodes (d 1970), of London, and Elly Brook (d 2015); *b* 2 August 1945; *Educ* St Paul's, Pembroke Coll Oxford (MA); *m* 16 March 1971 (m dis 1996), Georgina Caroline, da of Jack Gerald Clarfelt (d 2009); 2 s (Matthew b 1973, James b 1975), 1 da (Emily b 1983); *Career* called to the Bar Inner Temple 1968 (bencher 2007, Bar Cncl 2009); first prosecuting counsel to Inland Revenue at Central Criminal Court and Inner London Crown Courts 1981–89 (second prosecuting counsel 1979), recorder of the Crown Court 1987, head of chambers 1998–2003; dep chm IMRO Membership Tbnl Panel 1992–2001, memb Appeal Panel ICAEW 1998–2004, chm AIDB/AADB Disciplinary Tbnls 2004–11, chm FRC Tbnls 2011–14; memb: Panel of Advisors Financial Arbitration and ADR Center of Central Univ of Finance and Economics Beijing 2012, Panel of Mediators China Cncl for the Promotion of Int Trade 2013, Panel of Mediators and Arbitrators Lang Fang Arbitration Cmmn, Panel of Arbitrators Jinan Arbitration Cmmn, Panel of Arbitrators Chinese Arbitration Assoc, Panel of Arbitrators Thai Arbitration Inst, Global Panel of Distinguished Neutrals (arbitrators) Int Inst Conflict Prevention and Resolution; author of numerous legal pubns; FCIArb; *Recreations* reading, listening to opera, watching cricket, playing real tennis, theatre, ballet, art, former int fencer; *Clubs* MCC, Épée, Annabel's, Garrick; *Style—* Robert Rhodes, Esq, QC; ✉ Outer Temple, 222–225 Strand, London WC2R 1BA

RHODES, Prof Roderick Arthur William; s of Keith Firth Rhodes, and Irene, *née* Clegg; *b* 15 August 1944; *Educ* Fulneck Boys' Sch, Univ of Bradford (BSc), St Catherine's Coll Oxford (BLitt), Univ of Essex (PhD); *m* 7 Nov 2007, Jenny Fleming, *née* Lewis; 1 s (Edward Roderick b 25 June 1979), 1 da (Bethan Margaret b 30 Oct 1981); *Career* Univ of Birmingham 1970–76, Univ of Strathclyde 1976–79, Univ of Essex 1979–89, prof of politics and head of Dept Univ of York 1989–94, prof of politics Univ of Newcastle upon Tyne 1994–2002; ANU: prof of political science and head of dept 2003–07, distinguished prof of political science 2006–11, dir Research Sch of Social Sciences 2007–08; prof of govt Univ of Tasmania 2008–11, prof of govt (research) Univ of Southampton 2012–, Griffith Univ Brisbane 2012–15; adjungeret prof Institut for Statskundskab, Kobenhans Universitet 1998–2003, visiting research prof of politics and public policy Griffith Univ Brisbane 1999–2003; chm Public Admin Ctee Jt Univ Cncl for Social and Public Admin 1996–99; pres Political Studies Assoc 2002–05 (chm 1999–2002); research dir ESRC Whitehall Research Prog 1984–99, chair Local Governance Steering Ctee of ESRC 1992–98; ed Public Admin 1986–2011; Sam Richardson Prize for best article published in Australian Jl of Public Administration 2007, Int Research Assoc for Public Mgmnt and Routledge Prize for Outstanding Contrib to Public Mgmnt Research 2012, Special Recognition Award for Outstanding Contribution to Political Science Political Studies Assoc of the UK 2014, Lifetime Achievement Award European Consortium for Political Research (ECPR) 2015; fell Aust Acad of Social Sci 2004–, fell Acad of Social Sciences 2002–; *Books* Control and Power in Central-Local Government Relations (1981, 2 edn 1999), The National World of Local Government (1986), Beyond Westminster and Whitehall (1988), Policy Networks in British Government (ed, 1992), Prime Minister, Cabinet and Core Executive (jt ed, 1995), Understanding Governance (1997), United Kingdom (ed, 2 vols, 2000), Transforming British Government (ed 2 vols, 2000), Interpreting British Governance (jtly, 2003), Governance Stories (jtly, 2006), The Oxford Handbook of Political Institutions (jt ed, 2006), Observing Government Elites (jt ed, 2007), Comparing Westminter (jtly, 2009), The Australian Study of Politics (ed, 2009), The State as Cultural Practice (jtly, 2010), Everyday Life in British Government (2011), The Oxford Handbook of Political Leadership (jt ed, 2014), Lessons of Governing: A Profile of Prime Ministers' Chiefs of Staff (jtly, 2014), The Gatekeepers: Lessons from Prime Ministers' Chiefs of Staff (jtly, 2014), The Routledge Handbook of Interpretive Political Science (jt ed, 2015), Rethinking Governance: ruling rationalities and resistance (jt ed, 2016); *Recreations* cricket, rugby, crime fiction, popular music (jazz, rock); *Style—* Prof Roderick Rhodes

RHODES, Dame Zandra Lindsey; DBE (2014, CBE 1997); da of Albert James Rhodes (d 1988), of Chatham, Kent, and Beatrice Ellen, *née* Twigg (d 1968), fitter at Worth, Paris; *b* 19 September 1940; *Educ* Medway Technical Sch for Girls Chatham, Medway Coll of Art Rochester, Royal Coll of Art (DesRCA); *Career* started career as textile designer 1964, set up print factory and studio with Alexander McIntyre 1965, sold designs (and converted them into clothes) to Foale and Tuffin and Roger Nelson, transferred to fashion industry 1966, partnership with Sylvia Ayton producing dresses using own prints, opened Fulham Rd clothes shop (fndr ptnr and designer) 1967–68, first solo collection US 1969 (met with phenomenal response from Vogue and Women's Wear Daily), thereafter established as foremost influential designer (developed unique use of printed fabrics and treatment of jersey), prodr annual spectacular fantasy shows USA; fndr (with Anne Knight and Ronnie Stirling): Zandra Rhodes (UK) Ltd, Zandra Rhodes Shops 1975–86; md: Zandra Rhodes (UK) Ltd 1975–, ZLR Ltd (formerly Zandra Rhodes Shops); first shop London 1975 (others opened in Bloomingdales NY, Marshall Field Chicago, Seibu Tokyo and Harrods London), shops and licencees now worldwide; Zandra Rhodes designs currently incl: interior furnishing, wallpaper, scarves, hosiery, mens' ties, sheets and pillowcases, saris, jewellery, rugs, kitchen accessories, fine china figurines; launched fine arts and prints collections Dyanssen Galleries USA 1989, fur collection for Pologeorgis Furs 1995–; solo exhibitions incl: Texas Gallery Houston 1981, La Jolla Museum of Contemporary Art San Diego 1982, Barbican Centre 1982, Parson's Sch of Design NY 1982, Art Museum of Santa Cruz 1983, The Surface and Beyond Phoenix Art Museum 1997; work represented in numerous permanent costume collections incl:

V&A, City Museum & Art Gallery Stoke-on-Trent, Royal Pavilion Brighton Museum, City Art Gallery Leeds, Met Museum NY, Museum of Applied Arts & Sciences Sydney, Nat Museum of Victoria Melbourne; fndr Zandra Rhodes Fndn 1997–; notable licences incl: Eva Stillman Lingeria (USA) 1977, Wamsutta sheets and pillow cases (USA) 1976, CVP Designs interior fabrics and settings (UK) 1977, Philip Hockey Decorative Furs (UK) 1986, Zandra Rhodes Saris (India) 1987, Littlewoods Catalogues (UK) for printed t-shirt and Intasia sweaters 1988, Hilmet silk scarves and men's ties (UK) 1989, Bonnay perfumes 1993, Coats Patons needlepoint (UK) 1998, Pologeorgis Furs (USA) 1995, Zandra Rhodes II hand painted ready to wear collection (Hong Kong) 1995, Grattan Catalogue sheets and duvets (UK); set and costume designer Aida (ENO) 2007; acknowledged spokeswoman and personality of 60s and 70s (famous for green and later pink coloured hair), frequent speaker on fashion and design; subject of numerous documentaries and films incl: This is Your Life 1985, Classmates 1989, Colour Eye 1991; Designer of the Year English Fashion Trade UK 1972, Emmy Award for Best Costume Design Romeo and Juliet on Ice CBS TV 1984, Best Show of the Year New Orleans 1985, Woman of Distinction Award Northwood Inst Dallas Texas 1986, Lifetime Achievement Award (Hall of Fame) Br Fashion Awards 1995; key to Cities of: Miami, Hollywood, Philadelphia; hon fell Kent Inst of Art and Design 1992; Hon DFA Int Fine Arts Coll Miami, Hon Dr RCA, Hon DD CNAA 1987, Hon DLitt Univ of Westminster 2000; RDI 1977, FSIAD 1982; *Books* The Art of Zandra Rhodes (1984, US edn 1985, republished 1995); *Recreations* gardening, travelling, drawing, watercolours; *Style—* Dame Zandra Rhodes, DBE; ✉ The Zandra Rhodes Foundation, 79–85 Bermondsey Street, London SE1 3XF (☎ 020 7403 0222, fax 020 7403 0555), Zandra Rhodes Publications, 444 South Cedros, Studio 160, Solana Beach, CA 92075, USA (☎ 00 1 619 792 1814)

RHYS, Prof (David) Garel; CBE (2007, OBE 1989); s of Emyr Lewys Rhys, and Edith Phyllis, *née* Williams; *b* 28 February 1940; *Educ* Ystalyfera GS (Shepherd Award in Literature), Univ of Swansea (BA, Richard Price Prize in Economics), Univ of Birmingham (MCom); *m* (Charlotte) Mavis, da of Edward Colston Walters; 1 s (Jeremy Charles), 2 da (Angela Jayne, Gillian Mary); *Career* lectr Univ of Hull 1967–70 (asst lectr 1965–67); Univ Coll Cardiff 1970–87: lectr, sr lectr, prof; prof Cardiff Business Sch Univ of Wales 1987–2005, dir Centre for Automotive Industry Res Cardiff Business Sch Cardiff Univ (part of the Univ of Wales until 2005) 1991–2005, emeritus prof Univ of Cardiff 2005–; advsr to: Select Ctees House of Commons and House of Lords, Nat Audit Office; conslt to govt depts, lead conslt to UNIDO 1995–96; chm: Welsh Automotive Forum 2001–, Economic Res Advsy Panel Welsh Govt 2002–12, Saint Athan Cardiff Airport Enterprise Zone 2012–; pres Inst of the Motor Industry 2004–09; memb: Bd Welsh Devpt Agency 1994–98, UK Round Table on Sustainable Devpt 1996–2000, HE Funding Cncl for Wales 2003–10, Ministerial Advsy Gp Welsh Assembly Govt 2007–11, Bd Sector Devpt Wales Partnership 2013–; chair Low Carbon Vehicle Expert Panel 2013, co-chair Welsh Govt Green Growth Advsy Panel 2013; Freeman of Neath Port Talbot 1999, Freeman City of London 2000, Liveryman Worshipful Co of Carmen 2000; FITA 1987, FIMI 1989, FRSA, FLSW 2013; *Books* The Motor Industry: An Economic Survey (1971), The Motor Industry in the European Community (1989), Outsourcing and Human Resource Management (contrib, 2008); *Recreations* walking, gardening, still amusing my grandchildren, being outraged, reading; *Clubs* RAC; *Style—* Prof Garel Rhys, CBE; ✉ Cardiff University, Aberconway Building, Colum Drive, Cardiff CF10 3EU (☎ 029 2087 4281 or 029 2084 2714, e-mail rhysg@cf.ac.uk or charlotte.rhys@btinternet.com)

RHYS, Matthew (né Matthew Evans); s of Glyn Evans, and Helen Evans; *b* 1974, Cardiff; *Educ* Ysgol Gyfun Gymraeg Glantaf, RADA; *Career* actor; Patricia Rothermere Scholarship 1993, Welsh BAFTA Best Actor 1998 *Theatre* incl: The Graduate 2000, Romeo and Juliet (RSC) 2004–05; *Television* incl: Metropolis 2000, Partners and Crime 2003, Beau Brummell (BBC) 2006, Brothers and Sisters (ABC) 2006–11, The Mystery of Edwin Drood 2012, The Americas 2013–; *Film* incl: House of America 1997, Titus 1999, Whatever Happened to Harold Smith? 1999, Fakers 2004, Love and Other Disasters 2006, Virgin Territory 2007, The Edge of Love 2008, Luster 2010, Patagonia 2010; *Recreations* shooting; *Style—* Matthew Rhys, Esq; ✉ c/o United Agents Ltd, 12–26 Lexington Street, London W1F 0LE (☎ 020 3214 0800, fax 020 3214 0801, website www.unitedagents.co.uk)

RHYS EVANS, Peter Howell; s of Gwilym Rhys Evans, MC, of Rickledown, Durham, and Jean Marjorie, *née* Foord; *b* 17 May 1948; *Educ* Ampleforth, Bart's (MB BS, Cricket and Rugby colours), Univ of Paris, Gustave-Roussy Inst (DCC); *m* 1, 6 Jan 1973 (m dis), Irene Mossop; 2 s (Matthew b 1 Feb 1976, Marc b 2 May 1980), 1 da (Melissa b 2 March 1984); m 2, 30 Sept 1994, Frances Knight; 2 da (Olivia Frances b 5 April 1996, Sophie Katherine (twin) b 25 June 1998), 1 s (James Peter (twin) b 25 June 1998); *Career* qualified Bart's 1971, conslt and sr lectr ENT surgery Univ of Birmingham 1981–86, conslt ENT and head neck surgn The Royal Marsden Hosp 1986–; hon civilian conslt ENT surgn to the RN 1991–; visiting conslt ENT surgn St Bernard's Hosp Gibraltar; examiner RCS 1986–94, fndr memb Euro Acad of Facial Surgeons 1978 (vice-pres 1987), memb Nat Cncl Otolaryngological Res Soc 1984–88, memb Cncl RSM 1991–97; asst ed Jl of Laryngology & Otology 1986–96; Freeman City of London 1990, Freeman Worshipful Soc of Apothecaries; hon ENT surgn: St Mary's Hosp, King Edward VII Hosp for Officers; hon sr lectr Univ of London; memb BMA, MRCS 1971, LRCP, FRSM, FRCS 1978; *Publications* Cancer of Head and Neck (ed, 1983), Face and Neck Surgical Techniques – Problems and Limitations (ed, 1983), Facial Plastic Surgery – Otoplasty (guest ed, 1985), Principles and Practice of Head and Neck Oncology (ed, 2002), contrib to med jls and books on head and neck cancer and aquatic ape theory; *Recreations* skiing, golf, tennis, anthropology; *Style—* Peter Rhys Evans, Esq; ✉ 106 Harley Street, London W1N 1AF; The Royal Marsden Hospital, Fulham Road, London SW3 6JJ (☎ 020 7935 3525, 020 7352 8171 ext 2730 and 2731, fax 020 7351 3785)

RHYS JONES, Griffith (Griff); s of Elwyn Rhys Jones, and Gwyneth Margaret Jones; *b* 16 November 1953; *Educ* Brentwood Sch, Emmanuel Coll Cambridge (MA); *m* 21 Nov 1981, Joanna Frances, da of Alexander James Harris; 1 s (George Alexander b 1985), 1 da (Catherine Louisa b 1987); *Career* actor and writer; BBC radio prodr 1976–79; dir Talkback; chm Hackney Empire Appeal Ctee; FWCMD, FRSA; *Theatre* Charley's Aunt 1983, Trumpets and Raspberries 1985, The Alchemist 1986, Arturo Ui 1987, Thark 1989–90, Wind in the Willows 1990–91, The Revengers' Comedies 1991, An Absolute Turkey 1994, Plunder (Savoy) 1997, The Front Page 1998, Oliver! (Theatre Royal) 2009; dir Twelfth Night RSC 1989; *Opera* Die Fledermaus 1989; *Radio* Do Go On (Radio 4), The Griff Rhys Jones Show (Radio 2); *Television* comedy series incl: Not The Nine O'Clock News 1979–82, Alas Smith and Jones 1984, The World According to Smith and Jones 1986–87, Small Doses 1989, Smith and Jones 1991; co-presenter Comic Relief (BBC); presenter: Bookworm; plays incl: A View of Harry Clarke 1989, Ex (Screen One) 1991, Demob 1993; Restoration 2003–04, Mine All Mine 2004, Mountain 2007, Rivers, Three Men in a Boat; *Film* Morons From Outer Space 1985, Wilt 1989, Up N Under 1997, Puckoon; *Records* Bitter & Twisted, Scratch 'n' sniff, Alas Smith & Jones, Not the Nine O'Clock News; *Awards* Emmy Award for Alas Smith & Jones, Br Comedy Top Entertainment Series Award for Smith & Jones 1991, Br Comedy Top Entertainment Performer (with Mel Smith) for Smith & Jones 1991; Olivier Award for Best Comedy Performance for Charley's Aunt and Absolute Turkey, Sony Silver Award for Do Go On 2000, Mont Blanc Award for Arts Patronage 2003 (fundraising chm for Hackney Empire); *Books* The Lavishly Tooled Smith and Jones (1986), Janet Lives with Mel and Griff (1988), Smith and Jones Head to Head (1992), The Nation's Favourite Poems (ed, 1996), The Nation's Favourite Comic Poems (ed, 1998), The Nation's Favourite Twentieth Century Poems (ed, 1999), To the Baltic with Bob (2003), Semi-Detached, Rivers, Mountain; *Clubs* Groucho; *Style—* Griff Rhys Jones, Esq

RHYS WILLIAMS, Sir (Arthur) Gareth Ludovic Emrys; 3 Bt (UK 1918), of Miskin, Parish of Llantrisant, Co Glamorgan; s of Sir Brandon Rhys Williams, 2 Bt, MP (d 1988), and Caroline Susan, eldest da of Ludovic Anthony Foster (d 1990), of Greatham Manor, Pulborough, W Sussex; *b* 9 November 1961; *Educ* Eton, Univ of Durham, INSEAD; *m* 14 Sept 1996, Harriet, da of Maj Tom Codnor (d 2005); 2 s (Ludo Dhaulagiri b 12 Oct 2001, Hugo Thomas Casmir b 6 July 2003), 1 da (Tacita Clementine b 17 May 2006); *Heir* s, Ludo Rhys Williams; *Career* md: NFI Electronics 1990–93, Rexam Custom Europe 1993–96, BPB plc; dir Central Europe 1996–2000, ceo Vitec Gp plc 2001–08, ceo Capital Safety Ltd 2008–10, ceo Charter Int plc 2011–12, ceo PHS Gp 2012–14; chief commercial offr UK Govt 2016–; memb Cncl Fauna and Flora Int (FFI) 2013–; CEng, FIET, FIMechE, CCMI; *Recreations* conjuring, sailing, shooting; *Clubs* Garrick; *Style—* Sir Gareth Rhys Williams, Bt

RIBBANDS, Mark Jonathan; s of Henry Stephen Ribbands (d 2001), and Christina Ivy, *née* Saggers (d 1984); *b* 6 January 1959; *Educ* Forest Sch (expelled for making bombs), NE London Poly (BSc); *m* 30 May 1987 (m dis 1998), Maya, da of Flt Offr Wassoudeve Goriah, DFC (d 1969); 1 s (Adam b 27 Sept 1993); partner Mui Tsun; 1 s (James Ming b 26 July 2004); *Career* md Ribbands Explosives Ltd 1982–; involved with: explosives disposal, demolition, dealing in firearms, ammunition and explosives; video presenter: The Power of Explosives 1998, It Didn't Look Like a Bomb 2001, Power and Precision: An Introduction to Explosives 2003; memb Cncl Inst of Explosives Engrs 1988 and 1992–; tstee Entangled Bank 2013–; FGS 1983, FRGS 1983, MIExpE 1985, FRI (fell Royal Inst) 2012, FLS 2013; *Recreations* scuba diving, flying helicopters, motorcycling, driving fast cars, shooting, playing with fire, building things, growing things, the company of intelligent women, wallowing in sybaritic splendour; *Clubs* Milk & Honey; *Style—* Mark Ribbands, Esq; ✉ Dyson's Farm, Long Row, Tibenham, Norfolk NR16 1PD (e-mail mark@ribbands.co.uk, website www.ribbands.co.uk or www.entangled-bank.co.uk); 59 Greencoat Place, London SW1P 1DS

RIBBANS, Prof William; s of late Maurice Arthur Ribbans, MBE, of Ilmington, Warks, and Sheila Beryl, *née* Brightwell; *b* 28 November 1954; *Educ* Northampton GS for Boys, Royal Free Hosp Sch of Med London (BSc, MB BS), Univ of Liverpool (MChOrth), Univ of Glamorgan (PhD); *m* 10 Sept 1983, Siân Elizabeth, da of Phillip Noel Williams; 3 da (Rebecca Elizabeth b 3 Feb 1985, Hannah Alexandra b 31 Dec 1988, Abigail Victoria b 4 May 1992); *Career* house surgn and physician Royal Free Hosp London 1980–81; SHO: in orthopaedics and casualty Luton and Dunstable Hosp 1981–82, in gen surgery Northwick Park Hosp Harrow 1982–84; radiology registrar St Mary's Paddington 1984–85; orthopaedic registrar: Wexham Park Slough 1985–86, Northwick Park Hosp Harrow 1986–87; orthopaedic clinical fell Harvard Univ 1987–88; orthopaedic sr registrar: Central Middx Hosp 1988–89, Middx Hosp and UCH 1989–90; orthopaedic fell Sheffield Children's Hosp 1990, conslt in orthopaedic surgery (with special interests in sports injuries, post-traumatic limb reconstruction and foot and ankle) Royal Free Hosp 1991–95; chief medical offr Northants CCC 2012–; hon sr lectr Royal Free Hosp Sch of Med 1991–2001; reader in surgery: Univ of London 1991–95, Northampton Gen Hosp 1996–2012; memb Ct of Examiners RCS 2003– (tutor 1998–2001); hon orthopaedic surgn: English Nat Ballet 1991–, Northampton Saints RFC 1996–2010, Northampton Town FC 1999–; prof of sports medicine Univ of Northampton 2005–; medical dir Moulton Sports Rehabilitation; FRCSEd 1985, FRCSOrth 1990, MChOrth 1990, FBOA 1991, FRCS Eng 2001, FFSEM 2006; *Recreations* sports (especially rugby, cycling and athletics), antiques, philately; *Clubs* Old Northamptonians RFC; *Style—* Prof William J Ribbans; ✉ Chartlands, Cherry Tree Lane, Great Houghton, Northamptonshire NN4 7AT; The County Clinic, 57 Billing Road, Northampton NN1 5DB (☎ 01604 795414, e-mail wjribbans@uk-consultants.co.uk, website www.billribbans.com)

RIBEIRO, Baron (Life Peer UK 2010), of Achimota in the Republic of Ghana and of Ovington in the County of Hampshire; Sir Bernard Francisco Ribeiro; kt (2009), CBE (2004); s of Miguel Augustus Ribeiro (d 1995), and Matilda, *née* Ampiah (d 2000); *b* 20 January 1944, Achimota, Ghana; *Educ* Dean Close Sch Cheltenham, Middx Hosp Medical Sch; *m* 8 June 1968, Elisabeth Jean, *née* Orr; 1 s (Richard Francisco b 19 April 1973), 3 da (Nicola Helen b 22 July 1975, Joanna Charlotte, Tessa Elisabeth (twins) b 10 Nov 1978); *Career* registrar in surgery Orsett Hosp Essex 1970–72, registrar then sr registrar in surgery Middx Hosp London 1972–78, lectr in urology Accra 1974–75, conslt gen surgn Basildon Univ NHS Tst 1979–2008; surgical advsr to Expert Advsy Gp on AIDS and to UK Advsy Panel on Blood-Born Viruses 1994–2003; pres RCS 2005–08 (memb Cncl 1998–2008), pres Assoc of Surgns of GB and I 1999–2000 (hon sec 1991–96); medical vice-chm E of Eng Advsy Ctee on Clinical Excellence 2002–05, chm Ind Reconfiguration Panel 2012–; visiting prof of surgery UNC Chapel Hill 2006–07; memb Bd of Visitors HMP Chelmsford 1982–92; memb Cncl Dean Close Sch 2006– (pres 2016–); memb Test and Itchen Assoc; memb EU Sub-Ctee on Home Affrs House of Lords 2015–, memb Refreshment Ctee House of Lords 2015–, memb Select Ctee on the Long-term Sustainability of the NHS 2016–; Hon Liveryman Worshipful Co of Cutlers 2008, Master Worshipful Co of Barbers 2013–14; Hon DSc Anglia Ruskin Univ 2008, Hon DEng Univ of Bath 2012; memb Assoc of Surgns of GB and I, FRCS 1972 (patron 2011), FRCSEd 2001, FRCP 2006, hon fell Coll of Physicians and Surgeons of Ghana (FCPSG) 2006, fell Acad of Medicine of Malaysia (FAMM) 2006, hon fell Caribbean Coll of Surgeons 2007, hon memb Académie Chirurgie de Paris 2008, hon FRCSI 2008, hon FRCSGlas 2008, FCAnaes 2008, hon FACS 2008, hon FASA 2013; Offr Order of the Volta Ghana 2008; Concise Surgery (contrib, 1998), Surgery in the United Kingdom (2001), Emergency Surgery: Principles and Practice (contrib, 2006); *Recreations* field sports (shooting and fishing); *Clubs* Flyfishers', Surgical 60 Travellers; *Style—* The Lord Ribeiro, CBE

RICE, Janet; da of George Robert Whinham (d 1992), of Amble, Northumberland, and Ella, *née* Grey (d 1972); *b* 14 December 1949; *Educ* Duchess's County GS for Girls Alnwick, City of Leeds & Carnegie Coll of Educn (Cert Ed); *m* 7 Aug 1971, Martin Graham Rice, s of Alfred Victor Rice; *Career* pensions asst Clarke Chapman-John Thompson Ltd 1972–74, clerical offr DHSS 1974; British Gas plc (now BG Gp plc): pensions asst northern region 1974–78, pensions offr HQ 1978–85, asst pensions admin mangr 1985–86, pensions admin mangr 1986–89, mangr Pensions and Int Benefits 1989–96, gp head of pensions 1996–2001; dir ICL Pensions Tst Co 2002–; memb Advsy Cncl OPDU Ltd 1999–2005; memb Soc of Antiquaries of Newcastle upon Tyne 2000–; FPMI 1993 (assoc 1979, memb Cnl 1998–2001); *Recreations* walking, gardening, reading, family and local history; *Style—* Mrs Janet Rice; ✉ 17 Springfield Road, Pamber Heath, Tadley, Hampshire RG26 3DL

RICE, Peter Anthony; s of John Daniel Rice (d 1981), of Newry, Co Down, and Brigid Tina, *née* McVerry (d 1990); *b* 25 June 1950; *Educ* Abbey GS Newry, Lancaster Univ (BA), Univ of Buckingham (MA), Birkbeck Coll London (MA); *Career* Duncan C Fraser & Co 1971–74, Wood Mackenzie & Co 1974–88 (ptnr 1981), dir Hill Samuel & Co 1986–87, gp corp fin and planning mangr Commercial Union Assurance plc 1988–92, UK divnl dir Commercial Union 1993–98, dir Morley Fund Management 1998–2000; non-exec dir: Lloyd Thompson plc 1990–94, Gartmore Smaller Companies Investment Tst 2000–09, Rostrum Gp Ltd 2000–05; chm Edinburgh Central Cons Assoc 1977–79, fndr chm Scot Bow Group 1980–82; FIA 1974, memb Stock Exchange 1981; *Clubs* Athenaeum; *Style—*

R

Peter Rice, Esq; ✉ The Old Rectory, 6 Redington Road, Hampstead, London NW3 7RG (☎ 020 7431 3176)

RICE, Lady; Susan Ilene Rice; CBE (2005); da of Samuel Wunsch (d 1982), and Etta Waldman Wunsch (d 1992); *b* 7 March 1946, Providence, Rhode Island, USA; *Educ* Wellesley Coll Mass (BA), Univ of Aberdeen (MLitt); *m* 3 July 1967, Sir Duncan Rice, *qv*, s of Dr James Inglis Rice; 2 s (James b 10 Oct 1976, Sam b 3 May 1984), 1 da (Jane (Beady) b 24 Nov 1989); *Career* med researcher Yale Univ Med Sch 1970–73, dean Saybrook Coll Yale Univ 1973–79, staff aide to Pres Hamilton Coll 1980–81, dean of students Colgate Univ 1981–86; sr vice-pres and div head Nat Westminster Bancorp 1986–96; Bank of Scotland: dir of business projects 1997–98, head of branch banking 1998–99, md Personal Banking 1999–2000; chief exec Lloyds TSB Scotland plc 2000–09 (chm 2008–09), md Lloyds Banking Gp 2009–; non-exec dir: Scottish and Southern Energy plc 2003–14 (sr ind dir 2006–12), Bank of England 2007–14, Big Soc Capital 2011–, J Sainsbury's 2013–; chair: Ctee of Scottish Clearing Bankers 2001–03, Edinburgh Int Book Festival 2001–, Adsvy Ctee Scottish Centre for Research on Social Justice 2002–08, Consumer Affrs and Community Re-investment Ctee NY State Bankers Assoc, Edinburgh Festivals Forum 2008–, Chartered Banker Professional Standards Bd 2010–; dir: Scottish Business in the Community 2001–10, UK Charity Bank 2001–08, Scotland's Futures Forum 2005–13, Gtr Jamaica Devpt Corp, Neighborhood Housing Services of NYC, NY Community Investment Co, S Bronx Overall Economic Devpt Corp, Nat Centre for Universities and Business 2012–; tstee: David Hume Inst 2000–05, Lloyds TSB Fndn for Scotland 2009–10, Scotland's Cncl for Economic Advsrs 2011–; advsr: Community Re-investment Inst, Seton Hall Center for Public Service, Women's World Banking in N America; memb: HM Treasy Policy Action Team on Access to Fin Services, Foresight Sub-Ctee on Retail Fin Services, BP Scottish Advsy Bd 2002–03, HM Treasy Financial Inclusion Taskforce 2005–11, Univ of Oxford Saïd Business Sch Advsy Forum 2006–13, Cncl Chartered Inst of Bankers Scot 2001–, Scottish Advsy Task Force on The New Deal 2000–04, Aberdeen Common Purpose Advsy Bd 1999–2006, New Jersey Legislature Housing Advsy and Steering Ctees; HRH The Prince of Wales ambass for Scot for corporate responsibility 2005; hon pres Community Devpt Finance Assoc 2007–09; memb Nat Panel of Judges Rudy Bruner Award 1997, govr of patrons Nat Galleries of Scotland 2010–, dep chair Scotland's 2020 Climate Change Gp; patron Univ of Oxford Saïd Business Sch 2013–, memb of Ct Univ of Edinburgh 2014–; regent RCS(Ed) 2011, pres SCDI 2012–; induction American Acad of Women Achievers 1994, Business Person of Year Sunday Independent Award Ireland 1999, Corp Elite Business Award – Insider Corp Elite Business Woman of the Year 2002 and 2008, Spirit of Scotland Annual Business Award 2002, Lifetime Achievement Award Women in Banking and Finance 2005, Leadership Award Nat Business Awards Scotland 2007, Arts and Business Scotland Leadership Award 2011, Lifetime Achievement Award VIBES 2013; Burgess of Guild City of Aberdeen 1999; Hon DBA Robert Gordon Univ 2001, Dr (hc) Univ of Edinburgh 2003, Hon DLitt Heriot-Watt Univ 2004, Hon DUniv Paisley 2005, Hon DUniv Glasgow 2007, Hon DBA Queen Margaret Univ 2008, Hon LLD Univ of Aberdeen 2008; FCIBS 1998, FRSE 2002, CCMI 2003, FRSA 2004; *Recreations* hill walking, opera, modern art, reading, fly fishing; *Style—* Lady Rice, CBE; ✉ Lloyds Banking Group, The Mound, Edinburgh EH1 1YZ (☎ 0131 243 5503, fax 0131 243 7196, e-mail susan.rice@lloydsbanking.com)

RICE, Sir Timothy Miles Bindon (Tim); kt (1994); s of Hugh Gordon Rice (d 1988), and Joan Odette, *née* Bawden (d 2009); *b* 10 November 1944; *Educ* Lancing, La Sorbonne; *m* 1974, Jane, da of Col A H McIntosh, OBE (d 1979); 1 da (Eva Jane Florence b 1975), 1 s (Donald Alexander Hugh b 1977); 1 da (Zoe Joan Eleanor b 1998, with Nell Sully); *Career* writer and broadcaster; lyricist for stage shows: Joseph and the Amazing Technicolour Dreamcoat (music by Andrew Lloyd Webber) 1968, Jesus Christ Superstar (music by Andrew Lloyd Webber) 1970, Evita (music by ALW) 1976, Blondel (music by Stephen Oliver) 1983, Chess (music by Bjorn Ulvaeus and Benny Andersson) 1984, Cricket (music by Andrew Lloyd Webber) 1986, Starmania/Tycoon (music by Michel Berger) 1991, some lyrics for Beauty and the Beast (music by Alan Menken) 1994, Heathcliff (music by John Farrar) 1996, King David (music by Alan Menken) 1997, The Lion King (music by Elton John) 1997, Aida (music by Elton John) 1998, From Here to Eternity (music by Stuart Brayson) 2012; lyrics for animated film musicals: Aladdin (music by Alan Menken) 1992, The Lion King (music by Elton John) 1994, The Road to El Dorado (music by Elton John) 2000; major songs incl: Don't Cry For Me Argentina, Another Suitcase in Another Hall, Anthem from Chess, A Whole New World, The World is Stone, One Night in Bangkok, I Know Him So Well, Superstar, Any Dream Will Do, I Don't Know How To Love Him, Can You Feel The Love Tonight?, Circle of Life, All Time High, You Must Love Me, Hakuna Matata; writer and presenter American Pie (Radio 2) 2010–11 (52 part series); co-fndr: Pavilion Books, GRRR Books; chm Stars Organisation for Spastics 1983–85, pres Lord's Taverners 1988–90 and 2000, chm Fndn for Sport and the Arts 1991–2012, chm Richmond Park Cons Assoc 1996–2003; tstee Chance to Shine 2005–; Cameron Macintosh prof of contemporary theatre St Catherine's Coll Oxford 2003; memb Soc of Distinguished Songwriters (SODS), elected to Songwriters Hall of Fame US 1999; numerous gold and platinum discs, 13 Ivor Novello awards, 3 Tony awards, 6 Grammys, 3 Oscars, 3 Golden Globes, Olivier Special Award 2012; *Publications* incl: Guinness Book of British Hit Singles (10 vols) and many related books, Heartaches Cricketers' Almanack (annually since 1975), Evita (1978), Treasures of Lord's (1989), Oh What a Circus (memoirs, 1999), Debrett's People of Today 2007 (contrib article on Paul McCartney, 2006); *Recreations* cricket, history of popular music, chickens; *Clubs* MCC (pres 2002–03, tstee 2006–11), Garrick, Saints & Sinners (chm 1990–91), Groucho, Chelsea Arts, Dramatists', Heartaches Cricket; *Style—* Sir Tim Rice

RICH, Allan Jeffrey; s of Norman Rich, and Tessa, *née* Sawyer; *b* 9 October 1942; *m* 5 June 1966, Vivienne, da of Fred Ostro; 1 s (Jason b 8 May 1970), 2 da (Michaela b 6 May 1968, Natalie b 13 May 1972); *Career* TV buyer Masius Wynne Williams 1959–65, co fndr and media dir Davidson Pearce Berry & Spottiswoode 1965–74, fndr, chm and chief exec The Media Business plc 1975–, gp chm Mediacom TMB 1999, gp chm and vice-chm Europe Mediacom 2001–02; non-exec chm: Sports Revolution 2005–09, Michaelides & Bednash 2006–09, Esprit 2006–10; non-exec chm Cello 2004–; MAA 1966, MIPA 1966; *Recreations* tennis, football, cricket, golf; *Style—* Allan Rich, Esq

RICH, Nigel Mervyn Sutherland; CBE (1995); s of Charles Rich, and Mina Rich; *Educ* Sedbergh, New Coll Oxford (MA); *Career* articled clerk Deloitte Plender Griffiths 1967–71, accountant DH & S NY 1971–73, Jardine Matheson Hong Kong, Manila and South Africa 1974–94, md Hong Kong Land 1986–88, md Jardine Matheson 1988–94, ceo Trafalgar House 1994–96; chm: Exel 2002–05, Slough Estates Int 2006–; dep chm Xchanging 2006–; dir: KGR, John Armit Wines, Matheson & Co, Pacific Assets; dep chm Asia House; co-chm Philippine British Business Cncl; chm of govrs Downe House Sch; Freeman City of London, Renter Warden Worshipful Co of Tobacco Pipemakers and Tobacco Blenders; FCA 1971; *Recreations* golf, windsurfing, horseracing; *Clubs* Boodle's, Turf, MCC, R&A, Hurlingham, Denham Golf, NZ Golf; *Style—* Nigel Rich, Esq, CBE

RICHARD, Prof Dame Alison Fettes; DBE (2010), DL; da of Gavin Richard, and Joyce Richard; *b* 1 March 1948; *Educ* Queenswood Sch, Newnham Coll Cambridge (MA), Queen Elizabeth Coll Univ of London (PhD); *m* 1976, Robert E Dewar; 2 da, 1 s (decd); *Career* Yale Univ: asst prof 1972–80, assoc prof 1980–86, prof of anthropology 1986–2003, chair Dept of Anthropology 1986–90, dir Yale Peabody Museum of Natural History 1991–94, provost 1994–2002, Franklin Muzzy Crosby prof of the human environment 1998–2003, emeritus prof 2003–; vice-chllr Univ of Cambridge 2003–10, prof fell Newnham Coll Cambridge 2003–; pres Cambridge Network 2003–10; memb Editorial Bd: Folia Primatologica 1982–95, American Jl of Primatology 1988–97; author of numerous scientific articles on primate evolution, ecology and social behaviour in academic jls; co-dir Program of Conservation and Devpt in Southern Madagascar 1977–2003, conslt Species Survival Cmmn Int Union for the Conservation of Nature 1982–90, research fell Japan Soc for the Promotion of Science 1987; memb: External Advsy Ctee Duke Univ Primate Center 1980–94, Anthropology Visiting Ctee Harvard Bd of Overseers 1984–86, Int Advsy Gp of Scientists to Govt of Madagascar 1983–86, External Review Ctee for Anthropology Stanford Univ 1986, Duke Univ 1988 and State Univ of NY Stony Brook 1989, Scientific Advsy Cncl L B S Leakey Fndn 1986–96, Physical Anthropology Research Panel Nat Science Fndn 1988–91, Scientific Advsy Cncl Wenner-Gren Fndn for Anthropological Research 1991–94, Bd Liz Claiborne/Art Ortenberg Fndn 1998–, ESRC 2004–08, Advsy Bd Arcadia Fndn 2009–; memb Bd WWF-US 1995–2004 (memb Nat Cncl 1992–95), tstee WWF-Int Bd 2007–, tstee Howard Hughes Medical Inst 2009–; hon fell Wolfson Coll Cambridge 2003–, hon fell Lucy Cavendish Coll Cambridge 2003–; Verrill Medal Yale Univ 2008; hon degrees: Univ of Peking 2004, Univ of Antananarivo Madagascar 2005, York Univ Canada 2006, Univ of Edinburgh 2006, Queens Univ Belfast 2008, Anglia Ruskin Univ 2008, Yale Univ 2009, Chinese Univ of Hong Kong 2009, Ewha Womens Univ Korea 2009, Univ of Exeter 2010; Officier de l'Ordre National (Madagascar) 2005; *Publications* Behavioral Variation: case study of a Malagassy lemur (1978), Primates in Nature (1985); *Recreations* opera, gardening, cooking; *Clubs* Athenaeum; *Style—* Prof Dame Alison Richard, DBE, DL

RICHARD, Sir Cliff, né Harry Rodger Webb; kt (1995), OBE (1980); s of Rodger Oscar Webb (d 1961), and Dorothy Marie Bodkin (formerly Webb), *née* Beazley; *b* 14 October 1940; *Educ* Riversmead Sch Cheshunt; *Career* singer and actor; first hit record Move It 1958, own series on BBC and ITV, various repertory and variety seasons; 14 gold records, 35 silver records, celebrated 50th anniversary in music business 2008; films: Serious Charge 1959, Expresso Bongo 1960, The Young Ones 1961, Summer Holiday 1962, Wonderful Life 1964, Finders Keepers 1966, Two a Penny 1968, His Land 1970, Take Me High 1973; musicals: Time 1986, Heathcliff (title role) 1996; vice-pres: PHAB, Tear Fund, Princess Alice Hospice Tst, various other charitable orgns; Bernard Delfont Award for outstanding contribution to showbusiness 1995, South Bank Show's Outstanding Achievement Award 2000; *Books* Which One's Cliff (1977), Happy Christmas from Cliff (1980), You, Me and Jesus (1983), Jesus, Me and You (1985), Single-Minded (1988), My Life, My Way (2008); *Recreations* tennis, wine-making (own vineyards in Portugal); *Style—* Sir Cliff Richard, OBE; ✉ c/o PO Box 423, Leatherhead, Surrey KT22 2HJ (☎ 01372 467752, e-mail general@cliffrichard.org, website www.cliffrichard.org

RICHARD, Baron (Life Peer UK 1990), of Ammanford in the County of Dyfed; Ivor Seward Richard; PC (1993), QC (1971); s of Seward Thomas Richard, of Cardiff, and Isabella Irene Richard; *b* 30 May 1932; *Educ* St Michael's Sch Llanelly, Cheltenham Coll, Pembroke Coll Oxford (MA); *m* 1, 1956 (m dis 1962), Geraldine Maude, da of Alfred Moore, of Hartlepool, Co Durham; 1 s (Hon David Seward b 1959); m 2, 1962 (m dis 1985), Alison Mary, da of Joseph Imrie, of Alverstoke, Hants; 1 s (Hon Alun Seward b 1963), 1 da (Hon Isabel Margaret Katherine b 1966); m 3, 1989, Janet, da of John Jones, of Oxford; 1 s (Hon William John b 1990); *Career* called to the Bar Inner Temple 1955, Parly candidate (Lab) S Kensington Gen Election 1959 and LCC Election 1961, MP (Lab) Barons Court 1964–74, PPS to Sec of State for Def 1966–69, Parly under-sec of state for Def (Army) 1969–70, oppn spokesman Posts and Telecommunications 1970–71, dep oppn spokesman for Foreign Affrs 1971–74, UK perm rep at the UN 1974–79, chm Rhodesia Conf Geneva 1976; UK cmmr to the Cmmn of the European Communities 1981–85 responsible for: employment, social affrs, educn and vocational trg; Ldr of the Oppn in House of Lords 1992–97, Lord Privy Seal and ldr of the House of Lords 1997–98; chm Cmmn on the Powers and Electoral System of the Nat Assembly of Wales 2002–04; memb: Fabian Soc, Lab Lawyers; *Style—* The Rt Hon Lord Richard, PC, QC; ✉ House of Lords, London SW1A 0PW (☎ 020 7219 3000)

RICHARDS, (William Samuel) Clive; OBE (2000), DL (Herefordshire 2006); *b* 1 September 1937; *Educ* Bishop Vesey GS Sutton Coldfield; *m*; 3 c; *Career* articled clerk Peat Marwick Mitchell & Co Birmingham Office 1959–60, investment analyst rising to managing ptnr Wedd Durlacher & Co 1960–70, chief exec Rothschild Investment Tst 1970–75, gp fin dir N M Rothschild & Sons Ltd 1974–76, fndr Clive Richards & Co (investment and fin servs co, specialising in venture capital) 1976–; fndr and former chm Micro Business Systems plc 1978; former chm: Steel Burrill Jones Gp plc, Telephone Information Services plc, Security Archives plc, ESG Herefordshire Ltd; chm: Intelligent Environments Gp plc, Alpha Insurance Analysts Ltd, various other private cos; non-exec dir: Xpertise Gp plc, Corin Gp plc; former non-exec dir Minerva plc; commercial farm owner (2,059 acres); former pres Hereford Fedn of Young Farmers' Clubs; Top Fruit Grower of the Year 2010/11 and 2014; memb Cncl (representing Hereford) RASE 1995–; fndr Clive Richards Charity 1987, vice-pres Shaw Tst, memb Ctee Lord Mayor of London's Charity 1996–97; former chm of govrs Bishop Vesey GS, fndr and former chm Vesey Fndn; former chm Malvern Festival Theatre Tst; former treas and memb Ctee London Welsh RFC, patron and chm Bromyard Sports Assoc; High Sheriff Gtr London 1991–92; memb: Ct of Assts Worshipful Co of Chartered Accountants (Master 1996–97), Ct of Assts Worshipful Co of Gunmakers (Master 2011–12), Worshipful Co of Bowyers, Worshipful Co of Information Technologists, Worshipful Co of Gardeners; hon fell Univ of Worcester; FIMgt, FCMA 1960, FCA 1960; *Recreations* rugby, cricket, shooting, gardening, art, Nelsonia, Isambard Kingdom Brunel, breeding Hereford cattle and Black Labrador dogs; *Clubs* Reform, RAC, MCC; *Style—* Clive Richards, Esq, OBE, DL; ✉ Lower Hope, Ullingswick, Hereford HR1 3JF (☎ 01432 820557, fax 01432 820515, e-mail cliverichards@crco.co.uk)

RICHARDS, Dakota Blue; *b* 11 April 1994, Chelsea, London; *Career* actress; *Film* The Golden Compass 2007, The Secret of Moonacre 2008, The Fold 2013, The Quiet Hour 2014; *Television* Dustbin Baby 2008, Skins 2011–12, Lightfields 2013; *Style—* Ms Dakota Blue Richards; ✉ c/o Artists Rights Group Ltd, 4 Great Portland Street, London W1W 8PA (Twitter @DakotaBlueR)

RICHARDS, Rt Hon Lord Justice; Sir David Anthony Stewart Richards; kt (2003); s of late Kenneth Richards, of Heswall, Wirral, and late Winifred Edith, *née* Purdoe; *b* 9 June 1951; *Educ* Oundle, Trinity Coll Cambridge (MA); *m* 28 April 1979, Gilliam Moira, da of late Lt-Col W A Taylor; 1 s (Mark b 16 Oct 1981), 2 da (Sarah b 13 Jan 1985, Charlotte b 13 Jan 1985); *Career* called to the Bar Inner Temple 1974, jr counsel (Chancery) to DTI 1989–92, QC 1992, bencher Lincoln's Inn 2000, judge of the High Court of Justice (Chancery Div) 2003–15, a Lord Justice of the Court of Appeal 2015–; vice-chllr Co Palatine of Lancaster 2008–; *Clubs* Garrick; *Style—* The Rt Hon Lord Justice David Richards; ✉ Royal Courts of Justice, Strand, London WC2A 2LL

RICHARDS, David Thomas; s of Ralph Henry Richards (d 1990), of Cardiff, and Brenda Mary, *née* Brobin (d 2003); *b* 30 November 1954; *Educ* Whitchurch HS Cardiff, New Univ of Ulster Coleraine (BA); *m* 10 Aug 1979, Veryan Cumming, *née* Black, da of Griffith Black; 1 s (Adair b 19 June 1982), 2 da (Morna b 19 Aug 1984, Fiona b 6 Dec 1989); *Career* exec offr DTI 1978–79; Civil Service fast stream grad entry trainee 1979–83; Welsh Office: policy postings 1983–97, fin dir 1997–99; fin dir Welsh Govt 1999–2006, secondment to NHS Wales 2006–09, dir of governance Welsh Govt 2010– (princ accounting offr 2012); chair Steering Bd Intellectual Property Office 2002–11; *Recreations* books, playing the harp; *Style*— David Richards, Esq; ✉ National Assembly for Wales, Cathays Park, Cardiff CF1 3NQ (☎ 029 2082 5177, e-mail david.richards@wales.gsi.gov.uk)

RICHARDS, Derek William; s of William Albert Richards (d 1985), of Croydon, Surrey, and Mary Ann Ruby, *née* Bissell (d 1985); *b* 6 December 1943; *Educ* Wandsworth GS, Regent Street Poly Sch of Photography (Kodak scholarship, Dip Advtg Photography); *m* 10 June 1972, Rosemary Pauline, da of Reginald Arthur Sturman; *Career* photographer (specialising in people, travel and locations); initially asst to David Swann and Norman Parkinson, freelance advtg photographer 1967–, fndr Derek Richard Studios Ltd 1972, San Francisco 1982–84; numerous assignments for leading UK and USA based advtg agencies and design gps; memb Assoc of Photographers 1972 (memb Ctee 1973–75), fndr memb British Decoy and Wildfowl Carvers' Assoc (award winner 1989–2004); elected to Somerset Guild of Craftsmen 2006 (memb Gallery Ctee); *Books* one of the 80 craftsmen featured in Significant Figures in the Arts & Crafts Today (2011); *Recreations* restoring and 'trialing' vintage sports cars, decoy carving, film, theatre, walking, bird watching; *Clubs* Vintage Sports Car; *Style*— Derek Richards, Esq; ✉ Penn House, Hardington Mandeville, Somerset BA22 9PL (☎ 01935 862958, e-mail info@derekrichards.co.uk)

RICHARDS, Sir Francis Neville; KCMG (2002, CMG 1994), CVO (1991), DL (Glos 2007); o s of Sir (Francis) Brooks Richards, KCMG, DSC (d 2002); *b* 18 November 1945; *Educ* Eton, King's Coll Cambridge (MA); *m* 16 Jan 1971, Gillian Bruce, da of I S Nevill, MC (d 1948); 1 s (James b 1975), 1 da (Joanna b 1977); *Career* Royal Green Jackets 1967–69; HM Dip Serv: third sec to second sec Moscow 1971–73, second sec to first sec UK Delgn to MBFR talks Vienna 1973–76, FCO 1976–85, asst private sec to sec of state 1980–82, cnsllr (econ and commercial) New Delhi 1985–88, head of S Asian Dept FCO 1988–90, high cmmr to Namibia 1990–92, min Moscow 1992–95, asst under sec of state Central and Eastern Europe FCO 1995–96, dir Europe FCO 1996–97, dep under sec of state FCO 1998; dir GCHQ 1998–2003, govr and C-in-C Gibraltar 2003–06, chm Nat Security Inspectorate 2007–13; chm Int Advsy Bd Altimo 2007–13, memb Advsy Bd Sch of Mgmnt Univ of Bath 2014–; chm Bletchley Park Tst 2007–12, tstee Imperial War Museum 2007–16 (dep chm 2009–11, chm 2011–16); hon sr fell Univ of Birmingham, Hon DUniv Univ of Birmingham 2013; Hon Col Catering Support Regt RLC 2012–15; KStJ 2003; *Recreations* riding, walking, travel; *Clubs* Brooks's, Special Forces; *Style*— Sir Francis Richards, KCMG, CVO, DL

RICHARDS, Prof (William) Graham; CBE (2001); s of Percy Richards, and Julia, *née* Evans; *b* 1 October 1939, Hoylake, Merseyside; *Educ* Birkenhead Sch, BNC Oxford (MA, DPhil, DSc); *m* 1, 1970, Jessamy Kershaw (d 1988); m 2, 1996, Mary Phillips; *Career* jr res fell Balliol Coll Oxford 1964–66, CNRS Paris 1965–66; Univ of Oxford: lectr 1966–94, reader 1994–96, prof 1996–2007, chm of chemistry 1997–2007; Fulbright fell Stanford Univ 1975–76; dir: IP Gp plc, Inhibox Ltd; founding scientist Oxford Molecular Gp plc; ed Jl of Molecular Graphics 1984–96; Lloyd of Kilgerran Prize 1996, Mullard Award of Royal Soc 1998, Italgas Prize 2001, ACS Award for Computers in Chemical and Pharmaceutical Research 2004; memb American Chemistry Soc 1980; hon fell Balliol Coll Oxford 2006; FRSC 1966, fell AAAS 1998; *Publications* over 350 scientific papers, 19 books incl Spin-outs: creating businesses from university intellectual property (2009), 50 Years at Oxford (2011), University Intellectual Property: a source of finance and impact (2012); *Recreations* sport; *Clubs* Vincent's (Oxford); *Style*— Prof Graham Richards, CBE; ✉ Brasenose College, Oxford OX1 4AJ (☎ 01865 275908, fax 01865 275905, e-mail graham.richards@chem.ox.ac.uk)

RICHARDS, Prof Ivor James; s of Philip James Richards (d 1981), of Newmarket, Suffolk, and Ivy Gwenllian, *née* Kimber (d 1995); *b* 1 May 1943; *Educ* Newmarket GS, Univ of Wales (MA); *m* 5 June 1976 (m dis 1995), Anne Rostas; 1 da (Sarah Elizabeth b 13 March 1983), 1 s (Owen James b 30 Dec 1984); *Career* assoc architect Sir Leslie Martin Architects Cambridge 1969–90; works incl: Faculty of Music Univ of Cambridge 1975–85, Royal Concert Hall Glasgow 1978–90, Centro de Arte Moderna Gulbenkian Fndn Lisbon 1980–84, Royal Scottish Acad of Music and Drama Glasgow 1988, Ecumenical Church Cambridge 1991–, Masters' Houses Stowe Sch Buckingham 1993–, Orientation Centre Hadrian's Wall Steelrigg Northumberland National Park 1998–; exhibition Ivor Richards: retrospective 30 years (Univ of Newcastle) 1998; prof of architecture Sch of Architecture: Univ of Wales Cardiff 1986–95, Univ of Newcastle upon Tyne 1995–2004; emeritus prof of architecture Univ of Newcastle upon Tyne 2004–; visiting prof Dept of Architecture and History of Art Univ of Cambridge 2013–; external examiner: Sch of Architecture Univ of Newcastle upon Tyne, Sch of Architecture Univ of Nottingham, Sch of Architecture Univ of Central England, Sch of Architecture Univ of Singapore 1997–98; advsr Northumberland National Park 1998–2002; memb Advsy Bd Sch of Architecture Carnegie Mellon Univ Pittsburgh PA USA 1997–; RIBA Commendation Award (for Richards House Cambridge) 1985, RIBA Tstees' Medal (for Centro de Arte Moderna Gulbenkian Fndn Lisbon) 1991, Hyde Chair for Excellence in Architecture Univ of Nebraska 1991, RIBA Award (for Rostas House Cambridge) 1993; memb ARB, chartered memb ARIBA; *Publications* Manhattan Lofts (2000), Ecology of the Sky (2001), Groundscrapers and Subscrapers (2001), Eco Skyscrapers (ed, 2007); contrib to Architects Jl, Architectural Review, Architecture Today and Architecture Research Quarterly; *Recreations* writing, walking, cities and architecture; *Style*— Prof Ivor Richards; ✉ Apartment 12, Richard Newcombe Court, Rackham Close, Histon Road, Cambridge CB4 3EY (☎ 07517 934331, e-mail ivor_richards@hotmail.co.uk)

RICHARDS, Keith; *b* 18 December 1943; *Educ* Sidcup Art Sch; *Partner* (sep) Anita Pallenberg; 2 s (Marlon b 10 Aug 1969, Tara b 26 March 1976 d 4 June 1976), 1 da (Dandelion b 17 April 1972); m 1, 18 Dec 1983, Patti, *née* Hansen; 2 da (Theodora b 18 March 1985, Alexandra b 28 July 1986); *Career* guitarist and songwriter; Rolling Stones formed London 1962; signed recording contracts with: Impact Records/Decca 1963, London Records/Decca 1965, CBS 1983, Virgin 1992; has worked with Chuck Berry, Buddy Guy, Muddy Waters, Eric Clapton, Johnnie Johnson, John Lee Hooker and others; albums with Rolling Stones: The Rolling Stones (1964, reached UK no 1), The Rolling Stones No 2 (1965, UK no 1), Out Of Our Heads (1965, UK no 2), Aftermath (1966, UK no 1), Big Hits: High Tide and Green Grass (compilation, 1966, UK no 4), got LIVE if you want it! (live, 1967), Between The Buttons (1967, UK no 3), Flowers (US compilation, 1967, US no 3), Their Satanic Majesties Request (1967, UK no 3), Beggars Banquet (1968, UK no 3), Through The Past Darkly: Big Hits Vol 2 (compilation, 1969, UK no 2), Let It Bleed (1969, UK no 1), Get Yer Ya-Ya's Out! (live, 1970, UK no 1), Stone Age (compilation, 1971, UK no 4), Sticky Fingers (1971, UK no 1), Hot Rocks 1964–71 (US compilation, 1972, US no 4), Exile On Main Street (1972, UK no 1), More Hot Rocks (US compilation, 1973, US no 9), Goat's Head Soup (1973, UK no 1), It's Only Rock'n'Roll (1974, UK no 2), Made In The Shade (compilation, 1975, UK no 14), Rolled Gold – The Very Best of The Rolling Stones (compilation, 1975, UK no 7), Black and Blue (1976, UK no 2), Love You Live (live, 1977, UK no 3), Some Girls (1978, UK no 2), Emotional Rescue (1980, UK no 1), Tattoo You (1981, UK no 2), Still Life: American Concert 1981 (live, 1981, UK no 4), Undercover (1983, UK no 3), Rewind 1971–1984 (compilation, 1984, UK no 23), Dirty Work (1986, UK no 4), Steel Wheels (1989, UK no 2), Flashpoint (live, 1991, UK no 6), Voodoo Lounge (1994, UK no 1), Bridges to Babylon (1997, UK no 6), Forty Licks (2002); solo albums: Talk Is Cheap (1988, UK no 37), Live at the Hollywood Palladium December 15 1988 (1991), Main Offender (1992), Wingless Angels (1996); concert films: Sympathy For The Devil (dir Jean Luc Godard) 1969, Gimme Shelter 1970, Ladies and Gentlemen, The Rolling Stones 1977, Let's Spend The Night Together (dir Hal Ashby) 1983, Hail, Hail, Rock'n'Roll (with Chuck Berry) 1986, Flashpoint (film of 1990 Steel Wheels World Tour) 1991, Live at the Hollywood Palladium December 15 1988 (DVD, 2002); feature film: Michael Kohlhgaas 1969; *Style*— Keith Richards, Esq; ✉ c/o Munro Sounds, 5 Church Row, Wandsworth Plain, London SW18 1ES

RICHARDS, Prof Keith Sheldon; s of Maurice Richards (d 1973), of Cornwall, and Jean, *née* Young (d 2012); *b* 25 May 1949; *Educ* Falmouth GS, Jesus Coll Cambridge (MA, PhD); *m* 18 August 1973, Susan Mary, da of Frederick Brooks; *Career* lectr in geography Coventry Poly 1973–77 (sr lectr 1977), lectr Dept of Geography Univ of Hull 1978–84 (sr lectr 1984); Univ of Cambridge: lectr Dept of Geography 1984–, reader in physical geography 1995, prof of geography 1995–2014, head Dept of Geography 1994–99, exec sec Ctee for Interdisciplinary Environmental Studies 1995–99, dir Scott Polar Research Inst 1997–2002, emeritus prof 2014–; Emmanuel Coll Cambridge: fell 1984, dir of studies in geography 1984–96, asst bursar 1986–94 (dep bursar 1989); Br Geomorphological Research Gp: Ctee memb 1978–80, hon sec 1980–83, jr vice-chm 1992, vice-chm 1993–94, chm 1994–95; vice-pres (research) RGS/IBG 2004–07 (hon sec 2003–04), pres Geography Section BAAS 2005–06; memb: Br Hydrological Soc, Quaternary Research Assoc; NERC: memb Aquatic and Atmospheric Physical Sciences Ctee 1990–93, memb Steering Ctees 1995–97, memb Peer Review Coll 2004–; memb Peer Review Coll ESRC 2010–; BGRG ed 1984–89, memb ed bd and book review ed Earth Surface Processes and Landforms 1990–98; HEFCE: memb Geography Panel Research Assessment Panel (RAE) 2001, chair Geography and Environmental Studies Sub-Panel RAE 2008 and Research Excellence Framework (REF) 2014; assessor for Environment and Climate Prog DGXII EC 1996–; Cuthbert Peek Award RGS 1983, Leverhulme research fell 1985, Founder's Medal RGS 2013, Linton Award 2015; fell Br Soc for Geomorphology 2013; CGeog 2002, FRSA 2005; *Books* Stochastic Processes in One-Dimensional Series: An Introduction (1979), Geomorphological Techniques (ed with A S Goudie and others, 1982), Rivers: Form and Process in Alluvial Channels (1982), Geomorphology and Soils (ed with R R Arnett and S Ellis, 1985), River Channels: Environment and Process (ed, 1987), Slope Stability: Geotechnical Engineering and Geomorphology (ed with M Anderson, 1987), Landform Monitoring, Modelling and Analysis (ed with S Lane and J Chandler, 1998), Glacier Hydrology and Hydrochemistry (ed with M Sharp and M Tranter, 1998), Arsenic Pollution: A Global Synthesis (with P Ravenscroft and H Brammer, 2009); author of over 200 papers on geomorphology, hydrology, river and slope processes in various academic jls; *Recreations* reading, travel, opera; *Style*— Prof Keith Richards; ✉ Department of Geography, University of Cambridge, Cambridge CB2 3EN (☎ 01223 333393, e-mail ksr10@cam.ac.uk)

RICHARDS, Prof Martin Paul Meredith; s of Paul Westmacott Richards, and Sarah Anne, *née* Hotham; *b* 26 January 1940; *Educ* Westminster, Trinity Coll Cambridge (MA, PhD, ScD); *m* 1, 1961 (m dis 1966), Evelyn Cowdy; m 2, 1999, Sarah, *née* Smalley; *Career* SRC post-doctoral fell 1965–67; Univ of Cambridge: research fell Trinity Coll 1965–69, head Centre for Family Research 1967–2005, lectr in social psychology 1970–89, reader in human devpt 1989–97, head of dept Social and Political Scis Faculty 1996–99, prof of family research 1997–2005, emeritus prof 2005–; visiting fell Dept of Biology Princeton Univ 1966–67, visitor Center for Cognitive Studies Harvard Univ 1967 and 1968, Mental Health Research Fund fell 1970, Wineguard visiting prof Univ of Guelph 1987, visiting lectr NZ Fedn of Parents Centres 1984 and 1987, hon visiting prof Dept of Soc Scis City Univ 1992–94, de Lissa fell Univ of S Australia 1993, Williams Evans visiting fell Univ of Otago 1997; vice-chair UK Biobank and Governance Cncl 2008–14, memb Nuffield Cncl on Bioethics 2013–; *Books* Race, Culture, and Intelligence (ed jtly, 1972), The Integration of a Child into a Social World (ed, 1974), Benefits and Hazards of the New Obstetrics (ed jtly, 1977), Separation and Special Care Baby Units (jtly, 1978), Infancy: the World of the Newborn (1980), Parent-Baby Attachment in Premature Infants (ed jtly, 1983), Children in Social Worlds: Development in a Social Context (ed with Paul Light, 1986), Divorce Matters (jtly, 1987), Family Life (ed jtly), The Politics of Maternity Care (ed jtly, 1990), Sexual Arrangements: Marriage and Affairs (with J Reibstein, 1992), Obstetrics in the 1990s: Current Controversies (ed jtly, 1992), The Troubled Helix: Social and Psychological Implications of the New Human Genetics (ed jtly, 1996), What is a Parent? (ed with A Bainham and S Day Sclater, 1999), Body Lore and Laws (ed jtly, 2002), Children and their Families: Contact, Rights and Welfare (ed jtly, 2003), Blackwell Companion to the Sociology of Families (ed jtly, 2003), Supporting Children Through Family Change (jtly, 2003), Kinship Matters (ed jtly), Death Rites and Rights (ed jtly, 2007), The Limits of Consent (ed jtly, 2009), Regulating Autonomy (ed jtly, 2009), Birth Rites and Rights (ed jtly, 2011), Reproductive Donation (ed jtly, 2012), Relatedness in Assisted Reproduction (ed jtly, 2014); also author of numerous reviews and papers in learned jls; *Recreations* listening to country music, bird-watching, alpine gardening; *Style*— Prof Martin Richards; ✉ Centre for Family Research, University of Cambridge, Free School Lane, Cambridge CB2 3RF (☎ 01223 334510, e-mail mpmr@cam.ac.uk)

RICHARDS, Menna; OBE (2010); da of Penri Richards, of Maesteg, Mid Glamorgan, and Dilys, *née* Watkins; *b* 27 February 1953; *Educ* Maesteg GS, UCW Aberystwyth (BA); *m* 1985, Patrick Hannan; *Career* radio & TV journalist BBC Wales 1976–83; HTV Wales: journalist 1983–99, head of factual progs 1991, dir of progs 1993, md 1997–2000; controller BBC Wales 2000–; *Recreations* music, friends, family; *Style*— Ms Menna Richards, OBE; ✉ BBC Wales, Broadcasting House, Llandaf, Cardiff CF5 2YQ (☎ 029 2032 2001, fax 029 2055 5286)

RICHARDS, Prof Sir Michael Adrian; kt (2010), CBE (2001); s of Donald Richards (d 1994), and Peronelle, *née* Armitage-Smith; *b* 14 July 1951; *Educ* Radley, Trinity Coll Cambridge (MA), Bart's Med Coll London; *Career* ICRF research fell in med oncology Bart's London 1982–86, hon conslt in med oncology Guy's Hosp London 1986–95 (ICRF sr lectr 1986–91, ICRF reader 1991–95), clinical dir Cancer Services Guy's and St Thomas' Hosp London 1991–99, Sainsbury prof of palliative med St Thomas' Hosp London 1995–, head Academic Div of Oncology KCL 1998–99, nat cancer dir Dept of Health 1999–, chair Nat Cancer Research Inst 2006–08, currently chief inspector of hosps Care Quality Cmmn; former tstee: Science Museum, Marie Curie Cancer Care; FRCP 1993, Hon FRCR 2000, FFPHM 2002; *Publications* over 150 papers related to cancer and cancer services; *Recreations* hill walking, classical music; *Style*— Prof Sir Michael Richards, CBE

RICHARDS, Penny; da of Denis Richards, of London, and Barbara, *née* Smethurst; *b* 6 November 1950; *Educ* N London Collegiate Sch, AA Sch of Architecture (AADipl); *m* 28 June 1975, John Pringle, *qv*, s of Alexander (Sandy) Pringle; 1 s (Patrick b 24 Sept 1982), 1 da (Georgina b 28 Dec 1984); *Career* architect; with Rick Mather Architects 1977–81, ptnr Pringle + Richards Architects 1981–96, dir Pringle Richards Sharratt Architects 1996–; projects incl: Shrewsbury music sch and auditorium (RIBA Award 2001), Gallery Oldham (RIBA Award 2002), Sheffield Millennium Gallery and Winter Garden (Civic Tst Award and RIBA Award 2003), V&A Museum, Glass Gallery, Pitt Rivers Research Centre and Balfour Library, Pitt Rivers Museum main entrance (Oxford Preservation Tst Award 2009); first year tutor AA Sch of Architecture 1979–80, first year tutor (architecture) Oxford Poly 1990–91; external examiner: South Bank Univ 1990–94, Westminster Univ 1996–99, Bartlett Sch of Architecture UCL 2003–08, Univ of Lincoln 2010–; visiting prof Grad Sch of Architecture Univ of Pennsylvania 2000–01; vice-pres AA 2002–03 (memb Cncl 1998–2003), assessor Civic Tst 2000–03, reader Queen's Anniversary Prizes 2002–, memb RIBA Educn Ctee 1999–2004, memb RIBA Educn Tst Fund Ctee 1999–2008; RIBA 2000; *Recreations* everything to do with Italy: being there, speaking Italian, cooking Italian; growing English plants in Italy and Italian plants in

R

England; *Style*— Ms Penny Richards; ✉ The Old Lodge , Bishops Avenue, London SW6 6EE; Pringle Richards Sharratt Architects, Studio 2.01, Canterbury Court, Kennington Park, 1 Brixton Road, London SW9 6DE (✆ 020 7793 2828, fax 020 7793 2829, e-mail penny.richards@prsarchitects.com)

RICHARDS, Peter; s of Alfred James Clifford Richards (d 1969), of Stoke-sub-Hamdon, Somerset, and Eileen Mary Richards (d 2002); *b* 10 December 1954; *Educ* Yeovil GS, Plymouth Poly, Canterbury Sch of Architecture (DipArch), Univ of Reading (MSc); *m* 1, 1983 (m dis 1986), Elizabeth, *née* Wilmott; *m* 2, 1988, Isabel, *née* Miles; *Career* DOE PSA 1980–83; HOK Cecil Denny Highton: project architect 1983–88, assoc 1988–90, ptnr 1990–95, dir (i/c incl museums, further educn, higher educn and urban regeneration projects) 1996–2004; princ own architecture practice 2004–08, assoc dir Atkins Educn Architects 2007–09 (building schs for the future projects for Portsmouth, Bristol and NE Lincs), currently conslt for educn, cultural and govt office projects; Conservation Award for works to the Alfred Waterhouse bldg Royal Borough of Kensington and Chelsea; RIBA, memb Assoc of Project Mangrs (MAPM); *Recreations* conservation of historic buildings; *Style*— Peter Richards, Esq; ✉ 6 Hare Knapp, Bradford on Avon, Wiltshire BA15 1PJ (✆ 01225 864723, e-mail pr@peterrichards-architects.co.uk)

RICHARDS, Peter Charles; s of Geoff Richards, and Susan, *née* Baker; *b* 10 March 1978, Portsmouth, Hants; *Educ* Royal Hosp Sch Holbrook, Lord Wandsworth Coll Hants (England rugby schs cap); *m* Jo Wood; 1 da (Isabella Catherine b 11 Feb 2008), 1 s (Harry Valentine b 28 Nov 2011); *Career* sports TV and radio presenter, rugby coach and former professional rugby player; London Irish RFC 1996–99, Harlequins RFC 1999–2001, Benneton Treviso 2001–02, Bristol RFC 2002–03, Wasps RFC 2003–05, Gloucester RFC 2005–07, London Irish RFC 2007–10; England: Under 16s, Under 18s, Under 19s, Under 21s, England A, England 7s, first England cap 2006, memb squad World Cup 2007 (finalists); *Style*— Peter Richards, Esq; ✉ c/o Jo Wood (✆ 07979 673366, e-mail jomarywood@gmail.com)

RICHARDS, His Hon Judge Philip Brian; s of Glyn Bevan Richards (d 1976), of Ynysybwl, and Nancy Gwenhwyfar, *née* Evans (d 1992), of Bargoed; *b* 3 August 1946; *Educ* Cardiff HS, Univ of Bristol (LLB); *m* 1, 17 July 1971 (m dis 1988), Dorothy Louise, da of Victor George (d 2003), of Ystrad Mynach; 2 da (Rhuanedd b 1974, Lowri b 1978); *m* 2, 26 March 1994, Julia, da of Roy Jones (d 2002), of Tylorstown; 1 da (Megan b 1995), 1 step s (David b 1980); *Career* called to the Bar Inner Temple 1969; in practice 1969–2001, circuit jr Wales & Chester Circuit 1994, head of chambers 30 Park Place Cardiff 1994–99, recorder of the Crown Court 2000–01 (asst recorder 1995–99), circuit judge (Wales & Chester Circuit) 2001–; memb Parole Bd 2010–; Parly candidate (Plaid Cymru) 1974 and 1979; chm Parliament for Wales Campaign 1996–98, candidate Nat Assembly of Wales 1999; chm Judicial Welsh Language Trg Sub-Ctee of Lord Chllr's Standing Ctee on Welsh Language 2001–03 and 2005–; patron: Mountain Ash RFC, Neyland RFC; tstee Welsh Writers' Tst, chm Bd of Govrs Ysgol Gyfun Rhydfelen 1988–95, govr Ysgol Gynradd Gymraeg Abercynon 1999–2006; *Recreations* music, sport, literature, walking; *Clubs* Cardiff and County; *Style*— His Hon Judge Philip Richards; ✉ Cardiff Crown Court, The Law Courts, Cathays Park, Cardiff CF10 3PG

RICHARDS, Rt Hon Sir Stephen Price; kt (1997), PC (2005); s of Richard Alun Richards, of Llandre, Dyfed, and late Ann Elonwy Mary, *née* Price; *b* 8 December 1950; *Educ* KCS Wimbledon, St John's Coll Oxford (MA); *m* 29 May 1976, Lucy Elizabeth, da of Dr Frank Henry Stubbings, of Cambridge; 2 s (Matthew b 1979, Thomas b 1981), 1 da (Emily b 1984); *Career* called to the Bar Gray's Inn 1975 (bencher 1992); standing counsel to Dir Gen of Fair Trading 1989–91 (second jr counsel to DG 1987–89), a jr counsel to The Crown common law 1990–91, first jr Treasy counsel common law 1992–97; recorder of the Crown Court 1996–97, judge of the High Court of Justice (Queen's Bench Div) 1997–2005, presiding judge of the Wales & Chester Circuit 2000–03, a Lord Justice of Appeal 2005–16, dep head of civil justice 2013–15; dep chm Boundary Cmmn for Wales 2001–05; govr KCS Wimbledon 1998–2007 (chm Governing Body 2004–07); Hon LLD Univ of Glamorgan 2004, hon fell St John's Coll Oxford 2008–; *Books* Chitty on Contracts (co ed 25 and 26 edns); *Recreations* the Welsh hills; *Style*— The Rt Hon Sir Stephen Richards

RICHARDS OF HERSTMONCEUX, Baron (Life Peer UK 2014), of Emsworth in the County of Hampshire David Julian Richards; GCB (2011), KCB 2007), CBE (2000), DSO (2001); s of Col John Downie Richards, and Pamela Mary Richards; *b* 4 March 1952; *Educ* Eastbourne Coll (head boy, rugby capt), UC Cardiff (BA); *m* Caroline; 2 da (Joanna, Philippa); *Career* cmmnd RA 1971; regtl duty and staff 11 Armd Bde 1974–83, Staff Coll Camberley 1984, Cdr Field Battery 47 Field Regt 11 Armd Bde, COS Berlin Inf Bde 1986–88, instr Staff Coll 1988–91, CO 3 Regt RHA 1991–94, Col Army Plans MOD 1994–96, Higher Command and Staff Course 1996, Cdr 4 Armd Bde Germany 1996–98, Chief Jt Force Ops Permanent Jt HQ 1998–2001, Cdr UK Task Force East Timor 1999, Cdr UK Jt Task Force Sierra Leone 2000 (twice), Maj-Gen COS NATO ACE Rapid Reaction Corps Germany 2001–02, ACGS 2002–05, Lt-Gen Cdr Allied Rapid Reaction Corps Germany 2005–08, Cdr NATO/ISAF Afghanistan 2006–07, Gen C-in-C Land Forces 2008–09, CGS 2009–10, CDS 2010–13, sr advsr IISS 2013–16; exec chm Equilibrium Global 2014–16; dep grand pres Royal Commonwealth Ex-Services League 2014–16; *Publications* Victory Among People, Lessons from Countering Insurgency and Stabilising Fragile States (jt ed), Oxford Compendium of Modern Warfare (contrib), Taking Command (autobiography, 2014); *Recreations* military history, opera, riding, wine, offshore sailing; *Clubs* Royal Yacht Squadron, Royal Cruising, RA Yacht, British Kiel Yacht (Adm), Army and Navy, Cavalry and Guards; *Style*— The Lord Richards of Herstmonceux, GCB, CBE, DSO; ✉ House of Lords, London SW1A 0PW

RICHARDSON, Prof Brian Frederick; s of Ronald Frederick Richardson, CBE (d 1991), of London, and Anne Elizabeth, *née* McArdle (d 2005); *b* 6 December 1946, Woodford; *Educ* Ampleforth, Lincoln Coll Oxford, Bedford Coll London; *m* 31 March 1973, Catherine, da of Paul Normand; 3 da (Sophie b 24 Aug 1975, Alice b 23 Feb 1979, Laura b 25 Nov 1983); *Career* lectr in Italian: Univ of Strathclyde 1970–72, Univ of Aberdeen 1972–76, Univ of Leeds 1977–96; prof of Italian language Univ of Leeds 1996–2012; FBA 2003; *Style*— Prof Brian Richardson; ✉ School of Languages, Cultures and Societies, University of Leeds, Leeds LS2 9JT

RICHARDSON, David Ian; s of Jack Richardson (d 1997), and Betty, *née* Sandiford (d 2007); *b* 30 July 1958, Middleton, Lancs; *Educ* Wymondham Coll Norfolk, UC Durham (BA); *m* 4 Sept 1982, Victoria Mary, *née* Hannon; 1 da (Alice Jane b 20 Nov 1993), 1 s (Tobias Jack b 25 Feb 1998); *Career* HM Revenue and Customs (formerly Inland Revenue): joined as inspector of taxes 1979, press sec 1990–92, head Adjudicator's Office 1993–96, asst dir international 1996–2002, dir of central policy 2005–07, dir of specialist personal tax (formerly charity, assets and residence) 2008–13, dir of counter-avoidance 2014–; seconded: DTI 1985–87, head of EU and int tax HM Treasy 2002–04; *Recreations* family, hill walking, wine, Norwich City FC; *Style*— David Richardson, Esq; ✉ Counter-Avoidance, HM Revenue and Customs, 100 Parliament Street, London SW1A 2BQ (✆ 03000 585285, e-mail david.richardson@hmrc.gsi.gov.uk)

RICHARDSON, Prof David John; *b* 12 August 1964, Tynemouth; *Educ* Univ of Keele (BSc), Univ of Birmingham (PhD); *Career* UEA: joined 1991, dean Faculty of Science, pro-vice-chllr (Research, Enterprise and Engagement), dep vice-chllr, vice-chllr 2014–; *Style*— Prof David Richardson; ✉ University of East Anglia, Norwich Research Park, Norwich, Norfolk NR4 7TJ

RICHARDSON, Frank Anthony; s of Albert Edward Richardson, and Eileen, *née* Roberts; *b* 20 March 1933; *Educ* Leeds Central HS; *m* 6 Sept 1958, Patricia Elsie, da of Robert Stevenson Taylor; *Career* agent and organiser Cons Party 1956–73, sec Nat Union of Cons Agents 1971–73; assoc dir: John Addey Assocs 1973–77, Charles Barker Watney & Powell 1978–83; dir: Charles Barker Watney & Powell 1983, Shandwick Public Affairs 1990–94; sr ptnr Richardson Consultants 1994–; admin sec: Parly Info Tech Ctee 1985–2004, Parly Space Ctee 1989–2006, Parly Road Tport Study Gp 1987–99; jt sec Euro Inter-Parly Space Conference 2002; vice-pres Cons Group for Europe 1992–95; Freeman City of London 1993; memb Yorks Athletics Team 1958; *Recreations* tennis, swimming, travel; *Style*— Frank Richardson, Esq; ✉ 22 Gloucester Place Mews, London W1U 8BA (✆ 020 7487 4872)

RICHARDSON, Prof Genevra; CBE (2007); da of John Richardson (d 2002), of Broadshaw, W Lothian, and Josephine, *née* Henderson; *b* 1 September 1948; *Educ* KCL (LLB, LLM); *m* 12 April 1977, Sir Oliver Thorold, 16 Bt, qv, s of Sir Anthony Henry Thorold, 15 Bt (d 1999); 1 s, 1 da; *Career* lectr in law UEA 1979–87; Queen Mary Univ of London: lectr 1987–89, reader 1989–94, prof of public law 1994–2005, dean Faculty of Law 1996–99; prof of law King's Coll London 2005–; chair: Mgmnt Ctee Prisoners' Advice Service 1994–2003, Ind Enquiry into Care and Treatment of Darren Carr 1996–97, Expert Ctee advising Mins on Reform of Mental Health Legislation 1999, Appointing Authy for Phase 1 Ethics Ctees 2009–12; memb: Mental Health Act Cmmn 1987–92, Mgmnt Ctee Public Law Project 1991–2001, Animal Procedures Ctee 1998–2006, Administrative Justice and Tribunals Cncl (previously Cncl on Tribunals) 2001–, Cncl MRC 2001–08; tstee Med Research Fndn 2005–; author of books and jl articles in public law, criminal justice and mental health and the law; tstee: Med Coll of St Barts Hosp Tst 1999–2004, Nuffield Fndn 2002–; Hon FRCPsych 2004, FBA 2007; *Style*— Prof Genevra Richardson, CBE, FBA; ✉ School of Law, King's College, Strand, London WC2R 2LS

RICHARDSON, His Hon Judge Jeremy William; QC (2000); s of Thomas William Sydney Raymond Richardson (d 2000), of Retford, Notts, and Jean Mary, *née* Revill; *b* 3 April 1958; *Educ* Forest Sch, QMC London (LLB); *Partner* David Carruthers (civil partnership 2006); *Career* called to the Bar Inner Temple 1980 (bencher 2007); memb NE Circuit 1982–2009 (sec 1991–96), recorder 2000–09 (asst recorder 1998–2000), dep High Court judge (Family Div) 2004–09, designated civil judge for Humberside 2009–, resident judge at Hull Combined Court 2014–; memb Gen Cncl of the Bar 1992–94; *Style*— His Hon Judge Jeremy Richardson, QC; ✉ Kingston upon Hull Combined Court Centre, Lowgate, Hull HU1 2EZ (✆ 01482 586161, fax 01482 588257)

RICHARDSON, Dr Joanna; da of Capt Frederick Richardson, Intelligence Corps (d 1978), and Charlotte Elsa, *née* Benjamin (d 1978); *Educ* The Downs Sch Seaford, St Anne's Coll Oxford (MA, DLitt); *Career* author; FRSL 1959 (memb Cncl 1961–86); Chevalier de l'Ordre des Arts et des Lettres (France) 1987; *Books* Fanny Brawne: A Biography (1952), Théophile Gautier: His Life and Times (1958), Edward FitzGerald (1960), FitzGerald: Selected Works (ed, 1962), The Pre-Eminent Victorian: A Study of Tennyson (1962), The Everlasting Spell: A Study of Keats and His Friends (1963), Essays by Divers Hands (ed, 1963), Edward Lear (1965), George IV: A Portrait (1966), Creevey and Greville (1967), Princess Mathilde (1969), Verlaine (1971), Enid Starkie (1973), Verlaine, Poems (ed and translator, 1974), Stendhal: A Critical Biography (1974), Baudelaire, Poems (ed and translator, 1975), Victor Hugo (1976), Zola (1978), Keats and His Circle: An Album of Portraits (1980), Gautier, Mademoiselle de Maupin (translator, 1981), The Life and Letters of John Keats (1981), Letters from Lambeth: the Correspondence of the Reynolds Family with John Freeman Milward Dovaston 1808–1815 (1981), Colette (1983), Judith Gautier (1986, French edn 1989, awarded Prix Goncourt de la biographie, first time to a non-French writer), Portrait of a Bonaparte: the Life and Times of Joseph-Napoléon Primoli 1851–1927 (1987), Baudelaire (1994); *Style*— Dr Joanna Richardson; ✉ c/o Curtis Brown Ltd, 4th Floor, Haymarket House, 28–29 Haymarket, London SW1Y 4SP (✆ 020 7396 6600)

RICHARDSON, John; *Educ* Bromsgrove Sch, Univ of St Andrews (MA); *Career* assoc prodr Sonia Friedman Prodns 1999–2006 (prodns incl: Celebration, Shoot the Crow, Otherwise Engaged, As You Like It, The Home Place, Whose Life is it Anyway?, By the Bog of Cats, Guantanamo: Honour Bound to Defend Freedom, Endgame, Jumpers, Calico, See You Next Tuesday, Hitchcock Blonde, Absolutely! (Perhaps), Sexual Perversity in Chicago, Ragtime, Macbeth, What the Night Is For, A Day In the Death of Joe Egg (also Broadway), Afterplay, Up For Grabs, On An Average Day, Noises Off (also Broadway), Benefactors, Lobby Hero, Gagarin Way, Maria Friedman Live, A Servant to Two Masters, Port Authority, Spoonface Steinberg, Speed-the-Plow, In Flame, The Mystery of Charles Dickens, The Late Middle Classes, Last Dance at Dum Dum), prodr Old Vic Theatre 2006– (prodns incl: Electra, The Crucible, Clarence Darrow, Other Desert Cities, Fortune's Fool, Much Ado About Nothing, Sweet Bird of Youth, The Winslow Boy (also Broadway), Kiss Me Kate, Hedda Gabler, The Duchess of Malfi, Noises Off, The Playboy of the Western World, Richard III (also NY and int tour), The Tempest (also NY and int tour), The Real Thing, Six Degrees of Separation, Inherit the Wind, The Winter's Tale (also NY and int tour), The Cherry Orchard (also NY and int tour), Dancing at Lughnasa, Complicit, The Norman Conquests (also Broadway), Pygmalion, Speed-the-Plow, Cinderella, All About My Mother, Gaslight, The Entertainer, The Taming of the Shrew, Twelfth Night, A Moon for the Misbegotten (also Broadway); memb Soc of London Theatre 2008; *Style*— John Richardson, Esq; ✉ The Old Vic, 103 The Cut, London SE1 8NB (✆ 020 7928 2651, e-mail john.richardson@oldvictheatre.com, website www.oldvictheatre.com)

RICHARDSON, Very Rev John Stephen; s of James Geoffrey Richardson, of Rossendale, Lancs, and Myra, *née* Greenwood; *b* 2 April 1950, Rawtenstall; *Educ* Haslingden GS, Univ of Southampton (BA), St John's Coll Nottingham; *m* 29 July 1972, Elizabeth Susan (Sue), da of James Anness Wiltshire (d 1986), of Calne, Wilts; 2 da (Sarah Elizabeth b 1975, Ruth Mary b 1977), 2 s (Benjamin Stephen b and d 1981, Thomas Samuel John b 1982); *Career* various appts Cadbury Schweppes Bristol; asst curate St Michael and All Angels Bramcote Nottingham 1974–77, priest-in-charge Emmanuel Church Southill and curate Radipole and Melcombe Regis Team Miny 1977–80, asst missioner and lay trg advsr Dio of Salisbury and priest-in-charge Winterborne Monkton with Winterborne Came and Whitcombe with Stinsford 1980–83, vicar Christ Church Nailsea 1983–90, advsr in evangelism Dio of Bath and Wells 1986–90, provost and vicar of the Cathedral Church of St Peter Bradford 1990–2000, dean after the cathedral's measure 2000–01, vicar Wye, Brook and Hastingleigh 2001–09 (and Eastwell with Boughton Aluph 2004–09, and Hinxhill 2007–09), chaplain Imperial Coll London (Wye Campus) 2001–09, area dean West Bridge Dio of Canterbury 2003–09, priest-in-charge Holy Trinity Margate 2009–16, asst area dean Thanet Dio of Canterbury 2009–15, asst priest Benefice of New Romney 2016–; chm and dir Canterbury Diocesan Aquila Bd of Educn and Acad Tst 2013–; vice-pres Cncl Church's Ministry to the Jews 1994–2010; memb: Cncl St John's Theological Coll Nottingham 1988–94, Gen Synod 1993–2001 (memb Bd of Mission 1995–2000), Cncl Evangelical Alliance 1994–2000, Archbishop's Cncl and Bd of Fin Dio of Canterbury 2003–15; advsr of on deliverance miny Dio of Canterbury 2008–; govr: Bradford GS 1990–2001, Giggleswick Sch 1993–2002, Bolling Community Coll 1995–2001; tstee and vice-chm Acorn Christian Healing Tst 1990–2007, tstee Spennithorne House of Healing 1990–97; involved with local radio stations 1985–, memb Radio Leeds Local Broadcasting Cncl 1991–95; dir: Bradford Breakthrough 1992–2001, Spring Harvest 1998–2003 and 2007–10, Mildmay Mission Hosp 2004– (chm 2007–), Kent Community Housing Tst 2005–08; chm Spring Harvest Charitable Tst 2003–08; MInstD 1994; *Books* Ten Rural Churches (1988); *Recreations* football, cricket, spotting 1950s and 1960s municipal bus fleets; *Style*— The Very Rev John Richardson; ✉ The Rectory, 135, High Street, Dymchurch, Kent TW29 0LI (✆ 01843 294129 and 01843 221864, e-mail vicarjohnsrichardson@googlemail.com)

RICHARDSON, Keith William; s of Robert John David Richardson (d 1975), and Esmé Audrey, *née* Haynes (d 1990); *b* 1 November 1942; *Educ* Kelvinside Acad Glasgow, RSAMD Glasgow; *Children* 1 da (Taransay Jo Chisholm b 19 Nov 1972); *Career* television producer; stage mangr: Glasgow Citizens Theatre 1961–62, Pitlochry Festival Theatre 1963; theatrical agency dir SCOTTS 1963–69, asst stage mangr, stage mangr, floor mangr and production mangr Yorkshire Television 1969–77, prodr Tyne Tees Television 1977–78 (incl Paper Lads), prodr Yorkshire Television 1978–82 (incl Thundercloud, Second Chance, Horace, Harry's Game), head of drama Tyne Tees Television 1983–84 (exec prodr: Operation Julie, 4 Dramaramas; prodr: The Wedding, Supergran), dep controller of drama Yorkshire Television 1988–95 (exec prodr: Scab, May We Borrow Your Husband, Cloud Waltzer, 1914, All Out, Flying Lady Series I, Flying Lady Series II, Comeback, Mohicans, Climbing Out, Home Movies, The Contract, A Place of Safety, A Dinner of Herbs, Tears in the Rain, Magic Moments, The Beiderbecke Connection, Till We Meet Again, Talking Takes Two, Yellowthread Street, Missing Persons, Shoot to Kill, The World of Eddie Weary, Guests of the Emperor, Death Train, Mission Top Secret, Heartbeat I, Heartbeat II, III and IV, 15: The Life & Death of Philip Knight, The Wanderer, A Pinch of Snuff, The Dwelling Place, The Cinder Path, Firm Friend Series II, Ellington, Finney, Paparazzo; prodr A Day in Summer, original script cmmn Blood and Peaches), gp controller of drama Yorkshire Tyne Tees Television 1995–2004 (exec prodr: Heartbeat V, VI, VIII, IX, X, XI, XII and XIII, Ellington Series, Strike Force, Respect, The Governor II, Stiff Upper Lips, The Rag Nymph, The Moth, Supply and Demand, Trial and Retribution I, Black Velvet Band, Dingles Down Under, Changing Places, The Inspector Pitt Mysteries – The Cater Street Hangman, Lost for Words, Trial & Retribution II, Emmerdale – Revenge, Maisie Raine II, Fit, Fresh & Funky, Don't Look Now – The Dingles in Venice, The Secret, Emmerdale, Shipman, The Royal I, II and III), controller of drama Granada Yorkshire 2004– (exec prodr: Heartbeat XIV, XV, XVI, XVII and XVIII, The Royal IV, V, VI, VII and VIII, Steel River Blues, The Marchioness Disaster, Falling, The Royal Today); writer and dir Heartbeat: The Musical Celebration; chm TAPS 2007–10; former memb Bd Scottish Film Production Fund and Glasgow Film Fund; Int Emmy award for Supergran, BAFTA award for Emmerdale; for Lost for Words: Int Emmy, BAFTA award, Peabody award; Outstanding Contribution to RTS Yorkshire 2005; FRTS 2004; *Recreations* reading, whisky (collecting and drinking!); *Style*— Keith Richardson, Esq; ✉ e-mail k.w.richardson@hotmail.com

RICHARDSON, (William) Kenneth; s of James McNaughton Richardson, of Stirling, and Jane Ann McKay, *née* Monteith; *b* 16 November 1956; *Educ* HS of Stirling, Univ of St Andrews (MA); *m* 12 July 2014, Garry Steven Glover; *Career* planning asst Scot Opera 1983–87; Royal Opera: co-mangr 1987–90, gen mangr 1990–94, admin Royal Opera House Garden Venture 1987–91; artistic dir Dublin Grand Opera Soc 1990–91; arts dir Barbican Centre 1994, dir Covent Garden Festival 1996–2001, arts dir Chicago Humanities Festival 2002, assoc dir Greenwich Theatre 2002–05, dir 2008 Temple Festival 2006–08, exec prodr Temple Music 2009, artistic dir Oundle Int Festival 2014–; ind opera and music theatre dir and conslt; website designer 1995–, editorial dir Operaworld 2014–; tstee: Tête à Tête Opera 2003–, The Orgelbüchlein Project 2015–; FRSA 2005; *Books* Law & Soc: Which is to be Master? (jt ed); *Recreations* playing chamber music, gardening, figure skating; *Style*— Kenneth Richardson, Esq; ✆ 07713 487205, e-mail kenneth@kennethrichardson.co.uk, website www.kennethrichardson.co.uk

RICHARDSON, Prof Louise; *b* Repub of Ireland; *Educ* Trinity Coll Dublin (BA, MA), UCLA (MA), Harvard Univ (MA, PhD); *m* Dr Thomas Jevon; 2 da (Ciara, Fiona), 1 s (Rory); *Career* asst prof then assoc prof Harvard Govt Dept 1989–2001, exec dean Radcliffe Inst for Advanced Study Harvard Univ and lectr on law Harvard Law Sch 2001–08, princ and vice-chllr Univ of St Andrews 2009–15, vice-chllr Univ of Oxford 2016–; memb Scottish Govt's Cncl of Economic Advrs 2011–15; hon degrees: MGIMO (Moscow State Inst of Int Relations), Univ of Aberdeen, Queen's Univ Belfast, Univ of St Andrews; hon memb Royal Irish Acad 2015, memb American Acad of Arts and Sciences 2016; FRSE 2010, AcSS 2016; *Publications* When Allies Differ (1996), What Terrorists Want (2006), The Roots of Terrorism (ed, 2006), Democracy and Counterterrorism: Lessons from the Past (jt ed, 2007); *Style*— Prof Louise Richardson; ✉ Vice-Chancellors Office, University of Oxford, Clarendon Building, Broad Street, Oxford OX1 3BG (✆ 01865 270153, e-mail vice-chancellor@admin.ox.ac.uk)

RICHARDSON, Miranda; *b* 3 March 1958; *Career* actress; chair Women's Prize for Fiction 2013; *Theatre* incl: All My Sons (Derby Place), Educating Rita (Leicester Haymarket), The Designated Mourner (RNT), Insignificance (Bristol Old Vic), The Maids (Bristol Old Vic), Who's Afraid of Virginia Woolf? (Bristol Old Vic), Aunt Dan and Lemon (Almeida), Edmond (Royal Court), A Lie of the Mind (Royal Court), Etta Jenks (Royal Court), Pirasses (Royal Court), Grasses of a Thousand Colours (Royal Court) 2009; *Television* Agony 1979, The Comic Strip Presents 1982, A Woman of Substance 1983, Alas Smith and Jones 1984, The Death of the Heart 1985, Blackadder II 1986, The Storyteller 1987, Blackadder III 1987, Blackadder's Christmas Carol 1988, Blackadder Goes Forth 1989, Die Kinder 1990, Old Times 1991, Mr Wakefield's Crusade 1991, Absolutely Fabulous 1992, A Dance to the Music of Time 1997, Ted and Ralph 1998, Blackadder Back and Forth 1999, The Lost Prince (TV film for BBC) 2002, Merlin's Apprentice 2004, Gideon's Daughter 2005, Vivienne Vyle 2007, Rubicon 2010; *Film* Underworld 1985, The Innocent 1985, Dance with a Stranger 1985, Sweet as You Are 1987, Empire of the Sun 1987, Eat the Rich 1987, After Pilkington 1987, Ball-Trap on the Cote Sauvage 1989, The Fool 1990, Twisted Obsession 1990, The Bachelor 1991, Enchanted April 1991, The Crying Game 1992, Damage 1993, The Line, the Cross and the Curve 1993, Century 1993, The Night and the Moment 1994, Tom and Viv 1994, Fatherland 1994, Swann 1996, The Evening Star 1996, Kansas City 1996, Saint-Ex 1997, The Apostle 1997, The Designated Mourner 1997, St Ives 1998, The Scold's Bridle 1998, Merlin 1998, Jacob Two Two Meets the Hooded Fang 1999, Alice in Wonderland 1999, The King and I 1999, Sleepy Hollow 1999, Chicken Run 2000, Get Carter 2000, Snow White 2000, The Hours 2001, Spider 2002, The Rage in Lake Placid 2002, The Actors 2002, The Lost Prince 2002, Falling Angels 2003, The Hollywood Years 2003, The Prince and Me 2003, The Phantom of the Opera 2003, Wah-Wah 2004, Spinning Into Butter 2004, Harry Potter and the Goblet of Fire 2004, Southland Tales 2005, Paris, Je T'aime 2005, Provok'd 2005, Puffball 2006, Fred Claus 2006, Young Victoria 2007, Rubicon 2010, Made In Dagenham 2010, Harry Potter and the Deathly Hallows: Part 1 2010, Parade's End 2011, World Without End 2011, Belle 2014; *Style*— Ms Miranda Richardson; ✉ c/o Paul Lyon Maris, Independent Talent, Oxford House, 76 Oxford Street, London W1D 1BS (✆ 020 7636 6565, fax 020 7323 0101)

RICHARDSON, Dr Nicholas James; s of John William Richardson (d 1987), and Eileen, *née* Allan (d 1954); *b* 4 February 1940, Winchester, Hants; *Educ* Winchester (scholar), Magdalen Coll Oxford (Roberts Gawen scholar, BA, BPhil, DPhil, hon mention Conington Prize 1971); *m* 14 Dec 1968, Catherine Eugénie, *née* Vafopoulou; 2 s (Alexander William b 18 May 1969, Andrew John Nicholas b 28 July 1974), 2 da (Penelope Iona b 4 Feb 1973, Catherine Maria Elly b 22 Nov 1984); *Career* lectr in classics Pembroke Coll Oxford 1964–65, lectr in classics Trinity Coll Oxford 1965–66, HM Treasy 1967–68, fell and tutor in classics Merton Coll Oxford 1968–2004 (emeritus fell 2004–), warden Greyfriars Hall Oxford 2004–07; visiting fell: Center for Hellenic Studies Washington DC 1980–81, Princeton Univ 1989, Stanford Univ 2003; govr Plater Coll Oxford 1993–99, tstee Newman Tst Oxford 1997–2006, memb Oxford and Cambridge Catholic Educn Bd 1992–2004 (sec 1996–2000); FSA 1985–2015; *Books* The Homeric Hymn to Demeter (1974), The Iliad: A Commentary, Vol VI Books 21–24 (1993), The Homeric Hymns (contrib, 2003), Three Homeric Hymns: To Apollo, Hermes and Aphrodite (2010), Prudentius' Hymns for Hours and Seasons: Liber Cathemerinon (2015); *Recreations* real tennis, skiing, walking; *Clubs* Sloane, Oxford Antiquaries; *Style*— Dr Nicholas Richardson; ✉ The Old House, 72 High Street, Sutton Courtenay, Oxfordshire OX14 4AS (✆ 01235 848356, e-mail nicholasrichardson4@gmail.com)

RICHARDSON, Dr Nigel Peter Vincent; s of Vincent Boys Richardson (d 1965), and Jean Frances, *née* Wrangles; *b* 29 June 1948; *Educ* Highgate Sch, Trinity Hall Cambridge (MA), Univ of Bristol (PGCE), UCL (PhD); *m* 25 Aug 1979, (Averon) Joy, da of Rev Peter H James; 2 s (Matthew James b 11 Oct 1982, Thomas Stephen b 18 Oct 1984); *Career* Uppingham Sch: memb History Dept 1971–89, sixth form tutor 1977–83, second master 1983–89; headmaster Dragon Sch Oxford 1989–92, dep headmaster and dir of studies King's Sch Macclesfield 1992–94, headmaster The Perse Sch Cambridge 1994–2008, currently educn conslt and appraiser; course dir Summer Language Sch Sweden and Bell Sch Cambridge 1972–82; chm HMC 2007; ed Conference and Common Room 1999–2002; govr: Greycotes Sch Oxford 1989–92, King's Coll Sch Cambridge 1998–2004, King's Sch Ely 2008–13, Norwich Sch 2008–13, Magdalen Coll Sch Oxford 2008–; memb Educn Ctee Haileybury Coll 2009– (memb Cncl 2013–, chm Educn Ctee 2014–); BBC Radio 4: jt question compiler Top of the Form 1982–87, contrib Thought for the Day 1982–; syndic Cambridge Univ Press 2009–14; memb Bd Assoc of Governing Bodies of Ind Schs (AGBIS) 2014–; Walter Hines Page ESU scholar 2003; *Publications* The Effective Use of Time (1984, 2 edn 1989), First Steps in Leadership (1987), Typhoid in Uppingham: Analysis of a Victorian Town and School in Crisis 1875–7 (Br Assoc for Local History First Prize 2008), Thring of Uppingham: Victorian Educator (2014); ed Leading Schools series (Vol 1 2007, Vols 2 and 3 2008, Vol 4 2009, Vols 5 and 6 2010, Vol 7 2011 and Vol 8 2012); author of various histories and biographies for school use; contrib: TES, The Times, Daily Telegraph, Daily Mail, Social History of Medicine, Rutland Record; *Recreations* music, writing, sport, gardening, travel; *Clubs* East India, Lansdowne; *Style*— Dr Nigel Richardson; ✉ 6 High Meadow, Harston, Cambridge CB22 7TR (✆ 01223 872469, e-mail npvrichardson@btinternet.com)

RICHARDSON, (William) Norman Ballantyne; DL (Greater London 1985); s of Robert Richardson (d 1974), of Wishaw, Lanarkshire, and Sarah Maddick, *née* Shields; *b* 8 October 1947, Wishaw, Lanarkshire; *Educ* King Edward VI GS Birmingham (now King Edward VI Aston Sch), Goldsmiths Univ of London; *Partner* since 1984 Peter David Prost (civil partnership 24 May 2014); *Career* asst master Rosary RC Sch London 1970–78, dep head Emmanuel C of E Sch London 1979–81; headmaster: All Saints' C of E Sch London 1981–85, Christ Church C of E Sch London 1985–92, St Michael's C of E Sch London 1992–96; educn/headteacher conslt 1997–2010; chm: ILEA Divnl Consultative Ctee of Headteachers 1985–86 and 1989–90 (memb 1981–90), Local Advsy Ctee on Primary/Secdy Transfer 1987–88, ILEA Central Consultative Ctee of Headteachers 1989–90 (memb 1982–90), Consultative Ctee of Heads and Deputies in the Royal Borough of Kensington and Chelsea 1989–90, London Headteachers' Assoc (Kensington and Chelsea) 1990–91, London Diocesan Headteachers' Cncl 1991–92, 1993–94 and 1995–96 (memb 1984–96); memb: Colne/East Gade Advsy Ctee on Educn 1977–81, ILEA Standing Advsy Cncl on Religious Educn 1985–90, Royal Borough of Kensington and Chelsea Standing Advsy Cncl on Religions Educn 1989–92, London Borough of Haringey Standing Advsy Cncl on Religious Educn 1992–94; govr: Leavesden Green Infant Sch 1977–81, Leavesden Green Junior Sch 1977–81; life vice-pres Cheshire Agricultural Soc 2010–; chm London (South) Ctee: Royal Jubilee and Prince's Tsts 1984–90, The Prince's Tst 1990–95; sec: London Youth Involvement Ctee Queen's Silver Jubilee Tst 1981–83, Greater London Ctee Royal Jubilee and Prince's Tsts 1983–84; govr RNLI 1998–; life memb: Friends of St Columba's Church of Scotland, Friends of St George's Chapel Windsor, Friends of St Paul's Cathedral, Friends of Royal Free Hosp, Friends of York Minster, Friends of the John Rylands Univ Library, Friends of Lichfield Cathedral, Friends of Lincoln Cathedral, Friends of Winchester Cathedral, Friends of Cheshire Military Museum, Friends of Chester Cathedral; memb: RSL, Constitutional Monarchy Assoc, Monarchist League, European Atlantic Gp, Friends of the Prince's Tst, Friends of the Royal Acad, The Pilgrims, Queen's English Soc, St James's Branch Royal Br Legion, Manchester Literary and Philosophical Soc, Soc of Genealogists, ESU (sec Mid-Cheshire Ctee 2012–), Friends of St David's Cathedral, Historic Soc of Lancs and Cheshire, St Andrew Soc, Saltire Soc, Friends of Manchester Art Gallery, Friends of Romsey Abbey, Edinburgh HQ Branch Legion Scotland; featured in: The Observer Guide to Chelsea 1987, Good Schools Guide 1991; FRGS 1969 (long serving fell 2011), FRSA 1974 (life fell 2005), MBIM (later MIMgt, now MCMI) 1986, FCollT (formerly FCollP) 1989 (MCollP 1985, life fell 2010), MInstAM 1990, MIIM 1990, MISM (now MInstLM) 1990, MInstFM 1990; *Recreations* reading biographies, genealogy and travel; *Clubs* Royal Commonwealth Soc, Royal Over-Seas League, RSA, Manchester Literary and Philosophical Soc, ESU, Pilgrims; *Style*— W N B Richardson, Esq, DL; ✉ 16 Registry Close, Kingsmead, Northwich, Cheshire CW9 8UZ (e-mail richardwnbson@hotmail.co.uk)

R

RICHARDSON, Peter Edward Hugh; s of late Edward William Moreton Richardson, of Malvern, Worcs, and late Pamela Merle, *née* Case-Morris; *b* 12 April 1955; *Educ* Malvern Coll, The Queen's Coll Oxford (MA); *m* 22 Sept 1984, Miriam Elizabeth, da of late Dennis Brian Chance, of Chesham, Bucks; 1 s (Michael William b 1 Nov 1987), 1 da (Heather Caroline b 9 April 1990); *Career* trainee CA Price Waterhouse & Co 1976–77; Butterworth & Co (Publishers) Ltd: commissioning ed 1977–82, sr commissioning ed 1982–84, managing ed 1984–85; Churchill Livingstone (medical div of Pearson Professional): publisher 1985–87, publishing mangr 1987–90, publishing dir 1990–94, dir healthcare info and mgmnt 1994–97; md Royal Society of Medicine Press Ltd 1997–2010, md Br Editorial Soc of Bone and Jt Surgery (publishers of Bone and Joint Jl) 2010–; non-exec dir Portland Press Ltd 2015–, dir Publishers Licensing Soc 2016–; chm Medical Music Soc of London 2012–, hon treas Assoc of Learned and Professional Soc Publishers 2015–; fell Royal Soc of Medicine 2010 (elected memb Cncl 2013–); *Publications* E-Biomed and PubMed Central – a publisher's view (1999), How to Get Your Medical Book Published (2001), A Guide to Medical Publishing and Writing (2002); *Recreations* music, France; *Style*— Peter Richardson, Esq; ✉ 3 Butlers Close, Amersham, Buckinghamshire HP6 5PY (✆ 01494 722017); British Editorial Society of Bone and Joint Surgery, 22 Buckingham Street, London WC2N 6ET (✆ 020 7451 0900, e-mail p.richardson@boneandjoint.org.uk)

RICHARDSON, Ray; *b* 3 November 1964; *Educ* Roan Sch, St Martin's Sch of Art, Goldsmiths Coll London; *m* 1989; 2 s; *Career* artist; memb Assoc of Royal Engravers 2005; *Collections* Nat Portrait Gallery, De Beers London, J P Morgan London, Anglo American, Kasen-Summer Collection NYC, Tama Art Univ Tokyo, Ralph Lauren London and NY, V&A, RCA; *Selected Shows* Boycott Gallery Brussels 1989, 1992, 1995, 1998, 2000, 2001, 2003, 2004 and 2005, Galerie 31 Lille 1990, Galerie Alain Blondel Paris 1994, 1996, 1998, 2000 and 2003, Glasgow Print Studio 1992 and 1998, Beaux Arts London 1994, 1996 and 1999, Mendenhall Gallery LA 1998, Gallery Aoyama Tokyo 1999, Gallery Aoyama Tokyo 2002, Advanced Graphics London 2002 and 2004, Fabien Fryns Fine Art Puerto Banus 2002 and 2004, New Arts Gallery Litchfield Hills CT 2005, Mendenhall-Sobieski Gallery Pasadena CA 2005, Boycott Gallery 2006, Advanced Graphics 2006,

Eleven Fine Art London 2006, Advanced Graphics London 2007 and Boycott Gallery Brussels 2008; *Television and Radio* Oil on Canvas (BBC 2) 1997 and 1999, Fresh (LWT) 1998, Sampled (Channel 4) 1998, Grand Designs (Channel 4) 2004, Artists' Music (BBC Radio 3) 2006, Oil on Canvas (BBC 2) 2006, Artists and their Music (Radio 3) 2006; *Awards* BP Portrait Award 1990, Br Cncl Award 1989 and 1999, commemorative sculpture for Sir Matt Busby Scotland 1997; *Books* One Man on a Trip (1996), Oil on Canvas (1997), British Figurative Painting (1997), British Sporting Heroes (1998); *Recreations* football; *Clubs* King Vic Football, The Royal Brussels British Football, Old Roan FC, Old Tennisonians FC; *Style—* Ray Richardson, Esq; ✉ c/o Advanced Graphics, 32 Long Lane, London SE1 4AY

RICHARDSON, Robert Oliver; s of Robert Frederick Oliver (d 1987), and Marie, *née* Richardson (d 2001); *b* 26 September 1940; *Educ* Stretford GS; *m* 1, 1968 (m dis), Gwyneth Marilyn, *née* Hunt; m 2, 24 Aug 1974, Sheila Muriel Boustead, da of Cecil John Norman Miller, MBE; 1 s (James Malcolm b 8 April 1977), 1 step s (Michael John b 6 Oct 1961); *Career* journalist Daily Mail 1965–67 and 1968–72, ed Welwyn and Hatfield Times 1973–81, ed Herts Advertiser 1981–87, freelance journalist 1987–92 (contracted to The Independent 1990–92), staff journalist The Independent 1992–94, freelance journalist 1994–98, staff journalist Sunday Business 1998–2001, freelance journalist 2002–04, staff journalist The Observer 2004–05, freelance journalist The Observer and The Guardian 2005–; memb Crime Writers' Assoc 1985– (vice-chm 1992–93 and 2005–06, chm 1993–94 and 2006–07); *Books* The Book of Hatfield (1977), The Latimer Mercy (1985, John Creasey Meml Award for best first crime novel), Bellringer Street (1988), The Book of the Dead (1989), The Dying of the Light (1990), Sleeping in the Blood (1991), The Lazarus Tree (1992), The Hand of Strange Children (1993), Significant Others (1995), Victims (1997), An Act of Evil (e-book 2014), Skeleton Key (e-book 2014), The Dying of the Light (e-book 2015), Murder in Waiting (e-book 2015), Victims (e-book 2016); *Recreations* reading, walking, history, crosswords; *Style—* Robert Richardson, Esq; ✉ c/o Gregory and Company, 3 Barb Mews, London W6 7PA (☎ 020 7610 4676, fax 020 7610 4686)

RICHARDSON, Stephen Laurence; s of Laurence Richardson, of St Davids, Dyfed, and Rosalae, *née* Reilly; *b* 20 June 1959; *Educ* Maghull GS Liverpool, Ysgol Dewi Sant St David's, Faculty of Music Univ of Manchester, RNCM (Countess of Munster Award, Moores Fndn Award, Kay Opera Prize); *m* 19 July 1986, Colleen Delores, *née* Barsley; 2 da (Elise Delores b 3 Dec 1990, Abigail Rosina b 27 Sept 1992); *Career* bass; performed with orchs incl: LSO, City of Birmingham Symphony, Montreal Philharmonic, London Philharmonic, Hallé, Scottish National, London Sinfonietta, LSO, English String Orch, BBC Philharmonic, English Concert, Prague Symphony, BBC National Orch of Wales; worked with conductors incl: Sir John Pritchard, Neeme Järvi, Oliver Knussen, Trevor Pinnock, Sir Simon Rattle, Andrew Parrott, Jiri Belohlavec, Richard Hickox; appeared at festivals incl: Aldeburgh, Edinburgh, Frankfurt, Singapore, Brussels, Turin, Boston, Tanglewood, Hong Kong; *Performances* over 70 operatic roles incl: The King in Aida (ENO, Opera North), Colline in La Boheme (WNO), Priam in The Trojans (WNO), Da Silva in Ernani (WNO), Don Ferrando in Il Trovatore (Scottish Opera), Private Willis in Iolanthe (Scottish Opera), Ratcliffe in Billy Budd (Scottish Opera), Johann in Werther (Scottish Opera), Sarastro in The Magic Flute (Opera North), He-Ancient in A Midsummer Marriage (Opera North), Father in The Jewel Box (Opera North), Mongolian Soldier in Judith Weir's A Night at the Chinese Opera (Kent Opera), 150 anniversary performance of Mendelssohn's Elijah (BBC Proms) 1996; world premieres incl: Sir Joshua Cramer in Gerald Barry's The Intelligence Park, Where the Wild Things Are (Glyndebourne Festival Opera), Higglety Pigglety Pop (Glyndebourne Festival Opera), John Taverner's Eis Thanaton and Resurrection, Benedict Mason's Music for Three Charlie Chaplin Films; given recitals in Wigmore Hall London, Frankfurt, Prague, Berlin and Cologne; *Recordings* incl: Where the Wild Things Are, Goehr's The Death of Moses, Purcell's Ode for the Birthday of Queen Mary 1694, Mozart's Requiem, Macmillan's Vistitatio Sepulchri; *Recreations* sailing, fishing, painting, family life; *Style—* Stephen Richardson, Esq

RICHARDSON, Emeritus Prof Stephen Michael; CBE (2015); s of David Richardson, of Reigate, Surrey, and Frances Joan, *née* Pring; *b* 8 December 1951; *Educ* Wimbledon Coll, Imperial Coll London (BSc(Eng), PhD, Hinchley Medal IChemE); *m* 5 June 1976, Hilary Joy, da of Malcolm Graham Burgess; 2 da (Helen Alice b 23 Feb 1979, Susan Margaret Clare b 7 June 1984), 1 s (Martin David b 4 Oct 1980); *Career* Univ of Cambridge: Rolls-Royce research asst 1975–76, 1851 research fell 1976–77; Dept of Chemical Engrg Imperial Coll London: lectr 1978–87, Nuffield research fell 1984–85, sr lectr 1987–92, reader 1992–94, prof 1994–, head of dept 2001–08, princ Faculty of Engrg 2008–10, dep rector 2009–13, assoc provost 2013–15; visiting prof Loughborough Univ 1995–98; CEng 1988, FIChemE 1990 (MIChemE 1988), FREng 1996, FCGI 1999; *Publications* incl: Fluid Mechanics (Hemisphere NY, 1989), Blowdown of Pressure Vessels (Trans IChemE, 1992), Piper Alpha (Loss Prevention Bulletin, 1995); *Recreations* music, gardening, walking; *Style—* Emeritus Prof Stephen Richardson, CBE, FREng; ☎ 01737 766770; Department of Chemical Engineering, Imperial College, London SW7 2AZ (e-mail s.m.richardson@imperial.ac.uk)

RICHARDSON, Vicky; da of Anthony Richardson, and Margaret, *née* Ballard; *b* 16 October 1968, London; *Educ* N London Collegiate Sch, Central Sch of Art and Design, Chelsea Sch of Art, Univ of Westminster (BA), Napier Univ (NCTJ Cert), KCL (MA); *m* 6 Feb 1999, Adrian Friend; 3 da (Agnes b 4 March 2000, May b 3 Feb 2002, Eliza b 7 April 2007); *Career* asst ed Public Sector Building 1995–96, ed Public Service and Local Govt 1996–97, sr reporter RIBA Jl 1997–2000, dep ed RIBA Jl 2000–02, ed Blueprint 2004–10; dir of architecture, design and fashion Br Cncl 2010–16, co-dir London Festival of Architecture 2011–14, conslt 2016–; memb London Mayor's Cultural Strategy Gp 2008–, memb Cncl Architectural Assoc 2015–; tstee Campaign for Drawing 2006–11; Highly Commended PPA Editor of the Year 2007; Hon FRIBA 2014; *Publications* In Defence of the Dome (jtly, 1998), New Vernacular Architecture (2001); *Style—* Ms Vicky Richardson; ☎ 07496 727178, e-mail vicky@vickyrichardson.com)

RICHARDSON OF CALOW, Baroness (Life Peer UK 1998), of Calow in the County of Derbyshire; Rev Kathleen Margaret Richardson; OBE (1996); da of Francis William Fountain (d 1986), and Margaret, *née* Heron (d 1991); *b* 24 February 1938; *Educ* St Helena Sch Chesterfield, Stockwell Coll (teacher's cert), Wesley House Cambridge (theol trg); *m* 1964, Ian David Godfrey Richardson; 3 da (Hon Kathryn Jane b 1966, Hon Claire Margaret b 1968, Hon Anne Elizabeth b 1970); *Career* teacher Hollingwood Sec Sch Chesterfield 1958–61, Wesley deaconess Methodist Church 1961–64, pastoral worker Methodist/C of E Stevenage 1973–77, Methodist min W Yorks 1979–86, chm W Yorks District Methodist Church 1987–95, pres Methodist Conf 1992–93, co-ordinating sec Methodist Church 1995–99, moderator Free Churches Cncl and pres Churches Together in England 1995–99; Hon DLitt Univ of Bradford, Hon LLD Univ of Liverpool, Hon DD Univ of Birmingham 2000; *Recreations* reading, needlework; *Style—* The Rev Baroness Richardson of Calow, OBE; ✉ House of Lords, London SW1A 0PW (☎ 020 7219 0314)

RICHER, Julian; LVO (2007); s of Percy Isaac Richer, and Ursula Marion Haller; *b* 9 March 1959, London; *Educ* Clifton Coll; *m* 15 Oct 1982, Rosemary Louise, *née* Hamlet; *Career* salesman HiFi Markets Ltd 1977; fndr and md: Richer Sounds 1978– (Which? Best High Street Retailer 2010 and 2012, awarded Royal Warrant 2011, Which? Best Retailer 2015), JR Properties 1989–, Audio Partnership plc 1994–2010, The Richer Partnership 1997–2009, JR Publishing 1998–; dir Duchy Orginal 1998–2006; vice-pres RSPCA 2002–; fndr and chm Persula Fndn 1994–; fndr and tstee Acts 435 2009–, fndr and tstee ASB Help 2013–; Hon DBA: Bournemouth Univ, Kingston Univ; *Publications* The Richer Way (1995, 5 edn 2009), Richer on Leadership (1999), A Richer Life (2010); *Recreations* manages and plays drums in his own band, travel, cycling; *Style—* Julian Richer, Esq, LVO; ✉ Richer Sounds plc, Richer House, Hankey Place, London SE1 4BB (☎ 020 7403 1310, fax 020 7551 5353, e-mail teresac@richersounds.com, website www.richersounds.com); websites www.audiopartnership.com, http://asbhelp.co.uk, http://acts435.org.uk

RICHES, Naomi; MBE (2013); da of Robert Riches, of N Yorks, and Mary, *née* Ridley, of London; *b* 15 June 1983, Hammersmith, London; *Educ* Bucks New Univ (BA); *Partner* Tom Pacitto; *Career* Paralympic rower (professional athlete 2006–); achievements incl: five-time World Champion 2004, 2005, 2006, 2009 and 2011, Bronze medal (mixed coxed four) Paralympics Games 2008, Gold medal (mixed coxed four, with James Roe, MBE, *qv*, David Smith, MBE, Pamela Relph, MBE and Lily van den Broecke, MBE) Paralympic Games 2012; appeals ambass Royal Nat Orthopaedic Hosp Charity Stanmore; *Clubs* Marlow Rowing, Leander Rowing; *Style—* Miss Naomi Riches, MBE; ✉ c/o Amateur Rowing Association, 6 Lower Mall, Hammersmith, London W6 9DJ

RICHMOND, Barbara Mary; da of James Wallace Duff; *b* 28 July 1960; *Educ* St Aelred's RC HS, UMIST (BSc); *m* 25 Feb 1982, Alexander James Richmond; *Career* Arthur Andersen & Co Manchester 1981–87; GEC Alsthom: fin controller (Distribution Switchgear) 1987, fin controller (Transmission Switchgear) 1988, fin dir (Electrical Distribution Gp) 1989–92; gp fin dir: Whessoe plc 1994–97 (gp fin controller 1992–93), Croda International plc 1997–2006, Inchcape plc 2006–; non-exec dir: Carclo plc 2000–06, Scarborough Building Soc 2005–; FCA 1984; *Recreations* walking, gardening, travel, motor sport; *Style—* Mrs Barbara Richmond

RICHMOND, John; *b* 1960; *Educ* Kingston Poly (BA); *m* Angie Hill; *Career* fashion designer; began career in own co producing John Richmond collection, simultaneously worked freelance for Emporio Armani, Fiorucci, Joseph Tricot and 'Pin-Up' for Deni Cler, ptnr with Maria Cornejo producing Richmond/Cornejo label 1984–87 (shops in London and 16 in Japan), solo 1987–; int catwalk shows from 1991: The International Palace of Destroy, Dinner with Dali March 1992; estab diffusion range 'Destroy', clients incl Elton John, George Michael, Madonna and Prince; *Style—* John Richmond, Esq; ✉ 54 Conduit Street, London W1S 2YY

RICHMOND, LENNOX AND GORDON, 10 (and 5 respectively) Duke of (E 1675, UK 1876); Charles Henry Gordon Lennox; also Earl of March, Baron Settrington (both E 1675), Earl of Darnley, Lord Torbolton (all S 1675), Duc d'Aubigny (Fr 1684), Earl of Kinrara (UK 1876), and Hereditary Constable of Inverness Castle; s of 9 Duke of Richmond and (4 of) Gordon (d 1989), and Elizabeth Grace, *née* Hudson (d 1992); descended from King Charles II and Louise Renée de Penançoët de Kéroualle, who was cr Baroness Petersfield, Countess of Fareham and Duchess of Portsmouth for life by King Charles II and Duchesse d'Aubigny by King Louis XIV of France; *b* 19 September 1929; *Educ* Eton, William Temple Coll Rugby; *m* 26 May 1951, Susan Monica, o da of Col Cecil Everard Grenville-Grey, CBE, of Hall Barn, Blewbury, Berks, by his w, Louise Monica, eldest da of Lt-Col Ernest Fitzroy Morrison-Bell, OBE, JP, DL; 2 da (Lady Ellinor Caroline b 1952, Lady Louisa Elizabeth (Lady Louisa Collings) b 1967), 1 s (Charles Henry, Earl of March and Kinrara b 1955), and 2 adopted da (Maria b 1959, Naomi (Mrs Burke) b 1962); *Heir* s, Earl of March and Kinrara; *Career* late 2 Lt KRRC; FCA 1956–; chm: Dexam Int (Holdings) Ltd 1956–2009, Goodwood Gp of Cos 1969–2007; chm John Wiley & Sons Ltd 1991–98 (previously vice-chm and dir); dir: Industrial Studies William Temple Coll 1962–67, Country Gentlemen's Assoc Ltd 1975–89; memb: House of Laity Gen Synod 1960–80, Central and Exec Ctee World Cncl Churches 1968–75; church cmmr 1962–75; chm: Bd for Mission and Unity Gen Synod 1968–77, House of Laity Chichester Dio 1976–79, Chichester Cathedral Tst 1985–91; vice-chm Archbishops' Cmmn on Church and State 1966–70; memb: W Midlands Regnl Econ Planning Cncl 1965–68, W Sussex Economic Partnership Steering Ctee 1997–; pres: Sussex Rural Community Cncl (latterly Action in rural Sussex) 1973–2006 (chm Rural Housing Advsy Ctee 1996–2006), Chichester Festivities 1977–, S of England Agric Soc 1981–82, Br Horse Soc 1976–78, Sussex Enterprise (formerly Sussex C of C) 1980–, SE England Tourist Bd 1990–2003 (vice-pres 1974–90), AMREF (African Medical and Research Fndn) 2000–; chm: Rugby Cncl of Social Serv 1961–68, Dunford Coll (YMCA) 1969–82, Christian Orgns Res and Advsy Tst (CORAT) 1970–87, Tstees Sussex Heritage Tst 1978–2000, Assoc of Int Dressage Event Organisers 1987–94, Bognor Regis Regeneration and Vision Gp 2001–07, Sussex Community Fndn 2006–; chllr Univ of Sussex 1985–98 (treas 1979–82); hon treas and dep pres Historic Houses Assoc 1975–86; patron Sussex CCC 1991–; Lord-Lt of West Sussex 1990–94 (DL 1975–90); Freeman City of Chicester 2008; Hon LLD Univ of Sussex 1987; Medal of Honour Br Equestrian Fedn 1983; CIMgt 1982; *Style—* His Grace the Duke of Richmond, Lennox and Gordon; ✉ Molecomb, Goodwood, Chichester, West Sussex PO18 0PZ (☎ 01243 527861; office: 01243 755000, fax 01243 755005, e-mail richmond@goodwood.com)

RICHMOND-WATSON, Anthony Euan; s of Euan Owens Richmond-Watson (d 1954), and Hon Gladys Gordon, *née* Catto (d 1967); *b* 8 April 1941; *Educ* Westminster, Univ of Edinburgh (BCom); *m* 1, 1966, Angela, da of John Broadley, of Somerset (d 1979); 1 da (Tamsin b 1967), 1 s (Luke b 1971); m 2, 1976, Geraldine Ruth Helen, da of Charles Barrington, of Cornwall (d 1966); 1 da (Alice b 1976); *Career* merchant banker; dir Morgan Grenfell & Co Ltd 1975–96 (joined 1968), dir and dep chm Deutsche Morgan Grenfell Gp plc (formerly Morgan Grenfell Gp plc) 1989–96; dep chm Melrose Resources plc 1999–, chm Yule Catto & Co plc 2000–09 (dir 1978–2009), chm Norfolk Capital Gp plc 1986–90 (dir 1985–90); MICAS; *Style—* Anthony Richmond-Watson, Esq

RICKELL, Andrew David Rickell (Andy); s of David Rickell, and June Rickell; *b* 9 May 1963, York; *Educ* Huntington Sch York, Selwyn Coll Cambridge (BA), Univ of Southampton (Cert); *m* 26 Oct 1998, Ruth; 1 s (Mark); *Career* community devpt 1994–99, co-ordinator Disability Action Cheltenham 1999–2001, chief exec Br Cncl of Disabled People 2001–04, exec dir and disability cmmr Scope 2004–08, ceo Action on Disability and Work UK 2009–; Methodist church local preacher; Young Business Person of the Year 1986; memb Chartered Inst of Taxation 1989; *Style—* Andy Rickell, Esq; ✉ Action on Disability and Work UK, The Vassall Centre, Gill Avenue, Fishponds, Bristol BS16 2QQ

RICKER, Will; *b* Australia; *Career* restaurateur; proprietor: La Bodega Negra Soho and NY, XO Belsize Park, E&O Notting Hill, Eight Over Eight Chelsea, The Juice Well Soho; *Style—* Will Ricker, Esq; ✉ Ricker Restaurants Limited, 30–38 Dock Street, Leeds, West Yorkshire LS10 1JF

RICKETT, Brig John Francis; CBE (1990, OBE 1982, MBE 1967); s of Francis William Rickett (d 1981), and Lettice Anne, *née* Elliot (d 1985); *b* 7 September 1939, Laugharne, Carmarthenshire, S Wales; *Educ* Eton, RMCS, Def Servs Staff Coll India, RCDS; *m* June 1964, Frances (Fanny) Seton, da of Charles Francis Seton de Winton, CBE (d 2001); 2 da (Sophy Frances b 1965 d 1970, Emily Frances b 1974), 1 s (Charles Edward Francis (Charlie) b 1975); *Career* Welsh Guards, seconded for loan serv Fed Reg Army S Arab Emirates 1963–65; served: Aden, India, Hong Kong, Kenya, Germany, USA, NI, Falkland Islands; CO 1WG 1980–82; Cdr 19 Inf Brigade and Colchester Garrison 1984–86, Dep Cdr and COS HQ SE Dist Aldershot 1987–90, Mil Attaché Paris 1991–94, Regtl Lt-Col Welsh Guards 1988–94; ADC to HM The Queen 1993–95; Comptroller Union Jack Club 1995–2009, battlefield tour organiser 2009–; Pres: Colonie Franco-Britannique, Veterans Aid, Chipping Norton Air Cadets; Freeman City of London 2008, Liveryman Worshipful Co of Gunmakers 2008; Queen's Commendation for Brave Conduct 1964, mentioned in despatches 1974; FInstD 2000 (MInstD 1996); Knight of Magistral Grace SMOM, Chevalier of the Order of Danneborg (Denmark) 1975, Cdr Order of Merit (France) 1992; *Recreations* falconry, shooting, fishing, gardening, opera, touring battlefields; *Clubs* Institute of Directors; *Style—* Brig John Rickett, CBE; ✉ e-mail reddragon.barton@yahoo.co.uk, website www.battlefieldsdirect.com

RICKETT, William Francis Sebastian (Willy); CB (2010); s of Sir Denis Hubert Fletcher Rickett, KCMG, CB (d 1997), of Salisbury, and Ruth Pauline, *née* Armstrong (d 2003); *b* 23 February 1953; *Educ* Eton (Oppidan scholar), Trinity Coll Cambridge (MA); *m* 16 June 1979, Lucy Caroline, da of J H Clark (d 1997); 1 s ((Oliver Patrick) Oscar b 20 June 1983), 1 da (Rosanna Madeleine b 14 March 1986); *Career* Dept of Energy: joined 1975, private sec to perm sec 1977–78, princ 1978–81, private sec to Prime Minister 1981–83, seconded to Kleinwort Benson Ltd 1983–85, asst sec Electricity Privatisation 1987–90 (Oil Div 1985–87), under sec Energy Efficiency Office 1990–93; dir of fin DOE 1993–97, dir town & country planning DETR 1997–98, dep sec and head of econ and domestic affairs Secretariat Cabinet Office 1998–2000, head integrated tport taskforce DETR 2000, DG tport strategy and planning DETR 2000–01, DG transport strategy, roads, local and maritime transport DTLR 2001–02, DG strategy, fin and delivery Dept for Tport 2003–04, seconded to Ernst & Young 2004–06, DG energy DTI 2006–08, DG Energy Markets and Infrastructure Dept of Energy and Climate Change 2008–09, sr advsr Cambridge Economic Policy Assocs Ltd 2009–; chm Governing Bd Int Energy Agency 2007–09; chm Cambridge Economic Policy Associates Ltd 2013– (dir 2011–); non-exec dir Redland Roof Tiles 1994–97; dir: Nat Renewable Energy Centre Ltd 2010–13, Eggborough Power Ltd 2010–15, Impax Environmental Markets plc 2011–, Helius Energy plc 2011–15, Greencoat UK Wind plc 2012–, Smart DCC Ltd 2013–; sr advsr Cleveland Associates Ltd 2011–; ind energy expert Consumer Assoc 2011–12; FRSA, FIHT, FIE; *Recreations* photography, sports; *Style—* William Rickett, Esq, CB

RICKETTS, Prof Martin John; s of Leonard Alfred Ricketts (d 2000), and Gertrude Dorothy, *née* Elgar (d 1997); *b* 10 May 1948; *Educ* City of Bath Boys' Sch, Univ of Newcastle upon Tyne (BA), Univ of York (DPhil); *m* 1975, Diana Barbara, *née* Greenwood; 1 s, 1 da; *Career* econ asst Industrial Policy Gp 1970–72, research fell Inst of Econ and Social Research Univ of York 1975–77; Univ of Buckingham (formerly UC at Buckingham): lectr in econs 1977–82, sr lectr 1982–85, reader 1985–87, prof of econ orgn 1987–, dean Sch of Business 1993–97, pro-vice-chllr 1993, dean Sch of Humanities 2002–15; econ dir NEDO 1991–92; visiting prof Virginia Poly, Inst and State Univ 1984; tstee Inst of Econ Affrs 1992–, hon prof Heriot-Watt Univ 1996–2006; chm Buckingham Summer Festival 2004–; memb Royal Econ Soc, Scottish Econ Soc, American Econ Soc; FRSA; *Books* The Economics of Energy (with M G Webb, 1980), The Economics of Business Enterprise (1987, 3 edn 2002), The Many Ways of Governance (1999); also author of numerous papers on public finance, public choice, housing economics and economic organisation; *Recreations* music (especially playing piano and oboe); *Style—* Prof Martin Ricketts; ✉ Department of International Studies, University of Buckingham, Hunter Street, Buckingham MK18 1EG (☎ 01280 814080, fax 01280 822245, e-mail martin.ricketts@buckingham.ac.uk)

RICKETTS, HE Sir Peter Forbes; GCMG (2011, KCMG 2003, CMG 1999), GCVO (2014); s of late Maurice Alan Ricketts, of Lechlade, and Dilys, *née* Davies; *b* 30 September 1952; *Educ* Bishop Vesey's GS Sutton Coldfield, Pembroke Coll Oxford (BA); *m* 13 Sept 1980, Suzanne Julia, da of Ivor Horlington; 1 s (Edward b 1982), 1 da (Caroline b 1987); *Career* FCO: joined UK Mission to the UN 1974, third sec Singapore 1975–78, second sec UK Delgn to NATO 1978–81, first sec 1981–83, asst private sec to Foreign Sec 1983–85, first sec Washington 1986–89, dep head of Security Policy Dept 1989–91, head of Hong Kong Dept 1991–94, cnsllr (Financial and Euro Affairs) Paris 1994–97, dep political dir 1997–99, dir int security 1999–2000, chm Jt Intelligence Ctee Cabinet Office 2000–01, political dir FCO 2001–06, UK rep NATO 2003–06, perm under sec of state and head of the diplomatic serv FCO 2006–10, nat security advsr Cabinet Office 2010–11, ambass to France 2012–16; non-exec dir ENGIE Gp; *Recreations* Victorian art, Chinese porcelain; *Style—* HE Sir Peter Ricketts, GCMG, GCVO

RICKETTS, Robert Anthony; s of Robert Harold Ricketts (d 2003), and Mavis, *née* Harrington (d 2013); *b* 5 September 1962, London; *Educ* Emerson Park Sch, UCL (LLB), Law Soc Coll of Law; *m* 26 Aug 1990, Carole, *née* Pottinger; 1 s (Alexander b 22 March 1995), 1 da (Katherine b 15 Jan 1998); *Career* admitted slr 1987; Norton Rose 1985–89, Aviation Gp Frere Cholmeley 1989–95, founding ptnr Clark Ricketts 1995–2016, ptnr Holland & Knight UK LLP 2016–; memb Br Helicopter Advsy Bd, memb Br Business Gen Aviation Assoc; memb Law Soc 1987; Butterworth's Encyclopaedia of Forms and Precedents (Civil Aviation Section, 1993, 2006 and 2012); *Recreations* travel, cricket; *Clubs* Carlton, Royal Aeronautical Soc; *Style—* Robert Ricketts, Esq; ✉ Holland & Knight UK LLP, Waterman House, 41 Kingsway, London WC2B 6TP (☎ 020 7240 6767, e-mail robert.ricketts@hollandandknight.co.uk)

RICKFORD, Jonathan Braithwaite Keevil; CBE (2001); s of Richard Braithwaite Keevil Rickford (d 1990), and Dorothy Margaret, *née* Latham; *b* 7 December 1944; *Educ* Sherborne, Magdalen Coll Oxford (MA, BCL, Gibbs prize in law); *m* 20 July 1968, Dora Rose, da of Rt Rev Norman Sargant (d 1985); 1 s (Richard b 7 July 1971), 2 da (Margaret b 10 Dec 1973, Alice b 24 March 1975); *Career* barr 1970–85, slr 1985–; teaching assoc in law Univ of Calif Sch of Law 1968–69, lectr in law LSE 1969–72, sr legal asst Dept of Trade 1974 (asst 1972), Law Offrs Dept AG's Chambers 1976–79; DTI (formerly Dept of Trade): asst slr (co law) 1979–82, under sec (legal) 1982–84, the Slr 1984–87; British Telecommunications plc: slr and chief legal offr 1987–89, dir of govt rels 1989–93, dir of corp strategy 1993–96; sr fell Br Inst of Int and Comparative Law 1996–97, sr assoc European Public Policy Advisers (EPPA) 1997–98, project dir The Co Law Review 1998–2001, dir Co Law Centre 2003–06 (professorial fell 2006–); The Competition Cmmn (formerly Monopolies and Mergers Cmmn) 1997–2004; visiting prof in int corp law Leiden Univ The Netherlands 2002, visiting prof LSE 2003–09; FRSA 1991; *Recreations* sailing; *Clubs* Bosham Sailing; *Style—* Jonathan Rickford, Esq, CBE; ✉ e-mail jrickford@aol.com

RICKFORD, Dr William Jeremy Keevil; s of Richard Braithwaite Keevil Rickford (d 1990), of Dartmouth, Devon, and Dorothy Margaret Hart, *née* Latham; *b* 4 December 1949; *Educ* Sherborne, St Thomas' Hosp Med Sch London (MB BS); *m* 9 Oct 1982, Jacqueline Ann, da of Kenneth Cooke Burrow, MBE, of Sandgate, Folkestone, Kent; 1 da (Emma b 15 Dec 1983), 1 s (Thomas b 7 Jan 1986); *Career* asst prof Dept of Anaesthesiology Univ of Maryland Baltimore USA 1986–88, conslt anaesthetist E & N Hertfordshire NHS Health Tst 1988–; FRCA, FFARCSI; *Recreations* skiing, sailing; *Clubs* Royal Dart Yacht; *Style—* Dr W J K Rickford; ✉ Department of Anaesthetics, Lister Hospital, Corey's Mill, Stevenage, Hertfordshire SG1 4AB (☎ 01438 314333 and 01438 781086, e-mail rickfordwjk@aol.com)

RICKS, Dr Catherine Louise (Katy); da of Paul Koralek, CBE, of London, and Jenny, *née* Chadwick; *b* 16 March 1961; *Educ* Camden Sch for Girls, Balliol Coll Oxford (MA); *m* 1983, David Ricks; *Career* asst teacher: St Paul's Girls' Sch 1985–87, King Edward's Sch Edgbaston 1987–90, Latymer Upper Sch 1990–92; head of English St Edward's Sch Oxford 1992–97, dep head Highgate Sch 1997–2002, head Sevenoaks Sch 2002–; *Style—* Dr Katy Ricks; ✉ Sevenoaks School, Sevenoaks, Kent TN13 1HU (☎ 01732 467702, e-mail hm@sevenoaksschool.org)

RICKSON, Ian; s of Richard Rickson, and Eileen, *née* Frost; *b* 8 November 1963; *Educ* Univ of Essex (BA), Goldsmiths Coll London (PGTC); *Partner* Polly Teale; 2 c (Jack Gould b 6 Nov 1985, Eden Rickson b 2 Aug 2000); *Career* artistic dir Royal Court Theatre 1998–2006; prodns for the Royal Court incl: The Seagull, Krapp's Last Tape, The Winterling, Alice Trilogy, The Sweetest Swing in Baseball, Fallout, The Night Heron, Boy Gets Girl, Mouth to Mouth (and Albery), Dublin Carol, The Weir (Duke of Yorks and Broadway), The Lights, Pale Horse, Mojo (and Steppenwolf Theatre Chicago), Ashes and Sand, Some Voices, Killers, 1992 Young Writers' Festival, Wildfire, Jerusalem 2009; other prodns incl: The Hothouse (RNT), The Day I Stood Still (RNT), The House of Yes (The Gate), Me and My Friend (Chichester Festival Theatre), Queer Fish (BAC), First Strike (Soho Poly), La Serva Padrona (opera, Broomhill), The Seagull (Broadway), Hedda Gabler (Broadway), Parlour Song (Almeida) 2009, Jerusalem (Royal Court and West End) 2009–10 and (Broadway) 2011, The Children's Hour (West End) 2011, Betrayal (West End) 2011, Hamlet (Young Vic) 2011; films: dir Krapp's Last Tape (BBC 4) 2007, dir Fallout (Channel 4) 2008; hon fell Goldsmiths Coll London; *Clubs* Black's, The Hospital; *Style—* Ian Rickson; ✉ c/o Judy Daish, Judy Daish Associates, 2 St Charles Place, London W10 6EG

RIDDELL, Rt Hon Peter John Robert; CBE (2012), PC (2010); s of Kenneth Robert Riddell (d 1964), and Freda, *née* Young (d 2006); *b* 14 October 1948, Torquay, Devon; *Educ* Dulwich Coll, Sidney Sussex Coll Cambridge (BA); *m* 23 July 1994, Avril, da of late Richard Hillier Walker; 1 da (Emily Elizabeth b 16 July 1996); *Career* FT: city staff 1970–72, property corr 1972–74, Lex columnist 1975–76, econ corr 1976–81, political ed 1981–88, US ed 1989–91; The Times: political columnist and commentator 1991–2010, political ed 1992–93, asst ed (politics) 1993–2010; dir/chief exec Inst for Govt 2012–16 (sr fell 2008–11), public appts cmmr UK Govt 2016–; regular appearances on radio and TV current affairs progs such as Week in Westminster; visiting prof of political history Queen Mary & Westfield Coll London 2000–03; memb PC Inquiry into Treatment of UK Detainees 2010–11, memb Parly and Political Service Honours Ctee 2012–16; chm Hansard Soc 2007–12 (memb Cncl 1994–2012); Econ and Fin Journalist of the Year Wincott Awards 1981, Political Journalist of the Year 1985, Political Studies Assoc Political Columnist of the Year 2005, Br Acad's President's Medal 2010; Freedom City of London 2012; Hon DLitt: Univ of Greenwich 2001, Univ of Edinburgh 2007; hon fell Sidney Sussex Coll Cambridge 2005, hon fell Political Studies Assoc 2007; govr Dulwich Coll 2009– (chm of govrs 2015–); FRHistS 1998, AcSS 2012; *Books* The Thatcher Government (1983, 2 edn 1985), The Thatcher Decade (1989, 2 edn as The Thatcher Era and Its Legacy, 1991), Honest Opportunism – the rise of the career politician (1993, 2 edn 1996), Parliament Under Pressure (1998, 2 edn as Parliament Under Blair 2000), Hug Them Close (2003, Channel 4 Political Book of the Year), The Unfulfilled Prime Minister (2005, 2 edn 2006), In Defence of Politicians – in spite of themselves (2011); *Recreations* opera, theatre, watching cricket and baseball, reading; *Clubs* Garrick, Surrey CC, MCC; *Style—* The Rt Hon Peter Riddell, CBE; ✉ c/o Commissioner for Public Appointments, Room G/08, 1 Horse Guards Road, London SW1A 2HQ

RIDDICK, Graham Edward Galloway; s of late John Julian Riddick (d 1997), and late Cecilia Margaret (d 1991), da of Sir Edward Ruggles-Brise, 1 Bt, MC, TD, MP for Maldon (Essex) 1922–42 (d 1942); *b* 26 August 1955; *Educ* Stowe, Univ of Warwick; *m* 1988, Sarah Northcroft; 1 s (George John Galloway b 5 Jan 1991), 2 da (Rosannah Cecilia Mary b 10 April 1993, Charlotte Louise b 3 Jan 1996); *Career* MP (Cons) Colne Valley 1987–97, PPS to Hon Francis Maude as Fin Sec to the Treasy 1990–92, PPS to John MacGregor as Sec of State for Tport 1992–94; memb: Educn Select Ctee 1994–95, Deregulation Select Ctee 1995–97, Educn and Employment Select Ctee 1996–97; former vice-chm Cons Back Bench Employment Ctee; former sec: All-Pty Wool Textile Parly Gp, Cons Back Bench Trade and Industry Ctee; memb CBI London Regnl Cncl 1999–2005; gp marketing and communications dir Onyx Environmental Gp plc 1997–2000, business devpt dir DeHavilland Info Services plc 2000–05, commercial dir Adfero Ltd 2005–07, dir Norman Broadbent 2007–09, dir Ashurst Executives 2010–, dir Wild Search 2010–15; former memb Freedom Assoc Nat Cncl, former pres Yorks Cons Political Centre (CPC); *Recreations* shooting, fishing, tennis, squash, bridge, photography; *Style—* Graham Riddick, Esq

RIDDING, Caroline; da of Graham Ridding, of Bolton, and Carol Ann, *née* Power; *b* 6 August 1970, Bolton; *Educ* Canon Slade Sch Bolton, Univ of Westminster (HND), Univ of Plymouth (BSc); *m* 31 Dec 2001, Matthew Lamprell; 1 s (Charlie b 12 Nov 2007); *Career* book buying mangr Tesco Stores Ltd 1999–2006, md Avon Books Harper Collins Publishers 2006–; *Style—* Miss Caroline Ridding; ✉ HarperCollins Publishers, 77–85 Fulham Palace Road, London W6 8JB (☎ 020 8307 4659, e-mail caroline.ridding@harpercollins.co.uk)

RIDDING, John Joseph; *b* 25 June 1965; *Educ* Bedales, UC Oxford (BA); *m*; 3 c; *Career* journalist; Asia Pacific desk head Oxford Analytica 1996–97; Financial Times: Korea corr 1989–91, dep features ed 1991–93, Paris corr 1993–96, Hong Kong Bureau chief 1996–98, dep managing ed 1998–99, managing ed 1999–2001, dep ed 2001–03, ed and publisher FT Asia 2003–06, chief exec 2006–; *Style—* Mr J Ridding; ✉ Financial Times, 1 Southwark Bridge, London SE1 9HL

RIDDLE, Sr District Judge Howard Charles Frazer; s of Cecil Riddle (d 1987), of Sevenoaks, Kent, and Eithne, *née* McKenna (d 1997); *b* 13 August 1947; *Educ* Judd Sch Tonbridge, LSE (LLB); *m* 31 Aug 1974, (Susan) Hilary, da of Dr André Hurst (d 1992), of Ottawa, Canada; 2 da (Stephanie b 1979, Poppy b 1984); *Career* SSRC Canada 1971–76, sr ptnr Edward Fail Bradshaw & Waterson 1985–95; met stipendiary magistrate 1995–2000 (acting met stipendiary magistrate 1993–95), district judge (magistrates' court) 2000–10, memb Sentencing Advsy Panel 2004–10 (vice-chm 2007–10), chm Legal Ctee Cncl of HM District Judges (Magistrates' Courts) 2007–11, memb Law Cmmn Criminal Law Ctee 2009–, sr district judge and chief magistrate 2010–; vice-chm London Area Ctee Legal Aid Bd 1993–95; hon bencher Grays Inn 2012; memb Law Soc 1969; *Publications* Wilkinson's Road Traffic Offences (contributing ed, 2008–11), Blackstone's Criminal Practice (contrib and memb Editorial Bd); *Recreations* rugby football, walking, tennis, cycling; *Clubs* Druidstone, Tonbridge Juddian RFC; *Style—* Senior District Judge Riddle; ✉ Chief Magistrate's Office, Westminster Magistrates' Court, 181 Marylebone Road, London NW1 5BR (☎ 020 3126 3100)

RIDEL, David William; s of Maurice William Ridel (d 2008), and Violet Georgina, *née* Tull (d 1983); *b* 20 December 1947; *Educ* Forest GS Wokingham, Univ of Bristol (BA, BArch); *m* 23 Oct 1971, Felicity Laura, da of Rev Thomas Herbert Lewis; 2 s (Thomas William b 6 Jan 1976, Jack William b 7 Feb 1983), 1 da (Gemma Laura b 31 July 1977); *Career* architectural asst Marshall Macklin Monaghan Toronto Canada 1969–70, assoc architect Richard Lee Architect Bristol 1972–75, chief architect Community Housing Architects Team London 1975–79, chief exec Community Housing Assoc London 1979, sr architect YRM Architects London 1979–86, ptnr Building Design Partnership 1986–92, princ memb LSI architects LLP Norwich 1992–; corp memb RIBA 1974; govr Norwich Sch of Art & Design 1993–2007; *Recreations* skiing, ballet, opera, theatre; *Style—* David Ridel, Esq; ✉ LSI Architects, The Old Drill Hall, 23A Cattle Market Street, Norwich NR1 3DY (☎ 01603 660711, fax 01603 623213, e-mail david.ridel@lsiarchitects.co.uk)

RIDEOUT, Prof Roger William; s of Sidney Rideout (d 1949), of Bromham, Beds, and Hilda Rose, *née* Davies (d 1985); *b* 9 January 1935; *Educ* Bedford Sch, UCL (LLB, PhD); *m* 1, 30 July 1960 (m dis 1976), Marjorie Roberts, da of Albert Roberts, of Bedford; 1 da (Tania Mary b 1965); m 2, 24 Aug 1977, Gillian Margaret, *née* Cooper (d 2005); *Career* Nat Serv Lt RAEC 1958–60; lectr: Univ of Sheffield 1960–63, Univ of Bristol 1963–64; called to the Bar Gray's Inn 1964; UCL: sr lectr 1964–65, reader in Eng law 1965–73, prof of labour law 1973–2000, dean of faculty 1975–77, vice-dean and dep head Dept of Law

R

1982–89, dir of res studies 1993–99, fell 1997; memb Phelps-Brown Ctee 1967–68, chm Industrial Law Soc 1977–80 (vice-pres 1983–), pt/t chm Employment Tbnls 1983–2003 (salaried 2003–07), dep chm Central Arbitration Ctee 1978–2003; ILO Missions to: Gambia 1981–83, Somalia 1990–91, Egypt 1992–94; fell Soc for Advanced Legal Studies (FSALS); *Books* Trade Unions and the Law (1973), Industrial Tribunal Law (1980), Principles of Labour Law (5 edn, 1989), Bromham in Bedfordshire: A History (2003); *Recreations* local history; *Style*— Prof Roger Rideout; ✉ 255 Chipstead Way, Woodmansterne, Surrey SM7 3JW (☎ 01737 213489, e-mail rideout126@btinternet.com)

RIDER, Prof Barry Alexander Kenneth; OBE (2014); s of Kenneth Leopold Rider, of Cambridge, and Alexina Elsie, *née* Bremner; *b* 30 May 1952; *Educ* Bexleyheath Boys' Secdy Modern Sch, Univ of London (LLB, PhD), Univ of Cambridge (MA, PhD); *m* 1 Aug 1976, Normalita Furto, da of Don Isidro Rosales; 1 da (Mei Ling Antionette b 14 Dec 1979); *Career* called to the Bar Inner Temple 1977 (master of the bench 2010); fell (now fell commoner) Jesus Coll Cambridge 1976–, lectr in law Univ of Cambridge 1978–96, prof of law Univ of London 1996–2004, dir Inst of Advanced Legal Studies Univ of London 1996–2004, prof of mercantile law Univ of the Free State South Africa 1998–, hon sr research fell Inst of Advanced Legal Studies Univ of London 2004–, professorial fell Centre for Devpt Studies Univ of Cambridge 2007–, prof of law and dir LLM programmes BPP Law Sch 2007–, prof of comparative law Remnin Univ China 2011–; conslt Beechcroft LLP 2004–06, of counsel Bryan Cave LLP 2008–12; head Commercial Crime Unit Cwlth Secretariat 1981–89, specialist advsr Trade and Industry Select Ctee House of Cmmns 1989–93; conslt to Islamic Financial Services Bd and former conslt to UN, UNDP, UNCTAD, WHO, IMF, Asian Devpt Bank, World Bank, EU and CFTC; secondments to govts incl: Hong Kong, Singapore, Malaysia, Philippines, Barbados, Trinidad, South Africa, Zimbabwe, Mozambique, Zambia, India; int gen counsel Int Compliance Assoc 2007; visiting appts: Univ of Florida, Supreme People's Procuratorate Univ China, Univ of Hong Kong, Univ of Palermo; pres Br Inst of Securities Laws, exec dir Centre for Int Documentation on Organised and Economic Crime; memb Advsy Ctee Yicai Fndn China Overseas-Educated Scholars Fndn 2015–, special counselor on devpt Renmin Law Sch Beijing 2015–, memb Advsy Bd Centre for Financial Crime and Security Studies RUSI 2015–; int advsr: Centre for Criminology Univ of Hong Kong, Centre for Int Law and Policy New England Sch of Law, Faculty of Law Univ of Cyprus, Inst of Criminal Justice Beijing; chm: Hamlyn Tst 2001–04, Exec Ctee Soc of Advanced Legal Studies; gen ed of various jls incl: The Company Lawyer, Amicus Curiae, Jl of Financial Crime, International Jl of Disclosure and Governance, International and Comparative Corporate Law Jl; author, co-author and contrib to numerous books and works; Freeman City of London, memb Ct of Assts Worshipful Co of Pattenmakers (Warden 2005–07, Master 2007–08), Freeman Guild of Educators 2008, Liveryman Worshipful Co of Educators 2014; hon prof of laws Beijing Normal Univ 2006–, visiting prof Renmin Univ of China 2006–11; Hon LLD: Penn State Univ, Univ of the Free State South Africa; hon fell Soc of Advanced Legal Studies; FRSA, FIPI; *Recreations* riding, historic buildings, war games, paranormal; *Clubs* Oxford and Cambridge, Athenaeum, Civil Service; *Style*— Prof Barry Rider, OBE; ✉ Jesus College, Cambridge CB5 8BL (e-mail b.rider@jesus.cam.ac.uk)

RIDER, Steve; *Career* formerly: reporter and features writer Hayters, sports presenter and reporter LBC/IRM, sports ed Anglia TV, presenter and reporter Thames TV; presenter: Sportsnight (BBC) 1985–91, Grandstand (BBC) 1991–2005, ITV Sport 2005–10; presenter: Cwlth Games 1986, New Zealand 1990, Canada 1994 and Malaysia 1998 (BBC), Winter Olympics Calgary, Albertville, Lillehammer and Nagano (BBC), Olympic Games Moscow (ITV) 1980, Barcelona 1992 (BBC, Olympic Ctee Golden Rings Award, Sports Award RTS), Atlanta 1996 and Sydney 2000, Whitbread Round the World Race (BBC) 1997/98, Cricket World Cup (BBC) England 1999; presenter of several corp videos; host of several award ceremonies and press conferences; Sports Presenter of the Year TV and Radio Industries Club 1994, Sports Presenter of the Year RTS 1996; *Style*— Steve Rider, Esq

RIDGE, Rupert Leander Pattle; s of Maj Robert Vaughan Ridge (d 1987), of Brockley and Lacock, and Marian Ivy Edith, *née* Pattle (d 1977); *b* 18 May 1947; *Educ* King's Coll Taunton; *m* 1971, Mary Blanche, da of Maj Martin Gibbs (d 1994), of Chippenham, and Elsie Margaret Mary, *née* Hamilton Dalrymple (d 2012); 4 c (Thomas Leander Pattle b 1972, Marian Sophia b 1973, Edward Francis b 1976, Adeline Dyce Albinia Rose b 1979); *Career* offr Light Infantry 1968–73, with British Aerospace Defence (formerly British Aircraft Corporation) 1973–94 (numerous roles mostly as commercial exec), int dir Leonard Cheshire International 1994–2004, advsr Motivation Charitable Tst 2004–; tstee Action around Bethlehem Children with Disability (ABCD) 1994–2005 (chm 1998–2005), tstee Wellspring Counselling 2004–11 (chm 2006–09); former chm St Michael's Cheshire Home Axbridge; *Recreations* gardening and smallholding mgmnt; *Style*— Rupert Ridge, Esq; ✉ Motivation Charitable Trust, Brockley Academy, Brockley Lane, Backwell, Bristol BS48 4AQ (☎ 01275 464012, fax 01275 464019, e-mail ridge@motivation.org.uk)

RIDGWAY, George; s of John George Ridgway (d 1988), of Leicester, and Constance Winifred, *née* Bruce (d 1980); *b* 16 October 1945; *Educ* Wyggeston Sch, Leicester Poly; *m* 20 June 1970, Mary, da of John Chamberlain; 2 c (Imogen Kate b 6 Nov 1973, Julian George b 14 March 1978); *Career* chartered accountant; fin dir Ridgway & Co (Leicester) Ltd (machine tool manufacturers) 1980–98, sr ptnr Pole Arnold Leics 1986–2002, md HLB AV Audit plc 2002–05, ptnr Numerica LLP 2002–05, client ptnr Vantis plc; pres Leics and Northants Soc of CAs 1990–91, memb Cncl ICAEW 1994–2002, chair Business Law Ctee ICAEW; chair Leicester Coll; chair Leics Wooden Spoon Soc; dir Leicester Comedy Festival; FCA, ACiM; *Style*— George Ridgway, Esq; ✉ Alma House, Station Road, Attleborough, Norfolk NR17 2AS (e-mail georgeridgeway@btinternet.com)

RIDGWAY, Judith Anne (Judy); da of Dr Leslie Randal Ridgway, of Eastbourne, E Sussex, and Lavinia, *née* Bottomley; *b* Stalybridge, Manchester; *Educ* St Christopher Sch Letchworth, Keele Univ; *Career* former assoc dir Welbeck PR; cookery ed Woman's World Magazine 1984–90; freelance writer on: food, wine, cookery, catering, travel; int olive oil expert (author of EU papers on taste and flavour in olive oil 1993, 2002 and 2012); memb: Guild of Food Writers, Soc of Authors; Companion Guilde de Fromagers, Confrérie de St Uguzon 1990, Judges Panel Leone d'Oro Awards Verona 1996, 1998, 1999, 2000, 2001 and 2002; *Books* The Vegetarian Gourmet (1979), Salad Days (1979), Home Preserving (1980), The Seafood Kitchen (1980), The Colour Book of Chocolate Cookery (1981), Mixer, Blender, Processor Cookery (1981), The Breville Book of Toasted Sandwiches (1982), Waitrose Book of Pasta, Rice and Pulses (1982), Making the Most of: Rice, Pasta, Potatoes, Bread, Cheese, Eggs (1983), The Little Lemon Book, The Little Rice Book, The Little Bean Book (1983), Barbecues (1983), Cooking with German Food (1983), Frying Tonight (1984), Sprouting Beans and Seeds (1984), Man in the Kitchen (jtly, 1984), Nuts and Cereals (1985), The Vegetable Year (1985), Wining and Dining at Home (1985), Wheat and Gluten-Free Cookery (1986), Vegetarian Wok Cookery (1986), Cheese and Cheese Cookery (1986), 101 Ways with Chicken Pieces (1987), Pocket Book of Oils, Vinegars and Seasonings (jtly, 1989), Carr's Connoisseurs Cheese Guide (1989), The Vitamin and Mineral Diet Cookbook (1990), Catering for a Wedding (1991), The Vegetarian Delights (1992), The Quick After Work Pasta Cookbook (1993), Food for Sport (1994), Quick After-Work Vegetarian Cookbook (1994), The Noodle Cookbook (1994), Clearly Delicious (jtly, 1994), Quick After Work Winter Vegetarian Cookbook (1996), The Olive Oil Companion (1997), The Cheese Companion (1999), Optimum Nutrition Cookbook (jtly, 1999, 2 edn 2010), French Traditional Cheeses (2001), Judy Ridgway's Best Olive Oil Buys Round the World (2002 and 2005), Remarkable Recipes from the people who really know about extra virgin olive oil – the producers (2014, e-book 2013), A Banquet on a Budget (2016), The Olive Oil Diet (2016), Quick and Delicious Vegetarian Meals (jtly, 2016); wine: The Wine Lover's Record Book (1988), The Little Red Wine Book (1989), The Little White Wine Book (1989), Best Wine Buys in the High Street (1996), The Wine Tasting Class (1996), Best Wine Buys (1997); children's cookery: 101 Fun Foods to Make (1982), Cooking Round the World (1983), Festive Occasions (1986), Food and Cooking Round the World (jtly, 1986), Healthy Eating (jtly, 1990); how to books: Home Cooking for Money (1983), Running Your Own Wine Bar (1984), Successful Media Relations (1984), Running Your Own Catering Business (1993), Catering Management Handbook (jtly, 1994); *Recreations* opera, bridge, walking, reading; *Style*— Ms Judy Ridgway; ✉ 5E Sussex Heights, St Margaret's Place, Brighton BN1 2FQ (☎ 01273 733122, e-mail jridgway@oliveoil.org.uk, website www.oliveoil.org.uk, blog www.judyrigway-oliveoil.org.uk)

RIDING, Joanna; da of Alan Riding, of Longridge, Lancs, and Glenys Pauline, *née* Duxbury; *b* 9 November 1967; *Educ* Penwortham Girls HS, Blackpool & Fylde Coll of FE, Bristol Old Vic Theatre Sch; *Career* actress; spent three years whilst a student as solo and band vocalist; *Theatre* for Chichester incl: Dorothy in The Wizard of Oz, Anne in The Merry Wives of Windsor, Rosie in My Mother Said I Never Should; for RNT incl: Julie Jordan in Carousel, Anne Egerman in A Little Night Music, Sarah Brown in Guys and Dolls, Oh What a Lovely War; other credits incl: Happy as a Sandbag (Swan Worcester), Around the World in Eighty Days (Liverpool), Sally in Me and My Girl (Adelphi), Susie in Lady Be Good (Regents Park), The Picture of Dorian Day (Lyric Hammersmith and tour), Sarah Stone in No Way to Treat a Lady (Arts Theatre), Hey Mr Producer (Lyceum), Bertrande in Martin Guerre (Nat tour), Jane Smart in The Witches of Eastwick (Theatre Royal and Prince of Wales), Eliza Doolittle in My Fair Lady (Theatre Royal), Maggie Hobson in Hobson's Choice (Manchester Royal Exchange), Miss Gossage in The Happiest Days of our Life (Manchester Royal Exchange), Ruth in Blithe Spirit (Theatre Royal Bath and The Savoy London), Fenela in Playing for Time (Salisbury Playhouse); guest singer Jason Robert Brown concert (Players Theatre), own cabaret performance (Delfont Rooms and Prince of Wales), several musical workshops for new writers; cast album recordings of several shows; *Television* incl: Sean's Show (Channel X), The Brian Conley Show (LWT), Casualty (BBC), Strike Command (YTV), Wing and a Prayer (Thames), Holby City (BBC), The Royal (BBC), Midsomer Murders (ITV), Heart Beat (YTV), Terri in Where the Heart Is (YTV); *Radio* incl The Ruby in the Smoke (BBC7), The Shadow in the North (BBC7), Between Friends (BBC4), We (BBC4); *Awards* Olivier Award for Best Actress in a Musical for Carousel 1993, Olivier Award for Best Actress in a Musical for My Fair Lady 2003; nominated: Olivier Award for Best Actress in a Musical for Guys and Dolls 1997, Olivier Award for Best Actress in a Musical for The Witches of Eastwick 2001, Manchester Evening Standard Award for Best Actress, What's On Stage Award nomination for Best Actress for Blithe Spirit; *Recreations* music, reading, crosswords, keep fit; *Style*— Ms Joanna Riding

RIDING, (Frederick) Michael Peter; s of Frederick N Riding (d 2001), of Alton, Hants, and Elizabeth, *née* Lockwood (d 1999); *Educ* Barnard Castle Sch, Univ of Leeds (BA); *m* 31 May 2003, Ellie; 1 da, 2 s from previous m (Victoria b 10 Jan 1970, George b 20 Dec 1971, Samuel b 21 Feb 1973); *Career* sr vice-pres Asia Chemical Bank NY 1980–83; Lloyds Bank plc: princ mangr Far E Div Lloyds Bank International Ltd 1984–85, gen mangr Asia 1985–87, gen mangr trade finance 1987–89, gen mangr UK retail banking 1989–91, gen mangr commercial banking 1991–95, dir of commercial banking 1996–97, md Commercial Financial Servs 1997–99, md Corp Banking 2000–03, md Wholesale Banking 2004–; dir: Home Entertainment Corp plc 2004–, N Bristol NHS Tst 2004–; FCIB 1991; *Recreations* golf, theatre, art, opera; *Clubs* RAC, Royal Lytham St Anne's Golf, Weston-super-Mare Golf; *Style*— Michael Riding, Esq; ✉ Lloyds TSB Group plc, 25 Gresham Street, London EC2V 7HN (☎ 020 7356 2218)

RIDING, Robert Furniss; s of William Furniss Riding, FCA (d 1985), of Manchester, and Winifred, *née* Coupe (d 1993); *b* 5 May 1940; *Educ* Stockport GS, ChCh Oxford (MA); *Career* dir and later chm Nat Commercial Devpt Capital Ltd 1980–85, gen mangr Williams & Glyn's Bank plc 1982–85, treas and gen mangr The Royal Bank of Scotland plc 1985–86, dep chm and chief exec RoyScot Finance Gp plc 1986–90; chm: RoyScot Tst plc 1984–90, Royal Bank Leasing Ltd 1986–90, RoyScot Vehicle Contracts Ltd 1986–90, RoyScot Factors Ltd 1986–90, RoyScot Finance Services Ltd 1988–90, Conister Tst plc (IOM) 1992–2002 (dir 1991–2002), IOM Int Broadcasting plc 2004–05; non-exec dir: Int Commodities Clearing House Ltd 1985–86, Royal Bank of Scotland AG (Switzerland) 1985–86, Direct Line Insurance plc 1986–88, Royal Bank Gp Services Ltd 1987–90, A T Mays Gp plc 1988–90, Commercial Finance Ltd (IOM) 1992–2002, Rycroft Finance & Leasing Ltd (IOM) 1996–2001, The With Profits Plus Fund plc (IOM) 1996–2007, IOM Int Business Sch 2000–09, Neville James Int Funds PCC plc 2007–13; memb: Exec Ctee Assoc of Manx Bankers 1993–99 (pres 1997–99), Exec Ctee IOM Centre IOD 1994–2003 (chm 1999–2003), Cncl IOD 1999–2003, IOM Govt Boundary Cmmn 2010–13; tstee Seamanship Fndn 1990–96, tstee Island Tst 2000– (pres 2015–), tstee and former chm Assoc of Sea Trg Orgns 1981–2013; hon life memb RYA (memb Cncl 1983–99, chm of trg 1984–89, hon treas 1994–99), chm Derbyhaven Residents' Soc 2008–13, chm Soder & Man Prayer Book Soc 2010–, chm Sir Henry Royce Meml Fndn 2012–14; memb Sodor and Man Diocesan Synod 1997–2003 and 2005–07; chm Friends of St German's Cathedral 1996–2006, churchwarden St Bridget's Kirk Bride 2009–14; FCIB 1976; *Recreations* sailing, motoring; *Clubs* Island Cruising (vice-pres, cdre 1988–90), Manx Motor Racing (chm 1999–), Manx Classic Car (pres 2005–), Rolls-Royce Enthusiasts', Bentley Drivers'; *Style*— Robert Riding, Esq; ✉ Ballakeil House, Smeale, Isle of Man IM7 3EQ (☎ 01624 880151); Ashley House, Derbyhaven, Isle of Man IM9 1TZ (☎ 01624 822587, e-mail robertriding@manx.net); Middlewood, Old Banwell Road, Locking, North Somerset BS24 8BT (☎ 01934 822587)

RIDLEY, Sir Adam Nicholas; kt (1985); s of Jasper Ridley (s of Maj Hon Sir Jasper Ridley, KCVO, OBE, 2 s of 1 Viscount Ridley, by the Maj's w Countess Nathalie, da of Count Benckendorff, sometime Russian ambass in London) and Cressida Bonham Carter (d 1998) (da of Baroness Asquith of Yarnbury and gda of H H Asquith the Lib PM); nephew by marriage of Baron Grimond, TD, PC, of Firth, Co Orkney; *b* 14 May 1942; *Educ* Eton, Balliol Coll Oxford, Univ of Calif Berkeley; *m* 1, 1970 (m dis), Lady Katharine Rose Celestine Asquith, 2 da of 2 Earl of Oxford and Asquith; m 2, 1981, Margaret Anne (Biddy), da of Frederic Passmore, of Virginia Water, Surrey; 3 s (Jasper, Luke (twins) b 29 May 1987, Jo b 16 Aug 1988); *Career* Dept of Economic Affairs 1965–69, HM Treasy 1970–71, Central Policy Review Staff 1971–74; former econ advsr and asst dir CRD 1975–79, dir CRD 1979 election campaign; special advsr: to the Chllr of the Exchequer 1979–84, to Chllr of the Duchy of Lancaster; min in charge of the Office of Arts and Libraries (also mangr Personnel Office) 1985; memb EC Expert Gp on Economic and Social Concepts in the Community 1976–79; exec dir Hambros Bank Ltd and Hambros plc 1985–97, chm of tstees Equitas Tst 1990–2014 (tstee 2014–); DG London Investment Banking Assoc 2000–05; Lloyd's of London: chm Names Ctee 1994–95, dep chm Assoc of Lloyd's Membs 1995– (memb Bd 1990–), memb Cncl Lloyd's and memb Lloyd's Regulatory Bd 1997–99; memb Bd and chm: Sunday Newspaper Publishing plc 1989, Leopold Joseph plc 1998–2004; dep chm Nat Lottery Charities Bd 1995–99, non-exec dir: Morgan Stanley Bank Int Ltd 2006–13, Hampden Agencies Ltd 2007–12; dir Equitas Gp of Companies 2009–; tstee St Christopher's Hospice 1987–2009, tstee Br Sch at Athens

2002– (vice chm 2009–); *Style—* Sir Adam Ridley; ✉ Equitas Trust, c/o ALM Ltd, 22 Bevis Marks, London EC3A 7JB

RIDLEY, Prof Frederick Fernand; OBE (1978); *b* 11 August 1928; *Educ* The Hall Hampstead, Highgate Sch, LSE (BSc, PhD), Univ of Paris, Univ of Berlin; *m* 1967, Paula Frances Cooper Ridley, CBE, DL, *qv*; 2 s, 1 da; *Career* Univ of Liverpool: lectr 1958–65, prof of political theory and instns 1965–95, sr fell Inst of Public Admin & Mgmnt 1995–2006; visiting prof: Graduate Sch of Public Affairs Univ of Pittsburgh 1968, Coll of Europe Bruges 1975–83; chm: Job Creation Prog Manpower Servs Cmmn Merseyside 1975–77, Area Manpower Bd 1987–88 (vice-chm 1978–87); memb: Jt Univ Cncl for Social and Public Admin 1964– (chm 1972–74), Exec Political Studies Assoc 1967–75 (hon vice-pres 1995–), Cncl Hansard Soc 1970–94, Political Sci Ctee SSRC 1972–76, Ctee Euro Gp on Public Admin 1973–92, Public and Social Admin Bd CNAA 1975–82, Res Advsy Gp Arts Cncl 1979–82, Exec Merseyside Arts (Regnl Arts Assoc) 1979–84, Social Studies Res Ctee CNAA 1980–83 (chm), Advsy Cncl Granada Fndn 1984–98; vice-pres: Rencontres Européennes des Fonctions Publiques 1990–94, Acad Cncl Forschungsinst für Verwaltungswissenschaft Speyer 1992–2005, Entretiens pour l'Admin Publique en Europe 1994–2000; tstee Friends of Merseyside Museums and Galleries 1977–85; hon pres Politics Assoc 1976–81 (hon fell 1995–); ed: Political Studies 1969–75, Parliamentary Affairs 1975–2004; *Publications* numerous books and articles on political science and public admin; *Style—* Prof Frederick Ridley; ✉ 24 North Road, Grassendale Park, Liverpool L19 0LR (☎ 0151 427 1630)

RIDLEY, Ian Robert; s of Robert Edwin Ridley, of Weymouth, Dorset, and Barbara, *née* Fullbrook; *b* 23 January 1955; *Educ* Hardye's Sch Dorchester Dorset, Bedford Coll London (BA); *m* 22 Oct 1977, Josephine Anne, da of Gerald Leighton; 1 s (Jack William b 6 April 1990), 1 da (Alexandra Judith b 12 Feb 1986); *Career* editorial asst Building Magazine 1976, sports ed Worksop Guardian 1977–79, sports sub ed and reporter Evening Post Echo Hemel Hempstead 1979–80; The Guardian: sports sub ed 1980–85, asst sports ed 1985–87, dep sports ed 1987–88, sports writer 1988–90; sports feature writer The Daily Telegraph 1990–93, freelance writer and journalist 1993–94, football corr The Independent on Sunday 1994–98, football columnist The Observer 1998–; memb: NUJ, Football Writers' Assoc, SWA, Assoc Internationale de Presse Sportive; *Books* Season in the Cold: A journey through English football, Cantona: The Red and the Black, Tales from the Boot Camps (with Steve Claridge), Addicted (with Tony Adams, 1998), Hero and Villain (with Paul Merson, 1999), Floodlit Dreams: How to Save a Football Club (2006); *Style—* Ian Ridley, Esq

RIDLEY, Malcolm James; s of Eric Malcolm Thomas Ridley (d 1972), and Pauline Esther (d 1972); *b* 10 March 1941; *Educ* Trinity Sch Croydon, Univ of Bristol (LLB); *m* 1, 14 July 1962 (m dis 1976), Joan Margaret, da of Stanley Charles Martin (d 2001); 2 da (Camilla b 1970, Estelle b 1972); m 2, 9 April 1977, Bridget Mina, da of Dr Charles Edward O'Keeffe (d 1963); 1 da (Susannah b 1977), 1 s (John b 1979); *Career* chartered accountant; Price Waterhouse Vancouver 1962–68, Price Waterhouse London 1974–79, ptnr Coopers & Lybrand London 1981–96 (joined 1979), sole practitioner 1996–; CA Canada 1966, FCA 1980, ATII 1974; *Recreations* cricket, golf, bridge, theatre, music; *Clubs* MCC, Walton Heath Golf; *Style—* Malcolm Ridley, Esq; ☎ 01306 741457, fax 01306 741458, e-mail malcolm@mjridley.co.uk

RIDLEY, 5 Viscount (UK 1900); Dr Matthew White (Matt) Ridley; s of 4 Viscount Ridley, KG, GCVO, TD (d 2012); *b* 7 February 1958; *Educ* Eton, Magdalen Coll Oxford (DPhil); *m* 16 Dec 1989, Dr Anya Christine Hurlbert, da of Dr Robert Hurlbert, of Houston, TX; 1 s (Matthew White b 27 Sept 1993), 1 da (Iris Livia b 16 June 1997); *Heir* s, Hon Matthew Ridley; *Career* author and businessman; The Economist: sci ed 1984–87, Washington corr 1987–89, American ed 1990–92; chm: Int Centre for Life 1996–2003, Northern 2 Venture Capital Tst 1999–2008, Northern Rock plc 2004–07; dir: Northern Investors plc 1994–2007, P A Holdings 2000–08; FRSL, FMedSci; *Books* Warts and All (1989), The Red Queen (1993), The Origins of Virtue (1996), Genome (1999), Nature via Nurture (2003), Francis Crick (2006), The Rational Optimist (2010); *Style—* The Viscount Ridley; ✉ Blagdon, Seaton Burn, Newcastle upon Tyne NE13 6DD

RIDLEY, Paula Frances Cooper; CBE (2008, OBE 1996), JP (Liverpool City 1977), DL (Merseyside 1989); da of Ondrej Clyne, and Ellen, *née* Cooper; *b* 27 September 1944; *Educ* Greenhead HS Huddersfield, Kendal HS Westmorland, Univ of Liverpool (MA); *m* 21 Jan 1967, Prof Frederick Fernand Ridley, OBE, *qv*; 2 s (Joseph Francis b 12 July 1970, Dominic Andrew b 29 Sept 1974), 1 da (Caroline Rachel b 3 April 1976); *Career* lectr in politics and public admin Liverpool Poly 1966–72; project coordinator Regeneration Projects Ltd 1981–84, conslt BAT Industries Small Business 1983–95, dir Community Initiatives Res Tst 1983–90, memb Bd Brunswick Small Business Centre Ltd 1984–95, assoc CEI Consultants 1984–88, presenter and assoc ed Helpful Productions ind TV prodn co 1989–92; chm: Liverpool Housing Action Tst 1992–2007, V&A 1998–2007, Liverpool Biennial of Contemporary Art 2008–16, Nat Student Drama Festival 2009–12, Civic Voice 2010–13, Bd English Nat Ballet 2011–14; dir Calouste Gulbenkian Fndn (UK branch) 1999–2007; memb: Ct Univ of Liverpool 1972–2013 (memb Cncl 1998–2007), Bd Merseyside Development Corp 1991–98, IBA 1982–88, Royal Cmmn on Long Term Care of the Elderly 1998–99, Bd Nat Community Resource Centre; tstee: Tate Gallery 1988–98 (chm Tate Gallery Liverpool 1988–98), Granada Telethon Tst 1988–94, National Gallery 1995–98; chm Merseyside Civic Soc 1986–91, life govr Liverpool and Huyton Colls 1979–94; hon fell Liverpool John Moores Univ 2002, Hon LLD Univ of Liverpool 2003; FRSA, Hon FRIBA 2005; author of articles in various professional jls; *Recreations* art, architecture and heritage; *Style—* Mrs Paula Ridley, CBE, DL; ✉ 24 North Road, Grassendale Park, Liverpool L19 0LR (☎ 0151 427 1630); 69 Thomas More House, Barbican, London EC2Y 8BT

RIDLEY, Prof Tony Melville; CBE (1986); s of John Edward Ridley (d 1982), and Olive, *née* Armstrong (d 1997); *b* 10 November 1933, Castletown, Co Durham; *Educ* Durham Sch, King's Coll Durham (BSc), Northwestern Univ Illinois (MS), Univ of Calif Berkeley (PhD); *m* 20 June 1959, Jane, da of John William Dickinson (d 1984); 1 da (Sarah b 1962), 2 s (Jonathon b 1963, Michael b 1966); *Career* Nuclear Power Gp 1957–62, GLC 1965–69, DG Tyne & Wear Passenger Tport Exec 1969–75, md Hong Kong Mass Transit Railway Corp 1975–80, memb Bd London Regnl Tport (formerly London Tport Exec) 1980–88 (md Railways 1980–85), chm London Underground Ltd 1985–88; dir: Docklands Light Railway 1982–88 (chm 1987–88), London Tport International 1981–88 (chm 1982–87); md Eurotunnel 1989–90 (non-exec dir 1987–90); Imperial College London: prof of tport engrg 1991–99, head of Dept of Civil and Environmental Engrg 1997–99, emeritus prof of tport engrg 1999–; dir Univ of London Centre for Tport Studies 1994–95, sr tport advsr London 2012 Olympic Bid 2004–05, memb Ind Dispute Avoidance Panel for London 2012 2008–12; pres Light Rail Transit Assoc 1974–92, dir Major Projects Assoc 1995–2009, chm Steering Gp Global Tport Knowledge Partnership 2008–10; memb: Senate Engrg Cncl 1997–2000 (chm Bd for Engrg Profession 1997–99), Taskforce 10 (Science Technol and Innovation) UN Millennium Project 2002–05, Int Advsy Panel Miny of Tport Singapore 2007–11; pres: Assoc for Project Mgmnt 1999–2003, Commonwealth Engineers Cncl 2000–09, Exec Cncl World Fedn of Engrg Orgns 2000–09; int pres CILT 1999–2001; tstee RAC Fndn for Motoring 1999–2009 (memb Public Policy Ctee 1997–2010); chm Building Schs for the Future Investments LLP (BSFI) 2007–10; first recipient Highways Award of Inst of Highways and Transportation 1988, first recipient Herbert Crow Award Worshipful Co of Carmen 2001, President's Award Engrg Cncl 2002; Freeman City of London 1982, Liveryman Worshipful Co of Carmen 1982; Hon DTech Napier Univ 1996, Hon DEng Univ of Newcastle upon Tyne 1997; hon fell Worshipful Co of Paviors 2006; FICE (pres 1995–96, memb Cncl 1990–97), FCILT, FIHT, fell Hong Kong Inst of Engineers, fell Inst of Transportation Engrs, FRSA, FREng 1992, FCGI 1995, FAPM 1996, Hon FIA 1999; *Publications* articles in transport, engineering and other journals; *Recreations* theatre, music, international affairs; *Clubs* RAC, Hong Kong, Hong Kong Jockey; *Style—* Prof Tony M Ridley, CBE, FREng; ✉ Orchard Lodge, Stichens Green, Streatley, Berkshire RG8 9SU (☎ 01491 871075)

RIDPATH, Michael William Gerrans; s of Andrew Ridpath (d 2005), of Bircham, Norfolk, and Elizabeth, *née* Hinds Howell (d 1999); *b* 7 March 1961, Exeter; *Educ* Millfield, Merton Coll Oxford (exhibitioner, BA); *m* 1, 1985, Candy Ann Helman (d 1992); 2 da (Julia b 17 Feb 1990, Laura b 30 Dec 1992); m 2, 1994, Barbara Ann, da of James P Nunemaker (d 1999); 1 s (Nicholas b 19 May 1997); *Career* writer; trader Saudi Int Bank 1982–91, venture capitalist Apax Partners & Co 1991–94; author 1994–; treas Royal Literary Fund 1999; memb: Soc of Authors 1995, Crime Writers' Assoc 1995; *Books* Free to Trade (1995), Trading Reality (1996), The Marketmaker (1998), Final Venture (2000), The Predator (2001), Fatal Error (2003), On the Edge (2005), See No Evil (2006), Where The Shadows Lie (2010), 66 North (2011), Meltwater (2012), Traitor's Gate (2013), Sea of Stone (2014), Shadows of War (2015); *Style—* Michael Ridpath, Esq; ✉ c/o Oliver Munson, A M Heath & Co, 6 Warwick Court, London WC1R 5DJ (☎ 020 7242 2811, e-mail mail@michaelridpath.com, website www.michaelridpath.com)

RIDSDALE, (Robert) Peter; s of Arthur Ridsdale (d 1985), and Audrey Gwendoline, *née* Oakley (d 1974); *b* 11 March 1952; *Educ* Leeds Modern GS; *m* 1 (m dis), Shirley Ruth; 2 s (Simon Nicholas b 5 Sept 1976, Paul Anthony b 30 Jan 1979); m 2 (m dis), Jacqueline; 2 s (Matthew Peter b 30 Jan 1985, Joseph Michael b 23 May 1988); m 3, 22 April 1995, Sophie Victoria, *née* Hobhouse; 2 da (Charlotte Louise b 13 May 1996, Olivia Rose b 26 Dec 1997); *Career* personnel offr Appleyard of Leeds 1969–72, personnel mangr Baker Perkins 1972–78, industrial rels mangr ICL 1978–81, vice-pres HR International Div Schering Plough Corp 1981–85, md Top Man then md Evans Ltd Burton Group plc 1985–91, jt chief operating offr Alexon Group plc 1991–93, chief exec QVC – The Shopping Channel 1993–94, gp md then chief exec The Tulchan Group Ltd 1994–2000; chm: Leeds United FC 1997–2003 (former dir), Leeds United plc (parent co of Leeds United FC) 1998–2003, Education Leeds 2001–04, NSC Technology Group plc 2001–03, Motor Solutions Ltd 2001–03, Cardiff City Football Club Holdings 2006–10, Cardiff City FC Ltd 2006–10; founding ptnr Fearless Partnership 2011–; advsr to owner of Preston North End FC 2011–; non-exec dir: Fii plc 1997–2003, Ideal Shopping Direct plc 2000–01, Sports Card plc 2000–01; FInstD, memb Mktg Soc; *Recreations Publications:* United We Fall (autobiography, 2007); *Style—* Peter Ridsdale, Esq

RIEDL, Martin Paul; s of Kurt Riedl, and Ruth, *née* Schechner; *b* 12 September 1949; *Educ* Sutton Valence, Ealing Sch of Photography (Dip Photography); *m* 1, 18 April 1980 (m dis 1990), Patricia Kilbourn, *née* Dumond; 2 s (Alexander David b 17 Nov 1981, Arthur Jonathan b 15 June 1983); m 2, 7 June 2002, Annie Bronwen (d 2012), da of Edward Augustus Williams; 1 s (Harry Edward b 11 Sept 1990); *Career* photographer; asst to: Robert Dowling 1973–75, Derek Coutts 1975–77; freelance photographer 1978–, opened own studio 1979–; Chalk and Water (photography exhbn, Chichester Festival Theatre) 2006; fndr Film in Educn film prodn co 2004 (company has run The London Primary School Silent Film Festival Awards since 2010), clients incl: NHS (Exercise for Life cancer awareness film), DCSF (films on schools, academies and teacher devpt); awarded two merits and two silvers Assoc of Photographers, D & AD silver nomination, second place Polaroid European Final Art Awards, prizewinner London Photographic Awards; memb Assoc of Photographers 1976; *Recreations* sculpture, skiing, badminton, tennis; *Clubs* Chelsea Arts, Cobden; *Style—* Martin Riedl, Esq; ✉ Martin Riedl Photography, 59 Blomfield Road, London W9 2PA (☎ 07831 879095, e-mail martin@filmineducation.com); Film in Education (e-mail info@filmineducation.com, website www.filmineducation.com)

RIFFAT, Prof Saffa; *Educ* Univ of Oxford (DPhil, DSc); *m*; *Career* sr research fell Univ of Westminster 1986–88, lectr and reader Loughborough Univ of Technol 1988–92; Univ of Nottingham: British Gas prof of architectural technol and energy 1992–97, head Sch of the Built Environment 1996–, ICI prof of refrigeration technol 1998–2002, Baxi prof of sustainable energy systems 2002–, dir Inst of Bldg Technol, dir Inst of Sustainable Energy Technol (ISET); hon prof: Chongqing Univ, Dalian Univ of Technol; delivered keynote speeches at confs worldwide, author of over 350 papers for refereed jls and int confs; over 20 inventions related to heating, ventilation, power generation, lighting, heat recovery, refrigeration, air conditioning and renewable energy, currently desiging and raising funds for Nottingham Eco-Village (world's first eco-village driven by hydrogen); awarded Technol Transfer Fellowship; fndr memb Midlands Renewable Energy Technol Transfer (MRETT); memb Advsy Bd: Baxi Technologies, Premas International, MRETT, David Wilson Homes; CEng, FIMechE, FCIBSE, FInstE; *Style—* Prof Saffa Riffat; ✉ School of the Built Environment, University of Nottingham, Nottingham NG7 2RD

RIFKIND, Hugo James; s of Rt Hon Sir Malcolm Rifkind, KCMG, QC, MP,, *qv*, and Edith, *née* Steinberg; *b* 30 March 1977, Edinburgh; *Educ* Loretto, Emmanuel Coll Cambridge (BA); *m* 5 May 2007, Francisca Kellett; 1 da (b 2009); *Career* freelance journalist 2000–05, columnist The Herald 2002–05, features writer The Times 2005–, columnist The Spectator 2007–; Overexposure (2006); *Recreations* writing novels very slowly; *Style—* Hugo Rifkind, Esq; ✉ The Times, 1 Pennington Street, London E98 1TT (☎ 020 7782 7545, e-mail hugo.rifkind@thetimes.co.uk)

RIFKIND, Rt Hon Sir Malcolm Leslie; KCMG (1997), PC (1986), QC (Scot 1985); s of Elijah Rifkind, of Edinburgh; *b* 21 June 1946, Edinburgh; *Educ* George Watson's Coll Edinburgh, Univ of Edinburgh (LLB, MSc); *m* 1970, Edith Amalia, *née* Steinberg; 1 s, 1 da; *Career* advocate, called to the Bar Edinburgh 1970; MP (Cons): Edinburgh Pentlands Feb 1974–97, Kensington and Chelsea 2005–10, Kensington 2010–15 (Parly candidate Edinburgh Central 1970); memb Select Ctee Euro Secdy Legislation 1975–76, oppn front bench spokesman on Scottish affrs 1975–76, jt sec Cons Foreign and Cwlth Affrs Ctee 1978, memb Select Ctee on Overseas Devpt 1978–79, Parly under sec of state Scottish Office 1979–82, Parly under sec of state FCO 1982–83, min of state FCO 1983–86, sec of state for Scotland 1986–90, sec of state for transport 1990–92, sec of state for defence 1992–95, sec of state for foreign and Cwlth affrs 1995–97, shadow sec of state for work and pensions 2005, chm Intelligence & Security Ctee 2010–; memb Queen's Body Guard for Scotland (Royal Co of Archers) 1993–; Hon Col: 162 Movement Control Regt Royal Logistics Corps 1996–2005, City of Edinburgh Univs OTC; *Recreations* walking, reading, field sports; *Clubs* Pratt's, New (Edinburgh), White's; *Style—* The Rt Hon Sir Malcolm Rifkind, KCMG, QC; ✉ House of Commons, London SW1A 0AA

RIGBY, Jean Prescott; da of Thomas Boulton Rigby (d 1987), and Margaret Annie, *née* Whiteside; *Educ* Elmslie Girls' Sch Blackpool, Birmingham Sch of Music, RAM (Principal's prize), RSA (Peter Stuyvesant scholarships), Nat Opera Studio (Leverhulme & Munster scholar); *m* 21 Nov 1987, Jamie Hayes; 3 s (Daniel Thomas b 7 March 1989, Oliver James b 27 Nov 1990, Matthew Peter b 25 Sept 1992); *Career* opera singer (mezzo soprano); princ mezzo soprano ENO 1982–90; Royal Opera House debut 1983, Glyndebourne debut 1984; roles incl: title role in Carmen, Octavian in Der Rosenkavalier, Lucretia in The Rape of Lucretia, Penelope in Il Ritorno d'Ulisse in Patria, Magdalena in Die Meistersinger, Maddalena in Rigoletto, Dorabella in Cosi fan Tutte, Jocasta in Oedipus Rex, Nicklaus in Les Côntes d'Hoffman, Isabella in L'Italiana in Algeri, Charlotte in Werther, Helen in King Priam, Rosina in The Barber of Seville, Angelina in La

Cenerentola, Idamante in Idomeneo, Irene in Theodora, Marcellina in Figaro, Eduige in Rodelinda, Amastris in Xerxes; 150 anniversary performance of Mendelssohn's Elijah (BBC Proms) 1996; numerous TV appearances and recordings incl Bach (Birtwistle); vice-pres Young Epilepsy, ambass Momentum (children's charity); winner: bursary ROH, Royal Overseas League competition, ENO Young Artists competition, Silver medal Worshipful Co of Musicians; hon fell Birmingham Conservatoire; Hon ARAM 1984, Hon FRAM 1989, ARCM, ABSM; *Recreations* theatre, sport, cooking, British heritage, cinema; *Style*— Ms Jean Rigby

RIGBY, Jonathan Martyn; s of Patricia Ward; *b* 10 December 1968; *Educ* Univ of Stirling (BA); *m* Claire, *née* Unstead; *Career* acct dir AMV BBDO 1993–96, dir Bd WCRS 1996–2000, new business dir LOWE London 2000–03, md Draft FCB London 2003–05, strategy ptnr LOVE 2005–08, brand and mktg dir NetplayTV 2008–10, head of mktg Manchester United 2010–15, dir of mktg and fundraising BBC Children in Need 2015–; *Style*— Jonathan Rigby, Esq; ✉ Twitter @_jonathanrigby

RIGBY, Dr Michael Laurence; s of Thomas Rigby, of Burnley, and Kathleen, *née* Barker; *b* 19 March 1947; *Educ* Colne GS, Univ of Leeds Med Sch (MB ChB, MD); *Children* 3 da (Jessica Clair Louise b 27 March 1981, Olivia Jane b 22 Oct 1982, Claudia Anne b 16 April 1985); *Career* postgrad medical educn: Leeds, Birmingham, Oxford, Toronto, London; Canadian Heart Fndn research fell 1978–79, conslt paediatric cardiologist Brompton Hosp London 1983–; visiting prof of cardiology Univs of Singapore, Recife, Buenos Aires, Santiago and Cario; memb: Br Cardiac Soc, Argentian Soc of Cardiology, Brazilian Soc of Cardiology, Assoc for Euro Paediatric Cardiology; FRCP 1986, FRCPCH 1998; *Books* The Morphology of Congenital Heart Disease (1983), The Diagnosis of Congenital Heart Disease (1986), Paediatric Cardiology (2002, 2 edn 2010), Echocardiography in Congenital Heart Disease (2005), Handbook of Paediatric Cardiology (2011); *Recreations* piano, singing, music, writing, keep fit; *Style*— Dr Michael Rigby; ✉ Royal Brompton Hospital, Sydney Street, London SW3 6NP (☎ 020 7351 8542 , fax 020 7351 8547, e-mail michael.rigby@rbht.nhs.uk)

RIGBY, Sir Peter; kt (2002), DL (2000); s of John Yates Rigby (d 1972), and Phyllis, *née* Newman (d 2001); *b* 29 September 1943, Liverpool; *Educ* Waterloo GS Liverpool; *m* (m dis), Patricia Anne; 2 s (James Peter b 6 March 1971, Steven Paul b 6 Dec 1972); *Career* fndr, chm and ceo Rigby Gp (RG) plc 1975–, fndr, chm and ceo SCC EMEA plc UK, France, Holland, Spain, Romania and SCD Middle East (Dubai) and N Africa (Morocco), fndr and chm Eden Hotel Collection 1995–, fndr and chm Patriot Aerospace Gp 2002–, chm Coventry Airport 2010–, chm Br Int Helicopters Ltd, chm Regional and City Airports (Exeter Airport, Coventry Airport, Norwich Airport); dir Coventry and Warks Devpt Partnership 2011–, chm Coventry and Warks Local Enterprise Partnership 2012–14; tstee: Rigby Fndn 1995–, RAF Museums 2006–10; chm Millennium Point Tsts 1996–2003; patron Acorns Children's Hospice 1993–; Liveryman Guild of Air Pilots and Navigators 2009; Hon DUniv City of Birmingham Univ 2000, Hon DSc Aston Univ 2003; FRAeS 2014; *Recreations* flying (helicopter and fixed wing), classical music; *Style*— Sir Peter Rigby, DL; ✉ Rigby Group (RG) plc, James House, Warwick Road, Birmingham B11 2LE (☎ 0121 766 7000)

RIGBY, Peter Stephen; *b* 30 July 1955; *Educ* King George V GS Southport, Univ of Manchester (BA); *m* 1, 25 Aug 1979, Stasia Teresa; 1 s (Nicholas Ian b 1981); m 2; 2 da; *Career* asst factory accountant Metal Box 1978–80 (trainee accountant 1976–78), fin accountant Book Club Associates 1980–83, gp accountant Stonehart Publications 1983–86, chief exec International Business Communications (Holdings) plc 1989–98 (fin dir 1987, dep chief exec 1988), chm Informa 1998–2004, chief exec T&F Informa plc 2004–07, chm Informa plc 2007–; numerous co directorships; ACMA 1980; *Recreations* golfing, jogging, squash, weight training, soccer, rugby, reading, theatre, music; *Style*— Peter Rigby, Esq

RIGG, Prof Jonathan Digby; s of Nigel Rigg, of Tunbridge Wells, Kent, and Kathleen, *née* Foster; *b* 25 November 1959, Calcutta, India; *Educ* SOAS Univ of London (BA, PhD); *m* 1985, Janie, *née* Bickersteth; 2 s (Joshua Eliot b 1990, Samuel Morris b 2001), 2 da (Eleanor Grace b 1992, Francesca Poppy b 1998); *Career* SOAS Univ of London: British Acad research fell 1986–89, lectr in SE Asian geography 1989–93; Dept of Geography Univ of Durham: lectr 1993–95, reader 1995–2003, prof 2003–13; prof Geography Dept Univ of Singapore 2013–; FRGS, AcSS; *Books* Southeast Asia: A Region in Transition – A Thematic Human Geography of the Asean Region (1991), More than the Soil: Rural Change in Southeast Asia (2001), Southeast Asia: The Human Landscape of Modernization and Development (2003), Living with Transition in Laos: Market Integration in Southeast Asia (2005), An everyday geography of the Global South (2007), Unplanned Development: the hidden geometrics of change in Southeast Asia (2012); *Style*— Prof Jonathan Rigg; ✉ Department of Geography, University of Durham, South Road, Durham DH1 3LE (☎ 0191 334 1925, e-mail j.d.rigg@durham.ac.uk)

RIGHTON, Caroline Anne; da of Patrick Cornelius Donovan, and Maureen, *née* Doyle; *b* 26 February 1958; *Educ* La Retraite HS, Univ of Cardiff; *m* 1978, Mark; 2 s (Ben b 1981, James b 1989); *Career* journalist: rep Falmouth Packet 1977–79, chef The Seafood Restaurant Falmouth 1979–81, proprietor/publisher Carrick and West Cornwall Review 1980–82, sr prodr BBC Radio Cornwall 1982–84; presenter of various TV programmes 1982–98 incl: Matrix 1982–84, Good Morning Britain 1985–87, BBC Breakfast Time 1988, newsreader BBC News 1989, Good Health 1990, Business Daily (Channel 4)1991–93, various programmes for UK Living 1994, Good Morning with Anne and Nick (BBC1) 1995, Check it Out 1996, After Hours (Radio 5) 1997; md Visage TV 1998, controller of features and prog devpt Carlton Television 1999–2003, media mgmnt conslt 2004–; ind prodr for Really Vital Television Ltd; journalist: The Times, The Guardian, Woman and Home; columnist and assoc ed Popular Craft 1997–98, columnist Family Circle Magazine 1997; *Publications* The Life Audit (2005); *Recreations* cooking, walking, reading; *Style*— Ms Caroline Righton; ✉ e-mail caroline@carolinerighton.com

RIGLEY, Stephen James; s of Stuart Rigley, of Southwell, Notts, and Christine, *née* Jackson; *b* 11 December 1973, Nottingham; *Educ* Nottingham HS, Univ of Liverpool (BA); *m* Martina Antia, *née* Englebrecht; *Career* reporter Basingstoke Gazette 1996–2000, night news ed Southern Daily Echo 2000–02, reporter Daily Mail 2002–04, reporter Daily Star 2004–06, news ed Sunday Express 2006–13; acting dep ed Sunday Express 2013–14, dep ed Sunday Express 2014–; BT Home Counties News Reporter of the Year 1998; *Recreations* horse racing, Sheffield Wednesday FC, food and drink; *Style*— Stephen Rigley, Esq; ✉ Sunday Express, 10 Lower Thames Street, London EC3R 6EN (☎ 020 8612 7075, e-mail stephen.rigley@express.co.uk)

RILEY, Prof Alan John; s of Arthur Joseph Riley (d 1993), of Chestfield, Kent, and Edith Ada, *née* Rashbrook (d 1998); *b* 16 July 1943; *Educ* Bexley GS, Univ of London, Charing Cross Hosp Med Sch Univ of London (MB BS), Univ of Manchester (MSc); *m* 1, 14 Nov 1964 (m dis 1976), Pamela Margaret, da of Leonard George Allum, of London; 1 da (Veronica b 1968), 1 s (John b 1971); 2 adopted s (Grant b 1968, Robert b 1970); m 2, 11 Dec 1976, Elizabeth Jane, da of Capt Arthur Norman Robertson (d 1959); *Career* GP Bideford 1970–76, specialist in sexual med 1972–; sr lectr and hon conslt in human sexuality St George's Hosp Med Sch 1995–98, prof of sexual med Lancs Postgrad Sch of Med and Health Univ of Central Lancashire 1998–2008; dir: MAP Publishing Ltd 1991–95, Sexual Problems Services St George's Hosp London 1995–98; ptnr: SMC Developments 1986–, SMC Research 1985–; ed: British Jl of Sexual Med 1983–91, Sexual and Marital Therapy 1986–2007, The Jl of Sexual Health 1991–96; ed advsr Jl of Sex and Marital Therapy 1998–2010; author of over 100 pubns on aspects of sexual and reproductive med; dep co surgn St John Ambulance Bde (ret 1988); pres Br Soc for Sexual Impotence Research 2002; fell Assoc of Sexual and Marital Therapists 2008 (memb 1979), fell Coll of Sex and Relationship Therapy 2008; LRCP 1967, MRCS 1967, DObstRCOG 1969, FFPM RCP 1992 (MFPM RCP 1989); OStJ 1983; *Recreations* woodwork, photography, boating, natural history; *Style*— Prof Alan Riley; ✉ Kings Park, Cwmann, Lampeter, Ceridigion SA48 8HQ (☎ 01570 421264, e-mail alanriley@doctors.org.uk)

RILEY, Bridget; CH (1999), CBE (1974); da of John Fisher Riley (d 1991), of Cornwall and, Bessie Louise, *née* Gladstone (d 1975); *b* 24 April 1931; *Educ* Cheltenham Ladies' Coll, Goldsmiths Coll of Art, RCA; *Career* artist; AICA critics' prize 1963, John Moores Exhibition prize Liverpool 1963, Peter Stuyvesant Fndn travel bursary to USA 1964, int prize XXXIV Venice Biennale 1968, int prize Ohara Museum 8 Int Print Biennale Tokyo 1972, Praemium Imperiale Award for Painting 2003; colour projects for: Royal Liverpool Hosp 1980–83, St Mary's Hosp Paddington 1986–87; designed Colour Moves (Ballet Rambert) 1983; tstee Nat Gallery 1981–88, represented in major museums and art collections worldwide; Hon DLitt: Univ of Manchester 1976, Univ of Ulster 1986, Univ of Oxford 1994, Univ of Cambridge 1995, Univ of Exeter 1997, Univ of London 2005; Hon DA De Montfort Univ 1996; memb American Acad of Arts and Sciences 2006; *Exhibitions* Gallery One London 1962–63, Bridget Riley, Drawings (MOMA NY) 1966–67, Br Pavilion XXXIV Biennale Venice 1968, European Retrospective (Br Cncl touring exhbn Hanover, Berne, Dusseldorf, Turin and Prague) 1970–72, Retrospective Exhbn (Br Cncl touring US, Aust and Japan) 1978–80, Working with Colour (Arts Cncl of GB touring exhbn) 1984–85, According to Sensation 1982–1992 (Arts Cncl of GB touring exhbn Kunsthalle Nüberg, Quadrat Bottrop, Joseph Albers Museum and Hayward Gallery) 1992, Bridget Riley: Paintings from the 60s and 70s (Serpentine Gallery London) 2000, Bridget Riley: Paintings 1982–2000 and Early Works on Paper (PaceWildenstein NY) 2000, Bridget Riley: Reconnaissance (DIA Center for the Arts NY) 2001, Bridget Riley: Retrospective (Tate Britian) 2003, Bridget Riley: New Work (Museum Haus Esters and Kaiser Wilhelm Museum Krefeld) 2004, Bridget Riley (Museum of Contemporary Art Sydney) 2004–05; *Style*— Miss Bridget Riley, CH, CBE; ✉ c/o Karsten Schubert, 46 Lexington Street, London W1F 0LP (☎ 020 7734 9002, fax 020 7734 9008)

RILEY, Lt Gen Jonathon Peter; CB (2008), DSO (1996); s of John S Riley, and Joyce, *née* Outen; *b* 16 January 1955, W Sussex; *Educ* Kingston GS, UCL (BA), Univ of Leeds (MA), Cranfield Univ (PhD), RMA Sandhurst; *Career* cmmnd Queen's Royal Regt, served: 1 Bn 1974–76 and 1979–83, 6/7 Bn 1976–79, 3 Bn 1983–84, 1 Bn 1988–89; transferred Royal Welch Fusiliers 1990, served 1 Bn 1994–96, instr RMA Sandhurst 1984–86, student Staff Coll 1987 (instr 1993–94), COS 6 Armd Bde 1990–92, COS 1 Armd Div 1996–98, Cmd 1 Mechanized Bde 1998–2000, Jt Task Force Cdr Sierra Leone 2000–01, Asst Cmdt (Land) JSSC 2001–03, Dep Cmdg Gen CMATT (Iraq) and New Iraqi Army 2003, RCDS 2004, Cmdg Gen Multinational Div (SE) and GOC Br Forces Iraq 2004–05, Col RWF 2005–06, sr Br mil advsr US Central Cmd 2005–07, Dep Cdr NATO Force Afghanistan 2007–08, DG and Master Royal Armouries 2009–13; service in UK, Germany, NI (six tours), Central America, USA, Denmark, Sierra Leone, former Yugoslavia (five tours), Iraq (two tours) and Afghanistan; chm of tstees RWF 2005–, memb Historical Ctee advising Welsh Govt on World War 1 commemorations and chm Wales Military Ctee on World War 1 commemorations; visiting prof of war studies KCL, visiting fell Dept of History Univ of Birmingham 2009–14, visiting sr mentor Baltic Defence Coll 2016; external examiner Cranfield Univ 2004–14; memb: Catholic Record Soc 1988, Army Records Soc 2003–13, Countryside Alliance, Links (currently patron); memb Cncl RUSI 2004–14, patron Military Preparation Coll; tstee Strata Florida Project 2016; Offr Legion of Merit (USA) 2005; *Books* History of the Queen's Royal Regiment (1985), From Pole to Pole (1988, 2 edn 1999), Soldiers of the Queen (1992), White Dragon (1995), Napoleon and the World War, 1813 (2000), Regimental Records of the RWF Vols VI and VII (2001), The Life of General Hughie Stockwell (2006), Napoleon as a General (2007), That Astonishing Infantry (ed, 2008), Decisive Battle (2010), Up To Mametz (2010), A Matter of Honour (2011), Empire at Bay (2013), British Generals in Blair's Wars (contrib, 2013), The Last Ironsides (2014), The First Colonial Soldiers (2014), First Colonial Soldiers Vol 1 (2014), First Colonial Soldiers Vol 2 (2015), Oft In Danger: The Life of General Sir Anthony Farrar-Hockley (2015), British Army Guide to the Battlefields of the Great War, (Vol 2, contrib, 2016); *Recreations* field sports, rowing, walking, running, writing; *Clubs* Victory Services; *Style*— Lt Gen Jonathon Riley, CB, DSO; ✉ website www.generalship.org

RILEY, Marc; s of Albert Riley, and Josephine Riley; *Educ* St Gregory's GS Manchester; *Career* musician: The Fall 1978–83, The Creepers 1983–86; mangr In-Tape record label 1983–86, cartoonist Oink (children's comic) 1986–89, record promoter (incl Factory Records, 4AD, Circa) 1990–92; broadcaster BBC: Radio 1 (with Mark Radcliffe, *qv*) 1992–2004, Radio 5 1992–, 6 Music 2004–; *Awards* Sony Gold award (daytime) 1998, Sony Gold award (daytime music) 1999, Sony Gold award (daily sequences) 2001, Sony Silver award, Sony Bronze award; *Recreations* listening to/playing music, squash, five-a-side football, watching Manchester City FC; *Style*— Marc Riley, Esq; ✉ c/o PBJ Management, Soho Square, London (☎ 020 7434 6700, e-mail marc.riley@bbc.co.uk)

RILEY, Michael; *Career* trained as chartered surveyor Hillier Parker 1986–89; Chesterton Int 1989–97, HVB Real Estate Capital 1997–2001 (jt md 1999–2001), Quintain Estates and Devpt plc 2001–02 (chief exec 2002), dir Castlemore Securities Ltd 2002–05, jt chief exec The Local Shopping REIT plc (dir 2005–); *Style*— Michael Riley, Esq; ✉ Waypoint Asset Management, 3rd Floor, 10 Gees Court, St Christopher's Place, London W1U 1JJ

RILEY, Prof Norman; s of late Willie Riley, and late Minnie, *née* Parker; *Educ* Calder HS, Univ of Manchester (BSc, PhD); *m* 5 Sept 1959, Mary Ann, da of late Michael Mansfield; 1 s (Stephen b 1961), 1 da (Susan b 1964); *Career* asst lectr in mathematics Univ of Manchester 1959–60, lectr in mathematics Univ of Durham 1960–64; UEA: sr lectr in mathematics 1964–66, reader in mathematics 1966–71, prof of applied mathematics 1971–99, now emeritus; FIMA 1964; *Recreations* music, photography, travel; *Style*— Prof Norman Riley; ✉ School of Mathematics, University of East Anglia, Norwich NR4 7TJ (☎ 01603 592313)

RILEY, Prof Patrick Anthony; s of Bertram Hurrell Riley (d 1961), and Olive, *née* Stephenson (d 1987); *b* 22 March 1935, Neuilly-sur-Seine, France; *Educ* Manegg Sch Zurich, King Edward VII Sch King's Lynn, UCL, UCH Med Sch London (MB BS, PhD, DSc); *m* 5 July 1958, Christine Elizabeth, da of Dr Islwyn Morris (d 1972), of Treorchy, Glamorgan; 2 da (Sian b 12 Feb 1962, Caroline b 25 June 1963), 1 s (Benjamin b 20 Feb 1968); *Career* Rockefeller res scholar 1962–63, MRC jr clinical res fell 1963–66, Beit meml res fell 1966–68, Wellcome res fell 1968–70, sr lectr in biochemical pathology UCH Med Sch 1974–76 (lectr 1970–73), prof of cell pathology UCL 1984–2000 (reader 1976–84), emeritus prof of cell pathology Univ of London 2000–, dir Totteridge Inst for Advanced Studies 2001–; exec ed Melanoma Research 1990–2006; Myron Gordon Award 1993; Hon MD Charles Univ Prague 2011; CBiol, FSB 1976, FRCPath 1985; *Publications* Faber Pocket Medical Dictionary (with P J Cunningham, 1 edn 1966), Hydroxyanisole: Recent Advances in Anti-Melanoma Therapy (1984), Melanins and Melanosomes (ed with J Borovansky, 2011), Totteridge Institute Letters (with M Hobsley, 2011); over 250 scientific papers on free radical pathology, cancer and pigmentation; *Recreations* music, painting, astronomy, photography; *Clubs* Athenaeum, Linnean; *Style*— Prof Patrick Riley; ✉ 2 The Grange, Grange Avenue, London N20 8AB (☎ 020 8445 5687)

RILEY, Phil; *Educ* Columbia Business Sch (MBA); *m*; 3 c; *Career* grad trainee BRMB FM 1980; Chrysalis: md and launch dir 100.7 Heart FM W Midlands and Heart 106.2 FM

London 1994, chief exec 1999–2007; chm MXR consortium, memb Bd 4 Digital Gp Ltd; memb: Bd Digital Radio Devpt Bureau (DRDB), Radio Centre, RAJAR; *Recreations* keeping fit (completed a number of triathlons); *Style*— Phil Riley, Esq

RILEY, Simon James Blair; s of James Riley (d 1985), and Joanna, *née* Walker; *b* 27 February 1946; *Educ* Gordonstoun; *m* 1, 7 April 1973 (m dis 1984), Jacqueline Lila (Jackie), da of Col Henry Lancelot (Harry) Gullidge, of Taunton, Somerset; 2 da (Claire-Louise b 6 Sept 1975, Victoria b 19 Aug 1980); m 2, 29 Oct 1988, Estaire Joyce Danielle, da of Prof Johan De Vree; m 3, 9 June 1999, June Marion, da of Michael Farrell, of Arthurstown, Co Wexford; 2 c (Alexander Robert James, Jessica Joanna Margot (twins) b 14 June 2000); *Career* surveyor; Kirk & Kirk 1964–67, Grant Wilkinson & Co 1967–73 (dir 1970), dir James Riley & Associates 1973–83, conslt in Spain 1983–88, property developer 1988–; memb Ctee Br Automobile Racing Club; MNAEA 1965; *Recreations* racing motor cars, reading, collecting; *Clubs* Lighthouse, British Automobile Racing, Jaguar Drivers'; *Style*— Simon Riley, Esq; ✉ 23 Rossetti Garden Mansions, Flood Street, Chelsea, London SW3 5QX (✆ 020 7351 0248, fax 020 7622 7207, mobile 07974 669357)

RILEY-SMITH, Prof Jonathan Simon Christopher; s of Maj (William Henry) Douglas Riley-Smith (d 1981), of Tadcaster, N Yorks and Brewhurst, Loxwood, W Sussex, and Elspeth Agnes Mary, *née* Craik Henderson (d 1990); *b* 27 June 1938; *Educ* Eton, Trinity Coll Cambridge (BA, MA, PhD, DLitt); *m* 27 July 1968, Marie-Louise Jeannetta, da of Wilfred John Sutcliffe Field, of Norwich, Norfolk; 1 s (Tobias Augustine William b 19 Oct 1969), 2 da (Tamsin Elspeth Hermione b 10 Sept 1971, Hippolyta Clemency Magdalen b 10 Nov 1975); *Career* lectr in medieval history Univ of St Andrews 1966–72 (asst lectr 1964–65); Univ of Cambridge: asst lectr 1972–75, lectr 1975–78, fell Queens' Coll 1972–78, dir of studies in history 1972–78, praelector 1973–75, librarian 1973 and 1977–78; prof of history Royal Holloway and Bedford New Coll London 1978–94 (head Dept of History 1984–90), Dixie prof of ecclesiastical history Univ of Cambridge 1994–2005 (Dixie prof emeritus 2005–), fell Emmanuel Coll Cambridge 1994–2005, chm Bd of Faculty Univ of Cambridge 1997–99; librarian Priory of Scotland Most Ven Order of St John 1966–78, Grand Priory 1982–; hon fell Inst of Historical Res 1997–; corresponding fell Medieval Acad of America 2006; FRHistS 1971; KStJ 1969 (CStJ 1966), Knight Grand Cross of Grace and Devotion SMOM 2007 (Knight of Magistral Grace SMOM 1971, Officer of Merit Pro Merito Melitensi 1985); *Books* The Knights of St John in Jerusalem and Cyprus (1967), Ayyubids, Mamlukes and Crusaders (with U and M C Lyons, 1971), The Feudal Nobility and The Kingdom of Jerusalem (1973), What Were The Crusades? (1977, 4 edn 2009), The Crusades Idea and Reality (with L Riley-Smith, 1981), The First Crusade and The Idea of Crusading (1986), The Crusades: A Short History (1987, 2 edn 2005), Les Croisades (translation, 1990), Breve storia della Crociate (trans, 1994), The Atlas of the Crusades (ed, 1991), Grosser Bildatlas der Kreuzzüge (trans, 1992), The Oxford Illustrated History of the Crusades (ed, 1995), Cyprus and the Crusades (ed with N Coureas, 1995), Atlas des Croisades (trans, 1996), Montjoie. Studies in Crusade History in Honour of Hans Eberhard Mayer (ed jtly, 1997), The First Crusaders (1997), Hospitallers: The History of the Order of St John (1999), Al Seguito delle Crociate (trans, 2000), Dei Gesta per Francos, Etudes sur les croisades dédieés à Jean Richard (ed jtly, 2001), In Laudem Hierosolymitani: Studies in Honour of Benjamin Z Kedar (ed jtly, 2007), The Crusades, Christianity and Islam (2008), Crusaders and Settlers in the Latin East (2008), Templars and Hospitallers as Professed Religious in the Holy Land (2009), The Knights Hospitaller in the Levant c 1070–1309 (2012); *Recreations* the past and present of own family; *Style*— Prof Jonathan Riley-Smith; ✉ Emmanuel College, Cambridge CB2 3AP (✆ 01223 334200)

RIMER, Rt Hon Sir Colin Percy Farquharson; kt (1994), PC (2007); s of late Kenneth Rowland Rimer, of Beckenham, Kent, and late Maria Eugenia, *née* Farquharson; *b* 30 January 1944; *Educ* Dulwich Coll, Trinity Hall Cambridge (MA, LLB); *m* 3 Jan 1970, Penelope Ann, da of late Alfred William Gibbs; 1 da (Catherine b 1971), 2 s (David b 1972, Michael b 1974); *Career* res asst Inst of Comparative Law Paris 1967–68; called to the Bar Lincoln's Inn 1968 (bencher 1994); in practice 1969–94, QC 1988, judge of the High Court of Justice (Chancery Div) 1994–2007, a Lord Justice of Appeal 2007–14; hon fell Trinity Hall Cambridge 2009; *Recreations* music, novels, walking; *Style*— The Rt Hon Sir Colin Rimer

RIMINGTON, Dame Stella; DCB (1996); da of David Whitehouse, of Newstead; *b* 1935; *Educ* Nottingham HS for Girls, Univ of Edinburgh (MA); *Children* 2 da; *Career* DG Security Service 1992–96 (joined 1969); non-exec dir: Whitehead Mann GKR (formerly GKR Group) 1997–2001, Marks & Spencer plc 1997–2004, BG Group plc 1997–2005, Royal Marsden NHS Tst 1998–2001; chm Inst of Cancer Research 1997–2001; tstee: RAF Museum 1998–2001, Refuge; Hon Air Cdre 7006 (VR) Intelligence Squadron RAuxAF 1997–2001; Hon LLD: Univ of Nottingham 1995, Univ of Exeter 1996, London Metropolitan Univ 2004, Univ of Liverpool 2005; *Books* Open Secret (autobiography, 2001), At Risk (2004), Secret Asset (2006), Illegal Action (2007), Dead Line (2008), Present Danger (2009), Rip Tide (2011), The Geneva Trap (2012); *Style*— Dame Stella Rimington, DCB

RINGROSE, Adrian; *b* April 1967; *Educ* Univ of Liverpool (BA); *Career* Interserve plc (formerly Tilbury Douglas plc): business devpt dir Interservefm 2000–01, md 2001–03, memb Bd 2002–, dep chief exec 2003, chief exec 2003–; past chm Public Servs Strategy Bd CBI, emmb President's Ctee CBI; past pres Business Servs Assoc; CCMI, MCIM; *Style*— Adrian Ringrose, Esq; ✉ Interserve plc, Interserve House, Ruscombe Park, Twyford, Reading RG10 9JU

RINGROSE, Dr Peter Stuart; s of Arthur Ringrose, of Colchester, Essex, and Roma Margaret, *née* Roberts; *b* 9 October 1945, Leicester; *Educ* Alderman Newton Boys' GS Leicester, CCC Cambridge (MA, MPhil, PhD); *m* 11 March 1966, Nancy Elaine; 2 s (Simon Andrew b 16 Sept 1966, Timothy John b 6 Dec 1967), 1 da (Lucy Victoria b 3 April 1977); *Career* dept head Roche Pharmaceuticals 1970–79, div dir of chemotherapy, infectious diseases and molecular sciences Sandoz Forschungsinstitut Vienna 1979–82, sr vice-pres Worldwide Drug Discovery and Medicinal R&D Europe Pfizer Inc 1982–96, chief scientific offr Bristol-Myers Squibb and pres Pharmaceutical Research Inst Princeton 1997–2002, chm Biotechnology and Biosciences Reseach Cncl (BBSRC) 2003–09; non-exec dir: Cambridge Antibody Technology 2003–06, Astex Therapeutics 2005–11, Rigel Pharmaceuticals 2005–, Biotica 2007–12, Theravance Inc 2010–14, Thereavance Biopharma 2014–; memb Scientific Advsy Bd: Accenture Life Sciences 2003–06, Merlin Biosciences 2003–05, Cempra Pharmaceuticals 2006–10, Schering-Plough Inc 2007–09; memb Chemistry Advsy Bd Univ of Cambridge 1997–2013, William Pitt fell Pembroke Coll Cambridge 1998–2006 (hon fell 2006, chair Coll Corporate Partnership Program Bd); chm Hever Gp of Pharmaceutical R&D Heads 1999–2002; non-exec dir Technol Strategy Governing Bd 2007–09; memb: Governing Cncl NY Acad of Sciences 2001–05, Cncl Fndn for Science and Technology 2003–; former memb: Policy Advsy Bd Centre for Medicines Research International, Science and Regulatory Exec Pharmaceutical Research and Manufacturers of America, Center for Advanced Biotechnology and Medicine NJ, Scientific Ctee Assoc of Br Pharmaceutical Industries; memb Chllr's Ct of Benefactors Univ of Oxford 1998–2002; parish cncllr 2011–12; *Recreations* grandchildren, painting, archaeology, cartography; *Clubs* Athenaeum; *Style*— Dr Peter S Ringrose

RINK, John Stuart; s of Paul Lothar Max Rink (d 1977), and Mary Ida McCall, *née* Moore; *b* 25 October 1946; *Educ* Sedbergh, Univ of London (LLB); *m* 22 May 1971, Elizabeth Mary, da of Thomas Edgar Pitkethly; 1 s (Max Edgar b 2 Feb 1973), 1 da (Lucinda Mary b 1 Jan 1975); *Career* Allen & Overy: trainee slr 1970–72, asst slr 1972–77, ptnr 1977–, managing ptnr Litigation Dept 1989, managing ptnr 1994–2003, memb Bd 2003–04; legal dir British Aerospace plc 1994–95; dir Brixton plc 2003–06; memb Bd Eversheds 2004, Robson Rhodes 2004–06; memb Law Soc; *Recreations* golf, rugby, walking, opera; *Clubs* City Law, Royal Wimbledon Golf, Royal West Norfolk Golf, Windermere Motor Boat Racing, MCC; *Style*— John Rink, Esq; ✉ 2 Camp View, Wimbledon, London SW19 4UL (✆ 020 8947 4800)

RINTOUL, Dr Gordon Charles; CBE (2012); s of Henry Rintoul, and Janet, *née* Brown; *b* 29 May 1955; *Educ* Allan Glen's Sch Glasgow, Univ of Edinburgh (BSc), Univ of Manchester (MSc, PhD); *m* 1997, Stephanie Jane, *née* Budden; 1 s (Cameron Henry); *Career* res supervisor Chemical Museum Devpt Project 1982–84, conslt and tutor Open Univ 1984, curator Colour Museum 1984–87, dir Catalyst: The Museum of the Chemical Industry 1987–98, chief exec Sheffield Galleries and Museums Tst 1998–2002, dir Nat Museums Scotland 2002–; public engagement with science and engrg 2004–; pres (NW region) Assoc for Science Educn 1995–98, treas Assoc of Ind Museums 1991–97 (memb Cncl 1989–2002); memb: Registration Ctee Resource: The Cncl for Museums, Archives and Libraries 1995–2002, Cncl Museums Assoc 1998–2002, Bd SCRAN (Scottish Cultural Resources Access Network) 2002–06; hon prof Univ of Edinburgh; dip Museum Assoc; Hon DUniv Napier Univ 2013, Dr (hc) Univ of Edinburgh 2013; AMA; *Recreations* travel, reading, cooking; *Style*— Dr Gordon Rintoul, CBE; ✉ National Museums Scotland, Chambers Street, Edinburgh EH1 1JF (✆ 0131 247 4260, fax 0131 247 4308, e-mail g.rintoul@nms.ac.uk)

RIORDAN, Prof Colin; *b* 27 July 1959, Paderborn, Germany; *Educ* Liverpool Collegiate Sch, Univ of Manchester (BA, PhD); *m* (m dis 2013), Karin; 2 da; *Career* lectr Julius-Maximilians Universität Würzburg 1982–84; Univ of Wales Swansea: lectr in German 1986–94, sr lect in German 1994–98; Newcastle Univ: prof of German 1998–2007, head Sch of Modern Languages 2001–04, dean of postgrad studies Faculty of Humanities and Social Sciences 2004–05, pro-vice-chllr and provost Faculty of Humanities and Social Sciences 2005–07; vice-chllr Univ of Essex 2007–12, vice-chllr Cardiff Univ 2012–; *Style*— Prof Colin Riordan; ✉ Cardiff University, Main Building, Park Place, Cardiff CF10 3AT

RIORDAN, Linda; *b* 31 May 1953; *Educ* Univ of Bradford; *Career* private sec to Alice Mahon MP, cncllr Calderdale BC; MP (Lab/Co-op) Halifax 2005–15; non-exec dir Calderdale and Huddersfield NHS Tst, chair Ovenden Initiative, memb Bd Pennine Housing 2000–; *Style*— Ms Linda Riordan; ✉ House of Commons, London SW1A 0AA

RIORDAN, Stephen Vaughan; QC (1992); s of Charles Maurice Riordan, and Betty Morfydd, *née* Harries (d 1983); *b* 18 February 1950; *Educ* Wimbledon Coll, Univ of Liverpool (LLB); *m* 19 Feb 1983, Jane Elizabeth, da of Ernest Victor Thomas; 2 da (Alexandra Jane b 24 Aug 1983, Charlotte Ann b 2 March 1985); *Career* called to the Bar Inner Temple 1972, recorder of the Crown Court 1990– (asst recorder 1986–90), head of chambers; *Recreations* singing; *Style*— Stephen Riordan, Esq, QC; ✉ 19 Gwydrin Road, Liverpool L18 3HA (✆ 0151 722 1726)

RIPLEY, Prof Brian David; s of Eric Lewis Ripley, of Farnborough, Hants, and Sylvia May, *née* Gould; *b* 29 April 1952; *Educ* Farnborough GS, Churchill Coll Cambridge (MA, Smith's Prize, PhD); *m* 1973, Ruth Mary, *née* Appleton; *Career* Univ of London: lectr in statistics Imperial Coll 1976–80, reader in statistics 1980–83; prof of statistics Univ of Strathclyde 1983–90, prof of applied statistics Univ of Oxford 1990–2014, ret, professorial fell St Peter's Coll Oxford 1990–2014; Adams Prize Univ of Cambridge 1987; memb Int Statistical Inst 1982, fell Inst of Mathematical Statistics 1987, FRSE 1990; *Books* Spatial Statistics (1981), Stochastic Simulation (1987), Statistical Inference for Spatial Processes (1988), Modern Applied Statistics with S-Plus (with W N Venables, 1994 and 1997), Pattern Recognition and Neural Networks (1996), S Programming (with W N Venables, 2000); *Recreations* natural history; *Style*— Prof Brian Ripley, FRSE; ✉ Department of Statistics, University of Oxford, 1 South Parks Road, Oxford OX1 3TG (✆ 01865 272861, fax 01865 272595, e-mail ripley@stats.ox.ac.uk)

RIPPON, Her Hon Judge Amanda Jayne; *née* Field; da of Victor Field, and Jacqueline, *née* Cotton; *b* 16 December 1967, Leeds; *Educ* Lancaster Univ (BA), City Univ (DipLaw), Inns of Court Sch of Law; *m* 9 Sept 1996, Matthew James Rippon; 2 s (Elijah b 7 Dec 2001, Seth b 24 Oct 2005); *Career* called to the Bar Gray's Inn 1993; recorder 2008, circuit judge (NE Circuit) 2016–; memb Ctee Advocacy Trg Cncl (ATC) 2012–; *Recreations* cinema, music, opera, reading, travel; *Style*— Her Hon Judge Rippon; ✉ Newcastle upon Tyne Crown Court, The Law Courts, Quayside, Newcastle upon Tyne NE1 3LA (✆ 0191 201 2000, e-mail HHJ.Amanda.Rippon@ejudiciary.net)

RIPPON, Angela; OBE (2004); da of John and Edna Rippon; *b* 12 October 1944; *Career* journalist and television broadcaster; formerly with BBC Plymouth and Westward Television, joined BBC 1973, first woman journalist newsreader 1975, fndr memb TV-am 1982, with Channel 7 (USA) 1984, worked on BBC and ITV programmes, joined LBC Radio 1990, currently with BBC TV and ITV news; vice-pres: Br Red Cross, NCH Action for Children, Riding for the Disabled Assoc; patron Support Dogs; Barker Variety Club of GB; Hon Dr of Humanities American Int Univ 1994; *Television* BBC credits incl: Come Dancing, The Antiques Roadshow, Top Gear, Angela Rippon Meets..., The Morecambe and Wise Christmas Show, Eurovision Song Contest, 1979 General Election, Olivier Awards, Masterteam, Matchpoint, Angela Rippon's Summer Journey, In the Country, BBC Television News, Cash in the Attic, The Wedding of HRH Prince Charles and Lady Diana Spencer, Crufts, Watchdog Healthcheck, The Holiday Programme, Sun Sea and Bargain-Spotting (BBC2) 2005–; ITV and Channel 4 credits incl: What's My Line, A Game of War, The Windsors – sale of a lifetime, Open House, The Big Breakfast, Hidden Talents of the Rich and Famous, Live with Angela Roppon (ITV News Channel) 2003–05; overseas credits: The Nobel Prize (CNN – Turner Network), Those Were the Days (Sky), The Key to the White House (American Educnl TV), Simply Money, arts and entertainment corr CBS Boston, Channel 9 Aust; *Radio* credits incl: Breakfast with Angela Rippon (LBC), Angela Rippon's Drive Time (LBC), The Health Show (Radio 4), Friday Night with Angela Rippon (Radio 2), Friday Night is Music Night, numerous Radio 2 documentaries, compere Radio 2 music compilation progs and live transmissions with BBC Concert Orch; *Awards* New York Film Festival Silver Medal 1972, TV and Radio Industries Club Newsreader of the Year 1976, 1977 and 1987, TV Personality of the Year 1977, Emmy Award 1984 (for Channel 7 Boston), Entertainment Reporter of the Year 1984 (Boston), Sony Radio Award 1990, New York Radio Silver Medal 1992, Radio Personality of the Year 1993, RTS Roll of Honour 1997, European Woman of Achievement 2002; *Books* Riding (1980), In the Country (1980), Mark Phillips – The Man and his Horses (1982), Angela Rippon's Westcountry (1982), Victoria Plum (eight children's books, 1983), Badminton – a celebration (1983), Fabulous at 50 and Beyond (2003); *Style*— Ms Angela Rippon, OBE

RISBY, Baron (Life Peer UK 2010), of Haverhill in the County of Suffolk; Richard John Grenville Spring; s of late H J A Spring, and late Marjorie, *née* Watson-Morris; *b* 24 September 1946; *Educ* Rondebosch, Univ of Cape Town, Magdalene Coll Cambridge; *m* 13 Dec 1979 (m dis 1993), Hon Jane Henniker-Major, da of 8 Baron Henniker, KCMG, CVO, MC, DL (d 2004); 1 s, 1 da; *Career* vice-pres Merrill Lynch Ltd 1976–86 (joined 1971), dep md Hutton International Associates 1986–88, exec dir Shearson Lehman Hutton 1988–90, md Xerox Furman Selz 1990–92; Parly candidate (Cons) Ashton-under-Lyne 1983; MP (Cons): Bury St Edmunds 1992–97, Suffolk W 1997–2010; PPS to: Sir Patrick Mayhew (as Sec of State for NI) 1994–95, Rt Hon Tim Eggar (as Min of State DTI) 1996, Hon Nicholas Soames and James Arbuthnot (as Mins of State MOD) 1996–97; oppn frontbench spokesman on culture, media and sport 1997–2000, oppn frontbench spokesman on foreign and Cwlth affrs 2000–04, oppn frontbench treasury spokesman

2004–05, vice-chm Cons Pty 2006–10; PM's trade envoy to Algeria 2012–; memb House of Commons Select Ctee for Employment 1992–94, vice-chm Cons Backbench Arts and Heritage Ctee 1992–94, jt sec NI Cons Backbench Ctee 1993–95, memb House of Commons Select Ctee for NI 1994–97, vice-chm All Pty Racing and Bloodstock Gp 1996–97, co-chm Cons City Circle 2006–, memb Home Affrs Select Ctee 2006–07, chm All Pty Mauritius Gp 2008–, jt sec All Pty Drugs Misuse Gp, memb House of Lords EU Ctee (External Affrs); Small Business Bureau: vice-chm 1992–97, dep chm 1997–, chm of its Parly Advsy Gp 1992–; govr Westminster Fndn for Democracy 2001–10; held various offices Westminster Cons Assoc 1976–87; dir Br-Syrian Soc 2005–11, chm Br-Ukranian Soc 2007–; patron: The London Magazine, Open Reach; *Recreations* country pursuits, tennis, swimming; *Clubs* Boodle's; *Style*— The Lord Risby; ✉ House of Lords, London SW1A 0PW

RISDON, Prof (Rupert) Anthony; s of Capt Dennis Stanley Risdon (d 1986), and Olga Caris Argent, *née* Davis; *b* 5 March 1939; *Educ* Charing Cross Hosp Med Sch (MB BS, MD); *m* 15 April 1961, Phyllis Mary, da of Frederick Hough, of IOM; 2 s ((James) Mark b 1964, Simon Paul b 1967); *Career* lectr in histopathology Charing Cross Hosp Med Sch 1966–68, conslt pathologist Addenbrooke's Hosp Cambridge 1975–76, reader in morbid anatomy London Hosp Med Coll 1976–85, head Histopathology Dept Great Ormond St Hosp for Sick Children 1985–; memb: Pathology Soc of GB and I, Int Acad Pathology, Assoc of Clinical Pathologists; FRCPath; *Recreations* walking, swimming; *Style*— Prof Anthony Risdon; ✉ The Hospital for Sick Children, Department of Histopathology, Great Ormond Street, London WC1N 3JH (☎ 020 7405 9200)

RISHTON, John; *Career* with Ford of Europe 1979–94; British Airways plc: financial controller USA 1994–96, sales controller 1996–98, ops controller 1998–99, commercial controller 1999–2001, chief financial offr 2001–05, memb Exec Bd 2001–05, chief exec 2011–; finance dir Ahold 2006–11; non-exec dir: Allied Domecq plc 2003–, Rolls-Royce plc 2007–; *Style*— John Rishton, Esq; ✉ Rolls-Royce plc, 62 Buckingham Gate, London SW1E 6AT

RITBLAT, James (Jamie); s of Sir John Ritblat, *qv*, and Isabel Paja Steinberg (d 1979); *b* 18 February 1967, London; *Educ* Eton, Univ of Bristol; *m* 1995, Joanna Henrietta, *née* Jackson; 3 da, 1 s; *Career* fndr and ceo Delancey 1995– (sole sponsor Delancey UK Schs Chess Challenge 2011–, headline sponsor Delancey Br Nat Alpine Ski Championships 2011–, princ sponsor Br Ski and Snowboard 2014–); dir Maggie's Cancer Centres 2005–14, dep chm Real Estate Advsy Bd Tate Britain 2008–15, govr Southbank Centre 2009–16 (chm Property Ctee 2010–16), patron Gordon Russell Tst; tstee: Gordon Russell Tst 2002–11, Bathurst Estate 2013–; KCL: memb Governing Cncl 2006–14, chm Real Estate Advsy Bd 2008–15, memb Chm's Ctee 2008–15, vice-chm Governing Cncl 2014–15; *Recreations* skiing, farming, the arts, bee keeping, shooting, gardening; *Clubs* Boodles, Queens, RAC, MCC (memb Devpt Ctee and special advsr Real Estate 2008–11, memb Estates Ctee 2011–14); *Style*— Jamie Ritblat, Esq; ✉ Delancey, Lansdowne House, Berkeley Square, London W1J 6ER

RITBLAT, Lady; Jillian Rosemary (Jill) Ritblat; *née* Slotover; da of Max Leonard Slotover, FRCS, of Monte Carlo, Monaco, and Peggy Cherna, *née* Cohen; *b* 14 December 1942, Newcastle upon Tyne; *Educ* Newcastle upon Tyne Church HS, Roedean, Westfield Coll London (BA); *m* 1, 21 April 1966 (m dis 1981), Elie Zilkha; 1 s, 1 da; m 2, 27 Feb 1986, Sir John Ritblat, *qv*; *Career* called to the Bar Gray's Inn 1964; pupillage to Robin Simpson, QC, Victor Durand & Jeremy Hutchinson's Chambers 1964–65; alternate delegate for Int Cncl of Jewish Women UN Geneva 1977–79; Patrons of New Art Tate Gallery: founding memb 1982–, events organiser 1984–87, chm 1987–90, memb Acquisitions Sub-Ctee 1992–93 and 2000–01; memb Int Cncl Tate Gallery 1995– (vice-chm 1996–2001); co-curator: The Curator's Egg (Anthony Reynolds Gallery) 1994, One Woman's Wardrobe (V&A, Catalogue Design and Art Direction (D&AD) Silver Award for Graphic Design 1999) 1998–99; exec prodr Normal Conservative Rebels: Gilbert & George in China (Edinburgh Film Festival 1996, Gold Medal Chicago Film Festival 1996); memb: BFAMI Ctee 1980–, MAO (formerly MOMA) Museum of Modern Art Oxford 1986– (memb Cncl 1993–2010), Int Cncl Jerusalem Museum 1987–, Friends of the Tate Gallery Advsy Cncl 1990–2002, Nat Art Collections Fund Special Events Ctee 1991–92, William Townsend Meml Lectureship Ctee 1991–, Bd New Contemporaries 1991– (vice-chm 1992–), Bd Jerusalem Music Centre 1991–, Arts Cncl Appraisal for W Midlands Arts 1994, Int Cncl Wallace Collection 2008–; patron Nat Alliance for Art, Architecture and Design 1994–97, design tstee Public Art Cmmrs Agency 1996–99; memb Jury: Painting in the Eighties 1987, Turner Prize 1988, British Airways New Artist Award 1990, Swiss Bank Corporation Euro Art Competition 1994 and 1995, NatWest 90's Prize for Art 1994 and 1995, Financial Times Arts and Business Awards 2000 and 2001, Building Cmmn RIBA Regnl Award 2001, RIBA Manser Prize 2012; memb: Devpt Ctee Royal Acad of Music 2002–08 (Ctee of Honour 2010), Bd Br Architectural Tst (formerly RIBA Tst) 2006–12, Cncl Royal Coll of Art 2010–; tstee: Tate Fndn 2006–13 (hon memb 2013–), Design Museum 2010–, Garden Museum 2010–; Hon FRAM 2011, Hon FRIBA 2012; *Recreations* art, opera, travel, food, people; *Style*— Lady Ritblat; ✉ Lansdowne House, Berkeley Square, London W1J 6ER

RITBLAT, Sir John Henry; kt (2006); s of Montie Ritblat (d 1984), and Muriel, *née* Glaskie; *b* 3 October 1935; *Educ* Dulwich Coll, Univ of London, Coll of Estate Mgmnt; *m* 1, 1960, Isabel Paja Steinberg (d 1979); 2 s (Nicholas b 19 Aug 1961, James, *qv* b 18 Feb 1967), 1 da (Suzanne b 15 Sept 1962); m 2, 27 Feb 1986, Jill Ritblat, *qv*, *née* Slotover; *Career* articles West End firm of surveyors and valuers 1952–58, fndr ptnr and chm Conrad Ritblat and Co (conslt surveyors and valuers) 1958, md Union Property Holdings (London) Ltd 1969, chm The British Land Company plc 1970–2006 (md 1970–2004, hon pres 2007–), chm Milner Estates plc 1997–; cmmr Crown Estate Paving Cmmn 1969, memb Bd of Govrs The Weizmann Inst 1991, sole sponsor British Nat Ski Championships 1978–2001, hon surveyor King George's Fund for Sailors 1979, memb Cncl RGS 1984 (life memb 1982), pres British Ski Fedn 1994– (vice-pres 1984–89), dep chm and govr RAM; memb: Prince of Wales' Royal Parks Tree Appeal Ctee, Fin Devpt Bd NSPCC, British Library Bd 1995, Governing Body RAM 1998; dep chm and govr Hall Sch, govr London Business Sch (chm 2006–); hon life FRSA, life fell Royal Instn 2001 (memb Cncl 2002–); FSVA 1968, CIMgt, Hon RA; *Recreations* antiquarian books, old buildings, galleries, golf, skiing, real tennis; *Clubs* RAC, MCC, Carlton, Cresta (St Moritz), Queen's; *Style*— Sir John Ritblat

RITCHIE, Alasdair William; s of James Martin Ritchie (d 1993), and Noreen Mary Louise, *née* Johnston (d 2006); bro of Hamish Martin Johnston Ritchie, *qv*; *b* 10 March 1946; *Educ* Loretto; *m* 1, 4 April 1970 (m dis), Fiona Margaret, da of James Barr Richardson; 1 da (Sally Ann b 2 June 1973), 1 s (Cameron Glen b 28 April 1976); m 2, 31 Dec 2008, Janice Seidel; *Career* trainee Trumans Brewery 1964–66, mktg exec Scott Paper USA 1966–68, dir Lonsdale Crowther UK 1971–73 (dep md 1973–76), dir Grey Advertising UK 1976–79, fndr Holmes Knight Ritchie (md 1979–90); TBWA: UK chm 1990–96, UK chief exec 1990–97, pres Europe 1996–98; pres and ceo TBWA International 1997–98, sr vice-pres (ops) TBWA Worldwide (following merger with Omnicom's BDDP Worldwide gp) 1998; pres (worldwide) Octagon (sports mktg arm of Interpublic Group) 1998–2003; ptnr Tangerine consultancy NY 2003–, ceo Waterway (fire-hose testing nat franchise co) 2007–14, ceo Haven Consulting Gp (business consultancy) 2014–; MIPA; *Recreations* shooting, fishing, golf; *Clubs* Denham Golf, Trump Nat Hudson Valley; *Style*— Alasdair Ritchie, Esq; ✉ 32 Fieldstone Drive, Katonah, NY 10536, USA

RITCHIE, Andrew; QC (2009); *Educ* Magdalene Coll Cambridge (MA); *Career* qualified slr 1982; called to the Bar 1985; Personal Injuries Bar Assoc; fell and coll advocate Magdalene Coll Cambridge; *Style*— Andrew Ritchie, QC; ✉ The Chambers of Andrew Ritchie, QC, 9 Gough Square, London EC4A 3DG

RITCHIE, Maj-Gen Andrew Stephenson; CBE (1999); s of Rev Canon David Caldwell Ritchie (d 2000), and Dilys, *née* Stephenson (d 2010); *b* 30 July 1953, London; *Educ* Harrow Co Boys' Sch, RMA Sandhurst, Univ of Durham (BA); *m* 16 Dec 1981, Camilla, *née* Trollope; 2 da (Annabel b 3 Dec 1986, Charlotte b 30 Apr 1992), 1 s (Alexander b 12 Nov 1988); *Career* cmd RA 1973, regtl serv UK, Belize, Rhodesia and Germany 1974–84, Staff Coll 1985, SO Second Dir of Mil Ops MOD 1986–87, 3 RHA Germany, Cyprus and UK 1988–90, SO First Dir of Army Plans MOD 1990–92, CO 1 RHA UK 1992–95, COS 3 (UK) Div/Multinational Div SW Bosnia 1995–96, Higher Cmd and Staff Course 1997, Cdr RA 3 (UK) Div 1997–98, Dir Personal Servs (Army) 1998–2000, RCDS 2001, Dir Corporate Communications (Army) MOD 2001–02, GOC 4 Div 2002–03, Cmdt RMA Sandhurst 2003 06; dir: Goodenough Events Ltd 2006–, Goodenough Club Ltd 2013–; dir: Goodenough Coll 2006–, Regular Forces Employment Assoc 2010–; chm RA Steeplechase Ctee 2008–; tstee Larkhill Racecourse 2008–; memb Cncl Marlborough Coll 2006–15; *Recreations* hunting, opera, tennis, golf; *Clubs* Boodle's; *Style*— Maj-Gen Andrew Ritchie, CBE; ✉ Goodenough College, Mecklenburgh Square, London WC1N 2AB (☎ 020 7520 1520, e-mail andrew.ritchie@goodenough.ac.uk)

RITCHIE, Prof Donald Andrew; CBE (2005), DL (Merseyside 2002); s of Andrew Ritchie (d 1985), of Falkirk, and Winifred Laura, *née* Parkinson (d 1998); *b* 9 July 1938; *Educ* Latymer's Sch London, Univ of Leicester (BSc), Postgrad Med Sch Univ of London (PhD); *m* 22 Aug 1962, (Margaret) Jeanne, da of Henry Eden Collister, of Port St Mary, IOM; 1 da (Sarah b 1967), 1 s (Charles b 1969); *Career* research assoc Biophysics Dept Johns Hopkins Univ 1964–66, sr lectr Dept of Virology Univ of Glasgow 1972–78 (lectr 1966–72); Univ of Liverpool: prof of genetics 1978–2003, pro-vice-chllr 1992–95; Royal Soc Leverhulme Tst sr research fell 1991–92; Royal Acad of Engrg visiting prof Univ of Liverpool 2004–06; SERC: chm Molecular Biology and Genetics Ctee 1985–88, memb Science Bd 1988–91, chm Educn and Trg Panel 1988–91; NERC: memb Cncl 1990–95, chm Terrestrial and Freshwater Sciences Ctee 1992–95, chm Marine and Freshwater Microbial Biodiversity Steering Ctee 1999–2005; professional affrs offr Soc for Gen Microbiology 1998–2001; memb: DTI Biotechnol Jt Advsy Bd 1991–94, Food Res Ctee AFRC 1991–94, Cncl Marine Biological Assoc 1991–94, Fin and Environment Ctees Inst of Biology 1996–2002; Bd of Environment Agency: memb Bd 1998–2005, dep chm 2001–05; chm: Merseyside Nat Art Collections Fund 1996–2000, Liverpool Scottish Museum Tst 1999–, Cncl of Military Educn Ctees 2004–12, King's Regt Museum Tst 2006–; memb Cncl Liverpool Sch of Tropical Med 1993–98; memb: RFCA NW England and IOM 1995–2012, SaBRE Merseyside 2003–06; chm RSE Scotland Fndn Tst 2012– (tstee 2010–); govr: IOM Int Business Sch 2000–11, Shrewsbury Sch 2003–12 (dep chm 2006–12), Shrewsbury House Youth Club Liverpool 2006–; chm Friends of Shrewsbury House Everton 2015; Hon Col Univ of Liverpool OTC 2001–07; FRSB 1978, FRSE 1979, CBiol 1985; MStJ 2016; *Books* Molecular Virology (with T H Pennington, 1975), Introduction to Virology (with K M Smith FRS, 1980), over 100 papers in scientific journals; *Recreations* painting (one-man exhibition of paintings Shrewsbury Sch 2012), gardening, walking, photography; *Clubs* Athenaeum (Liverpool); *Style*— Prof Donald Ritchie, CBE, DL, FRSE; ✉ Allanbank, Gavinton, Duns, Berwickshire TD11 3QT (☎ 01361 882547, e-mail d.a.ritchie@liv.ac.uk)

RITCHIE, Hamish Martin Johnston; s of James Martin Ritchie (d 1993), and Noreen Mary Louise, *née* Johnston (d 2006); bro of Alasdair William Ritchie, *qv*; *b* 22 February 1942; *Educ* Loretto, ChCh Oxford (MA); *m* 20 Sept 1967, (Judith) Carol, da of Frank Knight Young (d 1992), of Bearsden, Scotland; 1 s (Stuart b 1970), 1 da (Susan b 1972); *Career* md Hogg Robinson UK Ltd 1980–81 (dir 1974–80); chm Marsh & McLennan Cos UK Ltd 2000–04 (joined 1983), dir Marsh Ltd 1997–2004; chm Br Insurance Brokers Assoc 2002–04; chm R&A Pension Fund; tstee: Eng Nat Ballet 2000–05, Princess Royal Tst for Carers 2000–05, Tower Hill Tst 2005–11; *Recreations* music and all sport (especially golf); *Clubs* MCC, RAC (dir 1990–99), R&A (capt 2008–09), Denham Golf, Pine Valley Golf (USA); *Style*— Hamish Ritchie, Esq; ✉ Oldhurst, Bulstrode Way, Gerrards Cross, Bucks SL9 7QT (☎ 01753 883262)

RITCHIE, Prof Ian Carl; CBE (2000); s of Christopher Charles Ritchie (d 1959), and Mabel Berenice, *née* Long (d 1981); *b* 24 June 1947, Hove, Sussex; *Educ* Varndean GS Brighton, Liverpool Sch of Architecture, Central London Poly (DipArch); *m* Jocelyne Van den Bossche; 1 s (Inti Timote Hugo b 1983); *Career* architect; ptnr Chrysalis Architects 1979–81, princ Ian Ritchie Architects 1981–, co-fndr and dir Rice Francis Ritchie (RFR) Paris (engrg design) 1981–88; projects incl: Fluy House Picardy 1976–77, Eagle Rock House Sussex 1980–82, La Villette Science City (with A Fainsilber) Paris 1981–86, The Louvre (sculpture courts and pyramids with I M Pei) Paris 1985–93, Roy Square Housing Limehouse 1986–88, L'Arche Cloud Paris 1986–90, Ecology Gallery at Natural History Museum 1989–90, Reina Sofia CARS Madrid (with Castro and Onzono) 1989–91, offices at Stockley Park London 1989–91, Jubilee Line Extension Bermondsey Station 1990–99, Albert Cultural Centre Somme 1991–93, Terrasson Cultural Greenhouse 1992–94, Leipzig Messe Central Glass Hall (with V Marg) 1992–96, HV Pylons for Electricité de France 1995, London Regatta Centre 1995–97, Crystal Palace Concert Platform 1997, Scotland's Home of Tomorrow Glasgow 1997, The Spire (Dublin's 21st century nat monument) 1998, ARTE TV HQ Strasbourg 1998, White City Redevelopment 1998–2005, Milan's Light Monument 1999, Plymouth Theatre Royal Prodn Centre 1999–2002, Wood Lane Station 2000–08, RSC Courtyard Theatre 2005, King Solomon Acad 2009, Sainsbury Wellcome Centre for Neuroscience UCL 2013, Royal Acad of Music New Theatre and Recital Hall 2015, Farson Business Park Malta 2015, RSC The Other Place 2016, Mercers Gardens Covent Garden 2016, Dylon housing London 2016; cmmr: Royal Fine Art Cmmn (RFAC) 1995–99, CABE 1999–2001 (now cmmr emeritus); advsr Nat History Museum 1991–95, advsr to the Lord Chllr 1999–2004, advsr Arup Fndn 2003–, masterplanner to British Museum 2004–06, govr and architectural advsr RSC 2001–16 (memb Int Cncl 2006–), advsr pres Columbia Univ NY Manhattanville Project 2007–11, advsr dean architecture and construction Greenwich Univ, advsr dir Centre for Urban Science and Progress NYU 2011–14, advsr Backstage Tst 2012–; designs exhibited and published worldwide; special prof Sch of Civil Engrg Univ of Leeds 2001–04, prof of architecture Royal Acad of Arts 2004–12; visiting prof: ; special visiting prof Univ of Liverpool 2009–; has taught at: Oita Univ Japan 1970, Planning Sch PCL 1972, Architectural Assoc 1979–82; DTI IBIS Project gatekeeper 1996–2001, chm Europan UK 1997–2003; memb: Urban Design Advsy Gp LDDC 1990–97, Cncl UK Steel Construction Inst 1994–97, Editorial Bd CITY jl 1994–99, Research Advsy Ctee Nat Maritime Museum 1995–97, UK Govt Foresight Construction Panel 1996–98, Spatial Devpt Strategy Policy Cmmn GLA 2000–01, Advsy Ctee Interdisciplinary Design for the Built Environment (IDBE) Univ of Cambridge 2001–04, Built Environment Panel and Design Panel ctees Royal Cmmn for the Exhbn of 1851 2001–, UK Nat Construction Technol Platform 2005–, European Construction Technol Platform High Level Gp 2005–08, Mayor of London's Design Panel 2007–08; RIBA: external examiner 1983–95, 2000–04 and 2007–, Pres's Medal assessor 1987, nat chm of awards 1988, Civic Tst assessor, chair RIBA Stirling Award 2006; Royal Acad of Arts: memb Cncl, chm Arts Collections and Library Ctee 2000–09, memb Mgmnt Ctee 2001–04, memb Magazine Editorial Bd, memb Enterprise Bd 2013–14; memb: IABSE, Scientists for Global Responsibility; registered ARB 1979, registered

German architect 1993, Tableau de L'Ordre des Architectes Français 1982; Hon DLitt Univ of Westminster 2000; RIBA 1979, FRSA 1981, RA 1998, RIAI 2008, Hon FRIAS 2009, Hon FAIA 2010; memb Akademie der Künste Berlin 2013; *Awards* Silver Medal Architectural Design 1982, Plus Beaux Ouvrages de Construction Metallique France 1986 and 1988, IRITECNA Prize for Europe 1991, Eric Lyons Meml Award for Euro Housing 1992, Robert Matthew Award for innovation and advancement of architecture Commonwealth Assoc of Architects 1994, RFAC Tst Arts Building of the Year 1998, Stephen Lawrence Award 1998, RIBA Awards 1998, 2000, 2003, 2004 and 2007, shortlisted Stirling Prize 1998, 2003, 2004 and 2007, Civic Tst Award 1998 and 2002, AIA Award London 1998, 2003 and 2008, RFAC Tst Sports Building of the Year 2000, Grand Silver Medal Académie d'Architecture France 2000, 2 Design Cncl Millennium Product Awards 2000, Regeneration of Scotland Supreme Award 2000, IABSE Int Outstanding Structure Award 2000, Copper Building of the Year 2000, Innovation in Copper Award 2000 and 2003, RFAC Tst Building of the Year 2003, Abercrombie Architectural Design Award 2004, shortlisted Mies van der Rohe Prize 2005, West Midlands Architect of the Year 2006, HSBC Rail Business Award 2009, RICS Award 2011, 3Rs Nat Award Heritage & Structure 2011, RIAI Award 2011, British Council for Offices (BCO) Award 2011; *Publications* (Well) Connected Architecture (1994), Architektur mit (Guten) Verbindungen (1994), The Biggest Glass Palace in the World (1997), subject of Ian Ritchie Tecnoecologia (A Rocca, 1998, in Italian, trans into English as Ian Ritchie Technoecology, 1998), Plymouth Theatre Royal Production Centre (2003), The Spire (2004), RSC Courtyard Theatre (2006), Leipzig Glass Hall (2007), Ian Ritchie Lines (2010), Being: An Architect (2013); *Recreations* art, swimming, reading, writing, theatre, poetry; *Clubs* Arts; *Style*— Professor Ian C Ritchie, CBE, RA; ✉ c/o Ian Ritchie Architects Limited, 110 Three Colt Street, London E14 8AZ (☎ 020 7338 1100, fax 020 7338 1199, e-mail iritchie@ianritchiearchitects.co.uk, website www.ianritchiearchitects.co.uk)

RITCHIE, Ian Russell; s of Hugh Russell Ritchie (d 1985), of Leeds, and Sheelah, *née* Mathews; *b* 27 November 1953; *Educ* Leeds GS, Trinity Coll Oxford (MA); *m* 10 June 1982, Jill Evelyn, da of Douglas Middleton-Walker, of Boston Spa, W Yorks; 2 s (Andrew Russell b 13 Jan 1987, Bruce Douglas b 6 March 1990); *Career* called to the Bar Middle Temple 1976 (Astbury law scholar), practising barr 1976–78; industrial rels advsr Engrg Employers' Assoc Yorks 1978–80, various posts rising to head of prodn servs Granada Television Manchester 1980–88; Tyne Tees Television: dir of resources 1988–91, md 1991–93, gp dep chief exec Yorkshire Tyne Tees Television Holdings plc (following merger) 1992–93; md The Television House 1993–94, md London News Network 1994–95, chief exec Channel 5 Broadcasting 1996–97, md Russell Reynolds Assocs exec search conslts 1997–98, chief exec Middle East Broadcasting Centre 1998–2000; Associated Press: ceo television news 2000–03, vice-pres global business and md Associated Press Int 2003–05; chief exec All England Lawn Tennis and Croquet Club 2005–11, chief exec Rugby Football Union 2011–; dir West Ham United plc 1999–2002, ind dir Football League 2004–12, dir Wembley Nat Stadium Ltd 2008–11; formerly: chm Newcastle Common Purpose, dir The Wearside Opportunity, govr Univ of Northumbria at Newcastle (formerly Newcastle Poly); FRSA; *Recreations* golf, tennis, theatre; *Clubs* Vincent's (Oxford); *Style*— Ian Ritchie, Esq; ✉ Rugby Football Union, Rugby House, Twickenham Stadium, 200 Whitton Road, Twickenham TW2 7BA

RITCHIE, Jean Harris; QC (1992); da of Walter Weir Ritchie (d 1979), and Lily, *née* Goodwin (d 2008); *b* 6 April 1947; *Educ* St Martin's Sch Solihull (scholar), King's Coll London (LLB, AKC), McGill Univ Montreal (LLM), Open Univ (BA); *m* Guy Thomas Knowles Boney, QC, *qv*, s of Dr Knowles Boney, MD; 2 s (R Oliver C b 21 Jan 1979, Christian V K b 29 March 1981); *Career* called to the Bar Gray's Inn 1970 (Churchill scholarship, Lord Justice Holker sr exhbn, bencher 2000); recorder W Circuit 1993–2008, head of chambers 2000–04; memb: Supreme Ct Rule Ctee 1993–97, Bd and Civil Ctee Judicial Studies Bd 1996–2001, QC Selection Panel 2006–11; chm of the inquiry into the care and treatment of Christopher Clunis 1993–94, chm Ritchie Inquiry into Quality and Practice within the NHS arising from the actions of Rodney Ledward 1999–2000; memb Medical Ethics Ctee King Edward Hosp London 2003–16, memb City Panel Treloar Tst 2005–08; chm of govrs Norman Court Prep Sch 1996–2000, tstee Bromley Tst 2006–, chm Wincester Cathedral Cncl 2011–; fell Winchester Coll 2008–; *Recreations* grandchildren, dog walking; *Style*— Miss Jean Ritchie, QC; ✉ King's Head House, Stockbridge, Hampshire SO20 6EU

RITCHIE, Prof Sir Lewis Duthie; kt (2011), OBE (2001); s of Lewis Duthie Ritchie, of Fraserburgh, and Sheila Gladys, *née* Noble; *b* 26 June 1952, Fraserburgh, Aberdeenshire; *Educ* Fraserburgh Acad, Univ of Aberdeen (Collie bursar, BSc, MB ChB, MD, John Watt prize, Smith Davidson Prize, Munday and Venn prize, RCGP Aberdeen and Kincardine prize), Univ of Edinburgh (MSc); *m* 8 July 1978, Heather, da of Arthur William Skelton; *Career* MO Aberdeen Hosps 1978–81, trainee in gen practice 1979–82, trainee in community med 1982–84, princ GP Peterhead Health Centre and Community Hosp 1984–2012, Sir James Mackenzie prof of gen practice Univ of Aberdeen 1992– (lectr in gen practice 1984–92, head Dept of Gen Practice and Primary Care 1992–2007, dir Undergrad Medical Prog 2008–13), hon conslt in public health med NHS Grampian 1993–2012 and 2014– (conslt in public health med Grampian Health Bd 1987–92, dir of public health NHS Grampian 2012–14), hon prof in primary care and public health Univ of Highlands and Islands 2014–, hon prof in gen practice Univ of Edinburgh 2015–; chair/past chair of Scottish Govt/NHS advsy ctees in: medical research, eHealth/IM&T, immunisation (MenC, Pneumococcal, H1N1, seasonal flu), community hosps, cardiovascular disease mngmnt/prevention (SIGN), cardiovascular nat standards (NHS QIS), telecare (NHS 24), community pharmacy; former chair Biomedical and Therapeutic Research Ctee Chief Scientist Office 2001–07; chair Scottish Medical and Scientific Advsy Ctee (SMASAC) 2007–15; chair: Inst of Remote Health Care 2014–, Ind Review of Primary Care Out of Hours Services in Scotland 2015, Queen's Nursing Inst Scotland 2015–; hon memb Aberdeen Medico-Chirurgical Soc 2015; John Perry Prize (Br Computer Soc) 1991, Ian Stokoe Meml Award RCGP 1992, Blackwell Prize Univ of Aberdeen 1995, Richard Scott lectr Univ of Edinburgh 2007, Eric Elder Medal Royal NZ Coll of GPs 2007, James Mackenzie lectr RCGP 2010, Provost Medal RCGP NE Scotland Faculty 2010, Stock Meml lectr Assoc of Port Health Authorities UK 2012, Fulton lectr RCGP W Scotland Faculty 2012, DARE lectr Faculty of Public Health UK 2014; chartered computer engr 1993, chartered IT professional 2004; DRCOG 1980, FRSM 1985, FFPHM 1993 (MFPHM 1983), FRCGP 1994 (MRCGP 1982), FRCPEd 1995, FRSA 2001, FBCS 2004 (MBCS 1985), Hon FRCPG 2015, FRSE 2016; *Books* Computers in Primary Care (1984, 2 edn 1986, Spanish edn 1991); author of pubns/reports on cardiovascular disease/prevention, community hospitals, computers, immunisation, oncology, academic GP careers, community pharmacy, professionalism and excellence in medicine; *Recreations* church, dog walking, swimming, reading military history and biography, classical music, art appreciation, civilian gallantry, RNLI; *Clubs* Harveian Soc; *Style*— Prof Sir Lewis Ritchie, OBE, FRSE; ✉ Cramond, 79 Strichen Road, Fraserburgh, Aberdeenshire AB43 9QJ (☎ 01346 510191, fax 01346 515598); Centre of Academic Primary Care, University of Aberdeen, School of Medicine and Dentistry, Polwarth Building, Foresterhill, Aberdeen AB25 2ZD (☎ 01224 437264, fax 01224 437285, e-mail l.d.ritchie@abdn.ac.uk)

RITCHIE, Margaret; MP; da of John Ritchie (d 1998), and Rose Anne, *née* Drumm (d 2000); *b* 25 March 1958, Downpatrick, Co Down; *Educ* St Mary's HS Downpatrick, Queen's Univ Belfast (BA, post-grad Dip); *Career* cncllr Down Dist Cncl 1985–2009 (vice-chm 1992–93, chair 1993–94); elected NI Forum 1996, MLA (SDLP) S Down 2003–12, min for social devpt 2007–10, ldr SDLP 2010–11; MP (SDLP) S Down 2010–, memb Environment Food and Rural Affrs Select Ctee, vice-chair All-Pty Parly Gp on Fisheries, co-chair All-Pty Parly Gp on the Visitor Economy; *Recreations* theatre, walking; *Style*— Ms Margaret Ritchie, MP; ✉ 32 Saul Street, Downpatrick, Co Down BT30 6NQ (☎ 028 4461 2882, fax 028 4461 9574, e-mail m.ritchie@sdlp.ie, Twitter @mritchiemp)

RITCHIE, Richard Bulkeley; s of W Ritchie (d 1984), of Dublin, and Ruth Mary, *née* Bulkeley; *b* 6 September 1952; *Educ* Shrewsbury, St Catherine's Coll Oxford (BA); *m* 28 Sept 1985, Dr Susan Rosemary Foister, da of Philip Foister, Hastings; 2 s (Felix b 1986, Joshua b 1992), 1 da (Isabella b 1988); *Career* called to the Bar Middle Temple 1978, standing counsel to the DTI in insolvency matters 1989, jr cncl to the Crown (Chancery A Panel) 1994–2004; *Style*— Richard Ritchie, Esq; ✉ 24 Old Buildings, Lincoln's Inn, London WC2A 3UJ (☎ 020 7404 0946, fax 020 7405 1360)

RITCHIE, Prof William; OBE (1994); s of Alexander Ritchie, and Rebecca Smith, *née* Caldwell; *b* 22 March 1940; *Educ* Wishaw High Sr Secdy Sch, Univ of Glasgow (BSc, PhD); *m* 29 March 1965, Elizabeth Armstrong Bell; 2 s (Derek Alexander b 26 June 1967, Craig William b 11 Dec 1968), 1 da (Lynne Elspeth b 10 Feb 1978); *Career* res asst Univ of Glasgow 1963; Univ of Aberdeen: asst lectr 1964–66, lectr 1966–72, sr lectr 1972–79, prof 1979–95, dean of Faculty of Arts and Social Sciences 1988–89, vice-princ 1990–95; vice-chllr Lancaster Univ 1995–2002; dir Aberdeen Inst for Coastal Science and Mgmnt 2002–11, Macaulay Land Use Research Inst 2006; adjunct prof World Maritime Univ Malmo 2002–; former hon prof Louisiana State Univ; hon ed Jl of Coastal Conservation; ind chm Scottish Aquaculture Research Forum 2004–, chm Monitoring Ctee Shetland Oil Terminal Environmental Advsy Gp, memb Bd of Tstees Nat Maritime Museum 2000–05, memb Advsy Bd Marine Scotland Science, memb Scot Coastal Forum, memb Advsy Bd Marine Alliance for Science and Technol for Scotland (MASTS) 2010–; nat chm Royal Scottish Geographical Soc 2005–08 (former chm Aberdeen Branch); sometime memb: Scot Examination Bd, Scot Univs Cncl of Entrance, Nature Conservancy Cncl (Scot); formerly: recorder and pres Section E BAAS, chm Scottish Office Ecological Steering Gps for the oil spill in Shetland, chm Sec of State for Scotland's Advsy Ctee on Sustainable Devpt, chm Sec of State for Scotland's Ctee on SSSIs, chm Sullom Voe Oil Terminal Environmental Advsy Gp, chm St Fergus Dunes Tech Mgmnt Ctee, convenor SCOVACT, memb Fulbright Cmmn; memb Cncl RSE; Hon DUniv Stirling, Hon DSc Lancaster Univ; FRSGS 1980, FRSE 1982, FRICS 1989; *Books* Mapping for Field Scientists (1977), Beaches of Highlands and Islands of Scotland (1978), Beaches of Scotland (1984), Surveying and Mapping for Field Scientists (1988), The Coastal Sand Dunes of Louisiana (Volume 1 Isles Dernieres (1989), Volume 2 Plaquemines (1990), Volume 3 Chandeleurs (1992), Volume 4 Bayou Lafourche Coastline (1995); *Style*— Prof William Ritchie, OBE, FRSE; ✉ SARF, PO Box 7223, Pitlochry PH16 9AF (☎ 01796 472829, website www.sarf.org.uk)

RITSON, Dr (Edward) Bruce; OBE (2013); s of Maj Harold Ritson (d 1979), of Edinburgh, and Ivy, *née* Catherall (d 1972); *b* 20 March 1937; *Educ* Edinburgh Acad, Univ of Edinburgh, Harvard Univ (MD, MB ChB, DPM); *m* 25 Sept 1965, Eileen Teresa, da of Leonard Carey, of Dublin; 1 da (Fenella b 1968), 1 s (Gavin b 1970); *Career* dir Sheffield Region Addiction Unit 1968–71, conslt and clinical dir Royal Edinburgh Hosp 1971–2002, sr lectr in psychiatry Univ of Edinburgh 1971–; memb Business Ctee Gen Cncl Univ of Edinburgh 2016–; advsr WHO 1977–, conslt W Australia Alcohol and Drug Authy 1983; vice-pres Med Cncl on Alcohol, former chm Substance Misuse Faculty RCPsych; chm: Howard League (Scotland) until 2006, DVLA Drug and Alcohol Advsy Ctee until 2006, Art in Healthcare, Scottish Health Action on Alcohol Problems; memb Parole Bd for Scotland 2004–10; FRCPsych 1979, FRCP (Edinburgh) 1987; *Books* The Management of Alcoholism (with C Hassall, 1970), Alcohol: The Prevention Debate (with M Grant, 1983), Alcohol Our Favourite Drug (1986), Tackling Alcohol Together (1999), Alcohol and Health (with M Y Morgan, 2010); *Recreations* theatre, travel, squash, cricket; *Clubs* New (Edinburgh); *Style*— Dr Bruce Ritson, OBE; ✉ 4 McLaren Road, Edinburgh EH9 2BH (☎ 0131 667 1735, e-mail bruce.ritson@talktalk.net)

RITTER, Prof Mary Alice; OBE (2014); *née* Buchanan Smith; da of Douglas Buchanan-Smith, and Iris Townsend; *Educ* Berkhamsted Sch for Girls, St Hilda's Coll Oxford (MA, Dip), Wolfson Coll Oxford (DPhil); *Family*; 3 s; *Career* post-doctoral research fell Dept of Zoology Univ of Oxford 1971–76, research assoc Dept of Pathology Univ of Connecticut 1976–78, research fell ICRF London 1978–84; Imperial College London (formerly Royal Postgrad Med Sch London): lectr in immunology 1982–86, sr lectr 1986–88, reader in immunology 1988–91, prof of immunology 1991–2012, vice-dean (educn) 1992–97, asst vice-princ (postgrad med) 1997–2000, dir Grad Sch of Life Scis and Med 2000–06, pro-rector (postgraduate affrs) 2004–05, chm Dept of Immunology Faculty of Medicine 2004–06, pro-rector (postgraduate and int affrs) 2005–07, pro-rector (int) 2007–11, emeritus prof of immunology 2012–; ceo Climate-KIC 2010–14 (int ambass 2015–); memb Cncl and chm Scientific Advsy Panel Action Research 1997–2000 (vice-chm Scientific Advsy Panel 1994–96); chm Nat Steering Ctee Research Cncls UK GRAD Prog 2005– (memb 2004–05), chm Govt UKIERI Evaluation Panel 2006–11, chair Advsy Bd Research Cncls' RCUK Vitae Prog 2008–10, memb high-lvel gp advising EC Cmmr for Research Carlos Moedas 2015–16; memb: Research Advsy Ctee Research into Ageing 2000–05, Prog Review Ctee Cambridge-MIT Inst 2004–07, Non-Clinical Trg and Career Devpt Panel MRC 2005–10, Non-Clinical Careers Ctee Acad of Medical Sciences 2006–11, PM's Initative 2 Ctee for HE 2006–11, German Excellence Initiative (Third Stream) 2006 and 2007, Europeans Unvs Assoc Cncl for doctoral education v-chair 2007–11, Univ Pierre et Marie Curie Paris VI Strat Advsy Bd 2011–, Lee Kong Chian Sch of Medicine Pro Tem Governing Bd 2010–11, A*STAR (Singapore Agency for Sci, Tech and Res) Grad Acad Int Advsy Panel 2007–11; Nat Res Fndn Singapoer memb Fellowship Evaluation Panel 2015–, Illuminate Cnsltng Gp Advsy Bd 2015–; FHEA (FILT 2001), FRSA 2004, FCGI 2006, FRCPath 2006, FRSB; *Publications* The Thymus (jtly, 1992); more than 100 research articles in scientific learned jls; *Recreations* travelling, gardening, cycling, biography, baroque music, ballet, opera, enjoying Grandchildren (1 grandson, 6 granddaughters); *Style*— Prof Mary Ritter, OBE; ✉ e-mail m.ritter@imperial.ac.uk

RITTERMAN, Dame Janet Elizabeth; DBE (2002); *née* Palmer; da of Charles Eric Palmer, of Sydney, Australia, and Laurie Helen, *née* Fuller; *b* 1 December 1941; *Educ* N Sydney Girls' HS, NSW State Conservatorium of Music (Frank Shirley Prize, Shadforth Hooper Prize, DSCM), Sydney Teachers' Coll Univ of Sydney, Univ of Durham (BMus), Univ of London (Hilda Margaret Watts Prize for Musicology, MMus, PhD); *m* 19 Dec 1970, Gerrard Peter Ritterman; *Career* teacher: Strathfield Girls' HS Sydney 1963–66, Swaffield Jr Mixed Infants Sch London 1967–68, Cheltenham Girls' HS Sydney 1968–69, Watford GS for Girls 1969–74; sr lectr in music: Middx Poly 1975–79, Goldsmiths London 1980–87; Dartington Coll of Arts: head of music 1987–90, dean 1988–90, princ 1990–93; dir Royal Coll of Music 1993–2005 (vice-pres 2005–); chllr Univ of Middx 2013–; visiting prof in music educn Univ of Plymouth 1993–2005; external examiner: BA Kingston Poly 1987–90, Univ of Glasgow 1991–95, KCL 1995–99; chief external examiner: PGCE Bradford and Ilkley Community Coll 1987–91, Welsh Coll of Music and Drama 1990–93, Manchester Metropolitan Univ 1991–93; chair: Arts Cncl Review of Training of Opera Singers 1992–93, ABRSM (Publishing) Ltd 1993–2005, Arts Cncl of England and BBC Nat Review of Orchestral Provision 1994–95, Subject Panel in Music Univ of London 1994–2000, The Mendelssohn and Boise Fndns 1996–98 and 2002–04, Advsy Cncl Arts Research Ltd 1997–2005, Fedn of Br Conservatoires 1998–2003, Postgrad Ctee AHRB 2002–04, HEFCE Funding Review Panel Small and Specialist Instns 2007–09, Arts

R

Research Bd PEEK, Austrian Science Fund 2009–, Int Advsy Bd Sibelius Acad Univ of the Arts Helsinki 2013–14; memb: Music Ctee Schs Examination and Assessment Cncl 1989–92, Exec Bd SW Arts 1991–93, Music Panel Arts Cncl of GB 1992–98, RMA Cncl 1994–2004, Exec Ctee ISM 1996–99, Bd ENO 1996–2004, Postgrad Panel AHRB 1998–2002, Euro Sci Fndn Humanities Programme 1999–2002, Steering Ctee London HE Consortium 1999–2005, Arts Cncl of England 2000–02, DfES Advsy Ctee Music and Dance Scheme 2001–05, Br Acad Review 'That Full Complement of Riches: the contributions of the arts, humanities and social sciences to the nation's wealth' 2002–03, Wissenschaftsrat Bundesministerium für Wissenschaft und Forschung (formerly Bundesministerium für Bildung Wissenschaft und Kultur Austria) 2003–12, Nominating Ctee AHRC 2005–07, Advsy Cncl Inst of Germanic and Romance Studies and Inst of Musical Research Sch of Advanced Study Univ of London 2005–12, Advsy Bd Inst of Advanced Studies in the Humanities Univ of Edinburgh 2005–13, Bd Sch of Advanced Study Univ of London 2007–14, Educn Advsy Ctee Nuffield Fndn 2007–10, Conseil de Fondation Haute École de Musique Geneva 2009–, Bd of Govrs Royal Welsh Coll of Music and Drama 2010–, Austrian Science Fund (FWF) Aufsichtsrat 2015–; tstee: The Countess of Munster Musical Tst 1993–, Plymouth Chamber Music Tst 2006–10, Belcea Quartet Tst 2012–, EU Chamber Orch Tst 2013–; conslt Govrs' Music Ctee Bd of Govrs of Wells Cathedral Sch 1993–2000, strategic devpt advsr Orpheus Inst Ghent 2009–; memb Bd of Dirs: Voices Fndn 2005–13, Anglo-Austrian Soc 2005–11; govr: Purcell Sch 1996–2000, Heythrop Coll London 1996–2006, Goldsmiths London 2002–2007, Dartington Coll of Arts 2005–08, Middlesex Univ 2006–13, Falmouth Univ 2008–16 (vice-chm 2013–16); memb Ct Worshipful Co of Musicians 2005–12; fell Heythrop Coll Univ of London 2008, fell Goldsmiths Univ of London 2009, assoc fell Inst of Musical Research Univ of London 2006–14; memb: RMA, RSM; Hon DUniv Univ of Central England Birmingham 1996, Hon DLitt Univ of Ulster 2004, Hon DUniv Middlesex 2005, Hon DMus Univ of Sydney 2010; fell: UC Northampton 1997, Dartington Coll of Arts 1997; sr fell RCA 2004; Hon RAM 1995, Hon GSMD 2000; FRNCM 1996, FHEA 2007; *Conference papers* incl: A Nineteenth Century Phoenix: the Concert Spirituel in Paris 1800–1830 (1986), Educating Tomorrow's Musicians (1988), Music History: its role in Higher Education Music (1989), Principle and Practice: the future of higher education in music (1991), First Impressions, Second Thoughts: Composers and their Reworkings (1993), Tradition and the individual talent: a musical perspective (1993), The Conservatoire within the Community: Challenging the Values (1994), Music Education National Debate 'Performing Music, Knowing Music' (1995), Learning What it is to Perform: A Key to Peer Learning for Musicians (1998), Teaching How to Learn, Learning How to Teach: Educating Musicians for the Twenty-first Century (1999), Grove as Director (2000), Making Music Work (2000), New Perspectives on Music Education (2008), Leading Arts Institutions in an Age of Uncertainty (2009); *Publications* Craft for Art's Sake: Variations on a Traditional Theme (1995), 'Gegensätze, Ecken und scharfe Kanten': Clara Schumanns Besuche in England, 1856–1888 (1996); contrib: Music for a Small Planet, Int Soc for Music Educn Yearbook (1984), Revue internationale de musique française (1985), Int Jl of Music Educn (1987), Music Teacher (1989), Br Jl of Music Educn (1990), Chopin Studies (1992), Musical Performance: A Guide to Understanding (2002), George Grove: Music and Victorian Culture (2003), Musical Life in Europe (1770–1914): Compositional, Institutional, and Political Challenges (2005), The Piano in Nineteenth-Century British Culture: Instruments, Performance and Repertoire (jtly, 2007), Musical Dimensions: A Festschrift for Doreen Bridges (2009), Art Futures: Current issues in higher arts education (2010); *Reports* National Review of Opera Training (Arts Cncl of GB 1993), ACE and BBC Review of National Orchestral Provision – Consultation Document (Arts Cncl 1995), The Conservatories of Finland (National Bd of Educn Finland) 1997, Learning What it is to Perform: a Key to Peer Learning for Musicians (2000); *Recreations* theatre, reading, country walking, bell-ringing; *Clubs* Athenaeum; *Style*— Dame Janet Ritterman, DBE; ✉ e-mail jritterman@blueyonder.co.uk

RITTNER, Luke Philip Hardwick; b 24 May 1947; *Educ* Blackfriars Sch, City of Bath Tech Coll, Dartington Coll of Arts, LAMDA; *m* 1974, Corinna Frances Edholm; 1 da; *Career* asst admin Bath Festival 1968, admin dir Bath Festival 1974–76, dir and fndr Assoc for Business Sponsorship of the Arts (now Arts and Business) 1976–83, sec-gen Arts Cncl of GB 1983–90, British cultural dir Expo '92 Seville 1990–92, dir of communications and public affrs Sotheby's 1992–99; currently chief exec Royal Acad of Dance; non-exec dir Carlton Television 1990–93; judge Theatre Panel Olivier Awards 1992–94, jury memb Shakespeare Prize 2000–06, judge Dance Panel Olivier Awards 2003–04, judge Theatre Panel Olivier Awards 2007–09; chm: English Shakespeare Co 1990–94, Exec Bd LAMDA 1994–, London Chorus (formerly London Choral Soc) 1994–2005; memb: Cncl Almeida Theatre 2000–02, Bd The Actors Centre 2000–02, Cultural Affrs Ctee English-Speaking Union 2010–, Advsy Devpt Bd Cambridge Summer Music Festival 2010–; patron: New London Orch 1998–2003, Dartington Coll of Arts Appeal 2002–; tstee: Victoria and Albert Museum 1980–83, The Hanover Band 1998–2002; Hon Doctor of Arts Univ of Bath 2004, Hon DCL Univ of Durham 2006; *Clubs* Garrick; *Style*— Luke Rittner, Esq; ✉ Royal Academy of Dance, 36 Battersea Square, London SW11 3RA

RIVERS, Prof Isabel; da of Anthony Haigh (d 1989), and Pippa, *née* Dodd (d 1976); b 9 May 1944; *Educ* St Helen's Sch Northwood, Girton Coll Cambridge (BA), Columbia Univ NY (MA, PhD); *m* 15 June 1963, Thomas Max Rivers, s of Erwin Rothbarth (d 1944), and Myfanwy, *née* Charles (d 2000); 1 s (Oliver Max 29 Nov 1966), 1 da (Frances Lucy b 28 Feb 1971); *Career* asst lectr Sch of English and American Studies UEA 1969–70, Ottilie Hancock research fell Girton Coll Cambridge 1970–73, lectr Dept of English Univ of Leicester 1973–84 (reader 1984–85), tutorial fell in English St Hugh's Coll Oxford 1985–2004; Univ of Oxford: lectr in English 1985–2004, titular reader 1996–2000, titular prof of English language and literature 2000–04; prof of eighteenth-century english literature and culture Queen Mary Univ of London 2004–, co-dir Dr Williams's Centre for Dissenting Studies 2004–12; Leverhulme major research fell 2000–03; memb Int Assoc of Univ Professors of English 2004, fell English Assoc 2004; hon fell Manchester Wesley Research Centre 2008; *Books* The Poetry of Conservatism, 1600–1745: A Study of Poets and Public Affairs from Jonson to Pope (1973), Classical and Christian Ideas in English Renaissance Poetry: A Students' Guide (1979, 2 edn 1994), Books and their Readers in Eighteenth-Century England (ed, 1982), Reason, Grace and Sentiment: A Study of the Language of Religion and Ethics in England, 1660–1780 (2 vols, 1991–2000), Books and their Readers in Eighteenth-Century England: New Essays (ed, 2001), Joseph Priestley: Scientist, Philosopher and Theologian (jt ed, 2008), Dissenting Praise: Religious Dissent and the Hymn in England and Wales (jt ed, 2011); *Recreations* opera, theatre, art galleries, looking at churches and houses, gardening; *Style*— Prof Isabel Rivers; ✉ School of English and Drama, Queen Mary University of London, Mile End Road, London E1 4NS (e-mail i.rivers@qmul.ac.uk)

RIVIERE, William D'Oyly; s of late Michael Valentine Briton Rivière, and Bridget D'Oyly, *née* D'Oyly-Hughes; b 15 May 1954; *Educ* Bradfield Coll, King's Coll Cambridge (MA); *m* 29 Aug 1992, Isabelle Sarah, *née* Corbett; 2 da (Camilla Isa b 4 May 1999, Miranda Josephine b 6 Aug 2002), 1 s from previous partner (Leo Forte b 27 June 1975); *Career* lectr: Univ of Verona 1980–84, Osaka Gakuin Univ 1985–89, Univ of Urbino 1990–; prof of modern English literature Univ of Urbino 1999–; author; memb Royal Soc of Asian Affairs 1990–; runner-up Trask Awards RSL 1989; Freeman Worshipful Co of Goldsmiths 1990; FRSL 2000; *Books* Watercolour Sky (1990), A Venetian Theory of Heaven (1992), Eros and Psyche (1994), Borneo Fire (1995), Echoes of War (1997), Kate

Caterina (2001), By the Grand Canal (2004); *Recreations* travelling, sailing and planting trees; *Clubs* Travellers; *Style*— William Rivière, Esq; ✉ Dilham Grange, North Walsham, Norfolk NR28 9PZ

RIVINGTON, James Maitland Hansard; s of Herbert Lawrence Rivington, of London, and Catherine Sybil, *née* Cooke; b 21 October 1959; *Educ* St Paul's Sch London (Fndn Scholar), Magdalen Coll Oxford (exhibitioner, BA), Oxford Poly; *Career* Blackwell Scientific Publications London and Oxford 1982–86, head of academic pubns and events British Acad 1986–; Liveryman Worshipful Co of Stationers & Newspaper Makers 1984; Freeman City of London 1982; *Recreations* playing cricket in the summer, supporting Brentford FC in the winter; *Style*— James Rivington, Esq; ✉ 7 Julien Road, Ealing, London W5 4XA (☎ 020 8579 4816); The British Academy, 10–11 Carlton House Terrace, London SW1Y 5AH (☎ 020 7969 5200)

RIVLIN, His Hon Geoffrey; QC (1979); s of Allenby Rivlin (d 1973), and May Rivlin (d 1980); b 28 November 1940; *Educ* Bootham Sch York, Univ of Leeds (LLB); *m* 1974, Maureen Smith, Hon ARAM, prof of violin RCM; 2 da (Emma b 30 Aug 1977, Sophie b 29 Nov 1981); *Career* called to the Bar Middle Temple 1963 (Colombus Prize in Int Law, bencher 1989, reader 2007); in practice NE Circuit 1963–89, jr of NE Circuit 1967–78, recorder of the Crown Court 1978–89, circuit judge (SE Circuit) 1989–2004, sr circuit judge 2004–11; advsr Serious Fraud Office 2012–; hon recorder of Westminster 2008–; chm Advsy Bd Computer Related Crime Research Centre Queen Mary & Westfield Coll London 1996–2003; govr: St Christopher's Sch Hampstead 1990–98, N London Collegiate Sch 1992–2002; *Books* Understanding the Law (5 edn, 2009); *Style*— His Hon Geoffrey Rivlin, QC

RIX, Prof Keith John Barkclay; s of Sgt Kenneth Benjamin Rix (d 2000), of Wisbech, Cambs, and Phyllis Irene, *née* Cousins (d 1984); b 21 April 1950; *Educ* Wisbech GS, Univ of Aberdeen (BMedBiol, MB ChB, MD), Univ of Edinburgh (MPhil), De Montfort Law Sch (LLM); *m* 31 Jan 1976, Elizabeth Murray, da of Robert Lumsden (d 1993), of Barrachnie; 3 da (Virginia b 1977, Marianne b 1981, Rowena b 1982); *Career* visiting res scientist Res Inst on Alcoholism NY State Dept of Mental Hygiene 1973, res fell Dept of Physiology Univ of Aberdeen 1975–76, registrar in psychiatry Royal Edinburgh Hosp 1976–79, lectr in psychiatry Univ of Manchester 1979–83, visiting lectr Alcohol Studies Centre Univ of Paisley 1979–2000, unit med advsr and conslt psychiatrist St James's Univ Hosp Leeds 1983–94, sr lectr in psychiatry Univ of Leeds 1983–2000, visiting conslt psychiatrist HMP Leeds 1983–2014, visiting prof of medical jurisprudence Inst of Med Univ of Chester 2013–; conslt forensic psychiatrist: Leeds Community and Mental Health Servs Teaching NHS Tst 1994–2000, The Grange 2000–15, Cygnet Hosp Wyke 2006–13; hon conslt forensic psychiatrist Norfolk and Suffolk NHS Fndn Tst 2014–; pt/t lectr De Montfort Law Sch 2010–14; fndr Aberdeen Cncl on Alcohol Problems, fndr memb Scottish Cncl on Alcohol Problems; past chm Ctee of Leeds Conslt Psychiatrists; RCPsych: former chm MCQ Clinical Topics Panel, memb Panel of Observers; memb British Acad of Forensic Sciences; past pres Leeds and W Riding Medico-Legal Soc; formerly assoc memb GMC (chm Fitness to Practise Panel); Expert Witness Award Lawyer Monthly 2016; MSB, CBiol 1985, FRCPsych 1992 (MRCPsych 1979), MAE 1995, FEWI 2002 (MEWI 1997), hon fell Faculty of Forensic and Legal Med RCP 2015; *Books* Alcohol and Alcoholism (1977), Alcohol Problems (with Elizabeth Lumsden Rix, 1983), A Handbook for Trainee Psychiatrists (1987), Expert Psychiatric Evidence (2011); *Recreations* bird watching, jazz, theatre, opera, collecting model military medics, nurses, paramedics and stretcher bearers; *Clubs* Ronnie Scott's, RSM, Sloane; *Style*— Prof Keith Rix; ✉ Fermoy Unit, Queen Elizabeth Hospital, Gayton Road, King's Lynn, Norfolk PE30 4ET (e-mail drrix@drkeithrix.co.uk, website www.drkeithrix.co.uk)

RIZA, Alper; QC (1991); s of Ali Riza (d 1985), and Elli, *née* Liasides; b 16 March 1948; *Educ* American Acad Larnaca Cyprus, English Sch Nicosia Cyprus; *m* 14 Aug 1981, Vanessa, da of Dr Patrick Hall-Smith, of Brighton; 2 da (Lily b 27 Dec 1981, Isabella b 20 July 1989); *Career* called to the Bar Gray's Inn 1973, appeals lawyer Jt Cncl for Welfare of Immigrants 1977–82, barr in private practice 1982–, recorder 2000– (asst recorder 1992–2000); *Recreations* music, chess; *Style*— Alper Riza, Esq, QC

ROACH, (Charles) Graham; s of Norman Charles Roach (d 1974), and Hazel, *née* Pascoe (d 1996); b 26 August 1947, Exeter, Devon; *m* 8 June 2005, Valerie Jayne, *née* Smith; 1 s (Shaun Charles b 21 April 1971), 2 da (Tanya Jane b 10 March 1972, Louise Ann b 5 June 1976); *Career* joined family business 1962 (dir 1968–), fndr and ceo Flagship Foods 1999–2004; *Recreations* horse racing, shooting; *Style*— Graham Roach, Esq; ✉ Prideaux House, St Blazey, Par, Cornwall PL24 2SS (☎ 01726 817304, fax 01726 817591, e-mail prideauxhouse@btconnect.com)

ROACHE, William Patrick; MBE (2001); s of Dr William Vincent Roache (d 1982), and Hester Vera, *née* Waddicor; b 25 April 1932; *Educ* Rydal Sch Colwyn Bay; *m* 1978, Sara McEwen (d 2009), da of Sidney Mottram; 2 s (Linus William Roache, William James), 1 da (Verity Elizabeth); *Career* army serv: joined RWF 1951, cmmnd 1952, served W Indies and Germany, seconded Trucial Oman Scouts, Capt Gulf 1955–56; actor in repertory film and TV; role of Ken Barlow in Coronation Street 1960–; pres St David's Hospice Llandudno; Hon MA Univ of Derby 2003, Hon DLitt Chester Univ 2007; *Recreations* golf; *Clubs* Wilmslow Golf; *Style*— William Roache, Esq, MBE; ✉ e-mail williamroache@talktalk.net

ROADS, Dr Christopher Herbert; s of Herbert Clifford Roads (d 1963), of Kneesworth, Cambs, and Vera Iris, *née* Clark (d 1986); b 3 January 1934; *Educ* Cambridge & County Sch, Trinity Hall Cambridge (open scholar, MA, PhD); *m* 24 April 1976 (m dis 1996), Charlotte Alicia Dorothy Mary, da of Neil Lothian (d 1996), of Minterne Magna, Dorset; 1 da (Cecilia Iris Muriel Lothian b 1981); *Career* Lt RA Egypt 1952–54; advsr to War Office on Disposal of Amnesty Arms 1961–62, keeper Dept of Records Imperial War Museum (IWM) 1962–70 (dep DG 1964–79); fndr and dir Cambridge Coral Starfish Res Gp 1968–, fndr and first dir Duxford Aviation Museum (IWM) 1970–79; tstee later dir HMS Belfast Pool of London 1970–79; UNESCO conslt in design and operation of audiovisual archives and museums in general 1976–; dir: Nat Sound Archive 1983–92, Historic Cable Ship John W Mackay 1986–; dir: Museums and Archives Development Associates Ltd 1977–85, Cedar Audio Ltd 1986–92, AVT Communications Ltd 1986–92, National Discography Ltd 1986–92, Symcom Ltd 1994–95; founding md and acting chm Historic Arms Exhibitions and Forts LLC (Oman) 2001–, Green Metals Ltd 2011–; assoc dir (consultancy) R&D Dept British Library 1992–94, advsr and dir-elect Jet Heritage Museum Hurn 1995–, dir-elect Baitar Rudaydah Small Arms Centre of Excellence and Museum 2000–; hon pres World Expeditionary Assoc 1971–; pres: Cambridge Numismatic Soc 1964–66, Archive and Cataloguing Commission of Int Film and TV Cncl (UNESCO category A) 1970–, Int Film and TV Cncl 1990–92; vice-pres: Duxford Aviation Soc 1974–, English Eight 1980–; memb Cncl of Scientific Exploration Soc 1971–82; life pres Historical Breech Loading Small Arms Assoc 1973–, chm Heritage Arms Rescue 1996–; pres Cambridge Univ Long Range Rifle Club 2008– (hon sec 1979–2008), vice-pres Cambridge Univ Rifle Assoc 1987– (memb Cncl 1955–87); Churchill fellowship 1971, visiting fell Centre of Int Studies Univ of Cambridge 1983–84; Silver Jubilee Medal 1977; Freeman City of London 1996, Liveryman Worshipful Co of Gunmakers 1996; FRGS; Order of Independence 2 Class (Jordan) 1977; *Recreations* rifle shooting (winner of various competitions incl Nat Match Rifle Championship Hopton 5 times), flying, marine and submarine exploration, wind surfing, cine and still photography; *Clubs* Hawks' (Cambridge), Oxford and Cambridge; *Style*— Dr Christopher Roads; ✉ The White House, 90 High Street, Melbourn, Royston, Hertfordshire SG8 6AL (☎ 01763 260866, fax 01763 262521); DX 12, Bahia Dorada, 29693 Estepona, Malaga, Spain (☎ and fax 00 34

952 76 9407, mobile 07803 129220); Historic Arms, Exhibitions and Forts LLC, PO Box 3726, Post Code 112 Ruwi, Muscat, Sultanate of Oman (office tel and fax 00 968 24501218, residence tel and fax 00 968 24596603, mobile 00 968 99797326)

ROADS, Elizabeth Ann; LVO (2012, MVO 1990); *née* Bruce; da of Lt-Col James Bruce, MC (d 1973), and Mary Hope, *née* Sinclair (d 1993); *b* 5 July 1951; *Educ* Lansdowne House Edinburgh, Cambs Coll of Technol, Study Centre for Fine Art London, Edinburgh Napier Univ (LLB); *m* 23 April 1983, Christopher George William Roads, TD, s of Dr Peter George Roads; 2 s (Timothy George Sinclair b 7 Sept 1986, William Peter Alexander b 22 Sept 1988), 1 da (Emily Ann Hope Clara b 3 Oct 1994); *Career* Inst of Educn Univ of London 1970, Christie's London 1970–74, Ct of The Lord Lyon 1975–, Lyon Clerk and Keeper of the Records 1986–, Linlithgow Pursuivant of Arms Extraordinary 1987, Carrick Pursuivant of Arms 1992–2010, Snawdoun Herald of Arms 2010–; sec Order of the Thistle 2014– (asst sec 2008–14); chm Scottish Records Assoc 2010–16, pres Old Edinburgh Club 2013–16, tstee and vice-chair Scottish Cncl on Archives; Queen's Silver Jubilee Medal 1977, Queen's Golden Jubilee Medal 2002, Queen's Diamond Jubilee Medal 2012; fell: Heraldry Soc of Scotland (memb 1977, chm 1997–2000, vice-pres 2016–), Royal Heraldry Soc of Canada 2004; academician Acad Int d'Heraldique 2008; FSA Scot 1986, FSA 2013; OStJ 1999; *Publications* The Thistle Chapel, within St Giles' Cathedral Edinburgh (co-author); articles in heraldic and genealogical jls, papers at heraldic congresses; *Recreations* history, reading, country pursuits, the family; *Style—* Mrs C G W Roads, LVO, FSA; ✉ Duchray, Aberfoyle, Stirlingshire FK8 3XL; Court of The Lord Lyon, HM New Register House, Edinburgh EH1 3YT (☎ 0131 556 7255, fax 0131 557 2148)

ROBARDS, Prof Anthony William; OBE (2002); s of Albert Charles Robards, of Lamberhurst, Kent, and Kathleen Emily Robards; *b* 9 April 1940, Lamberhurst, Kent; *Educ* The Skinners' Sch, UCL (BSc, PhD, DSc); *m* 1, 1962 (m dis 1985), Ruth, *née* Bulpett; 1 s (Martin David b 1967), 1 da (Helene Elizabeth b 1970); *m* 2, 1987, Eva Christina, da of Bo Knutson-Ek, of Lidingo, Sweden; *Career* currently dir AWR1 Associates; visiting res fell: ANU 1975, Univ of Stockholm 1986; chm York Science Park Ltd 1995–2012; pres: Royal Microscopical Soc 1982–84, York & N Yorks C of C 1996–97; dir N Yorks Business Link 1995–2004, non-exec chm York Test Gp Ltd 1999–2009, non-exec dir Avacta Gp plc 2005–14, exec chm York Science and Innovation Grand Tour Ltd 2010–13; Govr Co of Merchant Adventurers of the City of York 2008–09; tstee Yorks Cancer Research 2006– (dep chm 2009, chm 2010); FSB, DipRMS; *Books* Low Temperature Methods in Biological Electron Microscopy (with U B Sleytr, 1985); more than 130 scientific pubns; *Recreations* sailing, horology, photography, opera; *Style—* Prof Anthony Robards, OBE; ✉ Shrubbery Cottage, Nun Monkton, North Yorkshire YO26 8EW (☎ 01423 331023, e-mail anthonyrobards@aol.com); The Innovation Centre, York Science Park, York YO10 5DG (☎ 01904 435105, e-mail anthony.robards@york.ac.uk)

ROBARTS, (Anthony) Julian; s of Lt-Col Anthony Vere Cyprian Robarts (d 1982); *b* 6 May 1937; *Educ* Eton; *m* 1961, Edwina Beryl, da of Rt Hon Sir John Gardiner Sumner Hobson, OBE, TD, QC, MP (d 1967); 2 s, 1 da; *Career* banker; dir then md Coutts & Co 1963–91, dir Coutts Fin Co 1967–91, regnl dir NatWest Bank 1971–92; dir: The Int Fund for Insts Inc (USA) 1983–92, The F Bolton Group Ltd 1970–2008, Hill Martin 1992–2003 (chm 1993–2003), Wild Rose Holdings Ltd 2001–; chief exec The Iveagh Trustees Ltd 1993–98; tstee: Beit Med Meml Fellowships 1992–2001, Sargent Cancer Care 1997–2000; hon treas Union Jack Club 1970–2008 (also vice-pres); *Recreations* shooting, gardening, opera; *Clubs* Pratt's, MCC, Brooks's; *Style—* Julian Robarts, Esq; ✉ Bromley Hall, Standon, Ware, Hertfordshire SG11 1NY (☎ 01279 842422)

ROBATHAN, Baron (Life Peer UK 2015), of Poultney in the County of Leicestershire; Rt Hon Andrew Robert George Robathan; PC (2010); s of late Douglas Robathan, and late Sheena, *née* Gimson; *b* 17 July 1951; *Educ* Merchant Taylors' Sch Northwood, Oriel Coll Oxford; *m* 20 Dec 1991, Rachael, *née* Maunder; 1 s (Christopher Nicholas Andrew b 6 Dec 1996), 1 da (Camilla Mary Lavinia b 23 July 1999); *Career* offr Coldstream Gds and SAS 1974–89, rejoined for Gulf War 1991; cncllr London Borough of Hammersmith and Fulham 1990–92; MP (Cons): Blaby 1992–2010, Leics S 2010–15; PPS to Iain Sproat as min of state Dept of Nat Heritage 1995–97, shadow min for trade and industry 2002–03, int devpt 2003, shadow def min 2004–05, dep chief whip Cons Pty 2005–10, Parly under-sec of state Miny of Defence 2010–12, min of state for Armed Forces 2012–13, min of state NI Office 2013–14; chm Cons Backbench Defence Ctee 1994–95; vice-chm: Cons Backbench NI Ctee 1994–95 and 1997–2001, Cons Defence Ctee 1997–2001, Cons Backbench Policy Gp on Int Affrs and Defence 2001–02, All-Pty Cycling Gp (formerly chm) until 2010, Parly Renewable and Sustainable Energy Gp until 2010; chm Halo Tst 2003–06; *Recreations* mountain walking, tennis, skiing, wildlife, shooting; *Style—* The Rt Hon the Lord Robathan; ✉ House of Commons, London SW1A 0AA

ROBB, Prof Alan Macfarlane; s of Alexander Robb (d 1982), of Aberdeen, and Jane Margaret Robb (d 2011); *b* 24 February 1946, Glasgow; *Educ* Robert Gordon's Coll Aberdeen, Gray's Sch of Art (PGDip), RCA (MA); *m* 1969, Cynthia Jane, da of John Neilson, of Glasgow; 1 s (Daniel Alexander John b 1971), 1 da (Annabel Ellen Jane b 1974); *Career* artist and teacher; art master Oundle Sch Peterborough 1972–75; Crawford Sch of Art Cork Ireland: lectr in painting/printmaking 1975–78, head of painting 1978–80, head of fine art 1980–82; Duncan Jordanstone Coll of Art Dundee: head Sch of Fine Art 1983–2003, prof 1990–2007 (emeritus prof 2007–); speaker Context and Collaboration Int Public Art Symposium Birmingham 1990, main speaker Research Fine Art/Arts and Humanities Research Bd NAFAE Conf Tate Britain 2004; specialist advsr in fine art CNAA 1987– (memb Fine Art Bd); chief examiner in fine art NCEA Ireland, external examiner in painting and printmaking Sheffield Poly 1987–90; memb: Steering Gp Nat Assoc for Fine Art Educn 1988–, Chief Exec's Res Advsy Gp Ctee Scottish Higher Educn Funding Cncl 1994–98; lead assessor (quality assessment) in fine art SHEFC Kingston Univ London 2002–06; dir: Art in Partnership 1986–91, Workshop and Studio Provision for Artists Scotland (WASPS) 1984–94, Br Health Care Arts 1989–93, advsr Cwlth Cmmn 1998–2004; RSW 2010, memb Royal Scottish Acad of Arts and Architecture 2011; *Public Collections*: Aberdeen Art Gallery, Dundee Art Gallery, Crawford Gallery Cork, Fleming-Wyfold Art Fndn, Huntarian Glasgow Univ, Montgomery Securities New York, HRH Duke of Edinburgh – Arts Cncls of Ireland and Northern Ireland, Royal Coll of Art, Robert Gordon Univ, Univ of Dundee; *Exhibitions* regularly exhbns since 1968 at: Aberdeen Artists, Scot Soc of Artists, Royal Scot Acad, Royal Glasgow Inst, Royal Scottish Soc Watercolourists; solo incl: The New 57 Gallery Edinburgh 1972, Cork Art Soc 1976, Scot Arts Cncl touring exhibition 1978–79, Triskel Art Centre Cork 1979, Gallery 22 Cupar 1986, Francis Cooper Gallery Ducan Jordanstone Coll of Art Dundee 1991, Seagate Gallery 1996, EastWest Gallery London 1997 and 1999, The House of Miracles (EastWest Gallery London) 2005, Ayermanana/Yestermorrow (Fundacion Antonio Saura, Cuenca, Spain) 2006, Open Eye Edinburgh 2010, A Painted World – 40 Year Retrospective (McManus Galleries Dundee) 2012; group incl: Scot Young Contemporaries 1967–68, Univ of York 1970, RCA 1971, Architectural Assoc 1971, Napier Ct Trinity Coll Cambridge 1971, Eduardo Paolozzi's choice of the London postgrad sch shows 1972, Royal Acad 1972, E Midlands Arts 1973, EVA Limerick 1977–81, Clare Morris Open 1980 and 1982, Cork Art Soc 1978 and 1980, Peacock Printmakers touring exhibition The Art of Thinking 1985, 'Allegories of Desire' Small Mansion House London 1992, 'Five Scottish Artists' Centre D'Art En l'Ile Geneva 1994, Allan Stone Gallery NY 1996, Bruton St Gallery London 1996, 'I Live Now' Howard/Guild, Academie Gallery Utrecht 1999; *Awards* (painting) Arbroath Open 1968, (painting) Irish Open Exhibition of Visual Art Limerick 1977, (painting) Clare Morris Open 1982, Aberdeen Artists 1989, William J Macaulay RSA 2000; *Publications* Irish Contemporary Art (1982), In the Mind's Eye (1996), Fleming Wyfold Collection (2004), The House of Miracles (2005), Ayermanana (2005), History of Scottish Art (2007), A Painted World (2012); *Recreations* gardening, travel, walking; *Style—* Prof Alan Robb; ✉ website www.alanrobb.net

ROBB, Andrew MacKenzie; s of William MacKenzie Robb (d 1983), and Kathleen Rhona Harvey, *née* Gibbs (d 1990); *b* 2 September 1942; *Educ* Rugby; *Children* 2 da (Fiona b 1967, Erica b 1969); *Career* T Wall & Sons Ltd 1961–69, Hoskyns Gp Ltd 1969–71, gp finance dir P&O 1983–89 (finance controller Bulk Shipping Div 1971–75, finance controller 1975–83), exec dir Pilkington plc 1989–2003 (gp finance dir 1989–2001); non-exec dir: Alfred McAlpine plc 1993–2003, KESA Electricals 2003–, Corus plc 2003–, Laird Gp 2004–; memb Urgent Issues Task Force Accounting Standards Bd 1992–97; Freeman City of London, Liveryman Worshipful Co of Glaziers; JDipMA 1973; FCMA 1968, FCT 1992; *Recreations* fly fishing, golf; *Clubs* In & Out; *Style—* Andrew Robb, Esq

ROBB, Douglas; *b* 13 November 1970; *Educ* Birkenhead Sch, Univ of Edinburgh, Univ of Cambridge; *m* 28 March 1998, Lucinda, *née* McFerran; 1 da (Miranda b 23 March 2002), 2 s (Hector b 5 July 2004, Fergus b 18 Nov 2007); *Career* housemaster Oundle Sch, headmaster Oswestry Sch Shropshire until 2014, headmaster Gresham's Sch 2014–; *Recreations* cricket, skiing, shooting; *Clubs* East India, Lansdowne; *Style—* Douglas Robb, Esq; ✉ Gresham's School, Cromer Road, Holt, Norfolk NR25 6EA (☎ 01263 714511, e-mail headmaster@greshams.com, Twitter @Greshamshead)

ROBBÉ, Dr Iain J; s of Jack Robert Robbé (d 2007), and (Annette) Yvonne, *née* Conners (d 2002); *b* 3 November 1955; *Educ* Charterhouse, KCL (BSc), Westminster Med Sch (MB BS, MRCS, LRCP), Univ of London (MSc), Univ of Wales (MSc); *m* 1984, Gillian Nancy, da of Brig P Douglas Wickenden, RAMC (ret); *Career* jr hosp doctor 1980–84, specialist trg in public health med 1984–88, dir of public health and planning Worthing Health Authy 1988–91, dir of public health med Gwent Health Authy 1991–93, sr lectr in public health med Univ of Wales Coll of Med 1993–2012, clinical med educationist and conslt 2012–; FFPHM 1995–2012 (MFPHM 1987); *Recreations* wildlife and environmental protection, wine tasting, gardening; *Style—* Dr Iain J Robbé; ✉ Centre for Medical Education, University of Dundee, The Mackenzie Building, Kirsty Semple Way, Dundee DD2 4BF (e-mail robbemededu@aol.com, website www.iainrobbe.com)

ROBBIE, David Andrew; s of Frank Robbie, of Greenmount, Lancs, and Dorothy, *née* Holt; *b* 20 June 1963, Lancs; *Educ* Univ of St Andrews (MA); *Career* finance dir: CMG plc (now Logica CMG) 2000–03, Royal P&O Nedlloyd NV 2004–05, Rexam plc 2005–; non-exec dir BBC 2007–11; tstee Aldeburgh Music; ACA; *Recreations* theatre, travel; *Style—* David Robbie, Esq; ✉ Rexam plc, 4 Millbank, London SW1P 3XR (☎ 020 7227 4155, e-mail david.robbie@rexam.com)

ROBBIE, Victor Allan Cumming; s of W Allan Robbie (d 1995), of Aberdeen, and Mae, *née* Milne; *b* 22 March 1945; *Educ* Dumbarton Acad, Shawlands Acad; *m* 20 Jan 1968, Christine Elizabeth, da of Harold Featherby Jaggard (d 1987); 2 da (Gabrielle Sara b 3 Sept 1971, Kirsten Nicola b 7 May 74), 1 s (Nicholas Allan Graham b 13 June 1978); *Career* Sunday Post and Weekly News 1963–65, Scottish Daily Mail 1965–66, Daily Telegraph 1967–68, Daily and Sunday Telegraph (Sydney) 1969–71, Evening Standard 1971–73, athletics corr Daily Mirror 1980–86 (joined 1973), The Independent 1986–87, sports ed Scotland on Sunday 1988–89, sports ed The Independent 1989–91, asst ed and head of sport Daily Mail 1991–97; publisher: Golf Travel Magazine, PGA Yearbook; dir VR Assocs, fndr Scotlands-golf-Courses.com; *Books* Athletics Yearbook (1987), Scotland's Golf Courses: The Complete Guide (1997, revised edn, 2001), Tennis 98 (ed, 1998), Ireland's Golf Courses: The Complete Guide (2001, revised edn 2006); *Recreations* archaeology, travel, golf, watching my wife garden, Usquebaugh; *Clubs* Harris Golf, North Hants Golf; *Style—* Victor Robbie, Esq; ✉ e-mail vic@vrassociates.co.uk

ROBBINS, James; s of (Richard) Michael Robbins (d 2002), of London, and Elspeth, *née* Bannatyne (d 1993); *b* 19 January 1954; *Educ* Westminster, ChCh Oxford (BA, ed Isis magazine); *m* 30 Oct 1981, Gillian Elizabeth Cameron Gee, da of Dr Brian C Gee (d 2008); 1 da (Emily Maeve Cameron b 23 March 1991); *Career* BBC: news trainee 1977, Belfast newsroom 1979–83, reporter TV news (based London) 1983–87, Southern Africa corr (based Johannesburg) 1987–91, Europe corr (based Brussels) 1992–98, diplomatic corr (based London) 1998–; major assignments incl: hunger strikes Maze Prison, UK miners' strike, resignation of Pres P W Botha, rise of F W De Klerk, release of Nelson Mandela, political reforms and violence South Africa, Maastricht Treaty and aftermath, future of the European Union, attacks on USA Sept 11 2001, wars in Kosovo, Afghanistan, Iraq and Syria, crises at UN NY, Middle East peace process, Iran incl nuclear agreement, series on India and China (Race to the Top of the World); occasional radio presenting: The World at One, The World This Weekend, The World Tonight; frequent contrib to seminars and conferences as speaker or chair; *Recreations* family, opera, music, reading, walking, cooking and eating, tennis, looking out of train windows; *Style—* James Robbins; ✉ BBC World Affairs Unit, The Bridge on the 3rd Floor, Broadcasting House, London W1A 1AA (☎ 020 3614 3334, e-mail james.robbins@bbc.co.uk)

ROBBINS, Prof Keith Gilbert; s of Gilbert Henry John Robbins, and Edith Mary, *née* Carpenter; *b* 9 April 1940; *Educ* Bristol GS, Magdalen Coll and St Antony's Coll Oxford (MA, DPhil), Univ of Glasgow (DLitt); *m* 24 Aug 1963, Janet Carey, da of John Thomson, of Fulbrook, Oxon; 3 s (Paul b 1965, Daniel b 1967, Adam b 1972), 1 da (Lucy b 1970); *Career* lectr Univ of York 1963–71, dean of Faculty of Arts UCNW Bangor 1977–79 (prof of history 1971–79), prof of modern history Univ of Glasgow 1980–91, vice-chllr Univ of Wales Lampeter 1992–2003, sr vice-chllr Univ of Wales 1995–2001; vice-pres RHS 1984–88; pres: Historical Assoc 1988–91, Ecclesiastical History Soc 1980–81; Raleigh lectr Br Acad 1984, Ford lectr Oxford 1987, Winston Churchill travelling fell 1990; memb Humanities Research Bd Br Acad 1994–97 (memb Arts and Humanities Research Bd 1998–2003); ed History 1977–86; Hon DLitt: UWE, Univ of Wales; FRHistS 1970; FRSE 1991, FLSW 2010; *Books* Munich 1938 (1968), Sir Edward Grey (1971), The Abolition of War (1976), John Bright (1979), The Eclipse of a Great Power: Modern Britain 1870–1975 ((1983), 2 edn 1870–1992 (1994)), The First World War (1984), Nineteenth Century Britain: Integration and Diversity (1988), Appeasement (1988, 2 edn 1997), Churchill (1992), History, Religion and Identity in Modern Britain (1993), Politicians, Diplomacy and War in Modern British History (1994), Bibliography of British History 1914–89 (1996), Great Britain: Identities, Institutions and the Idea of Britishness (1997), The World since 1945: A Concise History (1998), The British Isles 1901–1951 (2002), Britain and Europe 1789–2005 (2005), England, Ireland, Scotland, Wales: The Christian Church 1900–2000 (2008), Pride of Place: A Modern History of Bristol Grammar School (2010), The Dynamics of Religious Reform in Northern Europe 1780–1920: Political and Legal Perspectives (2010), Religion and British Foreign Policy 1815 to 1941 (2010), Transforming the World: Global Political History since World War II (2013); *Recreations* music; *Style—* Prof Keith Robbins, FRSE; ✉ Gothic House, 48 Bridge Street, Pershore, Worcestershire WR10 1AT (☎ 01386 555709, e-mail profkgr@clara.co.uk)

ROBBINS, Oliver; CB (2015); s of Derek Robbins, and Diana, *née* Phillips; *b* 20 April 1975, London; *Educ* Colfe's Sch Lewisham, Hertford Coll Oxford (BA); *m* 2005, Sherry, *née* Birkbeck; 3 s (Fox b 2008, Saxon b 2010, Axel b 2012); *Career* policy advsr and sr civil servant HM Treasy 1996–2006, PPS to the PM 2006–07, dir Finance and Strategy (agency secondment) 2007–10, dep nat security advsr to the PM Cabinet Office 2010–14, DG Civil Service Cabinet Office 2014–15, second perm sec Home Office 2015–16, perm sec Dept for Exiting the EU and Europe advsr to the PM 2016–; *Style—* Oliver Robbins, Esq, CB

R

ROBBINS, Prof Peter Alistair; s of Michael John Robbins, and Shirley Dean, *née* Swift; *Educ* Univ of Oxford (BA, DPhil, BM BCh), Open Univ (BA); *Career* house surgn Gloucester Royal Hosp 1984–85, house physician John Radcliffe Hosp Oxford 1985; Univ of Oxford: fell The Queen's Coll 1985–, lectr (physiology) 1985–96, reader 1996–98, prof of physiology 1998–, head of dept 2011–; memb: Physiological Soc 1985, American Physiological Soc 1992; *Publications* contrib to scientific jls incl: Jl of Physiology, Jl of Applied Physiology, FASED, PNAS, PLoSMed; *Recreations* walking, fishing, piano, bridge, sailing; *Style*— Prof Peter Robbins; ✉ Department of Physiology, Anatomy and Genetics, Oxford University, Parks Road, Oxford OX1 3PT (☎ 01865 272490, e-mail peter.robbins@dpag.ox.ac.uk)

ROBBINS, His Hon Judge Stephen Dennis; s of Lt-Col J Dennis Robbins, OBE, TD (d 1986), of Essex, and Joan, *née* Mason; *b* 11 January 1948; *Educ* Orwell Park Suffolk, Marlborough, Coll of Europe Bruges; *m* 28 Sept 1974, Amanda Robbins, JP, da of J Michael Smith, of Cheshire; 3 da (Harriet b 1976, Victoria, Camilla (twins) b 1979); *Career* called to the Bar Gray's Inn 1969; in practice SE Circuit 1972–94, recorder Crown Court 1987–94, circuit judge (SE Circuit) 1994– (sitting Southwark, Maidstone and Central Criminal Court); London Common Law Bar Assoc and Senate Overseas Rels; chm: Disciplinary Ctee Potato Mktg Bd 1988–94, Mental Health Review Tbnls 1994–; memb Parole Bd 2001–; *Recreations* walking, swimming, shooting, music, collecting ephemera; *Style*— His Hon Judge Robbins; ✉ Hillcrest Farm, Sevington, Ashford, Kent TN24 0LJ (☎ 01233 502732); 2 The Studios, Edge Street, London W8 7PN (☎ 020 7727 7216)

ROBERTS, Prof Sir (Edward) Adam; KCMG (2002); s of Michael Roberts (d 1948), of London, and Janet, *née* Adam-Smith (d 1999); *b* 29 August 1940; *Educ* Westminster, Magdalen Coll Oxford (BA); *m* 16 Sept 1966, Frances Primrose, da of Raymond Horace Albany Dunn (d 1951), of Ludham, Norfolk; 1 da (Hannah b 1970), 1 s (Bayard b 1972); *Career* asst ed Peace News 1962–65, lectr int rels LSE 1968–81 (Noel Buxton student 1965–68); Univ of Oxford: Alastair Buchan reader in int rels 1981–86, professorial fell St Antony's Coll 1981–86, Montague Burton prof of int rels 1986–2007, fell Balliol Coll 1986–2007 (emeritus fell 2007–), sr research fell Dept of Politics and Int Rels 2008–; pres Br Acad 2009–13; memb: Cncl IISS 2002–08, Advsy Bd UK Defence Acad 2003–15, Cncl for Science and Technol 2010–13; Leverhulme major res fell 2000–03; govr Ditchley Fndn 2001–11; chm of govrs William Tyndale Sch 1976–78; Hon DSSc KCL 2010, Hon LLD Univ of Aberdeen 2012, hon doctorate Aoyama Gakuin Univ Tokyo 2012, Hon DLitt Univ of Bath 2014; hon fell: LSE 1997, St Antony's Coll Oxford 2006, Cumbria Univ 2014; foreign hon memb American Acad of Arts and Sciences 2011, memb American Philosophical Soc 2013, Univ of Cumbria 2014; FBA 1990; *Books* The Strategy of Civilian Defence: Non-violent Resistance to Aggression (ed, 1967), Nations in Arms: The Theory and Practice of Territorial Defence (1976, 2 edn, 1986), Documents on the Laws of War (with Richard Guelff, 1982, 3 edn 2000), United Nations, Divided World: The UN's Roles in International Relations (ed with Benedict Kingsbury, 1988, 2 edn 1993), Hugo Grotius and International Relations (ed with Hedley Bull and Benedict Kingsbury, 1990), Humanitarian Action in War (1996), The United Nations Security Council and War: The Evolution of Thought and Practice since 1945 (ed with Vaughan Lowe, Jennifer Welsh and Dominik Zaum, 2008), Civil Resistance and Power Politics: The Experience of Non-violent Action from Gandhi to the Present (ed with Timothy Garton Ash, 2009), Democracy, Sovereignty and Terror: Lakshman Kadirgamar on the Foundations of International Order (2012), Civil Resistance in the Arab Spring: Triumphs and Disasters (ed with Michael J Willis, Rory McCarthy and Timothy Garton Ash, 2016); *Recreations* mountaineering, cycling; *Clubs* Alpine; *Style*— Prof Sir Adam Roberts, KCMG, FBA; ✉ Balliol College, Oxford OX1 3BJ (e-mail adam.roberts@balliol.ox.ac.uk)

ROBERTS, Col Alan Clive; OBE (2001, MBE 1982), TD (1969), JP (1977), DL (W Yorks 1982); s of late Maj William Roberts, MBE, RA, and Kathleen Roberts; *b* 28 April 1934; *Educ* Askham House Sch Taunton, Rutherford Coll Newcastle, Manchester Poly (MPhil), Univ of Bradford (PhD); *m* 1956, Margaret Mary, *née* Shaw; 2 s (Martin b 9 Oct 1962, Adrian b 7 May 1971); *Career* Nat Serv 1954–56; TA: Lt 269 (W Riding) Field Regt RA 1956, Capt 1962, Maj 1968, Lt-Col cmdg Univ of Leeds OTC 1972–79, Col and Dep Cdr TA NE Dist 1980–, TA advsr to GOC NE Dist 1980–, Regtl Col Univ of Leeds OTC 1980–90 and 2000–; ADC to HM the Queen 1980–84; Hon Col: Univ of Leeds OTC 1990–99, Yorks ACF (N & W) 1993–, 269 (W Riding) Battery 101 (N) Regt RA 2000–; Hon Col Commandant RA 1996–; head of Biomaterials Lab Dept of Plastic and Maxillo-Facial Surgery St Lukes Hosp Bradford 1960–2000; Bradford Hosps NHS Tst and predecessors: conslt clinical scientist 1970–, dir of R&D 1992–2002; Univ of Leeds: Crown rep Cncl 1985, pro-chllr 1986–2000, chm Ct and Cncl 1986–2000, dir Univ of Leeds Fndn 1986–89, chm Advsy Bd Inst of Nursing 1994–96, convocation lectr 2000; Univ of Bradford: visiting sr research fell Plastic and Burns Research Unit 1988–, dir Biomaterials Research Unit 1990–94, memb Advsy Ctee Dept of Biomedical Sciences 1992–, hon prof 2000–, clinical dir Prosthetic Solutions Ltd 2005–, Advsy Bd Inst of Cancer Theraputics, chm Ethical Tissue Advsy Bd 2012–; Cncl of Europe fell Univs of Gothenburg, Malmö and Stockholm 1968, prof of biomaterials in surgery Academic Surgical Unit Univ of Hull 1994–; visiting prof/lectr: Univ of Indiana 1968, Univ of Texas 1968, 1974 and 1985, Dept of Polymer Technol Manchester Poly 1970–80, Stomatology Inst Univ of Bordeaux 1971, Plastic Surgery Inst Univ of Utrecht 1972, Univ of Pennsylvania 1975, Twente Univ of Technol Netherlands 1976, Univ of São Paulo 1976, Univ of Jakarta 1986, Trinity Coll Dublin 1987, Univ of Tokyo 1987, Univ of Moscow 1987, Univ of Malaysia 1988, Brunel Univ 2009–; guest lectr: Faculty of Dental Surgery RCS England 1969 and 1980, Faculty of Plastic Surgery RCS England 1976; dean's research lectr RMCS 1977, RSM-Stuart lectr RCSEd 2009, Stevens Lecture RSM 2016; numerous research and consultancy appts in the field of biomaterials and adhesives for plastic/reconstructive surgery; lead researcher/inventor Indermil tissue adhesive 1993 and Zeflosil prosthetic adhesive 2007; conslt Nuffield Hosp Leeds 2002–10, conslt Bradford Inst for Health Research 2012–; memb Br Standards Ctees on Cardio-Vascular Materials and Toxicology of Med Polymers; vice-chm Co of W Yorks Jt Emergency Exec Ctee 1983–88, chm Quality of Life Gp and memb Head and Neck Working Gp Yorks Regnl Cancer Orgn 1993–98, vice-chm Expert Working Gp Regnl R&D Ctee Yorks RHA 1994–95, memb Health Servs Res Gp Northern and Yorks RHA 1995–97, memb Research Advsy Ctee NHS Exec Northern and Yorks R&D Directorate 1998–99, chm Bradford Research Ethics Ctee 2003–11; ed Jl of the Inst of Br Surgical Technol 1965–69, assessor Jl of Biomedical Engrg 1979; CGLI: chief examiner in maxillo-facial technol 1968–98, hon life memb 1978, vice-chm Sr Awards Ctee 1991–97, pres CGLI Assoc (CGA) 1997–2003; moderator BTech higher technol courses 1985–97, examiner Univ of Sheffield Sch of Clinical Dentistry 1995–98, examiner Univ of Malta Medical-Dental Sch 2011–; chm Cncl of Mil Educn Ctees UK Univs 1990–96, dep chm Ctee of Chairmen of Univ Cncls 1993–97, memb Int Advsy Bd Med Sch Universiti Malaysia Sarawak 1993–; pres Leeds Boys' Bde 1972–2002, chm of tstees W Riding Artillery Tst 1983–; pres: Br Red Cross Soc W Yorks 1983–, W Yorks SSAFA – Forces Help 1998–, NSPCC Leeds 2001–; vice-chm Yorks and Humberside TAVRA 1987–89 and 1993–95; dir Weetwood Hall Ltd 1992–; govr: Gateways Sch 1992–2007, Pocklington Sch 2000–07; tstee: Edward Boyle Meml Tst 1986–98, Yorks Sculpture Park 1995–, ARNI Tst 2007–, Maritime Heritage Fndn 2010–; tstee and registrar League of Mercy 1999–; patron: Crime Stoppers 1995–, Age Concern 1995–; memb Cncl Br Red Cross Soc 1995–96; Denney Award for Innovation in Surgical Technol Inst of Surgical Technol 1960, Insignia Award in Technol CGLI 1969 and 1976, Prince Philip Medal for Outstanding Achievements in Science and Technol 1970, Merit and Achievement Award for Medical Materials Devpt Inst of Science and Technol 1972, Red Cross Badge of Honour 1992; hon sec Fellowship of Prince Philip Medallists 1993–, hon sub dean N Yorks RSM 2001–03; pres: Bradford Medico-Chirurgical Soc 1997–98, Br Inst of Surgical Technologists 1998–; hon life memb US Army Med Research Soc 1971; memb: Assoc of Clinical Biochemists, W Riding Medico Legal Soc, Leeds Med Chirogical Soc 2015–; non-regtl memb HAC 2000–; chm Cncl Order of St John S and W Yorks 2004–12, memb White Lion Soc 2007–; Grant of Arms Lancaster Herald 1993, Hon Liveryman Worshipful Co of Clothworkers 2000, Freeman City of London 2000, Gentleman Usher Imperial Soc of Knights Bachelor 2009; Hon LLD Univ of Leeds 2000, Hon DSc Univ of London 2005, Hon DSc Univ of Bradford 2007, Hon DTech Brunel Univ 2007; AIMechE 1967, CBiol 1971, FRSB 1987 (MSB 1970), memb NY Acad of Sciences 1987, FCGI 1990, FRSM 1993, CIMechE 1996, FLS 1999, fell Medical Soc of London 2009, hon fell RSM 2010 (hon treas 2003–07, vice-pres 2007–09, pres Technol Section 2010–, chm Academic Bd 2016–); Companion Order of the League of Mercy 2002, KStJ 2010 (OStJ 1994, CStJ 2001), Knight Cdr Military Constantinian Order of St George 2011, Knight Grand Offr Royal Order of the Eagle of Georgia 2015; *Books* Obturators and Prosthesis for Cleft Palate (1965), Facial Prosthesis: The Restoration of Facial Defects by Prosthetic Means (1972), Maxillo-Facial Prosthetics: A Multidisciplinary Practice (jtly, 1972), Adhesives in Surgery: How it Works Encyclopaedia (jtly, 1988); also author of numerous papers in med and scientific jls; *Recreations* silver, sculpture, music; *Clubs* Army and Navy (memb Gen Ctee 2009–11); *Style*— Col Alan Roberts, OBE, KStJ, TD, JP, DL; ✉ The Grange, Rein Road, Morley, Leeds LS27 0HZ (☎ 07836 253886, e-mail roberts@132acr.com)

ROBERTS, Aled R; AM; *Educ* Univ of Wales Aberystwyth; *m* Llinos; 2 s (Osian, Ifan); *Career* slr and ptnr Geoffrey Morris and Ashton until 2005, Mayor of Wrexham 2003–04, ldr Wrexham County Borough Cncl 2005–11, memb Nat Assembly for Wales (Lib Dem) N Wales 2011–; *Style*— Aled Roberts, Esq, AM; ✉ National Assembly for Wales, Cardiff Bay, Cardiff CF99 1NA; 18 High Street, Johnstown, Wrexham LL14 2SN

ROBERTS, Prof Andrew; s of Simon Roberts, of Cobham, Surrey, and late Katie Roberts; *b* 13 January 1963, London; *Educ* Gonville & Caius Coll Cambridge (exhibitioner, hon sr scholar, BA, PhD); *m* 1, (m dis); 1 s (Henry b 2 June 1997), 1 da (Cassia b 3 June 1999); m 2, 2007, Susan Gilchrist; *Career* author; visiting prof KCL 2015–; Wolfson Prize for History 1999, James Stern Silver Pen Award 1999, Intercollegiate Studies Inst prize, Br Army Military Book Prize 2012, LA Times Biography Prize 2015, Grand Prix of the Fondation Napoleon 2015, Bradley Foundation Prize 2016; Hon DHL Westminster Coll MO; FRSL 2000, FRHistS 2016; *Books* The Holy Fox (1991), Eminent Churchillians (1994), Salisbury: Victorian Titan (1999), Napoleon and Wellington (2001), Hitler and Churchill: Secrets of Leadership (2003), What Might Have Been (ed, 2004), Waterloo: Napoleon's Last Gamble (2005), A History of the English-Speaking Peoples Since 1900 (2006), The Correspondence Between Mr Disraeli and Mrs Sarah Brydges Willyams (ed, 2007), Masters and Commanders (2008), The Art of War (2008), The Storm of War (2009), Love, Tommy: Letters Home, from the Great War to the Present Day (2014), Napoleon the Great (2015), Elegy: The First Day on the Somme (2016); *Clubs* Beefsteak, Brooks's, Garrick, Aspinall's, Pratt's, Saintsbury, Pilgrims, Univ Pitt (Cambridge), Walbrook (hon memb), Other Other (Wisconsin, hon memb), Chaos (NY, hon memb), Brook (NY), Spectacle (hon memb), 5 Hertford St (hon memb); *Style*— Professor Andrew Roberts; ✉ 22 South Eaton Place, London SW1W 9TA (☎ 020 7730 3091, e-mail andrew@andrew-roberts.net, website www.andrew-roberts.net)

ROBERTS, Anthony Howard Norman; OBE (2012); s of Kenneth Arthur Norman Roberts (d 1982), and Ivy Beatrice Maude Roberts (d 1970); *b* 15 November 1938, Woodford Green, Essex; *Educ* Bancroft's Sch, Univ of Leeds (BSc), St Catharine's Coll Cambridge (MA), Worcester Coll Oxford (BM BCh, MA); *m* 24 March 1972, Dr (Fiona Edith) Vivian, da of Prof Richard Broxton Onians (d 1986), and Rosalind Lathbury Onians (d 2010); 2 da (Clare b 1974, Natasha b 1976); *Career* lectr in chemical engrg Univ of Surrey 1961–64; conslt plastic and hand surgn Stoke Mandeville Hosp and dir Oxford Region Burn Unit 1985–2001 (emeritus conslt 2001–), surgical tutor 1989–94, regnl advsr in plastic surgery 1996–99 (chm Specialist Trg Ctee Oxford and Wessex), med advsr St John Ambulance Nat HQ 2003–04; Restore – Burn and Wound Research (formerly Stoke Mandeville Burns and Reconstructive Surgery Research Tst, tstee 2001–12, chm of tstees 2007–10, pres 2012–), civilian conslt advsr to the RAF 1998–2001 (hon civilian conslt in surgery 2002–), medical advsr to HM Coroner (IOW), hon sr advsr Br Fndn for Int Reconstructive Surgery and Trg 2011–, UK Int Emergency Trauma Register 2013–, hon conslt Isle of Wight NHS Tst 2014–; hon sr lectr in surgery UCL 1999–; visiting prof: Chinese Univ of Hong Kong 1990– (C C Wu prof 1996), Dhaka Univ 2005–; visiting lectr/prof: Southern Africa 1988 and 1995, Australia 1990 and 1993, India 1990, 1993, 1999 and 2001, Israel 1992, Papua New Guinea 1993, Bosnia 1994, 1996, 2001 and 2003, Egypt 1995, 1997, 1999–2005 and 2009, Russia 1997, China 1998, Botswana 1998, Azerbaijan 1998, 1999 and 2000, Philippines 1999, Kosovo 2001 and 2007, Romania 2004, Bangladesh 2005, Cambodia 2008; examiner general surgery RCPSGlas 1997–2004, intercollegiate examiner MRCS 2004–10; author of articles in med, surgical and ornithological jls; second in command surgical team the Bradford disaster 1985; ldr disaster relief team: Athens Refinery Fire 1992, Operation Phoenix Bosnia 1994–96, Haiti Earthquake 2010, Philippines Typhoon Haiyan 2013 and South Sudan Explosion 2015; memb Cncl St John Ambulance IOW 2002–12 (dep county surgn 2003–10, acting county medical offr 2010–12, chm County Priory Gp 2014–); memb: Br Burn Assoc 1976–2007 (co-opted memb Ctee 1998–2002, chm Burn Prevention Ctee 1999–2002, hon memb 2007–), Br Assoc of Plastic Reconstructive and Aesthetic Surgns 1986–, Br Soc for Surgery of the Hand 1986– (memb Cncl 1996–2000), Int Soc for Burn Injuries 1990– (memb Disaster Planning Ctee), Int Soc of Surgery of the Hand (memb War Injuries Ctee), Military Surgical Soc 2006–; hon memb: Assoc of Plastic Surgeons of Southern Africa 1988–, Assoc of Kosovan Plastic Surgeons 2007–, UK Int Emergency Trauma Register 2012–; memb Ringing and Migration Ctee Br Tst for Ornithology 2006–09, life memb Br Exploring Soc 1957–; county cmmr IOW Scout Assoc 2009–14 (vice-pres 2014–); Freeman City of London 2007; FRCS 1976, FRCSGlas 2004, FRSB 2015; memb Order of St John 2014 (Serving Bro St John Ambulance 2012); *Books* contrib: Bander's Aid (A Guide to the Australian Bird in the Hand) (3 edn, 1994), Paediatric Care in Developing Countries (2002), Textbook of Hospital Care in Poorly Resourced Countries (2013), Autobiography of Dr H March Webb (foreword, 2015); author of papers on surgery, ornithology and engrg; *Recreations* ornithology, sport, travel; *Clubs* Hawks' (Cambridge), British Ornithological Union, Cambridge Univ Cruising, Seaview Yacht, RAF; *Style*— Mr Anthony Roberts, OBE, FRCS, FRSB; ✉ Haseley Manor, Arreton, Isle of Wight PO30 3AN (☎ 01983 865420)

ROBERTS, Antony Mabon (Tony); s of Lt Hylton Mabon Roberts (d 1987), and Phyllis Mary, *née* Dickinson; *b* 9 July 1939; *Educ* Birkenhead Sch, Univ of Hamburg, Univ of Cambridge (MA), Yale Univ (MA); *m* 7 Aug 1965, Angela Dale, da of Maj Eric William Huggins, of Southwold, Suffolk; 1 s (Benjamin Mabon b 1969), 1 da (Clare Joy b 1972); *Career* sr prodr BBC TV 1976–; prodns incl: English Law 1968, Avventura 1971, Ensemble 1975, The Living City 1977, Wainwright's Law 1980, Whatever Happened to Britain 1982, Honourable Members 1983, Politics of Pressure 1985, Téléjournal 1983, Heute Direkt 1984, Issues of Law 1986, Person to Person 1988, Give and Take 1989, When In Germany 1991; ptnr Gratus and Roberts Productions 1991–; addiction treatment cnsllr Priory Hosp Roehampton; accredited cnsllr; *Recreations* cricket, tennis, golf; *Clubs*

MCC; *Style—* Tony Roberts, Esq; ✉ 59 Breamwater Gardens, Ham, Richmond, Surrey TW10 7SG (☎ 020 8940 9631)

ROBERTS, Ben Andrew; *b* 1 April 1975, Coventry; *Educ* Coventry Sch Bablake, Univ of Leeds (BA); *Career* head of UK theatrical distribution and acquisitions Metrodome 1998–2003, vice-pres worldwide acquisitions Universal Int Pictures 2003–07, ceo Protagonist Pictures 2007–12, dir BFI Film Fund 2012–; *Style—* Ben Roberts, Esq; ✉ British Film Institute, 21 Stephen Street, London W1T 1LN

ROBERTS, Prof Bernard; s of John William Roberts (d 1985), and Annie Margaret, *née* Leahy (d 1996); *b* 19 February 1946, Cork City, Ireland; *Educ* Bletchley Road Sch, Bletchley GS, Univ of Hull (univ prize in applied maths, BSc), Univ of Sheffield (PhD); *m* 2 Oct 1971, Margaret Patricia, da of Ernest Cartlidge; 4 s (Alastair b 1977, James b 1979, Michael b 1981, Richard b 1986); *Career* jr research fell in applied mathematics Univ of Sheffield 1967–71; Univ of St Andrews: temp lectr applied mathematics 1971–73, lectr applied mathematics 1973–87, reader in applied mathematics 1987–94, prof of solar magnetohydrodynamics 1994–2010 (emeritus prof 2010–), head of applied mathematics 1997–98; one year leave of absence Enrico Fermi Inst Univ of Chicago 1974–75; consltin coronal physics American Science and Engineering Mass 1977; visiting prof: Univ of New Hampshire 1980–81 and 1985–86, Observatoire de Paris 1981, Univ of Leuven 1988–89, Univ of New Hampshire 1990 and 2002, Universitat de les Balears de Mallorca 1993; visiting scientist: Institut für Astronomie Zurich 1982, National Center for Atmospheric Research Colorado 1989; memb: NASA Skylab Workshop on Active Regions Colorado 1978–81, USA Global Oscillation Network Group 1987, Theory Research Assessment Panel PPARC 1998–2001; guest investigator USA Solar Maximum Mission 1980, 1984–86 and 1987–89; NASA res scientist Dept of Physics and Astronomy Univ of Iowa 1985–86; chm UK Solar Physics Community 1992–98, memb Solar System Advsy Panel PPARC 2001–03; Saltire Award For Distinguished Contributions to the Physical Sciences 1998, Chapman Medal Royal Astronomy Soc 2010; FRAS 1994, FRSE 1997; *Publications* numerous learned lectrs, reviews and articles in scientific jls, incl chapter 3 in Solar System Magnetic Fields (1985), chapter 6 in Advances in Solar System Magnetohydrodynamics (1991), articles in Encyclopedia of Astronomy and Astrophysics (2001); *Recreations* hill walking; *Style—* Prof Bernard Roberts, FRSE; ✉ School of Mathematics and Statistics, University of St Andrews, St Andrews, Fife KY16 9SS (☎ 01334 463716, fax 01334 463748)

ROBERTS, Colin; CVO (2006); *b* 31 July 1959; *Educ* King's Coll Cambridge (MA), Courtauld Inst of Art London (MPhil); *m* 2000, Camilla Frances Mary, *née* Blair; 2 s; *Career* diplomat; lectr Ritsumeikan Univ Kyoto 1983–84; called to the Bar 1986, in private practice 1986–89; entered HM Dip Serv 1989, Repub of Ireland Dept 1989–90, second sec FCO 1990, second sec (economic) then first sec (political) Tokyo 1990–94, EU Dept (Internal) FCO 1995–96, first sec (political/military) Paris 1997–98, head Common Foreign and Security Policy Dept FCO 1998–2000, cnsllr (political) Tokyo 2001–04, ambass to Lithuania 2004–08, dir Overseas Territories FCO and HM cmmr for Br Antarctic Territory and Br Indian Ocean Territory 2008–12, dir Eastern Europe and Central Asia FCO 2012–13, govr Falkland Islands and HM cmmr for S Georgia and S Sandwich Islands 2014–; *Recreations* mountain sports, natural history, tennis, reading; *Clubs* Travellers'; *Style—* Mr Colin Roberts, CVO; ✉ c/o Foreign & Commonwealth Office, King Charles Street, London SW1A 2AH

ROBERTS, Dr Colin; s of Theophilus Roberts (d 1991), of Wrexham, and Daisy, *née* Roberts (d 1989); *b* 25 January 1937; *Educ* Univ of Liverpool (med students undergrad scholar, BSc, MB ChB, MD), Victoria Univ of Manchester (DipBact); *m* 8 July 1961, Marjorie Frances, da of James Conway; 2 s (David Colin b 15 Oct 1962, Philip John b 10 Oct 1967); *Career* registrar in pathology Sefton Gen Hosp Liverpool 1964–66 (house physician and house surgn 1963–64), hon sr registrar United Liverpool Hosps 1966–70, lectr in med microbiology Univ of Liverpool 1969–70 (lectr in pathology 1966–69); Regnl Public Health Lab Fazakerley Hosp Liverpool: asst microbiologist (sr registrar) 1970–73, sr microbiologist 1973–75, consltmed microbiologist 1975–87, dep dir 1977–87; Public Health Lab Serv: dep dir 1987–93, consltmed microbiologist 1987–99, med and scientific postgrad dean 1993–99; John Radcliffe Hosp Oxford (now Oxford Univ Hosp): locum consltmicrobiologist 2000–07, hon conslt 2007–10, hon clinical scientist (non-medical) 2011–13; hon conslt med microbiologist Mersey RHA 1975–87; Univ of Liverpool: hon lectr in infectious diseases 1975–87, hon lectr Sch of Tropical Med and Infectious Diseases 1985–87; memb Cncl: Assoc of Clinical Pathologists (asst sec 1990–92), Assoc of Med Microbiologists (pres 1994–95), RCPath (asst registrar 1990–92, registrar 1992–96, vice-pres 1996–99), Pathology Section RSM 1999– (hon treas 2003–05, pres 2009–10); chm Med Microbiology Scientific Advsy Ctee Clinical Pathology Accreditation (UK) 1996–2000; sec Assoc of Academic Clinical Bacteriologists and Virologists 2000–07, study module tutor LSHTM distance learning in hosp infection 2004–08; asst ed Jl of Hosp Infection 2004–, memb Editorial Bd Int Jl of Environmental Health Research; Harold Ellis Award RCS 2012; hon life memb Central Sterilising Club 1996 (chm 1992–96); hon fell Liverpool John Moores Univ 2001; memb numerous professional socs incl: Br Soc for the Study of Infection, Pathological Soc of GB and I; Hon DipHic 1999; FRCPath 1986, FRIPH 1992, Hon FRCPCH 1996, Hon FFPH 1997, FMedSci 1998, FRCP 1999, Hon FFPathRCPI 2000, FAcadMEd 2010, Hon FRCS 2013; *Publications* contrib chapters/ed various books and proceedings incl: Infectious and Communicable Diseases in England and Wales (contrib, 1990), Quality Control: Principles and Practice in the Microbiology Laboratory (jt ed, 1991, 2 edn 1999), A Supervisor's Handbook of Food Hygiene and Safety (1995); also author of numerous pubns in academic jls; *Recreations* theatre, music, art, literature, sport (rep Wales at schoolboy level in soccer); *Clubs* RSM; *Style—* Dr Colin Roberts; ✉ Level 6, Microbiology Department, The John Radcliffe, Headington, Oxford OX3 9DU (☎ 01865 220886, fax 01865 220890, e-mail colin.roberts@orh.nhs.uk)

ROBERTS, Prof (Victor) Colin; s of Ernest Roberts (d 1993), and Marjorie Frances, *née* Edwards (d 1987); *b* 11 February 1943; *Educ* Christ's Hosp, KCL (BSc(Eng), AKC), Univ of Surrey (MSc, PhD); *m* 27 July 1968, Christine Joan, da of Walter Clifford Lake; 2 da (Tara Jane b 27 June 1972, Catherine Elizabeth b 30 Nov 1973); *Career* apprentice Associated Electrical Industries Rugby 1961, engr Associated Electrical Industries (Manchester) then Compagnie Française Thomson-Houston (Paris) until 1967, successively research asst, lectr, sr lectr then prof of biomedical engrg KCH Med Sch London 1967–90, fndn prof of med engrg and physics King's Coll Sch of Med and Dentistry London 1990–2003 (now emeritus), dir of med engrg KCH NHS Tst 1990–2003, dir Nat Centre of Rehabilitation Engrg 1991–2003, dir Cornwall Mobility Centre 2004– (chm 2012–), chm Royal Cornwall Hosps NHS Tst 2005–07 (non-exec dir 2003–05), chm Cornwall Medi-Park Ltd 2005–09, dir NHS Innovations SW Ltd 2007– (chm 2012–); visiting prof: Univ of Plovdiv Bulgaria 1997–, Peninsula Med Sch 2004–13, Exeter Med Sch 2012–; ed: Med and Biological Engineering and Computing 1985–92, Med Engrg and Physics 1993–99; memb: Bd of Surgical Specialties RCS 1977–82, Admin Cncl Int Fedn for Med and Biological Engrg 1991–97; chm: Med Electronics Ctee IEE 1976–77, Br Design Awards Panel for Med Equipment Design Cncl 1979–81, Working Gp on Clinical Engrg Int Fedn for Med and Biological Engrg 1982–85, Health and Wellbeing Innovation Centre Truro 2011–; memb Future Economy Bd Cornwall LEP 2015–; Pres's Prize Biological Engrg Soc 1980, distinguished overseas lectr Instn of Engrs Aust 1987, Nightingale Prize Inst of Physics and Engrg in Med 1996, 25th Jubilee Medal Bulgarian Soc of Med Physics and Biomedical Engrg 1997, EU Leonardo da Vinci Award 2004; govr James Allen's Girls' Sch 1998–2004; hon memb: Instn of Biomedical Engrs of Aust 1987, Romanian Soc for Clinical Engrg 1991; Hon MD Med Univ of Plovdiv 1998; FRSM 1973, FIEE 1981, FInstP 1981, FSIAD 1981, fell Biological Engrg Soc 1993 (pres 1976–78), founder fell Inst of Physics and Engrg in Med 1995, fell Int Acad of Med and Biological Engrg 2002; *Books* Blood Flow Measurement (1972), Doulton Ink Wares (1993), Amputee Management (1995), Medical Radiation Physics (1995); numerous papers in the scientific and medical press; *Recreations* classical music, opera, my Stanley steam car; *Style—* Prof Colin Roberts; ✉ Lower Penair Barn, St Clement, Truro, Cornwall TR1 1TF (e-mail stburyan@netscape.net)

ROBERTS, Dr Dafydd Llewellyn Lloyd; s of Capt William Jones Roberts (d 1981), of Holyhead, Gwynedd, and Kate, *née* Griffiths (d 1991); *b* 6 January 1949; *Educ* Holyhead Comp Sch, Univ of London (MB BS); *m* Mary Josephine, da of Richard Joseph Farrell; 1 da (Catherine Mary Lloyd b 17 Sept 1977), 1 s (Daniel William Lloyd b 12 Dec 1984); *Career* jr hosp appointments Royal London Hosp, Harold Wood Hosp Essex, Chase Farm Hosp Middx and Univ Hosp of Wales Cardiff 1972–75, med offr and GP 1975, dermatology trg posts Univ Hosp of Wales and N Staffs Hosps 1976–81, consltdermatologist West Glamorgan Health Authy 1981, currently consltdermatologist Swansea NHS Tst, current chm UK Skin Cancer Working Pty; former: sec Med Staff Ctee Swansea Hosps, memb W Glamorgan District Med Ctee, memb Welsh Med Ctee, chm Welsh Sub-Ctee of Dermatology, chm Welsh Audit Gp (Dermatology); author of various pubns relating to clinical dermatology especially on malignant melanoma and skin cancers; memb: BMA, Br Assoc of Dermatologists (former hon treas); fell American Acad of Dermatology, FRSM, FRCP 1994 (MRCP 1975); *Style—* Dr Dafydd Roberts; ✉ 49 Higher Lane, Langland, Swansea SA3 4NT (☎ 01792 369919); Singleton Hospital, Sketty, Swansea SA22 8QA (☎ and fax 01792 285324)

ROBERTS, David John Marling; MC (1965); s of John Edmund Marling Roberts (d 1980), of Checkendon, Oxon, and Jean, *née* Wheelock (d 1988); *b* 6 February 1943; *Educ* Marlborough, RMA Sandhurst, Manchester Business Sch; *m* 16 Dec 1967, Nicola Chamberlin; 2 da (Kate (Mrs Harries), Harriet d 1996), 1 s (Mark); *Career* served Army (Green Jackets) 1961–71 (ret as Capt); W H Smith plc 1971–96: md Wholesale Div 1980–85, md Retail 1985–91 (Main Bd 1988), dep gp md 1991–94, gp md 1994–96; non-exec chm NAAFI 1996–2001 (dir 1993–2001); non-exec dir: NPI 1993–99 (dep chm 1998–99), Martin Currie Enhanced Income Tst plc 1999–2005; chm Tomorrow's Net Ltd 2000–; memb: Br Retailers' Assoc 1986–91, Exec Cncl Army Benevolent Fund 1988–2009; JP Berks 1978–87, High Sheriff Berks 2001–02; CIMgt; *Recreations* country activities, tennis, golf, restoring old houses; *Clubs* MCC; *Style—* David Roberts, Esq, MC; ✉ e-mail dmarlingrob@gmail.com

ROBERTS, Dennis Laurie Harold; s of William Harold Roberts, of Meopham, Kent, and Gwendoline Vera, *née* Edwards; *b* 24 January 1949; *Educ* Univ of Sheffield (BA, MSc); *m* 1980, Anne Mary, *née* Hillhouse; 1 s (Edward William b 31 Dec 1985); *Career* civil servant; CSO 1972–76, DOE 1976–83, MOD 1983–85; DOE: head Local Govt Fin Div 1985–89, head Water Environment Div 1989–92, head Fin Div 1992–94; dir of statistics Office of Population Censuses and Surveys 1994–96, gp dir Socio-Economic Statistics Office for Nat Statistics 1996–98, gp dir Fin and Corp Services Office for NAT Statistics 1998–2000, dir Roads and Traffic Directorate 2000–03, exec dir of registration and corporate servs Office for Nat Statistics 2004–08, dir of statistical sources Office for Nat Statistics 2008–; memb RSS 1975; *Recreations* walking, reading, watching football; *Style—* Dennis Roberts, Esq

ROBERTS, Dr Dewi Wyn; MBE (2011), DL (Gwynedd, 2009); s of Capt John Roberts (d 1964), of Caernarvonshire, and Janet, *née* Griffith (d 1947); *b* 6 March 1939, Edern, Caernarvonshire; *Educ* David Hughes GS Anglesey, Downing Coll Cambridge (MA, MB, BChir, Athletics blue), Westminster Hosp Univ of London; *m* 10 Aug 1962, Dr Sheila Mary, *née* Benson; 1 s (John Griffith), 1 da (Catrin Ann Griffith Macey); *Career* house surgn and house physician Addenbrooke Hosp Cambridge; family doctor Daventry 1966–96; dir and chm Community Justice Intevention Wales; memb Cncl Bangor Univ; High Sheriff Gwynedd 2007–08; former athlete (rep Wales), team mangr Oxford/Cambridge Athletics 1990–2005, chm Pwllheli Sports Club, fndr memb Daventry rugby, squash and athletics clubs, tstee Ffestiniog and Welsh Highland Railway; MRCS, LRCP; OStJ 2009; *Clubs* Hawks' (Cambridge), Achilles (pres), RSM; *Style—* Dr Dewi Roberts, MBE, DL; ✉ Derwen Deg, Hwfa Road, Bangor, Gwynedd LL57 2BN (☎ 01248 354415)

ROBERTS, Elizabeth Jane (Liz); da of Martin Gwylfa Roberts, of Timperly, Cheshire, and Hilda Elizabeth, *née* Gilbert; *b* 10 June 1960; *Educ* Sale GS for Girls, Univ of Sussex; *m* Oct 2009, Steven Buckley; 1 da (Eve b Nov 1992); *Career* editorial asst Phaidon Press 1982–83, sub ed then chief sub ed Building Magazine 1984–86; Media Week: broadcast reporter 1986–87, broadcast ed 1987–88, news ed 1988–89, dep ed 1989–90, ed 1990–92; freelance journalist 1993–96: The Guardian, Sunday Telegraph, Esquire, She; ed Nursery World 1997– (features ed 1996–97); tstee Daycare Tst 2007–10; FRSA 2007; *Recreations* music, walking, travel, food, literature, singing; *Style—* Ms Liz Roberts

ROBERTS, Ferdy; s of Paul Malcolm Buckle Roberts, and Elizabeth Wendy Coombs, *née* Lodge; *b* 11 September 1975, Bradford, W Yorks; *Educ* Bingley GS, Park Lane Coll Leeds, GSM (BA); *m* Poppy Miller; *Career* actor and theatre dir; fndr and co-artistic dir with Oliver Dimsdale, *qv*, Filter Theatre 2000–, artistic assoc Lyric Theatre Hammersmith 2009–; prodns incl: Faster (Battersea Arts Centre) 2001, Twelfth Night (Filter and RSC) 2006–10, Caucasian Circle (RNT), Water (Lyric Hammersmith) 2007, Wallenstein (Chichester Festival Theatre) 2009, Three Sister (Filter and Lyric Hammersmith) 2010; film work incl: Sex and Drugs and Rock and Roll, Mr Nice, Honest; Chichester Festival Theatre 2000; *Style—* Ferdy Roberts, Esq; ✉ c/o Eamonn Bedford, Macfarland and Chard, 33 Percy Street, London W1T 2DF (☎ 020 7636 7750, e-mail ferdy@filtertheatre.com, website www.filtertheatre.com)

ROBERTS, Sir Hugh Ashley; GCVO (2010, KCVO 2001, CVO 1998, LVO 1995); s of Rt Rev Dr Edward Roberts (d 2001), and Dorothy Frances, *née* Bowser (d 1982); *b* 20 April 1948; *Educ* Winchester, CCC Cambridge (MA); *m* 13 Dec 1975, Hon (Priscilla) Jane Stephanie Low (Hon Lady Roberts, DCVO, *qv*), er da of late 1 Baron Aldington, KCMG, CBE, DSO, TD, PC, DL; 2 da (Sophie b 1978, Amelia b 1982); *Career* Christie Manson & Woods Ltd 1970–87 (dir 1978–87); The Queen's Works of Art: dep surveyor 1988–96, dir The Royal Collection and surveyor 1996–2010, surveyor emeritus 2010–; FSA; *Books* For the King's Pleasure (2001), The Queen's Diamonds (2012); *Recreations* gardening; *Style—* Sir Hugh Roberts, GCVO, FSA; ✉ The Royal Collection, St James's Palace, London SW1A 1BQ (☎ 020 7930 4832)

ROBERTS, Humphrey Richard Medwyn; s of Hugh Medwyn Roberts (d 1961), of Southport, Lancs, and Enid Marjorie, *née* Pochin (d 1987); *b* 29 May 1931; *Educ* Leas Sch Hoylake, Aldenham, King's Coll Cambridge (MA), Westminster Med Sch (MB BChir, Bulkeley medal, Arthur Evans prize); *m* 21 March 1964, Pamela Ruth, da of Robert Barker; 2 da (Caroline Jane Medwyn b 1 Aug 1965, Katharine Lucy Medwyn b 29 June 1967), 1 s (James Hugh Medwyn b 28 June 1969); *Career* SHO Chelsea Hosp for Women 1963–64, res obstetrician Queen Charlotte's Hosp 1966–67, consltobstetrician and gynaecologist Queen Mary's Hosp Roehampton 1968–79; Westminster Hosp: house surgn 1957–58, res obstetric asst 1958, registrar in obstetrics and gynaecology 1964–66, consltobstetrician and gynaecologist 1968–91; hon consltgynaecologist: Hosp of St John and Elizabeth 1971–80, St Luke's Hosp for the Clergy 1986–96; examiner: obstetrics and gynaecology Univs of Cambridge and London, diploma and membership RCOG, Central Midwives Bd; memb: BMA 1957, Medical Def Union 1957, Hospital Conslt and Staff Assoc 1982,

R

Chelsea Clinical Soc 1979 (pres 1993–94, sr tstee 1995–2002); FRCS(Eng) 1961, FRCOG 1978 (MRCOG 1965); *Recreations* Sherlock Holmes, bird watching, gardening; *Style*— Humphrey Roberts, Esq; ✉ 64 Chartfield Avenue, London SW15 6HQ (☎ 020 8789 1758)

ROBERTS, Prof Ian Gareth; s of Idris Michael Roberts (d 1971), and Dorothy Sybil, *née* Moody (d 1997); *b* 23 October 1957, Stamford, Lincs; *Educ* Univ of Wales Bangor (BA), Univ of Southern Calif (PhD), Univ of Cambridge (DLitt); *m* 10 July 1993, Lucia, da of Luigi Cavalli; 1 s (Julian Maxwell b 11 June 1996), 1 da (Lydia Iona b 14 March 2001); *Career* asst de linguistique Anglaise Département de Langue et Littérature Anglaises Université de Genève 1985–86, maître-asst Département de Linguistique Générale Université de Genève 1986–91, prof and head of linguistics Univ of Wales Bangor 1991–96, prof and head of English linguistics Universität Stuttgart 1996–2000; Univ of Cambridge: prof of linguistics 2000–, head of linguistics 2000–05, professorial fell Downing Coll 2000–, chair Faculty of Modern and Medieval Languages 2011–15; jt ed Jl of Linguistics 1994–2000 (asst ed 1996–2000); Prix Latsis de l'Université de Genève 1989; hon doctorate Univ of Bucharest 2013; memb: Linguistic Soc of America 1982, Generative Linguistics in the Old World 1983, Linguistics Assoc of GB 1991, Fndn for Endangered Languages 1992, Philological Soc 2001, Academia Europaea 2008; hon memb Linguistic Soc of America 2016–; FBA 2007; *Books* The Representation of Implicit and Dethematized Subjects (1987), Viagem Diacrônica pelas Fases do Português Brasileiro: Homagem a Fernando Tarallo (jt ed, 1993), Verbs and Diachronic Syntax: A Comparative History of English and French (1993), Clause Structure and Language Change (jt ed, 1994), Comparative Syntax (1996), The Syntax of the Celtic Languages (jt ed, 1996), Beyond Principles and Parameters: Essays in Memory of Osvaldo Jaeggli (jt ed, 1999), Syntactic Change: A Minimalist Approach to Grammaticalisation (jtly, 2003), Principles and Parameters in a VSO Language: A Case Study in Welsh (2005), Diachronic Syntax (2007), Comparative Grammar (ed, 6 vols, 2007), Agreement, Clitics and Defective Goals (2010), Parametric Variation: Null Subjects in Minimalist Theory (jtly, 2010), Syntactic Variation: The Dialects of Italy (jt ed, 2010); *Recreations* novels, music, fine wine; *Style*— Prof Ian Roberts; ✉ 4 Chancellor's Walk, Cambridge CB4 3JG (☎ and fax 01223 356931, mobile 07585 602847); Department of Linguistics, University of Cambridge, Sidgwick Avenue, Cambridge CB3 9DA (☎ and fax 01223 335010, e-mail igr20@cam.ac.uk)

ROBERTS, Sir Ivor Anthony; KCMG; s of Leonard Moore Roberts (d 1981), and Rosa Maria, *née* Fusco (d 1999); *b* 24 September 1946; *Educ* St Mary's Coll Crosby, Keble Coll Oxford (Gomm scholar, MA); *m* 4 May 1974, Elizabeth Bray, da of Norman Douglas Bernard Smith; 2 s (Huw Benedict Bernard b 1976, David Daniel Rowland b 1979), 1 da (Hannah Rebecca Louise b 1982); *Career* HM Dip Serv: joined 1968, ME Centre for Arabic Studies 1969, third then second sec Paris 1970–73, second then first sec FCO 1973–78, first sec Canberra 1978–82, dep head News Dept FCO 1982–86, cnsllr FCO 1986–88, min Madrid 1989–93, ambass to Yugoslavia 1996–97 (chargé d'affaires 1994–96), seconded as sr assoc memb St Antony's Coll Oxford 1998–99, ambass to Repub of Ireland 1999–2003, ambass to Italy 2003–06 (concurrently non-resident ambass to San Marino); pres Trinity Coll Oxford 2006–; pres Univ of Oxford RFC 2014–; patron Venice in Peril Fund; chm Cncl of the Br Sch in Rome 2008–12; hon fell Keble Coll Oxford 2001; Freeman City of London 2009; FCIL 1991; *Publications* Satow's Diplomatic Practice (ed, 7 edn 2017), Razgovori s Miloevi?em (2012), The Black Hand and the Sarajevo Conspiracy (chapter in Balkan Legacies of the Great War: The Past is Never Dead, eds Othon Athanastakis, David Madden and Elizabeth Roberts, 2015), Conversations with Miloevi?: Diplomacy in the Time of War (2015); *Recreations* opera, skiing, golf; *Clubs* Oxford and Cambridge, Downhill Only (Wengen), Beefsteak; *Style*— Sir Ivor Roberts, KCMG; ✉ President's Lodgings, Trinity College, Oxford OX1 3BH (☎ 01865 279900, fax 01865 279874, e-mail ivor.roberts@trinity.ox.ac.uk)

ROBERTS, John Edward; CBE (2004); s of Arthur Roberts (d 1976), and Dora, *née* Watkin (d 1987); *b* 2 March 1946; *Educ* Oldershaw GS Wallasey, Univ of Liverpool (BEng), St Helens Mgmnt Coll (DMS); *m* 20 June 1970, Pamela, da of William Baxter; 1 s (Richard b 1980), 1 da (Gemma b 1982); *Career* Manweb: fin dir 1984–91, md 1991–92, chief exec 1992–95; chief exec: S Wales Electricity 1996–97, Hyder Utilities 1997–99, United Utilities 1999–2006; chm: Halite Energy Gp Ltd 2010–, BlackRock New Energy Investment Tst 2011–14, Impello plc 2013–, Electricity NW 2014–; non-exec dir: Royal Bank of Canada (Europe) Ltd 2005– (chm 2009–), International Power plc 2006–11; DL Merseyside 2006–12; fell Liverpool John Moores Univ 2004, Hon DEng Univ of Liverpool 2004; FACCA 1983, FIEE 1992, FREng 2002; *Recreations* scuba diving, watching cricket, listening to opera; *Clubs* Reform; *Style*— Dr John Roberts, CBE

ROBERTS, John Frederick; *b* 30 March 1946; *Educ* Bristol GS, Univ of Bristol (BDS), Eastman Dental Center Rochester NY (Cert Paedodontics); *m* Gabriele Elizabeth; 2 s (Alexander John b 14 Oct 1979, Sebastian Frederick b 24 March 1983); *Career* house offr Bristol Dental Hosp 1971, assoc in gen dental practice Bristol 1972–74, princ in gen dental practice Johannesburg 1974–76, sr ptnr private paediatric dental practice London, sr demonstrator Dept of Orthodontics and Dentistry for Children UMDS Guy's Hosp 1978–1998; recognised teacher status in paediatrics Univ of London Faculty of Med and Dentistry 1990–; numerous invited lectures and courses UK and abroad; memb: BDA, Br Soc of Paediatric Dentistry, American Acad of Paedodontics, American Soc of Dentistry for Children, American Dental Soc of London, American Bd of Paedodontics, Euro Acad of Paediatric Dentistry; Specialist in Paediatric Dentistry 1998; *Publications* Kennedy's Paediatric Dentistry (co-author); author of various articles in Br Dental Jl; *Style*— John Roberts, Esq; ✉ 74 Bois Lane, Amersham, Buckinghamshire HP6 6BX (☎ 01494 725685); 33 Weymouth Street, London W1G 7BY (☎ 020 7580 5370, fax 020 7636 3094, website www.paediatric-dentistry.co.uk)

ROBERTS, His Hon John Houghton; s of John Noel Roberts, and Ida, *née* Houghton; *b* 14 December 1947; *Educ* Calday Grange GS, Trinity Hall Cambridge (MA); *m* 1, 1972 (m dis 1990), Anna Elizabeth, da of Peter Tooke Sheppard, of Essex; 3 s (James b 1974, Edward b 1976, William b 1978); m 2, 20 April 1991, Mary, da of Frederic Wilkinson, of Merseyside; *Career* called to the Bar Middle Temple 1970; recorder of the Crown Court 1988–93, circuit judge (Northern Circuit) 1993–2013, resident judge Bolton Crown Court 1997–2001, circuit judge Liverpool Crown Court 2002–; *Recreations* golf, rugby football, music; *Clubs* Athenaeum (Liverpool), Heswall Golf; *Style*— His Hon John Roberts; ✉ Liverpool Crown Court, Queen Elizabeth II Law Courts, Derby Square, Liverpool

ROBERTS, Dr John Maxwell; *b* 4 April 1948; *Educ* Henbury Sch Bristol, Univ of Sheffield (BEng, PhD, Mappin Medal and Premium 1969, Br Iron and Steel Inst Prize 1969); *m* 1969, Angela, *née* Willis; 3 s (Ben Matthew b 1976, David Maxwell b 1979, Thomas Edmund b 1984); *Career* site engr Sir Alfred McAlpine & Sons Ltd 1972–74, engr and assoc Bertram Done & Partners 1974–81, dir Allott & Lomax (later Babtie Gp, now Jacobs) 1985– (engr 1981–85); projects incl: Battersea Power Station redevelopment, Pepsi Max Big One Rollercoaster, Br Airways London Eye wheel, Brighton i360 viewing tower; James Forrest Medal and Premium ICE 1971–72, Lancashire and Cheshire Branch Prize IStructE 1984–85 and 1988–89, Sir Arnold Water Medal IStructE 1984–85, Gold Medal IStructE 2005; FICE, FIStructE (pres 1999–2000), FREng 1995; *Recreations* walking, gardening; *Style*— Dr John Roberts, FREng; ✉ Jacobs, 5 First Street, Manchester M15 4GU (☎ 0161 235 6000, e-mail johnm.roberts@jacobs.com)

ROBERTS, Keith; s of Cliff Roberts, andn Averay, *née* Collins; *Educ* Carshalton HS for Boys, Camberwell Sch of Art, Newcastle upon Tyne Poly (BA), RCA (MA); *Career* artist; commissions incl: Tindall, Riley & Co 1993, Br Airports Authy 1994, Defence of Britain Project Imperial War Museum London 1997, Egon Zhender Mgmnt Conslts 1998, AMBAC 1999, Crown Estates 2000; work in collections: Unilever, AMBAC, Pearsons, Tindall-Riley; memb: Parachute Regt Assoc, Flamenco Housing Co-op (chair 1997–2001); *Selected Solo Exhibitions* New Academy Gallery London 1993, 1996 and 1998, Blue Gallery London 1997, New Paintings (Curwen Gallery London) 1999, Adore the City (SM Gallery London) 2000, Keith Roberts (Boycott Gallery Brussels) 2000, Boycott Gallery Brussels 2002; *Selected Group Exhibitions* NEAC Annual (Mall Galleries London) 1990, Northern Graduates (New Academy Gallery London) 1990, Salon der Debutanten Holland 1991, Art London '91 (Olympia London) 1991, Discerning Eye (Mall Galleries London) 1991 and 1992, Contemporaries I (Eagle Gallery London) 1993, The Bridge Show (Lannan Gallery NY) 1994, What Happened Next? (Lannan Gallery NY) 1994, The Whitechapel Open (Whitechapel Gallery London) 1994, Making Marks (Mall Gallery London) 1994, 7th Oriel Mostyn Open (Mostyn Art Gallery Llandudno), Art '95 (London), Bureau de Change (Rustin Fndn Antwerp) 1996, 9th Oriel Mostyn Open (Mostyn Art Gallery Llandudno) 1997, Changing London (Eagle Gallery London) 1998, Bankside Browser (Tate Modern London) 1999, Art '99 (London Contemporary Art Fair) 1999, Crosscurrents (Lloyds Insurance Building London) 1999, Cheltenham & Gloucester Drawing Open (UK and Berlin) 1999–2000, The Crown Estates Projects London 2000, Holy Cow! (Clapham Art Gallery London) 2000, The Hunting Prize London 2000, Doughty & Sons London 2001, Urban Rhythms (SM Gallery London) 2001, Adapt Now (Art Gallery and Museum Glasgow) 2002, Headline (SM Gallery London) 2002, In Your Time (Percy Miller Gallery London) 2002; *Awards* Br Alcan Prize 1989, Marks & Spencer Prize NEAC 1990, Richard Ford Awards 1990, prizewinner Discerning Eye Mall Galleries London 1991, Barcelona Travel Award 1991, Delfina Studios Tst Scholarship 1992, Oppenheim-John Downes Meml Tst 1995, Triangle Artists Workshop Scholarship 1997; *Recreations* cycling; *Clubs* Surrey Road Cycling; *Style*— Keith Roberts, Esq

ROBERTS, Prof Kenneth; s of Ernest William Roberts, and Nancy, *née* Williams; *b* 24 September 1940, Stockport, Gtr Manchester; *Educ* Stockport Sch, LSE (BSc, MSc); *m* 8 Aug 1964, Patricia, da of Frank Newton, of Macclesfield; 1 s (Gavin Paul b 19 Feb 1968), 2 da (Susan Alexis b 18 Dec 1970, Vanessa Jane (twin) b 19 Dec 1970); *Career* successively asst lectr, sr lectr, reader then prof Univ of Liverpool 1966–; memb: Br Sociological Assoc, Int Sociological Assoc, Euro Sociological Assoc, Leisure Studies Assoc, Inst of Career Guidance; hon memb Leisure Studies Assoc, hon fell Inst of Career Guidance, life memb World Leisure Organisation, sr fell American Leisure Acad, academician Acad of Social Sciences; *Books* Youth and Leisure (1983), The Changing Structure of Youth Labour Markets (1987), Leisure and Lifestyle (1989), Youth and Work (1991), Careers and Identities (1992), Youth and Employment in Modern Britain (1995), Poland's First Post-Communist Generation (1995), Leisure in Contemporary Society (1999, 2 edn 2006), Surviving Post-Communism (2000), Class in Modern Britain (2001), The Leisure Industries (2004), Key Concepts in Sociology (2008), Youth in Transition: In Eastern Europe and the West (2008), Sociology: An Introduction (2012), The Business of Leisure (2016), Social Theory, Sport, Leisure (2016); *Recreations* football, Frank Sinatra; *Style*— Prof Kenneth Roberts; ✉ 2 County Road, Ormskirk, Lancashire L39 1QQ (☎ 01695 574962); School of Sociology and Social Policy, University of Liverpool, Eleanor Rathbone Building, Bedford Street South, Liverpool L69 7ZA (☎ 0151 794 2971, fax 0151 794 3001, e-mail k.roberts@liverpool.ac.uk)

ROBERTS, Lisa; QC (2015); da of Dr Geraint Roberts, and Mrs Shirley Roberts; *b* 2 February 1969, Manchester; *Educ* St Catherine's Coll Oxford (BA), Huddersfield Univ (CPE), Inns of Court Sch of Law; *m* 25 June 1994, Jonathan Bourne; 1 da (Emily Constance b 22 Jan 2000), 1 s (Daniel George William b 12 May 2002); *Career* called to the Bar 1993; memb: Criminal Bar Assoc, Health and Safety Lawyers Assoc, Northern Circuit; *Recreations* music, tennis, travel, MUFC; *Style*— Miss Lisa Roberts, QC; ✉ Lincoln House Chambers, 8th Floor, Tower 12, 18–22 Bridge Street, Spinningfields, Manchester M3 3BZ (☎ 0161 8325701, e-mail lisa.roberts@lincolnhousechambers.com)

ROBERTS, Malcolm John Binyon; s of Sqdn Ldr Kenneth Arthur Norman Roberts (d 1973), and Greta Kathleen, *née* Cooper (d 2010); *b* 3 July 1951, Nottingham; *Educ* St Edmund's Sch Canterbury; *m* 1, 28 April 1984 (m dis 2012), Caroline Mary, da of John Harry Scrutton; 2 s (Frederick, Charles), 1 da (Iona); m 2, 19 Sept 2015, Kate Murphy; *Career* ptnr Montagu Loebl Stanley 1979–86, dir Fleming Private Asset Management 1986–2000, JP Morgan Private Bank 2000–02, dir Rothschild Private Management 2002–12 (md 2007–12), md Kleinwort Benson Wealth Mgmnt 2012–; memb Stock Exchange Examination Ctee (Taxation) 1985–87; tstee Granville Sch Sevenoaks 1986–2009, special tstee Moorfields Eye Hosp 1996–2010 (chm 2005–10), memb Ctee Art for Youth 2003–09, tstee Household Cavalry Museum Tst 2007–, memb Cncl Assoc of NHS Charities 2009–10, govr Voluntary Hosp of St Bartholomew 2011–, memb Investment Ctee RSM 2012–, tstee Univ of London 2015–; Liveryman Worshipful Co of Barbers (memb Ct of Assts 2012); FCSI 2000 (memb Stock Exchange 1978), FRSA 2006; *Recreations* tennis, planting trees, game shooting; *Clubs* City; *Style*— Malcolm Roberts, Esq; ✉ 14 St George Street, London W1S 1FE

ROBERTS, Martin Charles; s of Denis Walter Wakem Roberts (d 1988), of Epsom, Surrey, and Joan Mary, *née* Saunders; *b* 11 April 1955; *Educ* City of London Freemen's Sch, Univ of Kingston upon Thames (BA), Guildford Law Sch; *m* 3 Sept 1988, Jane Rosalind, da of John Henderson; 1 s (James William b 27 Sept 1992), 1 da (Georgina Rosalind b 5 Sept 1994); *Career* Pinsent Masons: articled clerk 1977–79, asst slr 1979–83, ptnr 1983–, memb Partnership Bd 1992–98, dep head Construction and Engrg Law Dept 1994–97, head of Power and Energy Sector 1997–2000, managing ptnr Construction and Engrg Sector 2000–03, head London office 2004–; CEDR accredited mediator 1997; memb CBI London Rgnl Cncl 2012–, memb CBI Construction Cncl 2012–; Freeman City of London 1975, Liveryman City of London Slrs' Co 1985 (memb Ct 1999–, steward 2004–07, sr warden 2011–12, Master 2012–13); memb: Law Soc 1977, City of London Law Soc 1985 (memb Ctee 1997–, memb Ctee Litigation Sub Ctee 1991–2003, pres 2012–13); *Recreations* tennis, swimming, music, theatre, cinema; *Clubs* RAC; *Style*— Martin Roberts, Esq; ✉ Pinsent Masons, 30 Crown Place, London EC2A 4ES (☎ 020 7490 4000, fax 020 7490 2545, e-mail martin.roberts@pinsentmasons.com)

ROBERTS, Michael Andrew; s of Michael Francis Roberts, and Georgina Sara Olmos Adriazola; *b* 14 May 1966; *Educ* Prior Park Coll Bath, St Benet's Hall Oxford (BA); *m* 1, Michelle Cora Farrell (d 2008); m 2, 6 Oct 2012, Emma Kate, *née* Wild; 1 da, 1 s; *Career* Decision Makers Ltd 1989–91, CBI 1991–2008 (dir 2000–08), chief exec Assoc of Train Operating Cos 2008–, DG Rail Delivery Gp 2013–; non-exec dir The Carbon Tst 2001–08; memb: Standing Advsy Ctee on Trunk Road Assessment 1996–99, Dep PM's Panel on Transport White Paper 1997–98, Cmmn for Integrated Transport 2000–08; memb: Green Alliance, National Tst; *Recreations* football, running (London marathon 1999, 2001 and 2003), skiing, cinema, music; *Clubs* Molesey Boat; *Style*— Michael Roberts, Esq; ✉ ATOC/RDG, 2nd Floor, 200 Aldersgate Street, London EC1A 4HD(☎ 020 7841 8001)

ROBERTS, Michael Symmons; s of David Symmons Roberts, and Iris, *née* Corcoran; *b* 13 October 1963, Preston, Lancs; *Educ* St Bartholomew's HS Newbury, Univ of Oxford; *m* 1992, Ruth Humphreys; 3 s (Joseph, Patrick, Griffith); *Career* poet and dramatist; prodr and dir of numerous documentaries for radio and TV; prof of poetry Manchester Met Univ; Gregory Award for Br poets under 30 Soc of Authors 1988, Whitbread Poetry Award (for Corpus) 2004, Forward Prize for Poetry 2013, Costa Poetry Award 2013; shortlisted: T S Eliot Prize 2004, Forward Prize for Best Poetry Collection 2004, Griffin Int Poetry Prize 2005; fell English Assoc (FEA), FRSL 2014; *Radio* The Real Thing (BBC

Radio 3, Sony Award), A Damn Good Lie (BBC Radio 1, Sandford St Martin Award), Anno Domini (BBC Radio 2) 1999, A Fearful Symmetry (BBC Radio 4 and World Serv) 2000 (Sandford St Martin Premier Award), Behold the Man (BBC Radio 2) 2000, Brimstone (BBC Radio 4) 2000, The Wounds (BBC Radio 4) 2001, The Hurricane (BBC Radio 4) 2002, A Higher Place (BBC Radio 4) 2002, Last Words (BBC Radio 4) 2002, Soldiers in the Sun (BBC Radio 3) 2007 (winner Clarion Award, shortlisted Mental Health Award), Elegy (BBC Radio 3) 2008, Breath (BBC Radio 4) 2008, Worktown (BBC Radio 4) 2008; *Libretti* in collaboration with James MacMillan: Raising Sparks (song cycle, Royal Festival Hall and BBC Radio 3) 1997, Quickening (choral oratorio, Royal Albert Hall and BBC Radio 3) 1999, Parthenogenesis (chamber opera, Edinburgh Festival and BBC Radio 3) 2000, The Birds of Rhiannon (choral, Royal Albert Hall) 2001, The Sacrifice (opera) 2003 (RPS Award 2008), Zaide (re-translation and completion unfinished libretto for Mozart opera) 2003, Clemency (co-commissioned by ROH, Scottish Opera and Boston Symphony Opera) 2011; The Sleeper (opera with music by Stephen Deazley, commissioned by Welsh Nat Opera) 2011; *Poetry* Soft Keys (1993), Raising Sparks (1999), Burning Babylon (2001, shortlisted T S Eliot Prize), Corpus (2004, Whitbread Poetry Award; shortlisted: Griffin Int Poetry Prize, Forward Prize, T S Eliot Prize), The Half Healed (2008), Drysalter (2013, winner Forward Poetry Prize 2013, winner Costa Poetry Award 2013, shortlisted T S Eliot Prize), Selected Poems (2016); poems published in numerous jls and newspapers incl: The Observer, The Guardian, TLS, London Review of Books, The Independent, London Magazine; *Fiction* Patrick's Alphabet (2006), Breath (2008); *Non-Fiction* Edgelands (jtly, 2011, winner 2011 Jerwood Award, winner 2012 Foyles Book of Ideas Award, shortlisted Ondaatje Prize); *Recreations* playing and watching football with my sons; *Style—* Michael Symmons Roberts, Esq; ✉ c/o Anna Webber, United Agents, 12–26 Lexington Street, London W1F 0LE (☎ 020 3214 0876, website www.symmonsroberts.com, @symmonsroberts)

ROBERTS, Michèle Brigitte; da of Reginald George Roberts, of Felton, nr Bristol, and Monique Pauline Joseph, *née* Caulle; *b* 20 May 1949; *Educ* St Mary's Abbey London, St Michael's Convent London, Univ of Oxford (MA), UCL (ALA); *Career* author and poet; formerly: p/t journalist, p/t teacher, pregnancy tester, cnsllr, res asst, book reviewer; librarian British Council Bangkok (responsible for S Vietnam and Cambodia) 1972–73; poetry ed: Spare Rib 1974–76, City Limits 1981–83; writer in residence Univ of Essex 1987–88, writer in residence UEA 1992, visiting prof Nottingham Trent Univ 1996– (visiting fell 1995–96), prof of creative writing UEA 2001–06 (emeritus prof 2007–); various Arts Council fellowships; involved in Int Women's Liberation Movement 1970–; Gay News Literary Award 1978, Arts Council Grant 1978, W H Smith Literary Award 1993; FRSL; Chevalier de l'Ordre des Arts et des Lettres (France); *Novels* A Piece of the Night (1978), The Visitation (1983), The Wild Girl (1984), The Book of Mrs Noah (1987), In The Red Kitchen (1990), Daughters of the House (1992, shortlisted Booker Prize 1992, W H Smith Literary Award 1993), Flesh and Blood (1994), Impossible Saints (1997), Fair Exchange (1999), The Looking-Glass (2000), The Mistressclass (2002), Reader, I Married Him (2005), Ignorance (2012); *Poetry* The Mirror of the Mother (1986), Psyche And the Hurricane (1991), All the Selves I Was (1995); *Short stories* During Mother's Absence (1993), Playing Sardines (2001); *Other works* Paper Houses (memoir), Food, Sex and God (essays, 1988), contrib numerous stories and essays to anthologies, co-author numerous books of poetry and short stories, première of play The Journeywoman Colchester 1988, film script The Heavenly Twins (French TV and Channel 4); *Recreations* food, sex, foreign travel, gardening, reading; *Style—* Ms Michèle Roberts; ✉ c/o Aitken Alexander Associates, 18–21 Cavaye Place, London SW10 9PT (☎ 020 7373 8672, website www.aitkenalexander.co.uk); website www.micheleroberts.co.uk

ROBERTS, (David) Paul; OBE (2008); s of Percival Roberts (d 2011), and Nancy, *née* Samuel (d 1991); *b* 6 September 1947, Epsom; *Educ* Univ of Bristol (BSc, CertEd), Cambridge Inst of Educn (Dip); *m* 1969, Helen Margaret, *née* Shone; 2 da (Clare b 1973, Alison b 1975); *Career* teacher Ipswich Sch 1970–74, head of mathematics then dep head Harlington Upper Sch 1974–83; Notts CC: gen inspr then sr div inspr 1983–88, princ educn offr then sr asst dir 1989–92, princ inspr then dep dir of educn 1992–97; dir of educn Nottingham City Cncl 1997–2001; Capita Strategic Educn Servs: dir of educn Haringey Cncl 2001–03, dir 2003–04; Improvement and Devpt Agency: strategic advsr educn and children's servs 2004–05, dir strategy info and devpt 2005–09, md 2009–10; advsr on creativity in schools to Secs of State DCMS and DfES 2005–10, memb Creature and Culture Educe Bd DSCF and DCMS 2007–08; chair of tstees Creativity, Culture and Educn 2008–; cmmr Warwick Cmmn on the Future of Cultural Value 2014– (cmmr 2013–); NESTA: memb Fellowship Prog Ctee 2003–06, memb Innovation Ctee 2006–09, memb Bd Public Services Innovation Lab 2009; memb Editorial Panel Action Research Jl 1991–2002; memb Bd Guideline Careers Ltd 1997–2001, memb Bd Nottingham Playhouse 1997–2001; chair of Bd Nottingham Music Educ Hub 2014–; vice-chm Mountview Acad of Theatre Arts, vice-chm Nottingham Contemporary Art Gallery 2010–; memb Bd of Dirs: Greenwood Acads Tst 2010–14, Innovation Unit 2010– (chair 2014–); memb: Assoc of Chief Insprs and Advsrs 1992–97, Assoc of Chief Educn Offrs 1997–2003; FRSA 1999; *Publications* Nurturing Creativity in Young People (2006), Organisational Innovation in the Public Sector (2013), The Virtuous Circle – Why Creativity and Cultural Education Count (2014); reviews and articles in local govt, educn and mathematical jls 1978–; *Recreations* arts, hill walking; *Style—* Paul Roberts, Esq, OBE; ✉ 55 Dunster Road, West Bridgford, Nottingham NG2 6JE (☎ 07799 408229, email paulroberts9994@gmail.com)

ROBERTS, Peter David Thatcher; s of Leonard Charles Roberts (d 1978); *b* 1 March 1934; *Educ* Alleyn's Sch Dulwich, King Edward VII Nautical Coll; *m* 1959, Elizabeth June, da of Dr W A Dodds, of Johannesburg, South Africa; 2 da (Susannah b 1964, Angela b 1965), 1 s (James b 1969); *Career* MN 1951–59, Lt RNR; Leinster/Hispania Maritime Ltd: joined 1960, dir 1963, md 1965; Hays plc: joined 1969, dir 1983–93; former dir Shipowners P & I Assoc Ltd (chm 1993–97); Master Co of Watermen and Lightermen of the River Thames 1993–94, emeritus memb Ct of Assts Worshipful Co of Shipwrights; assoc Hon Co of Master Mariners; MICS 1962; *Recreations* offshore sailing, golf; *Clubs* Royal Ocean Racing, Wildernesse (capt 2000); *Style—* Peter Roberts, Esq; ✉ Callenders Cottage, Bidborough, Tunbridge Wells, Kent TN3 0XJ (☎ 01892 529053)

ROBERTS, Peter John; s of Reginald Sidney Roberts (d 1992), of Horsham, W Sussex, and Evelyn Isobel, *née* Turner (d 1998); *b* 27 November 1938; *Educ* St Dunstan's Coll, Trinity Coll Cambridge (MA); *m* 1, 9 July 1960, Ann Belinda Le Grys (d 1990), da of Albert Kenneth Rice (d 1969); 2 da (Rachel b 1961, Hannah b 1966), 2 s (Simon b 1963, Ben b 1965); m 2, 19 July 1991, Anne Veronica, da of Patrick Joseph Dillon (d 2000); *Career* C & J Clark Ltd 1960–93: md Neptune Shoes Ltd 1972–80, head of corp planning Clarks Shoes 1980–85, mktg and prodn servs dir Clarks Shoes 1985–86, md Torlink Ltd 1987–93, franchise dir C & J Clark Int 1992–93; chief exec DGAA Homelife (formerly Distressed Gentlefolks' Aid Assoc) 1993–98, chm and md Nutmeg UK Ltd 2000–, non-exec dir Somerset Partnership NHS & Social Care Tst 1999–2004 (vice-chair 2003–04); chm Somerset Relate Marriage Guidance 1979–82 and 1987–90, hon treas Mediation-UK 2002–03, memb Nat Cncl RELATE 1979–90, tstee Bishop Simeon Tst for Educn & Welfare of South African Students 1990–2003, chm VOICES (vol sector umbrella gp of charities in care of elderly) 1996–99, interim dir Nat Heart Forum 1999, govr Chartfield Delicate Sch 1997–2002, dir New Futures Project WRVS 2002–03; chm of govrs: Crispin Sch 1978–89, Strode Coll 1989–93; *Recreations* gardening, travel, music, skiing, bridge; *Clubs* Reform; *Style—* Peter Roberts, Esq; ✉ Nutmeg UK Ltd, 2 Queen Caroline Street, London W6 9DX (☎ 020 8323 8001, e-mail peter.roberts@nutmeg-uk.com)

ROBERTS, Peter John Martin; s of Alfred John Victor Roberts, and Pamela, *née* Dodd; *b* 31 May 1963; *Educ* Tiffin Boys' Sch Kingston-Upon-Thames, Merton Coll Oxford (MA), Inst of Educn London (PGCE); *m* 1990, Marie, *née* Toudic; 3 da (Camille b 1991, Sophie b 1993, Juliette b 1994); *Career* Winchester Coll: asst master 1986–90, head of history 1990–97, master in coll 1991–2003; headmaster Bradfield Coll 2003–11, headmaster King's Sch Canterbury 2011–; tstee: Folkestone Acad 2011–, Cumnor House Sch, Northbourne Park Sch; *Recreations* bookbinding, calligraphy, sailing; *Style—* Peter Roberts, Esq

ROBERTS, Prof Richard Henry; né Vodvarka; s of Ing Jindrich Vodvarka, and Beatrice Joan Redfern Roberts; *b* 6 March 1946, Manchester; *Educ* William Hulme's GS Manchester, Lancaster Univ (BA), Univ of Cambridge (MA, BD), Univ of Edinburgh (PhD), London Coll of Music (Dip); *m* 7 Sept 1968, Audrey, *née* Butterfield (d 2010); 1 s (Anthony James b 10 Aug 1982); *Career* temp lectr in theology and religious studies Univ of Leeds 1975–76, lectr in systematic theology Univ of Durham 1976–89 , Maurice B Reckitt res fell Dept of Religious Studies Lancaster Univ 1988–91, prof of divinity Univ of St Andrews 1991–95, prof of religious studies Lancaster Univ 1995–2003 (now emeritus); visiting emeritus prof Univ of Stirling; founding dir: Centre for the History of the Human Sciences Univ of Durham 1988–91, Inst for Religion and the Human Scis Univ of St Andrews 1991–95; sr hon res fell Dept of Religious Studies Lancaster Univ 1994–95; memb Sociology of Religion Advsy Bd Int Theological Jl Concilium 1992–; founding memb Scientific Ctee Assoc for Rhetoric and Communication in South Africa; rapporteur res projects in sociology of religion ESRC 1993–; memb Editorial Bd: Literature and Theology 1988–, Jl of Contemporary Religion 1994–: memb: Soc for the Study of Theology 1975–, Centre for the History of the Human Scis Univ of Durham 1985–, Br/Int Comparative Literature Assoc 1987–, Int Sociological Assoc 1995– (pres Research Ctee 22 1998); fell Centre for Human Ecology Edinburgh 2003; *Books* Hope and its Hieroglyph: a critical decipherment of Ernst Bloch's' Principle of Hope' (1990), A Theology on Its Way: Essays on Karl Barth (1992), The Recovery of Rhetoric: persuasive discourse and disciplinarity in the human sciences (co-ed with J M M Good, 1993), Religion and the Transformations of Capitalism: Comparative Approaches (1995), Nature Religion Today: Paganism in the Modern World (co-ed with Jo Pearson and Geoffrey Samuel (1998), Time and Value (co-ed with Scott Lash and Andrew Quick, 1998), Religion, Theology and the Human Sciences (2001); current research religion and theory, ritual, music and altered states of consciousness; *Recreations* ashtanga yoga, hill walking, music, singing; *Style—* Prof Richard H Roberts

ROBERTS, Dr Sir Richard John; kt (2008); s of John Walter, and Edna Wilhelmina, Roberts, of Saltford, Bristol; *b* 6 September 1943, Derby; *Educ* City of Bath Boys' Sch, Univ of Sheffield (BSc, PhD); *m* 1, 1965, Elizabeth, *née* Dyson; 1 da (Alison Elizabeth b 11 April 1967), 1 s ((Richard) Andrew b 30 Oct 1968); m 2, 1986, Jean Elizabeth Tagliabue; 1 s (Christopher John b 25 Jan 1987), 1 da (Amanda Rae b 10 Aug 1989); *Career* res assoc in biochemistry Harvard Univ 1971–72 (res fell 1969–70), asst dir for res Cold Spring Harbor Lab 1986–92 (sr staff investigator 1972–86); New England Biolabs: res dir 1992–2005, chief scientific offr 2005–, conslt and chm Scientific Advsy Bd 1974–92; chm Nat Advsy Ctee BIONET 1987–90 (memb 1984–86), sr exec ed Nucleic Acids Res 1987–2009; chm Bd of Scientific Counsellors Nat Center for Biotechnology Information (NCBI) 1996–2000, chm Steering Ctee on Genetics and Biotechnology ICSU 1998–2001, chm bd Univ of Sheffield in America 2003–, advsr to dir NASA Astrobiology Prog 2000–, scientific advsr to CIAR Evolutionary Biology 2002–04, pres Bd of Tstees Ocean Genome Legacy 2004–; memb: Scientific Advsy Bd Genex Corp 1977–85, Editorial Bd Nucleic Acids Research 1977–87, Editorial Bd Jl of Biological Chemistry 1979–84, Nat Advsy Ctee GENBANK 1982–89, panel NIH Study Section in Biochemistry 1985–88, Editorial Bd CABIOS (Computer Applications in the Biosciences) 1985–2002, panel NCI Cancer Centers Support Grant Review Ctee 1990–92, panel NLM Study Section 1993–95, Editorial Bd Current Opinion in Chemical Biology 1997–2001, Bd Albert Schweitzer Acad of Med 1998– (vice-pres 2003–), Scientific Cncl Advsy Ctee Inst of Molecular Biology and Biotechnology (IMBB) 2002–06, President's Cncl NY Acad of Sciences 2010–, Advsy Bd Nat Park System 2011–13, Advsy Bd JGI Microbial Genomics and Metagenomics 2011–, Cncl STS Forum 2011–, Scientific Advsy Bd Empiriko Corporation 2013–, Scientific Advsy Bd Elysium Health 2015–, Scientific Advsy Bd Int Centre for Genetic Engineering and Biotechnology (ICGEB) 2016–; chm Scientific Advsy Bd Celera Corp 1998–2002, chm Sci Advsy Bd Lynkeus Biotech 1998–2004, Sci Advsy Bd CFG SUNY 2002–; memb Sci Advsy Bd: Molecular Tool 1994–2000, Oxford Molecular Gp 1996–99, Conservation Law Fndn 1998–, PubMed Central 2000–03, Orchid Biosciences 2000–03, Diversa Corp 2003–05, PubChem 2004–, RainDance Technologies 2004–, ICGEB 2005–, InVivo Therapeutics 2007– (dir 2009–), Orwik 2009–; vice-chm Int Sci Advsy Bd JDW Inst of Genome Sciences Hangzhou China 2003–; visiting prof Univ of Bath 1996–98, hon prof 4th Mil Med Univ Xian 2002–, hon prof Dalian Inst of Chemical Physics 2002–, distinguished scientist and research scholar Boston Univ 2003–, hon prof Chinese Univ Hong Kong 2006– (Wei Lun visiting prof 1996), hon prof Nankai Univ China 2006–; advsr to the city of Yixing China 2012–13, hon citizen Yixing 2012, hon pres Richard J Roberts Inst of Biotech Yixing 2012–, hon prof Astana Med Univ Kazakhstan 2012–, distinguished prof Northeastern Univ 2013–; vice-pres Albert Schweitzer Acad of Med 2003–; memb: American Soc for Microbiology; patron Oxford Int Biomedical Center 1994–, tstee Gaddafi Int Charity and Devpt Fndn 2009–11; hon memb Int Raoul Wallenberg Fndn 2003; memb Bd Friends of the Nat Library of Medicine 2006–12, memb NRF Singapore Int Eval Panel 2007–; corresponding memb Nicaraguan Acad of Sciences 2009–, hon memb NY Acad of Sciences 2015; assoc memb EMBO 1995, fell Science Museum London 2009; John Simon Guggenheim fell 1979–80, ASM Fndn lectr 1988–89, Miller prof Univ of Calif Berkeley 1991, Nobel Prize for Physiology or Med 1993, Bourke lectr Boston Univ 1994, Dakin lectr Adelphi Univ 1994, Convocation Award Univ of Sheffield 1994, Golden Plate Award American Acad of Achievement 1994, Ada Doisy lectr Univ Illinois Urbana 1996, foreign fell Nat Acad Med Sci Pakistan 1996, Faye Robiner Award Ross Univ 1994, William Ferdinand lectr Purdue Univ 1997, Steinberg/Wylie lectr Univ of Maryland 1997, Knudson lectr Oregon State Univ 1997, Procter & Gamble Distinguished Lectr Purdue Univ 1997, Medicus Magnus of the Polish Acad of Med 1998, Robert Church lectr on biotechnology Univ of Calgary 1998, Albert Einstein meml lectr Princeton Univ 2000, Sutton Lecture Univ of Kansas Med Center 2002, Barry Berkowitz lect Northeastern Univ 2003, Robert Harris lectr MIT 2004, Dan Nathans lectr Johns Hopkins Univ 2006, Gabor Medal Royal Soc 2007, Lester O Krampitz lectr Case Western Reserve Univ 2009, TIE Boston Legends and Leaders Award 2011, Hans Krebs Medal FEBS 2013, TT Tchen Meml Lecture Wayne State Univ 2014, George H Boyd Distinguished Lecture Univ of Georgia 2016; Hon MD: Univ of Uppsala 1992, Univ of Bath 1994; Hon DSc: Univ of Sheffield 1994, Univ of Derby 1995, Chinese Univ Hong Kong 2005; hon Dr Univ of Athens 2009, Hon Dr Universidad Andres Bello Chile 20214; FRS 1995, fell American Acad of Microbiology 1997, FAAAS 1997, fell American Assoc for Cancer Research (AACR) Acad 2013; *Recreations* croquet; *Style—* Dr Sir Richard Roberts; ✉ New England Biolabs, 240 County Road, Ipswich, MA 01938, USA (☎ 00 1 978 380 7405, fax 00 1 978 412 9910, e-mail roberts@neb.com)

ROBERTS, Prof Ronald John; s of Ronald George Roberts, and Marjorie, *née* Kneale; *b* 28 March 1941; *Educ* The GS Campbeltown, Univ of Glasgow (BVMS, PhD); 17 July 1964, Helen, *née* Macgregor; 2 s (Ronald b 10 July 1967, Calum b 14 March 1969); *Career* lectr

R

in veterinary pathology Univ of Glasgow 1966–71 (asst in microbiology 1964–66); Univ of Stirling: sr lectr in biology and dir Aquatic Pathobiology Unit 1972–76, reader in aquatic pathobiology 1976–79, prof and dir Inst of Aquaculture 1979–96, emeritus prof 1996–; Hagerman distinguished visiting prof Univ of Idaho 1996–2016, adjunct prof Univ of Malaysia 2009–16, adjunct prof Washington State Univ Pullman 2010–16; advsr on fish pathology: Miny of Overseas Devpt UK 1973–99, FAO 1974–88; dir: Bradan Ltd, Heron Associates, Heron Pisces Ltd; chm Campbeltown and Kintyre Enterprise 1996–2006; sec Lady Linda McCartney Meml Tst 2001–; dep chm European Food Safety Authy Veterinary Panel 2003–09; memb: Animals Ctee AFRC 1989–92, Fisheries Strategy Advsy Ctee ODA 1989–96, Scientific Advsy Ctee Cabinet Office 1994–95; scientific advsr Lithgow Gp plc 1996–2011, Res Grants Ctee Scottish Higher Educn Funding Cncl 2001–10; chm Argyll and Bute Countryside Tst 1996–2006; ed: Jl of Fish Diseases 1977–2015, Aquaculture Research 1985–2000; Buckland Gold Medal 1985, Crookes Veterinary Award for res BVA 1989, Dalrymple-Champneys Cup and Medal 1990; cdr Most Noble Order of the Crown (Thailand) 1992; FRSE 1978 (memb Cncl 1980–83), FIBiol 1980, FRCPath 1985 (MRCPath 1974), FRCVS 1991 (MRCVS 1964); *Books* Fish Pathology (1978, 4 edn, 2012); author of numerous scientific papers; *Style*— Prof Ronald J Roberts, FRSE; ✉ Carrick Point, Ardnacross, Campbeltown, Argyll PA28 6QR

ROBERTS, Stephen Cheveley; s of Dr David Cheveley Roberts (d 1993), of Mill Hill, London, and Elizabeth, *née* Thornborough (d 1990); *b* 23 August 1956; *Educ* Mill Hill Sch, Univ Coll Oxford (MA, PGCE); *m* March 1985, Joanna Meryl, da of John Andrew Cunnison; 2 s (Matthew Timothy b 6 March 1986, Douglas Mark b 27 Sept 1987); *Career* credit analyst Orion Bank 1980–81, asst master Christ's Hosp Sch Horsham 1981–85, head of physics and housemaster Oundle Sch 1985–93, headmaster Felsted Sch 1993–2008, princ Stamford Endowed Schs 2008–16; memb: HMC 1993–2016, Secdy Heads Assoc 1993–2016; *Recreations* golf, walking, reading; *Clubs* Vincent's (Oxford), East India; *Style*— Stephen Roberts, Esq; ✉ The Forge, 2 London Road, Wansford PE8 6JB

ROBERTS, Stephen Pritchard; s of Edward Henry Roberts (d 1987), and Violet, *née* Pritchard (d 1998); *b* 8 February 1949; *Educ* Royal Coll of Music (ARCM 1969, GRSM 1971); *Career* professional singer (concert, oratorio and opera), baritone; memb Vocal Faculty Royal Coll of Music; regular performances Europe, tours to Far East, USA, Canada, S America, BBC recordings for radio and TV (Prom appearances); commercial recordings incl: St Matthew Passion, Carmina Burana, Sea Symphony, Elgar's The Apostles, Penderecki's St Luke Passion, Canterbury Pilgrims, Serenade to Music; opera repertoire incl: Marriage of Figaro and Die Fledermaus (Opera North), Gluck's Armide, Ravel's L'Heure Espagnole; opera recordings incl: Tippett's King Priam, Birtwistle's Punch and Judy; *Style*— Stephen Roberts, Esq; ✉ 144 Gleneagle Road, London SW16 6BA (☎ and fax 020 8516 8830, e-mail srobertsbaritone@aol.com, website www.stephenroberts.uk.com)

ROBERTS OF LLANDUDNO, Baron (Life Peer UK 2004), of Llandudno in the County of Gwynedd; Rev John Roger Roberts; s of late Thomas C Roberts; *b* 23 October 1935; *Educ* John Bright GS Llandudno, UCNW Bangor, Handsworth Methodist Coll Birmingham; *m* 1962, Eirlys Ann (d 1995); 1 s (Hon Gareth), 2 da (Hon Rhian, Hon Sian); *Career* ordained Methodist min 1962; supt min Llandudno 1982–2002, min Toronto 2003–04; memb Aberconway BC 1976–87, Parly candidate Conwy 1979, 1983, 1987, 1992 and 1997; pres Welsh Lib Dems 1990–96, memb European Lib, Democratic and Reform Pty (ELDR), ldr Welsh European list ELDR 1999; chair: Aberconwy Talking Newspaper, Welsh Water Lifeline; tstee Fund for Human Need; radio and TV broadcaster (Welsh and English); *Style*— The Rt Hon the Lord Roberts of Llandudno

ROBERTSON, Andrew James; QC (1996); s of Pearson Robertson (d 1958), and Zillah Robertson (d 1991); *b* 14 May 1953; *Educ* Bradford GS, Christ's Coll Cambridge (scholar, MA); *m* 1981 Gillian Amanda; 1 da (Rebecca Francesca b 1984), 2 s (Hamish Alexander b 1985, Joshua Edward Adam b 1994); *Career* called to the Bar Middle Temple 1975; currently head of chambers KBW; memb Criminal Bar Assoc; *Recreations* climbing, bloodstock; *Style*— Andrew Robertson, Esq, QC; ✉ KBW, The Engine House, 1 Foundry Square, Leeds LS11 5DL (☎ 0113 297 1200, fax 0113 297 1201, e-mail clerks@kbwchambers.com)

ROBERTSON, Andrew John; s of John Hector Robertson, and Jennifer Mary, *née* Cullen; *b* 17 November 1960; *Educ* Michaelhouse Balgowan Natal, City of London Poly, City Univ (BSc); *m* 13 Feb 1987, Susan Louise, da of Michael John Bayliss; 2 da (Amy Louise b 13 Aug 1988, Louisa Jane b 25 July 1991); *Career* Ogilvy & Mather: trainee media planner 1982, account dir 1986, memb Bd of Dirs 1987, mgmnt supervisor and new business dir 1988–89; gp dir J Walter Thompson Co 1989, chief exec WCRS 1990–95, md Abbott Mead Vickers BBDO Ltd 1995–2001, BBDO: ceo and pres North America 2001–04, global ceo 2004–; FIPA 1987; *Recreations* tennis, squash, opera, ballet; *Style*— Andrew Robertson, Esq

ROBERTSON, Andrew Ogilvie; OBE (1994); s of Alexander McArthur Ogilvie Robertson (d 1971), and Charlotte Rachel, *née* Cuthbert (d 1989); *b* 30 June 1943; *Educ* Glasgow Acad, Sedbergh, Univ of Edinburgh (LLB); *m* 4 July 1974, Sheila, da of Philip Sturton; 2 s (James Mungo Ogilvie b 9 Nov 1975, Alexander Philip Ogilvie b 11 Aug 1977); *Career* ptnr T C Young 1968–2006; sec and treas Clydeside Fedn of Community Based Housing Assocs 1978–93, sec The Briggait Co Ltd 1983–88, founding sec and legal advsr The Princess Royal Tst for Carers 1990–2006 (tstee 2006–12), vice-pres Carers Tst 2012–; chm: Post Office Users' Cncl for Scotland 1988–99, Scottish Housing Assocs Charitable Tst 1990–2009, Scottish Building Soc 2003–06; chm Gtr Glasgow Community & Mental Health Servs NHS Tst 1994–98, chm Glasgow Royal Infirmary Univ NHS Tst 1997–99, chm Gtr Glasgow Primary Care NHS Tst 1999–2005, chm Gtr Glasgow and Clyde NHS Bd 2007–15 (memb 1999–, vice-chair 2004–07), tstee Music in Hospitals 2007–13, chm Erskine Hosp Bishopston 2011– (sec 1976–2002, vice-chm 2006–11); dir: The Merchants House of Glasgow 1980–2006, Glasgow C of C 1981–94, Scotcash 2007–11; govr Sedbergh Sch 2000–08, chm LAR Housing Tst 2016–, Glasgow carers champion 2016–; Univ of Glasgow Hon DSc (2015); *Recreations* mountaineering, sailing, swimming, cycling, reading; *Clubs* East India, Western (Glasgow); *Style*— Andrew Robertson, Esq, OBE; ✉ Burnside Cottage, Main Street, Drymen, Stirlingshire G63 0BQ (☎ 0141 221 5562, fax 0141 221 5024, e-mail aor@tcyoung.co.uk)

ROBERTSON, Angus; MP; s of Struan Robertson, and Anna, *née* Haenlein; *b* 28 September 1969; *Educ* Broughton HS Edinburgh, Univ of Aberdeen (MA); *Career* news ed Austrian Broadcasting Corp (ORF) 1991–98, reporter BBC Vienna 1992–98, communications conslt Communications Skills Int (CSI) 1994–2001; contrib NPR USA, RTE Ireland and ABC Aust 1992–98; candidate (SNP) Midlothian Scot Parly elections 1999; MP (SNP) Moray 2001–; shadow Scot min for Defence and Foreign Affrs 2003– (memb Scot shadow Cabinet, shadow Scot min for Defence 2001–03); SNP Westminster spokesman on Europe and def 2001–; vice-chm All-Pty Whisky Industry Gp 2001–, vice-chm All-Pty Offshore Oil and Gas Gp, memb All-Pty Fishing Industry Gp 2001–; memb Nat Exec Young Scot Nationalists (YSN) 1986, jr vice-pres Univ of Aberdeen Students Rep Cncl 1987–88, nat organiser Fedn of Student Nationalists 1988; SNP: int press spokesman UK Parly election 1997 and Scot Parly election 1999, memb Int Bureau 1998–, advsr European and Int Affrs SNP Gp Scot Parl 1999–2001; memb NUJ; past memb: Works Cncl Austrian Broadcast Corp, UN Corrs Assoc Vienna, Austrian Guild of PR Conslts; *Recreations* football, rugby, skiing, playing golf badly, films, travel, books, socialising and whisky tasting in moderation; *Style*— Angus Robertson, Esq, MP; ✉ House of Commons, London SW1A 0AA (e-mail robertsona@parliament.uk); Constituency Office, 9 Wards Road, Elgin IV30 1NL (☎ 01343 551111, website www.moraymp.org)

ROBERTSON, Angus Frederick; s of Eric Desmond Robertson, OBE (d 1987), and Aileen Margaret, *née* Broadhead (d 2010); *b* 4 November 1954; *Educ* Westminster, Univ of Stirling (BA); *m* (m dis), Frances Ellen, da of Patrick Carroll Macnamara, of Ardgay, Sutherland; *Career* called to the Bar Middle Temple 1978; *Clubs* Naval and Military; *Style*— Angus Robertson, Esq; ✉ 2 King's Bench Walk, London EC4Y 7DE (☎ 020 7353 1746, fax 020 7583 2051)

ROBERTSON, (Charles) Archibald (Archie); OBE (2002); s of Donald Robertson, and Isabella, *née* Duncan; *b* 26 December 1953, Perth, Scotland; *Educ* Dingwall Acad, HS of Stirling, Univ of Stirling (BA); *m* 1977, Judith, *née* Cranston; 2 da (Iona b 1978, Katy b 1983), 1 s (Neil b 1981); *Career* BP Int 1976–96 (head of transport distribution BP Oil Europe 1994–96), dir of ops Environment Agency 1996–2003, chief exec Highways Agency 2003–08, gp chief exec David MacBrayne Ltd 2010–12, advsr to Buro Happold LLP 2013–; memb Bd Dept for Transport 2003–08; memb Cmmn for Integrated Transport 2003–08; chm: Via Verde Inc 2011–, Rapid5D Ltd 2012–, Living Streets 2013–; non-exec dir: Capita Symonds Ltd 2009–11, ASI Solutions Ltd 2009–10; dir Ardnish Experiences Ltd 2014–; tstee: Inst of Business Ethics 2008–10, Covent Garden Market Authy 2013–; memb Green Alliance; FCIHT 2005, CCMI 2011; *Recreations* sport, skiing, following rugby union, the Munros, the natural environment; *Clubs* Little Ship, Ski Club of GB, Herts Mountaineering, Scotch Malt Whisky Soc; *Style*— Archie Robertson, Esq, OBE; ✉ Rapid5D Ltd, Ford House, 31–34 Railway Street Chelmsford CM1 1QS (☎ 01245 218198, e-mail archie.robertson@rapid5d.com)

ROBERTSON, Rev Charles; LVO (2005); s of Thomas Robertson (d 1941), of Glasgow, and Elizabeth, *née* Halley (d 1942); *b* 22 October 1940; *Educ* Camphill Sch Paisley, Univ of Edinburgh, New Coll Edinburgh; *m* 30 July 1965, Alison Margaret, da of Rev John Strachan Malloch, MBE, of Aberdeen; 1 s (Duncan John b 6 June 1967), 2 da (Mary Blackadder b 29 Dec 1968, Margaret Isobel b 5 Feb 1976); *Career* asst minister N Morningside Church Edinburgh 1964–65; parish minister: Kiltearn Ross-shire 1965–78, Canongate Kirk (The Kirk of Holyroodhouse) Edinburgh 1978–2005, minister emeritus 2005–; chaplain to: HM The Queen in Scotland 1991–, the High Constables and Guard of Honour of Holyroodhouse 1993–, the Lord High Cmmr the Gen Assembly of the Church of Scotland 1990, 1991 and 1996 (HRH The Princess Royal); convenor Gen Assembly's Panel on Worship 1995–99 (sec 1982–95); Church of Scotland rep Jt Liturgical Gp 1984–99 (chm 1994–99), tstee Church Hymnary Tst 1987–, pres Church Service Soc 1988–91 (hon pres 1991–); chaplain to: Clan Donnachaidh Soc 1981–96, Elsie Inglis Maternity Hosp 1982–87, Moray House Coll of Educn 1986–98, New Club Edinburgh 1986–2015, No 2 (City of Edinburgh) Maritime HQ Unit RAAF 1987–99, Edinburgh Univ at Moray House 1998–2002, No 603 (City of Edinburgh) Squadron RAAF 1999–2015, Incorporation of Goldsmiths of the City of Edinburgh 2000–, Co of Merchants of the City of Edinburgh 2002–, Edinburgh and Lothians Scots Guard Assoc 2004; Convenery of Trades of Edinburgh 2005; JP City of Edinburgh 1980–2006; lectr in church praise St Colm's Coll Edinburgh 1980–93; tstee: Edinburgh Old Town Tst 1987–91, Edinburgh Old Town Charitable Tst 1991–, Carnegie Tst for the Univs of Scotland 2005–15; govr St Columba's Hospice 1986–2006; chm: Queensbury House Hosp 1989–95 (dir 1978–, vice-chm 1985–89), Queensbury House Tst 1996; memb: Exec Ctee Scot Veterans' Residences 1978–2005, Broadcasting Standards Cncl 1988–94, Historic Bldgs Cncl for Scotland 1990–99; sec Ctee to Revise the Church Hymnary 1995–2004, chm Soc for the Benefit of Sons & Daughters of the Clergy of the Church of Scotland (tstee 2003–); tstee Edinburgh World Heritage Tst 1999–2000; *Books* Singing the Faith (ed, 1990), Common Order (ed, 1994), St Margaret Queen of Scotland and Her Chapel (ed, 1994); sec of Ctees which compiled: Hymns for a Day (1983), Songs of God's People (1988), Worshipping Together (1991), Clann ag Urnaigh (1991), Common Ground (1998), By Lamplight (compiled with Elizabeth, Duchess of Hamilton, 2000); *Recreations* Scottish and Edinburgh history, hymnody, collecting Canongate miscellanea; *Clubs* Puffins, New (Edinburgh, hon memb), Royal Scots (Edinburgh, hon memb); *Style*— The Rev Charles Robertson, LVO; ✉ 3 Ross Gardens, Edinburgh EH9 3BS (☎ 0131 662 9025, e-mail canongate1@aol.com)

ROBERTSON, Prof Edmund Frederick; s of Edmund Jozef Chojnacki (d 1998), and Dorothy Mabel, *née* Warnes (d 1994); *b* 1 June 1943; *Educ* Madras Coll St Andrews (Tullis Prize, Sir William Robertson Prize, Dux), Univ of St Andrews (Taylor Thompson Bursary, BSc), Univ of Warwick (MSc, PhD); *m* 16 July 1970, Helena Francesca, da of Tadeusz Slebarski (d 2003); 2 s (Colin Edmund b 16 Nov 1974, David Anthony b 26 Sept 1978); *Career* Univ of St Andrews: lectr in mathematics 1968–84, sr lectr 1984–95, head Pure Mathematics Div 1988–91 and 2004–07, head Algebra Research Team 1988–2002, prof of mathematics 1995–2008, head Sch of Mathematical and Computational Sciences 1997–2000, chair Groups, Algorithms and Programming (GAP) Cncl 2003–09 (memb 1997–2003 and 2009–), head Sch of Mathematics and Statistics 2000–01, assoc dir Centre for Interdisciplinary Res in Computational Algebra (CIRCA) 2000–08, prof emeritus 2008–; chair Scientific Ctee BMC 2005–08 (memb 2003–05 and 2008–11); memb: EPSRC Mathematics Coll 1997–2000, EPSRC Peer Review Coll 2000–02, 2003–05 and 2006–10, Scottish Mathematical Cncl 1997–2004; ed Proceedings A Royal Soc of Edinburgh 2004–07, ed American Mathematical Soc/London Mathematical Soc History of Mathematics series 2007–11; memb: Edinburgh Mathematical Soc 1969– (memb Ctee 1986–89, memb Policy Advsy Ctee 1996–99 and 2007–10), London Mathematical Soc 1977–, European Mathematical Soc 2000–; Partnership Award (for innovation in mathematics teaching in higher educn) 1992, European Academic Software Award 1994, Undergraduate Computational Engrg and Science Award Dept of Energy USA 1995, Best Mathematics Website Award Scientific American 2002, Exemplary Online Resources Award Merlot 2002, Signum Pro Scientia Absoluta Vera Hungarian Sciences Soc 2008, Comenius Medal of Societas Comeniana Hungarica 2012, Certificate of Excellence Babes-Bolyai Univ Romania 2013, Hirst Prize and Lectureship London Mathematical Soc 2015; chair Madras Tst 2008–10 (vice-chair 1986–2008 and 2010–); govr Morrison's Acad 1999–2007, people's warden All Saints Church 2007–12, tstee St Andrew's Preservation Tst 2013–14; FRSE 1997; *Publications* author of over 140 papers and 25 books incl award-winning History of Mathematics; *Style*— Prof Edmund Robertson, FRSE; ✉ Mathematical Institute, University of St Andrews, North Haugh, St Andrews, Fife KY16 9SS (☎ 01334 463702, fax 01334 463748, e-mail efr@st-andrews.ac.uk, website www-history.mcs.st-and.ac.uk/history)

ROBERTSON, Dr Elizabeth Margaret; da of Alastair Robertson, of Aberdeen, and Dorothy Elizabeth, *née* Barron; *b* 7 October 1951; *Educ* St Margaret's Sch for Girls Aberdeen, Univ of Aberdeen (MB ChB, DMRD); *Career* conslt radiologies NHS Grampian 1982–2011, clinical dir of radiology Aberdeen Royal Hosps NHS Tst 1996–99, assoc med dir Grampian Univ Hospitals Tst 1999–2011 (dep med dir 2003–04), hon clinical sr lectr in radiology Univ of Aberdeen; pres Scottish Radiological Soc 2002–04; FRCR; *Style*— Dr Elizabeth Robertson; ✉ 95 King's Gate, Aberdeen AB15 4EN (☎ 01224 326831)

ROBERTSON, Geoffrey Ronald; QC (1988); s of Francis Albert Robertson, of Longueville, Sydney, Aust, and Bernice Joy, *née* Beattie; *b* 30 September 1946; *Educ* Epping Boys HS, Univ of Sydney (BA, LLB), Univ of Oxford (Rhodes scholar, BCL); *m* Kathy Lette, *qv*; 1 s (Julius Blake), 1 da (Georgina Blaise); *Career* called to the Bar Middle Temple 1973 (bencher 1997), fndr and head Doughty St Chambers 1990–, recorder 1999–2012 (asst recorder 1993–99); appeal judge UN Special Court for War Crimes Sierra Leone 2002–07 (first pres of Court 2002–04), distinguished jurist memb UN Internal Justice Cncl 2008–12; visiting prof: Univ of NSW Aust 1977, Univ of Warwick 1980–81, Birkbeck

Coll London 1998–, QMC 2003–, New Coll of the Humanities 2014–; memb Cncl JUSTICE; tstee: Capital Cases Tst, Sydney Univ Tst; govr SOAS 2015–; NY Bar Assoc Award for Distinction in Int Law and Affrs 2011; Hon LLD: Univ of Sydney, Brunel Univ, Romanian Nat Sch of Political Sci 2011; *Books* Reluctant Judas (1976), Obscenity (1979), People Against the Press (1983), Media Law (1984, 5 edn 2007), Hypotheticals (1986), Does Dracula Have Aids? (1987), Freedom, The Individual and the Law (1989, 2 edn 1993), The Justice Game (1998), Crimes Against Humanity (1999, 4 edn 2012), The Tyrannicide Brief (2005), The Levellers: The Putney Debates (2007), The Statute of Liberty (2009), Was There An Armenian Genocide? (2009), The Iranian Prison Massacres 1988 (2010), The Case of the Pope: Vatican Accountability for Human Rights Abuses (2010), Mullahs without Mercy: Human Rights and Nuclear Weapons (2013), Dreaming Too Loud: Reflections on a Race Apart (2013), An Inconvenient Genocide – Who Now Remembers the Armenians? (2014); *Plays* The Trials of Oz (BBC TV, 1991); *Recreations* tennis, opera, fishing; *Style*— Geoffrey Robertson, Esq, QC; ✉ Doughty Street Chambers, 53/54 Doughty Street, London WC1N 2LS (☎ 020 7404 1313, fax 020 7404 2283, e-mail g.robertson@doughtystreet.co.uk)

ROBERTSON, Grace; OBE (1999); da of James Fyfe Robertson (d 1987), and Elizabeth, *née* Muir (d 1973); *b* 13 July 1930; *Educ* Kendal HS for Girls, Eothen Sch Caterham, Maria Grey Teacher Trg Coll Twickenham; *m* 16 Dec 1954, (Godfrey) Thurston Hopkins, s of Robert Thurston Hopkins (d 1958); 1 da (Joanna b 15 Jan 1960), 1 s (Robert James b 27 Oct 1961); *Career* photographer, lectr and broadcaster; photojournalist Picture Post 1949–57, freelance 1957–60, teacher 1965–78; subject of: Channel 4 documentary 1986, Grace Robertson – Photojournalist of the 50's (monograph) 1989, Master Photographers (BBC Radio 3 series) 1991, The Nineties (BBC 2) 1993; Distinguished Photographers' Award American Women in Photography Int 1992; Hon DLitt Univ of Brighton 1995, Hon DEd Brunel Univ 2007; Hon FRPS 1996; *Exhibitions* Nat Museum of Photography, Film and TV 1986, Photographers Gallery 1987, Zelda Cheatle Gallery London 1989, Nat Museum of Wales Cardiff 1989, Gardner Centre Univ of Sussex 1990, Cathleen Ewing Gallery Washington DC 1992, RNT (retrospective exhbn) 1993, Watershed Bristol 1993, Univ of Brighton Sussex 1994, Leaving Their Mark: Sixteen Achieving Women of Eastbourne (Towner Gallery) 1995, Leica Gallery NY 1998, A Sympathetic Eye (retrospective exhbn, Univ of Brighton) 2002, Aberdeen Art Gallery 2002, The Lowry 2003, Breaking the Frame: Pioneering Women in Photojournalism (Museum of Photographic Arts San Diego) 2006; *Photographic Work in Collections* incl: V&A, Nat Museum of Photography, Film and TV Bradford, J Paul Getty Museum LA, Nat Museum of Women in the Arts Washington DC, Michigan State Univ, Akron Art Museum Ohio, Helmut Gernsheim Collection Univ of Texas, Nat Gallery of Aust, Hulton Getty Collection London; *Publications* A Sympathetic Eye (2002), Breaking the Frame: Pioneering Women in Photojournalism (2006); *Recreations* painting, reading, walking, listening to music; *Style*— Ms Grace Robertson, OBE; ✉ c/o The Photographers' Gallery, Halina House, 5 Great Newport Street, London WC2H 7HY (☎ 020 7831 1772); c/o Peter Fetterman, Gallery A7, 2525 Michigan Avenue, Santa Monica, California 90404, USA (☎ 00 131 04 536463)

ROBERTSON, Air Marshal Graeme Alan; CBE (1988, OBE 1985); s of Ronald James Harold Robertson, DFC (d 1999), and Constance Rosemary, *née* Freeman (d 2007), of Walton on the Naze, Essex; *b* 22 February 1945, Woodford, Essex; *Educ* Bancroft's Sch, RAF Coll Cranwell (Sir Philip Sassoon Meml Prize), Open Univ (BA); *m* Barbara Ellen, da of Frederick William Mardon (d 1975); 1 da (Nicole Jane b 17 Dec 1975); *Career* pilot No 8 Sqdn (Hunters) Bahrain 1968–69, pilot/weapons instr No 6 Sqdn RAF Coningsby (Phantoms) 1970–72, instr pilot 288 Operational Conversion Unit RAF Coningsby (Phantoms) 1972–73, instr pilot/Flt Cdr 550th Tactical Fighter Trg Sqdn Luke AFB Arizona (Phantoms) 1973–75, Flt Cdr No 56 Sqdn RAF Wattisham (Phantoms) 1975–77, RAF Staff Coll 1977–78, Operational Requirements/Plans Staff MOD 1978–82, CO No 92 Sqdn RAF Wildenrath Germany (Phantoms) 1982–84, CO No 23 Sqdn RAF Stanley Falkland Is (Phantoms) 1984–85, CO RAF Wattisham 1985–87, Dir of Air Staff Briefing and Co-ordination MOD 1987–88, RCDS 1989, Dir of Defence Progs MOD 1990–91, Dep Cdr RAF Germany 1991–93, AOC No 2 Group 1993–94, ACDS (Programmes) MOD 1994–96, COS and Dep C-in-C Strike Command 1996–98; def and air advsr Br Aerospace 1999–2000, sr military advsr BAE SYSTEMS 2000–03; Hon Col 77 Regiment (Vols) RE 1996–99; Hon ADC to HM the Queen 1986–87; QCVSA 1973; md Blackbourne Wells Ltd 2003–, co-ordinator Br-American Community Relations MOD 2004–10, md Tefkal Assocs Ltd 2010–; Freeman City of London, clerk and co sec Hon Co of Glos 2013–; FRAeS, FRSA; *Recreations* shooting, sailing, winter sports; *Clubs* MCC, RAF, Cheltenham; *Style*— Air Marshal G A Robertson, CBE; ✉ c/o National Westminster Bank plc, 4 Northgate, Sleaford, Lincolnshire NG34 7BJ

ROBERTSON, Rt Hon (Maj), Sir Hugh Michael; KCMG (2014), PC (2012); s of George Robertson, of Canterbury, and June, *née* McBryde; *b* 9 October 1962; *Educ* King's Sch Canterbury, RMA Sandhurst, Univ of Reading (BSc); *m* 17 May 2002, Anna Copson; 1 s (James); *Career* offr The Life Guards 1985–95; active serv: NI 1987, UN Cyprus 1988, Gulf War 1991, Bosnia 1994; commanded Household Cavalry: HM The Queen's Birthday Parade 1993, state opening of Parliament 1993, Silver Stick Adj 1994–95; Schroder Investment Mgmnt 1995–2001 (asst dir 1999–2001); MP (Cons) Faversham and Mid Kent 2001–15, sec Parly Fruit Gp 2001–, Cons whip 2002–04, shadow min for sport and Olympics 2005–10, chair Parly UN Gp 2005–08, parly under-sec of state for sport and Olympics 2010–12, min of state for sport, Olympic legacy and tourism 2012–13, min of state for foreign and Cwlth affairs 2013–14; govr Westminster Fndn for Democracy 2005–08; Armourers and Brasiers Prize 1986; distinguished fell Univ of Reading 2014; FRGS 1995; Sultan of Brunei's Personal Order of Merit 1992; *Recreations* cricket, hockey; *Clubs* Cavalry and Guards, MCC (playing member), Pratts; *Style*— The Rt Hon Sir Hugh Robertson KCMG MP; ✉ House of Commons, London SW1A 0AA (☎ 020 7219 2463); Constituency Office, 11 The Square, Lenham, Kent ME17 2PQ (☎ 01622 851616)

ROBERTSON, Iain Alasdair; CBE (1995); s of Rev R Robertson (d 1994), and Johanna, *née* Mackenzie (d 2004); *b* 30 October 1949, Perth; *Educ* Perth Acad, Univ of Aberdeen (LLB); *m* 12 March 1977, Judith Helen, *née* Stevenson; 2 s (Niall b 27 Sept 1979, Calum b 31 March 1982), 1 da (Johanna b 24 Feb 1983); *Career* admitted slr 1973; W&J Burness WS 1971–73, Maclay Murray and Spens 1973–75, Br Petroleum 1975–90, chief exec Highlands and Islands Enterprise 1990–2000, gp strategy dir AWG plc 2000–03, Accounts Cmmn 2003–10; non-exec dir Scottish Tourist Bd 1993–95; memb Supervisory Bd Locate in Scotland 1991–2000, chm Coal Liabilities Strategy Bd, chm Scottish Legal Aid Bd 2006–16, chm Keep Scotland Beautiful 2012–15; memb Law Soc of Scotland; *Recreations* skiing, reading, music; *Style*— Iain A Robertson, Esq, CBE; ☎ 07775 820850, e-mail ianrobertson@hotmail.com

ROBERTSON, Ian; s of James Love Robertson (d 1992), of Glasgow, and Mary Hughes Reid (d 1980); *b* 10 August 1947, Glasgow; *Educ* Queen's Park Secdy Sch Glasgow; *m* 6 May 2001, Fiona Ann, *née* Hervey; by earlier m, 1 da (Lorna b 3 Sept 1971), 2 s (Graeme, Douglas (twins) b 4 Aug 1977); *Career* dir J&A Ferguson 1976–81, factory chief accountant United Biscuits Glasgow 1982–84, financial controller Terrys of York 1984–87, finance dir Northern Dairies 1987–91, gp financial controller Northern Foods 1991–94; Wilson Bowden plc: finance dir 1994–2002, gp chief exec 2003–07; non-exec dir: Homes & Communities Agency 2008–, Leeds Building Soc 2008–15; external expert UN Jt Staff Pension Fund Audit Ctee 2010–14 (dep chair 2012–14); memb Financial Reporting Cncl 2004–07, memb Audit Advsy Bd Scottish Parl Corp Body 2007–14 (chair 2010–14), ind memb Audit Ctee Dept for Communities and Local Govt (DCLG); memb Eastwood DC 1973–84 (provost 1980–84); dep chair Elmet & Rothwell Cons Assoc 2016–; MICAS 1969 (pres 2004–05, convenor Investigations Ctee 2010–); *Recreations* reading, music, walking, politics; *Style*— Ian Robertson, Esq; ✉ 18 Hollybush Green, Collingham, West Yorkshire LS22 5BG (☎ 07768 996526, e-mail ianrobertsonca@gmail.com)

ROBERTSON, James Campbell; s of Surgn Lt James Robertson (ka 1942), of Edinburgh, and Mathilda Mary, *née* Campbell; *b* 15 October 1941; *Educ* Epsom Coll, Guy's Hosp, Univ of London (MB BS), RCP and RCS (DCH); *m* 2 May 1970, Dr Margaret Elizabeth Robertson, da of late Charles Edwin Kirkwood, of Salisbury, Wilts; 3 s (Charles James b 1971 d 1995, Andrew b 1973, Alistair b 1974); *Career* conslt physician in rheumatology and rehabilitation Salisbury and Southampton DHAs and Wessex Regnl Rehabilitation Unit 1974–2006, dir Wessex Regnl Rehabilitation Unit 1980–90, currently medico-legal practice; fndr ed Care Science and Practice (now Jl of Tissue Viability); author of papers on prevention of neck and back pain, osteoporosis, measurement of physical signs, patient support systems, bandaging and interface pressure mgmnt and burns scarring; former chm and fndr memb Soc for Tissue Viability; fndr sec Soc for Res in Rehabilitation; memb: BMA, Br Soc of Rheumatology, Br Inst of Musculoskeletal Medicine; FRCP, MRCS; *Books* Blueprint for a Clinical Grip Strength Monitor and Limb Strength Measurement System (1986); *Recreations* sailing, DIY; *Clubs* RSA, Salisbury Medical Soc; *Style*— Dr James Robertson; ✉ Rheumatology Department, Salisbury District Hospital, Salisbury, Wiltshire (☎ 01722 336262 ext 4218)

ROBERTSON, John; s of Charles Robertson, and Anges Millen, *née* Webster; *b* 17 April 1952, Anniesland, Glasgow; *Educ* Shawlands Acad Sr Secdy Sch, Langside Coll, Stow Coll; *m* Eleanor, *née* Wilkins Munro; 3 da; *Career* BT: joined 1969, tech offr 1973–87, special faults investigation offr 1987–91, customer service mangr 1991–95, field mangr 1995–99, local customer mangr 1999–2000; MP (Lab): Glasgow Anniesland 2000–05 (by-election), Glasgow NW 2005–15; PPS to Yvette Cooper, MP (as Sec of State for Dept for Work and Pensions), PPS to Kim Howells, MP (as Min for the ME) 2005–08, PPS to Yvette Cooper, MP (as shadow home sec) 2010–; House of Commons: Scottish Affrs Select Ctee 2001–05, European Scrutiny Select Ctee 2003–05, chair All Pty Communications Gp, chair All Pty Shipbuilding and Ship Repair Gp, hon sec and treas Scottish Parly Lab Pty Gp, vice-chair Smoking and Health All Pty Gp, chair All Pty Gp on Music 2005–, chair All Pty Gp on Nuclear Energy 2005–, vice-chair All Pty Nigeria Gp, vice-chair All Pty New Media Gp, chair All Pty Gp on Angola 2007–, sec All Pty Parly Gp on Water and Sanitation in the Third World, vice-chair All Pty Parly Gp on Cannabis and Children, vice-chair All Pty Parly Gp on Corporate Responsibility, memb Energy and Climate Change Select Ctee 2009–; constituency positions incl: branch chm 1987–89, constituency vice-chm 1989–94, chm 1995–2000, campaign co-ordinator 1987–2001, election agent 1994–2000; Communication Workers' Union (CWU): memb Glasgow Branch Ctee 1983–91, political and educn offr Glasgow Branch 1985–89; Soc of Telecom Executives (Connect): memb W of Scotland Ctee 1994–2000, chm W of Scotland Branch 1997–2000, nat negotiator 1998–2000; memb Lab Pty 1984–; *Recreations* football, cricket, reading, music; *Clubs* Garrowhill Cricket, Cambus Athletic, Old Kilpatrick Bowling; *Style*— John Robertson, Esq; ✉ Glasgow North West Parliamentary Office, 131 Dalsetter Avenue, Glasgow G15 8TE (☎ 0141 944 7298, fax 0141 944 7121, e-mail jrmpoffice@btinternet.com, website www.john-robertson.co.uk)

ROBERTSON, John William; s of Ian Middleton Strachan Robertson, of Broughty Ferry, Dundee, and Agnes Ramsey Seaton, *née* Findlay; *b* 27 August 1956; *Educ* The HS of Dundee, Univ of Dundee (BSc, Zinn Hunter Award, Henry Dickson Prize, Gordon Mathewson Award), Univ of Liverpool (BArch); *m* 27 July 1984, Judy Ann, da of Thomas Gordon John Peacock; 2 da (Charlotte Elizabeth b 21 April 1986, Georgina Emily b 10 Feb 1988); 1 s (Edward James b 4 June 1990); *Career* architect; Fitzroy Robinson Partnership: qualified architect 1980, assoc 1983, ptnr 1985; Hurley, Robertson & Associates 1993–2005, John Robertson Architects 2005–, currently specialises in interior architectural projects and the design and construction of well known architectural projects in the Cities of London and Westminster; Freeman City of London 1986; memb: City Architecture Forum, City Property Assoc; RIBA 1981; *Awards* commendation for high standard of design achieved in the Structural Steel Awards for Aviation House Gatwick Airport 1989, Br Cncl for Offices Award for One Great St Helens London 2000; City Heritage Award 2001, Royal Fine Art Cmmn Tst Award 2001 and Civic Trust Award 2002 Commendation for restoration of Daily Express Building Fleet Street, Br Cncl for Offices Award 2006 for 10 Queen Street Place London; *Recreations* bagpiping, golf, sailing, skiing, scuba diving; *Clubs* Berkshire Golf (Ascot), RAC; *Style*— John Robertson, Esq; ✉ John Robertson Architects, 111 Southwark Street, London SE1 0JF (☎ 020 7633 5102, website www.jra.co.uk)

ROBERTSON, Katharine Eleanor Hannah Maria (Kate); da of William Anthony Archibald Godfrey, of Hadleigh, Suffolk, and Eleanor Bedford, *née* Wilson; *b* 10 October 1955; *Educ* St John's Coll Houghton Johannesburg, Univ of Cape Town (BA, LLB); *m* 23 June 1990, Bruce Michael Edwin Granville Robertson, s of Kenneth Robertson; 1 da (Ella Katharine Marjorie b 27 Nov 1991); *Career* advtg exec; J Walter Thompson Johannesburg SA: account supr 1982–83, account dir 1983–84, client servs dir 1984–86; J Walter Thompson Europe: Euro account dir 1987–91, regional dir-in-charge 1992–94; dir and head of European new business Bates Europe 1995–97; fndr and chief exec London office Scholz & Friends 1997–2002; Euro RSCG Worldwide: joined as exec vice-pres Europe 2003–04, exec vice-pres global brands and global brand dir Reckitt Benckiser 2004–06, UK gp chm 2006– (incorporating Euro RSCG London, Euro RSCG Biss Lancaster, Euro RSCG KLP, Euro RSCG Skybridge, Euro RSCG Fuel, CGI Brand Sense, Maitland Consultancy, Conran Design Group and EHS Brann); judge Media and Mktg Europe Awards 2006; *Style*— Mrs Kate Robertson; ✉ Euro RSCG Worldwide, Cupola House, 15 Alfred Place, London WC1E 7EB

ROBERTSON, Dr Kevin William; s of James Alexander Robertson, of Thurso, Caithness, and Elizabeth Margaret, *née* Grant; *b* 22 August 1965; *Educ* Thurso HS, Univ of Glasgow (MB ChB, Livingstone prize for physiology, MD); *Career* jr house offr Univ Dept of Surgery then Univ Dept of Med Glasgow Royal Infirmary 1988–89, SHO Western Infirmary surgical specialities rotation Glasgow 1989–91, SHO W of Scotland rotation in surgery in gen 1991–93, SHO Dept of Vascular Surgery Glasgow Royal Infirmary 1993–94, SHERT (Scottish Hosps Endowment Research Tst) research fell and lectr Univ Dept of Surgery Glasgow Royal Infirmary and Beatson Inst for Cancer Research 1994–96, W of Scotland Higher Surgical trainee 1996–2002, conslt surgn N Glasgow Hosps NHS Univ Hospitals 2003–; memb: Amnesty Int, Médècins sans Frontière; fell Upper Gastro-Intestinal Surgical Unit St George's Hosp Sydney 2002–03, FRCSGlas 1992 (memb Cncl and Jr Advsy Ctee 1993–97, convenor Jr Advsy Ctee 1997–99), FRCS 2000; *Recreations* Lister, football, travel; *Clubs* Western Baths Swimming; *Style*— Dr Kevin Robertson; ✉ University Department of Surgery, Queen Elizabeth Building, Glasgow Royal Infirmary, Glasgow G31 2ER (☎ 0141 211 4000)

ROBERTSON, Laurence Anthony; MP; s of James Robertson, and Jean Christine, *née* Larkin; *b* 29 March 1958; *Educ* St James' CE Secdy Sch, Farnworth GS, Bolton Inst of HE; *m* 1, 1989 (m dis), Susan; 2 step da (Sarah b 1973, Jemma b 1981); m 2, 2015, Anne Marie; *Career* industrial conslt 1982–92, charity fundraising conslt 1992–97, MP (Cons) Tewkesbury 1997–; oppn whip 2001–03, shadow min for business 2003–05, shadow min for NI 2005–; memb House of Commons Select Ctees on: Jt Consolidated Acts 1997–2001, Social Security 1999–2001, European Scrutiny 1999–2001; former jt vice-chm Cons Backbench Ctee on Euro and Foreign Affrs, jt sec Cons Backbench Ctee on the

Constitution 1997–2001, former memb 1922 Exec Ctee, chm All Pty Parly Gp on Ethiopia and Djibouti 2009–, chm NI Affrs Select Ctee 2010–, jt-chm All Pty Parly Gp on Racing and Bloodstock 2010–; co-chm: Br Irish Parly Assembly 2012–, All Pty Parly Gp on Engineering, All Pty Parly Gp on Brazil; *Recreations* racing, golf, the countryside, reading; *Style—* Laurence Robertson, Esq, MP; ✉ House of Commons, London SW1A 0AA (☎ 020 7219 4196)

ROBERTSON, Prof Neil Patrick; s of Dennis Robertson, and Barbara Robertson; *Educ* Cranleigh Sch, St Thomas' Med Sch (MB BS), Univ of London (MD); *Career* registrar in neurology Bristol Royal Infirmary 1990–91; Addenbrooke's Hosp Cambridge: clinical res assoc and hon clinical registrar 1992–95 (also at Hitchingbrooke Hosp Huntingdon), hon sr registrar 1995–97, hon conslt 1998; sr lectr in neurology Univ of Cardiff 1999–2010, prof of clinical neurology Univ of Cardiff and hon conslt in neurology Univ Hosp of Wales Cardiff 2010–; hon conslt Heath Hosp Cardiff 1999–; Charles Symonds Prize 1995; memb Med Protection Soc, assoc memb Assoc of Br Neurologists; FRCP 2002 (MRCP 1992); *Publications* author of numerous editorials and chapters in books; *Recreations* skiing, rugby, art, horticulture; *Style—* Prof Neil Robertson

ROBERTSON, Nick; OBE (2011); *Career* fndr ASOS.com 2000–, chief exec ASOS plc 2001–; *Style—* Nick Robertson, Esq, OBE; ✉ ASOS plc, Greater London House, Hampstead Road, London NW1 7FB (executive assistant Charlotte Balin ☎ 020 7756 1017, e-mail helencarnall@asos.com)

ROBERTSON, Prof Pamela Beaumont; da of Charles Ian Barclay Reekie (d 2006), and Constance Marion, *née* Clarke (d 1979); *Educ* St George's Sch for Girls Edinburgh, UCL, Univ of Manchester; *m* 7 April 1984, William Robertson; 1 s (James Scott b 1986), 1 da (Elizabeth Clarke b 1988); *Career* sr curator Hunterian Art Gallery Univ of Glasgow; curator Whistler 2003 festival 2000–03, guest co-curator Charles Rennie Mackintosh (Glasgow Museums) 1996–97; princ investigator Mackintosh Architecture: Context, Making and Meaning 2010–; chair Charles Rennie Mackintosh Soc 2003–07; memb: Historic Buildings Cncl Scotland 1998–2002, Curatorial Ctee Nat Tst for Scotland 2001–, Export Review Ctee for Works of Art 2004–10; govr Glasgow Sch of Art 2006–10; first recipient Iris Fndn Award for Outstanding Contribution to the Decorative Arts Bard Grad Sch NY 1998; FRSE 2003, FRSA 2007; *Books* Charles Rennie Mackintosh: The Architectural Papers (ed, 1990), Charles Rennie Mackintosh: Art is the Flower (1994), The Mackintosh House (1998, Scottish Museum of the Year Award for Publications 1999), The Chronycle: The Letters of Charles Rennie Mackintosh to Margaret Macdonald Mackintosh, 1927 (2001), Beauty and the Butterfly: Whistler's Depictions of Women (2003), Doves and Dreams: The Art of Frances Macdonald and J Herbert McNair (2006); website Mackintosh Architecture (www.mackintosh-architecture.gla.ac.uk, 2014–); *Style—* Prof Pamela Robertson; ✉ Hunterian Art Gallery, University of Glasgow, 82 Hillhead Street, Glasgow G12 8QQ

ROBERTSON, Prof Paul; *Career* violinist; leader Medici String Quartet; Medici String Quartet: formed 1971, artists in residence and fells of Lancaster Univ, currently artists in residence Univ of Surrey, launched own record label Whitehall 1992; currently visiting prof: of music and psychiatry Kingston Univ, Bournemouth Univ; guest lectures incl: City Univ, Medical Soc of London, The Study Soc, Coll of Psychic Studies, Music and The Young Mind Conference New Coll Sch Oxford, Brain, Art, Mind, Music Conference Univ of Bath, Music, Brain Function, SEAL Conference Budapest, Brain Function and The Mind Conference (with concert by Medici Quartet) Geneva Cantonal Hosp, Holburne Museum (Bath Festival), The Art and Music of Business (with concert by Medici String Quartet) Roffey Park Mgmnt Ins, HM Whitemoor Prison, RSA, Acad Med Centre of Amsterdam Anatomy Lesson (with concert by Medici String Quartet); broadcasts incl: interview with Margaret Howard (Classic FM, nominated for Prix Italia 1993), The Mind of Music (series of six dialogues and concerts for Classic FM) 1995, Music & The Mind (Channel 4 Television) 1995; 1995–96 tours: Italy, Bulgaria, Germany, The Netherlands, Scandinavia, Spain; 1994–95 festival appearances incl: Bath, Lichfield, Salisbury, Three Choirs; BBC Lunchtime Recital St John's Smith Square, Glories of the String Quartet (series of 6 concerts) Braithwaite Hall Croydon Clocktower; *Recordings* with Medici String Quartet incl: Beethoven The Complete String Quartets Cycle, Alan Bush Dialectic Quartet Op 15, Elgar String Quartet, Franck Piano Quintet in F minor (with John Bingham), Janácek The Kreutzer Sonata and Intimate Letters, Mendelssohn String Quartet Op 13, Shostakovich Two Pieces for Octet (with Alberni String Quartet), Ravel String Quartet, Smetana From My Life, Vaughan Williams Phantasy Quintet (with Simon Rowland-Jones), Music and the Mind – Musical Illustrations from Channel 4 series, double CD of selected works for Koch International; recordings on own label incl: Brahms Piano Quintet in F minor Op 13 (with John Lill), Delius A Song before Sunrise, Haydn Six String Quartets Op 20, Mozart's Journey to Prague (with Dorothy Tutin and Richard McCabe), Mozart Clarinet Quintet in A major K 581 (with Jack Brymer), Schubert Death and the Maiden, Dvorák String Quartet in F major Op 96 American; *Style—* Prof Paul Robertson; ✉ c/o Georgina Ivor Associates, 28 Old Devonshire Road, London SW12 9RB (☎ 020 8673 7179, fax 020 8675 8058, e-mail GIvor@aol.com)

ROBERTSON, Robin; *Career* poet; ed Jonathan Cape; tstee Griffin Tst for Excellence in Poetry 2000–; Forward Prize for Best First Collection 1997 (for A Painted Field), E M Forster Award 2004, Forward Prize for Best Collection 2006 (for Swithering), Editor of the Year Br Book Industry Award 2008, Forward Prize for Best Single Poem 2009 (for At Roane Head), Cholmondeley Award 2012, Petrarch Prize 2013; FRSL 2009; *Publications* ed: Firebird 3: Writing Today (1984), Firebird 4: New Writing from Britain and Ireland (1985), 32 Countries: photographs of Ireland by Donovan Wylie with new writing by thiry-two Irish writers (1989), Mortification: Writers' Stories of Their Public Shame (2003); poetry: Camera Obscura (1996), A Painted Field (1997), Penguin Modern Poets Vol 13 (with Michael Hofmann and Michael Longley, 1998), Slow Air (2002), Actaeon: The Early Years (2006), Swithering (2006), The Wrecking Light (2010), Hill of Doors (2013), Sailing the Forest: Selected Poems (2014); translation: The Deleted World: versions of Tomas Tranströmer (2006), Medea (2008), Bacchae (2014); *Style—* Robin Robertson, Esq; ✉ Jonathan Cape, Random House, 20 Vauxhall Bridge Road, London SW1V 2SA; c/o Peter Straus (e-mail peters@rcwlitagency.co.uk)

ROBERTSON, Sir Simon Manwaring; kt (2010); s of David Lars Manwaring Robertson (d 1999), of Newick, E Sussex, and Pamela Lauderdale Manwaring, *née* Meares; *b* 4 March 1941; *Educ* Cothill Sch, Eton; *m* 26 June 1965, Virginia Stewart, da of Mark Richard Norman (d 1994), of Much Hadham, Herts; 1 s (Edward Manwaring b 1968), 2 da (Selina Manwaring b 1969, Lorna Manwaring b 1973); *Career* dir: Kleinwort Benson Ltd 1977–97, Kleinwort Benson Group plc 1988–97 (dep chm 1991–96, chm 1996–97); pres Goldman Sachs Europe Ltd 1997–2005, md Goldman Sachs Int 1997–2005; fndr Simon Robertson Associates 2005–; non-exec chm Rolls Royce 2005–; non-exec dir: Berry Bros & Rudd Ltd 1998, HSBC plc 2006–; dir Royal Opera House Covent Garden Ltd 2002–; tstee: Eden Project 2000–, Royal Opera House Endowment Fund 2001–; chm Royal Acad Tst 2002–; *Recreations* being in the Prättigau, tennis; *Clubs* White's, Boodle's, Racquet (NY); *Style—* Sir Simon Robertson

ROBERTSON, Stanley Stewart John; CBE (1998); s of Jock Stanley Robertson, and Florence Kathleen, *née* Carpenter; *b* 14 July 1938, London; *Educ* Wandsworth Tech Coll, Liverpool Poly (DipEE); *m* 1961, Valerie, *née* Housley; 2 s, 2 da; *Career* student engrg apprentice UKAEA 1956–62, asst electrical engr CEGB 1962–67, electrical engrg mangr Shell Chemicals UK 1967–74; Health and Safety Exec: sr electrical inspr 1974–77, superintending inspr 1980–91 (dep superintending inspr 1977–80), dep chief inspr and regnl dir 1991–93, chief inspecting offr Railways 1993–98, md Robertson Safety Engineering Servs Ltd 1998–2010, exec dir Metro Solutions Ltd 2005–13; conslt on safety and engrg 1998–, health and safety conslt to Taiwan High Speed Rail Corp 1998–2006, health and safety conslt Roads and Transport Authy Dubai 2008–09; non-exec dir NQA Ltd 1993–96; chm: HSE Technol Ctee investigating RF ignition hazards St Fergus Scot 1979, Railway Industry Advsy Ctee Health and Safety Cmmn 1993–98, Nat Inspection Cncl for Electrical Installation Contracting 1993–95, HSE Ctee investigating safety of Forth Rail Bridge 1995–96; memb HSE Tech Ctee investigating collapse of railway tunnels at Heathrow Airport and New Austrian Tunnelling Method 1994; author of various pubns and tech papers on electrical and railway safety matters; CEng 1973, FIEE 1987 (MIEE 1973), MCIT 1994, FCILT 1998; *Recreations* listening to music, gardening; *Style—* Stanley Robertson, Esq, CBE

ROBERTSON, Prof Stephen Edward; s of Prof Charles Martin Robertson (d 2004), and Theodosia Cecil, *née* Spring Rice (d 1984); *b* 6 April 1946, Woodbridge, Suffolk; *Educ* Westminster, Trinity Coll Cambridge (MA), City Univ (MSc), UCL (PhD); *m* 1, 25 June 1966, Judith Anne (d 2005), da of Edwin Donald Kirk (d 1943); 1 da (Magdalene b 1977), 1 s (Colin b 1979); m 2, 10 April 2010, Georgina Margaret, *née* Seddon, widow of David Hardie; *Career* Royal Soc Scientific Info res fell UCL 1973–78, Fulbright scholar Univ of Calif Berkeley 1981, prof of info systems City Univ 1988–2009 (prof emeritus 2010–), researcher Microsoft Research Ltd 1998–2013; visiting prof UCL 2007–; memb Universities' Research Assessment Panel for Library and Information Management 1996 and 2001; author of many scientific papers; Tony Kent Strix Award Inst of Information Scientists 1998, Gerard Salton Award Assoc for Computing Machinery 2000; fell Girton Coll Cambridge 2003–; fell Assoc for Computing Machinery 2014; *Style—* Prof Stephen Robertson; ✉ website http://staff.city.ac.uk/~sb317/

ROBERTSON, Stephen Peter; *Educ* Shenfield Sch, Univ of Nottingham (BSc Chemistry); *Career* sr brand mangr Brooke Bond Oxo Foods (Unilever) 1981–85, mktg devpt mangr Alberto-Culver Co Ltd 1985–86, European mktg mangr Mars Inc Drinks Gp 1986–92, mktg dir UK and Ireland Mattel Toys Ltd 1992–93, mktg dir B & Q plc (subsid of Kingfisher plc) 1993–2000, chm Screwfix Direct (subsid of Kingfisher plc) 1999–2002, dir communications Kingfisher plc 2002–03, mktg dir Woolworths plc 2004–07, DG Br Retail Consortium 2008–13; non-exec dir: Fresca 2005–08, Nat Portrait Gallery Co 2008–11, Hargreaves Lansdown 2011–, Timpson Gp 2011–, Clipper Retail Logistics plc 2014–; chm Business West Ltd 2012–, memb Advsy Bd Retail Week 2012–, advsr Bd Legend Exhbns Ltd 2014–16; visiting prof Bristol Business Sch 2015–; memb Mktg Gp of GB; fell Mktg Soc 1999 (memb 1991, chm 1997–98), FRSA 2012, FCIM; *Style—* Stephen Robertson, Esq; ✉ Chairman, Business West, Leigh Court, Abbots Leigh, Bristol BS8 3RA

ROBERTSON OF PORT ELLEN, Baron (Life Peer UK 1999), of Islay in Argyll and Bute; Sir George Islay MacNeill Robertson; KT (2004), GCMG (2004), PC (1997); s of George P Robertson (d 2002), of Dunoon, Argyll, and Marion I, *née* MacNeill (d 1996); *b* 12 April 1946; *Educ* Dunoon GS, Univ of Dundee (MA); *m* 1 June 1970, Sandra, da of late James U Wallace, of Dundee; 2 s (Malcolm b 1972, Martin b 1975), 1 da (Rachael b 1980); *Career* research asst Econs Gp Tayside Study 1968–69, Scottish organiser GMWU (now GMB) 1969–78; MP (Lab): Hamilton 1978–97, Hamilton S 1997–99; PPS to sec of state for Social Servs 1979; oppn spokesman on: Scotland 1979–80, Defence 1980–81, Foreign and Cwlth Affrs 1981–93 (dep FCO spokesman 1983, princ spokesman on Europe 1984–93); chief oppn spokesman on Scotland 1993–97, sec of state for defence 1997–99; sec-gen NATO 1999–2003; exec dep chm Cable and Wireless plc 2004–06, chm Cable and Wireless Int 2006–08; non-exec dir: Weir Gp plc 2003–15, Smiths Gp plc 2004–06, Western Ferries (Clyde) Ltd 2005–, Royal Edinburgh Military Tattoo 2015–; sr counsellor The Cohen Gp (Washington DC) 2004–; chm Scottish Lab Pty 1977–78; vice-chm Bd Br Cncl 1985–94; govr Ditchley Fndn 1988– (chm Cncl of Mgmnt 2009–); hon patron Glasgow-Islay Assoc 2000–, chm John Smith Memorial Tst 2004–08, co-chm British Russia Round Table 2005–, chm Cmmn on Global Road Safety 2006–, tstee Queen Elizabeth Diamond Jubilee Tst 2013–, memb Advsy Bd World War One Centenary Commemoration 2014–; chllr Order of St Michael and St George 2011–; Hon Col London Scottish (Vols) Regt 2000–; Golden Plate Award Int Acad of Achievement 2000, ESU Winston Churchill Medal of Hon 2003, Transatlantic Leadership Award European Inst Washington DC 2003, Award for Distinguished Int Leadership Atlantic Cncl of USA 2003, Global Leadership Award Chicago Cncl on Foreign Rels 2004, Hanno R Elenbogen Citizenship Award Prague Soc; Elder Bro Trinity House 2002, Hon Guild Bro Guildry of Stirling 2004; DSc (hc) Cranfield Univ RCMS 2000; LLD (hc): Univ of Dundee 2000, Univ of Bradford 2000, Baku State Univ Azerbaijan 2001, Nat Acad of Sciences Kyrkyz Repub 2002, Romanian Sch of Political and Administrative Studies 2003, Univ of St Andrews 2003, French Univ Armenia, Nat Acad of Sciences Azerbaijan, Glasgow Caledonian 2004, Univ of Paisley 2006, Univ of Lincoln 2010; Hon DUniv: Stirling 2007, Robert Gordons Univ 2011; hon prof Univ of Stirling 2009; FRSA 1999, jr pres RIIA 2002–11, Hon FRSE 2003; Grand Cross Order of the Star (Romania) 2000, Grand Cross Order of Orange-Nassau (Netherlands) 2003, Grand Cross Order of Jesus (Portugal) 2003, Grand Cross Order of Isabel the Catholic (Spain) 2003, Grand Cross Order of Merit (Poland, Luxembourg, Italy, Hungary) 2003, Grand Cross Order of the Stara Planina (Bulgaria) 2003, Grand Cross Order of Merit (Federal Republic of Germany) 2003 (Commander's Cross 1991), Presidential Medal of Freedom (USA) 2003, Grand Cordon Order of Leopold (Belgium) 2003, Grand Cross Order of Grand Duke Gedeminos (Lithuania) 2003, Grand Cross Order of King Petar Kresmir IV (Croatia) 2003, Distinguished Public Service Medal US Department of Defence 2003, First Class Order of the Cross of the Tarra Mariana (Estonia) 2004, Order of the White Two-Arm Cross First Class (Slovakia) 2004, Commander of the Grand Cross The Order of Three Stars (Latvia) 2004, Grand Cross Order of Yaroslav the Wise (Ukraine) 2005; *Publications* Islay and Jura (2006), Dunblane: its people in a century of change (jtly, 2012); *Recreations* photography, golf, family, reading; *Clubs* Army and Navy, Islay Golf, Dunblane New Golf; *Style—* The Rt Hon the Lord Robertson of Port Ellen, KT, GCMG, PC, Hon FRSE

ROBERTSON-MACLEOD, (Roderick) James Andrew; s of Col Roderick Cameron Robertson-Macleod, DSO, MC (d 1989), and Daphne Mary, *née* Bick (d 2014); *b* 5 March 1951; *Educ* St Aubyn's Rottingdean, Milton Abbey; *m* 1991, Karen Theodora, da of Petre Barclay; 2 da (Katrina Rose b 2 Jan 1992, Louisa Iona b 15 Dec 1995), 1 s (Jack Alexander b 30 Sept 1993); *Career* joined Royal Green Jackets HM Forces 1970, UN Forces Cyprus 1971, Regtl Serv 1971–74, served NI 1975–76, ADC to GOC NI 1976–78, Adj 4 Royal Green Jackets 1978–80, ADC to TSH Prince and Princess of Monaco 1980–83; dir sports sponsorship co (pt of Markham Gp) 1983–89, commercial dir Operation Raleigh 1990–92, chief exec Raleigh International 1992–2003, dir John D Wood 2004–05, dir Aegis Defence Services 2005–06, conslt G4S 2006–; *Recreations* tennis, skiing, politics; *Clubs* Rifles London; *Style—* James Robertson-Macleod, Esq; ✉ Hill House, Coneyhurst, West Sussex RH14 9DL (☎ 01403 786877, e-mail jrobmac@btinternet.com)

ROBERTSON-PEARCE, Dr Anthony Brian (Tony); Laird of Camster Burn Estate, Caithness, Scotland; s of John Gilbert Robertson-Pearce (d 1967), of Testwood House, Lyndhurst, Hants, and Damaris Aubrey, *née* Wilce (d 1946); *b* 3 April 1932; *Educ* Chideock Manor Sch, Christ's Coll Cambridge (BA), Univ of Stockholm (Dip Archaeological Photography), Alliance Française Paris (Dip French); *m* 1, 18 May 1956 (m dis 1973), (Ingrid) Christina, da of Erik Nystrom (d 1957), of Stockholm, Sweden; 2 da (Pamela b 22 April 1957, Penelope b 3 Oct 1965), 1 s (Michael b 3 Aug 1960); m 2, 7 June 1974 (m dis 1980),

Catharina Carlsdotter, da of Capt Soldan Carl Fredrik Henningsson Ridderstad (d 1973), of Linkoping, Sweden; *Career* supervisor and photographer excavations Motya Sicily 1965, Br Sch of Archaeology Baghdad 1966, supervisor and MO Tell-A-Rimah N Iraq 1967, photographer and MO Br Excavations Tawilan Jordan 1968; Central Bd of Nat Antiquities (Riksantikvarieambetet) Stockholm: field archaeological photographer 1969, joined Publishing Dept 1972, subsequently head of publishing; Swedish TV film debut The Inquiry 1990 as Cdre in Royal Swedish Navy; PRO Sollentuna Kommun Stockholm 1983–88; dep govr Bd of Govrs American Biographical Inst Research Assoc; Int Biographical Centre Cambridge: dep DG (Europe), awarded Int Order of Merit (IOM) 1990, vice-consul for Sweden 2003–, life memb World Peace and Diplomacy Forum 2004; memb Swedish Nat Ctee ICOMOS (Int Cncl on Monuments and Sites), dep memb Assembly (Region R33) UN Int Parliament for Safety and Peace 1991–; Hon DH London 1991; Duine Uasal of the Clan Dhonnachaidh (Scotland), Gentleman of the Bodyguard Balgonie Castle Fife Scotland 1997–, appointed lifetime Ambassador General of the United Cultural Convention (USA) 2006; Int Biographical Centre of Cambridge Man of the Year 2011; KStJ 1997; FRAI, FIBA; *Books* Dr James Robertson 1566–1652 (1972), The Prehistoric Enclosure of Ekornavallen Sweden (1974), The Ruins of Kronoberg Castle (1974), Kaseberg Ship-setting (1975), The Battle of Rotebro 1497 (1986), Klasroskolan 1804–1881 (1987), Living Science Volume 001 (author of Introduction on Iraq, 2003); provided most of the illustrative material for Assyrian Ivories from Nimrud (by Prof Sir M E L Mallowan, 1968); author of numerous Swedish archaeological reports 1970–79; *Recreations* riding, heraldic artwork, painting watercolours; *Clubs* Naval, Sallskapet Stockholm; *Style*— Dr Anthony B Robertson-Pearce; ✉ Ambassador-General Robertson-Pearce, UCC, Nybrogatan 54, S-11440 Stockholm, Sweden (✆ 00 46 8 661 02 68, fax 00 46 8 667 64 96)

ROBINS, David Anthony; s of John Anthony Robins (d 2012), and Ruth Wenefrede, *née* Thomas (d 1990); *b* 2 September 1949, Lazenby, Yorks; *Educ* Sir William Turners GS Redcar, UCL (BSc); *m* 11 Sept 1981, Joanna Christina, *née* Botting; 2 s (Joseph Edward Desmond b 15 March 1983, Timothy Anthony James b 10 Nov 1988), 1 da (Eleanor Mary b 8 May 1984); *Career* econ analyst Investment and Res Dept Cwlth Bank Sydney 1973–74, Japanese economist Overseas Dept Bank of England 1976–78, exec Japanese Dept James Capel 1978–80, Far Eastern economist then chief int economist Phillips & Drew 1980–86; Union Bank of Switzerland: head of res and sr mangr UBS Phillips & Drew Tokyo 1986, md UBS Securities Inc NY 1988, sr vice-pres and functional advsr on securities and res UBS Zurich 1990, ceo UBS Ltd London and dep to Head of Region Europe 1994, exec vice-pres Europe, chief operating offr region Europe and memb Enlarged Gp Exec Bd 1997–98; ING Gp: ceo ING Barings 1998–2000 (also chm 2000), memb Exec Bd 2000; non-exec dir: London Clearing House Ltd 2001–07, MPC Investors Ltd (now RWC Partners Ltd) 2001–07, Bending Light Ltd 2001–, Meggitt plc 2002–14, Asian Total Return Investment Co (formerly Henderson Asian Growth and before that Henderson TR Pacific Investment Tst) 2002–15 (chm 2004–15), Emerging Markets Gp Ltd 2004–10, Oriel Securities Ltd 2007–14 (chm), Fidelity Japanese Values Investment Tst plc 2010– (chm 2012–), Serralux Inc (formerly Serrasolar Inc) 2011–, SVG Capital plc 2013–, Pemberton Capital Advisers LLP 2013–14, NHBS Ltd 2014–; advsr Millennium Assocs AG 2015–; memb Investment Ctee Univs Superannuation Scheme 2004–08; dep chm East London Business Alliance 2000–06 (chm Hackney Bd 1996–2003), memb Bd Hackney Empire Ltd 2001–13 (chm 2003–13), chm of tstees New Philanthropy Capital 2001–10, govr Eltham Coll 2001–13 (chm of govrs 2004–13, chm Devpt Bd 2012–); memb: Chartered Inst of Securities and Investment (formerly Securities and Investment Inst), RIIA, IOD, RSA; *Recreations* walking, gardening, film, sport; *Clubs* Aston Martin Owners; *Style*— David Robins, Esq; ✆ 07774 732955, e-mail robrobins@aol.com

ROBINSON; *see also:* Lynch-Robinson

ROBINSON, (George) Adrian; s of Thomas Gerard Robinson, BEM (d 1994), of Preston, Lancs, and Elizabeth, *née* Gillow (d 1997); *b* 3 November 1949; *Educ* Preston Catholic Coll, Pembroke Coll Oxford (MA, Cricket blue); *m* 6 April 1974, Susan Margaret, da of James Hopwood Edmondson (d 1995), of Accrington, Lancs; 2 s (Philip Adrian b 9 Sept 1984, Andrew James b 3 May 1987); *Career* various appts Midland Bank Ltd 1971–80; Airbus Industrie: sales fin mangr 1980–82, dep sales fin dir 1982–84, sales fin dir 1984; corporate fin dir Midland Bank plc 1985; md special fin gp Chemical Bank 1987–89 (dir Aerospace 1986–87), dep gen mangr The Nippon Credit Bank 1990–92; aerospace conslt 1992–; dir: Aircraft Lease Securitisation Ltd (also chm), ALS Leasing Inc, Babcock & Brown Air Funding I Ltd; ACIB 1973; *Recreations* golf, tennis, shooting; *Clubs* Oxford Univ Cricket, Bearsted Golf; *Style*— Adrian Robinson, Esq

ROBINSON, (Richard) Andrew (Andy); OBE (2004); s of Raymond Thomas Robinson, of Taunton, Somerset, and Patricia Mary, *née* Beckett; *b* 3 April 1964; *Educ* Richard Huish Coll, Loughborough Univ; *m* Samantha Elizabeth, da of John Andrew Morrison; 3 s (Oliver James b 21 July 1991, Edward George b 1 Feb 1993, Henry John b 12 Aug 1995), 1 da (Charlotte Elizabeth b 6 Sept 1997); *Career* rugby union coach and former player (flanker); clubs: Taunton 1981–83, Loughborough Univ 1982–86 (capt 1986), Bath 1986–2000 (capt 1991–93, Courage League Champions 1996, winners Pilkington Cup 1996, coach 1997–2000); England: 8 caps, debut v Aust 1988, five nations debut v Scotland 1989, Player of the Year Five Nations Championship 1989, formerly asst coach Under 21s, coach full team 2000–04 (winners World Cup Aust 2003), head coach 2004–06; head coach Edinburgh Rugby 2007–09; Br and Irish Lions: 6 appearances tour Aust 1989, asst coach tour Aust 2001, coach tour NZ 2005; head coach Scotland 2009–; physical educn and maths teacher: Writhlington Sch 1986–89, King Edward Sch Bath 1989–94; sports dir Colstons Collegiate Sch 1994–96; *Recreations* all sports (especially golf and cricket), gambling; *Style*— Andrew Robinson, Esq, OBE

ROBINSON, (Moureen) Ann; *b* Blackpool; *Educ* Harris Tech Coll Preston, LSE; *m* Peter Crawford Robinson; *Career* civil servant 1958–93 (latterly dep chief exec Benefits Agency), chief exec Scope (formerly Spastics Soc) 1993–95, assoc dir Computer Sciences Corporation 1995–96, DG Br Retail Consortium 1997–99, chair Energywatch (Gas and Electric Consumer Cncl) 1999–2003, ptnr Rush Consultancy Servs 2004–, consumer policy dir uSwitch 2005–16, dir Public Awareness Health and Social Service Information Standard 2009–14, chair Ascertiva 2012–15; memb: GMC 2002–12, Prison Serv Pay Review Body 2004–08; tstee Fndn for Credit Counselling 2000–08; *Recreations* bridge; *Style*— Mrs Ann Robinson; ✉ 706 Duncan House, Dolphin Square, London SW1V 3PP (✆ 020 7798 6728, e-mail annrob@ntlworld.com)

ROBINSON, Anne; da of late Bernard Robinson, and late Anne, *née* Wilson; *b* 26 September 1944; *Educ* Farnborough Hill Convent, Les Ambassadrices Paris XVI; *m* 1, 1968 (m dis 1973), Charles Martin Wilson, *qv*; 1 da (Emma Alexandra Wilson b 18 July 1970); m 2, 1980, John Penrose (m dis 2007); *Career* journalist; Daily Mail 1966–68, The Sunday Times 1968–77, asst ed Daily Mirror 1980–93 (columnist 1983–93); columnist: Today 1993–95, The Times 1993–95, The Times 1998–2001, The Daily Telegraph 2003–; presenter: Anne Robinson Show (BBC Radio 2) 1988–93, Points of View (BBC TV) 1988–97, Watchdog (BBC TV) 1993–2001, Weekend Watchdog (BBC TV) 1997–2001, The Weakest Link (BBC TV) 2000–11, The Weakest Link (NBC TV) 2000–03, Great Britons (BBC TV) 2002, Test The Nation (BBC TV) 2002–07, Watchdog with Anne Robinson (BBC TV) 2009–15, My Life In Books (BBC TV) 2010–; hon fell Liverpool John Moores Univ 1996; *Books* Memoirs of an Unfit Mother (2001); *Recreations* newspapers, television, dogs, having opinions, decently cooked food; *Clubs* Bibury Cricket (vice-pres), Bibury Tennis (pres); *Style*— Ms Anne Robinson; ✆ 07595 047047, e-mail office@victoriagrove.co.uk

ROBINSON, Rt Rev Anthony William (Tony); *see:* Pontefract, Bishop of

ROBINSON, Dr Bill; s of Harold Desmond Robinson (d 1988), and Joyce Grover, *née* Liddington; *b* 6 January 1943; *Educ* Bryanston, Univ of Oxford (BA), Univ of Sussex (DPhil), LSE (MSc); *m* 19 Aug 1966, Heather Mary (d 1995), da of James Albert Jackson; 2 s (Nicholas, Matthew), 1 da (Rosemary); m 2, 1997, Priscilla Elizabeth, da of Cedric Ernest Stille; *Career* systems analyst IBM 1968–69, econ asst Cabinet Office 1969–70, econ advsr HM Treasy 1971–74, head of div Euro Cmmn 1974–78, ed Econ Outlook London Business Sch 1978–86, dir Inst of Fiscal Studies 1986–91; advsr Treasy Ctee House of Commons 1981–86, memb Retail Prices Advsy Ctee 1988–90; econ columnist The Independent 1989–91 and Independent on Sunday 2000–, special advsr to Chllr of Exchequer 1991–93, dir London Economics 1993–99, head UK business economist corporate finance and recovery PricewaterhouseCoopers 1999–2007; KPMG: head of economics Forensic 2007–12, chm of economics and regulation 2012–, chief economist 2015–; *Books* Medium Term Exchange Rate Guidelines for Business Planning (1983), Britain's Borrowing Problem (1993); *Recreations* the bassoon, skiing, opera, bridge, windsurfing, writing musicals; *Clubs* Reform; *Style*— Dr Bill Robinson; ✉ KPMG, 15 Canada Square, London E14 5GL (✆ 020 7311 3515, fax 020 7311 3630, mobile 07715 704743, e-mail bill.robinson@kpmg.co.uk)

ROBINSON, Maj (Alfred) Christopher; s of Col Annesley Robinson, DSO (d 1976), of Long Melford, Suffolk, and Doris Lilian, *née* Barrett (d 1988); *b* 18 November 1930; *Educ* Wellington, RMA Sandhurst; *m* 1, 17 Aug 1957 (m dis 1961), Caroline Stafford (d 1996), da of Maj Christopher Scott-Nicholson (ka 1945), of Ruthwell, Dumfriesshire; m 2, 31 March 1962 (m dis 1978), Amanda, da of Paul Boggis-Rolfe (d 1988), of Bampton, Oxon; 2 da (Nicola b 1963, Polly b 1964), 2 s (Charles b 1964, Barnaby b 1970); *Career* 16/5 The Queen's Royal Lancers 1951–65; Trade Indemnity Co Ltd 1966–70, Glanvill Enthoven & Co Ltd 1970–73, The Spastics Soc (now Scope) 1973–91; tstee: The Little Fndn, The Mother and Child Fndn; pres Ferriers Barn Disabled Centre; pres Bures & Dist Branch Royal Br Legion; Hon DSc London Met Univ 2008; MInstF (MCIFM 1986); *Recreations* country conservation, wine appreciation; *Clubs* Essex; *Style*— Maj Christopher Robinson; ✉ Water Lane Cottage, Bures, Suffolk CO8 5DE (✆ 01787 227179)

ROBINSON, Clare Lois; da of late (John) Aubrey Robinson, and Shirley Joan, *née* Lynas; *b* 1 March 1963, Larne, NI; *Educ* Belfast HS, Belfast Royal Acad, Univ of Bristol (LLB), Chester Law Sch; *m* 14 May 1994, Patrick McDonnell; 2 s (William Patrick b 7 Dec 1996, James Aubrey b 12 Feb 1998), 1 da (Megan Shirley b 19 Jan 2001); *Career* Osborne Clarke: slr 1987–, ptnr 1992–, head Litigation Dept 1999–2004, Partnership Cncl 2014–; ADR Gp accredited mediator 2005–; memb Law Soc 1987–; *Recreations* reading, sport; *Style*— Ms Clare Robinson; ✉ Osborne Clarke, 2 Temple Back East, Temple Quay, Bristol BS1 6EG (✆ 0117 917 4022, fax 0117 917 4023, email clare.robinson@osborneclarke.com)

ROBINSON, Prof Colin; s of James Robinson (d 1937), of Stretford, Lancs, and Elsie, *née* Brownhill (d 1959); *b* 7 September 1932; *Educ* Stretford GS, Univ of Manchester (BA); *m* 1, 13 July 1957 (m dis 1983), Olga, da of Harry West; 2 s (Julian b 1961, Stewart b 1964); m 2, 18 June 1983, Eileen Catherine, *née* Marshall; 2 s (Richard b 1966, Christopher b 1971), 2 da (Louise b 1967, Elaine b 1969); *Career* RAF 1950–53; head Economics Div Corp Planning Dept Esso Petroleum 1960–66, econ advsr natural gas Esso Europe 1966–68, prof of economics Univ of Surrey 1968–; editorial dir Inst of Econ Affrs 1992–2002; Br Inst of Energy Economists' Economist of the Year 1992; Int Assoc of Energy Economics' Outstanding Contrib to the Profession Award 1998; FSS 1969, FInstPet 1979, fell Soc of Business Economists 2000; *Books* Business Forecasting (1970), North Sea Oil in the Future (1977), The Economics of Energy Self Sufficiency (1984), Can Coal Be Saved? (1985), Energy Policy: Errors, Illusions and Market Realities (1993), Arthur Seldon: A Life for Liberty (2009); *Recreations* walking, music, home improvements; *Style*— Prof Colin Robinson; ✉ Department of Economics, University of Surrey, Guildford, Surrey GU2 5XH (✆ 01483 259171, e-mail c.robinson180@btinternet.com)

ROBINSON, Prof Daniel Nicholas; s of Henry S Robinson (d 1962), and Margaret, *née* Peters (d 1956); *b* 9 March 1937, NY; *Educ* Colgate Univ (BA), Hofstra Univ (MA), City Univ of NY (PhD); *m* 18 Sept 1967, Francine, *née* Malasko; *Career* Columbia Univ: res psychologist 1960–65, asst dir Sci Honors Program 1964–68, sr res psychologist 1965–68, asst dir of life sciences 1967–68; Amherst Coll MA: asst prof of psychology 1968–70, assoc prof of psychology 1970–71; Univ of Georgetown: assoc prof of psychology 1971–74, chm Psychology Dept 1973–76 and 1985–91, prof of psychology 1974–97, dir Graduate Program in Psychology 1981–83, adjunct prof of philosophy 1996–98, distinguished res prof 1997–2001, distinguished res prof emeritus 2001–; Philosophy Faculty fell Univ of Oxford 2002–, fell Oriel Coll Oxford 2002; visiting lectr in psychology Princeton Univ 1965–68, visiting prof Folger Shakespeare Inst 1977, visiting sr memb Linacre Coll Oxford 1990– (adjunct fell 2015–), visiting lectr in philosophy Univ of Oxford 1991–99, visiting prof of psychology Princeton Univ 2001–02, visiting prof of psychology Columbia Univ 2002–05; memb Bd of Consulting Scholars James Madison Program in American Ideals & Instns Princeton Univ 2001–; involvement with: Nat Sci Fndn 1965–75, Nat Insts of Health 1967–70, Public Broadcasting System (for The Brain series 1978–84 and PBS and BBC for The Mind series 1985–88), Attorney Gen's Task Force on Crime 1980, MacArthur Fndn 1985, Dept of Health and Human Services Special Panel on Fetal Tissue Transplant Research 1988, Dept of Health and Human Services Sec's Advistory Ctee on Genetic Testing 2002; conslt developmental psychology Nat Inst of Mental Health 1997–98; Pres's Medal Colgate Univ 1986, Public Service Award Gen Servs Administration 1986, Lifetime Achievement Award Div of the History of Psychology American Psychology Assoc 2001, Distinguished Contribution Award Div of Theoretical & Philosophical Psychology American Psychology Assoc 2001, Presidential Distinguished Alumni Award City Univ of NY, Joseph Gittler Award American Psychological Assoc 2011; memb: Br Philosophical Assoc, American Philosophical Assoc, Soc of Scholars; fell British Psychological Soc 1980–99, fell Divs 3, 24 and 26 American Psychological Assoc (pres: Div 26 (History of Psychology) 1984–85, Div 24 (Theoretical Psychology) 1989–90); *Publications* The Enlightened Machine: An Analytical Introduction to Neuropsychology (1973), An Intellectual History of Psychology (1976), Systems of Modern Psychology: A Critical Sketch (1979), Psychology and Law: Can Justice Survive the Social Sciences? (1980), Toward a Science of Human Nature: Essays on the Psychologies of Hegel, Mill, Wundt and James (1982), Foundations of Psychobiology jtly, 1983), The Wonder of Being Human: Our Mind and Our Brain (jtly, 1984), Philosophy of Psychology (1985), Aristotle's Psychology (1989), An Intellectual History of Psychology (1995), Wild Beasts and Idle Humours: The Insanity Defense from Antiquity to the Present (1996), Praise and Blame: Moral Realism and Its Applications (2002), Consciousness and Mental Life (2007), How Is Nature Possible? Kant's Project in the First Critique (2012); *Recreations* gardening, writing fiction; *Clubs* Cosmos (Washington DC); *Style*— Prof Daniel Robinson; ✉ 34 Thackley End, Oxford OX2 6LB (✆ 01865 556776); Philosophy Faculty, Radcliffe Humanities Centre, Woodstock Road, Oxford OX2 6GG (e-mail dan.robinson@philosophy.ox.ac.uk)

ROBINSON, David James Roper; s of Andrew Thomas Roper Robinson (d 2006), of Dulwich, London, and Barbara Anne, *née* Black; *b* 19 July 1955; *Educ* Westminster (Queen's scholar), Pembroke Coll Cambridge (fndn exhibitioner, MA); *m* 15 June 1996, Jennifer Jane, da of Sir Alan McLintock (d 2007); 1 s, 2 da; *Career* articled Bennett Welch

R

& Co 1979–81, asst slr Glover & Co 1982–85, ptnr Frere Cholmeley (later Frere Cholmeley Bischoff) 1989–98 (joined 1985), head Private Client Dept Frere Cholmeley Bischoff 1994–98, fndr ptnr Forsters 1998–, head Private Client Dept Forsters 1998–2013; *Recreations* music, art, collecting books, travel; *Style—* David Robinson, Esq; ✉ Forsters, 31 Hill Street, London W1J 5LS (☎ 020 7863 8333, fax 020 7863 8444, e-mail david.robinson@forsters.co.uk)

ROBINSON, (David) Duncan; CBE (2008); s of Tom Robinson (ka 1944), and Ann Elizabeth, *née* Clarke; *b* 27 June 1943; *Educ* King Edward VI Sch Macclesfield, Clare Coll Cambridge (scholar, MA), Yale Univ (Mellon fellowship, MA); *m* 7 Jan 1967, Elizabeth Anne (Lisa), da of Frederick Totten Sutton (d 1979), of Fairfield, Conn, USA; 2 da (Amanda Jane b 1971, Charlotte Elizabeth b 1989), 1 s (Thomas Edward b 1975); *Career* keeper of paintings and drawings Fitzwilliam Museum Cambridge 1976–81 (asst keeper 1970–76), fell and coll lectr Clare Coll Cambridge 1975–81; dir of studies in history of art Univ of Cambridge until 1981: Churchill, Clare, Lucy Cavendish, Queens' and Sidney Sussex Colls and New Hall; dir Yale Center for British Art New Haven 1981–95, ceo Paul Mellon Centre for Studies in British Art London, adjunct prof of history of art Yale Univ 1981–95, fell Berkeley Coll Yale Univ 1981–95, fell Clare Coll Cambridge 1995–2002, dir Fitzwilliam Museum Cambridge 1995–2007, master Magdalene Coll Cambridge 2002–12, dep vice-chllr Univ of Cambridge 2005–12; memb: Ctee of Mgmnt Kettle's Yard Univ of Cambridge 1970–81 and 1995–2007, Ct RCA 1975–78 and 1996–2007, Art Advsy Panel Arts Council of GB 1978–81 (memb Exhibitions Sub Ctee 1978–79, memb Art Fin Ctee 1979–80, memb Cncl and vice-chm Art Panel 1981), Assoc of Art Museum Dirs 1983–88; chair City of Cambridge Public Art Panel 2009–15; elector to Slade Professorship of Fine Art Univ of Cambridge 1978–81 and 1997–2007, govr Yale Univ Press 1987–95; pres Friends of Stanley Spencer Gallery Cookham 1998–2015, vice-pres NADFAS 2000–06; memb: Art and Artefacts Indemnity Advsy Panel to Fed Cncl on the Arts and the Humanities 1991–94 (chm 1992–94), Museums and Collections Advsy Ctee English Heritage 1996–2002, Fitzwilliam Museum Tst 1995–2007, Bd of Govrs SE Museums Serv 1997–99, Gainsborough's House Soc 1997–2002, Advsy Cncl Paul Mellon Centre for Studies in Br Art London 1997–2002 and 2005–10, AHRB 1998–2003, Wingfield Arts Tst 2001–03, NW Essex Collection Tst 2002–07 (chair 2002–03, hon treas 2003–07), Museum Serv East of England 2001–03, Burlington Magazine Tst 2003–11, Burlington Magazine Fndn 2003–, Royal Collection Tst 2006–12; chair Jardine Fndn Scholarship Ctee Hong Kong 2006–12; tstee: Yale Univ Press London 1990–2014, Charleston Tst (USA) 1990–92, American Friends of the Georgian Gp 1992–94, Henry Moore Fndn 2006–14 (chair 2008–14), Prince's Drawing Sch 2007–13 (chair), Chantrey Bequest 2009–15, Cambridge and County Folk Museum 2012–13 (chair); public, visiting and pt/t lectr UK and USA; memb Conn Acad of Arts & Scis 1991; hon fell Magdalene Coll Cambridge 2012; FRSA 1990, FSA 2006; *Publications* numerous catalogues, articles and reviews; author of: A Companion Volume to the Kelmscott Chaucer (1975, re-issued as Morris, Burne-Jones and the Kelmscott Chaucer, 1982), Stanley Spencer (1979, revised edn 1990), Man and Measure: the Paintings of Tom Wood (1996), The Yale Center for British Art: A Tribute to the Genius of Louis I Kahn (1997), The Fitzwilliam Museum Cambridge: One Hundred and Fifty Years of Collecting (1998); *Clubs* Oxford and Cambridge; *Style—* Duncan Robinson, Esq, CBE; ✉ Magdalene College, Cambridge CB3 0AG (e-mail dr206@cam.ac.uk)

ROBINSON, Gavin James; MP; s of John Calvert Robinson, of Belfast, and Claire Alison, *née* Nesbitt; *b* 22 November 1984, Belfast; *Educ* Grosvenor GS Belfast, Queen's Univ Belfast (MA), Univ of Ulster (LLB), Inst of Professional Legal Studies Belfast; *m* 5 March 2011, Lindsay Elizabeth, *née* Witherow; 1 s (Reubenn James b 13 Sept 2013); *Career* called to the Bar NI 2008, barr-at-law Inn of Court Belfast 2008–; Belfast City: cncllr 2010–15 (elected 2011 and 2014), alderman 2012–15, Lord Mayor 2012–13; MP (DUP) Belfast E 2015–; special advsr to first min of NI 2011–12 and 2013–15; *Style—* Gavin Robinson, Esq, MP; ✉ 96 Belmont Avenue, Belfast BT4 3DE (☎ 028 9047 3111, e-mail gavin.robinson.mp@parliament.uk); House of Commons, London SW1A 0AA

ROBINSON, Dr Geoffrey Walter; CBE (1998); s of George Robinson (d 1987), and Edith Margaret, *née* Wilson (d 1988); *b* 9 November 1945; *Educ* Aireborough GS Leeds, Univ of Nottingham (BSc, PhD); *m* 12 Aug 1967, Edwina, da of Thomas Ernest Jones (d 2003); 1 s (Richard Antony b 13 Oct 1970), 1 da (Catherine Louise b 29 April 1972); *Career* IBM: UK Labs 1969–82, scientific centre mangr 1982–84, tech programmes mangr 1984–85, UK tech dir 1985–86, dir of software devpt 1986–88, dir Hursley Lab 1988–92 and 1994–96, dir of technol 1996–97; DG and chief exec Ordnance Survey 1998–99; chief advsr on science and technol DTI 1992–94, chm Br Geological Survey 2002–04 (memb Bd 2001–05); non-exec dir Pirelli Gen plc 2002–05, Pirelli UK Tyres Ltd 2002–05; memb: Centre for Exploitation of Science and Technol 1986–92, NERC 1992–94, SERC 1992–94, PPARC 1994–98, Cncl for the Central Lab of the Research Cncls 1995–98, Bd Quality Assurance Agency for Higher Educn 1997–2000; ESRC: chm Innovation Research Prog 1994–2000, chm Virtual Soc Research Prog 1996–2000; pres BCS 1995–96, vice-pres IEE 1998–2000, dep chm Fndn for Science & Technol 1998–2000; memb Worshipful Co of Info Technologists 1988; Hon DTech King Alfred's Coll Winchester (CNAA) 1992, Hon DUniv Leeds Metropolitan Univ 1997; FIEE 1993, FREng 1994, FBCS 1994 (MBCS 1988); *Style—* Dr Geoffrey Robinson, CBE, FREng; ✉ Fardale, Hookwood Lane, Ampfield, Romsey, Hampshire SO51 9BZ

ROBINSON, George; MLA; *b* 30 May 1941; *Educ* Limavady Tech Coll; *Career* former civil servant; mayor of Limavady 2002–03, MLA (DUP) E Londonderry 2003–; *Style—* Alderman George Robinson, MLA; ✉ Northern Ireland Assembly, Parliament Buildings, Belfast BT4 3XX

ROBINSON, Helen; OBE; da of Dr John Christopher Wharton (d 1997), and Gertrude Margaret, *née* Dingwall (d 1996); *Educ* Roedean; *m* 1 (m dis 1979), Philip Robinson; m 2, Desmond Preston (d 1995); 1 s (decd), 1 da; m 3, Oliver Prenn; *Career* fashion asst, fashion ed and latterly exec ed Vogue Magazine London and New York 1960–75; Debenhams plc: joined 1975, dir Dept Store, mktg and design mgmnt dir (Main Bd) 1981–86; mktg dir Condé Nast Publications Ltd 1986–88, gp md Thomas Goode & Co Ltd 1988–93 (resigned upon sale of co), special projects and mktg full-time consultancy Asprey Gp 1996–98, business consultancy MIA Pty Aust 1998–2000, chief exec New West End Co Ltd 2000–05; non-exec dir: British Airports Authy 1978–95 (memb Chm's Design Ctee 1988–95), London Transport 1984–95 (chm Design Policy Ctee), London Electricity 1989–94, Churchill China plc 1996–98; vice-chm Cncl and chm Staff Ctee RCA 1982–2000; memb: Design Mgmnt Advsy Gp London Business Sch 1985–95, Cncl The Cottage Homes (retail trade charity) 1995–96; govr and tstee Cwlth Inst 1994–2007, tstee Cwlth Educn Tst 2007–16; WWF: tstee 1988–95, chm WWF UK Ltd 1988–95, memb Cncl of Ambassadors 1999–2006, fell 2006–; Sr FRCA, Hon FCSD, FRSA; *Style—* Helen Robinson, OBE; ✉ 47 Hyde Park Gate, London SW7 5DU (☎ 020 7584 8870)

ROBINSON, Prof Hilary Frances; da of Ivor Robinson, of Oxford, and Olive, *née* Trask; *b* 25 June 1956; *Educ* John Mason HS Abingdon, Univ of Newcastle upon Tyne (BA), RCA (MA, Allen Lane/Penguin Books award), Univ of Leeds (PhD); *m* 1995 (m dis), Alastair MacLennan; *Career* painted and exhibited 1979–85; freelance writer; tutor Glasgow Sch of Art 1987–92, ed Alba (Scottish visual art magazine) 1990–92; Univ of Ulster at Belfast: lectr in fine art 1992–2002, prof of the politics of art 2002–05, head Sch of Art & Design 2002–05 (research co-ordinator 1999–2002); dean Coll of Fine Arts Carnegie Mellon Univ USA 2005–10, prof of art theory and critisism Sch of Art Carnegie Mellon Univ 2010–; author of numerous pubns on feminist art; memb: Assoc of Art Historians 1988, Coll Art Assoc USA 1993, Assoc Int des Critiques d'Art 1996; *Books* Visibly Female (ed, 1987), The Rough Guide to Venice (co-author, 1989, 2 edn 1993), Feminism-Art-Theory 1968–2000 (2001), Reading Art, Reading Irigaray: The politics of art by women (2006); *Style—* Prof Hilary Robinson; ✉ School of Art, College of Fine Arts, Carnegie Mellon University, 5000 Forbes Avenue, Pittsburgh PA 15213, USA

ROBINSON, Sir Ian; kt (2000); s of Thomas Mottram Robinson (d 1972), and Eva Iris, *née* Bird (d 1984); *b* 3 May 1942; *Educ* Univ of Leeds (BSc), Harvard Univ (SMP); *m* 28 Oct 1967, Kathleen Crawford, da of James Leay, of Edinburgh; 1 s (Andrew John b 1977), 1 da (Caroline Anne b 1973); *Career* Ralph M Parsons Co Ltd: dir of ops 1979, vice-pres (USA) 1983, md 1985; md John Brown Engineering Constructors Ltd 1986–90, chief exec John Brown Engineers & Constructors 1990–92; chm and chief exec John Brown plc 1992–95, chm Engrg Div and main bd dir Trafalgar House plc 1992–95, chief exec Scottish Power plc 1995–2001; chm Scottish Enterprise 2001–03; non-exec chm: Amey plc 2001–03, Hilton Gp plc 2001–06, Ladbrokes plc 2006–09; non-exec dir: RMC Gp plc 2000–01, Siemens plc 2003–, Scottish Newcastle plc 2004–08, Compass Gp plc 2006–; FIChemE, FREng 1994, FRSE 2003; *Recreations* golf; *Clubs* RAC; *Style—* Sir Ian Robinson, FREng

ROBINSON, Jancis Mary (Mrs N L Lander); OBE (2003); da of Thomas Edward Robinson (d 2000), and Ann, *née* Conacher (d 2012); *b* 22 April 1950; *Educ* Carlisle HS, St Anne's Coll Oxford (MA); *m* 22 Oct 1981, Nicholas Laurence Lander, *qv*, s of Israel Lennard Lander; 2 da (Julia Margaux b 10 July 1982, Rose Ellen b 6 March 1991), 1 s (William Isaac b 5 Sept 1984); *Career* early career experience: mktg and producing skiing holidays for Thomson Holidays 1971–74, undertaking odd jobs while writing for Good Food Guide 1975; asst ed then ed Wine and Spirit 1975–80, fndr Drinker's Digest 1977 (became Which? Wine Monthly 1980), ed Which? Wine Monthly and Which? Wine Annual Guide 1980–82, Sunday Times 1980–86 (wine corr, food corr, gen features); wine corr: The Evening Standard 1987–88, Financial Times 1989–, www.jancisrobinson.com 2001–; presenter and writer The Wine Programme (1983, 1985 and 1987), presenter Jancis Robinson's Christmas Wine List 1985, presenter BBC Design Awards 1986–87, narrator Design Classics 1987; presenter and writer: Jancis Robinson Meets 1987, Matters of Taste 1989 and 1991, Vintners' Tales 1993 and 1998 (Glenfiddich Award), Grape Expectations (US) 1994 and 1995, Jancis Robinson's Wine Course 1995, The Food Chain 1996 and 1998, Taste 1999; dir Eden Productions Ltd; wine conslt British Airways; Glenfiddich Awards: Best Book on Wine (The Great Wine Book) 1983, Broadcaster of the Year and Glenfiddich Trophy 1984, Wine Writer 1986, Food Writer 1986, Best Book on Wine (The Oxford Companion to Wine) 1995, Drink Writer of the Year and Glenfiddich Trophy 1996, TV Personality of the Year 1999; other recent awards incl: Soc of Wine Educators Grand Award (US) 2009, Schweizer Silberlorbeeren Medaille Historia Gastronomica Halvetica (Switzerland) 2010 (for Hallwag Handbuch Wein, the German version of How to Taste), Goldene Traube Pannonien Award Burgenland (Austria) 2011; memb Inst of Masters of Wine 1984, hon pres Wine and Spirit Educn Tst 2012–14; Jurade de St Emilion, Commanderie de Bontemps de Médoc et Graves, Freedom (hc) of The Vintners' Co for services to wine 2013; Hon DUniv Open Univ 1997; Officier de l'Ordre du Mérite Agricole (France) 2010, Comendador da Ordem do Mérito Empresarial (Order of Merit Portugal) 2012; *Books* The Wine Book (1979), The Great Wine Book (1982), Masterglass (1983), How to Choose and Enjoy Wine (1984), Vines, Grapes and Wines (1986), Jancis Robinson's Food and Wine Adventures (1987), Jancis Robinson on The Demon Drink (1988), Vintage Timecharts (1989), The Oxford Companion to Wine (ed, 1994, 1999, 2006 and 2015), Jancis Robinson's Wine Course (1995 and 2003), Jancis Robinson's Guide to Wine Grapes (1996), Confessions of a Wine Lover (1997), Jancis Robinson's Wine Tasting Workbook (2000), The Oxford Companion to the Wines of North America (conslt ed, 2000), Jancis Robinson's Concise Wine Companion (2001), The World Atlas of Wine (5 edn with Hugh Johnson, 2001, 6 edn 2007, 7 edn 2013), How to Taste Wine (2008), Wine Grapes (with Julia Harding and Jose Vouillamoz, 2012), American Wine (with Linda Murphy, 2012); *Style—* Ms Jancis Robinson, OBE; ✉ website www.jancisrobinson.com

ROBINSON, Prof John; s of William Clifford Robinson (d 1982), and Annie, *née* Banks; *b* 11 July 1933; *Educ* Little Lever Secondary Sch, Radcliffe Jr Tech Coll, Salford Univ (BSc), Cranfield Univ (MSc), Inst of Sound and Vibration Res Univ of Southampton (PhD), Faculty of Engrg Sci and Mathematics Univ of Southampton (DSc); *m* 1, 3 Aug 1957 (m dis 1980), Cynthia, da of late Eric Nicholls; 2 s (Gary Edward b 16 Aug 1958, Lee John b 16 May 1961); m 2, 12 Sept 1984, Shirley Ann (decd), da of Roland Walter Bradley, of Bidford-on-Avon, Warks; *Career* Br and USA Aerospace Industry 1949–71, head Robinson and Associates 1971–95; conslt organiser World Congress and Exhibition on Finite Element Methods 1975–95 (ed and publisher World Congress Proceedings 1975–95), ed and publisher Finite Element News 1976–95, lectr of worldwide courses on Understanding Finite Element Stress Analysis 1980–95, fndr and memb Steering Ctee Nat Agency for Finite Element Methods and Standards 1983–95, dir Robinson FEMInst 1986–95, industrial res prof Univ of Exeter 1986–95; composer and lyricist; fndr GBM Prodns; prodr (own musicals): Lorna Doone 1992, Shipperbottom's Rocking Horses 1994, Behind the Iron Mask (Duchess Theatre London) 2005 and (New World Stages Theatre NY) 2007, Too Close to the Sun (Comedy Theatre (now Harold Pinter Theatre) London) 2009, A Midsummer Night's Dream (fully sung-through concert version to commemorate 400 years since Shakespeare's death, Wharf Theatre Devon) 2016; prodr (own ballets, in Vienna): The World of Bidlake Wood 1998, Alice Through the Looking Glass 2001; MRAeS 1962, MIMechE 1964, CEng; *Books* Structural Matrix Analysis for the Engineer (1966), Integrated Theory of Finite Element Methods (1973), Understanding Finite Element Stress Analysis (1981), Early FEM Pioneers (1985), articles; *Style—* Prof John Robinson

ROBINSON, John Harris; CBE (2014); *b* 22 December 1940; *Educ* Woodhouse Grove Sch, Univ of Birmingham (BSc); *m* 2 March 1963, Doreen Alice; 1 s (Mark John b 9 March 1965), 1 da (Karen Claire b 1 Nov 1968); *Career* ICI 1962–65, Fisons 1965–70, sr conslt PA Consulting Group 1970–75, chief exec Woodhouse & Rixon (Holdings) 1975–79; Smith & Nephew plc: md Smith & Nephew Medical 1979–85, gp dir UK and Europe 1985–90, chief exec 1990–97, chm 1997–2000; chm: Low & Bonar plc 1997–2001, UK Coal (formerly RJB Mining plc) 1997–2003, George Wimpey plc 1999–2007, Railtrack Gp plc 2001–02, Paragon Healthcare Gp Ltd 2002–06, Consort Medical plc (formerly Bespak plc) 2004–09, Affinity Healthcare Ltd 2005–10, Oasis Ltd 2007–10; chm Abbeyfield Soc 2009–15; non-exec dir Delta plc 1993–2001, operating ptnr Duke Street Capital 2001–10; pres: IChemE 1999–2000, Chartered Inst of Mgmnt 2002–03; memb Industrial Devpt Advsy Bd DTI 1998–2000; chm McRobert Award Royal Acad of Engrg 2010–14; pro-chllr and chm Cncl Univ of Hull 1998–2006; tstee: Methodist Independent Schs Tst 2011–, Royal Coll of Surgeons 2014–, Livability 2014–; govr: Hymers Coll Hull 1984–2012, Woodhouse Grove Sch 2004–13; Hon DEng Univ of Birmingham 2000, Hon DUniv Bradford 2000, Hon DBA Univ of Lincoln 2002, Hon DSc Univ of Hull 2006; memb Ct of Assts Worshipful Co of Engrs 2006 (Master 2010, chm Engrs Tst 2012–); CEng, FIChemE, CIMgt, FREng 1998; *Recreations* golf, cricket, walking; *Clubs* Athenaeum; *Style—* John Robinson, Esq, CBE; ✉ 146 Artillery Mansions, Victoria Street, London SW1H 0HX

ROBINSON, Prof John Joseph; s of James Reid Robinson (d 1983), and Elizabeth Mary, *née* Ennis (d 1985); *b* 11 June 1940; *Educ* Down HS Downpatrick, Queen's Univ Belfast (BAgr, PhD); *m* 26 Sept 1967, Margaret, da of Samuel James Magill; 1 da (Lyn Elizabeth b 29 Dec 1972), 1 s (Andrew James b 11 July 1974); *Career* postdoctoral research fell

Queen's Univ Belfast 1966–67, ARC postdoctoral researcher Wye Coll London 1967–68; Rowett Research Inst Bucksburn Aberdeen: sr scientific offr 1968–73, principal scientific offr 1973–83, sr principal scientific offr (individual merit) 1983–94; Scottish Agric Coll Aberdeen: sr scientist in animal reproduction 1994–98, prof of animal reproduction 1998–; pres British Soc of Animal Science 1993–94; Fish Meal Manufacturers' Annual Research Award 1979, Research Medal RASE 1982, Sir John Hammond Meml Prize British Soc of Animal Production 1984, Sir William Young Award Royal Highland Agric Soc of Scotland 1989, George Hedley Meml Award Nat Sheep Assoc 1991; FRSE 1996; *Publications* author and co-author of over 400 publications incl refereed scientific papers, invited scientific reviews, book chapters and technical bulletins; *Recreations* gardening, club rambling; *Style—* Prof John Robinson, FRSE; ✉ 4 Hopecroft Terrace, Bucksburn, Aberdeen AB21 9RL; Scotland's Rural College, The Ferguson Building, Craibstone Estate, Bucksburn, Aberdeen AB21 9YA (☎ 01224 711052, fax 01224 711291, e-mail john.robinson@sruc.ac.uk)

ROBINSON, John Martin; s of John Cotton Robinson, and Ellen Anne Cecilia (d 2003), eld da of George Adams, of Cape Town, South Africa; *b* 10 September 1948; *Educ* Fort Augustus Abbey, St Andrews, Oriel Coll Oxford (MA, DPhil, DLitt); *Career* librarian to Duke of Norfolk 1978–; architectural writer Country Life 1974–; vice-chm Georgian Gp 1994–2014; Maltravers Herald of Arms Extraordinary 1989–; heraldic advsr to Nat Tst; chm Art and Architecture Ctee Westminster Cathedral 1996–; tstee: Arundel Castle 1987–, Wilton House 2007–, Burghley House 2009–14; FSA; Knight SMOM; *Books* The Wyatts (1980), Dukes of Norfolk (1983, 2 edn 1995), Georgian Model Farms (1983), Latest Country Houses (1984), Cardinal Consalvi (1987), Oxford Guide to Heraldry (jtly with Thomas Woodcock, 1988, 3 edn 2001), Temples of Delight (1990), Country Houses of the North West (1991), Treasures of The English Churches (1995), Windsor Castle (1996), Francis Johnson Architect (jtly with David Neve, 2001), The Staffords (2002), The Regency Country House (2005), Grass Seed in June (2006), Felling The Ancient Oaks (2012), James Wyatt Architect to George III (2012), Requisitioned: The British Country House in the Second World War (2014); *Clubs* Travellers, Roxburghe, Pitt, XV, Beefsteak, Pratt's; *Style—* John Robinson, Esq, FSA, Maltravers Herald of Arms Extraordinary; ✉ Beckside House, Barbon, via Carnforth, Lancashire LA6 2LT (☎ 01524 276300, office 020 7831 4398, e-mail mentmore@historical-buildings.co.uk)

ROBINSON, Julian; *Educ* Brighton Sch of Architecture, London Metropolitan Univ, KCL; *Career* station architect Jubilee Line Extension Project 1995–99, princ architect TfL 2000–02, sr architect St Pancras Station RLE 2004–07, head of architecture Crossrail 2008–; *Style—* Julian Robinson, Esq; ✉ Crossrail, 25 Canada Square, Canary Wharf, London E14 5LQ

ROBINSON, Sir Kenneth (Ken); kt (2003); s of James Robinson (d 1977), of Liverpool, and Ethel, *née* Allen (d 2005); *b* 4 March 1950; *Educ* Liverpool Collegiate GS, Wade Deacon GS, Bretton Hall Coll, Univ of Leeds (BEd), Univ of London (PhD); *m* 30 Jan 1982, Marie-Thérèse, da of Frederick George Watts, of Liverpool; 1 s (James b 11 Oct 1984), 1 da (Katherine Marie b 4 May 1989); *Career* educationist; dir Nat Curriculum Cncl Arts in Schools project 1985–89, prof of arts educn Univ of Warwick 1989–2000 (prof emeritus 2001–); chm Nat Advsy Ctee on Creative and Cultural Educn 1998–99; dir Culture, Creativity and the Young Cncl of Europe project; sr advsr J Paul Getty Tst LA 2000–06; FRSA; *Books* Learning Through Drama (1977), Exploring Theatre and Education (ed, 1980), The Arts in Schools (princ author, 1982), The Arts and Higher Education (ed, 1983), The Arts 5–16 (1990), Arts Education in Europe (1997), All Our Futures: Creativity, Culture and Education (1999), Out of Our Minds: Learning to Be Creative (2001), The Element: How Finding Your Passion Changes Everything (2009); *Recreations* theatre, music, cinema; *Style—* Sir Ken Robinson

ROBINSON, Mark Nicholas; s of late Eric Robinson, of Leigh on Sea, Essex, and Kate Emily Robinson; *b* 24 January 1952; *Educ* Westcliff GS for Boys, Univ of Dundee (MA, vice-pres Students' Union); *m* 4 June 1976, Patricia Margaret, da of John Malone; 2 s (Matthew John b 31 July 1981, Rory Patrick b 20 Aug 1985), 1 da (Chloe Elizabeth b 16 Nov 1983); *Career* salesman Thomson Regional Newspapers 1975–76, Allardyce Advertising 1976–77, account exec Manton Woodyer Ketley 1977–78, account dir CDP/Aspect Advertising 1981–85 (account mangr 1978–81), dir Ted Bates 1985–87; business devpt dir: Dorland Advertising 1987–88, Horner Collis & Kirvan 1988–92, GGK 1992–93, Publicis 1993–97; mktg dir J Walter Thompson 1997–2001, md Miracle Media Gp 2001–2002, ceo Beatwax Communications 2002–05, worldwide head of mktg Vizeum 2005–; fndr and dir Radio Feltham 1994–, dir Prison Radio Assoc 2006–; dir Devpt Bd Royal Court Theatre 2000–, head London Advsy Gp Common Purpose 2004–; IPA: chm IPA Soc 1987–88, memb various ctees incl Devpt and Trg Ctee; chm NABS 1998–2000; FIPA 1991; *Recreations* cycling, films (fndr memb St Margarets Film Club); *Style—* Mark Robinson, Esq

ROBINSON, Martin; *Career* dep ed NME until 2011, ed ShortList 2011–; *Style—* Martin Robinson, Esq; ✉ Twitter @martin_rob, @ShorListEditor; ShortList, 26–34 Emerald Street, London WC1N 3QA (website www.shortlist.com, Twitter @ShortList)

ROBINSON, Michael Stuart; *b* 17 May 1964; *Educ* St Albans Sch, Portsmouth Poly (BSc); *m* 1994, Lucie Kate, *née* Bailey; 1 da, 1 s; *Career* audit mangr Pricewaterhouse 1986–92, chief internal auditor and head of business devpt Blackhorse Financial Servs 1992–97; chief exec: Clerical Medical Int 1997–2005, HBOS Europe Financial Servs 2005–06, UK Hydrographic Office 2006–11; ACA 1989; *Recreations* music, sailing, tennis, skiing; *Style—* Michael Robinson, Esq

ROBINSON, Mike; *Career* proprietor and chef The Pot Kiln Frilsham, co-proprietor Harwood Arms Fulham (Michelin star); television appearances incl: Great Food Live (UKTV Food), Saturday Kitchen (BBC2), Tales from the Country (ITV), Countrywise (ITV), Countrywise Kitchen (ITV); *Books* Wild Flavours (2005), Wild Flavours, Fit for Table (2008), Countrywise Kitchen Cookbook (2011); *Style—* Mike Robinson, Esq; ✉ The Pot Kiln, Frilsham, Nr Yattendon RG18 0XX

ROBINSON, Neil; s of Arthur Robinson, of Liverpool, and Margery Robinson (d 1989); *b* 25 April 1958; *Educ* Anfield Comp Sch Liverpool; *m* 1988, Susan Elizabeth, da of late John Carr Campbell FRCS; 1 s (Struan Campbell b 3 Oct 1994); *Career* journalist: S Yorkshire Times 1976, Evening Chronicle Newcastle 1979, Border Television 1986; Border Television: head of news and current affairs 1989, controller of programmes 1991, dir of programmes 2000; dir Cumbria Inward Invest Agency Ltd 1997–; Euro bd memb Co-operative International de la Recherche et d'Actions en Metiere de Communication 1998–; memb: Northern Production Fund Panel Northern Arts 1993–, Television Soc 1988, BAFTA Scot Ctee 1998–; FRSA 1995; *Clubs* Groucho; *Style—* Neil Robinson, Esq; ✉ Fayrefield, High Bank Hill, Kirkoswald, Cumbria

ROBINSON, Nicholas; s of Samuel Robinson (d 1987), and Sarah, *née* McCloy; *b* 7 November 1948; *Educ* The HS Greenock, Univ of Glasgow; *m* 15 April 1971, Elizabeth, da of Donald Campbell Service; 3 s (Gary b 16 Sept 1971, Graeme Campbell b 21 March 1974, Gordon Douglas b 15 July 1976); *Career* apprentice CA Wylie & Bisset CA's 1967–73, accountant then fin dir TAB Ltd 1973–76, accountant Fleming & Wilson CA's 1976–78, British National Oil Corporation 1978–79, fndr own practice 1979 (merged with Kidsons Impey 1982, now HLB Kidsons), currently dir of business devpt and North region managing ptnr HLB Kidsons; regular contrib to Business Press; MICAS 1973; *Recreations* motor cruising, golf, music; *Clubs* St James' (Manchester); *Style—* Nicholas Robinson, Esq

ROBINSON, Nicholas Anthony (Nick); *b* 5 October 1963, Macclesfield, Cheshire; *Educ* Cheadle Hulme Sch, Univ Coll Cambridge; *m* 1991, Pippa; 1 da (Alice), 2 s (Will, Harry); *Career* BBC: joined as prodn trainee 1986, dep ed Panorama 1993–96, presenter Weekend Breakfast and Late Night Live Radio 5 Live 1996–99, chief political corr News 24 1999–2002; political ed ITN 2002–05, political ed BBC 2005–15, presenter Today BBC Radio 4 2015–; *Style—* Nick Robinson, Esq; ✉ BBC Broadcasting House, Portland Place, London W1A 1AA

ROBINSON, Nicholas Ridley; s of late Capt Leslie Jack Robinson, JP, and late Eileen Mary, *née* Phillips; *b* 2 September 1952; *Educ* Dulwich Coll; *m* 1, 26 May 1976 (m dis 1980), Vivienne; m 2, 13 Sept 1980, Joanna Mary, da of late Wilford Henry Gibson, CBE, of Sanderstead, Surrey; 2 s (Stuart Laurence Ridley b 9 May 1984, Duncan Henry b 18 Aug 1987), 1 da (Felicity Mary b 1 April 1990); *Career* admitted slr 1977; sr ptnr Sandom Robinson 1988– (ptnr 1978–); chair The Isthmian Football League Ltd 2015– (vice-chair 2008–15); vice-chair Br Home and Hosp for Incurables 1996–2008; memb Cncl FA 2008–; chief finance offr Kent Soc of RFU Referees Ltd 2001–16; Freeman: City of London, Worshipful Co of Slrs, Worshipful Co of Farriers; memb Law Soc 1977, FCIArb 1993; *Publications* The First 100 Years of the Isthmian Football League (2009); *Recreations* soccer and rugby union; *Clubs* RAC; *Style—* Nicholas Robinson, Esq; ✉ Triumph House, Station Approach, Sanderstead Road, South Croydon CR2 0PL (☎ 020 8651 5053, fax 020 8651 9146, e-mail nickrob@clara.net)

ROBINSON, Nick; *Career* Phoenix IT Gp: fndr 1993, ceo 1997– (dep chm 2008–); *Style—* Nick Robinson, Esq; ✉ Phoenix IT Group plc, Technology House, Hunsbury Hill Avenue, Northampton NN4 8QS

ROBINSON, Oliver John à Beckett; s of Brian Robinson, and Jane, *née* Morris; *b* 2 September 1973, Djakarta, Indonesia; *Educ* Worth Abbey, Wimbledon Sch of Art (HND), Bucks Coll (John Hegarty Award, BA); *Career* art dir D'Arcy (formerly DMB&B) 1997–2002; Agency.com (formerly iTraffic): sr art dir then creative dir 2003–06, head of creative 2006–07; assoc creative dir GT 2007–08, assoc creative dir Dare 2008–10, creative dir J Walter Thompson 2010–15, sr creative dir FP7 McCanns Dubai 2015–; judge Microsite Category D&AD 2007, judge D&AD 2012; *Awards* overall winner Campaign Digital 2005 (category winner Silver Award 2005 and 2006, finalist Cannes Cyber Lion 2005, 2006 and 2007, Agency of the Year Revolution Magazine 2007 (Best Intergrated Mktg 2006), Gold Award IAB/Adweek Mixx Awards, Best Online Advtg Net Imperative, DMA Echo Award, two first places IAB Creative Showcase, Web Mktg Assocs Int Advtg Award, Creative Review The Annual Award 2010, Newspaper Awards, Grand Prix and Best in Class Int Food and Beverage Awards 2013; *Recreations* film, reading, shooting, new media, design, painting, typography, good eating; *Style—* Oliver Robinson, Esq; ✉ CROCKS, Bentley, Near Farnham, Surrey GU10 5NF

ROBINSON, Paul; *b* 15 October 1979, Beverley, Yorks; *Career* professional footballer; clubs: Leeds United 1996–2004 (first team debut 1998), Tottenham Hotspur 2004–08, Blackburn Rovers 2008–; England: 41 caps, debut v Australia 2003, memb squad European Championship 2004 and World Cup 2006, ret 2010; *Style—* Mr Paul Robinson

ROBINSON, Dr Paul Hyman; s of Maurice Isaac Robinson, of Finchley, London, and Stella Robinson, *née* Hymanson; *b* 14 February 1950; *Educ* Haberdashers' Aske's, UCH Med Sch London (BSc, MB BS), Univ of London (MD); *m* 1, 29 July 1974 (m dis 1992), Susan Deborah, da of Joseph Saffer, of Bournemouth, Dorset; 2 da (Jessica b 1979, Zoë b 1988), 2 s (Matthew b 1981, Daniel b 1986); m 2, 11 April 1998, Sonja, da of Liselotte Wilberg; *Career* jr hosp doctor UCH, Whittington Hosp and Nat Hosp Queen Sq 1975–80, trainee psychiatrist Bethlem Royal and Maudsley Hosps 1980–86, sr lectr and conslt psychiatrist KCH and Maudsley Hosp 1986–90, conslt psychiatrist Gordon and Westminster Hosps and head Eating Disorders Unit Gordon Hosp 1990–96; Royal Free Hosp: conslt psychiatrist 1997–2007, head Eating Disorders Service, St Ann's Eating Disorders Serv Russell Unit 2007–; hon sr lectr Royal Free and UC Sch of Med; numerous pubns on anorexia nervosa, bulimia nervosa, gastric function and biology of cholecystokinin; assoc memb Inst Family Therapy 1988; FRSM 1983, FRCPsych 1995 (MRCPsych 1982), FRCP 2001 (MRCP 1977); *Books* Community Treatment of Eating Disorders (2006); *Style—* Dr Paul Robinson; ☎ 020 7685 5904, fax 020 7685 1003, e-mail drpaulrobinson@gmail.com

ROBINSON, Rt Hon Peter David; PC (2007), MLA; s of David and Sheliah Robinson; *b* 29 December 1948; *Educ* Annadale GS, Castlereagh Coll of Further Educn; *m* 1970, Iris Robinson, *qv*, *née* Collins; 2 s, 1 da; *Career* MP (DUP) Belfast E 1979–2010, memb NI Assembly 1982–86; DUP: gen sec 1975–79, dep ldr 1980–2008 (resigned 1987, re-elected 1988), ldr 2008–; memb: NI Forum 1996–98, NI Assembly 1998–; NI Assembly: min for regnl devpt 2000–02, min for finance 2007–08, first min 2008–16; alderman Castlereagh Borough Cncl 1977–2007; *Style—* The Rt Hon Peter Robinson, MLA; ✉ 51 Gransha Road, Dundonald, Belfast BT16 2HB (☎ 028 9047 3111)

ROBINSON, Peter James Edmund; s of Tom Robinson, of Blockley, Glos, and Doreen, *née* Clingan; *b* 18 November 1965, Mombasa, Kenya; *Educ* St Catharine's Coll Cambridge (MA); *Children* 1 da (Eva b 26 Aug 1993); *Career* literary agent; ed Michael Joseph 1986–89, literary agent Curtis Brown 1989–2005, fndr and md Robinson Literary Agency Ltd; FRSA; *Recreations* music; *Clubs* Century; *Style—* Peter Robinson, Esq; ✉ Robinson Literary Agency Limited, 20 Powis Mews, London W11 1JN (☎ 020 7096 1460, e-mail peter@rlabooks.co.uk)

ROBINSON, Prof Peter Michael; s of Maurice Allan Robinson, and Brenda Margaret, *née* Ponsford; *b* 20 April 1947; *Educ* Brockenhurst GS, UCL (BSc), LSE (MSc), Australian Nat Univ (PhD); *m* 27 Feb 1981, Wendy Rhea, da of Morris Brandmark; 1 da; *Career* lectr LSE 1969–70; assoc prof: Harvard Univ 1977–79 (asst prof 1973–77), Univ of Br Columbia 1979–80; prof Univ of Surrey 1980–84, prof of econometrics LSE 1984–95, Tooke prof of economic science and statistics LSE 1995–, Leverhulme Tst personal research prof 1998–2003; author of numerous articles in learned jls and books; co-ed: Econometric Theory 1989–91, Econometrica 1991–96, Jl of Econometrics 1997–2013, Jl of Time Series Analysis 2013–; jt ed Time Series Analysis Vol II 1996, ed with Long Memory Time Series 2003; memb Editorial Bd Annals of Statistics, memb Advsy Bd Econometric Theory 2005–, memb Exec Cncl Jl of Econometrics 2014, involved with various other jls; Best Paper Award Japan Statistical Soc 2009; dr (hc) Carlos III Univ Madrid 2000; memb Int Statistical Inst 2005; fell: Econometric Soc 1989, Centre for Microdata Methods and Practice 2003, Spatial Econometrics Assoc 2006, Modelling and Simulation Soc of Australia and NZ 2007 (Biennial Medallist 2007), Granger Centre for Time Series Econometrics 2007; FIMS 2000, FRSA 1999, FBA 2000; *Recreations* walking; *Style—* Prof Peter M Robinson; ✉ London School of Economics and Political Science, Houghton Street, London WC2A 2AE

ROBINSON, Stephen Julian Roper; s of Andrew Thomas Roper Robinson, of London, and Barbara Anne, *née* Black; *b* 28 September 1961; *Educ* Westminster, The Queen's Coll Oxford (scholar, BA); *Career* reporter Natal Witness South Africa 1983–85, freelance writer Cape Town 1985–86; Daily Telegraph: joined 1986, Belfast corr 1987, Johannesburg corr 1987–90, Washington corr 1990–97, foreign ed 1997–2001, asst ed 2001–05, comment ed 2005–; contrib The Spectator 1985–; winner T E Utley Meml Prize 1990; *Recreations* tennis, reading; *Style—* Stephen Robinson, Esq; ✉ 2 Albert Terrace Mews, London NW1 7TA (☎ 020 7722 3332); The Daily Telegraph, 1 Canada Square, Canary Wharf, London E14 5DT (☎ 020 7538 5000, fax 020 7538 7270, e-mail stephen.robinson@telegraph.co.uk)

ROBINSON, Sir Tony; kt (2013); *Educ* Wanstead Co HS, Central Sch of Speech and Drama; *Children* 1 s (Luke), 1 da (Laura); *Career* actor and writer; vice-pres Br Actor's Equity

R

1996–2000; memb Lab Pty NEC 2000–04; Hon MA: Univ of E London, Univ of Bristol; Hon Dr: Univ of Exeter, Oxford Brookes Univ, Open Univ, Univ of Chester; hon fell Univ of Cardiff; *Theatre* numerous appearances as child actor incl original version of stage musical Oliver!, several years in rep theatre, theatre dir for 2 years, then successively with Chichester Festival Theatre, RSC and NT; Tony Robinson's Cunning Night Out Tour 2005–07; *Television* incl: Ernie Roberts in Horizon documentary Joey, Baldrick in Black Adder (4 series, BBC), Sheriff of Nottingham in Maid Marian and Her Merry Men (also writer, 4 series), Alan in My Wonderful Life (3 series, Granada); as presenter: Points of View, Stay Tooned, three African documentary features for Comic Relief, Time Team (20 series, Channel 4), Great Journey to the Caribbean, 2 series of Worst Jobs in History (Channel 4), The Real Da Vinci Code (Channel 4), Me and My Mum (Channel 4), Tony Robinson's Crime and Punishment, Man On Earth 2009, Blitz Street 2010, Tony Robinson's History Walks 2013–14, Man Down (sitcom, 2016); as writer: Fat Tulip's Garden (30 episodes, Central), Odysseus – the Greatest Hero of Them All (13-part series, BBC), Blood and Honey (26 episodes, BBC); *Awards* for writing: 2 RTS, BAFTA, Int Prix Jeunesse; *Publications* No Cunning Plan (autobiography, 2016); non-fiction: Archaeology is Rubbish (with Prof Mick Aston, 2002), In Search of British Heroes (2003), The Worst Jobs in History (with David Wilcock, 2004), The Worst Children's Jobs in History (2005, Blue Peter Factual Book of the Year); also author of 17 children's books incl: Tony Robinson's Kings & Queens (1999), Bad Kids (2009), Tony Robinson's Weird World of Wonders – World War Two (2014, Blue Peter Factual Book of the Year); also 7 other books in the Weird World of Wonders series; *Style*— Sir Tony Robinson; ✉ c/o JHA, 3 Stedham Place, London WC1A 1HU (website www.jeremyhicks.com)

ROBINSON, Trevor; OBE (2009); *b* 20 March 1964, Clapham, London; *Educ* Chelsea Coll of Art; *m* Rania; 2 s (Mylo Antoine b 17 Aug 2007, Reece b 17 June 1990), 1 da (Itsi b 6 Oct 2008); *Career* TBWA 1987–89, HHCL 1989–95, fndr and creative dir Quiet Storm 1995–; chair IPA Ethnic Diversity Forum; fndr Create Not Hate 2007–; Best TV Commercial RTS Award 1992, LACE Best Business Award 2004, 4 Creative Circle Awards, 5 Bronze and Silver D&AD Awards; *Recreations* cinema, music, film, cycling; *Clubs* Groucho, Soho House; *Style*— Trevor Robinson, Esq, OBE; ✉ Quiet Storm, 42–44 Beak Street, London W1F 9RH (☎ 020 7534 3870)

ROBINSON, Victor Philip; s of Francis Herbert Robinson (d 1962), and Constance Harriet, *née* Phillips (d 1975); *b* 26 November 1943; *Educ* Cranleigh Sch, St Mary's Hosp Med Sch (MB BS); *m* 30 Oct 1965, Elizabeth Margaret, da of Lt Cdr Kenneth Thomas Basset (d 1989); 4 da ((Anne) Michelle b 30 Aug 1966, Louise Frances b 27 Aug 1969, Charlotte Faye b 31 Jan 1972, Victoria Jane b 29 Aug 1974); *Career* conslt obstetrician and gynaecologist: Queen Charlotte's Maternity Hosp, St George's Hosp Med Sch, Hillingdon and Mount Vernon Hosps, Harefield Hosp 1982–; former conslt obstetrician and gynaecologist Hillingdon Hosp Tst 1982–2006; obstetrician reponsible for the care of first reported pregnancies in UK following heart and lung transplantations (presentation to World Congress); author of various pubns in obstetrics and gynaecology incl psychological issues and bereavement; former chair of tstees Child Bereavement UK; memb: Jubilee Sailing Tst, Youth Tst South; memb: RSM, BMA; FRCOG; *Recreations* sailing, flying, vintage and classic Bentley motor cars; *Clubs* Royal Solent Yacht; *Style*— Victor Robinson, Esq; ✉ Rectory Cottage, Cuxham, Watlington, Oxfordshire OX49 5NQ (e-mail drvicrobinson@aol.com)

ROBINSON, Vivian; QC (1986); s of William Robinson (d 1986), of Wakefield, and Ann, *née* Kidd (d 2000); *b* 29 July 1944; *Educ* Queen Elizabeth GS Wakefield, The Leys Sch Cambridge, Sidney Sussex Coll Cambridge (BA); *m* 19 April 1975, (Nora) Louise, da of Maj Peter Duncan Marriner, TD (d 1988), of Rayleigh; 2 da (Katherine Anne b 12 Sept 1977, Anna Ruth b 12 July 1981), 1 s (Edward Duncan b 30 Jan 1980); *Career* called to the Bar Inner Temple 1967 (bencher 1991, treas 2009); recorder of the Crown Court 1986–, gen counsel Serious Fraud Office 2009–11, ptnr McGuire Woods London LLP 2011–; Liveryman and memb Court of Assts Worshipful Co of Gardeners (Master 2000–01); *Recreations* gardening, reading; *Clubs* Garrick, MCC, Pilgrims; *Style*— Vivian Robinson, Esq, QC; ✉ McGuire Woods London LLP, 11 Pilgrim Street, London EC4V 6RN (☎ 020 7632 1600)

ROBINSON, Winifred; da of John Robinson, of Liverpool, and Mary Bernadette, *née* Whitehill; *b* 7 December 1957; *Educ* Notre Dame Collegiate Liverpool, Univ of Liverpool; *m* March 1998, Roger Wilkes; 1 s (Anthony John Roger b 1999); *Career* broadcaster; reporter and presenter North West Tonight (BBC TV) 1987–90, reporter File on Four (BBC Radio 4) 1990–91, local govt corr (BBC North West) 1991–94, reporter Today Programme (BBC Radio) 1995–98; presenter (BBC Radio): Today Programme 1998–2001, The World Today 1998–2001, You and Yours 2000–; reporter and presenter Radio 4 documentaries 2004–; Interview of the Year Radio Academy Award 2014 (for interview with Ralph Bulger, father of James Bulger, to mark 20th anniversary of his murder); hon degree Liverpool Hope Univ 2014; *Recreations* gardening, cooking, reading; *Style*— Ms Winifred Robinson; ✉ You and Yours, BBC, Third Floor, Dock House, MediaCityUK, Salford M50 2LH (☎ 0161 836 1346); c/o Maggie Pearlstine Associates Ltd, 31 Ashley Gardens, Ambrosden Avenue, London SW1P 1QE (☎ 020 7828 4212)

ROBINSON, Zoe; *b* 30 November 1989, Bury, Lancs; *Career* Paralympic boccia player; achievements incl: Gold medal mixed team (with David Smith, Dan Bentley and Nigel Murray, MBE, *qqv*) Paralympics Beijing 2008, Bronze medal mixed team (with David Smith, Dan Bentley and Nigel Murray, MBE, *qqv*) Paralympics London 2012; *Style*— Ms Zoe Robinson; ✉ c/o British Paralympic Association, 60 Charlotte Street, London W1T 2NU

ROBISON, Shona; MSP; da of Robin Robison, and Dorothy Robison; *b* 26 May 1966, Redcar, Yorks; *Educ* Alva Acad, Univ of Glasgow (MA), Jordanhill Coll; *m* 1997, Stewart Hosie, MP, *qv*; 1 da (Morag b 29 June 2003); *Career* homecare organiser Glasgow City Cncl; MSP (SNP): Scotland NE 1999–2003, Dundee E 2003–11, Dundee City E 2011–; shadow min for health 2003–07, min for public health and sport 2007–11, min for Cwlth Games and sport 2011–; *Recreations* hill walking, cooking; *Style*— Ms Shona Robison, MSP; ✉ The Scottish Parliament, Edinburgh EH99 1SP (☎ 0131 348 5707, e-mail shona.robison.msp@scottish.parliament.uk); Constituency Office (☎ 01382 623200, fax 01382 903205)

ROBOTHAM, (John) Michael; OBE (1997); s of Alpheus John Robotham, OBE, JP, DL (d 1994), of Quarndon, Derbys, and Gwendolyn Constance, *née* Bromet (d 1999); *b* 27 March 1933; *Educ* Clifton; *m* 29 June 1963 (m dis 1989), Diana Elizabeth, da of Alfred Thomas Webb (d 1967); 2 s (Guy Thomas Blews b 1967, Adam John Blews b 1971 d 1982); m 2, 1989 (m dis 2006), Victoria Mary Cronjé, da of Victor St Clair Yates; m 3, 2007, Celia Margaret Powiecki, da of Canon John Smyth; *Career* 2 Lt 12 Royal Lancers 1957–59; assoc J M Finn & Co (membs of FSA) 1980–2008; dir: Western Selection plc 1971–, London Finance & Investment Gp plc 1984–; chm Monteagle SA 1996–2012; vice-pres Inst of Advanced Motorists 2002– (chm 1989–2002); memb Worshipful Co of Carmen 2002–; FCA, MSI (memb Stock Exchange 1963); *Recreations* travel; *Clubs* Cavalry and Guards', HAC, City of London; *Style*— Michael Robotham, Esq; ✉ Brickwall Farm House, Clophill, Bedfordshire MK45 4DA (☎ 01525 861333, fax 01525 862477); City Group plc, 6 Middle Street, London EC1A 7JA (☎ 020 7796 1858)

ROBOZ, Zsuzsi; da of Imre Roboz (d 1945), and Edith, *née* Grosz (d 1976); *b* 15 August 1939; *Educ* Royal Acad of Arts London, Pietro Annigoni Florence; *m* 22 Jan 1964, (Alfred) Teddy Smith; *Career* artist; solo exhibitions incl: Hong Kong Arts Festival 1976, Revudeville (V&A) 1978, Drawn to Ballet (Royal Festival Hall) 1983, Budapest Spring Festival 1985 and 1988, Music Makers (Royal Festival Hall) 1987, Lincoln Center New York 1989, British Art Now – a personal view (ART 93, Business Design Centre) 1993, The Creators (Roy Miles Gallery London) 1994, The Spirit of Nature (David Messum Fine Art London) 1995, New Drawings (David Messum Fine Art London) 1997, XXth Century Illusions (David Messum Fine Art London) 1999, Drawn to Music (David Messum Fine Art London) 2002, Messum's Cork Street 2005, 2008 and 2011–; portraits incl: Lord Olivier in the Theatre Museum, Dame Ninette de Valois in Nat Portrait Gallery, Sir George Solti, Sir John Gielgud, Prince William of Gloucester in Barnwell Church; work in public collections incl: Tate Gallery London, Theatre Museum, V&A, Nat Portrait Gallery, Museum of Fine Arts Budapest, Pablo Casals Museum Puerto Rico, St John's Coll Cambridge, Royal Festival Hall London; memb Pastel Soc, FRSA; *Books* Women & Men's Daughters (1970), Chichester Ten, Portrait of a Decade (1975), British Ballet To-day (1980), British Art Now: A personal view (text by Edward Lucie-Smith, 1993), Roboz: A painter's paradox (text by John Russell Taylor, 2006); *Recreations* music, swimming, reading; *Clubs* Chelsea Arts, Arts; *Style*— Ms Zsuzsi Roboz; ✉ The Studio, 76 Eccleston Square Mews, London SW1V 1QN (☎ 020 7834 4617, fax 020 7724 6844)

ROBSON, Alexandra; da of Sir John Robson, KCMG, and Lady Robson; *b* 5 December 1963; *Educ* Sherborne Sch for Girls, KCL (BA); *m* 24 April 1993 (m dis 2011), Simon Brocklebank-Fowler, *qv*; 1 da (Honor b 1998); *Career* Trimedia 1985–88, GCI London 1988–91, head of PR Historic Royal Palaces 1991–95, md Aurelia PR 1999–2005, md APR Communications 2005–; MIPR 1990; *Recreations* entertaining; *Style*— Ms Alexandra Robson; ✉ APR Communications, Victoria House, 1A Gertrude Street, London SW10 0JN (☎ 020 7349 3801, fax 020 7376 5295, mobile 07768 992401, e-mail arobson@aprcommunications.com, website www.aprcommunications.com)

ROBSON, Prof Brian Turnbull; OBE (2008); s of Oswell Robson (d 1973), and Doris Lowes, *née* Ayre (d 1984); *b* 23 February 1939; *Educ* Royal GS Newcastle, St Catharine's Coll Cambridge (MA, PhD); *m* 21 Dec 1973, Glenna, da of Jack Leslie Ransom, MBE, DCM, Croix de Guerre (d 1974); *Career* lectr UCW Aberystwyth 1964–67, Harkness fell Univ of Chicago 1967–68, lectr Univ of Cambridge 1968–77, fell Fitzwilliam Coll Cambridge 1968–77; Univ of Manchester: prof of geography 1977–2004, dean Faculty of Arts 1988–90, pro-vice-chllr 1993–97, prof emeritus 2004–; dir Centre for Urban Policy Studies 1983–; pres Inst of Br Geographers 1992–93, hon sec Manchester Statistical Soc 2011–13 (pres 1995–97); chm Manchester Cncl for Voluntary Servs 1983–91; Fndr's Medal RGS 2000, Sir Peter Hall Award Regnl Studies Assoc 2015; FRGS 1973, AcSS 2000, FRSA 2007, hon MRTPI 2002; *Books* Urban Analysis (1969), Urban Growth (1973), Urban Social Areas (1975), Managing The City (1987), Those Inner Cities (1988), Assessing the Impact of Urban Policy (1994), Index of Local Conditions (1995), The Impact of Urban Development Corporations (1998), Regional Development Agencies and Local Area Regeneration (2000), The State of English Cities (2001), A Typology of Deprived Neighbourhoods (2008), John Wood, Urban Cartographer (2014), Maps and Maths in the 1832 Great Reform Act (2014), The Town Plans of William Stukeley (2016); *Recreations* theatre, watercolour painting, gardening, antique maps, classical music; *Style*— Prof Brian Robson, OBE; ✉ 32 Oaker Avenue, West Didsbury, Manchester M20 2XH (☎ 0161 448 7182); Department of Geography, University of Manchester, Manchester M13 9PL (☎ 0161 275 3639, e-mail brian.robson@manchester.ac.uk)

ROBSON, Bryan; OBE; s of Brian Jackson Robson, of Chester-Le-Street, Co Durham, and Maureen, *née* Lowther; *b* 11 January 1957; *Educ* Birtley Lord Lawson Comp; *m* 2 June 1979, Denise Kathleen, da of George Brindley, of Great Barr, Birmingham; 2 da (Claire b 17 Sept 1980, Charlotte b 17 June 1982), 1 s (Ben b 2 Sept 1988); *Career* professional footballer and mangr; player: West Bromwich Albion 1974–81, Manchester United 1981–94 (359 appearances and 99 goals, capt until 1994, FA Cup 1983, 1985 and 1990, Charity Shield 1983 and 1992, 1993, European Cup Winners' Cup 1991, Rumbelows Cup 1992, FA Premier League 1993 and 1994); player/mangr Middlesbrough FC 1994–2001 (promotion to Premier League 1995, finalists FA Cup and League Cup 1997); mangr: Bradford City 2003–04, West Bromwich Albion 2004–06, Sheffield United 2007–08; England: player 1980–92 (90 caps, 26 goals, appointed capt 1982), asst coach 1994; charity work incl: Wallness Hurdles and Adventure Farm, Bryan Robson Scanner Appeal; Hon MA: Univ of Manchester 1992, Univ of Salford 1992; *Books* United I Stand (1984), Robbo (autobiography, 2006); *Recreations* horse racing; *Style*— Bryan Robson, Esq, OBE

ROBSON, Christopher; s of John Thomas Robson, and Eva Elizabeth, *née* Leatham; *b* 9 December 1953, Falkirk, Scotland; *Educ* Cambridge Coll of Arts & Technol, Trinity Coll of Music London; *m* 1974 (m dis 1983), Laura Carin, da of Leonard Snelling, of Blackheath; partner, Marie Reich; 1 s (Fynn Eliot Reich-Robson b 23 June 2009); 1 s by Samantha Lambourne (Joel Robson-Lambourne b 9 Dec 1994); *Career* counter-tenor; studied with: Nigel Wickens, James Gaddarn, Paul Esswood, Helga Mott, Geoffrey Parsons, Sir Peter Pears, Laura Sarti, Thomas Helmsley, John Shirley Quirke; concert debut Queen Elizabeth Hall with London Orpheus Choir and Orch 1976, operatic debut as Argones in Sosarme with Barber Opera Birmingham 1979; memb: London Oratory Choir 1974–81, Monteverdi Choir 1974–85, King's Consort 1979–86, Westminster Cathedral Choir 1981–84, ENO 1981–, New London Consort 1985–; roles with ENO incl: Shepherd in Monteverdi's Orfeo (ENO debut) 1981, title role in Akhnaten (UK premiere), Edgar/Mad Tom in Lear (UK premiere), Arsamenes in Xerxes, title role in Julius Caesar, Polinesso in Ariodante 1993 and 1996, Oberon in Midsummer Night's Dream 1995; has also performed princ roles with opera cos incl: Royal Opera Co Covent Garden, Houston Grand Opera, NY City Opera, Northern Stage, Covent Garden Opera Festival, Opera Factory London, Opera Factory Zurich, Nancy Opera, Frankfurt Opera, Scottish Opera, Berlin Kammeroper, Bavarian State Opera, São Paulo Opera, Innsbruck Landestheater, Badisches Staatstheater Karlsruhe, Pfalzbautheater Ludwigshafen, Bayerisches Staatsoper Munich, Opera North, Chicago Lyric Opera, Flanders Opera, Glyndebourne Touring Opera, Glyndebourne Festival Opera (world premiere of Flight 1998), Lyric Theatre Hammersmith (world premiere of The Maids); has performed with orchs incl: Royal Philharmonic, English Chamber Orch, London Sinfonietta, London Bach Orch, BBC Philharmonic, Northern Sinfonia, Bournemouth Sinfonietta, London Baroque Orch, European Baroque Orch, Hanover Band, Concentus Musicus Vienna, Tonhalle Orch Zurich, Vienna Symphony, City of London Sinfonia, Rochester Symphony Orch, Sharoun Ensemble Berlin; worked with conductors incl: Sir Charles Mackerras, Walter Weller, Claudio Abbado, Gustav Leonhardt, Roy Goodman, Niklaus Harnoncourt, Richard Hickox, Mark Elder, Paul Daniel, Ton Koopman, Rene Jacobs, Howard Arman, David Atherton, Sir Neville Marriner, Noel Davies, Sir Peter Maxwell Davies, John de Main, Christopher Keene, Peter Neumann, Brenton Langbein, Zubin Mehta, Simone Young; performed at festivals incl: BBC Proms, Chichester, Three Choirs, Greenwich, Camden, Almeida (world premiere of Casken's Golem), Huddersfield Contemporary Music, Aix en Provence, Montpelier, Stuttgart, Den Haag, Bruges, Barcelona, San Sebastian, Zurich, Salzburg, Wiener Moderne, Warsaw; gala performances incl: Royal Opera House Covent Garden 1986, ENO 1987, Sadler's Wells 1991; *Recordings* Valls' Missa Scala Aretina (with Thames Chamber Orch), Vivaldi's Nisi Dominus (with Kings Consort), Biber's Marienvespers (with Salzburg Bachchor) and Requiem (with New London Consort), The Delights of Posilipo (with New London Consort), Monteverdi's 1610 Vespers (with New London Consort), Monteverdi's Orfeo (with New London Consort), Blow's Venus and Adonis (with New London Consort), Heinrich Schütz

Auferstehungs and Weinacht Historias, Tippett's The Ice Break (with London Sinfonietta), Maxwell-Davies' Resurrection (with BBC Philharmonic), Handel's Messiah (with Collegium Musicum 90), Casken's Golem (with Music Projects London), Locke's Psyche and Bach Magnificat (with New London Consort), Purcell's Odes (with the Orch of the Age of Enlightenment), Handel's Xerxes (Bavarian State Opera), Arne's Artaxerxes (PArley of Instruments), Vivaldi's Canatatas (New London Consort); *TV/Video* Xerxes (ENO), Ariodante (ENO), Orontea (Innsbruck Festival), Hail Bright Cecilia (Norrington), My Night with HAndel (Channel 4), Hell for Leather (DRS Television); *Awards* finalist Kathleen Ferrier Award 1978, winner GLAA Young Musician Award 1979, winner Wroclawskiego Szermierza Statuette Wroclaw Int Music Festival 1991, Opernfestspiel Prize Munich 1997 and 2002; awarded title Bayerischer Kammersänger by the Bavarian State 2003; *Recreations* films, theatre, food and wine, driving; *Clubs* Home House; *Style*— Ks Christopher Robson; ✉ c/o Music International, 13 Ardilaun Road, London N5 2QR (☎ 020 7359 5183, fax 020 7226 9792, e-mail contact@christopher-robson.com, websites www.christopher-robson.com and http://de.linkedin.com/pub/ks-christopher-robson/7/115/454)

ROBSON, Christopher William; s of Leonard Robson (d 1970), of Egglescliffe, Co Durham, and Irene Beatrice, *née* Punch (d 1984); *b* 13 August 1936; *Educ* Rugby; *m* 17 July 1965, Susan Jane, da of Maj John Davey Cooke-Hurle (d 1979), of Co Durham; 2 da (Sarah Louise b 1966, Lydia Katharine b 1969), 1 s (Andrew Leonard Feilding b 1973); *Career* Nat Serv Lt RASC 1955–57; admitted slr 1962, sr ptnr Punch Robson (formerly JWR Punch and Robson) 1971–95; chm Richmond (Yorks) Cons Assoc 1999–2001; fell Woodard Schs (Northern Div) Ltd 1974–85, chm Queen Mary's Sch Duncombe Park 1979–85; tstee Kiplin Hall 1989–; memb Br Astronomical Assoc; High Sheriff N Yorks 2008–09; FRAS; *Recreations* astronomy, skiing, walking; *Style*— Christopher Robson, Esq; ✉ Rudd Hall, East Appleton, Richmond, North Yorkshire DL10 7QD (☎ 01748 811339, fax 0845 638 1182, e-mail robsonrudd4@gmail.com)

ROBSON, David Ernest Henry; QC (1980); s of Joseph Robson (d 1979), and Caroline, *née* Bowmaker (d 2006); *b* 1 March 1940; *Educ* Robert Richardson GS Ryhope, ChCh Oxford (MA); *Partner* Leslie Colwell (civil partnership 2006); *Career* called to the Bar Inner Temple 1965, memb NE circuit 1965, recorder Crown Ct (NE circuit) 1979–2006, bencher Inner Temple 1988, head of chambers 1980–99; pres Herrington Burn (Sunderland) YMCA 1986–2001, artistic dir Royalty Studio Theatre Sunderland 1986–88; *Recreations* acting, Italy; *Clubs* County Durham; *Style*— David Robson, Esq, QC; ✉ 3 Broad Chare, Quayside, Newcastle upon Tyne NE1 3DQ (☎ 0191 232 2392)

ROBSON, Dr David John; s of Alan Victor Robson, TD, LDS, RCS(Ed), and Joan Dales, *née* Hawkins; *b* 23 February 1944; *Educ* Repton, Middx Hosp Med Sch (MB BS); *Career* conslt physician Greenwich HA 1978–2009, dir Greenwich HA HISS Project 1990–93; dir Greenwich Healthcare then Queen Elizabeth Hosp NHS Tst: med 1993–96, information 1996–2004, med dir 2004–08, ceo 2008–09; chm Greenwich and Bexley Community Hospice 2009–; tstee Quaker Social Action 2012–, tstee Six Week Meeting 2014–; FRCP 1986; *Clubs* Savage; *Style*— Dr David Robson; ✉ 37 Hassendean Road, Blackheath, London SE3 8TR

ROBSON, Derek; *b* 17 June 1967, Marlborough, Wilts; *m* Sarnia; 2 da (Millie, Evie); *Career* grad trainee Ogilvy & Mather Direct; Bartle Bogle Hegarty (BBH): account planner 1992–99, bd planner 1999–, dep UK planning dir 1999–2004, global business dir (Levi's and Interbrew) 2003–, md BBH London 2004–; *Style*— Derek Robson, Esq; ✉ BBH London, 60 Kingly Street, London W1B 5DS (☎ 020 7734 1677)

ROBSON, Euan; *Educ* Univ of Newcastle upon Tyne (BA), Univ of Strathclyde (MSc); *Career* Scottish mangr Gas Consumers Cncl 1986–99; MSP (Lib Dem) Roxburgh & Berwickshire 1999–2007; Scottish Parl: memb Audit Ctee 1999–2001, memb Justice and Home Affrs Ctee 1999–2001, Justice I and Justice II Ctees 2001, dep min for Parl (later Parly business) 2001–03, chief whip 2001–03, dep min for educn and young people 2003–05; assoc Caledonia Public Affrs Ltd 2008–, chm Water Engine Technols Ltd; memb River Tweed Cmmrs 1993–2001; pres Kelso Angling Assoc; cncllr Northumberland CC 1981–89 (hon alderman 1989–); writer of articles and books on Scottish art; *Style*— Euan Robson, Esq

ROBSON, Ian; s of Edward Robson, of Langport, Somerset, and Lucy, *née* Greatorex; *b* 21 July 1950; *Educ* Consett GS Co Durham, Bath Acad of Art (BA), Brighton Poly (Postgrad Dip), Univ of Westminster (MBA); *m* 1, 1974, Julia Mary, da of Thomas William Manning; 2 da (Sarah Rose b 4 June 1978, Tessa Imogen Eva b 10 April 1980); m 2, 1987, Ellen Alunwen Frances, da of Alun Williams; 3 da (Lois Amy b 2 Nov 1988, Miranda Lucy, Sophie Frances (twins) b 5 March 1991); *Career* princ Robson Dowry Associates (formerly Robson Design Associates) brand and communication design consultancy 1976–; pt/t lectr in printmaking Brighton Poly 1975, visiting lectr in graphic design Fndn Studies Dept Winchester Sch of Art 1975–79, pt/t lectr in graphic design Somerset Coll of Arts and Technol 1984–86, memb DBA Trg Task Gp 1988–89, advsy memb Yeovil Coll of Art Advsy Panel 1989, industry rep govr Somerset Coll of Arts and Technol (memb Art and Design Advsy and Liaison Ctees, chair Audit Ctee) 1990–2000; CSD: area rep and memb Cncl SW Region 1984–91, hon treas SW Region 1985–89, educn rep to Bath Coll of HE 1987–88, memb Cncl 1993–2000; head of regnl devpt Design Business Assoc 2009–; memb DMI 1999, memb Royal Photographic Soc; MInstD 1997, MSCD (MSIAD 1982); *Exhibitions and Awards* Gane meml travelling scholar (Italy, Germany and Switzerland) 1972, open field print exhbn (UK tour) 1974, print graphic exhbn (Thumb Gallery London) 1975, Bull meml scholar 1976, SW Arts Award for Photography 1979, design work selected for Graphics UK London 1983/for London and overseas 1984, report and accounts work selected for exhbn at World Trade Centre 1987 and 1988, finalist Rank Xerox DTP Document of the Year Award 1989, Creative Contact Award for Promotional Literature 1991, Best Commemorative Label Label of the Year Award The Labologists Soc 1998, Best Poster DRAMI Awards 1999, Award of Excellence UK Property Marketing & Design Awards 1999, Best Annual Report Charity and Public Service Publishing Awards 2002, 6th Most Efficient Accountancy Website Business 2www 2002, nominated Best Legal Knowledge Management/Information Portal LOTIE Awards 2002, commendation Best Annual Report S W Financial Communications Awards 2003, special mention/nomination VINITALY Int Packaging Competition 2003, Popcomm Award for Best Annual Report (Public Sector) 2003, Bronze Medal Wine and Spirit Int Design Award 2005, Silver Medal Wine and Spirit Int Design Awards 2006, Top 10 Regional Press Advertising Campaign Magazine 2007, Wine List of the Year IWC Awards 2009, Packaging Design Award The Dieline Awards 2016; *Recreations* family and home, the development of the design industry (art, architecture and design generally), gardening (practical as well as the history of gardens), photography (particularly rural and urban landscape), travelling in the UK and overseas, walking rural and coastline areas (with a particular interest in islands), tennis, films and reading, Gordon setters (showing and breeding), Clan Gunn; *Clubs* British Gordon Setter Club, Gordon Setter Assoc, Clan Gunn Soc; *Style*— Ian Robson, Esq; ✉ Robson Dowry Associates Ltd, 1 The Sanctuary, Eden Office Park, Ham Green, Bristol BS20 0DD (☎ 0117 929 8040, e-mail ian@robsondowry.co.uk, website www.robsondowry.co.uk, Twitter @IanRobson11)

ROBSON, John Malcolm; s of Edward Stephen Robson (d 1989), and Joan Barbara, *née* Burchett; *b* 16 March 1952; *Educ* KCS Wimbledon, Univ of London (LLB); *m* 30 Aug 1991, Jennifer Lillias, da of Bernard Seed, of Sutton, Surrey; 2 s (David, Aidan), 1 da (Lillias); *Career* called to the Bar Inner Temple 1974, pt/t chm Appeals Service; FCIArb; *Recreations* swimming, ceramics, wines; *Clubs* RAC; *Style*— John Robson, Esq; ✉ 265 Fir Tree Road, Epsom Downs, Surrey (☎ 01737 210121); Arden Chambers, 27 John Street, London WC1N 2BL (☎ 020 7242 4244, fax 020 7242 3224)

ROBSON, Laura; da of Andrew Robson, and Kathy Robson; *b* 21 January 1994, Melbourne, Australia; *Career* tennis player; achievements incl Silver medal (mixed doubles, with Andy Murray, *qv*) Olympic Games London 2012; *Style*— Ms Laura Robson; ✉ Twitter @laurarobson5

ROBSON, Peter Gordon; s of Donald Robson (d 1981), and Lette, *née* Brewer (d 1996); *b* 5 November 1937; *Educ* Scarborough HS; *Career* asst master Marton Hall Bridlington 1962–70, head of maths Cundall Manor York 1972–89 (sr master 1973–76), fndr Newby Books (publishers) 1990; *Books* Between the Laughing Fields (poems, 1966), Maths Dictionary (1979), Maths for Practice and Revision (5 vols, 1982–90), Fountains Abbey – a Cistercian Monastery (1983), The Fishing Robsons (1991), Everyday Graphs (1993), Coordinate Graphs (1993), Science Dictionary (1994), Early Maths (4 vols, 1999–2006), Car Registrations in the British Isles (2003), Eleven Plus Mathematics Practice Tests (CD-ROM, 2007), Car Registration Guide (2008), Scale Drawings, Plans and Bearings (2010), Fred Rowntree: Architect (2014), Maths Practice Papers for Senior School Entry (2016); *Recreations* music, genealogy, heraldry, photography; *Style*— Peter Robson, Esq; ✉ 31 Red Scar Lane, Scarborough, North Yorkshire YO12 5RH (e-mail petrov37@btinternet.com)

ROBSON, Rupert Hugo Wynne; s of C H W Robson (d 2005), and S A Robson, *née* Carnegie (d 2009); *b* 11 February 1961, London; *Educ* Eton (Oppidan scholar), Trinity Coll Oxford (exhibitioner, BA); *m* 1, 14 Dec 1991 (m dis 2011), Lucy, *née* Howe; 1 da (Imogen b 22 Aug 1994), 2 s (Alexander b 5 Oct 1996, Christian b 6 June 1999); m 2, 14 April 2012, Georgina, *née* Stourton; *Career* Bankers Tst 1983–86, dir J Henry Schroder Wagg 1986–96, dir J O Hambro Financial Brands 1997–98, ceo ie gp 1998–99, md Citigroup Global Markets 2000–03, md HSBC CIBM 2003–06; non-exec chm: Cattles plc 1997–99, Charles Taylor plc 2007–15, Silkroute Financial Gp 2008–12, Tullett Prebon plc 2013– (non-exec dir 2007–), EMF Capital Partners 2013–, Sanne Gp plc 2015–; non-exec dir: Tenet Gp 2006–10, London Metal Exchange Hldgs 2009–11, Nomos Bank 2011–13, Savills plc 2015–; memb Advsy Cncl Wilton Park 2005–12; govr: Sherborne Sch 2006–15, Sherborne Girls Sch 2007–15; *Recreations* reading, writing, shooting, tennis, travel; *Clubs* Boodles; *Style*— Rupert Robson, Esq; ✉ Clay Hill House, Browns Lane, East Stour, Gillingham, Dorset SP8 5JT

ROCHA, John; CBE (2002); *b* 23 August 1953, Hong Kong; *Educ* Croydon Art Coll; *m* 2, Odette Gleeson; 3 c; *Career* fashion designer; encouraged by Irish Trade Bd estab career in Dublin late 1970s, worked in Milan 1988–90, subsequently estab John Rocha, currently showing biannually at London Fashion Week, launched John Rocha at Waterford Crystal 1997, launched RochaJohn Rocha at Debenhams and John Rocha Jewellery 2002, opened shop at 15 Dover Street London 2007; British Fashion Designer of the Year 1994; hon doctorate Univ of Ulster 1994, Hon MA Univ of the Creative Arts 2008; *Style*— Mr John Rocha, CBE; ✉ website www.johnrocha.ie

ROCHE, Rt Rev Arthur; *see:* Leeds, Bishop of (RC)

ROCHE, David; s of Lawrence Roche (d 1983), and Jocelyn, *née* Baker (d 2008); *b* 8 May 1961, London; *Educ* Worth Sch Sussex, Hatfield Coll Univ of Durham (BA); *m* 20 June 1987, Johanna, *née* Kari; 3 s (Daniel b 19 Nov 1988, Maximilian b 20 Feb 1991, Benjamin b 23 Dec 1994); *Career* production planner Burlington Klopmann plc 1984–86, stock control mangr Horne Brothers plc 1986–89, product dir HMV Europe Ltd 1989–2001, product dir Waterstone's UK Ltd 2002–06, ceo Borders UK & Ireland Ltd 2006–08, gp sales and mktg dir HarperCollins Publishing 2008–11, owner David Roche Enterprises Ltd 2011–, chm Evanidus Ltd 2008–14; chm: London Book Fair 2012–, BookBrunch 2016–, New Writing North 2016–; conslt Entertainment Alliance 2015–; memb Advsy Bd MA in Publishing Univ of Kingston 2006–; pres Booksellers Assoc 2005–07, tstee Booktrust 2008–14; Retail Personality of the Year Bookseller Retail Awards 2005; *Recreations* golf, rugby, cooking, wine, reading, theatre, arts; *Clubs* MCC, Royal Wimbledon Golf, Soho House (fndr memb); *Style*— David Roche, Esq; ✉ 25 Kingston Hill Place, Kingston upon Thames, Surrey KT2 7QY (☎ 020 8546 1023, mobile 07962 667982, e-mail david@davidroche.co.uk, website www.davidroche.co.uk)

ROCHE, Sir David O'Grady; 5 Bt (UK 1838), of Carass, Limerick; s of Lt-Cdr Sir Standish O'Grady Roche, 4 Bt, DSO, RN (d 1977), and Evelyn Laura, only da of late Maj William Andon, of Jersey; *b* 21 September 1947, Dublin; *Educ* Wellington, Trinity Coll Dublin; *m* 1971, Hon (Helen) Alexandra Briscoe Gully, JP, da of late 3 Viscount Selby (d 1959), and formerly w of Roger Moreton Frewen (d 1972); 2 s (David Alexander O'Grady b 1976, 1 s decd), 1 da (Cecilia Evelyn Jonnë (Mrs Harvey) b 1979); *Heir* s, David Alexander Roche; *Career* CA, formerly with Peat Marwick Mitchell & Co; mangr Samuel Montagu & Co Ltd; chm: Carlton Real Estates plc 1978–82, Echo Hotel 1986–94, Plaza Holdings Ltd 2000–; cncllr London Borough of Hammersmith and Fulham 1978–82; memb Estonian Govt Tax Reform Cmmn 1993–94; memb Hon Artillery Co 1972–75; dep chm Standing Cncl of the Baronetcy 2012–; Freeman City of London, Freeman City of Glasgow; FCA; *Publications* The Silver Bullet – Reasons for Tax Reform; *Recreations* shooting, sailing, yacht (Aramis); *Clubs* Buck's, Kildare St and Univ (Dublin), Royal Yacht Squadron; *Style*— Sir David Roche, Bt; ✉ Bridge House, Starbotton, Skipton, North Yorkshire BD23 5HY; 20 Lancaster Mews, London W2 3QE (☎ 020 7402 2220, mobile 07836 783186, e-mail sdr@plaza-h.com)

R

ROCHE, (William) Martin; s of Albert Charles Roche (d 1973), and Josephine Francis Clare (d 1973); *b* 19 June 1952, Glasgow; *Educ* James Watt Coll Greenock, Univ of Aberdeen (MA); *m* 2 May 1992, Fiona, da of John G Temple; 2 da (Josie Ishbel Temple b 24 March 1993, Anna Caitlin Temple b 18 June 1995), 1 s (Franklin Dominic Temple b 15 Feb 1999); *Career* with family business 1970–76, in higher educn 1976–82, property mangr Cornellis Property Mgmnt 1982–83, econ devpt offr Borders Regional Cncl 1983–84, dir London Office Scottish New Town Devpt Corp 1984–86, public affrs dir Ash Gupta Communications 1986–87, with Bell Pottinger Communications (formerly Lowe Bell Communications) 1987–2000; fndr Anchor Reputation Management 2001–13, The Martin Roche Consultancy 2014–; advsr to small businesses and start-ups (particularly in the arts and culture sectors) 2005–; Etoile Ptnrs 2010–; speaker on reputation mgmnt, political and geopolitical communications, brand and reputation strategies, inward investment attraction and place marketing; author of numerous articles on communications, political and business issues; *Publications* newspaper articles in UK and int pubns, blogs and business chapters; *Recreations* political biography, history, literature, architecture, classical music, visual art, short story writing, cricket, travel; *Style*— Martin Roche, Esq; ✉ Court Barn, Stuppington Court Farm, Canterbury, Kent CT4 7BP (☎ 07715 749621, e-mail wmartinroche@btinternet.com)

ROCHE, Nicola; da of Laurence Roche, and Felicity, *née* Bawtree; *b* 4 August 1963, Victoria, BC; *Educ* St Columba's Coll Dublin, Trinity Coll Dublin (MB, BCh, BAO, MCh); *m* 22 June 2002, Keith Archer; 2 da (Lara b 12 Aug 2002, Louisa b 8 Aug 2005); *Career* conslt breast surgn Royal Free Hosp 2002–05, conslt breast surgn Royal Marsden NHS Fndn Tst 2005–; private consulting rooms Lister Hosp; memb Assoc of Breast Surgns; FRCS; *Style*— Ms Nicola Roche; ✉ Lister Hospital, Chelsea Bridge Road, London SW1W 8RH (☎ 020 7881 2059, fax 020 7881 4094, e-mail MissRoche.secretary@hcahealthcare.co.uk)

ROCHE, Peter Charles Kenneth; s of Dr (George) Kenneth Trevor Roche (d 1989), and Margaret Bridget, *née* Tyrrell (d 2006); *b* 27 January 1947; *Educ* Stonyhurst; *m* 24 April 1971, Gloria Evelyn Margarita, da of John Hugh Cogswell Hicks MBE (d 2006); 2 s

(Daniel Peter James b 19 May 1977, Simon Matthew John b 5 Nov 1981), 1 da (Lucy Georgina 16 Feb 1979); *Career* articled clerk then audit sr Barton Mayhew & Co 1965–71, audit supervisor Deloitte & Co Nairobi 1971–73, chief accountant then gen mangr East African Fine Spinners Nairobi 1973–75, fin dir then dep md Futura Publications Ltd London 1975–80, fin and admin dir MacDonald Futura Publishers Ltd 1980–81, fin dir MacDonald & Co 1981–82, co-fndr, fin dir and dep md Century Publishing Co Ltd 1982–85, fin dir and dep md Century Hutchinson Ltd 1985–89, fin dir then gp md Random Century Group Ltd (Century Hutchinson bought by Random House Inc) 1989–92; The Orion Publishing Group Ltd: co-fndr, gp md 1992–2003, chief exec 2003–13; Hachette UK Ltd dep chief exec 2005–13; chm Atlantic Books Ltd 2014–; non-exec chm Boxtree Ltd 1989–96; FCA 1976 (ACA 1971); *Recreations* cricket, rugby, tennis, books and newspapers; *Clubs* RAC, Kongonis Cricket, Surbiton Golf; *Style*— Peter Roche, Esq; ✉ Field House, 20 Leigh Hill Road, Cobham, Surrey KT11 2HX (✆ 01932 862713, e-mail pckroche@gmail.com)

ROCHESTER, Bishop of 2010–; Rt Rev James Henry Langstaff; s of late Harry Langstaff, and Jillian Harper, *née* Brooks; b 27 June 1956, Hostert, Germany; *Educ* Cheltenham Coll, St Catherine's Coll Oxford (MA), Univ of Nottingham (BA), St John's Theological Coll Nottingham (Dip); m 28 Aug 1977, Bridget, *née* Streatfeild; 1 s (Alasdair b 28 Oct 1983), 1 da (Helen b 23 Jan 1986); *Career* ordained: deacon 1981, priest 1982; asst curate St Peter Farnborough 1981–86, vicar St Matthew Duddeston and St Clement Nechells 1986–96, area dean of Birmingham City 1995–96, chaplain to Bishop of Birmingham 1996–2000, rector Holy Trinity Sutton Coldfield 2000–04, area dean of Sutton Coldfield 2002–04, Bishop of Lynn 2004–10; memb Bd FCH Housing and Care 1988–2002, non-exec dir Good Hope Hosp NHS Tst 2003–04, chair Flagship Housing Gp 2006–; memb E of Eng Regnl Assembly 2006–10; *Recreations* golf, skiing, theatre, choral singing, contemporary fiction; *Style*— The Rt Rev the Bishop of Rochester

ROCK, Angus James; s of Ian George Rock, and Anne Elizabeth, *née* Lyons; b 16 September 1964; *Educ* Cooper Sch Bicester, Gosford Hill Sch Kidlington; *Career* designer Cherwell Laboratories 1983–86, proprietor A J R Marketing (design and mktg an electronic instrumentation range for motorsport) 1986–88, sales and mktg mangr Stack Ltd 1988–91; ptnr: Design Graphique 1991–93, Head to Toe 1993–, www.httsalon.com 2010–; dir Arandar Ltd 2005–; Br Design Award 1990, DTI Smart Award 2004; *Recreations* squash, tennis, skiing, music, golf, classic cars; *Style*— Angus J Rock, Esq; ✉ Head to Toe, 6/8 Cumnor Road, Wootton, Boars Hill, Oxford OX1 5JP (✆ and fax 01865 326600)

ROCK, Kate Harriet Alexandra Rock; *Educ* Baroness (Life Peer UK 2015), of Stratton in the County of Dorset; *Career* vice-chm Cons Pty; *Style*— The Baroness Rock

ROCK, Lucy Jane Frances; da of John Francis Howard Rock, of Matfield, Kent, and Jane, *née* Hubbard; b 1 May 1970, Tunbridge Wells, Kent; *Educ* Tunbridge Wells Girls GS, Magdalen Coll Oxford (exhibitioner, BA); m 20 Nov 2004, Michael Joseph Lea; 3 da (Beatrix b 23 Jan 2007, Agnes b 12 Aug 2008, Elspeth b 6 Oct 2010); *Career* reporter Kent and Sussex Courier 1992–94, news ed nat news agency 1994–96, sr reporter Daily Mirror 1996–2002 (Reporting Team of the Year Br Press Awards 1999), dep news ed Daily Express 2002–04, news ed The Observer 2004–; co-fndr and ed She Said blog Observer 2014–; memb Advsy Bd ESRC Research Centre on Micro-Social Change, memb Scientific Advsy Ctee Int Centre for Lifecourse Studies in Soc and Health; *Recreations* music, ballet; *Style*— Ms Lucy Rock; ✉ The Observer, Kings Place, 90 York Way, London N1 9GU (✆ 020 7713 4650, e-mail lucy.rock@guardian.co.uk)

ROCK, Prof Paul Elliot; s of Ashley Rock (d 2002), of London, and Charlotte, *née* Dickson (d 1969); b 4 August 1943; *Educ* William Ellis GS, LSE (BSc), Nuffield Coll Oxford (DPhil); m 25 Sept 1965, Barbara (d 1998), da of Hayman Ravid (d 1989); 2 s (Matthew Charles b 1970, Oliver James b 1974); *Career* visiting prof Princeton Univ USA 1974–75, visiting scholar Miny of the Slr Gen of Canada; LSE: asst lectr 1967–70, lectr 1970–76, prof of sociology 1986–95, prof of social instns 1995–, emeritus prof 2008; visiting prof Univ of Pennsylvania 2006–10, visiting prof Univ of Macau 2016–; fell Center for Advanced Studies in Behavioral Sciences Stanford California 1996; dir The Mannheim Centre 1992–95; memb: Sociology and Social Admin Ctee SSRC 1976–80, Exec Ctee Br Sociological Assoc 1978–79, Parole Bd 1986–89; ed The British Journal of Sociology 1988–95; hon fell RegNet Australian Nat Univ 2005–; Hon DUniv Middlesex 2009; appointed official historian of criminal justice by the Prime Minister 2009; FRSA 1997, FBA 2000; *Books* Making People Pay (1973), The Making of Symbolic Interactionism (1979), Understanding Deviance (jtly, 1982–2011), A View From The Shadows (1987), Helping Victims of Crime (1990), The Social World of an English Crown Court (1993), Reconstructing a Women's Prison (1996), After Homicide (1998), Constructing Victims' Rights (2004), Victims, Policy-making and Criminological Theory (2010); *Style*— Prof Paul Rock; ✉ London School of Economics and Political Science, Houghton Street, Aldwych, London WC2A 2AE (✆ 020 7955 7296, fax 020 7955 7405, e-mail p.rock@lse.ac.uk)

ROCKCLIFFE, Melanie; b 16 March 1959, Altrincham, Cheshire; m 19 Dec 2004, Mark Rockcliffe; 1 s (Finley Miles b 29 June 2010); *Career* head Talkback Mgmnt until 2005, co-fndr (with Conor McCaughan and Michael Duff) and agent TROIKA 2005– (clients incl Graham Norton, Matt Lucas, Griff Rhys Jones, Kate Thornton *qqv*, Amanda Holden); *Style*— Ms Melanie Rockcliffe; ✉ TROIKA, 10a Christina Street, London EC2A 4PA (✆ 020 7336 7868, fax 020 7490 4642, e-mail melanie@troikatalent.com, website www.troikatalent.com)

ROCKER, David; s of Richard Frederick Rocker (d 1984), of Hatfield Peverel, Essex, and Elizabeth Ellen, *née* Lewis (d 2000); b 9 June 1944; *Educ* King Edward VI Sch Chelmsford; m 1972 (m dis 1992), Jacolyn Jane, da of John Geoffry Matthews, of Finchingfield, Essex; *Career* admitted slr; ptnr Leonard Gray & Co 1968–71; legal advsr: Hawker Siddeley Group Ltd 1971–73, Trident TV 1973–79; dir of legal affrs Guinness plc 1982–86, chm Guinness Superlatives Ltd 1984–85, Guinness Overseas Ltd 1985–86; sr ptnr David Rocker & Co 1986–; chm: Rocker Ltd 1989–2000, Scarab Property Ltd 1999–2000, Burton & Co (Thorney) Ltd 2003–, Cousin Ltd 2005–, Mirabeau Ltd 2005–, Cousin DE Ltd 2009–, Cousin VM Ltd; *Recreations* motor racing, riding, bridge; *Style*— David Rocker, Esq; ✉ The Maltings, 21 The Green, Writtle, Essex CM1 3DT (✆ 01245 420141)

ROCKLEY, Edward George (Ted); s of George Alfred Rockley (d 1982), and Catherine Rockley (d 1998); b 27 April 1952; *Educ* Quintin Kynaston, Hornsey Sch of Art, Middlesex Poly (DipAD); m 1983, Lyn Michelle Joniel, da of Colin Wakeley; 2 da (Camilla b 14 Sept 1984, Roseanna b 26 Nov 1992), 1 s (Joshua b 17 March 1987); *Career* animator and designer BBC Adult Literacy Project 1974–77, freelance animator 1977–81, co-dir Klactoveesedstene Animations Ltd 1981–; *Style*— Ted Rockley, Esq; ✉ Oscar Grillo & Ted Rockley Animations, 11 Gordon Road, London W5 2AD (✆ and fax 020 8991 6978, e-mail klacto@klacto.com)

RODDAM, Francis George (Franc); m Leila, *née* Ansari; *Career* director, screenwriter and producer; dir numerous commercials; chm: Ziji Prodns Ltd, Ziji Publishing Ltd; memb: Acad of Motion Picture Arts & Sciences, BAFTA, Soc of Authors; *Films* incl: K2, War Party, Aria, The Bride, The Lords of Discipline, Quadrophenia; *Television* incl: The Fight, Mini, The Family, Dummy, Making Out, Harry, An Ungentlemanly Act, The Crow Road, Moby Dick, Cleopatra, The Canterbury Tales, Auf Wiedersehen, Pet, MasterChef; *Style*— Franc Roddam, Esq; ✉ c/o Independent Talent Group, 40 Whitfield Street, London W1T 2RH

RODDICK, (Thomas) Gordon; *Educ* RAC Cirencester; m 1970, Dame Anita Roddick, DBE (d 2007); 2 da (Justine b 1969, Samantha b 1971); *Career* co-fndr The Body Shop International plc 1976; co-fndr The Big Issue; *Style*— Gordon Roddick, Esq

RODENBURG, Patsy; OBE (2005); da of Marius Rodenburg, of London, and Margaret Edna, *née* Moody; b 2 September 1953; *Educ* St Christopher's Sch Beckenham, Central Sch of Speech and Drama London; *Career* voice coach RSC 1981–90; formed The Voice and Speech Centre 1988; head of voice: Guildhall Sch of Music and Drama 1981–, RNT 1990–; appointed prof Guildhall Sch of Music 2014; LGSM (The City of London) 1982, distinguished visiting prof Southern Methodist Univ Dallas 1989, hon memb VASTA 1995, memb Bd RSC 2014–; assoc: The Michael Howard Studios New York 1996, Royal Court Theatre London 1999; works extensively in theatre, film, TV and opera incl: Europe, USA, Canada, Asia and Aust; coached many leading theatre and opera cos incl: Stratford Festival Theatre Canada, Kabuki Theatre Japan, NT of Greece, Lithuania, Norway, NT Sch of India, The Market Theatre Johannesburg, Peking Opera, Ex Machina (Robert Lepage); for GB: Royal Opera, ENO, Opera North, English Shakespeare Co, Cheek by Jowl, Theatre de Complicité; RNT 1990–2006; *Publications* The Right to Speak (1992), The Need for Words (1993), The Actor Speaks (1996), Speaking Shakespeare (2002), Presence (2007), Power Presentation (2009); *DVDs* Shakespeare in the Present (2011); *Recreations* reading, travelling; *Style*— Ms Patsy Rodenburg, OBE; ✉ website www.patsyrodenburg.com

RODENHURST, John Emberton; s of Jeffrey Royle Rodenhurst (d 1964), of Ellesmere, Shropshire, and Margaret Elizabeth, *née* Emberton, of Cockshutt, Shrewsbury; b 9 August 1941; *Educ* Oswestry HS for Boys; m 26 April 1967, Rosemary Barbara, da of Horace Harrison, of Moreton Say, Market Drayton; 1 s (Simon John b 29 Dec 1967), 1 da (Penelope-Jane b 30 Jan 1970); *Career* hotelier; proprietor Soughton Hall Hotel 1986–; *Recreations* shooting and country pursuits, good food and wine, a little golf, widespread travel, horse racing; *Style*— John Rodenhurst, Esq; ✉ Soughton Hall, Northop, Mold, Clwyd CH7 6AB (✆ 01352 840 811, fax 01352 840 382)

RODFORD, Neil John; *Educ* Preston Comp Sch, CIM (DipM); *Career* W H Smith: magazine sales mangr 1989–91, magazine mangr 1991–93, ops mangr 1993–94, gen mangr 1994–96; Harrods Hldgs: gen mangr Harrods Knightsbridge 1996–97, md Fulham FC 1997–2000; ptnr and business devpt mangr Keegan Partnership 2000–01, chief exec Formation Group plc 2001–09, chief exec James Grant Gp Ltd 2009–; *Recreations* soccer, squash, golf, horse racing; *Style*— Neil Rodford, Esq; ✉ James Grant Group, 94 Strand on the Green, Chiswick, London W4 3NN

RODGER, Nicholas Andrew Martin; s of Lt Cdr Ian Alexander Rodger, RN, of Arundel, W Sussex, and Sara Mary, *née* Perceval; b 12 November 1949; *Educ* Ampleforth, Univ Coll Oxford (MA, DPhil); m 28 Aug 1982, Susan Eleanor, da of Henry Meigs Farwell, of Ickenham, Middx; 1 da (Ellen b 1984), 3 s (Christopher b 1987, Alexander b 1989, Crispian b 1997); *Career* asst keeper of Public Records 1974–91; Anderson fell National Maritime Museum Greenwich 1992–99; Univ of Exeter: sr lectr in history 1999–2000, prof of naval history 2000–08; sr research fell All Souls Coll Oxford 2008–; hon sec Navy Records Soc 1976–90; FBA, FSA, FRHistS; *Books* The Admiralty (1979), The Wooden World, An Anatomy of the Georgian Navy (1986), The Insatiable Earl: A Life of John Montagu, Fourth Earl of Sandwich 1718–1792 (1993), The Safeguard of the Sea. A Naval History of Britain, Vol 1, 660–1649 (1997), The Command of the Ocean: A Naval History of Britain 1649–1815 (2004); *Recreations* hill walking, music; *Style*— N A M Rodger, Esq, FBA; ✉ All Souls College, Oxford OX1 4AL

RODGERS, Brid; *née* Stratford; da of Thomas Stratford (d 1947), of Co Donegal, and Josephine, *née* Coll (d 1996); b 20 February 1935; *Educ* St Louis Convent Monaghan, UC Dublin (BA, HDipEd); m 16 July 1960, Antoin Rodgers, s of James Rodgers; 3 da (Mary b 18 April 1961, Anne b 5 June 1962, Brid b 2 May 1965), 3 s (Séamus b 25 Oct 1963, Tom b 2 March 1971, Antoin b 24 April 1973); *Career* teacher 1957–60 and 1988–92; chairperson SDLP 1978–80, gen sec SDLP 1981–83, memb Irish Senate 1983–97, memb Craigavon Cncl 1985–93, ldr SDLP Cncl Gp Craigavon BC 1985–93, memb SDLP Talks Team Brooke-Mayhew Talks 1991, SDLP delg Forum for Peace and Reconciliation (Dublin Castle) 1994–95, elected to NI Forum for Political Dialogue 1996, chairperson SDLP Talks Team Castle Buildings Talks 1996–98, formerly pty spokesperson on Women, Cultural Affairs and Parades, dep ldr SDLP 2001–03; MLA (SDLP) Upper Bann 1998–2003; min of Agric and Rural Devpt NI Exec 1999–2002; former memb: Southern Educn & Library Bd, Standing Advsy Cmmn on Human Rights; dir Bord Bia 2004–10; Hon LLD NUI 2003, Hon DLitt Harper Adams Univ 2009; *Recreations* walking, reading, golf; *Style*— Ms Brid Rodgers; ✉ 34 Kilmore Road, Lurgan, Co Armagh BT67 9BP (e-mail b100rodgers@btinternet.com)

RODGERS, Joan; CBE (2001); da of Thomas Rodgers (d 1971), and Julia Rodgers; b 4 November 1956; *Educ* Whitehaven GS, Univ of Liverpool (BA), RNCM Manchester; m 1988, Paul Daniel, CBE, *qv*; 2 da (Eleanor b 4 Sept 1990, Rose b 14 May 1993); *Career* soprano; debut as Pamina in Die Zauberflöte at the Aix-en-Provence Festival; major roles incl: Zerlina in Don Giovanni (Royal Opera House Covent Garden, Paris), Pamina (Covent Garden, ENO, Paris Opera), Gilda in Rigoletto (ENO), Nannetta (ENO), Countess Almaviva in The Marriage of Figaro/Le Nozze di Figaro (ENO, Netherlands Opera Amsterdam), Susanna in Le Nozze di Figaro (Glyndebourne, Paris, Florence), Cleopatra in Giulio Cesare (Scottish Opera), Yolande (Edinburgh Festival), Despina in Cosi fan Tutte (Paris, Florence), Br premiere of Chabrier's Briséis (Edinburgh Festival), Fiordiligi in Cosi fan Tutte (Theatre de la Monnaie Brussels), Donna Elvira in Don Giovanni (Scottish Opera 1995, Paris 1996), Pamina in Die Zauberflöte (Met Opera NY 1995, Berlin 1996), Ginevra in Ariodante (ENO) 1996, Hero in Beatrice et Benedict (Brussels Opera), Blanche in Les Dialogues des Carmelites (Amsterdam), Governess in Britten's Turn of the Screw (Royal Opera House), Anne Truelove in The Rake's Progress (BBC Symphony Orchestra) 1997, Marschallin in Der Rosenkavalier for Scottish Opera, Ginevra in Ariodante (Munich) 2000; appeared at other operatic venues incl: Opera Bastille Paris, Zurich, Munich; given concerts in: London, Vienna, Madrid, Copenhagen, Salzburg, Paris, Lisbon; ABC tour of Australia 1995, BBC Proms; worked with conductors incl: Sir Colin Davis, Sir Georg Solti, Andrew Davis, Daniel Barenboim, Jeffrey Tate, Sir Simon Rattle, Zubin Mehta; winner Kathleen Ferrier Meml Scholarship 1981; *Recordings* incl: solo recital of Tchaikovsky Songs, Mozart Mass in C (under Harnoncourt), Mozart Da Ponte Operas (with the Berlin Philharmonic under Barenboim), Vaughan Williams Sea Symphony (with the Royal Liverpool Philharmonic under Vernon Handley), Beethoven 9th Symphony (with the Royal Liverpool Philharmonic under Charles Mackerras), Handel Messiah, Delius Mass of Life and Howells Hymns Paradisi (under Richard Hickox), Creation (with Frans Brüggen), Rachmaninov Songs (with Howard Shelley); *Recreations* walking, cooking, playing with my children; *Style*— Ms Joan Rodgers, CBE

RODGERS, Worshipful (Doris) June (Mrs Roger Evans); da of James A Rodgers, JP, of Craigavad, Co Down, and Margaret Doris, *née* Press; b 10 June 1945; *Educ* Victoria Coll Belfast, Trinity Coll Dublin (MA), Lady Margaret Hall Oxford (MA); m 6 Oct 1973, Roger Kenneth Evans, *qv*, s of Gerald Raymond Evans of Mere, Wilts; 2 s (Edward Arthur b 13 May 1981, Henry William b 8 Feb 1983); *Career* called to the Bar Middle Temple 1971; recorder of the Crown Court 1993–; chllr of the Dio of Gloucester 1990–; memb Court of Common Cncl City of London Ward Farringdon Without 1975–96, former memb City and East London Area HA; Freeman City of London 1975; memb: Hon Soc of Middle Temple, Ecclesiastical Law Soc; *Recreations* architectural history, Italy, tapestry; *Clubs* Oxford and Cambridge; *Style*— The Worshipful Miss June Rodgers; ✉ 2 Harcourt

Buildings, The Temple, London EC4Y 9DB (☎ 020 7353 6961, e-mail jrodgers@harcourtchambers.co.uk)

RODGERS, Susannah; da of Brian Rodgers, and Ann, *née* Groves; *b* 9 August 1983, Stockton-on-Tees, Co Durham; *Educ* Newcastle Univ; *Career* Paralympic swimmmer; achievements incl: Silver medal (50m butterfly) and Bronze medal (400m freestyle) Br Championships 2011, Silver (50m butterfly) Br Int Disability Swimming Championships 2011, 5 Gold medals (100m freestyle, 400m freestyle, 100m backstroke, 50m butterfly and 4x100m freestyle relay) and Silver medal (50m freestyle) European Championships 2011, Gold medal (50m butterfly) Br Championships 2012, 3 Bronze medals (400m freestyle, 4x100m freestyle and 100m freestyle) Paralympic Games 2012, Gold medal (4x100m freestyle relay) and 4 Silver medals (400m freestyle, 100m freestyle, 50m freestyle and 50m butterfly) IPC World Championships Montreal 2013, 5 Gold medals (50m, 100m and 400m freestyle, 50m butterfly, 34 point 4x100m freestyle relay) and 1 Silver medal (100m backstroke) IPC European Championships Eindhoven 2014, 1 Bronze medal (100m freestyle) and 1 Gold medal (4x100m medley relay) IPC World Championships Glasgow 2015, 5 Gold medals (50m, 100m and 400m freestyle, 50m butterfly and 4x100m medley relay) IPC European Championships Madeira 2016, 1 Gold medal (50m butterfly) Paralympics Rio 2016; Disability Swimmer of the Year Splash Award 2011; non-exec dir Br Athletes Cmmn; project mangr Br Cncl 2008–; tstee Spirit 2012 (chair Spirit of Achievement Panel); Freedom City of London 2013; *Clubs* Otter Swimming, Beckenham Swimming; *Style—* Miss Susannah Rodgers; ✉ e-mail sejrodgers@gmail.com, Twitter @susie_rodgers

RODNEY BENNETT; *see:* Bennett

RODRIGUES, Christopher John; CBE (2007); s of late Alfred John Rodrigues, and Joyce Margaret, *née* Farron-Smith; *b* 24 October 1949, London; *Educ* Univ Coll Sch, Jesus Coll Cambridge (MA, Rowing blue, pres CUBC), Harvard Business Sch (Baker scholar, MBA); *m* Priscilla Purcell Young; 1 s, 1 da; *Career* with Spillers Foods London 1971–72, Foster, Turner & Benson London 1972–74, MBA Harvard 1974–76, McKinsey & Co London 1976–79, American Express NY and London 1979–88; Thomas Cook Group Ltd: chief operating offr 1988–90, gp md 1990–92, gp chief exec 1992–95; gp chief exec Bradford & Bingley plc 1996–2004, pres and ceo Visa International 2004–06, chm VisitBritain 2007–; chm: International Personal Finance 2007–15, Openwork Hldgs Ltd 2014–; non-exec dir: Energis 1997–2002, FSA 1997–2003, Ladbrokes plc 2003–13; memb: Exec Ctee World Travel and Tourism Cncl 2006–, Cncl Nat Tst 2010–; chm: Windsor Leadership Tst 2007–15, Almeida Theatre 2008–, Br Bobsleigh & Skeleton Assoc 2013–, Port of London Authority 2015–; vice-chm World Travel and Tourism Cncl 2016–; tstee Nat Tst 2012–; steward Henley Royal Regatta 1998–; FRSA; *Recreations* cooking, skiing, rowing, shooting, opera, ballet; *Clubs* Leander (past chm), Hawks' (Cambridge), Brook (NY); *Style—* Christopher Rodrigues, Esq, CBE; ✉ VisitBritain, Sanctuary Buildings, 20 Great Smith Street, London SW1P 3BT

RODWELL, Dennis Graham; s of Albert James Rodwell, MBE (d 1991), and Constance Edith, *née* Scaddan (d 1999); *b* 24 January 1948; *Educ* Kingswood Sch Bath, Clare Coll Cambridge (MA, DipArch), Open Univ (Dip French); *m* 1, 10 May 1975 (m dis 2002), Rosemary Ann, *née* Rimmer; 2 s (Nicholas b 1978, Christopher b 1979), 1 da (Melanie b 1982); m 2, 22 Dec 2010, Dr Beria Bayizitlioglu, of Odemis, Turkey; *Career* architect, author and lectr; in practice Dennis Rodwell Architects 1975–98; works incl: historic building restorations, urban conservation and regeneration, heritage presentation, rescue and restoration of Melrose Station and its mgmnt as a mixed use commercial devpt 1985–2003; recipient numerous awards and commendations; int conslt on cultural heritage and sustainable urban devpt to World Heritage Centre and Div of Cultural Heritage UNESCO, German Agency for Tech Co-operation (GTZ), World Bank and Br Cncl 1998–; conservation offr/urban design City of Derby 1999–2003, princ planner (heritage and design) Burnley Borough Cncl 2009, Kelso townscape heritage initiative project offr Scottish Borders Cncl 2010–11; ptnr European Cmmn Seventh Framework Prog research project Energy Efficiency for EU Historic Districts Sustainability 2012–; memb The Edinburgh New Town Conservation Ctee 1981–84 and 1987–90, tstee The Trimontium Tst 1988–2000 (chm 1988–90); served ctees: Scottish Georgian Soc, Cncls of the Royal Incorporation of Architects in Scotland, Edinburgh Architectural Assoc; lecturing incl European Urban Conservation course Univ of Dundee 1991–93, speaking incl at int conservation confs 1975–; RIBA 1974, FRIAS 1982, FSA Scot 1990, FRSA 1991, memb Inst of Historic Building Conservation (IHBC) 1998, affiliate memb RTPI 2000; *Publications* Conservation and Sustainability in Historic Cities (2007); articles in jls and books upon historical, architectural and urban conservation subjects incl: European Heritage (1975), Architectural Conservation in Europe (1975), Context (1989–), Civilising the City (1991), Journal of Architectural Conservation (2002–), World Heritage (2002–), The Historic Environment: Policy and Practice (2010–); *Recreations* travel, modern languages, walking, reading, photography, gardening, music; *Style—* Dennis Rodwell, Esq; ✉ Greenside Park, St Boswells, Melrose, Roxburghshire TD6 0AH (☎ 01835 824625, mobile 07740 871043, e-mail dennis@dennisrodwell.co.uk, website www.dennisrodwell.co.uk)

RODWELL, Maj John Francis Meadows; s of Maj Percival Francis (Jim) Rodwell, MBE, TD (d 2010); *b* 11 July 1946; *m* 9 March 1974, Rosie, da of John Trevor Munden Brook (d 1981), of Meole Brace, Shrewsbury; *Career* joined Suffolk and Cambs Regt 1965, Mons OCS 1965, Grenadier Gds 1968, psc 1979, ret Army 1983; SG Warburg & Co Ltd: joined 1983, corp and community affrs dir Mercury Asset Mgmnt 1996–98 (admin dir 1989–96), corp and community affrs dir Merrill Lynch Mercury 1998–99; corp affrs conslt 1999–2002, dir Sponsorship Consulting Ltd 2002–08; chm: Hedley Foundation 2002– (tstee and dir 1984–), Fairhood Properties Ltd 2003–, Holbeck Properties Ltd 2003–, Mountbarrow Properties Ltd 2003–, Merewood Properties Ltd 2003–, Middlerigg Servs Ltd 2003–; HM Body Guard Hon Corps of Gentlemen at Arms 1998–2016, Worshipful Co of Skinners; DL London Borough of Enfield, Edmonton and Southgate 2013–14, Rep DL London Borough of Ealing 2014–15; *Recreations* gardening, golf; *Clubs* Cavalry and Guards' (chm 1996–2002, tstee 2002–15, vice-pres 2013–), Pratt's, City of London, Royal West Norfolk Golf; *Style—* Maj John F M Rodwell; ✉ The Hedley Foundation, 1–3 College Hill, London EC4R 2RA (e-mail jrodwell@hedleyfoundation.org.uk)

RODWELL, Prof Warwick James; OBE (2009); s of Thomas George Rodwell, and Olive Ellen *née* Nottage; *b* 24 October 1946, Rochford, Essex; *Educ* Southend-on-Sea HS for Boys, Loughborough Coll of Educn (BSc, DLC), Inst of Archaeology (BA), Worcester Coll Oxford (DPhil), Univ of Birmingham (MA), Univ of Oxford (DLitt), Univ of London (DLit); *m* 2004, Diane Marie Gibbs; *Career* architectural historian; conslt archaeologist: Glastonbury Abbey 1976–2005, Bristol Cathedral 1976–2010, Wells Cathedral 1977–2014, Lichfield Cathedral 1982–2009, Westminster Abbey 2004–; memb Coll of St Peter Westminster; visiting prof in archaeology Univ of Reading; FSAScot 1965, FSA 1977, FRHistS 1992; The Archaeology of Churches (2012), The Coronation Chair and Stone of Scone (2013); 300 other publications; *Recreations* visiting historic buildings, bibliophilia, writing; *Style—* Prof Warwick Rodwell, OBE; ✉ Westminster Abbey, 20 Dean's Yard, London SW1P 3PA (☎ 020 7654 4879, e-mail warwick.rodwell@westminster-abbey.org)

ROE, David John; CBE (2001); s of Malcolm Roe, and Pauline, *née* Baker; *b* 26 November 1958; *Educ* Selwyn Coll Cambridge (BA), Queen Mary Coll London (MA); *Partner* Alison Mary Sharpe; 1 s; *Career* civil servant; Export Credits Guarantee Dept 1983–85, DTI 1985–92; HM Treasy: joined 1992, head of int fin instns 1994–97, head of fin regulatory reform 1997–2000; on secondment to Charities Aid Fndn 2001–02, PM's Strategy Unit 2002–03; Dept for Culture, Media and Sport: head of strategy, policy and delivery 2003–05, dir of strategy 2005–07, dir of corporate servs and change 2007–10; dir public sector innovation Dept for Business, Innovation and Skills 2010–11, freelance conslt 2011–; assoc: Rema Consulting 2012–, Roffey Park Inst 2012–; pt/t UK alternate dir EBRD 1995–97, govr Fielding Primary Sch 2005–; memb ICA; *Recreations* playing the saxophone, watching Brentford FC, seaside holidays, books; *Style—* David Roe, Esq, CBE

ROE, James; MBE (2013); *b* 28 March 1988, Leamington Spa, Warks; *Educ* King Edward VI Sch Stratford-upon-Avon, Oxford Brookes Univ (BA); *Career* Paralympic rower; achievements incl: Gold medal (mixed coxed four) World Rowing Championships 2009 and 2011, Silver medal (mixed coxed four) World Rowing Championships 2010, Gold medal (mixed coxed four) World Cup 2012, Gold medal (mixed coxed four) Paralympic Games 2012; *Style—* Mr James Roe, MBE; ✉ Twitter @jamesroe2012

ROE, Dame Marion Audrey; DBE (2004); *née* Keyte; da of William Keyte (d 1977), and Grace Mary, *née* Bocking (d 1983); *b* 15 July 1936, London; *Educ* Bromley HS, Croydon HS (both GPDST), English Sch of Languages Vevey Switzerland; *m* 1958, James Roe, *qv*, s of Kenneth Roe; 2 da (Philippa b 1962, Jane b 1965), 1 s (William b 1969); *Career* Parly candidate (Cons) Barking 1979, MP (Cons) Broxbourne 1983–2005; PPS to Rt Hon John Moore as Sec of State for Tport 1986–87 (PPS to jr tport mins 1985–86), Parly under sec of state Dept of the Environment 1987–88; memb Commons Select Ctees on: Agric 1983–85, Social Servs 1988–89, Commons Procedure 1990–92, Sittings of the House 1991–92, Commons Liaison 1992–2005, House of Commons Admin 1991–97 (chm 1997–2005), Health 2000–01 (chm 1992–97); memb Speaker's Panel of Chm 1997–2005; managing tstee Parly Contributory Pension Fund 1990–97; jt sec Cons Pty Orgn 1985, memb 1922 Ctee Exec 1992–94, vice-chm 1922 Ctee 2001–2005 (sec 1997–2001); chm Cons House of Commons Benevolent Fund 1998–99; chm Cons Pty Parly Ctees on: Horticulture and Markets 1989–97 (sec 1983–85), Social Security Ctee 1990–97 (vice-chm 1988–90); vice-chm Cons Pty Parly: Environment Ctee 1990–97, Health Ctee 1997–99; sec All-Pty Br-Canadian Parly Gp 1991–97 (vice-chm 1997–2005); chm All-Pty Hospices Gp 1992–2005 (sec 1990–92), jt chm All-Pty Gp on Breast Cancer 1997–2005; vice-chm: All-Pty Fairs and Showgrounds Gp 1992–2005 (jt chm 1989–92), All-Pty Parly Garden Club 1995–2005, All-Pty Gp on Alcohol Misuse 1997–2005, All-Pty Parly Gp on Domestic Violence 1999–2005; memb Exec Ctee: UK Branch Cwlth Parly Assoc 1997–2005 (vice-chm 2003–04), Br Gp Inter-Parly Union 1997–98 and 2001–05 (vice-chm 1998–2001); memb Dept of the Environment Advsy Ctee on Women's Employment 1989–92, substitute memb UK Delgn to Cncl of Europe and WEU 1989–92, memb UK Parly Observer Gp monitoring elections in Angola 1992, UK rep on Cwlth Observer Gp monitoring elections in the Seychelles 1992, rep UK Branch Cwlth Parly Assoc Int Women Parliamentarians Ctee 2003–05; successfully sponsored Prohibition of Female Circumcision Act 1985 (Private Member's Bill), memb six-memb Inter-Parly Union Int Panel on Prohibition of Female Genital Mutilation 2002–05; Parly conslt to Horticultural Trades Assoc 1990–95; cncllr: London Borough of Bromley 1975–78, GLC (Ilford North Div) 1977–86; GLC: vice-chm Historic Bldgs Ctee 1977–78, whip for Planning and Communications Gp 1977–78, Cons dep chief whip 1978–82, vice-chm Gen Mgmnt Ctee 1978–81, leading Cons spokesman Police Ctee 1982–83, memb Cons Ldr's Ctee 1982–83, memb various other GLC ctees 1978–82; GLC rep on Gen Servs Ctee of AMA 1978–81, UK rep Conf of Local and Regnl Authorities of Europe 1981; chm Nat Cncl for Child Health and Well-being (formerly The Children's Health Gp) 2001–; memb: Gen Advsy Cncl BBC 1986–87, International Women's Forum 1992–2005, Euro Research Gp 1994–2005, NHS Confedn Parly Panel 2000–05, UNICEF Parly Advsy Ctee 2002–05, UNICEF UK Key Parly Supporters Gp 2002–05; govr Research into Ageing Tst 1988–97, hon regnl vice-pres Eastern Region Housebuilders Fedn 1993–2005; pres: Broxbourne Orgn for the Disabled (co-pres) 1991–2005, Save Temple Bar Campaign 1991–93, Lea Valley Arthritis Care 1993–2005, Hoddesdon Soc 2009–16 (vice-pres 2005–09), Broxbourne Parly Cons Assoc 2013– (pres Women's Section 1983–2015, patron 2006–13); vice-pres: Women's Nat Cancer Control Campaign 1985–87 and 1988–2001, Herts Chamber of Trade & Commerce 1983–87 and 1988–2005, E Herts Operatic Soc 1986–2005, Herts Alcohol Problems Advsy Serv 1991–2005, Herts Assoc of Local Cncls 1991–2005, Capel Manor Horticultural and Environmental Centre 1994– (chm Capel Manor Horticultural and Environmental Centre Tst Fund 1989–94), Assoc of Dist Cncls 1994–2005, Herts Cons Soc 1995–2005; patron: Herts St John Ambulance Appeal 1989, E Herts Hospice Care Serv 1994–2005, Oxford Int Centre for Palliative Care 1994–2005, Herts Co Youth Orchestras and Choirs 1995–2005, MOVE IT 1997–2005, UN Women UK Nat Ctee (formerly UK Nat Ctee UN Devpt Fund for Women) 2004–15, Int Centre for Child Studies, Hospices of Hope 2005–; vice-patron The Chaucer Clinic Appeal 2001–05; tstee Nat Benevolent Fund for the Aged 1999– (chm of tstees 2010–); life memb Showmen's Guild of GB 2005–, memb Cncl Wine Guild of UK 2007–; Freeman City of London 1981, Freeman Borough of Broxbourne 2005, Liveryman Worshipful Co of Gardeners 1993 (Freeman 1989); fell Industry and Parl Tst 1990, FRSA 1990–2008, Hon MIHort 1993, Hon Fellowship of Professional Business and Tech Mgmnt 1995; *Publications* The Labour Left in London – A Blueprint for a Socialist Britain (CPC pamphlet, 1985); *Recreations* opera, ballet, theatre, family; *Style—* Dame Marion Roe, DBE

ROE, Sally Jean; *b* 4 September 1956; *Educ* Wakefield Girls HS, St Hilda's Coll Oxford (BA); *Career* admitted slr 1981; slr specialising in construction and engrg law; Dawson & Co: trainee 1979–81, asst slr 1981–85, ptnr Dispute Resolution Dept 1985–88; Freshfields Bruckhaus Deringer LLP: joined dispute resolution practice as assoc slr 1988, ptnr 1990–; dir Major Projects Assoc 2005–; higher courts (civil proceedings) qualification 1995; Partnering and Alliancing in Construction Projects (with Jane Jenkins, 2003); *Recreations* skiing, walking, theatre, opera; *Style—* Mrs Sally Roe; ✉ Freshfields Bruckhaus Deringer LLP, 65 Fleet Street, London EC4Y 1HS (☎ 020 7832 7277, fax 020 7108 7277, e-mail sally.roe@freshfields.com)

ROEDY, William H (Bill); *b* 13 June 1948; *Educ* West Point, Harvard Univ (MBA); *Career* served US Military 10 years (incl as pilot and as Cdr NATO Missile Base); sometime vice-pres Nat Accounts LA, joined Home Box Office Cable TV and Cinemax 1979, various mktg appts and mgmnt conslt for TV stations in Boston Mass 1979–89, md and chief exec MTV Europe 1989–94, pres MTV Networks International 1994–2011; currently chair Staying Alive Fndn; memb CCTA; *Style—* Bill Roedy, Esq

ROFFE, Clive Brian; JP (1987); s of Philip Roffe (d 1961); *b* 4 June 1935; *Educ* Montpelier Coll Brighton; *m* 1966 (m dis 1997), Jacqueline Carole, *née* Branston; 2 da (Danielle Philippa Geraldine b 1970, Natasha Nicole b 1974); m 2, 4 June 2000, Michelle Nadler; *Career* Lloyd's underwriter 1966, fin conslt; chm: Melbo Petroleum Ltd 1970, Edinburgh Insurance Services 1971, Gemini Business Centre 1992, Hereford Investments Ltd 1998; co dir; Freeman City of London, Liveryman Worshipful Co of Bakers, Liveryman Worshipful Co of Feltmakers, memb Ct of Assts and Master Worshipful Co of Upholders; *Recreations* organ, philately, jogging; *Clubs* RAC, City Livery, City Livery Yacht, Ward of Cheap, Ward of Aldgate, Strangers Norwich; *Style—* Clive Roffe, Esq; ✉ 33 The Close, Norwich NR1 4DZ (e-mail clive@londonandnorfolk.co.uk)

ROFFE, Melvyn Westley; s of Brian Roffe, of Derby, and Vera, *née* Hickinbotham; *b* 15 June 1964, Derby; *Educ* Univ of York, Univ of Durham (PGCE); *m* 1988, Catherine Stratford; 1 da (Grace), 1 s (Edmund); *Career* English master Oundle 1986–93; Monmouth Sch: head of English 1993–97, dir of studies 1997–2001; headmaster Old Swinford Hosp Stourbridge 2001–07, princ Wymondham Coll Norfolk 2007–14, princ George Watson's Coll Edinburgh 2014–; chm Boarding Schs Assoc 2008–09; Mayor of Oundle 1993; tstee

R

English Speaking Union Scotland 2014–, memb Advsy Ctee for Scotland Duke of Edinburgh's Award Scheme 2015–; memb Co of Merchants City of Edinburgh 2015–; FRSA 2001, Hon FCOptom 2009; *Recreations* cultural pursuits, historic transport, current affairs; *Clubs* Nat Lib, Caledonian; *Style*— Melvyn Roffe, Esq; ✉ George Watson's College, Colinton Road, Edinburgh EH10 5EG (☎ 0131 446 6000, e-mail principal@gwc.org.uk)

ROGAN, Baron (Life Peer UK 1999), of Lower Iveagh in the County of Down; Dennis Robert David Rogan; s of Robert Henderson Rogan, and Florence, *née* Arbuthnott; *b* 30 June 1942, Banbridge, Co Down; *Educ* Wallace HS Lisburn, Belfast Coll of Technol, Open Univ (BA), Kennedy Sch of Govt Harvard Univ; *m* 7 Aug 1968, Lorna Elizabeth, *née* Colgan; 2 s (Timothy Robert John, Damian Ardis); *Career* mgmnt trainee Moygashel Ltd 1960–69, mktg and sales William Ewart & Sons Ltd 1969–72; Lamont Holdings plc: mktg and sales 1972–76, gen sales mangr 1976–78; fndr and md Dennis Rogan & Associates 1978–, fndr and exec chm Associated Processors Ltd 1985–, dir chm Stake Holder Communication Gp, dep chm Belfast Telegraph Newspapers 2000–, dir International Advsy Bd Independent News & Media Gp 2001–; memb Int Advsy Bd Parker Green Int 2008–; sits as cross-bench peer in House of Lords, pres UU Pty (former chm), ldr UU Pty House of Lords; memb: Inter Parly Union, Cwlth Parly Assoc, RFCA for NI; former chm: South Belfast UU Constituency Assoc, Ulster Young Unionist Cncl, Lisburn Unit of Mgmnt Eastern Health and Social Services Bd; patron The Somme Assoc 2000–; Hon Col 40 (Ulster) Signals Rgt 2009–; memb Textile Inst; MBIM; *Recreations* rugby, gardening, oriental carpets, shooting; *Clubs* Reform (Belfast), Army and Navy; *Style*— The Rt Hon the Lord Rogan; ✉ 31 Notting Hill, Malone Road, Belfast BT9 5NS (☎ 028 9066 2468, fax 028 9066 3410); 13 Little College Street, London SW1P 3SH (☎ 020 7219 8625, fax 020 7219 1657); House of Lords, London SW1A 0PW (fax 020 7219 5979)

ROGAN, Simon; *Career* chef patron L'Enclume Cumbria 2003– (2 Michelin stars); television appearances incl Great British Menu (BBC 2) 2012 (winner, cooked dessert for the Olympic Banquet); *Style*— Simon Rogan, Esq; ✉ L'Enclume Restaurant with Rooms, Cavendish Street, Cartmel, Nr Grange over Sands, Cumbria LA11 6PZ

ROGER, David Bernard; s of John Grant Roger, of Newstead, Scotland, and Margaret Jean, *née* Dymock; *b* 23 February 1951; *Educ* Melville Coll Edinburgh, Univ of Newcastle upon Tyne (BA), Univ of Bristol (MA), Univ of Paris (Scenographic Diploma), ENO theatre design course; *Career* theatre designer; designs incl: La Mort de Zarathustra (Lucernaire Paris) 1979–80, The Mission (Soho Poly) 1982, The Knot Garden (Opera Factory) 1984, Akhnaten (ENO) 1985, La Boheme (Opera North) 1986, Temptation (RSC The Other Place) 1987, Faust parts 1 and 2 (Lyric Hammersmith) 1988, Simplicius Simplicissimus 1989, Cosi Fan Tutte (TV version Channel 4) 1989, Figaro (Opera Factory Zurich) 1990, Morte d'Arthur (Lyric Hammersmith) 1990, Manon Lescaut (Opera Comique Paris) 1990, Don Giovanni (TV version Channel 4) 1990, The Fiery Angel (Kirov St Petersburg, Royal Opera House and NY Met Opera) 1991–92, The Return of Ulysses (ENO) 1992, The Coronation of Poppea (Opera Factory) 1992, The Bacchae (Opera Factory) 1993, Plunder (Savoy) 1995, Mr Worldly Wise (Royal Ballet) 1995, Madam Butterfly, Tosca, Aida and Carmen (Royal Albert Hall) 1997/98, Carmen (Royal Albert Hall) 1997/2001, Heat of the Sun (Carlton TV), Births Marriages and Deaths (BBC 2), Last Christmas (BBC 1), The Sins (BBC 1), Swallow (BBC1), Early Doors (BBC 2), Eroica (BBC 2), Riot at the Rite (BBC 2), Low Winter Sun (Channel 4), Sherlock Holmes (BBC 1), Persuasion (ITV); memb Soc of Br Theatre Designers; *Clubs* 2 Brydges Place; *Style*— David Roger, Esq; ✉ 52B College Road, London NW10 5ER (☎ 020 8969 8354)

ROGERS, Prof Chris; *Career* teaching posts: Queen Mary & Westfield Coll London, Univ of Cambridge, UC Swansea, Univ of Warwick; prof of probability Univ of Bath, prof of statistical science Univ of Cambridge 2002–; *Books* Diffusions, Markov Processes, and Martingales (with David Williams); *Style*— Prof Chris Rogers; ✉ Statistical Laboratory, Centre for Mathematical Sciences, Wilberforce Road, Cambridge CB3 0WB

ROGERS, Prof Colin; s of William Joseph Rogers (d 1952), and Margaret Anne Gwendoline, *née* Goodgame (d 1971); *b* 1 December 1940; *Educ* Magdalen Coll Sch Oxford, Univ of Oxford (BA), Univ of Toronto (MEd), Univ of Nottingham (MSc, PhD, DSc); *Career* lectr Univ of Nottingham 1968–71; assoc prof: Old Dominion Univ Virginia USA 1973–74, Univ of W Ontario Canada 1974–78 (asst prof 1971–73); prof Univ of Waterloo Canada 1981–88 (assoc prof 1978–81), chair mathematical engrg Loughborough Univ of Technol 1988–92, prof of applied mathematics Univ of NSW Aust 1992– (head Dept of Applied Mathematics 1998–2006); chair of engrg mathematics Hong Kong Polytechnic Univ 2007–11; currently: ptnr investigator Australian Research Cncl Centre of Excellence for Mathematics and Statistics of Complex Systems, visiting professorial fell Univ of New South Wales; visiting prof: Univ of Adelaide Aust 1975, Univ of Cambridge 2002, Univ of Rome 2005, Univ of Bologna 2006; sr visitor Dept of Applied Mathematics and Theoretical Physics Univ of Cambridge 1979, adjunct princ research scientist Georgia Inst Technol 1989– (visiting prof 1982 and 1984), membre associé Centre de Recherches Mathématiques Université de Montréal Canada 1998–, visiting fell Clare Hall Cambridge 2012–13; memb Editorial Bd: Jl of Mathematical Analysis and Applications, Int Jl of Nonlinear Mechanics, Studies in Applied Mathematics, Boundary Value Problems; Centenary Medal (Aust) 2003, Australian Acad of Science Hannan Medal 2011; FInstP, FAA; *Books* Bäcklund Transformations and Their Applications (with W F Shadwick, 1982), Wave Phenomena: Modern Theory and Applications (ed with T B Moodie, 1986), Nonlinear Boundary Value Problems in Science and Engineering (with W F Ames, 1989), Nonlinear Equations in the Applied Sciences (ed with W F Ames, 1991), Bäcklund and Darboux Transformations: Geometry and Modern Applications in Soliton Theory (with W K Schief, 2002); *Recreations* Argentinian dance (estilo milonguero), athletics (Canadian National Masters Cross Country and 10,000 metres champion 1981), Welsh language studies; *Clubs* Oxford and Cambridge; *Style*— Prof Colin Rogers, FAA; ✉ 4B/8 Hampden Street, Paddington, Sydney 2021, NSW (☎ 00 61 29 332 4137); School of Mathematics, University of New South Wales, Sydney 2052, NSW, Australia (e-mail c.rogers@unsw.edu.au)

ROGERS, Colin Stuart; s of George Stuart Rogers (d 1982), and Jean Ritchie Christian (d 2000), of Farningham, Kent; *b* 6 February 1947, Islington, London; *Educ* St Olave's GS London, Univ of Essex (BA, MA); *m* 24 Nov 1972, Deborah, *née* Mortimer; 2 s (Benedict Randall b 19 June 1973, Thomas Mortimer b 6 Feb 1977); *Career* with ATV Network then Central Independent Television 1972–80: variously head of scripts, prodr of children's drama, prodr of single plays, ATV rep on ITV Network Children's Prog Ctee and ITV Labour Rels Ctee, latterly prodr of drama series Central Television; freelance prodr 1980–85 (series incl Spyship and Anna of the Five Towns, films incl Three Minute Heroes, Atlantis and The Groundling and the Kite for Play for Today and Space Station Milton Keynes for Screen Two; dir three shorts for The Golden Oldie Picture Show); BBC TV: exec prodr 1986–90, dep head Drama Series and Serials Dept 1986–88, prodr of series incl All Passion Spent 1986 (nominated BAFTA Best Drama Series), A Perfect Spy 1987 (TRIC Best BBC TV Series Award 1988, nominated BAFTA Best Drama Series 1988 and Best Mini-series Emmy 1989), Summer's Lease 1989 (nominated BAFTA Best Drama Series 1990, John Gielgud awarded Best Actor Emmy 1990); exec prodr Thin Air 1987, Sophia and Constance 1988, Shadow of the Noose 1989, Portrait of a Marriage 1990 (Grand Prize Banff Festival 1991), Spender (created with Jimmy Nail and Ian la Frenais) 1991; estab independent film drama prodn co Deco Films and Television Ltd 1990 (prodns incl continuing series of Resnick drama serials for BBC 1992– (Bronze Medal NY Festival 1992)), concurrently controller of drama Meridian Broadcasting Ltd 1991–95; at Meridian exec prodr of: Harnessing Peacocks (Gold Nymph Award Best Film and Silver Nymph Award Best Screenplay Monte Carlo Festival 1994) 1993, Under the Hammer 1994, The Ruth Rendell Mysteries 1994 and 1995 (Master of the Moor Silver Medal NY Festival 1995), The Vacillations of Poppy Carew 1994, The English Wife 1995; chm and chief exec Deco Group of Companies 1995– (prodr film Peggy Su! 1997), dir Cornwall Film Fund 2001–03; exec prodr: The Way Things Work 2002, Jubilee Pool 2002, Birt Dyneley 2002, Cheap Rate Gravity 2002, Fishing Film 2003; country dir India BBC World Serv Tst 2003–05 (Global Business Coalition Award 2008), exec dir Nat Assoc for Literature Devpt 2005–06, country dir Nigeria BBC World Serv Tst 2007–08; exec prodr: Jasoos Vijay (Thriller Prog of the Year Indian TV Awards), Haath Se Haath Milaa (UNICEF/Cwlth Broadcasting Assoc Award 2003, Best Public Service Ad Campaign Indian TC Awards 2004); juror Monte-Carlo Television Festival 2012; vice-chair Cornwall and Isles of Scilly NHS PCT 2006–08; lectr UC Falmouth 2005–10; memb: Nat Advsy Ctee Kent Literature Festival 1993–98, Cncl RTS 1995–99, Media Centre for Cornwall Steering Gp 1999–2001 (dir 2001–), Ctee W Cornwall Branch CPRE 1999–2005, Cornwall CC Cultural Industries Task Force 2000–03, Bd of Tstees Cornwall Theatre Co Ltd 2005– (chair 2010–12); Mencap: memb Bd of Tstees 2005–14, memb Bd of Govrs Mencap Nat Coll 2006–10 (chair 2008–10), chair Educn and Learning Ctee 2010–14, memb Audit and Assurance Ctee 2011–14, memb Nominations, Employment and Remuneration Ctee 2013–; chair Cornwall and Isles of Scilly NHS PCT Special Cases Appeals Tbnl 2010–13; FRTS, FRSA; *Books* A Bunch of Fives (1977); *Clubs* Groucho; *Style*— Colin Rogers, Esq; ✉ e-mail office@decofilms.co.uk

ROGERS, Danny; s of Prof Alan Rogers, and Wendy, *née* Prince; *Educ* Lord Howard of Effingham Sch, Univ of Leicester (BA); *Career* journalist; PR conslt 1993–96, freelance journalist 1996–2001, assoc ed (news) Marketing 2001–04, dep ed Marketing 2004, ed PR Week 2004–12, ed Campaign 2013–14, ed-in-chief Brand Republic Gp 2014–; *Recreations* football, tennis; *Style*— Danny Rogers, Esq; ✉ PR Week, 174 Hammersmith Road, London W6 7JP

ROGERS, Jane Rosalind; da of Prof Andrew W Rogers (d 1989), and Margaret Kathleen, *née* Farmer; *b* 21 July 1952; *Educ* New Hall Cambridge (BA), Univ of Leicester (PGCE); *m* Michael L Harris; 1 da (Kate Lucy b 1981), 1 s (Laurence Jay b 1984); *Career* novelist and playwright; Arts Cncl writer in residence Northern Coll Barnsley 1985–86, writer in residence Sheffield Poly 1987, Judith E Wilson visiting writer/fell Univ of Cambridge 1991, prof of creative writing Sheffield Hallam Univ 1994–; memb Soc of Authors; FRSL 1994; *Books* Separate Tracks (1983), Her Living Image (1984, Somerset Maugham Award 1985), The Ice is Singing (1987), Mr Wroe's Virgins (1991), Promised Lands (1995, Writers' Guild Best Fiction Book Award), Island (1999), Good Fiction Guide (ed, 2001), The Voyage Home (2004), The Testament of Jessie Lamb (2011, Arthur C Clarke Award); *Television and Radio Work* Dawn and the Candidate (Channel 4, Samuel Beckett Award 1990), Mr Wroe's Virgins (BBC adaptation); radio adaptations incl: Shirley, Island; *Recreations* walking, travel, reading; *Style*— Ms Jane Rogers, FRSL; ✉ e-mail jane.rogers@btinternet.com, website www.janerogers.org

ROGERS, Juliet Mary; s of Edward Maxwell Rogers, of Christchurch, NZ (d 1997), and Lois Josephine, *née* Ablett; *b* 2 May 1957, NZ; *Educ* Univ of Canterbury Christchurch (BA, MA), Victoria Univ Wellington (DipBA); *m* 28 Aug 1982 (sep 2002), Perry Laurence Lennon; 1 da (Sophie Anna b 29 Feb 1984), 1 s (Chrisopher James Edward b 17 Jan 1987); *Career* sales rep William Collins Publishers 1978–80, probation offr Dept of Justice 1980–84, mktg mangr MacDonald Publishers 1987–90; md: Random House NZ 1990–98, Random House Aust 1998–2001, Murdoch Books Aust and UK 2002–11; proprietor and dir The Wild Colonial Company 2011–; pres Aust Publishers Assoc 2004–08; chair Indigenous Literacy Fndn 2011–; *Recreations* reading, film, gardening; *Style*— Ms Juliet Rogers; ✉ The Wild Colonial Company, PO Box 417, Balmain, NSW 20421, Australia (☎ 0061 419 606818, e-mail juliet@wildcolonialcompany.com.au, website www.wildcolonialcompany.com.au)

ROGERS, Keith Taylor; s of John Taylor Rogers, of Falkirk, Scotland, and Lilian, *née* Brown (d 2005); *b* 26 February 1961, Falkirk, Scotland; *Educ* Grangemouth HS, Univ of Strathclyde (BSc); *m* 1985, Natalie Sarah, *née* Pitt; 1 s (Jonathan Keith b 8 Sept 1987); *Career* fndr and ceo Anchor International Ltd 1987–99, fndr and ceo Goals Soccer Centres plc 2000–; Ernst and Young Entrepreneur of the Year (Scot) 2006, Ernst and Young Entrepeneur of the Year (UK) 2006, Entrepreneurial Exchange Entrepreneur of the Year 2010; *Recreations* reading, European cinema, opera, travel, jazz, cycling; *Style*— Keith Rogers, Esq; ✉ Over Lethame House, Lethame Road, Strathhaven, Scotland (☎ 01357 529443, keith@rogersfamily.eu); Keith Rogers Goals Soccer Centres, Orbital House, Peel Park, East Kilbride G7 5PR

ROGERS, Malcolm Austin; CBE (2004); s of James Eric Rogers, and Frances Anne, *née* Elsey; *b* 3 October 1948; *Educ* Oakham Sch, Magdalen Coll Oxford, ChCh Oxford (MA, DPhil); *Career* Nat Portrait Gallery: asst keeper 1974–83, dep dir 1983–94, keeper 1985–94; dir Museum of Fine Arts Boston 1994–2015 (dir emeritus 2015–); Humanitas visiting prof in museums, galleries and libraries Univ of Oxford 2012; Fndn for Italian Art and Culture Excellency Award 2010; Liveryman Worshipful Co of Girdlers; Hon DFA Emmanuel Coll Boston, Hon Dr of Humane Letters Boston Architectural Coll 2014; memb American Acad of Arts and Sciences 2011; FSA 1986; Chevalier L'Ordre des Arts et des Lettres (France) 2007, Commendatore al Merito della Repubblica Italiana 2009, Encomienda de la Orden de Isabel la Catolica (Spain) 2010; *Books* Dictionary of British Portraiture 4 Vols (jt ed, 1979–81), Museums and Galleries of London Blue Guide (1983, 3 edn 1992), William Dobson (1983), John and John Baptist Closterman: A Catalogue of their Works (1983), Elizabeth II: Portraits of Sixty Years (1986), Camera Portraits (1989), Montacute House (1991), Companion Guide to London (ed with Sir David Piper, 1992), The English Face (ed with Sir David Piper, 1992), Boughton House: The English Versailles (contrib, 1992), Master Drawings from the National Portrait Gallery (1993), Van Dyck 1599–1641 (contrib, 1999); *Recreations* food, wine, music, travel, gardening; *Clubs* Beefsteak, Wednesday Evening Club of 1777 (Boston), Thursday Evening (Boston); *Style*— Malcolm Rogers, Esq, CBE, FSA; ✉ Russell Court, Lower Green, Broadway, Worcestershire WR12 7BU (☎ 01386 854828)

ROGERS, Martin John; s of Douglas John Rogers (d 2008), and Mary, *née* Sayce (d 2008); *b* 21 July 1955; *Educ* Bargod GS, UC of Wales Aberystwyth (BSc); *m* 1977, Beth, da of Peter Jones (d 2000), and Amy Jones; 3 da (Lucy Elizabeth b 31 Jan 1981, Kate Elinore b 2 Feb 1983, Sophie Jane b 11 May 1987); *Career* Pannell Kerr Forster: joined Cardiff Office 1976, ptnr 1985, sr ptnr Derby 1989–96; sr ptnr PricewaterhouseCoopers Derby (formerly Coopers & Lybrand before merger) 1996–99, gp fin dir Ascot plc 1999–2001, chm and non-exec of a number of private cos 2001–05, managing ptnr E Midlands Mazars LLP 2005–14, sr ptnr 2014–; govr Univ of Derby 2005–; MInstD, FCA 1979; *Recreations* country sports, sailing, skiing; *Clubs* RAC; *Style*— Martin Rogers, Esq; ✉ Mazars LLP, Park View House, 58 The Ropewalk, Nottingham NG1 5DW (☎ 0115 964 4744)

ROGERS, Mary; *Career* chief exec Industry Forum 2002–11, jt ceo Urban Catalyst, jt ceo Gtr London Enterprise; chair Pensions and Investment Research Consultancy; dep chm: Guys & Lewisham Mental Health NHS Tst, Stonebridge Housing Action Tst, non-exec dir 21st Century ERA, cmmr Rgnl Policy Cmmn; tstee: One World Action, Big Issue Fndn; *Style*— Ms Mary Rogers

ROGERS, Prof (John) Michael; s of John Patrick Rogers (d 1961), of Dalton-in-Furness, Lancs, and Constance Mary, *née* Fisher (d 1994); *b* 25 January 1935; *Educ* Ulverston GS,

CCC Oxford (MA), Oriel Coll Oxford (BPhil), Pembroke Coll Oxford (DPhil); *Career* Nat Serv RA 1953–55, later Capt Intelligence Corps TA; res fell Oriel Coll Oxford 1958–61, philosophy tutor Pembroke and Wadham Coll Oxford 1961–65, asst then assoc prof American Univ in Cairo 1965–77, asst then dep keeper Dept of Oriental Antiquities Br Museum 1977–91, Slade prof Univ of Oxford 1991–92, Khalili prof of Islamic art and archaeology SOAS Univ of London 1991–2000, hon curator Khalili Collection of Islamic art 2001–; advsr NACF, memb Editorial Ctee Burlington Magazine, corr memb Deutsches Archäologisches Institut 1989; FSA 1974, FBA 1988; Order Egyptian Republic Class II 1969; *Books* The Spread of Islam (1976), Islamic Art and Design 1500–1700 (1983), Süleyman the Magnificent (with R M Ward, 1980), Mughal Painting (1993), The Uses of Anachronism on Methodological Diversity in the History of Islamic Art (1994), Empire of the Sultans: Ottoman art from the collection of Nasser D Khalili (Musée d'art et d'histoire Geneva, 1995), Sinan (2006), The Arts of Islam: Treasures from the Nasser D Khalili Collection (exhbn catalogue, 2007, revised edn 2010), Tale and Image: Persian paintings in the Khalili Collection, Volume 2 (with Manijeh Bayani, 2017); author of numerous articles on arts, architecture and economic and social history of Islam; *Recreations* music, mountains, botany; *Clubs* Beefsteak; *Style*— Prof Michael Rogers, FBA, FSA; ✉ The Nasser D Khalili Collection of Islamic Art, Unit 24, Victoria Road Estate, London W3 6UU (☎ 020 8992 5000, e-mail michael@nourhouse.com)

ROGERS, Nicholas Emerson (Nick); s of Reginald Emerson Rogers (d 1983), and Doreen, *née* Burbidge (d 1991); *b* 15 March 1946, Chislehurst, London; *m* 26 Oct 1973 (m dis 1997), Linda Jane; *Career* photographer: Sunday Independent Plymouth 1968–70, Reading Evening Post 1970–72; staff photographer Daily Mail 1973–78; dep picture ed The Observer 1983–86; feature photographer: The Times 1986–90, The European 1990, Sunday Telegraph 1990–96; freelance 1996–; Kodak Industrial and Commercial Photographer of the Year 1987, Feature Photographer of the Year Br Press Awards 1988, commended Nikon Awards 1988; FRPS; *Recreations* photography, sailing, walking, travel, watercolour painting, building model boats; *Style*— Nick Rogers, Esq; ✉ 25 Bishops Court, Newton Hill, Newton Ferrers, Near Plymouth, Devon PL8 1DT (☎ 01752 872738, e-mail nick@nickrogers.org.uk)

ROGERS, Nick; *b* 25 February 1967, Oxford; *Educ* Oxford Polytechnic (ONC, BTEC HNC), Coventry Univ (BEng), Warwick Manufacturing Gp (studying for PhD); *Career* Jaguar Land Rover (formerly Land Rover): apprentice technician Product Engrg 1984–88, body research and devpt engr 1988–90, project engr Body Engrg 1990–91, project ldr Midland Engineering Centre 1992–94, project team ldr Swindon/Longbridge 1994–95, chief engr Body Structures Design 1995–98, chief engr Re-Engineering Munich 1998–99, project ldr T5 2000–03, chief prog engr T5 Platform 2003–05, lean manufacturing mangr Range Rover, Defender and Powertrain Operations 2005–07, vehicle line dir Range Rover 2007–15, exec dir Product Engrg 2015–; FIMechE; *Recreations* motorsport, travel; *Style*— Nick Rogers, Esq; ✉ Jaguar Land Rover, Banbury Road, Gaydon, Warwickshire CV35 0RR (e-mail nrogers6@jaguarlandrover.com)

ROGERS, Peter; CBE (2011); *Educ* LLB; *Career* Babcock Int Gp plc: chief operating offr 2002–03, memb Bd 2002–, gp ceo 2003–; non-exec dir Galliford Try plc; former dir: Courtaulds plc, Acordis BV; FCA; *Style*— Peter Rogers, Esq, CBE; ✉ Babcock International Group plc, 33 Wigmore Street, London W1U 1QX

ROGERS, Professor Philip John; MBE (1990); s of John William Rogers (d 1990), and Lilian Fleet (d 1991); *b* 4 October 1942; *Educ* Poly of North London (HNC); *m* 24 Nov 1979, Wendy Joan, *née* Cross, da of Leonard George Cross and Joan Sylvester Romans; 2 da (Ffion Clare b 25 May 1982, Ceri Frances b 29 Sept 1983), 1 s (Trystan Philip b 16 April 1985); *Career* trainee and optical instrument designer Hilger and Watts London 1960–66; Pilkington Optronics (now Qioptiq Ltd) 1966–2005 (chief optical designer from 1969, chief engr Optics 1994–2000), fndr VNF Ltd 2006; visiting prof Cranfield Univ 2007–13, visiting prof Glyndwr Univ 2012–; Int Society for Optical Engrg (SPIE): memb Bd 1995–97, memb European Steering Ctee 1984–86, memb Strategic Planning Ctee 1999–2001, memb Nominating Ctee 1996, memb Awards Ctee 1996–2001; memb: UK Inst of Physics Optical Gp Ctee 1991–97, Thomson College Scientifique et Technique Paris 1992–98, Imperial Coll Optics Advisory Ctee 1995–2005, Welsh Opto-Electronics Forum Steering Ctee 1996–98, UK Consortium for Photonics and Optics Mgmnt Ctee 1997–2004; holder of numerous patents, presented numerous papers and lectures worldwide, presented Open Univ prog 1977; assessor: Engrg Leadership Awards Royal Acad of Engrg 2000, Queen's Anniversary Prizes for Higher and Further Educn 2000; fell: Int Soc for Optical Engrg USA (1991), Optical Soc of America (1998); FREng 1998, FInstP 1992; *Awards* Finalist UK Mfrg Industry Achievement Award, Design Innovation of the Year 1996, Finalist Royal Acad of Engrg MacRobert 1997; *Publications* author of numerous articles and contributions in professional jls and books; *Recreations* listening to classical music, astronomy, computing, family activities; *Style*— Professor Philip Rogers, MBE, FREng; ✉ 24 Cilgant Eglwys Wen, Bodelwyddan, Denbighshire LL18 5US (☎ 01745 582498, e-mail philjrog@aol.com)

ROGERS, Lady; Ruth; *b* 2 July 1948; *Educ* Colorado Rocky Mountain Sch, Bennington Coll Vermont, London Coll of Printing; *m* 1973, Baron Rogers of Riverside, *qv*; 2 s (Roo b 18 Jan 1975, Bo b 2 Dec 1983), 3 step s (Ben b 12 June 1963, Zad b 5 Nov 1965, Ab b 12 July 1968); *Career* Art Dept Penguin Books 1971–73, Richard Rogers Architects 1974–85, chef/owner (with Rose Gray, MBE (d 2010)) River Cafe 1987–; Italian Restaurant of the Year The Times 1988, Best New Restaurant Courvoisier Best of Best Awards 1989, Eros Awards Evening Standard 1994 and 1995; memb Bd Royal Court Theatre; *Books* with Rose Gray: The River Cafe Cook Book (1995, Food Book of the Year Glenfiddich Awards 1996), River Cafe Cook Book 2 (1997), River Cafe Italian Kitchen (1998), River Cafe Cook Book Green (2000), River Cafe Cook Book Easy (2003), River Cafe Two Easy (2005), River Cafe Pocket Books (2006), River Cafe Classic Italian (2009); *Style*— Lady Rogers, MBE; ✉ River Cafe, Thames Wharf, Rainville Road, London W6 9HA (☎ 020 7386 4200, fax 020 7386 4201)

ROGERS OF RIVERSIDE, Baron (Life Peer UK 1996), of Chelsea in the London Borough of Kensington and Chelsea; Richard George Rogers; CH (2008), kt (1991); s of Dada Geiringer Rogers, and Nino Rogers; *b* 23 July 1933, Florence, Italy; *Educ* Architectural Assoc London (AA Dip), Yale Univ (MArch, Fulbright and Yale scholar); *m* 1, 1960, Su Brumwel; 3 s; m 2, 1973, Ruth Rogers, MBE, *qv*; 2 s; *Career* architect; chm: Rogers Stirk Harbour & Ptnrs (formerly Richard Rogers Partnership) 1977–, Richard Rogers Architects Ltd London, Richard Rogers Japan KK Tokyo, Richard Rogers SL Spain; projects incl: house in Wimbledon 1968–69, PA Technol Centre phases 1, 2, 3 Cambridge 1970–84, ICRAM Paris 1971–77, Centre Pomidou 1971–77, Lloyd's of London 1978–84, Fleetguard Factory France 1979–81, Inmos Microprocessor Factory Newport 1982–87, PA Technol Science Lab Princeton USA 1982–85, Thames Reach Housing 1984–89, Billingsgate Market Conversion London 1985–88, Reuters Data Centre London 1987–92, European Courts of Human Rights Strasbourg 1989–95, Terminal 5 Heathrow Airport 1989–2008, Chiswick Park London 1989–, Bordeaux Law Courts 1992–98, Thames Valley Univ 1993–96, Daimler Chrysler Berlin 1993–99, 88 Wood Street London 1993–2000, Channel 4 Headquarters 1994, Montevetro London 1994–2000, Lloyd's Register of Shipping 1995–99, Minami Yamashiro Primary Sch Japan 1995–2003, Millennium Dome 1996–99, Broadwick Street London 1996–2002, T4 Madrid Barajas Airport 1997–2006 (Stirling Prize 2006), Paddington Waterside 1999–2004, Nat Assembly for Wales Cardiff 1999–2005, Barcelona Bullring 2000–10, Antwerp Law Cts 2000–2005, Canary Riverside South London 2001–, Maggie's Centre London 2001–08 (Stirling Prize 2009), Leadenhall Street London 2002–, Mossbourne Community Academy London 2002–04, Bodegas Protos Spain 2003–06, 300 New Jersey Ave Washington DC 2004–09, Oxley Woods Housing 2005–, NEO Bankside London 2005–, Campus Palmas Altas Seville 2005–09, One Hyde Park London 2005–10, World Trade Centre Tower 3 NY 2006–, Br Museum London 2007–, Grand Paris 2008–; masterplans: London Docklands Devpt 1984, South Bank London 1986, Shanghai 1994, Dunkirk France 1998, Mallorca 1998, Greenwich Peninsular London 2000, Tate Modern Bankside 2000, Wembley London 2000, Almada Portugal 2002, Canada Water London 2002, Lea Valley/Olympics London 2003, Lewisham Gateway 2003, Barangaroo Sydney 2009, Bercy Charenton Paris 2010–; vice-pres RIBA 1986–87, chm Architecture Fndn 1991–2001, dep chm Arts Cncl of England 1994–97, chm Urban Task Force 1998–2001; memb: RIBA Cncl 1984–87, UN Architects' Ctee 1984–87, Continuing Professional Devpt RIBA, UN World Cmmn on 21st Century Urbanisation, Congress of Int Modern Architects; chief advsr to the Mayor of London on architecture and urbanism 2000–08, advsr to the Mayor of Barcelona's Urban Strategies Cncl; UK business ambass 2008–; chm Bd Tate Gallery 1981–89; hon tstee MOMA NY; Reith lectr BBC (Cities for a Small Planet) 1995; Saarinen prof Yale Univ 1985; pres Nat Communities Resource Centre, tstee UK Bd Médecins du Monde, patron Soc of Black Architects, patron Maggie's Centres; Royal Gold Medal for Architecture 1985, Arnold W Brunner Meml Prize American Acad and Inst of Arts and Letters 1989, Thomas Jefferson Meml Fndn Medal in Architecture 1999, Praemium Imperiale Award 2000, Golden Lion for Lifetime Achievement 2006, Tau Sigma Delta Gold Medal 2007, Minerva Medal 2007, Pritzker Architecture Prize Laureate 2007; Hon Dr: Univ of Westminster 1992, South Bank Univ 1996, Czech Tech Univ Prague 1999; Hon DDes Oxford Brookes Univ 2000, Laurea (hc) Univ of Florence 2004; hon prof Tongi Univ China 2004; hon fell Univ of Wales Inst Cardiff 2007 and others; RIBA, hon memb Academie d'Architecture 1983, academician Int Acad of Architecture, RA 1984, Hon FAIA 1986, hon memb Bund Deutscher Architekten 1989, FRIAS 1999, Hon FREng 2005; Chevalier de l'Ordre National de la Legion d'Honneur 1986, Friend of Barcelona 1997; *Publications* Architecture – A Modern Review (1990), Cities for a Small Planet (with Philip Gumuchdjian, 1997), Cities for a Small Country (with Anne Power, 2000); subject of: By Their Own Design (Abbey Suckle Granada, 1980), Nine Projects – Japan – Richard Rogers Partnership (Blueprint Extra 3, 1991), The Architecture of Richard Rogers (Deyan Sudjic, 1994), Richard Rogers (Kenneth Powell, 1994), Richard Rogers Partnership – Works and Projects (ed Richard Burdett, 1996), Richard Rogers: Complete Works vols 1–2 (Kenneth Powell, 2001/2002) vol 3 (2005), Richard Rogers + Architects From the House to the City (2010); *Style*— The Lord Rogers of Riverside, CH; ✉ Thames Wharf, Rainville Road, London W6 9HA (☎ 020 7385 1235, e-mail enquiries@rsh-p.com, website www.rsh-p.com)

ROGERSON, Daniel John (Dan); s of Stephen John Rogerson, of Bodmin, Cornwall, and Patricia Anne, *née* Jones; *b* 23 July 1975, St Austell, Cornwall; *Educ* Bodmin Coll, Univ of Wales Aberystwyth; *m* 21 Aug 1999, Heidi Lee, *née* Purser; 2 s (Mawgan John b 24 Nov 2004, Jago John b 17 Sept 2007), 1 da (Elowen Ruby Rose b 19 Nov 2008); *Career* co-cncllr Bedford Borough Cncl 1999, dep ldr Lib Dem Cncl Gp; Parly candidate (Lib Dem) Bedfordshire NE 2001, MP (Cons) Cornwall N 2005–15; *Style*— Dan Rogerson, Esq; ✉ House of Commons, London SW1A 0AA (☎ 020 7219 4707, e-mail contact@danrogerson.org)

ROGERSON, Philip Graham; s of Henry Rogerson, and Florence, *née* Dalton; *b* 1 January 1945; *Educ* William Hulme's GS Manchester; *m* 21 Dec 1968, Susan Janet, da of Jack Kershaw, of Cleveleys, Lancs; 2 da (Penelope Rose b 2 Dec 1971, Hannah Rosemary b 7 April 1988), 1 s (Simon Andrew b 19 July 1974); *Career* various appts with the ICI Gp 1978–92 (gen mangr fin ICI plc 1989–92); British Gas plc (now BG plc): exec dir 1992–98, dep chm 1996–98; non-exec chm: PII Gp Ltd 1998–2002, Bertram Gp Ltd 1999–2001, Viridian Gp 1999–2005, KBC Advanced Technologies plc 1999–2004, Project Telecom plc 2000–2003, Copper Eye Ltd 2001–03, Aggreko plc 2002–12 (dep chm 1997–2002), Thus Gp plc 2004–08, Carillion plc 2005–14 (dep chm 2004–05), Northgate plc 2006–09 (non-exec dir 2003–), Bunzl plc 2010–, De La Rue plc 2012–; non-exec dep chm International Public Relations (formerly Shandwick International plc) 1997–98; non-exec dir: Halifax Building Society (now Halifax plc) 1995–98, LIMIT plc 1998–2000, Wates City of London Properties plc 1998–2000, British Biotech plc 1999–2003, Octopus Capital 2000–01, Celltech plc 2003–04, Davis Service Gp plc 2004–10; FCA, FCT; *Recreations* golf, tennis, theatre; *Style*— Philip Rogerson, Esq; ✉ 1 Providence Tower, Bermondsey Wall West, London SE16 4US (☎ 020 7237 8962)

ROGISTER, Prof John; s of J J A Rogister (d 1985), of Solihull, and A Rogister, *née* Smal (d 1992); *b* 26 March 1941; *Educ* Solihull Sch, Keble Coll Oxford (pres OU English Club), Univ of Birmingham (BA), Worcester Coll Oxford (DPhil); *m* 1972, Margaret Kathleen, da of late Harold Jury, of New Malden; *Career* sr lectr in modern history Univ of Durham 1982–2001 (lectr 1967–82); assoc prof of history Université de Paris X 1982–84; visiting prof: Collège de France Paris (Bronze Medal of the Collège) 1987, 1999 and 2006, Scuola Normale Superiore Pisa 1988, Università degli Studi di Roma La Sapienza 2003; assoc dir of studies École Pratique des Hautes Études (IV Section) Sorbonne Paris 1988–89, assoc prof of history Université Paul Valéry Montpellier III 1989–90 (guest prof 1996, 1998 and 1999); guest prof of history Université Lumière Lyon 2 2000; pres Int Cmmn for the History of Representative and Parliamentary Insts 1990–99 (hon pres 1999–); memb: Jury for the Prize (lit and history) of the Assoc de la Noblesse de France 1993–2006, French Govt Cmmn d'études de la Reconstruction des Tuileries 2006–, Br section Franco-Br Cncl 2007–12 (hon memb 2014–), Bureau of the Int Ctee of Historical Sciences 2010–15; memb Editorial Bd Parliaments, Estates and Representation 1990–; memb Scientific Cncl: Parlement(s) Revue Politique 2009–, Revue d'Histoire Diplomatique 2009–; Hon Dip Institul de Istorie 'Nicolae Iorga' Romanian Acad 1998; memb: Société de l'Histoire de France 1985, Société Royale des Archives Verviétoises (Belgium) 1989; corresponding memb Académie des Sciences Morales et Politiques Inst de France 2003; FRHistS 1978, FSA 1997; Commandeur Order of the Palmes Académiques (for services to French culture) 2015 (Chevalier 1984, Offr 1988), Grand Officier de l'Ordre National du Mérite (France) 2011 (Commandeur 2001), Accademico (hc) Accademia Siculo-Normanna di Palermo e Monreale (Italy) 2004, Officier de l'Ordre des Arts et des Lettres 2007, Commandeur de l'Ordre de la Couronne (Belgium) 2008; *Publications* Durham University Journal (ed, 1975–81), 1776 American Independence Bicentennial Exhibition Catalogue, National Maritime Museum Greenwich (leading contrib, 1976), Parliaments, Estates and Representation (fndr ed, 1981–90), 16th Biennale Exhibition Catalogue, 'Casa dell'Uomo' (Milan, 1986), Louis XV and the Parlement of Paris 1737–1755 (1994), Correspondance du Président de Brosses et de l'Abbé Marquis Antonio Niccolini (with Mireille Gille, 2016); leading contrib to GB Nini Exhibition Catalogues (Urbino and Blois, 2001); also ed of unpublished texts of George I Bratianu (1990 and 1997) and author of over 60 articles and reviews in pubns incl English Historical Review, French History, History, History Today, Revue Historique and TLS; *Recreations* travel, music; *Clubs* Beefsteak, Travellers, Oxford and Cambridge, City Univ, Fondation Universitaire (Brussels); *Style*— Prof J Rogister, FSA; ✉ 4 The Peth, Durham DH1 4PZ (e-mail john.rogister@btinternet.com)

RÖHL, Prof John Charles Gerald; s of Dr Hans-Gerhard Röhl (d 1976), of Frankfurt-am-Main, Germany, and Freda Kingsford, *née* Woulfe-Brenan; *b* 31 May 1938; *Educ* Stretford GS, Corpus Christi Coll Cambridge (MA, PhD); *m* 7 Aug 1964, Rosemarie Elfriede, da of Johann Werner von Berg (d 1946), of Hamburg; 1 da (Stephanie Angela b 1965), 2 s

R

(Nicholas John, Christoph Andreas (twins) b 1967); *Career* RAF 1956–58; prof of history Univ of Sussex 1979–99 (lectr 1964–73, reader 1973–79, dean Sch of Euro Studies 1982–85); visiting prof of history: Univ of Hamburg 1974, Univ of Freiburg 1977–78; fell: Alexander von Humboldt Fndn 1970–71, Historisches Kolleg Munich 1986–87, Woodrow Wilson Int Center for Scholars Washington DC 1989–90, Inst for Advanced Study Princeton NJ 1994, Moses Mendelssohn Zentrum Potsdam 1996, Nat Humanities Center NC 1997–98; *Books* Germany Without Bismarck: The Crisis of Government in the Second Reich 1890–1900 (1967), From Bismarck to Hitler: The Problem of Continuity in German History (1970), 1914 – Delusion or Design? The Testimony of Two German Diplomats (1973), Philipp Eulenburgs Politische Korrespondenz (3 vols, 1976–83), Kaiser Wilhelm II – New Interpretations (ed with N Sombart, 1982), Kaiser, Hof und Staat – Wilhelm II und die deutsche Politik (1987), Der Ort Kaiser Wilhelms II in der deutschen Geschichte (ed, 1991), Wilhelm II: Die Jugend des Kaisers 1859–1888 (1993), The Kaiser and his Court: Wilhelm II and the Government of Germany (1994, jt winner Wolfson History Prize 1994), Purple Secret: Genes, 'Madness' and the Royal Houses of Europe (with Martin Warren and David Hunt, 1998), Young Wilhelm: The Kaiser's Early Life 1859–1888 (1998), Wilhelm II: Der Aufbau der Persönlichen Monarchie 1888–1900 (2001, Gissings Prize 2003), Wilhelm II: The Kaiser's Personal Monarchy 1888–1900 (2004), Wilhelm II: Der Weg in den Abgrund 1900–41 (2008), Wilhelm II: Into the Abyss of War and Exile 1900–41 (2014, Einhard Prize 2013), Wilhelm II Eine Biographie (2013), Kaiser Wilhelm II: A Concise Life (2014), Aus dem Großen Hauptquartier. Kurt Riezlers Briefe an Käthe Liebermann, 1914–1915 (ed, with G Roth 2016); *Recreations* jazz, classical music, walking, bird watching; *Style*— Prof John C G Röhl; ✉ 11 Monckton Way, Kingston, Lewes, East Sussex BN7 3LD (☎ 01273 472778)

ROJO, Dr Tamara; CBE (2016); da of Pablo Rojo, of Madrid, and Sara Diez; *b* 1974, Montreal; *Educ* Centro de Danza da Victor Ullate, Universidad Rey Juan Carlos de Madrid (DA Magna Cum Laude); *Career* ballerina; Compañia de Danza Victor Ullate (Comunidad de Madrid) 1991–96, princ English Nat Ballet 1997–2000, princ Royal Ballet 2000–12, artistic dir English Nat Ballet 2012; guest dancer: Mariinsky Ballet, Mikhailovsky Ballet, Ballet Nacional de Cuba, Teatro alla Scala Ballet, Royal Swedish Ballet, Nat Ballet of Finland, Tokyo Ballet, New Nat Tokyo Ballet, Nat Ballet of China, English Nat Ballet, Birmingham Royal Ballet; has also danced at galas throughout Europe, Asia and the Americas; repertory incl all teh major roles in the classics as well as ballets by Macmillan, Ashton, Cranko, Makarova, Messerer, Kylian, Balanchine, Robbins, Fokine, Mats Ek, Van Mannen, Van Dantzig, Nils Christie, Roland Petit, Glen Tetley, Ben Stevenson, Lev Ivanov, Nureyev, Vassiliev and Alicia Alonso; has had works created for her by Derek Deane, Wayne McGregor, Kim Brandstrup, Liam Scarlett, Fei Bo, Christopher Hampson, Ricardo Cue, Christopher Bruce, Cathy Marston, Luca Veggetti and Victor Ullate; resident guest teacher Royal Ballet Sch 2008–; *Awards* Gold Medal and Critics' Award Paris Concours 1994, First Prize of Italian Critics 1996, Outstanding Achievements in Dance Barclays Theatre Award 2000, Best Female Dancer Critics Circle Dance Awards 2001, Spanish Gold Medal of Fine Arts 2002, The Prince of Asturias Arts Award 2005, Benois de la Danse 2008, Medalla Internacional de las Artes de la Comunidad de Madrid 2008, Laurence Olivier Award for Best New Dance Prodn 2010, Encomienda de Numero Spanish Order of Isabel la Catalica 2012, Kennedy Center Gold Medal in the Arts 2012, Santander Bank Fndn Award to Anglo-Spanish Relations 2013; *Recreations* theatre, reading, films; *Clubs* Hospital, Soho House; *Style*— Dr Tamara Rojo, CBE; ✉ English National Ballet, Markova House, 39 Jay Mews, London SW7 2ES (e-mail tamara.rojo@ballet.org.uk, website www.tamara-rojo.com)

ROLAND, Prof Martin; CBE (2003); s of Peter Ernest Roland, and Eileen Margaret, *née* Osborne; *b* 7 August 1951; *Educ* Rugby, Univ of Oxford (MA, BM BCh, DM); *m* 1, Gillian Rogers; 1 s (Christopher); m 2, Rosalind Jane, *née* Thorburn; 2 s (Duncan (decd), Jonathan), 1 da (Alison); *Career* house physician Radcliffe Infirmary Oxford 1975, house surgn Royal United Hosp Bath 1975–76, GP vocational scheme Cambridge 1976–79, lectr in gen practice St Thomas' Hosp Med Sch and princ in gen practice London 1979–83, princ in gen practice Cambridge 1983–93, dir of studies in gen practice Cambridge Univ Sch of Clinical Med 1987–93, prof of gen practice Univ of Manchester 1993–2009, prof of health services research Univ of Cambridge 2009–16 (emeritus prof of health services research 2016–); former dir Nat Primary Care R&D Centre, dir NIHR Sch for Primary Care Research 2006–09; author of numerous pubns on hosp referrals, back pain, use of time and quality of care in gen practice; MFPHM 1987, FRCGP 1994, FMedSci 2000, FRCP 2001 (MRCP 1978); *Style*— Prof Martin Roland, CBE; ✉ University of Cambridge, Institute of Public Health, Forvie Site, Robinson Way, Cambridge CB2 0SR (☎ 01223 330320, fax 01223 762515, e-mail martin.roland@medschl.cam.ac.uk)

ROLES, William Richard; s of Anthony John Howard Roles, of London, and Vanessa Jane, *née* Baldwin; *b* 4 September 1969, Eastbourne, Sussex; *Educ* Ardingly Coll, Mander Portman Woodward Coll London, Univ of Reading (BA), Coll of Law London (Dip); *m* 23 Aug 1997, Victoria Anne, *née* Dennison; 1 s (Alexander Richard Howard b 22 Sept 2001), 1 da (Eleanor Isobel b 27 Oct 2004); *Career* admitted slr 1997; trainee slr Steggles Palmer 1995–97, slr Wilde & Ptnrs 1997–99, slr Eversheds 1999–2004, ptnr and head Banking Dept Mills & Reeve 2004–; memb Law Soc 1997; *Recreations* Chelsea FC, history, family; *Style*— William Roles, Esq; ✉ Mills & Reeve, Botanic House,100 Hills Road, Cambridge CB2 1PH (☎ 01223 364422, fax 01223 324549, e-mail william.roles@mills-reeve.com)

ROLET, Xavier; KBE (2015); *Educ* Columbia Business Sch (MBA), Institut des Hautes Etudes de Défense Nationale (IHEDN, postgrad degree); *Career* Goldman Sachs 1984–94, Credit Suisse First Boston 1994–96, Dresdner Kleinwort Benson 1997–2000, sr exec Lehman Brothers 2000–08, ceo Lehman France 2008–09, chief exec London Stock Exchange 2009–; non-exec dir LCH Clearnet until 2010, memb Bd of Overseers Columbia Business Sch; Hon FCSI; Chevalier Légion D'Honneur France 2016; *Style*— Sir Xavier Rolet, KBE; ✉ London Stock Exchange, 10 Paternoster Square, London EC4M 7LS

ROLFE, David John; *b* 2 April 1939; *Educ* King Edward VII Sch Sheffield, Univ of Sheffield; *m*; 3 da; *Career* architect; jt fndr Rolfe Judd Group 1968; Freeman City of London, Liveryman Worshipful Co of Chartered Architects; RIBA 1965; *Recreations* vintage motor sport, travel, music; *Clubs* East India; *Style*— David Rolfe, Esq; ✉ Rolfe Judd Group, Old Church Court, Claylands Road, London SW8 1NZ (☎ 020 7556 1500, fax 020 7556 1501)

ROLINGTON, Alfred; *b* 31 December 1950; *Educ* BA; *Career* dir EMAP Business Publishing 1979–82, md Eastside Publishing 1982–84, chief exec Lloyd's of London Press Business Publishing 1984–92, group md Jane's Information Group 1993–2008, ceo Oxford Analytica 2008–; *Clubs* Ronnie Scott's; *Style*— Alfred Rolington, Esq

ROLL, Michael; *b* 17 July 1946, Leeds; *Educ* Roundhay GS Leeds; *m* Juliana Markova, the pianist; 1 s (Maximilian); *Career* pianist; debut aged twelve Royal Festival Hall playing Schumann's Concerto under Sir Malcolm Sargent, winner Leeds Int Pianoforte competition aged seventeen, US debut with Boston Symphony Orchestra 1974 (with Sir Colin Davis); worked with numerous major conductors incl: Pierre Boulez, Erich Leinsdorf, Kurt Masur, André Previn, Kurt Sanderling; appeared at festivals incl: Aldeburgh, Bath, Edinburgh, Granada, Hong Kong, Vienna, BBC Proms; given recitals in numerous venues incl: NY, Milan, Berlin, Dresden, Leipzig, London; concerto appearances with: Kurt Masur in Leipzig and London, Valery Gergiev in Leningrad and UK, Sergei Comissiona in Helsinki; performed Beethoven Concerti with Swedish Radio Orch, Rotterdam Philharmonic and Monte-Carlo orchs 1995–96; *Recordings* complete cycle of Beethoven Concerti (with RPO and Howard Shelley, first CD voted one of top CD releases for 1996 by BBC Music Magazine); *Style*— Michael Roll, Esq; ✉ c/o Martin Muller, Konzertdirektion, UHRS Knappken 8, D-59320 Ennigerloh-Ostenfelde, Germany (☎ 0049 25 24 263480, fax 0049 25 24 263481, e-mail info@kdmueller.de)

ROLLAND, Lawrence Anderson Lyon; s of Lawrence Anderson Rolland (d 1959), of Leven, and Winifred Anne, *née* Lyon (d 1978); *b* 6 November 1937; *Educ* George Watsons Coll Edinburgh, Duncan of Jordanstone Coll of Art Dundee (DipArch); *m* 30 April 1960, Mairi, da of John McIntyre Melville (d 1980), of Kirkcaldy; 2 da (Gillian b 1961, Katie b 1967), 2 s (Michael b 1963, Douglas b 1966); *Career* sole ptnr L A Rolland 1960, jt sr ptnr Robert Hurd 1965, ptnr L A Rolland & Partners 1965, sr ptnr Hurd Rolland Partnership 1985–97 (conslt 1997–); winner of more than 20 awards and commendations incl: Saltire Soc, Civic Tst, RIBA, Europa Nostra, Times Conservation, Stone Fedn; fndr chm Scottish Construction Industry Gp 1980, memb Bd and Cncl NTS 2005–; chm Ct Univ of Dundee 1998–2004 (memb 1993–2009), chllr's assessor Univ Dundee 2002–09; chm Bd of Govrs Duncan of Jordanstone Coll of Art 1993–94, convenor Advsy Ctee for Artistic Matters for Church of Scotland 1975–80, gen tstee Church of Scotland 1979–2013, memb Building EDC and NEDC 1982–88, chm Educn Tsts RIBA 1996–, memb Bd ARB 1997– (chm Educn and Practice Advsy Gp 1999–2003), memb Bd NTS 2005–; hon fell Bulgarian Inst of Architects 1987, hon dr Univ of Dundee 2004; pres: RIAS 1979–81, RIBA 1985–87; FRSA 1988, FRSE 1983; *Projects* incl: Queen's Hall concert hall Edinburgh, restoration and redesign of Bank of Scotland Head Office (original architect Sibbald, Reid & Crighton 1805, and later Bryce 1870), housing in Fife's Royal Burghs, Br Golf Museum St Andrews, General Accident Life Assurance York, Arch Const Royal Soc of Edinburgh, redesign of GMC Cncl Chambers London; *Recreations* music, fishing and more architecture; *Style*— Dr Lawrence Rolland, PPRIBA, PPRIAS, FRSE, FRSA; ✉ Blinkbonny Cottage, Newburn, nr Upper Largo, Leven, Fife KY8 6JF (☎ 01333 360383, e-mail rolland@newburn.org.uk)

ROLLES, Keith; s of Trevor Rolles, of Port Talbot, W Glamorgan, and Betty, *née* Hopkin; *b* 25 October 1947; *Educ* Quakers Yard GS Mid Glamorgan, The Royal London Hosp Med Coll (BSc, MB BS, MS); *m* 22 Aug 1970, Sharon, da of Thomas McGrath (d 1979); 2 s (David b 1981, Thomas b 1986); *Career* lectr in surgery and hon conslt surgn Univ of Cambridge and Addenbrooke's Hosp 1984–88, conslt surgn and dir Liver Transplant Unit The Royal Free Hosp 1988–; Hon MA Univ of Cambridge 1983; Hon MS Univ of London 1985; FRCS 1976; *Recreations* squash, tennis, skiing; *Style*— Keith Rolles, Esq; ✉ Academic Department of Surgery, The Royal Free and University College Medical School, Royal Free Campus, Rowland Hill Street, Hampstead, London NW3 2PF (☎ 020 7830 2198)

ROLLIN, Dr Anna-Maria; MBE (2014); *née* Tihanyi; da of George Tihanyi (d 1997), and Irene Tihanyi (d 1996); *b* Budapest, Hungary; *Educ* Northlea Sch Bulawayo Rhodesia, Guy's Hosp Med Sch London (MB BS); *m* 27 July 1973, Henry Rapoport Rollin; 1 s (Aron David Rapoport b 15 Jan 1976), 1 da (Rebecca Ilona b 21 May 1979); *Career* anaesthetist; pre-registration house physician St Helen's Hosp Hastings 1970, pre-registration house surgn Guy's Hosp London 1970–71; SHO: Mpilo Hosp Bulawayo 1971, Guy's Hosp London 1971–72, St Thomas' Hosp London 1972–73; registrar anaesthetics Guy's Hosp London and Queen Victoria Hosp E Grinstead 1973–75, sr registrar anaesthetics Guy's Hosp London and Lewisham Hosp London 1975–77, conslt anaesthetist Epsom Gen Hosp Surrey 1977–2011, visiting conslt anaesthetist Children's Tst Tadworth 1995–2006, hon conslt anaesthetist Royal Surrey Co Hosp 2001–, hon conslt anaesthetist Epsom and St Helier Univ Hosps NHS Tst 2011–; professional standards advsr Royal Coll of Anaesthetists; memb Cncl: RSM Section of Anaesthesia 1987–90 and 2000–12 (pres 2004–05), Assoc of Anaesthetists of GB and I 1990–96 (asst hon treas 1992–94, vice-pres 1994–96, chair Risk Mgmnt Working Party 1995–98, hon memb), Royal Coll of Anaesthetists 2001– (sr vice-pres 2007–08, faculty tutor 1980–87, ed Bulletin 2001–05, memb Editorial Bd Br Jl of Anaesthesia, chm Hosp Visits Ctee 2005–, prof standards advsr), Preoperative Assoc 2003–, Assoc of Paediatric Anaesthetists 2004– (hon memb 2012); lead assessor in anaethesia GMC 1998– (also Professional and Linguistic Assessments Bd (PLAB) examiner 2002–); memb Central Conslts and Specialists Ctee (CCSC) and chm Anaesthetic Sub-Ctee BMA 1993–96; Dept of Health: memb Bd New ways of working in anaesthesia 2003–, memb Working Gp on Paediatric Anaethesia and Emergency Care in the Dist Gen Hosp 2004–, memb Working Party on Choice for Children 2004–; pres Br Anaesthetic and Recovery Nurses Assoc 2003–05 (life memb 2005–); chm Southern Soc of Anaesthetists 1991–92; memb: Soc of Anaesthetists of the SW Region, History of Anaesthesia Soc, European Soc of Anaesthesiology 2005–; hon memb Assoc of Anaesthesiologists of Mauritius; LRCP 1970, MRCS 1970, FFARCS 1975, FRCA 1996; Raising the Standard (jt ed, 1999), Raising the Standard: Information for Patients (jt ed, 2003); author of chapters in books and numerous pubns in learned jls; *Style*— Dr Anna-Maria Rollin, MBE; ✉ Royal College of Anaesthetists, 35 Red Lion Square, London WC1R 4SG (☎ 020 7092 1500, e-mail arollin@rcoa.ac.uk); c/o Jackie Dove, Clockhouse Medical Practice, 4 Dorking Road, Epsom, Surrey KT18 7LX (☎ 01372 840836, e-mail jackie.dove@clockhouse.org)

ROLLINSON, Timothy John Denis; CBE (2012); s of William Edward Denis Rollinson (d 1963), and Ida Frances, *née* Marshall (d 2014); *b* 6 November 1953, Wanstead, London; *Educ* Chigwell Sch, Univ of Edinburgh (BSc); *m* 1, 1975 (m dis), Dominique Christine, *née* Favardin; 2 da (Marie-Claire Julie b 2 Feb 1981, Fiona Sophie b 10 Feb 1984), 1 s (William Benoit b 28 April 1986); m 2, 6 April 2013, Frances Isabel Smith; *Career* Forestry Cmmn: district offr Kent 1976–78, New Forest 1978–81, head of growth and yield studies 1981–88, land use planning 1988–90, Parly and policy 1990–93, sec 1994–97, chief conservator Eng 1997–2000, head of policy and practice 2000–03, dir Forestry Gp 2003–04, DG and dep chm 2004–13, ret; pres Inst of Chartered Foresters 2000–02, chair Global Partnership on Forest Landscape Restoration 2002–, chair Standing Ctee on Cwlth Forestry 2004–12; patron Tree Aid 2008–, tstee Royal Botanic Gardens Edinburgh 2009–, tstee Woodland Tst 2013–; FICFor 1978, FIAgrE 2004, chartered environmentalist 2005, CCMI 2006; *Recreations* golf, travel; *Clubs* Craigmillar Park Golf, Dunbar Golf; *Style*— Timothy Rollinson, Esq, CBE; ✉ e-mail tim.rollinson@talk21.com

ROLLS, Charles; *Career* formerly md Plymouth Gin, co-fndr (with Tim Warrillow) Fever-Tree 2005–; *Style*— Charles Rolls, Esq; ✉ Fever-Tree, The Plaza, 535 Kings Road, London SW10 0SZ

ROLLS, Prof Edmund Thomson; s of Eric Fergus Rolls, and May Martin, *née* Thomson; *b* 4 June 1945; *Educ* Hardye's Sch Dorchester, Jesus Coll Cambridge (MA), The Queen's Coll Oxford (Thomas Hardy scholar), Univ of Oxford (DPhil, DSc); *m* 1969 (m dis 1983), Barbara Jean, *née* Simons; 2 da (Melissa May, Juliet Helen); *Career* Univ of Oxford: fell by examination Magdalen Coll 1969–73, fell and tutor in psychology CCC 1973–2008, lectr in experimental psychology 1973–2008, prof of experimental psychology 1996–2008; Oxford Centre for Computational Neuroscience 2008–; sr research fell then prof of computational neuroscience Univ of Warwick 2008–; assoc dir MRC Oxford Interdisciplinary Research Centre for Cognitive Neuroscience 1990–2003; sec: European Brain and Behaviour Soc 1973–76, Cncl European Neuroscience Assoc 1985–88; Spearman Medal Br Psychological Soc 1977; Canadian Cwlth fell 1980–81; Hon DSc Toyama Medical Univ 2005; memb Academia Europaea, membre d'honneur Société Française de Neurologie 1994; *Books* The Brain and Reward (1975), Thirst (with B J Rolls, 1982), Neural Networks and Brain Function (with A Treves, 1998), Introduction to Connectionist Modelling of Cognitive Processes (with P McLeod and K Plunkett, 1998), The Brain and Emotion (1999), Computational Neuroscience of Vision (with G Deco, 2002), Emotion Explained (2005), Memory, Attention and Decision-Making (2008), The Noisy Brain: Stochastic Dynamics as a Principal of Brain Function (with G Deco, 2010), Neuroculture: On the Implications of Brain Science (2012), Emotion and Decision-Making Explained (2014), Cerebral Cortex: Principles of Operation (2016); 530 neuroscience research papers at www.oxcns.org; *Recreations* sailing, windsurfing; *Style—* Prof Edmund Rolls; ✉ Oxford Centre for Computational Neuroscience (e-mail edmund.rolls@oxcns.org, website www.oxcns.org)

ROMAINE, Prof Suzanne; *Educ* Bryn Mawr Coll (AB), Univ of Edinburgh (MLitt), Univ of Birmingham (PhD); *Career* early career: sr research scientist in linguistic anthropology Max-Planck-Institut-für-Psycholinguistik Nijmegen, lectr in linguistics Univ of Birmingham; Merton prof of English language Univ of Oxford 1984–; Kerstin Hesslegren prof Univ of Uppsala 1991–92, Rotary Int Fndn fell Univ of Edinburgh, Canada Cwlth scholar Ontario Inst for Studies in Educn Univ of Toronto; Hon Dr: Univ of Tromsø 1998, Univ of Uppsala 1999; fell Finnish Acad of Science and Letters Helsinki Finland; *Books* Socio-historical Linguistics: Its Status and Methodology (1982), Sociolinguistic Variation in Speech Communities (ed, 1982), The Language of Children and Adolescents: The Acquisition of Communicative Competence (1984), Pidgin and Creole Languages (1988), Bilingualism (1989, 2 edn 1995), Language in Australia (ed, 1991), Language, Education and Development: Urban and Rural Tok Pisin in Papua New Guinea (1992), Language in Society: An Introduction to Sociolinguistics (1994, 2 edn 2000), Communicating Gender (1999), Creole Genesis, Attitudes and Discourse. Studies Celebrating Charlene J Sato (ed with John Rickford, 1999), Vanishing Voices: The Extinction of the World's Languages (with Daniel Nettle, 2000); *Style—* Prof Suzanne Romaine; ✉ Merton College, Oxford OX1 4JD

ROMER, Stephen Charles Mark; s of late Mark Lemon Robert Romer, and Philippa Maynard, *née* Tomson (d 2010); *b* 20 August 1957, Herts; *Educ* King's Coll Sch Cambridge, Radley, Trinity Hall Cambridge (BA, PhD); *m* 17 July 1982 (sep), Bridget Julia, *Née* Strevens; 1 s (Thomas Mark Strevens b 19 June 1985); *Career* Henry fell Harvard Univ 1978–79, teacher British Inst Paris 1983–88 (postgrad scholar 1979–80), asst associé Univ of Paris X 1987–89, asst prof Univ of Lód? Poland (British Cncl post) 1989–90, maître de confs Univ of Tours 1990–; visiting prof in French Colgate Univ NY, visiting fell Sidney Sussex Coll Cambridge, visiting fell All Souls Oxford 2010; Gregory Award for Young Poets 1985, Prudence Farmer Award New Statesman 1985; FRSL 2011; *Poetry* Islay and other poems (1978), Idols (1986, Poetry Book Soc recommendation), Plato's Ladder (1992, Poetry Book Soc choice), Selected Poems of Jacques Dupin (trans, 1992), The New Poetry (contrib to anthology, 1993), Traductions, Passages: Le Domaine Anglais (ed, 1993), Tribute (1998), Twentieth-Century French Poems (ed, 2002), Anthologie Bilingue de la Poésie Anglaise (contrib, 2005), Tribut (selected poems in French translation, 2007), Yellow Studio (2008, shortlisted for T S Eliot Prize 2008), Into the Deep Street: 7 Modern French Poets 1938–2008 (co-ed, 2009); *Style—* Stephen Romer, Esq; ✉ c/o Carcanet Press (website www.carcanet.co.uk); c/o Faber & Faber (website www.faber.co.uk)

ROMER-LEE, Alexander Knyvett (Alex); s of Knyvett Romer-Lee, OBE (d 1996), of Hickling, Norfolk, and Jeanne Pamela, *née* Shaw (d 1982); *b* 18 August 1953; *Educ* Eton, Institut Universitaire de Technologie Dijon; *m* Janet Christine; 1 da (Katherine Pamela b 6 Jan 1985), 1 s (Jonathan Knyvett b 15 Oct 1987); *Career* PricewaterhouseCoopers (formerly Deloitte Haskins & Sells and then Coopers & Lybrand): chartered accountant 1980, ptnr Southampton 1988, ptnr Chm's Office London 1988–89, managing ptnr Budapest 1990–91, ptnr London 1992–2001, ldr Central and Eastern Europe Financial Services 1996–2001, chm AKRL Ltd and subsidiaries 2001–; dir: Sonali Bank (UK) Ltd 2001–14, FCE Bank plc 2006–15, QBurst Technologies (UK) Ltd 2011–, UBA Capital Europe Ltd 2015–, BCS Prime Brokerage Ltd 2015–; prop Les Amis de Whiteparish 1987–; FCA 1991; *Recreations* Burgundy wine, cricket, fishing, sailing; *Clubs* MCC, East India; *Style—* A K Romer-Lee, Esq; ✉ Nunns Orchard, Whiteparish, Salisbury, Wiltshire SP5 2RJ (☎ 01794 884255, e-mail akromerlee@btconnect.com)

ROMERO, Rebecca; MBE (2009); *b* 24 January 1980, Carshalton, Surrey; *Educ* Wallington HS for Girls, Richmond upon Thames Coll, St Mary's Coll Twickenham; *Career* rower and cyclist; memb: Kingston Rowing Club, Leander Club; sr int rowing debut 2001; rowing achievements incl: Silver medal quadruple sculls Cwlth Games 1998, Gold medal coxless pairs World Under 23 Championships 2000, winner quadruple sculls World Cup 2004 and 2005, Silver medal quadruple sculls Olympic Games Athens 2004, Gold medal quadruple sculls World Championships 2005; amateur cyclist 2006–, Silver medal individual pursuit World Track Cycling Championships 2007, 2 Gold medals (3000m individual pursuit and 3000m team pursuit) World Track Cycling Championships 2008, Gold medal individual pursuit Olympic Games Beijing 2008; *Style—* Miss Rebecca Romero, MBE; ✉ e-mail contact@rebeccaromero.co.uk, website www.rebeccaromero.co.uk

ROMERO-MARTINEZ, HE Ivan; *b* 1 August 1949, Olanchito, Honduras; *Educ* Nat Univ of Honduras, Catholic Univ of Santo Domingo (PhD), John Hopkins Univ US, Centre of Compared Studies Buenos Aires, Univ of Brussels; *m*; 2 c; *Career* Honduran diplomat 1971–; perm rep UN (NY) until 2008, ambass to the Ct of St James's 2008–; *Publications* Strikes in Honduran Legislation, Honduras and International Treaties, Cultural Aspects of Olanchito, Honduras is Another Thing, General Maximo Gomez in Honduras, Precendents and Perspectives of The Central American Common Market; various studies and articles in national and international newspapers and magazines; *Style—* HE Mr Ivan Romero-Martinez; ✉ Embassy of Honduras, 4th Floor, 136 Baker Street, London W1U 6UD

ROMNEY, 8 Earl of (UK 1801); Sir Julian Charles Marsham; 14 Bt (E 1663); also Baron of Romney (GB 1716) and Viscount Marsham (UK 1801); s of Col Peter Marsham, MBE (s of Hon Sydney Marsham, yst s of 4 Earl of Romney), and Hersey, da of Maj Hon Richard Coke (3 s of 2 Earl of Leicester, KG, JP, DL, by his 2 w, Hon Georgina Cavendish, da of 2 Baron Chesham); suc kinsman, 7 Earl of Romney 2004; *b* 28 March 1948; *Educ* Eton; *m* 1975, Catriona, da of Sir Robert Christie Stewart KCVO, CBE, TD; 2 s (David, Viscount Marsham b 1977, Hon Michael b 1979), 1 da (Lady Laura b 1984); *Heir* s, Viscount Marsham; *Career* land agent; farmer; High Sheriff Norfolk 2007–08; *Recreations* conservation, golf, field sports; *Style—* The Rt Hon the Earl of Romney; ✉ Wensum Farmhouse, West Rudham, King's Lynn, Norfolk PE31 8SZ (☎ 01485 528432, e-mail jcr@graytonestate.co.uk)

RONAN, Mark Edward; *b* 4 November 1968, Prescot, Merseyside; *Educ* Castle Rushen HS Isle of Man, Emmanuel Coll Cambridge (MA), Moray House Sch of Educ Edinburgh (PGCE); *Career* head of dept Rugby 1994–2003, dep head Trent Coll 2003–07, headmaster Pocklington Sch 2008–; memb York & North Yorks Chamber of Commerce Leadership Gp, memb Ind State Sch Partnership Forum; *Recreations* travel, walking; *Style—* Mark Ronan, Esq; ✉ Pocklington School, West Green, Pocklington, York YO42 2NJ (☎ 01759 321200, e-mail mainoffice@pocklingtonschool.com, website www.pocklingtonschool.com)

RONSON, Dame Gail; DBE (2004); *née* Cohen; da of Joseph Cohen, and Marie Cohen; *b* 3 July 1946, London; *m* 10 Sept 1967, Gerald Maurice Ronson, *qv*; 4 da (Lisa Debra (Mrs Althasen), Amanda Caroline, Nicole Julia (Mrs Ronson-Allalouf), Hayley Victoria (Mrs Paradise)); *Career* early career with Norwood Orphanage and Stepney Jewish Meals on Wheels, later involved as fundraiser with Central Br Fund for Jewish Refugees and Jewish Welfare Bd (sometime memb Cncl), former chm Women's Div Jt Israel Appeal, jt chair Cncl for a Beautiful Israel 1987–94, memb Bd Jewish Care 1992– (appeals chm and capital gifts chm 1998–, dep chm 2002–, hon pres 2010–); dep chm Gerald Ronson Fndn 2005, pres RNIB 2012; tstee: Ronson Fndns 1980–95, Winnington Charitable Fndn, Park Chase Charitable Fndn; dir ROH 2001–, tstee ROH Tst 1985–2014, ambass ROH 2014–; co-chm St Mary's Hosp Save the Baby Fund 1985–96, vice-pres Assoc for Research into Stammering in Childhood 1991–, tstee Home Farm Devpt Tst 1991–94, fundraiser Roundhouse Tst; *Style—* Dame Gail Ronson, DBE; ✉ 4 Bentinck Street, London W1U 2EF (☎ 020 7299 9777, fax 020 7487 2970)

RONSON, Gerald Maurice; CBE (2012); *b* 27 May 1939; *m* 10 Sept 1967, Dame Gail Ronson, DBE, *qv*; 4 da (Lisa, Amanda, Nicole, Hayley); *Career* chief exec: Heron Corporation plc 1976– (chm 1988–93), Heron International plc (fndr (as Heron Gp) 1956, chm 1983–93); chm and chief exec Snax 24 Corporation Ltd, chm Rontec, chm Ronson Capital Ptnrs; vice-pres NSPCC 1984–, ambass of Druse Community Mount Carmel 1990–, govr London Acad 2004–, chm of tstees Gerald Ronson Fndn 2005–; hon DCL Northumbria Univ 2009, Hon PhD Hebrew Univ of Jerusalem 2014; Hon FGSM 2013; Encomienda de Numero of the Order of Civil Merit (Spain) 2009; *Books* Gerald Ronson, Leading from the Front, My Story; *Clubs* Royal Southern Yacht; *Style—* Gerald M Ronson, Esq, CBE; ✉ c/o Heron International plc, 4 Bentinck Street, London W1U 2EF (☎ 020 7486 4477, fax 020 7487 2970)

RONSON, Mark Daniel; s of Laurence Ronson, and Ann Dexter-Jones; *b* 4 September 1975, London; *Educ* Collegiate Sch NY, Vassar Coll, NYU; *Career* music prodr; co-fndr Allido Records 2004; albums: Here Comes the Fuzz 2003, Version 2007; singles incl: Just (feat Alex Greenwald) 2006 (re-issued 2008), Stop Me (feat Daniel Merriweather) 2007, Oh My God (feat Lily Allen) 2007, Valerie (feat Amy Winehouse) 2007; other singles as prodr incl: Littlest Things (Lily Allen) 2006, Rehab 2006, You Know I'm No Good 2007 and Back to Black 2007 (all Amy Winehouse), Never Miss A Beat (Kaiser Chiefs) 2008; *Awards* Grammy Awards incl: Prodr of the Year (Non-Classical) 2008, Record of the Year 2008 (for Rehab (Amy Winehouse)), Best Pop Vocal Album 2008 (for Back to Black (Amy Winehouse)); Best British Male Solo Artist BRIT Award 2008; *Style—* Mr Mark Ronson

ROOCROFT, Amanda Jane; da of Roger Roocroft, of Coppull, Lancs, and Valerie, *née* Metcalfe; *b* 9 February 1966; *Educ* Southlands HS, Runshaw Tertiary Coll, Royal Northern Coll of Music; *m* David Gowland; *Career* soprano; winner Decca-Kathleen Ferrier Meml Prize and Silver Medal Worshipful Co of Musicians 1988, Royal Philharmonic Soc/Charles Heidsieck Award for operatic debut 1990; currently studies with Barbara Robotham; fell: Univ of Central Lancashire, Royal Northern Coll of Music; Hon Dr Univ of Manchester 2003; *Opera Performances* ROH incl: Fiordiligi in Cosi fan tutte, Guilietta in I Capuleti e i Montecchi, Mimi in La Boheme, Pamina in The Magic Flute, Cleopatra in Giulio Cesare, title role Madam Butterfly, Katya Kabanova, Desdemona in Otello; Bavarian State Opera Munich: Fiordiligi, Amelia in Simon Boccanegra, Donna Elvira in Don Giovanni, Desdomona in Otello; Glyndebourne Festival: Fiordiligi, Donna Elvira and title role in Katya Kabanova, title role in Jenufa; other performances incl: Don Elvira (Metropolitan Opera NY), Tatiana in Eugene Onegin (WNO); *Concert Performances* incl: The Proms, London's South Bank, Edinburgh Int Festival, City of Birmingham Symphony Orchestra with Sir Simon Rattle; *Recitals* incl: Wigmore Hall London, Concertgebouw Amsterdam, Musikverein Vienna, La Monnaie Brussels, Lincoln Center NY; appearances throughout the rest of the UK, Europe and NY (incl NY Philharmonic); *Recordings* incl: Vaughan Williams' Serenade to Music (Hyperion), Cosi fan Tutte (with Baroque English Soloists under John Eliot Gardiner, Deutsche Grammophon 1992), solo album Amanda Roocroft (EMI 1994), Mozart and his contemporaries (with the Academy of St Martin in the Fields and Sir Neville Marriner, 1996); *Recreations* reading, cooking, sewing; *Style—* Miss Amanda Roocroft

ROOLEY, Richard Herbert; s of George Arthur Rooley, CBE (d 2001), of Stoke Poges, Bucks, and Valeria, *née* Green (d 1994); *b* 24 April 1940; *Educ* Glasgow Acad, Morrisons Acad, Trinity Coll Dublin (BA, BAI); *m* 25 July 1964, (Ismena) Ruth Rooley, da of George Young (d 1956), of Eire; 1 s (George b 1966), 1 da (Ismena b 1968); *Career* Donald Smith & Rooley conslt engrs: joined 1964, assoc 1968, ptnr 1971–91; sr ptnr Rooley Consultants 1991–; ptnr Project Management Partnership 1978–; memb Cncl CIBSE 1972–81 and 1989–92, chm Bldg Servs Res and Info Assoc 1984–86, chm Nat Jt Consultative Ctee 1993; churchwarden Stoke Poges 1980–86, lay chm Burnham Deanery Synod 1985–86, reader C of E; Liveryman Worshipful Co of Engrs (Master 1999–2000), Master Worshipful Co of Constructors 1992–93; MConsE; American Soc of Heating Refrigerating and Air Conditioning Engrs (ASHRAE): memb Bd of Dirs 1980–83, vice-pres 1997–2001, pres 2003–04; FREng 1989 (hon sec Civil Engrg 1992–95, memb Cncl 1992–95), FICE, FIMechE, FCIBSE; *Recreations* golf; *Style—* Richard Rooley, Esq, FREng; ✉ Greenways, Church Lane, Stoke Poges, Buckinghamshire SL2 4PB (☎ 01753 648040, e-mail richard@rooley.com)

ROOM, Prof Graham; *b* 17 March 1947; *Educ* Christ's Coll Cambridge (MA), Balliol Coll Oxford (BPhil), Nuffield Coll Oxford (DPhil); *m* 31 March 1979, Susan; 2 c (Alison, Hywel); *Career* Univ of Bath: lectr in sociology 1973–86 (leave of absence as research fell Univ of Kent 1979–80), reader in social policy 1986–92, prof of European social policy 1992–, head Sch of Social Sciences 1995–97; conslt to EC on social action progs 1979–85, coordinator Evaluation of the Second European Prog to Combat Poverty 1985–89, coordinator EU Observatory on National Policies to Combat Social Exclusion 1990–93, memb Cncl of Europe Steering Gp on Poverty and Marginalisation 1990–91, special advsr House of Lords Select Ctee on the European Communities 1994; govr Swindon FE Coll 2002–03; AcSS 2004; *Books* The Sociology of Welfare: Social Policy, Stratification and Political Order (1979), Europe Against Poverty: The European Poverty Programme 1975–80 (jtly, 1982), Health and Welfare States of Britain: An Inter-Country Comparison (jt ed, 1983), Cross-National Innovation in Social Policy: European Perspectives on the Evaluation of Action-Research (1986), New Poverty in the European Community (1990), Towards a European Welfare State? (ed, 1991), Anti-Poverty Action-Research in Europe (1993), Beyond the Threshold: The Measurement and Analysis of Social Exclusion (ed, 1995), Poverty and Social Exclusion in Europe (jtly, 2002), Insecurity and Welfare Regimes in Asia, Africa and Latin America: Social Policy in Development Contexts (jtly, 2004), The European Challenge: Innovation, Policy Learning and Social Cohesion in the New Knowledge Economy (2005), Complexity, Institutions and Public Policy (2011), Agile Actors on Complex Terrains: Transformative Realism and Public Policy (2016); *Recreations* sailing (yachtmaster offshore); *Style—* Prof Graham Room; ✉ Department of Social and Policy Sciences, University of Bath, Bath BA2 7AY (☎ 01225 386090, e-mail hssgir@bath.ac.uk, website http://www.bath.ac.uk/sps/staff/graham-room/)

ROONEY, Michael (Mick) John; *b* 5 March 1944, Epsom, Surrey; *Educ* Sutton East Jr Art Sch, Sutton Art Sch, Wimbledon Sch of Art, RCA, British Sch at Rome (Abbey major scholarship); *m* 1, 1967, Patricia Lavender; 1 da (Claire b 1969), 1 s (Rory b 1971); m 2 (m dis), Alexandra Graescher; 1 s (Clement b 1989); *Career* painter; pt/t lectr in art 1968–88, head of painting RA Schs 1991–96; ARCA, RA 1991; *Solo Exhibitions* 1977–87: Galeria Petit Amsterdam, Nanki de Vries Amsterdam, The Hague, Groningen; 1985–2002: Mercury Gall London (4 exhbns), Santa Fe, Portland Oregon, Vienna, Salzburg, New York, Chicago, Holland; *Collections* Pallant House, Jerwood Fndn, RA Collection, Tower Art Gall Eastbourne, Hove Museum, Ashmolean Oxford, Ambro Bank

R

Amsterdam, Museo Ralli Switzerland, Wolfson Coll Cambridge, Transport for London, RCA Coll; numerous group exhibitions; *Recreations* cooking, playing guitar, interest in French, Italian, Spanish and German poetry and literature; *Clubs* Chelsea Arts; *Style*— Mick Rooney, Esq, RA

ROONEY, Wayne Mark; s of Thomas Wayne Rooney, and Jeanette Marie, *née* Morrey; *b* 24 October 1985, Croxteth, Liverpool; *Educ* De La Salle Sch Liverpool; *m* 12 June 2008, Coleen, *née* McLoughlin; 2 s (Kai Wayne b 2 Nov 2009, Klay Anthony b 21 May 2013); *Career* professional footballer; clubs: Everton until 2004 (joined as schoolboy, FA Youth Cup finalists May 2002, first team debut Aug 2002, 67 first team appearances, 15 goals), Manchester United 2004– (debut v Fenerbahçe 2004, over 400 appearances, 200 goals, winners League Cup 2006, 2009 and 2010, Premier League champions 2007, 2008, 2009, 2011 and 2013, winners UEFA Champions League 2008); England: debut v Australia 2003, 89 caps, 38 goals, memb squad European Championships 2004 and World Cup 2006, 2010 and 2014; BBC Sports Young Personality of the Year 2002, PFA Young Player of the Year 2005 and 2006, FIFPro World Young Player of the Year 2005, Sir Matt Busby Player of the Year 2006, PFA Player of the Year 2010, Footballer of the Year Football Writers' Assoc 2010; *Books* My Story So Far (autobiography, 2006), My Decade in the Premier League (2012); *Style*— Mr Wayne Rooney; ✉ Manchester United Football Club, Sir Matt Busby Way, Old Trafford, Manchester M16 0RA

ROOPE, Nicolas; s of Robert Roope, of St Albans, and Lisbet, *née* Algreen-Ussing; *b* 26 February 1972, Singapore; *Educ* Liverpool John Moores Univ (BA); *m* 24 June 2006, Violetta, *née* Boxill; *Career* designer CHBi Ltd 1995–96, ptnr and designer Antirom Ltd 1996–99, int creative dir Oven Digital 1999–2001, pntr and creative dir Poke 2001–, ptnr and creative dir Hulger Ltd 2004–; ambass UK Webby, memb Int Acad of Digital Arts and Sciences, co-chair Internet Week Europe, jury chair Lovie Awards; memb: Tech City Advsy Gp, Advsy Bd to MUBI, Tech City Advsy Bd to Number 10; Design SIG memb to the Technology Strategy Bd; D&A Pencil Award 1997, Oneshow Pencil Award 2004, Webby Award 2005, 2006, 2007, 2008, 2009, 2010 and 2011, iF Award (for Pip Phone) 2007, Gmark Award (for Pip Phone) 2007, D&A Black Pencil Award 2011, Brit Insurance Design of the Year (for Plumen 001 designer energy saving light bulb) 2011; *Recreations* hiking, skiing; *Clubs* Meat; *Style*— Nicolas Roope, Esq; ✉ Poke, 82 Baker Street, London W1U 6QS

ROOT, Jane; *b* 1957; *Educ* London Coll of Printing, Univ of Sussex; *Career* freelance journalist and film critic; with Cinema of Women (film distribution co) 1981–83, press offr and catalogue author Edinburgh Film Festival 1981–84, with BFI 1982–83 (wrote for The Cinema Book, Women's Guide to Film, Hollywood Now), writer and researcher Open the Box Beat Productions 1983, co-fndr Wall to Wall Productions 1987 (head of prog devpt and jt md until 1996), head Independent Commissioning Gp BBC 1997–98, controller BBC 2 1999–2004 (responsible for launching Great Britons initiative and series incl The Weakest Link and The Office); Discovery Channel USA: gen mangr 2004, exec vice-pres 2004–06, pres 2006–07; pres and gen mangr Science Channel USA 2006, fndr and ceo Nutopia 2009–; memb Exec Ctee Edinburgh Int TV Festival 2006 and 2007; *Style*— Ms Jane Root

ROOT, Jonathan Mark; s of Harold Root (d 2000), and Joan Elizabeth Root, *née* Towler; *Educ* Oakham Sch, Gloucester Coll of Art, St Alban's Coll of Art; *Career* fine art portrait and advertising photographer; lectr: Glasgow Sch of Art, Kingston Univ; cmmns incl: 'Twins' Liberty, J&B, Tennents, British Airways, Benson and Hedges, Body Shop, Mulberry, Harvey Nichols, Canon, Sony, Liverpool FC, BSkyB, Shakespeare's Globe, American Express; portraits incl: David Hockney, Peter Blake, Richard Rogers, Norman Foster, Philippe Starck, Lord Harwood, Lord March, The Marquis of Bath, Marc Newson, Taylor Wessing, NPG, David Hockney, Mark Rylance, Edmund De Waal, Camila Batmanghelidjh, James Blake; exhbns incl: John Kobal Photographic Portrait Awards 1995, 1996 and 2000, Lurzer's archive 1998 and 2000, American Photo 2000, Britart at Selfridges 2003, The Edwardian Drape Society (Tapestry Gallery) 2004, Lords and Ladies (Tapestry Gallery) 2004, Brit Art exhbn Selridges 2005, Selfridges' Sitting Pretty exhbn (Rabih Hage Gallery) 2007; 6 portraits chosen for collection N P Gallery; worked for numerous newspapers and magazines incl: The Independent, The Observer, Daily Telegraph, Financial Times, New Scientist, Sunday Times, Vanity Fair, Harpers & Queen, Tatler, Jack, The Economist, Management Today, Intelligent Life, Icon, Wall Street Journal; Erotic Photographer of the Year 2005, Most Original Car Salon Privé 2012; memb Assoc of Photographers 1995–; *Awards* winner Assoc of Photographers Silver and Merit Awards 1996 and 1997, Communication Arts Award of Excellence 1997, The Scottish Advertising Awards 1998, highly commended London Photographic Awards (LPA4) 2000, merit London Photographic Awards (LPA5) 2001, European Design Annual Certificate of Excellence 2000, Sony Campaign Cannes 2000, Management Today Veuve Clicquot Business Woman of the Year 2009, Feature Shoot Winner (for 'Twins') 2015; *Books* Ken Livingstone Memoir (2011); *Recreations* classic cars, cycling, cinema, motorsport, music, shooting, walking; *Clubs* Jupiter Owners Auto, De Tomaso Drivers; *Style*— Jonathan Root, Esq; ✉ Jonathan Root Photography (website www.jonathanroot.co.uk)

ROOTES, 3 Baron (UK 1959); Nicholas Geoffrey Rootes; o s of 2 Baron Rootes (d 1992), and Marian, *née* Hayter; gf 1 Baron Rootes, GBE, founded Rootes Motors; *b* 12 July 1951; *Educ* Harrow; *m* 1976, Dorothy Anne, da of Cyril Walter James Wood (d 1979), of Swansea, and formerly wife of Jonathan Burn-Forti; 1 step da (Lucinda Burn-Forti b 1963), 1 step s (Dante Burn-Forti b 1965); *Heir* cous, William Rootes; *Career* business owner Nick Rootes Associates; tstee Rootes Charity Tst, patron Assoc of Rootes Car Clubs; *Books* The Drinker's Companion (1987), Doing a Dyson (1995); *Recreations* fly fishing, skiing, tennis; *Clubs* Ski Club of GB, Bembridge Sailing; *Style*— The Rt Hon the Lord Rootes; ✉ 26 Solent Landing, Beach Road, Bembridge, Isle of Wight PO35 5NZ (website www.nickrootes.com)

ROOTS, Guy Robert Godfrey; QC (1989); s of William Lloyd Roots, TD, QC, MP (d 1971) of London, and Elizabeth Colquhoun Gow, *née* Gray (d 2000); *b* 26 August 1946; *Educ* Winchester, BNC Oxford (MA); *m* 17 May 1975, Caroline, da of (Alfred Saxon) Godfrey Clarkson (d 1970), of Herts; 3 s (William b 1978, Hamish b 1979, Sam b 1986); *Career* called to the Bar Middle Temple 1969 (Harmsworth scholar 1969, bencher 2000); chm Planning and Environment Bar Assoc 2000–04; Liveryman Worshipful Co of Drapers 1972; fell Soc of Advanced Legal Studies 1998; *Publications* Compulsory Purchase and Compensation Service (gen ed), Ryde on Rating and the Council Tax (gen ed); *Recreations* sailing, fishing, skiing, photography, woodworking; *Clubs* Itchenor Sailing; *Style*— Guy Roots, Esq, QC; ✉ Francis Taylor Building, Temple, London EC4Y 7BY (☎ 020 7353 8415, fax 020 7353 7622, e-mail clerks@ftb.eu.com)

ROPER, Brian; s of Harold Herbert Albert Roper, and Elizabeth, *née* Rooney; *b* 15 December 1949, London; *Educ* Univ of Wales (BSc Econ), Univ of Manchester (MA Econ), Swansea Met Univ (DipAD), Swansea Univ (MA); *m* 1971, Margaret Patricia, *née* Jones; 1 s (Sion b 1976), 1 da (Bethan b 1978); *Career* tutor in economics UWIST 1971–72, lectr in economics Teesside Poly 1973–75, sr lectr then princ lectr in economics Leicester Poly 1975–80; Newcastle upon Tyne Poly: head Sch of Economics 1980–85, actg head Faculty of Professional Studies 1985–87, head Dept of Economics and Govt 1987, dean Faculty of Social Sciences 1987–88 (actg dean 1987), actg asst dir (academic) 1988, asst dir (resources) 1988–90; dep vice-chllr (academic affrs) and dep chief exec Oxford Poly (later Oxford Brookes Univ) 1991–93, vice-chllr and chief exec Univ of North London 1994–2002; London Met Univ: chief exec 2002–04, vice-chllr and chief exec 2004–09; Hon DLitt, Hon DTech, Hon DSci; FSS; *Publications* author of numerous conference papers, book chapters, and articles in learned jls; *Recreations* thoughtful art, observing nature, flanerie, writing creatively; *Clubs* Porthcawl RFC; *Style*— Brian Roper, Esq

ROPER, Jeremy James; s of Robert Burnell Roper, CB, of Lindfield, W Sussex, and Mary, *née* Petyt; *b* 13 June 1954; *Educ* KCS Wimbledon, Univ of Birmingham (LLB); *m* 20 Sept 1980, Alison Mary, da of Bryan Peter Studwell Cleal, of Wotton-under-Edge, Glos; 2 da (Katharine Mary b 1984, Elizabeth Diana b 1992), 1 s (Richard James b 1987); *Career* admitted slr 1979; ptnr: Needham and James slrs 1983–93, Dibb Lupton Broomhead 1993–95, Wansbroughs Willey Hargrave (now DAC Beachcroft LLP) 1995–; tstee Birmingham Children's Hosp 2013–; memb Law Soc 1977; *Recreations* sport, vegetable gardening, theatre; *Style*— Jeremy Roper, Esq

ROPER, Baron (Life Peer UK 2000), of Thorney Island in the City of Westminster; John Francis Hodgess Roper; PC (2005); s of Rev Frederick Mabor Hodgess Roper, by his w Ellen Frances, *née* Brockway; *b* 10 September 1935; *Educ* William Hulme's GS Manchester, Reading Sch, Magdalen Coll Oxford, Univ of Chicago; *m* 1959, Valerie (d 2003), da of Rt Hon John Edwards, OBE, sometime MP; 1 da; *Career* former economics lectr Manchester Univ; Royal Inst of International Affairs: ed International Affairs 1983–88, head Int Security Prog 1985–88 and 1989–90, dir of studies 1988–89; head WEU Inst for Security Studies Paris 1990–95; Parly candidate: (Lab) Derbyshire High Peak 1964, (SDP) Worsley 1983; MP (Lab and Co-op 1970–81, SDP 1981–83) Farnworth 1970–83; PPS to Min of State for Industry 1978–79, Lab oppn spokesman on Defence (front bench), SDP chief whip 1981–83; Lib Dem chief whip House of Lords 2001–05; vice-chm: Anglo-German Parly Gp 1974–83, Anglo-Benelux Parly Gp 1979–83; Cncl of Europe: conslt 1965–66, memb Consultative Assembly 1973–80, chm Ctee on Culture and Educn 1979–80, memb WEU 1973–80, chm Ctee on Defence Questions and Armaments WEU 1977–80; chm: Lab Ctee for Europe 1976–80, Cncl on Christian Approaches to Defence and Disarmament 1983–89, GB/East Europe Centre 1987–90; hon treas Fabian Soc 1976–81; memb: Gen Advsy Cncl IBA 1974–79, Cncl Inst of Fiscal Studies 1975–90; vice-pres Manchester Statistical Soc 1971–, tstee History of Parliament Tst 1974–84; *Books* Towards Regional Co-operatives (with Lloyd Harrison, 1967), The Teaching of Economics at University Level (1970), The Future of British Defence Policy (1985), British-German Defence Co-operation (ed with Karl Kaiser, 1988), Franco-British Defence Co-operation (ed with Yves Boyer, 1988), Western Europe and the Gulf (ed with Nicole Gnesotto), Towards a New Partnership: US European Relations in the Post-Cold War Era (ed with Nanette Gantz); *Style*— The Rt Hon the Lord Roper, PC

ROSCOE, (John) Gareth; s of late John Roscoe, and late Ann, *née* Jones; *b* 28 January 1948; *Educ* Manchester Warehouseman and Clerks Orphan Sch (now Cheadle Hulme Sch), Stretford Tech Coll, LSE (LLB), Univ of Leicester (LLM) 2003; *m* 1, 29 Aug 1970 (m dis 1979), Helen Jane (d 2013), da of Geoffrey Duke Taylor, of Skipton, N Yorks; 1 da (Kate b 26 July 1974); m 2, 29 Aug 1980, Alexis Fayrer (Alex Brett-Holt, *qv*), da of late Raymond Arthur Brett-Holt, of Esher, Surrey; 1 da (Philippa Claire b 8 Feb 1982), 1 s (Jonathan Hugh b 1 Aug 1983); *Career* called to the Bar Gray's Inn 1972; in practice 1972–75, Law Offr's Dept Attorney Gen's Chambers 1979–83, dep slr DOE 1987–89 (legal asst 1975–79, sr legal asst 1979, asst slr 1983–87); legal advsr to BBC until 1998, co sec BBC Worldwide Ltd until 1998, dir BBC Worldwide Ltd 1989–96, dir Educational Recording Agency Limited until 1998; conslt advsr DTI 1999–2001, legal advsr Competition Cmmn 2001–04 and 2005–08, legal advsr Dept for Work and Pensions 2004–05; non-exec memb: Optimum NHS Tst 1995–97, KCH NHS Tst 2001–04; memb: Bar Cncl 1987–90 (memb Race Relations and Law Reform Ctees), Advsy Ctee Centre for Communications and Law UCL; tstee and dir Anglia Care Tst 2009– (chm 2011–15); *Recreations* music, gardening, company of friends; *Style*— Gareth Roscoe, Esq; ✉ e-mail garethroscoe@aol.com

ROSCOE, Dr Ingrid Mary; da of Dr Arthur Allen, CBE (d 1956), and Else Margaretha, *née* Markenstam (d 1968); adopted da of late Brig Kenneth Hargreaves, CBE; *b* 27 May 1944, Rugby; *Educ* St Helen's Northwood, Univ of Leeds (BA, PhD); *m* 5 Oct 1963, J R Marshall Roscoe, DL; 1 s (Nicholas b 20 June 1964), 2 da (Emma b 8 May 1966, Katherine b 9 July 1970); *Career* lectr in sculpture history Univ of Leeds 1990–96, ed Church Monuments Jl 1993–2000; author of articles on British sculpture in: Apollo, Gazette des Beaux-Arts, Grove Dictionary of Art, Walpole Soc Jl, Oxford DNB; memb Exec Ctee Walpole Soc 2000–05; tstee: Martin House Children's Hospice 1989–98, York Minster 2005–10, Yorkshire Sculpture Park 2006–; pres: Prince's Tst W Yorks, Nat Mining Museum, Yorks Historic Churches, Calderdale Community Fndn, Yorks Vols Regtl Assoc, Leeds Philharmonic Soc, W Yorks Scouts, Together Women Project, W Riding Woodcarvers; co rep NACF 1972–84; memb Governing Cncl Univ of Huddersfield; high steward Selby Abbey 2000–08; HM Lord-Lt W Yorks 2004– (DL 1994–99, Vice Lord-Lt 1999–2004); Hon Col Leeds UOTC 2007–14; Hon DCL Univ of Huddersfield 2007, Hon LLD Leeds Met Univ 2008, Hon DCL Univ of Leeds 2010, Hon DLitt Univ of Bradford 2010; FSA 1998; CStJ 2006; *Books* The Royal Exchange (contrib, 1997), A Biographical Dictionary of British Sculptors 1660–1851 (2009), Durham Cathedral: History, Fabric and Culture (contrib, 2014); *Recreations* family, the arts, British history, Shakespeare's plays, walking; *Style*— Dr Ingrid Roscoe; ✉ Church House, Nun Monkton, York YO26 8EW; West Yorkshire Lieutenancy Office, Bowcliffe Hall, Bramham, Wetherby LS23 6LP

ROSE, Anthony; *Career* vice-pres for technol Sega Australia New Devpts until 2001, chief technol offr Kazaa/Altnet 2001–07, head of digital media technol BBC 2007–10, chief technol offr YouView 2010, co-fndr and chief technol offr Zeebox 2011–; *Style*— Anthony Rose, Esq

ROSE, Anthony John Wynyard; s of John Donald Rose, FRS (d 1976), and Yvonne Valerie, *née* Evans (d 1996); *b* 22 January 1946; *Educ* Oundle; *m* 1972 (m dis 1990), Angela Katherine, da of Wing Cdr Thomas Kenneth Waite (d 1987), of Cheltenham, Glos; 1 da (Katherine Lucy b 19 March 1980), 3 s (Dominic John Wynyard, Alexander Richard Thomas (twins) b 4 Nov 1984, Oliver Louis Christopher b 2 Dec 1986); m 2, 1996, Beverly Jane Murray; *Career* Hon Artillery Co 1970–75; admitted slr 1970; slr Slaughter & May 1970–72 and ICI Ltd 1972–77, ed Aerostat 1975–82, ptnr Charles Russell 1978–92, ptnr Barlow Lyde & Gilbert 1992–98, princ Hampden Law; dir: Hampden Legal plc, Corporate Due Diligence Ltd, Corporate Reporting Ltd; memb Competition Ctee ICC; hon legal advsr Nat Army Museum; author of various articles on Euro competition law and hot air ballooning, awarded Aerostat medal; Freeman City of London 1975, Freeman Worshipful Co of Salters 1975; memb: Law Soc, Int Bar Assoc; *Recreations* ballooning, shooting, fishing, reading, tennis, dogs; *Clubs* Hon Artillery Co; *Style*— Anthony Rose, Esq; ✉ Bonnett Farm, Rendcomb, Gloucestershire GL7 7ET (☎ 01242 870016, mobile 07802 284297, e-mail ajwr@anthonyjwrose.com)

ROSE, Barry Michael; *b* 10 March 1945; *Educ* Univ of Manchester (BSc); *Career* asst investment mangr Co-operative Insurance Society Ltd 1971–76, investment mangr Scottish Life Assurance Co 1976–88, gen mangr investment Scottish Provident Institution 1988–93 (dir 1998–), chief exec Scottish Provident UK 1993–2001; dir: Baillie Gifford Shin Nippon Investment Tst 1998–, Wolfson Microelectronics plc 2001–10, Liverpool Victoria Friendly Soc; FIA 1970; *Style*— Barry Rose, Esq

ROSE, Rt Hon Sir Christopher Dudley Roger; kt (1985), PC (1992); s of Roger Rose (d 1987), of Morecambe, and Hilda, *née* Thickett (d 1986); *b* 10 February 1937; *Educ* Morecambe GS, Repton, Univ of Leeds (LLB), Wadham Coll Oxford (BCL); *m* 5 Aug 1964, Judith, *née* Brand; 1 s (Daniel b 1967), 1 da (Hilary b 1969); *Career* lectr in law Wadham Coll Oxford 1959–60 (hon fell 1993), Bigelow teaching fell Law Sch Univ of Chicago 1960–61, called to the Bar Middle Temple 1960 (bencher 1983, dep treas 2001, treas 2002), QC

1974, recorder of the Crown Court 1978–85, presiding judge Northern Circuit 1987–90 (practised 1961–85), judge of the High Court of Justice (Queen's Bench Div) 1985–92, a Lord Justice of Appeal 1992–2006; chief surveillance cmmr 2006–15; chm Criminal Justice Consultative Cncl 1994–2000, vice-pres Co Appeal (Criminal Div) 1997–2006; memb Senate Inns of Court and Bar 1983–85; govr Pownall Hall Sch 1977–89, UK tstee Harold G Fox Fndn 1995–2005; Hon LLD Univ of Leeds 2008; *Clubs* Garrick; *Style*— The Rt Hon Sir Christopher Rose; ✉ Office of the Surveillance Commissioners, PO Box 29105, London SW1V 1ZU

ROSE, David Leslie Whitfield; s of Leslie Rose (d 1980), of Leeds, and Joyce, *née* Whitfield (d 1981); *b* 27 February 1954; *Educ* Roundhay Sch Leeds, Downing Coll Cambridge, Inns of Court Sch of Law (MA, LLB); *m* 1, 14 April 1982 (m dis 2004), Genevieve Mary, da of Thomas Vernon Twigge, of Burley-in-Wharfedale, W Yorks; 1 s (Matthew b 1986), 1 da (Alice b 1989); m 2, 11 June 2016, Netsayi Nancy Price (da of late Enos Tapererwa Kambarami, of Harare, Zimbabwe); *Career* called to the Bar 1977, practicing barr specialising in property, wills and tsts 1979–, memb NE Circuit and Northern Chancery Bar Assoc; memb: Professional Negligence Bar Assoc, Northern Mediators 2000; dir No 6 Ltd 1998–2005; tstee St John's Church Moor Allerton 2000–10, vice-chair Leeds Youth Opera 2002–11 (tstee 2011–); memb Hon Soc of Middle Temple; *Recreations* music, reading, travel, walking, history; *Style*— David Rose, Esq; ✉ 6 Park Square East, Leeds LS1 2LW (☎ 0113 245 9763, fax 0113 242 4395, e-mail rose@psqb.co.uk)

ROSE, Dinah Gwen Lison; QC (2006); da of Michael Rose, and Susan, *née* Latham; *b* 16 July 1965, London; *Educ* City of London Sch for Girls, Magdalen Coll Oxford (BA), City Univ (Dip); *m* 10 Feb 1991, Peter Kessler; 2 da (Hannah b 21 April 1997, Katherine Lucy b 18 Dec 1999); *Career* called to the Bar Gray's Inn 1989 (Arden scholar 1988); barr Blackstone Chambers 1990–; *Style*— Miss Dinah Rose, QC; ✉ Blackstone Chambers, Blackstone House, Temple, London EC4Y 9BW

ROSE, Gregory; s of Bernard William George Rose, OBE (d 1996), and Molly Daphne Rose, OBE, JP, DL, *née* Marshall; *b* 18 April 1948; *Educ* Magdalen Coll Oxford (BA); *m* Helen Ireland; 1 s (Freddy Ireland); *Career* conductor; prof of conducting Trinity Laban; appts incl: princ conductor Jupiter Orch, Singcircle, Circle, Jupiter Singers, CoMA London Ensemble; guest appts incl: London Philharmonic, Ulster Orch, BBC Concert Orch, BBC Singers, Finnish Radio Symphony Orch, Polish Nat Radio Symphony, St Petersburg Symphony Orch, Estonian Philharmonic Chamber Choir, Netherland Radio Chamber Orch, Philharmonia, Royal Scottish Nat Orch, Netherland Radio Choir, Nederland Kamerkoor, Groupe Vocal de France, Westdeutscher Rundfunk Chor, Estonian Philharmonic Chamber Choir, Steve Reich and Musicians, Netherlands Wind Ensemble, and also orchs in Denmark, Norway, Finland, Holland, Poland, Latvia, Estonia, Ireland, Russia, India and Sri Lanka; series dir Almeida Festival (Cage at 70 1982, Reich at 50 1986); festivals have included BBC Proms 1978 and 1989, many TV and radio recordings throughout Europe; many compositions published incl: Birthday Ode for Aaron Copland, Tapiola Sunrise, Thambapani, Missa Sancta Pauli Apostoli, Missa Sancti Dunstani, Music For a Kytherian Amphitheatre, St Pancras Service, Clarifica me Pater, Sh'alu Shlom Yerushalayim, Missa Sacra Coeur, 5 Sets of Evening Canticles, Danse Macabre, Avebury Stone Circles, Garden of the Gods, Red Planet, Missa Sancti Vedasti, Dancing in the Sun-split Clouds; fndr ctee memb Assoc of Br Choral Dirs, memb SPNM; Br Composer Award (Liturgical Category) 2006; *Publications* Boosey & Hawkes: Everlasting Mary, God's Strange Ways, Animals etcetera, It's Snowing, Camrose Lord's Prayer, Copland, The Golden Willow Tree, Five Spanish Carols, Four Traditional English Carols, Colla Voce: Missa Sancta Pauli Apostoli, A Song for Judith, Hummell Violin Concerto (ed); novello: Vespers for Mary Magdalen; *Recreations* walking, listening to music, church bell ringing; *Style*— Gregory Rose; ✉ 57 White Horse Road, London E1 0ND (☎ 020 7790 5883, mobile 07765 957024, e-mail gr@gregoryrose.org, website www.gregoryrose.org)

ROSE, Guy Simon; s of Henry Rose (decd), and Georgina Clifford, *née* Elkan; *Educ* Royal GS Guildford, Michaelhouse Coll SA; *Career* arbitrageur Myers & Co (Stockbrokers) 1963–67, with 3M Co (UK) plc 1970–73, publisher with Exchange Telegraph Co 1974–79, md Bandwagon Music Ltd 1980–86, sr ptnr Futerman, Rose & Associates (Literary Agents) 1992–; memb: Equity 1975–, Assoc of Authors' Agents 1995–, BAFTA; *Recreations* jazz, a capella singing; *Style*— Guy Rose, Esq; ✉ Futerman, Rose & Associates, 91 St Leonards Road, London SW14 7BL (☎ 020 8255 7755, fax 020 8286 4860, e-mail guy@futermanrose.co.uk)

ROSE, Sir John E V; kt (2003); *b* 9 October 1952, Blantyre, Malawi; *Educ* Univ of St Andrews (MA); *m* Felicity; 3 c (Tom, Anne, Charlie); *Career* Rolls-Royce plc: joined 1984, memb Bd 1992–, chief exec 1996–2011; tstee Eden Project; Hon FREng, FRAeS, FIMechE; Commandeur de la Legion d'Honneur 2008, Singapore Public Service Star 2008; *Style*— Sir John Rose; ✉ Rothschild, New Court, St Swithin's Lane, London EC4N 8AL

ROSE, Justin Peter; *b* 30 July 1980, Johannesburg, South Africa; *Career* golfer; as amateur: winner England U16 and U18 aged 14, memb GB & I team Walker Cup 1997 (youngest ever player), winner St Andrews Links Trophy 1998, 4th place 127th Open Golf Championship 1998 (winner Silver Medal for Lowest Amateur Score, equalled all-time amateur scoring record); turned professional 1998; tournaments won: Victor Chandler British Masters 2002, Chunichi Crowns Japan 2002, Nashua Masters Southern African Tour 2002, Dunhill Championship 2002, Mastercard Masters 2006, Volvo Masters 2007, Morgan Stanley Meml Tournament 2010, AT&T Nat 2010; Gold medal Olympic Games 2016; winner European Order of Merit 2007; memb GB & I team Seve Trophy 2003 and 2007 (winners); *Recreations* tennis, soccer, cricket; *Style*— Justin Rose, Esq; ✉ website www.justinrose.com

ROSE, Kevin John; s of Thomas Rose, of Bletchley, Bucks, and Jeanette Iris, *née* Farman; *b* 10 July 1956; *Educ* Bletchley GS; *m* July 1979, Gillian, da of Thomas Lovett; 1 s (Alexander John b 20 Dec 1985); *Career* mktg offr BOC 1976–78 (sales offr 1974–76); VAG (UK) – Volkswagen/Audi: fin controller Sales & Mktg 1978–80, field support mangr 1980–81, fleet ops mangr 1981–84, fleet servs mangr 1984–88, distribution mangr 1988–90, customer servs mangr 1990–91, regnl mangr 1991–93, head of mktg 1993–95; dir Seat UK 1995–99, dir Audi UK 1999–; *Recreations* squash, tennis, soccer coaching; *Style*— Kevin Rose, Esq; ✉ Audi UK, Yeomans Drive, Blakelands, Milton Keynes MK14 5AN (☎ 01908 601313, fax 01908 601040, e-mail kevin.rose@audi.co.uk)

ROSE, Martin John; s of John Ewert Rose, of Chandlers Ford, Hants, and Margaret Mary, *née* Eames; *b* 21 March 1956; *Educ* St Mary's Coll Southampton, Univ of Warwick (LLB); *m* 7 May 1988, Emma Margaret Havilland, da of Robert Bernard Hutchinson, of Wimborne, Dorset; 2 s (George Edward b 1993, Simon Elliot b 2000), 1 da (Harriet Victoria b 1996); *Career* called to the Bar Middle Temple 1979; practising barr Western circuit 1980–86, legal conslt The Stock Exchange 1986, sr legal advsr The Securities Assoc 1986–89, sr asst slr Linklaters and Paines 1990–92, gp legal and compliance dir Smith & Williamson 1992–; FSI; *Recreations* gardening, naval history; *Style*— Martin Rose, Esq; ✉ Smith & Williamson, 25 Moorgate, London EC2R 6AY (☎ 020 7131 4000, e-mail mjr@smith.williamson.co.uk)

ROSE, Norman Hunter; WS; s of Rev David Douglas Rose, and Catherine Drummond, *née* Pow; *b* 11 March 1949; *Educ* Royal HS Edinburgh, Univ of Edinburgh (LLB); *m* 18 Oct 1980, Kay, da of Gordon Murray Sanderson; *Career* SSC; articled clerk A & W M Urquhart WS Edinburgh 1970–72, asst slr Dunfermline Town Cncl 1972–74, dep sec Law Soc of Scotland 1977–85 (asst sec 1974–76), dep dir of company affrs CBI 1985–88, dir of European affrs Electronic Data Systems Corp 1989–91 (assoc int gen counsel 1988–89), govt affrs conslt 1992–94, sec Br Paediatric Assoc 1995–96, conslt Jackaman Smith & Mulley Slrs Ipswich 1995–2002, DG Business Servs Assoc 1996–2007, ptnr VetA Government Affairs 2007–11, chm UKTF Ltd 2012–, ptnr New Paradigm Business Services LLP 2013–, sec gen European Centre for Facility Mgmnt 2013–; dir Fedn Against Software Theft 1986–90; chm Euro Business Services Round Table 2004–; memb: Bd American Electronics Assoc 1989–91, Nat Cncl CBI 1996–2002, CBI Trade Cncl Assoc 1997–2002, Bd SITPRO 1998–2011 (vice-chm 2003–05, chm 2006–11), Best Value Review Gp ODPM 2001–02, NHS Social Partnership Forum 2002–07, Bd Asset Skills 2005–07, European Forum for Business-Related Services 2004–05, European Forum on Services in Internal Market 2006–10, Workplace Advsy Gp DfES 2006–07, Widening Participation in Learning Sub-Gp Dept of Health 2006–07, Organising Ctee World Mgmnt Forum 2009–10, European Expert Network in Maintenance Educn 2009–, vice chm European Cmmn High Level Gp on Business Services 2012–14; vice-pres and chair of Bd European Soc of Assoc Execs 2006–09, sec gen NOMOS Lawyers Int 2008–10; DG Enterprise and Industry Working Gp on Standardisation and Services 2009–11; memb Editorial Advsy Bd: The Facilities Business 1999–2001, Government Opportunities 2000–11, UNECE PPP Alliance 2002–10; memb UK Delgn UNCEFACT 2015–, chair CEN TC 447 2016–; cnsllr on European govt affrs European Pest Control Assoc (CEPA) 2008–10; non-exec dir BiP Solutions Ltd 2007–09; dir: Nat Archives of Scotland 1981–88, Edinburgh Medical Missionary Soc 1981–90, Scottish Export Assoc 2000–02; pres Inst of Assoc Mgmnt 2014–16; tstee St Lazarus Fndn 2001–14, tstee St Lazarus Tst 2013–14; pres Edinburgh Univ Club of London 1999–2002; memb: Law Soc of Scotland 1972, Soc of Writers to HM Signet in Scotland 1972, Soc of Slrs to the Supreme Courts in Scotland 1977 (memb Cncl 1981–85 (fiscal 1982–85)); hon lay chaplain Felixstowe Coll 1992–94; memb: Freston Parish Cncl 1995–2002, St Edmundsbury & Ipswich Diocesan Synod 2000–05; vice-chair IPRCC 2015–; Liveryman Worshipful Co of World Traders 2003 (Almoner 2015–), Liveryman Worshipful Co of Educators 2013; FRSA 1997, FIAM 1997, FCMI 2012; Knight Commander of the Order of St Lazarus of Jerusalem (memb 1981–, receiver gen Commandery of Lochore 1983–87, justiciar England 1998–2014, Cdr City of London 2012–15, chllr England and Wales 2014–); *Recreations* music, cooking, wine, European history; *Style*— Norman Rose, Esq, WS; ✉ EFCM (☎ 08456 434232, mobile 07740 403181, e-mail norman.rose@ebsrt.eu)

ROSE, Prof Richard; s of late Charles Imse, and Mary Rose, of St Louis, MO; *b* 9 April 1933; *Educ* Clayton HS MO, Johns Hopkins Univ (BA), LSE, Univ of Oxford (DPhil); *m* 1956, Rosemary, da of late James Kenny, of Whitstable, Kent; 2 s, 1 da; *Career* political PR Mississippi River Road 1954–55, reporter St Louis Post – Dispatch 1955–57, lectr in govt Univ of Manchester 1961–66; Univ of Strathclyde: prof of politics 1966–75, dir Centre for the Study of Public Policy 1976–2005 and 2012–; prof and dir Centre for the Study of Public Policy Univ of Aberdeen 2005–11; visiting prof European Univ Inst Florence 1976–77 and 2011–; guest prof: Wissenschaftszentrum Berlin 1988–90 and 2006–07, Central Euro Univ Prague 1992–95; Ransone lectr Alabama 1990, sr fell Oxford Internet Inst 2003–05; fndr memb Exec Ctee Euro Consortium for Political Res 1970, US Ambassador's appointee US-UK Fulbright Educnl Cmmn 1970–75, sec Res Ctee on Political Sociology Int Political Sci Assoc and Int Sociological Assoc 1970–85, fndr memb Exec Ctee Br Politics Gp in the US 1974–95; memb: Steering Ctee Choice in Social Welfare Policy Cncl of Euro Studies 1974–77, Home Office Working Pty on the Electoral Register 1975–77; convenor Work Gp on UK Politics Political Studies Assoc 1976–88, conslt to Chm NI Constitutional Convention 1976, memb Cncl Int Political Sci Assoc 1976–82, co-dir 1982 World Congress Programme Rio de Janeiro; specialist advsr House of Commons Public Admin Ctee 2002–03; conslt: OECD 1980–, World Bank 1992–, Cncl of Europe 1999; UNDP conslt Pres of Colombia 1990, scientific advsr Paul Lazarsfeld Soc Vienna 1991–; dir Scotland in the World Forum 2008–11; ed Journal of Public Policy 1985–2011 (chm Bd 1981–84); memb Cncl British Irish Studies Assoc 1987; founding fell Soc for the Advancement of Socio-Economics 1989; fell: American SSRC Stanford Univ 1967, Woodrow Wilson Int Centre Washington DC 1974; Guggenheim fellowship 1973–74, foreign memb Finnish Acad of Sci and Letters 1985, hon vice-pres UK Political Studies Assoc 1986, foreign memb American Acad of Arts and Sciences 1994; Lasswell Lifetime Achievement Award in Public Policy 1999, Lifetime Achievement Award UK Political Studies Assoc 2000, Lifetime Achievement Award Comparative Study of Elections 2008, ECPR Dogan Fndn Lifetime Achievement Award 2009, Sir Isaiah Berlin Award UK Political Studies Assoc 2010; Hon Dr Örebro Univ 2005, Hon Dr European Univ Inst 2010; FBA 1992; *Books* incl: Politics in England (1965, 5 edn, 1989), Governing without Consensus – an Irish Perspective (1971), Electoral Behavior (1974), International Almanac of Electoral History (jtly, 1974, 3 edn, 1991), Presidents and Prime Ministers (jt ed, 1980), Do Parties Make a Difference? (1980, 2 edn, 1984), Understanding Big Government (1984), The Postmodern President (1988, 2 edn, 1991), Ordinary People in Public Policy (1989), Loyalties of Voters (jtly, 1990), Lesson – Drawing in Public Policy (1993), Inheritance in Public Policy (jtly, 1994), What is Europe? (1996), How Russia Votes (jtly, 1997), Democracy and Its Alternatives (jtly, 1998), International Encyclopedia of Elections 2000, The Prime Minister in a Shrinking World (2001), Elections without Order (jtly, 2002), Learning From Comparative Public Policy (2005), Russia Transformed (jtly, 2006), Elections and Parties in New European Democracies (jtly, 2009), Understanding Post-Communist Transformation (2009), Popular Support for an Undemocratic Regime (jtly, 2011), Representing Europeans (2013), Learning About Politics in Time and Space (2014); books and articles translated into 18 languages; *Recreations* enjoying architecture, music, writing; *Clubs* Reform, Cosmos (Washington DC); *Style*— Prof Richard Rose, FBA; ✉ 1 East Abercromby Street, Helensburgh, Argyll G84 7SP (☎ 01436 672164, website www.profrose.eu)

ROSE, Dr Stephen John; s of Bernard Rose (d 1967), of London, and Grace Alberta, *née* Hefford; *b* 20 March 1951; *Educ* Highgate Sch, Univ of Cambridge, Guy's Hosp Med Sch London (BA, MA, MB BChir, MD); *m* 1, 29 Jan 1983 (m dis 2008), Beatriz; 2 da (Sybilla Alessandra b 1985, Eilidh Veronica b 1986); m 2, 30 Aug 2010, Hannah; *Career* jr doctor Guy's Hosp, registrar Westminster Hosp Med Sch London, lectr Univ of Aberdeen, currently conslt and hon sr lectr Dept of Child Health Univ of Birmingham; memb Nat Exec Jr Hosp Drs; FRCP, FRCPCH; *Books* Case Histories in Paediatrics (1984), Early Recognition of Child Abuse (1984), Textbook of Medicine for Medical Students (1986), Paediatrics (2002), Legally Important Clinical Mistakes (2006); *Recreations* rackets, rowing; *Clubs* Cambridge Union, Stratford-upon-Avon Boat; *Style*— Dr Stephen Rose; ✉ Department of Paediatrics, Birmingham Heartlands Hospital, Bordesley Green East, Birmingham B9 5SS (☎ 0121 424 1687, fax 0121 773 6458, e-mail sbrose98@aol.com or stephen.rose@heartofengland.nhs.uk)

ROSE, Prof Steven Peter Russell; s of Lionel Sydney Rose (d 1959), and Ruth, *née* Waxman (d 1988); *b* 4 July 1938; *Educ* Haberdashers' Aske's, King's Coll Cambridge (state scholar, open scholar, BA), Maudsley Inst of Psychiatry London (MRC scholar, PhD); *m* Prof Hilary Ann Rose, *qv*; 2 s (Simon John Chantler b 2 Dec 1955, Benjamin Jacob b 9 March 1963); *Career* Beit meml fell and Guinness res fell Dept of Biochemistry and New Coll Oxford 1961–63, Nat Inst of Health postdoctoral fell Istituto Superiore di Sanita Rome 1963–64, MRC res staff Nat Inst for Med Res then MRC Metabolic Reactions Res Unit Dept of Biochemistry Imperial Coll London 1964–69, lectr Extramural Dept Univ of London 1965–69, prof of biology, chair Dept of Biology and dir Brain and Behaviour Res Gp Open Univ 1969–99 (currently emeritus prof of neuroscience), Gresham prof of physic (jtly with Hilary Rose) 1999–2002; visiting appts: res fell Hirnforschungsinstitut

R

Leipzig 1961, sr res fell Australian Nat Univ 1977, prof Univ of Queensland Inst for Med Res 1979, scholar Museum of Comparative Zoology Harvard Univ 1980, Hill visiting distinguished res prof Univ of Minnesota 1992, Osher fell The Exploratorium San Francisco 1993, prof UCL 1999–; scientific sec Science Res Cncl Neurobiology Panel 1968–69, memb Neurochemical Gp (Biochemical Soc) Ctee 1970–75, dir and scientific advsr Edinburgh Science Festival 1991–97; pres Biology Section Br Assoc for the Advancement of Science 1996; memb editorial bds of numerous pubns 1973–; medal of the Univ of Utrecht 1989, PK Anokhin medal Inst of Physiology Moscow 1990, Sechenov medal 1992, Ariens Kappers medal 1999, Biochemical Soc medal 2002, Edinburgh medal 2004, BNA Award for Outstanding Contributions to Neuroscience 2012; fndr memb: Brain Research Assoc (memb Ctee 1965–68, 1970–75 and 1988–90), Br Soc for Social Responsibility in Science (memb Ctee 1969–70 and 1974–76); memb: Biochemical Soc, Int Soc for Neurochemistry, Brain Res Assoc, European Brain and Behaviour Soc, European Neurosciences Assoc, European Soc for Neurochemistry, COPUS 1997–2000; FIBiol 1970, FRSA 1980; *Books* The Chemistry of Life (1966), Science and Society (with Hilary Rose, 1969), The Conscious Brain (1973), No Fire, No Thunder (with Sean Murphy and Alastair Hay, 1984), Not In Our Genes (with Richard Lewontin and Leo Kamin, 1984), Molecules and Minds – Essays on Biology and the Social Order (1988), The Making of Memory (1992, Science Book prize 1993, new edn 2003), Lifelines (1997), Brainbox (1997), Brains to Consciousness (1998), Alas, Poor Darwin (with Hilary Rose, 2000), The 21st Century Brain (2005), Genes, Cells and Brains: the Promethean Promises of the New Biology (with Hilary Rose, 2012, paperback 2013), Can Neuroscience Change our Minds (with Hilary Rose, 2016); ed of numerous books, author of numerous res papers; *Style*— Emeritus Prof Steven Rose; ✉ Department of Life Health and Chemical Sciences, Open University, Milton Keynes MK7 6AA (☎ 01908 652125, fax 01908 654167, e-mail s.p.r.rose@open.ac.uk)

ROSE, Susan; *Career* journalist; early career as newspaper journalist; former ed: Your Home, Perfect Home; ed Ideal Home 2003–; *Style*— Ms Susan Rose; ✉ Ideal Home, IPC Media Ltd, King's Reach Tower, Stamford Street, London SE1 9LS

ROSE, Hon Mrs Justice; Dame Vivien Judith; DBE (2013); da of Eric Rose (d 2000), and Jacqueline, *née* Sugarman; *b* 13 April 1960, London; *Educ* Newnham Coll Cambridge (BA), BNC Oxford (BCL); *m* 2002, Dr B J Bulkin; *Career* called to the Bar Gray's Inn 1984; barr Monckton Chambers Gray's Inn 1984–95, Govt legal service advsr 1996–2008, recorder 2009–13, dep High Court judge 2012–13, judge of the High Court of Justice (Chancery Div) 2013–; legal chm Competition Appeal Tbnl 2005–, pres Upper Tbnl Tax and Chancery Chamber 2015–; *Publications* Bellamy and Child European Union Law of Competition (jtly, 7 edn 2013); *Recreations* cinema, music, theatre; *Style*— The Hon Mrs Justice Rose; ✉ Royal Courts of Justice, 7 Rolls Building, Fetter Lane, London EC4A 1NL

ROSE OF MONEWDEN, Baron (Life Peer UK 2014), of Monewden in the County of Suffolk; Sir Stuart Alan Ransom Rose; kt (2008); *b* 17 March 1949, Havant, Hants; *Educ* St Joseph's Convent Dar es Salaam, Bootham Sch York; *Career* Marks & Spencer plc 1971–89: store departmental mangr 1971–75, head office merchandiser and buyer rising to head of dept and gp commercial exec 1976–87, commercial exec Europe 1987–89; Burton Gp: bd dir Debenhams 1989–91, md Evans 1991–93, md Dorothy Perkins 1993–94, memb Gp plc Bd and chief exec Burton Menswear, Evans, Dorothy Perkins and Principles 1994–97; chief exec: Argos plc 1998, Booker plc 1998–2000, Arcadia Gp plc 2000–02, Marks & Spencer plc 2004–10; non-exec dir Land Securities plc; chm Br Fashion Cncl; *Style*— The Lord Rose of Monewden

ROSEMONT, David John; s of Leslie Rosemont (d 1964), of Oxted, Surrey, and Elizabeth, *née* Williams (who m 2, 1974, Air Cdre Philip E Warcup, and d 1997); *b* 26 August 1945, Edgbaston, W Midlands; *Educ* Lancing, AA Sch of Architecture; *m* 1, 8 Aug 1975 (m dis 2000), Elizabeth Abbott (Abbey), da of Frederick Milne Booth Duncan (d 1995), of Ayr, Scotland; 2 s (Hugo David b 3 March 1979, Jonathan Duncan b 22 Dec 1980); m 2, 20 Dec 2002, Frances Margaret Steele, *née* Lowry (d 2007), da of Rev Richard Lowry (d 1960), of Funchal, Madeira; m 3, 2 June 2008, Udaliyah Cabrera, da of Verginie Toring, of Montebello, Kananga, Leyte, Philippines; 1 da (Anne-Sophie Claire b 23 April 2009); *Career* architect 1971; assoc: Fairhursts Manchester 1975–77, SKP Architects London 1977–81; private practice The Rosemont Gp 1981–2005, conslt Husband & Carpenter Ltd 2005–, conslt Akaal Assocs Ltd 2008–; chm Wandsworth Challenge Partnership 1994–2004; vice-chm Wandsworth C of C 1995–98 and 1999–2000, dir Business Link London South West 1995–98, memb Bd Wandsworth Strategic Local Partnership 2002–05; pres Assoc Dis-want France 2007–10, memb Bd Assoc de Patrimoine des Monts d'Arrée 2010–, memb Victorian Soc, memb Vielles Maisons de France, memb Maisons Paysannes de France; winner design awards Bath, Kingston upon Thames, Lambeth and Richmond upon Thames, winner Services to Business Community Civic Award London Borough of Wandsworth 2003; MAE 1988, memb AA, RIBA; *Books* Histoire de Scrignac (2012); *Recreations* opera, photography, gastronomy, classic cars, places; *Clubs* Berkshire Automobile, Association Dis-Want; *Style*— David Rosemont, Esq; ✉ e-mail davidjohn.rosemont@sfr.fr

ROSEN, Prof Michael; CBE (1989); s of Israel Rosen (d 1969), of Dundee, and Lily Rosen, *née* Hyman (d 1996); *b* 17 October 1927; *Educ* Dundee HS, Univ of St Andrews (MB ChB); *m* 17 Oct 1955, Sally Barbara, da of Leslie Israel Cohen (d 1960); 2 s (Timothy b 1956, Mark b 1962), 1 da (Amanda (Prof Kirby) b 1959); *Career* Nat Serv Capt RAMC, served UK, Egypt and Cyprus 1952–54; sr registrar Cardiff 1957, fell Case Western Reserve Univ Cleveland OH 1960–61, conslt anaesthetist Cardiff Teaching Hosp 1961–93, hon prof in anaesthetics Univ of Wales 1984–93; dean Faculty of Anaesthetists RCS 1988; pres: Assoc of Anaesthetists of GB and I 1986–88, Coll of Anaesthetists 1988–91; vice-pres World Fedn of Socs of Anaesthesiology 2000–04 (treas 1992–2000), chm World Fedn of Soc of Anaesthesiology Fndn 2001–04, chm Dyscovery Tst 2001–; Sir Ivan Magill Gold Medal 1993; Hon LLD Univ of Dundee 1996; hon memb: Aust Soc of Anaesthesiologists 1974, French Soc of Anaesthesiologists 1978, Japanese Soc of Anaesthesiologists 1989, Univ Anaesthetists (USA) 1989; memb Acad of Med Malaysia 1989; FRCOG 1989, Hon FFARCSI 1990, FRCS 1994; *Books* Handbook of Percutaneous Central Venous Catheterisation (with I P Latto and W S Ng, 1981, 2 edn 1992), Obstetric Anaesthesia and Analgesia: Safe Practice (contrib, 1982), Intubation: Practice and Problems (with I P Latto, K Murrin, W S Ng, R S Vaughan and W K Saunders, 1985), Difficulties in Tracheal Intubation (with I P Latto and B Tindall, 1985), Patient-Controlled Analgesia (with M Harmer and M D Vickers, 1985), Consciousness Awareness and Pain in General Anaesthesia (with J N Lunn, 1987); *Style*— Prof Michael Rosen, CBE; ✉ 45 Hollybush Road, Cardiff CF23 6TZ (☎ and fax 029 2075 3893, e-mail rosen@mrosen.plus.com)

ROSEN, Michael Wayne; s of Harold Rosen, of London, and Connie Ruby, *née* Isakofsky (d 1976); *b* 7 May 1946; *Educ* Harrow Weald Co GS, Watford Boys' GS, Middlesex Hosp Med Sch London (MB), Wadham Coll Oxford (BA), Nat Film Sch, Univ of Reading (MA), Univ of N London (PhD); *m* 1, 1976 (m dis 1987), Susanna, da of William Steele; 2 s (Joseph Steele Rosen b 7 July 1976, Eddie Steele Rosen b 9 June 1980 d 27 April 1999); m 2, 1987 (m dis 1997), Geraldine Clark, da of Jack Dingley; 1 s (Isaac Louis Rosen b 15 June 1987); m 3, 8 March 2003, Emma-Louise, da of Frederick Williams; 1 da (Elsie Lavender Ruby Rosen b 10 March 2001), 1 s (Emile Frederick Harold Rosen b 23 December 2004); *Career* writer/broadcaster; presenter: Poems by Post and Meridian Books (BBC World Serv), Treasure Islands (BBC Radio 4), Best Words (BBC Radio 3), Word of Mouth (BBC Radio 4), Readabout (YTV), True Lives; writer/presenter: Everybody Here (Channel 4, 1982), Black and White and Read All Over (Channel 4, 1983); performances in schs, colls, libraries and theatres throughout UK 1976–; Children's Laureate 2007–09; lectr in Singapore, Aust, USA and Canada; visiting prof: London Met Univ, Middlesex Univ; *Awards* Sunday Times Student Drama Award 1968, C Day Lewis fell 1976, Signal Poetry Award 1982, The Other Award 1982, Smarties Award 1990, Eleanor Farjeon Award 1997, Talkies Award 1998, Sony Radio Acad Award 2003; *Books* Mind Your Own Business (1974), You Can't Catch Me (1981), Quick Let's Get Out of Here (1983), Don't Put Mustard in the Custard (1985), Hairy Tales and Nursery Crimes (1985), The Wicked Tricks of Till Owlyglass (1989), The Golem of Old Prague (1990), Goodies and Daddies (1991), You Wait Till I'm Older Than You (1996), Michael Rosen's Book of Nonsense (1997), Snore! (1998), Rover (1999), Centrally Heated Knickers (2000), Michael Rosen's Sad Book (2004), Totally Wonderful Miss Plumberry (2006); anthologies: The Kingfisher Book of Children's Poetry (ed, 1985), A Spider Bought a Bicycle (ed, 1986), The Kingfisher Book of Funny Stories (ed, 1988), Rude Rhymes (ed, 1989), A World of Poetry (ed, 1991), The Chatto Book of Dissent (ed with David Widgery, 1991), The Vintage Book of Dissent (ed with David Widgery, 1996), Carrying the Elephant: A Memoir of Love and Loss (2002), This is Not My Nose (2004), In the Clonie (2005); *Plays* Backbone (1969, performed Royal Court), Regis Debray (1971, performed BBC Radio 4), Pinocchio in the Park (2001, Unicorn Theatre, performed Regents Park Open Air Theatre); *Recreations* Arsenal FC supporter, reading, second-hand book collecting; *Style*— Michael Rosen, Esq; ✉ c/o United Agents Limited, 12–26 Lexington Street, London W1F 0LE (☎ 020 3214 0800, fax 020 3214 0801, website www.unitedagents.co.uk)

ROSEN, Murray Hilary; QC (1993); s of Joseph Rosen, and Mercia, *née* Herman, of London; *b* 26 August 1953; *Educ* St Paul's, Trinity Coll Cambridge (MA), Brussels Free Univ (Dip); *m* 1975, Lesley, *née* Samuels; 3 da, 1 s; *Career* called to the Bar Inner Temple 1976, ad eundem Lincoln's Inn (bencher 2004); recorder 2000–, deemster Isle of Man High Court 2011–, dep High Court judge (Chancery Div) 2013–; ptnr and head of Advocacy Unit Herbert Smith Freehills 2005–14; chm: Bar Sports Law Gp 1997–2001, Br Assoc for Sport and the Law 2003–05; memb: Court of Arbitration for Sport, Sport Resolutions; mediator (CEDR and ADR-Gp accredited); FCIArb 1999; *Recreations* books, music, cricket, real tennis; *Style*— Murray Rosen, QC; ✉ 4 New Square, Lincoln's Inn, London WC2A 3RJ

ROSENCRANTZ, Claudia; da of Alfred Rosenkranz (d 1986), and Leonore, *née* Meyer; *b* 23 June 1959; *Educ* Queen's Coll London; *Career* picture ed/journalist The Telegraph Sunday Magazine, Sunday Magazine and Elle 1979–86; TV researcher: Aspel & Company, The Trouble with Michael Caine, An Audience with Victoria Wood, Dame Edna Experience (LWT, 1986); prodr: The Dame Edna Experience (series 2) 1989 (nominated for Br Acad Award), Incredibly Strange Film Show, A Late Lunch with Les (Channel 4) 1990, An Audience with Jackie Mason, A Night on Mount Edna (LWT) 1991 (Golden Rose of Montreux), Dame Edna's Hollywood (NBC), Edna Time (Fox), Elton John – Tantrums and Tiaras; prodr/dir Two Rooms, creator/prodr Dame Edna's Neighbourhood Watch (LWT, 1992); exec prodr: Don't Forget Your Toothbrush (Channel 4) 1994, Features Dept BBC (responsible for Out of This World and Prisoners in Time) 1994–95; controller Network Entertainment ITV 1995–2006 (responsible for 600 progs a year incl: WWT BAM, Ant & Dec's Saturday Night Take-Away, Popstars (Silver Rose of Montreux 2001), Pop Idol (Best Entertainment Programme TRIC Awards 2002), I'm A Celebrity Get Me Out of Here (BAFTA Award 2003), Ant and Dec's Saturday Night Takeaway, Dancing on Ice, Harry Hill's TV Burp, Britain's Got Talent), dir of programming LIVING and LIVING2 2006, dir of TV Virgin Media TV 2007–11 (progs incl: Dating in the Dark (RTS Prog Award for Best Multi-Channel Prog 2009), Four Weddings (nomination Best Multi-Channel Prog Broadcast Awards 2010); Woman of the Year 2003, nomination Channel of the Year Broadcast Awards 2010 (for LIVING); FRTS 2004; *Style*— Miss Claudia Rosencrantz

ROSENTHAL, Dennis; s of Hermann Rosenthal, and Ilse Rosenthal; *b* 18 August 1944, Johannesburg, SA; *Educ* King Edward VII HS Johannesburg (Jan Hofmeyr scholar), Univ of the Witwatersrand (BA, LLB), Univ of SA (BA); *m* 21 Dec 1971, Nadine, *née* Gehler; 4 s, 1 da; *Career* admitted attorney SA 1968, admitted slr England Wales 1978, called to the Bar Gray's Inn 2009; articled to Lubbers, Spitz, Block and Rubenstein, lectr in law Univ of the Witwatersrand, attorney Werksmans Johannesburg 1971–74, lawyer Nedbank Syfrets Johannesburg 1974; ptnr: Victor Mishcon & Co 1980–87 (joined 1975), Hill Bailey 1987–89, Saunders Sobell Leigh & Dobin (latterly Forsyte Saunders Kerman) 1989–98, Paisner & Co (latterly Berwin Leighton Paisner LLP) 1998–2009, barr Henderson Chambers 2010–; memb Int Bar Asscoc; former govr: Menorah Primary Sch, Kisharon Sch; *Books* Consumer Credit Law and Practice: A Guide, Financial Advertising Law, Goode: Consumer Credit Law and Practice (co-ed), Goode: Consumer Credit Reports (co-ed), Halsbury's Laws of England (contrib, 4 edn), Encyclopaedia of Forms and Precedents (contrib, 5 edn); *Recreations* music, art, gardening, reading; *Style*— Dennis Rosenthal, Esq; ✉ Henderson Chambers, 2 Harcourt Buildings, Temple, London EC4Y 9DB (☎ 020 7583 9020, fax 020 7583 2686, e-mail drosenthal@hendersonchambers.co.uk)

ROSENTHAL, Jim; s of Albi Rosenthal, of Oxford; *b* 6 November 1947; *Educ* Magdalen Coll Sch Oxford; *m* Chrissy; 1 s (Tom b 14 Jan 1988); *Career* TV sports presenter; Oxford Mail and Times 1968–72, BBC Radio Birmingham 1972–76, BBC Radio Sports Unit 1976–80, with ITV Sport 1980–; Sports Presenter of the Year (RTS) 1997 and 1999, Sports Presenter of the Year (TRIC) 1990; *Style*— Jim Rosenthal, Esq; ✉ ITV Sport, 200 Gray's Inn Road, London WC1X 8HF (☎ 020 7843 8116, fax 020 7843 8153)

ROSENTHAL, Sir Norman Leon; kt (2007); s of Paul Rosenthal, and Kate, *née* Zucker; *b* 8 November 1944; *Educ* Westminster City GS, Univ of Leicester (BA), Sch of Slavonic and E Euro Studies, Free Univ of Berlin (Kunsthistorisches Seminar); *m* 1989, Manuela Mena Marques; *Career* art exhibitions organiser; first exhibition Artists in Cornwall Leicester Museum and Art Gallery 1965, librarian and res Thomas S Agnew & Sons 1966–68, exhibition offr Brighton Museum and Art Gallery 1970–71 (organised Follies and Fantasies for Brighton Festival), organiser (with Vera Russell) Artists Market (non-profit making gallery Covent Garden) 1972–73, exhibition offr Inst of Contemporary Arts London 1973–76 (organised The German Month 1974, Art into Society – Society into Art, Seven German Artists, The Greek Month 1975), exhibitions sec Royal Acad of Arts 1977–2008, special advsr Royal Acad of Arts 2008–; memb: Bd Palazzo Grassi Venice 1985, Opera Board Royal Opera House Covent Garden 1995–99, Bd of Tstees Baltic Centre for Contemporary Art Gateshead 2004–, Comité Scientifique Réunion des Musées Nationaux Paris 2005–; German Br Forum Award 2003; Hon DLitt: Univ of Southampton, Univ of Leicester 2006; hon fell Royal Coll of Art London 1987, Chevalier de l'Ordre des Arts et des Lettres (France) (Cavaliere Ufficiale) 1992, Cross of the Order of Merit of the FRG 1993, Officier de l'Ordre des Arts et Lettres 2003, Order of the Aguila Azteca (Mexico) 2006; *Royal Academy Exhibitions* curator of loan exhbns incl: Robert Motherwell 1978, Post-Impressionism 1979, Stanley Spencer 1980, A New Spirit in Painting 1981, Great Japan Exhibition 1981–82, Painting in Naples, Caravaggio to Giordano 1982, Murillo 1983, The Genius of Venice 1983–84, From Vermeer to De Hooch, Dutch Genre Painting 1984, Chagall 1985, Joshua Reynolds 1986, New Architecture: Foster, Roger, Stirling 1986, The Age of Chivalry 1987, The Early Cézanne 1988, Henry Moore 1988, The Art of Photography 1989, Frans Hals 1990; other exhbn work at the Royal Acad (with Christos M Joachimides): German Art in the Twentieth Century 1985 (also shown at the Staatsgalerie Stuttgart), British Art in the Twentieth Century 1987 (also shown at the Staatsgalerie Stuttgart), Italian Art in the Twentieth Century 1989 (version shown at Palazzo Grassi Venice), American Art in the Twentieth Century 1993 (at Martin-Gropius-Bau Berlin 1994), Sensation: Young British Artists from the Saatchi Collection 1997, Charlotte Salomon 1998, Apocalypse 2000, The Genuis of Rome 2001, Botticelli's Dante 2001, Frank Auerbach 2001, 195 Rembrandt's Women 2001, Paris: Capital of the Arts 1900–1968 2002, Return of the Buddha 2002, The Galleries Show 2002, The Aztecs 2002, Masterpieces from Dresden 2003, Kirchner 2004, Illuminating the Renaissance 2004, Philip Guston 2004, Turks 600–1600 2005, Edvard Munch by Himself 2005, China: The Three Emperors 1662–1795 2005, Jacob van Ruisdael: Master of Landscape 2006, Modigliani and his Models 2006, USA TODAY: New American Art from the Saatchi Gallery 2006, Georg Baselitz Retrospective 2007; *Other Exhibitions*: Zeitgeist (Martin Gropius-Bau Berlin) 1982, Metropolis (Martin Gropius-Bau Berlin) 1991, The Age of Modernism – Art in the 20th Century (Martin-Gropius-Bau Berlin) 1997; *Style—* Sir Norman Rosenthal; ✉ The Royal Academy of Arts, Burlington House, Piccadilly, London W1J 0BD (☎ 020 7300 5742, fax 020 7300 5774)

ROSEWELL, Bridget; OBE (2013); da of Geoffrey Noel Mills (d 1978), and Helen Handescombe, *née* Rodd; *b* 19 September 1951; *Educ* Wimbledon HS, St Hugh's Coll Oxford (BA, MPhil); *m* (m dis); 1 s (Christopher Edward b 30 July 1978), 1 da (Harriet Sarah Louise b 6 April 1980); *Career* economist; Univ of Oxford: lectr St Hilda's Coll 1976–78, res offr Inst of Economics & Statistics 1976–81, lectr Somerville Coll 1978–81, tutor in economics Oriel Coll 1981–84; head Economic Trends Dept and dep dir Economic Affrs CBI 1984–86, chief Euro economist Wefa Ltd 1986–88, chm Business Strategies Ltd 1988–2000, founding dir and chm Volterra Partners 1999–; conslt chief economist GLA; non-exec dir: Network Rail, Ulster Bank Gp Ltd, Atom Bank; sometime memb: Res Priorities Bd ESRC, Ind Panel of Forecasters HM Treasy; author of numerous articles in various pubns; frequent lectr, presenter and broadcaster; *Books* Reinventing London (2013); *Style—* Mrs Bridget Rosewell, OBE; ✉ Volterra Partners, 56–58 Putney High Street, London SW15 1SF (☎ 020 8878 6333, fax 020 8878 6685, e-mail brosewell@volterra.co.uk)

ROSEWELL, Michael John (Mike); s of Frederick Jack Rosewell (d 1974), of Walton-on-Thames, Surrey, and Anne Emma, *née* Helps (d 1984); *b* 22 January 1937; *Educ* Woking GS, LSE (BSc), Westminster Coll (PGCE); *m* 1961, Jill Drusilla, da of Stanley William Orriss; 2 da (Anna-Marie b 1964, Michelle Jane b 1969 d 2012), 1 s (Daniel James b 1966); *Career* economics master, rowing coach and journalist: Ealing GS 1959–64, St George's Coll Weybridge 1964–76, St Edward's Sch Oxford 1976–95 (visiting coach 1999–2005); rowing journalist and writer: Surrey Herald 1963–76, Surrey Comet 1967–76, Evening Mail 1968–77, Oxford Times 1976–2014; features writer Rowing Magazine 1968–97, rowing corr The Times 1989–2007, feature writer Thames User 1992, ed Friends of the Boat Race 1995–2009, dep ed Regatta Magazine 1996–2001 (features writer 1987–); memb Cncl ARA 1968–2000 (chm Publicity Ctee, chm Jr Rowing Ctee, asst ed Br Rowing Almanack, Eng Rowing Team mangr, memb Exec Ctee, GB Jr Team delegate, GB Jr Crew coach); chief coach: ChCh Oxford 1978–90, Oxford Women's Boat Race Crew 1979–87, Wadham Coll Oxford 1995–98, Trinity Coll Oxford 1996; vice-chm Oxford Branch Parkinson's Disease Soc 1993–96; memb: Sports Writers' Assoc of GB 1990, Br Assoc of Rowing Journalists (BARJ) 1990 (chm 2002–05, pres 2005–); ARA Medal of Honour 1997, Journalist of the Year BARJ 2007; *Books* Beginners Guide to Rowing (1970); *Recreations* boating, golf, angling, gardening; *Clubs* Walton Rowing, Leander; *Style—* Mike Rosewell, Esq; ✉ 24 Greenway Road, Shipston-on-Stour, Warwickshire CV36 4EA (☎ 01608 664849)

ROSIER, (Frederick) David Stewart; s of Air Chief Marshal Sir Frederick Rosier, GCB, CBE, DSO (d 1998), and Hettie Denise, *née* Blackwell (d 2010); *b* 10 April 1951, Halton, Buckinghamshire; *Educ* Winchester Coll, Keble Coll Oxford (MA), RMA Sandhurst; *m* 1, (m dis 2007) Julia Gomme; 1 s (Charles Frederick James b 8 Dec 1990); m 2, 2015, Sarah Stanley; *Career* cmmnd 1st The Queen's Dragoon Gds 1973–78; resigned Capt 1978; exec dir S G Warburg & Co Ltd 1984–87 (joined 1978); dir: Warburg Investment Management Ltd 1982–87, Mercury Asset Management Group plc 1987–98, Mercury Bank AG 1990–95; dep chm Mercury Asset Management plc 1991–98, chm Merrill Lynch Channel Islands Ltd 1992–2002, md Merrill Lynch Investment Managers 1998–2002, chm Thurleigh Investment Managers LLP 2003–16, sr advsr Tilney 2016–; cmmr Royal Hosp Chelsea 2012–; chm Armed Forces Charities Advsy Co, dir Invesco Perpetual Select Tst; former dir: Threadneedle Asset Mgmnt, Forces Pension Soc Investment Co; cncllr Wandsworth BC 1982–86; tstee: Nuffield Tst for the Forces of the Crown, 1st The Queen's Dragoon Gds Heritage Tst, Battle of Britain Memorial Tst; former tstee: Burma Star Assoc, Victory Services Club, Winchester Coll 1945 War Memorial Fund; Liveryman Worshipful Co of Coachmakers and Coach Harness Makers; FCSI; *Books* Be Bold, a biography of Air Chief Marshal Sir Frederick Rosier, GCB, CBE, DSO (2011); *Recreations* golf, skiing, tennis; *Clubs* Cavalry and Guards' (chm 2007–11, tstee 2012–), Boodle's, Pratt's, Hurlingham, MCC, Swinley Forest; *Style—* David Rosier, Esq; ✉ e-mail fdsrosier@gmail.com

ROSIN, Prof (Richard) David; s of Isadore Rowland Rosin (d 1993), of Zimbabwe, and Muriel Ena, *née* Wolff (d 1999); *b* 29 April 1942, Harare, Zimbabwe; *Educ* St George's Coll Salisbury S Rhodesia, KCL, Westminster Hosp Sch of Med (MB BS, MS, LRCP, MRCS, DHMSA, Arthur Evans meml prize in surgery, Rogers prize); *m* Michele Shirley (d 2009), da of Ivor Moreton (d 1984); 2 da (Natasha Jane b 25 May 1972, Katya Sarah b 4 May 1983), 1 s (Alexei John b 8 Aug 1973); *Career* house physician then house surgn Westminster Hosp 1966–67, ship's surgn P&O Lines 1967, SHO in clinical pathology Westminster Hosp 1968, SHO (latterly Burns Unit) Birmingham Accident Hosp 1969, SHO (rotation) Westminster Hosp 1969–71; registrar: Sutton Hosp Surrey 1971–73, St Helier's Hosp Carshalton 1973–74; clinical asst St Mark's Hosp London 1974–75, sr registrar Kingston Hosp 1975–77, sr registrar Westminster Hosp 1977–79, consIt in gen surgery and surgical oncology St Mary's Hosp 1979–2007 (chm Div of Surgery 1992–95), former conslt surgn King Edward VII's Hosp for Offrs, clinical dir of surgery St Charles' Hosp 1990–92, prof of surgery Univ of West Indies Bridgetown 2007–; visiting lectr Univ of Hong Kong 1978, visiting fell Pearson Coll Yale Univ; Runcorn travelling fell 1976, Arris and Gale lectr RCS 1976, Ethicon Fndn scholar 1976 and 1978, Br Jl of Surgery travelling fell 1983, Penrose-May tutor RCS 1985–90, Hunterian prof RCS 1987, Arnott lectr RCS 1991, Gordon Taylor lectr 2005, Vicary lectr 2006, Standford Cade lectr 2006, Zachary Cope lectr 2008, BJS lectr ASGBI 2008; regnl advsr NW Thames Region RCS(Ed), examiner (MB BS) London and (FRCS) RCS(Ed), intercollegiate specialist examiner in gen surgery; past memb Cncl The Marie Curie Fndn; chm ICBSE 2003–06; pres Caribbean Soc of Endoscopic Surgns 2013–; memb: Soc of Minimally Invasive Gen Surgns (fndr and hon sec), Surgical Research Soc, Assoc of Surgns of GB and I (SMIGS rep on Surgical Gastroenterology Ctee), RSM (pres Clinical Section 1982–83, pres Section of Surgery 1992–93, memb Cncl 2003–05, memb Cncl Oncology Section), Br Soc of Gastroenterology, Br Assoc of Surgical Oncology (former hon sec, pres 2003–04), London Med Soc, Hunterian Soc, Melanoma Study Gp (first hon sec 1986–89, pres 1989–92), World Soc of Hepato-Biliary Surgery, Int Coll of Surgns, Euro Assoc of Endoscopic Surgns, Assoc of Endoscopic Surgns of GB and I (memb Cncl 1995–2001); Freeman: City of London 1972, Worshipful Soc of Apothecaries 1971, Worshipful Co of Barber Surgns 1978; fell Assoc Upper Gastro-Intestinal Surgeons of GB and I, fell Assoc of Surgns of GB and Ireland, first hon fell Caribbean Coll of Surgns, hon fell South Africa Soc of Endoscopic Surgns, hon fell Indian Assoc of Surgeons, hon fell Indian Assoc of Surgical Oncology, hon fell Sociedad De Cirujanod Generales Del Peru 2013; FRCS 1971 (memb Cncl 1994–2006, vice-pres 2004–06), FRCSE 1971, hon fell SAGES 1996 (memb 1994), FICS, DHMSA 2003; *Books* Cancer of the Bile Ducts and Pancreas (jt ed, 1989), Head and Neck Oncology for the General Surgeon (jt ed, 1991), Diagnosis and Management of Melanoma in Clinical Practice (jt ed, 1992), Minimal Access Medicine and Surgery – Principles and Practice (ed, 1993), Minimal Access General Surgery (ed, 1994), Minimal Access Surgical Oncology (ed, 1995), Minimal Access Thoracic Surgery (ed, 1998), ed-in-chief Int Jl of Surgery, ed-in-chief Int Jl of Surgical Case Reports and series ed Minimal Access textbooks; also author of various book chapters and published papers; *Recreations* particularly golf, opera, music and theatre, history of medicine and surgery, travelling, cinema, cricket, reading, tennis, skiing, shooting; *Clubs* Garrick, NZ Golf, Roehampton, MCC, Barbados Cricket Assoc, Barbados Golf Assoc, Barbados Scuba Diving Assoc, Barbados Cruising; *Style—* Prof R David Rosin; ✉ 302 Westcliffe Apartments, 1 South Wharf Road, London W2 1JB (☎ 020 7087 4260, e-mail rdavidrosin@gmail.com); Diagnostic Medical Services Ltd, Beccles Road, St Michael, Barbados (☎ 00 12 4642 65051)

ROSINDELL, Andrew Richard; MP; s of Frederick William Rosindell, and Eileen Rosina, *née* Clark; *b* 17 March 1966; *Educ* Marshalls Park Secdy Sch; *Career* researcher and freelance journalist 1986–97, res asst to Vivian Bendall, MP; European Fndn: memb 1997–2005, dir 1997–99, int dir 1999–2005; MP (Cons) Romford 2001– (Parly candidate (Cons) Glasgow Provan 1992 and Thurrock 1997); a vice-chm Cons Pty 2004–05, HM Oppn whip 2005–07, shadow home affrs min and spokesman on animal welfare 2007–10; memb Deregulation and Regulatory Reform Select Ctee 2001–05, memb Jt Ctee on Statutory Instruments 2002–03, sec Cons 92 Gp 2003–06; memb: Constitutional Affairs Select Ctee 2003–05, NI Grand Ctee 2006–07, Br-American Parly Gp, Foreign Affrs Select Ctee 2010–; chm All-Pty Parly Gp: Montseratt 2003–, Br-Manx (formerly Anglo-Manx) 2005–, Greyhound 2006–, St George's Day 2007–, Flag and Heraldry 2008–, Zoos & Aquariums 2010– (sec 2007–10), Br Overseas Territories 2010–, Australia and NZ 2010– (sec 2001–10), Canada 2010– (sec 2008–10), Turks and Caicos Islands 2010–, Mauritius 2010–, Pitcairn Islands 2010–, Liechtenstein 2010– (sec 2005–10), Polar Regis 2011–, Central America 2011– (sec 2010–11); co-chm: All-Pty Parly Mongolia Gp 2010–, All-Pty Parly St Lucia Gp 2012–; jt chm All-Pty Parly Br-Switzerland Gp 2010–; vice-chm All-Pty Parly Gp: Iceland 2005–, Bermuda 2005–, CI 2006–, Madagascar 2007–, Br Indian Ocean Territory (Chagos Islands) 2008–, Gibraltar 2010– (sec 2001–02), Queen's Diamond Jubilee 2010–; treas: All-Pty Parly Denmark Gp 2005– (jt treas 2001–05), All-Pty Parly Botswana Gp 2010–; sec All-Pty Parly Gp: Falkland Islands 2001–, Pacific Islands 2009–, Belize 2010–; vice-chm and sec All-Pty Parly Cayman Islands Gp 2010–; memb: Cwlth Parly Assoc 2001– (memb Exec Ctee 2010–), Inter-Parly Union (Br Gp) 2001– (memb Exec Ctee 2010–), Panel of Chairs 2010–; presented to Parl: St George's Day Bill 2006, Traditional Counties Towns and Villages Bill 2007, Union Flag Bill 2008, Br Overseas Territories and Crown Dependencies Bill 2008, Br History in Schs Bill 2009, Diamond Jubilee Bill 2009, Dog Control and Welfare Bill 2010, Public Festivals, Holidays and Commemorations Bill 2011, UK Borders Bill 2012, UK Register of Places Bill 2014, Constitutional & Parly Reform Bill 2014; Armed Forces Parly Scheme: Royal Marines 2002–03, RAF 2005–07, Br Army 2009–13; cncllr Havering BC 1990–2002; Cons Pty: joined 1981, chm Romford Young Cons 1983–84, memb Nat Union Exec Ctee 1986–88 and 1992–94, chm Gtr London Young Cons 1987–88 (chm anti-CND campaign 1983–84), chm Chase Cross Ward Cons 1988–99, int sec UK Young Cons 1991–98, chm Nat Young Cons 1993–94, chm European Young Cons 1993–97, chm Romford Cons Assoc 1998–2001, pres Havering Park Ward Cons 2000–, pres Gibraltar Branch 2004–, pres Cons Friends of Taiwan 2011–, dep chm Int Office 2014–; chm Int Young Dem Union 1998–2002 (UK Young Cons rep 1991–98, exec sec 1994–98), exec memb Int Dem Union (IDU) 1998–2002; co-ordinator Freedom Trg Prog 1993–98; memb: Cons Christian Fellowship, Cwlth Parly Assoc 2001–, Inter-Parly Union 2001–, Cons Parl Friends of Israel 2001–, Cons ME Cncl 2005–, Cons Friends of India 2005–, Cons Friends of America 2008–, Cons Friends of Australia and NZ 2010–, Bd Canadian-United Kingdom Cncl 2010–; parly advsr Guild of Travel and Tourism 2008–; chm: N Romford Community Area Forum 1998–2002, Cons Friends of Gibraltar 2002–, Norfolk Island-UK Friendship Gp 2009–, Zimbabwe-Rhodesia Relief Fund 2010–, Palace of Westminster Philatelic Soc 2010–; pres Caribbean Young Democrat Union 2001–, co-pres Br ME and N Africa Cncl 2012–; pres Romford Sqdn Air Trg Corps 2002–; vice-pres: Romford and Dist Scout Assoc 1995–, Constitutional Monarchy Assoc, Flag Inst (memb 2008–), Romford RBL Band and Corps of Drums 2010–, Romford FC, Retired Greyhound Trust; memb: Salvation Army Romford Citadel 1973–82, Church of St Edward the Confessor Romford 1988–, Standing Advsy Cncl for Religious Educn Havering 1990–2000, London Accident Prevention Cncl 1990–95, Hornchurch Theatre Tst 1990–2002, Royal Soc of St George (chm Houses of Parl branch 2009–), Friends of the UK Overseas Territories, Br Overseas Territories Conservation Forum 2003–, Essex Wildlife Tst 2008, St Alban Protomartyr Church Romford, Br Irish Parly Assembly 2010–, Cncl Freedom Assoc, Cncl Canada UK Colloquium 2010–, No Turning Back Gp; hon memb: SW Essex branch Burma Star Assoc, Romford Lions, Falkland Islands Assoc, Havering-atte-Bower CC, Romford Model Railway Soc, N Romford Community Assoc, Pitcairn & Norfolk Island Soc, HMS Antrim Assoc 2008–, Romford Rotary Club 2010– (vice-pres 2010–), Bd IMAN Fndn; hon assoc memb Br Veterinary Soc; patron: Br Monarchy Soc, Justice for Dogs, Remus Meml Horse Sanctuary, Lennox Children's Cancer Fund, Cons Cwlth Assoc (Branch No 1); govr: Bower Park Sch Romford 1989–90, Dame Tipping C of E Sch 1990–2002, Havering-atte-Bower 1990–2002, Westminster Fndn for Democracy 2010–; Mayor's Award for Community Action 1978, India Fellowship Industry and Parl Tst 2009; Freeman City of London 2003, Hon Alderman London Borough of Havering 2007; *Publications* Defending Our Great Heritage (co-author, 1993); *Recreations* cycling, travel, history, philately, dog owner (Buster); *Clubs* East Anglian Staffordshire Bull Terrier (hon memb), The Staffordshire Bull Terrier Soc (hon memb), Romford Conservative and Constitutional, RAF Assoc, Royal British Legion (Romford), Romford Golf (hon memb); *Style—* Andrew Rosindell, Esq, MP; ✉ House of Commons, London SW1A 0AA (☎ 020 7219 8475); Constituency Office, Margaret Thatcher House, 85 Western Road, Romford, Essex RM1 3LS (☎ 01708 766700, e-mail andrew@rosindell.com, website www.andrew-rosindell.com); Home ☎ 01708 761186

ROSKILL, Hon Julian Wentworth; s of Baron Roskill, PC, DL (d 1996), and Elisabeth Wallace, *née* Jackson; *b* 22 July 1950; *Educ* Winchester; *m* 1975, Catherine Elizabeth, 2 da of Maj William Francis Garnett (d 2004), of Quernmore Park, Lancaster; 2 s (Matthew b 1979, Oliver b 1981); *Career* admitted slr 1974; ptnr Mayer Brown International LLP 1988–2008 (former head Employment Gp, advsr 2009–); memb: Law Soc, City of London Slrs' Co (former chm Employment Sub-Ctee), Employment Lawyers Assoc; *Recreations* photography, music, theatre, tennis; *Style—* The Hon Julian W Roskill; ✉ Mayer Brown International LLP, 201 Bishopsgate, London EC2M 3AF (☎ 020 3130 3898, fax 020 3130 8944, e-mail jroskill@mayerbrown.com)

ROSLING, (Richard) Alan; OBE (1994); s of Derek Norman Rosling, of Bucklers Hard, and Joan Elizabeth, *née* Heseltine; *b* 16 August 1962; *Educ* Univ of Cambridge (Richmond exhibitioner, BA), Harvard Business Sch (Baker scholar, Harkness fell, MBA); *m* 1990, Sarmila, da of Dr S K Bose; 3 s (Aidan Samya b 2 June 1993, Kieran Shaurya b 19 Dec 1996, Euan Sharanya b 23 Aug 1999); *Career* investment banker S G Warburg & Co

Ltd 1983–86, chief exec Piersons (part of Courtaulds Textiles plc) 1988–90, memb PM's Policy Unit 1991–93, strategy devpt dir United Distillers 1993–97, Jardine Matheson Ltd 1998–2003 (latterly chm India), exec dir Tata Sons Ltd 2004–; chm: Br Business Gp Mumbai, City of London Advsy Bd for India, Indo-Br Business Ctee Bombay C of C; *Recreations* South Asia, travel, sailing; *Clubs* Bengal; *Style—* Alan Rosling, Esq, OBE

ROSS, Alastair; MLA; s of Samuel Ian Ross, and Jennifer, *née* Mawhinney; *b* 4 March 1981, Belfast; *Educ* Friends Sch Lisburn, Univ of Dundee (MA), Queen's Univ Belfast (MA); *Career* press offr DUP 2005, political res and Parly aide to Sammy Wilson, MP, MLA, *qv*, 2005–07, MLA (DUP) E Antrim 2007–, private sec to Arlene Foster, MLA, *qv* (as Min for Enterprise, Trade and Investment) 2011–14; former memb: Ctee for Justice, Ctee for Educn, Ctee for the Environment, Ctee for Regnl Devpt, ad hoce Ctee on Sexual Offences; chm: Standards and Privileges Ctee 2011–14, Employment and Learning Ctee, All Pty Gp on Rugby, Ctee for Justice 2014–, Ad Hoc Mental Capacity Bill 2015–; memb All Pty Gp on SMEs; chm DUP Young Democrats 2006–08, chm Larne Democratic Unionists 2008–, memb NI Policing Bd 2010–11; *Recreations* hockey, cricket, travel; *Clubs* Lisnagarvey Hockey; *Style—* Alastair Ross, Esq, MLA; ✉ DUP Office, 31 Lancasterian Street, Carrickfergus BT38 7AB (☎ 028 9332 9980, e-mail office@alastairross.org, website www.alastairross.org); Room 355, Parliament Buildings, Stormont BT4 3XX; 116 Main Street, Larne BT40 1RG (☎ 028 2826 7722)

ROSS, Dr Alastair Robertson; s of (Alexander) Alastair James Ross, FSAScot (d 1985), and Margaret Elizabeth McInnes, *née* Robertson (d 1983); *b* 8 August 1941, Perth, Scotland; *Educ* McLaren HS Callander, Duncan of Jordanstone Coll of Art Dundee (DA, PGDip), Nat Acad of Fine Art Athens (postgrad); *m* 12 April 1975, Kathryn Margaret Greig, da of late John Ferrier Greig Wilson, of Arbroath, Tayside; 1 da (Alexandra b 1981); *Career* artist; lectr Duncan of Jordanstone Coll Univ of Dundee 1969–2003 (pt/t 1966–69), tutor Sch of Scottish Artists in Malta 1991–93; works incl: bronze panel Royal Calcutta Golf Club, bronze for Blackness Devpt Project Dundee, portrait in bronze of Sir Iain Moncreiffe of that Ilk at HM New Register House Edinburgh 1988 (awarded Sir Otto Beit Medal of Royal Soc Br Sculptors 1988); cmmn of a twice life-size torso in bronze for new Rank Xerox HQ Marlow Bucks 1988–89, one-man touring exhbn (26 sculptures) UK and USA 1996–97, cmmnd by Scotland on Sunday in assoc with Glenfiddich to design and produce Spirit of Scotland Awards 1998, cmmnd by P&O Steam Navigation Co to create bronze sculpture for newly-built cruise liner Aurora 2000, cmmnd to design and sculpt bronze cast figure of St Andrew as finials on heraldic gonfannons for Univ of St Andrews and St Andrews Community Cncl 2006; invited guest artist Brechin Arts Festival 2006, visiting prof Univ of Texas 1996; hon vice-pres Paisley Art Inst 2010 (Dip of Paisley Art Inst 2010); work represented in public and private collections worldwide; accorded personal civic reception by City of Dundee 1999; awarded: Dickson Prize for Sculpture 1962, Holo-Krome (Dundee) Sculpture Prize and Cmmn 1962, Scottish Educn Dept Travelling Scholarship 1963, Royal Scottish Acad Chalmers Bursary 1964, Royal Scottish Acad Carnegie Travelling Scholarship 1965, Duncan of Drumfork Scholarship 1965, Post-Grad Scholarship Scottish Educn Dept 1965–66, award winner in sculpture Paris Salon Exhibition 1967, awarded Medailles de Bronze 1968 and d'Argent 1970 Société des Artistes Français (membre associé 1970), Sir William Gillies Bequest Fund Award RSA 1989, Paisley Art Inst Reid Kerr Coll Award for Sculpture 2006, Paisley Art Inst Glasgow Art Club Fellowship Award 2010; memb: Exec Ctee Fife Branch St John Assoc 1979–2010, RSA Alexander Nasmyth Fund Ctee 1986–89, RSA Spalding Fund Ctee 1986–89, Cncl Br Sch at Rome 1990–96, Fife Order Ctee Order of St John 1991–2010, Bd of Dirs Workshop and Artists' Studio Provision Scotland Ltd 1997–2005, Dundee Inst of Architects Architectural Awards Adjudication Panel RIAS 1998–2000, Saltire Soc Arts and Crafts in Architecture Awards Adjudication Panel 2001–05, Bd of Tstees The St Andrews Fund for Scots Heraldry 2001–, (Royal Scot Acad representative) Bd of Tstees for St John's Kirk of Perth 2001–05, Cncl RSA 1999–2001, Sculpture Advsy Panel Montrose Heritage Tst 2005–06, RSA Gen Purposes Ctee 2005–09, RSA Kinross Scholarship Ctee 2005–09, Bd of Tstees City of Dundee Burgess Charity 2015–; external assessor J D Fergusson Art Awards Tst 2005–06, assessor Scottish Drawing Competition 2009; elected librarian Royal Scottish Acad 2005–09; patron Univ of Abertay Dundee Fndn 2006–, memb Cncl Scottish Artists' Benevolent Assoc 2012; Paisley Art Inst Reid Kerr Coll Award for Sculpture 2008; Baron-Bailie Easter Moncreiffe 1974–, Burgess City of Dundee 2011; Freeman City of London 1989; Hon DArts Univ of Abertay Dundee 2003; hon life memb: Perthshire Art Assoc 2005, Paisley Art Inst 2007; memb Soc of Portrait Sculptors 1966, FRSA 1966, ARBS 1968 (vice-pres 1988–90, Scottish rep on Cncl 1972–92), professional memb SSA 1969 (memb Cncl 1972–75), FSA Scot 1971, FRBS 1975, ARSA 1980, MBIM 1989, Hon FRIAS 1992, RGI 2004, RSA 2005; SBStJ 1979, OStJ 1984 (Service Medal with Bar 2010), CStJ 1997 (memb Priory Cncl Priory of Scotland 1996–2004); Alastair Ross – Sculptures 1960–2000 (2001); *Recreations* heraldry, genealogy, Scottish history; *Clubs* Royal Perth, Puffin's (Edinburgh); *Style—* Dr Alastair Ross; ✉ Ravenscourt, 28 Albany Terrace, Dundee DD3 6HS (☎ 01382 224 235, e-mail a.r.ross@arross.co.uk, website www.arross.co.uk and www.arross.com)

ROSS, Alexander (Sandy); s of Alexander Coutts Ross (d 1978), and Charlotte Edwards, *née* Robertson (d 1978); *b* 17 April 1948, Grangemouth, Falkirk; *Educ* Grangemouth HS, Univ of Edinburgh (LLB), Moray House Coll; *m* Alison Joyce, *née* Fraser; 3 c (Andrew b 1 Sept 1983, Francis b 29 May 1986, Thomas b 13 July 1992); *Career* articled then slr Edinburgh 1970–74, lectr Paisley Coll of Technol 1974–76, prodr Granada Television Manchester 1977–86, controller of arts and entertainment Scottish Television 1986–97, dep chief exec Scottish Television Enterprises 1997–98, controller of regnl prodn Scottish Media Gp 1999–2000, md Scottish Television 2000–04, md Int Devpt Scottish Television 2004–07, chief exec MurrayfieldMedia 2007–; dir Assembly Theatre Ltd; cncllr: Edinburgh Town Cncl 1971–75, Edinburgh Dist Cncl 1974–78; former memb Ctee BAFTA Scotland (former chair), memb BAFTA, former chm Salford Conf on Television from the Nations and Regions; assoc Adam Smith Coll Fife 2012; *Recreations* reading, golf, music, watching football, curling; *Clubs* Glen Golf, Haunted Major Golf Soc (N Berwick), Oyster Club Edinburgh, Prestonfield Golf, Edinburgh Corporation Golf (capt 2012–13), East Linton Curling (pres 2016–); *Style—* Sandy Ross, Esq; ✉ 10 Campbell Avenue, Edinburgh EH12 6DS (☎ 0131 539 1192, mobile 07803 970107, e-mail sandy.ross@murrayfieldmedia.com)

ROSS, Alexander Guy Campbell; s of David Ross, and Gill, *née* Johnson; *b* 26 November 1959, London; *Educ* Westminster Sch, Univ of Sussex (BA); *m* 23 Sept 1995, Sophia, *née* Maltby; 1 da (Natasha b 29 July 1996 (twin)), 2 s (Jasper b 29 July 1996 (twin), Geordie b 28 Aug 1999); *Career* md Snipe & Grouse Ltd 1984–89, slr Theodore Goddard 1993–2004, ptnr Wiggin LLP 2004–; memb: Int Assoc of Entertainment Lawyers 1995 (memb Exec Ctee 2005–), Br Literary and Artistic Copyright Assoc 1997; *Recreations* sailing, hill walking; *Clubs* 2 Brydges Place, Bembridge Sailing Club; *Style—* Alexander Ross, Esq; ✉ Wiggin LLP, Jessop House, Jessop Avenue, Cheltenham, Gloucestershire GL50 3WG (☎ 01242 631291, e-mail alexander.ross@wiggin.co.uk)

ROSS, Alistair Charles; s of Alan Alistair Ross, OBE (d 1984), and Marjorie Evelyn, *née* Catch; *b* 29 November 1951; *Educ* Westminster, Charing Cross Hosp Med Sch, Univ of London (MB BS); *m* 19 Nov 1977, Alexandra Jane Elaine, da of Samuel Philippe Alexandre Holland; 2 da (Katherine Alexandra MacKenzie b 1980, Victoria Isobel MacKenzie b 1982), 1 s (James Alistair George MacKenzie b 1984); *Career* surgical registrar The London Hosp 1979–82, sr orthopaedic registrar St Mary's Hosp London 1982–88, conslt orthopaedic surgn Royal United Hosp and Royal Nat Hosp for Rheumatic Diseases Bath 1988–2012, dir Bath and Wessex Orthopaedic Res Unit 1988–2005, conslt orthopaedic surgeon Bath Clinic 1988–; Euro travelling scholar Br Orthopaedic Assoc 1987, hon sr lectr Sch of Postgrad Medicine Univ of Bath 1992–, John Charnley tutor in orthopaedics RCS 1999–2002; assoc ed Jl of Bone and Jt Surgery/Bone and Joint Jl 2006–, ed BON 2011–13; examiner FRCS (Tr & Orth) 2007–; tstee John Charnley Tst; memb: Int Soc of Limb Salvage (ISOLS), Eurospine, Br Orthopaedic Oncology Soc, Br Hip Soc, Br Assoc of Spinal Surgns, Rheumatoid Arthritis Surgical Soc (pres 1994, treas 1995–98, hon sec 1998–99), Br Orthopaedic Study Gp 1994– (editorial sec 1999–2009, hon sec 2010–12), Educn Ctee Br Orthopaedic Assoc 1995–2002, Bd of Specialist Socs Br Orthopaedic Assoc 1998–2002, ex officio memb Cncl Br Orthopaedic Assoc 2011–13; Freeman City of London 1977, Liveryman Worshipful Soc of Apothecaries 1993; LRCP, FRCS 1980 (MRCS 1976), FBOA 1988; *Publications* Wrist and Hand (Gray's Anatomy, 41 edn) papers and chapters on lower limb joint replacement, spinal surgery, surgery of the brachial plexus and surgical oncology; *Recreations* music; *Clubs* Leander, Athenaeum; *Style—* Alistair Ross, Esq; ✉ The Bath Clinic, Claverton Down Road, Bath BA2 7BR (☎ 01225 838859, fax 01225 838890)

ROSS, Amanda; *née* Stevens; *b* 4 August 1962, Rochford, Essex; *Educ* Furtherwick Park Sch Canvey Is, SE Essex Sixth Form Coll, Univ of Birmingham (BA); *m* 6 Oct 1990, Simon Ross; 2 s (Luciano Edward b 12 June 2006, Orlando John b 20 Dec 2008); *Career* researcher Central TV 1984, lead singer with big band touring Germany 1985, prodr, dir and format creation for ITV cos, BBC and VH1 until 1994, fndr (with husband, Simon) and jt md Cactus TV 1994–; TV prodns incl: Richard & Judy (Channel 4) 2001–08 (estab Richard & Judy Book Club), Saturday Kitchen (BBC 1), Hairy Bikers Food Tour of Britain (BBC 2), The Galaxy British Book Awards, ITV Crime Thriller Awards, The Roux Scholarship, The Roux Legacy, Weekend (ITV), Munch Box (ITV); fndr (with Michel Roux, Jr, *qv*) cookery sch Cactus Kitchens 2013; British Book Trade Award for inspiring wider reading 2005, Bookseller Retail Award for expanding the market 2006 and 2007, Best Campaign RTS Award 2008, Bookseller Award for Outstanding Achievement 2009, nominated 4 RTS awards (incl Best Campaign RTS Education Award 2008); tstee Kidscape; memb: UK Advsy Bd Room to Read, Selection Bd World Book Night; ambass: Nat Literacy Tst, Wellbeing of Women, Kidscape; memb: BAFTA, RTS; Richard & Judy's Wine Guide (2005), Saturday Kitchen Cookbook (2007), Saturday Kitchen Best Bites (2008), Saturday Kitchen at Home (2009), Saturday Kitchen Bible (2013); *Recreations* renovating house in Italy, my dogs, cooking; *Style—* Ms Amanda Ross; ✉ Cactus TV, Cactus Studios, 1 St Lukes Avenue, London SW4 7LG (e-mail amanda.ross@cactustv.co.uk)

ROSS, Anthony Lee (Tony); s of Eric Turle Lee Ross (d 1982), and Effie, *née* Griffiths (d 1981); *b* 10 August 1938; *Educ* Helsby Co GS, Liverpool Regnl Coll of Art (NND); *m* 1, 16 Sept 1961 (m dis 1971), Carole Dawn, *née* D'Arcy; m 2, 1971 (m dis 1976), Joan Lillian, *née* Allerton; 1 da (Alexandra Ruth b 10 Aug 1971); m 3, 30 June 1979, Zoë, da of Cyril Albert Goodwin, of Cuffley, Herts; 1 da (Katherine Lee b 12 April 1980); partner, Wendy; *Career* author and illustrator; drawings in magazines incl Punch, Time and Tide, Town 1962–75, sr lectr Manchester Poly 1965–86, first book published 1973; TV films incl: Towser 1983, Little Princess 2006; exhibitions: London, Holland, Germany, Japan, USA, France; patron: Malcolm Sargent Cancer Fund for Children Readathon, Chelsea Children's Hosp Sch, Assoc of Illustrators; *Awards* USA, Holland, Japan, Belgium, E Germany, W Germany; *Books* illustrator for over 900 children's books incl: The Reluctant Vampire (by Eric Morecambe, 1982), Limericks (by Michael Palin, 1985), Fantastic Mr Fox (by Roald Dahl, 1988), The Magic Finger (by Roald Dahl, 1989), Alice Through The Looking Glass (by Lewis Carroll, 1992), Meet Just William Series (by R Crompton, 1999), Susan Laughs (with Jeanne Willis, 1999), Pippi Longstocking (2000), Worzel Gummidge (2000), What did I look like when I was a baby? (with Jeanne Willis, 2000), I want to be a cowgirl (with Jeanne Willis, 2001), Horrid Henry series (by Francesca Simon); author of 90 children's books incl: I'm Coming to Get You (1984), I Want my Potty (1986), A Fairy Tale (1991); *Recreations* travel; *Clubs* Chelsea Arts; *Style—* Tony Ross, Esq; ✉ Andersen Press, 20 Vauxhall Bridge Road, London SW1V 2SA

ROSS, Charlotte Miranda; da of Nigel Ross, of Dunkeld, and Janice, *née* McEwen; *b* 19 October 1969; *Educ* Arran HS, Univ of Glasgow (MA); *Career* journalist; asst ed Sunday Herald 1998–2000, ed S2 2000–01; The Scotsman: asst ed 2001–02, exec ed Features 2002–03; dep ed Evening Standard 2012–; *Style—* Ms Charlotte Ross

ROSS, Daniel P (Dan); s of Stephen L Ross, *qv*; *b* 20 February 1979, London; *Educ* Mill Hill Sch London, UCL; *Career* Grant Thornton 1999–2001, Grant Thornton Corp Finance 2001–04, dir Golf in Dubai 2004–06, Ross Bennet-Smith 2007– (ptnr 2008–); tstee The McGinley Fndn 2014–; *Recreations* golf, music, skiing, travel; *Style—* Dan Ross, Esq; ✉ Ross Bennet-Smith, Charles House, 5–11 Regent Street, London SW1Y 4LR (☎ 020 7930 600, e-mail danr@rossbennetsmith.com)

ROSS, David Craib Hinshaw; s of Douglas Hinshaw Ross (d 1977), of Glasgow, and Jean Mitchell, *née* Blyth (d 1999); *b* 14 January 1948, Glasgow; *Educ* Kelvinside Acad Glasgow, Trinity Coll Glenalmond, Univ of Glasgow (LLB); *m* 5 Jan 1974, Helen Elizabeth, *née* Clark; 2 s (Peter David Hinshaw, Andrew Douglas), 1 da (Frances Elizabeth); *Career* slr Maclay Murray & Spens 1972–75 (apprentice 1970–72); Biggart Baillie (formerly Biggart Baillie & Gifford WS): slr 1975–77, ptnr 1977–, head of corporate 1997–2001, chm and sr ptnr 2001–08; dir APUC Ltd 2007–15, ret; chm Scottish Chambers of Commerce 2003–07, dir Br Chambers of Commerce 2004–07, former memb Scottish Euro Preparations Ctee, dir and memb Exec Ctee Scottish Cncl for Devpt and Industry 2003–07; hon life memb Euro-American Lawyers Gp (former chm); author of various articles on energy and corporate governance matters; sec Loganair Ltd 1998– (dir 2009–12); chm of panels for Youth Business Scotland; memb Ct (Governing Body) Univ of Glasgow 2004– (convener 2010–, chm Investment and Nomination Ctees until 2014, memb Finance Ctee 2010–, currently memb Remuneration Ctee), chair Ctee of Scottish Univ Chairs 2013–, memb Scottish Univ Advsy Forum 2013–; memb Advsy Bd Interface 2008–; memb Law Soc of Scotland 1973–2009; *Recreations* rhododendrons, swimming; *Clubs* Western (Glasgow); *Style—* David C H Ross; ✉ Eastfield, 10 Ledcameroch Road, Bearsden, Glasgow G61 4AB (☎ and fax 0141 570 0558)

ROSS, David Peter John; s of late John Malcolm Thomas Ross, and Linda Susan, *née* Thomas; *b* 10 July 1965, Grimsby, Lincs; *Educ* Uppingham, Univ of Nottingham (BA); *Family* 1 s (Carl Cosmo Thomas b 16 Jan 2003); *Career* chartered accountant Arthur Andersen 1988–91; Carphone Warehouse: co-fndr 1991, finance dir 1991–96, chief operating offr 1996–2003, non-exec dep chm 2003–08; chm: National Express Gp 2001–08, Gondola Holdings 2005–06, 2012 Legacy Bd of Advsrs to the Mayor 2008 and 2012–15; non-exec dir: Big Yellow Storage plc 2000–08, Wembley National Stadium Ltd 2002–07, Trinity Mirror plc 2004–07, Cosalt plc 2005–13 (chm 2008–13); memb: Home Office Audit Ctee 2004–07, Panel Lord Carter's Review of Legal Aid Procurement 2005–06; memb: Bd Sport England 1999–2005, Bd Olympic Lottery Distributor 2005–08, Bd London Organising Ctee of the Olympic Games 2008, Cncl Serpentine Gallery 2008–, Bd Cwlth Games England 2009–, Bd Br Olympic Assoc 2011– (chair Audit Ctee); fndr Nevill Holt Opera Festival 2012; chair: David Ross Fndn, David Ross Educn Tst 2007–15, New Schools Network 2015–; chair Devpt Ctee Univ of Nottingham 2009–; tstee Uppingham Sch 2001– (memb Fndn Bd, fell 2011–), tstee Nat Portrait Gallery 2006– (chair Audit and Compliance Ctee); Entrepreneur of the Year 1999; ACA 1991; *Recreations* opera, cycling; *Clubs* RAC, Carlton; *Style—* David Ross, Esq; ✉ e-mail eci@kandahar.co.uk

ROSS, David Thomas Mcleod; s of David Ross, and Margaret, *née* Mcleod; *b* 3 June 1949; *Educ* Boroughmuir Secdy Sch Edinburgh; *m* 25 Aug 1973 (m dis), Margaret Gordon Sharpe Ross, da of Robert Charters Russell, of Loanhead; 3 da (Lindsay b 1976, Louise b 1978, Heather b 1984); *Career* CA 1976; md Ivory and Sime plc 1988–90 (joined 1968, dir 1982), ptnr Aberforth Partners 1990–2015; non-exec dir: Aberforth Smaller Companies Trust plc 1990–94, Aberforth Split Level Trust plc 1990–94, US Smaller Companies Investment Trust plc 1991–98, JP Morgan US Smaller Cos Investment Tst plc, EP Global Opportunities Tst plc, F&C UK Real Estate Investments Ltd; memb: Co of Merchants of the City of Edinburgh, High Constables and Guard of Honour Holyrood House; FCCA; *Recreations* skiing, golfing; *Style*— David Ross, Esq; ✉ 5 Belgrave Crescent, Edinburgh EH4 3AQ (☎ 0131 447 332 2232, e-mail dtmross@hotmail.co.uk)

ROSS, Prof Euan Macdonald; s of Dr James Stirling Ross (d 1992), of Welwyn Garden City, Herts, and Frances, *née* Blaze (d 1999); *b* 13 December 1937, Welwyn Garden City, Herts; *Educ* Aldenham, Univ of Bristol (MD, DCH); *m* 11 June 1966, Dr Jean Mary Palmer, da of George Palmer (d 1984); 2 s (Rev Matthew b 1967, Dr James b 1972); *Career* house physician Bristol Royal Infirmary 1962–63, SHO Aberdeen and Dundee Teaching Hosps 1963–64, registrar in paediatrics Dundee Teaching Hosps 1964–69, lectr in paediatrics Univ of Bristol 1969–74, sr lectr Middx and St Mary's Med Schs Univ of London 1974–84, conslt paediatrician Central Middx Hosp London 1974–84 and Charing Cross Hosp London 1984–89, prof of community paediatrics King's Coll London (KCL) 1989–2000 (emeritus prof 2001–); co-dir Child Studies Unit KCL; paediatric adviser Mid-Western Health Bd Ireland 2002–04; expert witness on child health medico-legal issues; visiting lectr: Boston Children's Hosp Med Sch, Zamboanga Philippines 2000, Tirana Albania 2001; memb: Br Paediatric Surveillance Unit (fndr memb), Exec Bd Whizz-Kidz charity 1999–2008; examiner Sheffield Hallam Univ 2006–09; pres Br Soc for History of Paediatrics and Child Health 2015–; FRCP 1980, FRCPCH 1997, FFPH 1997, Hon FRCPH 2002; *Books* Paediatric Perspectives on Epilepsy (1985), Epilepsy in Young People (1987), Paediatric Epilepsy (1994), Management for Child Health Services (1998), Paediatrics and Child Health (2001); *Recreations* Scottish matters, design, art and photography; *Clubs* Athenaeum, Harvean; *Style*— Prof Euan Ross; ✉ Linklater House, Mount Park Road, Harrow Hill HA1 3JZ (☎ and fax 020 8864 4746)

ROSS, Hugh Robert; s of Flt Lt Robert James Ross, RAF (d 1954), and Marion Bertha, *née* Maidment; *b* 21 April 1953; *Educ* Christ's Hosp (RAF Benevolent Fund scholar), Univ of Durham (Kitchener scholar, BA), London Business Sch (NHS scholar, MBA); *m* 7 Aug 1981, Margaret Catherine, da of Joseph Martin Hehir; 1 da (Kate Mairead Hehir b 6 March 1984), 1 s (Robert Joseph Hehir b 10 May 1987); *Career* nat admin trainee Wessex RHA 1976–78, asst sector admin Princess Margaret Hosp Swindon 1978–80, patient servs offr Westminster Hosp London 1981–83 (asst admin 1980–81), dir of operational servs Bart's London 1985–86 (dep unit admin 1983–85); unit gen mangr: City Unit Coventry HA 1986–90, Leicester Gen Hosp 1990–93; chief exec: Leicester Gen Hosp NHS Tst 1993–95, United Bristol Healthcare NHS Tst 1995–2002; prog dir Bristol Health Serv Plan 2002–04, chief exec Cardiff and Vale NHS Tst 2004–09, dir NHS Wales Health Strategy Unit 2009–11, dir The Hehir-Ross Partnership 2011–14, dep-chair High Educn Funding Cncl for Eng 2014–; *Recreations* golf, Southampton FC, real ale; *Style*— Hugh Ross, Esq; ✉ 40 Alma Road, Clifton, Bristol BS8 2DB

ROSS, James Hood; *Educ* Univ of Oxford (BA), Manchester Business Sch (Dip Business Mgmnt); *m*; 3 c; *Career* served RN 1957–59; British Petroleum: joined 1959, worked variously in UK, France and Africa, involved in demerger Shell-Mex BP and creation of BP Oil Ltd, asst gen mangr BP Tanker Co, dep chm Stolt Tankers and Terminals USA, gen mangr corp planning BP Group, chief exec and md BP Oil International 1986–88, pres and chief exec BP America Inc and an md The British Petroleum Co plc 1988–92; chief exec Cable and Wireless plc 1992–95; chm The Littlewoods Organisation 1996–2002, non-exec chm National Grid 1999–2002 (dep chm March-July 1999), non-exec dep chm National Grid Transco plc (following merger) 2002–; non-exec dir: McGraw Hill Inc (USA), DataCard (USA), Groupe Schneider (France), Prudential plc 2004–; non-exec chm Liverpool Associates in Tropical Health; vice-chm N W Business Leadership Team, former chm Manchester Business Sch, memb Bd N W Devpt Agency, tsee Cleveland Orch; *Style*— James Ross, Esq

ROSS, Lt-Col Sir (Walter Hugh) Malcolm; GCVO (2005, KCVO 1999, CVO 1994), OBE (1988); s of Col Walter John Macdonald Ross, CB, OBE, MC, TD, JP, DL (d 1982), of Netherhall, Bridge-of-Dee, Castle-Douglas, Kirkcudbrightshire, and Josephine May, *née* Cross (d 1982); *b* 27 October 1943; *Educ* Eton, RMA Sandhurst; *m* 31 Jan 1969, Susan (Susie) Jane, da of Gen Sir Michael Gow, GCB, DL; 2 da (Tabitha b 1970, Flora b 1974), 1 s (Hector b 1983); *Career* Scots Gds 1964–87; mgmnt auditor The Royal Household 1987–89; sec Central Chancery of The Orders of Knighthood 1989–90, Comptroller Lord Chamberlain's Office 1991–2006 (Asst Comptroller 1987–90), Master of the Household to TRH The Prince of Wales and The Duchess of Cornwall 2006–08; extra equerry to HM The Queen 1988–; chm Westminster Gp plc 2007–; HM Lord-Lt Stewartry of Kirkcudbright 2006– (DL 2003); memb Queen's Body Guard for Scotland (Royal Co of Archers) 1981– (Brig 2003, Ensign 2012); Freeman City of London 1994; KStJ 2009 (CStJ 2007, Prior Order of St John Scotland 2009–15); *Clubs* Pratt's, New (Edinburgh); *Style*— Lt-Col Sir Malcolm Ross, GCVO, OBE

ROSS, Moira; *Career* ed of format entertainment BBC 2010–11 (progs incl: Strictly Come Dancing, Eurovision Song Contest, So You Think You Can Dance), head of entertainment Wall to Wall 2012– (exec prodr The Voice UK); *Style*— Ms Moira Ross; ✉ Wall to Wall Television, 85 Gray's Inn Road, London WC1X 8TX

ROSS, Nicholas David (Nick); s of John Caryl Ross, of Surrey, and Joy Dorothy, MBE, *née* Richmond; paternal gf Pinhas Rosen was signatory to Israel's Declaration of Independence and first Min of Justice; *b* 7 August 1947; *Educ* Wallington Co GS, Queen's Univ Belfast (BA); *m* 1 March 1985, Sarah Patricia Ann, da of Dr Max Caplin, OBE, of London; 3 s (Adam Michael b 1985, Samuel Max b 1987, Jack Felix b 1988); *Career* BBC freelance reporter and presenter N Ireland 1971–72; presenter radio: Newsdesk, The World Tonight 1972–74, World at One 1972–75 and 1984, Call Nick Ross 1986–97, Radio 4 Gulf News FM 1991, The Commission 1998–2005; prodr and dir documentaries incl The Fix and The Biggest Epidemic of Our Times 1981; presenter TV: fndr presenter BBC Breakfast TV, Sixty Minutes 1983–84, Man Alive, Out of Court, Fair Comment 1975–83, Watchdog, Star Memories, Crimewatch UK 1984–2007, Drugwatch 1985–86, A Week in Politics (Channel 4) 1986–88, various debates (BBC, ITV and BskyB), Crime Limited (BBC) 1993–94, Westminster with Nick Ross 1994–97, BBC TV political party conference coverage 1995, We Shall Overcome 1998 and 1999, So You Think You're a Good Driver 1999–2002, Destination Nightmares 1999–2000, Nick Ross (debates) 1999, Crime Museum (Sky) 2008–11, Truth About Crime with Nick Ross (BBC1) 2009; chm corp conferences; memb: Govt Ctee on Ethics of Gene Therapy 1990–93, Health of the Nation Working Gp 1991–98, Gene Therapy Advsy Ctee 1993–96, Nat Bd for Crime Prevention 1993–95, Crime Prevention Agency 1995–99, Property Crime Reduction Task Force 1999–2002, Ctee on the Public Understanding of Science, Med Audit Ctee RCP, Nuffield Cncl on Bioethics 1999–2006, NHS Nat Plan Action Team 2000, Medical Ethics Ctee RCP 2004–, Acad of Medical Sciences Inquiry into Use of Non-Human Primates 2007–08, Advsy Panel Egrg and Physical Sciences Research Cncl 2008–11; chm Science Book Prize 1991 and 2006; memb Advisory Bd: Crime Concern, Victim Support; pres: Healthwatch, London Accident Prevention Cncl 2007–14; vice-pres Inst of Advanced Motorists, chm Kensington Soc, ambass WWF 2004–11; patron: Prisoners Abroad, Missing Persons Helpline, Patients Assoc, Kidney Research Aid Fund, Animal Care Tst, Apex Tst, Br Wireless for the Blind Fund, Jewish Assc for the Mentally Ill, NICHS, Resources for Action, Simon Community of NI, Myasthenia Gravis Assoc, Tacade, Young At Heart; dir: Crimestoppers, UK Stem Cell Fndn, Dfuse, Sense About Science; chm: Jill Dando Inst of Crime Science UCL, Advsy Bd Wales Cancer Bank 2012–, Evidence Matters 2014–; Broadcasting Press Guild Radio Broadcaster of the Year 1997, Best Documentary Celtic Film Festival 1999; hon fell and visiting prof UCL; Hon Dr Queen's Univ Belfast; FRSA, FRSM, Hon FRCP; *Books* Crime, How to Solve It and Why So Much of What We're Told is Wrong (2013); *Recreations* influencing public policy, good food, scuba diving, skiing; *Clubs* BAFTA, RTS, RSM, Hospital; *Style*— Nick Ross, Esq; ✉ PO Box 999, London W2 4XT (e-mail nick@nickross.com, website www.nickross.com)

ROSS, (Carl) Philip Hartley; s of John Carl Ross (fndr Ross Foods Ltd); *b* 3 May 1943; *Educ* Shrewsbury; *m* 1, 1968, Pamela Jean, *née* Dixon; 3 da (Rachel b 1969, Kathryn b 1971, Amanda b 1975); m 2, 1985, Joanna Louise, *née* Norton; 2 s (Thomas b 1989, Samuel b 1991); m 3, 2009, Ann Margaret, *née* Askew; *Career* chartered accountant; Peat Marwick Mitchell & Co 1961–65, Forrester Boyd & Co 1965–68; dir Cosalt Ltd 1971–75, md Orbit Holdings Ltd 1972–75; chm: Bristol & West Cold Stores Ltd 1974–83, Philip Ross & Co Chartered Accountants 1982–, S Cartledge & Son Ltd 1995–; sec: The Grange and Links Hotel Ltd 2004–, Sandilands Golf Club Ltd 2004–; FCA; *Recreations* golf, football; *Style*— Philip Ross, Esq; ✉ Philip Ross & Co, 2A Knowle Street, Mablethorpe, Lincolnshire LN12 2QH (☎ 01507 472727, fax 01507 479280, e-mail philipross.accountants@virgin.net)

ROSS, Deputy Shane Peter Nathaniel; s of John Ross, of Knockmore, Enniskerry, and Ruth Isabel, *née* Cherrington; *b* 11 July 1949, Dublin; *Educ* Rugby, TCD, Univ of Geneva; *m* 20 April 1974, Ruth, *née* Buchanan; 1 s (Hugh), 1 da (Rebecca); *Career* memb Seanad Éireann (Ind) Univ of Dublin panel 1981–2011, TD (Ind) Dublin South (Dublin Rathdown) 2011–; ptnr Dillon & Waldren Stockbrokers 1980 (chair 1980–87), formerly stock exchange corr Irish Times, business ed Sunday Independent 1995–2011; chm: Kleinwort Benson European Privatisation Tst plc 1994–96, Close FTSE 100 Fund plc 1999–2004, SVM Global Tst plc 2005–; former memb Irish Stock Exchange; *Books* The Bankers (2009), Wasters (jtly, 2010); *Recreations* tennis, skiing; *Clubs* Kildare St and Univ (Dublin); *Style*— Deputy Shane Ross; ✉ Glenbrook, Enniskerry, Co Wicklow, Ireland (☎ 00 353 1 211 6692); Leinster House, Dublin 2, Ireland (☎ 00 353 1 6183014, fax 00 353 1 6184192, e-mail shane.ross@oireachtas.ie)

ROSS, Stephen Lawrence; s of Julian Ross (d 1988), of London, and Miriam, *née* Gimmack (d 1994); *b* 11 December 1950; *Educ* Woodhouse GS; *m* 1 (m dis); 1 s (Daniel Paul b 20 Feb 1979), 1 da (Nicola Jane b 2 Oct 1981); m 2, 2008, Dominique, *née* Clarke; *Career* CA 1974; audit mangr Deloitte Haskin & Sells (London) (now PricewaterhouseCoopers) 1976, ptnr Keane Shaw & Co (London) 1978, founding ptnr Ross Bennet-Smith (London) 1983–; tsee Teenage Cancer Tst 1998–2007; FCA; *Recreations* football, golf, horse racing, magic, music, opera; *Style*— Stephen L Ross, Esq; ✉ Ross Bennet-Smith, Charles House, 5–11 Regent Street, London SW1Y 4LR (☎ 020 7930 6000, fax 020 7930 7070, e-mail stephenr@rossbennetsmith.com, website www.rossbennetsmith.com)

ROSS, Dr Sue; da of Roy Ingram Craddock, of St Monans, Fife, and Eileen, *née* Lee; *b* 4 July 1952; *Educ* Nottingham Bluecoat Sch, Univ of St Andrews, CCC Oxford, Keele Univ (PhD), Univ of Northumbria; *Children* 2 da (Emma b 17 July 1986, Anna b 3 Oct 1991); *Career* dir of social work E Renfrewshire Cncl 1995–2001, chief exec Selby & York PCT 2001–2003, md Sue Ross Consulting Ltd 2004, professional head SSIA; *Books* Social Work Management and Practice-Systems Principles (jtly, 1989); *Style*— Dr Sue Ross

ROSS, Tessa; CBE (2010); da of Len Ross, of London, and Shannie, *née* Kingsley; *Educ* Westminster, Univ of Oxford (BA); *m* Dec 1987, Mark Scantlebury, s of Lester Scantlebury; 2 s (Joseph b 3 Aug 1989, Louis b 1 Aug 1996), 1 da (Matilda b 8 Feb 1993); *Career* head of devpt Br Screen 1989–93, head ind commissioning Drama BBC 1993–2000, head of drama Channel 4 2000–03, head Film 4 2003–14, controller film and drama Channel 4 2007–15, chief exec National Theatre 2015–; Outstanding Contribution to Cinema BAFTA 2013; *Style*— Ms Tessa Ross, CBE

ROSS, Thomas Mackenzie; OBE (1999); s of Duncan C Ross, of Muir of Ord, Ross-shire, Scotland, and Elsie, *née* Mackenzie; *b* 4 May 1944; *Educ* Dingwall Acad, Univ of Edinburgh (BSc); *m* Oct 1967, Margaret, da of Robert Dewar; 1 da (Elaine Caroline b 1968), 1 s (Steven Graeme b 1970); *Career* trainee actuary Scottish Life Assurance Co Edinburgh 1966–70, consulting actuary and later vice-pres Charles A Kench & Associates Vancouver Canada 1971–76, ptnr Clay & Partners Consulting Actuaries 1976–93, princ Aon Consulting 1993–2004; chm: Scottish Life Assurance Co 1999–2001, Profile Corporate Communications Ltd 1999–2003, Penta Capital Ptnrs (Holdings) 2000–07, Edinburgh UK Tracker Trust (now Aberdeen UK Tracker Tst) 2002–14, Pension Policy Inst 2001–08; dir Royal London 2001–10, pres Faculty of Actuaries 2002–04, Nat Assoc of Pension Funds 1989–99 (chm 1995–97); memb: CBI Pensions Panel 1983–95, Take-Over Panel Code Ctee 2002–08, Bd for Actuarial Standards 2006–09; chm Children's Liver Disease Fndn 2002–; fell: Faculty of Actuaries 1970, Pensions Management Inst 1987; hon fell Soc of Actuaries in Ireland 2011; ASA 1971; *Recreations* horse racing, golf, gardening, hill walking; *Style*— Thomas Ross, Esq, OBE; ✉ Beauchamp Barn, Drayton Beauchamp, Buckinghamshire HP22 5LS (☎ 01296 630098, e-mail tom@tomross.co.uk)

R

ROSS RUSSELL, Graham; *b* 3 January 1933; *Educ* Loretto, Trinity Hall Cambridge, Harvard Business Sch; *m* 1963, Jean Margaret, da of late Col K M Symington; 4 c; *Career* Laurence Priest & Co Stockbrokers 1963–88, chm Laurence Priest & Co Ltd 1986–88; chm: EMAP plc 1990–94, Securities Inst (now Chartered Inst for Securities and Investment) 1992–2000, F&C PEP Investment Trust plc (now F&C Capital Income Trust plc) 1993–2005; dir: UK Select Investment Tst 1995–, Foresight Technol 3 VCT plc 1996–, Barloworld Ltd 2001–03; chm UK Business Incubation 1998–; tsee Nesta 2001–07; Stock Exchange: memb 1965–91, memb Cncl 1973–91, dep chm 1984–88; chm and govr Sutton's Hosp Charterhouse 1997–2007; cmmr Public Works Loan Bd 1981–95, dir Securities and Investments Bd 1989–93; hon fell Trinity Hall Cambridge 2000; *Style*— Graham Ross Russell, Esq; ✉ 30 Ladbroke Square, London W11 3NB

ROSSBERG, Sara Jutta Maria; da of Manfred Rossberg (d 2004), of Darmstadt, Germany, and Josefine, *née* Kamps (d 1978); *b* 14 October 1952; *Educ* Viktoria Sch Darmstadt, Staedel Acad of Fine Art Frankfurt/Main, Camberwell Sch of Art and Crafts; *Career* painter (based London since 1976); travelling scholar: German Nat Fndn 1976–77, DAAD 1977–78; portraits incl Anita Roddick (cmmnd by Nat Portrait Gall 1995); *Solo Exhibitions* Acad of Fine Art Frankfurt/ Main 1973, Int Art Fair Basle 1986, Kunstkeller Bern 1987, Treadwell Gall 1987, Thumb Gall London 1988, Don't I Know You? retrospective museum touring show 1989, Rosenberg & Stiebel Inc NY 1990, Louis Newman Galleries LA 1990, Thumb Gall 1991, Stiebel Modern NY 1991, 1993 and 1994, Warrington Mus and Art Gall 1992, Turnpike Gall Leigh 1996, Julian Hartnoll Gall London 1997, Galerie Vielle du Temple Paris 2003, Newhall Cambridge 2005, Albemarle Gallery London 2007; *Group Exhibitions* incl: Summer Show Royal Acad 1978, Chelsea Art Soc 1978, Treadwell Gall 1982, various int art fairs UK and abroad 1982–, Art by Woman Wolverhampton Art Gall 1988, self-portrait touring show 1988, Nat Portrait Gall 1989, 1990 and 1993, John Moores 16 Liverpool 1989, Drawing Show Thumb Gall 1988, 1990 and 1995, European Artists Works on Paper Kunstkeller Bern 1990, Discerning Eye Mall Galleries, Portrait Now Nat Portrait Gall, Singer & Friedlander Watercolour touring exhibition 1995, Art 99 London 1999, Br Artists in Paris Galerie Vieille ou Temple 2000, Artists of the Ideal MOMA Verona Italy 2002, Espace Belleville Paris 2004,

Chateauroux: George Sand: A Modern View, What is Realism? (Albemarle Gallery) 2005, InG Discerning Eye Exhibition 2008, Threadneedle Prize Exhibition 2009, Face Value (Newport Museum and Art Gallery) 2010–11, ArtHouse Richmond 2014, Wow (Linz Austria) 2014, Drawings (Galerie Lattemann Darmstadt Germany) 2015, Columbia Threadneedle Prize Exhbn Mall Galleries London 2016; *Awards* Crown Award 1978, prizewinner 16th John Moore's Liverpool Exhbn 1989, commendation BP Awards Nat Portrait Gall 1990; *Recreations* music, running; *Style—* Ms Sara Rossberg; ✉ e-mail sararossberg@gmail.com, websites http://sararossberg.tumblr.com and http://www.saatchiart.com/sararossberg

ROSSDALE, Rt Rev David Douglas James; *b* 22 May 1953; *Educ* St John's Sch Leatherhead, KCL (MSc), Chichester Theol Coll, Westminster Coll Oxford (MA), Roehampton Inst Univ of Surrey (MSc); *m* 1982, Karen Jane, *née* Paul; 2 s (Christopher b 1986, Paul b 1989); *Career* curate St Laurance Upminster 1981–86, vicar of Moulsham St Luke 1986–90, vicar of Cookham 1990–2000, area dean of Maidenhead 1994–2000, canon ChCh Oxford 1999–2000, bishop of Grimsby 2000–13, canon and prebendary Lincoln Cathedral 2000–, asst bishop of Lincoln 2013–; dir Reach2 Educnl Tst 2013–; govr Wellington Coll 2004–10, Corp of the Sons of the Clergy 2008–, tstee Blue Cross 2015–; *Recreations* travelling, cooking, flying NPPL (M); *Clubs* Farmers; *Style—* The Rt Rev David Rossdale; ✉ Home Farm, Fen Lane, East Keal, Spilsby, Lincolnshire PE23 4AY (☎ 01472 371715, fax 01472 371716, e-mail rossdale@btinternet.com)

ROSSDALE, Fleur Viola; da of John Spencer Rossdale, and Lucie Marcelle Louise, *née* Bourcier (d 2013); *b* 20 March 1957, London; *Educ* Francis Holland Sch, Florence Univ (Dip); *m* 1, 1982 (m dis 1996), Fletcher Robinson; 2 s (George James Patrick b 1984, William Sydney b 1986); m 2, 2000 (m dis 2015), Peter Wadley, RIBA; *Career* originator of the British Interior Design Exhibition staging first show-house in UK 1982, subsequent series of purpose built interior design led exhbns at The Chelsea Town Hall during 1980s and 90s, estab The British Interior Design Exhibition at Cambridge Gate Regents Park showing work of 30 leading interior designers 1997, currently undertaking total interior design of Hambleden Manor Oxon, forthcoming exhbn of British interior design and fine art with fashion designers in a private house in London; *Books* Classic Meets Contemporary (1998); *Recreations* include walking, writing, painting, tennis, boating and reading; *Clubs* Hurlingham, Aspria (Brussels); *Style—* Miss Fleur Rossdale; ✉ Rue de la Vallee, 31, Ixelles 1000, Brussels, Belgium (e-mail fleur@fleurrossdale.com)

ROSSE, 7 Earl of (I 1806); Sir (William) Brendan Parsons; 10 Bt (I 1677); also Baron Ballybritt and Oxmantown (I 1795), Lord of the Manor of Womersley in England and of Parsonstown, Newtown and Roscomroe in Ireland; s of 6 Earl of Rosse, KBE (d 1979), and Anne, *née* Messel (d 1992); half-bro of 1 Earl of Snowdon, GCVO, *qv*; *b* 21 October 1936; *Educ* Aiglon Coll Switzerland, Grenoble Univ, ChCh Oxford (MA); *m* 1966, Alison, da of Maj John Cooke-Hurle, of Startforth Hall, Barnard Castle; 2 s ((Laurence) Patrick, Lord Oxmantown b 1969, Hon Michael b 1981), 1 da (Lady Alicia b 1971); *Heir* s, Lord Oxmantown; *Career* late 2 Lt Irish Gds; UN official: Ghana, Dahomey, Mid-W Africa, Iran, Bangladesh, Algeria 1963–80; dir: Historic Irish Houses and Gardens Assoc 1980–91, Agency for Personal Services Overseas 1981–89, Birr Scientific and Heritage Fndn 1985–, Lorne House Tst 1993–2001; memb Irish Govt Advsy Cncl on Devpt Co-operation 1983–88, fndr Ireland's Historic Science Centre; hon fell TCD; LLD (hc) Dublin; Hon FIEI; *Style—* The Earl of Rosse; ✉ Birr Castle, Co Offaly, Republic of Ireland (☎ 00 353 57 912 0023)

ROSSER, Bradley John (Brad); s of Thomas Rosser, and Valerie, *née* Tranter; *b* 21 October 1963, Aust; *Educ* Trinity Coll HS Perth, Univ of Western Australia (BComm, Hackett studentship, Cwlth scholar), Cornell Univ (MBA); *m* 7 Sept 2002, Kate, *née* Bone; 2 da (Grace Josephine b 18 Oct 2003, Madeleine Jade b 2 Nov 2006); *Career* exec asst Bond Corporation Holding Ltd: to Television Chief Exec 1987, to Bd of Dirs 1987–88, to MD 1988–90, to Chm 1991–92; mgmnt consulting McKinsey & Co Inc UK 1992–95 (mangr 1994–95), gp corporate devpt dir Virgin Gp 1995–98 (memb Bd, non-exec dir Virgin cos incl Victory Cooperation, Virgin Clothing, Virgin Vie, Virgin Exec Aviation and Virgin Bride), former gp vice-chm Instant Access Gp of Cos, fndr BSF Group; former vice-chm London Broncos Rugby League Club; *Recreations* tennis, golf, cricket, water sports, travel; *Style—* Brad Rosser, Esq

ROSSER, Michael John (Mike); s of John Desmond Rosser (d 1992), of Enfield, Middx, and Joan, *née* Oakley (d 2006); *b* 15 November 1943; *Educ* Edmonton Co GS; *m* Jo Haigh; 1 da (Katherine Joan b 31 Aug 1980), 1 s (David John b 18 March 1987), 2 step da (Jessica Daisy b 14 May 1986, Pollyanna Rose b 29 Nov 1988); *Career* media dir Allen Brady & Marsh 1975–77, md J Walter Thompson, JWT Direct and Conquest Media Manchester 1987–91 (media dir J Walter Thompson 1977–86), ptnr FDS Group 1994– (corp devpt and recovery trg conslt 1993–); dir The Network Ltd (Field Marketing) 2001–03; non-exec dir Cougar Industries Ltd Watford, Plant Glazing Services & Nationwide Plant Ltd Barnsley, R J Stokes & Sons Ltd (Paint Manufacturing Div) Sheffield 1996–2000, non-exec chm and dir English Rose Hotels, dir and sales and marketing director ACM Waste Mgmnt plc 2002–08; FIPA; *Recreations* watching soccer, cricket and squash; golf (playing and watching); *Style—* Mike Rosser, Esq; ✉ The Royds, 326 Wakefield Road, Denby Dale, Huddersfield HD8 8SD (home ☎ 01484 866731, office 01484 860501, mobile 07836 695613, fax 01484 861424, e-mail mike.rosser@fdsgroup.uk.com)

ROSSER, Baron (Life Peer UK 2004), of Ickenham in the London Borough of Hillingdon; Richard Andrew Rosser; JP (1978); s of Gordon William Rosser (d 1985), and Kathleen Mary, *née* Moon (d 1985); *b* 5 October 1944; *Educ* St Nicholas GS Northwood, Univ of London (BSc); *m* 17 Nov 1973, Sheena Margaret, da of Iain Denoon; 2 s (Hon Keith Malcolm b 1976, Hon Colin Michael b 1977), 1 da (Hon Rachel Anne b 1980); *Career* Transport Salaried Staffs' Assoc: res offr 1968–76, fin offr 1976–77, sec London Midland Regn 1977–82, asst gen sec 1982–89, gen sec 1989–2004; non-exec dir Nat Offender Mgmnt Serv Bd 2000–09, non-exec chm Nat Offender Mgmnt Service Audit Ctee 2003–09; cncllr London Borough of Hillingdon 1971–78 (chm Fin Ctee 1974–78), Parly candidate (Lab) Croydon Central Feb 1974, memb Lab Pty Nat Exec Ctee 1988–98 (chm 1997–98, vice-chm 1996–97); oppn whip House of Lords 2010–11, oppn front bench spokesman on defence House of Lords 2011–, memb of oppn front bench team on Home Office and transport House of Lords 2011–; memb Gen Cncl TUC 2000–04; chm Uxbridge Bench 1996–2000; CMILT 1968; *Style—* The Lord Rosser; ✉ House of Lords, London SW1A 0PW (☎ 020 7219 4589)

ROSSI, Mario; s of Carlo Rossi, of Glasgow, and Vitoria, *née* Bertoncini; *b* 11 February 1958; *Educ* Glasgow Sch of Art (BA) Royal Coll of Art (MA); *Partner* Lindsay Alker; 2 da (Vita Rossi, Stella); *Career* artist; lectr Goldsmiths Coll London 1985–90, currently sr lectr in painting Central St Martin's Sch of Art; work in the collections of: Arts Cncl Collection England, BBC Scotland, Contemporary Arts Soc, V&A, Gallery of Modern Art Edinburgh, Cleveland Art Gallery Middlesbrough, Unilever, Nordstern Cologne, British Council, Glaxo-Wellcome, EMI Worldwide, Tetrapak, DTI; Gulbenkian Rome scholar Br Sch at Rome 1982–83, fellowship in creative arts Trinity Coll Cambridge 1987–89, Coopers & Lybrand under 35 award Whitechapel Open 1988, Fulbright fell in visual art 1993–94, Artist Professional Devpt Scheme 1998–2000; *Solo Exhibitions* incl: The Archaeologist (Demarco Gallery, City Arts Centre) 1984, Interim Art 1985, Cleveland Gallery Middlesbrough 1987, Atelier 1 Hamburg 1987, Anderson O'Day Gallery London 1988, 1990 and 1993, Ozones (Wren Library, Trinity Coll Cambridge) 1989, Spacex Gallery Exeter 1990, Peter Scott Gallery Lancaster Univ 1991, Oldham Gallery 1991, Angel Row Gallery Nottingham 1991, Anderson O'Day Gallery Economist Bldg St James's 1992, Northern Arts Sunderland 1995, De La Warr Pavilion E Sussex 1999 and 2000, Cornerhouse Manchester 2000, Host (Hastings Museum and Art Gallery) 2001, Corridor of Mesmeric Transference (SEEDA Guildford) 2004, Wonderland (Media Centre Hastings) 2007, Latitude and Longitude (F-ish Hastings) 2008, Seascapes (Village Underground London) 2008, Heaven and Hell (Ivychurch Romney Marsh) 2010, AKA London, Metropole Galleries Folkestone; *Group Exhibitions* incl: Cross Currents (Third Eye Centre Glasgow) 1979, Scottish Young Contemporaries (Travelling Exhibition) 1981, Expressive Images (New 57 Gallery Edinburgh) 1982, 12 Artisti Britannici A Roma (Palazzo Barberini Rome) 1983, Five Painter (Riverside Studios) 1985, New Image Glasgow (Third Eye Centre Glasgow) 1985, New Art-New World (Sothebys London and NY) 1986, Contemporary British Woodcuts (Worcester Museum) 1986, The Vigorous Imagination-New Scottish Art (Scottish Nat Gallery of Modern Art Edinburgh and touring) 1987, Glasgow Garden Festival 1988, Fire and Metal (Goldsmiths' Gallery) 1988, Whitechapel Open (Whitechapel Gallery) 1988, John Moores 16 (Walker Art Gallery Liverpool) 1989, Scottish Art Since 1900 (Scottish Nat Gallery of Modern Art Edinburgh and The Barbican) 1989–90, Real Life Stories – The Cleveland Collection (Spacex Gallery Exeter) 1990, Post Morality (Kettle's Yard Cambridge) 1990, Post-Modern Prints (V&A) 1991, John Moores 17 (Walker Art Gallery Liverpool) 1991, Cleveland Drawing Bienale Middlesbrough 1991, Cross Over (Anderson O'Day Gallery) 1992, The Return of the Cadaure Equis (Drawing Centre NY) 1993, A Cloud Burst of Material Possessions (Towner Art Gallery Eastbourne, Worcester City Art Gallery, Purdy Hicks Gallery London, Mead Gallery Coventry) 1997, The Word (Addison Wesley Longman Harlow) 1997, Times of Our Lives (Whitworth Gallery Manchester) 2000, Shot on the Coast (film festival, St Mary in the Castle, Hastings) 2000, Host (Hastings Museum and Art Gallery) 2001, The Most Dangerous Game (Rhodes and Mann Gall London) 2002, Sanctuary (Gallery of Modern Art Glasgow) 2003, Smog (London Sch of Hygiene and Tropical Med) 2003, Strangers to Ourselves (South East of England) 2004, Something Strange (Fine Art Museum, Torino, Finland) 2004, Unspooling Artists and Cinema (Cornerhouse Manchester) 2010; The End (2000), Cinematic Decay and Architectural Dissolution (2000), Monsters, Ghettos and the Neo-Baroque (2000); *Clubs* Chelsea Arts; *Style—* Mario Rossi, Esq; ✉ Seaside, Cliff End, Pett Level, East Sussex TN35 4EE (☎ and fax 01424 813291)

ROSSITER, Mark Francis; Mark Edward Rossiter, of Warrington, and Kathleen, *née* Concannon; *b* 19 June 1962; *Educ* Boteler GS Warrington; *m* Elizabeth, *née* Farrow; *Career* journalist; Altrincham & Sale Guardian 1988–90, ed Warrington Guardian 1992–95, gp ed Guardian Series Newspapers 1995–96, ed dir Newsquest (Cheshire) Ltd 1996–97, ed-in-chief Bolton Evening News, Bury Times Gp & Leigh Jl, currently ed-in-chief N Wales Newspapers; *Awards* winner North West Young Journalist of the Year Br Guild of Editors 1985, winner Journalist of the Year Br Press Awards 1993; memb Soc of Editors; chm Fundraising Ctee Marie Curie Cancer Care (Bolton/Bury area); *Style—* Mark Rossiter, Esq; ✉ North Wales Newspapers, Mold Business Park, Wrexham Road, Mold, North Wales (☎ 01352 707721)

ROSSLYN, 7 Earl of (UK 1801); Sir Peter St Clair-Erskine; 10 Bt (S 1666), CVO (2014), QPM (2009); also Baron Loughborough (GB 1780); s of 6 Earl of Rosslyn (d 1977), and Comtesse Athenaïs de Rochechouart-Mortemart; *b* 31 March 1958; *Educ* Eton, Univ of Bristol, Univ of Cambridge; *m* 1982, Helen M, eld da C R Watters, of Sussex; 2 s (Jamie William, Lord Loughborough b 28 May 1986, Hon Harry b 9 May 1995), 2 da (Lady Alice b 14 June 1988, Lady Lucia b 1993); *Heir* s, Lord Loughborough; *Career* Met Police 1980–94, Thames Valley Police 1994–2000; Met Police: cdr 2000–03, head Royalty and Diplomatic Protection Dept 2003–14; master of the household to TRH The Prince of Wales and the Duchess of Cornwall 2014–; tstee Dunimarle Museum; Commandeur de la Legion d'Honneur 2014; *Clubs* White's; *Style—* The Rt Hon the Earl of Rosslyn, CVO, QPM

ROSSOR, Prof Martin Neil; s of late Harry Bruce Rossor, and late Eileen, *née* Curry; *b* 24 April 1950; *Educ* Watford GS, Jesus Coll Cambridge (MA, MD, Ralph Horton-Smith Prize), KCH Med Sch London (MB BChir); *m* 5 July 1973, Eve Beatrix, da of Prof Kurt Lipstein, of Cambridge; 2 s (Alexander b 28 Aug 1979, Thomas b 20 July 1981), 1 da (Charlotte b 31 July 1984); *Career* house offr in gen med KCH and house offr in gen surgery The Brook Hosp London 1974–75, SHO in gen med Bart's 1975–76, SHO in thoracic med The Brompton Hosp 1976–77, SHO in neurology Nat Hosp for Nervous Diseases London 1977–78, registrar in clinical pharmacology and gen med Royal Postgrad Med Sch and Hammersmith Hosp London 1978, clinical scientist MRC Neurochemical Pharmacology Unit and hon registrar in neurology Addenbrooke's Hosp Cambridge 1979–82, sr registrar in neurology Nat Hosp for Neurology and Neurosurgery London 1983–86 (registrar in neurology 1982–83), conslt neurologist to The Nat Hosps for Neurology and Neurosurgery, St Mary's Hosp and the Western Ophthalmic Hosp London 1986–, sr lectr Inst of Neurology London 1992–98, clinical dir for neurology Nat Hosp for Neurology and Neurosurgery 1993–98 (prof of clinical neurology 1998–); dir UK Clinical Research Network for Dementia and Neurodegenerative Diseases (DeNDRoN) 2005–14, nat dir for dementia research NIHR, dir NIHR Queen Square Dementia Biomedical Research Unit; memb Med Advsy Panel Alzheimer Disease Soc 1986–2000; ed Jl of Neurology, Neurosurgery and Psychiatry, Euro ed Alzheimer's Disease and Associated Orders 1992–2001, memb Editorial Bd Euro Jl of Neurology 1994–97; memb: Assoc of Br Neurologists (memb Cncl 1993–96, pres 2011–13), RCPsych (affiliate), RSM, World Fedn of Neurology Dementia (memb Exec Ctee), Dementia Panel Euro Fedn of Neurological Socs (chm 1994–2000); patron Dementia Relief Tst; vice-pres Alzheimer Soc 2001–; Freeman City of London, Liveryman Worshipful Soc of Apothecaries (memb Ct of Assts 1999–); FRCP 1990, FMedSci 2002; *Books* Unusual Dementias (ed, 1992), The Dementias (ed with Prof Growdon, 1998 and 2007), Neurology A Queen Square Textbook (ed with Clarke, Howard and Shorvon); also author of numerous book chapters and original papers on Alzheimer's disease and related dementias; *Recreations* English literature, sailing, equestrian sports; *Clubs* Athenaeum; *Style—* Prof Martin Rossor; ✉ National Hospital for Neurology and Neurosurgery, Queen Square, London WC1N 3BG (☎ 020 3448 3798, fax 020 3448 3104, e-mail m.rossor@ucl.ac.uk)

ROSTRON, Chad Kenneth; s of Kenneth William Briggs Rostron, and Rosemary Rostron; *b* 6 May 1951; *Educ* Sherborne, Univ of Newcastle upon Tyne (MB BS); *Career* conslt ophthalmologist St George's Hosp 1988, hon sr lectr Univ of London 1988; author of pubns on corneal and kerato-refractive surgery; DO 1979; memb RSM; FRCS 1983, FRCOphth 1989; *Style—* Chad Rostron, Esq; ✉ Arnott Eye Associates, 22a Harley Street, London W1G 9BP (☎ 020 7580 1074, e-mail rostron@doctors.org.uk, website www.chadrostron.co.uk)

ROSWALD, Ann-Louise; da of Björn Thomas Roswald, of Scarborough, N Yorks, and Judith Elizabeth Holt, *née* Gullen; *b* 26 May 1974; *Educ* Pindar Sch Scarborough, Scarborough Sixth Form Coll, York Coll of Further and Higher Educn, Central St Martins (BA, Grad Fashion Week Award 1997); *m* 19 June 1999, Nicholas Gerard Hartley, s of Keith Hartley; 1 s (Harry Fitz b 1 July 2007); *Career* fashion designer; dir and head designer Ann-Louise Roswald; exhibited London Fashion Week; catwalk shows: NY 2000, Korea 2001, Hong Kong 2002, Singapore 2003; featured in pubns incl: Vogue, Elle Decoration, Harpers & Queen; Marks and Spencer New Generation Award 1998 and 1999; Ann Louise Roswald Bridal Wear launched 2007; design collaborations incl: Love Rosa (with high street retailer Oasis) 2004–, Lou Lou and Law (with Natasha Law) 2006–, Ann Louise Roswald for Evans Swimwear and Resort collection, Lavender Tst Charity T-shirt design donation; supporter of numerous charities incl Gilda's Club and Breast Cancer Research;

memb Ctee My Favourite Dress Ball; *Recreations* photography, painting, walking, cycling, running, skiing, fishing, theatre and cinema; *Style—* Ms Ann-Louise Roswald; ✉ Moorgate Lees Farm, Hawsker, Whitby, North Yorkshire YO22 4JU (e-mail info@annlouiseroswald.com)

ROTH, Hon Mr Justice; Sir Peter Marcel Roth; kt (2009), QC (1997); s of Dr Stephen J Roth (d 1995), and Eva Marta, *née* Gondos; *b* 19 December 1952; *Educ* St Paul's (head boy), New Coll Oxford (open scholar, MA), Univ of Pennsylvania Law Sch (Thouron fell, LLM); *m* 2010, Tessa Margaret Fras; 1 da (Emily Eva); *Career* called to the Bar Middle Temple 1977 (Harmsworth scholar, bencher); recorder 2000, dep judge High Ct 2008, judge High Ct 2009–, pres Competition Appeal Tbnl 2013–; visiting assoc prof Univ of Pennsylvania Law Sch 1987, visiting prof KCL 2003–09; vice-pres Pennsylvania Law European Soc 1995–2003, chair Competition Law Assoc 2003–09, chair Lawyers Advsy Ctee Peach Brigades Int (UK) 2007–; tstee Br Inst of Int and Comparative Law 2006–08; govr Tel Aviv Univ 2006–10; *Publications* Bellamy & Child's European Community Law of Competition (jt ed, 2008); numerous articles in legal pubns; *Recreations* travel, music; *Style—* The Hon Mr Justice Roth

ROTH, Tim Simon; s of Ernie Roth (*né* Smith), and Ann Roth; *b* 14 May 1961, London; *Educ* Dick Shepherd Comp Sch Tulse Hill, Strand Comp Sch Brixton, Camberwell Sch of Art; *Family* 1 s (Jack b 1985) with Lori Baker; m 1993, Nikki Butler; 2 s (Timothy Hunter b 1995, Michael Cormac b 1996); *Career* actor; *Television* incl: Meantime 1981, Made in Britain 1982, Metamorphosis 1987, Common Pursuit 1992, Murder in the Heartland 1993, Heart of Darkness 1994, Tsunami: The Aftermath 2006, Lie To Me 2009–, Skellig 2009; *Film* incl: The Hit 1984 (BAFTA nomination, Evening Standard Best Newcomer), To Kill a Priest 1988, The Cook, The Thief, His Wife and Her Lover 1989, Vincent and Theo 1990, Rosencrantz and Guildenstern are Dead 1990, Reservoir Dogs 1992, The Perfect Husband 1993, Little Odessa 1994, Captives 1994, Pulp Fiction 1994, Four Rooms 1994, Rob Roy 1995 (Oscar nomination, BAFTA winner, Golden Globe nomination), Everyone Says I Love You 1996, Mocking the Cosmos 1996, Liar 1997, Animals 1997, No Way Home 1997, Gridlock'd 1997, Hoodlum 1997, The Legend of 1900 1998, The War Zone (dir) 1999, Vatel 2000, Lucky Numbers 2000, Invincible 2001, Planet of the Apes 2001, The Musketeer 2001, To Kill a King 2003, Silver City 2004, Nouvelle-France 2004, Don't Come Knocking 2005, Dark Water 2005, Funny Games 2007, Youth Without Youth 2007, The Incredible Hulk 2008; *Style—* Tim Roth, Esq; ✉ c/o Staci Wolfe, Polaris PR, 8135 West Fourth Street, 2nd Floor, Los Angeles, USA

ROTHENBERG, Robert Michael (Bob); MBE (2007); s of Helmut Rothenberg, OBE (d 2003), and Anna Amalia, *née* Hannes (d 1991); *b* 10 August 1950; *Educ* Highgate Sch, Univ of Exeter (BA); *m* 10 July 1981, Philippa Jane, da of Stephen Fraser White, of Great Doddington, Northants; 2 da (Katie b 1982, Joanna b 1987), 1 s (Simon b 1983); *Career* chartered accountant 1975–; ptnr Blick Rothenberg LLP Chartered Accountants 1979– (sr ptnr 1997–), dir Gatton Consulting Group Ltd 1987–92, lectr to professional audiences on taxation and co law 1981–; dir Think London 1997–2009, dir easyJet plc 2009–10, dir London First 2012– (treas 2013–); tstee Prince's Fndn for Building Community 2004–13, memb Regent's Park Theatre Devpt Cncl 2010–12, tstee Mayor's Music Fund 2011–, tstee Police Now 2016–; govr Highgate Sch 1998–; hon treas Camden CAB 1982–87; FCA, CTA, MAE; *Books* Mastering Business Information Technology (1989), Understanding Company Accounts (4 edn, 1995); *Recreations* travel, skiing, opera, theatre; *Clubs* Garrick, MCC; *Style—* Bob Rothenberg, Esq, MBE; ✉ 74 Hillway, Highgate, London N6 6DP (☎ 020 8348 7771, e-mail bob@rothenberg.co.uk); Blick Rothenberg LLP, 16 Great Queen Street, Covent Garden, London WC2B 5AH (☎ 020 7486 0111, e-mail bob.rothenberg@blickrothenberg.com, website www.blickrothenberg.com)

ROTHERHAM, Miles Edward; s of Leonard Rotherham, CBE, of Horningsham, Wilts, and Nora Mary, *née* Thompson (d 1991); *b* 23 November 1941; *Educ* Dulwich Coll, Christ's Coll Cambridge (BA, MA); *m* 8 April 1972, Anne Jennifer, da of Maj Alan Holier James, TD, DL (d 1983), of Northlands, Winterton, South Humberside; 1 s (James b 1976), 1 da (Joanna b 1978); *Career* tech offr Inco 1964–68, sales mangr Int Nickel 1968–78; dir: Amari World Metals 1978–, Br Petroleum Metals Marketing 1979–89, Olympic Dam Marketing 1989–93; chm Miles Metals Ltd 1993–; friend of Battersea Park; Freeman City of London 1978, Liveryman Worshipful Co of Goldsmiths 1981; CEng 1979, FIM 1979; *Recreations* antique collecting, boules; *Clubs* Athenaeum; *Style—* Miles Rotherham, Esq; ✉ 13 Soudan Road, London SW11 4HH

ROTHERMERE, 4 Viscount (UK 1919) Jonathan Harold Esmond Vere Harmsworth; 4 Bt (UK 1910); also Baron Rothermere (UK 1914); patron of three livings; s of 3 Viscount Rothermere (d 1998), and his 1 wife, Patricia Evelyn Beverley, *née* Matthews (d 1992); *b* 3 December 1967; *m* 15 July 1993, Claudia Caroline, da of T J and Patricia Clemence, of London; 2 s (Hon Vere Richard Jonathan Harold Harmsworth b 20 Oct 1994, Hon Alfred Northcliffe St John Harmsworth b 20 May 2010), 3 da (Hon Eleanor Patricia Margaret Harmsworth b 17 Oct 1996, Hon Theodora Mairi Ferne Harmsworth b 9 July 2001, Hon Iris Geraldine Lilian Harmsworth b 6 Jan 2004); *Career* md: Courier Printing and Publishing until 1997, Evening Standard 1997–98; chm Daily Mail and General Tst plc 1998–; *Style—* The Rt Hon the Viscount Rothermere; ✉ Daily Mail and General Trust plc, Northcliffe House, 2 Derry Street, London W8 5TT

ROTHEROE, Dominic Peter Alford (Dom); s of John William Rotheroe, of Gubblecote, Herts, and Jacqueline Patricia *née* Fearn; *b* 24 April 1964; *Educ* Aylesbury GS, Harrow Coll of HE (BA); *m* 1, 1983 (m dis 1987), Nataa, *née* Lueti?; m 2, 1994 (m dis 1996), Maja *née* Bogojevi?; *Career* writer and film dir; *Documentaries* dir and ed A Sarajevo Diary 1993 (nomination BAFTA Flaherty Award, special commendation Prix Europa), cameraman and ed Shadows on the Street 1996, cameraman and shoot dir Blockade 1996, dir and cameraman We Can Rebuild You 2000, writer, dir and cameraman The Coconut Revolution 2000 (Grand Prize FICA Film Festival Brazil 2001, Richard Keefe Meml Award Br Environmental Media Awards 2001, Silver Kite and Grand Prix Mar Del Plata Film Festival Argentina 2001), dir various documentaries Al Jazeera Int 2006–07; *Films* writer and dir My Brother Tom 2001 (Golden Rose Sochi Int Film Festival 2001, Best Debut St Petersburg Film Festival 2001, Herald Angel Award Edinburgh Film Festival 2001, Studio Bruxelles Award Flanders Film Festival 2001, Prix du Public Angers Premiersplans Film Festival France 2002, Artistic Contrib and Youth Jury Award Verona Film Festival 2002, Jury Prize Chatenay-Malabry Festival 2002), writer and dir Exhibit A 2006; *Publications* London Inn Signs (author and photographer, 1987); author of articles in various publications; *Recreations* films, music, literature, travel; *Style—* Dom Rotheroe, Esq

ROTHERWICK, 3 Baron (UK 1939); Sir (Herbert) Robin Cayzer; 3 Bt (UK 1924); eld s of 2 Baron Rotherwick (d 1996), and Sarah Jane, *née* Slade (d 1978); *b* 12 March 1954; *Educ* Harrow, RMAS, RAC Cirencester; *m* 1, 1982 (m dis 1994), Sara Jane M, o da of Robert James McAlpine, of Tilstone Fearnall, Cheshire, and late Mrs J McAlpine; 1 da (Hon Harriette Jane b 1986), 2 s (Hon Herbert Robin b 1989, Hon Henry Alexander b 1991); m 2, 2000, Tania Jane, o da of Christopher Fox and Jenny Atkinson; 1 s (Hon August Inigo b 2000, Hon Tommy Christopher b and d 2003), 1 da (Hon Clementine Eleanor b 2006); *Heir* s, Hon Herbert Cayzer; *Career* late The Life Guards; elected memb House of Lords 1999–, oppn spokesperson and whip 2001–05; memb Cncl of Europe 2000–01; dir: Cayzer Continuation PCC Ltd 2004–, Air Touring Ltd 2006–10, Cornbury Estates Co Ltd 2006–, Cornbury Maintenance Co Ltd 2012–; pres Gen Aviation Awareness Cncl (GAAC), dir PFA (Ulair) Ltd 1999–2003, dir Light Aviation Assoc (LLA) 2008–; *Recreations* aviation, sub-aqua, conservation; *Clubs* White's; *Style—* The Lord Rotherwick; ✉ Cornbury Park, Charlbury, Oxfordshire OX7 3EH (e-mail rr@cpark.co.uk)

ROTHSCHILD, Hon Emma Georgina; CMG (2000); da of 3 Baron Rothschild, GBE, GM, FRS (d 1990), and his 2 w, Teresa Georgina, MBE, JP, *née* Mayor; *b* 16 May 1948; *Educ* Somerville Coll Oxford (MA), MIT; *m* 1991, Prof Amartya Kumar Sen; *Career* MIT: assoc prof of humanities 1978–80, assoc prof of science technol and society 1979–88; directeur de recherche invité École des Hautes Études en Sciences Sociales Paris 1981–82, sr res fell King's Coll Cambridge 1988–96, dir Centre for History and Economics and fell King's Coll Cambridge 1996–; memb OECD Gp of Experts on Science and Technology in the New Socio-Economic Context 1976–80, OECD sci examiner Australia 1984–85; chm: UN Res Inst for Social Devpt 1999–, Rothschild Archive Tst 1999–, Kennedy Memorial Tst 2000–; memb: Governing Bd Stockholm Int Peace Res Inst 1983–93, Bd Olof Palme Meml Fund Stockholm 1986–, Royal Cmmn on Environmental Pollution 1986–93, Bd British Council 1993–, Bd UN Fndn 1998–, Cncl for Sci and Technol 1998–2001; *Books* Paradise Lost: the Decline of the Auto-Industrial Age (1973), Economic Sentiments (2001); author of articles in jls; *Style—* The Hon Emma Rothschild, CMG; ✉ King's College, Cambridge CB2 1ST

ROTHSCHILD, 4 Baron (UK 1885) Nathaniel Charles Jacob Rothschild; 5 Bt (UK 1847), OM (2002), GBE (1998); s of 3 Baron Rothschild, GBE, GM, FRS (d 1990), and his 1 w, Barbara, o da of late St John Hutchinson, KC; *b* 29 April 1936; *Educ* Eton, ChCh Oxford (BA); *m* 1961, Serena Mary, da of Sir Philip Dunn, 2 Bt, and Lady Mary St Clair-Erskine, da of 5 Earl of Rosslyn; 3 da (Hon Hannah Mary b 1962, Hon Beth Matilda b 1964, Hon Emily Magda b 1967), 1 s (Hon Nathaniel Philip Victor James b 1971); *Heir* s, Hon Nathaniel Rothschild; *Career* chm: Five Arrows Ltd 1980–2010 (pres 2010–), RIT Capital Partners, J Rothschild & Co Ltd; non-exec dep chm British Sky Broadcasting Gp plc 2003–08; chm Bd of Tstees: Nat Gallery 1985–91, National Heritage Meml Fund 1992–98, National Heritage Lottery Fund 1994–98, Gilbert Collection Tst 1998–2006, Hermitage Rooms at Somerset House 1999–2006; Hon DLitt Univ of Newcastle upon Tyne 1998, Hon LLD Univ of Exeter 1998, Hon Dr Univ of Keele 2000, Hon DCL Univ of Oxford 2002, Hon DLitt Univ of Warwick 2003, Hon DSc Univ of London 2004, hon student ChCh Oxford 2006; Hon FBA 1998, Hon FRIBA 1998, Hon FRAM 2002, FKC 2002; Cdr Order of Henry the Navigator (Portugal) 1985; hon fell City of Jerusalem 1992, PhD Hebrew Univ of Jerusalem of Jerusalem 1992, Weizmann Award for Humanities and Science 1997; fell Ashmolean Museum Oxford 2006; *Style—* The Rt Hon the Lord Rothschild, OM, GBE; ✉ 14 St James's Place, London SW1A 1NP (☎ 020 7493 8111); The Dairy Queen Street, Waddesdon, Aylesbury, Buckinghamshire HP18 0JW (☎ 01296 653235)

ROTHWELL, Prof Dame Nancy Jane; DBE (2005), DL (Gtr Manchester 2010); *Educ* Univ of London (BSc, PhD, DSc); *Career* Univ of Manchester: prof of physiology 1994, chm Div of Neuroscience 1998–2000, currently pres and vice-chllr and prof of physiology; pres British Neuroscience Assoc 2000–04, chair Research Defence Soc 2004–07, memb Cncl Acad of Med Sciences 2002–05, chair AZ Bd Science Ctee 2007–15, memb Gtr Manchester Local Enterprise Partnership Bd 2011–, co-chair Cncl for Science and Technol 2012–; tstee: NESTA 2002–05, CRUK 2002–07; non-exec dir AstraZeneca plc 2006–15; columnist Times Higher Educn Supplement 2004–06; delivered Royal Instn Christmas Lectures 1998, Pfizer Award for Innovative Science 2003; memb Cncl RS 2013–16; FMedSci 2000, FRS 2004; *Style—* Prof Dame Nancy Rothwell, DBE, DL; ✉ The University of Manchester, Oxford Road, Manchester M13 9PL

ROTHWELL, Peter Francis; s of Prof William Rothwell, and Margaret, *née* Meehan; *b* 13 September 1959; *Educ* Manchester Grammar, St Edmund Hall Oxford (MA); *m* Sara Anne, da of Prof G Randell; 1 da (Emily Laura b 1 Jan 1985); *Career* Thomson Holidays 1982–88 (joined as grad trainee, successively mktg asst, mktg exec, product mangr, mktg mangr), dir for Europe Jetset International 1988, gen mangr Thomson Worldwide and Citibreaks April-Aug 1989, mktg dir Lunn Poly Ltd Aug 1989–93, purchasing dir Thomson Tour Operations Ltd 1993–94, md Airtours Holidays 1995–2001, chief exec Thomson Holidays (TUI Northern Europe) 2001–06, md TUI UK 2004–06, chief operating offr TUI AG Tourism 2006–07, dep ceo TUI Travel plc 2007–09, ceo Kuoni Travel Hldg Ltd 2009–; MCIM 1989; *Recreations* skiing, squash, sailing; *Style—* Peter Rothwell, Esq

ROTTER, Prof (John) Michael; s of late Godfrey Cyril John Rotter, and late Gwendoline May Rotter; *b* 31 October 1948, Chesterfield, Derbys; *Educ* Clare Coll Cambridge (MA), Univ of Sydney (PhD); *Children* 1 s (Benedict Edward Godfrey b 1979), 1 da (Rebecca Victoria Elizabeth b 1981); *Career* lectr then sr lectr Univ of Sydney 1975–89, prof of civil engrg Univ of Edinburgh 1989– (head of dept 1989–92, head of div 1992–99); visiting prof (première classe) INSA Lyon 1996, 2000 & 2010 and (classe exceptionelle) 2012–13; visiting prof: Tech Univ Graz 1997, 2001 and 2005, Tech Univ Vienna 2000; author of five books and over 450 pubns in jls and confs; CEng, FIE(Aust) 1987, FICE 1996, FREng 2004, FRSE 2005, FASCE 2007, FIStructE 2007; *Publications* Structural Design of Steel Bins for Bulk Solids (jtly, 1983), Design of Steel Bins for the Storage of Bulk Solids (ed, 1985), Guidelines for the Assessment of Loads on Bulk Solids Containers (jt ed, 1986), Guide for the Economic Design of Circular Metal Silos (2001), Stability of Steel Shells: European Design Recommendations (jt ed, 5 edn 2008; 2013); over 450 scientific articles; *Recreations* hill walking, classical music, theatre; *Style—* Prof J Michael Rotter; ✉ 176 Mayfield Road, Edinburgh EH9 3AX (e-mail m.rotter@ed.ac.uk); 6 Montvallet, St Gengoux le National, 71460 France (☎ +33 385938354)

R

ROUCH, Peter Christopher; QC (1996); s of Rupert Trevelyan Rouch (d 1975), and Doris Linda, *née* Hayes (d 1982); *b* 15 June 1947; *Educ* Canton HS Cardiff, UC Wales Aberystwyth (LLB); *m* 1980, Carol Sandra, *née* Francis; 1 s (Robin Benjamin), 1 da (Hannah Jessica); *Career* called to the Bar Gray's Inn 1972, recorder 1992–; *Recreations* skiing, golf, fishing, cinema, reading; *Style—* Peter Rouch, Esq, QC; ✉ 9 Mayals Road, Mayals, Swansea SA3 5BT; 20 Archery Close, London W2 2BE; Apex Chambers, Cardiff CF11 9WB (☎ 02920 232032); 3 Temple Gardens, London EC4Y 9AU (☎ 020 7353 3102)

ROUECHÉ, Mossman (Jr); s of Col Mossman Roueché (d 2003), of Winter Park, Florida, and Elizabeth Molin, *née* Meier (d 2008); *b* 14 December 1947; *Educ* Montgomery Blair HS Maryland, Kenyon Coll Ohio (BA), SUNY Buffalo (MA); *m* 29 July 1972, Charlotte Mary, da of Charles Percy Tunnard Wrinch (d 1999), of Guernsey, CI; 1 da (Alice b 1979), 1 s (Thomas b 1986); *Career* trainee Standard Chartered Bank plc 1973–75, dir Samuel Montagu & Co Ltd (now subsid of HSBC) 1986–96 (joined 1975), md and European head of transaction devpt HSBC Bank plc (formerly HSBC Markets Ltd) 1994–2006, chm Montagu Pension Trustees Ltd 1995–2000; dir HSBC Bank Pension Tst (UK) Ltd 2000–, chm Asset and Liability Ctee 2004–12, chm Appeals and Discretionary Ctee 2012–; memb Advsy Cncl Warburg Inst Univ of London 2005–11, memb Finance and General Purposes Ctee Br Sch at Athens 2013–; tstee Lambeth Palace Library 2005–; *Recreations* travel, Byzantine philosophy; *Style—* Mossman Roueché, Esq; ✉ HSBC Bank plc, Level 27, 8 Canada Square, London E14 5HQ

ROUGHEAD, Malcolm; OBE (2005); *Educ* Univ of Glasgow; *Career* global sales and mktg dir Guinness World Records until 2001; VisitScotland: dir of mktg 2001–10, chief exec 2010–; *Style—* Malcolm Roughead, Esq, OBE; ✉ VisitScotland, Ocean Point One, 94 Ocean Drive, Edinburgh EH6 6JH

ROUND, Prof Nicholas Grenville; s of Isaac Eric Round, and Laura Christabel, *née* Poole; *b* 6 June 1938; *Educ* Launceston Coll, Pembroke Coll Oxford (MA, DPhil); *m* 2 April 1966, Ann, da of Louis Le Vin; 1 da (Grainne Ann b 1968); *Career* Queen's Univ Belfast: lectr in Spanish 1962–71, warden Alanbrooke Hall 1970–72, reader in Spanish 1971–72;

Stevenson prof of hispanic studies Univ of Glasgow 1972–94, Hughes prof of Spanish Univ of Sheffield 1994–2003 (emeritus prof 2003–); former exec memb and vice-chm Clydebank/Milngavie Constituency Lab Pty, chair Cornwall Lab Pty 2007–10; former exec memb: Strathclyde West Euro-Constituency Lab Pty, Strathclyde Regnl Lab Pty; pres Assoc Internac de Galdosistas 1999–2001; tstee Morrab Library Penzance 2011–; memb: ALL, MHRA, SSMLL, AHGBI, AIH; MITI 1990, FBA 1996; Oficial de la Orden de Isabel la Católica 1990; *Books* Unamuno: Abel Sánchez (1974), The Greatest Man Uncrowned: A Study of the Fall of Don Alvaro de Luna (1986), Tirso de Molina: Damned for Despair (1986), On Reasoning and Realism (1991), Libro llamado Fedrón (1993), Translation Studies in Hispanic Contexts (ed, 1998), New Galdo's Studies (ed, 2003); *Recreations* music, reading, drawing, hill walking, politics, all aspects of Cornwall; *Clubs* Queen's Univ Belfast Student's Union (hon life memb); *Style*— Prof Nicholas Round, FBA; ✉ 10 King's Road, Penzance, Cornwall TR18 4LG (☎ 01736 362365, e-mail nickround@blue-earth.co.uk)

ROUNDELL, James; s of Charles Wilbraham Roundell, and Ann, *née* Moore; *b* 23 October 1951; *Educ* Winchester, Magdalene Coll Cambridge (MA, Cricket blue); *m* 3 May 1975, Alexandra Jane, da of Sir Cyril Stanley Pickard; 1 s (Thomas b 1979), 1 da (Rebecca b 1982); *Career* Christie's Fine Art Auctioneers: joined 1973, i/c 18th and 19th century English Drawings and Watercolours 1974–76, dir Old Master & Modern Prints 1976–86, dir Impressionist and Modern Pictures 1986–95; proprietor James Roundell Ltd 1995–; dir Simon C Dickinson Ltd 1998–; chm Soc of London Art Dealers 2010–; vice-chm Pictura European Fine Art Fair 2007–; Master Worshipful Co of Grocers 2014 (Freeman 1972, Liveryman 1981, memb Ct of Assts 2009–); *Books* Thomas Shotter Boys (1975); *Recreations* cricket, sailing, opera, golf; *Clubs* Hurlingham, MCC, I Zingari, Bosham Sailing, various cricket clubs; *Style*— James Roundell, Esq; ✉ James Roundell Limited, 58 Jermyn Street, London SW1Y 6LX

ROURKE, Josie; da of Sean Joseph Rourke, and Vivienne Imelda, *née* Perrin; *b* 3 September 1976, Salford, Gtr Manchester; *Educ* St Patrick's RC HS Eccles, Eccles Coll of Further Educn, New Hall Cambridge (BA); *Career* freelance dir; resident trainee dir Donmar Warehouse 2000–01, trainee assoc dir Royal Court Theatre 2002–03, assoc dir Sheffield Theatres 2005–06, artistic dir Bush Theatre 2007–11, artistic dir Donmar Warehouse 2012–; non-exec dir Channel 4; *Style*— Ms Josie Rourke; ✉ c/o Fay Davies, The Agency (London) Ltd, 24 Pottery Lane, Holland Park, London W11 4LZ

ROUSE, Anne Barrett; da of William Dashiell Rouse, of Atlantic, Virginia, and Florence Irene, *née* Munson; *b* 26 September 1954; *Educ* W Springfield HS, Shimer Coll Ill, Bedford Coll London (BA); *Career* Islington MIND: employment worker 1988–91, dir 1991–94; state registered nurse 1982, registered mental nurse 1984; author of articles in The Independent and The Washington Post; poems published in: The Observer, TLS, New Statesman, London Review of Books, London Magazine, Atlantic Monthly; Hawthornden fell 1999, Royal Literary Fund writing fell Univ of Glasgow 2000–02; *Poetry* Sunset Grill (1993), Timing (1997); anthologies incl: New Women Poets (ed Carol Rumens, 1990), The Firebox (ed Sean O'Brien, 2000), The School of Night (2004); *Style*— Ms Anne Rouse; ✉ Bloodaxe Books, PO Box 1SN, Newcastle upon Tyne NE99 1SN (e-mail rouseanne@hotmail.com)

ROUSE, Jon; s of James Clement Rouse, of Kettering, Northants, and Barbara Jean, *née* Fowler; *b* 23 May 1968; *Educ* Latimer Sch Kettering, Univ of Manchester (LLB), Univ of N London (MA), Univ of Nottingham (MBA); *m* 13 July 1991, Heulwen Mary, *née* Evans; *Career* private sec to min for Housing 1994–95, policy and communications mangr English Partnerships 1995–98, sec Govt Urban Task Force 1998–99, chief exec CABE 2000–04, chief exec Housing Corp 2004–, bd dir English Partnerships 2004–; FA qualified referee 2004–; Hon DUniv Oxford Brookes; Hon FRIBA 2001, Hon MRTPI 2002; *Recreations* tennis, hiking, French cinema; *Clubs* Queens Park Rangers FC, Nottingham Ambassadors; *Style*— Jon Rouse, Esq; ✉ The Housing Corporation, Maple House, 149 Tottenham Court Road, London W1T 7BN

ROUSE, Justin Clive Douglas; QC (2015); s of Malcolm Rouse, of Bonchurch, IOW; *b* 21 May 1958, Horndean, Hants; *Educ* Ryde Sch, univ in London (BA), Inns of Court Law Sch; *m* 9 Dec 1989, Hilary, *née* Brader; 4 da (Camilla, Elizabeth b 15 March 1991 (twins), Josephine b 29 Feb 1992, Claudia b 19 May 1994 (twin)), 1 s (Maximilian b 19 May 1994 (twin)); *Career* called to the Bar 1982; recorder of the Crown Court 2005; memb Criminal Bar Assoc; winner Denning Cup for advocacy 1980; *Recreations* gardening, skiing, travel, countryside issues, fishing; *Clubs* Amersham and Chiltern Rugby; *Style*— Justin Rouse, Esq, QC; ✉ 9 Bedford Row, London WC1R 4BU (chambers); (☎ 020 7489 2727)

ROUSE, Lucy Jane; da of Julian Spencer Rouse, of Brighton, East Sussex, and Pauline Ann Rouse (d 2007); *b* 3 June 1971; *Educ* Tunbridge Wells Girls' GS, Univ of York (BA, news ed Vision), Birkbeck Coll London (MA); *Children* 2 da (Charlotte Eve Henrietta Perry b 2002, Honor Beatrice Olivia Perry b 2004); *Career* journalist; with Government Group Publications 1992–95 (rising to ed Government Purchasing); Emap: dep ed M&M Europe 1995–97, assoc ed Mediaweek 1997–98, dep ed TV World 1998–99, features ed then ed Broadcast 1999–2002, sr ed Broadcast 2002–03; freelance journalist 2003–12 (incl for: Broadcast, Media Guardian and Sunday Times); communications mangr Salisbury Festival 2012–; memb Broadcasting Press Guild; *Recreations* walking, reading, gardening, theatre and cinema; *Style*— Ms Lucy Rouse; ✉ mobile 07974 238386, e-mail rouse_lucy@hotmail.com and lucy@salisburyfestival.co.uk

ROUSSEAU, Prof George Sebastian; s of Hyman Victoire Rousseau (d 1993), of NYC, and Esther, *née* Zacuto (d 2005); *b* 23 February 1941, NYC; *Educ* Amherst Coll USA (BA), Princeton Univ USA (MA, PhD); *Career* Osgood fell in Eng lit then Woodrow Wilson dissertation fell Princeton Univ 1965–66, instr and asst prof Harvard Univ 1966–68, asst prof then assoc prof UCLA 1968–69, German state lectr W Germany univs 1970, hon fell Wolfson Coll Cambridge 1974–75, prof of Eng and eighteenth century studies UCLA 1976–93, Regius Chalmers prof of Eng Univ of Aberdeen 1994–98, research prof of humanities De Montfort Univ 1999–2002, prof Modern History Research Unit Univ of Oxford 2002–08; co-dir Centre for the History of Childhood Univ of Oxford, permanent memb Workgroup for Literature and Science Univ of Bergen Norway, Bd memb Edinburgh Univ Project for the History of Distributed Cognition 2015–18; overseas fell Univ of Cambridge 1979, visiting fell commoner Trinity Coll Cambridge 1982, sr Fulbright research scholar Sir Thomas Browne Inst The Netherlands 1983, visiting exchange prof King's Coll Cambridge 1984, Clark Library prof Univ of California 1985–86, sr fell Nat Endowment for the Humanities 1986–87, Nat Endowment for the Humanities and Westfield Center lectr National Mozart Symposium 1990–91, visiting fell Magdalen Coll Oxford 1993–94, sr US Fulbright prof Univ of Lausanne Switzerland 1994, visiting professorial fell New Coll and Merton Coll Oxford 1999, SAMKUL visiting prof of the humanities Univ of Bergen Noway 2016–20; chm Inst Memberships and prog chm annual meeting American Soc for Eighteenth Century Studies 1971–72, pres Western Soc for Eighteenth Century Studies 1985–86, chm and tstee Soc for Lit and Sci 1985–92; delg Museums, Libraries and Archives Cncl (MLA) Assembly 1971–74; memb Exec Ctee: Div on Lit and Sci MLA 1985–89, Div on Comparative Studies in Eighteenth Century Lit 1989–92; book reviewer NY Sunday Times 1967–; Louis Gottshalk Prize American Soc for Eighteenth Century Studies 1987; memb History of Science Soc 1966; Dr (hc) Univ of Bucharest 2007; FRSM 1967, fell American Cncl of Learned Socs 1970, FRSA 1973; *Books* This Long Disease My Life: Alexander Pope and the Sciences (co-author, 1968), English Poetic Satire (co-author, 1969), The Augustan Milieu: Essays Presented to Louis A Landa (jt ed, 1970), Tobias Smollett: Bicentennial Essays Presented to Lewis M Knapp (jt ed, 1971), Organic Form: The Life of an Idea (ed, 1972), Goldsmith: The Critical Heritage (1974), The Ferment of Knowledge: Studies in the Historiography of Science (1980), The Letters and Private Papers of Sir John Hill (1981), Tobias Smollett: Essays of Two Decades (1982), Science and Imagination: The Berkeley Conference (ed, 1987), Sexual Underworlds of the Enlightenment (co-author, 1987), The Enduring Legacy: Alexander Pope Tercentenary Essays (co-author, 1988), Exoticism in the Enlightenment (co-author, 1990), The Languages of Psyche: Mind and Body in Enlightenment Thought (1990), Perilous Enlightenment: Pre- and Post-Modern Discourses: Sexual, Historical (1991), Enlightenment Crossings: Pre- and Post-Modern Discourses: Anthropological (1991), Enlightenment Borders: Pre- and Post-Modern Discourses: Medical, Scientific (1991), Hysteria Before Freud (co-author, 1993), Gout: The Patrician Malady (co-author, 1998), Framing and Imagining Disease (2003), Marguerite Yourcenar: Life and Times (2004), Nervous Acts: Essays on Literature and Culture (2005), Children and Sexuality: The Greeks to The Great War (ed, 2007), The Notorious Sir John Hill: The Man Destroyed by Ambition in the Era of Celebrity (2012), Rachmaninoff's Cape: A Nostalgia Memoir (2015); 200 scholarly articles, papers and chapters, and frequent commentary in newspapers and discussions; *Recreations* chamber music, hillside walking, gardening; *Style*— Prof George Rousseau; ✉ c/o Jonathan Pegg Literary Agency, ☎ 02076 036830, e-mail info@jonathanpegg.com

ROUTLEDGE, (Katherine) Patricia; CBE (2004, OBE 1993); da of Isaac Edgar Routledge (d 1985), of Birkenhead, Cheshire, and Catherine, *née* Perry (d 1957); *b* 17 February 1929; *Educ* Birkenhead HS, Univ of Liverpool (BA); *Career* actress and singer; trained Bristol Old Vic Theatre Sch and with Walther Gruner Guildhall Sch of Music; Top TV Comedy Actress Award 1991, Grand Order of Water Rats Award 1991, Variety Club of GB Award 1993, BBC 60th Anniversary Award 1996; Hon DLitt: Univ of Liverpool 1999, Univ of Lancaster 2008; *Theatre* first professional appearance as Hippolyta in A Midsummer Night's Dream (Liverpool Playhouse) 1952, first West End appearance in Sheridan's The Duenna (Westminster Theatre) 1954, first Broadway appearance in How's the World Treating You? (Music Box NY) 1966 (Whitbread Award 1966), Darling of the Day (Broadway) 1968 (Antoinette Perry Award 1968), Love Match (Ahmanson Theatre Los Angeles) 1968–69, Cowardy Custard (Mermaid Theatre) 1972–73, Noises Off (Savoy Theatre) 1981, Mistress Quickly in Henry V, Queen Margaret in Richard III (RSC (Olivier Award Nomination)) 1984–85, The Old Lady in Candide (Old Vic) 1988–89 (Olivier Award 1989), Come for the Ride (solo show) 1988 and (tour) 1989, Carousel (RNT) 1993, The Rivals (Chichester) 1994, Beatrix (Chichester and tour) 1996, The Importance of Being Earnest (Chichester, Theatre Royal, Australian tour and Savoy Theatre) 1999–2001, Wild Orchids (Chichester) 2002, The Solid Gold Cadillac (Garrick Theatre) 2004, The Best of Friends (Hampstead and tour) 2006, Facing the Music (Menier Chocolate Factory) 2006 and (nat tour) 2007–14, Office Suite (Chichester and tour) 2007, Crown Matrimonial (Guildford and tour) 2008, Admission: One Shilling (Nat Gallery) 2009, (nat tour) 2010–14 and (Australian tour) 2014, An Ideal Husband (Chichester) 2014; *Television* incl: Sophia and Constance, A Woman of No Importance 1982 (Broadcasting Press Guild Critics Award), A Lady of Letters 1988 (BAFTA Nomination), First and Last, Missing Persons, Victoria Wood – As Seen on TV, Talking Heads (BBC, also staged Comedy Theatre) 1992, Hildegard of Bingen (BBC) 1994, Keeping Up Appearances (BBC) 1990–95, lead role in Hetty Wainthropp Investigates (BBC) 1995–98, Anybody's Nightmare (Carlton) 2001, The Brontës (BBC) 2003; *Clubs* Sloane; *Style*— Miss Patricia Routledge, CBE; ✉ 6 King George Gardens, Chichester, West Sussex, PO19 6LB

ROUX, Alain; s of Michel Roux, OBE, *qv*, and Françoise Marcelle, *née* Becquet (d 2004); *b* 27 March 1968, London; *Career* apprentice Pâtisserie Millet Paris 1984–86, commis de cuisine Débutant Restaurant Pic France, commis de cuisine Le Domaine d'Orvault France 1987–88, mil serv as commis de cuisine at Palais de l'Elysée Paris 1988–89, commis de cuisine La Bonne Etape France 1989–90, 1 commis de cuisine tournant Château de Montreuil France 1990, 1 commis de cuisine La Côte Saint-Jacques France 1990–91; The Waterside Inn Berks: demi-chef de partie 1992–95, sous-chef 1995–2000, jt chef patron 2000– (three Michelin stars); master pâtissier Int Assoc Relais et Desserts; *Style*— Alain Roux, Esq; ✉ c/o The Waterside Inn, Ferry Road, Bray, Berkshire SL6 2AT (☎ 01628 771966, fax 01628 789182, e-mail alainroux@btconnect.com)

ROUX, Albert Henri; OBE (2002); s of Henri Roux (d 1983), and Germaine Roux (d 2003); bro of Michel André Roux, *qv*; *b* 8 October 1935; *Educ* Ecole Primaire St Mandé France; *m* 1959, Monique; 1 s (Michel Albert b 1960), 1 da (Danielle b 1965); *Career* French Mil Serv Algeria; fndr (with bro) Le Gavroche Restaurant 1967 (moved to Mayfair 1981), fndr memb Académie Culinaire de Grande Bretagne, chm Chez Roux Ltd; Hon DSc Cncl for Nat Academic Awards 1987; Maitre Cuisinièr de France 1968, Officier du Mérite Agricole 1987 (Chevalier 1975), Chevalier Legion d'Honneur 2005, Knight of the Order of the Crown of Romania (KFO); *Books* with Michel Roux: New Classic Cuisine (1983), The Roux Brothers on Patisserie (1986), The Roux Brothers on French Country Cooking (1989), Cooking For Two (1991); *Recreations* fishing, racing; *Style*— Albert Roux, OBE, KFO; ✉ Chez Roux Ltd, 539 Wandsworth Road, London SW8 3JD

ROUX, Michel Albert; s of Albert Roux, *qv*, and Monique, *née* Merle; *b* 23 May 1960; *Educ* Emanuel Sch London; *m* 20 April 1990, Giselle Francoise, da of late Marcel Malbos; 1 da (Emily Amandine b 8 Feb 1991); *Career* chef; apprenticeship under Maître Patissier Paris 1976–79, trained under Alain Chapel at Mionay 1980–82; mil service Elysée Palace kitchens 1982–83; Boucherie Lamartine Paris 1983, Charcuterie Mothu Paris 1983, sous chef Gavers Restaurant London 1983–84, commis de cuisine Tante Claire London 1984, Mandarin Hotel Hong Kong 1984, Waterside Inn Bray 1985; chef of Roux Restaurants incl: Roux Patisserie, Roux Lamartine, Le Poulbot Brasserie, Le Gamin; chef de cuisine Le Gavroche London 1991– (three Michelin stars); presenter judge MasterChef Professionals (BBC 2) until 2014, presenter Food & Drink (BBC 2) until 2014; memb Traditions et Qualité, memb Relais et Chateaux; fundraiser for VICTA (Visually Impaired Children Taking Action); hon apprenticeship Apprenticeship Ambassadors Network; Maitre Cuisinèr de France 2002; *Awards* The Carlton London Restaurant Awards 1999, The Carlton London Restaurant Awards Laurent Perrier Award of Excellence 2000, The Academy of Food and Wine Services 2000, Restrauteurs Restaurant of the Year Awards 2000, Lifetime Achievement Red Ribbon Family Business Award, Catey Special Award; *Books* Le Gavroche Cookbook (2001), Marathon Chef Cookbook (2002), Matching Food and Wine Cookbook (2005), Vin de Constance Cookbook (2006), A Life in the Kitchen (2009), Cooking with a Masterchef (2010), The French Kitchen (2013); *Recreations* long-distance running, marathons, ultra endurance running, football and rugby fan (keen supporter of Manchester United FC and the Harlequins); *Style*— Michel Roux, Jr; ✉ Le Gavroche, 43 Upper Brook Street, London W1K 7QR (☎ 020 7408 0881, fax 020 7409 0939, e-mail bookings@le-gavroche.com, website www.le-gavroche.co.uk and www.michelroux.co.uk)

ROUX, Michel André; Hon OBE (2002); s of Henri Roux (d 1983), and Germaine, *née* Triger (d 2003); bro of Albert Henri Roux, *qv*; *b* 19 April 1941, Charolles, France; *Educ* Ecole Primaire Saint Mandé France, Brevet de Maîtrise (Pâtisserie); *m* 1 (m dis 1979), Françoise Marcelle, *née* Becquet; 1 s (Alain b 1968), 2 da (Christine b 1963, Françine b 1965); m 2, 21 May 1984, Robyn Margaret, *née* Joyce; *Career* French Mil Serv 1960–62; Versailles 1960, Colomb Béchar Algeria 1961–62, awarded the Médaille Commémorative des Opérations de Securité et de Maintien de l'Ordre en AFC avec Agiape Sahara BOPP no 42; commis pâtissier and cuisiniér at Br Embassy Paris 1955–57, commis cook to Miss Cécile de Rothschild Paris 1957–59 (chef 1962–67); restaurants opened in England: Le

Gavroche 1967, The Waterside Inn 1972 (3 Michelin stars 1985), Le Gavroche (moved to Mayfair) 1981, Roux Britannia 1986; memb: l'Académie Culinaire de France (UK branch), Assoc Relais et Desserts, Assoc Relais et Chateaux; Hon Dr of Culinary Arts Providence RI 2002; *Awards* Silver Medal des Cuisiniers Français (Paris) 1963, Silver Medal Ville de Paris 1966, Silver Medal Sucre Tiré et Soufflé (London) 1970, Prix International Taittinger (2nd, Paris) 1971, Gold Medal Cuisiniers Français (Paris) 1972, Meilleur Ouvrier de France en Pâtisserie (Paris) 1976, Vermeil Medal du Prestige des Cuisiniers Français (Paris) 1983, Lauréat Best Menu of the Year Prepared for a Private Function (Caterer and Hotel Keeper) 1984, Lauréat Restaurateur of the Year (Caterer and Hotel Keeper) 1985, Lauréat du Premier Hommage Veuve Cliquot aux Ambassadeurs de la Cuisine Française dans le Monde (Paris) 1985, Lauréat Personality of the Year Gastronomie dans le Monde (Paris) 1985, Lauréat Culinary Trophy Personality of the Year in Pâtisserie (Assoc of French Pâtissiers de la Saint-Michel) 1986, Chevalier de l'Ordre National du Mérite 1987, Officier du Mérite Agricole 1987, The Man of the Year award (RADAR) 1989, Chevalier de l'Ordre des Arts et des Lettres (France) 1990, Chevalier dans l'Ordre de la Légion d'Honneur 2004, Lifetime Achievement Award London 2006; *Books* New Classic Cuisine (1983), Roux Brothers on Pâtisserie (1986), At Home with the Roux Brothers (1987), French Country Cooking (1989, revised edn 2010), Cooking for Two (1991), Desserts, a Lifelong Passion (1994), Sauces (1996, 2 edn 2009), Life is a Menu (autobiography, 2000), Only the Best (2002), Eggs (2005), Pastry (2008), Sauces, Savoury and Sweet (2009), Desserts (2011), Michel Roux The Collection (2012), The Essence of French Cooking (2014); *Recreations* shooting, walking, skiing; *Style*— Michel Roux, Esq, OBE; ✉ Twitter @michelrouxobe

ROWALLAN, 4 Baron (UK 1911); John Polson Cameron Corbett; s of 3 Baron Rowallan (d 1993), and his 1 w, Eleanor Mary, *née* Boyle; *b* 8 March 1947; *Educ* Eton, RAC Cirencester; *m* 1, 1971 (m dis 1983), (Susan) Jane Dianne Green; 1 s (Hon Jason William Polson Cameron b 1972), 1 da (Hon Joanna Gwyn Alice Cameron b 1974); m 2, 17 April 1984 (m dis 1994), Sandrew Filomena Bryson; 1 s (Hon (Jonathan Arthur) Cameron b 1985), 1 da (Hon Soay Mairi Cameron b 1988); m 3, 1995, Claire Dinning, da of late Robert Laidler; *Heir* s, Hon Jason Corbett; *Career* estate agent; commentator; chm: Diamond Investments Ltd, Scotia Exploration Ltd, Fenwick Eco Park Ltd, Rowallan Renewables Ltd; chm Loch Goin Covenanters Tst; patron Depression Alliance; ARICS; *Recreations* cinema, equestrianism, horse racing, skiing, travel, solar power; *Style*— The Lord Rowallan; ✉ Meiklemosside, Fenwick, Ayrshire KA3 6AY (☎ 01560 600667, e-mail john.rowallan@gmail.com)

ROWAN, David; *b* 8 April 1965, London; *Educ* Haberdashers' Aske's, Gonville & Caius Coll Cambridge (MA); *Career* journalist; trainee journalist The Times 1988–89; launch ed Education and The Editor supplements and ed Comments and Letters, Analysis, Saturday Outlook and Guardian Unlimited The Guardian 1990–2000, writer, broadcaster and conslt ed (incl: launch ed Public Agenda and Career supplements and columnist The Times, media interviewer Evening Standard, contrib Sunday Times Magazine, The Times Magazine, Daily Telegraph Magazine and The Observer) 2001–05, ed Jewish Chronicle 2006–09, ed Wired 2009–; ind filmmaker Channel 4 News; *Style*— David Rowan, Esq; ✉ Wired, Conde Nast Publications Ltd, 1 Hanover Square, London W1R 0AD

ROWBOTHAM, Dr Hugo Dalyson; s of George Frederick Rowbotham (d 1975), and Monica Dalyson, *née* Boyle, of Upton, nr Blewbury, Oxon; *b* 30 March 1942; *Educ* Dragon Sch Oxford, Shrewsbury, King's Coll Durham (MB BS, Hockey colours); *m* 8 Sept 1973, Gloria Geraldine; 1 s (Richard b 23 Jan 1976), 2 da (Louisa b 12 Aug 1980, Emily b 23 Feb 1982); *Career* house surgn and physician Newcastle Gen Hosp 1965–66, ENT sr house offr Royal Victoria Infirmary 1966–67, surgical res asst Royal Marsden Hosp 1968–71, private GP 1971–; visiting med offr: King Edward VII Hosp 1975–, The London Clinic 1975–; memb: BMA, Soc of Occupational Med, Sloane Soc, Chelsea Clinical Soc; *Recreations* hockey; *Clubs* Surbiton Hockey, Llamas Hockey, English Nat Ballet Co (Gold Card memb); *Style*— Dr Hugo Rowbotham; ✉ 11 Cromwell Crescent, London SW5 9QW (☎ 020 7603 6967); 116 Harley Street, London W1G 7JL (☎ 020 7935 4444 or 020 3219 3273, fax 020 7486 3782)

ROWBOTHAM, Dr Thomas Robert (Tom); *b* 9 June 1941; *Educ* Queen's Univ Belfast (BSc, Cross Country capt and blue), Univ of Surrey (MSc), Univ of Nottingham (PhD); *Career* British Telecommunications plc (formerly GPO): exec engr London 1964–68, sr exec engr Microwave Radio Castleton S Wales 1968–74, head Digital Transmission Res Section Martlesham 1974–78, chief of communications R&D Intelsat Washington 1978–80, head Site Servs Div Martlesham 1980–83, head Optical Transmission System Res Div Martlesham 1983–87, gen mangr Network Systems Res Dept Martlesham 1987–89, dir of networks technol Martlesham 1989–93, sr vice-pres Concert (a BT/MCI jt venture) 1993–95, dir of tech strategy BT 1995–2000; chm KCC Ltd 1988–99, chm Teltier Technologies 2001–02, vice-chm Flomerics plc 1999–; dir: Aravox Inc 2000–02, ERA Technologies 2001–, ERA Fndn 2002–; non-exec dir Piping Hot Networks 2000–01; vice-pres int affrs IEEE Communications Soc 1992–93, vice-chm IEE Electronics Divnl Bd 1999, memb IEE Cncl, non-exec dir IEEE Fndn 1998–01, non-exec dir IEEE Inc 2000–01; venture ptnr St Paul Venture Capital 2000–, advsr Carlyle European Venture Partners 2001–; prof (special chair) Univ of Nottingham 1986–89, visiting prof KCL 1993–; Sporting All Ireland Youths Cross Country Championships Winners Medal 1958 and 1959, vice-pres British Telecom Research Football Club; FREng 1992, FIEE; *Books* Communications Systems Analysis (with P B Johns, 1972); *Recreations* marathon running; *Clubs* In & Out; *Style*— Dr Tom R Rowbotham, FREng

ROWE, Anthony; s of late Norman Oliver George Rowe, and Eunice Constance Mary Rowe; *b* 1945, Bristol; *Educ* W of Eng Acad of Art; *Career* artist and designer; scenic artist rising to theatre designer Bristol Old Vic Theatre Co 1971–75, head of design Bristol Old Vic Theatre Sch 1975–95, design co-ordinator RSC 1996–2003, jt dir Number 9 Gallery Winchcombe (with Judy Hill) 2004–; freelance design for opera, ballet and animation; design lectr: Shakespeare Inst, Univ of Birmingham; memb Panel SW Arts 1983–86; *Selected Exhibitions* The Gallery Upstairs Henley-in-Arden, Royal Birmingham Soc of Artists, Venice in Peril (WH Patterson London), Llewellyn Alexander Gallery London, The New English Art Club, The Mall Galleries, D'Arcy Gallery Cheltenham, Montpellier Gallery Stratford-upon-Avon, Affordable Arts fair London, Herbert Gallery Coventry; *Recreations* music, walking; *Style*— Anthony Rowe, Esq; ✉ 4 Corelli Close, Stratford-upon-Avon, Warwickshire CV37 9PU (e-mail anthonyrowe07@gmail.com, website www.anthonyrowe.co.uk)

ROWE, Crispin; s of Peter Whitmill Rowe, of Cranbrook, Kent, and Bridget, *née* Moyle; *b* 28 May 1955, Burton on Trent; *Educ* Bryanston, Univ of Newcastle upon Tyne (BA, PGCE); *m* Aug 1977, Jillian, *née* Highton (d 2008); 2 s (Thomas Patrick b 25 Oct 1981, Benjamin Peter b 16 May 1986), 1 da (Hannah Clare b 7 May 1983); *Career* history teacher: Watford Boys' GS 1978–80, Royal GS Newcastle upon Tyne 1980–92; King Edward's Sch Bath: dep head 1992–2004, headmaster 2004–08; headmaster St Paul's Sch Sao Paulo 2008–14; memb Assoc of Sch and Coll Ldrs; *Recreations* sport, music; *Style*— Crispin Rowe, Esq; ✉ R Dona Eponina Afonseca 142, Granja Julieta, São Paulo, Brazil (☎ 00 55 114328 6659)

ROWE, Heather; da of Leonard Richard Rowe, of Welwyn, Herts, and Enid, *née* Livermore; *b* 16 October 1957; *Educ* Welwyn Garden City GS, Univ of Manchester (LLB); *m* Tim Olsen; *Career* admitted slr 1981, articled clerk and slr Wilde Sapte 1979–83, SJ Berwin & Co 1983–85, Durrant Piesse 1985–88, ptnr Lovells (now Hogan Lovells) 1988–2004; former chm: ICC UK Ctee on Telecommunications and Information Technology, ICC Int Working Pty on Data Protection and Privacy; Freeman Worshipful Co of Slrs; memb Law Soc; *Publications* Data Protection Act 1988 – A Practical Guide, E-Finance: Law and Regulation (gen ed and co-author); *Recreations* fishing, birdwatching, gardening, ceramics, painting, cars; *Clubs* Piscatorial Soc, Historic Rally Car Register; *Style*— Miss Heather Rowe; ✉ 53A The Close, Salisbury, Wiltshire SP1 2EL (☎ 01722 331141, e-mail timandheatherolsen@gmail.com)

ROWE, John Richard; s of William Rowe (d 1990), of Wanstead, London, and Anne, *née* Radley (d 2000); *b* 1 August 1942; *Educ* St Barnabas Secdy Modern Sch; *m* 22 Oct 1966, Rosa Mary, da of Geoffrey Laurence Ball (d 1958), of Woodford Bridge, Essex; *Career* asst film librarian Twentieth Century Fox 1958–61, film researcher Rediffusion TV 1961–72 (progs incl: The Life and Times of Lord Mountbatten 1966–68, This Week), head of prodn res Thames TV 1972–82 (progs incl Emmy award winning World at War series 1972–74); Sky TV: head of programming 1982–84, head of prodn 1984–93; prodr Special Projects QVC The Shopping Channel 1994–95 (exec prodr 1993–94); fndr and exec prodr John Rowe Productions (ind prodr of film and TV prodns) 1995–; co-ordinating dir 1987 World Music Video Awards; prodr: The Pet Show series, Live from the Escape, Live from Rotterdam; prodr and dir: A Magical Disney Christmas, Ferry Aid Gala, Deadly Ernest Horror Show series 1989–91, Screeners 1997, Blues Clues 1997–2000 (6 series 2002–03), Havakazoo 2000; dir: The Gulf Aid Gala, Masters of History 1998, Reflections in the Eye: A documentary on the life of Anthony Quinn 2000, Monkey Makes 2002–04, Big Cook, Little Cook 2004 and 2005; writer, prodr and dir: Nickelodeon Live Tour 2002–04, The Big Story Book 2005; writer and dir Nickelodeon Jump Up Event 2006, 2007 and 2008; hon memb Research Bd of Advsrs American Biographical Inst; *Books* Little Stories for Little People (2013), The Casebook of Inspector Sniffabout (2014), The Casebook of Inspector Sniffabout Book Two (2014); *Recreations* cinema, walking, reading; *Style*— John Rowe, Esq; ✉ 24 Long Hill, Mere, Warminster, Wiltshire BA12 6LR (☎ and fax 01747 861 966, e-mail jrowe@btinternet.com, website sbpra.com/johnrowe)

ROWE, Michael; *Educ* High Wycombe Coll of Art (DipAD), RCA (MA); *Career* in own silversmithing workshop 1972, sunglasses designer Polaroid (UK) Ltd 1971–72; spectacle designer: Optica Info Cncl fashion promotion 1973, Merx International Optical Co 1974–76; visiting lectr: Bucks Coll of Higher Educn 1973–82, Camberwell Sch of Art and Crafts 1976–82; visiting lectr and tutor RCA 1978–84; researcher (with Richard Hughes) into: colouring, bronzing and patination of metals Camberwell Sch of Art and Crafts 1979–82 (work published as manual by Crafts Cncl 1982), ancient patinated surfaces British Museum 1984–87; course leader Dept of Metalwork and Jewellery RCA 1984–; guest lectr: colls in Düsseldorf, Cologne, Schwabisch Gmund, Pforzheim and Munich 1983, Gerrit Rietreld Académie Amsterdam 1984, Oslo Statens Handverks-Og Kunstindustriskole 1985, Bezalel Coll of Art Jerusalem 1987; guest speaker: Soc of N American Goldsmiths Conf Toronto 1985, Jewellers and Metalsmiths Gp of Aust Fourth Biennial Conf Perth, First International Metal Arts Symposium Won-Kwang Univ 1995; memb jury: Mecca Dante Stakes Trophy Competition 1981 and 1982, Perrier Trophy Competition 1982, Das Tablett (int silversmithing competition) 1983, Chongju Int Craft Bienniale Competition South Korea 1999; Freeman City of London 1983, Freeman Worshipful Co of Goldsmiths 1983; Hon Dr Buckinghamshire New Univ 2004, hon doctorate Hasselt Univ Belgium 2010; FRCA 1987, FRSA 1989; *Solo Exhibitions* Crafts Cncl Gallery London 1978, V&A Craft Show London 1985, Retrospective Exhibition (Princess of Museum Leeuwarden) 1988, Contemporary Applied Arts London 1988, The Eloquent Vessel (Museum für Angewandte Kunst Cologne, Museum für Angewandte Kunst Gera, and Deutsches Goldschmiedhaus Hanau) 1992, Studio Ton Berends The Hague 1993, Galerie Louise Smit Amsterdam 1995, Retrospective Exhibition (Birmingham Museum and Art Gallery, Manchester Art Gallery, City Art Gallery Leicester and tour) 2003–05; *Group Exhibitions* incl: Europalia '73 Brussels 1973, The Craftsman's Art (V&A) 1973, Collab '74 (Br Design and Craft and Philadelphia and World Crafts Exhibition Toronto) 1974, Sotheby Contemporary British Crafts at Auction Munich and London 1980, Galerie Ra Amsterdam 1983, Our Domestic Landscape (one of five selector/writer/exhibitors, London, Manchester and Aberystwyth) 1986, British Art and Design 1986 (Kunstlerhaus Vienna) 1986, Contemporary British Crafts (Br Cncl) 1988, Function Nonfunction (Rezac Gallery Chicago) 1989, New British Design Image and Object (Pompidou Centre Paris and Nat MOMA Kyoto) 1990, 20th Century Silver (Crafts Cncl London) 1993, The National Collection (Silver Tsts cmmns Goldsmiths Hall London) 1994, Design of the Times: 100 Years of the RCA (RCA) 1996, Objects of Our Time (Silver Jubilee exhibn Crafts Cncl London) 1996, First Choice (Museum Boymans van Beuningen Rotterdam) 1996, Design mit Zukunft (Focke Museum Bremen, Museum für Angewandte Kunst Cologne) 1997–98, European Prize for Contemporary Art and Design Led Crafts (Palais Harrach Vienna, Rohsska Museum Gothenburg, Musée des Arts Decoratifs Paris) 1998–99, Metalmorphosis: British Silver and Metalwork 1880–98 (Museum of Decorative Arts Prague, Brohan Museum Berlin) 1998–99, World Contemporary Craft Now (Cheongju Int Craft Biennale S Korea) 1999, Treasures of the 20th Century (Goldsmiths' Hall London) 2000, Cheongju Int Craft Biennale 2001, Torino 2002: Masterpieces 1902–2002 (Turin) 2002, Crafts Now: America, Europe and Asia (World Crafts Forum Kanazawa) 2003, Ars Ornata Europeana: Mais Perto/Closer (Nat Musuem of Art Lisbon) 2005, Transformations: The Language of Craft (Nat Gallery of Aust Canberra) 2005–06, Mindful of Silver (Goldsmiths Hall London) 2011; *Work in Public Collections* incl: Birmingham City Museum and Art Galleries, Crafts Cncl London, Leeds City Art Gallery, V&A, Karlsruhe Museum, Art Gallery of Western Aust Perth, Shipley Art Gallery Gateshead, Stedelijk Museum Amsterdam, Nat MOMA Tokyo, Museum Boymans van Beuningen Rotterdam, Royal Museum of Scotland Edinburgh, Musée des Arts Decoratifs Paris, Vestlanske Kunstindustrimuseum Bergen, Worshipful Co of Goldsmiths, Nordenfjeldske Kunstindustrimuseum Trondheim, Museum of 21st Centruy Art Kanazawa, Manchester Art Gallery, Nat Gallery of Aust Canberra, Millennium Galleries Sheffield; *Commissions* incl: silver pomander for The Craftman's Art exhbn (V&A, cmmned by Crafts Cncl) 1972, silver pomander (V&A, cmmned by Liberty & Co) 1975, pair of silver candelabra for 10 Downing St (cmmned by The Silver Tst) 1994, silver vase (cmmned by Worshipful Co of Goldsmiths) 1997, silver cup for Millennium Cmmns (Sheffield Millennium Galleries, cmmned by Sheffield Assay Office) 2002, perm installation (cmmned by Middlesbrough Inst of Modern Art) 2005, silver jug (cmmned by Worshipful Co of Goldsmiths) 2005, Cornwall Heartlands World Heritage Site commission for a perm wall installation; *Awards* Frogmoor Fndn travelling scholarship 1967, dip World Crafts Cncl 1974, res award Camberwell Sch of Art and Crafts 1978, Sotheby Decorative Arts award 1988, awarded Japan Fndn Artists Fellowship 1993, Prize Winner European Prize for Contemporary Art and Design Led Crafts 1998, Golden Ring of Honour Gesellschaft Für Goldschmiedekunst Germany 2002; *Publications* Michael Rowe (monograph, essays by Martina Margetts and Richard Hill, 2003); *Style*— Michael Rowe, Esq; ✉ Department of Metalwork and Jewellery, Royal College of Art, Kensington Gore, London SW7 2EU (☎ 020 7590 4263, e-mail michael.rowe@rca.ac.uk)

ROWE, Rita; *née* Mason; da of Cecil Mason (d 2004), and Marguarita Helen, *née* Dixon (d 1974); *b* Belfast; *Educ* St Helens Sch, St Helens Coll Merseyside; *m* 1, 1971, Gerald James Rowe; m 2, 1993, John Fagan Williams, s of Frank Thomas Williams; 1 step da (Kate Brannan); *Career* sales promotions exec Lancashire Evening Telegraph 1974–81,

R

freelance journalist and broadcaster 1980–96, publicity offr Manchester Theatres 1981–84, conslt Staniforth Williams PR 1984–86, fndr and jt md Mason Williams PR 1986–, ceo Muse Gp; recipient 60 industry awards for PR work incl for Boots Opticians, News International, Waddingtons Games, Vauxhall, Dale Farm, Hasbro, Express Dairy and for business achievements; FInstD, FRSA, FCIPR; *Recreations* cinema, fashion, motorsport, music, sailing, skiing, travel, walking; *Clubs* RAC, Soho House Gp, Bluebird; *Style—* Ms Rita Rowe; ✉ The Penthouse, Italian Building, Dockhead Road, Nr Butler's Wharf, London; Mason Williams PR, Universal Square, Devonshire Street, Manchester M12 6JH (✆ 0845 094 1007, website www.mason-williams.co.uk)

ROWE-BEDDOE, Baron (Life Peer UK 2006), of Kilgetty in the County of Dyfed; Sir David Sydney Rowe-Beddoe; kt (2000), DL (Gwent 2003); s of Sydney Rowe-Beddoe (d 1937), of Kilgetty, and Gwen Dolan, *née* Evans (d 1967); *b* 19 December 1937; *Educ* Llandaff Cathedral Sch, Stowe Sch, St John's Coll Cambridge (MA), Harvard Univ Grad Sch of Business Admin (PMD); *m* 1, 1962 (m dis 1982), Malinda, o da of Thomas Collison, of Calif; 3 da (Hon Lisa Dolan b 1964, Hon Samantha Olwen b 1967, Hon Amanda Sian b 1969); m 2, 1984, Madeleine Harrison, o da of late Walter Geminder; *Career* served RN, Sub-Lt Lt RNVR 1956–58, Lt RNR 1958–66; chief exec Thomas De La Rue & Co 1971–76 (joined 1961); Revlon Inc 1976–81 (pres: Latin America and Caribbean 1976–77, EMEA 1977–81); pres: GFTA Trendanalysen 1981–87, Morgan Stanley – GFTA Ltd 1983–91; chm: Cavendish Services Group 1987–93, EHC International Ltd 2001–, Mitel Corporation (Canada) 2002–06, Victoria Capital (UK) Ltd 2004–07, gfta The Euro/Dollar Technol Co Ltd (formerly gfta Analytics Ltd) 2005–, European Property Advsrs Ltd 2010–; dir: Development Securities plc 1994–2000, Toye & Co plc 2002– (dep chm 2003–); chm: Welsh Devpt Agency 1993–2001, Devpt Bd for Rural Wales 1994–98, N Wales Economic Forum 1996–2001, Mid Wales Partnership 1996–2001, SE Wales Economic Forum 1999–2001, Wales Millennium Centre 2001–10 (now life pres), Rep Body Church in Wales 2002–; dep chair UK Statistics Authy 2008–; memb: Welsh Economic Cncl 1994–96, Prince of Wales Ctee 1994–97, UK Regnl Policy Forum 1999–2002, House of Lords Sub-Ctee B (Internal Market) Select Ctee on EU 2007–12, House of Lords Select Ctee on the Barnett Formula 2008–09, House of Lords Administration and Works Ctee 2009–, Economic Affrs Ctee 2012–; dir: Int Film Festival of Wales 1998–2000, Cardiff Int Festival of Musical Theatre Ltd 2000–04, City of London Sinfonia 2000–03; pres: Welsh Centre for Int Affrs (WCIA) 1999–2005, Celtic Film Festival 2000, Llangollen Int Musical Eisteddfod 2000–05, Royal Welsh Coll of Music and Drama 2004– (govr 1993–2004, chm Bd of Govrs 2000–04), Cardiff Business Club 2006– (chm 2002–06), Johnian Soc 2007; pro-chllr Univ Glamorgan 2007–; patron: Prince's Trust Bro, Menuhin Competition 2008; Freeman: City of London, Worshipful Co of Broderers; Hon DUniv Glamorgan 1997, Hon DScEcon Univ of Wales 2004; hon fell: Univ of Wales Coll Newport 1998, Univ of Cardiff 1999, Univ of Wales Inst Cardiff 2002, Univ of Aberystwyth 2008; FRSA; Order of the Rising Sun Gold Rays with Neck Ribbon (Japan) 2008; *Recreations* music, theatre, country pursuits; *Clubs* Cardiff & County, Garrick, The Brook (NY); *Style—* The Lord Rowe-Beddoe, DL; ✉ Wales Millennium Centre, Bute Place, Cardiff CF10 5AL (✆ 029 2063 6400)

ROWE-HAM, Sir David Kenneth; GBE (1986); s of Kenneth Henry Rowe-Ham (d 1990), and Muriel Phyllis, *née* Mundy (d 2002); *b* 19 December 1935; *Educ* Dragon Sch, Charterhouse; *m* 1 (m dis 1980), Elizabeth, *née* Aston; 1 s (Adrian); m 2, 1980, Sandra Celia, widow of Ian Glover; 1 s (Mark b 1981), and 1 adopted step s (Gerald); *Career* CA 1962; cmmnd 3 King's Own Hussars; sr ptnr Smith Keen Cutler 1972–82, conslt to Touche Ross & Co 1984–93; chm: Asset Trust plc 1982–89, Jersey General Investment Trust Ltd 1988–89, Olayan Europe Ltd 1989–, Brewin Dolphin Holdings plc 1992–2003, APTA Healthcare plc 1994–96, Coral Products plc 1995–2006, Peninsular South Asia Investment Co Ltd (formerly BNP Paribas South Asia Investment Co Ltd) 1995–2008, Gradus Group plc (jt chm) 1995–97, Arden Partners plc 2006–10; dir: W Canning plc 1981–86, Savoy Theatre Ltd 1986–98, Williams plc 1992–2000, CLS Holdings plc 1994–99, Chubb plc 2000–03, Hikma Pharmaceuticals plc 2005–14; regnl dir (London) Lloyds Bank 1985–91, memb Advsy Panel Guinness Flight Unit Trust Mangrs Ltd 1985–99 (chm 1987); Alderman City of London Ward of Bridge and Bridge Without 1976–2004, Sheriff City of London 1984–85, Lord Mayor of London 1986–87; JP City of London 1976–94, chief magistrate 1986–87; chm: Birmingham Municipal Bank 1970–72, Political Cncl Jr Carlton Club 1977; dep chm Political Ctee Carlton Club 1977–79; memb: Stock Exchange 1964–84, Birmingham City Cncl 1965–72, Ct City Univ 1981–86 (chllr 1986–87), Ct HAC 1976–2004; govr Royal Shakespeare Co 1988–2003, former tstee Friends of D'Oyly Carte; pres: Black Country Museum Devpt Tst, The Crown Agents Fndn 1996–2002; Liveryman: Worshipful Co of CAs in England and Wales (Master 1985–86), Worshipful Co of Wheelwrights; hon memb Worshipful Co of Launderers; Hon DLitt City Univ 1986; FCA; Commandeur de l'Ordre Mérite (France) 1984, Cdr Order of the Lion (Malawi) 1985, Order of the Aztec Eagle (Class II) Mexico 1985, Order of King Abdul Aziz (Class I) 1987, Grand Officier Order of Wissam Alouite (Morocco) 1987, Order of Diego Losada of Caracas (Venezuela) 1987; Pedro Ernesto medal (Rio de Janeiro) 1987; HM's Cmmn of Lieutenancy for City of London 1987–2004; KJStJ 1986; *Recreations* theatre; *Clubs* Garrick; *Style—* Sir David Rowe-Ham, GBE; ✉ 140 Piccadilly, London W1J 7NS (✆ 020 7245 4000)

ROWELL, Jack; OBE (1998); s of Edwin Cecil Rowell (d 1956), of Hartlepool, and Monica Mary, *née* Day (d 1991); *Educ* West Hartlepool GS, Univ of Oxford (MA); *m* 26 May 1969, Susan Rowell, JP, da of Alan Cooper; 2 s (Dominic John b 27 Aug 1972, Christian Michael b 24 Dec 1974); *Career* with Procter & Gamble until 1976, Lucas Ingredients Bristol 1976–88 (fin dir, chief exec), chief exec Golden Wonder 1988–92, exec dir Dalgety plc 1993–96; chm: Dolphin Computer Services Ltd 1994–99, OSI Holdings Ltd 1994–99, Marlar Bennett International Ltd 1994–99, Lyons Seafoods Ltd 1994–2003, Turleigh Ltd 1995–, UKR Product Group plc 2004–; non-exec chm: Pilgrim Foods Ltd 1996–2004, Coppice Ltd 2002–06; dir: Celsis International plc 1994–2009 (ceo 1998–, chm 2000–10), Oliver Ashworth Group plc 1997–99; memb Bd Sport England 2006–10, chm of tstees Bath Rugby 2010–; memb SW Cncl Prince's Tst 2008–13, memb Advsy Bd Bath Univ Business Sch 2010–14; Hon LLD Univ of Bath 1994; FCA; *Rugby career* joined Gosforth (later Newcastle Gosforth), appointed capt and later coach (winners John Player Cup Final); coach Bath RFC 1977–94 (winners John Player Specials Cup (later Pilkington Cup) 1984, 1985, 1986, 1987, 1989, 1990, 1992 and 1994, winners Courage League Div 1 1989, 1991, 1992, 1993 and 1994, winners Middx Sevens 1994), mangr England RFU team 1994–97 (5 Nations Grand Slam 1995, semi-finalists World Cup South Africa 1995, 5 Nations champions and Triple Crown 1996 and 1997), dir Bristol Rugby Ltd until 2003, dir of rugby Bath RFC 2003–05, pres Bath Rugby 2007–09 (non-exec dir 2005–07, chm of tstees 2010–15); Hall of Fame Newcastle & Bath Rugby 2015; *Recreations* rugby, golf; *Style—* Jack Rowell, Esq, OBE; ✉ Middlehill House, Middlehill, Box, Wiltshire SN13 8QS (✆ 01225 744576)

ROWLAND, John; QC (1996); s of Peter Rowland (d 1976), and Marion Agnes *née* Guppy; *b* 17 January 1952; *Educ* Aquinas Coll Perth, Univ of Western Aust (BEcon), Univ of London (LLB); *m* 8 Dec 1979, Juliet Claire, da of Ernest John Hathaway; 3 s (Benjamin b 1985, Matthew b 1988, Luke b 1990), 2 da (Freya b 1992, Cassia b 1996); *Career* Pilot Offr RAAF 1971–72; tutor Kingswood Coll Univ of Western Aust 1973–74; called to the Bar: Middle Temple 1979, Victoria 2002; in practice 1979–; admitted to practice NSW and Victoria 2001; memb: London Common Law Bar Assoc 1984, COMBAR; *Recreations* cricket, walking, skiing; *Style—* Mr John Rowland, QC; ✉ 4 Pump Court, Temple, London EC4Y 7AN (✆ 020 7842 5555, fax 020 7583 2036, e-mail jrowland@4pumpcourt.com)

ROWLAND, Jonathan (Jon); s of David Rowland, and Sara, *née* Porush; *b* 7 November 1946; *Educ* Univ Coll Sch London, Architectural Assoc Sch of Architecture (AA Dipl), Univ of Sussex (MA); *m* 1 Feb 1972, Charlotte Ann, da of Gordon Scott Bessey; 1 da (Abigail Amber b 29 June 1976), 1 s (Adam Benjamin b 30 March 1979); *Career* conslt architect and urban designer; dir Jon Rowland Urban Design Ltd, owner John Rowland Ar 1992–2016; exhibitor at galleries in Oxford and London incl Capability Brown exhbn Blenheim Palace; responsible for urban design strategies in Liverpool, York, South Bank London, Newcastle, Leeds, Bracknell, and Lewisham, city centre masterplans for Cardiff, Lincoln, Gloucester and Bristol, masterplanner for Belfast's Shankill Road, Crumlin Road, Shore Road, Falls Road and E Belfast communities (with RPS); responsible for the Strategy for Architecture and the Built Environment in SW, urban design assistance to Crown Estates, urban design guidance for S Oxon, advsr spatial devpt strategy GLA, design advsr to Exeter City Cncl on expansion of city centre and Lewisham Cncl on devpt of town centre, new urban villages at Runcorn and Warrington, new Millennium community at Telford (Building for Life Gold Award); worked in Africa, S Asia, Far East, Caribbean on World Bank and ODA projects; other projects incl city centre masterplans in Lincoln, Cardiff and Bristol; urban extensions incl: Cottam Hall Preston (with Atkins, shortlisted for RTPI Award), West Summers Harlow (reinterpreting Sir Frederick Gibberd's design principles), Stranraer Waterfront (with Smith, Scott, Mullan Assocs, nominated Scottish Design Award 2011); memb: Ctee Urban Design Gp (chm 1992–97), Design Panel NWDA, Oxford Design Review Panel; former memb English Partnerships National Design Advsy Panel; vice-chair Urban Design Alliance, chair Hertfordshire County Council Design Review Panel 2016; enabler Cmmn for Architecture and the Built Environment (CABE) (rep SE Region, chair Berks Oxon Bucks-Milton Keynes (BOB-MK) Design Network 2004–14, memb Design Review Panel 2008, chair Design Review Design Cncl), chair and built environment expert Design Cncl/CABE Design Review Panel; former visiting lectr: Architectural Assoc, Oxford Brookes Univ; memb Editorial Bd: Open House, Urban Design International; exhibitor at: Royal Acad London, Green Coll Oxford, Wolfson Coll Oxford, Said Business Sch; pres Oxford Jewish Congregation 2013–15; winner (as part of Urbed team) Wolfson Economic Prize 2014; former memb: Land Use Soc, Landscape Fndn; memb: RIBA, ARCUK, Royal Anthropological Inst, Urban Design Gp; Academist Acad of Urbanism; FRSA (memb Ctee S Central Region); *Publications* Community Decay (1973), Urban Design Futures (2006), The Quality of Life in Cities: the 21st Century Suburb (jtly, 2012); author of numerous articles in various professional jls; *Recreations* music, art, walking; *Style—* Jon Rowland, Esq; ✉ Jon Rowland Urban Design, 65 Hurst Rise Road, Oxford OX2 9HE (✆ 01865 863642, e-mail jonrowland@jrud.co.uk, websites www.jrud.co.uk and www.jonrowlandart.co.uk)

ROWLAND, Prof Malcolm; s of Stanley Rowland (d 1973); *b* 5 August 1939; *Educ* Univ of London (BPharm, PhD, DSc); *m* 5 Sept 1965, Dawn; 2 da (Lisa Claire b 21 Dec 1968, Michelle b 1 July 1970); *Career* assoc prof of pharmacy and pharmaceutical chemistry Univ of Calif San Francisco 1970–75 (asst prof 1967–71); Univ of Manchester: prof of pharmacy 1975–2005, head Dept of Pharmacy 1988–91, dean Sch of Pharmacy 1998–2001, research prof 2002–04, prof emeritus 2004–; adjunct prof Dept of Bioengineering and Therapeutic Sciences Sch of Pharmacy and Medicine Univ of Calif San Francisco 2009–; chief exec Medeval Ltd 1983–93 (pres 1993–98), fndr and princ NDA Partners 2003–; ed Jl of Pharmacokinetics and Pharmacodynamics (formerly Jl of Pharmacokinetics and Biopharmaceutics) 1973–2006; pres European Fedn of Pharmaceutical Scientists 1996–2000, vice-pres Int Pharmaceutical Fedn 2001–08; Hon DSc Univ of Poitiers 1981, Hon DPh Univ of Uppsala 1989, Hon PhD Univ of Athens 2011; fell: Royal Pharmaceutical Soc of GB 1987 (memb 1965), American Assoc of Pharmaceutical Scientists 1988; hon fell: Acad of Pharmaceutical Sciences, American Coll of Clinical Pharmacology; Hon MRCP, FIMA 1978, FMedSci 2001, fell Br Pharmacological Soc; *Books* incl: Essentials in Pharmacokinetics and Pharmacodynamics (with Dr T N Tozer, 2006, 2 edn 2016), Clinical Pharmacokinetics and Pharmacodynamics: Concepts and Applications (with Dr T N Tozer, 4 edn 2010); author or co-author of more than 300 scientific pubns in the field of pharmacokinetics and pharmaceutical sciences; *Clubs* Athenaeum; *Style—* Prof Malcolm Rowland; ✉ 54c Belsize Avenue, London NW3 4AE (e-mail mrow190539@aol.com); Manchester School of Pharmacy, University of Manchester, Stopford Building, Manchester M13 9PT

ROWLAND PAYNE, Dr Christopher Melville Edwin; s of Maj Edwin Rowland Payne, and Rosemary Ann, *née* Bird; *b* 19 May 1955; *Educ* Clifton, Univ of London, St Bart's Med Coll (MB BS, MRCP); *m* 28 May 1994, Wendy Margaret, da of Maxwell Mair, of Bermuda; 3 da (Anoushka Poppy Joy b 24 Sept 1997, Alexandra Katinka Heather b 25 March 1999, Araminta Lily Bird Mair b 19 Jan 2004); *Career* conslt dermatologist and landowner; house surgn St Bart's Hosp London 1978; house physician: Med Prof Unit Royal Infirmary Edinburgh 1978, Royal Marsden Hosp 1979; dermatological registrar St Thomas's Hosp London 1980–83, dermatological sr registrar Westminster Hosp 1983–89; professeur universitaire Faculté de Medecine de Paris 1985–86; conslt dermatologist: Kent and Canterbury Hosp 1990–94, William Harvey Hosp Kent 1990–97, Cromwell Hosp London 1990–2000, The London Clinic 1994–, Royal Marsden Hosp 1997–2001; clinical prof of dermatology Ross Univ NY 1990, visiting prof of dermatology Univ of Sci and Technol Kumasi Ghana 1995, prof of academic cosmetic dermatology Università degli Studi Guglielmo Marconi 2011–; ed Jl of Cosmetic Dermatology 2000–04; Roxburgh prize 1977; Br Assoc of Dermatologists awards 1984, 1985, 1986, 1988, 1989 and 1993; Dowling Club prizes: 1985, 1986, 1987 and 1988, MRC project grant 1988–89; RCP award 1989; sec-gen Euro Soc for Cosmetic and Aesthetic Dermatology 1997–2014 (pres 1998–99); hon memb Société Française de Dermatologie; memb: Br Assoc of Dermatologists, Int Soc for Dermatological Surgery; UK co-ordinator Euro Soc for Laser Dermatology; HAC 1974–76; Freeman City of London, Liveryman Worshipful Soc of Apothecaries; *Publications* contrib: chapters on needle aponeurotomy for Dupuytren's contracture, skin cancer and melanoma, lasers, fillers and botulinum: BMJ, Lancet, British Jl of Dermatology, Jl of Cosmetic Dermatology and others; *Recreations* shooting, cycling, military history; *Clubs* Travellers'; *Style—* Dr Christopher Rowland Payne; ✉ The London Clinic, 27 Devonshire Place, London W1G 6JF (✆ 020 7224 1228, fax 020 7487 5479, e-mail crp@rowlandpayne.co.uk); 32 Warwick Square, London SW1V 2AD

ROWLANDS, Anthony Francis; s of Arthur Rowlands (d 1998), and Joan, *née* Shortt (d 2005); *b* 11 August 1952; *Educ* Ryde Sch, The Queen's Coll Oxford (open scholarship), Churchill Coll Cambridge, Inst of Educn Univ of London; *m* 1981, Harriet Jane (d 2014), da of late Alick Isaacs, FRS, and late Dr Susanna Isaacs Elmhirst; 1 da (Alice Louisa b 13 June 1983), 1 s (Samuel Peter Harold b 4 March 1986); *Career* history teacher: Bristol GS 1976–79, Haberdashers' Aske's Sch 1979–89, Dr Challoner's GS Amersham 1990–98; dir Centre for Reform 2000–05, exec dir CentreForum 2005–; cncllr (Lib Dem) St Albans City and Dist Cncl 1986–2003 and 2006–, cncllr Herts CC 1993–97; Parly candidate (Lib Dem): St Albans 1997, IOW 2005, Hertsmere 2010, Broxbourne 2015; *Recreations* running (completed 12 London marathons), cricket, football, supporting Burnley FC; *Clubs* MCC, National Liberal; *Style—* Anthony Rowlands; ✉ 106 Beaumont Avenue, St Albans, Hertfordshire AL1 4TP (✆ 07761 232064, e-mail anthonyrowlands@hotmail.com)

ROWLANDS, Prof Brian James; *b* 18 March 1945; *Educ* Wirral GS Cheshire, Guy's Hosp Med Sch (MB BS), Univ of Sheffield; *m* 16 Oct 1971, Judith Thomas (d 2008); 1 da

(Rachel b 14 March 1975); partner, Kalliope Valassiadou; 1 da (Sofia b 1 Aug 2007); *Career* lectr Dept of Surgery Univ of Sheffield 1974–77, fell surgical gastroenterology and nutrition Dept of Surgery Univ of Texas Med Sch Houston 1977–78; Univ of Texas Health Sci Centre Houston: instr surgery 1977–78, asst prof of surgery 1978–81, assoc prof of surgery 1981–86; prof and head Dept of Surgery Queen's Univ Belfast 1986–97, prof and head of Section of Surgery and Div of Gastrointestinal Surgery Queen's Medical Centre Univ of Nottingham 1997–2009, emeritus prof Univ of Nottingham 2009–; memb Surgical Res Soc, sec Assoc of Profs Surgery, chm Scientific Ctee Assoc of Surgns of GB and I 1997–, pres Assoc of Surgeons GB&I 2007–08, memb Cncl RCS England 2007–08, dir of professional affrs E Midlands SHA/RCS England 2009–14, memb E Midlands Clinical Senate Cncl 2012–; FRCS 1973, fell American Coll Surgns 1983; FRCSI 1988, FRCS (Ed) 1995, FRCPS (Glas) 1995; *Books* The Physiological Basis of Modern Surgical Care (jt ed, 1988), Critical Care for Postgraduate Trainees (jt ed, 2005), ABC of Tubes, Drains, Lines and Frames (jt ed, 2008); *Recreations* travel, gardening, sailing, golf, going to Greece; *Clubs* Lingdale Golf, Trent Offshore Group; *Style—* Prof Brian J Rowlands; ✉ 96 Station Road, Cropston, Leicestershire LE7 7HE (☎ 0116 234 0074); Queen's Medical Centre, University Hospital, Nottingham NG7 2UH (☎ 07786 731245, e-mail bjr.surgery@nottingham.ac.uk)

ROWLANDS, Chris; *Educ* Univ of London (LLB); *Career* early career with Barclays Bank, with 3i Gp plc 1984–96, ptnr and head of corp finance Arthur Andersen 1996–2002 (latterly memb UK Leadership Team); 3i Gp plc: former memb Exec Ctee, head of gp markets and growth capital 2002–05, head of gp markets 2005–07, managing ptnr Asia until 2009; non-exec dir Principality Building Soc 2005–; memb Bd of Dirs Finance Wales 2010–; *Style—* Mr Chris Rowlands

ROWLANDS, Baron (Life Peer UK 2004), of Merthyr Tydfil and Rhymney in the County of Mid Glamorgan; Edward (Ted) Rowlands; s of William Samuel Rowlands (d 1966), of Rhondda; *b* 23 January 1940; *Educ* Rhondda GS, Wirral GS, King's Coll London; *m* 1968, Janice Williams (d 2004); 2 s, 1 da; *Career* res asst History of Parly Tst 1963–65, lectr in modern history and govr Welsh Coll of Advanced Technol 1965–66; MP (Lab): Cardiff N 1966–70, Merthyr Tydfil 1972–83, Merthyr Tydfil and Rhymney 1983–2001; Parly under-sec of state: for Wales 1969–70 and 1974–75, FCO 1975–76; min of state FCO 1976–79; oppn front bench spokesman on: Foreign and Cwlth Affairs 1979–81, Energy 1981–87; chm: All-Pty Gp on Publishing 1983–84, Select Ctee on Defence Trade and Industry and Foreign Affairs; memb Select Ctee on Foreign Affairs 1987–2001; memb: Governing Body and Exec of Cwlth Inst 1980–91, Academic Cncl Wilton Park 1983–90; judge: Booker McConnell Novel of the Year Competition 1984, Manchester Oddfellows Social Award Book; *Style—* The Rt Hon the Lord Rowlands; ✉ 42 Station Road, Kidwelly, Carmathenshire SA17 4UT

ROWLEY, Paul Keith; s of James Keith Rowley (d 1988), and Christine Mabel Stableford, *née* Damp; *b* 17 March 1966, Preston, Lancs; *Educ* W R Tuson Coll Preston (ONC); *m* 25 Aug 1995, Sara Elizabeth, *née* Douglas; 2 s (George Alexander b 3 Nov 1997, Lucus James b 10 July 2001); *Career* apprentice bricklayer 1982–87, mgmnt trainee Alfred McAlpine 1987–93, land and sales mangr Fairclough Homes 1991–93, md Rowland Homes 1993–; Property Entrepeneur of the Year NW 2003 and 2005; *Recreations* fell walking, skiing; *Style—* Paul Rowley, Esq; ✉ Rowland Homes, Farington House, Stanifield Lane, Leyland, Lancashire PR25 4UA (☎ 01772 621166, fax 017772 623552, e-mail paul.rowley@rowland.co.uk)

ROWLEY, Rupert William Kinglsey; s of David William Rowley, and Irene, *née* Arksey; *b* 21 February 1977, Sheffield, S Yorks; *Educ* King Edward VII Sch Sheffield, The Sheffield Coll Castle Centre; *m* 3 April 2007, Marianne, *née* Soria; *Career* restaurateur; training: Restaurant Gordon Ramsay London, L'Ortolan Shinfield, Le Manoir aux Quat Saisons Great Milton; currently head chef Fischer's Hotel and Restaurant Baslowhall (1 Michelin star); dir Rowleys Restaurant and Bar Baslow; *Recreations* fishing (course and fly), photography, watercolour painting; *Style—* Rupert Rowley, Esq; ✉ 18 Shetland Road, Dronfield, Derbyshire S18 1WB (☎ 01246 413029, e-mail rupertrowley@tiscali.co.uk); Fischer's Baslowhall, Calver Road, Baslow, Derbyshire DE45 1RR (☎ 01246 583259, fax 01246 583818, e-mail reservations@fischers-baslowhall.co.uk)

ROWLING, JK (Joanne Kathleen); OBE (2000); *Educ* Univ of Exeter; *m* 26 Dec 2001, Dr Neil Murray; *Career* novelist; pres children's charity Lumos; commencement speaker Harvard Univ 2008, fell Exeter Coll Oxford 2014; Beacon Fellowship 2013; Freedom of the City of London 2012; hon degree: Napier Univ, Dartmouth Coll USA, Univ of Exeter, Univ of St Andrews, Harvard Univ, Univ of Aberdeen; FRSL; Prince of Asturias Award for Concord Spain 2003, Chevalier de la Légion d'Honneur 2009; *Books* Harry Potter and the Philosopher's Stone (1997), Harry Potter and the Chamber of Secrets (1998), Harry Potter and the Prisoner of Azkaban (1999), Harry Potter and the Goblet of Fire (2000), Quidditch Through the Ages (2001, in aid of Comic Relief), Fantastic Beasts & Where to Find Them (2001, in aid of Comic Relief), Harry Potter and the Order of the Phoenix (2003), Harry Potter and the Half-Blood Prince (2005), Harry Potter and the Deathly Hallows (2007), The Tales of Beedle the Bard (2008, in aid of Lumos), The Casual Vacancy (2012), The Cuckoo's Calling (2013, as Robert Galbraith), The Silkworm (2014, as Robert Galbraith); *Awards* incl: FCBG Children's Book Awards, Nestlé Smarties Book Prize Gold Medal 9–11 Years 1997, 1998 and 1999, British Book Awards' Children's Book of the Year 1998 and 1999, Prix Sorcières 1999, Author of the Year and Lifetime Achievement Award Br Book Award 1999 and 2008, Whitbread Children's Book of the Year 2000, W H Smith Children's Book of the Year 2000 and 2003, W H Smith Fiction Award 2004, W H Smith Book of the Year 2006, Outstanding Achievement Award South Bank Show Award 2008, The Edinburgh Award 2008, The James Joyce Award UC Dublin 2008, Outstanding British Contribution to Cinema BAFTA 2011; *Style—* J K Rowling

ROWLINSON, Stephen Richard; s of Henry Robert Rowlinson (d 1988), of Godalming; *b* 25 December 1939, Suffolk; *Educ* Wanstead HS, Univ of Nottingham (BA); *m* 17 Aug 1967, Kathleen Ann (Kathy); 2 s (Benjamin Toby, Thomas Henry), 1 da (Emily Kate Louise); *Career* Sullivan Stauffer Colwell Bayles Inc 1961–62, Harris Lebus Ltd 1962–67, McKinsey and Co Inc 1967–74, TCK Gp Ltd 1974–77, Rowlinson Tomala and Assocs Ltd 1977–80, Bickerton Rowlinson Ltd 1980–85, Korn/Ferry Int Ltd 1985–89, Penna plc 1989–91, Merton Associates Ltd 1991–2001, chm Bartlett Merton Ltd 1998–2001, chief exec Daric plc 1998–2001; chm: Exton Estates Ltd 2002–05, London Private Capital Ltd 2002–, Penna Consulting plc 2005–16; *Recreations* sailing, skiing; *Clubs* Royal Thames Yacht; *Style—* Stephen Rowlinson, Esq; ✉ Goodsoal Farm, Burwash Common, East Sussex TN19 7LX (e-mail stephen@londonprivatecapital.com)

ROWNTREE, Brian; CBE (2004); *Career* previous public appointments at chair and non-exec dir level in criminal justice, health and FE, chm NI Housing Exec 2004–12, chair Civil Service Cmmrs NI 2012–; past vice-pres Cecodhas European Social Housing Forum, memb Mgmnt Bd Assoc for Criminal Justice Reform and Devpt, non-exec ind memb NI Policing Bd 2011; chair Home of the Future Gp; memb: Bd Co-operation Ireland, NI Advsy Ctee Nat Access Mgmnt Agency, Bd Fair Share NI; hon MCIH 2008, FRSA; *Style—* Brian Rowntree, Esq, CBE

ROWSELL, Joanna; MBE (2013); *b* 5 December 1988, Surrey; *Educ* Nonsuch HS for Girls Cheam; *m* July 2015, Daniel Shand; *Career* track and road cyclist; team pursuit achievements incl: Gold medal World Championships 2008, 2009 and 2012, Silver medal World Championships 2010, Gold medal European Track Championships 2011, Gold medal Olympic Games 2012; *Style—* Ms Joanna Rowsell, MBE; ✉ website www.joannarowsell.com, Twitter @joannarowsell

ROXBURGH, Prof Ian Walter; s of Walter McRonald Roxburgh, and Kathleen Joyce, *née* Prescott; *b* 31 August 1939; *Educ* King Edward VII GS Sheffield, Univ of Nottingham (BSc), Univ of Cambridge (PhD); *m* 1960, Diana Patricia, *née* Dunn; 2 s, 1 da; *Career* research fell elect Churchill Coll Cambridge 1963, lectr in maths KCL 1964–66 (asst lectr 1963–64), reader in astronomy Univ of Sussex 1966–67; Queen Mary & Westfield Coll (formerly QMC) London: prof of applied maths 1967–87, head Sch of Mathematical Scis 1978–95, dir Astronomy Unit 1983–2001, prof of maths and astronomy 1987–2011 (emeritus prof of astronomy and maths 2011–), pro-princ 1987; chm Heads of Univ Depts of Mathematics & Statistics 1988–93; conslt European Space Agency; Parly candidate: (Liberal) Walthamstow W 1970, (SDP) Ilford North 1983; memb: European Physical Soc, European Astronomical Soc, Int Astronomical Union, Royal Astonomical Soc, Inst of Physics; CPhys, FInstP, FRAS; *Books* Physical Process in Astrophysics (jt ed, 1995), Stellar Structure and Habitable Planet Finding (jt ed, 2002), Convection in Astrophysics (jt ed, 2007); over 300 articles in jls: Monthly Notices Royal Astonomical Soc, Astonomy and Astrophysics, Astrophysical Jl, Nature, Science, Solar Physics, General Relativity and Gravitation, etc; *Clubs* Royal Astronomical Soc Club; *Style—* Prof Ian W Roxburgh; ✉ 37 Leicester Road, Wanstead, London E11 2DW (☎ 020 8989 7117)

ROXBURGH, Johnny; *b* 28 May 1949, Scotland; *Career* qualified CA; formerly: Touche Ross South Africa, BDO Stoy Hayward; fndr and prop The Admirable Crichton 1980–2014, fndr Johnny Roxburgh Designs Ltd 2014–; *Style—* Johnny Roxburgh, Esq; ✉ Johnny Roxburgh Designs Ltd, 29 Battersea Church Road, London SW11 3LY (e-mail johnny@johnnyroxburghdesigns.co.uk)

ROXBURGH, Dr Stuart Thomas Dalrymple; s of Robert Roxburgh (d 2002), and Helen Roxburgh (d 2000); *b* 10 May 1950; *Educ* Camphill Sch, Univ of Glasgow (MB ChB); *m* 25 June 1975, Christine MacLeod Campbell (d 2012), da of John Ramsay (d 1979); 1 s (Campbell b 27 March 1980), 1 da (Alison b 5 Oct 1982); *Career* conslt ophthalmologist Tayside Health Bd until 2013, hon sr lectr Dept of Ophthalmology Univ of Dundee (former head of Dept) until 2013; vice-chm Acad of Royal Colleges and Facilities in Scotland 2003–05; FRCSEd 1979, FRCOphth 1988 (vice-pres, chm Examination Ctee 2000–04); *Recreations* golf, hill walking, painting; *Style—* Dr Stuart Roxburgh; ✉ 13 Torwoodlee, Perth PH1 1SY (☎ 01738 634347, e-mail stuart.roxburgh@blueyonder.co.uk)

ROXBURGHE, 10 Duke of (S 1707); Sir Guy David Innes-Ker; 11 Bt (Premier Bt of Scotland or Nova Scotia, S 1625); also Lord Roxburghe (S before 31 March 1600), Earl of Roxburghe, Lord Ker of Cessford and Cavertoun (both S 1616), Marquis of Bowmont and Cessford, Earl of Kelso, Viscount of Broxmouth (S, with the Dukedom the last Peerages cr in the Peerage of Scotland, 1707), and Earl Innes (UK 1837); s of 9 Duke of Roxburghe (d 1974) and his 2 w (late Mrs Jocelyn Hambro); 1 Earl obtained a charter in 1648 of succession to the honour, to his gs 4 s of his da Countess of Perth, and after him the 3 s successively of his gda Countess of Wigton; Dukedom in remainder to whoever succeeds to Earldom; *b* 18 November 1954; *Educ* Eton, Magdalene Coll Cambridge; *m* 1, 1977 (m dis 1990), Lady Jane, *née* Grosvenor, da of 5 Duke of Westminster and Hon Viola Lyttelton, da of 9 Viscount Cobham;1 da (Lady Rosanagh Viola Alexandra b 1979), 2 s (Charles Robert George, Marquis of Bowmont and Cessford b 1981, Lord Edward Arthur Gerald b 1984); m 2, 3 Sept 1992, Virginia Mary, da of David Wynn-Williams; 1 da (Lady Isabella May b 1994), 1 s (Lord George Alastair b 1996); *Heir* s, Marquis of Bowmont and Cessford; *Career* formerly Lt RHG/1 Dragoons; landowner, co dir; Liveryman Worshipful Co of Fishmongers; *Recreations* fishing, shooting, golf, racing, skiing; *Clubs* White's; *Style—* His Grace the Duke of Roxburghe; ✉ Floors Castle, Kelso, Roxburghshire (☎ 01573 224288); Roxburghe Estate Office, Kelso, Roxburghshire (☎ 01573 223333, e-mail estate@floorscastle.com)

ROY, Frank; s of James Roy (d 1989), and Esther, *née* McMahon; *b* 29 August 1958; *Educ* St Josephs' HS Motherwell, Our Lady's HS Motherwell, Motherwell Coll (HNC), Glasgow Caledonian Univ (BA); *m* 17 Sept 1977, Ellen, da of Patrick Foy; 1 s (Brian), 1 da (Kelly-Anne); *Career* Ravenscraig Steelworks 1977–91, PA to Helen Liddell, MP 1994–97; MP (Lab) Motherwell and Wishaw 1997–2015, PPS to sec of state for Scotland Dr John Reid, MP 1999–2001, PPS to dep sec of state Helen Liddell, MP 1998–99, asst govt whip 2005–06, a Lord Cmmr of HM Treasy (Govt whip) 2006–; House of Commons: memb Social Security Select Ctee 1997–98, memb Defence Select Ctee 2001–05; *Recreations* gardening, reading, football; *Style—* Frank Roy, Esq; ✉ House of Commons, London SW1A 0AA (☎ 020 7219 3000)

ROY, Lindsay Allan; CBE (2004); s of John Roy (d 1966), and Margaret, *née* Allan (d 2004); *b* 19 January 1949, Perth; *Educ* Univ of Edinburgh (BSc); *m* 1 April 1972, Irene, *née* Patterson; 2 s (Allan b 27 May 1978, Kevin b 26 Aug 1983), 1 da (Jacqueline b 17 Nov 1980); *Career* princ teacher of modern studies Queen Anne HS Dunfermline 1974, asst rector Kirkcaldy HS 1983–86, depute rector Glenwood HS Glenrothes 1986, rector Inverkeithing HS 1990, rector Kirkcaldy HS 2008–; assoc assessor HM Inspectorate of Educn 1996, chm Curriculum and Student Affrs Ctee Carnegie Coll 1997, pres Headteachers Assoc of Scotland 2004–05, Int Confederation of Sch Principals 2006–, memb Cncl Sch Ldrs Scotland 2008–, exec memb Int Confederation of Principals 2009–; MP (Lab) Glenrothes 2008–15; FRSA; *Recreations* soccer, mountain biking, angling, reading; *Style—* Lindsay Roy, Esq, CBE; ✉ 1 Parliament Street, Westminster, London SW1A 0AA (☎ 020 7219 8273, e-mail royl@parliament.uk)

ROYALL, District Judge Martyn; s of late Frederick Bertram Royall, of Torquay, and Edna Doreen, *née* Ball; *b* 8 January 1948; *Educ* Bishop Wordsworth Sch Salisbury, Coll of Law Guildford; *m* 24 June 1972, Jacqueline Barbara, da of late Jack Thompson; 1 da (Anna Rebecca b 16 Jan 1974), 1 s (Jack Hain b 13 Oct 1975, Thomas Martyn b 2 July 1979); *Career* articled Thomas Eggar & Sons Chichester, qualified slr 1972, ptnr Hawkins 1973–92 (joined 1972), district judge 1992–, recorder 2000– (asst recorder 1997–2000); pres: Kings Lynn W Norfolk Law Soc 1988– (sec 1974–83), Assoc of District Judges 2004–05; chm Nat Young Slrs Gp 1982; memb The Law Soc; *Recreations* outdoor sports (incl shooting); *Style—* District Judge Martyn Royall; ✉ Norwich Combined Court, The Law Courts, Bishopsgate, Norfolk NR3 1UR (☎ 01603 728200)

ROYALL OF BLAISDON, Baroness (Life Peer UK 2004), of Blaisdon in the County of Gloucestershire; Janet Anne (Jan) Royall; PC (2008); da of Basil Oscar Royall (d 1993), and Myra Jessie, *née* Albutt (d 1995); *b* 20 August 1955, Glos; *Educ* Royal Forest of Dean GS, Westfield Coll Univ of London (BA), South Bank Poly (Dip); *m* 6 Sept 1980, late Stuart Henry James Hercock, s of late Henry Hercock; 1 da (Hon Charlotte Rebecca b 2 Sept 1984), 2 s (Hon Edwin Henry Frederick b 28 May 1986, Hon Henry Jonathan b 5 Feb 1989); *Career* Continental Farms Europe 1978, sec-gen Br Lab Gp European Parl 1979–85, Office of Ldr of the Oppn 1985–92, political advsr to Rt Hon Neil Kinnock MP 1992–94, cabinet memb to Rt Hon Neil Kinnock (as EU Cmmr) 1995–2001, Parly co-ordinator Press and Communications Dept European Cmmn 2001–03, head EC Office Cardiff 2003–04, Capt HM Body Guard of Hon Corps of Gentlemen-at-Arms (chief Govt whip, House of Lords) 2008–10, ldr House of Lords 2008–10, shadow ldr House of Lords 2010–15; vice-pres Party of European Socialists 2012–; pro-chllr Univ of Bath 2014–; visiting prof Inst of Global Health Innovation; chair People's History Museum Manchester; *Recreations* gardening, reading, swimming; *Style—* The Rt Hon the Baroness Royall of Blaisdon, PC; ✉ House of Lords, London SW1A 0PW (☎ 020 7219 8652, e-mail royallj@parliament.uk, Twitter @LabourRoyall)

R

ROYDON, Terry Rene; s of Leon Roydon, and Lyanne, *née* Hamoniere; *b* 26 December 1946; *Educ* Clifton, Univ of London (BSc), Univ of Pittsburgh (MBA); *m* 29 Sept 1972, Carol Joycelyn, da of Stanley Norris; 1 da (Karen b 1977); *Career* md Comben Group plc 1970–84, chief exec Prowting plc 1985–98; chm: Banner Homes Gp plc 1999–2002, Swallow Homes Ltd 2000–01, Inland plc 2007–; dir: Nat House Bldg Cncl 1981–2004, PPS Ltd 1996–2014, Dom Devpt SA (Poland) 1999–, County and Metropolitan plc 2003–05, McCann Homes Ltd 2003–11, Gladedale plc 2005–07, Kimberly Enterprise NV 2005–, Inland Homes plc 2007–, Adama Hldg Ltd 2009–12, Larkfleet Gp 2011–; pres: Housebuilder Fedn 1984, European Union of Housebuilders and Developers 1995–97 and 2015–17; govr St Helen's Sch Northwood 1988–2012; *Style—* Terry Roydon, Esq; ✉ Kingsmill, The Marlins, Northwood, Middlesex HA6 3NP

ROYDS, Richard George; s of Nicholas Clyne Royds, and Sally Royds; *b* 15 November 1957; *Educ* Charterhouse; *m* Lucinda, da of Richard McClean; 1 s (George), 1 da (Isabella); *Career* sales exec: LWT 1976–79, Capital Radio 1979–82; dir The Media Shop 1982–86; md: Wardley Unit Trust Managers 1986–89, John Govett Unit Trust Managers 1989–92, Mercury Fund Managers Ltd 1992–2000; dir: Mercury Asset Management plc 1992–98, Mercury Life Assurance Co Ltd 1992–2000, Mercury Asset Management Ltd 1998–2000, Merrill Lynch Fund Managers 2000–; md mktg communications Merrill Lynch Investment Managers 2000–; *Recreations* golf, fishing, art, wine, eating, shopping; *Clubs* Sunningdale Golf, Royal St George's Golf, The Golf Match; *Style—* Richard Royds, Esq; ✉ Merrill Lynch Investment Managers, 33 King William Street, London EC4R 9AS (☎ 020 7743 3000, fax 020 7743 1109)

ROYLE, Carol Buchanan (Mrs Julian Spear); da of Derek Stanley Royle (d 1990), and Jane Irene, *née* Shortt (d 2010); *b* 10 February 1954; *Educ* Streatham HS for Girls, Pitmans Sch Wimbledon, Royal Central Sch of Speech and Drama; *m* Julian David Barnaby Spear, s of Bernard Spear; 1 s (Taran Oliver Buchanan b 5 Nov 1983), 1 da (Talitha Mary-Jane Buchanan Royle Spear b 31 Aug 1995); *Career* actress; *Theatre* incl Harrogate Repertory Co 1976–77; RSC 1980–82 and 1990–92 incl: Ophelia in Hamlet and Cressida in Troilus and Cressida 1980–82, Princess of France in Love's Labour's Lost and Mrs Arbuthnot in A Woman of No Importance; other roles incl: Titania in A Midsummer Night's Dream (Regent's Park) 1988, Kate in Harold Pinter's Old Times (Birmingham Rep) 1993, May in Fay Weldon's Four Alice Bakers (Birmingham Rep) 1999, Private Lives (Theatre Clwyd), Arcadia (Theatre Clwyd), Mdm Ranevskya in The Cherry Orchard (Theatre Clwyd) 2007, Lady Bracknell in The Importance of Being Earnest (Northampton), See You Next Tuesday (West End), Festen (West End), Going Straight (nat tour), An Ideal Husband (nat tour), Flora Humble in Humble Boy (New Vic Stoke), Else in Festen (Lyric Theatre), Maria in Moonlight (Donmar Warehouse), Syrie Maugham in Storm in a Flower Vase (Arts Theatre) 2014, Last of the Duty Free (UK Tour) 2014, Gertrude in Hamlet (Theatre Clwyd) 2015, extensive work at Windsor Theatre Royal; *Television* for BBC incl: Blakes 7 1979, Possibilities 1982, Bergerac 1983, Oxbridge Blues 1984, A Still Small Shout 1985, Life Without George (three series) 1987–89, Hedgehog Wedding 1987, Blackeyes 1989, Casualty 1990, The Bill; for ITV incl: The Professionals, Waxwork 1980, Heartland 1980; for Thames incl: Judgement Day 1983, Ladies in Charge 1985–86, The London Embassy 1987; other credits incl: The Cedar Tree (three series, ATV) 1977–79, Girl Talk (ATV) 1980, The Racing Game (YTV) 1980, Feet Foremost (Granada) 1982, The Outsider (YTV) 1983, Crime Traveller 1996, Thief Takers 1997, stint in Heartbeat, stint in Crossroads, Gil Mayo, stint in Doctors, currently semi-regular in Casualty as Emilie, Huntington's Disease sufferer; *Films* incl: Tuxedo Warrior 1982–83, When the Wall Comes Tumbling Down (EMI) 1984, Deadline (RSPCA) 1988; *Awards* London Drama Critics' Award for Most Promising Actress (for Ophelia) 1980; *Style—* Ms Carol Royle; ✉ c/o Phil Belfield, Belfield & Ward, 26–28 Neal Street, London WC2H 9QQ (☎ 020 3416 5290)

ROYLE, Gavin Timothy; s of late Basil Victor Royle, and late Gwen Royle; *Educ* Epsom Coll, Charing Cross Med Sch Univ of London (entrance scholar, MB BS, MS, Cricket capt); *m* Katherine; 2 s (Matthew, Thomas), 1 da (Elisabeth); *Career* surgical trg Oxford and Harvard, former MRC research fell at MIT and lectr in surgery Massachusetts Gen Hosp 1980, conslt gen surgn specialising in breast and endocrine disease Southampton Univ Hosps 1983–, conslt surgn Southampton and Salisbury Breast Screning Unit 1988–, hon conslt surgn St Mary's Hosp IOW 2007–, currently hon sr lectr in surgery Univ of Southampton, breast and thyroid lead clinician Southampton Univ Hosps; pres Southampton Medical Soc 2011; memb: Br Breast Gp, Br Assoc of Surgical Oncology, Assoc of Surgery, BMA, Br Assoc of Endocrine Surgns; Oxford HA Surgery Prize 1977, Wessex Med Sch Tst TV South Award 1986; MRC fellowship 1980; LRCP 1970, FRCS 1974 (MRCS 1970); *Publications* author of papers on various aspects of gen surgery, especially breast disease and metabolism; *Recreations* fishing, reading, clay pigeon shooting; *Clubs* MCC; *Style—* Mr Gavin Royle, FRCS; ✉ Nuffield Hospital Hampshire, Winchester Road, Chandlers Ford, Hampshire SO53 2DW (☎ 023 8025 8434, fax 023 8025 8446)

ROZENBERG, Joshua Rufus; Hon QC; s of Zigmund Rozenberg (d 1982), and Beatrice Doris, *née* Davies (d 1995); *b* 30 May 1950, London; *Educ* Latymer Upper Sch, Wadham Coll Oxford (MA); *m* 31 March 1974, Melanie, da of Alfred Phillips; 1 s, 1 da; *Career* trainee journalist BBC 1975, admitted slr 1976; legal and constitutional affrs corr BBC News 1997–2000 (legal affrs corr 1985–1997), legal ed The Daily Telegraph 2000–08, legal journalist and commentator; hon bencher Gray's Inn 2003; Hon LLD: Univ of Hertfordshire 1999, Nottingham Trent Univ 2012, Univ of Lincoln 2014, Univ of Law 2014; *Books* Your Rights and The Law (with N Watkins, 1986), The Case For The Crown (1987), The Search For Justice (1994), Trial of Strength (1997), Privacy and the Press (2004); *Recreations* reading, writing, wrestling with computers; *Clubs* Garrick; *Style—* Joshua Rozenberg, QC; ✉ BCM Rozenberg, London WC1N 3XX (e-mail joshua@rozenberg.net, website www.rozenberg.net)

RUANE, Christopher Shaun (Chris); s of Michael Ruane (d 1974), and Esther, *née* Roberts; *b* 18 July 1958; *Educ* Blessed Edward Jones Comp Rhyl, Univ of Wales Aberystwyth, Univ of Liverpool (PGCE); *m* 1994, Gill Roberts: 2 c; *Career* dep headmaster Ysgol Mair Primary Sch Rhyl 1991–1997; MP (Lab) Vale of Clwyd 1997–2015, memb Welsh Affairs Select Ctee 1999–2002, PPS to Rt Hon Peter Hain, MP (as Sec of State for Wales) 2002–07, PPS to Rt Hon Caroline Flint, MP (as Min for Housing DCLG then Min Dept of Work and Pensions) 2007–08; chair All-Pty Gp on Heart Disease 2002–, treas All-Pty Objective One Gp; chair N Wales Gp of Lab MPs 2002–, chair Welsh Gp PLP; former local cncllr; fndr and pres Rhyl Environmental Assoc, pres N Wales Ramblers Assoc; memb NUT (pres Vale of Clwyd branch 1989 and 1998); *Style—* Chris Ruane; ✉ 25 Kinmel Street, Rhyl LL18 1AH (☎ 01745 354626, fax 01745 334827, e-mail ruanec@parliament.uk); House of Commons, London SW1A 0AA (☎ 020 7219 6378)

RUBENS, Prof Robert David; s of Joel Rubens, of London, and Dinah, *née* Hasseck; *b* 11 June 1943; *Educ* Quintin GS, King's Coll London (BSc), St George's Hosp Med Sch London (MB BS), Univ of London (MD); *m* 30 Oct 1970, Margaret, da of Alan Chamberlin, of Burncross, S Yorks; 2 da (Abigail b 15 Nov 1971, Carolyn b 10 June 1974); *Career* house and registrar appts St George's, Brompton, Hammersmith & Royal Marsden Hosps 1968–72, conslt physician Guy's Hosp 1975– (dir of oncology servs 1985–90), prof of clinical oncology Guy's and St Thomas' and King's Coll Hosps Sch of Med and Dentistry of King's Coll London 1985–2003 (chm Div of Oncology 1989–97); ICRF: memb scientific staff 1972–85, dir Clinical Oncology Unit 1985–97; chief med offr: Mercantile & General Reinsurance Co plc 1987–97 (conslt med offr 1977–97), Legal & General Assurance Society Ltd 1992– (conslt med offr 1978–), Swiss Re Life and Health Ltd 1997–; ed-in-chief Cancer Treatment Reviews 1992–2001; examiner RCP 1987–93; chm EORTC Breast Cancer Co-operative Gp 1991–93; pres Assurance Med Soc 2003–05 (memb Cncl 1982–90), memb Assoc of Cancer Physicians 1985; hon dir Inc Homes for Ladies with Limited Income 1983–2000; memb: BMA 1969, British Breast Gp 1976, American Assoc for Cancer Res 1977, American Soc of Clinical Oncology 1977; Freeman: City of London 1979, Worshipful Soc of Apothecaries 1978 (Liveryman 1983); FRCP 1984 (MRCP 1969); *Publications* A Short Textbook of Clinical Oncology (1980), Bone Metastases (1991), Cancer and the Skeleton (2000) pubns on experimental and clinical cancer therapy; *Recreations* golf, bridge; *Clubs* Royal Wimbledon Golf; *Style—* Prof Robert Rubens; ✉ 5 Currie Hill Close, Arthur Road, Wimbledon, London SW19 7DX (☎ 020 8946 0422)

RUBERY, Dr Eileen Doris; CB (1998), QHP (1993); *b* 16 May 1943; *Educ* Univ of Sheffield (MB, ChB), Univ of London (Dip Med Radiotherapy), Univ of Cambridge (PGC Chemical Microbiology, PhD), Univ of London (MA); *m*; 1 da; *Career* Sheffield Royal Infirmary: house physician (endocrinology and therapeutics) 1966–67, house surgn 1967; MRC research fell 1968–71, Meres' sr research student St John's Coll Cambridge 1971–73; Addenbrooke's Hosp: sr registrar Dept of Radiotherapy and Oncology 1976–78 (registrar 1973–76), Wellcome sr clinical res fell Dept of Clinical Biochemistry and hon conslt Dept of Radiotherapy and Oncology 1978–82; Girton Coll Cambridge: sr res fell and dir of med studies 1980–82, registrar of the roll 1997–2012, visiting fell 1997–2000, sr res fell 2000–12; DHSS (now Dept of Health): sr med offr Toxicology and Environmental Protection (TEP) Div 1983–88, princ med offr TEH and head of Food and Radiation Branch 1988, princ med offr and head Communicable Disease Branch 1988–89, sr princ med offr and head Communicable Disease and Immunisation Div 1989–91, seconded to E Anglian Regnl HA 1991, sr princ med offr and head of Health Promotion (Med) Div 1991–95, under sec and head of Health Aspects of Environment and Food Div 1995–97, under sec and head Protection of Health Div 1997–99; Univ of Cambridge: pt/t secondment as lectr in public health med Inst of Public Health 1993–95, pt/t sr res assoc Judge Inst of Mgmnt Studies 1997–2004, course dir MSt in community enterprise 2001–04, sr assoc Judge Inst 2004–08; memb GMC disciplinary ctees 2000–06; conslt to public sector and other orgns on food safety and other public health issues; tutor in art history: Univ of Cambridge Inst of Continuing Educn 2004–, Rewley House Univ of Oxford 2005–09; Helen P Tompkinson Award BMA, WHO Travelling Fellowship; memb Cncl Roedean Sch 2002–05; FFPHM, FRCR, FRSPH, FRCPath; *Publications* numerous articles in professional journals on art history, biochemistry, radiation, public health, professional devpt, risk and uncertainty; *Recreations* reading, theatre, music (classical and opera), travel, Byzantine, Romanesque, Gothic art and art history; *Style—* Dr Eileen Rubery, CB, QHP; ✉ e-mail edr1001@cam.ac.uk

RUBERY, His Hon (Reginald) John; s of Reginald Arthur Rubery (d 1964), and Phyllis Margaret, *née* Payne (d 1992); *b* 13 July 1937; *Educ* Wadham House Hale, King's Sch Worcester; *m* 1, 10 June 1961 (m dis), Diana, da of Maurice Wilcock Holgate; 1 s (Mark John b 7 Feb 1968); m 2, 15 March 1974, Frances Camille, da of Thomas Murphy; 1 step da (Leonie); *Career* admitted slr 1963, ptnr Whitworths Manchester then Taylor Kirkman & Mainprice Manchester 1963–68, cncllr Manchester City Cncl 1968–74, hon sec Law Soc Manchester 1974–78, county court registrar then dist judge 1978–95, recorder of the Crown Court 1991–95 (asst recorder 1987–91), circuit judge (Midland & Oxford Circuit) 1995–2010, judge Court of Appeal St Helena 1997–2012, justice of appeal Falklands Islands, Br Indian Ocean Territory and Br Antarctic Territory; pt/t chm Immigration Appeal Tbnl 1998–2005, pt/t chm Mental Health Review Tbnl 2001–10, memb Parole Bd 2010–; memb: Law Soc, District Judges Assoc, Cncl of Circuit Judges; *Recreations* golf, swimming, gardening; *Style—* His Hon John Rubery; ✉ Birkby, Charnes Road, Ashley, Market Drayton, Shropshire TF9 4LQ

RUBIN, Dr Anthony Paul; s of Henry Walter Rubin (d 1990), and Lily, *née* Hooberman (d 1999); *b* 20 September 1937, Wembley, Middx; *Educ* St Paul's, Gonville & Caius Coll Cambridge, London Hosp Med Sch (MA, MB BChir); *m* 14 June 1969, Gillian Mary, da of John Dolbear (d 1997); 2 da (Deborah Jane b 19 June 1971, Esther Louise b 12 June 1974); *Career* registrar then sr registrar in anaesthetics Charing Cross Hosp 1964–71, insr in anesthesiology Univ of Washington Seattle 1969–70; conslt anaesthetist: Charing Cross Hosp (later Chelsea and Westminster Hosp) 1971–97, Royal Nat Orthopaedic Hosp Stanmore 1975–2004; Royal Coll of Anaesthetists: former examiner, memb Cncl, gold medallist; memb Assoc of Anaesthetists 1964; FRCA 1966, FRSM 1969; *Books* Problems in Obstetric Anaesthesia (jtly, 1993); numerous chapters and scientific papers; *Recreations* association football, travel, music; *Clubs* Queen's; *Style—* Dr Anthony Rubin; ✉ 42 Menelik Road, London NW2 3RH (☎ 020 7794 8802, e-mail rubin@easynet.co.uk)

RUBIN, (Robert) Stephen; OBE; s of Berko Rubin, and Minnie Gould; *b* 3 December 1937, Liverpool; *Educ* Canford, UCL (LLB); *m* 1958, Angela; 4 c; *Career* called to the Bar Inner Temple; chm Pentland Gp plc; former dir: Reebok Int, Adidas AG, La Chemise Lacoste; chm World Short Course Swimming Championships Manchester 2008, hon pres World Fedn of the Sporting Goods Industry, past pres World Sports Fedn, former world pres Textile Inst; Lifetime Achievement Award Br Sports Industry; Hon LLD Lancaster Univ, Hon DArt Nottingham Trent Univ; FRSA, fell UCL, Companion Textile Inst; *Recreations* anything to do with water, reading; *Clubs* Athenaeum, Travellers; *Style—* Stephen Rubin, Esq; ✉ Pentland Group plc, 8 Manchester Square, London W1U 3PH

RUBINSTEIN, Felicity Kate; da of Hilary Rubinstein, *qv*, and Helge, *née* Kitzinger; *b* 27 July 1958; *Educ* Godolphin & Latymer Sch, Camden Sch for Girls, Univ of Warwick; *m* 1991, Hon Roland Alexander Philipps, *qv*, s of 3 Baron Milford (d 1999); 1 s (Nathaniel Alexander b Dec 1996); *Career* literary agent; Rosenstone/Wender lit agency NY USA 1980–84, Viking Penguin Inc publishers NY USA 1985–86, dir William Heinemann Ltd publishers UK 1987–88, md Macmillan London publishers UK 1989–93, ptnr Lutyens and Rubinstein literary agency and bookshop 1993–; *Recreations* more reading, food; *Style—* Ms Felicity Rubinstein; ✉ 21 Kensington Park Road, London W11 2EU

RUCKER, Chrissie; MBE (2010); *m* 2 Sept 1995, Nick Wheeler, *qv*; 1 s (Tom b 1996), 3 da (Ella b 1998, India b 2000, Bea b 2004); *Career* fndr White Company 1994–; *Style—* Ms Chrissie Rucker, MBE; ✉ The White Company, 1 Derry Street, London W8 5HY

RUCKER, Jane; *see:* Campbell Garratt, Jane Louise

RUDAIZKY, John Nicholas; s of Raymond Rudaizky, and Shirley Rudaizky; *b* 15 July 1964, Johannesburg, SA; *Educ* King Alfred Sch Hampstead, City Univ London (BSc); *m* Louise Rudaizky; 2 da (Eliana, Mia); *Career* managing ptnr Saatchi & Saatchi 1987–2001, fndr RudaizkyRyan 2001–05, global business dir Vodafone JWT, ceo Team Vodafone and Team GSK WPP plc 2005–14, ptnr Global Brand & External Communications EY 2014–; chair (mktg and commercial) SnowsportGB; fndr RudaizkyRyan 2002, global dir JWT, ceo Team GSK (prev WPP), ceo Team Vodafone 2007–14; *Recreations* snowboarding, golf, tennis; *Clubs* Soho House, MGGB; *Style—* John Rudaizky, Esq; ✉ blog www.rudaizky.com

RUDD, Amber; MP; *b* 1963, London; *Educ* Univ of Edinburgh; *m* (m dis), A A Gill, *qv*; 2 c; *Career* MP (Cons) Hastings & Rye 2010–; sec of state for energy and climate change 2015–16, home sec 2016–; *Style—* Ms Amber Rudd, MP; ✉ House of Commons, London SW1A 0AA

RUDD, Charlie Richard Cooper; s of Lewis Rudd, of Winchester, Hants, and Joan, *née* Bower; *b* 28 June 1967, London; *Educ* Bryanston, Royal Holloway Coll; *m* 17 June 1995, Katrina, *née* Woods; 2 s (Oliver b 27 July 1998, Toby b 11 Dec 2000); *Career* grad trainee rising to account mangr Ogilvy & Mather Ltd 1989–92, account mangr rising to bd dir

Simons Palmer Denton Clemmow & Johnson Ltd 1992–98, bd dir J Walter Thompson Ltd 1998, head of account mgmnt, dep md, md then chief operating offr Bartle Bogle Hegarty Ltd 1999–2015, ceo Ogilvy & Mather Ltd 2016–; *Recreations* family, sport, news junkie; *Style*— Charlie Rudd, Esq; ✉ Ogilvy & Mather, Sea Containers, 18 Upper Ground, London SE1 9RQ (☎ 020 3193 3201, e-mail charlie.rudd@ogilvy.com)

RUDD, Sir (Anthony) Nigel Russell; kt (1996), DL (Derbyshire); s of Samuel Rudd (d 1983), and Eileen, *née* Pinder (d 1999); *b* 31 December 1946; *Educ* Bemrose GS Derby; *m* 20 Sept 1969, Lesley Elizabeth, da of Bernard Thomas Hodgkinson (d 1990); 2 s (Timothy Nigel b 27 May 1971, Edward Thomas b 23 Sept 1973), 1 da (Jennifer Clare b 24 March 1978); *Career* chm: Williams plc 1982–2000, Pendragon plc 1989–2010, Pilkington plc 1995– (dir 1994–), Kidde plc 2000–03, Boots plc 2003–06 (non-exec dir 1999–2006, dep chm 2001–03), Alliance Boots plc 2006–07, BAA 2007–; non-exec dir: Barclays plc 1996– (dep chm 2004–), BAE Systems plc 2006–; memb CBI Preident's Ctee; chllr Loughborough Univ 2010–; Liveryman Worshipful Co of Chartered Accountants, Freeman City of London; Hon DTech Loughborough 1998, Hon DUniv Derby 1998; *Recreations* golf, field sports, skiing, tennis; *Clubs* Brooks's, RAC, Chevin Golf, Notts Golf, London Capital, The China; *Style*— Sir Nigel Rudd, DL

RUDD, Roland Dacre; s of Anthony Rudd, of London, and Ethne, *née* Fitzgerald (d 2008); *b* 24 April 1961, London; *Educ* Millfield Sch Somerset, Regent's Park Coll Oxford (BA, pres Oxford Union 1985); *m* July 1991, Sophie, *née* Hale; 2 s (Rory b 1993, Oliver b 1998), 1 da (Isabelle b 1995); *Career* worked for Lord Owen 1985, employment corr The Times 1985–89, dep City ed Sunday Correspondent 1989–97, financial and political writer Financial Times 1991–94, chm and fndr Finsbury 1994–; founding chm Business for New Europe 2006–; co-fndr Breakingviews, memb memb Exec Ctee Army Bd, memb Bd of Tstees ROH, chm Corporate Advsy Gp The Tate, memb Gt Ormond St Hosp Centre for Children's Rare Disease Research Bd, chm and fndr Legacy10; visiting fell Centre for Corporate Reputation Univ of Oxford; govr Wellington Coll; *Recreations* Chelsea FC, Wagner, modern art; *Style*— Roland Rudd, Esq; ✉ Finsbury, Tenter House, 45 Moorfields, London EC2Y 9AE (☎ 020 7073 6356, fax 020 7374 4133, website www.finsbury.com)

RUDDOCK, Rt Hon Dame Joan Mary; DBE (2012), PC (2011); da of Kenneth Charles Anthony (d 1981), and Eileen Messenger; *b* 28 December 1943; *Educ* Pontypool GS for Girls, Imperial Coll London (BSc); *m* 1, 1963 (sep), Keith Ruddock (d 1996), s of Charles Ruddock (d 1966); m 2, 18 Sept 2010, Frank Doran, MP, *qv*; *Career* mangr Citizens' Advice Bureau Reading, chairperson CND 1981–85; MP (Lab) Lewisham Deptford 1987–2015, shadow min for transport 1989–92, shadow min Home Office 1992–94, shadow min for environmental protection 1994–97, Parly under sec of state for women 1997–98, Parly under sec of state DEFRA 2007–08, Parly under sec of state Dept for Energy and Climate Change 2008–09, min of state Dept for Energy and Climate Change 2009–10; hon fell Goldsmiths Coll London, hon fell Laban Centre London, hon companion Trinity Laban 2014; *Style*— The Rt Hon Dame Joan Ruddock, DBE; ✉ e-mail damejoanruddock@gmail.com

RUDDOCK, Michael (Mike); OBE (2006); s of Vernon James Ruddock (d 1997), of Blaina, and Margaret Mary, *née* Carroll; *b* 5 September 1959, Blaina, Gwent; *Educ* Nantyglo Secdy Sch; *m* 11 June 1987, Bernadette Mary (Bernie); 2 s (Ciaran Terence James, Rhys James), 1 da (Katie Mary); *Career* rugby union player and coach; played as back row forward for Blaina, Tredegar, Swansea (Swansea Player of the Year 1982) and Wales B, ret following industrial accident 1985; coach: Blaina 1986–88 (winners Monmouthshire Premier League 1987), Cross Keys 1988–90, Bective Rangers 1990–91, Swansea 1991–97 (beat Aust nat team 1992, Welsh League 1992 and 1994, Welsh Challenge Cup 1995), Leinster 1997–2000 (winners Irish Provincial Championship 1997, also coach Ireland A and asst coach Ireland 1998), Ebbw Vale 2000–03, Newport Gwent Dragons 2003–04, Wales nat team 2004–06 (winners Six Nations Championship and Grand Slam 2005, former coach Emerging Wales and Wales A and former asst nat team coach); dir of rugby Worcester Warriors 2007–; Welsh Coach of the Year 1992 and 2005; hon fell: Cardiff Univ 2005, Newport Univ 2005; *Style*— Mr Mike Ruddock, OBE

RUDDOCK, Sir Paul; kt (2012); *Educ* Mansfield Coll Oxford (MA); *Career* formerly with Goldman Sachs then md and head of int Schroder & Co Inc, co-fndr and chief exec Lansdowne Ptnrs Ltd 1998–; cmmr Nat Infrastructure Cmmn; former chm V&A, former chm Gilbert Tst for the Arts, tstee Metropolitan Museum of Art NY, chm Expert Panel World War I Centenary Cathedral Repairs Fund, chm Oxford Univ Endowment Mgmnt; Bancroft fell Mansfield Coll Oxford 2008; FSA; *Recreations* art history, tennis, walking; *Clubs* Athenaeum; *Style*— Sir Paul Ruddock; ✉ 10 Colville Mews, London W11 2DA

RUDDOCK, Air Marshal Peter William David; CB (2011), CBE (2001); s of late William James Ruddock, and Evelyn Mary, *née* Besançon; *b* 5 February 1954, Carlow, Ireland; *Educ* Grosvenor HS Belfast, Advanced Staff Coll Bracknell, Ashridge Mgmnt Coll, Manchester Business Sch, Henley Mgmnt Coll; *m* 1; 1 da (Alison Margaret b 17 July 1984), 1 s (David Alexander b 24 June 1988); m 2, 27 Oct 2001, Joanna Elizabeth, *née* Mitchell; *Career* cmmnd RAF 1974, completed tours 1978–88, qualified weapons instr (air defence) 1982, cmd Phantom Qualified Weapons Instr (QWI) course RAF Coningsby then RAF Leuchars 1986–88, gp weapons and Phantom desk offr HQ No 11 Gp RAF Bentley Priory 1988–90, advanced staff trg 1990, posted Defence Intelligence Serv (DIS) 1991–93, OC Ops Wing RAF Coningsby 1993–96, asst dir DIS 1996–99, cmd RAF Coningsby 1999–2000, Air Cdre Defensive Ops HQ No 1 Gp 2000–02, Dir of Air Staff 2002–04, Air Sec 2004–06, DG Saudi Armed Forces Project 2006–11, business devpt dir Lockheed Martin UK 2011–16, chief exec Lockheed Martin UK 2016–; display pilot Battle of Britain Meml Flight 1993–2000; FRAeS, FCMI 2011; *Recreations* golf, sailing, equestrian activities, most sports, military and family history; *Clubs* RAF; *Style*— Air Marshal Peter Ruddock, CB, CBE, FRAeS, FCMI, RAF (Retd); ✉ Lockheed Martin UK, Cunard House, 15 Regent Street, London SW1Y 4LR

RUDGE, John Aulton; s of Kenneth James Rudge (d 1993), of Stivichall, Coventry, and Leigh, *née* Soames; *b* 29 August 1951; *Educ* Woodlands Sch Coventry, Sch of Architecture Univ of Nottingham (BA, BArch); *m* 19 Aug 1972, Christine, da of William Hollowood (d 1956); 2 da (Alexandra Jane b 25 Sept 1981, Sussanah Kate b 21 April 1987), 1 s (Robert Aulton b 7 May 1983); *Career* architect: Erewash DC Derbys 1975–79, de Brant Joyce and Partners London 1979–83; ptnr Percy Thomas Partnership 1986–94 (assoc 1983–86), chief exec Percy Thomas Partnership (Architects) Ltd 1996–2004 (dir 1994), dir of architecture Capita Percy Thomas 2004–07, dir of architecture Capita Architecture 2007–15, managing ptr Aulton LLP 2015–; drafting new Building Performance Standards for UK Armed Forces 2015–; most notable works incl: Kenstead Hall, London residence for HRH King Fahd of Saudi Arabia, conversion of Grade 2 listed building (7 Albemarle St) into business and fine arts sch for Univ of Notre Dame, Royal Hosp Muscat, Armed Forces Hosp Muscat, Int Convention Centre and Symphony Hall Birmingham, Procurement Exec HQ for the Miny of Defence in N Bristol, Dorset County Hosp (Ph2), Wales Millennium Centre project Cardiff, Russels Hall Hosp Dudley, Def Trg Review PFI, ExxonMobil Lagos masterplan, ExxonMobil Eket QIT masterplan; dir: The Bristol Initiative 1991–92, Bristol 97 1991–94, PTP Seward 1995–97, PTP Hong Kong 2004, Cycle to Cannes (C2C) 2008–15; 3 nominations RIBA Design Awards, 1 nomination BCO Awards; RIBA 1976, ARCUK 1975, FBE 1991, BCO 1996–2011; *Recreations* cycling; *Style*— John Rudge, Esq; ✉ Aulton LLP, 8 Forest Hills, Almondsbury, Bristol BS32 4DN (☎ 01454 613964, mobile 07881 504119, e-mail aulton.consultants@btinternet.com)

RUDIN, Richard Duncan (professional name Richard Duncan); s of Arthur Derek Rudin (d 1981), and Margaret, *née* Swale; *b* 24 May 1957; *Educ* John Willmott GS Sutton Coldfield, Sutton Coldfield Coll of FE, Highbury Tech Coll, Open Univ (BA), Univ of Leicester (MA), holder City & Guilds Cert Techer in Further and Adult Educn; *m* 30 July 1983, Alison Marjorie, da of David Hay; 1 s (David Duncan Rudin b 2 June 1990); *Career* trainee newspaper reporter (NCTJ) Midland News Assoc 1976–79, newscaster/reporter Beacon Radio 1979–80, presenter/prodr BFBS Germany 1980–84, presenter Metro Radio Newcastle 1984–86, sr presenter Red Rose Radio Preston 1986–89, prog organiser BBC Radio Leeds (and on attachment as prodr BBC Radio Sheffield) 1989–92, prog controller Radio City Gold 1992–95, with media trg and PR Co CAT 1995–, lectr in journalism, public affairs, radio prodn etc Liverpool Community Coll 1995–98, sr lectr radio and journalism Liverpool John Moores Univ; also freelance writer and broadcaster (work broadcast on Radio 4); nominated Best Outside Broadcast Sony Radio Award 1988; memb: Radio Acad, NUJ, NATFHE; *Publications* An Introduction to Journalism (with Trevor Ibbotson, 2002), Encyclopedia of Radio (contrib, 2004); *Recreations* writing, reading, political biographies, histories and theory, walking, playing with son; *Style*— Richard Rudin, Esq; ✉ 1 Oakleigh, Skelmersdale, Lancashire WN8 9QU (☎ and fax 01744 886505, e-mail richard@richardrudin.com, website www.richardrudin.com)

RUDKIN, (James) David; s of David Jonathan Rudkin (d 1995), of Bosham, W Sussex, and Anne Alice *née* Martin (d 1969), of Armagh, NI; *b* 29 June 1936; *Educ* King Edward's Sch Birmingham, Univ of Oxford (MA); *m* 3 May 1967, (Alexandra) Sandra Margaret, da of Donald Thompson (d 1969); 2 s (Jamie b 1972, Tom (twin) b 1972 d 1997), 2 da (Sophie b 1977, Jess b 1978); *Career* Nat Serv RCS 1955–57, schoolmaster (classics and music) Co HS Bromsgrove 1961–64; dramatist and screenwriter; Judith E Wilson fell Univ of Cambridge 1985, visiting prof Univ of Middlesex 2004–, hon prof Univ of Wales Aberystwyth 2006–; work incl: Afore Night Come 1960 (staged 1962), The Sons of Light 1964 (staged 1976), Ashes 1972 (staged 1974), Cries from Casement as his Bones are Brought to Dublin 1972 (radio 1973), Penda's Fen 1972 (TV film, shown 1974), The Triumph of Death 1976 (staged 1981), Hansel and Gretel 1979 (staged 1980), Artemis 81 1980 (TV film, shown 1981), The Saxon Shore 1983 (staged 1986), Testimony 1985 (film screenplay, released 1988), author/dir White Lady 1986 (TV film, shown 1987), December Bride 1988 (film screenplay, released 1990), John Piper in the House of Death 1985 (staged 1991), Broken Strings (libretto, staged 1992), The LoveSong of Alfred J Hitchcock 1989 (radio 1993, staged 2013), Sir Gawain 1990 (TV adaptation, 1991), Symphonie Pathétique 1993 (revised 2000, unstaged), The Haunting of Mahler (radio 1994), The Woodlanders (film screenplay, released 1997), Trade 1997 (revised as Angel of the Canals 2003, unstaged), Red Sun 2002 (staged 2003), The Master and Margarita (Bulgakov, adaptation staged 2004), The Giant's Cause... 2004 (radio 2005), Black Feather Rising 2007 (libretto, staged 2008), Merlin Unchained 2008 (staged 2009), Macedonia 2013 (radio 2015); translations: The Persians 1965 (Aeschylus, radio 1965), Moses and Aaron 1965 (Schoenberg opera, staged 1965), Hecuba 1974 (Euripides, radio 1975), Hippolytus 1978 (Euripides, staged 1978), Peer Gynt 1982 (Ibsen, staged 1982), Deathwatch and The Maids 1987 (Genet, staged 1987), Rosmersholm 1989 (Ibsen, broadcast 1990), When We Dead Waken 1989 (Ibsen, staged 1990); John Whiting Award 1974, NY OBIE 1977, NY Film Festival Gold Medal 1987, European Film Festival Jury Special Award 1990, Sony Radio Award 1994; *Publications* Dreyer's Vampyr (monograph, 2005); *Recreations* bridge, languages (now mainly Celtic), geology, music and piano, cliff walking; *Style*— David Rudkin; ✉ c/o Casarotto Ramsay & Associates Ltd, Waverley House, 7–12 Noel Street, London W1F 8GQ (e-mail agents@casarotto.co.uk, website www.davidrudkin.com)

RUDLAND, Malcolm; s of Harold William Rudland (d 1966), of Leeds, and Marika, *née* Széll (d 1943); *b* 17 August 1941; *Educ* Ashville Coll Harrogate, St Paul's Cheltenham, Royal Acad of Music (BMus); *Career* music teacher Cirencester Sch; conductor; works incl: Fiddler on the Roof, West Side Story, Peter Pan; pianist and organist; music critic for: The Times, Opera, Musical Times; hon sec Peter Warlock Soc; FRCO, ARAM; Pro Cultura Hungarica; *Recreations* gliding, walking, reading; *Style*— Malcolm Rudland, Esq; ✉ 31 Hammerfield House, Cale Street, London SW3 3SG (☎ and fax 020 7589 9595, e-mail mrudland2@gmail.com, website malcolmrudland.org)

RUDLAND, Margaret Florence; da of Ernest George Rudland (d 1979), and Florence Hilda, *née* Davies; *b* 15 June 1945; *Educ* Sweyne Sch Rayleigh, Bedford Coll London; *Career* asst mathematics mistress Godolphin & Latymer Sch 1967–70, VSO Ilorin Nigeria 1970–71, asst mathematics mistress Clapham Co Sch 1971–72, asst mathematics mistress and head of mathematics St Paul's Girls' Sch 1972–83, dep headmistress Norwich HS 1983–85, headmistress Godolphin & Latymer Sch 1986–; govr: St Margaret's Sch Bushey 1996–, Merchant Taylor's Sch 1999–, St Mary's Sch Ascot 2002–; memb: Cncl UCL, Bd UCAS 2002–, General Teaching Cncl (GTC) 2002–; pres GSA 1996, memb Cncl Nightingale Fund 1996–; *Recreations* opera, travel, cinema; *Style*— Miss Margaret Rudland; ✉ The Godolphin & Latymer School, Iffley Road, Hammersmith, London W6 0PG (☎ 020 8741 1936)

RUDLAND, His Hon Judge Martin William; s of Maurice Rudland, of Sheffield, S Yorks, and Patricia, *née* Crossley; *b* 13 March 1955; *Educ* Rowlinson Sch Sheffield, Univ of Sheffield (LLB); *m* 1, 1980, Norma Jane Lee; 2 s (Oliver William b 17 Dec 1983, Edward James Martin b 23 Jan 1987); m 3, 1997, Mrs Linda Sturgess Jackson, *née* Potter; 1 step s, 1 step da; *Career* called to the Bar Middle Temple 1977 (Harmsworth scholar 1977); in practice 1977–2002, jr NE Circuit 1985, recorder 1996–2002 (asst recorder 1992–96), circuit judge (Northern Circuit) 2002–; *Recreations* books, walking, cinema, travel; *Style*— His Hon Judge Rudland; ✉ Manchester Crown Court, Courts of Justice, Crown Square, Manchester M3 3FL (☎ 0161 954 1800)

RUDMAN, Shelley-Marie; da of Jack Rudman, of Pewsey, Wilts, and Josephine-Ann, *née* Goddard; *b* 23 March 1981, Swindon, Wilts; *Educ* Pewsey Vale Sch, New Coll Swindon (BTEC), Univ of Bath (HND, Tugendhat Chllrs Award, Full Blue Award), St Mary's Coll Twickenham (BSc); *Partner* Kristan Bromley; 2 da (Ella-Marie b 6 Oct 2007, Sofia Lee Rudman-Bromley b 19 Jan 2015); *Career* skeleton bobsleigh: World Student Champion 2005, Silver medal European Championships 2006, Silver medal Winter Olympic Games 2006, team capt Vancouver Olympic Winter Games 2010, overall World Cup Champion 2011–12, World Champion 2013–14, represented GB Sochi Olympic Winter Games 2014; athletics coach and gym instr Univ of Bath 1999–2001, cross country coach and gym instr American Community Int Sch Cobham Surrey 2001–02, classroom mangr Devizes Sch 2004–06; full time athlete 2006–; 100% Me Drugs Free in Sport ambass for UK; hon teaching fell Faculty of Health and Wellbeing Sheffield Hallam Univ; BBC West Sports Personality of the Year 2006; *Style*— Miss Shelley-Marie Rudman

RUDOFSKY, John Alec; s of Alexander Edward Rudofsky, and Ethel, *née* Frost; *b* 13 December 1951; *Educ* St Clement Danes Sch, Selwyn Coll Cambridge (MA); *m* 1978, Susan Judith, da of late James Ernest Riley; 3 s (James Alexander b 1980, Nicholas John b 1984, Joshua Lewis b 1987); *Career* fin journalist: City Press 1973–76, BBC radio 1973–76, Investors Chronicle 1976–79, Daily Telegraph 1979–86; asst dir and fin communications conslt Streets Communications 1987–88, fndr dir and communications conslt Citigate Dewe Rogerson (formerly Citigate Communications Ltd) 1988–2000, dir Helsen Communications 2000–12, dir J R Consulting 2012–; *Style*— John Rudofsky, Esq; ✉ e-mail john@jrconsulting.me

RUDOLF, Anthony; s of Henry Cyril Rudolf, (d 1986), and Esther, *née* Rosenberg (d 2011); *b* 6 September 1942; *Educ* City of London Sch, Institut Britannique Paris, Trinity Coll Cambridge; *m* (m dis); 1 s (Nathaniel b 1974), 1 da (Naomi b 1976); *Career* fndr and

R

publisher Menard Press 1969–; visiting lectr Faculty of Arts and Humanities London Metropolitan Univ 2001–03, Royal Literary Fund fell Univ of Hertfordshire 2003–05, Royal Literary Fund fell Univ of Westminster 2005–08; juror Neustadt Int Prize for Literature Oklahoma 1986, judge of translation prize Br Comparative Literature Assoc 1994–97; Adam lectr King's Coll London 1990, H H Wingate/Jewish Quarterly Prize for Non-Fiction 1991, Hawthornden fell 1993, Pierre Rouve meml lectr Univ of Sofia 2001; patron Safer World Fndn 1990–2000; FRSL 2005, fell English Assoc 2010; Chevalier de l'Ordre des Arts et des Lettres 2004; *Books* The Same River Twice: Poems (1976), After the Dream: Poems (1980), Selected Poems of Yves Bonnefoy (1985, 1995 and 2000), translations of Edmond Jabès, Claude Vigée and Yevgeni Vinokurov (various dates), The Unknown Masterpiece: translation with essay of Balzac's story (1988), Wine from Two Glasses: Poetry and Politics (The Adam Lecture for 1990), At an Uncertain Hour: Primo Levi's War Against Oblivion (1990), I'm Not Even a Grown-Up: The Diary of Jerzy Feliks Urman (1991), The Poet's Voice (poems and translations, 1994), Engraved in Flesh (on Piotr Rawicz) (1996, revised edn 2007), The Arithmetic of Memory: autobiography (1999), Mandorla (poems, 1999, illustrated edn 2007), Kitaj (2001), Piotr Rawicz: Blood from the Sky (ed and introduced, 2004), Rescue Work: Memory and Text, Pierre Rouve Memorial Lecture 2001 (2004), Kafka's Doll (2007), Songs of Absence (trans of Claude Vigée's poems, 2007), Zigzag: five sequences in prose and verse (2010), Silent Conversations: a Reader's Life (2013), A Vanished Hand (2013), My Word For It: Collected Poems 1963–2014 (forthcoming), Jerzyk (2016), Yves Bonnefoy Poetry and Poetic Prose (co-ed, 2016); *Recreations* listening to music, looking at paintings, watching cricket; *Clubs* Patisserie Valerie RIBA; *Style*— Anthony Rudolf, Esq; ✉ The Menard Press, 8 The Oaks, Woodside Avenue, London N12 8AR (e-mail anthony.rudolf@menardpress.co.uk)

RUEBAIN, David Ezra; *Educ* Lord Mayor Treloar Coll, Hampstead Sch, Oriel Coll Oxford (MA), Coll of Law (CPE); *Career* admitted slr 1989, with Levenes 1995– (head Dept of Educn and Disability Law); accredited mediator, non-exec dir Equality Works Consultancy; founding memb The Times Newspaper Law Panel, chair Mental Health and Disability Ctee Law Soc; memb: Educn Law Assoc, Educ Law Practitioners Gp, Disability Discrimination Act Advsrs Gp, Nat Autistic Soc panel of specialist educ law slrs, Disability Rights Cmmn panel of specialist disability discrimination slrs; memb Editorial Bd: Disability and Soc, Community Care Law Reports; peer reviewer Legal Servs Cmmn; conslt on disability discrimination law to FA Premier League; tstee Disability Discrimination Act Representation and Advice Project; hon legal advsr to ind panel for Special Educn Advice; RADAR Person of the Year 2002; fell Br American Project; *Books* Disability Discrimination Act Tool Kit (co-author), Taking Action, A Guide for Parents of Children with Special Educational Needs (co-author), Education Law and Practice (co-author), Atkin's Court Forms (co-author, vol on educ law), Disability Rights Law and Policy (contrib), Disability Discrimination: The Law and Practice (consltg ed), Disability Rights in Europe: From Theory to Practice (contrib), Disabled Children and the Law (co-author), The Good Schools Guide (contrib); *Recreations* swimming, exercise, watching Arsenal FC, socialising; *Style*— David Ruebain, Esq; ✉ Levenes Solicitors, Ashley House, 235–239 High Road, Wood Green, London N22 8HS (☎ 020 8881 7777)

RUFFELLE, Frances; da of Norman Albert Ruffell, and Sylvia, *née* Bakel; *b* 29 August 1966; *Educ* Gate House Learning Centre, Sylvia Young Theatre Sch; *m* 31 Aug 1990, John Newport Caird, s of George Bradford Caird; 1 da (Eliza Sophie b 15 April 1988), 2 s (Nathaniel George b 17 June 1990, Felix Manley b 24 May 1995); *Career* actress and singer; *Theatre* roles incl: The Sleeping Prince (Haymarket) 1983, Starlight Express (Apollo) 1984, Les Misérables (RSC and Palace) 1985 and (Broadway) 1987 (Tony Award for Best Featured Actress, Helen Hayes Award for Best Newcomer, Outer Circle Critics' Award for Best Newcomer, Theatre World Award), Apples (Royal Court) 1989, Chicago (Adelphi) 2003–04 and (Cambridge Theatre) 2005, Joseph and the Amazing Technicolor Dreamcoat (tour), Pippin (Menier Chocolate Factory), Congs from a Hotel Bedroom (ROH), Mathilde (Edinburgh), Make Me a Song (New Players), Lucky Stiff (Bridewell), An Evening with Jason Robert Brown (New Players), Beneath the Dress (Edinbugh Festival, Menier Chocolate Factory and Garrick); *Television* incl: The Equalizer (CBS) 1987, Further Adventures of Robin Hood (Channel 5) 1999, Headless (Channel 5) 2000 (also co-wrote soundtrack), Dream Team 2001–02, Strangers (ITV), SWALK (ITV), The Hard Word (ITV), Objects of Affection Marks (BBC); *Films* Wildcats of St Trinian's 1980, The Road to Ithaca 1999, The Invitation, Secrets and Lies, P'Tang Yang Kipperbang, Keep Off the Grass, Les Miserables 2012, Devil's Tower 2013; *Recordings* contrib incl: cast of Les Misérables London 1985 and Broadway 1987, cast of Starlight Express 1984, duet with Christopher Cross on Back of My Mind 1988, featured on Ian Dury's Apples 1989, cast of Children of Eden 1991, duet with Michael Crawford on Michael Crawford Sings Andrew Lloyd Webber 1991; solo albums: Fragile 1996, Frances Ruffelle 1998, Showgirl 2004, Imperfectly Me; Purif.y (as PaTala) 2005; *Style*— Ms Frances Ruffelle

RUFFER, Jonathan Garnier; DL (Co Durham); s of Maj J E M Ruffer (d 2010); *b* 17 August 1951; *Educ* Marlborough, Sidney Sussex Coll Cambridge; *m* 1982, Jane Mary, da of Dr P Sequeira; 1 da (Harriet b 16 Oct 1990); *Career* Myers and Co Stock Exchange; called to the Bar Middle Temple (jr Harmsworth exhibitioner, hon bencher 2015); J Henry Schroder Wagg 1977–79, Dunbar Group Ltd 1980–85 (dir Dunbar Fund Management Ltd 1981–85), dir CFS (Investment Management) Ltd 1985–88, md Rathbone Investment Management 1988–94, chief exec Ruffer LLP (formerly Ruffer Investment Management Ltd) 1994–2012 (chm 2011–); dir: Rathbone Bros plc 1989–94, Odey Asset Management 1992–2005, Fuel Tech NV 1994–98, Electric & General Investment Tst plc 2001–11; chm: Good Shepherd Mission Bethnal Green 1998–2008, Auckland Castle Tst 2012–, Eleven Arches Tst 2015–; *Books* The Big Shots (1977), Babel: the Breaking of the Banks (2009); *Recreations* opera, sleeping; *Clubs* Athenaeum, Beefsteak; *Style*— Jonathan Ruffer, Esq, DL; ✉ Castle Lodge, Market Place, Bishop Auckland, Co Durham DL14 7NP; 4 Brunswick Mews, London W1H 7FB; Ruffer LLP, 80 Victoria Street, London SW1E 5JL (☎ 020 7963 8138)

RUFFLES, Dr Philip Charles; CBE (2001); s of Charles Richard Ruffles (d 1980), and Emily Edith (d 1998); *b* 14 October 1939; *Educ* Sevenoaks Sch, Univ of Bristol (BSc); *m* 27 May 1967, Jane, *née* Connor; 2 da (Amy Jane b 12 June 1971, Laura Megan b 31 May 1974); *Career* Rolls-Royce: graduate apprentice 1961–63, engr preliminary design 1963–68, project devpt engr RB211 1968–75, mangr JT10D Team E Hartford 1976, chief engr RB211 1977–80, head of engrg Helicopters 1981–83, dir of technol 1984–87, dir of design engrg 1987–89, tech dir 1989–90, dir of engrg 1991–96, dir of engrg and technol 1997–2001; dir Domino Printing Sciences plc 2002–14; memb Cncl for Science and Technology 2007–10; Royal Aeronautical Soc: Ackroyd Stuart prize 1987, Gold medal 1996; MacRobert Award Royal Acad of Engrg 1996, Royal Designer for Industry (RDI) 1997, James Clayton Prize IMechE 1998, Prince Philip Medal Royal Acad of Engrg 2001, Francois-Xavier Bagnout Aerospace Prize 2001, RTO Sawyer Award ASME 2002, Premio Internazionale Barsanti & Matteucci Award 2002, Glazebrook Medal Inst of Physics 2011; hon prof Univ of Warwick, hon fell Imperial Coll London 2002; Hon DEng: Univ of Bristol 1995, Univ of Birmingham 1998, Univ of Sheffield 1999; Hon DSc City Univ 1998; Liveryman Worshipful Co of Engineers; FREng 1988, FRAeS, FIMechE, FRS 1998; *Recreations* rugby; *Style*— Dr Philip Ruffles, CBE, FRS, FREng; ✉ 5 Ford Lane, Allestree, Derby DE22 2EX (☎ 01332 553550)

RUGOFF, Ralph; *Career* dir Hayward Gallery 2006–; *Style*— Ralph Rugoff, Esq; ✉ Hayward Gallery, South Bank Centre, Belvedere Road, London SE1 8XX

RUMBELOW, His Hon (Arthur) Anthony; QC (1990); *b* 9 September 1943; *Educ* Salford GS, Queens' Coll Cambridge (Squire scholar, BA); *m* 1; 3 da (Joanna, Elspeth, Antonia); m 2, Vivienne Ashworth, *née* Fletcher; 1 da (Rosalind); *Career* called to the Bar Middle Temple 1967 (Harmsworth exhibitioner and Astbury scholar); recorder 1988, dep judge of the High Court (Family Div) 2000–14, circuit judge (Northern Circuit) 2002–14 (ret), sr judge Br Sovereign Bases Cyprus 2008–13; chm: Med Appeal Tbnl 1988–2002, Mental Health Review Tbnl 2000–13; memb Parole Bd 2010–; *Style*— His Hon Anthony Rumbelow, QC; ✉ Manchester Civil Justice Centre, Bridge Street West, Manchester M3 3FX (☎ 0161 240 5000)

RUMBELOW, (Roger) Martin; s of Leonard Douglas Rumbelow (d 1980), and Phyllis Mary, *née* Perkins (d 1984); *b* 3 June 1937; *Educ* Cardiff HS, Univ of Bristol (BSc), Cranfield Inst of Technol (MSc); *m* 24 July 1965, (Marjorie) Elizabeth, da of Charles Richard Glover, of Macclesfield, Cheshire (d 2015); *Career* Nat Serv RAF pilot and Flying Offr 1955–57; Concorde project mangr Br Aircraft Corp 1973–74 (tech sales 1960–67, dep prodn controller 1967–73); DTI: princ 1974–78, asst sec 1978–86, under sec Mgmnt Servs and Manpower Div 1987–92, under sec Electronics and Engrg Div 1992–96; freelance conslt and advsr 1996–; dir Knott Park RA Ltd 2001–; tstee and dir The Florestan Tst 2006–12; CEng, MRAeS; *Recreations* singing, tennis, theatre, electronics; *Clubs* RAF; *Style*— Martin Rumbelow, Esq; ✉ The Spinney, The Chase, Knott Park, Oxshott, Surrey KT22 0HR (☎ 01372 842144, e-mail mrumbelow@aol.com)

RUMFITT, Nigel John; QC (1994); s of Alan Rumfitt (d 2007), and Dorothy, *née* Ackroyd (d 2000); *b* 6 March 1950, Leeds; *Educ* Leeds Modern Sch, Pembroke Coll Oxford (MA, BCL); *m* 15 Sept 1984, Pamela, *née* Pouncey; *Career* teaching asst Northwestern Univ Sch of Law Chicago 1972–73; called to the Bar Middle Temple 1974 (Harmsworth law scholar); recorder of the Crown Court 1995–2010 (asst recorder 1991–95); memb: Criminal Bar Assoc, Midland Circuit; *Recreations* skiing, sailing; *Style*— Nigel Rumfitt, Esq, QC; ✉ Chambers of Simeon Masterey QC, 7 Bedford Row, London WC1R 4BS (☎ 020 7242 3555, fax 020 7242 2511, e-mail clerks@7br.co.uk)

RUNCIE, Hon James; s of Robert Runcie, former Archbishop of Canterbury (d 2000), and Rosalind Runcie (d 2012); *b* 1959; *Educ* Marlborough, Trinity Hall Cambridge, Bristol Old Vic Theatre Sch; *m* 1985, Marilyn Imrie; 1 da (Charlotte b 1989), 1 step-da (Rosie Kellagher b 1978); *Career* writer and dir Radio Drama BBC Scotland 1983–85, documentary producer and dir BBC 1988–2000, freelance dir Oxford Film and TV 2000–10, freelance dir IWC Media 2005–08, freelance dir Modern TV 2006–11, producer and dir Silver River Productions 2011–12, artistic dir Bath Festivals 2009–13, head of literature and the spoken word Southbank Centre 2013–15; visiting prof Bath Spa Univ; *Books* The Discovery of Chocolate (2001), The Colour of Heaven (2003), Canvey Island (2006), East Fortune (2009); The Granchester Mysteries: Sidney Chambers and the Shadow of Death (2012), Sidney Chambers and the Perils of the Night (2013), Sidney Chambers and the Problem of Evil (2014), Sidney Chambers and the Forgiveness of Sins (2015), Sidney Chambers and the Dangers of Temptation (2016); *Recreations* cinema, cricket, fashion; *Clubs* Athenaeum; *Style*— The Hon James Runcie; ✉ c/o DGA, 55 Monmouth Street, London WC2H 9DG (☎ 020 7240 9992, website www.jamesruncie.com, Twitter @James_Runcie)

RUNCIMAN OF DOXFORD, Viscountess; Ruth; DBE (1998, OBE 1991); da of Joseph Michael Hellmann (d 1941), and Dr Ellen Hellmann (d 1982); *b* 9 January 1936; *Educ* Roedean Sch Johannesburg, Univ of the Witwatersrand (BA), Girton Coll Cambridge (BA); *m* 1, 1959 (m dis 1962), Denis Mack Smith; m 2, 1963, 3 Viscount Runciman of Doxford, CBE, *qv*; 2 da (Lisa b 18 Aug 1965, Catherine b 18 July 1969), 1 s (David b 1 March 1967); *Career* memb Advsy Cnl on the Misuse of Drugs 1974–95, memb Cncl Nat Assoc of CAB 1978–83, dir ENO 1978–83, dep chm Prison Reform Tst 1981–; chm: Mental Health Act Cmmn 1994–98, Nat AIDS Tst 2000–06 (tstee 1989–93), Central and NW London NHS Fndn Tst 2001–13, UK Drug Policy Cmmn 2007–13; tstee: Prince's Tst Volunteers 1989–94, Mental Health Fndn 1990–96, The Pilgrim Tst 1999–2011, Sainsbury Centre for Mental Health 2001–03; memb PCC 1998–2001 (memb Charter Compliance Panel 2004–06); advice worker Kensington CAB 1986–2001; Hon LLD De Montfort Univ 1997, hon fell Univ of Central Lancs 2000, hon fell Girton Coll Cambridge 2001; *Recreations* gardening; *Style*— The Viscountess Runciman of Doxford, DBE; ✉ fax 020 7372 4668

RUNCIMAN OF DOXFORD, 3 Viscount (UK 1937); Sir Walter Garrison (Garry) Runciman; 4 Bt (UK 1906), CBE (1987); also Baron Runciman (UK 1933); s of 2 Viscount Runciman of Doxford, OBE, AFC, AE, DL (d 1989), and his 2 wife, Katharine Schuyler, *née* Garrison (d 1993); *b* 10 November 1934; *Educ* Eton, Trinity Coll Cambridge; *m* 17 April 1963, Ruth (Viscountess Runciman of Doxford, DBE, *qv*), da of Joseph Hellman, of Johannesburg, and former w of Denis Mack Smith; 2 da (Hon Lisa b 18 Aug 1965, Hon Catherine b 18 July 1969), 1 s (Hon David Walter b 1 March 1967); *Heir* s, Hon Prof David Runciman; *Career* fell Trinity Coll Cambridge 1959–63 and 1971–; chm: Andrew Weir and Co Ltd 1991–2005, Runciman Investments Ltd 1990–2012; memb FSA (formerly SIB) 1986–98 (dep chm 1998); treas Child Poverty Action Gp 1972–97; pres Gen Cncl Br Shipping 1986–87 (vice-pres 1985–86); chm Royal Cmmn on Criminal Justice 1991–93; pres Br Acad 2001–05; Hon DLitt Univ of Oxford 2000; FBA 1975; *Books* Plato's Later Epistemology (1962), Social Science and Political Theory (1963), Relative Deprivation and Social Justice (1966), A Critique of Max Weber's Philosophy of Social Science (1972), A Treatise on Social Theory Vol I (1983), Vol II (1989), Vol III (1997), The Social Animal (1998), The Theory of Cultural and Social Selection (2009), Great Books, Bad Arguments (2010), Very Different but Much the Same (2014); *Clubs* Brooks's; *Style*— The Rt Hon the Viscount Runciman of Doxford, CBE; ✉ Trinity College, Cambridge, CB2 1TQ

RUSBRIDGER, Alan Charles; s of G H Rusbridger, of Guildford, Surrey, and Barbara, *née* Wickham (d 1995); *b* 29 December 1953; *Educ* Cranleigh Sch, Magdalene Coll Cambridge (MA); *m* 1982, Lindsay, da of Baron Mackie of Benshie, CBE, DSO, DFC (Life Peer), *qv*; *Career* reporter Cambridge Evening News 1976–79, reporter, columnist and feature writer The Guardian 1979–86, TV critic The Observer 1986–87, Washington corr London Daily News 1987, features ed The Guardian 1989–93 (feature writer and ed Weekend Guardian 1987–93), ed The Guardian 1995–2015 (dep ed 1993–95), exec ed The Observer 1997–2015; chair Scott Tst 2015–; dir Bd: Guardian Newspapers Ltd (GNL) 1994, Guardian Media Group (GMG) 1999; memb: Code Ctee PCC 2004–09, NUJ, Scott Tst; commended Br Press Awards 1977 and 1978, What the Papers Say Award Newspaper Ed of the Year 1996, 2001 and 2005, Nat Newspaper Ed of the Year Newspaper Focus Awards 1996, Freedom of the Press Award London Press Club Awards 1998; chm: Photographer's Gallery 2001–04, Nat Youth Orch 2004–; visiting fell Nuffield Coll Oxford 2004–, visiting prof Queen Mary's Coll London; *Publications* The Guardian Year (ed, 1994), Fields of Gold (with Ronan Bennett) 2002; also author of three children's books; *Recreations* golf, music; *Clubs* Garrick, Soho House, Broadway Golf; *Style*— Alan Rusbridger, Esq; ✉ The Guardian, Kings Place, 90 York Way, London N1 9GU (☎ 020 3353 2000, fax 020 7837 4530)

RUSH, Caroline; *Career* British Fashion Council: chief exec 2009–; fndr Vogue Designer Fashion Fund; *Style*— Ms Caroline Rush; ✉ British Fashion Council, Somerset House, South Wing, Strand, London WC2R 1LA

RUSH, Prof Michael David; s of Wilfred George Rush (d 1983), of Richmond, Surrey, and Elizabeth May Winifred, *née* Gurney (d 1985); *b* 29 October 1937, Kingston upon Thames; *Educ* Shene GS Richmond, Univ of Sheffield (BA, PhD); *m* 25 July 1964, Jean Margaret, da of George Telford (d 1987), of Golcar, W Yorks; 2 s (Jonathan b 1968, Anthony b

1971); *Career* Nat Serv RASC 1957–59; Univ of Exeter: asst lectr 1964–67, lectr 1967–81, sr lectr 1981–90, head Dept of Politics 1985–92, reader in Parliamentary govt 1990–94, prof of politics 1994–2003, emeritus prof of politics 2003–; visiting lectr Univ of Western Ontario 1967–68, visiting prof Univ of Acadia Nova Scotia 1981, res fell Carleton Univ Ottawa 1975, 1992 and 1999; assoc ed Jl of Legislative Studies, memb Editorial Bd Br Jl of Canadian Studies; chm Study of Parliament Gp 1990–93; memb Cncl Hansard Soc 1992–2001, memb Governance Bd Hansard Soc Scholars 2013–; FRSA 1992; *Books* The Selection of Parliamentary Candidates (1969), The MP and his Information (jtly, 1970), An Introduction to Political Sociology (jtly, 1971), The House of Commons: Services and Facilities (co-ed, 1974), Parliamentary Government in Britain (1981), The House of Commons: Services and Facilities 1972–82 (ed, 1983), The Cabinet and Policy Formation (1984), Parliament and the Public (1976 and 1986), Parliament and Pressure Politics (ed, 1990), Politics and Society: An Introduction to Political Sociology (1992), British Government and Politics Since 1945: Changes in Perspective (co-ed, 1995), The Role of the Member of Parliament Since 1868: From Gentlemen to Players (2001), Parliament Today (2005), The Palgrave Review of British Politics 2005 (co-ed, 2006), The Palgrave Review of British Politics 2006 (co-ed, 2007), When Gordon Took the Helm: the Palgrave Review of British Politics 2007–08 (co-ed, 2008), Parliamentary Socialisation: Learning the Ropes or Determining Behaviour? (jtly, 2011); *Recreations* listening to classical music, theatre, travel; *Style*— Prof Michael Rush; ✉ 2 St Loyes Road, Heavitree, Exeter EX2 5HA (✆ 01392 254089, e-mail michael.rush4@tiscali.co.uk)

RUSHDIE, Sir (Ahmed) Salman; kt (2007); s of Anis Ahmed Rushdie (d 1987), and Negin, *née* Butt; *b* 19 June 1947, Bombay; *Educ* Rugby, King's Coll Cambridge; *m* 1, 1976 (m dis), Clarissa Luard; 1 s; *m* 2, 1988 (m dis), Marianne Wiggins; *m* 3, 1997 (m dis), Elizabeth West; 1 s; *m* 4, 2004, Padma Lakshmi; *Career* writer; former advertising copywriter; memb: Gen Cncl Camden Ctee for Community Relations 1975–82, Int PEN 1981–, Cncl ICA 1985–, Production Bd BFI 1986–; pres PEN American Center 2004–; Freedom of the City Mexico City 1999; hon prof of the humanities MIT 1993; FRSL 1983, Commandeur de l'Ordre des Arts et des Lettres (France) 1999; *Books* Grimus (1975), Midnight's Children (1981, Booker Prize, James Tait Black Meml Prize, E-SU Literary Award, Best of the Booker Prize), Shame (1983, Prix du Meilleur Livre Etranger 1984), The Jaguar Smile: a Nicaraguan Journey (1987), The Satanic Verses (1988, Whitbread Award), Haroun and the Sea of Stories (1990), Imaginary Homelands (essays, 1991), The Wizard of Oz (1992), East, West (1994), The Moor's Last Sigh (1995, Whitbread Fiction Award 1996, Book of the Year Br Book Awards 1996, The EU's Aristeion Prize for Literature 1996), The Ground Beneath Her Feet (1999, Commonwealth Prize (Eurasic Section) 2000), Fury (2001), Step Across This Line: Collected Non-Fiction 1992–2002 (2002), Shalimar the Clown (2005, shortlisted Whitbread Novel of the Year 2005); *Television films* The Painter and the Pest 1985, The Riddle of Midnight 1988; *Style*— Sir Salman Rushdie; ✉ c/o The Wylie Agency, 17 Bedford Square, London WC1B 3JA (✆ 020 7908 5900, fax 020 7908 5901)

RUSHGROVE, Ben; s of David Charles Rushgrove, and Alison Jane Rushgrove; *b* 23 February 1988, Bath; *Educ* BTech; *Career* Paralympic athlete; achievements incl: 6th 100m and 7th 200m European Open Championships 2005, Bronze medal 200m IPC World Championships 2006, European record 100m 2006, 2 Gold medals (100m and 200m) and world record 200m VISA Paralympic World Cup 2007, Silver medal 100m Paralympics Beijing 2008, Bronze medal 200m Paralympics London 2012; Susannah Ingram Award Br Athletic Supporters Club 2006, Disabled Sportsperson of the Year (19 and over) Banes Chair's Sports Award 2009; *Style*— Ben Rushgrove, Esq; ✉ TeamBath, The Department of Sports Development, University of Bath, Claverton Down, Bath BA2 7AY

RUSHMAN, Dr Geoffrey Boswall; s of William John Rushman (d 1967), of Northampton, and Violet Helen Elizabeth, *née* Richards (d 1999); *b* 20 August 1939; *Educ* Northampton GS, Univ of London, Bart's Med Coll London (MB BS); *m* 12 Oct 1963, Gillian Mary, da of George Leslie Rogers, of Alcester, Warks; 3 da (Alison b 1965, Ruth b 1967, Jacqueline b 1969); *Career* jr anaesthetist Bart's 1968–73, conslt anaesthetist Southend Hosp 1974–99; Assoc of Anaesthetists prize for contribs to anaesthesia; examiner final FRCA Royal Coll of Anaesthetists 1994–2000 (part I 1991–94) and Coll assessor 1993–99; memb Cncl Section of Anaesthesia RSM 1985–88 and 1991–2000 (sr sec 1992–93, pres 1999–2000), elected memb Cncl RSM 2001–05; lay reader Oxford Diocese; FFARCS 1970; *Books* Synopsis of Anaesthesia (ed 8–11, 1977, 1982, 1987, 1993), MCQ Self Test Companion (1994), A Short History of Anaesthesia (1996), Short Answer Questions in Anaesthesia (1997), Lee's Synopsis of Anaesthesia (12 edn, 1999); *Recreations* skiing, preaching The Gospel, mountain walking, fishing; *Clubs* RSM; *Style*— Dr Geoffrey Rushman; ✉ Aylesbury Road, Thame, Oxfordshire OX9 3AW

RUSHMAN, Nigel John; s of Maj Frederick William Edward Henry Rushman, and Irene Vera, *née* Beer; *b* 25 May 1956; *Educ* Gillingham Tech HS, Gravesend GS, Thanet Tech Coll; *m* 1, 21 Sept 1980 (m dis), Deborah Sally, da of Kenneth William White, of London; 1 da (Louise Amanda b 1986); *m* 2, 28 July 1989, Nicola Susan, da of David Polding, of Oare, Wilts; 1 da (Sophie b 1995); *Career* fndr Rushmans Ltd, fndr Venica; former dir: Cubavest Ltd, Modulec Ltd; *Recreations* thinking, fly fishing, shooting; *Clubs* Cavalry & Guards, Yacht Club de Monaco; *Style*— Nigel Rushman, Esq; ✉ Rushmans Ltd, PO Box 2391, Marlborough, Wiltshire SN8 3WJ (✆ 01264 852010, fax 01264 852011, website www.rushmans.com Twitter @nrushman)

RUSHTON, Kenneth John (Ken); s of Dr Martin Rushton (d 1996), and Halina, *née* Schoenfeld (d 2002); *b* 6 October 1944; *Educ* Uppingham, Trinity Coll Dublin (MA); *m* Sept 1970, Lesley Christine, da of Michael Jackson (d 2001); 2 s (Patrick b July 1973, Christopher b March 1982), 1 da (Jane b Feb 1976); *Career* ICI: joined 1968, various secretarial appts, asst co sec 1988–96, co sec 1996–99, ret; dir Inst of Business Ethics 2000–01, dir UK Listing Authority 2001–03; FICS, FRSA; *Recreations* theatre, music, opera, skiing, golf; *Clubs* RSA, IOD; *Style*— Ken Rushton, Esq

RUSHTON, Prof Neil; s of John Allen Rushton (d 1996), and Iris, *née* Street (d 1987); *b* 16 December 1945; *Educ* Oglethorpe Sch Tadcaster, Middx Hosp London (MB BS), Univ of Cambridge (MD); *m* 12 June 1971, Sheila Margaret, da of Capt Geoffrey Greville Johnson (d 1997), of Southwold, Suffolk; 2 s (Mark b 25 Sept 1973, Timothy b 24 Jan 1980), 1 da (Nicola b 15 Aug 1975); *Career* Univ of Cambridge: dir Orthopaedic Res Unit 1983–2013, fell Magdalene Coll 1984–, emeritus prof of orthopaedics; hon orthopaedic conslt Addenbrooke's Hosp; Hunterian prof RCS; examiner Univs of Cambridge, Oxford and London; dep ed for Research Jl of Bone & Joint Surgery (B) 1996–2006; Hon MA Univ of Cambridge 1979; pres Euro Orthopaedic Research Soc, fndr memb Br Hip Soc, memb Br Orthopaedic Assoc, Br Orthopaedic Research Soc, FIMMM, FRCS; *Books* Colour Atlas of Surgical Exposures of the Limbs (1985), Orthopaedics – The Principles and Practice of Musculoskeletal Surgery (contrib, 1987), Body Clock (contrib); *Recreations* sailing, snow skiing, scuba diving, wines; *Clubs* SCGB, Athenaeum; *Style*— Prof Neil Rushton; ✉ 37 Bentley Road, Cambridge CB2 8AW (✆ 01223 353624, fax 01223 365889, e-mail nr10000@cam.ac.uk)

RUSKIN, Paul; *b* 22 August 1958; *Educ* Hertford Coll Oxford (MA), Cranfield Sch of Mgmnt (MBA); *Career* Cambridge Consultants Ltd: joined 1980, business unit mangr Informatics 1995–2001, dir 1996–2001; dir and ind conslt Paul Ruskin Ltd 2001–05, dir of special projects Premier Performance Div UK Ford 2002–04, memb Mgmnt Gp PA Consulting 2005–; MIEE 1981, CEng; *Style*— Paul Ruskin, Esq

RUSSELL, Alec Charles Cumine; s of James Cecil Cumine Russell of Aden, CBE, and Diana Margaret, *née* White; *b* 21 October 1966; *Educ* Winchester, New Coll Oxford (BA); *Career*

Daily Telegraph: Bucharest corr Jan-Dec 1990 (Turkey during Gulf War and Kurdish crisis), Yugoslav War corr 1991–92, SE Europe staff corr (based Bucharest) 1992–93, South Africa corr (based Johannesburg) 1993–98, asst foreign ed 1998–99, dep foreign ed 2000–01, foreign ed 2001–02, asst ed (foreign) 2002–; highly commended: Young Journalist of the Year Award 1990, David Blundie Freelance Corr Award 1991; *Publications* Prejudice and Plum Brandy (1993), Big Men Little People (1999); *Style*— Alec Russell, Esq

RUSSELL, Hon Ms Justice; Dame Alison Hunter Russell; DBE (2014), QC (2008); *Career* called to the Bar Gray's Inn 1983; recorder 2004, judge of the High Court of Justice (Family Div) 2014–; *Style*— The Hon Ms Justice Russell; ✉ Royal Courts of Justice, Strand, London WC2A 2LL

RUSSELL, Angus Charles; s of Kenneth John Russell (d 2002), and Nora, *née* Liversidge (d 1977); *b* 2 January 1956; *Educ* Bablake Sch Coventry, Coventry Univ; *m* 11 Nov 2011, Nadine, *née* Mercier; 2 da (Harriet Emily b 7 Dec 1988, Sophie Francesca b 21 July 1990); *Career* trainee CA PricewaterhouseCoopers 1975–80, in fin, mktg and business devpt ICI plc 1980–93, gp treas Zeneca Gp plc 1993–99, vice-pres (corp fin) Astrazeneca plc 1999, chief financial offr Shire Pharmaceuticals Gp plc 1999–2008, ceo Shire plc 2008–13; non-exec dir: City of London Investment Tst plc 2003–09, Intermune Inc 2011–; memb ICA 1979, FACT 2001; *Recreations* sailing, cycling, skiing, collecting art, contemporary ceramics and classic cars; *Style*— Angus Russell, Esq; ✉ Shire plc, Hampshire International Business Park, Chineham, Basingstoke, Hampshire RG24 8EP (✆ 01256 894222, fax 01256 894713, e-mail arussell@shire.com)

RUSSELL, Rt Rev Dr Anthony John; *b* 25 January 1943; *Educ* Uppingham, Univ of Durham (BA), Trinity Coll Oxford (DPhil), Cuddesdon Theol Coll; *m* 1967, Sheila Alexandra; 2 da (Alexandra b 1969, Serena b 1975), 2 s (Jonathan b 1971, Timothy b 1981); *Career* ordained: deacon 1970, priest 1971; curate Hilborough Gp of Parishes 1970–73, rector Preston-on-Stour, Atherstone-on-Stour and Whitchurch 1973–88, canon theologian Coventry Cathedral 1977–88, chaplain to HM The Queen 1983–88, dir Arthur Rank Centre (Nat Agric Centre) 1983–88, area bishop of Dorchester Dio of Oxford 1988–2000, bishop of Ely 2000–10, hon asst bishop Diocese of Oxford 2010–; memb Gen Synod 1980–88 and 2000–10, hon chaplain Royal Agric Benevolent Inst 1983–2002; memb: Archbishops' Cmmn on Rural Affairs 1988–90, Rural Devpt Cmmn 1991–99; tstee Rural Housing Tst 2006; vice-patron RASE 2002– (chaplain 1982–91, vice-pres 1991–2002, pres 2004–05); pres East of England Agric Soc 2007; pres Woodward Corp 2003–; memb House of Lords 2007–10; govr Radley Coll 2003–14; Hulsean preacher Univ of Cambridge 2004, univ select preacher Oxford 2011; visitor: Jesus Coll Cambridge, St John's Coll Cambridge, Peterhouse Cambridge 2000–10; hon fell: Wolfson Coll Cambridge, St Edmund's Coll Cambridge 2000, St Chad's Coll Durham 2007, Trinity Coll Oxford 2011; FRAgS 2008; *Books* Groups and Teams in the Countryside (ed, 1975), The Clerical Profession (1980), The Country Parish (1986), The Country Parson (1993); *Clubs* Oxford and Cambridge, Farmers'; *Style*— The Rt Rev Dr Anthony Russell; ✉ Lyehill House, Holton, Oxford OX33 1QF (✆ 01865 876415, e-mail lyehill@hotmail.co.uk)

RUSSELL, His Hon Anthony Patrick; QC (1999); s of Dr Michael Hibberd Russell (d 1987), and Pamela, *née* Eyre (d 2011); *b* 11 April 1951; *Educ* The King's Sch Chester, Pembroke Coll Oxford (MA); *Career* called to the Bar Middle Temple 1974; jr Northern Circuit 1977, recorder 1993–96 and 2001–04 (asst recorder 1989–93), standing counsel (Criminal) to the Inland Revenue 1994–96, circuit judge (Northern Circuit) 2004–06, sr circuit judge 2006–15, hon recorder of Preston 2006–15, recorder Preston Guild 2012; memb Bar Cncl 1988–94; Guild of Church Musicians: memb Cncl 1985–93 and 1995–2004, hon fell 2001, vice-pres 2005; Hon Burgess City of Preston 2012; hon fell Univ of Central Lancs 2013; *Recreations* singing, listening to music, video photography, travel, the countryside, researching family history; *Clubs* Oxford and Cambridge; *Style*— His Hon Anthony Russell, QC; ✉ The Law Courts, Openshaw Place, Ring Way, Preston PR1 2LL (✆ 01772 844700)

RUSSELL, Sir Charles Dominic; 4 Bt (UK 1916), of Littleworth Corner, Burnham, Co Buckingham; s of Sir Charles Russell, 3 Bt (d 1997); *b* 28 May 1956, London; *Educ* Worth Abbey Sch; *m* 1, 24 May 1986 (m dis 1995), Sarah Jane Murray, da of Anthony Chandor, of Haslemere, Surrey; 1 s (Charles William b 8 Sept 1988); *m* 2, 6 Sept 2005, Wandee Ruanrakrao; *Heir* s, Charles Russell; *Career* antiquarian book dealer; *Clubs* Chelsea Arts; *Style*— Sir Charles Russell, Bt

RUSSELL, Charlotte; *b* 4 February 1988; *Career* cricketer; with clubs: Brighton and Hove WCC and Sussex WCCC; memb England touring squad Aust and NZ 2007 and 2008; memb ECB Coaches Assoc 2006, memb MCC Young Cricketers 2009–10; *Style*— Ms Charlotte Russell; ✉ The England and Wales Cricket Board, Lord's Cricket Ground, London NW8 8QZ

RUSSELL, Christopher Garnet; s of George Percival Jewett (d 1948), of Boscombe, Hants, and Marjorie Alice Boddam-Whetham, *née* Keeling-Bloxam; *b* 6 April 1943; *Educ* Westminster, New Coll Oxford (MA); *m* 23 June 1973, Agatha Mary, da of Stephen Joseph Culkin (d 1984); 2 da (Claire b 1974, Lucy b 1975), 1 s (Charles b 1976); *Career* called to the Bar Middle Temple 1971, ad eundum Lincoln's Inn 1985; *Style*— Christopher Russell, Esq; ✉ Penhayle, New Polzeath, Cornwall (✆ 01208 862041); Framfield Place, Framfield, East Sussex (✆ 01825 890021); 12 New Square, Lincoln's Inn, London WC2 (✆ 020 7419 9411 or 020 7419 8000, fax 020 7419 1313, e-mail christopher.russell@newsquarechambers.co.uk, website www.12newsquare.co.uk); Third Floor East, 7 Stone Buildings, Lincoln's Inn, London WC2 (✆ 020 7404 9739)

RUSSELL, Clare Nancy; da of Sir Ewan Macpherson-Grant, 6 Bt (d 1983), and Lady Macpherson-Grant; *b* 4 August 1944; *Educ* Scotland; *m* 1967, Oliver Henry Russell; 2 s, 1 da; *Career* head decorator Constance Spry 1962–65, sec to Fourth Clerk at the Table House of Commons 1965–67, dir Craigo Farms Ltd 1970–; estate owner and land mangr Ballindalloch 1979–, opened Ballindalloch Castle to the public 1993; chm Queen Mary's Clothing Guild 1990–93 (estab Queen Mary's Clothing Guild in Scotland 1986); memb: Cncl Nat Tst for Scotland 1985–88, Moray Health Cncl 1986–91, Exec Ctee Scotland's Garden Scheme 1987–93 (dist organiser Moray and Banff 1980–93), Bd Children's Hospice Assoc Scotland 1995–2002; Sunday sch teacher Inveraven Church 1982–2008; HM Lord-Lt Banffshire 2002– (DL 1991–98, Vice Lord-Lt 1998–2002); Hon MUniv Aberdeen 2010; *Books* Favourite Recipes, Dried Flowers and Pot Pourri from Ballindalloch Castle (1993), Favourite Puddings from Ballindalloch Castle (1995), Favourite First Courses from Ballindalloch Castle (1996), Favourite Recipes from Ballindalloch Castle (1998), I Love Food (2004), I Love Banffshire (2009), I Love Food 2 (2013); *Recreations* dog-handling, gardening, flower arranging, piano, tapestry, knitting, cooking, historic houses, antiques; *Clubs* Sloane; *Style*— Mrs Clare Russell; ✉ Pitchroy Lodge, Blacksboat, Ballindalloch, Banffshire AB37 9BQ (✆ 01807 500206, e-mail celmisia@googlemail.com)

RUSSELL, Prof Donald Andrew Frank Moore; s of Samuel Charles Russell (d 1979), and Laura, *née* Moore (d 1966); *b* 13 October 1920; *Educ* KCS Wimbledon, Balliol Coll Oxford (MA, DLitt); *m* 22 July 1967, Joycelyne Gledhill Dickinson (Joy) (d 1993), da of Percy Parkin Dickinson (d 1972); *Career* served WWII: Royal Signals 1941–43, Intelligence Corps 1943–45; St John's Coll Oxford: fell 1948–88 (emeritus fell 1988–), univ lectr in classical languages and lit 1952–78, reader in classical lit 1978–85, prof of classical lit 1985–88; J H Gray Lectures Univ of Cambridge 1981; visiting prof: Univ of N Carolina 1985, Stanford Univ 1989–91; FBA 1971; *Books* Longinus On the Sublime (1964), Plutarch (1972), Ancient Literary Criticism (with M Winterbottom, 1972), Criticism in Antiquity

(1981), Menander Rhetor (with N G Wilson, 1981), Greek Declamation (1983), Anthology of Latin Prose (1990), Anthology of Greek Prose (1991), Dio Chrysostom, Orations 7, 12, 36 (1992), Plutarch: Selected Essays and Dialogues (1993), Libanius: Imaginary Speeches (1996), Quintilian (2001), Heraclitus: Homeric Allegories (with D Konstan, 2005), Plutarch: How to Study Poetry (with R Hunter) 2011; *Style*— Prof Donald Russell, FBA; ✉ 35 Belsyre Court, Oxford OX2 6HU (✆ 01865 556135); St John's College, Oxford OX1 3JP

RUSSELL, Francis George Scott; s of Robert Scott Russell, CBE (d 2000), of East Hanney, Oxon, and Anne, née Ingle Finch; b 4 February 1949, Oxford; *Educ* Westminster, ChCh Oxford; *Career* Christie's: joined 1972, dir 1978, dep chm 2004; dir Mount Stuart Tst; memb: Arts Panel, Nat Tst 1995–2015; FSA; Portraits of Sir Walter Scott (1987), John, 3rd Earl of Bute: Patron and Collector (2004), 52 Italian Places: A Pocket Grand Tour (2007), Places in Turkey (2010), Places in Syria (2011), Places in Jordan (2012), 101 Places in Italy (2014); author of articles and reviews in magazines incl Burlington Magazine, Apollo, Master Drawings, Walpole Soc, National Trust Studies, Studi Tizianeschi, The Art Book Cornucopia and Country Life and of contributions to The Dictionary of Art, exhbn catalogues, festschrifts and symposium pubns; *Recreations* sightseeing; *Clubs* Beefsteak, Pratt's, Turf, White's; *Style*— Francis Russell, Esq; ✉ 30C Upper Montagu Street, London W1H 1RP (✆ 020 7724 0054); The Grange, East Hanney, Wantage, Oxfordshire OX12 0HQ; Christie's, 8 King Street, St James's, London SW1Y 6QT (✆ 020 7389 2075)

RUSSELL, Lord Francis Hastings; s (by 2 m) of 13 Duke of Bedford (d 2002), and Lydia, Duchess of Bedford, née Yarde-Buller (d 2006); b 27 February 1950, Paarl, S Africa; *Educ* Eton; m 1, 1971 (m dis); 1 da (Czarina b 14 July 1976); m 2, 1996 (m dis); 2 s (John Francis b 5 June 1997, Harry Evelyn Terence b 11 Nov 1999); *Career* chartered surveyor 1979; MRICS; *Recreations* skiing, golf; *Style*— Lord Francis Russell; ✉ Ribsden Cottage, Chertsey Road, Windlesham, Surrey GU20 6HX (✆ 01276 477478, fax 01276 473528, e-mail francis@lfr.co.uk)

RUSSELL, Prof Ian John; s of Phillip William George Russell (d 1975), of Chestfield, Kent, and Joan Lilian, née Snook (d 1984); b 19 June 1943, Chatham, Kent; *Educ* Chatham Tech Sch for Boys, QMC London (BSc), Univ of Br Columbia (NATO studentship, MSc), Univ of Cambridge (Trinity Hall research studentship, PhD); m 20 July 1968 (m dis 2007), Janice Marion, da of Gladstone Herbert Hall; 1 s (Simon Alexander b 14 Sept 1975), 1 da (Charlotte Louise b 3 Jan 1979); *Career* res fell Magdalene Coll Cambridge 1969–73, SRC res fell Univ of Cambridge 1969–71, Royal Soc res fell King Gustaf V Res Inst Stockholm 1970–71; Univ of Sussex: lectr in neurobiology 1971–79, MRC sr res fell 1979–81, reader 1979–87, prof of neurobiology 1987–2011, MRC sr res leave fell 1995–98; prof of neurobiology Univ of Brighton 2011–; memb: Physiological Soc 1972, Soc of Experimental Biology 1966–1990, Assoc for Res in Otolaryngology 1993–, Acoustical Soc of America 1998–; Award of Merit ARO USA 2010; FRS 1989, FRSB 2014; *Recreations* hockey, windsurfing, gardening, walking, music, reading and especially my family; *Style*— Prof Ian Russell, FRS; ✉ Little Ivy Cottage, Waldron, East Sussex TN21 0QX; School of Pharmacy and Biomolecular Sciences, University of Brighton, Brighton BN2 4GJ (✆ 01273 642103, e-mail I.Russell@brighton.ac.uk)

RUSSELL, Ian Simon MacGregor; CBE (2007); s of James MacGregor Russell, of Norwich, and Christine, née Clark; b 16 January 1953; *Educ* George Heriot's Sch Edinburgh, Univ of Edinburgh (BCom); m 25 Oct 1975, Fiona; 1 s (Ewan b 7 April 1982), 1 da (Lindsay b 9 July 1989); *Career* audit sr Thomson McLintock 1974–78, accountant Mars Ltd 1978–81, controller Pentos plc 1981–83, sub fin dir Hongkong and Shanghai Banking Corporation 1983–90, controller Tomkins plc 1990–94; Scottish Power plc: finance dir 1994–99, dep chief exec 1999–2001, chief exec 2001–06; advsr 3i Gp; non-exec dir: Johnston Press plc 2007–, JP Morgan Fleming Mercantile Tst plc, British Assets Tst plc 2008–; non-exec chm: Remploy Ltd 2007–, Advanced Power AG 2007–, Univ of Edinburgh Bd; dir Business in the Community Ltd; MICAS 1977; *Recreations* golf; *Clubs* RAC; *Style*— Ian Russell, Esq, CBE

RUSSELL, Jeremy Jonathan; QC (1994); s of Sidney Thomas Russell, of St Albans, Herts, and Maud Eugenie, née Davies; b 18 December 1950; *Educ* Watford Boys' GS, City of London Poly (BA), LSE (LLM); m 1987, Gillian Elizabeth, da of Hugh Giles; 1 s (Thomas Jonathan Giles b 8 Oct 1988), 1 da (Monica Eugenie Helen b 10 May 1990); *Career* called to the Bar Middle Temple 1975; in practice SE Circuit, salvage arbitrator Lloyd's 2000–05 and 2009–16, sitting solely as arbitrator and mediator in shipping and commercial matters 2015–, salvage appeal arbitrator 2016–; CEDR accredited mediator; *Recreations* reading (particularly military history), gliding, classic cars; *Style*— Jeremy Russell, Esq, QC; ✉ Quadrant Chambers, Quadrant House, 10 Fleet Street, London EC4Y 1AU (✆ 020 7583 4444, fax 020 7583 4455, e-mail jeremy.russell@quadrantchambers.com)

RUSSELL, John Bayley; s of Frederick Charles Russell (d 1987), of Brisbane, Aust, and Clarice Emily Mander, née Jones (d 1959); b 22 January 1942; *Educ* C of E GS Brisbane, Univ of Queensland (BComm); m 27 Sept 1968, Virginia; 1 s (Simon b 1972); *Career* Deutsche Securities Aust Ltd (formerly Bain & Co Securities): ptnr 1972–92, ptnr i/c London Office 1980–84 and 1986–99, ptnr i/c NY office 1984–86; chm: Cedar Estates Ltd 2000–06, Thirty Five Ltd 2002–10, Henderson Far East Income Ltd 2007–, Minster Pharmaceuticals plc 2007–10 (dir 2005–10); dir Henderson Far East Income Tst plc 2000–07, dir Herencia Resources plc 2006–; memb: Aust Business in Europe 1990–2005, Victorian Advsy Ctee 1992–97; MInstD 2006; *Recreations* reading; *Style*— John Russell, Esq; ✉ e-mail jbr@jbrussell.com

RUSSELL, Madeline Ann; da of Samuel Lewis Smith (d 1951), and Molly Rita Stimson, née Saunders (d 2007); b 26 January 1951, Biggleswade, Beds; *Educ* Stratton GS Biggleswade, Holborn Coll of Law, Languages and Commerce; m 1, 16 Sept 1972 (m dis 1985), Colin John Dawson; 2 da (Katherine b 27 Nov 1975, Jennifer b 17 Aug 1977); m 2, 5 Feb 1994, Stuart Archibald Russell; *Career* admin mangr Quantime Ltd 1985–89, ptnrship mangr Bindman & Ptnrs 1989–96, chambers mangr Fountain Ct Chambers 1996–98, conslt in legal practice mgmnt 1998–2002; Beds CC: cncllr 2001–09, cabinet memb for community devpt 2002–03, cabinet memb for children's servs 2003–05, ldr 2005–09; cncllr Biggleswade Town Cncl 2003–07 and 2011–; memb: Biggleswade Deanery Synod 1983–86, St Albans' Diocesan Synod 1986–88; tstee PACE UK Int Affrs 1986–94, govr Stratton Upper Sch 1989–12 (chm 2000–12), memb East of England Regnl Assembly 2005–09 (memb Regnl Exec 2005–09), memb Bd East of England Devpt Agency 2008–12, chm Stratton Educn Tst 2012–, PCC sec St Leonard Old Warden 2013–, tstee Beds Music Tst 2014–, tstee Beds & Herts Historic Churches Tst 2014–, chm Caldecote Lower Sch 2014–; FCMI 2009 (memb 1987); *Publications* Making the United Nations a Winner (co-author, 1987); *Recreations* cycling, walking, music, crosswords, sudoku; *Style*— Mrs Madeline Russell; ✉ Wychbrook, 31 Ivel Gardens, Biggleswade, Bedfordshire SG18 0AN (✆ 01767 312966, e-mail wychbrook@me.com)

RUSSELL, Michael William; MSP; s of Thomas Stevenson Russell (decd), and Jean Marjorie, née Haynes (decd), of Kirrcudbright; b 9 August 1953; *Educ* The Marr Coll Troon, Univ of Edinburgh (MA); m 30 March 1980, Cathleen Anne, née Macaskill; 1 s (b 13 Feb 1988); *Career* prodr and dir; creative prodr Church of Scotland 1974–77, dir Cinema Sgire 1977–81, exec dir Network Scotland Ltd 1983–91, dir Eala Bhan Ltd 1991–2009, sec gen Assoc of Film and TV in the Celtic Countries 1981–83; SNP: various branch offices 1974–87, candidate Clydsdale 1987, campaign manager Alex Salmond's leadership campaign 1990, vice-convenor publicity 1987–91, chief exec 1994–99, shadow min of parly, shadow min for culture, broadcasting and gaelic 1999–2000, shadow min for children and educn, incl culture 2000–03; MSP (SNP): Scotland South 1999–2003 and

2007–11, Argyll & Bute 2011–; contested SNP Leadership 2004; Scottish Parl: min for environment 2007–09, min for culture, external affrs and the constitution 2009, cabinet sec for educn and lifelong learning 2009–14, convener Finance Ctee 2016–; prof of Scottish culture and governance Univ of Glasgow 2015–; former dir Scottish Nat Photography Centre; former vice-chm Skeklers Theatre Co, former chair Save a Life in Scotland, former bd dir Glasgow Film Theatre, former tstee Celtic Film and TV Assoc, tstee Scottish Futures Forum 2015–; FRSA 2007; *Publications* Glasgow – The Book (ed, 1990), Edinburgh – A Celebration (ed, 1992), Poem of Remote Lives – The Enigma of Werner Kissling (1997), In Waiting: Travels in the Shadow of Edwin Muir (1998), A Different Country (2002), Stop the World – The Autobiography of Winnie Ewing (ed, 2004), Grasping the Thistle (with Dennis Macleod, 2006), The Next Big Thing (2007), The Price of Innocence (with Ian McKie, 2007); *Recreations* cookery, gardening; *Clubs* Glasgow Art; *Style*— Michael Russell, Esq, MSP

RUSSELL, Sir (Alastair) Muir; KCB (2001); s of Thomas Russell (d 1988), and Anne, née Muir (d 1977); b 9 January 1949; *Educ* HS of Glasgow, Univ of Glasgow (BSc); m 19 Aug 1983, Eileen Alison Mackay, CB, FRSE, qv, da of Alexander William Mackay OBE (d 1967), of Dingwall, Ross-shire; *Career* Scottish Office 1970–99: seconded as sec to Scottish Devpt Agency 1975–76, asst sec 1981, princ private sec to Sec of State for Scotland 1981–83, under sec 1990, seconded to Cabinet Office 1990–92, under sec (housing) Environment Dept 1992–95, dep sec 1995, sec and head Agric Environment and Fisheries Dept 1995–98, perm under sec of state Scottish Office 1998–99, perm sec Scottish Exec 1999–2003; princ and vice-chllr Univ of Glasgow 2003–09; chm Judicial Appointments Bd for Scotland 2008–16, memb Bd Moredun Research Inst 2009–; dir UCAS 2005–09, memb Cncl ACU 2006–10, convenor Univs Scotland 2006–08, memb Bd USS 2007–09, memb Bd of Govrs Glasgow Sch of Art 2009– (dep chair of govrs), non-exec dir Nat House-Building Cncl and chm Scottish Ctee; non-exec dir Stagecoach Holdings plc 1992–95; memb Cncl Edinburgh Int Festival Soc 2004–09, chm Dunedin Concerts Tst 2009–, chm Royal Botanic Garden Edinburgh 2011–; Hon LLD Univ of Strathclyde 2000, Hon DUniv Glasgow 2001, Dr (hc) Univ of Edinburgh 2009; Freeman City of London 2006; FRSE 2000 (memb Cncl 2013–16), FInstP 2003, Hon FRCPSGlas 2005; *Clubs* New (Edinburgh); *Style*— Sir Muir Russell, KCB, FRSE; ✉ e-mail muir.russell@btinternet.com

RUSSELL, Peter John; s of Capt Raymond Colston Frederick Russell, of Bristol, and late Marjorie Catherine, née Lock; b 14 December 1951; *Educ* Bedminster Down Sch Bristol, Univ of London (BA, LLM); m 7 April 1979, Dr Evelyn Mary, da of Sqdn Ldr Lorence Alan Scott, of Bridport, Dorset; 1 da (Sarah Anne b 1982), 1 s (Timothy Paul b 1985); *Career* called to the Bar Inner Temple 1975; in practice Northern Circuit 1979–93, lectr in law Univ of Manchester 1975–82; judge Employment Tbnls 1993– (pt/t 1992); memb: Manchester Wine Soc, La Commanderie de Bordeaux á Manchester, Hon Soc of the Inner Temple; *Recreations* wine tasting, gardening; *Style*— Peter Russell, Esq; ✉ Alexandra House, 14/22 The Parsonage, Manchester M3 2JA (✆ 0161 833 6167, fax 0161 832 0249)

RUSSELL, Dame Philippa Margaret; DBE (2009, CBE 2002, OBE 1999); née Stoneham; da of Garth Rivers Stoneham (d 1987), of Barrow-in-Furness, Cumbria, and Nancy Wooler, née Leslie (d 1997); b 4 February 1938, Sheffield; *Educ* Barrow-in-Furness GS for Girls, St Hilda's Coll Oxford (BA); m 22 Aug 1959, Dr Alan Russell, OBE; 2 s (Simon Fitzgerald b 3 Nov 1963, James Christopher b 18 Oct 1964), 1 da (Emma Caroline b 18 Nov 1971); *Career* dir Cncl for Disabled Children 1976–2003, disability policy advsr Nat Children's Bureau 2003–; cmmr Disability Rights Cmmn 2002–; chair MOVE, memb Nat Learning Disability Task Force; tstee: Disability Partnership, Mental Health Fndn, ICAN, 4Children, Centre for Studies in Inclusive Educn; patron: United Response, Contact a Family; Rose Fitzgerald Kennedy Centenary Int Award 1990; Lifetime Achievement Award: 4Children 2004, Royal Assoc for Disability and Human Rights, RADAR (Royal Assoc of Disability and Rehabilitation) 2005; Hon Dr: King Alfred's Coll of HE Winchester, Univ of York, Univ of Lincoln 2012; hon fell Univ of Central Lancs; Hon FRCPCH 1997, FRSA, Hon FRPsych 2013; *Publications* author of a wide range of articles, reports and books on disabled children, family support and carers, health and social care; *Recreations* art, music, walking, family life; *Style*— Dame Philippa Russell, DBE; ✉ 4 West Hill Court, Millfield Lane, Highgate, London N6 6JJ (✆ 020 8340 3376); Old Brewery House, 118 St Pancras, Chichester, West Sussex (✆ 01243 785579); National Children's Bureau, 8 Wakley Street, London EC1V 7QE (✆ 020 7843 9708, e-mail prussell@ncb.org.uk)

RUSSELL, Sir Robert Edward (Bob); kt (2012); s of Ewart James Russell (d 1989), and Muriel Alice, née Sawdy (d 1988); b 31 March 1946, Camberwell, London; *Educ* Myland Primary Colchester, St Helena Secdy Modern Colchester, North East Essex Tech Coll Colchester; m 1 April 1967, Audrey, da of Frank Blandon (d 1996); 2 s (Andrew, Mark (twins) b 5 March 1968), 2 da (Joanne b 16 May 1971 d 1978, Nicola b 9 April 1981); *Career* reporter Essex County Standard and also Colchester Gazette 1963–66, news ed Braintree and Witham Times 1966–68, ed Maldon and Burnham Standard 1968–69, sub-ed London Evening News 1969–72, sub-ed London Evening Standard 1972–73, press offr British Telecom (formerly Post Office Telecommunications) Eastern region 1973–85, publicity offr Univ of Essex 1986–97, MP (Lib Dem) Colchester 1997–2015, sports spokesman 1999–2005; memb: Home Affrs Ctee 1998–2005 and 2006–10, Draft Charities Bill (Jt Ctee) 2004, Regulatory Reform Ctee 2005–06, Armed Forces Bill Ctee 2005–06 and 2011–, Panel of Chairs 2009–10, Speaker's Ctee for the Independent Parly Standards Authy 2010–, Administration Ctee 2010–11, Defence Ctee 2011–15; memb Lib Dem Home and Legal Affairs Team 1997–99; mayor of Colchester 1986–87, ldr Colchester BC 1987–91 (cncllr 1971–2002); *Recreations* promoting the town of Colchester; *Style*— Sir Bob Russell; ✉ Magdalen Hall, Wimpole Road, Colchester CO1 2DE (e-mail sir.bob.russell@hotmail.com)

RUSSELL, Ronald; s of Samuel Russell (d 1988), of Glasgow, and Marion, née Hanley; b 14 January 1956, Glasgow; *Educ* St Mungo's Acad Glasgow, Caledonian Univ; m 1 Oct 1991, Sandra, née Cheyne; 2 da (Shonagh b 6 July 1992, Jill b 28 Feb 1996); *Career* finance dir: Southern Natural Gas (part of Sonat Inc) USA 1979–89, Healthcare Scotland Ltd 1989–2004; dir Affinity Hospitals Holdings Ltd, non-exec dir IPM plc; FCA 1976; *Recreations* supporting Celtic FC; *Style*— Ronald Russell, Esq; ✉ Healthcare Scotland, 35 Albert Street, Aberdeen AB25 1XU

RUSSELL, Rupert Edward Odo; s of David Hastings Gerald Russell (see Debrett's Peerage, Ampthill, B), of London, and Hester Clere, née Parsons; b 5 November 1944; *Educ* Selwyn House Sch Montreal, Rannoch Sch Perthshire; m 9 Dec 1981, Catherine Jill, former Lady Brougham and Vaux, da of William Daniel Gulliver (d 1970); *Career* admitted slr 1973; ptnr: Blount Petre and Co 1979–86, Amhurst Brown Martin and Nicholson 1986–87, Payne Hicks Beach 1988–92, REO Russell & Co (own practice) 1992–; vice-pres Cities of London and Westminster Cons Assoc (former chm); memb Law Soc 1973; *Recreations* skiing, sailing, fishing, gardening; *Clubs* Buck's (former chm); *Style*— Rupert Russell, Esq; ✉ Highleaze, Oare, Marlborough, Wiltshire SN8 4JE (✆ 01672 562487/564352, fax 01672 564163); Wassand Hall, Seaton, Hull HU11 5RJ (✆ 01672 564352)

RUSSELL BEALE, Simon; CBE (2003); s of Lt-Gen Sir Peter Beale, RAMC, and Dr Julia Beale, née Winter; b 12 January 1961; *Educ* St Paul's Cathedral Choir Sch, Clifton, Gonville & Caius Coll Cambridge, GSM; *Career* actor; assoc artist: RSC, RNT, Almeida Theatre; *Theatre* Traverse Theatre credits incl: Die Hose, The Death of Elias Sawney, Sandra Manon; others incl: Look to the Rainbow (Apollo), Women Beware Women (Royal Court),

A Winter's Tale, Everyman in His Humour, The Art of Success, The Fair Maid of the West, Speculators, The Storm, The Constant Couple, The Man of Mode, Restoration, Some Americans Abroad, Mary and Lizzie, Playing with Trains, Troilus and Cressida, Edward II, Love's Labour's Lost, The Seagull, Richard III, King Lear, The Tempest, Ghosts, The Duchess of Malfi (Greenwich and West End) 1995, Mosca in Volpone (RNT, Olivier Award for Best Supporting Performance 1996) 1995, Rosencrantz and Guildenstern are Dead (RNT) 1996, Othello (RNT) 1997–98, Candide, Money, Summerfolk, Battle Royal (RNT) 1999–2000, Hamlet 2001 (Evening Standard Best Actor Award 2001, Critics Circle Award 2001), Humble Boy (RNT) 2001, Twelfth Night, Uncle Vanya (Donmar Warehouse and NY, Evening Standard Best Actor Award 2003, Olivier Award 2003, Critics Circle Best Actor Award 2003), Jumpers 2003, Macbeth (Almeida) 2005, Julius Caesar (Barbican) 2005, The Philanthropist (Donmar Warehouse) 2005 (Evening Standard Best Actor Award 2005, Critics Circle Award 2005); *Television* A Very Peculiar Practice, The Mushroom Picker, Down Town Lagos, Persuasion, A Dance to the Music of Time (Best Actor: BAFTA 1998, RTS 1998), The Last Temptation of Franz Schubert, Alice inWonderland, Spooks, The Hollow Crown (Best Supporting Actor BAFTA 2013); *Film* incl: An Ideal Husband, Blackadder Back and Forth, The Gathering, My Week With Marilyn; *Style—* Simon Russell Beale, Esq, CBE; ✉ c/o The Richard Stone Partnership, 2 Henrietta Street, London WC2E 8PS (☎ 020 7497 0849, fax 020 7497 0869)

RUSSELL-JONES, Maj-Gen (Peter) John; OBE (1988); s of Lt-Col P R Russell-Jones (d 1986), and Margaret (Peggy), *née* Roberts (d 1998); *b* 31 May 1948; *Educ* Wellington, RMA Sandhurst, RMCS Shrivenham, Staff Coll, Royal Coll of Defence Studies; *m* 2 Oct 1976, Stella Margaret, da of D P R Barrett; 1 s (James b 1 April 1979), 1 da (Polly 2 Feb 1981); *Career* Lt-Col and CO Engr Tank Regt 1988–90, Col Defence Policy MoD London 1990, Brig and chief exec Royal Engr Trg Orgn 1991–94, RCDS 1995, dir Int Orgns MOD London 1996–97, Maj-Gen 1997, capability mangr Manoeuvre MoD London 1997–2001; Col Cmdt Royal Engr 1999; army advsr BAE Systems 2001–; *Recreations* golf, military history, rock and blues music, family, travel; *Style—* Maj-Gen P J Russell-Jones, OBE; ✉ RHQ RE, Brompton Barracks, Chatham, Kent ME4 4UG (☎ 01634 822355)

RUSSELL-JONES, Dr Robin David (né Rhidian David Russell Jones); s of John Lewis Russell-Jones, JP (d 1970), of Saundersfoot, Pembrokeshire, and Mary Elizabeth, *née* Ebsworth (d 1997); *b* 5 March 1948, Carmarthen, Wales; *Educ* Rugby (Leaving Exhibition), Peterhouse Cambridge (MA, MB BChir, Medical Scholar); *m* 1, 1 Nov 1975, Ann Hilary Fair (d 1991), da of Roger Brian Nixon (d 1988), of Cheltenham, Glos; 1 da (Joy b 1976), 1 s (Christopher b 1979); m 2, 18 Sept 1993 (m dis 2013), Nina, da of Kailash Salooja, of Goring-on-Thames, Oxon; 2 da (Eleanor b 1994, Lily b 1996); *Career* conslt dermatologist St Thomas' Hosp, Ealing Hosp and Hammersmith Hosp 1983–2008, lead clinician in dermato-oncology Guy's Kings and St Thomas's Med Sch 2003–08; sr lectr Dept of Med Royal Postgraduate Med Sch London; dir Skin Tumour Unit St John's Inst of Dermatology St Thomas' Hosp 1996–2005; chm: Friends of the Earth Pollution Advsy Ctee, Campaign for Lead Free Air 1984–89, UK Skin Lymphoma Gp 1999–2005, Planetary SOS 2012–15; fndr and int conference organiser Help Rescue the Planet (HRTP) 2012–15 (chair 2015–); produced, directed and edited documentary on ozone depletion and climate change broadcast on BBC 2; FRCP 1990 (MRCP 1973), FRCPath 2002; *Books* Lead Versus Health (1983), Radiation and Health (1987), Ozone Depletion (1989) and 210 peer-reviewed pubns in scientific literature incl Lancet, New England Jl of Med, Cancer, Blood and Jl of Clinical Oncology; *Recreations* skiing, sailing, golf, horse riding; *Style—* Dr Robin Russell-Jones; ✉ Atholl House, Church Lane, Stoke Poges, Buckinghamshire SL2 4NZ

RUSSILL, Patrick Joseph; s of John Leonard Russill, and Mitty, *née* Clarke; *b* 9 September 1953, Yeovil, Somerset; *Educ* Shaftesbury GS, New Coll Oxford (Margaret Bridges organ scholar, MA); *m* 28 April 1979, Jane Mary, *née* Rogers; 3 da (Francesca b 1981, Helen b 1985, Katherine b 1991), 2 s (Benjamin b 1983, Dominic b 1988); *Career* organist, choral conductor and church music educator; dir of music London Oratory 1999– (asst organist 1976–77, organist 1977–99), organist for Papal Mass Wembley Stadium 1982; dir: Oxford Chamber Choir 1977–79, London Oratory Jr Choir 1984–2003, Europa Singers of London 1985–89; Royal Acad of Music: teacher of music techniques 1982–87, head of church music studies 1987–97, head of choral conducting 1997–, prof of organ 1999–; visiting lectr St George's Coll Jerusalem 1994–95, visiting prof of choral conducting Leipzig Hochschule für Musik 2001–; chief examiner Royal Coll of Organists 2005–; external examiner: UEA 1991–97, Univ of Leeds 2004–05, Univ of Sheffield 2013; memb Exec Ctee Church Music Soc 1990–; given lectures to various bodies incl: Incorporated Assoc of Organists, Soc of St Gregory, Royal Sch of Church Music, Winchester Diocesan Synod, Yale Inst of Sacred Music, Hungarian Church Music Assoc, Br Inst of Organ Studies; tstee Nicholas Danby Tst 1999–; memb Ctee Organists' Charitable Tst 1994–, memb Cncl Royal Coll of Organists 1996–2008, vice-pres Herbert Howells Soc 2007 (hon patron 1993–2007), hon memb Cathedral Organists Assoc 2012; Award for Choral Leadership Assoc of Br Choral Dirs 2015; Hon RAM 1993 (Hon ARAM 1989), Hon FGCM 1997, Hon FRCO 2002 (ARCO 1971); *Performances* organ recitals in UK, France, Germany, Near East and Asia incl Royal Festival Hall (debut 1986) and Queen Elizabeth Hall, UK premières of works by Hakim and Grier, CD solo recordings for ASV and Herald; work as choral director on EMI, Hyperion, Herald and Deutsche Grammophon Archiv; *Publications* editions of Howells and Sweelinck; music ed The Catholic Hymnbook 1998; author of numerous articles mainly on church music for jls and periodicals incl: The Organist, Organists' Review, British Institute of Organ Studies (BIOS) Journal, Royal College of Organists (RCO) Yearbook, Choir and Organ, Gramophone, The Cambridge Companion to the Organ (1998), Laaber Enzyklopaedie der Kirchemusik (2011 and 2013); *Recreations* open air and family photography; *Style—* Patrick Russill, Esq; ✉ The Oratory, Brompton Road, London SW7 2RP; Royal Academy of Music, Marylebone Road, London NW1 5HT (e-mail p.russill@ram.ac.uk)

RUSTAGE, Christopher Charles; s of George Roland Rustage (d 1983), of Manchester, and Mary, *née* Killian (d 1993); *b* 7 June 1948; *Educ* Our Lady of Grace Coll Manchester, St Joseph's Coll Manchester; *m* 1, 1967 (m dis 1986), Ann, da of Herman Taylor; 2 da (Andre-Jayne b 1967, Joanne Marie b 1971), 1 s (Christopher George b 1974); m 2, Angela Parkin; *Career* property developer, master franchise specialist, owner and investor, and hotel owner; apprentice motor body fitter 1965–66, specialist importer of blending and roasting teas and coffees, labourer/driver 1968–69, grave digger, brewery asst, asst to lion tamer at Billy Smart's circus, watch assembler and shoe polish manufacturer 1969–73, fndr construction co 1973–79, livestock farmer 1979–83, inventor/manufacturer new health products 1983–87, property speculator and furniture manufacturer 1987–90, fndr Riverside International Ltd (largest privately owned franchising chain in Europe) 1990–, financial support group developer 2009; chm The Pet Club Great Britain Ltd; memb Manorial Soc of GB 1972, memb Confedn of Trades & Indust 1983, memb Prince's Tst 1983–84; Lord of the Manor of Edern; *Books* The Fax Book (1983); *Recreations* shooting, boating, travel, country pursuits; *Style—* Christopher Rustage, Esq

RUSTIN, Prof Gordon John Sampson; s of Maj Maurice Edward Rustin, MC (d 1972), of Hale, Cheshire, and (Barbara) Joan, *née* Goldstone; *Educ* Uppingham, Middx Hosp Med Sch (MB BS), Univ of London (MSc, MD); *m* 17 Feb 1977, Frances Phyllis, da of Lionel Rainsbury, of London; 1 s (Edward Samuel b 4 May 1981), 1 da (Jessica Leah b 3 Jan 1986); *Career* registrar Whittington Hosp and UCH 1974–76, res fell Hammersmith Hosp 1977–78, sr registrar Charing Cross Hosp 1978–84, sr lectr and hon conslt in med oncology Charing Cross Hosp and Mount Vernon Hosp 1984–95, dir of med oncology Mount Vernon Hosp 1995–, prof UCL, Univ of Herts and Inst of Cancer Research; over 300 pubns on: tumour markers, vascular targeting therapy, germ cell, trophoblastic and ovarian tumours; memb: BMA 1971, ACP 1985; FRCP 1992 (MRCP 1974), BACR 1979; *Recreations* sailing, golf, opera, skiing; *Style—* Prof Gordon Rustin; ✉ 15 Wellgarth Road, London NW11 7HP (☎ 020 8455 5943); Bishops Wood Hospital, Northwood, Middlesex HA6 2JW (☎ 01462 814409, fax 01462 287729, e-mail grustin@nhs.net)

RUSTIN, Prof Malcolm Howard Albert; s of Maurice Edward Rustin, MC (d 1972), and Barbara Joan, *née* Goldstone (d 2013); *b* Hale, Cheshire; *Educ* Uppingham, Middx Hosp Med Sch London (BSc, MB BS, MD); *m* Dr Joanna Rustin; 2 s (Jonathan b 1986, Benjamin b 1986), 1 da (Hannah b 1989); *Career* conslt dermatologist and hon prof Royal Free and University Coll Med Sch 1989–; special clinical interest in connective tissue diseases and both a clinical and research commitment to atopic eczema; UK dermatology rep to UEMS; chm Dermatitis and Allied Diseases Research Tst (Dermatrust), past chm and memb Dermatology Specialty Advsy Ctee JRCPTB; past pres Section of Dermatology Royal Soc of Med; Gold medal American Acad of Dermatology; hon memb Br Assoc of Dermatologists (former academic vice-pres), fell American Acad of Dermatology; previous appts: sr registrar (dermatology) UCHL and Middx Hosp London, Muir-Hambro res fell RCP; FRCP; *Publications* author of over 200 pubns on general dermatology and the pathogenesis and treatment of atopic eczema; *Recreations* walking, golf, skiing; *Style—* Prof Malcolm Rustin; ✉ The Physicians Clinic, 13–14 Devonshire Street, London W1G 7AE (☎ 07557 969960, fax 020 7034 8160, e-mail malcolmrustin@btconnect.com); Department of Dermatology, The Royal Free Hospital, Pond Street, London NW3 2QG (☎ 020 7830 2376, fax 020 7830 2247)

RUTHERFORD, His Hon Judge Andrew; DL (Somerset); s of Robert Mark Rutherford, and Alison Wellington, *née* Clark; *b* 25 March 1948; *Educ* Clifton, Univ of Exeter (LLB); *m* 7 April 1994, Lucy Elizabeth, da of Prof Edmund Bosworth; 2 da (Isobel b 1 Dec 1996, Alexandra b 12 Oct 1999); *Career* called to the Bar Middle Temple 1970, recorder of the Crown Court 1993–95, circuit judge (Western Circuit) 1995–; *Clubs* Bath and County; *Style—* His Hon Judge Rutherford, DL; ✉ Bristol Civil Justice Centre, 2 Redcliff Street, Bristol BS1 6GR

RUTHERFORD, Lyn Malcolm; s of Wilfred Rutherford, and Margaret, *née* Robinson; *b* 20 January 1948, Consett, Co Durham; *Educ* Hookergate GS, Univ of Liverpool; *Partner* Michelle Phipps; *Career* admitted slr 1972; articles McKeags and Co 1970–72, slr Clayton Mott 1973, Dickinson Dees 1974–2008 (ptnr and head Family Law Gp), family law conslt McDaniel & Co Slrs 2011–; tstee of cat and dog shelter; *Recreations* horse racing, football; *Style—* Lyn Rutherford, Esq; ✉ McDaniel & Co, 23 Portland Terrace, Jesmond, Newcastle upon Tyne NE2 1QS (☎ 0191 281 4000, fax 0191 281 4333, e-mail lr@mcdanielslaw.com. website www.mcdanielslaw.com)

RUTHERFORD, Michael John Cloette Crawford (Mike); s of Capt W H F Crawford Rutherford (d 1986), of Farnham, Surrey, and Annette, *née* Downing (d 1993); *b* 2 October 1950; *Educ* Charterhouse; *m* 13 Nov 1976, Angela Mary, da of Harry Downing; 2 s (Tom William b 4 Dec 1980, Harry John Crawford b 19 Nov 1987), 1 da (Kate Elizabeth b 19 Oct 1977); *Career* musician; fndr memb Genesis 1966 (with Peter Gabriel, *qv*, and Tony Banks), first single released 1969, seventeenth album released 1992; fndr Mike and the Mechanics gp 1985–; top ten single Over My Shoulder 1995 (from album Beggar on a Beach of Gold 1995); *Recreations* polo (Cowdray Park); *Style—* Mike Rutherford, Esq; ✉ c/o Hit & Run Music Ltd, 30 Ives Street, London SW3 2ND (☎ 020 7581 0261, fax 020 7584 5774)

RUTHVEN, Prof Kenneth Borthwick Howard; *b* 1 February 1952, Edinburgh; *Educ* Univ of Edinburgh (DipEd), Moray House Coll Edinburgh (PGCE), Univ of Oxford (MA), Univ of Stirling (PhD), Univ of Cambridge (MA); *Career* teacher of mathematics and computing at schs in Edinburgh, Brighton and Cambridge 1974–83; Univ of Cambridge: lectr in educn 1983–98, reader in educn 1998–2005, prof of educn 2005–; Educational Studies in Mathematics: ed 1994–95, ed-in-chief 1996–2000, advsy ed 2001–; author of 50 research papers in peer-reviewed jls; memb Br Soc for Res into Learning Mathematics 1983– (chair 2006–08); tstee Sch Mathematics Project 1996– (dep chair 2004–05, chair 2006–); AcSS 2011; *Style—* Prof Kenneth Ruthven; ✉ University of Cambridge, Faculty of Education, 184 Hills Road, Cambridge CB2 8PQ (☎ 01223 767600, fax 01223 767602, e-mail kr18@cam.ac.uk)

RUTLAND, 11 Duke of (E 1703); David Charles Robert Manners; also Earl of Rutland (E 1525), Baron Manners of Haddon (E 1679), Marquess of Granby (E 1703), and Baron Roos of Belvoir (E 1616); s of 10 Duke of Rutland (d 1999), by his 2 w, Frances, *née* Sweeny; *b* 8 May 1959; *Educ* Wellesley House Broadstairs, Stanbridge Earls; *m* 6 June 1992, Emma L, da of John Watkins, of Knighton, Powys; 3 da (Lady Violet Diana Louise b 18 Aug 1993, Lady Alice Louisa Lilly b 27 April 1995, Lady Eliza Charlotte b 27 July 1997), 2 s (Charles John Montague, Marquess of Granby b 3 July 1999, Lord Hugo William James b 24 July 2003); *Heir* s, Marquess of Granby; *Career* dir Belvoir Estate; chm Historic Houses Assoc in E Midlands until 1999; pres: Grantham branch Air Crew Assoc, Grantham Canal Restoration Soc; memb and dep chm Civilian Ctee ATC Sqdn Grantham Lincs (47F Sqdn); patron Benedictine Abbey Alton; memb Hereford Cattle Breeders Assoc; Freeman City of London, Liveryman Worshipful Co of Gunsmiths; *Recreations* shooting, fishing, flying; *Clubs* Turf, Annabel's; *Style—* His Grace the Duke of Rutland; ✉ Belvoir Castle, Grantham, Lincolnshire NG32 1PE (☎ 01476 871026)

RUTLEY, David Henry; MP; *b* 7 March 1961; *Educ* Lewes Priory Sch, LSE (BSc), Harvard Business Sch (MBA); *m* Rachel; 2 s, 2 da; *Career* business devpt dir PepsiCo Int 1991–94, special advsr to Cabinet Office Miny for Agriculture, Forestry and Fisheries and HM Treasy 1994–96, dir of business effectiveness Safeway Stores 1996–2000, dir of financial services and dir e-commerce Asda Stores 2000–05, sales and mktg dir Halifax Gen Insurance 2005–07, business conslt 2008–09, mktg dir Barclays Bank 2009–10; MP (Cons) Macclesfield 2010–, PPS to Damian Green, MP, *qv* (as Min of State for Immigration then Min of State for Policing and Criminal Justice) 2010–; memb Treasy Select Ctee 2010, sec All Party Parly Gp on Nat Parks 2010–, co-chm All Party Parly Gp on Mountaineering 2010–; *Style—* David Rutley, Esq, MP; ✉ House of Commons, London SW1A 0AA (☎ 020 7219 7106, e-mail david.rutley.mp@parliament.uk, website www.davidrutley.org.uk, Twitter @davidrutleymp

RUTNAM, Philip; *Educ* Univ of Cambridge, Harvard Univ; *Career* formerly private sec to Fin Sec, ptnr and memb Bd Ofcom 2003–09; Dept for Business, Innovation and Skills: DG of business 2009–10, DG of business and skills 2010–; *Style—* Philip Rutnam, Esq; ✉ Department for Business, Innovation and Skills, 1 Victoria Street, London SW1H 0ET

RUTTER, Claire; *Educ* Guildhall Sch of Music & Drama (AGSM), Nat Opera Studio (sponsored by Friends of Eng Nat Opera); *m* Stephen Gadd (baritone); *Career* soprano; Wigmore Hall recital debut 1994; *Roles* with Scottish Opera incl: Violetta in La Traviata, Countess Almaviva in The Marriage of Figaro, Elettra in Idomeneo, Gilda in Rigoletto, Fiordiligi in Cosi fan Tutte, Rosalinde in Die Fledermaus; other prodns incl: Violetta (WNO), Mimi in La Bohème (Hong Kong and Beijing International Festival), Beethoven No 9 Choral Symphony (BBC Scottish Symphony Orchestra), Songs of the Auvergne (with BBC Scottish Symphony Orch), Madama Butterfly (with Royal Liverpool Philharmonic Orch), Giovanna D'Arco in Ludwigshafen (Opera North), Violetta in La Traviata (ENO), Gilda in Rigoletto (ENO and WNO), Donna Anna in Don Giovanni (ENO and Montpellier), Verdi Requiem, Sea Symphony, Fiordiligi (Dallas, US debut) 2003, Amelia in Ballo in Maschera (ENO), Tosca (ENO), Elvira in Ernani (ENO), La Gioconda

R

(Opera North), Lucrezia Borgia (ENO), Donna Anna (Dallas and Bordeaux), Tosca and Norma (Grange Park Opera), Amelia in Ballo in Maschera (Finnish Nat Opera), Violetta (Oslo); *Recordings* highlights of Madame Butterfly and La Bohème (with RPO) 1997, Illustrated Man (film score by Jerry Goldsmith, with Royal Scottish Nat Orch), Holst's Mystic Trumpeter (with Royal Scot Nat Orch), Christmas Classics with Carl Davis and Hallé 2003, The Kingdom (with the Halle and Sir Mark Elder); *Style*— Miss Claire Rutter; ✉ c/o James Black, James Black Management Ltd, The Old Grammar School, High Street, Rye, East Sussex TN31 7JF

RUTTER, Hadyn Michael; s of Herbert Rutter (d 1985), of Winsford, Cheshire, and Mabel Rutter; *b* 29 December 1946; *Educ* Verdin GS Winsford, Lincoln Coll Oxford (BA, Hanbury Law Scholar); *m* 1 April 1970, Susan, da of Charles Robert Johnson, of Winsford; 3 da (Tanya b 1974, Amanda b 1977, Lisa b 1981); *Career* admitted slr 1971; Richards Butler & Co London 1969–72, sr ptnr Bruce Campbell & Co Cayman Islands 1977–80 (joined 1972), own practice 1980–; pres Cayman Islands Law Soc 1979 (sec 1975–79); dir: Golf Links Publishing Ltd, Golf Links Int Ltd, Golf Links Int Inc, Offshore Corporate Servs Ltd (IOM), Trusco SA (Geneva); organiser World Pro-Am: Arizona, Acapulco, Hong Kong, Dubai, Las Vegas, Sun City, Thailand; Duke of Edinburgh Award (Gold) 1965; memb Law Soc 1971; *Publications* Cayman Islands Handbook Tax Guide (1977), The Golf Rules Dictionary (1997, 4 edn 2004); *Recreations* cricket, golf; *Clubs* Oxford and Cambridge; *Style*— Hadyn Rutter, Esq; ✉ 18 Majestic Apartments, Onchan, Isle of Man IM3 2BD (☎ 01624 661800, e-mail hadynrutter@manx.net, website www.golfrulesdictionary.com)

RUTTER, John Milford; CBE (2007); *b* 1945, London; *Educ* Highgate Sch, Clare Coll Cambridge; *Career* composer and conductor; dir of music Clare Coll Cambridge 1975–79, fndr Cambridge Singers 1979; guest-conductor and lectr worldwide incl Europe, Scandinavia, N America and Australasia; major compositions incl: Requiem 1985, Magnificat 1990, Psalmfest 1993, Mass of the Children 2003; hon fell Westminster Choir Coll Princeton 1980, fell Guild of Church Musicians 1988, pres Bach Choir; Medal of the Royal Coll of Organists 2014; hon bencher Middle Temple 2008; Hon Freeman Worshipful Co of Barbers; DMus (Lambeth) 1996; Hon Dr: Anglia Ruskin Univ 1999, Univ of Leicester 2005, Univ of Hull 2009, Open Univ 2014; Hon DMus Durham Univ 2012; *Publications* Opera Choruses (1995), European Sacred Music (1996); *Style*— John Rutter, Esq, CBE

RUTTER, Dr (James) Michael; CBE (2002); s of James William Rutter (d 1996), of Kendal, Cumbria, and Lily, *née* Harriman (d 1986); *b* 20 August 1941; *Educ* Kendal GS, Royal (Dick) Sch of Vet Studies Univ of Edinburgh (BVM and S, BSc, PhD); *m* 1 July 1967, Jacqueline Patricia, da of late Thomas Anderson Watson; 1 da (Charlotte Sophie b 6 May 1977); *Career* Univ of Edinburgh: research scholar 1964–67, research asst 1967–69; Inst for Research on Animal Diseases Compton (later Inst for Animal Health): vet research offr 1969–73, princ vet research offr 1973–84, seconded to Dept of Educn and Science 1975–78, head Dept of Microbiology 1984–89, acting head Compton Lab 1986–89; dir of Vet Meds DEFRA (formerly MAFF) 1989–2002 (memb Mgmnt Bd MAFF 1992–99), chief exec Vet Meds Directorate 1990–2002, JMR Consultancy 2002–; expert conslt: ODA 1986, Food and Agric Orgn 1991–92, WHO 1997; assessor Animal Medicines Trg Regulatory Authy 2007–; memb EC Ctee for Vet Medicinal Products 1991–99, memb Mgmnt Bd European Meds Evaluation Agency 1996–2002, chair DEFRA/BPC Poultry Research Ctee 2008–; dir Vet Benevolent Fund 2004–13 (sec 2006–13), pres Vet Res Club 2007–08; MRCVS 1964, FRSM; *Books* Perinatal Ill Health in Calves (ed, 1973), Pasteurella and Pasteurellosis (co-ed, 1989); author of numerous scientific articles; *Recreations* gardening, ballet, theatre, outdoor sports; *Style*— Dr Michael Rutter, CBE

RUTTER, Prof Sir Michael Llewellyn; kt (1992), CBE (1985); s of Llewellyn Charles Rutter, and Winifred Olive, *née* Barber; *b* 15 August 1933, Lebanon; *Educ* Wolverhampton GS, Bootham Sch York, Univ of Birmingham Med Sch (MB ChB, MD); *m* 28 December 1958, Marjorie, da of Richard Heys (d 1983); 2 da (Sheila b 22 April 1960, Christine b 18 Sept 1964), 1 s (Stephen b 5 April 1963); *Career* memb scientific staff MRC Social Psychiatry Research Unit 1962–65; Inst of Psychiatry Univ of London: sr lectr (later reader) 1966–73, prof of child psychiatry 1973–98, prof of developmental psychopathology 1998–; hon conslt physician Bethlehem Royal and Maudsley Hosps 1966–; hon dir: MRC Child Psychiatry Unit Inst of Psychiatry 1984–98, Social, Genetic & Developmental Psychiatry Research Centre 1994–98; pres Int Soc for Research in Child and Adolescent Psychopathology 1997–99, pres Soc for Research in Child Devpt 1999–2001; Hon Dr: Univ of Leiden 1985, Catholic Univ Louvain 1990, Univ of Jyvaskyla 1996; Hon DSc: Univ of Birmingham 1990, Univ of Chicago 1991, Univ of Minnesota 1993, Univ of Ghent 1994, Univ of Warwick 1999, UEA 2000, Univ of Sussex 2014, Univ of St Andrew's 2013; Hon MD Univ of Edinburgh 1990, Hon DUniv N London, hon prof Univ of Amsterdam 2001; Distinguished Scientific Contribution Award American Psychological Association 1995, Castilla del Pino Prize for Achievement in Psychiatry Cordoba Spain 1995, Helmut Horten Research Award Helmut Horten Stiftung Switzerland 1997, Etienne de Greef Prize Int Soc for Criminology 1998, Ruane Prize 2000, Sarnat Prize 2001, IMFAR Award 2002, G Stanley Award 2003, Brooke Garber Nerdich Award 2004; foreign assoc memb: Inst of Med US Nat Acad of Sciences 1988, US Nat Acad of Educn 1990; foreign hon memb American Acad of Arts and Sciences 1989; founding memb Academia Europaea 1988, hon memb Br Paediatric Assoc 1994; hon FRSM 1996, hon fell Inst of Child Health 1996, Hon FRCPsych 1997; fell KCL 1998, fndr fell and memb Cncl Acad of Med Scis 1998; FRS 1987, Hon FBA 2002; *Books* incl: A Neuropsychiatric Study in Childhood (with P Graham and W Yule, 1970), Maternal Deprivation Reassessed (1972, 2 edn 1981), The Child With Delayed Speech (ed with J A M Martin, 1972), Cycles of Disadvantage: A Review of Research (with N Madge, 1976), Changing Youth in a Changing Society: Patterns of Adolescent Development and Disorder (1979), Developmental Neuropsychiatry (ed 1983), Juvenile Delinquency: Trends and Perspectives (with H Giller, 1983), Language Development and Disorders (ed with W Yule, 1987), Straight and Devious Pathways from Childhood to Adulthood (ed with L Robins, 1990), Developing Minds: Challenge and Continuity Across the Lifespan (with Majorie Rutter, 1993), Child and Adolescent Psychiatry: Modern Approaches (ed with E Taylor and L Hersov, 3 edn 1994), Development Through Life (ed with D Hay, 1994), Stress, Risk and Resilience in Children and Adolescents: Processes, Mechanisms and Interventions (ed with R J Haggerty, L R Sherrod and N Garmezy, 1994), Psychosocial Disorders in Young People: Time trends and their causes (co-edited with David Smith, 1995), Behavioral Genetics (with R Plomlin, J DeFries and G E McClearn, 3 edn, 1997), Antisocial Behaviour by Young People (with H Giller and A Hagell, 1998), Sex Differences in Antisocial Behaviour: Conduct, Disorder, Delinquency and Violence in the Dunedin Longitudinal Study (with T Moffitt, A Caspi and P Silva, 2001), Child and Adolescent Psychiatry (ed with Eric Taylor, 4 edn 2002), Genes & Behaviour: Nature-nurture interplay explained (2006), Rutter's Child & Adolescent Psychiatry (ed with D Bishop, D Pine, S Scott, J Stevenson, E Taylor and A Thapar, 5 edn 2008), Genetic Effects on Environmental Vulnerability to Disease (ed, 2008), Gene-Environment Interactions in Developmental Psychopathology (ed with Kenneth Dodge, 2011); *Recreations* grandchildren, fell walking, tennis, wine tasting, theatre; *Style*— Prof Sir Michael Rutter, CBE, FRS; ✉ 190 Court Lane, Dulwich, London SE21 7ED; Institute of Psychiatry, Psychology & Neuroscience, De Crespigny Park, Denmark Hill, London SE5 8AF (☎ 020 7848 0882, fax 020 7848 0881, e-mail michael.rutter@kcl.ac.uk)

RUTTLE, (Henry) Stephen Mayo; QC (1997); s of His Hon Henry Samuel Jacob Ruttle (d 1995), and Joyce Mayo, *née* Moriarty (d 1968); *b* 6 February 1953; *Educ* Westminster (Queen's scholar), Queens' Coll Cambridge (BA); *m* 24 Aug 1985, Fiona Jane, da of William Mitchell-Innes; 2 da (Emma Jane Mayo b 1988, Bethia Claire Mayo b 1993), 2 s (James Patrick Mayo b 1990, David Timothy Mayo b 1995); *Career* called to the Bar Gray's Inn 1976 (bencher 2004); currently practicing as specialist commercial and community mediator (also sits as reinsurance arbitrator); Lt Bailiff Guernsey 2007–; memb: Br Insurance Law Assoc, Lloyd's of London Arbitration Panel, Civil Justice Cncl ADR Sub-Ctee; CEDR accredited and registered mediator; contributor to numerous publications on mediation and conflict resolution; active church member, committed to dispute resolution at individual and community level; memb and accredited mediator Hong Kong Int Arbitration Centre 2006–; fell Int Acad of Mediation 2007; *Recreations* fly fishing, the countryside, mountains, oak furniture; *Clubs* Flyfishers'; *Style*— Stephen Ruttle, Esq, QC; ✉ Brick Court Chambers, 7–8 Essex Street, London WC2R 3LD (☎ 020 7379 3550, fax 020 7379 3558, e-mail stephen.ruttle@brickcourt.co.uk)

RYAN, Chris John; s of Henry Patrick Ryan, of Melton, Suffolk, and Evelyn May, *née* Hill; *b* 16 June 1954; *Educ* Farlingaye Sch Woodbridge, Colchester Sch of Art; *m* 22 June 1982, Vanessa Faith, da of Colin Day; *Career* photographer; trained with Phil Jude, Tony Copeland and Van Pariser; own studio 1981–; major assignments incl: covers for Radio Times and Telegraph, Aston Martin cars, Vogue España magazine, annual reports for Duke of Westminster and Société Générale de Belgique; awards from D & AD and Assoc of Photographers; memb Assoc of Photographers 1976; *Recreations* anything hedonistic; *Style*— Chris Ryan, Esq

RYAN, Sir Derek Gerald; 4 Bt (UK 1919), of Hintlesham, Suffolk; o s of Sir Derek Gerald Ryan, 3 Bt (d 1990), and his 1 w, Penelope Anne, *née* Hawkings; *b* 25 March 1954; *Educ* Univ of Calif Berkeley (BAED); *m* 1986 (m dis 1990), Maria Teresa, da of Juan G Rodriguez, of Lexington, Kentucky; *Heir* kinsman, Barry Ryan; *Career* with Fowler Ferguson Kingston Ruben architects Salt Lake City Utah 1977–79, Atelier d'Urbanisme en Montagne architects/urban planners Chambéry France 1979; NBBJ architects/planners Seattle Washington 1980–99, ptnr Williams Ptnrs Architects PC Ketchum Idaho 1999–2014, sole prop dgrArchitect Ketchum Idaho 2014–; memb Nat Cncl of Architects Registration Bd (NCARB) 1984, memb AIA 1999; *Recreations* skiing, guitar; *Style*— Sir Derek Ryan, Bt; ✉ PO Box 6966, Ketchum ID 83340, USA (☎ 00 1 208 720 4153, e-mail dgarchitect@gmail.com)

RYAN, Rt Hon Joan; PC (2007); *b* 8 September 1955, Warrington; *Educ* Liverpool Coll of HE, Southbank Poly; *m* Martin Hegarty; 1 s (Michael), 1 da (Julie); *Career* former teacher with Hammersmith and Fulham LEA; MP (Lab) Enfield N 1997–2010 and 2015–; PPS to Rt Hon Andrew Smith, MP, *qv*, until 2002, asst Govt whip 2002–03, Govt whip 2003–06, Parly under sec of state Home Office 2006–07, PM's rep for Cyprus 2007–08; Barnet Cncl: cncllr 1990–97, dep ldr 1994–97, chm Policy and Resources Ctee 1994–97; memb Panel of Chairs 2016–; *Recreations* reading, music, visiting historic buildings; *Style*— The Rt Hon Joan Ryan

RYAN, Michelle Claire; da of Craig Ryan, and Tina Ryan; *b* 22 April 1984; *Educ* Chace Community Sch Enfield (Govr's prize for outstanding achievement); *Career* actress; patron and completed Virgin London marathon for CLICSargent; performed in Nat Dance Comp and Finals (HM's Theatre London); memb: SAG, BAFTA; *Theatre* credits incl: The Stars in our Eyes (HM's Theatre London), Smash (London Palladium), Hollywood and Broadway (Millfield Theatre), Next Stop...Broadway (Millfield Theatre), Who's the Daddy (Kings Head Islington), 24 Hour Plays (Old Vic), The Talented Mr Ripley (Royal and Derngate Northampton), Sally Bowles in Cabaret (Savoy Theatre); *Television* credits incl: The Worst Witch (ITV), Burnside (ITV), Zoe Slater in Eastenders (BBC) 2000–05, Miss Marple (ITV), Mansfield Park (ITV), Jekyll (BBC 1), Comic Relief 2007 (BBC 1), Jaime Sommers in Bionic Woman (NBC), Mr Eleven (ITV), Merlin (BBC 1), Doctor Who (BBC 1) 2009, One Night In Emergency (BBC 3), Shelter Me (The Metal Hurlant Chronicles) 2012, Death in Paradise (BBC), Covert Affairs; *Film* Cashback, Suzy, I Want Candy, Lila Owens, Flick, Huge, 4. 3. 2. 1., Girl Walks into a Bar, Cleanskin, Cockneys vs Zombies, The Man Inside, Andron, The Last Photograph 2016, Somnium 2016, Confinement 2016; *Awards* BBC1 Best TV Moments of 2001, Best Single Episode British Soap Awards 2004, Glamour Magazine UK TV Actress of the Year 2009; *Recreations* reading, theatre, cinema, painting, yoga, running, dance, singing, horse riding, flying; *Clubs* BAFTA; *Style*— Miss Michelle Ryan; ✉ c/o Lindy King, United Agents, 12–26 Lexington Street, London W1F 0LE (☎ 020 3214 0800); c/o Jason Weinberg, Untitled Entertainment, 350 S Beverly Drive, Suite 200, Beverly Hills, CA 90212

RYAN, Dr Paul; s of John Joseph Ryan (d 2006), and Mary Cecilia, *née* Walsh (d 1992); *b* 14 January 1947, Northampton; *Educ* LSE (MSc, BSc), Harvard Univ (PhD); *m* 1, 30 June 1970 (m dis); 1 s (Jude Sebastien b 20 March 1974); m 2, 2 May 1986, Gale, *née* Smith; 1 s (Stephen Jacob b 31 Oct 1986); *Career* lectr and sr lectr Faculty of Economics Univ of Cambridge 1977–2004, fell King's Coll Cambridge 1977–, prof of labour economics Dept of Mgmnt KCL 2004–09; visiting prof Univ of California at Berkeley 1994–95; conslt: World Bank, ILO, OECD; memb American Economic Assoc; *Publications* The Problem of Youth (1991), The Roles of Evaluation for Vocational Education and Training (1999); *Recreations* swimming, film, music, history, walking; *Style*— Dr Paul Ryan; ✉ King's College, Cambridge CB2 1ST (☎ 01223 331100, e-mail paul.ryan@kings.cam.ac.uk)

RYAN, Sean Matthew; s of Brendan Manus Ryan, of London, and Marion Celia, *née* Hinkley; *b* 14 September 1959; *Educ* King's Sch Worcester, Pembroke Coll Oxford (scholar, MA); *m* 12 May 1984, Carmel Mary, da of Kevin Campbell; 1 s (Alastair Matthew b 24 Aug 1988), 2 da (Charlotte Anne b 21 April 1990, Anna Marion b 19 April 2000); *Career* reporter Reading Evening Post 1982–85; Daily Mail 1985–90; Sunday Times: environment corr 1991–94, science corr 1994–95, dep news ed and science ed 1995–96, Focus ed 1996–97, foreign ed 1997–2013, associate ed (digital, Focus, campaigns, regions) 2013–; memb Bd Watch Tst for Environmental Educn 1992–93, govr St Gabriel's Sch Newbury, chm Tom Walker Tst 2009–; Pfizer Award Young Journalist of the Year 1983, Team of the Year (Kosovo) British Press Awards 2000; Campaign of the Year (NHS) Br Journalism Awards 2013; *Recreations* walking, running; *Style*— Sean Ryan, Esq; ✉ The Sunday Times, 1 London Bridge Street, London SE1 9GF (☎ 020 7782 5667, fax 020 7782 5050, e-mail sean.ryan@sunday-times.co.uk, Twitter @seanmatthewryan)

RYCROFT, Matthew; CBE; *b* 16 June 1968; *m* 1997, Alison Emma Victoria; 3 da; *Career* diplomat; entered HM Dip Serv 1989, third sec Geneva 1990, asst desk offr Security Policy Dept 1990–91, third sec then second sec (Chancery) Paris 1991–95, head of section Eastern Adriatic Unit FCO 1995–96, desk offr Policy Planners FCO 1996–98, first sec (political) Washington DC 1998–2002, private sec (foreign affrs) to PM 2002–04, ambass to Bosnia and Herzegovina 2005–08, EU dir FCO 2008–11, chief operating offr FCO 2011–; *Style*— Matthew Rycroft, Esq, CBE; ✉ c/o Foreign & Commonwealth Office, King Charles Street, London SW1A 2AH (e-mail matthew.rycroft@fco.gov.uk)

RYCROFT, Philip John; CB (2014); s of John Rycroft, and Shirley, *née* Parsons, of Kirkby Malham, Yorkshire; *b* 22 May 1961, Skipton, Yorkshire; *Educ* Leys Sch Cambridge, Wadham Coll Oxford (MA, DPhil); *m* 19 Aug 1989, Kathleen, *née* Richards; 2 s (Ewan b 7 Jul 1994, Alexander b 22 Feb 1997); *Career* cabinet of Sir Leon Britain European Cmmn 1995–97; head of div, dep head Policy Unit Scottish Exec 1997–2000, public affairs mangr Scottish Newcastle plc 2000–02, head Schs Gp Scottish Exec 2002–06, head

Enterprise, Transport and Lifelong Learning Dept Scottish Exec 2006–07, DG educn Scottish Govt 2007–09, DG innovation and enterprise and chief exec Better Regulation Exec Dept for Business, Innovation and Skills 2009–11; corp affrs dir Hutchison Whampoa (Europe) Ltd until 2012, DG Dep PM's Office 2012–15, second permanent sec and head UK Governance Gp Cabinet Office 2015–; *Recreations* triathlon; *Style*— Mr Philip Rycroft, CB; ✉ 1 Horse Guards Road, London SW1A 2HQ

RYDER, Chris; s of late Dermod Ryder, and late Brigid, *née* Burns; *b* 9 May 1947; *Educ* St MacNissis Coll Garron Tower, St Mary's CBS Belfast; *m* 1, 1967 (m dis 1996), Anne, da of late John Henry; 3 s (Paul, Declan, Edward), 1 da (Michelle); m 2, 2000, Genevieve, da of Jack Belton; *Career* clerical offr Postmaster-Gen's Dept 1965–66, freelance journalist and publicist 1966–70, advtg and publicity mangr Bass Ireland Ltd 1970–71, freelance journalist 1971–72, news reporter The Sunday Times 1972–88, Irish corr The Daily Telegraph 1988–93, author, journalist and broadcaster 1993–; fndr memb NI Community Rels Cncl 1990–94, memb Police Authy for NI 1994–96; memb Ulster History Circle 2003–07 (sec 2007); *Books* The RUC: A Force Under Fire (1989), The UDR: An Instrument of Peace? (1991), Inside the Maze (2000), Drumcree: The Orange Order's Last Stand (with Vincent Kearney, 2001), The Fateful Split: Catholics and the RUC (2004), A Special Kind of Courage: 321EOD Squadron Battling the Bombers (2005), Fighting Fitt (2006); *Recreations* music, reading; *Style*— Chris Ryder, Esq; ✉ 1 Clontonacally Road, Carryduff, Belfast BT8 8AG (☎ 028 9081 3721, e-mail chris@chrisryder.co.uk)

RYDER, Rt Hon Lord Justice; Sir Ernest Nigel Ryder; kt (2004), PC (2013), TD (1996), DL (Gtr Manchester, 2009); s of Dr John Buckley Ryder, TD (d 1983), of Bolton, Lancs, and Constance, *née* Collier; *b* 9 December 1957, Bolton, Lancs; *Educ* Bolton Sch, Peterhouse Cambridge (MA, jr treas Cambridge Union Soc); *m* 1990, Janette Lynn Martin; 1 da; *Career* merchant banker Grindley Brandt & Co 1979–81; called to the Bar Gray's Inn 1981 (bencher 2004); QC 1997, recorder of the Crown Court 2000–04 (asst recorder 1997–2000), a dep judge of the High Court 2001–04, judge of the High Court of Justice (Family Div) 2004–13, liaison judge Family Div Northern Circuit 2005–09, presiding judge Northern Circuit 2009–13, judge in charge of the modernisation of family justice 2011–13, a Lord Justice of Appeal 2013–, sr pres Tbnls 2015–; boundary cmmr for England 2000–04; counsel North Wales Tbnl of Inquiry 1996–98; chllr Univ of Bolton 2014–, prof of strategic mgmnt of the law Univ of Bolton 2015–; tstee The Nuffield Fndn 2014–; TA: cmmnd Duke of Lancaster's Own Yeo 1981, Sqdn Ldr Duke of Lancaster's Yeo 1990, Sqdn Ldr Royal Mercian and Lancastrian Yeo 1992; Hon LLD Univ of Bolton 2013; FRSA 2010; *Publications* Clarke Hall and Morrison on Children (ed), Child Care Management Practice (2009); *Recreations* listening, walking; *Style*— The Rt Hon Lord Justice Ryder; ✉ Royal Courts of Justice, Strand, London WC2A 2LL

RYDER, Peter; CB (1994); s of Percival Henry Sussex Ryder (d 1976), and Bridget, *née* McCormack (d 1997); *b* 10 March 1942; *Educ* Yorebridge GS, Univ of Leeds (BSc, PhD); *m* 24 April 1965, Jacqueline Doris Sylvia, DL, da of Douglas Rigby; 2 s (Andrew Stephen b 9 April 1966, Mark James b 19 Aug 1970), 1 da (Louise Pauline b 4 Feb 1972); *Career* res asst Physics Dept Univ of Leeds 1966–67; Meteorological Office: asst dir Cloud Physics Res 1976–82, asst dir Systems Development 1982–84, dep dir Observational Servs 1984–88, dep dir Forecasting Servs 1988–89, dir of Servs 1989–90; dep chief exec and dir ops Meteorological Office Executive Agency 1990–96; conslt on environmental info servs 1996–; chm: Thames Regnl Flood Defence Ctee 2003–09, EuroGOOS 2003–08, Marine Protected Areas Science Advsy Panel 2009–11; William Gaskell Meml Medal 1981, L G Groves Meml Prize for Meteorology 1982; FRMetS 2004 (memb Cncl 1980–83, memb Editorial Bd Quarterley Jl 1981–84, gen sec 2001–06); *Recreations* gardening, walking, fishing, photography; *Style*— Dr Peter Ryder, CB, FRMetS; ✉ 8 Sherring Close, Bracknell, Berkshire RG42 2LD (☎ 01344 423380)

RYDER, Sophie Marie-Louise; da of Wilfred Ryder (d 1981), of Twickenham, and Jacqueline, *née* Bazin; *b* 1963, London; *Educ* Chiswick Comp, Kingston Poly, Royal Acad Schs (Dip); *m* 5 Nov 1989 (m dis 2011), Harry Scott, s of James Scott (d 2000); 2 da (Maud Augusta Ryder b 24 Aug 1989, Nell Ryder Lucy b 8 Aug 1991); *Career* sculptor; residencies: Yorkshire Sculpture Park 1986, Grizedale Forest Cumbria 1986, Salisbury Cathedral 1987, Forest of Dean 1988, Kilkenny Eire 1992, Boulogne France 1996, Cheltenham Art Gallery and Museum 1997, Cheltenham Music Fetival 1997, Cheekwood Sculpture Park Nashville 1998; *Solo Exhibitions* incl: Edward Totah Gallery London 1987, Salisbury Cathedral 1987, Courcoux & Courcoux Gallery Stockbridge 1987, 1988, 1990, 1992, 1998, 2000 and 2002, St Paul's Gallery Leeds 1988, Henley Festival Henley-on-Thames 1989, Berkeley Sq Gallery London 1989, 1995, 1997, 1999, 2001 and 2003, Newport City Museum & Art Gallery Newport 1990, Yorkshire Sculpture Park 1991 and 2008, Winchester Cathedral 1994, Red House Museum & Gardens Dorset 1994, The Allen Gallery Hampshire 1994, Belloc Lowndes Gallery Chicago 1996, O'Hara Gallery NY 1997, Cheltenham Art Gallery and Museum 1997, Victoria Art Gallery Bath 1999, Cartwright Hall Art Gallery Bradford 1999, Odapark Venray Holland 2000, Buschlen Mowatt Galleries Vancouver 2000, Gallerie de Bellefeuille Montreal 2001, Metropole Galleries Folkestone 2002, Buschlen Mowatt Galleries 2002, Pierrepoint Fine Art Oxford 2002, Imago Galleries Palm Desert 2004, 2007 and 2013, Storey Gallery Lancaster 2004, Victoria Art Gallery Bath 2004 and 2009, Canary Wharf London 2005, Atkinson Gallery Millfield Sch 2006, Frederick Meijer Gardens and Sculpture Park 2007, Cartwright Hall Art Gallery Bradford 2012, Villa D'arte Italy 2012, RWA Bristol 2013, Three Dimensions (Celia Lendis Contemporary Art Gallery Moreton-in-Marsh) 2013; *Group Exhibitions* incl: Inaugural Pick of the Graduates (Christies London) 1984, Dogwork (Interim Art London) 1984, Summer in the City (Gallery 24 London) 1985, Sophie Ryder & Harry Scott (Gallery 24 London) 1985, The Nature of the Beast (Henley Festival) 1985, Bretton Menagerie (Yorkshire Sculpture Park) 1986, Freedom to Touch (Laing Art Gallery Newcastle) 1986, Animal in Photography (Photographers Gallery London) 1986, Cats (Louise Hallet Gallery London) 1987, Glasgow Garden Festival 1988, Cleveland Gallery Middlesborough 1988, Winter Exhibition (Berkeley Sq Gallery London) 1988, The Cultivated Garden (Oxford Gallery Oxford) 1988, Chilford Hall Press Cambridge 1988, The Fabricated Landscape (Plymouth City Museum) 1988, Menagerie (Glasgow Print Studio) 1990, Hannah Peschar Gallery Surrey 1991, Art at Milton Keynes 1992, Women Artists – Critics' Choice (Bruton St Gallery London) 1992, Millfield 20th Century Sculpture Exhbn (Millfield Sch) 1992, Young British Art (Århus Festival Denmark) 1992, Art in the City (Finsbury Park) 1993, Sophie Ryder Collages (Oxford Gallery Oxford) 1993, Within Reach (Bury St Edmunds Gallery) 1993, Summer Show (Berkeley Sq Gallery London) 1994, Drawings (Artbus Fife) 1994, Sculpture at Goodwood (Chichester) 1994, Minotaurs Myths and Legends (Berkeley Sq Gallery London) 1994, Chelsea Harbour London 1996, Manchester Academy 1997, Wimpole Hall Cambridge 1997, The Scottish Gallery Edinburgh 1997, Animals in Art (Blue Cross, Sothebys London) 1997, Vancouver Sculpture Festival 1998, Shape of the Century – 100 Years of British Sculpture (Salisbury and Canary Wharf) 1999, Den Haag Sculptuur (The Hague Holland) 1999 and 2001, Veranneman Foundations Belgium 2000, Kirkland Int Outdoor Sculpture Exhbn Washington 2001, Éigse (Carlow Arts Festival) 2001, Art Miami 2002, Palm Beach 2002, Newbury Spring Festival 2003, Solomon Gallery Dublin 2005, Vancouver Biennale 2005, 2007, 2009 and 2011, Blickachsen 6 (Kurpark Bad Homburg) 2007, Aynhoe Park Banbury 2010 and 2011, Wet Paint Gallery Cirencester 2013; *Public Collections* Newport City Museum, Yorkshire Sculpture Park, Barings Bank Collection, De Beers Collection, Conoco Ltd, Gerard and National Bank, National Trust (Buckland Abbey), EFG Private Bank Ltd, Le Trion Secdy Sch France, Cheekwood Sculpture Park Nashville, Cheltenham BC, Cheltenham Art Gallery and Museum, Victoria Art Gall Bath; *Style*— Ms Sophie Ryder; ✉ The Studio, Lampits Farm, Winson, Cirencester, Gloucestershire GL7 5ER (e-mail enq@sophie-ryder.com, website www.sophie-ryder.com, Twitter @sophieryderart)

RYDER, Susan Myfanwy Prudence; da of Capt Robert Edward Dudley Ryder, VC (d 1986), and Hilaré Myfanwy, *née* Green-Wilkinson (d 1982); *b* 14 March 1944; *Educ* Beaufront Sch Camberley, Byam Shaw Sch of Art (David Murray travel scholar, NDD); *m* Martin Graves Bates; 1 s (Oliver Robert Hunter b 29 March 1969), 1 da (Susannah Hilaré Myfanwy b 15 May 1970); *Career* artist; regular exhibitor: Royal Academy Summer Exhbn, Royal Soc of Portrait Painters, New English Art Club (memb 1980–); RP 1992; *Solo Exhibitions* Haste Gallery 1979 and 1981, W H Patterson 1989, 1995 and 1999, Oakham Galleries 2004, Arthur Ackermann 2009 and 2010, Panter & Hall 2013; *Portraits* HRH The Princess of Wales 1981, Miss Pears 1984, Miss Nicola Paget 1991, Sir Eric Ash 1993, Lord Porter 1994, HM The Queen 1996, Sir Michael Scholar (pres St John's Coll Oxford) 2010; *Awards* Barney Wilkins prize 1990, winner Alexon Portrait Competition 1991, first prize New English Art Club Critic's prize 1993; *Recreations* family and friends; *Style*— Miss Susan Ryder, RP, NEAC; ✉ 48 Stratford Road, London W8 6QA (e-mail sue@susanryder.co.uk, website www.susanryder.co.uk)

RYDER OF WENSUM, Baron (Life Peer UK 1997), of Wensum in the County of Norfolk; Rt Hon Richard Andrew Ryder; PC (1990), OBE (1981); s of (Richard) Stephen Ryder, JP, DL (d 2003), and Margaret, *née* MacKenzie; *b* 4 February 1949; *Educ* Radley, Magdalene Coll Cambridge (BA); *m* 1981, Caroline Ryder, CVO, MBE, o da of late Sir David Stephens, KCB, CVO; 1 s (decd), 1 da; *Career* journalist; political sec to Ldr of the Oppn then to PM 1975–81; MP (Cons) Norfolk Mid 1983–97; PPS to: Fin Sec to the Treasy 1984, Sec of State for Foreign Affrs 1984–86; chm Cons Foreign and Cwlth Cncl 1984–89; Govt whip 1986–88, Parly sec MAFF 1988–89, econ sec to the Treasy 1989–90, paymaster-gen 1990, Parly sec to the Treasy (Govt chief whip) 1990–95; chm Eastern Counties Radio 1997–2001, vice-chm BBC 2002–04 (actg chm of govrs 2004); chm: Inst of Cancer Research 2005–13, Ucandoit 2011–14, Child Bereavement UK 2013–; dir of family businesses; *Style*— The Rt Hon Lord Ryder of Wensum, OBE, PC; ✉ House of Lords, London SW1A 0PW

RYDSTRÖM, Marilyn; OBE; da of Kenneth Oberg (d 2002), and Averil Irene, *née* Harding (d 1998); *b* 24 October 1947, Surbiton, Surrey; *Educ* Bedford Coll Univ of London (BSc); *m* 20 July 1985, Björn Lennart Rydström; *Career* probation offr Surrey, sr social worker Hillingdon Borough 1973–77, head of community projects Capital Radio plc 1977–87, dir of fundraising RNID 1987–89, sr conslt ChapterOne/Ketchum Fundraising 1989–92, mktg and commercial dir Stowe Sch Bucks 1992–95, client servs dir Guide Dogs for the Blind 1995–99, DG People's Dispensary for Sick Animals (PDSA) 1999–2008, dir Severn Promotions Co Ltd; currently dir and tstee Severn Hospice Ltd, dir; past voluntary positions with The Prince's Tst: memb and chm NW London Ctee, memb Marine Conservation Soc (dir and tstee 2010–14), memb Strategy Gp for London, memb Prince's Tst Cncl; other past voluntary positions: memb Lord Chancellor's Advsy Ctee W Mercia, memb Lord Chancellor's Advsy Sub-Ctee Salop; former tstee and memb: Artsline, Crime Prevention Advsy Ctee NACRO, Mgmnt Ctee Alone in London; Churchill fell 1984; memb Inst of Fundraising 1989, CCMI 2007; *Recreations* sailing, diving, marine conservation, wildlife photography; *Clubs* Kennel; *Style*— Mrs Marilyn Rydström, OBE, CCMI; ✉ e-mail marilynrydstrom@aol.com

RYE, Renny Michael Douglas; s of Douglas Rye, of Maidstone, Kent, and Pamela, *née* Whitmore; *b* 2 December 1947; *Educ* Maidstone GS, St Catherine's Coll Oxford (BA); *m* 8 Aug 1970, Ann, da of (Andrew Frank) Peter Lynn, of Maidstone, Kent; 1 da (Helen b 1974), 1 s (Thomas b 1977); *Career* BBC: prodn ops asst BBC radio 1971–73, asst floor mangr TV plays dept 1973–79, prodr and asst ed Blue Peter 1979–81; freelance drama dir: The Box of Delights (BBC) 1983–84, The December Rose (BBC) 1985, Casualty (BBC) 1986, The Gemini Factor 1987, All our Children (BBC) 1987–89, Agatha Christie's Poirot 1988–91, The Other Side of Paradise 1991, Lipstick on Your Collar (Channel 4) 1992, Midnight Movie (film) 1993, Chandler & Co (BBC), Kavanagh QC 1994, Karaoke, Cold Lazarus (BBC/Channel 4) 1995, Family Money (Channel 4) 1996, Big Women (Channel 4) 1997, Oliver Twist (ITV) 1999, Close & True (ITV) 2000, Two Thousand Acres of Sky (BBC) 2001–02, Silent Witness (BBC) 2002–03, Midsomer Murders (ITV) 2003–16, Vital Signs (ITV) 2006; memb: BAFTA, DGGB, Directors UK; *Recreations* cricket, films, music; *Style*— Renny Rye, Esq; ✉ c/o Jessica Sykes, Independent Talent Group Ltd, Oxford House, 76 Oxford Street, London W1D 1BS (☎ 020 7636 6565)

RYLANCE, His Hon John Randolph Trevor; s of Dr Ralph Curzon Rylance (d 1983), and Margaret Joan Clare, *née* Chambers (d 2005); *b* 26 February 1944, Mears Ashby, Northants; *Educ* Shrewsbury; *m* 14 Dec 1974, Philippa Anne, da of Philip Sidney Bailey (d 1975); 2 da (Georgina b 1976, Charlotte b 1978); *Career* called to the Bar Lincoln's Inn 1968; res asst to Sir Edward Gardner, QC, MP 1971–73, recorder 1993–2003 (asst recorder 1989–93), circuit judge (SE Circuit) 2003–14, dep circuit judge 2014–; memb Professional Conduct Ctee Bar Cncl 1992–94; govr Fulham Cross Sch 1977–88, branch chm Fulham Cons Assoc 1983–89 (memb Mgmnt Ctee 1980–90), memb Exec Ctee Fulham Soc 1988–2012, chm Fulham Palace Tst 1996–2011 (tstee 1991–2012); *Clubs* Hurlingham; *Style*— His Hon John Rylance

RYLAND, David Stuart; s of Sir William Ryland, CB (d 1988), of Croydon, Surrey, and Lady Sybil Ryland; *b* 27 October 1953; *Educ* Dulwich, Exeter Coll Oxford; *m* 18 July 1986, Anne Helen, da of Kenneth Wright, of Benfleet, Essex; *Career* admitted slr 1981; Clifford Chance 1981–88, ptnr SJ Berwin & Co 1988–2013, corp real estate ptnr Paul Hastings London 2013–; Freeman City of London; memb Law Soc; *Recreations* films, music, sport; *Style*— David Ryland, Esq; ✉ Paul Hastings, Ten Bishops Square, Eighth Floor, London E1 6EG

RYLANDS, Patrick; s of Leo Rylands (d 1978), and Ada, *née* Hyde (d 1992); *b* 12 September 1942; *Educ* Hull Coll of Art (NDD), RCA (DesRCA); *m* Ljiljana, *née* Mom?ilovi? (d 2009); *Career* toy designer; teacher: Sch of Ceramics Hornsey Sch of Art 1966–70, Sch of Architecture Poly of North London 1972–76; ceramic designer Grindley Hotel Ware Stoke-on-Trent 1966–70, visiting designer Creative Playthings USA 1970, freelance cmmns for Rosedale, Kurt Naef and Europlastic 1970–76, sole design conslt for Ambi Toys by Europlastic 1976–2002, conslt Tolo Toys Ltd (Hong Kong) 2003–04; memb juries: Design Cncl Design Index, Design Cncl Design Awards, RSA Burseries, Toymakers' Guild Prizes, Br Toy and Hobby Manufacturers' Assoc Prize Ctee; memb: Tstees Ctee V&A Bethnal Green Museum of Childhood 1998–2009, Artworkers Guild 1998; RDI 1999; *Recreations* drawing and photography; *Style*— Patrick Rylands, RDI; ✉ 76A Belsize Park Gardens, London NW3 4NG (☎ 020 7586 0878, e-mail patrickrylands@mac.com)

RYLE, Sallie Elizabeth; da of Barry Davidson Eaton Smith, MBE (d 1995), of Ilkley, W Yorks, and Mary Elizabeth, *née* Priest (d 1996); *b* 14 November 1950; *Educ* Ilkley GS; *m* 19 Sept 1981, Nicholas Peter Bodley Ryle, s of Michael Thomas Ryle, of Winsford, Somerset; 1 s (George David Bodley b 6 April 1987), 1 da (Vanessa Isabelle b 25 April 1990); *Career* Yorkshire TV: asst publicity offr 1982–84, head of publicity 1984–87, head of publicity and PR 1987–96; chief press offr Granada TV 1997–98, head of media relations (North) Granada and head of regnl affrs Yorkshire Television 1998–2004, dir Yorkshire Television 2004–; ITV: controller 2004–07, dir Prog Publicity 2007–08, sr press advsr Global Content 2008–09, communications conslt ITV Studios 2010; freelance communications conslt 2011–; assoc ptnr: ALDERmedia 2011–, Pagefield

R

Communications 2011–; *Recreations* equestrian sports, tennis, travel; *Style*— Ms Sallie Ryle

RYLE-HODGES, Carolyn; da of Harry Morton Neal, and Cecilia Elizabeth, *née* Crawford; *b* 10 June 1961; *Educ* Courtauld Inst of Art London (BA); *m* 2 June 1988, Rupert Ryle-Hodges, s of Edward Ryle-Hodges; 1 da (Eve b 1 May 1991), 1 s (William b 20 March 1993); *Career* ptnr Long & Ryle Art Gallery 1988–; corp clients incl: Lloyd Thompson, McKinsey's & Co, Cazenove & Co, Kreditbank, Morgan Grenfell, Société Générale, Mitsui Trust, HM Customs & Excise, Mitsubishi Corp plc, London Underground Ltd Canary Wharf, Barclays Bank, Paribas, Bank America Tst, Capsticks Slrs; memb: Worshipful Co of Carpenters, Friends of the Tate, Friends of the Royal Acad; *Recreations* visiting museums, walking; *Style*— Mrs Carolyn Ryle-Hodges; ✉ 4 Redesdale Street, London SW3; Long and Ryle Art Gallery, 4 John Islip Street, London SW1P 4PX (✆ 020 7834 1434, fax 020 7821 9409, e-mail carolyn@long-and-ryle.com, website www.long-and-ryle.com)

RYLEY, John Hamilton; s of Ted Ryley (d 2006), and Wanda, *née* Keston; *b* 21 December 1961, Chelmsford, Essex; *Educ* Eastbourne Coll, Univ of Durham (BA), Wharton Sch of Business Philadelphia (AMP); *m* Oct 1987, Harriet, *née* Constable; 1 s (Finn b 1994), 2 da (Stella b 1996, Oonagh b 1998); *Career* grad news trainee BBC 1987–89; ITN News at Ten: prog prodr 1990–92, prog ed 1992–95; Sky News: exec prodr 1995–2000, exec ed 2000–06, head of news 2006–; *Publications* 20 Years of Broadcast News (co-ed, 2009); *Recreations* cricket, cycling, fishing; *Clubs* MCC; *Style*— John Ryley; ✉ Sky News, British Sky Broadcasting Ltd, Grant Way, Isleworth, Middlesex TW7 5QD (✆ 020 7705 3000, e-mail john.ryley@bskyb.com, webste www.skynews.com)

RYOTT, Emma; *b* Leeds; *Educ* St James' Sch West Malvern, Francis Holland Sch, Trent Poly (BA); *Children* 1 s (Matthew); *Career* costume and set designer; asst to wardrobe supervisor and touring wardrobe asst Eng Nat Ballet 1981–85, costume supervisor and designer Royal Shakespeare Theatre 1985–97; *Productions* Kiss Me Kate (Old Vic and Savoy Theatre) 1986, Henceforward (Vaudeville Theatre) 1988, Macbeth (USA tour) 1988, Twelfth Night (Royal Shakespeare Theatre) 1989, Big Game (Nuffield Theatre Southampton) 1989, Sir Thomas More (Shaw Theatre) 1990, Archbishop Ceiling (Royal Shakespeare Theatre) 1990, Henry IV (Wyndhams Theatre)1990, Electra (Riverside Studios) 1992, Hamlet (Mediaeval Players) 1992, Francesca da Rimini (Bregenzerfestspiele Austria) 1994, Orlando (Flanders Opera) 1995, Rhapsody (Royal Ballet) 1995, Steptext (Royal Ballet) 1995, Shakespeare Revue (Vaudeville Theatre) 1995, Son of Man (Royal Shakespeare Theatre) 1995, The Entertainer (Hampstead Theatre) 1996, A Doll's House (Odeon Paris) 1997, Porgy and Bess (Bregenzerfestspiele) 1998, Hidden Variables (Royal Ballet) 1999, Un Ballo in Maschera (Bregenzerfestspiele) 1999 and 2000, The Merry Widow (Met Opera NY) 2000, Manon Lescaut (ENO) 2000, La Bohème (Bregenzerfestspiele) 2001, Manon Lescaut (Göteborg Operan Sweden) 2002, Nine (Malmo Musikteater Sweden) 2002, La Bohème (Bregenzerfestspiele) 2002, Ragtime (West End) 2003, Pearl Fishers (State Opera Kazan Russia) 2003, Lulu (Stuttgart Ballet) 2003, Marriage of Figaro (Savoy Opera) 2004, One Touch of Venus (Opera North) 2004, Le Peau Blanche (Stuttgart Ballet) 2005, Oedipus Rex (Epidaurus Festival Contemporary Theatre Athens) 2005, Berenice (Heidelberg Staattheater) 2005, Sandmann (Stuttgart Ballet) 2006, Rock & Roll (Royal Court and West End) 2006 and (Broadway) 2007, Barber of Seville (Grange Park Opera) 2006, The Return of Ulysses (Royal Flanders Ballet) 2006, Damnation of Faust (Semper Opera Dresden) 2007, Lost Tableau (Royal Swedish Ballet) 2008, Leonce and Lena (Aalto Ballet), Aida (WNO), Otello (Salzberg Festival), Sandmann (Latvian Nat Opera), Otello (Teatro dell'opera Rome), Orphee and Enydice (Staatstheater) 2009, Fallstaff 2009, Death of Penthus (film) 2009, Arhat Taming the Dragon (film) 2009; *Style*— Ms Emma Ryott; ✉ agent: Loesje Sanders, Pound Square, 1 North Hill, Woodbridge, Suffolk IP12 1HH (✆ 01394 385260, fax 01394 388734, e-mail loesjev@aol.com)

S

SAATCHI, Charles; s of Nathan David Saatchi (d 2000), and Daisy Saatchi, of London; *b* 9 June 1943; *Educ* Christ's Coll Finchley; *m* 1, 1973 (m dis 1990), Doris Jean, da of Jack Lockhart of USA; m 2, 1990 (m dis 2001), Kay Hartenstein; 1 da (Phoebe); m 3, 2003 (m dis 2013), Nigella Lawson, *qv*; *Career* assoc dir Collett Dickenson Pearce 1966–68, dir Cramer Saatchi 1968–70, dir Saatchi & Saatchi Co plc 1970–93 (hon pres 1993–95), fndr ptnr M&C Saatchi Ltd 1995–; Chm's Award for Outstanding Contribution to Commercials Indust (British TV Advtg Awards) 1994; *Recreations* karting; *Style*— Charles Saatchi, Esq; ✉ c/o Saatchi Gallery, Duke of York's HQ, King's Road, London, SW3 4RY

SAATCHI, Baron (Life Peer UK 1996), of Staplefield in the County of West Sussex; Maurice Saatchi; s of late Nathan Saatchi, and Daisy Saatchi; *b* 21 June 1946; *Educ* LSE (BSc); *m* 1984, Josephine Hart (d 2011), novelist; 1 s ((Hon) Edward b 1985), 1 step s; *Career* chm Saatchi & Saatchi Co plc 1984–94; fndr ptnr M&C Saatchi Ltd 1995–; House of Lords: oppn Treasy spokesman 1999–2003, oppn Cabinet Office spokesman 2001–03; co-chm Cons Pty 2003–05; dir Centre for Policy Studies 1999–; memb Cncl RCA 1997; govr LSE; *Publications* The War of Independence (1999), Happiness Can't Buy Money (1999), The Bad Samaritan (2000), Poor People! Stop Paying Tax ! (2001), The Science of Politics (2001), If this is Conservatism, I am a Conservative (2005), In Praise of Ideology (2006), Enemy of the People (2008), The Myth of Inflation Targeting (2009); *Style*— The Lord Saatchi; ✉ M&C Saatchi plc, 36 Golden Square, London W1F 9EE (☎ 020 7543 4510, fax 020 7543 4502)

SABIN, Paul Robert; DL (Kent 2001); s of Robert Reginald Sabin (d 1988), and Dorothy Maude, *née* Aston (d 1992); *b* 29 March 1943; *Educ* Oldbury GS, Aston Univ (DMS); *m* 19 June 1965, Vivien, da of Harry Furnival; 1 s (Martin Lawrence b 1969), 2 da (Ann Hazel b 1973, Caroline Jane b 1978); *Career* West Bromwich CBC 1959–69, chief fin offr Redditch Devpt Corp 1975–81 (joined 1969); City of Birmingham: joined 1981, city treas 1982–86, dep chief exec 1984–86; chief exec Kent CC 1986–97; chief exec Leeds Castle Foundation and Leeds Castle (Enterprises) Ltd 1998–2003; chm Veolia Water South East until 2012; hon citizen City of Baltimore USA 1985; Kent Ambass 2002–; CPFA 1966, FTS, DMS, FCMI; *Recreations* fine books, music; *Style*— Paul Sabin, Esq, DL

SABORIO DE ROCAFORT, HE Mrs Pilar; da of Dr Mario Saborio (d 1985), and Aurora de Rocafort (d 2002); *b* 20 July 1960, Limón, Costa Rica; *Educ* Scuola Superiore per Interpreti e Traduttori Rome (Dip), Univ of Miami (BA), Univ of Cambridge (MPhil); *Children* 2 da (Marie-Béatrice b 24 Nov 1988, Marianne b 31 July 1992), 1 s (Xavier b 15 April); *Career* Costa Rican diplomat; staff interpreter and translator Instituto Centroamericano de Administración de Empresas (INCAE) Costa Rica 1984–1985, certified translator Miny of Foreign Affrs Costa Rica 1985–90, program coordinator Central American Peace Scholarship INCAE/USAID 1986–1988, asst dir industrial devpt Costa Rica Investment and Devpt Program FL 1990–92, ind interpreter and translator FL 1992–96, adjunct prof of world regnl geography Univ of Miami 2003 and Florida Int Univ 2005, ambass to Ct of St James's 2007–;; *Style*— HE Mrs Pilar Saborio de Rocafort; ✉ Costa Rican Embassy, Flat 1, 14 Lancaster Gate, London W2 3LH (☎ 020 7706 8844, fax 020 7706 8655, psaborio@btconnect.com)

SACH, Keith Howard; JP (Warks 1989); s of Cyril James Sach (d 1989), of Warks, and Jessie Annie, *née* Andlaw (d 1990); *b* 13 May 1948; *Educ* Strode's Sch Egham, King George V Sch, St Peter's Coll Birmingham (pres Union), Open Univ; *m* 14 July 1990, Elizabeth Anne (Mrs Brierley), da of Geoffrey Ball (d 1990); 2 step da (Alexis b 1973, Kathryn b 1979), 1 step s (Jonathan b 1976); *Career* asst master Solihull Sch 1970–79, dir RLSS UK 1979–88 (chief Cwlth sec 1979–86, Cwlth vice-pres 1987, UK hon life govr 2007), md S & P Safety 1988–90, dir: Safety Mgmnt Partnership Ltd 1992–95, Scalefast Systems Ltd 1996–2010, IQL UK Ltd 2001–06 (chm 2001–06); leisure risk mgmnt conslt to: Overseas Govts, HSE, Sport England, RLSS Aust, 1Life Mgmnt Solutions, Sports and Leisure Management, Mosaic Spa & Health Clubs, 3D Leisure, Active Nation, local authorities; broadcaster and writer; swimming pool health and safety advsr Royal Life Saving Soc UK 2007–; tstee Warks Justices' Mess 2009–, Ind Advocacy 2011–12; memb: Magistrates Assoc (chm Warks Branch 1998–2004 and 2005–, memb Nat Cncl 2001–05, tstee 2005); Civil, Criminal and Coroners' Courts expert witness on swimming pool, leisure centre, sport and recreation accidents; chm: Nat Water Safety Ctee 1980–83, Nat Rescue Trg Cncl 1981–88 (tstee 1995–97); tstee Warks Crimebeat, patron Mary Ann Evans Hospice, ambass Heart of England Community Fndn; Hon Constable St Helier Jersey 1984, Hon Citizen Burlington Ontario 1985, High Sheriff Warks 2013–14; *Books* Safety in Swimming Pools (contrib, 1988), Recreation Management Factfile (contrib, 1991/92), Quality in the Leisure Industry (contrib, 1992), Handbook of Sports and Recreational Building Design (contrib, 1993), Guide to Risk Assessment (jtly, 1993), Managing Health and Safety in Swimming Pools (contrib, 1999 and 2003), Magistrates' Courts Security Guide (contrib, 2004); *Recreations* theatre, music, travel, swimming, history of the Warwickshire Shrievalty; *Style*— Keith H Sach, Esq, JP; ✉ Gardens Cottage, Wroxall Abbey, Warwick CV35 7NB (☎ 07831 608900, e-mail highashfarm@aol.com)

SACHRAJDA, Prof Christopher Tadeusz Czeslaw; s of Czeslaw Sachrajda (d 1959), and Hanna Teresa, *née* Grabowska; *b* 15 November 1949; *Educ* Finchley Catholic GS London, Univ of Sussex (BSc), Imperial Coll London (PhD); *m* 31 Aug 1974, Irena, da of Antoni Czyzewski, and Antonina Czyzewski; 2 s (Andrew Marian b 22 Sept 1978, Gregory Antoni Czeslaw b 23 Nov 1979), 1 da (Sophie Maria b 31 July 1992); *Career* Harkness fell (for study and travel in USA) Stanford Linear Accelerator Center Stanford Univ 1974–76, fell and staff memb CERN Geneva 1976–79; Dept of Physics and Astronomy Univ of Southampton: lectr 1979–86, sr lectr 1986–88, reader 1988–90, prof 1990–, head of dept 1997–2000; PPARC (formerly SERC): sr fell 1991–96, memb Cncl 1998–2004; author of numerous pubns in scientific lit; CPhys 1989, FInstP 1989, FRS 1996; *Recreations* family activities, tennis, philately (early Polish), walking; *Clubs* Portswood Lawn Tennis; *Style*— Prof Christopher Sachrajda, FRS; ✉ 20 Radway Road, Southampton SO15 7PW (☎ 023 8078 4208); School of Physics and Astronomy, University of Southampton, University Road, Highfield, Southampton SO17 1BJ (☎ 023 8059 2105, fax 023 8059 5359, e-mail cts@phys.soton.ac.uk)

SACKMAN, Simon Laurence; s of Bernard Sackman (d 1986), and Mamie, *née* Epstein (d 2003); *b* 16 January 1951; *Educ* St Paul's, Pembroke Coll Oxford (MA); *m* 7 Feb 1982, Donna, da of Hon Solomon Seruya, OBE (d 2015), and Frants Seruya (d 2007); 3 da (Sarah b 1984, Paloma b 1987, Claire b 1992); *Career* Norton Rose Fulbright LLP: articled clerk 1974–77, asst slr 1977–83, ptnr 1983–2014, legal conslt 2014–; memb: City of London Slrs Co 1982, Law Soc 1977, Int Bar Assoc 1989; *Recreations* theatre, opera, classical music, gardening; *Clubs* MCC; *Style*— Simon Sackman, Esq; ✉ Norton Rose Fulright LLP, 3 More London Riverside, London SE1 2AQ (☎ 020 7283 6000, fax 020 7283 6500, e-mail simsac99@gmail.com)

SACKS, John Harvey; s of late Joseph Gerald Sacks, of London, and late Yvonne, *née* Clayton; *b* 29 April 1946, London; *Educ* Perse Sch Cambridge, Univ of London (LLB); *m* 2 Dec 1969, Roberta Judith, da of late Archy Arenson, of Regent's Park, London; 2 da (Deborah b 7 Oct 1972, Rachel b 1 March 1976), 1 s (David b 19 Jan 1981); *Career* currently managing ptnr JSA Consultancy Services London; chief exec Arenson Group plc 1982–97, chm and md President Office Furniture Ltd, chm Bradley Gp Ltd 1999–, dir Luke Hughes and Co Ltd 1999–2000, md Samas Roneo Ltd 2000–01, md Roneo Systems Furniture Ltd 2001–07, prop JSA Consultancy Servs 2007–, dir Chair Compare Ltd; pres Fédération Européenne de Meubles de Bureau 1996–97; chm Office Furniture and Filing Mfrs' Assoc (OFFMA) 1990–96, past chm London & SE Furniture Manufacturing Assoc; Liveryman Worshipful Co of Furniture Makers; FCA, FRSA; *Recreations* cycling, angling, bridge, music; *Clubs* Savile; *Style*— John Sacks, Esq; ✉ JSA Consultancy Services, 4th Floor, Gray's Inn Square, Gray's Inn, London WC1R 5JA (Tel: 020 7242 8556) (☎ 020 7242 8556, e-mail john.sacks@jsacs.com, website www.jhsacs.com)

SACKS, Baron (UK Life Peer 2009), of Aldgate in the City of London; Chief Rabbi Sir Jonathan Henry Sacks; kt (2005); s of late Louis David Sacks, of London, and Louisa, *née* Frumkin; *b* 8 March 1948; *Educ* Christ's Coll Finchley, Gonville & Caius Coll Cambridge (MA), New Coll Oxford, Univ of London (PhD), Jews' Coll London, Yeshivat Etz Hayyim London; *m* 14 July 1970, Elaine, da of Philip Taylor (d 1986); 1 s (Joshua b 1975), 2 da (Dina b 1977, Gila b 1982); *Career* lectr in moral philosophy Middx Poly 1971–73; Jews' Coll London: lectr Jewish philosophy 1973–76, lectr Talmud and Jewish philosophy 1976–82, Chief Rabbi Lord Jakobovits prof (first incumbent) in modern Jewish thought 1982–, dir rabbinic faculty 1983–90, princ 1984–90, Chief Rabbi of the United Hebrew Congregations of the Cwlth 1991–2013; Sherman Lecture Univ of Manchester 1989, Reith Lecture 1990, Cook Lecture 1997; visiting prof of philosophy Univ of Essex 1989–90; currently visiting prof: of philosophy Hebrew Univ, of theology and religious studies KCL; rabbi: Golders Green Synagogue London 1978–82, Marble Arch Synagogue London 1983–90; editor Le'ela, A Journal of Judaism Today 1985–90; memb CRAC; The Jerusalem Prize 1995; Hon Doctorates: Middlesex 1993, Cambridge 1993, Haifa (Israel) 1996, Liverpool 1997, Yeshiva (NY) 1997, St Andrews 1998, Lambeth 2001, Glasgow 2001, Bar Ilan Israel 2004, Leeds Met 2004, Heythrop 2006, Roehampton 2009, Basel 2010, Ben Gurion Israel 2011, Aberdeen 2011, Liverpool Hope 2013, Salford 2013; hon fell Gonville & Caius Coll Cambridge 1993, hon fell KCL 1993; *Books* Torah Studies (1986), Tradition and Transition: Essays Presented to Chief Rabbi Sir Immanuel Jakobovits to Celebrate Twenty Years in Office (1986), Traditional Alternatives (1989), Tradition in an Untraditional Age (1990), The Reith Lectures 1990–, The Persistence of Faith (1991), Orthodoxy Confronts Modernity (ed, 1991), Crisis and Covenant (1992), One People? (1993), Will We Have Jewish Grandchildren? (1994), Community of Faith (1995), Faith in the Future (1995), The Politics of Hope (1997), Morals & Markets (1999), Celebrating Life (2000), A Letter in the Scroll (2000), Radical Then Radical Now (2001), The Dignity of Difference (2002), The Passover Haggadah (2003), From Optimism to Hope (2004), To Heal a Fractured World (2005), New Translation and Commentary of The Authorised Daily Prayer Book (4 edn, 2007), Koren Sacks Siddur (2009), Future Tense (2009), Covenant & Conversation: A Weekly Reading of the Jewish Bible: Genesis (2009), Covenant & Conversation: A Weekly Reading of the Jewish Bible: Exodus (2010), The Great Partnership (2011), The Koren Rosh Hashanah Mahzor (2011), The Koren Yom Kippur Mahzor (2012), The Koren Pesach Mahzor (2013), Covenant & Conversation: A Weekly Reading of the Jewish Bible: Leviticus (2015), Not In God's Name: Confronting Religious Violence (2015), Covenant & Conversation: Lessons in Leadership (2015), The Koren Sukkot Mahzor (2015), The Koren Shavuot Mahzor (2016); *Recreations* walking; *Style*— The Lord Sacks

SACKUR, Stephen John; s of Robert Neil Humphrys Sackur, of Spilsby, Lincs, and Sallie, *née* Caley; *b* 9 January 1964; *Educ* King Edward VI GS Spilsby, Emmanuel Coll Cambridge (BA), Harvard Univ (Henry fellowship); *m* May 1992, Zina, da of Saadallah Sabbagh; *Career* BBC: trainee 1986–87, prodr Current Affairs 1987–89, reporter World At One 1989–90, foreign affairs corr 1990–92, Middle East corr 1992–97, Washington corr 1997–2002, Europe corr 2002–05, presenter Hardtalk 2005–; Int TV Personality of the Year Assoc for Int Broadcasting 2010; FRSA; *Books* On the Basra Road (1991); *Recreations* football, cinema, books, walking, day dreaming; *Style*— Stephen Sackur, Esq; ✉ BBC News and Current Affairs, New Broadcasting House, Portland Place, London W1A 1AA

SACKVILLE, Hon Thomas Geoffrey (Tom); yr s of 10 Earl De La Warr, DL (d 1988); *b* 26 October 1950; *Educ* Eton, Lincoln Coll Oxford (BA); *m* 1979, Catherine, da of late Brig James Windsor Lewis; 1 s, 1 da; *Career* formerly merchant banker; MP (Cons) Bolton W 1983–97; PPS to Min of State Treasy 1985–86, PPS to Min of State NI Office 1986–87, PPS to min of state for Social Security 1987–88, an asst Govt whip 1988–89, a Lord Cmmr of the Treasy (Govt whip) 1989–92, jt Parly under-sec of state Dept of Health 1992–95, Parly under-sec of state Home Office 1995–97; dir NewMedia Investors Ltd 1997–2000, chief exec Int Fedn of Health Plans 1998–; tstee Royal Hosp for Neurodisability 2004–; *Style*— Tom Sackville

SACRANIE, Sir Iqbal; kt (2005), OBE (1999); s of Abdul Karim Mussa Sacranie (d 1982), and Mariam Mussa Sacranie (d 2008); *b* 6 September 1951, Malawi; *m* 30 Jan 1976, Yasmin, *née* Ismail; 2 da (Sameena (Mrs Ahmad), Raheena (Mrs Memi)), 3 s (Hamza, Mohammed, Abdul Karim); *Career* early career in accountancy, articled clerk 1972–77; sec gen Muslim Cncl of GB 2002–06 (founding sec gen 1997); dep pres World Memon Orgn 2004–, vice-pres Family Welfare Assoc, memb Bd Int Advsy Panel World Islamic Economic Forum; chair of tstees: Muslim Aid, Memon Assoc UK, Balham Mosque, Tooting Islamic Centre, Al Rissala Educn Tst; patron Cmmn on Multifaith Britain; Muslim News Award for Excellence, PM's Good Citizenship award; Hon LLD Leeds Met Univ 2005; FFA 1978; *Recreations* cricket, volleyball, golf; *Style*— Sir Iqbal

Sacranie, OBE; ✉ Unit 1, Red Lion Business Park, Red Lion Road, Surbiton, Surrey KT6 7QD

SADEQUE, Shahwar; *née* Imam; da of Ali Imam (d 1943), of Bangladesh, and Akhtar Imam (d 2010); *b* 31 August 1942; *Educ* Dhaka Univ Bangladesh (BSc), Bedford Coll London (MPhil), Kingston Poly (MSc); *m* 7 Oct 1962, Pharhad Sadeque (d 2010), s of Abdus Sadeque (d 1961); 1 da (Schehrezade b 13 Nov 1963), 1 s (Fahim b 26 Jan 1971); *Career* computer programmer BARIC Services Ltd 1969–73, physics teacher Nonsuch HS for Girls Sutton 1973–84, pt/t res into application of artificial intelligence and vision systems to mfrg processes Kingston Univ (formerly Kingston Poly) 1985–92; educnl and ICT conslt 1997–, special rep of the Secretary of State FCO (only person appointed from outside the Dip Serv) 1998–; md TriEs Ltd 1991–; vice-chair Immigration Advsy Serv 2002–07 (memb 2000–02); assoc Hosp mangr SW London and St George's Mental Health NHS Tst 2004– memb: Cmmn for Racial Equality 1989–93, Bd of Govrs BBC 1990–95, Bd Waltham Forest Housing Action Tst 1991–2002, VAT & Tax Tbnl/First Tier Tax Chambers 1991–2014, Income and Corporation Taxes Tbnl 1992–2010, Sch Curriculum and Assessment Authy 1993–97, Nat Cncl for Educnl Technol 1994–97, Metropolitan Police Ctee 1995–2000, Bd of Govrs Kingston Univ 1995–2002, Cncl C&G 1995–2011, Marshall Aid Commemoration Cmmn FCO 1998–2004, Panel 2000 FCO 1998, MRC Working Gp for Operational and Ethical Guidelines 1998–2001, RCP Ctee on Ethical Issues in Medicine 1998–2007, Lord Chancellor's Advsy Cncl on Nat Records and Archives 1999–2004, Dept of Health Good Practice in Consent Advsy Gp 2000–01, Nuffield Cncl on Bioethics Working Party on Healthcare Related Res in Developing Countries 2000–02, Patient Information Advsy Gp Dept of Health 2001–04, Panel of Independent Persons UCL 2003–, patient and carer network RCP 2004–07, MRC Ethics, Regulation and Public Involvement Ctee 2008–13, First Tier Tax Tbnls 2010–14; govr of Tstees Research into Ageing 1998–2001; tstee: Windsor Leadership Tst 1998–2005; involved with community work for the elderly and charity fundraising (Oxfam and UNICEF); formerly: memb various Cons Pty bodies incl Cons Women's Nat Ctee and Bow Gp Educn Standing Ctee, govr Riverview Co First Sch; voluntary worker St George's Hosp Tooting; hon fell City and Guilds of London Inst 2008, FRSA 1994–2000; *Publications* papers: Education and Ethnic Minorities (1988), Manufacturing – Towards the 21st Century (1988), A Knowledge-Based System for Sensor Interaction and Real-Time Component Control (1988); *Recreations* collecting thimbles and perfume bottles, cooking Indian-style, keeping up-to-date with current affairs; *Style*— Mrs Shahwar Sadeque

SADGROVE, Very Rev Michael; DL (Durham 2011); s of late Ralph Sadgrove, and Dorothea, *née* Leyser; *b* 13 April 1950; *Educ* UCS London, Balliol Coll Oxford (MA), Trinity Theol Coll Bristol; *m* 1974, Elizabeth Jennifer, *née* Suddes; 3 da (Joanna Elizabeth Marie b 1977, Philippa Thomasin Jane b 1979, Eleanor Jemima Clare b 1983), 1 s (Aidan Mark Daniel b 1982); *Career* ordained: deacon 1975, priest 1976; licensed to officiate Rural Deanery of Cowley 1975–77; Salisbury and Wells Theol Coll: lectr in Old Testament studies 1977–82, vice-princ 1980–82; hon vicar-choral Salisbury Cathedral 1978–82, vicar Alnwick Northumberland 1982–87, canon residentiary, precentor and vice-provost Coventry Cathedral 1987–95, provost of Sheffield 1995–2000, dean of Sheffield 2000–03, dean of Durham 2003–15, ret; memb Cathedrals Fabric Cmmn for England 1996–2006; Bishops' sr inspr of theol colls and courses 1982–2010; chm Univ of Durham Ethics Advsy Ctee 2004–14; pt/t lectr Dept of Theology and Religious Studies Univ of Durham; memb Soc for Old Testament Studies 1978; memb Gen Synod of the Church of England 2003–10; rector St Chad's Coll Durham 2009– (visitor 2003–09); memb Cncl: Univ of Durham 2003–15, Hatfield Coll Durham 2004–14; pres St Cuthbert's Hospice Durham 2003–, hon patron Durham City Tst 2009–; FRSA 1997; *Books* A Picture of Faith (1995), The Eight Words of Jesus (2006), Wisdom and Ministry (2008), I Will Trust in You: a companion to the evening Psalms (2009), Lost Sons: readings in the patriarchal stories (2012), Landscapes of Faith: the Christian Heritage of North East England (2013), Christ in a Choppie Box (2015); *Recreations* music, the arts, poetry and classical literature, walking the north-east of England, railways and trams, travels in Burgundy, European issues, photography; *Style*— The Very Rev Michael Sadgrove, Emeritus Dean of Durham; ✉ Barswell House, 27 Church Street, Haydon Bridge, Northumberland NE47 6JG (☎ 01434 688675, e-mail sadgrove@outlook.com)

SADLER, Brent Roderick; s of Philip Sadler (d 1959), and Ruth, *née* Dunkerley (d 1996); *b* 29 November 1950; *Educ* Royal Masonic Sch Bushey; *m* 15 Nov 2003, Dr Jelena Anicic; from previous marriages 2 s, 2 da; *Career* news reporter; formerly with: Harrow Observer, Reading Evening Post, Southern TV, Westward TV and HTV Bristol; ITN 1981–91 (ME corr 1986–91); assignments covered incl: hunger strikes Maze Prison Belfast 1981, Falklands war 1982, Israeli invasion of Lebanon 1982, Lebanese civil war 1981–89, Sabra and Chatila massacres 1983, US invasion of Grenada 1986, siege of Bourj al Barajneh Beirut 1987, Iran-Iraq war 1983–88, Gulf war 1991; sr int corr CNN (Lebanon) 1991–; assignments covered incl: release of Western hostages Beirut 1991, post-war Iraq (incl US missile strikes 1993), Somalia famine 1992–93, Bosnia Herzegovina 1993–96, PLO-Israeli peace agreement 1993, South African elections 1994, US intervention in Haiti 1994, Chechnya rebellion 1995–97, Israeli 'Grapes of Wrath' offensive against Lebanon 1996, death of Diana, Princess of Wales 1997, showdown in Iraq 1997, Kosovo 1998–99, NATO strikes on Yugoslavia 1999; bureau chief CNN Beirut 1997–2009, special corr Inside the Middle East (CNN) 2009; winner: Middx Co Press Journalist of the Year 1971, RTS Regional News Award 1980, RTS Int News Award 1987, BAFTA Awards (with ITN team) for Quality of Coverage from Lebanon 1983 and Best Actuality Coverage of Gulf War 1992, Emmy (US) for Somalia 1993, Overseas Press Club of America Award for Meritorious Reporting in Lebanon 1996, Cable Ace Award for Coverage of Russian Elections 1996; *Recreations* fly fishing, skiing, tennis, sailing; *Style*— Brent Sadler, Esq

SAFFMAN, His Hon Judge Andrew Maurice; s of Leonard Saffman (d 2000), and Rita Saffman; *Educ* Univ of Leeds (LLB); *m* 1980, Andrea; 2 s (Sam b 4 Jan 1982, John b 22 Aug 1986), 1 da (Hannah b 14 March 1983); *Career* admitted slr 1977; district judge 2001 (dep district judge 1995), circuit judge (North Eastern Circuit) 2013–; *Style*— His Hon Judge Saffman; ✉ Leeds Combined Court Centre, The Courthouse, 1 Oxford Row, Leeds LS1 3BG

SAGE, John George Patrick; s of Austin Sage, and Pauline, *née* Hussey; *Educ* Princethorpe Coll, Univ of Reading (BA); *m*; 1 s, 2 da; *Career* news ed Brighton Evening Argus 1993–95, asst news ed UK News 1995–96; Teletext Ltd: asst ed 1997–98, exec ed 1998–99, ed-in-chief 2000–; memb Soc of Editors 2000–; *Recreations* my family, squash, tennis, golf; *Style*— John Sage, Esq; ✉ Teletext Ltd, Building 10, Chiswick Business Park, 566 Chiswick High Road, London W4 5TS (☎ 020 8323 5000)

SAGGAR, Prof Shamit; s of Krishan Dev Saggar, of Nairobi, Kenya, and Kamala, *née* Bhakoo (d 1974); *b* 14 August 1963; *Educ* Finchley Manorhill Sch, Univ of Essex (BA, PhD); *m* 23 July 1988, Rita Alfred; 4 c (Shelley b 1994, Shaan b 1998, Symran b 2001, Reuben b 2008); *Career* early academic appts at Univ of Essex and Univ of Liverpool, reader in political behaviour Univ of London until 2001, seconded as sr policy advsr PM's Strategy Unit Cabinet Office 2001–03, prof of public policy Univ of Essex 2013–; visiting appts: Yale Univ, UCLA, ANU, Univ of Western Aust, NYU, visiting prof of public policy Univ of Toronto; chm UPP Gp Hldgs Ltd 2013–; sr fell: Demos, 21st Century Tst; chm Legal Complaints Serv Law Soc 2005–, cmmr Better Regulation Cmmn 2006–; non-exec dir: FSA, NCC, Whittington Hosp NHS Tst, Ethics Standards Bd Accountancy Fndn; cmmr: RSA Migration Cmmn, Ind Asylum Cmmn 2006–; sometime conslt to MIS, EHRC, Speaker's Conference on Parly Representation, Hansard Soc, Age Concern England, Cmmn for Racial Equality, Cwlth Cmmn on Respect and Understanding, BBC, Carlton Television and numerous UK and int govt depts; memb Advsy Cncl: Global Britons Prog Foreign Policy Centre, Inst for Citizenship, RNIB; memb Customer Impact Panel ABI 2006–; sr advsr Foreign Policy Centre and European Inclusion Index Br Cncl; govr Peabody Tst; Stein Rokkan postgrad fell 1988, Menzies fell 1992 and 1997, Harkness fell 1993, John Adams fell 2000, Yale world fell 2003–04; FRSA; *Books* incl: Race and Representation (2000), Pariah Politics (2008); *Recreations* travel, cooking, tennis, the company of my children; *Clubs* Cwlth; *Style*— Prof Shamit Saggar; ✉ c/o University of Essex, Wivenhoe Park, Essex CO4 3SQ (☎ 0206 874824, e-mail shamit@essex.ac.uk)

SAIDI, Samira Miriam (Sam); da of Hussein Ahmed Saidi, of Manchester, and Elizabeth Anne, *née* Bradshaw; *b* 8 July 1961; *Educ* Bush Davies Schs (ARAD), Royal Ballet Sch; *m* 28 Feb 1987, Alain Jacques Luis Dubreuil, s of Jacques E Dubreuil (d 1989), of Monaco; 2 s (Téo Jacques b April 1993, Louis Frederick b Jan 1996); *Career* dancer; Birmingham Royal Ballet (formerly Sadler's Wells Royal Ballet) 1979– (latterly first soloist); roles created incl: title role in David Bintley's The Snow Queen, Sybil Vane in The Picture of Dorian Gray, Giselle, Les Sylphides, Alice in Hobson's Choice, Kenneth Macmillan's Quartet, Odette/Odile in Swan Lake, and many other princ roles in co's repertoire; recreated second movement in Massine's Choreartium; ret dancing 1998; teacher: Dance Track prog Educ Dept Birmingham Royal Ballet, Royal Ballet Sch (teaching jr assocs); also choreographer Nat Youth Ballet; dir of dance English Nat Ballet Sch 2012–; *Recreations* theatre, interior design, antiques; *Style*— Miss Samira Saidi

SAIL, Lawrence Richard; s of Gustav Hellmut Sail, and Barbara, *née* Wright; *b* 29 October 1942, London; *Educ* Sherborne, St John's Coll Oxford (open scholar, Trevelyan scholar, BA); *m* 1, 1965 (m dis 1981), Teresa Luke; 1 s (Matthew Charles b Feb 1972), 1 da (Erica Jocelyn b April 1974); m 2, 1994, Helen Bird; 2 da (Rose Arlette, Grace Romola (twins) b June 2003); *Career* admin offr ILEA then Planning Dept GLC 1965–66, head of modern languages Lenana Sch Nairobi 1966–70, freelance writer 1971–73 and 1991–; teacher of French and German: Millfield Sch 1973–74, Blundell's Sch 1976–80 (visiting writer 1980–81), Exeter Sch 1982–91; course tutor and guest reader Arvon Fndn 1978– (chm 1990–94), participant WH Smith Poets in Schs Scheme 1978–, prog dir Cheltenham Festival of Literature 1991, judge Whitbread Book of the Year Awards 1991, memb jury European Literature Prize 1994–96, co-dir 50th Anniversary Cheltenham Festival of Literature 1999; visited for Br Cncl: India 1993, Egypt 1996, Bosnia 1996, Ukraine 1999, Portugal 2006 and 2007; participant: Anglo-French Poetry Festival Paris 1993, Trois Rivières Poetry Festival Quebec 2003, Medellin Int Poetry Festival Colombia 2004; poems broadcast on BBC radio and TV; compiler and presenter: Time for Verse series (BBC Radio 4), edition of Poetry Now (BBC Radio 3); Hawthornden fell 1992, Writer's Bursary Arts Cncl 1993, Cholmondeley Award 2004; memb SCR St John's Coll Oxford; FRSL 1998; *Poetry* Opposite Views (1974), The Drowned River (1978), The Kingdom of Atlas (1980), Devotions (1987), Aquamarine (1988), Out of Land: New & Selected Poems (1992), Building into Air (1995), The World Returning (2002), Eye-Baby (2006), Waking Dreams: New and Selected Poems (2010), Songs of the Darkness: Poems for Christmas (2010), The Quick (2015); *Other Works* Children in Hospital (with Teresa Sail, 1974), Death of an Echo (radio play, 1980), Cross-currents (essays, 2005), Sift: Memories of Childhood (2010), The Key to Clover and other essays (2013); as contrib: Mind Readings, Sightlines (short stories), work in numerous anthologies incl Palgrave's Golden Treasury and The Oxford Book of Christmas Poems; poems, reviews, articles and essays in various periodicals and newspapers; as ed: First and Always: Poems for Great Ormond Street Children's Hospital (1988), South West Review (1980–85), South West Review: A Celebration (1985), 100 Voices (1989); The New Exeter Book of Riddles (ed with Kevin Crossley-Holland, 1999), Light Unlocked: Christmas Card Poems (with Kevin Crossley-Holland, 2005); *Style*— Lawrence Sail; ✉ Richmond Villa, 7 Wonford Road, Exeter EX2 4LF

SAINI, Pushpinder; QC (2008); *Educ* Univ of Oxford (MA, BCL); *Career* called to the Bar Gray's Inn 1991 (bencher 2012); memb Blackstone Chambers; practice areas incl: commercial, banking and financial services, public law and human rights, media and entertainment, EU and competition; *Style*— Pushpinder Saini, Esq, QC; ✉ Blackstone Chambers, Blackstone House, Temple, London EC4Y 9BW

SAINSBURY, Prof (Richard) Mark; s of Richard Eric Sainsbury, and Freda Margaret, *née* Horne; *b* 2 July 1943; *Educ* CCC Oxford (scholar, MA, DPhil); *Career* Radcliffe lectr in philosophy Magdalen Coll Oxford 1968–70, lectr in philosophy St Hilda's Coll Oxford 1970–73, Radcliffe lectr in philosophy BNC Oxford 1973–75, lectr in philosophy Univ of Essex 1975–78, lectr in philosophy Bedford Coll London 1978–84 (actg head of Philosophy Dept 1981–84); KCL: lectr in philosophy 1984–87, reader 1987–89, head Dept of Philosophy 1988–95, Susan Stebbing prof of philosophy 1989–2008; prof Philosophy Dept Univ of Texas at Austin 2002–; visiting research fell ANU 1992, Wittgenstein lectr and visiting prof Bayreuth Univ 1994, Leverhulme sr res fell 2000–02; ed MIND 1990–2000; FBA 1998; *Books* Russell (1979), Paradoxes (1988, 3 edn 2009), Logical Forms (1991, 3 edn 2009), Departing from Frege (2002), Reference Without Referents (2005), Fiction and Fictionalism (2009), Seven Puzzles of Thought and How to Solve Them: An Originalist Theory of Concepts (with Michael Tye, 2013), Thinking About Things (2017); also author of numerous articles and reviews in learned jls; *Recreations* baking bread; *Style*— Prof Mark Sainsbury, FBA

SAINSBURY OF PRESTON CANDOVER, Baron (Life Peer UK 1989), of Preston Candover in the County of Hampshire; Sir John Davan Sainsbury; KG (1992), kt (1980); eldest s (by 1 m) of late Baron Sainsbury (Life Peer), of Drury Lane; *b* 2 November 1927; *Educ* Stowe, Worcester Coll Oxford; *m* 8 March 1963, Anya (Anya Linden, the Royal Ballet ballerina), da of George Charles Eltenton; 2 s, 1 da; *Career* J Sainsbury plc: dir 1958–92, vice-chm 1967–69, chm 1969–92, pres 1992–; dir The Economist 1972–80, dir Centre for Policy Studies 2009–12; hon vice-pres Royal Opera House Covent Garden 2009– (dir 1969–85, chm 1987–91), dir Royal Opera House Tst 1974–84 and 1987–97, chm of tstees Royal Opera House Endowment Fund 2001–05, memb Bd of Hon Dirs Royal Opera House 2016–; memb Cncl of Friends of Covent Garden 1969–91 (chm 1969–81); tstee: Nat Gallery 1976–83, Westminster Abbey Tst 1977–83, Tate Gallery 1982–83, Rhodes Tst 1984–98, Saïd Business Sch Fndn 2003–15; jt hon treas Euro Movement 1972–75; pres: Br Retail Consortium 1993–97 (memb Cncl 1975–79), Sparsholt Coll 1993–2000; memb President's Ctee CBI 1982–84; vice-pres Contemporary Arts Soc 1984–96 (hon sec 1965–71, vice-chm 1971–74, vice-patron 1998–2006); a dir Friends of Nelson Mandela Children's Fund 1996–2000; chm Benesh Inst of Choreology 1986–87, chm of govrs Royal Ballet 1995–2003 (govr 1987–2003); govr Royal Ballet Sch 1965–76 and 1987–91, dir Rambert Sch of Ballet and Contemporary Dance 2003–05 (chm Devpt Ctee 2002–03, chm Steering Ctee 2005–09, chm Rambert Sch Tst 2005–10); visitor Ashmolean Museum 2003–15, patron Dulwich Picture Gallery 2004– (chm of tstees 1994–2000), patron Sir Harold Hillier Gardens and Arboretum 2005–; memb Jt Parly Scrutiny Ctee on Draft Charities Bill 2004–05; Albert Medal RSA 1989, Hadrian Award 2000, Prince of Wales Medal for Arts Philanthropy 2008, Univ of Oxford Sheldon Medal 2010, Gjergj Kastrioti-Skenderbeg Presidential Award (Albania) 2014; hon bencher Inner Temple 1985; hon fell Worcester Coll Oxford 1982, hon fell British Sch at Rome 2002; Hon DScEcon Univ of London 1985, Hon DLitt South Bank Univ 1992, Hon LLD Univ of Bristol 1993, hon

DScEcon (hc) Univ of Cape Town 2000; FIGD 1973, Hon FRIBA 1993; *Clubs* Garrick, Beefsteak; *Style—* The Rt Hon Lord Sainsbury of Preston Candover, KG

SAINSBURY OF TURVILLE, Baron (Life Peer UK 1997), of Turville in the County of Buckinghamshire; David John Sainsbury; s of late Sir Robert Sainsbury, and of Lisa Ingebourg, *née* Van den Bergh; *b* 24 October 1940; *Educ* King's Coll Cambridge (BA), Columbia Grad Sch of Business NY (MBA); *m* 1973, Susan Carroll Reid; 3 da; *Career* J Sainsbury: joined 1963, dir 1966–98, fin controller 1971–73, fin dir 1973–90, dep chm 1988–92, chief exec 1992–97, chm 1992–98; Parly under sec of state for science and innovation DTI 1998–2006; memb: Ctee Review of the Post Office (Carter Ctee) 1975–77, Cmmn on Public Policy and Br Business IPPR 1995–97; author The Race to the Top (Govt review of sci and innovation policies) 2007; memb Governing Body London Business Sch 1985–98 (chm 1991–98), chm Transition Bd Univ for Industry 1998–99; tstee SDP 1982–90, chllr Univ of Cambridge 2011–; Andrew Carnegie Medal of Philanthropy (received on behalf of Sainsbury family) 2003; Hon LLD Univ of Cambridge 1997; Hon FREng (Hon FEng 1994); *Publications* Government and Industry: A New Partnership (1981), Wealth Creation and Jobs (with Christopher Smallwood, 1987), Progressive Capitalism: How to Achieve Economic Growth, Liberty and Social Justice (2013); *Style—* Lord Sainsbury of Turville; ✉ House of Lords, London SW1A 0BW (✆ 020 7219 3000)

SAINT, (Prof) Andrew John; s of Rev Arthur James Maxwell Saint, and Elisabeth Yvetta, *née* Butterfield; *b* 30 November 1946; *Educ* Christ's Hosp, Balliol Coll Oxford (BA), Warburg Inst Univ of London (MPhil); *Career* teacher Univ of Essex 1971–74, architectural ed The Survey of London 1974–86, historian English Heritage 1986–95, prof of architecture Univ of Cambridge 1995–2006, gen ed Survey of London English Heritage 2006–; Alice Davis Hitchcock Medallion Soc of Architectural Historians (GB) 1978 and 1989; Hon FRIBA; *Books* Richard Norman Shaw (1976), The Image of the Architect (1983), Towards A Social Architecture (1986), Architect and Engineer (2007); *Style—* Andrew Saint; ✉ 14 Denny Crescent, London SE11 4UY (✆ 020 7735 3863)

ST ALBANS, Bishop of 2009–; Rt Rev Dr Alan Gregory Clayton Smith; s of Frank Eric Smith (d 1985), and Rosemary Clayton, *née* Barker; *b* 14 February 1957; *Educ* Trowbridge GS for Boys, Univ of Birmingham (BA, MA), Wycliffe Hall Oxford (CertTheol), Univ of Wales Bangor (PhD); *Career* curate St Lawrence Pudsey 1981–84, chaplain Lee Abbey Fellowship 1984–90, diocesan missioner and team vicar St Matthew's Walsall 1990–97, archdeacon of Stoke-upon-Trent 1997–2001, hon canon of Lichfield Cathedral 1997–2009, bishop of Shrewsbury 2001–09; memb House of Lords 2013–; chair Shropshire Strategic Partnership 2006–09; Hon DD Univ of Birmingham 2010; *Books* Growing up in Multifaith Britain (2007), God-Shaped Mission: theological and practical perspectives from the rural church (2008), The Reflective Leader (2011), Saints and Pilgrims in the Diocese of St Albans (2013); *Recreations* travel, music, skiing, gardening; *Style—* The Rt Rev the Bishop of St Albans; ✉ Abbey Gate House, Abbey Mill Lane, St Albans, Hertfordshire AL3 4HD (✆ 01727 853305, fax 01727 846715 , e-mail bishop@stalbans.anglican.org)

ST ALBANS, 14 Duke of (E 1684); Murray de Vere Beauclerk; also Baron Hedington and Earl of Burford (E 1676), Baron Vere of Hanworth (GB 1750); Hereditary Grand Falconer and Hereditary Registrar of Court of Chancery; s of 13 Duke of St Albans, OBE (d 1988), and his 1 w, Nathalie Chatham (d 1985), da of Percival Walker; gggggs of 1 Duke of St Albans, who was natural s of King Charles II and Eleanor (Nell) Gwynn; *b* 19 January 1939; *Educ* Tonbridge; *m* 1, 1963 (m dis 1974), Rosemary Frances, o da of Francis Harold Scoones, MRCS, LRCP, JP; 1 da (Lady Emma Caroline de Vere (Lady Emma Smellie) b 22 July 1963), 1 s (Charles Francis Topham de Vere, Earl of Burford b 22 Feb 1965); m 2, 1974 (m dis 2001), Cynthia Theresa Mary (d 2002), da of late Lt-Col William James Holdsworth Howard, DSO, and former w of late Sir Anthony Robin Maurice Hooper, 2 Bt; m 3, 2002, Gillian Anita, da of late Lt-Col Cyril George Reginald Northam, and wid of Philip Nesfield Roberts; *Heir* s, Earl of Burford (Charles Beauclerk, *qv*); *Career* CA 1962; govr-gen Royal Stuart Soc 1989–; pres Beaufort Opera 1991–; patron Bestwood Male Voice Choir 2001–; Freeman City of London, Liveryman Worshipful Co of Drapers; FCA; *Style—* His Grace the Duke of St Albans; ✉ 16 Ovington Street, London SW3 2JB

ST ALDWYN, 3 Earl (UK 1915); Sir Michael Henry Hicks Beach; 11 Bt (E 1619); also Viscount St Aldwyn (UK 1906), Viscount Quenington (UK 1915); s of 2 Earl St Aldwyn, GBE, TD, PC (d Jan 1992), and Diana Mary Christian, *née* Mills (d July 1992); *b* 7 February 1950, Oxford; *Educ* Eton, Univ of Oxford (MA); *m* 1, 1982, Gilda Maria, o da of Barão Saavedra (d 1984), and Baronesa Saavedra, of Ipanema, Brazil; 2 da (Lady Atalanta Maria b 1983, Lady Aurora Ursula b 1988); m 2, 2005, Mrs Louise Wigan; *Heir* bro, Hon David Hicks Beach; *Career* dir The Rank Fndn; Liveryman Worshipful Co of Mercers; *Clubs* Leander, White's, Pratt's, Royal Yacht Squadron; *Style—* The Rt Hon the Earl St Aldwyn; ✉ The Mill House, Coln St Aldwyns, Cirencester GL7 5AJ (✆ 01285 750 226, e-mail mstaldwyn@infunmar.com); International Fund Marketing (UK) Ltd, 5th Floor - Suite 7A, Berkeley Square House, Berkeley Square, London W1J 6BY (✆ 020 7616 7400, fax 020 7616 7411)

ST ANDREWS, Earl of; George Philip Nicholas Windsor; er s and h of HRH The Duke of Kent, KG, GCMG, GCVO (*see Royal Family section*); *b* 26 June 1962; *Educ* Eton (Kings scholar), Downing Coll Cambridge; *m* 9 Jan 1988, Sylvana Palma (b 28 May 1957), da of Max(imilian) Karl Tomaselli and Josiane Preschez; 1 s (Edward Edmund Maximilian George, Lord Downpatrick b 2 Dec 1988), 2 da (Lady Marina-Charlotte Alexandra Katharine Helen b 30 Sept 1992, Lady Amelia Sophia Theodora Mary Margaret b 24 Aug 1995); *Heir* s, Lord Downpatrick; *Career* attached FCO 1987–88, Books and Manuscripts Dept Christie's 1996–98; chm: GB-Sasakawa Fndn 2005– (tstee 1995–), Golden Web Fndn 2006–12; tstee: SOS Children's Villages (UK) 1998, Global E-health Fndn 2013–; memb Advsy Bd Next Century Fndn 2010–; patron: Assoc for Worldwide Cancer Research 1995–, The Princess Margarita of Romania Tst 1997–, Prince George Galitzine Meml Library 2005–, Welsh Sinfonia 2011–, Friends Mongolia and Inner Asia Studies Unit Univ of Cambridge 2012–, The Chopin Soc UK 2013, Centre for Islamic Finance Univ of Bolton 2014–; *Style—* Earl of St Andrews; ✉ York House, St James's Palace, London SW1A 1BQ

ST ASAPH, Bishop of 2009–; Rt Rev Gregory Kenneth Cameron; s of Kenneth Hughes Cameron, and Irene Cameron; *b* 6 June 1959, Monmouthshire; *Educ* Croesyceiliog GS, Lincoln Coll Oxford, Downing Coll Cambridge, Univ of Wales Coll Cardiff, St Michael's Coll LLandaff; *m* 22 July 1995, Clare Margaret Catherine, *née* Lee; 3 s (Benedict b 9 July 1997, William b 29 April 1999, Edward b 10 May 2002); *Career* asst curate Parish of St Paul Newport 1983–86, ass priest/team vicar Rectorial Benefice of Llanmartin 1986–88, tutor St Michael's Theological Coll Llandaff and lectr in Old Testament UC Cardiff 1986–89, chaplain and head of religious studies Wycliffe Coll 1988–94, dir Bloxham Project 1994–2000, chaplain to Dr Rowan Willams (as Archbishop of Wales) and Monmouth Diocesan communication offr 2000–03, dir of ecumenical affrs and studies Anglican Consultative Cncl 2003–09 (dep sec gen 2004–09); co-chair Anglican-Oriental Orthodox Int Cmmn 2014–; research fell Centre for Law and Religion Cardiff Univ 1998–99 (hon research fell 1999–), hon fell Lincoln Coll Oxford 2010; DD Episcopal Divinity Sch Massachussets 2007; Cross of St Augustine; *Publications* Mary, Grace and Hope, Study Guide and Commentary (with Don Bolen, 2006); *Recreations* heraldry, Egyptology; *Style—* The Rt Rev the Bishop of St Asaph; ✉ Esgobty, Llanelwy, St Asaph LL17 0TW (✆ 01745 583503, e-mail bishop.stasaph@churchinwales.org.uk)

ST AUBIN de TERAN, Lisa Gioconda; da of Cuthbert Jan Alwin Rynveld Carew, of Guyana, and Joan Mary St Aubin (d 1981); *b* 2 October 1953; *Educ* James Allen's Girls' Sch Dulwich; *m* 1, 1970, Jaime Cesar Terán Mejia Cifuentes Terán; 1 da (Iseult Joanna Teran St Aubin (Mrs Iseult Terán Ysenburg) b 5 May 1973); m 2, 1982, George Mann Macbeth; 1 s (Alexander Morton George Macbeth b 30 Sept 1982); m 3, 1989, Robbie Charles Duff-Scott, s of Frederick Duff-Scott (d 1989); 1 da (Florence Cameron Alexandra Rose Duff-Scott b 10 July 1990); *Career* plantation mangr and sugar farmer Venezuelan Andes 1972–78; writer; *Awards* Somerset Maugham Award 1983, John Llewelyn Rhys Prize 1983, Eric Gregory Award for Poetry 1983; trans into many languages, public readings worldwide; *Books* Keepers of the House (1983), The Slow Train to Milan (1984), The Tiger (1984), The Bay of Silence (1985), The High Place (poetry, 1986), The Marble Mountain (short stories, 1989), Joanna (1990), Venice the Four Seasons (essays, 1992), A Valley In Italy: Confessions of a House Addict (1994), The Hacienda (memoirs, 1997), The Palace (novel, 1997), South Paw (short stories, 1999), Memory Maps (memoirs, 2001), Otto (2004), Mozambique Mysteries (2007); *Recreations* reading, falconry, herbal medicines; *Clubs* Groucho; *Style—* Mrs Lisa St Aubin de Terán

ST AUBYN, Edward; *b* 1960, London; *Educ* Westminster, Keble Coll Oxford; *Career* novelist; *Books* Never Mind (1992, Betty Trask Award), Bad News (1992), Some Hope (1994), On the Edge (1998), A Clue to the Exit (2000), Mother's Milk (2006, Prix Fermina Etranger 2007, South Bank Show Literature Award 2007, shortlisted Man Booker Prize 2006), At Last (2011), Lost For Words (2014, Bollinger Everyman Wodehouse Prize for Comic Fiction 2014, Prix Rive Gauche 2014); *Style—* Edward St Aubyn; ✉ c/o Aitken Alexander Associates, 291 Gray's Inn Road, London WC1X 8QJ

ST CLAIR, William Linn; *b* 7 December 1937; *Educ* Edinburgh Acad, St John's Coll Oxford; *Children* 2 da (Anna b 1967, Elisabeth b 1970); *Career* writer; formerly under sec HM Treasy, served Admiralty and FCO; chm Open Book Publishers 2009–; conslt: OECD 1992–95, EU 1996; int pres Byron Soc; fell: All Souls Coll Oxford 1992–96 (visiting fell 1981–82), Trinity Coll Cambridge 1998–2008 (visiting fell 1997–98); visiting fell Huntington Library Calif 1985, sr research fell Inst of English Studies Sch of Advanced Study Univ of London 2009–; memb Ctee London Library 1996–2000; patron English PEN Writers-in-Prison Ctee 2000; FRSL, FBA (memb Cncl 1997–2000); *Awards* Heinemann Prize for Lit 1973, Time Life Award for Br Non-Fiction 1990, Thalassa Forum Award for Culture 2000; *Publications* Lord Elgin and the Marbles (1967, revised edn 1998), That Greece Might Still Be Free (1972, 2 edn 2009), Trelawny (1978), Policy Evaluation – A Guide For Managers (1988), The Godwins and the Shelleys – The Biography of a Family (1989), Executive Agencies – A Guide to Setting Targets and Judging Performance (1992), Conduct Literature for Women 1500–1640 (jt ed with Irmgard Maassen, 2000), Mapping Lives: The Uses of Biography (jt ed with Peter France, 2002), Conduct Literature for Women 1640–1710 (jt ed with Imgard Maassen, 2002), The Reading Nation in the Romantic Period (2004), The Political Economy of Reading (2005, revised edn 2012), The Grand Slave Emporium, Cape Coast Castle and the British Slave Trade (2006, published in US as The Door of No Return (2007)), Looking at the Acropolis of Athens from Modern Times to Antiquity (in Cultural Ethics, ed Sandis, 2014), Romantic Biography (in Life-Writing, ed Leader, 2015); *Recreations* old books, Scottish mountains; *Style—* William St Clair; ✉ 52 Eaton Place, London SW1X 8AL (✆ 020 7235 8329, e-mail ws214@cam.ac.uk); c/o Deborah Rogers, 20 Powis Mews, London W11 1JN

ST CLEMENT, Pamela (Pam); *b* 11 May 1942; *Educ* The Warren Worthing, Rolle Coll, Rose Bruford Coll of Drama; *m* 1970 (m dis 1979), Andrew Gordon; *Career* actress and presenter; Lifetime Achievement Award Br Soap Awards 2012, Showbusiness Personality of 2012; involved in charity and other activities; vice-pres Scottish Terrier Emergency Care Scheme; patron: London Animal Day, Tusk Tst, Africat UK (SE), Pets as Therapy; ambass Hearing Dogs for Deaf People; supporter: Age UK, Blue Cross, PDSA, Battersea Dogs Home, Kennel Club and Good Citizen Dog Scheme, Environmental Investigation Agency, Project Life Lion, DSWF, WSPA, Animals Asia, Brooke Hosp for Animals, Int League for the Protection of Horses, Not Forgotten Assoc, Battle of Britain Memorial Tst, Royal Br Legion; memb Inst of Advanced Motorists; gave speech and awards Duke of Edinburgh Awards St James's Palace; hon doctorate Univ of Plymouth 2008, fell Rose Bruford Coll of Drama 2015; *Theatre* incl: Joan Littlewood's Theatre Royal Stratford, Royal Shakespeare Theatre Co; other credits incl: Stringberg and Chekov (Prospect Theatre Co), Macbeth (Thorndike Theatre), I Am A Camera (Yvonne Arnaud Guildford and tour), Once a Catholic (Leeds Playhouse); *Television* incl: Within These Walls (2 series, LWT), Shall I See You Now? (BBC play), A Horseman Riding By (BBC series), Emmerdale Farm (YTV), Shoestring (BBC), Partners in Crime (LWT), Cats Eyes (TVS), The Tripods (BBC), Not For The Likes Of Us (BBC Play for Today), Pat Butcher in EastEnders (BBC) 1986–2012 and 2016, Leonardo II (BBC) 2012, animal items presenter This Morning 2012, Whipsnade 13 part Wildlife Series (2 Series, Anglia TV), Animal Planet, Adopt-a-Wild Animal, Wild at Heart, BBC Animal Awards, Bull 2015, Casualty 2016; *Film* incl: Hedda, Dangerous Davies, The Bunker, Scrubbers; *Books* End of an Earring (autobiography, 2015); *Style—* Ms Pam St Clement; ✉ c/o Saraband Associates (e-mail brynnewton@btconnect.com)

ST DAVIDS, Bishop of 2008–; Rt Rev (John) Wyn Evans; s of Ven David Eifion Evans (d 1997), and Iris Elizabeth, *née* Gravelle (d 1973); *b* 4 October 1946; *Educ* Ardwyn GS Aberystwyth, UC Cardiff (BA), St Michael's Theol Coll Llandaff (BD), Jesus Coll Oxford; *m* 1997, Diane Katherine Baker; *Career* ordained deacon 1971, priest 1972; curate St Davids Pembs 1971–72, minor canon St Davids Cathedral 1972–75, graduate student Jesus Coll Oxford 1975–77, permission to officiate Oxford Dio 1975–77, diocesan advsr on archives St Davids 1976–82, rector Llanfallteg with Castell Dwyran and Clunderwen with Henllan Amgoed and Llangan 1977–82, examining chaplain to Bishop of St Davids 1977, diocesan warden of ordinands 1978–83, diocesan dir of educn 1982–92; Trinity Coll Carmarthen: chaplain and lectr 1982–90, dean of chapel 1990–94, head Dept of Theology and Religious Studies 1991–94; St Davids Cathedral: hon canon 1988–90, canon (4th cursal) 1990–94, dean and precentor 1994–2008; chm St Davids Diocesan Advsy Ctee 2006–08; Church in Wales: memb Rep Body 1998–2004, chm of deans 2001–08, memb Cathedrals and Churches Cmmn 2001–; chm Cathedral Libraries and Archives Assoc 2001–07; pres Trinity UC Carmarthen 2009; memb: Exec Friends of Friendless Churches 1995–2006 (episcopal patron 2008–), Ct Nat Library of Wales 1999–2006, Ct Univ of Wales Cardiff 2002–11; visitor Univ of Wales Trinity St David's 2010–; memb Gorsedd of Bards 1997; FSA 1989, FRHistS 1994; *Publications* St Davids Cathedral 1181–1981 (with Roger Worsley, 1981), St David of Wales (ed with Jonathan Wooding, 2007), contrib to various jls incl Jl of Welsh Ecclesiastical History, Carmarthen Antiquary, Diwinyddiaeth; *Recreations* reading, music, antiquities; *Clubs* Oxford and Cambridge; *Style—* The Rt Rev Bishop of St Davids

ST EDMUNDSBURY, Dean of; *see:* Collings, Very Rev Neil

ST GEORGE, Charles Reginald; s of William Acheson St George (d 1993), and Heather Atwood, *née* Brown (d 1978); *b* 20 April 1955; *Educ* Henley GS, Univ of Exeter (BA), Queen's Univ Kingston Ontario (MA); *m* 1, 19 July 1980 (m dis 1989); 1 da (Imogen Margaret b 15 Jan 1984), 1 s (Michael John b 31 Dec 1985); m 2, 17 Oct 1991; 2 s (Henry Peter b 19 May 1995, Edward Charles George b 23 April 1998); *Career* CBI: sec Smaller Firms Cncl 1979–82, head of secretariat 1982–83; account mangr Ian Greer Associates Ltd 1983–87, md Profile Political Relations Ltd 1989–90 (dir 1987–88), dir PPS Group Ltd 2001– (jt md 1990–2001); Parly candidate (Lib) Guildford 1980–82, Lib Alliance borough cncllr Guildford 1983–87; *Recreations* golf, tennis and skiing; *Style—* Charles St George, Esq; ✉ PPS Group Ltd, 5D West Wing, The Willow Brook Centre, Bristol BS32 8BS (✆ 01454 275630, e-mail charles.stgeorge@ppsgroup.co.uk)

S

ST GILES, Mark Valentine; s of late Austin Loudon Valentine St Giles, and Sybil Gladwin Sykes Thompson; *b* 4 June 1941; *Educ* Winchester, Clare Coll Cambridge (MA); *m* 1966, Susan Janet, da of late Edward Turner; 2 da (Emma b 1968, Lucy b 1970), 1 s (Edward b 1974); *Career* analyst Laurence Keen & Gardner stockbrokers 1964–69, dir Jessel Securities 1969–75, md Allied Hambro Ltd 1975–83, dir Hambros Bank 1975–83, dir (later md) GT Management plc 1983–88, chm Cadogan Management Ltd 1988–93, dir Framlington Group plc 1989–97, dir International Financial Strategy Ltd 1993–2000, ptnr Cadogan Financial 2000–; *Recreations* travel, sailing, gardening; *Clubs* Travellers; *Style*— Mark St Giles, Esq; ✉ Cadogan Financial, Higher House, West Lydford, Somerset TA11 7DG (☎ 01963 240664, fax 01963 240655, e-mail staegidius@yahoo.com)

ST HELENA, Lord Bishop of 2011–; Rt Rev Dr Richard David Fenwick; s of William Samuel and Ethel May Fenwick; *b* 3 December 1943; *Educ* Glantaf Secdy Modern Sch, Monkton House, Canton HS Cardiff, Univ of Wales Lampeter (BA, MA, PhD), Trinity Coll Dublin (MusB, MA), Fitzwilliam Coll Cambridge, Ridley Hall Cambridge; *m* 1975, Dr Jane Elizabeth Hughes; 1 s, 1 da; *Career* ordained: deacon 1968, priest 1969, bishop 2011; asst curate: Skewen 1968–72, Penarth with Lavernock 1972–74; priest-vicar, succentor and sacrist of Rochester Cathedral 1974–78; St Paul's Cathedral: minor canon 1978–83, succentor 1979–83, warden of the Coll of Minor Canons 1981–83; vicar St Martin's Ruislip 1983–90, priest-vicar of Westminster Abbey 1983–90; Guildford Cathedral: canon residentiary and precentor 1990–97, sub-dean 1996–97; dean of Monmouth 1997–2011; chm Liturgical Cmmn Church in Wales 1998–2011; Archbishop of Wales's Award in Church Music (hc) 2012; warden Guild of Church Musicians 1998–2011; Liveryman Worshipful Co of Musicians, Hon Liveryman and Master's Chaplain Worshipful Co of Gold and Silver Wyre Drawers 1981–2011; Hon DLitt Central Sch of Religion 2012; FLCM, FTCL, Hon FVCM, Hon FGCM; OStJ 2001; *Publications* contribs to various musical and theol jls; *Recreations* travel, reading, music; *Style*— The Rt Rev the Lord Bishop of St Helena; ✉ Bishopsholme, St Helena Island, South Atlantic Ocean (☎ 00 290 24471, e-mail richard.d.fenwick@googlemail.com)

ST JOHN OF BLETSO, 21 Baron (E 1559); Sir Anthony Tudor St John; 18 Bt (E 1660); s of 20 Baron, TD (d 1978), and Katharine Emily, *née* von Berg; *b* 16 May 1957; *Educ* Diocesan Coll Cape Town, Univ of Cape Town (BA, BSc, BProc), Univ of London (LLM); *m* 1, 16 Sept 1994 (m dis 2012), Dr Helen Jane Westlake, eldest da of Michael Westlake, of Bath, Avon; 2 s (Hon Oliver Beauchamp b 1995, Hon Alexander Andrew b 29 Aug 1996), 2 da (Athene b 24 Feb 1998, Chloe b 17 June 1999); m 2, Oct 2015; *Heir* s, Hon Oliver St John; *Career* sits as Independent Peer in Lords (Parly interests foreign affairs, environment, financial and legal services), Extra Lord-in-Waiting to HM The Queen 1998–; dep chm All-Pty Parly SA Gp; memb: EC Select Ctee A (Trade, Finance and Foreign Affairs 1996–99, EU Sub-Ctee B Energy Internal Markets; solicitor and stockbroker; md Globix (UK) 1998–2002; former chm: Eurotrust Ltd, Spiritel plc; former conslt to Merrill Lynch plc London; non-exec dir Regal Petroleum 2003–, chm IDH plc 2015–, chm Strand Hanson, dir GRIT, dir Falcon Gp, advsr Silicon Valley Bank, advsr Betway; *Recreations* tennis, golf, skiing, running; *Clubs* Sunningdale Golf (conslt), Beaverbrook Golf, Royal Cape, Hurlingham; *Style*— The Rt Hon The Lord St John of Bletso; ✉ House of Lords, London SW1A 0PW (e-mail asj1957@ocra.com)

ST JOHNSTON, Dr (Robert) Daniel; s of Colin David St Johnston, and Valerie Joyce, *née* Paget; *b* 24 April 1960, London; *Educ* Christ's Coll Cambridge (BA), Harvard Univ (PhD); *Partner* Bénédicte Sanson; 1 da (Emma b 18 Dec 2000), 1 s (Pierre b 13 Feb 2004); *Career* geneticist; European Molecular Biology Orgn (EMBO) fell 1988–90, Max Planct Gesellschaft research fell 1990–91, postdoctoral fell Max Planck Institut für Entwicklungsbiologie Tübingen 1991–98, Wellcome Tst sr fell Wellcome/Cancer Research Campaign Inst of Cancer and Developmental Biology and Dept of Genetics Univ of Cambridge 1991–97, Wellcome Tst princ fell Wellcome Tst/Cancer Research UK Gurdon Inst and Dept of Genetics Univ of Cambridge 1997–, EMBO dir Wellcome Tst and University of Cambridge PhD prog in developmental biology 2000, prof of developmental genetics Univ of Cambridge 2003–; dir Gurdon Inst 2009–; Balfour lectr Genetical Soc of GB 1995, bye fell Peterhouse Cambridge 1995–; memb Ctee Br Soc of Developmental Biology 1995–2000, dir Co of Biologists 1995–; memb Editorial Bd: Development 1999–, EMBO Jl 1999–, EMBO Reports 2000–; author of numerous articles in learned jls; Gold Medal EMBO 2000; fell EMBO 1997, FMedSci 2004, FRS 2005; contrib to various publications and learned jls; *Style*— Dr Daniel St Johnston; ✉ The Gurdon Institute, University of Cambridge, Tennis Court Road, Cambridge, CB2 1QN (☎ 01223 334127)

ST MAUR SHEIL, Michael Patrick; s of John St Maur Sheil, and Doreen Victoria, *née* Bradley; *b* 31 October 1946; *Educ* Bloxham Sch, St Edmund Hall Oxford; *m* Janet Susan, o da of Cdr F Allford, RN (ret); 1 s (Ross Patrick), 1 da (Fiona Jean); *Career* photographer (specialising in corp, industrial, and editorial photography); assoc Black Star photographers' agency NY 1971–; clients incl: Anti-Slavery Int, Bechtel, EC, Time, Nat Geographic, NY Times; exhbns: Child Trafficking in West Africa 2002, Fields of Battle – Messines and Passchendale 2007, Fields of Battle 1914–1918 (Canadian War Museum Ottawa) 2008, The Belgian Have Not Forgotten 1914–1918 (NZ War Meml Museum) 2009, Fields of Battle, Lands of Peace 14–18 (Great Hall of Westminster London) 2013, (Jardin du Luxembourg Paris, St James's Park London, Canadian Senate Ottawa, Nottingham, Strasbourg) 2014 and (Istanbul) 2015, Verdun – une siecle pour la Paix, 1916–2016 (Paris, Berlin & Verdun) 2016, Fields of Battle, Lands of Peace – Somme 100 (Guildhall, London) 2016; badged memb Int Guild of Battlefield Guides 2008, memb Br Cmmn for Military History 2011; numerous awards incl First Prize World Press Photo Awards 2002; FRGS 1983; *Publications* National Geographic Guide to Britain and Ireland (contrib photographer, 1983), Champs de Bataille de la Grand Guerre (2008), Fields of Battle, Lands of Peace 14–18 (2014), For the Fallen – Centenary book for the Commonwealth Graves Commission (2014), Fields of Battle, Lands of Peace 1914–1918 (2016); numerous magazine and annual reports; *Recreations* fishing, cricket, walking, photographing fields of battle; *Style*— Michael St Maur Sheil, Esq; ✉ websites www.westernfrontphotography.com and www.fieldsofbattle1418.org

ST OSWALD, 6 Baron (UK 1885); Charles Rowland Andrew Winn; DL (W Yorks 2004); s of 5 Baron St Oswald (d 1999); *b* 22 July 1959; *m* 1985, Louise Alexandra, da of Stewart Mackenzie Scott; 1 s (Hon Rowland Charles Sebastian Henry b 1986), 1 da (Hon Henrietta Sophia Alexandra b 1993); *Heir* s, Hon Rowland Winn; *Career* landowner; *Style*— The Rt Hon the Lord St Oswald, DL

ST PIERRE, Roger; s of Alexander Richard St Pierre, MBE (d 1999), and Caroline Amelia Borrett (d 1985); *b* 8 November 1941; *Educ* Ilford County HS; *m* 10 Nov 1975, Lesley, da of Bernard Constantine, of Sheffield; 1 s (Richard b 1976), 2 da (Danielle b 1978, Nicole b 1979); *Career* author and journalist; editor: Disco International 1977–79, Voyager Magazine (British Midland in-flight Magazine) 1986–90, European Hotelier 1992–95, Pocket Guide Series 1993–97, Holiday and Leisure World 1995–, Entertain Magazine 1995–97, Cycling Today 1996–98, American Express Great Golf Hotel Guide 1997–2001, Business Focus 2006–10, Incentive Travel 2010–; contrib to: Debrett's International Collection, London Evening Standard, The Dorchester Magazine, World Finance, European CEO, The Wealth Collection, Renaissance, The Times, Financial Weekly, Wish You Were Here, ABTA Magazine, Meridian, Conference and Incentive Travel, Incentive Travel and Corporate Meetings, DriveTime, Selling Long Haul, High Flyer, Essentially America, Independent Travel Trade News, Incentive Travel, Cycling Plus; sr writer www.allwaystraveller.com, our man on the ground Belfast Telegraph; formerly PR mangr for: Diana Ross, Glen Campbell, Jerry Lee Lewis, Don Williams, James Brown, Jackson 5, Frankie Lane; author of more than 1,000 record/album sleeve notes; broadcaster BBC and www.solarradio.com; cycle racer in many countries, mangr of int cycle teams; specialist writer on: travel (131 countries and all 50 US states visited), hotel industry, food and drink, music, motoring, cycling, leisure; memb Br Guild of Travel Writers, memb Travel Writers Alliance, memb Motoring Writers Guild; Hon Col Cwlth of Kentucky; *Books* incl: Book of The Bicycle (1973), The Rock Handbook (1986), Illustrated History of Black Music (1986), Marilyn Monroe (1987) Story of The Blues (1993), AA/Thomas Cook Guide to Orlando (1994), McDonalds – A History (1994), Tom Jones – In His Own Words (1996), Know the Game – Cycling (1996); *Recreations* cycling, music, travel; *Style*— Roger St Pierre, Esq; ✉ The Hoods, High Street, Wethersfield, Essex CM7 4BY (☎ 01371 850238, fax 01371 851714, e-mail stpierre.roger@gmail.com, website www.rogerstpierre.com)

ST QUINTON, Martin George; s of Eric St Quinton (d 2003), and Sybil, *née* Sanderson (d 1977); *b* 9 November 1957, Hull; *Educ* Univ of Durham (BA), Pacific Western Univ USA (MBA); *m* 6 August 1983, Judith, *née* Faughey; 2 da (Abigail b 17 Feb 1990, Caroline b 20 Sept 1991), 2 s (George b 8 Nov 1995, Charlie b 10 June 2000); *Career* ceo Saint Group 1980–93, ceo Danka International plc 1993–99, ceo and founder Azzurri Communications Ltd 2000–12; fndr Saint Fndn Charitable Tst, owner and chm Gloucester Rugby Club 2016–; Ernst & Young Technology Entrepreneur of the Year 2004; *Recreations* horseracing, travel; *Clubs* Roxburghe Golf, Racehorse Owners', Jockey; *Style*— Martin St Quinton, Esq; ✉ Gloucester Rugby Ltd, Kingsholm Stadium, Gloucester GL1 3AX (☎ 01452 300951, e-mail mstq123@gmail.com)

SAKO, Prof Mari (Lady Chakrabarti); da of Kanzo Sako, and Akemi, *née* Hiei; *b* 12 June 1960; *Educ* Univ of Oxford (BA), LSE (MSc(Econ)), Johns Hopkins Univ (Lessing-Rosenthal trg grant 1982–84, Univ fell 1982–84, MA), Univ of London (PhD); *m* Sir Sumantra Chakrabarti, *qv*; 1 da (Maya b 5 Sept 1995); *Career* research assoc The Technical Change Centre London 1984–86, research asst COMRES Imperial Coll London 1986–87; LSE: lectr in modern Japanese business 1987–92, lectr in industrial rels 1992–94, reader in industrial rels 1994–97; prof of mgmnt studies Univ of Oxford 1997–; fell Japanese Soc for the Promotion of Sci Econs Dept Kyoto Univ 1992, Japan Fndn fell Inst of Soc Sci Univ of Tokyo 1997, fell New Coll Oxford 2007–; pres Soc for the Advancement of Socio-Economics 2010–11, memb Acad of Mgmnt; FRSA 2001; *Books* How the Japanese Learn to Work (with R Dore, 1989, 2 edn 1998), Prices, Quality and Trust: Inter-firm Relations in Britain and Japan (1992), Japanese Labour and Management in Transition: Diversity, Flexibility and Participation (co-ed with H Sato, 1997), Are Skills the Answer? (jtly with C Crouch and D Finegold, 1999), Shifting Boundaries of the Firm (2006); also author of numerous book chapters and articles in learned jls; *Recreations* music, travel; *Style*— Prof Mari Sako; ✉ Saïd Business School, University of Oxford, Park End Street, Oxford OX1 1HP (☎ 01865 288925)

SALEM, Maurice; *b* 19 January 1970, Lebanon; *Educ* Br Sch of Brussels, Carmel Coll, Univ of London (BA); *Career* fixed income UBS 1991–94, fndr and md Wharton Asset Management UK LLP 1994–; FSA 2000; *Style*— Maurice Salem, Esq

SALES, Rt Hon Lord Justice; Rt Hon Sir Philip James Sales; kt (2008); *b* 11 February 1962; *Career* judge of the High Court of Justice (Chancery Div) 2008–14, Lord Justice of Appeal 2014–; *Style*— The Rt Hon Lord Justice Sales; ✉ Royal Courts of Justice, Strand, London WC2A 2LL

SALFORD, Bishop of 2014–; Rt Rev John Stanley Kenneth Arnold; s of (Stanley) Kenneth Arnold, and Mary, *née* Murray (d 2005); *b* 12 June 1953, Sheffield, S Yorks; *Educ* Ratcliffe Coll Leics, Trinity Coll Oxford (BA), Gregorian Univ Rome (BPhil, BTh, JCD); *Career* barr-at-law Cncl of Legal Educn 1975–76; Westminster Cathedral: hosp and cathedral chaplain 1985–88, cathedral sub-administrator 1988–93; parish priest Our Lady of Mount Carmel and St George Enfield 1993–2001, vicar gen and chllr Westminster RC Diocese 2001–06, moderator of the Curia 2005–14, auxiliary bishop of Westminster 2006–14 (titular bishop of Lindisfarne 2006–), chair of tstees Cafod 2011–; Bencher Middle Temple 2010; hon fell Trinity Coll Oxon 2015; *Publications* Quality of Mercy: A Re-evaluation of the Sacrament of Reconciliation (1993); *Style*— The Rt Rev the Bishop of Salford; ✉ Wardley Hall, Worsely, Manchester M28 2ND

SALIS; *see:* de Salis

SALISBURY, Dr Jonathan Richard; s of George Richard Salisbury (d 1971), and Patricia Doreen, *née* Jones; *b* 25 June 1956; *Educ* Hereford HS, UCL (BSc), UCH Med Sch (MB BS), King's Coll Sch of Med (MD); *m* 1, 19 May 1984 (m dis 2004), Alyson Frances, da of Lister Wilfred Bumby (d 1996), of Herne Bay, Kent; 1 da (Elizabeth b 1989), 1 s (Joseph b 1992); m 2, 1 Sept 2007, Marianna, da of Andreas Philippides, of Lemosos, Cyprus; 1 s (Andrew b 2009), 1 da (Sophia b 2012); *Career* GKT: sr lectr in histopathology 1987–97, reader in histopathology 1997–2004; conslt histopathologist KCH London 2004– (hon conslt 1987–2004); FRCPath 1997 (MRCPath 1986–97); *Style*— Dr Jonathan Salisbury; ✉ 84 Harbut Road, London SW11 2RE; Department of Histopathology, King's College Hospital, Bessemer Road, London SE5 9PJ (☎ 020 3299 3093, fax 020 3299 3670, e-mail jon.salisbury@nhs.net)

SALISBURY, Bishop of 2011–; Rt Rev Nicholas Roderick Holtam; s of Sydney Roderick Holtam, and Kathleen, *née* Freeberne; *b* 8 August 1954; *Educ* Latymer GS Edmonton, Collingwood Coll Durham (BA), KCL (BD, AKC, Tinniswood prize), Westcott House Cambridge, MA (Dunelm); *m* 1981, Helen, da of Esmond (Ted) Harris; 3 s (David b 1983, Timothy b 1984, Philip b 1989), 1 da (Sarah b 1986); *Career* asst curate St Dunstan and All Saints Stepney London 1979–82, lectr Lincoln Theol Coll 1983–87, vicar Christ and St John with St Luke Isle of Dogs London 1988–95, vicar St Martin in the Fields 1995–2011; *Books* A Room With A View – Ministry With the World at Your Door (2008), The Art of Worship (2011); *Clubs* Farmers (chaplain 1998–2011); *Style*— The Rev the Bishop of Salisbury; ✉ South Canonry, 71 The Close, Salisbury SP1 2ER (☎ 01722 334031)

SALISBURY, 7 Marquess of (GB 1789); Sir Robert Michael James Gascoyne-Cecil; KCVO (2012), PC (1994), DL (Herts 2007); also Baron Cecil (E 1603), Viscount Cranborne (E 1604), Earl of Salisbury (E 1605); and Baron Gascoyne-Cecil (Life Peer UK 1999), of Essendon, Co Rutland; s of 6 Marquess of Salisbury (d 2003); received a Writ in Acceleration summoning him to the House of Lords in his father's Barony of Cecil 1992; *b* 30 September 1946, London; *Educ* Eton, ChCh Oxford; *m* 1970, Hannah Ann, da of Lt-Col William Joseph Stirling of Keir, gs of Sir William Stirling-Maxwell, 9 Bt (a Baronetcy dormant since 1956); 2 s (Robert Edward William, Viscount Cranborne b 1970, Lord James Richard b 1973), 3 da (Lady Elizabeth Ann b 1972, Lady Georgiana, Lady Katherine (twins) b 1977); *Heir* s, Viscount Cranborne; *Career* MP (Cons) Dorset S 1979–87; chm Afghanistan Support Ctee; PPS to Cranley Onslow as Min of State FCO April-May 1982 (when resigned to be free to criticise Govt Ulster devolution plans), Parly under sec of state MOD 1992–94, Lord Privy Seal and ldr of the House of Lords 1994–97, shadow spokesman on NI and shadow ldr of the House of Lords 1997–98, leave of absence House of Lords 2002–; chm RVC Cncl 1998–2007, pres RASE 2007–08; chm Combined Clinical Science Fndn, pres Friends of the Br Library, chm Friends of Lambeth Palace Library, chm comparative clinical sci fndn 2004–, Thames Diamond Jubilee Fndn 2011–14; memb Hunterian Museum, Bd of Tstees of the Hunterian Collection 2014–, pres Game & Wildlife Conservation Tst, chllr Univ of Hertfordshire 2005–, govr The Charterhouse, chm Ct of Patrons Thrombosis Research Inst, chm Thames Diamond Jubilee Fndn 2011–15; DL Dorset 1998–2006; *Style*— The Most Hon the Marquess of Salisbury, KCVO, PC, DL; ✉ 2 Swan Walk, London SW3 4JJ

SALJE, Prof Ekhard Karl Hermann; s of Gerhard Salje, of Hanover, and Hildegard, *née* Drechsler; *b* 26 October 1946; *Educ* Herschel Sch Hanover, Univ of Hanover (Dip Physics, PhD); *m* 19 July 1952, Elisabeth, *née* Démaret; 1 s (Henrik b 26 June 1980), 4 da (Joelle b 16 Oct 1981, Jeanne b 2 April 1983, Léa-Cécile b 4 June 1985, Barbara b 25 April 1990); *Career* prof of crystallography Univ of Hanover 1978–87 (lectr in physics 1975–78); Univ of Cambridge: lectr in mineral physics 1987–88, reader 1988–92, prof 1992–94, prof of mineralogy and petrology 1994–2016, head Dept of Earth Sci 1999–2008, pres Clare Hall 2001–08; co-dir IRC in superconductivity 1987–98; prog dir Cambridge-MIT Inst 2000–03; visiting prof: Univ of Paris 1981–82, Univ of Grenoble 1990–92, Japan 1996 (Monbusho prof), Univ of Le Mans 1998, Bayerisches Geoinstitut Bayreuth 1998–, Univ of Bilbao 1999, Univ of Hamburg 2003–07, Univ of Leipzig 2008, Max Planck Inst of Mathematics Leipzig 2009; hon prof Xi'an Jiotong Univ 2012; Ulam fell Los Alamos US; memb Bd: Max Planck Inst of Mathematics Leipzig 2003–12, Univ of Hanover 2004 (senator 1980–82), Univ of Hamburg 2004–08, Parly Office of Science and Technol 2007–; pres Alexander von Humboldt Assoc UK 2004–08; Abraham Gottlieb Werner Medal 1994, Humboldt Prize 1999, Ernst Ising Prize for Physics 2002, Golden Medal Univ of Hamburg 2002, Agricola Medal for Applied Mineralogy 2006; hon fell Darwin Coll Cambridge 2002, hon fell Clare Hall 2008; fell: Mineralogical Soc 1990 (Schlumberger medal 1998), Acad of Science (Leopoldina) 1994, Acad Royal de Barcelona 2010; FInstP 1996, FGS 1996, FRS 1996, FRSA 1996; Chevalier dans l'Ordre des Palmes Académiques (France) 2003, First Class Cross of the Order of Merit Germany 2006; *Books* Phase Transitions in Ferroelastic and Co-elastic Crystals (1990, 2 edn 1993); author of over 600 scientific pubns; *Recreations* music, painting; *Style*— Prof Ekhard Salje, FRS; ✉ Department of Earth Sciences, University of Cambridge, Downing Street, Cambridge CB2 3EQ (☎ 01223 333481, fax 01223 333478, e-mail es10002@esc.cam.ac.uk)

SALKELD, David John; s of William (Bill) Salkeld, and Freda Salkeld; *b* 23 February 1956, Middlesbrough; *Educ* Middlesbrough HS, Univ of London (BSc); *m* Catherine; 3 s (Andrew, Nicholas, Christopher); *Career* co industrial rels mangr Findus 1981–83, gp employee rels mangr Grand Metropolitan Retail 1983–86, personnel dir then ops dir Northern Foods plc 1986–90, md Northern Dairies (div of Northern Foods plc) 1990–95, ceo Arla Foods plc 1995–2003, gp ceo Grampian Country Foods Gp Ltd 2003–05 (non-exec dir 2002–03), currently ceo Symington's Ltd; sr ind dir Kelda Gp plc 2000–; non-exec dir: Vircol plc, T2 Communications, Yorkshire Financial Mgmnt; FIGD; *Recreations* running, keep fit, Leeds United FC, golf, family; *Style*— David Salkeld, Esq; ✉ e-mail david.salkeld@btinternet.com

SALMON, Prof Michael John (Mike); s of Arthur Salmon (d 1972), and May, *née* Dadswell; *b* 22 June 1936, Leeds; *Educ* Roundhay Sch Leeds, Univ of Leeds (BA, PGCE), Univ of Leicester (MEd); *m* 1, 5 April 1958 (m dis 1973), Angela, da of Leslie Winstone Cookson; 1 s (Andrew John b 17 April 1964); m 2, 17 Aug 1973, Daphne Beatrice (d 1996), da of Albert Ernest Bird; 1 s (Christopher Michael b 14 Dec 1984); m 3, 25 April 1998, Sheila Frances, da of Edward John Patterson; *Career* Flt Lt RAF 1957–62; lectr Letchworth Coll of Technol 1962–65, sr then princ lectr Leeds Coll of Technol 1965–68, princ lectr NE London Poly 1968–71, head Dept of Applied Economics and head Int Office NE London Poly 1971–77, dep dir Chelmer Inst of Higher Educn 1977–83, dir Essex Inst of Higher Educn 1983–89, dir Anglia Higher Educn Coll 1989–91, dir Anglia Poly 1991–92, vice-chllr Anglia Poly Univ 1992–95; dir: Proshare Ltd 1991–93, Essex TEC 1989–93; non-exec dir Mid Essex Hosp Servs NHS Tst 1993–95, chm Essex Rivers NHS Trust 1995–2005; ptnr Salmons Reach Consultancy 2008–; chm Postgrad Medical Inst Anglia Ruskin Univ 2009–13; chm Tendring Community Renewal Forum 1998–2001; memb various ctees and bds Cncl for Nat Academic Awards 1971–92; memb: Electricity Industry Trg Bd 1973–75, Educn Advsy Cncl IBA 1973–83, Poly and Coll Funding Cncl 1989–93, E Regn Cncl CBI 1989–93, Forum 2000 1993–, CVCP (chm Student Affairs Ctee 1992–95), Academic Ctee Royal Coll of Music 1995–2000, General Optical Cncl 1999–2012 (vice-chm 2002–05, chm Educn 2002–05), Disciplinary Ctee Royal Pharmaceutical Soc of GB 2007–; govr: Norwich Sch of Art and Design 1996–2001 (chm of govrs 1999–2001), King Edward VI Sch Chelmsford (vice-chm 2000–01); Hon PhD Anglia Poly Univ 1995; memb Worshipful Co of Spectacle-Makers 2006–; hon fell: Fachhochschule für Wirtshaft Berlin 1994, Limburg Hogeschool Netherlands 1996; FRSA 1982, FIMgt 1982; *Recreations* travel, hill walking, gardening; *Style*— Prof Mike Salmon; ✉ Barberries, Russell Lane, Danbury, Essex CM3 4NZ (☎ 01245 223734, e-mail profmike.salmon@gmail.com)

SALMON, Nicholas Robin (Nick); *Career* formerly: ceo Babcock Int Gp plc, exec vice-pres Alstom SA; chief exec Cookson Gp plc 2004–; non-exec dir United Utilities plc 2005–; *Style*— Nick Salmon; ✉ Cookson Group plc, 165 Fleet Street, London EC4A 2AE

SALMON, Peter; s of late Patrick Joseph Salmon, and late Doreen Salmon; *b* 15 May 1956; *Educ* St Theodore's RC Comp Secdy Sch, Univ of Warwick, CAM (certificate in advtg and mktg), NCTJ qualification; *Family*; 4 s (Michael, David, Paul, Joseph), 2 step s (Thomas, Matthew); *Career* English teacher VSO Borneo 1977–78, with Miny of Overseas Devpt (now DFID) 1978–79, reporter Chatham News and Standard 1979–81, with BBC Radio & TV (series prodr Crimewatch, ed Nature, exec prodr 999) 1981–93, head of TV features BBC Bristol 1991–93, controller of factual progs Channel Four Television Corporation 1993–96, dir of progs Granada TV 1996–97, controller BBC 1 1997–2000, dir of sport BBC 2000–05, chief exec The Television Corporation 2005–06, chief creative offr BBC Vision Studios 2006–09, dir BBC North 2009–, memb Exec Bd BBC 2010; *Recreations* music, football, cycling, museums; *Clubs* Burnley FC; *Style*— Peter Salmon, Esq

SALMON, Timothy John (Tim); s of late John Frederick Salmon, and Esmé, *née* Lane; *b* 31 December 1960, Redhill, Surrey; *Educ* Caterham Sch, Univ of Exeter (BA); *m* 21 July 1990, Helen Sophia, da of late Anthony Jessup; 1 s (James Timothy (Jim) b 27 March 1997), 1 d (Georgina Helen (Gina) b 2 Feb 1999); *Career* Arthur Andersen: mangr 1987–93, ptnr 1993–2001, chief fin offr 1998–2001; interim finance dir Cons Central Office 2002, interim chief financial offr (business process mgmnt) Xansa plc 2003, finance dir Richards Butler 2004–07, head of performance mgmnt Barlow Lyde & Gilbert LLP 2007–08, chief operating offr McGrigors LLP 2008–12, interim dir finance & ops CET Primary Schools 2014, chief operating offr Rawlison Butler LLP 2015–16; FCA 1995 (ACA 1985); *Recreations* motoring, DIY, gardening, theatre, reading, watching sport; *Clubs* RAC; *Style*— Tim Salmon, Esq; ✉ Woodside, Slines Oak Road, Woldingham, Surrey CR3 7BH (☎ 07778 956508, e-mail salmons@ukgateway.net)

SALMOND, Rt Hon Alexander Elliot Anderson (Alex); PC (2007), MP; s of Robert Fyfe Findlay Salmond, of Linlithgow, Scotland, and Mary Stewart Milne; *b* 31 December 1954, Linlithgow, W Lothian; *Educ* Linlithgow Acad, Univ of St Andrews (MA); *m* 6 May 1981, Moira French McGlashan; *Career* asst economist Govt Econ Serv 1978–80, economist Royal Bank of Scotland 1980–87; MP (SNP): Banff and Buchan 1987–2010, Gordon 2015–; MSP (SNP): Banff and Buchan 1999–2001, Gordon 2007–11, Aberdeenshire E 2011–; ldr Opposition Scottish Parliament 1999–2000; ldr SNP 1990–2000 and 2004–14 (dep ldr 1987–90); first min Scottish Govt 2007–14; visiting prof of economics Univ of Strathclyde 2001–07; *Publications* numerous articles and conference papers on oil and gas economics; *Recreations* reading, golf; *Style*— The Rt Hon Alex Salmond, MSP; ✉ 84 North Street, Inverurie AB51 4QX (☎ 01467 670070)

SALMOND, Prof George Peacock Copland; s of John Brown Salmond (d 1998), and Joan Tennant Lambie, *née* Copland (d 1989); *b* 15 November 1952; *Educ* Bathgate Acad, Whitburn Acad West Lothian, Univ of Strathclyde (Malcolm Kerr Prize for Biology, BSc), Univ of Warwick (PhD), Univ of Cambridge (MA, ScD); *m* 1975 (m dis 1985), Christina Brown Adamson; partner, Carolyn Ann Alderson; 1 da (Kathryn Rebecca Salmond b 1996); *Career* post doctoral research fell Dept of Molecular Biology Univ of Edinburgh 1977–80, lectr in microbiology Biological Lab Univ of Kent 1980–83; Dept of Biological Sciences Univ of Warwick: lectr in microbiology 1983–89, sr lectr 1989–93, prof 1993–96; prof of molecular microbiology Dept of Biochemistry Univ of Cambridge 1996–, fell and memb Governing Body Wolfson Coll Cambridge 2000–; dir Cargenex Research Ltd 1997–2000; BBSRC: memb Plants and Microbial Sciences Ctees 1999–2001 (chm Natural Products Biology Steering Gp 2000–02), chm Plant and Microbial Sciences Panel for Scientific Quality Assessment of BBSRC Research Insts 2001, memb Integration Panel for BBSRC Inst Science Quality Assessment 2001, memb Cross Ctee Gp on Antimicrobial Research 2001, memb Sequencing Panel 2002–, memb Plant and Microbial Metabolomics Initiative Sift Panel 2002–, chm Research Equipment Initiative Ctee 2002, 2003 and 2004; Scot Exec Environment and Rural Affrs Dept (SEERAD): chm Quality of Science Assessment Panel (Plants) for Scot Research Insts 2002–, memb Integration Panel Quality of Science Assessment Panels 2002–; memb: Scientific Advsy Bd NSC Technologies Illinois 1996–2001, Panel for Jt Research Cncls Equipment Initiative (JREI) 2001, Pathogen Sequencing Advsy Gp Wellcome Tst Sanger Inst 2002–06, Cncl Fedn of European Microbiological Socs 2004–09, Science Unions Ctee Royal Soc 2005–09, Int Expert Review Gp FUGE Prog 2003 and 2007, Coll of Experts Medical Research Cncl 2005–, Int Expert Review Panel Visiting Gp Science Fndn of Ireland 2006, Scottish Science Advsy Cncl 2010–; dir, tstee and memb Governing Cncl John Innes Centre Norwich 2003–10, dir, tstee and memb Governing Body Scottish Crop Research Inst Dundee 2003–11 (memb Science Ctee 2006–11), Bd of Dirs James Hutton Inst 2011– (memb Advsy Ctee on Science 2011–); sr ed Jl of Molecular Microbiology and Biotechnology 1998–2008; memb Ed Bd: Molecular Microbiology 1988–97, Molecular Plant Pathology-On-Line 1996–, Molecular Plant Pathology 1999–2002, Microbiology 1999–2000, Future Microbiology 2006–; assoc ed: European Jl of Plant Pathology 1992–98, Molecular Plant-Microbe Interactions 1993–98; Soc for Gen Microbiology: memb Cncl 1997–2001 and 2004–09 (also dir and tstee), convener and chm Physiology, Biochemistry and Molecular Genetics Gp Ctee 2002–07, int sec 2004–09; Colworth Prize Lecture SGM 2011; Hon DSc Univ of Strathclyde 2010; memb: Genetical Soc, Biochemical Soc, American Soc of Microbiology, Br Soc for Plant Pathology (vice-pres 2009, pres-elect 2009–11, pres 2011), Br Soc for Antimicrobial Chemotherapy, Soc for Industrial Microbiology; fell Cambridge Philosophical Soc FRSA 2001, FFCS 2001, FSB 2009, FRSE 2012; *Publications* author of numerous articles in learned jls on molecular biology (incl studies on bacterial cell division, bacterial virulence, antibiotics, quorum sensing, protein secretion, bacteriophages, abortive infection, toxin-antitoxin systems and bacterial gas vesicles); *Recreations* poetry, philosophy, comedy; *Style*— Prof George Salmond; ✉ Department of Biochemistry, University of Cambridge, Tennis Court Road, Cambridge CB2 1QW (☎ 01223 333650, fax 01223 766108, e-mail gpcs@mole.bio.cam.ac.uk)

SALOMON, William Henry; s of Sir Walter Hans Salomon (d 1987), and Kaete Gerda, *née* Jacoby (d 2011); *b* 30 September 1957; *Educ* Lycée Français de Londres, Westminster, Magdalene Coll Cambridge (MA, LLB), Inns of Court Sch of Law; *m* 4 July 1992, Emma Georgina (Gigi), da of Maj H R Callander, MC (decd); 1 da (Bettina b 9 April 1994), 1 s (Alexander b 26 March 1996); *Career* trainee Welt am Sonntag Hamburg 1974, Brown Shipley & Co Ltd 1978–80, trainee Brown Brother Harriman NY 1980–81, Rea Brothers Ltd 1981–85, Finsbury Asset Management Ltd 1987–99; dir: Immuno International AG 1981–97, Manganese Bronze (Holdings) plc 1987–2002, Rea Brothers Group plc 1988–99 (dep chm until 1998, chm 1999), Adam & Harvey Group plc 1991–2002, Aquila International Fund Ltd 1994–2011, Ocean Wilson Holdings Ltd 1995– (dep chm 1999–), Hanseatic Asset Mgmnt LBG 1998–, Hansa Capital Ptnrs LLP 1998–, Aberdeen Emerging Markets Investment Tst 1999–2002, Close Asset Mgmnt Holdings Ltd 1999–2002 (vice-chm 1999–2000), Cathedral Capital plc 2002–06, New India Investment Tst plc 2004–14 (chm), Fleet Mortgages 2014–; memb Hon Soc of the Inner Temple 1986–; govr Chelsea Acad 2009–15; life pres Young Enterprise; *Recreations* reading, squash, shooting, fishing, tennis; *Clubs* Norddeutscher Regatta Verein Hamburg, Rio de Janeiro Country, Hurlingham, Bath and Racquets, Brooks's, 5 Hertford Street; *Style*— William Salomon, Esq; ✉ Hansa Capital Partners LLP, 50 Curzon Street, London W1J 7UW (☎ 020 7647 5750, fax 020 7647 5770, e-mail info@hansacap.com, website www.hansagrp.com)

SALOP, Archdeacon of; *see*: Hall, Ven John Barrie

SALSBURY, Peter Leslie; *Career* Marks and Spencer plc: jt md i/c clothing, home furnishings, direct mail, european retail, franchise operations, int franchise gp 1994–98 (previously dir i/c personnel and store operations), md i/c general merchandise 1998–99, chief exec 1998–2000; chm Molten Gp Ltd 2011–; non-exec dir: TR Property Investment Tst plc 1997–2013 (chm 2004–13), Highway Insurance Holdings 2006–08; currently with P&S Salsbury Ltd (Mgmnt Consultants); *Style*— Peter Salsbury; ✉ P&S Salsbury Ltd, 63 St Johns Avenue, London SW15 6AL

SALT, Dr (Robert) Barry; s of Francis Robert Salt (d 1975), and Margaret Jaffray, *née* Incoll (d 1965); *b* 15 December 1933; *Educ* Williamstown HS, Melbourne HS, Univ of Melbourne, NW Poly London, Birkbeck Coll London (BSc, PhD), London Sch of Film Technique; *Career* teacher Sunshine HS Melbourne 1955, dancer Ballet Guild Co Melbourne 1955–56, computist Cwlth Aeronautical Res Labs Melbourne 1956, dancer Western Theatre Ballet London 1957, computer programmer Int Computers & Tabulators London 1958–60, lectr in physics Sir John Cass Coll London 1965–66, dancer Ballet Minerva London 1966, freelance lighting cameraman 1968–71, supply teacher ILEA 1969–70, film teacher and res asst Slade Sch London 1970, lectr for post grad dip in film studies UCL 1973–78, pt/t lectr Slade Sch London 1978–82, tutor in film-making Sch of Film & TV RCA 1982–87, pt/t tutor in film-making for post grad dip Communications Dept Goldsmiths Coll London 1987–88, course dir London Int Film Sch 1988–2016; visiting lectr film schs and univs England and Europe 1977–; films directed incl: My Name is Errol Addison (documentary) 1965, Pop Up Into a New World (documentary) 1967, The Future Perfect (fictional short) 1968, Six Reels of Film to be Shown in any Order (fiction feature) 1971; organiser and presenter series of progs on film history Nat Film Theatre 1976–; invited speaker at many academic confs on film history in England and Europe 1976–; conslt and writer for Microsoft Encarta 1994–, author of numerous articles on dance, film and science subjects; *Books* Film Style and Technology – History and Analysis (1983, 3 edn 2009), Making Pictures: A Century of European Cinematography (jtly, 2003), Moving into Pictures (2006); *Recreations* reading, working; *Style*— Dr Barry Salt; ☎ 020 8749 5413

SALT, Julia Ann; da of Kenneth Gordon Richardson, and Nora, *née* McLachlan; *b* 4 May 1955; *Educ* St Mary's Senior HS Hull, St Hilda's Oxford (MA); *Family* 1 da (Freya b 12 Aug 1983), 1 s (Frederick b 17 July 1985); m 10 Aug 2000, Graham Bailey; *Career* ptnr Allen & Overy 1985–2009, ptnr and fndr Plane Legal LLP 2009–; memb The Law Soc 1977; govr Rugby Sch 2000–03; *Recreations* sailing, golf, languages; *Clubs* Royal Yacht Squadron, Royal Ocean Racing, Royal Corinthian Yacht; *Style*— Mrs Julia A Salt; ✉ Plane Legal LLP, Tower House, Quarr Road, Ryde PO33 4EL

SALTER, David Arthur; s of James Wardel Salter, and Kathleen Wright Salter; *b* 27 August 1948; *Educ* Ecclesfield GS, Pembroke Coll Cambridge (MA, LLM); *m* Anne Ruth; 2 s (Robin James Edward b 1 March 1977, William David Wardel b 17 April 1982), 1 da (Alice Rosemary b 9 May 1989); *Career* admitted slr 1972; asst slr: Mills & Reeve Norwich 1972–74 (formerly articled clerk), Barber Robinson Harrogate 1974–75, Booth

S

& Co 1975–78; ptnr: Addleshaw Goddard (formerly Addleshaw Booth & Co) 1978–2008 (latterly nat head Family Law Gp), Mills & Reeve 2008– (latterly jt nat head Family Law Gp); recorder of the Crown Court 1995–, dep judge of the High Court 2011–; sometime memb Family Procedure Rule Ctee, sometime memb Family Ctee Judicial Studies Bd, sometime chm Resolution; tstee Harrogate Int Festival, organist and choirmaster Knaresborough Parish Church, sometime chm Leeds Festival Chorus, sometime govr St Peter's Sch York, chm Northern Section Alvis Owner Club; past pres Int Acad of Matrimonial Lawyers (past pres European Chapter); ARCO; *Books* Matrimonial Consent Orders and Agreements (jtly), Humphreys' Family Proceedings (gen ed), Family Courts: Emergency Remedies in the Family Courts (jtly), Pensions and Insurance on Family Breakdown (gen ed), Debt and Insolvency on Family Breakdown (jtly), Butterworths Family Law Service (ed), Family Finance and Tax (jtly), The Family Court Practice (jtly), Pensions on Divorce (jtly), Family Law Precedents Service (gen ed); *Clubs* Royal Over-Seas League; *Style*— Mr David Salter; ✉ Mills & Reeve LLP, 1 City Square, Leeds LS1 3ES (☎ 0113 388 8442, fax 0113 388 8441, e-mail david.salter@mills-reeve.com, website www.mills-reeve.com and www.divorce.co.uk)

SALTER, Ian; s of Norman Salter, and Turid Salter; *b* 20 February 1968, Chatham, Kent; *Educ* King's Sch Rochester, Univ of Bristol (LLB), Coll of Law Guildford; *m* 27 Feb 1993, Caryn; 1 s (David), 1 da (Rhiannon); *Career* slr; Burges Salmon Solicitors 1990– (ptnr 1999–, currently head Nuclear Law Unit); memb: Law Soc 1990, Int Nuclear Lawyers' Assoc 1998; MRTPI 1996; *Clubs* Reform; *Style*— Ian Salter, Esq; ✉ Burges Salmon LLP, One Glass Wharf, Bristol BS2 0ZX (☎ 0117 939 2000, fax 0117 902 4400, e-mail ian.salter@burges-salmon.com)

SALTER, Ian George; s of late Desmond Salter, and Diane Salter (d 1992); *b* 7 March 1943; *Educ* Hutchins Sch Hobart; *Career* md SG Investment Mgmnt Ltd (formerly Strauss Turnbull then Société Générale Strauss Turnbull) 2001–03, chm CCH International (formerly Emdex Trade) 2001–09, dir Tilney Investment Mgmnt (London) 2003–05, conslt Deutsche Bank Private Wealth Mgmnt 2008–10; non-exec dir: Plus Markets Gp 2007–09, Pan Holdings 2008–12; memb Hobart Stock Exchange 1965–69; London Stock Exchange: memb 1970–, memb Cncl 1980–91, non-exec dir 1986–2004, dep chm 1990–2004; inspr DTI 1984–87, memb Fin Reporting Cncl 1994–2002, memb Code Ctee Takeover Panel 2002–04; *Recreations* gardening, opera, travel; *Style*— Ian Salter, Esq; ✉ 34 St Leonards Terrace, London SW3 4QQ

SALTER, Very Rev (Arthur Thomas Alexis) John; TD (1988); er s of Arthur Salter (d 1982), of The Tong-Norton Farm, Shropshire, and Dora May, *née* Wright (d 1985); the Salter family has been seated in Shropshire since the reign of King John, when John de le Sel is mentioned in the records of Shrewsbury Abbey 1211 (*see* Burke's Landed Gentry, 18 edn, vol III, 1972); *b* 22 November 1934; *Educ* Wellington GS (Careswell Exhibitioner), KCL (AKC 1960), St Boniface's Theol Coll Warminster; *Career* served Intelligence Corps 1954–55, RAMC 1955–56; ordained: deacon 1961, priest 1962; asst priest: St Peter's Mount Park Ealing 1961–65, St Stephen with St Thomas the Apostle Shepherd's Bush 1965–66, St Alban the Martyr Holborn with St Peter Saffron Hill 1966–70; priest-in-charge St Clement Barnsbury and St Michael the Archangel Islington 1970–79, vicar St Silas with All Saints Pentonville 1970–2000, guild vicar St Dunstan-in-the-West with St Thomas of Canterbury within the Liberty of the Rolls 1979–99; ordained Melkite Greek Catholic Patriarchal Priest 2002; cnsllr for Foreign Relations to his Sacred Beatitude the Melkite Greek Catholic Patriarch Gregory III of Antioch and all the East, of Alexandria and of Jerusalem 2002–; chm Wynford Estate's Old People's Club 1971–90, chaplain Law Courts Branch Edward Bear Fndn for Muscular Dystrophy 1979–99, chm Ctee Anglican and Eastern Churches Assoc 1990–2001 (gen sec 1975–90); Royal Army Chaplains' Dept 1975–94, CF IV (Capt) 1975–81, CF III (Maj); chaplain: 36 Signal Regt 1975–80, 257 (S) Gen Hosp RAMC (V) Duke of York's HQ 1980–94, Reg Army Reserve of Offrs 1994–96; hon chaplain HMTS Lancastria Assoc 1996–2007; memb: Ctee Nikaean Club Lambeth Palace 1999–2001, Societas Sanctae Crucis (SSC), Soc of Friends of St George's Windsor and Descendants of the Knights of the Garter, Coptic Cultural Centre Venice, Friends of the Holy Father, Maj-Gen the Duke of Westminster's Ulysses Tst 2008; fell Sion Coll 1979; sr chaplain of military and hospitaller Order of St Lazarus of Jerusalem (chaplain of jurisdiction and justice Order of St Lazarus of Jerusalem 1974, memb Spiritual Advsy Cncl Ordr of St Lazarus 2010), chaplain to HBM Consulate-Gen Istanbul 1975, Locum Tenens Apocrisarios to HAH The Ecumenical Patriarch and to His Sacred Beatitude the Patriarch of Constantinople of the Armenians, hereditary Lord of Choulton and Eton 1982–; chm Pontifical Soc of St John Chrysostom 2002; Freeman City of London 1990; Hon Archimandrite's Cross of Byelo-Russian Autocephalic Orthodox Church-in-Exile 1979, Archpriest's Cross of Ethiopian Catholic Uniate Church (Eparchy of Asmara Eritrea) 1980, Archpriest's Cross Exarchate of Pope Shenouda III (Coptic Orthodox Patriarchate of Alexandria) 1981, Hon Knight Order of St Michael of the Wing (Royal House of Braganza Portugal) 1984, Companion of Honour Order of Orthodox Hospitallers (Ethnarchy of Cyprus and Greek Patriarchate of Antioch) 1985; The Anglican Papalist: Life of Revd H J Fynes-Clinton (2013); *Recreations* travelling in Eastern Europe, genealogy, reading; *Clubs* Athenaeum, City Volunteers Officers'; *Style*— The Very Rev John Salter, TD, SSC, AKC, SChOLJ(J); ✉ 1 St James Close, 1 Bishop Street, Islington, London N1 8PH (☎ 020 7359 0250)

SALTER, Rebecca; *b* 24 February 1955; *Educ* Bristol Poly; *Career* artist; research student Kyoto City Univ of Arts Japan (Leverhulme scholarship) 1979–81, living and working: in Japan 1981–85, in London 1985–; artist in residence Josef and Anni Albers Fndn CT 2003; RA 2014; *Awards* incl: Greater London Arts Award 1985, Pollock-Krasner Fndn Award 1995 and 2003, Cheltenham Open Drawing Award 1997; *Solo Exhibitions* incl: Galerie Maronie Kyoto 1981, Amano Gall Osaka 1982, Gall Suzuki Kyoto 1983, Gall Te Tokyo 1984, Curwen Gall London 1984 and 1987, Art Forum Singapore 1985, Miller/Brown Gall San Francisco 1986, Ichikawa Gall Tokyo 1990, Greene Gall Connecticut 1991, Quay Arts Centre Isle of Wight 1992, Ishiyacho Gall Kyoto 1993, Jill George Gallery London 1994, 1996, 1998 and 2000, M-13/Howard Scott Gall NY 1997 and 1999, Galerie Pousse Tokyo 1998, Galerie Michael Sturm Stuttgart 1999, Feichtner & Mizrahi Vienna 1999, Gall Sowaka Kyoto 1999, Howard Scott Gall NY 2001 and 2004, Russell-Cotes Art Gall Bournemouth 2001, Hirschl Contemporary Art London 2002, Line Fosterart London 2004, Beardsmore Gall London 2006, Howard Scott Gall NY 2007, Beardsmore Gall London 2009, Into the Light of Things (Yale Center for Br Art) 2011, Howard Scott Gallery NY, Beardsmore Gallery London, Beardsmore Gallery London 2013; *Group Exhibitions* incl: Rijeka Drawing Biennale Yugoslavia 1982, Ryu Int Gall Tokyo 1982, Ljubljana Int Print Biennale Yugoslavia 1983 and 1985, Curwen Gall London 1984 and 1985, Osaka Contemporary Art Fair 1985, Norwegian Int Print Biennale 1986, Int Contemporary Art Fair London 1986, Chicago Int Art Exhibition 1986–92, Oxford Gall Oxford 1988, Art London '89 1989, RCA 1990, Basel Art Fair 1991, Cleveland Drawing Biennale 1991, Intaglio Gall London 1992, Mall Galleries London 1992, Eagle Gall London 1993, Jill George Gall 1994, Tate Gall London 1995, Turnpike Gall Leigh 1995, Cheltenham Open Drawing 1996, Galerie Michael Sturm Stuttgart 1996, Rubicon Gall Dublin 1997, 20th Century Art Fair London 1997 and 1998, Gainsborough's House Sudbury 1999, Art 2000 London 2000, Art 2001 London 2001, Working the Grid Lafayette Coll Easton PA 2002, Untitled: work on paper Hirschl Contemporary Art London 2003, Atlantic Fosterart London 2003, Yale Center for British Art 2005, Watercolour (Tate Britain) 2011; *Work in Collections* incl: Tate Gall London, British Museum, Cleveland County Cncl, Unilever London, WH Smith plc, Govt Art Coll, The Mortgage Corp, Arthur Anderson & Co London, MSP Ltd, Leslie & Godwin Gp London, Pearl Assurance Peterborough, Gartmore Investment Mgmnt Ltd, San Francisco MOMA, Portland MOMA, JP Morgan NYC, World Print Cncl San Francisco, Heithoff Family Collection Calif, Lake Tower Collection Chicago, American Telephone and Telegraph Co, California Coll of Arts and Crafts, Library of Congress Washington DC, Frechen Kunstverein Germany, Yale Center for British Art, Victoria and Albert Museum London, Yale Univ Art Gallery; *Commissions* incl: United Airlines, EPR Architects, St George's Hosp Tooting, Guy's Hosp London, 9–15 Sackville St London, many private cmmns; Japanese Woodblock Printing (2001), Japanese Popular Prints: From Votive Slips to Playing Cards (2006); *Style*— Ms Rebecca Salter; ✉ Park Studios, 34 Scarborough Road, London N4 4LT (e-mail info@rebeccasalter.com)

SALTER, Richard Stanley; QC (1995); s of Stanley James Salter (d 1980), and Betty Maud, *née* Topsom (d 1974); *b* 2 October 1951; *Educ* Harrow Co Sch, Balliol Coll Oxford (MA); *m* 11 May 1991, Shona Virginia Playfair, o da of (Jack) Philip Cannon, *qv*; *Career* called to the Bar Inner Temple 1975 (bencher 1991), asst recorder 1997–2000, recorder 2000 , asst boundary cmmr 2000–06, dep judge of the High Court (Queen's Bench Div) 2010– and (Commercial Court) 2016–; chm Inner Temple Scholarships Ctee 2002–09; chm London Common Law and Commercial Bar Assoc 2004–05 (memb Ctee 1986–2001, vice-chm 2002–03); memb: Cncl of Legal Educn 1990–96 (chm Bd of Examiners 1992–93), Advocacy Studies Bd 1996–2000, Advsy Bd City Univ Inst of Law 2001–08, Bar Cncl 2004–13 (chm Legal Services Ctee 2010–13), Devpt Bd Centre for Commercial Law Studies 2012–; tstee Oxford Law Fndn 2011–, tstee English Touring Opera 2015–; govr Inns of Court Sch of Law 1996–2001; visiting fell in financial law Oxford Univ Faculty of Law 2013–; Distinguished Friend of Oxford Award 2014; Freeman Worshipful Co of Musicians 2013–16, Liveryman Worshipful Co of Musicians 2016–; ACIArb 1983; *Publications* contrib: Banks, Liability and Risk (1990, 3 edn 2001), Halsbury's Laws of England: Guarantee and Indemnity (4 edn, 1993), Banks and Remedies (2 edn, 1999); ed: All England Commercial Cases (1999–), Legal Decisions Affecting Bankers (vols 12–14, 2001); *Recreations* books, music, theatre, cricket; *Clubs* Savile, Shoscombe Village Cricket; *Style*— Richard Salter, Esq, QC; ✉ 3 Verulam Buildings, Gray's Inn, London WC1R 5NT (☎ 020 7831 8441, fax 020 7831 8479)

SALTISSI, Dr Stephen; s of Victor Saltissi, of Leeds, and Betty, *née* Weinman; *b* 21 September 1950; *Educ* Roundhay Sch Leeds, King's Coll London (MB BS), Univ of London (MSc, MD); *m* 30 July 1972, Sandra Bernice, da of Maurice Aaron Bellman, of Leeds; 2 da (Nicola b 1978, Caroline b 1980); *Career* sr res fell St Thomas' Hosp 1979–80 (registrar 1977–78); sr registrar: N Tees 1981–82, Newcastle upon Tyne 1982–84; Royal Liverpool Univ Hosp: conslt physician and cardiologist 1984–, clinical sub dean 1991–2001, clinical dir of med 1992–96, head of cardiology 1998–2010 (also Broadgreen Univ Hosp), assoc medical dir 2001–04 (also Broadgreen Univ Hosp), lead for clincial risk mgmnt 2001–04 (also Broadgreen Univ Hosp), lead cardiologist Cheshire and Merseyside Cardiac Clinical Network, currently pt/t conslt cardiologist Royal Liverpool Univ Hosp; medico-legal expert Stephen Saltissi Medical Servs Ltd; hon lectr Univ of Liverpool 1984–; memb Appraisals Ctee Nat Inst for Clinical Excellence 2001–10; past chm Library Ctee Royal Liverpool Univ Hosp, chm Liverpool Cardiac Rehabilitation Services; memb: Br Cardiac Soc 1985, Merseyside and N Wales Assoc Physicians 1984, Royal Liverpool Univ Hosp Clinical Risk Mgmnt Gp, Cncl Br Soc of Echocardiography 1998–2000; FRCP 1991 (MRCP 1975); *Recreations* tennis, supporter Liverpool FC, travel; *Style*— Dr Stephen Saltissi; ✉ Wansfell, 25 Hillside Drive, Woolton, Liverpool L25 5NR (☎ 0151 428 2034, mobile 07979 770348, e-mail stephensaltissi@blueyonder.co.uk); Royal Liverpool University Hospital, Prescot Street, Liverpool L7 8XP (☎ 0151 706 3265 (sec), 0151 706 3574 (direct line), fax 0151 706 5833, e-mail stephen.saltissi@rlbuht.nhs.uk); 88 Rodney Street, Liverpool L1 9AR (☎ 0151 709 7066, fax 0151 709 7279)

SALTOUN, Rt Hon Lady (twenty-first holder of title; S 1445); Flora Marjory; Chief of the Name of Fraser; family granted right to own Univ of Fraserburgh by King James VI; *née* Fraser; da of 20 Lord Saltoun, MC (d 1979), and Dorothy, da of Sir Charles Welby, 5 Bt, CB, by Maria, sis of 4 Marquess of Bristol; *b* 18 October 1930; *Educ* St Mary's Wantage; *m* 1956, Capt Alexander Ramsay of Mar, DL (d 2000); 3 da; *Heir* da, Hon Mrs Nicolson; *Career* sat as Independent in House of Lords 1979–2014; *Clubs* New; *Style*— The Rt Hon the Lady Saltoun; ✉ Inverey House, Braemar AB35 5YB

SALUSBURY-TRELAWNY; *see:* Trelawny

SALVESEN, Alastair Eric Hotson; CBE (2010); s of Lt-Col Iver Ronald Stuart Salvesen (d 1957), and Marion Hamilton, *née* McClure (d 1997); Christian Salvesen (fndr of family business, no longer trading) emigrated from Norway to Edinburgh 1846; bro of Robin S Salvesen, DL, *qv*; *b* 28 July 1941; *Educ* Fettes, Cranfield (MBA); *m* 18 July 1979, Elizabeth Evelyn, da of Patrick Murray, WS, RNVR (d 2001), of Hawick, Roxburghshire; 1 da (Venetia Clare Johanna), 1 s (George Edward Thomas); *Career* chm: Dawnfresh Seafoods Ltd 1983– (md 1981–93), Dovecot Studios Ltd 2001–, Silvertrout Ltd 2004–; dir: Praha Investment Holdings Ltd 1985–, Richmond Foods plc 1994–2003, New Ingliston Ltd 1995–, Luing Cattle Soc 1996–99, Edinburgh New Town Cookery Sch 2009– (chm), Archangels Investors Ltd; pres Royal Highland & Agric Soc of Scot 2001–02; exec memb: UK Assoc of Frozen Food Prodrs 1990–2004 (chm Shellfish Ctee 1984–96), British Frozen Foods Fedn 1992–2015 (pres 1995–97); chm Shellfish Ctee Food & Drink Fedn 2007–08; memb: Deregulation Taskforce for Food, Drink and Agriculture 1993–94, Cncl Shellfish Assoc of GB 2003 (also memb Ctee); estab Alastair Salvesen Art Scholarship 1989; memb Cncl Royal Soc of Arts 2005; govr: The Fettes Tst 1994– (dep chm 2009–), Donaldson's Tst 1997–2009, Compass Sch 1994–2009 (chm 1996–2009); tstee Dovecot Fndn 2010, tstee Fet-Lor Youth Club; memb The Queen's Body Guard for Scotland (The Royal Company of Archers); Liveryman Worshipful Co of Fishmongers; CA; Queen's Jubilee Medal; HRSA, FCIM, FCMI, FRSA, FSA Scot, FRAgS 2004, FRIAS, memb Inst of Chartered Accountants of Scotland 1995; *Publications* Slekten Salvesen 1550–1995; *Recreations* shooting, archery, farming and forestry, contemporary Scottish art; *Clubs* New (Edinburgh), Farmers; *Style*— Alastair E H Salvesen, Esq, CBE; ✉ Whitburgh, Pathhead, Midlothian EH37 5SR (☎ 01875 320304, fax 01875 320766); Dawnfresh Seafoods Ltd, Bothwell Park Industrial Estate, Uddingston, Lanarkshire G71 6LS (☎ 01698 810008, fax 01698 810088, e-mail alastair.salvesen@dawnfresh.co.uk)

SALVIDANT, Sallie Christina Ellen; da of James Cooper (d 1990), and Nancy Cooper (d 2000); *b* 3 August 1950, Barnet, Herts; *Educ* Kenya HS, Univ of London (CertEd, BEd); *m* 1, 17 May 1968 (m dis 1970), Geoffrey Salvidant; 1 da (Rebecca Kirsty b 7 Aug 1969); *m* 2, 27 Dec 2001, Alan Lewis; *Career* teacher Taiz North Yemen 1970–72, class teacher Beckford Infants Sch West Hampstead 1977–81, class teacher Christchurch Primary Sch Regents Park 1981–85, head of lower sch Holmewood Boys Prep Sch 1985–87, headmistress Rupert House Prep Sch Henley 1987–93, headmistress Bute House Prep Sch for Girls (formerly St Paul's Girls' Prep Sch) Hammersmith 1993–2012; currently educnl conslt Salvus Ind Educnl Consultancy Ltd; trained head's mentor; govr: St Christopher's Sch Hampstead, Br Sch of Paris, West Buckland Sch, Headington Sch; former memb No10 Dist Cte, Policy and Promotions Ctee and Inspections Ctee IAPS, ISI inspector; Tatler Best Headmistress of a Prep School 2004; IAPS 1987, AHIS 1987; *Recreations* breeding Siamese cats, gardening, walking dogs; *Style*— Mrs Sallie Salvidant; ✉ e-mail sallie.salvidant@gmail.com

SALWAY, Francis; s of Toby Salway, and Ann Salway; *b* 5 October 1957; *Educ* Rugby, Univ of Cambridge (MA); *m* 1 June 1985, Sarah; 1 s (Hugh), 1 da (Rachael); *Career* Richard Ellis 1979–82, Abacus Devpt 1982–85, Coll of Estate Mgmnt Reading 1985–86,

Standard Life 1986–2000; Land Securities Gp plc: joined 2000, memb Bd 2001, gp chief exec 2004–12; dir: Next plc 2010, Cadogan Gp Ltd 2012; chm: London Community Fndn 2012, Town and Country Housing Gp 2012; past pres Br Property Fedn; visiting prof LSE 2012; *Books* Depreciation of Commercial Property (1986); *Recreations* walking; *Style*— Francis Salway, Esq

SALZ, Sir Anthony Michael Vaughan; kt (2013); s of Michael Salz, of Yelverton, Devon, and Veronica, *née* Hall; *b* 30 June 1950; *Educ* Radley, Univ of Exeter (LLB); *m* 17 May 1975, Sally Ruth, da of Harold J Hagger, of Broughton, Hants; 1 s (Christopher b 1978), 2 da (Emily b 1980, Rachel b 1982); *Career* admitted slr 1974; Freshfields Bruckhaus Deringer: joined 1975, seconded to Davis Polk and Wardwell NY 1977–78, ptnr 1980–2006, head of corporate finance 1990–94, head of corporate 1994–96, sr ptnr 1996–2000, jt sr ptnr 2000–06; vice-chm BBC 2004–06 (acting chm 2006), chm Bloomsbury Publishing plc 2013–; exec vice chm N M Rothschild & Sons Ltd 2006–; memb Advsy Panel Swiss Re Centre for Global Dialogue 2006–11, chair Ind Cmmn on Youth Crime and Antisocial Behaviour 2008–10, co-chair Educn and Employers Taskforce 2009–10, lead non-exec bd memb Dept for Educn 2010–12, lead Ind Review of Barclays Business Practices 2013; memb Corp Advsy Gp Tate Gallery 1997– (chm 1997–2002), memb Advsy Bd Financial Services Knowledge Transfer Network 2010–14; dir: Tate Fndn 2000–, Habitat for Humanity GB 2004–10, ROH 2008–, Scott Tst 2009–, Forward Inst 2014–; tstee: Eden Tst 2001– (chm 2009–), Paul Hamlyn Fndn 2005–, Conran Fndn 2007, Media Standards Tst 2007–, Reprieve 2011–, High Street Fund 2011–13, Foundation for FutureLondon 2015–, Supreme Court UK Arts Tst 2016–; chair: London Higher Skills Bd 2008–10, SHINE: Support and Help in Educn 2008–10, Teach First Business Ldrs Cncl 2012; advsr Advsy Bd Univ of Exeter Sch of Business and Economics 2003, govr Wellington Acad 2008–; Hon LLD Coll of Law 2008, Hon LLD Univ of Exeter 2003; FRSA 1996; contrib to various learned jls; *Recreations* fly fishing, tennis, golf, theatre, contemporary art, Southampton FC and the family generally; *Clubs* MCC, Berkshire Golf, Trevose Golf; *Style*— Sir Anthony Salz; ✉ N M Rothschild & Sons Ltd, St Swithin's Lane, New Court, London EC4N 8AL

SAMANI, Vinay; s of Amritlal Samani, of London, and Jayaben, *née* Madlani; *b* 4 June 1970, Eldoret, Kenya; *Educ* Univ of Birmingham (LLB); *m* 2 Nov 1997, Komal, *née* Ondhia; 2 s (Pranav b 21 Aug 2001, Keshav b 19 Sep 2003); *Career* admitted slr 1994; ptnr Linklaters 2004–; *Style*— Vinay Samani, Esq; ✉ Linklaters, One Silk Street, London EC2Y 8HQ (☎ 020 7456 2000)

SAMARAWICKRAMA, Prof Dayananda Yasasiri Dias; s of late Kornelis Dias Samarawickrama, of Galle, Sri Lanka, and late Alice, *née* Mirinchi Arachchi; *b* Sri Lanka; *Educ* Mahinda Coll Galle, Univ of Ceylon (BDS), The London Hosp Med Coll Univ of London (PhD); *m* August 1970, Padma Grace, *née* Kodithuwakku; 2 da (Amanda Kanchana Dias b Sept 1975, Samantha Thanuja Dias b Feb 1978); *Career* asst lectr in conservative dentistry Univ of Peradeniya Sri Lanka 1968, research fell Depts of Conservative Dentistry and Oral Pathology The London Hosp Med Coll 1970, sr lectr in restorative dentistry and dental materials sci Univ of Peradeniya 1981 (lectr in conservative dentistry 1975); The London Hosp Med Coll: lectr in conservative dentistry 1983, dir Dental Auxiliary Sch and sr lectr in conservative dentistry 1989–95; actg head Dept of Conservative Dentistry and sr lectr in conservative dentistry St Bartholomew's and the Royal London Sch of Med and Dentistry 1995, hon conslt in restorative dentistry Barts and The London NHS Tst 2000–10, prof of conservative dentistry Queen Mary's Sch of Med & Dentistry Univ of London 2004–10 (sr tutor 2002–10, hon prof 2009–10, emeritus prof 2011–); visiting prof and educnl advsr Oman Dental Coll Muscat 2011–, fell Oman Dental Coll Sultanate of Oman for outstanding service 2013–, visiting prof Faculty of Dental Sciences Univ of Peradeniya Sri Lanka 2014–; GDC: specialist in restorative dentistry 2000–, specialist in endodontics 2001–; exec sec Cwlth Dental Assoc 2012–; memb: Cncl Br Assoc of Teachers of Conservative Dentistry 1995– (pres 1996–97 and 2008–09), Cncl Sri Lankan Med and Dental Assoc in the UK (pres 1997–98), Dental Chapter Barts and The London Alumni Assoc (pres 2002–03); assessor int qualifying exam Gen Dental Cncl UK 2000–08, memb LDSRCS Examination Bd RCS 2009–; external examiner: Univ of Liverpool 2005–08, KCL 2005–09, Univ of Manchester 2006–09, Postgrad Inst of Medicine Sri Lanka 2006–08, Overseas Registration Exam Gen Dental Cncl UK 2008–, UCL Eastman Dental Inst 2009–, Univ of Warwick 2010–, KNUST Kumasi Ghana 2012–; author of more than 100 pubns incl original papers, reviews, chapters in books and conf papers; WHO: fell in oral health 1976–77, fell in med educn 1980, memb and reporter WHO/FDI Jt Working Gp on Dental Educn and Trg 1982–86, conslt and advsr on oral health care Sri Lanka 1980–82; conslt: Miny of Health Trinidad & Tobago 1992–96, Miny of Health Barbados and Barbados Dental Cncl 2001–03; Queen Mary Long Service Award 2008, DDU Dentist Teacher of the Year Award 2008, Geoffrey Slack Medal for outstanding service Inst of Dentistry Barts and The London Queen Mary Univ of London 2012; memb: BDA 1985–, Br Soc for Restorative Dentistry 1999–; FDSRCS 1992, FHEA 2007, FCGDP (Sri Lanka) 2011; *Publications* Oxford Handbook of Dental Nursing (jt ed, 2012); *Recreations* hiking, gardening, reading, writing; *Style*— Prof Dayananda Samarawickrama

SAMBROOK, Prof Richard Jeremy; s of (Philip) Michael Sambrook (d 1980), of Ashford, Kent, and Joan Hartridge (d 1983); *b* 24 April 1956; *Educ* Maidstone Sch for Boys, Univ of Reading (BA), Birkbeck Coll London (MSc); *m* 3 Oct 1987, Susan Jane, da of John Fisher; 1 s (Huw b 17 July 1992), 1 da (Freya b 20 Jan 1994); *Career* journalist with Thomson Regional Newspapers (on Rhondda Leader and South Wales Echo) 1977–80; BBC: chief sub ed BBC Radio News 1980–84, prodr BBC TV News 1984–88, dep ed Nine O'Clock News 1988–92, news ed BBC TV and Radio News 1992–96, head of newsgathering BBC News 1996–99, dep dir BBC News 1999–2001, dir BBC News 2001–04, dir BBC Global News 2004–10; global vice-chm and chief content offr Edelman 2010–12; prof of journalism and dir Centre for Journalism Cardiff Sch of Journalism, Media and Cultural Studies Univ of Cardiff; visiting fell Reuters Inst for the Study of Journalism 2010; FRSA, FRTS; *Recreations* music, novels, tennis; *Style*— Prof Richard Sambrook

SAMODUROV, Viacheslav; s of Vladimir Samodurov, of St Petersburg, and Irina Maimusova; *b* 19 May 1974, Tallin, Estonia; *Educ* Vaganova Acad of Ballet St Petersburg; *Career* ballet dancer; princ dancer Kirov Ballet Mariiensky Theatre St Petersburg 1998–2001 (joined 1992), Dutch Nat Ballet Amsterdam 2000–03, Royal Ballet Covent Garden 2003–; first prize Maya Plisetskaya Competition 1996; *Performances* with Kirov Ballet incl: Don Quixote, La Bayadère, La Sylphide, Le Corsaire, The Nutcracker, Giselle, Laurencia, Cinderella, Romeo and Juliet, Grand pas classique, Le Jeune Homme et la Mort, Petrushka, Schéhérazade, Tchaikovsky pas de deux, Symphony in C, Capriccio, The Fairy's Kiss, Middle Duet, Poem of Ecstasy; with Dutch Nat Ballet incl: La Sylphide, Sleeping Beauty, Apollo, Duo Concertante, Symphony in Three Movements, Violin Concerto, Brahms Schoenberg Quartet, The Four Temperaments, Les Noces, Choreartium, Symphonic Variations, Adagio Hammerklavier, Black Cake, Five Tangos, Andante Festivo, Four Last Songs, Approximate Sonata, The Vertiginous Thrill of Exactitude; with Royal Ballet: Romeo & Juliet, The Four Temperaments, Cinderella, Agon, Le Spectre de la Rose, L'Après-Midi d'Un Faune, Voices of Spring; *Recreations* watercolour painting, travel, reading; *Style*— Viacheslav Samodurov, Esq; ✉ c/o Suzanne Banki, 19 Tierney Road, London SW2 4QL (☎ 020 8674 1670); Royal Opera House, Covent Garden, London WC2E 9DD (☎ 020 7240 1200)

SAMPSON, Adam; *Educ* Maidstone GS, Brasenose Coll Oxford; *m*; 2 c; *Career* system probation offr Probation Service 1987–87, dep dir Prison Reform Tst 1989–94, dep prisons ombudsman Home Office 1994–97, chief exec Rehabilitation of Addicted Prisoners Tst (RAPt) 1998–2003, ceo Shelter 2003–; *Recreations* cinema, football, music; *Style*— Adam Sampson, Esq; ✉ Shelter, 88 Old Street, London EC1V 9HU (☎ 0844 515 2124, fax 0844 515 2176)

SAMPSON, Nicholas Alexander; s of Charles Sampson, of Faversham, Kent, and Patricia, *née* Burgess; *b* 27 August 1958, Gillingham, Kent; *Educ* Gillingham GS, Howard Sch Rainham, Selwyn Coll Cambridge (MA), Westminster Coll Oxford (PGCE); *Children* 2 da (Frances Isobel Rachel, Aurora Nancy Alys (twins) b 10 Apr 1994); *Career* HM inspr of taxes 1981–82, Wells Cathedral Sch 1984–94, headmaster Sutton Valence Sch 1994–2000, princ Geelong GS Australia 2000–04, master Marlborough Coll 2004–12, headmaster Cranbrook Sch Sydney 2012–; *Recreations* literature, drama, music, sport; *Clubs* Athenaeum; *Style*— Nicholas Sampson, Esq; ✉ Cranbrook School, 5 Victoria Road, Bellevue Hill, NSW 2023, Australia (☎ 0061 293 279426, fax 0061 293 630783, e-mail nsampson@cranbrook.nsw.edu.au)

SAMS, Craig; *b* 1944, Nebraska; *Educ* Wharton Sch Univ of Pennsylvania (BSc), Kingston Univ (DBA); *m* 1991, Josephine Fairley; *Career* opened Seed (macrobiotic restaurant) 1967, co-fndr and prop Whole Earth Foods 1967–2003; Green & Black's Organic Chocolate: co fndr (with w, Josephine Fairley) 1991, first product to carry Fairtrade mark, pres 1991–, non-exec dir 2005–; co-fndr Carbon Gold Ltd 2007 (exec chair), dir Duchy Originals Ltd 2009–; chm: Soil Assoc 2001–07 (hon treas 1990–2001), Judges Bakery Ltd, Soil Association Certification Ltd 2007– (also dir); former tstee Slow Food UK; About Macrobiotics (1972), The Brown Rice Cookbook (1982, 2 edn 1992), The Little Food Book (1993), The Story of Green & Black's (with Josephine Fairley, 2008); co-publisher Seed Magazine: The Journal of Organic Living 1972–77, contrib Natural Products News; *Clubs* Groucho; *Style*— Craig Sams, Esq; ✉ c (e-mail craig@craigsams.com)

SAMS, Jeremy Charles; s of late Eric Sams, of London, and late Enid, *née* Tidmarsh; *b* 12 January 1957; *Educ* Whitgift Sch Croydon, Magdalene Coll Cambridge, Guildhall Sch of Music; *Family* 1 s (Toby Oliver Sams-Friedman b 26 Nov 1994); *Career* composer, director, translator of opera and plays; freelance pianist 1977–82; *Theatre* dir: Schippel, The Plumber, Entertaining Mr Sloane (Greenwich), The Card (Newbury), Wind in the Willows (Tokyo) 1993, Neville's Island (Nottingham and West End) 1994, Enjoy (Nottingham), Wild Oats (RNT) 1995, The Wind in the Willows (Old Vic) 1995, Passion (Queen's) 1996, Marat/Sade (RNT) 1997, Enter the Guardsman (Donmar) 1997, Two Pianos Four Hands (Birmingham Rep and Comedy) 1999, Spend! Spend! Spend! (Piccadilly) 1999 (and tour 2001), Noises Off (RNT) 2000 (tour, West End and Broadway 2001), What The Butler Saw (Theatre Royal, Bath and tour) 2001, Benefactors (Albery and tour) 2002, The Water Babies (Chichester) 2003, Little Britain (UK tour) 2005, Donkey's Years (West End and UK tour) 2006, The Sound of Music (Palladium) 2006 and (UK tour) 2009, 13 The Musical (Broadway) 2008, The King and I (Royal Albert Hall) 2009, Educating Rita (Menier Chocolate Factory and Trafalgar Studios) 2010, The Wizard of Oz (Palladium) 2011; translations incl: The Rehearsal (Almeida and Garrick, Time Out Award 1991), Leonce and Lena (Sheffield Crucible), Becket (Theatre Royal Haymarket), The Miser (NT), Les Parents Terribles (RNT), Mary Stuart (RNT) 1996, Le Bourgeois Gentilhomme (Nottingham Playhouse) 1997, Colombe (Salisbury Playhouse) 1999, Waiting in the Wings (Broadway) 1999, Scapino (Chichester Festival Theatre) 2005; adaptations incl Chitty Chitty Bang Bang (London Palladium) 2002 and (Broadway) 2005, Amour (Broadway) 2002; *Opera* dir: The Reluctant King (Opera North), Opera Libretto: The Enchanted Island (Met Opera NY) 2011; translations incl: The Magic Flute, Macbeth, Figaro's Wedding, Force of Destiny, La Bohème, The Ring (ENO), Cosi fan Tutte (Opera 80), Johnny Strikes Up, L'Étoile, Orpheus in the Underworld, The Reluctant King (Opera North), The Merry Widow (Royal Opera), Don Giovanni (ENO) 2010; *Scores* over 30 scores for theatre and TV: Kean (Old Vic), The Sneeze, A Walk in the Woods (West End), Persuasion (BAFTA Award for Original TV Music 1996), Have your Cake (BBC) 1997, The Mother (BBC) 2003, Enduring Love (Pathé) 2004 (Ivor Novello Award); at the RSC: Temptation, The Tempest, Measure for Measure, Merry Wives of Windsor, Midsummer Night's Dream; at RNT: Sunday in the Park With George (music dir), Ghetto (also lyrics), The Wind in the Willows (also lyrics), Arcadia; *Books* The Miser (trans, 1991), The Rehearsal (trans, 1991), Les Parents Terribles (trans, 1995), Wild Oats (1995), The Merry Widow (trans, 2000), Enigma Variations (trans, 2003), The Visitor (trans, 2003), Don Juan (trans, 2003), Antigone (trans, 2003); *Clubs* Ivy; *Style*— Jeremy Sams, Esq; ✉ c/o The Agency, 24 Pottery Lane, Holland Park, London W11 4LZ (☎ 020 7727 1346, fax 020 7727 9037)

SAMSON, Prof Thomas James (Jim); s of Edward Samson, of NI, and Matilda Jane, *née* Smyth; *b* 6 July 1946; *Educ* Queen's Univ Belfast (BMus), UC Cardiff (MMus, PhD, LRAM); *Career* res fell in humanities Univ of Leicester 1972–73; Univ of Exeter: lectr in music 1973–87, head of dept 1986–92, reader in musicology 1987–92, prof of musicology 1992–94; prof of music Univ of Bristol 1994–2002, prof of music Royal Holloway Univ of London 2002–11, prof 2 Norwegian Univ of Science and Technol 2004–07: memb Cncl RMA; Order of Merit of the Polish Miny of Culture 1989; FBA 2000; *Books* Music in Transition: A Study in Tonal Expansion and Atonality (1977), The Music of Szymanowski (1980), The Music of Chopin (1985, German trans), Chopin Studies (1988), The Late Romantic Era, Man & Music 7 (1991), The Cambridge Companion to Chopin (1992), Chopin – the Four Ballades (1992, Polish trans), Chopin Studies 2 (with John Rink, 1994), Chopin (Master Musicians, 1996, Japanese trans), The Cambridge History of Nineteenth-Century Music (2002), Virtuosity and the Musical Work: The Transcendental Studies of Liszt (2003, winner Royal Philharmonic Book Prize 2004), Chopin Ballades (2008, winner Edn of the Year Int Piano Awards 2009), An Introduction to Music Studies (with J P E Harper-Scott, 2009, Korean trans), Music in the Balkans (2013); *Recreations* farming, astronomy; *Style*— Prof Jim Samson; ✉ Department of Music, Royal Holloway, University of London, Egham, Surrey TW20 0EX

SAMSWORTH, Jane Mary Catherine; da of James Gerard Brodie, and Elizabeth, *née* Griffiths; *b* 8 October 1951, London; *Educ* Univ of Sussex (BA), Coll of Law Lancaster Gate; *m* 30 May 1980, Robert Samsworth; 2 da (Eleanor Chloe b 18 Nov 1988, Esmée Verity Annabel b 25 Sept 1995); *Career* slr; Legal Dept GLC 1978–82, Legal Dept Br Telecom plc 1982–1987, Hogan Lovells (formerly Lovells) 1987–2014 (ptnr in Pensions Gp 1991–2014), tstee dir Hogan Lovells PLC Pension Tstees Ltd 2014–; pres Soc of Pension Conslts 1999–2001, chm Pension Advsrs Service 2004–06, memb Defined Benefits Ctee (formerly Retirement Policy Ctee) Nat Assoc of Pension Funds (NAPF) 2007–14; memb City of London Slrs Co; chm Harpenden Tangent Club 2004–05 (sec 2006–07); FPMI (APMI); Guide to the Pensions Act 1995 (jtly, 1995); *Recreations* books, restaurants, family, tourist guiding (qualified City of London and Camden guide); *Style*— Mrs Jane Samsworth

SAMUEL, Andrew William Dougall; s of Capt Andrew Samuel, RN (d 1952), and Letitia Shearer Samuel (d 1999); *b* 12 July 1937; *Educ* Hutchesons' Boys' GS Glasgow, Glasgow Sch of Architecture; *m* 1, 20 Feb 1962 (m dis 1981), Sybille Marie Luise; 1 s (Craig Andrew Alexander Porter b 1966), 1 da (Katja Lilian Hamilton b 1969); m 2, 2 Oct 1981, Mary Carswell, da of John Bisset (d 1978), of Carmunock, Glasgow; *Career* chartered architect; princ and dir Andrew Samuel & Co Ltd 1968, chm Townhead Properties Ltd 1980, md Gavin Watson Ltd 1983; holder (with entry in Guinness Book of World Records): World Canoeing Record Loch Ness 1975–85, World Canoeing Record English Channel 1976–2005, World Canoeing K2 Doubles Record English Channel 1980–86; World Masters Games (with A Wilson) 1989: first K2 500m, first K2 5000m, third K2

S

Marathon; Scottish Nat Canoeing Racing Coach 1976–83, registered Int Canoe Fedn (ICF) official; chm former E Central Tourist Assoc (Scotland), former chm Central Scotland Tourist Assoc, festival dir Trossachs Water Festival 1973–76, sec Trossachs Tourist Assoc 1969–76 (past pres), initiated formation of Loch Lomond and Trossachs Nat Park 1970 (opened 2002); memb SME Consultative Gp to Scottish Exec Scottish Parl; memb: Cncl CBI Scotland, Cncl CBI/SME; FRIAS, RIBA, FIPD, FFB; *Recreations* boating, travel, canoeing, photography; *Clubs* Trossachs Canoe and Boat, West Kilbride Golf; *Style*— Andrew Samuel, Esq; ✉ Woodside, Glazert Road, Dunlop, Ayrshire KA3 4DE (e-mail samuel.malibuinvestments@gmail.com)

SAMUEL, Christopher John Loraine (Chris); *b* 1 July 1958; *Educ* Marlborough, St Edmund Hall Oxford (MA); *m* 1988, Alison Oralia; 2 da (Harriet Lucy b 12 Dec 1989, Alexandra Mary b 9 Dec 1991), 1 s (Oliver John Loraine b 19 Jan 1996); *Career* gp fin controller Prudential-Bache Int (UK) Group 1985–90, dir of fin Prudential-Bache Securities (Canada) Ltd 1990–91, chief fin offr Prudential Securities (Japan) Ltd 1991, sr vice-pres/int controller Prudential Securities Inc NY 1991–94, dir and chief operating offr Hill Samuel Asset Mgmnt Group Ltd 1995–97, dir and chief operating offr Gartmore Investment Mgmnt plc 1997–2005, gp chief financial offr Cambridge Place Investment Mgmnt 2006–09; Ignis Asset Mgmnt: chief operating offr 2009, chief exec 2009–; ACA 1983; *Clubs* MCC, Leander; *Style*— Chris Samuel, Esq

SAMUEL, Sir John Michael Glen; 5 Bt (UK 1898), of Nevern Square, St Mary Abbots, Kensington, Co London; s of Sir John Oliver Cecil Samuel, 4 Bt (d 1962), and Charlotte Mary Desmond, *née* Hoyt (d 2006); *b* 25 January 1944, Saskatchewan, Canada; *Educ* Radley, UCL; *m* 1, 24 Sept 1966, Antoinette Sandra, da of late Capt Anthony Hewitt, RE; 2 s (Anthony John Fulton b 13 Oct 1972, Rupert Casper James b 9 March 1974); m 2, 25 Feb 1983, Mrs Elizabeth Ann Molinari, yst da of late Maj R G Curry, of Bournemouth; *Heir* s, Anthony Samuel; *Career* chm: Electric Auto Corporation (Detroit USA) 1978–82, Silver Volt Corporation (Freeport Bahamas) 1980–82, Whisper Electric Car A/S (Denmark) 1985–87, Synergy Research Ltd (UK) 1983–, Clean Air Transport (Hldgs) Ltd 1989–94, RE-fuel technology Ltd 1999–2008, RedT Energy plc 2009–; MIMechE, CEng; *Recreations* motor racing; *Style*— Sir John Samuel, Bt; ✉ website www.poweringnow.com

SAMUEL, William Edgar Foyle (Bill); s of Edgar Horace Samuel, and Winifred Olive, *née* Foyle; *b* 9 April 1941, Banstead, Surrey; *Educ* Harrow; *m* 1, 1964 (m dis 2010) Bente Pock; 3 da (Marina Ellen b 1965, Margaret Benta b 1968, Emma Mary b 1978); m 2, 2016, Vivienne Elizabeth Wordley; *Career* exec dir Investcorp Bank 1986–90; Turks and Caicos Islands: dir of tourism 1991, supt of banking and offshore fin 1992, dir Turks and Caicos Banking Ltd 1993–2000, UK rep Turks and Caicos Govt 1994–2004; dir W & G Foyle Ltd 1999–; dir Emirates Airline Festival of Literature Dubai 2008–12, dir Booksellers Assoc of UK and I 2009–; chm Batch UK Ltd 2009–; cncl memb UK Overseas Territories Conservation Forum 2002–, int cncl memb Minority Rights Gp 2009–15; FCA 1965; *Recreations* sailing, scuba, skiing, walking, reading, music; *Style*— Bill Samuel, Esq; ✉ c/o Foyles, 107 Charing Cross Road, London WC2H 0DT (e-mail bill@foyles.co.uk)

SAMUELS, His Hon John Edward Anthony; QC (1981); s of Albert Edward Samuels (d 1982), and Sadie Beatrice Samuels (d 1991); *b* 15 August 1940; *Educ* Charterhouse, Queens' Coll Cambridge (MA); *m* 1967, Maxine, da of Lt-Col F D Robertson, MC (d 1998); 2 s (David b 1970, Adam b 1973); *Career* called to the Bar Lincoln's Inn 1964 (bencher 1990); dep judge of the High Court 1981–97, recorder of the Crown Court 1985–97, circuit judge (SE Circuit) 1997–2006 (dep circuit judge 2006–10); chm Jt Regulations Ctee of the Inns' Cncl and the Bar Cncl 1987–90; memb: Senate of the Inns of Court and the Bar 1983–86, Bar Cncl 1992–97, Criminal Injuries Compensation Appeal Panel 1996–97, Ctee Cncl of HM Circuit Judges 2001–12 (chm Criminal Sub-Ctee 2002–06); asst Parly Boundary Cmmr 1992–95, lay chair NHS Complaints Panels 1996–97, judicial memb Parole Bd 2005–15, tstee Criminal Justice Alliance 2010– (chm 2012–); vice-pres Unlock (Nat Assoc of Ex-Offenders) 2006–, memb (Eng and Wales rep) Bd Int Assoc of Drug Treatment Courts 2006–, tstee Howard League for Penal Reform 2007–, tstee Centre for Crime and Justice Studies 2002–12, pres Prisoners' Educn Tst 2012– (tstee 2000–12, chm 2006–12), vice-pres Assoc of Membs of Ind Monitoring Bds (AMIMB) 2015–, patron Prisoners Advice Service 2015–; visiting prof Nottingham Trent Univ 2012–; *Publications* Action Pack: Counsel's Guide to Chambers Administration (1986 and 1988), Halsbury's Laws of England (contrib, 4 edn); *Recreations* conservation, restoration and serendipity; *Clubs* Garrick; *Style*— His Hon John Samuels, QC; ✉ Treasury Office, Lincoln's Inn, London WC2A 3TL (☎ 020 7405 1393)

SAMWORTH, Sir David Chetwode; kt (2009), CBE (1985), DL (1984); s of Frank Samworth; *b* 25 June 1935; *Educ* Uppingham; *m* 1969, Rosemary Grace, *née* Cadell; 1 s (Mark b 1970), 3 da (Mary b 1972, Susannah b 1975, Victoria b 1977); *Career* Lt Sudan and Cyprus; chm Pork Farms Ltd 1968–81, dir Northern Foods Ltd 1978–81; chm: Meat and Livestock Cmmn 1980–84, Samworth Brothers (Holdings) Ltd 1984–2005 (pres 2005–); non-exec dir: Imperial Group 1983–85, Thorntons plc 1988–93; pres: Br Meat Mfrs Assoc 1988–94, Leics Agric Soc 1996–99, RASE 2000–01, Young Enterprise Leics 2001–04; vice-chm Leics 33 Hosp Mgmnt Ctee 1970–74, memb Cncl of Univ of Nottingham 1975–76, chm Governing Body Uppingham Sch 1996–99 (vice chm 1980–89); High Sheriff of Leicestershire 1997, pres College of Canons Leicester Cathedral 2013–16; Liveryman Worshipful Co of Butchers; Hon LLD Univ of Leicester 2012; *Recreations* fishing; *Style*— Sir David Samworth, CBE, DL

SANCHEZ-IGLESIAS, Peter; s of Luis Sanchez-Iglesias, and Susan, *née* Lane; bro of Jonray Sanchez-Iglesias (d 2015); *b* 12 October 1985, Bristol; *Educ* Chew Valley Sch; *m* 23 Dec 2010, Hannah, *née* Cole; *Career* co-proprietor and chef Casamia Bristol 2006– (Michelin star 2009–); *Style*— Mr Peter Sanchez-Iglesias; ✉ Casamia, 38 High Street, Westbury Village, Westbury-on-Trym, Bristol BS9 3DZ (☎ 0117 959 2884, website www.casamiarestaurant.co.uk)

SANCROFT-BAKER, Raymond Samuel; s of Anthony Sancroft-Baker (d 1985), and Jean Norah, *née* Heron-Maxwell (d 1981); *b* 30 July 1950; *Educ* Bromsgrove Sch; *m* 29 Jan 1983 (m dis 1994), (Daphne) Caroline, da of Gp Capt Maurice Adams, OBE, AFC (d 1976); 2 s (Robert b 1985, Hugh b 1987); *Career* Christie's: head Coin and Metal Dept 1973, dir 1981–, dir Jewellery Dept 1988–; Freeman City of London 1972; Liveryman: Worshipful Co of Wax Chandlers 1973, Worshipful Co of Pattenmakers 1972 (memb Ct of Assts 1987, Master 1994); FRNS 1971, FGA 1992; *Recreations* tennis, squash, wood turning; *Style*— Raymond Sancroft-Baker, Esq; ✉ Christie's, 8 King Street, St James's, London SW1Y 6QT (☎ 020 7839 9060, e-mail rsancroft-baker@christies.com)

SANDBACH, Antoinette Geraldine; MP; da of Ian Mackeson-Sandbach (d 2012), and Annie Mackeson-Sandbach; *Educ* Univ of Nottingham (BA, LLM); *m* 31 March 2012, Matthew Robin Sherratt; 1 da (Sacha b 25 June 2002), 1 s (Sam b 19 Feb 2009 d 2009); *Career* called to the Bar (Lincoln's Inn) 1993, barr-at-law 9 Bedford Row 1995–2006; memb Nat Assembly for Wales (Cons) N Wales 2011–15, shadow min of rural affrs 2011–14, shadow min for environment and energy 2014–15; MP (Cons) Eddisbury 2015–; memb Bar Cncl 1997–2003; Liveryman Worshipful Co of Grocers; *Style*— Ms Antoinette Sandbach, MP; ✉ House of Commons, London SW1A 0AA (☎ 020 7219 3000, website www.antoinettesandbach.org.uk, Twitter @ASandbachMP)

SANDELL, Terry; OBE (1991); s of James William Sandell (d 2003), and Helen Elizabeth, *née* McCombie (d 1992); *b* 8 September 1948, Edgware, Middlesex; *Educ* Watford GS, Univ of Nottingham (BA), Univ of Edinburgh, City Univ London (MA); *m* 1986, Kate, *née* Ling; 2 s (Adam b 1976, Barnaby b 1978); *Career* VSO Sudan 1970–72; Br Cncl: dir Omdurman Centre Sudan 1974–78, regnl offr Soviet Union and Mongolia 1978–81, dir Austria 1983–89, dir Soviet Union/Cwlth of Ind States (CIS) 1989–92, dir Ukraine 2005–; first sec (cultural) Br embassy Moscow 1981–83, cultural counsellor Br Embassy Moscow 1989–92; dir Visiting Arts 1994–2005; memb bd: Academia Rossica 1998–, Festival of Muslim Cultures 2003–05; author of articles in books and learned jls; FRSA 1994; *Recreations* walking, swimming, performing and visual arts, reading; *Clubs* Lansdowne; *Style*— Terry Sandell Esq, OBE; ✉ British Council, VUL, Grigoriya Skovorodi 4/12, Kyiv 0470, Ukraine (☎ 0038 0444 905600, fax 0038 0444 905605, e-mail terry.sandell@britishcouncil.org.ua)

SANDEMAN, David Robert; s of Robert John Sandeman, of Bridge of Allan, Stirlingshire, and Enid, *née* Webb; *b* 3 August 1954; *Educ* Trinity Coll Glenalmond, UCL (BSc), Westminster Med Sch London (MB BS, pres Westminster Students' Union); *m* (m dis); 2 da (Isabel Laelia b 11 Oct 1988, Isla Alison b 13 Feb 2001), 1 s (Jonathan Donald b 17 Sept 1998); *Career* pre-registration houseman Westminster Hosp London 1979–80, A&E Luton and Dunstable Hosp 1980, gen surgery registrar (rotation) Birmingham 1980–83, SHO in neurosurgery Bristol 1984, registrar in neurosurgery Liverpool 1984–85 and 1986–87, research registrar UCH London and Inst of Neurology Queen's Square London 1985–86, sr registrar in neurosurgery Manchester Royal Infirmary and Hope Hosp Salford 1987–90, conslt neurosurgn Frenchay Hosp Bristol 1991–; research interests in neuro-oncology and laser application to neurosurgery, pioneer of interactive image directed surgical techniques, minimally invasive neurosurgery, neuro-endoscopy and surgical robotics; memb: Euro Laser Assoc 1987, Soc of Br Neurosurgeons 1991, French Neurosurgical Soc 1992, Euro Stereotactic Assoc 1992; *Books* Lasers in Neurosurgery (1990); *Recreations* skiing, cycling, swimming, triathlon, hill walking; *Style*— David R Sandeman, Esq; ✉ Department of Neurosurgery, Frenchay Hospital, Bristol BS16 1LE (☎ 0117 918 6614, fax 0117 970 1161, mobile 07831 451641, e-mail info@david-sandeman.com, website www.david-sandeman.com)

SANDERCOCK, Prof Peter Andrew Gale; s of Capt Michael John Gale Sandercock (d 1996), of Northwood, Middx, and Helen Betty, *née* Howland (d 1995); *b* 16 April 1951; *Educ* Shrewsbury, New Coll Oxford (MA, BMB Ch, DM); *m* 10 Sept 1977, Janet Mary, da of Peter Searell Andrews, of Little Addington, Northants; 3 s (David, Robert, Andrew), 1 da (Eleanor); *Career* actg clinical lectr Univ of Oxford 1981–85, lectr Univ of Liverpool 1985–87, sr lectr Univ of Edinburgh 1988–93, reader in Neurology Univ of Edinburgh 1993–99, prof 1999–; MRCP 1979, FRCP 1992, FMedSci 2001; *Books* Stroke (1987), Stroke: A Practical Guide to Management (3 edn, 2008); *Style*— Prof Peter Sandercock; ✉ Department of Clinical Neuroscience, Western General Hospital, Crewe Road, Edinburgh EH4 2XU (☎ 0131 537 2082 (secretary), fax 0131 332 5150)

SANDERS, Adrian; *b* 25 April 1959, Paignton, Devon; *Educ* Torquay Boys' GS; *Career* with Britannic Assurance 1978–85, joined Assoc of Lib (later Lib Dem) Cncllrs 1986–89, parly offr Lib Dem Whips' Office 1989–90, rejoined Assoc of Lib Dem Cncllrs 1990–92, with the office of Rt Hon Paddy Ashdown, MP 1992–93, with Nat Cncl for Voluntary Orgns (NCVO) 1993–94, joined Southern Assoc of Voluntary Action Gps for Europe (SAVAGE) 1994–97; MP (Lib Dem) Torbay 1997–2015, housing spokesman and regional whip (South and South West) 1997–99, local govt and housing spokesman 1999–2001, tourism spokesman 2001–05, dep chief whip 2005–10; chair All Pty Parly Gp for Diabetes 1999–2015, pres Parly Diabetes Global Network 2013–15, sec-gen Parly Diabetes Global Network 2016–; memb: Culture, Media and Sport Select Ctee 2005–13, Transport Select Ctee 2013–15, Panel of Chairs 2014–15; chm Soc of Ticket Agents and Retailers (STAR) 2015–; vice-pres League Against Cruel Sports 2014–, vice-pres Juvenile Diabetes Research Fndn (JDRF) UK 2015–; contested: Torbay 1992, Devon and East Plymouth Euro election 1994; cncllr Torbay Unitary Authority 2015–; *Recreations* soccer, music and films; *Style*— Adrian Sanders, Esq; ✉ 15 Oldway Road, Paignton, Devon TQ3 2TF

SANDERS, Prof Dale; s of Leslie G D Sanders, and Daphne M Sanders; *b* 13 May 1953, Scarborough, N Yorks; *Educ* Univ of York (BA), Univ of Cambridge (PhD, ScD); *Career* Yale Univ Sch of Med: James Hudson Brown res fell 1978–79, res assoc 1979–83; Univ of York: lectr 1983–89, reader 1989–92, prof of biology 1992–2010, head Biology Dept 2004–10; dir John Innes Centre 2010–; hon visiting prof Univ of York 2010–; author of over 100 pubns in learned in jls; President's Medal Soc for Experimental Biology 1987, Euro Sci Prize Körber Fndn 2001; FRS 2001; *Style*— Prof Dale Sanders; ✉ 3 Newmarket Road, Norwich NR2 2HG; John Innes Centre, Norwich Research Park, Colney, Norwich NR4 7UH (☎ 01603 450000, e-mail dale.sanders@jic.ac.uk)

SANDERS, (June) Deidre; da of Philip Ronald Heaton (d 1991), and Audrey Minton, *née* Harvey (d 1972); *b* 9 June 1945; *Educ* Harrow County GS for Girls, Univ of Sheffield (BA); *m* 12 Dec 1969, Richard James, 2 da (Susan b 1976, Phoebe b 1988); *Career* journalist, author, broadcaster; problem-page ed The Sun; memb: NSPCC Cncl, Br Assoc for Counselling; patron: Family Lives, Nat Family and Parenting Inst, Nat Assoc for People Abused in Childhood; Jubilee Medal 1977; FRSA, FRSM; *Books* Kitchen Sink or Swim? (1982), Women and Depression (1984), Woman Book of Love and Sex (1985), Woman Report on Men (1987); *Style*— Mrs Deidre Sanders; ✉ The Sun, The News Building, London SE1 9GF (☎ 020 7782 4000, e-mail problems@deardeidre.org)

SANDERS, Dr Eric; s of Albert Sanders, and Caroline, *née* Johnson; *b* 22 October 1946; *Educ* Stanley GS Co Durham, Univ of Wales (BSc, MB); *m* 10 July 1971, Dianne Marilyn, da of David Denzil Harris Thomas, of Carmarthen; 2 s (Gareth Wyn b 20 June 1974, Gethyn Huw b 21 Sept 1976), 1 da (Angharad Jane b 4 June 1980); *Career* pre-registration house offr Royal Infirmary Cardiff 1971, SHO Univ Hosp Wales 1972–74, research registrar and lectr Kruf Inst Renal Disease Royal Infirmary Cardiff 1974–80, conslt physician and dir of dialysis servs W Wales Hosp Carmarthen 1980–93, cons diabetologist N Durham Acute NHS Tst 1993–; dir of med servs W Wales Hosp 1992–; tstee and hon treas Kidney Research Unit Wales Fndn, memb Cncl Wales Diabetes Research Tst, former pres and regnl offr Lions Int Dist 105W; memb: Renal Assoc GB, EDTA; FRCP 1990 (MRCP 1974); *Books* Nephrology Illustrated (1981), Clinical Atlas of the Kidney (1993); *Recreations* local community service, music; *Style*— Dr Eric Sanders; ✉ Dryburn Hospital, North Road, Durham DH1 5TW (☎ 0191 333 2597)

SANDERS, Prof Jeremy Keith Morris; CBE (2014); s of Sidney Sanders, and Sylvia, *née* Rutman (d 1983); *b* 3 May 1948; *Educ* Wandsworth Sch, Imperial Coll London (Edmund White Prize, BSc), Churchill Coll Cambridge (PhD), Selwyn Coll Cambridge (ScD); *m* 1972, Louise Elliott; 1 s, 1 da; *Career* res assoc in pharmacology Stanford Univ 1972–73; Univ of Cambridge: demonstrator in chemistry 1973–78, lectr in chemistry 1978–92, reader and asst head Dept of Chemistry 1992–96, prof of chemistry 1996–2015, memb Cncl 1999–2002, head Dept of Chemistry 2000–06 (dep head 1998–2000), chm Allocations Ctee 1999–2000, dep vice-chllr 2006–10, chair Cambridge Prog for Industry 2003–07, head Sch of Physical Sciences 2009–11, pro-vice-chllr for institutional affrs 2011–15, emeritus prof 2015–; memb Cncl Imperial Coll London 2016–; fell: Christ's Coll Cambridge (Darwin Prize) 1972–76, Selwyn Coll Cambridge 1976–; visiting assoc prof and MRC fell Univ of Br Columbia 1979–80; pres Burgenstock Conference 2011 (vice-pres 2010); assoc ed New Journal of Chemistry 1998–2000, chm Editorial Bd Chemical Society Reviews 2000–02, chair Chemistry Sub-Panel 2008 UK Research Assessment Exercise 2004–08, ed-in-chief Royal Society Open Science 2016–; chair Storey's Field Community Tst 2016–; Meldola Medal 1975, Hickinbottom Award 1981, Pfizer Academic Award (on nuclear Overhauser effect) 1984, Pfizer Academic Award 1988 (on NMR of whole cells), Josef Loschmidt Prize 1994, Pedler Medal and Prize

1996, Izatt-Christensen Award in Macrocyclic Chemistry (USA) 2003, Davy Medal Royal Soc 2009; fell Japan Soc for the Promotion of Science 2002; FRSC, CChem 1978, FRS 1995, FRSA 1997; *Books* Modern NMR Spectroscopy (with B K Hunter, 1987, 2 edn 1993); Member, Council, Imperial College, London, 2016–; *Recreations* family, cooking, music; *Style—* Prof Jeremy Sanders, CBE, FRS; ✉ Department of Chemistry, University of Cambridge, Lensfield Road, Cambridge CB2 1EW (✆ 01223 336411, e-mail jkms@cam.ac.uk, website www.ch.cam.ac.uk/person/jkms)

SANDERS, Michael David; s of Norris Manley Sanders, of Farringdon, Hants, and Gertrude Florence, *née* Hayley; *b* 19 September 1935; *Educ* Tonbridge, Guy's Hosp Med Sch (MB BS, DO); *m* 1 Nov 1969, Thalia Margaret, da of Thomas Garlick (d 1961), of Ashover, Derbys; 1 s (Rupert Miles b 16 March 1971), 1 da (Melissa Tryce b 25 May 1973); *Career* house surgn Guy's Hosp 1959, resident Moorfields Eye Hosp 1963–67, Alexander Piggot Werner meml fell Univ of Calif San Francisco 1967–68; conslt ophthalmologist: Nat Hosp Nervous Diseases 1969–99, St Thomas' Hosp 1972–98; civil conslt ophthalmology RAF 1972; distinguished lectures: Middlemore 1985, Percival Hay 1986, Sir Stewart Duke-Elder 1987, Ida Mann 1987, Lettsomian 1988; Bowman Medal 1996, Montgomery Medal 1997; hon memb Pacific Coast Oto-Ophthalmological Soc, hon conslt Sydney Hosp Univ of Sydney; asst ed British Journal of Ophthalmology; past chm Frost Fndn, memb Cncl Iris Fund for Prevention of Blindness 1994–2003, chm Friends of Chawton Church 2004–, memb Cncl Gift of Sight Charity 2009–; pres Int Neuro-Ophthalmology Soc; FRCP, FRCS, FCOpth; *Books* Topics in Neuro-Ophthalmology (1979), Computerised Tomography in Neuro-Ophthalmology (1982), Common Problems in Neuro-Ophthalmology (1997); *Recreations* golf; *Clubs* RAF, Hankley Cmmn; *Style—* Michael Sanders, Esq; ✉ Chawton Lodge, Chawton, Alton, Hampshire GU34 1SL (✆ 01420 86681)

SANDERS, Prof Thomas Andrew Bruce (Tom); s of John Bruce Sanders (d 1992), of Eastbourne, E Sussex, and Annie, *née* Dewsberry (d 1990); *b* 29 December 1949, Eastbourne; *Educ* Eastbourne Coll, Queen Elizabeth Coll London (BSc), Univ of London (PhD, DSc); *m* 20 Oct 1973, Linda Marie, *née* Fassbender; 1 da (Mila b 30 March 1978), 1 s (Toby b 11 July 1981); *Career* prog assoc UNICEF (Indonesia) 1971–73; res nutritionist SW Thames RHA 1974–77; Queen Elizabeth Coll London: Rank Prize Funds fell 1977–79, res fell 1979–82, lectr in nutrition 1982–84; KCL: lectr in nutrition 1984–91, reader 1991–94, prof of nutrition and dietetics 1994–, head of Dept 1995–2001, head Research Div of Nutritional Sciences, memb Cncl, head Diabetes and Nutritional Sciences Div Sch of Medicine 2010–14, emeritus prof of nutrition and dietetics 2014–; chair Br Nutrition Fndn Task Force on Nutrition and Devpt: Short- and Long-Term Consequences for Health 2013; sci govr and tstee Br Nutrition Fndn, hon nutritional dir Heart UK, chair Assoc of Profs of Human Nutrition; memb: Advsy Ctee on Novel Foods and Processes Food Standards Agency 1994–2001, Nutrition Soc, British Atherosclerosis Soc, RSM, UK Sci Advsy Ctee Jt Health Claims Initiative, WHO/Food and Agriculture Orgn Expert Consultation on the Roles of Fats and Fatty Acdis in Human Nutrition 2008; frequent contrib to television and radio; fell HE Acad, fell Assoc for Nutrition 2013, FRSM 2014; *Books* The Vegetarian's Healthy Diet Book (1986), The Food Revolution (1991), You Don't Have to Diet (1994), Foods that Harm, Foods that Heal (1996), The Molecular Basis of Human Nutrition (2003), Nutrition and Development: Short- and Long-Term Consequences for Health (2013), Functional Dietary Lipids: Food Formulation, Consumer Issues and Innovation for Health (2016); over 260 publications in scientific journals.; *Recreations* surfing, windsurfing, cinema, theatre, opera, walking, travel, wildlife, sailing, reading, gardening; *Style—* Prof Tom Sanders; ✉ Diabetes and Nutritional Sciences Division, School of Medicine, King's College London, Franklin-Wilkins Building, 150 Stamford Street, London SE1 9NH (✆ 020 7848 4273, fax 020 7848 4171, mobile 07768 414337, e-mail tom.sanders@kcl.ac.uk, website www.kcl.ac.uk/schools/biohealth/research/nutritional/staff/tsanders.html)

SANDERS, Timothy Simon (Tim); s of Robert Ernest Sanders, and Patricia Anne, *née* Tracy; *b* 13 March 1959; *Educ* Llandovery Coll (Thomas Phillips scholar), Thames Valley GS, Univ of London (LLB); *m* Kathrine, da of Brian Thomas Firth; 1 s (James Thomas b 22 Sept 1986), 1 da (Alice Caroline b 22 March 1992); *Career* qualified 1984; assoc Allen and Overy; Theodore Goddard: assoc 1991–92, ptnr 1992, head Corp Tax Dept 1993–2000; ptnr and head of European tax Skadden, Arps, Slate, Meagher & Flom LLP 2001–; memb Law Soc 1984; CTA (fell) 1996; assoc memb ABA 2002; *Books* Tolley's Company Law (contrib), US Practising Law Handbook Series (contrib), Tottel's Tax Indemnities and Warranties (3 edn, 2009), Law Business Research's The Inward Investment and International Tax Review (ed and contrib); *Recreations* rowing, golf, theatre, sailing; *Clubs* Surrey CCC, Harlequins RFC, Tideway Scullers Sch; *Style—* Tim Sanders, Esq; ✉ Skadden, Arps, Slate, Meagher & Flom LLP, 40 Bank Street, Canary Wharf, London E14 5DS (✆ 020 7519 7000, e-mail tsanders@skadden.com)

SANDERS-CROOK, William Stanley; MBE (1972); s of William Charles Herbert Crook (d 1966), of Twickenham, Middx, and Mary Amelia, *née* Green (d 1986); *b* 2 November 1933; *Educ* Latymer Upper Sch, RMA Sandhurst; *m* 1, 5 May 1962; 1 s (William b 1963), 1 da (Deborah b 1972); m 2, 20 Dec 1982, Jean Rosemary, da of Eric Ernest Walker (d 1973), of Barnstaple, N Devon; *Career* Regular Army 1953–77; Maj; served infantry and para: BAOR, Cyprus, Suez, Malaya, Borneo, Singapore, MOD, NI, Brunei; writer; dir: John Roberts Conslts 1977–79, Jean Kittermaster PR 1981–; ceo Globe Run 1991–; *Novels* Four Days (1979), Death Run (1980), Triple Seven (1981), Fighting Back (1992); *Recreations* riding, scuba diving, dogs, cabinet making, painting; *Clubs* Special Forces, Mounted Infantry; *Style—* William Sanders-Crook, Esq, MBE; ✉ Hansdown House, Maesbury, Nr Wells, Somerset BA5 3HA (✆ 01749 840498, fax 01749 840921, e-mail wscjrk@gmail.com)

SANDERSON, Bryan Kaye; CBE (1999); s of Eric Sanderson (d 1973), and Anne, *née* Kaye; *b* 14 October 1940; *Educ* Dame Allan's Sch Newcastle upon Tyne, LSE (BSc(Econ)), IMEDE Business Sch Lausanne; *m* Oct 1966, Sirkka Aulikki, *née* Kärki; 1 da (Christina Elvira b Jan 1976), 1 s (Peter James Eric b Sept 1978); *Career* vol serv with UNA Peru 1962–64; BP Amoco plc (formerly British Petroleum): md and chief exec BP Nutrition 1987–90, chief exec BP Chemicals 1990–2000, an md (main bd dir) BP plc 1992–2000, chm BUPA 2001–06, chm Standard Chartered Bank 2003–06, chm Northern Rock 2007–08; chm Learning and Skills Cncl 2000–04; non-exec dir: Corus (formerly British Steel) 1994–2001, Six Continents 2001–03, Argus Media 2012–; pres CEFIC 1998–2000; memb DTI Steering Gp on Company Law Reform 1998–2001; non-exec dir: Sunderland FC Ltd (chm 1998–2004), Durham CCC 2005; chm Sunderland Area Regeneration Co 2001–08, non-exec chm Cella Energy until 2014; tstee Economist 2006–, chm Florence Nightingale Fndn 2008–; memb Ct of Govrs LSE 1999–2009 (vice-chm 1998–2003, emeritus govr 2009–); Hon DUniv: Sunderland 1998, York 1999; *Recreations* reading, golf, walking, gardening; *Style—* Bryan Sanderson, Esq, CBE; ✉ 40 Netherhall Gardens, Hampstead, London NW3 5TP (✆ 02077 942488, e-mail pa@40netherhall.com)

SANDERSON, Eric Fenton; s of late Francis Kirton Sanderson, of Dundee, and Margarita Shand, *née* Fenton; *b* 14 October 1951, Dundee; *Educ* Morgan Acad Dundee, Univ of Dundee (LLB, pres Students' Assoc), Harvard Business Sch (AMP); *m* 26 July 1975, Patricia Ann, da of late Lt-Cdr Donald Brian Shaw, and Mrs Pamela Shaw; 3 da (Anna b 1 June 1979, Caroline b 30 June 1982, Emma b 12 April 1985); *Career* articled clerk Touche Ross & Co Edinburgh, qualified CA 1976; The British Linen Bank Ltd: joined 1976, dir and head corp fin 1984, gp chief exec 1989–97; chief exec Bank of Scotland Treasury Services plc 1997–99 (also memb Bank of Scotland Mgmnt Bd); chm Kwik-Fit Insurance Services Ltd 2000–02; non-exec dir: MyTravel Group plc (formerly Airtours plc) 1987–2004 (dep chm 2001–02, chm 2003–04), English & Overseas Properties plc 1988–99, Oriel Leisure 1997–99, Docklands Light Railway Ltd 1999–2006, First Milk Ltd 2006–12, Schroder UK Mid Cap Fund plc 2011– (chm 2014–), Black Rock Greater European Fund plc 2013– (chm 2016–); chm MWB Group Hldgs plc 2005–12, memb British Railways Bd 1991–94; graduates assessor and memb Ct Univ of Dundee 2005–16 (chm 2010–16); FCIBS 1994 (MCIBS 1990); *Recreations* tennis, gardening, photography, art; *Clubs* New (Edinburgh); *Style—* Eric Sanderson, Esq; ✉ e-mail ericsanderson@blueyonder.co.uk

SANDERSON, Prof John Elsby; s of Arthur John Sanderson, of Rhoose Glamorgan, and Ruth Megan, *née* Griffiths; *b* 1 May 1949; *Educ* Blundell's, Univ of Cambridge (MA, MD), Bart's Med Coll London (MB BChir); *m* 1, 1972 (m dis 1977), Susanna Marion, da of Richard Tewson, of Hempstead, Essex; m 2, 1980, Dr Julia Dorothy Billingham, da of David Billingham, of Crowhurst, E Sussex; 1 da (Vanessa Maureen b 1980), 1 s (Henry John Elsby b 1981); *Career* house physician and surgn Bart's London 1973–74, sr house physician Brompton and Hammersmith Hosps 1974–75, res fell (cardiology) RPMS Hammersmith Hosp 1975–78, lectr in cardiovascular med Univ of Oxford and John Radcliffe Hosp Oxford 1978–81, Wellcome Tst lectr St Mary's Hosp and hon lectr Univ of Nairobi Kenya (St Marys/Univ of Nairobi Hypertension project) 1981–83, conslt physician and cardiologist Taunton and Somerset Hosp and clinical tutor Univ of Bristol 1983–92, sr lectr in med (cardiology) and conslt cardiologist The Chinese Univ of Hong Kong Prince of Wales Hosp 1992–96, prof of med and head Div of Cardiology Chinese Univ of Hong Kong 1996–2005, prof of cardiology and conslt cardiologist Keele Univ Med Sch and Univ Hosp of N Staffs NHS Tst 2005–07, prof of clinical cardiology Univ of Birmingham Med Sch 2007–09, hon prof (clinical) Dept of Medicine and Therapeutics Chinese Univ of Hong Kong 2009–; dep ed Heart jl 2004–09, hon prof (clinical) Dept of Medicine and Therapeutics and clinical professional conslt Clinical Skills Learning Centre Chinese Univ Hong Kong 2009–; memb: BMA, Br Cardiac Soc, Br Hypertension Soc, European Soc of Cardiology; fell American Coll of Cardiology; FRCP; *Publications* pubns and papers on heart failure, echocardiography, hypertension and Ischaemic heart disease; *Recreations* family, music, sailing, skiing and walking; *Clubs* Royal Hong Kong Yacht; *Style—* Prof John Sanderson

SANDERSON, Rupert; *Educ* Cordwainers Coll; *Career* shoe designer; co-fndr Fashion Fringe Shoes 2008; Accessory Designer of the Year Br Fashion Award 2008, Accessory Designer of the Year Elle Style Award 2009; *Style—* Rupert Sanderson, Esq; ✉ 19 Bruton Place, London W1J 6NP

SANDERSON, Timothy William; s of Dr Michael William Bristowe Sanderson, and Mrs Kay Glendinning, MBE, *née* Holman; *b* 3 March 1958; *Educ* Uppingham, UC Oxford (MA); *m* 9 Oct 1987, Damaris Stella Lavinia Margot Muir, da of Armitage Clifford Taylor (d 1967), of Hilden Hall, Penn, Bucks; 3 s (Hugh William Muir b 27 Nov 1990, Maximilian Henry Armitage b 14 July 1993, Alexander Edward Rohan b 6 Jan 1996); *Career* Hill Samuel Investment Management Group 1979–90, dir and chief investment offr Delaware International Advisers Ltd 1990–2000, chm and chief investment offr Sanderson Asset Management Ltd 2000–; tstee Inst of Int Monetary Research; fell Ashmolean Museum, tstee Southwark Cathedral Devpt Cncl, tstee Venice in Peril; memb: Chllr's Ct of Benefactors Univ of Oxford, Advsy Bd Faculty of History Univ of Oxford; assoc CFA (Chartered Financial Analyst) Inst; *Recreations* gardening, book collecting, literature, history, reading, wine, fine arts; *Clubs* Buck's, Hurlingham, Boodle's, Brooks's; *Style—* Timothy Sanderson, Esq; ✉ Sanderson Asset Management Ltd, 20 Savile Row, London W1S 3PR (✆ 020 7468 5970, fax 020 7468 5979, e-mail tsanderson@sandersonam.com); Marston House, Marston Bigot, Nr Frome, Somerset BA11 5DU

SANDHU, Prof Bhupinder Kaur; OBE (2013); da of Malkiat Singh Sandhu, and Swaran Kaur, *née* Garcha; *b* 24 April 1951; *Educ* Moat Girls' Sch Leicester, Wyggeston Girls' Sch Leicester, UCL (MB BS), Univ of London (MD); *m* 1980, Richard Whitburn; s of George Whitburn (d 1994) and Anna, *née* Evans; 2 da (Tara b 1 Feb 1983, Jess b 27 Jan 1986); *Career* res fell and hon sr registrar Hosp for Sick Children Gt Ormond St London 1981–84, lectr in child health and hon sr registrar Charing Cross and Westminster Hosp Med Sch 1984–88, conslt paediatric gastroenterologist and head Gastroenterology Unit Royal Hosp for Sick Children Bristol 1988–, hon sr clinical lectr Univ of Bristol 1988–; temp advsr WHO; visiting prof of child health, gastroenterology and nutrition UWE 2000–; examiner: Univ of London 1989–94 and 2005–, Addis Ababa Univ 1993–95, RCPCH 1997–, Univ of Birmingham 1999–2001, Univ of Cardiff 2007–; chm Div of Paediatrics 1991–96, sec SW Paediatric Soc 1991–96, chair Res Working Gp Euro Soc of Paediatric Gastroenterology, Nutrition and Hepatology, convenor and sec Br Soc of Paediatric Gastroenterology and Nutrition 1993–96, memb Nutrition Ctee RCPCH 2001–; United Bristol Healthcare Tst: memb Equal Opportunities Advsy Gp 1991–99, sec Hosp Med Ctee 1996–2000; pres elect Cwlth Soc of Paediatric Gastroentrology and Nutrition 2006–, memb Cwlth Advsy Ctee on Health 2004–06, pres Medical Women's Fedn 2005–06 (hon treas 2002–04), memb Cncl BMA 2006–08, co-chair Equal Opportunities Ctee BMA 2007–; delivered numerous invited guest lectures in UK and overseas, chaired int meetings and symposia; chair: Regnl Advsy Ctee BBC West 1992–96, Clifton Branch Bristol W Lab Pty 1999–2003; memb Bd: Bristol Old Vic Theatre Sch 1990–, VSO 1998–2005, Food Standards Agency 2000–02; memb Maternity and Health Links 1989–91; chair of govrs Highgate Primary Sch London 1984–88, govr Clifton HS 1994–2005, dep chair Governing Bd UWE 2004– (memb 1996–); Professional of the Year Asian Women of Achievement Awards 2002; FRCP 1996 (MRCP 1978), FRCPCH 1997; *Publications* author of over 80 papers in int jls on subjects related to child health, gastroenterology and nutrition; *Recreations* coastal walking, theatre, travel; *Style—* Prof Bhupinder Sandhu, OBE; ✉ Royal Hospital for Children, Upper Maudlin Street, Bristol BS2 8BJ (✆ 0117 342 8828, fax 0117 342 8845)

SANDHURST, 6 Baron (UK 1871); Guy Rhys John Mansfield; *see:* Guy Mansfield, QC

SANDIFER, Dr Quentin Dudley; s of Keith Dudley Sandifer (d 1982), and Joyce Eileen, *née* Lewis (d 1968); *b* 14 July 1960, Cardiff; *Educ* Univ of Wales (MB, BCh, MPH), London Business Sch (MBA), Columbia Univ NY (MBA); *m* 19 Jan 1985, Anne Griffiths, *née* Evans; 1 da (Charlotte b 11 Feb 1987), 2 s (Thomas b 22 June 1989, Christopher b 6 June 1991); *Career* house offr Singleton Hosp and North Tees Gen Hosp 1985–86; gen practice trainee: Royal Shewsbury Gp of Hosps 1986–89, St John's Hill Surgery Shrewsbury 1989–90; family physician and active staff physician Barrhead Clinic and Gen Hosp Alberta Canada 1990–92, specialist registrar in public health med South Glamorgan HA 1992–97; Iechyd Morgannwg (West/Mid Glamorgan) HA: conslt in public health med 1997–2000, exec dir of public health 2000–03; dir of public health Swansea Local Health Bd 2003–04, dir of public health and med dir Kent & Medway SHA 2004–05, exec dir of public health Kent & Medway SHA and Kent CC 2005–06, dep regnl dir of public health and med dir NHS SE Coast 2006–09, jt dir of public health NHS Camden and London Borough of Camden 2009–12, exec dir of public health services and med dir Public Health Wales NHS Tst 2012–; hon clinical sr lectr Univ of Kent 2005–10, hon sr lectr UCL 2010–; author various papers in learned jls; memb Advsy Ctee on Microbiological Safety of Food Food Standards Agency 2001–06; RSM: Janet Nash travelling fell 1996, pres Section of Gen Practice 1998–99, tstee 2001–08, hon sec 2004–08, hon vice-pres Section of Gen Practice with Primary Health Care 2004–07; DRCOG, FRCGP 2000 (MRCGP 1989), FRSH 2001, FFPH 2004 (MFPHM 1997), FRIPH 2005; *Recreations* opera, rugby; *Clubs* RSM; *Style—* Dr Quentin D Sandifer; ✉ 85 Henke Court, Schooner Way, Cardiff CF10 4EB

S

SANDILANDS, James Andrew Douglas; see: Torphichen, Lord

SANDISON, Francis Gunn; s of Capt Dr Andrew Tawse Sandison (d 1982), of Glasgow, and Dr Ann Brougham, née Austin; b 25 May 1949; Educ Glasgow Acad, Charterhouse, Magdalen Coll Oxford (MA, BCL); m 5 Sept 1981 (m dis 2007), Milva Lou, da of Prof John Emory McCaw, of Des Moines, Iowa; 1 s (Gavin b 1985); Career admitted slr 1974; ptnr Freshfields Bruckhaus Deringer 1980–2004 (asst slr 1974–80); memb: Law Soc 1974– (memb Tax Law Ctee 1992–2004, chm Corporation Tax Sub-Ctee 1993–99), City of London Law Soc 1980– (chm Revenue Law Sub-Ctee 1991–97), Addington Soc 1987–2004, Advsy Bd Fulbright Cmmn 1995–97, VAT Practitioners Gp 1996–2004, Tax Law Review Ctee 1997–2004, Tax Law Rewrite Consultative Ctee 2005–13; memb R Annan District Salmon Fishery Bd 2009– (vice-chm 2011–), tstee R Annan Tst 2011–; Distinguished Service Award City of London Law Soc 1997; Books Profit Sharing and Other Share Acquisition Schemes (1979), Whiteman on Income Tax (co-author 3 edn, 1988); Recreations fishing, wine, reading, cooking; Clubs Flyfishers', Yorkshire Fly Fishers'; Style— Francis Sandison, Esq; ✉ Cavendish Hill, Cavendish Terrace, Carlisle CA3 9NE (✆ 01228 520472, mobile 07801 782035, e-mail frankspeycaster253@btinternet.com)

SANDLER, Michael Stephen; s of Carl Bernard Sandler (d 1998), and Taube Irene Barash (d 1980); b 17 October 1947; Educ Leeds GS, Boston Univ (BA); m 1973, Gail Michele, da of late Dr David Granet, JP; 2 s (Andrew b 1975, Jonathan b 1978); Career qualified chartered surveyor; Conrad Ritblat & Co 1971–78, dir Streets Financial Ltd 1979–86, md Kingsway Financial Public Relations (Saatchi & Saatchi Co) 1986–88, chm Hudson Sandler Ltd 1988–; ARICS; Recreations theatre, cinema, golf, opera; Style— Michael Sandler, Esq; ✉ 2 Marston Close, London NW6 4EU (✆ 020 7328 7510); Hudson Sandler Ltd, 29 Cloth Fair, London EC1A 7JQ (✆ 020 7796 4133)

SANDS, (John) Derek; s of Reginald Sands (d 1971), of Manchester, and Elizabeth, née Whitlow (d 1988); b 26 January 1940; Educ Manchester Grammar, Univ of Manchester (LLB); m 1, 7 May 1966, Sylvia Rose (d 1981); 1 s (Christopher Andrew b 12 April 1967), 2 da (Amanda Melanie b 19 Dec 1968, Rachel Elizabeth b 15 Oct 1972); m 2, 7 Sept 1982, Kathleen; Career asst slr: Addleshaw Sons & Latham 1965–66 (articled clerk 1961–65), Cartwright & Backhouse 1966–67; ptnr Kirk Jackson (now Rowlands Slrs) 1968–2009 (asst slr 1967–68); Law Soc: memb Cncl 1986–2000, chm Family Law Ctee 1990–91, chm Courts and Legal Servs Ctee 1996–99, chm of various Law Soc working parties and task forces; chm Manchester Young Slrs' Assoc 1973–74, memb Cncl Manchester Law Soc 1974–2000 (pres 1985–86); author of numerous articles in legal jls incl Law Society's Gazette and Solicitor's Jl; memb: Law Soc 1965, Manchester Law Soc 1965; Recreations tennis, reading, music, gardening, travel, food, wine; Style— Derek Sands, Esq

SANDS, Jonathan Peter; OBE (2011); s of Peter Stuart Sands, of Buxton, Derbys, and Vivianne Anne, née Kidd; b 27 March 1961; Educ Normanton Sch, Stockport Coll of Technol; m 17 Sept 1983, Carolyn Jane, da of Norman Fletcher; 2 s (Thomas Charles b 9 March 1986, Henry George b 5 Oct 1993), 1 da (Polly Kate b 17 Sept 1992); Career IAS Advertising Macclesfield 1979–82, md Elmwood Design (pt of The Charles Wall Group before MBO 1989) 1985– (joined 1982); recipient numerous design awards incl Design Effectiveness, Clio, Mobius, Int Brand Packaging and NY Festivals; chm DBA 1995–97 (formerly dir), memb Cncl Design Cncl, former memb Cncl RSA; broadcaster and columnist; regular lectr at business confs, seminars and at univs on BA and MBA courses; memb DBA; memb Cncl RHS Yorkshire 2002–; Hon DSc Huddersfield Univ 2002; Recreations fast cars; Clubs Groucho, Harrogate Golf, Gullane Golf; Style— Jonathan Sands, Esq, OBE; ✉ Elmwood Design, 19–23 Fitzroy Street, London W1T 4BP

SANDS, Marc; s of Allan Sands and Ruth, née Buchholz; b 12 December 1963; Educ UC Sch London, Pembroke Coll Cambridge (MA), Univ of Bradford (MBA); m 11 Feb 1995, Lyndsay, née Griffiths; 2 s (Aldo, Emil); Career with: DMB & B London and NY offices 1987–91, SP Lintas 1992–93, Howell Henry Chaldecott Lury 1994–97; mktg dir Granada TV 1997–98, dir of brand mktg ONdigital (formerly BDB) 1998–2000, mktg dir Guardian Newspapers Ltd 2001–10, dir of audiences and media Tate 2010–; Recreations Arsenal FC (season-ticket holder), running, skiing; Style— Marc Sands, Esq; ✉ Tate, Millbank, London SW1P 4RG

SANDS, Peter; b 8 January 1962; Educ Univ of Oxford, Harvard Univ; Career McKinsey & Co: joined 1988, ptnr 1996–2002, dir 2000–02; Standard Chartered plc: gp fin dir 2002–06, gp chief exec 2006–; Style— Peter Sands, Esq; ✉ Standard Chartered Bank, 1 Basinghall Avenue, London EC2V 5DD

SANDS, Prof Philippe; QC; s of Alan Sands, of London, and Ruth, née Buchholz; b 17 October 1960, London; Educ Univ Coll Sch London, CCC Cambridge (BA, LLM); m 5 June 1993, Natalia Schiffrin; 1 s (Leo b 14 April 1995), 2 da (Lara b 16 May 1997, Katya b 11 April 2000); Career res fell St Catharine's Coll Cambridge 1984–88, lectr faculty of law KCL 1988–92, lectr, reader then prof SOAS Univ of London 1992–2001, prof of law UCL 2001–; Film My Nazi Legacy: What Our Fathers Did 2015; Publications Principles of International Environmental Law (2 edn 2003), Lawless World (2005), Torture Team (2008), Bowett's Law of International Institutions (6 edn 2009), East West Street: On the Origins of Genocide and Crimes against Humanity (2016), City of Lions (2016); Recreations skiing, Arsenal; Style— Prof Philippe Sands, QC; ✉ 50 Willow Road, London NW3 1TP (✆ 020 7404 3447, fax 020 7404 3448, e-mail p.sands@ucl.ac.uk)

SANDS, Sir Roger Blakemore; KCB (2006); s of Thomas Blakemore Sands (d 1980), and Edith Malyon, née Waldram (d 1986); b 6 May 1942; Educ UCS Hampstead, Oriel Coll Oxford (scholar, MA); m 24 Sept 1966, Jennifer Ann, da of Hugh T Cattell (d 1992); 1 da and 1 da decd; Career Clerks Dept House of Commons 1965–2006; princ clerk of: Overseas Office 1987–91, Select Ctees (and registrar of Members' Interests) 1991–94, Public Bills 1994–97, Legislation 1998–2001; clerk asst 2001–03, clerk and chief exec of House of Commons 2003–06; chm Study of Parliament Gp 1993–96; chm Standards Ctee Mid Sussex DC 2007–12, ind memb UK Public Affrs Cncl (UKPAC) 2010–14, ind person on standards issues Mid Sussex DC 2013–16; Style— Sir Roger Sands, KCB; ✉ No 4 (The Ashurst Suite), Woodbury House, Lewes Road, East Grinstead, West Sussex RH19 3UD (✆ 01342 302245)

SANDS, Sarah; Educ Goldsmiths Coll (BA); Career dep ed Daily Telegraph 1996–2004, ed Sunday Telegraph 2005, conslt ed Daily Mail 2006, ed-in-chief Reader's Digest UK 2008–09; Evening Standard: dep ed 2009–12, ed 2012–; Style— Ms Sarah Sands; ✉ London Evening Standard, Northcliffe House, 2 Derry Street, London W8 5EE

SANDWICH, 11 Earl of (E 1660); John Edward Hollister Montagu; also Viscount Hinchingbrooke and Baron Montagu, of St Neots (both E 1660); s of (Alexander) Victor Edward Paulet Montagu (10 Earl of Sandwich, who disclaimed peerages for life 1964; d 1995), and his 1 w, Rosemary (Maud), née Peto (d 1998); b 11 April 1943; Educ Eton, Trinity Coll Cambridge (MA); m 1 July 1968, (Susan) Caroline, o da of Rev Canon Perceval Ecroyd Cobham Hayman, of Rogate, W Sussex; 2 s (Luke Timothy Charles Montagu, Viscount Hinchingbrooke b 1969, Hon Orlando William b 1971), 1 da (Jemima Mary b 1973); Heir s, Viscount Hinchingbrooke; Career editorial conslt; info offr Christian Aid 1974–86 (memb Bd 1999–2004), conslt ed Save the Children Fund 1987–92, conslt CARE Int 1989–94, memb Cncl Anti Slavery Int 1997–2006, govr Beaminster Sch 1997–2004; jt owner/admin Mapperton Estate Dorset; elected hereditary peer House of Lords 1999–; memb: Constitution Ctee 2005–07, EU Ctee 2010–15, EU External Affrs Ctee 2013–15; pres: Samuel Pepys Club 1985–, Ind Asylum Cmmn 2006–08; Books Book of the World (1971), Prospects for Africa (jt ed, 1988), Prospects for Africa's Children (1990),

Children at Crisis Point (1992), Hinch: A Celebration (jt ed, 1997); Style— The Rt Hon the Earl of Sandwich; ✉ House of Lords, London SW1A 0PW

SANGER, Christopher; s of James Sanger, and Madeline Sanger; b 3 July 1970, London; Educ Shrewsbury, Lady Margaret Hall Oxford (MA), Warwick Business Sch (MBA); m 7 Sept 2002, Gillian; 1 da (Octavia b 28 Oct 2003), 1 s (Henry b 15 July 2005); Career chartered accountant Arthur Andersen 1992–98, head of business tax policy HM Treasy 1998–2001, head of tax policy devpt Deloitte & Touche 2002–04, ptnr and global head of tax policy Ernst & Young LLP 2005–; chm Tax Policy ICAEW, chm Tax Faculty ICAEW 2009–11, chm Mgmnt of Taxes Chartered Inst of Taxation 2011–13; memb Tax Law Review Ctee Inst for Fiscal Studies, memb HM Treasy Tax Professionals Forum 2011–, memb UN Subctee on Extractive Industries Taxation Issues for Developing Countries 2014–; CTA 1995, FCA 1996; Recreations tennis, family, Scottish dancing; Clubs Hurlingham; Style— Christopher Sanger, Esq; ✉ Ernst & Young LLP, 1 More London Place, London SE1 2AF (✆ 020 7951 0150, e-mail csanger@uk.ey.com or chris@csanger.com)

SANGER, James Gerald; s of Gerald Fountain Sanger, CBE, JP (d 1981), and (Margaret) Hope Sanger, MBE (d 1994); b 29 April 1939; Educ Shrewsbury, Worcester Coll Oxford (MA), Harvard Business Sch (MBA); m 21 Sept 1968, Madeline Mary, da of George William Jack Collis (d 1986); 1 s (Christopher James b 1970), 1 da (Katherine Hope b 1972); Career Farrow Bersey Gain Vincent & Co 1962–63 (articled 1957–59), asst to chm Associated Newspapers 1966–68 (joined 1963), md First Investors Ltd 1969–75, dir Henderson Administration 1974–75; fin dir: Blyth Greene Jourdain 1975–77, James Burrough plc 1977–84; exec dir: Tomkins plc 1985–88, Peek plc 1988–98, Associated Holdings Ltd 1998–2001, Liontrust Asset Mgmnt plc 1999–2010; dep chm: Stenoak Associated Services plc 1999–2001, Articon-Integralis AG 2000–05, DeRisk IT Ltd 2002–05, @Futsal Ltd 2009–, AtFutsal Gp Ltd 2010–; govr: Benenden Sch 1975–2002, Shrewsbury Sch 1985–99, Wellington Coll 2002–09; dep chm Farnham Castle 1998–2008; FCA 1973; Recreations real and lawn tennis, golf, travel, poetry, listening, Richard III; Clubs Hurlingham (chm 2007–10); Style— James Sanger, Esq; ✉ Moreton House, Brightwell-cum-Sotwell, Oxfordshire OX10 0PT (✆ 01491 833655, fax 01491 836599, e-mail jim@jimsanger.com)

SANGHERA, District Judge Pal Singh; s of Harbans Singh, of London, and Mohinder, née Kaur; b 15 December 1953; Educ Southall GS, Middx Poly (BA), Coll of Law Chester; m 10 April 1977, Mohinder; 1 da (Sangeet b 1982), 1 s (Bhopinder b 1983); Career admitted slr 1979 (articles with Chapman Wells); asst slr Whiteley & Pickering 1979–82, slr Ian Burr 1982, ptnr Ian Burr & Co 1982, appointed dep district judge 1995, gained higher court rights of advocacy 1998, apppointed full time Coventry Combined Court Centre 1999, recorder of the Crown Ct 2003–; memb Assoc of District Judges 1999, assoc memb of Commonwealth Magistrates and Judges Assoc; fndr chm British Asian Business and Professionals Assoc 1991; senator Jr Chamber Int; tstee Gursewak Tst; Recreations archery, voluntary organisations; Style— District Judge Sanghera

SANGHERA, Sathnam; Educ Wolverhampton GS, Christ's Coll Cambridge; Career journalist; with FT 1998–2006, columnist and feature writer The TImes 2007–, radio presenter BBC; Young Journalist of the Year British Press Awards 2002, Article of the Year Management Today 2005, Newspaper Feature of the Year Workworld Media Awards 2005, HR Journalist of the Year Watson Wyatt Awards for Excellence 2006 and 2009, Media Commentator of the Year Comment Awards 2015; Books The Boy with the Topknot: A Memoir of Love, Secrets and Lies in Wolverhampton (2009), Marriage Material (2014); Style— Mr Sathnam Sanghera

SANGSTER, Bruce; s of George Robertson Sangster, and Marie, née Davidson; b 12 March 1954; Educ Broxburn Acad Broxburn; m 22 Sept 1979, Jacqueline E R, da of John MacMillan Willison; 1 s (Jamie Sangster b 15 Aug 1982); Career commis chef then sr sous chef Old Course Hotel (British Transport Hotels) 1971–80, lectr Kingsway Tech Coll Dundee 1980–81; chef de cuisine: Kirroughtree Hotel Newton Stewart 1981–82, Rothley Court Hotel Rothley Leicestershire 1982–86, Balcraig House Hotel Scone Perthshire 1986–87; exec chef: Murrayshall Country House Hotel Scone Perthshire 1987–93, Lehman Brothers London 1993–2002; head chef and prop Sangster's Elie 2003–; memb Steering Ctee Scottish Chefs' Assoc 1993; CFA 1975; memb: Master Chefs of GB 1985– (chm Scot Div 1989–), Craft Guild of Chefs 1990; Awards Silver Catch Fish Cookery award 1977, Gold medal Cold Fish Dish 1979, Bronze medal Fat Sculpture 1979, Gold medal Gourmet Entrée Dish 1981, semi finalist Br Chef of The Year 1982, finalist Br Chef of The Year 1984 and 1988, third prize Br Chef of The Year 1986 and 1990, AA rosette 1986–87, 1989 and 1990, Michelin Red M award 1987 and 1988, Taste of Scotland Restaurant of the Year 1988, Scottish Hotel Guide Restaurant of the Year 1989, Silver and Bronze award as memb Br Culinary Team at Food Asia '90 1990, winner Egon Ronay British Lamb Chef 1990, Hotel awarded Newcomer of The Year 1990, memb Culinary Olympic Team for Frankfurt 1990, Gold medal St Andrews Food Festival 1991, Gold medal Fat Sculpture Scothot Glasgow 1991, 3 AA Rosettes at Murrayshall 1991, Gold and Bronze medals at Culinary Olympics in Frankfurt (capt Scottish team) 1992, capt British team for Food Asia in Singapore 1994 (Gold medal Nat Hot Kitchen, Silver medal Nat Team Buffet, Nayati Trophy for Most Outstanding Nat Hot Team), third Kikkomans Master Chef of Great Britain 1994 (and winner 1997), Best Competition Chef Award Craft Guild of Chefs 1995 and 1997, Gold medals Team Buffet and Hot Kitchen Hotel Olympia Open Grand Prix 1996, capt Br Nat Team Berlin Culinary Olympics 1996, capt Scottish Nat Team World Culinary Championships Scot Hot Glasgow 1997, World Culinary Cup (Gold medal Team Buffet Best Overall 1998, Gold medal Hot Kitchen 1998), Silver Medal Hot Kitchen and Gold Medal Cold Buffet Coupe Mondial Igheo Basle Switzerland 1999, Chef of the Year Craft Guild of Chefs 2000, 1 Gold medal 2 Silver medals for National Team Buffet and Silver medal Hot Kitchen Culinary Olympics Germany 2000, Gold National Hot Team Kitchen Chef Ireland 2001, 3 Gold medal for National team Buffet and 1 Gold National Hot Kitchen World Culinary Grand Prix Glasgow 2001, Chef of the Year CIS Award 2009, Michelin star 2009–, nat team coach Scottish Culinary Team Culinary Olympics Erfurt Germany 2012; entries in Good Food Guide and Egon Ronay 1981–, admitted into Scot-hot Hall of Fame 2011 (for contributions to the Scottish Hospitality Industry); Style— Bruce Sangster, Esq

SANGSTER, Nigel; QC (1998); s of Dr H B Singh; b 16 February 1954; Educ Repton, Univ of Leeds (LLB); Career called to the Bar Middle Temple 1976 (bencher 2007); in practice specialising in fraud 1977–, recorder of the Crown Court 1997–; memb Bar Cncl 1994–2004 and 2012–, memb Criminal Bar Assoc; Style— Nigel Sangster, Esq, QC; ✉ 25 Bedford Row, London WC1R 4HD (✆ 020 7067 1500, e-mail mail@nigelsangster.qc.com)

SANKEY, Vernon Louis; s of Edward Sankey (d 1982), and Marguerite Elizabeth Louise, née Van Maurik (d 1962); b 9 May 1949; Educ Harrow, Oriel Coll Oxford (MA); m 5 June 1976, Elizabeth, da of Tom Knights (d 2000); 3 s (James Edward b 12 May 1979, Mark Henry b 14 July 1981, William Thomas b 1 Feb 1985), 1 da (Angela Louise (twin) b 14 July 1981); Career Reckitt & Colman plc: mgmnt trainee Food & Drink UK 1971–74, asst mangr Fin & Planning HQ London 1974–76, dir of planning Europe France 1976–78, gen mangr Denmark 1978–80, PA to chm and chief Exec HQ 1980–81, md France 1981–85, md Food & Drink Norwich 1985–89, chm and chief exec Reckitt & Colman Inc USA 1989–99, gp dir N America 1989–91, bd memb 1989–99, chief exec 1992–99; chm: Thomson Travel Group plc 2000, Gala Gp Holdings plc 2000–02, Beltpacker plc 2000–04, The Really Effective Devpt Co Ltd 2000–06, Photo-Me Int plc 2000–07, Firmenich

SA 2006–13; non-exec dir: Pearson plc 1993–2006, Allied Zurich plc 1998–2000, Zurich Allied AG 1998–2000, Zurich Fin Services 1998–2012, Taylor Woodrow 2004–07, Vividas plc 2005–07, Atos SE 2006–; memb Int Advsy Bd Korn/Ferry International 1994–2005; memb Bd: Grocery Mfrs of America (GMA) 1995–99, Food Standards Agency 2000–05, Cofra Holdings AG (Switzerland) 2001–07; memb Advsy Bd Proudfoot UK plc 2001–06; memb Advsy Bd GLP LLP 2004–; govr Harrow Sch 2001– (dir and chm Harrow Sch Enterprises Ltd 2001–), tstee John Lyon Charity/Royal Charter 2001–; MInstD 1995; FRSA 1999; *Recreations* jogging, tennis, fitness; *Clubs* Leander; *Style*— Vernon Sankey, Esq; ✉ e-mail vernonsankey@outlook.com

SANT CASSIA, Louis Joseph; s of Maj Henri Emmanuel Sant Cassia, ED (d 1990), of St Paul's Bay, Malta, and Anna, *née* De Piro Gourgion (d 1995); *b* 19 September 1946; *Educ* Lyceum Malta, Royal Univ of Malta (MD), Univ of Nottingham (DM); *m* 11 July 1974, Antoinette, da of Gerald H Ferro, MVO, MBE (d 2005),of Sliema, Malta; 1 s (Henri b 1977), 1 da (Emma b 1980); *Career* cmmnd 1 Bn King's Own Malta Regt 1968–72; goalkeeper Malta water polo team Med Games 1967; res fell Dept of Obstetrics and Gynaecology Nottingham 1981–83, conslt obstetrician and gynaecologist Coventry 1987–2011, lead clinician for gynaecological oncology in Warwickshire 1999–2007; Coventry Dist tutor RCOG 1988–94; hon lectr Univ of Malta 1997, hon reader Univ of Warwick 2008–11; examiner MRCOG; chm: Coventry Med Res and Ethics Ctee 1993–2004, Med Advsy Ctee Warwickshire Nuffield Hosp 1995–2000, chm Sr Hosp Medical Staff Ctee Coventry 2004–09; hon pres Birmingham and Midlands Obstetrical and Gynaecological Soc 2009–10, hon pres Nuffield Visiting Soc 2013–15 (hon vice-pres 2012); author various pubns on gynaecological oncology, subfertility, recurrent spontaneous miscarriages and research ethics; FRCOG 1992 (MRCOG 1979); *Recreations* gardening, melitensia; *Style*— Louis Joseph Sant Cassia, Esq; ✉ Four Winds, Stoneleigh Road, Blackdown, Leamington Spa CV32 6QR (☎ 01926 422147, e-mail ljsantcassia@hotmail.co.uk)

SANTA-OLALLA, Brig David Manuel; DSO (1995), MC (1976); s of Manolo Santa-Olalla, of Spain, and Ann Santa-Olalla; *b* 10 February 1953, London; *Educ* Mount St Mary's Coll, KCL (MA), RMA Sandhurst; *m* 17 July 1976, Joanna Mary, *née* Gilbert; 2 da (Lydia b 18 March 1980, Zoe b 25 Oct 1981), 2 s (Thomas b 15 Dec 1984, Harry b 10 Jan 1987); *Career* cmmnd Green Howards 1973, served in NW Europe, NI, Cyprus, Brunei and Hong Kong 1973–84, Army Staff Coll 1985, served in Germany, NI and USA 1986–92 (despatches 1991), CO 1 Bn Duke of Wellington's Regt NW Europe and Balkans 1992–94, cmmnd 2 Inf Bde 2001–04, UK military advsr to Govt of Sierra Leone 2005, UK military forces Cyprus 2006–08; clerk Leathersellers' Co 2009–; *Recreations* golf, fishing, cricket, kitesurfing; *Clubs* Naval & Military; *Style*— Brig David Santa-Olalla, DSO, MC; ✉ The Leathersellers' Company, 21 Garlick Hill, London EC4V 2AU (☎ 020 7330 1440)

SANTER, Diederick John; s of Mark Santer, ret Bishop of Birmingham, and Henrietta, *née* Westrate (d 1994); *b* 3 July 1969, Cambridge; *Educ* Univ of Leeds (BA); *Children* 1 da (Henrietta Joy b 2 Nov 2004); *Career* TV prodr; early career as actor, freelance script reader United Prodns 1996, then script ed Where The Heart Is (series 1 and 2), A&E (series 1 and 2, Granada) and The Last Train (Granada), with BBC Drama Prodn 2000–, prodr Cutting It (series 1–3), The Taming of the Shrew, Much Ado About Nothing (BBC1, Bafta nomination) and Jane Eyre (BBC) 2006 (10 Emmy nominations), exec prodr EastEnders (BBC1) 2006–10 (Best Soap Award Nat TV, Br Soap and TV Quick Awards 2008, Best Continuing Drama RTS Awards 2009, Best Continuing Drama BAFTA 2010), md Lovely Day (TV prodn co) 2010–; Kudos TV jt-CEO (2015–); memb BAFTA 2003; *Style*— Diederick Santer, Esq; ✉ Kudos Film and TV, 12–14 Amwell Street, London EC1R 1UQ

SANTO DOMINGO, Alejandro; s of Julio Mario Santo Domingo, of NYC, and Beatrice, *née* Davila; *b* 13 February 1977; *Educ* Harvard Coll (BA); *Career* md Quadrant Capital Advisors Inc NYC, vice-chm Latin America SABMiller plc, chm Bd Bavaria SA, chm Backus & Johnston, memb Bd Valorem; memb Bd: Aid for AIDS, DKMS; *Recreations* squash, hunting, reading; *Style*— Alejandro Santo Domingo, Esq; ✉ Quadrant Capital Advisors Inc, 499 Park Avenue, 24th Floor, New York, NY 10022 USA (☎ 00 1 646 282 2600)

SANTS, Sir Hector William Hepburn; kt (2013); s of (Hector) John Sants, of Oxford, and Elsie Ann Watt Hepburn; *b* 15 December 1955; *Educ* Clifton, CCC Oxford (MA); *m* 21 Dec 1987, Caroline Jane, da of Kenneth Ord Mackenzie; 3 s (Hector Alexander b 9 Jan 1989, Edward Kenneth Richard b 16 Oct 1990, Arthur Frederick Joseph b 15 May 1994); *Career* ptnr Phillips & Drew stockbrokers 1977–87, head of int securities Union Bank of Switzerland Securities Inc NY 1987–88, head of research Union Bank of Switzerland 1988, head of equities and vice-chm UBS Ltd 1988–98, chm DLJ Int Securities, head of int equities Donaldson Lufkin & Jenrette 1998–2000, head of int equities and vice-chm Credit Suisse First Boston 2000–01, ceo EMEA Credit Suisse First Boston 2001–04, md Wholesale and Institutional Markets FSA 2004–07, chief exec FSA 2007–12, head of compliance Barclays plc 2013–; dep govr designate Bank of England 2010–; advsr Public Tstee Office 1996–2000; memb: Stock Exchange Settlement Servs Bd 1990, Securities and Futures Authy Bd 1993–94, EASDAQ Bd 1996–99, London Stock Exchange Bd 1997–2001, Fin Law Panel 2001–02, Europe Bd NASDAQ 2001–03, FSA Practitioners Bd 2001–04, LCH Clearnet Bd 2003–04, Fin Reporting Cncl 2004–07, Bd Nuffield Orthopaedic Centre NHS Tst 2002–07; chm Advsy Bd Saïd Business Sch Univ of Oxford 2007–; *Style*— Sir Hector Sants

SAPHIR, Nicholas Peter George; *b* 30 November 1944; *Educ* City of London, Univ of Manchester (LLB); *m* 1971, Ena, da of Raphael Bodin; 1 s; *Career* called to the Bar Lincoln's Inn 1967; dir Bodin and Nielsen Ltd 1975–; chm: Hunter Saphir plc 1987–97, Organic Milk Supplies Co-operative Ltd (OMSCO) 2003–, Rural Revival 2004–07, Coressence 2006–15, Epicore Health Ltd 2015–; non-exec dir: Dairy Crest Ltd 1987–93, Albert Fisher Gp plc 1993–97, San Miguel SA 1993–98 and 2001–07; pres Fresh Produce Consortium 1997–2000; chm: Central Cncl for Agricultural and Horticultural Corp (CCAHC) 1980–83, Food From Britain 1983–87, Agricultural Forum 2001–04; memb Food and Drinks EDC 1984–87; chm: Br Israel C of C 1991–94, New Israel Fund for Social Justice and Equality 2009–15; *Publications* Farmed Out (2001), London Wholesale Markets Review for DEFRA and Corpn of London (2002); *Recreations* sailing, carriage driving; *Clubs* Farmers'; *Style*— Nicholas Saphir, Esq

SAPOCHNIK, Carlos Luis; s of Leon Sapochnik (d 1985), of Argentina, and Clara Aronovich; *b* 18 July 1944; *Educ* Buenos Aires Nat Univ, Royal Coll of Art (MA), Univ of East London (MA); *m* 1966, Victoria, da of Vicente Rosenberg; 1 da (Manuela Maria b 8 Sept 1972), 1 s (Miguel Vicente b 21 July 1974); *Career* freelance graphic designer and illustrator 1970–92; art dir Free Association Books 1984–88, creative dir Burnett Associates 1988–90, dir The Running Head Ltd; publishing clients incl: Methuen & Co, Tavistock Publications, Routledge, Hutchinson Educnl; local govt clients incl: London Borough of Hackney, GLC; theatre clients incl: Royal Court Theatre, Haymarket Leicester, Lyric Hammersmith; other clients incl: Midland Bank, CBS Records; pt/t lectr in graphic design: Chelsea Sch of Art 1981–84, Bath Acad of Art 1982–86; princ lectr in postgraduate design studies Middx Univ 1990–2011; Quality Assurance Agency specialist reviewer art and design 1998–2000; solo drawing exhibitions: Vortex Gallery 1989, Argile Gallery 1990, Diorama Gallery 1994, Espace Amigorena Paris 1994; two-man drawing exhibitions: Boundary Gallery 1988, Ben Uri Gallery 1996; group exhibitions incl: Dublin Arts Festival 1975, Warsaw Poster Biennale 1976, 1978 and 1980, Lahti Poster Biennale Finland 1978, 1979 and 1983, Brno Graphic Design Biennale Czechoslovakia 1984, 1986, 1988 and 1992, London Group Open 1992, Riviera Gallery 1994, Rexel Derwent Open 1994, Pastel Soc 1994, Ben Uri Gallery 1996, Cheltenham Open 1996; ind organizational conslt 2001–; staff, assoc dir, dir Group Relations conferences Br Assoc of Psychotherapists 2010, 2011 and 2012, Northern Sch of Child and Adolescent Psychotherapy 2011, Br Psychotherapy Fndn (BPF) 2013 and Tavistock & Portman NHS Tst 2014, 2015 and 2016; memb Int Soc for the Psychoanalytic Study of Organizations 2003; fell Int Soc of Typographic Designers 2000; FCSD 1991, FHEA 2002; *Publications* contrib: Jl of Organisational and Social Dynamics (2003 and 2015), Psychodynamic Practice Jl (2005), Tracey Jl (Loughborough Univ, 2013); *Style*— Carlos Sapochnik, Esq; ✉ 106 Victoria Road, London N22 7XF (☎ 020 8340 4873, e-mail carlos@sapochnik.com)

SARGEANT, Mark; s of Brian Anthony Sargeant, of Swanley, Kent, and Joan Rita Mollins; *b* 25 August 1973; *Educ* Oakwood Park GS Maidstone, West Kent Coll Tonbridge; *Career* commis chef Boodle's 1993–94; chef: Reads Restaurant 1994–96, Le Soufflé 1996, Coast 1996–97, Aubergine 1997–98, Gordon Ramsay Restaurant 1998–2001; chef de cuisine Gordon Ramsay at Claridges 2001–08 (1 Michelin Star, 3 AA Rosettes, Tatler Restaurant of the Year 2002), mangr The Warrington 2008–; prop: Rocksalt Restaurant Folkestone 2011–, The Smokehouse Fish and Chips Folkestone 2011–; Young Chef of the Year 1996, Chef of the Year 2002; *Style*— Mark Sargeant, Esq

SARGENT, Kathryn; da of Anthony Sargent (d 2013), and Margaret, *née* Stevenson, of Leeds; *b* 7 June 1974, Leeds; *Educ* BA; *Career* master tailor; cutter Gieves and Hawkes 1996–2009, head cutter Gieves and Hawkes 2009–12, owner and head cutter Kathryn Sargent Ltd 2012–; technical judge Golden Shears Awards, external assessor Nat Tailoring Acad Dublin Ireland; Best Womenswear Winner Golden Shears Competition 1998; *Style*— Ms Kathryn Sargent; ✉ Kathryn Sargent Bespoke Tailoring, 6 Brook Street, London W1S 1BB (☎ 020 7493 2450, e-mail kathryn@kathrynsargent.com, website www.kathrynsargent.com, Twitter @KSargentBespoke)

SARNE, Tanya; OBE (2011); *see:* Gordon, Tanya Joan

SAROOSHI, Prof Dan; s of R and R Sarooshi; *Educ* Univ of NSW (LLB, BComm), KCL (LLM), LSE (PhD); *Career* legal asst to Prof Rosalyn Higgins, QC 1991–95, legal assoc Office of the Prosecutor UN War Crimes Tbnl for the Former Yugoslavia The Hague 1996–97, of counsel Tite & Lewis 2001–04, barr and door tenant Essex Court Chambers 2005–; teaching fell in public int law Dept of Law LSE 1993–96, sr lectr then reader in public int law and convenor of int law courses UCL 1997–2003, Herbert Smith Univ lectr in int economic law then reader in public int law Univ of Oxford 2003–06, prof of public int law Faculty of Law Univ of Oxford 2006–, sr research fell Queen's Coll Oxford 2012– (tutorial fell 2003–12); dir Hague Acad of Int Law Centre for Research in Int Law and Int Relations 2011; memb: World Trade Orgn Dispute Settlement List of Panellists 2006–, Exec Cncl American Soc of Int Law 2008–; Emile Noël Fellowship Jean Monnet Center for Int and Regnl Economic Law and Justice NY Univ Sch of Law 2002; Hon MA Univ of Oxford 2003; FRSA 2006; *Books* The United Nations and the Development of Collective Security: the Delegation by the United Nations Security Council of its Chapter VII Powers (1999, Guggenheim Prize 1999, American Soc of Int Law Cert of Merit 2001), Issues of State Responsibility before International Judicial Institutions (jt ed, 2004), International Organizations and their Exercise of Sovereign Powers (2005, American Soc of Int Law Book Prize 2006, American Soc for the Policy Sciences Myers S McDougal Prize 2006), Responsibility, Immunities, and Remedies for the Acts of Int Organizations (2014); *Recreations* jazz, opera; *Style*— Prof Dan Sarooshi; ✉ Essex Court Chambers, 24 Lincoln's Inn Fields, London WC2A 3EG (☎ 020 7813 8000, e-mail dsarooshi@essexcourt.net)

SARWAR, Anas; *b* 14 March 1983; *Educ* Hutchesons' GS Glasgow, Univ of Glasgow; *m* Furheen; 2 c; *Career* MP (Lab) Glasgow Central 2010–15, dep ldr Scottish Lab Pty 2011–; *Style*— Anas Sarwar, Esq; ✉ House of Commons, London SW1A 0AA

SASSOON, Adrian David; s of Hugh Meyer Sassoon, of London, and Marion Julia, *née* Schiff; *b* 1 February 1961; *Educ* Eton, Inchbald Sch of Design, Christie's Fine Arts Course; *Career* asst curator Dept of Decorative Arts J Paul Getty Museum Calif 1982–84 (curatorial asst 1980–82), dir Alexander & Berendt Ltd London 1990–92 (asst to md 1987–89); lectr on/dealer in French decorative arts, 18th century Sèvres porcelain and contemporary British ceramics and glass; treas and memb Ctee French Porcelain Soc 1989–95 (joined as memb 1985); memb: Cncl The Attingham Tst for the Study of the Country House 1990–95, Patrons of British Art Acquisitions Sub-Ctee Tate Gallery London 1997–99; tstee: Hermitage Fndn UK (formerly UK Friends of the Heritage Museum St Petersburg), Wallace Collection London 2007–15, Silver Tst 2013–; articles on French 18th century decorative arts in the J Paul Getty Museum Jls 1981–85; *Books* Decorative Arts: A Handbook of the J Paul Getty Museum (1986), Catalogue of Vincennes and Sèvres Porcelain in the J Paul Getty Museum (1991), Vincennes and Sèvres Porcelain from a European Collection (2001), Jewels by JAR (Metropolitan Museum of Art) (2013); *Clubs* Lyford Cay (Nassau), Brooks's; *Style*— Adrian Sassoon, Esq; ✉ e-mail email@adriansassoon.com

SASSOON, Baron (Life Peer UK 2010), of Ashley Park in the County of Surrey; Sir James Meyer Sassoon; kt (2007); s of Hugh Meyer Sassoon, of London, and Marion Julia, *née* Schiff; *b* 11 September 1955; *Educ* Eton, ChCh Oxford (exhibitioner, MA, Gibbs book prize); *m* 23 Oct 1981, Sarah Caroline Ray, da of Sir (Ernest) John Ward Barnes; 1 s (Frederick b 1 April 1987), 2 da (Alexandra b 6 Nov 1990, Victoria b 4 June 1994); *Career* Thomson McLintock & Co 1977–86, S G Warburg & Co Ltd 1987–95 (dir 1991–95); UBS Warburg (formerly Warburg Dillon Read): md 1995–2002, vice-chm Investment Banking 2000–02; HM Treasy: md Finance, Regulation and Industry 2002–06, Chllr's rep for promotion of the City 2006–08, commercial sec to the Treasy and Treasy spokesman House of Lords 2010–13; exec dir Jardine Matheson Hldgs 2013–; dir: HBV Enterprise 2000–02, Partnerships UK plc 2002–06, The Merchants Tst plc 2006–10 (chm 2010), Nuclear Liabilities Fund 2008–10, Dairy Farm Int 2013–, Hongkongland Hldgs 2013–, Jardine Lloyd Thompson 2013–, Mandarin Oriental Int 2013–; pres Financial Action Task Force 2007–08, memb Economic Recovery Ctee of the Shadow Cabinet 2009–10, memb Global Advsy Bd Mitsubishi UFJ Financial Gp 2013–, chm China-Britain Business Cncl 2013–; contrib articles to art and fin jls; tstee: Gerald Coke Handel Fndn 2001–10, Nat Gallery Tst 2002–09, Br Museum 2009–10 and 2013–; memb: Advsy Bd Resolution Fndn 2007–10, French Porcelain Soc, Ctee Hong Kong Assoc 2013–; govr Ashdown House Sch 2001–06, chm ifs Sch of Finance 2009–10; FCA 1991 (ACA 1980); *Publications* The Tripartite Review (2009); *Recreations* travel, the arts, watching sport; *Clubs* MCC; *Style*— The Rt Hon the Lord Sassoon; ✉ Matheson & Co, 3 Lombard Street, London EC3V 9AQ (☎ 020 7816 8100)

SATCH, William; *b* 9 June 1989; *Educ* Shiplake Coll Henley-on-Thames; *Career* rower; achievements incl: Bronze medal (eights) World Rowing U23 Championships 2010 and 2011, Bronze medal (coxless pair) Olympic Games 2012; *Clubs* Leander; *Style*— William Satch, Esq

SATTERTHWAITE, Christopher James; s of Col Richard George Satterthwaite, LVO, OBE (d 1993), of Petersfield, W Sussex, and Rosemary, *née* Messervy; *b* 21 May 1956; *Educ* Ampleforth, Lincoln Coll Oxford (MA); *m* 30 Jan 1988, Teresa Mary, da of Cdr L Bailey; 2 s (James Richard b 29 Oct 1988, Henry Frank b 8 Nov 1989), 1 da (Eleanor Sara b 6 Feb 1992); *Career* graduate trainee H J Heinz Ltd 1979–81, IMP Ltd 1981–93 (md 1987–93), dir HHCL and Partners 1993–99, chief exec Bell Pottinger Communications 1999–2000, chief exec Chime Communications 2000–; sr ind dir Centaur Media plc 2007–; dir Business in the Community; chm Roundhouse; former chm Mktg Soc; *Recreations* fly

S

fishing, escapology, bombology, motorbikes; *Style*— Christopher Satterthwaite, Esq; ✉ Chime Communications Ltd, 62 Buckingham Gate, London SW1E 6AJ (☎ 020 7096 5825, e-mail csatterthwaite@chimegroup.com)

SAUL, Christopher; *Career* Slaughter and May: joined as trainee slr 1977, ptnr 1986–, sr ptnr 2008–; *Style*— Christopher Saul, Esq; ✉ Slaughter and May, 1 Bunhill Row, London EC1Y 8YY

SAUL, Roger John; s of (Frederick) Michael Saul, of Chilcompton, Somerset, and Joan, *née* Legg; *b* 25 July 1950; *Educ* Kingswood Sch Bath, Westminster Coll London; *m* 23 July 1977, Marion Joan, da of Clifford Cameron; 3 s (William Michael, Cameron Robert, Frederick Jakes); *Career* fndr, creator, designer and pres Mulberry 1971–2002 (memb Bd until 2003), brand label in Br contemporary classic fashion worldwide; fndr Charlton House (restaurant and hotel) 1996 (Michelin star 1998–2003), launched Monty's (beauty product and spa range) 2004, co-fndr bottletop charity (with son Cameron) to raise funds and awareness for disadvantaged youth worldwide 2004, launched Sharpham Park (rare breed meat) and Spelt products (flour and cereal range) 2005, built first organic spelt flour mill in UK 2006, fndr and exec chm Kilver Court Designer Outlet Village, organic farm shop and gardens 2011; curator for eco cars Prince of Wales' Start initiative 2011, dir EV Cup electric car race series 2011; govr Kingswood Sch 2006; awarded Queen's Award for Export 1979, 1989 and 1996, BKCEC Exporter of the Year 1987–88, 1990 and 1996, Classic Designer of the Year 1992; *Publications* Mulberry At Home, The Spelt Cookbook, Spelt Recipe Book (2015); *Recreations* tennis, t'ai chi, gardening; *Style*— Roger Saul, Esq; ✉ Kilver Court, Shepton Mallet, Somerset BA4 5NF (☎ 01749 340428)

SAUMAREZ; *see:* de Saumarez

SAUMAREZ SMITH, Dr Charles Robert; CBE (2008); s of William Hanbury Saumarez Smith, OBE (d 1994), and Alice Elizabeth Harness, *née* Raven; *b* 28 May 1954; *Educ* Marlborough, King's Coll Cambridge (scholar, MA), Harvard Univ (Henry fellow), Warburg Inst Univ of London (PhD); *m* Romilly Le Quesne, *née* Savage; 2 s (Otto Livingstone b 1987, Ferdinand Le Quesne b 1990); *Career* Christie's research fell and dir of studies (history of art) Christ's Coll Cambridge 1979–82; V&A: asst keeper (responsible for V&A/RCA MA course in history of design) 1982–90, head of research 1990–94; dir National Portrait Gallery 1994–2002, dir National Gallery 2002–07, sec and ceo Royal Acad 2007–; visiting fell Yale Center for British Art 1983, Benno M Forman fellowship H F du Pont Winterthur Museum 1988, South Square fell RCA 1990, Slade prof Univ of Oxford 2002, visiting prof Grad Sch of Humanities Queen Mary Univ of London 2007–10 (visiting prof Sch of History 2010–); memb: Ctee Design History Soc 1985–89, Ctee Soc of Architectural Historians 1987–90, Editorial Bd Art History 1988–93, Exec Ctee Assoc of Art Historians 1990–94, Exec Ctee London Library 1992–96, Cncl Charleston Tst 1993–2015, Advsy Bd Fondazione Palazzo Strozzi 2008–13; tstee: Soane Monuments Tst 1988–2006, Prince's (now Royal) Drawing Sch 2003–16, Public Catalogue Fndn 2003–15; memb Advsy Cncl: Paul Mellon Centre for Studies in British Art 1995–99, Warburg Inst 1996–2003, Inst of Historical Research 1999–2003, Sch of Advanced Studies Univ of London 2003–07; pres Museums Assoc 2004–06 (memb Cncl 1998–2001, vice-pres 2002–04); govr Univ of the Arts 2001–13; Alice Davis Hitchcock medallion 1990; Hon DLitt: UEA 2001, Univ of Westminster 2002, Univ of London 2003, Univ of Sussex 2003, Univ of Essex 2005; hon fell Christ's Coll Cambridge 2002; Hon FRCA 1991, FRSA 1995, FSA 1997, Hon FRIBA 2000; *Publications* The Building of Castle Howard (1990), Eighteenth-Century Decoration: Design and the Domestic Interior in England (1993), The National Portrait Gallery (1997), The National Gallery: a short history (2009), The Company of Artists: the Origins of the Royal Academy of Arts in London (2012), New Annals of the Club (contrib, 2014); *Clubs* Brooks's; *Style*— Dr Charles Saumarez Smith, CBE, FSA; ✉ website www.charlessaumarezsmith.com; The Royal Academy of Arts, Burlington House, Piccadilly, London W1J 0BD (☎ 020 7300 8006, fax 020 7300 8026, e-mail chiefexecutive@royalacademy.org.uk)

SAUNDERS, Amanda Jane; da of Robin Saunders, of Worthing, W Sussex, and Angela, *née* Harman; *b* 1964, Rustington, W Sussex; *Educ* Gaisford HS Worthing, Univ of Warwick (BA); *m* 2005, Johnny Ellis; 2 s (Alfred Stanley b 2001, Frederick John b 2003); *Career* Royal Over-Seas League 1987–90, London Zoo 1990–93, Museum of London 1993–95, NSPCC 1995–2000, Br Museum 2000–02, ROH 2002– (dir of devpt 2005–); tstee Battersea Arts Centre 2007–, Clod Ensemble; *Recreations* walking by the sea, reading, family, friends, food; *Clubs* Soho House, Quo Vadis; *Style*— Ms Amanda Saunders; ✉ Royal Opera House, Bow Street, Covent Garden, London WC2E 9DD (☎ 020 7212 9193)

SAUNDERS, Dr Ann Loreille; MBE; da of George Cox-Johnson (d 1941), and Joan Loreille, *née* Clowser (d 1980); *b* 23 May 1930; *Educ* Henrietta Barnett Sch, Queen's Coll Harley St, UCL (BA), Univ of Leicester (PhD); *m* 4 June 1960, Bruce Kemp Saunders, s of Kemp Alexander Saunders (d 1973); 1 s (Matthew Kemp b 1964), 1 da (Katherine Sophia Loreille b 1967 d 1984); *Career* dep librarian Lambeth Palace Library 1952–55, asst keeper Br Museum 1955–56, borough archivist St Marylebone Public Library 1956–63, asst to the Hon Ed Jl of the British Archaeological Assoc 1963–75, hon ed Costume Soc 1967–2008, hon ed London Topographical Soc 1975–2015; pt/t lectr: Richmond Coll Kensington 1979–92, City Univ 1981–2007; contrib to various jls incl Geographical Magazine, Burlington Magazine and The London Journal; hon fell UCL 1991 (hon research fell Dept of History 1995–97); FSA; *Books* John Bacon RA, 1740–1799 (as Ann Cox-Johnson, 1961), Regent's Park: A Study of the Development of the Area from 1066 to the Present Day (1969), Arthur Mee's King's England Series: London North of the Thames (revised 1972), London: The City and Westminster (revised 1975), Regent's Park (revised, 1981), The Regent's Park Villas (1981), The Art and Architecture of London: An Illustrated Guide (won London Tourist Bd award for specialist guidebook of the year 1984, 2 edn 1988, reprinted 1992 and 1996), St Martin in the Fields: A Short History and Guide (1989), The Royal Exchange: a short history (1991, ed and co-wrote extended edn 1997), St Paul's: The Story of the Cathedral (2001), The History of the Merchant Taylors' Company (with Matthew Davies, 2004), Historic Views of London (2008), St Paul's Cathedral - 1400 Years at the Heart of London (2012); *Recreations* reading, embroidery, cooking, walking, studying London, going to exhibitions and the theatre and to churches; *Style*— Dr Ann Saunders, MBE, FSA; ✉ 3 Meadway Gate, London NW11 7LA

SAUNDERS, Dr (William) Anthony; s of Robert Valentine Saunders (d 1997), of Sneyd Park, Bristol, and Mary Isabel, *née* Kerr (d 2013); *b* 24 June 1940; *Educ* Clifton, Trinity Coll Cambridge (MA, MB BChir, MRCPsych, DPM, DCH); *m* 11 Feb 1967, Angela Pauline, da of Charles Alan Rapson (d 1971), of Topsham, Exeter; 2 da (Emma b 13 March 1968, Annabel b 29 July 1972), 1 s (Jonathan b 7 May 1970); *Career* conslt in child and adolescent pyschiatry 1973–2011, hon clinical lectr Univ of Southampton 1973–2011, conslt Marchwood Priory Hosp Southampton, conslt Winchester Coll, ret; former chm Wessex Child Psychiatrists, past nat chm Ctee of Mgmnt Assoc for Professionals in Servs for Adolescents; vol Stroke Assoc; Hospital Prize for Forensic Medicine; FRCPsych; *Publications* Tony Saunders Stroke Survivor (BMJ Blog, 2012); *Clubs* Wine Label Circle; *Style*— Dr Anthony Saunders; ✉ Meadow Cottage, Otterbourne, Winchester, Hampshire SO21 2EQ (☎ 01962 713129)

SAUNDERS, Dan; *Educ* Univ of Oxford (BA), Manchester Business Sch (MBA); *m* Sabita Gottumukkala; 2 s (Hal, Asoka); *Career* dir of mktg Nat Geographic Channels 2000–06, mktg conslt Sparrowhawk Media 2006–07, mktg mangr Packet Vision 2007–08, dir of content services Samsung Electronics Europe 2008–13, head Living Room Products Northern Europe Google 2013–; *Recreations* opera, walking, fly fishing; *Style*— Dan Saunders, Esq; ✉ Google, Central St Giles, 1–13 St Giles High Street, London WC2H 8AG

SAUNDERS, David John; s of James Saunders (d 1986), and Margaret, *née* Christy; *b* 4 August 1953; *Educ* Kingston Poly (BSc), Aston Univ (PhD); *m* 6 Sept 1975, Elizabeth Jean, da of Mandel Coutier Hodgson; 2 da (Zoë Alice b 1 March 1977, Jessica Elizabeth b 23 March 1988), 2 s (Robin Edward James b 23 May 1979, Tobias David Oliver b 4 Jan 1982); *Career* mgmnt trainee Serck Ltd 1975–78; DTI: trg posts then successively asst private sec to sec of state and private sec to jr min 1978–84, on loan to OFT 1984–87 (dep head Mergers Branch 1986–87), with Privatisation of Br Steel Unit 1987–88, export dir SE Office 1988–90, regnl mgmnt support offr 1990, sec BOTB and dir Jt Export Promotion Directorate (JEPD) 1990–95, dir Nuclear Power Privatisation Team 1995–96, dir Oil and Gas Div 1996–98; regnl dir Govt Office for the SE (GOSE) 1998–2002, dir business support DTI 2002–04, dir consumer and competition policy 2004–09, chief exec Competition Cmmn 2009–14, sr advsr Fin Conduct Authy 2014–, special advsr Europe Economics 2014–; *Recreations* swimming, cycling, photography, diving; *Clubs* Reform; *Style*— David Saunders, Esq; ✉ Financial Conduct Authority, 25 The North Colonnade, Canary Wharf, London E14 5HS

SAUNDERS, Dr Frances Carolyn; CB (2011); *née* Reger; da of Archibald John Christopher Reger, MBE (d 2006), and Joyce Anne, *née* Wood (d 2011); *b* 28 June 1954, Cambridge; *Educ* Univ of Nottingham (BSc, PhD); *m* 23 April 1977, Martin Vernon Saunders; *Career* grad trainee and electronic engr British Leyland 1975–78, research scientist RSRE 1978–88, manager Research Divs RSRE/Defence Research Agency 1988–92, head technical policy Technical Directorate Defence Research Agency 1992–95, Royal Coll of Defence Studies 1995, dir strategy and implementation Defence Test & Evaluation Orgn 1995–97, dir Centre for Defence Analysis 1997–2000, dir Research Cncls Office of Sci and Technol DTI 2000–03; pres Inst of Physics 2013–15; Defence Sci and Technol Lab MOD: tech dir 2003–05, acting chief exec and operations dir 2005–06, chief exec 2006–12; memb Steering Bd UK Space Agency 2015–; tstee Engrg Devpt Tst 2012, tstee Royal Acad of Engrg 2015–; memb Cncl Cranfield Univ 2008–16; DSc (hc) Univ of Nottingham 2015; FInstP 1999, FREng 2011; *Recreations* walking, cycling, sailing, music, guitar; *Style*— Dr Frances Saunders, CB, FREng, CEng, CPhys, FInstP; ✉ Institute of Physics, 76 Portland Place, London W1B 1NT

SAUNDERS, Graham Eric; s of Arthur Frank Saunders (d 1960), of York, and Ivy Ethel Saunders (d 2003); *b* 3 April 1945; *Educ* Archbishop Holgate's GS York, Univ of Durham (BSc, DipHSM); *m* 20 Dec 1969, Valerie, *née* Barton; 1 da (Elizabeth Helen b 23 Dec 1977), 1 s (Christopher Andrew b 25 Jan 1982); *Career* VSO 1966–67, nat admin trainee Sheffield Regnl Hosp Bd 1967–69, dep hosp sec Sunderland Gen Hosp 1969–70, sr admin asst Gp HQ Sunderland Hosp Mgmnt Ctee 1970–72, hosp sec Sunderland Royal Infirmary 1972–74, gen administrator (operational servs) Durham Health Dist 1974–77, dep chief administrator Leeds Eastern Health Dist 1977–81, dist gen mangr Harrogate HA 1985–92 (chief administrator 1982–85), chief exec Harrogate Health Care NHS Tst 1992–2001, chief exec W Yorks NHS Workforce Devpt Confedn 2001–05, policy advsr NHS Employers 2005–10, ind healthcare conslt 2005–10; ptnr Postgrad Medical Educn Trg Bd 2009–10, lay ptnr GMC 2010–; dir N Yorks TEC 1989–92, memb Nat Cncl Inst of Health Servs Mgmnt 1987–93, Yorks chm 1996–97; chm Magistrates Bench Trg Ctee 2009–12, dep chm Harrogate and Skipton Bench 2013–15; JP Harrogate and Skipton 1995–2015; govr Harrogate Coll 1985–97; FIHM 1999; *Recreations* walking, theatre, opera, good food; *Clubs* Rotary Club of Harrogate (pres 2015–16); *Style*— Graham Saunders, Esq; ✉ 36 Ayresome Terrace, Leeds LS8 1BH (☎ 0113 266 4729)

SAUNDERS, Iain Ogilvy Swain; s of Leslie Swain Saunders (d 1988), and Elizabeth, *née* Culme Seymour (d 1963); *b* 7 November 1947; *Educ* Radley, Univ of Bristol (BSc); *m* 1976, Roberta Ann, da of David Allen Phoenix; 1 da (Christina Ann Swain b 1983); *Career* Arbuthnot Latham 1968–71; Robert Fleming: joined 1971, Jardine Fleming Hong Kong 1976–78, gen mangr Jardine Fleming Tokyo 1978–84, dir Robert Fleming Holdings 1984–, pres and ceo NY office 1985–89, chm Fleming Investment Mgmnt London 1990–94, dep chm Robert Fleming Asset Mgmnt 1994–2001; dir: JP Morgan Fleming American Investment Tst plc 1990–2005, JP Morgan Fleming Indian Investment Tst plc 1994–2006, Aberdeen Asia Smaller Companies Investment Tst plc 2004–06; chm: Czech and Slovak Investment Co 1995–, JP Morgan European UCITS Funds 1996–, Baring Emerging Europe plc 2002–, MB Asia 2002–; memb Governing Cncl Euro Asset Mgmnt Assoc 1999–2001; *Recreations* sailing, gardening; *Style*— Iain Saunders, Esq; ✉ Duine, Ardfern, Argyll PA31 8QN (01852 500289)

SAUNDERS, Jennifer; *b* 6 July 1958, Sleaford, Lincolnshire; *m* 1985, Adrian Edmondson; 3 da; *Career* actress, writer and comedienne; Outstanding Contribution to Comedy Br Comedy Awards 2004; fell BAFTA 2009; *Theatre* An Evening With French and Saunders (nat tour) 1989, Me and Mamie O'Rourke 1993, French and Saunders Live in 2000 2000; writer Viva Forever! 2012; *Television* incl: The Comic Strip Presents... 1982–2000, The Young Ones 1982–84, The Dangerous Brothers 1986, French And Saunders (with Dawn French) 1987–2005, The Full Wax 1991–92, Absolutely Fabulous 1992–2005 and 2011– (Best Comedy BAFTA Award 1993 (nomination 1995, 1996 and 1997, Best Female Performance in a Comedy Prog BAFTA 2012), Best TV Sitcom Writers' Guild of GB 1993, Best New Comedy Br Comedy Awards 1993, Int Emmy 1994), Queen of the East 1995, Roseanne 1998, Friends 1998, The Magicians House 1999, Mirrorball 2000, The Vivienne Vyle Show 2006, Jam and Jerusalem 2006–09, The Vivienne Vyle Show 2007, The Life and Times of Vivienne Vyle 2007, A Bucket o' French and Saunders (with Dawn French) 2007, This Is Jinsy 2011; *Film* incl: The Supergrass 1985, Eat the Rich 1987, Prince Cinders 1993, In the Bleak Midwinter 1995, Muppet Treasure Island 1996, Spice World 1997, Fanny and Elvis 1999, Shrek 2 2004, L'Entente Cordiale 2006, Coraline 2009; *Style*— Ms Jennifer Saunders; ✉ c/o United Agents Ltd, 12–26 Lexington Street, London W1F 0LE (☎ 020 3214 0800, fax 020 3214 0801, website www.unitedagents.co.uk)

SAUNDERS, Prof John; s of John Saunders, and Queenie, *née* Thomas; *b* 27 August 1946; *Educ* Hatfield Secdy Modern Sch, Doncaster Tech Coll Loughborough Univ (BSc), Cranfield Inst of Technol (MBA), Univ of Bradford (DPhil); *m* 7 Aug 1981, Veronica Wai Yoke, da of Wong Peng Chow; 1 s (Paul), 1 da (Carolyne); *Career* successively: sales and marketing Hawker Siddeley Aviation, lectr Univ of Bradford Mgmnt Centre, lectr Univ of Warwick Business Sch, prof of marketing Loughborough Univ and dir Loughborough Univ Business Sch; currently dir Aston Business Sch and prof of mktg and pro-vice-chllr Aston Univ; fell European Mktg Acad, FBAM, FCIM, FRSA; *Books* Enterprise (1977), Practical Business Forecasting (1987), The Specification of Aggregate Marketing Phenomina (1987), The Best of Companies (1989), Competitive Positioning (1993), The Marketing Initiative (1994), Principles of Marketing: The European Edition (2001), Marketing Strategy and Competitive Positioning (2004); *Recreations* my family, travel, rock, literature, history, science and technology, exercise, DIY and gardening; *Style*— Prof John Saunders; ✉ Holme Leys Farm, Black Horse Hill, Appleby Magna, Leicestershire DE12 7AQ (☎ 01530 272759)

SAUNDERS, John David; s of John Alan Saunders (d 1995), and Gladys-Anne Triptree (d 1972); *b* 15 March 1953; *Educ* Brentwood Sch Essex, Univ of Bristol (LLB); *m* 2005, Elizabeth Anne Cumming; 1 s, 1 da; *Career* admitted slr 1977; Lord Chllr's Dept (now Miny of Justice): joined Legal Gp 1980, sec Cncl on Tbnls 1993–97, head of statute law repeals Law Cmmn 1997–; memb Law Soc 1977; *Recreations* Victorian music hall, cinema; *Clubs* Players Theatre, Scotch Malt Whisky Soc; *Style*— John Saunders, Esq; ✉ Law Commission, Steel House, 11 Tothill Street, London SW1H 9LJ

SAUNDERS, Hon Mr Justice; Sir John Henry Boulton Saunders; kt (2007); s of Henry George Boulton Saunders (d 1984), and Kathleen Mary, *née* Brandle; *b* 15 March 1949; *Educ* St John's Coll Sch Cambridge, Uppingham (music scholar), Magdalen Coll Oxford; *m* 20 Dec 1975, Susan Mary, da of Charles William Paull Chick (d 1989); 2 da (Sarah Kate b 30 Nov 1977, Hannah May b 21 May 1979), 1 s (Daniel Paull b 26 Nov 1985); *Career* called to the Bar 1972; prosecuting counsel to the DHSS (now DSS) Midland & Oxford Circuit 1983–91, recorder 1990–2004 (asst recorder 1987–90), QC 1991, dep judge of the High Court 2000, sr circuit judge (Midland Circuit) 2004–07, judge of the High Court of Justice (Queen's Bench Div) 2007–; hon recorder of Birmingham 2004–07; *Recreations* music, sailing; *Style*— The Hon Mr Justice John Saunders; ✉ c/o Royal Courts of Justice, Strand, London WC2A 2LL

SAUNDERS, Prof Max; s of Garry Saunders, and Diana Cohen, *née* Snow; *b* 24 June 1957, London; *Educ* Sevenoaks Sch, Queens' Coll Cambridge (entrance scholar, BA), Harvard Univ (AM), Selwyn Coll Cambridge (Le Bas Prize, PhD); *Career* research fell then coll lectr Selwyn Coll Cambridge 1983–89 (dir of studies for English Part II 1987, tutor 1988); KCL: univ lectr 1989–97, reader in English 1997–2000, prof of English 2000–, dir Centre of Life-Writing Research 2007, dir Arts and Humanities Research Inst 2012; chair Ford Madox Ford Soc 1997; fell English Assoc 2005; tstee Alfred Cohen Art Fndn; *Publications* Ford Madox Ford: A Dual Life (Vols 1 and 2, 1996), Ford Madox Ford: Selected Poems (ed, 1997), Ford Madox Ford: War Prose (ed, 1999), Ford Madox Ford: Critical Essays (jt ed, 2002), Self Impression: Life-Writing, Autobiografiction and the Forms of Modern Literature (2010), Ford Madox Ford: Parade's End, Vol 1: Some Do Not... (2010); *Style*— Prof Max Saunders; ✉ Department of English, King's College London, The Strand, London WC2R 2LS (e-mail max.saunders@kcl.ac.uk)

SAUNDERS, Prof Peter Robert; s of Albert Edward Saunders, of Orpington, Kent, and Joan Kathleen, *née* Swan; *b* 30 August 1950; *Educ* Selhurst GS Croydon, Univ of Kent (BA), Univ of London (PhD); *m* 15 April 1971 (m dis 1990), Susan Elisabeth, da of Dr Frank Ellis, of Redhill, Surrey; 1 s (Michael b 1971), 1 da (Claire Louise b 1973); *Career* res offr Univ of Essex 1973–76, prof of sociology Univ of Sussex 1988– (lectr 1976–84, reader 1984–88); research mangr Australian Institute of Family Studies 1999–2000; dir of social research Centre for Independent Studies 2002–08 (hon sr fell 2008–); FRSA 1987; *Books* Urban Politics: A Sociological Interpretation (1979), Social Theory and the Urban Question (1981 and 1986), An Introduction to British Politics (1984, new edn 2000), Social Class and Stratification (1989), A Nation of Home Owners (1990), Privatisation and Popular Capitalism (1994), Capitalism: A Social Audit (1995), Unequal but Fair? A Study of Class Barriers in Britain (1996), Reforming the Australian Welfare State (2000), The Survey Methods Workbook (2004), Australia's Welfare Habit (2004), The Government Giveth, and the Government Taketh Away (2007), Social Mobility Myths (2010); *Style*— Prof Peter Saunders; ✉ website www.petersaunders.org.uk

SAUNDERS, Robin Elizabeth; *b* 8 June 1962, North Carolina, USA; *Educ* Florida State Univ; *m* 1992, Matthew Roeser; 2 da (Ella, Savannah (twins)); *Career* financier; successively with Northern Tst, Citibank, Chemical Bank and Deutsche Bank, head Principal Finance Unit WestLB 1998–2003, fndr Clearbrook Investments Ltd 2004–, managing ptnr Clearbrook Scotland GP Ltd 2004–; dir: Swan Gp until 2003, Formula One Holdings Ltd until 2003, Pubmaster Ltd until 2003, Whyte and Mackay Gp Ltd until 2003, BHS Gp Ltd 1999–2003, Odeon Ltd 2003, Office of the Rail Regulator until 2004, Eclipse Scientific Gp Ltd 2005–07, Harbourmaster Capital Hldgs 2005–10, Hawk Gp 2005–; visiting fell Said Business Sch Oxford 2008–; memb Cncl Serpentine Gall 2002–, dir Sadler's Wells Tst 2011–; *Recreations* the Arts; *Style*— Ms Robin Saunders; ✉ Egyptian House, 170–173 Piccadilly, London W1J 9EJ

SAUNDERS, Steven Philip; s of David Saunders, of Ipswich, Suffolk, and Joy Saunders; *b* 8 June 1961; *Educ* St Joseph's Coll of HE nr Ipswich, Suffolk Coll of Higher and Further Educn; *Family* 2 da (Serena b 17 Sept 1988, Stefanie b 16 April 1991); *Career* mgmnt trainee The Savoy 1979–81, gen mangr White Hart Great Yeldham 1981–86; chef and proprietor: The Pink Geranium Restaurant Melbourn 1986–, The Sheene Mill Melbourn (hotel, brasserie and deli) 1997–, Steven Saunders at The Lowry 2000– (opened by HM The Queen 2000, awarded Best Building of the Year); proprietor: Hawthorn Ventures Ltd, Steven Saunders Enterprises, Steven Saunders Organic Cookery Sch UK; fndr: Organica 2001 (UK's first organic catering co), Steven Saunders at Home; chef presenter: Good Morning (BBC1), Ready Steady Cook (BBC2), Here's One I Made Earlier (Channel 4), Afternoon Live's Remote Control Cookery (Carlton), Sky Int, NBC; food writer Organic Life magazine; regular features in: Caterer and Hotelkeeper, Hello!, OK; resident chef/writer Organic & Natural Living magazine; presenter: own radio show BBC Radio Cambridgeshire 1987–, Talk Radio UK; launched Tibard (Steven Saunders Chefs clothing range) 2001, Organica (first organic catering co in UK); conslt Bonterra Organic Wines; introduced Work Based Degree for Chefs Master Chefs of GB; patron Born Free Fndn, vice-patron Addenbrooke's Hosp; memb Soil Assoc; fell Master Chef of GB; *Awards* Catey Award for Young Restaurateur of the Year 1991; for the Pink Geranium: Assoc of Catering Excellence Restaurant of the Year 1995, FT Top Ten Restaurants in the UK 1996, Michelin Red M, Ackerman Four Leaf Clover, Egon Ronay Arrow, Good Food Guide 7/10, 3 AA Rosettes, Business Person of the Year; *Books* Only the Best (1993), Chef's Secrets (1996), Here's One I Made Earlier (1997), Short Cuts (1998), Feng Shui Food '99 (1999), Manchester on a Plate (2001), Quick Cuisine (2001), Bonterra Organic Recipes (2002), Choose Your Food to Change Your Mood (2003); *Recreations* tennis, squash, theatre, diving, travel, entertaining; *Style*— Steven Saunders, Esq; ✉ c/o PR @ Sheene Mill Hotel & Brasserie, Station Road, Melbourn, Cambridgeshire SG8 6DX (☎ 01763 261393, fax 01763 261376, websites www.stevensaunders.com or www.sheenemill.co.uk)

SAUNT, Deborah; *Educ* Univ of Cambridge; *Career* architect; fndr DSDHA 1998–; *Style*— Ms Deborah Saunt; ✉ DSDHA, 357 Kennington Lane, London SE11 5QY (☎ 020 7703 3555, dsaunt@dsdha.co.uk, website www.dsdha.co.uk)

SAUVEN, John Bernard; s of Mauric Sauven (d 2009), and Mary Sauven; *b* 6 September 1954, London; *Educ* Univ of Cardiff (BSc); *Partner* Janet Convery; 2 s (Zachary b 1992, Dylan b 1996); *Career* exec dir Greenpeace 2007–; *Style*— John Sauven, Esq; ✉ Greenpeace, Canonbury Villas, London N1 2PN

SAVAGE, David Jack; s of Arthur Jack Savage (d 1953), of Farnborough, Hants, and Sylvia Maude, *née* Bacon (d 1993; descendant of Sir Nicholas Bacon, Lord Keeper of the Great Seal to Queen Elizabeth I); *b* 7 August 1939; *Educ* Hurstpierpoint Coll, Weissenhaus Holstein Germany, Alliance Francaise, Univ of London (LLB), Coll of Law; *m* 16 May 1981, Elizabeth Mary, da of late Dr and Mrs Ives; 2 s (Nicholas David St John b 1982, Louis Arthur Ives b 1983); *Career* admitted slr 1963; sr ptnr Foster, Savage & Gordon of Farnborough 1984–2001, conslt 2001–05, estab David Savage & Co (Notaries Public) 2005; NP 1988; cmmr of income tax 1969–90, vice-chm N Hants Local Valuation Tbnl 1984–90 (memb 1976–90); pres Hants Inc Law Soc 1983–84 (memb Ctee 1972–2002), dir Slrs' Benevolent Assoc 1984–96, chm Reading Legal Aid Funding Review Ctee 2000–02; memb: No 3 Southern Area Legal Aid Ctee 1989–2000 (vice-chm 1999–2000), Cncl Law Soc 1990–2002 (memb Criminal Law Ctee 1988–2002); life memb Berks Bucks and Oxon Law Soc (memb Ctee 1990–2002); Law Soc rep to UINL (Int Union of Latin Notaries) 1997–98; cncllr: Farnborough UDC 1964–73 (vice-chm 1972–73), Rushmoor BC 1973–80; Parly candidate (Cons): Birmingham Sparkbrook 1974, Birmingham Smallheath 1979; govr Swinton Cons Coll 1971–74, vice-pres Aldershot Divnl Cons Assoc 1973– (chm 1969–73); dir Aldershot FC 1971; chm of govrs Farnborough GS 1970–72; memb Ct Univ of Southampton 2000–; Freeman City of London 1989; Liveryman: Worshipful Co of Arbitrators 1989, Worshipful Co of Scriveners 1990, Worshipful Co of Woolmen 1991; ACIArb 1988; *Recreations* travel (preferably by train), browsing, bricklaying, ornithology; *Style*— David Savage, Esq; ✉ Ridgeway, 16 Clockhouse Road, Farnborough, Hampshire GU14 7QY; David Savage & Co, Ridgeway Chambers, Clockhouse Road, Farnborough, Hampshire GU14 7QY (☎ and fax 01252 372858)

SAVAGE, Dr Gary John; s of Keith Savage, of Halesworth, Suffolk, and Doreen, *née* Bloss; *b* 5 December 1970, Oulton Broad, Suffolk; *Educ* Bungay HS, Sidney Sussex Coll Cambridge (MA, PhD); *m* 1992, Natalie, *née* Watts; *Career* head of history and master-in-coll Eton 1996–2006, under master Westminster Sch 2006–10, headmaster Alleyn's Sch 2010–; govr Notting Hill Prep Sch 2004–14, govr Roedean Sch 2016–; memb HMC 2010; tstee Dulwich Picture Gallery 2014–; FRSA 2011; *Recreations* German, Ipswich Town FC, arts; *Clubs* Lansdowne, East India; *Style*— Dr Gary Savage; ✉ Alleyn's School, Townley Road, Dulwich, London SE22 8SU (☎ 020 8557 1493, e-mail headmaster@alleyns.org.uk, website www.alleyns.org.uk)

SAVAGE, Valerie (Mrs Paul Ridout); *b* 1944; *Educ* N London Collegiate Sch, Central Sch of Speech & Drama; *m* Paul Ridout; 1 da (Lucy); *Career* speech and language conslt in ind practice in London, int reputation for diagnosis and mgmnt of children with a variety of complex disorders incl Autistic Spectrum Disorder, Dyspraxia, Specific Language Impairment often complicated by multilingual and multiculural circumstances; wide experience in trg broadcast journalists for Sky News, Al Jazeera, etc; ptnr Ridouts LLP; RSM; *Publications* incl professional articles on speech disorders in the pre-school child and teaching progs to treat them; *Recreations* theatre, Indian cookery, opera, dancing Argentine Tango; *Clubs* RAC, Ind Doctors Fndn, By Invitation Only; *Style*— Miss Valerie Savage; ✉ Pinero House, 115A Harley Street, London W1G 6AR (☎ 020 7486 0503, fax 020 7034 4490, website www.valeriesavage.com)

SAVILL, Prof Sir John; kt (2008); s of Peter Edward Savill, and Jean Elizabeth, *née* Garland; *b* 25 April 1957; *m* Barbara Campbell; 2 s; *Career* former dir MRC/Univ of Edinburgh Centre for Inflammation Research, currently prof of experimental med and head Coll of Med and Vet Med Univ of Edinburgh; former pt/t chief scientist Scottish Govt Health Directorates; chief exec and dep chm Medical Research Cncl 2010–; former chair and govr Health Fndn, memb Clinical Interest Gp Wellcome Tst; former memb Lothian Health Bd; *Recreations* literature (20th century and crime novels), hockey, cricket; *Style*— Prof Sir John Savill; ✉ The Queen's Medical Research Institute, 47 Little France Crescent, Edinburgh EH16 4TJ

SAVILL, His Hon Judge Mark Ashley; *Career* called to the Bar 1993; fee-paid judge Health, Educn and Social Care Chamber First-tier Tbnl 2004, circuit judge (Northern Circuit) 2015–; *Style*— His Hon Judge Savill

SAVILLE, John; *Educ* Jesus Coll Oxford (MA); *m* 15 Dec 1992, Fabiola Moreno de Alboran; 1 da (Alexandra b 25 Oct 1993); *Career* diplomat; joined FCO 1981, desk offr Southern African Dept FCO 1981–82, 2 sec political Jakarta 1982–85, desk offr Southern European Dept FCO 1985–88, 2 then 1 sec press and public affrs Warsaw 1988–91, desk offr Non Proliferation Dept FCO 1991–94, 1 sec political Vienna 1995–98, head Cwlth and Burma Section SE Asia Dept FCO 1998–2000, dep head of mission Havana 2000–03, head WMD Review Unit FCO 2004–05, high cmmr to Brunei 2005–09, head Climate Change Project Climate Change Dept FCO 2009–10, dir Asia, Global High Growth, Markets and Mass Transport UKTI 2010–13, acting md UKTI 2013–14, ambass to Venezuela 2014–; *Clubs* Traveller's, Caracas Country; *Style*— HE Mr John Saville; ✉ c/o FCO (Caracas), King Charles Street, London SW1A 2AH

SAVILLE OF NEWDIGATE, Baron (Life Peer UK 1997), of Newdigate in the County of Surrey; Sir Mark Oliver Saville; kt (1985), PC (1994); s of Kenneth Vivian Saville, and Olivia Sarah Frances, *née* Gray; *b* 20 March 1936; *Educ* Rye GS, BNC Oxford (Vinerian scholar, BA, BCL); *m* 30 June 1961, Jill Whitworth; 2 s (William Christian b 8 March 1962, Henry Oliver b 8 Aug 1964); *Career* Nat Serv 2 Lt Royal Sussex Regt 1954–56; called to the Bar Middle Temple 1962 (bencher 1983); QC 1975, judge of the High Court of Justice (Queen's Bench Div) 1985–94, a Lord Justice of Appeal 1994–97, a Lord of Appeal in Ordinary 1997–2009, a Justice of the Supreme Court 2009–10; hon fell BNC Oxford 1998; Hon LLD London Guildhall Univ 1997, Hon LLD Nottingham Trent Univ 2008; *Recreations* sailing, flying, computers; *Clubs* Garrick; *Style*— The Rt Hon Lord Saville of Newdigate; ✉ House of Lords, London SW1A 0PW

SAVILLE ROBERTS, Liz; MP; *m* Dewi Roberts; 2 da (Lowri, Lisa); *Career* MP (Plaid Cymru) Dwyfor Meirionnydd 2015–; *Style*— Ms Liz Saville-Roberts, MP; ✉ House of Commons, London SW1A 0AA

SAVOURS; *see:* Campbell-Savours

SAVULESCU, Prof Julian; s of Radu Ion Savulescu (d 1998), and Valda Jean, *née* Thewlis; *b* 22 December 1963; *Educ* Haileybury Coll Melbourne (scholar), Monash Univ Melbourne (MB BS, PhD), Univ of Oxford (Sir Robert Menzies med scholar); *Career* clinical ethicist Oxford Radcliffe Hosps 1995–97, Logan research fell Monash Univ Melbourne 1997–98, dir Bioethics Prog Centre for Study of Health and Society Univ of Melbourne 1998–2002, Ethics of Genetics Prog Murdoch Children's Research Inst Royal Children's Hosp Melbourne 1998–2002, Uehiro chair in practical ethics Univ of Oxford 2002–, dir Oxford Uehiro Centre for Practical Ethics 2002–, dir Oxford Centre for Neuroethics 2009–; chm Dept of Human Services Victoria Ethics Ctee 1998–2002; ed Jl of Med Ethics 2001–04 and 2011–; *Publications* Medical Ethics and Law: The Core Curriculum (jtly, 2003); over 250 articles in BMJ, Lancet, Australian Jl of Philosophy, Bioethics, Jl of Med Ethics, American Jl of Bioethics, Med Jl of Australia, Philosophy, Psychiatry and Psychology, New Scientist etc; *Recreations* skiing, surfing, cycling, swimming, rollerblading, film, wine; *Style*— Prof Julian Savulescu; ✉ Oxford Uehiro Centre for Practical Ethics, Littlegate House, Oxford OX1 1PT (☎ 01865 286888, fax 01865 286886, e-mail ethics@philosophy.ox.ac.uk, website www.practicalethics.ox.ac.uk)

SAVVAS, Michael; s of Michael Savvas, of Cyprus, and Rebecca, *née* Hermogenou; *b* 16 March 1957, Aradippou, Cyprus; *Educ* Holloway Sch, London Hosp Med Coll (MB BS); *m* 1998, Jane Mary, *née* Biglin; 2 c (Savvas b 13 May 1998, Christopher b 25 Dec 1999); *Career* house surgn N Middx Hosp 1980–81, house physician Whipps Cross Hosp 1981, SHO A/E London Hosp 1982 (Dept of Obstetrics and Gynaecology 1981–82), SHO Dept of Obstetrics and Gynaecology Whipps Cross Hosp 1982–83, SHO/acting registrar Dept of Endocrinology Jessop Hosp for Women Sheffield 1983–84, registrar in obstetrics and gynaecology Westminster Hosp, St Stephen's Hosp and Hillingdon Hosp 1984–86, res registrar KCH and Dulwich Hosp 1986–88, sr registrar KCH, Lewisham Hosp and Greenwich District Hosp 1988–92, conslt Dept of Obstetrics and Gynaecology Lewisham Hosp and hon sr lectr UMDS (now GKT) 1992–2001, conslt obstetrician and gynaecologist KCH London 2002– (clinical lead Assisted Conception Unit); author of numerous scientific pubns; Galen Prize for advances in infertility Hellenic Med Soc; memb: Int Menopause Soc, Br Menopause Soc, Blair Bell Research Soc, Hellenic Med Soc, Int Soc of Gynaecological Endocrinology, BMA, Br Fertility Soc; MRCOG 1986, FRSM 1998 (memb Cncl, pres Section of Obstetrics and Gynaecology 2013–14); *Recreations* classical and medical history, theatre, classical music, cinema, gardening, reading; *Style*— Michael Savvas, Esq; ✉ Department of Gynaecology, The Blackheath Hospital, 40–42 Lee Terrace, London SE3 9UD (☎ 020 8318 7722); King's College Hospital, Denmark Hill, London SE5 9RS (☎ 020 3299 9000)

SAWBRIDGE, Edward Henry Ewen; s of Henry Raywood Sawbridge, CBE (d 1990), of Kingsgate, Kent, and Lilian, *née* Wood (d 1991); *b* 14 August 1953; *Educ* Radley, Balliol Coll Oxford (MA); *m* 23 July 1983, Angela Rose Louisa, da of Maj Anthony James MacDonald Watt (d 1991), of Longwood, Sunninghill, Berks; 3 s (Jack William Hugo b 1986, Hugh Anthony Edward b 1988, Arthur Henry James b 1991); *Career* Peat Marwick Mitchell & Co 1976–83, ACLI Metals (London) Ltd 1983–85, fin dir Lehman Brothers Commodities Ltd 1985–98, exec dir Lehman Brothers International Ltd 1991–98, fin dir Natixis Commodity Markets Ltd (formerly Natexis Metals Ltd) 1998–2011, chief operating offr Natixis London 2006–11; treas Bracknell Forest Voluntary Action 2012; govr Altwood Sch; FCA, FRSA; *Books* Capital Failure (contrib, 2014); *Recreations* bridge, fishing, cooking, lawns, golf, opera, ponds; *Clubs* Oxford and Cambridge; *Style*— Edward Sawbridge, Esq; ✉ e-mail edward@sawbridge.net

SAWCZUK, Basil; s of Petro Sawczuk (d 2000), and Maria, *née* Perik (d 2011); *b* 22 May 1954; *Educ* Chosen Hill GS Churchdown, Leicester Poly (DipArch), Open Univ (Dip Mgmnt, MBA), CEM Univ of Reading; *m* 19 May 1979, Sonia Elizabeth, da Stefan Szewczuk (d 1987), of Leicester; 1 s (Luke Sebastian b 24 Oct 1988); *Career* project architect Harper Fairley ptnrs Birmingham 1979–80, assoc Malcolm Payne and Assocs Birmingham 1980–83; DGI: joined 1983, exec dir DGI International plc 1986–91 and Overseas Business Devpt 1992–95, exec DGI Group plc 1991–92; divnl dir (following takeoverby W S Atkins) W S Atkins (Midlands)/Atkins DGI 1996–99, dir WS Atkins Architects Ltd 1999–2000; mktg dir: W S Atkins Property Design Gp 1999–2001, W S Atkins Property Services 2001–02, Lee Crowder Solicitors 2002–04; business devpt dir: Accord Housing Servs 2005–06, Accord Housing and Environmental Servs 2006–07; dir i/c Widdup Amer Achitects Ltd 2007–09; princ Potentialise Consulting 2009–; responsible for: computer centre GDS Swindon and SWEB HQ Bristol, various projects in Western Siberia, food distribution study in Tyumen region Russia for EC, Paediatric Polyclinic Nefteugansk Russia, several projects for the BBC; memb: Main Ctee Birmingham AA 1980–83 (ed BAA Gazette 1982–83), Ctee Housing Centre Tst 1980, Birmingham and Sutton Coldfield Crime Prevention Panel 1981–82, Ctee of Midland Study Centre 1984, RIBA Parly Action Lobby 1982–83; chm Midland Jr Liaison Organisation 1984; visiting prof Tyumen Univ Russia 1992–93; external examiner: Leicester Sch of Architecture 1990–94, Univ of Nottingham Sch of Architecture 1996–2000; visiting external lectr: De Montfort Univ Leicester, Univ of Nottingham, Univ of Central England, Cardiff Univ, Univ of Cambridge; memb W Midlands Arbitration Discussion Gp 1990–2001, registered mediator 1991, memb Acad of Experts 1990–99 (memb ADR Ctee 1993), memb Ctee Professional Marketing Forum 1997–99, memb Construction Ctee London C of C 2000–02, memb Fundraising Ctee Nat Inst of Conductive Education 2000–02; Freeman City of London 1983, Freeman Worshipful Co of Arbitrators 1983–94; MInstD 1999–2001, memb Br Soc of Clinical Hypnosis 2003; RIBA 1979, FCIArb 1989–2006 (ACIArb 1980, memb Panel of Arbitrators 1991, memb Ctee Midlands branch 1995–98), FCIM 2001; *Books* Risk Avoidance for the Building Team (1996), Marketing and Selling Professional Services in Architecture and Construction (2009), Creating Winning Bids (2013); various articles in professional jls; *Recreations* reading, fishing, photography; *Style*— Basil Sawczuk, Esq; ✉ e-mail basil@potentialise.com, website www.potentialise.com

SAWER, David Peter; *b* 14 September 1961, Stockport; *Educ* Univ of York (BA, DPhil), Staatliche Hochschule für Musik Rheinland Koln; *Career* composer in assoc Bournemouth Orchs 1995–96; Hon ARAM; *Awards* DAAD scholarship (to study with Mauricio Kagel in Köln) 1984, Sony Radio Award (for Swansong) 1990, Fulbright Fellowship 1992, Paul Hamlyn Fndn Award 1993, Arts Fndn Composer Fellowship 1995; *Compositions* for theatre: Etudes 1984, Food of Love 1988, The Panic 1991, Rumpelstiltskin 2009, The Lighthouse Keepers 2013; for orch: Byrnan Wood 1992, The Memory of Water 1993/1995, Trumpet Concerto 1994, Tiroirs 1996, the greatest happiness principle 1997, Musica ficta 1998, Piano Concerto 2002, Flesh and Blood 2011; chamber music: Cat's-Eye 1986, Take Off 1987, Good Night 1989, Rhetoric 1989, Hollywood Extra 1996, Rebus 2004, Rumpelstiltskin Suite 2011, Coachman Chronos 2014, Caravanserai 2015; choral music: Songs of Love and War 1990, Sounds Three Kandinsky Poems 1996 and 1999, Stramm Gedichte 2002, Mutability 2004; opera: From Morning to Midnight 1998–2001, Skin Deep 2005–08; instrumental: Solo Piano 1983, The Melancholy of Departure 1990, Between 1998; *Style*— David Sawer, Esq; ✉ c/o Rayfield Allied, Southbank House, Black Prince Road, London SE1 7SJ

SAWERS, Sir (Robert) John; GCMG (2015, KCMG 2007, CMG 1996); s of Colin Simon Sawers, and Daphne Anne, *née* Davis; *b* 26 July 1955; *Educ* Beechen Cliff Sch Bath, Univ of Nottingham (BSc); *Career* FCO appointments: Damascus 1982, London 1984, Pretoria/Cape Town 1988; head EU Presidency Unit 1992, princ private sec to foreign sec 1993, int fell Harvard Univ 1995–96, cnsllr Washington 1996, foreign affrs private sec to PM 1999, ambass Cairo 2001–03, UK special envoy to Iraq May-July 2003, political dir FCO 2003–07, UK Perm Rep to the UN NY 2007–09, chief Secret Intelligence Service (MI6) 2009–14, ret; chm and ptnr Macro Advsy Ptnrs 2015–, non-exec dir BP 2015–; *Recreations* theatre, tennis; *Style*— Sir John Sawers, GCMG

SAWLE, Dr Guy Victor; s of Victor Sawle, and Joan, *née* Roots; *Educ* Univ of Nottingham Med Sch (DM); *m* 18 July 1981, Fiona, *née* Alldis; 1 da (Chloe b 13 Sept 1983), 2 s (Oliver b 13 Oct 1985, Tristan b 5 Sept 1992); *Career* neurology trg Addenbrooke's Hosp Cambridge and St Thomas', Hammersmith and Nat Hosps London, currently conslt neurologist Queens Med Centre Nottingham; past pres Notts Medico Legal Soc; memb Assoc of Br Neurologists 1990, memb Movement Disorder Soc 1990; FRCP 1998; *Publications* Movement Disorders in Clinical Practice (ed, 1999); over 100 works incl pubns on functional brain imaging, movement disorders and neurological complications of pregnancy; *Recreations* music, koi, microscopy, astronomy; *Style*— Dr Guy Sawle; ✉ Department of Neurology, Queens Medical Centre, Nottingham NG7 2UH (☎ 0115 970 9792, fax 0115 960 4253)

SAWYER, Anthony Charles; CB (1999); s of Charles Bertram Sawyer (d 1999), and Elisabeth, *née* Spinks (d 1992); *b* 3 August 1939; *Educ* Redhill Tech Coll and AEC; *m* 1962, Kathleen Josephine, *née* McGill (d 2015); 2 s (Stephen b 1965, Andrew b 1967), 1 da (Sarah Ann b 1969); *Career* Customs and Excise: joined 1963, princ 1978–82, dep collector S Wales 1983–84, collector Edinburgh 1984–88, cmmr of Customs and Excise 1991–99, dir Outfield 1991–94 (dep dir 1988–91), dir Enforcement 1994–99; fiscal expert IMF 1999–2007 (expert missions to Bulgaria, Kenya, Kyrgyzstan, Nigeria, Romania, Tanzania, Tajikistan, Pakistan, the Philippines and Jordan); fiscal advsr to: Kyrgyz Repub 2000, Egypt 2003–04, Ethiopia 2004, Kenya 2005; non-exec dir Retail Banking Bd Royal Bank of Scotland plc 1994–97; dir Customs Annuity and Benevolent Fund 1998–2004; FCMI, FInstD, FRMetS, FRSA; *Recreations* walking, cricket, poetry; *Clubs* National Liberal, Royal Scots (Edinburgh), Sussex CCC; *Style*— Anthony C Sawyer, Esq, CB; ✉ e-mail acskjs@hotmail.com

SAX, Richard Noel; s of late Lt-Col George Hans Sax, and Yvonne Anna Marcelle, *née* Trausel (d 2011); *b* 26 December 1938; *Educ* Tonbridge, St John's Coll Oxford (MA); *m* 8 April 1967, Margaret, da of Ronald Frank Penny (d 1988); 3 da (Catherine b 1968, Josephine b 1971, Charlotte b 1974); *Career* Nat Serv cmmnd 2 Lt RASC 1957, attached 1 Gds Bde Irish Gds Cyprus (GSM Cyprus Clasp), Lt 1959; admitted slr 1967; managing ptnr Rubinstein Callingham 1984–93 (equity ptnr 1968–94), ptnr then conslt Manches 1994–2009; dep dist judge Princ Registry Family Div 1990–2009; chm Slrs Family Law Assoc 1987–89; memb: Law Cmmn Working Pty on Family Property 1974, Family Law Ctee Law Soc 1990–2000, Bd Children and Family Court Advsy Serv (CAFCASS) 2004–10; memb Law Soc 1967, past pres European Chapter and fell IAML, chair of govrs Skinners Kent Acad; third warden Ct Worshipful Co of Skinners; *Recreations* current affairs, gardening, history and archaeology, travel, art; *Clubs* MCC; *Style*— Richard Sax, Esq; ✉ 29 Kelsey Way, Beckenham, Kent BR3 3LP (☎ 020 8650 8272, e-mail saxpenny@ntlworld.com)

SAXBY, John; s of George Saxby, and Veronica, *née* Flynn; *b* 29 September 1949; *Educ* St Mary's Coll Crosby Liverpool, King's Coll London (BA), Univ of Cologne, MA (1992), MBA (1993); *m* 15 Nov 1986, Janet Adelyne, da of Harold Livesey; 1 da (Emily-Jane Christine b 7 Nov 1989); *Career* chief exec Co Durham and Darlington NHS Tst 2002–; *Recreations* distance running, fell running, cycling; *Style*— John Saxby, Esq; ✉ University of North Durham, Durham DH1 5TW (☎ 0191 333 2151)

SAXON, Prof David Harold; OBE (2005); s of Rev Canon Eric Saxon, of Bramhall, Manchester, and Ruth, *née* Higginbottom; *b* 27 October 1945, Stockport, Cheshire; *Educ* Manchester Grammar, Balliol Coll Oxford (Brackenbury scholar, BA, Scott prize, DSc), Jesus Coll Oxford (MA, DPhil); *m* 13 July 1968, Margaret, da of Rev John Flitcroft; 1 s (Philip Jeffrey b 28 Feb 1972), 1 da (Patricia Alice b 6 Dec 1974); *Career* Univ of Oxford: jr res fell Jesus Coll 1968–70, res offr Dept of Nuclear Physics 1969–70; res assoc Columbia Univ 1970–73; Rutherford Appleton Laboratory: res assoc 1974–75, sr scientific offr 1975–76, princ scientific offr 1976–89, grade 6 1989–90; Univ of Glasgow: Kelvin prof of physics 1990–2008, head Dept of Physics and Astronomy 1996–2001, vice-dean of physical sciences 2000–02, dean of physical sciences 2002–08, emeritus prof 2008–; chm Governing Ctee Scottish Univs Summer Sch in Physics 1997–2003 (dir 1993); chm STFC Calice Oversight Panel 2006–08; memb: Selection Panel SERC Particle Physics Experiment 1989–92, High Energy Particle Physics Ctee Inst of Physics 1989–93, Nuclear Physics Div Ctee Inst of Physics 1990–93, Detector R&D Ctee CERN 1990–93, Particle Physics Ctee SERC 1991–94 (chm 1992), Nuclear Physics Bd SERC 1992–93, UK Ctee on CERN 1992–95 and 1998–2004, Scientific Policy Ctee CERN 1993–98, Physics Res Ctee DESY Hamburg 1993–99, Research Assessment Physics Panel 1996, Cncl PPARC 1997–2001 (chm Particle Physics Ctee 1994–95, chm Public Understanding of Sci Panel 1997–2001), MRC Scientific Advsy Gp on Technol 1999 (Discipline Hopping Panel 2000 and 2006–09), Cncl Central Laboratories for Research Cncls 2000–01 and 2005–07 (chm Particle Physics Users Advsy Ctee 1998–2004, memb Resources Allocation Ctee 2006–07), External Review Ctee CERN 2001–02, Cncl RSE 2001–04 (res convener 2002–05), Univ of Trento Sci Advsy Panel 2002–04, Br Cncl Travel Awards Panel 2006–09, Cmmn C11 Int Union of Pure and Applied Physics (IUPAP) 2006–08; chm: UK Inst of Physics Conf 1993, 27th Int Conf on High Energy Physics 1994; chm Inst of Physics in Scotland 2003–05 (vice-chm 2001–03); CPhys, FInstP 1985, FRSE 1993, FRAS 2004; *Recreations* visiting grandchildren in Budapest; *Style*— Prof David H Saxon, OBE, FRSE; ✉ e-mail david.saxon@morespeed.net; c/o Miss V Flood, Kelvin Building, School of Physics and Astronomy, University of Glasgow, Glasgow G12 8QQ (☎ 0141 330 4702, e-mail valerie.flood@glasgow.ac.uk)

SAXON, Richard Gilbert; CBE (2001); s of Rev Canon Eric Saxon, QHC, of Stockport, and Ruth, *née* Higginbottom; *b* 14 April 1942; *Educ* Manchester Grammar, Univ of Liverpool (BArch, MCD); *m* 14 Sept 1968, (Elizabeth) Anne, da of Samuel Shaw Tatton, of Barwick in Elmet, Leeds; *Career* architect; Building Design Partnership (BDP): assoc 1970–77, ptnr 1977–97, head of architectural profession London Office 1991–96, chm London Office 1993–99, gp chm 1996–2002, dir 1997–2005, dir mktg 2000–05; princ Consultancy for the Built Environment (client and practice advsr) 2005–; design ptnr: J P Morgan HQ London 1986–91, Paddington Basin Redevelopment 1989–92, All England Lawn Tennis Club Redevelopment 1992–95, Adam Opel AG Headquarters Rüsselsheim Germany 1993–97; relationship dir Marks and Spencer 1995–2005, conslt Shell 2001, non-exec dir BLP Insurance Ltd 2013–, assoc dir Deploi BIM Strategies 2015–; awards incl: RIBA Halifax Bldg Soc HQ 1975 (listed Grade II 2013), Europa Nostra medal and Civic Tst Durham Milburngate Centre 1978, Civic Tst commendation Merseyside Maritime Museum Masterplan 1981, New City Architecture award JP Morgan HQ 1993, Civic Tst commendation All England Lawn Tennis Club No 1 Court 1998, BCO Award Halifax HQ 2000; bldg advsr EDC 1984–86; memb: Bldg Sub-Ctee Sci and Engrg Res Cncl 1987–90, Electronic Applications Sub-Ctee NEDO 1991–92, DTI Task Force on Construction Deregulation 1993, Bd Br Cncl for Offices 1990–99 (pres 1995–96), Bd Reading Construction Forum 1995–2002 (chair 1999–2002), Design Build Fndn 1997–2002, Building Ctee Univ of Cambridge 2004–; chm: Good Practice Panel Construction Industry Bd 1996–99, Collaborating for the Built Environment 2002–05, Ind Dispute Avoidance Panel for London 2012 2008–12, Jt Contracts Tbnl (JCT) 2015–; memb Strategic Forum for Construction 2001–02, memb The Bond (pres 2009–10), chm City of (London) Architecture Forum 2005–15, memb Exec Bd Construction Industry Cncl 2006–14 (also champion for research, innovation and knowledge), memb Govt BIM Steering Gp 2012–13, UK BIM ambass for growth 2012–13; memb Support Gp Nat Platform for Construction Research 2006–09, memb Research Reference Gp Cmmn for Architecture and the Built Environment 2008–11, memb Strategic Partnership Panel of Construction Skills 2009–, memb BIS Low Carbon Construction Innovation and Growth Team 2010; RIBA: vice-pres and memb Cncl 2002–08, memb Policy and Strategy Gp 2006–11, memb Client Service Panel 2008–11; Freeman City of London 1988, Master Worshipful Co of Chartered Architects 2005–06 (memb Ct of Assts 1992–); RIBA 1968, MCIM, FRSA 1987, MInstD, FRICS 2013; *Books* Atrium Buildings, Development and Design: Architectural Press (1983 and 1986), Moscow (1987), Kajima Press Japan (1988 and 1993), Bardon Chinese Agency ROC (1994), chapter Atrium Buildings Wiley/AIA Encyclopaedia of Architecture (1988), The Atrium Comes of Age (1993), Kenchiku Gijutsu Japan (1995), Be Valuable: A guide to creating value in the built environment: Constructing Excellence (2005), City Architecture: redesigning the City of London 1991–2011 (2011), Growth through BIM (2013), BIM for Construction Clients (2016); *Recreations* travel, photography, music, theatre, film, writing; *Style*— Richard Saxon, Esq, CBE; ✉ Consultancy for the Built Environment, 9 Whistlers Avenue, London SW11 3TS (☎ 07768 482838, e-mail richard@saxoncbe.com, website www.saxoncbe.com)

SAXTON, Joe Hugh Christopher; s of Hugh Michael Saxton, and Barbara Bevil Saxton; *b* Bristol; *Educ* Downsend Sch, Bedales Sch, Univ of Cambridge (MA), Univ of East Anglia (MA), Henley Mgmnt Coll (MBA); *m* June 1990, Julie Margaret; 2 s, 1 da; *Career* co-ordinator Harambee Centre Cambridge 1986–88, Fundraising Dept Oxfam 1988–91, account dir and dep client servs dir Brann Ltd 1991–96, dir of communications RNID 1997–2000, head of not for profit Future Fndn 2000–03, driver of ideas nfpSynergy (MBO from Future Fndn) 2003–; tstee: RSPCA 1991–96, Inst of Fundraising 2002–08 (chair 2005–08); chair People & Planet 2005–15, chair and co-fndr CharityComms 2007–13, chair PTA-UK 2015–; MMRS, MInstF; *Publications* It's Competition, But Not As We Know It? (1997), What Are Charities For? (1998), Polishing the Diamond (2002), Mission Impossible (2004), The 21st Century Volunteer (2005), The 21st Century Donor (2007), Sending Out an SMS (2011), Gimme, Gimme, Gimme (2011), A Chance to Give (2013), Strength in Numbers (2013), Ringing a Bell (2015), The New Alchemy (2015); *Recreations* ferrying my children to sports training, snuggling on the sofa with my wife, sending e-mails, planning walks on the Cumbrian fells that never happen; *Style*— Joe Saxton, Esq; ✉ nfpSynergy, 2–6 Tenter Ground, Spitalfields, London E1 7NH (☎ and fax 020 7426 8888, e-mail joe.saxton@nfpsynergy.net)

SAXTON, Prof Robert Louis Alfred; s of Capt Ian Sanders Saxton, barr-at-law, of London, and Dr Jean Augusta Saxton, *née* Infield; *b* 8 October 1953; *Educ* Bryanston, St

Catharine's Coll Cambridge (MA), Worcester Coll Oxford (BMus, DMus); *m* Teresa Cahill, *qv*; *Career* visiting tutor Univ of Oxford 1980–82, lectr Univ of Bristol 1984–85, visiting fell Princeton Univ 1986, composer in residence City Univ 1987–89, head of Composition Dept GSM 1990–98 (composition tutor 1979–84 and 1986–90), artisitic dir Opera Lab 1993–99, visiting fell in Composition Univ of Bristol 1995–2000, head Composition Dept RAM 1998–99, univ lectr and tutorial fell Worcester Coll Oxford 1999–; composer of over 40 published works, over 20 commercial recordings; contrib to various music jls; several radio and TV appearances; memb: Cncl SPNM 1978–90 (memb Exec Ctee 1979–82), Artistic Bd Blackheath Concert Halls 1987–89, BBC Score Reading Panel 1988–, Arts Cncl of GB Music Advsy Panel 1989–93, Site Devpt Bd South Bank Centre 1996–97, Governing Bd South Bank Centre 1997–; tstee Mendelssohn/Boise Fndn 2010–; hon pres Assoc of English Singers and Speakers 1997–; PRS 1976, FGSM 1986, MCPS 1990; *Recreations* theatre, cinema, reading biography, history and philosophy; *Style*— Prof Robert Saxton; ✉ c/o Music Sales, 8/9 Frith Street, London W1V 5TZ (☎ 020 7434 0066, fax 020 7278 6329); c/o University of York Music Press, Department of Music, University of York, Heslington, York Y10 5DD (☎ 01904 432434, fax 01904 432450, e-mail uymp@york.ac.uk); c/o Liz Webb Management, 3 Morley Close, Lewes BN7 1NQ

SAXTON, Robert Michael; s of Arthur Colin, and Joyce, *née* Dulson; *b* 12 August 1952; *Educ* Magdalen Coll Oxford (MA); *Career* publisher; Studio Vista 1975–80, exec ed Mitchell Beazley 1980–91 (responsible for lists on gardening, design, architecture and photography), editorial dir Duncan Baird Publishers UK 1991–2013 (int co-edn titles and illustrated reference); *Poetry* The Promise Clinic (1994), Manganese (2003), Local Honey (2007), Hesiod's Calendar (2010), The China Shop Pictures (2012), Six-way Mirror (2016); *Recreations* poetry, ornithology, bird photography, modern jazz, learning jazz piano, world music, Indian classical music; *Style*— Robert Saxton, Esq; ✉ website www.robertsaxton.co.uk

SAYCE, Dr (Lucy) Elizabeth (Liz); OBE (2009); da of Dr Richard Anthony Sayce (d 1977), and Dr Olive Lenore, *née* Davison (d 2013); *b* Oxford; *Partner* Dr Rachel Perkins (civil partnership 2007); *Career* policy dir Mind 1990–98, dir Lambeth, Southwark and Lewisham Health Action Zone 1998–2000, dir of policy and communications Disability Rights Cmmn 2000–07, chief exec RADAR 2007–12, chief exec Disability Rights UK 2012–; cmmr UK Cmmn for Employment and Skills; Independent Review Disability Employment Programmes 2010–11; Harkness fell 1995–96; memb Healthwatch England Ctee; *Publications* From Psychiatric Patient to Citizen (2000), From Psychiatric Patient to Citizen Revisited (2015); *Style*— Dr Liz Sayce, OBE; ✉ Disability Rights UK, CAN Mezzanine, 49–51 East Road, London N1 6AH (e-mail liz.sayce@disabilityrightsuk.org)

SAYER, Michael John; s of Maj Douglas James William Sayer, MBE, TD, JP (d 2005), of Sparham Hall, Norfolk, and Mary Elizabeth, *née* Weddall; *b* 11 October 1947; *Educ* Repton, Pembroke Coll Oxford (MA, BLitt); *Career* landowner, author; CLA: memb Norfolk Branch Ctee 1972, memb Water Sub-Ctee 1980–84, memb Tax Sub-Ctee 1989–93, memb Cncl 1993– (memb Exec 1999–2004), chm Norfolk Branch 1995–98, memb Environment Sub-Ctee 2005–; tax cmmr 1979–2009 (chm St Faith's and Aylsham Div 1988–2005, chm Central Norfolk Div 2006–09); memb: Norwich Diocesan Synod 1973–82 (Pastoral Ctee 1974–82), Tax Ctee Historic Houses Assoc 1990–; chm Norfolk Churches Tst 1984–86; jt rep Duke of Norfolk on Cmmn d'Information et de Liaison des Associations de Noblesse d'Europe (CILANE) 1994– (co-ordinator 2008–11), vice-pres Friends of the Countryside 1998–, delg European Landowners' Orgn UN Framework Convention on Climate Change 1999, 2001, 2008, 2009 and 2015; FSA 1982; *Books* English Nobility: The Gentry, The Heralds and The Continental Context (1979), Norfolk section of Burke's and Savill's Guide to Country Houses, vol III, East Anglia (1981), The Disintegration of a Heritage: Country Houses and their Collections 1979–1992 (1993), Sea-Level Rise and Coastal Defence in the Southern North Sea (jt ed, 2004), Climate Change and the European Countryside (jtly, 2006); *Recreations* history, architecture, shooting; *Clubs* Norfolk; *Style*— Michael J Sayer, Esq, FSA; ✉ Sparham House, Norwich NR9 5PJ

SAYER, Paul Anthony; s of John Sayer (d 1992), of South Milford, nr Leeds, and Adelaide, *née* Lambert (d 1985); *b* 4 October 1955; *Educ* Tadcaster GS; *m* 31 Jan 1981, Anne, da of James Bell (d 1997); 1 s (Simon b 19 Dec 1984); *Career* author; shop asst 1973–76, RMN 1979, psychiatric nurse 1976–81 and 1986–89, shop keeper 1981–84, storeman 1984–85, author 1989–; Royal Literary Fund Fell Univ of Leeds 2008–10; memb Soc of Authors 1988; *Books* The Comforts of Madness (1988, Constable Trophy for Fiction, Whitbread First Novel Award, Whitbread Book of the Year Award), Howling at the Moon (1990), The Absolution Game (1992), The Storm-Bringer (1994), The God Child (1996), Men in Rage (1998), Like So Totally (2010); *Recreations* lifelong supporter of York City FC, and other hopeless causes; *Style*— Paul Sayer, Esq; ✉ e-mail paulsayer@fsmail.net

SAYER, Philip William; s of Edward George Poulton Sayer, of Basingstoke, Hants, and Jean, *née* Kennedy; *b* 7 January 1947; *Educ* Queen Mary's GS Basingstoke; *m* Dec 1984, Joan Katherine, da of Ronald Frederick Taylor; 1 da (Rosie b Sept 1985), 1 s (Joseph b 21 July 1991); *Career* photographer; asst to Maurice Broomfield, photographer Butlins Holiday Camp Bognor 1965–67, photographic printer Derek Robinson Partnership 1967–70, freelance editorial photographer 1970–; currently contrib to various magazines incl: Domus (RA magazine), Crafts, Blueprint, World of Interiors, GQ (USA), Travel & Leisure (USA), ES, The Times – Saturday Review; currently photographer numerous design gps Europe and USA; solo exhibitions: Portraits for Print (Norwich Sch of Art) 1983, The Face of Craft (Br Crafts Centre) 1984, Portraits (Impressions Gallery York) 1985, permanent exhibition of portraits (The Blueprint Café Design Museum London) 1989, The 100 Mile City (exhibition Architectural Fndn London) 1992, The Making of the Modern World (Science Museum) 1993, The Hermitage, St Petersburg (Pentagram Gallery) 1995, Eye to Eye (Barrett Marsden Gallery London) 2002, Icons of Icons (RCA) 2003; FCSD 1983; *Books* Building of Faith – Westminster Cathedral (1995), Critical Mass (Royal Acad, 1998), Alexander 'Greek' Thompson (with Gavin Stamp, 1999), West Wing (2005), Studio, Ruthin Crafts Centre (2010), Gordon Baldwin Objects for a Landscape (with David Whiting, 2012); *Recreations* painting, cycling, music (jazz, country and western), reading; *Style*— Philip Sayer, Esq; ✉ e-mail philip.sayer@talk21.com, website http://www.philipsayerpartnership.com/

SAYER, Robert; s of Kenneth Sayer (d 1979) and Ellen; *b* 16 January 1952; *Educ* Salvatorian Coll Harrow Weald, Univ of Swansea (BA); *m* 1997, Catherine Hunt; *Career* founder and sr ptnr Sayer Moore & Co 1983; Law Soc: memb 1979–, vice-pres 1995–96 and 1998–99 (dep vice-pres 1997–98), dep treas 1996–97, treas 1997–99, pres 1999–2000; memb: Law Soc of Ireland 1996, Cwlth Law Assoc; assoc memb America's Bar Assoc 1995–, hon memb Inst of Advanced Legal Studies; *Publications* numerous articles in Law Soc Gazette, The Lawyer, New Law Journal, Solicitors Journal; *Recreations* sailing, writing; *Clubs* Naval and Military; *Style*— Robert Sayer, Esq; ✉ Sayer Moore & Company, 190 Horn Lane, Acton, London W3 6PL (☎ 020 8993 7571, fax 020 8993 7763)

SAYER, Stephen Thomas; s of late Charles Martin Sayer, of Epping, Essex, and late Justina, *née* Marsden Jones; *b* 8 July 1945; *Educ* Framlingham Coll, Coll of Law London; *m* 1, 20 July 1968 (m dis 1987), Gillian Susan, da of John Talbot Warwick, of Rustington, W Sussex; 2 s (Edward b 1971, Timothy b and d 1973), 1 da (Harriet b 1976); m 2, 30 Jan 1988, Aileen, da of Roy Victor Wegener, of Toowoomba, Aust; *Career* admitted slr 1968; articles Iliffe Sweet & Co, ptnr Richards Butler 1974–2005 (asst slr 1968), sr lawyer Said Al-Shahry Law Office Muscat, managing lawyer OhmLaw Kuwait 2011–12; memb Advsy Bd Inst of Law City Univ, memb Ctee Omari-Br Lawyers Assoc; Freeman City of London 1978, Liveryman Worshipful Co of Slrs 1975; memb: Law Soc 1968, Lawyers Club 1980, Soc of English and American Lawyers, UK Assoc of European Law; *Books* Joint Ventures with International Partners, International Joint Venture and Agency and Distribution sections of Longman's Commercial Precedents, Negotiating International Joint Ventures, Technology, Media and Telecommunications Review (jt contrib); *Recreations* real tennis, reading, theatre, history; *Clubs* Reform, Lansdowne, Hatfield House, Chelsea Soc; *Style*— Stephen Sayer, Esq; ✉ Saslo, PO Box 1288, PC112, Muscat, Oman (e-mail stephen.sayer@me.com)

SAYERS, Michael Patrick; QC (1988); s of Maj (Herbert James) Michael Sayers, RA (ka 1943), and Sheilah de Courcy Holroyd, *née* Stephenson (d 1969); *b* 28 March 1940; *Educ* Harrow, Fitzwilliam Coll Cambridge (Evelyn Rothschild scholar, MA); *m* 12 March 1976, Moussie Brougham, *née* Hallstrom; 1 da (Nicola b 27 Dec 1980), 1 s (Frederick b 3 Dec 1981), 1 step s (Henry Brougham b 12 Nov 1971); *Career* called to the Bar Inner Temple 1970 (bencher 1994); jr Central Criminal Court Bar Mess 1975–78, supplementary prosecuting counsel to the Crown Central Criminal Court 1977–88, dep circuit judge 1981, recorder of the Crown Court 1986–2005 (asst recorder 1982); memb Ctee Barrs' Benevolent Assoc 1991–2007; chm Harrow Assoc 1991–97 (vice-pres 1999), hon sec Anglo-Swedish Soc 2006– (vice-chm 2016); *Recreations* shooting, stalking, theatre, Sweden; *Clubs* Garrick, Pratt's, Swinley Forest Golf; *Style*— Michael Sayers, Esq, QC; ✉ 26 King's Quay, Chelsea Harbour, London SW10 0UX (fax 020 7351 4466)

SAYERS, Michael Warwick; s of Warwick Sayers (d 1977), and Sheila, *née* Carr (d 2008); *b* 25 August 1943; *Educ* Charterhouse, Univ of Oxford; *m* 23 Aug 1969, Elizabeth Ruth, *née* Wood; 1 da (Rachel b 26 Dec 1970), 1 s (Jeremy b 24 Feb 1973); *Career* called to the Bar 1967; legal advsr Central Criminal Court 1966–72, advocate Criminal Injuries Compensation Bd 1972–76, legal advsr Law Cmmn 1976–78, sec Cncl on Tbnls 1981–87 (legal advsr 1978–81); Lord Chllr's Dept: head Criminal Policy and Professional Practice Div 1987–88, head Judicial Appts Div 1988–91, head Family Law Div 1991–94; chief exec and sec Law Cmmn 1994–2003; chm Panel of Arbitrators UK Sport Resolutions 2000– (memb Panel Appts and Review Bd 2005–11), legal advsr Selection Panels for UK Athletics for Olympics and Paralympics 2004–12, chm Licensing Ctee LTA 2008–, chm Disciplinary Panel LTA 2011–, memb Panels on Integrity and Discipline and on Selection and Eligibility 2012–; gen sec Cwlth Assoc of Law Reform Agencies 2004–; law reform int conslt 2004–; legal chm NHS Tbnl 1996–2000, chm Parole Local Ctees 1987–95, memb Clergy Discipline Cmmn of the C of E 2004–13; first chm Editorial Bd Tribunals 1994; govr Aldro Sch 1983–2014 (chm 2006–14); FRSA; *Publications* Tribunals Practice and Procedure (jtly, 1985), The Council on Tribunals: New Developments in Research (1985), The Council on Tribunals (1986), Tribunals, Inquiries and Ombudsmen (jtly, 1987), Franks Revisited: A Model of the Ideal Tribunal (jtly, 1990), The Importance and Variety of Tribunals (1994), Co-operation between Commonwealth Law Reform Agencies (2000), International Co-operation in Law Reform (2003), Law Reform Across the Commonwealth: a New Voice (2005), Best Practices in Law Reform (2005), Law Reform: Co-operation Across Frontiers (2005), Small States and Law Refom (2008), Law Reform: in the Commonwealth, in Small States and in the Caribbean (2009); *Recreations* involvement in local church, sport; *Clubs* Surrey Sports Park Squash (Guildford); *Style*— Michael Sayers, Esq; ✉ e-mail thesayers@hotmail.com

SAYLE, Alexei David; s of Joseph Henry Sayle (d 1984), *née* Mendelson (d 2013); *b* 7 August 1952; *Educ* Alsop HS Liverpool, Southport Art Sch, Chelsea Sch of Art (DipAD), Garnet Coll Roehampton (CertEd); *m* Linda Eleanor, da of Noel Rawsthorn; *Career* comedian, actor and writer; master of ceremonies: Comedy Store Club 1979–80, Comic Strip Club 1980–81; various solo tours as stand-up comedian and residency at Edinburgh Festival; *Television* incl: The Young Ones 1982–85, The Strike 1987, Alexei Sayle's Stuff 1988–91, Night Voice 1990, Itch 1991, Selling Hitler 1991, The All-New Alexei Sayle Show 1994 and 1995, Paris 1995, Sorry About Last Night (writer and actor, BBC) 1995, Great Railway Journeys of the World 1996, Hospital! (Channel 5) 1997, Alexei Sayle's Merry Go Round (BBC) 1998, Alexei Sayle's Liverpool (documentary, BBC 2) 2008; *Films* Gorky Park 1983, Supergrass 1985, Siesta 1986, Indiana Jones and the Last Crusade 1989, Swing 1999; *Recordings* single released Ullo John! Gotta New Motor? 1984; *Radio* presenter Fourth Column (Radio 4) 1994; *Columnist* Time Out, Sunday Mirror, The Observer Magazine, The Independent, Esquire, Car; motoring corr Daily Telegraph; *Awards* Best Comedy Awards incl: Pye Radio 1981, RTS 1988, Broadcast Press Guild 1988, International Emmy 1988, Bronze Rose of Montreux; *Books* Train to Hell (1982), Geoffrey the Tube Train and the Fat Comedian (1987), Great Bus Journeys of the World (1988), Barcelona Plates (2000), The Dog Catcher (2001), Overtaker (2003), The Weeping Women Hotel (2006), Mister Roberts (2008), Stalin Ate My Homework (memoir, 2010); *Recreations* cycling; *Clubs* Chelsea Arts; *Style*— Alexei Sayle; ✉ c/o Cassie Mayer Ltd, 5 Old Garden House, The Lanterns, Bridge Lane, London SW11 3AD

SAYWELL, (John Anthony) Telfer; JP (Richmond 1985); s of John Rupert Saywell (d 1948), of London, and Winifred, *née* Green (d 1980); *b* 19 August 1939; *Educ* Abingdon Sch, Open Univ (BA); *m* 8 June 1968, June Mary, da of Maurice Thomas Hunnable (d 1972), of Rivenhall, Essex; 1 da (Polly b 1969), 2 s (Thomas b 1971, Henry b 1977); *Career* CA; Fincham Vallance & Co 1958–63, Tansley Witt & Co 1963–69; Layton Fern & Co Ltd (coffee and tea specialists): joined 1969, md 1970, chm 1975–2011; pres UK Coffee Trade Benevolent Soc 1983–91; chm Mediation in Divorce 1997–2001, chm Richmond upon Thames Magistrates Court 2004–06, chm London Bench Forum 2006; govr RSC 1982–; treas: Harlequin FC 1971–78, Union Soc City of Westminster 1985–98, St Luke's Educnl Centre 1989–99, Integrated Neurological Services 2009–; hon auditor Richmond upon Thames Disabled Assoc 1973–98, Master Billingsgate Ward Club 1987–88; Freeman City of London 1981, Master Worshipful Co of Carmen 1998, memb Worshipful Co of Parish Clerks 2000; FCA 1964; *Recreations* sailing, studying, skiing; *Clubs* Harlequin FC, Leander, Frinton Working Men's; *Style*— Telfer Saywell, Esq; ✉ 1 Cumberland Road, Kew Gardens, Richmond, Surrey TW9 3HJ (☎ 020 8940 0528)

S

SBIHI, Mohamed; *b* 27 March 1988; *Educ* Hollyfield Sch, St Mary's UC; *Career* rower; achievements incl: Silver medal (eights) World Championships 2010 and 2011, Bronze medal (eights) Olympic Games 2012; *Clubs* Molesey Boat; *Style*— Mohamed Sbihi, Esq

SCADDING, Dr Glenis Kathleen; *née* Dawes; *b* 3 October 1947; *Educ* Newnham Coll Cambridge (sr scholar, MA), Middx Hosp Med Sch (Florence Johnstone and Stoney clinical studentship, Freeman scholar in obstetrics, MB BChir), Univ of Cambridge (MD, Ralph Noble prize); *m*; 4 c; *Career* house physician Middx Hosp 1972–73, house surgn Kettering Gen Hosp 1972–73, SHO in neurology Walton Hosp Liverpool 1973–74, MO Shining Hosp Pokhara Nepal 1974–75, SHO Med Unit Brompton Hosp 1974–75, Abbott research fell and hon registrar in endocrinology Royal Free Hosp 1976–80, hon lectr in med Royal Free Med Unit 1978, Wellcome research fell Dept of Neurological Scis 1980–83, sr registrar Dept of Immunology Middx Hosp 1983–87, conslt physician in rhinology and allergy Royal Nat Throat, Nose and Ear Hosp and hon sr lectr Dept of Immunology UCL Sch of Med 1987–, Joseph Sr White fell RCP 1988–92; pres UK Semiochemistry Network; William Frankland Award for Servs to Clinical Allergy in the UK 2006, Clemens von Pirquet Award European Acad of Allergy and Immunology 2012, Walter Jobson Horne Award BMA 2012, World Allergy Orgn Distinguished Clinician Award 2013; pres Br Soc for Allergy and Clinical Immunology (sec 2006–09); memb: European Acad of Allergy and Clinical Immunology (former chair ENT Section), RSM (pres Section of Immunology), BMA, Br Soc for Immunology, Antibody Club, Euro Rhinological Soc, Br Assoc of Paediatric Otolaryngologists; assoc memb: RCPath, Zoological Soc; FRCP

1995 (MRCP); *Books* Clinical Immunology (co-ed), Immunology of ENT Disorders (ed, 1995), Investigative Rhinology (with Prof V J Lund, 2004), Paediatric ENT (co-ed, 2007), Fast Facts in Rhinitis (co-author, 2007); *Clubs* Athenaeum; *Style*— Dr Glenis K Scadding; ✉ Royal National Throat, Nose & Ear Hospital, Gray's Inn Road, London WC1X 8DA (☎ 020 7915 1542, fax 020 7915 1430, e-mail g.scadding@ucl.ac.uk)

SCALES, Prunella Margaret Rumney; CBE (1992); da of John Richardson Illingworth (d 1977), and Catherine, *née* Scales (d 1982); *Educ* Moira House Eastbourne, Old Vic Theatre Sch London; *m* 1963, Timothy West, *qv*, s of H Lockwood West, of Brighton, E Sussex; 2 s (Samuel, *qv*, b 1966, Joseph b 1969); *Career* actress, dir and teacher; frequent broadcasts, readings, poetry recitals and fringe productions, has directed plays at Bristol Old Vic, Arts Theatre Cambridge, Billingham Forum, Almost Free Theatre London, Nottingham Playhouse, West Yorkshire Playhouse and Nat Theatre of WA Perth; teacher at several drama schools; Hon DLitt: Univ of Bradford 1995, UEA 1996; *Theatre* seasons at Stratford-on-Avon and Chichester Festival Theatre 1967–68; credits incl: The Promise 1967, Hay Fever 1968, It's a Two-Foot-Six-Inches-Above-The-Ground-World 1970, The Wolf 1975, Breezeblock Park 1978, Make and Break (Haymarket) 1980, An Evening with Queen Victoria 1980, The Merchant of Venice 1981, Quartermaine's Terms (Queen's) 1981, When We Are Married (Whitehall) 1986, Single Spies (RNT) 1989, School for Scandal (RNT) 1990, Long Day's Journey into Night (RNT) 1991, Some Singing Blood (Royal Court) 1992, The Editing Process (Royal Court) 1995, Staying On 1997, Just the Three of Us 1997, The Birthday Party 1999, The Cherry Orchard 2000, The External 2001, A Day in the Death of Joe Egg 2001, Too Far to Walk (King's Head) 2002, A Woman of No Importance (Theatre Royal London) 2004, Gertrude's Secret (New End Theatre London) 2007–08, Carrie's War (Apollo Theatre) 2009; *Television* incl: Sybil Fawlty in Fawlty Towers (BBC) 1975–79, Doris and Doreen, A Wife like the Moon, Grand Duo, The Merry Wives of Windsor 1982, Outside Edge, Mapp and Lucia 1985, After Henry 1990, The Rector's Wife (Channel 4) 1994, Signs and Wonders (BBC) 1994, The World of Lee Evans (Channel 4) 1995, Searching (ITV) 1995, Emma (Meridian/ITV) 1996, Lord of Misrule (BBC) 1996, Breaking the Code (BBC) 1996, Midsomer Murders, The Ghost of Greville Lodge 2000, Looking for Victoria, Mr Loveday's Little Outing 2006, Miss Marple 2008, The Royal 2011; *Films* incl: Hobson's Choice 1951, Laxdale Hall 1952, The Lonely Passion of Judith Hearne 1989, A Chorus of Disapproval 1989, Howards End 1990, Wolf 1994, An Awfully Big Adventure 1994, Stiff Upper Lips 1996, An Ideal Husband 1999, Horrid Henry 2011, Sub Rosa 2013, The Phone Call 2013; *Recreations* gardening, canal boat; *Style*— Prunella Scales, CBE; ✉ c/o Conway van Gelder Ltd, Third Floor, 8–12 Broadwick Street, London W1F 8HW (☎ 020 7287 0077, fax 020 7287 1940, e-mail vena@conwayvg.co.uk)

SCALLY, Dr Gabriel John; s of Bernard Gabriel Scally, and Maureen, *née* Hopkins; *b* 24 September 1954; *Educ* St Mary's GS Belfast, Queen's Univ Belfast (MB BCh, BAO), London Sch of Hygiene and Tropical Med London (MSc), FFPHM, MFPHMI, MRCGP; *m* 1990, Rona Margaret, *née* Campbell; 2 da; *Career* trainee in gen practice 1980–81, sr tutor Dept of Community Med Queen's Univ Belfast 1984–86, chief admin MO and dir of public health Eastern Health and Social Servs Bd Belfast 1989–93 (conslt in public health med 1986–88); regnl dir of public health: SE Thames RHA 1993–94, S and W RHA 1994–96, SW Region 1996–; memb: NI Bd for Nursing, Health Visiting and Midwifery 1988–93, Cncl BMA 1985–86 and 1988–89 (chm Jr Membs Forum 1988–89), GMC 1989–99, Nat Treatment Agency for Substance Misuse 2004–; author of papers on med research and health policy in med jls; *Recreations* sailing, traditional and contemporary Irish music, theatre, London Irish RFC; *Style*— Dr Gabriel Scally; ✉ 11 Dowry Square, Bristol BS8 4SH (☎ 0117 926 8510); Regional Public Health Group, Government Office for the South West, 2 Rivergate Temple Quay, Bristol BS1 6ED (☎ 0117 900 3530, fax 0117 900 1911, e-mail gscally.gosw@go-regions.gsi.gov.uk)

SCANLON, Mary; da of John Charles Campbell (d 1981), and Anne, *née* O'Donnell (d 2001); *b* 25 May 1947; *Educ* Craigo Secdy Sch Montrose, Univ of Dundee (MA); *m* 26 Sept 1970, James Scanlon; 1 da (Claire b 26 Jan 1973), 1 s (Grant James b 11 Oct 1974); *Career* various admin and secretarial posts 1963–70; lectr: Abertay Univ Perth and Inverness Coll 1982–99; MSP (Cons) Highlands and Islands 1999–2016; MIPD; *Recreations* hill walking, swimming, pilates; *Style*— Mary Scanlon

SCANNELL, Rick; *Educ* Univ of East London (BA), Univ of Cambridge (LLM); *Career* called to the Bar 1986; practising barr specialising in EU free movement law and immigration, human rights and refugee law, currently memb Garden Court Chambers; notable cases in House of Lords incl: Oladehinde and Alexander v Sec of State for the Home Dept (SSHD) 1991, M v Home Office 1994, T v SSHD 1996, Sepet and Bulbul v SSHD 2001, Saadi and others v SSHD 2001, N v SSHD 2006; cases before European Court of Human Rights incl: Saadi v UK 2007, N v UK 2007; before European Court of Justice Bidar v UK 2005; chair Immigration Law Practitioners' Assoc (ILPA) 2000–05 (memb 1983–); special advocate Special Immigration Appeals Cmmn 1998–2005 (resigned over Govt's failure to release Belmarsh detainees despite contrary House of Lords decision); memb: Administrative Law Bar Assoc, Justice, Haldane Soc, Legal Action; Hon LLD Univ of E London 2005; *Publications* Immigration: Recent Developments (co-writer, 1985–2003), Current Law (edns 1996, 1997, 1999 and 2002), Butterworths Immigration Law Service (co-ed, 1997–), Immigration, Nationality and Asylum under the Human Rights Act 1998 (contrib, 1999), Macdonald's Immigration Law and Practice (contrib, 5 edn 2001, 6 edn 2004) Freedom of Movement of Persons in the Enlarged European Union (co-writer, 2004), Halsbury's Laws of England, Vol 4 (2): British Nationality, Immigration and Asylum (contrib); *Recreations* circus skills (flying trapeze, acro-balance, unicycling and juggling), car and motorbike racing; *Style*— Rick Scannell, Esq

SCARD, Dennis Leslie; s of late Charles Leslie Scard (d 1998), of Harrow, and Doris Annie Scard (d 1976); *b* 8 May 1943; *Educ* Lascelles County Secdy Sch, Trinity Coll of Music; *m* Linda Christine, *née* Perry; 2 s from prev m (Timothy Martin b 27 Feb 1969, Christopher Robin b 18 July 1974); *Career* professional musician (horn player) 1962–85 (worked with various symphony and chamber orchs and other musical combinations, opera, ballet, recording and theatre work); Musicians' Union: memb Exec Ctee 1979–85, dist official E and NE area 1985–90, gen sec 1990–2000; former chair Shoreham Port Authy; memb Bd Symphony Hall/Town Hall Birmingham; former memb Central Arbitration Ctee ACAS, former lay memb Employment Tbnl Serv; chair Henry Wood Accommodation Tst; Hon FTCL; memb Royal Soc of Musicians 1983; *Recreations* music, theatre, cooking, walking, lawn bowls; *Style*— Dennis Scard, Esq; ✉ 6 Cranborne Avenue, Meads, Eastbourne, East Sussex BN20 7TS (☎ 01323 648364, e-mail calverton100@hotmail.com)

SCARDINO, Dame Marjorie Morris; DBE (2002); da of Robert Weldon Morris (d 1990), of Texas, and Beth, *née* Lamb; *b* 25 January 1947; *Educ* Baylor Univ TX (BA), George Washington Univ Law Sch, Univ of San Francisco Law Sch (JD); *m* 1974, Albert J Scardino; 1 da (Adelaide b 1978), 2 s (William b 1979, Albert b 1984); *Career* ptnr Brannen Wessels Searcy law firm Savannah Ga 1975–85, publisher The Georgia Gazette 1978–85 (winner Pulitzer Prize), pres The Economist Newspaper Gp Inc New York 1985–92, chief exec The Economist Gp plc London 1992–96, gp chief exec Pearson plc 1997–; non-exec dir Nokia Corp; memb various charitable and advsy bds incl: The Carter Center, John D and Catherine T MacArthur Fndn, Oxfam; memb American Acad of Arts & Sciences 2010; *Style*— Dame Marjorie Scardino, DBE; ✉ Pearson plc, 80 Strand, London WC2R 0RL

SCARFE, Gerald Anthony; CBE (2008); s of Reginald Thomas Scarfe, and Dorothy Edna, *née* Gardner; *b* 1 June 1936; *m* Jane Asher, *qv*, da of Dr Richard Asher (d 1968), of London; 1 da (Katie Geraldine b 11 April 1974), 2 s (Alexander David b 16 Dec 1981, Rory Christopher b 10 Dec 1983); *Career* designer and director; political cartoonist of the Sunday Times 1967–; designer and dir of animation Pink Floyd's The Wall (MGM Film and live shows); exhbns: UK tour 2001 and 2003, Sheffield Galleries 2005, Fine Art Soc 2005, Portcullis House Westminster 2008, Portcullis House House of Commons 2008–09, work from Pink Floyd The Wall (Halle Germany) 2009, Milksnatcher – The Thatcher Drawings (Bowes Museum) 2015; projects and inflatables for Roger Waters worldwide live tour The Wall 2011–12; major retrospective exhbns: Wilhelm Busch Museum Hanover 2010, Egon Schiele Gallery Czech Repub 2012, Kampa Museum Prague 2013; 6 sculptures of the Br Character (Millennium Dome) 2000; creator of original murals for Scarfes Bar Rosewood Hotel London 2014; Hon Dr Arts Univ of Liverpool, Hon DLitt Univ of Kent, Hon DLitt Univ of Dundee 2007; *Theatre* numerous scenery and costume credits incl: Orpheus in the Underworld (London Coliseum), What a Lucky Boy (Manchester Royal Exchange), Ubu Unchained (Traverse Theatre), Magic Flute (LA Opera), An Absolute Turkey (Globe), Mind Millie for Me (Haymarket), designer of animation and inflatables Pink Floyd The Wall stage shows 1980, Scarfe at the NPG (one man show at Nat Portrait Gallery) 1998, Fantastic Mr Fox (LA Opera) 1998, The Magic Flute (Seattle Opera) 1999 and (San Francisco Opera) 2007, Peter and the Wolf (Holiday on Ice Paris and world tour) 2000, The Nutcracker (ENB London Coliseum and nat tour) 2002–09, animation sequence for Miss Saigon (UK tour) 2004–05, Miss Saigon (int tour) 2006–10, The Magic Flute (LA Opera) 2008; *Television* dir of films for the BBC: Hogarth 1970, Scarfe by Scarfe 1986, Scarfe's Follies 1987, I Like The Girls Who Do 1988, Scarfe on... 1989, Scarfe on Sex 1991, Scarfe on Art 1991, Scarfe in Paradise 1992, Scarfe on Class 1993; designed title sequence for Yes Minister series 1980 and Yes Prime Minister 1985 and 2012; *Film* designer of animated sequences Pink Floyd The Wall 1982, prodn designer and character design for Walt Disney's Hercules 1997; *Books* Scarfe by Scarfe (1986), Scarfe's Seven Deadly Sins (1987), Scarfe's Line of Attack (1988), Scarfeland (1989), Scarfe on Stage (1992), Scarfe Face (1993), Hades – The Truth at Last (1997), Heroes and Villains (2003), Gerald Scarfe: Drawing Blood (2005), Monsters (2008), Gerald Scarfe: The Making of Pink Floyd The Wall (2010); *Recreations* skiing; *Clubs* Brooks's; *Style*— Gerald Scarfe, Esq, CBE; ✉ e-mail info@geraldscarfe.com, website www.geraldscarfe.com

SCARISBRICK, Diana; da of Charles Wood (d 1994), and Genevieve, *née* Sutherland (d 1995); *b* 8 October 1928; *Educ* Christ's Hosp, St Hugh's Coll Oxford (exhibitioner, MA); *m* 5 July 1955, Peter Ewald Scarisbrick, s of Charles Ewald Scarisbrick (d 1966); 1 da (Sophie Hastings-Bass b 15 May 1956); *Career* freelance lectr and writer on jewellery and engraved gems; jewellery ed Harpers & Queen Magazine 1990–93, memb Editorial Advsy Panel Apollo magazine; contrib to: Burlington Magazine, Apollo Magazine, Country Life, Il Giornale Dell'Arte, exhibition and museum catalogues in Belgium, Britain, Sweden, Germany, France, USA and Japan; research assoc Beazley Archive Inst of Classical and Byzantine Studies Univ of Oxford; memb: Soc of Antiquaries; *Books* The Ralph Harari Collection of Finger Rings (with Prof John Boardman, 1977), Jewellery (1984), Il Valore Dei Gioielli e Degli Orologi da Collezione (1984 and 1987), 2500 Years of Rings (1988), Ancestral Jewels (1989), Rings (1993), Jewels in Britain 1066–1837 (1994), Classical Gems, Ancient and Modern Intaglios and Cameos in the Fitzwilliam Museum, Cambridge (with Dr Martin Henig and Mary Whiting, 1994), Tudor and Jacobean Jewellery (1995), Chaumet, Master Jewellers from 1780 (1995), Chaumet: Two Centuries of Fine Jewellery (catalogue of exhbn at Musée Carnavalet Paris, 1998), Crowning Glories: Two Centuries of Tiaras (catalogue of exhbn at Museum of Fine Arts Boston, 2000), Three Thousand Years of Rings (catalogue of exhbn of Hashimoto ring collection at Teien Met Art Museum Tokyo, 2000), From the Renaissance to Art Deco: Jewellery 1540–1940 (catalogue of exhbn at Teien Met Art Museum Tokyo 2003), Historic Rings: Four Thousand Years of Craftsmanship (2004), Napoléon Amoureux (exhbn at 12 Place Vendôme, Paris 2004), Dignity and Beauty: The Story of the Tiara (exhbn at Bunkamura Museum Tokyo 2007), Rings: Jewellery of Power, Love and Loyalty (2007), The Art of Gem Engraving from Alexander the Great to Napoleon III (exbhn catalogue Hakone Museum, 2008), Brilliant Europe: Jewels of the European Court (2008), Scottish Jewellery (2009), Brilliant Impressions: An Exhibition of Antique Paste and Other Jewellery (exhbn catalogue S J Phillips, 2010), Portrait Jewels: Opulence & Intimacy from the Medici to the Romanovs (2011), Indian Jewellery: Enchanting the West (contrib, exhbn Kremlin 2014), Elihu Yale: Merchant, Collector & Philanthropist (2014); *Recreations* walking, sight-seeing; *Style*— Mrs Diana Scarisbrick; ✉ 11 Chester Terrace, London NW1 4ND

SCARLETT, Sir John McLeod; KCMG (2007, CMG 2001), OBE (1987); s of Dr James Henri Stuart Scarlett (d 1961), of Bromley, Kent, and Clara Dunlop, *née* Morton (d 2006); *Educ* Epsom Coll, Magdalen Coll Oxford (MA); *m* 1970, Gwenda Mary Rachel, da of Norman Howard Stilliard; 3 da (Alexia b 1971, Victoria b 1976, Rhiannon b 1979), 1 s (John b 1986); *Career* joined HM Dip Serv 1971, third sec Nairobi 1973–74, second sec Moscow 1976–77; first sec: FCO 1977–84, Paris 1984–88, FCO 1988–91; political cnsllr Moscow 1991–94, cnsllr FCO 1994–2001, chm Jt Intelligence Ctee 2001–04, chief Secret Intelligence Service (MI6) 2004–09; memb Bd Times Newspapers Ltd, sr advsr Morgan Stanley, sr advsr Statoil; chm Bletchley Park Tst, tstee Imperial War Museum; *Clubs* Oxford and Cambridge; *Style*— Sir John McLeod Scarlett, KCMG, OBE

SCASE, Prof Richard; *Educ* Thetford GS, Univ of Leicester (MA), Univ of Kent (PhD); *m* 1967 (m dis 1987), Anita Scase; 2 da (Camilla b 23 June 1969, Katrina b 10 March 1976); *Career* research fell Univ of East Anglia 1965–67; Univ of Kent: asst lectr 1967–69, lectr 1969–76, sr lectr 1976–84, prof of organisational behaviour 1984–; currently prof of mgmnt Univ of Kent; visiting prof: Univ of London, Univ of Auckland, Monash Univ Aust, Tilburg Univ the Netherlands, Univ of Essex; fndr media co part of Capital Gp UK; fndr (with two others) business to business co providing on-line learning materials for corp mgmnt devpt progs; memb: DTI Retail and Consumer Services Panel, DTI Design for Living in an Ageing Soc Working Gp, EC Working Pty 1998–2000; keynote speaker at corp and indust events; voted by Personnel Today as ninth most influential person in Br on personnel and human resource mgmnt; *Publications* 23 authored and co-authored books incl Reluctant Managers (1989) and Corporate Realities (1995), Britain 2010: The Changing Business Landscape (2000), Living in the Corporate 200 (2002), Global Remix (2007); contrib to national newspapers, professional magazines, radio and tv progs; *Clubs* Athenaeum; *Style*— Prof Richard Scase; ✉ University of Kent, 10 St Stephen's Hill, Canterbury, Kent CT2 7AX (☎ 01227 463430, e-mail r.scase@kent.ac.uk, website www.richardscase.com)

SCHAEFER, Prof Stephen Martin; s of Gerhardt Martin Schaefer, OBE (d 1986), of Bramhall, Cheshire, and Helga Maria Schaefer (d 1992); *b* 18 November 1946; *Educ* Manchester Grammar, Univ of Cambridge (MA), Univ of London (PhD); *m* 26 July 1969 (m dis 2009), Teresa Evelyn; 2 s (Maximilian b 1974, Joshua b 1977); *Career* London Business Sch: research offr, sr research offr and lectr 1970–79; asst prof Stanford Univ 1979–81; London Business Sch: sr research fell and prof of finance 1981–, dir Inst of Fin and Accounting 1985–92, research dean 1992–95; visiting asst prof: Univ of Chicago, Univ of Calif Berkeley 1977; visiting prof: Univ of Venice 1991, Univ of Cape Town 1996; dir: Lawtex plc 1974–91, Securities Assoc 1990–91, Securities and Futures Authy 1991–96, Tokai Derivative Products Ltd 1998–99; non-exec dir: Tokai Bank Europe 2000–02, Leo Fund Managers 2004–11; tstee Smith Breeden Mutual Funds 1992–2000; memb American Fin

Assoc; *Style—* Prof Stephen Schaefer; ✉ London Business School, Sussex Place, Regents Park, London NW1 4SA (☎ 020 7000 8267, fax 020 7000 8201, e-mail sschaefer@london.edu)

SCHAFF, Alistair Graham; QC (1999); s of John Schaff, and Barbara Dorothy, *née* Williams; *b* 25 September 1959; *Educ* Bishop's Stortford Coll, Magdalene Coll Cambridge (MA); *m* 13 April 1991, (Marie) Leona, *née* Burley; 1 s (Dominic Michael b 21 Jan 1994), 1 da (Eleanor Marcella b 4 Sept 1996); *Career* called to the Bar 1983; *Recreations* family life, foreign travel, history, spectator sports; *Style—* Alistair Schaff, Esq, QC; ✉ 7 King's Bench Walk, Temple, London EC4Y 7DS (☎ 020 7583 0404, fax 020 7583 0950, e-mail clerks@7kbw.law.co.uk)

SCHAPIRA, Prof Anthony Henry Vernon; s of Marcus Schapira (d 1994), of Yorkshire, and Hannah Constance (d 1982); *Educ* Bradford GS, Westminster Med Sch (entrance scholar, Berridge research scholar, BSc, MB BS, MD, DSc, AKC); *m* 1; 1 da (Sarah Victoria Constance b 1983); m 2, 2003, Laura, da of Robert Swan Johnson; *Career* house physician to Sir Richard Bayliss, Chief Physician to HM The Queen 1979, med trg Hammersmith and Whittington Hosps, Nat Hosp for Neurology and Neurosurgery and St Thomas' Hosp 1980–84, trg in neurology Royal Free Hosp and Nat Hosp for Neurology and Neurosurgery 1983–88, Wellcome research fell 1985–87; Royal Free and UC Med Sch and Inst of Neurology London: sr lectr and conslt in neurology 1988–90, univ chair of clinical neurosciences 1990–; conslt neurologist Royal Free Hosp, Nat Hosp for Neurology and Neurosurgery; vice-dean UCL 2009– (dir UCL Royal Free Campus 2009), non-exec dir Bd Royal Free London Fndn Tst 2009–; non-exec dir Office of the Public Guardian Miny of Justice 2012–; co-ed-in-chief European Jl of Neurology 2006–12 (ed-in-chief 2012–); hon prof of neurology Mount Sinai Med Sch NY 1995; visiting prof: Harvard Univ 2009, Yale Univ 2010; Queen Square Prize 1986, Graham Bull Prize for Clinical Sci RCP 1995, European Prize for Clinical Science 1998, Buckston Browne Medal Harveian Soc 1995, Opprecht Prize 1999, Duchenne Prize 2005; memb: Movement Disorders Soc, Harveian Soc 1994; FRCP 1992, FMedSci 1999; *Books* Mitochondrial Disorders in Neurology (1994), Mitochondria: DNA, Protein and Disease (1994), Muscle Diseases (1999), Clinical Cases in Neurology (2001), Mitochondrial Disorders in Neurology 2 (2002), Mitochondrial Function and Dysfunction (2002), Current Treatment of Parkinson's Disease (2005), Textbook of Neurology and Clinical Neuroscience (2005), Parkinsonian Disorders (2008), Movement Disorders 4 (2009); *Recreations* chess (Yorkshire champion 1966), motor racing, European history, international affairs; *Clubs* Athenaeum; *Style—* Prof Anthony Schapira; ✉ University Department of Clinical Neurosciences, Institute of Neurology, University College London, Rowland Hill Street, London NW3 2PF (☎ 020 7830 2012, fax 020 7472 6829)

SCHEER, Cherrill Sheila; *née* Hille; da of Maurice Hille (d 1968), and Ray Hille (d 1986); *b* 29 March 1939; *Educ* Copthall Co GS, Architectural Assoc London, Architectural Dept Kingston Sch of Art; *m* 3 Dec 1961, Ian Scheer, s of Oscar Scheer (d 1988); 1 s (Ivan), 1 da (Danielle Ann (Mrs Benson)); *Career* mktg dir Hille International Ltd 1970–83 (mktg mangr 1961–70); dir: Print Forum Ltd 1965–, S Hille & Co (Holdings) Ltd 1970–; dir gp mktg: Hille Ergonom plc 1983–89, Scott Howard Furniture Ltd 1989–91, Cherrill Scheer & Associates 1991–; congress dir Design Renaissance 1993 Int Design Congress; vice-pres Design & Industry Assoc (chm 1976–78); past govr London Met Univ; past chm Office Furniture, Furniture and Filing Mfrs' Assoc; current memb Nat Sch of Furniture Bd; hon fell in design Arts Inst at Bournemouth; Mixology10 Lifetime Achievement Award; Liveryman Worshipful Co of Furniture Makers; FCSD (past memb Cncl), FInstSMM, FRSA; *Recreations* architecture, design and modern art; *Style—* Mrs Cherrill Scheer; ✉ 16 Kerry Avenue, Stanmore, Middlesex HA7 4NN (☎ 020 8954 3839); Cherrill Scheer & Associates, Hille House, 132 St Albans Road, Watford, Hertfordshire WD24 4AE (☎ 01923 242769, fax 01923 228110, e-mail csa@hillehouse.co.uk)

SCHIEMANN, Rt Hon Sir Konrad Hermann Theodor; kt (1986), PC (1995); s of Helmuth Schiemann (d 1945), and Beate, *née* von Simson (d 1946); *b* 15 September 1937, Berlin; *Educ* King Edward's Sch Birmingham, Freiburg Univ, Pembroke Coll Cambridge (MA, LLB); *m* 1965, Elisabeth Hanna Eleonore, da of late John Holroyd-Reece; 1 da (Juliet b 1966); *Career* called to the Bar Inner Temple 1962 (bencher 1985, reader 2002, treas 2003), jr counsel to the Crown (Common Law) 1978–80; QC 1980, recorder of the Crown Court 1985, judge of the High Court of Justice (Queen's Bench Div) 1986–95, a Lord Justice of Appeal 1995–2003, judge Court of Justice of the EU 2004–12; chm Cncl St John's Smith Square 1995–2003 (memb 1984–95, tstee 1990–95), vice-chm Parole Bd 1991–92 (memb 1990): memb advsy bd: Centre for Euro Legal Studies Univ of Cambridge 1996–, Centre of Euro Private Law Münster Univ 1999–, Acad of European Law 2004–11, European Competition Jl 2005–, European Law Review 2006–; memb Cncl of Mgmnt Br Inst of Int and Competition Law 2000–06; contrib to English and German legal books and journals; govr English Nat Ballet 1995–2001, dir Acad of Ancient Music 2001–03, vice-chm Temple Music Fndn 2002–03; patron Busoga Tst 1999– (chm 1989–99); hon fell Pembroke Coll Cambridge 1998; *Recreations* music, reading, walking, water sources in Uganda; *Clubs* Athenaeum; *Style—* The Rt Hon Sir Konrad Schiemann

SCHIFF, Sir András; kt (2014); s of Odon Schiff, and Klara, *née* Csengeri; *b* 21 December 1953; *Educ* Franz Liszt Acad of Music Budapest (with Pal Kadosa, Ferenc Rados and Gyorgy Kurtag), private study with George Malcolm; *m* Oct 1987, Yuuko, *née* Shiokawa; *Career* concert pianist; regular orchestral engagements: NY Philharmonic, Chicago Symphony, Vienna Philharmonic, Concertgebouw Orchestra, Orchestre de Paris, London Philharmonic, London Symphony, Royal Philharmonic, Philharmonia, Israel Philharmonic, Washington Nat Symphony; orchestral conductor: Baltimore Symphony, Chamber Orchestra of Europe, City of Birmingham Symphony, LA Philharmonic, Philadelphia, Philharmonia; cr Cappella Andrea Barca (own orch) 1999; festivals incl: Vienna, Feldkirch, Salzburg, Lucerne, Edinburgh; fndr and artistic dir Musiktage Mondsee Festival 1989–98, co-fndr (with Heinz Holliger) Ittinger Pfingst Konzerte Kartause Ittingen 1995, started Hommage to Palladio series Teatro Olimpico Vicenza 1998; hon prof Music Schs Budapest, Detmold and Munich; hon memb Beethoven House Bonn 2006; special supernumerary fell Balliol Coll Oxford; memb of honour Vienna Konzerthaus 2012; Oder pour le Merite for Science and Arts 2012; *Awards* Premio della Academia Chigiana Siena 1987, Wiener Flotenuhr (Mozart Prize of the City of Vienna) 1989, Bartók Prize 1991, Instrumentalist of the Year Int Classical Music Awards 1993, Claudio Arrau Meml Medal Robert Schumann Soc 1994, Instrumentalist of the Year Royal Philharmonic Soc 1994, Kossuth Prize 1996, Leonie Sonnings Music Prize Copenhagen 1997, Penna d'Oro della Cittá di Vicenza 2003, Musikfest-Preis Bremen 2003, Premio della critica Musicale Franco Abbiati Italy 2007, Royal Acad of Music Prize 2007, Wigmore Hall Medal 2008, Klavier-Festival Ruhr Prize 2009, Schumann Prize City of Zwickau 2011, Int Stiftung Mozarteum Golden Mozart-Medaille 2012, Grosse Verdienstkreuz mit Stern der Bundesrepublik Deutschland 2012, Solo Instrumental Recording of the Year Int Classical Music Award 2012 (for Geistervariationen), Gold Medal Royal Philharmonic Soc 2013; *Recordings* incl: all the Mozart Piano Concertos (with The Camerata Academica Salzburg and Sandor Vegh), Bach Concertos (with The Chamber Orchestra of Europe), all the Schubert Piano Sonatas, Mozart Sonatas and Chamber Music (on Mozart's own instruments), Beethoven Piano Concertos (with The Staatskapelle Dresden and Bernard Haitink), Bartok Piano Concertos (with The Budapest Festival Orchestra and Ivan Fischer), Lieder (with Peter Schreier, Robert Holl, Cecilia Bartoli and Juliane Banse), Geistervariationen (with works by Robert Schumann); *Recreations* theatre, art, cinema, literature, languages, soccer; *Style—* Sir András Schiff; ✉ Askonas Holt Limited, Lincoln House, 300 High Holborn, London WC1V 7JH (☎ 020 7400 1799, e-mail Gaetan.LeDivelec@askonasholt.co.uk)

SCHILD, Geoffrey Christopher; CBE (1993); s of Christopher Schild (d 1963), of Sheffield, and Georgina Schild (d 1970); *b* 28 November 1935; *Educ* High Storrs GS Sheffield, Univ of Reading (BSc), Univ of Sheffield (PhD), Univ of Reading (DSc); *m* 1 Aug 1961, Tora, da of Canon Peter Madland (d 1977), of Bergen, Norway; 2 s (Øystein Christopher b 1962, Peter Geoffrey b 1969), 1 da (Ingrid b 1965); *Career* lectr in virology Univ of Sheffield 1963–67; dir World Influenza Centre at MRC Nat Inst for Med Res 1969–75 (memb scientific staff MRC 1967–75), dir and chief exec Nat Inst for Biological Standards and Control 1985–2002 (head Div of Virology 1975–85), currently chief scientific offr iBioPharma Inc USA; visiting prof in vaccinology Univ of Bergen 1998–, academic attachment Imperial Coll London; dir MRC Directed Prog of AIDS Res 1987–94; chm: MRC Working Gp on Hepatitis Vaccines, European Community Working Pty on Biotechnology 1986–93, Bd Int Soc for Influenza and other Respiratory Viruses; memb: Dept of Health Jt Ctee on Vaccination and Immunisation 1975–, MRC Ctee on Vaccines and Immunological Procedures 1975–93, Ctee on Safety of Medicines, Sub-Ctee on Biologicals 1977–, Nat Biological Standards Bd 1985–, MRC Aids Research Co-ordinating Ctee; WHO: memb Special Advsy Gp on Vaccine Devpt 1989–, memb Steering Ctee on AIDS Res 1989–, memb Advsy Task Force WHO Global Prog on Vaccines and Immunization, memb Strategic Task Force Children's Vaccine Initiative; memb and vice-chm Bd of Tstees Int Vaccines Inst Seoul, memb Bd UK Health Protection Agency 2003–; professional affrs offr UK Soc for Gen Microbiology 2002–; Freeman City of London 1988; Hon DSc Univ of Sheffield 2002; Hon FRCP 1999; FIBiol 1977, FRCPath 1993, FRCPEd 1998, FMedSci 2001; *Recreations* ornithology, music; *Style—* Dr Geoffrey C Schild, CBE; ✉ 17 Sunnyfield, Mill Hill, London NW7 4RD (☎ 020 8959 5767, fax 020 8906 3978, e-mail the.schilds@btinternet.com)

SCHILLING, Keith; *b* 25 July 1956; *Educ* City of London Poly (MA); *Career* slr-advocate specialising in reputation management, privacy protection, commercial litigation, copyright, data protection, cyber and family; formerly Wright Webb Syrett, sr ptnr and co-fndr Schilling & Lom 1984–, chairman and sr ptnr Schillings 2001–, slr-advocate Schillings 2008–; memb: Law Soc, Int Acad of Matrimonial Lawyers; *Publications* Reputation – Corporate and Individual Reputation Law Westlaw UK Insight, The Laws of Privacy and Confidentiality Writers' and Artists' Yearbook; author of various articles and pubns in the press; *Recreations* trekking, cycling, water sports; *Clubs* Soho House, Groucho's; *Style—* Keith Schilling, Esq; ✉ Schillings, 41 Bedford Square, London WC1B 3HX

SCHLAGMAN, Richard Edward; s of Jack Schlagman, of London, and Shirley, *née* Goldston (d 1992); *b* 11 November 1953, London; *Educ* UCS Hampstead, Brunel Univ; *Partner* Mia Hägg; 2 s (Johan Otto b 2010, Gustav b 2012); *Career* publisher; co-fndr, jt chm and md Interstate Electronics Ltd 1973–86, purchased Bush name from Rank Organisation and renamed IEL Bush Radio Ltd 1981, floated Bush Radio on London Stock Exchange 1984, Bush Radio plc sold 1986; acquired Phaidon Press Ltd 1990 (sold 2012), chm and publisher Phaidon Press Ltd 1990–2012, pres Phaidon Press Inc 1998–2012, acquired Cahiers du Cinéma 2009 (chm and publisher Cahiers du Cinéma 2009–); memb Bd Judd Fndn Texas 1999–2009 (pres 1999–2001); memb Exec Ctee Patrons of New Art Tate Gallery 1994–97, jury memb City of Ascona Concert Hall Architecture Competition 2004; patron: Bayreuther Festspiele, Salzburger Festspiele, Schubertiade Festival, Salzburger Osterfestspiele; memb Glyndebourne Festival Soc; FRSA; *Recreations* music, art, architecture; *Clubs* Chelsea Arts, Annabel's; *Style—* Richard Schlagman, Esq

SCHMIDT, Prof Michael Norton; OBE (2006); s of Carl Bernhardt Schmidt (d 1971), and Elizabeth Norton, *née* Hill (d 1990); *b* 2 March 1947; *Educ* The Hill Sch Pottstown PA, Christ's Hosp (ESU scholar), Harvard Univ, Wadham Coll Oxford (exhibitioner, MA, pres OU Poetry Soc), St John's Coll Cambridge; *m* (m dis), Claire Patricia Harman; 2 s (Charles Bernhardt b 1980, Benedict William b 1985), 1 da (Isabel Claire b 1982); *Partner* Angel Garcia Gomez (civil partnership); *Career* fndr md and editorial dir Carcanet Press Ltd 1969–; Univ of Manchester: Gulbenkian fell of poetry 1971–74, special lectr and sr lectr in poetry Dept of English 1974–98, dir The Writing Sch (formerly The Poetry Centre) 1993–98, dir Writing Sch and prof of English Manchester Metropolitan Univ 1998–2005, prof of poetry Univ of Glasgow 2006–14; writer in residence St John's Coll Cambridge 2012–15; fndr and gen ed PN Review (formerly Poetry Nation) 1972–; NW theatre critic The Independent 1986–88, Northern theatre critic The Daily Telegraph 1988–93; Br delegate at literary congresses in Liège Murcia Valencia and Paris; memb Arts Cncl Touring Panel 1991–94; adjudicator Translation Awards Br Comparative Literature Assoc 1992; advsr Finnish Literature Bd 1990–; selector Globe Theatre Awards 1993–95; dir Modern Poetry Archive Project Rylands; memb Finnish Literature Soc; FRSL 1994; *Books* British Poetry since 1960 (with G Lindop, 1972), Ten English Poets (1976), Flower and Song: Aztec Poetry (trans with E Kissam, 1977), Fifty Modern British Poets (1979), Fifty English Poets 1300–1900 (1979), Five American Poets (with J Mathias, 1979), Eleven British Poets (1980), British Poetry since 1970 (1980), The Colonist (published as Green Island in USA, 1983, LA Times Book Award, 1984), On Poets & Others (trans, 1986), The Dresden Gate (1988), Reading Modern Poetry (1989), New Poetries (1994), Lives of the Poets (1998), The First Poets: Lives of the Ancient Greek Poets (2004), The Novel: A Biography (2014); *Poetry* Black Buildings (1969), It Was My Tree (1970), Bedlam and the Oakwood (1970), Desert of the Lions (1972), My Brother Gloucester (1976), A Change of Affairs (1978), Choosing a Guest (1983), The Love of Strangers (1988), Selected Poems (1996), The Harvill Book of Twentieth-Century Poetry in English (1999), The Story of Poetry I: From Caedmon to Caxton (2001), The Story of Poetry II: From Skelton to Dryden (2002), Lives of the First Poets (2004), Lives of the Ancient Poets: The Greeks (2004), The Story of Poetry III: From Pope to Burns (2007), The Resurrection of the Body (2007), The Poetry Archive, Michael Schmidt Reads His Poems (2008), Collected Poems (2010), The Stories of my Life (2014); *Clubs* PEN, Savile; *Style—* Prof Michael Schmidt, OBE, FRSL; ✉ c/o Carcanet Press Ltd, 4th Floor, Alliance House, 30 Cross Street, Manchester M2 7AQ (☎ 0161 834 8730, fax 0161 832 0084)

SCHMIEGELOW, Ian Lunn; *b* 16 March 1943; *Educ* Oundle, Magdalene Coll Cambridge (MA); *m* 1, 1966, Penelope (d 1992); 3 da (Alexandra, Catrina, Antonia); m 2, 1997, Samantha; *Career* called to the Bar Inner Temple 1967, in practice 1967–69; Hambros Bank Ltd: joined 1969, dir 1978–85, exec dir 1982–85; sr vice-pres and chm Mgmnt Cncl for EMEA First National Bank of Chicago 1985–87, chm Hamilton Lunn gp of cos 1988–, chm Trans Balkan Investments Ltd 2009, dep chm Jordan Int Bank 2010–; *Clubs* Turf; *Style—* Ian Schmiegelow, Esq; ✉ 33 Catherine Place, London SW1E 6DY (☎ 020 7630 3350. fax 020 7630 3360)

SCHOCHET, Rabbi Yitzchak; s of Immanuel Schochet, of Toronto, Canada, and Jette, *née* Elzas; *b* 6 July 1965, Toronto, Canada; *Educ* Ner Israel Coll US (Dip), Ohr Elchanan LA, Yeshiva Gedolah Miami, London and NY (BA), Kilel Avrechim NY, UCL (MA); *m* 8 Feb 1989, Hannah, *née* Herzog; 3 s (Mordechai b 2 April 1990, Dov Yehuda b 25 Dec 1992, Menachem b 31 July 1994), 2 da (Esti b 18 July 1999, Sarah b 18 July 2008); *Career* ordained as rabbi 1989; asst dean Oholei Torah Boy's Sch of NY 1990–91, rabbi Richmond Synagogue UK 1991–93, teacher Jews Free Sch Middx 1991–94, rabbi Mill Hill United Synagogue 1993–; chm Rabbanical Cncl United Synagogues 2008–; columnist: The Guardian 2002–04, Jewish News 2002–; int lectr and broadcaster; hon princ Rosh Pinah Jewish Primary Sch, chaplain Sydmar Lodge Retirement Home, hon princ Etz Chaim Primary Sch 2013–; conslt European Jewish Advocacy Gp, chm RCUS 2008;

S

Recreations swimming (3 miles a week), Muay Thai boxing; *Style*— Rabbi Yitzchak Schochet; ✉ Mill Hill Synagogue, Station Road, Mill Hill, London NW7 2JY (✆ 020 8959 1137, fax 020 8959 6484, e-mail office@millhillsynagogue.co.uk)

SCHOFIELD, Dr Jennifer Anne; *née* Goy; da of Stanley Stephen Goy (d 1979), and Mary Catherine, *née* Jones (d 2005); *b* 12 July 1946; *Educ* Rosebery GS Epsom, Middlesex Hospital Med Sch (MB BS); *m* 1 Oct 1977, Neil McCallum Schofield, s of Fred Schofield (d 2000); 3 s (Guy b 11 May 1980, Stuart b 25 Oct 1981, Max b 17 April 1992), 1 da (Olivia b 13 March 1983); *Career* ships surgn MN P&O Shipping Co 1973–74; anaesthetist Duchess of Kent Children's Hosp Hong Kong 1975–76, sr registrar in anaesthetics Hosp for Sick Children Gt Ormond St London 1977, med offr Grendon Underwood Prison Aylesbury 1979–81, conslt anaesthetist Stoke Mandeville Hosp Aylesbury 1981–2007 (clinical dir Critical Care Directorate 1996–99); chm Oxford Regnl Anaesthetic Advsy Ctee 1991–94; FRCA 1975; *Recreations* needlework, family life; *Style*— Dr Jennifer Goy; ✉ Perrotts Farm, Bicester Road, Long Crendon, Aylesbury, Buckinghamshire HP18 9BP (✆ 01844 201585)

SCHOFIELD, Jon; *b* 10 May 1985, Petersfield, Hants; *Educ* Clitheroe Royal GS, Loughborough Univ (BSc); *Career* sprint kayaker; achievements incl: Silver medal (K-1 200m relay) and Bronze medal (K-2 200m) World Championships 2010, Gold medal (K-2 200m) European Championships 2010, 2011 and 2012, Silver medal (K-2 200m) World Championships 2011, Bronze medal (K-2 200m) Olympic Games 2012; *Recreations* coffee, classic cars, guitar; *Style*— Mr Jon Schofield; ✉ website www.jon-schofield.co.uk, Twitter @jonscho

SCHOFIELD, Kenneth Douglas; CBE (1996); s of Douglas Joseph Schofield (d 1978), and Jessie, *née* Gray (d 1994); *b* 3 February 1946; *Educ* Auchterarder HS; *m* 12 June 1968, Evelyn May, da of Arthur Gordon Sharp (d 1973); 2 da (Susan b 28 Jan 1971, Evonne b 13 Nov 1973); *Career* mangr Dunblane branch Perth Trustee Savings Bank 1969–71 (joined 1962), dep to press and PR dir George Simms Organisation 1971–74, first exec dir PGA Tournament Players Div (now PGA European Tour) 1975–; memb Cncl Golf Fndn; assoc Savings Bank Inst 1966–71; *Books* Pro Golf (1972–75), John Player Golf Yearbook (1973–75); *Recreations* golf, all main sports, walking; *Clubs* Wentworth (hon memb), Crieff Golf (hon memb), Auchterarder Golf (hon memb), Foxhills Golf & County, Royal & Ancient, Caledonian; *Style*— Kenneth D Schofield, Esq, CBE; ✉ PGA European Tour, Wentworth Drive, Virginia Water, Surrey GU25 4LX (✆ 01344 840400, fax 01344 840451)

SCHOFIELD, Paul Robert; s of Robert Schofield, of Blackburn, Lancs (d 2008), and Margaret, *née* Platt; *b* 23 May 1955, Rossendale, Lancs; *Educ* St Mary's Coll GS Blackburn, Univ of Manchester (LLB), Coll of Law Chester; *m* Patricia, *née* Birkett; 2 da (Katy b 18 Feb 1982, Lucy b 15 July 1984), 1 s (James Paul b 14 Aug 1990); *Career* admitted slr 1980; Farleys Slrs: joined as trainee 1977, equity ptnr 1982–; supervisor Serious Fraud Panel 2000; duty slr 1984; memb: Law Soc 1980, Criminal Law Solicitors' Assoc 2000; *Recreations* travel, football, sailing, foreign property investment; *Clubs* Blackburn Rovers; *Style*— Paul Schofield, Esq; ✉ Farleys Solicitors, 22–27 Richmond Terrace, Blackburn BB1 7AQ (✆ 01254 606000, fax 01254 272319, e-mail paul.schofield@farleys.com)

SCHOFIELD, Phillip Bryan; s of Brian Homer Schofield, and Patricia, *née* Parry; *b* 1 April 1962, Oldham; *Educ* Newquay GS; *m* March 1993, Stephanie, da of John Lowe; 2 da (Molly b July 1993, Ruby b Jan 1996); *Career* bookings clerk Radio Outside Broadcasts BBC 1979, TV and radio presenter NZ 1981–84; BBC TV: Broom Cupboard anchorman Children's BBC 1985–87, co-presenter (with Sarah Greene) Going Live until 1993, presenter Schofield's Europe 1990–93, presenter Television's Greatest Hits 1992–93, also The Movie Game (3 series), Schofield's Europe, Take Two (4 series); presenter: Schofield's TV Gold 1993–96, Schofield's Quest 1994–96, Talking Telephone Numbers 1994–97, One in a Million 1996–97, National Lottery Winning Lines 2001–04 (BBC 1), The Cube (ITV 1); co-host: Test the Nation (ITV) 2002–04, This Morning (ITV) 2002– (Best Daytime Prog Nat TV Awards 2004 and 2013), Best Ever... (ITV) 2004–, Dancing on Ice (ITV) 2006–, Mr & Mrs (ITV 1) 2008–; anchor The Royal Wedding (ITV); performed title role in Joseph and the Amazing Technicolor Dreamcoat (London Palladium 1992–93, nationwide tour 1993–96), title role in Doctor Dolittle 1998–2001, Jack the Ripper in The Lodger (Windsor) 2000; Top Man on TV 1987–88, Number 1 TV personality in all maj teenage magazines 1987–88, Best Dressed Man of the Year 1992, Variety Club Show Business Personality of the Year 1992; involved in: Children's Royal Variety Performance 1987–88, Royal Variety Performance 1992, Stars Orgn for Spastics, NSPCC, Br Heart Fndn; *Style*— Phillip Schofield, Esq; ✉ c/o George Ashton, James Grant Media Ltd, 94 Strand on the Green, London W4 3NN (✆ 020 8742 4950, fax 020 8742 4951)

SCHOFIELD, Dr Roger Snowden; s of Ronald Snowden Schofield (d 1970), of Leeds, and Muriel Grace, *née* Braime (d 1972); *b* 26 August 1937; *Educ* Leighton Park Sch Reading, Clare Coll Cambridge (BA, PhD, LittD); *m* 3 Sept 1961; 1 da (Melanie b 1972); *Career* fell Clare Coll Cambridge 1969– (res fell 1962–65), sr res offr Cambridge Group 1966–73, dir SSRC Cambridge Group for the History of Population and Social Structure 1974–94, sr res assoc Cambridge Group for the History of Population and Social Structure 1994–97; hon readership in historical demography Univ of Cambridge 1991–97; ed: Local Population Studies 1968–97, Population Studies 1979–97; Br Soc for Population Studies: memb Cncl 1979–87, treas 1981–85, pres 1985–87; memb: Population Investigation Ctee 1976–97 (treas 1987–97), Historical Demography Ctee Int Union for the Scientific Study of Population 1983–91 (chm 1987–91); FRHistS 1970, FRSS 1987, FBA 1988; *Publications* The Population History of England 1541–1871: A reconstruction (with E A Wrigley, 1981, 2 edn 1989), English Marriage Patterns Revisited (Journal of Family History, 1985), The State of Population Theory: forward from Malthus (contrib, 1986), Famine, Disease and Crisis Mortality in Early Modern Society (contrib with J Walter, 1989), The Decline of Mortality in Europe (with David Reher and Alain Bideau, 1991), Old and New Methods in Historical Demography (with David Reher, 1993), English Population History from Family Reconstitution (with E A Wrigley et al, 1997), Through a Glass Darkly (Social Science History, 1998), Taxation under the Early Tudors, 1485–1547 (2004); various articles on historical demography and research methods; *Style*— Dr Roger Schofield, FBA; ✉ 17 Christs Lane, Cambridge CB1 1NP (✆ 01223 314823, e-mail rss1@cam.ac.uk)

SCHOLAR, Sir Michael Charles; KCB (1999, CB 1991); s of Richard Herbert Scholar (d 1993), of Grampound, Cornwall, and Mary Blodwen, *née* Jones (d 1985); *b* 3 January 1942; *Educ* St Olave's and St Saviour's GS Southwark, St John's Coll Cambridge (MA, PhD), Univ of Calif Berkeley, Harvard Univ; *m* 26 Aug 1964, Angela Mary, da of William Whinfield Sweet (d 1984), of Wylam, Northumberland; 3 s (Thomas b 1968, Richard b 1973, John b 1980), 1 da (Jane b 1976 d 1977); *Career* asst lectr in philosophy Univ of Leicester 1968, fell St John's Coll Cambridge 1969 (hon fell 1999), asst princ HM Treasy 1969, private sec to Chief Sec HM Treasy 1974–76, sr int mangr Barclays Bank plc 1979–81, private sec to PM 1981–83, dep sec HM Treasy 1987–93 (under sec 1983); perm sec: Welsh Office 1993–96, DTI 1996–2001; chm Civil Service Sports Cncl 1998–2001; pres St John's Coll Oxford 2001–12, pro-vice-chllr Univ of Oxford 2005–12; memb Cncl of Mgmnt NIESR 2001–05; non-exec dir Legal and General Investment Management (Holdings) plc 2002–07; chm Benton Fletcher Tst 2004–11, chair UK Statistics Authy 2008–12; fell: Univ of Wales Aberystwyth 1996, Univ of Cardiff 2003; Freeman City of London 2013; Hon Dr Univ of Glamorgan 1999; ARCO 1965; *Recreations* playing the piano and organ, walking, gardening; *Style*— Sir Michael Scholar, KCB; ✉ 9 Stanley Road, Oxford OX4 1QY (✆ 01865 427738, e-mail mcscholar@hotmail.com)

SCHOLEFIELD, Prof John Howard; s of Frank Scholefield, and Beryl Scholefield; *b* 28 September 1959; *Educ* Bradford GS, Univ of Liverpool (Bromley scholarship, MB ChB, ChM); *Career* house offr Broadgreen Hosp Liverpool 1983–84, SHO (A&E and orthopaedic surgery) Walton Hosp Liverpool 1984–85, SHO (oncology, gastroenterology, urology and gen surgery) Northern Gen Hosp Sheffield 1985–86, Peri-Fellowship registrar rotation Royal Hallamshire Hosp Sheffield 1986–87, clinical res fell Imperial Cancer Res Fund Colorectal Unit St Mark's Hosp London 1987–89 (hon clinical asst and postgrad tutor 1988–89), lectr in surgery (registrar rising to sr registrar) Univ Dept of Surgery Clinical Sciences Centre Northern Gen Hosp Sheffield 1989–93, res surgical offr St Mark's Hosp London 1993–94; Section of Surgery Univ of Nottingham: sr lectr 1994–97 reader 1997–99, prof of surgery 2000–; hon conslt surgn Univ Hosp NHS Tst 1994–; chm Nat Cancer Res Inst Colorectal Gp 2001–; memb: Cncl Assoc of Coloproctology of GB and Ireland 1997–2000, Ctee Soc of Academic Surgns 1997–2000, Cancer Ctee RCS 2000–; memb Editorial Bd: Aird's Companion to Surgical Studies, Surgery (speciality ed for gen surgery); presented papers and many nat and int meetings of learned socs; memb: Surgical Res Soc, Br Assoc of Coloproctology, Assoc of Surgns of GB and Ireland (regnl rep 2002–), American Soc of Colon and Rectal Surgns, Br Soc for Gastroenterology, RSM (Coloproctology, Surgery and Oncology Sections), St Mark's Assoc, E Midlands Surgical Soc; FRCSEd 1987, FRCS 1988 *Awards* Nordic Travel Scholarship RSM 1990, NY Travelling Scholarship RCS 1991, Ethicon Fndn Travel Award RCS 1991, Surgical Res Soc Travelling Fellowship 1992, Br Digestive Fndn Travel Award 1992, RSM Travelling Fellowship 1993 (to American Soc of Colon and Rectal Surgns 1994), Japan Surgical Soc Travelling Scholarship 1996, John Arderne Medal RSM Section of Coloproctology 1989, Raven Prize Br Assoc of Surgical Oncology 1989, N of England Gastroenterology Soc Res Prize 1990, Hunterian prof RCS 1991; *Publications* Challenges in Colorectal Cancer (ed, 2000 and 2005); numerous book chapters, refereed papers, reviews, letters and published abstracts; *Recreations* squash, golf; *Style*— Prof John Scholefield; ✉ Division of GI Surgery, Queen's Medical Centre, Nottingham NG7 2UH (✆ 0115 849 3323 or 0115 993 2009)

SCHOLEY, Sir David Gerald; kt (1987), CBE (1976); s of Dudley Scholey, and Lois Scholey; *b* 28 June 1935; *Educ* Wellington, ChCh Oxford; *m* 1960, Alexandra Beatrix, da of Hon George Drew, and Fiorenza Drew, of Canada; 1 s (Christopher), 1 da (Fiorenza); *Career* Nat Serv 9 Queen's Royal Lancers 1953–55; TA Yorks Dragoons 1955–57, 3/4 CLY (Sharpshooters 1957–61), Met Special Constabulary (Thames Div) 1961–65; with: Thompson Graham & Co (Lloyd's Brokers) 1956–58, Dale & Co (Insurance Brokers) Canada 1958–59, Guinness Mahon & Co Ltd 1959–64; UBS AG: joined S G Warburg & Co Ltd 1965 (dir 1967–95, dep chm 1977, jt chm 1980–84, chm 1985–95), chm SBC Warburg July–Nov 1995, sr advsr International Finance Corp World Bank Gp 1996–2005, sr advsr FSA 2010–13; advsr: Capgemini Financial Services UK Ltd 2005–10, Longreach Gp 2006–, MDM Bank Moscow 2008–12; memb Export Guarantees Advsy Cncl 1970–75 (dep chm 1974–75), chm Construction Exports Advsy Bd 1975–78, Anglo American plc: non exec-dir 1999–2005, memb Remuneration Ctee 1999–2002, chm Remuneration Ctee 1999–2000, memb Nomination Ctee 1999–2005, memb Safety and Sustainable Devpt Ctee 2003–05; dir: Orion Insurance Co Ltd 1963–87, Mercury Securities plc 1969–86 (chm 1984–96), Stewart Wrightson Holdings Ltd 1972–81, Union Discount Co of London Ltd 1976–81, Bank of England 1981–98, British Telecom plc 1986–94, The Chubb Corporation (USA) 1991–2008, The General Electric Company plc 1992–95, J Sainsbury plc 1996–2000, Vodafone Gp plc 1998–2005, Close Bros 1999–2006 (also chm), Good Governance Gp G3 2012–13; memb: Inst Int d'Etudes Bancaires 1976–94 (pres 1988), Ctee on Finance for Industry NEDO 1980–87, Cncl IIS 1984–93 (hon treas 1984–90), Pres's Ctee Business in the Community 1988–91, Industry and Commerce Gp 1989–95, Save the Children Fund 1989–95 and 2002–03 (chm Save the Children Fund 75th Birthday Private Appeal London First 1993–96), Ford Fndn Advsy Gp on UN Financing 1992–93, Bd of Banking Supervision 1996–98, Fitch Int Advsy Ctee 2001–07, Mitsubishi Int Advsy Ctee 2001–07, Sultanate of Oman Fin Advsy Gp 2002–06, Lord Mayor's Appeal Ctee 2002–03; dir: INSEAD 1991–2004 (chm UK Cncl 1992–97, chm Int Cncl 1995–2003 (hon chm 2005), hon alumnus 2005), LSE 1993–96, London Symphony Orch 2012– (memb Advsy Cncl 1998–2004), Cranmere Gp Ltd 2014–; a govr BBC 1994–2000; advsr: BBC Philharmonic Orch 2006–13, ROH Muscat Oman 2011–; chm of tstees Nat Portrait Gallery 2001–05 (tstee 1992–2005), tstee Glyndebourne Arts Tst 1989–2002; govr Wellington 1978–88 and 1996–2004 (vice-pres 1998–2004); Hon DLitt London Guildhall 1993, Hon DSc UMIST 1999, hon student ChCh Oxford 2003 (memb Devpt Bd 2002–15), distinguished friend Univ of Oxford 2011; memb National Inst of Economic and Social Research 1984–2014, FRSA; *Style*— Sir David Scholey, CBE; ✉ UBS Investment Bank, 1 Finsbury Avenue, London EC2M 2PP (✆ 020 7568 2400, fax 020 7568 4225, e-mail david.scholey@ubs.com)

SCHOLTES, Prof Stefan; *b* 22 November 1960, Trier, Germany; *Educ* Univ of Karlsruhe (Dip, PhD), Cornell Univ; *Career* post-doc and lectr Univ of Karlsruhe 1990–96; Judge Business Sch Univ of Cambridge: lectr and reader 1996–2002, prof of mgmnt science 2002–10, Dennis Gillings prof of health mgmnt 2010–; visiting positions: Stanford Univ, MIT, London Business Sch; author of 24 articles in professional jls; *Books* On Convex Bodies and Some Applications to Optimization (1990), System Modelling and Optimization: Methods, Theory and Applications (jt ed, 2000), Flexibility in Engineering Design (2011), Introduction to Piecewise Differentiable Equations (2012); *Style*— Prof Stefan Scholtes

SCHOTT, Ben; s of Dr Geoffrey D Schott, of London, and Judith C, *née* Ross; *b* 26 May 1974, London; *Educ* Gonville & Caius Coll Cambridge (MA); *Career* writer, designer, miscellanist and creative conslt; contributing columnist New York Times; *Publications* Schott's Original Miscellany (2002), Schott's Food & Drink Miscellany (2003), Schott's Sporting, Gaming & Idling Miscellany (2004), Schott's Almanac (annually, 2005–11), Schottenfreude: German Words for the Human Condition (2013); *Recreations* adsignification, gluttony; *Clubs* Garrick; *Style*— Ben Schott, Esq; ✉ website www.benschott.com

SCHRODER, (Baron) Bruno Lionel; s of Baron Helmut William Bruno Schroder (d 1969), s of Baron Bruno Schroder or von Schröder, sr ptnr the London branch of the Banking House of J Henry Schroder & Co, cr Freiherr by Kaiser Wilhelm II aboard the yacht 'Hohenzollern' on 27 July 1904; the Baron's er bro Rudolph was cr Freiherr eight months later, and Margaret Eleanor Phyllis (d 1994), eld da of Sir Lionel Darell, 6 Bt, DSO, JP, DL; *b* 17 January 1933; *Educ* Eton, Université de Tours, Sch of Languages Hamburg, UC Oxford (MA), Harvard Business Sch (MBA); *m* 30 May 1969, Patricia Leonie Mary (Piffa), da of Maj Adrian Holt (d 1984); 1 da (Leonie b 1974); *Career* 2 Lt The Life Gds 1951–53; dir: Schroders plc 1963– (joined 1960), Schröder Gebrüder Bank Hamburg 1954–55, J Henry Schroder & Co Ltd 1966–, Schroders Inc 1984–; tstee Schroder Charity Tst 1960–, tstee Schroder Fndn 2004–; dir Fine Art Fund 2002–; tstee Univ Coll Membs Tst 1992–98; memb Bd of Tstees Br Urological Fndn (chm 1998–2002, tstee 2002–), former memb Cncl of Mgmnt Educn Univ of Oxford, memb Exec Ctee The Air Sqdn 1996–2002, memb Cncl Household Cavalry of the Life Guards 2003–, memb Cncl Air League 2007–; vice-chm Br Friends of the Harvard Business Sch; govr English Nat Ballet 1994–2000; tstee Argyllshire Piping Tst 1995–; steward and sr steward Argyllshire Gathering 1985–2000; Prime Warden of Worshipful Co of Goldsmiths 2001–02 (Freeman 1973, Liveryman 1976, memb Ct of Assts 1987–), Liveryman Guild of Air Pilots and Air Navigators; Queen Beatrix of the Netherlands Wedding Medal, Cross of the Order of

Merit of the Federal Rep of Germany; *Recreations* flying, stalking, shooting; *Clubs* Brooks's, White's, Leander; *Style*— Bruno Schroder; ✉ Schroders plc, 31 Gresham Street, London EC2V 7QA (☎ 020 7658 6000, fax 020 7658 2006, telex 885029)

SCHRÖDER, Prof Martin; s of Hermann Schröder (d 1971), and Edith, *née* Kruusna (d 1999); *b* 14 April 1954; *Educ* Slough GS, Univ of Sheffield (BSc), Imperial Coll London (PhD, DIC); *m* Leena-Kreet, da of Härm Kore; *Career* Royal Society/Swiss Nat Fndn postdoctoral fell Laboratorium für Organische Chemie Eidgenössische Technische Hochschule Zurich 1978–80, postdoctoral research asst Univ Chemical Laboratories Cambridge 1980–82; Univ of Edinburgh: sr demonstrator in inorganic chemistry Dept of Chemistry 1982–83, lectr 1983–91, reader 1991–94, personal chair in inorganic chemistry Dept of Chemistry 1994–95; Univ of Nottingham: prof and head of inorganic chemistry Dept of Chemistry 1995–2015, head Sch of Chemistry 1999–2005, dean Faculty of Science 2011–15; Univ of Manchester: prof of chemistry 2015–, vice-pres and dean Faculty of Science and Engineering 2015–; visiting prof Lash Miller Laboratories Univ of Toronto 1990, Mellor visiting prof Univ of Dunedin 1995, visiting prof Sch of Chemistry Univ Louis Pasteur Strasbourg 2004; memb various SERC panels and ctees incl Inorganic Chemistry Sub-Ctee 1990–93; memb various EPSRC panels and ctees and also chm and memb Inorganic Synthesis Panel, memb Dalton Cncl and Conference Ctee RSC 1998–2007, memb Review Panel (Sr) Institut Universitaire de France 2011–12; author of over 500 publications in learned jls; support research fell RSE 1991–92, Leverhulme Tst sr research fell 2005–06, Wolfson Merit Award Royal Soc 2005–10; Corday-Morgan Medal and Prize RSC 1989, Tilden lectr RSC 2000–01, Transition Metal Chemistry Award RSC 2003, RSC Award for Chemistry of the Noble Metals and their Compounds 2008; Hon Dr Tech Univ of Tallinn 2005; CChem, FRSC 1994, FRSE 1994, memb Academia Europaea; *Recreations* classical music, opera; *Style*— Prof Martin Schröder; ✉ The University of Manchester, Sackville Street Building, Manchester M13 9PL (☎ 0161 306 9119, mobile 07767 238477, e-mail m.schroder@manchester.ac.uk)

SCHUSSER, Oliver; *Career* vice-pres iTunes Int; *Style*— Oliver Schusser, Esq; ✉ Apple, One Hanover Street, London W1S 1YZ

SCHUTZ, Prof Bernard Frederick; s of Bernard Frederick Schutz, of Plainview, NY, and Virginia M, *née* Lefebure (d 1986); *b* 11 August 1946; *Educ* Bethpage HS NY, Clarkson Coll of Technol NY (BSc), Caltech (PhD); *m* 1, 13 Aug 1968 (m dis 1973), Joan Catherine, *née* Rankie; m 2, 16 Sept 1977 (m dis 1981), Susan, *née* Whitelegg; m 3, 22 Dec 1985, Sian Lynette, da of John Alexander Easton Pouncy, of Neath, W Glamorgan; 3 da (Rachel b 1984, Catherine b 1986, Annalie b 1989); *Career* postdoctoral res fell Univ of Cambridge 1971–72, instructor in physics Yale Univ 1973–74 (postdoctoral res fell 1972–73), prof Univ of Wales Cardiff 1984– (lectr 1974–76, reader 1976–84), dir Max Planck Inst for Gravitational Physics (The Albert Einstein Inst) Golm Germany 1995–2014; pt/t prof Cardiff Univ and dir Data Innovation Inst 2014–; Amaldi Medal Italian Soc for Gravitation 2006; memb: German Physical Soc, Soc of Sigma XI, Royal Acad of Arts and Sciences Uppsala Sweden, Deutsche Acad Leopoldina; hon prof: Univ of Potsdam 1998–, Univ of Hanover; Hon DSc Univ of Glasgow 2011; fell American Physical Soc, FRAS, FInstP, memb Learned Soc of Wales, fell Int Soc of General Relativity and Gravitation 2013; *Books* Geometrical Methods of Mathematical Physics (1980), A First Course in General Relativity (1985), Gravitational Wave Data Analysis (1989), Gravity from the Ground Up (2003); over 200 research articles; *Recreations* singing, skiing, sailing; *Style*— Prof Bernard Schutz; ✉ MPI Gravitational Physics, Am Muehlenberg 1, D-14476 Golm, Germany (☎ 00 49 331 5677220, fax 00 49 331 5677298, e-mail bernard.schutz@aei.mpg.de)

SCHWAB, Ann Dorothy (Annie); MBE (1999); da of William Henry Clovis, and Dorothy, *née* Taylor; *b* 28 November 1946; *Educ* Burnholme Sch York; *m* 1; 3 s (Barry Devlin b 4 July 1965, Neil Devlin b 12 July 1966, Ian Devlin b 23 July 1968); m 2, 31 Oct 1977, Germain Eric Schwab, *qv*; *Career* hotelier; The Olde Worlde Club York 1972–74, Hans and Gerda's Restuarant Findlenhof Zermatt Switzerland 1976–83, Hotel Poste Zermatt Switzerland 1983–84, Beck Farm Restaurant York 1984–88, Winteringham Fields Winteringham 1988–2005 (2 Michelin stars 1999); memb: Restaurant Assoc 1993, Hospitality Assoc 1993, Food Writers' Guild, Acad of Food and Wine Serv, Writers' Guild of Great Britain 1994, Euro Toque '96, Exec Ctee Restaurant Assoc of Great Britain; cmmr Euro Toques UK; chair Young Chef and Young Waiter Competition; FRSA 2002; *Recreations* journalism; *Style*— Mrs Annie Schwab, MBE, FRSA; ✉ Le Faure, 19500 Collonges la Rouge, France (☎ 00 33 5 55 84 13 03, e-mail euroannie@aol.com)

SCHWAB, Germain Eric; s of Eric Herbert Schwab (d 1967), of Switzerland, and Therese Marie Anne, *née* Unternahrer; *b* 5 December 1950; *Educ* Ecole Chantemerle Moutier Suisse, Ecole D'Aptitude Professionnelle Delémont Suisse, Ecole De Formation Professionnelle de Cuisiner Bienne Suisse, Diplome De Fin D'Apprentis Palais Des Congres Bienne; *m* 31 Oct 1977, Ann Dorothy Schwab, MBE, *qv*, da of William Henry Clovis; *Career* chef; Hotel Central Tavanne Switzerland 1970, La Grenette Fribourg Switzerland 1970, Gstaad Palace Gstaad Switzerland 1970, Portledge Hotel Bideford England 1971, Frederick Restaurant Camden London 1971, Chesterfield Hotel Mayfair London 1971, Dorchester Hotel London 1972, St Moritz Club Wardour St London 1973, Seiler Haus Mount Cervin Zermatt Switzerland 1974, Le Mirabeau Hotel Zermatt 1975, Le Bristol Hotel Zermatt 1977, Beck Farm Restaurant Wilberfoss England 1980, Winteringham Fields Winteringham 1988–2005 (Michelin star 1994, Which? Good Hotel Guide Humberside Hotel of the Year 1996, 9 out of 10 Good Food Guide 1999, 2 Michelin stars 1999); County Restaurant of the Year: Good Food Guide 1990, La Ina 1990; Restaurant of the Year The Independent 1990, English Estates Humberside Rural Employment award 1990, English Estates Humberside county winner (Tourism) 1990, Booker Prize Best Chef and Best Restaurant 1995, AA Chef of the Year 2006; memb: Société Master Chefs (UK) Feb 1983, Euro Toque 1990, Académie Culinaire de France; *Recreations* sketching; *Clubs* Sloane; *Style*— Germain Schwab, Esq

SCHWARTZ, Jeremy; *Career* former chief mktg offr News Int, country mangr L'Oreal UK & I until 2013, chm and chief exec Body Shop Int 2013–; *Style*— Jeremy Schwartz, Esq; ✉ The Body Shop International plc, New City Court, 20 St Thomas Street, London SE1 9RG

SCHWARTZ, Emeritus Prof Steven; AM; s of Robert Schwartz, and Frances Schwartz; *b* 5 November 1946, NYC; *Educ* Brooklyn Coll City Univ NYC (BA), Syracuse Univ (MSc, PhD); *Family* 2 s (Seth b 25 May 1969, Greg b 23 Jan 1976), 1 da (Tricia b 18 April 1972); m, 9 Nov 2001, Claire Mary; *Career* offr and grad fell US Public Health Serv NIH Washington DC 1967–68, clinical psychologist Veteran Admin Hosp Syracuse 1969–70, asst prof Dept of Psychology Northern Illinois Univ DeKalb 1971–75, research scientist Depts of Psychiatry, Community Med and Public Health Univ of Texas Med Branch Galveston 1975–78, sr lectr Dept of Psychology Univ of WA 1978–79, prof and head Dept of Psychology Univ of Qld 1980–90, pres Academic Bd Univ of Qld 1991–93, exec dean Faculty of Med and Dentistry Univ of WA 1994–96, vice-chllr and pres Murdoch Univ 1996–2002, vice-chllr and princ Brunel Univ 2002–06, vice-chllr and pres Macquarie Univ Sydney 2006–, exec dir Cncl for the Humanities, Arts and Social Sciences Melbourne 2013–; visiting research fell: NATO Brussels 1978, Int Brain Research Orgn Lausanne 1982; visiting prof: Stanford Univ 1983, Dept of Health Policy and Mgmnt Harvard Sch of Public Health 1987; Royal Soc and Australian Acad of Science exchange fell ICRF Labs London 1988, visiting fell Wolfson Coll Oxford 1994, Morris Leibovitz fell Univ of Southern Calif 1995, Oliver Smithies fell Balliol Coll Oxford 2013–, sr fell Centre for Ind Studies Sydney 2013–; chair UK Govt Review into HE 2003–04, memb Productive Industries Cmmn GLA 2003–; pres Sigma Xi The Scientific Research Soc 1986–90; memb Bd: Cncl for Int Educn Exchange (CIEE) 1997–, Cncl for Industry and HE 2002–, Fndn for Int Educn 2003–; memb Editorial Bd: Texas Reports in Biology and Med 1976–78, Jl of Research in Personality 1978–90, Applied Psycholinguistics 1980–84, Brain and Cognition 1991–95, Med Decision Making, Australian Autism Review, Jl of Child Clinical Psychology (special ed), The Behavioural and Brain Sciences, Current Psychological Reviews and Reports, Psychological Bulletin; memb: NY Acad of Sciences, Public Health Assoc of Australia, Soc for Med Decision Making, AAAS, Judgement and Decision Making Soc, Int Assoc of Univ Presidents, American Psychological Assoc; Travel Fellowship American Psychological Assoc 1973, Career Scientist Devpt Award NIH 1977, Brain Research Award Br Red Cross Soc 1988, ALIS Award Br Cncl 1988; govr: Henley Mgmnt Coll 2002–, Richmond the American Univ in London 2003–; ambass City of Perth 1999–; fell: Acad of Social Sciences Australia 1991, Australian Inst of Mgmnt 2000, Australian Inst of Co Dirs 2001; *Publications* Human Judgement and Decision Processes (ed with M F Kaplan, 1975), Human Judgement and Decision Processes in Applied Settings (ed with M F Kaplan, 1977), Language and Cognition in Schizophrenia (ed, 1978, republished 2013), Psychopathology of Childhood: An Experimental Approach (with J H Johnson, 1981, revised edn 1985), Measuring Reading Competence (1984), Medical Thinking: The Psychology of Medical Judgement and Decision-Making (with T Griffin, 1986), Classic Studies in Psychology (1986), Pavlov's Heirs (1987), Case Studies in Abnormal Psychology (ed, 1992), Classic Studies in Abnormal Psychology (1993), Abnormal Pscyhology (2000); also author of book chapters, reviews, conf papers, and articles in newspapers, magazines and learned jls; *Recreations* theatre, rambling; *Clubs* The Australian (Sydney); *Style*— Emeritus Prof Steven Schwartz, AM; ✉ Australian Curriculum, Assessment and Reporting Authority, Level 13, Tower B, Centennial Plaza, 280 Elizabeth Street, Sydney NSW 2000 (☎ 00 61 414 063 872, mobile 00 61 499 499566, e-mail steven.schwartz@acara.edu.au)

SCICLUNA, Martin Anthony; s of late William Scicluna, and Miriam Scicluna; *b* 20 November 1950; *Educ* Berkhamsted Sch, Univ of Leeds (BCom); *m* 1979 (m dis 2000); 2 s (Mark William b 26 April 1984, Edward James b 2 Feb 1989), 1 da (Claire Alexandra b 11 Aug 1987); *Career* Touche Ross (now Deloitte): joined 1973, ptnr 1982–2008, head London Audit Div 1990–95, chm 1995–2007, memb Bd of Directors and Governance Ctee Deloitte Touche Tohmatsu 1999–2007, ret 2008; chm: Great Portland Estates plc 2009–, RSA Insurance Gp plc 2013–; non-exec dir and chm Audit Ctee Lloyds Banking Gp plc 2008–13, non-exec dir Worldpay 2013– (sr ind dir 2016–); chm: London Soc of Chartered Accountants ICAEW 1988–89, Cncl ICAEW 1990–95; memb Company Law Review Steering Gp and chm Accounting and Reporting Working Gp Company Law Review 1999–2001, govr NIESR, memb Cncl Univ of Leeds 2008–11, memb Bd of Govrs Berkhamsted Sch 2008–16; Freeman City of London; Hon LLD Univ of Leeds 2008; *Recreations* tennis, gardening, wine, Arsenal FC; *Style*— Martin A Scicluna, Esq; ✉ Parkways, Little Heath Lane, Potten End, Hertfordshire HP4 2RX

SCLATER, Prof John George; s of John George Sclater, and Margaret Bennet Glen; *b* 17 June 1940; *Educ* Stonyhurst, Univ of Edinburgh (BSc), Univ of Cambridge (PhD); *m* 1, 1968, Fredrica Rose Feleyn; 2 s, (Iain, Stuart); m 2, 1985, Paula Anne Edwards; m 3, Naila Gloria Burchett; *Career* asst res geophysicist Scripps Instn of Oceanography 1967–72 (postgrad res asst 1965–67), prof MIT 1977–83 (asst prof 1972–77), dir Joint Prog in Oceanography and Ocean Engrg (with Woods Hole Oceanographic Instn) MIT 1981–83, The Instn for Geophysics Univ of Texas at Austin 1983–91 (assoc dir, sr res scientist, Shell distinguished prof in geophysics), prof UCSD/Scripps Instn of Oceanography 1991–; assoc ed Jl of Geophysical Res 1971–74; memb: Ocean Sciences Ctee US Nat Acad of Sciences 1972–76, Nat Sci Review Ctee on Oceanography 1974–77, Review Ctee IDOE Nat Science Fndn 1974, Heat Flow Panel JOIDES 1968–74, Science Fndn 1974, Ocean Crisis Panel IPOD 1974–76, Indian Ocean Panel JOIDES 1968–74, Indian Ocean Panel Ocean Drilling Prog 1985–88 (Lithesphere panel 1984–86), Ocean Studies Bd/Naval Panel 1985–; chm Ocean Studies Bd US Nat Acad of Sciences 1988–91 (memb 1985–92); Rosenstiel Award 1979, Bucher Medal AGU 1985; Guggenheim fell 1998–99; fell: Geological Soc of America, American Geophysical Union; fell: AAPG, Nat Acad of Sciences; FRS; *Publications* numerous contribs to Jl of Geophysical Res, Bulletin Earthquake Res, Earth and Planetary Science Letters, Geophysical Jl RAS, Tectonophysics, and other learned jls; *Style*— Prof John Sclater, FRS

SCLATER, John Richard; CVO (1999); s of Arthur William Sclater, and Alice, *née* Collett; *b* 14 July 1940; *Educ* Charterhouse, Gonville & Caius Coll Cambridge, Yale Univ, Harvard Univ; *m* 1, 23 Aug 1967 (m dis), Nicola Mary Gloria, o da of late Anthony Charles Cropper, TD, JP, DL, of Tolson Hall, Kendal; 1 s (James Arthur b 17 April 1970), 1 da (Emma Mary b 18 Jan 1972 d 12 July 1993); m 2, 25 April 1985, Grizel Elizabeth Catherine, o da of Lt-Col Herbrand Vavasour Dawson, DL, of Weston Hall, Otley, Yorks; *Career* chm: Foreign & Colonial Investment Trust plc 1985– (dir 1981), Foreign and Colonial Enterprise Trust plc 1986–, Foreign & Colonial Private Equity Trust plc 1994–, Finsbury Life Sciences Investment Trust plc 1997–, Argent Group Europe Ltd 1998–, Biotech Growth Tst plc; dep chm: Millennium & Copthorne Hotels plc 1996–, Grosvenor Group Holdings Ltd 2000– (dir 1999); dir: Berner Nicol & Co Ltd 1968–, James Cropper plc 1972–, Holker Estates Co Ltd 1974–, Hypo Foreign & Colonial Management (Holdings) Ltd 1974–, Grosvenor Estate Holdings 1989–, Wates Group Ltd 1999–; tstee: The Grosvenor Estate 1973–, Coll of Arms 1994–; Liveryman Worshipful Co of Goldsmiths 1993; *Recreations* country pursuits; *Clubs* Brooks's, Pratt's, Pitt (Cambridge); *Style*— J R Sclater, Esq, CVO; ✉ Sutton Hall, Barcombe, nr Lewes, East Sussex BN8 5EB (☎ 01273 400450, fax 01273 401086)

SCLATER, Patrick Henry; s of Henry Nicolai Sclater (d 2003), of Stockbridge, Hants, and Suzanna Mary, *née* Agnew (d 1993); *b* 9 January 1944; *Educ* Charterhouse, RAU (formerly RAC) Cirencester; *m* 6 July 1968, Rosalyn Heather, da of Urban George Eric Stephenson, of Frith House, Stalbridge, Dorset; 3 s (William b 1969, Alastair b 1971, Peter b 1976), 1 da (Heather b 1978); *Career* estate agent: sole princ Sclater Real Estate Dorchester 1974–83, Symonds Sampson & Sclater 1983–87, local dir Fulljames & Still Dorchester 1987; relocation agent: princ Sclater Property Search 1988–2009, chm Compass Relocation Ltd 1995–2009; partner in family farm; FRICS; *Recreations* shooting, sailing, walking, gardening, reading, travel; *Clubs* Farmers'; *Style*— Patrick H Sclater, Esq; ✉ Frith Farm, Stalbridge, Sturminster Newton, Dorset DT10 2SD (☎ 01963 250232, e-mail patricksclater@frith.farm)

SCLATER WALL, Madeleine Elizabeth Ramsden; *Educ* Manchester HS for Girls, Victoria Univ of Manchester (LLB); *Career* admitted slr England & Wales 1972, admitted Attorney California Bar USA 1982, admitted Attorney US Supreme Ct Bar 2003; secretariat Int Chamber of Commerce Ct of Arbitration 1972–74, slr Hawker Sidley Aviation 1974–77, asst gen counsel ITEL Corp Inc USA 1978–82, vice-pres and gen counsel Clarendon Gp USA 1982–85, vice-pres and chief counsel McDonnell Douglas Corp International USA 1985–90, gp dir of legal and regulatory affairs Cable & Wireless plc 1990–99, sr vice-pres gen counsel Equant NV Holland 1999–2001, gen counsel The European Lawyer 2001–05, pres Elizabeth Wall Int LLC (NY) (estab 2005); non-exec dir Legal & General Assurance plc 1998–2001; memb: Bd of Govrs Coll of Law 1995–2006, Bd of Tstees Civilia Fndn 1996–1999; chair US Bd of Dirs Assoc of Corp Counsel 2002–03 (memb 1997–, vice-chm 2001–02), pres European Chaptor of American Corporate Counsel Assoc 2003–04; int seminar and conf speaker; The Lawyer Magazine In-House Co Commercial Lawyer of the Year Award 1994, American Soc of Int Law Prominent

S

Woman in Int Law Award 1994, Assoc of Corp Counsel Excellence in Corp Practice Award 1999; memb: Law Soc 1972– (chm Commerce & Indust Gp 1996–97), Assoc of Corporate Counsel; Designee First 100 Years Women in Law Project; MInstD; *Recreations* travel, the arts, interior design, watching professional golf and rugby; *Clubs* The Cook Soc; *Style*— Elizabeth Wall; ✉ Elizabeth Wall Partners International LLC, 57 West 38th Street, 3rd Floor, New York, NY 10018, USA (☏ 001 212 753 7576, e-mail elizabeth@elizabethwall.com)

SCOBIE, Kenneth Charles; s of Charles Smith Scobie (d 1965), and Shena Bertram, *née* Melrose (d 1990); *b* 29 July 1938; *Educ* Daniel Stewart's Coll, Univ of Edinburgh (CA); *m* 29 Sept 1973, (Adela) Jane, da of Keith Somers Hollebone (d 1991), of Bampton Castle, Oxon; 1 da (Deborah b 19 May 1975), 1 s (Charles b 11 Oct 1976); *Career* CA; profit planning BMC (Scotland) Ltd 1961–63, dep fin dir Motor Car Div Rolls Royce 1963–66, sr mgmnt conslt and ptnr Robson Morrow & Co 1966–70, memb Main Bd and Exec Ctee Black and Decker Euro Gp 1971–72, md Vavasseur SA Ltd 1972–76, chief exec and dir Vernon Orgn 1977, md H C Sleigh UK Ltd 1979–82, gp md Blackwood Hodge plc 1984–90, non-exec dir Albrighton plc 1990–93, dir Postern Executive Group Ltd 1991–97, actg chm, dep chm and chief exec Brent Walker Group plc 1991–93; chm: Lovells Confectionery Ltd 1991–98, William Hill Group 1992–93, Cardinal Data Ltd 1993–94, Allied Leisure plc 1994–2000, Chemring plc 1997–2010; dep chm/chief exec Addis Ltd 1993–94; non-exec dir: Gartmore Indosuez UK Recovery (Group) Ltd 1993–98, Gartmore 1990 Ltd; pres London Scottish Football Club Ltd 1997–2001, chm Exec Bd Scottish Rugby Union 2000–03; CA 1961, CIMgt 1987; *Recreations* rugby, golf, tennis, cricket; *Clubs* Stewart's Melville, London Scottish RFC, Huntercombe Golf, The Durban; *Style*— Kenneth Scobie, Esq

SCORER, Timothy Rowland (Tim); s of Derek Rowland Scorer, TD (d 2012), and Margaret Shirley, *née* Staveacre (d 1998); *b* 25 June 1941; *Educ* Repton; *m* 1, 10 Oct 1965 (m dis 1981), Wendy Ann, da of Edward Thomas Glazier (d 1978); 2 s (Craig b 29 Jan 1967, Jamie b 3 July 1969); m 2, 25 Sept 1982 (m dis 1989), Julia Jane, da of Jeremy John Booth; 1 da (Lucinda b 29 Oct 1987); m 3, 7 May 1993, Julie Emma, da of Alan Baker; 2 s (Alexander b 3 Sept 1992, Cameron b 2 July 1996); *Career* admitted slr 1965; ptnr Josselyn & Sons Ipswich 1967, asst sec Law Soc 1976; ptnr: Barlow Lyde & Gilbert London 1980, Jarvis & Bannister 1992, DLA 1997, Thomas Cooper & Stibbard 2001–07; conslt: Ince & Co 2007–12, Quercus Law 2012–14, Kennedys Law 2014–; chm and fndr Lawyers' Flying Assoc, int vice-pres Lawyer Pilots' Bar Assoc USA; hon slr: Hon Co of Air Pilots (Freeman 1985, Liveryman 1988), Helicopter Club of GB, Flying Farmers Assoc, Br Air Display Assoc, Historic Aircraft Assoc; Freeman City of London 1987; memb Law Soc 1966; MRAeS; *Publications* A Guide to General Aviation Claims Handling (2010); *Recreations* flying as PPL, photography, travel, cooking; *Style*— Tim Scorer, Esq; ✉ The Forge, 1 Church View, Colne Engaine, Colchester, Essex CO6 2EP (☏ 01787 224294, mobile 07860 557766, e-mail timscorer1@gmail.com); Kennedys Law LLP, 25 Fenchurch Avenue, London EC3M 5AD (☏ 020 7667 9372, fax 020 7667 9777, e-mail tim.scorer@kennedyslaw.com)

SCOREY, David; QC (2015); *Educ* St John's Coll Oxford (BA), Leiden Univ (LLM); *m* 2004, Katie Renwick; 1 da (b 2005), 2 s (b 2008, 2010); *Career* called to the Bar Lincoln's Inn 1997; memb American Law Inst; *Books* Human Rights Damages (with Tim Eicke, QC, 2001), The Bermuda Form: Interpretation and Dispute Resolution of Excess Liability Insurance (with C Harris and R Geddes, 2011); *Clubs* Garrick; *Style*— David Scorey, Esq, QC; ✉ Essex Court Chambers, 24 Lincoln's Inn Fields, London WC2A 3EG (☏ 020 7813 8000, e-mail dscorey@essexcourt.com)

SCOTLAND, Tony; s of Peter Whitmore Scotland (d 1997), and Elizabeth Ann, *née* Dunn (d 1954); *b* 29 May 1945, Bucks; *Career* reporter East Essex Gazette 1961–65, TV reporter ABC Hobart 1966–68, TV reporter Look East BBC Norwich 1968–69, sub ed BBC Radio News London 1969–72, prodr The Arts Worldwide BBC Radio 3 1972–80, announcer Radio 3 1972–92; conslt and presenter Classic FM 1992–98, freelance writer 1992–; articles published in The Spectator, Harpers & Queen, Sunday Telegraph, The Independent, House & Garden, Catholic Herald, Erotic Review; fndr Bulgarian Orphans Fund 2000–16; *Books* The Empty Throne – The Quest for an Imperial Heir in the People's Republic of China (1993), Six Story Ballets in Words and Music (writer and narrator, 1997), Lennox & Freda (2010); *Recreations* travel, music, gardening; *Style*— J A Scotland, Esq; ✉ e-mail jascotland@googlemail.com

SCOTLAND OF ASTHAL, The Rt Hon the Baroness (Life Peer UK 1997), of Asthal in the County of Oxfordshire; Patricia Janet Scotland; PC (2001), QC (1991); da of Arthur Leonard Scotland, of Ilford, Essex; *b* 19 August 1955; *Educ* Univ of London (LLB); *m* 1985, Richard Martin Mawhinney, s of Raymond Johnston Mawhinney; 2 s (Hon Matthew Jackson b 1992, Hon Benjamin James b 1994); *Career* called to the Bar Middle Temple 1977 (bencher 1997), memb Bar of Antigua and Cwlth of Dominica; recorder 2000 (asst recorder 1994), dep judge of the High Ct (Family Div) 2000, fndr memb and former head of chambers 1 Gray's Inn Sq, former door tenant Bridewell Chambers; Parly under-sec of state FCO 1999–2001, Parly sec Lord Chllr's Dept (now Miny of Justice) 2001–03, min of state for the criminal justice system and law reform Home Office 2003–05, min of state for the criminal justice system and offender mgmnt Home Office 2005–07, Attorney-Gen for England, Wales and NI 2007–10; shadow Attorney-Gen for England, Wales and NI 2010–11, Prime Ministerial Trade Envoy to South Africa 2011–; fdng patron of the Corporate Alliance Against Domestic Violence 2011, fndr the Eliminate Domestic Violence Global Fndn; alternate UK Govt rep European Convention 2002–03, spokesperson for DTI on women & equality issues House of Lords; memb: PLP Women's Gp, Advsy Panel of Br American Project, ICTIS; former chm: ILEA Disciplinary Tbnl, HMG Caribbean Advsy Gp; former memb: Millennium Cmmn 1994–99, House of Commons Working Party on Child Abduction, Ctee Cmmn for Racial Equality, Legal Advsy Panel Nat Consumer Cncl, Advsy Ctee on Mentally Disordered Offenders; former memb Bar Ctees incl: Public Rels, Race Rels, Judicial Studies Bd Ethnic Minority Advsy Ctee; memb: Thomas More Soc, Lawyer's Christian Fellowship; former hon pres Trinity Hall Law Soc; Black Woman of the the Year (Law) 1992, Peer of the Year House Magazine Awards and Channel 4 Political Awards 2004, Parliamentarian of the Year Political Studies Assoc Awards 2004, Spectator Parliamentarian of the Year 2005; hon fell: Soc of Advanced Legal Studies, Wolfson Coll Cambridge, Cardiff Univ; Hon Dr: Univ of Westminster, Univ of Buckingham, Univ of Leicester, Univ of E London, Univ of W Indies; Dame Sacred Mil Constantinian Order of St George 2003; alderman of Bishopsgate in the City of London 2014; *Style*— The Rt Hon the Baroness Scotland of Asthal, PC, QC; ✉ House of Lords, London SW1A 0PW

SCOTT, Rev Dr Adam; OBE (2008), TD (1979); s of Brig Fraser Scott, of Broxbourne, Herts, and Bridget Penelope, *née* Williams; *b* 6 May 1947; *Educ* Marlborough, ChCh Oxford (MA), City Univ Business Sch (MBA), St Andrews (PhD); *m* 30 Sept 1978, Prof Oona MacDonald, PhD, FCSP, da of Prof R J D Graham (d 1950), of St Andrews, Fife; *Career* OUOTC 1965–68, CVHQ RA, 94 Locating Regt 1968–81, cmd Reserve Meteorologists, Capt 1975, ret 1981; reader St Aldate's Oxford 1970–75; ordained (Southwark): deacon 1975, priest 1976; asst curate St Michael and All Angels Blackheath Park 1975–, House of St Barnabas Soho 1999–; dean: Ministers in Secular Employment, Woolwich Episcopal Area 1990–2000; officiating chaplain Nat Reserve HQ Royal Artillery (NRHQ RA) and Woolwich 2016–; trained as intellectual property lawyer 1970–74; called to the Bar Inner Temple 1972; with: ITT 1974–77, PO 1977–81; BT: corp planner 1981–86, dir Office of Iain Vallance (chm of BT) 1986–88, dir of int affairs 1988–92, chm apparatus supply business 1992–94, ret 1997; sr advsr Europe Economics 1998–2000; memb: Competition Cmmn Appeal Tbnls 2000–2003, Guernsey Utility Appeal Panel 2002–08, Competition Appeal Tbnl 2003–12 (dir of studies 2012–); Univ of St Andrews: fell St Andrews Mgmnt Inst 1994–96, professorial fell 1996–97, sr research fell 1998–2012; non-exec dir SAMI Consulting Ltd 2014– Freeman City of London 1993; CEng, FIET (FIEE 1994, MIEE 1981), FRSA 1995, FHEA 2007, MITP (memb Inst of Telecommunications Professionals) 2007; *Recreations* gardening, walking; *Clubs* Nuffield Health; *Style*— The Rev Dr Adam Scott, OBE, TD; ✉ 19 Blackheath Park, Blackheath, London SE3 9RW (☏ 020 8852 3286)

SCOTT, Adrian Eason Bailey; DL (Dorset, 2008); s of Deric Sidney Scott (d 1997), and Margaret Emeline, *née* Bailey (d 1993); *b* 12 February 1938, Bournemouth, Dorset; *Educ* Canford Sch; *Career* Nat Serv Royal Signals 1956–58 (Gen Serv Medal); dir, jt md then chm Deric S Scott Ltd Funeral Directors 1960–97; chm European Gp Selected Ind Funeral Homes 1976–77, pres Bournemouth and Dist Assoc of Funeral Dirs; fndr chm Bournemouth Jr Chamber 1967 (also chm 1974); co-chm Bournemouth Deanery Synod 1979–84 (memb 1970–98), memb Gen Synod C of E 1980–90 (memb Liturgical Cmmn and Diocesan Synod), churchwarden St Stephen's Church Bournemouth 1975–85 and 2002–07, churchwarden Major Parish of Bournemouth Town Centre 1986–87, 1995–2000 and 2012–13; memb The Samaritans 1968–93, govr Talbot Heath Sch 1982–95 (chm governing body 1994–95), tstee Vitalis Tst; Paul Harris fell Rotary Int; High Sheriff Dorset 2007–08; Pres Rotary Club of Boscombe & Southbourne 1995 & 2009; *Recreations* travel, dining out, music; *Clubs* East India; *Style*— Adrian Scott, Esq, DL; ✉ 7 Byron House, 28 Boscombe Cliff Road, Bournemouth, Dorset BH5 1JP (☏ and fax 01202 397983, e-mail adrian@ebscott.fsnet.co.uk)

SCOTT, Andrew John; CBE (2006); s of late Cyril John Scott, and Gertrude Ethel, *née* Miller; *b* 3 June 1949; *Educ* Bablake Sch Coventry, Univ of Newcastle upon Tyne (BSc, MSc), Univ of Huddersfield (DMS); *m* 1972, Margaret Anne, JP, *née* Benyon; *Career* civil engr Local Water Authy Tyneside, London and W Yorks 1971–84, actg dir W Yorks Tport Museum 1984–86, keeper of technol Bradford City Museums 1986–87, dir London Tport Museum 1988–94, head Nat Railway Museum 1994–2009 (winner Euro Museum of The Year Award 2001), dir Science Museum 2009–10; author various essays for museological jls; chm: York Civic Tst 2015–; tstee: N Yorks Moors Historical Railway Tst; chm York Tourism Bureau 1998–2008, vice-chm Festiniog Heritage Ltd, pres North Eastern Locomotive Preservation Gp, memb N York Moors Nat Park Authy 2012–, chair York Civic Tst 2015–; chm of advsrs Int Assoc of Tport Museums, vice-pres Assoc of Br Tport and Engrg Museums; MICE 1976, FMA 1993 (AMA 1987); *Books* North Eastern Renaissance (1991), Making Histories in Transport Museums (with C Divall, 2001); *Recreations* travel, railways, ecclesiastical architecture; *Style*— Andrew Scott, Esq, CBE; ✉ e-mail andrew@scottyork.net

SCOTT, Sir Anthony Percy; 3 Bt (UK 1913), of Witley, Surrey; s of Col Sir Douglas Scott, 2 Bt (d 1984), and Elizabeth Joyce, née Glanley (d 1983); *b* 1 May 1937, London; *Educ* Harrow, ChCh Oxford; *m* 1962, Caroline Teresa Anne, er da of (William Charles) Edward Bacon, of Mobberley, Cheshire; 2 s (Henry Douglas Edward b 1964, Simon James b 1965), 1 da (Miranda Claire b 1968); *Heir* s, Henry Scott; *Career* called to the Bar Inner Temple 1960; ptnr in stockbroking firm Laurie Milbank & Co 1974–; chm and md L M (Moneybrokers) Ltd 1986–1995; Liveryman Worshipful Co of Haberdashers; *Clubs* St Moritz Tobogganing; *Style*— Sir Anthony Scott, Bt; ✉ Chateau la Coste, 81140 Larroque, France

SCOTT, (John) Brough; MBE (2009); s of Mason Hogarth Scott (d 1971), of Broadway, Worcs, and Irene Florence, *née* Seely (d 1976); *b* 12 December 1942; *Educ* Radley, CCC Oxford; *m* 3 Nov 1973, Susan Eleanor, da of late Ronald Grant MacInnes, of Abinger Common, Surrey; 2 da (Sophie Diana b 20 July 1974, Tessa Irene b 3 Nov 1984), 2 s (Charles Ronald Brough b 21 Jan 1976, James Seely b 14 Feb 1979); *Career* amateur and professional jump jockey (100 winners incl Imperial Cup and Mandarin Chase) 1962–70; TV journalist: ITV 1971–84 (chief racing presenter 1979–), Channel 4 1985–2001; sports journalist: Evening Standard 1972–74, Sunday Times 1974–90, Independent on Sunday 1990–92, Sunday Times 1993–95, Sunday Telegraph 1995–2008; fndr dir Racing Post 1985–; Lord Derby Award (racing journalist of the year) 1980, Clive Graham Trophy (services to racing) 1982, Sports Feature Writer of the Year 1985, 1990 and 1992; vice-pres Jockeys' Assoc 1969–71; chm Injured Jockeys' Fund, tstee Moorcroft Racehorse Welfare Centre; *Books* World of Flat Racing (1983), On And Off The Rails (1984), Front Runners (1991), Racing Certainties (1995), Galloper Jack (2003), Of Horses and Heroes (2008), McCoy (2010); *Recreations* riding, books, making bonfires; *Style*— Brough Scott, MBE; ✉ Coneyhurst Ltd, Meadow House, Coneyhurst Lane, Ewhurst, Surrey GU6 7PL (☏ 01483 277379, website www.broughscott.com)

SCOTT, Prof Clive; s of Jesse Scott, of Outwell, Norfolk, and Nesta Vera, *née* Morton; *b* 13 November 1943; *Educ* Bishop's Stortford Coll, St John's Coll Oxford (state scholar, Casberd exhibitioner, MA, MPhil, DPhil); *m* 1, 13 Aug 1965 (m dis 1983), Elizabeth Anne, da of Rowland Drabble; 1 da (Katherine Sophie b 27 Nov 1969), 1 s (Benjamin Nicholas b 24 Aug 1972); m 2, 21 July 1984, Marie-Noëlle, da of Jean Guillot; 2 s (Samuel William b 28 July 1985, Thomas Alexander b 3 Feb 1991); *Career* UEA: asst lectr 1967–70, lectr 1970–88, reader 1988–91, prof of European literature 1991–2007, head Sch of Literature and Creative Writing 2004–05, emeritus prof of European literature 2008–; dir of studies Br Cncl summer sch for Soviet teachers of English 1983–88; Clark lectures Univ of Cambridge 2010; pres Modern Humanities Research Assoc 2014; FBA 1994; Officier dans l'Ordre des Palmes Académiques 2008; *Books* French Verse-Art: A Study (1980), Anthologie Éluard (1983), A Question of Syllables: Essays in Nineteenth-Century French Verse (1986), The Riches of Rhyme: Studies in French Verse (1988), Vers Libre: The Emergence of Free Verse in France 1886–1914 (1990), Reading the Rhythm: The Poetics of French Free Verse 1910–1930 (1993), The Poetics of French Verse: Studies in Reading (1998), The Spoken Image: Photography and Language (1999), Translating Baudelaire (2000), Channel Crossings: French and English Poetry in Dialogue 1550–2000 (2002, R H Gapper Book Prize 2004), Translating Rimbaud's Illuminations (2006), Street Photography: From Atget to Cartier-Bresson (2007), Literary Translation and the Rediscovery of Reading (2012), Translating the Perception of Text: Literary Translation and Phenomenology (2012, R H Gapper Book Prize commendation 2013), Translating Apollinaire (2014); *Style*— Prof Clive Scott, FBA; ✉ School of Literature, Drama and Creative Writing, University of East Anglia, University Plain, Norwich NR4 7TJ (☏ 01603 592135, fax 01603 250599)

SCOTT, David Griffiths; s of Wilfred Emberton Scott (d 1967), and Gwenith, *née* Griffiths (d 2000); *b* 15 February 1942; *Educ* Adams GS Newport, Christ's Coll Cambridge (MA), London Business Sch (MSc); *m* 1969, Alison Jane Fraser; 2 da (Helen b 1971, Katherine b 1976), 1 s (James b 1974); *Career* md: ISC Alloy Ltd 1975–84, Impalloy Ltd 1978–84, Kleen-e-ze Holdings plc 1984–88, Yale Security Products Ltd 1989–91; dir: Ops Bd Newman Tonks plc 1991–94, David Scott Associates Ltd 1994–; ops dir Intelek plc 1994–99; CEng, FIMechE; *Recreations* golf, sailing, cricket, watercolours; *Style*— David Scott, Esq; ✉ The Barn, Main Street, Wick, Pershore, Worcestershire WR10 3NZ (☏ 01386 554185, fax 01386 553713, e-mail dgscott@btinternet.com)

SCOTT, David Morris Fitzgerald; s of Rev Canon William Morris Fitzgerald Scott (d 1959), of Birkenhead, Cheshire, and Nora Compigné, *née* Shaw (d 1995); *b* 7 June 1946; *Educ* St Lawrence Coll Ramsgate, The Hotchkiss Sch Lakeville CT, CCC Oxford (scholar, MA); *m* 10 June 1972, Jacqueline Mary, da of Kenneth Percy Pool; 2 da (Elizabeth b 1976, Sarah b 1978), 1 s (Michael b 1981); *Career* ptnr Kitcat & Aitken 1974–80 (investment analyst 1967–74), vice-pres Bank of NY 1980–83; dir: Warburg Investment Mgmnt Int 1983–85, Mercury Warburg Investment Mgmnt 1985–87, Mercury Rowan Mullens 1987–89, Mercury Asset Mgmnt Private Investors Gp 1990–2000, Singer & Friedlander Investment Mgmnt 2000–08, OLIM Ltd 2008–12; memb Cncl Westcott House Cambridge; hon fell Sion Coll; chm Oliver Borthwick Meml Tst; tstee: Alexandra Tst, Stock Exchange Benevolent Fund; treas New England Co; Freeman City of London, Past Master Worshipful Co of Scriveners; *Recreations* reading, old silver, military and church history; *Clubs* Brooks's, City of London; *Style*— David Scott, Esq; ✉ Windmill House, Windmill Lane, Wadhurst, East Sussex TN5 6DJ (☎ 01892 782683)

SCOTT, Sir David Richard Alexander; kt (2013), CBE (2006); s of Lt Cdr Robert Irwin Maddin Scott, OBE (d 1968), of Lyddington, Rutland, and (Margaret Sylvia) Daphne, *née* Alexander; *b* 25 August 1954; *Educ* Wellington; *m* 1 Aug 1981, Moy, da of Air Chief Marshal Sir John Barraclough, KCB, CBE, DFC, AFC (d 2008); 1 s (Alexander b 8 Aug 1982), 1 da (Arabella b 11 Jan 1985); *Career* CA Peat Marwick Mitchell & Co Blackfriars 1972–81, Channel Four Television Corporation (Channel Four Television Co Ltd until 1993): controller of fin and co sec 1981–88, dir of fin 1988–97, md 1997–2002, md and dep chief exec 2002–05; chief exec Digital UK Ltd 2008–13; FCA 1976, FRTS 2004, FRSA 2008; *Recreations* opera, theatre, ballet, bridge, sailing, country pursuits; *Clubs* Guards Polo, Royal Thames Yacht, Boodles; *Style*— Sir David Scott, CBE

SCOTT, Douglas Keith (Doug); CBE (1994); s of George Douglas Scott, of Nottingham, and Edith Joyce Scott; *b* 29 May 1941; *Educ* Cottesmore Secdy Modern Sch, Mundella GS Nottingham, Loughborough Teachers' Trg Coll (Cert); *m* 1, 1962 (m dis 1988), Janice Elaine, da of Thomas Arthur Brook, of Notts; 1 s (Michael b 1963), 2 da (Martha b 1973, Rosie b 1978); m 2, 17 Sept 1993 (m dis 2002), Sharavati Prabhu; 2 s (Arran b 1994, Euan b 1996); m 3, 8 Dec 2007, Patricia Borland Lang; *Career* mountaineer; began climbing aged 12, visited Alps aged 17 and most years thereafter; pres Alpine Climbing Gp 1976–82, pres Alpine Club 1999–2001, vice-pres Br Mountaineering Cncl 1994–97; Hon MA: Univ of Nottingham 1991, Loughborough Univ 1994; Hon MEd Nottingham Trent Univ 1995; *Expeditions* first ascents incl: Tarso Teiroko Tibesti Mountains Sahara 1965, Cilo Dag Mountains SE Turkey 1966, S face Koh-i-Bandaka (6837m) Hindu Kush Afghanistan 1967, E pillar of Mt Asgard Baffin Island Expedition 1972, Changbang (6864m) 1974, SE spur Pic Lenin (7189m) 1974, Mt McKinley (6226m, first alpine ascent of S face via new route, with Dougal Haston) 1976, E face direct Mt Kenya 1976, Ogre (7330m) Karakoram Mountains 1977, N Ridge route Kangchenjunga 1977 (and without oxygen 1979), N summit Kussum Kangguru 1979, N face Nuptse 1979, Kangchungtse (7640m, alpine style) 1980, Shivling E pillar (13-day alpine style push) 1981, N face to central summit Changlang (with Rheinhold Messner) 1981, Pungpa Ri (7445m) 1982, Shishapangma S face (8046m) 1982, Lobsang Spire (Karakoram) 1983, Broad Peak (8047m) 1983, Mt Baruntse (7143m) 1984, E summit Mt Changlang (7287m, and traverse over unclimbed central summit alpine style to within 100m of summit) 1984, rock climbs Southern India 1986, rock climbs Wadi Rum Jordan 1986, S face Mt Jitchu Drake (6793m, alpine style) Bhutan 1988, Indian Arete Latok III 1990, Hanging Glacier Peak S (6294m, via S ridge) 1991, Chombu E (5745m) 1996, Drohmo Central Summit (6855m, via S pillar alpine style with Roger Mear) 1998, Targo Ri (6572m) 2000; first Br ascent Salathé Wall El Capitain Yosemite 1971, first alpine style ascent Diran (7260m) 1985, first Br ascent Chimtarga (5482m) Fansikye Mountains Tadzhikistan 1992, climed Mt Vinson (4897m, highest point in Antarctica) 1992, attempt on Nanga Parbat (8135m) via Mazeno Ridge 1992, climbed three Mazeno Peaks 1993 (also Mazeno Spire and West Peak), climbs and explorations in Tierra del Fuego 1994, original route and new route up N face V Carstenez Pyramid (4884m) 1995, second ascent NE ridge Teng Kongma (6215m) 1998, first ever foreigner (with Greg Child) to explore mountains of central Arunachal Pardesh 1999; memb other expdns incl: Euro Mt Everest Expedition to SW face 1972; Br Mt Everest Expedition to SW face 1972 (autumn), Br Mt Everest Expedition (reached summit with Dougal Haston, via SW face, first Britons on summit) 1975; *Publications* Big Wall Climbing (1974), Shishapangma, Tibet (with Alex McIntyre, 1984), Himalayan Climber (1992); contributor to Alpine Journal, American Alpine Journal and Mountain Magazine, Himal Magazine; *Recreations* rock climbing, organic gardening; *Clubs* Alpine, Alpine Climbing Gp, Nottingham Climbers; *Style*— Doug Scott, Esq, CBE; ✉ Stewart Hill Cottage, Hesket Newmarket, Wigton, Cumbria CA7 8HX

SCOTT, Dougray; *Educ* Kirkcaldy Coll of Technol (later Fife Coll), Welsh Coll of Music and Drama; *Career* actor; *Theatre* Wallace (Scottish Theatre), Welcome Home (Old Red Lion), To Kill A Mockingbird (SNAP Theatre Co), This Island's Mine (Gay Sweatshop), Indigo (Almedia), The Power and the Glory (Chichester Festival Theatre), Unidentified Human Remains (Traverse), And the True Nature of Love (Hampstead), The Rover (Jacob Street), To The Green Fields Beyond (Donmar Warehouse); *Television* incl: Crow Road 1996, Arabian Nights 2000, Heist 2006, Desperate Housewives 2006–07, Dr Jekyll and Mr Hyde 2008, Father & Son 2009, The Day of the Triffids 2009, The Diplomat 2009, Hemlock Grove 2013, Strike Back 2013, The Wrong Mans 2013; *Film* incl: Mission: Impossible II 2000, Enigma 2001, Ripley's Game 2002, To Kill A King 2003 (also assoc prodr), The Poet 2003, One Last Chance 2004 (also exec prodr), Things to Do Before You're 30 2004, Dark Water 2005, The Ten Commandments 2006, Perfect Creature 2007, Hitman 2007, Love Me Forever 2008, New Town Killers 2008, There Be Dragons 2011, United 2011, A Thousand Kisses Deep 2011, My Week with Marilyn 2011; *Style*— Dougray Scott, Esq; ✉ c/o Public Eye Communications, Suite 318, 535 King's Road, London SW10 0SZ (☎ 020 7351 1555, fax 020 7351 1010)

SCOTT, Dr Eleanor Roberta; da of late William Ettles, and Roberta, *née* Reid; *b* 23 July 1951; *Educ* Bearsden Acad, Univ of Glasgow (MB ChB); *m* 1977 (m dis 1994) David Scott; 1 da (Tania Emily 10 July 1982), 1 s (Robert David b 7 July 1985); partner, Rob Gibson, MSP, *qv*; *Career* various jr hosp dr posts 1974–78, trainee in gen practice Nairn 1979, community paediatrician Inverness 1980–87, community paediatrician Ross and Cromarty 1987–2003, MSP (Green) Highlands and Islands 2003–07; memb Scottish Green Pty 1989–; *Recreations* traditional music, gardening; *Style*— Dr Eleanor Scott; ✉ 8 Culcairn Road, Evanton IV16 9YT (☎ 01349 830388, e-mail eleanorsco@googlemail.com)

SCOTT, Finlay McMillan; CBE (2009), TD (1984); s of Finlay McMillan Scott (d 1985), and Anne Cameron Robertson, *née* Coutts (d 1972); *b* 25 May 1947; *Educ* Greenock HS, Open Univ (BA, LLB), Univ of Durham (MSc); *m* 1, 17 May 1969 (m dis 2001), Eileen Frances, da of Ronald Francis Marshall; 1 da (Karen Anne Coutts b 21 Dec 1972), 1 s (Finlay Alan McMillan b 18 July 1975); m 2, 5 Jan 2002, Prof Elizabeth Susan Perkins; *Career* Dept for Educn 1975–94 (under sec (grade 3) 1990), seconded as sec Univs Funding Cncl 1990–92, seconded as sec and dep chief exec HEFCE 1992–94, chief exec and registrar GMC 1994–2009; memb: NI Higher Educn Cncl 1994–2001, Med Workforce Standing Advsy Ctee 1996–2001, Postgrad Medical Educn and Trg Bd 2003–09; TA: Intelligence Corps 1973–76, RAOC 1976–94, Lt Col 1989, Royal Logistic Corps 1994–95, RARO 1995–; govr: London Guildhall Univ 1996–2002, London Metropolitan Univ 2003–09; *Recreations* horses; *Style*— Finlay Scott, Esq, CBE, TD; ✉ Kiln Farm, 122 Carr House Lane, Ince Blundell, Merseyside L38 1QQ

SCOTT, (Celia) Gay; da of Ivor Norman Bailey (d 1986), and Enid Alice, *née* Sherwood (d 1997); *b* 25 March 1944; *Educ* St Angela's Providence Convent London, NW London Poly, Brighton Coll of Librarianship; *m* 18 May 1967, Michael James Frederick Scott, s of Capt John Bristol Irwin Scott (d 1991), of Bedford; 1 s (Charles b 1982); *Career* Membs' Info Serv House of Commons 1973–74, head of Euro Unit Greater London Cncl 1976–80, fndr and dir European Information Ltd (acquired by Eurofi 1982) 1980–, dir Eurofi 1982–2006; assoc Library Assoc 1967, MIInfSc 1977; *Publications* The European Economic Community (1979), A Guide to European Community Grants and Loans, Money for Research and Development (jtly, 1986), Eurobrief (monthly 1981–83); *Recreations* riding, walking, cookery, tennis, theatre-going, gardening; *Style*— Mrs Michael Scott; ✉ Holly Lodge, Beetley, Norfolk NR20 4BT (☎ 01362 816267)

SCOTT, Graham Robert; s of Robert Alexander Scott, of Alness, Ross-shire, and Helen, *née* Tawse (d 1987); *b* 8 December 1944; *Educ* Bryanston, Univ of Nottingham (BSc); *m* 19 Aug 1967, Wendy Jean, da of Harry Mumford (d 1983); 1 s (Andrew), 1 da (Harriet); *Career* gen mangr Unitrition Int Ltd 1984–86, md BP Nutrition (UK) Ltd 1987–89, area chief exec BP Nutrition Specialities 1989–90, chief exec BP Nutrition Petfoods 1991–93, gp chief exec JLI Group plc 1994–95, chief exec NWF Group plc 1995–2007; non-exec dir: Buxton Arts Festival Ltd 1997–, Butcher's Pet Care Ltd 2001–; non-exec chm Dee Valley Group plc 1998–2002 and 2003–; CEng 1971, MIChemE 1971; *Style*— Graham Scott, Esq

SCOTT, Prof Hazel R; *née* Wyllie; da of Very Rev Dr Hugh R Wyllie, of Hamilton, Strathclyde, and Eileen, *née* Cameron; *b* 31 January 1965; *Educ* Hutchesons' GS, Univ of Glasgow (MB ChB, MD); *m* 16 Sept 1994, Alastair E Scott; 2 s (Iain b 1 April 1999, Alexander b 9 June 2004); *Career* sr registrar W Glasgow Hosps Univ NHS Tst until 1996, conslt physician (with an interest in respiratory med) Wishaw Gen Hosp NHS Tst 1996–; dir Med Educn Lanarkshire Acute Hosps Tst 2001–10; dir of medical educn and continuing professional devpt (CPD) RCPSGlas 2006–; dir of deanery devpt and assoc postgrad dean Dept of Postgrad Medicine Glasgow Univ, hon prof of medical educn Faculty of Medicine Univ of Glasgow; FRCP; *Publications* Davidson's Foundations of Clinical Practice (2009); *Recreations* music, gardening; *Style*— Prof Hazel R Scott; ✉ Department of Medicine, Wishaw General Hospital NHS Trust, Wishaw, Lanarkshire ML2 0DP (☎ 0141 223 1507)

SCOTT, Helen; *b* 25 July 1990, Birmingham; *Career* para-cyclist (sighted pilot); achievements (with Aileen McGlynn, OBE) incl: Silver medal (women's tandem kilo) Para-Cycling Track World Championships 2011, 3 Silver medals (pursuit, kilo and sprint) Para-Cycling Track World Championships 2012, 2 Silver medals (kilo and individual 1km time trial) and Bronze medal (individual pursuit) Paralympic Games 2012; *Style*— Ms Helen Scott; ✉ Twitter @Scottie2507

SCOTT, Hugh Johnstone; s of Hugh Johnstone Scott (d 1961), and Agnes Alison Leckie, *née* Storie (d 1994); *Educ* Paisley GS, Glasgow Sch of Art (DA), Jordanhill Coll (CertEd); *m* 23 Dec 1960, Mary Smith Craig, da of James Hamilton; 1 s (David b 7 Oct 1961), 1 da (Caroline b 18 Sept 1963); *Career* Nat Serv 1958–60; art teacher various schs 1971–84 (latterly head of art Lomond Sch Helensburgh); full time author 1984–; writer in residence City of Aberdeen 1991 (Scottish Arts Cncl bursary), pt/t lectr in creative writing Adult and Continuing Educn Dept Univ of Glasgow 1988–, tutor with the Arvon Fndn 1994, pt/t lectr in drawing and painting Adult and Continuing Educn Dept Univ of Glasgow 1998–2003, ind tutor of drawing and painting and of creative writing 2003–, columnist and cartoonist for The Park Weekly News (formerly The Press & Post then The Park Free Press) 2003–, columnist and cartoonist (writing as The Guru) Writers' Forum magazine 2007–; winner Woman's Realm Children's Story Competition 1982, Scottish Arts Cncl bursary 1988–89, Whitbread Children's Category Book of the Year 1989, Scottish Arts Cncl bursary 1993–94 and 1997; memb Soc of Authors 1988; *Books* incl: The Shaman's Stone (1988), The Plant That Ate The World (1989), Why Weeps The Brogan? (1989, short-listed for the McVitie prize 1990), Freddie and the Enormouse, The Haunted Sand, The Camera Obscura, The Summertime Santa, Something Watching, The Gargoyle (1991), Change the King! (1991), A Box of Tricks (1991), A Ghost Waiting (1993), The Place Between (1994), The Ghosts of Ravens Crag (1996), The Grave-Digger (1997), The Secret of the Pit (1998), Giants (1999), Likely Stories (2011); *Recreations* weight training, reading, exploring England, painting; *Style*— Hugh Scott, Esq; ✉ c/o Walker Books Ltd, 87 Vauxhall Walk, London SE11 5HJ (☎ 020 7793 0909, fax 020 7587 1123)

SCOTT, Prof Ian Richard; s of Ernest Richard Scott (d 1971), of Geelong, Aust, and Edith Miriam Scott (d 1976); *b* 8 January 1940; *Educ* Geelong Coll, Queen's Coll, Univ of Melbourne (LLB), King's Coll London (PhD); *m* 1 Oct 1971, Ecce Scott, da of Prof Boris Norman Cole, of Leeds; 2 da (Anneke b 1 Jan 1978, Kaatye b 3 Jan 1981); *Career* barr and slr Supreme Court of Victoria 1964–, called to the Bar Gray's Inn 1995 (hon bencher 1988, QC (hc) 2016); Univ of Birmingham: reader judicial admin 1976–78, dir Inst of Judicial Admin 1976–82, Barber prof of law 1978–2000, dean Faculty of Law 1985–94, prof of law 2000–05, emeritus prof 2005–; visiting research prof Whittier Coll California 1978–79, exec dir Victoria Law Fndn 1982–84, non-exec dir Royal Orthopaedic Hosp NHS Tst 1996–2000; gen ed The White Book 2007– (contributing ed 1989–2006); memb: Lord Chllr's Review Body on Civil Justice 1985–88, Policy Advsy Gp Nat Health Serv Litigation Authy 1997–2000, Alternative Dispute Resolution sub-ctee of Civil Justice Cncl 1998–2002; chm Home Sec's N Yorks Magistrates' Courts Inquiry 1989; *Style*— Prof I R Scott, QC(Hon); ✉ School of Law, University of Birmingham, Birmingham B15 2TT

SCOTT, Prof James; s of Robert Bentham Scott (d 1976), and Iris Olive, *née* Hill, of Melton Mowbray, Leics; *b* 13 September 1946; *Educ* Univ of London (scholar, BSc), London Hosp Med Coll (MB BS, MSc, MRCP); *m* 1976, Diane Marylin, da of Herbert Lowe; 2 s (William b 30 July 1981, Edward b 10 Sept 1984), 1 da (Lucy b 20 Jan 1990); *Career* house offr: London Hosp 1971–72, Hereford Co Hosp 1972; SHO Midland Centre for Neurosurgery and Neurology and Queen Elizabeth Hosp Birmingham 1972–73; registrar in med: Gen Hosp Birmingham 1973–74, Academic Dept of Med Royal Free Hosp London 1975–76; MRC research fell and hon sr registrar Royal Postgraduate Med Sch and Hammersmith Hosp London 1977–80, Euro Molecular Biology Orgn fell Dept of Biochemistry Univ of Calif San Francisco 1980–83, MRC clinical scientist and hon conslt physician MRC Clinical Research Inst and Northwick Park Hosp 1983–91, hon dir MRC Molecular Med Gp 1992–, prof of med and chm Dept of Med Imperial Coll Sch of Med at Hammersmith Hosp (Royal Postgraduate Med Sch until merger 1997) 1992, dir of med and chief of serv med cardiology Hammersmith Hosps NHS Tst 1994, dir Genetics and Genomics Research Inst Imperial Coll (dep princ Research); Humphrey Davy Rolleston lectr RCP 1989, guest lectr MRS 1990, Pfizer lectr Clinical Research Inst Montreal 1990, guest lectr Japan Atherosclerosis Soc 1992, medallist and visiting prof RSM/American Heart Assoc 1992, Montreal Merck Frosst-McGill lectr in lipid metabolism 1992, Simms lectr 1995; Graham Bull Prize RCP 1989, Squibb Bristol-Myers Award 1993 (for cardiovascular research); memb: Grants Ctee B MRC Systems Bd until 1990, Research Fund Ctee Br Heart Fndn until 1992, Research Ctee RCP 1988–; external examiner (BSc Clinical Scis) 1991 and internal examiner (MB BS) 1993 Univ of London; author of numerous book chapters, reviews and refereed papers; Euro ed Arteriosclerosis, Thrombosis and Vascular Biology (American Heart Assoc jl); fell Queen Mary & Westfield Coll London 1998; memb: Biochemical Soc, RSM, Euro Molecular Biology Orgn 1993; FRCP 1986, FRS 1997, FIBiol 1998, FMedSci 1998, hon fell Assoc of Physicians of GB and I 1998; *Recreations* family and friends, the twentieth century novel, British impressionist and modern painting, long distance running and swimming; *Style*— Prof James Scott, FRS; ✉ Genetics and Genomics Research Institute, Imperial College School of Medicine, South Kensington Campus, Exhibition Road, London SW7 2AZ (☎ 020 7594 3614, fax 020 7594 3653)

S

SCOTT, James Empson; s of James Christopher Scott (d 1979), and Phyllis Margaret, *née* Empson (d 1985); *b* 8 November 1942; *Educ* King's Sch Canterbury, Oriel Coll Oxford, Middx Hosp Med Sch (MA); *m* 1, 1967 (m dis), Mary, da of Sir Brian Fairfax-Lucy (d 1974); 2 da (Sophie b 1970, Charlotte b 1974); m 2, 1980, Katherine Henrietta, da of Sir Michael Cary (d 1978); 2 s (Matthew b 1984, Ned b 1985), 1 da (Molly b 1990); *Career* successively: sr registrar (orthopaedic surgery) Middx Hosp and Royal Nat Orthopaedic Hosp, Fulbright scholar and fell in orthopaedic surgery Massachusetts Gen Hosp, conslt orthopaedic surgn St Stephen's Hosp, St Mary Abbott's Hosp and Westminster Hosps, conslt orthopaedic surgn Chelsea and Westminster Hosp London; sr examiner (MB BS) Univ of London, memb Cncl Orthopaedic Section RSM; former ed Jl of Bone and Joint Surgery (currently emeritus ed); FRCS, FBOA; *Recreations* paintings; *Clubs* Athenaeum; *Style*— James Scott, Esq; ✉ 8 Rectory Grove, London SW4 0EA (☎ 020 7622 0571); The Lister Hospital, Chelsea Bridge Road, London SW1W 8RH (☎ 020 7259 9216, fax 020 7259 9221)

SCOTT, Sir James Jervoise; 3 Bt (UK 1962), of Rotherfield Park, Hants, DL (2013); s of Sir James Walter Scott, 2 Bt, DL (d 1993), and Anne Constantia, *née* Austin (d 2005); *b* 12 October 1952, Winchester; *Educ* Eton, Trinity Coll Cambridge; *m* 1, 13 Oct 1982, Judy Evelyn; 1 s (Arthur Jervoise Trafford b 2 Feb 1984); m 2, 2011, Emily Helen Wahlberg Thompson; 1 s (Wilfred Jervoise b 3 Dec 2014); *Heir* s, Arthur Scott; *Career* ed Big Farm Weekly 1984–88; memb Hants CC 2001–05; High Sheriff Hants 2004–05; pres Hants Branch CLA 2005–14 (chm 1996–98), chm Taxation and Political Ctee Historic Houses Assoc 2006–; Liveryman Worshipful Co of Mercers; *Style*— Sir James Scott, Bt, DL; ✉ Rotherfield Park, East Tisted, Alton, Hampshire GU34 3QE

SCOTT, John; JP, MSP; s of William Scott, of Ballantrae, Ayrshire, and Elizabeth Haddow, *née* Graham; *b* 7 June 1951; *Educ* George Watson's Coll Edinburgh, Univ of Edinburgh (BSc); *m* 7 June 1975, Charity Nadine Mary (d 2000), da of Lt-Col G M T Bousfield; 1 s (Gordon John b 12 June 1977), 1 da (Caroline Mary Elizabeth b 1 May 1979); *Career* farmer W Scott & Son partnership Balkissock 1973–, ptnr Doorstep Dishes and Events in Tents 1986–2000, estab fertiliser selling agency 1987–2000, fndr dir Ayrshire Country Lamb Ltd 1988–93, estab Ayrshire Farmers Markets 1999, MSP (Cons) Ayr 2000–; memb Tport and Environment Ctee Scot Parl 2001–03, Scot Cons spokesman on the environment 2001–03, memb Corporate Body Scot Parl 2003–07, dep convenor Petitions Ctee Scot Parl 2003–07; policy cmmr (rural affrs) Rifkind Policy Cmmn Scot Cons Pty 1998, dep chm Carrick Cumnock and Doon Valley Cons Pty 1999–2000; NFU of Scot: convenor Hill Farming Ctee 1993–99, pres Ayrshire Exec 1994–96; chm: Ayrshire and Arran Farming and Wildlife Advsy Gp 1993–99, S of Scot Regnl Wool Ctee 1996–99, Advsy Gp Hill Sheep and Native Woodland Project 1999–, Scot Area Ctee UK Cons Countryside Forum 1999–2000; fndr chm: Scot Assoc of Farmers' Markets 2001–05, Ayrshire Farmers' Markets 2001–08; *Recreations* geology, curling, bridge, rugby; *Style*— John Scott, Esq, MSP; ✉ Constituency Office, 17 Wellington Square, Ayr KA7 1EZ (☎ 01292 286251, fax 01292 280480); Scottish Parliament, Edinburgh EH99 1SP (☎ 0131 348 5664, fax 0131 348 5617, e-mail john.scott.msp@scottish.parliament.uk)

SCOTT, Sir (Walter) John; 5 Bt (UK 1907), of Beauclerc, Bywell St Andrews, Co Northumberland; s of Maj Sir Walter Scott, 4 Bt, JP, DL (d 1992), and Diana Mary, *née* Owen (d 1985); *b* 24 February 1948; *Educ* privately; *m* 1, 1969 (m dis 1971), Lowell Patria, da of late Gp Capt Pat Vaughan Goddard, of Auckland, NZ; 1 da (Rebecca b 1970); m 2, 1977, Mary Gavin, o da of Alexander Fairley Anderson, of Gartocharn, Dunbartonshire; 1 da (Diana Helen Rose b 1977), 1 s (Walter Samuel b 1984); *Heir* s, Walter Scott; *Career* farmer, columnist, author, TV broadcaster and snuff manufacturer; chm Sir Walter Scott Fine Border Snuffs; fndr memb Cholmondeley Coursing Club 1995; pres: Union of Country Sports Workers 2000, Tay Valley Wildfowlers Assoc 2001, Sporting Lucas Terrier Assoc 2007, Gamekeepers Welfare Tst 2008, Newcastle-upon-Tyne Wildfowlers Assoc 2009–, Assoc for the Working Lurcher/Longdog 2015; chm North Pennine Hunt 2008 (jt master 2009); memb Bd: Heather Tst 2004–08 (vice-pres 2008–13), The European Squirrel Fedn 2004; patron: Nat Org of Beaters and Pickers Up, Wildlife Art Tst 2008; centenary patron BASC 2008; *Publications* Clarissa and the Countryman (2000), Clarissa and the Countryman Sally Forth (2001), A Sunday Roast (2002), The Game Cookbook (2004), A Greener Life (2006), A Book of Britain (2010); *Recreations* field sports; *Clubs* Pratt's; *Style*— Sir John Scott, Bt

SCOTT, John Gavin; LVO (2004); s of Douglas Gavin Scott, and Hetty, *née* Murphy; *b* 18 June 1956; *Educ* Queen Elizabeth GS Wakefield, St John's Coll Cambridge (organ scholar, MA, MusB); *m* 1, 28 July 1979 (m dis 2010), Carolyn Jane, da of David James Lumsden; 1 da (Emma Jane b 27 Dec 1984), 1 s (Alexander Gavin b 29 Oct 1987); m 2, 25 May 2013, Lily Isabel Ardalan; *Career* asst organist: Wakefield Cathedral 1970–74, St Paul's and Southwark Cathedrals 1978–84; organist and dir of music St Paul's Cathedral 1990–2004 (sub-organist 1984–90), organist and dir of music St Thomas Church Fifth Avenue NY 2004–; debut Henry Wood Proms 1977, Royal Festival Hall debut March 1979; frequent solo tours, dir of St Paul's Cathedral Choir in numerous concerts, tours and recordings; awarded first prize: Manchester International Organ Competition 1978, Leipzig J S Bach Competition 1984; International Performer of the Year Award American Guild of Organists 1998; Liveryman Worshipful Co of Musicians; Hon DMus Nashotah House Seminary WI 2008; Hon RAM 1990, Hon FGCM 1996, Hon FRSCM 2006, Hon FTCL 2002; *Recordings* as soloist: Liszt's Ad Nos, Ad Salutarem Undam 1984, Organ Music by Marcel Dupré 1986, Organ Music by Maurice Duruflé 1989, Organ Music by Mendelssohn, Janácek's Glagolitic Mass 1990, Organ Music by Elgar, Harris and Bairstow 1992, Organ Music by William Mathias 1993, Great European Organs No 40 1996, 20th Century Masterpieces 1998, Marcel Dupré Vol II 1998, Organ Music by Percy Whitlock 2004, On a Sunday Afternoon 2007; as conductor with St Paul's Choir: Christmas Music 1986, My Soul Doth Magnify the Lord 1987, Herbert Howell's Church Music 1987, My Spirit Hath Rejoiced 1988, Praise to the Lord 1989, The English Anthem Vol 1–8 1989–2004, Stainer's Crucifixion 1990, Hear my Prayer 1991, Cathedral Music by Kenneth Leighton 1992, Music by William Croft 1993, RPO Christmas Concert 1993, Christmas Carols 1994, Psalms Vol 1–12 1994–2000, Passiontide 1996, Music for St Paul's 1998, Advent at St Paul's 1998, Epiphany at St Paul's 2001, Remembrance 2003; as conductor with St Thomas Choir: Christmas on 5th Avenue 2005, Easter on 5th Avenue 2006, Messiah (Mozart orchestration) 2008, Rachmaninoff Vespers 2008, American Voices 2009, O Sing Unto the Lord – Music of Henry Purcell 2010, Durufle and Howells Requiems 2011, Faure Requiem 2012, Bach Motets 2015; *Publications* The New St Paul's Cathedral Psalter (1997), Ash Wednesday to Easter for Choirs (1998), St Paul's Cathedral Descant Book (2001), Epiphany to All Saints for Choirs (2004), The Anglican Psalter (2009); *Recreations* reading, travel; *Style*— Dr John Scott, LVO; ✉ 202 West 58th Street, New York, NY 10019, USA (☎ 00 212 757 7013, e-mail jscott@saintthomaschurch.org)

SCOTT, John Philip Henry Schomberg; DL (Roxburgh, Ettrick & Lauderdale 2013); s of late Christopher Bartle Hugh Scott, and late Anne Margaret D'Arcy, *née* Kerr, of Galashiels, Scotland; *b* 1952; *Educ* Eton, Magdalene Coll Cambridge (MA), INSEAD Fontainebleau (MBA); *m* 6 Dec 1977, Jacqueline Dawn, da of Colin Rae, MC, of Bunbury, Cheshire; 2 s (Alexander Hugh Frere b 1982, James Julian Frere b 1985); *Career* Jardine Matheson & Co Ltd Hong Kong 1974–80; dir: Lazard Brothers & Co Ltd London 1988–2001 (joined 1981), Xaar plc 2001–10, Dunedin Income Growth Investment Tst plc 2001–12 (chm 2006–12), Miller Insurance Services Ltd 2001–12, Scottish Mortgage Investment Tst plc 2001– (chm 2010–), Martin Currie Pacific Tst plc 2002–15, JP Morgan Claverhouse Investment Tst plc 2004–, Schroder Japan Growth Fund plc 2004–15, Alternative Asset Opportunities PCC Ltd 2009–, Bluefield Solar Investment Fund Ltd 2013–; dep chm Endace Ltd 2005–13 (formerly chm); chm: Alpha Insurance Analysts 2013–, Impax Environmental Markets 2014– (formerly dep chm); memb Queen's Body Guard for Scotland (Royal Co of Archers); Freeman City of London 1981, Liveryman Worshipful Co of Grocers 1992 (memb Ct of Assts 2002–, Master 2007–08); FCII 1980, FCSI 2005 (MSI 1993); *Recreations* outdoor sports; *Clubs* New (Edinburgh), Boodle's, Pratt's, Farmers, Forest (Selkirk), '71 (Cambridge); *Style*— John Scott, Esq; ✉ Hollybush, by Galashiels, Selkirkshire TD1 3PU

SCOTT, Jonathan; *Career* Herbert Smith Freehills: joined as trainee 1979, ptnr 1988–, sr ptnr 2010–; *Style*— Jonathan Scott, Esq; ✉ Herbert Smith Freehills, Exchange House, Primrose Street, London EC2A 2EG

SCOTT, Lee; s of Sidney Scott (d 1997), and Rennee, *née* Cain (d 1983); *b* 6 April 1956, Stratford, London; *Educ* Clarkes Coll Ilford; *m* 18 May 1987, Estelle King; 3 da (Sara b 8 Dec 1977, Hana b 28 Oct 1981, Rachel b 24 July 1988), 2 s (Daniel b 28 June 1979, Ben b 16 May 1984); *Career* campaign dir United Jewish Israel Appeal 1988–98, former cncllr (Cons) Redbridge BC, Parly candidate (Cons) Waveney 2001, MP (Cons) Ilford N 2005–15; *Style*— Lee Scott, Esq; ✉ House of Commons, London SW1A 0AA (☎ 07712 437054, e-mail leescott.uk14@yahoo.co.uk)

SCOTT, Patricia Mary; *née* Rouse; da of Gordon James Rouse (d 1978), and Hilda May, *née* Marchant; *b* 28 November 1954; *Educ* Hreod Burna Sr HS, Portsmouth Poly; *m* 1 Aug 1975, Anthony Vincent Scott, s of Thomas Arthur David Scott; 1 s (Adam James b 27 May 1991), 1 adopted da (Anna Louise b 7 July 1995); *Career* various appts Thorn Television Rentals Ltd and Thorn EMI plc 1974–85, accountant Burmah Oil Exploration Ltd 1985; Thorn EMI plc: gp tax mangr 1986–89, dir Taxation and Treasury 1989–94; chief exec The Chieveley Consulting Group Ltd 1995–97 and 1998–2005, gp treas Redland plc 1997–98; dir: Woodbridge Ptnrs Ltd 2002–11, Scott Young Ltd 2002–07; dir and fndr: Leadership in Finance 2005–06, The Rivendell Centre Ltd incorporating Leading Edge Change 2006–; founding ptnr Scott Peters LLP (trading as Rivendell and Leading Edge Change) 2007–, chief exec Rivendell Publishing Ltd 2008–, princ ptnr Guides for High Achieveing Finance Directors 2012–; non-exec dir: Warden Housing Assoc 1995–2006, Housing Ops Bd Home Housing Gp 2006–10; fndr and author The Finance Director's Survival Guide 2011–; hon fin dir Swindon & Cricklade Railway 2009–; hon treas St Augustine's Church 1985–2002, tstee One Small Step charity for the disabled 1993–96; govr Downe House Sch 1995–97; fell Chartered Assoc of Certified Accountants 1989 (memb 1984); memb Tax Law Review Ctee 1994–2004; FCCA, FCT; *Publications* Having their Cake: How the City and Big Bosses are Consuming UK Business (co-author, 2004), Adam's Inheritance (as Alesana Fleetwood, 2008), Corporate Treasury Management Made Simple (2013), The Nuts and Bolts of Buying and Selling Companies and Businesses (2013), 121 Hints and Tips for High Achieving Finance Directors (2013); *Recreations* walking, fiction writing, PC gaming, meditation, personal growth; *Style*— Patricia Scott; ✉ Rivendell, 5 The Clays, Market Lavington, Devizes, Wiltshire SN10 4AY (☎ 01380 816077, fax 01380 816077, e-mail pat.scott@rivendellcentre.com, pat.scott@leadingedgechange.com or pat.scott@fdsguide.com)

SCOTT, Prof Sir (George) Peter; kt (2007); *b* 1 August 1946, Newcastle upon Tyne; *Educ* Merton Coll Oxford (BA), Univ of Calif Berkeley Graduate Sch of Public Policy (visiting scholar, Harkness fell); *Career* reporter then news ed TES 1967–69, reporter The Times 1969–71, dep ed The Times Higher Educational Supplement 1971–73, leader writer The Times 1974–76, ed The Times Higher Educational Supplement 1976–92; Univ of Leeds: prof of educn 1992–97, dir Centre for Policy Studies in Educn 1992–97, pro-vice-chllr (external affrs) 1996–97; vice-chllr Kingston Univ 1997–; chm: governing body S Thames Coll 1985–92, Exec Ctee UKCOSA 1992–98; memb: Continuing Educn Working Pty 1985–86, Nat Advsy Body for Public Sector Higher Educn 1985–86, Further Educn Unit 1993, Further Educn Staff College Review Gp, Further Educn Funding Cncl 1993, Lord Chllr's Advsy Ctee on Legal Educn and Conduct 1994–99 (vice-chm 1996), Bd of Mgmnt FE Devpt Assoc 1994–, HEFCE Working Pty on Higher Educn in Further Educn 1995 Advsy Ctee on Academic Standards Bolton Inst of Higher Educn 1996–, Nat Advsy Gp on Continuing Educn and Lifelong Learning (Fryer Ctee) 1997–, Bd of Directors Educn Counselling Service Br Cncl 1999–, Bd of Directors HESA 2000–, HEFCE Review Panel Inst of Educn Univ of London 2000, Bd HEFCE 2000–06, Cncl Euro Univ Assoc (EUA) 2002– (inagural pres 2008–10); Hon LLD Univ of Bath, Hon DLitt CNAA, Hon DLitt Grand Valley State Univ, Hon DPhil Anglia Poly Univ; hon fell UMIST, hon fell Bath Coll of HE; memb Academia Europaea; AcSS 2000, fell Soc for Research into HE, FRSA; *Books* Strategies for Postsecondary Education (1976), The Crisis of the University (1984), Knowledge and Nation (1990), The New Production of Knowledge: the dynamics of science and research in contemporary societies (jtly, 1994), The Meanings of Mass Higher Education (1995), Governing Universities: Changing the Culture? (jtly, 1996); also author of numerous book chapters and articles in learned jls; *Style*— Prof Sir Peter Scott; ✉ Kingston University, River House, 53–57 High Street, Kingston upon Thames, Surrey KT1 1LQ (☎ 020 8547 7010, fax 020 8547 7009, e-mail p.scott@kingston.ac.uk)

SCOTT, Peter Anthony; s of J Barclay Scott, and Doris Scott; *b* 24 April 1947; *Educ* Manchester Poly; *m* May 1969, Lynne Scott, *née* Smithies; 1 da (Deborah Ann b 26 July 1972) 1 s (Steven Anthony b 10 Oct 1975); *Career* fin accountant: Fothergill & Harvey plc 1962–75, Crane Fruehauf Ltd 1975–77; Peel Holdings plc: co sec 1977–84, fin dir 1984–85, md 1985–; FCCA 1979; *Style*— Peter A Scott, Esq; ✉ Peel Holdings plc, Peel Dome, The Trafford Centre, Manchester M17 8PL (☎ 0161 629 8200, fax 0161 629 8333, e-mail pscott@peel.co.uk)

SCOTT, Peter Denys John; CBE (2008), QC (1978); s of John Ernest Dudley Scott, and Joan Steinberg, *née* Clayton-Cooper; *b* 19 April 1935; *Educ* Monroe HS Rochester NY, Balliol Coll Oxford (MA); *Career* Nat Serv Lt RHA; called to the Bar Middle Temple 1960; chm Gen Cncl of the Bar 1987 (vice-chm 1985–86), judicial chm City Disputes Panel; chm The Takeover Panel 2000–10; memb Investigatory Powers Tbnl 2000–10; chm Bd of Tstees: Kensington Housing Tst 1998–2002, Nat Gallery 2000–08; *Style*— Peter Scott, Esq, CBE, QC; ✉ 4 Eldon Road, London W8 5PU (☎ 020 7937 3301, fax 020 7376 1169); Chateau Bellegarde, Maseube 32140, France (☎ 00 33 562 660027 or 00 33 685 464039, fax 00 33 562 661683)

SCOTT, Philip Edward Hannay; s of late Edward Beattie Scott, MBE, and Mary, *née* Potter (d 2013); *b* 6 April 1957; *Educ* Millfield, Cricklade Coll Andover; *m* 23 Sept 1989, Victoria, *née* Byles; 1 s (Frederick Charles Edward b 27 Nov 2001); *Career* formerly worked in film industry Tor Films Ltd (Tarka the Otter); paralysed in motor racing accident 1977; illustrator 1978–, freelance journalist and broadcaster BBC 1979–1986 (Radio 4, World Service, Local Radio); currently equity trader; co-fndr (with wife Victoria) Kudos Capital Ptnrs LLP 2003–; work with the disabled 1979–; achievements incl: fndr memb Project 81, fndr memb Hampshire Centre for Ind Living 1982, became one of first people to be completely supported in the community by a health authy; promotor of interests of the disabled through aviation achievements incl: fndr Operation Ability Ltd 1984, first tetraplegic to pass a Civil Aviation Authy medical to gain private pilot's licence 1999; involved in first G tests for tetraplegic person 1985; Man of the Year Award for servs to disabled community 1988, Gerald Frewer Meml Trophy 1992, Br Microlight Aircraft Assoc Chairman's Award 1999; Freeman: City of London, Worshipful Co of Haberdashers 1978; AMRAeS 1985, MIED 1992; *Recreations* art, engineering, travel, flying, calligraphy, aviation; *Style*— Philip Scott, Esq

SCOTT, Philip Gordon; s of John Theophilus Scott (d 1973), of Great Yarmouth, and Grace Virginia, *née* Cole (d 1999); *b* 6 January 1954; *Educ* Great Yarmouth GS, KCL; *m* 9 Feb 1974, Helen Rebecca Evelyn, da of James Richard Blair Fearnley (d 1985); 1 da (Rebecca Jane b 11 Dec 1978); *Career* Aviva plc: joined 1973, qualified as actuary 1979, asst actuary for NZ 1981–84, asst investment mangr 1984–87, investment mangr 1987–88, sr investment mangr 1988–92, gen mangr (Fin) 1992–93, gen mangr (Life and Pensions) 1993–98, dir 1993–, chief exec (Life) 1998–2002, gp exec dir Avivia Int and chm Morley Fund Mgmnt 2003–06, gp finance dir Aviva plc 2007–10, ret; non-exec dir: Diageo plc 2007–, RBS plc 2009–14; pres Inst and Faculty of Actuaries 2012–13; FIA 1979, FRSA, FCPA; *Recreations* sailing, gardening, apples; *Clubs* Annabel's, RAC; *Style—* Philip G Scott, Esq; ✉ Whitegate Farm, Burgh St Margaret, Great Yarmouth, Norfolk NR29 3DB (☎ 01493 369599)

SCOTT, Primrose Smith; da of Robert Scott (d 1978), of Uphall, W Lothian, and Jeannie McLaughlan, *née* Pollock (d 1962); *b* 21 September 1940; *Educ* Ayr Acad; *Career* trainee Stewart Gilmour & Co, qualified CA 1963, various managerial positions leading to ptnr Deloitte Haskins & Sells Edinburgh 1981–87, in own practice The McCabe Partnership (formerly Primrose McCabe & Co) 1987–99; dir: Dunfermline Building Society 1990–2005, Lothian and Edinburgh Enterprise Ltd 1995–99, Ecosse Unique Ltd 2004–; non-exec dir Northern Venture Trust plc 1995–2010; ICAS: memb Cncl 1987–95, chm Gen Practice Ctee 1990–93, pres 1994–95, head of Quality Review 1999–2002; tstee: New Lanark Tst 2002–06, Bield Housing Assoc 2005–08; cmmr Queen Victoria Sch Dunblane 1999–2006; hon treas Hospitality Industry Tst Scotland 1994–2002, hon treas Age Scotland 2004–14, treas Borders Youth Theatre 2008–14; hon fell SCOTVEC 1994; *Recreations* keep fit and dog walking; *Style—* Miss Primrose Scott; ✉ The Cleugh, Redpath, Earlston, Berwickshire TD4 6AD (☎ 01896 849042)

SCOTT, Sir Ridley; kt (2003); *b* 30 November 1937, South Shields; *Career* film dir and prodr; fell BFI 2009; *Films* as dir incl: The Duellists 1977, Alien 1979, Blade Runner 1982, Legend 1986, Someone To Watch Over Me 1987, Black Rain 1989; as dir and prodr: Thelma & Louise 1991 (BAFTA nomination for Best Dir 1991, Academy Award nomination for Best Dir 1991), 1492 – Conquest Of Paradise 1992, White Squall 1996, GI Jane 1997, Gladiator 2000 (Academy Award nomination for Best Dir 2001, BAFTA nomination for Best Dir 2001, Golden Globe nomination for Best Dir 2001; voted Best Film at BAFTA's 2001 and Academy Awards 2001), Hannibal 2001, Black Hawk Down 2001 (Oscar nomination for Best Director 2002), Matchstick Men 2003, Kingdom of Heaven 2005, A Good Year 2006, American Gangster 2007, Body of Lies 2008, Robin Hood 2010, Prometheus 2012, The Counsellor 2013; as prodr: In Her Shoes 2005, Tristan + Isolde 2006, The Assassination of Jesse James by the Coward Robert Ford 2007, The A-Team 2010; *Television* as prodr: Numb3rs 2005–10, The Good Wife 2009–; *Style—* Sir Ridley Scott; ✉ c/o Julie Payne, 42–44 Beak Street, London W1R 3DA

SCOTT, Sebastian Simon Frere; s of Christopher Hugh Bartle Frere Scott, and Anne Margret D'Arcy Kerr; *b* 1 August 1961, Galashiels, Scotland; *Educ* Univ of Bristol (BA), Harvard Business Sch (AMP); *Career* studio mangr and reporter BBC Radio 1983–86, researcher That's Life and Kilroy BBC TV 1986–87, researcher and reporter Network Seven Sunday Prodns 1989, reporter Six O'Clock Show and Eyewitness LWT 1989–90, ed and series prodr Reportage and Rough Guide BBC TV 1990; Planet 24: ed The Word Channel 4 1991, exec prodr (features) 1992, ed The Big Breakfast Channel 4 1992–96; md and exec prodr Princess Productions 1996–2010 (prodns incl: Model Behaviour, The Restaurant, Wright Stuff, Light Lunch, The Friday Night Project, Date My Mom), exec conslt creative dir Telegraph Media Gp 2010–12, ceo Predictable Media 2012–14; memb BAFTA 2003–; *Style—* Sebastian Scott, Esq

SCOTT, Prof Stephen Basil Cuthbert; CBE (2014); *Educ* Univ of Cambridge (BSc, MB BChir); *Career* conslt child adolescent psychiatrist; prof of child health and behaviour Inst of Psychiatry KCL; dir Nat Acad for Parenting Research; FRCP, FRCPsych; *Style—* Prof Stephen Scott, CBE; ✉ The National Academy for Parenting Research, King's College, London, Box P85, 16 De Crespigny Park, London SE5 8AF

SCOTT, Tavish Hamilton; MSP; s of John H Scott, of Bressay, Shetland, and Wendy Scott; *b* 6 May 1966, Inverness; *Educ* Anderson HS Lerwick, Napier Coll (BA); *m* 1, Margaret; 1 da (Lorna Katherine b 3 July 1992), 2 s (Alasdair Duncan b 10 Aug 1993, Cameron James John b 11 Feb 2000); m 2, Kirsten; 1 s (Archie Thomas Campbell b 2 Aug 2009); *Career* research asst to Jim Wallace MP 1989–90, press offr SLD 1990–92, cncllr Shetland Islands Cncl 1994–99 (vice-chm Roads and Tport Cmmn); MSP (Lib Dem) Shetland 1999–; dep min for parl 2000–01, dep min for finance, public services and parly business 2003–05, min for tport 2005–07, ldr Scottish Lib Dems 2008–11; chm Lerwick Harbour Tst 1997–99; *Recreations* golf, current affairs, Up-Helly-Aa, football, cinema, reading; *Style—* Tavish Scott, Esq, MSP; ✉ The Scottish Parliament, Edinburgh EH99 1SP (☎ 0131 348 6296, fax 0131 348 5807, e-mail tavish.scott.msp@parliament.scot)

SCOTT OF NEEDHAM MARKET, Baroness (Life Peer UK 2000), of Needham Market in the County of Suffolk; Rosalind Carol (Ros) Scott; *née* Leadbeater; da of Kenneth Leadbeater (d 1996), and Carol Leadbeater (d 2007); *b* 19 August 1957; *Educ* Whitby GS, UEA (BA); *Family* 1 da (Sally Rebecca b 1984), 1 s (Jamie Alan b 1987); m 22 April 2008, Mark Valladares; *Career* memb and ldr Suffolk CC 1993–, chair Local Govt Assoc Tport Exec 1997–2004, memb UK Delgn Ctee of Regions EU 1998–2002, memb Cmmn for Integrated Tport 2001–07, chair House of Lords EU Scrutiny Ctee Energy and Environment 2013–; tstee Industry and Parliament Tst 2014–; non-exec dir: Anglia TV 2002–05, Lloyds Register 2004–10; memb Bd: Entrust plc 2000–07, Audit Cmmn, Harwich Haven Authy 2012–; patron: E Coast Sailing Tst, Wings of Hope; *Recreations* choral singing, walking; *Style—* The Rt Hon the Baroness Scott of Needham Market; ✉ House of Lords, London SW1A 0PW (☎ 020 7219 8660, fax 020 7219 8602, e-mail scottrc@parliament.uk)

SCOTT THOMAS, Dame Kristin; DBE (2015); *b* 24 May 1960, Redruth, Cornwall; *m* (m dis); 3 c; *Career* actress; patron Hope and Homes for Children; *Theatre* La Lune déclinante sur 4 ou 5 personnes qui dansent (Festival de Semur en Auxois) 1983, The Seagull (Royal Court Theatre) 2007 (Best Actress Olivier Award), Betrayal (Comedy Theatre) 2011, Old Times (Harold Pinter Theatre) 2013, Electra (The Old Vic) 2014, The Audience (Apollo Theatre) 2015; *Television* incl: Titmuss Regained 1991, Look at it this Way 1992, Body and Soul 1994, Belle Époque 1995, Gulliver's Travels 1996; *Films* incl: Under the Cherry Moon 1986, Agent Trouble 1987, Djamal Et Juliette 1987, Lounge Chair 1998, A Handful of Dust 1988, Uncontrollable Circumstances 1989, Headstrong 1989, The Governor's Party 1990, In the Eyes of the World 1990, The Bachelor 1991, Bitter Moon 1992, Four Weddings and a Funeral (BAFTA winner), An Unforgettable Summer 1994, Richard III 1995, Angels and Insects 1995 (BAFTA nomination), Plaisir d'Offrir 1995, The Confessional 1995, Mission: Impossible 1996, Somebody to Love 1996, Microcosmos 1996, The English Patient 1996 (Oscar nomination, BAFTA nomination, Golden Globe nomination), Armour Et Confusions 1997, The Horse Whisperer 1998, Sweet Revenge 1998, Souvenier 1998, Random Hearts 1999, Up at the Villa 2000, Play 2000, Life as a House 2001, Gosford Park 2001, Tell No One 2007, The Other Boleyn Girl 2008, Easy Virtue 2008, Largo Winch 2008, I've Loved You So Long 2008 (BAFTA nominatin, Golden Globe nomination, London Critics' Circle Award), Confessions of a Shopaholic 2009, Partir 2009, Nowhere Boy 2009, Leaving 2010 (Best Actress Evening Standard Award 2011), Love Crime 2010, Sarah's Key 2010, In Your Hands 2010, Salmon Fishing in the Yemen 2011, The Woman in the Fifth 2011, Bel Ami 2012, In the House 2012, The Invisible Woman 2013, Only God Forgives 2013, Suite Francaise 2014; *Style—* Dame Kristin Scott Thomas, DBE; ✉ c/o Independent Talent Group, 40 Whitfield Street, London W1T 2RH

SCOTT-BARRETT, Jonathan; s of John Scott-Barrett (d 1968), and Doreen, *née* Robottom (d 1976); *b* 13 April 1944; *Educ* Prince of Wales Sch Nairobi, Ellesmere Coll; *m* 1, 1968 (m dis 1980), Jane, *née* Colchester; 2 s (Marcus b 25 Sept 1970, Dominic b 13 July 1972), 1 da (Miranda b 31 July 1977); m 2, 22 Sept 1983, Malise, *née* Menzies; *Career* Capt 15/19 King's Royal Hussars 1963–68; chartered surveyor Savills 1969–72, ptnr Knight Frank & Rutley (Paris) 1972–76, partner Kapnist International Cap d'Antibes 1976–81, dir Hong Kong Hi Speed Ferries Ltd 1982–86, dir Centaur Publishing Ltd (magazine titles incl Marketing Week, Money Marketing, Design Week, Creative Review) 1986–2002, chm Perfect Information Ltd 1996–2002, ceo Eureka Mining plc 2006–, ceo Rodeo Devpt Ltd Cameroon 2010–12; non-exec dir Hanson plc 1991–2000, exec dir Celtic Resources plc 2007–; FRICS 1971; *Recreations* tennis, shooting, historic motor racing; *Clubs* Cavalry and Guards', Annabel's; *Style—* Jonathan Scott-Barrett, Esq; ✉ 10/12 Brompton Square, London SW3 2AA (☎ 07770 303099, e-mail jsb@celticresources.com)

SCOTT-BOWDEN, Brig Robert Logan; MBE (1992); s of Maj-Gen L Scott-Bowden, CBE, DSO, MC*, and J H Scott-Bowden, *née* Price; *b* 6 June 1955; *Educ* Wellington, RMA Sandhurst, RMCS Shrivenham; *m* 16 Aug 1980, Nicola Frances Kimberley, *née* Phillips; 1 da (Camilla Frances b 20 Sept 1984), 1 s (Christopher William b 15 March 1987); *Career* cmmnd The Royal Scots (The Royal Regt) 1974 (mentioned in despatches 1976); Adj 1 Bn 1981–83, instr RMA Sandhurst 1983–85, SO3 G3 HQ Falkland Islands 1985, Staff Coll Camberley 1986–87, Co Cdr 1 Royal Scots 1988–89, SO2 G3 (Operational Requirements) 1990–91, Co Cdr and chief instr RMA Sandhurst 1992–93, instr Staff Coll Camberley 1994, CO 1 Royal Scots 1994–97 (Queen's Commendation for Valuable Serv 1996), SO1 J3 (Land) Perm Jt HQ 1997–98, integrated project team ldr Defence Procurement Agency 1998–2001, cmd 52 Lowland Bde 2001–02, cmd 52 Inf Bde 2002–04, Col The Royal Scots (The Royal Regt) 2005–06, Dir of Inf 2005–08, head Tech Div Def Acad Coll of Mgmnt and Technol 2009–10, ret from HM Forces; dir of regions ABF The Soldiers' Charity 2010–14; regnl gen mangr Europe and Africa EM&I (UK) Ltd 2014–; *Recreations* hill walking, skiing, sailing, rugby, Italian cooking, golf; *Style—* Brig Robert Scott-Bowden, MBE; ✉ 3 Bath Road, Lymington, Hampshire SO41 3RU

SCOTT-GALL, His Hon Judge Anthony Robert Gall; s of Sidney Robert Gall (d 1994), and Daphne Margaret, *née* Williamson (d 1990); *b* 30 March 1946; *Educ* Stowe, New Coll Oxford (BA); *m* 8 Sept 1973, Caroline Anne, da of David Charles Roger Scott; 1 s (Alexander David Robert b 6 Aug 1975), 1 da (Henrietta Charlotte Anne b 16 Dec 1976); *Career* called to the Bar Middle Temple 1971; recorder 1993–96, circuit judge (SE Circuit) 1996–; *Recreations* gardening, travel, music, rugby union, cricket, country pursuits, 5 grandchildren and the family dog; *Clubs* Richmond FC, Armadillos Cricket; *Style—* His Hon Judge Scott-Gall; ✉ Lewes Combined Court, High Street, Lewes, East Sussex BN7 1YB

SCOTT-MANDERSON, Marcus Charles William; QC (2006); s of Dr William Scott-Manderson (d 2001), and Pamela Scott-Manderson; *b* 10 February 1956; *Educ* Harrow, ChCh Oxford (BCL, MA), Dept of Forensic Med Univ of Glasgow, The Hague Acad of Int Law 1980; *m* 5 July 2003, Melinda Penelope Tillard; *Career* called to the Bar Lincoln's Inn 1980, Queen's Counsel 2006; sec Family Law Bar Assoc Conciliation Bd 1992–96, memb Legal Working Gp Reunite Int Child Abduction Centre 2004– (memb 1999–); memb: Br Acad of Forensic Sci, Forensisch Medisch Genootschap The Netherlands 1983–98; *Publications* Butterworths Essential Family Practice (contrib, 2001 and 2002 edns); *Recreations* ancient history, archaeology, fencing, travel; *Clubs* Lansdowne; *Style—* Marcus Scott-Manderson, QC; ✉ 17 Burlington Road, London SW6 4NP (☎ 020 7731 1476); Park House, The Strand, Ashton-in-Makerfield, Wigan, Lancashire; 4 Paper Buildings, Temple, London EC4Y 7EX (☎ 020 7427 5200, fax 020 7353 4979, e-mail msm@4pb.com, website www.4pb.com)

SCOTT-MONCRIEFF, Lucy Ann; CBE (2014); da of Lt Col William Scott-Moncrieff (d 1997), and Rosemary, *née* Knollys (d 2012); *b* 26 March 1954; *Educ* St Mary's Sch Calne, Guildford Tech Coll, Univ of Kent at Canterbury (BA); *Partner*, 1985–95, John Dowie; 2 s (Stephen Harry b 1 March 1987, Robert Arthur b 7 Nov 1989); *Career* admitted slr 1978; specialises in mental health law; asst slr Offenbach and Co 1978–83, asst slr Bradbury and Co 1983–85, ptnr Offenbach and Co 1985–87, sole practitioner 1987 (subsequent partnerships with Tony Harbour and then Lydia Sinclair), sr ptnr Scott-Moncrieff and Associates 1987– (subsequently md); judge Mental Health Tbnl 2007–; assoc Verita 2008–; cmmr: Mental Health Act Cmmn 1987–90, Postcomm 2008–11, Judicial Appointments Cmmn 2014–; memb QC Appointments Panel 2005–11, memb Ind Cmmn on Mental Health and Policing 2012–13, House of Lords cmmr for standards 2016–; Law Soc: fndr memb Mental Health and Disability Ctee 1983–2010 (co-chair 2003–04), memb Cncl 2002–, chair Access to Justice Ctee 2004–08 (memb 2002–), dep vice-pres and vice pres 2010–12, pres 2012–13; co-chair Legal Aid and Access to Justice Ctee Int Bar Assoc 2013–, tstee LawWorks 2010–, tstee Howard League for Penal Reform; hon lectr Univ of Kent at Canterbury; Hon LLD Univ of Kent 2009; *Recreations* gardening, avoiding housework, having ideas; *Style—* Ms Lucy Scott-Moncrieff, CBE; ✉ Scott-Moncrieff and Associates Ltd, 88 Kingsway, London WC2B 6AA (☎ 020 7841 1099, e-mail scomo@scomo.com, website www.scomo.com)

SCOURFIELD, Gareth John; s of Charles John Scourfield (d 2006), and Clara Margaret Joyce, *née* Adams (d 2002); *b* 23 December 1953, Pembroke, Wales; *Educ* Pembroke GS, Thames Poly London (DipArch); *m* 1, Nov 1987 (m dis); 1 da (Angharad Kate b 6 Apr 1988); m 2, Sept 2002 (m dis); *Career* architect; London Transport Architects Dept 1975–76, West Faulkner Architects London 1978–81, chm Pembroke Design Ltd Haverfordwest Architects and Surveyors 1981–; advsr to tstees Pembroke Castle 1985–, memb Cncl Royal Soc of Architects in Wales 1989– (pres 2007–09); founding memb Bd: Pembrokeshire Historic Buildings Tst 1990–, Pembroke Dock Museum Tst 1995–, Pembroke Dock Sunderland Tst 2010–; winner of 50 awards for architecture/built environment; RIBA 1980, ACIArb 1985, MRICS 2003; Castles and Strongholds of Pembrokeshire (1982), Conservation Master Plan for Pembroke Dock (2002); author of numerous articles and papers on the built environment and building in the national parks; *Recreations* reading, photography, rugby union (Lions and Wales), travel, music, cooking, horse riding; *Clubs* Rotary (Pembroke), Loyal Welsh Lodge; *Style—* Gareth J Scourfield, Esq; ✉ Pembroke Design Ltd, Architects and Surveyors, 5/7 Picton Place, Haverfordwest, Pembrokeshire SA61 2LE (☎ 01437 764135, mobile 07775 952951, fax 01437 764471, e-mail gareth@pembrokedesign.co.uk)

SCOVELL, Brian Souter; s of Percy Henry John Scovell (d 1991), of IOW, and Maude Janet Scovell (d 1978); *b* 21 November 1935; *Educ* Ventnor Coll, Elgin Acad, NCTJ (Cert, Dip); *m* 1 Oct 1965, Audrey Esther (d 2000), da of Eric William O'Sullivan; 1 da (Louise Jayne b 8 Oct 1967), 1 s (Gavin Richard Souter b 25 Oct 1969); *Career* journalist; trainee reporter Isle of Wight Guardian 1952–57, gen reporter Wolverhampton Express and Star 1957–58; sports reporter: Norwich Evening News and Eastern Daily Press 1958, Press Assoc 1959–60; cricket corr and dep football corr Daily Sketch 1960–71, cricket and football corr Daily Mail 1971–; maj events covered incl: football World Cups 1966, 1982, 1986 and 1990, cricket World Cups 1975, 1979 and 1983, over 280 test matches and 300 int football matches; chm Football Writers Assoc 1982, sec Cricket Writers Club 2004–06 (chm 1985–89, cm Facilities Ctee 2006–); Cricket Writer of the Year Wombwell Cricket Lovers Soc 1963, highly recommended in sports news section Sports Cncl Writing Awards 1991; FA soccer coach 1966, MCC cricket coach 1977; *Books* Everything That's

S

Cricket (1963), Whose Side Are You On Ref? (1973), The Big Match (1976), The Diary of a Season (1979), Not Out (1979), Trevor Brooking (1981), Ken Barrington – A Tribute (1982), Glory, Glory (1984), Revelations of a Soccer Manager (1985), The Big Match Soccer Anthology (1987), And the Next Voice You Will Hear (1987), Gary Sobers – Twenty Years at the Top (1988), Handbook of Soccer (1988), Beating the Field – Brian Lara's Story (1995), Dickie: A Tribute to Umpire Dickie Bird (1996), Chelsea Azzurri (1997), Sixty Years on the Back Foot: Sir Clyde Walcott's Life in Cricket (1999), Football Gentry (2005), The England Managers: The Impossible Job (2006), Jim Laker 19–90 (2006), Brian Lara: Cricket's Troubled Genius (2007), Bill Nicholson: Football's Perfectionist (2010), Thank You Hermann Goering – The Life of a Sports Writer (2011), Our Beloved Cricket – From Village Greens to Lords (2013), 1966's Sporting Conquests of Alf Ramsey and Gary Sobers (2016); *Recreations* watching and umpiring cricket, watching and writing on football, going on cricket tours abroad, reading, public speaking, walking, cinema; *Clubs* Woodpeckers CC; *Style—* Brian Scovell, Esq; ✉ Daily Mail, Northcliffe House, 2 Derry Street, London W8 5TT (☎ 020 8464 4133, mobile 07879 612690)

SCREECH, Rev Prof Michael Andrew; s of Richard John Screech, MM (d 1986), of Plymstock, Devon, and Nellie Ernestine, *née* Maunder (d 1977); *b* 2 May 1926; *Educ* Sutton HS Plymouth, UCL (BA); *m* 4 April 1956, (Ursula) Anne Grace, da of John William Reeve (d 1960), of Byfleet, Surrey; 3 s (Matthew Erasmus John b 30 Jan 1960, Timothy Benjamin Mark b 28 Sept 1961, Toby Daniel Luke b 3 Oct 1963); *Career* other rank Intelligence Corps (mainly Far East) 1944–48; successively asst lectr, lectr then sr lectr Univ of Birmingham 1951–61, reader then prof of French UCL 1961–71, Fielden prof of French language and literature UCL 1971–84, Johnson prof Inst for Res in the Humanities Madison Wisconsin 1978, Campion lectr Regina Saskatchewan 1983, Dorothy Ford Wiley prof of Renaissance culture N Carolina 1986, Zaharoff lectr Oxford 1988; visiting prof: Collège de France 1989, La Sorbonne 1990; fell and chaplain All Souls Coll Oxford 2001–03 (sr res fell 1984–93, emeritus fell 1993–2001 and 2003–), hon fell Wolfson Coll Oxford 2001– (extraordinary fell 1993–2001), occasional lectr Oxford Ministry Course 1994–96; ordained: deacon 1993, priest 1994; memb comité: d' Humanisme et Renaissance 1958–, des Textes Littéraires Français 1958–, du patronage des Textes Classiques de la Renaissance 1986–; corresponding memb: Inst Archéologique et Historique Geneva 1990, L'Académie des Inscriptions et Belles-Lettres 2000; tstee Lambeth Palace Library 1994–2006; formerly memb Whitchurch St Mary's PCC, Whitchurch Parish Cncl, formerly chm of Mangrs Whitchurch Primary Sch; Médaille de la Ville de Tours 1984; fell UCL 1982; DLitt: Birmingham 1960, London 1982, Oxford 1990; Hon DLitt Exeter 1993, hon doctorate Geneva 1998, hon doctorate Neuchâtel 2009; FBA 1981, FRSL 1989; Chevalier dans l'Ordre National du Mérite France 1983, Chevalier dans la Légion d'Honneur 1992; *Books* The Rabelaisian Marriage (1958), L'Evangélisme de Rabelais (1959), Marot Evangélique (1967); Rabelais edns: Tiers Livre (1964), Gargantua (1970), Prognostication (1975); Regrets and Antiquitez de Rome (by Du Bellay, ed 1964), Rabelais (1979), Erasmus – Ecstasy and the Praise of Folly (1980), Montaigne and Melancholy (1983), Apology for Raymond Sebond (by Montaigne, trans 1987), A New Rabelais Bibliography (1988), Montaigne – The Complete Essays (1991), Some Renaissance Studies (1992), Clément Marot, a Renaissance poet discovers the Gospel (1993), Warden Mocket of All Souls College: Doctrina et politia Ecclesiae anglicanae (ed, 1995), Monumental Inscriptions in All Souls Coll Oxford (1997), Laughter at the Foot of the Cross (1998), Montaigne's Copy of Lucretius (1998), Rabelais: Gargantua and Panagruel (translator, 2006); *Recreations* walking, gardening; *Clubs* Athenaeum, Pangbourne Working Men's; *Style—* The Rev Prof M A Screech, FBA, FRSL; ✉ 5 Swanston Field, Whitchurch-on-Thames, Reading RG8 7HP (e-mail michael.screech@btinternet.com)

SCRIMGEOUR, Alastair James; s of Robin Neville Carron Scrimgeour (d 1996), of Wilts, and Deirdre Elizabeth Blundell, *née* Brown (d 2014); *b* 17 April 1956, London; *Educ* Eton, Univ of Bristol (BSc); *Career* chartered accountant; ptnr: Binder Hamlyn London 1986–94 (joined 1978), Arthur Andersen 1994–2002, Deloitte 2002–10; chm Bury Water Co Ltd, non-exec dir LLW Repository Ltd, non-exec dir The Osborne Studio Gallery Ltd; dir Nuclear Industry Assoc; tstee The Police Fndn; FCA; *Recreations* shooting, racing, gardening, tennis; *Clubs* RAC, Turf; *Style—* Alastair Scrimgeour, Esq; ✉ 5 Elswick Street, London SW6 2QR; The Old School House, Bury, Dulverton, Somerset TA22 9NE (☎ 01398 323715, e-mail aj.scrimgeour@btinternet.com)

SCRIMGEOUR, Angus Muir Edington; s of Dr David Muir Scrimgeour (d 1977), and May Burton Clair, *née* Edington (d 1988); *b* 19 February 1945; *Educ* Westminster, New Coll Oxford (MA), UCL (MSc); *m* 21 Dec 1968, Clare Christian Gauvain, da of Dr Ronald Ormiston Murray, MBE; 1 s (Alexander b 1971); *Career* vice-pres Citibank NA 1974–84, chief exec Edington plc merchant bank 1984–90, dep chm Henry Cooke Group 1990–91 (jt chief exec 1988–90), chief exec Bankside Underwriting Agencies Ltd 1992–95; Corporation of Lloyds: dir CSU 1993–96, head of market mgmnt 1995–96; vice-pres and chief fin offr World Bank (MIGA) Washington DC 1997–02, chm Scrimgeour & Co 1983–, chm Solar Products Ltd 2003–12, chm Solaray Systems (Pty) Ltd S Africa 2010–; pres Int Assoc for Digital Pubns 2004–; *Recreations* design, chess, music; *Clubs* Oxford and Cambridge, IOD, Berkshire Golf; *Style—* Angus Scrimgeour, Esq; ✉ 3134 P Street NW, Washington DC 20007, USA (☎ 00 1 202 337 2781)

SCRIVEN, Jane Katherine; da of Sir Peter Gibbings, of London, and Elspeth, *née* Macintosh; *b* 5 October 1959, England; *Educ* Millfield, KCL (LLB); *m* 13 June 1987, Simon Scriven; 1 da (Harriet Clare b 22 Aug 1990), 1 s (Frederick Charles b 10 June 1994); *Career* slr Norton Rose 1986–87, commercial mangr Elders IXL Hong Kong 1987–89, strategy and investment mangr Elders Finance 1989–91; Geest plc: devpt dir 1991–2000, memb Bd 1996–2005, md Continental Europe 2000–05; non-exec dir Greene King plc 2005–11, chm Origin8 Deli-Cafés Ltd 2006–, chm Pension Tstee Co Bakkavor Gp 2011–; memb Law Soc 1986; *Recreations* skiing, equestrianism; *Style—* Mrs Jane Scriven; ✉ e-mail janescriven@aol.com

SCRIVEN, Pamela; QC (1992); da of Maurice Scriven (d 1979), and Evelyn Lavinia, *née* Stickney; *b* 5 April 1948; *Educ* UCL (LLB); *m*; 2 c; *Career* called to the Inner Temple Bar 1970, bencher 1995; recorder of the Crown Ct 1996– (asst recorder 1993–96), dep judge of the High Ct (Family Div); Chm Family Law Bar Assoc 1999–2001 (memb 1991–); *Recreations* theatre and travel; *Style—* Pamela Scriven, QC; ✉ 1 King's Bench Walk, 2nd Floor, Temple, London EC4Y 7DB

SCRIVEN, Peter John Keith; s of Sydney Verdun Scriven, of Dudley, W Midlands, and Mona Patricia, *née* Gaston (d 1974); *b* 25 July 1956; *Educ* Alexandra GS Midlands, UCW Aberystwyth (BScEcon), Leicester Poly (DMS); *m*; 3 s (Thomas Edward b Feb 1990, Matthew Alexander b Nov 1994, Oliver William b Dec 1996); *Career* UK mktg mangr Barclays Bank 1977–83, investment mktg mangr Charterhouse Merchant Bank 1983–84, strategic planning mangr Citicorp UK 1984–86, Euro business planning mangr Chase Manhattan Bank 1986–87, gp head of business devpt National and Provincial Building Society 1987–90, sr vice-pres and gen mangr Middle East Visa International Service Association 1990–; MInstM; *Recreations* flying, skiing, foreign travel, ocean sailing; *Clubs* MCIM, BMAA, RYA, DOSC; *Style—* Peter Scriven, Esq; ✉ PO Box 74751, Dubai, United Arab Emirates (e-mail scriveni@eim.ae)

SCRIVENER, Anthony Frank; QC (1975); s of Frank Bertram Scrivener (d 1995), of Kent, and Tonia, *née* Mather (d 2002); *b* 31 July 1935; *Educ* Kent Coll Canterbury, UCL; *m* m 1, Iren Becze; 1 da (Zsuzsa b 4 Oct 1966), 1 s (Zoltan b 10 Oct 1968); m 2, Ying Hui Tan; *Career* called to the Bar Gray's Inn 1959 (Holt scholar); lectr Ghana 1959–61, in practice 1961–, recorder of the Crown Court 1975, head of chambers 1992–2001; bencher Lincoln's Inn, chm Bar Cncl 1991; UK judge FIA Int Court of Appeal, RAC steward; Chambers UK Directories Lifetime Achievement Award 2008; *Recreations* walking with family dog Domino, chess, cards, croquet, car racing; *Style—* Anthony Scrivener, Esq, QC; ✉ 2–3 Gray's Inn Square, Gray's Inn, London WC1R 5JH (☎ 020 7242 4986, fax 020 7504 1166)

SCROPE, (Simon) Henry Richard (Harry); s of Simon Egerton Scrope (d 2010), and Jane, *née* Parkinson; *b* 3 September 1974, London; *Educ* Aysgarth Sch, Ampleforth Coll, Newcastle Univ, RMA Sandhurst, South Bank Univ; *Career* commissioned Coldstream Guards 1997, ret from Br Army as Maj 2005; qualified chartered surveyor 2008; CB Richard Ellis 2005–10, chief operating offr Stonehaven 2010–13, md Brompton Bike Hire Ltd 2013–; FRGS, MRICS 2008; *Recreations* mountains, countryside, history; *Clubs* Cavalry and Guards, Market; *Style—* S H R Scrope, Esq; ☎ 07885 854220, e-mail harryscrope@aol.com; Brompton Bicycle Ltd, Unit 1, Greenford Park, Ockham Drive, Greenford UB6 0FD

SCRUTON, Prof Sir Roger Vernon; kt (2016); s of John Scruton, of High Wycombe, Bucks, and Beryl Clarys, *née* Haines (d 1967); *b* 27 February 1944; *Educ* Royal GS High Wycombe, Jesus Coll Cambridge (MA, PhD); *m* 1, 1975 (m dis 1979), (Marie Genevieve) Danielle, da of Robert Laffitte, of Orthez, France; m 2, 1996, Sophie Jeffreys, da of late 2 Baron Jeffreys; *Career* called to the Bar Inner Temple 1974, fell Peterhouse Cambridge 1969–71, prof of aesthetics Dept of Philosophy Birkbeck Coll London (formerly lectr and reader), Univ Profs Prog Boston Univ 1992–94; ed Salisbury Review 1982–2000; FRSL 2003, FBA 2009; *Books* Art and Imagination (1974), The Aesthetics of Architecture (1979), The Meaning of Conservatism (1980), Fortnight's Anger (1981), A Dictionary of Political Thought (1983), Sexual Desire (1986), Thinkers of the New Left (1986), A Land Held Hostage (1987), The Philosopher on Dover Beach (1990), Francesca (1991), Xanthippic Dialogues (1993), Modern Philosophy: An Introduction and Survey (1994), Animal Rights and Wrongs (1996), An Intelligent Person's Guide to Philosophy (1996), The Aesthetics of Music (1997), On Hunting (1998), An Intelligent Person's Guide to Modern Culture (1998), Perictione in Colophon (2000), England: an Elegy (2000), The West and the Rest (2002), News From Somewhere (2004), Death-Devoted Heart (2004), Gentle Regrets (2005), A Political Philosophy (2006), Culture Counts (2007), Beauty (2009), I Drink Therefore I Am (2010), Green Philosophy (2012), The Face of God (2013), Notes from Underground (2014), The Soul of the World (2014), The Disappeared (2015), How to be a Conservative (2015), Fools, Frauds and Firebrands (2015), The Ring of Truth (2016); *Recreations* music, hunting; *Style—* Prof Sir Roger Scruton; ✉ Sunday Hill Farm, Brinkworth, Wiltshire SN15 5AS

SCUDAMORE, Richard; *Educ* Univ of Nottingham; *m* Catherine; 2 s (Patrick, Ned), 1 da (Lara); 2 c from previous m (Jamie, Chloe); *Career* chief exec Premier League 1999–; memb Bd Football Fndn; *Style—* Richard Scudamore, Esq; ✉ Premier League, 30 Gloucester Place, London W1U 8PL

SCULLY, Prof Crispian; CBE (2000); s of Patrick Scully and Rosaleen, *née* Richardson; *b* 24 May 1945; *Educ* Univ of London (BDS, BSc, MB BS, PhD), Univ of Bristol (MD, MDS); *m* 5 Oct 1977, Zoë Boucoumani; 1 da (Frances b 31 Jan 1982); *Career* lectr: Univ of London (oral immunology) 1977–79, Univ of Glasgow (oral med and pathology) 1979–81; sr lectr Univ of Glasgow (oral med and pathology) 1981–82, prof of oral med, surgery and pathology Univ of Bristol 1982–94, head Univ of Bristol Dental Sch 1986–90, dean Eastman Dental Inst Univ of London 1993–2008, prof of special needs dentistry Univ of London 1997–2010 (prof of oral med, pathology and microbiology 1994–), prof of oral medicine Univ of Bristol 2010–12; adjunct prof Univ of Helsinki 2005–10, visiting prof Univ of Edinburgh 2006–, emeritus prof UCL 2010–; conslt: UHBT, UCLH Tst, Gt Ormond St Hosp, Nuffield Orthopaedic Centre, John Radcliffe Hosp Oxford, Royal Free Hosp, Lothian Health Authy, HCA; dir WHO Collaborating Centre for Oral Health/General Health 2010–; past pres Int Acad of Oral Oncology, pres Soc for Oral Medicine, past pres European Assoc of Oral Med; past chm Central Examining Bd for Dental Hygienists; past pres Br Soc for Oral Med; past memb Central Research and Devpt Ctee Dept of Health; fell UCL; Hon DSc Univ of Athens, Hon DChD Univ of Santiago, Hon DMed Univ of Pretoria, Hon Dr Univ of Helsinki; FDSRCS, FDSRCSE, FDSRCPS, FFDRCSI, FRCPath, FMedSci, FHEA, FSB; *Books* incl: Multiple Choice Questions in Clinical Dentistry (jtly, 1985), Hospital Dental Surgeon's Guide (1985), Slide Interpretation in Oral Diseases and the Oral Manifestations of Systemic Disease (jtly, 1986), Dental Surgery Assistant's Handbook (jtly, 1986, 2 edn 1993), Colour Aids in Oral Medicine (jtly, 1988, 3 edn 1999), Dental Patient Care (1989), Atlas of Stomatology (jtly, 1989, 4 edn 2010), Occupational Hazards to Dental Staff (jtly, 1990), Radiographic Interpretation in Oral Disease (jtly, 1991), Clinical Virology in Oral Medicine and Dentistry (jtly, 1992), Colour Aids in Medicine and Surgery (jtly, 1993, 2 edn 1999), Colour Atlas of Orofacial Diseases in Childhood and Adolescence (jtly, 1993, 2 edn 2001), Colour Atlas of Oral Pathology (jtly, 1995), Oral Health Care for those with HIV Infection and Other Special Needs (jtly, 1995), Innovations and Development in Non-invasive Orofacial Health Care (jtly, 1996), Oxford Handbook of Dental Care (jtly, 1999), Diagnostic Handbook of Oral Disease (1999), Dermatology of the Lips (jtly, 2000), Applied Basic Science in Dentistry (2002), Periodontal Manifestations of Local and Systemic Disease (jtly, 2003), Textbook of General and Oral Medicine (jtly, 1999, 2 edn 2003), Orofacial Disease for the Dental Team (jtly, 2003), Oral and Maxillofacial Medicine (2004, 3 edn 2013), Oral Diseases (jtly, 3 edn 2004), Key Topics in Human Diseases (jtly, 2005), Medicina y Patologia Oral (jtly, 2006), Culturally Sensitive Oral Health Care (jtly, 2006), Special Care in Dentistry (jtly, 2007), Medical Problems in Dentistry (jtly, 1982, 7 edn 2014), Common Medical Conditions (jtly, 2010), Applied Medicine and Surgery in Dentistry (jtly, 2010), Pocketbook of Oral Disease (jtly, 2012), Oral Medicine and Pathology at a Glance (jtly, 2010, 2 edn 2016), Textbook of Dental Nursing (jtly, 2011, 2 edn 2015), Genetics of Dental and Orofacial Disease (jtly, 2012), Dental Mammoth; foundations of clinical dentistry (jtly, 2014, 2 edn 2016), Oral Medicine; update for the Dental Team (jtly, 2014), Scullys Handbook of Medical Problems in Dentistry (2016), Clinical Dentistry (2016); *Recreations* swimming, hill walking, skiing, travelling, music, windsurfing, sailing, playing music, cycling; *Style—* Prof Crispian Scully, CBE; ✉ e-mail crispian.scully@ucl.ac.uk

SCULLY, Paul; MP; s of Basil Scully (d 1989), and Joan, *née* Gray; *b* 29 April 1968, Rugby; *Educ* Bedford Sch, Univ of Reading; *m* 19 May 1990, Emma, *née* May; 1 s (Benjamin b 28 June 1992), 1 da (Josephine b 10 Feb 1998); *Career* cncllr London Borough of Sutton 2006–10; ptnr Nudge Factory Ltd 2011–; MP (Cons) Sutton and Cheam 2015–; *Style—* Paul Scully, Esq, MP; ✉ House of Commons, London SW1A 0AA (e-mail info@scully.org.uk website www.scully.org.uk, Twitter @scullyp)

SCULTHORPE, Paul; s of Douglas Rae Sculthorpe, and Linda Margaret, *née* Griffiths; *b* 22 September 1977, Burnley; *Educ* Counthill Sch Oldham; *m* Lindsay, *née* McCulloch; 1 s (Jake b 18 March 2000), 1 da (Lucy Jo b 11 Nov 2003); *Career* rugby league player; amateur clubs: Mayfield RLFC, Waterhead RLFC, Rosebridge RLFC; professional clubs: Warrington RLFC 1994–98, St Helens RLFC 1998– (transferred for £375,000, world record for a forward, capt 2004–); winner: Grand Final 1999, 2000, 2002 and 2006, World Club Championship 2001 and 2007, Challenge Cup 2001, 2004, 2006 and 2007); England 1995– (4 caps, also former capt under 16s), GB 1996– (26 caps, capt 2005–06), Lancashire (3 appearances); awarded full testimonial 2008; Rugby League drug free sport ambass to UK Sport; regular panelist and reporter on A Question of Sport (BBC); *Awards* Players' Player of the Year 2001, Liverpool Echo Rugby League Player of the Year 2001, Sky Viewers Player of the Year 2001, Rugby League Writers Player of the Year 2001,

Man of Steel 2001 and 2002, BBC NW Rugby League Player of the Year 2001 and 2002, Rugby League Express readers Player of the Year 2001 and 2002, memb Rugby League Dream Team 2001, 2002 and 2004, runner-up Golden Boot Award 2001 and 2002, BBC NW Sportsman of the Year 2002, memb Rugby League World Dream Team 2002, winner Opta Statistics 2002, Scouseology Award for Sport 2005, BBC Sports Personality Team of the Year 2006; Gillette Face of Rugby League 2004–08; *Books* Sculthorpe: Man of Steel (2007); *Recreations* golf, snooker, music; *Style—* Mr Paul Sculthorpe; ✉ c/o David Howes, Howes etc Ltd, 6 Canalside Studio, Roundhouse Business Park, Graingers Way, Leeds LS12 1AH (☎ 0113 243 1188, mobile 07814 937642, fax 0113 245 6608, e-mail david@howesetc.co.uk, website www.howesetc.co.uk); St Helens RLFC, Knowsley Road, St Helens, Merseyside WA10 4AD

SCUPHAM, John Peter; s of John Scupham, OBE (d 1990), of Thorpe St Andrew, Norwich, Norfolk, and Dorothy Lacey, *née* Clark (d 1987); *b* 24 February 1933; *Educ* Perse Sch Cambridge, St George's Harpenden, Emmanuel Coll Cambridge (BA); *m* 1, 10 Aug 1957 (m dis 2012), Carola Nance, da of Hermann Justus Braunholtz, CBE (d 1963); 3 s (Christopher, Giles, Roger), 1 da (Kate); m 2, 2012, Margaret Elizabeth Steward; *Career* Nat Serv 1952–54; head of English St Christopher Sch Letchworth 1961–80, fndr The Mandeville Press 1974–; Cholmondeley Award Society of Authors Awards 1996; FRSL; *Books* The Snowing Globe (1972), Prehistories (1975), The Hinterland (1977), Summer Palaces (1980), Winter Quarters (1983), Out Late (1986), The Air Show (1988), Watching the Perseids (1990), Selected Poems (1990), The Ark (1994), Night Watch (1999), Collected Poems (2002), Borrowed Landscapes (2011); *Recreations* book collecting; *Style—* Peter Scupham, Esq, FRSL; ✉ Old Hall, Norwich Road, South Burlingham, Norwich NR13 4EY (☎ 01493 750804)

SCURR, John Henry; s of Henry Scurr (d 1981), and Joyce, *née* Standerwick (d 2011); *b* 25 March 1947; *Educ* Langley GS, Middx Hosp Med Sch London (BSc, MB BS); *m* 1, 16 July 1969 (m dis 1986), Gillian Margaret Mason; 2 da (Ruth b 1971, Ingrid b 1972), 1 s (James b 1976); m 2, 5 April 1986 (sep 2000), Nicola Mary Alexandra, da of Ivor S Vincent (d 1994), of London; 2 s (Edward b 1984, Thomas b 1990), 1 da (Victoria b 1986); partner The Hon Persephone Brigstocke; 1 da (Flora b 17 Feb 2006 (twin)), 1 s (George b 17 Feb 2006 (twin)); *Career* conslt surgn Middx Hosp and UCH, sr lectr in surgery Univ of London, hon conslt surgn St Luke's Hosp for the Clergy; memb Aeromedical Practitioners Assoc; Freeman Worshipful Soc of Apothecaries 1989, Freeman Guild of Air Pilots and Air Navigators 1994 (Liveryman 1999); FRSM 1972, FRCS 1976; *Books* Microcomputer Applications in Medicine (1987); *Recreations* flying, walking; *Clubs* RAF; *Style—* John Scurr, Esq; ✉ The Grange, Cloatley Road, Hankerton SN16 9LQ (☎ 01666 577630); Lister Hospital, London SW1W 8RH (☎ 020 7730 9563, fax 020 7834 6315, e-mail jscurr@uk-consultants.co.uk, website www.jscurr.com)

SEABECK, Alison Jane; *née* Ward; da of late Michael Ward, and Lilian, *née* Lomas; *b* 20 January 1954, Dagenham; *Educ* Harold Hill GS Essex, NE London Poly; *m* 1, 1975 (m dis 2007), Denis Seabeck; 2 da; m 2, Oct 2012, Rt Hon Wyvill Richard Nicolls (Nick) Raynsford, MP, *qv*; *Career* Parly asst Rt Hon Roy Hattersley, MP 1987–92, advsr Rt Hon Nick Raynsford, MP 1992–2005; MP (Lab): Plymouth Devonport 2005–10, Plymouth Moor View 2010–15; asst Govt whip 2007–08, PPS to Sec of State for Transport 2008–09, shadow housing and planning min 2010–11, shadow min for defence procurement 2011–; memb ODPM Select Ctee, memb Regulatory Reform Select Ctee 2005–07, chm All Pty Parly Gp on Local Govt 2006–07, parly convenor Lab Housing Gp 2005–07, vice-chair PLP ODPM Ctee 2006–07, vice-chair SW Gp of Lab MPs 2006–07, chair SW Regnl Select Ctee 2009–10, memb Backbench Business Ctee 2010; memb: GMB, UNITE, SW Co-op Pty, Fawcett Soc, Lab Women's Network; patron Devon Lupus Gp, hon pres 47th Plymouth Scout Gp; *Recreations* reading, swimming, walking; *Style—* Ms Alison Seabeck; ✉ House of Commons, London SW1A 0AA (☎ 020 7219 6431, e-mail alison.seabeck.mp@parliament.uk); Constituency Office ☎ 01752 365617

SEABORN, Hugh Richard; CVO (2014); s of Richard Anthony Seaborn, and Wendy Nora, *née* Punt; *b* 24 May 1962, York; *Educ* Pocklington Sch Yorks, Newcastle Poly; *m* 10 June 2000, Michaela, *née* Scanlon; 3 s (Jacob b 27 August 2003, Thomas 18 Jan 2005, Oliver b 18 Aug 2007); *Career* Landmark Property Conslts Cape Town 1987–88, Richard Ellis Fleetwood Botswana 1988–91, dir and head of investment mgmnt Richard Ellis 1991–2000, ceo and agent to the tstees Portman Estate 2000–08, chief exec Cadogan Estate 2008–; memb: London Bd Royal and Sun Alliance 2004–08, Cncl Duchy of Lancaster 2005–; non-exec dir TR Property Investment Trust plc 2007–; chm Westminster Property Owners Assoc 2008; FRICS 1999; *Recreations* family, running, reading; *Clubs* Oriental, Home House, Sloane; *Style—* Hugh Seaborn, Esq, CVO; ✉ Cadogan, 18 Cadogan Gardens, London SW3 2RP

SEABROOK, Michael Richard; s of Robert Henry Seabrook (d 1983), of Solihull, and Clara, *née* Berry (d 2000); *b* 24 March 1952; *Educ* King Edward's Sch Birmingham, Univ of Exeter (LLB); *m* 1 Sept 1979, Hilary Margaret Seabrook, JP, da of Anthony John Pettitt, of Bromley, Kent (d 2007); 2 s (Nicholas b 1983, William b 1986); *Career* admitted slr 1976; articled clerk Lovell White & King 1974–76, asst slr Clifford-Turner 1976–79; ptnr: Needham & James 1981–86 (asst slr 1980), Eversheds 1986–2011 (dep sr ptnr 1994–2003); memb Cncl Birmingham C of C and Industry 1995–2003, non-exec dir W Midlands Enterprise; non-exec dir: Steelite Int Ltd, MC Trustees Ltd, Gateley (Holdings) plc, Alycidon Capital Ltd; non-exec chm Springboard Corp Fin Ltd; tstee Queen Elizabeth Hosp Birmingham Charity; memb Law Soc 1976; *Recreations* sporting; *Clubs* Blackwell Golf, East India and Public Schools, Warwickshire Imps Cricket, Knowle & Dorridge Cricket, Warwickshire Pilgrims Cricket; *Style—* Michael R Seabrook, Esq; ✉ 5 Broadacre Gardens, 236 Grange Road, Dorridge, Solihull, West Midlands BG3 8QB (☎ 01564 773732)

SEABROOK, Peter John; MBE (2005); s of Robert Henry Seabrook (d 1987), of Galleywood, Essex, and Emma Mary, *née* Cottey (d 1989); *b* 2 November 1935; *Educ* King Edward VI GS Chelmsford, Essex Inst of Agric Writtle (MHort, Dip Hort); *m* 14 May 1960, Margaret Ruth, da of Arthur Wilfred Risbey (d 1990), of Churchdown, Glos; 1 s (Roger b 9 Feb 1962), 1 da (Alison b 13 May 1964); *Career* Nat Serv RASC 1956–58; author of books and presenter of TV progs on gardening; horticultural advsr and dir Cramphorn plc 1958–66, tech rep Bord na Mona 1966–70, horticultural conslt 1971–; dir: William Strike Ltd 1972–95, Roger Harvey Ltd 1981–99; gardening corr: Nurseryman and Garden Centre 1964–2003, The Sun 1977–, The Yorkshire Post 1981–92, Amateur Gardening 1986–, Horticulture Week 2004–; hon fell Writtle Coll 1997, assoc of honour RHS 1996, Victoria Medal of Honour RHS 2003; FIHort; *Radio* presenter: In Your Garden 1965–70, Gardeners' Question Time 1981–82; *Television* presenter gardening features Pebble Mill at One BBC 1 1975–86; presenter: WGBH TV Boston USA 1975–97, Gardener's World BBC 2 1976–79, Chelsea Flower Show 1976–89, Gardeners' Direct Line BBC TV 1982–90, Peter Seabrook's Gardening Week BBC 1 1996, Great Gardeners HGTV 1997–98; *Books* Shrubs For Your Garden (1973), Complete Vegetable Gardener (1976), Book of the Garden (1979), Good Plant Guide (1981), Good Food Gardening (1983), Shrubs for Everyone (1997); *Recreations* gardening; *Clubs* Farmers'; *Style—* Peter Seabrook, Esq, MBE; ✉ 212A Baddow Road, Chelmsford, Essex CM2 9QR

SEABROOK, Robert John; QC (1983); s of Alan Thomas Pertwee Seabrook, MBE (d 2001), and Mary, *née* Parker (d 1977); *b* 6 October 1941; *Educ* St George's Coll Harare, UCL (LLB); *m* 1, 19 Oct 1965 (m dis 2008), Liv Karin, da of Rev Bjarne Djupvik (d 1983), of Bergen, Norway; 2 s (Justin b 20 Dec 1969, Magnus b 23 April 1975), 1 da (Marianne b 23 Oct 1971); m 2, 23 April 2016, Sarah, da of John Bird, of London; *Career* called to the Bar Middle Temple 1964 (bencher 1991, treas 2007); recorder 1984–2007, dep judge of the High Court 1991–2010, ldr SE Circuit 1989–92; chm Bar Cncl 1994; memb: Interception of Communications Tbnl 1995–2000, Criminal Justice Consultative Cncl 1995–2002, Investigating Powers Tbnl 2000–, Regulation of Investigatory Powers Guernsey Tbnl 2006–; memb Court Univ of Sussex 1988–93, vice-pres Brighton Coll (govr 1993–2004, chm 1998–2004); Master Worshipful Co of Curriers 1995 (Liveryman 1972); *Recreations* wine, listening to music, travel, skiing; *Clubs* Athenaeum (tstee 2016–), Les Six; *Style—* Robert Seabrook, QC; ✉ 1 Crown Office Row, Temple, London EC4Y 7HH (☎ 020 7797 7500, fax 020 7797 7550, DX 1020, e-mail robert.seabrook@1cor.com)

SEAFORD, 6 Baron (UK 1826); Colin Humphrey Felton Ellis; s of Maj William Felton Ellis (d 1977), and Edwina, *née* Bond (d 1976); *b* 19 April 1946, Sussex; *Educ* Sherborne, RAC Cirencester; *m* 1, 1971 (m dis 1992), Susan, *née* Magill; 2 da (Hon Harriett Fay b 4 April 1973, Hon Charlotte Susan b 17 Oct 1975), 2 s (Hon Benjamin Felton Thomas b 17 Dec 1976, Hon Humphrey Henry Guysulf b 10 March 1983); m 2, 1993, Penelope Mary Bastin, *née* Goulson; *Heir* s, Hon Benjamin Ellis; *Career* resident agent Ely Lodge Enniskillen 1968–70, farmer Dorset 1970–93 (dir Blackmore Farms 1982–92), farmer Wilts 1993–; sec Br Bison Assoc, memb various ctees; MRICS; *Recreations* shooting, fishing, writing limericks; *Style—* The Rt Hon the Lord Seaford; ✉ Bush Farm, West Knoyle, Warminster, Wiltshire BA12 6AE (☎ 01747 830263, e-mail info@bisonfarm.co.uk)

SEAGER, Chris; s of David Seager (d 2002), and Mamie, *née* Harrison (d 1973); *b* 10 November 1949; *Educ* Monks Park Comp Sch Bristol, Guildford Sch of Art (Dip Film and TV); *m* 3 March 1995, Erica Banks; 2 s (Daniel b 23 Feb 1983, Calum b 16 Sept 1995), 1 da (Rosana b 15 July 1989); *Career* cinematographer; Educational TV Unit Wessex TV, studio camera operator BBC Technical Ops, camera asst rising to lighting cameraman BBC Film Dept Ealing Studios; freelance dir of photography 1994–; memb BSC 1996 (memb Bd of Govrs 2002–); *Television* incl: Arena: Scarfe on Scarfe (BAFTA Award), Only Fools and Horses, Ashenden 1991, The Vampyr (opera) 1993 (winner Prix Italia Music and Arts), A Dance to the Music of Time 1997, Frenchman's Creek 1998 (nominated RTS Best Photography Drama Award 1999), Lorna Doone 2000 (nominated BAFTA Photography and Lighting Award 2002), The Way We Live Now 2001 (nominated BAFTA Photography and Lighting Award 2002), State of Play 2003 (RTS Best Photography – Drama Award 2003), The Young Visters 2003, Sex Traffic 2004 (BAFTA Photography and Lighting Award 2005), The Girl in the Café 2005 (BAFTA Photography and Lighting Drama Award 2006), Hamlet 2009 (nominated Photography and Lighting Award 2010), Five Daughters 2010 (nominated BAFTA Photography and Lighting Award 2011), The Hour 2011 (nominated BAFTA Photography and Lighting Award 2012), Call the Midwife (series 1) 2012, Game of Thrones (series 3) 2013, Dracula 2013, Tyrant (pilot) 2014, Galavant (pilot) 2014; *Film* Cold Comfort Farm 1994, Stonewall 1994, Beautiful Thing 1995, Fever Pitch 1996, Alive and Kicking 1996, White Noise 2003, Stormbreaker 2007, Straightheads 2007, The Walker 2007, The Merry Gentleman 2008, Wild Child 2008, New in Town 2009, Retreat 2011, Penthouse North 2012, Set Fire to the Stars 2014; *Recreations* gym; *Clubs* Soho House; *Style—* Chris Seager, Esq, BSC; ✉ c/o Alison Law, McKinney Macartney Management Ltd, Gable House, 18–24 Turnham Green Terrace, London W4 1QP (☎ 020 8995 4747, e-mail alison@mckinneymacartney.com); c/o Ryan Tracey, United Talent Agency, UTA Plaza, 9336 Civic Centre Drive, Beverly Hills, CA 90210 USA (☎ 001 310 860 3778, e-mail traceyr@unitedtalent.com)

SEAGROVE, Jennifer Ann (Jenny); da of Derek Claud Seagrove, of Penang, Malaysia (d 2014), and Pauline Marjorie, *née* Pilditch (d 1993); *b* Kuala Lumpur; *Educ* St Hilary's Godalming, Queen Anne's Caversham, Kirby Lodge Cambridge, Bristol Old Vic Theatre Sch; *m* 19 May 1984 (m dis 1988), Madhav Sharma; *Career* actress; fndr and chm Mane Chance Sanctuary; tstee Born free Fndn; Best Actress Michael Elliott Award 2006; FRSA *Theatre* incl: title role in Jane Eyre (Chichester Festival Theatre), King Lear in New York (Chichester), Present Laughter (Globe), The Miracle Worker (Comedy and Wyndhams), Dead Guilty (Apollo), Hurly Burly (Queen's), Hamlet (Ludlow Festival), Brief Encounter (Lyric), Female Odd Couple (Apollo), The Constant Wife (Apollo), The Secret Rapture (Apollo), The Night of the Iguana (Lyric), The Letter (Wyndhams), Absurd, Person, Singular (Garrick), Pack of Lies, A Daughter's A Daughter (Trafalgar Studios), Bedroom Farce (Duke of Yorks Theatre), The Country Girl (Apollo), Volcano (Duke of York Theatre), The Governess, Brief Encounter on Air, How the Other Half Loves (Theatre Royal Haymarket); *Television* incl: A Woman of Substance, Hold the Dream, Diana, Lucy Walker, The Woman in White, Judge John Deed, Identity, Lewis, Endeavour; for American television: The Hitchhiker, In Like Flynn, Deadly Games, Incident at Victoria Falls, The Betrothed, Camp X; *Films* incl: To Hell and Back in Time for Breakfast, A Shocking Accident, Local Hero, Savage Islands, Tattoo, Moonlighting, The Sign of Four, Appointment with Death, A Chorus of Disapproval, The Guardian, Miss Beatty's Children, Don't Go Breaking My Heart, Zoe, Pranks (short), Another Mother's Son; *Recreations* country walks with dog, running, writing poetry, gardening, theatre, cinema, campaigning for animal welfare and the environment; *Style—* Miss Jenny Seagrove; ✉ c/o Steve Potts, BKL House, 1 Venice Wal, London W2 1RR (☎ 020 7446 6200); voiceovers c/o Leigh Mattie, Just Voices (☎ 020 7881 2568)

SEAL, ne Sealhenry Samuel; *m* 2005 (sep), Heidi Klum, the model; 2 s (Henry, Johan), 1 da (Lou), 1 step-da (Leni); *Career* singer and songwriter; debut single Killer (with Adamski) reached UK number 1 for 4 weeks 1990, first solo single Crazy reached number 1 in 3 countries 1990; albums: Seal (UK no 1, US Top 20) 1991, Seal II (UK no 1) 1994, Human Being 1998, Seal IV 2003, System 2007, Soul 2008, Commitment 2010, Soul 2 2011; Best Male Artist, Best Album, Best Video (for Killer) BRIT Awards 1992, Best Song, Best Record, Best Male Pop Vocal (for Kiss From a Rose) Grammy Awards 1996, International Hit of the Year Ivor Novello Awards 1996; *Style—* Seal

SEAL, Dr Barry Herbert; s of Herbert Seal, and Rose Ann Seal; *b* 28 October 1937; *Educ* Univ of Bradford, Harvard Business Sch; *m* 1963, Frances Catherine Wilkinson; 1 s (Robert), 1 da (Catherine); *Career* chem engr, control engr, univ lectr; former ldr Bradford Cncl Labour Gp; MEP (Lab) Yorkshire W 1979–99; former ldr Br Lab Gp in European Parl; memb European Parly: Tport Ctee, Social Affairs Ctee; pres of Delgn to USA; chm: Brookfields Int 1999–2003, N Kirklees Primary Care Tst 2002–06, Bradford Dist NHS Care Tst 2007–12, Ucan Recycling CiC 2012–, AgeUK Leeds 2013–; Hon Freeman Borough of Calderdale 2000; *Books* Dissertations on Computer Control; *Recreations* walking, bridge, reading, cinema; *Style—* Dr Barry Seal; ✉ Brookfields Farm, Brookfields Road, Wyke, Bradford BD12 9LU (☎ 01274 671888, e-mail barry@ucanrecycling.co.uk)

SEALY, Prof Leonard Sedgwick; s of Alfred Desmond Sealy (d 1964), and Mary Louise, *née* Mark (d 1967); *b* 22 July 1930; *Educ* Stratford HS NZ, Univ of Auckland (MA, LLM), Univ of Cambridge (PhD, Yorke prize); *m* 11 Aug 1960, Beryl Mary, da of Richard Edwards; 2 da (Elizabeth Helena b 23 Jan 1963, Louise Caroline b 3 Dec 1969), 1 s (Mark Edward Byers b 4 Sept 1964); *Career* called to the Bar NZ and admitted barr and slr 1953; Univ of Cambridge: asst lectr 1959–61, lectr 1961–91, SJ Berwin prof of corp law 1991–97; Gonville & Caius Coll Cambridge: fell 1959–, tutor 1960–70, sr tutor 1970–75; ed Cambridge Law Jl 1982–88; gen ed: British Company Law and Practice 1989–2014, International Corporate Procedures 1991–2005; Cwlth ed Gore-Browne on Companies 1996–2005; *Books* Cases and Materials in Company Law (1971, 12 edn with S Worthington 2016), Benjamin's Sale of Goods (with A G Guest and others, 1974, 7 edn 2006), Company Law and Commercial Reality (1984), Disqualification and Personal

Liability of Directors (1986, 6 edn 2000), Annotated Guide to the Insolvency Legislation (with D Milman, 1987, 19 edn (with D Milman and P Bailey) 2016), Commercial Law, Text and Materials (with R J A Hooley, 1994, 4 edn 2008); *Style*— Prof Leonard Sealy; ✉ Gonville & Caius College, Cambridge CB2 1TA (☎ 01223 332400, fax 01223 332456)

SEALY, Nicholas John Elliot; OBE (2015); s of John Edward Sealy (d 1968), and Joan Ursula, *née* Pelham (d 1989); *b* 3 May 1938, Chobham, Surrey; *Educ* Eton, RMA Sandhurst; *m* 1 May 1971, Hon Lavinia Caroline, *née* Piercy; 1 s (Edward John Pelham b 25 Sept 1975), 1 da (Lucinda Clare (Mrs James Marsh) b 17 July 1977); *Career* 3 Bn Green Jackets (RB) 1959–65; Smith & Willamson 1966–2005 (chm 1992–2000); dir Ecclesiastical Insurance Gp 1999–2009 (chm 2003–09); dir: Allchurches Tst Ltd 2003–13 (chm 2009–13), Charities Investment Managers Ltd 2008– (chm 2009–16; tstee Charibond 2008– (chm 2009–); govr Royal Humane Soc until 2015; past tstee: Friends of the Elderly, Surrey Clubs for Young People, The Royal Green Jackets Museum Tst; High Sheriff Surrey 2007–08; FCA 1979 (ACA 1971); *Recreations* shooting; *Clubs* Boodle's; *Style*— Nicholas Sealy, Esq, OBE; ✉ Timber Hill, Chobham, Surrey GU24 8JF (☎ 01932 873875, office tel/fax 01932 873635, e-mail nicksealy@chobham.net)

SEAMAN, Christopher Bertram; s of Albert Edward Seaman (d 1960), of Canterbury, Kent, and Ethel Margery, *née* Chambers (d 1985); *b* 7 March 1942; *Educ* Canterbury Cathedral Choir Sch, King's Sch Canterbury, King's Coll Cambridge (Scholar, MA); *Career* princ timpanist and memb Bd London Philharmonic Orch 1964–68; princ conductor: BBC Scot Symphony Orch 1971–77 (asst conductor 1968–70), Northern Sinfonia Orch 1974–79; chief guest conductor Utrecht Symphony Orch 1979–82, conductor in res Baltimore Symphony Orch 1987–98, music dir Rochester Philharmonic 1998–; music dir Naples (Florida) Philharmonic Orch 1993–2004; appears as guest conductor worldwide; FGSM 1972; *Recreations* people, reading, shopping, theology; *Style*— Christopher Seaman

SEAMAN, Prof (Marvin) Roy; s of late Charles Seaman, of Harleston, Norfolk, and late Mary Elizabeth, *née* Goldsmith; *b* 11 September 1945; *Educ* Stradbroke Secdy Modern Sch, RAF Tech Trg Coll; *m* 19 Oct 1977, Judy, da of late Joseph Ragobar, of Marabella, Trinidad; 2 s (Christian b 1978, Jonathan b 1982), 1 da (Michelle-Anne b 1981); *Career* RAF 1961–67; int mgmnt conslt to Br firms 1968–81, fndr and chm Franchise Development Services Ltd 1981–2015 (established 21 offices in 14 countries worldwide); publisher: The UK Franchise Directory 1984–2015, The Franchise Magazine 1985–2015, Franchise International 1998–2015, The Irish Franchise Magazine 1999–2015, European Franchising 2000–15, The Scottish Franchise Magazine 2004–15; visiting lectr seminars and confs on franchising and licensing (servs to estab franchisors, prospective franchisors, franchise publications, public relations, seminars, exhibitions and marketing); acknowledged by IOD as Europe's franchise boss and Britain's greatest franchise mastermind; hon prof Beijing Normal Univ 2005; memb: Int Christian C of C, Full Gospel Businessmen's Fellowship Int, CBI; FInstD, MCIM, MInstEx, CFE 2007; *Recreations* deep sea fishing, walking, relaxing with family; *Style*— Prof Roy Seaman; ✉ Cedar Lodge, Ipswich Road, Tasburgh, Norfolk NR15 1NS (☎ 01508 470686); Franchise Development Services Ltd, Franchise House, 56 Surrey Street, Norwich NR1 3FD (☎ 07812 334561, e-mail roy@royseaman.com)

SEARLE, Adam Eric; s of Eric George Searle, DFC (d 2006), and Enid, *née* Dawe; *b* 9 August 1957, Copthorne, Sussex; *Educ* Hustpierpoint Coll, Guy's Hosp Dental Sch (BDS), Guy's Hosp Med Sch (MB BS); *m* 28 Sept 1991, Christina, *née* Ramage; 2 da (Daisy b 1992, Rosie 1997), 2 s (George b 1993, Freddie b 1994); *Career* plastic surgn; conslt: Charing Cross Hosp 1994, Royal Marsden Hosp 1999; past pres Plastic Surgery Section RSM, pres Br Assoc of Aesthetic Plastic Surgns 2004–06; contrib articles in scientific jls; Ian McGregor Medal RCS 1994; FRCS 1989, FRCS (Plas) 1994; *Recreations* smallholding, family, life and love; *Clubs* Wilks XV; *Style*— Adam Searle, Esq; ✉ The Consulting Suite, 82 Portland Place, London W1B 1NS (☎ 020 7927 6515, fax 020 7927 6511, e-mail adamsearle@theconsultingsuite.co.uk)

SEARLE, Gregory Mark Pascoe (Greg); MBE (1993); s of Paul Frederick Searle, of Chertsey, Surrey, and Judith Ann (Judy), *née* Brant; *b* 20 March 1972; *Educ* Hampton Sch, South Bank Univ (BSc); *m* 18 Oct 1997, Jennifer (Jenny) Anne, *née* Hickman; 1 da (Josephine Sasha b 1 March 2001), 1 s (Adam John b 30 April 2003); *Career* amateur rower; jr debut for Hampton Sch Club 1988, sr debut Molesey Boat Club 1990; achievements incl: winner schs triple of Schs Head, Nat Schs and Princess Elizabeth Cup Henley 1988, Gold medal Jr World Championships 1989 and 1990 (debut 1988), Bronze medal (eights) World Championships 1991 (debut 1990), Gold medal (coxed pairs, with bro Jonny) Olympic Games 1992, Bronze medal World Indoor Rowing Championships 1992, Gold medal (coxed pairs, with bro Jonny) World Championships 1993, Bronze medal (coxless fours) Olympic Games 1996, Bronze medal (single sculls) World Championships 1997, 4th place (coxless pairs) Olympic Games 2000, Silver medal (eights) World Championships 2010, Silver medal (eights) World Championships 2011, Bronze medal (eights) Olympic Games 2012; first person ever to compete in both Jr and Sr World Championships in same year 1990; memb GBR Challenge crew Americas Cup 2002–03; leadership devpt conslt Lane 4 Management 1997–2001 and 2003–; *Recreations* off-road Land Rover driving, rugby, scuba diving; *Style*— Greg Searle, Esq, MBE

SEARS, Dr Charles Alistair Newton; s of Dr (Harold) Trevor Newton Sears (d 1995), and Dr Janet Sorley, *née* Conn (d 1994); *b* 30 December 1952; *Educ* Sandbach Sch, Middx Hosp Med Sch London (MB BS); *m* 6 May 1978, Judith Lesley, da of Dr Leslie Victor Martin, of Oxbridge, Dorset; 3 s (James b 1979, Robert b 1982, Nicholas b 1986); *Career* house offr Middx Hosp 1978; SHO: neurosurgery Royal Free Hosp 1978–79, med Queen Elizabeth Hosp Birmingham 1979–82; ptnr in gen practice Salisbury 1983–2013, clinical asst Learning Disability 1986–2006 (clinical asst Rheumatology 1985–92); trainer in gen practice Salisbury Dist Vocational Trg Scheme 1987–2008; memb: Cncl RCGP 1991–95, Health Cncl of Disability Partnership 1992–2007, Med and Social Servs Ctee Muscular Dystrophy Campaign 1993–2003, NHS Exec Commissioning Gp for R&D in Complex and Physical Disability 1994–98, Jt Specialty Ctee for Rehabilitation Med RCP 1994–2011, Devpt Gp National Back Pain Guidelines RCGP 1996 and 1999, Devpt Gp Faculty of Occupational Med Back Pain Guidelines 1999–2000, Editorial Bd Guidelines in Practice 1999–2003, Ctee of Safety Devices 2001–09; vice-pres Backcare 2003– (tstee 1994–2002); RCGP nominee to Back Pain Sub-Gp Clinical Standards Advsy Gp 1992–95; FRCGP 2003 (MRCGP 1988), FRIPH 2005, FRSPH 2008; *Style*— Dr Charles Sears

SEARS, (Robert) David Murray; QC (2003); s of (Robert) Murray Sears, and Janet Leslie, *née* Heape; *b* 13 December 1957, Haslemere, Surrey; *Educ* Eton, Trinity Coll Oxford (MA); *m* 14 July 1984 (m dis 2007), Victoria Jane, *née* Morlock; 1 s (Benedict b 7 May 1994), 1 da (Cordelia b 31 Jan 1996); *Career* MOD 1979–83, barr 4 Pump Court Temple 1985–2007, barr Atkin Chambers 2007–10, barr 4 New Square 2010–12, barr Crown Office Chambers 2012–; *Recreations* sailing, motorcycling, supporting Ipswich Town FC; *Clubs* Leander, Vincent's (Oxford), Bucks; *Style*— David Sears, Esq, QC; ✉ Crown Office Chambers, 2 Crown Office Row, Temple, London EC4Y 7HJ

SEATON, Andrew; s of Albert William Seaton (d 2003), and Joan, *née* McKenzie (d 2004); *b* 20 April 1954; *Educ* Univ of Leeds, Beijing Univ; *m* Helen, *née* Pott; 3 s; *Career* FCO: 2 sec Dakar 1979–82, head China Trade Unit Br Trade Cmmn Hong Kong 1982–87, head of recruitment Personnel Policy Dept 1987–89, head of China section Far Eastern Dept 1989–92, dep head of overseas devpt admin Aid Policy Dept 1992–95, dep consul gen and trade cncllr Br Consulate Gen Hong Kong 1995–2000, head of China Hong Kong Dept 2000–03, HM consul gen Chicago 2003–07, HM consul gen to Hong Kong 2008–12, currently exec dir Br Chamber of Commerce Hong Kong; *Recreations* family, wine, walking; *Style*— Andrew Seaton, Esq

SEATON, Prof Anthony; CBE (1997); s of Dr Douglas Ronald Seaton (d 1986), of Ipswich, Suffolk, and Julia, *née* Harrison (d 2009); bro of Dr Douglas Seaton and James Ronald Seaton, *qqv*; *b* 20 August 1938; *Educ* Rossall Sch, King's Coll Cambridge (BA, MB, MD); *m* 4 April 1964, Jillian Margaret Duke; 2 s (Andrew b 1966, Jonathan b 1969); *Career* qualified in med 1962, asst prof of med Univ of W Virginia 1969–71, conslt chest physician Univ of Wales 1971–77, dir Inst of Occupational Med Edinburgh 1978–90, prof Univ of Aberdeen 1988–2003 (head Dept of Environmental and Occupational Med), emeritus prof Univ of Aberdeen 2003–, sr conslt Inst of Occupational Med Edinburgh 2004–; Tudor Edwards lectr RCP and RCS, Hunter lectr Faculty of Occupational Med, Gehrmann lectr American Coll of Occupational and Environmental Med, Warner lectr Br Occupational Hygiene Soc, Meiklejohn lectr Soc of Occupational Med, Thackrah lectr Soc of Occupational Med; author of numerous pubns in jls; memb: Br Occupational Med and Thoracic Socs (pres Br Thoracic Soc 1999), Ctee on Med Effects of Air Pollution Dept of Health, Industrial Injuries Advsy Ctee 2013–; chm expert panel on air quality standards DOE 1991–2001, memb Royal Soc and Royal Acad of Engrg Working Gp on Nanoscience 2003–04, chm NERC Research Advsy Ctee on Human Health and Environment 2006–; Br Thoracic Soc Medal 2006; DSc (hc) Univ of Aberdeen 2007; FRCP 1977 (MRCP 1964), FRCPE 1986, FFOM 1985, FMedSci 1998; *Publications* Occupational Lung Diseases (with W K C Morgan 1975, 3 edn 1995), Thorax (ed, 1977–81), Respiratory Diseases (with D Seaton and A G Leitch, 1989, 2 edn 2000), Practical Occupational Medicine (1994, 2 edn 2005); *Recreations* keeping fit, opera, painting, vol food bank worker; *Clubs* St Andrew Boat; *Style*— Prof Anthony Seaton, CBE; ✉ 8 Avon Grove, Cramond, Edinburgh EH4 6RF (☎ 0131 336 5113, e-mail a.seaton@abdn.ac.uk)

SEATON, Dr Douglas; s of Dr Douglas Ronald Seaton (d 1986), of Ipswich, Suffolk, and Julia, *née* Harrison; bro of Prof Anthony Seaton, CBE and James Ronald Seaton, *qqv*; *b* 5 February 1946; *Educ* Rossall Sch Fleetwood, Univ of Liverpool (MB ChB, MD); *m* 1 Aug 1970, Anja Elisabeth, da of Frits Coenraad Neervoort, of Bussum, Netherlands; 3 s (Edward b 31 Aug 1972, Bart b 8 Feb 1974, Michael b 20 May 1978); *Career* sr med registrar United Liverpool Hosps 1976, instr in med W Virginia Univ USA 1977, conslt physician in gen and respiratory med The Ipswich Hosp 1979–2006, asst ed Thorax 1980–82; author of med papers on respiratory diseases, contrib chapters in med textbooks; MRCS, FRCP (MRCP), FRCPEd; *Books* Crofton and Douglas's Respiratory Diseases (with A Seaton and A G Leitch, 1989 and 2000); *Recreations* country walking, church architecture; *Style*— Dr Douglas Seaton; ✉ King's Field, 23 Park Road, Ipswich, Suffolk IP1 3SX (☎ 01473 216671, fax 01473 212011)

SEATON, James Ronald; s of Douglas Ronald Seaton (d 1986), of Ipswich, Suffolk, and Julia, *née* Harrison; bro of Dr Douglas Seaton and Prof Anthony Seaton, CBE, *qqv*; *b* 3 March 1955; *Educ* Rossall Sch Fleetwood, Wirral GS Bebington, Univ of Birmingham (BA); *m* 7 Oct 1978, Jessica Ruth, da of Arthur Barwell Hampton; 1 da (Rachel Amelia b 2 Aug 1980), 1 s (Nicholas James b 12 March 1985); *Career* knitwear and clothing designer/mfr: J & J Seaton 1978– (2 collections annually), Seaton 1995– (2 collections annually), Toast (mail order) 1997– (2 collections annually); *Books* The Seaton Collection (1989); *Recreations* paleo-ethno botany; *Style*— James Seaton, Esq; ✉ J & J Seaton, Llanfynydd, Carmarthen, Dyfed SA32 7TT (☎ 01558 668825, fax 01558 668875)

SEAWARD, Prof Mark Richard David; *b* 10 August 1938; *Educ* City GS Lincoln, Univ of Birmingham (BSc, Dip Ed), Univ of Nottingham (MSc), Univ of Bradford (PhD, DSc); *Career* head of biology Brigg GS 1960–65, lectr Loughborough Trg Coll 1965–67, sr lectr Trinity and All Saints Colls 1967–73; Univ of Bradford: chm Post Grad Sch of Environmental Sci 1980–88, chm Bd of Studies and Higher Degrees Ctee 1981–84, memb Cncl 1984–90, memb Senate 1984–97, prof of environmental biology 1990–2010, head Dept of Environmental Sci 1991–95, emeritus prof 2010–; hon visiting prof Univ of Lincoln 2007–15; chm Ctee Heads of Environmental Sciences 1996–99; vice-pres Linnean Soc 1997–2001, 2006–07 and 2015–; hon memb: Br Lichen Soc (memb Cncl), Japan Lichenology Soc, Polish Lichenology Soc, Italian Lichenology Soc; ed The Naturalist 1975–2010; author of over 435 scientific papers and assoc ed of 2 jls; Ursula Duncan Award Br Lichen Soc, Acharius Medal Int Lichenology Assoc; pres Leeds Philosophical Literary Soc 2003–07; exec memb Tennyson Soc; Nummo Aureo Univ of Wroclaw, Dr (hc) Univ of Wroclaw; FSB, FLS; *Books* Lichen Ecology (1977), Lichenology in the British Isles 1568–1975 (1977), A Handbook for Naturalists (1980), Urban Ecology (1982), Atlas of the Lichens of the British Isles (1982), Lichen Atlas of the British Isles (1995–), Richard Spruce, Botanist and Explorer (1996), Lichenology in Latin America (1998), Ecology of the Chagos Archipelago (1999), Biodeterioration of Stone Surfaces (2004), Biodiversity and Ecology of Lichens (2009), Diversity of Lichenology – Anniversary Volume (2009), Census Catalogue of Irish Lichens (2010), Systematics Biodiversity and Ecology of Lichens (2012); *Recreations* book collecting, music, philately; *Clubs* Linnean; *Style*— Prof Mark Seaward; ✉ University of Bradford, Bradford BD7 1DP (☎ 01274 234212, e-mail m.r.d.seaward@bradford.ac.uk)

SEAWRIGHT, Paul; s of William James Seawright, and Isobel, *née* McComb; *Educ* Belfast Royal Acad, Univ of Ulster, W Surrey Coll of Art (BA); *Career* photographer; Univ of Ulster: pt/t lectr in art and design 1990–92, assoc lectr in photography 1991–94; Univ of Wales Coll Newport: sr lectr in documentary photography 1994–95, course ldr documentary photography 1995–97, head of res Dept of Media Arts 1997–2000, currently head Centre for Photographic Res; visiting prof Ecole Nationale Superior des Beaux Arts Paris 1996; founding ed Source; chm Photo Works North 1992–94; memb Visual Arts Panel Arts Cncl of NI 1992–94, advsr to bd Gall of Photography Dublin 1994–97; *Solo Exhibitions* Mikkelin Valokuvakesus Finland 1989, Gallery Vapauden Aukion Helsinki 1989, The Photographer's Gall London 1991 and 1995, The Gall of Photography Dublin 1992 and 1995, Impressions Gall York 1992, The Int Center of Photography NY 1992, The Old Museum Belfast 1993, Arts Cncl Gall Belfast 1993, UN Gen Assembly Building NY 1993, Blue Sky Gall Portland Oregon 1993 and 1997, Cornerhouse Manchester 1994, Ffotogallery Cardiff 1996, Houston Fotofest 1996, Françoise Knabe Gall Frankfurt 1997, Le Lieu l'Orient France 1997, Galerie du Jour / Agnes b Paris 1998 and 2001, Rena Bransten Gall San Francisco 1998 and 2000, Rhona Hoffman Gall Chicago 1998 and 2000, Angles Gall Santa Monica 1998 and 2001, Kerlin Gall Dublin 1999, Centro de Fotografia Univ of Salamanca 2000, Maureen Paley/Interim Art London 2000, Photo.doc Forum Box Helsinki 2000, Bonakdar Jancou Gall NY 2000, Grieder Von Puttkamer Berlin 2000, Museum of Contemporary Art Zagreb 2000, Hasselblad Centre Kunst Museum Gothenberg 2001, Douglas Hyde Gall Dublin 2001, Fndn Marangoni Florence 2002; *Group Exhibitions* Show of Hands (Photographers' Gall London) 1988, Death (Cambridge Darkroom Gall/Kettles Yard) 1988, Shocks to the System (Arts Cncl of GB RFH and Ikon Gall Birmingham) 1991, NI Cultural Counterpoint Conf (SUNY Binghamton) 1991, Current Account (RPS Bath and Mai de la Photo Riems) 1992–93, Through the Lens (Arts Cncl of NI touring exhbn) 1992, Recent Acquisitions (Ulster Museum Belfast) 1992, History of the Photographic Image (Rencontres Intls de la Photographie Arles) 1992, Godowsky Awards (PRC Gall Boston) 1993, Documentary Dilemmas (Brit Cncl touring Euro, S America and Ireland) 1993–94, Nervous Landscapes (Southeast Museum of Photography Florida) 1994, Different Stories (Photo Int and Nederlands Foto Instituut Rotterdam) 1994, Ceasefire (Wolverhampton Museum and Art Gall) 1994–95, L'Imaginaire Irlandais (Ecole des Beaux Arts Paris) 1996, Inside Out (Galerie du Jour/ Agnes b Paris) 1996, Kerlin Gall Dublin 1996, Lie of the Land (touring exhbn, Gall of

Photography Dublin, Centre Nationale de la Photographie Paris, Copenhagen, Salamanca, Athens and Prague) 1996–97, Irish MOMA/Glen Dimplex Artists Award (Irish MOMA) 1997, Recent Acquisitions (Irish MOMA) 1997, NGBK Contemporary British Photography (Berlin) 1997, Residue (Douglas Hyde Gall Dublin) 1997, Political Spaces – Three Person (Rena Bransten San Francisco) 1997, The Missing – Three Person Exhibition (Nederlands Foto Instituut Rotterdam) 1997, Photos Leurres (French Inst Prague) 1998, Le Primtemps (Cahor France) 1998, Sightings – New Photographic Art (ICA London) 1998, Europe in Decay (Light Hall Kuopio and Helsinki Cathedral) 1998, Troubled, Photography and Video from Northern Ireland (The Light Factory and Contemporary Art Museum Raleigh N Carolina) 1998, Declinations of the Boundaries (Galerie Lichtblick Cologne) 1999, Revealing Views; Images from Ireland (RFH) 1999, Under Exposed (Public Art Project Stockholm) 1999, Contemporary Art (Arts Cncl of Ireland Collection, Limerick City Art Gall) 1999, Silent Presence (Staatliche Kunsthalle Baden-Baden Germany) 1999, Concern for the Document (Vox Populi Le Mois de la Photo Montreal Canada) 1999, Contemporary Art (Ormeau Baths Gall Belfast) 1999, Fragments of Document & Memory (Tokyo Photo Bienalle, Tokyo Met Museum of Photography) 1999, Surveying the Landscape (Lombard/Fried Fine Arts NY) 1999, Engaging Tradition (Hotbath Gall Bath), 0044 (PS1 NY, Albright-Knox Art Gall Buffalo) 1999 and Ormeau Baths Gall Belfast and Crawford, Municipal Art Gall Cork) 2000, Lautlose Gegenwart (Bielefelder Kunstverein) 2000, Foto Biennale Rotterdam 2000, Irish Art Now: From the Poetic to the Political (McMullen Museum of Art Boston Coll, Art Gall of Newfoundland and Labrador Canada, Chicago Cultural Centre Chicago) 2000 and Irish MOMA 2001, British Art Show 5 (tour venues incl Scottish Nat Gall of Modern Art, Southampton City Art Gall, Ffotogallery Cardiff and Ikon Birmingham) 2000, Auto Werke (Deichtorhallen Hamburg, with Gillian Wearing, *qv*, et al) 2000, 50 Years of Irish Art (Irish MOMA) 2001, On the Margins (Barbara Krakow Gall Boston) 2001, Depicting Abscence/Implying Prescence (San Jose Inst of Contemporary Art Calif) 2001, Werner Mertz Prize (Centrum Beeldende Kunst Maastricht Netherlands) 2001, A470 (Oriel Gall Llandudno Wales and Chapter Cardiff) 2001, New Directions (Winston Wachter Fine Art Seattle) 2001, The Gap Show – Critical Art from Great Britain (Museum am Ostwall Dortmund Germany) 2002, Gewaltbilder – Gewalt in der Gegenwartskunst (Museum Bellerive Zurich) 2002; collections incl: Arts Cncl of GB, Cncl of Ireland, Int Center of Photography NY, Art Gall of Ontario Canada, Vereins-und Westbank Hamburg, Worcester City Art Gall and Museum, Deutsche Bank Frankfurt, AIB Collection Dublin, ACC Bank Dublin, Simmons and Simmons London, Waterford RTC, Museum of Contemporary Art Strasbourg, San Francisco MOMA, Art Inst Chicago, BMW Munich; *Awards* Photoworks in Progress Cmmn Netherlands Foto Inst 1997, Irish MOMA/Glen Dimplex Artists Award 1997, BMW Auto Werke Cmmn Munich 1998, Ville de Paris Artist Award 1999, In Context Cmmn S Dublin CC 2000, War Artist Cmmn Afghanistan Imp War Museum 2002; *Publications* numerous exhibition catalogues and features in magazines and jls; *Style*— Paul Seawright, Esq; ✉ University of Wales College Newport, PO Box 179, Newport NP18 3YG (✆ 01633 432642, fax 01633 432168, e-mail paul.seawright@newport.ac.uk)

SEBAG MONTEFIORE, Dr Simon Jonathan; *b* 27 June 1965, London; *Educ* Harrow, Gonville and Caius Coll Cambridge (PhD); *Career* historian, novelist and TV presenter; writer and presenter BBC TV series: Jerusalem (2012), Rome (2012), Byzantium/Istanbul (2013); FRSL; *Books* non-fiction incl: Catherine the Great and Potemkin (2004), Stalin: The Court of the Red Tsar (2004, History Book of the Year Br Book Award 2004), A History of Caucasus (2005), Speeches that Changed the World (2007), Young Stalin (2008, LA Times Book Prize for Best Biography, Costa Book Award), Jerusalem: The Biography (2011), Titans of History (2012); fiction incl: My Affair with Stalin (2004), Sashenka (2008), One Night in Winter (2013); *Style*— Dr Simon Sebag Montefiore; ✉ c/o Georgina Capel, Capel & Land Literary Agency, 29 Wardour Street, London W1D 6PS

SEBAG-MONTEFIORE, Charles Adam Laurie; s of Denzil Charles Sebag-Montefiore (d 1996), and Ruth Emily, *née* Magnus; *b* 25 October 1949; *Educ* Eton, Univ of St Andrews (MA); *m* 5 Oct 1979, Pamela Mary Diana, da of Archibald Tennant (d 1955); 2 da (Elizabeth Anne b 1982, Laura Rose b 1984), 1 s (Archibald Edward Charles b 1987); *Career* initial career with Touche Ross & Co CAs, ptnr Grieveson Grant & Co 1981–86, dir Kleinwort Benson Securities Ltd 1986–94, dep chm Harvill Press Ltd 1994–2002; dir: Euclidian plc 1994–99, Elderstreet Corporate Finance Ltd 1997–99, IDJ Ltd 1999–2004, Govett European Enhanced Investment Trust plc 1999–2004 (chm 2003–04), Kiln plc 2001–06; chm Community Careline Services Ltd 2001–02, non-exec dep chm West 175 Media Gp 2001–06 (dir 2000–06), non-exec dir Hightex Gp plc 2006–14; tstee HSBC Common Funds for Growth and Income 1994–2002; dir Ludgate Investments Ltd 2004–12 (non-exec dir 2013–), dir Scholium Gp plc 2014–; chm: Projects Ctee Nat Art-Collections Fund 1977–86, London Historic House Museums Tst 1992–2009 (tstee 1987–2009); hon treas: Friends of the Nat Libraries 1990–, Friends of the British Library 1990–95, Friends of Lambeth Palace Library 1990–, The London Library 1991–2003, The Walpole Soc 1992–; govr of Patrons of the Nat Gallery of Scotland 1992–2010, treas Roxburghe Club 2002–; tstee: Samuel Courtauld Tst 1992–2007, Nat Art Collections Fund ('Art Fund') 2000–11, Nat Manuscripts Conservation Tst 2000–, Montefiore Endowment 2004–07, Oxford Centre for Hebrew and Jewish Studies 2004–, Strawberry Hill Tst 2004–07, Nat Gallery 2012–, Wordsworth Tst 2013–, Harewood House Tst 2014–; jt sec Soc of Dilettanti 2002–; Liveryman Worshipful Co of Spectacle Makers 1973; FCA 1974, FRSA 1980, FSA 1995; *Publications* The British as Art Collectors: From the Tudors to the Present (jtly, 2012), A Dynasty of Dealers: John Smith and Successors 1801–1924 (2013), Brooks's 1764–2014: The Story of a Whig Club (jt ed, 2013); *Recreations* visiting picture galleries, collecting books, opera; *Clubs* Brooks's, Beefsteak, Roxburghe; *Style*— Charles Sebag-Montefiore, Esq, FSA; ✉ 21 Hazlewell Road, London SW15 6LT (✆ 020 8789 5999, e-mail csmontefiore@gmail.com)

SEBAGH, Dr Jean-Louis; s of Simon Sebagh of Paris, and Paule, *née* Levy; *b* 25 August 1954, Oran, Algeria; *m* July 1990, (m dis) Thalia Bloch; 1 s (Theo b 8 April 1991), 1 da (Emy b 10 Oct 1993); *Career* head and neck cosmetic surgn; fndr Cosmetic Doctor At Work Ltd; memb Societé Francaise de Chirurgie Esthetique; *Style*— Dr Jean-Louis Sebagh; ✉ French Cosmetic Medical Company Ltd, 25 Wimpole Street, London W1G 9GL (✆ 020 7637 0548, fax 020 7637 5110, e-mail drsebagh@gmail.com)

SEBASTIAN, Timothy (Tim); s of Peter Sebastian, CBE (d 2006), of Hove, E Sussex, and Pegitha, *née* Saunders (d 2006); *b* 13 March 1952; *Educ* Westminster, New Coll Oxford (BA), UC Cardiff (Dip Journalism); *m* 4 June 1977 (m dis 1995), Diane, da of John Buscombe, of Frensham, Surrey; 1 s (Peter b 1981), 2 da (Clare b 1983, Caroline b 1986); *Career* BBC TV: eastern Europe corr 1979–82, Moscow corr 1984–85, Washington corr 1986–89, presenter Hardtalk 1997–2004; presenter Conflict Zone DW TV 2015–; fndr and chm The Doha Debates 2004–12, fndr and chm The New Arab Debates 2012–15; fell commoner Corpus Christi Coll Cambridge 2015–16; *Books* Nice Promises (1984), I Spy in Russia (1985), The Spy in Question (1987), Spy Shadow (1989), Saviour's Gate (1990), Exit Berlin (1992), Last Rights (1993), Special Relations (1994), War Dance (1995), Ultra (1997); *Style*— Tim Sebastian, Esq

SECCOMBE, Georgina Claire; *née* Harland; da of Philip Harland, of Canterbury, Kent, and Claire, *née* Hunt; *b* 14 April 1978, Canterbury, Kent; *Educ* Benenden, Loughborough Univ (BSc); *m* Charles Seccombe; 1 da (Mollie); *Career* modern pentathlete 1996–2008; achievements as individual incl: Bronze medal World Championships 2001 and 2002, Gold medal European Championships 2003, Gold medal World Cup Final 2003, Bronze medal Olympic Games Athens 2004, World Cup series champion 2007; achievements in team relay events incl: Gold medal World Championships 1999, Gold medal European Championships 2000 (Silver medal 1999 and 2002); achievements in team events incl: Gold medal World Championships 1999, 2001, 2003 and 2004 (Silver medal 2000, 2006 and 2008), Gold medal European Championships 2000, 2001, 2002, 2006 and 2007 (Silver medal 1999, Bronze medal 2003); memb Exec Bd UIPM (Union Internationale de Pentathlon Moderne) 2008–15, sport engagement mangr BOA 2010–, dep chef de mission Team GB Rio 2016 2013–; memb Mgmnt Team Give Them a Sporting Chance charity 2005–; Sunday Times Student Sportswoman of the Year 2001, BBC SW Sportswoman of the Year 2003, Bath Chronicle Sportswoman of the Year 2004; *Recreations* mountain biking; *Style*— Mrs Georgina Seccombe

SECCOMBE, Baroness (Life Peer UK 1991), of Kineton in the County of Warwickshire; Dame Joan Anna Dalziel Seccombe; DBE (1984); *née* Owen; da of Robert John Owen (d 1941), of Solihull, W Midlands, and Olive Barlow Owen; *b* 3 May 1930; *Educ* St Martin's Sch Solihull; *m* 1950, Henry Lawrence Seccombe (d 2008), s of Herbert Stanley Seccombe (d 1951), of Lapworth, Warks; 2 s (Hon Philip Stanley b 1951, Hon Robert Murray b 1954); *Career* memb: W Midlands CC 1977–81 (chm Trading Standards 1979–81), Midlands Elec Consultative Cncl 1981–90; chm: Cons Womens Nat Ctee 1981–84, Nat Union of Cons & Unionists Assoc 1987–88 (vice-chm 1984–87), Lord Chllr's Advsy Ctee, Solihull Magistrates 1975–93, Solihull Bench 1981–84; vice-pres Inst of Trading Standards Admin 1992–; vice-chm Cons Party 1987–97; memb: W Midlands Police Ctee 1977–81 and 1985–91, Admin and Works Sub-Ctee 1991–94, Offices Ctee House of Lords 1991–94 and 1997–2000, Broadcasting Ctee 1994–97, Finance and Staff Sub-Ctee 1994–97, Personal Bills Ctee 1994–97, Information Ctee 2012–15, Liaison Ctee 2015–; oppn whip House of Lords 1997–2001, dep chief oppn whip House of Lords 2001–10, Cons Pty whip 2010–; Nuffield Hosps: govr 1988–2001, dep chm 1993–2001, chm tstees Pension Fund 1992–2001; extra Baroness in Waiting to HM the Queen 2004–; pres St Enedoc Golf Club 1991–; JP Solihull 1968–2000 (chair 1981–84); *Recreations* living a full life; *Style*— The Lady Seccombe, DBE; ✉ House of Lords, London SW1A 0PW (✆ 020 7219 4558)

SECKER, Prof Philip Edward; s of Cyril Edward Secker (d 1980); *b* 28 April 1936, Aylesbury, Bucks; *Educ* Haberdashers' Aske's, Univ of London; *m* 1968, Judith Andrea, da of Douglas Eric Lee (d 1981); 2 s; *Career* chartered engr; lectr Univ of London 1961–64, visiting asst prof MIT 1964–65; UCNW: lectr 1965–69, sr lectr 1969–73, reader 1973–75, prof 1975–80; md IDB (UCNW) Ltd 1971–80, engrg dir Royal Doulton Ltd 1980–87, visiting prof Dept of Physics Keele Univ 1985–; md IEE 1999–2001 (acting chief exec 1998–99, dep chief exec 1990–97); exec sec ERA Fndn 2002–05; dir: UWB Enterprises Ltd 2001–06, Young Engrs Ltd 2001–11; chm IDB Ltd 2006–10; *Publications* Science of Materials (jtly, 1965), Industrial Electrostatics (jtly, 1994); also 90 technical papers; *Recreations* refurbishing classic cars, gardening; *Style*— Prof Philip Secker; ✉ Gwel-y-Don, Cae Mair, Beaumaris, Anglesey LL58 8YN (✆ 01248 810771, e-mail psecker@hotmail.co.uk)

SECKER-WALKER, Dr Jonathan; s of Geoffrey Secker-Walker (d 1968), of Farnborough, Hants, and Joan Alice, *née* Diplock (d 1995); *b* 19 October 1942; *Educ* Sherborne, UCL (BSc), UCH Med Sch (MB BS); *m* 20 July 1968, Jan Lilian, da of Charles James Goodwin (d 1998), of Ryde, IOW; 1 da (Katherine Louise b 16 Aug 1971), 1 s (Thomas Adam b 30 April 1973); *Career* registrar (anaesthetics): UCH 1970–72, Gt Ormond St 1972; sr registrar (anaesthetics) St Thomas' Hosp 1973, clinical asst Toronto Sick Children's Hospital 1974, conslt anaesthetist and sr lectr UCH 1975, sr lectr in clinical audit UCL 1988–94, gen mangr UCL Hosps 1992–94, med dir Merrett Health Risk Management Ltd 1994–98, sr lect Univ of Wales Coll of Med 1999–2003, emeritus conslt UCL Hosps 1994–, public govr Taunton and Somerset NHS Tst 2007–; FRCA 1972, FRSM; *Publications* chapters and books on clinical risk management and clinical governance; *Recreations* skiing, sailing, walking, theatre; *Clubs* RSM; *Style*— Dr Jonathan Secker-Walker; ✉ Brook House, Stogumber, Somerset TA4 3SZ (✆ 01984 656701)

SECKL, Prof Jonathan Robert; s of Josef Seckl, and Zehava, *née* Segal; *b* 15 August 1956; *Educ* William Ellis Sch London, UCL (BSc, MB BS, Filliter Prize, Magrath scholarship, Fellowes Gold Medal, Achison exhbn), Westminster Hosp Med Sch London (PhD); *m* 9 Nov 1986, Molly, *née* Sifnugel; 1 s (Benjamin b 15 July 1988), 1 da (Joanna b 4 Nov 1989); *Career* Univ of Edinburgh: Sir Jules Thorn research fell 1984, Wellcome Tst/RSE sr clinical research fell 1989, hon conslt physician 1989, sr lectr in med 1993, prof of endocrinology 1996, Moncrieff-Arnott prof of molecular med 1997, head Dept of Med Sciences 2001, head Sch of Molecular and Clinical Med 2002, dir of research Coll of Medicine and Veterinary Med 2005– (exec dean 2010–), vice-princ (planning, resources, research policy) 2012–; memb: Lloyds TSB Ctee RSE, Scottish Science Advsy Ctee (SSAC), Cncl Acad of Medical Sciences 2008–11, Cncl Soc of Endocrinology 2012–16; Soc for Endocrinology Medal 1998, Geoffrey Harris Prize European Endocrine Societies 2012; PhD (hc) Umea Univ 2001; memb Assoc of Physicians 1991; MRCP 1983, FRCPEd 1993, FMedSci 1999, FRSE 2002; *Publications* approximately 400 papers, reviews and chapters on endocrinology, notably on glucocorticoid biology in relation to brain ageing and obesity/type 2 diabetes; author of several patents; *Recreations* tennis, skiing; *Style*— Prof Jonathan Seckl; ✉ Edinburgh University, The Queen's Medical Research Institute, 47 Little France Crescent, Edinburgh EH16 4TJ (✆ 0131 242 6777, fax 0131 242 6779, e-mail j.seckl@ed.ac.uk)

SECUNDE, Nadine Rekeszus; da of John Philip Secunde, of the USA, and Patricia Margaret, *née* Bousi; *b* 21 December 1951; *Educ* Oberlin Conservatory of Music Oberlin Ohio, Univ of Indiana; *m* Heiner Rekeusus; 1 da (Anja Maria b 1989), 1 s (Jan-Philipp b 1992); *Career* soprano; studied with Margaret Harshaw at Univ of Indiana, Fulbright scholarship to Germany 1979, memb Hessisches Staatstheater Ensemble Wiesbaden 1980–84, with Cologne Opera 1984–89, Bayreuth Festspiele 1987–92; numerous guest appearances at major opera houses incl Munich, Vienna, Berlin, San Francisco, Chicago, Paris, Barcelona; *Recordings* incl: Prokofiev's The Fiery Angel (DDG), Strauss' Elektra (Phillips), Bayreuther Ring (Sieglinde), laser disc of Britten's Turn of the Screw; *Recreations* rare books; *Style*— Ms Nadine Secunde; ✉ c/o Ingpen & Williams Ltd, 7 St George's Court, 131 Putney Bridge Road, London SW15 2PA (✆ 020 8874 3222, fax 020 8877 3113)

SEDDON, Nicholas Paul (Nick); s of Clive Seddon, of Congleton, Cheshire, and Alison Helen, *née* Dale; *b* 11 July 1960; *Educ* Sandbach GS, Univ of Birmingham (LLB); *m* 13 Nov 2010, Citra Susanto; 1 s (Frederick Clive Carbury b 24 Sept 2012); *Career* admitted slr 1984; ptnr: Needham & James Birmingham 1988–93 (joined 1982), DLA Piper (formerly Dibb Lupton Alsop) 1993–99 and 2003–08, Olivier Cheah & Partners Ltd 2014–, Beaton Capital Ltd 2014–; managing shareholder Asia Heller Ehrman LLP 2008, managing ptnr Asia Eversheds LLP 2008–13, dir Seddon and Co Ltd 2013–; memb Law Soc; Freeman City of London, Liveryman Worshipful Co of Basketmakers; *Recreations* motor sport, gardening, photography, wine, classic cars; *Clubs* Hong Kong, Foreign Correspondents (Hong Kong); *Style*— Nick Seddon, Esq; ✉ e-mail nick@oliviercheah.com, nick.seddon@beatoncapital.com

SEDDON, Patsy Frances Jane; da of Richard Hayes, of Pembrokeshire, and Cynthia, *née* Shelley; *Educ* Tudor Hall, Winkfield Coll; *m* 1971 (m dis 2002), Julian Seddon; 1 s (Alexander James Dyson b 2 May 1973), 1 da (Zoe Louisa b 8 May 1974); *Career* Browns South Molton St London 1970–73; Phase Eight Ltd (fashion and design): fndr 1979, chm 1979–2001, pres 2001–05; fndr Hazelbury Ltd (trades as Thyme & Spice) 2004; runner-up Entrepreneur of the Year 2001; *Recreations* plants, flowers, cooking, decoupage, skiing; *Style*— Mrs Patsy Seddon; ✉ 109 Hazlebury Road, London SW6 3HR

S

SEDGWICK, Peter Norman; s of late Norman Victor Sedgwick (d 1995), of Dorset, and late Lorna Clara, *née* Burton (d 2008); *b* 4 December 1943, Rickmansworth; *Educ* Westminster Cathedral Choir Sch, Downside, Lincoln Coll Oxford (MA, BPhil); *m* 17 Feb 1984, Catherine Jane, *née* Saunders, da of Barry Donald Thomas and Janet Saunders; 2 s (Richard b 30 Dec 1986, Christopher b 14 April 1988), 2 da (Victoria b 6 July 1989, Rebecca Elizabeth b 3 Dec 1990); *Career* HM Treasy: econ asst 1969, econ advsr 1971, sr econ advsr 1977, under-sec 1984, dep dir 1995–99; vice-pres and memb Mgmnt Ctee European Investment Bank Luxembourg 2000–06, dir European Investment Fund 2002–06, chm 3i Infrastructure plc 2007–15; memb London Symphony Chorus 1972– (chm 1979–84), tstee London Symphony Chorus Endowment Fund; dir and chair Governance Ctee Dyslexia Action 2007–11, chair Bowel Cancer UK 2013–; *Recreations* singing, gardening, walking; *Style*— Peter Sedgwick, Esq

SEDLEY, Rt Hon Sir Stephen John; kt (1992), PC (1999); s of William Sedley (d 1984), and Rachel Sedley (d 1987); *b* 9 October 1939; *Educ* Mill Hill Sch, Queens' Coll Cambridge (open scholar and exhibitioner, BA); *m* 1, 1968 (m dis), Ann Tate; 3 c (Jane May b 5 May 1970, Benjamin Anthony b 9 May 1972, Sarah Ann b 27 Sept 1975); m 2, 1996, Teresa (Tia) Cockrell; *Career* called to the Bar: Inner Temple 1964 (bencher 1989), Trinidad and Tobago 1986; QC 1983, asst recorder 1985–92, judge of the High Court of Justice (Queen's Bench Div) 1992–98, Lord Justice of Appeal 1999–2011; memb Int Cmmn on Mercenaries (Angola) 1976, pres Nat Reference Tbnls for coalmining industry 1983–87, chair Inquiry into the death of Tyra Henry (Lambeth) 1986–87, fndr memb and dir Public Law Project 1988–93, chm Sex Discrimination Ctee Bar Cncl 1992–95; pres Br Inst of Human Rights 2000–12, hon vice-pres Administrative Law Bar Assoc 1993– (memb Ctee 1987–92), chair Br Cncl Advsy Ctee on Governance 2002–05; ad hoc judge European Court of Human Rights 2000–01, cmmr Hammarskjöld Cmmn 2012–13; hon prof of law: Univ of Wales at Cardiff 1992–, Univ of Warwick 1993–; visiting professorial fell Univ of Warwick 1981, distinguished visitor Hong Kong Univ 1992, Bernard Simons Meml Lecture 1994, Paul Sieghart Meml Lecture on Human Rights 1995, Radcliffe lectr Univ of Warwick 1996, Hamlyn Lectures 1998, Laskin prof and lectr Osgoode Hall Toronto 1997 (visiting fell 1987), Atkin lectr 2002, Blackstone lectr 2006, visiting prof Univ of Oxford 2011–15, hon fell Mansfield Coll Oxford 2012–, Keeley fell Wadham Coll Oxford 2014–15, Adler lectr 2015; pres Holdsworth Soc Univ of Birmingham 2005; Hon Dr Univ of N London 1996; Hon LLD: Nottingham Trent Univ 1997, Univ of Bristol 1999, Univ of Warwick 1999, Univ of Durham 2001, Univ of Hull 2002, Univ of Southampton 2003, Univ of Exeter 2004, Univ of Essex 2007; *Publications* From Burgos Gaol (translation, 1964), The Seeds of Love (anthology, 1967), Inside the Myth (contrib, 1984), Civil Liberties (contrib, 1984), Police, the Constitution and the Community (contrib, 1985), Challenging Decisions (1986), Public Interest Law (contrib, 1987), Whose Child? (report of the Tyra Henry Inquiry, 1987), Civil Liberties in Conflict (contrib, 1988), Law in East and West (contrib, 1988), Citizenship (contrib, 1991), A Spark in the Ashes: the pamphlets of John Warr (ed with introduction, 1992), Administrative Law and Government Action (contrib, 1995), The Making and Remaking of the British Constitution (with Lord Nolan, 1997), The Golden Metwand and the Crooked Cord (contrib, 1998), Freedom, Law and Justice (1998 Hamlyn Lectures, 1999), Freedom of Expression and Freedom of Information (contrib, 2000), Judicial Review in International Perspective (contrib, 2000), Discriminating Lawyers (contrib, 2000), The New Brain Sciences (contrib, 2004), Le Council d'Etat et le Code Civil (contrib, 2004), A Simple Common Lawyer (contrib, 2009), Tom Bingham and the Transformation of the Law (contrib, 2009), Ashes and Sparks (essays, 2011); contrib Oxford DNB; also various articles in: Public Law, Modern Law Review, Journal of Law and Society, Civil Justice Quarterly, London Review of Books, Industrial Law Journal, Law Quarterly Review, Osgoode Hall Law Journal; *Style*— The Rt Hon Sir Stephen Sedley; ✉ c/o Cloisters, Temple, London EC4Y 7AA

SEED, Paul; *b* 18 September 1947; *Educ* Manchester Grammar, Univ of Manchester (BA); *Career* director; actor 1970–1981; credits as dir incl: Too Late to Talk to Billy (trilogy, BBC) 1982–83, Wynne & Penovsky (BBC, US title The Man from Moscow) 1984, Inappropriate Behaviour (BBC) 1986, Capital City (Euston Films) 1988–89, House of Cards (BBC) 1990, To Play the King (BBC) 1993, Disaster at Valdez (HBO/BBC, US title Dead Ahead) 1992, The Affair (HBO/BBC) 1994–95, Have your Cake and Eat It (BBC/Initial) 1996, Playing the Field (Tiger Aspect/BBC) 1997, A Rather English Marriage (Wall to Wall/BBC) 1998, Every Woman Knows a Secret (Carnival/ITV) 1998–99, Murder Rooms (BBC, US title The Dark Beginnings of Sherlock Holmes) 1999, Dirty Tricks (Little Bird/Carlton) 2000, My Beautiful Son (Showtime/Granada, US title Strange Relations) 2001, Auf Wiedersehen, Pet (BBC) 2001–02, Ready When You Are, Mr McGill (WTTV/ITV) 2002–03, The Booze Cruise (YTV) 2003, New Tricks (BBC) 2003–04, Christmas Lights (Granada) 2004, Northern Lights (Granada) 2005–06, Perfect Day (five) 2006, A Risk Worth Taking 2007; *Style*— Paul Seed, Esq; ✉ c/o Tim Corrie, United Agents, 12–26 Lexington Street, London W1F 0LE (☎ 020 3214 0800, fax 020 3214 0801, website www.unitedagents.co.uk)

SEED, Ven Richard Murray Crosland; s of Denis Briggs Seed (d 2012), and Mary Crosland, *née* Barrett (d 1986); *b* 9 May 1949, Leeds; *Educ* St Philips Sch Burley-in-Wharfedale, Univ of Leeds (MA), Edinburgh Theological Coll; *m* 1973, Jane Margaret, da of John Berry; 3 da (Emily b 1975, Lucy b 1977, Miriam b 1980), 1 s (Timothy b 1983); *Career* curate Christ Church Skipton 1972–75, curate Baildon 1975–77, team vicar Kidlington 1977–80, chaplain Campsfield House Detention Centre 1977–80, vicar of Boston Spa 1980–99, archdeacon of York 1999–2012 (archdeacon emeritus 2012–); fndr chm Martin House Hospice for Children 1982–2012 (designated fndr Martin House 2012–); *Recreations* walking, dogs, travel, gardening; *Style*— The Ven Richard Seed; ✉ Mill Cottage, Main Street, Allerston, Pickering, York YO18 7PG (☎ 01723 859011, e-mail randjseed@gmail.com)

SEEDS, Prof Alwyn John; s of Harry Seeds (d 1987), and Margaret Mary, *née* Ferguson (d 2007); *b* 1955; *Educ* Dover GS, Chelsea Coll London (BSc), UCL (PhD), Univ of London (DSc); *m* 1986, Angela Carolyn, da of Ronald Williams; 1 da (Caroline Emily Margaret b 1993); *Career* staff memb Lincoln Laboratory MIT 1980–83, lectr Dept of Electrical and Electronic Engrg QMC London 1983–86; Dept of Electronic and Electrical Engrg UCL: lectr 1986–91, sr lectr 1991–93, reader 1993–95, prof of optoelectronics 1995–, head of dept 2006–16; chm Lightwave Ctee IEEE Microwave Theory and Techniques Soc 1998–2001, chm Cmmn D Int Union for Radio Sci 1998–2001, chm IEE Photonics Professional Network 2001–07, memb and panel chm Peer Review Coll UK EPSRC 1995–, memb Technical Evaluation Ctee Agence Nationale de Recherche France 2007–12, memb Bd of Govrs IEEE Photonics Soc 2007–09 (vice-pres technical affrs 2008–10), dir SynOptika Ltd, dir SiQuand Ltd, fndr Zinwave Ltd, memb Sub-panel HEFCE Research Excellence Framework 2011–14; conslt: Alcatel, BBC, Euro Space Agency, Thales Ltd, Euro Cmmn, Lincoln Laboratory MIT, QinetiQ plc; chm Elm Park and Chelsea Park Residents Assoc 1991–; Gabor Medal and Prize Inst of Physics 2012; Liveryman Worshipful Co of Engrs; FIEE, FIEEE, FREng; *Publications* author of over 350 publications on microwave devices and circuits, lasers, optoelectronics and optical communications; *Recreations* audio engineering, music, opera, amateur radio; *Clubs* Athenaeum; *Style*— Prof Alwyn Seeds; ✉ Department of Electronic and Electrical Engineering, University College London, Gower Street, London WC1E 6BT (☎ 020 7679 7928, fax 020 7388 9325, e-mail a.seeds@ucl.ac.uk, website www.ee.ucl.ac.uk)

SEEISO, HRH Prince Seeiso Bereng; s of King Moshoeshoe II of Lesotho (d 1996), and Queen 'Mamohato, *née* Mojela (d 2003); *b* 16 April 1966; *Educ* Ampleforth, Nat Univ of Lesotho (BA), Univ of Birmingham (MA), Beijing Language Inst; *m* 15 Dec 2001, HRH Princess 'Mabereng, *née* Makara; 1 s (Prince Bereng Selala Seeiso), 1 da (Princess 'Masentle Thabitha Seeiso); *Career* appointed princ chief Matsieng 1991; Lesotho diplomat; memb: Nat Constituent Assembly 1991, Senate 1993; dep chairperson Coll of Chief 1994, high cmmr to UK 2005–; memb Parly Reform Ctee 2004; memb: CPA, Cncl of Traditional Ldrs Southern African Devpt Community (SADC); co-patron Sentebale Prince's Trust; *Recreations* horse riding, hiking, tennis; *Style*— HRH Prince Seeiso Bereng Seeiso; ✉ 4 Holne Chase, Hampstead Garden Suburb N2 0QN; Lesotho High Commission, 7 Chesham Place, London SW1X 8HN (☎ 020 7235 5686, fax 020 7235 5023, e-mail hicom@lesotholondon.org.uk)

SEEKINGS, John Charles; s of late Leonard Charles Seekings, of Shrewsbury, and late Joan Margaret, *née* Lemming; *b* 25 October 1955; *Educ* Worthing Technical HS, Univ of Southampton (BSc); *m* 1 June 1985, Andrea Katrina, da of late James Peter Hamilton MBE; 2 da (Charlotte Elise b 30 April 1986, Emily Alexandra b 1 March 1989), 2 s (Matthew Charles b 10 Sept 1991, Alexander James b 4 June 1999); *Career* freelance stage and prodn mangr 1977–78; ROH: tech mangr 1979–87, asst tech dir 1988–92, dep tech dir 1993–95, devpt dir 1995–98, dir of ops and devpt 1998–; co sec ROH Covent Garden Ltd 2002–08; dir: ROH Devpts Ltd 1996–, ROH Mgmnt Ltd 1997–, ROH Hldgs Ltd 1997–, ROH Trading Ltd 2000–; ROH Pensions tstee 2006–; TTTS Ltd: conslt to Bd 1992–95, dir and chm 1995–; chm Bd Arts Devpt Tst 2004–07, memb Cncl Nat Cncl for Drama Trg 2005–09, memb Soc of London Theatres 2006–; FRGS 1977; *Recreations* family, travel, reading; *Style*— John Seekings, Esq; ✉ Royal Opera House, Covent Garden, London WC2E 9DD (☎ 020 7212 9350, fax 020 7212 9512, e-mail john.seekings@roh.org.uk)

SEFTON, Catherine; *see:* Waddell, Martin

SEGAL, Prof Anthony Walter; s of Cyril Segal, and Doreen, *née* Hayden; *b* 24 February 1944; *Educ* Univ of Cape Town (MB ChB, MD), Univ of London (MSc, DSc, PhD); *m* 18 Dec 1966 (m dis), Barbara Ann, da of Justice Solomon Miller (d 1987), of Durban, South Africa; 3 da (Terry b 1969, Jessica b 1972, Penelope b 1975); *Career* Charles Dent prof of med UCL 1986–, fell UCL 2002; FRCP, FRS 1998, FMedSci 1998; *Recreations* golf, sailing, art, theatre; *Style*— Prof Anthony Segal, FRS; ✉ Department of Medicine, University College London, University Street, London WC1E 6JJ (☎ 020 7679 6175, fax 020 7679 6211)

SEGALL, Anne (Mrs David Evans); *b* 20 April 1948; *Educ* St Paul's Girls' Sch London, St Hilda's Coll Oxford (exhibitioner, MA); *m* David Howard Evans, QC; 2 s (Oliver, Edward); *Career* economics and banking corr Investors' Chronicle 1971–76, banking corr The Economist 1976–80, banking then economics corr Daily Telegraph 1980–2001, freelance journalist/writer 2001–; Harold Wincott award 1975; *Recreations* swimming, theatre, reading; *Style*— Ms Anne Segall; ✉ e-mail annesegall@hotmail.com

SEGARS, Joanne; OBE (2003); *b* 5 December 1964, London; *Educ* Liverpool John Moores Univ (BA), Univ of Warwick (MA); *Career* sr pensions offr TUC 1988–2001, head of pensions and savings Assoc of Br Insurers 2001–05; Nat Assoc of Pension Funds: dir of policy 2005–06, pres and ceo 2006–; chm PensionsEurope 2012–, dir Pensions Infrastructure Platform Ltd 2014–; dir TUC Stakeholder Tstees Ltd; founding govr and memb Bd Pensions Policy Inst, dir European Fedn for Retirement Provision 2007–; *Recreations* travel, skiing, photography; *Style*— Ms Joanne Segars, OBE; ✉ NAPF, Cheapside House, 138 Cheapside EC2V 6AE (Twitter @joannesegars)

SEIFERT, John Michael; s of Lt-Col Richard Seifert, and Josephine Jeanette, *née* Harding; *b* 17 February 1949; *Educ* Mill Hill Sch, Bartlett Sch of Architecture, UCL (BSc, Dip Arch); *m* 1 (m dis); 2 s (James, Edward), 1 da (Elizabeth), 1 step s (Marlon); m 2, Marina, *née* Prikhodko; 1 da (Sparkle); *Career* architect; co-fndr Seifert International 1984, fndr and dir Seifert Architects LLLC; major projects incl: Cutlers Gardens 1983, Mermaid Theatre 1983, Bank of Chicago House 1984, Sheraton Hotel Lagos 1985, Bishopsbridge 1985, MISR Bank Tower 1986, South Quay Plaza 1987, Swiss Banking Corporation 1988, Hambros Bank 1988, Sceptre Court 1988, Greenwich View 1989, Glengall Bridge 1989, Hilton Hotel Paris 1991, HMP Parc 1994, Hilton Frankfurt 2003, Imperial Dubrovnik 2004, Radisson Frankfurt 2005, Vilamoura Resort 2008, Intercontinental Cologne 2011, Conrad Algarve 2013, Corinthia London 2013, Hilton Kiev 2014, NHA Trang Resort 2014; major competitions won: Surrey Docks Shopping Centre 1983, Limehouse Basin 1985, Heathrow Hotel 1988, Sandwell Mall 1988, Frankfurt Hilton 1995, RAC HQ 1997, Westhafen Frankfurt 2004; memb ARB; *Recreations* painting, sculpture, numismatics; *Clubs* Carlton; *Style*— John Seifert, Esq

SEITLER, Jonathan; QC (2003); *Educ* Univ of Oxford (BA, Dip Law); *Career* called to the Bar Inner Temple 1985 (Duke of Edinburgh scholar); practising barr specialising in property law and professional negligence litigation, memb Wilberforce Chambers 1995–, qualified mediator 2003; memb: Commercial Bar Assoc, Professional Negligence Bar Assoc; Property Finance Negligence: Claims Against Solicitors and Valuers (co-author, 1996), Commercial Property Disputes: Law and Practice (1999); *Recreations* football (referee under-9's games); *Style*— Jonathan Seitler, Esq, QC; ✉ Wilberforce Chambers, 8 New Square, Lincoln's Inn, London WC2A 3QP (☎ 020 7306 0102, fax 020 7306 0095, e-mail jseitler@wilberforce.co.uk)

SEITZ, Hon Raymond George Hardenbergh; s of John Francis Regis Seitz, and Helen Stewart Johnson Hardenbergh; *b* 8 December 1940, Hawaii; *Educ* Yale Univ (BA); *m* 10 May 1985, Caroline, *née* Richardson; 2 s (Royce Manning Barr b 24 Sept 1966, Thomas McKeen Cutler b 10 April 1974), 1 da (Hillary Helen Brewster b 1 Jan 1969); *Career* American Dip Serv until 1994: consular offr Montreal 1968–69, political offr Nairobi and concurrently vice-consul Seychelles 1969–70, princ offr Bukavu Zaïre 1970–72, staff offr later dir Secretariat Staff Washington 1972, special asst to DG Foreign Serv 1972–75, political offr London 1975–79 (DG's Award for Reporting), dep exec sec Dept of State Washington 1979–81, dep asst sec for public affrs 1981–82, exec asst to Sec of State 1982–84, min London 1984–89, asst sec of state for Euro and Canadian affrs Washington 1989–91, ambass to Ct of St James's 1991–94; chm Authoriszor 1999–; vice-chm Lehman Brothers International (Europe) 1996–2003 (sr md 1995–96); non-exec dir: Telegraph Group plc 1994–, Chubb Corporation 1994–, Cable & Wireless plc 1995–2002, British Airways plc 1995–2002, Marconi plc (formerly GEC plc) 1995–2002, Rio Tinto plc 1996–2002; memb Special Ctee of the Bd Hollinger Int Inc 2003–; tstee: National Gallery 1996–2001, Royal Acad 1996–; chm Whitbread Book of the Year and Literary Awards 1999; Presidential Award for Meritorious Service 1986 and 1988; Knight Cdr's Cross (Germany) 1991; Benjamin Franklin Medal RSA 1996; hon doctorates: Univ of Reading 1992, Richmond Coll 1992, Univ of Bath 1993, Univ of Leeds 1994, Univ of Durham 1994, Heriot-Watt Univ 1994, Univ of Buckingham 1998; Over Here (1998); *Recreations* literature, architecture; *Clubs* Garrick, Beefsteak; *Style*— The Hon Raymond Seitz

SELBORNE, 4 Earl of (UK 1882); Sir John Roundell Palmer; GBE (2011, KBE 1987), DL (Hants 1982); also Baron Selborne (UK 1872), Viscount Wolmer (UK 1882); s of Viscount Wolmer (k on active service 1942; s of 3 Earl) and Priscilla (*see* Baron Newton); suc gf 1971. Lord Selborne's gggf, the 1 Earl, was Lord Chllr 1872–74 and 1880–85 and his ggf was First Lord of the Admiralty 1900–05 and helped establish the RNVR, the RFR, Osborne and Dartmouth Naval Colleges and the Designs Committee which resulted in the Royal Navy being equipped with Dreadnoughts; *b* 24 March 1940; *Educ* Eton, ChCh Oxford; *m* 1969, Joanna Van Antwerp, da of Evan James, of Upwood Park, Abingdon (and sis of late Countess Baldwin of Bewdley); 3 s (William Lewis, Viscount Wolmer b 1971, Hon George, Hon Luke (twins) b 1974), 1 da (Lady Emily b 1978); *Heir* s, Viscount Wolmer; *Career* sits as Cons in House of Lords, chm Sub-Ctee D (Agric and Food) House of Lords' Select Ctee on Euro Communities 1991–93 and 1999–2003, chm Select Ctee on Science and Technology 1993–97 and 2014–; chm: Hops Marketing Bd 1978–82, Agric and Food Res Cncl 1983–89 (memb 1975–89, dep chm 1982), Joint Nature Conservation Ctee 1991–97, Agricultural Mortgage Corporation 1994–2002; pres RIPHH 1991–98, pres RGS, with IBG 1997–2000, chm Fndn for Science and Technology 2006–, memb Royal Cmmn on Environmental Pollution 1993–98; non-exec dir: Lloyds Bank plc 1994–95, Lloyds TSB Group plc 1995–2004; chllr Univ of Southampton 1996–2006; chm Bd of Tstees Royal Botanic Gardens Kew 2003–09; former vice-chm Apple and Pear Devpt Cncl, treas Bridewell Royal Hosp (King Edward's Sch Witley) 1972–83; memb UNESCO World Cmmn on the Ethics of Scientific Knowledge and Technology 1999–2003; FRS 1991; *Clubs* Travellers; *Style*— The Earl of Selborne, GBE, DL, FRS; ✉ Temple Manor, Selborne, Alton, Hampshire GU34 3LR (☎ 01420 473646)

SELBY, Prof Peter John; CBE (2001); s of Joseph Selby, and Dorothy, *née* Cross; *b* 10 July 1950; *Educ* Lydney GS, Univ of Cambridge (MA, MB, MB BChir, MD, DSc); *m* 8 July 1972, Catherine Elisabeth, da of Peter Thomas, and Vera, *née* Wilson; 1 da (Alexandra b 1980), 1 s (David b 1985); *Career* conslt physician Royal Marsden Hosp London 1985–88, prof of cancer medicine and conslt physician Univ of Leeds and St James's Univ Hosp Leeds 1988– (dir Cancer Research UK Clinical Research Centre 1993–2010), dir of clinical research ICRF 1997–2001, lead clinician Leeds Cancer Centre 1997–2005, pro dean for research Leeds Faculty of Medicine of Health 2006–08, dir Biomedical and Health Research Centre Leeds 2009–13, dir Leeds Inst of Molecular Medicine 2010–13, dir Leeds NIHR Diagnostic Evidence Cooperative 2013–; ed Br Jl Cancer 1987–92; dir: Nat Cancer Research Network 2001–05, UK Clinical Research Network 2005–10, NIHR Clinical Research Networks 2008–10; pres Br Oncological Assoc 1992–94, pres Assoc of Cancer Physicians 2007–; NIHR sr investigator 2010–18; Cancer Research UK: tstee and memb Cncl and Research Strategy Ctee 2012–, chm Public Policy Ctee 2014–; pres European Cancer Concord 2014–17; Pfizer Excellence in Oncology Lifetime Achievement Award 2007; FRCP, FRCR, FMedSci; *Books* Hodgkin's Disease (1987), Confronting Cancer: Cause and Prevention (1993), Cancer in Adolescents (1995), Malignant Lymphomas (2002), Cell and Molecular Biology of Cancer (2005), Problem Solving in Oncology (2007), Problem Solving in Acute Oncology (2014), Problem Solving in Older Cancer Patients (2015), Problem Solving through Precision Oncology (2016); *Recreations* reading, music, walking; *Style*— Prof Peter Selby; ✉ Cancer Research Building, St James's University Hospital, Beckett Street, Leeds LS9 7TF (☎ 0113 206 5668, fax 0113 242 9886)

SELBY, Rona; *Educ* Beckenham GS for Girls, Univ of Exeter (BA); *m* 1978, David Selby; 1 s (Ben b 1983), 1 da (Tamsin Alexandra b 1985); *Career* The Bodley Head Publishers 1975–88 (memb Bd 1987–88), publisher Methuen Children's Books 1988–92, conslt S4C Wales 1992, children's book devpt conslt to BBC 1992–96, head of BBC Children's Publishing (Video, Books and Audio) 1996–97, fndr The Children's Media Consultancy 1997–2004, editorial dir Andersen Press Ltd 2004–14; *Books* Angela Anaconda: The Secret Life of Teachers (2002), Families and How to Survive Them (2002), Gordy Loves Gina (2003),Wallace and Gromit: Welcome to West Wallaby Street (2003); *Publications* articles on children's media published in The Author and The Bookseller; *Recreations* learning Mandarin, Chinese art and culture, travel, theatre; *Style*— Rona Selby

SELDON, Sir Anthony; kt (2014); *b* 2 August 1953; *Educ* Tonbridge, Worcester Coll Oxford (BA), LSE (PhD), KCL (PGCE, Blackwell Teaching Prize), PCL (MBA); *m*; 1 s, 2 da; *Career* research fell and tutor LSE 1980–82, head of politics Whitgift Sch Croydon 1983–89, head of history and sixth form gen educn Tonbridge Sch 1989–92, dep headmaster then actg headmaster St Dunstan's Coll Catford 1993–97, headmaster Brighton Coll 1997–2005, master Wellington Coll 2006–15; vice-chllr Univ of Buckingham 2015–; visiting fell Dept of Int History Univ of Kent 1992–94; founding dir Inst of Contemporary British History; historical advsr to orgns incl Rio Tinto-Zinc Corp; ed and fndr: Modern History Review, Politics Review, Contemporary Record, Making Contemporary Britain (book series); regular broadcaster and newspaper contrib; FRSA, FRHistS; *Publications* books incl: Churchill's Indian Summer (1981), By Word of Mouth (with Joanna Pappworth, 1983), Contemporary History (ed, 1987), Ruling Performance (ed with Peter Hennessy, 1987), Political Parties Since 1945 (ed, 1988), The Thatcher Effect (ed, with Dennis Kavanagh, 1989), Politics UK (jtly, 1991), The Conservative Century (ed, 1994), The Major Effect (ed with Dennis Kavanagh, 1994), The Heath Government 1970–1974 (ed with Stuart Ball, 1996), The Contemporary History Handbook (ed with Brian Brivati, 1996), The Ideas that Shaped Post-War Britain (ed with Davis Marquand, 1996), How Tory Governments Fall (ed, 1996), Major: A Political Life (1997), 10 Downing Street: An Illustrated History (1999), The Powers Behind the Prime Minister (with Dennis Kavanagh, 1999), Britain Under Thatcher (with Daniel Collings, 2000), The Foreign Office: An Illustrated History (2000), The Blair Effect 1997–2001 (ed, 2001), Public and Private Education: The Divide Must End (2001), Partnership not Paternalism (2002), Brave New City (2002), New Labour, Old Labour (ed with Kevin Hickson, 2004), Blair The Biography Vol I (2004), The Conservative Party: An Illustrated History (with Peter Snowdon, 2004), The Blair Effect 2001–05 (ed David Kavanagh, 2005), Recovering Power: The Conservatives in Opposition Since 1867 (ed with Stuart Ball, 2005), Blair Unbound. The Biography Vol II (2007), Blair's Britain (ed, 2007), An End to Factory Schools (2009), Trust. How we lost it and how we got it back (2009), Brown at 10 (with Guy Lodge, 2010), Why Schools? Why Universities? (Cass lecture 2010), The Great War and Public Schools (with David Walsh, 2013), The Independent School Problem (2014), The Architecture of Diplomacy, The Washington Embassy (with Daniel Collings, 2014), The Coalition Effect (ed with Mike Finn, 2015), Beyond Happiness (2015), Cameron at 10 (with Peter Snowdon, 2015), Downing Street: An Illustrated History (2016); regular book reviewer for academic jls and newspapers; *Recreations* drama, music, sport; *Style*— Sir Anthony Seldon; ✉ The University of Buckingham, Yeomanry House, Hunter Street, Buckingham MK18 1EG

SELF, William Woodard (Will); s of Peter John Otter Self, of Canberra, Aust, and Elaine, *née* Rosenbloom; *b* 26 September 1961; *Educ* Christ's Coll, Exeter Coll Oxford (MA); *m* June 1989 (m dis 1996), Katharine Sylvia Anthony, da of John Chancellor; 1 s (Alexis b June 1990), 1 da (Madeleine b Sept 1992); m 2, 1997, Deborah Jane Orr, *qv*; 2 s (Ivan William Scott b Sept 1997, Luther James David b Aug 2001); *Career* writer; columnist: The Observer 1995–97, The Times 1997–99, The Independent on Sunday 1999–2001, Evening Standard 2002–, New Statesman 2010–; Geoffrey Faber Meml Award 1992; prof of contemporary thought Brunel Univ 2011; *Books* The Quantity Theory of Insanity (1991), Cock and Bull (1992), My Idea of Fun (1993), Grey Area (1994), Junk Mail (1995), The Sweet Smell of Psychosis (1996), Great Apes (1997), Tough Tough Toys for Tough Tough Boys (1998), How the Dead Live (2000), Perfidious Man (2000), Sore Sites (2000), Feeling Frenzy (2001), Dorian (2002), Dr Mukti (2004), The Book of Dave (2006), Psychogeography (2007), The Butt (2008), Liver (2008), Walking to Hollywood (2010), Umbrella (2012); *Style*— Will Self, Esq

SELIGMAN, Mark Donald; s of Spencer Walter Oscar Seligman (d 2001), and Joanne Winifred Rhoda, *née* Bye (d 2010); *b* 24 January 1956; *Educ* Eton, Lincoln Coll Oxford (MA); *m* 17 April 1982, Louise Angela Mary, da of Sir Philip De Zulueta (d 1989); 1 s (Jocelyn David b 9 April 1983), 2 da (Lucinda Marie Joanne b 27 April 1985, Iona Louise b 22 Sept 1990); *Career* Price Waterhouse 1977–80, fin analyst Chloride Gp plc 1981–83, dir SG Warburg & Co Ltd 1989–95 (joined 1983); head UK investment banking BZW 1995; Credit Suisse First Boston: head UK investment banking 1997–99, dep chm Europe 1999–2005, chm UK investment banking 2003–05, sr advsr 2005–11; dep chm G4S plc 2011–15 (joined 2006), non-exec dir BG Gp plc 2010–16, sr ind dir Kingfisher plc 2012–; chm Corp Fin Ctee London Investment Bankers Assoc 1999–2001; memb Panel of Takeovers and Mergers 1999–2001 (alternate memb 2006–); memb Lord Mayor's Appeal Ctee 2003; memb Heart of the City Advsy Bd 2006–12, dir Industrial Development Advisory Bd 2005–12 (chm 2009–12); memb Regnl Growth Fund Advsy Panel 2011–15; chm Remuneration Ctee Lincoln Coll Oxford 2006–12, memb Rectors Cncl Lincoln Coll Oxford; co-pres Winchester House Sch Look to the Future Appeal 2005; tstee Aston Martin Heritage Tst 2004–11; Freeman City of London 2003, Immediate Past Master Worshipful Co of Int Bankers (Master 2014–15); ACA 1980; *Recreations* stalking, old cars, music; *Clubs* Northern Meeting, Beefsteak, Pilgrims; *Style*— Mark Seligman, Esq; ✉ 55 Victoria Road, London W8 5RH

SELIGMAN, Roderick; s of Madron Seligman, CBE, MEP (d 2002), and Nancy-Joan, *née* Marks (d 2012); *b* 16 November 1954, London; *Educ* Harrow Sch, Trinity Coll Oxford (capt Oxford Ski Team), INSEAD (MBA); *m* 15 October 2014, Susie Wesson; 1 s (Joe b 2000), 1 da (Emma b 2003); *Career* qualified CA Arthur Andersen, Lazard Bros 1985–88; former finance dir TVF plc; World Productions: commercial, legal and financial dir 1997–2004, md 2004– (television prodns incl: Ballykissangel 2001, Perfect Day 2005, Outlaws 2005, No Angels 2006, This Life 2007, Hancock and Joan 2008, United 2011, Line of Duty 2012, The Fear 2012, The Great Train Robbery 2013, The Bletchley Circle 2013, Code of a Killer 2014), The Secret Agent 2015, Dark Angel 2015, Line of Duty (series 3) 2016; Parly candidate Cons Pty 1983; memb ICAEW; *Recreations* skiing, photography, golf, sailing; *Clubs* MCC, Chelsea Arts, BAFTA, Hampstead Golf; *Style*— Roderick Seligman, Esq; ✉ 56 Cadogan Place, London SW1X 9RT

SELKIRK OF DOUGLAS, Baron (Life Peer UK 1997), of Cramond in the City of Edinburgh; James Alexander Douglas-Hamilton; PC (1996), QC (Scot 1996); disclaimed Earldom of Selkirk for life 1994; 2 s of 14 Duke of Hamilton and Brandon, KT, GCVO, AFC, PC (d 1973); *b* 31 July 1942; *Educ* Eton, Balliol Coll Oxford (MA, Boxing blue, pres Oxford Union, pres OUCA), Univ of Edinburgh (LLB); *m* 1974, Hon Priscilla Susan (Susie), *née* Buchan, da of 2 Baron Tweedsmuir (d 1996), and Baroness Tweedsmuir of Belhelvie (d 1978); 4 s (Hon John Andrew, Master of Selkirk b 8 Feb 1978, Hon Charles Douglas b 1979, Hon James Robert, Hon Harry Alexander (twins) b 1981); *Heir* s, Hon John Andrew, Master of Selkirk; *Career* offr TA 6/7 Bn Cameronians Scottish Rifles 1961–66, TAVR 1971–73, Capt 2 Bn Lowland Volunteers 1973; advocate 1968–76; MP (Cons) Edinburgh W Oct 1974–97 (Parly candidate (Cons) Hamilton Feb 1974); Scottish Cons whip 1977, a Lord Cmmr of the Treasy 1979–81, PPS to Malcolm Rifkind MP 1983–87 (as Min FO 1983–86, as sec of state for Scotland 1986–87), Parly under sec of state for home affrs and environment 1987–92 (incl local govt at Scottish Office 1987–89, additional responsibility for local govt fin 1989–90 and for the Arts in Scotland Sept 1990–92), Parly under sec of state for educn and housing Scottish Office 1992–95, min of state for home affrs and health (with responsibility for roads & tport and construction) Scottish Office 1995–97, appointed Scottish Cons spokesman for the Arts, culture and sport 1998; MSP (Cons) Lothians 1999–2007, chief whip and business mangr Scottish Cons Gp of MSPs 1999–2001, princ home affrs spokesman Scottish Cons Gp of MSPs 2001–03, Educn spokesman 2003–07; memb Scottish Select Ctee on Scottish Affrs 1981–83; chm Scottish Parly All-Pty Penal Affrs Ctee 1983; hon pres Scottish Amateur Boxing Assoc 1975–98; pres: Royal Cwlth Soc (Scotland) 1979–87, Scottish Nat Cncl UN Assoc 1981–87, Int Rescue Corps 1995–, Scottish Veterans Garden City Assoc 2003–, Trefoil House 2007; memb Queen's Body Guard for Scotland (Royal Co of Archers); patron Hope and Homes for Children 2002– (chm Edinburgh Support Gp 2002–07 (vice-chm 2007–09)); Hon Air Cdre No 2 Maritime HQ Unit (RAAF) 1995–99, Hon Air Cdre 603 (City of Edinburgh) Sqdn RAAF 1999–2015; cncllr Murrayfield and Cramond 1972–74; life memb Nat Tst for Scotland (memb Cncl 1977–82); *Books* Motive for a Mission: The Story Behind Hess's Flight to Britain (1971), The Air Battle for Malta: the Diaries of a Fighter Pilot (1981), Roof of the World: Man's First Flight over Everest (1983), The Truth About Rudolf Hess (1993), After You Prime Minister (2009); *Recreations* golf, forestry, debating, history, boxing; *Style*— The Rt Hon Lord Selkirk of Douglas, PC, QC; ✉ House of Lords, London SW1A 0PW

SELLAR, Irvine; *Career* fndr and chm Sellar Property Gp 1991–; creator, developer and shareholder London Bridge Quarter incl The Shard; *Style*— Irvine Sellar, Esq; ✉ Sellar Property Group, 110 Park Street, London W1K 6NX

SELLARS, John Ernest; CBE (1994); s of late Ernest Buttle Sellars, and late Edna Grace Mordaunt; *b* 5 February 1936; *Educ* Wintringham GS Grimsby, Univ of Manchester (BSc, MSc); *m* 20 Dec 1958, Dorothy Beatrice, da of late Maj Douglas Norman Morrison; 3 da (Karen b 1961, Fiona b 1962, Ann b 1964); *Career* res engr English Electric (GW) Ltd 1958–61, lectr Royal Coll of Advanced Technol (now Univ of Salford) 1961–67, head of mathematics Lanchester Coll of Technol 1967–71, head of computer science Lanchester Poly (now Coventry Univ) 1971–74, chief offr Business Educn Cncl 1974–83, dir and chief exec Business and Technology Educn Cncl 1983–94, dir City Technol Colls Tst 1989–94; London Guildhall Univ: govr 1994–2000, vice-chm of govrs 1995–2000, chm Fin and Employment Ctee 1995–2000; dir and tstee Gatsby Technical Educn Projects 1999–2005; memb Engrg Cncl 1994–95; memb RoSPA: Exec Ctee 1994–2002, Policy Ctee 1997–99, Fin Ctee 1997–2002; memb Br Accreditation Cncl for Independent Further and Higher Educn 1999–2002; hon fell Nene Coll of HE; Hon DUniv Sheffield Hallam Univ, Hon DTech London Guildhall Univ; *Recreations* walking, travel; *Clubs* Reform, Middlesex CCC, MCC; *Style*— John Sellars, Esq, CBE; ✉ 306 Cassiobury Drive, Watford, Hertfordshire WD17 3AW (☎ 01923 233055)

SELLERS, Paul; s of Joseph Sellers (d 1999), and Margaret, *née* Westland; *b* 16 August 1963, Fontainebleu, France; *Educ* Ampleforth, Univ of Manchester (BA), Univ of Leeds (MA), RSA (Dip); *m* 25 Aug 1995, Laura, *née* Clyde; 2 s (Tristan b 1 Nov 1997, Fabian b 29 Jan 2002); *Career* teacher Univ of Science and Technol China 1988–89, Br Cncl Milan 1990–93, Anglo-Mexican Cultural Inst Mexico 1993–95, Br Cncl 1995– (Barcelona, Cyprus, Madrid, Greece, UAE, currently dir S India); *Style*— Paul Sellers, Esq

SELLERS, Dr Susan Mary; da of Geoffrey Noel Sellers, of Esher, Surrey, and Mary McNeil, *née* Boswell; *b* 13 January 1949; *Educ* Birkenhead HS, Univ of Manchester (MB ChB, MD); *m* 16 July 1983, Andres Lopez, s of Andres Lopez Gil, of Murcia, Spain; 2 s (James b 3 Dec 1984, Teo b 10 Nov 1986), 1 da (Susannah b 24 May 1989); *Career* retired obstetrician and gynaecologist; registrar Southmead and Frenchay Hosps Bristol 1976–78; John Radcliffe Hosp Oxford: clinical lectr 1982–87, conslt 1988–2001; conslt obstetrician St Michael's Hosp Bristol 2001–14; former memb Expert Advsy Gp on AIDS, former chair Claims Advsy Ctee Medical Protection Soc, specialist advsr Care Quality Cmmn 2014–; FRCOG 1993 (MRCOG 1977); *Recreations* music, family, cookery, travelling, gardening; *Style*— Dr Susan Sellers; ✉ 8 Old Sneed Rd, Stoke Bishop, Bristol BS9 1ET

SELLEY, Clive; *Educ* Univ of Bristol; *Career* former chief exec BT Innovate & Design and chief info offr BT Gp, currently chief exec Openreach; *Style*— Clive Selley, Esq; ✉ Openreach, 123 Judd Street, London WC1H 9NP

SELLEY, Prof Richard Curtis; s of Harry Westcott Selley (d 1967), and Dorothy Joan, *née* Curtis (d 1999); *b* 21 September 1939; *Educ* Eastbourne Coll, Univ of London (BSc, PhD), Imperial Coll London (DIC); *m* 15 May 1965, Pauline, da of John Fletcher; 2 da (Helen b

S

24 Aug 1967, Andrea b 2 April 1969); *Career* Imperial Coll London: post doctoral res fell 1963–66, lectr in sedimentology 1966–69, reader in petroleum geology 1974–89, head Dept of Geology 1988–93, prof of applied sedimentology 1989–2000, emeritus prof in sedimentology and petroleum geology 2000–, sr res fell 2000–; visiting res fell Natural History Museum 1990–92; sr sedimentologist Oasis Oil Co of Libya 1969–71, sr geologist Conoco Europe Ltd 1971–74; dir: R C Selley & Co Ltd 1982–2000, Tooting Constitutional Club Ltd 1972–2007; chm SE Surrey Bench 2003–05 (dep chm 1999–2001); memb: Cncl Geological Soc of London 1992–97 (vice-pres 1992–94, hon sec Foreign and External Affairs 1994–97), Cncl Euro Fedn of Geologists 1994–97, Cncl Science and Technol Institutes 1994–97, Cncl Geologists' Assoc 2000–03; Hon DSc Kingston Univ 2006; hon memb Wine Guild of the UK 2005; Silver Medal Geological Soc of London 2003, Coke Medal Geological Soc of London 2010; hon memb Petroleum Exploration Soc of GB 2006; CGeol, FGS 1962, AAPG 1971, PESGB 1971, SPE 1981, JP 1981, EurGeol 2002, CSci 2004; *Books* Ancient Sedimentary Environments (1970, 4 edn 1996), Introduction to Sedimentology (1976, 2 edn 1982), Elements of Petroleum Geology (1985, 3 edn 2015), Applied Sedimentology (1988, 2 edn 2000), African Basins (1997), The Winelands of Britain (2004, 2 edn 2008, 3 edn 2015), The Box Hill and Mole Valley Book of Geology (2006); *Recreations* researching the geology of British vineyards; *Clubs* Chaps; *Style—* Prof Richard Selley, JP; ✉ Department of Earth Sciences and Engineering, Royal School of Mines, Imperial College, Prince Consort Road, London SW7 2BP (e-mail r.selley@imperial.ac.uk)

SELLS, Oliver Matthew; QC (1995); s of Sir David Perronet Sells (d 1993), of Royston, Herts, and Beryl Cecilia, *née* Charrington (d 1997); *b* 29 September 1950; *Educ* Wellington, Coll of Law London; *m* 30 Aug 1986, Lucinda Jane, da of Gerard William Mackworth-Young (d 1984), of Fisherton de la Mere, Wilts; 1 s (Hugo William b 17 June 1988), 1 da (Rosanna Mary b 30 June 1991); *Career* called to the Bar Inner Temple 1972 (bencher 1996); in practice SE Circuit, supplementary counsel to The Crown 1981–86, recorder of the Crown Court 1991– (asst recorder 1987–91); chm SE Circuit Liaison Ctee 2002-memb: Gen Cncl of the Bar 1977–80 and 1985–89, Cwlth Law Assoc; hon memb American Bar Assoc; dir Music for Charity; chm of tstees St Mary's Church Houghton-on-the-Hill 2000–, tstee Breckland Soc 2004–; *Recreations* shooting, cricket, fishing; *Clubs* Boodle's, MCC, Norfolk (Norwich), Royal W Norfolk Golf; *Style—* Oliver Sells, Esq, QC; ✉ 5 Paper Buildings, Temple, London EC4Y 7HB (✆ 020 7583 6117, fax 020 7353 0075)

SELLS, Prof Robert Anthony; s of Rev William Blyth Sells (d 1977), of Portsmouth, and Eleanor Mary Sells; *b* 13 April 1938, Leamington Spa, Warks; *Educ* Christ's Hosp, Univ of London Guy's Hosp (MB BS); *m* 1, 1964 (m dis 1976), Elizabeth Lucy, *née* Schryver; 2 s (Rupert William Blyth b 1967, Henry Perronet b 1968), 1 da (Katherine b 1970); *m* 2, 10 May 1977, Dr Paula Gilchrist, da of Stephen Muir (d 1988), of Denbigh, Clwyd; 2 s (Edward Anthony b 1981, Patrick David b 1982); *Career* lectr: Dept of Surgery Univ of London Guy's Hosp 1967–68, Dept of Surgery Cambridge Univ 1968–70; MRC travelling scholar Peter Bent-Brigham Hosp Harvard Univ 1970–71, dir Regnl Transplant Unit; conslt surgn: Royal Liverpool Hosp 1971, Liverpool HA 1978, ret; pres Liverpool Med Inst 1997–98; pres The British Transplantation Soc 1983–86, vice-pres The Transplantation Soc 1990–94 (cncllr 1982–88), chm Int Forum for Transplant Ethics 1995–2008, pres Moynihan Chirurgical Club 2000–01; conductor laureate Crosby Symphony Orchestra, memb Bd N Wales Int Music Festival 2005–, dir Royal Liverpool Philharmonic Soc 2006–12, fndr and dir Vale of Clwyd Singers 2010–; hon prof Univ of Liverpool (chair Immunology and Surgery Dept Faculty of Med); MA Cambridge Univ; Liveryman Welsh Livery Guild 2009; memb BMA 1962, FRCS, FRCSEd; *Books* Transplantation Today (1982), Organ Transplantation: Current Clinical and Immunological Concepts (1989); *Clubs* Moynihan Chirurgical (pres 2000–01); *Style—* Prof Robert Sells; ✉ Cil Llwyn, Llandyrnog, Denbighshire LL16 4HY (✆ 01745 710296)

SELOUS, Andrew; MP; s of Cdr G M B Selous, OBE, VRD (d 2007), of Langley, Norfolk, and Miranda, *née* Casey (d 1995); *b* 27 April 1962; *m* 28 Aug 1993, Harriet Victoria, da of late Jeremy Marston; 3 da (Camilla b 20 July 1995, Laetitia b 7 March 1997, Maria b 30 Oct 2000); *Career* MP (Cons) Bedfordshire SW 2001–; *Style—* Andrew Selous, Esq, MP; ✉ House of Commons, London SW1A 0AA

SELWAY-SWIFT, Paul; *b* 20 May 1944; *Educ* Allhallows Sch, Sloan Sch of Mgmnt MIT; *Family* 3 da; *Career* HSBC Gp: joined 1962, gp gen mangr Hong Kong and China HongKong and Shanghai Bank 1988–96 (appointed exec dir 1992), chm HSBC Investment Bank Asia until 1996, dir Hang Seng Bank until 1996, dep chm HSBC Investment Bank London 1996–98, chm Samuel Montagu 1996–98, chm HSBC Capital Markets India 1996–98, dep chm Guyerzeller Bank Zurich 1996–98; chm: Novae Group plc (formerly SVB Hldgs plc) 1998–, Singer and Friedlander Gp plc 2003–05 (non-exec dir 2000–05); non-exec chm Chivers Communications plc 2000–01 (non-exec dir 2000) currently dir: Alba plc, Asia Investment Corporation, Atlantis China Fund plc, Forman Hardy Hldgs Ltd (dep chm), Li & Fung Ltd, Temenos Gp AG; formerly dir: Cathay Pacific Airways Ltd, Hutchison Wampoa Ltd, Hong Kong Electric Co Ltd, Visa Int (Asia Pacific), Hong Kong Building and Loan Agency Ltd, Regent Int Hotels; formerly: chm Hong Kong Assoc of Banks, steward Royal Hong Kong Jockey Club, dir Hong Kong Trade Devpt Cncl, advsr Hong Kong SAR Land Fund; memb Sports Broadcasting Monitoring Ctee; *Recreations* golf, horse racing, rugby, fly fishing, wine, music; *Style—* Paul Selway-Swift, Esq; ✉ ; e-mail paul@selway-swift.com

SELWYN, Prof Julie; CBE (2016); *Educ* Univ of Wales (MSc), Univ of Bristol (PhD); *m* 30 Sept 1988, William Selwyn; 3 s (William b 26 April 1990, Anthony b 11 March 1992, Christopher b 20 Nov 1997); *Career* various social work posts in Avon CC, Wiltshire CC and Kent CC, prof of child and family social work Univ of Bristol 1993–; dir Hadley Centre for Adoption and Foster Care Studies; *Books* Selwyn J., Wood, M. and Newman T. (2016) Looked after Children and Young People in England: developing measures of subjective well-being. Child Indicators Research. First online DOI 10.1007/s12187–016–9375–1 Selwyn J & Meakings S (2015); *Publications* Beyond the Adoption Order: challenges, interventions and disruption (with S Meakings and D Wijedasa, BAAF 2015), Adolescent-to-Parent Violence in Adoptive Families (with S Meakings, British Journal of Social Work 2015), 'She just didnt smell right!' Odour and adoptive family life (with S Meakings, Adoption & Fostering 2015), Looked After Children and Young People in England: developing measures of subjective well-being (with M Wood and T Newman, Child Indicators Research 2016); *Style—* Prof Julie Selwyn, CBE

SELWYN GUMMER; see: Gummer

SEMPILL, 21 Lord (S 1489); James William Stuart Whitemore Sempill; s of Ann Moira, Lady Sempill (20 in line; d 1995), and her 2 husband Lt-Col Stuart Whitemore Chant-Sempill, OBE, MC, late Gordon Highlanders (d 1991); *b* 25 February 1949; *Educ* Oratory Sch, St Clare's Hall and Hertford Coll Oxford; *m* 1977, Josephine Ann Edith, da of Joseph Norman Rees, of Kelso; 1 s (Hon Francis, Master of Sempill b 4 Jan 1979), 1 da (Hon Cosima b 20 April 1983); *Heir* s, Master of Sempill; *Career* tobacco exec Gallaher Ltd 1972–80, brand mangr South African Breweries Johannesburg 1982–86; account dir: Bates Wells Pty Ltd (Advertising Agency) 1986–87, Partnership in Advertising Johannesburg 1988–90; client serv dir Ogilvy and Mather Cape Town 1990–92, trade mktg dir Scottish & Newcastle Breweries Edinburgh 1993–95, Angus Dundee Distillers plc 2001–03, dir of mktg Caledonian Brewing Co Edinburgh 2003–06, dir The Gathering 2009 Ltd; memb Standing Cncl of Scottish Chiefs 1996–; sat as cross-bench peer House of Lords 1996–99, prospective Parly candidate (Cons) Scottish Parl 1998–; chm Edinburgh N and Leith Cons Assoc 1999–2001; tour guide Clan Chief Tours; *Recreations*

walking, rugby, scuba diving; *Clubs* Royal Over-Seas League; *Style—* The Lord Sempill; ✉ 9 Westmill Haugh, Lasswade, Midlothian EH18 1BF (✆ 0131 531 9482, e-mail jamiesempill@gmail.com, website www.clanchieftours.com)

SEMPLE, Dr Colin Gordon; s of Dr Thomas Semple, and Elspeth Roubaix, *née* Dewar; *Educ* Loretto, BNC Oxford (MA), Univ of Glasgow (MB ChB, MD); *m* 31 March 1979, Elaine Elizabeth, *née* Rankin; 1 s (Alan b 1981), 1 da (Gillian b 1983); *Career* Southern Gen Hosp: conslt physician 1988–, assoc postgrad dean 2002–08; chm Specialist Advsy Ctee in Gen Med of the Jt Ctee of Higher Med Trg 1999–2003; author of various papers on diabetes and endocrinology; vice-pres RCPSGlas 2005–07 (hon sec 1998–2001); FRCP (Glasgow, Edinburgh, London); *Recreations* golf, fishing, gardening; *Style—* Dr Colin Semple; ✉ Diabetes Centre, Southern General Hosptial, Glasgow G51 4TF (✆ 0141 201 1100)

SEMPLE, Margaret Olivia (Maggie); OBE (2000); da of Robert Henry Semple, and Olivia Victorine Semple (d 1992); *b* 30 July 1954; *Educ* Shelburne Girls' HS London, UC Worcester, Univ of London (Advanced Dip), Univ of Sussex (MA); *Career* teacher Parliament Hill Girls' Sch London 1975–79, ILEA advsy dance teacher White Lion Centre London 1979–80, head of performing arts N Westminster Sch London 1980–88; Arts Cncl London: dir AEMS project 1988–91, dir of educn and trg 1991–97; nat prog dir of Learning Experience New Millennium Experience Co 1997–2001, chief exec and dir The Experience Corps 2001, sr assoc The King's Fund 2001–04, chm Nat R&D Centre Inst of Educn Univ of London 2004–10, chm Wellcome Wolfson Dana Centre Science Museum London 2004–11, owner Maggie Semple Ltd 2010–; res dir Extemporary Dance Theatre 1985–88; reader Open Univ; pres Laban Guild UK 1994–2000; external examiner Liverpool Inst for Performing Arts 1997–2000; memb Govt's Nat Advsy Gp for Continuing and Lifelong Learning, Civil Service cmmr 2001–07; chm Nat Youth Music Theatre 2001–12; memb Jury Bonnie Bird Choreographic Award 1991–97; memb Bd: Rambert Dance Co 1998–2006, Teacher Trg Agency 2000–03, The Roundhouse Tst 2000–06, The Women's Library 2000–04, The Arts Educnl Schs Tst 2000–09, De Montfort Univ 2000–09, Br Sch 2003–, Arts Cncl London 2003–06, South Bank Arts Centre 2011–; memb: Nat Curriculum Working Gp for Physical Educn 1989–90, Cwlth Inst Educn Ctee 1992–94, All Souls Gp Oxford 1994–2009, Further Educn Funding Cncl's Widening Participation Ctee 1995–97, e-Learning Task Force DfES 2002–03, Nat Policy Gp for the YMCA, Cncl of Europe's Expert Gp on Creativity and Youth Initiative, Cncl of Euro Cultural Centre of Delphi, Windsor Leadership Tst, Advsy Bd McDonald's Restaurants UK 2005–10, HM Ct Service 2007; non-exec dir Criminal Cases Review Cmmn 2011–; tstee: Barnado's 1997–2000, Nat Museums of Science and Industry (NMSI) 2003, Balance Fndn for Unclaimed Assets 2004–07, Br Library 2007–15; memb Cncl: RSA 1998–2003 (tstee 1992–98), Inst of Educn Univ of London 2003, City and Guilds 2006; chm Science Museum 2008–10, dir Sadlers Wells Theatre; memb Bd Southbank Arts Centre 2011; assoc memb Sr Common Room Exeter Coll Oxford; fell Br American Project (BAP) 1992–; UK expert on EC Kaleidoscope Ctee 1994–97; contrib to books and jls; Hon DEd De Montfort Univ; FCGI 2005; *Publications* Semple, Women, Fashion, Stories (2010); *Recreations* reading; *Clubs* The Club at the Ivy; *Style—* Dr Maggie Semple, OBE; ✉ 4 Goodwin's Court, off St Martin's Lane, London WC2N 4LL (mobile 07711 118386, e-mail maggie.semple@experience-corps.co.uk, website www.experiencecorps.co.uk and www.maggiesemple.com)

SENIOR, Grahame; s of Raymond Senior, of Huddersfield, W Yorks, and Evelyn, *née* Wood; *b* 21 October 1944; *Educ* King James Sch; *m* 10 July 1965, Prudence Elizabeth, da of William Holland; 2 da (Claire Elizabeth b 30 Oct 1967, Charlotte Elizabeth b 26 Sept 1980), 1 s (Adam Michael b 3 June 1970); *Career* mgmnt trainee then asst publicity exec Royal Insurance Group 1963–65, writer Radio Caroline 1965, copywriter Vernons 1965–66, devpt writer Royds 1966–67; Brunnings: copy chief 1967–69, creative dir 1969–73, md 1978–79; fndr Senior King Ltd 1980 (currently chm and chief exec), fndr MKA Films 1981, fndr Media Options Ltd (media independent) 1984 (currently chm); fndr and pres IN Int Network of Agencies; chm Bugscang & Associates Ltd, prop Howard's House Hotel Wilts 2009–, chm CREW Performance Enhancement 2010–; author of various articles and booklets on mktg, market targeting and tourism mktg 1973–87; chm Northern Publicity Assoc, organiser Northern NABS fundraising initiatives, fndr Liverpool Gold Medal Awards for Man of the Year; dir: Spaghetti House Restaurants Ltd, Associated Hotel Services Ltd; parish church warden, chm Friends of Tring Church, theological study to become a reader 2011–14, licensed min of religion C of E 2014; ACII 1965, MIPA 1967, MInstM 1969; *Recreations* dry fly fishing, gardening, ballet, tennis, painting, reading, wine, cooking; *Clubs* Reform, RAC, IOD; *Style—* Grahame Senior, Esq; ✉ Senior Partners, Greenways, Grove Road, Tring, Hertfordshire HP23 5PD (✆ 01442 822770, e-mail gsenior@seniorpartners.co.uk)

SENIOR, Dr Michael; DL (Gwynedd 1989); s of Geoffrey Senior (d 1957), of Glan Conwy, N Wales, and Julia Elaine, *née* Cotterell (d 1984); *b* 14 April 1940; *Educ* Uppingham, Open Univ (BA, PhD); *Career* writer and farmer; radio play The Coffee Table (1964); memb Bd of Tstees Civic Tst for Wales 1998–2004; Hon RCA 2000; *Books* Portrait of North Wales (1973), Portrait of South Wales (1974), Greece and its Myths (1978), Myths of Britain (1979), The Age of Myth and Legend in Heroes and Heroines (1980), Sir Thomas Malory's Tales of King Arthur (ed, 1980), The Life and Times of Richard II (1981), Who's Who in Mythology (1985), Conwy: The Town's Story (1977), The Crossing of the Conwy (1991), Son et Lumière Script: A Place in History (1991), Gods and Heroes in North Wales, a Mythological Guide (1992), North Wales in the Making (1995), Figures in a Landscape (part 1 1997, part 2 1999), Did Lewis Carroll Visit Llandudno? (2000), Llys Helig and the myth of lost lands (2002), Back from Catraeth (poems, 2002), The Standing Stones of North-Western Wales (2003), Did Prince Madog Discover America? (2004), Hillforts of Northern Wales (2005), Cromlechs and Cairns (2006), This Is Where You Live (2007), Faithful Hound (2009), Yr Wyddfa (2010), Gateways to Snowdonia (2012), The Vales of Clwyd and Llangollen (2013), The Vale of Ffestiniog (2014), Who Were The Druids? (2015); author of additional local history booklets 1982–99; *Recreations* hill walking, painting, croquet; *Style—* Dr Michael Senior, DL; ✉ Bryn Eisteddfod, Glan Conwy, Colwyn Bay, North Wales LL28 5LF; c/o David Higham Associates Ltd, 5–8 Lower John Street, London W1R 4HA

SENIOR, Robert; *b* 5 December 1964, Middlesbrough, Cleveland; *Educ* Univ of Durham; *m* Inge; 3 c (Lotte, Bas, Sanne); *Career* began career in advtg at Burkitt Weinreich Bryant; DMB&B: joined 1989, memb bd 1992–94; client services dir TBWA Simons Palmer 1994–98; co-fndr and managing ptnr Fallon 1998–2007, UK ceo SSF Gp 2007–11, EMEA ceo Saatchi & Saatchi Fallon Gp 2011–, worldwide ceo Saatchi & Saatchi 2015–; *Style—* Robert Senior, Esq

SENNETT, Prof Richard; s of Maurice Reid Sennett (d 1993), and Dorothy, *née* Vorontsov-Zhnezetsky; *b* 1943, Chicago; *Educ* Juliard Sch of Music, Univ of Chicago (BA), Harvard Univ (PhD); *m* 1982, Saskia, *née* Sassen; 1 c (Hilary b 1976); *Career* prof NY Univ 1972–97, dir NY Inst for the Humanities 1976–85 and 1997, chair and prof LSE 1998– (academic govr 2006–); chm UN Cmmn on Urban Studies 1988–93, pres American Cncl on Work 1993–97; Amalfi Award for Sociology 1999, Friedrich Ebert Award for Service to Social Democracy 1999, Hegel Prize 2008; Chevalier de l'Ordre des Arts et des Lettres (France) 1996; FRSL 1996, FRSA 2005; *Publications* incl: Flesh and Stone: The Body and the City in Western Civilization (1994), The Corrosion of Character: the Personal Consequences of Work in the New Capitalism (1998), Respect: The Formation of

Character in a World of Inequality (2003), The Culture of the New Capitalism (2006), The Craftsman (2007), Together: the Rituals, Pleasures, and Politics of Cooperation (2012); *Recreations* cooking, chamber music; *Clubs* Century Assoc (NY), Signet (Harvard); *Style—* Prof Richard Sennett; ✉ London School of Economics and Political Science, Houghton Street, London WC2A 2AE (☎ 020 7955 6076, fax 020 7955 7697, e-mail r.sennett@lse.ac.uk)

SENTAMU, Most Rev Dr John Tucker Mugabi; *see:* York, Archbishop of

SENTANCE, Andrew William; CBE (2012); s of William Thomas Wulfram Sentance, and Lillian, *née* Bointon; *b* 17 September 1958; *Educ* Eltham Coll London, Clare Coll Cambridge (MA), LSE (MSc, PhD); *m* 3 Aug 1985, Anne Margaret, da of Raymond Austin Penfold; 1 s (Timothy Michael b 4 March 1989), 1 da (Rebecca Louise b 21 March 1991); *Career* petrol station mangr Petrocell Ltd 1980–81, mgmnt trainee NCB 1982–83; CBI: economist with Economic Affrs Directorate 1986–89, dir economic affrs CBI 1989–93; sr res fell London Business Sch 1994–95, dir Centre for Economic Forecasting London Business Sch 1995–97, chief economic advsr Br Retail Consortium 1995–97; British Airways plc: chief economist 1998–2006, head of environmental affrs 2003–06; memb Cmmn for Integrated Transport 2006–10, memb Monetary Policy Ctee Bank of England 2006–11; sr economic advsr Pricewaterhouse Coopers 2011–; professorial fell Univ of Warwick 2006–; visiting prof of economics Royal Holloway Univ of London 1998–, visiting prof Cranfield Univ 2001–08; memb: RPI Advsy Ctee 1989 and 1992–94, CSO Advsy Ctee 1992–95, HM Treasy Ind Panel of Economic Forecasting Advsrs 1992–93, Cmmn on Wealth Creation and Social Cohesion 1994–95, NAPF Retirement Income Inquiry 1994–95, ONS Advsy Ctee 1996–99, Advsy Bd Air Transport Action Gp 2000–06; Soc of Business Economists: memb 1988–, memb Cncl 1991–2003, chm 1995–2000, dep chm 2000–03, fell 2001–, vice-pres 2013–; tstee: Harvest Help 1996–2006, Anglo-German Fndn 2001–09, BA Pension Funds 2002–06, BuilditInternational 2012–; FRAeS 2004; *Recreations* playing piano, guitar, writing and performing music; *Style—* Dr Andrew Sentance, CBE; ✉ e-mail andrewsentance@aol.com

SERGEANT, John; s of Ernest Sergeant (d 1985), and Olive Stevens, *née* Cook, of Devon (d 2004); *b* 14 April 1944; *Educ* Millfield, Magdalen Coll Oxford (BA); *m* 1969, Mary, *née* Smithies; 2 s (William b 1973, Michael b 1975); *Career* freelance writer and broadcaster; appeared with Alan Bennett in his comedy series On The Margin (BBC) 1966, trainee Liverpool Daily Post & Echo 1967–70; BBC TV and Radio: news reporter 1970–80, political corr 1980–88, chief political corr 1988–2000; political ed ITN 2000–02; assignments as reporter in 25 countries incl: Vietnam, Rhodesia, NI, Turkish invasion of Cyprus, Israeli invasion of Lebanon; also acting corr in Dublin, Paris and Washington; journalism incl travel pieces for Daily Mail; sometime presenter of Radio 4 current affrs programmes incl World at One, Today and PM, guest on light entertainment programmes incl Strictly Come Dancing 2008, QI, Parkinson, Room 101 as well as several appearances on Have I Got News For You, UK Theatre tour 'An Audience with John Sergeant' 2003–09, regular contrib to One Show (BBC), host Argumental (Dave) 2008–; presenter: John Sergeant's Tourist Trail (ITV) 2009, John Sergeant on Tracks of Empire (BBC) 2010, Britain's Flying Past: The Spitfire (BBC 2) 2011, Britain's Flying Past: Sea King (BBC 2) 2013, Britain's First Photo Album (BBC 2), Sergeant on Spike (ITV), Royal Greenwich (ITV), Barging Round Britain (ITV) 2015; appearances on Question Time (BBC TV) and Any Questions (BBC Radio); frequent after dinner speaker; winner Broadcasting Press Guild award for most memorable outside broadcast of 1990 (Mrs Thatcher interrupting live broadcast outside Paris Embassy to announce participation in second round of Cons Pty leadership ballot), winner Best Contribution to TV Award 2000 (Listener and Viewer Assoc); pres Johnson Soc 2003–04, memb Hansard Soc Cmmn on the Communication of Parliamentary Democracy; Hon DLitt Univ of Teesside, Hon DLitt Univ of Lincoln; *Books* Give Me Ten Seconds (memoirs, 2001), Maggie: Her Fatal Legacy (2005), Barging Round Britain (w David Bartley, 2015); author of play and short story for Radio 4; *Recreations* sailing; *Style—* John Sergeant; ✉ c/o Anita Land, Anita Land Ltd, 10 Wyndham Place, London W1H 2PU (☎ 07836 764139)

SERGEANT, Sir Patrick John Rushton; kt (1984); s of George Sergeant, and Rene Sergeant; *b* 17 March 1924; *Educ* Beaumont Coll; *m* 1952, Gillian, *née* Wilks; 2 da (Harriet, Emma); *Career* Lt RNVR 1945; asst city ed News Chronicle 1948, city ed Daily Mail 1960–84 (dep city ed 1953), fndr and md Euromoney Publications 1969–85 (chm 1985–92, pres 1992–); dir: Associated Newspapers Group 1971–83, Daily Mail and Gen Tst 1983–2003; Wincott Award Financial Journalist of the Year 1979; Freeman City of London; Domus fell St Catherine's Coll Oxford 1988; FRSA; *Books* Another Road to Samarkand (1955), Money Matters (1967), Inflation Fighters Handbook (1976); *Recreations* tennis, swimming, talking; *Clubs* RAC, Mark's, All England Lawn Tennis and Croquet, Queen's, Garrick; *Style—* Sir Patrick Sergeant; ✉ No 1 The Grove, Highgate Village, London N6 6JU; Euromoney Institutional Investor plc, 6–8 Bouverie Street, London EC4Y 8AX (*Tel* 020 7779 8879, e-mail psergeant@euromoneyplc.com)

SERMON, (Thomas) Richard; MBE (2010); s of Eric Thomas Sermon (d 1978), of Nottingham, and Marjorie Hilda, *née* Parsons (d 1969); *b* 25 February 1947; *Educ* Nottingham HS; *m* 10 Oct 1970, Rosemary Diane, da of Thomas Smith (d 1971), of Sheffield; 1 s (Thomas Christopher b 1971), 1 da (Catherine Marjorie b 1975); *Career* co sec Crest Hotels Ltd 1969–74, dep chm Good Relations Gp Ltd 1974–79; md: Shandwick Consultants Ltd 1979–87; chief exec: Shandwick Europe plc 1988–90, Shandwick International plc 1990–96; chm: Gryphon Corporate Counsel Ltd 1996–, Shandwick Consultants Ltd 1996–2000; PR advsr Goldman Sachs International 1992–96, sr advsr Agilitas Partners LLP 2011–; dir: Gryphon Ptnrs Ltd 1994–, Jardine Lloyd Thompson Group plc 1996–2006, Newmond plc 1997–2000, Defence Storage and Distribution Agency 1999–2006, Wrightson Wood Ltd 2002–05, The PBN Co Ltd 2003–08, Eloqui Public Relations Ltd 2003–09, Mgmnt Bd Def Acad of the UK 2007–10, China Eastsea Business Software Ltd 2008–09, Chairmen's Forum Ltd 2005–, IFB Research Fndn Ltd 2009–, VisionRe Ltd 2013–14, The UK Research Integrity Office 2013–; appointed memb PPP Healthcare 1994–98; vice-pres: RADAR 1987–, Providence Row 1997–; memb Nat Advsy Cncl on Employment of People with Disabilities (NACEPD) 1994–98; dir The City of London Sinfonia Ltd 1995–2001; chm: Fedn of London Youth Clubs 1996–2008 (hon treas 1995–96, dep chm 2008–09), The Home Improvement Tst 1997–2013; memb Cncl: Fndn for Mfrg and Industry 1994–98, City and Guilds of London Inst 1994– (memb Exec Ctee 1999–, jt hon sec 2005–, vice-chm 2013–); Sheriff City of London 2010–11; Freeman City of London 1968; memb Ct of Assts: Worshipful Co of Wheelwrights 1990 (Master 2000–01), Worshipful Co of Chartered Secs and Administrators 1991 (Master 2006–07); FCIS 1972, Hon FCGI 2004; *Recreations* shooting; *Clubs* City of London, City Livery, Mark's, Walbrook, Army and Navy; *Style—* Richard Sermon, Esq, MBE; ✉ Friars Well, Aynho, Banbury, Oxfordshire OX17 3BG (☎ 01869 810284, fax 01869 810634); Gryphon Corporate Counsel Ltd, Suite 1B, 17–20 Ironmonger Lane, London EC2V 8EP (☎ 020 7776 8828, fax 020 7323 9859, e-mail richardsermon@gryphoncorporate.com)

SEROTA, His Hon Judge Daniel; QC (1989); *b* 27 September 1945; *Educ* Univ of Oxford (MA); *m*; 2 da; *Career* called to the Bar Lincoln's Inn 1969; recorder of the Crown Court 1989–99, circuit judge (SE Circuit) 1999–; *Style—* His Hon Judge Serota, QC; ✉ Milton Keynes County Court, 351 Silbury Boulevard, Witan Gate East, Central Milton Keynes MK9 2DT (☎ 01908 302800)

SEROTA, (Hon) Sir Nicholas Andrew; kt (1999), CH (2013); o s of Baroness Serota (d 2002); does not use courtesy prefix of Hon; *b* 27 April 1946; *Educ* Haberdashers' Aske's, Christ's Coll Cambridge (BA), Courtauld Inst of Art London (MA); *m*; 2 da; *Career* regnl art offr and exhibition organizer Arts Council of GB 1970–73; dir: MOMA Oxford 1973–76, Whitechapel Art Gallery 1976–88, The Tate Gallery 1988–; chm VAAC British Cncl 1992–98 (memb 1976–98), cmmr Cmmn for Architecture and the Built Environment (CABE) 1999–2006; memb Olympic Delivery Authy 2006–12, memb Exec Bd BBC 2016–; tstee: Public Art Devpt Tst (PADT) 1983–87, Architecture Fndn 1991–99, Little Sparta Tst 1995–2008; Hon DArts: London Guildhall Univ 1990, Univ of Plymouth 1993; Hon DLitt: Keele Univ 1994, South Bank Univ 1996, Univ of Exeter 2000, London Inst 2001, Univ of Essex 2002, Univ of Cambridge 2016; Hon DUniv Wimbledon Sch of Art (Univ of Surrey) 1997; hon fell: Queen Mary & Westfield College London 1988, Goldsmiths Coll London 1994, Christ's Coll Cambridge 2002; sr fell RCA 1996; Hon FRIBA 1992; *Books* Experience or Interpretation: The Dilemma of Museums of Modern Art (1997); *Style—* Sir Nicholas Serota, CH; ✉ Tate, Millbank, London SW1P 4RG (☎ 020 7887 8004, fax 020 7887 8010)

SERRUYS, Andre Paul; s of Harry Serruys (d 2005), and Honor, *née* Shickle; *b* 5 November 1956; *m* 17 May 1997, Leticia, *née* Faez-Thope; 1 s (Jorge b 3 Sept 1994), 2 da (Annie b 16 Oct 1998, Ellie 17 Sept 2001); *Career* fndr SPC Hldgs Ltd 1995–; *Style—* Andre Serruys, Esq; ✉ Stanfield Hall, Norfolk NR18 9RJ; SPC Atlas Works, Norwich Road, Lenwade, Norfolk NR9 5SN (☎ 01603 872852 fax 01603 872793, e-mail andre@serruys.com)

SERVICE, Louisa Anne; OBE (1997); *née* Hemming; da of Lt-Col Henry Harold Hemming, OBE, MC (d 1976), of London, and Alice Louisa Hemming, OBE, *née* Weaver (d 1994); *b* 13 December 1931, Paris, France; *Educ* schs in Canada, France, USA and UK, St Hilda's Coll Oxford (MA); *m* 28 Feb 1959 (m dis 1984), Alastair Stanley Douglas Service, CBE, s of Lt Cdr Douglas Service (d 1976), of London; 1 s (Nicholas Alastair McFee Douglas b 9 May 1961 d 2013), 1 da (Sophia Alice Louisa Douglas b 20 April 1963); *Career* export dir Ladybird Electric 1955–59; dir Glass's Information Services Ltd 1971– (dep chm 1976–81, chm 1981–95); jt chm: Hemming Gp 1976–2011 (fin dir 1966–76, dir 2015–), Hemming Publishing 1985–; chm: Mayer-Lismann Opera Workshop 1976–91, Youth and Music 1990–2000, Jacqueline du Pré Music Bldg 2000–06; memb Cncl: Friends of Covent Garden 1982–2005 (memb Mgmnt Ctee 1982–95 and 1997–2002), Haydn/Mozart Soc 1990–92; memb Advsy Bd Rudolfe Kempe Soc; hon sec Women's India Assoc 1967–74, dep chm Paddington Probation Hostel 1976–86; chm: Hackney Juvenile Ct 1975–82, Westminster Juvenile Ct 1982–88, Hammersmith and Fulham Juvenile Ct 1988–92, Hammersmith and Fulham Family Proceedings Ct and Youth Ct 1992–94, Family Proceedings Ct and Youth Ct 1994–2001; memb: London Magistrates Cts Ctee 1995–2001 (chm Audit Ctee), Dept of Trade's Consumer Credit Appeals Panel 1981–2006, FIMBRA Appeals Tribunal 1989–92, Adjudication and Appeals Ctee Slrs' Complaints Bureau 1992–93; JP 1969–2001; tstee: Women's India Tst 1989–, Robert Mayer Tst 1990–2010, Performing Arts Lab 1996–99; judge Crime Writers' Assoc Historic Crime Fiction 2013; memb St Hilda's Coll Oxford Devpt Ctee, treas St Hilda's Coll Law Network 1998–2002; Cwlth Countries League: vice-pres 1992–2008, tstee Educn Fund 1992–2008, pres 2008–14, tstee 2013–, patron 2014; FRGS; *Recreations* music, travel, reading; *Clubs* Athenaeum (memb: Gen Ctee 2003–09, Exec Ctee 2004–09, Talks Dinners Ctee 2009–15, Music Ctee 2014–); *Style—* Ms Louisa A Service, OBE; ✉ c/o Hemming Publishing Ltd, 32 Vauxhall Bridge Road, London SW1V 2SS (☎ 020 7973 6404, fax 020 7233 5049)

SERVICE, Tom; *b* 1976, Glasgow; *Educ* Univ of York, Univ of Southampton; *Career* presenter Music Matters (BBC Radio 3) 2003–; music writer The Guardian 1999–; guest artistic dir Huddersfield Contemporary Music Festival 2005, chm Contemporary Music for All; *Publications* Music As Alchemy: Journeys with Great Conductors and their Orchestras (2012), Thomas Adès: Full of Noises: Conversations with Tom Service (2012); *Style—* Tom Service, Esq; ✉ Music Matters, BBC Radio 3, Broadcasting House, London W1A 1AA

SERWOTKA, Mark Henryk; s of Henryk Josef Serwotka, of Aberdare, S Wales, and Audrey Phylis Serwotka; *b* 26 April 1963, Cardiff; *Educ* Bishop Healey RC Comp Sch Merthyr Tydfil; *m* 6 April 2001, Ruth Louise, da of Robert Cockcroft; 1 da (Imogen b 6 Nov 1994), 1 s (Rhys b 26 June 1997); *Career* Public and Commercial Servs Union: lay rep 1980–2002, personal case offr 1995–98, gen sec 2001–; DHSS: clerical offr 1980–2000, exec offr 2000–02; *Recreations* sport, walking, reading; *Style—* Mark Serwotka, Esq; ✉ Public and Commercial Services Union, 160 Falcon Road, London SW11 2LN (☎ 020 7924 2727, fax 020 7924 6377, e-mail mark@pcs.org.uk)

SESSIONS, John Gibb; né Marshall; s of John Craig Marshall, of St Albans, Herts, and Esmé Richardson; *b* 11 January 1953; *Educ* Verulum Sch St Albans, Univ of Bangor (MA), RADA; *Career* actor; *Theatre* Liverpool Everyman: Chameleon Blue, A Midsummer Night's Dream; Phoenix: The American Napoleon, The Common Pursuit; Riverside Studios: Christmas Show, Salute to Doctor Johnson, Lives of the Great Composers, The Life of Napoleon; other credits incl: Limbo Tales (Gate), Waiting for Godot (Young Vic), One Flew Over the Cuckoo's Nest (Manchester Royal Exchange), Hamlet (Sheffield Crucible), Man is Man (Almeida), The Alchemist (Lyric Hammersmith), The Orton Diaries (NT), Die Fledermaus (Royal Opera House), Tartuffe (Playhouse), Chestnuts Old and New (King's Head), The Life of Napoleon (Albery), Travelling Tales (Haymarket and nat tour), The Soldier's Tale (Barbican), Daniel in My Night with Reg (Theatre Upstairs Royal Court and Criterion), Paint Said Fred (Royal Acad), The Soldier's Tale (Barbican, with LSO), Longing (Hampstead); *Solo Shows* at: Liverpool Everyman, Young Vic, Cottesloe, Royal Exchange, Gate; The Eleventh Hour (Donmar Warehouse) *Television* Channel 4 incl: Girls on Top, The Madness Museum, Porterhouse Blue, Gramsci, Whose Line Is It Anyway?, A History of Psychiatry, The Christmas Show; BBC: The Cellar Show, Saturday Review, Laugh I Nearly Paid My Licence Fee, Tender is the Night, The Lenny Henry Show, Jute City, Have I Got News for You, Life with Eliza, The Full Wax, Some Enchanted Evening, On the Spot, Tall Tales, Tom Jones, Likely Stories, In the Red, Stella Street (series I, II, III and IV), Splendour in the Grass: In the Footsteps of Wordsworth and Coleridge, The Man, Gormenghast, Randall and Hopkirk (Deceased), Murder Rooms, Well-Schooled in Murder; LWT: After Midnight, The Ackroyd Dickens; Yorkshire: The New Statesman, A Day in Summer; other credits incl: Boon (Central), Menace Unseen (Thames), The Treasure Seekers (Carlton), The Inspector Linley Mysteries, The Lost Prince, Judge John Deed, Midsomer Murders, Dalziel and Pascoe, George Eliot – A Life, Hawking, Absolute Power, QI 2005–06, The English Harem 2005, Jackanory Annivrsary Special 2006, The Moving Finger 2006, Low Winter Sun 2006, The Ronni Ancona Show 2006, New Tricks 2007, Hotel Babylon 2007, Reichenbach Falls (BBC 4) 2007, Oliver Twist 2007, Lewis 2010, Shameless 2012, Life Story 2012; *Radio* incl: New Premises, Whose Line Is It Anyway?, Beachcomber By the Way, Figaro gets Divorced, Poonsh, Aunt Julia and the Scriptwriter, Mightier than the Sword, The Reith Affair, Saturday Night Fry, Good Opera Bad Opera, The Destiny of Nathalie X, Season's Greetings, Reconstructing Louis, The Man Who Came To Dinner, The Haunting, The Titanic Enquiry, St Graham and St Evelyn, Pray for Us, In the Company of Men, The Possessed (BBC Radio 3), Atlee Confidential (BBC Radio 4), Hot Metal (BBC Radio 4), Zazie on the Metro (BBC Radio 4), From Russia With Love 2012, The Rivals 2013, Jonathan Strange and Mr Norrell 2014, Outlanders 2014; *Film* incl: Faith, The Sender, The Bounty, Gunbus, Whoops Apocalypse, Castaway, Henry V, Sweet Revenge, The Pope Must Die, Princess Caraboo, In the Bleak Midwinter, Pinocchio, My Night with Reg, Cousin Bette, A Midsummer Night's Dream, 1 of the Hollywood 10, The Gangs of New York, High Heels and Low Life, Flight of Fancy, Five Children and It, The Merchant of Venice, Stella Street: The Movie, Rag Tale, Funny Farm 2006, The

Good Shepherd 2006, Intervention 2007, Inconceivable 2008, The Last Station 2008, Dagenham Girls 2010, The Making of Plus One 2010, The Domino Effect 2010, The Real Joe McCarthy 2011, Filth 2012, The Silent Storm 2013, Mr Holmes 2015, Legend 2015, Florence Foster Jenkins 2015; *Recreations* socialising, reading, travelling; *Clubs* Groucho, 2 Brydges; *Style*— John Sessions, Esq; ✉ c/o Markham, Froggatt & Irwin Ltd, 4 Windmill Street, London W1P 1HF (☎ 020 7636 4412, fax 020 7637 5233)

SETCHELL, David Lloyd; s of Raymond Setchell (d 1967), and Phyllis Jane, *née* Lloyd (d 1952); *b* 16 April 1937; *Educ* Woodhouse GS, Jesus Coll Cambridge (MA); *m* 1, 11 Aug 1962, Muriel Mary, *née* Davies (d 2012); 1 da (Justine (Mrs Nicholas Panay) b 1967), 1 s (Andrew b 1970); m 2, 25 April 2015, Margaret Shirley, *née* Amphlett Lewis; *Career* Peat Marwick London 1960–64, Shawinigan Ltd 1964–71; mktg mangr Gulf Oil Chemicals (Europe) 1971–77 (vice-pres 1978–82), md Gulf Oil 1982–98; dir: RAF Personnel and Trg Cmd Bd 2000–06, Univ of Glos (chair 2002–07); hon doctorate Univ of Glos 2007; FEI (pres 1996–98), FCA; *Recreations* golf, music, theatre; *Clubs* Oriental, MCC, St George's Hill Golf, Cotswold Hills Golf, Rotary; *Style*— David Setchell, Esq; ✉ 8 Park Place, Cheltenham GL50 2QR

SETCHELL, Sir Marcus Edward; KCVO (2014, CVO 2004); s of Eric Headley Setchell (d 1980), of Cambridge, and Barbara Mary, *née* Whitworth (d 1992); *b* 4 October 1943; *Educ* Felsted, Univ of Cambridge, St Bartholomew's Hosp Med Coll (MA, MB BChir); *m* 1973, Dr Sarah Loveday, da of Vernon Alfred Robert French (d 1967), of Northwood, Middx, and Dr Margaret French, *née* Davies (d 1981); 2 da (Anna b 1974, Catherine b 1980), 2 s (Thomas b 1976, David b 1984); *Career* conslt gynaecologist and obstetrician: St Bartholomew's Hosp and Homerton Hosp 1975–2000, Whittington Hosp 2000–08, King Edward VII Hosp for Offrs; dir Fertility Unit Portland Hosp 1987–94, med dir Homerton Hosp 1994–97; surgn/gynaecologist to HM The Queen 1990–; regnl assessor Maternal Mortality Enquiry 1992–2010; speciality advsr (gynaecology) to Nat Patient Safety Agency 2003–06; chm Med Ctee King Edward VII Hosp 1998–2005; RSM: memb Cncl, pres Section of Obstetrics and Gynaecology 1994–95; memb Cncl RCOG 1994–2000; tstee and memb Cncl WellBeing 2003–, chm Voluntary Bd St Bartholomew's Hosp; Liveryman Worshipful Soc of Apothecaries; FRCS, FRCSEd, FRCOG; *Publications* Progress in Obstetrics and Gynaecology (1987), Scientific Foundations of Obstetrics and Gynaecology (ed, 1991), Reconstructive Urology (1993), Ten Teachers Gynaecology (1995), Ten Teachers Obstetrics (1995), MCQ's in Obstetrics and Gynaecology (1996), Shaw's Textbook of Operative Gynaecology (2001), Self-Assessment in Gynaecology and Obstetrics (2001), General Surgical Operations (2006); *Recreations* tennis, skiing, sailing, travel, gardening; *Clubs* All England Lawn Tennis & Croquet, RSM, Fountain, St Albans Medical, Garrick; *Style*— Sir Marcus Setchell, KCVO; ✉ 64 Wood Vale, London N10 3DN (☎ 020 8444 5266); 5 Devonshire Place, London W1G 6HL (☎ 020 7935 4444, fax 020 7486 3446)

SETH, Vikram; Hon CBE (2001); s of Premnath Seth, and Leila, also *née* Seth; *b* 20 June 1952; *Educ* Doon Sch Dehradun India, Tonbridge, Corpus Christi Coll Oxford (open scholarship, MA), Stanford Univ (MA, full fellowship), Nanjing Univ China; *Career* writer; sr ed Stanford Univ Press 1985–86; Guggenheim Fellowship 1986, Commonwealth Poetry Prize 1986, Sahitya Akademi Award 1988, W H Smith Literary Award and Cwlth Writers Prize (for A Suitable Boy) 1994; hon fell Corpus Christi Coll Oxford 1994; FRSL; Chevalier de l'Ordre des Arts et des Lettres (France) 2001, Padma Shri (India) 2007; *Books* Mappings (poems, Calcutta, 1982), From Heaven Lake – Travels Through Sinkiang and Tibet (1983, Thomas Cook Travel Book Award), The Humble Administrator's Garden (poems, 1985), The Golden Gate – A Novel in Verse (1986), All You Who Sleep Tonight (poems, 1990), Beastly Tales From Here and There – Fables in Verse (Penguin India, 1992), Three Chinese Poets (translations, 1992), A Suitable Boy (novel, 1993), Arion and the Dolphin (libretto, 1994), An Equal Music (1999), Two Lives (2005), A Suitable Girl (novel, 2012); *Recreations* Chinese calligraphy, swimming, music; *Style*— Vikram Seth; ✉ c/o David Godwin Associates, 55 Monmouth Street, London WC2H 9DG (☎ 020 7240 9992)

SETHI, Jyotin; bro of Sunaina Sethi, *qv*, and Karam Sethi, *qv*; *Educ* Haberdashers Aske's, Univ of Cambridge; *Career* private equity investor and restaurateur; dir Barclays Ventures 2003–13; co-fndr and md JKS Restaurants 2008–, co-fndr and dir Trishna Restaurants Ltd 2008–, dir Bubbledogs and Kitchen Table Ltd 2012–, co-fndr and dir Gymkhana Restaurants Ltd 2013–, dir Lyles Restaurants Ltd 2014–, dir Bao London Ltd 2014–, co-fndr and dir Hoppers Restaurants Ltd 2015–; *Style*— Mr Jyotin Sethi; ✉ JKS Restaurants, 67–69 George Street Marylebone, London W1U 8LT

SETHI, Karam; s of Harash Sethi, and Meenakshi, *née* Tandon; bro of Sunaina Sethi, *qv*, and Jyotin Sethi, *qv*; *b* London; *Educ* Haberdashers Askes, Univ of Nottingham; *m* Oct 2013, Tanya, *née* Ghai; *Career* chef and restaurateur; co-owner/fndr JKS Restaurants 2008–; owner: Trishna London 2008– (Michelin star 2012–), Gymkhana 2013– (Michelin star 2014–, Best Indian Restaurant National Restaurant Awards 2015), Hoppers 2015–; dir: Bubbledogs 2012–, Kitchen Table 2012– (Michelin star 2014–), Lyle's 2014– (Michelin star 2015–), Bao 2014–; *Style*— Mr Karam Sethi; ✉ JKS Restaurants, 67–69 George Street, Marylebone, London W1U 8LT

SETHI, Sunaina; da of Harash Sethi, and Meenakshi, *née* Tandon; sis of Karam Sethi, *qv*, and Jyotin Sethi, *qv*; *b* 31 October 1987, London; *Educ* Univ of Nottingham; *m* 24 Jan 2015, Karan Gokani; *Career* operations dir and wine buyer JKS Restaurants, gen mangr and sommelier Trishna Restaurants Ltd 2010–; Zagat 30 Under 30 2012, Imbibe Restaurant Personality of the Year 2016; *Recreations* cinema, music, opera, tennis, travel, walking; *Style*— Ms Sunaina Sethi; ✉ JKS Restaurants, 67–69 George Street, Marylebone, London W1U 8LT (Twitter @suesethi)

SEVER, Prof Peter Sedgwick; s of Harry Sedgwick Sever, of London, and Lillian Maria, *née* Moran (d 1990); *b* 23 July 1944; *Educ* Manchester Grammar, Trinity Hall Cambridge (MA, MB BChir), St Mary's Hosp Med Sch (Lord Moran schor), Univ of London (PhD); *Career* SHO: in gen med and cardiology St Mary's Hosp London 1969–70, in chest diseases The Brompton Hosp 1970; MRC jr research fell Dept of Biochemistry St Mary's Hosp Med Sch and hon med registrar to the Professorial Med Unit 1971–74, lectr in med and pharmacology St Mary's Hosp Med Sch and hon sr registrar St Mary's Hosp 1974–76, sr lectr in med St Mary's Hosp Med Sch and hon conslt physician 1976–89, prof of clinical pharmacology and therapeutics St Mary's Hosp Med Sch 1980– (Imperial Coll London since 1985); prog conslt Wellcome Tst/Kenya/St Mary's Research Unit 1980–85, chm Specialist Advsy Ctee on Clinical Pharmacology Jt Ctee on Higher Med Trg 1984–90, memb Br Heart Fndn Grant Awards Ctee 1988–92, govr Imperial Coll of Sci Technol and Med 1989–93, memb Exec Scientific Ctee Euro Soc of Cardiology 1991–93; ed: Clinical Science 1980–87, Jl of Hypertension 1983–89, Jl of Human Hypertension 1987, Jl of Drug Development 1988; jt ed-in-chief Jl of the Renin-Angiotensin Aldosterone System 2000–; co-chm Anglo-Scandinavian Cardiac Outcomes Trial; memb: Br Pharmacological Soc 1976, Int Soc of Hypertension 1978; sec: London Hypertension Soc 1977–85, Euro Blood Pressure Gp 1979–82; hon fell Trinity Hall Cambridge 2011–; pres: Br Hypertension Soc 1989–91, European Cncl for Blood Pressure and Cardiovascular Research 1998–99; memb Cncl Br Heart Fndn 2002– (chm Fellowships Ctee); fell Euro Soc of Cardiology, FRCP; *Books* Clinical Atlas of Hypertension (with Peart and Swales, 1992), Cardiovascular Disease – Practical Issues for Prevention (with Poulter and Thom, 1993), also editor of several books on cardiovascular disease and hypertension and author of over 300 papers on cardiovascular disease and clinical pharmacology; *Recreations* sport (tennis and rugby), theatre, travel; *Style*— Prof Peter Sever; ✉ Hedgerley House, Hedgerley, Buckinghamshire SL2 3UL; International Centre for Circulatory Health, Imperial College London, 59 North Wharf Road, London W2 1NY (☎ 020 7594 1100, e-mail p.sever@imperial.ac.uk)

SEVERIN, Prof Dorothy Sherman; Hon OBE (2003); da of late Wilbur Sherman, and late Virginia Sherman; *b* 1942; *Educ* Harvard Univ (AB, AM, PhD); *m* 24 March 1966 (m dis 1979), Giles Timothy Severin; 1 da; *Career* tutor Harvard Univ 1964–66, visiting lectr Univ of W Indies 1967–68, asst prof Vassar Coll NY 1968–69, lectr Westfield Coll London 1969–82, Gilmour prof of Spanish Univ of Liverpool 1982–2008 (emerita 2008–, ed Bulletin of Hispanic Studies 1982–2008); visiting prof: Harvard Univ 1982, Columbia Univ NY 1985, Yale Univ 1985, Univ of Calif Berkeley 1996; pro-vice-chllr Univ of Liverpool 1989–92; memb: NI HE Cncl 1993–2001, Int Courtly Lit Soc (former pres Br Branch), Peer Review AHRC 2005–09, Research Assessment Exercise Sub-Panel (Iberian) HEFCE 2005–08; founding chair Women in Spanish, Portuguese, Latin American Studies 2000–03; tstee: Modern Humanities Res Assoc 1979–2013 (hon treas 2009–13), Res Panel Humanities Res Bd Br Acad 1994–96, Junta Assoc Hispánica de Literatura Medieval 1997–99 (hon memb 2007–), Junta Convivio 2004–11, Junta Asociación Internacional de Hispanistas 2004–10; memb Assoc of Hispanists of GB and I, corresponding memb Real Academia Española; FSA; *Books* Celestina (edns 1969, 1987), Memory in La Celestina (1970), Diego de San Pedro, La pasión trobada (1973), La Lengua de Erasmo romançada por muy elegante estilo (ed, 1975), Diego de San Pedro, Poesía (ed with Keith Whinnom, 1979), Cosas sacadas de la crónica del rey Juan II (ed with Angus Mackay, 1982), Celestina with the Translation of James Mabbe 1631 (ed, 1987), Tragicomedy and Novelistic Discourse in Celestina (1989), Cancionero de Oñate-Castañeda (1990), The Paris Cancioneros (with F Maguire and M Garcia, 1993 and 1997), Witchcraft in Celestina (1995), Animals in Celestina (with Vicenta Blay, 1999), Two Spanish Songbooks (2000), Del manuscrito a la imprenta en la época de Isabel la Católica (2004), Religious Parody in the Spanish Sentimental Romance (2005), An Electronic Corpus of 15th Century Castilian Cancionero Manuscripts (with F Maguire, 2007), Religious Piety and Religious Parody (2013); *Style*— Prof Dorothy Sherman Severin, OBE, FSA; ✉ Modern Languages and Cultures, Cypress Building, University of Liverpool, Chatham Street, Liverpool L69 7ZR (☎ 0151 794 2774, e-mail d.s.severin@liv.ac.uk)

SEVERIN, Giles Timothy (Tim); s of Maurice Watkins, and Inge Severin; *b* 25 September 1940; *Educ* Tonbridge, Keble Coll Oxford (MA, BLitt); *m* 1966 (m dis 1979), Dorothy Virginia Sherman; 1 da; *Career* author, film maker, historian, traveller; expeditions: led motorcycle team along Marco Polo route 1961, river Mississippi by canoe and launch 1965, Brendan Voyage from W Ireland to N America 1977, Sindbad Voyage from Oman to China 1980–81, Jason Voyage from Iolkos to Colchis 1984, Ulysses Voyage from Troy to Ithaca 1985, First Crusade route by horse to Jerusalem 1987–88, travels on horseback in Mongolia 1990, trans-Pacific bamboo raft from Hong Kong 1993, Prahu voyage Eastern Indonesia 1996, Pacific Ocean travels in search of the white whale, Caribbean travels for castaway histories 1998; films: The Brendan Voyage, The Sindbad Voyage, The Jason Voyage, Crusader, In Search of Genghis Khan, The China Voyage, The Spice Islands Voyage, In Search of Moby Dick; Founder's medal RGS, Livingstone medal RGS (Scotland), Sir Percy Sykes medal RSAA; Hon DLitt: Univ of Dublin, UC Cork; *Books* Tracking Marco Polo (1964), Explorers of the Mississippi (1967), The Golden Antilles (1970), Vanishing Primitive Man (1973), The African Adventure (1973), The Oriental Adventure (1978), The Brendan Voyage (1978), The Sindbad Voyage (1982), The Jason Voyage (1985), The Ulysses Voyage (1987), Crusader (1989), In Search of Genghis Khan (1991), The China Voyage (1994), The Spice Islands Voyage (1997), In Search of Moby Dick (1999), Seeking Robinson Crusoe (2002), Viking (novel, 2005), Corsair (novel, 2007), Buccaneer (novel, 2008), Sea Robber (novel, 2009), The Book of Dreams (novel, 2012), The Emperor's Elephant (novel, 2013), Privateer (novel, 2014), The Pope's Assassin (2015); *Style*— Tim Severin, Esq

SEVERN, David Benjamin; s of Benjamin Henry Severn (d 1976), and Winifred, *née* Jackson (d 1985); *b* 17 June 1948; *Educ* Open Univ (BA); *m* 1 (m dis 1979), Claire Olivia Ann, *née* Grafe; m 2, Christine Mary, *née* O'Connor; *Career* formerly with: Barclays Bank, DHSS, Building Societies Cmmn, SIB, PIA, FSA; DG Assoc of Ind Fin Advsrs (AIFA), owner David Severn Consulting; govr Pensions Policy Inst; FRSA; *Publications* Safer Products (research report for Financial Services Consumer Panel), The Financial Ombudsman Service and Mortgage Endowment Complaints (report for the Financial Ombudsman Service), various articles for Money Management (FT business magazine); *Recreations* horse racing; *Style*— David Severn, Esq; ✉ e-mail david.severn.comment@gmail.com

SEVILLE, Prof Jonathan Peter Kyle; s of Peter Linton Seville, and Joan Kathleen, *née* Monks; *b* 5 February 1956, Aylesbury; *Educ* Gonville & Caius Coll Cambridge (entrance scholar, MA, MEng), Univ of Surrey (PhD); *m* 1994, Elizabeth Jane, *née* Pope; 2 da (Rosie Elizabeth b 1989, Alice Minnie Judith b 1993); *Career* chemical engr Res Div Courtaulds Ltd 1979–81; sr lectr Univ of Surrey 1991–94 (lectr 1984–91); Univ of Birmingham: prof of chemical engrg 1994–2008, head Dept of Chemical Engrg 1998–2008; dean of engrg Univ of Warwick 2008–11, dean and head Faculty of Engrg and Physical Sciences Univ of Surrey 2011–; visiting prof Univ of Br Columbia 1989–90, visiting prof Tech Univ of Denmark Copenhagen 1997–99, hon prof S China Univ of Technol Guangzhou 1999–2004; external examiner Universiti Putra Malaysia (UPM) 1999–2001, external examiner Univ of Mauritius 2003–07; co-fndr dir Particle Conslts Ltd; numerous consultancies incl conslt on particle technol Unilever Res 1985–2004; ed-in-chief Powder Technology 1995–2014; IChemE: memb Ctee Particle Technol Subject Gp 1985– (sec 1991–95, chm 1995–97), memb Pubns Ctee 1986–88, memb Product-Process Working Pty 1998–2000, memb Cncl 2003–09 and 2015–, chair Audit Ctee 2010–14, dep pres 2015–16, pres elect 2016–17; memb: Ctee Particle Characterisation Gp RSC 1984–88, Working Pty on Single Particle Light Interaction BSI 1985–86, Particulate and Coal Technol Sub-Ctee SERC 1988–91, Cncl Filtration Soc 1992–94 (memb Editorial Advsy Ctee Filtration and Separation 1992–94), Coll EPSRC 1994–, Steering Gp Particle Technol UK Forum 1998– (fndr memb), Exec Ctee Standing Conf of Profs and Heads of Dept of Chemical Engrg 1999–2006, Standing Ctee Educn and Trg Royal Acad of Engrg 2005–08 and 2013–, W Midlands Advanced Manufacturing Task Gp 2009–10, Advsy Bd Research Center Pharmaceutical Engrg Graz Austria 2010–; Engrg Cncl: memb Bd and tstee 2013–, chair Registration Standards Ctee 2015–; UK rep Agglomeration Working Pty Euro Fedn of Chemical Engrg 1994–2006; CEng, FIChemE 1997, FREng 2004; *Books* Gas Cleaning at High Temperatures (jt ed, 1993), Processing of Particulate Solids (jtly, 1997), Gas Cleaning in Demanding Applications (ed, 1997), Granulation (jt ed, 2007); author of numerous articles in learned jls; *Recreations* theatre; *Style*— Prof Jonathan Seville

SEWARD, Desmond; s of W E L Seward, MC (d 1975), and Eileen Bennett (d 2002); *b* 22 May 1935, Paris; *Educ* Ampleforth, St Catharine's Coll Cambridge (BA); *Career* author; Knight SMOM 1978, Knight Constantinian St George (Parma) 2001; *Books* The First Bourbon (1971), The Monks of War (1972, new edn 2000, Spanish trans 2004), Prince of the Renaissance (1973), The Bourbon Kings of France (1976), Eleanor of Aquitaine (1978), The Hundred Years War (1978, new edn 1996), Monks and Wine (1979, French trans 1982), Marie Antoinette (1981), Richard III (1983, new edn 1998), Naples (1984), Italy's Knights of St George (1986), Napoleon's Family (1986), Henry V (1987), Napoleon and Hitler (1988, Russian translation 1996), Byzantium (with Susan Mountgarret, 1988), Metternich (1991, German translation 1993), Brooks's: a social history (jt ed with Philip Ziegler, 1991), The Dancing Sun (1993); Sussex (1995), The Wars of the Roses (1995), Caravaggio (1998, Japanese translation 2000), Eugénie (2004), Savonarola (2006),

Jerusalem's Traitor (2009, Hebrew trans 2012), Wings over the Desert (2009), Old Puglia (with Susan Mountgarret, 2009), The Last White Rose (2010), The Demon's Brood (2014), Renishaw Hall: The Story of the Sitwells (2015); *Recreations* walking, France, Italy; *Clubs* Brooks's, Pratt's; *Style*— Desmond Seward, Esq

SEWARD, Dame Margaret Helen Elizabeth; DBE (1999, CBE 1994); da of Frederick Oldershaw, and Gwen, *née* Rappaporte; *b* 5 August 1935; *Educ* Latymer Sch London, London Hosp Dental Sch (BDS, FDS RCS, MCCD, MDS); *m* 5 May 1962, Prof Gordon Robert Seward, CBE; 1 da (Pamela Elizabeth b 31 May 1964), 1 s (Colin Robert b 9 Sept 1966); *Career* registrar Oral Surgery Dept and dental offr to the Nursing Staff London Hosp Whitechapel 1960–62 (resident dental house surgn 1959–60), sr hosp dental offr Highlands Gen Hosp London 1962–64, hon clinical asst Dental Health Study Unit London Hosp Med Coll 1967–75; locum conslt: Highlands Gen Hosp London 1969–70, N Middx Hosp London 1970; chief dental offr Dept of Health 2000–02; pt/t sch/community dental offr Cheshunt 1970–75, pt/t sr research fell Br Postgrad Med Fndn 1975–77, Cncl of Europe travelling fell The Netherlands 1978, ed Br Dental Jl 1979–92 (ed designate 1978–79); pres BDA 1993–94 (pres designate 1992), pres GDC 1994–99 (memb 1976–); ind dir Quality Assurance Agency in HE 1997–2000; vice-chm Standing Dental Advsy Ctee 1990–94 (memb 1984–94), vice-dean Bd of Faculty RCS 1990–91 (memb 1980–88), pres Section of Odontology RSM 1991–92; hon pres Women in Dentistry 1988–92; ed Int Dental Jl (Fédération Dentaire Internationale) 1990–2000; memb Advsy Bd DENPLAN 1999–2000 and 2002–; tstee EFFORT 1999–2000; memb: Br Paedodontic Soc 1969 (nat sec 1975–78), Br Assoc of Oral and Maxillofacial Surgns 1965, Br Assoc for the Study of Community Dentistry 1974 (fndr memb), Br Dental Eds Forum 1980 (chm 1983–85), Med Protection Soc – Dental Protection 2003–; hon memb Br Orthodontic Soc 1998; chm of govrs The Latymer Sch London 1983–94; author of various book chapters and of numerous papers in learned jls; hon memb American Dental Assoc 1992, fell American Coll of Dentists New Orleans 1994, hon fell Acad of Dentistry Int Vancouver 1994, hon fell Queen Mary & Westfield Coll London 1997–98; Hon DDSc Univ of Newcastle upon Tyne 1995, Hon DDS Univ of Birmingham 1995, Hon DSc Univ of Sheffield 2002, Hon DSc Univ of Portsmouth 2005, Hon DSc Univ of Plymouth 2011; Hon FDSRCSE 1995, Hon FDSRCPS 1998, Hon FRCA 2001, Hon FGDP 2001; *Books* Open Wide – Memoir of the Dental Dame (2009); *Video* Nothing but the Tooth (teething disturbances and treatment); *Recreations* walking, entertaining at home, United Reformed Church (Richmond Hill St Andrews Bournemouth); *Clubs* Lansdowne, RSM; *Style*— Dame Margaret Seward, DBE; ✉ 1 Wimpole Street, London W1M 8AL

SEWELL, Prof Herb; *Educ* Univ of Birmingham (BDS, MSc, PhD), Univ of Leicester (MB ChB); *Career* academic appts Univ of Glasgow and Univ of Aberdeen, prof of immunology Univ of Nottingham 1990– (head Div of Immunology until 2002, pro-vice-chllr (research) 2002–07); chair: Jt Ctee on Immunology and Allergy RCP and RCPath 1994–98, Special Advsy Ctee on Immunology RCPath; memb: UK Advsy Gp on Quarantine 1998, Advsy Cncl on Novel Foods 1998–2001, Cncl MRC 2004–11, Nuffield Cncl on Bioethics; UK rep WHO Consultation on Xenotransplantation, cmmr UK Meds Cmmn, non-exec dir Nottingham Univ Hosps NHS Tst 2013–17; Hon DDS Univ of Birmingham 2001, Hon DSc Univ of the WI 2003; FRCP, FRCPath, FMedSci; *Books* The Immunological Basis of Surgical Science and Practice (ed with Oleg Eremin, 1992), Essential Immunology for Surgeons (2011); *Style*— Prof Herb Sewell; ✉ Medical School, Queen's Medical Centre, Nottingham NG7 2UH

SEWELL, Prof John Isaac; s of Harry Sewell (d 1975), of Kirkby Stephen, Cumbria, and Dorothy, *née* Brunskill (d 1977); *b* 13 May 1942; *Educ* Kirkby Stephen GS, Univ of Durham (BSc, DSc), Univ of Newcastle upon Tyne (PhD); *m* 6 May 1989, Ruth Alexandra, da of Walter Baxter (d 1986), of Edinburgh; *Career* Univ of Hull: lectr 1968–76, sr lectr 1976–84, reader in integrated electronic systems 1984–85; Univ of Glasgow: prof of electronic systems 1985–2005 (emeritus prof 2005–), dean of engrg 1990–93, memb Univ Ct 2000–04; visiting research prof Univ of Toronto 1995; author of 161 publications; winner IEE J J Thomson Paper Premium 1992 (jtly); FIEE 1986, FIEEE 1992; *Recreations* climbing, swimming; *Style*— Prof John Sewell; ✉ 16 Paterson Place Bearsden, Glasgow G61 4RU (☎ 0141 586 5336); School of Engineering, University of Glasgow, Glasgow G12 8LT (☎ 0141 330 6125, fax 0141 330 4907, e-mail john.sewell@glasgow.ac.uk, website www.elec.gla.ac.uk)

SEWELL, Rufus Frederick; *b* 29 October 1967; *m* 1999, Yasmin Abdullah; *Career* actor; *Theatre* credits incl: Royal Hunt of the Sun, Comedians (both Compass Theatre Co), The Lost Domain (Watermill Theatre Newbury), Peter and the Captain (BAC), Pride and Prejudice (Royal Exchange Manchester), The Government Inspector, The Seagull, As you Like It (all Crucible Sheffield), Making it Better (Hampstead and Criterion), Arcadia (RNT), Translations (Plymouth Theatre NY), Rat in the Skull (Duke of Yorks), Macbeth (Queen's Theatre), Luther (NT), Rock'N'Roll (Royal Court and Duke of York) 2006 (Best Actor Critics Circle Awards 2006); *Television* credits incl: The Last Romantics (BBC), Gone to Seed (Central), Middlemarch (BBC), Dirty Something (Skreba), Citizen Locke, Cold Comfort Farm (Thames), Henry IV (BBC), Arabian Nights, Helen of Troy, Charles II: The Power and the Passion, John Adams, Eleventh Hour, The Pillars of the Earth, Zen, Parade's End; *Films* credits incl: Twenty-One, Dirty Weekend, A Man of No Importance, Carrington, Victory, Hamlet, The Woodlanders, The Honest Courtesan, Martha – Meet Frank, Daniel & Laurence, In a Savage Land, Bless the Child, A Knight's Tale, Extreme Ops, Tristan & Isolde, The Illusionist, Amazing Grace, The Holiday, The Tourist, Abraham Lincoln: Vampire Hunter, Hotel Noir, All Things to All Men, The Sea, I'll Follow You Down, Hercules; *Style*— Rufus Sewell, Esq

SEYFRIED, David John; *see:* Herbert, 19 Baron

SEYMOUR, Anya; *see:* Hindmarch, Anya

SEYMOUR, David; CB (2005); s of Graham Seymour (d 2011), and Beatrice (Betty), *née* Watson (d 1992); *b* 24 January 1951; *Educ* Trinity Sch Croydon, The Queen's Coll Oxford (open exhibitioner, BA), Fitzwilliam Coll Cambridge (LLB); *m* 1972, Elisabeth, da of Ronald and Muriel Huitson; 1 s (Nicholas b 16 Feb 1977), 2 da (Rachel b 10 June 1979, Charlotte b 21 Dec 1981); *Career* retired civil servant; law clerk Rosenfeld Meyer & Susman (attorneys) Beverly Hills Calif 1972–73; called to the Bar: Gray's Inn 1975 (Holt scholar, bencher 2001, memb Mgmnt Ctee 2012–15), NI 1997; Home Office: joined as legal asst 1976, princ asst legal advsr 1994–96, dep legal advsr 1996–97, legal advsr 2000–12; ind reviewer of justice and security in NI 2014–; legal sec (DG) to the Law Offrs 1997–2000; memb NI Criminal Justice Review 1998–2000; visiting lectr Sch of Law Univ of Connecticut 1986; govr Trinity Sch Croydon 2010– (chm of govrs 2015–), memb Ct of Govrs Whitgift Fndn 2015–; *Recreations* walking, watching cricket, gardening, golf; *Clubs* MCC; *Style*— David Seymour, Esq, CB; ✉ Home Office, 2 Marsham Street, London SW1P 4DF

SEYMOUR, Jane; da of late John Frankenberg, of Hillingdon, Middx, and Mieke, *née* van Tricht; *b* 15 February 1951; *Educ* Wimbledon HS, Arts Educnl Tst; *m* 1, 1971 (m dis), Michael John Attenborough, *qv*; m 2, 1977 (m dis), Geoffrey Planer; m 3, 1981, David Flynn, s of Lloyd Flynn, of Santa Barbara, California; 1 da (Katherine Jane b 1982), 1 s (Sean Michael b 1985); m 4, 1993 (sep), James Keach; 2 s (John Stacy, Kristopher Steven (twins) b 1995); *Career* actress; int ambassador Childhelp USA, ambassador UNICEF nat chm Cityhearts, active involvement in CLIC UK, hon chm RP Fndn USA (fighting blindness), hon citizen Illinois USA 1977; *Theatre* incl: Amadeus (Broadway) 1981, Not Now Darling (Canterbury Repertory), Ophelia in Hamlet (Harrogate Repertory), Lady Macbeth in Macbeth, Nora in A Dolls House; *Television* incl: The Onedin Line 1973, Strauss Family 1973, Captains and Kings 1976 (Emmy nomination), Seventh Avenue 1977, Awakening Land 1978, Battlestar Galactica 1978, Dallas Cowboy Cheerleaders 1979, East of Eden 1981 (Golden Globe Best Actress), The Scarlet Pimpernel 1982, The Haunting Passion 1983, The Phantom of the Opera 1983, The Sun Also Rises 1984, Dark Mirror 1984, The Leather Funnel 1984, Jamaica Inn 1985, The Hanged Man 1985, Obsessed with a Married Man 1985, The Woman He Loved (Golden Globe nomination) 1988, Onassis (Emmy Award) 1988, War and Remembrance (Emmy nomination) 1989, Jack the Ripper 1989, Angel of Death, Matters of the Heart, Are You Lonesome Tonight?; most recently Dr Quinn – Medicine Woman (160 episodes, Golden Globe winner), Sunstroke, Praying Mantis, A Passion for Justice – The Hazel Brannon -Smith Story, The Absolute Truth, A Marriage of Convenience, A Memory of the Heart, Murder in the Mirror, Enslavement – The True Story of Fanny Kemble, Blackout, Yesterday's Children; *Films* incl: Oh, What a Lovely War 1969, Sinbad and the Eye of the Tiger 1972, Young Winston 1973, Live and Let Die 1973, Four Feathers, Somewhere in Time 1980, Oh Heavenly Dog 1980, Lassiter 1984, Head Office 1986, The Tunnel 1987, Keys to Freedom 1989, Le Revolution Français, Swiss Family Robinson 1997, Dr Quinn the Movie 1999; *Books* Jane Seymour's Guide to Romantic Living (1987); This One and That One series: Yum (jtly, 1998), Splat (jtly, 1998), Boing (jtly, 1999), Eat (jtly, 1999), Me & Me (jtly, 1999), Play (jtly, 1999), Talk (jtly, 1999); *Style*— Miss Jane Seymour

SEYMOUR, Miranda; da of George Fitzroy Seymour, JP, DL (d 1994), of Thrumpton Hall, Notts, and Hon Rosemary Nest Scott Ellis, da of 8 Baron Howard de Walden; *b* 8 August 1948; *Educ* private sch, Bedford Coll London (BA); *m* 1, 1972 (m dis 1981), Andrew Sinclair; 1 s (Merlin b 1973); m 2, 1989 (m dis 2005), Anthony Gottlieb; m 3, 2005, Edward Lynch; *Career* writer; visiting prof Nottingham Trent Univ 1996; FRSL 1996, FRSA; *Books* for children: Mumtaz the Magical Cat (1984), The Vampire of Verdonia (1986), Caspar and the Secret Kingdom (1986), Pierre and the Pamplemousse (1990); The Madonna of the Island – Tales of Corfu (short stories, 1980); historical novels: The Stones of Maggiare (1974), Count Manfred (1976), Daughter of Darkness – Lucrezia Borgia (1977), The Goddess (1978), Medea (1981); modern novels: Carrying On (1984), The Reluctant Devil (1990), The Telling (1997, US edn The Summer of 39, 1999); other writing: A Ring of Conspirators – Henry James and his Literary Circle (biography, 1989, reissued 2004) Ottoline Morrell: A Life on the Grand Scale (1992, reissued 2008); Robert Graves: Life on the Edge (1995, reissued 2003), Mary Shelley: a Biography (2000), A Brief History of Thyme and Other Herbs (2002), The Bugatti Queen (2004), In My Father's House: Elegy for an Obsessive Love (memoir, 2007), Chaplin's Girl: The Life and Loves of Virginia Cherrill (2009); *Style*— Ms Miranda Seymour, FRSL, FRSA; ✉ c/o David Higham Literary Agency, 5–8 Lower John Street, London W1 (☎ 020 7437 7888, fax 020 7437 1072)

SEYMOUR, Prof Richard; s of Bertram Seymour, of Scarborough, N Yorks, and Annie Irenie, *née* Sherwood; *b* 1 May 1953; *Educ* Scarborough HS for Boys, Royal Coll of Art (MA(RCA)); *m* April 1980, Anne Margaret, da of Steven Hart; 1 da (Peggy Teresa b 12 June 1982), 1 s (Arthur William b 25 Sept 1985); *Career* product designer; freelance art dir within various London advtg agencies incl JWT, Holmes Knight Ritchie and Michael Bungey DFS 1977–79, creative dir Blazelynn Advertising London 1979–82 (various D&AD awards), freelance designer working specifically on advtg and new product devpt projects 1982–83, fndr designer Seymour-Furst specialising in film prodn design 1983–84, fndr (with Dick Powell, *qv*) Seymour-Powell 1984– (clients incl Yamaha, Tefal, Casio, Nokia, Ford and Aqualisa); external assessor BA Product Design course Central St Martin's Coll of Art and Design 1990– (memb Jt Course Advy Ctee Product Design Dept 1989–90), external examiner RCA Transportation Design course 1993–, visiting prof of product and transportation design RCA 1995–; inaugural product design judge BBC Design Awards 1987, memb Panel of Judges D&AD Product Design Section 1987, main speaker Blueprint Moving Up seminars 1988; memb: Exec Ctee Design Business Gp 1988–, Int Advsy Ctee Design Museum 1989–, Steering Ctee Lead Body for Design 1991–, Bd of Tstees Design Museum London 1994–, Exec Ctee D&AD 1997– (pres 1999); Hon Dr Coll for Creative Studies Michigan; FRSA 1993, FCSD 1993; regular contrib British design press; *Television* contrib BBC Design Classics, Designs on Britain and several children's progs featuring design and future thinking 1986, subject of Channel 4 Designs on Your... series 1998, Better By Design (six part series, Channel 4) 2000, Innovation Nation (BBC); *Awards* Best Overall Design and Product Design (for Norton F1 motorcycle) Design Week Awards 1990, D&AD Silver Award (for Technophone Cellular Telephone) 1991, ID Award and D&AD Silver Award (for MuZ Skorpion motorcycle) 1993, winner Product Design category BBC Design Awards 1994, CSD Minerva Award (for MuZ Skorpian) 1994, ID Award (for Sun Voyager) 1994, D&AD President's Award (for outstanding contribution to design) 1995, DBA Design Effectiveness Award 1995, 2002 and 2003, Special Commendation Prince Philip Designers Prize 1997, winner Janus (France) 1998, shortlisted Prince Philip Designers Prize 2003, Gerald Frewer Meml Trophy Inst of Engrg Designers 2003, Corp Film Samsung European Premium Design 2003, Star Pacic Award 2003; *Books* The Mirrorstone (conceived and designed 1985, words by Michael Palin, Smarties Award for Innovation in Book Design 1985, Hatchard's Top Ten Authors Award 1985); *Recreations* playing the cello, piano and organ, Early English music, motorcycles; *Style*— Prof Richard Seymour; ✉ Seymour Powell, The Factory, 265 Merton Road, London SW18 5JS (☎ 020 7381 6433, fax 020 7381 9081, e-mail design@seymourpowell.com, website www.seymourpowell.com)

SEYMOUR, His Hon Judge Richard William; QC (1991); s of late Albert Percy Seymour, and late Vera Maud, *née* Greenfield; *b* 4 May 1950; *Educ* Brentwood Sch, Royal Belfast Academical Instn, Christ's Coll Cambridge (scholar, De Hart prize, coll prize, MA); *m* 14 Aug 1971, Clare Veronica, da of Stanley Victor Peskett; 1 da (Victoria Jane Rebecca b 29 Aug 1979), 1 s (Edward Patrick James b 4 Nov 1981); *Career* called to the Bar Gray's Inn 1972 (Holker jr exhbn and sr scholarship); pupil barrister 5 Essex Court Temple 1972–73, chambers of R I Threlfall QC 1973, in practice 1973–2000, recorder of the Crown Court 1995–2000 (asst recorder 1991–95), judge of the Technol and Construction Court 2000–05, sr circuit judge (SE Circuit) 2000–, assigned to High Court of Justice (Queen's Bench Div) 2005–; pres Mental Health Review Tbnl 2000; govr Anglia Ruskin Univ 2011–; *Books* The Quantum of Damages (jt ed, 1975, 4 edn), Practice and Procedure for the Quantity Surveyor (contrib 8 edn, 1980), The Architect in Practice (contrib 6 edn, 1981), Courtroom Skills for Social Workers (with Clare Seymour, 2007), Courtroom and Report Writing Skills for Social Workers (with Clare Seymour, 2011), Practical Child Law for Social Workers (with Clare Seymour, 2013); *Recreations* archaeology, walking, foreign travel; *Style*— His Hon Judge Seymour, QC; ✉ Royal Courts of Justice, Strand, London WC2A 2LL

SHACKLE, Prof Christopher; s of Francis Mark Shackle (d 1943), and Diana Margaret, *née* Harrington (d 1990); *b* 4 March 1942; *Educ* Haileybury, Merton Coll Oxford (BA), St Antony's Coll Oxford (Dip Social Anthropology, BLitt), Univ of London (PhD); *m* 1 (m dis), Emma Margaret, *née* Richmond; 2 da (Mary b 15 Feb 1967, Zoe b 13 Sept 1974), 1 s (Guy b 16 April 1969); m 2, Shahrukh, *née* Husain; 1 s (Adam b 24 May 1982), 1 da (Samira b 16 July 1987); *Career* SOAS Univ of London: fell in Indian Studies 1966, lectr in Urdu and Panjabi 1969–79, reader 1979–85, prof of modern languages of S Asia 1985–2007, pro-dir for Academic Affrs 1997–2002, actg dir 2001, pro-dir 2002–03; Royal Asiatic Soc Medal 2006; FBA 1990 (memb Cncl 1995–96 and 2000–04); Sitara-i-Imtiaz 2005 (awarded by Pres of Pakistan); *Books* Teach Yourself Punjabi (1972), An Anthology of Classical Urdu Love Lyrics (1972), The Siraiki Language of Central Pakistan (1976), A

S

Guru Nanak Glossary (1981), An Introduction to the Sacred Language of the Sikhs (1983), The Sikhs (1984), Urdu Literature (1985), Ismaili Hymns from South Asia (1992), The Indian Narrative (1992), Qasida Poetry in Islamic Asia and Africa (1996), Hali's Musaddas (1997), Treasury of Indian Love Poetry (1999), Sikh Religion, Culture and Ethnicity (2001), SOAS Since the Sixties (2003), Teachings of the Sikh Gurus (2005), The Art of Spiritual Flight (2006), Stories of Mazhar ul Islam (2006), Bullhe Shah, Sufi Lyrics (trans, 2015); *Style*— Prof Christopher Shackle, FBA; ✉ 7 Hartley Court, Knole Road, Bexhill-on-Sea TN40 1LH

SHACKLETON OF BELGRAVIA, Baroness (Life Peer UK 2010), of Belgravia in the City of Westminster; Fiona Sara Shackleton; LVO (2006); da of Jonathan Philip Charkham, CBE (d 2006), of London, and late Moira Elizabeth Frances, *née* Salmon; *b* 26 May 1956; *Educ* Benenden, Univ of Exeter (LLB); *m* 26 Sept 1985, Ian Ridgeway, s of Lt-Col Richard John Shackleton, MBE (d 1977); 2 da (Cordelia Molly Louise b 25 May 1988, Lydia Elizabeth Moira b 6 July 1989); *Career* slr; articled clerk Herbert Smith & Co 1978–80, admitted slr 1980; ptnr: Brecher & Co 1981–84 (joined 1980), Farrer & Co 1986–2000 (joined 1984), Payne Hicks Beach 2001–; slr to HRH The Prince of Wales 1996–2005, slr to TRH Princes William and Harry of Wales 1996–; memb: Law Soc, International Acad Matrimonial Lawyers; govr Benenden Sch 1985–2007, tstee Endowment Fund ROH 2013–, memb Advsy Cncl London Philharmonic Orchestra 2013–; Citywealth Outstanding Individual of the Year Award 2008; Hon LLD Univ of Exeter 2010; *Books* The Divorce Handbook (with Olivia Timbs, 1992); *Recreations* bridge, food, opera and calligraphy; *Style*— The Baroness Shackleton of Belgravia, LVO; ✉ Payne Hicks Beach, 10 New Square, Lincoln's Inn, London WC2A 3QG (☎ 020 7465 4300, fax 020 7465 4380)

SHACKLOCK, Timothy Anthony (Tim); s of Anthony Shacklock (d 1976), and Netta Joan, *née* Payne (d 2010); *b* 12 July 1956, Nottingham; *Educ* Nottingham Boys' HS; *m* (m dis); 3 da (Antonia, Georgina (twins) b 26 Aug 1990, Daniella b 27 Oct 1995); *Career* CA 1980; Spicer & Pegler until 1980, Pannell Kerr Forster 1980–88 (ptnr 1985), dir Kleinwort Benson 1989 (joined 1988), head of corporate finance Dresdner Kleinwort Benson 1996–2001, dep chm Dresdner Kleinwort Wasserstein 2001–02, fndr and ceo Gleacher Shacklock 2003–; FCA; *Recreations* skiing; *Style*— Tim Shacklock, Esq; ✉ Gleacher Shacklock LLP, Cleveland House, 33 King Street, London SW1Y 6RJ (☎ 020 7484 1120, fax 020 7484 1160)

SHAFER, Prof Byron Edwin; *b* 8 January 1947; *Educ* Yale Univ (BA), Univ of Calif Berkeley (PhD, Peter B Odegard Prize); *m*; 1 s; *Career* resident scholar Russell Sage Fndn 1977–84, assoc prof of political science Florida State Univ 1984–85, Andrew W Mellon prof of American govt Univ of Oxford 1985–2001, acting warden Nuffield Coll Oxford 2000–01, Glenn B and Cleone Orr Hawkins prof of political science Univ of Wisconsin 2001–; memb Editorial Bd Jl of Policy History 1993–; ed The Forum: A Jl of Applied Research in Contemporary Politics; author of numerous pubns in learned professional jls; memb: American Political Science Assoc, American Historical Assoc, Political Studies Assoc UK, Br Assoc for American Studies; American Political Science Assoc: E E Schattschneider Award 1980, Franklin L Burdette Pi Sigma Alpha Award 1990, Jack L Walker Award 2000, V O Key Award 2007, Samuel Eldersveld Career Achievement Award 2015; Hon MA Univ of Oxford 1985; *Style*— Prof Byron Shafer; ✉ Department of Political Science, University of Wisconsin, Madison, WI 53706, USA (☎ 00 1 608 263 1909, fax 00 1 608 265 2663, e-mail bshafer@polisci.wisc.edu)

SHAFI, Dr Shuja; *b* 30 September 1943, Hyderabad, India; *m* 10 June 1970, Afsar, *née* Siddiq; 1 s (Faheem b 4 May 1971), 2 da (Bilquis b 27 Dec 1974, Amina b 1 April 1984); *Career* formerly dr, lectr, hospital conslt and clinical regnl post-grad advsr, dir Public Health Laboratory London 1991–2003; Muslim Council of Britain: joined 2000, dep sec-gen, sec-gen until 2016, currently chair Health and Medical Ctee, Healthcare Chaplaincy Ctee, Food Standards Ctee and Research and Documentation Ctee; lead conslt microbiologist Health Protection Agency 2003–08; distance learning module organiser London Sch of Hygiene and Tropical Medicine, regnl postgrad advsr RCPath; memb: BMA, Hospital Infection Soc, RSM; chair Halal Food Ctee BSI; memb Islamic Cultural Soc of Harrow, memb Hyderabad Deccan Assoc London; FRCPath (MRCPath); *Publications* over 80 pubns in medical jls incl Lancet and Int Jl of Infectious Diseases on hajj and health; *Recreations* gardening, reading, travel; *Style*— Dr Shuja Shafi

SHAFIK, Dame Nemat (Minouche); DBE; *b* Alexandria, Egypt; *Educ* Univ of Massachusetts-Amherst (BA), LSE (MSc), St Antony's Coll Oxford (DPhil); *Career* Dept for Int Devpt: DG country progs 2004–08, perm sec 2008–11, dep md IMF 2011–14, dep govr Bank of England 2014–; *Style*— Dame Nemat Shafik, DBE

SHAH, Bharat Kumar Hansraj; s of Hansraj D Shah, and Lalitaben H Shah; *b* 20 December 1949, Nairobi, Kenya; *Educ* Univ of Bath (BPharm); *m* 29 July 1974, Jayoti; 2 s (Hatul b 26 Oct 1978, Rajiv b 15 Jan 1985); *Career* Sigma Pharmaceuticals plc: retail pharmacy 1975–1985, wholesale and distribution of pharmaceuticals 1982–, md 1982–; memb: Pharmaceutical Soc of GB, Inst of Pharmaceutical Mgmnt; Ferris Gold Medal in Pharmacy, Glory of India Award, Ernst & Young Entrepreneur of Year (UK central region), GG2 Entrepreneur of the Year; memb Sigma Charitable Trust; hon doctorate Univ of Bath 2011; FRSA, fell Inst of Br Engrs, FRPharmS 2013; *Recreations* sports, travelling; *Style*— Dr Bharat Shah; ✉ Unit 1–7, Colonial Way, PO Box 233, Watford, Hertfordshire WD24 4YR (☎ 01923 444999, fax 01923 444998, e-mail bharat@sigmaplc.co.uk)

SHAH, Monisha; da of Amrit Shah, of India, and Rekha, *née* Pavagadhi; *b* 11 September 1969, Bombay, India; *Educ* Univ of Bombay (BA), SOAS Univ of London (MSc), London Business Sch (MBA); *Partner* Mark Young; 1 s (Rehan Alexander Coatsworth b 3 March 2009); *Career* BBC Worldwide: joined 2000, dir of sales emerging markets 2005–, acting dir of sales developed markets 2008–09; bd dir BBC World India, bd dir Worldwide Media Ltd, memb Bd Radio Mid-day West; tstee Tate 2007– (non-exec dir Tate Enterprises 2008–). young global ldr World Economic Forum 2009–; *Recreations* visual arts, media, current affairs, travel, food, dogs, books, Manchester United FC; *Style*— Ms Monisha Shah; ✉ Hogerty Hill, Lunghurst Road, Woldingham, Caterham CR3 7HE (e-mail hogerty.hill@live.co.uk); BBC Worldwide, MCIA3 Media Centre, 201 Wood Lane, London W12 0TT (☎ 020 8433 2000, fax 020 8433 3570, e-mail monisha.shah@bbc.co.uk)

SHAH, Naseem (Naz); MP; *Career* MP (Lab) Bradford W 2015–; *Style*— Ms Naz Shah, MP; ✉ House of Commons, London SW1A 0AA

SHAH, Navnit Shankerlal; *b* 9 December 1933; *Educ* Bombay Univ (MB BS), RCP (DLO), RCS (FRCS); *m* Frances, *née* Murphy; *Career* currently: hon conslt surgn Royal Nat Throat Nose and Ear Hosp London, hon conslt otologist Nuffield Hearing and Speech Centre London; former hon sr lectr Inst of Laryngology and Otology, hon prof Portmann Fond Bordeaux France, sr vice-pres Hearing Int; memb Sections of Laryngology and Otology RSM (pres Section of Otology 1990–91), former vice-chm and hon med advsr Cwlth Soc for the Deaf (latterly Sound Seekers); visiting prof in otolaryngology Madidol Univ Bangkok Thailand; formerly: vice-dean and chm Acad Bd Inst of Laryngology and Otology, sr lectr/dep dir Professorial Unit and chm Med Ctee Royal Nat ENT Hosp, pres Indian Med Assoc of GB; memb: Br Assoc of Otolaryngologists, Br Assoc of Audiological Physicians, BMA; FRSM; *Recreations* reading, current affairs; *Style*— Navnit Shah, Esq; ✉ 6 Holmdene Avenue, London NW7 2LX (☎ 020 8959 3711)

SHAH, Samir; OBE (2000); s of Amrit Shah, of Bombay, India, and Uma, *née* Chaudhary (d 1973); *b* 29 January 1952; *Educ* Latymer Upper Sch, Univ of Hull (BSc), St Catherine's Coll Oxford (DPhil); *m* 18 Dec 1983, Belkis Bhegani, da of Jan-Mohammed Hassam, of Kampala, Uganda; 1 s (Cimran Temur b 19 Oct 1986); *Career* Home Office 1978–79, LWT 1979–87, head of current affairs and political progs BBC 1987–98, ceo Juniper Communications 1998–; non-exec dir BBC 2007–10; special prof Univ of Nottingham 2006–, memb External Advsy Panel Humanities Div Univ of Oxford 2013–; chair Runnymede Tst 1999–2009; tstee and dep chair V&A 2004–; FRTS; *Clubs* Groucho; *Style*— Samir Shah, Esq, OBE; ✉ Juniper Communications, 52 Lant Street, London SE1 1RB (☎ 020 7407 9292)

SHAH, Sanjeev; *Career* fund mangr: Special Values PLC, Special Situations Fund, FIL Investments Int Ltd; *Style*— Sanjeev Shah, Esq; ✉ Fidelity Investments International, 25 Cannon Street, London EC4M 5TA

SHAHENSHAH, (Dr) Osman; *Educ* Brown Univ (BA), Columbia Univ (MA), Univ of Pennsylvania (PhD); *Career* fndr Afren plc 2004 (ceo 2007–); *Style*— Mr Osman Shahenshah; ✉ Afren plc, Kinnaird House, 1 Pall Mall East, London SW1Y 5AU

SHAKERLEY, Lady Elizabeth Georgiana; granted style, rank and precedence of an Earl's da 1961; *née* Anson; da of Lt-Col Thomas William Arnold, Viscount Anson (d 1958), and HH Princess Anne of Denmark, *née* Anne Bowes-Lyon (d 1980); sis of 5 Earl of Lichfield (d 2005); *b* 7 June 1941, Windsor (HM King George VI stood sponsor); *m* 1972, as his 2 wife, Sir Geoffrey Adam Shakerley, 6 Bt (d 2012); 1 da (Fiona Elizabeth Fenella b 1973); *Career* proprietor Party Planners; dir Mosimann's (a members only dining club); past pres Action for ME; ambass: DebRa (Middle East), Marco Pierre White, Grayshott Spa (Middle East); *Books* Lady Elizabeth Anson's Party Planners Book (1986); *Style*— The Lady Elizabeth Shakerley; ✉ 56 Ladbroke Grove, London W11 2PB (☎ 020 7727 7686, fax 020 7727 6001, e-mail ladyelizabeth@party-planners.co.uk and pa@party-planners.co.uk)

SHAKESPEARE, Nicholas William Richmond; s of John William Richmond Shakespeare, and Lalage Ann, *née* Mais; *b* 3 March 1957; *Educ* The Dragon Sch Oxford, Winchester, Magdalene Coll Cambridge (MA); *Career* asst prodr BBC TV 1980–84, dep arts/literary ed The Times 1985–87; literary ed: London Daily News 1987, Daily Telegraph 1988–91, Sunday Telegraph 1989–91; visiting fell All Souls 2016; FRS 1999, FRSL 1999; *Publications* The Men Who Would Be King (1984), Londoners (1986), The Vision of Elena Silves (1989, Somerset Maugham prize, Betty Tst Prize), The High Flyer (1993), The Dancer Upstairs (1995, American Library Assoc Award for Best Novel 1997), Bruce Chatwin (1999), Snowleg (2004), In Tasmania (2004, Tasmania Book Prize 2007), Secrets of the Sea (2007), Inheritance (2010), Under the Sun: the Collected Letters of Bruce Chatwin (ed, with Elizabeth Chatwin, 2011), Priscilla (2013), Stories from Other Places (2015); for television: The Waugh Trilogy (BBC), Return to the Sacred Ice (BBC), Iquitos (Channel 4), For the Sake of the Children (Granada, US Christopher Award), In the Footsteps of Bruce Chatwin (BBC), The Private Life of Dirk Bogarde (BBC, Best TV Documentary RTS Award 2001, Best Arts Documentary BAFTA 2001); *Recreations* travelling, drawing; *Clubs* Beefsteak, Literary Soc; *Style*— Nicholas Shakespeare, Esq

SHAKESPEARE, Stephan; *Educ* Univ of Oxford (MA); *Career* co-fndr and ceo YouGov 2000–, fndr PoliticsHome.com; chair Data Strategy Bd Dept for Business, Innovation and Skills 2012–13; memb Advsy Bd Oxford-Man Inst of Quantitative Finance 2014–; tstee Nat Portrait Gallery; *Style*— Stephan Shakespeare, Esq; ✉ YouGov, 50 Featherstone Street, London EC1Y 8RT

SHAKESPEARE, Prof (Sir) Thomas William; 3 Bt (UK 1942), of Lakenham, City of Norwich, but does not use the title; er s of Sir William Geoffrey Shakespeare, 2 Bt (d 1996), and Susan Mary, *née* Raffel; *b* 11 May 1966; *Educ* Radley, Pembroke Coll Cambridge (MA), King's Coll Cambridge (MPhil, PhD); *Family* by Lucy Ann Broadhead: 1 da (Ivy Connor Broadhead b 7 June 1988); by Judy Brown: 1 s (Robert Samuel Brown b 19 Nov 1988); m, 12 Oct 2002 (m dis 2008), Caroline Emily, da of Lloyd Bowditch, of Victoria, Aust; *Heir* bro, James Shakespeare; *Career* lectr in sociology Univ of Sunderland 1993–99, research fell in sociology Univ of Leeds 1996–99, dir of outreach Policy Ethics and Life Sciences Research Inst Newcastle 1999–2005 (research fell 2005–07); chair NE Regnl Arts Cncl and memb Arts Cncl England 2004–08; prof of disability research UEA; memb Nuffield Cncl on Bioethics 2004–; *Publications* The Sexual Politics of Disability (1996), The Disability Reader (1998), Exploring Disability (1999), Help (2000), Disability and Postmodernism (2002), Genetic Politics (2002), Disability Rights and Wrongs (2007), Arguing about Disability (2009); *Style*— Prof Thomas Shakespeare; ✉ e-mail tomshakespeare@blueyonder.co.uk; Medical School, UEA, Norwich Research Park, Norwich NR4 9JT

SHALE, Prof Dennis John; s of Samuel Edward Shale, of Leicester, and Winifred Beatrice, *née* Newstead (d 1986); *b* 19 February 1948; *Educ* Charles Keene Coll, Univ of Newcastle upon Tyne (BSc, MB BS, MD); *m* 1, 23 March 1970 (m dis 1993), Kathleen Patricia, da of Harry Clark, of Great Glen, Leics; 1 da (Victoria b 1975), 1 s (Matthew b 1978); m 2, 1 May 1993, Pamela Joan, da of Charles Lawrence, of Penarth, S Glamorgan; 1 s (George b 1994), 1 da (Rosie b 1996), 1 adopted da (Kate b 1987); *Career* lectr in physiology Univ of Newcastle upon Tyne 1976–78, jr trg posts in med Newcastle upon Tyne and Oxford 1978–81, sr registrar in respiratory med Oxford 1981–84, sr lectr in respiratory med Univ of Nottingham 1985–90, David Davies prof of respiratory and communicable diseases Univ of Wales Coll of Med 1991–; author of chapters in books on respiratory med and original articles in aspects of respiratory med incl shock lung and cystic fibrosis in int jls, contrib editorials and reviews to med jls; assoc ed Thorax 1986; hon regnl advsr to Cystic Fibrosis Tst; memb WHO Advsy Ctee on future mgmnt of cystic fibrosis; memb: Br Thoracic Soc 1983, Med Res Soc 1984, Societas Euro Pneumonology 1985, American Throacic Soc 1989; FRCP 1991 (MRCP 1980); *Recreations* gardening, archaeology, English and American literature, baroque music; *Style*— Prof Dennis Shale; ✉ University of Wales College of Medicine, Section of Respiratory Medicine, Llandough Hospital, Penarth, South Glamorgan CF64 2XX

SHALIT, Prof Jonathan Sigmund; OBE (2014); s of David Manuel Shalit, and Sophie Shalit, JP, *née* Gestetner; *b* 17 April 1962; *Educ* City of London Sch; *m* 31 Oct 2010, Katrina; 2 step-da (Jessica, Sofia); *Career* chm ROAR Global Entertainment + Management 1987–, chm Cole Kitchenn; prof Henley Sch of Business: Variety Club of GB (also vice-pres), Chickenshed Theatre Co; Freeman City of London, Liveryman Worshipful Co of Coachmakers and Harness Makers; MInstD; *Recreations* sailing, music, theatre, family, television, film; *Clubs* Annabel's, Ivy, RAC, Groucho, Soho House, 5 Herford St, Century, Arts, Electric, BAFTA; *Style*— Prof Jonathan Shalit, OBE; ✉ ROAR Global, ROAR House, 46 Charlotte Street, London W1T 2GS (Twitter @JonathanShalit)

SHAMTALLY, Bhye Mahmood (Danny); s of Hadjee Abdool Raffick Shamtally, of Mauritius, and Bibi Afroze, *née* Hisaindee; *b* 7 June 1951; *Educ* Mauritius Coll, Bhujoharry Coll, Univ of Durham Business Sch (MBA); *m* 19 Sept 1973, Carmelita Panaligan, da of late Francisco Panaligan; 1 s (Reza b 2 Dec 1976), 1 da (Natasha b 17 Jan 1979); *Career* staff nurse Belmont Hosp 1974–76, offr-in-charge London Borough of Sutton Social Serv 1977–85 (asst offr-in-charge 1976–77), princ ptnr Care Unlimited (Private Nursing Homes) 1983–; md Care Unlimited Gp Ltd; dir Solution Avant Ltd 1999–; memb: NSPCC, Nat Tst; gold friend Benjamin Waugh Fndn NSPCC; fell Durham Univ Soc 1994; RN 1974, FRSPH 1985, MCMI 1994, FIHE 1998, fell Royal Soc of Med 2013; *Recreations* country walks, antiques, collectors' cars, poetry; *Clubs* United and Cecil, Carlton, Rotary Reigate (pres 2009–10); *Style*— Danny Shamtally, Esq; ✉ Care Unlimited, Chaldon Rise Mews, Rockshaw Road, Merstham, Surrey RH1 3DB (☎ 01737 645171, fax 01737 644590, e-mail danny@careunlimited.co.uk)

SHAND, Dr Charles Stuart; s of Maj C W Shand, OBE, BEM (d 2006), and Sybil, *née* James (d 2005); *b* 10 July 1945, Stockton Heath, Cheshire; *Educ* Purbrook Park Liberal Arts Acad Portsmouth, The Sorbonne Paris (Dip, Leverhulme Tste Nat Sunlight Fellowship), North London Poly (MBA), Hendon Technical Coll (HND Mech Engrg, HND Chem Engrg, HND Textile Technol), INSEAD Fountainebleu and Magdalen Coll Oxford, Univ of Seattle (PhD), City of York Univ, Newcastle Univ (Dip); *m* 1977, Penelope Sue, da of Sydney John Valentine (d 1969), of Wimbledon, London; 1 s (Charles William Valentine b 1986); *Career* works mangr Emsworth Launderers & Drycleaners Ltd 1965–66, mktg mangr Patons & Baldwins Ltd 1966–70, dir Leo Burnett Ltd 1970–71, dir Childs Greene Public Relations Ltd 1971–73, md United Kingdom Sales Promotion Ltd 1971–73, jt md CGA Marketing Group Ltd 1971–73, dir/Euro mangr Young & Rubicam Group Ltd 1973–80, dir J Walter Thompson Ltd 1980–81, dir int mktg mangr Cadbury Schweppes plc 1981–84, dir of client servs Minale Tattersfield & Partners 1984–88, dir The Page Factory Ltd 1988–91, dep chm Field Wiley & Company Ltd 1988–91; chm: The Shand Group SC 1992–2003, Studio 36 International 1992–2003, Universal Shand Group Inc 2003–; non-exec chm Rowntree, James & Garner LLC 2008–; vice-chm Shand International Management Ltd 1986–; dir: Christian Shand BV 1995–2003, Mission Dynamics Group 1995–2003; involved with major design projects (corp and brand identities, new product devpt, architectural projects, etc); awards incl: 3 Silver Awards D&AD (for Irish Distillers Packaging, Gold Mastercard (NatWest Bank) and BP Int Packaging), 2 Certs of Distinction NY Art Dirs' Club (for Hundhaar Schnapps Packaging and Forte Hotels), Best Literature Award DBA/Mktg Design Effectiveness Awards (for MOMI), Best Brochure Award (for MOMI) and Best Poster Award (for Charlie Chaplin Exhbn, MOMI) NY Festivals; chm SwimStars Fndn 2003–, dir Team Swimstars USA 2007, chm SwimExcell SC 2008; chm Isabella Fndn 2014; memb Assoc of Masters in Business Admin, MIAA 1982, MIPR 1984, memb D&AD 1987, FInstD 1989, FRSA 1994; *Publications* The Italian Tomato Cookbook (jtly), Design a la Minale Tattersfield (jtly), The Best of British Packaging (jtly), The British and America (jtly), Sieze The Day (jtly), The Essence of A Man (jtly with David Weeks); *Recreations* cycling, gymnastics, motoring, swimming, triathlon; *Clubs* Cyclists Touring, Fellowship of Cycling Old Timers, Veteran Cycle, Headliners' (Austin TX, hon memb), Socio Merito, Societa del Passatore (Faenza), Velo Club St Raphaël (hon memb), Seattle Randonneurs, ZBW Delft, Marco Polo (Hong Kong), Cyclos Cyclotes – French Fedn of Cyclo Touristes, Gruppo Sportiva Modena; *Style—* Dr Charles Shand; ✉ Rowntree, James & Garner LLC, Scottsdale 16 B, Eversley Road, Surbiton, Surrey KT5 8BG (☎ 020 8399 8535, fax 020 8287 8096, e-mail swimstars@blueyonder.co.uk)

SHAND, Terence Richard; s of Terence James Shand, and Dorothy Joyce, *née* Shackell; *b* 27 October 1954; *Educ* Borehamwood GS; *m* 1 (m dis 1985) Maureen; 1 s (Elliot James b 1977); m 2 (m dis 1995), Arja, da of Paavo Saren; 1 s (Terence Elias b 1984), 2 da (Natalia Sirka b 1988, Eleanor Veronica Grace b 2000); *Career* dir Stage One Records Ltd 1978–83, chm Castle Communications plc 1983–97, chm and ceo Eagle Rock Entertainment Ltd 1997–; *Recreations* tennis, shooting, music, reading; *Clubs* Carlton, Saints and Sinners (London), Arts Club, Soho House; *Style—* Terence Shand, Esq; ✉ Eagle Rock Entertainment Ltd, Eagle House, 22 Armoury Way, London SW18 1EZ (☎ 020 8870 5670)

SHAND, William Stewart; s of William Paterson Shand (d 1990), of Derby, and Annabella Kirkland Stewart, *née* Waddell (d 1952); *b* 12 October 1936; *Educ* Repton, St John's Coll Cambridge (MA, MB BChir, MD); *m* 26 Aug 1972, (Anne) Caroline Dashwood (d 2005), da of late Patrice Edouard Charvet, of Cheltenham, Glos; 2 s (Robert b 1974, James b 1976), 2 step da (Claire b 1964, Sophie b 1966), 1 step s (Tom b 1967); *Career* hon consulting surgn Bart's and the Royal London Hosps 1997– (conslt surgn Bart's 1973–96); hon conslt surgn St Mark's Hosp for Diseases of the Colon and Rectum 1985–95; govr Sutton's Hosp in Charterhouse 1989–2009; Penrose-May teacher RCS (Penrose-May tutor 1980–85, memb Ct of Examiners RCS 1985–91); licensed reader C of E; memb Ct of Assts: Worshipful Soc of Apothecaries 1974 (Master 2004–05), Worshipful Co of Barbers 1981 (Master 2001–02); fell: Assoc of Surgns of GB and I, Hunterian Soc, Harveian Soc of London, Travelling Surgical Soc (pres 1994–97); FRCS 1969, FRCSEd 1970; *Books* The Art of Dying (jtly, 1989); *Recreations* stained glass window making, painting, fishing, walking; *Style—* William Shand, Esq; ✉ Fennel Cottage, 25 Station Road, Nassington, Peterborough PE8 6QB (☎ 01780 782933)

SHANES, Eric; s of Mark Shanes (d 1993), of London, and Dinah, *née* Cohen (d 1977); *b* 21 October 1944; *Educ* Whittingehame Coll Brighton, Regent Street Poly Sch of Art, Chelsea Sch of Art (DipAD); *m* Jacky, da of Kenneth Darville (d 1969), of Windsor; 1 da (Anna b 1976), 1 s (Mark b 1979); *Career* author, journalist and artist; classical music critic Daily Mail 1988–89, numerous contribs to Burlington Magazine, Apollo, and Modern Painters jls; fndr ed: Turner Studies, Art Book Review; lectr: Chelsea Sch of Art (pt/t) 1966–88, Dept of Art History Univ of Cambridge, Royal Coll of Music; lecture tours: N America 1982, 1983, 1984, 1986 and 2002, Switzerland 1987, Malaysia 1988; Br Cncl Cultural Exchange award as official visitor: Romania 1982, Czechoslovakia 1984; Yorkshire Post Art Book award 1979; vice-pres Turner Soc 1994– (chm 1988–94 and 2000–08); awarded Nuclear Electric scholarship 1995 (to research and exhibit Turner's Colour-Beginnings at Tate Gallery 1997); fndr chm Save Acton Swimming Baths campaign; *Exhibitions* numerous studio shows of paintings and prints; Splinter Gallery London 1992, Wall-to-Wall Gallery London 2004; guest exhibition curator: J M W Turner – the Foundations of Genius (Taft Museum Cincinnati) 1986, Masterpieces of English Watercolour from the Hickman Bacon Collection and the Fitzwilliam Museum Cambridge (touring Japan) 1990–91, Turner's Watercolour Explorations (Tate Gallery) 1997, Turner in 1066 Country (Hastings Art Gallery) 1998, J M W Turner: The Great Watercolours (Royal Acad of Arts London) 2000–01, The Golden Age of Watercolours: The Hickman Bacon Collection (Dulwich Picture Gallery) 2001–02, Yale Center for British Art 2002, Winslow Homer, Poet of the Sea (Dulwich Picture Gallery) 2006; *Books* Turner's Picturesque Views in England and Wales (1979), Turner's Rivers, Harbours and Coasts (1981), The Genius of the Royal Academy (1981), Hockney Posters (1987), Constantin Brancusi (1989), Turner's England (1990), Turner: The Masterworks (1990), Turner's Human Landscape (1990), Dali: The Masterworks (1990), Warhol: The Masterworks (1991), Jack Beal: American Realist (1992), Turner: The Master Painter (1992), Warhol: The Master Painter (1993), Dali: The Master Painter (1994), Impressionist London (1994), Jake's Legacy: A History of Whittingehame College (2000), Turner: The Life and Masterworks (2004), Warhol: The Life and Masterworks (2004), The Pop Art Tradition (2007), The Life and Masterworks of J M W Turner (2008), JMW Turner, A Life in Art I: Young Mr Turner, The First Forty Years 1775–1815 (2016); photographic essay in Gustav Mahler: Songs and Symphonies of Death (Donald Mitchell, 1985); *Recreations* music appreciation, swimming; *Style—* Eric Shanes, Esq; ✉ 7 Cumberland Road, Acton, London W3 6EX (☎ 020 8992 7985, e-mail ericshanes@aol.com, website www.ericshanes.com)

SHANKS, Duncan Faichney; s of Duncan Faichney Shanks (d 1956), of Uddingston, Strathclyde, and Elizabeth Provan, *née* Clark (d 1943); *b* 30 August 1937; *Educ* Uddingston GS, Glasgow Sch of Art (post dip, travelling scholarship to Italy); *m* 1 Aug 1966, Una Brown, da of Laurence George Gordon (d 1965), of Hartwood, Strathclyde; *Career* pt/t lectr Glasgow Sch of Art 1962–79, full time artist 1979–; memb RGI 1982, RSW 1987, RSA 1990 (ARSA 1972); *Recreations* music; *Style—* Duncan Shanks, Esq, RSA

SHANKS, Prof Ian Alexander; OBE (2012); s of Alexander Shanks, of Dumbarton, and Isabella Affleck, *née* Beaton; *b* 22 June 1948; *Educ* Dumbarton Acad, Univ of Glasgow (BSc), CNAA (PhD); *m* 14 May 1971, Janice Smillie, da of J Coulter, of Dumbarton, Dunbartonshire; 1 da (Emma b 1977); *Career* projects mangr Scottish Colorfoto Labs Alexandria 1970–72, princ sci offr RSRE Malvern 1973–82, princ scientist Unilever Research 1982–86, visiting prof of electrical and electronic engrg Univ of Glasgow 1985–, chief scientist Thorn EMI plc 1986–94; vice-pres physical and engrg sciences Unilever 2001–03; memb: Optoelectronics Ctee The Rank Prize Funds 1985–, Steering Gp for Science and Engrg Policy Studies Unit 1988–90, Sci Consultative Gp BBC 1989–91, Advsy Bd for the Res Cncls (ABRC) 1990–93, Royal Soc/Royal Acad of Engrg Science Advsy Gp for the Nat Physical Laboratory 1998–2007 (chm 2008–14), Advsy Bd for Inst of Nanotechnology 2001–06, Pres Assoc for Science Educn Scotland 2007–08; memb Cncl and vice-pres The Royal Soc 1989–91; chm Inter-Agency Ctee on Marine Science and Technol 1991–93; Clifford Paterson medal Inst of Physics 1984; Hon DEng Univ of Glasgow 2002; FIEE, FRS 1984, FREng 1992, FRSA 1993, FRSE 2000, Hon FIoN (hon fell Inst of Nanotechnology) 2005; *Recreations* music, antique clocks and pocket watches, Art Deco sculpture; *Style—* Prof Ian Shanks, OBE, FRS, FREng, FRSE; ✉ 23 Reres Road, Broughty Ferry DD5 2QA (e-mail ianshanks@mail.com)

SHANNON, Jim; MP; s of Richard James Shannon, and Mona Rhoda Rebecca, *née* Hamilton; *b* 25 March 1955; *Educ* Coleraine Academical Inst; *m* 6 June 1987, Sandra, da of Robert George; 3 s (Jamie b 3 March 1988, Ian b 29 Aug 1991, Luke b 10 June 1993); *Career* Ulster Def Regt 1973–74 and 1975–77 (GSM), 102 Royal Artillery Air-Def 1977–88; joined DUP 1977; memb Ards Cncl 1985– (mayor 1991–92), memb NI Forum for Political Dialogue 1996–98; MLA (DUP) Strangford 1998–2010, MP (DUP) Strangford 2010–; Apprentice Boys of Derry (Comber), sec Loyal Orange Inst Kircubbin LOL 1900, past dist master Royal Black Preceptory No 11 Dist, sec Royal Black Preceptory Ballywalter No 675; memb: Millisle branch Royal Br Legion, NSPCC, Mid Ards branch Ulster Farmers Union, Ulster-Scots Language Soc, Countryside Alliance 1973–, BASC; *Recreations* field sports, football, conservation, Ulster-Scots language; *Clubs* Carrowdore Shooting; *Style—* Jim Shannon, Esq, MP; ✉ Strangford Lodge, 40 Portaferry Road, Kircubbin BT22 2RY (☎ 028 4278 8581, fax 028 4278 8581, e-mail jim.shannon1@btopenworld.com); 34A Francis Street, Newtownards BT23 7DN (☎ 028 9182 7990, fax 028 9182 7991)

SHANNON, Keith; *m* Kate, *née* Levesley; *Career* diplomat; asst desk offr EC Dept (Internal) FCO 1989–90, desk offr Latin America Dept FCO 1990–91, 3 sec (aid/commercial) Maputo 1991–94, 2 sec (technol) Paris 1995–99, head of section Drugs and Int Crime Dept FCO 1999–2002, head of section Financial Planning and Performance Dept FCO 2002–03, dep head of mission and HM consul Vilnius 2004–08, ambass to Moldova 2009–13, dep dir of foreign policy Nat Security Secretariat Cabinet Office 2013, dep dir Eastern Europe and Central Asia Directorate FCO 2014–; *Style—* Mr Keith Shannon; ✉ c/o FCO, King Charles Street, London SW1A 2AH

SHAO, En; *b* 1954, Tianjin, China; *Educ* Beijing Centre Music Conservatory, RNCM (Lord Rhodes fellow); *Career* conductor; made to stop music studies due to Cultural Revolution 1966–70; awarded first Eduard Van Beinum Fndn Scholarship 1988, winner Hungarian Television Int Conductor's Competition 1989; second princ conductor Chinese Broadcasting Symphony Orch for 5 years, princ guest conductor Central Philharmonic Orch of China, princ guest conductor Nat Youth Orch China, conductor Hungarian Radio Orch and State Symphony Orch 1989, assoc conductor BBC Philharmonic Orch 1990–92, princ conductor and artistic advsr Ulster Orch 1992–95, princ guest conductor Euskadi Symphony Orch Spain 1994–97; currently: chief conductor RTV Slovenia Symphony Orch, princ guest conductor China Nat Symphony Orch , music dir and princ conductor Taipei Chinese Orch; guest conductor: Bournemouth Symphony Orch, all BBC Orchs, Northern Sinfonia, Royal Liverpool Philharmonic Orch, Hallé Orch, Royal Scottish Nat Orch, Oslo Philharmonic Orch, Helsinki Philharmonic Orch, Berlin Symphonic Orch, Czech Philharmonic Orch, ABC Orchs Australia 1991, 1993 and 1994, Toronto Symphony Orch, Vancouver Symphony, Colorado Symphony Orch, Nat Symphony Orch Johannesburg (debut 1996); debut BBC Proms 1995; *Recreations* Chinese cooking, contemporary interior design and architecture, ballet, jazz, environmental issues; *Style—* En Shao, Esq; ✉ c/o IMG Artists, London, The Light Box, 111 Power Road, London W4 5PY (☎ 020 8233 5814)

SHAPIRO, Dr Leonard Melvyn; s of Joseph Shapiro, of London, and Stella, *née* Solomon; *b* 9 March 1951; *Educ* Leyton County HS London, Univ of Manchester (BSc, MB ChB, MD); *Children*2 da (Laura b 10 Sept 1980, Kiana b 14 Aug 2010), 1 s (Paul b 3 May 1984); *Career* sr registrar Nat Heart Hosp 1983–88, conslt cardiologist Papworth and Addenbrooke's Hosps Cambridge 1988–; special interests: athlete's heart, coronary artery disease, structural interventional cardiology; med advsr FA, dir Cardiac Servs 1998–2002; co-fndr and founding pres Br Soc of Echocardiography; fell American Coll of Cardiology; FRCP 1993 (MRCP 1978); *Books* A Colour Atlas of Hypertension (with K M Fox, 1985, 2 edn with M Bucalter, 1991), A Colour Atlas of Angina Pectoris (with K M Fox and C Warnes, 1986), A Colour Atlas of Heart Failure (with K M Fox, 1987, 2 edn 1995), A Colour Atlas of Physical Signs in Cardiovascular Disease (with K M Fox, 1988), A Colour Atlas of Palpitations and Syncope (with K M Fox, 1989), A Colour Atlas of Congenital Heart Disease in the Adult (with K M Fox, 1989), A Colour Atlas of Coronary Artery Atherosclerosis (1990, 2 edn 1992), Mitral Valve Disease (with F C Wells, 1996), An atlas of echocardiography (with A Kenny, 1997); *Recreations* triathlon; *Style—* Dr Leonard Shapiro; ✉ Cardiac Unit, Papworth Hospital, Papworth Everard, Cambridge CB23 8RE (☎ 07442 502602, fax 01954 210696, e-mail sec@lmshapiro.com, website www.lmshapiro.com); Spire Cambridge Lea, New Road, Impington CB24 9EL

S

SHAPPS, Rt Hon Grant; PC (2010), MP; *b* 14 September 1968, Watford, Herts; *Educ* Watford GS, Manchester Poly (HND); *m* Belinda; 2 s (Hadley b 2001, Noa b 2004), 1 da (Tabytha (twin) b 2004); *Career* PrintHouse Ltd: fndr 1990, dir 1990–2000, chm 2000–; Parly candidate (Cons): N Southwark and Bermondsey 1997, Welwyn Hatfield 2001; MP (Cons) Welwyn Hatfield 2005–, vice-chm (campaigning) Cons Pty, shadow housing min 2007–10, min of state for housing and local govt Dept for Communities and Local Govt 2010–12, min without portfolio 2012–15, chm Cons Pty 2012–15; *Style—* The Rt Hon Grant Shapps, MP; ✉ House of Commons, London SW1A 0AA (e-mail grant@shapps.com, website www.shapps.com)

SHARIFF, Yasmin; da of Chottu Amirali Alibhai Shariff (d 1992), and Shirin Popat Jiwa; *b* 7 April 1956, Kampala, Uganda; *Educ* Kenya HS, AA Sch of Architecture, SOAS Univ of London (MA), Bartlett Sch of Architecture UCL (DipArch); *m* 8 Dec 1983, Dennis Charles Sharp (d 2010); 1 s (Deen b 1984); *Career* architect; former appts: Lobb Partnership (Populous), ACP, Pringle Brandon, Jestico and Whiles; architect dir Dennis Sharp Architects 1992–, head of design multi-academy sponsor 2009–11; conslt Eric Parry Architects; RIBA: cncllr 1998–2004, chair Eastern Regn 1999–2001, hon sec and memb Bd 2013–14; memb AA Cncl 2011–15 (hon sec 2013–15); sr lectr in architecture Univ of Westminster 1992–2009, EU Framework 5 evaluator 1999–2001, Civic Tst judge 1999–2009; memb: UK Round Table on Sustainable Devpt 1999–2001, Bd E of England Devpt Agency 2001–06, Cncl E England Arts 2003–06, Bd Architects Registration Bd 2003–06; memb: ARB, RIBA, AA, WCCA, FBUA; FRSA, RA; *Publications* contrib: The Illustrated Dictionary of Architecture (ed D Sharp, 1991), The Guinness Book of Records 1492 (ed D Manley, 1992), The Encyclopedia of Vernaculr Architecture (ed P Oliver, 1998), Towards a New Architect (2010); contrib articles to architectural jls, author of conf papers; *Recreations* theatre; *Style*— Ms Yasmin Shariff; ✉ 1 Woodcock Lodge, Epping Green, Hertfordshire SG1 3ND (☎ 01707 875253, e-mail yshariff@sharparchitects.co.uk)

SHARKEY, Baron (Life Peer UK 2010), of Niton Undercliff, in the County of the Isle of Wight; John Kevin Sharkey; *b* 24 September 1947; *Educ* Univ of Manchester (BSc); *m* 3 da; *Career* formerly with: Benton & Bowles, KMP; Saatchi & Saatchi: joined 1984, dep chm 1986, md 1987; chm: Broad Street Group, BDDP; fndr jt chm and ceo BST-BDDP (formerly Bainsfair Sharkey Trott) 1990–97, jt chm BDDP GGT (following merger with GGT Advertising) 1997–98; md Europe Manpower plc 1998; *Style*— The Lord Sharkey; ✉ House of Lords, London SW1A 0PW

SHARMA, Rita; OBE (2007); da of Varindar Kumar (d 1998), and Raj Rani, *née* Prakash Sangar (d 1995); *b* 29 July 1960, India; *m* 12 Jan 1987, Rahul Sharma; 1 da (Ria b 20 Oct 1988), 1 s (Rohan b 8 Feb 1991); *Career* founder and md www.bestattravel.co.uk 1986–; memb Bd TiE UK; Hon PhD Univ of E London 2005; *Style*— Mrs Rita Sharma, OBE; ✉ BestAtTravel plc, 7–9 Whitfield Street, London W1T 2AS website www.bestattravel.co.uk)

SHARMAN, Alison Jane; da of Frank Sharman (d 1995), and Bel, *née* Thompson (d 2010); *b* 18 March 1965; *Educ* Ellesmere Park Comp, Eccles Sixth Form Coll, Newcastle upon Tyne Poly (BA); *Children* 2 da (Abigail b 22 May 1995, Olivia b 11 Oct 1996); *Career* TV prodr; prodn sec Watchdog (BBC) 1986–88, sec and researcher TV-am 1988–89, prodr and presenter BSkyB 1989–90, researcher Travelog (Channel 4) 1990–92; BBC: successively researcher, dir, prodr and series prodr Holiday 1992–98, ed devpt Daytime 1998–2000, creative dir Gen Factual 2000–01, controller Daytime 2002–05, controller CBBC 2005–06; dir Factual & Daytime ITV 2006–13, head of commissioning SBS Australia 2013–; *Recreations* theatre, cinema, cooking, sport; *Style*— Ms Alison Sharman; ✉ SBS, 14 Herbert Street, Artarmon, NSW 2064, Australia (☎ 00 612 9430 2904, e-mail alisharman@btinternet.com)

SHARMAN, Baron (Life Peer UK 1999), of Redlynch in the County of Wiltshire Colin Morven; OBE (1980); *b* 19 February 1943; *m* Angela; 1 s (Richard b 1972), 1 da (Sarah b 1969); *Career* qualified chartered accountant Woolgar Hennel & Co 1965; KPMG (and predecessor firms): joined 1966, expanded practice Benelux Scandinavia and the Netherlands 1977–81, large scale investment London 1981–87, sr ptnr Nat Mktg and Industry Gps and chm KPMG Mktg Ctee 1987–90, sr mgmnt consultancy ptnr 1989–90, sr regnl ptnr for London and South East 1990–94, chm KPMG Management Consultancy International 1991–94, UK sr ptnr 1994–98, chm KPMG International 1997–99; chm: Aegis Gp plc 1999–2008, Aviva 2006– (non-exec dir 2005–), Le Gavroche Ltd; non-exec dir: AEA Technology plc 1996–2002, Young & Co's Brewery 1999–2002, BG Gp 2000–, Reed Elsevier 2002–, Group 4 Securicor 2003–05; memb Supervisory Bd ABN Amro NV; chair Foresight Crime Prevention Panel DTI; memb Advsy Bd The George Washington Inst for Mgmnt; hon memb Securities Inst; ambass for Merseyside 1998–; Hon Dr Cranfield Univ 1998; Hon MSI, FCA (ACA 1965), CIMgt; *Recreations* outdoor and field sports, shooting, sailing; *Clubs* Reform, Bembridge Sailing; *Style*— The Rt Hon the Lord Sharman, OBE

SHARMAN, Helen Patricia; OBE (1992); da of John David Sharman, of Sheffield, and Lyndis Mary, *née* Barrand; *b* 30 May 1963; *Educ* Jordanthorpe Comp Sch Sheffield, Univ of Sheffield (BSc), UCL (MA); *Career* dep head Coatings Section MOV Hammersmith (formerly Marconi-Osram Valve, GEC subsid) 1985–87 (joined 1984), res technologist Mars Confectionery Slough 1987–89; selected as UK astronaut for Project Juno (jt venture between USSR and Antequera Ltd) 1989, trained at Yuri Gagarin Cosmonaut Trg Centre USSR 1989–91, became first Br person in space during mission 1991, scientific lectr and presenter 1992–99; gp ldr Nat Physical Lab 2010–13, faculty technical mangr Kingston Univ 2013–15, departmental operations mangr Imperial Coll London 2015–; Geoffrey Pardoe award RAeS, Bronze medal Br Interplanetary Soc, Friendship of the People of the Soviet Union medal, The Worshipful Guild of Air Pilots and Air Navigators award, Gold Medal of the Royal Aero Club, Pres's Medal of the Soc Chemical Industry, Univ of Sheffield Chancellor's medal for achievement, Russian Fedn Medal for services to the exploration of space 2011; Freeman City of Sheffield; Hon MSc Univ of Birmingham 1991, Hon Master of Univ Univ of Surrey 1992; Hon DSc: Univ of Kent 1995, Southampton Inst 1997, Univ of Staffordshire 1998, Univ of Exeter 1999, Brunel Univ 2010; Hon DTech: Univ of Plymouth 1995, The Robert Gordon Univ 1996; hon memb Soc of Chemical Industry (SCI) 1992; fell Sheffield Hallam Univ, fell Science Museum London; hon memb Radio Soc of GB 1991, CChem, Hon FRSC 1993 (MRSC 1991), FRGS 1995, FRAeS 1995 (MRAeS 1991), FBIS 1996 (MBIS 1990), fell and pres Inst of Science and Technol 2016; *Recreations* music, travel; *Style*— Dr Helen Sharman, OBE; ✉ c/o DBA Speakers, 58 Station Avenue, Walton-on-Thames, Surrey KT12 INQ (☎ 01932 228544, e-mail diana@dbaspeakers.com, website www.dbaspeakers.com)

SHARMAN, Mark; s of Stanley Brian Sharman, of Leamington Spa, Warwicks, and Beryl Mary, *née* Brown; *b* 2 January 1950; *Educ* John Port GS Etwall; *m* 1981, Patricia, da of Ivor Goodier (d 1987); 2 s (Matthew b 7 Oct 1981, Luke b 4 Nov 1984); *Career* reporter Derby Evening Telegraph 1967–71, reporter Raymond's News Agency 1971, sports reporter Derby Evening Telegraph 1972, sports sub-ed then chief sub-ed Birmingham Evening Mail 1972–76, sports journalist ATV Ltd Birmingham 1976, sports prodr London Weekend Television 1977–81 (incl prog ed ITV coverage of 1978 World Cup and 1980 Olympics), head of sport, head of news and sport then contoller of news and sport TVS 1981–88 (responsible for ITV network progs incl Emergency 999 and Police International), ed ITV Olympics 1988, md Chrysalis Television plc 1988–91, head of progs London News Network 1992–94, dep head Sky Sports 1997–98 (dir of programming 1994–97), controller of sport Channel 4 TV 1998–2000, dir broadcasting prodn Sky Networks 2000–03, dep md Sky Networks 2003, conslt 2003–05, dir ITV Sport 2005–07, dir ITV News and Sport 2007–08; *Style*— Mark Sharman, Esq

SHARP, David John; s of Norman Sharp, of Viggory Lodge, Horsell Common, Woking, Surrey, and Freda Madeleine, *née* Wakeford; *b* 15 April 1949; *Educ* Lancing, St Mary's Hosp Med Sch London (MB BS, FRCS, MD); *m* 7 Sept 1982, Marisa Nicole, *née* Parnes; 2 s (Oliver b 1985, William b 1986), 1 da (Augusta b 1990); *Career* registrar on orthopaedic higher surgical trg scheme Royal Orthopaedic Hosp Birmingham 1981–83, sr registrar on orthopaedic higher surgical trg scheme Northampton and Royal Postgrad Med Sch London 1983–88, research fell Materials Dept QMC London 1986, conslt orthopaedic and spinal surgn The Ipswich Hosp 1988–; memb: Br Orthopaedic Research Soc, Br Assoc of Spinal Surgeons; tstee DISCS charity for spinal research; FBOA; *Recreations* vintage car, drawing, saxophone, opera, sailing; *Style*— David Sharp, Esq; ✉ Peartree, Farm, Charsfield, Woodbridge, Suffolk IP13 7QE (☎ 01473 737266, e-mail dj.m.sharp@btinternet.com)

SHARP, Prof Deborah; OBE (2016); *b* 11 November 1951; *Educ* Lady Margaret Hall Oxford (BA, BM BCh), DRCOG, Univ of London (PhD); *m* Dr Michael Roden Norman; *Career* currently prof of primary health care Univ of Bristol and head Sch of Clinical Academic Trg Severn Deanery; FRCGP; *Recreations* dressage; *Style*— Prof Deborah Sharp, OBE; ✉ Centre for Academic Primary Care, School of Social and Community Medicine, Canynge Hall, 39 Whatley Road, Bristol BS8 2PS (☎ 0117 3314543, e-mail debbie.sharp@bristol.ac.uk)

SHARP, Lesley; *Educ* Guildhall Sch of Music and Drama (Gold Medal); *Career* actress; AGSM; *Theatre* RSC: Cyrano de Bergerac, King Lear, Maydays, The Body, Macbeth, Mary and Lizzie, Playing with Trains; Royal Court: Gone, Who Knew McKenzie, Road, Shirley, Greenland, Our Country's Good/The Recruiting Officer, Top Girls (also tour), Ingredient X; National Theatre: Command or Promise, True Dare Kiss, Tin Tang Mine, Six Characters in Search of an Author, Fathers and Sons, Murmuring Judges, Uncle Vanya, Mother Courage, Harper Regan, A Taste of Honey; other credits incl: The God of Hell (Donmar Theatre), A Family Affair (Cheek by Jowl), Summerfolk (Chichester Festival Theatre), Ghosts (West End); *Television* Road, Tartuffe, Top Girls, Frank Stubbs, Dandelion Dead, Prime Suspect, Common as Muck, Moonstone, Playing the Field, Great Expectations, Daylight Robbery, Nature Boy, Clocking Off, Bob and Rose, The Second Coming, Carrie's War, Carla, Afterlife, Our Hidden Lives, True Voice of Murder, True Voice of Prostitution, The Diary of Ann Frank, The Children, Cranford, The Shadow Line, Shirley, Scott and Bailey, Starlings, Capital, Paranoid; *Film* The Love Child, Rita, Sue and Bob Too, The Rachel Papers, Close my Eyes, Priest, Naked, The Full Monty, From Hell, Cheeky, Inkheart, Vera Drake; *Awards* for Bob and Rose: Outstanding Dramatic Actress of the Year Monte Carlo Television Festival, RTS Best Actress Award, nominated Best Actress BAFTA, nominated Best Actress Br Comedy Awards; Broadcasting Press Guild TV Actress Award 2001 (for Bob and Rose and Clocking Off); for Afterlife: Best Female Actor RTS Awards, Outstanding Dramatic Actress of the Year Monte Carlo TV Festival 2006 (nominee 2007), Hamilton Deane Award for Outstanding Acting 2006; nominated: Olivier Award for Best Comedy Performance 1986, Olivier Award for Best Supporting Actress 1992, RTS Awards for Clocking Off, Best Actress in a Supporting Role BAFTA (for The Full Monty); *Style*— Ms Lesley Sharp

SHARP, Michael John Todkill; *Career* Debenhams plc (formerly Debenhams Ltd): trading dir 1997–2004, chief operating offr 2004–08, dep chief exec 2008–11, chief exec 2011–16; hon prof in fashion business Glasgow Caledonian Univ 2013; *Style*— Michael Sharp, Esq; ✉ e-mail michaelsharp.vantage@hotmail.com

SHARP, Peter John; s of John Frederick Sharp, of Plumstead, N Norfolk, and Joan Brimelow, *née* Hotchkiss; *b* 16 April 1956; *Educ* Berkhamsted, Univ of Oxford (BA); *m* 22 Dec 1984, Philippa Joanna, da of Sqdn Ldr William Ronald Stanley Body, of Drinkstone Green, Suffolk; 3 s (Samuel Frederick b 1985, William Rodric Peter b 1991, Christopher Patrick Brimelow b 1996), 2 da (Holly Rose b and d 1987, Florence Emily b 1989); *Career* admitted slr 1982; ptnr Wilde Sapte 1984–95 (memb Managing Bd 1990–92), ptnr Le Boeuf Lamb Greene & MacRae (founding English ptnr London office) 1995–2012, ptnr Morgan Lewis 2012–; dep chm Prince's Youth Business Tst S London 1993–94 (chm 1991–93); memb: Law Soc, Little Ship Club; *Recreations* yachting, motor racing, cycling; *Style*— Peter Sharp, Esq; ✉ Morgan Lewis, Condor House, 5–10 St. Paul's Churchyard, London EC4M 8AL

SHARP, Hon Richard Simon; s of Baron Sharp of Grimsdyke (d 1994), and Marion, *née* Freeman; *b* 8 February 1956; *Educ* Merchant Taylors', ChCh Oxford (MA); *m* 29 Aug 1987, Victoria Susan, da of Lloyd Nelson Hull; 1 da (Caroline Nicola b 17 Oct 1989), 2 s (James Eric Halle b 6 June 1992, Alexander Simon Lloyd b 30 April 1994); *Career* Morgan Guaranty Trust Co 1978–84, ptnr Goldman Sachs 1994–; non-exec chm Huntsworth plc 2008–; *Style*— The Hon Richard Sharp

SHARP, Steven Michael; s of Clarence Sharp, of Willerby, E Yorks, and Anne, *née* Price; *b* 5 July 1950; *Educ* Ainthorpe HS Kingston upon Hull, Hull Poly (Hotel and Catering Inst, City and Guilds of London Inst); *Family* 1 da (Emma Louise b 3 Feb 1978), 1 s (Daniel James b 21 Aug 1979); m, 18 Oct 1996, Lesley Sharp, *née* Mair; 2 da (Amelia Grace b 9 Jan 1997, Freya Rose b 16 Dec 2003); *Career* mktg mangr Bejam Gp plc 1978–83, head of retail mktg Argyll Gp plc 1983–87, mktg dir Asda Gp plc 1987–89, mktg dir Debenhams plc 1989–92, mktg dir The Burton Gp plc 1992–2004, chm Steven Sharp plc 1997–, gp mktg dir Arcadia plc 2001–04, exec dir mktg Marks & Spencer plc 2004–14; chm Imagineer London Ltd 2014–; visiting prof Glasgow Caledonian Univ; FCIM, fell Mktg Soc, FRSA; *Recreations* shooting, cycling, music, art, flying; *Clubs* RAC, IOD, Soho House; *Style*— Dr Steven Sharp

SHARP, Rt Hon the Lady Justice; Dame Victoria Madeleine Sharp; DBE (2009), QC (2001); *Career* called to the Bar Inner Temple 1979; recorder 1998, judge of the High Ct of Justice (Queen's Bench Div) 2009– (previously dep judge), presiding judge Western Circuit 2012, a Lady Justice of Appeal 2013; vice-pres Queen's Bench Div 2016–; *Style*— The Rt Hon the Lady Justice Sharp, DBE; ✉ Royal Courts of Justice, Strand, London WC2A 2LL

SHARP OF GUILDFORD, Baroness (Life Peer UK 1998), of Guildford in the County of Surrey; Margaret Lucy Sharp; da of Osmund Hailstone, and Sydney Mary Ellen, *née* White; *b* 21 November 1938; *Educ* Tonbridge Girls' GS, Newnham Coll Cambridge (MA); *m* 1962, Thomas Sharp; 2 da; *Career* asst princ Bd of Trade and HM Treasy 1960–63, lectr in economics LSE 1963–72, pt/t guest fell Brookings Instn Washington DC 1973–76, econ advsr NEDO 1977–81, res fell Sussex Euro Res Centre Univ of Sussex 1981–84, sr fell Science Policy Res Unit Univ of Sussex 1984–2000; Parly candidate (SDP/Alliance) Guildford 1983 and 1987, Parly candidate (Lib Dem) Guildford 1992 and 1997, memb Lib Dem Fed Policy Ctee 1992–2003; memb Advsy Cncl Save Br Sci, chair NIACE Cmmn on Colls in their Communities 2011–12; retired House of Lords 2016; tstee Transformation Tst, pres AOC Charitable Tst 2015–; memb Corporation of Guildford Coll 2004–13, govr Weyfield TKAT Acad Guildford; *Books* The State, the Enterprise and the Individual (1974), The New Biotechnology: European Governments in search of a strategy (1985), Europe and the New Technologies (ed, 1985), Managing Change in British Industry (with Geoffrey Shepherd, 1986), Strategies for New Technologies (ed with Peter Holmes, 1987), European Technological Collaboration (with Claire Shearman, 1987), Technology and the Future of Europe (jt ed, 1992), Technology Policy in the European Union (with John Peterson, 1998), Colleges in their Communities: a dynamic nucleus; author of articles in learned jls dealing with science and technology policy; *Recreations* walking, reading, theatre, listening to music; *Style*— The Rt Hon the Baroness Sharp of Guildford; ✉ 96 London Road, Guildford, Surrey GU1 1TH (☎ 01483 572669, e-mail margaretsharp@ntlworld.com)

SHARPE, Prof David Thomas; OBE (1986); s of Albert Edward Sharpe, of Swanscombe, Kent, and late Grace Emily, *née* Large; *b* 14 January 1946; *Educ* GS for Boys Gravesend, Downing Coll Cambridge, Univ of Oxford Med Sch (MB BChir); *m* 1, 23 Jan 1971 (m dis 2000), Patricia Lilian, da of Brinley Meredith (d 1965); 1 s (Timothy Richard Brinley b 4 Aug 1972), 2 da (Katherine Anna b 24 June 1974, Caroline Louise b 2 Nov 1978); m 2, 11 June 2004, Tracey Louise, da of Peter Bowman and Sandra Wade; *Career* plastic surgeon; house surgn Radcliffe Infirmary Oxford 1970–71, SHO in plastic surgery Churchill Hosp Oxford 1971–72, Pathology Dept Radcliffe Infirmary 1972–73 (Accident Service 1972), gen surgery Royal United Hosp Bath 1973–75; registrar: Plastic Surgery Unit Chepstow 1976–78 (plastic surgeon 1976), Canniesburn Hosp Glasgow 1978–80; sr registrar in plastic surgery Leeds and Bradford 1980–84, chm and md Plastech Research and Design Ltd 1984–, dir Plastic Surgery and Burns Research Unit Univ of Bradford 1986–, prof of plastic and reconstructive surgery Univ of Bradford, chm Breast Special Interest Gp Br Assoc of Plastic Surgns 1997–99; conslt plastic surgn St Luke's Hosp Bradford and Bradford Royal Infirmary, visiting conslt plastic surgn Yorkshire Clinic Bradford, BUPA Hosp Elland W Yorkshire; author of various chapters, leading articles and papers on plastic surgery topics, major burn disaster management, tissue expansion and breast reconstruction; memb Cncl British Assoc of Aesthetic Plastic Surgeons 1989– (pres 1997–99); former chm Yorks Air Ambulance; Br Design Award 1988, Prince of Wales Award for Innovation and Prodn 1988; Hon DSc Univ of Bradford 2012; FRCS 1975; *Recreations* painting, shooting, flying (PPL H), astronomy; *Style*— Prof David T Sharpe, OBE; ✉ Danby Low Mill, Ulshaw, Leyburn, North Yorkshire DL8 4PX (e-mail profsharpe@hotmail.com); The Yorkshire Clinic, Bradford Road, Bingley, West Yorkshire BD16 1TW (☎ 01274 560311, fax 01274 510760)

SHARPE, Thomas Anthony Edward; QC (1994); s of late James Sharpe (d 1981), and Lydia, *née* de Gegg; *b* 21 December 1949; *Educ* Trinity Hall Cambridge; *m* 1, (m dis), Sheena Carmichael, da of late Baron Carmichael of Kelvingrove (Life Peer); 2 c; m 2, Phillis, da of late W P Rogers; 2 c; *Career* called to the Bar Lincoln's Inn 1976 (bencher 2004); fell Wolfson Coll and Nuffield Coll Oxford 1987; chm New London Orch 1998–2000, tstee Help Musicians UK (formerly Musicians Benevolent Fund 1999–), memb Advsy Bd LPO; *Recreations* music, art, furniture, travelling; *Clubs* Beefsteak, Reform; *Style—* Thomas Sharpe, Esq, QC; ✉ 1 Essex Court, Ground Floor, Temple, London EC4Y 9AR (☎ 020 7583 2000, fax 020 7583 0118)

SHARPE-NEWTON, Geraldine; *née* Sharpe; da of late Jesse J Sharpe, of New York City, and Adrienne Rosaire; *b* NY; *Educ* Univ of Illinois (BA), Univ of Pittsburgh (MLS); *m* 1, 1962 (m dis 1974), Thomas Alan Newton; 1 da (Jennifer Jesse b 1965), 1 s (Matthew Ross b 1968); m 2, 1992, John Peter Bluff; *Career* assoc dir special projects Burson Marsteller PR 1974–77, vice-pres Niki Singer Inc 1977–79, vice-pres of PR Simon and Schuster 1979–80, dir Info Servs CBS News 1980–83, head of Press and Public Affrs ITN 1983–91, strategic dir of communications WWF UK 1991–94, sr vice-pres Int PR Turner Broadcasting System Inc 1994–98, md GSN Communications 1998–2001, ptnr Sharpe/McKenna Ltd 2002–06, md Sharpe Connections 2006–; dir First Take, memb Bd Critical Eye 2005–, assoc Clarity The Writing Experts 2013–; chm Int Women's Forum (formerly Forum UK) 1997–99; pres Media Soc 2006–10 and 2012, specialist mentor Prince's Tst 2011–, mentor Sch for Creative Startups, memb Bd and tstee Theatre 503, memb Bd Tricycle Theatre Devpt Ctee, ambass Editorial Intelligence; media advsr and trainer; memb: RTS, Int Women's Forum; pres The Media Soc 2012–; *Recreations* collecting art, theatre, reading, writing, adventure travel; *Clubs* Soho House, Groucho, Hurlingham, Arts, Authors (Bucks); *Style—* Mrs Geraldine Sharpe-Newton; ✉ 29 Albert Mansions, Albert Bridge Road, London SW11 4QB (☎ 07771 765989)

SHARPLES, Hon Christopher John; s of Baroness Sharples, *qv*, and Sir Richard Sharples, KCMG, OBE, MC (assass 1973); *b* 24 May 1947; *Educ* Eton, Business Sch of Neuchâtel; *m* 1, 1975 (m dis), Sharon, da of late Robert Sweeny, DFC; 3 c; m 2, 2010, Gaynor, da of Maj Rhidian Llewellyn, MC, and Lady Honor Llewellyn; *Career* VSO India 1965–66; C Czarnikow Ltd 1968–72, co fndr and dir Inter Commodities Ltd (renamed GNI Ltd in 1984 following partial acquisition by Gerrard & National plc) 1972–2000, fndr dir and chm ICV Ltd 1981–98, fndr dir and chm Royalblue plc 1982–90, vice-chm International Petroleum Exchange 1986–87 (dep chm 1986–); dir: Hiscox Dedicated Insurance Fund plc 1995–96, Gerrard Vivian Gray 1995–98, Futures and Options Assoc 1998–2000, Digital River Inc and Ltd 1998–2006, Unigestion (UK) Ltd 2000– (dep chm), Grandeye Ltd 2004–08, Seeker Wireless 2006–12, Wheatley Assocs Ltd 2010– (chm); chm: Assoc of Futures Brokers and Dealers 1987–92 (memb Rules Ctee 1987–91, chm Finance and General Purpose Ctee 1987–91), SFA 1991–95 (chm Exec Ctee 1991–95, chm Capital Rules Ctee 1991, memb Finance Ctee 1991–96), Lombard Street Research Ltd 1997–2000, Datastream International Ltd 1996–98, Membertrack Ltd 1999–2000; memb: Advsy Panel Securities and Investments Bd 1986–87, City Panel on Takeovers and Mergers 1991–95; MSI; *Recreations* sailing, flying; *Clubs* Royal Yacht Squadron, Air Squadron, White's, Pratt's; *Style—* Christopher Sharples; ✉ Unigestion Ltd, 105 Piccadilly, London W1J 7NJ

SHARPLES, Prof Mike; *b* 14 December 1952; *Educ* St Andrews Univ (BSc), Univ of Edinburgh (PhD); *Career* res fell Open Univ 1981–82, res fell Univ of Edinburgh 1982–84, lectr in artificial intelligence Univ of Sussex 1984–93, sr lectr Sch of Cognitive and Computing Sci Univ of Sussex 1993–97, Kodak/Royal Acad of Engrg res prof of educnl technol Univ of Birmingham 1997–2003, prof of educnl technol 2003–05, prof of learning sciences and dir Learning Sciences Research Inst Univ of Nottingham 2005–; founder mLearn int conference series on mobile learning; dep scientific mangr Kaleidoscope European Network of Excellence on Technol Enhanced Learning; memb Editorial Bd: Computers and Composition 1994–, Jl of Computer Assisted Learning 2001–; pres Int Assoc for Mobile Learning, fndr and memb Ctee Writing and Computers Assoc 1991–; memb: Soc for the Study of Artificial Intelligence and Simulation of Behaviour 1989–, Soc of Authors 1990–; MIEEE 1999, FRSA 2002; *Books* Cognition, Computers and Creative Writing (1985), Computers and Thought: a Practical Introduction to Artificial Intelligence (1989), Benefits and Risks of Knowledge-based Systems (1989), Computers and Writing: Issues and Implementations (ed, 1992), Computer Supported Collaborative Writing (ed, 1993), The New Writing Environment: Writers at Work in a World of Technology (ed with T van der Geest, 1996), How We Write: An Account of Writing as Creative Design (1999); also author of 35 articles in learned jls, 75 refereed conf papers, and 60 book chapters; *Recreations* sailing, skiing; *Style—* Prof Mike Sharples; ✉ Institute of Educational Technology, The Open University, Walton Hall, Milton Keynes MK7 6AA

SHARPLES, Baroness (Life Peer UK 1973), of Chawton in the County of Hampshire; Pamela Swan; da of Lt Cdr Keith William Newall, RN (d 1937), and Violet Ruby, *née* Ashton (who m 2, Lord Claud Nigel Hamilton, GCVO, CMG, DSO, s of 2 Duke of Abercorn, and d 1986); *b* 11 February 1923; *Educ* Southover Manor Lewes, Florence Italy; *m* 1, 1946, Sir Richard Christopher Sharples, KCMG, OBE, MC, govr of Bermuda (assass in Bermuda 1973), s of Richard William Sharples, OBE; 2 s ((Hon) Christopher John Sharples, *qv* b 1947, Hon David Richard b 1955), 2 da (Hon Fiona (Hon Mrs Paterson) b 1949, Hon Miranda (Hon Mrs Larkins) b 1951); m 2, 1977, Patrick David de Laszlo (d 1980); m 3, 1983, (Robert) Douglas Swan (d 1995); *Career* served WAAF 1941–46, Armed Forces Pay Review Bd 1979–81; sits as Cons peer in House of Lords; chm TVS Tst 1981–92; *Recreations* golf, gardening; *Clubs* Mid Ocean Bermuda, Parliamentary Golf Assoc, Rushmoor Golf; *Style—* The Rt Hon the Lady Sharples; ✉ 60 Westminster Gardens, Marsham Street, London SW1P 4JG (☎ 020 7821 1875)

SHARPLES, Prof Ray Martin; s of Wilfred Sharples, of Widnes, Cheshire, and Irene, *née* Lamb (d 1983); *b* 13 January 1955, Widnes, Cheshire; *Educ* Wade Deacon GS Widnes, Univ of St Andrews (BSc, class medal), Univ of Edinburgh (PhD); *m* 31 Oct 1988, Heather Webster Scott; 2 s (Alasdair Gordon Scott b 15 April 1992, Stuart David Scott b 17 Dec 1994); *Career* staff astronomer Anglo-Australian Observatory 1984–90; Univ of Durham: lectr 1990–95, reader 1995–2002, prof 2002–, head Astronomical Instrumentation Gp; author of 120 scientific pubns; memb Optical Soc of America; MInstP, FRAS; *Recreations* rock climbing, mountaineering; *Style—* Prof Ray Sharples; ✉ Department of Physics, Rochester Building, Science Laboratories, South Road, Durham DH1 3LE (☎ 0191 334 3719, fax 0191 334 3609, e-mail r.m.sharples@durham.ac.uk)

SHARPSTON, Eleanor Veronica Elizabeth; QC (1999); da of Charles Sharpston, and Pauline, *née* Bryant; *b* 13 July 1955; *Educ* St Paul's Girls' Sch (scholarship), Bedales (scholarship), Konservatorium der Stadt Wien Vienna, King's Coll Cambridge (MA), CCC Oxford (Rowing blue, pres Oxford Univ Women's Boat Club 1978–80; Squash blue), Inns of Court Sch of Law; *m* 1991, David John Lyon, naval historian (d 2000); *Career* called to the Bar Middle Temple 1980 (Jules Thorn scholar 1980, Sir Peter Bristow scholar 1981, bencher 2005), Bar of Ireland 1986, Bar of Gibraltar 1999; practising barr specialising in EC law, jt head Hailsham Chambers; référendaire to Advocate Gen Sir Gordon Slynn at EC Court of Justice Luxembourg 1987–90, lectr and dir European Legal Studies UCL 1990–92; Univ of Cambridge: fell in law King's Coll 1992–2010 (emeritus fell 2011–), lectr 1992–98, affiliated lectr 1998–2005, sr fell Centre for European Legal Studies 1998–2005, Yorke distinguished visiting fell 2006–; advocate gen European Court of Justice 2006–; chm Bar European Gp 2003–04; hon doctorate Univ of Glasgow 2010, hon doctorate Nottingham Trent Univ 2011, hon doctorate Univ of Stockholm 2014; hon fell CCC Oxford 2010; FSA; *Publications* numerous academic articles; *Recreations* theatre, classical music, european literature, sailing square riggers, karate, skiing; *Clubs* Leander, Athenaeum, Remenham; *Style—* Advocate General Eleanor Sharpston; ✉ Court of Justice of the European Union, L-2925 Luxembourg (☎ 00 352 4303 2215)

SHARROCK, Ivan; s of William Arthur Sharrock, and Gladys Muriel, *née* Roberts; *b* 17 July 1941; *Educ* Newquay GS, Cornwall Tech Coll; *m* 5 Oct 1974, Suzanne Jacqueline Clare, da of Jack Cecil Edward Haig, of Sutton Coldfield; 1 s (Sky Kelly Ivan b 1975); *Career* prodn sound mixer; memb: AMPAS, Assoc of Motion Picture Sound, Cinema Audio Soc (USA), BAFTA, BECTU; joined BBC 1961, trained in film sound techniques at Ealing Film Studios 1961–64, outside broadcasts BBC TV 1964–65, freelance sound mixer with Alan King Assocs 1965–81; fell Assoc of Motion Picture Sound 2014; *Film* has recorded over 90 feature films incl: The Shining 1980, The French Lieutenant's Woman 1981 (Br Acad Award), Greystoke 1984 (Br Acad nomination), The Last Emperor 1987 (Oscar), The Sheltering Sky 1990, Patriot Games 1992, Little Buddha 1993, Mary Shelly's Frankenstein 1994, The Saint 1996, The English Patient 1996 (Br Acad nomination), The Talented Mr Ripley 1999 (Br Acad nomination), U571 2000 (Oscar nomination), Gangs of New York 2002 (Oscar and Br Acad nominatons), Cold Mountain 2003 (Br Acad nomination), Brothers Grimm 2004, Closer 2004, The Da Vinci Code 2005, Blood Diamond 2006 (Oscar nomination), Speed Racer 2007, Clash of the Titans 2010, Pirates of the Caribbean: On Stranger Tides 2011, Cloud Atlas 2012 (German Film Acad nomination); *Recreations* sailing, music, reading, vintage car renovation and trialling; *Style—* Ivan Sharrock, Esq; ✉ 9 Burghley Road, London NW5 1UG (☎ 020 7267 3170, fax 020 7284 4306, e-mail ivan@raspberry-ss.com)

SHARROCK, Thea Zoe; da of Peter Sharrock, of London, and Victoria Brittain; *b* 11 December 1975; *Educ* King Alfred Sch London, St Paul's Girls' Sch, Univ of Oxford; *m* 11 Sept 2004, Paul Handley; *Career* theatre director; trained Anna Scher Theatre 1987–97, asst to head NT Studio 1996; artistic dir: Southwark Playhouse 2001–03, Gate Theatre 2004–07; tstee James Menzies-Kitchin Meml Tst, patron Anna Scher Theatre; sometime player Arsenal Ladies FC; *Plays* Top Girls (Battersea Arts Centre) 2000 (James Menzies-Kitchin Meml Tst Young Dir of the Year 2000), Art (assoc dir, Wyndham's Theatre, Whitehall Theatre and nat tour) 2001–02, The Sleepers Den (Southwark Playhouse) 2001, Top Girls (Oxford Stage Co nat tour) 2001, Top Girls (Aldwych Theatre and nat tour) 2002, Free (NT Loft) 2002, Trip's Cinch (Southwark Playhouse) 2002, Mongoose (Southwark Playhouse) 2003, The Fight for Barbara (Peter Hall Season Theatre Royal Bath) 2002, The Deep Blue Sea (Theatre Royal Bath) 2003, A Doll's House (Southwark Playhouse) 2003, Don Juan and Blithe Spirit (both Peter Hall Season Theatre Royal Bath) 2004, Tejas Verdes (Gate Theatre), Private Lives (Peter Hall Season Theatre Royal Bath), The Chairs (Gate Theatre) 2006, Equus (Gielgud Theatre) 2007, The Misanthrope (Comedy Theatre) 2009; *Recreations* Arsenal FC; *Style—* Miss Thea Sharrock; ✉ c/o Michael Foster, ARG, 4 Great Portland Street, London W1W 8PA (☎ 020 7436 6400, fax 020 7436 6700)

SHAUGHNESSY, 5 Baron (UK 1916); Charles George Patrick Shaughnessy; s of late Alfred James Shaughnessy, and Jean Lodge; *b* 9 February 1955, London; *Educ* Eton, Magdalene Coll Cambridge; *m* 1983, Susan, *née* Fallender; 2 da (Hon Jenny Johanna b 1990, Hon Madelyn Sarah b 1995); *Heir* bro, David James Bradford Shaughnessy; *Career* actor; co-fndr Bus Stop 31 Prodns; *Style—* The Lord Shaughnessy; ✉ PO Box 705, Santa Monica, California 90406, USA

SHAVE, Prof Terry; *b* 8 June 1952, Suffolk; *Educ* Ipswich Sch of Art, Loughborough Coll of Art (BA), Slade Sch London (Higher Dip Fine Art); *Career* artist; prof of fine art and head Fine Art Dept Staffordshire Univ; work subject of numerous exhibition catalogues, magazine and newspaper articles; *Solo Exhibitions* Staffordshire Poly Gallery 1983, Some Kind of Eden (Morley Gallery London) 1983, The Minories Colchester (and tour) 1985, Notes from an Ordinary Hell (Ikon Gallery Birmingham) 1986, The Fall to Pandemonium series (Gallery N Kirby Lonsdale) 1989, Anderson O'Day Gallery London 1990, Wolf-at-the-Door Gallery Penzance 1990, Accumulations (City Museum and Art Gallery Stoke-on-Trent) 1993, Tour to Mead Gallery (Univ of Warwick) 1993, Works on Paper (Midlands Contemporary Art Birmingham) 1993, Behind the View (Ainscough Gallery Liverpool) 1995, Loaded (Ikon Gallery Birmingham) 1996, Reloading (Real Gallery NY) 1997, Comes the Flood (Flaxman Studios Stoke-on-Trent); *Group Exhibitions* incl: British Printmaking Now (Thumb Gallery London) 1978, Six Attitudes to Print (Aspex Gallery Portsmouth) 1982, 4th Tolly Cobbold/Eastern Arts Nat Exhibition (prizewinner) 1983, Place (Gimpel Fils London) 1983, John Moores Liverpool Exhibition 15 (prizewinner) 1987, The Presence of Painting (S Bank Centre/Arts Cncl touring) 1989, The Language of Landscape (Anderson O'Day London) 1990, 4 UK Artists (Norlino Gallery NY) 1990, Landscape Visions (selected by Peter Fuller, Pears Gallery Aldeburgh) 1990, A Tribute to Peter Fuller (Beaux-Arts Bath) 1990, 11th Bradford Int Print Biennale (RCA London) 1991, Beyond the Wow Factor (New York State Univ) 1993, first Harlech Int Contemporary Art Exhibition (invited artist) 1994, Foreign Bodies (Shinjuki Cultural Centre Tokyo) 1996, Warming Up (Arcus Nurnberg) 1996, Aid (Hellenic American Union Gallery Athens) 2003; *Work in Public and Corporate Collections* Arts Cncl of GB, Ipswich Corp, Birmingham Museum and Art Gallery, Stoke-on-Trent Museum and Art Gallery, Bedfordshire CC, St Thomas' Hosp London, Colgate/Palmolive Ltd, Unilever Ltd, Coopers & Lybrand Ltd, Univ of Warwick; *Style—* Prof Terry Shave; ✉ 19 Park Avenue, Wolstanton, Newcastle-under-Lyme, Staffordshire ST5 8AX

SHAW, Antony Michael Ninian; QC (1994); s of Harold Anthony Shaw (d 2015), and Edith Beatrice Sandbach, *née* Holmes, of Iden Green, Kent; *b* 4 October 1948, Dublin, Repub of Ireland; *Educ* King's Sch Canterbury, Trinity Coll Oxford (major history scholar, BA); *m* Louise Göta (d 2006), da of Louis Carl Faugust (d 1971); 1 s (James William Hugo b 19 Jan 1984), 2 da (Antonia Elizabeth Göta b 21 June 1985, Olivia Louise Beatrice b 17 Aug 1990); *Career* res in constitutional law and human rights in Anglophonic Africa financed by Ford Fndn 1970–71, res offr Legal Res Unit Bedford Coll London 1972–75, called to the Bar Middle Temple 1975 (Astbury scholar 1976, bencher 2003), visiting lectr London Coll of Printing 1975–76, pupillage 1976, tenancy at 4 Brick Court chambers of Barbara Calvert, QC, 1977, head of chambers 4 Brick Court 1988–99; asst recorder 1997–2000, recorder 2000–07; corporate and serious fraud work; vice-chm Legal Aid and Fees Ctee Bar Cncl 1995–97, govr Int Students House 1999–2003, memb Criminal Bar Assoc, memb Bar Cncl Conduct Ctee 2007, vice-chm Remuneration Ctee Bar Cncl 2008–09, chm Remuneration Ctee Bar Cncl 2010–11; contrib to numerous publications and jls; *Books* Archbold's Criminal Pleadings and Practice (co-ed, 1990–), Fraud (contrib 2008–, dep ed 2011–); *Recreations* history, reading; *Style—* Antony Shaw, QC; ✉ 18 Red Lion Court, London EC4A 3EB (☎ 020 7520 6000, e-mail tony.shaw@18rlc.co.uk)

SHAW, Sir Charles de Vere; 8 Bt (UK 1821), of Bushy Park, Dublin; s of late Capt John Frederick de Vere Shaw, yr s of 6 Bt; suc unc, Sir Robert Shaw, 7 Bt (d 2002); *b* 1 March 1957; *Educ* Michaelhouse, RMA Sandhurst; *m* 1985 (m dis 2013), Sonia, elder da of Geoff Eden and Meera Eden, of Farnham, Surrey; 1 da (Alexandra Frances b 1986), 1 s (Robert Jonathan de Vere b 1988); *Heir* s, Robert Shaw; *Career* served Europe, Central America and Middle East with 5th Royal Inniskilling Dragoon Guards (subsequently the Royal Dragoon Guards) 1975–87, Major; dir of consultancy Safetynet plc 1989–94; md Morgan Lovell plc 1994–2000, ceo Intellispace 2001–05, md Arlington Property Services 2005–08, ceo Leadership Dynamics 2013–; non-exec chm Interiors Gp, non-exec dir Hurley

S

Palmer Flatt; *Recreations* leading expeditions including to the Geographic North Pole in 1997, most sports, photography, wine; *Clubs* Army and Navy, RGS; *Style—* Sir Charles Shaw, Bt; ✉ Bondoni, PO Box 34, CPU Al Bahjah, Muscat, Sultanate of Oman (e-mail charles@leadershipdynamics.co.uk)

SHAW, Chris Thomas; s of John Dennis Bolton Shaw (d 1989), of Sussex, and Isabel, *née* Loewe (d 1985); *b* 19 June 1957; *Educ* Westminster, Balliol Coll Oxford; *Career* trainee LBC 1980–81, bulletin ed Independent Radio News 1981–85, chief sub-ed ITN 1987–89 (writer 1985–87), sr prodr Sky News 1990–91; ITN: rejoined 1992, foreign and home news ed Channel 4 News 1992–93, prog ed News at Ten 1993–96, ed ITN news service for Channel Five 1996–98; Channel Five Broadcasting: controller of news, current affrs and documentaries 1998–2001, sr prog controller 2001–11; editorial dir ITN Prodns 2012–; *Style—* Chris Shaw, Esq; ✉ ITN Productions, 200 Grays Inn Road, London WC1X 8XZ (☎ 020 7421 7123)

SHAW, Christopher Nigel (Chris); s of Jack Shaw, of Clowne, Derbys, and Vera, *née* Gould; *b* 31 March 1962; *Educ* Cardiff High Sch, LSE (BSc); *m* 4 Sept 1993, Caroline Margaret, da of Francis Flynn; 2 da (Phoebe Helena b 15 March 1997, Isobel Louise b 7 Oct 1998); *Career* media trainee rising to media supr McCann-Erickson 1984–89; Publicis: sr media planner 1989–90, media mangr 1990–91, media account dir 1991–92; media account dir and bd dir Optimedia (following merger with Geers Gross and FCB) 1992–93, European media account dir Initiative Media 1993–95, jt md then pres EMEA Universal McCann 1997–2006 (fndr dir 1995), 19 Entertainment 2006–08 (working on Honda Racing F1 Team account), sr vice-pres commercial development EMEA Discovery Communications 2008–11, global head of advtg sales NBC Universal 2012–13,exec vice-pres and md Be Viacom Viacom Int Media Networks 2013–; *Style—* Chris Shaw, Esq; ✉ BE VIACOM, Elephant House, 17–29 Hawley Crescent, Camden, London NW1 8TT

SHAW, David Lawrence; *b* 14 November 1950; *Educ* KCS Wimbledon, City of London Poly; *m* 1986, Dr Lesley Christine Shaw, *née* Brown; 1 s (b 1989), 1 da (b 1994); *Career* with Coopers & Lybrand 1971–79, County Bank 1979–83, fndr and chm Sabrelance Ltd 1983–, dep chm The Adscene Group plc 1986–99, chm RRI plc 1994–2000, dir Business Cncl for Int Understanding (Europe) Ltd 2000–; sr advsr Inst for Global Economic Growth Washington DC; chm and tstee The David Shaw Charitable Tst 1994–, chm 2020 Strategy Ltd 1997–; fin dir Nettec plc 2003–05; MP (Cons) Dover 1987–97 (Parly Candidate (Cons) Leigh 1979 and Kingston & Surbiton 2001); memb Social Security Select Ctee House of Commons 1991–97, vice-chm Cons Pty Finance Ctee 1990–97, chm Cons Pty Smaller Businesses Ctee 1991–97, former co-chm All-Pty Dolphin Protection Gp, fndr Bow Gp/Ripon Soc Transatlantic Confs (chm Bow Gp 1983–84); joined Cons Pty 1970, cncllr Royal Borough of Kingston upon Thames 1974–78, vice-chm Kingston and Malden Cons Assoc 1979–86, chm Bow Gp 1983–84; memb Cncl PITCOM 1995–97; hon vice-pres IPI 1996–; MInstD, FCA (ACA 1974); *Clubs* Carlton; *Style—* David Shaw, Esq, FCA; ✉ 66 Richborne Terrace, London SW8 1AX (☎ 020 7735 6965, fax 020 7582 9380, e-mail david@davidshaw.net, website www.davidshaw.net)

SHAW, Donald Gordon Brian; *b* 14 January 1956; *Educ* Edinburgh Acad, Univ of Aberdeen (LLB); *m* May 2000, Susan Edith Shaw; 2 da (Alexandra, Georgia); *Career* admitted slr 1979 (articled Shepherd & Wedderburn); Dundas & Wilson LLP: ptnr 1985–14, Real Estate industry ldr 2000–06, managing ptnr 2006–12; ptnr Garretts 1997–2002, ptnr Cameron McKenna LLP 2014–, dir Four Quarters Devpt Ltd 2014–; ldr Real Estate Law Andersen Legal 1998–2002, ptnr Andersen Worldwide 1998–2002; memb Law Soc of Scotland; fell Soc Advanced Legal Studies 1998, WS, NP; *Recreations* psychology, music, history, art, wine, travel; *Style—* Donald Shaw, Esq; ✉ CMS Cameron McKenna LLP, Cannon Place, 78 Cannon Street, London EC4N 6AF (☎ 020 7367 2323, e-mail donald.shaw@cms-cmck.com)

SHAW, Fiona Mary; Hon CBE (2001); da of Dr Denis Joseph Wilson, of Cork, Ireland, and Mary Teresa, *née* Flynn; *b* 10 July 1958, Cork, Ireland; *Educ* Scoil Mhuire Cork, UC Cork, RADA; *Career* actress; hon prof of drama Trinity Coll Dublin, Hon LLD Nat Univ of Ireland 1996; Hon PhD: Open Univ 1997, Trinity Coll Dublin 2001, Univ of Ulster 2004; Officier de l'Ordre des Arts et des Lettres (France) 2000; *Theatre* Julia in The Rivals (NT) 1983, Mary Shelley in Bloody Poetry (Leicester and Hampstead) 1984; RSC 1985–88: Tatyana Vasilyevna in Philistines, Celia in As You Like It, Madame de Volange in Les Liaisons Dangereuses, Erika Brückner in Mephisto, Beatrice in Much Ado About Nothing, Portia in The Merchant of Venice, Mistress Carol in Hyde Park, Katherine in The Taming of the Shrew, Lady Frampul in New Inn, title role in Electra (Best Actress Olivier Awards 1989, Theatre Critics's Award 1989); title role in Mary Stuart (Greenwich) 1988, Rosalind in As You Like It (Old Vic, Best Actress Olivier Awards 1989), Shen Te/ Shui Ta in The Good Person of Sichuan (NT, London Theatre Critics' Award 1989, Best Actress Olivier Awards 1989), title role in Hedda Gabler 1991 (Abbey Theatre Dublin and Playhouse London, nominated Best Actress Olivier Awards 1992, winner London Theatre Critics' Award 1992), Machinal (RNT, Best Actress Evening Standard Award 1993, Best Actress Olivier Awards 1994), Footfalls (Garrick, 1 week) 1994, title role in Richard II (RNT) 1995, Millamant in The Way of the World (RNT) 1995, The Waste Land (Paris and Canada, winner Drama Desk Award NY 1997) 1996, speaker in Honegger's Joan of Arc at the Stake (BBC Proms) 1997, The Prime of Miss Jean Brodie (RNT) 1998; dir Widower's Houses (RNT) 1999, Medea (Abbey Theatre Dublin) 2000 (Irish Times Best Actress Award 2000), Medea (Queen's Theatre) 2001 (Best Actress Evening Standard Award 2002), The Powerbook (RNT) 2002, Medea (US tour) 2003 (Elliot Norton Award, Obie Award, NY Tony nomination), The Seagull (Edinburgh Festival) 2003, The Powerbook (Paris, Rome) 2003, Julius Caesar (Barbican) 2005, My Life is a Fairytale (NY) 2005, Readings (Theatre Nationale de Chaillot Paris) 2005, Dido and Anaeas (Vienna Festival) 2006 and 2009 and (Paris) 2008, Woman and Scarecrow (Royal Court) 2006, Happy Days (RNT, Paris, Epidaurus Madrid, Dublin, Amsterdam) 2007, Mother Courage (Nat Theatre) 2009, London Assurance (NT) 2012, Scenes from an Execution (NT) 2013, The Testament of Mary (Broadway) 2013 and (Barbican) 2014; *Opera* dir Riders to the Sea (ENO) 2008, Elegy for Young Lovers (ENO) 2010, Marriage of Figaro (ENO) 2011 and 2014, The Rape of Lucretia (Glyndebourne) 2013 and 2015 and (Berlin) 2014, Onegin (Met NY) 2013; *Television* incl: Elspeth in Fireworks for Elspeth 1983, Hedda Gabler 1993, Persuasion 1994, Jane Eyre 1994, The Waste Land 1995, Gormenghast 1999, The British Face 2005, True Blood 2011, Maigret 2015; *Film* My Left Foot 1988, The Mountains of the Moon 1988, Three Men and a Little Lady 1990, London Kills Me 1991, Super Mario Brothers 1993, Undercover Blues 1993, Anna Karenina 1996, The Butcher Boy 1996, The Avengers 1997, The Last September 1998, RKO 281 1999, The Triumph of Love 2000, Harry Potter and the Philosopher's Stone 2000, Harry Potter and the Chamber of Secrets 2002, Harry Potter and the Prisoner of Azkaban 2003, The Black Dahlia 2005, Catch and Release 2005, Fracture 2006, Harry Potter and the Order of the Phoenix 2007, Dorian Gray 2009, Harry Potter and the Deathly Hallows: Part 1 2010, Tree of Life 2011, Pixels 2014, The Countrywoman 2015, The White King 2015, The Hippopotamus 2015; *Books* Players of Shakespeare (1987), Clamorous Voices (contrib, 1988), Conversation with Actresses (1990); *Recreations* travel, reading, running, painting; *Style—* Miss Fiona Shaw; ✉ c/o Independent Talent Group Ltd, 40 Whitfield Street, London W1T 2RH (☎ 020 7636 6565, fax 020 7323 0101, e-mail shawassist@aol.com)

SHAW, (John) Howard; QC (2011); s of Arthur Shaw, and late Edith, *née* Richardson, of Oldham, Lancs; *b* 6 September 1948; *Educ* The Hulme GS Oldham, Bristol Univ (LLB); *m* 30 Dec 1972, Mary Charlotte, da of Rev Charles Strong, MBE (d 1959); 2 s (Alister Cameron, Duncan Howard); *Career* grad entry scheme Tstee and Income Tax Dept National Westminster Bank 1970–72; called to the Bar Inner Temple 1973; 3 Dr Johnson's Bldg: pupillage with Her Hon Judge Adrianne Uziell-Hamilton then His Hon Judge K Machin, QC, 1973–74, in practice 1973–87, admin of chambers 1987–90, head of chambers 1990–96; moved chambers to 29 Bedford Row; admitted to the Bar Rep of Ireland (King's Inn); arbitrator 2013; memb: Family Law Bar Assoc, Professional Negligence Bar Assoc, Personal Injury Bar Assoc; MCIArb 2013; *Recreations* music, opera, reading, travel, walking, theatre, rugby, football, walking the dogs; *Clubs* Wimbledon Village; *Style—* Howard Shaw, Esq, QC, MCIArb; ✉ Thornhill House, 1 Thornton Hill, Wimbledon, London SW19 4HU (☎ 020 8946 3465); 29 Bedford Row, London WC1R 4HE (☎ 020 7404 1044, e-mail hshaw@29br.co.uk)

SHAW, John Dennis; s of Frederick Shaw (d 2003), of Chapeltown, Sheffield, and Dorothy, *née* Wilson (d 1958); *b* 11 July 1938; *Educ* Ecclesfield GS, Univ of Sheffield Med Sch (MB ChB); *m* 5 Sept 1964, Margaret, da of William John Jones, of Dymock, Glos; 1 da (Susan b 1965), 1 s (Simon b 1966); *Career* rotating registrar United Sheffield Hosp 1965–67, sr registrar in otolaryngology Cardiff Royal Infirmary and Singleton Hosp Swansea 1967–70, res fell Wayne State Univ Detroit 1970, conslt ENT surgn Royal Hallamshire Hosp Sheffield 1971–94, currently hon conslt ENT surgn; memb Cncl Sections of Otology and Laryngology RSM, regnl advsr in otolaryngology RCS Trent, memb Ct of Examiners RCS; FRCSEd 1967, FRCS 1969; *Books* Fibreoptic Endoscopy of the Upper Respiratory Tract; *Style—* John Shaw, Esq; ✉ The Gables, Sandygate Road, Sheffield S10 5UE (☎ 0114 230 7784)

SHAW, Dr Mark Robert; s of William Shaw (d 1993), and Mabel Courtenay, *née* Bower (d 2010); *b* 11 May 1945; *Educ* Dartington Hall Sch, Oriel Coll Oxford (MA, DPhil); *m* 11 July 1970, Francesca Dennis, da of Rev Dennis Wilkinson (d 1971); 2 da (Zerynthia b 23 Dec 1972, Melitaea b 19 April 1978); *Career* research asst Dept of Zoology Univ of Manchester 1973–76, research fell Univ of Reading 1977–80; Nat Museums of Scotland (formerly Royal Scottish Museum): asst keeper Dept of Natural History 1980–83, keeper of natural history 1983–96, keeper of geology and zoology 1996–2005, hon research assoc 2005–; frequent contrib to various pubns on entomology; FRES 1974, FRSE 2004; *Recreations* field entomology, family life; *Style—* Dr Mark R Shaw; ✉ National Museums of Scotland, Chambers Street, Edinburgh EH1 1JF (☎ 0131 247 4246, fax 0131 220 4819, e-mail m.shaw@nms.ac.uk)

SHAW, Martin; s of Albert Cyril Shaw (d 1967), of Leeds, and Letitia Whitehead (d 1978); *b* 31 October 1944; *Educ* Leeds GS, UCL (LLB); *m* 1, 19 Aug 1967 (m dis 1995), Christine Helen, da of Maurice Grenville Whitwam (d 1986), of Leeds; 1 da (Sarah b 25 Nov 1970), 2 s (Simon b 17 March 1973, Jonathan b 4 Aug 1978); m 2, 2 Aug 1996, Christine Elizabeth St Lawrence, da of Ivor St Lawrence Morris (d 1991), of Collingham, W Yorks; *Career* Simpson Curtis (merged with Pinsent & Co to form Pinsent Curtis 1995, now Pinsent Masons): articled clerk 1966–69, slr 1969–71, ptnr 1971–2012, head Corporate Dept 1980–88, managing ptnr 1992–94, head Corporate Dept Leeds 1999–2007, head Corporate Europe 2007–14, conslt 2014–; chm: Minstergate plc 1985–89, ABI Caravans Ltd 1986–88, Minster Corporation plc 1988–90, Legal Resources Group 1988–91; dir Leeds Business Venture 1982–95; govr: Richmond House Sch 1977–92, Gateways Sch 1985–; memb Variety Club of GB (chm Yorks region 1995); *Recreations* running, golf, squash, tennis; *Style—* Martin Shaw, Esq; ✉ Cobblers Cottage, St John's Road, Bishop Monkton, Harrogate HG3 3QU (☎ 01765 676766); Pinsent Masons, 1 Park Row, Leeds LS1 5AB (☎ 0113 244 5000, fax 0113 244 8000)

SHAW, Murray William Anderson; s of Leslie Conway Shaw (d 1992), and Adeline Georgina, *née* Young; *b* 25 September 1957, Dundee; *Educ* Devonport GS, Bristol GS, Tudor Grange GS Solihull, Solihull Sixth Form Coll, Univ of Dundee (LLB); *m* 4 Oct 1986, Grace Yeun Hym, *née* Wong; 2 s (Adam David b 22 March 1990, Frazer Conway b 13 Oct 1992); *Career* slr specialising in construction and planning law; asst slr Biggart Baillie (formerly Biggart Baillie & Gifford) 1982–85 (apprentice 1980–82), asst Speechly Bircham 1985–86; Biggart Baillie & Gifford: asst slr 1986–87, ptnr 1987–2009, sr ptnr 2009–12; ptnr: DWF Biggart Baillie 2012–14, Gillespie Macandrew 2014–; chm ICAS Appeal Ctee 2012–, chm Glasgow Building Preservation Tst 2015– (vice-chm 2012–15), dir Scottish N American Business Cncl 2014–; memb: Licensing and Disciplinary Ctees ACCA 2003–12, Planning Law Ctee and Remuneration Ctee Law Soc, RTPI 2011; memb Ct Univ of Abertay Dundee 2013–; memb Law Soc of Scot 1982; ACIArb 2003; *Recreations* golf, watching sport, cinema, theatre, American history and politics; *Clubs* Whitecraigs Golf, New Golf, Glasgow Hutchesons' Aloysians (GHA) Rugby Football; *Style—* Murray Shaw, Esq; ✉ Gillespie Macandrew, 5 Atholl Crescent, Edinburgh EH3 8EJ (☎ 0131 225 1677, e-mail murray.shaw@gillespiemacandrew.co.uk)

SHAW, Prof Dame Pamela Jean; DBE (2014); *Career* Univ of Newcastle upon Tyne: Wellcome sr research fell in clinical science 1991–2000, hon conslt/sr lectr in neurology 1991–97, prof of neurological medicine 1997–2000; prof of neurology Univ of Sheffield 2000–; conslt neurologist Sheffield Teaching Hosps NHS Fndn Tst 2000–; dir: Sheffield Care and Research Centre for Motor Neuron Disorders 2002–, Sheffield Inst of Translational Neuroscience 2010; *Style—* Prof Dame Pamela Shaw, DBE; ✉ Academic Neurology Unit, Department of Neuroscience, Sheffield Institute of Translational Neuroscience, University of Sheffield, 385a Glossop Road, Sheffield S10 2HQ

SHAW, Dr Richard; s of Donald Shaw (d 1982), and Marion, *née* Hewitt (d 1998); *b* 20 January 1949, Ashton-under-Lyne, Lancs; *Educ* Sedbergh Sch, Univ of Sussex (BA), Univ of Exeter (CertEd), UCL (PhD); *m* 12 Jan 1983, Poorna, *née* Charles; 3 s (Bede b 20 Jan 1985, Benedict b 31 March 1989, Timothy b 6 Sept 1994); *Career* sr educn offr and field dir VSO 1976–81, Dept of the Environment 1988–97 (princ offr 1988–92, sr civil servant 1992–97), dir for the environment Surrey CC 1997–2001, chief exec Oxon CC 2001–04, chief exec Surrey CC 2005–09, interim chief exec S Downs Nat Park Authy 2009–12; chair Alliance for Int Devpt SOLACE, memb Whitehall Capability Review Team DfID; memb Cncl and Audit Ctee Univ of Surrey 2005–09, assoc Nat Sch of Govt; *Recreations* tennis, diving, gym; *Style—* Dr Richard Shaw; ✉ Norrels Corner, Forest Road, East Horsley, Surrey KT24 5DH

SHAW, Prof Richard Wright; CBE (1997); s of George Beeley Shaw (d 1965), and Bella, *née* Wright (d 1982); *b* 22 September 1941; *Educ* Lancaster Royal GS, Sidney Sussex Coll Cambridge (MA); *m* 2 April 1965, Susan Angela, da of Lewis Birchley; 2 s (David Lewis b 24 Sept 1970, James Lachlan b 29 July 1977); *Career* Univ of Leeds: asst lectr in mgmnt 1964–66, lectr in economics 1966–69; Univ of Stirling: lectr in economics 1969–75, sr lectr in economics 1975–84, head Dept of Economics 1982–84; Paisley Coll: prof and head Dept of Economics and Mgmnt 1984–86, vice-princ 1986, princ 1987–92; princ and vice-chllr Univ of Paisley 1992–2001; visiting lectr in economics Univ of Newcastle NSW 1982; dir: Renfrewshire Enterprise 1991–2000, Univs and Colls Employers Assoc 2000–01; chm Lead Scotland 2001–07; convenor Ctee of Scottish Higher Educn Principals 1996–98; memb: Scottish Economic Cncl 1995–97, Scottish Business Forum 1998–99; fell Scottish Vocational Educn Cncl 1995; Hon DUniv: Glasgow 2001, Univ of West of Scotland 2008; FRSA; *Books* Industry and Competition (with C J Sutton, 1976); *Recreations* walking, listening to music, sketching, painting; *Style—* Prof Richard Shaw, CBE

SHAW, Prof Robert Alfred; s of Walter Schlesinger (d 1964), and Lily Karoline, *née* Plahner (d 1954); *b* 2 November 1924, Vienna, Austria; *Educ* Univ of London (BSc, PhD, DSc); *m* 23 Aug 1980, Dr Leylâ Süheylâ Shaw, da of Yusuf Gözen and Bedia, *née* Akel, of Tarsus, Turkey; 1 s (Dr Robert Y H W b 28 March 1984), 1 da (Dr Lily B Z L b 30 May

1989); *Career* WWII Royal Fusiliers and Queen's Royal Regt UK, India, SE Asia command 1944–47; Birkbeck Coll Univ of London: asst lectr 1953–56, lectr 1956–65, prof of chemistry 1965–90, prof emeritus 1990–; co-dir of an EC sponsored int research project in chemistry with Poland 1994–2004, co-dir of int research projects in chemistry: with Indian Inst of Science Bangalore 1971–81, with Turkey 1998– and 2002–; pioneer in interdisciplinary and international res collaboration interested in teamwork and leadership issues; author of more than 350 pubns, mainly chemistry, some also on educn, third world countries and history of medicine; plenary lectr to Turkish Chemical Congress Konya 2002 and Kars 2004, delivered 13th Holocaust Meml Day Lecture 'A Life in Science – Gifted by the Kindertransport' Univ of Wolverhampton 2015; memb Academic Policy Ctee of the Inter-Univ Cncl for Higher Educn Overseas 1976–81, UNESCO conslt to Turkish Govt 1977, main speaker and memb Organising Ctee of Conf sponsored by Institut Mondial du Phosphate Rabat Morocco 1977, main speaker on life-long educn in Koblenz W Germany 1978, fndr memb and former memb Steering Ctee Univ of the Third Age London; Dr (hc): Univ Paul Sabatier Toulouse 1978, Gebze Inst of Technol Turkey 2005; memb Soc of Chemical Indust; CChem, FRSC; *Recreations* reading, music, travelling, skiing, fencing, history of medicine; *Style—* Prof Robert A Shaw; ✉ Brettargh Holt, Camden Way, Chislehurst, Kent BR7 5HT (☎ 020 8467 5656, e-mail brettargh.holt@dsl.pipex.com); School of Biological and Chemical Sciences, Birkbeck College (University of London), Malet Street, London WC1E 7HX

SHAW, Simon Dalton; MBE (2004); *b* 1 September 1973, Nairobi, Kenya; *Educ* King's Coll, Runneymede Coll, Godalming Sixth Form Coll, UWE; *m* Jane; 4 c (Samantha, Tyler, Beau, Sienna); *Career* rugby union player (lock); clubs: Otago NZ, Bristol RUFC 1993–97, London Wasps RUFC 1997–2011 (winners Tetley's Bitter Cup 1999 and 2000, Parker Pen Challenge Cup 2003, Zurich Championship 2003, 2004 and 2005, Heineken Cup 2004 and 2007), Toulon 2011– (Heineken Cup 2013); England: 71 caps, debut v Italy 1996, winners Six Nations Championship 2000, 2003 (Grand Slam 2003) and 2011, ranked no 1 team in world 2003, winners World Cup Aust 2003, finalists World Cup France 2007; memb squad British and Irish Lions tour to South Africa 1997, NZ 2005 and South Africa 2009; PRA Players Player of the Year 2004; *Books* Simon Shaw – The Hard Yards; *Style—* Simon Shaw, Esq, MBE; ✉ c/o Rugby Football Union, Rugby House, Rugby Road, Twickenham, Middlesex TW1 1DS

SHAW, Stephen; s of Ivan Shaw, and Phyllis, *née* Niechcicki; *b* 20 December 1952; *Educ* Harrow Co GS, Univ of Birmingham (LLB); *m* 26 Sept 1978, Fabia Melanie, da of John Alexander; 2 s (Gideon David b 20 Sept 1982, Aaron Alexander b 7 Jan 1987), 2 da (Gabrielle Leah b 25 March 1984, Rachel Rose Sybil b 24 July 1991); *Career* called to the Bar Gray's Inn 1975, currently judge of the First Tier Tbnl (Property Chamber) and dep district judge (London); accredited CEDR mediator specialising in mediation of property and commercial disputes; Legal 500 listed, recommended leading mediator Chambers & Partners Directory; MCIArb; *Books* contrib New Law Journal and Estates Gazette on landlord and tenant matters; *Recreations* amateur magic, jazz, cycling; *Style—* Stephen Shaw, Esq; ✉ website www.stephenshawmediation.com; Lamb Chambers, Lamb Building, Temple, London EC4Y 7AS (☎ 020 7797 8300, mobile 07775 944760, fax 020 7797 8308, e-mail stephenshaw@lambchambers.co.uk, website www.lambchambers.co.uk)

SHAW, (Dr) Stephen; CBE (2004); s of Walter Arthur Shaw (d 1976), and Gwendolyn Primrose, *née* Cottrell (d 2011); *b* 26 March 1953, London; *Educ* Rutlish Sch Merton, Univ of Warwick (BA), Univ of Leeds (MA), Univ of Kent (PhD); *m* 23 April 1977, Christine Elizabeth, da of Michael Robinson; 2 s (with Jane Angela Skinner); *Career* lectr: Coventry Tech Coll 1975–76, Mid-Kent Coll of Technol 1977–79, res offr Home Office 1980–81, dir Prison Reform Trust 1981–99; prisons ombudsman 1999–2001, prisons and probation ombudsman 2001–10; chief exec Office of the Health Professions Adjudicator 2010–12; independent assessor of complaints: CPS 2013–, Dept for Transport 2013–; memb Disciplinary Panel Nat Fedn of Property Professionals 2012–, chair Independent Advsy Panel on Non-compliance Mgmnt Home Office 2013–14, head Welfare in Detention Review Home Office 2015; sr assoc Verita Consultants LLP 2013–, dir Procordia Ltd 2013–; DUniv Univ of Central England 2000; *Publications* numerous publications on criminal justice and economic isssues; *Recreations* family life, watching Fulham FC; *Style—* Stephen Shaw, CBE; ✉ e-mail stephen.shaw999@gmail.com

SHAWCROSS, Conrad Hartley Pelham; s of (Hon) William Hartley Hume Shawcross, and Marina Warner, *qqv*; *b* 26 April 1977, London; *Educ* Chelsea Coll of Art (Foundation), Ruskin (BA), Slade (MFA); *m* 2013, Carolina Mazzolari Shawcross, *née* Mazzolari; 3 c; *Career* artist and sculptor; RA elect (youngest living artist) 2013; *Solo Exhibitions* incl: Oxford Science Park 2010, Turner Contemporary 2011, Victoria Miro Gallery London 2011, Journeys: Conrad Shawcross and Tavares Strachan (Museum of Art Rhode Island Sch of Design) 2011, Science Museum London 2011–12, Nat Gallery London 2012, MUDAM Luxembourg 2012, ROH London 2012, Roundhouse London 2013, Palais de Tokyo Paris 2013, Galerie Kluser Munich 2013, Galerie Gabriel Rolt Amsterdam 2013, ARTMIA Fndn Beijing 2014, MCA Sydney 2015, Sharjah Art Fndn 2015, The New Art Centre Roche Court 2015, Benaki Museum Athens 2016; *Group Exhibitions* incl: LUSTWARANDE '11 (int sculpture exhbn, RAW Park de Oude Warande Tilburg) 2011, 55th Venice Biennale 2013, Grand Palais Paris 2013, Light Show (Hayward Gallery London 2013) and (Auckland Art Gallery) 2014–15, RA Summer Exhbn 2014, MOFO (Museum of Old and New Art Tasmania) 2014, Epicentre: Conversations and discussions between artists (Parra & Romero Ibiza) 2014, Lexus Hybrid Art (Optika Pavilion Moscow) 2014, Victoria Miro (Schloss Sihlberg Zürich) 2014, Light Show (Auckland Art Gallery New Zealand) 2014, Primal Architecture (IMMA Dublin) 2014, Da Vinci: Shaping the Future (Art Science Museum Singapore) 2014, Proportio (Palazzo Fortuny Venice) 2015, Art Out Loud (Chatsworth House Derbyshire) 2015; *Public Commissions* incl: Paradigm Francis Crick Inst London 2016, The Optic Cloak Greenwich Peninsula London 2016; *Style—* Conrad Shawcross, Esq; ✉ c/o The Royal Academy, Burlington House, Piccadilly, London W1J 0BD; c/o Victoria Miro Gallery, 16 Wharf Road, London N1 7RW (☎ 020 7336 8109, e-mail info@victoria-miro.com, website www.victoria-miro.com)

SHAWCROSS, Eleanor Joan Georgina; da of William Shawcross, CVO, *qv*, and Michal, *née* Levin; *Educ* St Paul's Girls' Sch, Univ of Oxford; *m* Lord Wolfson of Aspley Guise, *qv*; *Career* former mgmnt conslt Boston Consulting Gp, currently special advsr to Rt Hon George Osborne, MP, *qv*; *Style—* Ms Eleanor Shawcross; ✉ Advisor to the Chancellor of the Exchequer 11 Downing Street London SW1A 2AB

SHAWCROSS, Valerie; CBE (2002), AM; *b* 1958; *Educ* Queen Elizabeth HS Manchester, Univ of Liverpool (BA), Univ of London (MA); *Career* dep pres Guild of Undergrads Univ of Liverpool 1980–81, exec offr UK Cncl for Overseas Students' Affrs 1981–84, ILEA Further and Higher Educn Div 1984–86, campaign offr World Univ Service (UK) 1986–87, project mangr Cwlth Secretariat 1987–91, head of Public Affairs Nat Fedn of Women's Insts 1991–92, Nat Women's Offr Lab Pty 1993, cncllr London Borough of Croydon 1994–2000 (chair Educn Ctee 1995–97, dep ldr 1996–97, ldr 1997–2000); GLA: memb London Assembly (Lab) Lambeth & Southwark 2000–16, chair Tport Ctee 2008–09, 2011–12, 2013–14 and 2015–16 (vice-chair 2009–10, 2012–13 and 2013–14), memb London Fire and Emergency Planning Authy 2013–15 (chair 2000–08); memb Lab Pty 1979–; *Recreations* swimming, poetry, theatre; *Style—* Ms Valerie Shawcross, CBE, AM; ✉ e-mail val@valshawcross.com, website www.valshawcross.com, Twitter @ValShawcross, Facebook Valerie Shawcross)

SHAWCROSS, (Hon) William Hartley Hume; CVO (2011); s (by 2 m) Baron Shawcross (Life Peer, d 2003); *b* 28 May 1946; *Educ* Eton, UC Oxford; *m* 1, 1972 (m dis 1980), Marina Warner, *qv*, da of Col Esmond Pelham Warner, TD (d 1982), of Cambridge; 1 s (Conrad Hartley Pelham b 1977); m 2, 1981 (m dis), Michal, da of late A J Levin by his w Leah; 1 da (Eleanor Joan Georgina b 1983); m 3, 1993, Olga Polizzi, CBE, *qv*, eldest da of Baron Forte (Life Peer) (d 2007), and wid of Marchese Alessandro Polizzi di Sorentino; *Career* writer and broadcaster; chm Article 19: The Int Centre on Censorship 1986–96; memb Bd Int Crisis Gp 1995–2006; memb Informal Advsy Gp UNHCR 1996–2001; memb Govr's World Service Consultative Gp BBC 1997–2004; memb Cncl Disasters Emergency Ctee 1998–2002; assoc prodr and presenter Queen and Country (BBC TV series) 2002; chm Charity Cmmn 2012–; patron The Wiener Library, memb Bd Anglo-Israel Assoc, memb Bd Henry Jackson Soc; *Books* Dubcek (1970), Crime and Compromise (1974), Sideshow (1979), The Quality of Mercy (1984), The Shah's Last Ride (1989), Rupert Murdoch (1992), Deliver Us from Evil: Warlords, Peacekeepers and a World of Endless Conflict (2001), Queen and Country (2002), Allies: The United States, Britain and the War in Iraq (2003), The Official Biography of Queen Elizabeth the Queen Mother (2009), Justice and the Enemy – Nuremberg 9/11 and the Trial of Khalid Sheikh Mohammed (2012); *Style—* William Shawcross, CVO; ✉ Janklow & Nesbit, 13A Hillgate Street, London W8 7SP (website www.williamshawcross.com)

SHAWYER, Peter Michael; s of Edward William Francis Shawyer (d 1986), of Brookmans Park Herts, and Marjorie Josephine Shawyer; *b* 11 September 1950; *Educ* Enfield GS, Univ of Sheffield (BA); *m* 23 June 1979, Margot Anne, da of Wing Cdr Norman Edwin Bishop (d 1975), of Sidmouth, Devon; 1 da (Emily b 3 Dec 1980), 1 s (Richard b 14 March 1984); *Career* CA; Deloitte & Touche (formerly Touche Ross): joined 1972, memb Bd, managing ptnr, memb Euro Mgmnt Bd, memb Central Europe Bd; specialist in taxation and author of numerous tax articles in specialist journals; FCA 1975; *Recreations* golf; *Clubs* Hadley Wood Golf, Brocket Hall Golf; *Style—* Peter Shawyer, Esq; ✉ Deloitte & Touche, Stonecutter Court, 1 Stonecutter Street, London EC4A 4TR (☎ 020 7303 5764, fax 020 7353 8648, telex 884739 TRLNDN G)

SHEA, Dr Jamie Patrick; *b* 11 September 1953; *Educ* Univ of Sussex (BA), Lincoln Coll Oxford (DPhil); *Family* m with 2 c; *Career* NATO: admin Cncl Ops Section of Exec Secretariat 1980–82, head of youth programmes 1982–85, head of external relations conferences and seminars 1985–98, asst to sec-gen 1988–91, dep head and sr planning offr Policy Planning Unit and Multilateral Affairs Section of Political Directorate 1991–93, spokesman and dep dir of info and press 1993–2000 (the public voice of NATO during the Kosovo conflict March-June 1999), dir of info and press 2000–, dep asst sec-gen 2003–; PR Week Euro Communicator of 1999; hon fell Atlantic Cncl of UK, external assoc Centre for Defence and Security Studies Univ of Manitoba Winnipeg Canada, fndn year fell, 21st Century Fndn, assoc memb Institut Royal des Relations Internationales Brussels; vice-pres and memb of bd of govrs Centre d'Etudes de Relations Internationales et Stratégiques Univ Libre de Bruxelles 1988– (Jean Monnet visiting prof), prof of int relations American Univ Washington DC 1985–99, lectr in defence studies Univ of Lille 1987–90, adjunct prof of int relations James Madison Coll Michigan State Univ 1987–, dir MSU Summer Sch Brussels 1987–, course instr Int Relations MA Boston Univ 1991–94, lectr in US/Euro Relations Univ of Antwerp 1993–; memb: Advsy Bd Centre d'Etudes et de Prospectives Stratégiques Paris, Trans-Atlantic Policy Network, Centre for Euro Policy Studies Brussels, Euro-Atlantic Movement, Int Studies Assoc USA; *Publications* The NATO Executive Secretariat (1983), NATO and Public Opinion (1986), The Myths of Anti-Americanism (1986), The Atlantic Gap: National Differences and the Future of the Alliance – Options for Action by the Private Sector (1987), NATO Public Opinion Survey (1987, 1988 and 1989), NATO's Future (1989), NATO 2000: The View from Brussels (1990), Moving on from the London Declaration: The Political Role of NATO in the new Europe (1992), The Impact of the Moscow Coup on NATO (1992), Coping with Disorder in Europe (1993), NATO in the 1990s (with Prof Michael Schechter, 2001); also articles in jls and book chapters; *Style—* Dr Jamie Shea; ✉ NATO, Division of Public Diplomacy, NATO Headquarters, Blvd Leopold III, 1110 Brussels, Belgium (☎ 02 707 44 13, fax 02 707 45 79, e-mail j.shea@hq.nato.int)

SHEADER, Timothy; *Career* artistic dir Regent's Park Open Air Theatre 2007–; *Style—* Timothy Sheader, Esq; ✉ Regent's Park Theatre Ltd, Stage Door Gate, Open Air Theatre, Inner Circle, Regent's Park, London NW1 4NU

SHEARD, Rodney Kilner (Rod); s of Saville Kilner Sheard (d 1990), and Margaret Helen, *née* Gibson; *b* 11 September 1951, Brisbane, Aust; *Educ* Indooroopilly HS Queensland, Queensland Inst of Technol (DipArch); *m* 30 July 1988, Catherine Marie Elisabeth, *née* Nouqueret; 2 s (Pierre Saville b 25 Nov 1989, Louis Alexandre b 21 July 1999); *Career* architect; specialist in stadia and creator of Stadia Generations concept; ptnr Howard Lobb and Ptnrs 1981 (joined 1975), chm LOBB 1993, currently sr princ and memb Bd HOK Sport+Venue+Event (formerly HOK+LOBB); work exhibited at Royal Acad and by Design Cncl; memb Venue Mgmnt Assoc; Hon DSc Univ of Luton 2002; RIBA 1977, FRSA, MRAIA; *Projects* incl: Croke Park Masterplan Dublin 1989–90, Royal Selangor Turf Club Kuala Lumpur 1989–93, Alfred McAlpine Stadium Huddersfield 1991–93 (RIBA Building of the Year Award 1995), Arsenal FC North Stand 1991–93, Chelsea FC North Stand 1993–94, Reebok Stadium Bolton Wanderers FC 1994–97, Millennium Stadium Cardiff 1995–99, Kempton Park Racecourse Main Stand 1995–97, Westpac Trust Stadium Wellington 1996–2000, Telstra Stadium (formerly Stadium Australia) Sydney 1996–99, Telstra Dome (formerly Colonial Stadium) Melbourne 1996–2000, Wembley National Stadium 1998–, Ipswich Town FC North Stand 1999–2002, Members' Facilities All England Lawn Tennis & Croquet Club Wimbledon 1999–2002, Arsenal Stadium Arsenal FC 1999–, Suncorp Stadium Brisbane 2000–03, Ascot Racecourse 2001–, Centre Court All England Lawn Tennis & Croquet Club Wimbledon 2002–; *Publications* Sports Architecture (2001), Stadia: A Design & Development Guide (with Prof Geraint John, *qv*, 1994); *Recreations* fly fishing, sailing, skiing, reading; *Clubs* RAC; *Style—* Rod Sheard, Esq; ✉ Populous, 14 Blades Court, Deodar Road, London SW15 2NU

S

SHEARER, Alan; CBE (2016, OBE 2001); s of Alan Shearer, and Anne, *née* Collins; *b* 13 August 1970; *Educ* Gosforth HS Newcastle upon Tyne; *m* Lainya; 1 s (Will), 2 da (Chloe, Hollie); *Career* football pundit and former professional footballer; clubs: Southampton FC 1988–92 (over 100 appearances), Blackburn Rovers 1992–96 (transferred for then Br record fee of £3.2 million, winners FA Premier League 1994/95), Newcastle United 1996–2006 (transferred for then world record fee of £15 million, player-coach 2005–06); England: 63 full caps (30 as captain) and 30 goals (scored on debut v France 1992), capt England 1996–2000, memb squad European Championships 1992, 1996 and 2000, memb squad World Cup 1998, ret 2000; temp mangr Newcastle United 2009; Sport Writers Player of the Year 1994, PFA Player of the Year 1995 and 1997, third FIFA World Player of 1996 Awards, Premier League Overall Player of the Decade 2003, Domestic Player of the Decade 2003; currently pundit Match of the Day (BBC); *Style—* Alan Shearer, Esq, CBE

SHEARER, Anthony Patrick (Tony); s of James Francis Shearer, CBE (d 1997), and Judith Margaret, *née* Bowman (d 2011); *b* 24 October 1948, Wimbledon, London; *Educ* Rugby; *m* 1, 1 Dec 1972 (m dis 2007), Jennifer, da of Alfred Dixon (d 1981); 2 da (Juliet b 19 Aug 1980, Lauretta b 30 March 1982); m 2, 31 March 2007, Pam, da of Ken Mapes (d 2003); *Career* chief exec Singer & Friedlander Gp 2003–05; ptnr Deloitte Haskins & Sells 1980–88 (joined 1967), chief operating offr M & G Group plc 1988–96, chief exec Electronic Share Information Ltd 1996–97, chief exec Mellon Fund Administration Ltd

1997–98, dep chief exec Old Mutual International 1998–2001; chm: Planet Recruit Ltd 2000–03, Updata plc 2001–03 and 2009–, Uruguay Mineral Exploration Inc 2002–09, Caxton FX 2006–11, Jerrold Hldgs 2006–07, UK Wealth Mgmnt 2007–11, Abbey Protection Gp 2007–14, IMAS Corporate Advsrs Ltd 2009, Gees Haulage 2009–11, Triple Plate Junction 2010–15, Sparkl 2012–, Orosur Mining Inc 2012–13; non-exec dir: Gremlin Group plc 1997–98, Wogen plc 2005–, Harvard Int plc (formerly Alba plc) 2008–12; govr Rugby Sch 1994–2004, chm of govrs Packwood Haugh Sch 2000–06; FCA; *Publications* numerous articles and letters; interviews on TV and radio; *Recreations* skiing, tennis, rock 'n' roll; *Clubs* Brooks's, Hurlingham, MCC; *Style—* Tony Shearer, Esq; ✉ 8 Kew Bridge Road, London TW8 0FG (e-mail tony@tonyshearer.com)

SHEARER, David James Buchanan; s of John Shearer (d 2012), of Glasgow, and Muriel, *née* Dunn (d 2003); *b* 24 March 1959, Dumfries; *Educ* Eastwood HS Glasgow, Univ of Glasgow (BAcc), Columbia Business Sch; *Partner* Virginia Helen Wallis Braid; *Career* qualified CA 1983; Deloitte & Touche: joined 1979, ptnr 1988, ptnr in charge Corporate Finance and exec memb Nat Corporate Finance 1992–99, global dir of corporate finance Deloitte Touche Tohmatsu 1996–99, sr ptnr Scotland and NI, memb UK Bd and memb UK Exec Gp 1999–2003; ptnr Buchanan Shearer Assocs LLP 2012–; chm: Crest Nicholson plc 2007–09, Mouchel Gp 2012–14, Aberdeen New Dawn Investment Tst plc 2012– (previously dep chm), Scottish Edge Fund 2014–, Liberty Living Gp 2015–; co-chm Martin Currie (Hldgs) Ltd 2012–14 (previously non-exec dir); non-exec dir: HBOS plc 2004–07, Scottish Financial Enterprise 2005–10, Mithras Investment Tst 2007–; sr ind dir: Renold plc 2007–12, STV Gp plc 2007–, Superglass Hldgs plc 2007–12; chief strategic advsr and non-exec dir City Inn Ltd 2010–11; govr Glasgow Sch of Art 2004–10; FRSA, FIoD; *Recreations* heli-skiing, yachting, rugby, golf, art, wine; *Clubs* Royal Western Yacht, Braemar Golf; *Style—* David Shearer, Esq; ✉ 32 Great Western Terrace Lane, Glasgow G12 9XB (☎ 0141 342 4243, e-mail djbshearer@btopenworld.com)

SHEARER, Patrick John; QPM (2007); *Educ* Univ of Aberdeen (MA, LLB); *Career* Grampian Police: joined 1983, asst chief constable 2001–05, dep chief constable 2005–07; chief constable Dumfries and Galloway Constabulary 2007–; *Style—* Patrick J Shearer, QPM; ✉ Dumfries and Galloway Constabulary, Cornwall Mount, Dumfries DG1 1PZ (☎ 01387 242201, e-mail executive@dg.pnn.police.uk)

SHEARS, Philip Peter; QC (1996); s of Arthur Geoffrey Shears (d 1969), of Hong Kong, and Olave, *née* Grain (d 1967); *b* 10 May 1947; *Educ* The Leys Sch Cambridge, Univ of Nottingham (LLB), Univ of Cambridge (LLB); *m* 2, 1990, Sarah; 3 c by prev m (James b 1977, Eleanor b 1980, Michael b 1981); *Career* called to the Bar Middle Temple 1972; memb Midland Circuit, recorder of the Crown Court 1990– (asst recorder 1985), specialist in commercial fraud and serious crime; Liveryman Worshipful Co of Fletchers; memb Criminal Bar Assoc; *Recreations* sailing, country sports; *Clubs* Royal Yacht Squadron, Royal London Yacht (past Cdre), Bar Yacht; *Style—* Philip Shears, Esq, QC; ✉ 7 Bedford Row, London WC1R 4BU (☎ 020 7242 3555, fax 020 7242 2511)

SHEARSMITH, Reeson Wayne (Reece); s of Reece Shearsmith, of Hull, and Christine, *née* Don; *b* 27 August 1969; *Educ* Bretton Hall Coll (BA); *m* 17 Feb 2001, Jane, *née* Welch; 1 da (Holly Madeline b 16 Sept 2002), 1 s (Daniel Finbar b 23 June 2004); *Career* comedian, actor and writer; Hon Dr Univ of Huddersfield 2003, Hon Dr Univ of Hull 2013; *Theatre* A Local Show for Local People (Theatre Royal London and UK tour) 2000–01, Art (Whitehall Theatre London) 2002–03, As You Like It (Wyndham's Theatre London) 2005, Leo Bloom in The Producers (Theatre Royal London) 2006, Nick Finchling in The Common Pursuit (Chocolate Factory) 2008, Phil Murray in Comedians (Lyric Hammersmith) 2009, Narrator in The Rocky Horror Show (Hull New Theatre, nat tour) 2010, Betty Blue Eyes (Novello) 2011, Ghost Stories (Duke of York) 2010, Colin in Absent Friends (Harold Pinter Theatre) 2012, Hangmen (Royal Court) 2015, The Dresser (Duke of York's Theatre) 2016; *Television* BBC: Alexei Sayle's Merry-Go-Round 1998, Lenny Goes to Town 1998, In the Red 1998, The League of Gentlemen 1999, 2000 and 2002, Randall & Hopkirk (Deceased) 2000, TLC 2002, Catterick 2003, New Tricks, Psychoville 2009 and 2010 (also writer), Victoria Wood's Midlife Christmas 2009, House of Fools 2013, Inside No 9 2013, Horrible Histories 2013, An Adventure in Space and Time 2013, Car Share 2014, Doctor Who 2015, Car Share (BBC 1) 2015, Inside No. 9 (bbc 2) 2015/16, Stag (BBC 2) 2016; other credits incl: Spaced (Channel 4) 1999, The All Star Comedy Show (ITV) 2004, Max and Paddy's Road to Nowhere (Channel 4) 2004, Ladies & Gentlemen (Channel 4), The Abbey (ITV), Christmas at the Riviera (ITV), Marple (ITV), Ickle Bill Um (Channel 4), Bad Sugar (Channel 4) 2012, Psychobitches (Sky Arts) 2013, The Widower (ITV) 2013, Chasing Shadows (ITV) 2014, Alan Partridge – Mid Morning Matters (Sky) 2014, Hunderby (Sky) 2015; *Radio* On the Town with the League of Gentlemen (Radio 4) 1997, Self Storage (BBC Radio 4), Reece Shearsmith's Haunted House (BBC Radio 4) 2009, Bird Island (Radio 4) 2012, Aonach Hourn (BBC Radio 4) 2014; *Film* This Year's Love 1999, Birthday Girl 2001, Shaun of the Dead 2003, The League of Gentlemen's Apocalypse 2005, The Cottage 2007, Burke & Hare 2010, A Field in England 2013, The World's End 2013, High Rise 2014; *Awards* Perrier Award 1997, Sony Silver Award for Radio Comedy 1998, Golden Rose of Montreux 1999, Best Entertainment Award RTS 2000, Best Comedy Series BAFTA 2000, NME Readers' Poll 2001, Best Comedy South Bank Show 2003, Best New TV Comedy Br Comedy Award 2009 (for Psychoville), nominated Olivier Award 2011 (for Betty Blue Eyes), Best Comedy Performance RTS Award (for Inside No. 9) 2014; *Publications* A Local Book for Local People (2000), The League of Gentlemen (script book, 2003), The League of Gentlemen's Book of Precious Things (2007); *Recreations* drawing (caricatures, cartoons), magic, conjuring; *Clubs* Soho House; *Style—* Reece Shearsmith, Esq; ✉ Twitter @reeceshearsmith; c/o Nick Forgacs, Independent Talent Group Ltd, 40 Whitfield Street, London W1T 2RH (☎ 020 7636 6565)

SHEBBEARE, Sir Thomas Andrew (Tom); KCVO (2003, CVO 1996); s of late Robert Austin Shebbeare, and Frances Dare Graham; *b* 25 January 1952; *Educ* Malvern, Univ of Exeter (BA); *m* 1976, Cynthia Jane Cottrell; 1 s, 1 da; *Career* World University Service (UK) 1973–75, gen sec British Youth Cncl 1975–80, admin Cncl of Europe 1980–85, exec dir Euro Youth Fndn 1985–88, chief exec The Prince's Tst 1998–2003 (dir 1988–98), dir of charities to HRH The Prince of Wales 2004–11; chm: Foundations Forum 2004–09, Virgin Money Giving 2012–, Virgin StartUp 2013–; dir: Gifts in Kind 1996–, UK Skills 1998–2004, Skills Festivals Co 1999–, Sch Food Tst 2005–10; tstee: The Nations Tst 1995–2004, The Prince's Charities Fndn China 2007–, Turquoise Mountain Fndn 2007–; chm Spring Films Ltd 2012–; dir: CIM Investment Mgmnt Ltd 2006–, Delphis-Eco Ltd 2012–; tstee: Queen's Coll London 2006–13, Royal Parks Fndn 2012–; fell Green Templeton Coll Oxford; Hon LLD Univ of Exeter 2005; *Recreations* family, cooking, gardening, food and drink; *Style—* Sir Tom Shebbeare

SHEDDEN, Dr (William) Ian Hamilton; s of George Shedden (d 1966), of Bathgate, Scotland, and Agnes Hamilton, *née* Heigh (d 1979); *b* 21 March 1934; *Educ* The Acad Bathgate, Univ of Edinburgh (BSc, MB ChB), Univ of Birmingham (MD), City Univ London (Dip Law); *m* 21 March 1960, Elma Joyce, da of Lewis M Jobson (d 1985), of Edinburgh; 3 s (Malcolm b 1960, Andrew b 1962, Colin b 1971), 1 da (Clare b 1968); *Career* cmmnd Capt RAMC 1961–67, regtl MO Hallamshire Bn York and Lancaster Regt 1961–67; lectr Univ of Sheffield 1960–64, sr res fell MRC 1964–67, dir R&D Lilly Industries Ltd 1968–77, vice-pres Eli Lilly & Co USA 1977–83, prof of med Univ of Indiana USA 1979–, md Glaxo Group Research Ltd 1983–86; dir: Speywood Group, The Speywood Laboratory 1991–97, Speywood Pharmaceuticals 1994–97; non-exec dir Evolutec Ltd 2000–01; asst dep coroner City of London 1987–99, conslt physician Institut Henri Beaufour Paris 1998–2001; Freeman City of London 1975, Liveryman Worshipful Soc of Apothecaries 1974; CBiol, FIBiol 1969, FRCPEd 1983, FACP 1981, FFPM 1990, FRCP 1991; *Books* Vinca Alkaloids in the Chemotherapy of Malignant Disease (ed vol 1–3, 1968–70); *Recreations* golf, travel (especially in the Antarctic); *Clubs* Naval and Military, The Dalmahoy; *Style—* Dr Ian Shedden; ✉ Beachamwell House, Beachamwell Road, Swaffham, Norfolk PE37 8BF (☎ 01760 724126, fax 01760 724135, e-mail ian.shedden@ukgateway.net)

SHEEHAN, Prof Antony; s of Thomas Sheehan (d 1977), of Cork, Ireland, and Mary Kerr, *née* Hood; *b* 10 September 1964, Cannock, Staffs; *Educ* Cardinal Griffin RC Sch Cannock, Staffs Coll (CertEd), St George's Psychiatric Sch Stafford, Manchester Met Univ (BEd), Univ of Nottingham (MPhil), Univ of Keele (DipHSM); *m* 26 March 2001, Andrea, *née* Coleman; 1 s (Ashley Thomas b 2 March 1984), 3 da (Bonnie Michelle b 2 Jan 1988, Ellie b 10 Aug 2006, Ava b 8 Nov 2009); *Career* mental health nurse; formerly: dir and mgmnt conslt European Nursing Devpt Agency, dir of serv devpt Fndn NHS Tst Staffs, asst regnl dir of public health NHS Exec W Midlands 1995–99, jt head of mental health then ceo Nat Inst for Mental Health in Eng (NIMHE) and dir of mental health Dept of Health 1999–2003, DG Care Servs Dept of Health 2003–06, DG Health and Care Partnerships Dept of Health 2006–07, chief exec Leicestershire Partnership NHS Tst 2007–; chair and memb numerous Govt, departmental and NHS ctees and gps incl memb Expert Bd on Mental Health and Learning Disabilities NI Dept of Health 2007–09; visiting prof of health and social care strategy De Montfort Univ; visiting prof Univ of Central England; memb Panel of Inquiry Gray Report 1995; conslt: Int Cncl of Nurses and WHO Geneva 1990, WHO Copenhagen 1994, Ivan Sechenov Acad Moscow 1994; memb Editorial Bd Public Serv Leadership Jl, author of more than 50 pubns; chair of tstees Together charity 2007–, patron AS-IT, former pres No Panic; registered nurse; IHI fell 2011–12; Hon DSc Univ of Wolverhampton 2003, Hon Dr Univ of Staffordshire 2005; MHSM, Hon MFPH, FRSA; *Recreations* walking with dogs, film, photography, fast cars; *Style—* Prof Antony Sheehan; ✉ Leicestershire Partnership NHS Trust, George Hine House, Gipsy Lane, Leicester LE5 0TD (☎ 0116 2256547, fax 0116 2256679, e-mail antony.sheehan@leicsport.nhs.uk)

SHEEHAN, Malcolm; QC (2015); s of John Sheehan (d 2013), and Mary Josephine, née Hyland, of Almondbury, W Yorks; *Educ* Univ of Oxford (MA); *Partner* Alexis Roberts; *Career* called to the Bar (Lincoln's Inn) 1993, judicial asst to the Ct of Appeal 1997, judge of the First Tier Tbnl 2009; AG's Panel of Jr Counsel to the Crown 2006–15; memb: London Common Law and Commercial Bar Assoc, Commercial Bar Assoc, Health and Safety Lawyers Assoc, Professional Negligence Bar Assoc, Personal Injury Bar Assoc; *Recreations* skiing, tennis, travel, swimming, theatre; *Style—* Malcolm Sheehan, Esq, QC; ✉ Henderson Chambers, 2 Harcourt Buildings, London EC4Y 9DB

SHEEHY, Sir Patrick; kt (1991); s of Sir John Francis Sheehy, CSI (d 1949), and Jean Newton Simpson (d 1993); *b* 2 September 1930; *Educ* Australia, Ampleforth; *m* 1964, Jill Patricia Tindall; 1 s, 1 da; *Career* Nat Serv 2 Lt Irish Gds 1948–50; British-American Tobacco Co: joined 1950, various appts Nigeria, Ghana, Ethiopia and West Indies, mktg advsr London 1962–67, gen mangr Holland 1967, memb Gp Bd 1970, memb Chm's Policy Ctee and chm Tobacco Div 1975; BAT Industries plc: dep chm 1976–81 (chm BATCo Bd), vice-chm 1981–82, chm 1982–95; chm: Marlborough Underwriting 1996, Perpetual Income Investment Trust Ltd 1996–2007; non-exec dir: British Petroleum Company plc 1984–98, Asda Property Holdings 1994–, Abdela Holdings UK Ltd 1996, Sherritt International Corp 1996–, Celtic plc 1996, EFG Private Bank Ltd 1996, Cluff Mining 1997–; memb Cncl of Int Advsrs Swiss Bank Corporation 1985–97, memb Bd The Spectator 1988–2004; formerly memb: President's Ctee CBI, European Roundtable of Industrialists, Action Ctee for Europe, Cncl RIIA; estab Franco British Colloque 1990–, chm Home Office Inquiry into Police Responsibility and Rewards; Chevalier de la Légion d'Honneur (France) 1995; *Recreations* golf, reading, skiing; *Style—* Sir Patrick Sheehy

SHEEN, Michael; OBE (2009); s of Meyrick Sheen, and Irene Sheen; *b* 5 February 1969, Newport, S Wales; *Educ* Glan Afan Comp Sch Port Talbot, Royal Acad of Dramatic Art; *Children* 1 da (Lily Mo); *Career* actor; *Television* incl: The Deal 2003, Dirty Filthy Love 2004, Kenneth Williams: Fantabulosa! 2006, Masters of Sex 2013–; *Film* incl: Kingdom of Heaven 2005, Underworld: Evolution 2006, The Queen 2006, Blood Diamond 2006, Frost/Nixon 2009 (Best Actor Evening Standard Br Film Award 2009 (jtly)), Underworld: Rise of the Lycans 2009, The Damned United 2009, Twilight: New Moon 2009, Alice In Wonderland 2010, Beautiful Boy 2010, The Special Relationship 2010, TRON: Legacy 2010, Admission 2013, Kill the Messenger 2014, Far from the Madding Crowd 2015; *Theatre* incl: Frost/Nixon, Caligula, Look Back In Anger, Peer Gynt, Moonlight, Romeo and Juliet, Hamlet; *Style—* Michael Sheen, Esq, OBE; ✉ Roxane Vacca, 61 Judd Street, London WC1H 9QT

SHEERMAN, Barry John; MP; s of William Sheerman; *b* 17 August 1940; *Educ* Hampton GS, LSE (BSc), Univ of London (MSc); *m* 1965, Pamela Elizabeth, *née* Brenchley; 1 s, 3 da; *Career* former univ lectr; MP (Lab): Huddersfield E 1979–83, Huddersfield 1983–; memb: Public Accounts Ctee 1980–83, Parly Univ Gp; chm: Parly Advsy Cncl for Tport Safety, Educn and Skills Ctee 1999–; chair: Parly Manufacturing Industry Gp, Parly Gp for Design and Innovation, Cross Pty Advsy Gp on Preparation for EMU, Policy Connect (formerly Made In The UK then Networking for Industry), Labour Party School to Work Cmmn, Gp on Sustainable Manufacturing, Cross-Pty Gp on European Economic Reform 2005–, Skills Cmmn 2006, EPSRC High Level 2012; oppn front bench spokesman on employment and educn with special responsibility for devpt of educn policy and trg for over-16s 1983–87, spokesman on employment 1987–97, home affairs front bench spokesman on police, prisons, crime prevention, drugs, civil defence and fire serv, dep to Rt Hon Roy Hattersley MP 1988–92, shadow min for disability rights 1992–94, memb Sec of State for Trade and Industry's Manufacturing Task Force, memb HE Cmmn 2011; chair World Bank Global Road Safety Partnership 2002–04, chair Urban Mines 2003, chair John Clare Educn and Environment Tst 2005–; Hon DEd: Kingston Univ 2006, Univ of Bradford 2006; *Books* Harold Laski (with Isaac Kramnick, 1993); *Recreations* social entrepreneuring, walking, music; *Style—* Barry Sheerman, Esq, MP; ✉ House of Commons, London SW1A 0AA (☎ 020 7219 5037, constituency office 01484 451382, e-mail sheermanb@parliament.uk, website www.barry4huddersfield.co.uk, Twitter @barrysheerman)

SHEFF, Sylvia Claire; MBE (1995), JP (1976); da of Isaac Glickman (d 1981), of Prestwich, Manchester, and Rita, *née* Bor (d 1976); *b* 9 November 1935; *Educ* Stand GS for Girls, Univ of Manchester (BA); *m* 28 Dec 1958, Alan Frederick Sheff (d 1986); 1 da (Janine Rachel b 1960), 1 s (Marcus Jeremy b 1963); *Career* teacher 1958–77; fndr and dir Friendship with Israel All-Pty Gp (in European Parl) 1979–90, asst nat dir Cons Friends of Israel 1985–89 (nat projects dir 1974–85), assoc dir Manchester Jewish Cultural Centre 1990–94; chm and pres Manchester 35 Gp Women's Campaign for Soviet Jewry 1980– (fndr chm 1972–80), fndr memb Bury Family Conciliation Serv Mgmnt Ctee 1985–87, hon sec Nat Cncl for Soviet Jewry UK 1987–89 (memb Cncl 1975–90), del Bd of Deps of Br Jews 1987–, int co-ordinator Yeled Yafeh Fellowship Children of Chernobyl Project 1990–94, memb UK Assoc of Jewish Lawyers and Jurists 2001–; delg and lectr Jewish Rep Cncl of Gtr Manchester; concert promoter/dir Manchester Jewish Community's Musical Tribute to HM The Queen on Her Golden Jubilee 2002–, memb Exec Ctee Jewish Rep Cncl of Gtr Manchester and Region 2009–, fndr and dir Orgn of Jewish Lawyers 2008–; *Recreations* bridge, theatre, opera, travel; *Style—* Mrs Sylvia Sheff, MBE; ✉ 6

The Meadows, Old Hall Lane, Whitefield, Manchester M45 7RZ (☎ 0161 766 4391, fax 0161 766 4391, e-mail sylvia@sheff.fsbusiness.co.uk)

SHEFFIELD, Graham; CBE (2010); *b* 12 February 1952, London; *Educ* Univ of Edinburgh (BA); *m*; 2 c; *Career* music prodr BBC Radio 1976–90 (series incl: Ragas and the Republic, Music Weekly and Tasting Notes (Sony Radio Award 1990)), music dir South Bank Centre 1990–95 (fndr Meltdown Festival), artistic dir Barbican 1995–; chair Int Soc of Performing Arts 2004–06, chm Royal Philharmonic Soc 2005–, cncl memb Arts Cncl Eng 2002–08, int artistic assoc Luminato Festival Toronto 2007–; Hon Dr of Arts City Univ; Chevalier de l'Ordre des Arts et des Lettres (France) 2005, Chevalier de Tastevin de Bourgogne (France) 2005; *Recreations* wine, cricket, skiing, piano; *Clubs* MCC; *Style—* Graham Sheffield, Esq, CBE; ✉ Barbican Centre, Silk Street, London EC2Y 8DS

SHEFFIELD, Sir Reginald Adrian Berkeley; 8 Bt (GB 1755), of Normanby, N Lincs; DL (Lincs 1985); s of Maj Edmund Sheffield, JP, DL (d 1977), of Sutton Park, Sutton-on-the-Forest, York; (s of 6 Bt), and Nancie Miriel Denise, wid of Lt Cdr Glen Kidston, RN, and yst da of Edward Roland Soames (d 1997); suc unc, Sir Robert Sheffield, 7 Bt 1977; *b* 9 May 1946; *Educ* Eton; *m* 1, 1969 (m dis 1975), Annabel Lucy Veronica, da of late Timothy Angus Jones, and late Hon Mrs Pandora Astor; 2 da (Samantha Gwendoline (Mrs David Cameron), *qv*, b 1971, Emily Julia (Mrs Tom Mullion) b 1973); m 2, 1977, Victoria Penelope, da of late Ronald Clive Walker, DFC; 1 s (Robert Charles Berkeley b 1984), 2 da (Alice Daisy Victoria (Mrs Etienne Cadestin) b 1980, Lucy Mary (Mrs Tom Jackson) b 1981); *Heir* s, Robert Sheffield; *Career* chm Normanby Estate Holdings and subsidiaries; cncllr (Cons) Ermine Ward Humberside CC 1981–89, vice-chm S Humberside Business Advice Centre Ltd 1984–2010; memb: CLA, IOD, HHA, RHS; *Recreations* shooting, stalking; *Clubs* White's, Pratt's, Lincolnshire; *Style—* Sir Reginald Sheffield, Bt, DL; ✉ Thealby Hall, Thealby, Scunthorpe, North Lincolnshire DN15 9AB; Estate Office, Normanby, Scunthorpe, North Lincolnshire DN15 9HS; Sutton Park, Sutton-on-the-Forest, York YO61 1DP (e-mail norestate@btconnect.com)

SHEIKH, Baron (Life Peer 2006), of Cornhill in the City of London; Mohamed Iltaf Sheikh; s of late Mohamed Abdullah Sheikh, and late Kalsum Ara Sheikh; *b* 13 June 1941; *Educ* Mbale Secdy Sch Uganda, City of London Coll, Holborn Coll; *m* 1986, Shaida Begum, da of late Mohamed Lateef Thantrey; 1 da from previous m (Hon Zarina b 23 May 1971); *Career* Sun Alliance Insurance Co 1962–66, Household and Gen Insurance Co 1966–69, Guardian Royal Exchange 1969–78, Camberford Law plc 1978–2009, chm Macmillan Sheikh plc 2010–14; pres Insurance Inst of Croydon 1981–82, memb Nat Cncl of Chartered Insurance Inst 1985–87, chm Life & Pensions Gp of Insurance Inst of Croydon 1989–90, memb Ctee Financial Intermediaries Mangrs and Brokers Regulatory Assoc 1991 and 1996, regnl chm Br Insurance Brokers Assoc 1998–2002 (dir Main Bd); chm Sheikh Abdullah Fndn 2003–, chm Cons Muslim Forum 2003–14; Freeman City of London 1995; hon fell Br Inst of Cleaning Science, FCII 1968 (ACII 1966); *Recreations* walking, countryside, keeping fit, travelling; *Clubs* Carlton; *Style—* The Rt Hon the Lord Sheikh; ✉ House of Lords, London SW1A 0PW

SHEIKHOLESLAMI, Prof (Ali) Reza; s of Sultan Ali Sultani Sheikholeslami (d 1972), and Shah Zadeh, *née* Mansuri; *b* 21 July 1941; *Educ* Hadaf HS Tehran, Columbia Univ (BA), Northwestern Univ (MA), UCLA (PhD); *m* 2, 1996, Scheherezade, da of Ibrahim Vigeh; *Career* asst prof of political science Univ of Washington 1975–85, sr research fell Harvard Univ 1985–88; Univ of Oxford: visiting sr fell St Antony's Coll 1988–90, Soudavar prof of Persian studies and professorial fell Wadham Coll 1990–; *Books* The Political Economy of Saudi-Arabia, The Structure of Central Authority in Qagar Iran 1871–1896; *Recreations* reading, cycling, travelling; *Style—* Prof Reza Sheikholeslami; ✉ Oriental Institute, University of Oxford, Pusey Lane, Oxford OX1 2LE (☎ 01865 278200, fax 01865 278190, e-mail ali.sheikholeslami@orinst.oxford.ac.uk)

SHEIL, Anthony Leonard; s of William Anthony Sheil (d 1945), and Flora Aileen, *née* MacDonnell (d 1982); *b* 18 May 1932, London; *Educ* Ampleforth, ChCh Oxford; *m* 23 Nov 1997, Annette, *née* Worsley-Taylor; *Career* fndr and chm Anthony Sheil Associates (literary agency) 1962–; co-fndr and dir: Sources of History Ltd 1970–75, Wallace Aitken & Sheil 1972–89; chm Sheil Land Associates 1990–99; chm Authors Agents Assoc 1981–84; *Recreations* walking, reading, philhellenism; *Clubs* Beefsteak; *Style—* Anthony Sheil, Esq; ✉ 3/57 Drayton Gardens, London SW10 9RU (☎ 020 7835 0221, fax 020 7835 0846, e-mail anthony.sheil@gmail.com); c/o Gillon Aitken Associates Ltd, 18 Cavaye Place, London SW10 9PT (☎ 020 7373 8672, fax 020 7373 6002, e-mail anthony@aitkenalexander.co.uk)

SHEINKMAN, Elizabeth; da of Shepard A Sheinkman, and Katherine, *née* Ruben; *b* 1 June 1971, NY; *Educ* Sidwell Friends HS Washington DC, Columbia Univ NY (BA); *m* 2 July 2005, Hon James Byng; *Career* asst ed: Oxford Univ Press NY 1993–94, Alfred A Knopf 1994–96; literary agent Elaine Markson Literary Agency NY 1996–2004, dir Elaine Markson Agency Ltd UK 2004–06, sr agent and dir Book Bd Curtis Brown Gp Ltd 2006–12, agent William Morris Entertainment 2012–; co-chair Young Lions Ctee NY Public Library 2003–05, visiting fell Bread Loaf Writers' Conf 2000, 2001 and 2006, visiting lectr Chenango Valley Writers' Conf 1998 and 1999; memb: PEN 1999–, Women in Publishing (NYC Chapter) 2001–04; *Recreations* music, yoga; *Clubs* Soho House; *Style—* Ms Elizabeth Sheinkman; ✉ 151 Chesterton Road, London W10 6ET (☎ 020 8964 8883, fax 020 8969 8524); William Morris Entertainment, 100 New Oxford Street, London WC1A 1HB

SHEINWALD, Sir Nigel; GCMG (2011, KCMG 2001); s of Leonard Sheinwald (d 2006), and Joyce, *née* Posener (d 2009); *b* 26 June 1953, London; *Educ* Harrow Co Sch for Boys, Balliol Coll Oxford (MA); *m* 20 Aug 1980, Julia, *née* Dunne; 3 s; *Career* HM Diplomatic Service 1976–2012: postings in Moscow, Washington DC, Brussels, London, press sec and head News Dept FCO 1995–98, dir Europe FCO 1998–2000, UK ambass and permanent rep to the EU Brussels 2000–03; foreign policy advsr to the PM and head of Cabinet Office Def and Overseas Secretariat 2003–07, ambass to USA 2007–12; dir Royal Dutch Shell 2012–, dir Invesco Ltd 2015–; visiting prof and memb Cncl KCL 2012–; *Style—* Sir Nigel Sheinwald, GCMG; ✉ c/o Foreign and Commonwealth Office, King Charles Street, London SW1A 2AH

SHEKERDEMIAN, Marcia; QC (2015); da of Hrant Shekerdemian, and Loretta Shekerdemian; *b* 16 November 1963, London; *Educ* Trinity Hall Cambridge (BA); *m* 30 Jan 1993, Roland Higgs (d 2009); 1 s (Leo Higgs b 3 Dec 1993), 1 da (Perdita Higgs b 8 Jan 1996); *Career* called to the Bar (Middle Temple) 1987; dep registrar in bankruptcy High Court 2002; memb: Barrister's Complaints Advsy Service, Chancery Bar Assoc, Insolvency Lawyers Assoc; *Recreations* cinema, fashion, music, family life, cooking, walking; *Clubs* Athenaeum; *Style—* Ms Marcia Shekerdemian, QC; ✉ 11 Stone Buildings, Lincolns Inn, London WC2A 3TG

SHEKHDAR, James (Jim); s of Nariman Shekhdar (d 1988), and Amy Doris Shekhdar (d 1965); *b* 13 November 1946, Leamington Spa, Warks; *Educ* Leamington Coll for Boys, QMC; *m* 13 Aug 1977, Jane, *née* Riley; 2 da (Anna b 28 May 1979, Sarah b 22 April 1981); *Career* ocean rower; civil engr UK, Africa, Aust, Middle East, NZ and New Guinea 1970–81, prop of own IT business then sales and mktg role Epson 1982–85, mgmnt conslt CEE Bratislava 1985– (pt/t 1997–), ocean rower, project planner and speaker 1997–; world record unassisted and solo row of the Pacific Ocean in 274 days; supporter: Williams Fund, Saving Faces, BASICS, Population Concern; *Books* Bold Man of the Sea (2001); *Recreations* sport, adventure and exploration; *Clubs* Northwood Cricket; *Style—* Jim Shekhdar, Esq; ✉ 35 Roy Road, Northwood Middlesex HA6 1EQ (☎ and fax 01923 822411, e-mail jim.shekhdar@btinternet.com)

SHELBROOKE, Alec Edward; MP; s of Cncllr Derek Shelbrooke, and Patricia Shelbrooke, JP; *b* 1976, Kent; *Educ* Brunel Univ; *m* 27 May 2011, Susan, *née* Spencer; *Career* projects offr Univ of Leeds 1999–2010; cncllr Leeds City Cncl 2004–10, MP (Cons) Elmet and Rothwell 2010–; assoc memb IMechE 1999; *Recreations* football, reading, cricket; *Style—* Alec Shelbrooke, Esq, MP; ✉ House of Commons, London SW1A 0AA; First Floor, 43 Market Place, Wetherby LS22 6LN (☎ 01937 589002, website www.alecshelbrooke.co.uk)

SHELDON, Brig Geoffrey Paul; s of William Sheldon, of Matlock, Derbys, and Margaret, *née* Aitken; *b* 9 October 1953; *Educ* Dunfermline HS, Magdalen Coll Oxford (MA); *Career* CO 1 Bn Queen's Lancashire Regt 1991–94, directing staff Army Staff Coll 1994–95, dir Kuwait Jt Command & Staff Coll 1995–98, RCDS 1999, Cdr Br Forces Falkland Is 2000, dir Land Digitalization MOD 2001–04, account dir Defence Consulting EDS 2007; Col Queen's Lancashire Regt 2001–06, memb Queen's Lanc Regtl Cncl; *Recreations* cricket, sailing, running, military history; *Style—* Brigadier Geoffrey Sheldon; ✉ EDS, 1–3 Bartley Wood Business Park, Barley Way, Hook, Hampshire RG27 9XA (☎ 01256 742000, fax 01256 742666)

SHELDON, Paul Christopher John; *b* 5 October 1953, Kent; *Educ* Marlborough, Durham Univ; *m* 1983, June; 2 da (Nicola b 1985, Felicity b 1996), 1 s (William b 1987); *Career* Hodder and Stoughton Publishers 1975–93, md Hodder and Stoughton NZ 1988–91, ceo Surrey CCC 1996–2011, fndr Paul Sheldon Consulting 2012–; *Clubs* MCC, RAC, Wildernesse, St Enodoc; *Style—* Paul Sheldon, Esq; ✉ Paul Sheldon Consulting, 1st Floor, 1 Suffolk Way, Sevenoaks, Kent TN13 1YL

SHELDON, Richard Michael; QC (1996); s of Ralph Maurice Sheldon, of Maidenhead, Berks, and Ady, *née* Jaudel; *b* 29 September 1955; *Educ* Bolton Sch, Maidenhead GS, Jesus Coll Cambridge (MA, pres CUMC); *m* 1983, Helen Mary, da of John Lake; 1 da (Laura Jane b 1986), 2 s (Nicholas James b 1988, William Mark b 1991); *Career* called to the Bar Gray's Inn 1979; *Publications* Halsbury's Laws of England (Vol 7 (3), Companies 4 edn, 1996); *Recreations* music, bassoon; *Style—* Richard Sheldon, Esq, QC; ✉ 3/4 South Square, Gray's Inn, London WC1R 5HP (☎ 020 7696 9900, fax 020 7696 9911)

SHELDRICK, Dr (Evelyn) Carol; da of Clement Gordon Sheldrick (d 1979), and Doris Evelyn, *née* Sackett (d 1982); *b* 29 March 1942; *Educ* Woodford HS, Univ of Oxford (MA, BM BChir), Univ of London (MPhil); *m* 17-Dec-83; *Career* conslt: Maudsley Hosp 1978–97 (formerly house offr, registrar then sr registrar), Blackheath Hosp 1997–2005; author of articles and chapters on changing diagnosis in psychiatry, delinquency, sexual abuse and risk; MRCP 1971, FRCPsych 1989; *Recreations* music, theatre, gardening, walking; *Style—* Dr Carol Sheldrick

SHELFORD, Peter Bengt McNeill; s of Leonard Vere McNeill Shelford (d 1993), and Kerstin Olivia, *née* Lindberg (d 1979); *b* 20 February 1951; *Educ* St John's Sch Leatherhead, Guildford Tech Coll, Univ of Southampton, Guildford Coll of Law; *m* 1, 2 July 1977 (m dis 2001), Patricia Evelyn, da of Comet Norman Pullen; 1 s (Andrew b 21 Sept 1979), 2 da (Sarah b 30 May 1983, Emma b 25 Oct 1985); m 2, 17 July 2006, Sharon Vendiola Tabar; 1 da (Kirsten b 11 Oct 2006); *Career* admitted slr: England and Wales 1975, Hong Kong 1996; Clyde & Co: articled clerk 1973–75, asst slr 1975–79, ptnr 1979–2001 (Hong Kong office 1996–2001); ptnr DLA Piper (formerly DLA Piper Rudnick Gray Cary) 2001– (cuurently managing ptnr Bangkok office); memb: Regnl Panel Singapore International Arbitration Centre, Panel Singapore Chamber of Maritime Arbitration, Panel Hong Kong Int Arbitration Centre; fell Singapore Inst of Arbitrators; *Recreations* tennis, golf, bridge, swimming; *Style—* Peter Shelford, Esq; ✉ DLA Piper (Thailand) Ltd, 47th Floor, Unit 4707, Empire Tower, 195 South Sathorn Road, Yannawa, Sathorn, Bangkok, 10120, Thailand

SHELLEY, David; *Educ* Univ of Oxford; *Career* publishing dir Allison & Busby 2000–05; editorial dir Little, Brown Book Gp 2005–07, publisher Sphere 2007–09, dep publisher Little, Brown 2009–11, publisher Little, Brown 2011–15; ceo Orion Publishing Gp & Little, Brown 2015–; *Style—* David Shelley, Esq; ✉ Little, Brown Book Group, 100 Victoria Embankment, London EC4Y 0DY

SHELLEY, Howard Gordon; OBE (2009); s of Frederick Gordon Shelley (d 1979), and Katharine Anne, *née* Taylor; *b* 9 March 1950; *Educ* scholar: Highgate Sch, RCM; *m* 7 June 1975, Hilary Mary Pauline, *née* Macnamara; 1 s (Alexander Gordon b 1979), 1 step s (Peter Cullivan b 1962); *Career* concert pianist and conductor; London debut Wigmore Hall 1971, Henry Wood Prom debut (TV) 1972, conducting debut London Symphony Orch Barbican 1985, concert performances worldwide; has had piano concertos written for him by Cowie, Chapple and Dickinson; performed first cycle of the complete solo piano works of Rachmaninov at Wigmore Hall 1983; Two-Piano duo with Hilary Macnamara (debut 1976); princ guest conductor London Mozart Players 1992–98 (assoc conductor 1990–92), musical dir and princ conductor Uppsala Chamber Orch 2000–03; memb Worshipful Co of Musicians; FRCM, ARCO; *Recordings* incl: complete solo piano works and concertos of Rachmaninov, piano concerto cycles of Mozart, Mendelssohn, Hummel, Herz, Moscheles and Cramer, Chopin recitals, Schumann recital, Gershwin piano concerto and rhapsodies, piano concertos by Vaughan Williams, Carwithen, Alwyn, Rubbra, Tippett, Howard Ferguson and Peter Dickinson, Mozart and Schubert symphonies with RPO, Reinecke symphonies; *Awards* Chappell Gold medal 1971, Silver medal of Worshipful Co of Musicians, Dannreuther Concerto prize; *Style—* Howard Shelley, Esq, OBE; ✉ 38 Cholmeley Park, Highgate, London N6 5ER; Caroline Baird Artists, Pinkhill House, Oxford Road, Eynsham, Oxfordshire OX29 4DA (☎ and fax 01865 882771, e-mail caroline@cbartists.com)

SHELTON, Graham John; s of Alfred Thomas Shelton (d 1987), of Derby, and Louisa Emily, *née* Clarke (d 1984); *b* 26 October 1950, Derby; *Educ* Bemrose GS for Boys Derby, Univ of Wolverhampton (BA), Univ of Birmingham (scholar, MSocSci), DipHSM, Univ of Cardiff (LLM); *m* 15 Dec 1979, Noelle Margaret, da of James Minihan, of Limerick, Ireland; 3 s (Matthew William Henry b 31 Dec 1982, James Eoin b 11 Oct 1984, Piers Thomas b 25 Jan 1992), 2 da (Lydia Louise b 9 April 1987, Naomi Marie b 18 July 1989); *Career* trainee in health servs mgmnt Trent RHA, subsequent appts in W Midlands and E Anglian regions, dep unit admin The Royal Hallamshire Hosp Sheffield 1983–85, unit admin Raigmore Hosp Inverness 1985–86, dir and unit gen mangr Mental Health Servs Norwich HA 1986–93 (acting dist gen mangr 1988–89), ceo Norfolk Mental Health Care NHS Tst 1993–2000, head Mental Health NHS Exec Eastern 2000–03, md Graham Shelton Partnership Ltd 2003–12 (princ 2014–); memb Mental Health Review Tbnl 2002–; formerly: hon research fell UEA, pt/t lectr in health servs mgmnt Sheffield Hallam Univ; author of jl pubns on mgmnt and mental health servs; resident Norwich and Kilkee Co Clare Ireland; MHSM 1976; FRSA 1999; *Recreations* family, church, music, theatre, memb Aylsham Town Band, memb Norwich Cathedral Chamber Choir, Jay Singers, Norfolk and Norwich Festival Chorus and Laudemus!; *Clubs* Norfolk; *Style—* Graham Shelton, Esq; ✉ e-mail g.j.shelton@btinternet.com

SHEMILT, Prof Elaine Katherine Mary; da of Harold J Shemilt, and Margarita Isabel Diaz Medina; *b* 7 May 1954; *Educ* Bloomfield Collegiate Sch Belfast, Brighton Sch of Art, Winchester Sch of Art (BA), Royal Coll of Art (MA); *m* 1, 1977 (m dis 1984) David A Duly; 2 s (Benjamin b 1979, Emile Josef b 1980); m 2, 1985 (sep 1997), Dr T J C Murphy; 1 da (Genevieve Clare b 1988); *Career* artist; art teacher 1979–80, artist and printmaker in residence South Hill Park Arts Centre Berks 1980–82, fell in fine art and printmaking Winchester Sch of Art 1982–84, sr lectr and course dir Dept of Printmaking Sch of Fine Art Duncan of Jordanstone Coll of Art Dundee 1989– (lectr 1985–88, reader in fine art 2003–), vice-chm and dir Dundee Printmakers Workshop/Seagate Gallery Dundee 1989–

S

96, external assessor for printmaking UWE 1991–95, external assessor for printmaking Humberside Univ 1996–99, external assessor for printmaking Norwich Sch of Art and Design 1999–2001, artist in residence Univ of Wollongong NSW Aust 2000, creative dir Centre for Remote Environments Univ of Dundee; visiting lectr: Univ of Sydney Aust, Univ of Canberra Aust; professional memb Scottish Soc of Artists 1992 (memb Cncl 1995–98), pres elect Soc of Scottish Artists; Shackleton scholar; FRSA, FRGS; *Exhibitions* incl: Serpentine Gallery 1976, ICA 1978, Minories Gallery Colchester 1979, Hayward Gallery 1979, Ikon Gallery Birmingham 1980, South Hill Park Main Gallery Berks 1981, The Winchester Gallery 1984, Aspects Gallery Exeter 1984, Tom Allen Centre London 1984, The London Group Barbican 1987, Gallery Twerenbold Lucerne Switzerland 1988, Bellfrie Gallery Copenhagen 1988, Courtauld Gallery 1993, Roger Billcliffe Gallery Glasgow 1993, Scotland National Gallery of Modern Art 1993, Gallerie Centre d'Arl en Lille Geneva 1993, The Demarco European Art Fndn Edinburgh Festival 1993, Gallerie Beeldspraak Amsterdam 1995, Lamont Gallery London 1996, Kansas State Univ Gallery 1997, Moorhead State Univ Minnesota 1997, Seagate Gallery Dundee 1997, Brazen Head Gallery Norfolk 1998, Cooper Gallery DJCAD 1999, CentreSpace Dundee Contemporary Arts 1999, Dick Institute Kilmarnock 1999, Peacock Aberdeen 2000, European Media Art Festival Osnabruck Germany, Traces of Conflict Imp War Museum London 2002; *Work in Collections* BBC, Landesbank Stuttgart, Arts Cncl, Dundee City Museums and Art Galleries, Lincoln and Humberside Arts, Scottish Arts Cncl, Southern Arts; *Important Works* incl: Hayward Annual Installation 1979, Behind Appearance (toured across midwest of USA) 1997, Chimera (with, Stephen Partridge, winner of Adobe Software Award) 1998; *Style*— Prof Elaine Shemilt; ✉ Duncan of Jordanstone College of Art and Design, College of Art Science and Engineering, University of Dundee, Perth Road, Visual Research Centre, DCA 152 Nethergate, Dundee DD1 4DY (✆ 01382 385145, website www.elaineshemilt.co.uk)

SHEMMANS, David; *Educ* UMIST (BEng), Harvard Business Sch; *Career* former ops dir and co-fndr Wavedriver Ltd; sr business devpt mangr Ricardo Consulting Engrs 1999–2002, business devpt dir Ricardo plc 2002–03, md Ricardo Consulting Engrs 2003–05, ceo designate and md int ops Ricardo plc 2005, ceo Ricardo plc 2005– (memb Bd); *Style*— David Shemmans, Esq; ✉ Ricardo plc, Shoreham Technical Centre, Shoreham-by-Sea, West Sussex BN43 5FG

SHENKIN, Prof Alan; *b* 3 September 1943, Glasgow; *Educ* Hutchesons' GS Glasgow, Univ of Glasgow (BSc, MB ChB, PhD); *m* 27 June 1967, Leonna Estelle; 2 da (Susie b 1970, Trudi b 1971), 1 s (Stephen b 1975); *Career* lectr in biochemistry Univ of Glasgow 1970–74, Royal Soc European exchange fell Karolinska Inst Stockholm 1976–77; conslt in clinical biochemistry Glasgow Royal Infirmary 1978–90 (sr registrar 1974–78), prof of clinical chemistry Univ of Liverpool 1990–2007; European ed Nutrition jl 1986–2007, author of various research papers and book chapters on nutritional support and micronutrients; pres Assoc of Clinical Biochemists 2000–03 (chm Scientific Ctee 1994–96); vice-pres: European Soc of Parenteral and Enteral Nutrition 2002 (treas 1988–92, hon memb 2010–), Br Nutrition Fndn 2005–10 (hon pres 2010–); memb Cncl and Exec RCPath 1995–98 (also chm Specialty Advsy Ctee on Chemical Pathology), memb Cncl Nutrition Soc 1995–98 and 2005–08 (ctee memb Clinical Metabolism and Nutritional Support Gp 1988–94), chm Intercollegiate Gp on Nutrition 1996–2006, chm Intercollegiate Ctee on Metabolic Med 2001–03; hon memb: Czechoslovakian Med Soc and Czechoslovakian Soc for Parenteral and Enteral Nutrition 1990, Assoc of Clinical Biochemists 2008; tstee Alkaptonuria Soc 2008–, memb Cncl and tstee Royal Philosophical Soc of Glasgow 2013–; FRCPath 1990, FRCPGlas 1990, FRCP 1993; *Recreations* golf, word games, travel; *Clubs* Glasgow Golf; *Style*— Prof Alan Shenkin; ✉ 9/3 Barcapel Avenue, Newton Mearns, Glasgow G77 6QJ

SHENNAN, Bob; *b* 18 March 1962, Wirral, Merseyside; *Educ* Royal GS Lancaster, CCC Cambridge; *Career* head BBC Radio Sport 1993–98, head BBC Sport 1998–2000, controller BBC Radio Five Live 2000–08, dir of radio Channel 4 2008, controller BBC Radio 2, BBC 6Music and Asia Network 2009–, dir BBC Music 2014–; chair, fell and tstee Radio Acad; *Style*— Bob Shennan, Esq; ✉ BBC Radio 2, BBC Broadcasting House, Portland Place, London W1A 1AA

SHENNAN, Francis Gerard; s of Thomas Gerard Shennan, of Tadley, Hants, and Cecelia Shennan; *b* 14 September 1949; *Educ* Preston Catholic Coll, St Joseph's Coll Dumfries, Univ of Edinburgh (LLB); *m* 1998, Marion Young; 1 da (Lorna Young b 4 Sept 1980), 1 s (Neil Young b 7 July 1984); *Career* writer and journalist; news sub ed: Daily Mirror Manchester 1975–76, Scottish Daily Record 1976–88; recruitment columnist the Scotsman 1988–89, fndr prop The Shennan Agency 1988–2007, Scot business ed The Sunday Times 1989–90, currently dir Casino Training UK Ltd, formerly dir Footie Index Ltd; law examiner for Scot Nat Cncl for the Trg of Journalists 1981–84, external examiner of media law Napier Poly Edinburgh 1984–92; law lectr: Napier Univ, Strathclyde Univ, Glasgow Caledonian Univ, Telford Coll Edinburgh, Glasgow Metropolitan Coll, Cardonald Coll, NUJ, Associated Newspapers, Johnstone Press; speaker: Law Soc of Scotland, Nat Employment Conf, Nat Investment Forum, NW Writers' Assoc, SE Writers' Assoc; contrib to: The Herald, The Times, The Guardian, Scotland on Sunday, The Scotsman, CA Magazine, Investors' Chronicle, Mail on Sunday, and various business, media and women's magazines in UK and abroad; also corp work for Govt and Scottish enterprise agencies; UK Regnl Finance Writer of the Year 2001 and 2005 (shortlisted 1999, runner-up 2000), runner-up Scottish Financial/Business Writer of the Year 1999, shortlisted BIBA Regnl Finance Writer 2007; *Books* The Life, Passions, and Legacies of John Napier (1990), Rebels in Paradise: The Inside Story of the Battle for Celtic Football Club (with D Low); *Recreations* travelling; *Style*— Francis Shennan, Esq; ✉ 64 Ashton Lane, Glasgow G12 8SJ (✆ 0141 579 5040, e-mail info@francisshennan.com)

SHENTON, Marilyn Jennifer; da of Ivan Harold Leak (d 1998), and June, *née* Dennett (d 1978); *b* 15 December 1950; *Educ* Fallowfield C of E HS Manchester, Northern Counties Teacher Trg Coll, Univ of Birmingham, Rotherham Coll of Art and Technol; *m* 15 Sept 1971, David Lister Shenton, s of William Shenton; 2 s (Andrew Lister b 26 Jan 1979, Simon Peter b 20 April 1980); *Career* photographer; work exhibited at Bircham Gallery Norfolk, provided images for Photonica, Alamy and Getty int picture libraries, work featured in int photography and art magazines; exhibited BIPP Int Photographic Awards Exhbn 2000–01, 2001–02 and 2002–03, On the Edge (fine art and photographic exhbn, Sheringham Norfolk, in conjunction with N Norfolk Exhbn Project) 2002, Social Documentary of Gypsy Horse Fairs exhbn Gressenhall Rural Life Museum Norfolk 2002–03, N Norfolk Coastline exhbn Fine Art Landscapes N Norfolk Cncl 2003; speaker on: photographic trg overseas Cyprus 2005, art in the landscape and passion for the horse 2005–; Master Photographers' Assoc awards: Press and PR Photographer of the Year 1999, 2000, 2001 and 2002, Pictorial Photographer of the Year 2000, Fashion and Illustrative Photographer of the Year 2001, Master Photographer of the Year 2001 (nominated 2002 and 2003), Black and White Photography Award 2002; BIPP Int Photographic Awards: winner Press and PR Category 2001 (nominated 2002, bronze 2003), Art of Illustration Award 2003 (gold), New Art of Science Award 2003 (gold); assoc Master Photographers' Assoc 1997, ARPS 1997, LBIPP 2000; *Recreations* photography and art (including digital art); *Style*— Mrs Marilyn Shenton

SHEPHARD, Benjamin Peter (Ben); *b* 11 December 1974; *Educ* Chigwell Sch, Univ of Birmingham; *Career* television presenter: Control Freaks (Channel 4) 1998, The Bigger Breakfast (Channel 4) 1998, T4 1998, Planet Pop (Channel 4) 2000, Entertainment Today then GMTV Today 2000–10, This Morning (ITV) 2005–11, Soapstar Superstar (ITV)

2006, 1 vs 100 (BBC 1) 2008, The Krypton Factor (ITV) 2009–10, Goals On Sunday (Sky Sports) 2010–, UEFA Champions League (Sky Sports) 2010–, Safebreakers (Sky 1) 2011, Tipping Point (ITV) 2012–, Good Morning Britain (ITV) 2014–; *Style*— Mr Ben Shephard; ✉ c/o James Grant Group Ltd, 94 Strand On The Green, Chiswick, London W4 3NN

SHEPHARD OF NORTHWOLD, Baroness (Life Peer UK 2005), of Northwold in the County of Norfolk; Gillian Patricia Shephard; PC (1992), DL (Norfolk 2003); *b* 22 January 1940; *Educ* North Walsham Girls' HS, St Hilda's Coll Oxford; *Career* MP (Cons) Norfolk South West 1987–2005; PPS to Economic Sec to Treasy 1988–89, Parly under-sec of state DSS 1989–90, min of state HM Treasy 1990–92, sec of state for employment 1992–93, min of agriculture, fisheries and food 1993–94, sec of state for educn 1994–95, sec of state for educn and employment 1995–97; shadow ldr of the House of Commons 1997–98, shadow sec of state for environment, tport and the regions 1998–99; Cons Pty: dep chm 1991–92 and 2002–04, head of candidate devpt 2001–03; chm Assoc of Cons Peers 2006–; memb Ctee on Standards in Public Life 2003–07; chm: E of Eng Bio-Fuels Forum 2003–, Video Standards Cncl 2005–, Franco-Br Soc 2006–; patron Workers Educnl Assoc 2006–; hon fell St Hilda's Coll Oxford 1991, memb Cncl Univ of Oxford 2000–06; *Style*— The Rt Hon the Baroness Shephard of Northwold, PC, JP, DL

SHEPHERD, Geoffrey Graham; s of Henry Martin Shepherd, and Margaret, *née* Clarke; *b* 4 June 1949, Sollihull, W Midlands; *Educ* Hodge Hill Sch Birmingham, Univ of London (BSc); *Career* grad trainee health serv mgmnt 1972–74, asst administrator KCH 1974–76, administrator St George's Hosp London 1976–85, gen mangr Islington HA 1985–89, chief exec Barking and Havering Family Health Servs Authy 1989–92, chief exec Redbridge and Waltham Forest HA 1992–95, assoc dir Kensington, Chelsea and Westminster HA 1995–98, chief exec Guy's and St Thomas's Charity 1998–2009, chm Young Dementia UK Homes 2012–; chm Chelsea Social Cncl 1995–98, vice-chm Assoc of Charitable Fndns 2004–07, chm Florence Nightingale Museum 2006–11; dir Westminster Gardens Ltd 2013–; MCIPD, MHSM, FKC; *Recreations* reading, art, country life, skiing; *Style*— Geoffrey Shepherd, Esq; ✉ 29 Westminster Gardens, Marsham Street, London SW1P 4JD (✆ 07850 850843, e-mail geoffgshepherd@gmail.com)

SHEPHERD, Prof James; s of James Bell Shepherd, of Ardbeg, Bute, and Margaret McCrum, *née* Camick; *b* 8 April 1944; *Educ* Hamilton Acad, Univ of Glasgow (BSc, MB ChB, PhD); *m* 5 July 1969, Jan Bulloch, da of William Bulloch Kelly, of Motherwell; 1 s (Ewen James b 7 Feb 1974), 1 da (Fiona Elizabeth b 7 July 1976); *Career* lectr in biochemistry Univ of Glasgow 1969–72; Dept of Pathological Biochemistry Univ of Glasgow and Glasgow Royal Infirmary: lectr 1973–77, sr lectr and hon conslt 1977–84, prof and head of dept 1988–2006, prof emeritus 2006–; clinical dir Laboratories Glasgow Royal Infirmary 1993–; asst prof of med Methodist Hosp Houston TX 1976–77, visiting prof of med Cantonal Hosp Geneva 1984; dir W of Scotland Coronary Prevention Study 1989–96, dir Prospective Study of Pravastatin in the Elderly at Risk (PROSPER) 1998–2002, exec memb Treating to New Targets Study 2005, exec memb Use of Statins in Primary Prevention: an Intervention Trial Evaluating Rosuvastatin 2008; chm Euro Atherosclerosis Soc 1993–96; memb: Coronary Prevention Gp, Int Atherosclerosis Soc; FRSE 1996, FMedSci 1998, FRCP, FRCPath; *Books* incl: Lipoproteins in Coronary Heart Disease (jtly, 1986), Atherosclerosis: Developments, Complications and Treatment (jtly, 1987), Lipoprotein Metabolism (1987), Coronary Risks Revisited (ed jtly, 1989), Human Plasma Lipoproteins (ed jtly, 1989), Preventive Cardiology (ed jtly, 1991), Lipoproteins and the Pathogenesis of Atherosclerosis (ed jtly, 1991), Cardiovascular Disease: Current perspectives on the Asian-Pacific Region (ed jtly, 1994), Clinical Biochemistry: An illustrated colour text (co-author, 1995, 4 edn 2008), Lipoproteins in Health and Disease (ed jtly, 1999), Statins: The HMGCoA reductase inhibitors in perspective (ed jtly, 2000, 2 edn 2004), Lipids and Atherosclerosis Annual 2001 (ed jtly, 2001), Lipids and Atherosclerosis Annual 2003 (ed jtly, 2003); *Style*— Prof James Shepherd, FRSE; ✉ 17 Barriedale Avenue, Hamilton ML3 9DB (✆ 01698 428259, fax 01698 286281, e-mail jamesshepherd844@btinternet.com)

SHEPHERD, Prof John H; s of Dr Henry Robert Shepherd, DSC, of Enfield, Middx, and Mimika, *née* Martaki; *b* 11 July 1948; *Educ* Blundell's, Bart's Med Coll (MB BS); *m* 27 May 1972, Alison Sheila, da of Capt Henry Stephen Brandram-Adams, MBE, of Wootton, IOW; 1 s (David b 1976), 2 da (Katy b 1978, Emily b 1985); *Career* conslt gynaecological surgn: Bart's 1981–2008, Chelsea Hosp for Women 1983–84, Royal Marsden Hosp 1983–2015; prof of surgical gynaecology Bart's and the London Sch of Medicine and Dentistry Queen Mary Westfield Coll London; hon conslt King Edward VII Hosp for Offrs 1993–2015; Hunterian prof RCS 2006–07; author of over 300 chapters and scientific articles on med topics relating to cancer, gynaecology and obstetrics; pres Section of Obstetrics and Gynaecology RSM 2006–07 (hon sec 1997–98); memb: Cncl RCOG 1984–87, 1989–95 and 2004–10, Cncl Soc of Pelvic Surgns 2004–09 (vice-pres 1999, pres 2007–08), Working Pty in Gynaecological Oncology MRC; chm Gynaecological Cancer Sub Ctee of UK Co-ordinating Ctee for Cancer Res 1994–97; memb: Soc of Gynaecologic Oncologists, Chelsea Clinical Soc, Academia Europaea, NY Acad of Science; Liveryman Worshipful Soc of Apothecaries; memb BMA 1971; fell: Belgian Royal Acad of Med 1986, Singaporian Acad of Med 1987; hon fell Flemish Soc of Obstetrics and Gynaecology (VVOG) 2002; FRSM 1972, FRCS 1975, MRCOG (Gold Medal) 1978, FACOG 1981, FRCOG 1996; *Books* Clinical Gynaecological Oncology (1985, 2 edn 1990), Ovarian Cancer (2002), Shaw's Textbook of Operative Gynaecology (7 edn 2013); *Recreations* skiing, sailing, cricket, squash, classical music; *Clubs* MCC, Royal Ocean Racing, Royal Corinthian Yacht; *Style*— Prof John Shepherd; ✉ Claremont House, Market Hill, Cowes, PO31 7TR Isle of Wight (✆ 01983 296843)

SHEPHERD, Michael Charles; s of Henry Robert Shepherd, and Mimika; *b* 1 October 1953; *Educ* Blundell's, Univ of Surrey (BSc); *m*; 3 c; *Career* London Hilton 1976–79, Lesotho Hilton 1979–81, asst to sr vice-pres for Europe Hilton International EMEA 1981–84, exec asst mangr Istanbul Hilton 1984–86, mangr Athens Hilton 1986–88, mangr Corfu Hilton 1987; gen mangr: Cyprus Hilton 1988–92, Nile Hilton 1992–93, The Langham Hilton 1993–97; md The Savoy Hotel London 1997–2003, gen mangr London Hilton on Park Lane 2003–; chm London Regnl Br Hospitality Assoc (BHA), memb Nat Exec BHA; trainer HCITB 1978–; int lifememb Soc of Golden Keys (Les Clef d'Or) 2013; memb Advsy Bd Dept of Mgmnt Univ of Surrey; Freeman Llantrisant Wales, Freeman City of London, Master Innholder; Hon DUniv W London; FIH; *Awards* Hilton Int Gp Hotel Gen Mangr of the Year 1990, nominated Hilton UK Gen Mangr of the Year 1996, Worldwide Exec Travel Awards Hotel of the Year (Savoy Hotel) 1997, National Catey Award Corp Hotel of the Year (Savoy Hotel) 1998, Condé Nast Travel Readers Award Top Business Hotel 1998, Best Br Hotel Telegraph Travel Awards 1999 and 2000, 5 Star RAC Gold Ribbon 2002 and 2003, 5 Star AA Red Star Award 2002 and 2003, Business Traveller Magazine Best Business Hotel in Western Europe 2005, Business Traveller Magazine Best Business Hotel in Europe 2006, Visit London Large Hotel of the Year 2006, Visit Britain/Enjoy England Excellence Silver Award Large Hotel of the Year 2007, Univ of Surrey Vice-Chllr's Alumni Award 2012; *Recreations* gardening, tennis, walking, reading, travel, int economical and political current affairs, sailing; *Style*— Michael Shepherd, Esq; ✉ The London Hilton on Park Lane, 22 Park Lane, London W1K 1BE

SHEPHERD, Philip Alexander; QC (2003); s of Col John Ernest Shepherd, of Cobham, Surrey, and Eve, *née* Zachariou; *b* 1 May 1950; *Educ* St Georges Coll Weybridge, LSE (BSc); *m* 31 May 2014, Francesca Kate Liebling; *Career* called to the Bar Gray's Inn 1975; recorder 2000–, memb of chambers and ldr Aviation and Travel Gp 24 Old Buildings; memb: Br Italian Law Assoc, Commercial Bar Assoc, Chancery Bar Assoc, European Air Law

Assoc, Geneva Panel of Arbitrators, Int Bar Assoc; LCIA arbitrator; MCIArb, MCIAeS; *Recreations* flying, opera, walking, skiing; *Clubs* RAC; *Style*— Philip Shepherd, Esq, QC; ✉ 24 Old Buildings, Lincoln's Inn, London WC2A 3UP (☎ 020 7691 2424, fax 0870 460 2178, e-mail philip.shepherd@xxiv.co.uk)

SHEPHERD, Sir Richard Charles Scrimgeour; kt (2013); s of Alfred Shepherd, and Davida Sophia, *née* Wallace; *b* 6 December 1942; *Educ* LSE, Johns Hopkins Sch of Advanced Int Studies (MSc Econ); *Career* dir: Partridges of Sloane Street Ltd, Shepherd Foods Ltd; memb SE Econ Planning Cncl 1970–74; MP (Cons) Aldridge Brownhills 1979–2015 (Parly candidate (Cons) Nottingham E Feb 1974); memb Select Ctee on: Treasy and CS 1979–83, Modernisation of the House of Commons 1997–, Public Admin 1997–2000; sec Cons Ctees on Euro Affairs and Indust 1980–81, vice-chm Cons Pty Ctee for Constitutional Affairs Scotland and Wales 1999– (jt vice-chm 1999–), memb All-Pty Br Cncl Gp 1999–, memb Jt Ctee on Human Rights; co-chm Campaign for Freedom of Information; memb: Cons Euro Reform Gp, Fresh Start Gp; sponsor: Crown Immunity Bill 1986, Protection of Official Information Bill 1988, Referendum Bill 1992, Public Interest Disclosure Bill; Cons Whip withdrawn 1994–95; Backbencher of the Year 1987, Campaign for Freedom of Information Award 1988, voted one of 10 most effective MPs 1988, Spectator-Highland Park Parliamentarian of the Year 1995; underwriting memb Lloyd's 1974–94; *Clubs* Carlton, Beefsteak, Chelsea Arts; *Style*— Sir Richard Shepherd; ✉ House of Commons, London SW1A 0AA (☎ 020 7219 3000, constituency ☎ and fax 01922 451449)

SHEPHERD, Dr Robert John; s of Reginald John Stuart Shepherd (d 1973), of Gloucester, and Ellen, *née* Pritchard; *b* 16 January 1946; *Educ* King's Sch Gloucester, Univ of Liverpool (MB ChB); *Career* med registrar Nat Heart Hosp London, sr med registrar Radcliffe Infirmary Oxford; conslt physician Dept of Med for the Elderly Leics DHA 1977–93, conslt physician Leicester General Hosp NHS Tst 1993–2000, conslt physician Leicester Univ Hospitals Tst 2000–03; locum conslt physician: Countess of Chester Hosp 2004–05, Univ Hosp of Coventry and Warwick 2005–06, James Cook Hosp Middlesborough 2006, James Paget Univ Hosp 2006–, Lorne and Islands Hosp Oban 2007, Furness Gen 2007, Borders Gen Melrose 2007, Dumfries and Galloway 2007, Royal Shrewsbury Hosp 2007–09, Pontefract Gen Infirmary 2009–, St George's Hosp London 2009, Pilgrim Hosp Boston 2010, Rugby Hosp 2010, Coventry and Warwick Hosps 2010, Harrogate District Hosp 2011, Bassetlaw Hosp 2011, Hereford Hosp 2011, Scarborough Hosp 2011, Barnstaple Hosp 2012, Macclesfield Hosp 2012, Queen's Medical Centre Nottingham 2013, Western Isles Hosp Stornaway 2013, Medway Maritime Hosp 2013, Pinderfields Hosp Pontefract 2014, Hinchingbrooke Hospital Huntingdon 2014, Whiston Hosp 2014, Roodlands Hosp Scotland 2014–15; conslt physician Norfolk and Norwich Hosp 2015– regional serv advsr (Trent region) for geriatric med 1997–99; memb Exec and Cncl Br Geriatric Soc 1996–2002 (hon dep treas 1996–99, dir and treas 1999–2002), chm Trent Br Geriatric Soc 1996–99 (hon treas 1991–93, hon sec 1993–96); memb BMA; MRCP (UK), FRCPEd 1992, FRCP 1995, FRCPGlas 1997; *Publications* Syncope in Myxoedema due to Transient Ventricular Fibrillation (PostGrad Med Jl), Normal Pressure Hydrocephalus Presenting as Parkinsonian Syndrome (Thorax), Unusual Presentation of Systemic Lupus Erythematosus (Hospital Update, 1996), Age Related Variations in Presentation and Outcome in Wegener's Granulomatosis (Jl of RCP, 1997), also author of various other papers; *Recreations* travel, photography, collecting antiques; *Style*— Dr R J Shepherd; ✉ Broadwas Hall, Broadwas, Worcestershire WR6 5NE

SHEPHERDSON, Jane Elizabeth; MBE (2007); da of John Shepherdson, and Margaret, *née* Smith; *b* 23 August 1963, Bristol; *Educ* Univ of N London; *m* 18 Sept 1993, Barry O'Connor; *Career* brand dir Topshop 1998–2006, ceo Whistles 2008–; creative advsr Oxfam 2007–, non exec dir People Tree, advsr Centre for Fashion Enterprise; hon doctorate Univ of the Arts London; *Recreations* cinema, reading, skiing, travel, walking, flying trapeze; *Clubs* Soho House; *Style*— Ms Jane Shepherdson, MBE; ✉ Whistles, 183 Eversholt Street, London NW1 1BU

SHEPPARD, Andy; s of Philip Charles Sheppard, of Salisbury, and Irene, *née* Rhymes; *b* 20 January 1957; *Educ* Bishop Wordsworth GS; *m* 2, Rebecca Sian, da of Rod Allerton; 1 da (Phoebe Rose b 30 Sept 1992), 1 s (Charles Benjamin b 12 Sept 1995); m 3, 2013, Sara Da Costa; *Career* jazz saxophonist; composer for TV, film, theatre and dance; self-taught at age of 18, busker Paris Metro; worked with numerous bands incl Urban Sax; musicians worked with incl: Gil Evans, George Russell, Carla Bley; formed several bands incl: In Co Motion, Big Co Motion, Inclassificable, Moving Image (world tour); patron: Music Space, Bristol Harbourside; Br Jazz Awards: best instrumentalist 1989 and 1990, best album 1990, best big band 1991; Hon MMus Univ of West of England 1993; *Recordings* Introductions in the Dark, Soft on the Inside, In Co Motion, Rhythm Method, Inclassificables, Songs with Legs, Moving Image, Delivery Suite, Learning to Wave, Dancing Man and Woman, Nocturnal Tourist, Music for a New Crossing, PS, On The Edge of a Perfect Moment, Deep River, Movements in Colour, Trio Libero; *Recreations* deck chair, gin and tonic; *Clubs* Ronnie Scott's; *Style*— Andy Sheppard, Esq; ✉ website www.andysheppard.co.uk; c/o Serious Ltd, 51 Kingsway Place, Sans Walk, Clerkenwell, London EC1R 0LU (website www.serious.org.uk)

SHEPPARD, Audley William; QC (2015); s of William Searle Sheppard (d 1977), and Joyce Marion Sheppard, *née* Audley (d 2014); *b* 19 August 1960, Hastings, New Zealand; *Educ* Victoria Univ of Wellington (BCA, LLB), Univ of Cambridge (LLM); *m* 4 Oct 1997, Amanda Caroline, *née* Carter; 1 s (William b 19 Dec 2002), 1 da (Iona b 19 April 2005); *Career* admitted barr and slr NZ 1985, Bell Gully NZ 1984–85, Clifford Chance LLP 1986– (ptnr 1995–), admitted slr Eng and Wales 1990; vice-pres London Ct of Int Arbitration; visiting prof School of Int Arbitration Queen Mary Univ of London; *Recreations* rugby, sailing, skiing, tennis; *Clubs* Roehampton Sports; *Style*— Audley Sheppard, Esq, QC; ✉ Clifford Chance LLP, 10 Upper Bank Street, London E14 5JJ (☎ 020 7006 1000, e-mail audley.sheppard@cliffordchance.com)

SHEPPARD, Howard William; *b* 2 November 1944; *Educ* Kingston Sch of Architecture (DArch), Heriot-Watt Univ (MSc), Birkbeck Coll London (MA); *m*; 3 c; *Career* asst architect Marani Routhwaith & Dick Architects Toronto 1966–67, architect with various private practices 1969–72; GLC: architect planner Transportation and Planning (Central London) 1972–76, project architect Dept of Architecture (Housing) 1976–79, devpt planner Transportation and Planning (NW London) 1979–81; London Docklands Devpt Corp: sr architect planner 1981–86, area dir (Devpt) Wapping and Limehouse 1986–89 (Isle of Dogs and Wapping 1989–91), dir City Design and Planning 1991–97, planning advsr Canary Wharf Gp London 1998–2009, planning conslt 2010–; cmmr Town and Country Planning Assoc 2004–06; visiting prof of architecture and urban studies Virginia Poly Inst and State Univ 1976–77, memb Awards Panel American Inst of Planning (Virginia) Williamsburg 1977, memb Planning Ctee Br Property Fedn 2002–, chair Local Advsy Gp London Festival of Architecture 2008 and 2010; tstee Tower Hamlets and Canary Wharf Further Educn Tst 2001–; speaker: Int Forum Waterfront 2001 Osaka 1991, Seoul Int Conf 2007, Paris World Business Districts Network Conf 2008; panelist: Expo Real 2009, Munich 2009; memb: Nat Tst, Consumer Assoc; corp memb: RIBA, RTPI; *Style*— Howard Sheppard, Esq; ✉ Number One, St Agatha's Drive, Kingston upon Thames, Surrey KT2 5SH (☎ 020 8541 4081, e-mail howardwsheppard@yahoo.co.uk)

SHEPPARD, Maurice Raymond; s of Wilfred Ernest Sheppard (d 1976), and Florence Hilda Sheppard (d 2002); *b* 25 February 1947; *Educ* Haverfordwest GS, Eisteddfod Maldwyn, Loughborough Coll of Art, Kingston Coll of Art (DipAD), RCA (MA); *Career* artist, draughtsman and watercolourist; cmmnd to paint The Golden Valley (for Lord Attenborough's film Shadowlands) 1993; Br Instn Award 1971, David Murray Landscape Award 1972, Geoffrey Crawshay Meml travelling scholar Univ of Wales 1973; memb Nat Art Collection Fund; Casgliad Maurice Sheppard PPRWS Collection – the artist's private collection of Br and Continental artists (600 drawings) gifted to Nat Library of Wales Aberystwyth 2007; ARWS 1974, RWS 1977, VPRWS 1979, PRWS 1984–87 (tstee 1983–95, hon retired memb 2002), NEAC 2000; *Major Exhibitions* Fairfax-Lucy, Hayes, Sheppard (New Grafton Gallery) 1976, Maurice Sheppard (New Grafton Gallery) 1979, Maurice Sheppard (Christopher Wood Gallery) 1989, Beard, Jane Carpanini, Sheppard (Attic Gallery Swansea) 2007, Aled Prichard Jones and Maurice Sheppard (Attic Gallery Swansea) 2013; *Group Exhibitions* incl: Royal Acad Summer Exhibition 1971–2013, Royal Watercolour Soc 1974–2002, Mall Gallery, Agnews, John Nevil Gallery Canterbury, Leonie Jonleigh Gallery Guildford, Tom Caldwell Belfast and Dublin, Prouds Pty Sydney, Mitsokoshi Japan; formed gp with Pamela Kay, Paul Newland and Jacqueline Rizvi showing at Alresford Gallery 2003 and Abbott and Holder 2004 and 2005, Alpha House Gallery Sherbourne 2007; *Collections* public collections: Royal Watercolour Soc Diploma Collection, V&A, Nat Museum of Wales, City of Birmingham Museum and Art Gallery, Beecroft Museum and Art Gallery Westcliffe-on-Sea, Tullie House Museum Carlisle, UCW Aberystwyth, Nat Library of Wales, Topsham Museum Devon, Maidstone Museum and Bentlif Art Gallery, Bedford Museum and the Cecil Higgins Art Gallery, Towner Art Gallery Eastbourne; private collections: HM The Queen, Lord Pym, Lord Inglewood, Lady Jane Wellesley, Lady Serena Rothchild, Lady Alice Fairfax-Lucy, Sir Francis Beaumont, Andrew Wilton, Lord Young; corporate collections: Boots plc, WH Smith, Blue Circle plc, HOR Oil (UK) plc, MBNA International Bank of America Ltd (11 works, 1972–95), Canary Wharf Devpt Corp, Federated Tst Corp, Mobil Oil Co; *Recreations* cycling, music, a small garden, quiet; *Style*— Maurice Sheppard, Esq; ✉ 33 St Martin's Park, Crow Hill, Haverfordwest, Pembrokeshire SA61 2HP

SHEPPARD, Tommy; MP; *Career* MP (SNP) Edinburgh E 2015–; *Style*— Tommy Sheppard, Esq, MP; ✉ House of Commons, London SW1A 0AA

SHEPSTONE, Dr Basil John; s of James John Shepstone (d 1957), of Bloemfontein, South Africa, and Letitia Isabel, *née* Robinson (d 1984); *b* 4 August 1935; *Educ* Brebner HS Bloemfontein, Univ of the Orange Free State (BSc, MSc, DSc), Univ of South Africa (BA), Univ of Oxford (BM BCh, MA, DPhil), Univ of Cape Town (MD); *m* 23 Sept 1961, (Brenda) Victoria, da of James Dudley Alen, of Cambridge; 1 s (Jonathan James b 21 Nov 1962), 1 da (Charlotte Isabel b 8 Dec 1965); *Career* jr lectr in radiation physics Univ of The Orange Free State and hosp physicist Nat Prov Hosp Bloemfontein SA 1958–60, house offr in paediatrics and thoracic surgery United Oxford Hosps 1969, head of Dept of Nuclear Med Univ of Cape Town and Groote Shuur Hosp Cape Town 1972–78 (sr specialist Dept of Radiotherapy 1970–72), dean of degrees Wolfson Coll Oxford 1980–, univ lectr and hon conslt in radiology Oxford Univ and Oxfordshire Health Authy 1981–, head of Dept of Radiology Oxford Univ 1984– (clinical lectr 1978–81), dir of clinical studies Oxford Univ Med Sch 1988–91 (dep dir 1985–88); contrib to jls and books on solid state physics, radiobiology, radiotherapy, radiodiagnosis, nuclear med and med educn; memb: Br Inst of Radiology, Br Nuclear Med Soc; fell Wolfson Coll Oxford; FInstP, LRCP, MRCS, FRCR; *Recreations* art history, reading, travelling; *Style*— Dr Basil Shepstone; ✉ Department of Radiology, University of Oxford, The Radcliffe Infirmary, Woodstock Road, Oxford OX2 6HE (☎ 01865 224679)

SHER, Sir Antony; KBE (2000); s of Emanuel Sher, and Margery, *née* Abramowitz; *b* 14 June 1949; *Educ* Sea Point Boys HS Cape Town, Webber-Douglas Acad of Dramatic Art London, Post Grad drama course Manchester Univ Drama Dept and Manchester Poly Sch of Theatre; *partner* (civil partnership 2005) Gregory Doran, *qv*; *Career* actor, author and artist; DLitt (hc) Univ of Liverpool 1998, Hon DUniv Exeter 2004, Hon DLitt Univ of Warwick 2007, Hon DLitt Univ of Cape Town 2010; *Theatre* hon assoc artist RSC, roles incl: Richard III (Best Actor Awards: Drama Magazine Awards 1984, Evening Standard Awards 1985 and Olivier Awards 1985), Shylock in Merchant of Venice, The Fool in King Lear, Vindice in The Revenger's Tragedy, Tartuffe, Johnnie in Hello and Goodbye, title role in Singer, title role in Tamburlaine 1993, title role in Cyrano de Bergerac 1997, Leontes in The Winter's Tale 1999, title role in Macbeth 1999, Domitian Caesar in The Roman Actor 2002, Malevole in The Malcontent 2002, Iago in Othello 2004, Prospero in The Tempest 2009 (co-prodn with Baxter Theatre Cape Town), Falstaff in Henry IV Parts One and Two (Best Shakespearean Performance, Critics Circle Award), Willy Loman in Death of a Salesman 2015; other roles incl: Arnold in Torch Song Trilogy (Albery) 1985 (Best Actor Olivier Awards 1985), title role in Arturo Ui (RNT) 1991, Astrov in Uncle Vanya (RNT) 1992, Henry Carr in Travesties (Savoy) 1994, Titus Andronicus (Market Theatre Johannesburg, transfered to RNT, TMA Best Actor Award) 1995, Stanley (RNT and Broadway) 1996 (Best Actor Olivier Awards 1997), Tsafendas in ID (Almeida) 2003, Primo (Cape Town RNT and Broadway) 2004–05 (Best Solo Performance NY Drama Desk Awards, Outer Critics Circle Awards and South African Fleur du Cap Awards 2006), title role in Kean (Apollo) 2007, Stockmann in Enemy of the People (Sheffield Crucible) 2010, Gellburg in Broken Glass (Tricycle Theatre) 2010 and (Vaudeville Theatre) 2011, Jacob in Travelling Light (NT) 2012, Freud in Hysteria (Bath Theatre Royal and Hampstead Theatre) 2013, Voigt in The Captain of Köpenick (Royal Nat Theatre) 2013; dir Breakfast with Mugabe (RSC); *Television* incl: Howard Kirk in The History Man (BBC) 1980, Genghis Cohn (BBC) 1993, Macbeth (Channel 4) 2001, The Jury (Granda) 2002, Home (BBC4) 2003, Primo (BBC and HBO) 2007, God on Trial (BBC) 2008, The Shadow Line (BBC) 2011; *Films* incl: Alive and Kicking 1996, Mrs Brown 1997, Churchill the Hollywood Years 2004; *Exhibitions* A Cast of Characters (London Jewish Cultural Centre) 2007, The Audience (Nat Theatre) 2009 and (Sheffield Crucible and Coventry Herbert Gallery) 2010; *Books* Year of the King (actor's diary and sketchbook, 1985), Middlepost (1988), Characters (painting and drawings, 1989), The Indoor Boy (1991), Cheap Lives (1995), Woza Shakespeare! (with Gregory Doran, 1996), The Feast (1998), Beside Myself (autobiography, 2001), ID (stage play, 2003), Primo Time (2005), Primo (stage play, 2005), The Giant (stage play, 2007), Year of the Fat Knight: the Falstaff Diaries (2015); *Style*— Sir Antony Sher, KBE; ✉ c/o Paul Lyon-Maris, Independent Talent, 40 Whitfield Street, London W1T 2RH (☎ 020 7636 6565)

SHER, Samuel Julius (Jules); QC (1981); s of Philip Sher (d 1985), and Isa Phyllis, *née* Hesselson (d 1994); *b* 22 October 1941; *Educ* Athlone HS, Univ of the Witwatersrand (BCom, LLB), Univ of Oxford (BCL); *m* 29 Aug 1965, Sandra, da of Michael Maris, of Johannesburg, South Africa; 1 s (Brian b 10 July 1967), 2 da (Joanne b 8 Aug 1969, Debby b 6 May 1974); *Career* called to the Bar Inner Temple 1968 (bencher 1988), recorder 1987–2005, dep judge of the High Ct, head of chambers Wilberforce Chambers 2006–10, ret (arbitrator 2014–); actg High Court judge E Caribbean Supreme Court 2016; special advsr on the mgmnt of complex disputes to Attorney-Gen of Singapore 2012–; qualified mediator 2012–; memb Ethics Ctee Tate 2007–; *Recreations* tennis; *Style*— Jules Sher, Esq, QC; ✉ 12 Constable Close, London NW11 6TY (☎ 020 8455 2753, e-mail jules.sher@talktalk.net)

SHERBORNE, Bishop of 2016–; Rt Rev Karen Marisa Gorham; *Career* ordained: deacon 1995, priest 1996; curate Parish of Northallerton with Kirby Sigston Dio of York 1995–99, priest-in-charge St Paul's Church Maidstone 1999–2007, archdeacon of Buckingham 2007–16; FRSA 2012; *Style*— The Rt Rev the Bishop of Sherborne

SHERBOURNE OF DIDSBURY, Baron (Life Peer UK 2013), of Didsbury in the City of Manchester; Sir Stephen Ashley Sherbourne; kt (2006), CBE; *Educ* Univ of Oxford; *Career* political sec to PM Margaret Thatcher 1983–87, dir Chime Communications plc 2001–03, COS to the Ldr of the Oppn 2003–05, dir Smithfield Consultants 2006–15, chm

S

Interel UK 2012–13, memb Advsy Bd Edelman 2016–; *Style—* The Lord Sherbourne of Didsbury, CBE; ✉ House of Lords, London SW1A 0PW

SHERIDAN, Christopher Julian; s of Mark Sheridan, and Olive Maud, *née* Hobbs; *b* 18 February 1943; *Educ* Berkhamsted Sch; *m* 1972, Diane Virginia, *née* Wadey; 1 da (Kate b 20 April 1974); *Career* Samuel Montagu & Co Ltd: joined International Div 1962, exec dir responsible for Dealing Div activities 1974–81, md Dealing Div 1981–84, chief exec 1984–94, dep chm 1988–94; chm Yorkshire Building Society 1995–2006; non-exec dir: Hanover Acceptances Ltd 1995–, Minerva plc 1996–2008, Coutts Consulting Gp 1997–99, Willmott Dixon Ltd 1999–2003, ICBCStandard Bank plc (formerly Standard Bank London Ltd) 1999–, Alpha Bank London Ltd 2004– (currently chm); dep chm Inspace plc 2005–08, Willmott Dixon Hldgs Ltd 2008–; FCIB, CIMgt; *Recreations* theatre, tennis; *Style—* Christopher Sheridan, Esq

SHERIDAN, David Martin; s of Vernon Arthur Sheridan (d 1990), and Ruth Eleanor, *née* Caminer (d 2003); *b* 31 August 1950; *Educ* Haberdashers' Aske's, King's Coll London (BSc); *m* 1 July 1978, Christine Lesley, *née* White; 2 da (Hillary Ann b 17 June 1984, Deborah Lynn b 15 April 1987); *Career* chartered accountant; i/c Statistics Dept Marians Bloodstock Agency 1972–74, buyer Racal-BPL 1974–75, articles Mercer & Hole 1975–78, qualified ACA 1978, exec dir Brand Packaging Jefferson Smurfit Group 1980–82 (joined as PA to divnl fin dir 1978), chm Veruth Holdings Ltd 1991–, md Europa Components & Equipment plc 1991–2015 (fin & mktg dir 1982–90, chm 2015–), dir SIBA (UK) Ltd 1995–; pres Beds, Bucks & Herts Soc of Chartered Accountants 1988–89, memb Cncl ICAEW 1993–96 (past memb of numerous ctees), ICAEW rep jt ICAEW/ICAS Working Pty Breaking the Code 1999; Bd of Chartered Accountants in Business (BCAB): chm Working Pty 1992, co-vice-chm 1993–96, co-opted memb 1996–2000; treas: Owens Sch Assoc 1997–2002, Friends of St Albans Music Sch 2002–, Friends of Herts County Youth Music 2015–, Herts County Youth Orchestra 2015–; tstee Children's Int Voices of Enfield 2014–, dir The Shared Learning Tst (formerly Barnfield Multi Academy Tst) 2015–; memb St Albans Round Table 1983–91, sports offr Area 28 (Round Table) 1989–91, chm Elstree and Borehamwood Twin Town 20th Anniversary 2001–02; *Recreations* work, more work, my family,badminton, riding, crosswords, cinema, music, travel; *Clubs* 41 (St Albans, chm 2010–11), XLI Investment (chm 2015–); *Style—* David Sheridan, Esq; ✉ Europa Components & Equipment plc, Europa House, Airport Way, Luton LU2 9NH (☎ 01582 692440, mobile 07711 699096, e-mail daivd@europacomponents.com or david@lynton-ave.demon.co.uk, website www.europacomponents.com)

SHERIDAN, James; s of Frank Sheridan (d 1995), of Glasgow, and Annie Burke (d 1990); *b* 24 November 1952; *m* 15 Oct 1977, Jean McDowell, da of William McDowell; 1 s (Alan b 19 Nov 1980), 1 da (Joanne b 3 Sept 1984); *Career* cncllr Renfrewshire Cncl 1995–2003; MP (Lab): Renfrewshire W 2001–05 (constituency abolished), Paisley and Renfrewshire North 2005–15; *Recreations* golf, exercise; *Style—* Mr James Sheridan; ✉ Mirren Court Three, 123 Renfrew Road, Paisley, Renfrewshire PA3 4EA (☎ 0141 847 1457, fax 0141 847 1395, e-mail enquiries@jimsheridanmp.org.uk, website www.jimsheridanmp.org.uk); House of Commons, London SW1A 0AA

SHERIDAN, Paul Francis; s of Stanislaus Sheridan (d 1994), and Mary Patricia, *née* Keown; *b* 4 July 1960, Kesh, Co Fermanagh; *Educ* St Patrick's Coll Belfast, Richard Huish GS Taunton, Univ of Southampton (LLB); *m* 30 Jan 1999, Alice Naomi Jane; 1 s (Theo Huxley b 20 Oct 2001), 1 da (Amy Natasha b 16 Jan 2005); *Career* slr specialising in environment law; ptnr CMS Cameron McKenna LLP; *Style—* Paul Sheridan, Esq; ✉ CMS Cameron McKenna LLP, Cannon Place, 78 Cannon Street, London EC4N 6AF (☎ 020 7367 2186, e-mail paul.sheridan@cms-cmck.com)

SHERIDAN, Paul Richard; TD (1982, Bar 1991); s of Patrick William Sheridan (d 1991), of Grimsby, and Claire Sheridan, JP, *née* Marklew (d 1990); *b* 19 July 1951, Cleethorpes, Lincolnshire, UK; *Educ* Havelock Sch Grimsby, Grimsby Coll of Technol, Univ of Kent (BA); *m* 30 June 1985, Beverley, *née* Seagger; 1 da (Cordelia Scarlet b 17 Dec 1996); *Career* RCT TA, Maj 1985–93 (Cadet 1969, 2 Lt 1970, Lt 1972, Capt 1977), Staff Coll (TA) 1991, RARO II 1993–2006; admitted slr 1979; ptnr Wilkin Chapman 1982–2011, NP 1985; Cmmr for Oaths 1990; pres: Grimsby & Cleethorpes Law Soc 2005–06, Lincs Law Soc 2009–10; chm League of Friends of Grimsby Hosps 1985–88 (hon membership offr 1988–95), chm Community Fund Raising Panel MRI £1m Scanner Appeal 1992–94; patron Nat Domesday Ctee 1986; Lord of the Manor of Aspenden Herts 1985–; memb: Law Soc 1979, Notaries Soc 1985; ind memb Standards Ctee West Lindsey DC 2007–10; Freeman City of London 1985, Liveryman Worshipful Co of Carmen 1986; *Recreations* heraldry; *Clubs* Victory Services, London; *Style—* Paul R Sheridan, Esq, TD; ✉ Folly Cottage, 9 Church Street, Caistor, Lincolnshire LN7 6UG (☎ 01472 852070)

SHERIDAN, Richard Jonathan; s of late Dr Morris (Roger) Sheridan, of London, and late Yvonne, *née* Brook; *b* 20 December 1956; *Educ* City of London Sch, Guy's Hosp Med Sch Univ of London; *Career* former conslt obstetrician and gynaecologist Watford Gen Hosp (now ret), hon conslt obstetrician and gynaecologist Queen Charlotte's and Chelsea Hosps; memb Cncl and former vice-pres Obstetrics and Gynaecology Section Royal Soc of Med; Freeman City of London, Liveryman Worshipful Soc of Apothecaries; FRCS 1985, FRCOG 1998 (MRCOG 1985); *Papers* Fertility in a Male with Trisomy 21 (1989); *Recreations* squash, skiing, riding; *Style—* Richard Sheridan, Esq; ✉ Spire Hospital, Heathbourne Road, Bushey, Hertfordshire WD2 1RD (☎ and fax 020 8421 8537)

SHERIDAN, Sylvia; OBE (2001); adopted da of Joseph Ford, and Margaret Ford; *b* 26 March 1948, Manchester; *Educ* Pendower HS for Girls Newcastle upon Tyne, Shepherd's Commercial Coll Newcastle upon Tyne, Open Univ (BA); *m* 1969, Chris Sheridan (d 2013); 1 da (Victoria b 2 Oct 1973); *Career* newsdesk copy taker BBC Newcastle 1970–71, sales exec Tyne Tees TV 1971, prodn sec Granada TV 1972–81, prodn sec, community educn offr and prog researcher Thames TV 1981–86, community educn offr Anglia TV 1986–87, head of community affrs TV-am 1987–89, fndr, chm and chief exec Independent Media Support Ltd 1989–2013; memb Cncl of Mgmnt BBFC 1999–2008; memb Bd of Tstees RNID 1999–2002, tstee Herts Hearing Advsy Serv 2001–02; *Recreations* flying light aircraft, travel, cooking, golf, motor cruising day skipper; *Clubs* Naval and Military, Home House, Royal Solent Yacht; *Style—* Mrs Sylvia Sheridan, OBE; ✉ Garstons, Gatcombe, Isle of Wight PO30 3EQ (mobile 07796 690980, e-mail sysh@live.co.uk)

SHERLING, Clive Richard; s of late Philip Sherling, and Maureen Vivienne, *née* Gulperin, of Northwood, Middx,; *b* 20 October 1949; *Educ* Woodhouse GS, LSE (BSc Econ); *m* 3 March 1993, Sally Ann; 2 s (Adrian Mark, William David (twins) b 31 Oct 1977); *Career* articled clerk then ptnr Arthur Andersen 1970–87, with Apax Partners Worldwide 1987–2004; former chm: Football Fndn, Sports Aid Fndn Charitable Tst, Football Licensing Authy, BVCA; former vice-chm Wembley National Stadium Ltd; tstee Nat Theatre, tstee Nat Theatre Fndn, chm Jr Tennis Coaching Fndn; FCA (ACA 1973); *Recreations* soccer, theatre, walking, cycling, tennis; *Style—* Clive Sherling, Esq; ✉ Lincoln House, Woodside Hill, Chalfont St Peter, Buckinghamshire SL9 9TF (☎ 01753 887454)

SHERLOCK, David Christopher; CBE (2006); s of Frank Ernest Sherlock (d 1987), and (Emily) Edna, *née* Johnson (d 1993); *b* 6 November 1943; *Educ* Blakesley Sch, Rutlish Sch Merton, Coll of Art & Industrial Design Newcastle upon Tyne, Univ of Nottingham (BA, MPhil); *m* 1, 1969 (m dis 1975) Jean, *née* Earl; m 2, 1976, Cynthia Mary, da of Norman Lovell Hood; 1 da (Zoë Virginia Mary b 10 Feb 1977), 1 s (Nicholas David b 12 Oct 1978); *Career* Nottingham Coll of Art & Design 1967–70, Trent Poly 1970–74, dep dir Nat Coll of Art & Design Dublin 1975–80; princ: Winchester Sch of Art 1980–87, Central St Martin's Coll of Art & Design 1988–91; asst rector London Inst 1988–91, dir of devpt RCA 1991–93, regnl sr inspr and nat sr inspr for art and design Further Educn Funding Cncl 1993–97, chief exec and chief inspr Training Standards Cncl 1997–2001, chief inspr Adult Learning for England and chief exec Adult Learning Inspectorate 2000–07, dir Beyond Standards Ltd 2007–; memb Nat Apprenticeship Task Force 2004–06, memb Bd Qualifications and Curriculum Authy (QCA) 2006–10, pres Nat Inst for Adult Continuing Educn (NIACE) 2007–12, cmmr Nat Inquiry into Lifelong Learning 2007–08, chair Nat Skills Acad for Social Care 2008–12, professional lead Govt Ind Review of Professionalism in Futher Educn 2012, sec and vice-chm Instn for FE 2013–15, dep cmmr for FE 2015–; chm: GTA England 2008–13, Prospects Coll of Advanced Technol 2013–, Quality and Standards Cmmn City and Guilds 2014–; editorial advsr Ind Cmmn into Adult Vocational Educn and Trg 2013, advsr 157 Gp DELPHI Study Further Educn in 2020 2013; regular columnist Times Educational Supplement 2003–07; assoc Br Cncl 2007–; conslt industrial designer and sometime advsr to EC, UN and govts of Bangladesh, Somalia, Ghana, Portugal and Turkey; FRSA 1975, FCGLI 2007; Quality Improvement in Adult Vocational Education and Training: Transforming Skills for the Global Economy (jtly, 2008), The Coming of Age for FE? (contrib, 2015); *Recreations* mountain biking; *Style—* David Sherlock, Esq, CBE; ✉ Poplar Farm, West Tytherley, Salisbury SP5 1NR (e-mail info@beyondstandards.net)

SHERLOCK, Baroness (Life Peer UK 2010), of Durham in the County of Durham; Maeve Christina Mary Sherlock; OBE (2001); *Educ* Our Lady's Sr Sch Abingdon, Univ of Liverpool (BA), Open Univ (MBA), Univ of Durham (MA); *Career* various roles Nat Union of Students 1985–90 (incl pres 1988–90); dir: UKCOSA 1990–97 (previously dep dir), Nat Cncl for One Parent Families 1997–2000; memb Cncl of Economic Advsrs HM Treasy and advsr to The Rt Hon Gordon Brown, MP, *qv*, as Chllr of the Exchequer 2000–03, chief exec Br Refugee Cncl 2003–06, cmmr Equality and Human Rights Cmmn 2007–10; non-exec dir: Child Maintenance and Enforcement Cmmn 2008–10, Financial Ombudsman Serv 2008– (sr ind dir 2011–); chair HM Treasy Advsy Panel on the future role of the Third Sector in Economic and Social Regeneration 2006–07, memb Carnegie Cmmn on the Future of Civil Soc 2007–10; memb Bd European Assoc for Int Educn 1995–97, chair Nat Student Forum 2007–10, founding tstee Nat Family and Parenting Inst 1999–2000, tstee DEMOS thinktank 2004–06; chair of judges Charity Awards 2008–10; bd dir Endsleigh Insurance Servs 1986–90; govr Sheffield Hallam Univ 1997–98, hon fell St Chad's Coll Univ of Durham 2006–, memb Cncl St John's Coll Univ of Durham 2009–; Hon DUniv Sheffield Hallam Univ 1999; *Recreations* politics, books, cookery, music, theology; *Style—* The Baroness Sherlock, OBE; ✉ House of Lords, London SW1A 0PW (e-mail sherlockm@parliament.uk)

SHERLOCK, Sir Nigel; KCVO (2014), OBE (2003); s of Horace Sherlock (d 1967), and Dorothea, *née* Robinson (d 1980); *b* 12 January 1940, Carlisle; *Educ* Barnard Castle Sch, Univ of Nottingham (BA); *m* 3 Sept 1966, Helen Diana Frances, da of M Sigmund (d 2004); 2 s (Andrew b 27 July 1968, Mark b 7 July 1976), 1 da (Emma b 5 Sept 1970); *Career* stockbroker; chief exec Wise Speke (Div) 1993–2000, dir Ockham Holdings 1993–98, dir Brewin Dolphin Securities 1998–2005, dir Brewin Dolphin Holdings plc 1998–2002; non-exec memb: Cncl Nat Assoc of Pension Funds 1988–90, London Stock Exchange plc 1995–2001 (memb Bd), Skipton Building Soc 1998–2007, Church of England Pensions Bd 1998–2009; non-exec dep chm Assoc of Private Client Investment Managers and Stockbrokers 1995–2003; memb Cncl NE Regional C of C 1997–2004 (pres 2000–01); memb Bd of Govrs Royal GS Newcastle upon Tyne 1998–2005 (chm 2000–05); Univ of Newcastle upon Tyne: pro-chllr and chm 1993–2002, memb Ct 2002–09, hon memb Ct 2009–; pres Northumberland Co Scouts 2000–12 (memb Cncl 1980–98, silver wolf 2007), patron Northumbria Coalition Against Crime 2001–15 (vice-patron 1995–2001); Community Fndn of Tyne & Wear: fndr memb 1988, vice-pres 2001–15, vice-patron 2015–; tstee: William Leech Charity 1990–, Bede Museum Tst (now Fndn) 1980–90 (chm 1985–90); memb Bd Royal Northern Sinfonia Orchestral Soc 1974–95 (chm 1990–95), memb Royal Northern Sinfonia Devpt Tst 1980–2001 (chm 1981–2001, tstee 1980–2001), memb Bd Royal Northern Sinfonia Orchestra 1984–96, memb Bd and chm Fundraising Ctee North Music Tst (The Sage Gateshead) 2000–05, jt pres St John Ambulance Northumbria 2001–12, pres N of England Reserve Forest Cadet Assoc 2009–14 (vice-pres 2001–09); memb Newcastle Diocesan Bd of Fin 1973–87 (chm 1978–87), memb Bishop's Cncl Dio of Newcastle 1975–94, memb Finance Advsy Ctee of Dean and Chapter Durham Cathedral 1987–2014 (chm 1997–2009), chm Newcastle Cathedral Cncl 2002–05, hon lay canon Newcastle Cathedral 2007–10 (canon emeritus 2010–), chm Crown Nominations Cmmn for the Appt of the Archbishop of York 2005; High Sheriff Tyne & Wear 1990–91, HM Lord-Lt Tyne & Wear 2000–15 (DL 1995–2000), JP Tyne & Wear 2000–15; North-East Businessman of the Year Lifetime Achievement Award 2014; Freeman: City of Newcastle, City of London, Hostmen's Co; Liveryman Worshipful Co of Scriveners (Newcastle); Hon Col RMR Tyne 2003–12, Hon Col Northumbrian Univs OTC 2003–09; hon fell St John's Coll Durham 1997 (memb Cncl 1984–95), hon memb Trinity House Newcastle upon Tyne 1995, Winterbottom Fellowship S Tyneside Coll 2015; Hon DCL: Univ of Newcastle upon Tyne 2002, Univ of Northumbria 2006; Hon DBA Univ of Sunderland 2015; CCMI 2000; K St J 2002; *Recreations* music, theatre, countryside pursuits; *Clubs* Brooks's, Northern Counties (Newcastle); *Style—* Sir Nigel Sherlock, KCVO, OBE; ✉ 14 North Avenue, Gosforth, Newcastle upon Tyne NE3 4DS

SHERRARD, Scott Rathman; s of John Alfred Sherrard (d 1999), of Buckhaven, Fife, and Mary Stephen, *née* Stiven; *b* 19 May 1954; *Educ* Dundee HS, Galashiels Acad, Gonville & Caius Coll Cambridge (BA, vice-pres JCR); *m* 1, 7 July 1978, Lorna Jane (d 1985), da of Allan William Clark; 1 s (Nicholas Clark Stiven b 25 Dec 1982); m 2, 29 Aug 1987, Susan Elizabeth, da of William Graham Clark; 1 da (Katherine Jane b 15 Sept 1988); *Career* Scottish & Newcastle Breweries Ltd: joined as mgmnt trainee 1975, brand mangr 1976–78, mktg mangr 1978–81; fndr ptnr: Cockman Thompson Wilding Ltd 1981–83, Grierson Cockman Craig & Druiff Ltd 1983–85; Grey London Ltd advtg agency: planning dir 1985–88, creative devpt dir 1988–90, md 1990–95; chief exec The Cambridge Centre 1995–, chm Collett Dickenson Pearce 1995–2000, dir Theatre of Ideas Ltd 1999–, commercial dir Durham CCC 2012–14, exec dir Alnwick Garden 2014–15; writer/prodr of musical for Edinburgh Festival, creator A Garden of Fairy Tales; chm Borders Young Libs; tstee Maltings Theatre and Cinema Berwick upon Tweed 2016–; memb: Devpt Ctee Bridget's Tst, Mktg Soc, Bd Berwick Film and Media Arts Festival 2012–; *Recreations* children, piano, golf, fishing; *Clubs* Tyneside Anglers Syndicate, Durham CCC; *Style—* Scott Sherrard, Esq; ✉ Gordon House, Polwarth Rhodes, Duns, Berwickshire TD10 6YP (☎ 01361 884966, e-mail scott.sherrard@thecambridgecentre.co.uk, website www.scottsherrard.com)

SHERRARD, Simon Patrick; DL (Cornwall 2014); s of Patrick Sherrard (d 1997), and Angela Beatrice, *née* Stacey (d 1988); *b* 22 September 1947; *Educ* Eton; *m* 23 Aug 1975, Sara Anne, da of Maj Peter Pain Stancliffe, MBE; 3 da (Emma b 11 Jan 1977, Kate b 4 Aug 1978, Polly b 6 April 1983), 1 s (James b 19 Oct 1984); *Career* Samuel Montagu & Co Ltd 1968–74, Jardine Matheson & Co Ltd Hong Kong 1974–84; Bibby Line Group Ltd Liverpool: md 1985–97, chm 1997–2015; chm: Port of London Authy 2001–09, chm A&P Gp 2002–09, Cornwall Multiple Sclerosis Therapy Centre Ltd 2009–; non-exec dir: Cooke Bros (Tattenhall) Ltd 1991–2005 (chm 2005), Lloyd's Register 1992–2008 (dep chm 2002–08), Johnson Service Gp plc 2000–08 (chm 2004–08), Bolesworth Estate Co Ltd 2007–10; pres Chamber of Shipping 2000–01; memb Bd of Tstees Liverpool Sch of Tropical Medicine 1998–2007 (dep chm 2002–07), tstee Mission to Seafarers 2000–15, memb Cncl White Ensign Assoc, tstee Royal Liverpool Philharmonic Hall Diamond Jubilee Fndn 1996–2005, memb Cncl RNLI 2006–16 (vice-pres 2016–), tstee Plymouth Marine Lab, tstee Nat Maritime Museum Cornwall 2014–; elder bro Trinity House; High Sheriff Cheshire 2004–05; Freeman Worshipful Co of Watermen and Lightermen of the River Thames, Liveryman Worshipful Co of Shipwrights (Prime Warden 2010–11); *Recreations* tennis, golf, breeding rare sheep; *Clubs* Boodle's, MCC, Beefsteak; *Style*— Simon Sherrard, Esq, DL; ✉ Willapark, Bossiney, Tintagel, Cornwall PL34 0BA (☎ 01840 770467, e-mail simon@sherrard1.demon.co.uk)

SHERRATT, Dr Brian Walter; OBE (1995), JP (Nottingham); s of late Walter Eric Sherratt, and Violet Florence, *née* Cox-Smith; *b* 28 May 1942, Oxford; *Educ* Univ of Leeds (BA, PGCE), Univ of London (AcDipEd, MA), Univ of Birmingham (PhD); *m* 1966, (Pauline) Brenda Hargreaves; 2 s, 2 da; *Career* asst master Normanton GS 1965–67, head Religious Studies Dept Selby GS 1967–70, sr lectr in religious studies and warden Avery Hill Coll of Educn 1970–73, asst master Kidbrooke Sch 1970–71, warden Mile End Teachers' Centre Avery Hill Coll 1971–73, dep head Sandown Court Sch Tunbridge Wells 1976–79 (sr master 1973–76), headmaster and warden Kirk Hallam Sch and Community Centre 1979–84, headmaster Great Barr Sch Birmingham 1984–2005; hon lectr Sch of Educn Univ of Birmingham 1988–; chm: Eco-Schs Advsy Panel 1997–2001, Green Code Prog for Schs Advsy Panel 1998–2005; memb: Ct Univ of Birmingham 1986–90, Organising Ctee Going for Green 1994–96, Sutton Coldfield Coll Corporation 1994–98, Centre for Policy Studies 1994–, Politeia 1995–, Civitas 2000–; non-exec dir: Going for Green Limited 1996–2000, ENCAMS (Environmental Campaigns) 1998–2005 (vice-chm 2003–05, memb Resources Ctee 2002–03 and Audit Ctee 2003–05, chm Devolution Ctee 2004–05); memb: Educn Cmmn 2002–, Academic Advsy Cncl Univ of Buckingham 2005–12, T S Eliot Soc (UK) 2013–; tstee ENCAMS Pension Funds 1999–2005, dir Nottingham Park Estate Ltd 2005–11 (chm 2008–11); magistrate trg observer Nottingham Bench 2008–12; Queen Mother's Birthday Award for the Environment 1999, George Cadbury Prize in Educn 2005, British Educnl Leadership Mgmnt and Admin Soc (BELMAS) Best PhD Thesis of the Year Award 2005; Freeman Guild of Educators 2003, Freeman City of London 2012, Liveryman Worshipful Co of Educators 2014; FIMgt 1984, FRSA 1984; *Publications* Gods and Men: a survey of world religions (1971), Local Education Authorities Project: Locally Managed Schools (1998), Opting for Freedom: a stronger policy on grant-maintained schools (Centre for Policy Studies, Policy Study No 138, 1994), Grant-Maintained Status: considering the options (1994), A Structured Approach to School and Staff Development: from theory to practice (co-author, 1996), Radical Educational Policies and Conservative Secretaries of State (co-author, 1997), Headteacher Appraisal (co-author, 1997), Leadership and Professional Knowledge in Education (contrib, 1999), The Role of the Chancellor of the Exchequer in the Making of Educational Policy: Kenneth Baker and the Lawson Factor (co-author, 2004), Permanent Secretaries, Consensus and Centrism in National Policy-making in Education: Sir David Hancock and the Reform Act 1988: A Place for a Humanistic Research Dimension? (co-author, 2012), The Permanent Secretary as Policy Maker, Shaper, Taker, Sharer and Resister in Education: Reflectins on Sir James Hamilton as a Centralising Outsider (co-author, 2013), Leading Education in the United Kingdom: a study of the policy and personal relationship of selected permanent secretaries and their secretaries of state (co-author, 2013), Reforming the Civil Service and Revising the Role of the Mandarin in Britain: a view from the perspective of a study of eight permanent secretaries at the Ministry of Education between 1976 and 2011 (co-author, 2013), Centrism and the Mandarin Class: understanding the meta-politics of Whitehall bureaucratic neutrality (co-author, 2015), Portrait of a Mandarin: Biography in the Study of Public Administration? (forthcoming); contrib TES; *Recreations* classical music, literature, antiques, buildings; *Clubs* Athenaeum; *Style*— Dr Brian Sherratt, OBE, JP; ✉ Oakhurst, 17 Lenton Road, The Park, Nottingham NG7 1DQ (e-mail brian.sherratt@ntlworld.com, website www.schoolleadershiplab.co.uk and www.briansherratt.org, Twitter @briansherratt)

SHERRATT, Brindley; s of Jack Sherratt (d 1996), of Manchester, and Jean, *née* Crowhurst; *b* 20 July 1962, Manchester; *Educ* Irlam HS Lancs, Salford Coll of Technol, RAM (Dip); *m* 1983, Christina, *née* Cook; 1 da (Amy b 1 April 1990), 1 s (Matthew b 1 June 1994); *Career* opera singer (bass); operatic debut Leparello in Don Giovanni (WNO); roles with ENO incl: debut as Sarastro in Die Zauberflöte, Sparafucile in Rigoletto, Ramfis in Aida, Ramfis in Aida; roles with ROH incl: debut as Publio in La Clemenza di Tito 2002, Jeronimus in Maskerade, He-Ancient in The Midsummer Marriage, Marchese di Calatrava in La forza del Destino, Prince Gremin in Onegin 2008 (also WNO), Bartolo in Le nozze di Figaro; BBC Proms: St Matthew Passion, Judas Maccabeus, Les Noces and the St John Passion; performances at notable venues incl: Handel's Messiah with Mozarteum Orch Salzburg Festival, Mozart's Vespers opening of Birmingham Symphony Hall, Commendatore in Don Giovanni (Santa Fe Festival) 2004, Rocco in Fidelis (Glyndebourne Festival) 2006, Sarastro (Hamburg Stat Opera de Lausanne), Theseus in A Midsummer Night's Dream (La Monnaie Brussels), Wurm in Luisa Miller (Opera de Lausanne), Melisso in Alcina (Opera de Montpellier), Il Re in Ariodante (Reis Opera), Balducci in Benvenuto Cellinni (Salzburg), Bartolo in Le Nozze di Figaro (Salzburg); broadcasts for radio incl: Mozart's Mass in C Minor, Rossini's Petite Messe Solennelle, Stravinsky's Canticum Sacrum; ARAM; *Recreations* walking, cycling, kayaking; *Style*— Brindley Sherratt, Esq; ✉ c/o Sue Spence, Askonas Holt Ltd, Lincoln House, 300 High Holborn, London WC1V 7JH (☎ 020 7400 1700, e-mail sue.spence@askonasholt.co.uk)

SHERRIFF, Paula; MP; *b* 1975, Alexandria, Scotland; *Career* MP (Lab) Dewsbury 2015–; *Style*— Miss Paula Sherriff, MP; ✉ House of Commons, London SW1A 0AA

SHERRINGTON, Prof David; s of James Arthur Sherrington, KSG (d 1986), of Middlesbrough, and Elfreda, *née* Cameron (d 1996); *b* 29 October 1941, Blackpool, Lancs; *Educ* St Mary's Coll Middlesbrough, Univ of Manchester (BSc, Dip, PhD); *m* 20 July 1966, Margaret, da of Richard Gee-Clough (d 1980), of Blackpool, Lancashire; 1 s (Andrew Damian), 1 da (Lesley Jane); *Career* lectr in theoretical physics Univ of Manchester 1967–69 (asst lectr 1964–67), prof of physics Imperial Coll London 1983–89 (lectr in theoretical solid state physics 1969–74, reader 1974–83), Wykeham prof of physics Univ of Oxford 1989–2008, Ulam scholar Los Alamos Nat Laboratory 1995–96, external prof Santa Fe Inst 2004–, emeritus prof 2008–; jls ed: Communications on Physics 1975–78, Advances in Physics 1984–, Journal of Physics A: Mathematical and General 1989–93; contrib many papers in scientific jls; Bakerian Lecture Royal Soc (premier prize lecture in physical sciences) 2001, Scott Lectures Cambridge 2009; Dirac Medal and Prize Inst of Physics 2007, Blaise Pascal Medal in Physics European Acad of Sciences 2011; fell New Coll Oxford 1989–; hon MA Univ of Oxford 1989; FInstP 1974, fell American Physical Soc 1984, FRS 1994, fell European Acad of Sciences 2008 (chm Physics Div 2011–, chm Academic Cncl 2012–); *Books* Phase Transitions in Soft Condensed Matter (co-ed, 1989), Spontaneous Formation of Space – Time Structures and Criticality (co-ed, 1991), Phase Transitions and Relaxation in Systems with Competing Energy Scales (co-ed, 1993), Physics of Biomaterials: Fluctuations, Selfassembly and Evolution (co-ed, 1995), Dynamical Properties of Unconventional Magnets (co-ed, 1997), Landscape Paradigms in Physics and Biology: Concepts, Structures and Dynamics (co-ed, 1997), Stealing the Gold: A Celebration of the Pioneering Physics of Sam Edwards (co-ed, 2005); *Style*— Prof David Sherrington, FRS; ✉ Rudolf Peierls Centre for Theoretical Physics, University of Oxford, 1 Keble Road, Oxford OX1 3NP (☎ 01865 273963, fax 01865 273947, e-mail d.sherrington1@physics.ox.ac.uk)

SHERRY, Dr Norman; s of Michael Sherry, and Sarah, *née* Taylor; *b* 6 July 1935; *Educ* Univ of Durham (BA), Univ of Singapore (PhD); *m* 1, June 1960, Dulcie Sylvia, da of Samuel William Brunt; m 2, Sept 1990, Carmen Sherry, *née* Flores; 1 s (John Michael Graham b 6 June 1990), 1 da (Ileana Taylor b 29 Dec 1993); m 3, Dec 2012, Pat Sherry, *née* Villalon; *Career* lectr in English literature Univ of Singapore 1961–66, Mitchell distinguished prof of lit Trinity Univ San Antonio TX 1983–; fell Humanities Res Center N Carolina 1982, fell Guggenheim Fndn 1989–90, first holder of Roydon B Davis Chair Georgetown Univ Washington DC 1998; FRSL 1986; *Books* Conrad's Eastern World (1966, reprinted 1971, reissued 2005), Jane Austen (1966), Charlotte and Emily Bronte (1969), Conrad's Western World (1971, reissued 2005), Conrad and His World (1972), Conrad – The Critical Heritage (1973), Conrad in Conference (1976), The Life of Graham Greene Vol One 1904–39 (1989, Edgar Allan Poe Award 1990), The Life of Graham Greene Vol Two 1939–55 (1994, nominated Edgar Allan Poe Award 1994, included in NY Times as one of Best Eleven Books of 1995, featured in NY Times Books of the Century 1998), The Life of Graham Greene Vol Three 1955–91 (2004, nominated Edgar Allan Poe Award 2005); ed Conrad Edns: Lord Jim (1967, 1974), An Outpost of Progress, Heart of Darkness (1973), Nostromo (1974), The Secret Agent (1974), The Nigger of The Narcissus, Typhoon, Falk and Other Stories (1975); contrib: The Academic American Encyclopedia, Guardian, Daily Telegraph, Oxford Magazine, Modern Language Review, Review of English Studies, Notes and Queries; BBC book contrib: Kenneth Muir Festschrift (1987), Creativity (1989); TV and radios; Conrad and His Critics BBC Radio 3 1981, film on Graham Greene Arena BBC TV 1989, in-depth TV interview on Greene's Life and Letters Global Catholic Network 2005, TV interview with LA Theater Works on play The Living Room 2005; *Recreations* talking, writing, reading, public speaking, jogging, table tennis; *Clubs* Savile; *Style*— Dr Norman Sherry; ✉ PO Box 6108, San Antonio, Texas 78209, USA (e-mail nsherry@trinity.edu)

SHERWELL, Elise; *née* Laverick; da of Peter M Laverick, *qv*, and Elaine, *née* Steckler; *b* 27 July 1975, Rustington, W Sussex; *Educ* Guildhall Sch of Music and Drama; *Career* amateur rower; memb Thames Rowing Club; achievements incl: Bronze medal single sculls World Under 23 Championships 1997, Bronze medal eights World Championships 1997, seventh place eights Olympic Games Sydney 2000, Bronze medal double sculls Olympic Games Athens 2004 and Beijing 2008; trainee slr Ashurst LLP; *Recreations* playing the double bass, climbing, sailing; *Clubs* Thames Rowing, London Rowing; *Style*— Mrs Elise Sherwell

SHERWOOD, Bishop of 2006–; Rt Rev Anthony Porter; *b* 10 February 1952; *Educ* Gravesend Sch for Boys, Hertford Coll Oxford, Ridley Hall Cambridge; *Career* curate Edgware 1977–80, curate Haughton St Mary 1980–83, priest i/c Bacup Christ Church 1983–87, vicar Bacup 1987–91, rector Rusholme Holy Trinity 1991–2006, hon canon Machester Cathedral 2004–06, hon canon Southwell Minster 2006–; Archbishops' sport ambass 2014–; *Books* Prince of Thieves (2006), Chips (2007), Super Jack (2008), Seed Scattering (2014); *Style*— The Rt Rev the Bishop of Sherwood; ✉ Jubilee House, Westgate, Southwell, Nottinghamshire NG25 0JL (☎ 01636 819133, e-mail bishopsherwood@southwell.anglican.org)

SHERWOOD, Charles N C; *b* 30 September 1959; *Educ* Univ of Cambridge (Whittaker scholar, MA), Harvard Univ Grad Sch of Business Admin (Baker scholar, MBA); *m* ; 3 c; *Career* assoc conslt Boston Consulting Gp 1981–1983, gen ptnr Business Sch Travel 1984–85, ptnr Permira (formerly Schroder Ventures) 1985–; non-exec dir: Homebase 2001–02, The AA 2004–, Sea Containers Inc 1996–; *Recreations* snow, rock and ice climbing, skiing and ski mountaineering, scuba diving, paragliding, guitar, reading; *Style*— Charles Sherwood, Esq

SHERWOOD, James Blair; s of William Earl (d 1996), and Florence Balph Sherwood (d 2005); *b* 8 August 1933; *Educ* Yale Univ (BA); *m* 31 Dec 1977, Shirley Angela, da of Geoffrey Masser Briggs (d 1993), of Hinton Waldrist, Oxon; 2 step s (Charles Nigel Cross Sherwood b 1959, Simon Michael Cross Sherwood b 1960); *Career* Lt (jr grade) US Naval Reserve 1955–58; mangr French Ports and asst gen freight traffic mangr United States Lines Co (Le Havre and NY) 1959–62, gen mangr Container Transport International Inc 1963–64, fndr and pres Sea Containers Ltd (Bermuda) 1965–2006, fndr Orient-Express Hotels Ltd (chm 1987–2007, dir 2007–11, chm emeritus 2011–); estab Harry's Bar (with Mark Birley) London 1979; restored and brought into regular service Venic e Simplon-Orient-Express 1982; prop Capannelle Wine Estate Gaiole in Chianti Italy 1997–, prop Panorama Farms (Tulbagh Cape Province S Africa) 2014–; memb Cncl Save Venice Inc; tstee Solomon R Guggenheim Fndn NY, memb Pres's Cncl on Int Activities Yale Univ, tstee Oxford Philharmonic; hon citizen Venice; Order of the Southern Cross (Brazil); *Publications* Orient-Express, a personal journey (2012); *Recreations* tennis, skiing, golf, sailing; *Clubs* Pilgrims, Mory's, Hurlingham, Mark's, Idle Hour Country, Garrick; *Style*— James Sherwood, Esq; ☎ 020 7373 2216

SHERWOOD, Martin William; s of Peter Louis Sherwood (d 1992), and Mervyn, *née* De Toll (d 2005); *Educ* Westminster, New Coll Oxford (BA); *Career* grad trainee, account exec and supervisor Ogilvy Benson & Mather advtg agency 1967–74, mktg mangr, sales mangr, controller shop-in-shops, then md (subsid) Debenhams plc 1974–85, md Retail Detail Ltd 1985–87, md MMI plc financial mktg gp 1987–94, chief exec Investment Finance Div Mills & Reeve 1994–97, dir Teather & Greenwood Ltd Stockbrokers 1997–2004, dir Smith & Williamson 2004–10, ptnr Enterprise Investment Partners LLP 2011–, dir EIS companies; non-exec dir Notting Hill Housing Tst 1981–1997 (memb Fundraising Ctee), non-exec dir and chm Audit Ctee Chelsea & Westminster Hospital NHS Tst 2000–03; memb NEDO Ctee 'Better Made in Britain' 1984, fndr memb: Cncl and dir Enterprise Investment Scheme Assoc, Securities Inst; fndr and tstee CRUSAID 1986–97; *Recreations* charity, bridge, opera, horse racing, travel; *Clubs* Home House; *Style*— Martin Sherwood; ☎ 07768 764542, e-mail martinsherwood@hotmail.com

S

SHERWOOD, Oliver Martin Carwardine; s of Nathaniel Edward Carwardine Sherwood (d 1998), of Easthorpe, nr Colchester, Essex, and Heather Patricia Motion, *née* Carolin; *b* 23 March 1955; *Educ* Radley; *Children* 2 da (Davina Ruth b 7 July 1984, Sabrina Coral b 14 Oct 1994), 2 s (Peter Frederick Carwardine b 27 Oct 1986, Archie William Nathaniel b 17 April 1997); *Career* racehorse trainer; asst trainer to: G Pritchard-Gordon Newmarket 1975–76, Arthur Moore Ireland 1976–79, Fred Winter Lambourn 1979–84; racehorse trainer Rhonehurst Upper Lambourn 1984–; trainer of 500 winners incl winners of: EBF Novice Hurdle Final Cheltenham 1986, Glenlivet Hurdle Liverpool 1987, Sun Alliance Novices Hurdle Cheltenham 1987 and 1988, Sun Alliance Novices Steeplechase Cheltenham 1988, Bic Razor Gold Cup Handicap Hurdle Lingfield 1989, Rapid Raceline Scottish Champion Hurdle Ayr 1989, Gerry Fielden Hurdle Newbury 1989, Charles Heidsieck Champagne Bula Hurdle Newbury 1989, New Year's Day Hurdle Windsor 1990, ASW Hurdle Ascot 1990, Ekbalco Handicap Hurdle Newcastle 1990, Hennessy Cognac Gold Cup Steeplechase Newbury 1990, Tingle Creek Handicap Chase Sandown 1990, Baring Securities Tolworth Hurdle Sandown 1990, First Nat Steeplechase Ascot 1990, Cheltenham Grand Annual Challenge Cup Handicap Chase Cheltenham 1991, BMW Champion Novices' Hurdle Punchestown 1991, Challow Hurdle 1994, Tote Gold Trophy 1994; champion amateur rider (ridden 95 winners incl 3 Nat Hunt Cheltenham Festival winners); *Recreations* shooting, cricket; *Style*— Oliver Sherwood, Esq; ✉ Rhonehurst, Upper Lambourn, Hungerford, Berkshire RG16 8RG (☎ 01488 71411, fax 01488 72786, e-mail oliver.sherwood@virgin.net, website www.oliversherwood.co.uk)

SHETTY, His Hon Judge Rajeev Rama; *Career* called to the Bar 1996, recorder 2009, legal assessor GMC/ Medical Practitioners Tribunal Service (MPTS) 2010–14, circuit judge (Northern Circuit) 2014–; dir Bar Mutual Indemnity Fund 2010–14; *Recreations* cinema, golf; *Clubs* Woking Golf; *Style*— His Hon Judge Shetty

SHETTY, Salil; *Educ* LSE (MSc), Indian Inst of Mgmnt Ahmedabad (MBA); *Career* ActionAid: dir India 1985–95, dir Kenya 1995–98, chief exec 1998–2003; dir UN Millennium Campaign 2003–10, sec gen Amnesty Int 2010–; *Style*— Salil Shetty, Esq; ✉ Amnesty International, 1 Easton Street, London WC1X 0DW

SHIELDS, Frank Cox; s of Joseph F Shields (d 1973), of Dublin, and Alice, *née* Cox (d 1972); *b* 10 September 1944, Dublin; *Educ* Harvard Univ (AB), Wharton Sch of Fin and Commerce (MBA); *m* 9 Oct 1971, Elizabeth Jean, da of John Blythe Kinross, CBE, of London; 1 da (Henrietta b 1973), 2 s (Oliver b 1975, Alexander b 1980); *Career* res staff LSE 1969–71; stockbroker: Cazenove & Co 1971–73, Grieveson Grant & Co 1973–78; exec dir: European Banking Co Ltd 1978–85, EBC AMRO Bank Ltd 1985–86; sr rep Maruman Securities Co Ltd London 1987, dir and gen mangr Maruman Securities (Europe) Ltd 1987–92; sr private banker and vice-pres Merrill Lynch International Bank Ltd 1992–94; head of real estate and tstee services National Bank of Kuwait (International) plc 1995–99; dir of investor rels and mktg: Emerging Markets Partnership (Europe) Ltd 2000–05, Mid Europa Partners LLP 2005–06, EMP Global 2006–07; dir of investor rels Abris Capital Ptnrs 2007–15; *Recreations* architecture, reading, travel; *Clubs* Brooks's, The Nassau (Princeton NJ), The Fly (Cambridge Mass); *Style*— Frank Shields, Esq; ✉ 5 Youngs Court, Hampstead, London NW3 1DD (✆ 020 7435 1175, e-mail fcshields@msn.com)

SHIELDS, Baroness (Life Peer UK 2014), of Maida Vale in the City of Westminster Joanna Shields; OBE (2014); *Educ* Pennsylvania State Univ, George Washington Univ (MBA); *Career* mktg mangr Nat Digital 1987–89, product mngr and VP Prodn Systems Electronics for Imaging 1989–97, CEO Veon 1997–2000, Int vice-pres Real Networks 2000–03, VPMD Decru EMEA 2003–05 (MD Syndication & Ptnrships Google EMEA 2005–07), ceo Bebo & Pres AOL People Networks 2007–09, vice-pres and md Facebook EMEA 2010–12, ceo & chm Tech City 2012–15, non-exec dir LSEG 2014–15; min for Internet Safety and Security 2015–; memb: Cncl BAFTA, Fundraising Bd There4Me NSPCC; *Style*— The Baroness Shields, OBE

SHIELDS, (Robert) Michael Coverdale; CBE (2002); s of Thomas Shields, and Dorothy Shields; *b* 23 January 1943; *Educ* Durham Johnston Grammar Tech Sch, Univ of Durham (BSc), Univ of Newcastle upon Tyne (DipTP); *m* 1965, Dorothy Jean Dennison; 2 s, 1 da; *Career* with Planning Depts: Newcastle upon Tyne 1964–65, Durham CC 1965–69, Nottingham 1969–73; dep dir of planning Leeds City Cncl 1973–78, city tech servs offr and dep chief exec Salford City Cncl 1978–83; chief exec: Trafford BC 1983–87, Trafford Park Devpt Corp 1987–98, NW RDA 1998–2003; dir Innvotec NW Tst Ltd 1998–2001, inaugural chief exec Manchester Knowledge Capital 2003–05, princ URC Associates 2003–11, assoc Amion Consltg 2004–11, chm United Utilities Trust Fund 2005–09, chm Liverpool Land Devpt Co 2005–08, chm Merseycare Ltd 2012; non-exec dir and dep chm Mersey Care NHS Tst 2009–12; tstee and dep chair Mfrg Inst 2006–; memb Bd Altrincham Forward 2011–14, chair working group preparing Altrincham Town Centre neighbourhood business plan 2013–; govr Altrincham GS 1988–98 (chm 1988–93); Univ of Salford: pro-chllr 1993–99, chm Cncl 1997–99, dep 1999–2003; hon fell Hesletine Inst Univ of Liverpool Sch of Mgmnt 2014–; Hon DSc Univ of Salford, Hon DLitt UMIST, Hon LLD Univ of Manchester; MRTPI (ret); *Recreations* family, books; *Style*— Michael Shields, Esq; ✆ 0161 928 2320, e-mail mike.shields@urca.co.uk

SHILLING, David; s of late Ronald Shilling, and Gertrude Shilling (d 1999); *b* 27 June 1953; *Educ* St Paul's; *Career* designer, artist; designs incl: menswear, womenswear, lingerie, furs, jewellery, fine china limited edition pieces, ceramic tiles, wallpapers, upholstery fabrics and designs for film, theatre, ballet and opera; important solo shows incl: The Hats (Ulster Museum exhibition, exhibited Worthing, Plymouth, Salisbury, Durham, Leeds and Exeter Museums) 1981–, David Shilling – A Decade of Design (Chester Museum) 1991; other solo exhibitions incl: Angela Flowers London, Tino Ghelfi Vicenza Italy, Rendezvous Gallery Aberdeen, Phillip Francis Sheffield, Richard Demarco Gallery Edinburgh, Sotheby's Stockholm, Salamo-Caro Gallery Cork St London 1993, British Cncl Köln 1995, Dubai 1999, Hatworks Museum Stockport 2001, National Horseracing Museum Newmarket 2001, Int Museum of the Horse Lexington KY 2002, Newmarket Racecourse 2002, Henley Festival 2003, Galerie Ferrero Nice 2004, Musee Chapeau Lyon 2004–05, Ferrero Gallery Nice 2005, Regent's Park London 2005, Holdenby Northampton 2006, Museu da Chapelaria Portugal 2008, Beijing 2009, Monaco 2012; work in museum collections: V&A, Met NY, Los Angeles County, Mappin Gallery Sheffield, Musée de l'Art Décoratif Paris, Philadelphia Museum of Art; UN sr conslt for design and product adaptation for developing countries (projects in S America, Asia and Africa) 1990–; pres Valdivia Ecuador; Lifetime Achievement Award Robb Report Shanghai 2014; *Publications* Thinking Rich (1986); recordings incl: Fashion Darling (EP, 2015); *Recreations* sleeping on aeroplanes, exploring, jet-skiing, jam making, 3D photography; *Style*— David Shilling, Esq; ✉ website www.davidshilling.com

SHILSON, Stuart James; LVO (2004); s of David Shilson, and Gillian, *née* Harford; *b* 1966, Surrey; *Educ* St Paul's Sch Barnes (Foundation scholar), Balliol Coll Oxford (BA, MSc), St John's Coll Cambridge (MPhil); *m* 1992, Sarah Catherine Mary, *née* Coleman; 2 da (Alexandra b 1998, Helena b 2000), 1 s (Hugh b 2004); *Career* called to the Bar (Middle Temple) 1992, barr in private practice 1992–97; McKinsey & Co: 1997–2001 and 2005– (princ 1998–2012, dir 2012–); sr civil servant Cabinet Office 1990–2000, asst private sec to HM The Queen 2001–04 (asst keeper of The Queen's Archives 2002–04); business advsr The Prince's Youth Business Tst 1994–97; Freeman City of London 2005, Liveryman Drapers' Co 2008– (memb Ct of Assts 2014–); FRGS 1989, FRSA 1996, FRI 2011, FLS 2015; GCStJ (Order of St John tstee 2011–); *Clubs* Athenaeum; *Style*— Stuart Shilson, Esq, LVO; ✉ McKinsey & Company Inc, 1 Jermyn Street, London SW1Y 4UH

SHILSTON, Andrew Barkley; s of Alan Shilston, and Patricia Shilston; *b* 20 October 1955; *Educ* Epsom Coll, Keble Coll Oxford (MA); *m* 30 Aug 1980, Catherine; 2 da (Sophie b 1985, Emma b 1988), 1 s (James b 1987); *Career* Arthur Andersen 1977–81, BP 1981–83, Abbott Laboratories 1983–84, fin dir Enterprise Oil plc 1985–2002, fin dir Rolls-Royce plc 2003–11; chm: Morgan Advanced Materials 2012–, Circle Hldgs plc 2012–; non-exec dir: AEA Technology plc 1996–2004, Cairn Energy 2004–08, BP plc 2012–; ACA 1980, FCT 1989; *Recreations* tennis, skiing, rugby, opera; *Clubs* RAC; *Style*— Andrew Shilston, Esq; ✉ Morgan Advanced Materials plc, Quadrant, 55–57 High Street, Windsor SL4 1LP (✆ 01753 837000)

SHIMELL, William Douglas John; s of William George Shimell, of Cawsand, Cornwall, and F Elizabeth Bowen; *b* 23 September 1952; *Educ* Westminster Abbey Choir Sch, St Edward's Sch Oxford, Guildhall Sch of Music, National Opera Studio; *m* 1996, Olga Slavka; *Career* baritone; *Roles* incl: Count Almaviva in The Marriage of Figaro (Glyndebourne Festival 1984, La Scala Milan 1987 and 1989, Geneva Opera 1989, Vienna Staatsoper 1990, 1993, 1994 and 1995, Zurich Opera 1990, Chicago Lyric Opera 1991, Champs Elysees Theatre Paris 1997), Marcello in La Bohème (Royal Opera House Covent Garden 1990, Vienna Staatsoper 1991, San Francisco 1993, Metropolitan NY 1996), title role in Don Giovanni (WNO 1984, ENO 1985, Amsterdam 1989 and 1992, Zurich 1991, Aix-en-Provence Festival 1993, Munich 1994, Berlin 1994, San Francisco 1995, Vienna Straatsoper 1997), Dandini in La Cenerentola (Glyndebourne Touring Opera 1983, Le Châtalet Paris 1986), Malatesta in Don Pasquale (Netherlands Opera) 1987, Nick Shadow in The Rake's Progress (San Francisco Opera 1988, Opèra de Lyon 1995, Munich 2002, Metropolitan NY 2003), Guglielmo in Cosi fan Tutte (Covent Garden, Geneva Opera, Zurich Opera, Tokyo, Bolshoi Theatre Moscow with La Scala Co 1989), Dourlinski in Lodoiska (La Scala Milan under Riccardo Muti, also recorded live for Sony) 1991, Don

Alfonso in Cosi fan Tutte (Rome 1995, Paris 1996, Metropolitan NY 1997), Sharpless in Madame Butterfly (Rome 1996, Metropolitan NY 1999 and 2002), title role in Hercules (Aix-en-Provence Festival) 2004; *Recordings* Joseph in Berlioz L'Enfance du Christ (with English Chamber Orch under Léger, Thames Television), Bach B minor Mass (with Chicago Symphony Orch under Sir Georg Solti, Decca), Vaughan Williams Sea Symphony (with Royal Liverpool Philharmonic under Vernon Handley, EMI), Lambert Summer's Last Will and Testament (with English Northern Philharmonic under David Lloyd-Jones), Stravinsky Pulcinella (with Amsterdam Concertgebouw under Chailly, Decca), title role in Don Giovanni (with Vienna Philharmonic under Riccardo Muti, EMI); *Films* Certified Copy 2010, Amour 2012; *Style*— William Shimell, Esq; ✉ c/o IMG Artists (UK) Ltd, The Light Box, 111 Power Road, London W4 5PY (✆ 020 7957 5811, fax 020 7957 5801)

SHINDLER, Dr Colin; s of Israel Shindler, of Prestwich, Manchester, and Florence, *née* Weidberg; *b* 28 June 1949; *Educ* Bury GS, Gonville & Caius Coll Cambridge (MA, PhD); *m* 23 Sept 1972, (Nancy) Lynn, da of Prof Robert Stephen White (d 2005), of Santa Barbara, CA; 1 da (Amy b 1975), 1 s (David b 1977); *Career* film, television writer and producer: res fell American Film Inst Beverly Hills 1972; as prodr incl: Love Story series (BBC) 1981, East Lynne (BBC) 1982, The Worst Witch (Central, American Cable Emmy) 1985, A Little Princess (LWT, BAFTA) 1986, Lovejoy (BBC, series V 1993, series VI 1994), Wish Me Luck (LWT) 1987, 1914 All Out (YTV, first prize Reims Int Film Festival) 1989; as writer and prodr: Young Charlie Chaplin (Thames/PBS, US Prime Time Emmy nomination), The Scarlet Thread (NBC) 1992, Madson (BBC) 1995, Manchester United Ruined My Life (BBC) 1998, Footballers' Lives 2003; author of screenplay Buster (feature film) 1988; Radio: Warner Bros Goes to War (BBC Radio 3) 1995, Second City Blues (BBC Radio 4) 1999, Mothers, Daughters and Chicken Soup (BBC Radio 4) 2002; memb BAFTA; lectr Faculty of History Univ of Cambridge 1998–; *Books* Hollywood Goes to War (1979), Buster (1988), Hollywood in Crisis (1996), Manchester United Ruined My Life (1998), High on a Cliff (1999), Fathers, Sons and Football (2001), First Love, Second Chance (2002), George Best and 21 Others (2004), The Worst of Friends (2008), National Service (2012), Manchester City Ruined My Life (2012), R W Barber: The Professional Amateur (2015), Four Lions (2016); *Recreations* cricket, soccer, golf, tennis, badminton, theatre, music, fell walking in the Lake District; *Style*— Dr Colin Shindler; ✉ c/o LBA, 91 Great Russell Street, London, WC1B 3PS (✆ 020 7637 1234)

SHINDLER, Geoffrey Arnold; OBE (2007); s of Israel Shindler (d 2004), of Manchester, and Florence, *née* Weidberg (d 1962); *b* 21 October 1942, Manchester; *Educ* Bury GS, Gonville & Caius Coll Cambridge (W M Tapp scholar, MA, LLM); *m* 20 Feb 1966, Gay, da of late Harry Kenton; 3 da (Freya b 29 Dec 1966, Nicola b 8 Oct 1968, Caroline b 29 Jan 1971); *Career* ptnr March Pearson & Skelton 1971–86 (articled clerk 1966–68, asst slr 1968–71), ptnr Halliwell Landau Manchester 1986–2005, sr memb Halliwells LLP 2005–06, ptnr Lane-Smith & Shindler LLP 2006–11, conslt DWF LLP 2011–14, ptnr Nova Private Client LLP 2014–; dir Old Trafford Consultants Ltd 2010–, memb: Bd of Visitors HM Prison Manchester 1973–84, Salford FPC 1984–89, Exec Ctee NW Arts 1984–91; chm: Local Review Ctee (Parole) HM Prison Manchester 1979–84, Soc of Tst and Estate Practitioners 1994–98, Inst for Fiscal Studies NW region 1996–98; pres Soc of Tst and Estate Practitioners 2006– (vice-pres 1998–2006); memb Tst Law Ctee, memb Bd of Advsrs and chm Int Advsy Bd Int Compliance Assoc; hon assoc Centre For Law and Business Univ of Manchester 1990–; dir: Opera North 1995–97, Royal Exchange Theatre Manchester 2003– (chm Devpt Ctee 2000–12), Manchester Camerata 2005–12 (chm 2007–12); chm Manchester Camerata Charity 2012–; vice-chm Lancs CCC 2009–12 (chm Business Ctee 2008–12, memb Bd of Dirs 2012–); recipient Muriel Goodwin trophy 1993; Freeman Worshipful Co of Tax Advsrs; visiting fell Centre for Legal Studies Univ of Bournemouth; memb: Manchester Literary and Philosophical Soc, Soc of Legal Scholars, Int Academy of Estate and Tst Law; *Books* Law of Trusts (with K Hodkinson, 1984); *Publications* Trusts and Estates Law and Tax Jl (conslt ed), Wills and Trusts Law Reports (memb Bd), Practical Inheritance Tax Planning (11 edn 2013, with M McLaughlin and P Davies, 13 edn 2016, with M McLaughlin, P Davies and R Ray); *Recreations* theatre, music, opera, books; *Clubs* Lancashire CCC (memb Ctee 2006–13, Bd dir 2013–), MCC; *Style*— Geoffrey A Shindler, Esq, OBE; ✉ 10 Bury Old Road, Prestwich, Manchester M25 0EX (✆ 0161 740 2291); Old Trafford Consultants Ltd, The Copper Room, Deva Centre, Trinity Way, Manchester M3 7BQ

SHINDLER, Nicola; da of Geoffrey Shindler, of Manchester, and Gay, *née* Kenton; *b* 8 October 1968; *Educ* Bury GS, Gonville & Caius Coll Cambridge (BA); *Children* 2 da (Abby b 8 March 2003, Jessica b 5 Sept 2005), 1 s (Sam Ringo b 9 June 2008); *Career* early work incl: script ed Cracker 1993, asst prodr Our Friends in the North 1994–95, prodr Hillsborough 1995–96, prodr Heart 1997; fndr Red Prodn Co 1998–, co-fndr Red Wall Prodn Co; prodr/exec: Queer As Folk (2 series), Love in the 21st Century, Clocking Off (4 series), Linda Green (2 series), Bob & Rose, The Second Coming, Sparkhouse, Flesh and Blood, Burn It (2 series), Mine all Mine, Jane Hall's Big Bad Bus Ride, Conviction, Casanova, Dead Man Weds, Big Dippers, Legless, New Street Law, Playhouse, The Mark of Cain, Unforgiven, Worried About the Boy, Single Father, Bedlam (2 series), Exile, Scott & Bailey (4 series), Love Life, Blackout, BBC Learning Life Stories, Last Tango In Halifax (3 series), Leaving, Blood, Heading Out, A Nice Arrangement, The Last Witch (pilot), Pat & Cabbage, Prey, Happy Valley, Cucumber, Banana, Tofu; *Awards* BAFTA: Best Single Drama 1996 and 2007, Best Series 2000, Best Drama (for Last Tango in Halifax) 2013; RTS: Drama Series 2001, Best Drama 2002, Best Drama Series 2002, Best Single Drama 2008 (for The Mark of Cain); RTS NW: Best Drama Series 2001, Best Prog 2001, Best Drama 2001, Best Network Drama 2001, Best Drama 2002, Best Prog Produced by NW Independent 2003, Best Network Drama Prog 2003, Best Cable Prog 2003, Best Drama (for Last Tango in Halifax) 2013; Indies: Drama Award 2001, Best Drama 2002, Best TV Prog of Year 2002; Indie-vidual Award 2002, TV Prog of the Year Prix Europe TV Fiction 2003, Best Single Drama Broadcast Awards 2003, Best Drama South Bank Show Awards 2007, Rotterdam Film Festival 2007, Movies That Matter Award Amnesty International, Golden Nymph Award for Best TV Film at Monte Carlo, Women in Film and TV Award 2012; *Clubs* Manchester United FC (season ticket holder); *Style*— Ms Nicola Shindler; ✉ Red Production Company, Level 3 White, Media City UK, Salford M50 2NT (✆ 0161 886 2340, e-mail info@redlimited.co.uk)

SHINGLER, Timothy Hugh; s of Hugh Shingler (d 1993), and Enid Mary, *née* Stuffins; *b* 10 August 1955; *Educ* Bromley Tech HS for Boys; *m* 1, 1979 (m dis 1985), Laura Muriel, *née* Mill; 1 da (Sarah Laura b 23 Dec 1983); *m* 2, 11 June 1988, Susan, da of Dennis Arthur Edgar Elmes; 2 da (Helen Elizabeth b 21 April 1992, Nicola Joanne b 27 Jan 1998); *Career* geological data supervisor and co scout Shell UK Exploration and Production 1973–81, sr project co-ordinator Petroleum Information Ltd 1981–86, assoc Petroleum Servs Div James Capel & Co 1990–91 (oil exec 1986–89), business devpt/mktg dir Petroleum Servs Gp Arthur Andersen (now Andersen) 2000–02 (sr mangr 1991–99), head of FSU/Asia Business Devpt CWC Gp 2002–03, business mangr EAME MNA Global 2003–12, vice-pres Western Hemisphere MNA Global 2012–13, ptnr Grosvenor Clive & Stokes 2013–; dir Borough 19 Motor Club Ltd; memb: Petroleum Exploration Soc of Great Britain 1986–, London Oil Analyst Gp, SE Asia Petroleum Exploration Soc; MInstPet 1986; *Recreations* motor sport, skiing, gardening, cooking; *Style*— Timothy Shingler, Esq; ✉ Grosvenor Clive & Stokes, 63 Catherine Place, London SW1E 6DY

SHINGLES, Godfrey Stephen (Geoff); CBE (1987); s of Sidney Shingles, and Winifred, *née* Moss; *b* 9 April 1939, Blofield, Norfolk; *Educ* Paston Sch North Walsham, Univ of Leeds (BSc); *m* 1, (m dis); 2 s (Jonathan b 19 Feb 1968, James b 29 April 1970); m 2, 2 Jan 1997, Frances Margaret; 1 da (Emma b 9 March 1998); *Career* Digital Equipment Co 1965–94 (latterly chm and chief exec), chm Imagination Technologies Group plc 1996–2015 (dep chm 1994–96); chm Speed-Trap Hldgs Ltd 2007–15, non-exec dir IS Solutions 2015–16; FInstD, FBCS, FIEE (now FIET); *Recreations* painting, skiing, sailing, rugby, golf, cricket; *Clubs* Royal Ocean Racing, MCC; *Style—* Geoff Shingles, Esq, CBE

SHINGLETON, Andrew Philip; s of Wilfrid James Shingleton (d 1984), and Grace Bernadina Shingleton, *née* Pole; *b* 28 June 1943; *Educ* Douai Sch; *m* 1, 1967, Vanessa Jane (d 1977), da of Capt John Liley, of Marbella, Spain; 3 s (Toby John-James b 1972, Alexander William, Barnaby Andrew (twins) b 1975); m 2, 1982, Wendy Elizabeth, da of Alec Barnes, of South Lancing, W Sussex; *Career* McCann Erickson Advertising: dir 1987–94, vice-pres McCann Erickson Worldwide 1994–; MIPA 1972, memb CAM 1973; *Recreations* walking the Cornish cliffs, golf, 18th century French history, guide lectr at the Wallace Collection; *Style—* Andrew P Shingleton, Esq; ✉ Bossiney, 75 Orchehill Avenue, Gerrards Cross, Buckinghamshire SL9 8QH (☎ 01753 887985)

SHIP, Chris; *b* 10 October 1973, Southampton; *Educ* Univ of Sussex (BA), Leeds Trinity Univ (PGDip); *Career* BBC Radio Solent 1996–97, BBC Surrey 1997–98, Wave 105 Hampshire 1998–2000; ITV News: news corr 2000–06, political corr then sr political corr 2006–12, dep political ed 2012–; part of news coverage award BAFTA 2014; *Style—* Chris Ship, Esq; ✉ ITN Ltd, 200 Gray's Inn Road, London WC1X 8XZ (website www.itv.com/news, Twitter @ChrisShipITV)

SHIPLEY, Her Hon Judge Jane; da of John Roberts Shipley, and late Maureen Anne Shipley; *b* 5 January 1952; *Educ* Maltby GS (head girl), St Hugh's Coll Oxford (MA, pres Oxford Law Soc); *m* 22 May 1977, David Arthur Farnsworth; 2 da (Emma, Sarah); *Career* called to the Bar Gray's Inn 1974, joined NE Circuit 1974, recorder of the Crown Court 1995–2000 (asst recorder 1991–95), circuit judge (NE Circuit) 2000–; *Recreations* gardening; *Style—* Her Hon Judge Jane Shipley; ✉ Sheffield Law Courts, 50 West Bar, Sheffield S3 8PH (☎ 0114 281 2400)

SHIPLEY, Baron (Life Peer UK 2010), of Gosforth in the County of Tyne and Wear; John Warren Shipley; OBE (1995); s of Edward Shipley (d 1987), and Grace, *née* Horton (d 2000); *b* 5 July 1946, Whitby, N Yorks; *Educ* Whitby GS, UCL (BA, pres Student Union); *m* 16 Aug 1969, Margaret, *née* Pattison; 1 s (Jonathan b 4 Sept 1974), 1 da (Helen b 5 Jan 1977); *Career* Procter and Gamble 1969–71, Open Univ 1971–2005 (regnl dir (North and EU) 1997–2005); Newcastle City Cncl: cncllr 1975–2003 and 2004–12, oppn ldr 1988–98, ldr 2006–10; memb Bd One North East 2005–12; vice-pres Local Govt Assoc 2010–; *Style—* The Lord Shipley, OBE; ✉ House of Lords, London SW1A 0PW (e-mail shipleyj@parliament.uk)

SHIPMAN, Timothy James (Tim); *b* 13 May 1975, Basingstoke, Hants; *Educ* Queen Elizabeth's GS Horncastle, Churchill Coll Cambridge (MA, MPhil); *m* 25 July 2015, Charlotte Todman; *Career* trainee then dep foreign ed Daily Express 1997–2001, dep political ed Sunday Express 2001–05, political corr Daily Mail 2005–07, Washington corr Sunday Telegraph 2007–09, dep political ed Daily Mail 2009–14, political ed Sunday Times 2014–; dir Shippers Media Ltd; chm Parly Press Gallery 2012; shortlisted Political Journalist of the Year British Press Awards 2015 and 2016; *Books* All Out War: The Full Story of How Brexit Sank Britain's Political Class (2016); *Recreations* cricket, motorsport, reading, travel; *Clubs* Groucho, White City All Stars Cricket; *Style—* Tim Shipman, Esq; ✉ e-mail tim.shipman@sunday-times.co.uk, Twitter @ShippersUnbound; c/o Victoria Hobbs (literary agent), AM Heath, 6 Warwick Court, London WC1R 5DJ (☎ 020 7242 2811, e-mail pippa.mccarthy@amheath.com); c/o Kirby Jones Management (speaking agent)(☎ 020 3713 7291, e-mail penny@kirbyjones.co.uk)

SHIPPEY, Prof Thomas Alan; s of Ernest Shippey (d 1962), and Christina Emily, *née* Kjelgaard (d 2012); *b* 9 September 1943, Calcutta, India; *Educ* King Edward's Sch Birmingham, Queens' Coll Cambridge (MA, PhD); *m* 1, 27 Dec 1966 (m dis 1983), Susan Margaret, da of John Veale, of Bingley, W Yorks; 2 da (Louise b 1970, Gillian b 1972), 1 s (John b 1973); m 2, 19 June 1993, Catherine Elizabeth, da of John Barton, of Bromley, Kent; *Career* lectr Univ of Birmingham 1965–72, fell St John's Coll Oxford 1972–79, prof of English language and medieval English literature Univ of Leeds 1979–93, Walter Ong chair Dept of English St Louis Univ 1993–2008; *Publications* Old English Verse (1972), Poems of Wisdom and Learning in Old English (1976), Beowulf (1978), The Road to Middle-Earth (1982), Fictional Space (1991), Fiction 2000 (1992), Oxford Book of Science Fiction Stories (1992), Oxford Book of Fantasy Stories (1994), Beowulf: The Critical Heritage (1998), Tolkien: Author of the Century (2000), The Shadow-walkers (2005), Roots and Branches (2007); Heroes and Legends (DVD, 2014), Hard Reading: learning from science fiction (2016); *Recreations* walking, science fiction; *Style—* Prof Thomas Shippey; ✉ May Cottage, 3 Stevens Walk, Buckland Newton, Dorset DT2 7BQ (e-mail shippey@slu.edu)

SHIPWRIGHT, Adrian John; s of Jack Shipwright, and Jennie, *née* Eastman; *b* 2 July 1950, Southampton; *Educ* King Edward VI Sch Southampton, ChCh Oxford (MA, BCL); *m* 17 Aug 1974, Diana Evelyn, da of Percival Denys Treseder (d 1971); 1 s (Henry b 1983), 1 da (Fiona b 1985); *Career* asst slr Linklaters & Paines 1977, official student and tutor in law ChCh Oxford 1977–82, ptnr Denton Hall Burgin & Warrens 1984–87 (asst slr 1982–84), ptnr SJ Berwin & Co 1987–92 (conslt 1992); called to the Bar Lincoln's Inn 1993, in practice Pump Court Tax Chambers 1993–2004, with Moore & Blatch 2004–07, conslt Clarke Willmott 2007–08, Pump Ct Tax Chambers 2008–11, dir Allington Eames Ltd 2011–12, conslt MLaw LLP 2012–, dir Montagu Business Services Ltd 2012–; judge First Tier and dep judge Upper Tier Finance and Tax Chamber 2002–15; memb Tst Law Ctee; KCL: hon lectr in laws 1986–90, prof of business law 1992–96, visiting prof 1996–2010; govr King Edward VI Sch Southampton 1982–96; fell CTA, FRSA, AIIT, TEP; *Books* CCH British Tax Reporter Vol 5 (1986) Tax Planning and UK Land Development (1988, 3 edn 2001), Capital Gains Tax Strategies in the New Regime (1989), UK Tax and Intellectual Property (1990, 2 edn 1996), VAT, Property and the New Rules (1990), UK Tax and Trusts (1991, 2 edn 2000), Strategic Tax Planning (ed and contrib), Textbook on Revenue Law (1997, 3 edn 2000), Tolley's Tax Digest on the Gaar Dec 2013; *Recreations* music; *Style—* Adrian Shipwright, Esq; ✉ MLaw, 3A Montagu Row, London W1U 6DZ

SHIRAISHI, Yuko; da of Masahiro Shinoda, of Tokyo, Japan, and Kazuko Shiraishi; *b* 6 March 1956; *Educ* Shinmei Jr Sch Tokyo, Myojyo HS Tokyo, Chelsea Sch of Art (Br Cncl scholar, BA, MA); *m* 1983, David Juda, *qv*; *Career* artist; projects: Field Inst Hombroich, Stiftung Insel Hombroich Museum Neuss 2001, BBC White City Project 2001–03, Moorfields Eye Hosp London 2006, Canal Wall Regent's Canal London 2008; curator Kyoto Art Walk Japan 2008; *Solo Exhibitions* Edward Totah Gallery 1988, 1990 and 1992, Shigeru Yokota Gallery Tokyo 1989, 1992, 1997, 2001 and 2011, Galerie Konstruktiv Tendens Stockholm 1990, 1994, 1997 and 2006, Gallery Kasahara 1993, 1996 and 2001, Galerie Hans Mayer Düsseldorf 1996, EAF Adelaide 1996, Annely Juda Fine Art 1997, 2001, 2005 and 2009, Ernst Museum Budapest 1998, Tate Gallery St Ives 1999, Museum Wiesbaden 2002, Mead Gallery Warwick Arts Centre Coventry 2002, Leeds City Art Gallery 2003, Crawford Municipal Art Gallery Cork 2003, Waygood Gallery Newcastle 2003, Leonard Hutton Galerie NY (with Joseph Albers) 2006; *Group Exhibitions* incl: New Contemporaries (ICA) 1980, The Presence of Painting: Aspects of British Abstraction 1957–88 (Arts Cncl Mappin Gallery Sheffield and touring) 1988, Kunstlerinnen des 20 Jahrhunderts (Museum Wiesbaden Germany) 1990, Geteilte Bilder (Folkwang Museum, Germany) 1992, A Sense of Purpose (Mappin Art Gallery Sheffield) 1992, Recent British Painting (Arts Cncl touring exhbn) 1993, Zwei Energie Haus fur Konstructive und Konkrete Kunst (Zurich) 1993; Jerwood Painting Prize Royal Scottish Acad Edinburgh/The Royal Acad of Arts London 1994, Clear and Saturated (arti et Amicitiae Amsterdam) 1998, Geometrie als Gestalt (Neue Nationalgalerie Berlin) 1999, Blue (New Art Gallery Walsall) 2000, Monochrome (Mucsarnok Budapest) 2002, Art Unlimited Basel 2003, Kyoto Art Walk Nijo Castle 2005, MOT London 2006, Busan Biennale Sea Art Festival 2006, Alles Wilhelm-Hack Museum Germany 2009; *Work in Public Collections* Unilever, Br Museum, IBM, Arthur Andersen collection, Seibu Japan, McCrory Corporations NY, Arts Cncl of GB, Contemporary Art Soc, Graves City Art Gallery Sheffield, Ohara Museum Japan, Weishaupt Forum Germany, Daimler Benz Stuttgart Germany, British Cncl London, Govt Collection London, Sammlung Albertina Vienna, Ludwig Museum Budapest, Nat Museum of Art Osaka, Wilhelm-Hack Museum Germany, Kunsthalle Wirth Germany; *Style—* Ms Yuko Shiraishi; ✉ Acme Studio, Studio F, 15 Orsman Road, London N1 5RA (website www.yukoshiraishi.com)

SHIRCORE, Jenny; *Career* make-up artist; *Film* The Dreamchild, Wish You Were Here, On The Black Hill, Stormy Monday, Eric The Viking, The Secret Garden, My Sister My Sister, Mary Reilly, In The Bleak Midwinter, The Secret Agent, Rasputin, Land Girls, Complicity, Blow Dry, Elizabeth (Best Make-Up and Hair Acad Award, Best Make-Up and Hair BAFTA), Notting Hill, Gangster No 1, Enigma, The Four Feathers, The Good Thief, Dirty Pretty Things, Ned Kelly, Girl With A Pearl Earring, Vanity Fair, The Phantom of the Opera, Ask The Dust, Mrs Henderson Presents, As You Like It, Starter For Ten, Amazing Grace, Elizabeth: The Golden Age, Inkheart, The Young Victoria (Best Make-Up and Hair BAFTA), 1939, Clash of the Titans, Bel Ami, WE, My Week With Marilyn, Great Expectations, The Invisible Woman; *Style—* Ms Jenny Shircore; ✉ c/o McKinney Macartney Management Ltd, Gable House, 18–24 Turnham Green Terrace, London W4 1QP

SHIRLEY, Malcolm Christopher; s of Lt Cdr Leonard Noel Shirley, RN (d 1988), of Burford, Oxon, and Edith Florence, *née* Bullen (d 1999); *b* 10 April 1945; *Educ* Churcher's Coll Petersfield, BRNC Dartmouth, RN Engrg Coll (BSc); *m* 18 April 1970, Lucilla Rose Geary, da of Cdr Thomas Geary Dyer, RN (d 2008); 3 s (Guy b 1 March 1975, Ben b 1 March 1977, Hugo b 2 Jan 1979); *Career* RN: Midshipman 1964, Sub Lt 1965–69, Lt 1969, dep marine engr offr HMS Zulu 1970–73, trg offr HMS Eastbourne 1973–75, sr engr offr HM Yacht Britannia 1975–77, Lt Cdr 1976, RN Staff Coll 1977–78, Ship Design Authy MOD Bath 1978–79, marine engr off HMS Coventry 1980–81, asst naval attaché Paris (1982–84), manning and trg policy desk offr MOD Whitehall 1984–86, OC Machinery Trials Unit 1987–89, Capt 1989, asst dir MOD Bath 1989–91, UK military rep NATO (SHAPE) Belgium 1992–94, Cdre 1995, i/c Rating Study Gp, cmdg offr HMS Sultan 1995–98; DG Engrg Cncl 1998–2001, sec Royal Cmmn for the Exhbn of 1851 2002–10; Freeman City of London, Liveryman Worshipful Co of Engineers 1999 (Asst 2002); CEng 1973, FIMarEST (FIMarE 1980), hon FRCA 2009; *Recreations* sailing, music, fine wine; *Clubs* RNSA, Royal Yacht Sqdn, Royal London Yacht; *Style—* Mr Malcolm Shirley

SHIRLEY, Dame Stephanie (Steve); DBE, (2000, OBE 1980); *née* Buchtal; da of late Arnold Buchthal, and Margaret, *née* Schick; arrived in UK on Kindertransport as unaccompanied child refugee in 1939; f moved from being friendly enemy alien (one of the Dunera boys) prior to UK Army, to US Army (serving at Nuremberg trials) later German equivalent of High Ct Judge, changed name on naturalisation to Brook to honour Rupert Brooke; *b* 16 September 1933, Dortmund, Germany; *Educ* Sir John Cass Coll London (BSc); *m* 14 Nov 1959, Derek George Millington Shirley, s of George Millington Shirley (d 1970); 1 s (Giles Millington d 1998); *Career* PO Res Station Dollis Hill 1951–59, CDL 1959–62; Xansa (previously FI Gp plc, now part of Sopra Gp): fndr dir 1962–93, ceded control to workforce 1991, pres 1993–2007, memb CSR Advsy Bd Steria 2008; non-exec dir: AEA Technology plc (formerly UKAEA) 1992–2000, Tandem Computers Inc 1992–97, John Lewis Partnership plc 1999–2001; European Advsy Bd Korn/Ferry Int 2001–04; chair Women of Influence 1993; vice-pres City & Guilds Inst 2000–05; memb: Computer, Systems and Electronics Requirements Bd 1979–81, Electronics and Avionics Requirements Bd 1981–83, Cncl Work Fndn 1984–90, NCVQ 1986–89, Br-N American Ctee 1991–2001, Cncl 1992 Cwlth Studies Conf; founding ambass for philanthropy 2009–10; RITA Award (recognition of IT achievement) 1985, Inst of Mgmnt Gold Medal 1991, Mountbatten Medal 1999, Autism Advocate Award 2013; US Nat Women's Hall of Fame 1995, Beacon Fellowship 2003, Br Computer Soc Lifetime Achievement Award 2004, Spears 2010, Oxford Internet Inst Lifetime Award 2014; tstee Help The Aged 1987–90, pres Br Computer Soc 1989–90; fndr: The Kingwood Tst 1994, The Shirley Fndn 1996–, Prior's Ct Fndn 1997, Autism Cymru 2001, Autistica 2004, Nat Autism Project 2015–; co-fndr Ambassadorsforphilanthropy.com 2011; patron: Disablement Income Gp 1989–2001, Centre for Tomorrow's Company 1997–; memb Cncl Buckingham Univ 1993–96, fell Ct of Benefactors Univ of Oxford 2001–, companion Guild of Cambridge Benefactors 2006–; Freeman City of London 1987, Master Worshipful Co of Info Technologists 1992–93; fndn fell Balliol Coll Oxford 2001, Distinction of Univ of Edinburgh 2013; hon fellowships or doctorates from 23 English univs and 4 Scottish univs; Hon FCGI 1989, FBCS 1971, CCMI (CIMgt 1984), CEng 1990, FREng 2001; *Publications* Sponsor: Designing for Special Needs, The Art of Prior's Court School, History of Autism, Let IT Go (memoir, www.let-it-go.co.uk); articles in professional jls; *Recreations* wishful thinking; *Clubs* Royal Soc of Med; *Style—* Dame Stephanie Shirley, DBE; ✉ 47 Thames House, Phyllis Court Drive, Henley-on-Thames, Oxfordshire RG9 2NA (☎ 01491 579004, fax 01491 574995, e-mail steve@steveshirley.com, websites www.steveshirley.com, www.let-it-go.co.uk)

SHLAIM, Prof Avi; s of Joseph Shlaim, and Aida, *née* Obadiah; *b* 31 October 1945; *Educ* Jesus Coll Cambridge (BA), LSE (MSc), Univ of Reading (PhD); *Career* Nat Serv 1964–66; lectr and reader in politics Univ of Reading 1970–87; Alistair Buchan reader in international relations Univ of Oxford 1987–96, fell St Antony's Coll Oxford 1987–2011, prof of international relations Univ of Oxford 1996–2011; Royal Soc for Asian Affrs Sir Percy Cox Medal 2011; memb: RIIA, Br Soc for Middle Eastern Studies; fell Br Acad 2006; *Books* British Foreign Secretaries since 1945 (jtly, 1977), The United States and the Berlin Blockade, 1948–49: A Study in Crisis Decision Making (1983), Collusion Across the Jordan: King Abdullah, the Zionist Movement, and the Partition of Palestine (1988), The Politics of Partition (1990), War and Peace in the Middle East: A Concise History (1995), The Iron Wall: Israel and the Arab World (2000), Lion of Jordan: King Hussein's Life in War and Peace (2007), Israel and Palestine: Reappraisals, Revisions, Refutations (2009); *Recreations* tennis, travel; *Style—* Prof Avi Shlaim; ✉ 10 Brindley Close, Oxford OX2 6XN (☎ 01865 556244); St Antony's College, Oxford OX2 6JF (☎ 01865 274460, e-mail avi.shlaim@sant.ox.ac.uk)

SHNEERSON, Dr John Michael; s of Gregory Shneerson (d 2004), of Orpington, Kent, and Alfreda, *née* Ledger (d 1980); *b* 27 September 1946; *Educ* St Paul's, St Edmund Hall Oxford (MA, DM), St Mary's Hosp London; *m* 15 March 1975, Dr Anne Shneerson, da of Dr Kenneth Maclean, of Oxted, Surrey; 2 da (Joanna b 1979, Catherine b 1981), 1 s (Robert b 1983); *Career* sr registrar Westminster & Brompton Hosps London 1978–80; conslt physician: Newmarket Gen Hosp 1980–2012, Papworth Hosp 1980–2013, Addenbrooke's Hosp 1980–96, W Suffolk Hosp 1983–2002; dir: Assisted Ventilation Unit Newmarket Gen Hosp 1981–92, Respiratory Support and Sleep Centre Papworth Hosp 1992–2012; FRCP 1986, FCCP 1993; *Books* Manual of Chest Medicine (1986), Disorders

S

of Ventilation (1988), Two Centuries of Real Tennis (1998), Handbook of Sleep Medicine (2000), Sleep Medicine: A Guide to Sleep and its Disorders (2005), Real Tennis Today and Yesterday (2015); *Recreations* golf, tennis, gardening; *Style*— Dr John Shneerson; ✉ Papworth Hospital, Papworth Everard, Cambridge CB23 3RE (✆ 01480 364384, fax 01480 364558)

SHONE, Richard Noel; *b* 8 May 1949; *Educ* Wrekin Coll, Clare Coll Cambridge (BA); *Career* writer and exhbn curator; ed The Burlington Magazine 2003–15 (assoc ed 1979–2003); selected and catalogued: Portraits by Duncan Grant 1969, Portraits by Walter Sickert 1990, co-selector Sickert exhbn Royal Acad 1992–93, purchaser Arts Cncl Collection 1994–96, selector New Contemporaries exhbn Liverpool and London 1996; curator: Head First (Arts Cncl tour) 1998–99, The Art of Bloomsbury (Tate and US tour) 1999–2000; contrib numerous articles on modern Br art and Bloomsbury to: The Spectator, The Observer, Artforum, The Burlington Magazine; closely involved in restoration and opening of Charleston Farmhouse Sussex (home of Vanessa Bell and Duncan Grant) 1980–; memb: Jury Turner Prize 1988, Advsy Ctee Govt Art Collection 1990–94; *Publications* Bloomsbury Portraits: Vanessa Bell, Duncan Grant and their Circle (1976, new edn 1993), The Century of Change: British Painting Since 1900 (1977), Sisley (1979), Augustus John (1979), The Post Impressionists (1980), Walter Sickert (1988), Rodrigo Moynihan (1988), Alfred Sisley (1992), Damien Hirst (2001); *Style*— Richard Shone, Esq; ✉ 87 Holbein House, Holbein Place, London SW1W 8PW (e-mail rnshone@gmail.com)

SHORE, Andrew; *s* of Frank Shore (d 1969), of Oldham, Lancs, and Edith, *née* Ashton (d 1963); *b* 30 September 1952; *Educ* Counthill GS Oldham, Univ of Bristol (BA), Royal Northern Coll of Music, London Opera Centre; *m* 1976, Fiona Mary, da of John Macdonald; 3 da (Sarah Jane b 12 Sept 1983, Emily Ann b 22 Sept 1985, Harriet Mary Edith b 16 March 1990); *Career* stage mangr and singer Opera for All tours (Frosch in Die Fledermaus, Fiorello in The Barber of Seville, Giacomo in Fra Diavolo, Marquis in La Traviata) 1977–79; Kent Opera: joined chorus 1979, subsequent roles incl Antonio in Marriage of Figaro, Pasha Selim in Il Seraglio, Dr Bartolo in The Barber of Seville and Papageno in The Magic Flute, deviser and presenter of educnl material; Opera North roles incl: King Dodon in The Golden Cockerel (debut 1985), Sacristan in Tosca, Leander in The Love for Three Oranges, Varlaam in Boris Godunov, Don Inigo in L'Heure Espagnole, Dr Bartolo, The Mayor in The Thieving Magpie, Don Jerome in Gerhard's Duenna, Geronimo in Cimarosa's Secret Marriage, title roles in Don Pasquale, Gianni Schicchi, King Priam, Wozzeck and Falstaff; Scottish Opera roles incl: Mr Flint in Billy Budd (debut 1987), Baron in La Vie Parisienne, Don Alfonso in Cosi Fan Tutte; ENO roles incl: Cappadocian in Salome (debut 1987), Doeg in Philip Glass's Planet 8, Don Alfonso, Falstaff, Papageno, Frank in Die Fledermaus, Dr Bartolo, Don Pasquale, Gianni Schicchi, Shishkov in House of the Dead, Dulcamara in Elixir of Love, Faninal in Der Rosenkavalier, Alberich in The Ring; Glyndebourne Festival roles incl: Baron Douphol in La Traviata (debut 1988), Vicar in Albert Herring, Falstaff, Kolenaty in Makropulos Case, Dikoj in Katya Kabanova, Dr Bartolo and Don Alfonso with Glyndebourne Touring Opera; WNO roles incl: Dr Bartolo (debut 1990, also Vancouver and Ottawa 1991), Sacristan in Tosca, Kolenaty, Papageno; debuts: Royal Opera House Covent Garden as Baron Trombonok in Rossini's Il Viaggio a Reims 1992, Paris Opera Bastille as Sacristan in Tosca 1995, Dulcamara in L'Elisir d'amore San Diego 1996 and Copenhagen 1999, Barcelona and Hamburg as Kolenaty 1999, La Monnaie Brussels as Kothner in Die Meistersinger, Chicago Lyric Opera in The Great Gatsby 2000, Santa Fe Festival as Falstaff 2001, Met Opera NY as Dulcamara 2006, Bayreuth Festival as Alberich in The Ring 2006; prodr for various amateur and professional gps: Nabucco, Manon Lescaut, Carmen, Orpheus in the Underworld, Bastien and Bastienne, Der Freischütz, Hugh the Drover, La Traviata, Romeo & Juliet, Handel's Faramondo, Wolf-Ferrari's School for Fathers; Tim Brandt Award in Opera Prodn 1977, nominated Olivier Award for Outstanding Achievement in Opera 1999; *Recordings* Nightingale by Charles Strouse 1983, Barber of Seville (role of Dr Bartolo) 1995, Don Pasquale (title role) 1998, L'Elisir d'amore (role of Dulcamara) 1999, Don Giovanni (role of Leporello) 2001, Falstaff (role of Falstaff) 2002, Andrew Shore Great Operatic Arias 2002, Wozzeck (title role) 2003; *Style*— Andrew Shore, Esq; ✉ c/o Ingpen & Williams Ltd, 7 St George's Court, 131 Putney Bridge Road, London SW15 2PA (✆ 020 8874 3222, fax 020 8877 3113)

SHORE, Darryl Francis; *b* 30 August 1946; *Educ* De La Salle Coll Sheffield, Sheffield Univ Med Sch (MB ChB); *Career* house surgn Royal Infirmary Sheffield 1972 (house physician 1971–72), demonstrator in pathology Univ of Sheffield 1972–73, sr house offr orthopaedic surgery Royal Hosp Sheffield 1973, sr house offr in gen surgery Bristol Royal Infirmary 1974 (sr house offr in urology 1973–74), sr house offr in orthopaedic surgery Dept of Orthopaedics Bristol 1974–75, registrar in paediatric surgery Children's Hosp Sheffield 1975–76, registrar in gen and vascular surgery Royal Infirmary Sheffield 1976 (registrar in gen surgery 1975); registrar in cardiothoracic surgery: Royal Infirmary and Children's Hosp and Cardiothoracic Unit Northern Gen Hosp Sheffield 1976–78, Brompton Hosp London 1978; res fell in cardiothoracic surgery Albert Einstein Coll of Med NY USA 1979; sr registrar in cardiothoracic surgery: Brompton Hosp London 1980, Hosp for Sick Children Gt Ormond St London 1981; sr registrar in cardiac surgery Nat Heart Hosp London 1982, conslt in cardiac surgery to the Southampton and SW Hampshire Health Authy and clinical teacher Univ of Southampton 1982–87; Royal Brompton Hosp: conslt cardiac surgn in adult and paediatric cardiac surgery 1987–, clinical dir of surgery 1990–95; *Publications* incl: Urinary Lithiasis in Childhood in the Bristol Clinical Area (jtly in Br Jl of Urology, 1975), Results of Mitral Valvuloplasty with Suture Plication Technique (jtly in Jl of Thoracic and Cardiovascular Surgery, 1980), Atresia in Left Atrio-Ventricular Connection (jtly in Br Heart Jl, 1982), Oral Veraparmil Fails to Prevent Supraventricular Tachycardia Following Coronary Artery Surgery (jtly in Int Jl of Cardiology, 1985), Thirteen Years Evaluation of the Bjork-Shiley Isolated Mitral Valve Prosthesis (jtly in Jl of Cardiovascular Surgery, 1989), Surgical Treatment for Infarct-Related Ventricular Septal Defects (jtly in Jl of Thoracic Surgery, 1990); *Style*— Darryl Shore, Esq; ✉ Royal Brompton Hospital, Sydney Street, London SW3 6NP (✆ 020 7351 8211)

SHORROCK, (John) Michael; QC (1988); *s* of James Godby Shorrock (d 1987), and Mary Patricia, *née* Lings (d 2001); *b* 25 May 1943; *Educ* Clifton, Pembroke Coll Cambridge (MA); *m* 25 Nov 1971, Marianne, da of Jack Mills (d 1983); 2 da (Amabel b 13 Dec 1971, Rose b 1 Sept 1974); *Career* called to the Bar Inner Temple 1965 (bencher 1995); recorder of the Crown Court 1982–, head of chambers 1992–2005, judge First Tier Tbnl (Social Entitlement Chamber) 2008–; memb: Criminal Injuries Compensation Bd 1995–2000, Criminal Injuries Compensation Appeals Panel 1997–2008; govr William Hulme's GS 1999–2006; *Style*— Michael Shorrock, Esq, QC; ✉ Atkinson Bevan Chambers, 2 Harcourt Buildings, Temple, London EC4Y 9DB (✆ 020 7353 2112, fax 020 7353 8339)

SHORT, Prof (Charles) Alan; *s* of Charles Ronald Short, and Dorothea Henrietta Winterfeldt; *b* 23 March 1955; *Educ* Lower Sch of John Lyon Harrow, Trinity Coll Cambridge (MA), Harvard Univ Graduate Sch of Design; *m* 2003, Slaine Catherine Campbell; 1 da (Georgia Grace Short b 2003); *Career* architect; ptnr Edward Cullinan Architects 1981–86; fndr: Peake, Short & Ptnrs 1986, Short and Associates 1997–; dean Faculty of Art and Design De Montfort Univ 1998–2001, elected prof of architecture and head of dept Univ of Cambridge 2001, academic ldr and min of educn distinguished prof Nat Centre for Int Research in Low-Carbon and Green Buildings Chongqing Univ China 2013–, distinguished prof Min of Educn China; winner Green Building of the Year Award (for Queens Building Leicester) 1995, High Architecture Low Energy Award (for Simonds Farsons CISK Malta) 1995, Building Magazine Building of the Year (for Lanchester

Library Coventry) 2000, CIBSE Environmental Initiation of the Year, BDA Public Building of the Year (for Sch of Slavonic and E European Studies) 2006, Global Sustainability Film Award tv/e 2013; RIBA Awards: Contact Theatre 2000, Poole Arts Centre 2003, Sch of Slavonic and E European Studies 2006, Pres's Award for Research 2007, Pres's Commendation for Research 2009; George Collins Fellow Soc of Architectural HIstorians 2014, Geddes Fellow Univ of Edinburgh 2014, fell Clare Hall Cambridge; DipArch, RIBA, FRSA; *Recreations* collecting drawings; *Clubs* Oxford and Cambridge, Chelsea Arts; *Style*— Prof Alan Short; ✉ Dept of Architecture, University of Cambridge, 1–5 Scroope Terrace, Cambridge CB2 1PX (e-mail cas64@cam.ac.uk, website shortandassociates.co.uk)

SHORT, Rt Hon Clare; PC (1997); da of Frank Short, and Joan Short; *b* 15 February 1946, Birmingham; *Educ* Keele Univ, Univ of Leeds (BA); *m* 1981, Alexander Ward Lyon (d 1993), former MP (Lab) York; *Career* civil servant Home Office 1970–75; dir: All Faiths for One Race Birmingham 1976–78, Youth Aid and the Unemployment Unit 1979–83; MP: (Lab) Birmingham Ladywood 1983–2006, (Ind Lab) Birmingham Ladywood 2006–10; front bench spokesperson on: employment 1985–88, social security 1988–91, environmental protection 1992–93, women 1993–95; elected to Shadow Cabinet 1995; chief oppn spokesperson on: tport 1995–96, overseas devpt 1996–97; sec of state for International Devpt 1997–2003; chm All-Pty Parly Gp on Race Rels 1985–86, memb Home Affrs Select Ctee 1983–85; memb Lab Pty NEC 1988–98; resigned from govt 2003, resigned Lab whip 2006; chair Policy Advsy Forum Cities Alliance 2008–, chair Extractive Industries Transparency Initiative (EITI) 2011–; tstee: Welfare Assoc, Africa Humanitarian Action, Hope Projects serving desitute asylum seekers; *Publications* Talking Blues – A Study of Young West Indians' Views of Policing (1978), Handbook of Immigration Law (1978), Dear Clare (1991), An Honourable Deception? New Labour, Iraq and the Misuse of Power (2004); *Recreations* family and friends, swimming; *Clubs* Two Brydges; *Style*— The Rt Hon Clare Short; ✉ 23 Larkhall Rise, London SW4 6JB (e-mail shortclare@gmail.com)

SHORT, David; WS; *s* of Maurice Short (d 1990), and Nancy, *née* Straker; *b* 25 January 1958, North Shields, Tyne & Wear; *Educ* Blyth Ridley HS, Univ of Dundee (MA), Univ of Strathclyde Univ (DipLP); *Children* 1 s (Tom b 31 Dec 1994); *Career* managing ptnr Lawford Kidd slrs until 2012 (joined 1982), ptnr Balfour+Manson LLP 2012–; Scottish sec Assoc of Personal Injury Lawyers; NP, memb Law Soc of Scotland 1986; *Recreations* golf, travel; *Style*— David Short, Esq, WS; ✉ 10 Ravelrig Drive, Balerno, Midlothian EH14 7NQ (✆ 0131 449 9521, e-mail ds.mail@btinternet.com); Balfour+Manson LLP, 54–66 Frederick Street, Edinburgh EH2 1LS (✆ 0131 200 1285, e-mail david.short@balfour-manson.co.uk)

SHORT, Philip; *s* of Wilfred Short (d 1976), and Marion, *née* Edgar (d 2008); *b* 17 April 1945; *Educ* Sherborne, Queens' Coll Cambridge (MA); *m* 1, 9 Aug 1968 (m dis), Christine Victoria, da of (Francis) Donald Baring-Gould; 1 s (Sengan b 1 March 1971); *m* 2, 1 Dec 1995 (m dis), Renquan, da of Zhen Gu; 1 s (Benedict b 10 May 1993); *m* 3, 8 July 2011, Ging, da of Danilo Daguyo Sr; 1 da (Romy b 7 Oct 2013); *Career* journalist and author; corr BBC (postings incl Moscow, Peking, Paris, Tokyo and Washington) 1972–97; sometime prof of comparative politics Univ of Iowa; *Books* Banda (1974), The Dragon and The Bear (1982), Mao: A Life (1999), Pol Pot: Anatomy of a Nightmare (2005), Mitterand: A Study in Ambiguity (2013); *Recreations* Chinese porcelain; *Style*— Philip Short, Esq

SHORTHOUSE, Prof Andrew John; *s* of George Sydney Shorthouse, and Dorothy Enid, *née* Baxter; *b* 25 April 1947, Market Bosworth, Leics; *Educ* Univ of London (BSc, MS), St Mary's Hosp London (MB BS); *m* 21 Jan 1977, Christine Elizabeth, *née* Tyrrell-Gray; 1 s (Dr James Richard Shorthouse b 3 Jan 1979), 1 da (Dr Alice Mary b 26 March 1982); *Career* sr surgical registrar St George's Hosp London 1981–86, hon sr lectr Univ of Sheffield 1986–, conslt gen and colorectal surgn Royal Hallamshire Hosp Sheffield 1986–2004, conslt colorectal surgn Northern Gen Hosp Sheffield 2004–, lead colorectal clinician Sheffield Teaching Hosps NHS Tst 2002–07, hon prof Sheffield Hallam Univ 2005–; author of book chapters and over 60 articles in med jls; hon sec Br Assoc of Surgical Oncology 1995–96, pres: Grey Turner Surgical Club 2002–03, Assoc of Coloproctology of GB and I 2005–06 (hon sec 1997–2000), European Soc of Coloproctology 2007–08 (fndr memb 2001, hon sec 2001–04), Section of Coloproctology RSM 2009–10; ACCEA Gold Award; memb Worshipful Co of Apothecaries; memb: Assoc of Surgns of GB and I, St Mark's Assoc, American Soc of Colon and Rectal Surgns; FRCS 1975; *Recreations* flyfishing, painting, gardening, music, travel, German, running; *Clubs* Derwent Flyfishing, Smithston Fishings; *Style*— Prof Andrew Shorthouse; ✉ e-mail shorthouse@doctors.org.uk

SHORTHOUSE, Dominic; *s* of Derek Shorthouse, of Highnam, Glos (d 2012), and Yvonne, *née* Leflaive; *b* 25 December 1961, Lincoln; *Educ* Univ of Oxford (MA), Stanford Grad Sch of Business (MBA); *m* 1, 23 Aug 1986 (m dis), Cathy, *née* Enmarch; 2 s (Tommy b 27 April 1996, Sam b 10 July 1998); *m* 2, July 2014, Amanda, *née* Rudman; 1 s (Dylan Jack Wolf b 11 Dec 2011); *Career* ptnr Warburg Pincus & Co 1988–2001, fndr and managing ptnr Englefield Capital 2002–; tstee: Anna Freud Cenre, Tommy's; advsr: ManoCap, Lennox Investment Mgmnt, Resolution Property; *Recreations* equitation, cycling, skiing, reading; *Clubs* Queens, Sunningdale Golf; *Style*— Dominic Shorthouse, Esq; ✉ Englefield Capital LLP, Michelin House, 81 Fulham Road, London SW3 6RD (✆ 020 7591 4208, fax 020 7591 4245, e-mail dominic@engcap.com)

SHORTRIDGE, Sir Jon Deacon; KCB (2002); *s* of Eric Creber Deacon Shortridge (d 1979), and Audrey Joan, *née* Hunt (d 1990); *b* 10 April 1947; *Educ* Chichester HS, St Edmund Hall Oxford (MA), Univ of Edinburgh (MSc); *m* 1972, Diana Jean, da of Dr E G Gordon; 1 da (Clare b 2 Dec 1975), 1 s (James b 9 Oct 1978); *Career* various jobs Miny of Housing, Countryside Cmmn and DOE 1969–75, various planning jobs Shropshire CC 1975–84; Welsh Office: joined 1984, private sec to Sec of State for Wales 1987–88, head Fin Div (grade 5) 1988–92, Head Local Govt Re-Organisation Gp (grade 3) 1992–95, head Local Govt Gp 1995–97, dir Econ Affairs (grade 2) 1997–99 (perm sec 1999); perm sec: Nat Assembly for Wales 1999–2007, Welsh Assembly Govt 2007–08; interim perm sec Dept of Innovation, Univs and Skills then Dept of Business, Innovation and Skills 2009, chair Audit Ctee Office of the Parly and Health Service Ombudsman 2010–16 (memb Bd 2013–); memb UK Statistics Authy 2010–12; chair: Audit Panel Ctee Cardiff CC 2009–15, Volunteering Matters (formerly Community Service Volunteers) 2010–15; chair Audit Ctee and advsy memb Cmmn for Local Administration in England 2012–; memb Cncl Cardiff Univ 2008–12, memb Audit and Scrutiny Ctee Univ of Oxford 2012–, memb Audit Ctee Royal Soc 2014–; hon fell: Glynd?r Univ (chllr and chair 2012–15), St Edmund Hall Oxford, Aberystwyth Univ, Cardiff Met Univ; hon doctorate Univ of Glamorgan; MRTPI 1974–96; *Books* Information Systems for Policy Planning in Local Government (jt ed, 1984); *Recreations* family, tennis, modern history; *Clubs* Oxford and Cambridge; *Style*— Sir Jon Shortridge, KCB; ✆ 01743 366670, e-mail jon.shortridge@btinternet.com

SHORTT, Denys Christopher; OBE (2013); *s* of Peter Shortt (d 2008), and Rosemary, *née* Meredith (d 2001); *b* 30 May 1964, Cheltenham; *Educ* Eagle House Sch, Warwick Sch; *m* 21 April 1990, Deborah, *née* Moty; 1 s (Charles b 10 Oct 1991), 1 da (Lydia b 20 Oct 1993); *Career* with Shakespeare Tea & Coffee Co (family business) 1982–94; fndr: DCS Europe 1994, Enable Software 2000, Enable Infomatrix Ltd 2004 (sold 2010), Deal-Track Ltd 2013; fndr EnableID 2015, www.supportingstratford.co.uk 2016; chm Coventry and Warks Local Enterprise Partnership, memb Bd Warwick Business Sch, dir Stratford Town FC, former memb Business Devpt Bd Scope, former memb Bd WMG Academy, advsr Royal Agricultural Univ; govr Cheltenham Coll, chair Agri-Tech Bd Royal Agricultural Univ Cirencester 2016; *Awards* Entrepreneur of the Year 2000, CBI Growing Business Award 2001, IOD Young Dir of the Year, CBI Growing Business Awards (Local Hero) 2011; ranked tenth in Management Today's Britain's Top 100 Entrepreneurs 2004, DCS listed in Fast Track 100, Enable listed in Tech Track 100, Top Track 250 (2013 and 2014), The Maserati 100 (2015); *Recreations* helicopter pilot, hockey (England under 21 int), farming, shooting, 4x4; *Clubs* Helicopter Club of GB, Ladykillers Hockey (chm), Goodwood Aviation; *Style*— Denys C Shortt, OBE; ✉ DCS Group UK Ltd, Timothy's Bridge Road, Stratford-upon-Avon, Warwickshire CV37 9YL (☎ 01789 208000, e-mail denys@dcsgroup.com, website www.dcsgroup.com); websites www.denysshortt.com, www.mystrategyplan.com, www.enableid.com and www.deal-track.com

SHOSTAK, Ray; CBE; *Career* head PM's Delivery Unit 2007–, DG of performance HM Treasury 2007–; *Style*— Ray Shostak, Esq, CBE; ✉ HM Treasury, 1 Horse Guards Road, London SW1A 2HQ

SHOTTER, Very Rev Edward Frank; s of Frank Edward Shotter (d 1970), and Minnetta, *née* Gaskill (d 1976); *b* 29 June 1933; *Educ* Humberstone Fndn Sch Clee, Sch of Architecture King's Coll Newcastle, St David's Coll Lampeter, Univ of Wales (BA), St Stephen's House Oxford; *m* 9 Dec 1978, Dr Jane Edgcumbe, da of Dr John Oliver Pearce Edgcumbe; 2 s (James b 1982, Piers b 1984), 1 da (Emma b 1987); *Career* ordained: deacon 1960, priest 1961; asst curate St Peter's Plymouth 1960–62, intercollegiate sec Student Christian Movement London 1962–66; dir: London Medical Gp 1963–89, Inst of Medical Ethics 1974–89; chaplain Univ of London 1969–89, prebendary St Paul's Cathedral London 1977–89, dean of Rochester 1989–2003 (now emeritus), memb Gen Synod 1994–2003, sec Assoc of English Cathedrals 1994–2002, chm Diocese of Rochester Thames Gateway Co-ordinating Gp 1997–2000; jt chm Kent Ecumenical Police Chaplaincy Ctee 1993–2001 (Force chaplain 1995–2001); chm Governing Body King's Sch Rochester 1989–2003, pres St Bartholomew's Hosp Rochester 1989–2003, dir Firmstart Medway 1991–2001; chm: Medway Enterprise Agency 1993–98, Medway Business Support Partnership 1994–98, Medway Business Point Ltd 1996–98, HMS Cavalier Meml Steering Gp 2000–07; vice-pres Inst of Med Ethics 1999– (Amulree fell 1991–99 and 2003–); chm: East Europe Subcommittee Liberal Party Foreign Affrs Panel 1974–81, Working Party on Ethics of Prolonging Life and Assisting Death 1993–97, Univ of Greenwich Research Ethics Ctee 1995–2003, Ctee on Welfare of Czech and Slovak Med Students in Britain 1968–69; fndr Journal of Medical Ethics 1975, memb Archbishop of Canterbury's Cnsllrs on Foreign Rels 1971–82, BCC East West Rels Advsy Ctee 1971–81, Educn Ctee St Christopher's Hospice 1982–89, Church Heritage Forum 1999–2003; FRSM 1976, Hon FRCP 2007; Patriarchal Cross Romanian Orthodox Church (Oeconomos Stavrophor) 1975; *Books* Matters of Life and Death (ed, 1970), Life Before Birth (jt author, 1986), The Saints of Rochester (2003), Medical Ethics Education in Britain 1963–1993 (jt author, 2007), A Benefice of Saints (2013); *Recreations* East European affairs, domestic architecture, gardening; *Clubs* Reform; *Style*— The Very Rev Edward Shotter; ✉ Hill House, Westhall, Suffolk IP19 8QZ (☎ 01502 575364)

SHOVELTON, Dame Helena; DBE (1999); *née* Richards; da of the late Denis George Richards, OBE, of Highgate, London, and the late Barbara, *née* Smethurst; *b* 28 May 1945; *Educ* N London Collegiate Sch, Regent St Poly (HND Business Studies), Strathclyde Grad Business Sch Univ of Strathclyde (MBA); *m* 1968, Walter Patrick Shovelton, CB, CMG (d 2012), s of Sydney Taverner Shovelton, CBE (d 1968); *Career* mgmnt trainee then industrial market research asst Urwick Orr & Partners 1965–67, in-house magazine and business digest writer/PR handler Alfred Pemberton Ltd (advtg agency) 1967–69, PA to Accountant then to MD Computer Sciences International 1969–71, bursar Wellgarth Nursary Trg Coll 1972–74, vol work 1978–85 (chair City of London Appeal for King George's Fund for Sailors 1984); md Good Companions Ltd 1985–87, mangr Tunbridge Wells CAB 1987–94; chair Nat Assoc of Citizens Advice Bureaux 1994–99 (vice-chair 1990–94); cmmr then dep chair Local Govt Cmmn for England 1995–98, chair Continuing Care Review Panel for E Sussex Brighton and Hove HA 1996–98; ind memb: Dept of Health's Panel for Recruitment of Non-Exec Dirs 1996–98, Cabinet Office's Better Regulation Task Force 1997–99, Banking Code Standards Bd (formerly Ind Review Body for the banking and mortgage lending codes) 1997–2000; cmmr then chair: Audit Cmmn 1995–2001, Nat Lottery Cmmn 1999–2000; memb Competition Cmmn (formerly Monopolies and Mergers Cmmn) 1997–2004, non-exec dir NHBC (Nat House-Building Cncl) 2012, chair 2020health 2012; chief exec Br Lung Fndn 2002–12; dir Energy Saving Tst 1998–2009, tstee RAF Benevolent Fund 1998–2006, tstee Independent Age 2013; Br Thoracic Soc Medal 2011; CIMgt 2000; FRSA 1995, hon FRCP 2006; *Recreations* reading, friends and family; *Clubs* RSA; *Style*— Dame Helena Shovelton, DBE; ✉ e-mail helena.shovelton@gmail.com

SHRAPNEL, John Morley; s of Norman Shrapnel, of Far Oakridge, Glos, and Mary Lillian Myfanwy, *née* Edwards; *b* 27 April 1942; *Educ* Stockport Sch Cheshire, City of London Sch, St Catharine's Coll Cambridge (MA); *m* 1975, Francesca Anne, da of Sqdn Ldr Anthony Charles Bartley, and Deborah Kerr, the actress; 3 s (Joe Sebastian b 1976, Alexander Carey b 1979, Thomas Heydon b 1981); *Career* actor; fndr memb Nat Youth Theatre; Merit Award for narration (Int Wildlife Film Festival) 1997; *Theatre* rep at Birmingham and Nottingham Playhouse; NT: Charles Surface in The School For Scandal, Banquo in Macbeth, Pentheus in The Bacchae, Endicott in Front Page, Orsino in Twelfth Night 1973–75; Leonard Brazil in City Sugar (Bush Theatre) 1976, Andrey in Three Sisters (Cambridge Theatre) 1976, Tesman in Hedda Gabler (Albery Theatre) 1977, Timon in Timon of Athens (Bristol Old Vic) 1979, Vaguin in Children of the Sun (RSC, Aldwych Theatre) 1979, Brutus in Julius Casear (Riverside Theatre) 1980, Agamemnon in John Barton's The Greeks (RSC) 1980; RSC 1985–93: Jeremy in Maydays, Sigmund in The Archbishop's Ceiling, Foustka in Vaclav Havel's Temptation, Oedipus Rex, Angelo in Measure for Measure, Creon in The Thebans, Azriel in The Dybbuk, Claudius in Hamlet; Gibbs in The Hothouse (with Pinter, Chichester Minerva and Comedy Theatre) 1995, Caesar in Julius Caesar (Barbican European tour) 2005, Gloucester in King Lear (Liverpool Everyman/Young Vic) 2008–09, Phèdre (with Helen Mirren, Nat Theatre, Washington and Epidaurus) 2009, Oliver in The School For Scandal (Barbican and Holland Festival) 2011, Lear in King Lear (Tobacco Factory Bristol) 2012, Duncan in Macbeth (with Kenneth Branagh, Manchester Int Festival and New York) 2013–14, Salter in Caryl Churchill's A Number (with son Lex, Nuffield Southampton and Young Vic) 2014–15, Claudius/Ghost in Hamlet (with Maxine Peake, Royal Exchange Manchester) 2014, Camillo in The Winter's Tale and George Chudleigh in Harlequinade (The Kenneth Branagh Co, Garrick Theatre) 2015–16; *Television* The Earl of Suffolk in Elizabeth R, McKendrick in Stoppard's Professional Foul, Erzberger in Gossip from the Forest, Hardinge in Edward and Mrs Simpson, Sakharov in People from the Forest, Glyde in Woman in White, Myshlaevsky in White Guard, Cyril Burt in The Intelligence Man, Creon in Sophocles' Theban Plays, BBC Shakespeare Series (Hector in Troilus and Cressida, Alcibiades in Timon of Athens, Kent in King Lear), Rev Eland in the Burston Rebellion, Steyne in Vanity Fair, Blake in Dennis Potter's Black-Eyes, Schulte-Hiller in Selling Hitler, Dr Jacobs in GBH, Dunning in Between The Lines, Archibald Hall in The Ladies' Man, Kavanagh QC, Black Easter, McIntyre in Bodyguards, Rev Glasson in True Tilda, Morse, Marshall Bentley in Invasion Earth, Midsummer Murders, Hornblower, Jonathan Creek, Mary and Jesus, Tenth Kingdom, Monty Sinclair in Gentleman Thief, Nick in The Fairy Godfather, Raymond Brooks in Foyle's War, Billy Palmer in the Last Detective, McCaffrey in The Inspector Lynley Mysteries, Prime Minister Shaw in The Palace, Cardinal Bukovac in Apparitions, New Tricks, Merlin, Waking the Dead; extensive commentaries and narrations for Wildlife progs; *Radio* extensive radio work incl: Morse in Inspector Morse, Death and the Maiden, Gielgud's celebratory King Lear, Pinter's 70th birthday celebratory Moonlight, Compte de Guiche in Cyrano de Bergerac, Radio 3 Proms readings 2012 and 2013; *Film* Petya in Nicholas and Alexandra, Fr James in Pope Joan, Semper in Wagner, Lionel in Personal Services, Zdhanov in Testimony, Mendalbaum in How to Get Ahead in Advertising, Cinca in Two Deaths, Skinner in 101 Dalmatians, Cain in Solo Shuttle, Jeremy in Notting Hill, Gaius in Gladiator, Cohen in The Body, Vandenberg in Claim, Hannah in Alone, Bratayev in K-19 the Widowmaker, The General in Mathilde, Nestor in Troy, Archbishop in The Hangman's Tale, Michael Kuhn in Alien Autopsy, Bernie in Sparkle, Lord Howard in The Golden Age, Lorenzo in Mirrors, Aleister Crowley in A Chemical Wedding, General Grey in The Duchess, Rev Purslow in The Awakening; *Recreations* walking, cycling, music, reading, cooking, family; *Clubs* Soho House; *Style*— John Shrapnel, Esq; ✉ c/o Lucy Johnson or Mary Fitzgerald, Curtis Brown, Haymarket House, 28/29 Haymarket, London SW1Y 4SP (☎ 020 7287 0077)

SHREEVE, Robert (Rob); s of Frank William Shreeve (d 1986), of Derby, and Dorothy, *née* Hill (d 1987); *b* 6 March 1950; *Educ* Bemrose GS Derby, Univ of Sussex (BA); *m* 13 August 1982, Margaret Mary, da of Alfred Sommi; 2 s (Daniel Gresley b 16 Dec 1982, Jack Hamilton b 27 Oct 1986), 1 step s (Lindsay Thomas Sharp b 21 Nov 1975); *Career* coll dir Hutchinson Publishing Group 1972–77, univ publisher (social science) Macmillan 1977–79, publisher Papermac 1979–82, editorial dir Sphere Books 1982–86, md The Network Club 1986–88, ind conslt 1988–90, md Virgin Publishing Ltd 1990–2000, md The Content Agency 2004–, co-fndr and chief exec One Alfred Place 2008–; *Recreations* trout fishing, boating, food and drink, photography, cinema, collecting contemporary art; *Clubs* One Alfred Place, Soho House; *Style*— Rob Shreeve, Esq

SHREWSBURY AND WATERFORD, 22 Earl of (E 1442, I 1446 respectively); Charles Henry John Benedict Crofton Chetwynd Chetwynd-Talbot; DL (Staffs); Premier Earl (on the Roll) in peerages both of England and Ireland; Baron Talbot (GB 1723), Earl Talbot and Viscount Ingestre (GB 1784); Hereditary Lord High Steward of Ireland and Great Seneschal; patron of 11 lvings; s of 21 Earl (d 1980) by 1 w, Nadine, Countess of Shrewsbury (d 2003); *b* 18 December 1952; *Educ* Harrow; *m* 1974, Deborah Jane, da of Noel Staughton Hutchinson, of Ellerton House, Sambrook, Salop; 1 da (Lady Victoria Jane b 7 Sept 1975), 2 s (James Richard Charles John, Viscount Ingestre b 11 Jan 1978, Hon Edward William Henry Alexander b 18 Sept 1981); *Heir* s, Viscount Ingestre; *Career* dep chm Britannia Building Soc 1988–91 (dir 1983–92); patron St Giles Hospice, hon pres SSAFA – Forces Help (Wolverhampton); pres: Shropshire Bldg Preservation Tst, Staffordshire Small-bore Rifle Assoc; pres: Bldg Socs Assoc 1992–97, British Institute of Innkeepers 1996–97, Gun Trade Assoc; chm Firearms Consultative Ctee 1994–99, dir Minibus Plus Ltd 1997–2001, chm Br Shooting Sports Cncl 2001–08 (pres 2008–14); patron Albrighton Moat Project; chllr Univ of Wolverhampton 1993–99; Hon LLD Univ of Wolverhampton 1994; *Recreations* all field sports; *Clubs* Army & Navy, Pratts; *Style*— The Rt Hon the Earl of Shrewsbury and Waterford, DL; ✉ Throstles House, Birdsgrove Lane, Ashbourne, Derbyshire DE6 2BP (e-mail shrewsburyc@parliament.uk)

SHRIGLEY, David; *b* 17 September 1968, Macclesfield, Cheshire; *Educ* Glasgow Sch of Art; *Career* artist; *Solo Exhibitions* Transmission Gallery Glasgow 1995, Catalyst Arts Belfast 1996, Photographers' Gallery London 1997, Galleri Nicolai Wallner Copenhagen 1997, 1998 and 2000, Stephen Friedman Gallery London 1997, 1999 and 2001, Francesca Pia Bern 1997 and 1999, CCA Glasgow 1997, Hermetic Gallery Milwaukee 1997, Galerie Yvon Lambert Paris 1998, 1999 and 2001, Bloom Gallery Amsterdam 1998, CCS Museum Bard Coll NY 2001, Camden Arts Centre 2002; *Group Exhibitions* In Here (Transmission Gallery Glasgow) 1992, New Art in Scotland (CCA Glasgow) 1994, Some of My Friends (Galerie Campbells Occaisionally Copenhagen) 1994, Scottish Autumn (Bartok 32 Galeria Budapest) 1995, Toons (Galerie Campbells Occaisionally Copenhagen) 1996, White Hysteria (Contemporary Art Centre of S Aust Melbourne) 1996, Big Girl/Little Girl (Collective Gallery Edinburgh) 1996, Fucking Biscuits and other drawings (Bloom Gallery Amsterdam) 1996, The Unbelievable Truth (Stedelijk Museum Bureau Amsterdam and Tramway Glasgow) 1996, Absolute Blue & White (Inverleith House Edinburgh) 1996, Sarah Staton Superstore (Up & Co NY) 1996, Slight (Norwich Gallery) 1997, Appetizer (Free Parking Toronto) 1997, Young British Photography (Stadthaus Ulm) 1997, About Life in the Periphery (Wacker Kunst Darmstadt) 1997, Caldas Biennale (Caldas de Rainha Portugal) 1997, Blueprint (De Appel Amsterdam) 1997, Tales of the City (Stills Gallery Edinburgh) 1997, Real Life (Galleria SALES Rome) 1998, Works on Paper (Alexander & Bonin NY) 1998, Habitat (Centre for Contemporary Photography Melbourne) 1998, Surfacing (ICA London) 1998, Common People: British Art Between Phenomenon & Reality (Fondazione Sandretto Rebaudengo Per L'Arte Guarene D'Alba) 1999, Bildung (Kunstverien Graz) 1999, Green (Exedra Hilversum) 1999, Zac 99 (Musee D'Art Moderne de la Ville de Paris) 1999, Diary (Cornerhouse Manchester) 1999, Love Bites (Ikon Gallery Birmingham and tour) 1999, Becks Futures (ICA London and tour) 2000, The British Art Show 5 (City Art Centre Edinburgh and tour) 2000, Open Country (Musee Cantonal des Beaux Arts Lausanne) 2000, The Fantastic Repetition of Certain Situations (Isabell II Madrid and tour) 2001, Under Bridges and Along the River (Casino Luxembourg) 2001, Rendezvous III (Collection Lambert Avignon) 2001; *Magazine Projects* insert in Parkett (number 53) 1998, weekly cartoon Independent on Sunday Review 1999–2000, Cabinet magazine (issue 1) 2001; *Publications* Slug Trails (1991), Merry Eczema (1992), Blanket of Filth (1994), Enquire Within (1995), Let Not These Shadows Fall Upon Thee (1996), Err (1996), Drawings Done Whilst On Phone To Idiot (1996), Blank Page and Other Pages (1998), Centre Parting (1998), This (1998), To Make Meringue You Must Beat The Egg Whites Until They Look Like This (1998), Why We Got The Sack From The Museum (1998), The Beast Is Near (1999), Hard Work (2000), Grip (2000), Do Not Bend (2001), Human Achievement (2002), Evil Thoughts (2003), Who I Am and What I Want (2003), Yellow Bird with Worm (2003), Kill Your Pets (2004), Let's Wrestle (2004), Joy (2005); *Style*— David Shrigley, Esq; ✉ Stephen Friedman Gallery, 25–28 Old Burlington Street, London W1S 3AN (☎ 020 7494 1434)

SHRIMPLIN, Roger Clifford; s of Clifford Walter Shrimplin (d 1987), and Grace Florence, *née* Davis; *b* 9 September 1948; *Educ* St Albans Sch, Jesus Coll Cambridge (MA, DipArch); *m* 21 Sept 1974, Catalina Maria Eugenia, da of L Alomar-Josa (d 1982); 3 s (Robert b 1977, Richard b 1980, Edward b 1985); *Career* architect; ptnr and princ C W & R C Shrimplin (Chartered Architects and Chartered Town Planners) 1975–; occasional lectr: Univ of Cambridge Sch of Architecture, AA, UCL, Manchester and Liverpool Univs Jt Sch, Kingston Univ; external examiner: Bartlett Sch of Architecture Univ of London, Oxford Brookes Univ; memb Cncl: ARCUK 1985–88 and 1994–97, RIBA 1995–2001, 2004–10 and 2013–; memb various ctees of RIBA, ARCUK, ACE and ARB (hon sec RIBA 1999–2001, 2007–09 and 2014–, hon treas 2009–10), dir RIBA Insurance Agency 2002–10, chm RIBA East 2011–13; tstee Temple Island Henley (chm 1987–99), chm Beds Architectural Heritage Tst 2001–08; hon sec and vice-pres (Europe) Cwlth Assoc of Architects (CAA) 2000–03 (tstee 2003–10); tstee The London Stained Glass Repository 1996–2012 (chm Mgmnt Ctee 1994–99), dir Glaziers Hall Ltd 2002–08; memb Bd Stoll Fndn 2015–; Lord of the Manor of Shimpling Norfolk 1987; Freeman and Liveryman: City of London, Worshipful Co of Glaziers & Painters of Glass 1974 (Master 2001–02); memb Ct City Univ 2007–; RIBA 1974, FRTPI 1985, FCIArb 1986, MIL 1994; Arquitecto

S

Colegiado (Baleares) 1990; *Style*— Roger Shrimplin, Esq; ✉ 11 Cardiff Road, Luton, Bedfordshire LU1 1PP

SHRIMPTON, David Everard; s of late Col G H T Shrimpton, CBE, TD, of Dulwich, and Joyce Margaret, *née* Little; *b* 19 May 1943; *Educ* Dulwich Coll; *m* 25 Oct 1969, Rosemary Sarah, da of Frank Victor Fone; 3 s (Matthew John b 3 Nov 1972, Benjamin James b 24 May 1975, Daniel Thomas b 11 April 1978); *Career* student trainee mangr Deloitte Haskins & Sells 1961–75, princ Industrial Devpt Unit DTI 1975–77, corp fin exec Midland Bank plc 1977–79; BDO Stoy Hayward: ptnr in charge corp fin 1979–89, gen practice ptnr 1989–2001; memb Exec Ctee Quoted Companies Alliance 2000–02; dir: Mark Warner Ltd 2002–07, Ruxley Holdings Ltd 2002–, Cashtec Services Ltd 2002–06, RWS Gp 2010–; non-exec dir FD Solutions; dep chair Affinity Sutton 2005–; Freeman City of London, Liveryman Worshipful Co of Chartered Accountants; FCA 1967; *Recreations* tennis, rugby and Fulham FC; *Style*— David Shrimpton, Esq

SHROPSHIRE, John Bourne; OBE (1996); s of Guy Stuart Shropshire, and Joan, *née* Olivant (d 1962); *b* 6 April 1955, Newmarket; *Educ* Oundle, Univ of Newcastle upon Tyne (BSc); *m* 14 July 1979, Patricia Sheila, *née* Wallis; 1 da (Davina Helen b 19 Feb 1981), 3 s (Guy William b 25 May 1983, Charles John b 27 March 1986, Henry James b 13 Aug 1991); *Career* joined GS Shropshire & Sons (family business) 1976; FRAgS, FIHort; memb Worshipful Co of Fruiterers; National Agricultural Award 2001; *Recreations* reading, walking, travel, countryside, shooting, skiing, tennis; *Clubs* Farmers'; *Style*— John Shropshire, Esq, OBE; ✉ Hainey Farm, Barway, Ely, Cambridgeshire CB7 5TZ (☎ 01353 727200)

SHUBROOK, Brian Ralph; s of Ronald Kenneth Shubrook, and Audrey Gwendoline, *née* Jones; *b* 22 June 1950; *m* 20 May 1972, Pauline, da of George Frederick Edgill, MBE, of Leigh-on-Sea, Essex; 2 da (Nicola Jane b 9 Aug 1974, Jessica Anne b 8 Jan 1979); *Career* sr foreign exchange dealer Lloyds Bank Int London 1968–74, foreign exchange mangr Banco de Santander London 1974–81, treas Bayerische Hypotheken und Wechsel Bank London 1981–86, first vice-pres and treas Swiss Volksbank London 1986–93, treas mangr Bayersiche Hypotheken-und Wechsel Bank AG (Hypobank) 1993–94, asst gen mangr Treasury Banco Santander London 1994–95, asst gen mangr and treas Bank Brussels Lambert London 1995–2001; co dir: Bowerpark Ltd 2001–04, Shubrook Developments Ltd 2002–, Quest End Devpts Ltd 2005–; memb Foreign Exchange Ctee Foreign Banks Assoc London; *Recreations* golf, squash, tennis; *Style*— Brian Shubrook, Esq; ✉ 10 High Elms, Chigwell, Essex IG7 6NF (☎ 020 8502 6715, fax 020 8502 6715, e-mail brian@shubrook.com)

SHUCKBURGH, Julian John Evelyn; s of Sir Evelyn Shuckburgh, GCMG, CB (d 1994), and Hon Nancy, *née* Brett (d 1999), da of 3 Viscount Esher (d 1963); *b* 30 July 1940; *Educ* Winchester, Peterhouse Cambridge; *m* 1, 1963 (m dis 1969), Faith, da of Sir Paul Wright, KCMG, OBE; 1 da (Matilda b 1964), 1 s (Benjamin b 1967); *m* 2, 1976 (m dis 1992), Sarah, eld da of Sir David Willcocks, CBE, MC, *qv*; 2 da (Amy b 1977, Hannah b 1979), 1 s (Alexander b 1982); *Career* publisher; Methuen & Co: publicity asst 1961, asst ed Academic Dept 1963, commissioning ed Academic Dept 1964–65; Weidenfeld & Nicolson Ltd: sr ed Reference Books 1965, sr ed Academic Dept 1966–68, dir Academic Dept 1968–72; read for the Bar Middle Temple 1972–73; editorial dir W H Allen Ltd 1973–75, publishing dir and md of Pitkin Pictorials Ltd Garrod & Lofthouse (Printers) 1975–78, md and fndr Shuckburgh Reynolds Ltd 1978–87, md Barrie & Jenkins Ltd 1987–2000, assoc publisher Ebury Press 1992–2000; *Books* The Bedside Book (1979), The Second Bedside Book (1981), London Revealed (2003), Spectacular London (2005), Harmony and Discord: The real life of Johann Sebastian Bach (2009); *Recreations* music (memb Bach Choir), walking, food and wine; *Style*— Julian Shuckburgh, Esq; ✉ 22 Ellingham Road, London W12 9PR (☎ 020 8749 7197)

SHUCKSMITH, Prof Mark; OBE (2009); s of Thomas David Shucksmith (d 2005), and Inga Shucksmith; *b* 25 August 1953, Hillingdon; *Educ* Sidney Sussex Coll Cambridge (MA), Univ of Newcastle upon Tyne (MSc, PhD); *m* 1979, Janet Susan Shucksmith; 2 da (Clare Louise b 29 Aug 1984, Anna Katherine b 10 May 1989); *Career* asst lectr in agricultural economics Univ of Newcastle upon Tyne 1977–81; Univ of Aberdeen: lectr, sr lectr then reader Dept of Land Economy 1981–93, prof of land economy 1993–2004, dir Arkleton Centre for Rural Devpt Research 1995–2004; dir Scottish Centre for Research on Social Justice 2001–04, prof of planning Univ of Newcastle upon Tyne 2005–, dir Newcastle Inst for Social Renewal Newcastle Univ 2012–; visiting prof Centre for Rural Research Univ of Trondheim Norway 2014–17; memb Bd Countryside Agency 2005–06, memb Affordable Rural Housing Cmmn 2005–06, cmmr Cmmn for Rural Communities 2006–13; chair Ctee of Inquiry on Crofting 2007–08; tstee: Arkleton Tst 2011–14, Action with Communities in Rural England (ACRE) 2014–, Carnegie UK Tst 2016–; memb: European Soc of Rural Sociology (chair Scientific Ctee 2014–15), Int Rural Sociological Assoc (first vice-pres 2004–08); FAcSS 2010, FRSA 2016; No Homes for Locals? (1981), Rural Housing in Scotland (1987), Housebuilding in Britain's Countryside (1990), Rural Scotland Today (1996), Exclusive Countryside? Social Inclusion and Regeneration in Rural Britain (2000), Housing in the European Countryside (2002), Young People in Rural Europe (2003), The CAP and the Regions: The Territorial Impact of the Common Agricultural Policy (2005), Comparing Rural Development: Continuity and Change in the Countryside of Western Europe (2009), Rural Transformations and Rural Policies in the US and UK (2012), Future Directions in Rural Development (2012), International Handbook of Rural Studies (2016); author of more than 100 articles in learned jls and chapters in books; *Recreations* listening to music, reading novels, hill-walking, drinking coffee; *Style*— Prof Mark Shucksmith, OBE; ✉ School of Architecture, Planning and Landscape, University of Newcastle upon Tyne, Newcastle upon Tyne NE1 7RU (☎ 0191 208 6808, e-mail mark.shucksmith@ncl.ac.uk)

SHUKER, Gavin; MP; *Educ* Icknield HS Luton, Luton Sixth Form Coll, Girton Coll Cambridge; *m* Lucie; 1 da (Ruby b 16 June 2013); *Career* MP (Lab) Luton S 2010–; *Style*— Gavin Shuker, MP; ✉ House of Commons, London SW1A 0AA

SHUKMAN, David Roderick; s of Dr Harold Shukman, of St Antony's Coll Oxford, and Rev Dr Ann Shukman, *née* King-Farlow; *b* 30 May 1958; *Educ* Eton, Univ of Durham (BA); *m* Jessica Therese, da of David Pryce-Jones; 2 s (Jack b 5 Dec 1989, Harry b 20 April 1992), 1 da (Kitty b 3 Nov 1994); *Career* reporter Coventry Evening Telegraph 1980–83; BBC TV: news trainee 1983–85, reporter BBC TV Northern Ireland 1985–87, defence and foreign affrs corr News and Current Affrs 1987–95, Europe corr 1995–99, world affrs corr 1999–2003, environment and sci corr 2003–; memb: Int Inst for Strategic Studies 1988, Royal Inst for Int Affrs 1988; FRGS, FRSA; *Books* All Necessary Means: Inside the Gulf War (with Ben Brown, 1991), The Sorcerer's Challenge: Fears and Hopes for the Weapons of the Next Millenium (1995); *Recreations* diving, cooking; *Clubs* Frontline; *Style*— David Shukman, Esq; ✉ BBC News and Current Affairs, BBC Television Centre, Wood Lane, London W12 7RJ (☎ 020 8743 8000)

SHULMAN, Alexandra; OBE (2005); da of Milton Shulman (d 2004), and Drusilla Beyfus, *qv*; *m* 26 May 1994 (m dis 2005), Paul Spike, s of late Rev Dr Robert W Spike, of NYC, and Alice Spike of El Paso TX; 1 s (Samuel Robert b 6 April 1995); *Career* successively: features ed Tatler Magazine, women's ed Sunday Telegraph, features ed Vogue Magazine; ed: GQ Magazine 1990–92, Vogue Magazine 1992–; visiting prof Univ of the Arts London 2003–; tstee National Portrait Gallery 1999–2008, tstee Royal Marsden Cancer Charity 2009–14; PPA Magazine Ed of the Year 1997 and 2008; *Books* Can We Still Be Friends (2012), The Parrots (2015); *Style*— Ms Alexandra Shulman, OBE;

✉ Vogue Magazine, Vogue House, Hanover Square, London W1R 1JU (☎ 020 7152 3635, fax 020 7408 0559)

SHULMAN, Jeremy Ian; s of David Shulman (d 1974), of Leeds, and Lilo Shulman; *b* 3 March 1952; *Educ* Leeds GS, Univ of Birmingham (LLB); *m* 6 Nov 1977, Angela Elaine Lewin; 1 s (David Charles b 1 Oct 1979); *Career* admitted slr 1975; currently sr ptnr Shulmans (fndr 1981); nat chm Young Slrs' Gp 1986–87, memb Cncl Law Soc 1991–97; past memb Law Soc Employment Law Ctee; pt/t judge Employment Tbnls, pres Interlegal Network 1999–2001, pres Leeds Law Soc 2001–02, vice-chm Park Lane Coll Leeds 2000–04, pres Yorkshire Lawyer Awards, sec Interlegal Network 2006–15; former memb Gen Advsy Cncl IBA, chm Local Radio Advsy Ctee; ambass Chamber International; memb Law Soc 1975; *Recreations* playing tennis and golf, walking (particularly in Yorkshire Dales), bird watching, watching cricket and rugby, music, reading; *Clubs* MCC, Moor Allerton Golf, Chapel Allerton Lawn Tennis and Squash; *Style*— Jeremy Shulman, Esq; ✉ Shulmans, 10 Wellington Place, Leeds LS1 4AP (☎ 0113 245 2833, fax 0113 246 7326, e-mail jshulman@shulmans.co.uk)

SHULMAN, Neville; CBE (2005, OBE 1990); *Career* mangr actors and film dirs 1973–, prodr theatrical prodns, documentaries and short films; chm and dir Int Theatre Inst 1985–2013, tstee Camden Arts Centre 1988–2000; offr and memb Theatres Advsy Cncl 1985–2002, chm Theatres Forum 2002, dir Int Inst of Dance and Theatre 2013–; vice-pres now ambass Action for Children (formerly NCH) 1989–; pres Rotary Club of London 1992–93 (vice-pres 1991–92); name given to: Neville Shulman Charity Cup Rotary Club 1992–, Neville Shulman Challenge Award RGS 2000–, Neville Shulman Conservation Award Earthwatch 2008–, Neville Shulman Film Award Scientific Exploration Soc 2014; Liveryman of the Worshipful Co of Blacksmiths 1992; Freeman of the City of London 1992; Hon Col Tennessee Army 1977–; memb: NUJ 1967–, Bhutan Soc 1995; fell Explorers Club 2002 (memb 1993); FRGS 1990, FRSA 1992; *Books* Exit of a Dragonfly (1985), Zen In the Art of Climbing Mountains (1992), On Top of Africa (1995), Zen Explorations in Remotest New Guinea (1997), Some Like It Cold (2001), Climbing the Equator (2005), Maybe Your Father's Inside (2016); *Recreations* contemporary art, travel, film, theatre, mountaineering; *Style*— Neville Shulman, Esq, CBE; ✉ 35A Huntsworth Mews, Gloucester Place, London NW1 6DB (☎ 020 7616 0777, fax 020 7724 8266)

SHUTT OF GREETLAND, Baron (Life Peer UK 2000), of Greetland and Stainland in the County of West Yorkshire; David Trevor Shutt; OBE (1993), PC; s of Edward Angus Shutt, of Stanningley, W Yorks; *b* 16 March 1942; *Educ* Pudsey GS; *m* 1965, Margaret, da of late Stanley Robert Pemberton, of Guiseley, W Yorks; 1 da (Hon Christine Ruth b 1969), 2 s (Hon Richard Alastair b 1971, Hon Andrew Edward Robert b 1979); *Career* chartered accountant; memb Calderdale BC 1973–90 and 1995–2003; dir Joseph Rowntree Reform Tst 1975–2010, tstee Joseph Rowntree Charitable Tst 1985–2010; *Style*— The Rt Hon the Lord Shutt of Greetland, OBE; ✉ House of Lords, London SW1A 0PW

SHUTTLE, Penelope Diane; da of Jack Frederick Shuttle, of Middlesex, and Joan Shepherdess Lipscombe; *b* 12 May 1947; *m* Peter William Redgrove (d 2003), s of G J Redgrove, of Hampstead; 1 da (Zoe b 1976); *Career* writer and poet; poetry recorded for Poetry Room Harvard and The Poetry Archive; Arts Cncl Award 1969, 1972 and 1985, Greenwood Poetry Prize 1972, EC Gregory Award for Poetry 1974, Authors' Fndn Grant 1993, Hawthornden fell 2005; chair Falmouth Poetry Gp; Cholmondeley Award 2007; *Radio* plays: The Girl who Lost her Glove 1975 (jt third prize winner Radio Times Drama Bursaries Competition 1974), The Dauntless Girl 1978; *Novels* An Excusable Vengeance (1967), All the Usual Hours of Sleeping (1969), Wailing Monkey Embracing a Tree (1974), The Terrors of Dr Treviles (with Peter Redgrove, 1974), Rainsplitter in the Zodiac Garden (1976), Mirror of the Giant (1979); *Poetry* Nostalgia Neurosis (1968), Midwinter Mandala (1973), Photographs of Persephone (1973), Autumn Piano (1973), Songbook of the Snow (1973), The Hermaphrodite Album (with Peter Redgrove, 1973), Webs on Fire (1977), The Orchard Upstairs (1981), The Child-Stealer (1983), The Lion from Rio (1986), Adventures with my Horse (PBS Recommendation 1988), Taxing The Rain (1992), Building a City for Jamie (1996), Selected Poems (PBS Recommendation 1998), A Leaf out of His Book (PBS Recommendation 1999), Redgrove's Wife (2006 reprinted 2007; shortlisted: The Forward Prize, the T S Eliot Award), Adventures with my Horse (2007), Sandgrain and Hourglass (PBS Recommendation 2010), Unsent: New and Selected Poems 1980–2012 (2012), In the Snowy Air (pamphlet, 2014), Heath (with John Greening, 2016), Four Portions of Everything on the Menu for M'sieur Monet! (pamphlet, 2016), Will You Walk A Little Faster? (2017); *Psychology* The Wise Wound (with Peter Redgrove, 1978 re-issued 1986, 1994,1999 and 2005), Alchemy for Women (with Peter Redgrove, 1995); *Recreations* cinema, gardening, music, opera, walking, yoga, travel, reading; *Style*— Ms Penelope Shuttle; ✉ c/o David Higham Associates, 7th Floor, Waverley House, 7–12 Noel Street, London W1F 8GQ (☎ 020 7434 5900, e-mail dha@davidhigham.co.uk, website www.davidhigham.co.uk)

SHUTTLEWORTH, 5 Baron (UK 1902); Sir Charles Geoffrey Nicholas Kay-Shuttleworth; 6 Bt (UK 1850); KG (2016), KCVO (2011), JP 1997; s of 4 Baron Shuttleworth, MC (d 1975), and Anne Elizabeth (d 1991), da of late Col Geoffrey Francis Phillips, CBE, DSO; *b* 2 August 1948; *Educ* Eton; *m* 1975, Ann Mary, da of James Whatman and former w of late Daniel Henry Barclay; 3 s; *Heir* s, Hon Thomas Kay-Shuttleworth; *Career* chartered surveyor; ptnr Burton Barnes and Vigers 1977–96; dir Burnley Building Society 1978–82, chm National and Provincial Building Society 1994–96 (dir and dep chm 1982–93), dep chm Abbey National plc 1996–99 (dir until 2004), chm Abbey National Gp Pensions Funds Tstee Co 2002–12, chm Santander (UK) Gp Pension Fund Tstee Co 2012–; memb House of Lords 1975–99; HM Lord-Lt and Custos Rotulorum of Lancashire 1997–, chm Duchy of Lancaster 2006–14 (memb Cncl 1998–2014), chm Assoc of Lord Lts 2008–; dir Rank Fndn 1993–2015; chm: Rural Devpt Cmmn 1990–97, Yorks Dales Millennium Tst 2000–05; memb Bd Skelmersdale Devpt Corp 1982–85; pres Reserve Forces and Cadets Assoc NW England and Isle of Man 2011–15; govr Giggleswick Sch 1982–2006 (chm of govrs 1983–97), memb Cncl Lancaster Univ 1990–93; Hon Col 4 Bn The Queen's Lancashire Regt 1996–99, Hon Col Lancastrian and Cumbrian Volunteers 1999–2005; hon fell Univ of Central Lancashire 1996, hon fell Myerscough Coll 2002 (patron 2002–10); KStJ 1997; *Clubs* Brooks's; *Style*— The Rt Hon the Lord Shuttleworth, KG, KCVO; ✉ Heber House, Leck, Carnforth, Lancashire LA6 2JG (☎ 01542 71445)

SHUTTLEWORTH, Dr Kenneth Owen; s of Owen William Shuttleworth, of Birmingham; *Educ* Handsworth GS Birmingham, City of Leicester Poly (Dip Arch); *Career* architect; ptnr/dir Foster & Partners (formerly Sir Norman Foster & Partners, joined 1974) until 2003, fndr Make 2003–; current projects incl: Crescent House Wiltshire, City of London Information Centre, Jubilee Campus Univ of Nottingham, Grosvenor Waterside London, London 2012 Olympic Handball Arena; cmmr CABE 2002–11; Hon Dr of Design De Montfort Univ 1994, Hon DSc Westminster Univ 2007, Hon DLitt Univ of Nottingham 2009; memb: ARCUK 1977, RIBA 1977; *Awards* Nottingham Science City Devpt Project Nottingham Evening Post Commercial Property Award 2008 (for Sir Colin Campbell Building), Bronze medal Best Visitor Information Initiative Visit London Awards 2008 (for City of London Information Centre), commendation Improvement to the Environment Nottingham Civil Soc Award 2008, Interiors/Private Residence London Natural Stone Award 2008, AJ100 Employer of the Year 2008, Concrete Soc Award for Sustainability 2008 (for 55 Baker St), Cert of Merit Structural Steel Design Awards 2008 (for 55 Baker St), commendation Office category MIPIM Architectural Review Future Project Award 2008 (for EDC HQ), commendation David Alsop Sustainability Award IStructE Structural Award 2008 (for 55 Baker St), Br Cncl for Offices Award for Refurbished/Recycled

Workplace (London and SE) 2009 (for 55 Baker St), Civic Tst Award (Gtr London region) 2009 (for City of London Information Centre), commendation Best Built Project London Planning Awards 2009 (for City of London Information Centre); *Recreations* drawing, design, photography, painting, landscape design; *Style*— Dr Kenneth Shuttleworth; ✉ Make, 55 Whitfield Street, London W1T 4HE

SHUTTLEWORTH, Maj Noel Charles; s of Rev Richard Charles Shuttleworth (d 1955), and Doris Marian, *née* Sims (d 1978); *b* 4 January 1933; *Educ* Haileybury and ISC, RMA Sandhurst; *Career* Scots Guards 1953–63, served Germany, Canada, Kenya, UK, ret Maj 1963; fndr The English Courtyard Assoc 1979– (winners of 6 Civic Tst Commendations, 10 Housing Design awards from DOE, RIBA and NHBC for excellence in housing design), dir Les Blancs Bois Ltd Guernsey 1987–2010, jt fndr Retirement Plus Ltd 2004, life pres Cognatum Ltd 2009, life pres Director Cognatum Property Ltd 2009; life pres The Elderly Accommodation Cncl 2004– (govr 1987–, chm 1992–2004); vice-pres Devizes Constituency Cons Assoc 1980–2009 (chm 1977–80); *Books* The Best Kept Secret of Retirement (2013); *Recreations* cricket (played for Kenya and E Africa 1962–63), tennis; *Clubs* Cavalry and Guards'; *Style*— Maj Noel Shuttleworth; ✉ Crabtree, Savernake Forest, Marlborough, Wiltshire (☎ 01672 870429); Cognatum Ltd, Glebe Barn, Cuxham Road, Watlington, Oxford OX49 5NB (☎ 01491 615960)

SHUTZ, Roy Martin; s of Joseph Shutz (d 1969), of Birmingham, and Alice, *née* Susz (d 1989); *b* 23 January 1943; *Educ* King Edward's Five Ways Sch Birmingham, Univ of Birmingham (LLB), Coll of Law; *Career* teacher Longsands Sch Cambridge 1966–68, admin asst Univ of Warwick 1968–69, asst to Academic and Fin Secs LSE 1969–74, chm Romar Investments Ltd 1969–; barr 1974–90; Barnet BC: memb 1982–98, chm Educn Ctee 1985–90, mayor 1990–91, leader 1991–94; chm Mill Hill RFC 1996–99, memb Corporation of Hendon Coll 1998–2000, memb Middx Area Probation Ctee 1986–94, non-exec dir Barnet Community Healthcare Tst 1991–94; dir Maze Restaurants Ltd 2001–06; memb Gen Advsy Cncl Br Property Fedn (BPF) 2002–06; FInstD, chm Cambs Branch Ctee IoD 2003–05 (memb 2001–06); *Books* History of Huntingdon Rugby Club (2015); *Recreations* golf, rugby union, singing, opera; *Clubs* Reform, Huntingdon RUFC (pres 2010–12); *Style*— Roy Shutz, Esq; ✉ Dean Courtyard, High Street, Lower Dean, Huntingdon PE28 0LL (☎ 01480 860874)

SIBBALD, Graham; s of Walter Inglis Sibbald, and Eileen Hilda, *née* Waddell; *b* 20 February 1961, Inverness; *Educ* George Heriot's Sch Edinburgh, Univ of Edinburgh (LLB, DipLP); *m* 21 June 1996, Diane Elizabeth, *née* Nicol; 1 da (Catherine Elsie), 1 s (James William Inglis); *Career* slr; NP; head Corp Gp Bird Semple (now DLA Piper) until 1997, ptnr Dundas & Wilson CS LLP 1997– (head Media Gp and practice area ldr Corp Gp Glasgow); memb Law Soc of Scot; *Recreations* family, golf, skiing, walking, reading; *Style*— Graham Sibbald, Esq; ✉ Dundas & Wilson CS LLP, 191 West George Street, Glasgow G2 2LD (☎ 0141 304 6025)

SIBBETT, Prof Wilson; CBE (2001); s of John Sibbett (d 1985), and Margaret, *née* McLeister (d 1983); *b* 15 March 1948; *Educ* Ballymena Tech Coll, Queen's Univ Belfast (BSc, PhD); *m* 20 Sept 1979, Barbara Anne, *née* Brown; 3 da (Hannah Margaret b 8 Dec 1980, Ruth Anne b 16 May 1983, Rachael Annette b 30 April 1985); *Career* Imperial Coll London: lectr in physics 1977–84, reader in physics 1984–85; Univ of St Andrews: head Dept of Physics 1985–87, head Sch of Physics and Astronomy 1987–94, dir of research Sch of Physics and Astronomy 1994–2003, Wardlaw prof of physics 1997–; chair Scot Sci Advsy Ctee 2002–06; Rank Prize in Optoelectronics 1997, Rumford Medal Royal Soc 2000, European Physical Soc Prize and Medal 2002, Royal Medal RSE 2009, Charles Hard Townes Award and Medal Optical Soc of America 2011; Hon LLD Univ of Dundee, Hon DSc TCD, Hon DSc Univ of Glasgow 2012, Hon DUniv Strathclyde 2012; FInstP 1986, FRSE 1988, FRS 1997, fell Optical Soc of America 1998, fell European Optical Soc 2007; *Publications* author of around 380 pubns in laser physics and optoelectronics; *Recreations* golf; *Clubs* Rotary (St Andrews), New Golf (St Andrews), Royal and Ancient Golf; *Style*— Prof Wilson Sibbett, CBE, FRS, FRSE; ✉ School of Physics and Astronomy, University of St Andrews, North Haugh, St Andrews, Fife KY16 9SS (☎ 01334 463100, fax 01334 463104, e-mail ws@st-and.ac.uk); The R&A, St Andrews, Fife KY16 9JD

SIBLEY, Dame Antoinette; DBE (1996, CBE 1973); da of Edward George Sibley, of Kent, and Winifred Maude, *née* Smith; *b* 27 February 1939; *Educ* Arts Educnl Sch Tring, Royal Ballet Sch; *m* 1, 1964 (m dis 1973), Michael George Somes, CBE (d 1994); m 2, 1974, Richard Panton Corbett, *qv*, s of William Corbett, of Shropshire; 1 da (Eloise b 1975), 1 s (Isambard b 1980); *Career* graduated into the Royal Ballet 1956, took over the role of Odette/Odile in Swan Lake at short notice Covent Garden 1959, promoted to soloist 1959 and to princ dancer 1960; famous partnership with Anthony Dowell, *qv*, spanning the 1960s, 1970s and 1980s; noted for interpretation of Aurora in Sleeping Beauty, title role in Giselle, title role in Ashton's Cinderella, Juliet in Macmillan's Romeo and Juliet, Titania in The Dream (created for her by Ashton), title role in Manon (created for her by Macmillan), Dorabella (created for her by Ashton), Chloë in Ashton's Daphnis and Chloë, Ashton's A Month in the Country, numerous other roles; has toured N and S America, USSR, Aust and Europe; prima ballerina role in film The Turning Point; pres Royal Acad of Dance 1991–2012 (vice-pres 1989–91); *Publications* Sibley and Dowell (1976), Antoinette Sibley (1981), Antoinette Sibley – Reflections of a Ballerina (1986); *Recreations* opera-going, reading, music, gardening; *Style*— Dame Antoinette Sibley, DBE; ✉ c/o The Royal Opera House, Covent Garden, London WC2

SIBLEY, Richard Edmonde Miles Phillippe; s of William Alfred Sibley, JP (d 1992), of Crowfield, Suffolk, and Florence May, *née* Marsh (d 2004); *b* 23 May 1949; *Educ* Clark's Coll London, Anglican Regnl Coll; *m* 5 June 1976, Hannelore, da of Hans Njammasch, of Germany; 1 s (Alexander b 21 March 1979); *Career* chief exec Ogilby Housing Society Ltd 1987–, chm Calderwood Housing Assoc 1992–2004; dir Sibley Property Co Ltd; chm NE London Valuation Court (rating) 1981–90; chm London (NE) Valuation and Community Charge Tbnl 1990–; Rotarian 1982– (pres 1993–94); Freeman City of London 1980, Liveryman and memb Court of Assts Worshipful Co of Coopers (Master 2007–08); *Recreations* painting, volcanology, fungi; *Clubs* Bishopsgate Ward; *Style*— R E M P Sibley, Esq; ✉ Ogilby Housing Society Ltd, Estate Office, Greenways Court, Butts Green Road, Hornchurch, Essex RM11 2JL (☎ 01708 475115/6)

SICHEL, Ronald James; s of Walter Adolf Sichel (d 1989), Chalfont St Peter, Bucks, and Thea Anna, *née* Tuchler (d 2005); *b* 22 May 1940; *Educ* Repton, L'Ecole Superieure Neuchâtel; *m* 16 Jan 1965 (m dis 1979), Colette Jeannine, da of Dr Charles Stagnaro (d 1983), of St Raphael, France; 1 s (Edward b 27 June 1973); *Career* wine shipper: H Sichel and Sons Ltd 1960, dir 1969–79, vice-chm 1979–88, chm 1988–94; dir John Rigby & Co (Gunmakers) Ltd 1995–98, dir J Roberts & Son (Gunmakers) Ltd 1998–; memb Worshipful Co of Founders 1963 (memb Ct 1997–, Master 2008–09, wine purchasing dir 2009–), Freeman City of London 1963; *Recreations* fly fishing, competition rifle shooting, game shooting, skiing, painting, golf, photography; *Style*— Ronald Sichel, Esq; ✉ Russell Mill House, Russell Mill Lane, Littleton Panell, Devizes, Wiltshire SN10 4ET (☎ 01380 818183, fax 01380 813 478); J Roberts & Son (Gunmakers) Ltd, Solelands Farm, Harbolets Road, West Chilington, West Sussex RH20 2LG (☎ 01403 741786)

SIDDALL, Robert Guy; s of Sir Norman Siddall (d 2002), of Mansfield, Notts, and Pauline, *née* Arthur (d 2009); *b* 28 January 1945; *Educ* Nottingham HS, Univ of Nottingham (BSc); *m* 1970, Gillian Elaine, da of Philip Morley, and Violet, *née* Fenton; 4 da (Anna-Louise b 1973, Naomi Sarah b 1975, Charlotte Elaine b 1978, Laura Mary b 1980); *Career* National Coal Board 1968–95; trainee 1966–68, various jr mgmnt positions 1968–71, undermangr Sherwood Colliery 1971–73, dep mangr Rufford Colliery 1973–75, colliery mangr Blidworth Colliery 1975–80, sr mining engr Planning & Surveying North Notts 1980–83, chief mining engr Doncaster area 1983–85; dep dir: Mining North Derbys 1985–87, Selby North Yorks 1987–88, Mining North Yorks area 1988–90; gp dir: North Yorks Gp 1990–91, South Yorks Gp 1991–93; dir Opencast 1991–93; conslt 1996–; dir Shelton Trenching Systems Ltd 1996–97; conslt mining engr; pres: Midland Inst of Mining Engrs 1992–93, Instn of Mining Engrs 1995–96; winner Futers Medal Instn of Mining Engrs 1992; author of several pubns in tech jls; FIMMM, FREng 1995; *Recreations* industrial archaeology; *Style*— Robert Siddall, FREng; ✉ Stud Farm House, Castle Hill, Carlton-on-Trent, Nottinghamshire NG23 6NX (☎ 01636 821991, 01636 822677, e-mail rgsiddall@aol.com)

SIDDALL, Victoria; *Educ* Univ of Bristol; *Career* Christie's 2000–03; Frieze: joined 2003, head of sponsorship, head of devpt, launched Frieze Masters 2010, dir Frieze Art Fairs 2014–; *Style*— Ms Victoria Siddall; ✉ Frieze, 1 Montclare Street, London E2 7EU

SIDDIQ, Tulip; MP; *Career* MP (Lab) Hampstead & Kilburn 2015–; *Style*— Ms Tulip Siddiq, MP; ✉ House of Commons, London SW1A 0AA

SIDDIQUI, Prof Mona; OBE (2011); da of Abdul Ali (d 1999), and Hasina Khatoon (d 1997); *b* 3 May 1963; *Educ* Univ of Leeds (BA), Univ of Manchester (MA, PhD); *m* 29 June 1991, Farhaj Siddiqui; 3 s (Suhaib b 2 Jan 1995, Zuhayr b 27 June 1996, Fayz b 23 Nov 2000); *Career* Univ of Glasgow: lectr in Islamic studies 1995–2002, sr lectr in Islamic studies 2002–05, prof of Islamic studies and public understanding 2006–; external examiner Univ of Aberdeen; chair Scottish Religious Advsy Cncl and memb Central Religious Advsy Cncl BBC; cmmr Calman Cmmn 2008–; Hon DLitt Univ of Wolverhampton 2002, hon doctorate Univ of Leicester 2009, hon doctorate Univ of Huddersfield 2009; FRSE 2005, FRSA 2005; How to Read the Qur'an (2007); author of articles in learned jls and books incl Encyclopaedia of the Qur'an and Jl of the American Academy of Religion; *Recreations* cooking, interior design; *Style*— Prof Mona Siddiqui, OBE

SIDDLE, Prof Kenneth; s of Fred Siddle, of Morecambe, Lancs, and Vera, *née* Sunderland; *b* 30 March 1947; *Educ* Morecambe GS, Downing Coll Cambridge (scholar, Bye fell, MA, PhD); *m* 1, 1971 (m dis 1994), Yvonne Marie, *née* Kennedy; 1 s (Paul b 1977); m 2, 1996, Anne Elizabeth Willis; 1 s (Edward John Willis b 2000); *Career* lectr Dept of Med Biochemistry Welsh Nat Sch of Med 1971–78; Univ of Cambridge: Meres sr student for med res St John's Coll 1978–81, fell Churchill Coll 1982–, Wellcome lectr Dept of Clinical Biochemistry 1981–90, prof of molecular endocrinology 1990–; visiting scientist Joslin Diabetes Center and Harvard Med Sch 1989–90; chm Biochemical Jl 1995–99; memb: Biochemical Soc 1970–, Diabetes UK (formerly Br Diabetic Assoc) 1972–, Br Soc for Cell Biology 1980–, Assoc of Clinical Biochemists 1985–; sr treas Cricket Club Univ of Cambridge; author of over 100 articles in scientific jls; *Recreations* mountaineering, cricket, gardening; *Clubs* Lancashire CCC, MCC, Hawks' (Cambridge); *Style*— Prof Kenneth Siddle; ✉ Department of Clinical Biochemistry, University of Cambridge, Addenbrooke's Hospital, Cambridge CB2 2QR (☎ 01223 336789, fax 01223 330598, e-mail ks14@mole.bio.cam.ac.uk)

SIDDLE, Roger; s of William Siddle, and Mary Siddle; *b* 1961; *Educ* Hampton Sch, Sidney Sussex Coll Cambridge (MA), Harvard Business Sch (MBA); *m* July 1992, Helen; 2 s (Huw, Gareth), 1 da (Carys); *Career* Andersen Consulting 1983–88; Bain & Co Inc UK: joined 1990, ptnr 1995–2007, managing ptnr UK 2001–07, chm European Operating Ctee 2006–07; gp chief exec BPP Hldgs plc 2007–09, gp chief exec Findel plc 2010–15; chm Cordium 2015–, chm Estera 2016–; cncllr London Region CBI 2004–07; memb: Exec Steering Ctee Advanced Inst of Mgmnt Research 2007–11, sr corporate advsr and Nat Devpt Bd NSPCC, chm Corporate Devpt Bd NSPCC 2009–12; *Recreations* family, wine, skiing, Newcastle United; *Style*— Roger Siddle, Esq; ✉ e-mail rogersiddle@hotmail.co.uk

SIDOLI, Franco; *Educ* BSc; *Career* investment agent CBRE Ltd; MRICS; *Style*— Franco Sidoli, Esq; ✉ CBRE Ltd, Henrietta House, Henrietta Place, London W1G 0NB

SIDOLI, Robert Andrew; s of Primo Sidoli, of Merthyr Tydfil, Glamorgan, and Barbara, *née* Bryant; *b* 21 June 1979; *Educ* Bishop Hedley HS, Univ of Cardiff (BSc); Nicola; *Career* rugby union player; domestic: Crawshays RFC, Pontypridd RFC 1998–2003 (player of the year 2000–01 and 2002–03), Celtic Warriors 2003–04, Cardiff Blues 2004–08, Bristol Rugby 2008–09, Newport Gwent Dragons 2009–14 (Player of the Year 2011–12); international: Wales Youth 1998 (played in FIRA Jr World Cup), Wales U21 2000, Wales A 2002, Wales 2002–07 (42 caps, debut v South Africa 2002, memb squad World Cup Aust 2003, winners Six Nations Grand Slam 2005); pres Cefn Coed RFC; *Recreations* snooker, cards, socialising; *Clubs* Merthyr RFC, Pontypridd RFC, Celtic Warriors; *Style*— Robert Sidoli, Esq

SIDOR, Neven Joseph; s of Kreo Sidor, of Wimbledon, London, and Blanka, *née* Novak; *b* 8 May 1953; *Educ* Univ of Nottingham (BA, BArch), RIBA (part III exam); *m* Hanya Chlala; 1 da (Alexa); *Career* architect Rock Townsend London 1978–81; Grimshaw Architects LLP (formerly Nicholas Grimshaw & Partners Ltd): joined 1981, assoc 1984–92, dir 1992–; projects incl: LSE, Lincoln's Inn Fields, Frankfurt Trade Hall, Engineering Building UCL, KPMG HQ Berlin, The Minerva Building London, Ijburg bridge Amsterdam, Bijlmer Station Amsterdam, Ludwig Erhard Haus Berlin, Waterloo International Terminal London, Lloyds TSB HQ London, Sainsbury Devpt Camden Town, Oxford Ice Rink, Herman Miller distribution facility; winning competition entries incl: Frankfurt Trade Hall, bridges Ijburg Devpt, Pusan High Speed Rail Complex, Berlin Stock Exchange & Communications Centre, UK Pavilion at EXPO 92; FRIBA; *Recreations* music, jazz guitarist; *Style*— Neven Sidor, Esq; ✉ Grimshaw Architects LLP, 57 Clerkenwell Road, London EC1M 5NG

S

SIEFKEN, Prof Hinrich Gerhard; s of Werner Johann Hinrich Siefken (d 1968), and Lisel, *née* Menne (d 1963); *b* 21 April 1939; *Educ* Carl Duisberg Gymnasium Leverkusen, Univ of Tübingen (DPhil), Univ of Nottingham (DLitt); *m* 1 Aug 1968, Marcia Corinne, da of Harry Birch (d 1989), of Sheffield; 1 da (Brigitte Christiane 14 March 1970), 1 s (Kristian Hinrich b 8 August 1973); *Career* tutor Univ of Tübingen 1962–65, lectr Univ Coll of N Wales Bangor 1965–66, wissenschaftlicher asst Univ of Tübingen 1966–67, sr lectr St David's Univ Coll Lampeter 1973–79 (asst lectr 1967–68, lectr 1968–73); Univ of Nottingham: prof of German 1979–97 (prof emeritus 1997–), head Sch of Modern Languages 1986–88, dean Faculty of Arts 1988–92, dir Inst of German, Austrian and Swiss Affrs 1992–94; hon prof of modern languages Univ of Wales Bangor 1999–; ed Trivium 1978–79 (subject ed 1974–79), gen ed Renaissance and Modern Studies 1986–88, memb Editorial Bd New Manchester German Texts 1986–91; *Books* Kudrunepos (1967), Ungeduld und Lässigkeit – Kafka (1977), Thomas Mann – Goethe Ideal der Deutschheit (1981), Theodor Haecker (1989), Theodor Haecker, Tag- und Nachtbücher (ed, 1989), Die Weisse Rose, Student Resistance to National Socialism (ed, 1991), Resistance to National Socialism: Arbeiter, Christen, Jugendliche, Eliten (ed, 1993), Die Weisse Rose und ihre Flugblätter (1994), Theodor Haecker: Leben und Werk (ed, 1995), Kunst und Widerstand (ed, 1995), Experiencing Tradition – Essays of Discovery (ed, 2003); *Recreations* music, walking, gardening; *Style*— Prof Hinrich Siefken; ✉ 6 Mountsorrel Drive, West-Bridgford, Nottingham NG2 6LJ (☎ 0115 981 1617, e-mail hinrichsiefken@hotmail.com)

SIEGHART, Mary Ann Corinna Howard; da of Paul Sieghart (d 1988), and Felicity Ann, *née* Baer; *b* 6 August 1961; *Educ* Cobham Hall, Bedales, Wadham Coll Oxford (major scholarship); *m* 17 June 1989, David Stephens Prichard, s of Maj Michael Prichard; 2 da;

Career writer and broadcaster; journalist Eye to Eye Publishing 1978–79, reporter Sunday Express 1979, arts ed rising to news ed Cherwell 1979–80, ldr and feature writer Daily Telegraph 1980–82, Eurobond corr rising to Lex Columnist Financial Times 1982–86, city ed Today 1986, political corr The Economist 1986–88, presenter The World This Week 1988, presenter The Week in Westminster (Radio 4); The Times: ed op-ed page 1988–91, arts ed 1989–90, acting ed Monday edn 1997–99, asst ed, columnist and political leader writer 1998–2007; currently: occasional presenter BBC Radio 4, chair Social Market Fndn, memb Cncl Tate Modern, non-exec dir Henderson Smaller Companies Investment Tst, non-exec dir The Merchants Tst plc, non-exec dir Ofcom Content Bd; chairwoman The Brains Trust (BBC 2), contrib Start the Week (Radio 4); treas Nat Cncl for One-Parent Families 1986–89; memb: Steering Ctee and Advsy Cncl New Europe 1999–2006, Social Studies Advsy Bd Univ of Oxford 1999–2003, Steering Ctee No Campaign 1999–2004; vice-chair N Fulham New Deal for Communities 2000–06; founding ctee memb Women in Journalism 1995–98; ptnr The Browser website 2008–; memb Cncl Tate Modern 2008–; vice-pres Nat Assoc for Gifted Children, tstee Kennedy Meml Tst, tstee Heritage Lottery Fund 1997–2002, tstee Inst of Art and Ideas; runner up young journalist of the year Br Press Awards 1983, Harold Wincott prize for Young Financial Journalist of the Year 1983, winner Laurence Stern fellowship 1984 (worked for the Washington Post); *Recreations* rollerblading, trekking in remote places, doodling, choral singing, classic cars, reading novels on holiday, listening to music, art, architecture; *Clubs* Groucho, Chelsea Arts, The Ivy; *Style*— Ms Mary Ann Sieghart; ✉ website www.maryannsieghart.com

SIEGHART, William Matthew Timothy Stephen; CBE (2016); s of Paul Sieghart (d 1988), and Felicity Ann, *née* Baer; bro of Mary Ann Sieghart, *qv*; *b* 14 April 1960, London; *Educ* Eton Coll, St Anne's Coll Oxford (MA); *m* 1996, Molly Dineen; 1 s, 1 da; *Career* fndr and chm Forward Publishing 1986–2001; dir: Groucho Club 1995–2001, Forward Gp 1998–2006, Hammer Films 1998–2007, Vrumi 2014–; fndr and chm Forward Arts Fndn 1993–, memb Cncl Arts Cncl England 2000–06 (chm Lottery Panel 2000–05), vice-pres Arts and Business 2001–10, chm Arts Fndn 2002–; chm: Forward Thinking 2004–, Somerset House Tst 2015–; dir Index on Censorship 1999–2000, author of ind review for DCMS (E-Lending in Public Libraries in England) 2013, chm Govt Advsy Panel on public library service in England (report published 2014); fndr and chm StreetSmart (Action for the Homeless) 1998–; govr Br Inst of Human Rights 1998–2013; fndr: Nat Poetry Day 1995–, Forward Poetry Prize, Bedtime Reading Week 2000–05, Big Arts Week 2001–08; tstee: Citizenship Fndn 1994–2011, Esmée Fairbairn Fndn 1998–, YCTV 1998–2001, Writer's and Scholar's Educnl Tst 1999–2000, The Poetry Archive 2001–05, Int Prize for Arab Fiction 2007–14, Free Word 2008–15, Reprieve 2008–16, Brit Docs 2013–; sr advsy fell UK Defence Acad 2004–10; *Books* The Forward Book of Poetry (ed, annually, 1993–), Poems of the Decade (ed, 2001, 2 edn 2011), The Swing Factory (2004), Winning Words (2012); *Recreations* travelling, playing and watching sport, poetry; *Clubs* Brooks, Groucho, MCC, Queenwood Golf, Aldeburgh Golf; *Style*— William Sieghart, Esq, CBE; ✉ 50 Albemarle Street, London W1S 4BD ✆ 020 7493 4361, e-mail sieghart1@mac.com)

SIGWART, Prof Ulrich; s of Dr August Robert Sigwart, and Elizabeth Augusta Sigwart; *b* 9 March 1941; *Educ* Univ of Basel, Univ of Munster Medical Sch, Univ of Freiburg; *m* 2 Sept 1967, Christine Rosemary, da of Peter Sartorius; 2 da (Ann Elizabeth b 27 Feb 1969, Catherine Isabel b 16 Oct 1976), 2 s (Philip Martin Christopher b 10 Aug 1970, Jan Michael Pierre b 27 April 1973); *Career* intern Community Hosp Lörrach, res Framingham Union Hosp 1968–71, chief of cath lab Gollwitzer Meier Inst Bad Oeynhausen 1973–79, chief of invasive cardiology Univ Hosp Lausanne 1979–89, conslt cardiologist and dir of invasive cardiology Royal Brompton London; academic career: prof of med Univ of Düsseldorf, assoc prof of cardiology Univ of Lausanne, prof and chief of cardiology Univ Hosp Geneva 2001–06; memb Editorial Bd: Clinical Cardiology, JACC (Jl of the American Coll of Cardiologists), Interventional Cardiology (asst ed), Frontiers in Cardiology, Handbook of Cardiovascular Interventions, Stent, Egyptian Heart Jl, Int Jl of Cardiovascular Interventions, Indian Jl of Cardiology, Asean Heart Jl, Jl of American Coll of Cardiology, Heart Views, Circulation (guest ed); assoc ed JACC-Interv; memb: Br Cardiac Soc, American Heart Assoc, Swiss Soc of Cardiology, German Soc of Cardiology; past chm: Working Gp on Myocardial Function, Working Gp on PTCA & Lysis SSC; co-fndr Jonas Fndn; ESC Grüntzig Award 1996 and 2006, King Faisal Prize for Medicine 2004, Sven Effert Prize 2004, Polzer Prize 2007, ACC Int Award 2007, ACC Paul Dudly White Award 2012, ACC Distinguished Scientist Award 2013; memb Swiss Nat Acad of Medical Sciences, hon memb Polish Soc of Cardiology, hon fell Russian Soc of Interventional Cardiology, hon memb Swiss Soc of Cardiology; Dr (hc) Univ of Lausanne 1999; FRCP, FACC, FESC; *Books* Automation in Cardiac Diagnosis (1978), Ventricular Wall Motion (1984), Coronary Stents (1992), Endoluminal Stents (1995), Handbook on Cardiocascular Interventions (1996); *Recreations* flying, sailing, music, skiing, photography; *Style*— Prof Ulrich Sigwart; ✉ 1 Avenue de Miremont, CH-1206, Geneva, Switzerland (e-mail ulrich.sigwart@unige.ch)

SIKORA, Prof Karol; s of Witold Karol Sikora (d 1966), and Thomasina Sikora; *b* 17 June 1948; *Educ* Dulwich Coll, Univ of Cambridge (MA, PhD, MB BChir), Middx Hosp; *m* 6 Dec 1975, Alison Mary; 1 s (Simon b 1977), 2 da (Emma b 1980, Lucy b 1982); *Career* formerly: prof and head Dept of Clinical Oncology Imperial Coll Sch of Med at Hammersmith Hosp (Royal Postgrad Med Sch until merger 1997), jt dir of cancer servs Hammersmith and Charing Cross Hosps; former chief WHO Cancer Prog; currently: dean Univ of Buckingham Med Sch, visiting prof of cancer med Hammersmith Hosp, medical dir Cancer Ptnrs UK, medical dir Proton Ptnrs Int; FRCR 1980, FRCP 1987, FFPM 2001; *Books* Monoclonal Antibodies (1984), Fight Cancer (1989), Cancer: a positive approach (1995), Treatment of Cancer (6 edn 2015), The Streetwise Patient's Guide to Surviving Cancer (2016); *Recreations* boating, climbing; *Clubs* Athenaeum, Polish Hearth; *Style*— Prof Karol Sikora; ✉ 21 Dorset Square, London NW1 6QG ✆ 020 7724 8086, fax 020 7724 8086, e-mail karolsikora@hotmail.com)

SILBURN, Paul; *Career* former dep creative dir TBWALondon, creative ptnr Saatchi & Saatchi 2008–; *Style*— Paul Silburn, Esq; ✉ Saatchi & Saatchi, 80 Charlotte Street, London W1A 1AQ

SILK; *see also:* Kilroy-Silk

SILK, Prof David Baxter A; *b* 14 April 1944; *Educ* Univ of London (MB BS, LRCP); *Career* gastroenterologist; lectr in med Dept of Med and Gastroenterology Bart's 1971–75, MRC Travelling fell and visiting assoc prof Univ of Calif San Francisco 1975–76, sr lectr and conslt Liver Unit KCL 1976–78, conslt physician Central Middx Hosp London 1978–2004, conslt physican St Marys Hosp London, prof of clinical nutrition Imperial Coll London 2002–; conslt in private practice 1978–; appointed to Editorial Bd: Gut 1978, Jl of Clinical Nutrition and Gastroenterology 1985, Gastroenterology in Practice 1987, Clinical Nutrition, Jl of Parenteral and Enteral Nutrition, Int Jl of Gastroenterology; chm Br Assoc of Parenteral and Enteral Nutrition (BAPEN) 1994–99 (tstee 2000–), pres Chelsea Clinical Soc 1996, past chm Centre for Gastroenterology and Hepatology Princess Grace Hosp (chm Medical Advsy Ctee 1986–2002); British Soc of Gastroenterology Res Medal 1978, Arvid Wretlind lectr European Soc of Parenteral and Enteral Nutrition 1987, John Lennard Jones Medal BAPEN 1999, Nutricia Int Clinical Nutrician Award 2000; memb: European Soc of Parenteral and Enteral Nutrition, American Soc of Parenteral and Enteral Nutrition, Assoc of Physicians; MRCS 1968, MD 1974, FRCP 1983 (MRCP); *Books* Nutritional Support in Hospital Practice (1983), Artificial Nutrition Support in Clinical Practice (1994), Coping with IBS (1997), Understanding Your IBS (1998); author of over 300 articles in learned jls; *Style*— Prof David Silk; ✉ 144 Harley Street, London W1G 7LD (✆ 020 935 0023, e-mail profsilk@hotmail.com, website www.dbasilk.co.uk); IBS Research Appeal (website www.ibsresearchupdate.org)

SILVER, Prof Ian Adair; s of Capt George James Silver (d 1937), and Nora Adair, *née* Seckham (d 1979); *b* 28 December 1927, Poona, India; *Educ* Rugby, CCC Cambridge (MA), Royal Vet Coll London (BVetMed, FRCVS); *m* 1, 30 June 1950, Marian (d 1994), da of Dr Frederick John Scrase (d 1981); 2 da (Alison b 1956 (who m Andrew Lorimer Hunter, *qv*), Fiona (Mrs Rainer Grün) b 1959), 2 s (Alastair b 1960, Angus b 1963); *m* 2, 6 May 1996, Maria, da of Prof Kazimierz Ereci?ski (d 1980); *Career* RN 'Y' Scheme 1945, Cambridge Univ, trans to Tech and Scientific Regt 1948; Univ of Cambridge: demonstrator in zoology 1952–57, lectr in anatomy 1957–70, fell and sr grad tutor Churchill Coll 1965–70; Univ of Bristol: prof of comparative pathology 1970–81, prof and chm Dept of Pathology and Microbiology 1981–93 (emeritus prof of pathology 1993–), dean Faculty of Med 1987–90, sr research fell 1995–; prof of neurology Univ of Pennsylvania 1977–2006; visiting prof: Louisiana Tech Univ 1973, Cayetana Heredia Univ Lima 1976, Royal Soc prof Federal Univ Rio de Janeiro 1977; chm: Inst of Clinical Neurosciences 2000–, Burden Neurological Inst 2006–; chm Southmead Health Servs NHS Tst 1992–99 (non-exec dir 1991–92); memb Research Cncl Ctees: MRC, SERC, AFRC, ARC; chm Laminitis Tst 2002–; pres: RCVS 1985–86 and 1987, Int Soc for Study of O Transport to Tissue 1977 and 1986; FRCVS; *Books* edited 7 scientific books, published over 200 learned papers; *Recreations* exploration, DIY, fishing; *Style*— Prof Ian Silver; ✉ c/o Centre for Clinical and Comparative Anatomy, School of Veterinary Science, Southwell Street, University of Bristol, Bristol BS2 8EJ (✆ 0117 928 8362, fax 0117 925 4794, e-mail ian.a.silver@bris.ac.uk)

SILVERMAN, Prof Bernard Walter; s of Elias Silverman (d 2008), and Helen, *née* Korn (d 1989); *b* 22 February 1952; *Educ* City of London Sch, Univ of Cambridge (MA, MMath, PhD, ScD); *m* 9 March 1985, Dr Rowena Fowler; 1 s (Matthew b 1989); *Career* res fell Jesus Coll Cambridge 1975–77, devpt mangr Sinclair Radionics Ltd 1976–77, lectr Univ of Oxford 1977–78; Univ of Bath: lectr 1978–80, reader 1981–84, prof of statistics 1984–93, head Sch of Mathematical Sciences 1988–91; Univ of Bristol: prof of statistics 1993–2003, Henry Overton Wills prof of mathematics 1999–2003, provost Inst for Advanced Studies 2000–03, prof emeritus 2003; prof of statistics Univ of Oxford 2003–, master St Peter's Coll Oxford 2003–09, memb Cncl Univ of Oxford 2007–10, fell Green Templeton Coll Oxford 2010–; chief scientific advsr Home Office 2010–; professorial research assoc Wellcome Tst Centre for Human Genetics Oxford 2009–15, sr research fell Smith Sch of Enterprise and the Environment Oxford 2009–; ed International Statistical Review 1991–94, ed Annals of Statistics 2007–09, author of over one hundred papers in jls; Chartered Statistician; pres Royal Statistical Soc 2010 (hon sec 1984–90), pres Inst of Mathematical Statistics USA 2000–01; chair: Jt Mathematical Cncl of the UK 2003–06, UK Mathematics Tst 2004–10, Peer Review Panel Dept for Tport Project for the Sustainable Devpt of Heathrow 2005–06, Statistics Panel HEFCE Research Assessment Exercise 2008; non-exec dir Defence Analytical Services Agency 2003–08, memb Govt GM Science Review Panel 2002–03; Guy Medal in Bronze Royal Statistical Soc 1984, President's Award Ctee of Presidents of Statistical Socs USA 1991, Guy Medal in Silver Royal Statistical Soc 1995; ordained C of E: deacon 1999, priest 2000; assoc parish priest St Paul's Clifton and St Mary's Cotham 2003–05 (curate 1999–2003), proctor in convocation (Gen Synod) 2000–03, assoc parish priest St Margaret's and St Giles' Oxford 2009–15; memb Arts and Humanities Research Cncl 2012–, chair UK Research Integrity Office 2014–; hon fell Jesus Coll Cambridge 2003, hon fell St Chad's Coll Durham 2010, Hon DSc Univ of St Andrews 2014, Hon DSc Lancaster Univ 2016; FRS 1997 (memb Cncl 2009–10), Academia Europea 2001, FAcSS; *Books* Density Estimation for Statistics and Data Analysis (1986), Nonparametric Regression and Generalized Linear Models (with P J Green, 1994), Functional Data Analysis (with J O Ramsay, 1997, 2 edn 2006), Applied Functional Data Analysis (jtly, 2002); *Clubs* Athenaeum; *Style*— Prof Bernard Silverman, FRS; ✉ website www.bernardsilverman.com

SILVERMAN, Emeritus Prof (Hugh) Richard; OBE (2000); s of S G Silverman (d 1985), and N E Silverman, of New South Wales; *b* 23 September 1940; *Educ* Brighton Coll of Art and Craft (DipArch), Univ of Edinburgh (MSc); *m* 24 Feb 1963, Aase Kay, da of Knud Sonderskov Madsen; 2 da (Jennifer Solvej b 24 April 1971, Sophia Annelise b 23 Nov 1974); *Career* dir Alec French Partnership (Architects) Bristol 1984–86, head The Welsh Sch of Architecture Cardiff 1986–97; memb: Bd Cardiff Bay Devpt Corp 1990–2000 (chm Devpt Advsy Panel); dir Edward Ware Homes Ltd 2002–04; dir Under The Sky Urban Renewal; emeritus prof Univ of Cardiff 2001–; ARIBA 1965–2013; *Style*— Emeritus Prof Richard Silverman

SILVERTON, Kate; da of Terry Silverton, and Patricia Silverton; *Educ* West Hatch HS Chigwell, Durham Univ; *m* 2010, Mike Heron; 1 da (Clemency Florence Rose b 2011), 1 s (Wilbur Ernest George b 2014); *Career* journalist: BBC News 24 2005–07, BBC News at One 2008–, BBC Weekend News Late Bulletin 2009–; *Recreations* travel, walking, cycling; *Style*— Ms Kate Silverton

SILVESTER, Simon Charles Arthur; *Educ* The King's Sch Chester, Trinity Hall Cambridge (MA, ed Cantab magazine); *Career* account planner Boase Massimi Pollitt 1983–87, copywriter Delaney Fletcher Delaney 1987–89, sr planner Gold Greenlees Trott 1989–90; planning dir: Burkitt Weinreich Bryant 1990–95; md Silvester Research 1996–98, global planning dir Ammirati Puris Lintas 1998–2000, head of planning McCann Erickson Germany 2000–02, exec planning dir Young and Rubicam EMEA 2002–; awards: Merit NY One Show 1988, Silver ILR Radio Awards 1988, Pyramid Epica Awards 1988, Merit Euro Awards 1988, WPP Atticus prizes 2003, 2004, 2005, 2006 and 2007; memb: MRS 1983, Mktg Soc 1992; *Publications* Spoilt Brats (1990), Invasion of Essex Men (1991), Eurokids – The Single Youth of the Single Market (1992), Is Research Killing Advertising? (1992), World Waves (1997), So You Think You Have a Global Brand? (2002), You're Getting Old (2002), How to Become an Icon (2003), Service With a Snarl (2004), Spam (2005), All You Need is Envy (2005), My Brain Hurts (2006), How To Think Digital (2007), Aaagh! (2008), Day of the Clones (2008), Mobile Mania (2009); *Recreations* travel, art; *Style*— Simon Silvester, Esq; ✉ e-mail simonsilvester@gmail.com, website www.silvester.com

SIM, Prof Edith; *née* Strachan; da of Joseph Dunbar Strachan, and Edith Mary Hay, *née* Pont; *b* 25 September 1951, Dundee; *Educ* Morgan Acad Dundee, Univ of Edinburgh (BSc), Univ of Oxford (DPhil); *m* 29 March 1975, Robert Braidwood Sim; 1 da (Grace Edith Margaret b 1982), 1 s (Francis Charles Joseph b 1987); *Career* Centre d'Etudes Nucleaires 1976–78, fell Royal Soc European Exchange Grenoble; Univ of Oxford: demonstrator Dept of Biochemistry 1978–83, Florey res fell LMH 1981–84, fell in biochemistry St Peter's Coll 1990, Wellcome sr lectr Dept of Pharmacology 1983–99, head Dept of Pharmacology 1999–2005, dir of grad trg Div of Medical Sciences 2006–10, sr research fell St Peter's Coll 2011, emeritus prof Dept of Pharmacology 2011; dean Faculty of Science, Engrg and Computing Kingston Univ 2011–14, emeritus prof Kingston Univ 2014–; scientific advsr Saturday Club Tst 2014–; SAC Arthritis and Rheumatism Cncl 1985–89; chair Doctoral Training Panel MRC 2011–15; tstee St Peter's Coll Fndn 2009, tstee Daphne Jackson Tst 2015, memb Bd of Govrs Edge Hill Univ 2016–, speaker volunteer Parkinson's UK 2016–; memb: Biochemical Soc 1976, Br Biophysical Soc 1978, BSI 1979, Int Soc for the Study of Xenobiotics (ISSX) 2000, RSM 2007; MCMB memb MRC 2004–08, fell Br Toxicology Soc 2008 (memb 1983), fell Br

Pharmacological Soc 2012 (memb 2000); Biological Membranes (1982), Humoral Factors in Natural Immunity (ed, 1993); over 200 res articles in learned jls; *Recreations* gardening, dancing; *Clubs* National Science and Engineering Saturday Club (ldr 2015); *Style—* Prof Edith Sim; ✉ Department of Pharmacology, Mansfield Road, Oxford OX1 3QT (☎ 01865 271884, e-mail edith.sim@pharm.ox.ac.uk); Faculty of Science, Engineering and Computing, Penrhyn Road, Kingston KT1 1LQ (☎ 020 8417 2598, e-mail e.sim@kingston.ac.uk)

SIMM, Ian; *Educ* Univ of Cambridge, Harvard Univ; *Career* project mangr McKinsey & Co Netherlands until 1996; Impax Gp: joined 1996, dir Bd 1997–, fndr and chief exec Impax Asset Mgmnt 1998–; non-exec dir Nat Environment Research Cncl 2013–; *Style—* Ian Simm, Esq; ✉ Impax Asset Management Group plc, Norfolk House, 31 St James's Square, London SW1Y 4JR

SIMM, John; eld s of Ronald James Simm, and Brenda Lily, *née* Chamberlain; *b* 10 July 1970; *Educ* Edge End HS, Blackpool and Fylde Coll of Further and Higher Educn, Drama Centre London (Dip); *m* 22 April 2004, Katie Victoria, *née* Magowan; 1 s (Ryan John Magowan b 13 Aug 2001), 1 da (Molly Victoria Lola Magowan b 9 Feb 2007); *Career* actor; *Theatre* Goldhawk Road (Bush Theatre), Danny Rule (Royal Court), Elling (Bush Theatre and Trafalgar Studios) 2007, Speaking in Tongues (Duke of Yorks Theatre) 2009, Hamlet (Sheffield Crucible Theatre) 2010, Betrayal (Sheffield Crucible) 2012, The Hot House (Trafalgar Studios) 2013, The Homecoming (Trafalgar Studios) 2015, Three Days in the Country (NT) 2015; *Television* Rumpole of the Bailey, Men of the World (two series), Chillers – The Mirror Man, Meat, Cracker, The Lakes (two series), Forgive and Forget, Never Never, Crime and Punishment, State of Play, Canterbury Tales: The Knight's Tale, Sex Traffic, Life on Mars (two series), The Yellow House 2007, Dr Who 2007, 2009, 2010 and 2012, The Devil's Whore 2008, Mad Dogs 2010–, Exile 2011, The Village (seasons 1 and 2) 2013–14, Prey (season 1) 2014, Intruders 2014, Code of a Killer 2015, The Catch 2016; *Films* Understanding Jane, Diana & Me, Boston Kickout (Best Actor Valencia Film Festival 1996), Human Traffic, Wonderland, 24 Hour Party People, Miranda, Skellig 2009, Everyday 2012; *Recreations* music, football (Manchester United), reading; *Clubs* Ivy, Soho House; *Style—* John Simm, Esq; ✉ c/o Sally Long-Innes, c/o Independent Talent Group, Oxford House, 76 Oxford Street, London W1D 1BS (☎ 020 7636 6565, fax 020 7323 0101)

SIMMERS, Graeme Maxwell; CBE (1998, OBE 1982); s of William Maxwell Simmers (the Scottish rugby int, d 1972), and Gwenyth Reinagle, *née* Sterry (Wightman Cup tennis champion); gm Mrs C R Sterry, *née* Cooper (5 times Wimbledon tennis champion); *b* 2 May 1935; *Educ* Glasgow Acad, Loretto; *m* 10 Sept 1965, Jennifer Margaret Hunter, da of William Roxburgh, OBE, of Fife; 2 s (Mark William b 1967, Peter Hunter Maxwell b 1973), 2 da (Corinne Charlotte b 1969, Kirstin Margaret b 1970); *Career* Nat Serv Lt RM 1959–61; CA 1959, ptnr Kidson Simmers 1959–88, chm Scottish Highland Hotels Group Ltd 1972–92, non-exec Forth Valley Health Bd 2002–10; chm Hotel and Catering Benevolent Assoc Scotland 1984–87; memb: Scottish Tourist Bd 1979–86, Nat Exec Br Hospitality Assoc 1991–97; chm Championship Ctee Royal and Ancient Golf Club 1988–91, govr The Queen's Coll Glasgow 1989–93, chm Scottish Sports Cncl 1992–99; chm of govrs Loretto Sch, elder and treas of Killearn Kirk; memb Ct Univ of Stirling 2001–10; Hon Col RMR Scotland 2000–06; Hon Dr Stirling Univ 2012; *Recreations* golf, tennis, skiing; *Clubs* Royal & Ancient (capt 2001–02), All England Lawn Tennis; *Style—* Graeme M Simmers, Esq, CBE; ✉ 11 Crawford Gardens, St Andrews, Fife KY16 8XG (☎ 01334 475519, e-mail graeme.simmers@btinternet.com)

SIMMONDS, Adam Christopher; s of George Simmonds, of Leighton Buzzard, Beds, and Christine, *née* White; *b* 12 February 1971, Welwyn Garden City, Herts; *Educ* Vandyke Upper Sch Leighton Buzzard, Barnfield Catering Coll Beds; *Career* chef; FortySeven Park Street London 1989, Halkin Hotel London 1990–91, Ritz Hotel London and Ritz Carlton Colorado USA 1991–92, demi chef then chef de partie The Lanesbrough London 1992–94 and Les Saveurs London 1994–95, jr sous chef L'Escargot London 1995–96, sous chef Jean-Christophe Novelli de Les Saveurs London 1996–97 and Heathcote's Longridge 1997–98, successively chef de partie, sr chef de partie and jr sous chef Le Manoir aux Quat Saisons 1998–2001, head chef The Greenway 2001–02 (3 AA Rosettes), head chef Ynyshir Hall Powys 2003–07 (1 Michelin Star 2006, 4 AA Rosettes, 2 Egon Ronay Stars, 8 out of 10 Good Food Guide), exec chef Adam Simmonds at Danesfield House (formerly Oak Room Restaurant Danesfield House Hotel) 2007–13 (Michelin Star 2011–13, 4 AA Red Rosettes, ranked 13th Best Restaurant in the UK Good Food Guide 2013), chef conslt Pavilion Restaurant London 2013–; chef Obsession Northcote 2014, chef Raymond Blanc's Diner des Protégés Le Manoir Aux Quat Saisons 2015; currently raising investment for Simmonds Restaurant; nat winner Chaine des Rotisseurs competition 1995, Br Meat Chef of the Year 1998, Gold medal class winner Hospitality Week cook and serve 1999, runner up Cotswold Chef of the Year 2003, Catey Hotel Chef of the Year 2011, contestant Great British Menu 2013 and 2014, winner of starter course 2014 (cooked at St Paul's Cathedral in honour of D-Day Anniversary); fell Master Chefs of GB; *Recreations* snowboarding, scuba diving, football, wake boarding, kite surfing; *Style—* Adam Simmonds, Esq; ✉ e-mail info@adamsimmonds.com, website www.adamsimmonds.com

SIMMONDS, Andrew John; QC (1999); s of Ernest Simmonds (d 1992), and Sybil Vera Erica Allen, *née* Hedley; *b* 9 May 1957; *Educ* Sevenoaks Sch, St John's Coll Cambridge (MA), Coll of Law (Astbury scholar of the Middle Temple); *m* 15 Aug 1981, Kathleen Claire, da of late David Moyse; 1 da (Imogen Ria Hedley b 23 July 1994); *Career* called to the Bar 1980, bencher Middle Temple 2012; practising barr specialising in contentious pensions and professional negligence litigation, dep High Court judge 2006–; *Recreations* skiing, running; *Style—* Andrew Simmonds, Esq, QC; ✉ 5 Stone Buildings, Lincoln's Inn, London WC2A 3XT (☎ 020 7242 6201, fax 020 7831 8102)

SIMMONDS, Andrew Keith John (Andy); s of Reginald Arthur Simmonds (d 1989), and Hilda Violet, *née* Hunnisett; *b* 10 August 1952; *Educ* Rye GS, Univ of Manchester (BSc); *m* 1978, Janet, da of A Stanley Hore; 2 da (Beth b 1981, Laura b 1984); *Career* articled clerk Deloitte & Co CAs 1973–77, sr lectr Accountancy Tuition Centre 1977–85 (lectr in financial accounting 1977–80), princ Tech Dept Touche Ross (now Deloitte LLP) 1985–, ptnr Deloitte LLP 1999–; memb Accounting Standards Bd 2007–; chm Financial Reporting Faculty ICAEW (memb Urgent Issues Task Force until 2007), memb EFRAG Technical Expert Gp 2010–; FCA (ACA 1977); *Books* Mastering Financial Accounting (Macmillan, 1986), Accounting for Europe (Touche Ross, 1989), Accountants Digest: Accounting for Subsidiary Undertakings (Accountancy Books, 1992), FRS 9 – A Practical Guide (1999); *Recreations* music, golf; *Style—* Andy Simmonds, Esq; ✉ Deloitte LLP, 2 New Street Square, London EC4A 3BZ (☎ 020 7007 0896, fax 020 70070158, e-mail asimmonds@deloitte.co.uk)

SIMMONDS, Eleanor May; OBE (2013, MBE 2009); *b* 11 November 1994, Walsall, W Midlands; *Career* Paralympic swimmer; achievements incl 2 Gold medals (100m freestyle and 400m freestyle) Paralympics Beijing 2008, 6 Gold medals (100m freestyle, 400m freestyle, 200m individual medley, 4x100m medley, 4x100m freestyle and 50m freestyle) World Championships 2009, 5 Gold medals (50m freestyle, 100m freestyle, 400m freestyle, 200m individual medley and 4x100m freestyle) European Championships 2009, Gold medal (200m individual medley) Paralympic World Cup 2010, 4 Gold medals (100m freestyle, 200m individual medley, 50m freestyle and 400m freestyle) World Championships 2010, 2 Gold medals (400m freestyle and 200m individual medley), Silver

medal (100m freestyle) and Bronze medal (50m freestyle) Paralympic Games 2012; BBC Young Sports Personality of the Year 2008; *Style—* Miss Eleanor Simmonds, OBE

SIMMONDS, Prof Kenneth; s of Herbert Marshall Simmonds, and Margaret, *née* Trevurza; *b* 17 February 1935, Christchurch, NZ; *Educ* Univ of NZ (BCom, MCom), Harvard Univ (DBA), LSE (PhD), Univ of de Deusto Spain (MGCE), JDipMA; *m* 19 June 1960, Nancy Miriam, *née* Bunai; 2 s (John, Peter), 1 da (Jane); *Career* clerk Guardian Trust Co Wellington 1950–53, asst co sec Gordon & Gotch Ltd Wellington 1953–55, chief accountant William Cable Ltd Wellington 1955–59; conslt: Arthur D Little Inc Cambridge Mass 1959–60, Harbridge House Inc Boston 1962–64; sr lectr Cranfield Inst of Tech 1963–64, asst prof of int business Indiana Univ Bloomington 1964–66, prof of mktg Univ of Manchester 1966–69, Ford Fndn prof of int business Univ of Chicago 1974–75, prof of mktg and int business London Business Sch 1969–2000 (emeritus prof 2000–), fell Said Business Sch Univ of Oxford 2002–05, visiting prof of global enterprise Univ of Auckland 2005–08; mktg advsr International Publishing Corp 1967–78; dir: British Steel Corp 1970–72, Redpath Dorman Long Ltd 1972–74, EMAP plc 1981–96, MIL Research Gp plc 1986–89, Aerostructures Hamble Ltd 1990–92, Enviros Ltd 1996–98, Diagnology Ltd 1997–2000, Manor House Gp Ltd 1997–2005; chm Planners Collaborative 1985–88; govr London Business Sch 1980–86, chm London Business Gp 1988–91, chief ed Int Jl of Advertising 1982–96; Chartered Inst of Mktg: memb senate 1994–2008, vice-dean 1996–2008; memb: Textile Cncl UK 1968–70, Ctee Social Science Res Cncl UK 1971–72, Ctee CBI 1971–74, Electrical Engrg Econ Devpt Ctee UK 1982–86; fell: CAs Aust and NZ, NZ Inst of Cost and Mgmnt Accountants, Acad of Int Business, Acad of Mktg; FCIS, FCMA, CGMA, FCIM; *Books* International Business and Multinational Enterprises (1973, 4 edn 1989), Case Problems in Marketing (1973), Strategy and Marketing (1982, 2 edn 1986), Short Cases in Marketing (1987); *Style—* Prof Kenneth Simmonds; ✉ London Business School, Regents Park, London NW1 4SA (☎ 020 7000 7000, e-mail ksimmonds@london.edu)

SIMMONDS, Mark Jonathan Mortlock; s of Neil Mortlock Simmonds, and Mary Griffith, *née* Morgan; *b* 12 April 1964; *Educ* Worksop Coll, Trent Poly (BSc); *m* 1994, Lizbeth Josefina, *née* Hanomancin-Garcia; 3 c; *Career* surveyor Savills 1986–88, ptnr Strutt and Parker 1988–96, dir Hillier Parker 1997–99, chm Mortlock Simmonds Brown 1999–; memb Wandsworth BC 1990–94 (chm Property Ctee 1991–92, chm Housing Ctee 1992–94); Parly candidate (Cons) Ashfield 1997, MP (Cons) Boston and Skegness 2001–15; sec All-Pty Latin America Gp 2001–; memb Select Ctee on Educn and Skills 2001–03, shadow min for educn 2003–04, shadow min for foreign affrs 2004–05, shadow min for int devpt 2005–07, shadow min for health 2007–10, Parly under sec of state FCO 2012–; *Recreations* family, rugby, tennis, hockey, history, reading; *Clubs* Naval and Military; *Style—* Mark Simmonds, Esq; ✉ House of Commons, London SW1A 0AA (☎ 020 7219 6254, fax 020 7219 1746, e-mail simmondsm@parliament.uk)

SIMMONS, Paul; s of John Simmons, and Jennifer Simmons; *b* 28 April 1967, Brighton; *Educ* Glasgow Sch of Art (BA), RCA (MA); *m* Emma, *née* Grehan; 2 da (Mila, Esme), 1 s (Hugo); *Career* co-fndr (with Alistair McAuley), ptnr and designer Timorous Beasties 1990–; clients incl: Famous Grouse, Nike, Fortnum & Mason, Philip Treacy, Penguin, Magna, Granta, Scottish Nat Portrait Gallery, Brintons Carpets, Liberty London, John Lewis; Scottish Style Award 2005, Best Textile Designer Elle Decoration 2006, Walpole Award 2007; *Recreations* cinema, music, reading, walking, birdwatching; *Style—* Paul Simmons, Esq

SIMMONS, Richard John; CBE (1995); s of John Eric Simmons, and Joy Mary, *née* Foat; *b* 2 June 1947; *Educ* Moseley GS Birmingham, LSE (BSc Econ), Univ of Calif Berkeley Business Sch; *m* 23 April 1983, Veronica, da of Richard Sinkins; 1 s, 1 da; *Career* chartered accountant; asst sec to IASC 1973–75, sr ptnr Arthur Andersen 1996–2001; chm: The Constable Educational Trust Ltd 2003–13, Green Acre Films Ltd 2010–14, Inclusive Learning Ltd and Skill Boosters Ltd 2010–, CET Primary Schs Ltd 2011–14; non-exec dir: Cranfield Info Technol Inst 1987–89, Westminster Forum Ltd 1999–2013; chm: Advsy Bd BPP Hldgs plc 2010–, Risk Mosaic 2014–; tstee Fndn for Social and Economic Thinking 2003–, chm BPP University 2010; memb: Devpt Bd Royal Acad of Arts 1990–2002, Shadow National Accounts Cmmn 2000–01, Bd of Treasurers Cons Pty 2001–03; hon treas Political Ctee Carlton Club 1992–2001; chm Bow Gp 1980–81 (tstee); chm and govr Moat Sch 2003–13; FCA 1971, FRSA, memb IOD; *Recreations* horse racing, tennis, gardening; *Clubs* Carlton; *Style—* Richard Simmons, Esq, CBE; ✉ BPP University, 68–90 Red Lion Street, London WC1R 4NY (e-mail richardsimmons@bpp.com)

SIMMS, Alan John Gordon; s of Edward Gordon Clark, formerly Januszkiewiscz (d 1981), of Aigburth, Liverpool, and Hilda Mary, *née* Gordon; *b* 3 April 1954; *Educ* Liverpool Collegiate GS, Univ of London (LLB, MA, BL); *m* 2 Aug 1980, Julia Jane, da of Paul Ferguson, of Leintwardine, Salop; 2 c (Jack Edward Paul Januszkiewiscz, Charlotte Jane Januszkiewiscz (twins) b 28 Feb 1996); *Career* called to the Bar: Lincoln's Inn 1976, King's Inn 2002; ad eundum Northern Circuit 1980–; memb Criminal Bar Assoc; sec Inst of Advanced Motorists 1986–88, chm RoSPA Chester (RoSPA Advanced Drivers Assoc Class One and Diploma holder), memb's rep Nat Exec Ctee RoSPA, legal memb Mental Health Review Tbnl 1994–; univ external examiner in forensic sci 1998–; advocacy tutor Northern Circuit; memb: Br Motor Racing Marshals Club, Br Automobile Racing Club (Oulton Park), Hon Soc of Lincoln's Inn 1976, Br Acad of Forensic Sci 1978, Bar Assoc of Commerce Fin and Industry 1980, Br Psychological Soc 1994, Forensic Sci Soc 1995, Philological Soc 1996, Hon Soc of King's Inn 2002, RUSI; qualified memb London Chauffeurs Guild; assoc fell Soc of Advanced Legal Studies 2001; *Recreations* reading, motor racing, motor racing marshalling, road safety, blues and jazz music, guitar playing, chess, crime (theory only); *Style—* Alan Simms, Esq; ✉ Chavasse Court Chambers, 2nd Floor, Chavasse Court, 24 Lord Street, Liverpool (☎ 0151 707 1191, e-mail clerks@chavassecounsel.plus.com)

SIMMS, (Dr) Brendan Peter; s of David John Simms, of Dublin, and Anngret, *née* Erichson; *b* 3 September 1967; *Educ* St Kilian's German Sch Dublin, Heinrich-Hertz Gymnasium Bonn, Trinity Coll Dublin (scholar, Gold medal), Univ of Tubingen, Peterhouse Cambridge; *m* 3 Sept 1993, Anita Mary, da of Richard John Bunyan; 1 da (Constance Maria b 21 April 1998), 1 s (Hugh Edward b 10 June 2002); *Career* res fell ChCh Oxford 1992–93; fell and dir of studies in history Peterhouse Cambridge 1993– (admissions tutor (humanities) 1997–2002), Newton Sheehy teaching fell in int rels Univ of Cambridge Centre of Int Studies 1998–; tstee Bosnian Inst London 1998–, memb Exec Ctee Br Irish Assoc 1998–2002, memb Editorial Bd German History; *Books* The Impact of Napoleon (1997), The Struggle for Mastery in Germany, 1780–1850 (1998), Unfinest Hour: Britain and the Destruction of Bosnia (2001); *Recreations* hill walking, football; *Style—* Brendan Simms; ✉ Peterhouse, Cambridge CB2 1RD (☎ 01223 338200, fax 01223 337578)

SIMMS, Sir Neville Ian; kt (1998); *Educ* Univ of Newcastle upon Tyne (BSc), Univ of Glasgow (MEng); *Career* structural engr Ove Arup and Partners 1966–69, with AM Carmichael Ltd Edinburgh 1969–70; Tarmac Gp: joined 1970, chief exec Tarmac Construction Ltd 1988–92, dir Bd Tarmac plc 1988–99, gp chief exec Tarmac plc 1992–99, dep chm Tarmac plc 1994–99; chm: Carillion plc 1999–2005, International Power plc 2000–11 (dep chm 2011–), Adelie Food Hldgs Ltd 2006–09; currently: co-chm Transmanche Link, chm Int Power plc 2000–, chm Equiniti 2009–; non-exec dir: Bank of England 1995–2002, National Power plc 1998–2000; memb Pres's Ctee CBI 1996–2009, Business Advsy Panel Trade Partners UK 2001–03; chm: Balsall Heath Birmingham Employers Forum 1994–97, Regnl Leadership Team Business in the Community West

Midlands 1998–2001, Regnl Leadership Team Business in the Community Solent 2005–07, HM Govt's Sustainable Procurement Task Force 2005–07; former chm National Contractors Gp; former memb: Overseas Project Bd DTI, Chancellor of Exchequer's Private Finance Panel 1993–97; chm Bretrust 2005–; govr: Stafford GS 1998–2004, Ashridge Mgmnt Coll 2000–; former govr Brooklands Sch Stafford; Hon DTech Univ of Wolverhampton 1997, Dr (hc) Univ of Edinburgh 2000, Hon DEng Univ of Glasgow 2001; MIHT, CIMgt, FICE, FCIBS, FREng; *Style*— Sir Neville Simms, FREng

SIMON, Crispin; *Career* chief exec Biocompatibles Int plc 1998–2011, dir Dept of Business Innovation and Skills 2012–14, ceo Rex Bionics 2014–; non-exec dir Imperial Coll Healthcare NHS Tst; govr Port Regis Sch; *Style*— Crispin Simon, Esq; ✉ Rex Bionics, Thame Park, Thame Park Road, Thame, Oxfordshire OX9 3PU

SIMON, 3 Viscount (UK 1940); Jan David Simon; s of 2 Viscount Simon, CMG (d 1993); *b* 20 July 1940; *Educ* Westminster, Dept of Navigation Univ of Southampton, Sydney Tech Coll; *m* 26 April 1969, Mary Elizabeth, da of late John J Burns (d 1966), of Sydney, NSW; 1 da (Fiona Elizabeth b 1971); *Heir* none; *Career* dep chm ctees House of Lords 1998–, dep speaker House of Lords 1999–; memb Select Ctee on: Dangerous Dogs (Amendment) Bill 1996, London Local Authy Bill 1998, Procedure of the House of Lords 1999–2002, Personal Bills 2004–10, Standing Orders (Private Bills) 2004–; co-opted memb Science and Technol Sub-Ctee 1 (Allergy) 2006–07; vice-chm Parly Advsy Cncl for Transport Safety; pres Driving Instructors Assoc 2000–14, pres GEM Motoring Assist, tstee Safety House 2015, tstee Road Safety Tst 2015; fell Univ of Herts; Younger Brother Trinity House; *Style*— The Viscount Simon; ✉ House of Lords, London SW1A 0PW (☎ 020 7219 5353)

SIMON, Josette; OBE (2000); da of Charles Simon, of Leicester, and Eileen, *née* Petty; *Educ* Alderman Newton's GS for Girls, Central Sch of Speech Training and Dramatic Art; *m* 27 Oct 1996, Mark Padmore; 1 da (Maisie b Sept 2000); *Career* actress; Hon MA Univ of Leicester (for services to the Arts) 1995, Pioneers and Achievers Award for services to the Arts 1998; *Theatre* RSC: Macbeth, Antony and Cleopatra, Much Ado About Nothing, The Tempest, Peer Gynt, The Custom of the Country, The Merchant of Venice, Love's Labour's Lost, Golden Girls, The Party, The War Plays, The Mystery of the Charity of Joan of Arc, Measure for Measure, A Midsummer Night's Dream, Don Carlos; RNT: The White Devil, After the Fall (Best Actress Evening Standard Drama Awards 1990, Plays and Players Awards 1990, Critics' Circle Awards 1991, London Theatre Awards 1991, Laurence Olivier Awards 1991); others incl Ibsen's The Lady from the Sea (Lyric Hammersmith) 1994, The Taming of the Shrew (Leicester Haymarket) 1995, The Maids (Donmar) 1997; concert performances: The Fairy Queen (with The Sixteen, conducted by Harry Christophers, Tel Aviv) 1994, King Arthur (with Les Arts Florrissante, conducted by William Christie, France) 1995; *Television* incl: The Squad, The Cuckoo Waltz, Pob's Programme, 123 Go, Umbrella, The Sharpeville Six, Somewhere to Run, Trumpet of a Prophesy, Here is the News, King, Tecx, Two Dogs and Freedom, Thompson, The Pyrates, When Love Dies, Capital City, Runaways, Nice Town, Seekers, Henry IV, Bodyguards, Kavanagh QC, Silent Witness, Dalziel and Pascoe, The Last Detective, Harry Enfield's 'Celeb'; *Radio* incl: Goldoni's Mirandolina, Cromwell Mansions, Dictator Gal (nominated Prix Futura Award Berlin 1993), Gertrude Stein's Listen to Me, The Roads of Freedom, Sealed with a Kiss, Medea, Selections from the Old Testament, Something Understood, Poetry Please, Twelfth Night; *Film* incl: Dardanelle, Cry Freedom, Milk and Honey (Best Actress: Atlantic Film Festival Canada 1988, Paris Film Festival 1990; nominated Best Actress Canadian Acad Award 1989), A Child from the South, Bitter Harvest, Bridge of Time; *Recreations* learning French and Italian, reading, cinema, music, travel, gardening, cooking; *Style*— Josette Simon, OBE

SIMON, Hon Mr Justice; Sir Peregrine Charles Hugo Simon; kt (2002); s (by 2 m) of Baron Simon of Glaisdale, PC, DL (Life Peer) (d 2006); *b* 1950; *Educ* Westminster, Trinity Hall Cambridge (MA); *m* 1980, Francesca, da of Maj T W E Fortescue Hitchins, of Brewham, Somerset; 2 da (Polly Harriet Artemis b 1982, Lucy Persephone Frances b 1984), 2 s ((Alexander Edward) Orlando b 1986, Ferdinand William Hugo b 1989); *Career* called to the Bar Middle Temple 1973 (bencher 1999); memb Midland & Oxford Circuit, QC 1991, recorder NE Circuit 1998, dep judge of the High Court 1999, judge of the High Court of Justice (Queen's Bench Division) 2002–; FLS; *Style*— The Hon Mr Justice Simon

SIMON, Peter; *b* 4 August 1949, Columbo; *Career* founded Monsoon 1973, created Accessorize 1984, fndr Monsoon Accessorize plc; fndr and tstee Monsoon Tst, tstee Tate; *Style*— Peter Simon, Esq; ✉ Monsoon Accessorize Ltd, Notting Dale Village, 1 Nicholas Road, London W11 4AN

SIMON, Dr Robin John Hughes; s of Most Rev William Glyn Hughes Simon, Archbishop of Wales (d 1972), and Sarah Ellen (Sheila), *née* Roberts (d 1963); *b* 23 July 1947; *Educ* Cardiff HS, Univ of Exeter (BA), Courtauld Inst of Art (MA), Univ of Exeter (DLitt); *m* 1, 1971, Margaret, *née* Brooke; m 2, 1979, Joanna, *née* Ross; 1 s (Benet Glyn Hughes b 1974), 2 da (Alice Emily Hughes b 1976, Poppy Candida Hughes b 1991); *Career* art historian; lectr in history of art and English Univ of Nottingham 1972–78, hist bldgs rep The Nat Tst 1979–80, dir Inst of European Studies London 1980–90, art critic The Daily Mail 1990– (arts corr 1987–90), ed Apollo magazine 1990–97, head of publications NACF, ed Art Quarterly and Review 1997–98, founding ed The Br Art Jl 1999–; selector: The Discerning Eye 1992, The Critics' Choice: New British Art 1993, Royal Watercolour Soc Summer Exhbn 1996; visiting prof of history of art and architecture Westminster Coll 1989, visiting prof of English UCL 2007–13 (hon prof of English 2013–); Paul Mellon lectr in British art Nat Gallery London and Yale Center for British Art New Haven 2013; memb: Ctee Courtauld Inst Assoc of Former Students 1991– (chm 1998–2010), Advsy Cncl Paul Mellon Centre for Studies in British Art 1993–98, Exec Ctee Assoc of Art Historians 1993–96, Ctee of Honour Lord Leighton Centenary Tst 1994–96, The Johnson Club 1995–, Exec Ctee Walpole Soc 2005–10 (memb Cncl 1991–96); tstee Foundling Museum 2008; Delmas fndn fell Venice 1978; FSA 1998; *Books* The Art of Cricket (jtly, 1983), The Portrait in Britain and America (1987), Buckingham Palace: A complete guide (ed, 1993), The King's Apartments, Hampton Court Palace (ed, 1994), The National Trust 1895–1995: 100 great treasures (jt ed, 1995), Lord Leighton 1830–1896 and Leighton House (ed, 1996), A Rake's Progress: From Hogarth to Hockney (jt ed, 1997), Enlightened Self-interest: The Foundling Hospital and Hogarth (jt ed, 1997), Oxford: Art and architecture (ed, 1997), Somerset House: The building and collections (ed, 2001), Public Artist, Private Passions: The world of Edward Linley Sambourne (ed, 2001) The Tyranny of Treatment: Samuel Johnson, his friends, and Georgian medicine (jt ed, 2003), Hogarth, France and British Art (2007), Johan Zoffany: Society Observed (contrib, 2011), Richard Wilson and the Transformation of European Landscape Painting (jt ed, 2014), Venice and the Veneto in the Renaissance: the Legacy of Benjamin Kohl (contrib, 2015); articles in various jls, papers and magazines; *Recreations* cricket (capt Poor Fred's XI), music; *Clubs* Garrick, MCC; *Style*— Dr Robin Simon, FSA, DLitt; ✉ The British Art Journal, 46 Grove Lane, London SE5 8ST; www.britishartjournal.co.uk, (Media Agent) c/o Francine Fletcher Associates www.fletcherassociates.net

SIMON OF HIGHBURY, Baron (Life Peer UK 1997), of Canonbury in the London Borough of Islington; Sir David Alec Gwyn Simon; kt (1995), CBE (1991); s of Roger A Simon (d 1993), of Shoreham, W Sussex, and Barbara, *née* Hudd (d 2000); *b* 24 July 1939, London; *Educ* Christ's Hosp, Gonville & Caius Coll Cambridge (MA), INSEAD (MBA); *m* 1, 1964 (m dis 1987), Hanne, da of Ehrling Mohn, of Oslo, Norway; 2 s (Hon Nicholas b 1964, Hon Alexander b 1967); m 2, 1992, Sarah, da of Frederick Roderick Smith (d 1994), of Much Wenlock, Salop; *Career* British Petroleum plc: mktg dir BP Oil UK 1980–82, md BP Oil International 1982–85, a gp md 1986–95, chief operating offr 1990–92, gp dep chm 1990–95, gp chief exec 1992–95, chm 1995–97; memb Court of Bank of England 1995–97; non-exec dir: Grand Metropolitan plc 1989–96, The RTZ Corporation plc 1995–97 (non-exec dir CRA Ltd Dec 1995–97); dep chm Unilever plc 2006–09 (advsy dir 2000–09), sr advsr Morgan Stanley 2000–14; memb: Advsy Cncl Deutsche Bank 1991–97, Supervisory Bd Allianz AG 1996–97, Int Cncl and UK Advsy Bd INSEAD 2000–08, Advsy Bd LEK Consulting 2000–05, Advsy Bd Fortis 2001–04, Bd Suez Gp 2001–, Fitch Int Advsy Ctee 2001–06, Supervisory Bd Volkswagen AG 2002–05, Int Advsy Bd Dana Gas 2006–; min for Trade and Competitiveness in Europe DTI and HM Treasy 1997–99, advsr to the PM on Modernisation of Govt 1999–2003; memb: Cncl Centre for European Reform 1996–, Advsy Gp on Reform of the EU 1999 and 2003, Centre for European Policy Studies 2002–; chm Cambridge Univ Fndn 2000–05, memb Univ of Cambridge Cncl 2005–10; tstee: Hertie Fndn 2001–15, Cicely Saunders Int 2001–10; Liveryman: Worshipful Co of Tallow Chandlers, Worshipful Co of Carmen; *Recreations* music, golf, reading; *Style*— Lord Simon of Highbury; ✉ House of Lords, London SW1A 1PW

SIMONS, Jonquil Edwina; da of Jack Albert Simons (d 1996), of London, and Rose, *née* Parish (d 2010); *b* 3 March 1953, Brighton; *Educ* Brighton & Hove HS for Girls GPDST; *m* 1990, Robert David Tracy, s of Arthur Herbert Tracy (d 1962); *Career* asst to Publicity Mangr Robert Hale & Co publishers 1971–72, publicity asst Evans Bros educnl publishers 1972–73, PR asst Sussex Police 1973–76, PRO Gardner Centre Theatre Sussex 1976–77, assoc dir Public Relations Counsel Ltd PR consultancy 1980–82 (account exec 1977–80), head of PR Alan Pascoe Associates Ltd 1982–84, freelance PR conslt 1984–88, ptnr The Matthews Simons Partnership 1988–93, sr ptnr The Simons Partnership 1993–; dir Eastbourne Designed for All 2013; accredited PR practitioner; CIPR: chm London & SE Gp Ctee 1986 and 1987 (memb 1983–93, hon sec 1983–85), memb Cncl 1989, 1990 and 1991, memb Educn and Trg Ctee 1989–95, chm Student Devpt Working Pty 1993, judge Sword of Excellence 1992 and 1993, memb Fells Forum Working Pty 1996–98, judge CIPR Excellence Awards 2012; memb Bexhill College Careers Acad Local Advsy Cncl 2011–13; memb tstee St Margaret's Hospice Somerset 2002–06; memb British Mensa; FCIPR 1991 (MCIPR 1981); *Recreations* theatre, travel, motorsport, reading; *Style*— Ms Jonquil Simons; ✉ The Simons Partnership, The Old Chapel, North Road, Tattershall Thorpe, Lincs LN4 4PQ(☎ 01526 200020, e-mail jonquilsimons@thesimonspartnership.co.uk, website www.thesimonspartnership.co.uk)

SIMONS, Paul; s of Francis Simons (d 1966), and Kathleen, *née* Ruddy (d 1983); *b* 11 March 1948; *Educ* Bridley Moor HS, Kingston Poly, Lancaster Univ (MA); *m* 1 (m dis), Lesley Bailey; 2 s (Neil b 27 Dec 1968, Nicholas b 6 Sept 1971); m 2 (m dis), Ann, da of William Perry, of Long Ashton, Bristol; 1 da (Kate b 7 Dec 1984), 1 s (Harry Jonathan b 27 Oct 1991 d 7 Jan 1993); *Career* Cadbury Schweppes 1972–75 (asst product mangr, product mangr), gp product mangr Imperial Tobacco Foods 1975–76, mktg mangr United Biscuits 1976–78, Cogent Elliott 1978–84 (account dir, client serv dir); Gold Greenlees Trott 1984–88 (client serv dir, dep md, vice-chm), chm and chief exec Simons Palmer Clemmow Johnson Ltd 1988–97, chief exec TBWA Simons Palmer (following merger) 1997–98, chm TBWA UK Group (following merger of TBWA International and BDDP Worldwide) 1998–99, chm and chief exec Ogilvy & Mather 1999–2002 (also chm Ogilvy & Mather Holdings Ltd), estab Paul Simons and Partners strategic consultancy 2002 (currently managing ptnr), chief exec Cagney Gp plc, managing ptnr More About Advertising (online publisher) 2013–; rock musician (guitar) 1963–67, played with several bands (started first band with late John Bonham of Led Zeppelin), released various unsuccessful records; author of numerous articles; memb Senate Lancaster Univ, memb Advsy Bd Lancaster Univ Mgmnt Sch; estab Harry Simons Tst to provide funds for res into Reyes Syndrome 1993; FIPA, FInstD, fell Marketing Soc; *Publications* Day 1 to Day 2555 (or seven years in the life of an advertising agency) (2011); *Recreations* golf, gym, sailing, concerts, travel; *Clubs* Home House; *Style*— Paul Simons, Esq; ✉ Bridge Cottage, Dursden Lane, Pewsey SN9 5JN (☎ 07831 820399, e-mail paul.simons@live.co.uk)

SIMONS, Prof Peter Murray; s of Jack Simons (d 1990), and Marjorie Nita, *née* Brown (d 1972); *b* 23 March 1950, London; *Educ* Univ of Manchester (BSc, MA, PhD), Univ of Salzburg (Diplôme d'Habilitation); *m* 21 July 1973, Susan Jane, *née* Walker; 1 s (Rupert Daniel b 17 Sept 1981), 1 da (Rebecca May b 7 Jan 1984); *Career* asst librarian Univ of Manchester 1975–77, lectr in philosophy Bolton Inst of Technol 1977–80, lectr in philosophy Univ of Salzburg 1980–95, prof of philosophy Univ of Leeds 1995–2009, prof of philosophy Trinity Coll Dublin 2009–; hon prof of philosophy Univ of Salzburg 1996–, hon prof of philosophy Univ of Nottingham 2011–; pres: European Soc for Analytic Philosophy 1993–96, Int Bernard Bolzano Soc 1993–98; ed History and Philosophy of Logic 1993–2001, author of 200 essays, articles and reviews; dir Franz Brentano Fndn, industrial conslt Ontek Corp Calif 1989–2001; Cultural Prize City of Salzburg 1986; Hon Dr Univ of Bolton 2012; fell Trinity Coll Dublin 2010; FBA 2004; memb Academia Europaea 2006, memb Royal Irish Acad 2013; *Books* Das Naturrecht heute and morgen: Gedächtnisschrift für Rene Marcic (ed with Dorothea Mayer-Maly, 1983), Parts: A Study in Ontology (1987), Philosophy and Logic in Central Europe from Bolzano to Tarski: Selected Essays (1992), Metaphysik – neue Zugänge zu alten Fragen (ed with J Brandl and A Hieke, 1996), Formal Ontology (ed with R Poli, 1996), Applied Ethics in a Troubled World (ed with E Morscher and O Neumaier, 1998), Routledge Companion to Metaphysics (ed with R Le Poidevin, A McGonigal and R P Cameron, 2009), Joint Ventures In Philosophy (with E Morscher, 2014); *Recreations* walking, choral singing, skiing; *Style*— Prof Peter Simons; ✉ Department of Philosophy, Trinity College Dublin, College Green, Dublin 2, Ireland (website http://sites.google.com/site/petermsimons)

SIMONS, Richard Brian; s of Harry Simons (d 1984), of High Wycombe, Bucks, and Ann Lily, *née* Gold; *b* 5 November 1952; *Educ* Royal GS High Wycombe, Exeter Coll Oxford (BA); *Children* 1 s (Harry b 26 Oct 1985), 1 da (Kate b 19 April 1988); *Career* ITN 1974–91: joined as grad trainee TV journalist 1974, news ed News at One 1977, news ed News at Ten 1979, news ed General Election 1983 and 1987, sports ed 1985–86, special productions exec 1989; head of features Carlton TV 1991–96; cmmns with Carlton incl: Hollywood Women, Hollywood Kids (BAFTA nominee for Best Documentary), Hollywood Men, Hollywood Pets, The Visit I, II and III (NY Film Festival Gold Award), Special Babies, Blues & Twos, Sport in Question, Animal Detectives, The Day I Nearly Died, Paranormal World of Paul McKenna I and II, SAS – Soldier's Story, Police Camera Action, Oddballs, Beyond Belief I and II, Champion Children, ITV Panasonic Sports Award, Police Stop!; Meridian Broadcasting Ltd (now part of ITV plc): controller of Programmes and Production 1996–2000, memb Bd 1997–2001; md Squirrel Networks Ltd 2001–, consltg head of devpt GMTV, devpt dir New Media Prodn United Broadcasting and Entertainment; memb RTS; *Recreations* tennis, TV, piano, cinema; *Clubs* Groucho; *Style*— Richard Simons, Esq

SIMONS, Susannah Catherine; da of Peter Simons, of Windsor, and Betty, *née* Edwards; *b* 19 April 1948; *Educ* Langley GS, GSM; *m* 17 July 1976 (m dis 2009), Richard Percival Taylor, s of Percival Taylor; 1 da (Sarah Kate b 7 May 1980), 1 s (Sebastian Richard b 29 Oct 1982); *Career* TV and radio presenter; radio drama studio mangr BBC 1970–73 (BBC trainee 1969), prodr and presenter Capital Radio 1973; presenter: IRN 1975, Tonight (BBC) 1977, PM (BBC Radio) 1977, various BBC Radio 4 news and current affairs progs 1977–87 (The World at One, The World This Weekend, Radio 4 Budget Special, 1981 Royal Wedding, 1987 General Election, also The Jimmy Young Show on Radio 2 and The News Quiz), The Business Programme (Channel 4) 1986, Business Daily (Channel

4) 1987–92, Today (Radio 4), Answering Back (Channel 4) 1992, Classic FM 1992–2002, Around Westminster (BBC 2) 1993, TUC Conf coverage (BBC 2) 1995; GWR Gp: head of Corporate Liaison Dept 1998–2001, dir of communications 2001–; head of public affrs and outreach BBC Radio and Music 2002–08, project exec BBC 2012 Cultural Olympiad 2008–, head of devpt The Space (BBC) 2011–13, dir Arts and Outreach Canvas 2015–; arts strategist and conference moderator; dir Business Television 1990–92; memb: Bd Orch of the Age of Enlightenment, Youth Dance England, B-Eat (Eating Disorders Assoc); currently dir Strategy Showcase; former chair: Nat Youth Dance Tst, London Advsy Bd Arts & Business; memb Royal Ballet Advsy Bd 1998–99, vice-chair New Music Biennial; tstee: More House Sch, Orchestra of the Age of Enlightenment, One Dance UK, Orchestras for All; Variety Club Female Radio Personality of the Year 1984, Broadcasting Press Best Radio Prog 1992; AGSM, FRSA; *Recreations* concert going, theatre, opera, reading, walking, cooking; *Clubs* RSA; *Style—* Ms Susannah Simons; ✉ Canvas, 1 Neal Street, London WC2H 9QL (e-mail susannah.simons@bravebison.io, website www.youtube.com/canvasarts)

SIMPKIN, Dr Paul; *b* 17 August 1945; *Educ* Queen Elizabeth GS Wakefield, St Thomas' Hosp Med Sch London (scholar, MB BS); *m* 1980, Marie-Louise, da of Dr Albert Edward Meechan Sieger; 2 da (Arabella Louise b 1981, Victoria Lucy b 1983); *Career* hon clinical asst Chest Dept St Thomas' Hosp 1975–80 (jr med appts 1970–75); conslt staff physician: GLC 1975–86, ILEA 1975–90; consulting occupational health physician 1980–, med advsr London Residuary Body 1986–93, md Medicine At Work Ltd 1989–, occupational health physician King Edward VII's Hosp London 2015–; med advsr to numerous cos, professional instns and local govt authorities; MRCP (UK) 1974, AFOM 1982; *Style—* Dr Paul Simpkin; ✉ 2 Upper Wimpole Street, London W1G 6LD (☎ 020 7935 5614)

SIMPKINS, Dr Chris; DL; *b* 28 January 1952, Hornchurch, Essex; *Educ* DMA; *Career* former chief exec South Holland DC, chief exec Falkland Islands Govt and head Falkland Islands Civil Service until 2007, DG Royal Br Legion 2007–16; tstee: Poppyscotland, Nat Meml Arboretum, Royal Br Legion ROI; Hon DUniv Loughborough Univ; FIoD; *Recreations* horticulture, cycling; *Clubs* Royal Overseas League; *Style—* Dr Chris Simpkins, DL; ✉ Royal British Legion, 199 Borough High Street, London SE1 1AA

SIMPSON, Alasdair John; s of James White Simpson (d 1987), and Joan Margaret, *née* Ebsworth (d 1997); *b* 10 March 1943; *Educ* Queen Elizabeth GS Carmarthen, Univ of London (LLB); *m* 1, 11 March 1966 (m dis 1998), (Judith) Jane, da of Sidney Zebulun Manches (d 1999), of St John's Wood, London; 1 s (Thomas), 2 da (Emily, Sarah); m 2, 16 July 1999, Tanya *née* Rose; 1 s (Jake); *Career* admitted slr 1967; sr ptnr Manches 1982–2003 (asst slr 1967, ptnr 1968), ptnr Addleshaw Goddard 2003–; memb Law Soc 1967; *Recreations* tennis, thoroughbreds, claret, Provençe and Arsenal FC; *Clubs* RAC, Turf; *Style—* Alasdair Simpson, Esq; ✉ Addleshaw Goddard LLP, Milton Gate, 60 Chiswell Street, London EC1Y 4AG (☎ 020 7606 8855, fax 020 7606 4390, website www.addleshawgoddard.com)

SIMPSON, David; MP; *Educ* Killicomaine HS, Coll of Business Studies Belfast; *Career* cncllr (DUP) Craigavon BC 2001–, memb NI Assembly (DUP) Upper Bann until 2010, MP (DUP) Upper Bann 2005– (Parly candidate (DUP) Upper Bann 2001); *Style—* David Simpson, Esq, MP; ✉ House of Commons, London SW1A 0AA

SIMPSON, David Richard Salisbury; OBE (1989); s of late Richard Salisbury Simpson, and late Joan Margaret, *née* Braund; *b* 1 October 1945; *Educ* Merchiston Castle Sch Edinburgh; *Career* VSO teacher W Pakistan 1963–64; CA; joined Peat Marwick Mitchell & Co 1964–72, Scottish dir Shelter (Campaign for the Homeless) 1972–74; dir: Amnesty Int (Br Section) 1974–79, Action on Smoking and Health (ASH) 1979–90; fndr and dir International Agency on Tobacco and Health 1991–, hon prof London Sch of Hygiene and Tropical Med; tstee Pier Arts Centre Stromness 1994–2012; *Books* Doctors and Tobacco, Medicine's Big Challenge (2000), Tobacco: A Global Threat (with J Crofton, 2002); *Recreations* reading, music, hill walking, Orkney; *Style—* David Simpson, OBE; ✉ c/o Clinical Trial Service Unit, Richard Doll Building, Old Road Campus, Roosevelt Drive, Oxford OX3 7LF

SIMPSON, Deborah (Debbie); QPM (2014); *Career* Asst Chief Constable Devon and Cornwall Constabulary 2008–11; Dorset Police: Dep Chief Constable 2011–12, Acting Chief Constable 2012, Chief Constable 2013–; *Style—* Ms Debbie Simpson, QPM; ✉ Dorset Police, Force Headquarters, Winfrith, Dorchester, Dorset DT2 8DZ

SIMPSON, Dr Graeme Kenneth; s of late Kenneth Caird Simpson, of Grangemouth, Stirlingshire, and Edna Muriel, *née* Graham; *b* 25 September 1956; *Educ* Grangemouth HS, Univ of Edinburgh Med Sch (BSc, MB ChB); *m* 6 May 1978, Jacqueline Sara, da of late Andrew Auchterlonie, of Edinburgh; 1 s (David Malcolm b 1978), 2 da (Elspeth Margaret b 1981, Patricia Hannah b 1984); *Career* SHO: Med Renal Unit Royal Infirmary Edinburgh 1981–82, Med Unit Roodlands Hosp Haddington 1982–83 (house surgn 1981); registrar in med Eastern Gen Hosp Edinburgh 1983–86 (house physician 1980–81), sr registrar in gen and geriatric med Newcastle upon Tyne 1986–89, conslt physician and clinical dir geriatric med Royal Alexandra Hosp Paisley 1989–; memb: Collegiate Membs Ctee RCP 1985–89 (chm and memb Coll Cncl 1988–89), Br Geriatric Soc; life memb Royal Med Soc; MRCP 1983, FRCPE 1995, FRCPGlas 2001; *Books* contrib Body Weight Control (1988); *Recreations* golf, swimming, gardening; *Style—* Dr Graeme Simpson; ✉ Weybridge, 18 Stanely Drive, Paisley, Strathclyde; Royal Alexandra Hospital, Paisley, Strathclyde

SIMPSON, Graham; *b* 5 September 1951; *Educ* Torells Boys' Sch, Univ of Southern Calif, AA Sch of Architecture (AADipl), Univ of Westminster (RIBA); *m* 1, 16 Aug 1980 (m dis 1990); 1 s (Bertram Rupert Oscar), 1 da (Chloë March Louise); m 2, 25 Nov 1995 (m dis 2012), Pauline Lucy Watson; *Career* architect; CZWG 1987–90 (projects incl The Circle London SE1 apartments, houses, business units, shops and courtyards), Prince Turki Abdullah Abdulrahman 1991–95 (projects incl private residences in Riyadh), Sir Norman Foster and Partners 1995–2000 (projects incl Al Faisaliah Centre, Riyadh, hotel, apartments, office, banquet hall and retail centre), Equestrian Acad Doha Qatar 2006–16, Houses Apartments Hotels (projects incl private residences in Sydney and New Zealand) 2007–16; RAIA, RIBA; *Recreations* history, travel; *Clubs* Travellers; *Style—* Graham Simpson, Esq; ☎ 00974 5583 2696, e-mail gplsimpson@aol.com

SIMPSON, Prof Hugh Walter; s of Rev Ian Simpson (d 1976), and Dr Elenora Simpson, *née* Howie (d 1989); *b* 4 April 1931; *Educ* Bryanston, Univ of Edinburgh (MB ChB, MD), Univ of Glasgow (PhD); *m* 21 March 1959, Myrtle Lilias, da of Maj H Emslie; 3 s (Prof Brig R G Simpson OStJ, FRCGP b 5 Jan 1960, Bruce Brian b 7 Feb 1961, Rory Drummond b 13 Jan 1968), 1 da (Rona O'Clanis b 17 June 1962); *Career* MO Br Antarctic Survey Hope Bay 1955–58, leader of many scientific expeditions to polar regns, pathologist then prof and head of div Glasgow Royal Infirmary and Univ of Glasgow 1959–93, sr res fell Univ of Glasgow and Dept of Surgery Royal Infirmary 1993–; inventor of Chronobra for detection of breast pre-cancer risk and breast cancer survival (UK and USA patents awarded); author of over 280 scientific pubns; examiner RCPath 1984–93, chm Ethical Ctee Glasgow Royal Infirmary 1987–92; Polar Medal 1964, Mungo Park Medal RSGS 1970, J Y Simpson Medal Lecture RCS(Ed) 1995, Pery Medal SCGB 1996; FRCPath, FRCP; *Recreations* polar exploration, skiing; *Style—* Prof Hugh Simpson; ✉ Farleiter, Kincraig, Inverness-shire PH21 1NU (☎ 01540 651 288, fax 01540 651813, e-mail h.simpson257@btinternet.com)

SIMPSON, James; s of late William Watson Simpson, and Beatrice Hilda, *née* Dixon; *b* 16 April 1944; *Educ* Barton Peveril GS Eastleigh, Univ of London (LLB); *m* 28 Dec 1968 (m dis 1982), Patricia Vivian (Tricia), da of late Michael Joseph Sheridan, of Southampton; 1 s (Toby b 1973), 1 da (Charlotte b 1975); *Career* RNR 1965, cmmnd Sub Lt 1966, Lt 1969, resigned cmmn 1974; admitted slr 1969, asst litigation slr Coffin Mew & Clover Southampton 1969–70, prosecuting slr Hants CC Portsmouth 1970–72; Brutton & Co Fareham: asst slr 1972–73, ptnr 1973–87, sr ptnr 1987–89; dep High and Co Ct registrar 1978–89; called to the Bar Middle Temple 1990; hon sec Hants Inc Law Soc 1987–89, fee paid employment judge 1996–2014, fee paid immigration judge 1998–2014; fndr chm Hamble Valley Round Table 1975–76 (chm Area I 1981–82); ward cncllr Fareham Borough Cncl 1978–82; *Recreations* foreign travel, photography, motorcycling; *Clubs* Hamble Valley Stick; *Style—* James Simpson, Esq; ✉ 40 Newtown Road, Warsash, Southampton SO31 9FZ (☎ 07850 332286, e-mail englishflyer@aol.com)

SIMPSON, Prof (William) James; s of Ronald, and Margaret Simpson; *b* 16 March 1954; *Educ* Scotch Coll Melbourne, Univ of Melbourne (BA), Univ of Oxford (Paget Toynbee Dante prize, MPhil), Univ of Cambridge (MPhil, PhD); *Career* tutor Univ of Melbourne 1977–78, lectr Westfield Coll London 1981–89; Univ of Cambridge: lectr 1989–99, prof of medieval and Renaissance English 1999–2003; Girton Coll Cambridge: official fell and coll lectr 1989–99, professorial fell 1999–2003, life fell 2004–; Donald P and Katherine B Loker prof of English and American literature Harvard Univ 2004–, prof Harvard Coll 2008–; visiting distinguished prof Univ of Connecticut 1997, visiting prof Chaucer-Langland Nat Endowment for the Humanities Inst Boulder Colorado 1995, visiting distinguished prof Stanford Univ 1999; *Publications* Medieval English Religious and Ethical Literature: Essays in Honour of G H Russell (jt ed, 1986), Parisian Libraries (1989), Piers Plowman: An Introduction to the B-Text (1990), Sciences and the Self in Medieval Poetry: Alan of Lille's 'Anticlaudianus' and John Gower's 'Confessio amantis' (1995), Images, Idolatory and Iconoclasm in Late Medieval England (jt ed), Reform and Cultural Revolution 1350–1547 (2002), Burning to Read: English Fundamentalism and its Reformation Opponents (2007), Under the Hammer: Iconoclasm in the Anglo-American Tradition (2010); author of numerous articles in books and learned jls; *Recreations* conversation; *Style—* Prof James Simpson; ✉ Harvard University Department of English and American Literature and Language, Barker Center, 12 Quincy Street, Cambridge, MA 02138, USA

SIMPSON, Joe; s of Lt-Col I L Simpson, and Geraldine Elizabeth, *née* McGuire; *b* 13 August 1960; *Educ* Ampleforth, Univ of Edinburgh (MA); *Career* author, mountaineer, guide and motivational speaker; memb Alpine Climbing Gp; ASC Speaker of the Year 2003; Hon Dr: Univ of Sheffield 2005, Sheffield Hallam Univ 2005, Leeds Metropolitan Univ 2005, Univ of Edinburgh 2006; *Books* Touching the Void (non-fiction, 1988, trans into 14 foreign languages, Boardman Tasker Prize 1988, NCR Book Award for Non-Fiction 1990, Literaturpreis des Deutschen Alpenvereins 1990, Cardo d'argento Premio ITAS del libro di Montagna 1993), The Water People (novel, 1992), This Game of Ghosts (autobiography, 1993), Storms of Silence (non-fiction, 1996), Dark Shadows Falling (non-fiction, 1997), The Beckoning Silence (non-fiction, 2002, winner Nat Outdoor Book Award USA 2003); *Film* Touching the Void (drama documentary, 2004, Outstanding Br Film of the Year BAFTA Awards 2004, Evening Standard Best Film of the Year 2004, Best Feature Film Banff Mountain Film Festival, Prix Special du Jury Festival International du Film d'Autrans Montagne & Aventure, Grand Prize Kendal Mountain Film Festival, People's Choice Kendal Mountain Film Festival, People's Choice Llanberis Mountain Film Festival), The Beckoning Silence (2008, Best Documentary Int Emmy, Special Jury Award Banff Mountain Film Festival, Best Mountaineering Award, special mention Grand Prix category and runner-up People's Choice Award Kendall Mountain Film Festival, Festival Grand Prize Vancouver Int Mountain Festival, Grand Prize Mountains and City Festival Slovakia); *Recreations* mountaineering, photography, paragliding, gardening, rock climbing, fly fishing, travel; *Style—* Joe Simpson; ✉ c/o Vivienne Schuster, Curtis Brown, 4th Floor, Haymarket House, 28–29 Haymarket, London SW1Y 4SP (☎ 020 7396 6600); Corporate Motivational Speaking, Parliament Communications Ltd, Marek Kriwald, Suite 16, Roddis House, 12 Old Christchurch Road, Bournemouth BH1 1LG (☎ 01202 242424, e-mail parlcom@aol.com); website www.noordinaryjoe.co.uk

SIMPSON, John Andrew; OBE (2014); s of Robert Morris Simpson, and Joan Margaret, *née* Sersale; *b* 13 October 1953; *Educ* Dean Close Sch Cheltenham, Univ of York (BA, Hockey colours), Univ of Reading (MA); *m* 25 Sept 1976, Dr Hilary Simpson, da of Edmund Wilfred Croxford; 2 da (Katharine Jane b 1982, Eleanor Grace b 1990); *Career* editorial asst Supplement to the Oxford English Dictionary 1976–79, ed Concise Oxford Dictionary of Proverbs 1979–81, sr ed Supplement to the Oxford English Dictionary 1981–84; Oxford English Dictionary: ed new words 1984–86, co-ed 1986–93, ed 1994–2013; contrib Balderdash & Piffle (BBC TV series) 2006 and 2007, co-ed James Joyce Online Notes (www.jjon.org) 2011–, project ldr Pittville History Works (pittvillehistory.org.uk) 2014–; visiting asst prof Dept of English Univ of Waterloo Ontario 1985, fell Kellogg Coll Oxford 1991– (emeritus fell 2013–); memb: English Faculty Univ of Oxford 1993–, Philological Soc 1994–, Advsy Bd Opera del Vocabolario Italiano 2003–05; founding memb and memb Exec Ctee European Fedn of Nat Institutions for Language 2002–; Hon DLitt ANU 1999, Hon DLitt Univ of Leicester 2014; FRSA 2007; *Publications* ed: Concise Oxford Dictionary of Proverbs (1982, 3 edn 1998), Oxford English Dictionary (2 edn with Edmund Weiner 1989, 3 edn online 2000–), Oxford Dictionary of Modern Slang (with John Ayto 1992, 2 edn 2008), OED Additions series vols 1 and 2 (with Edmund Weiner 1993, gen ed vol 3 1997); contrib: Oxford English (1986), Words (1989), Wörterbücher: ein internationales Handbuch zur Lexikographie (1990), The First English Dictionary 1604 (2007), The First English Slang Dictionary 1699 (2010), Superstitions: Omens, Charms, Cures 1787 (2011), Ware's Victorian Dictionary of Slang and Phrase (2013), The Word Detective (2016); articles in various lexicographical, linguistic and literary pubns; *Recreations* Gloucestershire local history; *Clubs* Athenaeum; *Style—* Mr John Simpson, OBE; ✉ 67 Prestbury Road, Cheltenham, Gloucestershire GL52 2BY (☎ 01242 255908, e-mail john.simpson@kellogg.ox.ac.uk)

SIMPSON, John Cody (FIDLER-); CBE (1991); s of Roy Simpson Fidler-Simpson (d 1980), of Dunwich, Suffolk, and Joyce Leila Vivienne, *née* Cody (d 1983); *b* 9 August 1944; *Educ* St Paul's, Magdalene Coll Cambridge (MA); *m* 1, 14 Aug 1965 (m dis 1996), Diane Jean, da of Dr Manville Petteys, of La Jolla, Calif, USA; 2 da (Julia Anne b 1969, Eleanor Mary b 1971); m 2, 8 May 1996, Adèle Krüger, da of Johan Krüger, of Johannesburg, South Africa; 1 s (Rafe b 2006); *Career* with the BBC; sub ed Radio News 1966, corr Dublin 1972; foreign corr: Brussels 1975, Johannesburg 1977; diplomatic corr TV News 1978, political ed 1980, presenter Nine O'Clock News 1981, diplomatic ed 1982–88, foreign affrs ed then world affrs ed 1988–; assoc ed The Spectator 1991–95, columnist The Sunday Telegraph 1995–; chm Chelsea Soc; awards: Golden Nymph Award for news reporting on Ayatollah Khomeini 1979, RTS TV Journalist of the Year 1990 and 2000, BAFTA Richard Dimbleby Award 1992, Columnist of the Year Nat Magazine Awards 1993, Best News Coverage BAFTA nomination 1994, RTS Award for Best Foreign Documentary 1997, Peabody Award USA 1997 and 2000, Peabody Tst Award 1999, BAFTA and RTS Awards for reporting from Belgrade 1999, 2 RTS Awards for reporting from Afghanistan 2002, Int Emmy 2002 for Fall of Kabul for BBC 10 O'Clock News 2002, War Corr Award Bayeux 2002, GQ Writer of the Year Award 2003, RTS Current Affairs Award for Panorama: In the Line of Fire 2004, Audio Book of the Year Pan Macmillan 2004, Int Ischia Journalism Prize 2010, The Churchillian Award 2012, BrandLaureate Int Brand Personality Award 2016; chllr Roehampton Univ 2005–; Hon DLitt: De Montfort Univ 1995, Univ of Nottingham 2001, Univ of Dundee 2003, St Andrews Univ 2005,

S

Roehampton Univ 2005 (hon fell 2014); Hon DUniv Southampton 2003; Hon Dr: UEA 2002, Univ of Leeds 2010, Sussex Univ 2015; hon fell: Magdalene Coll Cambridge 1999, Literary and Historical Soc UCD 2004, Coll of Teachers 2009; fell Int Visual Communications Assoc 2009; Freedom City of London 2011; FRGS 1990; *Books* The Best of Granta (jt ed, 1966), Moscow Requiem (novel, 1980), A Fine and Private Place (novel, 1982), The Disappeared (1985), Behind Iranian Lines (1988), Despatches from the Barricades (1990), From the House of War (1991), The Darkness Crumbles (1992), In the Forests of the Night (1993), Lifting the Veil (jtly, 1995), Oxford Book of Exile (1995), Strange Places, Questionable People (autobiography, 1998), A Mad World My Masters (2000), News from No Man's Land (2002), The Wars Against Saddam (2003), Days from a Different World (2006), Not Quite World's End (2007), Unreliable Sources (2010), We Chose to Speak of War and Strife (2016); *Recreations* books, travelling, diving; *Clubs* Garrick, Travellers, Chelsea Arts, Nat Yacht, Dun Laoghaire; *Style*— John Simpson, Esq, CBE; ✉ Twitter @JohnSimpsonNews; c/o Kruger Cowne Ltd, 7 Chelsea Wharf,15 Lots Road, London SW10 0QJ (☎ 020 7352 2277, e-mail gina@krugercrowne.com, website www.krugercrowne.com)

SIMPSON, Prof John Harold; s of Frederick Harold Simpson (d 1990), and Margaret Morrison, *née* Lees-Wallace (d 2008); *b* 21 May 1940; *Educ* Bootham Sch York, Exeter Coll Oxford (BA), Univ of Liverpool (PhD, DSc); *m* 31 Aug 1964, Frances Mary, da of Thomas Estell Peacock (d 1989); 3 da (Amanda b 1967, Rachel b 1968, Joanna b 1970); *Career* Univ of Wales Bangor: lectr in physical oceanography 1965, res fell Nat Inst of Oceanography 1969–70, personal chair in physical oceanography 1982, established chair in physical oceanography 1986–2005, head Sch of Ocean Scis 1996–2000, research prof of oceanography 2005–; visiting prof of physical oceanography Virginia Inst of Marine Sciences USA 1989; NERC: memb Ctee AAPS 1975–79, memb Cncl 1982–88, chm North Sea Project Scientific Steering Gp 1987–92, chm LOIS Shelf Edge Study Steering Gp 1992–98; memb: Cncl Scottish Marine Biological Assoc 1985–91, Cncl Netherlands Inst for Sea Research 2000–08; pres Challenger Soc for Marine Sci 1994–96; Nansen Medal for distinguished research in oceanography European Geosciences Union 2008, Challenger Medal for an exceptional contribution to marine science; *Publications* Physical and Biological Oceanography of the Shelf Seas (jtly, 2012); *Recreations* hill walking, sailing, gardening; *Style*— Prof John Simpson; ✉ Bangor University School of Ocean Sciences, Menai Bridge, Anglesey LL59 5AB (☎ 01248 382844, e-mail j.h.simpson@bangor.ac.uk)

SIMPSON, Rt Hon Keith Robert; PC (2015), MP; s of Harry Simpson, and Jean Betty, *née* Day; *b* 29 March 1949; *Educ* Thorpe GS Norfolk, Univ of Hull (BA), King's Coll London (postgrad research); *m* 1984, Pepita Maria, da of Norman Hollingsworth; 1 s (George Harry b 1991); *Career* sr lectr in war studies RMA Sandhurst 1973–86, head of foreign affrs and defence Cons Research Dept 1986–88, special advsr to sec of state for defence 1988–90, dir Cranfield Security Studies Inst Cranfield Univ 1991–97; MP (Cons): Norfolk Mid 1997–2010, Broadland 2010–; oppn frontbench spokesman for defence 1998–99, oppn whip Treasy and Health 1999–2001, oppn frontbench spokesman for environment, food and rural affrs 2001–02, shadow min for Def 2002–05, shadow min for FO (Middle East) 2005–08, shadow min for FO 2008–10, PPS to Foreign Sec 2010–15; parly cmmr Cwlth War Graves Cmmn 2008–; sec Cons Parly Backbench Defence Ctee 1997–98, memb PM's Advsy Bd Commemorating the First World War 2012–, memb Parly Intelligence and Security Ctee 2015–; memb: RUSI 1971–, IISS 1976–, Br Cmmn for Military History 1973–, House of Commons Catering Ctee 1997–98; Hon Col RMP; *Books* The Old Contemptibles (1981), A Nation in Arms (ed, 1982), History of the German Army (1985), The War the Infantry Knew 1914–1919 (1986), Waffen SS (1991); *Recreations* walking dogs, cinema, collecting books, walking battlefields, observing ambitious people; *Style*— The Rt Hon Keith Simpson, Esq, MP; ✉ House of Commons, London SW1A 0AA (☎ 020 7219 4053, fax 020 7219 0975)

SIMPSON, Paul Graham; s of Graham James Simpson, of Nuneaton, Warks, and Valerie Ann, *née* Chilton; *b* 27 August 1961; *Educ* Manor Park GS Nuneaton, King Edward VI Coll Nuneaton, Univ of Kent at Canterbury (BA); *m* Lesley Ann Simpson, *née* Turner; 1 s (Jack Aaron Bickerton); *Career* editorial asst MW Publishers Edgware 1982–84; Litho Week (Haymarket Publishing): reporter 1984–85, features ed 1985, news ed 1985, dep ed 1986–87, ed 1987–90 (youngest ever ed); ed: Newspaper Focus magazine (Haymarket Publishing) 1990–94, Four Four Two magazine (Haymarket Publishing) 1994–96, The Box 1996–, Demon magazine 1999–2000, Army magazine 2000–01, Freedom magazine 2001–06, Champions magazine 2004–15, FA Cup Final Prog 2005, DCM magazine 2006–09, KPMG Agenda 2008–10, KPMG Consumer Currents 2013–; ed-in-chief: Four Four Two magazine 1997–98, Haymarket R&D 1997–98, Focus magazine (Gruner and Jahr) 1998–99, UEFA Champions League Final progs 2009–15; conslt ed work and supply mgmnt magazines 2015– *Awards* for Newspaper Focus: nominated Business Magazine of the Year Media Week Awards 1991, Business Magazine of the Year PPA Awards 1992; nominated Ed of the Year PPA Awards 1992, Consumer Magazine of the Year PPA Awards (for Four Four Two), Customer Magazine of the Year PPA Awards 2002 (for Army), BSME Customer Magazine Ed of the Year 2008; *Books* Construction Yearbook (1983), British Printing Industry (1987), European Printing Industry (1992), European Newapaper Industry (1993), Football Intelligence (1997), Rough Guide to Online Shopping (2000), Paul Gascoigne (2001), Rough Guide to Cult Movies (2001), Rough Guide to Elvis (2002), Rough Guide to Cult TV (2002), Rough Guide to James Bond (2002), Rough Guide to Cult Pop (2003), Rough Guide to Cult Football (2003), Rough Guide to Lord of the Rings (2003), Rough Guide to Superheroes (2004), Rough Guide to Cult Fiction (2004), Rough Guide to Kids' Movies (2004), Rough Guide to Westerns (2005), Rough Guide to His Dark Materials (2007), 397 Ways To Pick A Movie (2009), Who Invented the Stepover? (with Uli Hesse, 2013), Elvis Films FAQ (2013); *Recreations* reading American thrillers, writing, listening to Elvis Presley records; *Style*— Paul Simpson, Esq; ✉ 64 Crescent Road, Shepperton, Middlesex TW17 8BP

SIMPSON, Prof Peter; *Educ* Bournemouth and Poole Coll of Art; *m* Dec 1970, Jennifer Carol, *née* Johnson; 2 da (Rebecca Caroline b 21 Sept 1972, Naomi Rosalind Mary b 18 July 1975); *Career* ceramic designer; currently emeritus prof of art Sch of Art and Design Univ of Derby (asst dean until 1999); visiting tutor and lectr in ceramics; memb Craftsmen Bursary Panel Southern Arts Assoc 1976–79 (memb Visual Arts Panel 1976–78), exhibition memb The Contemporary Applied Arts London; *Exhibitions* incl: one-man exhibition (Pace Gallery and Design Centre London) 1970, Ceramics '71 (Bradford City Art Gallery and Design Centre London) 1971, More British Potters (Keetles Yard Cambridge) 1972, International Ceramics '72 (V&A) 1972, Craftsman's Art (V&A) 1973, Modern British Crafts (Royal Scottish Museum Edinburgh) 1973, Gordon Baldwin, Peter Simpson (British Crafts Centre London) 1974, Chunichi 3 Int Exhibition of Ceramic Art Tokyo 1975, 6 Studio Potters (V&A) 1976, 2-man show (British Crafts Centre London) 1979, 4-man show (CPA London) 1980, Pottery Now (Sotheby's Gallery Belgravia London) 1985; numerous works in public collections incl Royal Scottish Museum (Edinburgh) and V&A (London); *Style*— Prof Peter Simpson

SIMPSON, Dr Sir Peter Jeffery; kt (2006); s of Thomas Simpson (d 1991), and Barbara, *née* Greenwood (d 2007); *b* 17 December 1946, London; *Educ* Bryanston (Closed Scholar), Bart's Hosp Univ of London (MB BS, MD), Radcliffe Infirmary Oxford; *m* 19 April 1969, Jane, *née* Carpenter-Jacobs; 3 da (Rachel Margaret b 23 June 1972, Anna Louise b 21 Dec 1973, Elizabeth Claire b 11 Nov 1976), 1 s (James Anthony b 21 July 1979); *Career* sr lectr Univ of Bristol and hon conslt Bristol Royal Infirmary and Southmead Hosps 1978–82, conslt anaesthetist Frenchay Hosp Bristol 1982–2007 (med dir); jtly created Euro Dip of Anaesthetists and Intensive Care 1984, examiner physiology Royal Coll of Anaesthetists 1984–96 (chm Examination Ctee), chm and tstee Nat Confidential Enquiry into Patient Outcome and Death 2002–05, dep chm and memb Postgraduate Educn and Trg Bd (chair 2004–05), memb Bd and Senate European Acad of Anaesthesiology until 2005; pres: European Soc of Anaesthesiology 2006–08, Tri-Serv Anaesthetic Soc 2003–05; chm UK Donation Ethics Ctee 2010–13; author of numerous articles published in scientific jls; FRCA 1970 (cncl memb 1997, vice pres 2001–02, pres 2003–06), FRCP 2005, FCARCSI 2006 (hon), FRCS 2007 (hon); *Publications* Understanding Anaesthesia (jtly, 4 edns), 600 MCQ's in Anaesthesia (jtly, 2 vols); *Recreations* golf, walking, photography, travel, choral singing; *Clubs* Bristol and Clifton Golf; *Style*— Dr Sir Peter Simpson; ✉ 2 St Hilary Close, Stoke Bishop, Bristol BS9 1DA (☎ 0117 9681537, mobile 07768 732373, fax 0117 9048725, e-mail pjsimpson@blueyonder.co.uk)

SIMPSON, Dr Richard John; s of John Taylor Simpson, and Margaret Norah *née* Coates; *b* 1942; *Educ* Univ of Edinburgh; *m* m, 2 s; *Career* princ in gen practice 1970–99 (sr ptnr 1987–99), psychiatrist Forth Valley Health Bd Area 1970–99, dir Forth Valley Primary Care Res Gp, med advsr on adoption and fostering Clackmannanshire Stirling and Falkirk Authorities 1982–2000, conslt in addictions; pt/t lectr on social work Univ of Stirling 1972–1990, hon prof of psychology Univ of Stirling; MSP (Lab): Ochil 1999–2003, Mid Scotland and Fife 2007–16; dep min for Justice 2001–02, shadow public min for Health 2007–16; chair Strathcarron Hospice 1988–92, memb Med Section (Scot) Br Agencies for Adoption and Fostering 1982– (chair 1985–89), pres Scot Union of Students 1967–69, memb Ct Heriot-Watt Univ 1969–78; hon pres Heriot-Watt Students Assoc 1969–75; FRCPsych 1994, MRCGP; *Recreations* golf, music, rugby, gardening; *Style*— Dr Richard Simpson

SIMPSON, Dr Roderick Howard Wallace; s of Dr Robert Wallace Simpson (d 1991), of Salisbury, and Betty Noreen, *née* Mollett (d 1994); *b* 10 January 1951; *Educ* King's Sch Bruton, Univ of St Andrews (BSc), Univ of Dundee (MB ChB), Univ of Stellenbosch (MMed); *m* 10 Nov 1979, (Alethea) Avrille, da of Cecil Alfred Milborrow, of Johannesburg, South Africa (d 1993); 3 s (Andrew b 1980, Richard b 1983, Nicholas b 1993), 1 da (Eleanor b 1987); *Career* registrar in pathology Guy's Hosp 1976–79, lectr in pathology Univ of Stellenbosch 1980–82, sr lectr in pathology and neuropathology Univ of the Witwatersrand 1982–85, conslt pathologist and sr lectr Univ of Exeter and Royal Devon and Exeter Hosps 1985–2013, currently prof of pathology Univ of Calgary Canada; invited lectr at nat and int conferences incl: Int Acad of Pathology Nice 1998, Dubai 2000, Amsterdam 2002, Brisbane 2004, Beijing 2005, Montreal 2006 and Pune 2008, Pakistan Soc of Pathology Peshawar 1996, UAE Pathology Congress Dubai 1999, Euro Soc congresses 1995, 1997, 1999, 2001, 2003, 2005, 2007 and 2009–15, Intercontinental Congress of Pathology Madeira 2000, Iguaçu 2004 and Barcelona 2008; sec European Soc of Pathology 2003–09 (memb Exec Ctee 1997–2001), memb Expert Panel for Revised WHO Histopathological Classification of Head and Neck Tumors, chm elect European Head and Neck Pathology Working Gp; FRCPath 1996 (MRCPath 1983); *Publications* Choroby slinných áz (Diseases of the salivary glands, with I Stárek); author of several chapters and over 110 pubns in med jls on aspects of histopathology (in particular tumours of the head and neck); *Recreations* cricket, travel, the past; *Clubs* East India, Somerset CCC; *Style*— Dr Roderick Simpson; ✉ Iron Pool, Dry Lane, Christow, Exeter, Devon EX6 7PF (☎ 01647 252034); University of Calgary, Department of Anatomical Pathology, Foothills Medical Centre, 1403 29th St NW, Calgary, Alberta, T2N 2T9 (☎ 001 403 944 8506)

SIMPSON, Prof Stephen James; s of Arthur Leonard Simpson, and Patricia Simpson; *b* 26 June 1957; *Educ* C of E GS Brisbane, Univ of Qld (BSc), Univ of London (PhD), Univ of Oxford (MA); *m* 1984, Lesley Kathryn; 2 s (Nicholas, Alastair); *Career* Univ of Oxford: MRC post-doctoral res asst Dept of Experimental Psychology 1982–83, demonstrator Dept of Zoology 1983–86, curator Hope Entomological Collections 1986–2005, lectr in entomology 1986–98, princ curator Univ Museum of Nat History 1989–92, reader in zoology 1996–98, prof 1998–2004, assoc head Dept of Zoology 2000–04, visiting prof 2005–08; fell: Linacre Coll Oxford 1986–88, Jesus Coll Oxford 1988–2004; fedn fell Sch of Biological Sciences Univ of Sydney 2005–09, ARC laureate fell Sch of Biological Sciences Univ of Sydney 2010–, academic dir Charles Perkins Centre Univ of Sydney; guest prof in animal behaviour Univ of Basel 1990, distinguished visiting prof Univ of Arizona 1999; NSW Scientist of the Year 2009, Wigglesworth Medal Royal Entomological Soc of London 2010; fell Wissenschaftskolleg (Inst for Advanced Study) Berlin 2002–03, fell Aust Acad of Sci 2007, hon fell Royal Entomological Soc 2013, FRS 2013; AC; *Publications* The Angler's Fly Identifier: The Complete Guide to Insects and Artificials (1996), The Right Fly: An Angler's Guide to Identifying and Matching Natural Insects (1996), Identifying Anglers' Flies: The new compact study guide and identifier (1997), The Nature of Nutrition: A Unifying Framework from Animal Adaptation to Human Obesity (2012); ed of 20 books and 313 scientific papers; *Recreations* fishing, cooking; *Style*— Prof Stephen Simpson, AC

SIMPSON, William George; s of William Anion Simpson (d 1961), of Liverpool, and Sarah Jane Simpson (d 1972); *b* 27 June 1945, Liverpool; *Educ* Liverpool Inst, Univ of Liverpool (BA), Univ of Aberdeen (Gilroy scholar), Univ of Dublin (MA); *m* 2 Nov 1968, Margaret Lilian, da of Bertram Pollard, of Liverpool; 2 da (Nicola Margaret b 1969, Fiona Sarah b 1974); *Career* asst librarian Univ of Durham 1969–73, John Rylands Library Univ of Manchester 1973–85 (asst librarian, sub-librarian, sr sub-librarian); univ librarian: Univ of Surrey 1985–90, Univ of London 1990–94; librarian and coll archivist Trinity Coll Dublin 1994–2002, dir John Rylands Library and univ librarian Univ of Manchester 2002–07, int library and heritage conslt 2008–; curator Oxford Univ Libraries 2002–07; UK advsr Br Univ in Egypt 2008–11; memb: SCONUL 1985–2007, Br Library London Servs Advsy Ctee 1990–94, Nat Cncl for Orientalist Library Resources 1991–96, An Chomhairle Leabharlanna 1995–2002, COLICO 1995–2002 (chair 1998–2000), Mgmnt Ctee Nat Preservation Office 1996–2002 (chair 1999–2002), Consultative Cncl on National Policy for Libraries and Information Services (Ireland) 1997–99; chm: American Studies Library Gp 1987–94, Guildford Inst 1987–90, CONUL 1997–99, Standing Ctee on Legal Deposit 1998–2001; dir: CURL 1992–97 and 2003–05, IRIS 1994–2004; sec LIBER Div of Library Mgmnt and Admin 2002–07, memb Int Editorial Bd Jl of Library Administration 2004–12; tstee: The Worth Library 1997–, The People's History Museum 2003–05, Working Class Movement Library 2007–, Frome Heritage Museum 2014– (vice-chair 2015–); fell Salzburg Fndn 2004; Memorial Medal Charles Univ Prague 1998; MCLIP, FRSA, FRAS; *Publications* Libraries, Languages and the Interpretation of the Past (1988), The Book of Kells on CD-ROM (ed, 2000); author of articles and reviews in learned and professional jls; *Recreations* astronomy, genealogy, languages, travel, Everton FC; *Style*— William Simpson, Esq; ✉ 1 Woolmer Villas, Petersfield Road, Greatham, Liss, Hampshire GU33 6AY

SIMPSON OF DUNKELD, Baron (Life Peer UK 1997), of Dunkeld in Perth and Kinross; George Simpson; s of William Simpson (d 1979), of Dundee, Scotland, and Eliza Jane, *née* Wilkie (d 1982); *b* 2 July 1942; *Educ* Morgan Acad Dundee, Dundee Inst of Technol (Dip Business Admin); *m* 5 Sept 1963, Eva, da of William Chalmers, of Dundee; 1 s (Hon George Anthony b 22 Feb 1965), 1 da (Hon Gillian b 23 Oct 1966); *Career* sr accountant Scottish Gas 1964–68, sr fin position British Leyland 1969–77, fin dir Leyland Truck & Bus Ltd 1978–79; md: Coventry Climax 1980–82, Freight Rover 1983–85, Rover Group Commercial Vehicles 1986–87; chief exec Leyland DAF 1987–88, chm and chief exec

Rover Group plc 1989–92, memb Supervisory Bd DAF NV 1989–94, chm Rover Group and dep chief exec British Aerospace plc (parent co) 1992–94; chief exec Lucas Industries plc 1994–96; Marconi plc (formerly GEC plc): md 1996–99, chief exec 1999–2001; non-exec dir: Pilkington plc 1992–99, ICI plc 1995–2001, Alstom SA 1998–, Nestlé SA 1999–, NW Venture Capital Fund Ltd, Bank of Scotland 2001–; pres: SMMT 1995–96 (formerly vice-pres), West Midlands Development Agency 1993–95; industrial prof Univ of Warwick 1991–, memb Govt Advsy Ctee on Business and Environment 1991–93; memb Cmmn on Public Policy and Br Business Inst of Public Policy Research 1995–97; memb Senate Engrg Cncl, memb Euro Round Table, govr London Business Sch; FCCA, ACIS, FIMI, FCIT, FRSA; *Recreations* golf; *Clubs* Royal Birkdale Golf, New Zealand Golf, Pine Valley Golf, Blaircowrie Golf; *Style*— The Rt Hon Lord Simpson of Dunkeld

SIMS, Prof Andrew Charles Petter; s of Dr Charles Henry Sims (d 1994), of Exeter, and Dr Norah Winnifred Kennan, *née* Petter (d 1998); *b* 5 November 1938; *Educ* Monkton Combe Sch, Emmanuel Coll Cambridge (MA, MB BChir, MD), Westminster Hosp Med Sch London; *m* 25 April 1964, Ruth Marie, da of Dr John Cuthbert Harvey (d 1988), of Birmingham; 2 s (David b 1965, John b 1968), 2 da (Mary b 1966, Ann b 1970); *Career* house surgn Westminster Hosp 1963–64, registrar Manchester Royal Infirmary 1965–68, conslt psychiatrist All Saints' Hosp Birmingham 1971–76, sr lectr and hon conslt psychiatrist Univ of Birmingham 1976–79, prof of psychiatry Univ of Leeds 1979–2000; ed Advances in Psychiatric Treatment 1993–2003, asst ed Br Jl of Psychiatry 1994–2005, ed Developing Mental Health 2002–05; pres RCPsych 1990–93 (dean 1987–90); chm: Confidential Inquiry into Homicides and Suicides of Mentally Ill People 1992–95, Schizophrenia Report of Clinical Standards Advsy Gp 1993–95, Spirituality and Psychiatry Special Interest Gp RCPsych 2003–05; memb GMC 1994–99; patron: Interhealth, Leeds Faith in Schs, Assoc for Pastoral Care for Mental Health; former patron John Young Fndn; MD (Lambeth) 1995; FRCPsych 1979 (Hon FRCPsych 1994), FRCPEd 1993, FRCP 1997; fell Coll of Physicians and Surgns Pakistan 1994, fell Coll of Psychiatrists South Africa 1997, fell Assoc of European Psychiatrists 2002; *Books* Neurosis in Society (1983), Psychiatry CMT (5 edn, 1983), Lecture Notes in Behavioural Science (1984), Symptoms in the Mind (1988), Anxiety in Clinical Practice (1988), Angsttherapie in der Klinischen Praxis (1993), Psychiatry (6 edn, 1993), Speech and Language Disorders in Psychiatry (1995), Symptoms in the Mind (1988, 3 edn 2003), Disorders of Volition (1998), Spirituality and Psychiatry (jt ed, 2009), Is Faith Delusion? (2009), Geloof: waan of werkelijkheid? (2010), Spiritual Narrative in Clinical Psychiatry (jt ed, 2016); *Recreations* music, theatre, gardening; *Clubs* Christian Medical Fellowship, RSM; *Style*— Prof Andrew Sims; ✉ Church Farm House, Alveley, Bridgnorth, Shropshire WV15 6ND

SIMS, John Haesaert Mancel; s of Harold Mancel Sims (d 1958), and Jeanie Emilie Anne, *née* Haesaert (d 1965); *b* 16 December 1929; *Educ* Highfield Sch Wandsworth, Brixton Sch of Bldg; *Career* Nat Serv RE 1948–50; various appts with quantity surveyors' firms in private practice 1950–73, in sole practice as bldg contracts conslt; lectr, writer, arbitrator, adjudicator and mediator 1973–, author of numerous articles on bldg contracts for Building 1975–89; pres Soc of Construction Arbitrators 1992–95, chm CIArb 1994–95 (vice-pres 1991–95), memb DTI Departmental Advsy Ctee on Arbitration Law 1990–96; Soc of Construction Law President's Medal for outstanding services to construction law 2008; Freeman City of London 1981, Liveryman Worshipful Co of Arbitrators 1982; FRICS 1967 (ARICS 1954), FCIArb 1970, MAE 1988, FRSA 1995; *Books* with Vincent Powell-Smith: Building Contract Claims (1983, 4 edn by David Chappell 2004), Contract Documentation for Contractors (1985, 3 edn with Christopher Dancaster 2000), Determination and Suspension of Construction Contracts (1985), The JCT Management Contract: A Practical Guide (1988), Construction Arbitrations: A Practical Guide (1989, 2 edn with Christopher Dancaster 1998); The Arbitration Act 1996: A Practical Guide (with Margaret Rutherford, QC, 1996); *Recreations* classical music, choral singing, reading; *Style*— John H M Sims, Esq; ✉ Common Farm, The Common, Leiston, Suffolk IP16 4UN (✆ 01728 833852, e-mail jhmsims@toucansurf.com)

SIMS-WILLIAMS, Prof Nicholas John; s of Rev Michael Vernon Sims Sims-Williams (d 1992), and Kathleen Marjorie, *née* Wenborn (d 1996); twin bro of Prof Patrick Sims-Williams, FBA, *qv*; *b* 11 April 1949, Chatham, Kent; *Educ* Borden GS Sittingbourne, Trinity Hall Cambridge (MA, PhD); *m* 1 July 1972, Ursula Mary Judith, da of (George) Hugh Nicholas Seton-Watson, CBE, FBA (d 1984); 2 da ((Jennifer) Helen Seton b 1986, Frances Mary Seton b 1989); *Career* research fell Gonville & Caius Coll Cambridge 1975–76; Univ of London: lectr in Iranian languages SOAS 1976–89, reader in Iranian studies 1989–94, prof of Iranian and Central Asian studies 1994–2004, research prof of Iranian and Central Asian studies 2004–07 and 2012–15 (emeritus prof 2015–), professional researcher 2008–12; research reader British Acad 1992–94, Leverhulme maj research fellowship 2002–04; visiting prof: Collège de France 1998–99, Macquarie Univ Sydney 1998–2000, Univ La Sapienza Rome 2001; adjunct prof Macquarie Univ Sydney 2004–06; assoc ed Encyclopaedia Iranica NY 2002–; chair Corpus Inscriptionum Iranicarum 2002– (sec 1985–2002), pres Philological Soc 2003–07 (sec 1998–2001), chair Section H4 (Linguistics and Philology) Br Acad 2004–07, vice-pres Int Union of Academies Brussels 2010–13 (memb Bd 2006–09); Prix Ghirshman Institut de France 1988; Hirayama prize Inst of Silk Road Studies 1996, World Prize for the Book of the Year of the Islamic Repub of Iran 2009, Denis Sinor Medal for Inner Asian Studies Royal Asiatic Soc 2015; corresponding fell Aust Acad of Scis 1989, associé étranger Académie des Inscriptions et Belles-Lettres Institut de France 2002 (correspondant étranger 2000), hon memb American Oriental Soc 2011, memb American Philosophical Soc 2014; FBA 1988, MAE 2012; *Books* The Christian Sogdian Manuscript C2 (1985), Sogdian and Other Iranian Inscriptions of the Upper Indus, I (1989) and II (1992), Documents Turco-Sogdiens du IXe-Xe Siècle de Touen-Houang (with James Hamilton, 1990, revised English edn, Turco-Sogdian Documents from 9th-10th century Dunhuang, 2015), Partita (1993), Serenade for ten wind instruments (1997), New Light on Ancient Afghanistan: the decipherment of Bactrian (1997), Bactrian documents from Northern Afghanistan, I (2001, revised edn 2012), II (2007) and III (2012), In Memoriam for string trio (2002), Bactrian Personal Names (2010), Seals, Sealings and Tokens from Bactria to Gandhara, 4th to 8th Century CE (jtly, 2011), Iranian manuscripts in Syriac script in the Berlin Turfan collection (2012), Dictionary of Manichaean Sogdian and Bactrian (jtly, 2012), Biblical and Christian Sogdian Texts from the Turfan Collection (2014), The Life of Serapion and other Christian Sogdian Texts from the Manuscripts E25 and E26 (2015), A Dictionary: Christian Sogdian, Syriac and English (2016); *Recreations* composing music, playing French horn; *Style*— Prof Nicholas Sims-Williams, FBA, MAE; ✉ 11 Park Parade, Cambridge CB5 8AL; c/o Ancient India and Iran Trust, 23 Brooklands Avenue, Cambridge CB2 8BG

SIMS-WILLIAMS, Prof Patrick; s of Rev Michael Vernon Sims-Williams (d 1992), and Kathleen Marjorie, *née* Wenborn (d 1996); twin bro of Prof Nicholas Sims-Williams, FBA, *qv*; *b* 11 April 1949; *Educ* Borden GS Sittingbourne, Trinity Hall Cambridge (MA), Univ of Birmingham (PhD); *m* 1986, Prof Marged Haycock, da of Emrys J Haycock; 1 da (Gwen Kathleen b 11 Nov 1990), 1 s (Gwilym Emrys b 10 Sept 1993); *Career* Univ of Cambridge: fell St John's Coll 1977–93, lectr Dept of Anglo-Saxon, Norse and Celtic 1977–93, reader in Celtic and Anglo-Saxon 1993; prof of Celtic studies Univ of Wales Aberystwyth 1994–2014 (emeritus prof 2014–); Br Acad research reader 1988–90, dir Br Acad project The Development of the Welsh Language; ed Cambrian Medieval Celtic Studies; O'Donnell lectr: Univ of Oxford 1981–82, Univ of Edinburgh 1986, Univ of Wales 2000–01; pres Int Congress of Celtic Studies 2011–; Leverhulme Tst Major Research Fellowship 2003–06; Sir Israel Gollancz prize British Acad, Antiquity prize, GT Clark Award, Vernam Hull Prize Univ of Wales; FBA 1996; *Books* Religion and Literature in Western England, 600–800 (1990), Britain and Early Christian Europe (1995), Ptolemy: Towards a Linguistic Atlas of the Earliest Celtic Place-Names of Europe (2000), The Celtic Inscriptions of Britain (2003), New Approaches to Celtic Place-Names in Ptolemy's Geography (2005), Ancient Celtic Place-Names in Europe and Asia Minor (2006), The Iron House in Ireland (2006), Additions to Alfred Holder's Celtic Thesaurus (2006), Studies on Celtic Languages Before the Year 1000 (2007), The Geography of Celtic Personal Names in the Latin Inscriptions of the Roman Empire (2007), A Corpus of Latin Inscriptions of the Roman Empire Containing Celtic Personal Names (2007), Introduction and Supplement to the Corpus of Latin Inscriptions of the Roman Empire Containing Celtic Personal Names (2009), Irish Influence on Medieval Welsh Literature (2010); *Recreations* music, sailing, carpentry; *Style*— Prof Patrick Sims-Williams, FBA; ✉ Department of Welsh, Aberystwyth University, Ceredigion SY23 3DY

SINCLAIR, Dr Andrew Annandale; s of Stanley Charles Sinclair, CBE (d 1973), and Kathleen, *née* Nash-Webber; *b* 21 January 1935; *Educ* Eton, Trinity Coll Cambridge, Harvard Univ, Columbia Univ NY; *m* 1 (m dis 1971), Marianne Alexandre; 1 s (Timon Alexandre); m 2 (m dis 1984), Miranda Seymour; 1 s (Merlin George); m 3, Sonia, Lady Melchett; *Career* Ensign Coldstream Gds 1953–55; ed and publisher Lorrimer Publishing 1968–87, md Timon Films 1968–; FRSL 1970, fell Soc of American Historians 1970, FRSA 2007; *Novels* The Breaking of Bumbo (1957), My Friend Judas (1958), The Project (1960), The Hallelujah Bum (1963), The Raker (1964), Gog (1967), Magog (1972), A Patriot for Hire (1978), The Facts in the Case of E A Poe (1980), Beau Bumbo (1985), King Ludd (1988), In Love and Anger (1994); *Non-Fiction* Prohibition The Era of Excess (1962), The Available Man The Life Behind the Mask of Warren Gamaliel Harding (1965), The Better Half The Emancipation of the American Woman (1965), A Concise History of the United States (1967), The Last of the Best – The Aristocracy of Europe in the Twentieth Century (1969), Che Guevara (1970), Jack – A Biography of Jack London (1977), John Ford (1979), Corsair – The Life of J Pierpoint Morgan (1981), The Other Victoria – The Princess Royal and the Great Game of Europe (1981), The Red and the Blue (1986), Speigel (1987), War Like a Wasp (1989), The War Decade (1989), The Need to Give the Patrons and the Arts (1990), The Naked Savage (1991), The Sword and the Grail (1992), Francis Bacon, His Life and Violent Times (1993), In Love and Anger: A View of the 'Sixties (1994), Arts & Cultures: A History of the Fifty Years of the Arts Council of Great Britain (1995), Jerusalem: The Endless Crusade (1996), Death by Fame: A Life of Elisabeth, Empress of Austria (1998), The Discovery of the Grail (1998), Dylan the Bard: a Life of Dylan Thomas (1999), The Secret Scroll (2001), Blood & Kin (2002), The Anatomy of Terror (2003), Rosslyn (2005), Viva Che! (2006), The Grail (2007), Man and Horse (2008), Down Under Milk Wood (2014); *Films* Under Milk Wood, Dylan on Dylan; *Recreations* visiting ruins; *Clubs* Chelsea Arts, Garrick; *Style*— Dr Andrew Sinclair; ✉ Flat 20, Millennium House, 132 Grosvenor Road, London SW1V 3JY (✆ 020 7976 5454, website www.filmisart.com)

SINCLAIR, Dr Bruce David; s of William Sinclair, of Comins Coch, Aberystwyth, and Muriel Elma, *née* Bruce; *b* 18 April 1961; *Educ* Ardwyn GS and Penglais Comp Aberystwyth, Univ of St Andrews (Thomson entrance bursary, BSc, PhD, J F Allen prize, Neil Arnot prize, class medal); *m* 17 Aug 1991, Marina Elizabeth, da of John Kenneth Blair, and Carita Blair; 2 s (Callum Dennis b 28 June 1993, Paul Bruce b 30 Oct 1995); *Career* Sch of Physics and Astronomy Univ of St Andrews: res asst in nonlinear optics in fibres 1986–87 then in diode pumped lasers 1987–89, Wolfson lectr (temp) in laser physics 1989, lectr 1989–96, sr lectr 1996–2001, reader 2001–, dir of teaching 2006–; Inst of Physics: local organiser Scot branch 1991–, hon sec Quantum Electronics Group 1994–98 (ctee memb 1992–95), chair Advsrs Ctee to Physical Scis Centre of UK Learning and Teaching Support Network 2002–04; dir 1998 EU-sponsored int summer sch on advances in lasers and applications; hon pres Students Voluntary Serv Univ of St Andrews; *Books* contrib chapter to Optoelectronic Devices (ed Des Smith, 1995), Advances in Lasers and Applications (ed, 1999); also author of over 40 publications in refereed jls and over 80 papers at confs and tech meetings; *Recreations* family, tandem, gardening, walking, swimming, DIY; *Style*— Dr Bruce Sinclair; ✉ School of Physics and Astronomy, University of St Andrews, North Haugh, St Andrews, Fife KY16 9SS (✆ 01334 463118, fax 01334 463104, e-mail b.d.sinclair@st-andrews.ac.uk)

SINCLAIR, Charles James Francis; CBE (2009); s of late Sir George Evelyn Sinclair, CMG, OBE, and Katharine Jane Sinclair (d 1971); *b* 4 April 1948; *Educ* Winchester, Magdalen Coll Oxford (BA); *m* 1974, Nicola, da of Maj W R Bayliss, RM; 2 s (Jeremy b 1977, Robert b 1979); *Career* VSO Zambia 1966–67, Dearden Farrow CAs London 1970–75; Associated Newspapers Holdings Ltd: joined 1975, asst md 1986, dep md 1987, md 1988, md and gp chief exec Daily Mail and General Trust plc 1988–2008; chm Associated British Foods plc 2009– (non-exec dir 2008–09); non-exec dir: Euromoney Institutional Investor plc 1985–2008, Schroders plc 1990–2004, Reuters Gp plc 1994–2005, SVG Capital plc 2005–13; memb Advsy Bd: Spencer Stuart 2006–12 (chm 2009–12), Reuters Inst for the Study of Journalism Univ of Oxford 2007–10; chm of tstees Minack Theatre Tst (Porthcurno Cornwall) 1985–; memb UK Ctee VSO 2006–11; govr Courtauld Inst of Art 2011–14, warden Winchester Coll 2014– (fell 2010–); FCA 1980 (ACA 1974); *Recreations* opera, fishing, skiing, theatre; *Clubs* Athenaeum, Vincent's, Flyfishers'; *Style*— Charles Sinclair, Esq, CBE, FCA; ✉ Associated British Foods plc, Weston Centre, 10 Grosvenor Street, London W1K 4QY

SINCLAIR, Dr Clive John; s of David Sinclair, of Hendon, and Betty, *née* Jacobovitch; *b* 19 February 1948; *Educ* UEA (BA), Univ of Calif Santa Cruz, Univ of Exeter, UEA (PhD); *m* 1979, Frances, da of Sydney Redhouse (d 1994); 1 s (Seth Benjamin b 1981); partner Haidee Becker Kenedy, da of John Becker (d 1981); *Career* writer; copywriter Young & Rubicam 1973–76, literary ed The Jewish Chronicle 1983–87, British Cncl writer in residence Univ of Uppsala Sweden 1988; judge: Int IMPAC Dublin Lit Award 2013, Frank O'Connor Int Short Story Award 2015; Bicentennial Arts fell 1980–81, Somerset Maugham prize 1981, one of 20 Best Young British Novelists 1983, Br Library Penguin Writer's fell 1996, Jewish Quarterly Prize for fiction 1997, PEN Silver pen for fiction 1997, Royal Literary Fund fell UEA 2005–07; memb: Soc of Authors, PEN 1979–; FRSL 1983; *Fiction* Bibliosexuality (1973), Hearts of Gold (short stories, 1979), Bedbugs (short stories, 1982), Blood Libels (1985), Cosmetic Effects (1989), For Good or Evil (short stories, 1991), Augustus Rex (1992), The Lady with the Laptop (short stories, 1996), Meet the Wife (2002), Death & Texas (short stories, 2014); *Non-Fiction* The Brothers Singer (biography, 1983), Diaspora Blues (travel, 1987), A Soap Opera from Hell (essays, 1998), Clive Sinclair's True Tales of the Wild West (short stories, history and travel, 2008); *Recreations* travel, football, cinema; *Style*— Dr Clive Sinclair, FRSL; ✉ 16 Canonbury Grove, London N1 2HR (✆ 07778 260516, e-mail clivejsinclair@gmail.com); Jonathan Pegg Literacy Agency, 32 Batoum Gardens, London W6 7QD (✆ 020 7603 6830, e-mail jonathan@jonathanpegg.com, website www.jonathanpegg.com)

SINCLAIR, Sir Clive Marles; kt (1983); s of late George William Carter Sinclair, and late Thora Edith Ella, *née* Marles; *b* 30 July 1940; *Educ* Highgate Sch, Reading Sch, St George's Coll Weybridge; *m* 1, 1962 (m dis 1985), Ann, *née* Trevor Briscoe (d 2004); 2 s, 1 da; m 2, 16 April 2010, Angie Bowness; *Career* ed Bernards (publishers) 1958–61; chm: Sinclair Radionics 1962–79 (produced pocket TV), Sinclair Research Ltd 1979–, Cambridge Computer Ltd 1986–90; fndr Sinclair Browne (publishers) 1981–85 (annual

S

Sinclair Prize for Fiction); dir: Shaye Communications Ltd 1986–91, Anamartic Ltd; visiting fell Robinson Coll Cambridge 1982–85; visiting prof: Imperial Coll of Science and Technol London 1984–92 (hon fell 1984), UMIST 1984 (hon fell); chm Br Mensa 1980–98; Mullard Award Royal Soc 1984; Hon DSc: Univ of Bath 1983, Univ of Warwick 1983, Heriot-Watt Univ 1983; *Publications* Practical Transistor Receivers (1959), British Semiconductor Survey (1963); *Recreations* music, poetry, mathematics, science, poker; *Clubs* RAC, Nat Liberal; *Style*— Sir Clive Sinclair; ✉ 1A Spring Gardens, Trafalgar Square, London SW1A 2BB (☎ 020 7839 7744)

SINCLAIR, David Grant; s of Leslie Sinclair (d 1978), of London, and Beatrice Zena (d 1979); *b* 12 February 1948; *Educ* Latymer Upper Sch; *m* 7 June 1970, Susan Carol, da of Alexander Merkin (d 1963), of London; 2 s (Alexander James b 1972, Julian Lloyd b 1974); 1 da (Olivia Lesley b 1982); *Career* fndr and sr ptnr Sinclair Assocs Chartered Accountants 1972–; jt fndr and dir International Corporate Compliance Ltd and assoc cos 1991–, fndr Axiom Capital Ltd 2001–; recognised expert in forensic accounting; CF 2005; FCA 1978 (ACA 1972); *Recreations* bridge, charity work; *Style*— David G Sinclair, Esq; ✉ Churchill House, 120 Bunns Lane, London NW7 2BA (☎ 020 3114 2128, fax 020 3004 1348, mobile 07977 466121, e-mail david@sinclairuk.com)

SINCLAIR, David William Jonathan; s of James Daniel Sinclair, of Glasgow, and Barbara Kathleen, *née* Barclay-Bishop; *b* 24 October 1952; *Educ* Eltham Coll London, Univ of Warwick (BA); *m* 1 May 1986, Prudence Evelyn, da of late Sir Evelyn Hone; 1 s (Jack b 23 Dec 1990), 1 da ((Josephine) Faith b 23 Aug 1989); *Career* music writer and broadcaster; former drummer/vocalist in groups incl: Empire Made 1976–77, Tidal Waveband 1977–78, Blunt Instrument 1978–79, London Zoo 1979–81, TV Smith's Explorers 1981–82, Laughing Sam's Dice 1983–85; contrib to magazines and newspapers incl: One Two Testing 1983–85, Guitar Heroes 1983–84, The History of Rock 1983–84, Kerrang! 1983–85, The Times 1985–, Q Magazine 1986–, Billboard (ed Global Music Pulse column) 1991–, Rolling Stone 1992–97, Mojo 1999–; researcher BBC TV (progs incl Eight Days A Week, Wogan, The Rock'n'Roll Years and Rock School) 1984–86; regular appearances on: Sunday Edition (BBC Radio 5) 1991–92, Sunrise Morning News (Sky TV) 1991–92, The Breakfast Show (BBC GLR) 1992–96; judge Mercury Music Prize 1994–; *Books* Tres Hombres – The Story of ZZ Top (1986), Rock on CD – The Essential Guide (1992, revised and updated 1993); *Recreations* tennis, badminton, bridge; *Clubs* Polytechnic of Central London; *Style*— David Sinclair, Esq; ✉ c/o The Arts Desk, The Times, 1 Pennington Street, Wapping, London E1 9XN (☎ 020 7782 5000, fax 020 7782 5046)

SINCLAIR, Franklin; s of Eddie Sinclair (d 1988), and Sheila, *née* Cohen (d 1995); *b* 28 June 1958, Manchester; *Educ* Manchester Grammar, Univ of Manchester (LLB), Coll of Law Chester; *m* 26 Oct 1989 (m dis 2000); 1 s (Miles b 8 April 1990), 2 da (Mica b 5 July 1992, Nikita b 23 Sept 1993); *Career* admitted slr 1982; sr ptnr Tuckers Slrs 1984– (joined 1983); higher courts advocate 2002; chm Criminal Law Slrs Assoc 1999–2002, pres Manchester Law Soc 2005; *Recreations* golf, music (disc jockey 1975–89); *Clubs* Durham Forest Golf (Cheshire); *Style*— Franklin Sinclair, Esq; ✉ Tuckers Solicitors, 63–65 Mosley Street, Manchester M2 3HZ (☎ 0161 233 4321, fax 0161 233 4344, e-mail sinclairf@tuckerssolicitors.com)

SINCLAIR, Iain Macgregor; s of Dr Henry Macgregor Sinclair (d 1989), and Doris, *née* Jones (d 1991); *b* 11 June 1943; *Educ* Cheltenham Coll, London Sch of Film Technique, Trinity Coll Dublin, Courtauld Inst of Art London; *m* (Mary) Annabel Rose, *née* Hadman; 2 da (Farne b 8 July 1972, Madeleine b 14 Jan 1980), 1 s (William Llewelyn b 21 Oct 1975); *Career* writer; *Books* incl: The Kodak Mantra Diaries (historical documentary, 1971), Lud Heat (poetry/essays, 1975), Suicide Bridge (poetry/essays, 1979), White Chappell, Scarlet Tracings (fiction, 1987), Flesh Eggs and Scalp Metal (poetry, 1989), Downriver (fiction, 1991), Radon Daughters (fiction, 1994), Lights Out for the Territory: Nine Excursions in the Secret History of London (1997), Slow Chocolate Autopsy (stories, 1997), Crash (film essay, 1999), Rodinsky's Room (documentary investigation, 1999), Landor's Tower (novel, 2001), London Orbital (2002), Dining on Stones (novel, 2004), Edge of the Orison (2005), London: City of Disappearances (ed, 2006), Hackney, That Rose-Red Empire (2009), Ghost Milk (2011); *Style*— Iain Sinclair, Esq; ✉ c/o John Parker, MBA Literary Agents, 62 Grafton Way, London W1P 5ZD (☎ 020 7387 2076, fax 020 7387 2042)

SINCLAIR, Jeremy; s of Donald Alan Forrester Sinclair (d 1987), of London; *b* 4 November 1946; *m* Jan 1976, Jacqueline Margaret, da of Jack Metcalfe (d 1994); 1 da (Naomi b 26 Jan 1979), 2 s (Leon b 21 Oct 1981, David b 13 March 1985); *Career* worldwide creative dir and chm Saatchi & Saatchi plc until 1995 (resigned); M&C Saatchi: ptnr 1995–, chm 2004–; *Style*— Jeremy Sinclair, Esq; ✉ M&C Saatchi plc, 36 Golden Square, London W1R 4EE (☎ 020 7543 4500)

SINCLAIR, 18 Lord (S *c* 1449, confirmed 1488–9); Matthew Murray Kennedy St Clair; DL (Stewartry of Kirkcudbright 2016); s of 17 Lord Sinclair, CVO (d 2004), and Anne Lettice, *née* Cotterell; 1 Lord resigned the Earldoms of Orkney and Caithness to the crown 1470, 10 Lord obtained Charter under Great Seal 1677 confirming his honours with remainders to male heirs whatsoever; *b* 9 December 1968; *Educ* Glenalmond, RAC Cirencester; *m* 2005, Laura Cicely, *née* Coode; 2 s (Harry Murray Kennedy St Clair (Master of Sinclair) b 6 Oct 2007, James Jonathan Kennedy St Clair b 24 May 2009); *Career* Smiths Gore 1992–2002, md Saint Property Ltd 2002–; memb Royal Co of Archers; MRICS 1994; *Recreations* sport; *Clubs* New (Edinburgh); *Style*— The Rt Hon the Lord Sinclair, DL; ✉ Knocknalling, St Johnstown of Dalry, Castle Douglas DG7 3ST (☎ 01644 430221); Saint Property Ltd, 61A Queen Street, Edinburgh EH2 4NA (☎ 0131 478 4533, fax 0870 889 5102, e-mail mstc@saintproperty.com)

SINCLAIR, Michael; *see*: Shea, Michael Sinclair MacAuslan

SINCLAIR, Murray; *b* 29 May 1961; *Educ* ChCh Oxford (MA), Univ of Edinburgh (LLB); *Career* slr to the Scottish Govt, head Govt Legal Service for Scotland; *Recreations* walking, football, astronomy; *Style*— Murray Sinclair, Esq; ✉ Scottish Government Legal Directorate, Victoria Quay, Edinburgh EH6 6QQ

SINCLAIR, Nicholas Hilary; s of Hugh Sinclair (d 1962), actor, of Sussex, and Rosalie, *née* Williams; *b* 28 January 1954; *Educ* Christ's Hosp, Univ of Newcastle upon Tyne; *Career* photographer; chm North Star Studios 1983–93; *Solo Exhibitions* Gardner Arts Centre Univ of Sussex 1983, Photogallery St Leonards-on-Sea 1985, Photography Centre of Athens 1986, Brighton Museum and Art Gallery 1995, Tom Blau Gallery London 1996, Brighton Museum and Art Gallery 1995, 1997, 2004 and 2007, Luciano Inga Pin Gallery Milan 1999, Focus Gallery London 2000, Pallant House Gallery Chichester 2014; *Selected Group Exhibitions* Nat Theatre 1985, Northern Centre for Contemporary Art Sunderland 1989, Br Cncl touring exhibition W Germany 1990–91, Angela Flowers Gallery London 1993, Nat Portrait Gallery London 1994, 1998–99, 2000 and 2001, Joseloff Gallery Univ of Hartford USA 1995, Tom Blau Gallery 1995, Kunsthalle Vienna 1997, Galerie Rudolfinum Prague 1997, Padglione d'Art Contemporanea Milan 1999, Culturgest Lisbon 1999, Caterina Gualco Gallery Genova 2000, Muée de l'Elysée Lausanne 2000, Giacomo Zaza Gallery Bisceglie 2001, Kunsthalle Wurth Kunzelsau 2003, Musee d'Art et Histoire Fribourg 2004, UBS Zurich 2005, Nat Museum of Wales Cardiff 2006, Kettle's Yard Cambridge 2006, Nat Portrait Gallery London 2014; *Public Collections* incl: Nat Portrait Gallery, V&A, Nat Museum and Galleries of Wales Cardiff, Nat Library of Wales Aberystwyth, Brighton Museum and Art Gallery, Staatsgalerie Stuttgart, Folkwang Museum Essen, Kunsthalle Wurth Kunzelsau, Musée de l'Elysée Lausanne, Galerie Kurt Im Hirsch Berlin 2009; *Books* Sussex Churches and Chapels (1989), The Chameleon Body (1996), Franko B (1998), Portraits of Artists (2000), Crossing the Water (2002), Kyffin Williams (2004); *Monographs* The Chameleon Body (1996), Franko B (1998), Portraits of Artists (2000), Crossing the Water (2002, Berlin: Imagining the Tri Chord (2007), Five Cities (2010); *Recreations* swimming, music, theatre, cinema; *Style*— Nicholas Sinclair, Esq; ✉ 56 Denmark Villas, Hove, East Sussex BN3 3TE (☎ 01273 730289, e-mail nicholas.sinclair@virgin.net, website www.nicholassinclair.com)

SINCLAIR, Ross; *b* 12 April 1966, Glasgow; *Educ* Glasgow Sch of Art (BA, MFA), Calif Inst of the Arts LA; *Career* artist; Paul Hamlyn Award 1998–2000, Arendt Oetker Atelier Stipendium Galerie für Zeitgenossische Kunst Leipzig 1999, Baloise Prize 2001; *Solo Exhibitions* incl: Fanclub (Stills Gallery Edinburgh) 1991, National Virus (Transmission Gallery Glasgow) 1991, Black Flags for USA '92 (Lime Gallery LA) 1992, We Don't Love You Anymore (Transmission Gallery Glasgow) 1993, Galerie Knoll Vienna 1993–94 and 2000, Art Zombies (Catalyst Arts Belfast) 1994, As Good As New (Smart Gallery Amsterdam) 1995, Studio Real Life (Galerie Campbells Occasionally Copenhagen) 1995, I Never Felt More Like Singin the Blues (De Paraplujfabrik Nijmegen) 1995, Real Life Rocky Mountain (CCA Glasgow) 1996, Containerize (Kunstwerke Berlin) 1997, Mercer Union (Toronto) 1997, Irving Gallery Aberdeen 1997, The Agency Contemporary Art London 1997, 1998, 2001, 2002 and 2004, Galerie Walcheturm Zurich 1998, Pier Arts Centre Stromness 1998, Fruitmarket Gallery Edinburgh 1999, Journey to the Edge of the World (Aspex Gallery Portsmouth) 2000, South London Gallery 2001, Badischer Kunstverein Karlsruhe 2001, Kunsthalle Hamburg (room installation) 2002, Galerie Yvon Lambert Paris 2002, Galleria Raffaella Cortese Milan 2002, Wewerka Pavillion Muenster 2002, Dundee Centre for Contemporary Arts 2003, Van Ram Gallery Gent 2004, The Agency 2004, Art Metropole Toronto 2004, Galerie KnapperBaumgarten Stockholm 2006, CCA Glasgow 2006; *Group Exhibitions* incl: International Departures (Gesellschaft für Aktuelle Kunst Bremen) 1993, Return of the Exquisite Corpse (Drawing Center NY) 1993, Left Luggage (Hou Hanru Paris and HU Obrist Vienna) 1993, 3+3+3 (Fruitmarket Gallery Edinburgh) 1994, GOL (Mark Boote Gallery NY) 1994, Easter Show, Summer Show LA 1994, Some Of My Friends (Galerie Campbells Occasionally Copenhagen) 1994, Wish You Were Here (Leeds) 1994, Modern Art (Transmission Gallery Glasgow) 1994, Museum of Despair (The Royal Mile (Aerial) Edinburgh) 1994, It is not Like it Used to be (Bartok 32 Galeria Budapest) 1994, Institute of Cultural Anxiety (ICA London) 1994, Eigen + Art at IAS (Independent Artspace London) 1995, Club Berlin (Kunstwerke at the Venice Biennale) 1995, Shift (De Appel Fndn Amsterdam) 1995, How to Dress (Kunsthalle Vienna) 1995, Shopping (CAPC Museum Bordeaux) 1995, Scottish Autumn (Uljak Exhbn Hall Budapest) 1995, 30 seconds plus Title (Art Gallery of Ontario Toronto) 1995, Fairytale in the Supermarket (Fotofeis Glasgow) 1995, 6eme Semaine Internationale de Video (Geneva) 1995, Make me Clean Again (Alpenmilchzentrale Vienna) 1996, Art for People (Transmission Gallery Glasgow) 1996, A4 Favours (Three Month Gallery Liverpool) 1996, Notell Hotel (Moat House Glasgow) 1996, Host (OB Projects Amsterdam) 1996, City Limits (Staffs Univ Stafford) 1996, Shopping (SoHo Art Week NY) 1996, Sarah Staton's Supastore De-Luxe (Up & Co NY) 1996, Speel (Artis Den Bosch) 1997, One Night Stands (The Norwich Gallery) 1997, Glasgow (Kunsthalle Bern) 1997, New Art from Glasgow (Museet For Samtidskunst Oslo) 1998, Do All Oceans Have Walls? (GAK & Kunstlerhaus Bremen) 1998, This Island Earth (An Turrain Art Centre Isle of Skye) 1998, From Here (High St project Christchurch NZ) 1998, Word Enough To Save a Life (Dilston Gove Church London) 1999, If I Ruled the World (Living Art Museum Iceland) 1999, LKW (OK Centre for Contemporary Arts Linz) 1999, For Those About to Rock (Galerie der Stadt Schwaz) 2000, The Blue Chamber (Duff House Banff) 2000, If I Ruled the World (CCA Glasgow) 2000, New Life (Expo Leipzig) 2000, Living in the Real World (Museum Dhont Dhanens Ghent) 2000, Video Vibe (Br Sch of Rome) 2000, LKW (Kunstverein Bregenz and Centre Pasquart Biel) 2000, A Shot in the Head (Lisson Gallery London) 2000, PICAF 2000 (Pusan Art Festival Korea) 2000, Landscape (Br Cncl touring exhbn) 2000–01, Black Box Recorder (Br Cncl London) 2000–01, PS1 NY 2001, City Racing, 10 Years (ICA London) 2001, Aesthetic Terrorism (The Agency London) 2001, Circles (ZKM Karlsruhe) 2001, G3 NY (Casey Kaplan NY) 2001, Gravita Zero (Fondazione Olivetti Rome) 2001, Dundee Centre for the Arts 2001, Air Guitar (MKG Milton Keynes) 2002, No One Ever Dies Here (Hartware projects Dortmund) 2002, Tent (Rotterdam) 2002, Arte Contemporanea & Montagu Aosta 2003, Glasgow MOMA 2003, Home at Last (Harewood House) 2003, Independence (South London Gallery) 2003, Words (Arts Cncl Collection, touring exhbn) 2003, Air Guitar (Milton Keynes Gallery) 2003, Skin Deep (MART Museum Rovereto) 2003, Galleria Sonia Rossi Pardone 2004, Villa Arson Nice 2004, Aichi Expo Nagoya Japan 2005, God is Bored With Us, Fast Moving Consumer Goods (London) 2005, Flag Project (Bethnal Green London) 2005, Critical Societies (Badischer Kunstverein Karlsruhe) 2005, cmmn for Radiance Light festival Glasgow 2005, sculpture project Wiesbaden 2006; *Style*— Ross Sinclair, Esq; ✉ website www.rosssinclair.co.uk

SINCLAIR, Rt Rev (Gordon) Keith; *see*: Bishop of Birkenhead

SINCLAIR TAYLOR, (Robin) James; s of late Bob Sinclair Taylor, and Wendy, *née* Cox; *b* 9 March 1948, Hastings, Sussex; *Educ* Grenville Coll, Univ of Leicester (BSc); *Children* 1 da (Jessica); *Career* admitted slr 1976; trained with Vivash Hunt, slr North Kensington Law Centre 1976–80, researcher American Legal Servs Cmmn 1980, sr slr Hounslow Law Centre 1981, fndr Sinclair Taylor & Martin 1981, ptnr Russell-Cooke (following merger) 1983–; tstee: Camden Charities, Ajahma Tst, Prairie Tst; govr Kensington and Chelsea Coll; memb Lord Chancellor's Legal Aid Advsy Ctee; treas Law Centre Fedn; chair Pregnancy Advsy Service; memb: Law Soc, Charity Law Assoc; *Books* Voluntary Sector Legal Handbook (1996 and 2001), Company Handbook and Register for Voluntary Sector Companies Limited by Guarantee (2002); *Recreations* sailing cruisers and dinghies, gardening, walking, fringe theatre; *Clubs* London Corinthian Sailing, Swanage Sailing; *Style*— James Sinclair Taylor, Esq; ✉ Russell-Cooke, 2 Putney Hill, Putney, London SW15 6AB (☎ 020 8394 6480, fax 020 8394 6535, e-mail james.taylor@russell-cooke.co.uk)

SINCLAIR-JONES, Ruth E; *née* Knopp; da of Philip Knopp (d 1975), and Ellen, *née* Sinclair; *b* 9 October 1957, Kent; *Educ* Bromley HS GPDST, Hertford Coll Oxford (scholar, MA); *m* 1982, David E Sinclair-Jones; 2 da (Catherine b 1989, Christina b 2002), 1 s (Philip b 1992); *Career* London Borough of the City of Westminster 1982–85, London Borough of Hammersmith and Fulham 1985–87; British Cncl: joined 1987, postings incl Bangkok, Warsaw, Vienna, Brussels, Sao Paulo; currently dir Erasmus+ UK Nat Agency; memb CIPFA 1986; *Recreations* reading, music, countryside, Scottish country dancing; *Clubs* British (Bangkok); *Style*— Mrs Ruth Sinclair-Jones; ✉ British Council, 10 Spring Gardens, London SW1A 2BN

SINDALL, Barry John; s of Reginald Sindall (d 1978), and Kathleen, *née* Kellison (d 2002); *b* 20 October 1945, Birkenhead, Cheshire; *Educ* Rock Ferry HS Birkenhead, Univ of Exeter (MEd); *m* 1975, Margaret, da of Fredrick Barker; 1 da (Roberta Karen b 6 March 1977), 1 s (Jon Grendon b 1 Sept 1978); *Career* teacher Duncan Bowen Sch Ashford 1967–68, head of humanities R M Bailey Sch Nassau 1968–76, dir of studies Colyton GS 1976–88, dep headteacher Torquay Boys' GS 1988–90, headteacher Colyton GS 1990–2008, chief exec GS Heads Assoc 2008–; memb Leading Edge Nat Steering Ctee, regnl co-ordinator Gaining Ground Prog, tstee W of England Sch for Children with Little or No Sight; FRSA 1992; *Recreations* amateur dramatics, skiing, fell walking, cricket; *Style*— Barry Sindall, Esq; ✉ Lower Hampton Cottage, Shute, Axminster, Devon EX13 7PA (e-mail bsindall@aol.com)

SINDEN, Marcus Andrew (Marc); s of Sir Donald Alfred Sinden, CBE, *qv*, of London, and Diana, *née* Mahony (d 2004); *b* 9 May 1954, London; *Educ* Hall Sch Hampstead, Edgeborough Sch, Stanbridge Earls Sch, Bristol Old Vic Theatre Sch; *m* 20 Aug 1977 (m dis 1997), Joanne Lesley, da of Geoffrey Gilbert (decd), of Dorset; 1 s (Henry (Hal) b 6 Feb 1980), 1 da (Bridie b 1 Sept 1990); *Career* actor, dir and theatre prodr; jeweller and goldsmith H Knowles-Brown Ltd Hampstead 1973–78; actor 1978–, artistic dir Mermaid Theatre 1993–94, prodr md Smallhythe Productions Ltd 1996–97, assoc prodr Bill Kenwright Ltd 1997–98, prodr md Marc Sinden Productions 2000–, md The One Night Booking Co Ltd 2003–, md UK Theatre Availabity Ltd 2003–, md Great Productions Ltd 2011–; Freedom of the City of London, Liveryman Worshipful Co of Innholders; memb Lodge of St Julian; memb Br Humanist Assoc, memb Directors Guild; FZS; *Theatre* as prodr: Br Theatre Season Monaco 2007 (High Patronage of HSH Prince Albert of Monaco), Jeffrey Archer's Prison Diaries, Seven Deadly Sins Four Deadly Sinners, An Evening With: Julian Clary, Gyles Brandreth, Nicholas Parsons, Sir Donald Sinden, etc, Asking For Trouble, Sex Wars, The Glee Club, East (Stage Award Best Ensemble Work), Shakespeare's Villains (also co-dir, nominated Soc of London Theatre Olivier Award for Best Entertainment), Lady Windermere's Fan, An Ideal Husband, Pygmalion (also co-dir), Just The Three of Us, Catch Me If You Can, My Fat Friend, Huckleberry Finn, Canaries Sometimes Sing, Dangerous to Know, Aladdin, Noel & Gertie, Passion (in concert for CD recording), Fallen Angels, Woman in Black, Move Over Mrs Markham, That Good Night; as actor West End incl: The Beaux Stratagem, Over my Dead Body, Ross, Two into One, School for Scandal, Underground, Her Royal Highness, Enjoy; as actor in other prodns: over 40 plays on tour and in rep incl Death and the Maiden, Sting in the Tale, Mansfield Park, Private Lives, Dangerous Obsession, There's a Girl in my Soup, John Bull's Other Island (Gaiety Dublin), Major Barbara (Chichester Festival), Death on the Nile, Chorus Girls (Stratford East), Importance of Being Earnest, Under Milk Wood, While the Sun Shines, Pygmalion, Privates on Parade, Julius Caesar, Norman Conquests and Pools Paradise; *Television* exec prodr: Business Profiles, Euronews, etc; dir and prodr Great West End Theatres; as actor: Judge John Deed, The Island, The Politicians Wife, Against All Odds, Century Falls, The Country Boy, Emmerdale, Magnum PI, Never the Twain, Bergerac, Rumpole of the Bailey, If You Go Down to the Woods Today, All at No 20, Wolf to the Slaughter, Crossroads, Home Front, Dick Turpin; *Film* as actor: Puckoon, The Brylcreem Boys, The Mystery of Edwin Drood, Carry on Columbus, Decadence, Piccolo Grande Amore, Mangeuses d'Homme, White Nights, The Wicked Lady, al-Mas' Ala Al-Kubra, Property of the State; as prodr: That Good Night; as dir: Jeffrey Archer's Prison Diary; *DVD* prodr and dir Great West End Theatres (40-part documentary series); *Other Work* many voice-overs on radio and TV incl: Fosters Lager, Apple Computers (nominated for Sony Award), Bassetts Allsorts; actor on numerous radio plays and audio-visual commentaries; prodr and dir of audio-tapes incl: The Ballad of Reading Gaol, The Fairy Tales of Oscar Wilde; *Publications* Seven Deadly Sins Four Deadly Sinners (play, co-author); *Recreations* Noël Coward, exploring Provence, clay pigeon shooting, polo, history of film stunt work, smoking cigars (nominated for The Spectator Cigar Smoker of the Year Award 2013 and 2015); *Clubs* Guards Polo, London Rowing, The Ivy; *Style—* Marc Sinden, Esq; ✉ Marc Sinden Productions, 1 Hogarth Hill, London NW11 6AY (☎ 020 8455 3278, e-mail marc@sindenproductions.com, website www.sindenproductions.com); agent: Berlin Associates, 7 Tyers Gate, London SE1 3HX (☎ 020 7632 5282, e-mail marcb@berlinassociates.com)

SINFIELD, (Robert) Adrian; s of Robert Ernest Sinfield (d 1983), of Diss, Norfolk, and Agnes Joy, *née* Fouracre (d 1995); *b* 3 November 1938; *Educ* Mercers' Sch, Balliol Coll Oxford (BA), LSE (Dip); *m* 17 Sept 1964, Dorothy Anne, da of George Stanley Palmer (d 1992), of Watford, Herts; 2 da (Beth b 1965 d 2013, Laura b 1969); *Career* jr admin Lutheran World Service Hong Kong 1961–62, res asst LSE 1963–64, res assoc NY State Mental Health Res Unit Syracuse 1964–65, Univ of Essex 1965–79 (asst lectr, lectr, sr lectr, reader sociology); prof of social policy Univ of Edinburgh 1979–95 (emeritus 1995–); visiting posts: Graduate Sch of Social Work and Soc Res Bryn Mawr Coll Pa 1969, NY Sch of Social Work Univ of Columbia 1969, Euro Chair of Social Policy Eötvös Loránd Univ Budapest 1996, 1999, 2001 and 2005, Dept of Applied Social Studies City Univ of Hong Kong 1999, Inst of Public Policy Auckland Univ of Technol 2004; conslt: on long term unemployed OECD Paris 1965–68, on industrial social welfare UN NY 1970–72, on income maintenance servs N Tyneside CDP 1975–78, on tax benefits ILO Geneva 1999; exec Child Poverty Action Gp 1974–78 and 2001–10 (vice-chair 2003–10), co-fndr and chair Mgmnt Ctee Unemployment Unit 1981–91; pres: Sociology and Social Policy BAAS 1993, Social Policy Assoc 1996–2001 (chair 1986–89); SPA Lifetime Achievement Award 2006; Hon PhD Eötvös Loránd Univ Budapest 2004; *Books* The Long-Term Unemployed (1968), Industrial Social Welfare (1971), What Unemployment Means (1981), The Workless State (co-ed with Brian Showler, 1981), Excluding Youth (co-author, 1991), The Sociology of Social Security (co-ed, 1991), Poverty, Inequality and Justice (ed, 1993), Tax Routes to Welfare in Denmark and the United Kingdom (co-author, 1996); *Recreations* reading, walking, travel; *Style—* Adrian Sinfield; ✉ 12 Eden Lane, Edinburgh EH10 4SD (☎ 0131 447 2182, e-mail adrian.sinfield@ed.ac.uk)

SINGER, Emeritus Prof Albert; s of Jacob Singer (Capt in Polish Army, d 1989), of Sydney, Aust, and Gertie, *née* Sadik (d 1986); *b* 4 January 1938; *Educ* Sydney GS, Univ of Sydney (MB BS, PhD), Univ of Oxford (DPhil); *m* 27 June 1976, Talya, da of Maurice Goodman (d 1991); 3 da (Leora b 1978, Rebecca b 1980, Alexandra b 1983); *Career* Nat Serv Royal Aust Air Force 1956–57, Univ Sqdn Flt Lt 1960, active serv with RAAF Reserve in Vietnam 1968–69; Commonwealth fell Oxford 1970, visiting fell to Europe and USA 1968–69, pt/t consIt WHO 1969–70, in res 1970–73, sr lectr then reader Univ of Sheffield 1973–80, consIt gynaecologist Whittington Hosp London 1980–, prof emeritus UCL; has published extensively on subject of gynaecological surgery and res into causes of female cancer; served on numerous govt panels and ctees primarily concerned with female cancer; memb RSM, FRCOG; *Books* The Cervix (with J Jordan), The Colour Atlas of Gynaecological Surgery (6 vols with David Lees), Lower Genital Tract Pre-Cancer (with J Monaghan); *Recreations* sport, especially tennis, swimming and sailing; *Clubs* Oxford and Cambridge; *Style—* Prof Albert Singer; ✉ First Floor Consulting Rooms, 212–214 Great Portland Street, London W1N 5HG (☎ 020 7390 8442, fax 020 8458 0168)

SINGER, Nicky Margaret; da of Geoffrey William Singer (d 1970), and Sheila Anne, *née* King (d 1987); *b* 22 July 1956; *Educ* Queen Anne's Caversham, Univ of Bristol (BA); *m* 17 Sept 1983, (Timothy) James Stephen King-Smith; 2 s (Roland James Singer-Kingsmith 28 Dec 1987, Edmund John Singer-Kingsmith b 26 Sept 1991), 1 da (Molly Rose Singer-Kingsmith b 23 July 1996); *Career* assoc dir of lectures and seminars ICA 1980–83, researcher Voices (Channel 4) 1983–84, programme consIt for David Puttnam at Enigma Film and TV 1984–85, literature offr SE Arts 1985–86, co-fndr and co-dir Performing Arts Labs charity 1987–96; presenter six films Labours of Eve (BBC) 1995; chair Literature Ctee Brighton Festival 1988–93, memb Bd SE Arts Bd 2000–02; *Books* novels: To Still the Child (1992), To Have and to Hold (1993), What She Wanted (1996), My Mother's Daughter (1998); children's fiction: Feather Boy (2002, Blue Peter Book of the Year 2002, BBC dramatisation 2004 (winner BAFTA Best Drama), Feather Boy the Musical (written jtly) 2006), Doll (2003, shortlisted Booktrust Teenage Prize), The Innocent's Story (2005), GemX (2006), Knight Crew (2009, commissioned as opera (Glyndebourne) 2010 (libretto written with Julian Philips as composer)), The Flask (2012), Island (with Chris Riddell as illustrator, 2015); non-fiction: The Tiny Book of Time (with Kim Pickin, 1999), The Little Book of the Millenium (with Jackie Singer, 1999); drama: Heartland (2011, collaboration with Scarabeus Aerial Theatre and Candoco Dance Co), Island (NT) 2012; *Style—* Ms Nicky Singer; ✉ c/o Conville and Walsh, Haymarket House, 28–29 Haymarket, London SW1Y 4SP

SINGH, Karamjit Sukhminder; CBE (2000); s of Tara Singh (d 1986), of Punjab, India, and Chanan, *née* Kaur (d 2001); *b* 11 March 1950; *Educ* Univ of Warwick (MA); *m* 1972, Jaswir Kaur (d 2014), da of Malkit Singh; 2 s; *Career* res assoc Industrial Rels Res Unit Univ of Warwick 1971–75, caseworker Leicester Community Rels Cncl 1975–78, sr exec offr Cmmn for Racial Equality 1978–82, princ offr W Midlands CC 1982–84, asst co clerk Leics CC 1984–87, memb Police Complaints Authy (England and Wales) 1987–90 and 1991–94, memb Parole Bd for England and Wales 1994–97, memb Criminal Cases Review Cmmn 1997–2006, memb Data Protection Tbnl 1997–2003, cmmr Electoral Cmmn 2001–10, memb QC Selection Panel for England and Wales 2005–11, NI Judicial Appts Ombudsman 2006–, chm Coventry and Warks NHS Partnership Tst 2006–10, social fund cmmr for GB 2009–13, social fund cmmr for NI 2009–; pt/t Civil Serv cmmr 1996–2000; memb: Area Manpower Bd for Coventry and Warks 1984–87, Industrial Tbnls Panel for England and Wales 1986–96, W Midlands Police Authy 1994–96, Complaints Audit Ctee Immigration and Nationality Dept 1994–97, Judicial Studies Bd 1994–99, Regulatory Decisions Ctee FSA 2002–06; non-exec dir Coventry HA 1996–2001; hon memb Working Gp Justice 1993–94; hon tstee Citizenship Fndn 1993–2000; tstee: Lloyds TSB Fndn for England and Wales 2001–06, Br Lung Fndn 2006–09, Joseph Rowntree Fndn 2014–; govr Coventry Univ 1994–99; Harkness Fellowship 1990–91; *Recreations* family, reading, charity work in India; *Clubs* Reform; *Style—* Karamjit Singh, Esq, CBE; ✉ Office of the Social Fund Commission, 2nd Floor, James House, 2–4 Cromac Avenue, Gasworks Business Park, Belfast BT7 2JA (☎ 02890 819827, e-mail sfc@osfcni.org.uk)

SINGH, HE Laleshwar Kumar Narayan; s of late Mr and Mrs Narayan, of Windsor Forest, Guyana; *b* 2 April 1941; *Educ* Windsor Forest Govt Sch, Indian Educn Tst Coll, Clerk to the Justices; *m* 10 Sept 1971, Latchmin, *née* Ramrattan; 2 c (Ashwindra b 22 Nov 1976, Vashti b 17 Oct 1987); *Career* Guyanese diplomat; migrated to Britain 1961; clerk to the justices, Inner London Magistrates' Courts 1971–93, high cmmr to UK 1993–2015 (concurrently non-resident ambass to the Netherlands, France, Russian Fedn, Czech Republic and the Holy See); dean of the Cwlth, dean of Caribbean High Cmmrs, dep to the Doyen of the Diplomatic Corps; Cacique's Crown of Honour Guyana Nat Award; *Style—* HE Mr Laleshwar Singh; ✉ Guyana High Commission, 3 Palace Court, Bayswater Road, London W2 4LP (☎ 020 7229 7684, fax 020 7727 9809, e-mail guyanahc1@btconnect.com)

SINGH, Dr Simon Lehna; MBE; s of Mengha Singh, and Sawarn, *née* Kaur; *b* 19 September 1964, Wellington, Somerset; *Educ* Imperial Coll London (BSc), Univ of Cambridge (PhD); *m* Anita Anand; 1 s (Hari); *Career* TV producer and dir 1991–96, writer and broadcaster 1997–; *Books* Fermat's Last Theorem (1997), The Code Book (1999), Big Bang (2004), Trick or Treatment? (2008), The Simpsons and Their Mathematical Secrets (2013); *Style—* Dr Simon Singh, MBE; ✉ c/o Patrick Walsh, Conville and Walsh Ltd, 2 Ganton Street, London W1F 7QL (☎ 020 7287 3030, e-mail patrick@convilleandwalsh.com)

SINGH OF WIMBLEDON, Baron (Life Peer UK 2011), of Wimbledon in the London Borough of Merton; Indarjit Singh; CBE (2009, OBE 1996), JP (Wimbledon 1984); *Educ* MBA; *Career* journalist and broadcaster; hon dir Network of Sikh Orgns UK, hon ed Sikh Messenger; fndr memb and former co-chair Interfaith Network UK, chair Sikh Cncl for Interfaith Rels, tstee World Congress of Faiths; memb: Religious Advsy Cncl UN Assoc, Inner Cities Religious Advsy Cncl DETR, Gene Therapy Advsy Ctee, Central Religious Advsy Ctee BBC and Independent Broadcasting Authy; Home Office consIt on the pastoral care of Sikhs in penal estabs 1976–; former memb: Home Sec's Advsy Cncl on Race Rels, Bd of Visitors Brixton Prison 1981–84, Med Ethics Ctee BMA 1993–98; frequent lectr on race rels at maj univs and other instns in UK and abroad; World Congress of Faiths Sir Francis Younghusband Meml Lecture 1990; frequent contrib: The Times, The Independent, and other newspapers and magazines in UK and abroad, Pause for Thought (BBC World Serv), Thought for the Day (BBC Radio 4); recipient: UK Templeton Prize (for furtherance of spiritual and ethical understanding) 1989, Interfaith Medallion (for servs to religious broadcasting) 1991, included in The Independent's Good List 2006; Hon LLD Univ of Leicester, Hon DLit Univ of Coventry; MComm, CEng, MIMinE; *Style—* The Lord Singh of Wimbledon, CBE, JP; ✉ Network of Sikh Organisations UK, 43 Dorset Road, Merton Park, London SW19 3EZ (☎ 020 8540 4148); House of Lords, London SW1A 0PW

SINGLETON, (Richard John) Basil; s of Richard Carl Thomas Singleton (d 2002), of Crumlin, Co Antrim, and Marion Frances, *née* Campbell (d 1981); *b* 25 April 1935; *Educ* Foyle Coll Londonderry, Campbell Coll Belfast, Hong Kong Univ; *m* 14 Sept 1957, Florence Elizabeth, da of Albert McRoberts, of Dunmurry, Co Antrim (d 1981); 1 s (Richard David b 1961 d 1975), 1 da (Wendy Marion Jane b 1964); *Career* RA 1953–55; Ulster TV Ltd: mktg exec 1959–64, mktg mangr 1965–73; md AV Browne Advertising Ltd 1973–82, chm and chief exec Basil Singleton Ltd 1982–2010; pres Publicity Assoc of NI 2007–16 (chm 1969–70); memb Belfast Jr C of C 1961–75; memb Ulster Branch Irish Hockey Union 1976–88, pres NI Civil Serv Hockey Club 1973–78; pres Old Campbellian Soc 1999; MCIM, MCIPR; *Recreations* hockey, tennis; *Clubs* Ulster Reform; *Style—* Basil Singleton, Esq; ✉ 72 Circular Road, Belfast, County Antrim BT4 2GD (☎ 028 9076 8330)

SINGLETON, Sir Roger; kt (2006), CBE (1997); s of Malcolm Singleton (ka 1944), and late Ethel, *née* Drew; *b* 6 November 1942; *Educ* City GS Sheffield, Univ of Durham (MA), Univ of Bath (MSc), Univ of London (Dip Soc Studies), Univ of Leeds (CertEd); *m* 30 July 1966, Ann, da of late Lawrence Edmond Hasler; 2 da (Jane b 1968, Katharine b 1969); *Career* various appts in care and educn of deprived and delinquent young people 1961–71, professional advsr to Children's Regnl Planning Ctee 1971–74, chief exec Barnardo's 1984–2006 (dep dir 1974–84), consIt and govt advsr 2006–, Govt's chief advsr on the safety of children 2009–10; chm Ind Safeguarding Authy 2007–12, chair Panel on the Indpendence of the Voluntary Sector, memb Home Office Independent Family Returns Panel; dir Safeguardingfirst Ltd; accredited mediator; assoc prof Univ of New Bucks; contribs to various jls; chm Perennial (Gardeners' Royal Benevolent Soc); md Lumos Fndn 2014–, pres Friends of St Andrew's Shalford; memb various Govt ctees and inquiries; Hon LLD Univ of Bath; CCMI 1994, FRSA 1991; Keeping our School Safe (209), Drawing the Line (2009), Physical punishment: improving consistency and protection (2010); *Recreations* timber framed buildings; *Clubs* Reform; *Style—* Sir Roger Singleton, CBE; ✉ e-mail rogersingleton42@gmail.com

SINGLETON, Her Hon Judge Sarah Louise; QC (2006); da of James Singleton, and Beryl Singleton; *b* 9 March 1962; *Educ* Roedean, Lancaster Girls' GS, Hertford Coll Oxford, Inns of Ct Sch of Law; *m*; 1 da, 1 s; *Career* called to the Bar 1983; practised from 28 St John St Chambers (now St John's Buildings) Manchester until 2012, asst recorder 1999, recorder 2000, dep judge of the High Court 2011, circuit judge (Northern Circuit) 2012; designated family judge for Lancs 2016–; chllr Dio of Sheffield 2013–; *Style—* HHJ Singleton, QC; ✉ Sessions House, Lancaster Road, Preston, Lancashire PR1 2PD

SINHA, Indra; s of Capt Bhagvati Prasad Sinha, of Bombay and Goa, India, and Irene Elizabeth, *née* Phare (d 1986); *b* 10 February 1950; *Educ* Mayo Coll Ajmer Rajasthan India, Oakham Sch, Pembroke Coll Cambridge (BA); *m* 9 Sept 1978, Viktoria Jane Yvette, da of Maj Arthur Henry Lionel Pilkington; 1 da (Tara Pauline Elizabeth b 6 Oct 1981), 2 s (Dan Alexander Iqbal b 28 Aug 1984, Samuel Barnaby Prem b 14 May 1988); *Career* writer; advtg copywriter: The Creative Business 1976–79, Ogilvy & Mather 1980–83; with Collett Dickenson Pearce & Partners 1984–95, chm and creative ptnr Chaos

S

Communication Ltd 1995; memb D&AD; *Books* Kama Sutra (new trans, 1980), Tantra (1994), The CyberGypsies (1998); *Recreations* travel, reading, cybertravel, folk music, butterflies; *Clubs* Sussex CCC, Cassoulet; *Style*— Indra Sinha, Esq

SINNETT, Prof Dudley Hugh; s of Hugh Sinnett, and Ruth, *née* Matthews; *Educ* Dynevor GS Swansea, Charing Cross Med Sch London, Univ of London (MS); *m* 27 Sept 1975, Jill Christine, *née* Morris-Jackson; 1 s (Tim), 1 da (Katie); *Career* sr surgical registrar Bart's London 1980–84, conslt surgn and hon sr lectr Royal Marsden Hosp London 1984–89, conslt breast surgn Charing Cross Hosp London 1989–2009, prof of breast surgery Imperial Coll London 2005; assoc postgrad dean for surgery London Deanery; examiner Univ of London, memb Ct of Examiners RCS (also memb Intercollegiate Bd of Examiners for FRCS); jt author of papers on magmnt of breast disease in learned jls; supporter: Royal Med Benevolent Fund, Haven Tst for Women with Breast Cancer, Women's Nat Cancer Control Campaign, Breast Cancer Care Med Advsy Panel; Freeman City of London, Liveryman Worshipful Soc of Apothecaries; FRCS 1976; *Recreations* watching sport, playing golf, reading, travel; *Clubs* MCC, RAC, Walton Heath Golf; *Style*— Prof Dudley Sinnett; ☎ 020 8642 1551, e-mail d.sinnett@imperial.ac.uk

SINNOTT, Kevin Fergus; s of Myles Vincent Sinnott (d 1974), of Wales, and Honora, *née* Burke (d 1993); *b* 4 December 1947; *Educ* St Roberts Aberkenfig, Cardiff Coll of Art (fndn course), Glos Coll of Art and Design (DipAD), RCA (MA); *m* 30 Aug 1969, Susan Margaret, da of Lawrence Hadyn Forward, and Rita, *née* Terry; 3 s (Matthew b 22 Aug 1971, Gavin b 6 June 1975, Thomas b 4 March 1983), 1 da (Lucy Anne b 24 Aug 1984); *Career* artist; visiting lectr: Ruskin Sch of Drawing Oxford 1975–76, Canterbury Coll of Art 1981–88; pt/t teacher St Martin's Sch of Art London 1981–93; *Solo Exhibitions* House Gallery London 1980 and 1983, Ikon Gallery Birmingham 1980, Riverside Studios London 1981, St Paul's Gallery Leeds 1981, Blond Fine Art London 1982 and 1984, Chapter Arts Centre Cardiff 1984, Bernard Jacobson Gallery (London 1986, London and NY 1987, NY 1988, London 1990), Jan Turner Gallery LA 1987, Roger Ramsay Gallery Chicago 1988, Anne Berthoud Gallery London 1990, Flowers East London 1992, 1994 and 1996, Gallery Henrik Kampmann Copenhagen 1996, Flowers East London 1998, Martin Tinney Gallery 1999, 2001, 2003, 2005, 2007, 2009, 2011 and 2013, Caldwell/Snyder NY 2000, Caldwell/Snyder San Francisco 2001 and 2002, Depot Haus Grafenwald Germany 2004 and 2006, Flowers Gallery London 2012 and 2014; *Group Exhibitions* incl: Whitechapel Open London 1978 and 1980, John Moores Liverpool 1978, 1980 and 1991, Ruskin Sch of Art Oxford 1981, Blond Fine Art London 1982–85, LA Louver Gallery 1986, Bernard Jacobson Gallery London 1986, Lefevre Gallery London 1988, The Contemporary Arts Centre Cincinnati 1988, Oriel Mostyn 2002; *Work in Public Collections* Br Cncl, Arts Cncl of GB, IOM Arts Cncl, RCA, The Whitworth Manchester, Br Museum, Wolverhampton City Art Gallery, Metropolitan Museum of Art NY, Deutsche Bank AG London, Unilever, Contemporary Art Soc of Wales, The Nat Museum of Wales, Univ Catholic Chaplaincy Oxford, Ashmolean Museum Oxford, Nat Library of Wales Aberystwyth; *Publications* Turkish Bath Paintings (1992), Paintings From Wales (1996), Hectic Days (1998), Behind the Canvas (autobiography, 2007); *Clubs* Chelsea Arts, Ogmore; *Style*— Kevin Sinnott, Esq; ✉ Ty'r Santes Fair, Pont-y-Rhyl, Bridgend, Mid Glamorgan CF32 8LJ (☎ 01656 871 854, e-mail mail@kevinsinnott.co.uk)

SINYOR, Joe; s of Samuel Joseph Sinyor, and Claire, *née* Mizrahi; *b* 16 August 1957; *Educ* Manchester Grammar, Jesus Coll Cambridge (BA), London Business Sch (MBA); *m* 22 Dec 1987, Pamela Caroline Neild, da of Michael Collis; 2 s (Joshua Samuel Michael b 17 Nov 1988, Benjamin Jonathan b 30 June 1990), 1 da (Jessica Claire Rachel b 1 Jan 1994); *Career* slr Nabarro Nathanson London 1979–81, corp fin exec J Henry Schroder Wagg 1984–85, sr engagement mangr McKinsey & Co Inc 1985–90, gp chief exec Pepe Group plc 1990–93, md Dillons The Bookstore 1994–98, md Sony United Kingdom Ltd 1998–2000, chief exec (newspapers) Trinity Mirror plc 2000–03, md Terra Firma Capital Partners 2003–06, md Strategic Value Partners LLP 2007–11, operating ptnr Actis 2011–14; non-exec dir Ideal Standard Int 2014–15, chm Global Garden Products 2014–; memb: Cncl Booksellers' Assoc 1995–98, Bd Channel Four TV Corp 1998–2004; *Recreations* family, opera, walking, skiing; *Style*— Joe Sinyor, Esq; ✉ 70 Sheldon Avenue, London N6 4ND

SISSONS, Dr Clifford Ernest; s of George Robert Percival Sissons (d 1964), and Elsie Emma, *née* Evans (d 1993); *b* 26 January 1934; *Educ* Liverpool Inst HS for Boys, Univ of Liverpool Med Sch (MB ChB); *m* 1, 28 Dec 1956 (m dis 1997), Mary Beryl, da of James Davies (d 1941); 2 s (Mark Christopher John, Guy Richard James), 1 da (Amanda Jane Elizabeth); m 2, 29 Nov 1997, Gweneth Dianne, da of Roy Williams; *Career* Nat Serv Capt RAMC 1959–61; house physician and house surgn Liverpool Stanley Hosp 1958–59; med registrar: Birkenhead Gen Hosp 1962–67, Professorial Med Unit Liverpool Royal Infirmary 1967–69; sr med registrar David Lewis Northern and Sefton Gen Hosp Liverpool 1969–72, conslt physician Wrexham War Memorial and Maelor Hosps 1972–98, conslt physician Spire Yale Hosp, Wrexham and Grosvenor Nuffield Hosp 1974–2014; memb Cncl RCP 1985–87 (regnl advsr 1982–87), examiner in med RCP (London) 1991–2014; memb: BMA, Royal Soc of Med, HEART UK, Welsh Cardiovascular Soc, Soc of Physicians in Wales; FRCP 1977 (MRCP 1966); *Recreations* languages, travel, reading, painting; *Style*— Dr Clifford Sissons; ✉ Spire Yale Hospital, Croesnewyd Road, Wrexham LL13 7YP (☎ 01978 291306, fax 01978 291397)

SISSONS, (Thomas) Michael Beswick; s of Capt T E B Sissons (ka 1940), and Marjorie, *née* Shepherd; *b* 13 October 1934; *Educ* Winchester, Exeter Coll Oxford (MA); *m* 1, 1960 (m dis), Nicola Ann, *née* Fowler; 1 s, 1 da; m 2, 1974 (m dis), Ilze, *née* Kadegis; 2 da; m 3, 1992, Serena, *née* Palmer; *Career* Nat Serv 2 Lt 13/18 Royal Hussars 1953–55; lectr in history Tulane Univ New Orleans 1958–59, AD Peters & Co Ltd Literary Agency 1959–88 (dir 1965, chm and md 1973–88), jt chm The Peters Fraser & Dunlop Group (PFD) Ltd 1994–99 (jt chm and md 1988–94, sr conslt 1999–), dir London Broadcasting Co 1973–75; pres Assoc of Authors' Agents 1978–81, memb Ctee MCC 1984–87 and 1993–2000 (chm Arts and Library Sub-Ctee 1985–93, chm Mktg and Public Affrs Sub-ctee 1995–2000); memb Bd: Groucho Club plc 1985–2001, BFSS 1994–95, Countryside Movement 1995–97; chm The Cardinall's Musick 2006–11; *Books* Age of Austerity (ed with Philip French, 1963, 2 edn 1986), A Countryside For All (ed, 2001); *Recreations* gardening, cricket, music, football; *Clubs* Groucho, MCC, Boodle's; *Style*— Michael Sissons, Esq; ✉ Raceyard House, Fawler Road, Kingston Lisle, Wantage OX12 9QH (☎ 01367 820581/724); PFD, Drury House, 34–43 Russell Street, London WC2B 5HA (☎ 020 7344 1022, fax 020 7836 9539, e-mail msissons@pfd.co.uk)

SISSONS, Sir (John Gerald) Patrick; kt (2012); s of Gerald William Sissons (d 1966), and Georgina Margaret, *née* Cockin (d 1960); *b* 28 June 1945; *Educ* Felsted, St Mary's Hosp Med Sch London (MB BS, MD); *m* April 1971 (m dis 1985), Jennifer Anne Scovell; 2 da (Sarah b 1973, Rebecca b 1974); *Career* registrar and hon lectr Royal Postgrad Med Sch London 1973–76, NIH Fogarty fell and asst memb Scripps Clinic San Diego 1977–80, reader in infectious diseases Royal Postgrad Med Sch 1987 (Wellcome sr lectr 1980–86); Univ of Cambridge: prof of med 1988–2005, Regius prof of physic 2005–12; vice-pres Acad of Medical Sciences 2010–; author of pubns on pathogenesis of virus infections; fell Darwin Coll Cambridge; FRCP, FRCPath, FMedSci 1998; *Recreations* travel; *Style*— Sir Patrick Sissons; ✉ University of Cambridge School of Clinical Medicine, Hills Road, Cambridge CB2 2SP (☎ 01223 336938)

SISSONS, Peter George; s of George Robert Percival Sissons (d 1964), and Elsie Emma, *née* Evans (d 1993); *b* 17 July 1942; *Educ* Liverpool Inst HS for Boys, Univ Coll Oxford (MA); *m* Sylvia; 2 s (Michael Peter, Jonathan Richard), 1 da (Kate Victoria); *Career* TV journalist and presenter; ITN 1964–89: gen trainee then script writer, gen reporter, foreign correspondent, news ed, industry correspondent, industry ed, presenter News at One 1978–82, presenter Channel Four News 1982–89; chm Question Time BBC TV 1989–93, presenter 6 O'Clock News BBC 1989–93, presenter 9 O'Clock News BBC 1994–2000, presenter 10 O'Clock News BBC 2000–03, presenter BBC News 24 (latterly BBC News) 2003–09, presenter Breakfast with Frost 2003–05; Broadcasting Press Guild's Best Front of Camera Performer 1984, RTS's Judges Award 1989, TRIC Newscaster of the Year 2001; hon fell Liverpool John Moores Univ 1997 (Roscoe lectr 2008); vice-pres Liverpool Sch of Tropical Med 2013; Hon LLD Univ of Liverpool 2002; *Books* When One Door Closes (autobiography, 2011); *Recreations* relaxing; *Style*— Peter Sissons, Esq; ✉ c/o Agent Knight Ayton Management (☎ 020 3795 1806)

SITKOVETSKY, Dmitry; s of Julian Sitkovetsky, violinist, and Bella Davidovich, pianist; *b* 1954, Baku, USSR; *Educ* Moscow Conservatoire, Juilliard Sch NY; *Career* violinist and conductor; winner Kreisler competition Vienna 1979; fndr and music dir New European Strings 1990–, princ conductor Ulster Orchestra 1996–2001 (now conductor laureate), music dir Greenboro Symphony Orch 2003–, princ guest conductor Russian State Orch 2003–; artist-in-residence: Orchestre de Castilla and Leon 2006, Bodensee Festival 2007; artistic dir: Korsholm Festival Finland 1983–93, Umea Festival Sweden 1991–93, Seattle International Music Festival 1993–; a founding artist Tuscan Sun Festival 2003–; guest conductor: Stuttgart Chamber Orch, MDR Leipzig Orch, chamber ensemble of St Martin in the Fields (tour of Germany) 1994, Vienna Virtuosi, Academia di Santa Cecilia, New York Chamber Symphony, Detroitt Symphony, BBC Philharmonic; worked with numerous major conductors incl Claudio Abbado, Vladimir Ashkenazy, Andrew Davis, Sir Colin Davis, Christoph Dohnányi, Sir Neville Marriner, Gennadi Rozhdestvensky, Wolfgang Sawallisch, Michael Tilson Thomas, Mariss Jansons, Yuri Temirkanov and Kurt Masur; given recital performances at various international venues and festivals incl Salzburg, Lucerne, Edinburgh, Ravinia and Mostly Mozart, BBC Proms (première of Casken's Violin Concerto) 1995; was the first postwar Russian emigré musician to return to Moscow at the official invitation in 1988; subject of South Bank Show 1993; *Recordings* incl: Bach (sonatas and partitas for solo violin), Haydn, Mozart, Beethoven, Mendelssohn, Brahms, Elgar, Bartók, Prokofiev and Shostakovich violin concerti; *Publications* author of over 20 transcriptions incl: Bach Goldberg Variations for String Trio and Goldberg Variations for String Orch, Dohnányi Serenade, Shostakovich String Symphony Opus 73 for String Orch, Tchaikovsky String Symphony Opus 30; *Style*— Dmitry Sitkovetsky, Esq; ✉ Greensboro Symphony Orchestra, 200 North Davie Street, Greensboro, NC 27401, USA

SIXSMITH, (George) Martin; s of George Francis Sixsmith, of Walton, Cheshire, and Joyce Lythgoe, *née* Sutton; *b* 24 September 1954; *Educ* Manchester Grammar, Sorbonne, New Coll Oxford (open scholar, MA), Leningrad Polytechnical Inst, Harvard Univ, St Antony's Coll Oxford; *m* 4 Sept 1976, Mary Winifred, da of Francis Cooney; 2 da (Joanna Mary b 19 Dec 1979, Rebecca Helen b 11 Oct 1988), 2 s (Patrick Martin b 7 Jan 1983, Daniel Thomas b 30 Oct 1985); *Career* Harkness fell and tutor in slavics Harvard Univ 1977–79; BBC: trainee journalist London 1980–82, Western Europe reporter Brussels 1982–85 then Geneva 1985–86, Eastern Europe corr Warsaw 1986–88, Moscow corr TV News 1988–91, Washington corr TV News 1991–95, Moscow corr TV News 1995–97; dir of information DSS until 1999, dir of communications Marconi plc 1999–2001, dir of communications DTLR 2001–02, freelance journalist and author 2002–; memb Young Königswinter Confs 1986; *Books* Vladislav Xodasevic: k 40-letiju so dnja smerti (critical biog of Vladislav Khodasevich the Russian poet, 1979), The Harvard Guide to France (1980), Jobit's Journal: A history of the French campaigns in Ireland (trans, 1982), Moscow Coup: the death of the Soviet system (1991), Spin, a novel (2004), I Heard Lenin Laugh (2006), The Litvinenko File: the true story of a death foretold (2007), The Lost Child of Philomena Lee: A Mother, Her Son and a Fifty Year Search (2009), Putin's Oil: The Yukos Affair and the Struggle for Russia (2010), Russia: a 1,000 Year Chronicle of the Wild East (2011); *Recreations* music, literature, psychology, Liverpool FC; *Style*— Martin Sixsmith, Esq

SKAN, Martin; s of Reginald Norman Skan (d 1985), of Worcester, and Millicent May, *née* Vaughan (d 1977); *b* 28 December 1934; *Educ* Haileybury, Harvard Sch Calif (exchange scholar); *m* 1, 1970 (m dis 1988), Sally Elizabeth Margaret, da of John Eric Wade; 2 da (Lara Julie b 1971, Tilly Matina b 1975); m 2, 1989, Brigitte Berta, da of late Erwin Heinrich Joos, of Winterthur, Switzerland; *Career* cmmnd Dorset Regt 1955–57; British Market Research Bureau Ltd (subsid of JWT Advertising) 1957–58, Kinloch (PM) Ltd 1958–89; dir: Skan Taylor & Co Ltd 1959–65, J A & P Holland Ltd 1962–65, Parkinsons (Doncaster) Ltd 1962–65, Holland Distributors Ltd 1962–65, Harper Paper Group (and subsid cos) 1962–65, LMS (Consultants) Ltd 1986–91; chm Chewton Glen (Hotels) Ltd 1966–2005 (pres 2005–); for Chewton Glen Hotel: Egon Ronay Hotel of The Year 1976, Michelin Star 1981–2005, The Hoteliers' Hotelier The Observer 1988, Times Hotel Restaurant of the Year 1990, Tourism Catey award 1990, American Express Country Hotel of the Year 1991 and 1992, 5 Red Stars (AA and RAC) 1993–2009, Condé Nast Traveller Magazine Best Resort Hotel in Britain 1998, Booker Award of Excellence for Best British Hotel 1998, Gourmet Magazine Best Country House Hotel in the World 2000, Best Small Hotel (under 60 rooms) World Gallivanters Guide 2003, Best Hotel Spa in Europe Gala Magazine Germany 2003, Best Hotel (under 100 rooms) Worldwide Gallivanters Guide 2004, Best Hotel in Britain Conde Nast USA 2006; Personality of the Year 1990, Master Innholder 1991–2005, Hotelier of the Year 1991, Director of the Year 1999 (PricewaterhouseCoopers), AA/AXA Lifetime Hospitality Award 2006–07; memb: Relais Château 1972–2009, Leading Hotels of the World 1972–99; fndr memb The Walpole Ctee 1991–2005; hon memb Académie Culinaire de France; Freeman City of London 1991; *Recreations* tennis, golf, cycling, skiing; *Clubs* Ascona Golf (Switzerland); *Style*— Martin Skan, Esq; ✉ Honeysuckle Cottage, Bramshaw, Hampshire SO43 7JH (☎ 023 8081 2149, e-mail mskan@skanenterprises.com)

SKELDING, Barry Howard; s of late Denis Howard Skelding, and Stella, *née* Scott Elliott; *b* 2 January 1945; *Educ* The Stationers' Co's Sch; *m* 27 Aug 1977, Margaret Marion, da of Gordon David Carnegie (d 1969); 2 da (Katie b 1981, Sarah b 1983); *Career* admitted slr 1970; assoc ptnr Gamlens 1970, gp property slr EMI Ltd 1970–80, ptnr Rowe and Maw 1980–92, assoc Jaques & Lewis and Eversheds 1993–95, ptnr Park Nelson 1995–2004, conslt Lester Aldridge LLP (incorporating Park Nelson) 2004–05 and 2007–08; memb Law Soc 1970; Freeman City of London 1996; *Recreations* lawn tennis, squash rackets, music, golf; *Clubs* Cumberland LT, Radlett LT and SRC, Veterans' Squash Club of GB, Veterans' Lawn Tennis Club of GB, Select; *Style*— Barry H Skelding, Esq; ✉ 2 Folly Pathway, Radlett, Hertfordshire WD7 8DS

SKELLERN, Peter; s of John Skellern, of Lancs (d 2007), and Margaret, *née* Spencer (d 1987); *b* 14 March 1947; *Educ* The Derby Sch Bury, Guildhall Sch of Music and Drama (AGSM); *m* 1970, Diana Elizabeth, da of Edward Dampier Seare (d 1997); 1 s (Timothy Seare b 29 Nov 1971), 1 da (Katherine Daisy b 22 June 1974); *Career* pianist, singer, composer; trombonist Nat Youth Brass Band 1963, memb March Hare pop gp 1968–70; wrote song You're a Lady (reached No 1 in 6 countries) 1972, writer for Stop the Week (BBC Radio 4) 1970s, made autobiographical TV series 1981, scriptwriter, composer and actor Happy Endings TV series of mini-musicals 1982, co-wrote (with Richard Stilgoe) and appeared in Who Plays Wins (Vaudeville) 1985 and toured with their two-man show every year until 2001; *Recordings* 15 albums incl: Astaire (1980), Oasis (with Julian Lloyd Webber and Mary Hopkin, 1982); *Publications* Trolls (musical for children, 1990, published by J

B Cramer), Six Simple Carols for SATB Choirs (published by Novello & Co, 1998); other anthems and sacred music published by Royal Sch of Church Music for whom he holds choral workshops throughout the country; *Recreations* painting, golf; *Clubs* MCC, Lord's Taverners, Soc for All Artists, Carlyon Bay Golf; *Style*— Peter Skellern, Esq

SKELLETT, Dr Colin Frank; OBE (2012); *b* 13 June 1945; *Educ* City Univ, North Staffordshire Poly (MSc); *Career* various operational mgmnt positions in water and sewerage industry until 1986; Wessex Water (previously Wessex Water Authy): div mangr 1986–88, gp md 1988–94, gp chief exec 1995–99, chm 1996–; chm Jarvis plc 2000–02, vice-chm Azurix 1999–2001, dir YTL Utilities UK 2002–; non-exec chm European Connoisseurs Travel 2006–, jt chm GWE Business West 2008–13, chm Future Bath Plus 2008–12, chair West of England Enterprise Partnership 2011–16, chair Bath Hotel and Spa Ltd 2013–; tstee Wateraid 1995–2003; memb Soc of Merchant Venturers; Hon DEng UWE 2014; fell Assoc of Churchill Fells 1983; CChem, FRSC, FCIWEM; *Recreations* walking, theatre, music; *Style*— Dr Colin Skellett, OBE; ✉ Wessex Water, Claverton Down, Bath BA2 7WW (☎ 01225 526000, fax 01225 528000)

SKELMERSDALE, 7 Baron (UK 1828); Roger Bootle-Wilbraham; s of Brig 6 Baron Skelmersdale, DSO, MC (d 1973), and Ann (d 1974), da of Percy Quilter and gda of Sir Cuthbert Quilter, 1 Bt; *b* 2 April 1945, Cove, Farnborough, Hants; *Educ* Eton, Lord Wandsworth Coll, Somerset Coll of Agriculture, Hadlow Coll; *m* 1972, Christine, da of Roy Morgan, of Hamel Evercreech, Somerset; 1 da (Hon Carolyn Ann (Dr Staton) b 1974), 1 s (Hon Andrew b 1977); *Heir* s, Hon Andrew Bootle-Wilbraham; *Career* horticulturist; dir Broadleigh Nurseries 1991– (md 1973–81); pres Somerset Tst for Nature Conservation 1980–, pres Br Naturalists Assoc 1980–95; Lord-in-Waiting to HM The Queen 1981–86; Parly under sec of state: DOE 1986–87, DHSS 1987–88, DSS 1988–89, NI Office (DHSS and Agric) 1989–90; dep chm of Ctees House of Lords 1991–95, dep speaker House of Lords 1995–2003, elected to sit in House of Lords 1999, oppn whip 2003–05, spokesman on work and pensions 2005–10, dep chm of ctees 2010–15; parly conslt 1991–96; memb Jt Ctee on Statutory Instruments 1991–2003, memb Sub-Ctee B (Euro energy, industry and tport) 1996–2003, memb House of Lords Procedure Ctee 1997–2000, memb Communications Ctee 2010–14; pres Taunton Dene Cons Assoc 2011–; vice-chm co-En-Co (Cncl for Environmental Conservation) 1979–81, pres Somerset Opera 1980–, chm The Stroke Assoc 1993–2004, pres Somerset Contract Bridge Assoc 2008–; govr Castle Sch Taunton 1992–96; memb RHS, tstee Hestercombe Gardens Tst 2001–08; FLS; *Recreations* gardening, reading, bridge, walking; *Style*— The Rt Hon Lord Skelmersdale; ✉ House of Lords, London SW1A 0PW (☎ 020 7219 3224, fax 020 7630 0088, e-mail skelmersdaler@parliament.uk)

SKELTON, Nick David; OBE (2012); s of David Frank Skelton, of Odnull Farm, Wase Lane, Berkswell, and Norma, *née* Brindley; *Children* 2 s (Daniel b 9 April 1985, Harry b 20 Sept 1989); *Career* show jumper; ridden 100 World Cup classes and 116 Nations Cup teams; jr Euro champion 1975, Br champion 1981, winner 10 classes Wembley 1981, Gold medal (team jumping) Olympic Games 2012, 3 team Gold medals Euro Championships (individual Bronze), 4 team Silver medals and 4 team Bronze medals World Championships (individual Bronze), winner Hickstead Derby 3 times (runner up twice), Gold medal (team jumping) Olympic Games 2016; Grand Prix wins: Dublin 4 times, NY twice, Aachen 3 times; GB high jump record Olympia 1975; *Recreations* skiing, farming; *Style*— Nick Skelton, Esq, OBE; ✉ c/o British Show Jumping Association, British Equestrian Centre, Stoneleigh, Kenilworth, Warwickshire CV8 2LR

SKEMPTON, Maj-Gen Keith; CBE, DL (Cheshire 2006); s of Dr Ivor Skempton (decd), and Leslie Skempton (decd), of Little Sutton, Cheshire; *b* 22 February 1949, Chester; *Educ* Birkenhead Sch, Liverpool Coll of Building, Army Staff Coll Camberley; *m* 1971, Sue, *née* Lawrence; 1 da (Kyra b 1979); *Career* cmmnd Cheshire Regt 1969; served UK, Europe, Middle East and Far East; COS HQ 33 Armoured Bde Germany 1982–83, mil asst to GOC NI 1986–88, CO 1 Bn Cheshire Regt 1988–91, Deputy COS 1 Armoured Div 1991–93, DACOS G4 Ops and Plans HQ Land Command 1993–96, COS Br Forces Cyprus 1996–98, Deputy COS Support HQ ARRC, Asst COS HQ AFSOUTH 2001–03; Col Cheshire Regt 1999–2006; business devpt dir Denis Ferranti Gp 2006–07, dir of ops Chester Cathedral 2007–08; conslt 2009– (for Capita Symonds 2010–13), defence sector lead Capita Property and Infrastructure Ltd 2013–; pres SSAFA Cheshire 2011–, tstee Cheshire Military Museum Chester; Queen's Commendation for Valuable Service (Kosovo), twice mentioned in despatches; FCMI 2003–13; *Recreations* interest in most sports, motor vehicles, travel, architecture, walking, shooting, sailing, skiing; *Clubs* Army and Navy, Chester City, Cheshire Pitt; *Style*— Major General Keith Skempton, CBE, DL; ✉ RHQ The Mercian Regiment (Cheshire), The Castle, Chester (☎ 01244 327617, website www.skempton.info); Capita Defence (e-mail keith.skempton@capita.co.uk)

SKENE, Charles Pirie; OBE (1992); *b* 30 April 1935; *Educ* Loretto, Robert Gordon Univ (DBA); *m* 9 May 1964, Alison Jean Katherine Lamont; 2 da (Jennifer b 1966, Pamela b 1972), 1 s (Richard b 1967); *Career* gp chm and chief exec of The Skene Group of Companies; pres: Jr Chamber Aberdeen 1967, Aberdeen C of C 1983–85, Assoc of Scot Chambers of Commerce 1985–86; fndr Aberdeen Civic Soc 1968, nat sec Jr Chamber Scot 1970 (dir 1969); chm: NE Branch of Lorettonian Soc 1976–86, Royal Northern and Univ Club 1981–82, Industry Year Grampian Area 1986, Industry Matters Grampian Area 1987–89; dir Aberdeen and NE Soc for the Deaf 1973–97, assessor to Dean of Guild 1983–95, industry conslt Scot Educn Indust Ctee 1986–87, former memb Exec Ctee Scot Cncl Devpt and Industry; Robert Gordon Univ: govr 1985–96, visiting prof of entrepreneurship, endowed chair of entrepreneurship 2001, Centre of Enterprise renamed Charles P Skene Centre of Entrepreneurship 2002; memb: Economic Affrs Ctee SCUA 1986–97, Exec Ctee CBI (Scot) 1988–94, 1996–2002, 2004–10 and 2011–, Open Univ Enterprise in Higher Educn Advsy Ctee for Scot 1990–92; chm: RGIT Enterprise Mgmnt Ctee 1988–93, Scot Industrialists' Cncl Grampian Branch, Scotland Educn Ctee CBI 1993–94, Enterprise Gp CBI (Scot) 1994–96; donor of the annual Skene Aberdeen Int Youth Festival Award 1976–2000; initiator Skene Young Entrepreneurs Award Scotland 1987–2004; author of paper Educating Scotsmen and Women 1987; MSC Fit for Work Award, European Year of the Environment (conservation award, design award commendation), Queen's Award for Enterprise Promotion 2005; Hon DBA Robert Gordon Univ 2000; FRSA, FBIPP; *Style*— Charles P Skene, Esq, OBE; ✉ The Skene Group, 96 Rosemount Viaduct, Aberdeen AB25 1AX (☎ 01224 627171, fax 01224 626866)

SKENE, Prudence; CBE (2000); da of Robert Worboys Skene (d 1988), and Phyllis Monica, *née* Langley (d 1982); *b* 9 January 1944; *Educ* Francis Holland Sch, Open Univ (BA); *m* 12 Sept 1986, Brian Henry Wray (d 2002); 2 step c (Nicholas Wray, Jacqueline Plant); *Career* admin Granada Films 1967–69, tour mgmnt UK and Australia 1969–71, mangr Castle Opera 1972, dep admin Round House Chalk Farm 1973–75, admin rising to exec dir Ballet Rambert 1975–86, exec prodr English Shakespeare Co 1987–90, freelance conslt 1991–, dir The Arts Fndn 1993–98, advsy dir Performing Arts Labs 1998–99; non-exec dir Theatre Royal Bath Ltd 1998–2003, chm Rambert Dance Co 2000–09; Arts Cncl of England: chm Dance Advsy Panel 1992–96, ACE/Royal Opera House Monitoring Ctee 1994–96, chm Lottery Advsy Panel 1996–2000, memb Audit Ctee; chm Arvon Fndn 2001–05, chair Free Word 2010–14; chm Dancers' Resettlement Tst and vice-chm and tstee Dancers' Resettlement Fund 1988–92; non-exec dir RUH NHS Tst Bath 1999–2003; tstee: Cardiff Old Library Tst 1996–2000, Stephen Spender Tst (formerly Stephen Spender Meml Fund) 2000– (chair 2013–), Friends of the V&A 2004–10, NESTA 2006–07, Nureyev Fndn 2007–; memb Cncl of Mgmnt Theatrical Management Assoc 1984–96 (pres 1991–92, vice-pres and chm Fin Ctee 1985–89); FRSA 1992; *Publications* Pride of Place (ed, 2002); *Recreations* travel, reading, food; *Style*— Ms Prudence Skene, CBE; ✉ 19A Eccleston Street, London SW1W 9LX (☎ 020 7259 9174, e-mail prue.skene@gmail.com)

SKENE CATLING, Charlotte Merilyn; da of Patrick Skene Catling, and Diane Wheeler Nicholson; *b* London; *Educ* Univ of Westminster, Architectural Assoc; *m* 22 Sept 2016, Adam Lowe; *Career* architect; illustrator for various magazines and books New York 1991–93, Studio Axel Kufus Berlin 1993, Elz & Rothkegel Architeken Berlin 1993; 1994–2000: set designer, contrib to pubns incl Burlington Magazine, Telegraph Magazine and The New Yorker, illustrator and writer, collabs with Marc Quinn and Malcolm McLaren; conceived and dir Eco Lab plc (nuturition, fashion and cosmetics co) with Jeremy King and Chris Corbin 2000–01, architectural/brand identity Agent Provocateur (designed over 50 sites in the UK and overseas) 2001–08, co-fndr Skene Catling de la Peña Architects 2002–; set designer and film dir; ran postgrad architecture studio ADS3 RCA 2007–12, external examiner Univ of Greenwich 2013–16, lectr Postgrad Architecture Karlsruhe Inst of Technol (KIT) Germany; ambass London Sch of Architecture 2013–14; contrib: Sunday Telegraph, Burlington Magazine, Architectural Review, ARCH+ 2011–; fndr Biennial Architectural Film Festival London 2017–; memb: Architects Registration Bd 2014, RIBA 2014; *Awards* RIBA Award 2007, winner Private Category Wood Awards, shortlisted RIBA Stephen Lawrence Award 2007, winner Record Houses Award Architectural Record 2008, Best One-off House British Home Awards 2008, World Architectural Award 2008, Britain's Top Notch Architects Daily Telegraph 2008, Top 50 Young Architects in the World Wallpaper* Magazine's Design Directory 2008, Honourable Mention Barbara Cappochin Architecture Prize 2009, Int Design Awards (Architecture) US 2009, Perm Regional Prize for Arts and Culture Russia 2011, Best Film (InShadow) 4th Int Festival of Video Performance and Technol Lisbon 2012, shortlisted Best House World Architecture Festival 2015, Best Building AVDC Awards 2015, RIBA South Award 2015, Building of the Year RIBA South 2015, RIBA National Award 2015, RIBA House of the Year 2015 (former Manser Medal), shortlisted Woman Architect of the Year Architectural Review 2016, Debrett's 500 Most Influential 2016, Progress 1000 London's Most Influential People Evening Standard 2016; *Books* featured in: Home: Investing in Design (2008), Encyclopaedia of Contemporary Residential Design (2009), 100 Country Houses: New Rural Architecture (2009), Spacecraft II (2009), Arcadia (2009), Reuse Architecture (2011) and numerous pubns incl Vogue UK, Vogue US, Architectural Review, Independent Magazine, FT, Spaces, Newsweek International, Wallpaper* Magazine, Architectural Record, World of Interiors, Vogue Living; *Recreations* drifting through cities; *Clubs* 5 Hertford Street, Chelsea Arts, The Academy, The Union; *Style*— Ms Charlotte Skene Catling; ✉ Skene Catling de la Peña, 3/71 Elm Park Gardens, London SW10 9QE (☎ 020 7262 2806, e-mail admin@scdlp.net, www.scdlp.net)

SKIDELSKY, Baron (Life Peer UK 1991), of Tilton in the County of East Sussex; Robert Jacob Alexander Skidelsky; s of Boris J Skidelsky (d 1982), and Galia V, *née* Sapelkin (d 1987); *b* 25 April 1939; *Educ* Brighton Coll, Jesus Coll Oxford (MA, DPhil); *m* 2 Sept 1970, Augusta Mary Clarissa, da of John Humphrey Hope (d 1974); 2 s (Hon Edward b 1973, Hon William b 1976), 1 da (Hon Juliet b 1981); *Career* res fell Nuffield Coll Oxford 1965–68, assoc prof Johns Hopkins Univ 1970–76; Univ of Warwick: prof of int studies 1978–90, prof of political economy 1990–2006; memb: Lord Chllr's Advsy Cncl on Public Records 1987–92, Schools Examination and Assessment Cncl 1992–93 (resigned); chm: Charleston Tst 1987–92, Social Market Fndn 1991–2001, Hands Off Reading Campaign 1994–97; tstee Manhatten Inst 1994–2006; dir: Stillwell Fin Servs 2000–02, Janus Capital Gp 2003–11, Greater Europe Fund 2005–09, Sistema Financial Corp 2008–10, Rusnano Capital AG 2010–15; advsr Deutsche Bank 2006–07; tstee: Humanitas 1991–2000, Moscow Sch of Political Studies 1999–, Daedalus Tst 2011–; govr Brighton Coll 1998– (chm Bd of Govrs 2004–); memb Wilton Park Acad Cncl 2002–09; sits in House of Lords (as Cons until 2001, then as cross-bencher), oppn spokesman on culture, media and sport House of Lords 1997–98, princ oppn spokesman on treasy affairs House of Lords 1998–99; memb Cncl Royal Econ Soc 2007–; FRHistS 1973, FRSL 1978, FBA 1994; *Books* Politicians and the Slump (1967), English Progressive Schools (1970), Oswald Mosley (1975), John Maynard Keynes (I 1983, II 1992, III 2000, single vol edn 2003), World After Communism (1994), Beyond the Welfare State (1997), John Maynard Keynes: The Return of the Master (2009), How Much is Enough? The Love of Money and the Case for the Good Life (jtly, 2012), Britain Since 1900 A Success Story (2014), The Essential Keynes (ed, 2015); *Recreations* tennis, bridge, opera; *Style*— The Rt Hon Lord Skidelsky, FBA; ✉ Saxon Lodge, Saxon Lane, Seaford BN25 1QL (e-mail skidelskyr@parliament.uk); Centre for Global Studies ☎ 020 7219 8721

SKIDMORE, Christopher James (Chris); MP; s of Robert Skidmore, and Elaine, *née* Packer; *b* 17 May 1981, Bristol; *Educ* Bristol GS, ChCh Oxford (BA, MSt); *m* 29 Nov 2014, Lydia, *née* Wilson; 1 da (Clementine b 2014), 1 s (Henry b 2016); *Career* MP (Cons) Kingswood 2010–; FRSA 2008, FRHistS 2010, FSA 2014; *Books* Edward VI: The Lost King of England (2007), Death and The Virgin: Elizabeth, Dudley and the Mysterious Death of Amy Robsart (2010), After the Coalition (2011), Britannia Unchained (2012), Bosworth: the Birth of the Tudors (2013); *Style*— Chris Skidmore, Esq, MP; ✉ House of Commons, London SW1A 0AA

SKIDMORE, (Frederic) David; OBE (1984); s of Frederick Ernest Skidmore (d 1990), of Bexhill on Sea, E Sussex, and Mary Elizabeth Skidmore (d 1980); *b* 10 December 1939; *Educ* Solihull Sch, Gonville & Caius Coll Cambridge (MA, MB BChir, MD), Birmingham Med Sch; *m* 2 July 1966 (m dis 1983), Yvonne, da of John Steel (d 1979); 1 da (Rebecca Mary b 1969), 1 s (David James Benedict b 1970); m 2, 1983, Diana Sarah; *Career* former: demonstrator in anatomy Cambridge, Br Heart Fndn res fell, lectr in surgery Univ of Manchester; currently conslt surgn, former hon sr clinical lectr Dept of Surgery Royal Free UC Med Sch, former examiner in surgery Univ of London, bd advsr and visiting prof Khartoum Breast Care Centre Khartoum (Mo Ibrahim Fndn); chief medical advsr (medicolegal) UK Medical Conslts; Freeman: City of London, Worshipful Soc of Apothecaries; memb: RIIA, RSM, Br Assoc for Surgical Oncology; FRCSEd 1968, FRCS 1970; *Books* Studies on Development of the Heart and Great Vessels (1973); *Publications* Cardiac Embryology, Trauma and Intensive Care; 37 papers on various surgical and cancer topics in peer-reviewed jls; *Recreations* swimming, windsurfing, ornithology; *Clubs* Hawks' (Cambridge), Otter, Lansdowne, Athenaeum; *Style*— David Skidmore, Esq, OBE; ✉ 2 The Close, London SE3 0UR; Wellington Hospital, London NW8 9LE (☎ 020 8318 6923, car 07836 714137 (emergencies only), fax 020 8852 6919, e-mail dskidmore@doctors.org.uk, website www.cancersurgeonconsultant.co.uk)

SKILTON, Prof David John; s of Henry Charles Stanley Skilton (d 1999), of London, and Iris Flora Marion Skilton (d 1975); *b* 10 July 1942, London; *Educ* Tollington GS London, King's Coll Cambridge (MA, MLitt), Univ of Copenhagen; *m* 1, 29 Oct 1976 (m dis 1981), Marvid Elaine Graham Wilson; m 2, 12 April 1984, Joanne Vivien Papworth; 1 da (Hannah Catherine b 1985), 1 s (Adam Jonathan b 1989); *Career* sr lectr Univ of Glasgow 1978–80 (lectr 1970–80), dean Faculty of Arts St David's Univ Coll Lampeter 1983–86 (prof of English 1980–86), prof of English and head Dept of English UWIST 1986–88; Cardiff Univ: prof of English 1988–2009, head Sch of English, Communication and Philosophy 1988–2002, dep princ 1992–95, pro-vice-chllr 1995–96, dean of Humanities and Social Studies 1997–2000, dir Centre for Editorial and Intertextual Research 2004–07, emeritus prof 2009–; founding ed Jl of Illustration Studies 2007–; memb Nat Curriculum English Working Gp 1988–89, literary advsr to Trollope Soc 1988–, chair Brianwave Project Tst; FRSA 2001, fell English Assoc 2002; *Books* Anthony Trollope

S

and his Contemporaries (1972), Defoe to the Victorians: Two Centuries of the English Novel (1978), The Complete Novels of Anthony Trollope (gen ed), Critical Approaches: The Early and Mid-Victorian Novel (1992), Anthony Trollope, An Autobiography (ed 1996); *Publications* Anthony Trollope and his Contemporaries (1972), Defoe to the Victorians: Two Centuries of the English Novel (1978), The Complete Novels of Anthony Trollope (gen ed), Critical Approaches: The Early and Mid-Victorian Novel (1992), Anthony Trollope, An Autobiography (ed 1996); Database of Mid-Victorian Illustration (http://dmvi.org.uk, with J Thomas and A Mandal), The Illustration Archive (illustrationarchive.ac.uk, with J Thomas, N Lloyd, O Rana, P Rosen and I Harvey); *Recreations* music; *Style—* Prof David Skilton; ✉ Cardiff University, Humanities Building, Colum Drive, Cardiff CF10 3EU (e-mail skilton@cf.ac.uk)

SKINNER, Alan Kenneth; s of Kenneth Alfred Skinner of Byfleet, Surrey, and Millicent Louise, *née* Chapman; *b* 27 August 1948, Cambridge; *Educ* Sutton Valence; *m* 24 March 1973, Heather, da of Peter Campbell; 1 da (Hannah b 13 June 1978); *Career* Edward Moore & Sons (now Menzies): articled clerk 1966–70, qualified 1970, ptnr 1975, sr ptnr Kingston upon Thames office 1975–2010; chm Accreditation of Trg Offices Surrey Bd ICAEW 1984–93, chm SW London Dist Soc of CAs 1981–82, external examiner Accountancy Fndn Course Kingston Univ 1986–94; non-exec dir Kingston Hosp 1990–97; dir: Holmshaw Property Co Ltd, Holmshaw Hldgs Ltd, Holmshaw Forestry Ltd, Limje Hldgs Ltd, Limje Industrial Ltd, Jesyem Medicare Ltd; memb: Kingston Round Table 1976–89, Kingston Rotary 1998–2013; FCA 1979 (ACA 1970); *Recreations* travel, walking, golf, rugby and cricket; *Style—* Alan Skinner, Esq; ✉ Green Hayes, Forest Road, Pyrford, Woking, Surrey GU22 8LU (e-mail aksgreenhayes@msn.com)

SKINNER, Prof Angus; s of Dr Theodore Skinner (d 1988), and Morag, *née* MacKinnon (d 1989); *b* 4 January 1950; *Educ* Univ of Edinburgh (BSc), Univ of London, Univ of Strathclyde (MBA), Univ of Pennsylvania (Master of Applied Positive Psychology (MAPP)), Open Univ (MA); *m* Sep 1995 (m diss 2001); 1 s (Aidan b 11 July 1980), 2 da (Jenny b 20 Sept 1982, Caitlin b 9 May 1985); *Career* social worker Cheshire and Kent Cncls 1971–75, social work mangr Lothian and Borders Cncls 1975–91, chief inspr Scottish Office 1992–2005 (chief social work advsr 1991–2005), chief knowledge offr (C&H) 2005–07; memb RSL; FRSA, FFICS, FIPPA; *Books* Another Kind of Home (1992), The Same As You (1999), Leadership in Social Care (2009); *Recreations* family, friends, learning, theatre, art history; *Style—* Prof Angus Skinner; ✉ 32A West Werberside, Edinburgh, EH4 1SU

SKINNER, Caroline Mary Louise; da of Robin Mark Hill Griffiths, of Glan-y-Wern, Llandyrnog, and Rosemary Alison, *née* Collins; *b* 30 January 1969; *Educ* Wycombe Abbey, Homerton Coll Cambridge (BEd), London Sch of Publishing and PR (DipPR); *m* 28 July 2001, Justin Skinner, s of Peter Skinner; *Career* teacher Burdett Coutts Primary Sch Westminster 1991–94, Phipps PR 1994–95, Consumer Mktg Team Charles Barker BSMG 1995–99, dir Counsel PR 1999–; *Recreations* tennis, skiing, golf; *Clubs* Campden Hill Lawn Tennis, David Lloyd Health and Fitness; *Style—* Mrs Caroline Skinner

SKINNER, Prof Christopher John (Chris); CBE (2010); s of Richard N Skinner, of Bexhill-on-Sea, East Sussex, and Daphne R, *née* Edginton; *b* 12 March 1953, London; *Educ* St Dunstan's Coll London, Trinity Coll Cambridge (BA), LSE (MSc), Univ of Southampton (PhD); *m* 1, 1979; 2 s (Thomas b 18 May 1976, Samuel b 5 March 1980); *m* 2, 1998, Sheila; *Career* asst statistician Central Statistical Office 1976–77, research asst LSE 1977–78, temp lectr rising to sr lectr Univ of Southampton 1978–94, prof Div of Social Statistics Univ of Southampton 1994–2011, prof of statistics LSE 2011–; dir ESRC Centre for Applied Social Surveys 2001–05, dir ESRC Nat Centre for Research Methods 2004–09; series ed Wiley Survey Methodology Series 1997–; ed: Jl of the Royal Statistical Soc 2007–11, Jl of Privacy and Confidentiality 2008–; vice-pres Int Assoc of Survey Statisticians 1995–97 (scientific sec 1993–95), memb Cncl Royal Statistical Soc 2005–09; ordinary memb Int Statistical Inst 2001; FRSS 1977, fell American Statistical Assoc 1994, AcSS 2001, FBA 2004; *Style—* Prof Chris Skinner, CBE; ✉ Department of Statistics, London School of Economics and Political Science, London WC2A 2AE

SKINNER, Dennis Edward; MP; s of Edward Skinner; *b* 11 February 1932; *Educ* Tupton Hall GS, Ruskin Coll Oxford; *m* 12 March 1960, Mary, da of James Parker; 1 s, 2 da; *Career* former miner; joined Lab Pty 1950, MP (Lab) Bolsover 1970–; NEC: memb Lab Pty Home Policy Ctee 1978–, memb Lab Pty Orgn Policy Ctee 1978, Lab Pty chm 1988–89; memb: Campaign Gp Labour MPs 1982–, Lab Pty Youth Ctee until 1982, Tribune Gp until 1982; memb Clay Cross Cncl 1960–72, pres Derbyshire Miners 1966–70; *Style—* Dennis Skinner, Esq, MP; ✉ House of Commons, London SW1A 0AA

SKINNER, Frank (né Chris Collins); *b* 28 January 1957; *Career* comedian, presenter and writer; sometime English tutor Halesowen Coll Birmingham, first stand-up gig at the Birmingham Anglers' Association 1987; stand-up incl: Frank Skinner Live at the Apollo 1994, Frank Skinner Live at the London Palladium 1996, Frank Skinner Live in Birmingham 1998, UK tour 2007 and 2014, The Man With No Show (Soho Theatre) 2016; columnist The Times 2009–11; pres Dr Johnson Soc 2010–11; Hon DUniv Central England in Birmingham, Hon DUniv Wolverhampton 2009; *Theatre* incl: Art 1999, Cooking with Elvis 2000, host Credit Crunch Caberet (Lyric Theatre London) 2009; *Television* incl: Packet of Three 1991, Fantasy Football League 1994, The Frank Skinner Show 1995–2005, Fantasy World Cup 1998, Baddiel and Skinner Unplanned 2000–05, Shane 2004–05, Frank Skinner's Opinionated 2010–11, Room 101 2012–, Frank Skinner on George Formby 2011, I Love My Country 2013, Portrait Artist of the Year (Sky Arts) 2013–, Doctor Who (as Perkins) 2014, Landscape Artist of the Year (Sky Arts) 2015–, Taskmaster 2015, What a Performance 2015; *Radio* incl: host Saturday Morning Frank Skinner's Absolute Radio Show 2009–, host Desert Island Discs 2010, host Baddiel and Skinner's Absolute Radio Podcasts SA World Cup 2010, host Don't Start 2011, 2012 and 2014, host The Rest is History (Radio 4) 2014–; *Awards* incl: Perrier Award 1991, Best Comedy Entertainment Personality British Comedy Awards 2001, Variety Club Award for Comedy 2001, London Favourite Comedy Act Capital Awards 2005, Sony Radio Award nomination 2006 (for Baddiel and Skinner World Cup Podcast), Sony Radio Silver Award 2010 (for Absolute Radio Show), Sony Award for Best Entertainment Prog 2011 (for Frank Skinner on Absolute Radio), Best Entertainment Prog Sony Radio Acad Silver Award 2012 (for Absolute Radio Show), Best Speech Programme Radio Acad Award 2014, Radio Hall of Fame 2015; *Books* Frank Skinner on Frank Skinner (2001), Frank Skinner On the Road (2008), Dispatches from the Sofa (2011); *Singles* writer and singer (with David Baddiel, qv, and The Lightning Seeds): Three Lions (official song for Euro '96, UK no 1 (twice), Germany no 17, NME Brat Award 1996), Three Lions '98 (UK no 1); *Recreations* supporting West Bromwich Albion FC; *Style—* Frank Skinner; ✉ c/o Avalon Public Relations, 4A Exmoor Street, London W10 6BD (☎ 020 7598 8000, fax 020 7598 7300)

SKINNER, Michael Gordon (Mick); s of Geordie Skinner, of Newcastle upon Tyne, and Chrissie, *née* Jackson; *b* 26 November 1958; *Educ* Wallbottle GS; *m* Anna, *née* Palmer; 1 da (Emily Elizabeth b 4 July 1995), 3 s (Maximilian George b 7 Sept 1997, Zachary Jack, Barnaby John (twins b 16 Oct 1998); *Career* former rugby union flanker; clubs: Blaydon RFC 1974–79, Blackheath RFC 1979–84 and 1992–94, Harlequins FC 1984–92 (winner John Player Cup 1988 and Pilkington Cup 1991); capt Barbarians' Easter tour of Wales 1990; rep: Blaydon Colts (winner Durham Co Colts Cup), Northumberland U21, Kent, London Div, England B (debut v France 1987); England: debut v France 1988, memb World Cup runners-up team 1991 (was the only England forward to score a try in the

World Cup), memb Grand Slam winning team 1992, 21 caps; currently TV and newspaper rugby pundit; freelance computer conslt; *Style—* Mick Skinner, Esq

SKINNER, Paul David; CBE (2014); s of William Skinner, and Elizabeth Skinner; *Educ* Palmer's Sch Grays, Pembroke Coll Cambridge (BA, Association Football blue), Manchester Business Sch (MBA); *m* 1971, Rita Jacqueline Oldak; 2 s; *Career* Royal Dutch/Shell Gp of Cos: joined 1966, assigned UK, Greece 1974–76 and Nigeria 1976–78, chm Shell NZ 1984–87, md Norske Shell 1987–91, pres Shell Int Trading and Shipping Co Ltd 1991–96, pres Shell Europe Oil Products 1998–99, chief exec Oil Products 1999–2003, gp md Royal Dutch/Shell 2000–03; chm Rio Tinto plc 2003–09 (non-exec dir 2001–); non-exec dir: Standard Chartered plc 2003–, Tetra Laval Gp 2005–, Air Liquide SA 2006–; pres UK Chamber of Shipping 1997–98; memb Bd INSEAD Business Sch Fontainebleu 1999–, chm ICC UK 2005–08, memb Def Bd (formerly Mgmnt Bd) MOD 2006–, chm Cwlth Business Cncl 2007–, non-exec chm Infrastructure UK; Liveryman Worshipful Co of Shipwrights; *Recreations* golf, skiing, fly fishing, opera, boating; *Clubs* Hawks' (Cambridge), Roehampton, RAC; *Style—* Paul Skinner, Esq, CBE

SKINNER, Peter; MEP; s of James Skinner, and Jean Skinner (d 2009); *Educ* Univ of Bradford (BSc), Univ of Warwick (postgrad cert industrial rels), Univ of Greenwich (PGCE); *m* 1, 14 July 1990 (m dis 2006), Julie Doreen; *m* 2, Nov 2006, Kim Strycharz-Skinner; *Career* industrial rels offr 1982–84, union organiser 1984–86, lectr NW Kent Coll and Univ of Greenwich 1989–94; MEP (Lab): Kent W 1994–99, SE England 1999–; *Recreations* most sports, especially football; *Style—* Peter Skinner, Esq, MEP; ✉ Fort Pitt House Business Centre, New Road, Rochester, ME1 1DU

SKINNER, Prof Quentin Robert Duthie; s of Alexander Skinner, CBE (d 1979), and Winifred Rose Margaret, *née* Duthie (d 1982); *b* 26 November 1940; *Educ* Bedford Sch, Gonville & Caius Coll Cambridge (MA); *m* 31 Aug 1979, Prof Susan Deborah Thorpe James, da of Prof Derrick James, of London; 1 da (Olivia b 7 Dec 1979), 1 s (Marcus b 13 July 1982); *Career* Univ of Cambridge: fell Christ's Coll 1962–2008, prof of political sci 1978–96, regius prof of modern history 1996–2008, pro-vice-chllr 1999; prof of humanities Univ of London 2008–; Hon LittD: Univ of Chicago 1992, UEA 1992, Univ of Helsinki 1997, Univ of Oxford 2000, Univ of Leuven 2004, Harvard Univ 2005, Univ of St Andrews 2005, Univ of Athens 2007, Univ of Aberdeen 2007, Alfonso Ibáxez Univ Santiago 2009, Univ of Oslo 2011, Univ of Copenhagen 2014; hon fell: Gonville & Caius Coll Cambridge 1997, QMC London 2000, Christ's Coll Cambridge 2008; FRHS 1970, FBA 1980; *Books* The Foundations of Modern Political Thought (2 vols, 1978), Machiavelli (1981), Meaning and Context (1988), Reason and Rhetoric in the Philosophy of Hobbes (1996), Liberty Before Liberalism (1998), Visions of Politics (3 vols, 2002), Hobbes and Republican Liberty (2008), Forensic Shakespeare (2014); *Style—* Prof Quentin Skinner, FBA; ✉ School of History, Queen Mary, University of London, Mile End Road, London E1 4NS (e-mail q.skinner@qmul.ac.uk)

SKIPWITH, Sir Patrick Alexander d'Estoteville; 12 Bt (E 1622), of Prestwould, Leicestershire; s of Grey d'Estoteville Townsend Skipwith (ka 1942), and Sofka (d 1994), da of Prince Peter Alexandrovitch Dolgorouky; suc gf, Sir Grey Humberston d'Estoteville Skipwith 1950; *b* 1 September 1938; *Educ* Harrow, TCD (MA), Imperial Coll London (PhD); *m* 1, 1964 (m dis 1970), Gillian Patricia (d 2012), adopted da of late Charles Frederick Harwood; 1 da (Zara Alexandra Jane d'Estoteville b 1967), 1 s (Alexander Sebastian Grey d'Estoteville b 1969); *m* 2, 1972 (m dis 1997), Ashkhain (d 2006), da of late Bedros Atikian; *m* 3, 1997 (m dis 2011), Martine Sophie Yvonne, da of late Joseph de Wilde; 2 s (Grey Camille d'Estoteville, Louis Peyton d'Estoteville (twins b 1997); *m* 4, 2012, Katherine Jane Mahon, da of Derek Mahon; 1 s (Nicholas James Mahon d'Estoteville b 2011); *Heir* s, Alexander Skipwith; *Career* marine geologist Ocean Mining Inc 1966–70, Directorate-Gen of Mineral Resources Jeddah Saudi Arabia 1970–73, geological ed Bureau de Recherches Géologiques et Minières Jeddah Saudi Arabia 1973–86; md Immel Publishing Ltd 1988–89; freelance editing (GeoEdit), translating and public relations 1986–96; head of translation BRGM Orléans France 1996–2003; freelance editing/translation (Traduscience) 2003–; Aprotrad; *Recreations* hill walking, golf; *Clubs* Chelsea Arts; *Style—* Sir Patrick Skipwith, Bt; ✉ 14 Wilton Rise, York YO24 4BW (e-mail patrick@donnery.com)

SKIPWORTH, Mark; s of George Skipworth, of Kingston upon Hull, E Yorks, and Jean Marjorie Skipworth; *b* 27 January 1959; *Educ* Sydney Smith Sch Hull, St John's Coll Oxford (BA); *m* 29 Aug 1981, Julie Alison Patricia, da of Frank Deegan; 2 s (Hunter b 31 Oct 1987, Patrick b 2 May 1992), 1 da (Zoe b 16 April 1994); *Career* reporter Sheffield Star 1980–84, writer Which? Magazine 1984–89, reporter Daily Telegraph 1989; Sunday Times: consumer affairs corr 1990–93, dep ed Insight 1994–95, news ed 1995–97, managing ed (news) 1998–2008; Telegraph Media Gp: exec ed (sport) 2008, exec ed 2009–14, dep ed 2014–16; *Awards* Yorkshire Young Journalist of the Year 1982, Nat Newspapers' Consumer Journalist of the Year 1991, commended Reporter of the Year Br Press Awards 1991, Scoop of the Year 1994, What the Papers Say Investigations of the Year 1994, Br Press Awards Exclusive of the Year 1994, Br Press Awards Team Journalism Award 1994, What the Papers Say Scoop of the Year 2006, Br Press Awards Team of the Year 2007, Sport Newspaper of the Year Sport Industry Award 2010; *Books* Oxford Type: The Best of ISIS (with Andrew Billen, 1984), The Scotch Whisky Book (1987), Class (with Greg Hadfield, 1994); *Recreations* piano and piano accordion; *Style—* Mark Skipworth, Esq

SKLAR, Dr Jonathan; s of Vivian Sklar (d 2007), of London, and Joyce, *née* Longworth (d 1991); *b* 9 June 1949; *Educ* Latymer Upper Sch, Royal Free Hosp Univ of London (MB BS), Inst of Psychoanalysis London; *Family* 2 da (Clea b 1 Aug 1978, Livia b 31 Oct 1981); *Career* psychoanalyst; sr registrar in psychiatry Friern and Royal Free Hosps 1978–79, sr registrar in psychotherapy Tavistock Clinic 1979–83, conslt psychotherapist Cambridge HA 1983–95; head of Dept of Psychotherapy Addenbrooke's Hosp 1989–95, visiting prof Århus Univ and Psychiatric Hosp 1991–92, in private psychoanalytic practice; sec Psychotherapy Exec of Joint Ctee of Higher Psychiatric Trg 1990–92; Freedom City of Cusco Peru 1989; hon medical degree awarded by Serbian Medical Soc 2012; trg analyst Br Psychoanalytical Soc 1998 (assoc memb 1984, memb 1991); vice-pres European Psychoanalytic Fedn 2007–11, memb Bd Int Psychoanalytic Assoc (IPA) 2015–; hon memb South African Psychoanalytic Soc 2016, hon memb Psychoanalytic Soc of Serbia 2016; LRCP, MRCS, FRCPsych 2010 (MRCPsych 1977); Hysteria and Mourning – A Psychosomatic Case (2008), Landscapes of the Dark (2011); *Recreations* reading, opera; *Clubs* Athenaeum; *Style—* Dr Jonathan Sklar; ✉ Flat 4, 33 Priory Terrace, London NW6 4DG (☎ 020 7485 6974, e-mail jonathan@sklar.co.uk, Twitter @IndepPsychoAn)

SKOLL, Lindsay Samantha; *b* 26 September 1970; *Educ* Univ of Nottingham; *m* 2005, Richard; 1 s, 2 step-c; *Career* diplomat; Japan Exchange and Teaching Prog Japan 1992–95, Lewis Int PR Communications 1995–96; FCO: visits and media services offr Info Dept 1996–97, Protocol Dept 1997–98, head VIP visits 1999–2001, head Korean and Mongolian Section NE Asia Pacific Dept 2001–02; seconded as sr regnl analyst E Asia Cabinet Office 2002–04, dep head of mission Pyongyang 2004–06, Whitehall Liaison Dept FCO 2006–07, policy sec UAE and Gulf initiatives ME and N Africa Directorate FCO 2010, dep head Climate Change and Energy Dept FCO 2010–12, high cmmr to the Seychelles 2012–15, min-cnsllr FCO 2016–; *Recreations* Scottish hill-walking, equestrianism, skiing, singing, piano; *Style—* Mrs Lindsay Skoll; ✉ c/o FCO, King Charles Street, London SW1A 2AH (e-mail lindsay.skoll@fco.gov.uk)

SKORUPSKI, Prof John Maria; s of Wactaw Skorupski (d 1991), of Warsaw, Poland, and late Wanda, *née* Pankiewicz; *b* 19 September 1946; *Educ* St Benedict's Sch Ealing, Christ's Coll Cambridge (MA), Univ of Cambridge (PhD); *m* 18 Sept 1971, Barbara, da of Ernest Robert Taylor; 2 da (Katharine Wanda Taylor b 3 Nov 1978, Julia Zofia Taylor b 9 Feb 1982); *Career* visiting lectr Univ of Ife Nigeria 1971–72, visiting prof Univ of Louvain Belgium 1974; res fell UC Swansea Univ of Wales 1974–76, lectr Dept of Philosophy Univ of Glasgow 1976–84, prof of philosophy Univ of Sheffield 1984–90, prof of moral philosophy Univ of St Andrews 1990–; gen ed: OUP OPUS paperbacks, The International Research Library of Philosophy; memb Editorial Bd: Ratio, The Philosophical Quarterly, Utilitas; pres Aristotelian Soc 1990–91; hon fell Centre for the Study of Political Thought Jagiellonian Univ Kraków Poland 1991–; memb Exec Ctee Mind Assoc 1992–; FRSE 1992; *Books* Symbol and Theory, A Philosophical Study of Theories of Religion in Social Anthropology (1975), John Stuart Mill (1989), English Language Philosophy 1750–1945 (1993), Ethical Explorations (1999), Why Read Mill Today? (2006), The Routledge Companion to Ethics (2010), The Domain of Reasons (2010); *Recreations* walking, skiing, music; *Style—* Prof John Skorupski, FRSE; ✉ Department of Moral Philosophy, University of St Andrews, St Andrews, Fife KY16 9AL (☎ 01334 462178)

SKREIN, (Stephen Peter) Michael; *b* 1947; *Educ* UCS, Univ of Oxford (MA), Univ of Southern Calif (AM), Coll of Law; *Career* Richards, Butler & Co: admitted slr 1973, ptnr Richards Butler 1976–2006, head Commercial Litigation Gp 1990–96; ptnr Reed Smith LLP (formerly Reed Smith Richards Butler LLP) 2007–; elected Honor Soc of Phi Kappa Phi; Freeman City of London, Liveryman City of London Slrs' Co; memb: Law Soc, Int Bar Assoc, Int Trademark Assoc, RTS, Br Literary and Artistic Copyright Assoc, The Media Soc; *Style—* Michael Skrein, Esq; ✉ Reed Smith LLP, The Broadgate Tower, 20 Primrose Street, London EC2A 2RS (☎ 020 3116 3000, fax 020 3116 3999)

SLACK, Prof Paul; *Career* Univ of Oxford: princ Linacre Coll 1996–2010, prof emeritus of early modern social history; FBA; *Books* incl: Crisis and Order in English Towns, 1500–1700: Essays in Urban History (ed with Peter Clark, 1972), Poverty in Early-Stuart Salisbury (1975), English Towns in Transition 1500–1700 (with Peter Clark, 1976), Rebellion, Popular Protest, and the Social Order in Early Modern England (ed, 1984), The Impact of Plague in Tudor and Stuart England (1985), Poverty and Policy in Tudor and Stuart England (1988), The English Poor Law, 1531–1782 (1990), Epidemics and Ideas: Essays on the Historical Perception of Pestilence (ed with Terence Ranger, 1992), From Reformation to Improvement: Public Welfare in Early Modern England (1999), Environments and Historical Change (1999), The Peopling of Britain: The Shaping of a Human Landscape (ed with Ryk Ward, 2002), Managing Water Resources Past and Present (ed with Julie Trottier, 2004), Plague: A Very Short Introduction (2012), The Invention of Improvement: Information and Material Progress in Seventeenth Century England (2015); *Style—* Prof Paul Slack; ✉ Linacre College, St Cross Road, Oxford OX1 3JA

SLACK, Robert William Talbot; s of Sir William Slack, of Somerset, and Lady (Joan) Slack; *b* 29 August 1953; *Educ* Winchester, Bart's Med Sch, Univ of Bristol; *m* 18 June 1982, Dr Nicola Slack, *née* Caporn; 1 da (Amy b 15 June 1984), 1 s (Edward b 9 Feb 1986); *Career* sr registrar ENT Surgery Bristol and Bath 1985–90, conslt ENT surgn Royal United Hosp Bath 1990–2012; sr clinical lectr Univ of Bristol 2004–13; lay memb Qualifications Ctee Bar Standards Bd 2012–; memb: GMC 1999–2008, Slr's Disciplinary Tbnl 2009–; Liveryman Worshipful Co of Barbers; FRCS 1984; *Recreations* real tennis, golf, sailing; *Style—* Robert Slack, Esq

SLADE, Sir Benjamin Julian Alfred; 7 Bt (UK 1831), of Maunsel House, Somerset; s of Capt Sir Michael Niall Slade, 6 Bt (d 1962), and Angela (d 1959), da of Capt Orlando Chichester; *b* 21 May 1956; *Educ* Millfield; *m* 1977 (m dis 1991), Pauline Carol, da of Maj Claude Myburgh; *Career* chm and md Shirlstar Holdings Ltd, dir Pyman Bell Ltd; Freeman City of London 1979, memb Worshipful Co of Ironmongers; *Recreations* racing, polo, bridge, shooting; *Style—* Sir Benjamin Slade, Bt; ✉ Maunsel House, North Newton, Bridgwater, Somerset (☎ secretaries 01278 663107, sales and events office 01278 661076 or main house 01278 661074, e-mail bensladebt@aol.com, website www.maunselhouse.co.uk); Woodlands Castle, Ruishton, Taunton, Somerset TA3 5LU (☎ 01823 444955, e-mail info@woodlandscastle.co.uk, website www.woodlandscastle.co.uk)

SLADE, Hon Mrs Justice; Dame Elizabeth Ann Slade; DBE (2008), QC (1992); da of late Dr Charles Slade, and Henriette Slade; *b* 12 May 1949; *Educ* Wycombe Abbey, LMH Oxford (exhibitioner, MA); *m* 1975; 2 da; *Career* called to the Bar Inner Temple 1972 (bencher 1990); recorder 1998–2008 (asst recorder 1995–98), dep judge of the High Court 1998–2008, pt/t judge Employment Appeal Tbnl 2000–03, judge of the High Court 2008–; chm Employment Law Bar Assoc 1995–97 (hon vice-pres 1997–); chm Bar Cncl Sex Discrimination Ctee 2000–02; tstee Free Representation Unit 1998–2002; memb Admin Tbnl of the Bank for Int Settlements 1999–2008 (vice-pres 2008), memb Admin Tbnl European Bank for Reconstruction and Devpt 2008; hon fell LMH Oxford 2009–; *Books* Tolleys Employment Handbook (ed then co-ed, 1–7 edn, 1978–90); *Recreations* theatre, art, music; *Style—* Hon Mrs Justice Slade, DBE; ✉ Royal Courts of Justice, Strand, London WC2A 2LL

SLADEK, Nancy; da of Dr Milan Sladek, of Geneva, Switzerland, and Hana, *née* Kozeluhova; *Educ* Heathfield Sch Ascot, Univ of Geneva (LèsL); *Children* 1 s (Lorenzo Michael b 21 Oct 2004); *Career* ed Literary Review 1999– (dep ed 1996–99); Benson Medal 2015; *Clubs* Academy; *Style—* Ms Nancy Sladek; ✉ Literary Review, 44 Lexington Street, London W1F 0LW (☎ 020 7437 9392, fax 020 7734 1844, e-mail nancy@literaryreview.co.uk)

SLARK, Gavin; s of Vincent Slark, of Leicestershire, and Moira Rose, *née* Smith; *b* 6 April 1965, Sunderland; *Educ* North Leamington Sch Royal Leamington Spa, London Business Sch; *m* 12 July 1986, Lori Mary, *née* Hall; 2 s (Daniel James b 30 March 1993, Jacob William b 18 Oct 1995); *Career* BSS Gp plc: md PTS Plumbing Trade Supplies and exec dir 2002–05, chief operating offr 2005–06, chief exec 2006–11; ceo Grafton Gp plc 2011–; *Recreations* travel, golf, Sunderland FC; *Style—* Gavin Slark, Esq

SLATER, Arnold; s of Arnold Slater, of Holmfirth, W Yorks, and Pauline Margaret, *née* Shaw-Parker; *b* 26 March 1948; *Educ* Hadham Hall Sch, Regent St Poly; *m* 21 Oct 1972, Judith Helen, da of Philip Ellison, of Bishop's Stortford, Herts; 1 s (Ross Adrian b 24 Sept 1973), 1 da (Anthea Helen b 15 Feb 1978); *Career* chief photographer Herts and Essex Observer 1973–78; photographer: Press Assoc 1978–87, London Daily News 1987, Sunday People 1987–88, The Mirror; winner: Simeon Edmunds award for best young press photographer, Ilford Press Photographer of the Year 1987; *Recreations* squash, skiing, fly tying, fly fishing; *Style—* Arnold Slater, Esq

SLATER, Barbara; OBE (2014); da of William John (Bill) Slater, CBE, former professional footballer; *Educ* Univ of Birmingham, Univ of Oxford; m; 3 c; *Career* BBC: joined as trainee asst prodr Natural History Unit 1983, subsequently head of prodn and head of gen sports, dir of sport 2009–; appointed expert Int Olympic Ctee Radio and TV Cmmn 2014; Inspirational Woman Prize Women in Film and TV Awards 2012; *Style—* Ms Barbara Slater, OBE; ✉ BBC Sport, Quay House, MediaCityUK, Salford, Greater Manchester M50 2QH

SLATER, David; *b* 21 October 1960; *Educ* Vyne Sch Basingstoke, Basingstoke Tech Coll, Bournemouth and Poole Coll of Art; *Career* designer; Raymond Loewy 1983, Allied International Designers 1983–86, Lansdown Euro 1986–87, assoc dir Fitch & Co 1987–89, creative dir Wolff Olins Hall 1989–90, freelance designer 1990–92; creative dir: Tango Design Consultancy 1992–95, Vista Design 1995–96, e-fact 1996–98, Saatchi & Saatchi Design 1998–2000, Addison Design 2000–01; md and creative dir David Slater Design 2002–; *Style—* David Slater, Esq; ✉ David Slater Design ☎ 01424 812256

SLATER, Dr David Homfray; CB (1996); s of William Dennis Slater, and Edna Florence, *née* Homfray; *b* 16 October 1940; *Educ* Ardwyn GS, UCW (BSc), Univ of Wales (PhD); *m* 18 April 1964, Edith Mildred, da of Geoffrey Edward Price; 4 da (Ellen Louise b 7 March 1965, Sian Juliet b 1 July 1966, Melanie Lynne b 18 March 1968, Emma Wynne b 22 Feb 1970); *Career* res asst Ohio State Univ 1966–69, sr res fell Univ of Southampton 1969–70, lectr Dept of Chemical Engrg and Technol Imperial Coll London 1970–75, ptnr Cremer & Warner 1979–81 (conslt 1975–79), fndr dir Technica Ltd (London) 1981, chm and chief exec Technica Inc (USA) 1987–91, dir and chief inspr HM Inspectorate of Pollution 1991–95, dir Pollution Prevention and Control and chm Policy Gp Environment Agency 1995–97; chm Task Force on Risk Assessment DETR 1997–98; conseiller DGXI E Euro Cmmn 1997–98; specialist advsr House of Commons Environment Tport and Regional Affrs Select Ctee 1999–2000; environmental advsr to Cabinet Office's Better Regulation Taskforce 2000–; md OXERA Environmental 1998–2001, princ ptnr ACONA Gp 2001–, dir Cambrensis 2002–, chm RLtec 2003–09, chm NIREX CLG 2005–07, dir Willworth Ltd 2008–; prof Warren Centre for Advanced Engineering Univ of Sydney 1985–86, hon prof of life sciences UCW 1991–, assoc fell Environmental Change Unit Univ of Oxford 1998–, chm Environmental Gp Regulatory Policy Inst Oxford 2001–2002, Royal Acad of Engrg prof UMIST 2002–06, adjunct prof Centre for Risk Mgmnt KCL 2003–06, hon visiting prof Cardiff Univ 2009–; CChem, CEng, FRSC; *Recreations* breeding dressage and showjumping horses, Ruxton Stud; *Clubs* Athenaeum; *Style—* Dr David Slater, CB; ✉ Ruxton Farm, King's Caple, Herefordshire HR1 4TX (☎ 01432 840568, fax 01432 840731)

SLATER, Adm Sir John Cunningham Kirkwood (Jock); GCB (1992, KCB 1988), LVO (1971), DL (Hants 2000); s of Dr James K Slater, OBE, MD, FRCPE (d 1965), of Edinburgh, and Margaret Claire Byrom, *née* Bramwell (d 2007); *b* 27 March 1938; *Educ* Edinburgh Acad, Sedbergh, Dartmouth; *m* 1972, Ann Frances, da of late William Patrick Scott, OBE, DL, of Orkney Islands; 2 s (Charles b 1974, Rory b 1977); *Career* RN; Equerry to HM The Queen 1968–71; CO: HMS Soberton (minesweeper) 1965, HMS Jupiter (frigate) 1972–73, HMS Kent (guided missile destroyer) 1976–77; Royal Coll of Def Studies 1978; CO: HMS Illustrious (aircraft carrier) 1981–83, HMS Dryad & Capt Sch of Maritime Ops 1983–85; ACDS (Policy and Nuclear) 1985–87; Flag Offr Scotland and N Ireland, Naval Base Cdr Rosyth, NATO Cdr N sub area E Atlantic, Cdr Nore sub area Channel 1987–89, Chief of Fleet Support 1989–91, C-in-C Fleet, Allied C-in-C Channel and C-in-C Eastern Atlantic 1991–92, Vice Chief of the Def Staff 1993–95, First Sea Lord and Chief of Naval Staff 1995–98, First and Princ Naval ADC to HM The Queen 1995–98; vice-chm RUSI 1993–95 (vice-pres 1995–98); non-exec dir: VT Gp plc 1999–2004, Lockheed Martin (UK) 2000–08; conslt Bristow Helicopters Ltd 2001–04; chm: Imperial War Museum 2001–06 (tstee 1999–2006), RN Club (1765–85) 2001–04, White Ensign Assoc 2002–05 (memb Cncl 1999–); pres American Air Museum in Britain 2001–06; currently vice-pres and chm emeritus RNLI (memb Cncl 1999–, chm Ops, Ctee 2001–02, dep chm 2002–04, chm 2004–08); memb Nat Youth Orchestra 1955; govr Sedbergh Sch 1997–2002, vice-patron St Dunstans 1998–2009, patron Treloar Tst 1999–; Hon DSc: Univ of Cranfield 1998, Univ of Southampton 2008; Elder Bro Trinity House 1995 (Yr Bro 1978), Freeman City of London 1989, Liveryman Worshipful Co of Shipwrights 1991 (memb Ct of Assts 2005–, Fourth Warden 2008, Third Warden 2009–, Renter Warden 2010, Prime Warden 2011–12); Cdr Legion of Merit (US) 1997; *Recreations* the outdoors; *Clubs* Army and Navy, Liphook Golf; *Style—* Adm Sir Jock Slater, GCB, LVO, DL; ✉ c/o The Naval Secretary, Leach Building, Whale Island, Portsmouth, Hants PO2 8BY (☎ 023 9262 5538, fax 023 9262 5100, e-mail jock.slater@talk21.com)

SLATER, Dr John Morton; s of Rev Percy William Slater (d 1988), of Winston, and Evelyn Maude Morton Slater (d 1978); *b* 21 August 1938; *Educ* Durham Sch, Univ of Nottingham (BSc), Univ of Toronto (MS), Univ of Illinois (PhD, L J Norton Memorial fell); *m* 30 Sept 1972, Susan Mary Black, da of Rev Dr John Park, of Stormont, Belfast; 2 s (William John Park b 28 April 1974, Philip James Morton b 10 May 1976), 1 da (Helen Mary Elizabeth b 15 Sept 1979); *Career* lectr Univ of Manchester 1965–70, conslt FAO 1966–67; MAFF: econ advsr 1970–84, head Econ and Stats (Food) Div 1984–92, head Econ (Int) Div 1992–96, head Econ and Stats Gp 1996–98, special advsr House of Lords Select Ctee on Sci and Technol 1999–2000; independent agric economic conslt 1998–; chm Millennium Masters Assoc 2003–06; govr Corporation of the Sons and Friends of the Clergy (formerly Corp of the Sons of the Clergy, merged with the Friends of the Clergy 2013) 2001–; Freeman City of London 1972, Master Worshipful Co of Turners 1999–2000 (memb Ct of Assts 1990); MRI; *Books* Fifty Years of the National Food Survey 1940–1990 (ed); *Recreations* squash (Durham Co squash 1971–73), cricket, golf, bridge; *Clubs* City Livery (hon sec 2002–03), MCC, United Wards; *Style—* Dr John M Slater; ✉ 28 Swain's Lane, London N6 6QR (☎ 020 7485 1238, e-mail slaterconsult@gmail.com)

SLATER, Mark William; s of James Derrick Slater, of Cranleigh, Surrey, and Helen Slater; *b* 13 May 1969, London; *Educ* Oundle, Peterhouse Cambridge (MA); *m* July 2005, Maritzina, *née* Caltagirone; 3 s; *Career* chm and fndr Slater Investments Ltd 1994–, fndr Internet Indirect plc 1998–2000 (subsequently non-exec dir New Media Spark 2000–01), chm Galahad Capital plc 2001–03 (non-exec dir 2003–06), dir Union Investment Mgmnt 2006–10; *Recreations* salmon fishing, cinema; *Clubs* Brooks's, Mark's, George, Annabel's, Aspinalls, 5 Hertford St; *Style—* Mark Slater, Esq; ✉ Slater Investments Limited, Nicholas House, 3 Laurence Pountney Hill, London EC4R 0EU (☎ 020 7220 9460)

SLATER, Nigel; *Career* cookery writer; food ed Marie Claire 1988–93, food columnist The Observer 1993–; *Awards* Glenfiddich Award 1989, 1995, 1999 and 2004, Cookery Writer of the Year Award 1995 and 1999, Glenfiddich Trophy 1995, BBC Media Personality of the Year 1997, Guild of Food Writers Broadcaster of the Year 1999, André Simon 2001 and 2004, People's Choice Book of the Year 2004, British Biography of the Year 2004; *Books* Real Fast Food (1992), Real Fast Puddings (1993), The 30-Minute Cook (1994), Real Good Food (1995), Real Cooking (1997), Nigel Slater's Real Food (to accompany eight-part television series 1998), Appetite (2000), Thirst (2002), Toast: The Story of a Boy's Hunger (2003), The Kitchen Diaries (2005), Eating for England (2007); *Style—* Nigel Slater, Esq; ✉ website www.nigelslater.com; c/o United Agents, 12–26 Lexington Street, London W1F 0LE (☎ 020 3214 0800, fax 020 3214 0801, website www.unitedagents.co.uk)

SLATER, Prof Nigel Kenneth Henry; *Educ* Univ of Cambridge (MA, PhD); *Career* lectr in chemical engrg Univ of Cambridge 1979–85, bioprocessing section mangr Unilever, head of bioprocess devpt Wellcome plc, currently prof of chemical engrg Univ of Cambridge and fell Fitzwilliam Coll Cambridge; former chair BBSRC Chemicals and Pharmaceuticals Directorate; memb: BBSRC Biochemical Engrg Review Panel, BBSRC Technol Interaction Bd, EPSRC Process Engrg Coll, SERC Process Engrg Ctee, SERC Separations Sub-Ctee; non-exec memb Bd Cobra Bio-manufacturing plc; FIChemE 1996, FREng 2004; *Style—* Prof Nigel Slater; ✉ Department of Chemical Engineering, University of Cambridge, New Museums Site, Pembroke Street, Cambridge CB2 3RA

SLATER, Richard; s of Dennis Slater (d 1979), and Freida, *née* Hodgson; *b* 18 August 1948; *Educ* UCS, Pembroke Coll Cambridge (MA); *m* Julie Norma, da of Gordon Jolley Ward; 2 s (Samuel Rupert b 1980, Frederick James b 1985), 1 da (Amy Louise b 1982); *Career* Slaughter and May: articled clerk 1970–72, asst slr 1972–79, ptnr 1979–2005; professional freelance photographer 2005–; FRGS; *Books* People in London (2014); *Recreations* tennis, theatre, cinema, opera, ballet, horse racing, watching football, rugby and cricket; *Clubs*

S

MCC; *Style—* Richard Slater, Esq; ✉ Richard Slater Photography, 105 Clifton Hill, London NW8 0JR (☎ 020 7328 8513, e-mail richardslater@photographyrs.com, www.richardslater.net, www.peopleinlondon.com)

SLATFORD, Rodney Gerald Yorke; OBE (2007); s of Frederick Charles Slatford (d 1951), and (Irene) Vida Yorke, *née* Robinson (d 1991); *b* 18 July 1944; *Educ* Bishop's Stortford Coll, Royal Coll of Music; *Career* double bassist, broadcaster; memb Nat Youth Orch of GB 1961–62, RCM 1963–65; princ bass: London Soloist's Ensemble 1965, Midland Sinfonia (later English Sinfonia) 1965–74, Nash Ensemble of London 1965–94, Purcell Room recital debut 1969, freelance Acad of St Martin-in-the-Fields 1972–74, co-princ double bass English Chamber Orch 1974–81, soloist Henry Wood Promenade Concert 1974, Wigmore Hall Double Bass Forum 1974, world recital tour (India, Sri Lanka, Singapore, Aust, NZ, Nepal) 1975, soloist Aix Festival English Chamber Orch 1977, artist in residence (one month) Cairo Conservatoire 1981, artist in residence Kusatsu Int Summer Acad Japan 1984; md and fndr Yorke Edn 1969–, prof RCM 1974–84, fndr and dir Isle of Man Int Double Bass Competition and Workshop 1978, examiner for Assoc Bd Royal Schs of Music 1979–96 and 2002–, admin Young Musicians Scheme Greater London Arts Assoc 1980–82, chm ESTA Music Competition Report 1982, head of School of Strings RNCM 1984–2001 (sr tutor in double bass 1980–84), fndr and chm The Yorke Tst 1984–, guest tutor Beijing Conservatoire 1984, organiser Manchester Bass Week 1985, reg presenter BBC Radio 3 1986–96, guest tutor Toho Sch of Music Tokyo 1988, chm ESTA Int Conf Manchester 1989, Portsmouth 1999; memb: Advsy Ctee Br Cncl Music 1989, Gowrie Ctee review of the London Music Conservatoires 1990, Exec Ctee European String Teachers' Assoc; chm Br Branch ESTA 1992–96; tstee Loan Fund for Musical Instruments 2005–; has made numerous broadcasts and recordings, juror and examiner at numerous nat and int venues, has lectured extensively since 1964, author of various reports and contrib to Grove's Dictionary of Music; Hon RCM 1976, FRNCM 1987; *Recreations* music publishing, gardening, cooking, walking; *Style—* Rodney Slatford, Esq, OBE; ✉ Grove Cottage, Southgate Road, South Creake, Norfolk NR21 9PA

SLATKIN, Leonard; s of Felix Slatkin, and Eleanor Aller; *b* 9 January 1944, LA; *Educ* Aspen Music Sch, Juilliard Sch; *m* 20 Nov 2011, Cindy McTee; 1 s (Daniel); *Career* conductor; music dir Nat Symphony Orch Washington DC 1996–2008, chief conductor BBC Symphony Orch 2000–04, music dir Detroit Symphony Orchestra 2008–, music dir Orchestre National de Lyon 2011–; conductor laureate St Louis Symphony Orch 1996– (music dir 1979–96); princ guest conductor: Philharmonia Orch 1997–2000, Royal Philharmonic Orch 2005–10; performed with numerous orchs incl: NY Philharmonic, NHK Symphony, Royal Concertgebouw, Berlin Philharmonic, Orchestre de Paris, Vienna Symphony, Czech Philharmonic, Orchestra del Teatro Comunale di Firenze; dir Cleveland Orch Blossom Festival 1992–99, fndr and dir Nat Conducting Inst USA; over 100 recordings and winner 7 Grammy Awards (64 nominations); *Books* Conducting Business: Unveiling the Mystery Behind the Maestro (2012); *Style—* Leonard Slatkin, Esq; ✉ website www.leonardslatkin.com

SLAUGHTER, Andrew Francis; MP; *b* 29 September 1960, Fulham, London; *Educ* Univ of Exeter; *Career* barrister; Hammersmith and Fulham BC: cncllr 1986–2006, dep cncl ldr 1991–96, cncl ldr 1996–2005; MP (Lab): Ealing Acton and Shepherd's Bush 2005–10 (Parly candidate (Lab) Uxbridge 1997 (by-election)), Hammersmith 2010–; PPS to Dr Stephen Ladyman MP 2005–07, PPS to Lord Malloch-Brown 2007–; memb: Co-op Pty, Unite; *Style—* Andrew Slaughter, Esq, MP; ✉ House of Commons, London SW1A 0AA (e-mail andy@andyslaughter.com, website www.andyslaughter.com)

SLEATH, David John Rivers; *b* 1 March 1961, Leamington Spa, Warks; *Educ* Univ of Warwick (BSc); *Career* Arthur Andersen 1982–98 (ptnr 1992–98), fin dir Wagon plc 1998–2005; SEGRO plc: fin dir 2005–11, chief exec 2011–; non-exec dir Bunzl plc 2007–; FCA; *Style—* David Sleath, Esq; ✉ SEGRO plc, 15 Regent Street, London SW17 4LR (☎ 020 7451 9100)

SLEEMAN, Prof Brian David; s of Richard Kinsman Sleeman (d 2002), and Gertrude Cecilia, *née* Gamble (d 1998); *b* 4 August 1939; *Educ* Canterbury Rd Sch Morden, Tiffin Boy's Sch Kingston upon Thames, Battersea Coll of Technol (BSc), Univ of London (PhD), Univ of Dundee (DSc); *m* 7 Sept 1963, Juliet Mary, da of Frederick James John (d 1972); 1 da (Elizabeth b 15 Sept 1966), 2 s (Matthew b 19 Feb 1969, David b 12 June 1972); *Career* Univ of Dundee: asst lectr 1965–67, lectr 1967–71, reader 1971–78, prof of applied analysis 1978–93, head Dept of Mathematics and Computer Sci 1986–89, Ivory prof of mathematics 1993–95, hon prof of mathematics 1995–; Univ of Leeds: prof of applied mathematics 1995–2004, prof emeritus 2004–; various hon visiting professorships at univs in USA, Canada, Sweden, France, Chile and China; visiting prof mathematical biology Univ of Abertay Dundee 2004–; chm Scot Branch IMA 1982–84, pres of Edinburgh Mathematical Soc 1988–89; life memb Clare Hall Cambridge 2002–; Erskine Fell Univ of Canterbury Christchurch NZ 2003 and 2008, Endowment Fund for the Future Fell Univ of Alberta Canada 2003; FIMA 1972, FRSE 1976, CMath 1991; *Books* Multiparameter Spectral Theory in Hilbert Space (1978), Differential Equations and Mathematical Biology (1983, 3 edn 2010); *Recreations* choral music, hill walking; *Style—* Prof Brian Sleeman, FRSE; ✉ 3 Campfield Road, Broughty Ferry, Dundee DD5 2NG (☎ 01382 775389, e-mail brian.sleeman@btinternet.com)

SLEEMAN, John Keith; s of John Sleeman, and Elsie, *née* Galloway; *b* 24 July 1949, London; *Educ* Univ of Durham (BSc); *m* 19 April 1975, Gail, *née* Blair; 1 da (Helena), 2 s (Christopher, Anthony); *Career* dir Samuel Montagu & Co Ltd 1989–94, md HSBC Bank plc 1994–2003; dir: Power Machines 2003–08, Open Investments 2006–09, PV Crystalox Solar plc 2007– (chm), UCP (formerly Unitech Corporate Parks) plc 2013–; ptnr then sr advsr S P Angel Corporate Finance LLP 2006–; Master Worshipful Co of Wax Chandlers 2011–12; FCA 1973, ACIB 1977; *Recreations* opera, reading, piano; *Style—* John Sleeman, Esq; ✉ S P Angel Corporate Finance LLP, 35–39 Maddox Street, London W1S 2PP (☎ 020 3463 2271, fax 020 7629 1341, e-mail john.sleeman@spangel.co.uk)

SLEEP, Dr Wayne Philip Colin; OBE (1998); s of stepfather Stanley Sleep, of Plymouth, Devon, and Joan Gwendoline Maude Sleep (d 1994); *b* 17 July 1948; *Educ* West Hartlepool Tech Sch, Royal Ballet Sch Richmond Park (Leverhulme scholarship); *Career* dancer, choreographer; joined Royal Ballet 1966 and in 1973 became princ dancer in over 50 leading roles incl: Puck in The Dream, Jester in Cinderella, Blue Boy in Les Patineurs, Petrushka, Alain and Widow Simone in La Fille Mal Gardée, Dr Coppélius in Coppélia (ENB tour) 1994; roles created for him by Sir Frederick Ashton incl: Koila in A Month in the Country, G R Sinclair in Elgar's Enigma Variations, Squirrel Nutkin and one of the Bad Mice in the film The Tales of Beatrix Potter; worked with other choreographers incl: Dame Ninette De Valois, Sir Kenneth Macmillan, Rudolph Nureyev, Joe Layton, Norman Main, Nigel Lythgoe; choreographer of: David and Goliath (London Contemporary Dance), dance sequence in Death on the Nile, The Hot Shoe Show (BBC TV), Harry Nilsson's The Point (and played leading role, Mermaid), Savoy Suite (Savoy Theatre reopening benefit for ENB) 1993, Promenade (for ENB Sch Festival) 1994, Alice in Wonderland (Nat Youth Ballet) 1997; acting roles incl: Ariel in The Tempest (New Shakespeare Co), Truffelino in The Servant of Two Masters, title role in Pinocchio (Birmingham rep), Tony Lumpkin in She Stoops to Conquer (BBC Radio), the Soldier in The Soldiers Tale (Festival Hall), The First Great Train Robbery, The Virgin Soldiers, original co of Cats 1981, Song and Dance 1982, Emcee in Gillian Lynn's Cabaret (West End), Puck in A Midsummer Night's Dream (Shakespeare Festival Brighton, Leeds and Nottingham) 2002, played in numerous pantomime seasons; formed own dance gp with nat and int tours under the names of Dash, The Hot Shoe Show and Bits and Pieces 1982–85, made several guest appearances, directed Carnival for the Birds (Royal Opera House), toured UK with cabaret show, revival of Song and Dance (West End and UK tour) 1992, Hollywood and Broadway – The Musicals (with Lorna Luft) 1992, directed royal ballet gala for Benesh Dance Notation charity 1993, Wayne's World of Dance tour 1993, Hollywood and Broadway Part II (UK tour) 1994, starred in and choreographed royal charity gala 90 Years of Dance 1995, own dance company tour Dance 1995, directed and starred in royal charity gala A Night of Stars (HM's Theatre) 1997, Hollywood and Broadway Part III (UK tour) 1997, starred in Le Fil Mal Gardé (Scottish Ballet) 1997, directed and starred in Lord Mayor of London charity gala A Celebration of Dance (Britten Theatre) 1997, directed and starred in Wayne Sleep Gala 50 Winks at Wayne Sleep 1998, directed and starred in Dash to the Coliseum 1998, Wayne's World of Classic Ballet tour 1998, starred in Aladdin Blackpool Grand 1998, directed and starred in Aspects of Dance (UK tour) 1999, choreographed Carousel (nat tour) 2000, star and choreographer Ready Steady Dance (UK tour) 2001, directed Dame Beryls Gray's 75th Birthday Gala (Sadlers Wells) 2002; fndr Wayne Sleep Dance Scholarship 1998, jazz ballet and tap teacher and coach; compere own radio show LBC 1987–97, subject of Special South Bank Show 1998; Show Business Personality of the Year 1983, two entries in Guinness Book of Records; Hon DUniv Exeter, Hon BA Teesside Univ 1999; FRSA; *Books* Variations on Wayne Sleep (1982), Precious Little Sleep (autobiography); *Clubs* Groucho; *Style—* Dr Wayne Sleep, OBE; ✉ c/o Burnett Crowther Ltd, 3 Clifford Street, London, W1S 2LF (e-mail associates@bgcltd.org)

SLEVIN, Dr Maurice Louis; s of David Slevin, of Cape Town, South Africa, and Nita, *née* Rosenbaum; *b* 2 July 1949; *Educ* De La Salle Coll East London, Univ of Cape Town (MB ChB); *m* 1, 5 Jan 1975 (m dis 1988), Cherry Lynn; 2 da (Lindi b 1978, Amy b 1981); m 2, 1993, Nicola Jane Harris; 1 da (Susannah b 1996), 1 s (Jamie b 1997); *Career* med registrar Groote Schuur Hosp Cape Town 1977, registrar and sr registrar Dept of Med Oncology Bart's London 1978–82, conslt physician and med oncologist Depts of Med Oncology Bart's and Homerton Hosps London 1982–2007, hon conslt physician and med oncologist Depts of Med Oncology Bart's and London NHS Tst 2007–; chm Cancerbacup (formerly Br Assoc Cancer United Patients), founder memb Doctors of Reform; MD 1984, FRCP 1989 (MRCP 1978); *Books* Randomised Trials in Cancer: A Critical Review by Sites (jt ed, with Maurice Staquet), Challenging Cancer: From Chaos to Control, Cancer: The Facts (with Michael Whitehouse, 1996), Cancer: How Worthwhile is Non Curative Treatment (1998), Challenging Cancer: Fighting Back, Taking Control, Finding Options (2002); *Style—* Dr Maurice Slevin; ✉ London Oncology Clinic, 95 Harley Street, London W1G 6AF (☎ 020 7317 2525, fax 020 7009 4225)

SLIM, 2 Viscount (UK 1960), of Yarralumla, ACT, and Bishopston, City and Co of Bristol; John Douglas Slim; OBE (Mil 1973), DL (Greater London 1988); s of Field Marshal 1 Viscount (Sir William Joseph) Slim, KG, GCB, GCMG, GCVO, GBE, DSO, MC, sometime GOC Allied Land Forces SE Asia, govr-gen Aust and govr and constable Windsor Castle (d 1970), and Aileen, *née* Robertson (d 1993); *b* 20 July 1927; *Educ* Prince of Wales Royal Indian Mil Coll Dehra Dun; *m* 1958, Elisabeth, da of Arthur Rawdon Spinney, CBE (decd); 2 s, 1 da; *Heir* s, Hon Mark Slim, *qv*; *Career* cmmnd Indian Army 6 Gurkha Rifles 1945–48, Lt Argyll and Sutherland Highlanders 1948, SAS 1952, Staff Coll 1961, Jt Serv Staff Coll 1964, Cdr 22 SAS Regt 1967–70, GSO1 (Special Forces) HQ UK Land Forces 1970–72, ret 1972; Morgan Crucible Co 1973–76, chm Peek plc 1977–91 (dep chm 1991–97); dir Trailfinders Ltd 1984–2007, dir various other cos; pres Burma Star Assoc, vice-pres Br-Aust Soc, vice-chm Arab-Br C of C and Industry 1977–96, tstee Royal Cwlth Ex-Services League 1996–2016, pres Special Air Serv Assoc 2000–11 (patron 2011–); memb House of Lords 1971, elected memb House of Lords 1999; Master Worshipful Co of Clothworkers 1995–96; FRGS 1983; *Clubs* White's, Special Forces; *Style—* The Rt Hon the Viscount Slim, OBE, DL; ✉ House of Lords, London SW1A 0PW

SLIM, Hon Mark William Rawdon; s and h of 2 Viscount Slim, OBE, DL, *qv*; *b* 13 February 1960; *m* 15 Feb 1992, Harriet Laura, yr da of Jonathan Harrison, of Beds; 3 s (Rufus William Rawdon b 15 April 1995, William James Harrison b 6 July 1999, Kit Cosmo John b 20 Aug 2004); *Career* fndr Mark Slim and Partners (real estate consltss), merged into CB Richard Ellis Ltd (currently exec dir); non-exec dir: Muntons Hldgs, Oakley Properties; chm of tstees Burma Star Assoc; Liveryman Worshipful Co of Clothworkers; *Recreations* shooting, fishing, history; *Clubs* White's, Aldeburgh Yacht; *Style—* The Hon Mark Slim

SLINN, David Arthur; CMG (2008), OBE (2000); s of Ronald Geoffrey Slinn, of Northampton, and Christine Mary, *née* Kingston; *b* 16 April 1959, Northampton; *Educ* Northampton GS, Univ of Salford (BA); *m* Heidi Alberta Hulan; 1 da; *Career* diplomat; joined FCO 1981, third sec UK Perm Rep to Conf on Disarmament (UKDis) Geneva 1983, second sec Ulaanbaatar 1987, second sec Pretoria and Cape Town 1990, FCO 1993, chargé d'affaires Tirana 1995, first sec Belgrade 1996, head Br Govt Office Pristina 1999, on loan to NATO/EU Macedonia 2001, ambass to North Korea 2002–06, head provincial reconstruction team Lashkar Gah Helmand Province Afghanistan 2007–08, seconded to Int Civilian Office Pristina Kosovo 2008–09, head Afghanistan Drugs and Justice Unit FCO 2009–11, ambass to Croatia 2012–15; ret; sr assoc Centre for Int Policy Studies Univ of Ottowa, fell Norman Paterson Sch of Int Affrs Carleton Univ; FRSA 2005; *Recreations* rugby, golf, malt whisky; *Style—* Mr David Slinn, CMG, OBE; ✉ e-mail davidslinn@gmail.com

SLIPMAN, Sue; OBE (1994); da of Max Slipman (d 1971), of London, and Doris *née* Barham (d 1972); *b* 3 August 1949; *Educ* Stockwell Manor Sch, Univ of Wales (BA), Univ of London (PGCE); *Children* 1 s (Gideon Max b 1988); *Career* pres NUS 1977–78, vice-chm Br Youth Cncl 1977–78, memb Cncl Open Univ 1978–81; memb: Nat Union of Public Employees 1970–85, EC Econ and Social Ctee 1990–92; dir: Nat Cncl for One Parent Families 1985–95, London East TEC 1989–, London TEC Cncl 1995–96, Gas Consumers' Cncl 1996–98; dir for social responsibility Camelot Gp plc 1998–2003, chm Bd Financial Ombudsman Service 2003–04, dir Foundation Trust Network NHS Confedn 2004–; chair: Better Regulation Task Force 1997–2001, Corporate Responsibility Gp 2002; memb Working Gp on Women's Issues to Sec of State for Employment; *Books* Helping Ourselves to Power: A Training Manual for Women in Public Life Skills (1986), Helping One Parent Families to Work (1988), Maintainance: A System to Benefit Children (1989), Making Maintainance Pay (1990); *Style—* Ms Sue Slipman, OBE

SLIWERSKI, Trevor Zygmunt; s of Zdzislaw Andrzej Sliwerski (d 2002), and Irene Sliwerski (d 1990); *b* 30 December 1950; *Educ* John Fisher Sch Purley; *m* Lynn, da of Leonard Arthur Francis (d 1991); 1 da (Claire Louise b 1983), 1 s (Jeremy Andrew Zbigniew b 1987); *Career* dealer: Savory Milln 1968–71, R Layton 1971–74, Nomura 1978–80; dir RBT Fleming 1980–85, dir i/c Japanese equity warrants Baring Securities 1985–95, AJG Investments Ltd 1995–96, head of convertible and warrant sales Investec Bank (UK) Ltd (formerly Guinness Mahon & Co Ltd) 1996–2001, dir MSG and Partners Ltd 2001–; proprietor Noah's Ark Nursery 1990–2004; *Recreations* walking, flying; *Clubs* Surrey Walking, Stock Exchange Athletic; *Style—* Trevor Z Sliwerski, Esq; ✉ Stratton Street Capital LLP, 200 Aldersgate, London EC1A 4HD (☎ 020 7766 0810, e-mail trevorsliwerski@strattonstreet.com)

SLOAM, Nigel Spencer; s of Maurice Sloam (d 1991), of London, and Ruth, *née* Davis (d 1998); *b* 17 December 1950; *Educ* Haberdashers' Aske's, Corpus Christi Coll Oxford (MA); *m* 3 Sept 1978, Elizabeth Augusta, da of Arnold Hertzberg; 1 da (Natalia Sylvia Caroline b 1979), 1 s (Oliver Julian Richard b 1983); *Career* trainee actuary Messrs Bacon & Woodrow 1972–76, actuary Sahar Insurance Co of Israel 1976–77, mangr Actuarial Dept

Charterhouse Magna Assurance Co 1977–78, dir Messrs Bevington Lowndes Ltd 1978–79, sr ptnr Nigel Sloam & Co 1979–, gérant NSS Actuarial Monaco Sarl 2010; Freeman City of London, Liveryman Worshipful Co of Basketmakers, Liveryman Worshipful Co of Actuaries; FIA 1977, ASA 1987, CMath 1991, MIMA; *Clubs* Oxford and Cambridge, City Livery, Goose and Beast (pres), The Maccabeans; *Style*— Nigel Sloam, Esq; ✉ Nigel Sloam & Co, Roman House, 296 Golders Green Road, London NW11 9PY (☎ 020 8209 1222, fax 020 8455 3973, e-mail nigel@nigelsloam.co.uk)

SLOAN, Anna; da of Ian Sloan, and Christine Miller; *b* 5 February 1991, Dumfries; *Educ* Glasgow Caledonian Univ (BA); *Career* curler; achievements incl: Silver medals European Curling Championships 2010, 2012 and 2013, Gold medal European Curling Championships 2011, Gold medal World Championships 2013, Bronze medal Winter Olympic Games 2014; involved with Active Schools; Hon Dr Glasgow Caledonian Univ; *Recreations* fashion, horse riding; *Clubs* Royal Caledonian Curling; *Style*— Ms Anna Sloan; ✉ c/o Red Sky Management, George Street, Edinburgh (www.redskymanagement.co.uk, Twitter @annasloan1)

SLOAN, Eur Ing Gordon McMillan; s of Samuel Sloan, of Muirkirk, Ayrshire, and Christine McMillan, *née* Turner; *b* 30 December 1934; *Educ* Muirkirk Sch, Kilmarnock Acad, Glasgow Royal Tech Coll; *m* 5 Aug 1961, Patricia Mary, da of William Stewart McKim (d 1979); 1 s (John), 4 da (Christine, Elizabeth, Mary, Rachel); *Career* sr engr Sir Bruce White, Wolfe Barry and Ptnrs Consulting Engrs 1956–73, dir Parsons Brown & Newton Consulting Engrs 1973–81, chief engr McMillan Sloan & Partners Consulting Engrs 1981–; notable works incl: studies, master plans, reports and detailed plans for major new ports at Dammam (Saudi Arabia), and Muara (Brunei), study and re-devpt plan with designs for Cardiff Port, design of floating port Aqaba (Jordan), alternative plan and detailed design for Nava Sheva new port Mumbai, detailed study of abandonment and removal of major N Sea prodn platform; advsr to developers of energy and transportation projects in Far East and to London Underground; professional examiner IMechE 1996–2001; Freeman City of London 1967, Liveryman Worshipful Co of Turners 1968 (memb Ct of Assts 1987, Upper Warden 1994–95, Master 1995–96, Dep Master 1996–97); CEng 1967, FInstPet 1974, FIMechE 1978, MSocIS (France) 1978, FPWI 1988, Eur Ing 1989, MIET 2006; *Recreations* music appreciation, property restoration; *Style*— Eur Ing Gordon Sloan; ✉ Douglas House, Soames Walk, New Malden, Surrey KT3 4RZ (e-mail gmsloan@mcmillan-sloan.co.uk)

SLOAN, His Hon Judge Paul Kay; QC (2001); s of Stanley Buchanan Sloan (d 2005), and Susan Ann, *née* Usherwood; *b* Essex; *Educ* City of London Sch, Queen Mary Coll Univ of London (LLB); *Career* called to the Bar 1981; asst recorder 1998, recorder 2000, circuit judge (North Eastern Circuit) 2011–, sr circuit judge, resident judge Newcastle upon Tyne Combined Court Centre and hon recorder of Newcastle 2014–; chm Barmark 2004–07; tutor judge Judicial Coll 2007–; *Style*— His Hon Judge Sloan, QC; ✉ Newcastle upon Tyne Combined Court Centre, Law Courts, Quayside, Newcastle upon Tyne NE1 3LA

SLOAN, Ronald Kenneth (Ronnie); *b* 21 July 1943; *Educ* Edinburgh Acad; *m* 29 May 1965, Sandra; 2 s (Elliot b 1969, Moray b 1971), 1 da (Hazel b 1978); *Career* Standard Life 1960–67, Friends Provident 1967–70; dir: Antony Gibbs Pensions Ltd 1970–71, Martin Paterson Assocs Ltd 1972–87; divnl dir and actuary Buck Paterson Conslts Ltd 1987–93, ptnr Punter Southall & Co 1994–2000, ind consulting actuary 2000–; chm Scottish Gp NAPF 1997–99 (Nat Assoc of Pension Funds), chm Scottish Actuaries Club 2000–01; pres Edinburgh Academical RFC 1992–94 (capt 1973–74), chm SportsAid Scotland 2009–, chm Raeburn Place Appeal; fundraiser for Children 1st (formerly RSSPCC) running 33 marathons around the world dressed as tartan Superman raising over £220,000; FFA 1967, FPMI 1977, FInstD 1980; *Recreations* tennis, rugby, running, Scottish country dancing; *Clubs* Edinburgh Acad, Royal Scots; *Style*— Ronnie Sloan, Esq; ✉ 20 Lomond Road, Edinburgh EH5 3JR (☎ 0131 551 5471)

SLOANE, Prof Peter James; s of John Joseph Sloane (d 1992), and Elizabeth, *née* Clarke (d 2004); *b* 6 August 1942; *Educ* Cheadle Hulme Sch, Univ of Sheffield (BA), Univ of Strathclyde (PhD); *m* 30 July 1969, Avril Mary, da of Kenneth Urquhart (d 1984); 1 s (Christopher Peter b 1971); *Career* asst lectr and lectr in political economy Univ of Aberdeen 1966–69, lectr in industrial economics Univ of Nottingham 1969–75, econ advsr Unit for Manpower Studies Dept of Employment 1973–74, prof of economics and mgmnt Paisley Coll 1975–84; Univ of Aberdeen: prof of political economy 1984–2002 (now emeritus), Jaffrey prof of political economy 1985–2002, vice-princ and dean of social scis and law 1996–2002; dir Welsh Economy Labour Market Evaluation and Research Centre (WELMERC) Dept of Economics Univ of Wales Swansea 2002–08 (emeritus prof 2008); visiting prof: McMaster Univ Hamilton Ontario 1978 (Cwlth fell), Indiana Univ 1996; hon professorial fell Univ of Melbourne 2007–10, pt/t adjunct prof Nat Inst of Labour Studies Flinders Univ Adelaide 2010–; hon res fell Inst for Labor Studies Bonn 2001–; vice-pres Int Assoc of Sports Economists 2000–10; memb: ESRC 1979–85, Sec of State for Scotland's Panel of Econ Conslts 1981–91, Cncl Scottish Econ Soc 1983–2001, Ct Univ of Aberdeen 1987–91 and 1993–2002, Royal Economic Soc, Euro Assoc of Labour Economists; FRSA 1997, FRSE 1997; *Books* Changing Patterns of Working Hours (1975), Sex Discrimination in the Labour Market (with B Chiplin, 1975), Sport in the Market? (1980), Women and Low Pay (ed 1980), The Earnings Gap Between Men and Women in Great Britain (1981), Equal Employment Issues (with H C Jain, 1981), Tackling Discrimination in the Workplace (with B Chiplin, 1982), Labour Economics (with D Carline, et al 1985), Sex at Work: Equal Pay and the Comparable Worth Controversy (1985), Low Pay and Earnings Mobility in Europe (ed with R Asplund and I Theodossiou, 1998), Employment Equity and Affirmative Action (with H Jain and F Horwitz, 2003), The Economics of Sport (with M Rosentraub and R Sandy, 2004), Modern Labour Economics (with P Latreille and N O'Leary, 2013), Handbook on the Economics of Professional Football (ed, with J Goddard, 2014); plus contributions to various academic jls; *Recreations* sport; *Clubs* Pennard Golf; *Style*— Prof Peter Sloane, FRSE; ✉ 5 Willowbrook Gardens, Mayals, Swansea SA3 5EB (☎ 01792 517511)

SLOBODA, Prof John Anthony; s of Mieczyslaw Sloboda (d 1981), and Mary, *née* Bregazzi; *b* 13 June 1950, London; *Educ* St Benedict's Sch Ealing, The Queen's Coll Oxford (MA), UCL (PhD); *m* 1980 (m dis 1991), Judith, *née* Nussbaum; 1 da (Miriam Anne b 14 Feb 1982); *Career* Keele Univ: memb Sch of Psychology 1974–2008, dir Unit for the Study of Musical Skill and Devpt 1991–2008, emeritus prof 2008–; research prof GSM 2009–; sometime pres: Psychology Section and Gen Section BAAS, European Soc for the Cognitive Sciences of Music; memb Editorial Bd: Musicae Scientiae (jl of European Soc for the Cognitive Sciences of Music), Psychology of Music, Music Perception, Psychology Teaching Review; Pres's Award for Distinguished Contributions to Psychological Knowledge Br Psychological Soc 1998; Oxford Research Gp: exec dir 2004–09, co-dir Every Casualty Prog 2007–14, co-dir Every Casualty Worldwide 2014–; co-fndr Iraq Body Count Project; FBPsS, FBA; *Publications* The Musical Mind: The Cognitive Psychology of Music (1985), Generative Processes in Music: The Psychology of Performance, Improvisation and Composition (1988), Musical Beginnings: Origins and Development of Musical Competence (jtly, 1996), Perception and Cognition of Music (jtly, 1997), Music and Emotion: Theory and Research (ed jtly, 2001), Exploring the Musical Mind (2004), Psychology for Musicians (jtly, 2007), Beyond Terror: The truth about the real threats to our world (jtly, 2007), Handbook of Music and Emotion (ed jtly, 2010); also author of research papers and jl articles; *Recreations* choral singing; *Style*— Prof John Sloboda; ✉ Guildhall School of Music and Drama, Silk Street, Barbican, London EC2Y 8DT (e-mail john.sloboda@gsmd.ac.uk)

SLOCOCK, Caroline Ann; da of Horace Slocock, and (Florence) Joyce, *née* Wheelton; *b* 30 December 1956, Wimborne, Dorset; *Educ* Talbot Heath Sch Bournemouth, UCL (BA); *m* John Nightingale; *Career* joined Dept of Employment 1982, private sec to sec of state for Employment 1985–87, memb Next Steps Project Team Cabinet Office 1988–89, private sec (home affrs) to PM 1989–91, head of Treasy personnel 1993–96, sr policy advsr on expenditure HM Treasy 1997–2000, jt head Early Years and Childcare Unit DfES 2000–02, chief exec Equal Opportunities Cmmn 2002–07, chief exec Refugee and Migrant Justice (formerly Refugee Legal Centre) 2007–10, dir Civil Exchange 2011–; *Publications* The Big Society Audit (2012, 3 edn 2015), Making Good: the Future of the Voluntary Sector (collection of essays, ed 2015), Independence in Question: the voluntary sector in 2016 (2016); *Recreations* gardening, photography, reading, swimming; *Style*— Ms Caroline Slocock; ✉ e-mail carolineslocock@civilexchange.org.uk

SLOCOCK, (David) Michael; s of Maj Arthur Anthony Slocock (d 1995), and Elizabeth Anthea, *née* Sturdy (d 1990); *b* 1 February 1945; *Educ* Radley, Lincoln Coll Oxford (BA); *m* 12 April 1969, Theresa Mary, da of Maj Anthony Clyde-Smith (d 1989), of Jersey, CI; 1 da (Lucinda Sheila Mary b 1971), 2 s (Julian Mark Anthony b 1973, Mark David Philip b 1976); *Career* The Sunday Telegraph 1967–69, Hill Samuel & Co Ltd merchant bankers 1969–71, dir various cos including Normans Group plc, Empire Plantations & Investments, L K Industrial Investments 1971–79; chief exec: Normans Group plc 1973–90, Selections Mail Order 1991–; *Recreations* sailing, skiing, golf, gardening; *Style*— Michael Slocock, Esq; ✉ Southover House, Tolpuddle, Dorchester, Dorset DT2 7HF (☎ 01305 848220)

SLOCOMBE, Sue; OBE (1994); da of Capt Leonard William Ellis, MBE (d 1977), and Phyllis Muriel, *née* Chick (d 1984); *b* 8 June 1949; *Educ* Nailsea GS, Bedford Coll of Physical Educ, Univ of Bristol; *m* 1, 5 Aug 1972, Martin Charles Slocombe, s of Charles Slocombe (d 1976); m 2, 30 June 2000, David Whitaker, OBE; *Career* teacher Clifton HS for Girls 1970–74; lectr: Coll of St Matthias 1974–76, Faculty of Educn Bristol Poly 1976–98; princ lectr and dir of studies UWE (formerly Bristol Poly); currently ptnr Performance Conslts LLP; course dir MSc in coaching and devpt in business 2002–10; sportswoman; int hockey player: Outdoor World Cup 1979, Euro Bronze medallist 1985, indoor capt 1985–88; coach England Ladies Sr Hockey Team 1986–94 (Euro Silver medal 1987, 4th in World Cup 1990, Euro Gold medal 1991), coach GB Ladies Olympic Hockey Squad 1993– (asst coach 1989–90, 4th in Atlanta Olympic Games 1996); memb: Coaches Advsy Panel Br Olympic Assoc, Exec Bd Nat Coaches Assoc 1993–98, Exec Bd Nat Coaching Fndn 1993–98, Sports Cncl Women in Coaching Advsy Gp 1993–96; involved in hockey coaching to club and int standard (also children's hockey coach); winner Coach of the Year award 1991; expert advsr Sport England 2000–06; prog dir Business, Women & Success in the 21st Century 2000; tstee Children our Ultimate Investment; memb: NASC, PE Assoc of GB and NI, BAALPE; *Books* Indoor Hockey (1985), Make Hockey Fun – Hockey for 8–12 year olds (1985); *Style*— Mrs Sue Slocombe, OBE; ✉ Brackenwood, 2 Folleigh Close, Long Ashton, Bristol BS41 9HX (☎ 01275 394116, e-mail sue.whitaker13@hotmail.co.uk)

SLOGROVE, Richard Paul; s of Wing Cdr A P Slogrove (d 1974), and Margaret Anne (Margot), *née* Hannam-Clark (d 1997); *b* 1 November 1945; *Educ* King's Ely (chorister, King's scholar), RAF Coll Cranwell (Sword of Honour, Queen's Medal), Univ of London (BA); *m* 6 June 1970, Judyth Anne (Jo), da of James Peacock (d 1999); 1 da (Emma b 1 June 1972); *Career* RAF 1963–76 (Sqdn Ldr); md Telex UK Ltd 1985–88; Memorex Telex: vice-pres Personal Computer Div 1988–90, pres Canada 1990–92, vice-pres N America Sales and Serv 1992–94; British Telecommunications plc: dir Global Mktg 1994–97, pres Asia Pacific 1997–2000, pres Operations BT Ignite 2000–01; memb Cncl Inst of Educ Univ of London 1996–2000, govr King's Ely 1998–2012 (chm Bd of Govrs 2005–12); chm of tstees Ely Cathedral Tst 2013–, dep chm Cranwellian Assoc 2014–; *Clubs* RAF, Leander; *Style*— Richard Slogrove, Esq; ✉ 9 Houghton Gardens, Ely, Cambridgeshire CB7 4JN (e-mail richardslogrove@btinternet.com)

SMALL, Harry; s of Eric James Small, of London, and Brenda, *née* Bedford; *b* 20 April 1957; *Educ* St Alban's Boys' GS, Oriel Coll Oxford (MA); *m* 7 April 2006, Jonathan Brough (civil partnership converted); *Career* asst slr Linklaters & Paines 1981–86 (articled clerk 1979–81); Baker & McKenzie: assoc Hong Kong 1986–87, assoc London 1987–89, ptnr Intellectual Property IT Dept 1989–, head IT and Communications Gp 2002–08, chair Global IT/Communications Gp 2008–14; chair Baker & Mckenzie LGBT+ Initiative 2012–; visiting lectr in trade mark law Queen Mary Coll London 1984–85, lectr in designs law Intellectual Property Dip Univ of Bristol 1993–2005, expert EU Economic and Social Ctee on various EU copyright and IT law proposals 1990–; author of numerous articles on IT matters; chm Soc for Computers and Law 1997–2000 (fell 2005); memb: Law Soc England 1981–, Law Soc Hong Kong 1986–87, Computer Law Gp 1990–2011; *Recreations* travel, food, drink, sleeping; *Clubs* Lansdowne; *Style*— Harry Small, Esq; ✉ Baker & McKenzie, 100 New Bridge Street, London EC4V 7JA (☎ 020 7919 1000, e-mail harry.small@bakermckenzie.com)

SMALLMAN, Timothy Gilpin; s of Stanley Cottrell Smallman (d 1965), of Kenilworth, Warks, and Grace Mary Louise, *née* Wilson (d 1990); *b* 6 November 1938; *Educ* Stowe; *m* 18 April 1964, Jane, da of Edward Holloway (d 1988), of Acocks Green, Birmingham; 2 s (Guy b 1965, Simon b 1967); *Career* chm: Smallman Lubricants (Hereford) Ltd 1972–2000, WF Smallman and Son Ltd 1978–2000 (md 1965–2000), Smallman Lubricants Ltd 1978–2000 (md 1978–96), Coronet Oil Refineries Ltd 1979–2000, Needwood Oils and Solvents Ltd 1984–2000, ret; nat pres Br Lubricants Fedn Ltd 1983–85 (dir 1977–89); FInstD 1965, FInstPet 1968; *Recreations* bridge, ornithology, nature and wildlife conservation; *Style*— Timothy Smallman, Esq; ✉ Luddington Manor, Stratford-upon-Avon, Warwickshire CV37 9SJ

SMALLWOOD, Christopher Rafton; s of James Rafton Smallwood, of Sandbach, Cheshire, and Josephine, *née* Mortimer; *b* 13 August 1947, Morecambe, Lancs; *Educ* Royal GS Lancaster, Exeter Coll Oxford (open exhibitioner, BA), Nuffield Coll Oxford (MPhil); *m* 28 July 1979, Ingeborg Hedwig Eva, *née* Wiesler; 1 s (Nicholas Joseph Christopher b 20 Sept 1982), 1 da (Stephanie Ingeborg b 22 Nov 1985); *Career* Harkness fell Harvard Univ 1968–69, lectr in economics Exeter Coll Oxford 1971–72, lectr in economics Univ of Edinburgh 1972–76, special advsr Cabinet Office Constitution Unit 1974–75, economic advsr HM Treasy 1976–81, dir of policy SDP 1981–83, chief economist British Petroleum Co plc 1983–86, economics ed Sunday Times 1986–89, gp economist and strategic devpt dir TSB Gp 1989–94 (also dir TSB Bank), ptnr Makinson Cowell Ltd 1994–98, ptnr Brunswick Gp Ltd 1998–2001, chief economic advsr Barclays plc 2001–05, dir Lombard Street Assocs 2005–; memb Competition Cmmn 2001–09; policy advsr Prince of Wales Charitable Fndns 2005–09; chm: Hounslow PCT 2007–09, Kingston Hosp NHS Tst 2009–11, St George's Healthcare NHS Tst 2011–; memb Advsy Cncl ECGD 1991–94; visiting fell Centre for Business Strategy London Business Sch 1987–88; dir UnLTD 2001– (chm Investment Ctee); *Recreations* opera, theatre, golf; *Clubs* Reform; *Style*— Christopher Smallwood, Esq

SMALLWOOD, Prof Rodney Harris (Rod); s of William Frederick Smallwood (d 1997), and Muriel, *née* Smith (d 2006); *b* 14 July 1945; *Educ* Withernsea HS, UCL (BSc), Lancaster Univ (MSc), Univ of Sheffield (PhD); *m* 3 Aug 1968, Anna Mary, *née* Treharne; 1 s (Ben b 15 Nov 1984); *Career* basic grade, sr grade, princ grade then top grade med physicist NHS 1970–96; Univ of Sheffield: prof of med engrg 1995–2003, prof of computational systems biology 2003–, dir of research (engrg) 2003–; author of and contrib to books and sci pubns; pres Inst of Physics and Engrg in Med 1999–2001; FREng 2001, Hon

S

FRCP 2002, FIEE, FInstP, fell Inst of Physics and Engrg in Med (FIPEM); *Recreations* fell running, mountaineering, cycling; *Style—* Prof Rod Smallwood; ✉ Department of Computer Science, University of Sheffield, Regent Court, 211 Portobello Road, Sheffield S1 4DP (☎ 0114 222 1840, e-mail r.smallwood@dcs.shef.ac.uk, website www.dcs.shef.ac.uk/~rod)

SMALLWOOD, Dr Stuart David; s of James Smallwood, of Canterbury, Kent, and Pamela Smallwood; *b* 21 February 1962; *Educ* Harvey GS Folkestone, Univ of Leeds (BSc), Univ of Cambridge (PhD), Univ of Bristol (PGCE, NPQH); *m* 9 April 1988, Charlotte, *née* Burlend; 1 da (Eleanor b 1991), 2 s (Oliver b 1995, Benedict b 2000); *Career* teacher of geography, head of geography and head of humanities Sir Thomas Rich's Sch Gloucester 1989–98, headmaster Bishop Wordsworth's Sch Salisbury 2002– (dep headmaster 1998–2002); memb: HMC, ASCL; *Recreations* ornithology, running, classical music, clarinet; *Style—* Dr Stuart Smallwood; ✉ Bishop Wordsworth's School, 11 The Close, Salisbury, Wiltshire SP1 2EB (☎ 01722 333851, fax 01722 325899, e-mail sds@bws.wilts.sch.uk)

SMART, Edward Christopher (Ted); *b* 9 April 1943, Twickenham; *Educ* St Edward's Sch Oxford; *m* Nicola; 3 s (Alex b 1976, Tim b 1978, Mat b 1982); *Career* with Royal Hong Kong Police 1963–71, fndr Eurasia Publishing 1972, with Color Library 1973–88, fndr The Book People Ltd 1988–; patron Deaf and Blind Children's Home Sreepur Bangladesh; *Recreations* reading, travel, keeping parrots; *Style—* Ted Smart, Esq; ✉ The Book People Ltd, Catteshall Manor, Godalming, Surrey GU7 1UU (☎ 01483 860215)

SMART, John Robert; s of Arthur Smart, and Amy, *née* Williams; *b* 18 June 1944; *Educ* Glan Taf HS Cardiff; *m* m 1, Janet (decd); 2 s (Alexander b 17 Jan 1973, Gareth b 17 March 1979); m 2, Kathy; *Career* articled to HMR Burgess & Ptnrs architects, then with various leading architects in Cardiff; fndr (with w, Janet) J R Smart (Builders) Ltd; dir Cardiff RFC; *Style—* John Smart, Esq; ✉ J R Smart (Builders) Ltd, 7–8 Park Place, Cardiff CF10 3DP (☎ 02920 398844, fax 02920 398855)

SMART, HE Timothy Spencer; *m* Veronika Smart (*née* Kantorovitch); *Career* diplomat; desk offr OSCE Dept FCO 1999–2000, second sec political Tel Aviv 2001–04, head of chancery Consulate Gen Basra 2004–05; FCO: team leader EU Middle East North Africa 2005–06, press sec to Perm Under Sec 2006–07, dep head Public Diplomacy Gp and head Strategic Communication Unit 2007–08; high cmmr, dean of diplomatic corps and local rep of presidency EU Cncl of Ministers Honaira 2008–11, chargé d'affaires and head South Pacific Network Suva 2011–12, ambass to Repub of Madagascar 2012–; *Style—* HE Mr Timothy Smart; ✉ c/o Foreign and Commonwealth Office (Antananarivo), King Charles Street, London SW1A 2AH

SMEDDLE, Geoffrey; *Educ* Oundle, Univ of Southampton (BA); *m* Katherine; *Career* head chef Étain Glasgow until 2006 (AA Restaurant Guide Restaurant of the Year 2006, Best City Chef Scottish Chef Award 2005), proprietor and head chef The Peat Inn Fife 2006– (Michelin star, Chef of the Year and Restaurant of the Year Scottish Restaurant Awards 2010); food and recipe columnist The Sunday Herald; fell Masterchefs of GB; *Style—* Geoffrey Smeddle, Esq; ✉ The Peat Inn, By St Andrews, Fife KY15 5LH (e-mail stay@thepeatinn.co.uk)

SMEDLEY, Brig John Edward Bruce; CVO (2014, LVO 2010); s of Edward Smedley (d 1986), and Veronica, *née* McCabe (d 1976); *b* 14 December 1946; *Educ* Felsted (scholar, head of sch), Univ of Reading (BA); *m* 3 April 1976, Lavinia, *née* Lane; 2 s (Rupert b 26 Jan 1979, Charles b 30 March 1981); *Career* cmmnd 3 Royal Tank Regt 1966; Cdr UN Peacekeeping Force in Cyprus (UNFICYP) Support Regt 1988–91, ACOS HQ Br Army of Rhine 1992–94, Cdr Armd Reconnaissance Ace Rapid Reaction Corps 1995, COS Staff Coll Camberley 1996, Dep Cdr 1 (UK) Armd Div 1997–2001; private sec to TRH The Earl and Countess of Wessex 2002–14; chm Int Golf for Youth Ltd 2015–; Freeman Worshipful Co of Haberdashers; FInstM; *Recreations* offshore sailing (RYA Yachtmaster), cricket, golf; *Clubs* Army and Navy; *Style—* Brigadier John Smedley, CVO; ✉ Holmrooke House, Chitterne, Wiltshire BA12 0LG

SMEETH, Ruth; MP; da of Lucy Kelly, *née* Bobrovitch; *b* 29 June 1979, Edinburgh, Scotland; *m* 18 Nov 2004, Michael Smeeth; *Career* sr researcher Amicus/AEEU 2000–04, head of govt relations Sodexo 2004–05, dir of public affrs BICOM 2005–07, public affrs mangr Nestlé 2007, campaign co-ordinator CST 2008–10, dep dir Hope not Hate 2010–15 (currently memb Bd), MP (Lab) Stoke-on-Trent (North) 2015–; memb RSA; *Recreations* cinema, reading, travel; *Clubs* Naval & Military; *Style—* Ms Ruth Smeeth, MP; ✉ House of Commons, London SW1A 0AA (☎ 020 7219 4844, e-mail ruth.smeeth.mp@parliament.uk, website www.ruthsmeeth.org.uk, Twitter @RuthSmeeth)

SMERDON, Richard William; s of late John Conran Smerdon, of Cheltenham, and late Monica Rosewarne, *née* Woollen; *b* 20 May 1942; *Educ* King Edward GS Aston Birmingham, ChCh Oxford (open Smith choral scholar, MA); *m* 1, 13 Aug 1966 (m dis 1991), Alison Lorna, *née* Webb; 1 s (Edward b 14 May 1968), 2 da (Helen b 2 Jan 1970, Jane b 26 August 1972); m 2, 19 Oct 1991, Dr Caroline Mary Kynaston Bowden, da of John Kynaston Williams; *Career* asst slr Slaughter and May 1965–69 (articled 1963–65), ptnr Osborne Clarke 1970–2004; assoc Stephen Platt and Assocs LLP 2012–; memb: Stock Exchange (Midland and Western) Working Pty on Smaller Co Markets 1994, Sub-Ctee on Corp Governance Int Devpts and Ctee on Negotiated Acquisitions American Bar Assoc 1998–2001; rapporteur: All Pty Parly Gp on Corporate Governance 2007–12, Genesis Initiative 2007–14, All Pty Parly Engrg Gp 2009–12; lectr FT Non-Exec Dirs Club 2008–11, visiting lectr Jersey Int Business Sch 2010–14, online tutor for Financial Times non-exec dirs' diploma 2014–; contributing ed European Corp Governance Inst research newsletter 2010–; founding chm Coach House Small Business Centre 1982–85, chm Bath Festival Fndn 1988–91; tstee Nat Fndn for Educn and Research 2003–07, memb Bd Henri Oguike Dance Co 2003–07; volunteer: The Passage Centre for Homeless 2007–, green gown guide Westminster Abbey 2008–, Hammersmith and Fulham Foodbank 2013–; *Books* Butterworth's Company Law Service (co-ed, 1987), Palmer's Company Law Manual (ed, 2001), A Practical Guide to Corporate Governance (4 edn 2010); *Recreations* singing early music, trekking with wife, grandchildren, allotment, gardening; *Clubs* Athenaeum; *Style—* Richard Smerdon, Esq; ✉ 5 Merthyr Terrace, London SW13 9DL (☎ 020 8741 0630, email richard.smerdon@mailbox.co.uk)

SMETHURST, Richard Good; s of Thomas Good Smethurst (d 1981), of Abingdon, Oxon, and Madeleine Nora, *née* Foulkes (d 1987); *b* 17 January 1941; *Educ* Liverpool Coll, Worcester Coll Oxford (Henriques scholar), Nuffield Coll Oxford (G Webb Medley jr scholar, BA, MA); *m* 1, 1964 (m dis), (Dorothy) Joan, da of William James Mitchenall (d 1951), of Shrewsbury; 2 da (Katharine b 1969, Frances b 1976), 2 s (James b 1971, Jonathan b 1979); m 2, 2000, Prof Susan Gillingham, da of Lance Mull (d 1965), of Bradford; 2 step da (Abigail b 1980, Esther b 1984); *Career* fell and tutor in econs St Edmund Hall Oxford 1965–66 (res fell 1964–65), consIt UN/FAO World Food Prog Inst for Cwlth Studies Oxford 1965–66; Univ of Oxford: fell and tutor in econs Worcester Coll and univ lectr in econs 1967–76, dir Dept for External Studies and professorial fell Worcester Coll 1976–86; dep chm Monopolies and Mergers Cmmn 1986–89 (pt/t memb 1978–86); Univ of Oxford: chm Gen Bd of the Faculties 1989–91, provost Worcester Coll 1991–2011, pro-vice-chllr 1997–2011, chm Conf of Colls 2001–03; pt/t econ advsr HM Treasy 1969–71, pt/t policy advsr PM's Policy Unit 1975–76; non-exec dir Investment Mgmnt Regulatory Orgn 1987–2000, Nuffield Orthopaedic Centre NHS Tst 1992–2000; memb: Advsy Cncl for Adult and Continuing Educn DES 1977–83, Continuing Educn Standing Ctee UGC/NAB 1984–88, Cncl Templeton Coll Oxford Centre for Mgmnt Studies 1982–2001, Consumer Panel FSA 1998–2005; chm: Unit for Devpt of Adult Continuing Educn 1991–92, Academic Consultative Ctee Open Univ 1986–92, Advsy Bd Music at Oxford 1988–94; tstee: Euro Community Baroque Orchestra 1986–93, Oxford Philomusica 2003–15; pres: WEA Thames and Solent 1992–2002, Nat Inst for Adult Continuing Educn (NIACE) 1994–2001; fndn hon fell Kellogg Coll Oxford 1990, hon fell St Edmund Hall Oxford 1991, hon fell St Catharine's Coll Cambridge 2002, hon fell Worcester Coll Oxford 2011; *Publications* Impact of Food Aid on Donor Countries (with G R Allen, 1967); contrib: New Thinking About Welfare (1969), The Economic System in the UK (1977, 2 edn 1979), New Directions in Adult and Continuing Education (1979), Continuing Education in Universities and Polytechnics (1982); various articles in Jl of Development Studies and Oxford Review of Education; *Recreations* good food, eating and occasionally cooking it; *Style—* Richard Smethurst, Esq; ✉ 43 Cranham Street, Oxford OX2 6DD (☎ 01865 552837, e-mail richard.smethurst@worc.ox.ac.uk)

SMIDDY, (Francis) Paul; s of Francis Geoffrey Smiddy, of Leeds, and Thelma Vivenne Smiddy; *b* 13 November 1953; *Educ* Winchester, Univ of Manchester; *m* 2009; 2 s (Francis Oliver b 1980, Stewart Alexander b 1982); *Career* mangr Price Waterhouse 1978–82, fin analyst J Sainsbury 1982–84, res analyst Capel-Cure Myers 1984–85, assoc dir Wood Mackenzie 1985–88; dir: Retail Res Kleinwort Benson Securities 1988–93, Retail Res Nomura Research Institute – Europe Ltd 1993–95, Credit Lyonnais Securities Europe 1995–2002, RW Baird Ltd 2002–05, European retail research HSBC 2006–09; writer 2009–; non-exec dir Royal Br Legion Trading Ltd 2010–15; ed Air Pilot magazine 2016–; Liveryman and Asst to the Ct Honourable Co of Air Pilots; FCA 1988; *Publications* Quick Look@Flying (2010); *Recreations* flying, sailing, military history, skiing; *Clubs* RAF; *Style—* Paul Smiddy, Esq

SMIETANA, Krzysztof; Wlodzimierz Smietana, of Kraków, Poland, and Irena, *née* Ludwig (d 1985); *b* 11 October 1956; *Educ* Secdy Music Sch Kraków, Kraków Acad of Music, Guildhall Sch of Music and Drama; *Career* violinist; formerly soloist with the Polish Chamber Orch, came to London 1980 to study under Yfrah Neaman at (and now teacher at) the Guildhall Sch of Music; performed throughout Europe, made several tours of Germany, appeared at most major London venues, appeared at Proms Festival 1997, appeared at BBC Proms Festival, regularly broadcast on BBC Radio 3, guest leader LSO; memb London Mozart Trio 1999–; prizewinner numerous int competitions, winner numerous Polish honours; FGSM 1996; *Recordings incl* Panufnik's Violin Concerto (CD Review magazine CD of the Month) 1989, Fauré Sonantas (CD for Meridian, Retailers Assoc Award for Best Chamber Music Recording 1995) 1993, Brahms Violin Sonatas (CD for ASV), Stravinsky Violin Concerto conducted by Robert Craft (CD for Music Masters), Polish XX Century Music for Piano Trio (CD for Polygram); *Style—* Krzysztof Smietana, Esq; ✉ 14 Kersley Road, London N16 0NP (☎ 020 7254 8876, fax 020 7254 8860, e-mail ksmietana@aol.com)

SMILEY, Philip David; s of late Col David de Crespigny Smiley, LVO, OBE, MC, and Moyra Eileen, *née* Montagu-Douglas-Scott; bro of Xan de Crespigny Smiley, *qv*; *b* 26 August 1951, W Germany; *Educ* Eton, Univ of St Andrews (MA); *m* 3 March 1995, Sohyung, da of Gen and Mrs Young-Woo Kim; 2 s (Francis Hugh Kim b 13 Jan 1996, Dominic David b 14 Dec 1998), 1 da (Flora Ruby b 3 Nov 2000); *Career* HM Overseas Colonial Serv 1974–85: Miny of Home Affrs Solomon Islands 1974–76, Judicial Dept Solomon Islands 1976–80, Civil Serv Branch Hong Kong 1981–83, Economic Servs Branch Hong Kong 1983–85; WI Carr Group 1985–90: research co-ordinator and dir Hong Kong 1985–87, md WI Carr (Far East) Ltd Hong Kong 1988–89, gp dir of fin and admin London 1989–90; Jardine Fleming Group 1990–2001: dir Jardine Fleming International Holdings Ltd, dir JF Asia Select Ltd, dir JF Asian Realty Inc, md Jardine Fleming International Securities Ltd Singapore, branch mangr Seoul Office 1990–96; chm: Jardine Matheson (Thailand) Ltd 2001–06, PXP Vietnam Fund 2004–15, Vietnam Emerging Equity Fund 2006–08 and 2015–, Vietnam Lotus Fund 2007–09, Advsy Bd Emerging Beachfront Land Investment Fund 2007–, Fidelity Asian Values plc 2010–; dir: Hyundai International Merchant Bank 1990–95, Arisaig India Fund 1999–, Asia Commercial Bank 2002–06, Tantallon BRIC Fund 2006–08, Tantallon Asian Smaller Cos Fund 2006–08, Endowment Fund 2007–; chm: Br C of C Korea, Bd Euro C of C Korea 1995–96; Solomon Islands Independence Medal 1976; *Recreations* books, travel, dogs; *Clubs* White's, Special Forces, Foreign Correspondents (Hong Kong), Hong Kong; *Style—* Philip Smiley, Esq; ✉ Chateau St Jean d'Anglès, St Araílles 32350, France (☎ and fax 00 33 5 62 64 19 69, e-mail pds@smileys.cc)

SMILEY, Xan de Crespigny; s of late Col David de Crespigny Smiley, LVO, OBE, MC and Bar, and late Moyra, widow of Maj Hugo Tweedie, and da of Lt-Col Lord Francis Montagu-Douglas-Scott, KCMG, DSO (6 s of 6 Duke of Buccleuch and Queensberry); bro of Philip David Smiley, *qv*; *b* 1 May 1949, Hanover, Germany; *Educ* Eton, New Coll Oxford (MA); *m* 1983, Hon Jane Lyon-Dalberg-Acton, 6 and yst da of 3 Baron Acton, CMG, MBE, TD (d 1989); 2 s (Ben Richard Philip de Crespigny b 1985, Adam David Emerich b 1988), 2 step da (Charlotte Pugh b 1978, Mrs Rebecca Ladenburg b 1979); *Career* journalist and broadcaster; commentator BBC Radio External Serv current affrs 1974–75, corr Spectator and Observer in Africa 1975–77, ed Africa Confidential newsletter 1977–81 (dir 1981–2004), ldr writer The Times 1982–83, foreign affrs staff writer then Middle East ed The Economist 1983–86, Moscow corr Daily Telegraph 1986–89, Washington corr The Sunday Telegraph 1990–92; The Economist: political ed and Bagehot columnist 1992–94, Europe corr 1994–95, Europe ed 1995–2003, Middle East and Africa ed 2003–14, ed-at-large 2014–; publisher The Soviet Analyst 1990–91; Noel Buxton lectr in African politics 1980; memb Cncl Chatham House 2010–; *Recreations* food, sport (memb Br ski team 1969, winner of Downhill Oxford v Cambridge 1969), shooting, travel, genealogy; *Clubs* Pratt's, Beefsteak, Polish Hearth, Grillion's, Special Forces, Cranium; *Style—* Xan Smiley, Esq; ✉ Lower Farm, Taston, Chipping Norton, Oxfordshire OX7 3JL; c/o The Economist, 25 St James's Street, London SW1A 1HG (☎ 020 7830 7000, e-mail xansmiley@economist.com)

SMILLIE, Carol Patricia; da of George Smillie, of Glasgow, and Isobel, *née* Blackstock; *b* 23 December 1961; *m* 30 Aug 1991, Alex Knight; 2 c; *Career* television presenter; BBC credits incl: Hearts of Gold, The Travel Show, Holiday Memories, National Lottery Live, Smillie's People (talk show), Changing Rooms, Star Secrets, Holiday Swaps, Holiday, Summer Holiday; other credits incl: The Big Breakfast (Channel Four), The Jamesons (Radio 2), Radio Clyde (own talk show), Get It On (STV), Wheel of Fortune (ITV), Dream Holiday Home (Channel 5); subject of This is Your Life, winner 2 Gotcha Oscars Noel's House Party; *Style—* Ms Carol Smillie; ✉ c/o David Anthony Promotions, PO Box 286, Warrington, Cheshire WA2 8GA (☎ 01925 632496, fax 01925 416589)

SMITH, His Hon Adrian Charles; s of Fred Smith (d 1993), and Jenny Smith (d 1994); *b* 25 November 1950; *Educ* Blackpool GS, Queen Mary Coll London (LLB); *m* 14 July 1973, Sally Ann, da of Peter Derek Monteverde Palmer; 2 da (Sophie Louise Elizabeth b 1977, Olivia Rose b 3 Aug 1979); *Career* called to the Bar Lincoln's Inn 1973; barr Northern Circuit 1974–96, recorder of the Crown Court 1994–96, circuit judge (Northern Circuit) 1996–2014; Crown Court liaison judge to Oldham Justices; memb Mgmnt Ctee Liverpool Witness Support 1990–93, legal memb NW Mental Health Review Tbnl 1994– (memb Restricted Panel 2000–); *Recreations* world travel, theatre, fell walking; *Clubs* Waterloo RUFC; *Style—* His Hon Adrian Smith; ✉ c/o Manchester Crown Court, Minshull Street, Manchester M1 3FS (☎ 0161 954 7500)

SMITH, Alan Frederick; *b* 21 July 1944; *Children* 1 da (Julia Ann 1971), 1 s (Michael b 1973); *Career* Colchester Borough Cncl 1961–66, Ipswich Borough Cncl 1966–73, asst county treas Suffolk CC 1973–74, fin mangr Anglian Water 1974–75, asst fin dir Southern Water Authy 1975–80, fin dir Anglian Water Authy 1980–90, gp md Anglian Water plc 1990–

97 (gp fin dir 1989–90); chm: Acambis plc (formerly Peptide Therapeutics Group plc) 1995–2006, Avlar Bioventures Ltd (formerly Quantum Healthcare Fund Manager Ltd) 1999–; memb CIPFA; *Style—* Alan Smith, Esq

SMITH, Prof Alan Gordon Rae; s of Alan Fife Smith (d 1976), and Jean Reid, *née* Lightbody (d 1971); *b* 22 December 1936; *Educ* Glasgow HS, Univ of Glasgow (Macfarlane scholar, MA), Univ of London (PhD); *m* 1972, Isabel, da of Neil McKechnie Robertson and Helen Brown; 1 da (Stella Jean b 1975), 1 s (Donald Alan Neil b 1979); *Career* research fell Inst of Historical Research Univ of London 1961–62; Univ of Glasgow: asst lectr in modern history 1962–64, lectr 1964–75, sr lectr 1975–85, reader 1985–92, head Dept of Modern History 1991–94, prof in modern history 1992–95, chm of history examiners 1993–94, head Sch of History and Archaeology 1993–95, prof of early modern history 1995–2002, emeritus prof 2002–; memb Governing Bd Inst of Historical Research Univ of London 1994–99 and 2003–08; FRHistS (memb Cncl 1990–94), FRSE 1996, FRAS 1997; *Publications* author or ed of ten books incl: Servant of the Cecils (1977), The Emergence of a Nation State (1984); *Recreations* watching sport, travel; *Style—* Prof Alan Smith, FRSE; ✉ 5 Cargil Avenue, Kilmacolm, Inverclyde PA13 4LS; Department of Modern History, University of Glasgow, Glasgow G12 8QQ (☎ 0141 330 4509)

SMITH, Rt Rev Alan Gregory Clayton; *see:* St Albans, Bishop of

SMITH, Alan Keith Patrick; *Educ* Univ of Edinburgh; *Career* exec dir Marks & Spencer plc 1978–93 (joined 1964), chief exec Kingfisher plc 1993–95, non-exec chm Mothercare plc 1996–2002, non-exec chm Space NK Ltd 1997–; non-exec dir: Colefax & Fowler Group plc 1994–, Whitehead Mann plc 1997–2006; memb Bd South Bank Centre 1995–; tstee Arts & Business 1999–; *Style—* Alan Smith, Esq

SMITH, Prof (Murdo) Alasdair Macdonald; DL (East Sussex 2001); s of John Smith (d 1970), and Isabella, *née* Mackenzie (d 2004); *b* 9 February 1949, Stornoway; *Educ* Nicolson Inst Stornoway, Univ of Glasgow (MA), LSE (MSc, Ely Devons Prize), Univ of Oxford (DPhil); *m* Sherry, *née* Ferdman; 2 da (Katie b 1979, Laura b 1981); *Career* lectr in econs: Univ Coll Oxford 1970–72, LSE 1972–81; Univ of Sussex: prof of econs 1981–, dean Sch of European Studies 1991–94, sr pro-vice-chllr 1997–98, vice-chllr 1998–2007; research fell Centre for Economic Policy Research 1983–2002; visiting positions: Columbia Univ, Univ of Rochester, Univ of California San Diego, Univ of Michigan, Coll of Europe Bruges and Natolin, European Univ Inst; convenor 1994 Gp of Univs 2001–05; memb Bd: Univ of Brighton 1998–2006, Univs and Colls Employers Assoc 2000–07, Univs UK 2003–07; chair of tstees Inst Devpt Studies 1998–2008; chm Armed Forces Pay Review Body 2010–13, dep chair Competition Cmmn 2012–14, inquiry chair Competition and Markets Authy 2014–; memb: Prison Serv Pay Review Body 2001–04, Doctors and Dentists Remuneration Review Body 2007–10, Sr Salaries Review Body 2010–13; govr: Holloway Sch London 1973–81 (vice-chm 1973–78, chm 1978–79); memb: SE Eng Regnl Assembly 1993–2003, Brighton and Hove Econ Partnership 2001–07; Hon DSc Univ of Warsaw 2004, Hon LLD Univ of Sussex 2008; *Recreations* gardening, twittering; *Style—* Prof Alasdair Smith, DL; ✉ 11 Gundreda Road, Lewes, East Sussex BN7 1PT (☎ 07740 091106, e-mail alasdair@sussex.ac.uk, Twitter @AlasdairMSmith)

SMITH, Dr Andrew Benjamin; s of Benjamin Butler Smith, of Stonehaven, Grampian, and Elsie Marjory, *née* Flemming; *b* 6 February 1954; *Educ* Mackie Acad Stonehaven, Univ of Edinburgh (BSc), Univ of Exeter (PhD); *m* 18 Aug 1976, Mary Patricia Cumming, da of David Cumming Simpson; 2 da (Katherine Heather b 22 Jan 1985, Fiona Margaret b 18 April 1987); *Career* postdoctoral research asst Univ of Liverpool 1979–81 and 1982–83 (temp lectr in geology 1981–82), research scientist Dept of Palaeontology The Natural History Museum 1983–; Bicentenary Medal Linnean Soc 1993, Bigsby Medal Geological Soc 1995, Lyell Medal Geological Soc 2002, Linnean Medal Linnean Soc 2005; Hon DSc Univ of Edinburgh 1989; FRSE 1996, FRS 2002; *Books* Echinoid Palaeobiology (1984), Systematics and the fossil record: discovering evolutionary patterns (1994); *Style—* Dr Andrew Smith, FRS, FRSE; ✉ Department of Palaeontology, The Natural History Museum, Cromwell Road, London SW7 5BD (☎ 020 7938 8925, fax 020 7938 9277, e-mail a.smith@nhm.ac.uk)

SMITH, Sir Andrew Charles; kt (2000); *Educ* Univ of Oxford (BA); *Career* called to the Bar Middle Temple 1974 (bencher 1999), QC 1990, judge of the High Court of Justice (Queen's Bench Div) 2000–2016, presiding judge North Eastern Circuit 2003–06, judge in charge of Commercial Court 2008–09; *Clubs* Reform; *Style—* Sir Andrew Smith; ✉ Royal Courts of Justice, Strand, London WC2A 2LL

SMITH, Rt Hon Andrew David; PC (1997), MP; s of late David E C Smith, and Georgina H J Smith; *b* 1 February 1951; *Educ* Reading Sch, St John's Coll Oxford (BA, BPhil); *m* 26 March 1976, Valerie, da of William Labert; 1 s; *Career* Oxford City Cncl: cncllr 1976–87, chm Recreation and Amenities Ctee 1980–83, chm Planning Ctee 1985–87, chm Race and Community Relations Ctee 1985–87; relations offr Oxford and Swindon Co-op Soc 1979–87; MP (Lab) Oxford E 1987–; oppn front bench spokesman: on higher educn 1988–92, on Treasy & econ affrs 1992–94; shadow chief sec to Treasy 1994–96, shadow sec of state for tport 1996–97; min of state Dept for Educn and Employment (employment, welfare to work and equal opportunities) 1997–99, chief sec to Treasy 1999–2002, sec of state for Work and Pensions 2002–04; memb Social Servs Select Ctee 1988–89, jt sec All-Pty Gp for Overseas Devpt 1987–94; memb USDAW; chm Govrs of Oxford Brookes Univ (formerly Oxford Poly) 1987–93; *Clubs* Blackbird Leys Community Assoc; *Style—* The Rt Hon Andrew Smith, MP; ✉ 4 Flaxfield Road, Blackbird Leys, Oxford OX4 5QD; Unit 1, Newtec Place, Magdalen Road, Oxford OX4 1RE; Constituency (☎ 01865 305080); House of Commons, London SW1A 0AA (☎ 020 7219 5102)

SMITH, Prof Andrew Paul (Andy); *b* 3 August 1952, Liss, Hampshire; *Educ* Cambridgeshire HS, UCL (BSc, PhD); *m*; 1 s, 2 da; *Career* post-doctoral res fell Dept of Experimental Psychology Univ of Oxford 1976–82, scientist MRC Perceptual and Cognitive Performance Unit Univ of Sussex 1982–88, Charles Hunnisett res fell Laboratory of Experimental Psychology Univ of Sussex 1989–90, dir Health Psychology Res Unit and reader Sch of Psychology UWCC 1990–93, prof Dept of Psychology Univ of Bristol 1993–99, prof Sch of Psychology and dir Centre for Occupational and Health Psychology Univ of Cardiff 1999–; CPsychol, FBPsS, FRSM; *Publications* author of numerous articles in learned periodicals; *Style—* Prof Andy Smith; ☎ 029 2087 4757, fax 029 2087 4758, e-mail smithap@cardiff.ac.uk

SMITH, Angela; MP; *b* 16 August 1961; *Educ* Univ of Nottingham, Newnham Coll Cambridge; *Career* MP (Lab): Sheffield Hillsborough 2005–10, Penistone and Stockbridge 2010–; oppn whip 2010–11, shadow dep ldr of House 2011–14, shadow water min 2014–15, shadow min for food, farming and animal welfare 2015–; Sheffield City Cncl: cncllr, cabinet memb for Educn; memb Unison; *Style—* Ms Angela Smith, MP; ✉ House of Commons, London SW1A 0AA; Maria House, 3 Fox Valley Way, Stocksbridge, S36 2AA (☎ 0114 283 1855, e-mail smithac@parliament.uk)

SMITH, Rt Hon Lady; Anne; PC (2013); da of John Mather (d 1965), of London, and Jessica, *née* Douglas; *b* 16 March 1955; *Educ* Jordanhill Coll Glasgow, Cheadle County GS for Girls, Univ of Edinburgh (LLB, medallist in Criminal Law); *m* 22 Sept 1979, David Alexander Smith, WS, s of William Duncan Smith (d 1998); 1 s (William Iain b 6 Aug 1983), 1 da (Charlotte Alexandra b 14 Aug 1985); *Career* apprenticed Shepherd & Wedderburn, WS 1977–79, pupil of Lord McGhie 1979–80, admitted Faculty of Advocates 1980, in practice 1980–2001, QC (Scot) 1993, senator Coll of Justice 2001–, judge of the Employment Appeal Tbnl 2004–12, pres Scottish Tbnls 2015–; chm Cncl St George's Sch for Girls 2003–11, chm RSNO Fndn 2007–15, pres Friends of the Music of St Giles Cathedral, chair Scottish Cncl of Ind Schs 2016–; *Recreations* music, hill walking, gardening; *Style—* The Rt Hon Lady Smith; ✉ Court of Session, Parliament House, Edinburgh EH1 1RF (☎ 0131 225 2595)

SMITH, Anthony David; CBE (1987); s of Henry Smith (d 1951), and Esther Smith; *b* 14 March 1938; *Educ* Harrow Co Sch, BNC Oxford (BA); *Career* current affrs prodr BBC TV 1960–71, fell St Antony's Coll Oxford 1971–76, dir BFI 1979–88, memb Bd Channel Four TV Co 1980–84, pres Magdalen Coll Oxford 1988–2005, memb Bd The Sixteen 2005–; memb: Writers and Scholars Educn Tst 1982–99, Arts Cncl of GB 1990–94; chm: Hill Fndn 2000–, Oxford-Russia Fund 2004–; memb Cncl Royal Acad of Dramatic Arts 2007–; tstee Prince of Wales Sch of Traditional Arts 2004–09; Hon Dr of Arts: Oxford Brookes Univ 1997, Univ of Lincoln 2008; *Books* The Shadow in the Cave: The Broadcaster, the Audience and the State (1973), British Broadcasting (1974), The British Press since the War (1976), Subsidies and the Press in Europe (1977), The Politics of Information (1978), Television and Political Life (1979), The Newspaper: An International History (1979), Newspapers and Democracy (1980), Goodbye Gutenberg – The Newspaper Revolution of the 1980's (1980), The Geopolitics of Information (1980), The Age of Behemoths – the Globalisation of Mass Media Firms (1991), From Books to Bytes (1993), Software for the Self (1995), Television – An International History (1998); *Clubs* Beefsteak, Garrick; *Style—* Anthony Smith, Esq, CBE; ✉ Albany, Piccadilly, London W1J 0AX (e-mail anthony.smith@magd.ox.ac.uk)

SMITH, (Brian) Arthur John; s of Sydney Frederick Smith, of Bath, and Hazel Nora, *née* Kirk; *b* 27 November 1954; *Educ* Roan Sch, UEA (BA); *Career* writer and comedian; former teacher and road sweeper, fndr memb National Revue Co, hosted First Exposure (BBC) and Paramount City (BBC), reg contrib Loose Ends (Radio 4), fndr comedy double act Fiasco Job Job with Phil Nice (C4 series Arthur and Phil Go Off 1985); author of plays: Live Bed Show (nominated for Perrier and Independent Theatre Awards 1989, Garrick Theatre 1995), Trench Kiss, An Evening With Gary Lineker (with Chris England, Edinburgh Festival then Duchess Theatre and Vaudeville Theatre (nominated Best Comedy Olivier Awards 1992)) 1991–92, Arthur Smith sings Andy Williams (Edinburgh, London, NY) 1992–93, Sod (with Nigel Cole) 1993; presenter: Sentimental Journeys (BBC Radio 4) 1994–2000, Excess Baggage (BBC Radio 4), Arthur Smith's Balham Bash (Radio 4) 2010, Arthur Smith's Pissed Up Chat Show (Edinburgh) 2011, Comedy Club (BBC Radio 4 Extra) 2011–, Arthur Smith Sings Leonard Cohen (vol 2, Edinburgh and tour) 2013; wrote and performed: Hamlet 1995, The Smith Lectures (BBC Radio 2) 1996–; screenplay My Summer with Des (BBC 1) 1998, Arthur Smith sings Leonard Cohen (Edinburgh) 2000, Dante's Inferno 2003, Arthur Smith's Swan Lake 2005; self-proclaimed Greatest Artist in the World, Artwart (exhibition Edinbugh, 2007), artutart (exhibition, 2007); winner If Comedy Award 2008; Hon DLitt UEA 2015; *Books* Trench Kiss (1990), An Evening With Gary Lineker (with Chris England, 1992), Pointless Hoax (1997), Sit-Down Comedy (2003), That Which Is Not Said (poetry, 2006), My Name is Daphne Fairfax (autobiography, 2009); *Recreations* giving up smoking, sleeping; *Clubs* Kilcoynes; *Style—* Arthur Smith, Esq

SMITH, (Donald) Barry; *b* 22 May 1948; *m* 1 Nov 1975, Sophie Janina, *née* Pasko (Rachel b 1978, Claire b 1980, Alice b 1986); *Career* divnl fin accountant Showerings Vine Products & Whiteways Ltd 1971–73, accountant CH Beazer Holdings plc 1973–78, sr ptnr Rossiter Smith & Co Chartered Accountants 1978–; Dolphin Packaging plc: fin dir 1987–89, chm 1989–90, dep chm 1990–2000; FCA 1971, ATII 1972; *Style—* Barry Smith, Esq; ✉ Rossiter Smith & Co, Bank House, 1 Burlington Road, Bristol BS6 6TJ (☎ 0117 973 0863, fax 0117 923 7929, e-mail barrysmith@rossitersmith.co.uk)

SMITH, Barry Howard; *b* 8 September 1949; *Educ* QMC London (LLB); *Career* admitted slr 1974; media and entertainment ptnr Richards Butler 1980–2007, ptnr Reed Smith Richards Butler 2007–08, ptnr Reed Smith 2008–; *Recreations* art, cinema, theatre; *Style—* Barry Smith, Esq; ✉ Reed Smith, The Broadgate Tower, 20 Primrose Street, London EC2A 2RS (☎ 020 3116 3586, fax 020 3116 3999)

SMITH, Betty (Liz); MBE (2009); da of Wilfred Gleadle, and Nellie, *née* Foster (d 1924); *b* 11 December 1921, Scunthorpe, Lincs; *Educ* Scunthorpe Modern Sch, Gateway Theatre; *m* 1945 (m dis 1959), Jack Thomas Smith; 1 da (Sarah Elizabeth b 1950), 1 s (Robert Wystagon Henry Nener b 1954); *Career* actress; WRNS 1940–45; various jobs in shops and summer seasons at Butlins 1957–71; *Films* incl: Bleak Moments 1971, Hard Labour 1973, The Duellists 1977, The French Lieutenant's Woman 1981, Trail of The Pink Panther 1982, A Private Function 1984, Bert Rigby You're a Fool 1989, Haunted 1995, Secrets and Lies 1996, Keep the Apidistra Flying 1997, A Christmas Carol 1999, Charlie and the Chocolate Factory 2005, Wallace and Gromit in the Curse of the Were Rabbit, Flick 2007, City of Ember 2008; *Television* incl: David Copperfield 1974, It Shouldn't Happen to a Vet 1975, It's a Lovely Day Tomorrow 1975, I Didn't Know You Cared 1975–79 (27 episodes), Nicholas Nickelby 1977, Now and Then (12 episodes) 1983–84, A Bit of Fry and Laurie (1 episode) 1990, The Vicar of Dibley (7 episodes) 1994–96, Alice in Wonderland 1999, The Bill (4 episodes) 1984–2002, The Royle Family (12 episodes) 1998–2006, Lark Rise to Candleford 2008; *Awards* Best Supporting Actress BAFTA for A Private Function 1984, Royle of the Year Oldie Magazine 2007, Best TV Comedy Actress Br Comedy Awards for the Royle Family 2007; *Books* Our Betty (autobiography, 2005), Jottings (short stories, 2007); *Recreations* just dreaming (preferably by the sea); *Style—* Mrs Liz Smith, MBE; ✉ c/o Conway Van Gelder Grant Ltd, 18–21 Jermyn Street, London SW14 6HP (☎ 020 7287 0077, fax 020 7287 1940)

SMITH, Bob; s of Frederick Brill, and Deirdre, *née* Borlaise; *Educ* Wandsworth Comp, Univ of Reading (BA), Goldsmiths Coll London (MA); *Career* artist, one half of Bob and Roberta Smith; memb Bd Chisenhale Gallery, dir and fndr (with Jessica Voorsanger, *qv*) Leytonstone Center for Contemporary Art; Rome scholarship 1985–87, Harkness fell 1987–90; trumpeter in Ken Ardley Playboys; *Exhibitions* Don't Hate Sculpt (Chisenhale Gallery) 1997, Intelligence (Tate Britain) 2000, Improve the Cat (Galleria Carbone Turin) 2001, It's not Easy being a famous Artist (Galleria Praz Delavacade Paris) 2002, Useless Women/Stupid Men (Anthony Wilkinson Gallery London) 2002, Art Amnesty (Pieroggi 2000 NY) 2003, Independance (South London Gallery) 2003, No Man is an Island (GAK Breman) 2003, Help Build the Ruins of Democracy (The Baltic Gatehead) 2004; *Publications* A is for book (2001), Inconsistant (2001), Make Your Own Damn Art (2004); *Recreations* going to work; *Style—* Bob Smith, Esq; ✉ c/o Hales Gallery, Tea Building G3, 5–11 Bethnal Green Road, London E1 6JJ

SMITH, Brenda; *Educ* Merchant Taylors', Univ of Manchester, Manchester Business Sch (MBA); *m*; 2 da; *Career* sr accountant Business Consultancy Div Arthur Andersen 1978–91; Granada Television: various financial roles 1981–83, prog mangr then operational line mangr Granada Film 1983–89, gen mangr Facilities Div 1989–93, dir of resources 1993–97, md Granada Television Ltd 1997–2004, md Granada Studios 1997–2004; EMEA gp md Ascent Media Gp 2004–; dir: Castlefield Properties Ltd (subsid of Granada Television), NW Regnl Devpt Agency, Liverpool European Capital of Culture 2008, Jt Industry Grading Scheme Ltd; non-exec dir: Liverpool Vision, MIDAS, Manchester Airport Aviation Services Ltd, AFM Lighting Ltd; chm London Forum Skillset; memb: NW Business Leadership Team, NW Vision, Business in the Community, CAMPUS, Cultural Consortium, Community Loan Fund NW, Ravensbourne Advsy Bd, Int Media Centre (IMC) Advsy Bd Univ of Salford, Bd Women in Film; non-exec memb NW Regnl Economic Panel; formerly: dir NW Film Television Cmmn, memb Manchester:Liverpool Vision Study, Skillset Steering Gp; other non-exec roles: Manchester HA 1992–96, Mental Health Services of Salford 1996–2000; Hon DLitt Univ of Salford; ACA, FRSA; *Recreations* all sports, theatre; *Style—* Ms Brenda Smith

SMITH, (William Wilson) Campbell; s of Stanley Smith (d 1993), of Glasgow, and Winifred Agnes Erskine, *née* Wilson (d 2002); *b* 17 May 1946; *Educ* Glasgow Acad, St Catharine's Coll Cambridge (exhibitioner, MA), Univ of Glasgow (LLB); *m* 13 April 1974, Elizabeth Margaret, da of Maj Tom Richards (d 1994); 2 da (Emma Jane Campbell b 24 May 1977, Kate Elizabeth Campbell b 30 Oct 1979); *Career* trainee slr Biggart Lumsden & Co Glasgow (qualified 1972), asst slr Herbert Smith & Co London 1972–73, ptnr Biggart Baillie Slrs Glasgow and Edinburgh 1974–2009 (managing ptnr 1997–2003); tstee The Lennoxlove Tst 2000–04, chm Glassford Sheltered Housing Tst 2002–04, dir Scottish Int Piano Competition 2008–11; Freeman City of Glasgow; memb: Incorporation of Barbers Glasgow 1970– (deacon 1989–90), Incorporation of Cordiners Glasgow 1975–; *Recreations* choral singing, barbershop singing, golf, croquet; *Clubs* Bognor Golf, The Bognor; *Style—* Campbell Smith; ✉ 6 West Drive, Aldwick, West Sussex PO21 4LY (☎ 01243 266968, e-mail campbell@dargarvel.co.uk)

SMITH, Catherine; MP; *b* 16 June 1985, Barrow-in-Furness, Cumbria; *Educ* Lancaster Univ (BA); *Career* MP (Lab) Lancaster and Fleetwood 2015–; shadow min (Voter Engagement and Youth Affrs) 2016–; *Style—* Ms Cat Smith, MP; ✉ House of Commons, London SW1A 0AA (☎ 020 7219 6001, e-mail cat.smith.mp@parliament.uk, website www.catsmith.co.uk)

SMITH, Sir Charles Bracewell; *see:* Bracewell-Smith, Sir Charles

SMITH, Charles William Peter; s of Peter Christopher Smith, of Windermere, FL, and Simone Hilary, *née* Collett; *b* 5 August 1969, Lowestoft, Suffolk; *Educ* St Joseph's Coll Ipswich, Cannock House Chelsfield; *m* 25 Aug 1998, Jane Elizabeth, *née* Thomas; 1 da (Rosie Isobel b 25 Dec 2001), 2 s (William Clifford Peter b 3 June 2003, Oliver James b 2 Aug 2005); *Career* Hiscox 1988–93, Foxtons 1993–98, Sotheby's International Realty 1998–; *Recreations* family, travel, art, classic literature; *Style—* Charles Smith, Esq; ✉ Lockbridge House, Lockbridge Road, Bourne End, Buckinghamshire SL8 5QT (☎ 01628 523851); Sotheby's International Realty, 26A Conduit Street, Mayfair, London W1S 2XY (☎ 020 7495 9580, fax 020 7495 9589, e-mail charles.smith@sothebysrealty.com, websites www.sothebyshomes.com and www.sothebysrealty.com)

SMITH, Chloe Rebecca; MP; *b* 17 May 1982, Ashford, Kent; *Educ* Univ of York; *Career* MP (Cons) Norwich North 2009–, economic sec to the Treasy 2011–12, min for political and constitutional reform Cabinet Office 2012–13; *Style—* Ms Chloe Smith, MP; ✉ House of Commons, London SW1A 0AA

SMITH, Colin Deverell; OBE (2011); *b* 21 May 1947, Lincolnshire; *Educ* Univ of Liverpool; *m* 1971, Kathy Morgan; 2 s; *Career* early career with Arthur Andersen; Safeway plc (formerly Argyll Group plc): joined 1979, financial controller and co sec Argyll Foods 1980–83, co sec and gp financial controller 1983–89, main bd dir 1984–99, finance dir 1989–93, gp chief exec 1993–99; chm: Poundland Gp Holdings 2002–12, Assured Food Standards 2003–09, Masstock Gp Hldgs 2007–08; non-exec dir: McBride plc 2002–11, Hilton Food Gp plc 2010–16 (chm 2016–), Poundland Gp Hldgs 2012–14; tstee Save the Children Fund 2001–05, chair of tstees The Challenge Network 2012–; FCA; *Style—* Colin Smith, Esq, OBE; ✉ Pyes, Penn Road, Beaconsfield, Buckinghamshire HP9 2TS

SMITH, Colin Hilton; s of Reginald Walter Smith (d 1982), and Barbara, *née* Milligan; *b* 21 February 1953; *Educ* Falmouth Sch of Arts, RCA, Yale Univ; *m* 1, 1976 (m dis 1980), Barbara Ann, da of William Henry Spicer; m 2, 1983 (m dis 1992), Rosemary Victoria, da of Gerald Henry Dean; 1 s (William Lawrence Hilton b 1986); *Career* artist; Great London Arts Assoc Award 1982, London Arts Bd Award 1995, Abbey Award in Painting Br Sch at Rome 1996; Harkness fell and res assoc Faculty of Fine Art Yale Univ 1983–86; *Solo Exhibitions* Nicola Jacobs Gallery London 1982, 1984, 1987 and 1989, Ruth Siegal NY 1986, Anderson O'Day Gallery London 1991, Kunstlandschaft Europa Kunstverein Freiburg 1991, Gallery Three Zero NYC 1993, Big Paintings for the Barbican London 1993, Galleri M Stockholm 1995, Univ of Northumbria Gallery 1995, Wilmer Cutler and Pickering Berlin 1995, The Chelsea Arts Club 1995 and 2004, Galleria Arte X Arte Buenos Aires 1996, Galleri M Stockholm 1997, Six Chapel Row Contemporary Art Bath 1998, Br Cncl Art Centre Buenos Aires 1998, Adair Margo Gallery Elpaso TX 1999, Rockwell Gallery London 2004, Reigate Sch of Art Gallery 2004; *Group Exhibitions* The First Exhbn (Nicola Jacobs Gallery) 1979, Sculpture and works on paper (Nicola Jacobs Gallery) 1980, Fourteenth Int Festival of Painting Cagnes-sur-Mer-France 1982, Tolly Cobbold Eastern Arts Fourth Nat Exhbn and tour 1983, The Figurative Exhibition II (Nicola Jacobs Gallery) 1983, New Talent (Hal Bromm NYC) 1984, The Image as Catalyst (Ashmolean Museum Oxford) 1984, Royal Over-Seas League Annual Exhbn (jt first prize winner) 1987, Academicians Choice (Mall Galleries London and The Eye Gallery Bristol) 1990, The London Gp Exhbn (RCA) 1990, Foregrounds and Distances (touring) 1992–93, Retour à la Peinture Montreal 1992, The Figure The City NYC 1993, Ian Jones and Colin Smith (Barbican) 1993, John Moores Exhbn 18 (Walker Art Gallery Liverpool) 1993, Painting The City (Corr Contemporary Art London) 1995, Mostra (Br Sch at Rome) 1996, The Motor Show – Cars in Art (touring exhbn) 1996; *Work in Collections* Tate Gallery London, Royal Palm Hotel Phoenix Arizona, NatWest Gp London, Br Cncl Buenos Aires, RCA, Unilever London, Arts Cncl of GB, Prudential Holborn, Pepsi Cola London, Contemporary Art Soc, Arthur Andersen Ltd, British Airways, EMI Ltd, Kettering Art Gallery, Carlton Communications, Coopers Lybrand, Virgin Airways London, The Duke and Duchess of Westminster, Amerivox Scandanavia Stockholm, Arthur Andersen Newcastle, Wilmer Cutler and Pickering Berlin, BML Corp Mgmnt Frankfurt, Scottish Equitable Edinburgh; *Publications* An Interview with Richard Diebenkorn (Artscribe 1992), Karl Weschice (The Whistler Magazine, 1996); *Recreations* reading, films; *Clubs* Chelsea Arts; *Style—* Colin Smith, Esq; ✉ 27 Orsman Road, Hoxton, London N1 5RA (☎ 020 7739 3067)

SMITH, Colin Roland Francis; s of Roland Smith (d 1993), of Sutton Coldfield, and Annie, *née* Colley (d 1954); *b* 6 September 1944, Birmingham; *Educ* John Willmott GS; *m* Sylvia, da of Sydney Skillett, of Guernsey; 1 da (Helena), 1 s (Gavin); *Career* Royal Signals Jr Leaders' Regt; harbour corr Guernsey Evening Press 1962–63; reporter on several local newspapers and Daily Sketch until 1968; The Observer: joined 1968, chief roving corr 1972–77, ME corr (based in Cyprus, Cairo and Jerusalem) 1977–85, chief roving corr 1985–88, Asia ed based in Bangkok 1988–90, asst ed and roving corr 1990, Washington corr 1993; roving corr The Sunday Times 1993–94; contrib: The Sunday Times 1995–, Prospect magazine 1997–, New Statesman 1999–, The Oldie 2005, The Literary Review 2006–, London Review of Books, Daily Mail; Int Reporter of the Year 1975 and 1985; *Books* The Palestinians (1975), Carlos – Portrait of a Terrorist (1976, revised edns 1995 and 2011), Fire in the Night: Wingate of Burma, Ethiopia and Zion (with John Bierman, 1999), Alamein – War Without Hate (with John Bierman, 2002), Singapore Burning: Heroism and Surrender in World War Two (2005), England's Last War Against France – Fighting Vichy 1940–42 (2009), Warsaw Boy (collaboration with Andrew Borowiec, 2014); *Novels* Cut-Out (1980, republished as Collateral Damage 2013), The Last Crusade (1991, republished as Spies of Jerusalem 2013), Let Us Do Evil (2014); *Recreations* tennis, military history; *Clubs* Frontline, Travellers; *Style—* Colin Smith, Esq; ✉ c/o Gillon Aitken Associates, 18–21 Cavaye Place, London SW10 9PT (☎ 020 7373 8672, e-mail gillon@gillonaitken.co.uk)

SMITH, (William) Dallas; s of William Smith, and Estelle Smith; *Educ* Aldenham, Univ of Ulster (BA); *Career* talent agent; worked in theatre admin: Mayfair Theatre London, Arts Theatre Cambridge, Royal Exchange Manchester, Palace Theatre Watford, Roundhouse Theatre London; gen mangr Hampstead Theatre London 1980–90, talent agent 1990–, dir PFD 1999–2007, United Agents 2008–; memb Advsy Panel LAMDA; FRSA; *Recreations* travel, food, theatre, cinema; *Style—* Dallas Smith, Esq; ✉ United Agents, 12–26 Lexington Street, London W1F 0LE (☎ 020 3214 0800, e-mail dsmith@unitedagents.co.uk)

SMITH, Prof (Anthony) David; s of Rev William Beddard Smith (d 1985), and Evelyn, *née* Eagle (d 1987); *b* 16 September 1938, Kunming, China; *Educ* Kingswood Sch Bath, ChCh Oxford (Bostock exhibitioner, MA, DPhil); *m* 1, 1962 (m dis 1974), Wendy Diana, *née* Lee; 1 da (Catherine Anne b 1965), 1 s (Richard David b 1968); m 2, 1975, Dr Ingegerd Östman; 1 s (Niklas Carl William b 1987); *Career* Univ of Oxford: Royal Soc Stothert res fell 1966–70, res lectr ChCh 1966–71, Wellcome res fell 1970–71, univ lectr in pharmacology and student of ChCh 1971–84, prof and head Dept of Pharmacology 1984–2005, hon dir MRC Anatomical Neuropharmacology Unit 1985–98, fell LMH Oxford 1984–, dir Oxford Project to Investigate Memory and Ageing (OPTIMA) 1988–, dep head Div of Med Sciences 2000–05; founding chief ed Neuroscience 1976–2001, ed and contrib articles in various jls; memb: Gen Bd of the Faculties Oxford 1980–84, Neurosciences Bd MRC 1983–85; chair Scientific Advsy Bd Alzheimer's Res Tst 1997–2002; Hon Dr Szeged Univ 1993, Hon Dr Med Lund Univ 1998; seventh Gaddum Meml Prize Br Pharmacological Soc 1979, Decade of the Brain lectr 1993, memb Norwegian Acad of Sci and Letters 1996, hon memb Hungarian Acad of Scis 1998, Dana Alliance for the Brain 2000; hon res fell Alzheimer's Res Tst 2006; FMedSci 2000; *Recreations* music, travel, Pre-Raphaelites, Art Nouveau, aboriginal art; *Style—* Prof David Smith; ✉ Department of Pharmacology, Mansfield Road, Oxford OX1 3QT (☎ 01865 271617, e-mail david.smith@pharm.ox.ac.uk)

SMITH, David Andrew; s of John William Smith (d 1968), of London, and Patricia Mary Smith; *b* 5 March 1952; *Educ* Finchley GS, Lincoln Coll Oxford (MA, ed Cherwell (univ newspaper)); *m* 1, 18 Oct 1980 (m dis 1994), Pamela, da of Douglas Keith Reading; 2 s (Mark Patrick Reading b 30 Dec 1982, Matthew Louis Reading b 29 May 1986); m 2, 16 Nov 1996, Sonia, da of Francisco Ruseler; 1 da (Alegria Ruseler-Smith b 14 Jan 1998), 1 s (Nelson Ruseler-Smith b 15 July 2000); *Career* corr Italy Reuters 1977–78 (Spain 1975–76); ITN corr: Africa 1979–81, Israel 1982–86, Soviet Union 1988–90, USA 1991–2004; UN: dep dir Info Office Washington DC 2004–10, dir Info Office Buenos Aires 2010–; visiting prof Univ of Michigan 1986–87; International Reporter of the Year (for despatches from Lebanon) RTS Awards 1983; *Books* Mugabe (1981), Prisoners of God – The Conflict of Arab and Jew (1987); *Style—* David Smith, Esq

SMITH, Cdre David Andrew Harry McGregor; CBE (2002); *b* Hampstead, London; *Educ* Lancing, RCDS; *m* Monique; *Career* served HMY Britannia 1986–88, staff of Naval Sec 1988–91, dir (Future Devpts) Navy Logistics Staff 1992–95, EA/DEPSACLANT USA 1995–98, RCDS 1998, Cdre HMS Nelson 1999–2000, dir Navy Personnel Corporate Programming 2000–01; memb Advsy Bd Origo Inc 2002; dir of markets City of London 2003–11, dir of markets and consumer protection City of London Corporation 2011–; chm King William IV Naval Fndn 2003, tstee RMC 2002; memb Ct Worshipful Co of Cooks of London; Freeman City of London; FIH 1994, FCIPD 2001; *Publications* Confucianism – Signpost to China's Future Relations with her East Asian Neighbours (1998); *Recreations* golf, fly-fishing, shooting, occasional sailing; *Clubs* Royal Thames Yacht, Royal Naval and Royal Albert Yacht, Anchorites; *Style—* Cdre David A H McG Smith, CBE; ✉ PO Box 270, Guildhall, London EC2P 2EJ (mobile 07760 352233)

SMITH, David Henry; s of Charles Henry Smith (d 1990), and Elizabeth Mary, *née* Williams (d 1963); *b* 3 April 1954; *Educ* West Bromwich GS, UC Cardiff (BSc(Econ), Tassie medallion), Birkbeck Coll London (MSc(Econ)); *m* 1980, Jane Howells; 2 s (Richard Howell b 1981, Thomas David b 1983), 2 da (Emily Victoria b 1987, Elizabeth Jane b 1992); *Career* econ report writer Lloyds Bank 1976–77, economist Henley Centre 1977–79, econ writer Now! magazine 1979–81, asst ed Financial Weekly 1981–84, econ corr The Times 1984–89, econ ed The Sunday Times 1989– (currently also policy advsr and asst ed); visiting prof Cardiff Business Sch Univ of Cardiff 2007–, visiting prof Univ of Nottingham 2011–; commended Journalist of the Year Br Press Awards 1992 and 1999, Business Columnist of the Year PPA Awards 1995 and 1996, Wincott Fndn Sr Financial Journalist of the Year 2004, Editorial Intelligence Economics Commentator of the Year 2013, Economic Commentator of the Year Comment Awards 2013; FRSA 1999; *Books* The Rise and Fall of Monetarism (1987), North and South (1989, 2 edn, 1994), Mrs Thatcher's Economics (1989), Mrs Thatcher's Economics: Her Legacy (1991), From Boom to Bust (1992), UK Current Economic Policy (1995, 2 edn 1999), Eurofutures (1997), Will Europe Work? (1999), Welfare, Work and Poverty (ed, 2000), Free Lunch (2003, 2 edn 2012), The Dragon and the Elephant: China, India and the New World Order (2007), The Age of Instability (2010), Something Will Turn Up; *Recreations* golf, squash; *Clubs* Bexley Tennis & Squash; *Style—* David Smith, Esq, FRSA; ✉ The Sunday Times, 1 London Bridge Street, London SE1 9GF (☎ 020 7782 5750, e-mail david.smith@sunday-times.co.uk, website www.economicsuk.com/blog)

SMITH, David John; s of Clive Norman Smith, of Eastleigh, Hants, and Mary Rose Windless; *b* 2 March 1989, Eastleigh, Hants; *Educ* Treloar Sch Alton, Treloar Coll, Alton Coll, Swansea Univ; *Career* Paralympic boccia player; achievements incl: Silver medal mixed team European Championships Portugal 2005, Bronze medal mixed team World Championships Rio de Janeiro 2006, 2 Gold medals individual and mixed team (with Ali Lalani, Zoe Robinson and Nigel Murray, MBE, *qqv*) World Cup Vancouver 2007, Gold medal mixed team (with Dan Bentley, *qv*, Zoe Robinson and Nigel Murray, MBE) Paralympics Beijing 2008, Gold medal individual and Silver medal mixed team (with Nigel Murray, MBE, Dan Bentley and Zoe Robinson) European Championships Portugal 2009, Bronze medal mixed team (with Nigel Murray, MBE, Dan Bentley and Zoe Robinson) World Cup Belfast 2011, Silver medal individual and Bronze medal mixed team (with Nigel Murray, MBE, Dan Bentley and Zoe Robinson) Paralympics London 2012, Gold medal individual and Gold medal mixed team (with Nigel Murray, MBE, Joshua Rowe, Dan Bentley, Martin Davies and Emma Goodchild) European Championships Portugal 2013, Gold medal individual and Bronze medal team (with Nigel Murray, MBE, Martin Davies and Joshua Rowe) World Championships Beijing 2014, Gold medal mixed team European Team and Pairs Championships Guildford 2015; youngest ever British champion, British champion 10 years running, unbeaten in UK since 2004; BBC South Sports Disabled Sportsman of the Year 2007, Hants and IOW Disabled Sportsman of the Year 2008; Freeman of the Borough of Eastleigh 2012; *Recreations* reading, watching football, rugby and snooker, traveling, walking (in my wheelchair), aircraft (especially British WW2); *Style—* David Smith, Esq; ✉ c/o British Paralympic Association, 40 Bernard Street, London WC1N 1ST (website www.gb-boccia.org)

SMITH, Derek Graham; s of Albert Edward Smith (d 1993), and Rosetta Alexandra, *née* Lyme (d 2001); *b* 16 May 1947; *Educ* Royal Liberty Sch Romford, Univ of Kent (BA); *m* 25 April 1981, Margaret Elizabeth, *née* Harris; 1 da (Michelle Helen b 7 Sept 1982), 1 s (Fraser James b 8 June 1987); *Career* Coopers and Lybrand 1969–77: joined as articled clerk 1969, subsequently supervisor then mangr; Mazars Neville Russell (formerly Neville Russell) 1977–: mangr then sr mangr, ptnr 1980–, chm Mgmnt Bd London Office 1991–, nat managing ptnr 1993; memb Exec Gp Mazars & Guérard Gp; sr ptnr The Damas Partnership 2005–, sr conslt Foulger Underwood Associates Ltd 2005–; memb Cncl St Mary's Church High Ongar, chm Houses Ctee and memb Finance Ctee and Finance Exec Chelmsford Diocese; tstee: Kent Union, Friendly Almshouses, Diocese of Chelmsford; Freeman City of London 1992; FCA 1972, FIMC 1987; *Books* Management and Control of Time in an Accountancy Practice (1982); *Recreations* DIY, local church; *Style—* Derek

Smith, Esq; ✉ 12 Meeson Meadows, Maldon, Essex CM9 6YS (☎ 07801 347554, e-mail dereksmithdamas@aol.com)

SMITH, Prof (Stanley) Desmond; OBE; s of Henry George Stanley Smith (d 1969), and Sarah Emily Ruth Weare; *b* 3 March 1931; *Educ* Cotham Bristol, Univ of Bristol (BSc, DSc), Univ of Reading (PhD); *m* 1 July 1956, Gillian Anne, da of Howard Stanley Parish; 1 s (David), 1 da (Nicola); *Career* SSO RAE Farnborough 1956–59; research asst Meteorology Dept Imperial Coll London 1959–60, reader Univ of Reading 1966–70 (lectr 1960–66), prof of physics and dept head Heriot-Watt Univ 1970–96; fndr, chm and dir Edinburgh Instruments Ltd 1971–2012, chief scientific offr Techcomp (Europe) 2013–, chm and dir Edinburgh Biosciences Ltd 2013–; dir Edinburgh C of C 1981–84; memb: cabinet ACOST 1987–88 (formerly ACARD 1985–87), Def Science Advsy Cncl MOD 1985–91; Hon DSc Heriot-Watt Univ 2003; FRMetS 1962, FRSE 1973 (Royal Medal 2012), FInstP 1976, FRS 1976; *Publications* Infrared Physics (jtly, 1966), Optoelectronic Devices (1995); *Recreations* mountaineering, skiing, tennis, golf, climate sceptic; *Clubs* Royal Soc; *Style—* Prof Desmond Smith, OBE, FRS, FRSE; ✉ Tree Tops, 29D Gillespie Road, Colinton, Edinburgh EH13 0NW (☎ 0131 441 7225); 106 Corniche du Pinateau, 05260 Chaillol 1600, Hautes Alpes, France (☎ 00 33 492 50 08 81, e-mail desmond.smith@wanadoo.fr); Edinburgh Biosciences Ltd, 2.2 Quantum Court, Heriot Watt Research Park South, Riccarton, Edinbugh EH14 4AP (☎ 0131 602 7010, e-mail des@edinbio.com)

SMITH, Drew; MSP; *Educ* Univ of Aberdeen, Univ of Glasgow, Open Univ; *Career* MSP (Lab) Glasgow 2011–; chair Scottish Young Lab 2005–06, memb Scottish TUC Gen Cncl 2007–10, chair Young Workers Ctee Scottish TUC 2008–09; *Style—* Drew Smith, Esq, MSP; ✉ The Scottish Parliament, Edinburgh EH99 1SP

SMITH, Edith Eleanor Bowman; da of Sandy Bowman, and Eleanor Bowman; *b* 15 January 1974, Anstruther, Fife; *Educ* Waid Acad Anstruther, Queen Margaret UC Edinburgh; *m* 22 Dec 2013, Thomas Michael Henry Smith; 2 s (Rudy Brae Bowman Smith b 10 June 2008, Spike Stanley Bowman Smith b 25 Feb 2013); *Career* TV and radio broadcaster; memb BAFTA; *Television* as presenter incl: Hitlist UK (MTV), Roadtipping (BBC Choice) 2002, Make My Day (Channel 4), RI:SE (Channel 4) 2002–03, BAFTAs (BBC3), Vue Film Show (Channel 4), Saving Planet Earth (BBC1), Glastonbury and Reading coverage (BBC2 and BBC3); as host: red carpet Britannia Awards 2014, Guitar Star (Sky Arts), Guitar Greats (Sky Arts); *Radio* presenter Hit Music Sunday (Capital FM) 2001–02; BBC Radio 1: co-presenter (with Colin Murray) Colin and Edith Show 2003–06, presenter afternoon show 2006–08, presenter Weekend Breakfast 2009–12, presenter Review Show 2012–; co-presenter (with Adam Buxton) BBC 6 Music 2012–, presenter The Bump Club (BBC Radio 5 Live) 2013, presenter The Album Show (BBC Radio Scotland), presenter The Quay Sessions (BBC Scotland); *Books* Edith Bowman's Great British Music Festivals (2015); *Recreations* cinema, music, film; *Style—* Edith Bowman; ✉ Radio 1, London W1W 6AJ; c/o Caroline Ridley, Money, 42a Berwick Street, London W1F 8RZ (e-mail megan@moneymanagement.uk.com, Twitter @edibow)

SMITH, (John) Edward Kitson (Ed); CBE (2014); s of Jack Kitson Smith (d 1992), and Edith, *née* Taylor (d 2010); *b* 24 October 1954, Calcutta, India; *Educ* St Dunstan's Coll Catford, London Met Univ (BA); *m* 11 July 1981, Jennifer Maude, *née* Linton; 1 s (Nicholas b 27 Feb 1987), 2 da (Jessica b 28 Nov 1988, Anna b 13 Sept 1997); *Career* PricewaterhouseCoopers: joined 1977, head of educn practice 1989–93, exec ptnr UK audit 1994–97, global ldr learning and devpt 1998–99, memb UK Bd 2000–03, sr ptnr and global assurance chief operating offr and ldr strategy 2004–07; fin advsr DES 1987–89, memb Accounting for People Taskforce DTI 2003; govr Univ of N London 1991–95, pro-chllr and chm Univ of Birmingham 2010–; chm: WWF-UK 2008–14 (memb Bd WWF-International), (sport) Br Univs and Colls 2008–14, Student Loans Co 2010–13, Crown Commercial Services (Cabinet Office) 2014–; dep chm NHS England 2011–; memb: Audit Ctee Poly and Colls Funding Cncl 1990–92, Advsy Bd Opportunity Now 2001–13, Bd Dept for Transport 2009–, UK Competition Cmmn 2009–14 (Competition and Markets Authy 2014–), Cmmn on Future of Women's Sport 2009–13, Civil Service Reform Bd – Accountability 2013–14; dep chm and memb Bd HEFCE 2004–11; treas and tstee The Work Fndn 2007–10, treas Chatham House 2008–, tstee Demos 2008–10; Liveryman Worshipful Co of Educators 2014–; Hon LLD: Univ of Bath 2009, Univ of Roehampton 2013, Univ of Aberdeen 2014; Hon DUniv Univ of Birmingham 2015; FCA 2000 (ACA 1980), FRSA, CPFA 2013; *Publications* Breakpoint/Breakthrough Strategies for Worklife Balance in the 21st Century (co-author, 1999), Accounting for People (2003), Diversity Dimensions (2004), Papering Over the Cracks? (co-author, 2006); *Recreations* golf, cooking, wine collecting, opera; *Clubs* Athenaeum, Lansdowne, Wildernesse Golf; *Style—* Ed Smith, Esq, CBE; ✉ Old Mill Leat, Vicarage Hill, Westerham, Kent TN16 1TJ (☎ 01959 564008, e-mail ed.smith@jeks.co.uk)

SMITH, Elaine; MSP; da of late William Dornan, and Mary McGill; *b* 7 May 1963, Coatbridge; *Educ* St Patrick's HS Coatbridge, Glasgow Coll, St Andrews Teacher Trg Coll; *m* 31 Dec 1986, James Vann Smith; 1 s (Vann b 5 May 1996); *Career* MSP (Lab) Coatbridge and Chryston 1999–, dep presiding offr Scottish Parl 2011–; convenor Lab's Campaign for Socialism; memb: Gen Teaching Cncl, TGWU; Free Spirit Award Scottish Politician of the Year 2002; *Recreations* swimming, bowling, reading, family; *Style—* Mrs Elaine Smith, MSP; ✉ The Scottish Parliament, Edinburgh EH99 1SP

SMITH, Elizabeth Jane; MSP; da of James Smith (d 1979), and Thelma, *née* Moncrieff; *b* 27 February 1960, Edinburgh; *Educ* George Watson's Coll Edinburgh, Univ of Edinburgh (MA), Moray House Coll of Educn Edinburgh (DipEd); *Career* teacher of econs and modern studies George Watson's Coll Edinburgh 1983–98, head of chm's office Scottish Cons Pty 1998–2003, pt/t teacher and political conslt 2003–07, MSP (Cons) Mid Scotland and Fife 2007–; past pres Watsonian Club; fell commoner CCC Cambridge 1992; memb Gen Teaching Cncl for Scotland 1983–, women's devpt offr Cricket Scotland, pres Scottish Women's Cricket Assoc; *Publications* Outdoor Adventures (2003), History of George Watson's Ladies' College (2006); *Recreations* cricket, hill-walking, photography, travel; *Clubs* New (Edinburgh); *Style—* Miss Elizabeth Smith, MSP; ✉ The Scottish Parliament, Holyrood Road, Edinburgh EH99 1SP (☎ 0131 348 6762, fax 0131 348 5933, e-mail elizabeth.smith.msp@scottish.parliament.uk)

SMITH, Elizabeth Jean; OBE (2004); *née* Hay; da of Lt-Gen Sir Robert Hay, KCIE (d 1980); *b* 15 August 1936; *Educ* St George's Sch Edinburgh, Univ of Edinburgh (MA); *m* 23 Feb 1960, Geoffrey Peter Smith, s of William Stanley Smith (d 1958), of Wallasey, Cheshire; 1 da (Catherine b 1965), 1 s (Graham b 1968); *Career* BBC: studio mangr 1958–61, prodr radio news 1961–70, dep ed consumer affrs Radio 4 1970–78, prodr TV current affrs 1978–79, sr asst Secretariat 1979–81, Cwlth fellowship to study the impact of satellite TV on India 1984, asst head central talks and features World Service 1981–84, head current affrs World Service 1984–88, controller English Services World Service 1988–94; sec gen Cwlth Broadcasting Assoc 1994–2010, chair Commonwealth Media Gp 2010–15, conslt Transforming Broadcasting (advising state broadcasters on moving towards public service broadcasting) 2011– (recent consultancies incl South Sudan, Sierra Leone, Bhutan and Namibia); visiting fell Univ of Westminster 2011–; monthly columnist The Listener 1975–78; tstee: One World Broadcasting Tst 1994–2000, Television Tst for the Environment 2000–04, Royal Cwlth Soc 2010–14; chair Voice of the Listener and Viewer Tst 2006–08; tstee London Ctee Cwlth Human Rights Initiative 1998–2010; memb: Cncl RIIA 1992–95, Bd Westminster Fndn for Democracy 1998–2001; Hon DLitt; fell Radio Acad; *Books* Healing Herbs (jtly, 1978), Sambo Sahib (as Elizabeth Hay, 1981), A Road Map to Public Service Broadcasting (2012); *Clubs* Reform, Royal Over-seas League; *Style—* Mrs Elizabeth Smith, OBE; ✉ e-mail elizabeth.smith226@gmail.com, website www.transformingbroadcasting.org.uk

SMITH, Emily Frances; da of late Oliver Ronald Smith, and late Moyra Elizabeth, *née* Blandy; *Educ* Cranborne Chase Sch, New Hall Cambridge (BA); *m* 1982, Sir Michael Wheeler-Booth, KCB , *qv*; 2 da (Kate b 1985, Charlotte b 1987), 1 s (Alfred James b 1990); *Career* author; called to the Bar Inner Temple 1975; legal advsr Dairy Trade Fedn 1976–80; reporter East Anglian Daily Times 1980–82, reporter and sub-ed Windsor Express Series 1982–85; *Books* Astrid the Au Pair from Outer Space (1999, Smarties Silver Award, 6–8 category), The Shrimp (2001, Smarties Gold Award, 6–8 category), Annie and the Aliens (2001), What Howls at the Moon in Frilly Knickers? (2001), Robomum (2003), When Mum Threw Out The Telly (2003), Patrick the Party Hater (2004), Joe v The Fairies (2005), A Stain on the Stone: A Jack Young Mystery (2006); *Style—* Ms Emily Smith; ✉ c/o David Higham Associates, 5–8 Lower John Street, Golden Square, London W1R 4HA (☎ 020 7437 7888, fax 020 7437 1072, e-mail dha@davidhigham.co.uk)

SMITH, Prof Francis William; s of Capt William Smith, RAMC (d 1978) of Harare, Zimbabwe, and Frances Marrianne May, *née* Emslie (d 1992); *b* 8 January 1943, Colchester, Essex; *Educ* Prince Edward Sch Harare, Univ of Aberdeen (MB ChB, DMRD, MD); *m* 5 Dec 1970, Pamela Anne, da of James Cox (d 1958), of Gateshead, Co Durham; 1 da (Jane b 1971), 1 s (James b 1976); *Career* dir of clinical magnetic resonance res Aberdeen Royal Infirmary 1980 (conslt in nuclear med 1979–97); conslt radiologist Grampain Univ Hospitals NHS Tst 1997–; prof of health sciences Robert Gordon Univ 1999–, prof of radiology Univ of Aberdeen 2005–; chief ed Magnetic Resonance Imaging 1985–91, assoc ed Jl of Magnetic Resonance Imaging 1991–2001; club dr: Montrose FC 1990–95, Dundee United FC 1995–; clinical dir Medserena 2010–; pres Soc for Magnetic Resonance Imaging 1983; FFR RCSI 1978, FRCPEd 1992, Dip in Sports Med 1992, FRCR 1997, FRCSEd 2005, FFSEM 2007; *Books* Magnetic Resonance in Medicine and Biology (1984), Practical Nuclear Medicine (1989); *Recreations* swimming, walking, entomology, fly fishing, golf; *Style—* Prof Francis Smith; ✉ 7 Primrosehill Road, Cults, Aberdeen AB15 9ND (☎ 01224 868745, e-mail franciswsmith@hotmail.com); Department of Radiology, Woodend Hospital, Eday Road, Aberdeen AB15 6XS (☎ 01224 681818 ext 56040, fax 01224 556232); Medserena Upright MRI, 114a Cromwell Road, London SW7 4ES (☎ 020 7370 6003, e-mail f.smith@medserena.com)

SMITH, Prof Frank Thomas; s of Leslie Maxwell Smith, of Havant, Hants, and Catherine Matilda, *née* Wilken; *b* 24 February 1948; *Educ* Kinson CP Sch, Bournemouth GS, Jesus Coll Oxford (BA, DPhil); *m* 16 Sept 1972, Valerie Sheila, da of Albert Alfred Hearn; 3 da (Helen b 1976, Natalie b 1978, Amy b 1987); *Career* res fell Theoretical Aerodynamics Unit Southampton 1972–73, lectr Imperial Coll London 1973–78, visiting prof Univ of W Ontario 1978–79, reader and prof Imperial Coll London 1979–84, Goldsmid prof in applied maths UCL 1984–, dir Lighthill Inst 2006–, dir London Taught Course Centre 2007–; FRS 1984; *Books* Boundary – Layer Separation (with Prof Susan Brown 1987); *Recreations* sports, reading, family; *Style—* Prof Frank T Smith, FRS; ✉ Mathematics Department, University College, Gower Street, London WC1E 6BT (☎ 020 7679 2839, fax 020 7383 5519, e-mail f.smith@ucl.ac.uk)

SMITH, Prof George David William; s of George Alfred William Smith (d 1989), and Grace Violet Hannah Dayton, *née* Bloom (d 2006); *b* 28 March 1943, Aldershot, Hants; *Educ* St Benedict's Sch Aldershot, Salesian Coll Farnborough, CCC Oxford (open scholar, graduate scholar, MA, DPhil); *m* 1968, Josephine Ann (d 2014), da of Edwin Walter Halford; 2 s (Timothy George Edwin b 1969, Richard Charles Edwin b 1972); *Career* Univ of Oxford: SRC research fell 1968–70, postdoctoral research fell 1970–75, sr research fell 1975–77, lectr in metallurgy 1977–92, George Kelley reader in metallurgy 1992–96, prof of materials science 1996–2010, head Dept of Materials 2000–05, emeritus prof 2010–; research fell Wolfson Coll Oxford 1972–77 (jr research fell 1968–72), fell St Cross Coll Oxford 1977–91 (emeritus fell 1992–), professorial fell Trinity Coll Oxford 1996–2010 (tutorial fell 1991–95, emeritus fell 2010–), hon prof Univ of Science and Technology Beijing 2005, advsy prof Chongqing Univ China 2005; Oxford Nanoscience Ltd (formerly Kindbrisk Ltd): md 1987–2002, chm 2002–04, R&D 100 award 1993, Prince of Wales' Award for Innovation 1997, Millennium Product Designation 1998, Nat Award for Innovative Measurement 2004; non-exec chm Polaron plc 2004–06; co-chm UK Materials Congress 1998, chair Int Review of UK Research Cncls Nanoscience Prog 2009; memb: Materials Research Soc (USA) 1987–, Minerals, Metals and Materials Soc (USA) 1992– (William Hume Rothery Award 2017), Office of Science and Technol Foresight Panel for Materials 1999–2003, HE Funding Cncl Research Assessment Panel for Materials 1999–2001, DTI Energy Materials Advsy Gp 2006–09, Exec Ctee of European Materials Research Soc 2007–10, Advsy Cncl Br Library 2005–11; ldr Materials Science and Nanotechnology sectors UK-China Partnership in Science 2007–09, scientific advsr Tokamak Solutions UK Ltd 2010–; dir Healthwatch Oxfordshire 2015–; Sir George Beilby Medal and Prize 1985, Acta Materialia Gold Medal 2005, Hatfield Lecture 2011, Hume Rothery Lecture 2014, Inaugural Fellowship Int Field Emission Soc 2016, Distinguished Physical Scientist Award Microscopy Soc of America 2016; Inst of Materials: memb 1963–, Vanadium Award (jtly) 1985, Rosenhain Medal and Prize 1991, memb Cncl 1997–2002, vice-pres 2002, Platinum Medal 2006; memb Exec Cncl Royal Soc 2002–04; memb Oxfordshire Health and Social Care Panel 2014–; hon fell CCC Oxford 2008; Liveryman Worshipful Co of Armourers and Braziers 2003 (Freeman 1998), Freeman City of London 1999; CEng 1978, CPhys 1996; assoc memb IOD 2015–; FInstP 1996 (MInstP 1978), FIM 1996, FRS 1996, FRSA 1997, FRSC 2003; *Books* Atom Probe Microanalysis: Principles and Application to Materials Problems (with M K Miller, 1989), Atom Probe Field Ion Microscopy (jtly, 1996); over 400 original scientific research papers 1968–; *Recreations* walking, fishing, bird watching, travel, grandchildren; *Style—* Prof George Smith, FRS; ✉ Department of Materials, University of Oxford, Parks Road, Oxford OX1 3PH (☎ 01865 273762, fax 01865 273738, e-mail george.smith@materials.ox.ac.uk)

SMITH, Giles; *Educ* RCA (MA), Univ of Cambridge (MA); *Career* urban and architectural designer; co-fndr Assemble (Turner Prize 2015); *Style—* Giles Smith, Esq

SMITH, Gillian Sara; da of Nathan Abraham Oppenheim, of Edinburgh, and Eve Renee, *née* Halson; *b* 26 January 1953; *Educ* St George's Sch for Girls Edinburgh, Newnham Coll Cambridge (MA, Roman Law Prize); *Children* 1 s (Simon Alexander b 25 May 1989); *Career* Linklaters & Paines 1977–81, in-house counsel Nordic Bank 1981–83; SJ Berwin: ptnr 1985–2010, seconded Watchell Lipton Rosen & Katz New York 1987–89, head of banking 1992–2008; of counsel Orrick Herrington and Sutcliffe (Europe) LLP 2012; tstee Plan Int (UK); *Recreations* reading, entertaining, gardening, travel, music, theatre; *Style—* Gillian Smith; ✉ 107 Cheapside, London EC2V 6DN (☎ 020 7862 4722, e-mail gsmith@orrick.com)

SMITH, Prof Gordon Campbell Sinclair; s of late Robert S Smith, of Glasgow, and Peggy M, *née* Fergusson; *b* 11 May 1965, Glasgow; *Educ* Stonelaw HS Glasgow, Univ of Glasgow (BSc, MB ChB, MD, PhD, DSc); *m* 2 Aug 1986, Nicola Wilkinson; 2 da (Jessica b Sept 1991, Alice b June 1994); *Career* jr hosp positions obstetrics and gynaecology Glasgow 1991–96, Wellcome Tst clinical research fell Univ of Glasgow 1992–93, Wellcome Tst advanced clinical research fell Cornell Univ 1996–99, trainee maternal-foetal med Glasgow 1999–2001, prof of obstetrics and gynaecology Univ of Cambridge 2001– (head Dept of Obstetrics and Gynaecology 2004–); memb: Perinatal Research Soc USA 2000, Soc of Gynaecological Investigation USA 2002, Gynaecological Visiting Soc 2004, Soc for Maternal Fetal Medicine USA; fell Hughes Hall Cambridge 2014; FRCOG 2008 (MRCOG 1995), FMedSci 2010; author of articles in learned jls incl: New England

S

Jl of Med, Nature, Lancet, Jl of the American Med Assoc, BMJ; *Style*— Prof Gordon Smith; ✉ Department of Obstetrics and Gynaecology, University of Cambridge, The Rosie Hospital, Robinson Way, Cambridge CB2 2SW (✆ 01223 336871, fax 01223 215327, e-mail obgyn-headofdept@lists.cam.ac.uk)

SMITH, Graham Alan; s of Sydney Horace Smith (d 1970), and Joan Olive, *née* Tame; *b* 29 October 1947; *Educ* Beckenham GS for Boys; *m* Aug 1978, Joan Louise; 1 s (Patrick Henry James Smith b Nov 1984); *Career* sales asst then exec ABC TV/Thames TV 1966–70, media gp head Boase Massimi Pollitt Advertising 1970–73, successively business devpt mangr, business devpt dir then vice-chm Saatchi & Saatchi Advertising 1973–92, exec vice-pres Ogilvy & Mather Europe 1992–94, dir and ptnr Warman & Bannister 1994– (formerly Leopard Advertising Ltd until 1997); memb Mktg Soc 1986; *Recreations* motor racing, photography, cricket; *Style*— Graham Smith, Esq; ✉ Warman & Bannister Ltd, 40 Marsh Wall, London E14 9TP (✆ 020 7512 1000, fax 020 7512 1999)

SMITH, Graham Paul; s of James Alfred Smith (d 1985), and Elsie Winifred, *née* Cleathero; *b* 25 December 1949; *Educ* Royal GS High Wycombe, Univ of Durham (BA), Osgoode Hall Law Sch Toronto (LLM); *m* 14 Sept 1991, Mary, da of Edward T Ray (d 1986), of Southwold, Suffolk; 1 da (Charlotte b 1994); *Career* slr Supreme Court 1975; ptnr: Clifford-Turner 1981–87, Clifford Chance 1987–2000; conslt Clifford Chance 2000–; Liveryman City of London Slrs' Co; memb Law Soc 1975; *Books* contrib chapters to: The Encyclopaedia of Information Technology Law (1990), Computer Law (3 edn, 1996); *Recreations* opera, cricket; *Clubs* MCC, RAC; *Style*— Graham Smith, Esq; ✉ Clifford Chance, 10 Upper Bank Street, London E14 5JJ (✆ 020 7006 1000, fax 020 7006 5555, e-mail graham.smith@cliffordchance.com)

SMITH, Graham Richard Elliott; s of Donald Smith (d 1978), and Betty Lillian, *née* Elliott; *b* 24 February 1958; *Educ* Royal GS Guildford, Univ of Nottingham (BA); *m* 19 Sept 1987, Sh?ron Elizabeth Peterson, da of Aubrey Owen Mulroney (d 2005); 2 s (Sebastian Guy Elliott b 5 November 1991, Willem Peter Elliott b 5 April 1994), 1 da (Leone Jane Peterson b 4 June 1990); *Career* admitted slr 1982; Wilde Sapte: articled clerk 1980–82, slr 1982–87, ptnr 1987–98; ptnr Allen & Overy 1998–13 (conslt 2013–); Freeman Worshipful Co of Slrs 1986–; memb Law Soc; *Recreations* golf, fine wine, travel; *Style*— Graham Smith, Esq; ✉ Allen & Overy LLP, One Bishop Square, London E1 6AD

SMITH, Henry Edward Millar; MP; s of John Smith (d 2006), and Josephine, *née* Millar (d 2012); *b* 14 May 1969, Epsom, Surrey; *Educ* UCL (BA); *m* 18 June 1994 (m dis 2016), Jennifer; 1 da, 1 s (and 1 s decd); *Career* ldr W Sussex CC 2003–10, MP (Cons) Crawley 2010–; *Style*— Henry Smith, Esq, MP; ✉ House of Commons, London SW1A 0AA

SMITH, Iain Alastair Robertson; OBE (2008); s of Nathaniel Lawrence Albert Smith, and Anne Cameron, *née* Urquhart; *b* 8 January 1949, Glasgow; *Educ* Jordanhill Coll Sch, London Film Sch; *m* Isabel J Smith; 1 s (Benjamin N M Smith), 2 da (Allie Smith, Claire Page); *Career* film prodr; prodr My Childhood (BFI), fndr prodn co (with Jon Schorstein) working on TV commercials, documentaries, children's feature films and low budget dramas; prodn mangr Deathwatch 1978, unit location mangr Chariots of Fire 1979; line prodr: Local Hero, The Killing Fields, The Mission; prodr: The Frog Prince, Seven Years in Tibet, Entrapment; fndr Applecross Productions 1987; co-prodr: Hearts of Fire, Killing Dad, City of Joy, Mary Reilly, The Fifth Element, 24: Live Another Day (TV series); exec prodr: 1492 – Conquest of Paradise, Spy Game, Cold Mountain, Mad Max: Fury Road (winner 4 BAFTAs and 6 Academy Awards); prodr: Alexander, The Fountain, Children of Men, Wanted, The A Team; dir Children's Film and TV Fndn, vice-pres Prodn Guild of GB; chair: Film Industry Trg Bd, Film Skills Cncl, Skillset Crafts and Technical Skills Acad, Br Film Cmmn; dep chm Br Film Advsy Gp; founding memb Scottish Film Trg Tst, memb: Br Screen Advsy Cncl and Skillset, Bd UK Film Cncl, Bd Scottish Screen, BAFTA, BFI; former memb: Scottish Film Cncl, Scottish Film Prodn Fund, Trade Ctee BFTPA, Trade Ctee AIP, Trade Ctee PACT; former govr Nat Film and TV Sch; *Recreations* reading, theatre, cinema, Scottish painting, walking, philosophy, travel; *Clubs* Groucho, Glasgow Art, BAFTA; *Style*— Iain Smith, Esq, OBE; ✉ c/o Sandra Marsh, Marsh Management, 9150 Wilshire Boulevard, Beverly Hills, CA 90212, USA (✆ 00 1 310 285 0303, fax 00 1 310 285 0218); Applecross Productions Ltd, Pinewood Studios, Pinewood Road, Iver Heath, Buckinghamshire SL0 0NH

SMITH, Ian Anderson; s of Sidney Victor Smith, and Mary, *née* Anderson; *b* 13 June 1948, Edinburgh; *Educ* London Business Sch (Sr Exec Prog), Inst of Electrical Engineers (HNC); *Children* 2 s (Robert Duncan b 29 July 1977, Andrew Douglas b 11 Dec 1981); *Career* customer service dir Digital UK, Ireland and Middle East 1987–90, dir European office Digital USA 1990–91, dir business ptnrs customer service dir Digital Equipment Corp 1991–94, md customer service BT UK 1994–99, regnl sr vice-pres and md Oracle Corporation Ltd UK, Ireland, Israel and South Africa 1999–2008, managing ptnr AndersonBick Consultants LLP; chm Young Enterprise, pres Inst Customer Service, chair Leadership & Mgmnt Advsy Panel; memb Bd: Specialist Schs and Acads Tst (SSAT), Business in the Community; hon fell Liverpool John Moores Univ; FIET, FBCS, FCGI; *Recreations* football, rugby; *Clubs* Caledonian; *Style*— Ian Smith, Esq; ✉ AndersonBick Consultants LLP, 47 Bridge House, St George Wharf, Wandsworth Road, London SW8 2LP (e-mail ian.smith@andersonbick.com, website www.andersonbick.com)

SMITH, Prof Ian Edward; s of David N Smith, of Dundee, and Netty T, *née* Millar; *b* 16 May 1946; *Educ* Dundee HS, Univ of Edinburgh (Bsc, MB ChB, MD, Ettles scholar, Leslie Gold medal), Univ of Illinois (Carnegie scholar), Harvard Univ; *m* 1978, Suzanne D, *née* Mackey; 3 da (Emily b 31 Oct 1979, Rebecca b 24 March 1982, Katy b 12 Dec 1984); *Career* Edinburgh Royal Infirmary: house physician 1971–72, house surgn 1972, SHO Dept of Med 1972–73, med registrar Med Professorial Unit Royal Marsden Hosp 1974–75, Royal Marsden res fell Dept of Med and Biophysics Inst of Cancer Research 1975–76, UICC travelling fell Sidney Farber Cancer Inst Harvard Med Sch 1976–77, lectr in med Inst of Cancer Research and hon sr med registrar Royal Marsden Hosp 1977–78, conslt med oncologist Royal Marsden Hosp 1978–2000, med dir Royal Marsden Hosp 2000–, prof of cancer med Inst of Cancer Research 2000–; invited lectrs worldwide on various aspects of lung and breast cancer treatment and biology; chm MRC Lung Cancer Working Party 1997, head Section of Med Inst of Cancer Research 1991– (hon sr lectr 1979–); chm: Assoc of Cancer Physicians 1996–, Sub-Ctee UK Coordinating Ctee on Cancer Research, Specialist Advsy Ctee on Med Oncology RCP; pres Euro Winter Oncology Conf 1997–98; former pres Edinburgh Royal Med Soc; memb: American Soc of Clinical Oncology 1980, Br Assoc for Cancer Research 1981, Br Assoc for Cancer Physicians 1982, Br Breast Gp 1982, Euro Soc of Med Oncology 1986, Br Oncological Assoc 1986; FRCP Edin 1986, FRCP 1988; *Books* Autologous Bone Marrow Transplantation in Solid Tumours (jt ed, 1984), Medical Management of Breast Cancer (jt ed, 1991); author of over 300 pubns on breast cancer, lung cancer and cancer biology; *Recreations* skiing, outdoors, reading; *Style*— Prof Ian Smith; ✉ Royal Marsden Hospital, Fulham Road, London SW3 6JJ (✆ 020 7808 2751, fax 020 7352 5441, e-mail ian.smith@rmh.nhs.uk)

SMITH, Ian Richard; *b* 22 January 1954; *Educ* Univ of Oxford (MA), Univ of Hull (PhD), Harvard Business Sch (MBA); *Career* early career Royal Dutch/Shell Group of Cos, md Monitor Co Europe until 1998; Exel plc: gp commercial dir Ocean Gp plc (subsequently merged with Exel) 1998, memb Exec Bd 2001, ceo consumer, retail and health (Europe) until 2003, ceo EMEA 2003–04; chief exec: General Healthcare Gp 2004–07, Taylor Woodrow plc 2007–08, Reed Elsevier 2008–09; economic and business advsr Office of the Quartet Representative 2010–; non-exec dir Galiform plc (formerly MFI Furniture Gp

plc); memb Competitiveness Cncl, advsr to govt on industrial policy; *Style*— Ian Smith, Esq

SMITH, Dr Ian Robertson; s of Robert Smith (d 1988), and Mary Elizabeth Boyd, *née* Loudon (d 1951); *b* 1 August 1943; *Educ* Paisley GS, Univ of Glasgow (MB ChB); *m* 1968, Margaret Foster, da of Provost Harry Clunie (d 1993); 1 da (Angela Elizabeth b 9 Nov 1969), 1 s (Michael Stuart, *qv* b 31 July 1971); *Career* house physician Paisley Infirmary 1968–69, house surgn Inverness Royal Infirmary 1969, SHO in obstetrics Inverness Raigmore 1969–70, GP Inverness 1970–2006, ret; chm Ness DOC (GP Cooperative) 1996–98 (dir 1998–2001); dir Highland Hospice 1998–2005; gen practice trainer 1986–95, assoc advsr in gen practice 1987–92; memb Highland Health Bd Gp Educn Ctee 1978–2001, ambass Highland Hospice 2008–; memb: BMA 1970, Highland Med Soc 1970 (pres 1994–95); FRCGP 1991 (N of Scotland Faculty: hon sec 1975–87, chm 1991–93, provost 2003–10, treas 2003–13); medical advsr Inverness Caledonian Thistle FC and Scottish FA 1998–2013, ret; *Clubs* Torness Curling, Inverness Golf; *Style*— Dr Ian Smith; ✉ Dromard, 43 Midmills Road, Inverness IV2 3NZ (✆ 01463 236741)

SMITH, Ivo; s of Guy Sydney Smith (d 1972), of Market Rasen, Lincs, and Florence Maud, *née* Titmarsh (d 1981); *b* 31 May 1931; *Educ* De Aston GS Market Rasen, Jesus Coll Cambridge (MA, MChir), St Mary's Hosp Med Sch Univ of London; *m* 17 Feb 1962, Janet, da of George James Twyman (d 1936), of Deal, Kent; 1 da (Mary b 1965), 2 s (Robin b 1966, Simon b 1969); *Career* Nat Serv RAF (Educn Branch) 1950–51; conslt surgn, lectr and author on surgery of the breast and the breast in art; med chm Pension Appeals Tbnls; Freeman City of London 1965, Liveryman Worshipful Soc of Apothecaries 1964; FRCS; *Recreations* my family, fishing; *Style*— Ivo Smith, Esq; ✉ 229 Princes Gardens, London W3 0LU (✆ 020 8992 0939)

SMITH, Prof Ivor Ramsay; s of Howard Smith (d 1966), of Birmingham, and Elsie Emily, *née* Underhill (d 1980); *b* 8 October 1929, Birmingham; *Educ* Univ of Bristol (BSc, PhD, DSc); *m* 3 Jan 1962, Pamela Mary, da of Alfred Voake (d 1976), of Birmingham; 3 s (Laurence David b 12 May 1963, Andrew Paul b 25 June 1965, Michael Jonathan b 8 Nov 1968); *Career* design and devpt engr GEC Birmingham 1956–59, reader (also lectr and sr lectr) Univ of Birmingham 1959–74; Loughborough Univ: prof of electrical power engrg 1974–, head Dept of Electronic and Electrical Engrg 1980–90, dean of engrg 1983–86, pro-vice-chllr 1987–91; memb Ctee: Royal Acad of Engrg, Headstart and Global Research Awards, Miny of Defence; CEng 1974, FIEE 1974, FREng 1988; *Publications* author/co-author of around 400 pubns (incl 2 books) in the areas of electrical machine control and the production, conditioning and use of high voltage and high current pulses of electrical energy; *Recreations* gardening, walking, reading; *Style*— Prof Ivor Smith, FREng; ✉ 83 Nanpantan Road, Loughborough, Leicestershire LE11 3ST; School of Electronic, Electrical and Systems Engineering, Loughborough University, Leicestershire LE11 3TU (✆ 01509 227005, fax 01509 227014, e-mail i.r.smith@lboro.ac.uk)

SMITH, Dr James Cuthbert (Jim); s of Leslie Cuthbert Smith (d 2000), and Freda Sarah, *née* Wragg (d 2011); *b* 31 December 1954; *Educ* Latymer Upper Sch, Christ's Coll Cambridge (MA, Frank Smart prize in zoology), Univ of London (PhD); *m* 22 Sept 1979, Fiona Mary, da of David Mackie Watt (d 2000); 2 s (Angus James MacDougall b 15 May 1994, Gavin Robert Benedict b 3 May 2002), 1 da (Kirsty Flora Elizabeth (twin) b 3 May 2002); *Career* NATO postdoctoral fell Sidney Farber Cancer Inst and Harvard Med Sch 1979–81; ICRF postdoctoral fell 1981–84; Nat Inst for Med Research: memb scientific staff 1984, sr scientist 1990, head Div of Developmental Biology 1991–2000, head Genes and Cellular Controls Gp 1997–2000; dir Wellcome Tst/Cancer Research UK Gurdon Inst Cambridge and John Humphrey Plummer prof of developmental biology 2000–09, dir Med Research Cncl Nat Inst for Med Research 2009–15, dir of research Francis Crick Inst 2013– (memb Bd 2014–), dep ceo and chief of strategy Med Research Cncl 2014–; scientific fell Zoological Soc, Wellcome visiting prof 1991–92, int res scholar Howard Hughes Med Inst 1993–98, hon prof Dept of Anatomy and Developmental Biology UCL 2009–, hon fell Christ's Coll Cambridge 2009–; ed-in-chief Development; author of numerous pubns and articles in scientific jls; chm British Soc for Developmental Biology 1994–99; memb: EMBO 1992 (medal 1993), Academia Europaea 2000; memb Advsy Cncl Br Library; Scientific Medal Zoological Soc 1989, Otto Mangold Prize German Soc for Developmental Biology 1991, Feldberg Fndn Award 2000, William Bate Harvey Prize 2001, Waddington Medal Br Soc for Devpt Biology 2013; FRS 1993, FIBiol 1997, FMedSci 1998, FRSA 2009, fell European Acad of Cancer Sciences 2009; *Publications* Principles of Development (jtly, 3 edn 2006); *Recreations* reading, family, cycling, running; *Clubs* Serpentine Running; *Style*— Dr Jim Smith, FRS; ✉ Francis Crick Institute, Mill Hill Laboratory, The Ridgeway, London NW7 1AA (✆ 020 8816 2048, fax 020 8816 2041, e-mail jim.smith@crick.ac.uk)

SMITH, James Edward; s of James Joseph Smith, of Liverpool, and Dorothy, *née* Roberts; *b* 31 March 1950; *Educ* Univ of Liverpool (BA, Duke of Edinburgh Gold award), Liverpool Univ Business Sch (Post Grad Degree in Mktg), Inst of Mktg (Dip MInstM); *m* 1979, Celia Margaret, da of John Nairm; 2 da (Emma Lindsey b 25 Sept 1980, Rebecca Caroline b 20 July 1982); *Career* articled clerk Harwood Banner & Co 1968–71, mktg mangr Mobil Oil 1971–73, student 1973–74, mktg mangr Lonrho 1974–76, mktg dir rising to md Graham Poulter Group 1976–85, client servs dir J Walter Thompson 1988–90 (bd dir 1985–88); chm: JWT Group Manchester until 1996, Conquest Creative Services; md Clear Marketing Communications Ltd (formerly Nairn Smith Partnership Ltd); dir: Onside Northwest, The Factory Youth Zone; MInstM; *Recreations* music, wine, skiing, basketball (10 caps England Youth Int), travel; *Clubs* Young Presidents' Organisation; *Style*— James Smith, Esq

SMITH, Jan Eileen; da of Harold Douglas Smith (decd), of Morecambe, and Lena, *née* Barrett; *b* 5 April 1947; *Educ* Casterton Sch Kirkby Lonsdale, Univ Coll of Rhodesia Salisbury (BA London); *Career* TSB Bank 1980–86, Lloyds Bank plc 1986–88, mktg dir First Direct 1989–90, dir of network mktg TSB Bank plc 1990–92; mktg dir Mazda Cars (UK) Ltd 1992–95, gp strategic dir RAC 1995–98, md The Virtual Co Ltd 1998–2015; currently: non-exec dir Cncl for Licensed Conveyancers, vice-chm Saffron Building Soc, non-exec dir Which? Fin Servs, non-exec dir Colchester Hosp Univ NHS Fndn Tst; memb Cncl and tstee AQA; Product Excellence Award Mktg Soc 1990; MAoC, MInstD, FIDM; *Recreations* motor racing, classic car rallying, reading, yoga; *Clubs* Brand Exchange; *Style*— Miss Jan E Smith

SMITH, Rt Hon Dame Janet Hilary (Dame Janet Mathieson); DBE (1992), PC (2002); da of Alexander Roe Holt (d 1970), and Margaret Holt, *née* Birchall (d 1991); *b* 29 November 1940; *Educ* Bolton Sch; *m* 1, 6 June 1959 (m dis 1982), Edward Stuart Smith, s of Edward Austin Carruthers Smith (d 1990); 2 s (Richard b 1959, Alasdair b 1963), 1 da (Rachel b 1962); *m* 2, 12 Oct 1984, Robin Edward Alexander Mathieson, s of Alexander John Mathieson, MC (d 1974), of Yoxall, Staffs; *Career* called to the Bar Lincoln's Inn 1972; QC 1986, recorder of the Crown Court 1988, memb Criminal Injuries Compensation Bd 1988–92, judge of the High Court of Justice (Queen's Bench Div) 1992–2002, judge Employment Appeal Tbnl 1994–2002, presiding judge (NE Circuit) 1995–98, Lord Justice of Appeal 2002–11, ind assessor of compensation for miscarriages of justice 2011–16; pres Cncl of the Inns of Court 2006–09; chm: Civil Ctee Judicial Studies Bd 2000–04, Security Vetting Appeals Panel 2000–09, Shipman Inquiry 2001–05; lead BBC Jimmy Savile Inquiry 2012–15 (Savile Report published 2016); chllr Manchester Metropolitan Univ 2003–09; chm Buxton Arts Festival 2007–14; *Style*— The Rt Hon Dame Janet Smith, DBE; ✉ Royal Courts of Justice, Strand, London WC2A 2LL

SMITH, Janice Ann; da of Frank Charles Henry Smith, MBE, of Tunbridge Wells, Kent, and Mary Elizabeth, *née* Bridges (d 1989); *b* 24 March 1960, Chiswick, London; *Educ* Tunbridge Wells Girls' GS, Univ of Leeds (LLB), Guildford Coll of Law; *m* 9 March 1996, Rev Robert John Dando; *Career* admitted slr; specialises in clinical negligence cases and risk mgmnt; Herbert Smith 1983–86, Beckman & Beckman 1987–89, Capsticks 1990– (ptnr 1991–); assoc non-exec dir Milton Keynes Gen NHS Tst, memb Clinical Negligence and Serious Injury Ctee Civil Justice Cncl; vice-pres London Dist Boys' Brigade, chair Baptist World Congress Ctee; memb Law Soc 1985; *Recreations* theatre, good food, shopping; *Style—* Miss Janice Smith; ✉ Capsticks Solicitors LLP, 1 St George's Road, Wimbledon, London SW19 4DR (☎ 020 8780 4712, e-mail jsmith@capsticks.co.uk)

SMITH, Jeff; *b* 24 December 1960; *Educ* Baines' GS Poulton-le-Fylde, North Cheshire Coll Warrington (BA); *m* Deborah; 1 s (Callum), 1 da (Ellie); *Career* prodr Popular Music Dept BBC World Service 1986–88, prog mangr Metro Radio Gp 1989–90, prodr and creator Evening Session BBC Radio 1 1990–93, ed of mainstream progs Radio 1 1993–95, dir of progs Wise Buddah ind prodn 1995–97, head of music policy Radio 11997–2000, prog controller 95.8 Capital FM 2000–02, head of music and programming strategy Capital FM Network 2002–03, music and media conslt 2003–04, programming dir Napster UK and Napster Int 2004–07, head of music BBC Radio 2 and BBC Radio 6 Music 2007–; creator Shout to the Top/ Queens of Noise (music drama, BBC Radio), cmmnd Sir Tom Stoppard's Darkside (BBC Radio 2); memb: Steering Ctee Radio Acad's Music Radio event 2000 and 2001, Ctee Sony Awards 2000 and 2001, Bd Mgmnt Ctee Pepsi Chart 2000–02; panellist NAB Europe conference Prague 2002, judge BBC Post Prodn Awards 2003, judge Mercury Music Prize 2013–; *Style—* Jeff Smith, Esq; ✉ c/o BBC Radio 2, Room 314, Western House, 99 Great Portland Street, London W1A 1AA (☎ 020 7765 3433, e-mail jeff.smith@bbc.co.uk, website www.bbc.co.uk/radio2)

SMITH, Joan Alison; da of Alan Smith (d 1985), and Ann Anita, *née* Coltman (d 2014); *b* 27 August 1953; *Educ* Girls GS Stevenage, HS for Girls Basingstoke, Univ of Reading (BA); *Career* journalist: Evening Gazette Blackpool 1976–78, Piccadilly Radio Manchester 1978–79, Sunday Times 1979–84; freelance writer 1984–; chair Writers in Prison Ctee English Pen 2000–04; associate prof Sch of Communications and Multi-Media Edith Cowan Univ WA 2002–05; memb FCO Freedom of Expression Panel 2002–04, pres Creators' Rights Alliance 2010–12, co-chair Mayor of London's Violence Against Women and Girls Panel 2013–, exec dir Hacked Off 2014–15; non-exec dir ALCS 2010–15; hon assoc Nat Secular Soc, patron Br Humanist Assoc 2013; FRSA; *Books* Clouds of Deceit (1985), A Masculine Ending (1987), Why Aren't They Screaming? (1988), Misogynies (1989), Don't Leave Me This Way (1990), Femmes de Siècle (ed, 1992), What Men Say (1993), Full Stop (1995), Hungry For You: From Cannibalism to Seduction – A Book of Food (1996), Different For Girls: How Culture Creates Women (1997), Moralities: Sex, Money and Power in the 21st Century (2001), What Will Survive (2007), The Public Woman (2013), Down with the Royals (2015); *Style—* Ms Joan Smith; ✉ c/o PFD, Drury House, 34–43 Russell Street, London WC2B 5HA

SMITH, John; OBE (2009); s of Ernest Sidney Smith (d 1983), and Marjorie Irene Nelly, *née* Hyde (d 1989); *b* 17 September 1942, Evesham, Worcs; *Educ* Evesham County Secdy Sch, N Glos Tech Coll; *m* 30 April 1966, Frances Sabina, *née* Newman; 2 da (Joanne Louise (Mrs Webb) b 15 Dec 1968, Claire Marie (Mrs Beaman) b 11 May 1972); *Career* electrical apprenticeship Booth & Bomford then Wathes until 1962, repairs and distribution mangr Midlands Electricity Bd until 1996 (ret); cncllr: Wychavon DC 1983–2015 (ldr 1989–92, vice-chm 2001, chm 2002), Evesham Town Cncl 1987– (mayor 1992–93), Hereford & Worcester CC 1995–96, Worcs CC 1996– (vice-chm 2006, chm 2007–08, cabinet memb for heath improvement 2008–11, cabinet memb for highways and transportation 2011–16, cabinet memb for public health and wellbeing 2016–); fndr memb Evesham & Pershore Housing Assoc, chm Evesham Arts Centre Ctee, chm Evesham Twinning Assoc, memb Friends of Evesham Community Hosp; tstee: John Martin Charity, Hampton Educational Charity, Wallace House Mgmnt Ctee (former memb), Rudge Charity, Deacle & Prince Henry's Educational Fndn; memb Royal Br Legion, pres Sea Cadet Unit; *Recreations* gardening, DIY; *Style—* John Smith, Esq, OBE; ✉ The Orchard, Malinshill Road, Hampton, Evesham, Worcestershire WR11 2QG (☎ 01386 443157, e-mail jhsmith@jhsmith.plus.com); Worcestershire County Council, County Hall, Spetchley Road, Worcester WR5 2NP

SMITH, (Edward Ernest) John; s of Ernest Frederick Smith, DCM, of Chiswick, London, and Elizabeth, *née* Reilly; *b* 13 August 1950; *Educ* Latymer Upper Sch London, Emmanuel Coll Cambridge (MA, MD, BChir), St Thomas' Hosp Med Sch London; *m* 23 April 1984, Muriel Susan, da of Daniel Shannon, of Ayr; 2 da (Susan b 1985, Katherine b 1987), 1 s (David b 1989); *Career* conslt cardiothoracic surgn St George's Hosp London and Royal Surrey Co Hosp Guildford; memb BMA 1974; FRCS 1978; *Recreations* opera, golf, skiing; *Clubs* London Rowing, Royal Wimbledon Golf; *Style—* John Smith, Esq; ✉ Homewood, 4A Drax Avenue, Wimbledon SW20 0EH (☎ 020 8946 1893, fax 020 8946 3130, e-mail eejsmith@btinternet.com); St Anthony's Hospital, North Cheam SM3 9DW (☎ 020 8725 3551)

SMITH, John Barry; s of Kenneth William Smith, and Elsie, *née* Jackson; *Educ* Derby Shelton Sch, S London Coll, Harvard Business Sch; *Career* audit clerk Bocock Bew Chartered Accountants 1973–75; BR Gp Commercial Subsidiaries: mgmnt trainee 1975–81, fin manager and head customer serv Seaspeed Hovercraft 1981–83; head of insurance rising to corp fin manager BR Board 1983–89; BBC: gp chief accountant 1989–92, fin controller Network TV 1992–96, dep fin dir 1996–97, dir of fin 1997–2000, dir of fin, property and business affrs then chief operating offr 2000–04, formerly chief exec BBC Worldwide; non-exec dir: Severn Trent 2003–08, Burberry Gp plc; former memb: Accounting Standards Bd, Public Services Productivity Panel HM Treasy, 100 Gp of Fin Dirs; dir UK Enterprise Advsy Bd Zurich Fin Services until 2001; dir Henley Festival, vice-pres RTS; *Recreations* country pursuits, opera, cinema, sports cars, skiing, sailing; *Style—* John Smith, Esq; ✉ BBC Broadcasting House, Portland Place, London W1A 1AA (☎ 020 8433 3533, mobile 07850 717762, e-mail john.smith@bbc.com)

SMITH, John William; s of William Stanley Smith, of Bromley, Kent (d 1981), and Stella, *née* Etherington (d 1998); *b* 14 January 1945, Bromley, Kent; *Educ* Univ of Newcastle upon Tyne (BA), LSE (MScEcon); *m* 15 Dec 1978, Yvonne, *née* Lukey; 2 da (Alice Lukey-Smith b 14 Nov 1979, Sara Lukey-Smith b 9 March 1983); *Career* Dept of Environment London 1977–90 (posts incl sr economic advsr Local Govt Finance, head Water Quality Div and head Waste Mgmnt Div), dir of regnl servs then dir of regulation Anglian Water Services Ltd 1990–97, dir of regulation & govt Railtrack plc 1997–2002, princ conslt Indepen Consulting Ltd 2004–06 (assoc 2006–), ind economic conslt 2006–; non-exec memb Steering Bd Marine & Fisheries Agency 2005–10, memb Competition Cmmn 2005–13; tstee and memb Bd Groundwork London 2010–, tstee Michaelhouse Centre Cambridge 2012–; MInstD 2002; Structure of the Water Industry in England: Does It Remain Fit for Purpose? (co-author DEFRA and OFWAT report, 2003); studies for RAC Fndn incl: Governance and Administration of National and Local Roads in GB (2009), Providing and Funding Strategic Roads – An International Perspective (jtly with Arup, 2011); *Recreations* choral singing, country walking, travel, films, theatre, preserved railways; *Style—* John Smith, Esq; ✉ e-mail jws141@btopenworld.com

SMITH, Jon; s of Michael Smith, of Toronto, Canada, and Rosemary, *née* Leavey (d 1968); *Educ* Orange Hill GS, Kingsway Coll of FE; *m* 1, Lee (decd); m 2, 20 July 1986, Janine, da of Martin Jaffe (d 1992), and Bernice Jaffe; 2 s (Ross Alexander b 10 Nov 1988, Scott b 12 April 1991); *Career* ptnr Anglo House Estates 1980–86, owner Green Light prodn co (sold 1981), fndr First Artist Corp plc 1986; chief exec London Monarchs 1990s; patron Br Stammering Assoc, tstee Lee Smith Research Fndn, former memb Bd Inst of Child Health; FInstD 1987; *Recreations* sports, the Arts, polar marathon running; *Style—* Jon Smith, Esq; ✉ First Artist Corporation, First Artist House, 85a Wembley Hill Road, Middlesex HA9 8BU (☎ 020 8900 1818, fax 020 8903 2964, e-mail jons@firstartist.com)

SMITH, Julian Arthur Vaughan; s of Neil Lindsey Vaughan Smith, of Appledore, Kent, and Frances Marguerite Katharine, *née* Coleridge; *b* 7 February 1969, London; *Educ* Charterhouse (fndn and sr fndn scholar), Peterhouse Cambridge (Lord North scholar, BA), Coll of Law London; *m* 10 Sept 1994, Suzanne Elaine, *née* Hearne; 2 da (Emma Frances Vaughan b 18 Aug 1998, Katherine Grace Vaughan b 18 Aug 1998); *Career* admitted slr 1994; Farrer & Co slrs: trainee 1992–94, asst slr Charities Team 1994–2000, ptnr 2000–; visiting lectr Centre for Charity Effectiveness Cass Business Sch; memb Advsy Bd European Assoc for Philanthropy and Giving; memb Advsy Ctee: Charinco, Charishare, Charishare Tobacco Restricted Common Investment Funds; chm Carthusian Tst; memb: Law Soc 1994, Charity Law Assoc 1994 (currently memb Ctee); *Publications* The Charities Act 2006 (jtly); *Recreations* family and friends; *Style—* Julian Smith, Esq; ✉ Farrer & Co, 66 Lincoln's Inn Fields, London WC2A 3LH (☎ 020 7242 2022, fax 020 7917 7408, e-mail jas@farrer.co.uk)

SMITH, Julian Richard; MP; *b* 1971; *Educ* Univ of Birmingham; *Career* MP (Cons) Skipton and Ripon and asst Govt whip 2010–; *Style—* Julian Smith, Esq, MP; ✉ House of Commons, London SW1A 0AA (☎ 020 7219 4866, e-mail julian.smith.mp@parliament.uk, website www.juliansmith.org.uk)

SMITH, Kate; da of Reginald Ernest Bayston, of Co Durham, and Mabel, *née* Jackson; *b* 8 May 1951; *Educ* Orpington Co Secdy Sch, Wilby Carr HS Doncaster, Doncaster Coll of Technol, Univ of Leeds (BA), Wine & Spirit Educn Tst (higher cert in wines & spirits, instructors cert in wines & spirits Dip pt A&B); *m* 14 Oct 1973, Richard Francis Smith, s of late William Henry Bernard Smith; 2 s (Giles Edward b 25 April 1983, Rupert James b 29 Aug 1995); *Career* asst mangr Restaurant and Banqueting Div Trust House Forte London 1974–75, lectr in food and beverages North Devon Coll 1976–77; Royal Garden Hotel London: project mangr Garden Cafe 1978, acting banqueting mangr 1978–80, promotions mangr 1980; sales and mktg dir Hyatt Carlton Tower London 1982, conslt Rank Hotels Ltd 1982–84, dir Smith Giddings Ltd (parent co of The Beetle & Wedge Hotel Moulsford-on-Thames Oxon); winner: Pub of the Year Award The Royal Oak 1985, Badoit Restaurant of the Year Award Beetle & Wedge 1991, Gonzalez Byass Customer Care Award Beetle & Wedge 1992, Good Hotel Guide César Award 1993, Hosts of the Year Egon Ronay Guide Beetle & Wedge 1995; Master Innholder until 1995, memb Académie Culinaire de France; *Recreations* skiing, theatre, interior design, wine and food; *Style—* Mrs Kate Smith; ✉ The Beetle & Wedge Hotel, Moulsford-on-Thames, Oxfordshire OX10 9JF (☎ 01491 651381, fax 01491 651376)

SMITH, Prof Keith; s of Joseph Smith (d 1972), and Catherine Maria, *née* Carr (d 1985); *b* 9 January 1938; *Educ* Hyde Co GS, Univ of Hull (BA, PhD); *m* 29 July 1961, Muriel Doris, da of George Hyde (d 1988); 1 da (Fiona b 1966), 1 s (Matthew b 1968); *Career* tutor in geography Univ of Liverpool 1963–65, lectr in geography Univ of Durham 1965–70, prof of geography Univ of Strathclyde 1982–86 (sr lectr 1971–75, reader 1975–82); Univ of Stirling: prof of environmental science 1986–98, head Sch of Natural Sciences 1994–96, dean Faculty of Natural Sciences 1996–97, emeritus prof of environmental science 1998–; FRSE 1988; *Books* Water in Britain (1972), Principles of Applied Climatology (1975), Human Adjustment to The Flood Hazard (1979), Environmental Hazards (with D N Petley, 1991, 6 edn 2013), Floods (with R C Ward, 1998); *Recreations* gardening, hill walking, painting; *Style—* Prof Keith Smith, FRSE; ✉ 11 Grinnan Road, Braco, By Dunblane, Perthshire FK15 9RF (☎ 01786 880359, e-mail keithandmuriel.smith@gmail.com); Department of Biological and Environmental Sciences, University of Stirling, Stirling FK9 4LA (☎ 01786 467750, fax 01786 446896)

SMITH, Dr Lindsay Frederick Paul; s of Frederick Jean Orlando Smith and Audrey Joyce Smith, of Yeovil, Somerset; *Educ* Univ of Bristol (BSc, MB ChB, MD, PhD), Univ of Western Ontario Canada (MClinSci); *m* 1990, Caroline Patricia, da of David Taylor; 4 s (William b 14 March 1992, James b 1 Oct 1993, Charles b 22 Feb 1996, Henry b 5 Jan 1998); *Career* princ in gen med practice Somerset 1988–; research fell Univ of Bristol 1988–94, RCGP research trg fell 1990–91, lectr Inst of Gen Practice Univ of Exeter 1995–96, hon conslt sr lectr Queen Mary & Westfield Coll London 1996–99, sr clinical res fell Peninsula Medical Sch 2006–10; chm Assoc for Community Based Maternity Care 1995–2000; author of original research/academic papers in scientific jls; memb Editorial Bd Br Jl of Gen Practice 1997–2008; memb: Health Technology Appraisal Ctee NICE 2003–10, vice-chair 2014, Health Technology Appeals Ctee NICE 2010–14, memb NICE Quality Standards Ctee 2012–14, NIC early cancer guidelines update gp 2013–15; FRCP, FRCGP, FHEA; *Recreations* duplicate bridge, badminton; *Style—* Dr Lindsay Smith; ✉ ESReC, Westlake Surgery, West Coker, Somerset BA22 9AH (☎ 01935 862624, fax 01935 862042, e-mail research@esrec.nhs.uk)

SMITH, Emeritus Prof Lorraine Nancy; da of Geoffrey Leonard Millington, and Ida May, *née* Attfield; *b* 29 June 1949; *Educ* Univ of Ottawa (BScN), Univ of Manchester (MEd, PhD); *m* Christopher Murray, s of Herbert Murray Smith (d 1990); 1 s (Nicholas Geoffrey Murray b 13 Nov 1979), 1 da (Jennifer Eugenie b 17 Dec 1983); *Career* staff nurse 1971–75, sister 1975–76; lectr Dept of Nursing Studies Univ of Manchester 1976–90; Univ of Glasgow: prof 1990–2011, head of sch 1990–2001; chair RCN Research Soc (Scot) 1999–2005, chair Workgroup of Euro Nurse Researchers 2005–08, chair SIGN 118 and SIGN 119 2008–10; memb: Members Advsy Bd MRC, Acute Healthcare Res Ctee 1991–94, UK Clinical Standards Advsy Gp 1994–99, Turning Point (Scotland) 1996, RCN (UK), Bd RCN Scotland 2009–10; memb Editorial Bd Hellenic Jl of Nursing Science; *Recreations* bridge, sailing, golf, skiing; *Clubs* S Caernarvonshire Yacht, Golff Abersoch; *Style—* Emeritus Prof Lorraine N Smith; ✉ Nursing & Health Care, University of Glasgow, 59 Oakfield Avenue, Glasgow G12 8LL (e-mail lorraine.smith2000@gmail.com)

SMITH, Louis; MBE (2013); *b* 22 April 1989, Peterborough; *Career* gymnast; memb Huntingdon Gymnastics Club; achievements on pommel horse incl: jr European champion 2004 and 2006, Br champion 2006, Gold medal Cwlth Games 2006, Gold medal Australian Youth Olympic Festival 2007, Bronze medal World Championships 2007, Bronze medal Olympic Games Beijing 2008, Silver medal World Championships 2010, 2 Silver medals European Championships 2010, Bronze medal World Championships 2011, Gold and Silver medal European Championships 2012, Silver medal Olympic Games 2012, Bronze medal (team event) Olympic Games 2012, Silver medal (pommel horse) Olympic Games 2016; winner Strictly Come Dancing (BBC 1) 2012; *Style—* Louis Smith, Esq, MBE

SMITH, Dr Malcolm; s of Ralph Smith (d 1988), and Hilda, *née* Joseph (d 1998); *b* 11 March 1949, Mid Wales; *Educ* Univ of London (BSc), Univ of Kent and Tropical Products Inst London (PhD); *m* 25 Oct 2002, Vivien Conway; *Children* 2 da (Clare b 24 July 1975, Annabel b 7 Dec 1981), 1 s (Thomas b 24 May 1979); *Career* research mangr Unilever plc 1973–75; Nature Conservancy Cncl: asst regnl offr N Wales 1975–86, dep head Sci and Policy Unit Wales HQ 1986–89, head Sci and Policy Branch Wales HQ 1989–91; Countryside Cncl for Wales: chief ecologist 1991–95, dir of policy and sci 1995–98, sr dir and chief scientist 1998–2004; memb: Terrestrial and Freshwater Sciences Bd NERC 1999–2000, Welsh Consumers Cncl 2004–08, Bd Environment Agency 2004–10 (memb with special responsibility for Wales), Consumer Focus Wales Bd 2008–13, Advsy Ctee Consumer Futures Wales 2013–14, Sustainability First Public Information Network

S

2016–; freelance writer on environment, wildlife, travel and sci 1982–; Life with Birds: A Story of Mutual Exploitation (2011), Back From The Brink (2015); numerous feature articles on environment, wildlife, heritage and travel in a range of UK and int pubns; *Recreations* gardening, wildlife, travel; *Style*— Dr Malcolm Smith; ☎ 07810 355921, e-mail malcolmsmith@penybryn203.wanadoo.co.uk

SMITH, Dame Margaret Natalie Cross (Maggie); CH (2014), DBE (1990, CBE 1970); da of Nathaniel Smith, and Margaret Little, *née* Hutton; *b* 28 December 1934; *Educ* Oxford HS for Girls, Oxford Playhouse Sch; *m* 1, 1967 (m dis 1975), Robert Stephens, actor (later Sir Robert Stephens; d 1995); 2 s (Christopher (actor under name of Chris Larkin), Toby); m 2, 1975, Beverley Cross (d 1998); *Career* actress; debut as Viola in Twelfth Night (OUDS) 1952, NY debut as comedienne in New Faces (Ethel Barrymore Theatre) 1956; dir United Br Artists 1982–; Hon DLitt: Univ of St Andrews 1971, Univ of London 1991, Univ of Cambridge 1994; Shakespeare Prize 1991, BAFTA Special Achievement Award 1993, Channel 4 Lifetime Achievement Award 1995, Laurence Olivier SOLT Special Award 2010; *Theatre* for Old Vic Co 1959–60 credits incl: The Double Dealer, As You Like it, Richard II, The Merry Wives of Windsor, What Every Woman Knows; NT credits incl: The Recruiting Officer 1963, Othello, The Master Builder, Hay Fever 1964, Much Ado About Nothing, Miss Julie 1965, A Bond Honoured 1966, The Beaux' Stratagem 1970 (also USA), Hedda Gabler 1970 (Evening Standard Best Actress Award), War Plays 1985, Coming in to Land 1986; at Festival Theatre Stratford Ontario: Antony and Cleopatra, The Way of the World, Measure for Measure, The Three Sisters 1976, A Midsummer Night's Dream, Richard II, The Guardsman, As You Like it, Hay Fever 1977, As You Like It, Macbeth, Private Lives 1978, Virginia, Much Ado About Nothing 1980; other credits incl: Share My Lettuce (Lyric Hammersmith) 1957, The Stepmother (St Martin's) 1958, Rhinoceros (Strand) 1960, Strip the Willow (Cambridge) 1960, The Rehearsal (Globe) 1961, The Private Ear and the Public Eye (Globe) 1962 (Evening Standard Drama Award Best Actress), Mary Mary (Queen's) 1963 (Variety Club of GB Best Actress of the Year), The Country Wife (Chichester) 1969, Design for Living (LA) 1971, Private Lives (Queen's) 1972 (also Globe 1973, NY 1975, Variety Club of GB Stage Actress Award 1972), Peter Pan (Coliseum) 1973, Snap (Vaudeville) 1974, Night and Day (Phoenix) 1979, Virginia (Haymarket) 1981 (Evening Standard Best Actress Award 1982), The Way of the World (Chichester and Haymarket) 1984 (Evening Standard Best Actress Award 1985), Interpreters (Queen's) 1985, Lettice and Lovage (Globe) 1987 (also NY 1990, Tony Award Best Leading Actress 1990), The Importance of Being Earnest (Aldwych) 1993, Three Tall Women (Wyndhams) 1994 and 1995 (Evening Standard Best Actress Award 1994), Talking Heads (Chichester) 1996 (also London 1997), A Delicate Balance (Haymarket) 1997, The Lady in the Van (Queen's) 1999, Breath of Life (Haymarket) 2002–03, Talking Heads (Aust and NZ tour) 2004, The Lady from Dubuque (Haymarket Theatre) 2007; *Television* incl: Bed Among the Lentils (as part of Alan Bennett's Talking Heads, BBC (RTS Award)) 1989, Memento Mori (BBC) 1992, Suddenly Last Summer (BBC) 1993, David Copperfield (BBC) 1999, All The King's Men (BBC) 1999, Capturing Mary 2007, Downton Abbey 2010– (Best Supporting Actress in a Mini-Series Emmy Award 2011, Outstanding Supporting Actress in a Drama Series Emmy Award 2012, Best Performance by an Actress in a Supporting Role in a Series, Mini-Series or Motion Picture Made for Television Golden Globe 2013); *Film* The VIP's 1963, The Pumpkin Eater 1964, Young Cassidy 1965, Othello 1966, The Honey Pot 1967, Hot Millions 1968 (Variety Club of GB Award), The Prime of Miss Jean Brodie 1968 (Oscar, SFTA Award), Oh! What a Lovely War 1968, Love and Pain (and the Whole Damned Thing) 1973, Travels with my Aunt 1973, Murder by Death 1976, California Suite 1977 (Oscar), Death on the Nile 1978, Quartet 1981, Clash of the Titans 1981, Evil Under the Sun 1982, The Missionary 1982, A Private Function 1984 (BAFTA Award Best Actress 1985), The Loves of Lily 1985, A Room with a View 1986 (Variety Club of GB Award, BAFTA Award Best Actress 1986), The Lonely Passion of Judith Hearne 1989 (Evening Standard British Films Award 1988, BAFTA Award Best Film Actress 1988), Hook 1992, Sister Act 1992, The Secret Garden 1993, Richard III 1996, First Wives Club 1996, Washington Square 1998, Tea With Mussolini 1999, The Last September 2000, Harry Potter and the Philosopher's Stone 2001, Gosford Park 2001 (Oscar nomination for Best Supporting Actress 2002), Divine Secrets of the Ya-Ya Sisterhood 2002, Harry Potter and the Chamber of Secrets 2002, Harry Potter and the Prisoner of Azkaban 2004, My House in Umbria 2004, Ladies in Lavender 2004, Harry Potter and the Goblet of Fire 2005, Keeping Mum 2005, Becoming Jane 2007, Harry Potter and the Order of the Phoenix 2007, Harry Potter and the Half-Blood Prince 2009, From Time to Time 2009, Harry Potter and the Deathly Hallows: Part 1 2010, Harry Potter and the Deathly Hallows: Part 2 2011, The Best Exotic Marigold Hotel 2012, Quartet 2013, My Old Lady 2014, The Second Best Exotic Marigold Hotel 2015, The Lady in the Van 2015; *Style*— Dame Maggie Smith, CH, DBE; ✉ c/o Independent Talent Group Ltd, 40 Whitfield Street, London W1T 2RH (☎ 020 7636 6565, fax 020 7323 0101)

SMITH, Sir Martin Gregory; kt (2013); s of late Archibald Gregory Smith, OBE, and Mary Eleanor, *née* Malone; *b* 2 February 1943; *Educ* St Albans Sch, St Edmund Hall Oxford (MA), Stanford Univ (MBA, AM Econ); *m* Elise Barr Becket, OBE; 1 s, 1 da; *Career* brewer Arthur Guinness Son and Co (Dublin) Ltd 1964–69, McKinsey and Co Inc 1971–73, dir Citicorp Int Bank Ltd 1974–80, chm Bankers Trust International Ltd 1980–83, co-fndr Phoenix Securities Ltd 1983–97; chm: Phoenix Partnership 1990–97, Phoenix Fund Managers Ltd 1990–97; European Investment Banking Donaldson, Lufkin & Jenrette 1997–2000, Amerindo Internet Fund plc 2000–06, GP Bullhound 2005–, Worldwide Healthcare Tst plc 2008–; dir: New Star Asset Management Ltd 2000–09, Phoenix Equity Partners 2000–06, Odgers, Ray & Berndtson plc 2001–09, Oxford Capital Partners 2010–, Energy Works plc 2014–; ptnr Beaumont Partners LLP 2009–16; sr advsr Bain Capital 2001–09, memb Advsy Bd IDDAS Ltd 2005–08, chm Advsy Bd Episode 1 Ventures 2010–15; chm: Bath Mozartfest 2000–2009, ENO 2001–05, Orchestra of the Age of Enlightenment 2011– (chm Bd of Advsrs 1985–2011); dep chm: South Bank Centre 1992–97, Science Museum 1999–2009; tstee: IMS Prussia Cove 1999–, Becket Collection 1999–2012, Wigmore Hall 2000–15, Tetbury Music Festival 2006–; dir Glyndebourne Arts Tst 2007–; visitor Ashmolean Museum 2006–14, govr Royal Acad of Music 2006–16, memb Princes Cncl of Charities 2009–10, memb Chancellor's Ct of Benefactors Univ of Oxford 2009, govr Ditchley Fndn 2010–; fndr Smith Sch of Enterprise and Environment Univ of Oxford 2007; Liveryman Hon Co of Musicians 2000; hon fell St Edmund Hall Oxford 2001, hon fell Science Museum 2009–; Hon FRAM 2003, FRGS 2015; *Recreations* music, conducting, riding, skiing, golf, sailing, real tennis; *Clubs* Brooks's, Garrick, MCC, Eastward Ho! (USA), Huntercombe Golf; *Style*— Sir Martin Smith; ✉ 29 Beaumont Street, Oxford OX1 2NP (e-mail mgs@martingsmith.com)

SMITH, Martin Stephen; s of Cyril George Smith, of Southampton, and Irene Mildred, *née* Harrison; *b* 1 July 1952; *Educ* Purley GS, Fitzwilliam Coll Cambridge (MA); *m* 24 Feb 1979, Krystyna Maria, da of Josef Parkitny; 2 da (Louisa Aniela b 10 Nov 1982, Natalia Maria b 24 Sept 1985); *Career* freelance writer and actor 1974, account mangr Ogilvy Benson & Mather advtg 1976–78 (copywriter 1975–76), account supervisor Saatchi & Saatchi 1978–80, account dir TBWA 1980–82; Bartle Bogle Hegarty: fndr ptnr 1982–2000, chm Lexington Street (below-the-line gp) 1989, md 1996–98, dep-chm 1998–2000; chief exec Grey Worldwide London 2000–02, fndr ptnr Rapley Smith & Jones Ltd 2002, ind communication strategist 2003, fndr ptnr Grounds Morris Smith 2004, worldwide ceo The Law Firm 2005–07, head of public affrs Inst of Cancer Research 2007–10, currently md Marketing PivotX; chm RedRoute Agency; non-exec dir Ovivo Mobile Communications Ltd, conslt Acanchi Ltd, creative conslt Candid Ltd, assoc Inaccord; lay memb Inst of Cancer Research; *Style*— Martin Smith, Esq; ✉ 19 Grand Avenue, London N10 3AY

SMITH, Most Rev Michael; *see:* Meath, Bishop of (RC)

SMITH, Michael Forbes; s of Forbes Weir Smith (d 2000), and Elizabeth, *née* Mackie (d 1972); *b* 4 June 1948, Aberdeen; *Educ* Aberdeen GS, Univ of Southampton (BSc), Heythrop Coll London (MA); *m* 1986, Claire Helen, *née* Stubbs; 1 da (Amelia b 1989), 1 s (Alastair b 1992), 1 other da (Sabina b 1965); *Career* Bd of Trade 1966–68, cmmnd Gordon Highlanders 1971 (ret as Capt 1978); entered HM Dip Serv 1978, second sec FCO 1978–79, second later first sec and head of Chancery Addis Ababa 1979–83, political advsr to govr Port Stanley 1983–85, SE Asia Dept then FO spokesman FCO 1985–89, consul (commercial) Zürich 1990–94, head of press and public affrs Bonn 1994–99, dep high cmmr Islamabad 1999–2003, first resident ambass to Tajikistan 2002–04, ret; fndr Tempered and True Consultancy (dip skills devpt) 2004, advsr Gulf International Minerals Ltd 2004–06, DG Chartered Inst of Arbitrators 2006–12; dir: IDRS Ltd 2007–11, City Disputes Panel 2010–12 (chm 2012), 12 Bloomsbury Square 2011–12; vice-pres St Thomas More PC Bonn 1996–99, memb Appeal Ctee and Church Cncl Farm St Church Mayfair 1986–90, memb Northern Meeting 2006, memb Highland Soc of London 2008, pres St Francis Lebrosy Guild 2014–; chm Bonn Caledonian Soc 1995–99; contrib Piping Times; FRGS 1971, FRSA 1991, FSA Scot 1995, DipIoD 2010; *Publications* Piping Times (contrib, 1999), Arbitration (contrib, 2011); *Recreations* music, Scotland, sailing, field and winter sports, entertaining and conviviality; *Clubs* Army and Navy, Royal Findhorn Yacht, Little Ship (Vice-Cdre 2014, Cdre 2015–); *Style*— Michael Forbes Smith, Esq; ✉ c/o Little Ship Club, Bell Wharf Lane, Upper Thames Street, London EC4R 3TB

SMITH, Michael (Paul) Marshall; s of Prof David M Smith, of Loughton, Essex, and Margaret, *née* Harrup; *b* 3 May 1965; *Educ* Chigwell Sch, King's Coll Cambridge (MA); *m* Paula Grainger; *Career* writer; ptnr Smith & Jones Film Production; Cambridge Footlights: memb 1984–87, memb Ctee 1987, performer/writer nat tour 1987 and tour of USA 1988; memb: Equity, Musicians Union; *Awards* Icarus Award 1990, BFS Award for Best Short Story 1990, 1991 and 1996, August Delerth Award for Best Novel 1995, Philip K Dick Award 2001; *Books* Only Forward (1994), Spares (1996), One of Us (1998), What You Make It (1999), The Straw Men (2002); short stories incl: Dark Terrors, Dark Voices, Dark Lands, The Mammoth Books, Omni; film and television adaptations: Clive Barker's Weaveworld, Robert Faulcon's Nighthunter, Jay Russell's Celestial Dogs; writer/performer (as Michael Rutger) And Now In Colour (BBC Radio 4, 2 series and 2 Christmas specials); *Recreations* music, art and design, foreign travel, cats (owner Spangle and Lintilla); *Clubs* Soho House, Groucho; *Style*— Michael Marshall Smith, Esq; ✉ c/o Jonny Geller, Curtis Brown, Haymarket House, 28–29 Haymarket, London SW1Y 4SP (☎ 020 7396 6600)

SMITH, Michael Stuart; s of Dr Ian Robertson Smith, *qv*, and Margaret, *née* Clunie; *b* 31 July 1971, Inverness; *Educ* Milburn Acad Inverness; *m* 17 Oct 1997, Laurence Simone, *née* Faruch; 1 da (Margot Lola b 22 July 1998), 1 s (Oscar Clunie b 3 June 2005); *Career* commis chef Riviera Restaurant The Glenmoriston Hotel Inverness 1984–86, sous chef Arisaig House Inverness 1987–91, sr chef de partie Le Pont de la Tour London 1991–94, sr sous chef Euphorium/Blueprint Cafe Design Museum 1994–98; head chef: Blue Bar Café Glasgow 1998–99, Arta/Gong Glasgow 2000–03, The Three Chimneys Skye 2004– (3 AA Rosettes 2004–, Observer Food Award 2005, Visit Scotland Gold Award 2006, CIS Award for Excellence 2006, 1 Michelin star 2014); involved with Great British Menu (BBC) 2008 and 2011; memb Slow Food Assoc 2005–; *Recreations* family holidays, dining, music, fishing, painting, mountain biking, wild food foraging; *Style*— Michael Smith, Esq; ✉ The Old Post Office, 8 Borreraig, By Dunvegan, Isle of Skye IV55 8ZY (☎ 01470 511362); The Three Chimneys and House Over-by, Colbost, Dunvegan, Isle of Skye IV55 8ZT (☎ 01470 511258)

SMITH, Prof Neilson Voyne (Neil); s of Voyne Smith (d 1991), and Lilian Freda, *née* Rose (d 1973); *b* 21 June 1939; *Educ* Trinity Coll Cambridge (MA), UCL (PhD); *m* 2 July 1966, Dr Saraswati Keskar, da of Dr Govind Raghunath (d 1963); 2 s (Amahl b 4 June 1967, Ivan b 13 July 1973); *Career* lectr in linguistics and W African languages SOAS Univ of London 1970–72 (lectr in W African languages 1964–70); UCL: reader in linguistics 1972–81, prof of linguistics 1981–2006, head Dept of Phonetics and Linguistics 1982–90, emeritus prof 2006–; memb: Linguistics Assoc of GB (pres 1980–86), Philological Soc 1964– (sometime memb Cncl), SSRC 1973–89; pres Assoc of Heads and Profs of Linguistics 1993–94; hon memb Linguistic Soc of America 2000; FBA 1999; *Books* An Outline Grammar of Nupe (1967), The Acquisition of Phonology (1973), Modern Linguistics (with Deirdre Wilson, 1979), Mutual Knowledge (ed, 1982), The Twitter Machine (1989), The Mind of a Savant (with I Tsimpli, 1995), Chomsky: Ideas and Ideals (1999, 3 edn (with N Allott) 2016), Language, Bananas and Bonobos (2002), Language, Frogs and Savants (2005), Acquiring Phonology (2010), The Signs of a Savant (with I Tsimpli, G Morgan and B Woll, 2011); *Recreations* travel, music, walking; *Style*— Prof Neil Smith; ✉ 32 Long Buftlers, Harpenden, Hertfordshire AL5 1JE (☎ 01582 761313 or 020 7580 5928, e-mail smithnv@gmail.com); Department of Linguistics, University College London, Chandler House, London WC1N 1PF

SMITH, Nicholas Desmond John (Nick); MP; *b* Jan 1960; *Educ* Birkbeck Coll London (MSc); *Career* former dir of policy Royal Coll of Speech and Language Therapists; cncllr London Borough of Camden 1998–2005, MP (Lab) Blaenau Gwent 2010–, PPS to Rt Hon Douglas Alexander, MP, *qv*, memb Public Accounts Ctee; *Style*— Nick Smith, MP; ✉ House of Commons, London SW1A 1AA

SMITH, Dr Norman Jack; s of Maurice Leslie Smith (d 1967), and Ellen Dorothy, *née* Solly (d 1994); *b* 14 April 1936, Ramsgate, Kent; *Educ* Henley GS, Oriel Coll Oxford (MA), City Univ (MPhil), Univ of Aberdeen (PhD); *m* 4 March 1967, Valerie Ann, da of Capt Arthur Ernest Frost (d 1978), and Marjorie, *née* Pilgrim (d 1996); 1 s (Malcolm b 1970), 1 da (Gail b 1974); *Career* market analyst Dexion Ltd 1957–60, commercial evaluation mangr Vickers Ltd 1960–69, business devpt mangr Baring Bros and Co Ltd 1969–80; md Smith Rea Energy Associates Ltd 1981–98; dir: Burntisland Engineers and Fabricators Ltd 1974–76, Zenith Reed Ltd 1975–76, International Economic Services Ltd 1975–76, SAI Tubular Services Ltd 1983–88, Atkins Oil and Gas Engineering Ltd 1984–86, Smith Rea Energy Analysts Ltd 1985–98, Gas Transmission Ltd 1989–95, Smith Rea Energy Aberdeen Ltd 1990–98, Capcis Ltd 1998–2000, Smith Rea Energy Ltd 1999–2000; DG Offshore Supplies Office 1978–80; chm: British Underwater Engineering Ltd 1981–83, Mentor Engineering Consultants Ltd 1988–92, Petroleum Venture Mgmnt Ltd 2001–05; chm Friends of the Canterbury Archaeological Tst 2003–07, memb Tst Cncl Canterbury Archaeological Tst 2003–07; patron Oriel Coll Devpt Tst 2003–11; FEI (fell Energy Inst), FSBE (fell Soc of Business Economists); *Publications* The Sea of Lost Opportunity: North Sea Oil and Gas, British Industry and the Offshore Supplies Office (2011), Losing Control: A study of mergers and acquisitions in the British aerospace supply chain (with Joseph Wright, 2015); numerous papers and articles in various jls, magazines and newspapers; *Recreations* archaeology, history, walking, swimming, gardening, writing; *Clubs* Oxford and Cambridge; *Style*— Dr Norman Jack Smith; ✉ c/o Oxford and Cambridge Club, 71 Pall Mall, London SW1Y 5HD (☎ 020 7930 5151, fax 020 7930 9490, website http://normanjsmith.wordpress.com)

SMITH, Owen; MP; *b* 2 May 1970, Morecambe, Lancs; *Educ* Univ of Sussex; *Career* early career as journalist BBC, subsequently Govt special advsr NI Office, latterly dir Amgen; MP (Lab) Pontypridd 2010–, shadow min for Wales 2010–11, shadow health min 2011, shadow Treasy min 2011–12, shadow sec of state for Wales 2012–15, shadow sec of state for DWP 2015–; *Style*— Owen Smith, Esq, MP; ✉ House of Commons, London SW1A 0AA

SMITH, Paul Adrian; CBE (2012); s of Clifford Bryce Smith, and Marjorie Doreen, *née* Walker; *b* 16 January 1947, Belfast; *Educ* Royal Belfast Academical Instn; *m* (m dis 2015) Sarah; 1 da (Lucy), 1 s (Sam); *Career* trainee projectionist rising to dir BBC 1966–73, freelance TV prodr and dir 1973–81, fndr chm and md Complete Video 1981–95, also estab The Edit Works and The Shooting Crew, former head of A&R LWT's record label, sold Celador Int and Celador Prodns 2006; currently: chm Celador Entertainment Ltd (estab 1988), chm Celador Films (estab 2000), chm Celador Radio Broadcasting (estab 2008); launched UK radio stations The Coast 2008 and The Breeze 2010, owns and operates 20 UK radio licences in South of England under brand names The Breeze, Sam FM and Fire Radio; Hon DSc Univ of Ulster 2012, Hon DMedia Southampton Solent Univ 2014; *Television* creator It'll Be Alright on the Night (winner Silver Rose of Montreux and nomination Br Acad Award for It'll Be Alright on the Night 2 1980); prodr and dir of shows in UK and US incl: An Audience with Jasper Carrott (LWT), The Pink Medicine Show (LWT), London Night Out (Thames), Bruce's Big Night (LWT), Oh Boy (ATV), Peter Cook and Company (LWT, Gold Medal NY TV Festival), TV's Censored Bloopers (NBC); Celador prodns incl: Who Wants to be a Millionaire? (ITV1, Best Light Entertainment Prog BAFTA Awards 1999, Outstanding Game or Audience Participation Prog Emmy Awards 2000 and 2001), Winning Lines (BBC 1), Jasper Carrott – Back to the Front (BBC 1), The Detectives (BBC 1), Ruby Wax's Commercial Breakdown (BBC 1), Talking Telephone Numbers (ITV), Auntie's Bloomers (BBC 1), The Hypnotic World of Paul McKenna (ITV), All About Me (BBC 1), You Are What You Eat (Channel 4); *Film* exec prodr Dirty Pretty Things 2002 (nominated Best Original Screenplay Oscars, won Best Film Evening Standard Film Awards 2002, nominated Best British Film BAFTA Awards 2002, Best Film Br Ind Film Awards 2003, special for excellence in film making Nat Bd of Review), The Descent 2005, Separate Lies 2005, Slumdog Millionaire 2008 (4 Golden Globes, 8 Oscars, 7 BAFTAs and numerous other worldwide industry awards), The Descent: Part 2 2009, The Scouting Book for Boys 2010, Centurion 2010; *Recreations* photography, cinema, collecting original sixties records, motor yachting, family and home, travelling; *Style*— Paul Smith, Esq, CBE; ✉ Celador Entertainment, 39 Long Acre, London WC2E 9LG (☎ 020 7845 6802, e-mail psmith@celador.co.uk)

SMITH, Paul Alick; s of Walter Alick Smith, and Valerie, *née* Cupit; *b* 31 October 1960, Carshalton, Surrey; *Educ* Greenshaw Comp Sutton, Colchester Inst (HND); *m* 22 June 1985, Jackie, *née* Shelley; 2 da (Felicity b 15 March 1987, Verity b 30 Jan 2001), 1 s (James b 12 April 1989); *Career* photojournalist Anglia Press Agency 1978–82, opened Brewsters 1982–84, Strutt Daughters 1984–86 (acquired 4 branches and opened further 16); Spicerhaart: currently chief exec, opened Spicer McColl 1989, launched Mortgages Direct 1990, acquired 72 Cornerstone Branches (renamed Spicer McColl) 1995, acquired Wolton Chartered Surveyors 1996, opened Felicity J Lord 1998, acquired 173 Woolwich Property Services branches (renamed Haart) 1999, acquired 47 Darlows branches 2000; Colchester Businessman of the Year 2005–06, Essex Countywide Businessman of the Year 2006–07; fell Inst of Sales & Mktg Mgmnt; *Recreations* Chelsea FC supporter; *Clubs* Colchester Colne Round Table (chm 1993–94 and 2005–06); *Style*— Paul Smith, Esq; ✉ Spicerhaart, Colwyn House, Sheepen Place, Colchester, Essex CO3 3LD (☎ 01206 732429, fax 01206 366984, e-mail paul.smith@spicerhaart.com)

SMITH, Sir Paul Brierley; kt (2000), CBE (1994); s of late Harold Smith, and late Marjorie Smith; *b* 5 July 1946; *Educ* Beeston Fields Sch; *m* 24 Nov 2000, Pauline Denyer; *Career* clothes designer; fndr and chm Paul Smith Ltd Nottingham 1970; currently wholesales in 73 countries around the world with Paul Smith shops in 23 countries; memb Design Cncl; finalist Design Cncl's Prince Philip Prize for the Designer of the Year 1992 and 1993; Hon MDes Nottingham Poly (now Nottingham Trent Univ) 1991; Hon Freedom City of Nottingham 1997; RDI 1991, Hon FRIBA 2007; *Style*— Sir Paul Smith, CBE; ✉ Paul Smith Ltd, 20 Kean Street, London WC2B 4AS (☎ 020 7836 7828)

SMITH, Paul David John; s of Ernest Smith, of Walton on the Naze, Essex, and Margaret Lillian, *née* Taylor; *b* 6 June 1949, London; *m* Helen Mary, *née* Verlander; 2 s (Joel Julian Verlander, Giles James Verlander); *Career* art dir Collet Dickenson and Pearce 1973–87 (bd dir 1975–87), creative dir Allen Brady & Marsh 1987–91, int creative dir Lowe Howard-Spink 1991–94, exec int creative dir Grey Advertising 1994–99; Ogilvy: regnl creative dir EMEA 1999–, vice-chm Ogilvy Europe 1999–; vice-chm S D Lime Sustainable Business Development Co; all nat and int awards incl: 4 D&AD, Cannes Lions (Gold, Silver and Bronze), New York One Show; FRSA; *Recreations* tennis, horse riding; *Clubs* Soho House; *Style*— Paul Smith, Esq; ✉ Ogilvy, 10 Cabot Square, Canary Wharf, London E14 4QB (☎ 020 7345 3205, e-mail paul.smith@ogilvy.com)

SMITH, Paul John; *Educ* Ampleforth, Univ of Newcastle upon Tyne (MB BS); *Career* asst lectr in anatomy 1969–71; surgical registrar: Glasgow Western Infirmary 1971–76, Wexham Park Hosp 1976–78; res asst Microsurgical Laboratory Univ of Louisville 1978; Christine Kleinert fell in hand surgery Louisville 1978, resident and instructor in plastic surgery Duke Univ N Carolina 1979; conslt plastic surgn: Mount Vernon Hosp 1982–, Gt Ormond St Hosp for Sick Children 1988–; memb: Cncl Br Hand Soc 1988–90, Editorial Bd Journal of Hand Surgery 1989–91; sec Plastic Surgery Royal Soc of Med 1990; FRCSGlas 1974; Hayward foundation scholar 1978, 1st prize American Assoc Hand Surgery Toronto 1979, Pulvertaft Prize British Hand Soc 1983; memb: BMA, RSM, BSSH, BAPS, BAAPS, American Soc of Surgery of the Hand; *Books* Principles of Hand Surgery (1990), Lister's The Hand – Diagnosis and Indications (2002); *Recreations* skiing; *Style*— Paul Smith, Esq; ✉ office 01923 828100

SMITH, Paul Jonathan; OBE (1999); s of late Arthur Godfrey Smith (d 1987), and Constance Mildred, *née* Phelps (d 2001); *b* 30 May 1956; *Educ* King Edward's Sch Birmingham, Queens' Coll Cambridge (MA, PhD); *m* 30 Aug 1997, Viveka Kumari; 3 c (Mrinal Sinh Smith b 4 Dec 1985, Nikhil Arthur Sinh Smith b 5 Nov 1994, Radheka Farah Kumari b 19 Oct 1996); *Career* lectr in English literature St Stephen's Coll Delhi Univ 1978–80, tripos supervisor Faculty of English Univ of Cambridge 1980–83; Br Cncl: asst dir Kano Nigeria 1983, asst rep Lagos Nigeria 1985, dep dir Drama and Dance 1987, AG rep Chile 1990, AG dir Berlin 1990, arts conslt 1991, AG dir Burma 1991, dep dir Bangladesh 1992, dir NZ 1995, dir Arts 1999, dir W India 2000–05, dir Egypt 2005–10, dir Afghanistan 2010–12, dir USA 2012, memb Bd of Tstees US Friends 2012–; memb Bd of Tstees: American Sch of Bombay 2003–05, Modern Arts and Science Univ Cairo 2009–10, Turquoise Mountain Fndn Afghanistan 2010–12 and 2012–; fndr memb Bd of Tstees Br Univ of Egypt 2008–1010; pres EU Nat Insts of Culture Washington DC Cluster 2013–14; memb Advsy Bd Caravan 2013–; theatre dir: Twelfth Night, Rosencrantz and Guildenstern are Dead, Love's Labour's Lost, Murder in the Cathedral, Everyman, Krapp's Last Tape, A Midsummer Night's Dream, Hamlet; *Publications* The St James Press Reference Guide to English Literature (contrib, 1990), Colonial and Postcolonial Shakespeares (contrib, 2001), British-Egyptian Relations from Suez to the Present Day (contrib, 2007), Full Fathom Five: Shakespeare's Old Seas and New Oceans (2010), Vintage Shakespeare: New Perspectives from India and Abroad (contrib, 2010); *Recreations* literature, theatre, cinema, theology, music; *Style*— Paul Smith, Esq, OBE; ✉ Paul Smith (591123), BFPO 5445, West End Road, Ruislip, Middlesex HA4 6EP (e-mail paul.smith@britishcouncil.org)

SMITH, Peter Alan; s of Dudley Vaughan Smith (d 1983), and Beatrice Ellen, *née* Sketcher; *b* 5 August 1946; *Educ* Mill Hill Sch, Univ of Southampton (BSc), Wharton Sch Univ of Pennsylvania (AMP); *m* 2 Oct 1971, Cherry, da of Thomas A Blandford (d 1986); 2 s (Nicholas David b 1975, Richard James b 1977); *Career* RAFVR 1964–67, cmmnd actg PO 1967; PricewaterhouseCoopers (formerly Coopers & Lybrand before merger): joined 1967, ptnr 1975–2000, managing ptnr London City Office 1989–94, memb Partnership Bd 1990–2000, chm Coopers & Lybrand 1994–98, sr ptnr 1998–2000; chm: RAC plc 2003–05, Savills 2004–16, Templeton Emerging Markets Investment Tst plc 2007–15 (non-exec dir 2004–15); non-exec dir: N M Rothschild & Sons 2001–, Equitable Life Assurance Soc 2001–10 (dep chm), Safeway plc 2002–04, Associated British Foods plc 2007–16, Rothschild & Co SCA 2012–; chm Land Restoration Tst 2010–; memb: Fin Ctee The Nat Tst 1991–98 and 2001–05, Prince of Wales Business Leaders' Forum 1994–2000, President's Ctee CBI 1994–98, Fin and Gen Purpose Ctee/Bd 1999–2008, Ctee on Corp Governance 1996–98; memb Cncl ICAEW 1997–2003 (treas 2001–03); former hon treas UK Housing Tst; Liveryman Worshipful Co of Chartered Accountants 1993; CCMI, FCA, FRSA; *Books* Housing Association Accounts and their Audit (1980); *Recreations* golf, gardens; *Clubs* Carlton, Walbrook, Beaconsfield Golf; *Style*— Peter Smith, Esq; ✉ New Court, St Swithins Lane, London EC4P 4DU (☎ 020 7280 5419, fax 020 7280 5562)

SMITH, Most Rev Peter David; *see:* Southwark, Archbishop of (RC)

SMITH, Prof Peter Frederick; s of Harold Frederick Smith (d 1987), and Irene May, *née* Shepherd (d 1990); *b* 24 December 1930, Liverpool; *Educ* Liverpool Inst HS, Queens' Coll Cambridge (MA), Univ of Manchester (PhD); *m* 1958, Jeannette Alexandra, da of Alexander Ferguson; 2 da (Karen Ann b May 1960, Pamela Jane b August 1962), 1 s (Michael James b March 1965); *Career* princ in architectural practice Ferguson Smith and Associates (later Partners) Sheffield 1968–89 (projects incl low energy housing devpts and churches as well as the restoration of listed bldgs such as the President's Lodge Queens' Coll Cambridge); chm and md Equity Homes Ltd (designers and builders of low cost extendible homes) 1983–87; sr lectr Univ of Sheffield 1974–86 (lectr 1965–74); Leeds Metropolitan Univ (formerly Leeds Poly): prof and head Dept of Architecture and Landscape 1986–90, actg head Dept of Construction 1988–90, prof and head Dept of Architecture and asst dean 1990, emeritus prof of architecture 1990; prof of architecture Sheffield Hallam Univ 1997–2002, special prof of sustainable energy Univ of Nottingham 2004–; research activity incl: EC contract to conduct intensive univ staff workshops in the UK, Ireland and Sweden on sustainability issues 1998–2000, EPSRC contract to investigate the feasibility of measures to upgrade the housing stock of England and Wales 1998–2001; memb Construction Indust Cncl Energy and Environment Ctee 1989–; RIBA: memb Yorks Regnl Cncl 1986– (chm 1990–91), chm Nat Environment and Energy Ctee 1988–96, memb Nat Cncl 1988–91 and 1997–, chm Euro Educn Ctee 1990–92, chm Jt RIBA/Dept of Energy Steering Ctee for the commissioning and prodn of Best Practice pubns and CPD environment and energy progs for the UK 1991–93, chm Sustainable Futures Ctee 1997–2002, vice-pres for Sustainable Development 2000–03; dir Pilkington Energy Efficiency Tst 1998–2008; lectr and keynote speaker at numerous architectural confs in Europe and the US; various interviews on environmental issues for BBC 1, Radio 4 and BBC World TV; script writer and presenter: Frank Lloyd Wright (ITV) 1972, Future Trends in Urbanism (ITV) 1972, The Soul of the City (BBC 1) 1973; FRIBA 1970; *Books* Third Millennium Churches (1973), The Dynamics of Urbanism (1975), The Syntax of Cities (1977), Architecture and the Human Dimension (1979), Architecktur und Asthetik (1981), Architecture and the Principal of Harmony (1987), Options for a Flexible Planet (1996), Concepts in Practice: Energy – Building for the Third Millennium (with A C Pitts, 1997), Architecture in a Climate of Change (2001, expanded 2 edn 2005, Mandarin trans 2009), Sustainability at the Cutting Edge – Emerging Technologies for Low Energy Buildings (2002, 2 edn 2007), Eco-Refurbishment – a Practical Guide to Creating an Energy Efficient Home (2003), The Dynamics of Delight – Architecture and Aesthetics (2003), Building for a Changing Climate – the Challenge for Construction, Planning and Energy (2009), Climate Change and Cultural Heritage – A Race Against Time (2013); written evidence to House of Commons Environment, Food and Rural Affrs Cmmn report 2005; contribs to other books and author of articles, papers and submissions to govt on energy related topics; *Recreations* painting, writing, travel; *Clubs* Oxford and Cambridge; *Style*— Prof Peter F Smith; ✉ 50 Endcliffe Hall Avenue, Sheffield S10 3EL (☎ 0114 266 1722, e-mail p.frederick.smith@gmail.com)

SMITH, Peter Michael; s of Peter William Smith (d 1944), of Reading, and Margaret, *née* Gilchrist (d 1971); *b* 10 January 1938; *Educ* St George's Coll Weybridge; *m* 1, 6 Dec 1975 (m dis 1998), Sarah Diana, da of John Seyfried; 2 s (Benjamin b 18 June 1977, Matthew b 17 Oct 1981); m 2, 19 July 2003, Carolyn Marie Noel-Johnson, da of Anthony Petit; *Career* served BSA Police Rhodesia 1956–59; Barclays Bank plc 1955–56, Barclays Bank Int 1959–62; PR and mktg mgmnt: Total Oil Products Central Africa 1962–66, Gallaher plc 1966–70; PR advsr Booker McConnell plc, exec sec Mgmnt Ctee Booker Prize for Fiction 1970–78, public affrs mangr Powell Duffryn plc 1978–85, dir of corp rels Reed Int plc 1985–87, jt managing ptnr City and Corporate Counsel (co-fndr 1987) 1987–93, dir UK Radio Devpts 1990–92, tstee One World Broadcasting Tst 1991–96, fndr chief exec The Strategic Partnership (London) Ltd 1994–2004; dir: Threadneedle Gp plc (co-fndr) 1987–2000, Elixir Mktg Communications Ltd 1992–2008, A T Hudson Ltd 1993–2013; chm Worldaware (Centre for World Devpt Educn) 1992–95; chm RSA Tomorrow's Company Inquiry Network 1993–95; BESO: dep pres and chm Fin and Gen Purposes Ctee 1997–2003, dep chm and chm Audit Ctee 2003–05; cncllr London Borough of Camden 1968–71; Parly candidate (Cons): Rowley Regis and Tipton 1970, West Bromwich W Feb 1974; joined SDP 1982, memb Lib Dem Party 1988–2015; memb Nat Cncl and Exec Ctee European Movement in UK 1981–82; chm PR Educn and Res Tst 1984–89; Royal Cwlth Soc: vice-pres, fndr and chm Focus Gp 1975–78, pres Focus Gp 1978–83, dep chm 1980–83; pres CIPR 1984 (chm City and Fin Gp 1981–82, chm Govt Affrs Gp 1991–95, awarded Stephen Tallents Medal 1995); Investor Rels Soc: co-fndr 1980, memb Ctee 1980–92, chm 1986–89, memb Professional Affrs Ctee 1989–2004; memb Worshipful Co of Mgmnt Conslts 2000–04 (memb Ct of Assts 2002–04); Freeman City of London 2000; Hon FCIPR (Hon FIPR 1998), FRSA 1985–2005, FInstD 1987–2005, MIRS (Hon MIRS 1989), MIMC 1990–2005, CMC; *Publications* Financial Public Relations: Investor Relations (1989); chapters and articles in books and jls; *Recreations* golf, reading, music; *Style*— Peter Smith, Esq; ✉ La Grange, Liffernet, 46100 Lunan, Figeac, France (☎ 00 33 5 65 34 99 36, e-mail psmith@lagrangeliffernet.com)

SMITH, Hon Mr Justice; Sir Peter Winston Smith; kt (2002); s of George Arthur Smith (d 1993), and Iris Muriel, *née* Winstanley (d 1986); *b* 1 May 1952; *Educ* Bridlington Sch, Selwyn Coll Cambridge (MA), Coll of Law Chancery Lane London (Hardwicke scholar, Tancred scholar, Megarry pupillage award); *m* 13 Sept 1980, Diane, da of Charles Webster Dalgliesh; 2 da (Laura b 13 July 1980, Katy b 15 Feb 1982), 1 s (James b 3 May 1983); *Career* called to the Bar Lincoln's Inn 1975 (bencher 2000); QC 1992; examiner of title HM Land Registry 1976–82, lectr Univ of Manchester 1977–83; practising N Circuit: 460 Royal Exchange Manchester 1979–87, 40 King St Manchester 1987–2002; dep High Court judge 1996–2002, recorder 1997–2002 (asst recorder 1994–97), judge of the High Court of Justice (Chancery Div) 2002–; acting deemster IOM 2000; *Books* Conveyancing Law-Practice (2 edn 1982); *Recreations* reading military history, avid student of Jackie Fisher, football, memb Titanic Historical Soc and Br Titanic Soc; *Style*— The Hon Mr

S

Justice Peter Smith; ✉ Royal Courts of Justice, 7 Rolls Buildings, Fetter Lane, London EC4A 1NL

SMITH, Phil; s of Emmanuel Smith, and Rosemary Smith; *Career* promotion asst Pinnacle Records 1976–79, head of regnl promotion Pye Records 1979–81, head of promotion Magnet Records 1981–82, head of promotion MCA/Universal Records 1982–92, prop Double Impact Ltd 1992–95, with First Artist Corp plc 1993– (currently chief operating offr); patron Lee Smith Leukaemia Orgn; football coach: Wealdstone FC, Maccabi GB; *Recreations* football (player and coach); *Style*— Phil Smith, Esq; ✉ First Artist Corporation plc, First Artist House, 87 Wembley Hill Road, Wembley, Middlesex HA9 8BU (☎ 020 8900 1818, fax 020 8903 2984, mobile 07831 527804, e-mail phils@firstartist.com)

SMITH, Philip Henry; s of Reginald Smith, and Grace, *née* Howgate; *b* 14 July 1934; *Educ* Leeds GS, Univ of Leeds (MB ChB); *m* 13 Aug 1960, Margaret, da of Wilfred Glover (d 1967); 4 da (Alison (Mrs Belfield) b 1962, Catherine b 1964 d 1964, Anne (Mrs Johnson) b 1967, Rosemary b 1967), 1 s (Richard b 1965 d 1988); *Career* Nat Serv and OC 50 FST Br Cameroons, OC Surgical Div Tidworth Mil Hosp; head Dept of Urology St James Hosp Leeds 1967–98, urologist to Regnl Spinal Injuries Unit Pinderfields Hosp Wakefield 1967–91; sec Urology Gp of European Orgn for Research on Treatment of Cancer 1979–82 (chm 1976–79); chm: Prostatic Cancer Sub Gp MRC 1985, Urology Working Party MRC 1988–91, Data Monitoring Ctee European Randomised Study for Screening for Prostate Cancer 1994–; memb: BAUS, European Assoc of Urology, Bd European Orgn for Research on Treatment of Cancer 1997–2000; FRCS 1960; *Books* Bladder Cancer (ed, 1984), Combination Therapy in Urological Malignancy (ed, 1988); *Recreations* grandchildren, gardening; *Style*— Mr Philip Smith; ☎ 0113 267 0966

SMITH, Dr Philip Henry; MBE (2016); s of Alfred Henry Smith (d 1977), of Leicester, and Georgina May, *née* Ives (d 1969); *b* 24 November 1946; *Educ* Loughborough Coll GS, Leicester Regnl Coll of Technol, Nottingham Poly; *m* 27 Dec 1968, Sonia Idena (d 2010), da of Ivan Garnet Moody (d 1964); 1 da (Melissa b 21 June 1969), 2 s (Christian Philip b 13 June 1972, Philip Raoul b 28 Feb 1975); *Career* sr audit asst Leics CC 1964–69, gp accountant Lusaka City Cncl Zambia 1969–72, branch accountant Dairy Produce Bd Zambia 1972–74, divnl dir and sec Dorada Holdings plc 1974–81, divnl fin dir Brook Tool Engineering Holdings plc 1981–83, gp treas Asda Group plc 1983–91, dir of treasy National Power plc 1991–99; non-exec chm: Environmental Tst Scheme Regulatory Body Ltd 2002–14, Milton Keynes Business Ldrs Partnership Ltd 2008–, Milton Keynes Business Cncl 2012–, Milton Keynes Sports Bd 2012–; non-exec dir: Leading Edge Technologies BVI 2002–, Stables Events Ltd 2011–, MK and Bucks County Sports Partnership 2012–, Destination MK 2012–, chm Milton Keynes Transport Partnership 2014–; tstee Wavendon Allmusic Plan Ltd 2012–; chm Milton Keynes Acad 2009–, tstee De Montfort Univ Students Union 2009–, govr Univ of Beds 2012–, patron Willen Hospice 2012–, memb Ouse Valley Ctee Lords Taverners 2013–, tstee Milton Keynes City Orchestra 2015–; Hon DBA De Montfort Univ 2010; memb IPFA 1971, FCMA 1974, FIMgt 1974, FCT 1988 (memb Cncl 1996–2001); *Recreations* sports, wine, gardening, economic affairs; *Clubs* Royal Navy, Royal Yacht Portsmouth, Lords Taverners, Milton Keynes Rotary; *Style*— Dr Philip H Smith, MBE; ✉ The Old White Horse, Main Street, Padbury, Buckingham MK18 2AY (☎ 01280 814848, e-mail phs@phsconsultancy.com)

SMITH, Phillip; s of Jeffrey Smith, and Rene Smith; *b* 3 June 1949; *Educ* Quarry Bank HS Liverpool, Univ of Southampton (BA), Loughborough Coll (CertEd); *Career* teacher 1972–95; Br Horseracing Bd: handicapper 1995–98, sr jumps handicapper 1998–2006, head of handicapping 2007–; footballer: Br Univs 1970–72, Altrincham FC 1973–75, Northwich Victoria 1976–78; *Publications* 21 Years of the Pattern (1992); *Recreations* golf; *Clubs* Broadway Golf; *Style*— Phillip Smith, Esq; ✉ c/o British Horseracing Authority, 75 High Holborn, London WC1V 6LS (e-mail psmith@britishhorseracing.com)

SMITH, Richard Lloyd; QC (2001); *b* 28 January 1963; *Educ* Wellsway Sch Keynsham, KCL (LLB); *m* 1990, Anna Sara; 1 da (Giorgia), 1 s (Joe Luca); *Career* called to the Bar Middle Temple 1986; recorder of the Crown Court (crime and sports) 2000–; lawyer: England rugby team Rugby World Cup Aust 2003, France 2007, NZ 2011 and England 2015, Br and Irish Lions rugby team tour NZ 2005 and S Africa 2009; memb: Chm's Panel, Sports Dispute Resolution Panel; *Style*— Richard Smith, Esq, QC; ✉ Guildhall Chambers, 23 Broad Street, Bristol BS1 2HG

SMITH, Prof Richard Michael; s of Louis Gordon Smith (d 1971), of Essex, and Elsie Fanny, *née* Ward; *Educ* Earls Colne GS Essex, UCL (BA, Rosa Morison prize), St Catharine's Coll Cambridge (MA, PhD); *m* 1971, Margaret Anne, da of William D McFadden; *Career* post doctoral res fell Univ of Chicago 1971–73, lectr in population studies Plymouth Poly 1973–74; Univ of Cambridge: asst lectr in population and historical geography 1974–76, fell Fitzwilliam Coll 1977–83; Univ of Oxford: lectr in historical demography 1983–89, professorial fell All Souls Coll 1983–94, reader in history of med and dir Wellcome Unit for the History of Med 1990–94; Univ of Cambridge: fell Downing Coll, reader in historical demography and dir Cambridge Gp for the History of Population and Social Structure 1994–2003 (sr res offr 1976–81, asst dir 1981), prof of historical geography and demography 2003–; fndn lectr Fitzwilliam Coll Cambridge 1989, Sir John Neal's lectr UCL 1995; fell UCL 2004; pres Economic History Soc 2007–; FRHistS 1985, FBA 1991; *Books* Sources on English Society 1250–1800: The Sir Nicholas Bacon Collection (1973), Bastardy and its Comparative History (1980), Land, Kinship and Life-Cycle (1984), The World We Have Gained: Histories of Population and Social Structures (1986), Life, Death and the Elderly: Historical Perspectives (1991), Medieval Society and the Manor Court (1996), The Locus of Care: Families, communities, institutions and the provision of welfare since antiquity (1997); *Recreations* walking in Norfolk, listening to music; *Style*— Prof Richard Smith, FBA; ✉ Cambridge Group for the History of Population and Social Structure, Sir William Hardy Building, Department of Geography, Downing Place, Cambridge CB2 3EN (☎ 01223 333181, fax 01223 333183, e-mail rms20@cam.ac.uk)

SMITH, Prof Richard Sydney William; CBE (2000); s of Sydney Frederick Smith, and Hazel Nora, *née* Kirk; *b* 11 March 1952; *Educ* Roan GS for Boys, Univ of Edinburgh Med Sch (BSc, MB ChB), Graduate Sch of Business Stanford Univ (MSc); *m* Oct 1977, Linda Jean, da of Alexander Rae Arnott; 2 s (Freddie Paris b April 1982, James Arthur b Feb 1984), 1 da (Florence Harriet Rose b March 1991); *Career* house offr: Eastern Gen Hosp Edinburgh 1976–77, Dunfermline and West Fife Hosp 1977; jr doctor Auckland and Green Lane Hosps Auckland NZ 1977–78, chief exec BMJ Publishing Group and ed British Medical Journal 1991–2004 (asst ed 1979–91), chief exec UnitedHealth Europe 2004–07, dir UnitedHealth Chronic Disease Initiative 2007–15; prof of medical journalism Dept of Med Univ of Nottingham 1993–2001, visiting prof: LSHTM 1996–2004, Warwick Medical Sch 2009–14, adjunct prof Imperial Coll Inst for Global Health Innovation 2011–; television doctor: BBC Breakfast Time 1982–86, TV-AM 1988–89; chair Patient Knows Best 2008–; chm Foresight Ctee on Info and Health 2020 2000; memb: BMA 1979–2004, Med Journalists' Assoc 1980, RCP working pty on alcohol 1985–87, RCP working pty on prison med 1987–90, bd ed Nat Med Jl of India 1991–2001, Int Ctee Med Jl Eds 1991–2004, Bd World Assoc of Med Eds 1994–2000, RCOG ind ctee Inquiry 1995, Bd Project HOPE UK 1996–2002, Editorial Bd Canadian Med Assoc Jl 1997–2001, Scientific Advsy Ctee of Univ of Lausanne 1997–2002, RCP working pty into Structure and Functions of RCP 1998, Bd Public Library of Science 2004–11, Governing Cncl St George's Univ of London 2004–12, Advsy Bd Global Trial Bank 2005–07, Medicines Partnership Task Force Nat Prescribing Centre 2006–08, UK Panel for Health and Biomedical Research Integrity 2006–14, Bd C3 Collaborating for Health 2009–15, Int Scientific Advsy Bd Children's Heartlink 2010–, Bd ICDDR.B 2012– (chair Bd of Tstees 2013–), Ind Cmmn on Whole Person Care 2013–14; advsr: Dept of Health Ind Inquiry into Inequalities in Health 1998, F1000Research 2015–, Medial 2015–; contrib Comment is Free The Guardian website 2006–10, blogger for BMJ 2009–; chair Cochrane Library Oversight Ctee 2010–; tstee Klevis Kola Fndn 2009–15; fell Acad of Gen Educn Manipal Karnataka India 1993; MFPHM 1991, FRCPE 1992, FRCP 1995–2010 (MRCP 1993), FRCGP 1997, FFPHM 1997, FAMS 1998, FRCSEd 1999; *Awards* Med Journalists' Assoc Young Journalist of the Year 1980, Periodical Publishers' Assoc Specialist Writer of the Year 1981, runner up Med Journalists' Assoc Journalist of the Year 1983 and 1985; *Books* Alcohol Problems (1982), Prison Health Care (1984), Unemployment and Health (1987), The Good Health Kit (1987), Health of the Nation (ed, 1991), Rationing in Action (1993), Management for Doctors (ed jtly, 1995), Scientific Basis of Health Services (1996), The Trouble with Medical Journals (2006); *Television* That's Family Life (BBC1, 1983), Compulsions (Thames, 1987), Fashion Victims (BBC2, 1991), Breakthrough or Ballyhoo (BBC2, 1992); *Recreations* music (particularly jazz and chamber), theatre, wine, hill walking, making soup, porridge, marmalade and trouble; *Style*— Prof Richard Smith, CBE; ✉ 35 Orlando Road, London SW4 0LD (☎ 07736 346940, e-mail richardswsmith@yahoo.co.uk)

SMITH, Sir Robert Hill; 3 Bt (UK 1945), of Crowmallie, Co Aberdeen; s (by 2 m) of Sir Gordon Smith, 2 Bt, VRD (d 1983); *b* 15 April 1958; *Educ* Merchant Taylors', Aberdeen Univ; *m* 13 Aug 1993, Fiona, da of Col J D Cormack; 3 da (Helen, Kirsty, Elizabeth); *Heir* bro, Charles Smith; *Career* MP (Lib Dem) W Aberdeenshire and Kincardine 2001–15; memb Lib Dem Tport and Environment Team 1997–98, memb Lib Dem Scot Affrs Team (police, prisons, tport and environment) 1998–99, vice-chm Parly All-Pty UK Offshore Oil and Gas Industry Gp 1998–99, memb Scottish Affrs Select Ctee 1999–, Scottish Affrs spokesman 1999–2001, memb Trade and Industry Select Ctee 1999–2001, memb Procedure Ctee 2001–, dep chief whip 2001–06, memb Int Devpt Select Ctee 2007–, memb Energy & Climate Change Ctee, memb Procedures Ctee, vice-chair Warm Homes Gp; *Recreations* sailing; *Clubs* Royal Thames Yacht; *Style*— Sir Robert Smith, Bt; ✉ Constituency Office, 6 Dee Street, Banchory, Kincardinshire, AB31 5ST (☎ 01330 8203300, fax 01330 820338, e-mail robert.smith.mp@parliament.uk)

SMITH, Robert James; s of Mervyn Daniel Smith (d 1982), and Marjorie Irene, *née* Griffin (d 2009); *b* 22 July 1945, Bristol; *Educ* King's Coll Taunton, Univ of Worcester (DipEd), Royal Holloway, Univ of London (BA); *m* 20 Aug 1970, Anne Rosemary, da of Brendan Fitzpatrick (d 1993), of London; 1 da (Kate b 1979), 1 s (Daniel b 1983); *Career* English teacher Hatfield Sch 1970–71, managing ed Gower Press Ltd, Xerox Corp Inc 1971–75, editorial mangr Octopus Books Ltd 1975–78, editorial dir Ebury Press Nat Magazine Co Ltd 1979–85, publishing dir Sidgwick and Jackson, Macmillan Publishers Ltd 1985–90, chm and md Smith Gryphon Ltd 1990–97, chm and md Robert Smith Literary Agency Ltd 1997–; memb Assoc of Authors' Agents 2000–; *Recreations* conservation, theatre, music, local history, collecting antiques and antiquarian books; *Clubs* Groucho; *Style*— Robert Smith, Esq; ✉ Robert Smith Literary Agency Ltd, 12 Bridge Wharf, 156 Caledonian Road, London N1 9UU (☎ 020 7278 2444, fax 020 7833 5680, e-mail robert@robertsmithliteraryagency.com)

SMITH, Robin Anthony; MBE (2015), TD (1978, Bar 1984), DL (W Yorks 1991); s of Tom Sumerfield Smith (d 1990), of Wetherby, W Yorks, and Mary, *née* Taylor (d 1998); *b* 15 February 1943; *Educ* St Michael's Coll Leeds, Univ of Manchester (LLB); *m* 5 Oct 1967, Jennifer Elizabeth, da of Eric Anthony Roslington (d 1978), of Leeds; 1 s (Jonathan b 1969), 1 da (Sarah b 1972); *Career* cmmnd KOYLI 1966, 5 Bn The Light Inf 1967–86, ret as Lt-Col 1986; admitted slr 1966; DLA Piper (formerly Dibb Lupton Alsop): ptnr 1968–87, managing ptnr 1987–93, sr ptnr 1993–98, conslt 1998–2007; non-exec dir: Leeds Building Soc 1998–13 (chm 2007–13), Town Centre Securities plc 1998–2009; local dir Coutts & Co 1999–2006; memb Law Soc 1966–2007 (memb Cncl 1982–91); govr Stonyhurst Coll 1990–98; KSG 2002; *Recreations* cricket, golf; *Clubs* Army and Navy, Alwoodley Golf, MCC, Yorkshire CCC (pres 2000–04, chm 2003–06), Western Province Cricket (SA), Scarborough Cricket (pres 2010); *Style*— Robin Smith, Esq, MBE, TD, DL; ✉ 15 Gateland Drive, Shadwell, Leeds LS17 8HU (e-mail robin.smith40@btinternet.com)

SMITH, Prof Roderick Arthur; *b* 26 December 1947, Oldham, Lancs; *Educ* The Hulme GS Oldham, St John's Coll Oxford (BA), Queens' Coll Cambridge (PhD, Gas Cncl res scholar); *m* 1975, Yayoi Yamanoi, of Tokyo; *Career* student engr apprentice and serv engr David Brown Corp 1966–71, Godfrey Mitchell res fell Queens' Coll Cambridge 1975–78, lectr Engrg Dept Univ of Cambridge 1980–88 (asst lectr 1977–80), official fell and dir of studies in engrg Queens' Coll Cambridge 1978–88; Univ of Sheffield: prof of mechanical and process engrg 1988–2000, head of dept 1992–95, warden Stephenson Hall 1992–2000 (sr warden 1997–2000), chm Advanced Railway Res Centre (ARRC) 1993–2000, Royal Acad of Engrg/Br Rail res prof of advanced railway engrg 1995–2000; Imperial Coll London: head Dept of Mechanical Engrg 2000–05, Royal Acad of Engrg Network Rail research prof and chm Future Rail Research Centre 2006–13; visiting prof Univ of York and Univ of Kyushu 1997–99, visiting chair of tport systems engrg Univ of Tokyo 1998–99, hon prof Central Queensland Univ 1999–, hon prof Chinese Acad of Railway Sci Beijing 2002–, sr visiting research fell St John's Coll Oxford 2005–06, visiting prof Univ of Oxford 2012–; chief scientific advsr Dept for Transport 2012–14; chm and non-exec dir Coll of Railway Technol Derby 1996–97; conslt: Br Steel plc 1987–90, HSE, BR (memb Res and Tech Ctee 1992–96); chief scientific advsr Dept for Tport 2012–; chm BR Crashworthiness Devpt Steering Gp 1993–96, chm Japanese Railway Soc 1996–, dir AEA Technol Engrg Dept Univ of Cambridge, Advanced Technol Centre 1998–, memb AEA Technol Sci and Engrg Ctee 1997–, chair Heathrow Airport Consultation Ctee 2015–; memb Editorial Bd: Int Jl of Fatigue, Fatigue of Engrg Materials, Condition Monitoring and Diagnostic Technol; memb Cncl IMechE 1999– (pres 2011–12); vice-pres Instn of Mechanical Engrs 2008–11, pres Engrg Integrity Soc 2016–; tstee Nat Museum of Sci and Industry 2002–; hon fell Queen's Coll Cambridge 2015–; ScD Univ of Cambridge 1998, Hon DEng Univ of Lincoln 2012, Hon DEng Univ of Sheffield 2015; FREng, CEng, FIMechE, FIM, FCGI 2000; *Publications* ed books on: fatigue and fracture mechanics, innovative teaching, engrg for crowd safety, railway engrg, condition monitoring; approx 350 published papers in areas of fatigue and fracture mechanics, finite element stress analysis railway and environmental engrg; *Recreations* mountaineering: ldr of expeditions to Arctic Norway, Everest region and Karakoram; *Clubs* Alpine, Oxford and Cambridge; *Style*— Prof Roderick Smith, FREng; ✉ website www.rodericksmith.synthasite.com; Department of Mechanical Engineering, Imperial College of Science, Technology and Medicine, South Kensington, London SW7 2AZ (☎ 020 7594 7007, e-mail roderick.smith@imperial.ac.uk)

SMITH, Dr Roger; s of Sylvanus Joseph Smith (d 1973), of Newcastle-under-Lyme, Staffs, and Winifred Beatrice, *née* Adams (d 1979); *b* 3 February 1930; *Educ* Newcastle-under-Lyme HS, Trinity Coll Cambridge (MA, MD), UCH London (PhD); *m* 1, 25 June 1955, Barbara Ann (d 2001), da of Harold Willatt (d 1987); 3 da (Philippa b 7 Dec 1956, Clare b 6 April 1962, Katharine b 3 April 1966), 1 s (Julian b 22 May 1960); m 2, 4 July 2008, Ann Valerie, da of Norman Wood (d 1973); *Career* served: Rifle Bde 1948, Intelligence Corps 1949; sr Wellcome res fell UCH London 1965–68, clinical reader Nuffield Depts of Med and Orthopaedic Surgery Oxford 1969–77, fell Nuffield Coll Oxford 1971–77, conslt physician in metabolic med John Radcliffe Hosp and Nuffield Orthopaedic Centre Oxford 1977–95, hon conslt physician Nuffield Orthopaedic Centre Oxford 1995–; fell Green Coll

Oxford 1984–95 (emeritus fell 1995); memb Cncl RCP 1985–89 (regnl advsr 1981–85), chm Med Staff Cncl and Med Exec Ctee Oxford Hosps 1987–89; memb: Cncl Nat Osteoporosis Soc, Assoc of Physicians; FRCP; *Books* Electrolyte Metabolism in Severe Infantile Malnutrition (1968), Biochemical Disorders of the Skeleton (1979), Osteoporosis (1990), Clinical and Biochemical Disorders of the Skeleton (2005, 2016); *Recreations* painting; *Style—* Dr Roger Smith; ✉ 24 Woodlands Brook, Wantage, Oxfordshire OX12 8FS (☎ 01235 771906, e-mail roger4.smith@outlook.com); Nuffield Orthopaedic Centre, Headington, Oxford OX3 7LD

SMITH, Ronald; OBE (2009); s of William Smith (d 2012), and Daisy, *née* Manson (d 2005); *b* 9 June 1951, Lerwick, Shetland Islands; *Educ* Anderson Educnl Inst, Univ of Aberdeen (MA), Aberdeen Coll of Educn (PGCE); *m* 10 April 1976, Mae, *née* Lambie; 1 da (Kirstin b 17 April 1982), 1 s (Craig b 9 Oct 1984); *Career* teacher then princ teacher of Latin and modern studies Broxburn Acad 1973–88; Educnl Inst of Scotland: asst sec 1988–95, gen sec 1995–2012; pres: Educn Int (Europe) 2006–12 (memb European Ctee 1995–2012), European Trade Union Ctee for Educn 2006–12 (memb Exec Bd 1995–2012); FEIS 2003; *Recreations* Livingston FC, Island of Foula; *Style—* Ronald Smith, Esq, OBE

SMITH, Sean; *b* 1 January 1959, London; *Family* 3 c; *Career* photographer and filmmaker; Garnham's Abbatoir Cambridge 1978–79; The Guardian 1988–; video work broadcast on BBC, Newsnight, Channel 4, ABC America and in other countries around the world; exhibitions: Iraq Photos (Imperial War Museum), On the Margins (The Dissenters' Chapel Kensel Green Cemetery), Frontlines (Kings Place Gall London and Northumbria Univ Gallery); Br Press Photographers' Year Photo of the Year 2006 and 2007 and Sports Feature 2009; RTS Award for Best Int News (for Iraq: Apache Company) 2008; memb: British Press Photographers Assoc, RSA; memb Burt Bacharach and Hal David Fan Club; *Publications* Five Thousand Days (contrib, 2004, also exhbn RNT), Frontlines Conflict in the 21st Century; *Recreations* cinema, music, opera, reading, sailing, travel, walking, drinking and other associated pleasures; *Style—* Sean Smith, Esq; ✉ e-mail sean.smith@guardian.co.uk, Twitter @seanphotosmith

SMITH, Sheridan; OBE (2015); *b* 25 June 1981, Epworth, Lincs; *Career* actress; *Television* incl: Dark Ages 1999, The Royle Family 1999–2000, Holby City 2001, Two Pints of Lager and a Packet of Crisps 2001–09, Eyes Down 2003–04, The Lenny Henry Show 2005, Love Soup 2005–08, Grownups 2006–09, Gavin and Stacey 2008–10, Benidorm 2009, Jonathan Creek 2009, 2010 and 2013, Mrs Biggs 2012 (Leading Actress BAFTA 2013), Dates 2013, The 7.39 2013, Cilla 2014, The C Word 2015; *Theatre* incl: Into the Woods (Donmar Warehouse), The Taming of the Shrew (Open Air Theatre Regent's Park), A Midsummer Night's Dream (Open Air Theatre Regent's Park), Little Shop of Horrors (Menier Chocolate Factory) 2006 and (Duke of York's Theatre and New Ambassadors Theatre) 2007, Tinderbox: a Revenge Comedy (Bush Theatre Shepherd's Bush) 2008, Legally Blonde (West End) 2009–11 (Best Actress in a Muscial What's On Stage Choice Award 2011, Best Actress in a Musical Laurence Olivier Award 2011), Flare Path (Theatre Royal Haymarket) 2011 (Evening Standard Natasha Richardson Award for Best Actress 2011, Best Performance in a Supporting Role Laurence Olivier Award 2012), Hedda Gabler (Old Vic) 2012 (Best Actress in a Play Whatsonstage Award 2013), Funny Girl (Menier Chocolate Factory and West End) 2015–; *Style—* Ms Sheridan Smith, OBE; ✉ c/o Independent Talent Group, 40 Whitfield Street, London W1T 2RH

SMITH, Simon; CMG (2015); *b* 14 January 1958, Wegberg, Germany; *Educ* Wadham Coll Oxford; *m* Sian Stickings; 2 da; *Career* FCO: joined 1986, 2 then 1 sec Tokyo 1989–92, dep head Southern European Dept 1995–97, cnsllr (economic/commercial) Moscow 1998–2002, head North East Asia and Pacific Dept 2002–04, head Eastern Dept 2004–05, dir for Russia, South Caucasus and Central Asia 2005–07, UK perm rep to UN Orgns Vienna 2007–12, ambass to Austria 2007–12, ambass to Ukraine 2012–15; *Recreations* sport (especially cricket), cooking, reading, music; *Clubs* Athenaeum; *Style—* Mr Simon Smith, CMG; ✉ c/o FCO, King Charles Street, London SW1A 2AH

SMITH, Prof Stephen Kevin; s of Albert Smith, DFC, of Birkenhead, and Drusilla, *née* Hills; *b* 8 March 1951; *Educ* Birkenhead Sch, Univ of London (MB BS, MD, DSc), Univ of Cambridge (MA); *m* 8 July 1978, Catriona Maclean, da of Alan Maclean Hobkirk, of Edinburgh; 1 s (Richard Alan), 2 da (Lucinda Jane, Alice Charlotte); *Career* lectr Univ of Sheffield 1982–85, conslt in obstetrics and gynaecology MRC Reproductive Biology Unit and Lothian Health Bd 1985–88, prof of obstetrics and gynaecology Univ of Cambridge 1988–2003 (fell Fitzwilliam Coll), princ Faculty of Med Imperial Coll London 2003–; ceo Imperial Coll Healthcare NHS Tst; author of various scientific and med pubns; FRCOG, FIBiol, FMedSci; *Recreations* walking, flying, politics, history, music; *Style—* Prof Stephen Smith; ✉ Faculty of Medicine, Imperial College London, Level 2 Faculty Building, South Kensington Campus, London SW7 2AZ (☎ 020 7594 8800, fax 020 7594 9833)

SMITH, Prof Sir Steven Murray (Steve); kt (2011); s of William Smith, and Doris Smith; *b* 4 February 1952; *Educ* Univ of Southampton (BSc, MSc, PhD, DSc); *m* Dr Jeannie Forbes; *Career* lectr in politics Huddersfield Poly 1976–78, lectr, sr lectr then prof of int relations UEA 1979–92, prof of int politics UCW Aberystwyth (later Univ of Wales Aberystwyth) 1992–2002 (pro-vice-chllr 1999–2002), vice-chllr Univ of Exeter 2002–; pres Int Studies Assoc 2003–04, pres Univs UK 2009–11, chair Bd UCAS; AcSS 2000; *Books* Foreign Policy Adaptation (1981), Politics and Human Nature (ed jtly, 1983), Foreign Policy Implementation (ed jtly, 1985), International Relations (ed, 1985), The Cold War Past and Present (ed jtly, 1987), British Foreign Policy: Tradition, Change, and Transformation (ed jtly, 1988), Belief Systems and International Relations (ed jtly, 1988), Explaining and Understanding International Relations (jtly, 1990), Deciding Factors in British Politics: A Case-Studies Approach (jtly, 1992), European Foreign Policy (ed jtly, 1994), International Relations Theory Today (ed jtly, 1995), International Theory: Positivism and Beyond (ed jtly, 1996), The Globalization of World Politics (ed jtly, 1997, 4 edn 2008), International Relations Theories: Discipline and Diversity (ed jtly, 2007), Foreign Policy: Theories, Actors, Cases (ed jtly, 2008); *Recreations* Norwich City FC, theatre, music, firework displays, arctophile; *Style—* Prof Sir Steve Smith; ✉ Vice-Chancellor's Office, University of Exeter, Northcote House, Queen's Drive, Exeter EX4 4QJ (☎ 01392 723000, e-mail vice-chancellor@ex.ac.uk)

SMITH, Stuart Crawford; s of David Norman Smith, of Spain, and Sheila Marie, *née* Hallowes; *b* 17 September 1953; *Educ* City of Bath Boys' Sch, Wadham Coll Oxford (major scholar, BA), Univ of Sussex (MA); *m* 23 Dec 1987, Hilary Joy Phillips; *Career* ed Marketing Week Magazine 1988– (joined as sub ed 1982); *Recreations* skiing, reading, riding; *Style—* Stuart Smith, Esq; ✉ Centaur Publishing, St Giles House, 49–50 Poland Street, London W1F 7AX (☎ 020 7970 4000, fax 020 7970 6721)

SMITH, Susan Lorraine (Susy); da of Clifford Bryce Smith (d 1999), and Marjorie Doreen Walker (d 1991); *b* 15 August 1957; *Educ* Grosvenor HS Belfast, Central Sch of Art London (BA); *m* Alex Evans; 2 da (Constance Marjorie (Connie), Harriet Anne (Hattie) (twins) b 6 March 1998); *Career* layout artist My Guy 1980, jr designer Ideal Home 1982, homes asst Homes & Gardens 1983, style ed In Store 1985, freelance stylist and design conslt 1987; House Beautiful magazine: style and design ed 1988–93, assoc ed 1993–95; ed Country Living 1995–; Innovation of the Year BSME 1999 (for Country Living's Farmer Wants a Wife), Best Coverage of Environmental Issues by a Consumer Magazine British Environment and Media Awards (BEMAS) 2003, Consumer Lifestyle Magazine of the Year PPA 2004, Ed of the Year Lifestyle Magazines BSME 2006, Consumer Lifestyle Magazine of the Year PPA 2006, Best Coverage of Environmental Issues by a Consumer Magazine Br Environment and Media Award 2006; *Recreations* gardening, walking, birdwatching; *Clubs* Blacks; *Style—* Ms Susy Smith; ✉ National Magazine Company, 72 Broadwick Street, London W1F 9EP (☎ 020 7439 5294, e-mail susy.smith@natmags.co.uk)

SMITH, Terence Charles (Terry); s of Ernest George Smith (d 1985), of London, and Eva Ada, *née* Bruce (d 2001); *b* 15 May 1953; *Educ* Stratford GS, UC Cardiff (BA), Mgmnt Coll Henley (MBA); *m* 31 Aug 1974, Barbara Mary, da of Ivor Thomas George, of Ebbw Vale; 2 da (Katy b 1981, Emily b 1984); *Career* mgmnt trainee, branch mangr, fin mangr Barclays Bank 1974–83, bank analyst W Greenwell and Co 1984–86, dir, bank analyst, head of fin desk Barclays de Zoete Wedd 1986–88, bank analyst James Capel and Co 1989–90, dep md and head of UK company research UBS Phillips & Drew 1990–92 (dismissed following publication of book on suspect UK financial accounting techniques), dir Collins Stewart stockbrokers 1992–, ceo Collins Stewart Inc 1999–, ceo Collins Stewart Tullett plc 2000–06, chm Collins Stewart plc 2006–, ceo Tullett Prebon plc 2006–; rated leading banking sector analyst 1984–90; ACIB, MSI; *Books* Accounting for Growth (1992, 2 edn 1996); *Recreations* boxing, shooting, flying; *Style—* Terry Smith, Esq; ✉ Collins Stewart plc, 9th Floor, 88 Wood Street, London EC2V 7QR (☎ 020 7200 7337)

SMITH, Thomas William David; s of George Ernest Smith, of Sheffield, and Dora Staniforth; *b* 4 August 1939; *Educ* Selwyn Coll Cambridge (MA, MB BChir), St Mary's Hosp Med Sch; *m* 24 Nov 1967, Christina Mary, da of William O'Connor, of Dublin; 3 s (Nicholas William Patrick b 1968, Thomas Fitzgerald George b 1972, Hugh Francis Niall b 1974), 2 da (Gillian Mary b 1970, Alexandra Gwen b 1972); *Career* orthopaedic registrar Oxford 1968–70, sr orthopaedic registrar Sheffield 1970–73, lectr Univ of Sheffield 1973–76, conslt orthopaedic surgn Sheffield 1976–; Liveryman Worshipful Co of Pattenmakers; FRCS, FRCSEd; *Recreations* fly fishing; *Clubs* Flyfishers'; *Style—* Thomas Smith, Esq; ✉ Cleveland House, 3 Whitworth Road, Sheffield S10 3HD (☎ 0114 230 8398)

SMITH, Timothy John; s of late Capt Norman Wesley Smith, CBE (sometime Cdre Orient Steam Navigation Co), and late Nancy Phyllis, da of Engr Capt F J Pedrick, RN; *b* 5 October 1947; *Educ* Harrow, St Peter's Coll Oxford (MA); *m* 1980, Jennifer Jane, da of late Maj Sir James Sidney Rawdon Scott-Hopkins, MP, MEP; 2 s (Henry b 1982, Charles b 1984); *Career* articled Gibson Harris & Turnbull 1969–71, sr auditor Peat Marwick Mitchell 1971–73, co sec Coubro & Scrutton Holdings 1973–79, sec Parly and Law Ctee ICAEW 1979–82, ptnr HM Williams CAs 2001–13, dir Nevill Hovey & Co Ltd CAs 2002–; chm Abbeyfield Launceston Soc 2003–10; MP (Cons): Ashfield 1977–79, Beaconsfield 1982–97; PPS to Rt Hon Leon Brittan 1983–85, Parly under-sec NI Office 1994; memb: NI Select Ctee 1994–97, HM Treasury Financial Reporting Advsy Bd 1996–97, Inland Revenue Tax Law Rewrite Steering Ctee 1996–97; vice-chm Cons Backbench Fin Ctee 1987–92, sec Cons Backbench Trade and Industry Ctee 1987–92, memb Public Accounts Ctee 1987–92 and 1995–97, vice-chm and jt treas Cons Pty 1992–94; treas: St Petrocs Soc 2005–14, Cornwall Community Fndn 2009–; chm N Cornwall Cons Assoc 2016–; memb Bishops Diocesan Cncl Truro 2015–; FCA, CTA; *Style—* Timothy Smith, Esq

SMITH, Will; *Educ* Wycliffe Coll Glos, Kingston Poly, Manchester Poly; *m* Lynn; *Career* jt prop (with Anthony Demetre): Arbutus 2006– (Harden's/Remy Martin Excellence Award 2007, Best New Restaurant Time Out Eating and Drinking Guide 2007, London Newcomer of the Year Good Food Guide 2007, Newcomer of 2006 Decanter Magazine, Newcomer of the Year Tatler, Michelin star), Wild Honey 2007– (Michelin star), Les Deux Salon 2011–; *Style—* Will Smith, Esq; ✉ Arbutus, 63–64 Frith Street, London W1D 3JW

SMITH OF BASILDON, Baroness (Life Peer UK 2010), of Basildon in the County of Essex; Rt Hon Angela Evans Smith; PC (2009); da of Patrick and Emily Evans; *b* 7 January 1959; *Educ* Chalvedon Sch Basildon, Leicester Poly (BA); *m* Dec 1978, Nigel Smith; *Career* trainee accountant London Borough of Newham 1981–83, sometime head of political and public relations League Against Cruel Sports 1983–95, Parly researcher to Alun Michael MP, *qv*, as Shadow Min for Home Affrs 1995–97; MP (Lab) Basildon 1997–2010; PPS to Paul Boateng, *qv* (Home Office Min) 1999–2001, asst Govt whip 2001–02, Parly under-sec of state NI Office 2002–06, Parly under sec of state Dept for Communities and Local Govt 2006–07, Parly prive sec to the PM 2007–09, min of state Cabinet Office 2009–10, shadow ldr of House of Lords 2015–; cncllr Essex CC 1989–97; memb: Amnesty Int, T&GWU; *Style—* The Rt Hon the Baroness Smith of Basildon; ✉ House of Lords, London SW1A 0PW

SMITH OF CLIFTON, Baron (Life Peer UK 1997), of Mountsandel in the County of Londonderry; Prof Sir Trevor Arthur Smith; kt (1996); s of late Arthur James Smith, and late Vera Gladys, *née* Cross; *b* 14 June 1937; *Educ* LSE (BSc); *m* 1, 14 Feb 1960 (m dis 1973), Brenda Susan, *née* Eustace; 2 s (Hon Adam James William b 6 June 1964, Hon Gideon Matthew Kingsley b 14 May 1966); m 2, 9 Aug 1979, Julia Donnithorne, *née* Bullock; 1 da (Hon Naomi Thérèse b 8 June 1981); *Career* school teacher LCC 1958–59, temp asst lectr Univ of Exeter 1959–60, res offr Acton Soc Tst 1960–62, lectr in politics Univ of Hull 1962–67 visiting assoc prof California State Univ Los Angeles 1969; QMC (later Queen Mary & Westfield Coll) London: lectr (later sr lectr) in political studies 1967–83, head of dept 1972–85, dean of social studies 1979–82, fndn prof 1983–91, pro-princ 1985–87, sr pro-princ 1987–89, sr vice-princ 1989–91; vice-chllr Univ of Ulster 1991–99; dir: Job Ownership Ltd 1978–85, New Society Ltd 1986–88, Statesman and Nation Publishing Co Ltd 1988–90, Gerald Duckworth & Co Ltd 1990–95; chm Conf of Rectors in Ireland 1987, chm Political Studies Assoc of UK 1988–89 (vice-pres 1989–91 and 1993–, pres 1991–93); govr: Sir John Cass and Redcoats Sch 1979–84, Univ of Haifa 1985–92, Bell Educn Tst 1988–93; memb Tower Hamlets DHA 1987–91 (vice-chm 1989–91), vice-pres Patients Assoc of UK 1988–97, dep pres Inst of Citizenship Studies 1991–99, non-exec dir N Yorks HA 2000–02; pres Belfast Civic Tst 1995–99; memb: Administrative Bd Int Assoc of Univs 1995–96, Editorial Bd Government and Opposition 1995–2013, Bd A Taste of Ulster 1996–99, Bd of Opera Northern Ireland, UK Socrates Cncl 1993–99 (chm 1996–99); Parliamentary candidate (Lib) Lewisham West 1959; House of Lords: Lib Dem Spokesperson on NI 1991–2011, memb Select Ctee on Science and Technology Sub-Ctee on Complementary and Alternative Med 1999–2000, memb British-Irish Inter-Parliamentary Assembly 2000–11, memb EU Select Ctee E (Law and Institutions) 2001, chm Select Ctee on Animals in Scientific Proceedures 2001–02, memb Select Ctee on Communications 2004–06, memb Select Ctee on Constitution 2005–08, memb Sub-Ctee on Lords' Interests 2006–08, memb Ad-Hoc Ctee on Barnett Formula 2008–09, memb Economic Affrs Select Ctee 2010–15; dir Joseph Rowntree Reform Trust Ltd 1975–2006 (chm 1987–99), dir Democratic Audit Ltd 2007–11; Hon LLD: Dublin 1992, Hull 1993, Belfast 1995, NUI 1996; Hon DHL Alabama 1998, Hon DLitt Univ of Ulster 2002; hon memb Senate Fachhochschule Augsburg 1994, hon fell Queen Mary Univ of London 2003; FAcSS 2001; FRHistS 1986, CIMgt 1992, FRSA 1994, FICPD 1998; *Clubs* Reform; *Style—* Prof Lord Smith of Clifton; ✉ House of Lords, London SW1A 0PW

SMITH OF FINSBURY, Baron (Life Peer UK 2005), of Finsbury in the London Borough of Islington; Christopher Robert (Chris) Smith; PC (1997); s of Colin Smith, and Gladys, *née* Luscombe; *b* 24 July 1951; *Educ* George Watson's Coll Edinburgh, Pembroke Coll Cambridge (PhD), Harvard Univ (Kennedy scholar); *Career* housing devpt worker 1976–83, MP (Lab) Islington S and Finsbury 1983–2005 (Parly candidate (Lab) Epsom and Ewell 1979); oppn front bench spokesman on Treasy and econ affrs 1987–92, memb Shadow Cabinet 1992–97, chief oppn spokesman on environmental protection 1992–94, shadow sec of state for Nat Heritage 1994–95; chief oppn spokesman on: social security 1995–96, health 1996–97; sec of state DCMS 1997–2001; dir Clore Leadership Programme 2003–08; chm Environment Agency 2008–14; memb Environment Select Ctee 1983–87;

S

chm: Tribune Group of MPs 1988–89 (sec 1984–88), Lab Campaign for criminal justice 1985–88; memb Ctee on Standards in Public Life 2001–04; pres Lab Environment Campaign (SERA) 1992–2007; visiting prof Univ of the Arts London 2002–; sr advsr Walt Disney Co 2001–07; cncllr London Borough of Islington 1978–83 (chief whip 1978–79, chm Housing Ctee 1981–83); ASTMS branch: sec 1978–80, chm 1980–83; chm Bd Tribune Newspaper 1990–93, chm Bd New Century Magazine 1993–96; chm: Classic FM Consumer Panel 2002–07, Wordsworth Tst 2002– (tstee 2001–02), Man Booker Prize 2004, Donmar Warehouse Theatre 2004–15 (memb Bd 2002–04), London Cultural Consortium 2004–08, Advertising Standards Authy 2007–, Film Policy Review 2011–12, art Fund Prize for Museums 2012, Inmidtown Business Improvement District 2014; non-exec memb Bd Phonographic Performance Ltd 2006–, non-exec memb Bd Spencer Ogden 2014–; tstee John Muir Tst 1991–97, tstee The Sixteen 2013–; memb: Cncl for Nat Parks 1978–88, Bd Shelter 1987–92, Exec Ctee NCCL 1986–88, Bd Sadler's Wells Theatre 1986–93, Exec Ctee Fabian Soc 1992–97 (vice-chm 1995–96, chm 1996–97), Exec Ctee Nat Tst 1995 97, Bd RNT 2001–09; chm The Art Fund 2014–; hon fell Pembroke Coll Cambridge 2004– (Master 2015–), visiting fell Ashridge Business Sch 2007–10; Sr FRCA 2007; *Publications* Creative Britain (1998), Suicide of the West (jtly, 2006); *Recreations* literature, music, theatre, mountaineering; *Style*— The Rt Hon the Lord Smith of Finsbury, PC; ✉ House of Lords, London SW1A 0PW

SMITH OF GILMOREHILL, Baroness (Life Peer UK 1995), of Gilmorehill in the District of the City of Glasgow; Elizabeth Margaret Smith; DL (City of Edinburgh); da of late Frederick William Moncrieff Bennett; *b* 4 June 1940; *Educ* Univ of Glasgow; *m* 5 July 1967, Rt Hon John Smith, QC, MP (d 1994), son of late Archibald Leitch Smith, of Dunoon, Argyll; 3 da (Hon Sarah b 22 Nov 1968, Hon Jane b 28 July 1971, Hon Catherine b 4 May 1973); *Career* memb PCC 1995–2001; non-exec dir: Deutsche (Scotland) Ltd 1996–2003, Hakluyt Fndn 1998–2001, City Inn 2001–11; memb BP Advsy Bd for Scotland 1996–2003, chm Edinburgh Festival Fringe Soc 1996–2012; cncl memb Russo-British Chamber of Commerce; pres: Scottish Opera 1996–2012, Birkbeck Coll London 1996–2002; govr ESU; tstee: Centre for Euro Reform 1997–2004, John Smith Meml Tst, 21st Century Tst 2002–08; memb Advsy Bd Beacon Fellowship 2002–05; *Style*— The Rt Hon Lady Smith of Gilmorehill, DL; ✉ House of Lords, London SW1A 0PW

SMITH OF LEIGH, Baron (Life Peer UK 1999), of Wigan in the County of Greater Manchester; Peter Richard Charles Smith; s of Ronald Ernest Smith, and Kathleen, *née* Hocken; *b* 24 July 1945; *Educ* Bolton Sch, LSE (BSc), Garnet Coll London (CertEd), Univ of Salford (MSc); *m* 1968, Joy Lesley Booth; 1 da; *Career* lectr: Walbrook Coll London 1969–74, Manchester Coll of Art and Technol 1974–2001; Wigan MBC: cncllr 1978–, chair of fin 1982–91, ldr 1991–; ldr Assoc of Gtr Manchester Authys 2000–, chm NW Regnl Assembly (latterly 4NW) 2006–08, chm Gtr Manchester Combined Authy 2011–; treas All Pty Rugby League Gp; vice-pres Br Epilepsy Assoc; Freedom of Wigan 2011; Hon LLD Manchester Met Univ 2012; *Recreations* gardening, jazz, sport (particularly rugby league); *Style*— The Lord Smith of Leigh; ✉ Mysevin, Old Hall Mill Lane, Atherton, Manchester M46 0RG (☎ 01942 676127); Wigan Council, Town Hall, Library Street, Wigan WN1 1YN (☎ 01942 827001, e-mail leader@wiganmbc.gov.uk)

SMITH OF NEWNHAM, Baroness (Life Peer UK 2014), of Newnham, of Crosby in the County of Merseyside; Julie Elizabeth Smith; da of Hugh Francis Smith, and Eileen Elizabeth, *née* Murphy; *b* 1 June 1969, Liverpool; *Educ* Merchant Taylors' Girls' Sch Crosby, Brasenose Coll Oxford (MA), St Antony's Coll Oxford (MPhil, DPhil); *Career* Hansiatic scholarship Hamburg 1995–97; Univ of Cambridge: currently sr lectr in int relations, dir European Centre @ POLIS 2013–, fell Robinson Coll; tstee: Gladstone's Library Hawarden, Cambridge Univ Catholic Assoc; cncllr (Lib Dem) Cambridge City Cncl 2003–15, vice chair Lib Dem Fed Policy Ctee 2012–; *Books* Voice of the People: The European Parliament in the 1990s (1995), Eminent Europeans: Personalities Who Shaped Contemporary Europe (ed with Martyn Bond and William Wallace, 1996), A Sense of Liberty: A Short History of the Liberal International 1947–97 (1997), Democracy in the New Europe (ed with Elizabeth Teague, 1999), Europe's Elected Parliament (1999), The New Bilateralism: The UK's Bilateral Relations Within the EU (with Mariana Tsatsas, 2002), Through the Paper Curtain: Insiders and Outsiders in the New Europe (co-ed with Charles Jenkins, 2003), Reinvigorating European Elections: the Implications of Electing the European Commission (2005), New Horizons in European Politics (2011), Palgrave Handbook on National Parliaments and the European Union (co-ed and contrib, 2015); articles in jls and books; *Recreations* music, travel, theatre, ballet, yoga; *Style*— The Baroness Smith of Newnham; ✉ 7 West Road, Cambridge CB3 9DT (☎ 01223 767229, e-mail jes42@cam.ac.uk, website www.juliesmithcambridge.co.uk, Twitter @DrJulieSmith1)

SMITHAM, Peter; s of Brinley James Smitham, and Violet May, *née* Linden; *b* 11 May 1942; *Educ* Univ Coll Swansea (BSc), Univ of Salford (DMS), Stanford Univ (Sr Exec Prog); *m* Lynne Helen, *née* Wolfendale; 2 da (Andrea, Samantha); *Career* mgmnt Co-operative Wholesale Society 1964–67, ops dir then gen mangr ITT 1967–71, gen mangr Barclay Securities 1971–73, md Jermyn Holdings 1973–83, md European electronics Lex Service plc 1983–85, ptnr Permira Advisers (formerly Schroder Ventures) 1985– (managing ptnr London office 1994–98, ldr European business 1998–2000); non-exec chm Memec Inc 2001–, dir various other companies; *Style*— Peter Smitham, Esq

SMITHERS, Prof Alan George; s of Alfred Edward (d 1976), of London, and Queenie Lilian, *née* Carmichael (d 1994); *b* 20 May 1938, London; *Educ* Barking Abbey, KCL (BSc, PhD), Univ of Bradford (MSc, PhD), Univ of Manchester (MEd); *m* 27 Aug 1962 (m dis 2003), Angela Grace, da of David Wykes, of Exeter; 2 da (Vaila Helen b 1967, Rachel Hilary b 1969); *Career* lectr in biology Coll of St Mark and St John 1962–64, lectr in botany Birkbeck Coll London 1964–67, sr lectr in educn Univ of Bradford 1969–75 (research fell 1967–69), prof of educn Univ of Manchester 1976–96, prof of educn (policy research) Brunel Univ 1996–98, Sydney Jones prof of educn Univ of Liverpool 1998–2004, prof of educn and dir Centre for Educn and Employment Research Univ of Buckingham 2004–; standing advsr House of Commons Educn Select Ctee; former memb Nat Curriculum Cncl, memb Beaumont Ctee on Nat Vocational Qualifications; CPsychol, fell Soc for Research in HE; *Books* Sandwich Courses: An Integrated Education? (1976), The Progress of Mature Students (jtly, 1986), The Growth of Mixed A Levels (jtly, 1988), The Shortage of Mathematics and Physics Teachers (jtly, 1988), Increasing Participation in Higher Education (jtly, 1989), Graduates in the Police Service (jtly, 1990), Teacher Provision in the Sciences (jtly, 1990), Gender, Primary Schools and the National Curriculum (jtly, 1991), The Vocational Route into Higher Education (1991), Teacher Provision: Trends and Perceptions (jtly, 1991), Staffing Secondary Schools in the Nineties (jtly, 1991), Every Child in Britain (Report of Channel 4 Education Commission, 1991), Beyond Compulsory Schooling (jtly, 1991), Technology in the National Curriculum (jtly, 1992), Technology at A Level (jtly, 1992), Assessing the Value (jtly, 1992), General Studies: Breadth at Level? (jtly, 1993), Changing Colleges: Further Education in the Market Place (jtly, 1993), All Our Futures: Britain's Education Revolution (1993), Technology Teachers (jtly, 1994), The Impact of Double Science (jtly, 1994), Post-18 Education: Growth, Change, Prospect (jtly, 1995), Affording Teachers (jtly, 1995), Co-educational and Single Sex Schooling (jtly, 1995), Trends in Higher Education (jtly, 1996), Technology in Secondary Schools (jtly, 1997), Staffing Our Schools (jtly, 1997), The New Zealand Qualifications Framework (1997), Co-educational and Single Sex Schooling Revisited (jtly, 1998), Degrees of Choice (jtly, 1998), Assessment in Primary Schools (1998), annual Good Teacher Training Guide (jtly, 1998–), Teacher Supply: Old Story or New Chapter? (jtly, 1999), Further Education Re-Formed (jtly, 2000), Coping with Teacher Shortages (jtly, 2000), Talking Heads (jtly, 2000), Attracting Teachers (jtly, 2000), Teachers Leaving (jtly, 2001), Teacher Qualifications (jtly, 2003), Factors Affecting Teachers' Decisions to Leave the Profession (jtly, 2003), The Reality of School Staffing (jtly, 2003), England's Education (2004), Teacher Turnover: Wastage and Movements Between Schools (jtly, 2005), Physics in Schools and Colleges (jtly, 2005, Five Years On (jtly, 2006), Patterns and Policies in Physics Education (jtly, 2006), The Paradox of Single Sex and Coeducation (jtly, 2006), Bucking the Trend (jtly, 2007), School Headship: Present and Future (jtly, 2007), Blair's Education (2007), The Diploma (jtly, 2008), Physics Teachers (jtly, 2008), HMC Schools (jtly, 2008), Specialist Science Schools (jtly, 2009), Physics Participation and Policies (jtly, 2009), Worlds Apart (jtly, 2010), Choice and Selection in Education (jtly, 2010), Educating the Highly Able (jtly, 2012), Confusion in the Ranks (2013), The Science and Mathematics Teaching Workforce (jtly, 2014), GCSE and A-Level Trends (2015), HEFCE's Blunder (2015), Social Disadvantage and Widening Access to Universities (2015); *Recreations* theatre, strolling; *Style*— Prof Alan Smithers; ✉ Centre for Education and Employment Research, University of Buckingham, Buckingham MK18 1EG (☎ 01280 820270, e-mail alan.smithers@buckingham.ac.uk)

SMITHERS, Andrew Reeve Waldron; s of Prof Sir David Waldron Smithers, MD, FRCP, FRCS, FRCR (d 1995), of Knockholt, Kent, and Gwladys Margaret, *née* Angel; gs of Sir Waldron Smithers, MP for 30 yrs Chislehurst and Orpington; *b* 21 September 1937; *Educ* Winchester, Clare Coll Cambridge (MA); *m* 8 June 1963, (Amanda) Jill, da of Edward Gilbert Kennedy; 2 s ((Matthew) Pelham b 10 Oct 1964, (Jonathan) Kit b 6 Dec 1967); *Career* chm: Whatman plc (formerly Whatman Reeve Angel plc) 1969–2002 (dir 1960–2002), Smithers & Co Ltd (Economic Conslts) 1989–; dir S G Warburg Securities 1967–89 (joined co 1962); *Books* Japan's Key Challenges for the 21st Century (jtly, 1998), Valuing Wall Street (jtly, 2000), Wall Street Revalued – Imperfect Markets and Inept Central Bankers (2009), The Road to Recovery: How and Why Economic Policy Must Change (2013); *Recreations* conversation, reading, performing arts; *Clubs* Brooks's, Yokohama Cricket, Tuesday, Political Economy; *Style*— Andrew Smithers, Esq; ✉ Smithers & Co Ltd, 20 St Dunstan's Hill, London EC3R 8HL (☎ 020 7283 3344, fax 020 7283 3345, e-mail info@smithers.co.uk)

SMITHSON, Dr (William) Henry; s of Ronald Geoffrey Smithson (d 1965), of Wetherby, W Yorks, and Harriet, *née* Gregson (d 2005); *b* 12 March 1951, Tadcaster, N Yorks; *Educ* Leeds GS, Univ of Dundee (MB ChB, MD), Univ of York (MSc); *m* 24 June 1982 (sep 2006), Jeanne Rachael, da of John Edmund Smales, of Roos, E Yorks; 1 s (William John b 6 May 1984), 1 da (Elizabeth Anne b 13 June 1988); *Career* GP trainee York Vocational Trg Scheme 1977–80, assoc family physician The Pas Manitoba Canada 1980–82, princ in gen practice Escrick York 1982–2008, sr clinical univ teacher Academic Unit of Primary Medical Care Univ of Sheffield 2008–; GP trainer 1986–91, vol trg course organiser York 1991–2000, prescribing lead and memb Bd Selby Primary Care Gp 1999–2001; hon clinical sr lectr Hull York Med Sch 2003–; RCGP: memb Yorks Faculty 1989–, chm Yorks Faculty 1996–99, Prince of Wales educnl fell in epilepsy 1996–98; memb: BMA 1982, York Med Soc 1983; professional memb Br Epilepsy Assoc 1994; chair Epilepsy Guidelines Gp Nat Inst for Clinical Excellence (NICE) 2002–04, Leading Practice Through Research grant holder Health Fndn 2003–05; DRCOG, FRCGP (MRCGP); *Publications* Epilepsy: A General Practice Problem (1997), Integrating the Algorithm into Community Practice (1999), Net Based Education (2000), Neuropathic Pain (2001), National Clinical Sentinel Audit on Epilepsy Related Death (2001), Epilepsy: Death in the Shadows (2002), The ABC of Epilepsy (2012); *Recreations* cricket, writing, foreign travel; *Clubs* York Wanderers Cricket; *Style*— Dr W H Smithson; ✉ Academic Unit of Primary Medical Care, Samuel Fox House, Northern General Hospital, Herries Road, Sheffield S5 7AU (e-mail henry.smithson@sheffield.ac.uk)

SMITHSON, Simon; s of Peter D Smithson (d 2003), and Alison M, *née* Gill (d 1997); *b* 28 June 1954; *Educ* Univ of Cambridge (BA, DipArch), Harvard Univ Graduate Sch of Design (MA); *Career* architect; George Candelis Paris 1976–77, Foster Associates 1979–80, Cambridge Seven Associates USA 1982–85, Civitas Inc USA 1985–88, Nicholas Hare Architects 1989–91, Richard Rogers Partnership 1991– (assoc dir 1996–), dir Richard Rogers SL (Spain) 2005, ptnr RSH-P 2011; lectr: Harvard Univ, Univ of Colorado Denver, Univ of Madrid, Royal Acad 2005, Univ of Valladolid Spain 2006 and 2008, Univ of Valencia 2006, Univ of Alcalde Henares Madrid 2007, Sch of Technol Focus-Abengoa Fndn Seville 2007, Habitat Futura Madrid 2007, RIBA 2007, Lisbon, TUDelft Netherlands 2008; *Projects* incl: General Cinema Corp refurbishment strategy, Williams Coll Athletic Facilities USA, street furniture for 16th Street Mall Denver USA, BAT HQ Staines, Shanghai Masterplan, Heathrow Airport Terminal 5, Daiwa Europe House, Lloyd's Register of Shipping, ParcBIT Masterplan Palma, Welsh Assembly Building, Antwerp Law Courts, T4 Madrid Barajas Airport, Pabilion de Estado Madrid Barajas, Abengoa HQ Seville, multi use building Campus de Justicia Madrid, Mixed Uses Building Campus of Justice Madrid; masterplans: Coto de Macairena Granada, Vallodolid Este, Castilla Leon Spain, El Calaveral Madrid, Valladolid Alta Velocidad Spain, La Cartuja Sevilla, bathrooms for Noken, Centro International Towers Bogotá, La Rinconada masterplan and transport interchange Caracas; *Clubs* London Rowing; *Style*— Simon Smithson, Esq

SMOSARSKI, Lisa; *m* 5 Sept 2009, Richard Woods; 2 s (Dylan b 30 Dec 2010, Jude b 6 Jan 2013); *Career* ed: Smash Hits 2003–05, Bliss 2005–06, More! 2006–09, Stylist 2009–; *Style*— Ms Lisa Smosarski; ✉ Stylist, 26–34 Emerald Street, London WC1N 3QA

SMOUHA, Joe; QC (2003); s of Brian Smouha, and Hana, *née* Btesh; *b* 20 January 1963; *Educ* Magdalene Coll Cambridge (MA), NYU Sch of Law (Fulbright Scholar, LLM); *Career* called to the Bar Middle Temple 1986 (bencher 2010); practising barr specialising in int commercial law, memb Essex Court Chambers 1987–; former chm Commercial Bar Assoc; dir English Concert, tstee Hebrew Univ of Jerusalem UK; *Style*— Joe Smouha, Esq, QC; ✉ Essex Court Chambers, 24 Lincoln's Inn Fields, London WC2A 3EG

SMOUT, Prof (Thomas) Christopher; CBE (1994); s of Arthur Smout (d 1961), of Sheriffs Lench, Worcs, and Hilda, *née* Follows (d 1979); *b* 19 December 1933; *Educ* Leys Sch Cambridge, Clare Coll Cambridge (MA, PhD); *m* 15 Aug 1959, Anne-Marie, da of Alfred Schøning, of Charlottenlund, Denmark; 1 da (Pernille Anne b 1961), 1 s (Andrew b 1963); *Career* prof of econ history Univ of Edinburgh 1971 (asst lectr 1959); Univ of St Andrews: prof of Scottish history 1980–91, dir St John's House Centre for Advanced Historical Studies 1992–97, dir Inst for Environmental History 1992–2000; historiographer Royal Scotland 1993–; memb Royal Cmmn on Ancient and Historical Monuments (Scotland) 1986–2000, dep chm Bd Scottish Nat Heritage until 1996, memb Royal Cmmn on Historic Manuscripts until 2003, memb Advsy Ctee on Public and Historical Records 2003, chm SCAPE (Scottish Coastal Archaeology and the Problem of Erosion Tst) until 2012, chm Strathmartine Tst 2013–; tstee Nat Museum of Scotland until 1995; Geddes Environmental Medal RSGS 2013; hon fell Trinity Coll Dublin 1995, Hon DSocSc Queen's Univ Belfast 1995, Hon DSSS Univ of Edinburgh 1996, Hon DLitt Univ of St Andrews 1999, Hon DLitt Univ of Glasgow 2001, Hon DUniv Stirling 2002; FRSE 1978, FBA 1988, FSA Scot 1991; *Books* A History of the Scottish People (1969), A Century of the Scottish People (1986), Scottish Voices (with Sydney Wood, 1990), Prices, Food and Wages in Scotland 1550–1780 (with A J S Gibson, 1995), Nature Contested (2000), A History of the Native Woodlands of Scotland 1500–1920 (with A R MacDonald and F Watson, 2005), Exploring Environmental History (2009), The Firth of Forth: An Environmental History (with Mairi Stewart, 2012); *Recreations* birds, butterflies, moths, dragonflies and bees;

Style— Prof Christopher Smout, CBE, FBA, FRSE; ✉ Chesterhill, Shore Road, Anstruther, Fife KY10 3DZ (☎ 01333 310330, e-mail christopher@smout.org)

SMOUT, (Peter Alun) Clifford; s of Peter Smout (d 2006), and Mary Patricia, *née* Chadbourne; *b* 26 July 1956; *Educ* Kimbolton Sch, Clare Coll Cambridge (BA); *m* 26 Oct 1985, Eileen Frances, *née* Roots (d 2005); 1 da (Jennifer Frances b 17 May 1988), 1 s (Alistair David b 17 Aug 1991); *Career* Bank of England: Int Div 1978–83, Money Markets Div 1983–86, fndr memb Wholesale Markets Supervision Div 1986–87, dep govr's private sec 1987–89, portfolio mangr Foreign Exchange Div 1989–91, sr mangr Supervision of US Banks 1991–93, head of Supervisory Policy Div 1993–98, head of Foreign Exchange 1998–2002, fin dir 2002–06; ptnr Centre for Regulatory Strategy Deloitte 2006–16; memb: RSPB, Herts & Middx Wildlife Tst,; *Recreations* birdwatching, football; *Clubs* Herts Bird; *Style—* Clifford Smout, Esq; ✉ e-mail psmout@btinternet.com

SMYTH, Clare; MBE (2013); da of William James Boyce Smyth, and Doreen Brenda Margaret Smyth; *b* 6 September 1978, Ballymoney, NI; *Career* head chef Gordon Ramsay Royal Hospital Road 2007–; *Style—* Ms Clare Smyth, MBE; ✉ Restaurant Gordon Ramsay, 68 Royal Hospital Road, London SW3 4HP

SMYTH, His Hon Judge David William; QC (1989); s of William McKeag Smyth (d 1954), and Eva Maud, *née* Moran (d 1992); *b* 12 November 1948; *Educ* Methodist Coll Belfast, Queen's Univ Belfast (Porter scholar, LLB); *m* 23 July 1977, Anthea Linda Hall-Thompson, DL, da of Lloyd Hall-Thompson (former MP, d 1992); 3 da (Rachel Anthea b 13 Feb 1979, Hannah Sophia b 31 Dec 1983 d 1984, Rebecca Charlotte b 21 May 1987), 1 s (Alasdair Lloyd William b 26 Aug 1980); *Career* called to the NI Bar 1972 (bencher 1997), political res London 1972–74, called to the Bar Gray's Inn 1978, called to the Bar of Ireland 1989; County Court judge: Fermanagh and Tyrone 1990–97, Antrim 1997–2011, Ards 2011–; chm: Legal Aid Advsy Bd NI 1994–2005, NI Cncl on Alcohol 1996–98, Bd of Advsrs Inst of Criminology Queen's Univ Belfast 2002, Cncl of County Court Judges 2005–; memb: Criminal Justice Working Gp on Drugs 2002, Ctee Anglo-French Judicial Gp 2002, Youth Conferencing Advsy Gp 2003; chm Bd of Advsrs Inst of Criminology Queen's Univ Belfast 2002; treas Inn of Court of NI 2009; Winston Churchill fell 2002, chm Winston Churchill Fellowship 2015; pres NI Community Addiction Service 1998, tstee N Belfast Working Mens' Club 1974–, pres Methodist Coll Belfast Former Pupils' Assoc (MCB FPA) 2011, pres Addiction NI 2010; *Recreations* cycling, history, opera, theatre; *Style—* His Hon Judge Smyth, QC; ✉ Royal Courts of Justice, Chichester Street, Belfast BT1 3JE (e-mail davidsmyth80@icloud.com)

SMYTH, Michael Thomas; CBE (2009); 2 s of Rev Kenneth Smyth, and Freda, *née* Boucher (d 2008); *b* 3 March 1957, Newtownards, Co Down; *Educ* Royal Belfast Academical Inst, Clare Coll Cambridge (MA); *m* 10 Sept 1983, Joyce, *née* Young; 1 s (William b 8 Sept 1990), 1 da (Rachel b 27 Feb 1993); *Career* former ptnr and head of govt practice Clifford Chance; former memb Press Complaints Cmmn; chm: Community Links, Law for Life; memb: Int Advsy Bd Project Assocs Ltd, Advsy Bd Wesleyan Assurance Ltd, Legal Service Bd, Fundraising Regulator; visiting prof: Queen Mary Univ of London, Univ of Essex; FRSA; *Books* Business and the Human Rights Act (2000), The Law of Political Donations (with P Barratt and F Campbell, 2012); *Clubs* Reform; *Style—* Michael Smyth, Esq, CBE; ✉ e-mail michaelsmyth@mtsmyth.com

SMYTH, Peterjohn Jeremy Vignaux; s of late Eric Thomas William Smyth, and Olive Cecily Smyth; *b* 14 April 1940; *Educ* Ampleforth (Cambridge exhibitioner), Clare Coll Cambridge (BA, Dip Arch); *m* Jan 1966, Julia, da of Hubert Alwyn Child; 1 s (Timothy Christian b 15 Sept 1966), 2 da (Rhoda b 9 Jan 1970, Dorothy Vignaux b 21 April 1973); *Career* architect; Morton Lupton & Smith Wallingford Berks 1963–66; Percy Thomas Partnership (Architects) Ltd (formerly Sir Percy Thomas & Son then Percy Thomas Partnership): joined 1966, assoc 1972–80, ptnr 1980–94, dir 1994, chm 2003; currently ptnr ESHA Architects; ldr and co-ordinating architect Prince of Wales' new urban village Poundbury (Dorchester) 1993; memb: Urban Villages Forum 1994–, Princes Fndn; work experience incl healthcare, university, housing, urban design and gen architecture projects; contrib articles to various pubns and sometime speaker and lectr; RIBA 1966; *Awards* winner: int competition for 600 bed hosp Cairo 1975, int competition for 1000 bed hosp Avellino (Italy) 1992, competition for The Prince of Wales Hospice Pontefract 2009; *Recreations* golf; *Style—* Peterjohn Smyth, Esq

SMYTH, Stephen Mark James Athelstan; s of Marcus Smyth (d 1965), of Ditchling, E Sussex, and Ann, *née* Symons; *b* 28 December 1946; *Educ* Hurstpierpoint Coll, Alliance Française; *m* 22 May 1981, Bridget Rosemary Diana, da of Maj (Arthur) Creagh Gibson (d 1970), of Glenburn Hall, Jedburgh; 2 da (Lalage Vivien b 5 Jan 1986, India b 24 May 1989); *Career* worked way around world 1966–67, PA to Greville Janner, MP 1973; called to the Bar Inner Temple 1974, recorder 2001–16 (asst recorder 1994–2001); chm Churchill Clinic IVF Ethical Ctee 1995; tstee Chichester Harbour Tst 2007; *Recreations* books, sailing; *Clubs* Bosham Sailing; *Style—* Stephen Smyth, Esq; ✉ Saltmill House, Mill Lane, Fishbourne, West Sussex PO19 3JN (☎ 020 7353 2112)

SNAPE, Baron (Life Peer UK 2004), of Wednesbury in the County of West Midlands; Peter Charles Snape; s of Thomas Snape, and Kathleen Snape; *b* 12 February 1942; *Educ* St Joseph's Stockport, St Winifred's Stockport; *m* 1963 (m dis 1980); 2 da; *Career* former railway signalman then guard, soldier (RE & RCT), British Rail clerk; chm Travel West Midlands 1977–2001, conslt TUI 2002–06, conslt FirstGroup plc 2006–; MP (Lab) West Bromwich E Feb 1974–2001, memb Cncl of Europe and WEU 1975, asst Govt whip 1975–77, Lord Cmmr of the Treasury (Govt whip) 1977–79; oppn front bench spokesman: on defence and disarmament 1981–82, home affrs 1982–83, transport 1983–92; *Style—* The Rt Hon the Lord Snape

SNASHALL, Prof David Charles; s of Cyril Francis Snashall (d 1998), of London, and Phyllis Mary, *née* Hibbitt (d 1970); *b* 3 February 1943; *Educ* Haberdashers' Aske's, Univ of Edinburgh (MB ChB), LSHTM (MSc, DIH, DTM&H), Univ of Wales Cardiff (LLM); *Children* (Lesley b 1963, Rebecca b 1978, Corinna b 1996); *Career* resident posts in hosp med and gen practice UK, Canada and France 1968–75, chief MO Majes Consortium Peru 1975–76, chief med advsr Tarmac 1977–81, project MO Mufindi Project 1981–82, chief MO Costain Group of Companies 1982–89, med advsr to House of Commons 1982–91, hon conslt and clinical dir of staff occupational health servs W Lambeth HA 1982–93, sr lectr in occupational health GKT 1982–2011, prof of occupational medicine KCL 2011–14 (emeritus prof 2014–), chief med advsr FCO 1989–98, chief med advsr Health and Safety Exec 1998–2003; clinical dir occupational health servs Guy's and St Thomas' Hosp Tst 1993–2015 (hon conslt physician 2015–); pres Faculty of Occupational Medicine RCP 2005–08, chair Research Ethics Ctee Health and Safety Exec 2003–15; memb: Health Servs Advsy Ctee HSE (BMA nominated) 1987–92, GMC 1989–96 and 1999–2003, Editorial Ctee Occupational and Environmental Med 1994–, GMC Fitness to Practise Panel 2003–06, Cncl BMA 2008–11, Ind Med Expert Gp Armed Forces Compensation Scheme 2009–; SE Thames regnl speciality advsr 1989–2005; FFOM 1987 (AFOM 1981, MFOM 1983), FRCP 1993 (MRCP 1972), FFOM(I) 2004, FFTMGlas 2006; *Publications* incl: Searching for Causes of Work-related Diseases: An Introduction to Epidemiology at the Work Site (jtly, 1991), ABC of Work-related Disorders (ed, 1997), ABC of Occupational and Environmental Medicine (ed, 2003, 2 edn 2012); *Recreations* travel, European languages, jazz music, mountaineering, cooking, gardening; *Style—* Prof David Snashall; ✉ 2 Charity Cottages, Petsoe End, Olney, Buckinghamshire MK46 5JL; Occupational Health and Safety Services, The Education Centre, St Thomas' Hospital, Westminster Bridge Road, London SE1 7EH (☎ 020 7188 4147)

SNEATH, Christopher George; s of Arthur George Sneath (d 1972), and Dorothy, *née* Knight (d 1989); *b* 27 June 1933; *Educ* Canford Sch; *m* 12 May 1962, Patricia Lesley, da of Anthony Spinks (d 1982); 1 da (Deborah Jane b 16 July 1963), 1 s (James Rupert b 19 Jan 1966); *Career* CA 1957; sr ptnr specialising in int business matters KPMG Peat Marwick 1978–94 (ptnr 1971–94), dep sec gen Peat Marwick Int 1978–80; receiver gen Order of St John 1991–98; dir: Spirax-Sarco Engineering plc 1994–2002, Millennium & Copthorne Hotels plc 1999–2010; vice-pres Saracens RFC (hon treas 1980–2005), dir Saracens Ltd 1996–2003; chm of govrs Queenswood Sch Herts 1999–2005 (govr 1989–2005), tstee The Sir Thomas Lipton Meml Home 1995–2009, dep chm Eastbourne Constituency Cons Assoc 2009–13, tstee Eastbourne Food Bank (chm 2014–); FCA; KStJ 1991; *Books* Guide to Acquisitions in the US (1989); *Recreations* watching cricket and rugby football, maintaining Lotus motor cars; *Clubs* Carlton, MCC, Pilgrims; *Style—* Christopher Sneath, Esq; ✉ Ascot House, Paradise Drive, Eastbourne, East Sussex BN20 7SX (☎ 01323 725709 (home), e-mail csneath@aol.com); ☎ 01323 725709 (office)

SNEATH, Christopher Gilbert; MBE (2013); s of Colin Frank Sneath, of Brookmans Park; *b* 25 June 1938; *Educ* Framlingham Coll; *m* 25 May 1963, Elizabeth Mary, da of Bernard Stephen Copson, of Potters Bar, Herts; 2 da (Lucy Jane b 1965, Julia Elizabeth b 1967); *Career* Nat Serv RCS 1957–59; md Barrett & Wright Group Ltd 1971–92, dir Phab UK Ltd 1991, sales and mktg dir A G Manly Group Ltd 1992–1999, dir C J Bartley & Co Ltd 1995–2000, conslt BSC Consulting; pres Heating & Ventilating Contractors Assoc 1990–91 and 1996; assessor Latham Review of Construction Industry 1994, conslt Building Services Research and Information Assoc 1998–2001, chm Construction Industry Sector Advsy Gp 1999–2001, dep chm Construction Industry Bd 1999–2001, chm Plumbing and Heating Industry Alliance 2001–08, chm Dep PM's Construction Health and Safety Task Ctee 1999–2001, chm WaterSafe Installers Scheme 2011–, chm Water Related Livery Companies 2013–14; chm Potters Bar and Dist Abbeyfield Soc 2002–03; tstee and memb Bd PHAB 2013– (chm London Area Clubs 1987); govr Mount Grace Sch; Master Worshipful Co of Plumbers 2010–11 (memb 1991, memb Ct of Assts 2006, Upper Warden 2009–10); CEng, FCIBSE, FCGI, hon fell Soc of Public Health Engrs, fell Chartered Inst of Plumbing and Heating Engrg; *Recreations* golf, marathon running; *Clubs* Brookmans Park Golf (capt 1980–81, pres 1994–99), Thorpeness Golf, RAC; *Style—* Christopher Sneath, Esq, MBE; ✉ 23 Shrublands, Brookmans Park, Hatfield, Hertfordshire AL9 7AL (☎ 01707 658709, e-mail cgsneath@dsl.pipex.com)

SNELL, HE Arthur Gordon; s of Roderick Saxon Snell, and Cecilia Mary, *née* Gordon Clark; *b* 30 October 1975, Brighton, E Sussex; *Educ* Bedales, Magdalen Coll Oxford (MA), Birkbeck Coll London (MSc); *m* Dr Charlotte Bigland; 1 da, 1 s; *Career* diplomat; joined FCO 1998, second sec (political) Harare 2000–01, second sec (political/economic) Abuja 2001–03, first sec (political) Sana'a 2003–05, first sec (political) Baghdad 2005–06, head of section ME Dept FCO 2006–08, dep head Counter Terrorism Dept FCO 2008–10, dep head of mission Helmand Civil-Military Mission Lashkar Gah 2010–11, high cmmr to Repub of Trinidad and Tobago 2011–15; *Publications* articles in Asian Affairs and Caribbean Journal of International Affairs; *Recreations* climbing mountains and skiing down them; *Clubs* Alpine, Savile, Travellers; *Style—* HE Mr Arthur Snell; ✉ c/o PGI, Level 2, 3 Sheldon Square, London W2 6HY

SNELL, Richard Owen; s of Richard Henry Snell, and Mildred, *née* Ratcliffe; *b* 5 September 1947, Colchester, Essex; *Educ* Univ of Leeds (BSc); *m* Sheila; 1 s (Richard James b 1976); *Career* Halcrow 1969–80; BP Exploration: joined 1980, head of UK civil engrg 1983–86, sr conslt 1986–92, ldr Structures and Naval Architecture 1992–2000, sr advsr 2000–04, Technical Authy 2004–07; dir Richard Snell Consulting Ltd; memb Standing Ctee on Structural Safety; Royal Acad of Engrg visiting prof Univ of Oxford; FREng, FICE 1996, FIStructE 2007; *Publications* author of several learned jls; *Recreations* yachting, travel, history; *Clubs* RYA, WMYC, RNVRYC (Rear Cdre); *Style—* Richard Snell, Esq, FREng; ✉ Richard Snell Consulting Ltd, 17 Links Road, Flackwell Heath, Buckinghamshire (☎ 01628 520161, e-mail richard@rosnell.co.uk)

SNELSON, Rear Adm David George; CB (2003); s of Mr and Mrs WM Snelson; *Educ* Alleyne's GS Uttoxeter, Britannia RN Coll Dartmouth; *Career* former CO HMS Ark Royal, former Cdr UK Maritime Forces; Chief Harbour Master Port of London Authy 2006; non exec dir Maritime and Coastguard agency 2012; non exec dir Milford Haven Port authy 2012; former tstee Marine Soc Sea Cadets 2012; Elder Brother Trinity House; former specialist advsr House of Commons Defence Ctee; memb Hon Co of Master Mariners; FNI (memb Cncl); Legion of Mert (US); *Recreations* sailing, reading; *Style—* Rear Adm David Snelson, CB; ✉ Maritime and Coastguard Agency, Spring Place, 105 Commercial Road, Southampton SO15 1EG

SNOOK, John Thomas; s of Bert Snook, and Elice, *née* Brew (d 1967); *b* 22 March 1954, Manchester; *Educ* Trinity Coll Cambridge (MA); *Partner* Amanda Chumas; *Career* chartered accountant; Deloitte, Haskins & Sells 1975–79, 3i 1979–83, Cinven 1983–85, co-fndr and managing ptnr CBPE Capital LLP 1985–; ACA 1979, MSI 1996; *Recreations* golf, vintage sports cars, reading; *Clubs* Royal Automobile; *Style—* John Snook, Esq; ✉ e-mail john@jsnook.plus.com

SNOW, Daniel Robert (Dan); s of Peter Snow, CBE, *qv*, and Ann Elizabeth MacMillan; *b* 3 December 1978, London; *Educ* St Paul's Sch Barnes, Balliol Coll Oxford; *m* Nov 2010, Lady Edwina Grosvenor, 2 da of Duke of Westminster, KG, CB, OBE, TD, DL, *qv*; *Career* television presenter and historian; *Television* incl: Beating Retreat (BBC 2) 2006, 20th Century Battlefields (BBC 2) 2006–08, Britain's Lost World (BBC 1) 2008, Hadrian (BBC 2) 2008, My Family at War (BBC 1) 2008, How the Celts Saved Britain (BBC 4) 2009, Montezuma (BBC 2) 2009, Battle for North America: The Battle of Quebec (BBC 2) 2010, The Empire of the Seas (BBC 2) 2010, Little Ships (BBC 2) 2010, Norman Walks (BBC 4) 2010, Filthy Cities (BBC 2) 2011, National Treasures Live (BBC 1) 2011, China's Terracotta Army (BBC 1) 2011, Rome's Lost Empire (BBC 1) 2012, Locomotion: Dan Snow's History of Railways (BBC 2) 2013, D Day: The Last Heroes (BBC 1) 2013; BAFTA Cymru, Voice of Listener and Viewer Special Award 2013; tstee The Tank Museum, pres Cncl for Br Archaeology, patron UK Armed Forces Humanist Assoc, ambass Electoral Reform Soc; hon Lt Cdr Royal Navy; *Books* Battlefield Britain (with Peter Snow, 2004), The World's Greatest Twentieth-century Battlefields (with Peter Snow, 2007), Death or Victory: the Battle of Quebec and the Birth of Empire (2009), Battle Castles: 500 Years of Knights and Siege Warfare (2012); *Style—* Mr Dan Snow; ✉ c/o United Agents, 12–26 Lexington Street, London W1F 0LE (Twitter @thehistoryguy)

SNOW, Jonathan George (Jon); s of Rt Rev George D'Oyly Snow, Bishop of Whitby (d 1977), and Joan Monica, *née* Way; *b* 28 September 1947; *Educ* St Edward's Sch Oxford, Univ of Liverpool; *m* 2010, Dr Precious Lunga; *Children* from previous relationship with Madeleine Colvin: 2 da (Leila Snow Colvin b 1982, Freya Snow Colvin b 1986); *Career* dir New Horizon Youth Centre Covent Garden 1970–73; journalist: LBC and IRN 1973–76, ITN 1976– (Washington corr 1983–86, diplomatic ed 1986–89); presenter Channel Four News 1989–; visiting prof: Nottingham Trent Univ 1992–2001, Univ of Stirling 2001–06; chllr Oxford Brookes Univ 2001–08; tstee: Nat Gallery 1999–, Tate Gallery 1999–04 (chair Members' Cncl Tate); dep chair Media Tst 1997–2015; chair New Horizon Youth Centre 1986–2016; *Books* Atlas of Today (1987), Sons and Mothers (1996), Shooting History: A Personal Journey (2004); *Style—* Jon Snow; ✉ ITN Ltd, 200 Gray's Inn Road, London WC1X 8XZ (☎ 020 7430 4237, fax 020 7430 4609)

SNOW, Peter John; CBE (2006); s of Brig John Fitzgerald Snow, CBE (Somerset LI, d 1973), and Peggy Mary, *née* Pringle (d 1970); *b* 20 April 1938; *Educ* Wellington, Balliol Coll Oxford (BA); *m* 1, 30 Sept 1964 (m dis 1975), Alison Mary, da of late George Fairlie

S

Carter, of Piltdown, E Sussex; 1 s (Shane Fitzgerald b 1966), 1 da (Shuna Justine b 1968); m 2, 15 May 1976, Ann Elizabeth, da of Dr Robert Laidlaw MacMillan, of Toronto, Canada; 1 s (Daniel Robert b 1978), 2 da (Rebecca Olwen b 1980, Katherine Peggy b 1983); *Career* Nat Serv 2 Lt Somerset LI 1956–58; dip and def corr ITN 1966–79 (reporter and newscaster 1962–66); presenter BBC TV: Newsnight and election progs 1979–97, Tomorrow's World 1997–2001, election progs 1997–2005; presenter (with s, Dan Snow) BBC TV: Battlefield Britain 2004, 20th Century Battles 2007, What Makes Britain Rich? 2007; BBC Radio 4: question master Mastermind, question master Masterteam 1998–2005, presenter Random Edition; Judges' Award for Outstanding Contribution to TV Journalism RTS Sports and Journalism Awards 1998; vice-patron Jubilee Sailing Tst; *Books* Leila's Hijack War (1970), Hussein: A Biography (1972), Battlefield Britain (with Dan Snow, 2004), The World's Greatest 20th Century Battlefields (with Dan Snow, 2007), To War with Wellington, from the Peninsula to Waterloo (2010), When Britain Burned the White House, the 1814 Invasion of Washington (2013), The Waterloo Experience (with Dan Snow, 2015); *Recreations* tennis, sailing, skiing, model railways; *Clubs* Athanaeum, Royal Cruising; *Style—* Peter Snow, Esq, CBE; ✉ c/o Athenaeum Club, 100 Pall Mall, London SW1Y 5ER

SNOWBALL, Joseph; s of Joseph Snowball (d 1960), and Gwendoline Alice, *née* Miles (d 1990); *b* 30 April 1946; *Educ* Cardiff HS; *m* 24 Oct 1970, Priscilla, da of Joseph Bennett; 1 s (Joseph Philip b 7 Sept 1973), 1 da (Carys Anne b 17 March 1976); *Career* Coopers & Lybrand CAs: articled clerk with predecessor firm 1962–68, ptnr in associate firm Lagos Nigeria 1978–81, ptnr in UK firm S Wales 1981–88, ptnr Gloucester office 1988–94; ptnr Gloucester office Guilfoyle Sage & Co 1994–2010 ret; FCA 1978 (ACA 1968); *Recreations* golf, rugby; *Clubs* Ross on Wye Golf; *Style—* Joseph Snowball, Esq; ✉ 33 Meek Road, Newent, Glos GL18 1UA(☎ 01531 828505, e-mail joseph.snowball@yahoo.co.uk)

SNOWBALL, Priscilla (Cilla); CBE (2009); *b* 1 October 1958; *Educ* Univ of Birmingham; *m* Geoff; 2 s (Fred, Albert), 1 da (Rosie); *Career* Abbott Mead Vickers BBDO: joined as new business dir 1992, rising to md then chief exec and gp chm 2006–; chm Women's Business Cncl 2016–; *Style—* Ms Cilla Snowball, CBE; ✉ Abbott Mead Vickers BBDO, Bankside 3, 90–100 Southwark Street, London SE1 0SW

SNOWDEN, Prof Sir Christopher Maxwell; kt (2012); s of William Arthur Snowden, of Cottingham, and Barbara Jeanne, *née* Locking; *b* 5 March 1956; *Educ* Univ of Leeds (BSc, MSc, PhD); *m* 8 Jan 1993, Irena, *née* Lewandowska; 2 s (James b 12 March 1994, William b 6 Aug 1996); *Career* applications engr Mullard Applications Lab Surrey 1977–78, lectr Dept of Electronics Univ of York 1982–83; Univ of Leeds: lectr rising to sr lectr Dept of Electronic and Electrical Engrg 1983–92, prof of microwave engrg (personal chair) 1992–2005, head Sch of Electronic and Electrical Engrg 1995–98, dir Inst of Microwaves and Photonics 1997–98; Filtronic plc: exec dir of technol 1998–99, jt chief exec 1999–2001, ceo compound semiconductors 2001–03, ceo Filtronic ICS 2003–05; pres and vice-chllr Univ of Surrey 2005–15, pres and vice-chllr Univ of Southampton 2015–; visiting prof physics Univ of Durham 2004–05; staff scientist M/A-COM Inc Corp R&D MA 1990–91; vice-chm European Microwave Assoc 2003–07; tstee Inst of Engrg and Technol (vice-pres 2006–07, dep pres 2007–09, pres 2009–10); dir: Engrg Technol Bd 2006–09, Defence Scientific Advsy Cncl 2007–; chair: S E England Science Engrg and Technol Advsy Cncl 2005–11, Engr Physical Sciences User Panel 2008–09; memb: Engrg and Physical Sciences Research Cncl 2006–12, Governing Body UK Technol Strategy Bd 2009–15, PM's Advsy Cncl for Science and Technol 2011–, UK Govt Foresight Advsy Bd 2011–; UK memb EU Cmmn Governing Bd Jt Research Centre 2011–12; chm Egrg Policy Gp and vice-pres Royal Acad of Egrg 2008–13; non-exec dir: Cenamps Ltd 2003–06, Intense Ltd 2004–09; chm The Daphne Jackson Charitable Tst 2005–09, chm Hero Ltd 2006–08; advsr First Ventures 2005–; patron: Surrey Community Devpt Tst 2005–09, Daphne Jackson Tst 2009–15, Surrey Youth Focus 2009–15; memb Cncl for Industry and HE 2006–, memb Bd Univs UK 2007– (chair Employability, Business and Industry Policy Gp Univs UK 2007–11, chm England and NI Cncl Univs UK 2011–13, vice-pres 2011–13, pres 2013–15), memb Governing Body Royal Surrey County Hosp NHS Tst 2009–11, dir Bd ERA Fndn 2010–; IEEE distinguished lectr (electron devices) 1996–2006, IEEE Microwave Prize 1999, Silver Medal Royal Acad of Engrg 2004, IEEE Distinguished Educator Award 2009, Outstanding Career Award European Microwave Assoc 2012; Hon DSc Univ of Strathclyde 2015, hon dr Univ of Leeds 2016; memb MIT Electromagnetics Acad; FIEE 1993, FIEEE 1996, FRSA 2000, FREng 2000, FRS 2005, FCGI 2005; *Publications* author of eight books and over 330 refereed journal and conference papers incl: Introduction to Semiconductor Device Modelling (1986, Japanese trans 1988), INCA Interactive Circuit Analysis (1988), Semiconductor Device Modelling (1988), Compound Semiconductor Device Modelling (1993); *Recreations* photography, oil painting; *Clubs* Athenaeum; *Style—* Prof Sir Christopher Snowden; ✉ Vice-Chancellor's Office, University of Southampton, University Road, Southampton SO17 1BJ (☎ 023 8059 5000, e-mail vice-chancellor@soton.ac.uk)

SNOWDEN, Hon Mr Justice; Sir Richard Andrew; kt (2015), QC (2003); s of Dr Paul Snowden, and Patricia, *née* Gatenby; *b* 22 March 1962, Reading; *Educ* Sir William Turner's Sixth Form Coll Redcar Cleveland, Downing Coll Cambridge (MA), Harvard Law Sch (LLM); *m* 3 Sept 1988, Kirsti Niinisalo-Snowden, *née* Niinisalo; 2 s (William b 16 Oct 1991, James b 14 Jan 1994); *Career* called to the Bar Lincoln's Inn (Denning Scholar, bencher) 1986, recorder 2007, dep judge of the High Court 2008, judge of the High Court of Justice (Chancery Div) 2015–; *Books* Lightman & Moss: The Law of Administrators and Receivers of Companies (5 edn); *Recreations* rowing, golf, cricket, rugby refereeing, opera; *Clubs* Rye Golf, Bewl Bridge Rowing; *Style—* The Hon Mr Justice Snowden; ✉ Royal Courts of Justice, Fetter Lane, London EC4A INL (☎ 020 7073 0304, e-mail wendy.simpson@hmcts.gsi.gov.uk)

SNOWDON, 1 Earl of (UK 1961); Sir Antony Charles Robert Armstrong-Jones; GCVO (1969); also Viscount Linley (UK 1961), and Baron Armstrong-Jones (Life Peer UK 1999), of Nymans in the County of West Sussex; sits as Baron Armstrong-Jones; s of Ronald Owen Lloyd Armstrong-Jones, MBE, QC, DL (d 1966), of Plas Dinas, Caernarfon, and Anne, *née* Messel, later Countess of Rosse (d 1992); *b* 7 March 1930; *Educ* Eton, Jesus Coll Cambridge; *m* 1, 6 May 1960 (m dis 1978), HRH The Princess Margaret Rose (d 2002), yr da of HM the late King George VI; 1 s, 1 da; m 2, 15 Dec 1978, Lucy Mary, da of Donald Brook Davies, of Hemingstone Hall, Ipswich, and formerly w of Michael Lindsay-Hogg (film dir, s of Edward Lindsay-Hogg, gs of Sir Lindsay Lindsay-Hogg, 1 Bt, JP); 1 da (Lady Frances b 17 July 1979); *Heir* s, Viscount Linley (*see* Royal Family section); *Career* photographer and designer; artistic advsr Sunday Times and Sunday Times Publications 1962–90, The Telegraph Magazine 1990–95, consultative advsr to Design Cncl London 1962–87, editorial advsr Design Magazine 1962–87; designer: Snowdon Aviary for London Zoo (in collaboration with Cedric Price and Frank Newby, Grade 2 listed 1998) 1965, for investiture of HRH the Prince of Wales at Caernarfon Castle (in collaboration with Carl Toms, CBE and John Pound, CBE) 1969, electrically-powered wheelchair for disabled people (Chairmobile) 1972; pres: Contemporary Art Soc for Wales until 1995, Civic Tst for Wales, Welsh Theatre Co, Gtr London Arts Assoc, Int Year of Disabled People England (1981), ADAPT (Access for Disabled People to Arts Premises Today) 1995–; vice-pres Bristol Univ Photographic Soc; memb: Cncl of Nat Fund for Research into Crippling Diseases, Faculty of Designers for Industry, The Prince of Wales Advsy Gp on Disability; patron: Metropolitan Union of YMCAs, British Water Ski Fedn, Welsh Nat Rowing Club, Physically Handicapped and Able-Bodied, Circle of Guide Dog Owners, Demand, Disabled Water Skiing Assoc; fndr Snowdon Award Scheme for Disabled Students 1980; provost RCA 1995– (sr fell 1986); Constable of Caernarfon Castle 1963–; Liveryman Worshipful Co of Clothworkers; fell Manchester Coll of Art and Design, hon fell Inst of Br Photographers; Hon DUniv Bradford 1989; Hon LLD: Univ of Bath 1989, Univ of Southampton 1993; RDI, FRSA, FSIAD, FRPS; *Exhibitions* Photocall London 1958, Assignments (Photokina) 1972, London 1973, Brussels 1974, Los Angeles, St Louis, Kansas, New York and Tokyo 1975, Sydney and Melbourne 1976, Copenhagen 1976, Paris 1977, Amsterdam 1977; Serendipity Brighton 1989 (also at Bradford 1989, Bath 1990), Photographs by Snowdon – a retrospective (Nat Portrait Gallery) 2000 (also at City Arts Centre Edinburgh 2000, Kunst Haus Wien Vienna 2001, Yale Center for British Art New Haven 2001); *Television* TV films: Don't Count the Candles (CBS 1968, winner two Hollywood Emmys, St George Prix, Venice Dip, Prague and Barcelona Film Festival award), Love of a Kind (BBC 1969), Born to be Small (ATV 1971, Chicago Hugo award), Happy being Happy (ATV 1973), Mary Kingsley (BBC 1975), Burke and Wills (1975), Peter, Tina and Steve (ATV 1977), Snowdon on Camera (BBC 1981, BAFTA nomination); *Awards* Art Dirs Club of NY Certificate of Merit 1969; Soc of Publication Designers: Cert of Merit 1970, Designers Award of Excellence 1973; Wilson Hicks Cert of Merit for Photocommunication 1971, Design and Art Directors Award 1978, Royal Photographic Soc Hood Award 1979; *Books* Malta (in collaboration with Sacheverell Sitwell, 1958), London (1958), Private View (in collaboration with John Russell and Bryan Robertson, 1965), Assignments (1972), A View of Venice (1972), The Sack of Bath (1972), Inchcape Review (1977), Pride of the Shire (in collaboration with John Oaksey, 1979), Personal View (1979), Tasmania Essay (1981), Sittings (1983), My Wales (in collaboration with Viscount Tonypandy, 1986), Israel – a First View (1986), Stills 1984–1987 (1987), Public Appearances 1987–1991 (1991), Wild Flowers (1995), Snowdon on Stage (1996), Wild Fruit (1997), London Sight Unseen (1999), Snowdon – a Retrospective (2000), Snowdon on Russia (2005), India by Snowdon (2008), Snowdon – A Life in View (2014); *Style—* The Rt Hon the Earl of Snowdon, GCVO; ✉ 22 Launceston Place, London W8 5LR (☎ 020 7937 1524, fax 020 7938 1727)

SNOWDON, Clive John; s of Harry Stanley Snowdon (d 1993), and Elizabeth Florence, *née* Taylor; *b* 7 June 1953, Stockport, Cheshire; *Educ* Univ of Leeds (BA); *m* 5 Aug 1978, Ann Louise, *née* Brimble; 2 s (Thomas b 10 Sept 1985, Jack b 27 Aug 1993), 1 da (Amy b 9 July 1986); *Career* md Burnfield plc 1992–97, chief exec Umeco plc 1997–; dir: Hill and Smith Gp plc, Midlands Aerospace Alliance; FT Entrepreneur of the Year 2008; FCA 1977; *Style—* Clive Snowdon, Esq; ✉ UMECO plc, Concorde House, Warwick New Road, Leamington Spa, Warwickshire CV32 5JG (☎ 01926 331800, e-mail clivesnowdon@umeco.com)

SNOWDON, Graham Richard; s of Thomas Richard Snowdon (d 1970), of Doncaster, S Yorks, and Edna Mary, *née* Storm (d 1997); *b* 8 February 1944; *Educ* Doncaster GS; *m* 5 Aug 1967, Peta Dawn, da of Frederick Alfred Rawlings (d 1992), of Lowestoft, Suffolk; 1 da (Jessica Louise (Mrs Andrew Friend) b 21 March 1972), 1 s (Frazer Richard b 6 March 1974); *Career* jr reporter: Barnsley Chronicle 1960–61, Yorkshire Evening News 1961–63; family sports agency Doncaster 1963–64, competitions press offr RAC Motor Sport Div London 1964–66, northern press offr RAC Manchester 1966–70, freelance sports journalist 1969–, regular contrib Daily Telegraph 1969–2007; cycling corr: The Guardian 1985–97, Press Assoc 1990–2007; ptnr Snowdon Sports Editorial 1970–2007, dir Snowdon Sports Media Ptnrs Ltd 2002– (md 2002–07); conslt Guinness Book of Records 1971–95; *Books* Pieces In A Jigsaw – A Family Perspective (2014); *Recreations* food and drink, walking, travel, motoring, autonumerology, heritage railways, wildlife (Companion WWF-UK), genealogy; *Clubs* Sports Journalists' Assoc of GB, Assoc Internationale des Journalistes du Cyclisme, Assoc Internationale de la Presse Sportive, NUJ (life memb 2006), Yorks Soc, North York Moors Historical Railway Tst, Hallam Wine Guild, CAMRA, Fulwood Sports, Stumperlowe Probus; *Style—* Graham Snowdon, Esq; ✉ 6 Hallam Grange Croft, Fulwood, Sheffield S10 4BP (☎ 0114 230 2233, e-mail mail@snowdon.gr); 43 Eastgate, Pickering, North Yorkshire YO18 7DU (☎ 01751 477581); Snowdon Sports Media Partners Ltd, PO Box 100, Sheffield S6 6YB (☎ 0114 232 5555, e-mail graham@snowdons.co.uk, website www.snowdons.com)

SNOWDON, Lisa; *b* 23 January 1972; *Career* model and presenter; cover shots for pubns incl: Vogue, Marie Claire, Elle; model for Marks and Spencer advertising campaign 2010, face of Belvita campaign; television presenting incl: MTV Select (MTV), Britain's Next Top Model, Something for the Weekend, Waitrose Weekend (Channel 4) 2014; co-presenter (with Johnny Vaughan, *qv*, then Dave Berry) breakfast show Capital London 2008–; Breakfast Show of the Year 2014 Radio Academy Award (Gold); *Style—* Miss Lisa Snowdon; ✉ Capital FM, 30 Leicester Square, London WC2H 7LA; c/o Money Talent Management, 42A Berwick Street, London W1F 8RZ

SNOWIE, Malcolm McDonald; s of James Tait Snowie, of East Gogar, Stirling (d 1977), and Sheila Fenwick, *née* McDonald; *b* 31 March 1959, Bridge of Allan, Stirlingshire; *Educ* Morrisons Acad Crieff; *m* 1, 25 June 1982 (m dis 2003), Heather, *née* Raeburn; 1 da (Lesley b 30 June 1987), 1 s (Calum b 3 March 1990); m 2, 6 May 2006, Amanda, *née* Buitelaar; 1 step s (James b 3 Aug 1985), 1 step da (Sarah b 3 Aug 1994); *Career* farmer; md and shareholder: Snowie Holdings Ltd, Snowie Ltd, Northern Hydroseeding Ltd, Barnhill Estates, Uphall Estates Ltd; dir and shareholder: M&A Ind Trading Co Ltd, Scot Heating Co Ltd; former dir Royal Highland Agricultural Soc, memb Bd Oatridge Agric Coll; memb Inst of Waste Mgmnt; *Recreations* hunting, shooting, sailing; *Style—* Malcolm Snowie, Esq; ✉ Tree Tops, Storrs Park, Windermere, Cumbria LA23 3LY (☎ 01506 444255, e-mail malcolm@scotheating.co.uk); Uphall Business Park, Uphall, Broxburn EH52 5NT (website www.scotheating.co.uk)

SNOWMAN, Daniel; s of Arthur Mortimer Snowman (d 1982), and Bertha, *née* Lazarus (d 1997); *b* 4 November 1938; *Educ* Jesus Coll Cambridge, Cornell Univ NY (MA); *m* 1975 (m dis 2014), Janet Linda, *née* Levison; 1 s (Benjamin b 1977), 1 da (Anna b 1978); *Career* broadcaster, writer and lectr; lectr Univ of Sussex 1963–67; prodr features arts and education BBC Radio 1968–95; prodns incl: A World in Common, The Vatican, Reith Lectures, Northern Lights (BBC Arctic Festival), variety of historical and cultural programmes; visiting prof of history Calif State Univ 1972–73, sr research fell Inst of Historical Research London; contrib to British and US newspapers and jls; *Books* America Since 1920 (1968), Eleanor Roosevelt (1970), Kissing Cousins: An Interpretation of British and American Culture, 1945–75 (1977), If I Had Been ... Ten Historical Fantasies (1979), The Amadeus Quartet: The Men and the Music (1981), The World of Plácido Domingo (1985), Beyond the Tunnel of History (1990), Pole Positions: The Polar Regions and the Future of the Planet (1993), Plácido Domingo's Tales from the Opera (1994), Fins de Siècle (with Lord Briggs, *qv*, 1996), PastMasters: The Best of History Today (2001), The Hitler Emigrés: The Cultural Impact on Britain of Refugees from Nazism (2002), Historians (2007), Hallelujah! An Informal History of the London Philharmonic Choir (2007), The Gilded Stage: A Social History of Opera (2009), Giuseppe Verdi (2014); *Recreations* singing with London Philharmonic Choir (former chm); *Style—* Daniel Snowman, Esq; ✉ website www.danielsnowman.org.uk

SNOWMAN, (Michael) Nicholas; s of Kenneth Snowman (d 2002), and Sallie, *née* Moghi-Levkine (d 1995); *b* 18 March 1944; *Educ* Hall Sch, Highgate Sch, Magdalene Coll Cambridge (BA); *m* 1983, Margo Michelle Rouard; 1 s; *Career* asst to Head of Music Staff Glyndebourne Festival Opera 1967–69, co-fndr and gen mangr London Sinfonietta 1968–72, admin Music Theatre Ensemble 1968–71, artistic dir Institut de Recherche et de Co-ordination Acoustique/Musique (IRCAM) Centre d'Art et de Culture Georges

Pompidou 1972–86; Ensemble InterContemporain Paris: co-fndr 1975, artistic advsr 1975–92, memb Bd 1992–, vice-chm 1998–; The South Bank Centre: gen dir (Arts) 1986–92, chief exec 1992–98; gen dir Glyndebourne Festival Opera 1998–2000, chm Wartski 2002– (co-chm 1997–2002), gen dir Opéra National du Rhin (Strasbourg, Mulhouse, Colmar) 2002–; govr Royal Acad of Music 1998– (Hon RAM); memb Music Ctee Venice Biennale 1979–86; Festival d'Automne de Paris: artistic dir Stravinsky 1980, Webern 1981, Boulez 1983; prog conslt Cité de la Musique La Villette Paris 1991; memb Br Section Franco-Br Cncl 1995–2000; tstee New Berlioz Edn 1996–, memb Comité Hector Berlioz 2000–; Officier de l'Ordre des Arts et des Lettres (France) 1990 (Chevalier 1985), Order of Cultural Merit (Poland) 1990, Chevalier dans l'Ordre National du Mérite (France) 1995; *Books* The Best of Granta (co-ed, 1967), The Contemporary Composers (series ed); author of papers and articles on music, architecture and cultural policy; *Recreations* films, eating, spy novels, France; *Clubs* Garrick; *Style*— Nicholas Snowman

SNYDER, Sir Michael John; kt (2008); s of Percy Elsworth Snyder (d 1953), and Pauline Edith, *née* Davenport; *b* 30 July 1950; *Educ* Brentwood Sch, City of London Coll; *m* 14 Dec 1974, Mary Barbara, da of Rev Wilfrid Edgar Dickinson; 2 da (Julia Caroline b 10 Nov 1976, Susanna Jane b 9 Sept 1978); *Career* chartered accountant; sr ptnr until 2016: Kingston Smith LLP, Kingston Smith Consulting LLP, Kingston Smith & Ptnrs LLP, Devonshire Corporate Services LLP; chm: KS International, Kingston Smith Ltd, Devonshire Corp Fin Ltd, Balance People Ltd, HR Insight Ltd, London Wholesales Business Loans Ltd, Gateway to London; dir GLE Loan Finance Ltd; former chm: Professional and Business Services Gp, National Business Angels Network, Cheviot Capital Ltd; Corp of London: former chm Policy and Resources Ctee, dep ward of Cordwainer, memb Finance Ctee, chm Guildhall Improvement Ctee; memb Securities Inst; chm Assoc of Practising Accountants, co-chm Professional and Business Services Cncl until 2015; memb Bd Thames Gateway London Partnership, former co-chm Chancellor's Professional Services Competitiveness Gp, memb Chancellor's High Level Taskforce in Financial Services; govr City of London Sch for Girls until 2016, vice-chm, hon treas and govr Brentwood Sch; common councilman City of London; Past Master, Liveryman and Memb of the Ct of Tallow Chandlers, Past Master Worshipful Co of Needlemakers; DSc City Univ 2001; FCA 1978 (ACA 1973), FInstD, MSI, FRSA, fell Royal Acad of Arts; Grand Cross Order of Merit (Germany) 1998; *Recreations* inland waterways, music, bridge; *Clubs* City Livery, Cordwainer Ward (vice-pres), City Pickwick; *Style*— Sir Michael Snyder

SOAMES, Hon Emma Mary; da of Baron Soames, GCMG, GCVO, CH, CBE, PC (Life Peer; d 1987), and Lady Soames, DBE, *née* Spencer-Churchill (d 2014); sis of Hon Rupert Soames, OBE, *qv* and Hon Nicholas Soames, MP, *qv*; *b* 6 September 1949; *m* 4 July 1981 (m dis 1989), James MacManus, assist ed The Times, s of Dr Niall MacManus, of London; 1 da (Emily Fiona b 1983); *Career* formerly: journalist Evening Standard, ed Literary Review, features ed Vogue, ed Tatler, freelance journalist, dep ed The Oldie 1991–92, ed ES Magazine (Evening Standard) 1992–94; ed Telegraph Magazine 1994–2002; Saga Magazine: ed 2002–08, ed-at-large 2008–; tstee: Rehabilitation of Addicted Prisoners Tst (RAPT), Fine Cell Work; *Clubs* Groucho, Other; *Style*— The Hon Emma Soames; ✉ 26 Eland Road, London SW11 5JY

SOAMES, Rt Hon Sir (Arthur) Nicholas Winston; kt (2014), PC (2011), MP; s of Baron Soames, GCMG, GCVO, CH, CBE, PC (Life Peer; d 1987), and Lady Soames, DBE, *née* Spencer-Churchill (d 2014), da of late Sir Winston Churchill and Baroness Spencer-Churchill; bro of Hon Rupert Soames, OBE, *qv* and Hon Emma Soames, *qv*; *b* 12 February 1948; *Educ* Eton; *m* 1, 1981 (m dis 1988), Catherine, da of Capt Tony Weatherall, of Dumfries; 1 s (Arthur Harry David b 1985); m 2, 21 Dec 1993, Serena Mary, da of Sir John Lindsay Eric Smith, CBE, JP, DL, of Shottesbrooke Park, Maidenhead, Berks; 1 da (Isabella b 1996), 1 s (Christopher b 2001); *Career* served 11 Hussars 1967–72, extra equerry to HRH The Prince of Wales 1970–72, Lloyd's insurance broker 1972–74, PA to Sir James Goldsmith 1974–76, PA to US Senator Mark Hatfield 1976–78, asst dir Sedgwick Group 1979–81; Parly candidate (Cons) Central Dumbartonshire 1979; MP (Cons): Crawley 1983–97, Sussex Mid 1997–; PPS to Rt Hon John Selwyn Gummer as Min of State for Employment and Chm of the Cons Party 1984–86, sec Cons Foreign Affrs Ctee 1986–87, PPS to the Rt Hon Nicholas Ridley 1987–89, PPS to Sec of State DTI 1989–92, Parly sec Min of Agric Fisheries and Food 1992–94, min of state (armed forces) MOD 1994–97, shadow sec of state for defence 2003–05; pres Cons ME Cncl; *Clubs* White's, Turf, Pratt's, Beefsteak; *Style*— The Rt Hon Sir Nicholas Soames, MP; ✉ House of Commons, London SW1A 0AA (☏ 020 7219 4143, e-mail nicholas.soames.mp@parliament.uk, website www.nicholassoames.org.uk)

SOAMES, Hon Rupert Christopher; OBE (2010); s of Baron Soames, GCMG, GCVO, CH, CBE, PC (Life Peer; d 1987), and Lady Soames, DBE, *qv*, *née* Spencer-Churchill; bro of Hon Emma Soames, *qv* and Hon Nicholas Soames, MP, *qv*; *b* 18 May 1959; *Educ* Eton, Worcester Coll Oxford (BA, pres Oxford Union 1980); *m* 1988, Camilla Rose, eldest da of Sir Thomas Raymond Dunne, of Gatley Park, Leominster, Herefordshire; 2 s (Arthur Christopher b 3 Feb 1990, Jack Winston b 20 Sept 1994), 1 da (Daisy b 2 April 1992); *Career* GEC plc: joined 1981, former md subsid Avery Berkel UK; Misys plc: joined 1997, chief exec Misys Banking and Securities Div, chief exec Aggreko plc 2003–14, chief exec Serco plc 2014–; non-exec dir Electrocomponents plc 2007–; *Clubs* Turf, White's, Pratt's; *Style*— The Hon Rupert Soames, OBE

SOANE, James; s of Alastair Soane, and Elizabeth Soane; *b* 31 August 1966; *Educ* Univ of Cambridge (MA), Bartlett Sch of Architecture UCL (DipArch, RIBA); *Partner* Christopher Ash; *Career* architect and designer; dir Project Orange 2001–; projects incl: Park Hotel Mumba India 2007, Orange Cottage Lavenham 2007, Whitechapel Gallery Dining Room 2009, I-talia restaurant Delhi, Jerwood Sch of Art and Technol Oakham, Zone Hotels India 2015, 1 Zhukov Moscow 2016; dir Conran & Partners 1999–2001 (joined 1992), studio master Bartlett 2001–04; studio teacher Kingston Univ 1992–97, visiting lectr Univ of Cape Town; visiting critic: Univ of Cambridge, RCA, South Bank Univ; chair RIBA New Courses 2010–15, dir of critical practice London Sch of Architecture 2015–; contrib: Evening Standard, Architect's Jl; *Publications* New Homes (2003), Catalogue (2003), PO Box (2010), A Gendered Profession (2016); *Recreations* walking, travelling, eating out, gardening, saunas, shopping; *Clubs* Shoreditch House; *Style*— James Soane, Esq; ✉ Project Orange, 1st Floor, Cosmopolitan House, 10A Christina Street, London EC2A 4PA (☏ 020 7739 3035, fax 020 7739 0103, e-mail mail@projectorange.com, website www.projectorange.com)

SOANES, Quentin Bruce; s of Bryan John Soanes (d 1974), and Beverley Charlotte, *née* Taylor (d 1977); *b* 20 January 1955, Australia; *Educ* Monmouth Sch, Univ of London (BA); *m* 22 Oct 1977, Verra, *née* Pavlovic; 2 s (Dorian Alexander b 15 Sept 1981, Dominik Bruce b 20 May 1984); *Career* H Clarkson & Co Ltd 1976–83, md Braemar Seascope Ltd (formerly Braemar Shipbrokers Ltd) 1983–2012, exec dir Braemar Shipping Servs plc 2007–12, md Dragon Shipping Servs Ltd 2012–14; chm: Cory Brothers Shipping Agency Ltd 2003–12, Braemar Howells Ltd 2005–12, Braemar Engrg Ltd 2009–12, Braemar Technical Servs 2011–12, Baltic Exchange Ltd 2012–14, Sterling Shipping Servs Ltd 2014–; *Recreations* long distance triathlon, indoor rowing, skiing; *Style*— Quentin Soanes, Esq; ✉ Thorneycroft, 17 Greenway, Hutton Mount, Brentwood, Essex CM13 2NR (☏ 01277 212888, e-mail qbsoanes@hotmail.com)

SOAR, Sarah Jane Spencer; *née* Lund; da of William Lund (d 2010), and Patricia, *née* Miles; *b* 1 January 1962, Oxford; *Educ* Headington Sch Oxford, Sherborne, Univ Coll of North Wales (BSc), Securities Inst (Dip); *m* 21 May 1988, Jonathan Soar; 2 da (Emily Mary b 10 Jan 1993, Sophie Jane b 28 May 1995); *Career* Brewin Dolphin Hldgs plc 1984–91 and 1994–2013 (memb Bd 2007–13, nat dir and business devpt dir), head Marlborough Office Seymour Pierce Butterfield 1991–94, head of investment mgmnt J M Finn and Co 2014–; memb Bd Wealth Mgmnt Assoc (WMA) 2016–; former chm Bd of Govrs St Francis Sch Pewsey; memb Securities Inst 1987, memb Cncl Inst of Dirs 2013–; *Recreations* walking, yoga, swimming, travel, theatre, reading; *Clubs* St Mary's Sports; *Style*— Mrs Sarah Soar; ✉ 1 Forsyte House, Chelsea Manor Street, London SW3 3TR (☏ 07786 195055, e-mail sarah.soar@icloud.com); J M Finn & Co, 4 Coleman Street, London EC2R 5TA

SOBOLEWSKI, Dr Stanislaw; s of Kazimierz Sobolewski (d 1979), of Scunthorpe, and Bronislawa Sobolewska (d 1989); *b* 9 February 1943; *Educ* Bialystok GS Poland, Med Acad of Bialystok Poland (MB BS), Univ of Bradford (PhD); *m* 1, 1968 (m dis 1976), Elizabeth, *née* Olszewska; 2 da (Marta b 1970, Anastasia b 1972), 1 s (Edward b 1974); m 2, Patricia, da of George Pearson (decd), of Rawmarsh, Rotherham, S Yorks; *Career* Grajewo Hosp Poland 1967, Olecko Hosp Poland 1968–70, sr house offr in rheumatology Harrogate 1971–72, registrar in pathology Sheffield 1974–77 (registrar in clinical haematology 1972–74), sr registrar in haematology Leeds and Bradford, conslt haematologist Trent RHA S Lincs Dist Boston; regnl rep RCPath, fndr chm Trent Region Haematology Sub Ctee, chm Boston Leukaemia and Cancer Fund, memb Med Exec Ctee Pilgrim Hosp; ACP 1974, memb Br Soc of Haematology 1976, MRCS 1976, LRCP 1976, MRCPath 1979; *Books* A New Function of Megakaryoctes in Malignancy (1986); *Recreations* classic cars restoration, swimming, football; *Clubs* Polish Social (Scunthorpe); *Style*— Dr Stanislaw Sobolewski; ✉ Pinewood, 32 Linden Way, Boston, Lincolnshire PE21 9DS (☏ 01205 351655); Consultant Haematologist, Pilgrim Hospital, Sibsey Road, Boston Lincolnshire PE21 9QS (☏ 012053 64801)

SODANO, Sandro; s of Massimo Sodano, and Alfonsina, *née* De Vita; *b* Newport, Wales; *Educ* St Joseph's RC Comp Sch Newport, Newport Coll of Art and Design, St Martin's Sch of Art (BA); *m* 4 Sept 1998 (m dis 2003), Piera Beradi; 1 da (Constanza Velvet b 19 June 2001); *Career* photographer; estab ABOUD SODANO with Alan K Aboud, *qv* 1990 (currently creative dir); photographer Royal Mail Stamp collection 2001; subject of documentary: Shillouette (Japan) 2001, Jigsaw (ITV) 2003; *Awards* D&AD Silver 1997; *Publications* Growing (co-author, 1995), subject of The End (2002); *Recreations* film, cooking; *Style*— Sandro Sodano, Esq; ✉ ABOUD SODANO, Studio 26, Pall Mall Deposit, 124–128 Barlby Road, London W10 6BL (☏ 020 8968 6142, fax 020 8968 6143, e-mail mail@aboud-sodano.com, www.aboud-sodano.com)

SODOR AND MAN, Bishop of 2008–; Rt Rev Robert Mar Erskine Paterson; s of David Donaldson Paterson (d 1969), and Letitia, *née* Jones (d 1997); *b* 27 February 1949, Cardiff; *Educ* King Henry VIII Sch Coventry, Univ of Durham (BA, DipTh, MA); *m* 17 July 1971, Pauline Anne, *née* Laing; 1 s (Simeon b 14 Sept 1975), 2 da (Naomi b 17 Aug 1977, Rebecca b 27 Nov 1979); *Career* princ offr Church of Wales Cncl for Mission and Miny 2000–06, canon Province of Wales 2004, chaplain and researcher to Archbishop of York 2006; *Recreations* gardening, reading, walking; *Style*— The Rt Rev the Lord Bishop of Sodor and Man; ✉ Thie yn Aspick, 4 The Falls, Douglas, Isle of Man IM4 4PZ (☏ 01624 622108, e-mail bishop@sodorandman.im, website www.sodorandman.im)

SOLARI, Vivien Juliet Emma; da of Victor Solari (d 2004), of Hants, and Annette Anderson, of Cheshire; *b* 11 November 1978, Aruba; *Educ* Ridge Danyers Coll Stockport, Univ of Leicester; *m* 20 July 2001, Nick Mills; *Career* fashion model 1998–; face of Radical Fashion exhbn V&A 2001–02; campaigns incl: Giorgio Armani cosmetics, Versace Versus perfume, Giorgio Armani Mania perfume, Calvin Klein, Christian Dior cosmetics, Jil Sander perfume, Vera Wang perfume, DKNY, Ralph Lauren, GAP, Sportmax, Bottega Veneta, Missoni, Burberry, Hermes, Patek Phillipe, Evian, Joop, Oil of Olay, Issey Miyake, Clarins skincare, Very Valentino perfume; catwalk shows (NY, Paris, Milan and London) incl: Calvin Klein, DKNY, Bottega Veneta, Christian Dior, Kenzo, Paul Smith, Burberry, Helmut Lang, Christian Lacroix, Fendi, Chanel, Nicole Farhi, Julien MacDonald, Diane von Furstenberg, VH1 Fashion Awards, Prince's Tst Fashion Rocks; appeared on cover of int magazines incl: Vogue (France, UK, Aust and Spain), Numero (France), Marie Claire (Italy and France), Elle (Italy and France), Surface (USA), Oyster (Aust), Amica (Italy), Donna (Italy), L'Officiel (France); featured in numerous editorials for magazines incl: W, Vogue (USA, UK, Italy, France, Aust, Russia and Germany), Elle (UK, USA and France), ID, Dazed and Confused, The Face, Visionnaire, Marie Claire (UK, Italy and France), 10; *Recreations* running, music, gardening; *Clubs* New Forest Runners; *Style*— Ms Vivien Solari; ✉ c/o ICM Models, 2nd Floor, 2 Henrietta Street, London WC2E 8PS (☏ 020 775 5110)

SOLEY, Baron (Life Peer UK 2005), of Hammersmith in the London Borough of Hammersmith and Fulham; Clive Stafford Soley; *b* 7 May 1939; *Educ* Downshal Secdy Modern, Newbattle Abbey Adult Educn Coll, Univ of Strathclyde (BA), Univ of Southampton (Dip Applied Soc Studies); *Career* probation offr 1970–75, sr probation offr 1975–79; MP (Lab): Hammersmith N 1979–83, Hammersmith 1983–97, Ealing, Acton and Shepherd's Bush 1997–2005; chm PLP 1997–2001; oppn front bench spokesman: on NI 1982–85, on home affrs 1985–87, on housing and local govt 1987–89, on housing and planning 1989–92; chm NI Affairs Select Ctee 1995–97 (memb 1994–97), memb Modernisation House of Commons Select Ctee 1998–2001, memb Jt Ctee on House of Lords Reform House of Commons 2002–05, memb Delegated Powers and Regulatory Reform Select Ctee House of Lords 2002–05, memb Constitutional Affrs Ctee House of Commons 2003–05, chm Draft Children (Contact) and Adoption Bill Jt Ctee House of Commons 2005, chm Intergovernmental Orgns Select Ctee House of Lords 2007–08, memb Inquiries Act 2005 Select Ctee House of Commons 2013–14, memb Arctic Select Ctee House of Commons 2014–15, memb EU Sub-Ctee on Home Affrs House of Lords 2015–; memb Standing Ctee: Prevention of Terrorism Bill 1983–84, Criminal Justice Bill 1987–88, Housing Bill 1987–88, Local Govt and Housing Bill 1988–89, Planning and Compensation Bill 1990–91, Freedom and Responsibility of the Press Bill 1992–93; memb NEC Lab Pty; fell Industry and Parliament Tst; memb GMB; campaign dir Future Heathrow 2005–10; chair: Mary Seacole Meml Statue Appeal 2004–, Arab-Jewish Forum 2005–14; chm and dir Good Governance Fndn 2010–15; *Publications* Regulating the Press (with Tom O'Malley); *Recreations* walking, photography, scuba diving; *Style*— The Rt Hon the Lord Soley; ✉ House of Lords, London SW1A 0PW

SOLOMON, David; s of Leslie Ezekiel Solomon, of London, and Peggy, *née* Shatzman; *b* 6 August 1948; *Educ* Clarks Coll, City of London Coll; *m* 1, 15 July 1973 (m dis 1986), Sarah-Lou Reekie; 1 s (Tony Daniel b 1980); m 2, 25 Nov 1997, Carol Stern; *Career* began in advertising with Garland-Compton, fndr Pink-Soda Fashion Co 1983 (opened Euro Office in Paris 1988, sold 2009), currently runs fashion and beauty product consultancy and mature model agency; winner Queen's Award for Export Achievement 1987, BKCEC Award for Export Achievement (awarded by HRH The Princess Royal); MInstMSM; *Recreations* running, boxing; *Style*— David Solomon, Esq; ✉ e-mail davidsolomon3@gmail.com

SOLOMON, Prof David Henry; AM (1990); s of H J Solomon, and Mary Solomon; *b* 19 November 1929, Adelaide, Aust; *Educ* Sydney Tech Coll (Dip), NSW Univ of Technol (BSc, MSc), Univ of NSW (PhD, DSc); *m* 28 Jan 1954, Harriet Valerie Dawn, da of Albert Henry Charles Newport; 3 da; *Career* with BALM Paints Ltd 1946–63 (ldr Resin and Polymer Resin 1955–63), demonstrator and teaching fell NSW Inst of Technol 1953–55; CSIRO: chief research scientist Div of Applied Mineralogy 1963–70, chief research

S

scientist Div of Applied Chemistry 1970–74, chief Div of Chemicals and Polymers 1974–89, dep dir Inst of Industrial Technol 1989–90; ICI Aust-Masson prof of chemistry and head Sch of Chemistry Univ of Melbourne 1990–94, professorial fell Dept of Chemical and Biomolecular Engrg Univ of Melbourne 1996–; dir Gradipore Ltd 1989–91; memb: Steering Ctee Strategic Review of Chemistry Research in Aust RACI 1991–92, Selection Ctee Aust Acad of Sci 1991–, Pubns Ctee and Activities Ctee Aust Acad of Technological Sci and Engrg 1991–; pres RACI 1979–80; Archibald D Olle Prize RACI 1967, H G Smith Meml Medal RACI 1971, David Syme Research Prize Univ of Melbourne 1976, Polymer Medal RACI 1977, Applied Research Medal RACI 1980, Leighton Meml Medal and Lecture RACI 1985, CSIRO Medal 1987 and 1990, Australian Bicentennial Science Achievement Award 1988, Ian William Wark Medal and Lecture Australian Acad of Science 1989, Clunies Ross Science and Technol Award 1994, Centenary Medal 2003, Victoria Prize 2006, PM's Prize for Science (Australia) 2011; numerous named lectrs; Hon Dr of Applied Sci Univ of Melbourne; FRACI 1966, fndn fell Aust Acad of Technological Sci and Engrg (FTSE) 1975, FAA 1975, FRS 2004, FIChemE 2007; AC 2016; *Books* Chemistry of Organic Film Formers (1967, 2 edn 1977), Step-Growth Polymerizations: Kinetics and Mechanisms (ed, 1972), The Catalytic Properties of Pigments: Technical Association of the Pulp and Paper Industry Inc (1977), Chemistry of Pigments and Fillers (1983), The Chemistry of Free Radical Polymerization (1995), The Chemistry of Radical Polymerization (2006), Australia's Plastic Banknote: From Concept to Reality (2014); *Recreations* fishing; *Style*— Prof David Solomon, AC; ✉ Department of Chemical and Biomolecular Engineering, University of Melbourne, Victoria 3010, Australia (☎ 00 61 3 8344 8200, fax 00 61 3 8344 4153, e-mail davids@unimelb.edu.au)

SOLOMON, David Joseph; s of Sydney Solomon (d 1963), of Bournemouth, and Rosie, *née* Joseph (d 1978); *b* 31 December 1930; *Educ* Torquay GS, Univ of Manchester (LLB); *m* 5 April 1959, Hazel, da of Joseph Boam, of London; 1 s (Jonathan b 1961), 2 da (Ruth b 1963, Joanne b 1966); *Career* slr; ptnr Nabarro Nathanson 1961–68; D J Freeman: head Property Dept 1976–90, chief exec 1990–93, sr ptnr 1992–96; tstee Highgate Literary and Scientific Instn 1999–2006 (pres 1993–98); memb Cncl Oriental Ceramics Soc 1989–92, 1994–97, 1998–2001 and 2002–06; tstee Public Art Devpt Tst 2000–02 (chm 1997–2000); *Recreations* Chinese ceramics, music, architecture, art, wine, literature; *Clubs* Athenaeum; *Style*— Mr David Solomon; ✉ Russell House, 9 South Grove, London N6 6BS (☎ 020 8341 6454, e-mail david@russellhouse.fsworld.co.uk); Longecourt les Culetre, 21230 Arnay le Duc, France (☎ 00 33 3 80 90 05 55)

SOLOMON, Nicola; da of Aaron Kenneth Solomon (d 2014), and Rosalie Ursula, *née* Sugarman; *b* 1 May 1960, Pembury, Kent; *Educ* Tonbridge GS for Girls, Univ of Warwick (LLB); *m* 3 Feb 1991, Rabbi Jonathan Wittenberg; 1 s (Amos Gershom Wittenberg b 20 March 1993), 2 da (Libbi Shulamit Wittenberg b 30 Oct 1995, Kadya Rachel Wittenberg b 30 July 1997); *Career* slr: Taylor Tyrrell Lewis and Craig 1982–84, Norton Rose Fulbright 1984–85, Stephens Innocent (subsequently Finers Stephens Innocent) 1985–2011 (ptnr 1988–2011), chief exec Soc of Authors 2011–; dep dist judge 1997–; memb: Bd Br Copyright Cncl, Law Soc; memb Worshipful Co of Stationers; *Recreations* gardening, reading, walking; *Style*— Ms Nicola Solomon; ✉ The Society of Authors, 84 Drayton Gardens, London SW10 9SB (☎ 020 7373 6642, e-mail nsolomon@societyofauthors.org, website www.societyofauthors.org)

SOLOMON, Stephen Edward; s of Maj William Edward Solomon (d 1977), and Winifred Constance, *née* Day (d 2005); *b* 29 November 1947; *Educ* Royal GS Guildford, Univ of Manchester, Coll of Law Guildford; *m* (m dis 1995) Maureen Diane, da of William Robert Wilkins, of Tenby, Dyfed; 2 s (Robert William Petrie b 1980, John Christopher Petrie b 1981); partner Alison Jane Mouser, da of Barry Mouser, of Rayne, Essex; 1 da (Emma Kate Mouser b 2008); *Career* admitted slr 1973; ptnr: Crossman Block and Keith slrs 1978–87 (joined 1976), Withers Crossman Block 1988–89, Crossman Block 1989–93; tstee The Law Debenture Corp plc 1994–95, ptnr W Davies Slrs 1996–2012; memb: Guildford Round Table 1979–89, Guildford XRT; memb Surrey Law Club; *Recreations* microlight flying, skiing, gliding, astronomy, plumbing, boating; *Clubs* Airborne Aviation; *Style*— Stephen Solomon, Esq

SOLTMANN, Diana-Margaret (Diana); da of HE Dr Otto Soltmann (d 2001), of Koblenz, W Germany, and Ethel Margaret, *née* Oakleigh-Walker; *b* 29 October 1952; *Educ* Rosemead Sch Littlehampton, Keele Univ (BA), LSE (Dip Personnel Mgmnt); *m* 16 June 1980, Timothy Congreve Stephenson, *qv*; 3 s (Christopher (Kit) b 2 Feb 1983, William b 8 July 1985, James b 1 Dec 1989); *Career* dir: Good Relations Technol 1978–85, The Communication Group 1985–89; head corp communications Blue Arrow plc 1988–89, md Millbank Public Relations 1990–99, currently gp chief exec Flagship Group; chm S London Ctee for the Employment of People with Disabilities 1994–97; memb Strategic Advsy Gp Mencap 1998–; AIPM, MIPR; *Recreations* reading, theatre; *Style*— Miss Diana Soltmann; ✉ Flagship Consulting, The Media Centre, 19 Bolsover Street, London W1W 5NA

SOLYMAR, Prof Laszlo; *b* 24 January 1930; *Educ* Tech Univ of Budapest (Dip Electrical Engrg, PhD); *m*; 2 da (Gillian Kathy Lacey-Solymar b 1963, Lucy Suzanne Solymar b 1970); *Career* lectr Tech Univ Budapest 1952–53; research engr: Research Inst for Telecommunications Budapest 1953–56, Standard Telecommunications Laboratories Ltd Harlow 1956–66; Univ of Oxford: fell and tutor BNC 1966–86, lectr Dept of Engrg Sci 1971–86, Donald Pollock reader in engrg sci Dept of Engrg Sci 1986–, professorial fell Hertford Coll 1986–, prof of applied electromagnetism 1992–97 (prof emeritus 1997–, Leverhulme emeritus fell 1997–99); visiting positions and consultancies: visiting prof Laboratoire de Physique École Normale Superieure Univ of Paris 1965–66, visiting prof Tech Univ of Denmark 1972–73, conslt Tech Univ of Denmark 1973–76, visiting scientist Thomson-CSF Research Laboratories Orsay France 1984, conslt BT Research Laboratories 1986–88, conslt Hirst Research Laboratories GEC 1986–88, visiting prof Dept of Physics Univ of Osnabruck Germany 1987, visiting prof Optical Inst Tech Univ Berlin 1990, conslt Pilkington plc 1990, visiting prof Dept of Physics of Materials Univ Autónoma Madrid 1993 and 1995, visiting prof Dept of Electrical and Electronic Engrg Imperial Coll London 2003–; Faraday Medal IEE 1992; author of 3 radio plays for BBC Radio 4 (with late John Wain) 1991: Anaxagoras, Archimedes, Hypatia; FIEE 1978, FRS 1995; *Books* Lectures on the Electrical Properties of Materials (with D Walsh, 1 edn 1970), Superconductive Tunnelling and Applications (1972), A Review of the Principles of Electrical and Electronic Engineering (4 volumes, ed, 1974), Lectures on Electromagnetic Theory (1 edn 1976), Volume Holography and Volume Gratings (with D J Cooke, 1981), Solutions Manual to Accompany Lectures on the Electrical Properties of Materials (1988) Lectures on Fourier Series (1989), The Physics and Applications of Photorefractive Materials (1996), Getting the Message; a History of Communications (1999), Waves in Metamaterials (2008, with E Shamonina), The Rhineland War: 1936 (2012), The Portrait of a Genius (2013), Three Scientists of the Ancient World (with John Wain, 2013), Anatomy of Assasinations (2013), Past, Present and Future (2014); over 300 articles in learned jls; *Recreations* languages, twentieth century history particularly that of the Soviet Union, theatre, chess, swimming, bridge; *Style*— Prof Laszlo Solymar; ✉ Department of Engineering Science, University of Oxford, Oxford OX1 3PJ (e-mail laszlo.solymar@hertford.ox.ac.uk)

SOMEN, David; s of Michael Somen, of Kenya, and Vera, *née* Gellert; bro of Jonathan Somen, *qv*; *b* 6 July 1965, Nairobi, Kenya; *Educ* Univ of Oxford (BA), Harvard Business Sch (MBA); *Career* assoc McKinsey & Co 1989–90 and 1991–94, fndr and ceo LCR Telecom Gp 1994–2000, md Primus Europe 2000–01, fndr and md Virtual IT 2002–, fndr and dep chm AccessKenya Gp 2002–; non-exec dir CIM Finance Mauritius, fndr and non-exec dir AccessWind Ltd Kenya; *Recreations* motorsport, cooking, fine dining; *Clubs* Muthaiga Country (Nairobi), Soho House; *Style*— David Somen, Esq; ✉ Virtual IT, The Lime House, Quadrant Business Centre, 135 Salusbury Road, London, NW6 6RJ (☎ +44 20 7644 2800)

SOMEN, Jonathan; s of Michael Somen, of Kenya, and Vera, *née* Gellert; bro of David Somen, *qv*; *b* 27 June 1969, Nairobi, Kenya; *Educ* Univ of Bristol (BSc); *m* 20 Dec 2001, Petra, *née* Meinzingen; 1 da (Talia b 29 Oct 2002), 2 s (Jaden b 16 Aug 2004, Noah b 14 Dec 2006); *Career* chief operating offr Kilimanjaro Mineral Water Kenya 1992–94, fndr and dir LCR Telecom Gp 1994–2000, fndr and gp md AccessKenya Gp 2000–15, fndr and dir Virtual IT Ltd UK, fndr and md AccessWind Ltd Kenya, fndr and md Eldama Technols Ltd Kenya; *Recreations* flying, rallying, motorsport; *Clubs* Muthaiga Country (Nairobi); *Style*— Jonathan Somen, Esq; ✉ c/o 41 Randolph Avenue, London W9 1BQ; PO Box 43588–00100, Nairobi, Kenya (☎ +254 20 360 0000, fax +254 20 360 0001, e-mail jsomen@accesskenya.com)

SOMERS, Chip; s of Walter Somers (d 2010), and Daphne, *née* Owen; *b* 2 March 1948, Kidderminster, Worcs; *Educ* Radley; *m* 1 Dec 2004, Heidi, *née* de la Rue; 1 da (Sophie), 1 s (Seth); *Career* mangr Thurston House 1987–93, treatment dir Dukes Priory Hosp Chelmsford 1993–96, fndr and chief exec Focus12 1997–; memb eATA, PDAP; Community Champion 2005; *Recreations* golf; *Style*— Chip Somers, Esq; ✉ Focus12, 82 Risbygate Street, Bury St Edmunds, Suffolk IP33 3AQ (☎ 01284 701702, e-mail chip@focus12.co.uk, website www.focus12.co.uk, Twitter @focus12rehab)

SOMERS COCKS, Hon Anna Gwenllian (Mrs Umberto Allemandi); OBE (2011); da of John Sebastian Somers Cocks, CVO, CBE (d 1964), and Marjorie Olive, *née* Weller (d 2002), and sister of 9 Baron Somers; raised to the rank of a baron's da 1996; *b* 18 April 1950, Rome; *Educ* Convent of the Sacred Heart Woldingham, St Anne's Coll Oxford (MA), Courtauld Inst Univ of London (MA); *m* 1, 1971 (m dis 1977), Martin Alan Walker; m 2, 1978 (m dis 1990), John Julian Savile Lee Hardy; 1 s (Maximilian John Lee b 10 Feb 1980), 1 da (Katherine Isabella Eugenia b 15 Feb 1982); m 3, 30 Nov 1991, Umberto Allemandi; *Career* asst keeper: Dept of Metalwork V&A 1973–85, Dept of Ceramics V&A 1985–87; ed Apollo 1987–90, ed-in-chief The Art Newspaper 1994–95, chm Umberto Allemandi & Co Publishing (publishers of The Art Newspaper) 1995–96, ed-in-chief The Art Newspaper 1996–2003, gp editorial dir Umberto Allemandi Publishing 2003 (ceo 2011–); chm Venice in Peril Fund 1999–2012; tstee The Gilbert Collection 1998–; memb Advsy Bd Sotheby's Inst 2002–, chm Bd Antarctic Biennale 2016–; tstee Cass Sculpture Fndn 2004–13; European Women of Achievement Award (Art and Media) 2006, Int Inst for Conservation (IIC) Advocate Award 2011, Istituto Veneto Journalism Award (for best article of the year on Venice) 2013; Liveryman Worshipful Co of Goldsmiths 2009; FSA; Commendatore Ordine della Stella della Solidarietá Italiana 2004; *Publications* The Victoria and Albert Museum – The Making of the Collection (1980), Princely Magnificence – Court Jewels of the Renaissance (ed and jt author, 1980), Renaissance Jewels, Gold Boxes and Objets de Vertu in the Thyssen Bornemisza Collection (1985), The Coming Death of Venice? (article in New York Review of Books, 2013), Venice: Devious and Destructive (article in New York Review of Books, 2014); *Recreations* learning Arabic, travelling; *Clubs* Academy (London); *Style*— The Hon Anna Somers Cocks, OBE, FSA; ✉ The Art Newspaper, 70 South Lambeth Road, London SW8 1RL

SOMERSET WEBB, Merryn; *Educ* Wycombe Abbey Sch, Gonville and Caius Coll Cambridge, SOAS London; *Career* institutional broker SBC Warburg Tokyo 1993–98, currently ed in chief MoneyWeek (joined 2000); contrib: FT, Sunday Post, Saga Magazine, Spectator; tstee Daiwa Anglo Japanese Fndn; hon doc Business Admin BPP Univ; affiliate Chartered Inst for Securities and Investment (CISI); *Style*— Ms Merryn Somerset Webb; ✉ MoneyWeek, 8th Floor, Friars Bridge Court, 41–45 Blackfriars Road, London SE1 8NZ

SOMERVILLE, Prof Jane; da of Capt Bertram Platnauer, MC, of London, and Pearl Annie, *née* Backler (d 1969); *b* 24 January 1933, London; *Educ* Queen's Coll London, Guy's Hosp Med Sch London (MB BS, MD); *m* 2 Feb 1957, Walter Somerville (d 2005), s of Patrick Somerville (d 1954), of Dublin; 1 da (Kate b 1961), 3 s (Lorne b 1963, Rowan b 1966, Crispin b 1972); *Career* sr lectr Inst of Cardiology London 1964–74, hon conslt physician Hosp For Sick Children 1968–88; hon sr lectr: Nat Heart and Lung Inst Univ of London 1974–98, Inst of Child Health until 1988; conslt physician and cardiologist Royal Brompton and Nat Heart Hosp (formerly Nat Heart Hosp) 1974–99, conslt cardiologist St Bartholomew's 1988–91, conslt physician for congenital heart diseases and dir Grown Up Congenital Heart Unit Royal Brompton and Nat Heart and Lung Hosp 1991–99, ret; currently conslt Cardiology Mater Die Hosp Malta Guch Clinic; hon conslt cardiologist Grown Up Congenital Heart Unit Middx Hosp/UCL, hon conslt advsr Congenital Heart Centre, emeritus prof of cardiology Imperial Coll London; memb Ctee on Cardiology RCP 1985–90, advsr on congenital heart disease for Sec of State's Hon Med Advsy Panel On Driving And Disorders Of The Cardiovascular System 1986 (published Heart Supplement 2002), advsr Congenital Heart Servs NATO Project Baltic States 2002–, chm Working Party Grown Up Congenital Heart Defects for British Cardiac Soc, chm Working Gp Grown Up Congenital Heart Disease European Soc of Cardiologists, pres Grown Up Congenital Heart Patients Assoc 2004–, memb Bd Beaconhouse Educnl Services Ltd 2008–; chm Bd of Govrs Queen's Coll London 1990–96; hon pres World Congress Pediatric Cardiology and Cardio Surgery 2004 and 2008; Gold Medal for servs to cardiovascular medicine European Soc of Cardiologists 2008, Distinguished Service Award American Coll of Cardiology 2009, awarded Legend status American Coll of Cardiology 2012; FACC 1972, FRCP 1973, FESC 1993; 300 papers, medical jls related to congenital heart disease, guest lectures and chapters in books on cardiology; *Recreations* collecting objets d'art, opera, roof gardening; *Style*— Prof Jane Somerville; ✉ 30 York House, 39 Upper Montagu Street, London W1H 1FR (☎ 07720 285715); 81 Harley Street, London W1G 8PP (☎ 020 7262 2144)

SOMERVILLE, Julia; OBE (2013); *b* 1947; *Career* journalist and broadcaster; BBC: joined 1973, news reporter then industrial/labour corr BBC Radio News 1979–1984, newscaster BBC TV 1984–87; newscaster with ITN 1987–2001, presenter LBC Radio 1999–2001, presenter Rip Off Britain (BBC) 2011–; chm Govt Art Collection Advsy Ctee 2003–; *Style*— Ms Julia Somerville, OBE

SOMERVILLE, Dr Kevin William; *b* 21 November 1950; *Educ* Lynfield Coll Auckland, Univ of Auckland (sr scholar in human biology, BSc, MB ChB, Beecham prize in physiology, sr prize in med, T W J Johnson prize in postgrad med), Univ of Nottingham (DM); *Career* physician with special interests in insurance med and risk assessment; house offr posts in Auckland and Nelson 1974–76, med registrar Auckland and Greenlane Hosps 1976–79, clinical research fell Gastrointestinal Unit Western General Hosp Edinburgh 1979–80, lectr and hon sr registrar Dept of Therapeutics Univ of Nottingham 1981–85, conslt gen physician Middlemore Hosp Auckland 1986, sr registrar Div of Geriatric Med Radcliffe Infirmary Oxford 1986–89, sr lectr Dept of Med Barts Med Coll and hon conslt physician Barts 1989–97, clinical dir Dept of Med for the Elderly Barts NHS Gp 1989–95, med conslt to Swiss Re 1997–; research and pubns on disease aetiology and pharmaco-epidemiology in older people; Elizabeth Brown prize Br Geriatrics Soc 1987; memb: Br Geriatrics Soc, Christian Med Fellowship, Br Soc of Gastroenterology, Assurance Med Soc, American Acad of Insurance Med; FRACP 1981, FRCP 1995; *Style*— Dr Kevin Somerville; ✉ 33 Oxhey Road, Watford, Hertfordshire WD19 4QG (☎ 01923 240827, fax 020 7933 5749, e-mail kevin_somerville@swissre.com)

SOMMERS, Paul; s of Arthur Sommers (d 1998), and Nesta Sommers (d 2000); *m* 18 Dec 1993, Jenny, *née* Zamit; 2 da (Holly b 17 Feb 1998, Scarlet b 18 March 2000); *Career* television prodr; former dir Aspect Film and Television, head Factual & Documentary Tiger Aspect Productions until 2009, co-fndr Alaska TV 2011–; prodr: The Real Don Giovanni (Channel 4, Best Music Documentary Award Midem Cannes) 1999, Cop Shop (ITV) 1999, Howard Goodall's Big Bangs (BAFTA Award 2000, Peabody Award 2000, nominee Int Emmy, nominee RTS) 2000, Harry Enfield's Real Kevins (BBC1) 2000, Kevin and Perry's Girlfriends (BBC1) 2000, Country House (four series, BBC2) 2002–04, A Place in France (two series, Channel 4) 2002 and 2004, When She Died the Death of a Princess (Channel 4 and Trio Channel USA) 2002; exec prodr: Omnibus: The Billy Elliott Boy (nominee RTS) 2001, Future Fighting Machines (2 series, Bravo and Tech TV USA) 2001, Doubletake and Doubletake Xmas Special (BBC2, BAFTA Award 2002, nominee Golden Rose) 2001 and 2003, The Crucified Soldier (Channel 4) 2002, Howard Goodall's Great Dates (Channel 4, 2002), The Men from the Agency (BBC4) 2003, Heist (Court TV USA) 2003, The Highest Bidder (BBC2) 2003, Country Parish (2 series, BBC2) 2003 and 2004, More than Love (Channel 4) 2003, A Place in Italy, A Place in Spain, A Place in Greece (Channel 4) 2004, Howard Goodall's 20C Greats (Channel 4) 2004, The Body of JFK, Hitler, Marilyn Monroe (Discovery US and BBC3) 2004; *Recreations* sky diving, polo; *Clubs* Groucho, Electric; *Style*— Paul Sommers, Esq

SONDHI, Ranjit; CBE (1999); s of Prem Lal Sondhi (d 2004), and Kanta Sondhi; *b* 22 October 1950, Ferozepur, India; *Educ* St John's HS Chandigarh, Bedford Sch, Univ of Birmingham (BSc); *m* 1979, Anita Bhalla; 1 da (Maya Zareen b 1983), 1 s (Kabir Prem b 1985); *Career* worked on inner city community projects incl Handsworth Action Centre 1972–76, fndr Asian Resource Centre Handsworth 1976–85, sr lectr Dept of Community and Youth Studies Westhill Coll Univ of Birmingham 1985–2007 (co-ordinator undergrad degree in race and ethnic studies 1997–2001); cmmr then dep chair Cmmn for Racial Equality 1989–95, chm Refugee Employment, Trg and Educn Forum 1990–95, cmmr Judicial Appointments Cmmn 2012–, cmmr Criminal Cases Review Cmmn 2012–; memb: Ethnic Minority Ctee Judicial Studies Bd 1991–95, Lord Chllr's Advsy Ctee on Legal Educn and Conduct 1996–2000, Home Sec's Race Rels Forum 1998–2002, Race Equality Advsy Panel 2003–; former memb: Birmingham TEC, Disability Task Force on Disability Rights DfEE, Strategic Gp on Tackling Racial Harassment in the NHS Dept of Health; visiting prof of diversity, cohesion and intercultural relations Univ of Coventry 2010; memb: Ind Broadcasting Authy 1987–90, Radio Authy 1990–95, Bd of Govrs BBC 1998–2006 (chm English Nat Forum), Civil Serv Cmmn 2006–10, Bd Tenant Services Authy 2009–12; non-exec dir Birmingham HA 1998–2002, chm Heart of Birmingham Teaching Primary Care Tst 2002–11, vice-chm Sandwell and W Birmingham Clinical Commissioning Gp 2012–; tstee: Nat Gall 2000–09, Baring Fndn 2002–, Bryant Tst 2003–, Teaching Awards Tst until 2006, Nat Educn Tst 2006–; former tstee: Prince's Tst, Feeney Tst; chm sampad 1998–; involved with projects incl Second City Second Chance and Birmingham Focus on Blindness; fell Nat Leadership Cncl NHS 2009–; lay memb Cncl Univ of Birmingham 2011–; Hon DUniv Univ of Central England 2003, Hon DLitt Univ of Wolverhampton 2007, Hon DUniv Birmingham 2010; FRSA; *Publications* Ethnicity and the Media (jtly, 1977), Asian Resource Centre: Problems, Perspectives, Progress (ed, 1979), Divided Families (ed, 1985), Educational Interventions (jtly, 1997), An Experiment in Moral Education (jtly, 1997), Twenty Years after the Act (jt ed, 1999); contrib to books and author of articles in jls; *Recreations* music, books, travel; *Style*— Ranjit Sondhi, Esq, CBE; ✉ Criminal Cases Review Commission, 5 St Philip's Place, Birmingham

SOOKE, Thomas Peter (Tom); *b* 8 January 1945; *Educ* Westminster, Pembroke Coll Cambridge (MA), Columbia Univ NY (MBA); *m* 6 June 1975, Ceridwen Leeuwke Bathurst, da of Derek Matthews (d 2009); 1 s (Alastair b 1981), 1 da (Leonie b 1985); *Career* Price Waterhouse 1967–70, Wallace Bros Bank 1972–76, dir Granville Holdings plc and Venture Funds 1976–87 (co fndr Br Venture Capital Assoc 1983), corp fin ptnr Deloitte 1988–91, CitiCourt Assocs 1991; chm Travel a la Carte Ltd, sr ind dir Mobeus Income and Growth VCT plc; FCA 1979; *Recreations* tennis, golf, British modern art; *Clubs* Oxford and Cambridge, MCC, Isle of Purbeck Golf; *Style*— Tom Sooke, Esq; ✉ 45 Faroe Road, London W14 0EL (☎ 020 7602 6910, e-mail tom.citicourt@btconnect.com)

SOOLE, Michael Alexander; QC (2002); s of Brian Alfred Seymour Soole (d 1974), and Rosemary Una, *née* Salt; *b* 18 July 1954; *Educ* Berkhamsted Sch (scholar), UC Oxford (scholar, MA, pres Oxford Union); *m* 2002, Catherine Gavine Marshall, *née* Gardiner; 3 step s, 2 step da; *Career* called to the Bar Inner Temple 1977; practising barr 1978–, recorder of the Crown Court 2000–; Parly candidate Aylesbury (SDP/Liberal Alliance) general elections 1983 and 1987; memb Bd Christian Aid 1991–2002, tstee Oxford Literary and Debating Union Tst 2005–; *Recreations* conversation; *Style*— Michael Soole, Esq, QC; ✉ 4 New Square, Lincolns Inn, London WC2A 3RJ (☎ 020 7822 2000, fax 020 7822 2001)

SOOTHILL, Prof Peter William; *b* 30 October 1957; *Educ* Guy's Hosp Med Sch London (MB BS), Univ of London (BSc, MD, MRCOG); *m* ; 3 c; *Career* KCH London: lectr then hon sr registrar in obstetrics and gynaecology and dir Day Assessment Unit 1989–91, subspeciality fell/sr registrar in fetal med 1991–92; sr lectr in obstetrics and gynaecology UCL Med Sch and Inst of Child Health Univ of London 1992–95, hon conslt UCH (dir Fetal Med Unit) and Gt Ormond St Hosp London 1992–95, prof of maternal and fetal med Univ of Bristol 1995– (now emeritus), conslt in maternal and fetal medicine Univ Hosp Bristol, visiting prof UWE; chm Fetal Anomaly Screening Prog Advsy Ctee UK Nat Screening Ctee; author of numerous articles in learned jls; hon fell South African Coll of Medicine; *Books* Alloimmune Diseases of Pregnancy; *Recreations* Cello; *Style*— Prof P W Soothill; ✉ University Department of Obstetrics and Gynaecology, Fetal Medicine Research Unit, St Michael's Hospital, Southwell Street, Bristol BS2 8EG (☎ 0117 928 5513, fax 0117 928 5683, e-mail peter.soothill@bristol.ac.uk)

SOPER, Rt Rev (Andrew) Laurence; OSB; s of Alan Soper, and late Anne, *née* Morris; *Educ* St Benedict's Sch Ealing, St Benet's Hall Oxford, Collegio Sant Anselmo Rome (STL, STD), St Mary's Coll Twickenham (PGCE); *Career* Barclays Bank 1960–64; entered monastery Ealing 1964; ordained: deacon (Assisi) 1969, priest 1970; St Benedict's Sch Ealing: teacher 1973–83, bursar 1975–91, prior 1984–91, ruling abbot 1991–2000; titular abbot St Albans 2000–; episcopal vicar for Religious in Archdiocese of Westminster Western Area 1995–2000; delg to Gen Chapter (sec) 1985 and 1989; pt/t chaplain Harrow Sch 1981–91, visiting chaplain Feltham YOI 1988–2000; chm Union of Monastic Superiors 1995–99, gen treas Int Benedictine Confedn 2002–; Freeman City of Norcia Italy; FRSA 1975; *Books* The Thoughts of Jesus Christ (1970), T H Green as Theologian (1972); *Recreations* walking; *Style*— The Rt Rev Laurence Soper, OSB; ✉ Badia Primaziale S Anselmo, Piazza Cavalieri di Malta 5, I-00153, Rome, Italy

SORABJI, Prof Sir Richard Rustom Kharsedji; kt (2014), CBE (1999); s of Prof Richard Kaikushru Sorabji (d 1950), of Oxford, and Mary Katharine Monkhouse (d 1990); *b* 8 November 1934; *Educ* Charterhouse, Pembroke Coll Oxford (BA, BPhil); *m* 1958, Margaret Anne Catherine, da of Kenneth Taster (d 1958); 1 s (Richard Jon Francis b 29 March 1959), 2 da (Cornelia Katharine b 23 Dec 1961, Tahmina Lucy b 28 Dec 1964); *Career* positions rising to assoc prof with tenure Sage Sch of Philosophy Cornell Univ NY 1962–69; KCL: joined Dept of Philosophy 1970, prof of ancient philosophy 1981– (now emeritus), chm Bd of Philosophical Studies 1979–82, head Philosophy Dept 1984–85 (acting head 1975, 1983 and 1987), designer and first dir King's Coll Centre for Philosophical Studies 1989–91, FKC 1990–, dir Inst of Classical Studies 1991–96 (now research fell); sr fell Cncl of Humanities Princeton Univ 1985, sr res fell Soc of the Humanities Cornell Univ 1979, memb SCR Pembroke Coll Oxford 1992–, fell Wolfson Coll Oxford 1996–, Br Acad research prof 1996–99, Gresham prof of rhetoric Gresham Coll London 2000–03 (fell 2003–04), adjunct prof Univ of Texas at Austin 2000–, distinguished visiting scholar NYU 2000–03, visiting prof City Univ of NY 2004–07, Cyprus global distinguished prof in the history and theory of justice NYU 2008–; pres Aristotelian Soc 1985–86, fndr and organiser Int Project on the Aristotle Commentators with 24 research assts and 99 published vols 1985–; Townsend lectr Cornell Univ 1991; Gifford lectr St Andrews Univ 1997, Gifford lectr Edinburgh Univ 1997; hon foreign memb American Acad of Arts and Scis 1997–, foreign memb Royal Flemish Acad of Arts and Sciences of Belgium 2008–; Choice Award for Outstanding Academic Books 1989–90; Hon DLitt Union Coll Schenectady 2007, Hon DLitt McGill Univ Canada 2009; FBA 1989; *Books* Aristotle on Memory (1972, 2 edn 2004), Articles on Aristotle (co-ed, 4 vols, 1975–79), Necessity, Cause and Blame (1980), Time, Creation and the Continuum (1983), Philoponus and the Rejection of Aristotelian Science (ed, 1987, 2 edn 2010), Translations of the Ancient Commentators on Aristotle (ed of 94 vols of trans and 5 of exposition, 1987–), Aristotle Transformed: The Ancient Commentators and Their Influence (ed, 1989), Matter, Space and Motion (1988), Animal Minds and Human Morals (1993), Aristotle and After (ed 1997), Emotion and Peace of Mind: From Stoic Agitation to Christian Temptation (2000), Sourcebook: The Philosophy of the Commentators 200–600AD (3 vols, 2004), Self: Ancient and Modern Insights about Individuality, Life and Death (2006), The Ethics of War: Shared Problems in Different Traditions (co-ed, 2006), Greek and Roman Philosophy 100 BC to 200 AD (co-ed, 2 vols, 2007), Opening Doors: The Untold Story of Cornelia Sorabji, Reformer, Lawyer and Champion of Women's Rights in India (2010), Gandhi and the Stoics: Modern Experiments on Ancient Values (2012); *Recreations* archaeology, architecture; *Style*— Prof Sir Richard Sorabji, CBE, FBA

SORBIE, Trevor; MBE (2004); s of Robert Sorbie (d 1992), of Harlow New Town, and Edna, *née* Saxby (d 1979); *b* 13 March 1949; *Educ* Richard Henry Sch of Hairdressing; *m* 1, Susan Harré; *m* 2 (m dis), Kris Szewczyk; 1 c (Jade b 12 Oct 1978); *Career* hair stylist; apprentice barber Ilford 1964, opened own shop Edmonton 1969; stylist: Henri Loughton 1971, Selfridges Ilford 1971, Vidal Sassoon 1972–73; artistic dir Vidal Sassoon 1973–78, stylist and session hairdresser Toni & Guy then John Frieda 1978, opened own salons Covent Garden 1979 and 1999, created Trevor Sorbie Professional product line 1986 (relaunched 1999); launched: Mg product range 2000, Style Solutions product line 2001, The Professional Range 2001, Long Hair Range 2002, Professional Rejuvenate Range 2003, Electrical Range 2005; subject of: Visions in Hair by Kris Sorbie and Jacki Wadeson, Legends, Trevor Sorbie by Jacki Wadeson (2003); patron: Terrence Higgins Tst, Headlines; patron of honour Fellowship of Australian Hairdressers 2003; ambass Hairdressers of the World Against Aids 2006; fell City & Guilds 2002; FCGI 2003; *Awards* British Hairdresser of the Year 1985, 1986, 1991, and 1992 (finalist 1995 and 1996), Nat Hairdresser of the Year 1985, London Stylist of the Year 1986 and 1989, Avant Garde Stylist of the Year 1989, Peluquerias magazine Foreign Stylist of the Year 1990 and 1991, British Hairdressing Hall of Fame 1991, Patron D'Honneur Lifetime Hairdressing Award 1993, Best Educn Award (USA) 1993, Living Legend Award NY 1995, World Congress Hall of Fame 1995, Most Newsworthy Male Worldwide (Int Beauty Show Award) 1996 and 1997, Best Haircutter Worldwide 1997, Grand Trophy of the Professional Press AIPP 2001, Aveda Master of the Arts 2002, Pantene Pro-V Celebrity Hairdresser of the Year 2002, British Master Award AHFA 2003, Most Wanted! Influential Hairdresser 2003 and 2004, Winner AIPP Trophy (Best Photo Category) 2003, Inspirational Leader Fellowship for British Hairdressing 2003, AIPP Grand Trophy of the Professional Press 2004, Global Icon Award 2006, International Icon Hall of Leaders Award 2006, Creative Head Award (Most Innovative Concept) My New Hair 2007, My New Hair Magazine Awards 2009, Salon Group of the Year Fellowship 2010, International Icon Hair of Leaders Award Irish Hairdresser Federation 2011, Legends of Industry Award Variety 2012, AH Awards 2012, Lifetime Achievement Scottish Hair and Beauty Awards 2012, Lifetime Achievement Award NHF Central England Hairdressing Awards 2012, Tribute: 50 Years of True Inspiration and Leading Creativity 2014, China Hairdressing Hair Fashion Awards 2015; *Recreations* cooking, walking, motor racing; *Clubs* The Wellington; *Style*— Trevor Sorbie, Esq, MBE; ✉ 27 Floral Street, Covent Garden, London WC2E 9DP (☎ 020 7379 6901)

SØRENSEN, (Nils Jorgen) Philip; *see:* Philip-Sørensen, Nils Jorgen

SORIANO, Kathleen; da of Salvador Soriano, of London and Valencia, and Kathleen, *née* O'Neill; *b* 18 July 1963, London; *Educ* Putney HS, Spalding Univ Louisville KY (ESU scholar), Univ of Leicester (BA); *m* 22 July 1995, Peter Greenhough; 1 da (Martha Amelia Scarlett b 3 June 1998); *Career* Royal Academy of Arts 1985–89, head of exhbns and collections Nat Portrait Gallery 1989–2006, dir Compton Verney 2006–08, dir of exhbns Royal Acad of Arts 2009–; Clore Leadership Prog fell 2004–05, Salzburg Seminar fell 2007; memb Bd: Tourism W Midlands 2006–08, Museums, Libraries and Archives W Midlands 2006–09, Wellcome Coll Exhbns Steering Gp 2007–, Sainsbury Centre UEA 2008–10, Nat Tst Contemporary Art Panel 2009–; Kentucky Col, hon capt Louisville Belle paddle steamer 1982; memb Women Ldrs in Museums; FRSA 2004; *Recreations* red wine, reading, film, theatre and contemporary dance; *Clubs* Arts; *Style*— Kathleen Soriano; ✉ Royal Academy of Arts, Piccadilly, London W1J 0BD (e-mail kathleen.soriano@royalacademy.org.uk, website www.royalacademy.org.uk)

SORKIN, (Alexander) Michael; s of Joseph Sorkin (d 1984), and Hilda Ruth, *née* Fiebusch; *b* 2 March 1943; *Educ* St Paul's Manchester Univ (BA); *m* 27 Nov 1977, Angela Lucille, da of Leon Berman (MC), of London; 2 da (Zoe b 1979, Kim b 1980), 1 s (Jacob b 1983); *Career* Hambros Bank Ltd: joined 1968, dir 1973, exec dir 1983, vice-chm 1987–95, dep chm 1995–98; dir Hambros plc 1986–98, md SG Hambros 1998–2001, vice-chm N M Rothschild 2001– (sr advsr 2015–); *Recreations* opera, golf, tennis; *Style*— Michael Sorkin, Esq; ✉ N M Rothschild & Sons, New Court, St Swithin's Lane, London EC4N 8AL (☎ 020 7280 5000, fax 020 7623 1788)

SORRELL, Lady Frances M; OBE (2016); *née* Newell; *m* Sir John Sorrell, CBE, *qv*; 3 c; *Career* fndr and co chm Newell and Sorrell Ltd (identity and brand conslts) 1976–97, chair Interbrand Fndn (following merger) 1997–2000, fndr and tstee The Sorrell Fndn 1999–; dir: Bd Royal Acad Enterprises 1996–99, Bd Inst for Employment Studies 2000–02; memb: City & Guilds Nat Advsy Ctee for Craft Design and Art 1994–96, Advsy Bd Nat Museum of Photography, Film & TV 1997–2003, City & Guilds Affairs & Awards Ctee 1999–2001, Arts Advsy Gp QCA 2000–03, Colour Gp, NHS Design Advsy Gp, Br Cncl Design Advsy Gp; tstee Mencap 1999–2005; godparent to the NMEC Millennium Dome Garden Zone 1999; judge: BBC Design Awards, D&AD Awards, RIBA Awards; chllr Univ of Westminster 2015–; visiting prof Univ of the Arts London; hon fell Univ College Falmouth, hon fell Hereford Coll of Arts; hon doctorate Open Univ, hon Dr of Arts Coventry Univ, hon MA Univ of Creative Arts Farnham 2015; hon memb City & Guilds; FRSA, FCD, FRIBA; *Awards* 11 Design Effectiveness Awards, five Silver D&AD Awards, five Clios, five Gold Awards NY Festival, Grand Award for BA Corporate Identity, two Art Director's Club of Euro Awards; *Style*— Lady Frances Sorrell, OBE; ✉ The Sorrell Foundation (☎ 020 7845 5680)

SORRELL, Sir John William; kt (2008), CBE (1996); s of late John William Sorrell, and Elizabeth Jane, *née* Taylor; *b* 28 February 1945; *Educ* Hornsey Coll of Art (NDD); *m* 1974, Frances Sorrell, *qv*, *née* Newell; 2 s, 1 da; *Career* designer Main Wolff & Partners 1964, ptnr Goodwin Sorrell 1964–71, design mangr Wolff Olins 1971–76; Newell & Sorrell Ltd (identity and design conslts, subsequently Interbrand Newell & Sorrell): fndr 1976,

S

ptnr 1976–83, chm 1983–2000; chm The Sorrell Fndn 1999–; chm: DBA 1990–92, Design Cncl 1994–2000, NHS London Design Advsy Gp 2001–03, CABE 2004–09; vice-pres CSD 1989–92; co-chm Br Abroad Task Force 2000–03; memb: BR Architecture and Design Panel 1991–93, RSA Design Advsy Gp 1991–93, Panel 2000 FCO 1998–2000, London Design Festival 2002–; govr Design Dimension 1991–93; chair Victory Ceremonies Medal Panel 2012 Olympics 2010–12, chair Univ of the Arts London 2013–; pres London Design Biennale 2015–; memb: Encouraging Innovation Competitiveness working party DTI 1998, Qualifications and Curriculum Authority Advsy Gp for Media and Culture 1998–, Culture and Creativity Advsy Gp DCMS 2002–03, London Challenge Ministerial Advsy Gp DfES 2002–06, Public Diplomacy Strategy Bd FCO 2002–06, Advsy Gp on Design of Sch Bldgs DfES 2002–04, Home Office Design and Technol Alliance 2007–12, Creative Industries Adsy Bd UKT&I (chair 2007–12), Creative Economy Prog Ministerial Steering Bd DCMS 2008–09; chair Creative Industries Fedn 2014–; UK business ambass 2009–; tstee RIBA Tst 2004–05; 'godparent' to the NMEC National Identity Zone; vice-pres CSD 1989–92; RSA Bicentenary Medal 1998; Hon DDes: De Montfort Univ 1997, Greenwich Univ 2007; Hon Dr London Inst 1999, Hon Dr Middlesex Univ 2006, Hon PhD London Met 2006, Hon Dr Univ of Huddersfield 2014; hon memb Romanian Design Fndn 1996, hon fell UC Falmouth 2006; memb: D&AD, Strategic Planning Soc, IOD; FCSD, FRSA, Hon FRIBA 2002, CCMI 2006, Hon FREng 2009; *Publications* Creative Island (2002), Joined up Design for Schools (2005), Creative Island II (2009), The Virtuous Circle (2014); *Recreations* architecture, Arsenal, art, film; *Clubs* Groucho, Chelsea Arts; *Style—* Sir John Sorrell, CBE

SORRELL, Sir Martin Stuart; kt (2000); s of Jack Sorrell, of Mill Hill, London, and Sally Sorrell; *b* 14 February 1945; *Educ* Haberdashers' Aske's, Christ's Coll Cambridge, Harvard Business Sch; *m* 1, 1971 (m dis 2005), Sandra Carol Ann, *née* Finestone; 3 s; m 2, 2008, Cristiana Falcone; *Career* assoc Glendinning Assocs 1968–69, vice-pres Mark McCormack Orgn 1970–74, dir James Gulliver Assocs 1975–77, gp fin dir Saatchi & Saatchi Co plc (mktg serv) 1977–86, gp chief exec WPP Group plc (communications servs) 1986–; non-exec dir: Storehouse plc 1994–97, Colefax & Fowler 1997–2003, Nasdaq 2001–04; chm Int Advsy Bd Br-American Business Inc; memb: Governing Body London Business Sch (dep chm), Advsy Bd Instituto de Estudios Superiores de la Empresa (IESE), Panel 2000, Advsy Bd Harvard Univ Grad Sch of Business and Administration until 2005, Advsy Bd Boston Univ Sch of Mgmnt, Bd Indian Sch of Business, Bd Engrg and Technol Bd, Cncl for Excellence in Mgmnt in Leadership DfEE, Ctee Special Olympics (memb Bd until 2005), Int Advsy Bd CBI; tstee: Univ of Cambridge Fndn, The Conference Bd, RCA Fndn; Br ambass for business until 2010; *Recreations* skiing, cricket; *Clubs* Harvard, MCC; *Style—* Sir Martin Sorrell; ✉ WPP, 27 Farm Street, London W1J 5RJ (☎ 020 7408 2204)

SORRELL, Richard; s of Alan Sorrell (d 1974), of Thundersley, Essex, and Elizabeth, *née* Tanner (d 1991); *b* 24 September 1948; *Educ* Eton House Sch Thorpe Bay, Walthamstow Art Sch, Kingston Coll of Art (DipAD), Royal Acad Schs (Post Grad Cert, bronze and silver medals); *m* 1, 1974 (m dis), Dodie, da of Michael Burke; 2 s (William b 1978, Edmund b 1981); m 2, 2015, Sue Ross; *Career* artist (painter, draughtsman and printmaker) 1972–; memb Art Workers' Guild, memb Ctee Nat Artists' Assoc 1995–96; chief hanger RWS 1999–2001; govr Mall Galleries 2000–; RBA De Lazlo medal 2002; RBA 1989 (ARBA 1988), NEAC 1995 (memb Ctee), VPRWS 2002 (ARWS 1975, RWS 1978, pres RWS 2006–09); *Works* aerial views incl: Blickling Hall, Ickworth and Uppark (all for National Tst), Stonor Park for Lord Camoys, Antony House for Sir Richard Carew-Pole, Settrington House for Sir Richard Storey, Buscot Park for Lord Faringdon, Summer Fields Sch Oxford, Channel Tunnel workings Shakespeare Cliff for V&A, model of Charlecote Park and Gatehouse 1998; painting of HM Queen Elizabeth the Queen Mother's 100th birthday parade 2001 (presented to HM Queen Elizabeth the Queen Mother) *Exhibitions* incl: Royal Acad 1971–, Royal Watercolour Soc 1975–, Royal Soc of Br Artists 1988–, Nat Portrait Gallery 1980, 1983 and 1984, Lutyens Exhbn Hayward Gallery 1980, Artists in National Parks (V&A) 1988, Agnews 1990, Cadogan Gallery 1992, Leamington Spa Art Gallery and Museum 1997, Bourne Gallery Reigate 2000, The Sheen Gallery 2001, Thompsons Gallery Stow-on-the-Wold 2002, Galleries Sternberg Chicago 2004, Chappel Galleries Essex 2008; *Collections* work in public collections incl: V&A, Museum of London, National Tst, Worshipful Co of Fishmongers; *Books* Alan Sorrell: The Life and Works of an English Neo-Romantic Artist (ed, with Sacha Llewellyn, 2013); *Recreations* planting trees; *Clubs* Chelsea Arts; *Style—* Richard Sorrell, Esq; ✉ Higher Hellangove Farm, Badgers Cross, Gulval, Penzance, Cornwall TR20 8XD (☎ 01736 369613, e-mail sorrellr@aol.com, website www.richardsorrell.co.uk)

SORRELL, Stephen Terence; s of Terence Sorrell, of Stockport, Cheshire, and Christine Mary, *née* Smith; *b* 5 October 1959, Stockport, Cheshire; *Educ* Marple Hall GS Stockport, Univ of Manchester (LLB), Chester Law Sch; *m* 23 June 1984, Jane Louise, *née* Goodman; 2 da (Ruth Hannah b 15 Aug 1986, Imogen Anne b 16 April 1989); *Career* sr; ptnr: Abson Hall & Co 1987–89, Eversheds LLP 1989–2016; projects incl: Cwlth Games Manchester, Manchester FC stadium, Olympic Games London, Earls Court devpt London; dir and shareholder 4D Pictures; tstee Home (new purpose-built centre for international contemporary art, theatre and film), memb Sr Leadership Team Arts and Business; ind memb Cncl Univ of Salford; memb Law Soc 1984; author of numerous articles on regeneration in property periodicals; *Recreations* contemporary art, theatre, cinema, Manchester City FC; *Style—* Stephen Sorrell, Esq; ✉ Weavers House, 42 Ack Lane East, Bramhall, Stockport SK7 2BY

SOUBRY, Anna Mary; MP; da of David Stuart Soubry (d 1985), and Frances Margaret, *née* Coward; *b* 7 December 1956; *Educ* Hartland Comp Worksop Notts, Univ of Birmingham (LLB); *Partner* Neil Davidson, CBE; 2 da (Amelia Anne Soubry Gordon b 8 July 1990, Rosamund Mary Soubry Gordon b 22 August 1991); *Career* journalist (Grampian TV then Central TV): Heart of the Country, Central Weekend, This Morning, The Time The Place, Speak Out; criminal barr 1995–2010; MP (Cons) Broxtowe 2010–; exec NUS 1980, hon pres Univ of Stirling 1981; *Recreations* cooking, rugby, football, music, cricket, food; *Style—* Miss Anna Soubry, MP; ✉ House of Commons, London SW1A 0AA

SOUEIF, (Dr) Ahdaf; da of M I Soueif, of Cairo, and Fatma Moussa; *b* Cairo; *Educ* Cairo Univ (BA), American Univ Cairo (MA), Lancaster Univ (PhD); *m* 1981, Ian Hamilton (d 2001); 2 s (Omar Robert b 1984, Ismail Richard b 1989); *Career* author; numerous appearances on Arab, American and Br TV and radio; memb: Bd Int Prize for Arab Fiction, Egyptian Writers' Union, PEN Egypt, PEN UK, Ctee for the Advancment of Arab-Br Understanding, Amnesty Int; patron: Caine Prize for African Lit, Palestine Solidarity Campaign; tstee Br Museum, fndr and chair Engaged Events charity 2007; Mahmoud Darwich Award 2010, Constantin Cavafis Award 2012, Blue Metropolis Award 2012; Hon PhD Lancaster Univ 2004, Hon DLitt London Met Univ, Hon DLitt Univ of Exeter 2008; fell Lannan Fndn 2002, fell Bogliasco Fndn 2002, FRSL; *Publications* incl: Aisha (short stories, 1983, shortlisted Guardian Fiction Prize 1983), In the Eye of the Sun (novel, 1992), Sandpiper (short stories, 1996, Best Collection of Short Stories Cairo Int Book Fair 1996), The Map of Love (novel, 1999, shortlisted Booker Prize for Fiction 1999), Mezzaterra: Fragments from the Common Ground (essays, 2004), I Think of You (short stories, 2007), Cairo, my City our Revolution (memoir, 2012, new edn Cairo: Memoir of A City Transformed 2013), Reflections on Islamic Art (essays, ed, 2012); translations incl: In Deepest Night (1998), I Saw Ramallah (2004 (by Mourid al-Barghouti 2000)); author of numerous essays, short stories and reviews in English and Arabic published in various newspapers and jls; *Clubs* Gezira (Cairo), Frontline; *Style—* Ahdaf Soueif; ✉ c/o Wylie Agency, 17 Bedford Square, London WC1B 3JA (☎ 020 7908 5900, fax 020 7843 2151, e-mail cbuchan@wylieagency.co.uk)

SOUNDY, Andrew John; s of Maj Harold Cecil Soundy, MBE, MC, TD (d 1969), and Adele Monica Templeton, *née* Westley (d 2005); *b* 29 March 1940; *Educ* Boxgrove Sch Guildford, Shrewsbury, Trinity Coll Cambridge (MA); *m* 12 Oct 1963, Jill Marion, da of Frank Nathaniel Steiner, of Gerrards Cross, Bucks; 1 s (Mark b 1964), 2 da (Emma b 1967, Victoria b 1969); *Career* admitted slr 1966; former sr ptnr Ashurst Morris Crisp slrs; former chm EW Fact plc; vice-pres The Lord Slynn of Hadley Euro Law Fndn 1998–2011; dir: St Michael's Hospice Basingstoke 1996– (chm 2007–11, pres 2011–), Anglo-Russian Opera and Ballet Tst 2001–; memb Bd of Govrs De Montfort Univ 2001–05; churchwarden parish of Mattingley 2002–10 (churchwarden emeritus 2010); FRSA; *Recreations* farming, countryside, opera, tennis, fellowship; *Clubs* Cavalry and Guards', City Law, Bishopsgate Ward; *Style—* Andrew J Soundy, Esq; ✉ Gainsborough House, 69 High Street, Odiham, Hampshire RG29 1LB (☎ 01256 704290, e-mail andrew.soundy@btconnect.com)

SOUTAR, Michael James (Mike); s of David Soutar, of Dundee, and Patricia Shanks, *née* Buik; *b* 8 November 1966; *Educ* Glenrothes HS, Univ of Michigan Exec Business Sch; *m* 8 April 1994, Beverly; 1 s (Alfie b 18 June 1991), 1 step s (Jai Francois b 25 Aug 1987); *Career* ed: Smash Hits 1990–94, FHM 1994–97; md Kiss FM Radio Ltd 1997–99, ed-in-chief Maxim (USA) 1999–2000, md Men's Div IPC Media 2000–03, chm Wallpaper Magazine Gp 2001–03, gp editorial dir IPC Media 2003–06, founding dir Crash Test Media 2006–, ceo ShortList Media 2007–16 (launched ShortList magazine Sept 2007, launched Stylist magazine Oct 2009), chm ShortList Media 2016–; Magazine of the Year UK (for FHM) 1997, Sony Gold Award (for Kiss FM) 1999, Magazine of the Year USA (for Maxim) 2000, Launch of the Year Award UK (for ShortList) 2008 and (for Stylist) 2010, PPA Publisher of the Year 2009, SME of the Year Nat Business Award (for Shortlist Media Ltd) 2011; tstee bd memb Comic Relief 2003–10; *Recreations* golf, watching Arsenal FC, gourmet cooking, running, cycling, travel; *Clubs* Soho House, Ivy; *Style—* Mike Soutar, Esq; ✉ ShortList Media Limited, 26–34 Emerald Street, London WC1N 3QA (☎ 020 7611 9702, e-mail mike.soutar@shortlist.com)

SOUTER, Sir Brian; kt (2011); *Career* co-fndr and chm Stagecoach Gp (chief exec until 2013); Businessman of the Year Insider Elite Award 2004, UK Master Entrepreneur of the Year Ernst & Young Entrepreneur of the Year Award 2010; *Style—* Sir Brian Souter; ✉ Stagecoach Group, 10 Dunkeld Road, Perth PH1 5TW

SOUTHALL, Anna; OBE (2013); da of Stephen Southall, of Herefordshire, and Philippa, *née* Cadbury; *b* 9 June 1948; *Educ* The Mount Sch York, UEA (BA), Gateshead Tech Coll (Postgrad Dip Picture Conservation); *m* 1983 (m dis), Chris Serle, *qv*; 2 s (Harry b 1983, Jack b 1987); *Career* Ecclesiastical Insurance Office 1970, Advsy Bd for Redundant Churches Church Cmmrs 1970–71, secdy school teacher in Shoreditch 1972–74, sr conservation offr Area Museum Service for SE England 1975–81, sr conservator Tate Gallery 1981–96, dir Nat Museums & Galleries of Wales 1998–2002 (asst dir 1996–98), chief exec Museums Libraries and Archives Cncl 2002–03; chair Icon (Inst of Conservation) 2005–06; vice-chair Big Lottery Fund 2006–; memb: Spoliation Advsy Panel 2000–, Exec Bd Assoc of Charitable Fndns 2004–, Advsy Panel Futurebuilders 2005–07; memb: Fawcett Cmmn on Women 2004, Barrow Cadbury's Cmmn on Young People 2005; tstee Barrow Cadbury Tst (chair 1996–2006); *Publications* author of several articles on painting conservation and artists' materials and techniques; *Recreations* family, museums, conservation, countryside; *Style—* Anna Southall, OBE

SOUTHERN, (Colin) Graham; *b* 21 September 1960, Liskeard, Cornwall; *m* Antje; 2 da (Anneke, Caitlin); *Career* Modern and Impressionist Dept and Modern Br Dept Christie's London 1985–90, dir Christie, Manson & Woods 1990–2001, dir Christie's Contemporary London 1997–2001, dir Anthony D'Offay Gallery 2001–; fndr (with Harry Blain, *qv*): Haunch of Venison 2002–, Blain/Southern 2010–; memb Exec Ctee Soc of London Art Dealers, tstee Public Catalogue Fndn 2009–, chm Assessment Bd Royal Drawing Sch 2015–; *Clubs* Chelsea Arts; *Style—* Graham Southern, Esq; ✉ Blain/Southern, 4 Hanover Square, London W1S 1BP (☎ 020 7493 4492, e-mail graham@blainsouthern.com)

SOUTHERN, Rt Rev Humphrey; *see:* Repton, Bishop of

SOUTHGATE, Crispin John; s of Brig John Terence Southgate, OBE, and Stancia Lillian, *née* Collins; *b* 16 February 1955; *Educ* Christ's Hosp, Merton Coll Oxford (MA); *m* 15 Sept 1979, Joanna Mary, da of Gerald Norman Donaldson, TD; 1 da (Eleanor b 1985), 2 s (William b 1987, Richard b 1990); *Career* Price Waterhouse & Co 1977–82; Charterhouse Bank Ltd: joined 1982, dir 1987, md 1992–94; dir S G Warburg 1994–95, md Merrill Lynch 2001–05 (dir 1996–2001), Pentangle Pensions Consltg 2005–; dir Institutional Investment Advrs 2007–; Corp Reporting Users Forum 2005–, Financial Reporting Cncl Working Party on Actuarial Standards 2006–08, IASB Employee Benefits Working Gp 2007–, Financial Stability Bd Enhanced Disclosure Task Force 2012–; treas Rainer Fndn 1984–97, memb Finance Ctee Dulwich Picture Gallery 2007–; ACA 1980; *Books* Instrumentos Financieros Para La Jubilacion (contrib, 2008); *Style—* Crispin Southgate, Esq

SOUTHGATE, Gareth; s of Clive Stanley Southgate, and Barbara Ann, *née* Toll; *b* 3 September 1970; *Educ* Hazelwick Sch W Sussex; *Career* professional footballer; player: Crystal Palace FC 1987–95 (capt 1993–95, champions Div One 1993–94), Aston Villa FC 1995–2001 (capt 1997–2001, winners Coca Cola Cup 1996, finalists FA Cup 2000), Middlesbrough FC 2001–06 (winners Carling Cup 2004, finalists UEFA Cup 2006); England: 50 full caps (1 goal), debut v Portugal 1995, memb squad European Championship 1996 and 2000, World Cup 1998 and 2002; mangr Middlesbrough FC 2006–09; head of elite devpt FA 2011–12; football pundit ITV; *Style—* Gareth Southgate

SOUTHGATE, Dr Vaughan Robert; DL (Beds 2009); s of Stanley Robert Double Southgate, of Kempston, Beds, and Peggy, *née* Dean; *b* 13 May 1944, Kempston, Beds; *Educ* Bedford Modern Sch, Univ of Wales Aberystwyth (BSc), Christ's Coll Cambridge (PhD); *m* 13 Aug 1966, Marilyn, *née* Kuhn; 1 da (Antonia Claire b 10 July 1969), 1 s (Crispin Robert William b 22 Dec 1971); *Career* Nat History Museum: jr res fell 1968, band 4 1971, band 3 1974, head Experimental Taxonomy Div 1983, head Biomedical Parasitology Div and band 2 (special merit) 1992–2004; CBiol 1980; memb Cncl and chm Autumn Symposium Ctee Br Soc for Parasitology; Zoological Soc of London: memb Publications Ctee 1975–80 and 1981–85, memb and chm Zoological Record Advsy Ctee 1982–86, memb Zoological Record Editorial Bd 1983–87; RSTMH: memb Cncl 1979–82 (ex-officio memb 1982–86), memb Meetings Ctee 1980 (chm 1981–85), hon sec 1986–91, vice-pres 1993–95, chm Electronic Publishing Working Pty 1996–98; WHO: dir Collaborating Centre for the Identification and Characterisation of Schistosome Strains and their Snail Intermediate Hosts 1983–2004, memb Working Gp on Schistosomiasis 1986–91, memb Expert Panel on Parasitic Diseases 2003–09; Linnean Soc of London: memb Cncl 1989–92 and 1997–2012, zoology sec 1997–2007, vice-pres 1997–2007, pres-elect 2008–09, pres 2009–12; ed Jl of Natural History 1972–83; memb Editorial Bd: Parasitology 1985–95, Transactions of the Royal Society of Tropical Medicine & Hygiene 1983–90 (chm 1990–91); author and co-author of 160 scientific papers and book chapters; external examiner for higher degrees in univs in UK, France, Belgium, Spain and the Netherlands; High Sheriff Beds 2007–08; pres Old Bedford Modernian Club 2013–14, pres Bedford Millennium Probus Club 2014–15; chm of tstees Friends of Cople Church 2004–14; tstee: John Spedan Lewis Tst 2002–, Beds and Luton Crimebeat 2007–16, Bedford Hospitals Charity 2008–, patron Higgins Bedford 2009–, pres London Soc of Old Aberystwythians 2012–14; hon fell Dept of Biology UCL; C A Wright Meml Medal Br Soc of Parasitology 1990; FRSM 2003,

FRSB 2009 (MIBiol 1980, FIBiol 1988); *Recreations* family, game fishing (trout and salmon), game shooting, photography, walking, travel; *Clubs* Biggleswade Ivel Rotary (fndr memb 2000–12, hon memb 2014–), Roxton Park Trout Fishery, Bedford Camera, Sheerhatch Syndicate Shoot, RSM, Bedford Forum 71; *Style*— Dr Vaughan Southgate, DL; ✉ The Coach House, Woodlands Close, Cople, Bedford MK44 3UE (✆ 01234 838714, e-mail v.southgate714@btinternet.com)

SOUTHWARK, Dean of; *see:* Slee, Very Rev Colin B

SOUTHWARK, Archbishop of (RC) 2010–; Most Rev Peter David Smith; *b* 21 October 1943, Battersea, London; *Educ* Clapham Coll, Univ of Exeter (LLB), St John's Seminary, Pontifical Univ of St Thomas Aquinas Rome (JCD); *Career* ordained priest St John's Seminary RC Archdiocese of Southwark 1972, asst priest Stockwell S London 1972–74, prof of canon law St John's Seminary 1977–84, vice-judicial vicar and judge Southwark Met Tbnl 1977, judicial vicar Southwark Met Tbnl 1980–85, admin St Andrew's Parish Thornton Heath 1984–85, judge Interdiocesan Tbnl of Second Instance Southwark 1985–95, rector St John's Seminary 1985–95, bishop of East Anglia 1995–2001, archbishop of Cardiff 2001–10; chm: Catholic Truth Soc 1993–2007, Bishops' Ctee for Marriage and Family Life 1995–2001, Catholic Assoc Pilgrimage Tst 1998–2001, Bishops' Conf Dept for Christian Responsibilty and Citizenship 1998–, Central Religious Advsy Ctee (CRAC) of the BBC and ITC 2001–04; vice-chm Catholic Agency for Social Concern 1996–2001, memb Mgmnt Ctee Catholic Educn Serv 1998–2001, vice-pres Catholic Bishops' Conf of England and Wales 2009–; hon fell Univ of Wales Lampeter 2004, hon fell Cardiff Univ 2006; Sub-Prelate and Chaplain Order of St John of Jerusalem 2002; Knight Cdr with Star Knights of the Holy Sepulchre 2010; *Style*— The Most Rev the Archbishop of Southwark; ✉ Archbishop's House, 150 St George's Road, London SE1 6HX (✆ 020 7928 2495, e-mail archbishop@rcsouthwark.co.uk, website www.rcsouthwark.co.uk)

SOUTHWELL, Dean of; *see:* Guille, Ven John Arthur

SOUTHWELL, Richard Charles; QC (1977); s of late Sir Philip Southwell, CBE, MC, and Mary, *née* Scarratt; *Educ* Winchester, Trinity Coll Cambridge; *m* 1962, Belinda Mary, da of late Col F H Pownall, MC; 2 s, 1 da; *Career* called to the Bar Inner Temple 1959 (reader 2001, treas 2002); Commercial Bar 1961–2003; past judge of the Courts of Appeal of Jersey and Guernsey, past Lt Bailiff Royal Ct of Guernsey; past pres Lloyd's Appeal Tbnl; past chm House of Laity Salisbury Diocesan Synod; lay canon emeritus Salisbury Cathedral; past govr and chm: St Mary's Sch Calne, Warminster Sch; founding tstee Tropical Health and Educn Tst (THET), tstee Community of St Denys, vice-chm and tstee Hosp of St John and St Katherine Heytesbury; chm Wessex Multiple Sclerosis Therapy Centre; *Publications* Quality of Justice, Quality of Justice: The Way Forward; *Recreations* helping charities and the Church of England; *Style*— Richard Southwell, QC; ✉ Manor House, Upton Lovell, Warminster, Wiltshire BA12 0JW (e-mail rcs@rcs-qc.com); Serle Court Chambers, 6 New Square, Lincoln's Inn, London WC2A 3QS (✆ 020 7242 6105, fax 020 7405 4004, e-mail clerks@serlecourt.co.uk)

SOUTHWELL AND NOTTINGHAM, Bishop of 2015–; Rt Rev Paul Gavin Williams; *Career* ordained 1992; curate St James and St Matthew's Muswell Hill, curate Christ Church Clifton, rector St James's Gerrard Cross, bishop of Kensington 2009–15; *Style*— The Rt Rev the Bishop of Southwell and Nottingham

SOWARD, Prof Andrew Michael; *b* 20 October 1943, London; *Educ* St Edward's Sch Oxford, Queens Coll Cambridge (open exhibition, BA, PhD), Univ of Cambridge (ScD); *m* 1968; 1 da, 1 s; *Career* visiting memb Univ of NY Courant Inst of Mathematical Sciences 1969–70; visiting fell Co-op Inst for Res in Environmental Sciences Boulder Colorado 1970–71; Univ of Newcastle upon Tyne: SRC res fell 1971, lectr 1971–81, reader in fluid mechanics 1981–86, head Dept of Applied Mathematics 1985–88, prof of fluid dynamics 1986–95, head Div of Applied Mathematics 1989–95, strategic research advsr 2011–; prof of applied mathematics Univ of Exeter 1996–2009 (emeritus prof 2009–); res and teacher Inst of Geophysics and Planetary Physics UCLA 1977–78; on staff Geophysical Fluid Dynamics Summer Sch Woods Hole Oceanographic Instn MA 1978 and 1987; ed Jl of Geophysical and Astrophysical Fluid Dynamics 1991– (memb Editorial Bd 1986–89, assoc ed 1989–90); FRAS, FIMA, FRS 1991; *Publications* book series ed The Fluid Mechanics of Astrophysics and Geophysics (jtly, 1994–2010); author of over 100 scientific papers; *Clubs* Fell and Rock Climbing; *Style*— Prof Andrew Soward, FRS; ✉ School of Mathematics & Statistics, Newcastle University, Newcastle upon Tyne, NE1 7RU (✆ 0191 208 7311, e-mail andrew.soward@ncl.ac.uk)

SOWDEN, Prof David Stewart; s of John Stewart Sowden (d 1980), and Elisabeth Ann, *née* Barford (d 1991); *b* 27 April 1956; *Educ* Cranbourne Bilateral Sch, Queen Marys Sixth Form Coll, Leeds Med Sch (MB ChB, DCH, DFFP); *m* 1981, Dr Maureen Patricia Burnett; *Career* house offr: (surgery) Leeds Gen Infirmary 1979–80, (med) Chapel Allerton Hosp Leeds 1980; GP vocational trg scheme Lincoln 1980–83, ptnr and full time princ in gen practice Measham 1983–2000; Univ of Leicester: clinical tutor to Dept of Gen Practice 1983–97, dir Gen Practice Postgraduate Educn Dept 1995–2000 (assoc regnl advsr 1991–95, chm Summative Assessment Bd 1997–2000); Leicester Vocational Trg Scheme: vocational trainer 1986–97, vocational course organiser 1988–91; postgrad dean of med Univ of Nottingham 2000–12, dean dir Trent Multi-Professional Deanery 2005–07, dean dir E Midlands Healthcare Workforce Deanery 2007–12, seconded as sr responsible owner (SRO) for Modernising Medical Careers (MMC) prog Dept of Health 2008–09; lead visitor Jt Ctee on Postgrad Trg for Gen Practice (JCPTGP) 2000–05 (nat lead dean obstetrics and gynaecology 2001–10, nat lead dean cardiothoracic surgery 2001–08, nat lead dean sport and exercise medicine 2005–10, nat lead dean genito-urinary med 2009–10), lead visitor Postgraduate Medical Educn and Trg Bd (PMETB) 2006–10 (memb Quality Assurance Sub-Ctee 2004–05), quality assurance visitor GMC 2010–11; educational advsr pandemic flu Dept of Health 2008–10, dir of medical educn (England) 2012, sr clinical advsr Centre for Workforce Intelligence 2012–; memb Educn and Trg Advsy Bd GMC 2013–; chair English Deans Ctee 2006–08, co-chair English Prog Bd Modernising Medical Careers (MMC) 2007–09, chair COPMeD (UK) 2010–12; non-exec dir Jt Mgmnt Bd WRT and NWP 2005–08; visiting prof Univ of Lincoln 2006–; FRCGP, FFSEM, FRCOG ad eundem, fell Acad of Medical Educators; *Recreations* golf, photography, travel; *Clubs* Willesley Park Golf, Arabella Country Estate SA; *Style*— Prof David Sowden; ✉ 18 Tower Gardens, Ashby de la Zouch, Leicestershire LE65 2GZ (✆ 01530 411119, e-mail sowden.burnett@sky.com)

SOWDEN, Susan; *née* Letley; da of Albert Henry Letley, and Ethel May Letley; *b* 10 June 1951, Margate, Kent; *Educ* Clarendon House GS for Girls, KCL (BSc, AKC, PGCE), Open Univ (Advanced Dip Educational Mgmnt); *m* 1, 18 Aug 1973; 3 c; m 2, 19 Aug 2000; *Career* teacher of geography, geology and environmental sci Peers Sch Oxford 1973–77 and 1984–85; various posts incl geography teacher, head of geography, housemistress (day girls), head of year and second dep head Headington Sch Oxford 1985–94; headmistress St Mary's Sch Wantage 1994–2006, registrar Headington Sch Oxford 2007–15; examination work 1973–94; chief examiner CSE (E Midlands Regnl Examinations Bd (EMREB)) 1983–87 and GCSE (Southern Examinations Gp (SEG)) 1987–89, sr asst chief examiner A Level (Jt Matriculation Bd (JMB)/Northern Examinations and Assessment Bd (NEAB)) 1988–94, team ldr for Teacher In Serv Trg (INSET) for SEG and NEAB; memb: Central ISIS Fin and Gen Purposes Ctee 1995–98, GSA Membership Ctee 1996–2001, The Bloxham Project Steering Ctee 1998–2005 (chm 1999–2005); voluntary teacher Leafield Primary Sch 1984–85; community serv work 1997–: Rotary Club, Dist Cncl Safety Ctee and Drugs Sub-Ctee; parish duties St Giles' Church Horspath 1988–94, asst ldr of Young Church Wychwood Parishes 1984–88; memb Leafield PC 1983–85; Anglican lay min 1993–; *Recreations* touring, canoeing, camping, walking with my family, visiting Nat Tst and Heritage sites, music, concerts, theatre, reading, cooking, handicrafts, watching sport (especially motor racing); *Style*— Mrs Sue Sowden

SOWERBY, Rt Rev Mark Crispin Rake; *see:* Horsham, Bishop of

SPACKMAN, Kim; da of Arthur Albert Spackman (d 1983), and Hilary Denise, *née* Maidment; *b* 29 October 1957; *Educ* Walthamstow Hall Kent; *Career* Thames TV plc 1980–92: sometime prog mangr, prodn mangr, assoc prodr, line prodr; line prodr Dark Horse Productions 1992; Reg Grundy Productions: prodn mangr 1992–94, head of prog mgmnt 1994–97; head of prog mgmnt Pearson TV UK Productions 1997–2001, head of prog mgmnt Thames TV Ltd 2001–; *Recreations* swimming, opera, reading, cinema; *Style*— Ms Kim Spackman; ✉ Thames Television Ltd, 1 Stephen Street, London W1T 1AL (✆ 020 7691 6504, fax 020 7691 6086)

SPACKMAN, Michael John; s of Geoffrey Bertram Spackman (d 1976), and Audrey Ivy Elizabeth, *née* Morecombe (d 1998); *b* 8 October 1936, Richmond, Surrey; *Educ* Malvern Coll, Clare Coll Cambridge (MA), Queen Mary Coll London (MScEcon); *m* 27 Feb 1965, Judith Ann, da of Walter Henry Leathem (d 1966); 2 s (Sean Michael b 1968, Keir David b 1972), 2 da (Juliet Sarah Helen Christina b 1977, Helena Claire Nicola b 1982); *Career* Mil Serv 2 Lt RA 1955–57; physicist UKAEA Capenhurst 1960–69, sr physicist/engr The Nuclear Power Group Ltd 1969–71, princ scientific offr then economic advsr Dept of Energy 1971–77, dir of economics and accountancy Civil Serv Coll 1979–80; HM Treasy: economic advsr 1977–79, head Public Servs Economics Div 1980–85, under sec and head Public Expenditure Economics Gp 1985–91 and 1993–95; chief economic advsr Dept of Tport 1991–93; Gwilym Gibbon fell Nuffield Coll Oxford 1995–96, affiliated conslt NERA Economic Consulting 1996–, visiting fell Centre for Analysis of Risk and Regulation LSE 2001–10, visiting sr fell Grantham Research Inst on Climate Change and the Environment LSE 2010–; *Recreations* walking, climbing; *Style*— Michael Spackman; ✉ 44 Gibson Square, Islington, London N1 0RA (✆ 020 7359 1053)

SPALDING, Alistair William; CBE (2012); s of Robert Spalding (d 1997), and Pauline, *née* Kenny; *b* 25 August 1957, Stotfold, Beds; *Educ* Hatfield Poly (BA), Edge Hill Coll (PGCE); *Children* 2 s (William b 18 June 2001, Casper b 25 Oct 2008); *Career* head of dance and performance South Bank Centre 1994–2000, dir of programming Sadler's Wells 2000–04, ceo and artistic dir Sadler's Wells 2004–; chair Dance UK, memb Cncl Arts Cncl of England 2009–; Chevalier de l'Ordre des Arts et des Lettres; *Recreations* swimming; *Clubs* Two Brydges; *Style*— Alistair Spalding, Esq, CBE; ✉ Sadler's Wells Theatre, Roseberry Avenue, London EC1R 4TN (✆ 020 7863 8034, e-mail artisticdirector@sadlerswells.com)

SPALDING, Frances; CBE (2005); da of Hedley Stinston Crabtree (d 1985), and Margaret, *née* Holiday (d 1989); *b* 16 July 1950; *Educ* Farringtons Sch Chislehurst, Univ of Nottingham (BA, PhD); *m* 20 April 1974 (m dis 1991), Julian Spalding; 1 s (Daniel b 11 Aug 1983); *Career* art historian and biographer; lectr Sheffield City Poly 1978–88, indep scholar 1989–2000, research co-ordinator for the Writers-in-Prison Ctee English PEN 1991–93, ed The Charleston Magazine 1992–2000, reader Newcastle Univ 2002 (lectr 2000, prof 2007); Paul Mellon sr research fell and visiting research fell Newnham Coll Cambridge 2005–06; ed Burlington Magazine 2015–16; memb: Soc of Authors, PEN, Charleston Tst 1991–2012, Exec Ctee English PEN 1997–2000; Hon FRCA, FRSL 1984 (memb Cncl 2006–11); *Publications* Magnificent Dreams: Burne-Jones and the late Victorians (1978), Whistler (1979, revised edn 1994), Roger Fry: Art and Life (1980), Vanessa Bell (1983), British Art since 1900 (1986), Stevie Smith: A Critical Biography (1988, revised edn 2002), Twentieth Century Painters and Sculptors (Dictionary of British Art series, 1990), Dance till the Stars Come Down: A Biography of John Minton (1991, revised edn 2005), Virginia Woolf: Paper Darts (selected and introduced, 1991), Duncan Grant (1997), The Bloomsbury Group (1997, revised edn 2005), The Tate: A Centenary History (1998), Gwen Raverat: Friends, Family and Affections (2001), John Piper in the 1930s: Abstraction on the Beach (with David Fraser Jenkins, 2003), Ravilious in Public (2003), John Piper, Myfanwy Piper: Lives in Art (2009), Prunella Clough: Regions Unmapped (2012), Virginia Woolf: Art, Life & Vision (2014); *Recreations* music; *Style*— Frances Spalding, CBE, FRSL; ✉ c/o Rogers, Coleridge & White Ltd, 20 Powis Mews, London W11 1JN (✆ 020 7226 5876)

SPALDING, Julian; s of Eric Spalding, and Margaret Grace, *née* Savager; *b* 15 June 1947; *Educ* Chislehurst and Sidcup GS for Boys, Univ of Nottingham (BA, Dip Museums Assoc); *m* 1, 1974 (m dis 1991), Frances; 1 s; m 2, 1991, Gillian, *née* Tait; *Career* art asst: Leicester Museum and Art Gallery 1970–71, Durham Light Infantry Museum and Arts Centre 1971–72; keeper Mappin Art Gallery 1972–76; dir: Sheffield City Cncl 1982–85 (dep dir 1976–82), Manchester City Art Galleries 1985–89, Glasgow Museums 1989–98; acting dir Nat Museum of Labour History 1987–88; dir: Scottish Football Museum Tst 1995–99, Niki de Saint Phalle Fndn 1995–; BBC broadcaster (talks and reviews incl Third Ear (BBC Radio 3) 1988); res fell Museum of Denmark 1999–2000; chm: Exhibitions Sub-Ctee Arts Cncl 1981–82 and 1986, Drawing Power 2000–; memb: Art Panel 1978–82, Art Galleries Assoc 1987– (fndr and memb Ctee 1976–), Visual Arts Advsy Ctee Br Cncl 1990–; master Guild of St George John Ruskin's Guild 1996–2005 (companion 1978, dir 1983); Crafts Cncl: memb Projects and Orgn Ctee 1985–87, memb 1986–90, memb Purchasing Ctee 1986, memb Exhibitions Ctee 1986–90; Lord Provost's Prize for Services to the Visual Arts in Glasgow 1999; FMA 1983; *Books* L S Lowry (1979), Three Little Books on Painting (1984), Is There Life in Museums? (1990), The Poetic Museum – Reviving Historic Collections (2002), The Eclipse of Art – Tackling the Crisis in Art Today (2003), The Art of Wonder: A History of Seeing (2005, Bannister Fletcher Prize 2006), Peter Angermann: Art and Life (2009), The Best Art You've Never Seen: 101 Hidden Treasures from Around the World (2010), Con Art – Why You Should Sell Your Damien Hirsts While You Can (2012), Nothing On – a satirical novel on contemporary art (2012), Elizabeth Frink Catalogue Raisonne (2013), Summers of Discontent – the Purpose of the Arts Today (with Raymond Tallis, 2014), Realisation – from Seeing to Understanding: The Origins of Art (2015); exhibition catalogues incl: Modern British Painting (1975), Glasgow's Great British Art Exhibition (1990), Gallery of Modern Art Glasgow (1996); contrib Burlington Magazine; *Style*— Julian Spalding, Esq; ✉ 90 Grassmarket, Edinburgh EH1 2JR (✆ and fax 0131 226 3798)

SPALL, Timothy; OBE (2000); *Career* actor; hon vice-pres The Archie and Gwen Smith Meml Tst Fund; FRSA 2000; *Theatre* NT incl: Bottom in A Midsummer's Night Dream, Ligurio in Mandragola, Dauphin in Saint Joan, Le Bourgeois Gentilhomme; RSC incl: Andre in The Three Sisters, Rafe in Knight of the Burning Pestle, Waxford Squeers/Mr Folair in Nicholas Nickleby, Simple in The Merry Wives of Windsor, Ivan in Suicide, Mech in Baal; Birmingham Rep incl: Boucicault in Heavenly Bodies, Gratiano in The Merchant of Venice, Harry Trevor/Baptista in Kiss Me Kate, Lawrence in Mary Barns (also Royal Court); other credits incl: Martin in Aunt Mary (Warehouse), Khelstakov in The Government Inspector (Greenwich), Vic Maggot in Smelling A Rat (Hampstead), Derek in Screamers (Playhouse Studio Edinburgh); *Television* BBC incl: Phil in A Nice Day at the Office, Jimmy Beales in Roots, Chico in La Nona, Francis Meakes in Broke, Paul in Body Contact, Clevor Trevor in Arena – Night Moves, Hawkins in Guest of the Nation, Gordon in Home Sweet Home, Sgt Baxter in A Cotswold Death, Yepikhodov in The Cherry Orchard, Shorty in The Brylcreem Boys, Wainwright in Vanishing Army, Pathologist in Murder Most Horrid, Dread Poets Society, Our Mutual Friend; other credits incl: Barry in Auf Wiedersehen Pet, Webster in Boon (Central), Frank Stubbs in Frank Stubbs Promotes (2 series), Kevin in Outside Edge (3 series, Best TV Comedy Drama

S

Br Comedy Awards 1994 for series 1 and 2), Donald Caudell in Stolen, Porfiry in Great Writers – Dostoyevsky, Lyndon in Dutch Girls, Pilot in A Class Act, Andrei in The Three Sisters, Pig Robinson in The Tale of Little Pig Robinson, Gordon Neville's Island, Oswold Bates, Shooting the Past, Vince in The Thing About Vince, Cunningham in Young Indiana Jones, Tommy Rag in Vacuuming Completely Nude in Paradise, Irving in Perfect Strangers, Barry in Auf Wiedersehen Pet 2002 and 2004, Mitchel Greenfield in Bodily Harm 2002, Malcolm Harvey in Mr Harvey Lights a Candle 2005, Terry Cannings in Cherished 2005, Eddie McEvoy in The Street 2006, Bill Ainscow in Mysterious Creatures 2006, The Fattest Man in Britain 2009; *Film* incl: Harry in Quadrophenia 1979, Jim in SOS Titanic 1979, Douglas in Remembrance 1982, Paulus in The Bride 1985, Polidari in Gothic 1986, Igor in To Kill A Priest 1988, Peck in Dream Demon 1988, Reverant Miln in Crusoe 1988, Aubrey in Life is Sweet 1990, Eric Lyle in The Sheltering Sky 1990, Ramborde in 1871 1990, Hodkins in White Hunter Black Heart 1990, Nick Watt in The Nihilist's Double Vision, African Footsteps, Maurice in Secrets and Lies 1996, Rosencrantz in Hamlet 1996, Det Inspr Healey in Wisdom of Crocodiles 1997, Beano Bagot in Still Crazy 1998, Mr Stirling in Clandestine Marriage 1998, Richard Temple in Topsy Turvy 1999, Don Armado in Love's Labour's Lost 1999, Gourville in Vatel 1999, The Mayor in The Old Man who read Love Stories 2001, Andy in Intimacy 2001, Mats in Rock Star 2001, Cliff Gumble in Lucky Break 2001, Thomas in Vanilla Sky 2001, Charles Cheeryble in Nicholas Nickleby 2002, Phil Basset in All or Nothing 2002, Quinty in My House in Umbria 2003, Darren Barrington in Getting Square 2003, Simon Graham in The Last Samurai 2003, Peter Pettigrew in Harry Potter and the Prisoner of Azkaban 2004, Mr Poe in Lemony Snicket's A Series of Unfortunate Events 2004, Peter Pettigrew in Harry Potter and the Goblet of Fire 2005, Albert Pierrepoint in Pierrepoint 2006, Sugarman in Death Defying Acts 2007, Nathaniel in Enchanted 2007, Beadle Bamford in Sweeney Todd 2008, Voice and Churchill in Jackboots in Whitehall 2008, Peter Taylor in The Damned United 2009, Harry Potter and the Half-Blood Prince 2009, Heartless 2009, Desert Flower 2009, From Time to Time 2009, Alice in Wonderland 2010, The King's Speech 2010, Harry Potter and the Deathly Hallows: Part 1 2010, Upside Down 2010, Sofia 2010, Comes a Bright Day 2011; *Clubs* Colony, Dean Street Soho; *Style*— Timothy Spall, OBE; ✉ c/o Markham & Froggatt Ltd, Julian House, 4 Windmill Street, London W1P 1HF (☎ 020 7636 4412, fax 020 7637 5233)

SPALTON, Prof David John; *Educ* Buxton Coll, Westminster Med Sch (MB BS); *m* 26 May 1979, Catherine, da of Donald George Bompas, CMG, of Petts Wood, Kent; 3 s (George b 1980, James b 1983, Benjamin b 1992); *Career* sr registrar Moorfields Eye Hosp 1976–77; prof and conslt ophthalmic surgn: Charing Cross Hosp 1981–83, St Thomas' Hosp 1983, King Edward VII Hosp for Offrs London; hon conslt ophthalmic surgn Royal Hosp Chelsea, ophthalmic advsr to the Met Police, prof of ophthalmology KCL; Liveryman Worshipful Soc of Apothecaries; past president UK and Ireland Soc of Cataract and Refractive Surgery, pres-elct European Soc of Cataract and Refractive Surgery; FRCS 1975, FRCOphth 1988, FRCP 1990; *Books* Atlas of Clinical Ophthalmology (1985, 3 edn 2004, BMA Award for Best Medical Textbook of the Year); *Recreations* fly fishing; *Clubs* Garrick; *Style*— Prof David Spalton; ✉ The London Clinic Eye Centre, 119 Harley Street, London W1G 6AU (☎ 020 7935 6174, e-mail profspalton@gmail.com)

SPARKES, HE Andrew; CMG (2007); *b* 4 July 1959; *Educ* Manchester Grammar, Trinity Hall Cambridge; *m* 1985, Jean Mary, *née* Meakin; 1 s (Edward b 1988), 1 da (Laura b 1992); *Career* diplomat; entered HM Dip Serv 1982, second sec (Chancery) Ankara 1985–88, first sec FCO 1988–92, first sec (political) Bangkok 1992–95, first sec rising to cnsllr FCO 1995–97, on loan to DTI 1997–99, dep head of mission Jakarta 1999–2001, dep high cmmr Pretoria 2001–04, ambass to Democratic Repub of Congo 2004–07 (concurrently non-resident ambass to Congo), ambass to Repub of Kosovo 2008–10, dep head EULEX Kosovo 2010–12, ambass to Nepal 2013–; *Style*— HE Mr Andrew Sparkes, CMG

SPARKES, David; OBE (2011); *b* 11 November 1948, Droitwich, Worcs; *m* Bettina; 4 c; *Career* qualified as engr specialising in fluid mechanics and thermodynamics; chief exec Br Swimming 1994–; gen sec Lige Européen de Natation (LEN); *Books* Swimming for All; *Recreations* cycling; *Clubs* Droitwich Dolphins Swimming (pres); *Style*— David Sparkes, Esq, OBE; ✉ British Swimming, SportPark, 3 Oakwood Drive, Loughborough, Leicestershire LE11 3QF (☎ 01509 618700, fax 01509 618701, website www.swimming.org)

SPARKS, Leslie Thomas (Les); OBE (1997); s of Eric Sparks (d 1977), of Yeovil, and Dorothy Leonie, *née* McQuillen (d 1987); *b* 3 March 1943; *Educ* Kingston Coll of Art (DipArch), Central London Poly (Dip Town and Country Planning); *m* 26 Aug 1967, Yvonne Ann, da of Alfred George Sawyer; 1 da (Heidi Jane b 15 March 1969), 1 s (Richard James b 12 Oct 1972); *Career* princ planning offr London Borough of Lambeth 1968–73, architect/planner for Hugh Wilson and Lewis Womersley 1973–74, chief planner New Ideal Homes 1974–75, Severn Gorge projects mangr Telford Devpt Corp 1975–80, dir of environmental services Bath City Cncl 1980–91, dir of planning and architecture Birmingham City Cncl 1991–99, pt/t planning inspr 1999–2002, cmmr Cmmn for Architecture and the Built Environment (CABE) 1999–2006 (chm Design Review Panel 2004–06, chm Crossrail Design Review Panel 2009–), cmmr English Heritage 2001–08 (memb Advsy Ctee, regnl cmmr for E Midlands, chm English Heritage/CABE Urban Panel); conslt Terence O'Rourke plc 1999–2006, planning advsr Joseph Rowntree Fndn 1999–2007, advsr Nottingham City Cncl 2001–12, architectural advsr Crown Estate 2002–12; visiting prof: Faculty of Built Environment UCE 1995–99, UWE 1999– (external examiner Faculty of Built Environment 1991–94); chm: Historic Buildings and Land Panel Heritage Lottery Fund 1999–2001, Bath and NE Somerset Urban Regeneration Panel 2004–14, W Midlands Region Design Review Panel 2007–, Plymouth Design Review Panel 2007–10, W Midlands Ctee Heritage Lottery Fund 2010–16, Ironbridge Gorge World Heritage Site Strategy Gp; memb: Urban Villages Forum Steering Ctee 1992–96, Historic Buildings Advsy Gp MOD 1994–99, Mgmnt Ctee Nat Cncl for Habitat II (The City Summit) Conf 1995–96, Urban Capacity Sub-Gp Sec of State's UK Round Table on Sustainability 1996–97, Process Sub-Gp Dep PM's Urban Task Force 1998–99, Town Planning Panel Research Assessment Exercise 2001 HEFCE 1999–2001, Review of Heritage Protection Steering Gp DCMS 2003–06, HS2 Design Panel 2015–; memb DOE/DETR/DTLR Steering Gps 1996–2002 (Planning for Sustainability, The Role and Effectiveness of Planning Briefs, Design in the Planning System, Urban Green Spaces Task Force); patron Urban Design Gp 1997–2011, tstee Birmingham Conservation Tst 1999–2012, chm Chamberlain Highbury Tst 2016–; non-exec dir Birmingham Groundwork 1999–2001; hon life memb Historic Towns Forum 1992; Hon DDes UWE 2000; corp memb RIBA 1971; MRTPI 1974, FRSA 1982; *Style*— Les Sparks, Esq, OBE; ☎ 0121 415 4547

SPARKS, Prof (Robert) Stephen John; CBE (2012); s of Kenneth Grenfell Sparks, and late Ruth Joan, *née* Rugman; *b* 15 May 1949; *Educ* Wellington, Bingley GS, Imperial Coll London (BSc, PhD); *m* 19 June 1971, Ann Elizabeth, da of Frederick Currie Talbot (d 1986); 2 s (Andrew Robert James b 24 Aug 1978, Daniel Joseph b 1 May 1982); *Career* Royal Exhibition of 1951 fell Lancaster Univ 1974–76, NATO fell Univ of Rhode Island 1976–78, lectr in geology Univ of Cambridge 1978–89, prof of geology Univ of Bristol 1989–; pres: Geological Soc of London 1994–, Int Assoc of Volcanology and Chemistry of the Earth's Interior 1999–2003; chief scientist Montserrat Volcano Observatory, prof NERC Research 1998–2003, European Research Cncl advanced researcher 2009–; chair Advsy Ctee for Mathematics Educn (ACME); memb: Grants Ctee NERC 1985–88 and 2001–05, various ctees Royal Soc; Bakerian Lecture Royal Soc 2000; Wager Medal Int Assoc of Volcanology and Chemistry of the Earth's Interior 1983, Bigsby Medal Geological Soc London, Murchison Medal Geological Soc London, Arthur Day Medal Geological Soc America, Arthur Holmes Medal European Geosciences Union, Thorarinsson Medal Int Assoc of Volcanology and Chemistry of the Earth's Interior 2008, Wollaston Medal Geological Soc London 2011, Vetlesen Prize 2015; Hon Dr: Lancaster Univ, Blaise Pascal Université, Institut de Physique du Globe de Paris; FRS 1988, FGS, fell American Geophysical Union; *Books* Tephra Studies (co-ed with S Self, 1980), Volcanic Plumes (with John Wiley, 1997), Physics of Explosive Volcanic Eruptions (co-ed with J Gilbert, 1998), Santorini Volcano (1999), State of the Planet (monograph); author of 400 published scientific papers; *Recreations* cricket, music, theatre; *Style*— Prof Stephen Sparks, CBE, FRS; ✉ Walnut Cottage, 19 Brinsea Road, Congresbury BS49 5JF (☎ 01934 834306); Department of Earth Sciences, University of Bristol, Bristol BS8 1RJ (☎ 0117 928 7789, e-mail steve.sparks@bristol.ac.uk)

SPARROW, Andrew; *b* 13 August 1966; *Educ* Univ of Edinburgh (MA); *Career* trained as journalist South Wales Echo, political corr Daily Mail 1995–98, political corr Daily Telegraph 1998–2005, sr political corr The Guardian 2008–; Political Journalist of the Year Br Press Award 2011, Mainstream Blogger in Comment Awards 2012; *Books* Obscure Scribblers: A History of Parliamentary Journalism; *Style*— Andrew Sparrow, Esq; ✉ The Guardian, Kings Place, 90 York Way, London N1 9GU (☎ 020 7219 6769, e-mail andrew.sparrow@theguardian.com)

SPAVEN, Dr Patrick John; OBE (1997); s of John Basil Spaven (d 1960), and Marie, *née* Burford; *b* 2 November 1949; *Educ* Felsted, Univ of Sussex (MA), Univ of Warwick (PhD); *m* 1976, Kirsti, da of Hans-Jacob Hallvang; 1 s (Thomas b 8 June 1983), 1 da (Rebecca b 10 Oct 1990); *Career* tutor in industrial studies Univ of Sheffield 1974–76, Nuffield research assoc Univ of Warwick 1976–77, industrial relations offr Advisory Conciliation and Arbitration Service 1977–80; British Council: industrial relations advsr 1980–84, asst rep Kenya 1984–88, head of employment relations 1988–91, dir Barcelona 1991–96, dir Sweden 1997–2000, head of research and evaluation 2000–05; lead conslt Spaven Research and Evalutation 2005–; hon memb Anglo-Catalan Soc 1993–; MCIPD; *Style*— Dr Patrick Spaven, OBE; ✉ Spaven Research and Evaluation, 7 Lloyd Close, Hove BN3 6LZ

SPEAIGHT, Anthony Hugh; QC (1995); s of George Victor Speaight (d 2005), of Kew Gardens, Surrey, and Mary Olive, *née* Mudd (d 2005); *b* 31 July 1948; *Educ* St Benedict's Sch Ealing, Lincoln Coll Oxford (MA); *m* 3 Aug 1991, Gabrielle Anne Kooy-Lister; 2 s (Edmund William Laurier b 18 July 1992, Lawrence Frederick Joseph b 28 May 1996), 1 da (Isabella Louise Annunziata b 14 Sept 1994); *Career* called to the Bar Middle Temple 1973 (bencher); elected memb Gen Cncl of the Bar 1987–91 and 1998–2000, memb Bar Cncl Working Pty on Televising Cts 1988; cmmr Govt Cmmn on a UK Bill of Rights 2011–12; chm Editorial Bd Counsel (Jl of the Bar of Eng and Wales) 1991–95, chm Bar Cncl Access to the Bar Ctee 2004–06; nat chm Fedn of Cons Students 1972–73, chm Youth Bd of the Euro Movement (UK) 1974–75, dep chm Cons Gp for Europe 1977, chm of research Soc of Conservative Lawyers 2016; Freeman City of London; Schuman Silver medal (awarded by FVS Fndn of Germany) 1976; *Books* The Law of Defective Premises (with G Stone, 1982), The Architects Journal Legal Handbook (jtly, 1985–2010), Butterworths Professional Negligence Service (jt ed, 2000); *Recreations* theatre, cricket, growing vegetables; *Clubs* Carlton (chm Political Ctee 2009–13), Hurlingham; *Style*— Anthony Speaight, Esq, QC; ✉ 4 Pump Court, Temple, London EC4 (☎ 020 7842 5555, fax 020 7583 2036)

SPEAKMAN, Prof John Roger; s of Ernest Wilcock Speakman, and (Miriam) Freda Speakman; *b* 29 November 1958, Leigh, Lancs; *Educ* Univ of Stirling (BSc, PhD), Univ of Aberdeen (DSc); *m* 9 Aug 1980, Mary Magdelene; 1 da (Emily Ann b 14 April 1993), 1 s ((Alasdair) Jack b 17 July 1995); *Career* Univ of Aberdeen: successively lectr, sr lectr and reader 1989–97, prof 1997–, head of integrative physiology 2003–; seconded pt/t to Rowett Research Inst 2000–05; memb Advsy Bd Mars Masterfoods 2001–; dir Co of Biologists 2004–; Scientific Medal Zoological Soc of London 1997, Scottish Science Medal Saltire Soc 2004; FRSE 2004; *Publications* Doubly Labelled Water: Theory and Practice (1997), Body Composition in Animals: A Handbook of Non-Invasive Methods (ed, 2001); author of more than 225 articles and papers in scientific pubns; *Recreations* photography; *Style*— Prof John Speakman

SPEARING, Prof Anthony Colin; s of Frederick Spearing, and Gertrude, *née* Calnin; *b* 31 January 1936; *Educ* Alleyn's Sch Dulwich, Jesus Coll Cambridge (MA), Univ of Cambridge (LittD); *m* 1961; 1 s, 1 da; *Career* research on Piers Plowman under supervision of C S Lewis and Elizabeth Salter 1957–60; Univ of Cambridge: W M Tapp fell Gonville & Caius Coll 1959–60, asst lectr in English 1960–64, supernumerary fell Gonville & Caius Coll 1960; Queens' Coll Cambridge: asst dir of studies in English 1960–67, lectr in English 1964–85, dir of studies in English 1967–85, sec Faculty of English 1970–71, chm Degree Ctee Faculty of English 1977–79, reader in Medieval English literature 1985–87, chm Faculty of English 1986–87, official fell 1960–87, life fell 1987–; Univ of Virginia: visiting prof of English 1979–80 and 1984, Center for Advanced Studies 1987–89, prof of English 1987–89, William R Kenan prof of English 1989–2016 (prof emeritus 2016–); external examiner: Univ of Bristol 1974, MA in Medieval Studies Univ of York 1974–76; Studentship Selection Ctee UK Dept of Educn and Science 1976–79; William Matthews lectr Birkbeck Coll London 1983–84; Lansdowne visiting fell Univ of Victoria BC 1993, Benjamin Meaker visiting prof Univ of Bristol 2003, Conway lectr Univ of Notre Dame 2007, visiting lectr at numerous univs in Britain, Europe, Canada and USA; PhD (hc) Lund Univ Sweden 2011; *Publications* Criticism and Medieval Poetry (1964, 2 edn 1972), An Introduction to Chaucer (with Maurice Hussey and James Winny, 1965), The Gawain Poet: A Critical Study (1970), Chaucer: Troilus and Criseyde (1976), Medieval Dream-Poetry (1976), Medieval to Renaissance in English Poetry (1985), Readings in Medieval Poetry (1987), The Medieval Poet as Voyeur (1993), The Cloud of Unknowing (trans, 2001), Textual Subjectivity: The Encoding of Subjectivity in Medieval Romances and Lyrics (2005), Medieval Autographies: The 'I' of the Text (2012); contrib to numerous learned jls; *Style*— Prof A C Spearing

SPEARING, (David) Nicholas; s of late George David Spearing, and Josephine Mary, *née* Newbould, of Kingston, Surrey; *b* 4 May 1954; *Educ* Caterham Sch, Hertford Coll Oxford (MA); *Family* 2 da (Laura b 1982, Elizabeth b 1987), 3 s (James b 1989, George b 1992); m, 2004, Caroline, *née* Butler; 1 s (Frederick b 2008); *Career* slr; articled Gordon Dadds & Co 1976–78; Freshfields: asst slr 1978–84, ptnr 1984–2012; ptnr Milbank, Tweed, Hadley & McCloy 2012–15, counsel Davis Polk & Wardwell 2015–; past chm Law Soc Slrs' Euro Gp; past pres Fielding Soc; memb City of London Slrs' Co; *Publications* contrib: Encyclopaedia of Forms and Precedents, Butterworths Competition Law; author of articles in professional jls; *Recreations* modern art, reading, antiques; *Style*— Nicholas Spearing, Esq; ✉ 21 Shooters Hill Road, Blackheath, London SE3 7AS (☎ 020 8293 1727, email nspearing@btinternet.com)

SPEARMAN, John Litting; s of Thomas Spearman, and Elizabeth Alexandra, *née* Leadbeater; *b* 25 November 1941; *Educ* Trinity Coll Dublin (MA); *m* 1, 1966, Susan Elizabeth, *née* Elmes; 1 s (Thomas Crawford John), 1 da (Laragh Elizabeth Jane); m 2, 1988, Angela Josephine, *née* van Praag; 1 da (Ottoline); *Career* graduate trainee Unilever 1964, account dir Lintas Advtg 1969, account dir and assoc bd dir Leo Burnett 1969–73, account dir, md then chm and chief exec Collett Dickenson Pearce 1973–90, chm Lazer Sales (sales and mktg subsid of LWT) 1990–92, chief exec Classic FM Radio 1992–97 (dep chm 1997–98); chm Playback (mgmnt trg video co) 1990–, operating ptnr Electra 1998–, chm FrameStore Gp 2001–; bd dir Royal Philharmonic Orch 1993–96, memb

Industry Lead Body for Design, patron dir RIBA, tstee World Monuments Fund, pres Music Therapy Appeal Ctee; memb Arts Cncl 1996–98; *Recreations* music, theatre, reading, gardening, walking, skiing, sailing; *Clubs* Athenaeum, Royal Irish Yacht, Hurlingham; *Style*— John Spearman, Esq

SPEARMAN, Richard; QC (1996); s of late Clement Spearman, CBE, and late Olwen Regina, *née* Morgan; *b* 19 January 1953; *Educ* Bedales, King's Coll Cambridge (MA); *m* 30 April 1983, Alexandra Elizabeth, da of late Bryan A Harris; 3 da (Olivia b 6 July 1985, Annabel b 11 Oct 1987, Lucinda b 16 Jan 1992); *Career* called to the Bar Middle Temple 1977 (bencher 2006), dep judge of the High Court of Justice 2013–; recorder 2000– (asst recorder 1998–2000), head of chambers 4–5 Gray's Inn Square 2012, memb 39 Essex Chambers 2013–; *Books* Sale of Goods Litigation (with F A Philpott, 1983, 2 edn 1994), Information Rights (contrib, 2004, 3 edn 2010); *Recreations* lawn tennis, real tennis, skiing, family; *Clubs* Brooks's, Hurlingham, MCC; *Style*— Richard Spearman, Esq, QC; ✉ 39 Essex Chambers, 81 Chancery Lane, London WC2A 1DD (☎ 020 7832 1111, fax 020 7353 3978, e-mail clerks@39essex.com)

SPEIRS, Robert (Bob); s of John Speirs (d 1967), and Isabella, *née* Clark (d 1993); *b* 23 October 1936; *Educ* Alleynes GS Uttoxeter; *m* 15 March 1958, Patricia; 2 s (John b 29 Aug 1967, Julian b 28 May 1971); *Career* Inland Revenue 1954–58, Dept of Taxes Fed of Rhodesia and Nyasaland 1958–64, sr tax mangr Coopers & Lybrand 1964–68, UK tax administrator Texaco Ltd 1968–77, fin dir BNOC/Britoil plc 1977–88, fin dir Olympia York Canary Wharf Ltd 1988–93, fin dir Royal Bank of Scotland Gp plc 1993–98; chm: Bell Gp plc 1999–2004, Miller Gp Ltd 1999–2008, Stagecoach Gp plc 2002–10 (non-exec dir 1995–2010); non-exec dir Canary Wharf Gp plc 1999–2004; *Recreations* gardening, travel, history, family (6 grandchildren); *Style*— Robert Speirs, Esq; ✉ Arden, Pitts Haven, Pitts Lane, Binstead, Isle of Wight PO33 3AX (☎ 01983 568708, mobile 07713 155735)

SPELLAR, Rt Hon John Francis; PC (2001), MP; s of William David Spellar; *b* 5 August 1947; *Educ* Dulwich Coll, St Edmund Hall Oxford; *m* 1981, Anne (d 2003); 1 da; *Career* nat offr EETPU 1969–82 and 1983–92; MP (Lab): Birmingham Northfield 1982–83, Warley W 1992–97, Warley 1997– (Parly candidate (Lab): Bromley 1970, Birmingham Northfield 1983 and 1987); memb Commons Select Ctee on Energy 1982–83, sec All-Pty Construction Ctee 1992–, oppn whip (Employment and Trade and Industry) 1992–94; oppn spokesman on: NI 1994–95, Defence 1995–97; Parly under sec of state MOD 1997–99, min of state for Armed Forces 1999–2001, min for Tport 2001–03, min of state for NI 2003–05, asst chief whip 2008–10, dep chief whip (oppn) 2010, oppn spokesman on foreign affrs 2010–; *Recreations* reading, gardening; *Clubs* Rowley Regis and Blackheath Labour; *Style*— The Rt Hon John Spellar, MP; ✉ House of Commons, London SW1A 0AA (☎ 020 7219 0674, e-mail spellarj@parliament.uk)

SPELLER, Prof Vivienne Marilyn (Viv); da of Edward Speller (d 1998), and Rosina Clara, *née* Bell (d 2012); *b* 28 July 1953; *Educ* Univ of Manchester (BSc, PhD); *Children* 1 da (Laura Jane Pottinger b 8 May 1983), 1 s (Matthew Bowman Pottinger b 6 July 1987); *Career* health educn Manchester and London 1978–84, dist health promotion mangr Wandsworth HA 1984–86 and Winchester HA 1986–92, regnl health promotion mangr and regnl Health of the Nation co-ordinator Wessex RHA and Wessex Inst for Public Health Med 1992–96, sr lectr in health promotion Univ of Southampton 1996–2000, exec dir of public health devpt and memb Bd Health Devpt Agency 2000–04; temp advsr WHO 2002–04, ind public health conslt 2004–, dir Health Devpt Consulting Ltd 2006–, visiting sr research fell Univ of Southampton 2007–, visiting prof South Bank Univ 2013; generalist specialist UK Voluntary Register for Public Health Specialists 2006; FFPH 2006; *Publications* author of numerous books, reports, peer-reviewed articles and book chapters; *Recreations* yoga, horses, gardening, reading; *Style*— Professor Viv Speller; ✉ Denmead, Hampshire (☎ 023 9223 2741, e-mail viv.speller@healthdevelopment.co.uk)

SPELLMAN, (Irene) Ruth; OBE (2007); *née* Hewlett; *b* Pyle, Glamorgan; *Educ* Croesyceiliug GS, Girton Coll Cambridge (MA); *m* 14 April 1979, Dr William Spellman; 3 c (Fiona, William, Rhiannon); *Career* NCB 1972–76, NEDO 1976–86, HR dir Eastern Region Coopers & Lybrand 1986–91, HR dir NSPCC 1991–98, chief exec Investors in People UK 1998–2006, chief exec IMechE 2006–08, chief exec CMI 2008–; FCIPD (FIPD 1996), FRSA 2000; *Recreations* music, politics, English literature; *Style*— Mrs Ruth Spellman, OBE; ✉ Chartered Management Institute, 2 Savoy Court, Strand, London WC2R 0EZ

SPELMAN, Rt Hon Caroline Alice; DBE (2016), PC (2010), MP; *née* Cormack; da of Marshall Cormack (d 2000), and Helen Margaret, *née* Greenfield (d 1994); *b* 4 May 1958; *Educ* Herts and Essex GS (Joan Ashdown Scholar), Queen Mary Coll London (DAAD Scholarship to Freiburg, Drapers' Co Prize, BA); *m* 25 April 1987, Mark Gerald Spelman, s of Denis Gerald Spelman (d 2001); 1 da (Eleanor b 27 April 1991), 2 s (David b 12 Sept 1992, Jonathan b 7 Nov 1994); *Career* sugar beet advsr to NFU of England and Wales 1981–84, dep dir Int Confdn of Euro Beetgrowers 1984–89, dir Spelman, Cormack & Assocs (agric conslts) 1989–2009; MP (Cons) Meriden 1997–; oppn whip 1998–1999, oppn spokesman health 1999–2001, shadow min for women 1999–01, shadow sec of state for int devpt 2001–03, shadow secretary of state for the environment 2003–04, shadow sec of state for local and devolved govt affrs 2004–06, shadow sec of state for communities and local govt 2006–07, chm Cons Pty 2007–09, shadow sec of state for communities and local govt 2009–10, sec of state for environment, food and rural affrs 2010–12, memb Environmental Audit Select Ctee 2013; vice pres Tearfund 2013; second church estates cmmr 2015–; *Publications* A Green and Pleasant Land (Bow Gp paper, 1991), Non Food Uses of Agricultural Raw Materials (1994); *Recreations* tennis, skiing, choral singing; *Style*— The Rt Hon Dame Caroline Spelman, DBE, MP; ✉ House of Commons, London SW1A 0AA (☎ 020 7219 2886, e-mail caroline@carolinespelman.com)

SPENCE, Christopher Alexander; CBE (2006, MBE 1992); s of Robert Donald Spence (d 1993), and Margaret, *née* Summerford (d 1994); *b* 24 April 1944; *Educ* Bromsgrove Sch; *m* 1990, Nancy Corbin, da of late Max Meadors; *Career* freelance cnsllr 1976–86; London Lighthouse: fndr dir 1986–96, pres 1997–2000; fndr chair Pan London HIV/AIDS Providers Consortium 1992–96, chair The HIV Project 1997–2000; chief exec: Nat Centre for Volunteering 1998–2004, Volunteering England 2004–07; tstee and chair Grants Ctee Diana, Princess of Wales Meml Fund 1998–2006 (chm of bd 1999–2006), tstee and vice-chm Timebank 1999–2002, pres Euro Volunteer Centre Brussels 2001–07; private sec to Speaker of the House of Commons; dir of courses Urban Ministry Project, dir Task Force; non-exec dir Oxfordshire Learning Disability NHS Tst 1996–2002 (vice-chair 1998–2002); lectr Counselling Dip Course London; hon fell Univ of Wales; FRSA 1998; *Publications* A Homecoming and the Harvest: A Counsellor's View of Death, Dying and Bereavement, At Least 100 Principles of Love (with Nancy Kline), AIDS: An Issue for Everyone, AIDS: Time to Reclaim Our Power, On Watch: Views from the Lighthouse; *Style*— Christopher Spence, Esq, CBE; ✉ Lower Farm Orchard, Preston Crowmarsh, Wallingford, Oxfordshire OX10 6SL (☎ 01491 835266, e-mail casp123@btinternet.com)

SPENCE, James William (Bill); DL (Orkney 1988); s of James William Spence (d 2002), of Stromness, Orkney, and Margaret Duncan, *née* Peace (d 2004); *b* 19 January 1945; *Educ* Firth Jr Secdy Sch Orkney, Leith Nautical Coll Edinburgh, Robert Gordon's Inst of Technol Aberdeen (Master Mariner), Univ of Wales Cardiff (BSc); *m* 1, 31 July 1971, Margaret Paplay (d 2000), da of Henry Stevenson (d 1983), of Stromness, Orkney; 3 s (James b 1976 d 2007, Steven b 1978, Thomas b 1980); m 2, 1 Nov 2003, Susan Mary, da of Air Vice-Marshal Robert George Price, CB, of W Heslerton, N Yorks; *Career* Merchant Navy 1961–74; apprentice deck offr Watts Watts & Co Ltd 1961–65, certificated deck offr P&O Steam Navigation Co Ltd 1965–74; Micoperi SpA 1974–75, temp asst site co-ordinator Scapa Flow Project; John Jolly: mangr 1975, jr ptnr 1976–77, sr ptnr 1977–78, md and proprietor 1978–, chm 2003–; consul Norway 1978 (vice-consul 1976–78), vice-consul The Netherlands 1978–94, chm Assoc of Hon Norwegian Consuls in the UK and Ireland 1993–95 (vice-chm 1991–93); chm RNLI Kirkwall Lifeboat Station Branch Ctee 1997–2004 (dep Launching Authy 1976–87, Station hon sec 1987–96); memb: Kirkwall Community Cncl 1978–82, Orkney Pilotage Ctee 1979–88; chm: Kirkwall Port Employers' Assoc 1979–87 (memb 1975), BHS Orkney Riding Club 1985–92 (memb 1984), Bd of Tstees Pier Arts Centre Tst Orkney 1989–91 (tstee 1980–91); Hon Sheriff Grampian, Highland and Islands (Kirkwall) 2000, Lord-Lt Orkney 2014– (Vice Lord-Lt 2011–14); MNI 1972, MICS 1979; Cdr Royal Norwegian Order of Merit 1987, Chevalier in the Order of Orange-Nassau (Netherlands) 1994; *Recreations* oenophilist, equestrian matters, Orcadian history, vintage motoring; *Clubs* Caledonian; *Style*— J William Spence, Esq; ✉ Alton House, Kirkwall, Orkney KW15 1NA; John Jolly, PO Box 2, Kiln Corner, Kirkwall, Orkney KW15 1HS (☎ 01856 872268, fax 01856 875002, mobile 07885 200860, e-mail cons.kirkwall@johnjolly.co.uk and bs3920@yahoo.com)

SPENCE, John Alexander; OBE (2005), DL (Kent 2001); s of James Alexander Spence (d 1960), of Maidstone, Kent, and Edith Charlotte, *née* Barden; *b* 11 April 1936; *Educ* Maidstone Tech Sch, Royal Dockyard Sch Chatham; *m* 2 July 1973, Patricia (d 2015), o da of Oliver G A Pocock; *Career* engr (ret 1984); non-exec dir Radio Invicta Ltd 1995–2000, non-exec chm/dir various small private cos; chm: Kent Ambulance Serv 1986–93, Medway HA 1986–93, Medway NHS Tst 1993–97; memb Shadow Bd W Kent Health Commissioning Agency 1991–93, formerly memb Cncl NAHA; pres Gillingham Cons Assoc 2002–06 (chm 1963–66, hon treas 1966–73, vice-pres 1973–); memb Gillingham BC 1961–72 (chm various ctees), memb Kent CC 1973–93 (chief whip Cons Gp 1985–92, chm various ctees incl Finance and Kent Superannuation Fund), memb ACC 1982–93 (memb Police Ctee 1982–93, chm Local Govt Fin Ctee 1991–93), chm UK Standing Ctee on Local Govt Superannuation 1992–93; Kent Police Authy: memb 1973–93, vice-chm 1973–77, chm 1981–86; memb Ashford Police Trg Centre 1973–89 (chm 1981–89), memb Police Negotiating Bd and Central Ctee for Common Police Servs 1982–89, memb Police Trg Cncl and Bd of Govrs Bramshill Police Staff Coll 1989–93; memb: Exec Bd Kent Inst of Med and Health Scis 1995–2001, Cncl Univ of Kent 1995–2003 (chm Audit Ctee), Ct Univ of Kent 1995–, Chatham Historic Dockyard Tst 1984–, Ct Rochester Bridge Tst 1987– (Jr Warden 1991–92 and 2001–03, Sr Warden 1992–94 and 2003–05), Rochester Cathedral Cncl 2001– (chm 2009–), Historic Dockyard Property (2005) Ltd 2005– (chm 2013–); tstee New Coll of Cobham 1991–2007 (pres 1991–94 and 2001–05), Rochester Cathedral Tst 2003–, chm Rochester Cathedral Business Guild 2009–; chm: Bridge Wardens Coll Univ of Kent 1996–2005, Medway Educn Business Partnership 1998–2006, Medway Learning Partnership 2000–08; ptnr govr Medway NHS Fndn Tst 2008–14, chm Lower Lines Park Tst 2010–, chm Br Transplant Games 2012; varied charitable work; Hon Alderman Kent CC 2010; hon fell South Bank Univ 1993; Hon DCL Univ of Kent 2003; FRSA; *Recreations* The National Trust; *Style*— John A Spence, Esq, OBE, DL; ✉ 175 Fairview Avenue, Gillingham, Kent ME8 0PX (☎ 01634 232538)

SPENCE, John Andrew; MBE (1999); *b* 30 January 1951; *Educ* George Watson's Coll Edinburgh, Trinity Coll Dublin (BA), Harvard Business Sch (PMD); *m* 26 Oct 1974, Yvonne; 1 s (Euan b 6 Oct 1977), 2 da (Lindsay b 8 March 1979, Catherine b 2 Nov 1981); *Career* Lloyds TSB Gp plc (formerly Lloyds Bank plc): joined 1973, head of business banking 1994–96, md 1996–98, chief exec Lloyds TSB Bank Scotland plc 1998–2000, dir of branch network 2000, dir of distribution 2001, dir of policy co-ordination and risk 2003; non-exec dir Edrington Gp 2001–; pres Enable, dep fin chm Business in the Community, tstee Blind in Business; chm Fin Ctee Chelmsford Cathedral; church cmmr 2005–; FRSA 1996, fell Chartered Inst of Bankers in Scotland (FCIOBS) 2001, FCIB 2003 (ACIB 1976); *Recreations* committees, cooking, swimming, motorcycling, theatre; *Style*— John Spence, MBE; ✉ Essex County Council, County Hall, Market Road, Chelmsford CM1 1QH

SPENCE, Prof John Edward (Jack); OBE (2002); s of John Herbert Spence (d 1946), of Krugersdorp, South Africa, and Violet, *née* Brown (d 1976); *b* 11 June 1931; *Educ* Boys' HS Pretoria, Univ of the Witwatersrand (BA), LSE (BSc); *m* 27 June 1959, Susanne Hilary Spence; 1 da (Rachel b 1967); *Career* lectr Dept of History and Politics Univ of Natal Pietermaritzburg 1958–60, Rockefeller jr res fell LSE 1960–62, reader Dept of Governmental Political Theory UC Swansea 1972–73 (asst lectr 1962–63, lectr 1963–68, sr lectr 1968–72), prof Dept of Politics Univ of Leicester 1973–91 (head of Dept of Politics 1974–81 and 1986–91, pro-vice-chllr 1981–85), dir of studies RIIA 1991–97 (assoc fell 1997–2003); academic advsr RCDS 1997–2007; visiting prof: Univ of California LA 1965 and 1976, Univ of Zimbabwe 1978, Univ of Witwatersrand 1980, Univ of Cape Town 1984, Univ of Natal 1985 and 1987, KCL 1997–, Univ of Reading 2010–15; pres African Studies Assoc UK 1977–78, chm Br Int Studies Assoc 1986–88, memb Hong Kong Cncl for Academic Awards 1986–90; memb RIIA 1961; hon fell: Univ of Staffs 1992, UC Swansea 1993, Nene Coll 1995, KCL 2014; Bradlow fell SA Inst of Int Affrs 1986; memb Governing Body: Uppingham Sch 1985–92, Haileybury Sch 1986–90; Hon LLD Univ of Witwatersrand 1997, Hon DLitt Nottingham Trent Univ 1998, Hon DLitt Univ of Leicester 2001; *Books* Republic Under Pressure (1965), Lesotho – Politics of Dependence (1968), Political and Military Framework of Investment in South Africa (1976), British Politics in Perspective (ed with R Borthwick, 1985), Change in South Africa (1994), Violence in Southern Africa (1997), After Mandela: The 1999 South African Election (1999), Seaford House Papers (2000–08), Ending Apartheid (with D Welsh, 2011); *Recreations* collecting Faber poetry volumes, walking dogs; *Style*— Prof J E Spence, OBE; ✉ 143 Corve Street, Ludlow, Shropshire SY8 2PG (e-mail suespence321@gmail.com); c/o Department of War Studies, King's College, The Strand, London WC2R 2LS

SPENCE, Dr Joseph Arthur Francis; s of Joseph Arthur Cuthbert Spence (d 1987), and Lenice, *née* Woolley (d 1992); *b* 18 December 1959, Coventry; *Educ* St Philip's GS Edgbaston, The Salesian Coll Battersea, Univ of Reading (BA), Birkbeck Coll Univ of London (PhD); *m* 29 June 1985, Angela Margaret Alexander, *née* Fiddes; 1 da (Katharine (Kitty) b 27 June 1987), 2 s (William b 28 June 1989, James b 19 Dec 1992); *Career* asst master Eton Coll 1988–2002 (master in coll 1992–2002), headmaster Oakham Sch 2002–09, master Dulwich Coll 2009–; govr of schs incl St George's Windsor Castle, St John's Coll Sch Cambridge and St Anselm's Bakewell; tstee Demarco Archive Tst; ed vols on Yeats, Shaw and Swift (Duckworth's The Sayings of... series) 1991–93; *Recreations* theatre, music, art, football, reading, writing; *Clubs* East India; *Style*— Dr Joseph Spence; ✉ Dulwich College, Dulwich Common, London SE21 7LD

SPENCE, Julie Anne; OBE (2006), QPM (2010), DL (2011); da of Alan Edwin Thomas Miller (d 2004), and Rita Margaret, *née* Moore; *b* 7 August 1955, Framlingham, Suffolk; *Educ* Colchester Co HS for Girls, I M Marsh Coll of PE, Univ of Liverpool (BEd), UWE (LLB), Univ of Exeter (MA), Henley Mgmnt Coll, Brunel Univ (MBA), Univ of Cambridge (Dip), IOD (Cert); *m* 18 April 1987, (Alfred) John Spence; *Career* head of girls' PE Sidcot Sch Winscombe 1977–78; Constable rising to Supt Avon and Somerset Constabulary 1978–99, Asst Chief Constable Thames Valley Police 1999–2004; Cambridgeshire Constabulary: Dep Chief Constable 2004–05, Chief Constable 2005–10, cmmr Press Complaints Cmmn 2011–12; pres British Assoc of Women in Policing; Network Woman of Achievement Award 1997, Leadership Award Int Assoc of Women Police 2002, Champions Award

S

Opportunity Now 2006, First Women Public Service Award 2009; hon doctorate Anglia Ruskin Univ 2008; *Recreations* walking, travelling, keeping fit, listening to smooth jazz; *Style*— Mrs Julie Spence, OBE, QPM, DL; ✉ Jule Spence Ltd (☎ and fax 01223 571848, e-mail jspence964@hotmail.co.uk)

SPENCE, Emeritus Prof Robert; s of Robert Whitehair Spence (d 1988), and Minnie Grace, *née* Wood (d 1984); *b* 11 July 1933; *Educ* Hymers Coll Hull, Hull Coll of Technol (BSc), Imperial Coll London (DIC, PhD, DSc); *m* 18 April 1960, Kathleen (d 2003), da of George Potts; 1 s (Robert b 1963), 1 da (Merin b 1966); *Career* Imperial Coll London: lectr 1962, reader 1968, prof of info engrg 1984–, head of Dept of Electrical and Electronic Engrg 1997–99, sr res investigator 2000–, emeritus prof 2000; Erskine fell Univ of Canterbury NZ 2002, visiting fell Univ of Manchester 2003–; founding dir and chm Interactive Solutions Ltd 1985–90; author of numerous papers; Dr RCA 1998; hon prof Univ of Waikato 2007–; FIEEE, FCGI, FREng 1990; Officier De L'ordre Du Palme Académique (France) 1996; *Books* Linear Active Networks (1970), Tellegen's Theorem and Electrical Networks (1970), Resistive Circuit Theory (1974), Modern Network Theory – An Introduction (1978), Sensitivity and Optimisation (1980), Circuit Analysis by Computer (1986), Tolerance Design of Electronic Circuits (1988), Information Visualization (2001, 2007, 2014), Introductory Circuits (2008), Rapid Serial Visual Presentation: Design for Cognition (2013); *Recreations* mosaic sculpture; *Style*— Emeritus Prof Robert Spence, FREng; ✉ Department of Electrical and Electronic Engineering, Imperial College of Science Technology and Medicine, Exhibition Road, London SW7 2BT (☎ 020 7594 6259, fax 020 7581 4419, e-mail r.spence@ic.ac.uk)

SPENCE, Prof Robin John Summerford; s of Donald Spence (d 1993), and Margaret, *née* Summerford (d 1994); *b* 7 August 1941; *Educ* Univ of Cambridge (MA, PhD), Cornell Univ (MSc); *m* 1, 12 Feb 1966 (m dis 1983), Fenella, da of Jock Butler; 2 s (Peter b 9 April 1969, Andrew b 30 Sept 1971); *m* 2, 30 May 1986, Bridget, da of Peter McKeigue; 1 da (Emily b 16 Dec 1986); *Career* structural engr Ove Arup & Partners 1963–69, lectr in civil engrg Univ of Zambia 1969–71, research asst Engrg Dept Univ of Cambridge 1971–73, research offr Intermediate Technol Devpt Gp 1973–75; Univ of Cambridge: lectr in architecture 1975–96, dir (later jt dir) Martin Centre for Architectural and Urban Studies 1987–2000, dir Cambridge Univ Centre for Risk in the Built Environment (CURBE) 1997–2008, prof of architectural engrg 2002–08; fell and dir of studies in architecture Magdalene Coll Cambridge 1975–2008 (tutor 1993–96); visiting posts: Islamic Architecture Prog MIT 1987, Architecture Dept UCLA 1991, Faculty of Architecure Georgia Inst of Technol Atlanta 1994, Earth Sciences Dept Macquarie Univ Sydney 1997; Li Ka Shing Fndn visiting lectr TsingHua Univ Beijing, Xi'an Univ of Architecture and Technol, Tong Ji Univ Shanghai and Hong Kong Univ 2001; dir Cambridge Architectural Research Ltd 1987– (chm 1990–2001), dir CARtograph Ltd 1990–97; pres European Assoc for Earthquake Engrg 2002–06; memb: Built Environment Coll EPSRC 1995–97, Royal Soc Steering Gp for the Int Decade for Nat Disaster Reduction 1997–99; Murray Buxton Award IStructE 1987; *Books* incl: Building Materials in Developing Countries (with D J Cook, 1983), Earthquake Protection (with A Coburn, 1992, 2 edn 2002), Interdisciplinary Design in Practice (ed with S Macmillan and P Kirby, 2001); *Style*— Prof Robin Spence; ✉ Cambridge Architectural Research Ltd, Unit 6, 25, Gwyder Street, Cambridge CB1 2LG (e-mail rspence@carltd.com)

SPENCE, Ronald Blackwood; CB (1997); s of Samuel Harold Spence (d 1980), and Margaret Galway, *née* McClure (d 1991); *b* 13 July 1941; *Educ* Methodist Coll Belfast, Queens Univ Belfast (BA); *m* 1, 1964 (m dis 1989), Julia, *née* Fitton; 1 da (Jacqueline b 27 Jan 1968), 1 s (Brian Neil b 2 Feb 1970); *m* 2, 1989, Sarah, *née* Steenson; *Career* asst princ Miny of Health 1963–67, princ Miny of Devpt 1967–74, asst sec Dept of the Environment 1974–80; NI Office: head Econ and Social Div 1980–82, under sec Dept of Fin and Personnel 1982–85, head Central Secretariat 1985–90, under sec Econ Devpt Dept 1990–94; perm sec: DOE (NI) 1994–99, DRD 1999–2001; chm: NI Partnership Bd 1996–2001, NI Events Co 1997–2001, Probation Bd for NI 2004–12, Ulster Sports Museum 2008–; dep chm Nat Heritage Lottery Fund 2006–13, memb NI Legal Servs Cmmn 2003–15 (chm 2010–15), memb NI Community Relations Cncl 2013–; *Recreations* golf; *Style*— Ronald Spence, Esq, CB

SPENCE, Prof Roy Archibald Joseph; OBE (2001), JP (1998); s of Robert Spence (d 1988), of Belfast, and Margaret, *née* Gilmore; *b* 15 July 1952; *Educ* Queen's Univ Belfast (MB BCh, MA, MD); *m* 26 Sept 1979, Diana Mary, da of Dr C Burns, OBE (d 1989), of Ballymoney; 2 s (Robert b 20 July 1982, Andrew b 14 Sept 1984), 1 da (Katharine b 11 Feb 1987); *Career* conslt surgn Belfast City Hosp 1986–; exec dir Belfast City Hosp Tst Bd 1993–97; hon lectr in surgery, anatomy and oncology and prof Queen's Univ of Belfast; Univ of Ulster: hon prof 1998–, pro-chllr 2002–09; prof and head Dept of Surgery Queen's Univ Belfast 2008–; Penman visiting prof Univ of Cape Town 2005, Peter Lowe lectr Coll of Surgeons Glasgow 2010, McEwan lectr Assoc of Surgeons 2011, Ravdin lectr American Coll of Surgeons Washington USA 2013; examiner: MRCS RCS(Ed) 2000–, Intercolliegate FRCS in Surgery 2000– (sec Bd 2009–13); chm Cancer Focus 2009–, pres Ulster Medical Soc 2012–13; memb: BMA, Assoc of Surgns; memb: Police Authy NI 1994–2001 (chm Community Rels Ctee 1996–98), Bd Crimestoppers NI, Bd of Govrs and Bd of Tstees Wallace HS Lisburn 1993–99; Moynihan Medal 1984; Hon LLD Univ of Ulster 2009; FRCSEd 1981, FRCSI 1981, FRCS (ad eundum) 2006, Hon FRCSGlas 2010; *Books* 18 books incl: Pathology for Surgeons (1986, 2 edn 1993), Colorectal Disease for Physicians and Surgeons (1997), Synopsis of Systematic Pathology for Surgeons (2001), Oncology – a Core Text (2001), Oncologic Emergencies (2002), Handbook of Oncology (2002, 4 edn 2015), Genetics for Surgeons (2005), Illustrated Clinical Anatomy (2005), Emergencies in Oncology (2006), Infection in Oncological Patients (2006); also author of 200 jl papers and 14 chapters in books; *Recreations* history; *Clubs* Moynihan, Ulster Reform; *Style*— Prof Roy Spence, OBE; ✉ 7 Downshire Crescent, Hillsborough, Co Down BT26 6DD (☎ 028 9268 2362, fax 028 9268 2418); Level 2, Belfast City Hospital, Lisburn Road, Belfast BT9 7AB (☎ 028 9032 9241, e-mail roy.spence@belfasttrust.hscni.net)

SPENCE, Stephen Frederick; s of Frederick Spence, of Tyne & Wear, and Veronica, *née* Scullion; *b* 23 December 1961; *Educ* Univ of Manchester (BA), AA Sch of Architecture London (Dip); *m* 9 Dec 1995, Yasmin, da of Awni Al-Ani; 2 s (Cooper b 13 Oct 1999, Mac b 13 July 2001), 1 da (Sadie b 15 Aug 2004); *Career* architect; Richard Rogers Architects Ltd 1987–98; architectural asst projects incl: Royal Docks 1987, Terminal 5 competition Heathrow 1988, Tokyo Forum 1988, Canary Wharf 1988; project architect: Farnborough Air Terminal 1989, Grosvenor Road 1989–90, Chiswick Park 1990, Stockley Park 1990, Daiwa HQ 1990–91, Inland Revenue competition (runner-up) 1991–92, Berlin Underground competition (winner) 1992, VR Techno Japan 1993–94, TVU Resource Centre 1994–96, Stephen Strasse Frankfurt 1995–98; assoc dir: Broadwick St London 1996–98, Visual Control Tower Heathrow 1996, Pusan Station competition Korea (runner-up) 1996, Pilkington plc HQ 1997; dir Spence Associates Ltd 1998–; projects incl: TVU Masterplan Feasability 1998, TVU Media Centre 1998, NEC Pavillion competition 1998, River Café Reception 1999, private residence Kensington London 2000, LSE 2001, Turner Gallery Margate 2001, Northbank pedestrian bridge 2003, New Wear crossing 2005; tutor AA 1989–90, advsr RIBA 2003; AA Dip Year Prize 1986–87; RIBA 2002; *Exhibitions* The New Breed-Sydney Aust 1988, Zurich Architecural Museum 1990, AA 1991, Sci Museum London 1999, RA 2000, Cube Gallery Manchester 2001, V&A 2003; *Style*— Stephen Spence, Esq; ✉ Spence Associates, 53 Dymock Street, London SW6 3ET (☎ 020 7224 9294, e-mail post@spenceassociates.co.uk)

SPENCE, Toby; s of Dr Magnus Peter Spence, of Datchworth, Herts, and Gillian Sara, *née* Squire (d 1991); *b* 22 May 1969; *Educ* Uppingham, New Coll Oxford (choral scholar), Guildhall Sch of Music and Drama; *m* (m dis) Suzanne Elizabeth, da of Brandon Vaughan Edwards; *Career* opera singer; tenor; princ operatic roles incl: Idamante in Mozart's Idomeneo, Tamino in Mozart's Die Zauberflöte, Ferrando in Mozart's Cosi Fan Tutte, Don Ottavio in Mozart's Don Giovanni, Tito in Mozart's La Clemenza di Tito, Tom Rakewell in Stravinsky's The Rake's Progress, David in Wagner's Die Meistersing von Nuremberg, Pylade in Gluck's Iphigenie en Tauride, Faust in Gounod's Faust; sung with all the great orchestras of the world incl: Berlin Philharmonic, Vienna Philharmonic, Cleveland Orchestra, London Symphony Orchestra; performed at various festivals incl: Brighton, Cheltenham, Salzburg, Edinburgh, Montreux, BBC Proms; *Recordings* incl: Philips Classics , Deutsche Gramaphon, Decca, BMG, Collins, Hyperion, EMI, Chandos, Opera Rara, Naxos; *Style*— Toby Spence, Esq

SPENCER, 9 Earl (GB 1765); Charles Edward Maurice Spencer; also Viscount Spencer, Baron Spencer (both GB 1761), and Viscount Althorp (GB 1765 and UK 1905); s of 8 Earl Spencer, LVO, DL (d 1992), and his 1 w, Hon Frances Ruth Burke Roche (d 2004), da of 4 Baron Fermoy; bro of late Diana, Princess of Wales (d 1997); *b* 20 May 1964; *Educ* Maidwell Hall, Eton, Magdalen Coll Oxford; *m* 1, 16 Sept 1989 (m dis 1997), (Catherine) Victoria, o da of John Lockwood, of Barnes, London; 3 da (Lady Kitty Eleanor b 28 Dec 1990, Lady Eliza Victoria, Lady Katya Amelia (twins) b 10 July 1992), 1 s (Louis Frederick John, Viscount Althorp b 14 March 1994); *m* 2, 15 Dec 2001 (m dis 2009), Caroline Freud, *née* Hutton; 1 s (Hon Edmund Charles b 6 Oct 2003), 1 da (Lady Lara Caroline b 16 March 2006); *m* 3, 18 June 2011, Karen Gordon, *née* Villeneuve; 1 da (Lady Charlotte Diana b 23 July 2012); *Heir* s, Viscount Althorp; *Career* page of honour to HM The Queen 1977–79; TV correspondent NBC News 1987–91 and 1993–96, reporter Granada Television 1991–93; *Publications* Althorp: The Story of an English House (1998), The Spencer Family (1999), Blenheim: Battle for Europe (2004), Prince Rupert: Last of the Cavaliers (2007), Killers of the King (2014); *Style*— The Rt Hon the Earl Spencer, DL; ✉ Althorp, Northampton NN7 4HQ

SPENCER, Dr David Anthony; s of late Henry William George Spencer, and late Veronica Clare, *née* Bonanno; *b* 7 November 1963; *Educ* Raine's Fndn GS London, Univ of Exeter (BSc), Imperial Coll London (MSc, DIC), Swiss Fed Inst of Technol Zurich (DrScNat); *m* m (m dis), Prof PD Dr Cinzia Cervato; 1 da (Francesca Louise b 13 April 1998); 1 s (Conrad Francis b 25 May 2003), 1 da (Tara Serena b 18 Dec 2005) by Christina Beales; 1 s (Damian Patrick b 6 April 2015) by Melissa Treby; *Career* visiting scientist Univ of Beijing and ldr Exeter Univ Geological Expdn to China 1986; Swiss Fed Inst of Technol Zurich (ETH-Zurich): pre-doctoral research fell 1988–89, research and teaching asst and doctoral research fell 1989–92, visiting ETH doctoral research fell 1992–93, visiting postdoctoral research fell 1993–94 and 1997, postdoctoral research fell 1994–97; visiting scientist Tokyo Inst of Technol 1996, Swiss Nat Science Fndn sr research fell 1997–99, research asst prof and lectr in structural geology Univ of Maine 1997–98, visiting prof Univ of the Punjab Lahore 1997–2000 (visiting lectr 1995), hon assoc prof Albert Schweitzer Int Univ Geneva 2001; sr reservoir geologist Roxar Sofware Solutions Roxar Ltd 2003–05, princ geologist BG Int (seconded to Trinidad and Tobago) 2005–07, princ geologist Woodside Energy Ltd Perth Australia 2008, chief geologist OMV Petrom Bucharest 2008–11, dept mangr oil reservoir studies OMV Petrom Bucharest 2001–13; gifted and talented mentor, learning mentor and learning support asst Behaviour Unit Raine's Fndn Sch London 2002–03 (also publicity offr and devpt offr); delivered scientific lectures at numerous univs, also made over 150 scientific presentations at int scientific confs worldwide; platinum exploration geologist Impala Platinum Ltd SA 1986–87, hydrogeological conslt Philippines 1992–94, staff geologist/reservoir devpt structural geologist Section for Reservoir Geology and Geophysics Dept of Reservoir Devpt Saga Petroleum ASA Norway 1998–99 (worked in Section for Wells Dept of Petroleum Technol and Drilling 1999–2000), estab Spencer Structural Conslts 2000; currently assoc ed The Professional Geologist, European regnl ed Himalayan Notes 1994–97; Imperial Coll/Swiss Fed Inst of Technol Scholarship 1988–89, Geochron Research Award 1991, Swiss Acad of Natural Sciences Travel Scholarship 1992, Huber-Kudlich Fndn Visiting Lectureship 1996, Outstanding Young Scientist Award Swiss Fed Inst of Technol 1996; memb Research Bd of Advsrs (Int Div) American Biographical Inst, nat and int advsr American Biographical Inst Research Assoc, hon memb Advsy Cncl Int Biographical Centre; tstee Raine's Fndn 2002–, fndn govr Raine's Fndn Sch London 2002–; climbed to south summit of Mt Everest 2000; Freeman City of London 2001, Liveryman Worshipful Co of Scientific Instrument Makers 2001 (Freeman 2001); fell: Geological Assoc of Canada, Geological Soc of India, Geological Soc of SA, Mineralogical Soc of GB and I, American Inst of Chemists, American Geographic Soc; memb: Soc of Petroleum Engrs, American Inst of Mining, Metallurgical and Petroleum Engrs, SA Instn of Mining and Metallurgy, Energy Inst (MEI), SocAcad; CGeol, EurGeol (European Geologist), AIPG-CPG (Certified Professional Geologist), AAPG-CPG (Certified Petroleum Geologist), PrSciNat (Professional Natural Scientist), PGeo (Professional Geologist), CHGeol (Certified Swiss Geologist), CIPES (Certified Ind Professional Earth Scientist), CPhys, EurPhys (European Physicist), CSci, CChem, EurChem (European Chemist), ARSGS (Professional Assoc of RSGS), RegSciTech (Registered Sci Technician), LCGI, MRI, MISTC, MIEnvSc MInstP, MInstPet, MIMMM, MRSC, MACS, FGS, FRAS, FRGS, FRSA, FLS, FICPD, FMinSoc; *Recreations* mountaineering, playing guitar, long distance walking, campanology, flying, reading travel books, skiing, family history research, travelling, listening to the BBC World Service, reading the Times, scuba diving; *Style*— Dr David A Spencer; ✉ e-mail david@spencer.name

SPENCER, Prof John Rason; Hon QC (2003); s of Donald Spencer, and Mary Spencer; *Educ* Univ of Cambridge (LLB, MA, LLD); *m* Rosemary, *née* Stewartson; 1 s, 2 da; *Career* Univ of Cambridge: asst lectr Law Faculty 1973–76, lectr 1976–91, reader 1991–95, prof 1995–2013, chm Faculty 1995–97, prof emeritus 2013–, dep vice-chllr 2014–16; fell Selwyn Coll Cambridge 1970–, bye fell Murray Edwards Coll Cambridge 2014–; academic bencher Inner Temple 2003; hon memb of chambers: Hardwicke Building 2003, 15 New Bridge St 2014–; Docteur en droit (hc) Univ of Poitiers 2004; Chevalier de l'Ordre des Palmes Académiques 1999; *Style*— Prof J R Spencer; ✉ Murray Edwards College, Cambridge CB3 0DF

SPENCER, John William James; s of Capt John Lawrence Spencer, DSO, MC (d 1967), and Jane Lilian, *née* Duff (d 2004); *b* 26 December 1957; *Educ* Sedbergh, Magdalene Coll Cambridge (MA), Open Univ Business Sch (MBA); *m* 2 Oct 1987, Jane Elizabeth, da of Andrew Young (d 1974); 1 s (Charles b 1990), 2 da (Rosanagh b 1991, Caitlin b 1996); *Career* dir: Dewey Warren & Co Ltd 1986–88, PWS North America 1988–89, BMS Special Risk Services Ltd 1989–95, Lloyd's America Ltd 1995–97; BMS Associates Ltd: dir 1997–2008, gp chief exec 2002–08; dir Argo Managing Agency Ltd 2008– (non-exec chm 2011–), non-exec dir Newline Underwriting Mgmnt Ltd 2010–, non-exec dir Thompson Heath & Bond Ltd 2012–, non-exec dir Markel Int 2016–; *Style*— J W J Spencer, Esq; ✉ Ghyllas, Sedbergh, Cumbria LA10 5LT; 8 Bushwood Road, Kew, Surrey TW9 3BQ

SPENCER, Johnny; s of Charles Thomas Spencer, and Ellen Patricia Spencer; *Educ* Goldsmiths Coll London, Camberwell Sch of Arts and Crafts (BA); *Career* artist; assoc researcher Copenhagen Free Univ 2001–; *Exhibitions* The Golden Age (ICA London) 1999, British Art Show 5 2000, Century Cities (Tate Modern) 2001; *Publications* New Neurotic Realism (1998), Young British Art: the Saatchi Decade (2000), Here, There and Elsewhere (2002); *Recreations* music; *Clubs* RFH; *Style*— Johnny Spencer, Esq; ✉ 57

Nithdale Road, Plumstead, London SE18 3PE (☎ 020 8244 0962, e-mail johnny@artio.demon.co.uk); c/o Anthony Wilkinson Gallery, 242 Cambridge Heath Road, London E2 9DA (☎ 020 8980 2662, fax 020 8980 0028, e-mail info@anthonywilkinsongallery)

SPENCER, Dr Jonathan Page; CB (2002); s of John Austin Spencer (d 2004), of Bath, and Doreen, *née* Page (d 1991); *b* 24 April 1949; *Educ* Bournemouth Sch, Downing Coll Cambridge (MA), Univ of Oxford (ICI res fell, jr res fell ChCh, DPhil); *m* 1976, Caroline Sarah, *née* Armitage; 2 da, 1 s; *Career* DTI: admin trainee 1974–77, princ 1977–83, private sec to Secs of State 1982–83, asst sec 1983–91, under sec and head Insurance Div 1991–97, DG Resources and Services 1997–2000, DG Business Competitiveness 2000–01; DG Clients and Policy Lord Chancellor's Dept (latterly Dept for Constitutional Affrs) 2002–05; currently public policy conslt and co dir; memb: Administrative Justice and Tbnls Cncl (formerly Cncl on Tbnls) 2005–13, Slrs Regulation Authy 2006–09, E Kent Hosps Univ Fndn Tst 2007–15, Strategic Advsy Bd on Intellectual Property 2008–10; chair C of E Pensions Bd 2009–, memb Gibraltar Financial Services Cmmn 2011– (chair 2016–); author of various articles in scientific jls; chair of govrs of two schs; *Recreations* making and listening to music, keeping the house up and the garden down; *Style—* Dr Jonathan Spencer, CB; ✉ Little Eggarton, Godmersham, Canterbury, Kent CT4 7DY

SPENCER, Michael Alan; s of Oscar Alan Spencer (d 1983), and Diana, *née* Walker; *b* 30 May 1955; *Educ* Worth Abbey, CCC Oxford (MA); *m* 9 July 1983 (m dis 2012), Lorraine Geraldine, da of Ronald Murphy; 2 s (Patrick b 8 May 1988, Thomas b 20 Feb 1990), 1 da (Alexandra b 17 June 1992); *Career* analyst Simon & Coats 1976–80, vice-pres Drexel Burnham Lambert 1981–83, dir Charles Fulton 1983–86, chm Intercapital 1986–99, ceo ICAP 1999–, chm Numis 2003–09; treas Cons Pty 2007–; *Recreations* running, riding, shooting, wine, art, politics; *Clubs* Whites; *Style—* Michael Spencer, Esq; ✉ ICAP plc, 1–2 Broadgate, London EC2M 7UR (☎ 020 7050 7400, fax 020 7050 7116)

SPENCER, Paul; CBE (2010); s of Dr Seymour Spencer, of Oxford, and Margaret Spencer (d 1999); *b* 3 January 1950, Oxford; *Educ* Ampleforth, Thames Poly (BA); *m* Sept 1975, Lorna, *née* Nykerk; 1 da (Deborah b 1977), 2 s (Richard b 1980, Charles b 1986); *Career* analyst ICI Pension Fund 1970–75, overseas fin mangr British Leyland plc 1975–80, gp treas Rolls Royce plc 1980–86, gp treas and assoc dir Hanson plc 1986–96; Royal and Sun Alliance plc: gp fin dir 1996–99, chief exec UK 1999–2003; currently chm: NS&I (Nat Savings and Investments), State Street Managed Pension Fund Ltd, Sovereign Reversions plc; non-exec dir: Resolution plc, WPP Gp plc; FCMA 1978, FCT 1982; *Clubs* Hurlingham; *Style—* Paul Spencer, Esq, CBE; ☎ 07768 462077, e-mail paulspencer120@hotmail.com

SPENCER, Raine, Countess; Raine; da of Alexander McCorquodale (1 cous of 1 Baron McCorquodale of Newton, PC) by his 1 w Dame Barbara Cartland, DBE (d 2000); *b* 9 September 1929; *m* 1, 1948 (m dis 1976), as his 1 w, 9 Earl of Dartmouth (d 1997); 3 s (William (10 Earl of Dartmouth, MEP, *qv*, Hon Rupert, Hon Henry, QC), 1 da (Lady Charlotte (Duchesa di Carcaci)); m 2, 1976, as his 2 w, 8 Earl Spencer, LVO, DL (d 1992); m 3, 1993 (m dis 1996), as his 2 w, Comte Jean-François Pineton de Chambrun, 3 s of Marquis de Chambrun; *Career* formerly a LCC Voluntary Care Ctee worker in Wandsworth and Vauxhall, and actively involved in the welfare of the elderly in other areas; memb Lewisham W LCC 1958–65; memb: GLC (Richmond) 1967–73, GLC Gen Purposes Ctee 1971–73; former memb BBC Nat Agric Advsy Ctee, chm Govt Working Pty on the Human Habitat for UN Conference on the Environment (which produced The Dartmouth Report, How Do You Want To Live?), and a UK delegate at the Conf in Stockholm 1972; chm: GLC Historic Bldgs Bd 1968–71, Covent Gdn Devpt Ctee 1971–75, UK Exec Ctee of European Architectural Heritage Year 1975; memb: English Tourist Bd 1971–75, BTA Infrastructure Ctee 1972–, Advsy Cncl V&A 1980–, BTA 1982–93 (Ctee Prestige Tourism for City of Nice, Special Jury for the Improvement of the Promenade des Anglais Nice 1994–96); chm: BTA Spas Ctee 1981–83, BTA Commendation Schemes Panel 1982–89, BTA Hotels and Restaurants Ctee 1983–87, BTA Accommodation Ctee 1987–93, BTA Devpt Ctee 1987–93, BTA Britain Welcomes Japan Ctee of Honour and Exec Ctee 1989, BTA Come to Britain Awards 1990–93, Ctee for Business Sponsorship of the Arts; dir Harrods International 1996– (with special interest in the 70 shops abroad, airport duty free shops and the devpt and licensing of new products), dir Harrods Management Ltd 2001–, dir Harrods Estates 2006–; awarded a gold medal for public speaking, and a former guest speaker at Univ of London, LSE and Univ of Cambridge debates; lectr at Holloway, Maidstone and Wandsworth Prisons and several thousand functions in UK, France, Austria, Belgium, Portugal, Holland and Switzerland; Hon LLD Dartmouth Coll USA; *Books* The Spencers on Spas (with photographs by Earl Spencer); *Style—* Raine, Countess Spencer; ✉ Sprimont Lodge, 2A Sprimont Place, London SW3 3HU (mobile 07917 000941, fax 020 7225 2021); Whiteway House, Chudleigh, nr Newton Abbot, Devon TQ13 0DY

SPENCER, Ritchie Lloyd; s of Capt P Lloyd Spencer; *b* 27 September 1942, Sunderland; *Educ* St Bees Sch, Univ of Manchester (BA), LSE; *m* 1965, Catherine Dilys, da of Dr John Naish; 3 s (Hal b 1968, Patrick b 1969, James b 1972); *Career* dir Sunderland Shipbuilders Ltd 1972–76, md Reliant Motors plc 1976–86, dir Nash Industries plc 1980–86, chief exec GKN Powder Metallurgy Div 1986–90; chm: Bound Brook Lichfield Ltd 1986–90, Firth Cleveland Sintered Products Ltd 1986–90, Sheepbridge Sintered Products Ltd 1986–90; pres: Bound Brook Italia SpA Brunico 1986–90, Saini SpA Milan 1986–90; dir: Mahindra Sintered Products Pune Ltd India 1986–90, Sintermex SA de CV Mexico 1986–90; md: European Industrial Services Ltd 1990–94, Nettlefolds Ltd 1990–94, Unifix Ltd 1990–94, Unifix (Belgium) NV/SA 1990–94, Unifix (Netherlands) BV 1990–94, EIS Depots Ltd 1990–94; chief exec ThyssenKrupp Woodhead Ltd 1994–2007, gen dir ThyssenKrupp Indusa Mure SLU Spain 2003–07; memb Cncl Soc Motor Manufacturers & Traders 1978–87, dir Motor Industry Res Assoc 1997–2011 (chm 1984–97); MIPM; *Recreations* theatre, music, gardening; *Style—* Ritchie Spencer, Esq; ✉ Skelbrooke Hall, Skelbrooke, Doncaster, South Yorkshire (☎ and fax 01302 728408); Dorlinn View, Argyll Terrace, Tobermory, Isle of Mull (☎ 01688 302324)

SPENCER, Hon Mr Justice; Sir Robin Godfrey Spencer; kt (2010); s of Eric Spencer (d 1992), of Chester, and Audrey Elaine, *née* Brown; *b* 8 July 1955; *Educ* King's Sch Chester, Emmanuel Coll Cambridge (MA); *m* 5 Aug 1978, Julia Margaret Eileen, da of Eric John Bennet Burley, of Chester; 3 da (Jennifer b 1983, Susanna b 1984, Laura b 1987); *Career* called to the Bar Gray's Inn 1978 (bencher 2004); in practice Wales & Chester Circuit, recorder of the Crown Court 1998–2010 (asst recorder 1993–98), QC 1999, dep judge of the High Court 2001–10, ldr Wales & Chester Circuit 2004–06, judge of the High Court 2010–; *Recreations* cricket, football, music, Methodist history; *Style—* The Hon Mr Justice Spencer; ✉ Royal Courts of Justice, Strand, London WC2A 2LL

SPENCER, Dr Sarah Ann; CBE (2007); da of Dr Ian Osborne Bradford Spencer (d 1978), of Tynemouth, and Elspeth, *née* Strang; *b* 11 December 1952; *Educ* Univ of Nottingham (BA), UCL (MPhil), Erasmus Univ Rotterdam (PhD); *m* 1978, Brian Hackland; 2 s (James b 30 Aug 1986, Nick b 24 July 1989); *Career* researcher Law Faculty UCL 1977–79; Cobden Tst: research offr 1979–84, dir 1984–85; dir Nat Cncl for Civil Liberties 1985–89; IPPR: research fell 1990–95, dir Citizenship and Governance Prog 1999–2002, sr assoc 2002–03, seconded as pt/t advsr PM's Strategy Unit Cabinet Office 2000 and 2003; Centre on Migration, Policy and Society (COMPAS) Univ of Oxford: dir of policy research 2003–05, assoc dir 2005–08, dep dir 2008–12 (now dir Global Exchange on Migration and Diversity), Open Soc fell 2012–13; assoc memb Nuffield Coll Oxford 2004–07, visiting prof Human Rights Centre Univ of Essex 2002–; chair Equality and Diversity Forum 2002–12, cmmr Cmmn for Racial Equality 2002–06 (dep chair 2003–05); memb: Cmmn on the Future of Multi-Ethnic Britain (Parekh Cmmn) Runnymede Tst 1998–2000, Human Rights Act Taskforce Home Office 1998–2001, Advsy Bd Transnational Communities Prog ESRC 1998–2002, Advsy Ctee Effective Govt Structures for Children Gulbenkian Fndn 1999–2000, Governance Advsy Ctee Br Cncl 1999–2006, Citizenship Educn Ctee Br Cncl 2000–02, Advsy Ctee on Ethnic Minorities in the Labour Market Cabinet Office 2001–02, Human Rights Forum DCA 2002–06, Taskforce Cmmn on Equality and Human Rights DTI 2003–05, Reference Gp on the Discrimination Law Review and Equalities Review Dept of Trade and Industry 2003–05, Task Gp on Gypsies and Travellers Dept of Communities and Local Govt 2006–07, Advsy Ctee Nat Employment Panel on English Language Tuition for Migrants Dept of Work and Pensions 2007, Sr Stakeholder Gp Govt Equality Office 2008–11, Royal Soc People and the Planet Working Gp 2010–12, Diana Princess of Wales Meml Fund Ctee on Refugees 2008–09; advsr Cambridge Ind Review of UK Anti-Discrimination Legislation 2000–01, advsr Atlantic Philanthopies (Ireland) 2006–; govr Br Inst of Human Rights 2002–; FRSA 1999; *Books* incl: Police Authorities during the Miners' Strike (1985), The Constitution of the United Kingdom (co-author, 1991), Immigration as an Economic Asset, the German Experience (ed, 1994), Strangers and Citizens: A positive approach to migrants and refugees (ed, 1994), Migrants, Refugees and the Boundaries of Citizenship (1995), Mainstreaming Human Rights in Whitehall and Westminster (co-author, 1999), Reluctant Witness (co-author, 2001), Age Equality Comes of Age (co-author 2003), Age as an Equality Issue: Legal and Policy Perspectives (jt ed, 2003), The Politics of Migration: Managing Opportunity, Conflict and Change (ed, 2003), Migrant Care Workers in Ageing Societies (jtly, 2009), The Migration Debate (2011); *Style—* Dr Sarah Spencer, CBE; ✉ COMPAS, University of Oxford, 58 Banbury Road, Oxford, OX2 6QS (e-mail sarah.spencer@compas.ox.ac.uk, www.compass.ox.ac.uk/people/staff/sarah-spencer)

SPENCER, His Hon Shaun Michael; QC (1988); s of late Edward Michael Spencer, of Leeds, and late Barbara Joan Patricia Spencer; *b* 4 February 1944; *Educ* Cockburn HS, Univ of Durham (LLB), Open Univ (Dip); *m* 9 June 1971, Nicola, da of Frederick George Greenwood, of Tockwith, N Yorks; 3 s (Robert Phillip b 1972, Samuel James Edward b 1982, Edward Frederick Claudio b 1993), 2 da (Eleanor Jane b 1979, Elizabeth Anne b 1980); *Career* lectr in law Univ of Sheffield 1966–68 (asst lectr in law 1965–66), called to the Bar Lincoln's Inn 1968 (Hardwicke & Mansfield scholar, bencher 1997), barr NE Circuit 1969, recorder of the Crown Ct 1985–2002, circuit judge (NE Circuit) 2002–14, designated civil judge Bradford Gp of Courts 2008–12; Master of Hounds Claro Beagles 1982–88; *Recreations* cookery, books, singing; *Style—* His Hon Shaun Spencer, QC; ✉ 34A Rutland Drive, Harrogate, North Yorkshire HG1 2NX (☎ 01423 523162); Snook House, Holy Island, Northumberland TD15 2SS (☎ 01289 389229)

SPENCER, Thomas Newnham Bayley (Tom); s of Thomas Henry Newnham Spencer (d 1979); *b* 10 April 1948; *Educ* Nautical Coll Pangbourne, Univ of Southampton; *m* 1979, Elizabeth Nan, *née* Bath; 2 da and 1 step da; *Career* Peat Marwick Mitchell CAs 1972–75, asst dir Britain in Europe referedum campaign 1975, J Walter Thompson advtg 1975–79; MEP (EPP): Derbyshire 1979–84, Surrey West 1989–94, Surrey 1994–99; Cons spokesman on: Social Affairs and Employment 1979–82, External Trade 1982–84; Cons dep chief whip Euro Parl 1989–91, permanent rapporteur on climate change EPP 1991–99, chm British Section EPP Gp Euro Parl 1994–97; former chm Euro Parl's Ctee on Foreign Affrs, Security and Defence Policy, pres GLOBE Int (Global Legislators for a Balanced Environment) 1995–99, chm Euro Union of Cons and Christian Democratic Students 1971–74; currently: exec dir Euro Centre for Public Affrs (founding exec dir 1987–89), visiting prof of global governance Surrey Euro Mgmnt Sch Univ of Surrey Guildford 2000–03, visiting prof of public affrs Brunel Univ 2003–; memb Religious and Scientific Ctee Religion, Science and Environment Symposia; memb Advsy Cncl Centre for Corp and Public Affrs Manchester Met Univ; writer, lectr and broadcaster; memb Editorial Bd: Jl of Public Affrs; assoc dean Templeton Coll Oxford 1984–89, memb Ct Univ of Surrey; Forum for the Future Green Ribbon Award 1999; Great Golden Medal for Merit (Austria) 1996; *Books* Public Affairs and Power: Essays in a Time of Fear (2003), Everything Flows: Essays on Public Affairs and Change (2005); *Recreations* gardening, opera; *Clubs* Carlton; *Style—* Tom Spencer, Esq; ✉ Barford Court, Lampard Lane, Churt, Surrey GU10 2HJ (☎ 01428 712375, website www.tomspencer.info)

SPENCER, His Hon Judge Timothy John; QC (2001); *Career* called to the Bar 1982; asst recorder 1998, recorder 2000, circuit judge (Midland Circuit) 2015–; *Style—* His Hon Judge Spencer, QC

SPENCER-CHURCHILL; *see:* Churchill

SPENS, David Patrick; QC (1995); s of Lt-Col Hugh Stuart Spens, MC, MBE, TD (d 1988), and Mary Jean Drake, *née* Reinhold (d 2006); *b* 2 May 1950; *Educ* Rugby, Univ of Kent (BA); *m* 7 April 1979 (m dis 2003), Daniele, da of Robert William Irving, MBE (d 1994); 2 da (Dominique b 1982, Sophie-Claire b 1986); *Career* called to the Bar Inner Temple 1973; jr counsel to the Crown at the Central Criminal Court 1988–95, recorder of the Crown Court 1994–, ldr South Eastern Circuit 2007–08; chm: Central Bar Mess 1997–2000, Criminal Bar Assoc 2004–05; *Style—* David Spens, Esq, QC; ✉ Garden Court Chambers, 57–60 Lincoln's Inn Fields, London WC2A 3LS (☎ 020 7993 7600, fax 020 7993 7700, e-mail david.sp@gclaw.co.uk)

SPENS, Michael Colin Barkley; s of Richard Vernon Spens (d 1996), and Margaret, *née* Barkley; *b* 22 September 1950; *Educ* Marlborough, Selwyn Coll Cambridge (MA); *m* Deborah Susan, da of A George Lane; 1 s (William b 21 Jan 1993), 2 da (Tatiana b 8 Oct 1994, Georgina b 18 Feb 1997); *Career* with United Biscuits 1972–74; housemaster and head of careers Radley Coll 1974–93, headmaster Caldicott Sch 1993–98, headmaster Fettes Coll 1998–; Freeman City of London, Liveryman Worshipful Co of Grocers; *Recreations* running, golf, crosswords, electronics, bridge, gardening, wood turning; *Clubs* Hawks' (Cambridge), New (Edinburgh), R&A, HCEG, Denham Golf; *Style—* Michael Spens, Esq; ✉ Headmaster's Lodge, Fettes College, Edinburgh EH4 1QX (☎ 0131 311 6701, fax 0131 311 6714, e-mail mcb.spens@fettes.com)

S

SPERRYN, Simon George; s of late George Roland Neville Sperryn (d 2013), and late Wendy, *née* King; *b* 7 April 1946; *Educ* Rydal Sch Clwyd, Pembroke Coll Cambridge (MA), Cranfield Sch of Mgmnt (MBA); *m* 11 Sept 1993 (m dis 2008), Jessica Alice Hayes; 2 s, 1 da; *Career* Chamber of Commerce and Industry: Birmingham 1967–77, chief exec Northants 1979–85, chief exec Manchester 1986–92, chief exec London 1992–2000; chm Manchester Camerata Ltd 1989–92; dir: Manchester TEC 1990–92, Business Link London 1995–2000, Stylites Ltd 2010–; chief exec Lloyd's Market Assoc 2001–07, chief exec Chartered Inst of Purchasing and Supply 2008–09; pres Br Chambers of Commerce Executives 1994–95; Br Chambers of Commerce: memb Bd of Dirs 1998–2000, ind assessor (nat accreditation) 2012–; dep chm World Chambers Fedn 2000; chm City of London Early Years Devpt and Childcare Partnership 1998–2000, non-exec dir Professional Assocs Research Network 2011–; memb: Met Police Serv Jt Steering Gp for Community Safety in London 1998–2000, Greater London Ctee FEFC 1996–2000, Cncl CII 2004–07, Bd Int Fedn of Purchasing and Supply Mgmnt 2008–09; chair South Staffs and Cambridge Water Customer Panel 2016–; tstee UNIAID Fndn 2003–10; CCMI (CIMgt), FRSA; *Style—* Simon Sperryn, Esq; ✉ 33 Halifax Road, Cambridge CB4 3QB, (☎ 01223 213821, mobile 07950 269296, e-mail simon@sperryn.org)

SPICER, Baron (Life Peer UK 2010), of Cropthorne in the County of Worcestershire; Rt Hon Sir (William) Michael Hardy Spicer; kt (1996), PC (2013); s of Brig Leslie Hardy Spicer (d 1981), and Muriel Winifred Alice Spicer (d 2004); *b* 22 January 1943; *Educ* Wellington (head of college), Emmanuel Coll Cambridge (MA); *m* 1967, Patricia Ann, da of Patrick

Sinclair Hunter (d 1981); 1 s, 2 da; *Career* asst to ed The Statist, dir Cons Systems Res Centre 1968–70, md Economic Models Ltd 1970–80; MP (Cons): Worcs S 1974–97, Worcs W 1997–2010; PPS to Trade Mins 1979–81, vice-chm Cons Pty 1981–83, dep chm Cons Pty 1983–84, Parly under sec of state Dept of Transport 1985–86, min for aviation 1986–87, Parly under sec of state Dept of Energy 1987–90, min of state for housing and planning 1990, chm Parly Office of Sci and Technol 1992, chm Parly and Scientific Ctee 1996–99, memb Treasy Select Ctee 1997–2001, chm Treasy Sub-Ctee 1998–2001, chm 1922 Ctee 2001–10 (memb Exec Ctee 1997–98), memb Bd Cons Pty 2001–10 (chm Finance Ctee 2007–10); pres Assoc of Electricity Prodrs 1991–2015; govr Wellington Coll 1992–2005; *Books* Final Act (1983), Prime Minister, Spy (1986), Cotswold Manners (1989), Cotswold Murders (1991), Cotswold Mistress (1992), A Treaty Too Far – A New Policy for Europe (1992), Cotswolds Moles (1993), The Challenge of the East (1996), The Spicer Diaries (2012); *Recreations* painting, writing, tennis, bridge; *Clubs* Garrick, Pratt's, Lords and Commons Tennis (capt/chm 1997–2006); *Style—* The Rt Hon the Lord Spicer; ✉ House of Lords, London SW1A 0PW

SPICER, Paul Cridland; s of late John Harold Vincent Spicer, and late Joan Sallie, *née* Hickling; *b* 6 June 1952; *Educ* New Coll Sch Oxford, Oakham Sch, Univ of London (BMus), Univ of Durham (PGCE), Royal Coll of Music (ARCO, ARCM, Walford Davies prize, top organ award); *Partner* Reinaldo de Santana Ribeiro (civil partnership 2011); *Career* asst dir of music Uppingham Sch 1974–78, dir of music Ellesmere Coll 1978–84, prodr BBC Radio Three 1984–86, sr prodr Radio Three Midlands 1986–90, artistic dir Lichfield Int Arts Festival 1990–2001; dir: Chester Bach Singers 1982–84, Leicester Bach Choir 1984–92, Birmingham Bach Choir 1992–, Royal Coll of Music Chorus 1996–97; fndr dir Finzi Singers 1987–2001; princ conductor: Royal Coll of Music Chamber Choir 1995–2008, Birmingham Conservatoire Chamber Choir 2002–, Petersfield Festival 2004–; guest conductor: Netherlands Radio Choir 1995–96, Nat Chamber Choir of Ireland 2006–07; prof of choral conducting: Royal Coll of Music 1998–2008, Birmingham Conservatoire 2003–; choral conducting teaching: St Peter's Coll Oxford 2006–, Durham Univ 2013–; memb Cncl: Assoc of Br Choral Dirs 1989–92 and 2004–05, Birmingham Contemporary Music Gp 1991–94; memb: RCO, Assoc of Br Choral Conductors, Victorian Soc; vice-chm British Arts Festivals Assoc 1994–97; tstee Finzi Tst, chm Finzi Friends until 2015, tstee Ellesmere Coll Schulze Tst 2007–, dir Abbotsholme Arts Soc 1990–2001, memb Cncl Lichfield Cathedral 2000–09, chm Sir George Dyson Tst 2009–, vice-pres Herbert Howells Soc; freelance record prodr; freelance conductor, conductor of choral workshops and masterclasses in UK, USA, Europe and Far East; frequent broadcaster and organ recitalist Radio 3; composer of choral, organ, instrumental and chamber music; memb Chapter Lichfield Cathedral 2015; hon res fell Univ of Birmingham, hon fell Birmingham Conservatoire, hon fell Univ Coll Durham Univ; FRSA; *Compositions* princ works incl: Easter Oratorio (chorus, soloists and orchestra), Advent Oratorio (chorus, orchestra and soloists), The Deciduous Cross (choir and winds), On The Power of Sound (chorus, soloists and orchestra), The Darling of The World (chorus, soloist and orchestra), Piano Sonata, Song for Birds (cycle), Dies Natalis (a Capella), Kiwi Fireworks (organ), Man, Wretched Man (chorus and organ), Pilgrimages (piano), Suite for Organ, Beyond Imagination Fair (song cycle for tenor and piano), Unfinished Remembering (choral symphony for 2 soloists, chorus and orchestra for World War I centenary); church music incl: Come Out Lazar, Magnificat and Nunc Dimittis (New Coll service), Prayer of St Cuthbert (for enthronement of Bishop of Durham), Four Carols for Dark Times (R S Thomas), Alive (R S Thomas), Tu es Petrus, Love is Beautiful Indeed, Pied Beauty, His Heart's Desire, Michael the Great Prince, Alive; *Publications* music published principally by Boosey & Hawkes, Novello (Music Sales), Banks and Triumph: English Pastoral Partsongs, Guides to Benjamin Britten's and James MacMillan's choral works; contrib Dictionary of Nat Biography; author of articles in many periodicals and recording booklets; Biographies: Herbert Howells (1998), Sir George Dyson (2014), The Music of Herbert Howells (contrib, 2014), Sir Arthur Bliss (in preparation); *Recreations* architecture (especially church vaulting), preserving mystery, promoting British music, running; *Clubs* Athenaeum; *Style—* Paul Spicer, Esq; ✉ Parkside, Burnthill Lane, Rugeley, Staffordshire WS15 2HX (☎ 01889 801929, e-mail paul@paulspicer.com, website www.paulspicer.com); c/o Val Withams, Choral Connections, 14 Stevens Close, Prestwood, Great Missenden, Buckinghamshire HP16 0SQ (☎ 01494 866389)

SPICER, Lt-Col Tim; OBE (1992); *Career* Br Army until 1994; fndr and chm Aegis 2002–15; fndr Aegis Charitable Fndn 2004–; FRGS; *Books* An Unorthodox Soldier; *Recreations* art, music, shooting, skiing, game fishing, big game hunting, conservation; *Clubs* Whites, SF, Frontline, Blacks, Beefsteak; *Style—* Lt-Col Tim Spicer, OBE, FRGS; ✉ e-mail ts@firegap.co.uk

SPIEGELBERG, Richard George; s of Francis Edward Frederick Spiegelberg (d 1979), and Margaret Neville, *née* Clegg (d 1999); *b* 21 January 1944; *Educ* Marlborough, Hotchkiss Sch USA, New Coll Oxford (MA); *m* 1, 1970 (m dis 1979), Coralie Eve, *née* Dreyfus; 2 s (Rupert b 1971, Maximilian b 1974); m 2, 1980, Suzanne Louise *née* Dodd; 1 s (Assheton b 1981), 1 da (Henrietta b 1984); *Career* Economist Intelligence Unit 1965–67, business journalist and mgmnt ed The Times 1967–74, princ Dept of Indust 1974–75, NEDO 1975–76; assoc dir: J Walter Thompson & Co 1976–80, Coopers & Lybrand 1980–84; dir and jt md Streets Financial 1984–87; exec dir corp communications Merrill Lynch Europe/Middle East and Merrill Lynch International Bank Ltd 1987–98, dir Chancery Communications Ltd 1999–2003, dir Cardew Group Ltd 2003–11; dep chm City of London Sinfonia 2011–; *Books* The City (1973); *Recreations* walking, golf, opera; *Clubs* Brooks's, Berkshire Golf; *Style—* Richard Spiegelberg, Esq; ✉ 27 Rowan Road, London W6 7DT

SPIERS, (John) Anthony (Tony); MBE (2005); *b* 19 September 1944; *Educ* Bishop Vesey's GS; *m* 1; 1 s; m 2, Anne; 2 s, 2 da; *Career* slr; formerly ptnr Peter Peter & Wright, Michelmores and Withy King; clerk to Blanchminster Charity 1976–84; memb Cornwall CC 1981–88, dir Slrs' Benevolent Assoc 1991–93, fndr chm W of England Soc of Tst and Estate Practitioners 1992–94, sec Devon and Somerset Law Soc 1994–2014, tribunal judge Social Entitlement Chamber 1997–2014, sec Bath Law Soc 2001–02; memb Assoc of Contentious Tst and Probate Specialists; memb Law Soc Wills and Equity Ctee 2004–14; memb Cncl RSA 1995–97 (chm SW Regnl Ctee 1996–97); *Recreations* walking, driving, fishing, family; *Style—* Tony Spiers, Esq, MBE; ✉ 2 Claremont Grove, Exeter EX2 4LY (e-mail tony@aspiers.com)

SPIERS, Sir Donald Maurice; kt (1993), CB (1987), TD (1966); s of Harold Herbert Spiers (d 1968), and Emma, *née* Foster (d 1978); *b* 27 January 1934, Wimbledon; *Educ* Trinity Coll Cambridge (MA); *m* 13 Dec 1958, Sylvia Mary (d 2014), da of Samuel Lowman (d 1963); 2 s (Simon b 1965, Philip b 1969); *Career* 2 Lt RE 1952–54, devpt engr de Havilland 1957–60, operational res Air Miny 1961–66, scientific advsr Far East AF 1967–70, asst chief scientist RAF 1971–78, MOD PE 1978–84, dep controller Aircraft 1984–86, Controller Estab Res & Nuclear Programmes 1987–89, Controller Aircraft 1989–94; aerospace conslt 1994–; chm: Computing Devices Co Ltd 1997–2001 (non-exec dir 1994–2001), European Helicopter Industries Ltd 1997–2003, Meggitt plc 1998–2001 (non-exec dir 1995–2003), Agusta Westland Int Ltd 2003–10, Farnborough Aerospace Consortium 2003–; non-exec dir: Smiths Industries Aerospace and Defence Ltd 1995–97, Messier-Dowty Int Ltd 1998–2004, TAG Aviation (UK) Ltd 1999–2005, General Dynamics UK Ltd 2001–10; pres: RAeS 1995–96, Popular Flying Assoc 1997–2000; *Clubs* RAF; *Style—* Sir Donald Spiers, CB, TD; ✉ 20 Paddock Close, Camberley, Surrey GU15 2BN (☎ 01276 28164, e-mail donald.spiers@ntlworld.com)

SPIERS, Prof John Raymond; s of H H Spiers (d 1956), and Kate, *née* Root (d 1976); *b* 30 September 1941; *Educ* Red Hill Sch E Sutton, Hornsey Coll of Art and Design, Catford Coll of Commerce, Univ of Sussex (BA); *m* 1, 24 June 1967 (m dis 1981), Prof Margaret Ann Boden, OBE, *qv*, da of Leonard Forbes Boden, OBE (d 1987); 1 s (Ruskin b 19 June 1968), 1 da (Jehane b 21 Jan 1972); m 2, 14 Jan 2003, Leigh Richardson, MBE, *née* Radford; 1 da (Lorna b 6 Aug 1978), 1 s (Philip b 6 April 1982); *Career* publisher and author 1960–; fndr, chm and md: The Harvester Press Ltd 1970–88, Harvester Microform Publications Ltd 1973–87, Wheatsheaf Books Ltd 1980–88; fndr and chm John Spiers Publishing Ltd 1988–, fndr chm Civitas Inst for the Study of Civil Society 1999–2000; chm Soc of Young Publishers 1972–73 (treas 1971–72), exec Independent Publishers Guild 1972–77; Parly candidate (Lab) Dorking 1974, resigned Lab Pty 1977, memb Cons Pty 1979–99; a special advsr to Rt Hon Sir Peter Morrison, MP (dep chm) Cons Central Office 1989–90, conslt dir Cons Central Office 1990–95; pres Brighton Kemp Town Cons Assoc 1991–95, dep treas Cons Pty SE Area England 1990–92; chm: Brighton Theatre Ltd 1984, Brighton Business Group 1989–95, Brighton Health Authy 1991–92, Brighton Healthcare NHS Tst 1992–94, David Salomon's Mgmnt Devpt Centre (SETRHA) 1993–94, Brighton Healthcare Arts Tst 1993–94, Advsy Bd Centre for Health Care Mgmnt Univ of Nottingham 1994–96, The Patients' Assoc 1995–97 (actg chief exec 1995–96), Health Policy Gp Centre for Policy Studies 1997–99; memb: Advsy Cncl IEA Health Unit 1989–92 and 1997–99, Communications Advsy Gp and Patients' Charter Advsy Gp NHS Mgmnt Exec 1991–94, Strategic Ctee on Women's Issues SE Thames RHA 1992–94, King's Fund NAHAT Public Participation Advsy Gp 1992, Governance in the NHS (Induction and Trg) Working Pty NHS Mgmnt Exec 1993, Ministerial Advsy Gp on Design in Healthcare 1993–98, PM's Advsy Panel on The Citizen's Charter 1994, Policy Advsy Gp Inst of Health Services Mgmnt 1994–98, NHSME Working Pty on Open Govt 1994, Bd Int Health Care Mgmnt Inst 1994–98, NHS Exec Patient Responsiveness Gp 1996–97, memb Bd Nat Cmmn on Care Standards 2001–03, Advsy Cncl Reform 2001–10; Nat Assoc of Health Authorities and Tsts: memb Cncl 1992–94, memb Exec 1993–94, vice-chm Provider Ctee 1993–94, chm Conf Ctee 1993–94 (memb 1992); health policy advsr The Social Market Fndn 1994–99; visiting fell: NHS Staff Coll Wales 1995–2010, King's Fund Mgmnt Coll 1996–2010; research fell Inst of Economic Affrs 1997–99 (sr research fell 1999–2000 and 2003–11), head of health care studies 1999–2000, adjunct scholar Cascade Policy Centre Portland OR 1999; external prof: Business Sch Univ of Glamorgan 1998–2001, Humanities and Social Studies Sch Univ of Glamorgan 2001–13; sr research fell Inst of English Studies Univ of London 2003–, visiting fell Ruskin Prog Lancaster Univ 2005–, professorial research fell Global Policy Inst London Met Univ 2013–; fndr and chm Edward Everett Root Publishers Co Ltd 2015–; founding dir Southern Sound Radio plc 1980–87; dir: Radical Soc 1988–2000 (co chm 1990–2000), Center for Intelligence Studies Washington DC 1990–93; pres The Gissing Fndn 2005–; tstee: Brighton Int Arts Festival 1989–96, Choice in Educn (grant maintained schs) 1989–92, Grant Maintained Schs Fndn 1992–99 (vice-chm 1992–99), The Trident Tst 1992–99 (vice-chm 1993, chm 1994–97), English Schs Orchestra and Choir 1998–2005, The League of Mercy 1999–2005 (companion 2002), Shakespeare Authorship Tst 2002–2005, The Ruskin Fndn 2002–09; organiser Victorian Popular Fiction Exhbn 2016; distinguished sr fell Center for Cons Studies Washington DC 1992 (assoc 2005–); librarian and memb Nat Cncl Francis Bacon Soc 1998–2005; organiser: The Rediscovery of George Gissing Exhbn 1971, Centenary Conference, Gissing and the City 2003; memb: Exec Ctee William Morris Soc 1973–76, Advsy Bd Centre for Study of Social History Univ of Warwick 1979–82, RSA; Univ of Sussex: memb Ct 1987–, vice-pres Univ of Sussex Alumni Soc 2002– (chm 1983–2004), memb Chllr's Advsy Gp 1986–98, hon fell Univ of Sussex Soc 1999–; JP (E Sussex) 1989–91; Queen's Award for Export Achievement 1986; Freeman City of London 2000; Hon DUniv Sussex 1994; Companion of the Guild of St George 1979 (fndr and ed The Companion 2001–05, dir 2002–05); FRSA 1994; hon fell Inst of Econ Affrs 2003–11; Knight Cdr with Star Order of St Stanislaus 1997 (Knight Grand Cross 1998); *Books* The Rediscovery of George Gissing (with Pierre Coustillas, 1971), The Invisible Hospital and The Secret Garden: An Insider's Account of the NHS Reforms (1995), Sense and Sensibility in Health Care (co-author, 1996), Who Owns Our Bodies: Making Moral Choices in Health Care (1997), Dilemmas in Health Policy (ed, 1998), The Realities of Rationing (1999), Coming, Ready or Not: The Politics, Present and Future of the NHS (2002), Patients, Power and Responsibility. The First Principles of Consumer-Driven Reform (2003), Gissing and the City (ed, 2006), Serious About Series (2007), Who Decides Who Decides? (2008), The Culture of the Publishers' Series (2 Vols, 2011), Just the Ticket! (2015), This Will Only Hurt a Little: Achieving Patient Benefit and the Reform of Clinical Practice, The Papers of Dr William G Pickering (ed, 2016); *Recreations* collecting Victorian books, reading them, supporting The Arsenal, canal boats, walking, travelling in railway carriages, natural history; *Clubs* Hoxton Hawks Vintage Cycling (pres 2006–), RSA; *Style—* Prof John Spiers; ✉ e-mail jr.spiers@btinternet.com

SPIERS, Shaun Mark; s of (Charles) Gordon Spiers (d 1990), and Ann Kathleen, *née* Hutton; *b* 23 April 1962; *Educ* Brentwood Sch, St John's Coll Oxford (BA), King's Coll London (MA); *Career* political offr SE Co-op 1987–94, MEP (Lab Co-op) London SE 1994–99; chief exec Assoc of Br Credit Unions 1999–2004; chief exec Campaign to Protect Rural England (CPRE) 2004–; *Style—* Shaun Spiers

SPILLER, David; *b* 28 August 1942; *Educ* Slade Sch of Art; *Career* artist; *Exhibitions* Zeitkunst Gall Innsbruck and Cologne 1987 and 1988, Eugene Lendel Gall Gras 1987, Kunstverein Mannheim 1987, Woord and Reeld (Museum Hedendaagse Kunst Utrecht) 1987, Twinings Gall NY 1988 and 1989, Kana Contemporary Arts Gall Berlin 1988, Alexander Roussos Gall 1990, Ariadne Gall Vienna 1990 and 1991, Willy Schoots Gall Eindhoven 1991, Reflex Gall Amsterdam 1992, Pop Artvertising (Museum Van Bommel Venlo) 1992, Gall Naviglio Milan and Venice 1992 and 1993, Gall Moderne Silkeborg 1994, Gall Cotthem Knokke 1995, 1998, 2000 and 2003, Gall Cotthem Barcelona 1997, Rokoko Gallery Stuttgart 1998, Beaux Arts London 1998, 1999, 2000, 2001, 2002, 2004 and 2005, Cartoons and Comics (Virgin Atlantic) 1999, Gall Moderne Silkeborg 1999, Gall Moderne Denmark 2000, Guy Pieters Belgium 2000 and 2003, Gallery Camino Real Boca Raton 2000, Galerie Klaus Peter Goebel Stuttgart 2000, Galerie Wild Frankfurt 2001, Museum Espace Belleville Paris 2002, Royal West of England Acad 2003, Ernst Hilger Vienna 2004, Raab Galerie Berlin 2004, Wild Gallery Frankfurt 2005, 2007 and 2008, Love for Sale (Bankside Gallery London, Gallery Moderne Silkeborg Denmark, Beaux Arts London and Midwest Kunst Herning Museum Denmark) 2005, Gallery Moderne Silkeborg Denmark 2006 and 2008, Apart Media Amsterdam 2006, Artcurial Paris 2006, Mannheim Kunstverein Germany 2007, Guy Pieters Gallery Knokke Belgium 2007 and 2009, Tournesol Gallery Lyon 2008, Gallery Willy Schoots Eindhoven 2008, Interatrium Gallery Porto 2008, Beaux Arts London 2008 and 2009, St Paul de Vence France 2009; art fairs incl: Chicago, Cologne, Frankfurt, Miami, Los Angeles, FIAC Paris, Art98, Art99; *Style—* David Spiller, Esq

SPILLER, Richard John; s of Capt Michael Macnaughton Spiller, of Belfast, and Agnes Gall, *née* Algie; *b* 31 December 1953; *Educ* Royal Belfast Academical Inst, Univ of Exeter (LLB), London Guildhall Univ (MA); *m* 17 Sept 1982, Hilary, da of William Wright, of Kingston upon Thames; 1 s (James b 1984), 1 da (Emily b 1987); *Career* admitted slr 1980; ptnr: D J Freeman/Kendall Freeman 1985–2007, Edwards Angell Palmer & Dodge 2008–11, Holman Fenwick Willan LLP 2011–; chm Insurance Law Ctee City of London Law Soc 2012–; Freeman: City of London 1986, Worshipful Co of Slrs 1986 (memb Insurance Law Ctee); memb Law Soc; *Style—* Richard Spiller, Esq

SPINDLER, Angela; da of Frank Jones (d 1995), and Rita, *née* Kelly, of Chester; *b* 30 August 1962, Chester; 30 Dec 2007, Prof Michael Luger; 1 s (Lewis Spindler b 8 Nov 1989), 1 da (Abigail Spindler b 14 March 1992); *Career* md George clothing Asda 2004–07, md Debenhams plc 2007–08, ceo Factory Shop Gp 2009–13, ceo N Brown Gp plc 2013–; non-exec dir and Remco chair Manchester Airport Gp; *Recreations* fashion, reading, tennis, travel, walking; *Clubs* Prestbury Tennis; *Style—* Ms Angela Spindler; ✉ N Brown Group plc, 40 Lever Street, Manchester M60 6ES (☎ 0161 238 2203, e-mail angela.spindler@nbrowngroup.co.uk, website www.nbrown.co.uk, Twitter @ALLuger)

SPINK, Air Marshal Clifford Rodney; CB (2002), CBE (1992, OBE 1989); s of Ronald Charles Spink (d 1990), and Beryl, *née* Phillips (d 2002); *b* 17 May 1946; *Educ* RAF Coll Cranwell; *m* 1, 3 April 1971, Christine Janet Grove (d 1973); m 2, 9 April 1977, Caroline Anne, da of Anthony Francis Smith; 1 da (Laura Claire b 2 Dec 1978), 1 s (Robert Alun b 13 Jan 1982); *Career* cmmnd RAF 1968, subsequently 111 (Fighter) Sqdn RAF Wattisham 1970–73, 56 (Fighter) Sqdn Akrotiri Cyprus 1974 (involved in conflict), 56 (Fighter) Sqdn Wattisham until 1976, instr RMAS 1976–79 (following courses at RMAS and Sch of Infantry Warminster), Flight Cdr 111 (Fighter) Sqdn RAF Leuchars 1979–82, NDC Latimer and subsequently HQ RAF Germany, Cdr 74 (Fighter) Sqdn RAF Wattisham 1986–89, Cdr RAF Mount Pleasant and Dep Cdr British Forces Falklands 1989–90, Cdr RAF Coningsby 1990–92, Detachment Cdr Dhahran (Gulf conflict) 1991, Air Cdre 1993, RCDS 1993 subsequently SASO HQ 11 Gp 1993–95, COS HQ 18 Gp, Air Vice-Marshal and First Air OC 11/18 Gp 1996–98, DG MOD Saudi Armed Forces Project 1998–2002; non-exec dir Eastern Airways; dir Contingency Planning Associates Ltd, md Clifford Spink Associates Ltd; pres: Royal Observer Corps Assoc, Battle of Britain Flight Assoc; Liveryman Hon Co of Air Pilots (Master 2012–13); FRAeS 1997; *Recreations* vintage aircraft, golf, garden; *Clubs* RAF; *Style—* Air Marshal Clifford Spink, CB, CBE, FCMI, FRAeS, RAF; ✉ Clifford Spink Associates Ltd, April Lodge, Loop Road, Keyston, Huntingdon, Cambridgeshire PE28 0RE

SPINK, Ian Alexander; s of John Arthur Spink, of Melbourne, Australia, and Lorna Kathleen, *née* Hart; *b* 8 October 1947; *Educ* Highett HS, Aust Ballet Sch; *m* 1, 1972 (m dis 1975), Gail Mae Ferguson; m 2, 1986 (m dis 1992), Michele Ashmore Smith; m 3, Lucinda Adele Bevan 1998; *Career* dancer Australian Ballet Co 1968–74, dancer and choreographer Dance Co of NSW 1975–77, dancer Richard Alston & Dancers Co 1978–79, fndr, dancer, dir and choreographer Ian Spink Dance Group 1978–82, co-fndr Second Stride (dance theatre) 1982–97 (became sole dir 1988), currently artistic dir CityMoves Dance Agency Aberdeen; theatre choreography for RSC, Ro Theatre (Holland) and The Crucible (Sheffield), opera choreography for Opera North, WNO, Royal Opera House, Scot Opera, Opera de Nice, ENO and Glyndebourne Festival Opera; dir: Fugue by Caryl Churchill (Channel Four) 1988, Judith Weir's The Vanishing Bridegroom (Scot Opera) 1990, The Pelican (Glasgow Citizens Theatre) 1992, Orlando (Batignano Opera Festival) 1992, Daughter of the Regiment (ETO) 1998–99, The Striker (Caryl Churchill, Aberystwyth) 2000, Orfeo (Purcell Sinfonia Japan) 2001, L'Enfant et les Sortilege and L'Heure Espagnole (Opera Zuid Maastricht) 2002, Private Lives (Glasgow Citizens Theatre) 2003, A Tragedy of Fashion (Rambert Dance Co) 2004; *Recreations* music, cooking, choreographing, growing avocado trees, thinking; *Style—* Ian Spink

SPITTLE, Dr Margaret Flora; OBE (2004); da of Edwin William Spittle (d 1977), and Ada Florence, *née* Axam; *b* 10 November 1939; *Educ* KCL (MSc, AKC), Westminster Hosp Med Sch; *m* 1, 2 Jan 1965 (m dis 1977), Clive Lucas Harmer, s of Cecil Norman Harmer (d 1986); 2 da (Kasha Jane Lucas b 1968, Victoria Margaret Lucas b 1971); m 2, 31 May 1986, David John Hare (d 2009), s of John Robinson Hare (d 1982); *Career* conslt clinical oncologist Meyerstein Inst of Clinical Oncology The Middx Hosp, St John's Dermatology Centre St Thomas' Hosp and Cromwell Hosp, Harley Street Cancer Centre 1971–; vice-pres and dean RCR 1994–97, vice-pres RSM 1994– (pres Oncology Section 1987, pres Radiology Section 1989, pres Open Section 2000), pres Head and Neck Oncologists of GB 1991; memb: Govt Ctee on Breast Screening, Nat Radiological Protection Bd, Govt Ctee on Med Aspects of Radiation in the Environment; tstee of many cancer charities; Freeman City of London, Liveryman Worshipful Soc of Apothecaries (memb Ctee); memb RSM; FRCP, FRCR; *Publications* many articles and chapters on breast cancer, head and neck and skin cancer and AIDS-related malignancies; *Recreations* family, golf, music, flying; *Clubs* RAC; *Style—* Dr Margaret Spittle, OBE; ✉ The Manor House, Beaconsfield Road, Claygate, Surrey KT10 0PW (☎ 01372 465540, fax 01372 470470); The Harley Street Cancer Centre, 81 Harley Street, London W1G 3AA

SPIVEY, Dr Nigel Jonathan; s of Rev A J Spivey, and Jennifer, *née* Norman; *Educ* Caterham Sch, Emmanuel Coll Cambridge (Athletics blue), Br Sch Rome, Univ of Pisa; *Career* Emmanuel Coll Cambridge: res fell 1986–89, lectr in classics 1991–, fell 1991–; lectr in classics St David's Univ Coll 1989–91; Runciman Prize 1997; *Books* Understanding Greek Sculpture (1996), Greek Art (1997), Etruscan Art (1997), Enduring Creation (2001), The Ancient Olympics (2004), How Art Made the World (2005), Songs on Bronze (2005); *Recreations* discus throwing, vegetable growing, family; *Clubs* Achilles; *Style—* Dr Nigel Spivey; ✉ Emmanuel College, Cambridge CB2 3AP (☎ 01223 334224, e-mail njs11@cam.ac.uk; c/o PFD, Drury House, 34–43 Russell Street, London WC2B 5HA

SPOFFORTH, (David) Mark; OBE (2014); s of Michael Gordon Spofforth (d 1987), and Joan Mary, *née* Marsh; *b* 26 July 1956; *Educ* Bradfield Coll, Univ of Durham (BSc); *m* 1, 31 July 1983, Dorothy Lesley, *née* Payne (d 2007); 1 da (Gemma Mary b 17 Nov 1987), 1 s (Peter Michael b 25 Jan 1990); m 2, 8 May 2015, Veronica Anne, *née* Walker; *Career* articled clerk Coopers & Lybrand 1980–82, managing ptnr Spofforths Chartered Accountants 1997–2000 (joined 1983, ptnr 1984–); ICAEW: memb Tech Ctee 1985–94, memb Cncl 1993–2015 (chm 2003–05), memb Gen Practitioner Bd 1993–99 (chm 1995–98), memb Exec Ctee 1998–2007, memb Members' Directorate 1998–2000, chm Educn and Trg 2000–03 and 2005–07, memb Regulation Review Working Pty, 2005 Working Pty, memb Practice Ctee 2009–12, memb Bd 2010–13, memb Remuneration Ctee 2010–13, vice-pres 2010–11, dep pres 2011–12, pres 2012–13; SE Soc of Chartered Accountants: memb Main Ctee 1990–2015, dep pres 1998–99, pres 1999–2000; dep chm Int Accounting Educn Standards Bd 2005–10, bd observer Int Fedn of Accountants 2014–; broadcaster BBC Southern Counties Radio; memb Ctee Charities SORP 2014–, tstee Thalidomide Tst 2014–; Freeman City of London, Master Worshipful Co of Horners 2009, Master Worshipful Co of Chartered Accountants; High Sheriff West Sussex 2016–17; FCA 1982, CTA 2005; FRSA 1994; Profitable and Sustainable Practice (report, 2003); *Recreations* rugby, skiing, scuba diving, watching international swimming; *Clubs* City Livery, Carlton; *Style—* Mark Spofforth, Esq, OBE; ✉ Spofforths, Donnington Park, Birdham Road, Chichester, West Sussex PO20 7AJ (☎ 01243 787627, fax 01243 532757, e-mail markspofforth@spofforths.co.uk)

SPOONER, Dr David; s of Rev Reginald H Spooner (d 1982), and Lucy Ellen, *née* Read; *b* 12 January 1949; *Educ* Magdalen Coll Sch Brackley, Univ of Birmingham (MB, BSc); *m* Diana Lilian, da of Frederick John Mason, of Banbury; 2 s (John, Andrew), 1 da (Rebecca); *Career* res fell Cancer Res Inst Sutton Surrey 1979–81, sr registrar in radiotherapy Royal Marsden Hosp London 1981–82 (registrar 1976–79); conslt in radiotherapy and oncology: Queen Elizabeth Hosp, Birmingham Children's Hosp, Royal Orthopaedic Hosp Birmingham; memb Cncl Royal Coll of Radiologists; FRCP, FRCR; *Style—* Dr David Spooner

SPOONER, Graham Michael; s of Ronald Sidney Spooner (d 1968), of Westcliff-on-Sea, Essex, and Kitty Margaret, *née* Cole (d 1985); *b* 23 August 1953; *Educ* Westcliff HS, St John's Coll Cambridge (MA); *m* Virginia Mary, *née* Barker; *Career* ICFC (now part of 3i Group plc): joined 1974, area mangr Nottingham 1983, local dir in London 1986, dir 3i plc 1987–93; head of corp fin Olliff & Partners plc 1993–95, dir Rea Brothers Limited 1995–96, nat dir of corp fin HLB Kidsons 1996–2000; dir: Downing Classic VCT plc 1999–2003, Downing Classic VCT 2 plc 2000–03, Downing Classic VCT 3 plc 2000–03, Classic Fund Mgmnt Ltd 2000–04, Mentor UK Ltd 2000–05 (princ 2004–), Dunn-Line plc 2004–06, Dowgate Capital plc 2007–08; venture capital advsr to Cwlth Devpt Corporation 1993, special advsr UN Devpt Prog 1993, assoc Amberley Advsy 2009–; memb Treasy and Strategy Ctees Metropolitan Housing Tst 1998–99; tstee BDA Pension & Life Assurance Scheme 2005–11; sr vice-patron Diabetes UK 2004–10 (memb Advsy Cncl 2003–11, treas 2005–11), dir Br Diabetic Assoc 2005–11, chm Diabetes UK Servs Ltd 2006–11, memb Ctee Johnian Soc 2007– (hon sec 2009–12, chm 2013–), vice-chm NACUE 2013–14; memb Devpt Bd RSA 2006–07, memb Campaign Bd St John's Coll 2008–12, memb Alumni Bd Henley Business Sch 2008–11, memb Devpt Bd Univ of Reading 2010–12, memb Advsy Bd KCL Business Club 2010–14, memb Advsy Bd Cambridge Univ Venture Club 2010–14; tstee Hon Treasurers Forum 2014–; FRSA 1998; *Publications* Raising Venture Capital, A Guide to Venture Capital for Accountants, The Corporate Finance Manual (ed, 2000–03), Venture Capital and Private Equity: A Practitioner's Manual (ed), A Practitioner's Guide to Venture Capital Law (contrib), The Director's Manual (contrib); memb ed bd Accountants Digest 1999–2002, memb Editorial Bd Corporate Money 1997–2000; *Recreations* classic cars, heritage; *Clubs* Oxford and Cambridge; *Style—* Graham Spooner, Esq; ✉ 4 Barrow Court, Barrow Gurney, North Somerset BS48 3RP (☎ 01275 463690, mobile 07769 674005, fax 01275 463690, e-mail gmspooner@mentoruk.com)

SPOONER, Richard Hamilton; s of Derek Richard Spooner (d 1978), and Patricia Sackville, *née* Hamilton (d 2013); *b* 17 February 1952; *Educ* King's Sch Ely, Lanchester Sch of Business Studies (BA); *m* 8 April 1978, Susan Elizabeth Ann, da of Anthony John Rowntree (d 1998); 3 da (Victoria, Catherine, Elizabeth); *Career* audit mangr Howard Tilly 1976–79, chief accountant Yeoman Aggregates Ltd 1979–83; dir: Yeoman Heavy Haulage Ltd 1980–83, Buckingham Computers Ltd 1981–84, HTA 1983–88; md: Howard Tilly Associates Ltd 1984–88, H T A Property Systems Ltd 1987–97; chm Baker Tilly Consulting 1988–; ptnr: Howard Tilly 1986–88, Baker Tilly 1988–; memb Acad of Experts; ACA, MInstD, MIMgt; *Recreations* golf, cricket, bridge, good food; *Clubs* MCC; *Style—* Richard Spooner, Esq; ✉ Orchard House, off Elkins Road, Hedgerley, Buckinghamshire (☎ and fax 01753 645357); Baker Tilly, 25 Farringdon Street, London EC4A 4AB (☎ 020 3201 8000, mobile 07918 080070, e-mail richard.spooner@bakertilly.co.uk)

SPOTTISWOODE, Clare Mary Joan; CBE (1999); da of Tony Spottiswoode, and Charlotte Spottiswoode; *b* 20 March 1953; *Educ* Cheltenham Ladies' Coll, Clare Coll Cambridge (MA), Yale Univ (Mellon fellowship, MPhil); *m* 1977, Oliver Richards, s of Robin Richards; 3 da (Imogen b 15 Sept 1980, Camilla b 13 April 1982, Olivia b 8 May 1990), 1 s (Dominic b 9 Dec 1991); *Career* economist HM Treasy 1977–80, sole proprietor Spottiswoode Trading (import business) 1980–84, chm and md Spottiswoode & Spottiswoode (microcomputer software house) 1984–90, tutor London Business Sch and software conslt 1990–93, DG Ofgas 1994–98, sr vice-pres European Water Azurix 1998–99; chm: Buyenergyonline.com 2000–01, Economatters 2000–, Bergesen AG 2003–; non-exec dir: Booker plc 1995–2000, Caminus 2000–03, Advanced Technology UK 2000–, British Energy plc 2001–07 (ind dep chm 2002–07), Tullow Oil plc 2002–, Busy Bees 2002–05, Biofuels Corporation 2004–07; memb Mgmnt Gp PA Consulting Gp 1999–2000, memb Bd of Dirs Bergesen AG 2003–; policy holder advocate Aviva 2006–; Hon DSSc Brunel Univ 1997; CIGE 1994; *Books* Quill (1984), Abacus (1984); *Recreations* children, gardening, theatre; *Style—* Ms Clare Spottiswoode, CBE

SPRAGG, His Hon Judge Robert Forrester; s of Francis John Forrester Spragg, and Vanessa Jane, *née* Cass, of Herts; *b* 1 February 1968, Welwyn Garden City; *Educ* Oundle, Newcastle Univ; *m* 1 Nov 1997, Jennifer Ann Sinclair; 2 da (Rosie b 13 Nov 2000, Annie b 6 Feb 2003), 1 s (Louis b 26 July 2007); *Career* admitted slr 1995; called to the Bar 2003; recorder 2012, circuit judge (NE Circuit) 2016–; *Recreations* cricket, football coach, walking; *Style—* His Hon Judge Spragg; ✉ Sheffield Crown Court, 50 W Bar, Sheffield S3 8PH (☎ 0114 281 2415)

SPRAGUE, Christopher William; s of Coulam Alfred Joseph Sprague (d 1997), and Joan Gertrude, *née* Jackson (d 1986); *b* 19 August 1943; *Educ* St Edward's Sch Oxford, ChCh Oxford (MA); *m* 24 April 1971, Clare, da of Dr John Russell Bradshaw (d 1968), and Jennie Winifred, *née* Bruce-Rayner (d 2005); 4 da (Katharine b 1972, Alison b 1974, Hannah b 1979, Alexandra b 1981); *Career* articled Simmons & Simmons, admitted slr 1970; Ince & Co: asst slr 1970–75, ptnr 1975–2004, conslt 2006–12; specialist in insurance and maritime law; memb Law Soc; holder FISA int rowing umpire's license 1993–2008, pres Thames Regnl Rowing Cncl 2005–06, chm Thames Regnl Umpires Cmmn 2003–08 (memb 1981–2008, sec 1981–88); govr Royal Sch Haslemere 2001–, pres St Edward's Sch Soc 2008–09; tstee Phyllis Tuckwell Hospice Farnham 2005–14; Freeman City of London, memb Ct of Assts Worshipful Co of Barbers (Master 2004–05), Liveryman City of London Solicitors' Co, Craft Owning Freeman Co of Watermen and Lightermen; FSA 2011; *Publications* Damages for Personal Injury and Loss of Life – The English Approach (1997), Notable Barber Surgeons (contrib, 2008); *Recreations* reading, history, rowing; *Clubs* Garrick, London Rowing, Leander; *Style—* C W Sprague, Esq, FSA; ✉ Pasturewood, Woodhill Lane, Shamley Green, Guildford, Surrey GU5 0SP (e-mail chris.sprague1@btinternet.com)

SPRANGE, Thomas Kimpton; QC (2015); *b* 21 February 1972, Sydney, Aust; *Educ* Cranbrook Sch, Univ of Sydney, University of NSW (LLM); *Children* 1 da (Zara Cole b 18 Feb 2005), 2 s (James Kimpton b 5 Dec 2006, Oliver Benjamin b 6 Aug 2008); *Career* admitted Law Soc of New South Wales, admitted slr advocate (England and Wales) 2001; ptnr Steptoe & Johnson 2002–11, ptnr and slr advocate King & Spalding 2011–; *Recreations* cinema, cricket, sailing, skiing, travel, swimming, Muay Thai; *Clubs* KO Muay Thai, Red Top Swim; *Style—* Thomas Sprange, Esq, QC; ✉ King & Spalding, 125 Old Broad Street, London EC2N 1AR

SPRATT, Prof Brian Geoffrey; CBE (2008); s of Clarence Albert Spratt (d 1966), of Rye, E Sussex, and Marjory Alice, *née* Jeffreys (d 1999); *b* 21 March 1947, Margate, Kent; *Educ* Tonbridge, UCL (BSc, PhD); *m* 1, (m dis 1995), Jennifer Broome-Smith; 1 s (Timothy Peter b 22 April 1988); m 2, Jiaji Zhou; 1 s (Henry Jestyn b 16 Feb 1995); *Career* res fell Dept of Biochemical Scis Princeton Univ 1973–75, res fell Dept of Genetics Univ of Leicester 1975–80; Univ of Sussex: lectr in biochemistry 1980–87, reader 1987–89, prof of molecular genetics 1989–97; princ res fell Wellcome Tst 1989–, prof of biology Univ of Oxford 1997–2001, prof of molecular microbiology Imperial Coll London 2001–; hon prof LSHTM 2002–12; chair: Wellcome Tst Infection and Immunity Panel 1995–98, Acad of Med Sciences Report on Academic Bacteriology in the 21st Century 2001, chair Royal Soc Report on Health Hazards of Depleted Uranium Munitions 2001–02, Independent Review of the Safety of UK Facilities Handling Foot and Mouth Disease Virus 2007; author of numerous publications on microbiology in learned jls; Squibb lectures Rutgers Univ 1985, RS Leeuwenhoek lecture 2003; Fleming Award Soc for Gen Microbiology 1982, Pfizer Academic Award 1983, Hoechst-Roussel Award American Soc for Microbiology 1993, Kitasato Medal for Microbial Chemistry 1995, Garrod Medal Br Soc Antimicrobial Chemotherapy 2011, GlaxoSmithKline Int Award American Soc for Microbiology 2011; FRS 1993, FMedSci 1998, fell American Acad of Microbiology 2003; *Style—* Prof Brian Spratt, CBE, FRS; ✉ Department of Infectious Disease Epidemiology,

S

Imperial College London, St Mary's Hospital, London W2 1PG (☎ 020 7594 3625, fax 020 7494 8321, e-mail b.spratt@imperial.ac.uk)

SPRATT, Jimmy; MLA; *Career* MLA (DUP) Belfast S 2007–; *Style—* Jimmy Spratt, Esq, MLA; ✉ Northern Ireland Assembly, Parliament Buildings, Belfast BT4 3XX

SPRAY, Martin Coulson; CBE (2013); s of Lionel Spray, and Constance; *b* 16 June 1951, London; *Educ* Tiffin Boys Sch Kingston-upon-Thames, Univ of Wales Swansea (BSc); *m* Marian; 1 s (Matthew), 1 da (Caroline); *Career* Educn Dept Royal Borough of Kingston-upon-Thames 1973–74, Science and Engrg Research Cncl 1974–88, area mangr London & SE WWF UK 1988–91, chief exec Berks, Bucks and Oxon Wildlife Tst 1991–2004 (currently vice-pres), acting DG The Wildlife Tsts and acting chief exec Royal Soc of Wildlife Tsts 2003–04, chief exec Wildfowl and Wetlands Tst 2004–; chm Marine Conservation Soc 2010–15; formerly: memb Bd and tstee Veolia Environmental Tst, chair North Wessex Downs Area of Outstanding Natural Beauty Cncl of Ptnrs, memb Cncl Br Assoc of Zoos and Aquaria, tstee Wildlife and Countryside Link, memb Rgnl Environmental Protection Advsy Ctee Environment Agency, memb Oxon Country Landowners Assoc Ctee, founder memb Bd Ponds Conservation, chm Oxon Environment Forum, UK Exec Ctee Int Union for Nature Conservation; Hon DSc Univ of Roehampton 2013; *Recreations* family, walking, cooking, eating out, friends, watching sport; *Style—* Martin Spray, Esq, CBE; ✉ Wildfowl & Wetlands Trust, Slimbridge, Gloucestershire GL2 7BT (☎ 01453 891131, e-mail martin.spray@wwt.org.uk)

SPRENT, Prof Janet Irene; OBE (1996); da of James William Findlater, and Dorothy May Findlater; *b* 10 January 1934; *Educ* Slough HS for Girls, Imperial Coll of Science and Technol London (BSc, ARCS), Univ of Tasmania (PhD), Univ of London (DSc); *m* 1955, Peter Sprent; *Career* scientific offr Rothamsted Experimental Station 1954–55, ICIANZ research fell Univ of Tasmania 1955–58, botany mistress Rochester Girl's GS 1959–61, lectr then sr lectr Goldsmiths Coll London 1960–67; Univ of Dundee: successively research fell, lectr, sr lectr and reader 1967–89, dean Faculty of Sci and Engineering 1987–89, prof of plant biology 1989–, head Dept of Biological Scis 1992–95, dep princ 1995–98; hon research fell James Hutton Inst (formerly Scottish Crop Research Inst) 1991–; chm of govrs Macaulay Land Use Research Inst 1995–2001 (govr 1990–); various overseas visits and int meetings in respect of nitrogen fixing crops and tree research, participatory researcher in major projects at Murdoch Univ W Australia; memb: NERC 1991–95, Scottish HEFC 1992–96, Jt Nature Conservation Ctee 1993–2000 and 2005–07, Panel for Individual Merit Promotions UK Research Cncl 1992–98, Bd Scottish Natural Heritage 2001–, Royal Cmmn on Environmental Pollution 2002–10, Scottish Cncl for Marine Science 2005–08, Strategic Science Advsy Panel RERAD 2006–07; tstee Royal Botanic Gardens Edinburgh 2007–15 (memb Scientific Advsy Ctee 2014–, research assoc 2015–); hon doctorate Swedish Univ of Agriculture Sciences (SLU) Uppsala 2010; hon memb Br Ecological Soc, memb Soc for Experimental Biology, memb Soc for Gen Microbiology, hon memb Botanical Soc of Scotland; emeritus prof, Leverhulme fell 1998–2000; FLS, FRSE 1990; *Books* The Ecology of the Nitrogen Cycle (1987), Nitrogen Fixing Organisms: Pure and Applied Aspects (with P Sprent, 1990), Advances in Legume Systematics, 5. The Nitrogen Factor (co-ed with D McKey, 1994), Nodulation in Legumes (2001), Legume Nodulation: a global perspective (2009); numerous book chapters and papers in scientific jls; *Recreations* walking, gardening, music; *Clubs* Farmers; *Style—* Prof Janet Sprent, OBE, FRSE; ✉ 32 Birkhill Avenue, Wormit, Newport on Tay, Fife DD6 8PW (☎ 01382 541706, e-mail jisprent@btinternet.com); Division of Plant Science, University of Dundee at James Hutton Institute, Dundee DD2 5DA

SPRING, Stephanie (Stevie); da of William Harold Spring (d 2001), and Marlene Green, *née* Coleman (d 2013); *b* 10 June 1957, London; *Educ* Eggars GS Alton, Univ of Kent (LLB); *Career* mktg mangr Alpine Holdings 1978–82, devpt mangr TVam 1982–84, business dir Grey Advertising 1984–88, dep md GGT 1988–92; md: WMGO 1992–94, Young & Rubicam 1994–99; ceo: Clear Channel UK 1999–2006, Future plc 2006–12; chm: ITG Gp 2014–, Kino-mo 2014–, Remco Co-operative Gp 2015–; memb Cncl UKC 2014–, sr ind dir ALCS 2014–; chm: Groundwork Fedn 2000–08, BBC Children in Need 2008–; Hon DUniv Kent 2011; fell: Inst of Practitioners in Advtg 1996, Mktg Soc 2004; *Recreations* travel, running, theatre and the arts; *Clubs* Soho House, WACL, MGGB, Thirty; *Style—* Ms Stevie Spring; ✉ e-mail stevie@steviespring.com, Twitter @steviespring1

SPRINGMAN, Prof Sarah Marcella; CBE (2012, OBE 1997); da of Paul Michael Eyre Springman (d 2013), and Dame Ann Marcella, *née* Mulloy (d 1987); *b* 26 December 1956, London; *Educ* Wycombe Abbey, Univ of Cambridge (Roscoe meml prize, coll prize, MA, MPhil, PhD, Squash blue, played in 11 Varsity matches in 6 different sports); *Career* Univ of Cambridge OTC TA: commissioned 1978, trg offr 1978, cmd Royal Engineer Wing 1980 and 1983–86, Lt 1980, Capt 1983–86 (officially ret 1997); Sir Alexander Gibb & Partners: various positions Geotechnical Dept, seconded to Public Works Dept and Monasavu Hydro-Electric Scheme Fiji, Adelaide and Canberra Offices 1975–83; Univ of Cambridge: SERC studentship Dept of Engrg 1983–84, research asst Soil Mechanics Gp Dept of Engrg 1985–89, res fell Magdalene Coll 1988–90, lectr Soil Mechanics Gp 1993–96 (asst lectr 1990–93), fell and college lectr in soil mechanics Magdalene Coll 1991–96, chair and initiator Language Prog for Engrs 1992–96; prof of geotechnical engrg Inst for Geotechnical Engrg Eidgenössische Technische Hochschule (ETH) Zürich 1997– (rector 2015–), head Inst of Geotechnical Engrg 2001–05 and 2009–11, jt dep head Dept of Civil Environmental & Geomatic Engrg 2013–14; memb EPSRC Peer Review Coll 2006–09 and 2012–, memb Search Ctee Queen Elizabeth Prize for Engrg 2012; memb Bd Implenia 2013–14, memb Exec Bd ETH Zürich 2015–; memb: Women's Engrg Soc 1983, British Geotechnical Assoc 1988, Swiss Geotechnical Soc 1998, Swiss Natural Hazards Competence Centre 1998–2010, Swiss Engineers and Architects 1999, Swiss Sci and Technol Cncl 2000–07, Royal Acad of Engrg Research Cmmn 2011, Stiftung Studentisches Wohnen 2015–; vice-pres kihz 2015–, pres Kuratorium Collegium Helveticum 2015–; govr: Marlborough Coll 1991–96, Wycombe Abbey Sch 1993–96; Hon DSc Univ of Bath 2013; hon fell Magdalene Coll Cambridge 2014, hon fell Girton Coll 2015, hon fell St Catharine's Coll 2015; CEng, MInstRE, memb Swiss Soc of Engrs and Architects 1990, life fell RSA 2005, FICE 2006 (MICE 1983), FREng 2009; *Sporting Career* 11 times British Triathlon champion, European Triathlon champion 1985, 1986 and 1988, 5 European Team Gold medals, S Pacific Squash champion 1982, champion Swiss Open Quadruple Sculls 1998, 2000 and 2003, champion Swiss Open Eights 1999, 2000, 2001, 2002 and 2003, vice-pres Int Triathlon Union 1992–96, 2008–12 and 2013–16 (co-chair Women's Cmmn 1990–92), govr World Masters Games 1992–2002, memb GB Sports Cncl 1993–96 (UK Sports Cncl 1997–2001 and 2014–), memb Exec Bd Br Triathlon Assoc 2005–06, pres and chair Bd Br Triathlon Fedn 2007–12, chair ETHZ Natural Hazards Gp, memb Mgmnt Bd ETH Competence Centre for Environmental Sustainability 2007–08, memb Nat Olympic Ctee 2008–12, memb Bd Schweizer Studienstitung Swiss Univ Sport Fedn 2015–, memb Hochschule-Gymnasium Ctee Zürich 2015–; Cosmopolitan-Clairol Women of Achievement Award 1991, Jane Tomlinson Award for Outstanding Contrib to Triathlon 220 Magazine 2011, Lifetime Award Sportswoman of the Year 2013; *Publications* Constitutive and Centrifuge Modelling: Two Extremes (ed, 2002), Permafrost (jt ed, 2003), Physical Modelling in Geotechnics (jt (first) ed, 2010, Telford Premium Prize 2013, Br Geotechnical Medal for best paper published by a member 2013); *Clubs* Cambridge Triathlon, Belvoir Ruder, Leander; *Style—* Prof Sarah Springman, CBE, FREng, FICE; ✉ HG F61, Institute for Geotechnical Engineering, ETH Zurich (Eidgenössische Technische Hochschule), Zürich CH 8093, Switzerland (☎ 00 41 44 633 3805, e-mail sarah.springman@igt.baug.ethz.ch); c/o Marianne Schwyter (assistant), e-mail marianne.schwyter@sl.ethz.ch

SPROTT, Duncan; s of Hugh Sprott (d 2014), and Brenda, *née* Grieves (d 2007); *b* 2 December 1952, Chipping Ongar, Essex; *Educ* Newport GS Essex, Univ of St Andrews, Heatherley Sch of Art; *Career* writer; freelance feature writer (travel) Sunday Times 2004–; *Books* 1784 (1984), The Clopton Hercules (1991, US title The Rise of Mr Warde), Our Lady of the Potatoes (1995), Sprottichronicon (2000), The Ptolemies Quartet: The House of the Eagle (2004), Daughter of the Crocodile (2006), Writing Historical Fiction (jtly, 2014); *Style—* Duncan Sprott, Esq; ✉ c/o Rogers, Coleridge & White Ltd, 20 Powis Mews, London W11 1JN (☎ 020 7221 3717, fax 020 7229 9084)

SPROUL, David; *Career* managing ptnr for operations Andersen until 2002; Deloitte: memb Global Exec, md for tax EMEA and UK until 2011, sr ptnr and ceo UK 2011–; *Style—* David Sproul, Esq; ✉ Deloitte, Stonecutter Court, 1 Stonecutter Street, London EC4A 4TR

SPRY, Christopher John; CBE (2002); s of Reginald Charles Spry (d 1962), and Kathleen Edith, *née* Hobart (d 2005); *b* 29 August 1946; *Educ* Sir Roger Manwood's Sch Sandwich, Univ of Exeter (BA); *m* 1, 1968 (m dis 1989), Jean Banks; 2 s (Matthew Alan b 16 Aug 1974, Michael John b 24 Nov 1978); m 2, 1989, Judith Christina, *née* Ryder; *Career* nat trainee 1967–69, admin asst Doncaster Royal Infirmary 1969–70, dep hosp sec Lewisham Hosp 1970–73, hosp sec Nottingham Gen Hosp 1973–75, dist admin S Nottingham 1978–81 (asst dist admin 1975–78), dist gen mangr Newcastle HA 1984–89 (dist admin 1981–84), regnl gen mangr SW Thames RHA 1989–94, regnl dir S Thames Region of NHS Executive 1994–96, chief exec Gtr Glasgow Health Bd 1996–2001, dir OD Partnerships Network 2001–11, dir Redwood House Mgmnt Co 2011–14; visiting prof Univ of Glasgow 2001–, non-exec dir Dorset County Hosp NHS Fndn Tst 2005–10; MIHSM 1972; *Recreations* books, enjoying townscapes, travel, keeping fit; *Style—* Christopher J Spry, Esq, CBE; ✉ 31 Redwood House, Charlton Down, Dorchester DT2 9UH (☎ 07788 714386, e-mail chrisjspry@gmail.com)

SPUFFORD, Francis; s of Prof Peter Spufford, *qv*, and Margaret Spufford, LittD, FBA; *b* 1964; *Career* freelance author and broadcaster; regular appearances on BBC Radio 4; regular contrib Condé Nast Traveller magazine; Young Writer of the Year Sunday Times 1977; FRSL 2007; *Publications* as ed: The Chatto Book of Cabbages and Kings: Lists in Literature (1989), The Chatto Book of the Devil (1992), Cultural Babbage: Technology, Time and Invention (with Jenny Uglow, 1996), The Vintage Book of the Devil (1997); as author: I May Be Some Time: Ice and the English Imagination (1996, Best Non-Fiction Book Writers' Guild Award 1996, Somerset Maugham Award 1997), The Child That Books Built (2002), The Backroom Boys: The Secret Return of the British Boffin (2003), Red Plenty (2010); *Style—* Francis Spufford, Esq

SPUFFORD, Prof Peter; s of Douglas Henry Spufford (d 1967), and Nancy Gwendoline, *née* Battagel (d 2010); *b* 18 August 1934, Hutton, Somerset; *Educ* Kingswood Sch Bath, Jesus Coll Cambridge (MA, PhD, LittD); *m* 7 July 1962, Prof Margaret Spufford, *née* Clark (d 2014); 1 s (Francis Spufford, *qv*, b 22 April 1964), 1 da (Bridget Margaret b 17 April 1967 d 1989); *Career* research fell Jesus Coll Cambridge 1958–60, asst lectr rising to reader Dept of History Keele Univ 1960–79 (sometime actg head of dept), lectr, reader in economic history then prof of European history Faculty of History Univ of Cambridge 1979–2001 (emeritus prof 2001–), fell Queens' Coll Cambridge 1979–; vice-pres Br Records Soc 2010– (sec 1960–79, chm 1985–2010, sometime gen ed), vice-pres Soc of Genealogists 1997–2014; Medal Royal Numismatic Soc 2005; FRHistS 1968, FSA 1990, FBA 1994; *Books* incl: Origins of the English Parliament (1967), Monetary Problems in the Burgundian Netherlands (1970), Handbook of Medieval Exchange (1986), Money and its use in Medieval Europe (1988), Power and Profit: The Merchant in Medieval Europe (2002); 6 other books and 76 articles and chapters in edited books incl Cambridge Economic History of Europe and New Cambridge Medieval History; *Style—* Prof Peter Spufford; ✉ Queens' College, Cambridge CB3 9ET (☎ 01223 335511, fax 01223 335522, e-mail ps44@cam.ac.uk)

SPURLING, (Susan) Hilary; CBE (2007); da of Judge Gilbert Alexander Forrest (d 1977), and Emily Maureen, *née* Armstrong; *b* 25 December 1940; *Educ* Clifton HS Bristol, Somerville Coll Oxford; *m* 4 April 1961, John Spurling; 1 da (Amy Maria b 1972), 2 s (Nathaniel Stobart b 1974, Gilbert Alexander Fettiplace b 1977); *Career* Spectator: theatre critic and arts ed 1964–69, lit ed 1966–69; book reviewer: The Observer 1970–87 and 2006–08, Daily Telegraph 1987–2006; tstee Royal Literary Fund 1999–2007 (chair Fellowship Ctee, hon memb 2007); hon fell Somerville Coll Oxford; Hon Dr Anglia Ruskin Univ; FRSL; *Books* Ivy When Young – The Early Life of I Compton-Burnett 1884–1919 (1974), Handbook to Anthony Powell's Music of Time (1977), Secrets of a Women's Heart – The Later Life of I Compton-Burnett 1919–69 (1984), Elinor Fettiplace's Receipt Book (1986), Paul Scott: a life (1990), Paper Spirits (1992), The Unknown Matisse – A Life of Henri Matisse, Vol 1 1869–1908 (1998), La Grande Thérèse (1999), The Girl from the Fiction Dept (2002), Matisse The Master: A Life of Henri Matisse vol 2 1909–1954 (2005, Whitbread Book of the Year, Whitbread Biography Prize, LA Times Biography Prize), Burying the Bones: Pearl Buck in China (2010, James Tait Black Prize 2011); *Style—* Ms Hilary Spurling, CBE; ✉ David Higham Associates, 5–8 Lower John Street, Golden Square, London W1R 4HA

SPURLING, John Antony; s of Antony Cuthbert Spurling (d 1984), and Elizabeth Frances, *née* Stobart (d 1990); *b* 17 July 1936, Kisumu, Kenya; *Educ* Dragon Sch, Marlborough, St John's Coll Oxford (BA); *m* 4 April 1961, Susan Hilary, da of Gilbert Alexander Forrest; 1 da (Amy Maria b 6 May 1972), 2 s (Nathaniel Stobart b 31 May 1974, Gilbert Alexander Fettiplace b 2 Dec 1977); *Career* Nat Serv 2 Lt RA 1955–57; plebiscite offr Southern Cameroons 1960–61, BBC Radio announcer 1963–66, freelance writer and broadcaster 1966–, Henfield writing fell Univ of E Anglia 1973, art critic The New Statesman 1976–88; playwright and novelist; FRSL 2010; *Plays* for stage: Macrune's Guevara (NT) 1969, In the Heart of the British Museum (Traverse Edinburgh) 1971, The British Empire Part One (Birmingham Repertory) 1980, Coming Ashore in Guadeloupe (Cherub Co Harrogate, Edinburgh and London) 1982–83, Racine at the Girls' Sch (Cheltenham Literary Festival) 1992, King Arthur in Avalon (Cheltenham Literary Festival) 1999, Robinson Crusoe Meets His Maker (HM Prison Albany) 2003; for BBC Radio 3: Dominion Over Palm and Pine 1982, The Christian Hero 1982, The Day of Reckoning 1985, Discobolus 1989, The Butcher of Baghdad 1993 (also staged by Cherub Co London 1993), Macrune's Guevara 1993, Heresy 2001; for BBC Radio 4: Fancy Pictures 1988, A Household in Hove 2002; *Novels* The Ragged End (1989), After Zenda (1995), A Book of Liszts (2011), The Ten Thousand Things (2014, Walter Scott Prize for Historical Fiction 2015), Arcadian Nights: Greek Myths Reimagined (2015); *Style—* John Spurling, Esq; ✉ website www.johnspurling.com; MacNaughton Lord Representation (plays), 44 South Molton Street, London W1K 5RT (☎ 020 7499 1411, fax 020 7493 2444, e-mail info@mlrep.com); Marshall Rights (novels), 19 Tennyson Road, London E17 8PR (☎ 020 8521 5489, e-mail david@marshallrights.co.uk)

SPURR, Dr (M) Stephen; *b* 9 October 1953; *Educ* King's Coll Sch Canterbury, Sidney GS Australia, Univ of Sydney (BA), CCC Oxford (Oxford Ancient History Prize, DPhil), Br Sch Rome (Rome Scholar); *m*; 2 c; *Career* lectr in ancient classics and ancient history Australian Nat Univ 1982–83; Eton Coll: joined 1984, Myers Museum of Egyptian Art 1989–2000, head of classics 1992–96, housemaster 1996–2000; head of coll and head master Upper Sch Clifton Coll Bristol 2000–05, head master Westminster Sch 2005–; *Publications* Arable Cultivation in Roman Italy (1986), Another Sea by Claudio Magris (trans, 1993), Egyptian Art at Eton College (1995), The Oxford Classical Dictionary (contrib, 1996); various articles and reviews; *Recreations* Roman archaeology, Egyptology, mountaineering, Mediterranean agriculture; *Style*— Dr Stephen Spurr; ✉ Westminster School, 17 Dean's Yard, Westminster, London SW1P 3PB

SPURRIER, Steven; s of John Spurrier (d 1988), of Derbys, and Pamela, *née* Neame (d 2002); *b* 5 October 1941, Cambridge; *Educ* Rugby, LSE (BSc); *m* 31 Jan 1968, Arabella, *née* Lawson; 1 s (Christian b 21 Feb 1971), 1 da (Kate b 10 July 1973); *Career* entered London wine trade 1964; prop: Caves de la Madeleine Paris (wine shop) 1970–88, L'Academie du Vin Paris 1973–88 (hosted California wine tasting 'The Judgement of Paris' 1976); ind wine conslt 1988–, clients incl Singapore Airlines; fndr Christie's Wine Course London 1982; conslt ed Decanter magazine; chm Decanter Wine Awards, co-chm Decanter Asia Wine Awards, judge int wine competitions; pres Circle of Wine Writers (formerly chm and vice-pres); *Books* incl: L'Academie du Vin Wine Course, L'Academie du Vin Guide to French Wines, How to Buy Fine Wine, The Clarke-Spurrier Fine Wine Guide (with Oz Clarke, *qv*, 1999, new edn 2001); *Recreations* looking at and collecting art, drinking wine; *Clubs* Boodle's, Chelsea Arts; *Style*— Steven Spurrier, Esq; ✉ 10 Playfair Mansions, Queen's Club Gardens, London W14 9TR (☎ 020 7385 3855, fax 020 7385 4059, e-mail steven@stevenspurrier.com); Decanter, The Blue Fin Building, 110 Southwark Street, London SE1 0SU (☎ 020 3148 5000, fax 020 3148 8524, website www.decanter.com)

SPURWAY, (Marcus) John; s of Marcus Humphrey Spurway (d 1994), of Goudhurst, Kent, and Eva, *née* Mann (d 1980); *b* 28 October 1938; *Educ* Archbishop Tenison's Sch Croydon; *m* 23 Oct 1963, Christine Kate, da of Robert Charles Townshend (d 1981), of Canterbury, Kent; 2 s (Marcus John Charles b 1967, Edward Lewis David b 1969); *Career* Nat Serv 4 Regt RHA; insurance broker; dir Morgan Reid & Sharman Ltd (Lloyd's brokers, formerly B & C Aviation Insurance Brokers), ret 1999; specialist in aviation insurance; *Books* Aviation Insurance Abbreviations, Organisations and Institutions (1983), Aviation Insurance, The Market and Underwriting Practice (1991), Aviation Law and Claims (1992); *Style*— John Spurway, Esq; ✉ Lomeer, Common Road, Sissinghurst, Kent TN17 2JR

SPYER, Prof (Kenneth) Michael (Mike); s of Harris Spyer (d 1982), and Rebecca, *née* Jacobs (d 1982); *b* 15 September 1943; *Educ* Coopers Company's Sch, Univ of Sheffield (BSc), Univ of Birmingham (PhD, DSc); *m* 25 Aug 1971, Christine, da of John Roland Spalton; 2 s (Simon Jeremy b 20 Nov 1976, Nicholas Henry b 26 Oct 1979); *Career* res fell Dept of Physiology Univ of Birmingham Med Sch 1969–72, Royal Soc Euro prog fell Instituto di Fisiologia Umana Pisa 1972–73, sr res fell Department of Physiology Univ of Birmingham Med Sch 1978–80 (res fell 1973–78); Royal Free Hosp Sch of Med (RFHSM): Sophia Jex-Blake prof of physiology Dept of Physiology 1980–2012 (emeritus 2012–), dir British Heart Fndn Neural Control Gp 1985–, chm Basic Med Sciences 1991–94; head Depts of Physiology RFHSM and UCL 1994–99, dir Autonomic Neuroscience Inst RFHSM 1997–; dean Royal Free & UC Med Sch 2001–06 (dean Royal Free Campus 1998–2001), vice-provost (enterprise) UCL 2006–10 (vice-provost (biomedicine) 2002–07), chair NHS London 2010–13; Crisp lectr Univ of Leeds 1988, Glaxo lectr Dept of Pharmacology Univ of Edinburgh 1993; visiting prof: Univ of Shanghai 1989, Georg-August Univ Göttingen 1990, Northwestern Univ Chicago 1990, Univ Vittoria Brazil 1991; Annual Review Lecture Physiological Soc 1994, Carl Ludwig Lecture American Physiological Society 1998; chm: Physiological/Pharmacological Panel Wellcome Tst 1993–96, Euro Biomedical Research Assoc 1996–; memb Ctee: Animal Procedures Home Office 1990–98, Benevolent Fund Physiological Soc 1993–99; memb Scientific Panel Brain Research Tst 1993–99, hon life memb Centre for Neuroscience UCL 1984, field ed News in Physiological Science 1992–96; chair Cncl St George's Univ of London 2012–, memb Cncl Brunel Univ London 2012–; Wolfson Univ Award 1989–92; Hon MD Univ of Lisbon 1991; memb: Physiological Soc 1972– (pres 2010–12), Brain Research Assoc 1973–, Euro Neuroscience Assoc 1976–, Research Defence Soc 1976–98 (hon sec 1986–89), Int Brain Research Orgn 1980–, Harveian Soc 1983– (hon sec 1987–89), Zoological 1983–96, Clinical Autonomic Soc 1983–, German Physiological Soc 1984–93, Soc for Neuroscience 1986–2010, American Physiological Soc 1997–; hon memb Physiological Soc 2003; author of numerous pubns in learned jls; Hon FRCP 2002, FMedSci; *Recreations* armchair sports, fly fishing, travelling (particularly in Italy), gardening, books, fine arts, bookbinding; *Clubs* Scotch Whisky Soc; *Style*— Prof Mike Spyer; ✉ University College London, Gower Street, London WC1E 6BT (☎ 020 8348 2354, e-mail k.spyer@ucl.ac.uk)

SQUIRE, Prof John Michael; s of George Victor Vincent Squire (d 1998), and Mary Hilton, *née* Clarke (d 1999); *b* 27 June 1945, Grappenhall, Cheshire; *Educ* Fettes, KCL (BSc, AKC, PhD); *m* 12 Aug 1969, Melanie Rae, *née* Chandy; 4 da (Deborah Rae b 1 Nov 1970, Emily Jane b 17 July 1973, Katherine Emma b 29 Sept 1975, Beth Mary b 30 Dec 1979); *Career* amanuensis and lektor Biophysics Inst Aarhus Univ 1969–71 (chm Governing Body Biophysics Inst 1971), visitor Biophysics Dept KCL 1971, higher scientific offr AFRC Muscle Unit Dept of Zoology Univ of Oxford 1972; Imperial Coll London: lectr and head Biopolymer Gp 1972–82, MRC fell 1982–84, reader in biophysics and head Muscle Gp Dept of Materials Science 1982–83 and Dept of Physics 1983–95, prof of structural biophysics Biophysics Gp Dept of Physics 1995–99, prof of structural biophysics Biomedical Sciences Division 1999, dep head of div (teaching) 2000–03, head Biological Structure and Function Section, visiting prof Dept of Surgery and Cancer 2006–; currently hon fell Sch of Physiology and Pharmacology Univ of Bristol; Univ of London: memb Bd of Studies in Biophysics, memb Special Advsy Ctee in Crystallography; visiting scientist NIH Washington DC 1986, Japan Soc for the Promotion of Science fell Tohoku Univ 1987; fndr and chm Imperial Muscle Initiative 2002–, fndr and occasional organiser London Muscle Conf; invited lectr at numerous courses and confs; chm: SRFC Beam Allocation Panel F 1989–92, Biological Structures Gp Br Crystallographic Assoc (BCA) 1990–94, MRC/EPSRC/BBSRC Biology Section Panel 1994–97; memb: SERC Biological Sciences Ctee Advsy Gp IV 1979–82, MRC Assessment Panel for Research and Advanced Course Studentships 1985–88, Cncl BCA 1987–95, SERC Synchrotron Radiation Facilities Ctee 1989–92, MRC/SERC Jt Review Ctee for Biology at Daresbury 1992–94, SERC Biological Sciences Ctee 1993–94, MRC/EPSRC/BBSRC/CCLRC Biology Jt Review Ctee 1994–97, EPSRC/BBSRC Collaborative Computing Projects Panel 1995–99 and 2002–, Synchrotron Radiation Users Forum (SRSUF) 1996–97; former ed The Fibre Diffraction Review, former ed Crystallography News; memb Editorial Bd: Jl of Muscle Research and Motility, Jl of Structural Biology; memb: AUT 1972–2007, BCA 1982, Anatomical Soc 1999; emeritus memb Biophysical Soc of America (memb 1977), hon fell Br Biophysical Soc 1974; CPhys, CBiol, FRMS 1977, FInstP 1999, FRSB 2001; *Publications* The Structural Basis of Muscular Contraction (1981), Muscle: Design, Diversity and Disease (1986), Fibrous Protein Structure (ed with P J Vibert, 1987), Molecular Mechanisms in Muscular Contraction (ed, 1990), Advances in Protein Chemistry Vol 70: Fibrous Proteins: Coiled-Coils, Collagen and Elastomers (2005), Advances in Protein Chemistry Vol 71: Fibrous Proteins: Muscle and Molecular Motors (2005), Advances in Protein Chemistry Vol 73: Fibrous Proteins: Amyloids, Prions and Beta Proteins (2006); also author of over 100 scientific pubns incl articles in The Encyclopedia of Life Sciences and The Encyclopedia of Neuroscience; *Recreations* music (piano, cello, composition), DIY, gardening, films, choral singing; *Style*— Prof John Squire; ✉ Muscle Contraction Group, School of Physiology, Pharmacology and Neuroscience, University of Bristol, Bristol BS8 1TD (☎ 0117 331 1465, fax 0117 331 2288, e-mail j.m.squire@bristol.ac.uk); e-mail j.squire@imperial.ac.uk

SQUIRE, Rosemary; OBE (2007); *Educ* Nottingham HS for Girls, Univ of Southampton (BA); *m* 1; 1 da (Jenny b 1986), 1 s (Dan b 1987); m 2, 1994, Howard Panter, *qv*; 1 da (Kate b 2002); *Career* co-fndr Ambassador Theatre Gp 1992– (jt md 2000–); *Style*— Ms Rosemary Squire, OBE; ✉ Ambassador Theatre Group, 2nd Floor, Alexander House, Church Path, Woking, Surrey GU21 6EJ

STABLEFORD, Brian Michael; s of William Ernest Stableford, of Denton, Lancs, and Joyce Wilkinson; *b* 25 July 1948; *Educ* Manchester Grammar, Univ of York (BA, DPhil); *m* 1, 1973 (m dis 1985), Vivien Wynne, da of Caradog Owen; 1 s (Leo Michael b 5 April 1975), 1 da (Katharine Margaret b 21 Oct 1978); m 2, 1987 (m dis 2011), Roberta Jane, da of Charles Cragg; *Career* lectr Sociology Dept Univ of Reading 1976–88; freelance writer (latterly full time); pt/t lectr in cultural and media studies UWE 1995–97, pt/t lectr in creative writing UC Winchester 2000–05; *Awards* incl: European SF Award 1984, Distinguished Scholarship Award Int Assoc for the Fantastic in the Arts 1987, J Lloyd Eaton Award 1987, Pioneer Award Science Fiction Research Assoc 1996, Science Fiction Research Assoc Pilgrim Award 1999; *Fiction and Science Fiction* incl: Hooded Swan (series, 1972–78), Man In a Cage (1976), The Mind Riders (1976), Daedalus (series, 1976–79), Realms of Tartarus (1977), The Last Days of the Edge of the World (1978), The Walking Shadow (1979), Asgard (trilogy, 1982–90), The Empire of Fear (1988), The Werewolves of London (trilogy, 1990–94), Sexual Chemistry – Sardonic Tales of the Genetic Revolution (1991), Young Blood (1992), Genesys (trilogy, 1995–97), The Hunger and Ecstasy of Vampires (1996), Inherit the Earth (1998), Architects of Emortality (1999), The Fountains of Youth (2000), Year Zero (2000), The Cassandra Complex (2001), Dark Ararat (2002), The Omega Expedition (2002), The Stones of Camelot (2006), The Moment of Truth (2009), The Womb of Time (2011), The Quintessence of August (2011); *Non-Fiction* incl: The Science in Science Fiction (1982), The Third Millennium (1985), Scientific Romance in Britain (1985), Yesterday's Bestsellers (1998), Glorious Perversity: The Decline and Fall of Literary Decadence (1999), Science Fact and Fiction: An Encyclopedia (2006), The Devil's Party: A Brief History of Satanic Abuse (2009), New Atlantis: A Narrative History of Scientific Romance (2016), The Plurality of Imaginary Worlds: The Evolution of French Roman Scientifique (2016); *Reference* contribs incl: The Encyclopedia of Science Fiction, The Survey of Science Fiction Literature, Anatomy of Wonder, Science Fiction Writers, The Survey of Modern Fantasy Literature, Supernatural Fiction Writers, The Cambridge Guide to Literature In English, Fantasy Literature, Horror Literature; *Style*— Brian Stableford, Esq; ✉ 8 Burnt Oak Lodge, 711 London Road, Hadleigh, Essex SS7 2EE (☎ 01702 557380)

STABLEFORTH, Dr David Edward; s of Edward Victor Stableforth (d 1975), of Weymouth, Dorset, and Una Alice Stableforth; *b* 23 February 1942; *Educ* Truro Sch, St Catharine's Coll Cambridge, St Mary's Hosp Paddington; *m* 11 May 1967, Penelope Jane, da of David Ivor Phillips, MC (d 1976), of Finchley, London; 2 da (Abigail b 1972, Emily b 1979), 1 s (William b 1973); *Career* sr med registrar Brompton Hosp and St James' Hosp Balham 1973–77, conslt physician Birmingham Heartlands Hosp Tst and hon sr lectr Univ of Birmingham 1977–2004, currently hon conslt physician Birmingham Heart of England NHS Fndn Tst; dir W Midlands Adult Cystic Fibrosis Centre 1990–2004; pres Midland Thoracic Soc 1995–98; tstee W Midlands Adult Cystic Fibrosis Centre Appeal; memb: Br Thoracic Soc; FRCP 1985; *Recreations* walking, cycling, sailing and canoeing, cooking, theatre and concert-going; *Style*— Dr David Stableforth; ✉ Spire Parkway Hospital, Damson Parkway, Solihull, West Midlands B91 2PP (☎ 0121 704 1451, e-mail docs@stableforth.fslife.co.uk)

STACE, Victoria Penelope (Vikki); da of Leonard H Stace (d 1981), of Cheltenham, and Gina, *née* Pluckrose; *b* 21 August 1950; *Educ* Malvern Girls' Coll, Univ of Bristol; *m* (m dis 1990), Gavin J Graham; 1 da (Chloe Alexandra b 23 July 1982), 1 s (Toby James Christopher b 8 June 1984); m 2, Tom F Tremlett; *Career* PR conslt; formerly: English teacher Nepal, journalist; publisher; mktg dir Sidgwick & Jackson, fndr Vikki Stace Associates subsequently Powerhouse 1985–98 (consumer and corp PR consultancy), md MacLaurin (following merger with Powerhouse) 1998–, dir hatch-group 2001–, ceo Trimedia Communications UK (following acquisition by Huntsworth plc) 2004–06, chm Trimedia 2007–10, dir of business devpt Huntsworth plc 2007–09, dir of client service Grayling 2010–; dir Atomic Int 2009–; chm Internet Learning Tst, former memb London Bd Princess Royal Tst for Carers; former chm Publishers Publicity Assoc; memb Cncl Univ of Bristol 2010–; MIPR, FRSA; *Recreations* golf, skiing, opera, theatre; *Clubs* Beaufort Polo, Groucho; *Style*— Ms Vikki Stace; ✉ Yew Tree House, Sopworth, Wiltshire SN14 6PR (☎ 01454 238344); Grayling, 29 Lexington Street, London W1F 9AH (☎ 020 7025 7500, e-mail vikki.stace@grayling.com)

STACEY, Prof Derek Norton; s of Albert Edward Stacey, and Rose, *née* Norton; *Educ* Tettenhall Coll, Balliol Coll Oxford (MA, DPhil); *Career* Univ of Oxford: dept demonstrator Clarendon Lab 1963–65, res fell Ford Fndn St Catherine's Coll 1965–68, univ lectr Clarendon Lab 1969–2005, tutorial fell University Coll 1969–87, student ChCh 1989–2005 (emeritus 2005–), prof of physics 1996–; visiting fell Jt Inst for Lab Astrophysics Boulder Colorado 1968–69, sr fell SERC 1982–87; sec Atomic and Molecular Sub-Ctee Inst of Physics 1972–5, memb Euro Gp for Atomic Spectroscopy (memb Bd 1972–75, chm 1975–79); Euro Physical Soc: memb Bd Atomic and Molecular Div 1975–89, memb Cncl 1987–91; *Publications* author of papers on experimental and theoretical physics incl quantum information processing, measurements of quantum electrodynamic effects in hydrogen and parity-violating optical rotation; *Recreations* squash, tennis, music, literature; *Style*— Prof Derek Stacey; ✉ 14 Barlow Close, Wheatley, Oxford OX33 1NL; Clarendon Laboratory, Parks Road, Oxford OX1 3PU (☎ 01865 272293, fax 01865 272400, e-mail d.stacey1@physics.oxford.ac.uk)

STACEY, Thomas Charles Gerard (Tom); s of David Henry Stacey (d 1986), and Isobel Gwen, *née* Part; *b* 11 January 1930, Bletchingley, Surrey; *Educ* Eton (fndr Wotton's Soc 1947, ed Eton Coll Chronicle 1948), Worcester Coll Oxford; *m* 5 Jan 1952, Caroline Susan, da of Charles Nightingale Clay (d 1961); 4 da (Emma b 1952, Mathilda b 1954, Isabella b 1957, Tomasina b 1967), 1 s (Sam b 1966); *Career* formerly: staff writer Picture Post, chief roving corr Sunday Times and others; co-initiated self-determination of Bakonzo tribe of Ruwenzori Mountains Uganda 1954 (leading to ultimate recognition of Rwenzururu as one of 5 constituent Ugandan kingdoms 2009); author, screenwriter, publisher and penal reformer; fndr and pres Stacey International (publishers) 1974–2011, fndr Capuchin Classics 2008; spearheaded Return of Narrative History campaign with republication of Carter and Mears' A History of Britain (9 Vols 2010–12); Parly candidate (Cons): Hammersmith N 1964, Dover 1966; initiator of offender electronic tagging 1981, fndr and dir Offender's Tag Assoc 1982–; fndr Pilgrimage 2000; John Llewelyn Rhys Meml Prize 1954, Granada Award (as foreign corr) 1961; tstee English PEN 2008–09; FRSL 1977 (memb Cncl 1987–92); *Books* The Hostile Sun (1953), The Brothers M (1960, ebook 2014), Summons to Ruwenzori (1963), To-day's World (1970), Immigration and Enoch Powell (1972), Peoples of the Earth (deviser and supervisor, 20 vols, 1973–74), The Living and The Dying (1976, ebook 2013), The Pandemonium (1980, ebook 2013), The Twelfth Night of Ramadan (under nom de plume Kendal J Peel, 1983, ebook 2014 as Tom Stacey), The Worm in the Rose (1985, ebook 2015), Deadline (novel and screenplay, 1988), Bodies and Souls (short stories, 1989, ebook 2014), Decline (1991, ebook 2014), Tribe: the Hidden History of the Mountains of the Moon (2003), Thomas Brassey, 1805–70: Greatest Railway Builder in the World (2005), The First Dog to be Somebody's Best Friend (children's book, 2007), The Man Who Knew Everything (2008, ebook 2011) A Dark and Stormy Night (2016); *Shorter Fiction* The Same Old Story (1999), The Tether

S

of the Flesh (2001), Golden Rain (2002), Grief (2004), The Swap (2006), Boredom, Or, the Yellow Trousers (2007), Mary's Visit (2008), The Kelpie from Rhum (2009), Extended Essays Islam and its Future (2015), The Metaphysics of Brexit (2016); *Recreations* trees, music; *Clubs* White's, Beefsteak, Pratt's; *Style*— Tom Stacey, Esq, FRSL; ✉ Clementi House, 128 Kensington Church Street, London W8 4BH (☎ 020 7229 4098, e-mail tomstacey1930@gmail.com, website www.tomstacey.com)

STACY, Neil Edwin; s of Edwin Frank Dixon Stacy (d 1997), of Hinton, Glos, and Gladys Emily, *née* Wallis (d 1980); *b* 15 May 1941; *Educ* Hampton GS, Magdalen Coll Oxford (MA, DPhil); *Career* actor; historian; FRHistS; *Theatre* incl: The Soldier's Fortune, A Room with a View, The Importance of Being Earnest, Richard II (Prospect Prodns) 1964–68, Enemy (Saville) 1969, The Recruiting Offr (Bristol and Edinburgh Festival) 1979, A Patriot for Me (Chichester Festival) 1983, Canaries Sometimes Sing (Albery) 1987, Captain Carvallo (Greenwich) 1988, Blithe Spirit (Lyric Hammersmith) 1989, Single Spies (RNT tour) 1990, The Letter (Lyric Hammersmith) 1995, Mrs Warren's Profession (Lyric Hammersmith) 1996, Cause Célèbre (Lyric Hammersmith) 1998, Real Inspector Hound (Comedy Theatre) 1998, Gasping (nat tour) 2000, A Perfect Gentleman (King's Head) 2001, Luther (RNT) 2001, The Deep Blue Sea (nat tour) 2003, Three Men in a Boat (nat tour) 2006, The Woman in White (nat tour) 2011, Dry Rot (nat tour) 2012, The Last of Duty Free (nat tour) 2014, And Then There Were None (nat tour) 2015; *Television* incl: War and Peace, Barlow at Large, Colditz, The Pallisers, To Serve Them All My Days, Shackleton, The Fourth Arm, Duty Free, Three Up Two Down, The House of Windsor, Get Well Soon; *Publications* Henry of Blois and the Lordship of Glastonbury (1999), Surveys of the Estates of Glastonbury Abbey (2001), Charters and Custumals of Shaftesbury Abbey (2006); contributions to the Oxford Dictionary of National Biography (2013); *Style*— Neil Stacy, Esq; ✉ c/o Shepherd Management, 4th Floor, 45 Maddox Street, London W1S 2PE (☎ 020 7495 7813, fax 020 7499 7535)

STAFF, Jamie Alan; MBE (2009); s of Alan James Staff, of Ashford, Kent, and Christine Ann, *née* Wright; *b* 30 April 1973, Ashford, Kent; *Educ* Dip; *Career* cyclist; early career as BMX rider (Gold medal elite men World BMX Championships 1996), moved to track cycling 2001–; World Track Championships: Gold medal team sprint 2002 and 2005 (Silver medal 2006 and 2008, Bronze medal 2003 and 2004), Gold medal keirin 2004, Bronze medal 1 km 2007; Cwlth Games: Silver medal team sprint 2002 and 2006, Bronze medal 1 km 2002; Gold medal team sprint Olympic Games Beijing 2008; *Style*— Jamie Staff, Esq, MBE; ✉ Mission Sports Management, First Floor, Park House, 14 Northfields, London SW18 1DD (☎ 020 87044165)

STAFFORD, Andrew Bruce; QC (2000); s of Cyril Stafford, of Newcastle upon Tyne, and Audrey, *née* Burman; *b* 30 March 1957; *Educ* Royal GS Newcastle upon Tyne, Trinity Hall Cambridge; *m* 2 Oct 1982, Catherine Anne, da of Derek Johnson; 4 da (Rebecca b 30 Sept 1983, Charlotte b 21 July 1985, Flora b 11 Dec 1986, Holly b 10 Dec 1988), 1 s (Benjamin b 29 May 1994); *Style*— Andrew Stafford, Esq, QC

STAFFORD, 15 Baron (E 1640); Francis Melfort William Fitzherbert; DL (Staffs 1994); s of 14 Baron (d 1986), and Morag Nada, da of late Lt-Col Alastair Campbell, of Altries, Milltimber, Aberdeenshire; *b* 13 March 1954; *Educ* Ampleforth, Univ of Reading, RAC Cirencester; *m* 1980, Katharine Mary, 3 da of John Codrington, of Barnes, London; 2 s (Hon Benjamin John Basil b 1983, Hon Toby Francis b 1985), 2 da (Hon Teresa Emily b 1987, Hon Camilla Rose Jane b 1989); *Heir* s, Hon Benjamin Fitzherbert; *Career* pro-chllr Keele Univ 1993–2004; non-exec dir: Tarmac Ind Products Div 1987–93, The Fndn NHS Tst 1991–99, Hanley Economic Building Soc 1993–2014 (vice-chm 2000–14); Staffordshire Univ chncllr: 2014–; pres: Staffs Environmental Fund 2002–12 (dir 1997–2002), Lord's Taverners (NW 1996–2007), Staffs CCC 1999–2008; chm Harper Adams Agric Coll 2004–07 (vice-chm 1990–2004), chm Countryside Learning 2010–; fell Keele Univ 2013, chllr Staffs Univ 2014–; High Sheriff Staffs 2005; Hon DUniv: Keele, Staffs; Hon DLitt Harper Adams Univ, Hon DSc Aston Univ; *Recreations* cricket, shooting, golf; *Style*— The Rt Hon the Lord Stafford, DL, FRAgS; ✉ Swynnerton Park, Stone, Staffordshire ST15 0QE

STAFFORD, Bishop of 2010–; Rt Rev Geoffrey Peter (Geoff) Annas; s of Derek Annas, of Gt Bookham, Surrey, and Betty, *née* Deverill (d 2012); *b* 29 November 1953, London; *Educ* Therfield County Secdy Sch Leatherhead, Univ of Leicester (BA), Salisbury and Wells Theological Coll; *m* 14 March 1987, Dr Ann Annas, *née* Clover; 1 da (Katie (Mrs David Furby) b 2 Oct 1989), 1 s (Ben b 19 Aug 1991); *Career* social worker Surrey CC 1975–80, curate St Matthews Elephant and Castle Dio Southwark 1983–87, vicar St Christopher's Walworth 1987–94, vicar St Christopher's Thornhill Southampton Dio Winchester 1997–2010; chaplain: Mayflower Theatre 1996–2010, Regent Theatre Stoke 2011–; memb Cncl of Mgmnt Theatre Chaplaincy UK (formerly Actors' Church Union) 2009–; *Style*— The Rt Rev the Bishop of Stafford; ✉ Ash Garth, 6 Broughton Crescent, Barlaston, Stoke-on-Trent ST12 9DD (☎ 01782 373308, e-mail bishop.stafford@lichfield.anglican.org)

STAFFORD, Jeremy; *Educ* Univ of Manchester (BSc); *Career* chief exec Phoenix IT Gp plc 2008–11, md Serco plc 2011–13, chief exec John Menzies 2013–; *Style*— Jeremy Stafford, Esq

STAFFORD, Julia; *Educ* Queen Mary Univ of London (BA), Imperial Coll London (MSc); *Career* fndr and dir Wine Pantry (London's specialist English wine merchant) 2011–; *Style*— Ms Julia Stafford; ✉ Wine Pantry, 1 Stoney Street, Borough Market, London SE1 9AA

STAFFORD-CLARK, Maxwell Robert Guthrie Stewart (Max); s of David Stafford-Clark, and Dorothy Oldfield; *b* 17 March 1941; *Educ* Felsted, Riverdale Country Day Sch NYC, Trinity Coll Dublin; *m* 1, 1971, Carole, *née* Hayman; m 2, 1981, Ann, *née* Pennington; 1 da (Kitty b 28 Aug 1988); *Career* artistic director; Traverse Theatre Edinburgh 1968–70, Traverse Theatre Workshop 1971–72, Joint Stock Theatre Group 1974–79, Royal Court Theatre 1979–93, Out of Joint Theatre Co 1993–; visiting prof Royal Holloway and Bedford New Coll London 1993–94, Maisie Glass prof Univ of Sheffield 1995–96, visiting prof Univ of Herts 1999–, hon prof Univ of York 2002–; Hon DLitt: Oxford Brookes Univ 2000, Univ of Herts 2000, Univ of Warwick 2006; *Books* Letters to George (1988), Taking Stock (2006); *Clubs* Frontline, Groucho; *Style*— Max Stafford-Clark, Esq; ✉ c/o Out of Joint, 7 Thane Works, Thane Villas, London N7 7PH (☎ 020 7609 0207, fax 020 7609 0203)

STAGG, Sir (Charles) Richard Vernon; KCMG (2008, CMG 2001); s of Walter Stagg, and Elise Patricia, *née* Maxwell; *Educ* Winchester, Oriel Coll Oxford; *m* 1982, Arabella Clare Faber; 3 s, 2 da; *Career* joined FCO 1977; served: Sofia 1979, The Hague 1982; first sec FCO 1985, UK rep to EU Brussels 1987, FCO 1988, UK rep to EU (press spokesman) Brussels 1991, private sec to foreign sec 1993, head EU (External) Dept 1996, ambass to Bulgaria 1998–2001, dir public servs and info FCO 2001–03, DG of corp affrs FCO 2003–07, high cmmr to India 2007–11, ambass to Afghanistan 2012–15, ret; chm Rothschild India 2015–; *Recreations* racing, gardening; *Clubs* Turf, Millennium; *Style*— Sir Richard Stagg, KCMG; ✉ 103 Piramal Tower, GK Marg, Lower Parel, Mumbai 400013, India

STAHEL, Rolf; s of Hermann Stahel (d 1997), of Jona, Switzerland, and Bluette Stahel; *b* 21 April 1944; *Educ* Handels Matura Lucerne, Harvard Univ (AMP); *m* Ewa; 2 s (Martin, Philip); *Career* sales admin Rhone Poulenc Switzerland 1963–67; Wellcome: rep UK 1967, asst mangr Switzerland 1968, gen mangr Italy 1969–74, md Thailand 1974–79, md Singapore 1979–90, dir of mktg Wellcome plc 1990–94; chief exec Shire Pharmaceuticals Gp plc 1994–2003, fndr chm Chesyl Pharma Ltd 2003–; non-exec chm: Newron Pharmaceuticals 2004–13, Cosmo Pharmceuticals 2006–12, Eusa Pharma Inc 2007–12, Connexios Life Sciences (Bangalore) 2010–, Midatech 2014–, Ergomed Clinical Research Ltd 2014–; CEO of the Year (pharmaceutical industry global award) 2001, techMARK Mediscience Award (for most significant contribution to UK lifesciences) 2003, Bioindustry Assoc Lifetime Achievement Award; memb Advsy Bd Imperial Business Sch Imperial Coll London 2007–; *Recreations* golf, classical music; *Clubs* RAC, Chaine des Rotisseurs; *Style*— Rolf Stahel, Esq; ✉ Neatham, Sleepers Hill, Winchester, Hampshire SO22 4NB (☎ 01962 868224, fax 01962 861441, e-mail rstahel@chesyl.com)

STAHL, Andrew; s of Adam Jack Stahl, of London, and Sheena Penelope, *née* Simms; *b* 4 July 1954; *Educ* Slade Sch of Fine Art; *m* 1, 1988 (dis 1999), Jean Oh Mei Yen, da of Henry Oh Sui Hong; 1 s (Matthew b 1992), 2 da (Rosie, Juno (twins) b 1995); m 2, 2001, Kumiko, da of Wataru Tsuna; 1 da (Miyu b 2002); *Career* artist; prof of fine art head of undergraduate painting UCL Slade Sch of Fine Art; Abbey Major Rome scholar 1979–81, fell in printmaking RCA 1989, Rome Award in painting Br Sch at Rome 1989, Wingate scholar 1991; artist in residence: Chiangmai Univ Thailand 2000, Silpakorn Univ Bangkok 2003, Univ of NSW 2004, Mahasarakarm Univ Thailand 2005, Br Cncl Bangkok 2006; *Solo Exhibitions* Air Gallery London 1981 and 1983, Paton Gallery London 1984 and 1988, Flowers East 1992, 1995 and 1998, Worthing Museum and Art Gallery 1993, Prints and Drawings (Flowers East) 1993, Maidstone Library Gallery 1994, Wolverhampton Art Gallery and Museum 1995, Fenderesky Gallery Belfast 1999, Chiangmai Univ Museum Thailand 2000, ac.t art Zirndorf Germany 2000–01, Silapakorn Univ Bangkok 2002, Tonson Gallery Thailand 2003–04, 2 weeks in Sydney (COFA Univ of NSW) 2004, Panya Vijinthanasarn & Andrew Stahl: Conversations, Collaborations and New Paintings (100 Tonson Gallery Bangkok) 2006, New Paintings (Robert Steel Gallery NY) 2007, Matthew Brown Gallery London 2007, Ardel Gallery Bangkok 2009, Robert Steele Gallery NY 2010, The Vivid Real Panya Vijinthanasarn and Andrew Stahl Thavibu Gallery Bangkok; *Group Exhibitions* incl: British Drawing (Hayward Gallery) 1982, Pagan Echoes (Riverside Studios) 1983, selections from 10 years at Air (Air Gallery) 1985, 17 International Festival of Painting Cagnes France 1985, Walking & Falling (Interim Art & Kettles Yard Cambridge) 1986, British Painting (touring Malaysia, Singapore, Hong Kong, Thailand) 1987, Artists Choice (V&A) 1987, London Group (RCA) 1988, Figuring out the 80's (Laing Art Gallery Newcastle), Whitechapel Open 1989, Rome Scholars 1980–90 (RCA) 1990, Selected Line (William Jackson Gallery) 1992, Biella Print Biennale 1993, 5 Artists (Angela Flowers Gallery) 1994, East Open Exhbn (Norwich Art Gallery) 1994, John Moores Liverpool Exhibition 1995, 3 Painters (Plymouth Arts Centre) 1996, Sad (Gasworks Studio) 1996, Life Live (MOMA Paris, invitation by David Medalla) 1996, Angela Flowers Gallery 1997 (Flowers East Gallery) 1997, Artists Camp (Nat Gallery Sri Lanka, selected by Br Cncl) 1997, British Figuration (Angela Flowers Gallery) 1997, Flowers West LA 1998, Millennium (Flowers East Gallery), London Bienniale 3 Artists Domingo St London 2000, Artists Choice (Flowers East Gallery) 2000, Small is Beautiful (Flowers East Gallery) 2002–04, Artskool (ENSBA Paris, Dover, Calais, Nimes and Central St Martins Coll of Art and Design) 2004, Figure, Place and Time (Art Space Gallery London) 2005, Royal Acad Summer Exhbn 2005, Painting from the 90s (Flowers Central) 2005, Monologue/Dialogue UK-Thai art today (Bangkok Univ Gallery) 2006, Heads (Flowers East Gallery) 2006, Portraits Small is Beautiful (Flowers Central) 2006, Small is Beautiful (Flowers Central) 2007, Stew (Artspace Gallery London) 2008, ...Same as it ever was Painting at Chelsea (Triangle Space Univ of the Arts London) 2008, Monologue/Dialogue part 2 (Bischoff/Weiss Gallery London) 2008, Paintings of the 80s (Matthew Bonn Gallerie Berlin) 2009, Art Below Zero (Sneeze Art Fair) 2009, Select (Peppercanister Gallery Dublin) 2010, Royal Acad Summer Exhibition 2011, Unearthed (London) 2011, WhaTTodip (Chiangmai Museum Thailand) 2011, The Perfect Nude (Wimbledon Space and Phoenix Gallery Exeter) 2012, Conficts of Interest (3 person show, H Gallery Bangkok) 2012, London 100 Prints Flowers (London) 2012, Circus Terminal (The Tabernacle London) 2012, RA Summer Exhibition 2012, 'Not Another Srt Project' The Barefoot Gallery Colombo Sri Lanka 2013, Br Art Festival Siam Paragon Bangkok 2013, 'You Are Not Alone' Stoke Newington Library Gallery 2014, 'The Artists Folio' Cartwright Hall Art Gallery Bradford 2014, '100 Tonson Gallery 10th Anniversary Exhibition' curated by Rirkrit Tiravanija Bangkok 2014, '(Detail)' H Gallery Bangkok & Transition Gallery London 2014, Monologue/Dialogue 3 Fragility and Monumentality Bangkok Art and Cultural Centre (BACC), Bangkok, Thailand 2014; *Work in Public Collections* Metropolitan Museum of Art New York, Arts Cncl of GB, Br Cncl, Contemporary Arts Soc, Br Museum, City Museum Peterborough, Leicestershire Educn Authy, Govt Art Collection, Bradford Museums and Galleries; *Style*— Andrew Stahl; ✉ e-mail andrewstahl@hotmail.com, website www.andrewstahl.co.uk

STAINES, Christopher John (Chris); s of Trevor John Staines, of Bury St Edmunds, Suffolk, and Susan Anne, *née* Bugg; *b* 20 February 1975; *Educ* Thurston Upper Sch Bury St Edmunds, West Suffolk Coll (NVQ); *Career* commis chef Angel Hotel Bury St Edmunds 1993–94, chef de partie Llangoed Hall Powys 1994–95, work placement Keswick Hall Keswick VA and Inn at Perry Cabin St Michaels MD 1995, jr sous chef Lucknam Park Country House Hotel 1995–99, Chez Nico at 90 Park Lane 1998–2000, chef de cuisine The Oakroom Marco Pierre White 2000–02, chef de cuisine Foliage Restaurant Mandarin Oriental Hotel (1 Michelin Star) 2002–09, exec chef Heckfield Place Hants 2009–, currently chef/dir The Abbey Hotel Bath; *Books* featured in Relish South West (2013); *Recreations* reading, music; *Style*— Chris Staines, Esq; ✉ The Abbey Hotel, 1–3 North Parade, Bath BA1 1LF

STALLARD, Thomas Alexander (Tom); s of Matthew Charles Stallard, and Dr Noelle Christine Stallard; *b* 11 September 1978, London; *Educ* Oundle, Jesus Coll Cambridge (Rowing blue, MA, MEng), Brunel Univ (MSc); *m* 23 April 2010, Dr Amanda, *née* Gemmill; *Career* rower; memb Leander Club; debut GB sr team 2002; achievements incl: Bronze medal coxed fours World Rowing Under 23 Championships 1999, Gold medal coxed fours World Rowing Championships 2002 (Silver medal 2003), Bronze medal eights World Rowing Championships 2007, Silver medal eights Olympic Games Beijing 2008, ninth mens eights Olympic Games Athens 2004; memb Cambridge crew Oxford v Cambridge Boat Race 1999, 2000, 2001 and 2002, pres Univ of Cambridge Boat Club 2002; race engr McLaren Formula 1 Team 2008–; *Clubs* Hawks; *Style*— Tom Stallard, Esq; ✉ e-mail tas@cantab.net

STALLWORTHY, Jon Howie; s of Sir John Arthur Stallworthy (d 1993), and Margaret Wright, *née* Howie (d 1980); *b* 18 January 1935; *Educ* Rugby, Univ of Oxford (MA, BLitt); *m* 25 June 1960, Gillian (Jill), da of Sir Claude Humphrey Meredith Waldock, CMG, OBE, QC (d 1981); 2 s (Jonathan b 1965, Nicolas, *qv*, b 1970), 1 da (Pippa b 1967); *Career* Nat Serv 1953–55, 2 Lt Oxon and Bucks LI, seconded Royal W African Frontier Force; visiting fell All Souls Coll Oxford 1971–72, dep academic publisher OUP 1972–77, Anderson prof of Eng lit Cornell Univ 1977–86, professorial fell Wolfson Coll and reader in Eng lit Univ of Oxford 1986–92, ad hominem prof of English lit Univ of Oxford 1992–2000, sr fell Wolfson Coll Oxford 2000–; Hon DUniv Surrey, Hon DLitt Westminster Coll USA; FRSL, FBA 1990; *Books* incl: Between the Lines, WB Yeats's Poetry in the Making (1963), Vision and Revision in Yeats's Last Poems (1969), Alexander Blok, The Twelve and Other Poems (trans with Peter France, 1970), Wilfred Owen (winner Duff Cooper Meml Prize, W H Smith & Son Literary Award, E M Forster Award, 1974), The Penguin Book of Love Poetry (ed, 1973, 2 edn 2003), Wilfred Owen – The Complete Poems and Fragments (ed, 1983, revised edn 2013), Boris Pasternak, Selected Poems (trans with Peter France, 1984), The Oxford Book of War Poetry (ed, 1984), The Anzac Sonata – New and Selected Poems (1986), First Lines – Poems Written in Youth from Herbert to Heaney (ed, 1987), Henry Reed – Collected Poems (ed, 1991), Louis MacNeice (1995, winner Southern Arts Lit Prize), The Guest from the Future (1995), The Norton Anthology of Poetry (4 edn, ed with Margaret Ferguson and Mary Jo Salter, 1996), Singing School: the Making of a Poet (1998), Rounding the Horn: Collected Poems (1998), The Norton Anthology of English Literature (7 edn, with M H Abrams and others, 2000), Anthem for Doomed Youth (ed, 2002), Body Language (2004), Survivors' Songs from Maldon to the Somme (2008), The New Oxford Book of War Poetry (ed, 2014), War Poet (2014); *Style*— Prof Jon Stallworthy; ✉ Long Farm, Elsfield Road, Old Marston, Oxford OX3 0PR; Wolfson College, Oxford OX2 6UD (☎ 01865 274100)

STALLWORTHY, Nicolas; QC (2011); s of Prof Jon Stallworthy, FBA, FRSL , *qv*, of Oxford, and Jill, *née* Waldock; *b* 10 June 1970; *Educ* Radley, ChCh Oxford; *m* 10 April 1999, Blaise Dawn, da of Nicholas Dudley, FRCS; 1 s (Macnair Jon b 11 Nov 2001), 2 da (Constance Alba b 26 April 2003, Penelope Dawn b 18 May 2008); *Career* called to the Bar 1993; specialist in law relating to occupational pension schemes; *Style*— Nicolas Stallworthy, Esq, QC; ✉ Outer Temple Chambers, 222 Strand, London WC2R 1BA

STAMP, Gavin Mark; s of Barry Hartnell Stamp, and Norah Clare, *née* Rich; *b* 15 March 1948; *Educ* Dulwich Coll, Gonville & Caius Coll Cambridge (MA, PhD); *m* 1, 12 Feb 1982 (m dis 2007), Alexandra Frances, da of Frank Artley, of Redcar; 2 da (Agnes Mary b 1984, Cecilia Jane b 1986); m 2, 10 April 2014, Dr Rosemary Hill, FSA, da of Edward and Barbara Hill, of Oxted; *Career* architectural historian and author; sr lectr Mackintosh Sch of Architecture Glasgow until 2003; hon prof Univ of Glasgow, Mellon sr fell and bye-fell Gonville & Caius Coll Cambridge 2003–04; contrib: The Spectator, Daily Telegraph, Independent, Herald, Architects Jl, Private Eye, Apollo, Country Life; chm Thirties Soc (now the Twentieth Century Soc) 1983–2007, fndr and chm Alexander Thomson Soc 1991; Hon FRIAS 1994, Hon FRIBA, FSA 1998; *Books* The Architects Calendar (1974), The Victorian Buildings of London (with C Amery, 1980), Temples of Power (with G Boyd Harte, 1979), Robert Weir Schultz and His Work for The Marquesses of Bute (1981), The Great Perspectivists (1982), The Changing Metropolis (1984), The English House 1860–1914 (1986), Telephone Boxes (1989), Greek Thomson (ed with S McKinstry, 1994), Alexander 'Greek' Thomson (1999), Edwin Lutyens: Country Houses (2001), Lutyens Abroad (ed with A Hopkins, 2002), An Architect of Promise (2002), The Memorial to the Missing of the Somme (2006, revised edn 2016), Britain's Lost Cities (2007), Lost Victorian Britain (2010), Anti-Ugly (2013), Gothic for the Steam Age: an illustrated biography of George Gilbert Scott (2015); *Style*— Gavin Stamp; ✉ 15 Belle Vue Court, Devonshire Road, London SE23 3SY

STAMP, Dr Gillian Penelope; da of late Guy St John Tatham, of Johannesburg, South Africa; *Educ* Univ of the Witwatersrand (BA), Brunel Univ (MA) BIOSS Brunel Univ (PhD); *m* 27 Dec 1958, Hon (Jos) Colin Stamp (d 2001), s of 1 Baron Stamp, GCB, GBE (d 1941); 2 s (Robbie, Jonathan); *Career* dir Brunel Inst of Orgn and Social Studies (BIOSS); res consultancy work for numerous nat and int cos; visiting prof Indian Inst of Technol New Delhi; memb Ed Bd Indian Journal of Training and Development; memb: Cncl St George's House Windsor 1995–2001, Bd Nat Sch of Govt 2006; fell: Windsor Leadership Tst 2000, Sunningdale Inst 2006; Hon DPhil 1991; FRSA 1992; *Publications* Well-Being at Work (with Colin Stamp, 1993); *Style*— Dr Gillian Stamp; ✉ 12 Ullswater Road, London SW13 (☎ 020 8748 2782, fax 020 8255 7579); Brunel Institute of Organisation and Social Studies, Brunel University, Uxbridge, Middlesex (☎ 01895 270072, fax 01895 254760)

STAMP, Malcolm Frederick; CBE (2002); s of Frederick Stamp, and Elizabeth Stamp; *b* 29 December 1952, Radcliffe, Manchester; *Educ* Stand GS; *m* (m dis); *Career* joined NHS 1974, unit gen mangr (Acute) N Manchester HA 1985–88, dist gen mangr Crewe HA 1988–90, dist gen mangr Liverpool HA 1990–92; chief exec: Royal Liverpool Univ Hosp Tst 1992–94, Norfolk & Norwich Health Care NHS Tst 1994–2002, Cambridge Univ Hosps 2002–06, Waikato Dist Health Bd NZ 2006–07, Provider Agency NHS London 2007–09 (also memb Bd NHS London), chief exec Univ Hospitals of Coventry and Warks Tst 2009–10, ceo Mid Essex Hosp Service NHS Tst 2010–13, ceo Metro North Hospitals and Health Services Brisbane Aust 2013–15; memb Bd Fndn Tst Network; former chm of govrs Peel Brow Primary Sch; Hon DCL UEA 2000; memb: Inst of Mgmnt Servs, Inst of Health Service Mgmnt; MHSM; *Publications* Consultant Appraisal (with Jack Sanger); *Recreations* football, reading, family; *Clubs* Commonwealth; *Style*— Malcolm F Stamp, Esq, CBE

STAMP, Terence Henry; s of Thomas Stamp (d 1983), and Ethel Esther *née* Perrot (d 1985); *b* 22 July 1938; *Educ* Plaistow Co GS; *Career* actor; Doctor of Arts (hc) 1993; *Films* incl: Billy Budd 1960, The Collector 1964, Far from the Madding Crowd 1966, Tales of Mystery 1967, Theorom 1968, Meeting with Remarkable Men 1977, Superman I and II 1977, The Hit 1984, Legal Eagles 1985, Wall Street 1987, Young Guns 1988, The Sicilain 1988, Prince of Shadows 1991, Priscilla, Queen of the Desert 1994, Limited Edition 1998, Bowfinger 1999, The Limey 1999, My Boss's Daughter 2002, My Wife is an Actress 2003, Get Smart 2008, Wanted 2009, Valkyrie 2009, Yes Man 2009, The Adjustment Bureau 2010; *Books* Stamp Album (1987), Coming Attractions (1988), Double Feature (1989), The Night (novel, 1992), Wheat and Dairy Free Cook Book (with Elizabeth Buxton, 1998); provided voice of God for The New Testament (audio book, 2007); *Recreations* film; *Clubs* New York Athletic; *Style*— Terence Stamp, Esq; ✉ c/o Untitled Entertainment, 1801 Century Park East, Suite 100, Los Angeles, CA 90067, USA

STAMP, 4 Baron (UK 1938) Trevor Charles Bosworth Stamp; s of 3 Baron Stamp (d 1987); *Educ* Leys Sch, Gonville & Caius Cambridge (BA), St Mary's Hosp Med Sch (MB BCh); *m* 1, 1963 (m dis 1971), Anne Carolynn, da of John Kenneth Churchill, of Tunbridge Wells; 2 da; m 2, 1975 (m dis 1997), Carol Anne, da of Robert Keith Russell, of Farnham, Surrey; 1 s, 1 da; *Heir* s, Hon Nicholas Stamp; *Career* med registrar Professorial Med Unit St Mary's Hosp 1964–66; Dept of Human Metabolism UCH and Med Sch: hon sr registrar 1968–73, hon sr lectr 1972–73; conslt physician and dir Dept of Bone and Mineral Metabolism Inst of Orthopaedics Royal Nat Orthopaedic Hosp 1974–99; hon conslt physician and sr lectr Middx Hosp and UCL Sch of Med 1974–99; emeritus conslt UCL Hosps 1999–; hon conslt physician RNOH 1999–; Prix André Lichtwitz France 1973; FRCP 1978; *Style*— The Lord Stamp; ✉ 91c Addison Road, London W14 8DB

STANBROOK, Clive St George Clement; OBE (1988), QC (1989); s of Ivor Robert Stanbrook, former MP for Orpington, and Joan, *née* Clement; *b* 10 April 1948; *Educ* Dragon Sch Oxford, Westminster, UCL (LLB); *m* 3 April 1971, Julia Suzanne, da of Victor Hillary; 1 s (Ivor Victor Hillary), 3 da (Fleur Elizabeth, Sophie Noelette, Isabella Grace); *Career* called to: the Bar Inner Temple 1972, the Turks and Caicos Bar 1986, the NY Bar 1988; memb Bd World Trade Center Assoc (London) 1977–83, fndr and sr ptnr Stanbrook & Hooper (int lawyers, now McDermott Will & Emery LLP following merger) Brussels 1977–; pres Br C of C for Belgium and Luxembourg 1985–87; *Books* Extradition the Law and Practice (jtly, 1980, 2 edn 2000), Dumping Manual on the EEC Anti Dumping Law (1980), International Trade Law and Practice (co ed, 1984), Dumping and Subsidies (jtly, 1996); *Recreations* tennis, sailing; *Style*— Clive Stanbrook, Esq, OBE, QC; ✉ McDermott Will & Emery Belgium LLP, Avenue des Nerviens 9–31, Brussels 1040, Belgium

STANCER, Rosie; da of Samuel Witterong Clayton, of The Great Park, Windsor, and Lady Mary, *née* Leveson Gower; *b* 25 January 1960; *Educ* Heathfield Sch Ascot, King James Coll Henley-on-Thames, Oxford and County Sch; *m* 9 July 1993, William Wordie Stancer, s of John Stancer; 1 s ('Jock' Wordie Stancer b 4 June 2001); *Career* jobs incl: developing The Princess Royal Tst for Carers 1991, dir of PR The Park Lane Hotel London 1992–97, lectr, travel writer and freelance journalist based in Prague 1997–2001; trained and worked in Polar expdns incl first all-women expdn to the N Pole (McVities Penguin North Pole Relay) 1997, first Br all-women expdn to the S Pole (M&G ISA Challenge) 1999–2000 and Snickers S Pole solo and unsupported expdn 2004; actively involved with Special Olympics; FRGS; *Recreations* writing accounts of own expeditions, cross country running, skiing, fencing, collecting Polar memorabilia, travelling anywhere off the track, shooting and missing overhead birds; *Style*— Ms Rosie Stancer; ✉ 44 Clavering Avenue, Barnes, London SW13 8DY (☎ 020 8748 1481)

STANDAGE, Simon; *Career* fndr memb: English Concert 1973, Salomon String Quartet 1981, Collegium Musicum 90 1990; prof of baroque violin: Royal Acad of Music, Liszt Acad Budapest; assoc dir Academy of Ancient Music 1991–95; recordings incl: Vivaldi Four Seasons (nominated for Grammy Award), Mozart Concertos, numerous works by Vivaldi, Telemann and Haydn; Medal for Services to Polish Culture 2008, Georg Philipp Telemann Prize 2010; hon RAM 2009; *Style*— Simon Standage, Esq; ✉ Collegium Musicum 90, 106 Hervey Road, Blackheath, London SE3 8BX (☎ 020 8319 3372, e-mail standages@pobox.com)

STANDEN, John Francis; s of Dr Edward Standen, and Margaret Standen; *b* 1948; *Educ* St James' Sch Burnt Oak, Univ of Durham (BA); *m* 9 Aug 1975, Kathleen Mary; 1 da (Aine b 1979), 2 s (Luke b 1981, Owen b 1984); *Career* Barclays de Zoete Wedd Ltd: ceo corp finance 1993–95, ceo emerging markets 1995–96; dir special projects Barclays plc 1997–98; non-exec chm: Reg Vardy plc 2002–06, Chapelthorpe plc 2002–07, Biome Technologies plc 2007–, Lavendon plc 2010–; chm Cncl Univ of Hull 2006–13; *Recreations* running, sailing, golf, family fun, theatre, opera; *Clubs* Glandore Harbour Yacht (Cork); *Style*— John Standen, Esq; ☎ 01455 206736

STANDING, John Ronald; Sir John Ronald Leon, 4 Bt, but prefers to be known by professional name of John Standing; s of Sir Ronald George Leon, 3 Bt (d 1964), and his 1 w, Dorothy Katharine (the actress Kay Hammond; d 1980), da of Cdr Sir Guy Standing, KBE (d 1937), and who m 2, Sir John Clements, CBE; *b* 16 August 1934; *Educ* Eton, Millfield, Byam Shaw Sch of Art; *m* 1, 1961 (m dis 1972), Jill, da of Jack Melford, actor; 1 s (Alexander John b 1965); m 2, 7 April 1984, Sarah Kate, da of Bryan Forbes, film dir; 2 da (India b 25 June 1985, Octavia b 3 Nov 1989), 1 s (Archie b 28 July 1986); *Heir* s, Alexander Leon; *Career* actor; 2 Lt KRRC 1953–55; artist (watercolours); *Theatre* incl: The Importance of Being Earnest 1968, Ring Round the Moon 1969, Arms and the Man 1970, Sense of Detachment 1972, Private Lives 1973, St Joan 1973, Jingo 1976, The Philanderer 1978, Plunder 1978, Close of Play 1979 (nomination Olivier Award), Tonight at 8.30 1981, Biko Inquest 1984, Rough Crossing 1985, Hayfever (Albery) 1992, A Month in the Country (Albery) 1994, Son of Man (RSC) 1996, A Delicate Balance 1998, Shadowlands (West End), Noel Coward Cabaret (Bellamy's, Pizza on the Park and Cafe Carlyle NY); *Television* UK incl: The First Churchills, Charley's Aunt, Tinker Tailor Soldier Spy, King Solomon's Mines; USA incl: Lime Street 1985, Murder She Wrote 1989, LA Law 1990, St Joan 1999, Longitude 1999, Gulliver's Travels 1997, Love in a Cold Climate 2001, The Falklands War 2002, The Real Jane Austin 2002, A Line of Beauty; *Film* incl: King Rat 1965, Walk Don't Run 1965, The Eagle Has Landed 1976, Rogue Male 1976, The Legacy 1977, Mrs Dalloway, Rogue Trader 1998, Mad Cows 1998, Eight and a Half Women 1998, Queens Messenger 2000, The Good Woman, V for Vendetta, Kerala, The Shooter, Oui Law, Before the Rains; *Recreations* painting, fishing; *Clubs* MCC; *Style*— John Standing, Esq

STANES, Sara Jayne; OBE (2007); *b* London; *Educ* Convent of St Marie Auxiliatrice London; *m* 1994, Richard James Stanes; *Career* early career as television advtg and documentary prodr; Royal Acad of Culinary Arts: dir of marketing and PR 1986–95, dir 1996–2009, ceo 2010–; food writer specialising in chocolate; Guild of Food Writers: memb 1987–, memb Ctee 1994–98, vice-chm 1996–98; chm Acad of Chocolate 2004–; judge: Organic Food Awards 2000–, Nat Training Awards 2002–08; Caterer & Hotelkeeper Special Award 2011, Top 100 Women First List 2012, nomination Lifetime Achievement Women First Award 2013; Hon Freeman Worshipful Co of Cooks 2006, Freeman City of London 2007; hon fell Thames Valley Univ 2004; hon doctorate Univ of West London 2013; *Publications* Chocolate: The Definitive Guide (2000, revised edn 2005, winner Guild Food Writers Jeremy Round Award 2000, Best Book in the English Language World Cookbook Fair Award 2000, nomination Andre Simon Award 2000, Ladle nomination Australian Jacob's Creek Media Award 2001), Chocolate (2005, Best Book in its category World Cookbook Fair 2006); *Recreations* chocolate, music, books, tennis, provenance of food, drink, the environment; *Clubs* Arts, Sloane; *Style*— Mrs Sara Jayne Stanes; ✉ Royal Academy of Culinary Arts, 53 Cavendish Road, London SW12 0BL (☎ 020 8673 6300, mobile 07789 874808, e-mail sarajaynestanes@raoca.org.uk)

STANFIELD, Prof Peter Robert; s of late Robert Ainslie Stanfield, and late Irene Louisa, *née* Walker; *b* 13 July 1944; *Educ* Portsmouth GS, Univ of Cambridge (MA, PhD, ScD); *m* 21 Sept 1987, Philippa (d 2004), da of Eric Moss (d 2005), of Leicester; 2 step s (Edward McMillan Barrie b 1968, William McMillan Barrie b 1970); *Career* SRC res fell MBA laboratory Plymouth 1968–69, fell Clare Coll Cambridge, univ demonstrator in physiology Univ of Cambridge 1969–74; Univ of Leicester: lectr in physiology 1974–81, reader 1981–87, prof 1987–2001, head Dept of Physiology 1989–93; prof of molecular physiology Univ of Warwick 2001–09 (emeritus prof 2009–); visiting prof: Purdue Univ Indiana 1984–85, Univ of Illinois at Chicago 1993–98; ed Journal of Physiology 1980–88, assoc ed Pflügers Archiv (European Jl of Physiology) 1993–2009; memb Physiological Soc 1973– (memb Ctee 1985–90 and 1995–99, hon sec 1996–99, hon memb 2010), hon memb Hungarian Physiological Soc 2001–; FMedSci 2003, FRSB 2012; *Books* Ion Channels: Molecules in Action (with D J Aidley, 1996); author of scientific papers on physiology of cell membranes; *Style*— Prof Peter Stanfield; ✉ School of Life Sciences, University of Warwick, Coventry CV4 7AL (☎ 07891 633 065, e-mail p.r.stanfield@warwick.ac.uk)

STANFORD, Rear Adm Christopher David (Chris); CB (2002); s of Joseph Gerald Stanford, and Dr Elspeth Stanford, *née* Harrison; *b* 15 February 1950; *Educ* St Paul's, BRNC Dartmouth, Merton Coll Oxford (MA), RN Staff Coll Greenwich, RCDS; *m* 1972, Angela Mary, da of Cdr Derek G M Gardner, VRD, RSMA; 3 da (Emmie b 1977, Liz b 1978, Hen b 1983), 1 s (Lt Thomas Stanford, RN, b 1987); *Career* joined RN 1967; various sea appts in navigational and warfare posts 1967–94; served HM Ships: Puma, Jupiter, Hubberston, Exmouth, Newcastle, Antrim, Brilliant (second in command), Fife (second in command); CO HMS Boxer 1988–89, CO HMS Coventry and 1 Frigate Sqdn 1993–94; MOD: dir of Naval Staff 1995–97, dir of Operational Capability 1997–99, COS to Surgeon General 1999–2002; ptnr Odgers Berndtson 2002– (global practice ldr healthcare 2002–15); chm Somerset and Dorset Sea Cadet Assoc 2003–12, memb Cncl and Finance and Gen Purposes Ctee White Ensign Assoc 2009–; vice-pres N Dorset Rugby Club; govr King Edward VII's Hosp (Sister Agnes) 2008–; yr bro Trinity House; Freeman City of London, Freeman Hon Co of Master Mariners; Hon DUniv Central England 2002; FNI 1999 (MNI 1988, sr vice-pres and memb Cncl until 2007), FRSA 2003–15; OStJ 2001; *Publications* contrib articles on maritime, environmental, leadership and medical issues to learned and professional journals; *Recreations* rugby, art, maritime affairs, Cornish industrial history, British railway history; *Clubs* Anchorites (past pres), Royal Navy of 1765 and 1785, Chelsea Arts; *Style*— Rear Adm Chris Stanford, CB; ✉ Church Farm Cottage, Cucklington, Wincanton, Somerset BA9 9PT (e-mail chrisstanford01@gmail.com)

STANFORD, Peter James; s of Reginald James Hughes Stanford (d 2004), and Mary Catherine, *née* Fleming (d 1998); *b* 23 November 1961; *Educ* St Anselm's Coll Birkenhead, Merton Coll Oxford (BA); *m* 1995, Siobhan Cross; 1 s, 1 da; *Career* reporter The Tablet

S

1983–84, ed The Catholic Herald 1988–92 (news ed 1984–88), freelance journalist and broadcaster 1984– (incl BBC, Daily Telegraph, The Guardian, The Observer, The Independent, The Independent on Sunday, The Tablet, presenter C4 series Catholics and Sex and on BBC Radio2, BBC Radio 4, Channel 5 and BBC World Service); vice-pres ASPIRE (Assoc for Spinal Res, Rehabilitation and Reintegration, chm 1991–2001 and 2005–12); patron: CandoCo Dance Co, Ways With Words; dir Frank Longford Charitable Tst; tstee Circles UK 2015–; *Books* Hidden Hands: Child Workers Around the World (1988), Believing Bishops (with Simon Lee, 1990), The Seven Deadly Sins (ed, 1990), Catholics and Sex (with Kate Saunders, 1992), Basil Hume (1993), Lord Longford (1994, revised and reissued as The Outcasts' Outcast 2003), The Catholics and Their Houses (with Leanda de Lisle, 1995), The Devil: A Biography (1996, televised 1998), The She-Pope (1998, televised 1998), Bronwen Astor: Her Life and Times (2000), Heaven: A Traveller's Guide (2002), Being a Dad (2004), Why I'm Still a Catholic (ed, 2005), C Day-Lewis: A Biography (2007), Teach Yourself Catholicism (2008), A Life of Christ (2009), The Extra Mile: A 21st Century Pilgrimage (2010), The Death of a Child (ed, 2011), How to Read a Graveyard: Journeys in the Company of the Dead (2013), Judas Iscariot: The Troubling History of the Renegade Apostle (2015); *Recreations* north Norfolk beaches, old Jaguars, old friends; *Clubs* PEN; *Style—* Peter Stanford, Esq; ✉ c/o Sheil Land Associates, 52 Doughty Street, London WC1N 2LS (website www.peterstanford.co.uk)

STANGER, David Harry; OBE (1987); s of Charles Harry Stanger, CBE (d 1987), of Knole, Somerset, and Florence Bessie Hepworth, *née* Bowden (d 2001); *b* 14 February 1939; *Educ* Oundle, Millfield; *m* 20 July 1963, Jill Patricia, da of Reginald Arthur Barnes, of Brussels, Belgium; 2 da (Vanessa b 1966, Miranda b 1967), 1 s (Edward b 1972); *Career* served RE 1960–66, seconded Malaysian Engrs 1963–66, operational serv Kenya, Northern Malaysia and Sarawak, Capt RE; joined R H Harry Stanger 1966, ptnr Al Hoty Stanger Ltd Saudia Arabia 1975–; ptnr/chm Harry Stanger Ltd 1972–90, chm Stanger Consultants Ltd 1990–93; first sec-gen European Orgn for Testing and Certification 1993–97 (UK rep on Cncl 1990–93), dir David H Stanger sprl 1997–2001, conslt materials engr 2001–08; chm: Assoc of Consulting Scientists 1981–83, NAMAS Advsy Ctee 1985–87, Standards Quality Measurement Advsy Ctee 1987–91, Advsy Bd Brunel Centre for Mfrg Metrology 1991–93, Lab Ctee Int Lab Accreditation Co-Operation 1996–2008 (ILAC, memb Exec Ctee 1998–2002); memb: Steering Ctee NATLAS 1981–85, Advsy Cncl for Calibration and Measurement 1982–87, Br C of C in Belguim 1997–2009, Advsy and Tech Ctee Dubai Municipality Accreditation Center 2008–10; memb Br Section Conseil National des Inqenieurs et des Scientifiques de France (CNISF) 1975–; Union Int des Laboratoires Independent (UILI): memb Governing Bd 1997–2010, sec-gen 1984–93 and 2001–03, rep to ISO/CASCO 2001–10; IQA 1969–2007 (chm Cncl 1990–93); chm Br Measurement and Testing Assoc 1990–93 (memb 1990–); Freeman City of London 1985, Freeman Worshipful Co of Water Conservators 1989; FRSA 1987 (memb Belgium section), life memb IOD 1987, fell Chartered Quality Inst 2007– (memb Advsy Bd 2007–10), Chartered Quality Professional 2008–; Malaysian Commorative Medal (Bronze) 1970, Pinqat Jasa Malaysia 2009; *Publications* Responsibility for Quality within British Industry (1989), Supporting European Quality Policies (1995), Customer Connection to a Global Laboratory Service (2000), Laboratory Services in a Global Marketplace (2002); *Recreations* collecting vintage wines; *Style—* D H Stanger, Esq, OBE; ✉ 7C Forth Mansions, Ta' Xbiex Seafront, Ta' Xbiex XBX 1027, Malta (e-mail stangerd14@gmail.com, website www.alhotystanger.com)

STANHOPE, Adm Sir Mark; GCB (2010, KCB 2004), OBE (1990), DL; *b* 26 March 1952, London; *Educ* London Nautical Sch, Worthing HS for Boys, St Peter's Coll Oxford (MA); *m* 1975, Jan Anne Flynn; 1 da; *Career* joined Royal Navy 1970; Deputy Supreme Allied Commander Transformation NATO 2005–07, Cdr-in-Chief Fleet 2007–09, First Sea Lord and Chief of Naval Staff 2009–13; pres Marine Soc and Sea Cadets 2014–, pres Britannia Assoc 2014–; pres Assoc of RN Offrs 2015–; tstee Royal Museums Greenwich 2015–; ret; *Recreations* Boating; *Clubs* Army and Navy; *Style—* Adm Sir Mark Stanhope, GCB, OBE, DL; ✉ Following Seas, 6 Barton Close, Exton, Exeter EX3 0PE

STANIER, Capt Sir Beville Douglas; 3 Bt (UK 1917), of Peplow Hall, Market Drayton, Shropshire; s of Brig Sir Alexander Beville Gibbons Stanier, 2 Bt, DSO, MC, JP, DL (d 1995), and Dorothy Gladys, *née* Miller (d 1973); *b* 20 April 1934; *Educ* Eton; *m* 1, 23 Feb 1963, (Violet) Shelagh (d 2007), da of Maj James Stockley Sinnott (ka 1941), of Tetbury, Glos; 2 da (Henrietta (Mrs Henrietta Stanier-Morgan) b 1965, Lucinda (Mrs James Stanier-Martin) b 1967), 1 s (Alexander James Sinnott b 1970); m 2, 15 May 2010, Nerena Anne Hyde (d 2015), da of Maj the Hon Nicholas Villiers; *Heir* s, Alexander Stanier; *Career* serv Welsh Gds 1952–60 (2 Lt 1953, Lt 1955, Capt 1958), UK, Egypt, Aust; ADC to Govr-Gen of Aust (Field Marshal Viscount Slim) 1959–60; stockbroker, ptnr Kitcat & Aitken 1960–76; farmer 1974–2012; conslt Hales Snails Ltd 1976–88; chm Buckingham Constituency Cons Assoc 1999–2003, chm Oxfordshire and Buckinghamshire Area Conservatives 2003–04, pres Buckingham Constituency Cons Assoc 2013–; memb Aylesbury Vale DC 1999– (cabinet 2001–); memb Whaddon Parish Cncl 1976– (chm 1986–); *Recreations* shooting, cricket; *Clubs* MCC; *Style—* Capt Sir Beville Stanier, Bt; ✉ Kings Close House, Whaddon, Buckinghamshire MK17 0NG (☎ 01908 501738, mobile 07778 305419, e-mail bdstanier@aol.com)

STANLEY, Barbara Elizabeth; *née* Hunter; da of Master John Morrison Hunter, CBE (d 1999), of Bangor, NI, and Elizabeth, *née* McKeag; *b* 2 July 1950, Belfast; *Educ* Glenlola Collegiate Sch Bangor NI, Queen's Univ Belfast (foundation scholar, BA), Univ of Leicester (PGCE); *m* 1978, Graham Stanley; 2 da (Louise b 25 Oct 1979, Jillian b 25 May 1982); *Career* in educn 1973–78 and 1986–; head of house Forest Sch Snaresbrook 1986–90, head of geography St Bernard's Convent Slough 1990–92, dep head Channing Sch Highgate 1992–95, headmistress Bedford HS 1995–2000, princ Alexandra Coll Dublin 2000–02, headmistress The Abbey Sch Reading 2002–14; independent schs specialist Assoc of Sch and Coll Ldrs (ASCL) 2015–; tstee Bishop Kivengere Sch for Girls Uganda, involved with Corrymeela Community NI and Benefice Cncl; churchwarden; HMC, GSA; FRGS 2001; *Recreations* outdoor activities, travel, community involvement, book group; *Style—* Mrs Barbara E Stanley; ✉ ASCL, 130 Regent Road, Leicester, LE1 7PG (☎ 0116 299 1122, e-mail barbara.stanley@ascl.org.uk)

STANLEY, Clare Fiona Louise; QC (2015); da of Dr Philip Edward Stanley, and Prof Margaret Anne Stanley, OBE, *née* Coutts, of Cambridge; *b* 25 January 1967, Adelaide, Australia; *Educ* Business Enterprise Centre Adelaide, Downing Coll Cambridge (BA); *m* 12 Sept 1998, Geoffrey Chapman; 1 da (Serena Margaret Grace Chapman b 12 July 1999), 1 s (Benjamin Philip Matthew Chapman b 16 Dec 2002); *Career* called to the Bar 1994; *Recreations* music, travel, walking, swimming; *Style—* Miss Clare Stanley, QC; ✉ Wilberforce Chambers, 8 New Square, Lincoln's Inn, London WC2A 3QP (☎ 020 7306 0102, e-mail cstanley@wilberforce.co.uk, website www.wilberforce.co.uk)

STANLEY, Rt Hon Sir John Paul; kt (1988), PC (1984); s of Harry Stanley (d 1956), and Maud Stanley (d 1993); *b* 19 January 1942; *Educ* Repton, Lincoln Coll Oxford; *m* 1968, Susan Elizabeth Giles; 2 s, 1 da; *Career* Cons Res Dept (Housing) 1967–68, res assoc IISS 1968–69, fin exec RTZ Corporation 1969–74; MP (Cons) Tonbridge and Malling Feb 1974–2015, memb Parly Select Ctee on Nationalised Industries 1974–76, PPS to Rt Hon Margaret Thatcher 1976–79, min for housing and construction with rank of min of state (DOE) 1979–83, min of state for armed forces MOD 1983–87, min of state for NI 1987–88; memb Parly Select Ctee on Foreign Affrs 1992–; *Recreations* music, arts, sailing; *Style—* The Rt Hon Sir John Stanley; ✉ House of Commons, London SW1A 0AA

STANLEY, Martin Edward; s of Edward Alan Stanley, of Northumberland, and Dorothy, *née* Lewis; *b* 1 November 1948; *Educ* Royal GS Newcastle upon Tyne, Magdalen Coll Oxford (exhibitioner, BA); *m* 1971 (m dis 1991), Marilyn Joan, *née* Lewis; 1 s (Edward b 8 April 1983); partner Janice Munday, CBE; 2 s (Nicholas decd, Joshua b 4 July 1998); *Career* various positions Inland Revenue 1971–80; DTI: various positions 1980–90, princ private sec 1990–92, head Engrg, Automotive and Metals Div 1992–96, dir of infrastructure and energy projects 1996–98; dir Regulatory Impact Unit Cabinet Office 1998–99, chief exec Postal Services Cmmn 2000–04, chief exec Competition Cmmn 2004–09, latterly chief exec Turks and Caicos Islands Govt; ed: www.civilservant.org.uk, www.regulation.org.uk, www.vauxhallandkennington.org.uk, www.andersonshelters.org.uk; *Books* How to be a Civil Servant (3 edn, 2016); *Recreations* travel, walking, sailing; *Style—* Mr Martin Stanley

STANLEY, Peter Henry Arthur; s of Col F A Stanley, OBE (d 1979), of Liphook, Hants, and Ann Jane, *née* Collins (d 1997); *b* 17 March 1933; *Educ* Eton; *m* 1, 7 May 1965 (m dis), Gunilla Margaretha Antonia Sophie, da of Count Wilhelm Douglas (d 1987), of Schloss Langenstein, Baden Wurttemberg; 1 da (Louisa b 1966), 1 s (Robin b 1968); m 2, 21 May 1990 (m dis), Mrs Lucy Campbell, da of James A Barnett, of Bel Air, CA; m 3, 29 May 1999, Hon Mrs Caroline Parr, da of Baron Renton, KBE, TD, PC, QC, DL (Life Peer) (d 2007); *Career* Grenadier Gds 1951–53; CA; trainee Dixon Wilson 1953–58, Peat Marwick (NY and Toronto) 1959–60, ptnr Hill Chaplin & Co (stockbrokers) 1961–68, chm and ceo Williams de Broë plc 1984–93 (dir 1968–93), chm BWD Securities plc 1995–2000 (dir 1994–2000), chm Manchester & London Investment Tst 2001– (dir 1997–); memb Cncl Stock Exchange 1979–86, dir Securities Assoc 1986–91 (chm Capital Ctee); FCA 1958; *Recreations* tennis, golf, shooting; *Clubs* White's, Swinley Forest Golf; *Style—* Peter Stanley, Esq; ✉ Cundall Hall, Helperby, North Yorkshire YO61 2RP (☎ 01423 360252, e-mail pstanyork@hotmail.com)

STANNARD, Ian; *b* 25 May 1987, Chelmsford, Essex; *Career* track and road cyclist; memb: Landbouwkrediet-Tonissteiner 2008, ISD 2009, Team Sky 2010–; Nat Road Race Champion 2012; *Style—* Mr Ian Stannard; ✉ website http://ianstannard.com, Twitter @istannard

STANNERS, Kate; *Career* former exec creative dir St Luke's, exec creative dir Saatchi & Saatchi 2005–; *Style—* Ms Kate Stanners; ✉ Saatchi & Saatchi, 80 Charlotte Street, London W1A 1AQ

STANNING, Heather; MBE (2013); *b* 26 January 1985, Yeovil, Somerset; *Educ* Univ of Bath (BSc); *Career* rower; achievements incl: Silver medal (coxless pair) World Championships 2010, Silver medal (coxless pair) World Championships 2011, Gold medal (coxless pair) Olympic Games 2012, Gold medal (coxless pair) World Championships 2014 and 2015, Gold medal (coxless pair) European Championships 2015 and 2016, Gold medal (coxless pair) Olympic Games Rio 2016; *Clubs* Army Rowing; *Style—* Ms Heather Stanning, MBE

STANSALL, Paul James; s of James Douglas Stansall (d 1984), of Newark, Notts, and Vera Jean, *née* Hall (d 2002); *b* 21 September 1946; *Educ* Winifred Portland Secdy Tech Sch Worksop, RCA (MA), Leicester Poly (DipArch); *m* 1, 1 Jan 1970 (m dis 1993), Angela Mary, da of Alexander Burgon (d 1954), of Beeston, Notts; 1 da (Alexandra b 1984); m 2, 15 July 2000, Moira Alison, da of Basil Fionn Young, of Thurso, Scotland; *Career* res asst UCL (memb Space Syntax Res Team) 1975–80, assoc DEGW Architects Planners and Designers (memb ORBIT 2 Team) 1980–89, visiting prof Cornell Univ 1987–88, dir Tectus Architecture Ltd 1991–2003, dir Tectus Space Mgmnt 2003–07, strategic workplace advsr OGC 2007–10, dir Dustlands 2010–; project mangr Energy Efficient Whitehall, memb Steering Gp CIBSE Energy BM; visiting lectr in property mgmnt Civil Service Coll 1991–2003, visiting lectr various UK univs; former memb Editorial Bd Jl of Property Mgmnt 1993; conslt to int cos, govt depts and local authorities (incl: Nat Audit Office, BA, The Wellcome Tst, Nomura Bank, DTI, City Univ, Winchester City Cncl) on space mgmnt; published numerous res papers and articles 1974–; tstee Transition Bath 2011–; memb Amnesty Int 2003–; RIBA 1987; *Publications* Getting the Best from Public Sector Office Accommodation (jtly, 2006), Working Beyond Walls (jtly, 2008); *Recreations* history of science, walking, Tai Chi, memb Vivavoices; *Style—* Paul Stansall, Esq; ✉ 2 Frankley Buildings, Bath BA1 6EG (☎ 01225 444217 (personal) and 07712 890041 (business), e-mail paul.stansall@virgin.net)

STANSBIE, (John) Michael; s of John Albert Stansbie, MBE, of Willersey, Worcs, and Norah Lydia, *née* Hopkins; *b* 2 October 1941; *Educ* Bolton Sch, ChCh Oxford (MA), Middlesex Hosp Med Sch (BM BCh); *m* 12 April 1969, Patricia, da of Joseph Arthur Dunn of St Arvans, Gwent; 2 s (Nicholas b 1973, Nigel b 1975); *Career* house surgn Middx Hosp London 1967, house physican Hillingdon Hosp Middx 1967–68, casualty offr Kettering Gen Hosp 1969, ENT registrar and sr ENT house offr Queen Elizabeth Hosp Birmingham 1970–71, sr ENT registrar W Midlands Trg Scheme 1972–76, conslt ENT surgn Walsgrave Hosps NHS Tst Coventry 1977–2001; lectr in anatomy Leicester/Warwick Med Sch 2001–14, lectr Warwick Med Sch 2005–14; W Midlands regnl advsr in otolaryngology RCS 1988–94, chm W Midlands Region Trg Sub-Ctee in Otolaryngology 1991–94, sec Midland Inst of Otology 1981–90; memb Panel of Examiners Intercollegiate Specialty Bd in Otolaryngology RCS 1996–2001; sec Shows Ctee Br Cactus and Succulent Soc 2004– (chm Coventry and Dist Branch 1987–90), vice-chm Friends of Coventry Cathedral 2009–15; FRCS 1972, FRSM 1977; *Publications* Clinical ENT Radiology (1993); *Recreations* natural history, cactus collecting and judging; *Style—* Michael Stansbie, Esq; ✉ 76 Bransford Avenue, Cannon Park, Coventry CV4 7EB (☎ 024 7641 6755, e-mail mstansbie@doctors.org.uk)

STANSGATE, Viscountcy of; *see:* Benn, Rt Hon Anthony Neil Wedgwood, MP

STANTON, David Leslie; CMG (2014); s of Leslie Stanton (d 1981), of Birmingham, and C Mary, *née* Staynes (d 2001); *b* 29 April 1943, Birmingham; *Educ* Bootham Sch York, Balliol Coll Oxford (BA); *m* 6 May 1989, Rosemary Jane, da of Kenneth Brown; 1 da (Acadia Elena b 27 April 1995); *Career* asst princ ODM 1965–69, SSRC sr scholarship Univ of Oxford 1969–71, princ ODA 1971–75, first sec Office of UK Perm Rep to EC 1975–77, memb Bd of Dirs Asian Devpt Bank 1979–82, head of dept ODA 1982–92, fin and admin advsr (on secondment) EBRD 1990–91, memb Bd of Dirs World Bank Gp 1992–97, memb Exec Bd and UK perm delg (with personal rank of ambass) UNESCO 1997–2003 (chair Fin and Admin Cmmn 2000–01); chair Exec Ctee Int Campaign for the Establishment of the Nubia Museum in Aswan and the Nat Museum of Egyptian Civilization in Cairo 2002–03, chair of tstees UNICEF UK 2004–13; govr Canonbury Sch 2003–06 (vice-chair 2005–06), dir Friends Trusts Ltd 2009–15, memb Quaker Peace and Social Witness Central Ctee 2014–, govr Bootham Sch York 2016–; *Recreations* mountains, gardens, painting; *Style—* David Stanton, Esq, CMG; ✉ e-mail davidstanton@canonburypark.plus.com

STANTON, Dr Lyndon; s of Joseph Reginald Stanton (d 1986), and Violet Hazel, *née* Sears; *b* 1942, Newport, Monmouthshire; *Educ* Newport HS for Boys, Univ of Wales (BSc, PhD); *m* 1964, Carol Ann, *née* Smith; 2 da (Victoria Jane (Dr McLean) b 1969, Leonie Alexandra b 1971); *Career* Salters' research fell Emmanuel Coll Cambridge, various commercial and technical appts ICI Ltd 1969–79; Arco Chemical Europe: gen mangr sales and mktg 1979–81, mangr M&A 1981–83, business mangr Urethanes 1983–88, dir Business Devpt 1988–91, vice-pres Business Mgmnt 1991–94, pres and ceo 1994–98; pres and ceo Lyondell Chemical Europe (following merger) 1998–2000; non-exec dir: Environment Agency 2002–09 (chm Industry Sub-Ctee, chm Southern Region Advsy Panel), Nuclear Decommissioning Authy 2004–08; author of scientific papers on nonlinear light scattering and atomic and molecular physics in learned jls; tstee: Prince of Wales's

Phoenix Tst 1996–2004 (chm 2003–04), Earthwatch Europe 1997–2002, Churches Conservation Tst 1999–2005 (dep chm 2001–05), Norden Farm Centre for the Arts 2002–12 (chm Finance and Mgmnt Ctee); *Recreations* watersports (especially scuba diving), collecting antique furniture and antiquarian scientific textbooks, photography and music; *Clubs* Athenaeum; *Style—* Dr Lyndon Stanton; ✉ Broadley, 11 Woodlands Ride, Ascot, Berkshire SL5 9HP (☎ 01344 626904, e-mail lyndon.stanton@btinternet.com)

STANTON, Prof Stuart Lawrence; s of Michael Arthur Stanton (d 1968), and Sarah, *née* Joseph (d 1992); *b* 24 October 1938, London; *Educ* City of London Sch, London Hosp Med Sch (MB BS); *m* 1, 25 Feb 1965; 3 da (Claire b 1967, Talia b 1970, Joanna b 1972); m 2, 17 Feb 1991; 1 da (Tamara b 1991), 1 s (Noah b 1994); *Career* conslt urogynaecologist St George's Hosp 1984–2003, prof St George's Med Sch 1997–2003 (hon sr lectr 1984–97); pres Br Soc of Urogynaecology 2003–; assoc: Br Assoc of Urological Surgns, European Assoc of Urologists; chair Hadassah UK 2010–12; patron: British Friends of Hebrew Univ 2004–; memb: Blair Bell Res Soc, Int Continence Soc; tstee Brit Friends of Boys Town Jerusalem 2012–; MRCS LRCP 1961, FRCS 1966, FRCOG 1987; *Books* Clinical Gynaecologic Urology (1984), Surgery of Female Incontinence (co-ed with Emil Tanagho, 1986, 2 edn 1986), Principles of Gynaecological Surgery (1987), Gynaecology in the Elderly (1988), Gynaecology (co-ed, 1992, 3 edn 2003), Pelvic Floor Re-education (co-ed, 1994, 2 edn 2008), Clinical Urogynaecology (co-ed, 1999), Urinary Tract Infection in the Female (co-ed, 2000), Female Pelvic Reconstructive Surgery (co-ed, 2002); *Recreations* photography, travel, opera, theatre, modern ceramics, grandchildren; *Style—* Prof Stuart Stanton; ✉ 1 Church Hill, London SW19 7BN (☎ 07796 697779, e-mail stuartstanton@hotmail.co.uk)

STAPLE, George Warren; CB (1996), Hon QC (1997); s of Kenneth Harry Staple, OBE (d 1978), and Betty Mary, *née* Lemon (d 2000); bro of William Philip Staple, *qv*; *b* 13 September 1940; *Educ* Haileybury; *m* Jan 1968, Olivia Deirdre, da of William James Lowry (d 1952), of Mtoko, Southern Rhodesia; 2 da (Alice b 1969, Polly b 1970), 2 s (Harry b 1976, Edward b 1978); *Career* admitted slr 1964; conslt Clifford Chance 2001– (ptnr 1967–92 and 1997–2001); DTI inspr: Consolidated Gold Fields plc 1986, Aldermanbury Trust plc 1988 (reported Dec 1990); dir the Serious Fraud Office 1992–97; chm of tbnls Securities and Futures Authy 1988–92, chm Fraud Advsy Panel 1998–2003; chm Review Bd for Govt Contracts 2002–09; memb: Commercial Court Ctee 1978–92, Court of Govrs London Guildhall Univ 1982–94, Cncl Law Soc 1986–2000 (treas 1989–92), Law Advsy Ctee Br Cncl 1998–2001, Sr Salaries Review Body 2000–04, Accountants Disciplinary Tribunal 2005–; tstee Royal Humane Soc, tstee Romney Marsh Historic Churches Tst; chm of govrs Haileybury 2000–08; hon bencher Inner Temple 2000; *Recreations* cricket, hill walking; *Clubs* Brooks's, City of London, MCC; *Style—* George Staple, Esq, CB, QC; ✉ Clifford Chance, 10 Upper Bank Street, London E14 5JJ (☎ 020 7006 1000, fax 020 7006 5555)

STAPLE, William Philip (Bill); s of Kenneth Harry Staple, OBE (d 1978), and Betty Mary, *née* Lemon (d 2000); bro of George Warren Staple, CB, QC, *qv*; *b* 28 September 1947; *Educ* Haileybury, Coll of Law; *m* 14 May 1977 (m dis 1986), Jennifer Frances, da of Brig James Douglas Walker, OBE, of Farnham; 1 s (Oliver b 1980), 1 da (Sophia b 1982); *Career* called to the Bar 1970; exec Cazenove & Co 1972–81; N M Rothschild and Sons Ltd: asst dir 1982–86, dir 1986–94 and 1996–99, seconded as DG to Panel on Takeovers and Mergers 1994–96; md Benfield Advisory 1999–2001, dir Brown, Shipley Corp Fin 2001–04, md Westhouse Securities LLP 2005–06, chief exec Hanson Westhouse Ltd 2006–09; Westhouse Hldgs plc: chief exec 2009–10, dep chm 2011–14; *Recreations* a variety of sports, theatre; *Clubs* White's, City of London; *Style—* William Staple, Esq; ✉ 18 Calico House, Clove Hitch Quay, London SW11 3TN (e-mail billstaple@hotmail.co.uk)

STAPLETON, Nigel John; s of Capt Frederick Ernest John Stapleton, of Winchmore Hill, London, and Katie Margaret, *née* Tyson; *b* 1 November 1946, London; *Educ* City of London Sch, Fitzwilliam Coll Cambridge (MA); *m* 20 Dec 1982, Johanna Augusta, da of Johan Molhoek, of Vienna, Austria; 1 s (Henry James b 1988), 1 da (Elizabeth Jane Cornelia b 1990); *Career* Unilever plc: various commercial appts 1968–83, vice-pres fin Unilever (United States) Inc 1983–86; Reed International plc: fin dir 1986–96, dep chm 1994–97, chm 1997–99; co-chief exec Reed Elsevier plc 1996–99 (chief fin offr 1993–96, chm 1996–98); chm: Veronis Suhler Int Ltd 1999–2002, Uniq plc 2001–, Cordiant Communications Gp plc 2003; non-exec dir: Allied Domecq plc (Allied-Lyons plc until 1994) 1993–99, Marconi plc 1997–2002, Sun Life and Provincial Holdings plc 1999–2000, AXA UK plc 2000–02, Royal Opera House Tst 2000–01, London Stock Exchange plc 2001–10, Reliance Security Gp plc 2002–11, KazPost Kazakhstan 2008–14, Samruk Energo Kazakhstan 2008–09, Real Estate Fund Samruk Kazyna Kazakhstan 2011–14, Sovereign Wealth Fund Samruk Kazyna 2014–15; chm: Postal Services Cmmn 2004–11, Ctee of Mgmnt Mineworkers Pension Scheme 2009–; ind tstee National Grid UK Pension Scheme 2013– (chair of tstees 2014–); chair of govrs Ashley C of E Primary Sch 2011–; Master Worshipful Co of Stationers & Newspaper Makers 2012; hon fell Fitzwilliam Coll Cambridge 1998–; FCMA 1987 (ACMA 1972); *Recreations* classical music, travel, tennis, opera; *Clubs* Oxford and Cambridge; *Style—* Nigel Stapleton, Esq; ✉ Coal Pension Trustees, 41 Moorgate, London EC2R 6PP (☎ 01932 226809, mobile 07901 715811, e-mail nigel.stapleton@btinternet.com)

STARK, Peter Harry Geoffrey; s of Geoffrey Stark (d 1981), and Barbara, *née* Willis (d 2012); *b* Guildford, Surrey; *Educ* Bournemouth Sch, Royal Coll of Music, Vienna Meisterkurse; *Family* 1 s (Harry b 1983), 1 da (Joanna b 1986); *Career* violinist: WNO 1978–88 (princ 2nd violin 1985–88), RPO 1981–83; freelance conductor 1990–; conductor-in-residence Nat Youth Orch of GB 1985–2010, prof of conducting Jr Acad Royal Acad of Music 1989–2010, sr fell of conducting and orchestral studies Trinity Coll of Music 1997–2004, prof of conducting Royal Coll of Music 2007–; artistic dir: Parnassus 1999–2009, W of Eng Philharmonic Orch 2000–10 (also conductor); princ conductor: Ernest Read Symphony Orch 1989–2010, Herts Co Youth Orch 1995–, Cambridge Univ Chamber Orch 2002–; conducted orchs incl: BBC Concert Orch, BBC Nat Orch of Wales, Berlin Symphony Orch, Bournemouth Symphony Orch, English Chamber Orch, EU Youth Orch, Guildford Philhamonic Orch, Hallé, LSO, Malaysian Philharmonic Orch, Nat Youth Orch of GB, Orch of the Age of Enlightenment, Orch of the Maggio Musicale Fiorentino, WNO, Nat Youth Chamber Orch, Nat Children's Orch, Royal Symphony Orch of Oman; worked with soloists incl: Prof Nicholas Daniel, Stephen Isserlis, CBE, John Lill, CBE, *qqv*; performed in major concert halls in London (incl Royal Festival Hall and Barbican) and UK; toured: Austria, Belguim, Bermuda, Denmark, France, Germany, Holland, Italy, Japan, Malaysia, Malta, New Zealand, Poland, Sultenate of Oman, Sweden, Switzerland, USA; asst to conductors incl: Sir Colin Davis, CH, CBE, Sir Andrew Davis, CBE, Sir Simon Rattle, CBE, *qqv*, Baron Menuhin, OM, KBE, Klaus Tennstedt; rehearsal dir EU Youth Orch 2009–; series conslt Maestro (BBC) 2008–10; numerous recordings for BBC Radio; prizewinner Third Leeds Comp for Conductors 1987, finalist Vittorio Gui Int Comp 1980; Royal Coll of Music: Adrian Boult Conducting Scholarship 1977, Theodore Steir Conducting Prize 1977, Arthur Bliss Prize 1977, Tagore Gold Medal 1977; Allcard Grant Worshipful Co of Musicians 1979; Hon DMus UWE 2000; GRSM 1976, ARCM 1977, Hon ARAM 1996, Hon FTCL 1996; *Clubs* Savile; *Style—* Dr Peter Stark; ✉ Bay Tree Cottage, Fordingbridge, Hampshire SP6 3NL (e-mail pstark@mac.com); c/o Sue Walker (PA), ☎ 01256 772122 or 07740 518509, e-mail wandelaar@btinternet.com)

STARKEY, Dr David; CBE (2007); *b* 1945; *Educ* Kendal GS, Fitzwilliam Coll Cambridge (open scholar, major state studentship, MA, PhD); *Career* research fell Fitzwilliam Coll Cambridge 1970–72, lectr in history Dept of Int History LSE 1972–98, visiting fell Fitzwilliam Coll Cambridge 1998–2001 (bye-fell 2001–); visiting Vernon prof of biography Dartmouth Coll NH 1987 and 1989, Br Cncl specialist visitor Australia 1989; contrib various newspapers, diary columnist The Sunday Times and Spectator, reg panellist Moral Maze (BBC Radio 4) 1992–2001, presenter weekend show Talk Radio 1995–98; presenter/writer: This Land of England (3 part series, Channel Four) 1985, Henry VIII (3 part series, Channel Four) 1998, Elizabeth I (4 part series, Channel Four) 2000, The Six Wives of Henry VIII (Channel Four) 2001, David Starkey's Henry VIII (Channel 4) 2002 (Indie Documentary Award 2002), The Unknown Tudors (Channel 4) 2002, Monarchy (Channel 4) 2004–07; memb Editorial Bd History Today 1980–, memb Commemorative Plaques Working Gp English Heritage 1993–2007, pres Soc for Court Studies 1996–2004; vice-pres Tory Campaign for Homosexual Equality (TORCHE) 1994–, hon assoc Rationalist Press Assoc 1995–, hon assoc Nat Secular Soc 1999–; historical advsr to quincentennial exhbn Henry VIII at Greenwich Nat Maritime Museum 1991; guest curator: Elizabeth exhbn Greenwich Nat Maritime Museum 2003, Lost Facts exhbn Philip Mould Gallery 2007; Norton Medlicott Medal for Services to History Historical Assoc 2001; Freeman Worshipful Co of Barbers 1992 (Liveryman 1999); Hon DLitt Lancaster Univ 2004, Hon DLitt Univ of Kent 2006; FRHistS 1984, FSA 1994; *Books* This Land of England (with David Souden, 1985), The Reign of Henry VIII: Personalities and Politics (1985, 2 edn 1991), Revolution Reassessed: Revisions in the History of Tudor Government and Administration (ed with Christopher Coleman, 1986), The English Court from the Wars of the Roses to the Civil War (ed, 1987), Rivals in Power: the Lives and Letters of the Great Tudor Dynasties (ed, 1990), Henry VIII: a European Court in England (1991), The Inventory of Henry VIII: Vol 1 (ed with Philip Ward, 1998), Elizabeth: Apprenticeship (2000, W H Smith Book Award), Six Wives: The Queens of Henry VIII (2003), Monarchy: the Beginnings (2004), Monarchy: from the Middle Ages to Modernity (2006); also author of numerous articles in learned jls; *Style—* Dr David Starkey, CBE, FSA; ✉ Fitzwilliam College, Cambridge CB3 0DG

STARKEY, Hannah; da of George Howard Stalberger (d 1994), and Elizabeth Bernadette, *née* Starkey; *b* 12 July 1971; *Educ* Napier Univ (BA), RCA (MA); *m* Sept 1998, Nathaniel Paul Sharman; 2 da (Molly Elizabeth b 19 Nov 2000, Ella Kate b 14 April 2002); *Career* artist; *Solo Exhibitions* Hannah Starkey, Scottish Homes (Stills Gallery Edinburgh) 1995, Maureen Paley Interim Art London 1998, 2000, 2002 and 2004, Galleria Raucci/Santamaria Naples 1999, Cornerhouse Manchester 1999, Nederlands Foto Institut Rotterdam 1999, Progetto (Castello di Rivoli Turin) 2000, Irish MOMA Dublin 2000, Monica de Cardenas Milan 2002, Lisboa Photo 2005, Tankya Bonakdar Gallery NY 2006, Maureen Paley London 2007, Twenty Nine Pictures (Warwick Arts Centre) 2011, Ormeau Road Gallery Belfast 2011; *Group Exhibitions* John Kobal Foundation (Nat Portrait Gallery London) 1997, Modern Narratives: The domestic and the social (Artsway London) 1998, Shine, Photo '98 (Nat Museum of Film and Photography Bradford) 1998, Sightings, New Photographic Art (ICA London) 1998, Real Life (Galleria SALES Rome) 1998, Look at me (Kunsthal Rotterdam (Br Cncl touring exhbn) 1998, Remix: Images Photographiques (Musée des Beaux-Arts Nantes) 1998, Silver & Syrup: A Selection from the History of Photography (V&A) 1998, 3rd International Tokyo Photo Bienalle (Tokyo Met Museum of Photography) 1999, Clues (Monte Video Netherlands Media Art Inst Amsterdam) 1999, Galerie Rodolphe Janssen Brussels 1999, Give and Take: The Contemporary Art Society at the Jerwood (JerwoodSpace London) 2000, Imago (Universidad de Salamanca) 2000, Suspendidos (Centro de Fotograffa Universidad de Salamanca) 2000, Citibank Private Bank Photography Prize (The Photographers' Gallery London) 2001, Instant City (MuseoPecci Prato) 2001, Extended Painting (Monica de Cardenas Milan) 2001, No World Without You, Reflections of Indentity in New British Art (Herzliya Museum of Art Tel Aviv) 2001, Telling Tales: Narrative Impulses in Recent Art (Tate Liverpool) 2001, Melancholy (Northern Gallery for Contemporary Art Sunderland) 2001, Painted, Printed and Produced in Great Britain (Grant Selwyn Fine Art NY) 2002, Landscape (Saatchi Gallery London) 2002, Comin of Age (New Art Gallery Walsall) 2002, The St James Group Ltd Photography Prize 2002 (Flowers East London) 2002, Sodium Dreams (Center for Curatorial Studies Museum Bard Coll NY) 2003, Take Five! (Huis Marsellie Amsterdam) 2004, Berlin Photography Festival 2005, The Portrait (Harris Museum and Art Gallery Preston) 2006, Jugend von heute (Schim Kunsthalle Frankfurt) 2006, Between Today and Yesterday (Turnpike Gallery Wigan) 2007, Visual Dialogues (Manchester Art Gallery) 2007, Something That I'll Never Really See (Sainsbury Centre for Visual Art Norwich) 2007; *Commissions* Scottish Homes Nat Housing Agency for Scotland 1995, Nat Museum of Photography, Film and Television 1998, 1st Commission Level 1 Bookstore Tate Modern London 2000; *Awards* Nat Housing Body for Scotland 1995, John Kobal Portrait Award 1997, Deloitte and Touche Fine Art Award 1997, The Sunday Times Award 1997, Vogue Condé Nast Award 1997, The Photographers' Gallery Award 1997, Award for Excellence 3rd Int Tokyo Photo Bienalle 1999, City Bank shortlist 2001, Arts Fndn 10th Anniversary Award 2000, Vic Odden Award Royal Photographic Soc 2003; *Publications* Hannah Starkey Photographs 1997–2007 (monograph, 2007); *Style—* Ms Hannah Starkey; ✉ c/o Maureen Paley, 21 Herald Street, London E2 6JT (☎ 020 7729 4112)

STARLING, Melvin James; s of James Albert Starling, and Jean, *née* Craddock; *b* 15 July 1954; *Educ* Vyners GS Andover, UCL (BSc, DipArch); *m* (sep); 1 da (Jemma Alice b 23 May 1984), 1 s (Thomas William b 15 May 1986); *Career* ptnr Pringle Brandon Architects 1986–2011, ret; RIBA 1985; *Recreations* golf, sport, architecture, building my own home; *Clubs* Betchworth Park Golf; *Style—* Melvin Starling, Esq; ✉ e-mail melvin@melvinstarling.com

STARMER, Sir Keir; KCB (2014), QC (2002), MP; *b* 1962; *Educ* Univ of Leeds (LLB), Univ of Oxford (BCL); *m* Victoria Alexander; *Career* called to the Bar 1987; legal offr Liberty until 1990; practising barr specialising in human rights law, memb Doughty Street Chambers 1990–2008; dir of public prosecutions 2008–13; MP (Lab) Holborn and St Pancras 2015–; fell Human Rights Centre Univ of Essex; Justice/Liberty Human Rights Lawyer of the Year Award 2000, Chamber and Partners Human Rights QC of the Year 2007; *Publications* incl: Justice in Error (ed, 1995), Three Pillars of Liberty, Political Rights and Freedoms in the United Kingdom (1996), Miscarriages of Justice (ed, 1999), European Human Rights Law (1999), Blackstone's Human Rights Digest (2001), Criminal Justice, Police Powers and Human Rights (2001), Human Rights Principles (contrib, 2001), Mithani's Directors' Disqualification (contrib, 2001), Human Rights and Civil Practice (contrib, 2001); author of numerous articles in newspapers and jls; *Style—* Sir Keir Starmer, KCB, QC, MP

STARMER-SMITH, Nigel Christopher; s of Harry Starmer-Smith (d 2002), and Joan Mary, *née* Keep (d 1985); *b* 25 December 1944; *Educ* Magdalen Coll Sch Oxford, UC Oxford (MA, Rugby blues); *m* 25 Aug 1973, Rosamund Mary, da of Wallace Bartlett; 1 da (Charlotte Alice Mary b 2 May 1975 d 1991); 2 s (Charles Jeremy Nigel b 5 June 1978, Julian Edward Giles b 9 April 1982 d 2001); *Career* schoolmaster Epsom Coll 1967–70, BBC Radio Outside Broadcasts 1970–73, sports commentator and presenter BBC TV (mainly rugby union and hockey) 1973–2002, ed-in-chief Rugby World magazine 1984–93, conslt/offical commentator Int Rugby Bd 2002–; minister's rep on Southern Sports Cncl 1989–93; tstee Reading and District Hospitals Charity 1992–, govr Shiplake Coll 2002–09; *Former Sportsman* rugby: Oxford Univ, Oxfordshire, Harlequins, Surrey, Barbarians, England; hockey: Oxford Univ, Oxfordshire; cricket: Territorial Army; *Books* The Official History of the Barbarians (1977), Rugby – A Way of Life (1986); numerous rugby annuals and books; *Recreations* tennis, golf, piano-playing, family; *Clubs* Leander,

S

Harlequin FC; *Style—* Nigel Starmer-Smith, Esq; ✉ Cobblers Cottage, Skirmett, Henley-on-Thames, Oxfordshire RG9 6TD (e-mail nstarmersmith@aol.com)

STARR, Nicholas Frederick (Nick); CBE (2013); s of Anthony Starr, and Marian *née* Coombs (d 2012); *b* 23 October 1957, Swanley, Kent; *Educ* Chislehurst and Sidcup GS, Merton Coll Oxford (BA); *Career* exec dir National Theatre 2002–14; fndr dir London Theatre Company 2014–; chair: Battersea Arts Centre, Bush Theatre 2009–; memb Bd Soc of London Theatre; tstee NESTA 2009–13; Tony Award 2011, Special Award Olivier Awards 2014; *Recreations* gardening, music, walking; *Style—* Nick Starr, Esq, CBE; ✉ London Theatre Company, NickStarr@londontheatrecompany.co.uk

STARY, Erica Frances Margaret; da of Eric Halstead Smith (d 1987), and Barbara Maud, *née* Creeke (d 1947); *b* 20 January 1943; *Educ* Hunmanby Hall, LSE (LLM); *m* 1, 1966; m 2, 1971, Michael McKirdy Anthony Stary (d 2012), s of Joseph Jind?ich Starý (presumed dead 1939); 1 da (Philippa b 1977); *Career* admitted slr 1965; lectr then sr lectr Coll of Law 1966–73, Inland Revenue 1974–75, successively asst ed, ed and consulting ed British Tax Review 1976–, tech offr Inst of Taxation 1981–86, city lawyer 1986–98, district judge 1998–2013, asst recorder then recorder 1996–2013; memb Nat Ctee of Young Slrs 1969–77, chm London Young Slrs Gp 1972, dir Slrs Benevolent Assoc 1973–77, dir and tstee London Suzuki Group and Tst 1984–89, asst clerk then clerk Second East Brixton Gen Cmmrs of Income Tax 1987–98; memb Cncl: Chartered Inst of Taxation 1989–98 (chm Technical Ctee 1993–94), Assoc of Taxation Technicians 1991–98 (pres 1994–95); tstee: Nat Children's Orch 1989–98, Tax Advrs Benevolent Fund 1996–98; Liveryman: Worshipful Co of Tinplate Workers alias Wire Workers, City of London Solicitors' Co, Worshipful Co of Tax Advrs (memb Ct of Assts 1995–, Master 2005–06), Worshipful Co of Plumbers (Sr Asst 2014, Upper Warden 2014–15, Master 2015–16); CTA (fell) 1984, fell Assoc of Taxation Technicians (ATT); *Recreations* sailing, cycling, music, theatre; *Clubs* Athenaeum; *Style—* Mrs Erica Stary; ✉ c/o Barclays Bank, 3 Church Street, Weybridge KT13 8DD

STATMAN, His Hon Judge Philip Richard; s of Martin Statman, of Thorpe Bay, Essex, and Evelyn Statman, *née* Silver; *b* 28 March 1953; *Educ* Westcliff HS for Boys, Mid-Essex Tech Coll (LLB), Inns of Court Sch of Law; *m* 18 Oct 1997, Dr Mary Louise Cameron (d 2006); 2 s (Samuel Alexander b 1 June 1999, Angus Joseph David b 19 Nov 2001); *Career* called to the Bar 1975; tenant Chambers of Barbara Calvert, QC 1976–89, tenant Chambers of Rock Tansey, QC, *qv*, 1989–2002, asst recorder 1997, recorder 2000, circuit judge (SE Circuit) 2002–, diversity and community rels judge; *Recreations* travel, cinema, antiques, reading, association football; *Style—* His Hon Judge Statman; ✉ Maidstone Combined Court Centre, Barker Road, Maidstone ME16 8EQ (☎ 01622 202000)

STATON, Roger Anthony; s of Harry James Staton (d 1977), of Coventry, and Janet, *née* Palmer; *b* 25 November 1945; *Educ* Bablake Sch Coventry, Univ of Manchester (BSc); *m* 23 May 1970, Angela, da of Joseph Armstrong; 2 s (David b 14 Sept 1971, Adam b 5 Aug 1973); *Career* trg offr GEC Telecommunications Ltd Coventry 1968–69 (apprentice 1963–68), prodn ed The Rugby Review 1969–71, dep ed Radio Communication magazine 1971–73; account exec: Scott Mactaggart Associates 1973–74, Golley Slater Public Relations 1974–76; fndr md Roger Staton Associates (renamed Six Degrees Ltd 2004) 1976–; dir: The Pegasus Press Ltd 1984–, ArtHaus Visual Communications Ltd 1987–, The RSA Group Ltd 1995–; FCIPR 2004 (MIPR); *Recreations* art history, reading, classic cars, cooking, walking; *Style—* Roger Staton, Esq; ✉ Six Degrees Ltd, Davidson House, Forbury Square Reading, RG1 3EU(☎ 01628 480280, fax 01628 487223, e-mail roger.staton@sixdegreespr.com)

STAUGHTON, Lady; Joanna Susan Elizabeth; OBE (2014), DL (Herts 1998); da of George Frederick Arthur Burgess (d 1963), and Lilian Margaret Colvin, *née* Bovill (d 1999); *b* 29 December 1937; *m* 16 Aug 1960, Rt Hon Sir Christopher Stephen Thomas Jonathan Thayer Staughton, *qv*; 2 da (Catharine Elizabeth b 11 June 1961, Sarah Louisa Margaret (Mrs Niall Donaldson) b 17 May 1963); *Career* sch care worker Inner London 1966–71; chm Herts Family Health Services Authy 1987–96; ind assessor Dept of Health 1996–; memb: Inner London Juvenile Panel 1970–99 (chm 1992–94), Police Complaints Bd 1976–85, S Westminster PSD 1980–90, Cncl Child Accident Prevention Tst 1991–97, Cncl Nat Children's Bureau 1991–97, Cncl NAHAT (now NHS Confedn) 1993–96, Cncl Br Heart Fndn 1994–; pres: Relate (Watford) 1992–98, Rickmansworth Scouts 1994–98, Herts Soc for the Blind; memb St Albans Abbey Music Tst 1995–2000; vice-pres Herts Alcohol Prevention Advsy Service, advsy memb Herts Community Fndn; govr various schs incl Francis Holland Schs 1971–; chm of govrs Princess Helena Coll Hitchin 1997–; Univ of Hertfordshire: memb Bd of Govrs 2004–, chm Devpt Ctee 2005– (memb 1995–); tstee Royal Patriotic Fund 1997–; High Sheriff Herts 1994–95; Freeman City of London 1995; *Recreations* swimming, walking, needlework; *Style—* Lady Staughton, OBE, DL; ✉ c/o 20 Essex Street, London WC2R 3AL

STAUGHTON, Dr Richard Charles David; LVO; s of Thomas Richard Staughton (d 1989), and Bardi Dorothy, *née* Cole (1989); *b* 15 August 1944; *Educ* Wellingborough Sch, Emmanuel Coll Cambridge (MA), Bart's Med Coll (MB BChir); *m* 1, 1979 (m dis 1988), Jenny, da of Sir Anthony Quayle (d 1989); 1 s (Dr Jack Anthony b 29 Dec 1982); m 2, 1991, Clare, o da of late Sir Mark Evelyn Heath, KCVO, CMG; *Career* successively: house surgn then SHO Bart's, registrar King Edward VII Hosp Windsor, registrar (dermatology) St Thomas' Hosp, sr registrar (dermatology) Westminster Hosp, conslt dermatologist Addenbrooke's Hosp Cambridge; conslt dermatologist Chelsea and Westminster Hosp and hon conslt to King Edward VII Hosp Beaumont St, Royal Hosp Chelsea and The Royal Brompton Hosp 1978–2008, ret from NHS; currently in private practice Lister Hosp; hon corresponding memb Soc Français de Dermatologie; memb: Br Assoc of Dermatologists (Archibald Gray Medal 2013), St John's Soc (pres 1987); FRCP; *Books* Cutaneous Manifestations of HIV Disease (1988, 2 edn 1994), Atopic Skin Disease (1996), Vulval Disease (1994, 2 edn 1997); *Recreations* gardening, fly fishing; *Clubs* Garrick, Chelsea Arts, Flyfishers', Piscatorial Soc; *Style—* Dr Richard Staughton, LVO; ✉ Lister Hospital, Chelsea Bridge Road, London SW1W 8RH (☎ 020 7881 4135, fax 020 7730 8016, e-mail rstaughton@lineone.net)

STAUNTON, Henry Eric; s of Henry Staunton (d 1976), and Joy Evelyn, *née* Brownlow; *b* 20 May 1948; *Educ* Univ of Exeter; *m* Karen; 1 s (James b 1977), 1 da (Clare b 1980); *Career* audit ptnr Price Waterhouse 1970–93, gp finance dir Granada Compass plc (following merger between Granada Gp plc and Compass Gp plc in 2000) 1993–2004, finance dir and dep chm Media Ventures Granada plc 2000–04, finance dir ITV plc 2004–06; non-exec chm WH Smith 2013–; non-exec dir: EMAP plc 1995–2002, Ashtead Gp plc 1997–2004 (chm 2001–04), Legal & General Gp plc 2004–, Ladbrokes plc 2006–; former non-exec dir: BSkyB plc, ITN Ltd; FCA; *Recreations* tennis, golf, theatre, travel; *Clubs* RAC; *Style—* Henry Staunton, Esq; ✉ WHSmith plc, Victoria House 4th Floor, 37–63 Southampton Row, Bloomsbury Square, London WC1B 4DA

STAUNTON, Marie; CBE (2013); da of Austin Staunton, of Grange-over-Sands, Cumbria, and Ann, *née* McAuley; *b* 28 May 1952; *Educ* Larkhill House Sch Preston, Lancaster Univ (BA), Coll of Law; *m* 15 March 1986, James Albert Provan, s of William Provan, of Wallaceton, Perthshire; 2 da (Lucy Maryanne b 1987, Amy Clare b 1994); *Career* slr; successively: legal offr Nat Cncl for Civil Liberties, dir Br Section Amnesty Int (memb Int Exec Ctee), ed Solicitors Jl, publishing dir FT Law and Tax, dep exec dir UK Ctee UNICEF; ceo Plan International UK 2000–13, interim ceo International Fedn of Anti-Leprosy Assocs (ILEP) 2014–15; UK ind memb EU Fundamental Rights Agency 2007–12; non-exec dir Crown Agents 2013–; chair Equality and Diversity Forum 2012–, chair Raleigh International 2013–, tstee Baring Fndn 2013–; FRSA; *Books* Data Protection – Setting the Record Straight Public Order Act – A Guide; *Recreations* children, theatre, gardening; *Clubs* Two Brydges Place; *Style—* Ms Marie Staunton, CBE; ✉ 18 Grove Lane, London SE5 8ST (☎ 020 7701 9191)

STEADMAN, Alison; OBE (2000); da of George Percival Steadman (d 1991), and Marjorie, *née* Evans (d 1996); *b* 26 August 1946; *Educ* Childwall Valley HS for Girls, East 15 Acting Sch; *Children* 2 s (Toby Leigh b 3 Feb 1979, Leo Leigh b 15 Aug 1981); *Career* actress; patron: Haringey Phoenix Gp (people with visual impairment), Friends of Carers (Nat Carers Assoc); Hon MA Univ of E London, Hon DUniv Essex 2003, Hon DLitt Univ of Liverpool 2006; *Theatre* credits incl: The Prime of Miss Jean Brodie (Theatre Royal, Lincoln), Soft for a Girl, The Fish in the Sea, The Foursome (all Everyman, Liverpool), Othello, Travesties (both Nottingham Playhouse), The Sea Achor (Upstairs, Royal Court), The King (Shaw Theatre), Wholesome Glory (Upstairs, Royal Court), The Pope's Wedding (Exeter/Bush Theatre), Abigail's Party (Hampstead), Joking Apart (Globe), Uncle Vanya (Hampstead), Cinderella and Her Naughty Sisters, A Handful of Dust (both Lyric, Hammersmith), Tartuffe (RSC/Pit), Maydays (RSC/Barbican), Kafka's Dick (Royal Court), Cat on A Hot Tin Roof (RNT), The Rise and Fall of Little Voice (RNT and Aldwych), Marvin's Room (Hampstead and Comedy Theatre), When We Are Married (Chichester and Savoy Theatre), The Provok'd Wife (Old Vic), The Memory of Water (Vaudeville Theatre), Entertaining Mr Sloane (Arts Theatre and tour), Horse and Carriage (W Yorks Playhouse), The Woman Who Cooked Her Husband (New Ambassadors Theatre), Losing Louis (Whitehall Theatre, Hampstead Theatre and Trafalgar Studios), Enjoy (Gielgud Theatre), Blithe Spirit (Apollo Theatre), Here (Rose Theatre Kingston); *Television* BBC credits incl: Girl, Hard Labour, He's Gone, Nuts in May, Flesh and Blood, Esther Waters, Through the Night, Pasmore, Abigail's Party, Nature in Focus, The Singing Detective, Virtuoso, Newshound, Pride and Prejudice, No Bananas, A Small Morning, The Cappuccino Years, Dalziel and Pascoe, Let Them Eat Cake, The Worst Week of My Life, Gavin and Stacey, Civil Arrangement; other credits incl: The Caucasian Chalk Circle (Thames), Coming Through (Central), The Finding (Thames), Monster Maker (Henson Organisation), Selling Hitler (Euston), Gone to Seed (Central), Without Walls: Degas and Pissaro Fall Out (Channel Four), Wimbledon Poisoner (BBC/ABTV), Six Sides of Coogan – The Curator (Pozzitive Television), Rory Bremnar Who Else (Vera Prodns), The Missing Postman (BBC Scotland), Fat Friends (Yorkshire TV), Fat Friends (Series 2, 3 and 4, Yorkshire TV), Celeb (Tiger Aspect), Gone to the Dogs (Central), Who Gets the Dog (ITV), Miss Marple, Fanny Hill, Come Rain, Come Shine (ITV), King of the Teds (Sky Arts), A Civil Arrangement (BBC4), The Autograph (Sky Arts), The Syndicate (BBC), Love and Marriage (ITV); *Radio* Gloomsbury (series 1 and 2); *Film* Champions, P'Tang Yang Kipperbang, Number One, A Private Function, Clockwise, The Short & Curlies, Stormy Monday, The Adventures of Baron Munchausen, Shirley Valentine, Wilt, Life is Sweet, Blame it on the Bellboy, Topsy Turvy, Happy Now, Chunky Monkey, The Life and Death of Peter Sellers, Confetti; *Short* DIY Hard; *Radio* Tale of Two Cities (BBC Radio 4); *Awards* Evening Standard Best Actress Award 1979, Olivier Award for Best Actress 1993; *Style—* Ms Alison Steadman, OBE; ✉ c/o ARG, 4 Great Portland Street, London W1W 8PA

STEADMAN, Dr Philip; s of late Melvyn Steadman, and Mary Elisabeth, *née* Jenkins (now Mrs Davies); *b* 3 April 1953, South Wales; *Educ* Ystalyfera GS, Cwmtawe Comp Sch, UCL (BSc), Imperial Coll London (MSc, Dip), Guy's Medical Sch (MB BS); *m* 26 Dec 1978, Kay, *née* Manning; 2 s (Jared b 27 Sept 1982, Jack b 14 June 1989), 3 da (Lucy b 3 Aug 1984, Emily b 19 Oct 1987, Katie b 12 Dec 1992); *Career* psychiatrist; hosp house positions then various jobs in psychiatric health 1990–99, conslt psychiatrist Oxleas Mental Health NHS Fndn Tst 1999– (chair Local Negotiating Ctee); former memb Cncl and dir BMA, chair BMA Regnl Local Negotiating Ctee, lead for mental health BMA Bd of Sci and Educn; contrib to various jls and pubns in particular for BMA Bd of Sci and Educn; FRCPsych 2009 (MRCPsych 1996); *Recreations* current affairs, films, reading, listening to music (mainly 1960s and 70s), playing with my grandchildren; *Style—* Dr Philip Steadman

STEADMAN, Timothy; s of Ronald Herbert Steadman, and Beatrice Dorothy, *née* Hunt; *b* 13 January 1955, Birmingham; *Educ* Ludlow GS, Hertford Coll Oxford (MA); *m* 6 Sept 1986, Alison Claire, *née* Spankie; 1 da (Anna), 2 s (Jack, Robert); *Career* slr; Lovells 1976–82, Baker & McKenzie 1982–97, Clifford Chance 1997–; author of articles in professional and firm pubns; memb: Law Soc, Int Bar Assoc; *Recreations* family, cooking, travel; *Style—* Timothy Steadman, Esq; ✉ Clifford Chance, 10 Upper Bank Street, Canary Wharf, London E14 5JJ (☎ 020 7006 1000, fax 020 7006 5555, e-mail tim.steadman@cliffordchance.com)

STEARNS, Michael Patrick; s of Cdr Eric Gascoyne Stearns, OBE, and Evelyn, *née* Sherry; *b* 19 January 1947; *Educ* Guy's Hosp London (BDS, MB BS); *m* Elizabeth Jane Elford Smith; *Career* registrar (later sr registrar) Guy's Hosp 1977–84; conslt head and neck surgn and otolaryngologist: Royal Free Hosp 1984–, Barnet Gen Hosp 1984–; sec Euro Acad of Facial Surgery 1989–98, treas Int Fedn of Facial Plastic Surgical Socs 2000–01; fell: Univ of Washington 1982, Univ of Oregon 1983; FRCS 1978, FRSM 1982; *Style—* Michael Stearns, Esq; ✉ Suite 14, 30 Harley Street, London W1G 9PW (☎ 020 7631 4448)

STEDMAN JONES, Prof Gareth; s of Lewis and Joan Olive Stedman Jones; *b* 17 December 1942; *Educ* St Paul's, Lincoln Coll Oxford (BA), Nuffield Coll Oxford (DPhil); *Children* 1 s by Prof Sally Alexander, 1 s by Prof Miri Rubin; *Career* research fell Nuffield Coll Oxford 1967–70, sr assoc memb St Antony's Coll Oxford 1971–72, Humboldt Stiftung Dept of Philosophy Goethe Univ Frankfurt 1973–74; Univ of Cambridge: fell King's Coll 1974–, lectr in history 1979–86, reader in history of social thought 1986–97, prof of political thought (formerly prof of political sci) 1997–2010; prof of the history of ideas Queen Mary Univ of London 2010–; memb Conseil Scientifique CNRS (Centre National de Recherche Scientifique) 2005–10; memb Editorial Bd New Left Review 1964–81, jt fndr and jt ed History Workshop Jl 1976–; FBA 2013; *Publications* Outcast London (1971), Languages of Class (1983), Klassen, Politik, Sprache (1988), Charles Fourier, The Theory of the Four Movements – trans 1: Patterson (ed, 1994), Karl Marx and Friedrich Engels, The Communist Manifesto (2002), An End to Poverty? A Historical Debate (2004), Religion and the Political Imagination (ed, 2010), Cambridge History of Nineteenth-Century Political Thought (jt ed, 2011), Karl Marx: Greatness and Illusion. A Life (2016); *Recreations* country walks, collecting old books, cricket; *Style—* Prof Gareth Stedman Jones; ✉ King's College, Cambridge CB2 1ST (☎ 01223 331120)

STEDMAN-SCOTT, Baroness (Life Peer UK), of Rolvenden in the County of Kent; Deborah Stedman-Scott; OBE, DL (E Sussex); da of Jack Scott, and Doreen, *née* Harry; *b* 23 November 1955, Paddington, London; *Partner* Gabrielle Stedman-Scott (civil partnership); *Career* Salvation Army 1978–83, Royal Tunbridge Wells C of C 1983–84, Tomorrow's People Tst Ltd 1984–2015 (ceo 2007–15); tstee New Devon Opera until 2012, tstee New Philanthropy Capital 2011–, govr Bexhill Acad 2015–; *Style—* The Baroness Stedman-Scott, OBE, DL, FRSA; ✉ House of Lords, London SW1A 0PW

STEED, Mark Stephen; s of David Paul Steed, and Pamela, *née* Lloyd; *b* 22 September 1965; *Educ* King Edward VI GS Chelmsford, Fitzwilliam Coll Cambridge (MA, Athletics blue), Univ of Nottingham (MA); *m* 31 July 2014, Samantha; 1 da (Anastasia Patricia Catharine b 29 Aug 1992), 2 s (William Mark Sebastian b 28 Aug 1994, Jeremy Charles Sandle b 11 Feb 1998); *Career* teacher: The Leys Sch Cambridge 1987–88, Radley Coll 1988–91, Oundle Sch 1991–2001 (head of religious studies 1993–98, housemaster 1997–2001); headmaster Kelly Coll Tavistock 2001–2008, princ Berkhamsted Sch 2008–15; chm ISC ICT Strategy Gp 2007–; govr Wren Acad Barnet 2008–15, dir Jumeirah English Speaking

Sch 2015–; *Recreations* running marathons, fives, stained glass, art and architecture; *Clubs* East India, Hawks' (Cambridge), Achilles, Lansdowne; *Style*— Mark S Steed, Esq; ✉ PO Box 24942, Dubai UAE (☎ 00 971 4361 9019, e-mail director@jess.sch.ae, blog http://independenthead.blogspot.com, Twitter @independenthead and @JESS_director)

STEED, Mark Wickham; s of Richard David Steed, and Jennifer Mary, *née* Hugh-Jones; gs of Henry Wickham Steed, editor of The Times; *b* 31 October 1952; *Educ* Downside; *m* 1, 3 June 1989 (m dis 1994), Carola Dawn, da of Dorian Joseph Williams, of Foscote Manor, Buckingham; m 2, 6 Aug 2011, Deborah Maxwell Veiller, of Bearsden, Glasgow; *Career* CA; dir: Oxford Investments Ltd 1981–86, Beckdest Ltd 1981–88, Colt Securities Ltd 1983–95, Global Portfolio Management Ltd 1996–98, Amstel Securities 2002–, Rocktron Ltd 2007–08, Sion Hall Family Office 2012–; vice-pres St Gregory's Soc; ACA, MSI, MCIM; *Recreations* shooting, realising dreams; *Clubs* Naval and Military; *Style*— Mark Steed, Esq; ✉ Keepers Cottage, The Shaw, Leckhampstead, Buckingham MK18 5PA

STEEDMAN, Prof Carolyn Kay; *née* Pilling; da of Ellis Kay Pilling (d 1977), of Streatham Hill and Gypsy Hill, London, and Edna Dawson (d 1983); *b* 20 March 1947; *Educ* Rosa Bassett GS for Girls London, Univ of Sussex (BA), Newnham Coll Cambridge (MLitt, PhD); *m* 1971 (m dis 1986), Mark Jerome Steedman, s of George Steedman (d 1998); *Career* class teacher in primary schs E Sussex and Warks 1974–81, project asst Schs Cncl Language in the Multicultural Primary Classroom Project Dept of Eng Inst of Educn Univ of London 1982–83, fell Sociological Research Unit Inst of Educn Univ of London 1983–84, reader Dept of Arts Educn Univ of Warwick 1991–93 (lectr 1984–88, sr lectr 1988–91), prof of social history Centre for the Study of Social History Univ of Warwick 1995– (reader 1993–95), prof History Dept Univ of Warwick 1998–2012 (emeritus prof 2013–); Helen Gamble research student Newnham Coll Cambridge 1970–71, visiting prof of history Univ of Michigan Ann Arbor 1992, Sir Simon research fell Dept of Sociology Univ of Manchester 1990–91, ESRC research prof 2004–07; ed History Workshop Jl 1983–1990; memb Panel for Validation and Review Cncl for Nat Academic Awards; external examiner: Univ of Portsmouth (formerly Portsmouth Poly) 1990–93, Keele Univ 1992–95, Univ of Leicester 1997–2000, Univ of Manchester 2002–; Nuffield Fndn small grant in social scis for work on Margaret McMillan (1860–1931) and the idea of childhood 1983, History Twenty Seven Fndn grant Inst of History Research 1983; FBA 2011; *Publications* incl: The Tidy House: Little Girls Writing (1982, awarded Fawcett Soc Book prize 1983), Policing the Victorian Community: the Formation of English Provincial Police Forces 1856–1880 (1984), Language Gender and Childhood (jt ed, 1985), Landscape for a Good Woman (1986), The Radical Soldier's Tale (1988), Childhood Culture and Class In Britain: Margaret McMillan 1860–1931 (1990), Past Tenses: Essays on Writing, Autobiography and History 1980–90 (1992), Strange Dislocations: Childhood and the Idea of Human Interiority 1780–1930 (1995), Dust (2001), Master and Servant: Love and Labour in the English Industrial Age (2007), Labours Lost: Domestic Service and the Making of Modern England (2009), An Everyday Life of the English Working Class. Work, Self and Sociability in the Early Nineteenth Century (2013); *Style*— Prof Carolyn Steedman; ✉ e-mail c.k.steedman@warwick.ac.uk

STEEDMAN, Prof Mark; s of George Steedman (d 1998), and Nan, *née* Saunders; *b* 18 September 1946; *Educ* Univ of Sussex (BSc), Univ of Edinburgh (PhD); *m* 1987, Prof Bonnie Lynn Webber, *née* Gerzog; *Career* research fell Univ of Sussex 1974–77, lectr Univ of Warwick 1977–83, lectr then reader Univ of Edinburgh 1983–88, assoc prof then prof Univ of Pennsylvania 1988–98, prof of cognitive science Univ of Edinburgh 1998–; fell American Assoc for Artificial Intelligence 1993, FRSE 2002, FBA 2002, fell Assoc for Computational Linguistics (ACL) 2012, fell Cognitive Science Soc 2013; *Books* Surface Structure and Interpretation (1996), The Syntactic Process (2000), Taking Scope (2012); *Recreations* hill climbing, jazz; *Clubs* Ortlieb's Jazzhaus, Philadelphia; *Style*— Prof Mark Steedman; ✉ School of Informatics, University of Edinburgh, 10 Crichton Street, Edinburgh EH8 9AB (☎ 0131 650 4631, fax 0131 650 6626)

STEEDMAN, Dr (Robert) Scott; CBE (2010); s of Robert Russell Steedman, OBE, of Blebocraigs, Fife, and Susan Elizabeth Sym, *née* Scott (d 2013); *b* 10 September 1958; *Educ* Edinburgh Acad, UMIST (BSc), Queens' Coll Cambridge (MPhil), St Catharine's Coll Cambridge (PhD); *m* 1, 5 Sept 1981 (m dis 2002), Zoreh, da of Dr Ebrahim Kazemzadeh (d 1993), of Mashad, Iran; 1 s (Nicholas Robert Cyrus b 1985), 1 da (Hannah Hope Eliza b 1990); m 2, 18 Nov 2005, Hon Deborah Jane, da of Lord Keith of Kinkel, GBE (Life Peer, d 2001), of Perthshire; *Career* fell St Catharine's Coll Cambridge 1983–93, lectr Dept of Engrg Univ of Cambridge 1983–90; with: EQE (safety and risk mgmnt conslts) 1990–92, Gibb Ltd (engrg consltss) 1993–2000, Whitby Bird & Partners Ltd (engrg design consltss) 2000–03, High-Point Rendel Ltd (capital project consltss) 2006–09; Foster Wheeler Energy (EPC contractor) 2009–10, non-exec dir Port of London Authy 2009–15, BRE Global 2010–11, dir BSI Gp 2012–; visiting prof MIT 1987; ed-in-chief Ingenia Royal Acad of Engrg 2004–; ind memb Defence Scientific Advsy Cncl 2005–11; vice-pres: Royal Acad of Engrg 2003–09, ICE 2005–09; chm Thomas Telford Ltd (publishers) 2003–07; CEng 1988, FICE 1994 (MICE 1988), FREng 2001, FInstRE 2009; *Books* Geotechnical Centrifuge Modelling (contrib, 1995), Environment, Construction and Sustainable Development (contrib, 2001), Geotechnics and Earthquake Geotechnics Towards Global Sustainability (contrib, 2011), Introduction to English for Global Communication of Civil and Environmental Engineering (with S Iai, 2013); *Recreations* the family, Bhutan, skiing, sailing; *Clubs* New (Edinburgh); *Style*— Dr Scott Steedman, CBE; ✉ 42 Hillgate Place, London W8 7ST (☎ 020 7727 9663)

STEEL, Her Hon Elizabeth Mary; DL (Merseyside 1991); da of His Hon Judge Edward Steel (d 1976), of Warrington, Cheshire, and Mary Evelyn Griffith, *née* Roberts (d 1987); *b* 28 November 1936; *Educ* Howells Sch Denbigh, Univ of Liverpool (LLB); *m* 8 April 1972, Stuart Christie (d 2011), s of Samuel Albert Christie; 1 da (Elspeth Victoria b 19 Nov 1976), 1 s (Iain Duncan b 17 Feb 1978); *Career* asst slr Percy Hughes & Roberts 1960–67 (articled clerk 1955–60); ptnr: John A Behn Twyford & Co 1968–80 (asst slr 1967–68), Cuff Roberts North Kirk 1980–91; recorder 1989–91, circuit judge (Northern Circuit) 1991–2007; nat vice-chm Young Cons 1965–67; memb: Cripps Ctee 1967–69, Race Relations Bd 1970–78, Gen Advsy Cncl BBC 1979–82; chm: NW Advsy Cncl BBC 1979–82, Steering Ctee Hillsborough Slrs Gp 1989–91, Royal Court Liverpool Tst Ltd 2008–13; dep and vice-chm Bd of Dirs Liverpool Playhouse 1980–88 (memb Bd 1968–94, vice-pres 1994–99); Liverpool Law Soc: vice-pres 1988–89, pres 1989–90, memb Ctee, former chm Legal Educn Sub-Ctee; non-exec dir Bd Royal Liverpool Univ Hosp Tst 1990–91, govr Liverpool John Moores Univ 2001–12, pres Merseyside branch ESU 2006–; tstee Liverpool Cathedral Centenary Tst 2003–10; hon fell Liverpool John Moores Univ 2013; Hon LLD Liverpool Univ 2007; memb: Law Soc 1960, Liverpool Law Soc 1960; *Recreations* theatre (watching professional and performing/directing amateur), music, needlework, cooking, reading, entertaining, being entertained; *Clubs* Athenaeum (Liverpool, vice-pres 2001–02, pres 2002–03); *Style*— Her Hon Elizabeth Steel, DL

STEEL, John Brychan; QC (1993); s of late Lt-Col John Exton Steel, of Swindon Hall, nr Cheltenham, Glos, and late Marianne Valentine, *née* Brychan Rees; *b* 4 June 1954; *Educ* Harrow, Durham Univ (BSc, capt ski club, pres athletic union); *m* 6 June 1981, Susan Rebecca, da of Dr Robert Fraser (d 1979), of Yarm, Co Durham; 2 s (Charles John Robert b 1984, Henry James Edward b 1989), 1 da (Sophie Rosanagh b 1986); *Career* Lt Inns of Court and City Yeomanry TA 1977–81; called to the Bar Gray's Inn 1978 (bencher 2007, chm Gray's Inn Mgmnt Ctee 2012–13), appointed to Attorney General's List of Counsel (Common Law) 1989, recorder 2000–; hon legal advsr and tstee The Air League, hon legal advsr to Mission Aviation Fellowship; memb Ctee Planning and Environmental Bar Assoc 2008–13; Gray's Inn prizewinner 1978; tstee and dir Busoga Tst 1982–2000, tstee Blenheim Palace; chm: Gray's Inn Field Club 1978–79, Kandahar Ski Club 1992–97, K Racing 1998–2000; dep chm Durham Global Security Inst Durham Univ (currently memb Bd); chm Oxford Airport General Aviation Gp, dep chm Ski Club of GB 1989–91; tstee Bentley Priory Battle of Britain Tst, memb The Air Sqdn; hon fell of law Durham Univ Law Sch; Freeman GAPAN; FRGS, FRAeS, FRSA; *Recreations* skiing, walking, flying; *Clubs* Boodle's, Kandahar; *Style*— John Steel, Esq, QC; ✉ 39 Essex Street, London WC2R 3AT (☎ 020 7832 1111, e-mail john.steel@39essex.com)

STEEL, Prof (Christopher) Michael; s of Very Rev Dr David Steel (d 2002), of Edinburgh, and Sheila Eunice Nanette, *née* Martin (d 1993); *b* 25 January 1940; *Educ* Prince of Wales Sch Nairobi, George Watson's Coll Edinburgh, Univ of Edinburgh (Ettles scholar, BSc, MB ChB, PhD, DSc, Leslie Gold Medal in Med); *m* 1 Aug 1962, Judith Margaret, da of Frederick David Spratt; 2 s (Andrew David b 15 Feb 1968, Robert Michael b 22 Nov 1969), 1 da (Heather Judith b 3 May 1974); *Career* jr hosp appts Edinburgh Teaching Hosps 1965–68, univ research fell Edinburgh Med Sch 1968–71, MRC travelling research fell Univ of Nairobi Med Sch 1972–73, memb Clinical Scientific Staff MRC Human Genetics Unit Edinburgh 1973–94 (asst dir 1979–94), prof of med sci Univ of St Andrews 1994–2004 (emeritus prof 2005–); T P Gunton Award BMA (for research and educn in the cancer field) 1993–94; memb: UK Gene Therapy Advsy Ctee 1994–2000, MRC Advsy Bd 1999–2005; FRCPE, FRCSEd, FRCPath, FRSE 1994, FMedSci 1998; *Books* Biochemistry: A Concise Text for Medical Students (1992); *Recreations* golf, skiing, theatre; *Clubs* RSM; *Style*— Prof Michael Steel, FRSE; ✉ The Medical School, University of St Andrews, North Haugh, St Andrews, Fife KY16 9TF (☎ 01334 463599, fax 01334 463482, mobile 07582 811487, e-mail cms4@st-and.ac.uk)

STEEL OF AIKWOOD, Baron (Life Peer UK 1997), of Ettrick Forest in The Scottish Borders; Sir David Martin Scott Steel; KT (2004), KBE (1990), PC (1977), DL (Ettrick and Lauderdale and Roxburghshire 1990–2013); s of Very Rev Dr David Steel, Moderator of the Gen Assembly of the Church of Scotland 1974–75; *b* 31 March 1938; *Educ* James Gillespie's Boys' Sch, Prince of Wales Sch Nairobi, George Watson's Coll Edinburgh, Univ of Edinburgh (MA, LLB); *m* 1962, Judith Mary, MBE, da of W D MacGregor, CBE; 2 s, 1 da; *Career* sometime journalist, asst sec Scottish Lib Pty 1962–64, BBC TV interviewer in Scotland 1964–65 and later presenter of religious programmes for STV, Granada and BBC; MP (Lib until 1988, then Lib Dem): Roxburgh, Selkirk and Peebles 1965–83, Tweeddale, Ettrick and Lauderdale 1983–97 (stood down); MSP (Lib Dem) Lothians 1999–2003; pres Anti-Apartheid Movement of GB 1966–69, memb Parly Delgn to UN 1967, sponsored Abortion Act 1967, Lib chief whip 1970–75, spokesman on foreign affrs 1975–76, ldr of Lib Pty 1976–88, memb Select Ctee on Privileges 1979–86, pres Lib International 1994–96, pres All Pty Parly Gp on Africa 2011–; presiding offr Scot Parl 1999–2003; fndr bd memb Int Inst for Democracy and Electoral Assistance (Stockholm) 1995; non-exec dir: Hall Advertising Ltd Edinburgh 1971–76, Border Television plc 1993–99, Heritage Oil & Gas Co Ltd 1995–97, General Mediterranean Holding SA 1996–, Blue Planet European Financials Investment Tst 1999–2010, Lycamoney Ltd 2015–; vice-pres The Countryside Alliance 1998–99; hon pres The Stationery Office Scotland 1997–98; chm Shelter Scotland 1969–73, memb Br Cncl of Churches 1971–74, rector Univ of Edinburgh 1982–85; regular contribs to newspapers incl The Scotsman and The Guardian; Freedom of Tweeddale 1988, Freedom of Ettrick and Lauderdale 1990; Chubb fell Yale Univ 1987, Hon Dr Univ of Stirling 1991, Hon DLitt Univ of Buckingham 1993, Hon DUniv Heriot-Watt 1996, Hon LLD Univ of Edinburgh 1997, Hon Dr Univ of Strathclyde 2000, Hon DUniv Open Univ 2001, Hon LLD Univ of Aberdeen 2001, Hon LLD Univ of St Andrews 2003, Hon LLD Glasgow Caledonian Univ 2004, Hon LLD Brunel Univ 2010; FRCOG 2013; Cdr's Cross of the Order of Merit (Germany) 1992; Chevalier de la Legion d'Honneur 2004; *Books* Boost for the Borders (1964), Out of Control (1968), No Entry (1969), The Liberal Way Forward (1975), A New Political Agenda (1976), Militant for the Reasonable Man (1977), A House Divided (1980), Partners in One Nation (1985), Border Country (with Judy Steel, 1985), The Time Has Come (1987), Mary Stuart's Scotland (with Judy Steel, 1987), Against Goliath (autobiography, 1989); *Recreations* classic cars, fishing; *Style*— The Rt Hon the Lord Steel of Aikwood, KT, KBE; ✉ House of Lords, London SW1A 0PW

STEELE, Prof Robert James Campbell; s of Robert Steele, and Elizabeth Sheridan, *née* Campbell; *b* 5 March 1952; *Educ* Daniel Stewart's Coll Edinburgh, Univ of Edinburgh (BSc, MB ChB, MD); *Career* research fell, registrar and lectr in surgery Univ of Edinburgh 1980–85, lectr in surgery Chinese Univ of Hong Kong 1985–86, lectr in surgery Univ of Aberdeen 1986–90, sr lectr and reader in surgery Univ of Nottingham 1990–96, prof of surgical oncology Univ of Dundee 1996–2003, prof of surgery and head Cancer Research Div Univ of Dundee 2003–; dir Scottish Colorectal Cancer Screening Cancer Pilot; chair: Colorectal Cancer Screening Project Bd, UK Colorectal Cancer Screening Exec Gp, Colorectal Cancer Focus Gp Scottish Intercollegiate Guidelines Network, Scottish Cancer Fndn; memb MRC Advsy Bd, memb Colorectal Clinical Studies Gp Nat Cancer Research Inst; pres Assoc of Coloproctology of GB and I (ACPGBI) 2014–16; FRCSEd 1984 (Gold Medal, memb Cncl), FRCS (ad eundem), 1995, fell Coll of Surgns Hong Kong 1995; FRCPE 2013; *Publications* five books, four guidelines, 47 book chapters and 253 peer reviewed publications; *Style*— Prof R J C Steele; ✉ Division of Surgery and Oncology, Mailbox 4, Level 7, Ninewells Hospital, Dundee DD1 9SY (☎ 01382 383542, fax 01382 496361, e-mail r.j.c.steele@dundee.ac.uk)

STEELE-PERKINS, Christopher Horace (Chris); s of Alfred Horace Steele-Perkins (d 1963), and Mary, *née* Lloyd (d 2001); *b* 28 July 1947; *Educ* Christ's Hosp, Univ of Newcastle upon Tyne (BSc); *m* 17 July 1999, Miyako Yamada, da of Shinsei Lee; 2 s (Cedric Angelo b 16 Nov 1990, Cameron Benjamin b 18 June 1992); *Career* photographer; Magnum Photos: memb 1982, pres 1995–98; vice-pres Magnum Photos Japan 1998–2003; visiting prof Musashino Art Univ Tokyo 2000; hon FRPS 2014; *Exhibitions* The Pleasure Principle (FNAC Paris) 1990, Africa (Perpignon France) 1992, Cross Section (Hong Kong Festival) 1993, No Mans Land (PGI Tokyo) 1999, Afghanistan (UK tour) 2000, Fuji (MAC Birmingham and Grandship Japan) 2001, Teds (Howard Greenburg Gall NY) 2003, Echoes (FNAC Paris) 2004; *Awards* Oskar Barnak Award 1988, Robert Capa Gold Medal 1989, Tom Hopkinson Award 1989, La nacion Premier Photojournalism Award 1994, Co-operative Soc and One World Award (for film Dying for Publicity) 1994, Sasakawa Fndn Grant 1999 and 2004, World Press Award 2000, Terence Donovan Award RPS 2008; *Books* The Teds (1979), About 70 Photographs (1980), Survival Programmes (jtly, 1982), Beirut: Frontline Story (1983), The Pleasure Principle (1989), Afghanistan (2000), Fuji (2001), Echoes (2004), Tokyo Love Hello (2007), Northern Exposures (2007), England, My England (2009), Fading Light: portraits of centenarians (2012), A Place in the Country (2014); *Recreations* chess, walking, music, literature, film; *Style*— Chris Steele-Perkins, Esq; ✉ Magnum Photos, 63 Gee Street, London EC1V 3RS (☎ 020 7490 1771, website www.chrissteeleperkins.com)

STEELE-PERKINS, Crispian; s of Dr Guy Steele-Perkins, and Sylvia de Courcey Steele-Perkins; *b* 18 December 1944; *Educ* Marlborough, Guildhall Sch of Music; *m* 1, 29 April 1967, Angela (d 1991), da of William Scambler Hall (d 1967); 2 da (Emma Victoria b 20 March 1968, Kathleen b 28 Oct 1970), ((Michael) Guy (twin) b 28 Oct 1970); m 2, 6 April 1995, Jane Steele-Perkins (second cous); *Career* trumpeter, specialising in Baroque period; with Sadler's Wells Opera/ENO 1966–73, dir London Gabrieli Brass Ensemble 1973–84, with English Chamber Orch 1973–76, asst princ trumpeter Royal Philharmonic Orch

S

1976–80, prof of trumpet Guildhall Sch of Music 1980–90, solo trumpeter with The English Baroque and The King's Consort 1980–, gives about 50 solo recitals and masterclasses a year; made over 800 recordings (incl 80 film soundtracks and 20 solo albums) incl: The English Trumpet, Trumpets Ancient and Modern, Classical Trumpet Concertos; *Books* The Trumpet (2001); *Recreations* classic motorcycles; *Style*— Crispian Steele-Perkins, Esq; ✉ 5 Westfield Gardens, Dorking, Surrey RH4 3DX (e-mail crispiansp@trumpet1.co.uk, website www.crispiansteele-perkins.co.uk)

STEEN, (David) Michael Cochrane Elsworth; OBE (2007); s of Prof Robert Elsworth Steen, MD (d 1981), and Elizabeth Margaret, *née* Cochrane (d 2002); *b* 5 March 1945; *Educ* Eton, RCM, Oriel Coll Oxford (MA); *m* 18 Dec 1971, Rosemary Florence, da of Maj William Bellingham Denis Dobbs; 3 da (Jane b 1973, Lucy b 1975, Rosalie b 1977), 1 s (Peter b 1977); *Career* KPMG (formerly Peat Marwick Mitchell & Co): joined 1968, ptnr 1982–98, head of audit servs 1987–90, head of UK insurance practice 1991–92, bd memb 1992–98, head of risk mgmnt 1996–98; dir: Old Mutual South Africa Trust plc 1998–2007, Molins plc 2000–08; memb Gaming Bd for GB 1999–2005, cmmr Gambling Cmmn 2005–07; tstee: The King's Consort 1998–99, Friends of the V&A 2003–07 (chm 2005–07), Gerald Coke Handel Fndn 2006–15, Anvil Arts 2007–13; memb Cncl Open Univ 2006–14 (treas 2009–14); chm RCM Soc 1998–2005; Liveryman Worshipful Co of Musicians 2013; Hon RCM 2006 (ARCM); *Books* Guide to Directors Transactions (1983), Audits & Auditors: What the Public Thinks (1989), The Lives and Times of the Great Composers (2003), Enchantress of Nations: Pauline Viardot – Soprano Muse and Lover (2007), Great Operas (2012), Short Guides to Great Operas (e-books, 2012), More Great Operas (2016); *Recreations* music (organ playing), bicycling, reading; *Clubs* Carlton, Leander; *Style*— Michael Steen, Esq, OBE; ✉ Nevilles, Mattingley, Hampshire RG27 8JU (☎ 01256 762144, e-mail dmc.steen@gmail.com)

STEER, Sir Alan; *Career* behaviour advsr Dept for Children, Schs and Families 2005–; memb Bd Ofsted 2011–; *Style*— Sir Alan Steer

STEER, Clive Allen; s of Allan Edwin Steer (d 1986), of Guildford, Surrey, and Majorie, *née* Allen (d 1976); *b* 11 May 1938; *Educ* Northmead Sch Guildford, Royal Aircraft Estab Coll Farnborough, Central Sch of Art and Design London; *m* 24 Feb 1962, Janet, da of Arthur F E Evans, OBE; 3 da (Rebecca b 8 Feb 1966, Georgina b 27 Oct 1970, Jacqueline b 23 Sept 1972), 1 s (Jonathan b 21 Sept 1967); *Career* industrial designer; Rediffusion Vision Limited London 1964–69, head of industrial design Philips Electrical (UK) Ltd 1969–79, Philips Singapore 1979–82, assoc Business Design Group 1985–89, dir On the Line Design (conslts) 1989–90, princ Steer Associates 1990–94, accompanying offr FCO 1994–95, business advsr Business Link 1995–2005, freelance conslt 2005–; speaker on design and mktg at Design Cncl courses; awards: Design Cncl award for Philips Design Team Product (consumer and contract goods) 1975, 1984 Oscar for Invention and Gold medal Int Exposition of Invention Geneva; former: memb Judging Panel Design Cncl Consumer and Contract Goods Awards, memb Jury Bursary Awards RSA, chm Product Gp (A1) CSD, chm Membership Bd CSD, memb Fellowship Bd CSD, govr St Martin's Sch of Art, vice-pres and memb Cncl CSD; FRSA 1978, FCSD 1979; *Recreations* gardening, walking; *Clubs* Beaujolais Old Friends Soc (BOFS); *Style*— Clive Steer, Esq; ✉ Beverley, 1 Greyford Close, Leatherhead, Surrey KT22 8DS (☎ 01372 386819)

STEFANOU, Stelio H; OBE (2004), DL (Hertfordshire 2011); s of George Stefanou (d 1979), of Surbiton, Surrey, and Katina, *née* Heracleiou (d 2014); *b* 6 November 1952; *Educ* Hollyfield Sch Surbiton, Tiffin GS Kingston upon Thames, Imperial Coll London (BSc), RCS (ARCS); *m* 1, 3 Sept 1977 (m dis), Rosemarie Ann, da of Sydney Gordon, of London; m 2, 26 April 2008, Susie, da of Clive Omer, of Codicote Herts; *Career* product devpt Johnson Matthey 1974–77, mktg exec Esso UK plc 1977–80, dir John Doyle Construction Ltd 1980–87, gp md and chief exec John Doyle Group plc 1987–99; Accord plc: chief exec 1999–2005, chm 2005–07; CBI: memb Nat Cncl 1994–97, chm Eastern Regnl Cncl 1995–97, memb Pres's Ctee 1996–97, memb Public Servs Strategy Bd 1997–2007, chm Local Govt Panel 1997–2007; non-exec dir East of England Investment Agency 1997–2001, memb East of England Devpt Agency 1999–2001; chm Herts Learning and Skills Cncl 2001–03, tstee The Tomorrow's People Tst Ltd 2008–14; currently: chm The Stefanou Fndn 2008, chm The Stefanou Fndn Cyprus 2013, vice-chm UK-Cyprus Enterprise Cncl 2013, chm WAVE Tst 2015; High Sheriff of Herts 2016; Freeman City of London 1994, Liveryman Worshipful Co of Founders; Hon DLitt Univ of Westminster 2007, Hon LLD Univ of Hertfordshire 2013; *Recreations* tennis, photography, cooking; *Clubs* RAC; *Style*— Stelio H Stefanou, Esq, OBE, DL; ✉ The Stefanou Foundation, Suite 106, 29 Broadwater Road, Welwyn Garden City, Hertfordshire AL73BQ

STEIN, Brian; s of Abraham Stein (d 1994), and Lillian Stein (d 1991); *b* 28 August 1943, Johannesburg, SA; *Educ* King Edward VII Johannesburg, Johannesburg Sch of Art; *Career* vol Israeli Def Force 1964–66, Frugal Sound Folk Music 1967–70, fashion photographer 1969–72, fndr Maxwells Restaurant Gp (incl Café de Paris nightclub) 1972–; vol pilot St John's Ambulance Air Wing 1985–1992; Freeman Guild of Air Pilots and Navigators 1985; *Recreations* polo, aviation, painting, shooting; *Clubs* Guards Polo (memb Bd of Dirs 2000), Royal Co of Berks (RCB) Polo, Stoke Park; *Style*— Brian Stein, Esq; ✉ 22 Henrietta Street, London WC2E 8ND (☎ 020 7379 6132, fax 020 7379 5025, e-mail post@maxwells.co.uk)

STEIN, Christopher Richard (Rick); OBE (2003); s of Eric Stein (d 1965), of Cornwall, and Dorothy Gertrude, *née* Jackson (d 1999); *b* 4 January 1947; *Educ* Uppingham, New Coll Oxford (BA); *m* 1, 21 Sept 1975 (m dis 2007), Jill, da of Jack Newstead; 3 s (Edward b 16 Jan 1979, Jack b 31 Oct 1980, Charles b 14 Sept 1985); m 2, Oct 2011, Sarah Burns, da of Anthony Gale; *Career* chef and restaurateur; estab (with Jill Stein) The Seafood Restaurant Cornwall 1975–; other business interests: St Petroc's Hotel and Bistro, Rick Stein's Café, Stein's Delicatessen, The Padstow Seafood School, Stein's Gift Shop, Stein's Patisserie, Stein's Fisheries, The Cornish Arms St Merryn, Rick Stein's Fish Falmouth; presenter: Rick Stein's Taste of the Sea (BBC 2) 1995 (Television Programme of the Year Glenfiddich Awards 1996), Rick Stein's Fruits of the Sea (BBC 2) 1997, Rick Stein's Seafood Odyssey (BBC 2) 1999, Fresh Food (BBC 2) 1999, The Seafood Lover's Guide 2000, Rick Stein's Food Heroes (BBC 2) 2002, Rick Stein's Food Heroes, Another Helping (BBC 2) 2003 and 2004, Rick Stein's French Odyssey (BBC 2) 2005, Rick Stein's Mediterranean Escapes (BBC 2) 2007, Rick Stein's Far Eastern Odyssey 2009, Rick Stein's Spain (BBC 2) 2011, Rick Stein's India 2013, Rick Stein Venice to Istanbul (BBC 2) 2015; BBC Good Food TV Personality of the Year 1996, winner Glenfiddich Trophy 2001; *Books* English Seafood Cookery (1988, Glenfiddich Food Book of the Year 1989), Rick Stein's Taste of the Sea (1995, André Simon Cookery Book of the Year 1996, BBC Good Food of the Year 1996), Fish (1996), Fruits of the Sea (1997), Rick Stein Cooks Fish (1997), Rick Stein Cooks Seafood (1998), Rick Stein's Seafood Odyssey (1999), Rick Stein's Seafood Lover's Guide (2000), Rick Stein's Seafood (2001, James Beard Award for US edn 2005), Rick Stein's Food Heroes (2002), Rick Stein's Guide to the Food Heroes of Britain (2003), Rick Stein's Food Heroes, Another Helping (2004), Rick Stein's French Odyssey (2005), Rick Stein's Mediterranean Escapes (2007), Rick Stein Coast to Coast (2008), Rick Stein's Far Eastern Odyssey (2009), Rick Stein's Spain (2011), Rick Stein's Indian Odyssey (2013), Under a Mackerel Sky, A Memoir (2013), Fish and Shellfish (2014), Rick Stein Venice to Istanbul (2015); *Recreations* swimming; *Style*— Rick Stein, Esq, OBE; ✉ The Seafood Restaurant, Riverside, Padstow PL28 8BY (☎ 01841 532700, fax 01841 533344, e-mail viviennetaylor@rickstein.com, website www.rickstein.com)

STEIN, Prof John Frederick; s of Eric Stein (d 1965), of Churchill, Oxon, and Dorothy, *née* Jackson (d 1999); *b* 20 February 1941; *Educ* Winchester, New Coll Oxford, St Thomas' Hosp Med Sch London (univ scholar); *m* 1, July 1964, Frances, *née* Hill; 1 s (William b 16 Nov 1965), 1 da (Polly b 8 July 1970); m 2, 14 Jan 1978, Clare, *née* Watson; 2 da (Lucy b 29 April 1979, Kate b 7 June 1981); *Career* med house appts St Thomas' Hosp London and Oxford and Leicester Hosps 1966–68, MRC research fell Radcliffe Infirmary Oxford 1968–70, fell and tutor in med Magdalen Coll Oxford 1970–2008, emeritus prof 2008–; memb: BMA 1966, AUT 1970, Physiological Soc 1975, Assoc of Br Neurologists 1980, Br Dyslexia Assoc 1980, Movement Disorders Soc 1990, US Soc for Neuroscience; FRCP 1995 (MRCP 1966), FRSM 2009, FMedSci 2014; *Books* Introduction to Neurophysiology (1980), Cerebellum and Control of Movement (1985), Sensory Basis of Dyslexia (1995), Visual Aspects of Dyslexia (2012); *Recreations* gardening, squash, music, opera, theatre, art; *Style*— Prof John Stein; ✉ Magdalen College, Oxford OX1 3AU; University Laboratory of Physiology, Parks Road, Oxford OX1 3PT (☎ 01865 272552, e-mail john.stein@dpag.ox.ac.uk)

STEIN, Thea; *Educ* Univ of Oxford; *Career* chief exec: NE Leeds PCT 2002–06, Yorkshire Forward 2006–12, Carers Tst 2012–14, Leeds Community Healthcare Tst 2014–; non-exec dir Great Places 2013–14; govr Leeds Met Univ 2011–13; *Recreations* beekeeping; *Style*— Ms Thea Stein; ✉ e-mail theastein@nhs.net

STEINBERG, Prof Hannah; da of late Dr Michael Steinberg, and Marie, *née* Wein; *Educ* Putney HS, Queen Anne's Sch Caversham, Univ of Reading (Cert Commerce), Denton Secretarial Coll, UCL (BA, PhD, Troughton scholar), Univ of London (postgrad studentship in psychology, pres Students Union); *Career* sec to md Omes Ltd 1943–44; UCL: joined 1950 as hon research asst, asst lectr then lectr in pharmacology, reader in psychopharmacology, prof of psychopharmacology (first in Western Europe and USA) 1970–92, head of Psychopharmacology Gp 1979–92, hon research fell in psychology 1992–; prof emeritus in psychopharmacology Univ of London 1989–; visiting research prof Sch of Social Science Middx Univ 1992–2001; hon consltg clinical psychologist Dept of Psychological Med Royal Free Hosp 1970, visiting prof in psychiatry McMaster Univ Ontario (briefly) 1971; discovered mutual potentiation of amphetamine and barbituate drugs ('purple hearts') 1963 (with E A Sykes); vice-pres: Collegium Internationale Neuro-Psychopharmacologicum 1968–74 (emeritus fell 1995–), Br Assoc for Psychopharmacology 1974–76 (hon memb 1989–); convener Academic Women's Achievement Gp 1979–92, special tstee Middx Hosp 1988–92; memb Editorial Bd: Br Jl of Pharmacology 1965–72, Psychopharmacologia 1965–80, Pharmacopsychoecologia 1987; memb: MRC Working Parties, Experimental Psychological Soc, Br Pharmacological Soc, Euro Behavioural Pharmacology Soc (fndr memb 1986), Euro Coll of Neuro-Psychopharmacology (fndr memb 1986), Br Assoc of Sport and Exercise Sciences (accredited sport and exercise scientist 1992–), European Health Psychology Soc; distinguished affiliate American Psychological Assoc Div of Psychopharmacology 1978, launch of the Br Assoc of Psychopharmacology Hannah Steinberg/Worlfson Fndn Annual Bursary 2011; Br Assoc for Psychopharmacology / AstraZeneca Lifetime Achievement Award 2001, CINP Pioneer Award 2008; Hon DSc Univ of London 2002; memb Br Psychological Soc 1954, CPsychol 1990, FBPsS 1959 (ed Bulletin 1955–62, hon fell 2007); *Publications* Animals and Men (trans and jt ed, 1951), Animal Behaviour and Drug Action (jt ed, 1963), Scientific Basis of Drug Dependence (1968), Psychopharmacology: Sexual Disorders and Drug Abuse (jt ed, 1972), Exercise Addiction (1995), Quality and Quantity in Sport and Exercise Psychology (1996), How Teams Work (1996), Cognitive Enhancement (1997), What Sport Psychologists Do (1998), Sport Psychology in Practice: the Early Stages (2000); author of numerous scientific and semi-popular articles and chapters on psychopharmacology, drug addiction, drug combinations, psychological benefits and risks of physical exercise, exercise addiction, creativity and writer's block, academic women's issues, and also planning law in conservation areas: initiator with E A Sykes of The Steinberg Principle on new devpts in conservation areas (Town and Country Planning Act, Listed Buildings Act, 1990); *Style*— Prof Hannah Steinberg; ✉ c/o Pharmacology Department, University College London, London WC1E 6BT (☎ 020 7267 4783, fax 020 7267 4780)

STEINBY, Prof Eva Margareta; da of Kaarlo Erkki Wilén and Doris Margareta Steinby; *b* 21 November 1938; *Educ* Univ of Helsinki (Hum Kand, Fil Kand, Fil Lic, Fil Dr), Univ of Oxford (MA); *Career* Institutum Romanum Finlandiae Rome: asst 1973–77, dir 1979–82 and 1992–94; docent in history Univ of Helsinki 1977–, sr research fell Finnish Acad Helsinki 1985–92, prof of archaeology of the Roman Empire and fell All Souls Coll Oxford 1994–; visiting fell All Souls Coll Oxford 1990–91; fell: Suomen Historiallinen Seura 1978, Societas Scientiarum Fennica 1983, Pontificia Accademia Romana di Archeologia 1993–95 (corresponding fell 1982); corresponding fell Deutsches Archäologisches Institut 1984, foreign hon fell Archaeological Inst of America, fell Academia Scientiarum Fennica 2000 Medaglia d'Oro per Benemeriti Culturali (Italy) 1983, Medaglia Daria Borghese 2002, prize of Finnish Cultural Fndn 2003; FSA 1997; Offr 1st class Order of White Rose (Finland) 1991; *Books* La cronologia delle figlinae doliari urbane (1976), Lateres signati Ostienses (vols I-II, 1977–78), Indici complementari ai bolli doliari urbani (CIL, XV, 1, 1987), Lacus Iurturnae I (ed, 1989), Lexicon Topographicum Urbis Romae (6 vols, 1993–2000), Ianiculum – Gianicolo (ed, 1997), La necropoli della Via Triumphalis Roma (2003); also author of numerous articles in Italian, German and Finnish learned jls; *Style*— Prof Eva Margareta Steinby, FSA

STEINER, Tim; OBE (2016); *Educ* Univ of Manchester; *Career* Goldman Sachs until 2000, co-fndr and ceo Ocado 2000–; *Style*— Mr Tim Steiner, OBE; ✉ Ocado, Titan Court, 3 Bishop Square, Hatfield Business Park, Hatfield AL10 9NE

STEINFELD, Alan Geoffrey; QC (1987); s of Henry C Steinfeld (d 1967), of London, and Deborah, *née* Brickman; *b* 13 July 1946; *Educ* City of London Sch, Downing Coll Cambridge (BA, LLB); *m* 19 Feb 1976, Josephine Nicole, da of Eugene Gros, of London; 2 s (Martin b 28 Jan 1980, Sebastian b 1 Nov 1981); *Career* called to the Bar Lincoln's Inn 1968 (bencher 1996), barr specialising in commercial Chancery law, dep judge of the High Court (Chancery and Queen's Bench Divs) 1994–; memb: Bar Cncl 1997, Assoc of Contentious Tst and Probate Specialists, Chancery Bar Assoc, Commercial Bar Assoc, Hong Kong Bar Assoc, Insolvency Lawyers Assoc; *Publications* Palmers Company Law Manual (conslt ed), Professional Negligence and Liability (contrib); *Recreations* lawn tennis, skiing, sailing, opera, cinema, lying in Turkish baths; *Clubs* RAC; *Style*— Alan Steinfeld, Esq, QC; ✉ 21 Wadham Gardens, London NW3 3DN (☎ 020 7483 3450); Villa Raphael, Cap d'Antibes, France; 24 Old Buildings, Lincoln's Inn, London WC2A 3UJ (☎ 020 7404 0946, fax 020 7405 1360, e-mail alan.steinfeld@xxiv.co.uk)

STEINFELD, Michael Robert; *b* 3 December 1943; *Educ* William Ellis Sch London, Pembroke Coll Oxford (BA); *m* 28 May 1980, Elizabeth Ann, *née* Watson; 2 da (Rebecca Hannah b 25 Feb 1981, Jemimah Francine b 15 Oct 1983), 1 s (Jonathon Henry b 29 Oct 1992); *Career* Titmuss Sainer & Webb (now Dechert): articled clerk 1968–70, asst slr 1970–72, made ptnr; currently sr ptnr Steinfeld Slrs; memb Law Soc; *Recreations* sport, food, cinema, newspapers, music, France; *Style*— Michael Steinfeld, Esq

STELLA-SAWICKI, Dr Marek Andrzej; MBE (2012); s of Jan Stella-Sawicki (offr 5 Lancers (Polish Cavalry) 1939 and lawyer, d 1984), of Poland, and Stanislawa, *née* Lissowska (offr AK (Home Army) Battle for Warsaw (Warsaw Rising) 1944, d 2002); *b* 21 February 1948; *Educ* Henry Jordan Sch, Tech Univ Cracow (MSc), KCL (PhD), The Buckingham Univ; *m* 27 July 1974, Teresa Francesca, da of Capt Antoni Witczak (d 1973), and Helena, *née* Skrzyszowska (d 2005); 2 da (Dominika Helena b 1976, Joanna Jadwiga b 1978); *Career* sr systems engr United Biscuits (McVities) Ltd 1975–78, sr projects engr Metal Box plc 1978–82, projects engrg mangr Computer Field Maintenance Ltd 1982–85, gen mangr DPCE Computer Servs plc 1985–86, dir engrg ops MBS plc 1986–88, dir Computacenter Ltd 1988–95, strategic mktg and tech dir Computeraid Services Ltd 1995–2001, UK tech dir and chief tech offr Pink Roccade 2001–04, chief technol offr Services Architecture Global Services Delivery Logica plc 2004–13, ptnr MSS Consulting 2013–; developer of corp and global strategy WASP and KNOWLEDGEfirst; launched e-Services Portal Platform V&A 2000; conslt Cover Pubns 1976–79, ed Video World 1979–81, publishing dir and editorial dir Video Press 1981–85; visiting prof Dept of Computer Science UCL 2007–; chm Polish Armed Forces War Memorial Project Nat Museum Arboretum Staffs 2008–09 (memb Ctee Br-Polish Memorial Appeal 2008–09), chm Fryderyk Chopin Meml Ctee Southbank Centre 2010–11, chm Polish Heritage Soc UK 2010, memb Polish Landowners Assoc; sponsorship: W Middx Lawn Tennis Club, Video Press Falklands Appeal; memb Cncl: Engrg Inst, AFSM (USA); life memb Ognisko Polskie (memb Ctee 2012), hon treas Assoc Polonaise des Chevaliers de Malte UK (chm 2012); memb Stewards Enclosure Henley Royal Regatta; Freeman City of London 2011; MCIM, FIET, CEng, RUSI; KM 2008, Knight of Grace and Devotion SMOM 2008, Polish Army Gold Medal 2010, Officer's Cross Polonia Restituta 2010, SMOM Officer's Cross Pro Merito Melitensi 2011, Pro Memoria Medal Office of Ex-Combatants and Victims of Oppression 2011, SPK Cross of Polish Ex-Combatants Assoc of Polish Ex-Combatants in London 2011, Silver Cross Gloria Artis Polish Min of Culture 2011, UK Airborne Forces Assoc Medal Utrinque Paratus-Ad Unum Omnes 2013; *Books* Investigation into Computer Modelling Simulation and Control of the Stirling Engine (1978), Video A-Z (10 vols, 1981–83), A-Z of Personal Computers (10 vols, 1983–86), Which Appliance (2 edns, 1984–86), Business Process Re-Engineering (6 vols, 1996–97), First to Fight (2009, DVD 2010, MP3 audio book 2010), Rozwiane Marzenia-Moje Wspomnienia 1831–1910 (Dr Jan Stella-Sawicki, 2011), A Debt of Dishonour (documentary film, 2013), Mass in F (AD 1867) by Prince Joseph Poniatowski, British Premiere at Westminster Cathedral Hall June 2015 (DVD and CD, 2015); *Recreations* skiing, shooting, bridge, target shooting (Bisley), figurative sculptures and monuments; *Clubs* Hurlingham, Ognisko Polskie, Henley Royal Regatta Stewards Enclosure, Nat Rifle Assoc, Classic Rally Assoc; *Style*— Dr Marek Stella-Sawicki, MBE, KM; ✉ e-mail drmarksawicki@hotmail.com

STEMBRIDGE, Andrew William; s of David William Stembridge, of Melrose, Roxburghshire, and Edith Jean, *née* Banks; *b* 27 April 1971, Ratho, Midlothian; *Educ* Edinburgh Acad, Selkirk HS, Earlston HS, Univ of Strathclyde (BA), Cornell Univ; *m* 17 July 1999, Alison Charlotte; 1 s (Harry Logan b 7 March 2004), 1 da (Charlotte Emma b 1 May 2006); *Career* front of house mangr One Devonshire Gardens Glasgow 1994, food and beverage mangr Malmaison Glasgow and Edinburgh 1995, asst gen mangr Blantyre Lenox MA 1995, ops mangr Chewton Glen 1997, gen mangr Scotsman Hotel Edinburgh 2001, md Chewton Glen 2003–; FHCIMA 2005; Master Innholder 2005; *Style*— Andrew Stembridge, Esq; ✉ Chewton Glen, Christchurch Road, New Milton, Hampshire BH25 6QS (☎ 01425 275341, fax 01425 272310, e-mail astembridge@chewtonglen.com)

STEMMER, Philip; s of Emanuel Stemmer, of London, and Regina Stemmer; *b* 12 December 1949; *Educ* Manchester Jewish GS, Turner Dental Sch Manchester (BDS, represented Univ of Manchester soccer team); *m* 22 Dec 1976, Elissa, da of Myer Freedman; 4 da (Shiri Debra b 12 Aug 1979, Daniella Civia b 15 Dec 1981, Natalie Ruth b 30 Nov 1985, Anna Sophie Rose b 14 Dec 1994), 1 s (Raphael Steven b 2 Dec 1993); *Career* dental surgn; gen practice (with Phillip Wander) Manchester 1974–76, opened new practice Manchester 1976–84, opened branch practice Droylsden 1982–84, practised in Israel 1984–86 (affiliated to Periodontal Dept Tel Aviv Dental Sch), in private practice Harley St then Devonshire Place 1986–, owner of practice North Finchley 1987–89, opened UK's first fresh breath centre to combat oral malodour 1995; memb: BDA, Alpha Omega, Dental Post Grad Soc of Manchester, Insight Gp, Int Soc of Breath Odor Res (ISBOR); rep Lancs Chess Team 1964; *Recreations* swimming, music (opera, cantorial, good modern), chess; *Style*— Philip Stemmer, Esq; ✉ 2 Devonshire Place, London W1G 6HJ (☎ 020 7935 7511/0407, mobile 07977 990490)

STENNING, Christopher John William (Kit); s of Col Philip Dives Stenning, of Sunnyside, Elie, Fife, and Cynthia Margaret, *née* Rycroft; *b* 16 October 1950; *Educ* Marlborough; *m* 1, 19 Sept 1981, Ruth Marian, da of late George Thomas Chenery Draper; 1 da (Rachel b 1983), 1 s (Jonathan b 1985); m 2, 21 April 2001, Christine Louise, da of John Walter Baxter; *Career* slr 1970–82, slr to Prudential Corp 1982–88, dir of corp fin David Garrick 1988–90, proprietor Kit Stenning Assocs 1990–91, ptnr Messrs Kennedys Slrs 1991–96; conslt McFadden 1996–; Freeman: City of London 1971, Worshipful Co of Haberdashers 1971; *Books* The Takeover Guide (1988); *Recreations* sport; *Clubs* Hurlingham; *Style*— Kit Stenning, Esq

STENSON, Jules Angus; s of Roger Stenson, and Janet, *née* McCall; *b* 24 April 1966, Sherborne, Dorset; *Educ* Tudor Grange Sch Solihull, Solihull Sixth Form Coll, Univ of Sheffield (BA); *Partner* Sarah Booth; *Career* trainee then sr reporter Swindon Evening Advertiser 1989–92, local govt reporter then chief reporter Liverpool Echo 1992–94, showbusiness reporter Sunday People 1994–96, asst ed (features) News of the World 1996–2011; *Books* Big Secrets of Big Brother (with Lewis Panther, 2001); *Recreations* skiing, poker; *Style*— Jules Stenson, Esq

STEPHEN, Dr (George) Martin; s of Sir Andrew Stephen, KB (d 1980), of Sheffield, and Frances, *née* Barker (d 1999); *b* 18 July 1949; *Educ* Uppingham, Univ of Leeds (BA), Univ of Sheffield (DipEd, DPhil, PhD); *m* 21 Aug 1971, Jennifer Elaine, da of George Fisher, of Polloch, Invernesshire; 3 s (Neill b 22 July 1976, Simon b 31 Aug 1978, Henry b 20 March 1981); *Career* various posts in remand homes 1966–71, teacher of English Uppingham Sch 1971–72, housemaster and teacher of English Haileybury Coll and ISC 1972–83, second master Sedbergh Sch 1983–87, headmaster The Perse Sch 1987–94, high master The Manchester Grammar Sch 1994–2004, high master St Paul's Sch 2004–; assoc memb of the room Gonville & Caius Coll Cambridge 1988–94; HMC: memb 1987–, chm Community Serv Ctee 1992–95, memb HMC/GSA Univ Working Pty 1994–2000, chm 2004–; memb: The Naval Review 1991–2004, CSU Educn Advsr Ctee, Cncl The Project Tst, Bd Royal Exchange Theatre 1999–2004, Bd LAMDA 2004–; govr: Withington Sch Manchester 1994–2002, Pownall Hall Sch Wilmslow 1994–2004, Ducie HS, The Hall Sch Hampstead, Orley Farm Harrow, Durston House Ealing; memb Ct Univ of Salford 2001–04; visiting lectr Dept of English and American Studies Univ of Manchester 2001–04; Hon Dr in Educn De Montfort Univ 1997; FRSA 1996; *Books* An Introductory Guide to English Literature (1982), Studying Shakespeare (1982), British Warship Designs Since 1906 (1984), English Literature (1986, 3 edn 1999), Sea Battles in Close Up (1987, 2 edn 1996), Never Such Innocence (1988, 3 edn 1993), The Fighting Admirals (1990), The Best of Saki (1993, 2 edn 1996), The Price of Pity (1996), The Desperate Remedy (2002), The Conscience of the King (2003), The Galleon's Grave (2004), The Rebel Heart (2006), The Diary of a Stroke (2006); *Recreations* sailing, scuba diving, rough shooting, writing, theatre; *Clubs* Athenaeum, East India Devonshire Sports & Public Sch (hon memb); *Style*— Dr Martin Stephen; ✉ St Paul's School, Lonsdale Road, Barnes, London SW13 9JT

STEPHEN, Michael; s of late Harry L Stephen; *b* 25 September 1942; *Educ* King Henry VIII Sch Coventry, Stanford Univ, Harvard Univ; *m* 27 May 1989, Virginia Mary, da of late Charles de Trensé; *Career* admitted slr 1964, called to the Bar Inner Temple 1966; Lt The Life Gds 1966–70; Harkness Fellowship USA (LLM Stanford) 1970–72, research fell Harvard 1972, asst legal advsr to UK Ambassador to UN 1972, practising barr 1972–92, MP (Cons) Shoreham 1992–97 (Parly candidate (Cons) Doncaster N 1983), PPS at Miny of Agric 1996–97, int lawyer 1997–2007, gp dep chm Symphony Environmental Technols plc 2007–; author: Section 36 Criminal Justice Act 1988 (appeals against lenient sentences), Bail (Amendment) Act 1993 (appeals against grant of bail); memb Trade and Industry and Environment Select Ctees House of Commons 1992–97, vice-chm Cons Parly Home Affairs and Legal Ctees; chm Constitutional Ctee Soc of Cons Lawyers 1997–2000; chm Severnside Airport Consortium 2000–06; Industry and Parliament Tst Fellowship (British Rail) 1993–94; co cnclr Dunmow Div Essex 1985–91, memb Nat Exec Assoc of CCs 1989–91; memb Chatham House 1984–; author of pamphlets and articles on Home Office and legal affrs, and foreign affrs; Evelyn Wrench meml lectr on Anglo-American rels USA; *Style*— Michael Stephen, Esq; ✉ e-mail kkrkyz@gmail.com

STEPHEN, Baron (Life Peer UK 2011), of Lower Deeside in the City of Aberdeen; Nicol Ross Stephen; s of R A Nicol Stephen, and Sheila G Stephen; *b* 23 March 1960, Aberdeen; *Educ* Robert Gordon's Coll Aberdeen, Univ of Aberdeen (LLB), Univ of Edinburgh (DipLP); *Partner* Caris Doig; 2 s, 2 da; *Career* slr, sr corp mangr, project mangr, co dir; cnclr Grampian Regnl Cncl 1982–91, MP (Lib Dem) Kincardine and Deeside 1991–92, MSP (Lib Dem) Aberdeen South 1999–2011, dep min of enterprise and lifelong learning 1999–2000, dep min for educn and young people 2000–03, min for tport 2003–05, dep first min and min for enterprise and lifelong learning 2005–07, ldr Scot Lib Dems 2005–08; *Recreations* golf, swimming; *Style*— The Lord Stephen; ✉ House of Lords, London SW1A 0PW (e-mail stephenn@parliament.uk)

STEPHENS, Barbara Marion; OBE (2002); da of late Sydney Davis Webb, and Edna Marion, *née* Finch; *b* 25 August 1951; *Educ* Colchester Co HS, Mid-Essex Tech Coll (HNC Engineering), NE London Poly (Dip Mgmnt Studies), City Univ (MBA); *m* 28 March 1970, Trevor James Stephens; *Career* mech technician apprentice Marconi Co 1969–73, various tech and managerial posts Marconi Communication Systems Ltd 1973–88, asst industry advsr then industry advsr NEDO 1988–92; W Cumbria Devpt Agency: dir of ops 1993–95, chief exec 1995–98; chief exec Local Govt Cmmn for England 1998–2002, head of public sector practice KMC International 2002–07, head of HE practice Carbon Search 2007–08, co sec and dir Carbon NFP Ltd 2008–14; regnl dir Open Univ London 2009–11, dir Student Casework Open Univ 2014–16; memb Cncl (now Senate) Engrg Cncl 1990–96; dir and tstee: Assoc of MBAs 2001–06 (memb Advsy Cncl 1998–2001), Educnl Broadcasting Services Tst 2002–08; external tstee Univ of Cumbria Students' Union 2015–, govr Central Acad Carlisle 2015–; chair NHSU 2003–05; memb: HEFCE 1995–2001, Advsy Forum for the Devpt of RN Personnel 1995–2002 (chm 2001–02), Bd New Opportunities Fund 2001–04, Bd Univ of Cumbria 2007–12; non-exec dir Cumbria Ambulance Service NHS Tst 1996–98; lay memb Professional Conduct and Complaints Ctee Gen Cncl of the Bar 2000–05 (lay vice-chair Standards Bd 2006–09), memb Bd Equality Challenge Unit 2008–15; Hon DUniv Bradford 2005, hon fell Univ of Cumbria 2015; IEng 1976, AMIPE 1976, MIEIE 1992, FIMgt 1994 (MBIM 1978), FRSA 1992; *Style*— Ms Barbara Stephens, OBE; ✉ Edgefield, 120A Stainburn Road, Workington, Cumbria CA14 1ST (☎ 01900 871095, e-mail contact@crook-hall.com)

STEPHENS, Huw; s of Prof Meic Stephens, *qv*, and Ruth Wynn Stephens; *b* 1981, Cardiff; *Career* radio presenter; presenter C2 (BBC Radio Cymru), presenter weekend afternoon 1–4pm slot and Thursday midnight till 2am slot BBC Radio 1 2011– (joined 1997 as youngest ever presenter); fndr SWN festival Cardiff 2007–; *Style*— Huw Stephens, Esq; ✉ BBC Radio 1, Clipstone Street, London W1N 4DJ

STEPHENS, John Lindsay; s of Rev Grosvenor Stephens (d 1992), and Olive, *née* Voysey-Martin (d 1987); *b* 23 July 1951; *Educ* Christ's Hosp, Coventry Univ (BA); *m* 30 Aug 1975, Nicola Elizabeth (Nikki), da of Neville Brouard, of St Saviour, Guernsey, CI; 1 s (David b 1982), 1 da (Joanna b 1980); *Career* admitted slr 1977; former ptnr Clarke Willmott & Clarke; *Recreations* family, music, food and wine, photography, working out; *Clubs* City of London, King George's Sports and Social; *Style*— John Stephens, Esq

STEPHENS, Malcolm George; CB (1991); s of late Frank Ernest Stephens, and Annie Mary Janet, *née* Macqueen; *b* 14 July 1937, London; *Educ* St Michael and All Angels and Shooters Hill GS, St John's Coll Oxford (Casberd scholar, MA); *m* 5 Dec 1975, Lynette Marie, da of late John Patrick Caffery; *Career* army service RAOC 1956–58; Dip Serv: joined 1953, Ghana 1959–62, Kenya 1963–65, Exports Credits Guarantee Dept 1965–82, princ 1970, seconded to Civil Service Staff Coll as dir of economics and social admin course 1971–72, asst sec 1974, estab offr 1977, under sec 1978, head project gp 1978–79, princ fin offr 1979–82; int fin dir Barclays Bank International 1982, export fin dir and dir Barclays Export Servs with Barclays Bank 1982–87, chief exec Export Credits Guarantee Dept (ECGD) 1987–92, chief exec London C of C and Industry 1992–93, sec gen Int Union of Credit and Investment Insurers (Berne Union) 1992–98 (pres 1989–92), md and dep chm Commonwealth Investment Guarantee Agency (CIGA) Ltd 1998–99, gp chm International Financial Consulting 1998–, first exec dir Int Inst for Practitioners in Credit Insurance and Surety 2000–01, chm Del Credere Insurance Services Ltd until 2001, chm IFC Training 2001–07; dir: European Capital 1992–2000, Berry Palmer & Lyle 1994–2001, Maj Projects Assoc 1996–99, Euler Int 1998–2000; advsr CDR International 1998–2000; exec vice-pres SGA International Florida 1998–2000; visiting scholar IMF 1998–99; conslt: World Bank 1997–98 and 1999, EU PHARE Prog 1997, 1998 and 1999, EU Cmmn 1998, 1999, 2000 and 2011, OECD (Russia) 2000 and 2001; conslt to govts of: Chile 1999, Bangladesh 1999, Sri Lanka 2000, Iran 2000–01, South Africa 2000–01, Australia 2000–03 and 2007–08, New Zealand 2001, Turkey 2001, Canada 2001, 2003, 2007–08 and 2008–09, Fiji 2003; special advsr Sinosure (Chinese export credit agency) 2000–; memb: Overseas Projects Bd 1985–87, British Overseas Trade Bd 1987–92, Zurich Emerging Markets Advsy Cncl 1997–2015, Inst of Credit Mgmnt; memb Cook Soc 2001–, chm Australian Fine and Decorative Soc 2006–08, nat sec Assoc of Australian Decorative and Fine Arts Socs 2012–14 (dep chm 2010–11); treas: Australia Britain Soc Southern Highlands 2008–14 (chm 2014), Order of Australia Assoc Southern Highlands 2004–; pres Southern Highlands Opera Appreciation Gp (SHOAG) 2013–; FIEx, FIB; *Publications* The Changing Role of Expore Credit Agencies (1999); *Recreations* gardening, fitness centre, reading, tapestry, watching cricket and football (Charlton Athletic); *Clubs* Union, Univ and Schs; *Style*— Malcolm Stephens, Esq, CB; ✉ 38 Argyle Street, Bong Bong Hill, Moss Vale, NSW 2577, Australia (e-mail malcolmstephens@hotmail.com)

STEPHENS, Mark Howard; CBE (2011); s of Howard Stephens, and Eve, *née* Banks; *b* 7 April 1957, Old Windsor, Berks; *Educ* St Paul's Secdy Modern, Cambridge Manor Acad for Dramatic Arts, Strodes GS, NE London Poly (BA), Coll of Law Lancaster Gate; *m* 1982, Donna Michelle Coote; 3 da (Eleanor Frances Jane, Olivia Catherine Ann, Sheridan Georgia Rose); *Career* admitted slr 1982; co-fndr Artlaw (legal dir 1982–84); HowardKennedyFSI LLP (subsequently Howard Kennedy LLP): fndr and sr ptnr 1983–99, sr memb 1999–; mediator ADR Chambers 2007–14; also broadcaster, writer and lectr; founding tstee Slrs' Pro Bono Gp Law Works 1997–2004; chair: Mgmnt Ctee Prog in Comparative Media Law & Policy Centre for Socio-Legal Studies Univ of Oxford 1997–, Slrs' Law Festival 1998–2001; memb Exec Ctee and dir Cwlth Lawyers Assoc 2007–13 (immediate past pres), memb Human Rights Cncl Int Bar Assoc 2009–, tstee Bd Int Law Book Tst; founding chair Policy Bd Internet Watch Fndn 1996–99 (vice-chair 1999–2003); memb: Br Copyright Cncl 1986–98, Bd ICSTIS (now Phone Pay Plus) 1990–96, FCO Free Expression Advsy Bd 2002–, Cncl Copyright Licensing Agency, Bd Internews 2015–; ind dir Ind Schs Inspectorate 2011–; chair Design Artists' Copyright Soc 2012–; tstee: Contemporary Art Soc 1992–2009 (hon slr 2002–09, chair 2009–14), Index on Censorship 2002–12 (hon slr 2012–), Bianca Jagger Human Rights Fndn 2007– (chair 2015–); chair Greenwich & Docklands Int Festivals 1999–2004, ind chair Global Network Initiative Washington DC 2014–; govr Wanstead C of E Primary Sch 1996–2002, govr Rose

S

Bruford Coll of Theatre & Performance 2002–05, chair Univ of E London 2009–, ExCo patron Int Alert Bd Ind Schs Inspectorate 2011; Freeman City of London, Liveryman Stationers Co, Freeman Slrs Co; LLD (hc) Univ of E London 2001; *Publications* Miscarriages of Justice – a review of justice in error (contrib, 1999), International Libel & Privacy Handbook (contrib, 2005 and 2013), La Presunción de Inocenicia Y Los Juicios Paralelos (contrib, 2013), Media Law & Ethics in the 21st Century – protecting free expression and curbing abuses (contrib, 2014), This is Not a Book About Gavin Turk (contrib, 2014); *Recreations* bees, theatre; *Clubs* Chelsea FC, Aston Martin Owners; *Style—* Mark Stephens, Esq, CBE; ✉ Howard Kennedy LLP, No 1 London Bridge, London SE1 9BG (☎ 020 7344 7650 or 020 7323 4000, fax 020 7344 5600, e-mail mark.stephens@hkfsi.com)

STEPHENS, Prof Meic; s of Herbert Arthur Lloyd Stephens (d 1984), and Alma, *née* Symes (d 1994); *b* 23 July 1938; *Educ* Pontypridd Boys' GS, UCW Aberystwyth (BA), Univ of Rennes (DipFrench), UCNW Bangor (DipEd), Univ of Wales (DLitt); *m* 14 Aug 1965, Ruth Wynn, da of Rev John Ellis Meredith (d 1981); 3 da (Lowri b 1966, Heledd b 1968, Brengain b 1969), 1 s (Huw, *qv*, b 1981); *Career* teacher of French Ebbw Vale GS 1962–66, ed Poetry Wales 1965–73, journalist Western Mail Cardiff 1966–67, lit dir Welsh Arts Cncl 1967–90; ed, journalist, literary conslt 1990–, columnist Western Mail 1991–; dir Combrógos Literary Agency; visiting prof of English Brigham Young Univ UT 1991; lectr: Univ of Glamorgan 1994–2001, Centre for Journalism Studies Univ of Cardiff 1998–99; prof of Welsh writing in English Univ of Glamorgan 2001–06 (emeritus 2006–); hon fell St David's UC Lampeter 1986–, life memb the Welsh Acad 1990 (fell 1999); sec Rhys Davies Tst 1990–; hon memb (White Robe) Gorsedd of Bards 1976; Hon MA Univ of Wales 2000; FLSW 2016; *Books* Triad (1963), The Lilting House (co-ed, 1969), Writers of Wales (co-ed, 110 vols, 1970–), Artists in Wales (ed, 3 vols, 1971/73/77), The Welsh Language Today (ed, 1973), Exiles All (1973), A Reader's Guide to Wales (ed, 1973), Linguistic Minorities in Western Europe (1976), Green Horse (co-ed, 1978), The Arts in Wales 1950–75 (ed, 1979), The Curate of Clyro (ed, 1983), The Oxford Companion to the Literature of Wales (ed, 1986), A Cardiff Anthology (ed, 1987), The White Stone (trans, 1987), A Book of Wales (ed, 1988), A Dictionary of Literary Quotations (1989), The Gregynog Poets (ed, 12 vols 1989–90), The Bright Field (ed, 1991), The Oxford Illustrated Literary Guide to Great Britain and Ireland (ed, 1992), A Most Peculiar People (ed, 1992), Changing Wales (ed, 12 vols 1992–97), A Rhondda Anthology (ed, 1993), Take Wales: Cinema in Wales (1993), Literature in 20th Century Wales: a Select Bibliography (1995), The Collected Poems of Harri Webb (ed, 1995), For the Sake of Wales (trans, 1996), The Basques (trans, 1996), The Collected Poems of Glyn Jones (ed, 1996), The Collected Stories of Rhys Davies (ed, 3 vols, 1996–98), Ponies, Twynyrodyn (1997), No Half-Way House: Selected Political Journalism of Harri Webb (ed, 1997), Cydymaith i Lenyddiaeth Cymru (ed, 1997), How Green Was My Valley (ed, 1997), Monica (trans, 1997), A Little Book of Welsh Quotations (1997), The New Companion to the Literature of Wales (ed, 1998), A Militant Muse: Selected Literary Journalism of Harri Webb (ed, 1998), A Little Book of Welsh Sayings (1998), Illuminations: An Anthology of Welsh Short Prose (trans, 1998), A White Afternoon (trans, 1998), Shadow of the Sickle (trans, 1998), Return to Lleifior (trans, 1999), Welsh Names for Your Children (1999), Wales in Quotation (1999), The Literary Pilgrim in Wales (2000), Looking Up England's Arsehole: the Patriotic Poems and Boozy Ballads of Harri Webb (ed, 2000), Rhys Davies: Decoding the Hare (ed, 2001), A History of the Parish of Llanegryn (trans, 2002), The Corgi Series (ed, 24 vols, 2003–05), A Community and its University: Glamorgan 1913:2003 (co-ed, 2003), A Semester in Zion (2003), The Plum Tree (trans, 2004), Poetry 1900–2000 (ed, 2007), The Complete Poems of Leslie Norris (ed, 2008), Necrologies: Obituaries of eminent Welsh people (2008), Eagle in the Maze (co-ed, 2008), Yeah, Dai Dando: A Novel (2008), A Bard for Highgrove: a Likely Story (2010), Cofnodion: Hunangofiant (2012), Welsh Lives: Gone but not Forgotten (2012), Rhys Davies: a Writer's Life (2013), Wilia, Cerddi 2003–13 (2014), My Shoulder to the Wheel (2015); *Recreations* the world of Wales; *Style—* Prof Meic Stephens; ✉ 10 Heol Don, Whitchurch, Cardiff CF14 2AU (☎ 029 20 623359)

STEPHENS, Nicholas Edward Egerton; DL (Shropshire 2000); s of Brian Alexis Fenwick Stephens, and Cynthia Mary Denise, *née* Prideaux-Brune; *b* 12 May 1946; *Educ* Charterhouse; *m* 10 Sept 1970, Avril Rose, da of Morgan Henry Birch Reynardson; 2 da (Samantha Jane (Mrs Adrian Boyes) b 12 June 1975, Clare Diana (Mrs Henry Cecil) b 17 June 1978); *Career* articled clerk R H March Son & Co (chartered accountants) 1965–69, Ionian Bank 1969–72, ptnr James Capel & Co 1978–80 (joined 1972), ptnr then dir (on incorporation) Albert E Sharp & Co (now Arbuthnot) 1980–2006; Parly candidate (Cons) Walsall North Gen Election 1983; High Sheriff of Shropshire 1995–96; chm st John Cncl Salop 2001–08, tstee Hospital Mgmnt Tst 2004–, treas Nat Cncl for the Conservation of Plants and Gardens 2008–13; Co Cmmr of Scouts 1983–88, fell Woodard Corp 1987–2006 (vice-provost Midlands Div 1998–2000), custos Ellesmere Coll 1992–99; patron of two livings; *Recreations* shooting, fishing, golf, opera, sailing; *Clubs* Boodle's, Pratt's, Turf; *Style—* Nicholas Stephens, Esq, DL; ✉ Grafton Lodge, Montford Bridge, Shrewsbury SY4 1HE (☎ 01743 850262)

STEPHENS, Philip Francis Christopher; s of Haydn Stephens, of London, and Teresa, *née* Martin; *b* 2 June 1953; *Educ* Wimbledon Coll, Worcester Coll Oxford (BA); *Children* 1 da (Jessica Rose b 24 Nov 1989), 1 s (Benedict Haydn b 24 March 1993); *Career* asst ed Europa Publications 1974–76, ed Commerce International 1976–79, corr Reuters London and Brussels 1979–83; Financial Times: econs corr 1983–88, political ed 1988–94, assoc ed and political commentator 1995–99, ed UK Edition 1999–2003, chief political commentator 2003–; govr Ditchley Fndn 2006– (memb Cncl 2008–, vice-chair Cncl 2013–); Fulbright fell; commended Br Press Awards 1991, David Watt Award for Outstanding Political Journalism 2002, Political Journalist of the Year Political Studies Assoc 2004, Political Journalist of the Year Br Press Award 2008; *Books* Politics and the Pound: The Conservatives' Struggle with Sterling (1996), Tony Blair, The Price of Leadership (2004); *Style—* Philip Stephens, Esq

STEPHENS, Simon William; s of Graham Stephens (d 2001), of Stockport, and Carole Stephens; *b* 6 February 1971; *Educ* Stockport Sch, Univ of York (BA), Inst of Educn Univ of London (PGCE); *m* Polly Heath; 2 s (Oscar Dylan b 6 Oct 1998, Stanley Samuel b 6 Feb 2002), 1 da (Scarlett Georgie Grace b 30 Jan 2007); *Career* writer; schoolteacher Eastbrook Sch Dagenham 1998–2000; Royal Court Theatre: resident dramatist 2000, writers' tutor Young Writers' Prog 2001–05; Pearson attached playwright Royal Exchange Theatre Manchester 2000, resident dramatist Nat Theatre 2006, assoc artist Lyric Hammersmith 2009–; musician and fndr memb The Country Teasers 1993– (tours of America and Europe, several single and album releases); *Plays* Bring Me Sunshine (Assembly Rooms Edinburgh, Riverside Studios London) 1997, Bring Me Sunshine (Royal Exchange) 2000, Bluebird (Royal Court Young Writers Festival) 1998, Herons (Royal Court) 2001 and (Stuttgart Staatstheater) 2003 (nomination Most Promising Playwright Olivier Awards 2001), Five Letters Home to Elizabeth (radio play, BBC Radio 4) 2001, Port (Royal Exchange) 2002 and (Graz Staatstheater) 2004 (Pearson Award for Best New Play), One Minute (Sheffield Crucible/Actors Touring Co) 2003 and (Stuttgart Staatstheater) 2004, Christmas (Ape Theatre Co/Bush Theatre) 2003–04, Country Music (Actors Touring Co/Royal Court Theatre) 2004 and (Essen Staatstheater) 2005, On the Shore of the Wide World (Royal Exchange/RNT) 2005 (Olivier Award for Best Play 2006), Motortown (Royal Court Theatre and Schauspielhaus Zurich) 2006 (Theater Heute Overseas Playwright of 2006), Pornography (Deutsche Schauspielhaus Hamburg) 2007 and (Traverse Theatre Edinburgh) 2008, Harper Regan (RNT, Deutsche Schauspielhaus Hamburg and Salzberg Festival) 2008, Punk Rock (Lyric Hammersmith) 2009, Sea Wall (Bush Theatre, Traverse) 2009, Marine Parade (Brighton Festival) 2010, A Thousand Stars Explode in the Sky (with Robert Holman and David Eldridge, Lyric Hammersmith) 2010, The Trial of Ubu (Toneelgroep Amsterdam/Essen Schauspielhaus and Hampstead Theatre) 2010, Wastwater (Royal Court) 2011 (Theater Heute Best Foreign Playwright), I Am The Wind (version of play by Jon Fosse, Young Vic and touring) 2011, Three Kingdoms (No99 Tallinn, Kammerspiel Munich and Lyric Hammersmith) 2011–12 (Theater Heute Best Foreign Playwright), A Doll's House (version of play by Henrik Ibsen) 2012, The Curious Incident of the Dog in the Nighttime (adaptation of novel by Mark Haddon, NT) 2012 (Best Play Olivier Award, Best Play What's On Stage Award, Best Theatre South Bank Award), Morning (Lyric Hammersmith and Traverse Theatre) 2012, London (Paines Plough) 2012; *Publications* Herons (2001), Port (2002), One Minute (2003), Christmas (2003), Country Music (2004), Collected Plays 1 (2005), On the Shore of the Wide World (2005), Motortown (2006), Harper Regan (2008), Pornography (2008), Collected Plays 2 (2009), Collected Plays 3 (2011); *Clubs* Blacks; *Style—* Simon Stephens, Esq; ✉ c/o Mel Kenyon, Casarotto Ramsay & Associates, National House, 60–66 Wardour Street, London W1V 3HP (☎ 020 7287 4450)

STEPHENSON, Andrew; MP; *b* 17 February 1981, Manchester; *Educ* Poynton HS, Royal Holloway Coll London; *Career* cncllr Macclesfield Borough Cncl 2003–07, MP (Cons) Pendle 2010–, PPS to Rt Hon Robert Halfon, MP *qv*, 2015–16, PPS to Rt Hon Mike Penning, MP (min for policing, fire and criminal justice and victims) and Rt Hon John Hayes, MP (min for security), *qqv*, 2016–; vice-chm Cons Pty (Youth) 2010–13; *Clubs* Carlton; *Style—* Andrew Stephenson, Esq, MP; ✉ House of Commons, London SW1A 0AA (☎ 020 7217 7222, e-mail andrew.stephenson.mp@parliament.uk)

STEPHENSON, Frank; s of Edward Stephenson (d 1990), and Maria, *née* Santos; *b* 3 October 1959, Casablanca, Morocco; *Educ* Art Center Coll of Design Calif (BSc); *m* 12 Oct 2009, Linda, *née* Norris; *Career* designer Ford Motor Co 1986–91, sr designer BMW, chief designer MINI 1996–2002, dir of design Ferrari and Maserati, dir of design Fiat Lancia, dir of design Alfa Romeo 2007–08, design dir McLaren 2008–; personal awards incl: La Bella Macchina Award Concourso Italiano 2004, Creative Spirit Award Art Center Pasadena 2010, Hills Millennium Award Inst of Engineering Designers 2014; *Recreations* motorsport, music, sailing, travel, walking; *Style—* Frank Stephenson, Esq; ✉ e-mail frank@frankstephenson.com; McLaren Technology Centre, Chertsey Road, Woking, Surrey GU21 4YH (e-mail frank.stephenson@mclaren.com, website www.mclarenautomotive.com)

STEPHENSON, Prof (Marjorie) Gail; *née* Midgley; da of James Midgley (d 1978), and Ina, *née* Simpson (d 1992); *b* 28 July 1953, Salford, Gtr Manchester; *Educ* Pendleon HS for Girls Salford, Manchester Sch of Orthoptics Manchester Royal Eye Hosp (DBO), Manchester Poly; *Career* sr orthoptist Royal Albert Edward Infirmary Wigan 1974–76, student teacher Manchester Royal Eye Hosp 1976–78; orthoptic teacher Manchester Royal Eye Hosp: full time 1978–81, pt/t 1982–91; pt/t locum head of Trg Sch Leeds Gen Infirmary 1987–89, pt/t research orthoptist St Paul's Eye Hosp Liverpool 1989–91, full time head Dept of Orthoptics Univ of Liverpool 1991– (responsible for writing and introducing one of UK's two 3 year honours degree courses in orthoptics); vision science advsr: Manchester United FC 1997–, Subaru World Rally Team 1998, Lawn Tennis Assoc 1998, Benetton Formula One 1998–; UK rep: World Cncl of Orthoptists 2005–, Int Orthoptic Cncl 2005–, European Orthoptic Cncl 2011; invited memb Woman of the Year Lunch 1993, 1994, 1995 and 1997; Br Orthoptic Soc: chm Nat Scientific Ctee 1989–92, chm Nat Educn Ctee 1990–92, memb Nat Exec Cncl 1989–, memb Working Pty into Post-Basic Orthoptic Qualifications 1989–, Br rep on selection panel for Int Orthoptic Assoc Fellowship 1990–, chm Professional Devpt Ctee 1992–; Orthoptists Bd Cncl for Professions Supplementary to Med: memb 1990–, memb Registration Ctee 1990–, memb Disciplinary Ctee 1990–, chm Educn Ctee 1994–95; vice-pres-elect Int Orthoptic Assoc 2012–, pres-elect European Orthoptic Assoc 2013 (first Br orthoptist to hold the position), awarded personal chair 2013; examiner (final examination) DBO 1991, external examiner (BSc Orthoptics) Glasgow Caledonian Univ 1994; memb Editorial Bd Br Orthoptic Jl 1991–, reviewer of neuro-ophthalmology papers submitted to Br Jl of Ophthalmology 1993–, memb Editorial Review Bd Strabismus Supplement Int Orthoptic Congress 2008, ed Strabismus Supplement Int Orthoptic Congress 2012, memb Editorial Bd Int Jl of Ophthalmic Practice 2012–, author of various pubns, book reviews and presentations; *Recreations* all sport, watching tennis and football, playing tennis and squash, swimming; *Style—* Prof Gail Stephenson; ✉ Head of the Directorate of Orthoptics and Vision Science, President of the OCE (European Orthoptic Association), University of Liverpool, Thompson Yates Building, Brownlow Hill, Liverpool L69 3GB (☎ 0151 794 5730, mobile 07807 106901)

STEPHENSON, Geoffrey Charles; s of Edmund Charles Stephenson, and Hilda Rose, *née* Bates; *b* 19 August 1943; *Educ* Bromley GS; *m* 3 Sept 1966, Margaret, da of Frank Wirth (d 1989); 2 da (Louise Elizabeth b 26 March 1970, Rebecca Dorothy b 8 Feb 1972), 1 s (Alistair James b 2 May 1974); *Career* Legal and General Assurance Society Ltd 1964–72; called to the Bar Gray's Inn 1971, ad eundem Lincoln's Inn 1991, admitted to State Bar Texas 1991; FCII; *Recreations* sport; *Clubs* Sundridge Park Lawn Tennis and Squash Rackets; *Style—* Geoffrey Stephenson, Esq; ✉ 42 Madeira Avenue, Bromley, Kent BR1 4AY (☎ 020 8460 8809, mobile 07932 683702, e-mail gstephenson@barristernet.co.uk)

STEPHENSON, Prof Geoffrey Michael; s of Maurice Stephenson (d 1958), of Kenton, Middx, and Laura, *née* Sharp (d 1975); *b* 16 April 1939; *Educ* Harrow Co Sch for Boys, Univ of Nottingham (BA, PhD); *m* 14 April 1962 (m dis 1981), Marguerite Ida, da of James Lindsay (d 1986), of Kettering; 1 s (Lawrence James b 1963), 1 da (Katherine b 1965); m, 10 Jan 1989, Jennifer Ann, da of Frederick Williams, of St Mellon, Cardiff, and Elsie Williams; 1 s (David Field William b 1989); *Career* prof of social psychology and head of dept Univ of Kent Canterbury 1978–98 (emeritus prof 1998–); visiting prof of psychology Heriot-Watt Univ 1997–2001; res prof of psychology Univ of Greenwich 2000–, hon prof of psychology London South Bank Univ 2005–; ed Community and Applied Social Psychology 1991–; chm Social Psychology Section Br Psychological Soc 1977–80; memb Euro Assoc of Experimental Social Psychology 1972– (pres 1984–87); chm: IBA Advtg Advsy Ctee 1988–90, ITC Advtg Advsy Ctee 1991–92; CPsychol, FBPsS 1980; *Books* incl: The Development of Conscience (1966), The Social Psychology of Bargaining (with Ian Morley, 1976), The Psychology of Criminal Justice (1992); *Recreations* sailing, violin playing, choral singing; *Style—* Prof Geoffrey Stephenson; ✉ e-mail gmstephenson@gmail.com

STEPHENSON, John William; JP (1980); s of Kenneth George Stephenson (d 1979), and Madeline Alice, *née* Ounsworth (d 1974); *b* 23 June 1938; *Educ* Harrow Co Sch; *m* 7 Sept 1963, Lesley Helen, da of Flt Lt Harold Douglas Hopper (d 1980); 2 da (Joanna Margaret b 1968, Sarah Elizabeth b 1970); *Career* chartered surveyor; Fuller Peiser: joined 1959, ptnr 1970–99, sr ptnr 1998–99; memb Wood Ctee: to review rating of plant and machinery 1991, to review rating of plant and machinery in prescribed industries 1996; chm Music in the Round Ltd 1993–2006 (dir and vice-chm 1988–93); chm Cncl St John Ambulance Derbys 2004–07 (memb Co Mgmnt Bd 2001–03), chm Sheffield GS Exhbn Fund 2005– (tstee 1999–); tstee Sheffield Town 1986– (town collector 2008–11); FRICS 1970; SBStJ; *Recreations* music, literature, walking; *Clubs* Royal Over-Seas League; *Style—* John Stephenson, Esq; ✉ Borgen, Grindleford, Hope Valley S32 2HT (☎ 01433 630288)

STEPHENSON, Kate Frances; da of Air Vice Marshal Tom Birkett Stephenson, and Rosemary Patricia, *née* Thornton Kaye; *Educ* Wadhurst Coll, Univ of Nottingham (Wells Award for Industrial Relations); *Career* regnl media dir (Greater China) Leo Burnett 1991–96, client serv dir and founding memb Carat Asia Pacific 1996–98, md OMD SE Asia 1998–2001, md OMD International 2001–; memb Young Presidents Orgn Singapore 2000–; *Recreations* water skiing, riding, skiing, cycling; *Style*— Ms Kate Stephenson; ✉ OMD Europe, Seymour Mews House, 26–37 Seymour Mews, London W1H 6BN

STEPHENSON, Martin Richard; s of Richard Stephenson (d 1986), and Gladys, *née* Wheatley (d 1975); *b* 20 February 1959, London; *Educ* Therfield Secdy Modern Leatherhead; *Partner* Belinda Morgan; 1 s (Henry b 1992), 2 da (Beatrice b 1994, Jemima b 1999); *Career* estab first co SSC Ltd 1984–, took over the running of Stephenson Shuttering Ltd 1987–; estab: Stephenson Holdings Ltd 1995–, Stephenson Devpts Ltd 2001–, M R Stephenson Ltd 2003–, Stephenson Gp 2007–; Webbliworld Ltd 2006–, Sparkzmedia Ltd 2006–; chm Construct 2007–, memb Bd Cares; *Recreations* classic car motor racing, tennis, golf, wine, travel, design; *Clubs* Goodwood Road Racing, IOD; *Style*— Martin Stephenson, Esq; ✉ Stephenson Group, Provinder Mill, Mill Bay Lane, Horsham, West Sussex RH12 1SS (☎ 01403 217000, fax 01403 215750, e-mail m.s@ stephenson-ssc.co.uk, website www.stephenson-ssc.co.uk)

STEPHENSON, Sir Paul Robert; kt (2008), QPM (2000); s of Jack Stephenson (d 1999), and Rose Catherine, *née* Sullivan; *b* 26 September 1953; *Educ* Fearns Co Secdy Sch, Bacup and Rawtenstall GS; *m* 8 June 1974, Lynda, da of James Alexander Parker (d 1995); 3 da (Shelley Marie b 18 April 1975, Lisa Kathryn b 31 Aug 1977, Rebecca Faye b 9 Nov 1983); *Career* Lancs Constabulary: Constable 1975, Sgt 1982, Inspr 1983, Chief Inspr 1986, Supt 1988, Sub-Divnl Cdr Accrington, on secondment Banbridge RUC, Divnl Cdr Preston (previously Sub-Divnl Cdr); Asst Chief Constable Merseyside 1994–99, Dep Chief Constable Lancs 1999–2002, Chief Constable Lancs 2002–05, Dep Cmmr Met Police 2005–09, Cmmr Met Police 2009–11 (acting Cmmr 2008–09); hon fell Univ of Central Lancashire 2007; *Recreations* music, reading, family pursuits; *Style*— Sir Paul Stephenson, QPM

STEPHENSON, Richard; *Educ* Univ of London (BSc), EDHEC Risk Inst (MSc), Booth Sch of Business Univ of Chicago (MBA); *Career* portfolio mgmnt Merrill Lynch Investment Mgmnt 1998–2000, vice-pres cap structure arbitrage Enron Credit Hedge Fund 2000–02, dir Arbor Research and Trading (UK/US) 2002–04, md event driven emerging markets Fimat Societe Generale 2004–07, sr advsr AISM Sal Oppenheim 2007–10, fndr, chm and ceo Altern8 Investment Mangrs (Monaco/UK) 2007–; memb Bd: Valor Capital Luxembourg, Senior Assist Belgium, Manufacture de Monaco; corp memb Alternative Investment Mangrs Assoc, assoc memb Center for Policy Studies, assoc memb Royal Inst of Int Affrs, ptnr memb Adam Smith Inst; patron Royal Soc of Literature 2013–; *Recreations* cigars, fine wine, Formula 1, golf, modern art, skiing, shooting, history, tennis; *Clubs* Arts, Bisley Shooting, Friends of the Royal Acad, Monaco Cigar, Monaco Epicurean Soc; *Style*— Richard Stephenson, Esq; ✉ website www.altern8invest.com

STEPHENSON, Timothy Congreve; s of Augustus William Stephenson (d 2000), of Cowden, Kent, and Mary Gloria (d 1992), only and posthumous child of Maj William La T Congreve, VC, DSO, MC; *b* 7 March 1940; *Educ* Harrow, London Business Sch; *m* 1, 14 April 1966 (m dis 1980), Nerena Anne, da of Maj the Hon William Nicholas Somers Laurence Hyde Villiers; 2 da (Lucinda (Mrs Guy Denison-Smith) b 1967, Henrietta (Mrs Ben Dyer) b 1975), 2 s (Guy b 1969, Frederick d 2009); *m* 2, 16 June 1980, Diana-Margaret Soltmann, *qv*, da of HE Dr Otto Soltmann (d 2001), of Koblenz, Germany; 3 s (Christopher b 1983, William b 1985, James b 1989); *Career* Welsh Gds 1959–65; Gallaher Ltd 1965–79, md Grafton Ltd and chm Grafton Office Products Inc 1980–86, md Stephenson Cobbold Ltd 1987–95, chm Stephenson and Co 1996–, chm Stephenson Executive Search Ltd 2012–; former memb Industrial Tbnls, fndr memb Bd of Lab Rels (ACAS) NI; *Recreations* shooting, gardening; *Clubs* Brooks's, Beefsteak, Pratt's, City of London, MCC; *Style*— T C Stephenson, Esq; ✉ Stephenson and Co, Linden House, Sarson Lane, Amport, Hampshire SP11 8HX (☎ 01264 771355, fax 01264 771595, e-mail tcs@ stephensonandco.com)

STEPNEY, Bishop of 2011–; Rt Rev Adrian Newman; s of John Henry Newman, of Barnet, and Ruth Doreen, *née* Henderson; *b* 21 December 1958; *Educ* Rickmansworth Sch, Univ of Bristol, Trinity Coll Bristol; *m* 1981, Gillian Ann; 3 s (Peter b 1986, Jack b 1989, Daniel b 1992); *Career* curate St Mark's Forest Gate 1985–89, vicar Christ Church Hillsborough and Wadsley Bridge Sheffield 1989–96, rector St Martin in the Bull Ring Birmingham 1996–2005, dean of Rochester 2005–11; *Style*— The Rt Rev the Bishop of Stepney; ✉ 63 Coborn Road, London E3 2DB

STEPTOE, Prof Andrew Patrick Arthur; s of Patrick Christopher Steptoe, CBE (d 1988), and Sheena McLeod, *née* Kennedy (d 1990); *b* 24 April 1951; *Educ* Uppingham, Gonville & Caius Coll Cambridge (choral exhibitioner, hon sr scholar and Swann prize for biology, MA), Magdalen Coll Oxford (DPhil, MA (incorporated)), Univ of London (DSc); *m* 1, 1980 (m dis 1984), Jane Furneaux, da of Hugh Horncastle; 1 s (William Arthur Hugh b 1981); *m* 2, 1991, Frances Jane, da of Peter Wardle; 1 s (Matthew Peter Steptoe Wardle b 1984); *Career* Dept of Psychiatry Univ of Oxford: MRC research student 1972–75, MRC trg fell 1975–77; St George's Hosp Med Sch London: lectr in psychology 1977–81, sr lectr 1981–87, reader 1987–88, prof of psychology 1988–2000; Br Heart Fndn prof of psychology UCL 2000– (dir Inst of Epidemiology and Health Care 2011–); visiting prof Dept of Public Health Univ of Tokyo 1992; memb: Research Progs Bd ESRC 1994–96, Educn and Psychosocial Research Ctee Cancer Research Campaign 1994–2000, Population and Systems Medicine Bd MRC 2009–13, Research Ctee ESRC 2015–; assoc ed: Health Psychology, Psychophysiology 1982–86, Jl of Psychophysiology 1987–89, Annals of Behavioral Med 1991–97, Br Jl of Clinical Psychology 1992–95, Jl of Psychosomatic Research 1994–97 (asst ed 1989–93), Int Jl of Rehabilitation and Health 1995–2002; ed Br Jl of Health Psychology 1995–2001; memb Editorial Bd: Int Jl of Behavioral Med, Psychoneuroendocrinology, Psychosomatic Med, Brain Behavior and Immunity, Stress; essay prize in clinical psychology (Mental Health Fndn) 1972, Kenneth Reeves essay prize (Soc for Psychosomatic Research) 1977; hon fell Swedish Soc of Behavioural Med 1988, fell Academiae Europaeae 2003; memb: Int Soc of Behavioural Med (pres 1994–96), Soc for Psychosomatic Research (pres 1983–85), Soc for Psychophysiological Research USA (memb Bd of Dirs 1984–87); FBPsS (memb Scientific Affrs Bd 1991–93); FAcSS, FMedSci; *Books* Psychological Factors in Cardiovascular Disorders (1981), Problems of Pain and Stress (1984), Health Care and Human Behaviour (with A Mathews, 1984), Essential Psychology for Medical Practice (with A Mathews, 1988), Stress, Personal Control and Health (with A Appels, 1989), Psychosocial Processes and Health (with J Wardle, 1994), Depression and Physical Illness (2006), Handbook of Behavioral Medicine (2010), Stress and Cardiovascular Disease (2012); non-medical: The Mozart-Da Ponte Operas: The Cultural and Musical Background to Le nozze di Figaro, Don Giovanni and Cosi fan tutte (1988), Mozart: Everyman – EMI Music Companion (1997), Genius and the Mind (1998); *Recreations* music, theatre, reading, family; *Style*— Prof Andrew Steptoe; ✉ Department of Epidemiology and Public Health, University College London, 1–19 Torrington Place, London WC1E 6UT (☎ 020 7679 1804, fax 020 7916 8542, e-mail a.steptoe@ucl.ac.uk)

STEPTOE, Roger Guy; s of Charles Steptoe, of Winchester, and Norah Constance, *née* Shaw; *b* 25 January 1953; *Educ* Univ of Reading (BA), Royal Acad of Music (LRAM); *Career* composer and pianist; composer-in-residence Charterhouse 1976–79; RAM: admin Int Composer Festivals 1987–93, prof of composition 1980–91; prof Harmony and Composition Analysis Ecole Nationale de Musique de Danse et d'Art Dramatique Brive-

la-Gaillarde France 2001–; freelance composer, works regularly as a soloist, chamber pianist and accompanist, compositions performed internationally, artistic dir Festival de Musique Classique d'Uzerche France; has performed in: UK, IOM, Russia, Sweden, Portugal, France, Spain, Scotland, Germany, USA; 50th birthday celebrations in UK, USA and France; memb: Inc Soc of Musicians, RAM Club; ARAM 1986; *Compositions* incl: King of Macedon (opera), Concertos for cello, oboe, tuba, clarinet and flute, Sinfonia Concertante for violin and string orchestra, Aubade for clarinet and string orchestra, 4 String Quartets, Piano Trio, Piano Quartet (Quatre romances sans paroles d'après Paul Verlaine), Four Sonnets for brass quintet, various song cycles for all voices and piano, instrumental works for different combinations, Oboe Quartet, 3 Piano Sonatas, Prélude for piano La Dame de Labenche (en hommage à Claude Debussy), Prélude for viola and piano (en hommage à Toru Takemitsu), 2 Violin Sonatas, In Winter's Cold Embraces Dye (for soprano, tenor, chorus and chamber orch), Life's Unquiet Dream (for baritone, chorus and chamber orch), Cheers! (for chamber orch), The Passionate Shepherd to his Love (for childrens' voices), Impressions Corrèziennes, nineteen variations for orchestra, This Side of Winter (symphonic poem), Clarinet Sonata, Dance Music for symphonic brass, Three-Tango Rhapsody for Symphony Orch, Sinfonietta for organ and 15 strings, Sonata for tuba, Dourando as trevas for two tubas and vibraphone, L'angélus du matin à l'angélus du soir for four Cristal Baschet, Seven Miniatures for piano trio, Sonata for trumpet and organ, Sonatine 1 for solo viola, Sonatine 2 for cello and piano, Sonatine 3 for organ solo, Sonatine 4 for oboe and piano, Sonatine 5 for violin and piano, Sonata for viola and piano, New York Fanfares for brass quintet, Toccata for organ, Five Shakespeare Songs for tenor and piano, Ballade for horn and chamber orch, Three Dances for solo horn, Motet for Stephen, Fall Music for violin and piano, Spring Music for brass quartet, Four Shakespeare Sonnets for baritone and string orch, Brive Dances for string orch, Intrada for organ, As You Like It (opera); *Recordings* incl: the Songs of Ralph Vaughan Williams with Peter Savidge, the Piano Quartets of Walton and Frank Bridge, Elegy on the Death and Burial of Cock Robin (James Bowman), Sinfonietta for organ and strings, oboe and clarinet concertos, Tuba Concerto, Dourando as trevas for two tubas and vibraphone, L'angélus du matin à l'angélus du soir, Seven Miniatures for piano trio, Sonata for trumpet and organ, Toccata for organ; principal pubishers: Stainer & Bell Ltd (London), Editions BIM (Switzerland); *Recreations* travel, music, gardening, food and drink and seeing friends; *Style*— Roger Steptoe, Esq; ✉ c/o 6 bis rue Jean Gentet, 19140 Uzerche, France (☎ 00 33 555 73 75 99, e-mail roger.steptoe@nordnet.fr, website www.rogersteptoe.com); professional enquiries c/o Jeremy Mathez, Editions BIM, CP 300, Route des Echelettes 51, CH-1674 Vuarmarens, Switzerland (☎ 021 909 1000, e-mail jm@editions-bim.com, website www.editions-bim.com)

STERLING, David; *Career* formerly perm sec Dept of Enterprise, Trade and Investment NI, currently perm sec Dept of Finance (DoF) NI; *Style*— David Sterling, Esq; ✉ Department of Finance, Clare House, 303 Airport Road, Belfast BT3 9ED

STERLING, Dr (Isobel Jane) Nuala; CBE (1993); *née* Bradbury; da of Prof Fred Bradbury (d 1948), and Florence Jane, *née* Ratcliff (d 1982); *b* 12 February 1937; *Educ* Friends' Sch Saffron Walden, KCL, St George's Hosp London (MB BS); *m* 26 August 1961, Dr Graham Murray, s of George Sterling (d 1987); 5 s (Charles b 1963, Guy b 1967, Andrew b 1974, Mark b 1977, Thomas b 1981), 1 da (b and d 1972); *Career* St George's Hosp London: house physician/surgn 1960–61, SHO 1961–62, med registrar 1965–67; in gen practice Oxford 1968–69, lectr Dept of Med Univ of Calif San Francisco 1969–70; Southampton Univ Hosps: sr registrar then lectr Dept of Med 1972–79, conslt physician in geriatric med 1979–2002 (emeritus 2002–); pres Med Women's Fedn 1989–90, chm Standing Med Advsy Ctee 1990–94 (memb 1984–96), vice-chm Regnl Advsy Ctee Distinction Awards (Wessex) 1999–2000 (Southern) 2000–03, memb Clinical Standards Advsy Gp 1992–94, memb Independent Review Panel on Advtg of Med 2000–, tstee Wessex Med Tst 1999–2004, tstee King Edward VII Hosp Midhurst 2002–06, memb RHS Lily Gp Ctee 2006– (chm 2012–), memb RHS Bulb Ctee 2013– (vice-chm 2014–); FRCP 1982 (MRCP 1971); *Publications* incl research papers on immunology, endocrinology, geriatric medicine, medical education and reports on medical services: Palliative Care (jtly with SNAC, 1990), Cystic Fibrosis (1993), Review of prescribing, supply and administration of medicines (under Dr June Crown, 1999), Prevention of strokes neurological update (Sri Lankan Medical Jl, 1999); *Recreations* golf, music, orchids, lilies, gardening; *Style*— Dr Nuala Sterling, CBE, FRCP; ✉ Vermont House, East Boldre, Hampshire SO42 7WX

STERLING OF PLAISTOW, Baron (Life Peer UK 1991), of Pall Mall in the City of Westminster; Sir Jeffrey Maurice Sterling; GCVO (2002), CBE (1977); s of late Harry Sterling, and Alice Sterling; *b* 27 December 1934; *Educ* Reigate GS, Preston Manor Co Sch, Guildhall Sch of Music; *m* 1985, Dorothy Ann, *née* Smith; 1 da; *Career* Paul Schweder & Co (Stock Exchange) 1955–57, G Eberstadt & Co 1957–62, fin dir General Guarantee Corp 1962–64, md Gula Investments Ltd 1964–69, chm Sterling Guarantee Trust plc 1969 (merged with P&O 1985), memb Bd of Dirs British Airways 1979–82, exec chm The Peninsular and Oriental Steam Navigation Company 1983–2005 (dir 1980–2005), chm P&O Princess Cruises 2000–03; special advsr to Sec of State for Industry (later Trade and Industry) 1982–90; World ORT Union: memb Exec 1966–, chm Orgn Ctee 1969–73, chm ORT Technical Servs 1974–, vice-pres British ORT 1978–; pres: Gen Cncl of Br Shipping 1990–91, EC Shipowners' Assocs 1992–94; chm The Queen's Golden Jubilee Weekend Tst 2002, dep chm and hon treas London Celebrations Ctee for Queen's Silver Jubilee; Motability: co-fndr 1977, chm Exec Ctee 1977–, vice-chm 1977–94, chm 1994–; chm: Young Vic Co 1975–83, Bd of Govrs Royal Ballet Sch 1983–99; govr Royal Ballet 1986–99; tstee Nat Maritime Museum 2005–, chm of tstees Royal Museums Greenwich 2005–13; Hon Vice Adm RNR 2015 (Hon Capt 1991), elder brother Trinity House 1991; Freeman City of London; Hon DBA Nottingham Trent Univ 1995, Hon DCL Univ of Durham 1996; Hon FIMarE 1991, Hon FICS 1992, Hon MRICS 1993, FISVA 1995, Hon FRINA 1997; KStJ 1998, Grand Offr Order of the May (Argentina) 2002, Officer's Cross of the Order of Merit (Germany) 2004; *Recreations* music; *Clubs* Garrick, Hurlingham, RAC; *Style*— The Rt Hon the Lord Sterling of Plaistow, GCVO, CBE

STERN, (John) Chester; s of Julius Charles Stern (d 1983), of Littlehampton, W Sussex, and Bertha Margaret, *née* Baker (d 2001); *b* 6 September 1944; *Educ* Parktown Boys' HS Johannesburg, Broad Green Coll Croydon; *m* 25 March 1967, Rosemary Ann, da of Wilfred Harold Symons; 2 da (Carolyn Joy b 28 Sept 1969, Paula Jane b 26 Feb 1972); *Career* asst librarian Wills Library Guy's Hospital Medical Sch 1964–65, ed asst Food Processing & Marketing 1965–66, freelance broadcaster BBC Radio London 1970–74, freelance sportswriter The Sunday Telegraph 1973–76; Metropolitan Police New Scotland Yard: publicity asst 1966–68, head of News Gp 1968–71, PRO Traffic Warden Service 1971–74, press and publicity offr London Airport Heathrow 1974–75, press and publicity offr S London 1975–77, head Press Bureau 1977–82; crime corr The Mail on Sunday 1982–2001, controller of public affrs Harrods 2001–04, dir of corp affrs Fulham FC 2001–04; freelance sportswriter and media conslt 2004–15; pres Crime Reporters' Assoc 1995 (chm 1993), capt Press Golfing Soc 1999; memb: Sports Journalists' Assoc, Football Writers' Assoc; Winston Churchill fell 1975; FRGS 1964, MIPR 1971; *Books* Dr Iain West's Casebook (1996), The Black Widow (2002), The Decoy (2012), The Green-Inker (2012), Code Zulu (2012); *Recreations* golf, acting; *Clubs* Mensa, Croham Hurst Golf (capt 2013–14); *Style*— Chester Stern, Esq; ✉ 101 Norfolk Avenue, Sanderstead, Surrey CR2 8BY (☎ 020 8657 3649, mobile 07841 697834, e-mail chesrose.stern@ btinternet.com)

STERN, Dr Jeremy Samuel; *Educ* Christ's Coll Cambridge (MA), UCL, Middx Sch of Med London (MB BChir); *Career* house surgn Basildon and Orsett Hosps 1991–92, house physician Southampton Gen Hosp 1992, SHO in med Guy's Hosp 1992–94, registrar in geriatrics St George's Hosp London 1994–95; registrar in neurology: Atkinson Morley's Hosp 1995–96, Chelsea & Westminster Hosp 1996–97; research fell (neurology) Hammersmith Hosp 1997–2000, specialist registar in neurology Nat Hosp for Neurology and Neurosurgery and Addenbrooke's Hosp 2000–03, conslt neurologist Frimley Park Hosp and St George's Hosp 2004–; Tourette Syndrome Assoc: tstee 1990–2000, chair 2002–07, medical dir 2007–; asst sec Assoc of Br Neurology Trainees 1998–2001; memb (youngest ever) GMC 1994–99; memb Br Neuropsychiatry Assoc 1992, memb Assoc of Br Neurologists 1995; memb Worshipful Soc of Apothecaries 2000 (Dip in History of Med 1995); FRCP 2008 (MRCP 1994); *Publications* On Tourette Syndrome; *Recreations* music, theatre, film, mandarin; *Clubs* Chopin Soc; *Style—* Dr Jeremy Stern; ✉ Ground Floor, Atkinson Morley's Wing, St Geroge's Hospital, Blackshaw Road, London SW17 0QT (☎ 020 8725 4631, fax 020 8725 2470, e-mail jeremy.stern@stgeorges.nhs.uk)

STERN, John Andrew; s of Peter Stern (d 2002), and Gillian, *née* Bannister; *b* 12 March 1970, London; *Educ* King's Sch Canterbury, Univ of Manchester (BA); *m* 17 April 2004, Clare Alison, *née* Henderson; 2 step da (Eloise b 19 Oct 1994, Georgie b 16 Oct 1997); *Career* reporter Hayters Sports Agency 1992–97, freelance sports writer 1997–2001, contrib Wisden Cricketers' Almanack 1999–, dep ed Wisden Cricket Monthly 2001–03, ed The Wisden Cricketer 2003–; cricket columnist Sunday Times 2003–; tstee Primary Club; *Recreations* football, cricket (Wendover CC) travel, food and wine; *Clubs* MCC, Lord's Taverners, Cricket Writers'; *Style—* John Stern, Esq; ✉ The Wisden Cricketer, 2nd Floor, 123 Buckingham Palace Road, London SW1W 9SL (e-mail john.stern@wisdencricketer.com)

STERN, Nadia; da of David Stern (d 2012), and Samantha, *née* Betty-June Brine (d 2008); *b* London; *Educ* BEd; *m* 2002, John Richard Young; *Career* centre dir Arvon Fndn at Lumb Bank, Action Projects in Educn, gen mangr Sadler's Wells, exec dir Hampstead Theatre, chief exec Talawa Theatre, chief exec Rambert 2007–; tstee and memb Bd Hampstead Theatre Fndn; *Recreations* arts (performing, visual, film), walking, birding; *Style—* Ms Nadia Stern; ✉ Rambert, 99 Upper Ground, London SE1 9PP (e-mail nadia.stern@rambert.org.uk)

STERN OF BRENTFORD, Baron (Life Peer UK 2007), of Elsted in the County of West Sussex and of Wimbledon in the London Borough of Merton; Prof Sir Nicholas Herbert (Nick) Stern; kt (2004); s of Adalbert Stern, and Marion Fatima, *née* Swann; *b* 22 April 1946; *Educ* Latymer Upper Sch, Peterhouse Cambridge (MA), Nuffield Coll Oxford (DPhilEcon); *m* 7 Sept 1968, Susan Ruth, da of Albert Edward Chesterton (d 1978); 1 da (Helen b 1976), 2 s (Daniel b 1979, Michael b 1980); *Career* jr res fell Queen's Coll Oxford (hon fell 2007), fell and tutor in econs St Catherine's Coll Oxford 1970–77 (hon fell 2000), prof of economics Univ of Warwick 1978–85, Sir John Hicks prof of econs LSE 1986–94, chief economist and special advsr EBRD 1994–99, sch prof of economics LSE 1999 (on leave 2000–03), chief economist and sr vice-pres World Bank 2000–03, second perm sec HM Treasy and head Govt Economic Serv 2003–07 (dir of policy and research PM's Cmmn for Africa 2004–05, ldr and author Stern Review on the Economics of Climate Change HM Treasy 2005–06), IG Patel prof of economics and govt, chair Grantham Inst on Climate Change and the Environment and dir India Observatory LSE 2007–, prof Collège de France 2009–10; ed Jl of Public Economics 1981–97; res assoc/visiting prof: MIT 1972, Ecole Poly 1977, People's Univ China Beijing 1988 (hon prof 2001); Ford Fndn visiting prof Indian Statistical Inst 1981–82, visiting fell Nuffield Coll Oxford 2004, hon fell Peterhouse Cambridge 2006; foreign hon memb American Acad of Arts and Scis 1998–; Great Briton of the Year (Environment) 2006, Patron's Royal Medal RGS 2009, Asahi Glass Fndn Blue Planet Prize 2009, BBVA Fndn Frontiers of Knowledge Award Climate Change 2010, Leontief Prize for Advancing the Frontiers of Economic Thought 2011; 12 hon doctorates incl: Univ of Warwick 2006, Univ of Cambridge 2008; fell Econometric Soc 1978, FBA 1993; *Books* An Appraisal of Tea Production on Smallholdings in Kenya (1972), Theories of Economic Growth (ed jtly, 1973), Crime, the Police and Criminal Statistics (jtly, 1979), Palanpur: The Economy of an Indian Village (jtly, 1982), The Theory of Taxation for Developing Countries (jtly, 1987), Economic Development in Palanpur over Five Decades (jtly, 1998), Growth and Empowerment (jtly, 2005), A Blueprint for a Safer Planet (2009); numerous articles in learned jls; *Recreations* walking, reading, watching football (particularly AFC Wimbledon); *Style—* The Lord Stern of Brentford

STERNBERG, Michael Vivian; QC (2008); s of Sir Sigmund Sternberg, *qv*, and Beartrice Ruth, *née* Schiff (d 1994); *b* 12 September 1951; *Educ* Carmel Coll, Queens' Coll Cambridge (MA, LLM); *m* 20 July 1975, Janine Lois, da of Harold Levinson; 2 da (Rachel Serena b 2 Feb 1980, Sarah Jessica b 4 Jan 1988), 1 s (Daniel Isaiah b 24 Sept 1982); *Career* called to the Bar Gray's Inn 1975, (bencher 2013); asst sec Family Law Bar Assoc 1986–88; qualified colaborator lawyer 2010, qualified family law mediator 2011; tstee: London Jewish East End Museum 1984–94, Sternberg Charitable Settlement; memb Cncl of Christians and Jews 1988, chm of tstees Three Faiths Forum 2010–; govr N London Collegiate Sch 1994–2009; Lloyd's underwriter 1978–96; Freeman City of London 1983, Liveryman Worshipful Co of Horners 1987; FRSA 2009, MCIArb 2012; Medaglia D'Argento di Benemerenza of the Sacred Military Constantinian Order of St George 1990, Knight of the Royal Order of King Francis I 2011; *Recreations* walking, reading, theatre; *Clubs* Reform; *Style—* Michael Sternberg, Esq, QC; ✉ 4 Paper Buildings, Temple, London EC4Y 7EX (☎ 020 7583 0816, fax 020 7353 4979)

STERNBERG, Sir Sigmund; kt (1976), JP (Middx, 1965); s of late Abraham Sternberg, and Elizabeth Sternberg; *b* 2 June 1921, Budapest; *m* 1970, Hazel, *née* Everett-Jones (d 2014); 1 step s, 1 step da; 1 s and 1 da from previous marriage; *Career* chm: Martin Slowe Estates Ltd 1971–; dep chm Lab Fin and Industry Gp 1972–93 (hon life pres 2002–); chm St Charles Gp HMC 1974; life vice-pres Royal Coll of Speech and Language Therapists 2002–; hon life pres Inst for Archaeo-Metallurgical Studies; patron Int Cncl of Christians and Jews; patron Charitable Tst Bd of Deputies of Br Jews, hon govr Hebrew Univ of Jerusalem 2012–; life pres Sternberg Centre for Judaism 1996–, life pres Movement of Reform Judaism 2011–; fndr: Three Faiths Forum (Christians, Muslims and Jews Dialogue Gp) 1997; hon vice-pres Inst of Business Ethics 2010–, sr regligious advsr World Economic Forum 2002–, life memb Magistrates Assoc 1965, vice-pres Keston Inst 2003–, memb John Templeton Fndn 1998– (Templeton Prize for Progress in Religion 1998); fndg patron Anne Frank Tst UK 1991–; Paul Harris fell 1989; offr Wissam Alouite (Morocco) 2009; Liveryman Worshipful Co of Horners, Freeman City of London 1965; Medal of Merit Warsaw Univ 1995, FIRST Lifetime Achievement Award 2008, Rotary Int Award for Progress in Religion 1998; Hon DUniv: Essex 1996, Open Univ 1998, Hebrew Union Coll Cincinnati 2000; Hon DHL Richmond American Int Univ 2008; hon fell UCL 2001; FRSA 1979, Hon FCST 1989, life fell RSM 2002; Order of the Orthodox Hospitallers 1st Class with Star and Badge of Religion 1986, OStJ 1988, KCSG 1985 (Star 2009), Silver Pontifical Medal 1986, Benemerenti Medal (Vatican) 1988 (in Silver 1990), Order of Merit (Poland) 1989, Order of the Gold Star (Hungary) 1990, Medaglia d'Argento di Benemerenza Sacred Mil Constantinian Order of St George 1991, Cdr's Cross 1st Class (Austria) 1992, Cdr's Cross Order of Merit (Poland) 1992, Cdr of the Order of Civil Merit (Spain) 1993, Cdr's Cross Order of Merit (Germany) 1993, Cdr Order of Honour (Greece) 1996, Cdr of the Royal Order of the Polar Star (Sweden) 1997, Wilhelm Leuschner Medal (Wiesbaden) 1998, Order of Commandatore of the Italian Republic (Italy) 1999, Cdr's Cross with a Star of the Order of Merit (Poland) 1999, Order de Mayo al Merito en el Gardo de Gran Oficial (Argentina) 1999, Order of Bernardo O'Higgins Grado de Gran Cruz (Chile) 2000, Order of Ukraine for Public Services (Ukraine) 2001, Order of Merit (Portugal) 2002, Order of the Madara Horsemen (Bulgaria) 2003, Order of the White Two-Armed Cross (Slovakia) 2003, Légion d'Honneur (France) 2003, Order of Francisco de Miranda (Venezuela) 2004, Knight Cdr's Cross Order of Merit (Germany) 2006, Order Pentru Merit (Romania) 2007, St Mellitus Medal 2008; *Books* subject of The Knight with Many Hats (biography by Emma Klein, 2012); *Recreations* reading the religious press, swimming; *Clubs* City Livery; *Style—* Sir Sigmund Sternberg; ✉ Star House, London NW5 4BA (fax 020 7485 4512)

STERRY, David; OBE (2005); *Career* May Gurney: chief exec 2000–08, non-exec chm 2008–; *Style—* David Sterry, Esq, OBE; ✉ KIER GROUP PLC, TEMPSFORD HALL, SANDY, BEDFORDSHIRE, SG19 2BD

STEUART FOTHRINGHAM OF GRANTULLY, Henry; OBE (1995); yst s of Maj Thomas Scrymsoure Steuart Fothringham, 21 of Pourie-Fothringham, MC, DL, JP, TD (d 1979), of Fothringham, Forfar, Angus, and Carola Mary (d 1989), da of Maj the Hon Charles Hubert Francis Noel, OBE (d 1947); *b* 15 February 1944, Edinburgh; *Educ* Fort Augustus Abbey, RAC Cirencester; *m* 20 May 1972, Cherry Linnhe Stewart, 14 of Achnacone (d 2001), da of Brig Ian Macalister Stewart, 13 of Achnacone, DSO, OBE, MC, DL (d 1987), of Achnacone, Appin, Argyll; 3 s (Patrick yr of Grantully b 1973, Charles 15 of Achnacone b 1974, Ian b 1976); *Career* specialist in Scottish silver, writer and researcher; memb: Tay District Salmon Fisheries Bd 1977–80, Reviewing Ctee on the Export of Works of Art 1982–94, Advsy Cncl on the Export of Works of Art 1982–94, Hist Ctee Scottish Goldsmiths Tst 2001–; co-curator Silver: Made in Scotland 2008; govr: Heartland Radio Fndn Ltd 1995–2000, Trades Maiden Hospital and Fund (Edinburgh) 2004–15, Edinburgh Trades Fund 2015–; Freeman: Worshipful Co of Goldsmiths 1993, City of London 1994, Incorporation of Bonnetmakers and Dyers of Edinburgh 2006– (boxmaster 2013–15), Inc of Candlemakers of Edinburgh 2009– (candlemaster 2009–13), Inc of Hammermen of Edinburgh 2012; Burgess City of Edinburgh 2007; memb: The Silver Soc 1977 (chm 1993–94), The Stewart Soc 1963 (hon vice-pres 1971–, pres 1995–98), Incorporation of Goldsmiths of the City of Edinburgh 1990 (Freeman 2000, Deacon's rep to Convenery of the Trades of Edinburgh 2004–14), Scottish Medievalists 2004–; hon historian Convenery of Trades of Edinburgh 2004–; FRSA, FSA Scot; *Books and Publications* The Family of Fothringham of Pourie (1990, 3 edn 1995), Edinburgh Goldsmiths' Minutes 1525–1700 (2007), Silver: Made in Scotland (jtly, 2008) Act Book of the Convenery of Deacons of the Trades of Edinburgh 1577–1755 (2010), The Trades of Edinburgh: Celebrating 450 Years (2012), Flodden and the Blue Blanket (jtly, 2013), We That is Tradds: The Incorporated Trades of Edinburgh (2013), The Ashfield Collection (2013), Heraldry of the Incorporated Trades (2013); contrib: Jackson's Silver and Gold Marks of England, Scotland and Ireland (1989), Scottish Gold and Silver Work (ed and co-author, 1991 edn), Bradbury's Book of Hallmarks (1991 edn); author of numerous articles in learned jls, book and exhbn reviews; regular contrib The Stewarts magazine; articles in Jl of The Silver Soc and Silver Studies; *Recordings* Pieces of the Past (1995), Pieces of the Past from Blair Castle (1997); *Recreations* Scottish silver studies, books, history, Scotland, the countryside, the Forth Bridge, gardening, music, reading; *Clubs* Royal Over-Seas League, Antiquaries Dining (Edinburgh), Puffins (Edinburgh); *Style—* Henry Steuart Fothringham, OBE; ✉ The Lagg, Aberfeldy, Perthshire PH15 2EE (☎ 01887 829582, e-mail henryfoth@hotmail.co.uk)

STEVENS, Alan Michael; s of Raymond Alfred George Stevens, of Bournemouth, Dorset, and Joan Patricia, *née* Drury; *b* 8 April 1955; *Educ* Malvern Coll, Selwyn Coll Cambridge (MA); *m* 2 May 1987, Lynn Sarah, da of Henry B Hopfinger, of Coventry, Warks; 2 da (Eloise b 1988, Natalia b 1993), 2 s (Thomas b 1990, Benjamin b 1992); *Career* admitted slr 1980; ptnr Linklaters 1987–2003 (joined 1978), ptnr Carey Olsen LLP 2003–15; memb Law Soc; Freeman Worshipful Co of Slrs; *Recreations* tennis, skiing, sailing, golf; *Clubs* Royal Hong Kong Yacht, St Helier Yacht, Hurlingham, Royal Channel Islands Yacht, La Moye Golf; *Style—* Alan Stevens, Esq

STEVENS, Brian Turnbull Julius; s of Maj John Osmond Julius Stevens, MBE, and Kathleen, *née* Forman; *b* 3 November 1938; *Educ* Eton; *m* 5 Dec 1970, Hon Henrietta Maria, da of Lt-Col 1 Baron St Helens, MC (d 1980); 3 da (Flora Matilda Julius b 25 Feb 1973, Harriet Maria Julius b 11 Jan 1975, Louisa Elizabeth Julius b 15 Oct 1976); *Career* admitted slr 1962; currently conslt Withers; memb Law Soc; *Recreations* field sports, gardening; *Clubs* Boodle's, Pratt's; *Style—* Brian Stevens, Esq; ✉ Withers, 16 Old Bailey, London EC4M 7EG (☎ 020 7597 6000, fax 020 7597 6543)

STEVENS, Dr Handley Michael Gambrell; s of Dr Ernest Norman Stevens (d 1991), and Dr Kathleen Emily Gambrell (d 1986); *b* 29 June 1941; *Educ* The Leys Sch, Phillips Acad Andover Mass, King's Coll Cambridge (MA, PhD); *m* 5 March 1966, Anne Frances, da of Robert Ross (d 2005); 3 da (Hilary b 1970 d 2010, Lucy b 1971, Mary b 1980); *Career* Dip Serv 1964–70 (Kuala Lumpur 1966–69); asst private sec Lord Privy Seal 1970–71, Civil Serv Dept 1970–73, DTI 1973–83, under sec Dept of Tport 1983–94 (Int Aviation 1983–87, Finance 1988–91, Public Tport in London 1991–94); research assoc Euro Inst LSE 1994–2008; *Publications* Tport Policy in Britain (1998), Brussels Bureaucrats? (2000), Transport Policy in Europe (2004), Air Transport and the European Union (2010); *Recreations* Anglican lay reader, music, walking; *Style—* Dr Handley M G Stevens; ✉ Flat One, 20 Netherhall Gardens, London NW3 5TH (☎ 020 7794 0874)

STEVENS, Prof Heather; CBE (2010); *Career* co-fndr (with husb David) Admiral Gp; chair of tstees Waterloo Fndn; *Style—* Prof Heather Stevens, CBE; ✉ The Waterloo Foundation, 46–48 Cardiff Road, Llandaff, Cardiff CF5 2DT

STEVENS, John Christopher Courtenay; *b* 23 May 1955; *Educ* Winchester, Magdalen Coll Oxford (BA); *Career* foreign exchange dealer Bayerische Hypotheken Wechselbank Munich 1976–77; fin corr Il Messaggiero Rome 1978; foreign exchange dealer: Banque Indosuez Paris 1979–80, Morgan Grenfell & Co Ltd London 1980–84; dir Morgan Grenfell International (and head of Euro Govt Bond Trading) 1985–89, advsr on foreign exchange and interest rates to J Rothschild Investment Management 1989–2005; MEP (Cons) Thames Valley 1989–99; advsr THS Ptnrs 1999–; *Books* A Conservative European Monetary Union (1990), On Line in Time – The Case for a Smart Citizen's Card for Britain; *Style—* John Stevens, Esq; ✉ 40 Smith Square, London SW1P 3HL (☎ 020 7222 0770)

STEVENS, Dr (Katharine) Lindsey Haughton; da of Richard Haughton Stevens (d 1977), and Rachel Vera Joyce, *née* Huxstep; *b* 17 July 1954; *Educ* Harrogate Ladies' Coll, Runton Hill Sch, Gresham's Sch, Churchill Coll Cambridge (MA), Middx Hosp Med Sch (MB BChir); *m* 1989, David Barrett McCausland, s of John McCausland, of Pett, E Sussex; 2 s (Duncan James Stevens b 1989, Theodore Richard Stevens b 1994), 1 da (Beth Mary Stevens b 1991); *Career* conslt/mangr A&E St George's Hosp 1985–96, clinical dir A&E Services St Helier Hosp 1996–99: Epsom and St Helier NHS Tst: dir A&E Services 1999–2008, dir Fndn Prog 2006–; hon sr lectr Univ of London 1985–, course dir and instr in advanced trauma life support RCS 1989–; research into: psychological effects of trauma and bereavement, domestic violence, teaching by simulation, water safety, resuscitation, cardiac illness, physiotherapy; dep dist surgn St John Ambulance Bde; sec S Thames A&E Conslts Ctee 2000–; A&E Section Royal Soc of Med: treas 1992–95, editorial rep 1995–97, library rep 1997–99; regnl sub-speciality advsr RCS 1990–93, assoc clinical advsr Health Service Ombudsman 2013–; memb: Nat Steering Gp Violence Against

Women and Children 2009–10, Nat MARACS Steering Gp 2010–; memb RSM 1989; FCEM 1993, FRCP 1994 (MRCP 1983), FRSA 2002; *Books* Emergencies in Obstetrics and Gynaecology, Violence against Women (contrib), Rape (contrib), ABC of Domestic and Sexual Violence (contrib), Challenging Concepts in Emergency Medicine (contrib); *Style*— Dr Lindsey Stevens; ✉ Emergency Services, Epsom and St Helier NHS Trust, Wrythe Lane, Carshalton SM5 1AA (☎ 020 8296 2276)

STEVENS, Matthew John Hamilton (Matt); s of Russell John Stevens, and Georgina Hamilton Kelly; *b* 1 October 1982, Durban, South Africa; *Educ* Kearsney Coll Durban, Univ of Cape Town, Univ of Bath; *Career* rugby union player (front row forward); clubs: South Africa Univs (capt), Western Province, Bath Rugby 2002–09, Saracens 2011–; England: 39 caps, debut v NZ 2004, finalists World Cup France 2007; memb British and Irish Lions touring squad NZ 2005, memb British and Irish Lions touring squad Australia 2013; also played for and captained South Africa under 18 and under 19 teams; *Recreations* scuba diving, horse riding, guitar playing; *Style*— Mr Matt Stevens

STEVENS, Melinda; da of Jolelyn Stevens, of Hungerford, Berks, and Jane, *née* Sheffield; *b* 18 January 1972, London; *Educ* St Mary's Calne, Univ of Manchester; *m* 7 July 2001, Marcus Langlands Pearse; 3 da (Ottilie b 16 July 2003, Nell b 2 July 2007, Willow b 24 Oct 2009); *Career* features ed Tatler 1995–97, hotel and restaurant critic People News 1997–99, columnist Sunday Times Style 2000–01, reviewer Evening Standard 2001–03, travel ed Tatler 2004–11, ed Condé Nast Traveller 2012–; *Recreations* reading, travel, dancing; *Clubs* Eagle (Gstaad); *Style*— Ms Melinda Stevens; ✉ Condé Nast Traveller, Vogue House, Hanover Square, London W1S 1JU (☎ 020 7152 3924, website www.cntraveller.com, Twitter @melindastevens3)

STEVENS, Patrick Tom; s of Tom Stevens, of Norfolk, and Gwendoline, *née* Nurse; *b* 21 August 1949; *Educ* Paston GS; *Career* tax specialist Coopers & Lybrand 1975–79, tax ptnr BDO Stoy Hayward (and predecessor firms) 1979–96, tax ptnr and managing ptnr (entrepreneurial services) Ernst & Young 1996–2013; Chartered Inst of Taxation: pres and memb Cncl 2005–13, tax policy dir Chartered 2013–15, ret; Liveryman: Worshipful Co of Tax Advsrs, Worshipful Co of Glass Sellers; FCA 1972, CTA (fell) 2003 (ATII 1975); *Recreations* theatre, cricket; *Style*— Patrick Stevens, Esq; ✉ Longacre, Sandhurst Road, Bodiam, East Sussex; (☎ 07775 818926)

STEVENS, Rear Adm Robert Patrick; CB (2000); s of late Major Phillip Joseph Stevens, RMP, and late Peggy, *née* Marshall; *b* 14 March 1948; *Educ* Prince Rupert Sch Wilhelmshaven, BRNC Dartmouth; *m* 1973, Vivien Roberts; 1 s, 1 da; *Career* CO HMS Odin 1979–81, CO qualifying course HMS Dolphin 1983–85, CO HMS Torbay 1985–88, USN War Coll 1988–89, asst dir Strategic Systems MOD 1989–91, Capt 7 Frigate Sqdn and CO HMS Argonaut 1992–93, memb Navy Presentation Team 1993–94, dir Jt Warfare MOD 1994–98, Flag Offr Submarines 1998–2001, Cdr Submarines (NATO) E Atlantic 1998–2001, COS (Ops) to C-in-C Fleet 1998–2001, COS COMNAVSOUTH 2002–05; ceo Br Marine Fedn 2006–; pres RN Football Assoc 1998–2004; *Recreations* skiing, sailing, tennis, golf; *Clubs* Royal Navy of 1765 and 1785, RNSA, SW Shingles Yacht, Royal Thames Yacht; *Style*— Rear Adm Robert Stevens, CB

STEVENS, Simon Laurence; s of Laurence Stevens, and Vivien Stevens; *b* 4 August 1966, Birmingham; *Educ* St Bartholomew's Comp Sch, Balliol Coll Oxford (BA, MA), Univ of Strathclyde (MBA); *m* 1998, Maggie Thurer; 1 s (Samuel b 2003), 1 da (Hannah b 2008); *Career* economic devpt mangr Guyana 1987–88, mgmnt UK NHS 1988–94, NY City Health Dept 1994–5, mgmnt UK NHS 1995–97, policy advsr to Sec of State for Health UK Dept of Health 1997–2001, PM's health advsr 2001–04, United Health Gp USA 2004–14, ceo NHS England 2014–; dir Commonwealth Fund of NY; Harkness fell Columbia Univ NY, hon doctorate Univ of Birmingham 2015; *Recreations* family, books, cooking without recipes; *Style*— Simon Stevens, Esq; ✉ NHS England, 80 London Road, London SE1 6LH

STEVENS, Stuart Standish; s of Maj Edward Aloysious Stevens (d 1948), and Virginia Mary, *née* D'Vaz (d 2008); *Educ* St Joseph's Euro HS Bangalore, Acton County GS, Royal Holloway Coll London; *Children* 4 s (Uther Edward b 1984, Stuart William b 1989, Alexander George b 1993, Maximilian Richard b 1994), 1 da (Isabella Eda b 1986); *Career* called to the Bar Gray's Inn 1970 (Inner Temple 1982); head of chambers; specialist in white collar and corp fraud; Freeman City of London 1991; *Style*— Stuart Stevens, Esq; ✉ Holborn Chambers, The Chambers of Stuart Stevens, 6 Gate Street, Lincoln's Inn Fields, London WC2 (☎ 020 7242 6060, fax 020 7242 2777, e-mail stuart.stevens@holbornchambers.co.uk)

STEVENS, Rt Rev Timothy John; CBE (2016); s of Ralph Stevens, and Jean Ursula Stevens; *b* 31 December 1946, Dagenham; *Educ* Chigwell Sch, Selwyn Coll Cambridge, Ealing Business Sch (Dip Mgmnt Studies), Ripon Coll Cuddesdon (DipTh, CertTheol); *m* 1973, Wendi Kathleen; 1 s, 1 da; *Career* grad mgmnt trainee BOAC 1968–72, second sec S Asian Dep FCO 1972–73; curate East Ham Team Miny 1976–79, team vicar St Albans Upton Park 1979–80, team rector Canvey Island 1980–88, urban offr to Bishop of Chelmsford 1988–91, archdeacon of West Ham 1991–95, bishop of Dunwich 1995–99, bishop of Leicester 1999–2015; memb Crown Appts Cmmn for See of Canterbury 2002, memb Archbishop's Cncl 2006–10, memb Standing Ctee House of Bishops 2006–10; chair Community and Voluntary Forum for Eastern Religion 1997–99, pres Leicester Cncl of Faiths 2001–, chair Cncl The Children's Soc 2003–10, chair of tstees Common Purpose UK 2013–, tstee United Learning Tst 2013–15; memb House of Lords 2003–15; Convenor of Lords Spiritual 2009–15; visiting prof in faith and society De Montfort Univ 2013–; govr De Montfort Univ 2005–12, chair Cncl Westcott House 2006–12; non-exec dir Norfolk and Suffolk NHS Tst 2015–; Hon LLD De Montfort Univ 2002, Hon DLitt Leicester Univ 2003; *Recreations* cricket, golf, swimming, North Yorkshire Moors; *Clubs* Royal Cwlth Soc; *Style*— The Rt Rev Timothy Stevens, CBE; ✉ 62 Horringer Road, Bury St Edmunds, Suffolk IP33 2DR (e-mail tjs46@icloud.com)

STEVENS CURL, Prof James; s of George Stevens Curl (d 1974), and Sarah, *née* McKinney (d 1995); *b* 26 March 1937; *Educ* Cabin Hill, Campbell Coll, Queen's Univ Belfast, Belfast Coll of Art, Oxford Sch of Architecture, UCL (DiplArch, DipTP, PhD); *m* 1, 1960 (m dis 1986), Eileen Elizabeth, da of John Blackstock (d 1984), of Belfast; 2 da (Dr Astrid James b 1962, Ingrid Teesdale b 1964); m 2, 1993, Prof Dorota Iwaniec, *qv*; *Career* architect, town planner, antiquarian, architectural historian; architectural ed Survey of London 1970–73, conslt architect to Scottish Ctee for European Architectural Heritage Year 1973–75, sr architect Herts CC 1975–77; De Montfort Univ Leicester: sr lectr 1978–88, prof of architectural history Dept of Architecture 1988–95, prof of architectural history and research Centre for Conservation Studies 1995–98, prof emeritus of architectural history 1998–, research fell Sch of Architecture 1998–2000; Queen's Univ Belfast: sr res fell Sch of Architecture 2000–02 (hon sr res fell 2002–), prof of architectural history 2000–02; practising assoc Acad of Experts; visiting fell Peterhouse Cambridge 1991–92 and 2002, visiting prof Univ of Ulster 2010–13 and 2015–, prof of architecture Univ of Ulster 2013–15; historic buildings conslt Adam Architecture Winchester 2015–; memb Advsy Cncl Friends of Kensal Green Cemetery 1998–2003 (memb Fabric Ctee 2003–08); memb: Fabric Advsy Ctee Leicester Cathedral 1992–2000, Educn Ctee Royal Soc of Ulster Architects 1997–99, Conservation Ctee Royal Soc of Ulster Architects 2000–01; pres Friends of Old Southampton Cemetery 2006–, jt patron Mausolea and Monuments Tst 2008–, vice-pres Friends of Kensal Green Cemetery 2014–; author of numerous articles and reviews; Liveryman Worshipful Co of Chartered Architects; hon Doctor of Arts De Montfort Univ 2014; MRIA, FSA, FSAScot, FRIAS, MRIAI, RIBA, Hon AABC; *Books* The Erosion of Oxford (1977), The Life and Work of Henry Roberts 1803–76, Architect (1983), The Londonderry Plantation 1609–1914 (1986), English Architecture (1987), The Art and Architecture of Freemasonry (1991, new edn 2002, Sir Banister Fletcher Award 1992), Encyclopaedia of Architectural Terms (1993), Egyptomania (1994), Victorian Churches (1995), Dictionary of Architecture (1999 and 2000), The Honourable The Irish Society and the Plantation of Ulster, 1608–2000: The City of London and the Colonisation of County Londonderry in the Province of Ulster in Ireland (2000), The Victorian Celebration of Death (2000 and 2004), Kensal Green Cemetery 1824–2001 (2001), Classical Architecture (2001), Piety Proclaimed (2002), Death and Architecture (2002), Georgian Architecture (2002), The Egyptian Revival (2005), Oxford Dictionary of Architecture and Landscape Architecture (2006), Victorian Architecture: Diversity and Invention (2007), Spas, Wells and Pleasure-Gardens of London (2010), Freemasonry & the Enlightenment: Architecture, Symbols, & Influences (2011), Georgian Architecture in the British Isles 1714–1830 (2011), The Practice of Architecture: Eight Architects 1830–1930 (contrib, 2012), Funerary Monuments & Memorials in St Patrick's Cathedral Armagh (2013), The Oxford Dictionary of Architecture (with Susan Wilson, 2015, paperback edn 2016), The Victorian Celebration of Death (ebook, 2015); *Recreations* music, opera, travel, literature, ecclesiology, food, wine, poetry, painting, conviviality; *Clubs* Art Workers' Guild, Oxford and Cambridge; *Style*— Professor James Stevens Curl, MRIA, FSA; ✉ 15 Torgrange, Holywood, Co Down BT18 0NG (☎ and fax 028 90 425 141, e-mail jscurl@btinternet.com, website www.jamesstevenscurl.com)

STEVENS OF KIRKWHELPINGTON, Baron (Life Peer UK 2005), of Kirkwhelpington in the County of Northumberland; Sir John Arthur Stevens; kt (2000), QPM, DL (Gtr London 2001); *Educ* St Lawrence Coll Ramsgate, Univ of Leicester (LLB), Univ of Southampton (MPhil); *Career* joined Met Police Force 1964, Asst Chief Constable Hampshire 1986–88, Dep Chief Constable Cambridgeshire 1988–91, Chief Constable Northumbria 1991–98, Metropolitan Police Cmmr 2000–05 (Dep Cmmr 1998–2000); HM Insp of Constabulary 1996–98; head of inquiries into: alleged malpractice at NCIS 1989–92, alleged collusion between paramilitaries and security forces in NI 1989–2003, the deaths of Diana, Princess of Wales and Dodi Fayed 2004–06, alleged corruption in football Premier League player transfers 2006; former: chm ACPO Crime Prevention Ctee, chm Behavioural Science Ctee, advsr to Forensic Science Service, visiting prof City Univ NY, memb directing staff Police Staff Coll; advsr on policing to SA, Jamaican, Bugarian, Romanian, Quatar and Greek govts; non-exec chm MonitorQuest 2005–, exec chm Axiom Ltd; non-exec dir: Travelex 2005–, BAA 2007–; chair Federation Equestre Internationale Ethics Panel 2009–; Hon Col Northumbria Army Cadets, Hon Air Cdre RAAF; fell Wolfson Coll Cambridge, hon fell Soc of Advanced Legal Studies; Freeman City of London 2002; LLD Univ of Leicester 2000, Hon PhD London Met Univ, Hon DLit Newcastle Univ, Hon DCL Univ of Northumbria 2001; Rotary Paul Harris Fell 2000; Star of Romania 2000; *Recreations* sport as both spectator and participant; *Style*— The Rt Hon the Lord Stevens of Kirkwhelpington, QPM, DL

STEVENS OF LUDGATE, Baron (Life Peer UK 1987), of Ludgate in the City of London; David Robert Stevens; s of late Arthur Edwin Stevens, CBE; *b* 26 May 1936; *Educ* Stowe, Sidney Sussex Coll Cambridge (MA); *m* 1, (m dis 1971), Patricia Rose; 1 da, 1 s; m 2, 1977, Melissa Milicevich (d 1989); m 3, 1990, Meriza Giori; *Career* mgmnt trainee Elliott Automation 1959; dir: Hill Samuel Securities 1959–68, Drayton Gp 1968–74; chm: English & International 1976–79, Drayton Far East 1976–93, Alexander Proudfoot Hldgs (formerly City & Foreign) 1976–95, Consolidated Venture (formerly Montagu Boston) 1979–93, Drayton Consolidated 1980–92, United News & Media (formerly United Newspapers plc) 1981–99 (dir 1974–99), EDC for Civil Engrg 1984–86, Express Newspapers 1985–99 (dep chm 2014–), INVESCO MIM (formerly Britannia Arrow Hldgs) 1989–93 (dep chm 1987–89), Drayton Japan 1980–88, Mid States 1989–95, Oak Industries 1989–96, Premier Asset Mgmnt plc 1997–2001, PNC Tele.Com (formerly Personal Number Co) 1998–2002, MIM Britannia Ltd (formerly Montagu Investment Mgmnt Ltd) 1980–93; chm EDC for Civil Engrg 1984–86, fndr, chm and dir Helicopter Emergency Rescue Service 1988–90; fell Sidney Sussex Coll Cambridge 1991; patron RCS 1998; Grand Official Order of Southern Cross Brazil 1993; *Recreations* golf, gardening; *Clubs* White's, Sunningdale Golf, Swinley Golf; *Style*— The Lord Stevens of Ludgate; ✉ House of Lords, London SW1A 0PW

STEVENSON, Sir Hugh Alexander; kt (2010); *b* 7 September 1942; *Educ* Harrow, UC Oxford (BA); *m* 23 Oct 1965, Catherine, *née* Peacock; 2 s, 2 da; *Career* Linklaters & Paines slrs 1964–70, joined S G Warburg & Co 1970, dir S G Warburg Group plc 1987–95; chm: Mercury Asset Management Group plc 1992–98 (dir 1986–98), Equitas Ltd 1998–2009, The Merchants Tst plc 2000–10; non-exec dir: Standard Life plc 1999–2008, FSA 2004–10 (dep chm 2009–10); memb Advsy Ctee on Business Appointments 2010–15; tstee: Stevenson Family's Charitable Trust, Welton Fndn, Sir Siegmund Warburg's Voluntary Settlement; *Style*— Sir Hugh Stevenson

STEVENSON, Jessica; *see:* Hynes, (Tallulah) Jessica Elina

STEVENSON, (Andrew) John; MP; *b* 4 July 1963; *Educ* Univ of Dundee, Coll of Law Chester; *Career* slr; ptnr Bendles; cncllr Carlisle City Cncl 1999–2010, MP (Cons) Carlisle 2010–; *Style*— John Stevenson, MP; ✉ House of Commons, London SW1A 0AA

STEVENSON, Juliet Anne Virginia; CBE (1999); da of Brig Michael Guy Stevens, MBE, and Virginia Ruth, *née* Marshall; *b* 30 October 1956, Kelvedon, Essex; *Educ* Hurst Lodge Sch, St Catherine's Sch Bramley, RADA (Gold Bancroft Medal); *Partner* Hugh Brody; 1 da (Rosalind b 1994), 1 s (Gabriel b 2000); *Career* actress; currently assoc artist RSC; *Theatre* RSC 1978–86 incl: Madame de Tourvel in Les Liaisons Dangereuses, Rosalind in As You Like It, Cressida in Troilus and Cressida (nominated for Olivier Best Actress Award), Isabella in Measure for Measure (nominated for Best Actress Award, winner Drama Magazine Best Actress Award), Titania/Hippolyta in A Midsummer Night's Dream, Susan in The Witch of Edmonton, Clara Douglas in Money, Lady Percy in Henry IV Parts I and II, Miss Chasen in Once in a Lifetime, Yeliena in The White Guard, Aphrodite/Artemis in Hippolytus, Octavia/Iras in Antony and Cleopatra, Caroline Thompson in The Churchill Play; other credits incl: Emma/Betsy in Other Worlds (Royal Court) 1982, Paulina in Death and the Maiden (Royal Court and Duke of York's, Best Actress Time Out Awards and Olivier Awards 1992), Anna in Burn This (Hampstead/Lyric), Fanny in On the Verge (Sadler's Wells), title role in Yerma (NT) 1987 (nominated for Olivier Best Actress Award), Hedda in Hedda Gabler (NT) 1989, Galactia in Scenes from an Execution (Mark Taper Forum Los Angeles), The Duchess of Malfi (Wyndham's) 1995, The Caucasian Chalk Circle (RNT) 1997, Not I 1997, Footfalls 1997, Amanda in Private Lives (RNT) 1999, Corinne in The Country (Royal Court) 2000, A Little Night Music (NYC Opera) 2003, We Happy Few (Gielguld Theatre) 2004, The Alice Trilogy (Royal Court) 2005, The Seagull (RNT) 2006, Duet for One (Almeida Theatre and Vaudeville Theatre) 2009 (nominated Best Actress Evening Standard Award and Olivier Award), The Heretic (Royal Court) 2011, Happy Days (Young Vic) 2014; *Television* for BBC incl: Nora in A Dolls House, Claire in The March, Rape Victim in Omnibus – Rape, Lucy Sadler in Aimée, Ruth in Out of Love, Hilda Spencer in Stanley, Rosalind in Life Story (winner Ace Cable TV Network Award Best Supporting Actress), Antigone in Oedipus at Colonus, title role in Antigone, Elizabeth Von Reitburg in Freud, Fliss in Bazaar and Rummage, Joanna Langton in Maybury, Stone Scissors Paper, Ten Days to War 2008, Dustbin Baby 2008, The Hour 2011, White Heat 2012, The Village 2013, Atlantis 2013; other credits incl: Margaret in In The Border Country (Channel Four), Vicky in Living With Dinosaurs (Jim Henson Organisation, winner Emmy Award for Best Children's Film), Barbara Mallen in The Mallens (Granada), The Politician's Wife

S

(Channel Four, The Broadcasting Press Guild Award for Best Actress 1996) 1995 (nominated Best Actress BAFTA Award), Mother in Cider with Rosie (Carlton) 1998, Trial By Fire (ITV) 1999, The Road from Coorain 2001, The Pact (Lifetime TV) 2002, Hear the Silence 2003, Ordeal by Innocence 2007, Place of Execution (ITV) 2008 (Best Actress Crime Thriller Award), Law and Order (ITV) 2009, Accused 2010, Ghost Story (Sky Arts) 2010, Lewis (ITV) 2011; *Films* incl: Nina in Truly Madly Deeply, Alice in Ladder of Swords, Cissie II in Drowning By Numbers, Fraulein Burstner in The Trial, Isobel in The Secret Rapture 1994, Mrs Elton in Emma 1996, Play (part of the Beckett on Film series) 2000, Bend It Like Beckham 2002, Food of Love 2002, Nicholas Nickleby 2002, Mona Lisa Smile 2003, Infamous 2005, Red Mercury Rising 2005, Pierrepoint 2005, Breaking and Entering 2006, When Did You Last See Your Father? 2007, The Secret of Moonacre 2008, A Previous Engagement 2008, Desert Flower 2010, Diana 2013; *Books* Clamorous Voices (co-author, 1988), Shall I See You Again (co-ed, 1994); *Recreations* talking, walking, reading, piano, travelling, cinema, theatre, music; *Style—* Juliet Stevenson, CBE

STEVENSON, Michael Charles; s of Michael Anthony Stevenson, and Ena Elizabeth Stevenson, of Doncaster; *b* 14 August 1960; *Educ* Doncaster GS, ChCh Oxford (open scholarship, MA); *m* 1987, Deborah Frances, da of Baron Taylor of Gosforth (Life Peer, d 1997); 1 s (Thomas b 1991), 2 da (Celia b 1994, Beatrice b 1998); *Career* BBC: trainee BBC Radio Sport 1983–84, prodr Talks & Documentaries BBC Radio 1984–88, prodr On the Record BBC1 1988–90, chief asst Policy & Planning 1990–91, dep ed On the Record 1991–92, sec 1992–96, dep dir Regional Broadcasting 1996–99, dir Educn 1999–2003, jt dir Factual and Learning 2000–2003; DfES: dir Strategy and Communications 2003, dir technol and chief info offr 2005–06; Cisco Systems: vice-pres global educn 2007–13, vice-pres global public sector (strategy, educn and healthcare) 2012–13; educn conslt 2013–; prof Glasgow Caledonian Univ 2013–; sr research fell Nat Centre for Univs and Business 2013–; memb Bd Resource (Cncl for museums, archives and libraries) 2000–06, non-exec dir Granada Learning 2007–10, non-exec dir Surrey and Borders Partnership NHS Fndn Tst 2011–, assoc Nesta 2014–; *Recreations* travel, sport, reading; *Style—* Michael Stevenson, Esq

STEVENSON, Patricia Mary; *née* Anstey; da of Dr Frank Bernard Anstey (d 1985), and Muriel Elizabeth, *née* Goodwin; *b* 17 December 1957, Bradfield, Berks; *Educ* Queen Anne's Sch Caversham, Univ of Surrey (BSc); *m* 29 June 1991, Gordon Cunningham Stevenson; 2 s (Luke Alexander Blackwood b 18 Oct 1994, Theodore James Anstey b 17 Aug 2000); *Career* sales exec Thomson Regnl Newspapers 1980–81, sr sales exec Mind Your Own Business Magazine 1981–84, advertisement mangr A La Carte magazine IPC Magazines 1984–87, head of business devpt Thames TV 1987–92; Condé Nast Pubns: promotions dir Tatler and Vanity Fair 1993–2000, publisher Tatler 2001–07, publishing dir Tatler 2008–; *Recreations* skiing, horse riding, art, travelling, friends; *Style—* Mrs Patricia Stevenson; ✉ Tatler, Condé Nast Publications Limited, Vogue House, Hanover Square, London W1S 1JU (☎ 020 7152 3006)

STEVENSON, (George) Raymond (Ray); s of Derek Stevenson (d 2007), and Margret Ann, *née* Sloan; *b* 25 May 1964, Lisburn, NI; *Educ* Bristol Old Vic Theatre Sch; *Partner* Elisabetta Caraccia; 1 s (Sebastiano Derek b 24 Dec 2007); *Career* actor; *Theatre* Jesus in York Mystery Plays (York Minster) 2000, Cardinal in The Duchess of Malfi (National Theatre) 2003; *Film* incl: King Arthur 2004, Punisher: War Zone 2008, Cirque du Freak 2010, The Book of Eli 2010, The Three Musketeers 2011, Thor 2011, GI Joe: Retaliation: 2013, Thor: The Dark World 2013; *Television* incl Rome 2005–07, Dexter 2012; *Recreations* painting (oils, fine art), golf, travel (insatiable gypsy!); *Style—* Ray Stevenson, Esq; ✉ c/o Brian Swardstrom, Endeavor, Los Angeles, California, USA (☎ 00 1 310 248 2000)

STEVENSON, (James Alexander) Stewart; MSP; s of James Thomas Middleton Stevenson (d 1990), and Helen Mary Berry, *née* MacGregor (d 1984); *b* 15 October 1946, Edinburgh; *Educ* Bell-Baxter Sch, Univ of Aberdeen (MA); *m* 1969, Sandra Isabel, *née* Pirie; *Career* with Bank of Scotland 1969–99 (positions incl: head of devpt servs, head of technol planning, dir of technol innovation), lectr Heriot-Watt Univ 1999–2002; MSP (SNP): Banff & Buchan (by-election) 2001–11, Banffshire and Buchan Coast 2011– (Scot Parl candidate Linlithgow 1999); min of transport, infrastructure and climate change 2007–10, min of environment and climate change 2011–12; convenor Standards, Procedures and Public Appts Ctee Scottish Parliament 2013–16; memb SNP 1961–; *Recreations* photography, public speaking, reading, genealogy; *Clubs* Town and County Banff; *Style—* Stewart Stevenson, Esq, MSP; ✉ Reidside, Ord, Banffshire AB45 3BL; Office 8, Burnside Business Centre, Peterhead AB42 3AW (☎ 01779 470444, e-mail msp@stewartstevenson.scot, website www.stewartstevenson.scot)

STEVENSON, Struan John Stirton; s of Robert Harvey Ure Stevenson (d 1992), and Elizabeth, *née* Robertson Stirton (d 1986); *b* 4 April 1948, Ballantrae, Ayrshire; *Educ* Strathallan Sch Perthshire, West of Scotland Agric Coll Auchincruive Ayr (DipAg); *m* 9 Sept 1974, Patricia Anne, da of late Dr Alastair Taylor; 2 s (Ryan b 30 April 1977, Gregor b 2 July 1980); *Career* MEP (Cons) Scotland 1999–2014; Parly candidate (Cons): Carrick Cumnock & Doon Valley 1987, Edinburgh S 1992, Dumfries 1997; Euro Parly candidate (Cons) NE Scotland (by-election) 1998); sr vice-pres Fisheries Ctee Euro Parl 2009–14 (pres 2002–04), pres Euro Parl's Delgn for Relations with Iraq 2009–14; personal rep of the Chm in Office Organization for Security and Co-operation in Europe 2010; author and political conslt 2014–; cncllr and gp ldr Convention of Scottish Local Authorities (COSLA) 1986–88; cncllr: Kyle & Carrick DC 1974–92 (ldr 1986–88), Girvan DC 1970–74; chm Scottish Cons Parly Candidates Assoc 1992–97; dir: J&R Stevenson Ltd 1968–2007, PS Communication Conslts Ltd 1994–99, Saferworld 1992–94; vice-pres European People's Party-European Democrats (EPP-ED) European Parly 2005–09; pres European Iraqi Freedom Assoc 2014–; memb NFU of Scotland, memb Advsy Ctee BBC Broadcasting Cncl 1984–88; hon prof Semey State Shakarim Univ Kazakhstan 2007; Hon DSc State Medical Acad Semipalatinsk Kazakhstan 2000; Freeman City of Semipalatinsk Kazakhstan 2003, State Shapagat (Charity) Medal Repub of Kazakhstan 2007, memb Order of Shapagat (Charity) Repub of Kazakhstan; *Books* Crying Forever: A Nuclear Diary (2006, Russian version 2007), Stalin's Legacy – The Soviet War on Nature (2012), So Much Wind – The Myth of Green Energy (2013), Self-Sacrifice – Life with the Iranian Mojahedin (2015); *Recreations* contemporary art, music, opera, theatre, cinema, poetry, cycling, dogs; *Clubs* New (Edinburgh); *Style—* Struan Stevenson, Esq; ✉ website www.struanstevenson.com, Twitter @StruanMEP

STEVENSON, Timothy Edwin Paul (Tim); OBE (2004); s of Derek Stevenson, and Pamela, *née* Jervelund; *b* 14 May 1948; *Educ* Canford Sch, Worcester Coll Oxford (MA), London Business Sch (Sloan fell); *m* 1973, Marion Emma Lander, da of Robin Johnston; 3 da (Molly b 29 April 1979, Beatrice b 15 May 1982, Isobel b 12 July 1984); *Career* called to the Bar Inner Temple (Duke of Edinburgh scholar); Burmah Castrol plc: asst gp legal advsr 1975–77, gp planning mangr 1977–81, chief exec Castrol Spain 1981–85, mktg mangr 1985–86, corp devpt mangr 1986–88, chief exec Expandite Gp 1988–90, chief exec Fuels Gp 1990–93, dir Lubricants 1993–98, chief exec 1998–2000; chm: Travis Perkins plc 2001–10, Morgan Crucible 2006–12, Johnson Matthey plc 2011–; non-exec dir: DfES 1997–2004, National Express Gp plc 2001–05, Partnerships UK plc 2001–04, Tribal Gp plc 2004–10; chm of govrs Oxford Brookes Univ 2004–08; memb Cncl of Mgmnt Oxford MOMA (latterly Modern Art Oxford) 1996–2004; Lord-Lt Oxon 2008– (DL 2007–08); Hon DUniv Oxford Brookes 2009; *Recreations* hill walking, reading, music; *Clubs* Oxford and Cambridge; *Style—* Tim Stevenson, Esq, OBE, DL; ✉ 263 Woodstock Road, Oxford OX2 7AE (☎ 01865 515477, e-mail office@stevenson-oxford.co.uk); Johnson Matthey plc, 5th Floor, 25 Farringdon Street, London EC4A 4AB (☎ 020 7269 8400, website www.matthey.com)

STEVENSON OF BALMACARA, Baron (Life Peer UK 2010), of Little Missenden in the County of Buckinghamshire; Robert Wilfrid (Wilf) Stevenson; s of James Alexander Stevenson (d 1993), and Elizabeth Anne, *née* Macrae (d 2006); *b* 19 April 1947, Lochalsh, Ross-shire; *Educ* Edinburgh Acad, UC Oxford (MA), Napier Poly pt/t (FCCA); *m* 1, 15 April 1972 (m dis 1979), Jennifer Grace, da of David Grace Antonio (d 1986), of Edinburgh; m 2, 19 April 1991, Elizabeth Ann, da of John Cavin Minogue, of Harrogate; 2 da (Iona Jane Minogue b 13 March 1992, Flora Kathleen Minogue b 19 Dec 1994), 1 s (Tobin James Minogue b 28 July 1993); *Career* res offr Univ of Edinburgh Students' Assoc 1970–74, sec Edinburgh Napier Univ 1974–87, dir: Br Film Inst 1988–97 (dep dir 1987–88), The Smith Inst 1997–2008, special advsr to the PM 2008–10; hon prof Univ of Stirling 1991–96; chair Consumer Credit Counselling Service 2010–12, chair StepChange Debt Charity 2012–15; govr Prestwood Lodge Sch 2008–10, govr Chiltern Way Fedn Sch 2010–14, memb Chiltern Way Fedn 2016–; Hon DA Napier Univ 2008; *Books* Gordon Brown Speeches 1997–2006 (ed, 2006), Moving Britain Forward (ed, 2006), The Change We Choose: Speeches 2007–2009 (ed, 2010); *Recreations* cinema, bee keeping, gardening; *Style—* The Lord Stevenson of Balmacara; ✉ Missenden House, Little Missenden, Amersham, Buckinghamshire HP7 0RD (☎ 01494 890689, e-mail wilf@wilfstevenson.co.uk)

STEVENSON OF CODDENHAM, Baron (Life Peer UK 1999), of Coddenham in the County of Suffolk; Sir (Henry) Dennistoun (Dennis) Stevenson; kt (1998), CBE (1981), DL (Suffolk 2008); s of Alexander James Stevenson, and Sylvia Florence, *née* Ingleby; *b* 19 July 1945; *Educ* Glenalmond Coll, King's Coll Cambridge (MA); *m* 1972, Charlotte Susan, da of Hon Sir Peter Beckford Rutgers Vanneck, GBE, CB, AFC, AE; 4 s; *Career* chm: SRU Gp of Cos 1972–96, GPA then AerFi Gp plc 1993–2000, Pearson plc 1997–2005 (dir 1986–97); dir Halifax plc 1999–2009; chm HBOS plc 2001–09, govr Bank of Scotland 2006–09; dir: British Technology Group 1979–89, Tyne Tees TV 1982–87, Manpower Inc (formerly Blue Arrow) 1988–2006, Thames Television plc 1991–93, J Rothschild Assurance plc 1991–97, J Rothschild Assurance Holdings plc 1991–99, English Partnerships 1993–99, BSkyB Gp plc 1994–2000, Lazard Brothers 1997–2000, Whitehall Tst Ltd 1997–2004, St James's Place Capital 1997–2002 (hon pres 2002–04), Economist Newspapers 1998–2011, Western Union Co 2006–12, Loudwater Investment Partners Ltd 2007–12, Culture and Sport Glasgow 2007–09, Cloaca Maxima Ltd 2010–13, Waterstones Hldgs Ltd 2011–, Inter Mediate 2011–; chm: Aycliffe & Peterlee Corporation 1971–80, Intermediate Technology Devpt Gp 1983–90, Tstees of Tate Gallery 1989–98; dir: Nat Building Agency 1977–81, LDDC 1981–88; chm 50 Million Volunteers (govt working party on role of voluntary movements and youth in the environment (HMSO)) 1971, ind advsr Ctee on Pop Festivals (Pop Festivals, Report and Code of Practice (HMSO)) 1972–76, advsr on agricultural mktg to Min of Agriculture 1979–83, special advsr to PM and Sec of State for Educn on the use of Information Technology in Educn 1997–2000; chm: House of Lords Appointments Cmmn 2000–09, Arts and Media Honours Ctee 2008–12; memb Panel on Takeovers and Mergers 1992–2000, memb Bd British Cncl 1996–2003, memb Standards Ctee Westminster CC 2008–12, memb House of Lords Works of Arts Ctee 2009–14; memb Inst for Govt 2008–13; chm: NAYC 1973–81, Sinfonia 21 (formerly Docklands Sinfonietta) 1989–99, London Docklands Devpt Corp 1984–88; dir: Aldeburgh Music Ltd (formerly Aldeburgh Prodns) 2000–12 (pres 2012–), Glyndebourne Prodns 1998–, London Music Masters 2011–; tstee Tate Gallery Fndn 1998–, tstee Horse's Mouth 2006–15, founding chm MQ: Transforming Mental Health 2010–15; memb Admin Cncl Royal Jubilee Tst 1978–80; pres Aldeburgh Music 2012–; govr: LSE 1995–99, London Business Sch 1999–2002; chllr Univ of the Arts London (now London Inst) 2000–10; *Recreations* home; *Clubs* MCC, Brooks's, Garrick; *Style—* The Lord Stevenson of Coddenham, CBE

STEW, HE Tim; MBE (1996); *Career* diplomat; joined FCO 1988, press offr Riyadh 1991–95, third sec Sarajevo 1995–96, dep high cmmr Belize 1996–99, head Iraq Sanctions/Humanitarian Team ME and N Africa Directorate FCO 2000–03, head Political and Economic Team Cairo 2003–06, dep head of mission Kuwait 2007–10, sr strategist Finance Directorate FCO 2010, head Arab Partnership Dept ME and N Africa Directorate FCO 2010–15, high cmmr to Repub of Trinidad and Tobago 2015–; *Style—* HE Mr Tim Stew, MBE; ✉ c/o FCO (Port of Spain), King Charles Street, London SW1A 2AH (e-mail tim.stew@fco.gov.uk)

STEWART, Alastair James; OBE (2006); s of late Gp Capt James Frederick Stewart, and late Joan Mary, *née* Lord; *b* 22 June 1952; *Educ* St Augustine's Abbey Sch, Univ of Bristol; *m* 8 April 1978, Sally Ann, da of Frederick Harold Rudolph Jung (d 1968); 3 s (Alexander b 1982, Frederick b 1993, Oscar b 1997), 1 da (Clementine b 1985); *Career* dep pres NUS 1974–76; Southern Independent TV: editorial trainee 1976, industrial reporter and presenter of progs (incl Energy – What Crisis?) 1976–80; ITN: industrial corr 1980–82, newscaster (incl News at Ten and Channel 4 News) 1982–89 and 1990–92, Washington corr 1990; news anchor London News Network 1993–2004, presenter ITV Lunchtime News 2007–, presenter ITV News at 6.30 2009–, presenter ITV News at Ten 2009–; presenter: Missing (LWT/ITV Network) 1993–96, Alastair Stewart's Sunday (BBC Radio 5) 1994, The Sunday Programme with Alastair Stewart (GMTV) 1994, Police Stop! (Carlton TV/ITV Network) 1994, The Carlton Debates (Carlton TV) 1995, Police, Camera, Action! (Carlton TV/ITV Network) 1995–2003 and 2007–09, Fire Live! (LWT/ITV Network) 1996, Devolution: The Future of the Union (LWT/ITV Network) 1997, Who Wants to be a London Mayor? (Carlton TV/LWT) 2000, 2004 and 2008, King of the Castle (Carlton TV) 2001, ITV News Channel 2003, Live with Alastair Stewart (ITV News Channel), Cities at War (with Walter Cronkite, ITV) 2006, Legacy of War (with Walter Cronkite, ITV) 2007, ITV News at 1030 2007, The Moral of the Story (ITV) 2007–10, Battle for London Mayor Debate (ITV) 2012; presenter various news progs incl: The Budget 1982–92, 2004–06 and 2008–14, General Election 1987, 1992, 1997, 2005, 2010 and 2015, State Opening of Parliament 1988–89 and 2004–05 weddings of Prince of Wales and Duke of York, funeral of Pope John Paul II; moderated first ever TV election debate between pty ldrs 2010; subject of This is Your Life (BBC TV) 1999; Face of London Award RTS 2002, Presenter of the Year RTS 2004, Broadcasting Press Guild Innovation Award (for Leaders' Debate), ITV News Gp Achievement Award (for Leaders' Debate), Political Studies Associate Jubilee Award (for Leaders' Debate); vice-pres: Homestart UK, NCH Action for Children; patron: The Zito Tst, Lord Mayor Treloar Coll, HOPE, Samantha Dixon Tst; patron: Just a Drop (former tstee), The Brooke, Crisis; vice-patron: Mental Health Fndn, SANE; ambass Crisis; memb Scrutiny Panel N and Mid Hants HA; govr Ravensbourne Coll; Hon LLD: Univ of Bristol 2008, Univ of Plymouth 2010, Univ of Winchester 2012, Univ of Sunderland 2012; *Recreations* reading, music, antique maps; *Clubs* Ivy, Century; *Style—* Alastair Stewart, OBE; ✉ ITN, 200 Gray's Inn Road, London WC1X 8XZ (☎ 020 7833 3000)

STEWART, Sheriff Alastair Lindsay; QC (Scot 1995); s of Alexander Lindsay Stewart (d 1977); *b* 28 November 1938; *Educ* Edinburgh Acad, St Edmund Hall Oxford, Univ of Edinburgh; *m* 1, 1968 (m dis), Annabel Claire, da of Prof William McCausland Stewart (d 1989); 2 s; m 2, 1991, Sheila Anne, da of David Hynd Flockhart (d 1999), wid of William Neil Mackinnon; *Career* tutor Faculty of Law Univ of Edinburgh 1963–73, standing jr counsel Registrar of Restrictive Trading Agreements 1968–70, advocate depute 1970–73; Sheriff: South Strathclyde, Dumfries and Galloway at Airdrie 1973–79, Grampian, Highland and Islands at Aberdeen 1979–90, Tayside, Central and Fife at

Dundee 1990–2004; temp judge Supreme Courts of Scotland 1996–2013, interim Sheriff Princ Lothian and Borders, Glasgow and Strathkelvin 2005; govr Robert Gordon's Inst of Technol 1982–90; hon prof Sch of Law Univ of Dundee 2001–12; chm: Grampian Family Conciliation Serv 1984–87, Scottish Assoc of Family Conciliation Servs 1986–89; memb Judicial Studies Ctee 2000–04; ed Scottish Civil Law Reports 1992–95; *Books* The Scottish Criminal Courts in Action (1 edn 1990, 2 edn 1997), Macphail's Sheriff Court Practice (jt ed, 2 edn, vol 1 1998, vol 2 2002), Stair Memorial Encyclopaedia of the Laws of Scotland (Evidence reissue, 2006); *Recreations* reading, music, walking; *Clubs* Western (Glasgow); *Style—* Sheriff Alastair L Stewart, QC; ✉ 86 Albany Road, Broughty Ferry, Dundee DD5 1JQ (✆ 01382 477580, e-mail als281138@aol.com)

STEWART, Andrew Marshall (Andy); s of Dr John Stewart (d 1982), of Essex and Dr Mabel Stewart, *née* Linscott (d 1980); *b* 15 August 1951, London; *Educ* Felsted Sch, Mid-Essex Tech; *m* 4 Oct 1975, Judith, *née* Stewart; 2 s (Mark b 3 Aug 1978, Paul b 22 Jan 1981); *Career* stockbroker and ptnr Simon and Coates 1968–86, chief exec Chase Manhattan Securities (following merger) 1986–90, fndr and chief exec Collins Stewart 1991–2003 (led MBO and IPO 2000), fndr Cenkos Securities (now Ravenscroft) 2005–; memb London Stock Exchange; *Recreations* National Hunt horse racing (owner of 25 race horses); *Clubs* Mullins Beach, Barbados, Guernsey, Aero Club; *Style—* Andy Stewart, Esq; ✉ Ravenscroft, The Market Building, Fountain Street, St Peter Port, Guernsey GY1 4JG (✆ 01481 729100, e-mail astewart@ravenscroft.gg, website www.ravenscroft.gg)

STEWART, Hon Lord; Angus Stewart; QC (Scot 1988); s of Archibald Ian Balfour Stewart, CBE, FSA Scot (d 1998), and Ailsa Rosamund Mary Massey; bro of Patrick Stewart, *qv*; *b* 14 December 1946; *Educ* Edinburgh Acad, Balliol Coll Oxford (BA), Univ of Edinburgh (LLB); *m* 14 June 1975, Jennifer Margaret, da of John Faulds Stewart (d 1980), of Edinburgh; 1 da (Flora b 13 Sept 1981); *Career* barr 1975–, sr advocate depute 2005–08, leading counsel Billy Wright Inquiry NI 2008–10, senator Coll of Justice 2010–; keeper of the Advocates Library 1994–2002; chm: Abbotsford Library Project 1995–2002, Scottish Cncl of Law Reporting 1997–2001; convenor Human Rights Ctee of Faculty of Advocates 2000–02; pres Stair Soc 2013–; tstee: Int E Boat Class Assoc 1993–, Nat Library of Scotland 1994–2005, Stewart Heritage Tst 1994–2001, Stewart Soc 1998– (pres 2001–04), Robert Louis Stevenson Club 2001–08; Hon Sheriff Campbeltown 2014–; *Publications* articles on law, history and literature; *Style—* The Hon Lord Stewart; ✉ The Court of Session, Parliament House, Edinburgh EH1 1RQ (✆ 0131 225 2595)

STEWART, Sir Brian John; kt (2002), CBE (1996); s of Ian Mann Stewart, and Christina Stewart; *b* 9 April 1945; *Educ* Perth Acad, Univ of Edinburgh (MSc); *m* 16 July 1971, Seonaid; 2 s (Alistair b 1974, Duncan b 1980), 1 da (Emily b 1976); *Career* articled clerk J & R Morison CAs Perth 1962–67, chief mgmnt accountant Ethicon Ltd Edinburgh 1969–76; Scottish and Newcastle plc: joined 1976, various commercial and financial positions in Scottish Brewers and William Younger subsids and Retail and Beer Prodn divisions, corp devpt dir 1985–88, gp fin dir 1988–91, gp chief exec 1991–2003, dep chm 1997–2000, exec chm 2000–03, non-exec chm 2003–07; chm C&C Gp 2010–; non-exec dir: Booker plc 1993–99, Standard Life Assurance Company 1993–2007 (non-exec chm 2003–07), Miller Gp 2008– (non-exec chm 2009–11); chm Brewers' and Licensed Retailers' Assoc (formerly Brewers' Soc) 1996–98 (vice-chm 1994–96), vice-pres Br Beer & Pub Assoc; memb Ct Univ of Edinburgh 1991–98; MICAS 1967; *Recreations* golf, skiing; *Style—* Sir Brian Stewart, CBE

STEWART, Danielle Caroline; OBE (2013); da of Edward Elieza Harris, of London, and Deanna Sylvia, *née* Levy (now Mrs Morgan-Russell); *b* 6 November 1961; *Educ* Sutton HS for Girls GPDST, Nonsuch HS for Girls, Kingston Poly; *Children* 2 da (Francesca Anne Forristal b 19 Dec 1995, Isabelle Roberta Forristal b 8 Oct 1998); *Career* Myers Davis Chartered Accountants 1980–82, Halpern & Woolf Chartered Accountants 1982–84, Bright Grahame Murray 1985–87, self-employed 1987–88, ptnr Warrener Stewart 1988–2004 (conslt 2004–); dir: A Plus Ltd, A Plus Software Ltd, God in the Boardroom Ltd, Stratethica Ltd, Pentagon Protection plc; co sec Campus Media plc; devised and released Auditplus audit system 1991; memb: Accounting Standards Bd Ctee on Accounting for Smaller Entities (CASE) 1997–, Auditing Practices Bd Tech Advsy Gp; industrial fell Kingston Univ; winner Young Accountant of the Year Award 1994; FCA, FCCA; *Books* Auditplus (1991), A Practitioner's Guide to the Company Law Review (2002); *Recreations* spiritual matters generally; *Style—* Ms Danielle C Stewart, OBE; ✆ 07876 032222, e-mail daniellestewart@hotmail.com

STEWART, David John; MSP; s of John and Alice Stewart; *b* 5 May 1956; *Educ* Inverness HS, Paisley Coll (BA), Univ of Stirling (Dip Social Work, CQSW), Open Univ Business Sch (Dip Mgmnt); *m* 6 Aug 1982, Linda Ann, *née* MacDonald; 1 s (Andrew b 14 Jan 1987), 1 da (Kirsty b 1 Jan 1993), 1 s decd (Liam d 1991); *Career* social work asst Edinburgh 1980; social worker: Dumfries 1981–86, Dingwall 1986–87; team mangr Inverness 1987–97; asst dir Scottish Cncl for Voluntary Orgns 2005–07; MP (Lab) Inverness E, Nairn and Lochaber 1997–2005, MSP (Lab) Highlands and Islands 2007–; Lab chief whip Scottish Parl 2008–11, convener Public Petitions Ctee 2011–, memb Scottish Parl Corp Body 2011–, shadow min for environment, climate change and land reform 2016–; cncllr Inverness DC 1988–96, govr Eden Court Theatre 1992–96; *Recreations* keep fit, sport, football, travel; *Style—* David Stewart, Esq, MSP; ✉ Highlands & Islands MPs Office, PO Box 5717, Inverness IV1 1YT (✆ 01463 716299)

STEWART, Capt Sir David John Christopher; 7 Bt (UK 1803), of Athenree, Tyrone; s of Sir Hugh Charlie Godfray Stewart, 6 Bt (d 1994), and his 1 w, Rosemary Elinor Dorothy, *née* Peacocke (d 1986); *b* 19 June 1935; *Educ* Bradfield, RMA Sandhurst; *m* 7 Nov 1959, Bridget Anne, er da of late Patrick Wood Sim; 3 da (Siobhan Amanda (Mrs Martin Thomas) b 1961, Selina Godfray (Mrs Jeremy West) b 1964, Sophie Caroline (Mrs Jonathan A'Court-Wills) b 1966); *Heir* half-bro, Hugh Nicholas Stewart; *Career* Capt (ret) Royal Inniskilling Fus (seconded Trucial Oman Scouts); hon pres Trucial Oman Scouts Assoc 2014–; sometime dir Maurice James (Hldgs) Ltd; Medal of the Order of the Tower of Al Qasimi 2003; *Recreations* cricket, golf, music; *Style—* Capt Sir David Stewart, Bt

STEWART, David Purcell; OBE (2015); s of Maurice Edward Stewart (d 1967), and Joyce Ethel Stewart (d 2000); *b* 8 September 1941; *Educ* Rutlish Sch Merton Park; *m* 14 Sept 1968, Judith Esther, da of Charles Owen (d 1983), of Bexleyheath, Kent; 1 da (Susannah Celia b 23 April 1977); *Career* chartered accountant; PricewaterhouseCoopers (formerly Deloitte Haskins & Sells and then Coopers & Lybrand): joined 1958, ptnr 1967–96, nat tax ptnr 1982–90, exec ptnr i/c Central London office 1990–94; chm Euro Human Resource Advsy Gp Coopers & Lybrand Europe 1994–98; dep chm Asda Property Holdings plc 1998–2001; dir ECB 2002–10, chm Surrey CCC 2003–10 (treas 1997–2003), dir Homerton Univ Hosp 2008–14; chm: Haig Housing 2000–, Tomorrow's People 2004–13; Freeman City of London 1982; FCA 1963, FInstD 1982; *Recreations* numismatics, theatre, opera, cricket; *Clubs* RAC, MCC; *Style—* David Stewart, Esq, OBE, FCA; ✉ 21 St Michaels, Wolfs Row, Limpsfield, Oxted, Surrey RH8 0QL

STEWART, Prof Frances Julia; da of Nicholas Kaldor (d 1986), and Clarissa, *née* Goldschmidt (d 1995); *b* 4 August 1940, Kaldor; *Educ* Univ of Oxford (MA, DPhil, Webb Medley jr and sr prizes); *m* 23 June 1962, Michael Stewart, s of J I M Stewart; 3 da (Lucy b 1964, Anna b 1966 (decd), Kitty b 1970), 1 s (David b 1974); *Career* econ asst HM Treasy 1961–62, econ asst then advsr NEDO and Dept of Econ Affrs 1962–67, lectr Univ of Nairobi 1967–69; Queen Elizabeth House Univ of Oxford: sr research offr 1972–93, dir 1993–2003, dir Centre for Research on Inequality, Human Security and Ethnicity 2003–10; fell Somerville Coll Oxford 1975–2008, emeritus prof of development economics and emeritus fell Somerville Coll Oxford 2010–; overseer Thomas Watson Inst Brown Univ RI; pres Devpt Studies Assoc 1990–92, chair UN Ctee for Devpt Policy, pres Human Devpt and Capability Assoc 2008–10, tstee Inst of Devpt Studies Univ of Sussex; UN Mahbub ul Haq Award 2009, Leontief Prize for Advancing the Frontiers of Economic Thought 2013; hon doctorate Univ of Sussex; *Books* Technology and Underdevelopment (1976), Adjustment with a Human Face (jtly, 1987), War and Underdevelopment (jtly, 2001), Defining Poverty in the Developing World (jtly), Horizontal Inequalities and Conflict: Understanding Group Violence in Multethnic Societies (jtly, 2008); *Recreations* gym, walking, children and grandchildren; *Style—* Prof Frances Stewart; ✉ Queen Elizabeth House, 3 Mansfield Road, Oxford OX1 3TB (✆ 01865 281800, fax 01865 281801, e-mail frances.stewart@qeh.ox.ac.uk)

STEWART, Gordon; s of Archibald Leitch Stewart (d 1997), of Luton, Beds, and Christina Macpherson, *née* Taylor (d 1976); *b* 18 April 1953; *Educ* Luton GS, Univ of Durham (BA); *m* 2 Oct 1982, Teresa Violet, da of Sir James Holmes Henry, 2 Bt, CMG, MC, TD, QC (d 1997), of Hampton, Middx; 2 s (Edmund James b 24 May 1985, Roland Valentine b 16 Jan 1988); *Career* asst slr Slaughter & May 1978–83 (articled clerk 1976–78); ptnr: Simmons & Simmons 1985–99 (asst slr 1983–85), Richards Butler 1999–2004, Haarmann Hemmelrath 2004–06, conslt Squire, Sanders & Dempsey 2006–07, counsel Ashurst 2007–; memb Law Soc; *Recreations* motoring, food and wine; *Style—* Gordon Stewart, Esq; ✉ Ashurst LLP, Broadwalk House, 5 Appold Street, London EC2A 2HA (✆ 020 7859 3077, fax 020 7638 1112, e-mail gordon.stewart@ashurst.com)

STEWART, Gordon Colin; s of Alan Alexander Fergus Stewart, of Glasgow, and Helen Somerville, *née* Curr (d 2015); *b* 16 May 1956; *Educ* Buckhurst Hill Co HS, Hutchesons' Boys GS Glasgow, UC Oxford (MA); *m* 1987, Fiona Annabel, da of Jack Gatchfield (d 2003), of Welwyn Garden City, Herts; 2 da (Jessica b 1989, Amelia b 1995), 1 s (Alexander b 1992); *Career* ptnr: Cameron Markby 1983–88 (articled and asst slr 1978–83), Allen & Overy LLP 1989–2016 (pt/t conslt 2016–); pres Soc of Practitioners of Insolvency 1996–97; memb: City of London Slrs' Co, Int Bar Assoc 1995, pres INSOL International 2011–13; hon memb Assoc of Business Recovery Professionals; *Books* Administrative Receivers and Administrators (1987), Leasing Law in the European Union (contrib, 1994), Directors in the Twilight Zone (ed and contrib, 2001, 4 edn 2013); *Recreations* running, literature, humour; *Clubs* Roehampton; *Style—* Gordon Stewart, Esq; ✉ Allen & Overy LLP, One Bishops Square, London E1 6AD (✆ 020 3088 0000, fax 020 3088 0088, e-mail gordon.stewart@allenovery.com)

STEWART, Iain Aitken; MP; s of James Stewart, and Leila, *née* Aitken; *b* 18 September 1972, Glasgow; *Educ* Hutchesons' GS Glasgow, Univ of Exeter; *Career* accountant Coopers & Lybrand 1993–94, head of research Scottish Cons Pty 1994–98, dep dir then dir Parly Resources Unit 1998–2006, headhunter Odgers Berndtson 2006–10; MP (Cons) Milton Keynes S 2010–, PPS to Rt Hon Patrick McLoughlin, MP, *qv*, as Sec of State for Tport 2013–15, PPS to Rt Hon David Mundell, MP, *qv*, as Sec of State for Scotland 2015–; memb Tport Select Ctee House of Commons 2010–13; cncllr Shenley Brook End and Tattenhoe Parish Cncl 2005–11; *Publications* Barnett and Beyond (jtly, 2003); *Recreations* opera, keep fit, cooking; *Style—* Iain Stewart, Esq, MP; ✉ House of Commons, London SW1A 0AA

STEWART, Prof Ian Nicholas; s of Arthur Reginald Stewart (d 2004), of Folkestone, Kent, and Marjorie Kathleen, *née* Diwell (d 2001); *b* 24 September 1945; *Educ* Univ of Cambridge (MA), Univ of Warwick (PhD); *m* 4 July 1970, Avril Bernice, *née* Montgomery; 2 s (James Andrew b 15 Nov 1973, Christopher Michael b 13 Jan 1976); *Career* Univ of Warwick: lectr 1969–84, reader 1984–90, prof 1990–2009, emeritus prof 2009–; Humboldt fell Tübingen Univ 1974, visting fell Univ of Auckland 1976, assoc prof Univ of Connecticut Storrs 1977–78, prof Univ of Southern Illinois Carbondale 1978, prof Univ of Houston 1983–84; Gresham prof of geometry Gresham Coll 1994–98; delivered televised Royal Instn Christmas Lectures 1997; Michael Faraday Medal Royal Soc 1995, Jt Policy Bd for Mathematics Communications Award 1999, Gold Medal IMA 2000, Ferran Sunyer i Balaguer Prize Institut d'Estudis Catalans 2001, Chaos Award Liege 2001, Award for the Public Understanding of Science and Technol AAAS 2001, Zeeman Medal 2010, Lewis Thomas Prize 2015; Hon DSc: Univ of Westminster 1998, Université Catholique de Louvain 2000, Kingston Univ 2003, Univ of Brighton 2014; DUniv Open Univ 2005; fell AAAS 2001, FRS 2001; *Books* Nut-Crackers (with J Jaworski, 1971), Concepts of Modern Mathematics (1975), Get Knotted! (with J Jaworski, 1976), Catastrophe Theory and its Applications (with T Poston, 1978), The Problems of Mathematics (1987), Singularities and Groups in Bifurcation Theory (with M Golubitsky and D Schaeffer, 1988), Game, Set and Math (1989), Fearful Symmetry (with M Golubitsky, 1992), Another Fine Math You've Got Me Into (1992), The Collapse of Chaos (with J Cohen, 1994), Nature's Numbers (1995), From Here to Infinity (1996), Figments of Reality (with J Cohen, 1997), The Magical Maze (1997), Life's Other Secret (1998), The Science of Discworld (with Terry Pratchett and J Cohen, 1999), Wheelers (with J Cohen, 2000), Flatterland (2000), What Shape is a Snowflake? (2001), The Annotated Flatland (2001), The Symmetry Perspective (with M Golubitsky, 2002), The Science of Discworld 2: The Globe (with Terry Pratchett and J Cohen, 2002), Evolving the Alien (with J Cohen, 2002), Math Hysteria (2004), Heaven (with J Cohen, 2004), The Science of Discworld 3: Darwin's Watch (with Terry Pratchett and J Cohen, 2005), The Mayor of Uglyville's Dilemma (2005), Letters to a Young Mathematician (2006), How to Cut a Cake (2006), Why Beauty is Truth (2007), Taming the Infinite (2008), Professor Stewart's Cabinet of Mathematical Curiosities (2008), Professor Stewart's Hoard of Mathematical Treasures (2009), Cows in the Maze (2010), Mathematics of Life (2011), Seventeen Equations that Changed the World (2012), The Great Mathematical Problems (2013), The Science of Discworld 4: Judgement Day (with T Pratchett and J Cohen, 2013), Symmetry: A Very Short Introduction (2013), Professor Stewart's Incredible Numbers (2015), Professor Stewart's Casebook of Mathematical Mysteries (2015); *Recreations* science fiction, guitar, geology, Egyptology; *Style—* Prof Ian Stewart; ✉ Mathematics Institute, University of Warwick, Coventry CV4 7AL (✆ 024 7652 2677, fax 024 7652 4182, e-mail i.n.stewart@warwick.ac.uk)

STEWART, John; *m* Sylvia; 1 s, 1 da; *Career* Woolwich: joined 1977, gp operations dir 1995–96, gp chief exec 1996–2000; dep ceo Barclays 2000–03, chief exec Nat Australia Bank 2004–08, chm Legal & General Gp plc 2010– (memb Nominations Ctee and Risk Ctee); non-exec dir Telstra Corp 2008–11, non-exec dir Financial Reporting Cncl 2014–15; memb Ct Bank of England 2009–15; past memb: Australian PM's Task Gp on Emmissions Trading, Australian Fed Attorney Gen's Business Govt Advsy Gp, Int Advsy Bd Scottish Enterprise; past dir Business Cncl Australia, past pres Int of Financial Servs, past chm Australian Bankers Assoc; chm Southern Cross Stud, chm Guide Dogs for the Blind 2012–15; *Recreations* sailing, three granddaughters; *Style—* John Stewart, Esq; ✉ Legal & General Group plc, One Coleman Street, London EC2R 5AA

STEWART, Sheriff John Hall; s of Cecil Francis Wilson Stewart (d 1964), and Mary Fyffe, *née* Hall; *b* 15 March 1944; *Educ* Airdrie Acad, Univ of St Andrews (LLB); *m* 29 Nov 1968, Marion, da of Donald MacCalman (d 1978); 1 s (Alan Breck b 1973) 2 da (Rohan Mhairi b 1975, Katryn MacCalman b 1978); *Career* enrolled slr 1971–77, advocate 1978–85; sheriff S Strathclyde Dumfries and Galloway: at Airdrie 1985–96, at Hamilton 1996–; memb Faculty of Advocates 1978; *Recreations* scuba diving, golf, spectator rugby football and soccer; *Clubs* Uddinton Rugby Football (past pres), Uddington Cricket and Sports (past pres); *Style—* Sheriff John H Stewart; ✉ 43 Grieve Croft, Bothwell, Glasgow G71 8LU (✆ 01698 853854); Sheriff's Chambers, Sheriff Court House, Hamilton (✆ 01698 282957)

S

STEWART, Sir John Young (Jackie); kt (2001), OBE (1972); s of Robert Paul Stewart (d 1972), and Jean Clark Young; *b* 11 June 1939; *Educ* Dumbarton Acad; *m* 1962, Helen McGregor; 2 s (Paul b 1965, Mark b 1968); *Career* former racing driver; memb Scottish and Br Team for clay pigeon shooting; former Scottish, English, Irish, Welsh and Br Grand Prix in Olympic Trap, won Coupe des Nations 1959 and 1960; first raced 1961, competed in 4 meetings driving for Barry Filer Glasgow 1961–62, drove for Ecurie Ecosse and Barry Filer winning 14 out of 23 starts 1963, 28 wins out of 53 starts 1964, drove Formula One for Br Racing Motors (BRM) 1965–67 then Br and European Championships for Ken Tyrrell in F3 1964 and 1968–73, has won Australian, NZ, Swedish, Mediterranean, Japanese and many other non-championship Grand Prix, maj int motor races, set new world record by winning 26 World Championship Grand Prix (Zandvoort) 1973, 27 (Nürburgring) 1973, third in World Championship 1965, second in 1968 and 1972, World Champion 1969, 1971 and 1973; fndr Stewart Grand Prix 1996; Br Automobile Racing Club Gold Medal 1971 and 1973, Daily Express Sportsman of the Year 1971 and 1973, BBC Sports Personality of the Year 1973, Segrave Trophy 1973 and 2000, Scottish Sportsman of the Year 1968 and 1973, USA Sportsman of the Year 1973; film: Weekend of a Champion 1972, Stewart Grand Prix 1997; pres Dyslexia Scotland, vice-pres Br Dyslexia Assoc; fndr, tstee and chm Grand Prix Tst, vice-pres Scottish Int Educn Tst; global ambass Royal Bank of Scotland 2004–12, ambass Rolex; global ambassador Moët Hennessy UK Ltd; pres Springfield Club; hon prof St Andrews Univ; Hon PhD Lawrence Inst of Technol USA 1986, Hon PhD Glasgow Caledonian Univ 1993, hon degree Cranfield Univ 1998, hon dr Univ of Edinburgh 2006; Hon DEng: Heriot-Watt Univ 1996, Univ of Stirling 2001 (also hon prof); *Books* World Champion (with Eric Dymock, 1970), Faster! (with Peter Manso, 1972), On the Road (1983), Jackie Stewart's Principles of Performance Driving (with Alan Henry, 1986), The Jackie Stewart Book of Shooting (1991), Racing Stewart – The Birth of a Grand Prix Team (with Jon Nicholson & Maurice Hamilton, 1997), Winning Is Not Enough (autobiography, 2007); *Recreations* shooting, golf; *Clubs* RAC, Br Racing Drivers' (pres 2000–06, vice-pres 2006–), Scottish Motor Racing, R&A, Gleneagles Golf, Loch Lomond Golf, Sunningdale Golf, Geneva Golf, Domain & Imperial Golf; *Style*— Sir Jackie Stewart, OBE; ✉ The Office, Clayton House, Butlers Cross, Ellesborough, Buckinghamshire HP17 0UR

STEWART, Joseph Martin (Joe); OBE (1994); s of Joseph A Stewart (d 1990), and Annie M, *née* Friel; *b* 5 November 1955; *Educ* St Patrick's Coll Belfast, Queen's Univ Belfast (LLB), Univ of Ulster (DMS); *m* Sept 1978, Deirdre Ann, *née* Ritchie; *Career* dir Engrg Employers Fed NI Assoc Belfast 1985–90 (joined 1978), dir Harland & Wolff Shipbuilding and Heavy Industries Ltd Belfast 1990–95, sec and chief exec Police Authy for NI 1995–2001 (authy memb 1988–94, vice-chm 1990–94), sr dir of human resources Police Service of NI 2001–; dir Police Rehabilitation and Retraining Tst; memb Bd: Labour Relations Agency 1986–90, Justice Sector Skills Cncl; chm chm NI Country Gp; fndr memb NI Growth Challenge; former JP; FCIPD; *Recreations* game shooting, motorcycling, country pursuits; *Clubs* Reform; *Style*— Joe Stewart, Esq, OBE; ✉ Police Service of Northern Ireland, Department of Human Resources, 42 Montgomery Road, Belfast BT6 9LD (☎ 028 9070 0928, fax 028 9070 0943)

STEWART, Kevin Morrice; MSP; s of Michael Stewart, of Aberdeen, and Sandra, *née* Morrice; *b* 3 June 1968, Aberdeen; *Career* cncllr and dep ldr Aberdeen City Cncl until 2011, MSP (SNP) Aberdeen Central 2011–; *Style*— Kevin Stewart, Esq, MSP; ✉ Scottish Parliament, Edinburgh EH99 1SP

STEWART, His Hon Judge Neill Alastair; yr s of late James Robertson Stewart, CBE, and late Grace Margaret, *née* Kirsop; *b* 8 June 1947; *Educ* Whitgift Sch, Clare Coll Cambridge, Inns of Court Sch of Law; *m* 2000, Tiffany, da of His Hon W L Monro-Davies; 1 s, 1 da; *Career* grad engr Sir Alexander Gibb & Partners 1968–70; practising barr 1975–99; circuit judge (SE Circuit) 1999–; *Style*— His Hon Judge Stewart; ✉ Guildford Crown Court, Bedford Road, Guildford, Surrey GU1 4ST

STEWART, Sir Patrick; kt (2010), OBE (2001); s of Alfred Stewart (d 1984), of Mirfield, W Yorks, and Gladys, *née* Barrowclough (d 1979); *b* 13 July 1940; *Educ* Mirfield Secdy Modern, Bristol Old Vic Theatre Sch; *m* 1966 (m dis 1992), Sheila Falconer; 1 s (Daniel b 20 Oct 1968), 1 da (Sophie b 29 June 1973); m 2, 2000 (m dis 2004), Wendy Neuss; m 3, 2013, Sunny Ozell Michelson; *Career* actor and dir; ceo Flying Freehold Productions; assoc artist RSC 1967 (now hon artist); chllr Univ of Huddersfield 2004–15 (prof of performing arts 2008–15, emeritus chllr 2015–); Hon DLit Pomona Coll, Hon DFA Santa Clara Univ, Hon DFA Julliard Sch NY; GQ Man of the Year (theatre) 1998; *Theatre* roles incl: King John, Shylock, Henry IV, Cassius, Titus Andronicus, Oberon, Othello, Leontes, Enobarbus (SWET Award), Touchstone and Launce, title role in Yonadab (NT) 1986; other credits incl: Who's Afraid of Virginia Woolf? (Young Vic) 1987 (London Fringe Best Actor Award), A Christmas Carol 1993 (Oliver Award Best Entertainment), The Tempest (NY) 1996, Othello (Washington DC) 1997, The Ride Down Mount Morgan (NY) 1998 and 2000 (Drama Desk Nomination), The Master Builder (Albery) 2003, The Caretaker (NY) 2003, A Life in the Theatre (Apollo) 2005, The Tempest (RSC) 2007, Macbeth (Best Actor Evening Standard Theatre Award 2007, Best Shakespearean Performance Critics' Circle Theatre 2008 (jtly, with Chiwetel Ejiofor), nomination Best Actor Tony Award), Hamlet (RSC) 2008 (Laurence Olivier Award 2009), Waiting for Godot (nat tour, Theatre Royal) 2009, Bingo (Chichester Festival Theatre), A Life in the Theatre (NY), The Merchant of Venice (RSC), Waiting for Godot/ No Man's Land (Broadway) 2013; *Television* incl: I Claudius, Tinker Tailor Soldier Spy, Smiley's People, The Mozart Inquest, Oedipus Rex, The Devil's Disciple, Miss Julie, Hamlet, Star Trek: The Next Generation (two Best Actor Awards and a nomination American TV Awards, also dir various episodes of The Next Generation), The Canterville Ghost, Moby Dick (Emmy Best Actor nomination, Golden Globe Best Actor nomination), A Christmas Carol (Screen Actors Guild Nomination), Animal Farm, King of Texas, The Lion in Winter (nomination Best Actor Golden Globe and Screen Actors Guild Awards), Mysterious Island, Eleventh Hour, Extras (nomination Emmy Award), Hamlet (nomination Emmy Award), Macbeth (Peabody Award), Richard II, High Spirits with Shirley Ghostman, Extras, Eleventh Hour, Hamlet, The Hollow Crown, Family Guy, American Dad, Blunt Talk; *Films* incl: Hedda, Dune, Lady Jane, Excalibur, LA Story, Death Train 1993, Robin Hood: Men in Tights 1993, Gun Men 1993, Jeffrey 1996, Star Trek: First Contact 1996, Dad Savage 1997, Conspiracy Theory 1997, Star Trek: Insurrection 1998, The Prince of Egypt 1998, X Men 2000, Jimmy Neutron: Boy Genius 2001, Star Trek: Nemesis 2002, X2 2003, Steamboy 2004, The Game of Their Lives 2005, Chicken Little 2005, X Men: The Last Stand 2006, Gnomeo and Juliet 2011, Ice Age: Continental Drift 2012, Legends of Oz: Dorothy's Return 2013, Hunting Elephants 2013, Match 2013, X Men: Days of Future Past 2014, Green Room; *Recreations* walking, scuba, travel; *Style*— Sir Patrick Stewart, OBE; ✉ c/o Independent Talent Group, 40 Whitfield Street, London W1T 2RH (☎ 020 7636 6565)

STEWART, Patrick Loudon Mclain; MBE, WS; s of Archibald Ian Balfour Stewart, CBE (d 1998), and Ailsa Rosamund Mary Massey; bro of Hon Lord Stewart, *qv*; *b* 25 July 1945, Campbeltown, Argyll; *Educ* Univ of Edinburgh (LLB); *m* Mary Anne; 1 s, 1 da; *Career* Lord-Lt Argyll and Bute 2011– (Vice Lord-Lt 2002–11); slr; FSA Scot; *Style*— Patrick Stewart, Esq, MBE, WS; ✉ Craigadam, Campbeltown, Argyll PA28 6EP; Clerk of Lieutenancy, 2 Castlehill, Campbeltown, Argyll PA28 6AW

STEWART, Robert Alexander (Bob); DSO, MP; *b* 7 July 1949; *Educ* Chigwell Sch, RMA Sandhurst, Univ of Wales; *Career* offr (rising to the rank of Col) Br Army 1969–96; MP (Cons) Beckenham 2010–; *Style*— Bob Stewart, DSO, MP; ✉ House of Commons, London SW1A 0AA

STEWART, Sir Roderick David (Rod); kt (2016), CBE (2007); *b* 10 January 1945; *Career* singer and songwriter; apprentice Brentford FC 1961; performed with bands The Five Dimensions, The Hoochie Coochie Men, The Soul Agents, Steampacket, The Shotgun Express; albums: Truth (with Jeff Beck Group, 1967, reached UK no 8), Cosa Nostra – Beck Ola (with Jeff Beck Group, 1969, UK no 39), An Old Raincoat Won't Ever Let You Down (1969), First Step (with The Faces, 1970, UK no 45), Gasoline Alley (1970, UK no 62), Long Player (with The Faces, 1971, UK no 31), Every Picture Tells A Story (1971, UK no 1), A Nod's As Good As A Wink...To A Blind Horse (with The Small Faces, 1971, UK no 2), Never A Dull Moment (1972, UK no 1), Sing It Again Rod (compilation, 1973, UK no 1), Ooh La La (with Small Faces, 1973, UK no 1), Coast to Coast Overture And Beginners (live, with The Faces, 1974, UK no 3), Smiler (1974, UK no 1), Atlantic Crossing (1975, UK no 1), A Night On The Town (1976, UK no 1), The Best of The Faces (compilation, 1977, UK no 24), The Best of Rod Stewart (compilation, 1977, UK no 1), Foot Loose And Fancy Free (1977, UK no 3), Blondes Have More Fun (1978, UK no 3), Rod Stewart's Greatest Hits (1980, UK no 1), Foolish Behaviour (1980, UK no 4), Tonight I'm Yours (1981, UK no 8), Absolutely Live (1982, UK no 35), Body Wishes (1983, UK no 5), Love Touch (1986, UK no 5), Out of Order (1988, UK no 11), The Best of Rod Stewart (1989, UK no 3), Storyteller 1964–90 (box set, 1989), Vagabond Heart (1991, UK no 2), The Best of Rod Stewart (compilation, 1993, UK no 3), Unplugged...and Seated (live, 1993), Spanner in the Works (1995), When We Were the New Boys (1998), Every Beat of My Heart (2000), Human (2000), It Had To Be You...The Great American Songbook (2002), Sweet Little Rock N Roller (2002), As Time Goes By...The Great American Songbook, Vol 2 (2003), Stardust...The Great American Songbook, Vol 3 (2004), Time (2013, UK no 1); recipient of numerous awards, incl Best Traditional Pop Vocal Album (for Stardust...The Great American Songbook, Vol 3) Grammy Awards 2005; *Style*— Sir Rod Stewart, CBE; ✉ c/o Warner Music, 28 Kensington Church Street, London W8 4EP (☎ 020 7937 8844)

STEWART, Roderick James Nugent (Rory); OBE (2004), MP; s of Brian Stewart, CMG, and Sally, *née* Rose; *b* 3 January 1973, Hong Kong; *Educ* Eton, Balliol Coll Oxford (MA); *m* Shoshana Clark; *Career* 2 Lt Black Watch (RHR) 1991; FCO 1995, second sec Jakarta 1997, Br rep Montenegro 1999, walked from Iran to Nepal 2000–02, dep governate co-ordinator Amara Iraq 2003, sr advsr Nasiriyah Iraq 2004, ceo Turqoise Mountain Fndn Afghanistan 2006; dir Carr Center, prof of practice and Ryan chair Harvard Univ (fell Carr Center 2004); MP (Cons) Penrith and The Border 2010–; The Places in Between (2004), Occupational Hazards (2006), Can Intervention Work (2011); *Style*— Rory Stewart, Esq, OBE, MP; ✉ House of Commons, London SW1A 0AA (e-mail rory@rorystewart.co.uk)

STEWART, Roger Paul Davidson; QC (2001); s of Martin Neil Davidson Stewart (d 1983), and (Elizabeth) Janet King, *née* Porter; *b* 17 August 1963, London; *Educ* Oundle, Jesus Coll Cambridge (MA, LLM); *m* 1, 18 June 1988 (m dis 2011), Georgina Louise, da of Dr Michael Pearce Smith; 2 s (Alexander b 16 Nov 1992, Samuel b 24 July 1995), 1 da (Victoria b 28 Nov 1997); m 2, Elizabeth Jane, da of late Norman Brick; 1 da (Mini b 7 Feb 2011), 2 step-s (Oliver, Jonathan), 2 step-da (Celeste, Amy); *Career* called to the Bar Inner Temple 1986 (bencher 2003); recorder 2002–; *Books* Jackson & Powell on Professional Negligence (ed 3 edn 1992, 4 edn 1997, gen ed 5 edn 2002, 6 edn 2006, 7 edn 2011); *Recreations* sailing, skiing; *Clubs* Nat Liberal, Lost Valley Mountaineering Assoc; *Style*— Roger Stewart, Esq, QC; ✉ 4 New Square, Lincoln's Inn, London WC2A 3RJ (☎ 020 7822 2000, fax 020 7822 2001, mobile 07973 542981, e-mail r.stewart@4newsquare.com)

STEWART, Dr Sir (John) Simon Watson; 6 Bt (UK 1920), of Balgownie; er s of Sir (John) Keith Watson Stewart, 5 Bt (d 1990), and Mary Elizabeth, *née* Moxon; *b* 5 July 1955; *Educ* Uppingham, Charing Cross Hosp Med Sch (MD); *m* 3 June 1978, Catherine Stewart, da of (Henry) Gordon Bond, of Shiplake, Oxon; 1 s ((John) Hamish Watson b 12 Dec 1983), 1 da (Anna Rebecca Watson b 1 May 1987); *Heir* s, Hamish Stewart; *Career* conslt in clinical oncology Charing Cross Hosp; Freeman City of London 1980, memb Worshipful Co of Merchant Taylors 1980; FRCP, FRCR; *Recreations* skiing, kite surfing, sailing; *Clubs* Oriental; *Style*— Dr Sir Simon Stewart, Bt; ✉ 8 Chiswick Wharf, London W4 2SR; Department of Oncology, Charing Cross Hospital, Fulham Palace Road, London W6 8RF (☎ 020 3311 1742)

STEWART, Stanley Charles; s of Rev William Henry Hawthorne Stewart (d 2003), of Kingston, Ontario, and Winifred Louise, *née* Ward (d 1994); *b* 14 November 1952, Ahoghill, NI; *Career* writer; Persian Royal Road expdn 1974–75, freelance feature writer Daily Telegraph and Sunday Times 1990–; FRGS 1980, FRSL 2002; *Books* Old Serpent Nile (1991), Frontiers of Heaven (1995, Thomas Cook Travel Book Award 1996), In the Empire of Ghengis Khan (2000, Thomas Cook Travel Book Award 2001, Benjamin Franklin Award 2003); *Clubs* Blacks; *Style*— Stanley Stewart, Esq; ✉ c/o The Sayle Agency, 8A King's Parade, Cambridge CB2 1SJ

STEWART, Hon Mr Justice; Sir Stephen Paul Stewart; kt (2013), QC (1996); s of Cyril Stewart (d 1994), and Phyllis Mary, *née* Hough (d 2008); *b* 9 October 1953; *Educ* Stand GS Whitefield, St Peter's Coll Oxford (MA), Open Univ (BA); *m* 5 July 1980, Prof M Felicity Dyer, da of (Anthony) Martyn Dyer; 1 da (Eleanor Catherine Anne b 3 Oct 1984), 1 s (Peter Edward John b 21 Dec 1989); *Career* called to the Bar Middle Temple 1975 (Harmsworth major exhibitioner and scholar, bencher 2013), in practice Northern Circuit, recorder 1999–2003 (asst recorder 1995–99), dep judge of the Technol and Construction Ct 2000–03, designated civil judge and sr circuit judge (Northern Circuit) 2003–13, judge of the High Court of Justice (Queen's Bench Div) 2013–, Queen's Bench administrative court liaison judge (Northern and North-Eastern Circuits) 2014–16; hon lectr in law Univ of Manchester 2012–, hon fell St Peter's Coll Oxford 2015; *Recreations* running, music, languages; *Clubs* East India; *Style*— The Hon Mr Justice Stewart; ✉ Royal Courts of Justice, Strand, London WC2A 2LL

STEWART, Prof Sir William Duncan Paterson; kt (1994); s of John Stewart, and Margaret, *née* Paterson; *b* 7 June 1935; *Educ* Dunoon GS, Univ of Glasgow (BSc, PhD, DSc); *m* 1, 8 Aug 1958, Catherine MacLeod (d 1998); 1 s (John b 6 Jan 1964 d 2007); m 2, 1 July 2000, Elizabeth, *née* Evans; *Career* asst lectr Univ of Nottingham 1961–63, lectr Univ of London 1963–68; Univ of Dundee: prof of biology 1968–94, vice-princ 1985–87; chief exec AFRC 1988–90; Cabinet Office: chief scientific advsr 1990–95, head of Office of Science and Technol 1992–95; ind conslt on science and technol; chm Dundee Teaching Hosps NHS Tst 1997–2000; pres Bioindustry Assoc 1995–98, chm Health Protection Agency 2003–09; non-exec chm Cyclacel plc 1998–2002; non-exec dir Water Research Centre; memb: NERC, AFRC, Advsy Bd for Res Cncls, Advsy Cncl on Science and Technol, Royal Cmmn on Environmental Pollution, NEDO Working Pty on Biotechnology, Cabinet Ctee on Science and Technol, Official Ctee on Science and Technol, MAFF Priorities Bd, Def Scientific Advsy Ctee, DTI Innovation Advsy Bd, Energy Advsy Ctee on R&D, BNSC Res Bd, Natural Environment Res Cncl, corp technol Bd SmithKline Beecham, Science, Industry and Translation Ctee Royal Soc 2014–; tstee Royal Botanic Gardens Kew 2006–11; author of over 300 scientific pubns; President's Medal Royal Acad of Engrg 1995; 25 hon degrees and fellowships from univs incl Univ of Edinburgh and Univ of Glasgow; CBiol; FRS 1977 (vice-pres 1995–97), FRSE 1973 (pres 1999–2002); *Recreations* observing Homo sapiens; *Clubs* Dundee United; *Style*— Prof Sir William

Stewart, FRS, FRSE; ✉ 1 Clarendon Drive, Dundee DD2 1JU (e-mail wdpses@btinternet.com)

STEWART, William Gladstone; *b* 15 July 1933; *Educ* Shooters Hill GS London, Woolwich Poly London; *m* 1, 1960 (m dis 1976), Audrey Ann, da of Charles Harrison; 1 s (Nicholas b 1961); 2 other c (Barnaby b 1976, Hayley b 1980); m 2, 1997, Laura, da of John Calland; 2 da (Isobel b 1989, Hannah b 1994); *Career* RAEC King's African Rifles 1952–55; Redcoat Butlins 1958, BBC TV 1958–67 (directors' course 1965), dir series with Al Read, Eric Sykes, freelance prodr, broadcaster and writer 1967–; co-fndr (with Colin Frewin) Sunset and Vine 1976, fndr md Regent Productions 1982 (sold to Pearsons 1999); prodns incl: The Frost Programme, David Frost, Live from London, Father Dear Father, Bless This House, The Price is Right, Family Fortunes, Don't Forget Your Toothbrush (winner: Bafta, Golden Rose at Montreux), Wanted (winner Silver Rose at Montreux), The Thoughts of Chairman Alf, Tickets for the Titanic, The Lady is a Tramp, The Nineteenth Hole, prod/dir series and specials with Max Bygraves, Bruce Forsyth, Reg Varney, Eric Sykes, Frankie Howerd, Warren Mitchell, Bob Monkhouse, Tommy Cooper 1988–2003, Fifteen-to-One (also presenter); presenter Georgian Giants – 19th Century Sport (BBC Radio 4) 2005, regular conslt and guest appearances on radio and television 2006–08, judge The People's Quiz 2007, guest on Radio Five Live, Heart Radio and The Daily Politics Show (BBC2) 2009, presenter Tom Driberg and Me, A Personal Portait by William G Stewart (BBC4) 2009 (private sec to Tom Driberg during 1960s), appearances on BBC, The One Show, Radio 4, Daily Politics and Radio 5 Live 2010; lectures: on Restitution of the Parthenon Marbles (EP Strasbourg, UNESCO Paris, Smithsonian Inst Washington, NY, Athens and London), Inst of Art and Law Annual Lecture 2000, lecture tour USA and Canada (8 cities) 2003; pres The Media Soc 2003–05; FRTS 1996 (elected to Hall of Fame 2000); *Recreations* the English language, classical history, music, tennis, gardening, riding; *Clubs* Reform; *Style*— William G Stewart, Esq; ✉ PO Box 429, New Malden, Surrey KT3 9AW (☎ 020 8942 4280)

STEWART, Prof William James; s of James W Stewart, of Hindhead, Surrey, and Margaret M Stewart; *b* 13 July 1947; *Educ* Blundell's, Imperial Coll London (BSc, MSc); *m* 1976, Dr Jill A Stewart, da of F E Chapman; 2 c (Alexander b 6 June 1983, Antonia b 1 May 1986); *Career* conslt, chief scientist Marconi plc (joined 1971), chm Innos 2004–; visiting prof: UCL, Univ of Southampton; contrib to numerous books and jls; granted numerous patents for inventions in field of optics; memb Editorial Advsy Bd Science; chm ECOC IOOC 1997; Worshipful Co of Scientific Instrument Makers award for achievement; fell Optical Soc of America, MIEEE LEOS, MIEE, MInstD; FREng 1989; *Recreations* woodwork; *Style*— Prof William Stewart, FREng; ✉ Manor House, High Street, Blakesley, Northamptonshire NN12 8RE (mobile 07801 716578, e-mail w.stewart@ieee.org)

STEWART-CLARK, Sir John (Jack); 3 Bt (UK 1918), of Dundas, W Lothian; s of Sir Stewart Stewart-Clark, 2 Bt (d 1971), and Jane Pamela, *née* Clarke (d 1993); *b* 17 September 1929; *Educ* Eton, Balliol Coll Oxford, Harvard Business Sch; *m* 1958, Lydia, da of James William Loudon, of Valkenswaard, The Netherlands; 4 da (Daphne (Mrs Nicholas Stephenson) b 1959, Nadia (Mrs Patrick J Waterfield) b 1963, Zarina (Mrs Richard S Noel) b 1965, Natalie (Mrs Andrew Bird) b 1969, 1 s (Alexander Dudley b 1960); *Heir* s, Alexander Stewart-Clark; *Career* late Coldstream Gds; Parly candidate (Cons & Unionist) Aberdeen N 1959; MEP (EDG): E Sussex 1979–94, E Sussex and Kent S 1994–99; treas European Democratic Gp 1979–92, vice-pres European Parliament 1992–97; chm EP Delgn to Canada 1979–82, vice-chm EP Delgn to Japan 1986–89; ctee spokesman on: external affrs 1979–83, institutional affrs 1983–85, youth, culture, educn and media 1989–92, civil liberties 1992–99; md: J & P Coats (Pakistan) Ltd 1961–67, J A Carp's Garenfabrieken (Helmond) Holland 1967–70, Philips Electrical Ltd London 1971–75, Pye of Cambridge Ltd 1975–79; dir: Cope Allman International Ltd 1980–83, Oppenheimer International Ltd 1980–84, Low & Bonar 1982–95, AT Kearney Management Consultants 1985–92, Pioneer Concrete Holdings Ltd 1989–2000; chm Dundas Castle Ltd 1999–; memb Bd Tstee Savings Bank Scotland 1986–89; former memb Cncl RUSI, chm Supervisory Bd European Inst for Security 1984–86, tstee dir European Centre for Work and Soc 1983–; chm: EPIC (European Parliamentarians and Industrialists Cncl) 1984–99, European Action Cncl for Peace in the Balkans 1994–96; pres CRONWE (Conf Regnl Orgns of NW Europe) 1987–93; memb Bd of Govrs European Inst for the Media, memb Bd of Mgmnt European Monitoring Centre for Drugs and Drug Addiction (EMCDDA) 2000–06; jt prodr open air play The Life of Jesus Christ (annually) 2003–15; tstee Mentor Fndn (UK), assoc Royal Photographic Soc; memb Queen's Bodyguard for Scotland (Royal Co of Archers); *Publications* European Competition Law (jtly), It's My Problem as Well: Drugs Prevention and Education (jtly); *Recreations* golf, tennis, music, travel, vintage cars, photography; *Clubs* White's; *Style*— Sir Jack Stewart-Clark, Bt; ✉ Dundas Castle, South Queensferry, Edinburgh EH30 9SP (☎ 0131 331 1114, fax 0131 331 2670)

STEWART-SMITH, John Ronald; s of Maj James Geoffrey Stewart-Smith (d 1938), of Falcon Hill Kinver, Worcs, and Bertha Mabel Milner, *née* Roberts (d 2006); *b* 23 February 1932; *Educ* Marlborough, New Zealand; *m* 22 Oct 1955, Catherine May, da of Walter Douglas Montgomery Clarke, JP (d 1948), of Bombay, India; 1 s (Geoffrey b 1958), 2 da (Joanna b 1960, Nicola b 1962); *Career* gp mktg dir Glover Gp Ltd 1976–79, projects dir and co sec Dashwood Finance Co Ltd 1983–, dir Kowloon Shipyard Co Ltd 1983–2003; CEng, MIMechE 1967, MIEx 1974, FIMarE 1989 (MIMarE 1969); *Recreations* opera, bridge; *Style*— John Stewart-Smith, Esq; ✉ Dashwood Finance Co Ltd, 65 London Wall, London EC2M 5TU (☎ 020 7588 3215, fax 020 7588 4818)

STEWARTBY, Baron (Life Peer UK 1992), of Portmoak in the District of Perth and Kinross; Sir (Bernard Harold) Ian Halley Stewart of Stewartby; kt (1991), RD (1972), PC (1989); s of Prof Harold Charles Stewart of Stewartby, CBE, DL (d 2001), and his 1 w Dorothy Irene, *née* Löwen (d 1969); *b* 10 August 1935; *Educ* Haileybury, Jesus Coll Cambridge (MA), Univ of Cambridge (LittD); *m* 8 Oct 1966, Hon Deborah Charlotte Stewart, 2 da of 3 Baron Tweedsmuir (2 s of 1 Baron Tweedsmuir, otherwise known as John Buchan, the author); 2 da (Hon Lydia Barbara Rose Anne Phoebe (Mrs Charles Pretzlik) b 1969, Hon (Dorothy) Louisa Charlotte Amabel (Mrs Andrew Elder) b 1970), 1 s (Hon Henry Ernest Alexander Halley b 1972); *Career* served RNVR 1954–56, Lt-Cdr RNR; with Seccombe Marshall & Campion (bill brokers) 1959–60; chm: The Throgmorton Trust plc 1990–2005, Delian Lloyd's Investment Trust plc 1993–95; dep chm: Standard Chartered plc 1993–2004, Amlin plc 1995–2006; dir: Brown Shipley & Co (merchant bankers) 1971–83, Diploma plc 1990–2007, Portman Building Society 1995–2002; dir FSA 1993–97; MP (Cons): Hitchin Feb 1974–83, N Herts 1983–92; oppn spokesman Banking Bill 1978–79, PPS to Rt Hon Sir Geoffrey Howe (as Chllr of the Exchequer) 1979–83, under sec MOD (Def Procurement) Jan-Oct 1983, econ sec Treasy with special responsibility for monetary policy and fin instns 1983–87, min of state for the Armed Forces 1987–88, min of state NI 1988–89; memb: Public Expenditure Ctee 1977–79, Public Accounts Ctee 1991–92; former jt sec Cons Parly Fin Ctee, tstee Parly Pension Fund 2000–05; chm Br Acad Ctee for Sylloge of Coins of Br Isles 1993–2003 (memb 1967–), chm Treasure Valuation Ctee 1996–2001, vice-chm Westminster Ctee Protection of Children 1975–92; memb House of Lords 1992–2015 (ret); vice-pres Herts Soc 1974–, vice-pres St John Ambulance Herts 1978–; memb Cncl Haileybury 1980–95 (life govr 1977); tstee Sir Halley Stewart Tst 1978– (pres 2002–); hon fell Jesus Coll Cambridge 1994, hon keeper of medieval coins Fitzwilliam Museum Cambridge 2008–; FBA 1981, FRSE 1986, FSA, FSA Scot, KStJ 1992 (CStJ 1986); *Books* The Scottish Coinage (1955, 2 edn 1967), Coinage in Tenth-century England (with C E Blunt and C S S Lyon, 1989), English Coins 1180–1551 (2009); *Recreations* history, real tennis; *Clubs* New (Edinburgh), Beefsteak, MCC, Hawks' (Cambridge); *Style*— The Rt Hon Lord Stewartby, PC, RD, FRSE, FSA, FBA; ✉ e-mail stewartby@btconnect.com

STEYN, David Andrew; s of John Hofmeyr Steyn, and Daphne Mary, *née* Nelson; *b* 13 September 1959; *Educ* Robert Gordon's Coll Aberdeen, Univ of Aberdeen (LLB); *m* 9 June 1990, Tanya Susan, da of Elisabeth and Lyon Roussel; 3 da (Elisabeth Daphne b 28 March 1991, Sophie Rebecca b 1 Oct 1996, Emily Charlotte b 10 Oct 1998), 1 s (James Philip b 17 Oct 1992); *Career* chief operating offr Alliance Bernstein LP; dir Tangent Communications plc; *Recreations* theatre, opera, chess; *Clubs* Athenaeum; *Style*— David Steyn, Esq; ✉ 18 Stanhope Terrace, London W2 2TU

STHEEMAN, Sir Robert; kt (2016), CB; *Career* chief exec UK Debt Mgmnt Office; *Style*— Sir Robert Stheeman, CB; ✉ The United Kingdom Debt Management Office, Eastcheap Court, 11 Philpot Lane, London EC3M 8UD

STIBY, Robert Andrew; OBE (2007), JP (1976); s of Maj Arthur Robert Charles Stiby, TD, JP (d 1987), and Peggy, *née* Hartley (d 1973); *b* 25 May 1937; *Educ* Marlborough, London Coll of Printing (Dip Printing Mgmnt); *m* 1, 1962; 1 s (Jonathan b 10 May 1963), 1 da (Emma b 17 Sept 1965); m 2, 1980; m 3, 1986, Julia, da of Sidney Fuller (d 2005); m 4, 2 July 2011, Kathy Waghorn; *Career* Nat Serv 1955–57; md and chm Croydon Advertiser Group of Newspapers 1969–83; chm: Radio Investments Ltd 1972–99, The Local Radio Company Ltd 1996–99, Tindle Radio Ltd 2000–06; dir: Capital Radio 1972–2001, Talk Radio UK 1994–99, Channel 103 2000–06, Midlands Radio 3 (Ireland) 2002–09; chm and dir Idyllwild Town Crier (US) 2004–10; pres: Newspaper Soc 1983–84, Croydon Boys' Club 1988–93; dir Fairfield Halls 1993–96; chm: Jesse Ward Fndn, Rosetti Fndn; chm of govrs London Coll of Printing 1979, govr BRIT Sch 2001–07; fell Radio Acad 2001; *Recreations* hill walking, sailing, painting; *Clubs* Reform, MCC; *Style*— Robert Stiby, Esq, OBE; ✉ Priory Barn, Old Standlynch Farm, Downton, Salisbury, Wiltshire SP5 3QR (☎ 01722 711959, e-mail rs@priorybarn.com)

STICHBURY, Jane; CBE (2004), QPM (2000); *Career* Met Police Serv 1977–99 (latterly Dep Asst Cmmr Central Area), Chief Constable Dorset 1999–2004, HM Inspr of Constabulary 2004–09; vice-chair Skills for Justice; tstee Streetwise/Police Partnership Tst; chm Royal Bournemouth and Christchurch Hospitals NHS Fndn Tst, memb St John Cncl Dorset; *Style*— Mrs Jane Stichbury, CBE, QPM

STICKLAND, Prof Neil Charles; s of Henry Frank Stickland (d 1997), of Torquay, Devon, and Audrey Fay, *née* Pinney; *b* 17 October 1949; *Educ* Torquay Boys' GS, Bedford Coll London (BSc), Univ of Hull (PhD), Univ of Edinburgh (DSc); *m* 27 Oct 1973, Margaret Rosamund, da of Arthur Robert Oliver; 3 da (Elizabeth Emma b 28 April 1976, Sarah Caroline b 10 Oct 1978, Rosemary Laura b 20 June 1982); *Career* research asst Zoology Dept Univ of Hull 1970–73; lectr in veterinary anatomy: Univ of Nairobi Kenya 1974–77, Royal (Dick) Sch of Veterinary Studies Univ of Edinburgh 1977–83; RVC Univ of London: sr lectr in veterinary anatomy 1984–94, prof of veterinary anatomy 1994–2011, head Dept of Veterinary Basic Sciences 1996–2001, 2003–05 and 2008–10, vice-princ research 2002–03, emeritus prof of comparative biomedical sciences 2013–; visiting lectr Dept of Veterinary Science Univ of Dar es Salaam Tanzania 1979, visiting assoc prof in anatomy and cellular biology Tufts Univ Boston USA 1982–83; Share-Jones Lecture 1995; author of approx 100 pubns in scientific jls and books (mostly on devpt and growth of skeletal muscle); memb: Anatomical Soc of GB and I 1980 (memb Cncl 1995–99), World Assoc of Veterinary Anatomists 1985, Euro Assoc of Veterinary Anatomists 1990; *Books* Color Atlas of Veterinary Anatomy: Vol 3: The Dog and Cat (jtly, 1996); *Recreations* walking, theatre, art exhibitions, travel; *Style*— Prof N C Stickland; ✉ The Royal Veterinary College, Royal College Street, London NW1 0TU (☎ 020 7468 5200, fax 020 7468 5204, e-mail nstickland@rvc.ac.uk)

STIHLER, Catherine; MEP (Lab) Scotland; da of Gordon McLeish Taylor, of Wishaw, and Catherine Doreen, *née* Sanders; *b* 30 July 1973; *Educ* Coltness HS Wishaw, Univ of St Andrews (MA, MLitt); *m* 14 April 2000, David Thomas Stihler, of Salinas, CA; 2 s (Alexander, Andrew); *Career* rep Young Labour Scottish Labour Pty Exec 1993–95, pres Univ of St Andrews Students' Assoc 1994–95, rep Young Labour NEC Labour Pty 1995–97, Parly candidate (Lab) Angus 1997, PA to Anne Begg, MP, *qv*, 1997–99; MEP (Lab) Scotland 1999–, health spokesperson Lab Pty 1999–2004, chair All-Pty Health Gp 2000–02, fisheries spokesperson Lab Pty 2000–09, dep ldr EPLP 2004–06, regnl spokesperson Lab Pty 2004–09, consumer spokesperson Lap Pty 2009–, EPLP whip 2014–; vice-chair IMCO Ctee 2014–, substitute memb ECON Ctee, co-chair European Parliament Prayer Breakfast; ed Parliament magazine 2002–11; hon pres CAVOC (Lanarkshire based umbrella voluntary organisation); memb: Community the Union, UNITE, Co-op Pty, Fabian Soc, Lab Movement for Europe, SERA, Christian Socialist Movement; rector Univ of St Andrews 2014–; *Publications* A Soldier and a Woman, chapter in Women and the Military (2000); *Recreations* films, running, yoga, tennis, music, studying languages; *Style*— Mrs Catherine Stihler, MEP; ✉ Constituency Office, 25 Church Street, Inverkeithing, Fife KY11 1LG (website www.catherinestihlermep.com)

STILES, George; s of John Leslie Stiles (d 1967), of Haywards Heath, W Sussex, and Joy Irene, *née* Baker (d 1985); *b* 9 August 1961; *Educ* Gresham's, Univ of Exeter (BA); *partner* Hugh Vanstone, *qv*; *Career* composer; memb: BASCA, Musicians Union, Equity, PRS, Mercury Musical Developments; *Theatre* credits with lyricist Anthony Drewe incl: Tutankhamun (Northcott Theatre & Imagination Building London) 1984, Just So (produced by Cameron Mackintosh 1989 and 1990, North Shore Music Theatre 2001, Chichester Festival Theatre 2004) 1985, Honk! (Watermill Theatre 1993, Stephen Joseph Theatre Scarborough 1997, RNT Olivier 1999, UK Tour 2001 (dir Julia McKenzie, *qv*) productions worldwide incl USA, Japan, Far East, South Africa, Israel, Scandinavia), Peter Pan (Copenhagen) 1999 and (Royal Festival Hall, recorded for BBC Radio 3) 2001, Christmas Season at Royal Festival Hall 2002, new songs and additional music Mary Poppins (Prince Edward Theatre and New Amsterdam Broadway) 2004 and (New Amsterdam Broadway) 2006–12; song contribs incl: The Challenge (Shaw Theatre) 1992, The Mercury Workshop Musical Revue (Jermyn Street) 1994, The Shakespeare Revue (RSC, Barbican, Vaudeville, nat tour); credits with lyricist Paul Leigh incl: Moll Flanders (Lyric Hammersmith 1993, Theatre Royal York 1995 and 1996), Tom Jones (Theatre Royal York 1996 and North Shore Music Theatre 2004), The Three Musketeers (premiere Stadttheater St Gallen Switzerland 2000, San Jose California 2001); other credits incl: composer for Twelfth Night and Uncle Vanya (Sam Mendes' farewell season at Donmar Warehouse) 2002, musical dir and composer for Barry Humphries' Look at me when I'm Talking to You, composer for Habeas Corpus (Donmar Warehouse); musical supervisor: Peter Pan (Birmingham Rep) 2007 and (W Yorks Playhouse) 2008, A Spoonful of Stiles and Drewe concert (HM Theatre) 2008, The Three Musketeers (Rose Theatre Kingston) 2010; composer Betty Blue Eyes (Novello Theatre) 2011 and (UK tour) 2014, composer Soho Cinders (concert recording) 2011 and (Soho Theatre) 2012, composer The Three Little Pigs and Goldilocks and the Three Bears (Singapore Repertory Theatre) 2012–13; forthcoming projects incl: adaption of The Wind in the Willows (with Julian Fellowes) 2015, adaptation of Graham Greene's Travels With My Aunt 2016; *Recordings* Honk!, Moll Flanders, The Shakespeare Revue, The Challenge, We Can Be Kind, Musical of the Year, Hey Mr Producer, The Three Musketeers (US cast album), Mary Poppins (London cast album), Soho Cinders concert recording 2011, Betty Blue Eyes 2012, Peter Pan – A Musical Adventure, The Three Little Pigs 2013, Honk! Original Demo Cast; *Awards* Vivian Ellis Prize (for Just So), TMA Regional Theatre Award for Best Musical (for Moll Flanders) 1995, The Orchestra's Prize and Best Song (for Peter Pan), 2nd Prize Musical

S

of the Year (for The Three Musketeers) 1996, Lawrence Olivier Award for Best New Musical 2000, Elliot Norton Award for Outstanding Musical (for Honk!) 2001, Olivier Award nomination (for Betty Blue Eyes) 2012; *Publications* Moll Flanders (Samuel French, 1995), Honk! (Weinberger's, 1998), The Three Musketeers (Weinberger's, 1999), Just So (MTI, 2000), Betty Blue Eyes (Weinberger's, 2013), The Three Little Pigs (Weinberger's, 2014), Goldilocks and the Three Bears (Weinberger's, 2014), Soho Cinders (Weinberger's, 2014); *Style*— George Stiles, Esq; ✉ c/o John Cohen, Clinton's, 55 Drury Lane, London WC2B 5RZ (☎ 020 8741 0606, e-mail jcohen@clintons.co.uk, website www.stilesanddrewe.com)

STILL, Simon; *b* 7 June 1949, London; *Educ* Univ of Durham; *m* Sally, *née* Arnett; 1 da (Tania), 2 s (George, Sam); *Career* chief operating offr Brewin Dolphin Hldgs plc 2001–09; dir Salmon Business Services Ltd 2009–15, chm Equipos Ltd 2012–14, sr advsr Simcorp Coric Ltd 2014–, currently dir DZ Environmental and Training Ltd; non-exec dir Assoc of Private Client and Investment Managers 2005–10; Durham Cathedral: chair Investment Ctee, memb Cncl, memb Finance Ctee, memb Gen Purposes Ctee, memb Audit Ctee; High Sheriff County Palatine of Durham 2005; FIoD; *Recreations* rural activities; *Clubs* Northern Counties; *Style*— Simon Still, Esq; ✉ DZ Environmental and Training Ltd, Rowlands House, Portobello Road, Birtley, Chester-Le-Street DH3 2RY

STIMPSON, Robin Mackay; WS; *Educ* Dundee HS, Univ of St Andrews (LLB); *Career* admitted slr 1971 (ret 2015); specialised in property and charity law; ptnr: Farquharson Craig & Co 1973–74, Anderson Strathern 1975–2015 (managing ptnr 1996–2009, head Residential Property Dept 1975–2012, const 2012–15); sometime tutor in practical conveyancing and legal practice as a business Univ of Edinburgh Legal Practice Unit; legal advsr Nat Tst for Scot 1982–2012; memb Legal Questions Ctee Church of Scotland 2012–; chm Edinburgh Slrs Property Centre (ESPC) 2002–13 (dir 1997–2001), dir Investors in People Scotland 2005–12, chm Edinburgh Clothing Store 2009–; govr Jewel & Esk Coll 2011–12, memb Bd Edinburgh Coll 2012–, gen tstee Church of Scotland 2014–; *Style*— Robin Stimpson, Esq, WS; ✉ Anderson Strathern, 1 Rutland Court, Edinburgh EH3 8EY (☎ 0131 270 7700, fax 0131 270 7788, e-mail robin.stimpson@andersonstrathern.co.uk)

STIMSON, Theresa Josephine (Tess); da of Michael Stimson (d 2012), and Jane, *née* Bower (d 2001); *Educ* Notre Dame Convent Sch Lingfield, St Hilda's Coll Oxford; *m* 1, 17 July 1993 (m dis 2002), Brent Sadler, *qv*; 2 s (Henry Louis Brent Stimson Sadler b 7 Sept 1994, Matthew Alexander Brent Stimson Sadler b 12 Sept 1997), 1 da (Lily Jane Isabeau Stimson Oliver b 12 Sept 2002); m 2, 23 Dec 2005, Erik Oliver; *Career* prodr ITN 1987–91; assignments incl: King's Cross fire 1987, Purley rail disaster 1988, European elections 1989, Thatcher resignation 1990, Gulf war 1990–91, McCarthy and Mann Beirut hostage releases 1991, Northern Ireland 1987–91; author, freelance journalist and lectr 1991–; assignments incl: Waite release 1991, South Africa 1992–94, Somalia famine 1992–93, Iraq 1992–93, Lebanon 1997–99, UK features and book reviews 2000–; prof of creative writing Univ of South Florida 2002–05, prof of media, journalism and digital arts St Michael's Coll 2015–; *Books* Yours Till the End (Sunnie and Jackie Mann biography, 1992), Beat the Bitch! How to Stop Other Women Stealing Your Man (2009); *Novels* Hard News (1993), Soft Focus (1995), Pole Position (1996), The Adultery Club (2007), The Infidelity Chain (2008), The Cradle Snatcher (2009), What's Yours Is Mine (2010), The Wife Who Ran Away (2012), The Lying Game (2013), An Open Marriage (2014); *Recreations* scuba diving, rock climbing, tennis, water and snow skiing, yoga; *Style*— Tess Stimson; ✉ 266 South Union Street, Burlington, Vermont 05401, USA (e-mail tessjstimson@gmail.com, website www.tessstimson.com); agent: Carole Blake, Blake Friedmann (☎ 020 7284 0408)

STING, né Gordon Matthew Sumner; CBE (2003); *b* 2 October 1951; *m* 20 Aug 1992, Trudie Styler, *qv*; 2 s, 2 da; 1 s and 1 da from previous m; *Career* musician and actor; teacher St Paul's Primary Sch Cramlington 1971–74, memb The Police 1977–86; Police albums: Outlandos D'Amour (1978, reached UK no 6), Regatta De Blanc (1979, UK no 1), Zenyatta Mondatta (1980, UK no 1), Ghost In The Machine (1982, UK no 1), Synchronicity (1983, UK no 1), Every Breath You Take – The Singles (compilation, 1986, UK no 1), Message In A Box – Complete Recording Sessions (1993), The Police Live (1995); solo albums: Dream Of the Blue Turtles (1985, UK no 1), Bring On The Night (live, 1986), Nothing Like The Sun (1987, UK no 1), The Soul Cages (1991, UK no 1), Ten Summoner's Tales (1993), Demolition Man (1993), Fields of Gold – The Best of Sting 1984–94 (1994), The Living Sea (IMAX movie soundtrack), Mercury Falling (1996), Brand New Day (1999), All This Time (live, 2001), Sacred Love (2003); films: Quadrophenia 1979, Radio On 1980, Brimstone And Treacle 1982, Dune 1984, The Bride 1985, Plenty 1985, Bring On The Night (concert) 1985, Julia and Julia 1987, Stormy Monday 1988, Julia 1988, Mercury Falling 1996, Gentlemen Don't Eat Poets 1997, Lock Stock and Two Smoking Barrels 1999; winner of numerous awards incl: Ivor Novello, BRIT, Grammy (16 awarded in total 1980–2000), BMI (10 awarded in total 1984–2000), Oscar nomination for Best Song for Until (from the film Kate and Leopold) 2002; co-fndr Rainforest Fndn; Hon DMus Univ of Northumbria at Newcastle; *Style*— Sting; ✉ c/o Publicity Department, Polydor Records, 72–80 Black Lion Lane, London W6 9BE

STIRK, Graham; *Educ* Oxford Poly (BA), AA Sch of Architecture (Dip Arch), Kingston Poly; *Career* architect; Richard Rogers Partnership: joined 1983, dir 1988, sr dir 1995; *Projects* incl: Wellcome Fndn HQ Cobham, London Patternoster Sq Competition, Tokyo Forum Competition, Potsdammer Platz Masterplan, Zoofenster Berlin, Lloyds Register of Shipping Liphook, SmithKline Beecham Masterplan, Montevetro apartments Battersea, Padre Pio Pilgrimage Cathedral Foggia Italy, Daiwa II, Rome Congress Hall Competition, Waterside Paddington, 22 Hanover Square; *Style*— Graham Stirk, Esq; ✉ Rogers Stirk Harbour and Partners, Thames Wharf, Rainville Road, London W6 9HA

STIRLING, Sir Angus Duncan Aeneas; kt (1994); s of Duncan Alexander Stirling (d 1990), and Lady Marjorie Stirling (d 2000); *b* 1933; *Educ* Eton, Trinity Coll Cambridge, Univ of London (Dip History of Art); *m* 1959, Armyne Morar Helen, er da of William and Hon Mrs Schofield, of Masham, N Yorks; 1 s, 2 da; *Career* former dep sec Gen Arts Cncl of GB, DG The Nat Tst 1983–95 (dep dir 1979–83), chm ROH Covent Garden 1991–96 (dir 1979–96), sr policy advsr Nat Heritage Meml Fund 1996, chm Greenwich Fndn for the Royal Naval Coll 1996–2003; pres Somerset Branch CPRE 2001–07; chm: Friends of Covent Garden 1981–91, Policy Ctee CPRE 1996–2001, Jt Nature Conservation Ctee 1997–2002; memb: Bd of Govrs Byam Shaw Sch of Art 1965–90, Advsy Cncl LSO 1979–, Crafts Cncl 1980–85, Bd of Govrs Courtauld Inst of of Art 1981–83 and 2002–14, Live Music Now 1982–89, Theatres' Trust 1983–90, Heritage of London Trust 1983–95, Heritage Educn Trust 1985–96, Samuel Courtauld Trust 1990–2012, Govt Task Force on Tourism and the Environment 1991, Tourism Ctee Int Cncl on Monuments and Sites (ICOMOS) UK 1993–2002, Cncl Royal Sch of Church Music 1996–98, Fabric Advsy Ctee Wells Cathedral 2001–; Royal Ballet: memb Bd 1979–96 (dep chm 1989–91), govr 1988–96; tstee: World Monuments Fund in Britain 1996–2007, Stowe House Preservation Trust 1998–2012; memb Bd of Govrs: Gresham's Sch 1999–2007, City and Guilds of London Art Sch 2003–11; pres: Friends of Holland Park 2003–, Kensington and Chelsea Nat Assoc of Decorative & Fine Arts Socs 2008–15; vice-patron Almshouses Assoc 1999–2009, memb Cncl Kensington Soc 2002–; hon fell Trinity Coll of Music 2004, hon fell Courtauld Inst of Art 2015; memb Ct of Assts Worshipful Co of Fishmongers 1991– (Prime Warden 2004–05); Hon DLit: Univ of Leicester 1995, Univ of Greenwich 2002; *Recreations* painting (exhibited regularly in London and Somerset since 2010); *Clubs* Beefsteak, Garrick, Brooks's, Grillions; *Style*— Sir Angus Stirling; ✉ 30 Upper Addison Gardens, London W14 8AJ (website www.angusstirlingartist.com)

STIRLING, Prof (William) James; CBE (2006); s of John Easton Stirling (d 1972), and Margaret Eleanor, *née* Norris; *b* 4 February 1953, Belfast; *Educ* Belfast Royal Acad, Peterhouse Cambridge (entrance scholarship, Thomas Parke scholar in mathematics, John Worthington student in mathematics, MA), Univ of Cambridge (Smith's Prize in mathematics, PhD); *m* 30 July 1975, Paula Helene, *née* Close; 1 s (Thomas John b 5 July 1981), 1 da (Helena Rachael b 3 March 1983); *Career* research assoc Physics Dept Univ of Washington Seattle 1979–81, research fell Dept of Applied Mathematics and Theoretical Physics Univ of Cambridge 1981–83; Theory Div CERN Geneva: fell 1983–85, staff memb 1985–86; Univ of Durham: lectr 1986–89, sr lectr 1989–90, reader 1990–92, prof of mathematical sciences and physics 1992–2008, dir Inst for Particle Physics Phenomenology (IPPP) 2000–05, pro-vice-chllr (research) 2005–08; Jacksonian prof of natural philosophy Cavendish Lab Univ of Cambridge 2008– (head of dept 2011–), professorial fell Peterhouse Cambridge 2008–; memb: Ctee Nuclear and Particle Physics Div Inst of Physics 1997–99, Physics Panel Research Assessment Ctees 2001 and 2008, Cncl STFC 2009–, HEFCE Science and Innovation Strategic Advsy Ctee 2010–; Royal Soc: memb Research Fellowships Panel A(i) 2002–05, memb Sectional Ctee 2 2000–03 (chm 2003), memb Cncl 2008; PPARC: memb Theory Sub-Ctee 1987–90, memb Particle Physics Ctee 1987–90 and 1998–2001, memb Educn and Trg Ctee 1998–2001, memb CERN Fellowship Panel 1998–2001, memb Panel to Review Sr Research Physicists in the Particle Physics Dept at Rutherford Appleton Lab 2001, chm Science Ctee 2001–03; memb numerous int conf advsy ctees; SERC/PPARC Sr Fellowship 1993–98, Humboldt Research Award 1997; pres Soc of Fells Univ of Durham 2003–08, memb Bd of Govrs Royal GS Newcastle upon Tyne 1998–2005; FInstP 1992, FRS 1999; *Publications* QCD and Collider Physics (1996); numerous research pubns in learned jls; *Recreations* listening to and playing Irish music; *Clubs* Royal Dublin Soc; *Style*— Prof W James Stirling, CBE, FRS; ✉ Department of Physics, Cavendish Laboratory, J J Thomson Avenue, Cambridge CB3 0HE (☎ 01223 337429, fax 01223 760520, e-mail wjs2@cam.ac.uk)

STIRRAT, Canon Prof Gordon Macmillan; s of Alexander Stirrat (d 1989), and Mary Caroline, *née* Hutchinson (d 1987); *b* 12 March 1940; *Educ* Hutchesons GS Glasgow, Univ of Glasgow (MB ChB), Univ of Oxford (MA), Univ of London (MD); *m* 2 April 1965, Janeen Mary, da of Hugh Brown (d 1983); 3 da (Lorna Margaret b 1966, Carolyn Jane b 1967, Lindsay Ann b 1970); *Career* lectr Univ of London 1970–75, clinical reader Univ of Oxford 1975–82; Univ of Bristol: prof of obstetrics and gynaecology 1982–2000, dean Faculty of Med 1990–93, pro-vice-chllr 1993–97, vice-provost Inst for Advanced Studies 1998–2003, res fell Centre for Ethics in Medicine 2000–14; hon vice-pres Inst of Medical Ethics 2012– (chair Medical Educn Working Gp 2007–12); memb: South West RHA 1984–90, Bristol & Weston Health Authy 1990–91, Bristol & Dist Health Authy 1991–96, GMC 1993–97, Christian Med Fellowship; chm House of Laity Anglican Dio of Bristol 2003–12, hon lay canon Bristol Cathedral 2008–10 (lay canon emeritus 2010–); FRCOG 1981; *Books* Obstetrics Pocket Consultant: Aids to Obstetrics & Gynaecology, Notes on Obstetrics and Gynaecology, Medical Ethics and Law for Doctors of Tomorrow; *Recreations* fly fishing, walking, reading, photography; *Style*— Prof Gordon Stirrat; ✉ Malpas Lodge, 24 Henbury Road, Westbury-on-Trym, Bristol BS9 3HJ (☎ 0117 950 5310, e-mail g.m.stirrat@bristol.ac.uk)

STIRRUP, Baron (Life Peer UK 2011), of Marylebone in the City of Westminster; Air Chief Marshal Sir Graham Eric (Jock) Stirrup; KG (2013), GCB (2005, KCB 2002, CB 2000), AFC (1983); s of William Hamilton Stirrup, and Jacqueline Brenda, *née* Coulson; *b* 4 December 1949; *Educ* Merchant Taylors', RAF Coll Cranwell, JSDC (1984), RCDS (1993), Higher Command and Staff Course (1994); *m* 4 Sept 1976, Mary Alexandra, da of James Elliott; 1 s (James Elliott b 13 June 1978); *Career* cmmnd RAF 1970, various flying appts UK, Middle East and USA 1971–84, OC 2 Sqn RAF Laarbruch Germany 1985–87, PSO to CAS 1987–90, CO RAF Marham 1990–92, dir Air Force Plans and Progs MOD 1994–97, AOC No 1 Gp RAF 1997–98, Asst Chief of Air Staff 1998–2000, Dep C-in-C Strike Command 2000–02, DCDS (Equipment Capability) 2002–03, CAS 2003–06, CDS 2006–10; ADC; DSc 2005; FIMgt 1983, FRAeS 1991; *Recreations* music, theatre, history; *Clubs* RAF, Beefsteak; *Style*— The Lord Stirrup, KG, GCB, AFC, ADC

STIRTON, Prof Charles Howard; s of late Dr Charles Aubrey Stirton, and Elizabeth Maud, *née* Inglesby; *b* 25 November 1946, Pietermaritzburg, SA; *Educ* St Charles's Coll Pietermaritzburg, Univ of Natal (MSc), Univ of Cape Town (PhD, South African Assoc of Botanists Jr Medal), Naval Gymnasium South Africa (Dip Engine Room Mechanics); *m* Jana (d 2015), da of late Vratislav antovsky; 1 da (Elishka); *Career* PRO Natal branch Wildlife Soc of South Africa 1966, lawyers' clerk Paola & Wright 1966, asst mangr Pobana Trading Store 1966–1967, chief professional offr Botanical Research Inst South Africa 1979–82 (sr professional offr 1975–78, South African liaison botanist London 1979–82), B A Krukoff botanist for neotropical legume research Royal Botanic Gardens Kew 1982–87, assoc prof Dept of Botany Univ of Natal 1988–90, freelance writer 1990, author of 139scientific papers in learned jls; Royal Botanic Gardens Kew: research co-ordinator for economic botany progs 1990–92, dep dir and dep dir of science 1992–95, dep dir and dir of science and horticulture 1995–96; fndr dir National Botanic Garden of Wales 1996–2002, chm Contextua Ltd 2002–05, dir St Vincent Gp Ltd and subsidiaries, dir Matara Gardens of Wellbeing 2011–13; strategic dir Ouroboros Research and Educn Tst 2005–07 (also tstee); sr res fell Univ of Birmingham 1992–96; hon prof: Univ of Reading 1995–97, Univ of Wales 1997–2005; genera 'Stirtonia' and 'Stirtonanthus' named; futurist; memb Steering Gp Species Survival Cmmn (IUCN) (chair Plants Sub-Ctee 1994–96), memb Sci Panel Nat Museum and Galleries of Wales; fndr pres and hon life memb Natal Evolutionary Biology Soc; govr Trinity Coll Carmarthen 1997–2000; tstee: ILDIS, Bentham-Moxon Tst 1990–96, Pat Brenan Meml Fund 1990–96, Gateway Gardens Tst 2003–10, Overberg Lowlands Conservation Tst (also scientific advsr); mentor Mellon Fndn 2007–09; new British tree named 'Sorbus stirtoniana Rich' 2009; Hon Dr Univ of Glamorgan 2001; hon research assoc Univ of Cape Town 2006–; FLS; *Books* Plant Invaders – Beautiful But Dangerous, Advances in Legume Biology, Advances in Legume Systematics 3, Problem Plants of Southern Africa, Weeds in a Changing World; *Recreations* gardening, reading, postal history, postcards, cinema, philately, history, philosophy; *Style*— Prof Charles Stirton; ✉ website http://chstirton.wordpress.com

STOBART, Paul Lancelot; s of George Lancelot Stobart, of La Massana Parc, Andorra, and Elizabeth Carla, *née* Bruxby; *b* 31 May 1957; *Educ* Peterhouse Sch Zimbabwe, Oriel Coll Oxford (BA); *Children* 5 da (Alice Lucy b 14 Dec 1995, Hannah Elizabeth, Grace Georgia (twins) b 6 Jan 2005, Imogen Scarlett, Honor Dulcie (twins) b 2 April 2006); *Career* Price Waterhouse London 1980–84, Hill Samuel London & NY 1984–88; Interbrand Group plc: dir 1988–94, chm Europe 1995–96; Sage Group plc: dir 1996–1997, chief operating offr 1997–2003, md Sage UK and Ireland 2003–; non-exec dir Capital & Regional plc; ACA 1983; *Books* Brand Power (ed, 1994); *Recreations* golf, cricket, theatre; *Clubs* Oxford and Cambridge Golfing Soc, Royal St George's Golf; *Style*— Paul Stobart, Esq; ✉ The Sage Group plc, North Park, Newcastle upon Tyne NE13 9AA (☎ 0191 294 3000, fax 0191 294 0001, e-mail paul.stobart@sage.com)

STOCK, Rt Rev (William) Nigel; s of Ian Heath Stock, MC (d 1975), and Elizabeth Mary, *née* Bell (d 1999); *Educ* Durham Sch, Univ of Durham (BA), Ripon Coll Cuddesdon (DipTh); *m* 1973, Carolyne Grace, *née* Greswell; 3 s (Michael George b 1977, Patrick Richard b 1979, Thomas Edward b 1982); *Career* ordained: deacon 1976, priest 1977; curate Stockton St Peter Durham 1976–79, priest-in-charge Taraka Lae Papua New

Guinea 1979–84, vicar of Shiremoor Newcastle 1985–91, team rector North Shields 1991–98, rural dean of Tynemouth 1992–98, hon canon Newcastle Cathedral 1997–98, canon residentiary Durham Cathedral 1998–2000, chaplain Grey Coll Durham 1999–2000, bishop of Stockport 2000–07, bishop of St Edmundsbury and Ipswich 2007–13, bishop at Lambeth 2013– (Bishop to HM Forces 2014–, Bishop for the Falkland Islands 2014–); hon asst bishop: Dio of Southwark 2013, Dio of London 2014, Dio of Bath and Wells 2016; memb House of Lords 2011–13; *Recreations* reading, walking, music, art, history; *Style*— The Rt Rev Nigel Stock; ✉ Lambeth Palace, London SE1 7JU (☎ 020 7898 1211, e-mail nigel.stock@lambethpalace.org.uk)

STOCKDALE, His Hon Judge David Andrew; QC (1995); s of John Ramsden Stockdale (d 1987), and Jean Stewart, *née* Shelley (d 2004); *b* 9 May 1951; *Educ* Giggleswick Sch, Pembroke Coll Oxford (MA); *m* 1 June 1985, Melanie Jane, da of late Anthony Newis Benson; 1 s, 3 da; *Career* called to the Bar Middle Temple 1975 (bencher 2003); Northern Circuit: in practice 1976–2010, jr 1978, treas 2008–10; recorder of the Crown Court 1993–2010 (asst recorder 1990–93), dep High Court judge 2008–, circuit judge (Northern Circuit) 2010–, sr circuit judge and hon recorder of Manchester 2013–; govr: Giggleswick Sch 1982– (chm 1997–2007), Terra Nova Sch 2000–08; *Recreations* the outdoors, motorcycling, remote Scotland; *Clubs* Sloane; *Style*— His Hon Judge Stockdale, QC; ✉ Courts of Justice, Crown Square, Manchester M3 3FL (☎ 0161 954 1800)

STOCKDALE, Dr Elizabeth Joan Noël; *Educ* Bentley GS, Cambridgeshire Coll of Arts and Technol, Univ of Aberdeen Faculty of Med (MB ChB), Univ of London (Dip Med Radiodiagnosis), Univ of Strathclyde Grad Business Sch (MBA), Univ of Aberdeen Coll of Arts and Social Science Grad Sch and Walter Scott Research Centre (MLitt); *m* 26 May 1979, Christopher Leo Stockdale; 1 da (Jane Frances b 1981), 2 s (David Leo Andrew b 1983, Alexander James b 1984); *Career* house surgn Aberdeen Royal Infirmary and house physician Woodend Gen Hosp Aberdeen 1972–73, sr house surgn Professorial Surgical Unit Great Ormond St Hosp London 1974, registrar and sr registrar Dept of Diagnostic Radiology St George's Hosp London 1975–79 (with appts to The Royal Nat Orthopaedic Hosp, Atkinson Morley's Hosp, The Royal Marsden Hosp and St James's Hosp), conslt radiologist to Grampian Health Bd 1980–2008, hon clinical sr lectr Univ of Aberdeen 1980–2008; BMA: chm Grampian Div 1995–97, memb Scottish Cncl 1997–2000, memb Scottish Ctee for Hosp Med Servs 1997–2000; former pres Aberdeen and NE Branch Med Women's Fedn; memb: Scottish Radiological Soc 1980, European Soc of Paediatric Radiologists 1980, Br Paediatric Radiology Soc 1982, Br Paediatric Assoc 1986, Scottish Surgical Paediatric Soc 1986, Br Inst Radiology 1990, Br Med Ultrasound Soc 1990–2008, Scottish Medico-Legal Soc 1997–, Scottish Standing Ctee RCR 1997–2002, Radiology Section UK Children's Cancer Study Gp (UKCCSG) 1998–2006; FRCR 1979, FRCPCH 1997; *Clubs* RSM, Edinburgh Sir Walter Scott; *Style*— Dr Elizabeth Stockdale; ✉ 1 Grant Road, Banchory, Kincardineshire AB31 5UW (☎ 01330 823096)

STOCKDALE, Sir Thomas Minshull; 2 Bt (UK 1960), of Hoddington, Co Southampton; er s of Sir Edmund Villiers Minshull Stockdale, 1 Bt, JP (d 1989), and Hon Louise Fermor-Hesketh (d 1994), da of 1 Baron Hesketh; *b* 7 January 1940; *Educ* Eton, Worcester Coll Oxford (MA); *m* 1965, Jacqueline, da of Ha-Van-Vuong, of Saigon (d 2010); 1 s (John Minshull b 1967), 1 da (Charlotte Fermor b 1970); *Heir* s, John Stockdale; *Career* called to the Bar Inner Temple 1966, bencher Lincoln's Inn 1994; memb Ct of Assts Worshipful Co of Fishmongers (Prime Warden 2001–02); *Recreations* shooting, travel; *Clubs* Turf, MCC; *Style*— Sir Thomas Stockdale, Bt; ✉ Manor Farm, Weston Patrick, Basingstoke, Hampshire RG25 2NT (☎ 01256 862841)

STOCKEN, Oliver Henry James; CBE (2013); s of Henry Edmund West Stocken (d 1980), and Sheila Guisard, *née* Steele (d 1998); *b* 22 December 1941; *Educ* Felsted, UC Oxford; *m* 1967, Sally Forbes, da of John Dishon, of Aust; 2 s, 1 da; *Career* md Barclays Aust 1982–84; dir: N M Rothschild & Sons 1972–77, Esperanza Ltd 1977–79, Barclays Merchant Bank Ltd 1979–86, Barclays de Zoete Wedd 1986–93 (fin dir 1991–93); fin dir Barclays plc 1993–99; non-exec chm Stanhope plc; chm MCC, chair Care Int (UK), dir Chicester Festival Theatre; tstee: Belvoir Castle Cricket Club, Friends of Arundel Cricket Club; FCA 1967; *Clubs* Brooks's, Garrick, MCC; *Style*— Oliver Stocken Esq, CBE; ✉ 25c Marryat Road Wimbledon London SW19 5BB (☎ 07860 448384, e-mail oliverstocken@yahoo.co.uk)

STOCKHAM TURNER, Dr Margaret Jean; *née* King; da of David Hugh Eveleigh King (d 2001), and Joan Elizabeth Mary (d 2016), *née* Thompson; *b* 11 December 1954, Leeds; *Educ* Convent of St Louis Bury St Edmunds, Cheltenham Ladies Coll, Co Upper Sch Bury St Edmunds, Princess Mary's RAF Hosp Physiotherapy Sch, Univ of Leicester (MSc), Brownsville Univ TX (PhD); *Family* 1 s (James b 13 Jan 1978), 1 da (Danielle b 21 Aug 1986); m, 29 March 1994, Donald Turner; *Career* clinical physiotherapy posts UK and overseas 1978–87, dist physiotherapist Kettering 1987–90, dir Elderly and Therapy Div Priority Services Unit Kettering 1990–94, dir Strategy and Ops Bedford and Shires NHS Tst 1994–98; chief exec: E Berks Community NHS Tst 1998–99, Bedford Primary Care Gp 1999–2001, Bedford PCT 2001–06, Beds PCT 2006–07; md Ptnrs in Practice Ltd 2007–; chm European Union of Women (EUW) 2013–; vice-chair Mind BLMK; lifetime memb Worldwide Who's Who; memb: Inst of Dirs, Inst of Health Mgmnt 1987; FRSM (memb 2010), FRSA; *Recreations* antiques, gardening, athletics, cinema and theatre, travel; *Clubs* Br Section European Union of Women (EUW); *Style*— Dr Margaret Stockham Turner; ✉ Partners in Practice Ltd, 3 Waltham Drive, Abbeyfields, Elstow, Bedfordshire MK42 9FY (☎ 01234 293486, e-mail margaret.stockham@ntlworld.com, Twitter @margstockham)

STOCKING, Dame Barbara Mary; DBE (2008); da of Percy Frederick Stocking (d 2001), of Rugby, Warwickshire, and Mary, *née* Catling (d 1993); *b* 28 July 1951; *Educ* Univ of Wisconsin Madison (MS), Univ of Illinois Urbana, New Hall Cambridge (BA); *m* 3 Oct 1981, Dr Robert John MacInnes, s of Dr Iain MacInnes, of Maidenhead; 2 s (Andrew Tom b 3 June 1986, Stephen Courtney b 12 Sept 1989); *Career* fell Kings Fund Coll 1983–86, dir Kings Fund Centre for Health Servs Devpt 1987–93; chief exec: Oxford RHA 1993–94, Anglia and Oxford RHA 1994–96; regional dir: Anglia and Oxford NHS Exec 1996–99, South-East NHS Exec 1999–2000; head Modernisation Agency NHS Executive 2000–01; chief exec Oxfam 2001–13; memb: Riverside Health Authy 1985–89, Advsy Ctee UK Harkness Fellowships 1989–95, Central R&D Ctee NHS 1991–96; Hon DSc: Univ of Luton 1998, Oxford Brookes Univ 1999; CIMgt 1996; *Books* The Image and the Reality: A Case Study of the Impacts of Medical Technology (with S L Morrison, 1978), Initiative and Inertia – Case Studies in the Health Service (1985), Expensive Medical Technologies (ed, 1988), A Study of the Diffusion of Medical Technology in Europe (series ed, 1991), Medical Advances (the future shape of acute services, 1992); *Recreations* music; *Style*— Dame Barbara Stocking, DBE

STOCKPORT, Bishop of 2015–; Rt Rev Libby Lane; *b* 8 December 1966, High Wycombe; *Educ* St Peter's Coll Oxford (MA), St John's Coll Cranmer Hall Durham (dip in ministry); *m* 1990, George Lane; *Career* ordained: deacon 1993, priest 1994; curate St James Blackburn 1993–96, permission to officiate Dio of York 1996–99, hospital chaplain Hull 1998–99, social responsibility offr Dio of Chester 2000–02, team vicar St George's Stockport 2002–07, vicar St Peter's Hale and St Elizabeth's Ashley 2007–14; asst dir of ordinands Dio of Chester 2005–07, dean of women in ministry Dio of Chester 2010–14; memb Gen Synod as elected memb House of Bishops 2016; chair Cranmer Ctee 2016; tstee Children's Soc 2016; Hon DD Univ of Wales Trinity St David; *Style*— The Rt Rev the Bishop of Stockport

STOCKTING, Charlotte; *Educ* MA; *Career* began career as media planner buyer Saatchi & Saatchi, subsequently sales exec Country Homes & Interiors, dir of mktg Condé Nast Pubns and Carlton Screen Advertising 2000; HELLO!: joined as magazine commercial dir 2000, rising to publisher, then publishing dir 2006–; *Style*— Ms Charlotte Stockting; ✉ HELLO! Magazine, London SE1 9PQ

STOCKTON, 2 Earl of (UK 1984); Alexander Daniel Alan Macmillan; also Viscount Macmillan of Ovenden; s of Rt Hon Maurice Victor Macmillan, PC, MP (Viscount Macmillan of Ovenden, d 1984), and Katharine, Viscountess Macmillan of Ovenden, DBE; gs of 1 Earl of Stockton (d 1986); *b* 10 October 1943; *Educ* Eton, Ecole Politique Université de Paris, Univ of Strathclyde; *m* 1, 1970 (m dis 1991), Hélène Birgitte (Bitta), da of late Alan Douglas Christie Hamilton, of Stable Green, Mitford, Northumberland; 1 s (Daniel Maurice Alan, Viscount Macmillan of Ovenden b 1974), 2 da (Lady Rebecca Elizabeth b 1980, Lady Louisa Alexandra b 1982); m 2, 1995 (m dis 2010), Miranda Elizabeth Louise, formerly w of late Sir Nicholas Keith Lillington Nuttall, 3 Bt, and previously of late Peter Richard Henry Sellers, CBE, and da of Richard St John Quarry and Diana, Lady Mancroft; *Heir* s, Viscount Macmillan of Ovenden; *Career* book and magazine publisher; journalist Glasgow Herald 1965–66, reporter Daily Telegraph 1967, foreign corr Daily Telegraph 1968–69, chief Euro corr Sunday Telegraph 1969–70; dep chm Macmillan Ltd 1972–80, chm Macmillan Publishers 1980–90, pres Macmillan Ltd 1990–2008; govr English Speaking Union 1978–84 and 1986–93; chm: Central London TEC 1990–95, London TEC Gp 1991–94, Campaign for Shooting 1996–2000; memb Sec of State's TEC Advsy Gp 1991–94; contested (Cons) Bristol Euro Parly Election 1994, MEP (Cons) SW England 1990–2004, district cncllr S Bucks District Cncl 2011–; Liveryman Worshipful Co of Merchant Taylors 1972 (memb Ct of Assts 1987, Master 1992–93); Liveryman Worshipful Co of Stationers & Newspaper Makers 1973 (memb Ct of Assts 1996); Hon DUniv Strathclyde 1993; Hon DLitt: De Montfort Univ 1993, Univ of Westminster 1995; hon fell London Inst 2003; FIMgt, FRSA, Hon FISVA 1996, Hon FRICS 1996; *Recreations* fishing, conversation; *Clubs* Beefsteak, Pratt's; *Style*— The Rt Hon the Earl of Stockton; ✉ The Priory, Denham Village, Buckinghamshire UB9 5AS (☎ 01895 834181, mobile 07860 461497, e-mail thepriory@dbac.co.uk)

STOCKWIN, Prof James Arthur Ainscow; OBE (2009); s of Wilfred Arthur Stockwin (d 1991), of Sutton Coldfield, and Dr Edith Mary, *née* Ainscow (d 1983); *b* 28 November 1935, Sutton Coldfield; *Educ* King Edward's Sch Birmingham, Exeter Coll Oxford (MA), ANU Canberra (PhD); *m* 30 Jan 1960, Audrey Lucretia Hobson, da of Eric Stuart Wood (d 1996); 2 da (Katrina Mary (Mrs Bennett) b 19 Nov 1961, Jane Clare (Mrs Skirrow) b 26 Jan 1964), 2 s (Rupert Arthur b 1 Oct 1966, Timothy James b 20 Dec 1968 d 1987); *Career* lectr, sr lectr, reader ANU Canberra 1964–81, Nissan prof of modern Japanese studies and dir Nissan Inst of Japanese Studies Univ of Oxford 1982–2003; St Antony's Coll Oxford: professorial fell 1982–2003, sub-warden 1999–2001, emeritus fell 2003–; pres Br Assoc of Japanese Studies 1994–95; Order of the Rising Sun Gold Rays with Neck Ribbon 2004, Japan Fndn Award 2009; *Books* The Japanese Socialist Party and Neutralism (1968), Japan: Divided Politics in a Growth Economy (1975, 4 edn (as Governing Japan: Divided Politics in a Resurgent Economy) 2008), Dynamic and Immobilist Politics in Japan (ed and part-author, 1988), The Establishment of the Japanese Constitutional System (by Junji Banno, trans 1992), The Story of Tim (1993), Dictionary of the Modern Politics of Japan (2003), Collected Writings of J A A Stockwin, Part I (2004), Thirty-Odd Feet Below Belgium: An Affair of Letters in the Great War, 1915–1916 (2005, revised edn 2016), Japan's Postwar (by Michael Lucken et al, trans 2011), Japanese Foreign Policy and Understanding Japanese Politics: The Writings of J A A Stockwin (2 Vols, 2012), The Great Transformation of Japanese Capitalism (Sébastien Lechevalier ed, trans 2014), Japan's Modern History, 1857–1937: A New Political Narrative (by Junji Banno, trans 2014), The Abe Experiment and the Future of Japan: Don't Repeat History (by Junji Banno and Jiro Yamaguchi, trans 2016); *Recreations* languages, collecting modern ceramics; *Style*— Prof J A A Stockwin, OBE; ✉ Nissan Institute of Japanese Studies, 27 Winchester Road, Oxford OX2 6NA (☎ 01865 274570, fax 01865 274574, e-mail arthur.stockwin@nissan.ox.ac.uk)

STODDARD, Christopher James; s of Frederick Stoddard, of Congleton, Cheshire, and Millicent, *née* Barnett; *b* 2 June 1947; *Educ* Newcastle HS, Univ of Sheffield (MB ChB, MD); *m* 26 June 1971, Margaret Elizabeth, da of Reginald Bailey (d 1977); 1 da (Emma Louise b 3 Oct 1975), 1 s (James Edward b 12 Oct 1977); *Career* surgical registrar Royal Infirmary Sheffield 1974–76, clinical fell in surgery McMaster Med Centre Hamilton Ontario 1978–79, sr lectr in surgery Liverpool 1981–86, conslt surgn Royal Hallamshire Hosp Sheffield 1986–2013 (lectr in surgery 1977–78), regnl specialty advsr in gen surgery Trent Region 1998–2005; memb Cncl Assoc Surgeons GB and I 2009–; sec Assoc of Upper Gastrointestinal Surgeons 2001–05; memb: Surgical Research Soc, Br Soc of Gastroenterology; FRCS 1976; *Books* Complications of Minor Surgery (1986), Complications of Upper Gastrointestinal Surgery (1987); *Recreations* golf, gardening; *Style*— Christopher Stoddard, Esq; ✉ Blaenwern, 12 Slayleigh Lane, Fulwood, Sheffield (☎ 0114 230 9284, e-mail christopherstoddard@btinternet.com); Claremont Hospital, Sandygate Road, Sheffield S10 5UB (☎ 0141 263 0330)

STODDART, John Joseph; s of John Stoddart, of Liverpool, and Patricia, *née* Taylor; *b* 6 June 1957; *Educ* St Joan of Arc RC Secdy Modern; *m* 27 March 2009 (m dis 2009), Tara, *née* Hamilton-Miller; *Career* served Grenadier Gds 1972–78 (joined aged 15); photographer 1978– (based Liverpool until 1984, London thereafter); early editorial work for magazines incl The Face and NME, currently working throughout Europe and USA; numerous exhibitions incl: Punks, Poets and other Stars 1995, It's Nothing Personal 1997, Peep World 2004, Society 2006, Flowers in a Dark Room 2009; Portrait Photographer of the Year 1989; *Publications* It's Nothing Personal (1997), Peep World (2004); *Recreations* photography, art; *Clubs* Chelsea Arts, Cavalry, Guards; *Style*— John Stoddart, Esq; ✉ Pearl Lodge, Clare Road, Whitstable, Kent CT5 2EL

STODDART, John Maurice; CBE (1995); s of Gordon Stoddart (d 1983), of Wallasey, and May, *née* Ledder (d 1969); *b* 18 September 1938; *Educ* Wallasey GS, Univ of Reading (BA); *Career* head Dept of Econ and Business Studies Sheffield Poly 1970–72, asst dir NE London Poly 1972–76, dir Humberside Coll 1976–83, vice-chllr and princ Sheffield Hallam Univ (previously Sheffield City Poly) 1983–98; dir: Sheffield Sci Park 1988–98, Sheffield TEC 1990–98; memb: CNAA 1980–86, Nat Forum Mgmnt Educn and Devpt 1987–96, Cncl for Educn and Trg in Social Work 1989–93, Cncl for Indust and Higher Educn 1990–94; chm: Ctee of Dirs of Polys 1990–93 (vice-chm 1988–90), Higher Educn Quality Cncl 1992–97, Defence Accreditation Bd 1999–2004, Northern General NHS Tst Bd 1999–2001; non-exec dir Sheffield Teaching Hosps Tst Bd 2001–06; Hon DEd CNAA 1992, Hon DLitt Coventry 1993, Hon DUniv Middx 1993; hon fell Humberside Coll 1983, companion Br Business Graduates Soc 1984; Hon LLD Univ of Sheffield 1998, Hon DUniv Sheffield Hallam 1998, Hon MA Univ of Northampton 1999, hon fell Univ of Bolton 2005; CIMgt 1990, FRSA 1980; author of various articles on education, business education and management; *Recreations* biography, hill walking, rowing; *Clubs* Reform; *Style*— John Stoddart, Esq, CBE; ✉ 6 Tapton Park Gardens, Sheffield S10 3FP (☎ 0144 2305467)

STODDART, Patrick Thomas; s of Thomas Stoddart (d 1987), of Leith, Scotland, and Anne Theresa Power (d 1979); *b* 23 November 1944; *Educ* Watford Boys' GS; *m* Nicolette, da of late Gp Capt A D Murray, RAF (ret); *Career* jr reporter Watford Observer 1962, Evening Echo Herts 1967–72, TV columnist London Evening News 1975–80 (joined as reporter 1972); freelance 1980–85 (various TV series as writer/presenter at TVS and Anglia), TV critic Channel 4 Daily 1989–91, broadcasting ed and TV critic Sunday Times

S

1986–92, freelance writer on broadcasting affrs The Times and Daily Telegraph, conslt ed Broadcast magazine, script conslt various TV cos; ptnr Keighley Stoddart media consultancy until 1998; TV critic Express Saturday Magazine 1997–2000; sr lectr in journalism Univ of Westminster 2005– (lectr in cultural journalism 2004–05), adjunct prof of int journalism and media Richmond Univ 2011–; media conslt to: Rory Bremner, London Radio, Yorkshire Television, Domaine Productions, Virgin Television, Bronson Knight, LWT and Reuters Television 1993–98; creative conslt to: Talent Television, Paul Knight Productions; editorial dir News World Ltd (conf chair 1997 and 1998); memb RIIA; *Recreations* rugby, cricket, military history, music; *Clubs* Fullerians RFC (chm), Fleet Street Strollers Cricket, Groucho; *Style—* Patrick Stoddart, Esq; ✉ 28 Sherwoods Road, Watford, Hertfordshire WD1 4AZ (☎ 01923 229901, fax 01923 351363, e-mail patrick.stoddart@virgin.net)

STODDART, Peter; eld s of Peter Cowe (d 1947), and Amelia McQuillan (d 1985); adopted s of Stanley Stoddart; *b* 23 August 1945, Sunderland; *Educ* Sunderland Tech Coll; *m* 1, 1971 (m dis 1975), Carol Ann, da of late Brian Goodfellow; 1 s (Neil Robert); m 2, 1977 (m dis 1980), Sandie, da of late Wah Loung Yuen; m 3, 2002, Angela Claire Kirton, da of late Frank Reavley; 2 da (Emmeline Claire Kirton, Sarah Ruth); *Career* articled clerk Metcalf McKenzie & Co 1963–68, gp financial accountant T Cowie plc 1968–70, tax mangr Price Waterhouse & Co 1970–74, corporate finance mangr Jennings Johnson & Co 1974–75, co sec Edward Thompson Gp 1975–77, various finance mangr roles 1977–78, various roles British Shipbuilders Corporation 1978–85, finance mangr rising to finance dir Nissan Motor Manfacturing (UK) Ltd 1985–2000 (tstee and latterly dep chm Nissan pension plans 1989–2000), interim ops dir One NE RDA 2000–01, memb Competition Cmmn 2001–09, CA in public practice 2009–; non-exec dir Wirrall C of C 1983–85, memb Cncl and chm Economic Affrs Ctee NE C of C 1996–99; chm: City of Sunderland Common Purpose Forum 1996–2000, NE Euro Forum 1998–2000, Audit Ctee United Learning 2013; dep chm Royal Victoria Infirmary and Associated Hosps NHS Tst 1991–97; chm Wearside Coll of FE 1990–96, dep chm City of Sunderland Coll 1996–97; FCA 1979 (ACA 1969); *Recreations* travel, local history studies, books; *Style—* Peter Stoddart, FCA

STODDART OF SWINDON, Baron (Life Peer UK 1983), of Reading in the Royal County of Berkshire; David Leonard Stoddart; s of late Arthur Leonard Stoddart, and Queenie Victoria, *née* Price; *b* 4 May 1926; *Educ* St Clement Danes GS, Henley GS; *m* 1, 1946 (m dis 1960), late Doreen M Maynard; 1 da (Hon Janet Victoria (Hon Mrs Cousins) b 1947); m 2, 1961, Jennifer, adopted da of late Mrs Lois Percival-Alwyn, of Battle, E Sussex; 2 s (Hon Howard David b 1966 (decd), Hon Mathwyn Hugh b 1969); *Career* clerical offr CEGB 1957–70 (previous employment in PO Telephones, railways and hosp service); ldr Lab Gp Reading Cncl 1964–72 (ldr Cncl 1965–72), memb Reading CBC 1954–72; Parly candidate (Lab): Newbury 1959 and 1964, Swindon by-election 1969; MP (Lab) Swindon 1970–83; PPS to Min of Housing and Construction 1974–75, asst Govt whip 1975, Lord Cmmr of the Treasury 1976–77, jr oppn spokesman on Industry 1982–83, oppn spokesman on Energy (Lords) 1983–88, oppn whip (Lords) 1983–88; Lab whip withdrawn 2001, now Ind Lab; trade unions: UNITE (formerly EETPU) 1953–, NALGO 1951–70; memb Nat Jt Cncl Electricity Supply Industry 1967–70; vice-pres Assoc of District Cncls 1994–98; chm: Campaign for an Independent Britain 1991–2007 (jt pres 2007–11), Alliance Against the European Constitution (AAEC, formerly Anti-Maastricht Alliance) 1992–2004, Global Britain 1998–2008; memb Cncl Freedom Assoc 2006–; *Style—* The Rt Hon the Lord Stoddart of Swindon; ✉ Sintra, 37A Bath Road, Reading, Berkshire (☎ 0118 957 6726); House of Lords, London SW1A 0PW

STOKE-ON-TRENT, Archdeacon of; *see:* Stone, Ven Godfrey

STOKELY, Guy Robert; *b* 30 October 1943; *Educ* Forest Sch, Univ of Oxford (MA); *m* 4 Oct 1968, Wendy Anne; 3 s (Robert b 1970, Tom b 1979, Tim b 1983), 1 da (Sarah b 1973); *Career* fin vice-pres Manufacturers Life Insurance Co 1966–78, gen mangr Saudi Int Bank 1978–91, dir Barclays de Zoete Wedd 1991–97, dir Barclays Capital 1997–; *Recreations* golf, water sports, gardening; *Clubs* RAC; *Style—* Guy Stokely, Esq

STOKER, Dr Dennis James; s of Dr George Morris Stoker (d 1949), of Mitcham, Surrey, and Elsie Margaret, *née* Macqueen (d 1986); *b* London; *Educ* Oundle, Guy's Hosp Med Sch Univ of London (MB BS); *m* 1, 22 Sept 1951, Anne Sylvia Nelson (d 1997), da of Norman Forster (d 1962), of Haywards Heath, W Sussex; 2 da (Claire b 1952, Catherine b 1958), 2 s (Philip b 1954, Neil b 1956); m 2, 30 Oct 1999, Sheila Mary Mercer, da of Philip Baines (d 1973), of Wirral, Cheshire; *Career* house physician Guy's Hosp 1951; cmmnd Med Branch RAF 1952: RAF Brampton 1952–53, RAF Bridgnorth 1953–55, RAF Hosp W Kirby 1955–56, Med Div RAF Hosp Wroughton 1956–58, i/c Med Div RAF Hosp Akrotiri Cyprus 1958–61, physician i/c Chest Unit RAF Hosp Wroughton 1961–64, Metabolic Unit St Mary's Hosp London 1964–65, i/c Med Div RAF Hosp Steamer Point Aden 1965–67, i/c Med Div RAF Hosp Cosford Staffs 1967–68, ret Wing Cdr 1968; conslt radiologist: St George's Hosp 1972–87, Royal Nat Orthopaedic Hosp 1972–93 and 1997–2002 (special tstee 1984–2000, chm 1992–98); dean Inst of Orthopaedics 1987–91 (dir of radiological studies 1975–93); ed Skeletal Radiology 1984–96, dean Faculty of Clinical Radiology, vice-pres Royal Coll of Radiologists 1990–91 (memb Faculty Bd 1983–85, memb Cncl 1985–88, Knox medal 1992); Int Skeletal Soc: fndr memb 1974, medal 1993; FRSM 1958, FRCP 1976, FRCR 1975, FRCS 1992; *Books* Knee Arthrography (1980), Orthopaedics: self assessment in radiology (jtly, 1988), Radiology of Skeletal Disorders (jtly, 5 edn 2007); *Recreations* medical history, gardening, genealogy, philology; *Clubs* RAF, Phyllis Court Henley; *Style—* Dr Dennis Stoker; ✉ 3 Pearces Orchard, Henley-on-Thames, Oxfordshire RG9 2LF (☎ and fax 01491 575756, e-mail dennis.stoker@btinternet.com)

STOKER, Prof Richard; s of Capt Bower Morrell Stoker (d 1983), of Scarborough, N Yorks, and Winifred, *née* Harling (d 2006), of Castleford, W Yorks; *b* 8 November 1938; *Educ* Breadalbane House Sch Castleford, Huddersfield Sch of Music (with Harold Truscott), Huddersfield Sch of Art, Royal Acad of Music (with Sir Lennox Berkeley), Nadia Boulanger Paris (Mendelssohn Scholarship), privately with Arthur Benjamin, Eric Fenby and Benjamin Britten; *m* 1, 1 Sept 1962 (m dis 1985), Jacqueline Margaret Trelfer; m 2, 10 July 1986, Dr Gillian Patricia Watson, da of Kenneth Walter Watson (d 1989), of Littleover, Derby; *Career* composer, actor, conductor, author, painter, pianist and poet; conducting debut Huddersfield Town Hall 1956, broadcasted and performed at Welsh Nat Eisteddfod 1955 and 1956 and Int Eisteddfod 1957; asst librarian LSO 1962–63, prof of composition RAM 1963–87 (tutor 1970–80); visiting prof: Binghamton NY 1970, State Univ of NY 1970; composition teacher: St Paul's Sch 1972–74, Magdalen Coll Cambridge 1974–76; composition teacher to: Paul Patterson, Joe Jackson, Malcolm Singer, the late Paul Reade, June Palmer, and many others; compositions incl: Johnson Preserv'd (Opera in 3 acts), Three String Quartets, Three Piano Trios, Polemics (for oboe quartet), Partita (for violin and piano), Music that Brings Sweet Sleep, Aspects 1 in 3, Aspects of Flight, Canticle 1: Canticle of the Rose, Canticle 2: Make me a Willow Cabin, Canticle 3: Chinese Canticle, A Little Organ Book, Three Improvisations, Organ Symphony, Three Pieces, Organ Partita, Contemporary Organ Technique, Variants, Three Preludes, Sonate Symphonique, Piano Concerto, Piano Variations, Two Piano Sonatas, A York Suite, A Poet's Notebook, Twelve Nocturnes, Duologue, Diversions, Portrait of a Town, Assemblages (4 pianos), Partita for Mandolin and Harp, Three Overtures, Benedictus, Ecce Homo, Proverbs, Three Violin Sonatas, Prelude and Toccata, Monologue, (Guitar) Sonatina, Improvisation, Diversions, Pastoral, Sonata, Concerto (vocal), 5 Songs of Love and Loss, 4 Yeats Songs, 4 Shakespeare Songs, Kristallnächt Monody, Bassoon Quartet, Sonata for Flute, Monody for Mary Magdalene (recorder and strings), 3 Carols (I Saw A Fair Maiden, Creator Lord and Jesu Holy Child), A Green Pleasant Land (for voice and recorder), A Garrick Round, Chorale Prelude no. 3 for organ, Concerto for recorder (or flute) and strings, 3 Asanas, 6 pieces for flute (Monody of Waterfalls, Peacocks, Whisper of Waves, Sonnet on Rainbow, Soliloquy of Clouds, Indian Blues); featured festival composer at: Buxton 1962, Harlow 1965 and 1968, Camden 1965, Farnham 1964, Cheltenham 1966, 1973 and 1981, Denmark 1980; recordings incl: Complete Solo Piano Music (Priory/Parkin), Complete Vocal Music Vol 1 & Piano Duos (ASC CD's), Complete Guitar Music (Vishnick, ASC), Vocal Music Vol 2 (ASC), Tribute to Hoagy Carmichael 2 vols (ACS), Sonatina for clarinet and piano (Chandos), 3 string quartets and string trio (Gaudeamus), Aspects of Flight (Gaudeamus), Piano Variations, Sonata & Concerto for 2 guitars (Gaudeamus), Improvisation (Fonal), Chorale for Strings (Saydisc), Fine and Mellow (JSO), Two Preludes (Royal), Polemics (oboe and string trio), Trio for oboe, bassoon and piano; over 250 film, TV and stage credits incl: Troilus and Cressida (Old Vic), Portrait of a Town (Standard), End of the Line (Nat Film Sch), Garden Party (Coliseum), My Friend-My Enemy (The Place), In Control (Movie-craft), The Innocent Sleep (Starlight), Mirror (Lionheart Productions); numerous film and TV credits as actor incl: The Queen, Red Mercury Rising, The Da Vinci Code, The Golden Compass, Miss Austen Regrets, The Telltale Heart, The Woolfman, Sherlock Holmes, Uncut, My Name is David Linley, Pirates of the Caribbean, Dark Shadows, Dredd, Big Man – Little Man, Malifecent, Sense 8, Apocalypse Slough, 6 short Indian films, Friday Night Dinner, 4007 (Bollywood film), Hurcules (with John Hurt), Downton Abbey (body double), Seconds from Disaster; as artist exhibited at: Lewisham Soc of Arts Summer Exhibition 1992, Lewisham Arts Festival 1992, Blackheath Soc 1993, Laurence House (one-man show) 1992; ed Composer Magazine 1969–80; memb and treas Steering Ctee Lewisham Arts Festival 1990 and 1992; fndr memb RAM Guild (memb Ctee 1994–, hon treas 1995–); Mendelssohn scholar 1962–63, PRS 1962, MCPS 1970, APC 1977– (memb Promotions Ctee 1995–), BASCA 1980 (professional memb), exec memb Composers' Guild 1962– (memb Exec Ctee 1969–80); memb: RSM 1984, Blackheath Art Soc 1988, Public Lending Right Soc 1990–, Lewisham Soc of Arts 1991, Poetry Soc 1992–, European-Atlantic Gp 1993–, U3A (London) 1994–, Magistrates' Assoc 1995–2002, English PEN 1996–, Int PEN 1996–, Crown Court 1998–2003, Br Assoc Composers and Song Writers 1999 (memb Exec Ctee 1999–, memb Legal Affairs Review Cmmn 2000–, memb Gold Badge Awards Cmmn 2002–), Royal Soc of Lit 1999–; adjudicator: Cyprus Orch Composers' Award for Miny of Culture 2001–, RPS Award 2003, BBC Br Composers' Award 2003, 2004, 2005 and 2014; fndr memb: Atlantic Cncl 1993, PAMRA 2000, PPL 2000, Creative Rights Alliance 2001–; social work: 'Mind' 1989–91, Samaritans 1991–94; JP Inner London 1995–2003; finalist Int Poetry Competition Nat Lib of Poetry Maryland USA 1994, Editors' Choice Award 1995, 1996 and 1997; winner of various music awards 1960s, winner Man of the Year Award American Biographical Inst 1997 and 1999; ARCM 1962, FRAM 1978 (ARAM 1971); *Books* Portrait of a Town (1974, film version 1976), Words Without Music (1974), Strolling Players (1978), Open Window-Open Door (1985, film version 1987), Tanglewood (1990, film version 1992), Between the Lines (1991), Diva (1992), Collected Short Stories (1993), Sir Thomas Armstrong – A Celebration (jtly, 1998), Turn Back the Clock (1998), Travellers Tales (1999), A Passage of Time (1999), The Way Of It (2001), A Magic Carpet Ride (2002); poetry anthologised 44 times; stories anthologised 14 times; 8 commissioned contributions Oxford DNB 2004– (advsr 2003–); *Plays*: Screened-Take Five, Super-Mark; *Recreations* squash, skiing, tennis, swimming, golf, windsurfing, judo, cricket, rowing, yoga, nodding off; *Clubs* Garrick, Debrett Society, RAM Guild; *Style—* Prof Richard Stoker, FRAM; ✉ c/o The Garrick Club (e-mail office@garrickclub.co.uk)

STOKES, Adam Oliver Green; s of David George Stokes, and Anne, *née* Rennoldson; *b* 8 October 1981, Northampton; *Educ* Stamford Coll; *m* 4 Aug 2008, Natasha, *née* Green; 2 s (Jenson Adam Green Stokes b 19 July 2013, Hugo Edward Green Stokes b 14 Oct 2015); *Career* sous chef Hambleton Hall 2001–08, head chef Glenapp Castle Hotel Ballantrae 2008–13 (Gourmet Menu of the Year Scottish Chef Award 2009, 6/10 Good Food Guide 2011–15, Catering in Scotland Restaurant of the Year 2011, 4 AA Rosettes 2012 and 2013, 3 AA Rosettes 2014, 2015 and 2016, Michelin star 2012, 2013, 2014, 2015 and 2016), Adam's Restaurant Birmingham 2013– (Tripadvisor Traveller's Choice Award – 4th Best Restaurant in the World 2015, Tripadvisor Traveller's Choice Award – No. 1 Restaurant in the UK and Europe 2015); memb: Hospitality Action 2012–, Slow Food Orgn 2012–; fundraising for NSPCC (Adam's Restaurant Birmingham) and Street Smart (Great Br Chefs' Charity Dinner) 2013; *Books* Relish Midlands Second Helping (introduction, 2015), Signature Dishes (2015); *Publications* contrib: A Taste of Relais & Chateaux (2009), Relish Scotland (2010), 36 Inspirational Chefs (2011), Relish Midlands Second Helping (2015), Signature Dishes (foreword, 2015); *Recreations* travelling, wine, restaurants, golf, motorsport, music; *Style—* Adam Stokes, Esq; ✉ e-mail adam@adamsrestaurant.co.uk, Twitter @adamstokeschef; Adam's, 16 Waterloo Street, Birmingham B2 5UG (☎ 0121 643 3745, e-mail adam@adamsrestaurant.co.uk, website www.adamsrestaurant.co.uk, Twitter @restaurantadams)

STOKES, Dr Adrian Victor; OBE (1983); s of Alfred Samuel Stokes, of London, and Edna, *née* Kerrison; *b* 25 June 1945, Mill Hill, London; *Educ* Orange Hill GS, UCL (BSc, PhD), Univ of Hertfordshire (LLB, PGCert); *m* 3 Oct 1970 (m dis 1978), Caroline Therese, da of Arthur Campbell Miles, of London; *Career* res programmer GEC Computers Ltd 1969–71, res asst/res fell Inst of Computer Sci/Dept of Statistics and Computer Sci UCL 1971–77, sr res fell and sr lectr Sch of Info Sci Hatfield Poly 1977–81, dir computing St Thomas' Hosp 1981–88 (King's Fund fell 1981–84); NHS Info Mgmnt Centre/NHS Info Authy: princ conslt 1989–97, asst dir 1997–99, jt dir 1999–2000; chief exec CAT Ltd 2000–, md Elvis Memories (UK) Ltd 2001–15; non-exec dir: Barnet Primary Care Tst (NHS Barnet) 2001–11, Nat Clinical Assessment Authy 2001–05; special tstee Royal Nat Orthopaedic Hosp NHS Tst 2003–13; chm: Euro Workshop for Open Systems Expert Gp Healthcare 1991–97, Disabled Drivers' Motor Club 1972–82, 1991–94 and 1997–2000, BSI Info Systems Technol Assembly 2000–, Disabled Motoring UK (formerly Mobilise Orgn) 2009–12 and 2015–18 (also life vice-pres 2005–); vice-pres Disabled Drivers' Motor Club 1982–2005, chm Exec Ctee Royal Assoc for Disability and Rehabilitation 1985–92, govr and memb Cncl of Mgmnt Motability 1977–, memb Exec Ctee Assoc for Spina Bifida and Hydrocephalus 1978–85, tstee and memb Cncl of Mgmnt PHAB 1982–90, tstee Ind Living Funds 1993–2002, tstee Mobility Choice 1988–2013; memb: DHSS Working Party on Mobility Allowance 1975, DHSS Working Party on the Invalid Tricycle Repair Serv 1976–80, DHSS Silver Jubilee Ctee On Improving Access for Disabled People 1977–78, DHSS Ctee on Restrictions Against Disabled People 1979–81, Social Security Advsy Ctee 1980–2001, Dept of Tport Panel of Advsrs on Disability 1983–85, Disabled Persons' Tport Advsy Ctee 1986–89, Social Entitlement Chamber First Tier Tbnl (formerly Disability Appeal Tbnl) 1993–, Cncl on Tbnls 2003–07, Adminstrative Justice and Tbnls Cncl 2007–11, Editorial Bd Tbnls Jl 2015–; pres Hendon North Lib Assoc, 1981–83, candidate for London Borough of Barnet Cncl Mill Hill Ward 1968, 1971, 1974 and 1978; hon res fell Dept of Computer Sci UCL 1988–90, hon visiting prof of info mgmnt UC Northampton 1994–1999, hon res fell King Alfred's Coll Winchester 2001–04, govr Univ of Hertfordshire 2005–11, memb Ct Univ of Hertfordshire 2005–16; Hon DSc Univ of Hertfordshire 1994; Freeman City of London 1988, Liveryman Worshipful Co of Info Technologists 1992 (Freeman 1988); CChem 1976, MRSC 1976, FBCS 1979, MCMI (MIMgt 1986), FIoD 1986, CEng 1990, FRSA 1997, CSci 2004, CITP 2004; *Books* An Introduction to Data Processing Networks (1978), Viewdata: A Public Information Utility (1978, 2 edn

1980), The Concise Encyclopaedia of Computer Terminology (1981), Networks (1981), What to Read in Microcomputing (with C Saiady, 1982), A Concise Encyclopaedia of Information Technology (1982, 3 edn 1986), Integrated Office Systems (1982), Computer Networks: Fundamentals and Practice (with M D and J M Bacon, 1984), Overview of Data Communications (1985), Communications Standards (1986), The A-Z of Business Computing (1986), OSI Standards and Acronyms (1987, 3 edn 1991), The BJHC Abbreviary (with H de Glanville, 1995); *Recreations* philately, science fiction, computer programming, collecting Elvis Presley records; *Style*— Dr Adrian V Stokes, OBE; ✉ 97 Millway, Mill Hill, London NW7 3JL (☎ 020 8959 6665, e-mail adrian.stokes@cat-ltd.demon.co.uk)

STOKES, Dr Alistair; *b* 22 July 1948; *Educ* Univ of Wales (BSc, PhD), Univ of Oxford (SRC res fellowship); *m* 22 Aug 1970, Stephanie Mary, da of B H Garland, of Fordingbridge, Hants; 2 da (Charlotte, Samantha); *Career* commercial dir Monsato Co St Louis MO 1980–82 (joined 1976); Glaxo Pharmaceuticals Ltd: int product mangr 1982–83, mktg and sales dir Duncan Flockhart Ltd 1983–85; gen mangr Yorks RHA 1985–87; Glaxo Pharmaceuticals Ltd: dir business devpt 1987–88, md Glaxo Labs Ltd 1988–89, regnl dir Glaxo Holdings plc 1989–90; dir and chief operating offr Porton International 1990–94, chm Ipsen Ltd (formerly Speywood Pharmaceuticals Ltd) 1994–; chm: E Berks Community Health Tst 1992–98, Stowic plc 1998–99; non-exec dir: Octagen Corp 1998–, Quadrant Healthcare plc 1999–2000, Spirogen Ltd 2003–; *Books* Plasma Proteins (1977); *Recreations* reading, walking, music; *Clubs* Naval and Military; *Style*— Dr Alistair Stokes; ✉ Ipsen Ltd, 190 Bath Road, Slough, Berkshire SL1 3XE

STOKES, David; *Educ* Univ of Sydney; *Career* chief exec IBM UK and Ireland 2013–; *Style*— David Stokes, Esq; ✉ IBM United Kingdom Limited, PO Box 41, North Harbour, Portsmouth, Hampshire PO6 3AU

STOKES, Leslie James; s of William James Stokes, and Peggy Florence, *née* Blunsom; *b* 22 May 1951; *Educ* Abbs Cross Tech HS, Sir John Cass Coll, Newcastle upon Tyne Poly (DipAD, RSA travelling bursary prize), RCA (MDes, Braun prize); *m* 1973, Janet Barbara, da of Alfred Johns Victor Hayes; 1 s (William James b 1987), 1 da (Kathryn Louise b 1982); *Career* lectr in 3D design Herts Coll of Art and Design 1976–79, industrial design conslt London and Upjohn 1976–81, ptnr London Associates (industrial design and product devpt) 1981–2011, dir LA-design 2011–; dir BDI 2007–; Br Design Award 1990, three Design Effectiveness Awards; responsible for five Millennium projects; memb various jury panels for Design Cncl Design awards, external examiner Univ of Northumbria 2003, course advsr Cranfield Business Sch; memb Design Business Assoc 1986; FCSD 1989 (MCSD 1981); *Style*— Leslie Stokes, Esq; ✉ London Associates, 105 High Street, Berkhamsted, Hertfordshire HP4 2DG (☎ 01442 862631, fax 01442 874354, e-mail office@la-design.co.uk, website www.la-design.co.uk)

STOKES, His Hon Judge Michael George Thomas; QC (1994), DL (Notts 2016); s of Michael Philip Stokes (d 1988); *b* 30 May 1948, Preston, Lancs; *Educ* Preston Catholic Coll, Univ of Leeds (LLB); *m* 9 July 1994, Alison H Pollock; 1 da (Anna Elizabeth Hamilton b 19 July 1995), 1 s (Henry James Kerr b 30 May 1999); *Career* called to the Bar Gray's Inn 1971 (Holt scholar, Macaskie scholar, master of the bench 2013); asst lectr Univ of Nottingham 1970–72, in practice Midland & Oxford Circuit 1973–2001, recorder of the Crown Court 1990–2001 (asst recorder 1986–90), circuit judge (Midland Circuit) 2001–, resident judge Leicester Crown Court 2002–06, sr circuit judge and resident judge Nottingham Crown Court 2006–, recorder Nottingham 2007–, dep judge High Court 2010–; recorder of Nottingham 2007–; pres Leics and Rutland Magistrates' Assoc 2005–; memb Remuneration and Terms of Work Ctee (formerly Fees and Legal Aid Ctee) Bar Cncl 1996–2000, memb Public Affairs Ctee 2000–01; pres Mental Health Tbnl 1999–2008; visiting prof of law Nottingham Trent Univ 2013; govr: Haddon Park HS Nottingham 2007–10, Sycamore Primary Sch Nottingham 2010–13, Ratcliffe Coll Leics 2012; *Books* Blackmail (novel, 2016); *Recreations* France, travel, writing; *Style*— His Hon Judge Michael Stokes, QC, DL; ✉ Nottingham Crown Court, Canal Street, Nottingham (e-mail mstokes1@btinternet.com)

STOLLER, Anthony David (Tony); CBE (2004); s of Louis Stoller (d 1973), and Pearl, *née* Poster (d 1992); *b* 14 May 1947; *Educ* Hendon Co GS, Gonville & Caius Coll Cambridge (MA, LLB), Bournemouth Univ (PhD); *m* 1969, Andrea (Andy), *née* Lewisohn; 1 da (Juliette Louise b 1975), 1 s (Timothy b 1976); *Career* grad trainee Thomson Regnl Newspapers 1969–72, mktg mangr Liverpool Daily Post and Echo Ltd 1972–74, sr offr radio then head radio programming IBA 1974–79, dir AIRC 1979–81, md Thames Valley Broadcasting plc 1981–85, md Tyrrell & Green John Lewis Partnership 1985–95, chief exec Radio Authy 1995–2003, external rels dir Ofcom 2003–06; lay memb Information Tbnl 2007–11, memb Competition Cmmn 2009–14, memb Competition and Markets Authy 2014–15; visiting prof Bournemouth Univ 2015–; chair: Joseph Rowntree Fndn, Joseph Rowntree Housing Tst 2011–, Winchester Action on Climate Change 2014–; ed the Friends Quartley 2008–; *Publications* Wrestling with the Angel (Swarthmore Lecture, 2001), Sounds of Your Life, the history of independent radio in the UK (2010), Classical Music on UK Radio 1939–45 (doctoral thesis); *Recreations* music, cricket, sailing; *Style*— Dr Tony Stoller, CBE; ✉ e-mail tonystoller@yahoo.co.uk

STONE, Alice; da of Charles Stone, and Angela Stone; *b* 21 August 1983; *Educ* BA; *Career* designer; PR mangr Pressroom PR 2005–08, fndr and creative dir Lily and Lionel Ltd 2008–; involved with Kids Company 2013–15; Walpole Brand of Tomorrow 2012, Drapers Accessory Brand of the Year 2014; *Recreations* cinema, fashion, gardening, music, reading, skiing, travel, walking; *Clubs* Soho House; *Style*— Ms Alice Stone; ✉ Flat 5, 8 South Hill Park Gardens, London NW3 2TG (☎ 07956 529988, e-mail alice@lilyandlionel.com, Twitter @LilyandLionel, website www.lilyandlionel.com)

STONE, Maj Gen Anthony Charles Peter; CB (1994); s of Maj Charles Cecil Stone (d 2002), of Somerton, Somerset, and Kathleen Mons, *née* Grogan (d 2003); *b* 25 March 1939; *Educ* St Joseph's Coll, RMA Sandhurst, Staff Coll Camberley; *m* 29 July 1967, (Elizabeth) Mary Eirlys, da of Rev Canon Gideon Davies (d 1987), of Little Comberton, Worcs; 2 s (Guy b 1972, Mark b 1979); *Career* RA: cmmd 1960, serv in Far East, Middle East, BAOR and UK (light, field, medium, heavy, locating and air def artillery), Battery Cdr Q (Sanna's Post) Battery and 2 i/c 5 Regt RA 1974–75, GSO 2 DASD MOD 1976, DS RMCS 1977, CO 5 Regt RA 1980; founded Special OP Troop 1982, Col GS Def Progs Staff MOD 1983, Mil Dir of Studies RMCS 1985, Dir of Operational Requirements (Land) MOD 1986, Dir Light Weapons Projects MOD 1989, VMGO/DG Policy and Special Projects MOD 1990, DG Land Fighting Systems MOD 1992, DG Land Systems MOD 1994–95, ret Army; Hon Col 5 Regt RA 1990–2008, Col Cmdt Royal Regt of Artillery 1993–2001, Rep Col Cmdt 1998–99; chm Nash Partnership Ltd 1996–2006, def advsr/ptnr Gracemoor Consultants (UK) 1996–2006, conslt PricewaterhouseCoopers 2006–08, ind defence analyst 2009–; memb Mil Advsy Bd Simrad Optronics Norway 2007–09; memb Ctee UK Defence Forum 1997–, memb Euro-Atlantic Gp 1997–, int conference chm IQPC 2002–09, memb Military Commentators' Circle 2013–; visiting research fell Dept of Def Studies Univ of York 1996–97; fell RUSI 1997; *Publications* Thoughts on 21st Century Warfare (1999), Trading Freedom for Security (2002), Lessons from Two Gulf Wars (2003), The Numbers Game (2003), The UK's Future Rapid Effects System (2004), Smaller Still & Still Better? Analysis of a reduced army (2005), Prepared or Not Prepared? Is that the question? (2006); *Recreations* family, sudoku, writing; *Clubs* Army and Navy; *Style*— Maj Gen Anthony Stone, CB

STONE, Carole; CBE (2015); *née* Conroy; da of Harry A Stone (d 1976), and Kathleen Jacques, *née* Conroy (d 1993); *b* 30 May 1942, Maidstone, Kent; *Educ* Ashford County GS for Girls, Southampton Tech Coll; *m* Richard Lindley, s of Lt Col Herbert Guy Lindley, and Penelope Lindley; *Career* joined BBC in 1963 as copy-taker in Newsroom BBC South, asst prodr BBC Radio Brighton 1967–70, gen talks prodr BBC Radio 4 1970, prodr BBC Radio 4's Any Questions? programme 1977–89, freelance TV/media conslt 1990–2007; tstee The Church of England Newspaper 2007–11; dir Lindley Stone Ltd (independent TV prodn co) 2007–, md YouGovStone Ltd 2007–11; pres The Media Soc 1997–99; memb Ctee Women in Journalism 2000–06, dir London Press Club 2001–06, chair External Advsy Bd YouGov Centre Univ of Cambridge 2016–; former ptnr The Intelligence Squared Debating Forum; tstee The Wallace Collection 2001–10; govr Tavistock and Portman NHS Fndn Tst; fndr TheStoneClub 2008–11; patron: SANE, TOP UK, Global Fndn to Eliminate Domestic Violence 2016–, Centre for Peaceful Solutions 2016–; chair Ambassadors of the Tutu Fndn UK 2015–; counsellor One Young World 2010–; sr fellowship Regent's Univ London 2014–; *Books* Networking – The Art of Making Friends (2001), The Ultimate Guide to Successful Networking (2004); *Recreations* bringing people together to discuss issues of the day; *Clubs* House of St Barnabas, Soho House, Groucho, Reform; *Style*— Ms Carole Stone, CBE; ✉ Flat 1, 19 Henrietta Street, London WC2E 8QH (☎ 020 7267 5870, mobile 07770 236398, fax 020 7267 2668, e-mail carole.stone@yougov.com)

STONE, David; MBE (2009); *b* 30 April 1981; *Career* Paralympic cyclist; achievements incl: Gold medal team sprint World Disability Championships 2005, 2 Bronze medals (road race and time trial) World Disability Championships 2005, Gold medal road race World Disability Championships 2006 and 2007, Gold medal road time trial World Disability Championships 2006 and 2007, 2 Gold medals (time trial and mixed individual road race) Paralympics Beijing 2008, Gold medal road race and Bronze medal time trial Paralympics London 2012; *Style*— David Stone, Esq, MBE; ✉ c/o British Cycling, Stuart Street, Manchester M11 4DQ

STONE, Martin; s of Abraham Stone (d 1971), of Cardiff, S Wales, and Eva Priscilla, *née* Anstee (d 1988); *b* 28 February 1945, Cardiff; *Educ* The Cathedral Sch Llandaff, Canton HS Cardiff, Univ of Liverpool (MB ChB, MD); *m* 4 July 1970, Jane, da of Tudor Lloyd-Williams (d 1978), of Mold, N Wales; 2 s (Andrew Martin b 1971, Robert Charles b 1975), 1 da (Louise Jane b 1980); *Career* jr doctor Liverpool Hosps 1968–72, SHO Torbay Hosp 1972–73, registrar Charing Cross Hosp 1973–75, res registrar MRC 1975–76; sr registrar: St George's Hosp 1976–77, Southampton Hosp 1977–80; conslt gynaecologist Royal Gwent Hosp NHS Trust 1980–2011; dir Fedn of Ind Practitioner Orgns (FIPO) 2002; memb: Med Advsy Ctee BUPA Hosp Cardiff (chm 1989), London Obstetric and Gynaecological Soc (chm 1992), Med Advsy Ctee St Joseph's Private Hosp (chm 2000–07), Welsh Obstetric and Gynaecological Soc (treas 1981–92, pres 2004); pres Caerleon Rotary Club 1992; memb: BMA, Acad of Experts; FRCOG 1986 (MRCOG 1973); *Recreations* red wine, theatre, golf; *Clubs* Celtic Manor Golf and Country; *Style*— Martin Stone, Esq; ✉ Ye Olde Forge, Llanmartin, Newport, Gwent NP18 2EB (☎ 01633 413073, fax 01633 411148, e-mail marjan@globalnet.co.uk); St Joseph's Private Hospital, Harding Avenue, Malpas, Newport, Gwent NP20 6ZE (☎ 01633 820300)

STONE, Michael John Christopher; DL (Glos 2002); s of Henry Frederick Stone (d 1979), and Joan Barbara, *née* Da Silva; *b* 10 May 1936; *Educ* Bradfield Coll, Hamburg (Language Course); *m* 8 Jan 1966, Louisa, da of Robert Dyson, of Peru; 2 s (Charles b 9 Oct 1966, Andrew b 21 Nov 1970), 1 da (Nicola (Mrs Edward Farquhar) b 11 Jan 1968); *Career* cmmnd RHA 1955–57, served Germany, cmmnd HAC 1957–63; gp chm E D & F Man 1983–2000 (commodity broker 1957); chm: E D & F Man Sugar Ltd, London Sugar Futures Market 1981–84, Wentworth Wooden Jigsaw Co Ltd 1998–, E D & F Man (Holdings) Ltd 2000–03; dir: Alistair Sampson Antiques 1991–2011, Standard Bank Jersey Ltd 1992–95, Calcot Manor Hotel 1993–, Redhill Aerodrome Ventures Ltd 1995–2008; chm: Bradfield Fndn 1991–2006, Nat Hosp for Neurology and Neurosurgery Devpt Fndn 1993–98; govr Bradfield Coll 1991–2006; *Recreations* shooting, fishing, skiing; *Clubs* White's; *Style*— Michael Stone, Esq, DL; ✉ The Old Rectory, Ozleworth, Wotton-under-Edge, Gloucestershire GL12 7QA (☎ 01453 845591)

STONE, Prof Nicholas James (Nick); s of Frederick James Stone (d 1996), and Edith Mary, *née* Ingham (d 2008); *b* 1 April 1938, Portsmouth, Hants; *Educ* Portsmouth GS, ChCh Oxford (BA, DPhil); *m* 1, July 1963 (m dis 1984), Mary Christine Gregory; 2 s (Graham Nicholas b 16 Nov 1964, Adrian Richard Ingham b 25 Oct 1969), 1 da (Deborah Frances b 12 Nov 1966); m 2, 30 Nov 1985, Jirina Rikovska; *Career* research physicist Lawrence Berkeley Laboratory 1963–65; Univ of Oxford: research asst Clarendon Laboratory 1965–69, head Low Temperature Nuclear Orientation Research Gp Clarendon Laboratory 1965–2005, lectr in physics 1969–97, prof of physics 1997–2005 (prof emeritus 2005–); tutorial fell in physics St Edmund Hall Oxford 1969–2005 (fell emeritus 2005–); visiting prof: Univ of Br Columbia 1976–77, Univ of Lyons 1986, Univ of NSW 1987; visiting scientist Los Alamos Nat Laboratory 1977, research assoc CERN Geneva 1990 and 1999, research prof Univ of Tennessee 2002–, research prof Univ of Maryland 2004–05; memb UK nat research ctees SERC, memb Bd Int Research Jls and Int Research Confs; compiler Int Table of Nuclear Moments IAEA Vienna 1996–; Pressed Steel Fellowship 1963–65, DSIR Fellowship 1966–69; *Publications* Low Temperature Nuclear Orientation (1986); over 250 papers on hyperfine interactions and low energy nuclear structure physics; *Recreations* travelling, reading, philately; *Style*— Prof Nick Stone; ✉ Clarendon Laboratory, Department of Physics, Oxford University, Parks Road, Oxford OX1 3PU (☎ 01865 272325, fax 01865 272400, e-mail n.stone1@physics.ox.ac.uk)

STONE, Prof Norman; s of Flt Lt Norman Stone, RAF (ka 1942), and Mary Robertson, *née* Pettigrew (d 1991); *b* 8 March 1941; *Educ* Glasgow Acad, Gonville & Caius Coll Cambridge (BA, MA); *m* 1, 2 July 1966 (m dis 1977), Marie Nicole Aubry; 2 s (Nicholas b 1966, Sebastian b 1972); m 2, 11 Aug 1982, Christine Margaret Booker, *née* Verity; 1 s (Rupert b 1983); *Career* Univ of Cambridge: fell Gonville & Caius Coll 1965–71, lectr in Russian history 1968–84, fell Jesus Coll 1971–79, fell Trinity Coll 1979–84; Univ of Oxford: prof of modern history 1984–97, fell Worcester Coll 1984–97; prof of int relations Bilkent Univ Ankara 1997–; *Books* The Eastern Front 1914–1917 (1975, Wolfson Prize 1976), Hitler (1980), Europe Transformed 1878–1919 (1983), The Other Russia (with Michael Glenny, 1990), World War One: A Short History (2007), The Atlantic and its Enemies (2010), Turkey: A Short History (2011), World War Two: A Short History (2013); *Recreations* Eastern Europe, Turkey, music; *Style*— Prof Norman Stone; ✉ 22 St Margarets Road, Oxford OX2 6RX (☎ 01865 439481); Department of International Relations, Bilkent University, 06533 Bilkent, Ankara, Turkey

STONE, Philippa Jane; da of (Vivian) Harry George Stubbs (d 1997), of Duston, Northants, and Merle Josephine Mure McKerrell Stubbs, *née* Carver (d 1992); *Educ* Notre Dame HS Northampton, Univ of St Andrews (BSc), Univ of Oxford (DipEd); statements of accomplishment: Univ of Edinburgh, Georgia Tech, Univ of Melbourne, Maryland Technology Enterprise Institute (MTech) Univ of Maryland, Darden Sch of Business Univ of Virginia, Univ of Florida, Univ of Tokyo, Stanford Univ, Univ of Geneva, Columbia Univ NY, IE Business Sch Madrid, Wharton Business Sch Univ of Pennsylvania, Higher Economics Sch Nat Research Univ Moscow, Rutgers Univ, Nat Univ of Singapore, Univ of Leiden, Duke Univ, Yale Univ (verified certificate); *m* (m dis), David Robert Stone, s of Robert Charles Stone (d 2003); 1 da; *Career* business conslt; dir: P J Stone Ltd 1984–2002 and 2006–, Sharepoint Ltd 1984–88, City Child Ltd (chm 1985–86), Children of High Intelligence Ltd 1991–94; tstee Self Esteem Network 1992–96 (chm 1994–95); memb: Redbridge HA 1989–91, European Union of Women (chm London E 1991–95, hon sec Gtr London Area 1992–95), London Cycling Campaign 1996–

S

97; chair Clapham Park West Residents Assoc 2003–04; FMS; *Recreations* art, opera, coursera, travel; *Clubs* Univ of St Andrews Alumni (London, chm 1993–2001, vice-chm 2003–04); *Style*— Mrs Philippa Stone

STONE, Rex; s of Hiram Stone, of Belper, Derbys, and Elsie Lorraine, *née* Taylor; *b* 13 August 1938; *Educ* Herbert Strutt GS; *m* 16 Oct 1965, Anita Kay, da of Albert Arthur Hammond (d 1974), of London; 1 s (Alistair b 7 May 1971), 1 da (Rachel b 23 March 1969); *Career* CA; audit mangr Peat Marwick Mitchell & Co (Jamaica) 1961–65, co sec RB MacMillan Ltd 1965–69; chm: Firestone Investments Ltd 1972–, Alida Holdings plc 1974–92 (fin dir 1969–72, jt md 1972–74), Chevin Holdings Ltd 1975–; dep chm: Derbyshire Building Society 1985–, British Polythene Industries plc 1989–98; FCA 1961; *Recreations* wine, travel, game shooting, golf; *Style*— Rex Stone, Esq; ✉ Firestone Investments Ltd, 29 Bridge Street, Belper, Derby DE56 1AY (☎ 01773 827151, fax 01773 829843)

STONE, Richard Anthony; s of Jack Stone (d 1990), and Margaret Elizabeth, *née* Baraclough (d 1983); *b* 3 March 1943; *Educ* Univ of Cambridge (MA), Darden Business Sch Virginia USA; *m* 26 Jan 1975, Susan Joan, da of Ronald James; 2 da (Natasha Louise b 4 Oct 1980, Katrina Elizabeth b 27 June 1984); *Career* W H Cork Gully & Co (merged with Coopers & Lybrand 1980): 1965–68, rejoined 1975, insolvency ptnr 1977–87, head Corp Fin UK 1987–95; Outwich Ltd 1969–72, fin dir Regional Properties Ltd 1972–74; dep chm Coopers &Lybrand UK 1995–98, memb Global Bd PricewaterhouseCoopers 1998–2000; dir: British Nuclear Fuel Ltd 2001–05, Halma plc 2001–, TR Property Investment Tst 2001–, Gartmore Global Tst 2003–, Candover Investments plc 2005–; chm: Shearings Gp Ltd 2001–05, Drambuie Ltd 2004–; Master Worshipful Co of Glaziers 2000–01, Freeman Worshipful Co of CAs; FCA (ACA 1968); *Recreations* opera, ballet, golf, horse racing, travel, gardening; *Clubs* IOD, Moor Park Golf; *Style*— Richard A Stone, Esq; ✉ e-mail richard.a.stone@talk21.com

STONE, Richard William; s of Leonard William Stone, of Colchester, Essex, and Thelma May, *née* Sparkes; *b* 5 June 1951; *Educ* Colchester Stanway Secdy Sch, Gilberd Sch Colchester; *m* 1, 1975 (m dis 1990), Anthea Margaret, da of Capt Frank Harvey Stephenson, DFC; 2 da (Flavia Xanthe b 28 Oct 1980, Chloe Beatrice b 5 Nov 1984); m 2, 1991, Rhonda Marie, da of Curtis E Miller, MD; 1 s (William Russell b 3 May 1994); *Career* portrait painter; teacher: Copford Glebe School Colchester 1970–71, Colchester Inst 1977–83, Art Centre Pasadena CA 1987–88; delivered numerous invited lectures; subject of many film and TV reports and numerous newspaper articles; vice-pres Colchester Cncl for Voluntary Serv, tstee Minories Art Gallery Colchester 1996, memb Heritage Ctee Royal London Insurance 1998; Paul Harris Fellowship Aust 2001; Freeman City of London 1985, Liveryman Worshipful Co of Painter Stainers; Hon Citizen Austin TX 1989, Hon Texan 1990; *Major Commissions* subjects incl: Sir Arthur Bliss, Sir Adrian Boult, Sir Yehudi Menuhin, HM Queen Elizabeth The Queen Mother, Chief Red Fox, Burmese Nat Dance Co, HRH Princess Margaret, HRH Princess Alice Duchess of Gloucester, HRH Prince Michael of Kent, HRH Princess Michael of Kent, Eric Morecambe, Lord Boothby, Prof Donald Denman, Leo McKern, Viscount De L'Isle, Sir Robert Carswell, Prof Ivor A Richards, Prof Clive Parry, Prof Jeremy Cowan, Prof Stuart Sutherland, Dame Mary Donaldson, Sir Allan Davis, Sir Ralph Perring, Lord Home, Lord Wilson of Rievaulx, Lord Callaghan, US ambass Charles H Price II, Beth Chatto, Dr Marvin Goldberger, HRH The Princess Royal, Ronald Lancaster, Lord Grey of Naunton, Sir James Miskin, Dr James Hooley, HM The Queen, Joseph Maitland Robinson, Neil Foster, Lady Holt, Lady Buck, The Marquess of Tavistock, Lord James Russell, Lord and Lady Robin Russell, Sir Evelyn de Rothschild, William Lese, Bruno Schroder, US ambass William Crowe, Nina Wang, Earl Cadogan, HRH The Duke of York, Michael Pickard, Stanley Booth, HRH The Duke of Edinburgh, HRH The Prince of Wales, the wedding of HRH Prince Edward and Sophie Rhys-Jones, Dame Joan Sutherland, Geng Zhao Jie, Baroness Thatcher, HRH The Duchess of Gloucester, Archbishop Desmond Tutu, Dr James Watson, Richard Wheeler, Gerald Milsom, Luciano Pavarotti, HRH The Countess of Wessex, HRH The Duke of Gloucester, Dame Julie Andrews, Mrs Michael Howard, Lord Sterling of Plaistow, Sir Neil Thorne, Baroness Thatcher (for The Ronald Reagan Library), Rt Hon Michael Howard, Sir Simon Jenkins, Hanabi-ko (Koko), Nancy Reagan, Judy Naake, Michael Grade, Christopher Pertwee, HRH The Duchess of Cornwall, Bernard Ribeiro, Nelson Mandela, Aubrey Ngcungama, Ambassador and Mrs Robert Tuttle, Mr F W de Klerk, South African High Cmmr Dr Lindiwe Mabuza, Sir John Ritblat, Sir Michael Marshall, Sir John Madejski, Sir Anwar Pervez, President Stejpan Mesic, Elizabeth Ward; *Exhibitions* Plymouth City Art Gallery 1974, Digby Gallery Colchester 1977, QEII (transatlantic liner) 1983–86, Pembroke Coll Cambridge 1984, English Speaking Union of the US 1986 (touring exhbn), Huntington Library and Art Gallery CA 1987, UK/LA Festival Univ of Southern Calif and Woodbury Univ Calif 1988, Laguna Gloria Art Museum Austin TX 1989, Br Consul-Gen's residence LA 1991, Nat Portrait Gall 1992, Faces and Figures (Nassau Co Museum NY) 1997, Westwood Park Colchester 1998, Met Museum of Art NY 2000, Camberwell Rotary Art Show Melbourne 2001, Notable Portraits (Partridge Fine Arts London) 2004, Cold Spring Harbour Lab Long Island NY 2004, Politics of Portraits (J Paul Getty Museum) 2005, LA Regency Club 2005; *Recreations* classical music, gardening; *Style*— Richard Stone, Esq; ✉ West Bergholt Lodge, Colchester, Essex CO6 3EA (☎ 01206 241241, fax 01206 240783, e-mail richard.stone@richardstoneuk.com, website www.richardstoneuk.com)

STONE, Terence Reginald; s of Harry Victor Stone, of Grey Stones, Dawlish, Devon, and Hilda Mary, *née* Western; *b* 18 August 1928; *Educ* Willesden Coll of Technol, Regent St Coll of Architecture, Westminster Univ; *m* 1 (m dis); 4 s, 2 da; m 2, 1 Sept 2011, Elizabeth Ann, da of William Gordon McKie; *Career* sr architect RAF Air Works Sqdn Air Miny 1947–49, asst architect Orlit and Reema Ltd 1952, asst architect Sr Richard Constain Ltd 1953; chief architect Costain (W Africa) Ltd 1956–60, chm Terence Stone Gp of Companies 1970–, sr ptnr Stewart Stone Design Conslts 1988–; md: Terence Stone (Devpt) Ltd 1962–, Terence Stone (Construction) Ltd 1975–; Lord of the Manor Earl Stone Hants; FCIOB, FRSH, FIAS, FCIM, FFB, MRICS; *Recreations* swimming, tennis, badminton, running, motor rallying, skiing, sponsorship and promotion of sport, travel, arts; *Clubs* Rolls Royce Enthusiasts, RROC, Rolls Royce Silver Ghost Assoc (European dir 2000–), RAC; *Style*— Terence Stone, Esq

STONE, Prof Trevor William; s of Thomas William Stone, and Alice, *née* Reynolds; *b* 7 October 1947; *Educ* Mexborough GS, Univ of London (BPharm, DSc), Univ of Aberdeen (PhD); *m* 1, 1971, Anne, da of late Dr Lewis Corina; m 2, 2005, Gail, da of late William Darlington; *Career* lectr in physiology Univ of Aberdeen 1970–77; Univ of London: sr lectr in neurosciences 1977–83, reader 1983–86, prof of neurosciences 1986–88; prof of pharmacology Univ of Glasgow 1989–; research fell Nat Inst Mental Health Washington DC 1974 and 1977; scientific dir ShinKanco 2002–09, dir PharmaLinks 2003–09; fell NY Acad of Sci, FRSM, fell Br Pharmacology Soc; Hon FRCP 2013; *Books* Microiontophoresis (1985), Purines: Basic & Clinical (1991), Adenosine in the Nervous System (1991), Neuropharmacology (1995), Pills, Potions, Poisons (2000); *Recreations* piano, music, photography, painting, snooker; *Style*— Prof T W Stone; ✉ Institute of Neuroscience and Psychology, College of Medical, Veterinary and Life Sciences, University of Glasgow, West Medical Building, Glasgow G12 8QQ (☎ 0141 330 4481, e-mail trevor.stone@glasgow.ac.uk)

STONE OF BLACKHEATH, Baron (Life Peer UK 1997), of Blackheath in the London Borough of Greenwich; Andrew Zelig Stone; *b* 7 September 1942; *Educ* Cardiff HS; *m* 1973, Vivienne Wendy, da of Bernard Lee; 1 s (Hon Daniel Marcus b 1976), 2 da (Hon Jessica Alexandra b 1980, Hon Susannah Naomi b 1984); *Career* Marks & Spencer: joined as mgmnt trainee 1966, dir 1990–99, jt md 1994–99; non-exec chm Deal Gp Media plc until 2007, non-exec dir N Brown Gp plc 2002–13; *Style*— The Lord Stone of Blackheath; ✉ House of Lords, London SW1A 0PW

STONEFROST, Hilary; da of Maurice Frank Stonefrost, CBE, DL, and Audrey Jean, *née* Fishlock; *b* 12 November 1955; *Educ* LSE (MSc), City Univ (Dip Law), Inns of Court Sch of Law; *m* 1, Aug 1981 (m dis), Nourollah Nourshargh; m 2, Oct 1992, William James Gregory Keegan , *qv*, s of William Keegan (d 1995); 2 da (Caitlin Clare b 5 Sept 1994, Lucinda Grace Julia b 18 Dec 1997), 1 s (James Patrick William (twin) b 18 Dec 1997); *Career* economist Bank of England 1979–89, report for British Bankers Assoc on Euro Central Bank 1990; called to the Bar Middle Temple 1991; visiting tutor in law City Univ 1991–92, ad hoc work for conslts London Economics 1991–92, practising barr and memb Chambers 3–4 South Square 1992–; *Books* The Law of Receivers and Companies (contrib), Debt Restructuring (jtly); *Style*— Ms Hilary Stonefrost; ✉ 3–4 South Square, Gray's Inn, London WC1R 5HP (☎ 020 7696 9900, fax 020 7696 9911, e-mail clerks@southsquare.com)

STONEHAM OF DROXFORD, Baron (Life Peer UK 2011), of the Meon Valley in the County of Hampshire; Benjamin Russell Mackintosh Stoneham; s of Benjamin John Russell Stoneham (d 1977), and Beryl Marty, *née* Eccles (d 2007); *b* 24 August 1948, Tunbridge Wells, Kent; *Educ* Harrow, Christ's Coll Cambridge (BA), Univ of Warwick (MA); *m* 11 Oct 1975, Anne Kristine, *née* Mackintosh; 2 s (Daniel b 29 Nov 1981, Adam 18 April 1984), 1 da (Eleanor b 2 Sept 1987); *Career* research offr Dept of Social and Administrative Studies Univ of Oxford 1971–74; NCB: grad trainee 1974–76, staff offr to Chm 1976–78; nat offr Nat Union of Railwaymen 1979–82; Portsmouth and Sunderland Newspapers plc: ind rels exec 1982–87, devpt dir 1987–89; md Portsmouth Publishing and Printing Ltd 1989–99, gp prodn dir and personnel dir News Int 2000–03, ops dir Lib Dems 2003–10; chair: Portsmouth and SE Hants Business Partnership Ltd 1994–2001, Portsmouth Harbour Renaissance Ltd 1996–2005; chair and dir: Portsmouth Housing Assoc 2004–07, First Wessex Housing Gp 2007–12; dir Thames Gateway Thurrock Urban Devpt Corp 2004–10, chair and dir HousingandCare21 2011–; *Recreations* family, gardening, sport; *Style*— The Lord Stoneham of Droxford; ✉ House of Lords, London SW1A 0PW (☎ 020 7219 3000, e-mail stonehamb@parliament.uk)

STONHOUSE, Rev Canon Sir Michael Philip; 19 (E 1628) and 16 Bt (E 1670), of Radley, Berkshire; s of Sir Philip Allan Stonhouse, 18 and 15 Bt (d 1993), and (Winnifred) Emily, *née* Shield (d 1989); *b* 4 September 1948; *Educ* Medicine Hat Coll, Univ of Alberta (BA), Wycliffe Coll (MDiv); *m* 1977, (Rev) Colleen Eleanor, da of James Albert Coucill (d 1969), of Toronto, Canada; 3 s (Allan James b 1981, David Michael b 1983, Philip Radley b 1987); *Heir* s, Allan Stonhouse; *Career* ordained: deacon 1977, priest 1978 (both Diocese of Calgary, Canada); asst curate St Peter's Calgary Alberta 1977–80; rector and incumbent: Parkland Parish Alberta 1980–87, St Mark's Innisfail and St Matthew's Bowden Alberta 1987–92, St James Saskatoon Saskatchewan 1992–2007, St John's Minster and Associated Churches Lloydminster Saskatchewan 2007–; canon Diocese of Saskatoon 2006; prolocuter Synod of the Province of Rupert's Land 2009–; *Publications* Getting The Small Rural Church Out of Trouble (1988); *Recreations* walking/hiking, geneaology; *Style*— The Rev Canon Sir Michael Stonhouse, Bt; ✉ 202–4827–46 Street, Lloydminster, SK S9V 0J6, Canada (☎ 00 1 306 825 8942, e-mail michaelstonhouse@hotmail.com); 4709–49th Avenue, Lloydminster, Saskatchewan S9V 0T3 (☎ 00 1 306 825 3116, e-mail lloydanglicanchurch@sasktel.net)

STONIER, Prof Peter D; s of Frederic Stonier (d 1981), and Phyllis Stonier; *b* 29 April 1945; *Educ* Cheadle Hulme Sch, Univ of Birmingham (BSc), Univ of Sheffield (PhD), Univ of Manchester (MB ChB), Open Univ (BA); *m* 13 May 1989, Elizabeth Margaret, *née* Thomas; 1 s (Thomas William b 10 April 1990), 1 da (Helen Elizabeth b 29 April 1993); *Career* NHS: house offr gen med and gen surgery Manchester Royal Infirmary 1974–75, SHO psychiatry Univ Hosp S Manchester 1975–76, SHO A&E, orthopaedics, gen surgery Leicester Royal Infirmary 1976–77; Hoechst UK Ltd: med advsr 1977–80, head of med services 1980–81, med dir 1982–94; Hoechst Roussel Ltd: med dir 1994–96, bd memb 1994–96; Hoechst Marion Roussel Ltd: med dir 1996–2000, memb Bd 1996–2000, conslt in pharmaceutical med 2000–; visiting prof in pharmaceutical med: Univ of Surrey 1992–2010, KCL 1998–; chm: Br Assoc of Pharmaceutical Physicians (BrAPP) 1988–90, Walton Manor Research Ethics Ctee 1982–88; memb cncl and treas Tst for Educn and Research in Therapeutics (TERT) 1990–93, memb Cncl Medical Benefit-Risk Fndn 1990–96, memb Cncl RCP 1998–2001, memb Cncl Alternate Medico-Pharmaceutical Forum; memb ABPI Med Ctee 1990–2000, memb Cncl Br Assoc of Psychopharmacology 1993–97, Appeal Panel Nat Inst for Clinical Excellence (NICE); pres: RSM Section of Pharmaceutical Med & Research 1994–96, Int Fedn of Associations of Pharmaceutical Physicians (IFAPP) 1996–98; Faculty of Pharmaceutical Med: memb Educn Ctee 1989–, memb Bd of Examiners 1994–98, convener and chair Task Force for Higher Specialist Trg in Pharmaceutical Med 1995–2002, chm Fellowship Ctee 1997–2001, vice-pres 1992–96, pres 1997–2001, dir of educn and trg 2003–; Univ of Surrey: course dir MSc in Pharmaceutical Med 1993–2001, med dir Human Psychopharmacology Research Unit (HPRU) 2001–04; med dir: Axess Ltd 2001–, Amdipharm plc 2003–13; non-exec dir: Phototherapeutics Ltd, Reneuron Ltd 2000–03; memb Bd and work package ldr IMI JU PharmaTrain 2009–; memb: Euro Coll of Neuropsychopharmacology (ECNP), Collegium Internationale Neuro-psychopharmacologicum (CINP), Br Pharmacological Soc, Int Med Club; hon research fell Dept Psychology Univ of Leeds 1983–90; MInstD; FFPM 1989, FRCPE 1993, MRCPsych 1994, FRCP 1998, FRSM, FRSA; *Publications* Human Psychopharmacology vol 1–6 (ed, 1987–97), Pharmaceutical Physician (fndr ed, 1989–98), Human Psychopharmacology Clinical and Experimental (ed, 1994–96), Clinical Research Manual (ed, 1994–2013), Careers with the Pharmaceutical Industry (ed, 1994, 2 edn 2003), Medical Marketing Manual (ed, 2001), Principles and Practices of Pharmaceutical Medicine (ed, 2002, 3 edn 2011); journals: Pharmaceutical Medicine (assoc ed, 1986–97, editorial advsr 1986–), Pharmaceutical Visions (ed advsr, 1995–2001), IFAPP News (ed, 1996–2000); *Recreations* opera, European travel; *Style*— Professor Peter Stonier; ✉ 5 Branstone Road, Kew, Richmond, Surrey TW9 3LB (☎ and fax 020 8948 5069, e-mail pstonier@btinternet.com)

STONOR, Air Marshal Sir Thomas Henry; KCB (1989); s of Alphonsus Stonor (d 1959), and Ann Stonor (d 1994); *b* 5 March 1936; *Educ* St Cuthbert's GS Newcastle upon Tyne, Kings Coll Durham (BSc); *m* 31 March 1964, Robin Antoinette, da of Wilfrid Budd (d 1980); 1 da (Alexandra Clare b 1965), 2 s (Jeremy Thomas b 1966, Giles Wilfrid b 1969); *Career* cmmnd RAF 1959, No 3 Sqdn 2 ATAF 1961–64, CFS, No 6 FTS, RAF Coll Cranwell 1964–67, No 231 OCU 1967–69, RAF Staff Coll 1970, HQ RAF Germany 1971–73, OC 31 Sqdn 1974–76, MA to VCDS 1976–78, OC RAF Coltishall 1978–80, RCDS 1981, Inspr Flight Safety 1982–84, Dir of Control (Airspace Policy) 1985–86, Dep Controller Nat Air Traffic Servs 1987–88, Gp Dir CAA and Controller Nat Air Traffic Servs 1988–91; aviation conslt 1991–2003; *Recreations* music, gardening; *Clubs* RAF; *Style*— Sir Thomas Stonor, KCB; ✉ 213 Woodstock Road, Oxford OX2 7AD (☎ 01865 557640, e-mail tandrstonor@talktalk.net)

STOPPARD, Dr Miriam; OBE (2010); da of Sydney Stern, and Jenny Stern; *b* 12 May 1937; *Educ* Newcastle upon Tyne Central HS, Royal Free Hosp Sch of Med London (prize for experimental physiology), King's Coll Med Sch Univ of Durham (MB BS), Univ of Newcastle upon Tyne (MD, MRCP); *Career* Royal Victorian Infirmary King's Coll Hosp

Newcastle upon Tyne: house surgn 1961, house physician 1962, SHO in med 1962–63; Univ of Bristol: res fell Dept of Chemical Pathology 1963–65 (MRC scholar in chemical pathology 1963–65), registrar in dermatology 1965–66 (MRC scholar in dermatology), sr registrar in dermatology 1966–68; Syntex Pharmaceuticals Ltd: assoc med dir 1968–71, dep med dir 1971–74, med dir 1974–76, dep md 1976, md 1977–81, dir Syntex Corp 1991–; hon clinical lectr Inst of Dermatology Univ of London; memb: Heberden Soc, Br Assoc of Rheumatology and Rehabilitation; Hon DSc Univ of Durham 2000, Hon LLD Univ of Newcastle upon Tyne 2004; memb RSM, FRCP 1998; *Television* series: Where There's Life (5 series) 1981–, Baby and Co (2 series) 1984–, Woman to Woman 1985, Miriam Stoppard's Health and Beauty Show 1988 and 1992, Dear Miriam 1989, People Today 1991 and 1992; *Publications* Miriam Stoppard's Book of Baby Care (1977), My Medical School (contrib, 1978), Miriam Stoppard's Book of Health Care (1979), The Face and Body Book (1980), Everywoman's Lifeguide (1982), Your Baby (1982), Fifty Plus Lifeguide (1982), Your Growing Child (1983), Baby Care Book (1983), Pregnancy and Birth Book (1984), Baby and Child Medical Handbook (1986), Everygirl's Lifeguide (1987), Feeding Your Family (1987), Miriam Stoppard's Health and Beauty Book (1988), Every Woman's Medical Handbook (1988), 7 lbs in 7 days (1991), Test Your Child (1991), The Magic of Sex (1991), Conception, Pregnancy and Birth (1992), Menopause (1994), A Woman's Body (1994), Complete Baby and Childcare (1995), Questions Children Ask (1997), Sex Education – Growing Up, Relationships and Sex (1997), The New Parent (1999), Teach Your Child (2001), Family Health Guide (2002), Defying Age (2003), New Pregnancy and Birth Book (2004), Toddler Play Series (I Love Shapes, On the Move, My Busy Day, Amazing Colours, 2006), The Grandparents' Book (2006), Baby Play Skills Series (Baby Senses, Baby Talking, Baby Games, Happy Baby, 2007), Bonding with Your Bump (2008), Trusted Advice series (2011), Grandparents – Enjoying and Caring for your Grandchild (2011); over 40 publications in med jls, daily column health page Daily Mirror; *Recreations* family, skiing, gardening; *Style*— Dr Miriam Stoppard, OBE; ✉ Miriam Stoppard Lifetime Ltd, The Media Village, 131–151 Great Titchfield Street, London W1W 5BB

STOPS, Leigh Warwick; s of Dr Denis Warwick Stops, of Kingston, Surrey, and Patricia, *née* Hill; *b* 29 May 1946; *Educ* Latymer Upper Sch, Univ of Sussex (BSc), Lancaster Univ (MA); *m* 3 Dec 1976, Patricia Jane, da of F H J Terry; 2 s (Caspar b 1986, Galen b 1988); *Career* advertising exec; dir: Colman RSCG & Ptnrs 1984–85, research and planning Allen Brady & Marsh Ltd 1985–90, planning Yellowhammer Advertising Ltd 1991–92; conslt The Business Devpt Gp 1992–96, sr lectr Bournemouth Univ 1992–95, dir of planning Publicis Ltd 1994–99, sr planner McCann-Erickson 1999–2003, ceo The Blonde Mouse Gp Ltd 2003–, mktg dir Watermans 2006–14; *Recreations* sailing, theatre, media, advertisements; *Style*— Leigh W Stops, Esq; ✉ 22 Old Deer Park Gardens, Richmond TW9 2TL (☎ 020 8287 1784, e-mail leighstops@blueyonder.co.uk)

STORER, Andrew; s of Thomas Storer (d 1978), and Anne, *née* Slimmon; *Educ* Bishop Wand Sch Sunbury-upon-Thames (memb Chapel Royal Choir Hampton Court Palace), Wimbledon Sch of Art (BA); *m* 1985, Jennifer (d 2006), da of Graham Law, and Isobel Drysdale; *Career* ballet and opera designer; worked for various dance and opera cos worldwide incl: Hannover Opera, Stuttgart Ballet, Theatre du Capitole Toulouse, Ballet du Nord, Teatro dell'Opera Rome, Teatro San Carlo Naples, Teatro Regio Turin, Nat Ballet of Portugal, New Jersey Ballet, Nevada Dance Theatre, Ballet de Santiago; work included in exhbns and pubns incl: Picasso and the Theatre (Brighton Festival) 1982, Design for Dance (Arnolfini Gallery Bristol) 1985, British Theatre Design: The Modern Age 1990, Make Space 1995, 2D-3D Design for Theatre (Soc of British Theatre Designers) 2002; head of prodn Royal Conservatoire of Scotland 2007–12, technical dir Scottish Opera 2012; memb Soc of British Theatre Designers; *Productions* London Contemporary Dance Theatre: Songs and Dances, Motorcade, Shadows in the Sun, Unfolding Field; Ballet Rambert: Lonely Town, Lonely Street, Pribaoutki, Colour Moves (with Bridget Riley , *qv*), Entre Dos Aguas, Light and Shade; Gothenburg Musikteater: Living in America, Love, Life and Death, Russian Story, Eva; other credits incl: Elvira Madigan (Royal Danish Ballet), Romeo and Juliet (Grand Theatre Geneva, Gothenburg Ballet, Arena di Verona and Scottish Ballet), Offenbach (Grand Theatre Geneva, Arena di Verona and Scottish Ballet), Petrouchka (Grand Theatre de Bordeaux), Short Cuts (Arena di Verona), Bach Dances (Semperoper Dresden), The Snowman (Scottish Ballet), Savoy Suite (Eng Nat Ballet), The Fairy Queen (English Consort), Mata Hari (Deutsche Oper Berlin), Tempus Fugit, Verschollen (Theater Krefeld Möchengladbach), Five: Fifteen (Scottish Opera); *Television and Video* For My Daughter (Danish Royal Ballet/Denmark's Radio/ZDF), Lonely Town, Lonely Street (Ballet Rambert/Denmark's Radio/RM Arts/ Virgin Classic Video); lighting designs: Tryst (Scottish Chamber Orch/BBC 1), Sound Bites Two (BBC Scottish Symphony Orch/BBC 2), Red Forecast Orchestral Theatre III (BBC Symphony Orch/BBC 2); *Recreations* walking, painting, Italian cuisine; *Style*— Andrew Storer, Esq; ✉ Scottish Opera, 40 Edington Street, Glasgow G4 9RD (☎ 0141 332 9559)

STOREY, (George) Anthony (Tony); OBE (1990); s of George William Storey (d 1956), of Haltwhistle, Northumberland, and Edna Mary, *née* Bell (d 2002); *b* 20 February 1939; *Educ* Queen Elizabeth GS Hexham, Univ of Nottingham (BA), Univ of Exeter (DipEd); *m* (m dis), Pamela May, *née* Trapnell; 1 s (Guy Keith b 30 May 1971), 1 da (Anne-Louise b 30 Oct 1972); *Career* Wallasey GS 1961–64, tutor Dept of Educn Univ of Oxford 1964–68, curriculum devpt Bicester Sch 1964–68, warden Cwlth Lodge 1964–68, visiting lectr in education Univ of Botswana Lesotho and Swaziland 1967, asst dir of educn Westmoreland LEA (Kendal) 1968–71, headmaster The Hayfield Sch Doncaster 1971–2008 (UK's longest serving secondary headteacher in one school); Lifetime Achievement Award North of England Region Teaching Awards 2004; Freeman of Doncaster 2008; *Books* Haltwhistle and South Tynedale (1972), Hope of Our Sires: QEGS Hexham in the 1950's (1998), Bishop Ridley and the Reiving Ridleys (1999), Altwessel in 1000AD (1999), Ridley and Ridley Hall (2000), Haltwhistle Church (2001), Medieval Haltwhistle (2001), A West End Boy's Own Story (2001), Transport Across the North Pennines from Romans to Railways (2007), The Alston Arches (2007), Haltwhistle 1750–1950 (2008), Doncaster: Romans to Railways (2008), Coalmining: South Tynedale and East Cumbria (2010); also a range of writing on educnl issues; *Recreations* local history, theatre, Northumberland; *Style*— Tony Storey, Esq, OBE; ✉ 9 The Paddocks, Lound, Retford, Nottinghamshire DN22 8RR (☎ 01777 818627)

STOREY, (Richard) Barnaby (Barney); MBE (2009); *b* 13 March 1977; *m* Dame Sarah Storey, DBE, *qv*; 1 da (Louisa Marie b 2013); *Career* Paralympic cyclist (sighted pilot); Nat Tandem Sprint Champion 2003, 2005, 2006, 2010, 2011 and 2012, Nat Keirin Champion 2003, Nat Team Sprint Champion 2004; achievements with Anthony Kappes, MBE, incl: 2 Gold medals (men's 1km time trial and men's sprint) World Disability Championships 2006, 2 Gold medals (men's 1km time trial and men's sprint) World Disability Championships 2007, 2 Gold medals (men's 1km time trial and men's sprint) Paralympics 2008; 2 Gold medals (tamdem 1km time trial and tamdem sprint, both with Neil Fachie, MBE) World Track Championships 2009, Nat Team Pursuit Champion 2010, Gold medal (individual sprint) and Silver medal (individual sprint, both with Neil Fachie, MBE, *qqv*) Paralympic Games 2012; *Style*— Mr Barney Storey, MBE; ✉ website www.teamstoreysport.com, Twitter @barneystorey

STOREY, Christopher Thomas; QC (1995); s of Leslie Hall Storey (d 1974), and Joan, *née* Walsh (d 2003); *b* 13 February 1945; *Educ* Rugby; *m* 1968, Hilary Enid, da of Robert Cushing Johnston; 2 s (Stephen Douglas Edward b 1976, Peter Stuart Desmond b 1978); *Career* CA 1967–82, barr NE Circuit 1982–2007, recorder of the Crown Court 2000–15; memb Hon Soc Lincoln's Inn 1977; FCA 1967–85; *Recreations* music, classic cars, instructor light aeroplanes, cricket, reading, undergardening; *Style*— Christopher Storey, Esq, QC; ✉ Park Lane Plowden, Westgate, Leeds LS1 2RD (☎ 01132 285000)

STOREY, Jeremy Brian; QC (1994); s of Capt James Mackie Storey (d 1976), of Harrogate, N Yorks, and Veronica, *née* Walmsley (d 1978); *b* 21 October 1952; *Educ* Uppingham, Downing Coll Cambridge (MA); *m* 19 September 1981, Carolyn, da of Eric Raymond Ansell (d 1996), of Edenbridge, Kent; 2 da (Alexis Erica b 1991, Sasha Louise b 1994); *Career* called to the Bar Inner Temple 1974; recorder of the Crown Court (Western Circuit) 1995– (asst recorder 1990–95), dep judge of the Technology and Construction Ct 1995–, actg deemster (judge) IOM Cts 1999–, dep judge of the High Ct of Justice (Queen's Bench Div) 2008–; asst boundary cmmr for Eng and Wales 2000–; TECBAR approved adjudicator 1999–, MCIArb 1999 (ACIArb 1997); *Recreations* travel, theatre, cricket; *Clubs* MCC, Glamorgan CCC; *Style*— Jeremy Storey, Esq, QC; ✉ 4 Pump Court, Temple, London EC4Y 7AN (☎ 020 7842 5555, fax 020 7583 2036)

STOREY, Maurice; CB (2003); s of Albert Henry Storey (d 1984), of Chelmsford, Essex, and Violet Ester, *née* Fisher (d 1984); *b* 14 June 1943; *m* 1, 8 Oct 1966, Hazel (d 1985), da of Joseph F Williams; 1 da (Jennifer b 6 Dec 1973); m 2, 30 May 1987, Linda, da of John Mears; 2 s (Shane Thomas b 17 Aug 1987, Karl Alan b 5 April 1989); *Career* apprentice Swan Hunter Shipbuilders 1958–62, ship repair mangr Swan Hunter Ship Repairers 1962–67, asst to marine supt rising to tech supt Shaw Savill Line 1967–72, head Technical Dept Kuwait Oil Tanker Co 1972–76, dir Sea Containers Ltd 1976–90, dir (ship and port mgmnt) Stena Line Ltd 1990–98, chief exec Maritime and Coastguard Agency 1998–2003, chm Hatsu Marine Ltd (now Evergreen Marine UK Ltd) 2003–07 (hon chm 2007–); dir: Stena Line Ltd, Stena Line UK Ltd, Stena Line Ports Ltd, Societe du Terminal Transmanche de Dieppe (STTD) 1990–98; pres UK Chamber of Shipping 2006–07 (chm Marine Policy Ctee, vice-chm Cruise Ship and Ferry Section); chm and dir Fishguard and Rosslare Railways and Harbours Co 1990–98, vice-chm Br Ctee Bureau Veritas, non-exec dir James Fisher plc 2003–13 (sr non-exec dir 2012–13); RNLI: memb Cncl and Tech Ctee 2002–14, vice pres 2014–; tstee Chatham Historic Dockyard 2007–; Millennium Lecture IMarE 2000; MBA (hc) 2001; memb Soc of Consulting Marine Engrs and Ship Surveyors 1976–, pres Inst of Marine Engrg Science and Technol 2005–06; CEng, FRINA 1969, FIMarEst 1972; *Books* The Design, Construction and Introduction of the Stena HSS (1997); *Recreations* golf, walking; *Style*— Maurice Storey, Esq, CB

STOREY, Baron (Life Peer UK 2011), of Childwall in the City of Liverpool; Michael John (Mike) Storey; CBE (2002, OBE 1992); *m* 30 July 1994, Carole; 1 da (Rachel); *Career* Liverpool City Cncl: elected cncllr 1973, dep ldr 1980–93, ldr 1998–2005; Lord Mayor of Liverpool 2009–10; Lib Dem educn spokesperson House of Lords; *Style*— The Lord Storey, CBE; ✉ 36 Countisbury Drive, Liverpool L16 0JJ (Twitter @lordstorey); House of Lords, London SW1A 0PW (e-mail storeym@parliament.uk)

Storey, Hon Sir Richard; 2 Bt (UK 1960) of Settrington, Co York; CBE (1996), DL; s of Baron Buckton (Life Peer, d 1978), and Elisabeth (d 1951), da of late Brig-Gen W J Woodcock, DSO; *b* 23 January 1937; *Educ* Winchester, Trinity Coll Cambridge (BA, LLB); *m* 1961, Virginia Anne, da of late Sir Kenelm Henry Ernest Cayley, 10 Bt; 1 s, 2 da; *Heir* s, Kenelm Storey; *Career* Nat Serv RNVR 1956; called to the Bar Inner Temple 1962; practised until 1969; chm Portsmouth and Sunderland Newspapers plc 1973–98 (dir 1962–99, chief exec 1973–86); contested (Cons) Don Valley 1966 and Huddersfield W 1970; dir: One Stop Community Stores Ltd 1971–98, Croydon Cable 1983–89, Reuters Hldgs plc 1986–92, Press Assoc Ltd 1986–95 (chm 1991–95), The Fleming Mid Cap Investment Tst plc 1989–2002 (chm 1996–2002), Foreign & Colonial Smaller Companies plc 1993–2002, Sunderland plc 1996–2004, Castle Howard Arboretum Tst (CHAT) 1997–2013, eFinancialNews 2000–06; memb: Regnl Cncl Yorks and Humberside CBI 1974–79, Nat Cncl and Exec Ctee CLA 1980–84 (chm Yorks Exec 1974–76), Press Cncl 1980–86, Cncl Newspaper Soc 1980–98 (pres 1990–91), Cncl INCA-FIEJ Res Assoc 1983–88, CBI Employment Policy Ctee 1984–88, BUPA Assoc 2002–04; fndr chm Regnl Daily Advertising Cncl 1988–90 (dir 1988–91), chm Sir Harold Hillier Gardens and Arboretum Mgmnt Ctee 1989–2005; chm York Health Services NHS Tst 1991–97; tstee: The Royal Botanic Gardens Kew Fndn 1990–2003, Hope & Homes for Children 2002–09; rep European Newspaper Publishers' Assoc 1990–96; chm Int Dendrology Soc 2007–12; memb Ct Univ of York 2006–10; Veitch Meml Medal 2005; High Sheriff N Yorks 1992–93; hon fell Univ of Portsmouth, Hon DLitt Univ of Sunderland; FRSA; *Recreations* silviculture, arboriculture; *Style*— The Hon Sir Richard Storey, Bt, CBE; ✉ 11 Zetland House, Marloes Road, London W8 5LB (☎ 020 7937 8823); Settrington Grange, Malton, North Yorkshire YO17 8NU (☎ 01944 768200, fax 01944 768484)

STOREY, Dame Sarah Joanne; DBE (2013, OBE 2009, MBE 1998); *née* Bailey; *b* 26 October 1977, Manchester; *Educ* Leeds Met Univ (BSc); *m* Barney Storey, MBE, *qv*; 1 da (Louisa Marie b 2013); *Career* Paralympic cyclist and former swimmer; memb: Stockport Metro SC 1988–98, City of Salford SC 1998–2002, Stretford ASC 2002–05, VC St Raphael 2005–; memb GB swim team 1992–2005, memb Br cycling team 2005–; swimming achievements incl: 2 Gold medals (100m backstroke and 200m individual medley) Paralympics Barcelona 1992, 3 Silver medals Paralympics Barcelona 1992, Bronze medal Paralympics Barcelona 1992, 2 Gold medals (200m individual medley and freestyle relay) World Swimming Championships 1994, 3 Silver medals World Swimming Championships 1994, Bronze medal World Swimming Championships 1994, 3 Gold medals (100m backstroke, 200m individual medley and 100m breaststroke) European Swimming Championships 1995, 2 Silver medals European Swimming Championships 1995, Bronze medal European Swimming Championships 1995, 3 Gold medals (100m backstroke, 200m individual medley and 100m breaststroke) Paralympics Atlanta 1996, Silver medal Paralympics Atlanta 1996, Bronze medal Paralympics Atlanta 1996, 6 Gold medals European Swimming Championships 1997, 2 Silver medals European Swimming Championships 1997, 2 Silver medals World Swimming Championships 1998, 4 Bronze medals World Swimming Championships 1998, 3 Gold medals European Swimming Championships 1999, 3 Silver medals European Swimming Championships 1999, Bronze medal European Swimming Championships 1999, 2 Silver medals (100m backstroke and medley relay) Paralympics Sydney 2000, 5 Gold medals European Swimming Championships 2001, Silver medal European Swimming Championships 2001, 3 Gold medals (100m freestyle, 400m freestyle and 200m individual medley) World Swimming Championships 2002, 2 Silver medals World Swimming Championships 2002, Bronze medal World Swimming Championships 2002, 2 Silver medals (200m individual medly and 100m breaststroke) Paralympics Athens 2004, Bronze medal 100m freestyle Paralympics Athens 2004; cycling achievements incl: 3 Gold medals (3000m individual pursuit, 500m time trial and road race) European Cycling Championships 2005, Silver medal road time trial European Cycling Championships 2005, Gold medal 3000m individual pursuit World Cycling Championships 2006 and 2007, 2 Silver medals (road race and road time trial) World Disability Championships 2006, Bronze medal time trial World Disability Championships 2006 and 2007, Gold medal 3000m individual pursuit British Track Championships (able-bodied) 2008, 2 Gold medals (women's individual pursuit and time trial) Paralympics Beijing 2008, 4 Gold medals (individual pursuit, individual road time trial, 500m time trial and individual road race) Paralympics London 2012, Gold medal 3000m Olympic Games 2016; head coach NW Disability Swim Squad 1996–2006; patron: Macclesfield Seals SC 1997–, St Dominics Girls' Sch 2004–, Children's Adventure Farm Tst 2006–; Hon MSc Manchester Met Univ 2003, Hon DSc Manchester Met Univ 2009; *Style*— Dame

S

Sarah Storey, DBE; ✉ Team Storey Sport, PO Box 80, Disley, Stockport SK12 2WF (website www.teamstoreysport.com, Twitter @mrssarahstorey and @teamstoreysport)

STOREY, Stuart Ellis; DL (Herts); s of Charles Ellis Storey (d 1995), of Holbeach, Lincs, and Kathleen Mary Storey (d 1982); *b* 16 September 1942; *Educ* Spalding GS, Loughborough Coll (Dip PE), Western Kentucky Univ (MA); *m* 28 Nov 1970, Shirley, da of Donald Hugh Godfrey Gardner; 2 s (Benjamin Ellis b 24 Feb 1974, James Stuart b 26 Nov 1976); *Career* TV sports commentator (athletics and other sports); teacher PE and maths Dr Challoner's GS Amersham 1965–67, grad asst coach (swimming, judo, volleyball) Western Univ Kentucky 1967–68, supply teacher in PE Kitwood Sch Boston 1968–69, head of PE Loughton Coll of Further Educn 1969–73 (also dep warden Debden Community Assoc), head of PE Thames Poly 1973 (dir of PE until 1989); with BBC TV Sports Dept 1974–90 and 1991–, with Eurosport 1990–91; covered 10 Olympic Games, 10 World Championships, 7 Cwlth Games and 10 European Championships; athletics career: winner All England Schs 100m hurdles 1959, winner All England Schs 110m hurdles 1961 (runner up 1960), first sr int England v GDR (110m hurdles) 1965, memb GB team Olympic Games Mexico 1968 and European Championships 1969, memb England team Cwlth Games 1970 (all at 110m hurdles); also coach to Geoff Capes (former shot put champion) for 17 years; chm tstees Wodson Park Sport and Recreation Tst, patron SPARKS, chair Ron Pickering Meml Tst; hon doctorate Univ of Greenwich 2008; *Recreations* golf, gym, cycling; *Style—* Stuart Storey, Esq, DL; ✉ c/o IMG (Sweden) AB, Ingmar Bergmans Gata 4, SE-114, 34 Stockholm, Sweden

STORMONTH DARLING, Peter; s of Patrick Stormonth Darling (d 1960), and Edith, *née* Lamb (d 1980); *b* 29 September 1932; *Educ* Winchester, New Coll Oxford (MA); *m* 1, 1958 (m dis), Candis Hitzig; 3 da (Candis Christa b 1959, Elizabeth Iona b 1960, Arabella b 1962); m 2, 1970 (m dis), Maureen O'Leary; *Career* 2 Lt Black Watch 1950–53, served Korean War, Flying Offr RAFVR 1953–56; chm Mercury Asset Management Group 1979–92; *Books* City Cinderella, The Life and Times of Mercury Asset Management (1999); *Clubs* MCC, White's, Hurlingham, New York Racquet and Tennis, Toronto; *Style—* Peter Stormonth Darling, Esq; ✉ c/o Soditic Limited, 12 Charles II Street, London SW1Y 4QU

STORY, Mark Trafford; s of John Story (d 1991), of Co Kildare, and Elaine Story; *b* 10 May 1955; *Educ* Dublin HS, Sch of Law Trinity Coll Dublin (BA, LLB); *Career* prodr RTE Radio 1978–83; sr prodr: Capital Radio 1983–88, BBC Radio 1 1988–90; prog dir: Piccadilly Radio 1990–95, Virgin Radio 1995–97; md Magic 105.4 1998–2011, md Kiss 100 FM 1999 and Magic 105.4fm, fndr RadioStory 2011–; Sony Award winner, New York Radio Gold Medal, Premios Ondos Gold winner; fell Radio Acad 1999; *Recreations* collecting Oriental art; *Style—* Mark Story, Esq

STOTHARD, Sir Peter Michael; kt (2003); s of Wilfred Max Stothard, and Patricia Jean, *née* Savage; *b* 28 February 1951; *Educ* Brentwood Sch, Trinity Coll Oxford (MA); *m* 1980, Sally Ceris, *née* Emerson; 1 da (Anna Ceris b 22 Nov 1983), 1 s (Michael Peter b 20 Dec 1987); *Career* journalist BBC 1974–77, business and political writer Sunday Times 1979–80; The Times: features ed and leader writer 1980–85, dep ed 1985–92, ed 1992–2002; ed TLS 2002–16; head Jury Man Booker Prize 2012; pres Classical Assoc 2011; President's Medal, Br Acad 2013, Criticos Prize 2013; hon fell Trinity Coll Oxford 2000; *Publications* Thirty Days: A Month at the Heart of Blair's War (2003), On the Spartacus Road, a Spectacular Journey Through Ancient Italy (2010), Alexandria, The Last Nights of Cleopatra (2013), The Senecans, Four Men and Margaret Thatcher (2016); *Recreations* ancient and modern literature; *Clubs* Garrick; *Style—* Sir Peter Stothard; ✉ The Times Literary Supplement, 1 London Bridge Street, London SE1 9GF (e-mail peter.stothard@gmail.com)

STOTT, Etienne; MBE (2013); *b* 30 June 1979, Manchester; *Educ* Univ of Nottingham (BSc); *Career* slalom canoeist; achievements incl: Bronze medal World Championships 2009, Silver medal (team) European Championships 2009, Bronze medal (team) European Championships 2010, Bronze medal (team) World Championships 2011, Gold medal (team) European Championships 2012, Gold medal Olympic Games 2012; *Clubs* Viking Kayak (Bedford); *Style—* Mr Etienne Stott, MBE; ✉ e-mail etistott@gmail.com, website www.bailliestottc2.co.uk, Twitter @etiennestott

STOTT, Ian Hood; s of Alan James Stott, and Mae, *née* Hood; *b* 29 January 1934; *Educ* Shrewsbury (1st XV rugby, capt fives); *m* 1, 1957, Gabrielle Mary, da of Rev W S Tuke; 2 s (Robert Ian b 1958, Simon Andrew b 1960 d 1989); m 2, 1979, Patricia Mary, da of Dr M Wynroe; 2 da (Ailsa Jane b 1980, Catherine Mally b 1982); *Career* Nat Serv Green Jackets and Lancs Fus (Lt) 1952–54; James Stott Ltd cotton spinners and weavers Oldham 1954–57, John Bright & Sons Ltd Rochdale 1957–62, proprietor garage gp/caravan park/hotels/property 1962–86, chm and md Oldham Athletic AFC 1986– (chm 1982–); memb: FA Cncl 1986–, Football League Mgmnt Ctee 1986–92 and 1995–, FA Exec 1992–94 and 1999–; vice-chm FA 1999–; *Recreations* cooking, food and drink, bridge, music; *Style—* Ian Stott, Esq; ✉ Oldham Athletic FC, Boundary Park, Oldham, Lancashire OL1 2PA (☎ 0161 624 4972, fax 0161 627 5915)

STOTT, Kathryn; da of Desmond Stott, of Nelson, Lancs, and Elsie, *née* Cheetham; *b* 10 December 1958; *Educ* Yehudi Menuhin Sch, Royal Coll of Music (ARCM, Tagore Golden Medal); *Children* 1 da (Lucy b 9 Nov 1984); *Career* pianist; studied under Vlado Perlemuter, Louis Kentner and Kendall Taylor; fifth place Leeds Int Piano Competition 1978, awarded Churchill scholarship 1979; recitals incl: Int Piano Series Wigmore Hall, Michael Nyman Festival South Bank, Gabriel Fauré Festival (artistic leader) Manchester 1995, Britten Concerto with Netherlands Philharmonic Orch Concertgebouw 1995, Beethoven Triple concerto with BBC Scottish Symphony Orch BBC Proms 1995; also played throughout Europe, USA, Australasia, Hong Kong, Singapore, Japan, Saudi Arabia, Zimbabwe (frequent touring partner of Yo-Yo Ma); solo recordings incl: works by Chabrier, Debussy, Liszt, Rachmaninov, Frank Bridge, Fauré complete piano works, Chopin complete Nocturnes; other recordings incl: John Ireland Concerto and Walton Sinfonia Concertante with RPO and Vernon Handley, George Lloyd Concerto No 3 with BBC Philharmonic, Herbert Howells Concerto No 2 with Royal Liverpool Philharmonic Orch and Vernon Handley, Michael Nyman Piano Concerto, Fauré Orchestral Works with Yan Pascal Tortelier and BBC Philharmonic, Graham Fitkin Circuit with Noriko Ogawa, Tokyo Symphony Orch, Otomo; artistic dir Piano 2000 Festival Manchester (and Piano 2003); memb Bd: Halle Concert Soc, Nordoff-Robbins Music Therapy; Chevalier de l'Ordre des Arts et des Lettres (France) 1995; *Recreations* horse riding, travel, Italian language; *Style—* Ms Kathryn Stott; ✉ c/o Jane Ward, 60 Shrewsbury Road, Oxton, Wirral CH43 2HY (☎ 0151 513 2716, e-mail jane@kathrynstott.com, website www.kathrynstott.com)

STOURTON, Edward John Ivo; s of Nigel John Ivo Stourton, CBE, of N Yorks, and Rosemary Jennifer Rushworth Abbott, JP; *b* 24 November 1957; *Educ* Ampleforth, Trinity Coll Cambridge (MA, pres Cambridge Union); *m* 1, 5 July 1980 (m dis), Margaret, da of late Sir James Napier Finney McEwen Bt; 2 s (Ivo b 11 June 1982, Thomas b 28 Sept 1987), 1 da (Eleanor b 1 June 1984); m 2, Nov 2002, Fiona Margaret, *née* Murch (Fiona Stourton, *qv*); *Career* TV journalist 1979–; Washington corr Channel Four News 1986 (fndr memb 1982), Paris corr BBC TV 1988, diplomatic ed ITN 1990–93, presenter BBC One O'Clock News and presenter radio and television documentaries BBC 1993–99, presenter Today Programme (BBC Radio 4) 1999–2009, presenter Sunday (BBC Radio 4) 2002–; *Books* Absolute Truth: The Catholic Church in the Modern World (1998), In the Footsteps of St Paul (2004), John Paul II: Man of History (2006); It's a PC World: What it means to live in a land gone politically correct (2008), Trinity, A Portrait (ed, 2011), Diary of a Dogwalker (2011), Cruel Crossing: Escaping Hitler across the Pyrenees (2013); *Recreations* reading; *Clubs* Travellers, Hurlingham; *Style—* Edward Stourton, Esq

STOURTON, Fiona Margaret; da of John Edward King, of Llandaff, Cardiff, and Mary Margaret, *née* Beaton; *b* 14 August 1957; *Educ* Godolphin & Latymer Sch, Howells Sch Llandaff, SOAS Univ of London (Rhuvon Guest prize, BA); *m* 1, 1980 (m dis 2002); 1 da (Rosalind Lesley Margaret b 27 Oct 1993); m 2, Nov 2002, Edward Stourton, *qv*; *Career* prodr Hausa/African section BBC World Service 1978–81, trainee BBC News 1981, prodr Newsnight 1985–86 (asst prodr 1981–85); sr prodr: BBC Breakfast Time 1986–87, Newsnight 1987–88, The Late Show 1988–89; political corr and news presenter C4 News/ITN 1992–94 (arts corr and news presenter 1989–92), dep ed Assignment BBC TV 1994–97, ed Correspondent BBC TV 1997–2002, sr exec prodr current affrs BBC Two 2002–06; Ten Alps plc: joined 2006, md Blakeway 2008–11, creative dir 2011–; memb BAFTA 2006–; *Recreations* reading, tennis; *Clubs* Hurlingham; *Style—* Ms Fiona Stourton

STOURTON, Hon James Alastair; yr s of 26 Baron Mowbray, 27 Segrave and 23 Stourton, CBE, and Jane Faith, *née* de Yarburgh-Bateson, da of 5 Baron Deramore; *b* 3 July 1956; *Educ* Ampleforth, Magdalene Coll Cambridge (MA); *m* 9 Oct 1993 (m dis 1997), Hon Sophia Ulla Stonor, yst da of 7 Baron Camoys; *Career* writer and historian; Sotheby's: joined 1979, dir Sotheby's London 1987, dep chm Sotheby's Europe 1997, chm Sotheby's Inst (Educn) 2002, chm Sotheby's UK 2006–12; prop The Stourton Press; panel memb Acceptance in Lieu Ctee, panel memb Heritage Meml Fund, tstee Strawberry Hill House; sr fell Inst of Historical Research; FSA; *Books* Great Smaller Museums of Europe (2003), Great Collectors of our Time: Art Collecting since 1945 (2007), The British as Art Collectors: From the Tudors to the Present (2012), Great Houses of London (2012), Kenneth Clark: Life, Art and Civilisation (2016); *Clubs* Roxburghe, White's, Beefsteak; *Style—* The Hon James Stourton; ✉ 21 Moreton Place, London SW1V 2NL (e-mail james@jamesstourton.com)

STOUT, Prof Robert William; s of William Ferguson Stout, CB (d 2005), of Belfast, and Muriel Stout, *née* Kilner (d 2004); *b* 6 March 1942, Belfast; *Educ* Campbell Coll Belfast (scholar), Queen's Univ Belfast (MD DSc); *m* 31 Dec 1969, Helena Patricia (d 2015), da of Frederick William Willis (d 1959), of Comber, Co Down; 2 s (Brian b 1971, Alan b 1972), 1 da (Caroline b 1974); *Career* MRC Eli Lilly foreign educn fell Univ of Washington Seattle 1971–73, sr research fell British Heart Fndn 1974–75; Queen's Univ Belfast: sr lectr Dept of Med 1975–76, prof of geriatric med Dept of Geriatric Med 1976–2007, dean Faculty of Med and Health Sciences 1991–2001, head Sch of Med 1998–2001; conslt physician Belfast City Hosp 1975–2007, dir of R&D NI Health and Personal Social Services 2001–08; chm: Specialty Advsy Ctee on Geriatric Med Jt Ctee on Higher Med Trg 1988–92, QAA Benchmarking Gp for Medicine 2000–02 and Main Panel B Research Assessment Exercise 2008; pres Ulster Med Soc 1999–2000 (hon treas 1979–83); vice-pres: Age Concern NI 1988–2001 (chm 1986–88), Research Into Ageing 1992–2001; RCP: NI regnl advsr 1984–90, examiner 1990–98; memb Royal Cmmn on Long Term Care 1997–99; Br Geriatrics Soc: memb Cncl 1984–90, memb Exec 1987–90, chm Scientific Ctee 1999–2001, pres 2002–04; memb: Bd UK Clinical Research Collaboration 2004–07, HEFCE Expert Advsy Gp on Research Excellence Framework 2009, NI Public Inquiry into Clostridium Difficile Outbreak in Northern HSC Tst 2009–10; chm: Editorial Bd Age & Ageing 1999–2002, Centre for Ageing Research and Devpt in Ireland 2003–15; memb: Bd of Govrs Methodist Coll Belfast 1983–2002 (hon lay sec 1988–91, chm 1994–97), Southern Health and Social Services Bd 1982–91, NI Health and Social Servs Cncl 1982–85, Eastern Health and Social Services Bd 1992–2002, NI Distinction and Meritorious Service Awards Ctee 2001–04, Health Research Bd Ireland 2002–07, Bd of Dirs Extra Care for Elderly People NI 2008–14, Cncl Stroke Assoc 2009–15 (chm NI Ctee 2009–15); vice-chm and medical dir NI Clinical Excellence Awards Ctee 2005–14; chm Bd of Govrs Edgehill Theological Coll Belfast 2005–11, NI chm Abbeyfield Soc 2015–; memb GMC 1991–2002; FRCP 1979, FRCPEd 1988–2014, FRCPI 1989–2014, FRCPSG 1995, FMedSci 1998; *Publications* Hormones and Atherosclerosis (1982), Arterial Disease in the Elderly (ed, 1984), Diabetes and Atherosclerosis (ed, 1992); scientific papers on geriatric medicine and related topics; *Recreations* golf, gardening, reading; *Clubs* Royal Belfast Golf; *Style—* Prof Robert Stout; ✉ 3 Larch Hill Drive, Holywood, Co Down BT18 0JS (☎ 028 9042 2253, e-mail rwstout@btinternet.com)

STOUTE, Sir Michael Ronald; s of late Maj Ronald Audley Stoute, OBE, of Barbados, and late Mildred Dorothy, *née* Bowen; *b* 22 October 1945; *Educ* Harrison Coll Barbados; *Children* 1 da (Caroline Elizabeth b 23 Jan 1972), 1 s (James Robert Michael b 6 June 1974); *Career* racehorse trainer 1972–, leading flat racing trainer 1981, 1986, 1989, 1994, 1997, 2000, 2003, 2005, 2006 and 2009, 26 classics won in England and Ireland; trained Derby winners: Shergar 1981, Shahrastani 1986, Kris Kin 2003, North Light 2004, Workforce 2010; Irish Derby winners: Shergar 1981, Shareef Dancer 1983, Shahrastani 1986; other major races won incl: Breeders Cup (Pilsudski) 1996, Japan Cup (Singspiel) 1996, Dubai World Cup (Singspiel) 1997, Japan Cup (Pilsudski) 1997, Breeders Cup (Kalanisi) 2000, Dubai Sheema Classic (Fantastic Light) 2000, Hong Kong Vase (Daliapour) 2000, Breeders Cup (Islington) 2003, Breeders Cup Turf (Conduit) 2008 and 2009; *Recreations* golf, deep sea fishing; *Style—* Sir Michael Stoute; ✉ Freemason Lodge, Bury Road, Newmarket, Suffolk CB8 7BT (☎ 01638 663801, fax 01638 667276)

STOW, His Hon Timothy Montague Fenwick; QC (1989); s of Geoffrey Montague Fenwick Stow, LVO (d 1990), of Portugal, and Joan Fortescue, *née* Flannery (d 1984); *b* 31 January 1943; *Educ* Eton; *m* 29 May 1965, Alisoun Mary Francis, da of Paul Walter Homberger, OBE (d 1978); 1 s (Richard Montague Fenwick b 15 Dec 1968), 1 da (Emma Mary b 15 Dec 1972); *Career* called to the Bar 1965 (bencher Gray's Inn 1998); recorder 1989–, head of chambers 1998–, circuit judge (SE Circuit) 2000–13; memb Bar Cncl 1982–85; *Recreations* looking after our country property, sailing, foreign travel, skiing, chain sawing; *Style—* His Hon Timothy Stow, QC

STOWE, Grahame Conway; s of Harry Stowe (d 1968), and Evelyn, *née* Pester (d 1990); *b* 22 May 1949; *Educ* Allerton Grange Sch Leeds, Univ of Leeds (LLB); *m* 27 Dec 1981, Marilyn Joyce, da of Arnold Morris; 1 s (Benjamin Harry George b 21 May 1988); *Career* admitted slr 1974, commenced own practice 1981; gained Higher Rights of Audience (Criminal Proceedings) qualification 1996; judge Benefit Appeal Tbnl 1985, judge Mental Health Tbnl 1987; memb Law Soc; *Recreations* gym; *Style—* Grahame Stowe, Esq; ✉ Stowe Family Law, 5 Portland Street, Leeds LS1 3DR (e-mail gcs@stowefamilylaw.co.uk)

STOWELL OF BEESTON, Baroness (Life Peer UK 2011), of Beeston in the County of Nottinghamshire; Tina Wendy Stowell; MBE (1996); *b* 2 July 1967, Nottingham; *Educ* Chilwell Comp, Broxtowe Coll of FE; *Career* MoD 1986–88, Br Embassy Washington 1988–91, Press Office Downing St 1991–96, various commercial sector positions at companies incl Paradine Prodns and Granada Media 1996–98, dep COS to Rt Hon William Hague, MP, *qv* (as Ldr of Cons and Oppn) 1998–2001; BBC: dep sec 2001–03, head of communications to Chm and Bd of Govrs (later BBC Tst) 2003–08, head of corp affrs 2008–10; communications conslt Tina Stowell Assocs 2010–11, Govt whip and Baroness-in-Waiting to HM The Queen 2011–13, House of Lords spokesperson Women and Equalities and Dept for Work and Pensions 2012–13, Parly under-sec Dept for Communities and Local Govt 2013–14, ldr House of Lords and Lord Privy Seal 2014–; *Style—* The Rt Hon Baroness Stowell, MBE; ✉ website www.tinastowell.co.uk; House of Lords, London SW1A 0PW

STRACEY, Sir John Simon; 9 Bt (UK 1818), of Rackheath, Norfolk; s of Capt Algernon Augustus Henry Stracey (d 1940), and Olive Beryl Stracey (d 1972); Sir John Stracey, 1

Bt, was a Recorder of The City of London; suc cous, Sir Michael George Motley Stracey, 8 Bt, 1971; *b* 30 November 1938; *Educ* Wellington, McGill Univ Montreal; *m* 1968, Martha Maria, da of Johann Egger (d 1936), of Innsbruck, Austria; 2 da; *Heir* cous, Henry Stracey; *Career* conslt and designer; *Clubs* Royal St Lawrence Yacht; *Style*— Sir John Stracey, Bt

STRACHAN, (John) Crispian; CBE (2003), QPM (1996), DL (2002); s of late Dr M N Strachan, of Worcestershire, and late Mrs B J Strachan; *b* 5 July 1949; *Educ* King's Sch Macclesfield, Jesus Coll Oxford (MA), Univ of Sheffield (MA); *m* 1974, Denise, da of late Tom Farmer; 3 da, 1 s; *Career* Met Police 1972–93, Sr Cmd Course Police Staff Coll 1992, asst chief constable Strathclyde Police 1993–98, chief constable Northumbria Police 1998–2005; visiting scholar in applied criminology and police mgmnt Cambridge Inst of Criminology 2011–; memb of various community gps in Northumbria; OStJ 2005; *Books* A Guide to Policing in the UK (co-author, 1992), Clinical Forensic Medicine (contrib, 2009); *Recreations* photography, woodwork, country walks; *Style*— Crispian Strachan, Esq, CBE, QPM, DL; ✉ 4 Rectory Close, High Wycombe, Buckinghamshire HP13 6HF (e-mail crispianstrachan@gmail.com)

STRACHAN, David John; *b* 24 June 1963, Peterhead, Grampian; *Educ* Elgin Acad, The Queen's Coll Oxford (MA), Wolfson Coll Cambridge (Dip Economics); *Career* early career in banking supervision and market ops with Bank of England; FSA: head of market conduct and infrastructure 1998–2001, dir of deposit-takers 2001–02, dir of insurance firms 2002–04, dir of retail firms and insurance sector ldr 2004–06, dir of maj retail gps and financial stability sector ldr 2006–08, dir financial stability 2008–11; head EMEA Centre for Regulatory Strategy Deloitte LLP 2011–; *Style*— Mr David Strachan; ✉ Deloitte LLP, Hill House, 1 Little New Street, London

STRACHAN, Prof Sir Hew Francis Anthony; kt (2013); s of Michael Francis Strachan, CBE, FRSE (d 2000), and Iris Winifred, *née* Hemingway (d 2007); *b* 1 September 1949; *Educ* Rugby, CCC Cambridge (MA, PhD); *m* 1, 26 June 1971 (m dis 1980), Catherine Blackburn; 2 da (Emily b 1973, Olivia b 1976); m 2, 12 July 1982, Pamela Dorothy Tennant, da of Felix Rowley Symes; 1 s (Mungo b 1990), 1 step s (Jack b 1973), 1 step da (Olivia b 1975); *Career* shipping trainee The Ben Line Steamers Ltd 1971–72; res fell CCC Cambridge 1975–78, sr lectr Dept of War Studies and Int Affairs RMA Sandhurst 1978–79; CCC Cambridge: fell 1979– (life fell 1992–), dean of coll 1981–86, tutor for admissions 1981–88, dir of studies in history 1986–92, sr tutor 1987 and 1989–92; prof of modern history Univ of Glasgow 1992–2001, Chichele prof of the history of war Univ of Oxford 2002–15, fell All Souls Coll Oxford 2002–15 (emeritus fell 2015–), dir Leverhulme Programme on the Changing Character of War Univ of Oxford 2004–12, Humanitas visiting prof in war studies Univ of Cambridge 2011, prof of int relations Univ of St Andrews 2015–; major research fellowship Leverhulme Tst 2008–11, dir Scottish Centre for War Studies 1996–2001; jt ed War in History jl 1994–2013; memb Cncl: Soc for Army Historical Res 1980–95, Lancing Coll 1982–90, Nat Army Museum 1994–2003; cmmr Cwlth War Graves Cmmn 2006–, memb Advsy Bd Def Acad 2008–, memb Chief of the Defence Staff's Strategic Advsy Panel 2010–, chair Task Force on Rebuilding the Military Covenant for the PM 2010, advsr Jt Parly Ctee on the Nat Security Strategy 2011–; DL Tweeddale 2006–14, Lord Lt Tweeddale 2014–; govr: Rugby Sch 1985–2007, Stowe Sch 1990–2002; Brig Queen's Body Guard for Scotland (Royal Co of Archers) 2008 (memb Cncl 2003–12); tstee Imperial War Museum 2010–, memb UK Advsy Ctee on the Centenary of the First World War 2012–; Br Acad Thank Offering to Britain fell 1998–99; Pritzker Award for Lifetime Achievement in Military Writing 2016; Hon DUniv Paisley 2005; FRHistS, FRSE 2003; *Books* British Military Uniforms 1768–1796 (1975), History of the Cambridge University Officers Training Corps (1976), European Armies and the Conduct of War (1983), Wellington's Legacy: The Reform of the British Army 1830–54 (1984), From Waterloo to Balaclava: Tactics, Technology and the British Army (1985, Templer Medal), The Politics of the British Army (1997, Westminster Medal), The Oxford Illustrated History of the First World War (ed, 1998), The British Army, Manpower and Society into the 21st Century (ed, 2000), The First World War, Vol I, To Arms (2001), Military Lives (ed, 2002), The First World War: a new illustrated history (2003), Big Wars and Small Wars: The British Army and the Lessons of War in the 20th Century (ed, 2006), Clausewitz on War (2007), Clausewitz in the 21st Century (ed, 2007), The Changing Character of War (ed, 2011), La Guerre Irregulière (ed, 2011), How Fighting Ends: A History of Surrender (ed, 2012), British Generals in Blair's Wars (ed, 2013), The Direction of War (2013); *Recreations* shooting, rugby football (now spectating); *Clubs* New (Edinburgh), Hawks' (Cambridge); *Style*— Prof Sir Hew Strachan; ✉ Glenhighton, Broughton, Biggar ML12 6JF

STRACHAN, Ian Charles; s of Dr Charles Strachan, of Wilmslow, Cheshire, and Margaret, *née* Craig; *b* 7 April 1943; *Educ* Fettes, Christ's Coll Cambridge (MA), Princeton Univ (MPA), Harvard Univ; *m* 1, 29 July 1967 (m dis 1987), Diane Shafer, da of Raymond P Shafer, of Washington DC, USA; 1 da (Shona Elizabeth b 15 Feb 1970); m 2, 28 Nov 1987, Margaret, da of Dr Hugh Auchincloss, of New Jersey, USA; *Career* assoc Ford Fndn Malaysia 1967–69, various positions Exxon Corporation 1970–86, fin dir Gen Sekiyu Tokyo Japan 1979–82, chm and chief exec Esso Hong Kong and Esso China 1982–83, corp strategy mangr Exxon Corpn NY 1984–86, chief fin offr and sr vice-pres Johnson and Higgins NY 1986–87, dep chief exec RTZ Corporation plc London 1991–95 (fin dir 1987–91); BTR plc: dir 1995–99, md July-Dec 1995, chief exec 1996–99; dep chm Invensys plc 1999–2000; non-exec dir: Commercial Union plc 1992–95, Transocean Sedco Forex Inc Houston TX 2000–, Reuters Gp plc 2000–, Instinet Gp 2000–05 (non-exec chm 2003–05), Johnson Matthey plc 2002–, Xstrata plc 2003–; *Recreations* tennis, reading, oriental antiques; *Style*— Ian Strachan

STRACHAN, James Murray; s of Eric Alexander Howieson Strachan, and Jacqueline Georgina, *née* Langoussis; *b* 10 November 1953; *Educ* King's Sch Canterbury, Christ's Coll Cambridge (exhibitioner, BA), London Coll of Printing; *Career* Chase Manhattan Bank 1976–77; Merrill Lynch: joined 1977, ed Merrill Lynch Int 1982–86, md Merrill Lynch Capital Markets and Merrill Lynch Europe 1986–89; photographer and writer (numerous books published and contribs to Sunday Times, FT and The Times) 1989–97, assoc photographer Getty Images 1990–; RNID: tstee and memb Fin Ctee 1994–96, chief exec 1997–2002, chm 2002–07, vice-pres 2008–; chm Audit Cmmn 2002–06; non-exec dir: Legal and General Gp 2003–11, Bank of England 2006–09, Care UK plc 2006–10, Welsh Water Ltd 2007–15, Sarasin & Ptnrs LLP 2008–, Social Finance Ltd 2008–12, FSA 2009–13, JPMorgan Asian Investment Tst plc 2009–, Towergate Insurance Ltd 2011–14; sr visiting fell (risk and regulation) LSE 2005–13; rotating chair Disability Charities Consortium 1997–2002, co-chair Task Force on Social Services Provision for Deaf and Hard of Hearing People 1998–2002, co-chair NHS Modernising Hearing Aid Services Gp 1999–2002, cmmr Disability Rights Cmmn 1999–2002, chair Task Force on Audiology Services 2000–02; memb: Ministerial Disability Rights Task Force 1997–99, Ministerial Disability Benefits Forum 1998–99, NCVO Advsy Gp on Diversity 2001–03; pres Midland Regnl Assoc for the Deaf 2001–; external memb Transition Gp (Energy) DTI 2001–02; memb Bd and Audit Ctee Office of Gas and Electricity Markets 2000–04, ind memb Business Bd DTI 2002–04; memb Bd Community Fund 2001–03; tstee: Save the Children 1999–2002, Somerset House Tst 2003–08 (chair Audit and Finance Ctee 2006–08); leadership patron Nat Coll of Sch Leadership 2003–13; hon fell Univ of the Arts London 2002; *Recreations* film, reading, swimming, tennis; *Style*— James Strachan, Esq; ✉ 10B Wedderburn Road, London NW3 5QG (e-mail james.strachan@mac.com)

STRACHAN, (Douglas) Mark Arthur; QC (1987); s of Flt Lt William Arthur Watkin Strachan (d 1998), and Joyce, *née* Smith; *b* 25 September 1946; *Educ* Orange Hill GS Edgware, St Catherine's Coll Oxford (BCL, MA), Nancy Univ France; *Career* called to the Bar Inner Temple 1969; head of chambers; recorder 1990– (asst recorder 1987–90), dep High Court Judge 1993–; contrib to legal jls: Modern Law Review, New Law Journal, Solicitors Journal; *Recreations* fatherhood, France, food, antiques; *Style*— Mark Strachan, Esq, QC; ✉ 3 Hare Court, Temple, London EC4Y 7BJ (☎ 020 7415 7800)

STRACHAN, Dame Valerie Patricia Marie; DCB (1998, CB 1991); *b* 10 January 1940; *Educ* Newland HS, Hull Univ, Manchester Univ; *m* John Strachan; *Career* Customs and Excise: joined as asst princ 1961, seconded to Dept of Economic Affairs, Home Office and Treasury, princ 1966–74, asst sec 1974–80, cmmr (under sec) 1980–87 (also head Treasy/Cabinet Office Jt Mgmnt Unit), dep chm (dep sec) 1987–93, DG Internal Taxation and Customs Gp 1989–93, chm of the Bd 1993–2000, dep chair Community Fund 2000–04; dep chair Big Lottery Fund 2004–06; Judicial Appointments cmmr 2012–; chair of govrs James Allen's Girls' Sch 2004–09, chair Cncl Univ of Southampton 2006–12; *Style*— Dame Valerie Strachan, DCB

STRAKER, Nicholas David Barclay; s of Hugh Charles Straker (d 1993), and Elaine Felicia, *née* Peat (d 2013); *b* 6 May 1952; *Educ* Eton, Durham Agric Coll, Lakeland Agric Coll Alberta; *m* 6 Sept 1980, Victoria Eyre, *née* Gray; 1 s (Sam Charles Barclay), 3 da (Jacquetta Lucy Eyre, Chloë Victoria Piffard, Selina Storm Felicia-Rose); *Career* 9/12 Royal Lancers 1971–75; farmer Little Hutton Farms 1975–76, conslt Towry Law & Co 1978–80; dir: Whitehouse Financial Services Ltd 1980–82, Lycetts Insurance Brokers and Financial Services 1982–; High Sheriff Co Durham 1994–95; ACII, FPFS; *Recreations* golf, riding, skiing, country sports, tennis, gardening, shooting, travel, hunting; *Clubs* Northern Counties, Eton Vikings; *Style*— Nicholas Straker, Esq; ✉ Lycetts, Milburn House, Dean Street, Newcastle upon Tyne NE1 1PP (☎ 0191 232 1151, e-mail nick.straker@lycetts.co.uk)

STRAKER, Timothy Derrick; QC (1996); s of Derrick Straker (d 1976), and Dorothy Elizabeth, *née* Rogers; *b* 25 May 1955; *Educ* Malvern Coll, Downing Coll Cambridge (MA); *m* 17 April 1982 (m dis 2007), Ann, da of late Michael Horton Baylis, of Highgate, London; 2 (Rosemary Elizabeth b 1985, Penelope Ann b 1987); *Career* called to the Bar: Gray's Inn 1977 (bencher 2003), ad eundem Lincoln's Inn 1979, Trinidad and Tobago 2001, NI 2001; asst recorder 1998, recorder 2000–, jt head of chambers 2002–08, 2008–12 and 2013–15, head of chambers 2015–; dep High Court judge 2010–; acting justice Falklands Court of Appeal, ad hoc election cmmr; Planning and Environmental Silk of the Year 2009, Times Lawyer of the Week 2013, Environmental Barrister of the Year Finance Monthly 2015; memb: Local Govt and Planning Bar Assoc, Admin Law Bar Assoc, Crown Office Users' Assoc, Admin Court Users' Assoc, Parly Bar Mess; memb Governing Cncl Malvern Coll 2011–; *Publications* articles: Judicial Review, Rights of Way Law Review; contrib to Halsbury's Laws of England: Public Health and Environmental Protection, Local Government, Markets; Intelligence Services Act, A Guide to Registration of Political Parties Act, Human Rights and Judical Review: Case Studies in Context (with Ian Goldrein, QC); The Civil Court Practice (conslt ed); *Recreations* history, reading, rackets (winner with Steve Tulley Tonbridge Tournament 2013 and finalist Winchester Invitation Doubles 2011 and 2013); *Clubs* Lansdowne, Oxford and Cambridge, Cwlth, Manchester Tennis and Racquet, St Paul's Rackets; *Style*— Timothy Straker, Esq, QC; ✉ 4–5 Gray's Inn Square, Gray's Inn, London WC1R 5AH (☎ 020 7404 5252, fax 020 7242 7803, e-mail ts@4-5.co.uk)

STRANG, Prof Sir John Stanley; kt (2016); s of William John Strang, CBE, FRS, of Castle Combe, Wilts, and Margaret Nicholas Strang; *b* 12 May 1950; *Educ* Bryanston, Guy's Hosp Med Sch Univ of London (MB BS); *m* 21 April 1984, Jennifer, da of Edwin Austin Campbell Abbey (d 1975); 2 s (Samuel John b 1985, Robert Luke b 1988), 1 da (Jasmine Rebecca b 1991, d 1998); *Career* regnl conslt in drug dependence Manchester 1982–86; Maudsley Bethlem Royal Hosp: conslt psychiatrist in drug dependence 1986–, prof of addiction behaviour and dir of Addiction Research Unit 1995–; conslt advsr on drug dependence to Dept of Health 1986–2003; FRCPsych 1994 (MRCPsych 1977), MD 1995, Hon fell Australasian Chapter of Addiction Medicine, FRCP 2006, FMedSci 2015; *Books* AIDS and Drug Misuse: the challenge for policy and practice in the 1990s (ed with G Stimson, 1990), Drugs, Alcohol and Tobacco: the science and policy connections (ed with G Edwards and J Jaffe, 1993), Heroin Addiction and Drug Policy: the British system (ed with M Gossop, 1994), Drug Misuse and Community Pharmacy (ed with J Sheridan, 2002), Methadone Matters: Evolving Community Methadone Treatment of Opiate Addiction (ed with G Tober, 2003), Heroin Addiction and the 'British System' (ed with M Gossop, 2005); *Style*— Prof Sir John Strang; ✉ National Addiction Centre, The Maudsley/Institute of Psychiatry, Denmark Hill, London SE5 8AF (☎ 020 7848 0438)

STRANGE, 17 Baron (E 1628); Adam Humphrey Drummond; eld s of Capt Humphrey Drummond of Megginch, MC (d 2009), and Lady Strange (16 holder of title, d 2005); *b* 20 April 1953, Dundee; *Educ* Eton, Sandhurst, Heriot Watt Univ (MSc); *m* 14 May 1988, Hon Mary Emma Jeronima, *née* Dewar, eld da of 4 Baron Forteviot, *qv*; 1 da (Hon Sophia Frances b 1991), 1 s (Hon John Adam Humphrey b 1992); *Heir* s, Hon John Drummond; *Career* Grenadier Gds 1973–94, Maj, ret; Perthshire Housing Assoc 1994–2011; farmer Balmyre Farms; MCIH; *Clubs* Perth; *Style*— The Lord Strange; ✉ The Mains of Megginch, Errol, Perthshire PH2 7RN

STRANGER-JONES, Anthony John; s of Leonard Ivan Stranger-Jones (d 1983), and Iris Christine, *née* Truscott (d 1991); *b* 30 December 1944; *Educ* Westminster, ChCh Oxford (MA); *m* 19 June 1976, Kazumi, da of Kazuo Matsuo, of Japan; 2 da (Amiko b 1977, Yukiko b 1980), 1 s (David b 1983); *Career* md Amex Finance (Hong Kong) Ltd 1974–76; dir: Amex Bank Ltd 1976–79, Korea Merchant Banking Corporation 1979–82, Barclays Merchant Bank Ltd 1979–86, Barclays de Zoete Wedd Ltd 1986–97 (md Corp and Investment Banking 1995–97); md Corp and Investment Banking Credit Suisse First Boston 1997–98, dir Barclays Private Bank Ltd 1999–2001, chm Essjay Consultants 2002–; ACIB 1971; *Clubs* Asia House, Gloucestershire CCC, IISS, Japan Soc, MCC, Savile; *Style*— Anthony Stranger-Jones, Esq; ✉ 33 Randolph Crescent, London W9 1DP (☎ 020 7286 7342, e-mail anthony@stranger-jones.com)

STRANRAER-MULL, The Very Rev Gerald Hugh; s of Capt Gerald Stranraer-Mull (d 1955), and Dolena Mackenzie, *née* Workman (d 1986); *b* 24 November 1942; *Educ* Woodhouse Grove Sch, King's Coll London (AKC); *m* 30 Dec 1967, Glynis Mary (d 2015), da of Capt David Kempe, of Iden Green, Kent; 1 da (Clare b 1970), 2 s (Michael Paul b and d 1974, Jamie b 1977); *Career* journalist 1960–66; curate: Hexham Abbey 1970–72, Corbridge 1972; rector Ellon and Cruden Bay 1972–2008, canon Aberdeen Cathedral 1981–2008, dean of Aberdeen and Orkney 1988–2008 (dean emeritus 2008–); chm: Ellon Schs Cncl 1982–86, Gordon Health Cncl 1982–86; tstee: Oil Chaplaincy Tst 1993–2008, Duncraig Iona (formerly Iona Cornerstone Fndn) 1994–2008; warden Community of Our Lady of the Isles Shetland 2005–, hon priest in charge Strathnairn 2009–11, hon priest St Michael and All Angels Inverness 2011–; FSA Scot 2011; *Books* A Turbulent House: The Augustinians at Hexham (1970), View of the Diocese of Aberdeen and Orkney (1977), A Church for Scotland: the story of the Scottish Episcopal Church (2000), Steps on the Way: the History of the Scottish Episcopal Church 1513–2013 (2013); *Style*— The Very Rev the Dean Emeritus of Aberdeen and Orkney; ✉ 75 The Cairns, Muir of Ord, Ross-shire IV6 7AT (☎ 01463 870986, e-mail DeanGerald@kclalumni.net)

STRASBURGER, Baron (Life Peer UK 2011), of Langridge in the County of Somerset; Paul Cline Strasburger; *b* 31 July 1946; *Career* entrepreneur and philanthropist; *Recreations*

sports, music, theatre, freedom, privacy; *Clubs* MCC; *Style—* The Lord Strasburger; ✉ House of Lords, London SW1A 0PW (Twitter @lordstras)

STRATFORD, (Howard) Muir; JP (1978); s of Dr Martin Gould Stratford, VRD (d 1993), of London, and Dr Mavis Winifred Muir Stratford, JP, *née* Beddall (d 1993); *b* 6 June 1936; *Educ* Marlborough; *m* 8 July 1961, Margaret Reid, da of Robert Linton Roderick Ballantine (d 1957); 2 da (Gail b 1964, Fiona b 1967), 1 s (Duncan b 1971); *Career* insurance broker, memb Lloyd's; dir Bowring London Ltd 1980–85 and 1986–91, chief exec Bowring M K Ltd 1985–86; dir Watford FC 1971–90; Liveryman Worshipful Company of Haberdashers 1959, Liveryman Worshipful Company of Insurers 1986; *Recreations* golf, watching football and cricket; *Clubs* MCC, Moor Park Golf; *Style—* Muir Stratford, Esq; ✉ Flint Cottage, Deadmans Ash Lane, Sarratt, Rickmansworth, Hertfordshire WD3 6AL (☎ 01923 260475)

STRATFORD, Neil Martin; s of Dr Martin Gould Stratford, VRD (d 1993), of London, and Dr Mavis Winifred Muir Stratford, JP, *née* Beddall (d 1993); *b* 26 April 1938; *Educ* Marlborough, Magdalene Coll Cambridge (MA), Courtauld Inst (BA); *m* 28 Sept 1966, Anita Jennifer (Jenny), da of Peter Edwin Lewis (d 1980); 2 da (Jemima b 1968, Rebecca b 1971); *Career* Coldstream Gds 1956, 2 Lt 1957–58, Lt 1958; trainee Kleinwort Benson Lonsdale 1961–63, lectr Westfield Coll London 1969–75, Keeper of medieval and later antiquities British Museum 1975–98 (emeritus 1998–2001); visiting memb Inst for Advanced Study Princeton 1998–99, visiting prof Paris Ecole Pratique des Hautes Etudes 1999, Appleton prof Univ of Florida Tallahassee 2000, prof de l'histoire de l'art médiéval Paris Ecole Nationale des Chartes 2000–03, visiting sr lecturing fell Duke Univ N Carolina 2006; chm St Albans Cathedral Fabric Advsy Ctee 1995–; Grand Prix de la Société Française d'Archéologie 2011; Liveryman Worshipful Co of Haberdashers 1959; hon memb Académie de Dijon 1975, foreign memb Soc Nat des Antiquaires de France 1985, associé étranger Académie des Inscriptions et Belles-Lettres 2012– (correspondant étranger 2002–12); FSA 1976; Commandeur Ordre des Arts et des Lettres (France) 2013 (Officier 2006); *Books* La Sculpture Oubliée de Vézelay (1984), Catalogue of Medieval Enamels in the British Museum, II. Northern Romanesque Enamel (1993), Studies in Burgundian Romanesque Sculpture (1998), La frise monumentale romane de Souvigny (2002), Chronos et Cosmos: Le pilier roman de Souvigny (2005), Cluny 910–2010: Onze siecles de rayonnement (ed and author of 8 chapters, 2010), Corpus de la Sculpture de Cluny Vol 1 Les Parties Orientales de la Grande Eglise Cluny III (ed and princ author, 2010); *Recreations* cricket and football, food and wine, music, particularly opera; *Clubs* Garrick, Beefsteak, MCC, IZ, Cambridge Univ, Pitt, Hawks' (Cambridge); *Style—* Neil Stratford, Esq, FSA; ✉ 17 Church Row, London NW3 6UP

STRATHALMOND, 3 Baron (UK 1955); William Roberton Fraser; o s of 2 Baron Strathalmond, CMG, OBE, TD (d 1976), and Letitia, *née* Krementz (d 2010); *b* 22 July 1947; *Educ* Loretto; *m* 1973, Amanda Rose, da of Rev Gordon Clifford Taylor, of St Giles-in-the-Fields Rectory, London; 2 s (Hon William b 24 Sept 1976, Hon George b 10 March 1979), 1 da (Hon Virginia (Mrs Oliver Chadwyck-Healey) b 22 Dec 1982); *Heir* s, Hon William Fraser; *Career* md London Wall Members Agency Ltd 1986–91, dir London Wall Holdings plc 1986–91, chm R W Sturge Ltd 1991–94, dir Gerling at Lloyd's Ltd (formerly Owen & Wilby Underwriting Agency Ltd) 1995–2000; pres RSAS Age Care 2008– (vice-pres 1989–2008), tstee The Medusa Tst 2014–; Liveryman Worshipful Co of Girdlers (Master 2010–11); MICAS 1972; *Recreations* golf, fishing; *Style—* The Lord Strathalmond; ✉ Holt House, Elstead, Surrey GU8 6LF

STRATHCLYDE, 2 Baron (UK 1955); Thomas Galloway Dunlop du Roy de Blicquy Galbraith; CH (2013), PC (1995); er s of Hon Sir Thomas Galbraith, KBE, MP (Cons and Unionist) Glasgow Hillhead 1948–82 (d 1982), by his w, Simone Clothilde Fernande Marie Ghislaine (d 1991), eldest da of late Jean du Roy de Blicquy, of Bois d'Hautmont, Brabant, whose marriage with Sir Thomas was dissolved 1974; suc gf, 1 Baron Strathclyde, PC, JP (d 1985); *b* 22 February 1960, Glasgow; *Educ* Sussex House London, Wellington, UEA (BA), Univ of Aix-en-Provence; *m* 27 June 1992, Jane, er da of John Skinner, of Chenies, Herts; 3 da (Hon Elizabeth Ida Skinner b 1 Dec 1993, Hon Annabel Jane Simone Skinner b 15 May 1996, Hon Rose Marie Louise Skinner Galbraith); *Heir* his brother, The Hon Charles Galbraith; *Career* insurance broker Bain Clarkson Ltd (formerly Bain Dawes) 1982–88; Lord in Waiting (Govt Whip House of Lords) 1988–89; spokesman for DTI; Parly under sec of state: Dept of Employment (and min for tourism) 1989–90, DOE July-Sept 1990, Scottish Office (min for agric, fish, Highlands and Islands) 1990–92, DOE 1992, DTI 1993; min of state DTI 1994; Capt HM Body Guard of Hon Corps of Gentlemen at Arms (chief Govt whip) 1994–97, oppn chief whip in the Lords 1997–98, oppn spokesman and shadow ldr of the House of Lords 1998–2010, ldr of the House of Lords and Chllr of the Duchy of Lancaster 2010–13; chm Trafalgar Capital Mgmnt Ltd 2001–10, dir Scottish Mortgage Investment Tst plc 2004–10; non-exec dir: Galena Capital 2004–10 and 2013–, Marketform 2004–10, Hampden Agencies Ltd 2008–10, non-exec dir Galena Asset Mgmnt SA Switzerland 2013–, chm Bank & Clients plc 2016–; pres Quoted Cos Alliance 2004–10; memb Bd Cons Fndn, Cons candidate Euro election Merseyside East 1984; memb Supervisory Bd Trafigura Beheer BV 2013–16; patron Pakistan Human Devpt Fund UK; govr Wellington Coll 2010–; Channel 4 Peer of the Year 2000, Spectator Peer of the Year 2004; *Style—* The Rt Hon Lord Strathclyde, CH, PC; ✉ House of Lords, London, SW1A 0PW (☎ 020 7219 5353)

STRATHERN, Prof Andrew Jamieson; s of Robert Strathern (d 1972), and Mary, *née* Sharp (d 1992); *b* 19 January 1939; *Educ* Colchester Royal GS, Trinity Coll Cambridge (major entrance scholar, BA, MA, PhD); *m* 1, 20 July 1973 (m dis 1986), Ann Marilyn Evans; 1 da (Barbara Helen Mary b 1969), 2 s (Alan Leiper b 1975, Hugh Thomas b 1975); m 2, 21 April 1997, Dr Pamela J Stewart; *Career* res fell Trinity Coll Cambridge 1965–68, fell Res Sch of Paufic Studies ANU 1970–72 (res fell 1969–70), prof of social anthropology Univ of Papua New Guinea 1973–76, prof and head of Dept of Anthropology UCL 1976–83, dir Inst of PNG Studies Port Moresby PNG 1981–86, emeritus prof Univ of London 1987–, Andrew W Mellon Distinguished prof of anthropology Univ of Pittsburgh 1987–, dir Center for Pacific Studies James Cook Univ Townsville 1996–; memb Cncl RAI 1977–80, vice-chm Social Anthropology Ctee SSRC 1979–81 (memb 1977–81); Rivers Meml Medal 1976, PNG 10 Anniversary of Ind Medal 1987; memb: Assoc of Social Anthropologists of GB and the Cwlth 1967, Assoc for Social Anthropology in Oceania 1987, European Assoc of Soc Anthropologists 1989, Euro Soc of Oceanists 1993; fell American Anthropological Assoc 1983, FRAI; *Books* The Rope of Moka (1971), Self - Decoration in Mt Hagen (jtly 1971), One Father, One Blood (1972), Ongka (1979), Inequality in Highlands New Guinea Societies (ed, 1982), A Line of Power (1984), The Mi-Culture of the Mt Hagen People (co-ed, 1990), Landmarks (1993), Ru (1993), Voices of Conflict (1993), Migration and Transformations (co-ed, 1994), Body Thoughts (1996), Millennial Markers (co-ed, 1997), Bodies and Persons (co-ed, 1998), Cultural Anthropology, a Contemporary Perspective (co-author 3 edn, 1998), Kuk Heritage: Issues and Debates (co-ed, 1998), Curing and Healing: Medical Anthropology in Global Perspective (jtly, 1999), The Spirit is Coming! A Photographic-Textual Documentation of the Female Spirit Cult in Mt Hagen (jtly, 1999); *Recreations* travel, poetry; *Style—* Prof Andrew Strathern; ✉ 1103 Winterton Street, Pittsburgh, PA 15206, USA (☎ 00 1 412 441 5778); Department of Anthropology, University of Pittsburgh, Pittsburgh PA 15260, USA (☎ 00 1 412 648 7519, fax 00 1 412 648 7535, e-mail strather@pitt.edu)

STRATTON, David; s of Lawrence James William Stratton (d 1989), and Muriel Elizabeth, *née* Hunt (d 2004); *b* 16 May 1947; *Educ* Altrincham GS for Boys, Colwyn Bay GS, Univ of Leeds (LLB); *m* 29 May 1971, Ruth Hazel, da of John Eric Delhanty; 3 s (James Anthony b 1 March 1976, Charles Edward b 21 April 1978, Oliver John b 26 Nov 1979), 3 da (Rachael Joanna b 6 May 1981, Rebecca Alice b 30 March 1987, Jessica Rose b 17 June 1990); *Career* admitted slr 1971; articled clerk to Town Clerk Warrington 1969–71, asst rising to princ asst slr Warrington Borough Cncl 1971–72, gp slr Christian Salvesen Properties Limited 1975–79 (asst gp slr 1972–75), head Commercial Property Dept and dep sr ptnr Halliwell Landau Solicitors Manchester 1979–95, sr ptnr Field Cunningham Solicitors Manchester 1995–2010, memb Rowlands Field Cunningham LLP 2010–11, ptnr Linder Myers 2011–; *Style—* David Stratton, Esq; ✉ Linder Myers LLP, 19 Spring Gardens, Manchester M2 1FB (☎ 0844 984 6400, e-mail david.stratton@lindermyers.co.uk)

STRATTON, Prof Sir Michael; kt (2013); *Career* dir Wellcome Tst Sanger Inst; FRS; *Style—* Prof Sir Michael Stratton; ✉ Wellcome Trust Sanger Institute, Gibbs Building, 215 Euston Road, London NW1 2BE

STRAUS, Peter Quentin; CBE (2016); s of Dr Ronnie Straus, and Graziella Straus, of Wimbledon, London; *b* 10 September 1960; *Educ* KCS Wimbledon, Christ's Coll Cambridge (MA, capt squash and tennis teams); *Career* publisher; Hodder and Stoughton Publishers: graduate trainee 1982–84, sales and marketing asst 1984–86, asst ed New English Library later jr ed, ed then sr ed Hodder and Stoughton Paperbacks 1986–88; editorial dir Hamish Hamilton 1990 (sr ed 1988–90); Macmillan Publishers Ltd: publishing dir and publisher Picador 1990–94, gp literary publisher Macmillan, Picador and Papermac 1994–95, ed-in-chief Macmillan, Pan, Picador, Papermac and Sidgwick & Jackson 1995–96, US scout 1996–97, publisher Picador 1997–, ed-in-chief Pan Macmillan, Macmillan, Pan, Sidgwick & Jackson, Boxtree, Channel 4 Books and Picador 2000–02, literary agent and dir Rogers, Coleridge & White Ltd 2002–; memb Booker Prize Mgmnt Ctee Booker plc 1991–2002, memb Mgmnt Ctee Samuel Johnson Prize 1998–; *Books* 20 Under 35 (ed, 1988); *Recreations* sport, film, theatre, reading; *Clubs* Beerhunters (Player of the Year 1992), Soho House; *Style—* Peter Straus, Esq, CBE; ✉ Rogers, Coleridge & White Ltd, 20 Powis Mews, London W1P 1JN (e-mail peters@rcwlitagency.co.uk)

STRAW, Rt Hon John Whitaker (Jack); PC (1997); s of Walter Straw, and Joan Straw; *b* 3 August 1946; *Educ* Brentwood Sch, Univ of Leeds, Inns of Court Sch of Law; *m* 1, 1968 (m dis 1978), Anthea Weston; 1 da (decd); m 2, 1978, Alice Elizabeth Perkins, CB, *qv*; 1 s, 1 da; *Career* called to the Bar Inner Temple 1972 (bencher 1997), barrister 1972–74; pres NUS 1969–71, memb Islington Cncl 1971–78, dep ldr ILEA 1973–74, contested (Lab) Tonbridge and Malling 1974; political advsr to Sec of State for: Social Servs 1974–76, Environment 1976–77, Granada TV (World in Action) 1977–79; MP (Lab) Blackburn 1979–2015; oppn front bench spokesman on: Treasy and econ affrs 1980–83, environment 1983–87; elected to Shadow Cabinet 1987; chief oppn spokesman on: educn 1987–92, housing and local govt 1992–94, home affrs 1994–97; sec of state Home Office 1997–2001, sec of state FCO 2001–06, ldr House of Commons 2006–07, sec of state for justice and Lord Chllr 2007–10; visiting fell Nuffield Coll Oxford 1990–98, visiting prof in public policy UCL 2011–; chm Pimlico Sch 1995–2000; Hon LLD: Univ of Leeds 1999, Brunel Univ 2007; FRSS 1995; *Publications* Last Man Standing (2012), Hamlyn Lectures (2013); *Style—* The Rt Hon Jack Straw; ✉ House of Commons, London SW1A 0AA

STREAT, Prof Michael; s of George Streat (d 1978), and Lore Streat (d 2000); *b* 23 July 1937; *Educ* UMIST (BSc), Imperial Coll London (PhD, DIC); *m* 3 Dec 1961, Carole Doreen, da of Joseph Bertram Robinson; 1 da (Denise (Mrs Shahar) b 16 June 1963), 1 s (Simon b 12 April 1966); *Career* successively lectr, sr lectr and reader Imperial Coll London 1961–89 (visiting prof 2003–13), prof of chemical engrg Loughborough Univ 1989–2002 (now emeritus, head Dept of Chemical Engrg 1992–2000); AMCT; CEng, FIChemE 1973, FREng 2000; *Publications* co-author of numerous articles and papers in learned jls on the application of adsorption and ion exchange technol; *Recreations* antique collecting (especially maps and prints), travelling, armchair sports, family and friends; *Style—* Prof Michael Streat; ✉ 5 Compass Close, Glendale Avenue, Edgware HA8 8HU (e-mail michael.streat@btopenworld.com)

STREATHER, Bruce Godfrey; s of William Godfrey Streather (d 1995), of Staffs, and Pamela Mary, *née* Revell (d 1993); *b* 3 June 1946, Sutton Coldfield; *Educ* Malvern, Univ of Oxford (MA); *m* 15 Dec 1973, Geraldine Susan, da of Colin Herbert Clout (d 1995), of San Francisco, USA; 3 da (Charlotte, Annabel, Miranda); *Career* admitted slr 1971; sr ptnr: Streathers LLP, Meaby & Co LLP; memb Law Soc; *Recreations* family, golf, Christianity; *Clubs* R&A, Sunningdale Golf, Vincent's (Oxford), Littlestone Golf, Moor Hall Golf; *Style—* Bruce Streather, Esq; ✉ Streathers, 44 Baker Street, London W1U 7AL (☎ 020 7034 4200, fax 020 7034 4301, e-mail bstreather@streathers.co.uk)

STREET, Dr Andrew Maurice; s of Harry Maurice Street, of Swadlincote, Derbys, and Patricia, *née* Wilson; *b* 30 September 1961; *Educ* Burton-on-Trent GS, St Hild and St Bede Coll Durham (BSc, Univ Prize), Lady Margaret Hall Oxford (DPhil); *m* 14 Oct 2005, Ruth Margaret, *née* Jackson; 1 s (Harry Andrew Alan b 9 Jan 2007); *Career* pt/t researcher AERE Harwell 1986, analyst Baring Brothers & Co Ltd 1986–88, options trader then sr trader Paribas Capital Markets Ltd 1988–91, head of equity derivatives trading Nomura International plc 1991–92, head of equity and commodity risk mgmnt and bd dir Mitsubishi Finance International plc 1992–95 (exec dir/head of arbitrage 1993–95); head of market risk mgmnt and asst dir SFA 1995–98; co-head Traded Risk Dept FSA 1998–2000, md Value Consultants Ltd 2000–; pt/t lectr Thames Valley Univ 2003–, pt/t lectr ICMA Centre Henley Business Sch Univ of Reading 2006–, pt/t lectr Judge Business Sch Univ of Cambridge 2013–; MInstP 1986, MSI; *Publications* Methods of Calculation of Cross Sections for Nuclear Reactors (DPhil thesis, 1987), Handbook of Risk Management and Analysis (2000), PRMIA Risk Handbook (2008), Financial Markets 2015 Edition – PRMIA Risk Handbook (2015); articles in Nuclear Science & Engineering magazine and Risk magazine; *Recreations* flying (PPL), theatre, cinema, sailing, reading, tinkering with computers, clay pigeon shooting, golf; *Clubs* Union Jack; *Style—* Dr Andrew Street; ✉ Value Consultants Ltd, 36 Elm Grove Road, London W5 3JJ (☎ 020 8566 0383, fax 020 8932 2591, e-mail andrew.street@value-consultants.co.uk)

STREET, Prof Sarah; da of D L Street, and C Street; *b* 1 February 1958, Cardiff; *Educ* Univ of Warwick (BA), St Peter's Coll Oxford (DPhil); *Career* archivist Dept of Western Manuscripts Bodleian Library Univ of Oxford 1985–93, Univ of Bristol 1993– (currently prof of film); *Books* Cinema and State (jtly, 1985), British National Cinema (1997), British Cinema in Documents (2000), Moving Performance (ed jtly, 2000), European Cinema: An Introduction (ed with Jill Forbes, 2000), Costume and Cinema: Dress Codes in Popular Film (2001), Transatlantic Crossings: British Feature Films in the USA (2002), The Titanic in Myth and Memory (ed jtly, 2004), Black Narcissus (2005), Film Architecture and the Transnational Imagination: Set Design in 1930s European Cinema (jtly, 2007), Queer Screen: The Screen Reader (ed jtly, 2007), British National Cinema (2009, expanded edition), Colour Films in Britain: The Negotiation of Innovation 1900–55 (2012, Best Book Prize British Assoc of Fim, TV and Screen Studies), Color and the Moving Image: History, Theory, Aesthetics, Archive (ed jtly, 2012), British Colour Cinema: Practices and Theories (ed jtly, 2013); *Style—* Prof Sarah Street; ✉ Department of Film and Television, School of Arts, University of Bristol, Cantocks Close, Woodland Road, Bristol BS8 1UP

STREET, Dame Susan Ruth (Sue); DCB (2005); *née* Galeski; da of Stefan Galeski, and Anna, *née* Galin; *b* 11 August 1949, London; *Educ* Camden Sch, Univ of St Andrews (MA); *m* 22 July 1972, Richard Street; 1 s (Robin b 5 Dec 1976), 1 da (Rebecca b 22 Sept 1978); *Career* Home Office 1972–74, British Cncl Bogota 1974–81, Home Office 1982–89, dir Top Mgmnt Prog Cabinet Office 1989–92, Price Waterhouse 1992–94, Cabinet Office 1994–96, Fire Serv 1996–99, dir Criminal Policy Gp Home Office 1999–2001, perm sec

DCMS 2001–06; advsr Deloitte 2007–12, non-exec dir Adlens 2014–; memb Bd: HMRC 2009–10, Min of Justice 2011–15; author of articles in Westminster and Whitehall jls; tstee ROH 2006–15, govr Royal Ballet 2007–; assoc fell Inst for Govt; memb Worshipful Co of Firefighters 2014–; exec coach Praesta 2014–; *Recreations* ballet, theatre, family life, poor golf; *Style*— Dame Sue Street, DCB; ✉ 85 South Lodge, Circus Road, London NW8 9EU (☎ 020 3737 1071, e-mail suestreet@damesuestreet.com)

STREET-PORTER, Janet; CBE (2016); *b* 27 December 1946; *Educ* Lady Margaret GS, Architectural Assoc; *m* 1, 1967 (m dis 1975), Tim Street-Porter; m 2, 1975 (m dis 1977), Tony Elliott; m 3, 1979 (m dis 1981), Frank Cvitanovich (d 1988); *Career* journalist, broadcaster and tv prodr; writer for: Petticoat Magazine 1968, Daily Mail 1969–71, Evening Standard 1971–73; contrib to Queen, Vogue, etc; LBC Radio 1973; presented numerous series for LWT 1975–81 incl: London Weekend Show, Saturday Night People, Around Midnight, Six O'Clock Show; produced and devised series from 1981 incl: Twentieth Century Box, Network 7; BBC TV: joined 1988, head of Youth and Entertainment Features then head of Independent Production for Entertainment; md Live TV for Mirror Group 1994–95; ed The Independent on Sunday 1999–2001; currently columnist Independent Newspaper and feature writer Daily Mail; presented numerous TV series incl: Travels with Pevsner (BBC 2) 1997, Coast to Coast (BBC 2) 1998, As the Crow Flies (BBC 2) 1999, All the Rage (one-woman show, Edinburgh Festival) 2003 and (tour) 2004, So You Think You Can Teach (five) 2004, Michael and Me (Sky One) 2005, Janet Saves the Monarchy (Sky One) 2005, The F Word with Gordon Ramsay 2006–08 (3 series), Grand Design Live 2008, Loose Women (ITV), Taste of Britain (BBC 1); tstee Sci Museum 2008–14; winner BAFTA award for originality 1988, Prix Italia for opera The Vampyr 1993; pres: Ramblers' Assoc 1994–96; *Publications* Baggage (autobiography, 2004), Fall Out (memoir, 2006), Life's Too F*****g Short (2008), Don't Let The B*****ds Get You Down (2009); *Recreations* walking, modern art; *Style*— Ms Janet Street-Porter, CBE; ✉ c/o Sophie Laurence, Factual Management, Golden Cross House, 8 Duncannon Street, London WC2N 4JF (☎ 020 7484 5133, e-mail sl@factualmanagement.com)

STREETER, David Thomas; MBE (2007); s of Reginald David Streeter (d 1976), of East Grinstead, W Sussex, and Dorothy Alice, *née* Fairhurst (d 1994); *b* 20 May 1937; *Educ* Cranbrook Sch, QMC London (BSc); *m* 1, 9 Sept 1967 (m dis 1979), Althea Elizabeth, da of Andrew Haig, of Waldringfield, Suffolk; 1 s (James b 1970); m 2, 5 Jan 1980, Penelope Sheila Dale, da of Gordon Kippax, of Netherfield, E Sussex; 2 da (Katharine b 1981, Olivia b 1987); *Career* Univ of Sussex: lectr in ecology 1965–76, reader in ecology 1976–2014, dean Sch of Biological Scis 1984–88, pro-vice-chllr 1989–97; lectr and broadcaster; memb: Gen Advsy Cncl BBC 1975–80, Cncl RSNC 1963–83, Advsy Ctee for England Nature Conservancy Cncl 1973–83, Countryside Cmmn 1978–84, SE Regnl Ctee Nat Tst 1989–2001, Nat Park Review Panel 1990–91, Sussex Downs Conservation Bd 1992–2006, Cncl Botanical Soc Br Isles 1994–99, Governing Body Hurstpierpoint Coll 1994–2005, Conservation Panel Nat Tst 1999–2011, Historic Buildings and Land Panel/Heritage Lottery Fund 1999–2005, Environmental Advsy Panel National Grid plc 2000–03; pres Sussex Wildlife Tst 2004–, pres Friends of Ashdown Forest 2012–; tstee Weald and Downland Open Air Museum 1993–2016; hon memb Botanical Soc of Britain and Ireland (BSBI) 2014; FRSB 1986, FLS 1996; *Books* Discovering Hedgerows (with R Richardson, 1982), The Wild Flowers of The British Isles (with I Garrard, 1983), The Natural History of the Oak Tree (with R Lewington, 1993), Collins Flower Guide (2009), Collins Wild Flower Guide (2016); *Recreations* natural history, visiting other people's gardens; *Style*— David Streeter, Esq, MBE; ✉ The Holt, Sheepsetting Lane, Heathfield, East Sussex TN21 0UY (☎ 01435 862849, e-mail davidtstreeter@gmail.com), The University of Sussex, John Maynard Smith Building, Falmer, Brighton BN1 9QG (☎ 01273 877306, fax 01273 678433, e-mail d.t.streeter@sussex.ac.uk)

STREETER, Gary; MP; *Career* MP (Cons): Plymouth Sutton 1992–97, Devon SW 1997–; asst Govt whip 1995–96, Parly sec Lord Chancellor's Department 1996–97; shadow min for Europe 1997–98, shadow sec of state for int devpt 1998–2001, a vice-chm Cons Pty 2001–02, shadow foreign min 2003–04, chm Cons Pty Int Office 2005–; *Style*— Gary Streeter, Esq, MP; ✉ House of Commons, London SW1A 0AA (☎ 020 7219 3000)

STREETER, Penny; OBE (2005); da of Peter Stiff, of S Africa, and Marion Hewson, *née* Hammonds; *b* 1 August 1967, Zimbabwe; *Educ* Alberton HS S Africa; *Family* 1 s (Adam b 18 Dec 1986), 2 da (Giselle b 22 Feb 1992, Bonnie b 27 Feb 1994); partner Nick Rea; 1 da (Matilda b 13 March 2001); *Career* owner, fndr and md Ambition 24hours 1996–, owner Nursing Services of S Africa 2006–, fndr QA Calling 2006–; placed first in Virgin Atlantic Fast Track 100 Companies 2002, CBI Entrepreneur of the Year 2003; *Style*— Ms Penny Streeter; ✉ Ambition 24hours, Ambition House, 92–96 Lind Road, Sutton, Surrey SM1 4PL (☎ 020 7112 4549, fax 020 8288 8993, e-mail penny.streeter@ambition24hours.co.uk)

STREETS, Paul Richard; OBE (2003); *b* 25 July 1959; *Educ* UCL (BSc), Univ of Reading (MSc), Loughborough Univ (DipCS), Univ of Warwick (MBA); *m* 27 Aug 1993, Alison; 3 c; *Career* field dir Africa Sight Savers 1988–92, head of business and devpt Quantum Care 1993–95, dep dir Amnesty Int UK 1996–98, chief exec Diabetes UK 1998–2003, chief exec Health Devpt Agency 2003–05, chief exec Postgrad Medical Educn and Trg Bd 2005–09, dir Patient and Public Experience Dept of Health 2009–13, chief exec Lloyds Bank Fndn 2013–; health care cmmr 2002–, dep chair Health Care Cmmn 2004–; lead memb NHS Modernisation Bd 2000–03, chair Contact a Family 2011–, chair UK Rare Diseases Advsy Gp 2014–; *Recreations* my children; *Style*— Paul Streets, OBE

STRELITZ, Paloma; *b* 20 November 1987; *Educ* N London Collegiate School, Univ of Cambridge, RCA; *Career* urban and architectural designer; co-fndr Assemble (Turner Prize 2015); *Style*— Ms Paloma Strelitz

STRETTON, Prof Graham Roy; *b* 22 October 1949; *Educ* Leicester Coll of Art, Trent Poly (Dip ID); *m* Susan Marie, chartered designer; *Career* asst designer Carter Deign Group Ltd 1971–72, designer Howard Sant Partnership 1972–73, designer Lennon and Partners 1973–77, head of interior design section Carter Design Group Ltd 1977–78, co-fndr (with wife) Design & Co 1978, dir Design & Co Consultants Ltd 1987–93, design mangr under contract Interior Consultancy Services Ltd 1989–94; memb Advsy Bd for Interior Design Trent Poly, special project visiting lectr De Montfort Univ; Br Inst of Interior Design (merged with CSD 1988): memb Gen Cncl 1981–86, chm Midland dist 1983–84, chm Publications Ctee until 1986, jr vice-pres 1987, liaison offr with SIAD, Bronze Medal 1988; memb Ctee Interior Educators Forum; prof Br Acad of Fencing, sr coach Br Fencing Assoc; FCSD 1980, FBID 1982, FRSA 1987; *Recreations* fencing coach (foil, épée and sabre dips); *Style*— Prof Graham Stretton; ✉ Design & Co, 64 The Ridgeway, Market Harborough, Leicestershire LE16 7HQ (☎ 01858 462507, e-mail design.co@btconnect.com)

STRICKLAND, Benjamin Vincent Michael (Ben); s of Maj-Gen Eugene Vincent Michael Strickland, CMG, DSO, OBE, CStJ, MM, Star of Jordan (d 1982), and Barbara Lamb, da of Maj Benjamin Lamb, RFA; *b* 20 September 1939; *Educ* Mayfield Coll, UC Oxford (MA), Harvard Business Sch (Dip AMP); *m* 1965, Tessa Mary Edwina Grant, da of Rear-Adm John Grant, CB, DSO (d 1996); 1 s (Benjamin b 1968), 1 da (Columbine b 1971); *Career* Lt 17/21 Lancers BAOR 1959–60, Lt Inns of Ct and City Yeomanry TA 1964–67; Price Waterhouse & Co 1963–68, dir J Henry Schroder Wagg & Co 1974–91, chief exec Schroders Australia 1978–82, dir and gp md Schroders plc 1983–91; chm Insurance Gp (formerly Iron Trades) 1996–; review of mission and finances Westminster Cathedral 1991; memb Steering Gp for Vision for London 1991–97; advsr on strategy to leading City law firm 1992–95, advsr on strategic issues to chief execs in service and financial businesses 1994–2012, mentor to chief execs 2005–12; volunteer for reading help and organiser of book and history clubs 2004–; FCA, FRSA; *Publications* Bow Group Book on Resources of the Sea (with Laurance Reed, 1965), chapter on globalisation in Financial Services Handbook (1986); *Recreations* travel, history, films, theatre, family; *Clubs* Boodle's, Hurlingham; *Style*— Ben Strickland, Esq; ✉ 23 Juer Street, London SW11 4RE (☎ 020 7585 2970, mobile 07949 850040, fax 020 7924 5269, e-mail bvmstrickland@icloud.com)

STRIDE, Melvyn John (Mel); MP; *b* 30 September 1961, Perivale, Middx; *Educ* Portsmouth GS, Univ of Oxford; *m* Michelle, *née* Hughes; *Career* MP (Cons) Central Devon 2010–; pres Univ of Oxford Cons Assoc 1982, pres Oxford Union 1984; Tourist Bd Guide of the Year 2005; *Recreations* history, qualified tourist guide; *Clubs* RAC; *Style*— Mel Stride, Esq, MP; ✉ House of Commons, London SW1A 0AA

STRINGER, Prof Christopher Brian; s of late George Albert Stringer, and late Evelyn Beatrice, *née* Brien; *b* 31 December 1947; *Educ* East Ham GS for Boys, UCL (BSc), Univ of Bristol (PhD, DSc); *m* 2 April 1977 (m dis 2004), Rosemary Susan Margaret, da of late Leonard Peter Frank Lee; 1 da (Katherine Ann b 25 July 1979), 2 s (Paul Nicholas David b 21 Oct 1981, Thomas Peter b 9 April 1986); *Career* temp secdy sch teacher London Borough of Newham 1966; The Natural History Museum (formerly Br Museum (Natural History)): temp scientific offr 1969–70, sr res fell 1973–76, sr scientific offr 1976–86, princ scientific offr (Grade 7) 1986–, head Human Origins Gp 1990–, individual merit promotion (Grade 6) 1993–, individual merit promotion (Band 1) 2013–; visiting lectr Dept of Anthropology Harvard Univ 1979, visiting prof Royal Holloway Coll London 1995–; Br rep Int Assoc for Human Palaeontology 1986–; distinguished lectr Amer Anthropological Assoc 2000; memb: The Primate Soc 1975–, The Quaternary Research Assoc 1975–, Palaeoanthropology Soc; Lyell lectureship Br Assoc for the Advancement of Science 1988, Radcliffe lectr Green Coll Oxford 1996, Osman Hill medal 1998, Henry Stopes medal 2000, Mulvaney lectr ANU 2001, Dalrymple lectr Univ of Glasgow 2001, Rivers meml medal RAI, Frink Medal ZSL 2009, Mandela science lectr Cape Town 2009, Coke Medal Geological Soc 2011, Galton lectr Galton Soc 2011, James Croll Medal Quaternary Research Assoc 2012; Hon LLD Univ of Bristol 2000, Hon DSc Univ of Kent 2009; FRS 2004, Hon FSA 2010, fell AAAS 2011 (memb 2005); *Books* Our Fossil Relatives (with A Gray, 1983), Human Evolution – An Illustrated Guide (with P Andrews, 1989), In Search of the Neanderthals (with C Gamble, 1993, Best Archaeological Book 1994), African Exodus (with R McKie, 1996), The Complete World of Human Evolution (with P Andrews, 2005, 2 ed 2011), Homo Britannicus (2006, Kistler Award 2008, Best Archaeological Book 2008), The Origin of Our Species (2011), Lone Survivors: How We Came to be the Only Humans on Earth (2012), Britain: One Million Years of the Human Story (with R Dinnis, 2014); *Recreations* listening to music, soccer, astronomy, current affairs, travel; *Clubs* West Ham United FC; *Style*— Prof Christopher Stringer; ✉ Department of Earth Sciences, The Natural History Museum, London SW7 5BD (☎ 020 7942 5539, e-mail c.stringer@nhm.ac.uk, website www.nhm.ac.uk/our-science/departments-and-staff/staff-directory/chris-stringer)

STRINGER, Graham; MP; *Career* MP (Lab): Manchester Blackley 1997–2010, Blackley & Broughton 2010–; Parly sec Cabinet Office 1999–2001, a Lord Cmmr to HM Treasy (Govt whip) 2001–02; *Style*— Graham Stringer, Esq, MP; ✉ House of Commons, London SW1A 0AA (☎ 020 7219 3000)

STRINGER, Sir Howard; kt (2000); s of Harry Stringer, MBE, and Marjorie Mary, *née* Pook; *b* 19 February 1942, Cardiff (became a US citizen 1985); *Educ* Oundle, Univ of Oxford (MA); *m* 29 July 1978, Dr Jennifer A K Patterson; 1 s (David Ridley), 1 da (Harriet Kinmond); *Career* served US Army Vietnam 1965–67 (US Army Commendation Medal); journalist, prodr and exec CBS Inc 1965–95 (pres 1988–95, numerous awards for progs incl 9 individual Emmys), chm and ceo TELE-TV 1995–97; Sony Corporation: joined 1997, chm Sony Canada 1997–2013, chm Sony Electronics Ltd 1998–2013, chm and ceo Sony Corporation of America 1998–2013, memb Bd 1999–2013, gp vice-chm 2003–05, corporate head Sony Entertainment Business Gp 2003–13, chm and gp ceo 2005–13, rep corp exec offr, memb Bd Sony BMG Music, memb Bd Sony Ericsson, ret 2013; chm of tstees American Film Inst 1999–; memb Bd: NY Presbyterian Hosp, American Theater Wing, American Friends of the British Museum, Carnegie Hall, Teach for America, Center for Communication; memb Bd of Tstees Paley Center for Media (formerly the Museum of Television and Radio), memb Corporate Leadership Ctee Lincoln Center for the Performing Arts; hon fell: Merton Coll Oxford 2000, Welsh Coll of Music and Drama 2001; hon dr: London Inst 2003, Univ of Glamorgan 2005; honored Alliance for Lupus Res; *Awards*; Fndn Award Int Radio and TV Soc 1994, memb Broadcasting and Cable Hall of Fame 1996, First Amendment Leadership Award Radio and TV News Directors Fndn 1996, Steven J Ross Humanitarian Award UJA Fedn of NY 1999, memb Welsh Hall of Fame RTS 1999, Communication Award Centre for Communication 2000, Teach for America Annual Award 2001, Phoenix House Award 2002, Int Emmy Fndrs Award 2002, Distinguished Leadership Award NY Hall of Science 2003, Medal of Honor St George's Soc 2004; other honours from: Museum of the Moving Image 1994, Literacy Ptnrs 2002, Nat Multiple Sclerosis Soc 2002, Big Brothers and Big Sisters of NY City 2005, NY Landmarks Conservancy 2005, named one of the World's 100 Most Infulential People Time Magazine 2005, Lincoln Center for the Performing Arts 2006, Visionary Award for Innovative Leadership in Media & Entertainment Paley Center for Media 2007; *Style*— Sir Howard Stringer

STRINGER, Prof Dame Joan K; DBE (2009, CBE 2001); da of Frank Bourne, and Doris, *née* Ayres; *b* 12 May 1948, Stoke-on-Trent; *Educ* Univ of Keele (BA, PhD); *m* Roel Mali; *Career* Robert Gordon Univ: lectr then sr lectr in public admin 1980–88, head Sch of Public Admin and Law 1988–91, asst princ 1991–96; princ and vice-patron Queen Margaret UC 1996–2002, princ and vice-chllr Napier Univ 2003–13; chair Education UK Scotland 2006–11, chair Int Ctee Univs Scotland 2005–12, sr HE advsr Br Cncl 2013–; memb: Bd of Mgmnt Aberdeen Coll of FE 1992–96, Scottish Ctee Nat Ctee of Inquiry into HE (Dearing Ctee) 1996–97, Human Fertilisation and Embryology Authy 1996–99, Cncl World Assoc Cooperative Educn 1998–2002, Scottish Cncl for Postgrad Medical and Dental Educn 1999–2002, Bd HE Careers Servs Unit 2000–05, Working Gp on the Modernisation of the SHO Dept of Health 2000–02, Advsy Gp Scottish Nursing and Midwifery Educn Cncl (SNMEC) 2000–01, Scottish Health Min's Learning Together Strategy Implementation Gp 2000–01, Bd UCEA 2001–11, Equality Challenge Steering Gp Univs UK 2001–03, Bd Quality Assurance Agency for HE 2002–06, Bd HE Statistics Agency 2003–13, Bd Leadership Fndn for HE 2005–10, Royal Soc Working Gp on HE, Shadow Bd Sector Skills Cncl for Lifelong Learning; former memb Shadow Ministerial Jt Supervisory Gp Careers Scotland; auditor HEQC 1992–97; non-exec dir City Refrigeration Holdings 2013–; cmmr for Scottish Equal Opportunities Cmmn 1995–2001, chair NI Equality Cmmn Working Gp 1998–99, chair Scottish Exec's Strategic Expert Gp on Women 2003–04; non-exec dir Grampian Health Bd 1994–96; memb: Govt's Consultative Steering Gp on the Scottish Parl 1998, Exec Ctee Scottish Cncl Devpt and Industry 1998–2013, Scottish Ctee Br Cncl 2000–12, Scottish Selection Ctee Queen's Golden Jubilee Award 2001–12, Bd Judicial Appts Bd for Scotland 2002–07, China Forward Planning Gp Scottish Exec 2005–, Br C of C Hong Kong; convener: Product Standards Ctee Scottish Salmon 2001–03, Scottish Cncl for Voluntary Orgns 2001–07; memb: Cncl Edinburgh Int Festival Soc 1999–2005, Devpt Advsy Bd Scottish Opera and Scottish Ballet 2000–02, Bd HESA 2003–13, Bd Nat Theatre of Scotland 2009–, Bd UCAS

2009–13, Cncl RSE 2013–, IOD 2013–; tstee David Hume Inst, ex-officio tstee Carnegie Tst for the Univs of Scotland, tstee Community Integrated Care 2013–; fell 48 Gp Club 2006–; Hon DLitt Univ of Keele 2001, Hon Dr Univ of Edinburgh 2011, Hon Dr Open Univ 2014; MInstD, CCMI, FRSE, FRSA; hon citizen Shandong China 2007, Yellow River Friendship Award Henan Province China 2007; *Style*— Prof Dame Joan Stringer, DBE

STRONACH, Prof David Brian; OBE (1975); s of Ian David Stronach, MB, FRCS (d 1955), and Marjorie Jessie Duncan, *née* Minto (d 1997); *b* 10 June 1931; *Educ* Gordonstoun, St John's Coll Cambridge (MA); *m* 30 June 1966, Ruth Vaadia; 2 da (Keren b 1967, Tami b 1972); *Career* Nat Serv Lt 1 Bn Duke of Wellington's Regt 1950–51; Br Acad archaeological attaché in Iran 1960–61, dir Br Inst of Persian Studies 1961–80, prof of Near Eastern archaeology Univ of Calif Berkeley 1981–2004 (emeritus prof 2004–), curator of Near Eastern archaeology Hearst Museum of Anthropology Univ of Calif Berkeley 1983–2004; fell: Br Sch of Archaeology in Iraq 1957–59, Br Inst of Archaeology at Ankara 1958–59; lectureships incl: Hagop Kevorkian visiting lectr in Iranian art and archaeology Univ of Pennsylvania 1967, Rhind lectr Univ of Edinburgh 1973, Charles Eliot Norton lectr American Inst of Archaeology 1980, visiting prof of archaeology and Iranian studies Univ of Arizona 1980–81, Columbia lectr in Iranian studies Columbia Univ 1986, Charles K Wilkinson lectr Metropolitan Museum of Art NY 1990, Victor M Leventritt lectr in art history Harvard Univ 1991, visiting prof Collège de France 1999; dir of excavations at: Ras al 'Amiya Iraq 1960, Yarim Tepe Iran 1960–62, Pasargadae Iran 1961–63, Tepe Nush-i Jan Iran 1967–78, Shahr-i Qumis/Hecatompylos Iran 1967–78, Nineveh Iraq 1987–90, Erebuni Armenia 2007–10; advsy ed: The Jl of Mithraic Studies 1976–79, Iran 1981–96, Iranica Antiqua 1985–, Bulletin of the Asia Institute 1987–, American Journal of Archaeology 1989–96, Ancient West and East 2002–; Ghirshman Prize of Acad des Inscriptions et Belles Lettres Paris 1979, Sir Percy Sykes Medal Royal Soc for Asian Affrs 1980, Gold Medal of the Archaeological Inst of America for Distinguished Archaeological Achievement 2004, Northern California Phi Beta Kappa Excellence in Teaching Award 2006; corr memb German Archaeological Inst 1966–73; first hon vice-pres Br Inst of Persian Studies 1981–; assoc memb Royal Belgian Acad 1988; fell: German Archaeological Inst 1973, Explorers Club NY 1980; FSA 1963; *Books* Pasargadae A Report On The Excavations Conducted By The British Institute of Persian Studies from 1961 to 1963 (1978), Festschrift, Neo-Assyrian, Median, Achaemenian and Other Studies in Honour of D S (1998, 1999), Tepe Nush-i Jan: The Major Buildings of the Median Settlement (with Michael Roaf, 2007), Irans Erbe in Flugbildern Von Georg Gerster (with Ali Mousavi, 2009), Ancient Iran from the Air (with Ali Mousavi, 2012); *Recreations* tribal carpets, represented Univ of Cambridge in athletics 1953; *Clubs* Hawks' (Cambridge), Explorers (NY); *Style*— Prof David Stronach, OBE, FSA; ✉ Department of Near Eastern Studies, University of California, Berkeley, CA 94720–1940, USA (☎ 00 1 510 527 8663, fax 00 1 510 643 8430, e-mail stronach@berkeley.edu)

STRONG, Michael John; s of Frank James Strong (d 1987), and Ivy Rose, *née* Fruin (d 1964); *b* 27 December 1947; *Educ* Rutlish Sch Merton, Coll of Estate Mgmnt; *m* 25 April 1970, Anne Mary, da of Rev William Hurst Nightingale (d 1996); 1 s (Jonathan Alexander b 1977); *Career* chartered surveyor; early career with Prudential Assurance Co and Healey & Baker; C B Richard Ellis: joined 1972, ptnr 1977, gp dir 1997, chm Europe 2001, pres EMEA 2005; currently princ Michael Strong Consulting; Freeman: City of London 1981, Worshipful Co of Chartered Surveyors 2002; memb: Royal Acad, RHS; FRICS; *Recreations* golf, music, travel, gardens; *Clubs* RAC; *Style*— Michael Strong, Esq; ✉ The Coolins, Manor House Lane, Little Bookham, Surrey (☎ 01372 452196, mobile 07785 114787, e-mail michaelstrongconsulting@gmail.com (☎ 020 7182 2000)

STRONG, Sir Roy Colin; CH (2016), kt (1981); yst s of George Edward Clement Strong (d 1984), of Winchmore Hill, London, and Mabel Ada, *née* Smart; *b* 23 August 1935; *Educ* Edmonton Co GS, Queen Mary Coll London, Warburg Inst (PhD); *m* Sept 1971, Julia Trevelyan Oman, CBE (d 2003); *Career* writer, historian, critic (radio, TV and lectures in England and America); Nat Portrait Gallery: asst keeper 1959, dir, keeper and sec 1967–73; dir and sec V&A 1974–87; Ferens prof of fine art Univ of Hull 1972, Walls Lectures Pierpont Morgan Library 1974, Andrew Carnduff Ritchie Lectures Yale Univ 1999; vice-chm South Bank Bd 1986–90; memb: Arts Cncl of GB 1983–87 (chm Arts Panel 1983–87), Fine Arts Advsy Ctee Br Cncl 1974–87, Craft Advsy Cncl, RCA Cncl 1979–87, Br Film Inst Archive Advsy Ctee, Westminster Abbey Architectural Panel 1975–89, Historic Bldgs Cncl Historic Houses Ctee; former tstee: Arundel Castle, Chevening; Shakespeare Prize FVS Fndn Hamburg 1980; pres Garden History Soc 2004–06; High Bailiff and Searcher of the Sanctuary of Westminster Abbey 2000; Liveryman Worshipful Company of Goldsmiths; fell Queen Mary Coll London 1975, sr fell RCA 1983; Hon DLitt: Univ of Leeds 1983, Keele Univ 1984; Hon MA Univ of Worcester 2004; FSA, FRSL 1999; *Television* Royal Gardens (BBC) 1992, The Diets Time Forgot (Channel 4) 2008, The Genius of British Art 2010; *Publications* Portraits of Queen Elizabeth I (1963), Leicester's Triumph (with J A van Dorsten, 1964), Holbein and Henry VIII (1967), Tudor and Jacobean Portraits (1969), The English Icon: Elizabethan and Jacobean Portraiture (1969), Elizabeth R (with Julia Trevelyan Oman, 1971), Van Dyck – Charles I on Horseback (1972), Mary Queen of Scots (with Julia Trevelyan Oman, 1972), Inigo Jones – The Theatre of the Stuart Court (with Stephen Orgel, 1973), Splendour at Court – Renaissance Spectacle and Illusion (1973), An Early Victorian Album, The Hill/Adamson Collection (with Colin Ford, 1974), Nicholas Hilliard (1975), The Cult of Elizabeth: Elizabethan Portraiture and Pageantry (1977), And When Did You Last See Your Father? The Victorian Painter and the British Past (1978), The Renaissance Garden in England (1979), Britannia Triumphans: Inigo Jones, Rubens and Whitehall Palace (1980), Designing for the Dancer (contrib, 1981), The English Miniature (contrib, 1981), The New Pelican Guide to English Literature (contrib, 1982), The English Year (with Julia Trevelyan Oman, 1982), The English Renaissance Miniature (1983), Artists of the Tudor Court (catalogue 1983), Art and Power: Renaissance Festivals 1450–1650 (1984), Glyndebourne – A Celebration (contrib, 1984), Strong Points (1985), Henry Prince of Wales (1986), For Veronica Wedgewood These (contrib, 1986), Creating Small Gardens (1986), Gloriana (1987), A Small Garden Designer's Handbook (1987), Cecil Beaton The Royal Portraits (1988), Creating Small Formal Gardens (1989), British Theatre Arts Design (contrib, 1989), Lost Treasures of Britain (1990), England and the Continental Renaissance (contrib, 1990), Sir Philip Sidney's Achievements (contrib, 1990), A Celebration of Gardens (1991), The Garden Trellis (1991), The British Portrait (contrib, 1991), Versace Il Teatro (1991), Small Period Gardens (1992), Royal Gardens (1992), The Art of the Emblem (contrib, 1993), William Larkin (1994), A Country Life (1994), Successful Small Gardens (1994), The Tudor and Stuart Monarchy (3 vols, 1995–97), The Story of Britain (1996), Country Life 1897–1997 – The English Vision (1996), The Roy Strong Diaries 1967–1987 (1997), Happiness (1997), The Spirit of Britain: A Narrative History of the Arts (1999, reissued as The Arts in Britain. A History 2003), Garden Party (2000), The Artist and the Garden (2000), Ornament in the Small Garden (2001), Feast: A History of Grand Eating (2002), The Laskett: The Story of a Garden (2003), Coronation: A History of Kingship and the British Monarchy (2005), A Little History of the English Country Church (2007), Visions of England (2011), Self-Portrait as a Young Man (2013), Remaking a Garden, The Laskett Transformed (2014); *Recreations* gardening, weight training; *Clubs* Garrick; *Style*— Sir Roy Strong, CH, FSA, FRSL; ✉ The Laskett, Much Birch, Herefordshire HR2 8HZ

STROUD, Dr Michael (Mike); OBE (1993); s of Victor Stroud, of Ridley, Kent, and Vivienne Richardson, *née* Zelegman; *b* 17 April 1955, London; *Educ* Trinity Sch Croydon, UCL (BSc), St George's Hosp Med Sch (MB BS), Univ of London (MD); *m* 1987, Thea, *née* de Moel; 1 s (Callan b 2 Dec 1987), 1 da (Tarn b 17 April 1990); *Career* doctor and explorer; various NHS trg posts 1979–85, NHS registrar in med 1987–89, research in human performance 1989–95 (latterly chief scientist in physiology Defence Research Agency Centre for Human Scis), research fell in nutrition and sr registrar in gastroenterology Southampton Univ Hosps NHS Tst 1995–98, conslt gastroenterologist and sr lectr in med, gastroenterology and nutrition Southampton Univ Hosps NHS Tst 1998–; Footsteps of Scott Antarctic expdn 1985–86, 5 North Pole expdns 1986–90, crossed Antarctic with Sir Ranulph Fiennes 1992–93 (first unsupported crossing in history), ldr UK team Marathon of the Sands Sahara Desert 1994, Eco-Challenge adventure race 1995 and 1996, first unsupported, non-stop desert crossing of Qatar 2002, seven full marathons on seven continents in seven days with Sir Ranulph Fiennes 2003; various TV and radio appearances incl as endurance expert Are You Tough Enough for the SAS (BBC) and presenter The Challenge (BBC); Polar Medal 1994; memb Physiology Soc 1994; MRCP (UK) 1984, FRCP (London and Edinburgh) 1995; FRGS 1994; *Books* Shadows on The Wasteland (1993), Survival of The Fittest (1998); *Recreations* Polar travel, mountaineering, sea kayaking; *Style*— Dr Mike Stroud, OBE

STROWGER, Clive; OBE (2013); s of Gaston Jack Strowger, CBE, and Kathleen, *née* Gilbert; *b* 4 July 1941; *Educ* Univ Coll Sch Hampstead; *m* 23 Jan 1965, Deirdre Majorie, da of Col Bertram Stuart Trevelyan Archer, GC, OBE; 3 s (Timothy b 26 Aug 1968, Andrew b 18 Dec 1969, Stephen b 29 Sept 1980), 1 da (Louise b 2 June 1975); *Career* various managerial positions Ford Motor Co 1966–71, sr fin mgmnt positions then fin dir BL Int British Leyland Corp 1971–77, Grand Metropolitan 1977–90 (md brewing, chief exec consumer servs, chm and chief exec foods, gp fin dir and chief exec retail and property), chief exec Mountleigh Group plc 1990–91, mgmnt conslt 1991–92, chief exec APV plc 1992–94; chm: London First Centre 1997, Walters Hexagon Ltd 1998, Starpoint Electrics 1998, Focus Central London TEC 1999; chm Advsy Bd Merchant International Gp 1998, memb Bd London First 1995– (treas); advsr and conslt to various companies; non-exec dir deltaDOT Ltd 2005–; Freeman Worshipful Co of Brewers; FCA 1965, ATII 1965, CIMgt 1990; *Recreations* choral singing, family, tennis, skiing; *Style*— Clive Strowger, Esq, OBE

STRUDLEY, Brig David; CBE (1991, OBE 1988, MBE 1986); s of Frank Walter Henry Strudley, and Peggy Doris Strudley; *b* 10 October 1947, Portsmouth; *Educ* Portsmouth Sch, RMA Sandhurst (Commandant's Commendation), Army Tech Staff Coll (MSc), Open Univ (MBA), Univ of Leeds (MA); *m* Tracey Jane; 3 da (Rachel, Hannah, Emily); *Career* cmmnd RSigs 1968, transferred to 9/12 Royal Lancers (Prince of Wales's) 1972; CO 2 (Co Armagh) Bn Ulster Defence Regt 1986–88, directing staff RMCS 1988–89, Dir of Ops HQ NI 1989–91, sr mil advsr Defence Res Agency 1991–93, COS HQ NI 1993–96; Dep Col Royal Irish Regt 1997–2008, pres Royal Br Legion NI 1997–2007, md Police Rehabilitation and Retraining Tst 2000–03, ceo Naomi House 2003–05, dir and princ Police Acad NI 2005–06, ceo Acorns 2006–; registrar Methodist Coll 1997–2000; chm Together for Short Lives UK Transition Taskforce 2012–; memb Inst of Counselling 1992, MInstD 1996; FIMgt 1987 (MIMgt 1982), FRSA 2008; *Books* Military Technology Handbook (ed, 1988); *Recreations* walking, field sports, furniture restoration; *Style*— Mr David Strudley, CBE, FRSA; ✉ Acorns Children's Hospice Trust, Drake's Court, Alcester Road, Wythall, West Midlands B47 6JR (☎ 01564 825009, e-mail david.strudley@acorns.org.uk)

STRUDWICK, Maj-Gen Mark Jeremy; CBE (1990); s of late Ronald Strudwick, and late Mary, *née* Beresford; *b* 19 April 1945; *Educ* St Edmund's Sch Canterbury, RMAS; *m* 1, 1970, Janet Elizabeth Coleridge (d 2013), da of late Lt Col J R Vivers; 1 s, 1 da; m 2, 2015, Susan Jennifer, da of Dr Douglas Guest, CVO; 2 step-s, 1 step-da; *Career* cmmnd The Royal Scots (The Royal Regiment) 1966 (Col 1995–2005), served in UK, BAOR, Cyprus, Canada, India, NI (despatches twice), cmd 1 Bn Royal Scots 1984–87, instr Staff Coll Camberley 1987–88, ACOS G1/G4 HQ NI 1988–90, Higher Command and Staff Course 1989, cmd 3 Inf Bde 1990–91, NDC New Delhi 1992, Dep Mil Sec MOD 1993–95, Dir of Inf 1996–97, ADC to HM The Queen 1996–97, Col Cmdt The Scottish Div 1997–2000, GOC Scotland and Govr Edinburgh Castle 1997–2000; memb Queen's Body Guard for Scotland (Royal Co of Archers) 1994– (Brig 2006, Ensign 2016); cmmr Queen Victoria Sch Dunblane 1997–2000; govr: Royal Sch Bath 1993–2000, Gordonstoun 1999–2007, Excelsior Acad Newcastle 2009–15; dir Edinburgh Military Tattoo 2007–15; chief exec The Prince's Scottish Youth Business Tst 2000–12, tstee Historic Scotland Fndn 2001–15, chm Scottish Veterans Residences 2001–16, chm Scottish Nat War Meml 2009–; Cdre Infantry Sailing Assoc 1997–2000; Prior Order of St John Scotland 2015–; CCMI 2002; KStJ 2015; *Recreations* golf, shooting, fishing, sailing; *Clubs* The Royal Scots (tstee 1995–, chm of tsetse 2015–), Highlands and Lowland Brigades' (pres 2007–); *Style*— Maj-Gen Mark Strudwick, CBE; ✉ Scottish National War Memorial, The Castle, Edinburgh EH1 2YT (☎ 0131 226 7393)

STRUTHERS, Prof Allan David; s of Dr David Struthers (d 1987), of Glasgow, and Margaret Thompson, *née* Adams (d 1989); *b* 14 August 1952; *Educ* Hutchesons' Boys' GS Glasgow, Univ of Glasgow (BSc, MB ChB, MD); *m* Julia Elizabeth Anne, da of Robert Diggens (d 1993); 1 da (Kate Lisa b 1980), 1 s (Gordon Allan Benjamin b 1982); *Career* jr then SHO Glasgow Teaching Hosps 1977–80, registrar then research fell Dept of Materia Medica Stobhill Hosp Glasgow 1980–82, sr med registrar Royal Postgraduate Med Sch and Hammersmith Hosp London 1982–85, sr lectr, reader then prof Dept of Clinical Pharmacology Ninewells Hosp and Med Sch Dundee 1985–, prof of cardiovascular med Univ of Dundee; SKB Prize for Research in Clinical Pharmacology (Br Pharmacological Soc) 1990; memb Assoc of Physicians of GB and I 1992; FRCP, FRCPE, FESC 1994, FRSE 2010, FMedSci 2011; *Books* Atrial Natriuretic Factor (1990); *Recreations* cycling, travel, walking, opera; *Style*— Prof Allan Struthers

STUART, HE Christopher Charles; *m* 1986, Isabelle Julie Louise; 1 s (William Charles Oliver b 9 July 1993); *Career* diplomat; devpt chemist 1982–86, HM inspr of heath and safety Health and Safety Exec 1986–96, pt/t lectr Basford Hall Coll 1993–97, first sec science and technol Tokyo 1997–2001, head Nr East and North Africa Unit UKTI 2001–02, Japanese language trg 2003–04, head of investment and dep consul gen W Japan 2004–07, consul gen and head UKTI Osaka 2007–09, on secondment as dir corp devpt Energy Technologies Inst 2009–12, ambass to Mongolia 2012–; *Style*— HE Mr Christopher Stuart; ✉ c/o Foreign & Commonwealth Office (Ulaanbaatar), King Charles Street, London SW1A 2AH

STUART, Rt Hon Gisela Gschaider; PC (2015), MP; *b* 26 November 1955; *Educ* Realschule Vilsbiburg, Manchester Poly, Univ of London (LLB); *m* 1, 1980 (m dis 2000), Robert Scott Stuart; 2 s; m 2, 2010, Derek Scott (d 2012); *Career* MP (Lab) Birmingham Edgbaston 1997–; memb House of Commons Social Security Select Ctee 1997–98, PPS to Paul Boateng, MP, *qv*, as min of state at the Home Office 1998–99, Parly under-sec Dept of Health 1999–2001; memb: Foreign Affairs Select Ctee 2001–10, Defence Select Ctee 2010–, Intelligence and Security Ctee 2015–; ed The House magazine; rep Convention on Future of Europe; tstee: Westminster Fndn, Henry Jackson Soc; *Publications* The Making of Europe's Constitution (2003); *Style*— The Rt Hon Gisela Stuart, MP; ✉ House of Commons, London SW1A 0AA (☎ 020 7219 3000)

STUART, Graham; MP; s of Peter Stuart (d 2005), and Joan Stuart; *b* 1962, Carlisle; *Educ* Glenalmond Coll, Selwyn Coll Cambridge; *m* Anne; 2 da (Sophie, Katie); *Career* chm Cambridge Univ Cons Assoc 1985; sole proprietor Go Enterprises 1984–, dir CSL Publishing 1987–; ldr Cons Gp Cambridge CC 2000; Parly candidate (Cons) Cambridge

2001, MP (Cons) Beverley and Holderness 2005–; project dir Cons Pty Yorks and Humberside 2006–07; memb Cons Pty Bd 2006–10; chm Educn Select Ctee 2010–; fndr Beverley and Holderness Pensioners' Action Gp, chm Community Hosps Acting Nationally Together, chm East Riding Health Action Gp 2007; *Style—* Graham Stuart, Esq, MP; ✉ House of Commons, London SW1A 0AA (e-mail graham@grahamstuart.com, website www.grahamstuart.com)

STUART, Sir (James) Keith; kt (1986); s of James Stuart, and Marjorie Stuart; *b* 4 March 1940; *Educ* King George V Sch Southport, Gonville & Caius Coll Cambridge (MA); *m* 1966, Kathleen Anne Pinder, *née* Woodman; 3 s, 1 da; *Career* dist mangr S Western Electricity Bd 1970–72; sec British Transport Docks Bd 1972–75, gen mangr 1976–77, md 1977–82, dep chm 1980–82, chm 1982–83; chm: Associated British Ports Holdings plc 1983–2002, Seeboard plc 1992–96; pres Inst of Freight Forwarders 1983–84, dir Int Assoc of Ports and Harbors 1983–2000 (vice-pres 1985–87); dir: Royal Ordnance Factories 1983–85, BAA plc 1986–92, City of London Investment Tst 1999–2011, RMC Gp plc 1999–2005, Mallett plc 2005–06; advsr Gas and Electricity Markets Authy 2007– (memb 2000–06); pres Br Quality Fndn 1997–2000; chm UK–South Africa Trade Assoc 1988–93, vice-chm Southern Africa Business Assoc 1995–2002; memb Cncl CIT 1979–88 (vice-pres 1982–83, pres 1985–86); chm Trinity Coll London 2009–15 (dir 1992–, pres emeritus 2015–), chm of tstees Trinity Coll of Music 2008– (tstee 2001–, govr 1991–2003), chm of tstees Cambridge Univ Musical Soc 2012–; govr Nat Youth Orch of GB 1997–2004; vice-chm Mgmnt Bd and chm Advsy Cncl London Mozart Players 2002–09; Freeman City of London 1985, Liveryman Worshipful Co of Clockmakers 1987 (memb Ct of Assts 1998–); FCILT, FRSA, Hon FTCL 1998; *Recreations* music; *Clubs* Brooks's, Oxford and Cambridge (tstee 1989–94); *Style—* Sir Keith Stuart

STUART, Prof Mary; da of Isobel Thompson, and Thomas Cleary; *b* 4 March 1957, Cape Town; *Educ* Chisipite Senior Sch Harare Zimbabwe, Univ of Cape Town (BA), Open Univ (BA, DPhil); *m* 1978, Douglas Ian Stuart; 2 d (Adryon, Myra b 8 Aug 1982 (twins)); *Career* community theatre co-ordinator and people's educn worker The People's Space Theatre Cape Town 1979–81, drama teacher Westminster Play Assoc 1981–82, dir Cast Underground Community Theatre London 1984–87, lectr in women's educn Streatham and Tooting Adult Educn Inst 1987–89, sr lectr in special educn Lambeth Community Coll 1990–91, lectr in continuing educn Univ of Sussex 1991–95, asst dir Centre for Continuing Educn Univ of Sussex 1995–2000, dir Inst of Educn Univ of Sussex 2000–01, assoc research dir Nat Co-ordinating Team for the HEFCE, DfES and the LSC 2001–05, pro-vice-chllr Univ of Sussex 2000–05, dep vice-chllr Kingston Univ, vice-chllr Univ of Lincoln 2009–; memb Bd HEFCE, chair Social Mobility Advsy Gp UUK, chair Academic Reference Gp UUK; dir greater Lincolnshire Local Enterprise Partnership; FHEA, FRSA; *Publications* incl: Engaging with Difference: The 'Other' in Adult Education (with A Thomson, 1995), Collaborating for Change? Managing Widening Participation in Further and Higher Education (2002), Not Quite Sisters: Women with Learning Difficulties and Social Policy (2002), Social Mobility and Higher Education: the Life Experience of First Generation Entrants in Higher Education (2012); numerous chapters in pubns and articles in jls on education, adult learning, learning difficulties, social mobility and widening participation in HE; *Recreations* cinema, music, opera, modern art, travel, jazz, theatre, film; *Style—* Prof Mary Stuart; ✉ University of Lincoln, Brayford Pool, Lincoln LN6 7TS (☎ 01522 886100, e-mail mstuart@lincoln.ac.uk, website www.lincoln.ac.uk)

STUART, Nicholas Willoughby; CB (1992); s of Douglas Willoughby Stuart (d 2013), and Margaret Eileen, *née* Holms (d 2013); *b* 2 October 1942; *Educ* Harrow, ChCh Oxford (MA); *m* 1, July 1963 (m dis 1974), Sarah, *née* Mustard; 1 s (Sebastian b 26 Dec 1963 d 1976), 1 da (Henrietta b 21 March 1965); m 2, 30 Dec 1974, Susan Jane Fletcher, *qv*; 1 da (Emily Fletcher b 12 Sept 1983), 1 s (Alexander Fletcher b 1 Feb 1989); *Career* asst princ DES 1964–68, private sec to Min of Arts 1968–69, princ DES 1969–73; private sec to: Head of Civil Serv 1973, PM 1973–76; asst sec DES 1976–79, memb Cabinet of Pres of Euro Cmmn 1979–81, under sec DES 1981–87, dep sec DES 1987–92, dir of resources and strategy Dept of Employment 1992–95, DG for Employment and Lifelong Learning DfEE 1995–2000, DG for Lifelong Learning DfEE 2000–01; pres Nat Inst for Adult Continuing Educn (NIACE) 2012 (chm 2003–12), pres Nat Inst for Learning and Work 2012–; memb: Bd Univ for Industry (UFI) 2001–07, Cncl Inst of Educn Univ of London 2001–10, Curriculum and Qualifications Authy 2002–10, CAFCASS 2003–12, Cncl GDST 2003–12; tstee: Policy Studies Inst 2002–09, Harrow Mission 2000–, Primary Shakespeare Company 2014–; hon treas Br Assoc for Adoption and Fostering 2015–; chm Specialist Schs and Acads Tst 2009–11 (memb 2005–08), chm John Lyon's Charity 2002–10 (memb Ctee 1996–); chair of govrs Edward Wilson Primary Sch 2002–12, govr Harrow Sch 1996–2009; *Recreations* allotment gardening, english canals; *Style—* Nicholas Stuart, Esq, CB; ✉ 181 Chevening Road, London NW6 6DT (e-mail nwstuart@gmail.com)

STUART (aka CHOW-STUART), Alexander Charles; s of Alfred William Noble Stuart, of Sussex, and Eileen Lucy Stuart; *b* 27 January 1955, Bexley, London; *Educ* Bexley GS; *m* 1998, Charong Chow; 1 s (Hudson b 2004), 1 da (Paradise Rose b 2009); 1 s by Ann Totterdell (Joe Buffalo b 15 Aug 1983 d 1989); *Career* writer; author of film criticism and various screenplays; exec prodr Insignificance (film, dir Nicolas Roeg) 1985; screenwriter: Agatha Christie's Ordeal By Innocence (film, dir Desmond Davis) 1985, The War Zone (film, dir Tim Roth) 1999, Under The Skin (film, dir Jonathan Glazer) 2014, Love Me Haiti (short film, dir Hugues Gentillon) 2014; writer and presenter TV documentary The End of America (dir Laura Ashton) 1999; prof of film Univ of Miami 1994–97; exhbn Words & Images (Pérez Art Museum) 1997; film writing workshops Central Sierra Arts Cncl 2012; *Books* novels: Glory B (1983), The War Zone (1989, short-listed Whitbread award 1989), Tribes (1992); children's books: Joe, Jo-Jo and the Monkey Masks (1988), Henry and the Sea (with Joe Buffalo Stuart, 1989); non-fiction: Five and a Half Times Three: The Short Life and Death of Joe Buffalo Stuart (with Ann Totterdell, 1990), Life on Mars (1996), The War Zone (published screenplay, 1999); *Recreations* family, Buddhism, China, swimming, bodyboarding, gardening, peace, our dogs Husky Go-Go and Orzo and our lovebird, Miso; *Clubs* Groucho, Writers Guild of America, Shanghai Business, Connected Shanghai; *Style—* Alexander Chow-Stuart, Esq; ✉ e-mail tranquilbuddha@gmail.com, website www.alexanderstuart.com; c/o Charles Walker, United Agents, 12–26 Lexington Street, London W1F 0LE (☎ 020 3214 0800, fax 020 3214 0801, website www.unitedagents.co.uk)

STUART TAYLOR, Sir Nicholas Richard; 4 Bt (UK 1917), of Kennington, Co London; s of Sir Richard Laurence Stuart Taylor, 3 Bt (d 1978), and Lady Stuart Taylor; Sir Frederick Taylor, 1 Bt was pres of RCP; *b* 14 January 1952; *Educ* Bradfield; *m* 1984 (m dis 1999), Malvena Elizabeth Sullivan; 2 da (Virginia Caterina b 1989, Olivia Malvena b 1991); *Heir* none; *Career* slr 1977; *Recreations* skiing and other sports; *Style—* Sir Nicholas Stuart Taylor, Bt; ✉ 30 Siskin Close, Bishops Waltham, Hampshire SO32 1RQ

STUART-MOORE, Hon Mr Justice; Hon Michael Stuart-Moore; QC; s of Kenneth Basil Moore (d 1987), and Marjorie Elizabeth, *née* Hodges; *b* 7 July 1944; *Educ* Cranleigh Sch; *m* 8 Dec 1973, Katherine Ann, da of Kenneth William and Ruth Scott; 1 s (James b 1976), 1 da (Zoe-Olivia b 1978); *Career* called to the Bar Middle Temple 1966; dep circuit judge 1981, recorder of the Crown Court 1985–, QC 1990, judge of the High Court Hong Kong 1993–97, judge of the Court of Appeal Hong Kong 1997–99, vice-pres of the Court of Appeal Hong Kong 1999–2009, dep judge of the High Court Hong Kong 2010–; chm: Market Misconduct Bd 2011–15, Securities and Futures Appeals Tbnl 2012–14, Mandatory Provident Fund Schemes Appeal Bd 2012–14; Gold Bauhinia Star 2009;

Recreations photography, flute, tennis, travel; *Clubs* Hong Kong, Hong Kong Cricket; *Style—* The Hon Mr Justice Stuart-Moore, QC, GBS; ✉ e-mail michaelstuartmoore@hotmail.com

STUART-SMITH, Rt Hon Sir Murray; KCMG (2012), kt (1981), PC (1988); s of Edward Stuart-Smith, and Doris, *née* Laughland; *b* 18 November 1927, Enfield; *Educ* Radley, CCC Cambridge; *m* 1953, Joan; 3 s, 3 da; *Career* called to the Bar Gray's Inn 1952 (bencher 1978, vice-treas 1997–98, treas 1998–99); QC 1970, recorder of the Crown Court 1972–81, judge of the High Court of Justice (Queen's Bench Div) 1981–87, presiding judge Western Circuit 1982–86, a Lord Justice of Appeal 1987–2000; pres Court of Appeal of Gibraltar 2007– (judge 2001–), judge Court of Appeal of Bermuda 2004–; cmmr for Security Service 1989, cmmr for Intelligence Services 1994, chm Proscribed Organisations Appeal Cmmn 2001, chm Pathogens Access Appeal Cmmn 2002; memb Criminal Injuries Compensation Bd 1979–81; hon fell CCC Cambridge 1994; *Recreations* playing cello, shooting, building, playing bridge; *Style—* The Rt Hon Sir Murray Stuart-Smith, KCMG; ✉ Royal Courts of Justice, Strand, London WC2A 2LL

STUART-SMITH, Stephen James Adrian; s of D M Stuart-Smith, of Leics; *b* 18 August 1954; *Educ* Smallwood Manor, Denstone Coll, KCL (BA), Inst of Educn Univ of London (PGCE), Univ of Reading (MA); *Partner* Marco Livingstone, *qv* (civil partnership 20 Jan 2006); *Career* bookseller 1977–78, teacher 1978–85; head History Dept: Lord Wandsworth Coll Long Sutton 1985–88, Ditcham Park Sch Petersfield 1988–89; md Enitharmon Press Ltd 1987–, md Enitharmon Editions Ltd 2001–; administrator Ben Nicholson, David Hockney and Aubrey Beardsley exhibitions for Japan 1992–98; literature assessor London Arts Bd 1994–96, memb Literature Advsy Gp London Arts Bd 1996–2000; memb Ctee Edward Thomas Fellowship 1986–94, memb London Philharmonic Choir 1999–2007; chair The Poetry Sch 1997–2003; memb Assoc Internationale des Critiques d'Art 1997–; FRSA 1990; *Publications* An Enitharmon Anthology (1990); contrib The Times, The Independent and literary jls; *Recreations* music, theatre; *Style—* Stephen Stuart-Smith, Esq; ✉ Enitharmon Editions Ltd, 10 Bury Place, London WC1A 2JL (e-mail stephen@enitharmon.co.uk)

STUART-SMITH, Tom; s of Sir Murray Stuart-Smith, *qv*, and Joan, *née* Motion; *b* 14 February 1960, Watford, Herts; *Educ* Univ of Cambridge, Univ of Manchester; *m* 30 May 1986, Dr Sue, *née* Evans; 1 da (Rose b 1988), 2 s (Ben b 1990, Harry b 1992); *Career* landscape architect 1984–; dir Elizabeth Banks Assocs, fndr Tom Stuart-Smith Ltd 1998–; 8 Gold Medals Chelsea Flower Show (incl Best in Show 2003, 2006 and 2008); memb Landscape Inst 1987; *Projects* incl: Broughton Grange 2000, Woodperry 2000, Windsor Castle (new garden to mark the Queen's Golden Jubilee) 2002, Italian Garden Trentham Staffs, Mount St John 2006, Bicentenary Glasshouse Garden Wisley 2007, The Garden of Illusion at the Connaught 2013, Keeper's House Garden RA 2013; *Books* The Barn Garden: Making a Place (2011); *Recreations* music (violin); *Style—* Tom Stuart-Smith, Esq; ✉ Greenhill House, 90–93 Cowcross Street, London EC1M 6BF (website www.tomstuartsmith.co.uk)

STUBBS, Dawne Alison; da of William Thomas Telford, of Thrapston, Northamptonshire, and Janet Christine, *née* Smith; *b* 8 June 1967; *Educ* Prince William Sch Oundle, Tresham Coll Kettering, Huddersfield Poly (BSc, awards for design in knitwear); *m* 6 July 1996, Philip Michael Stubbs; 2 s (Elliott Edward b 1 March 1999, Henry William b 19 Sept 2002); *Career* asst designer Lister & Co plc colour yarn spinners 1987–88, designer Pierre Sangan Leicester and CI 1989–92, head of design John Smedley Ltd knitwear design 1992–2001, product/design mangr Sara Lee Courtaulds 2003–05; John Smedley Ltd: brand mangr 2005–08, creative dir 2008–; winner Br Fashion Award for Classics Royal Albert Hall 1997; *Recreations* dressmaking, languages, knitting, swimming; *Style—* Mrs Philip Stubbs

STUBBS, Imogen Mary; da of Robin Desmond Scrivener Stubbs (d 1974), and Heather Mary, *née* McCracken (d 1986); *b* 20 February 1961; *Educ* St Paul's Girls', Westminster, Exeter Coll Oxford (scholar, BA), RADA (Silver medallist, John Barton Award in Stagefighting); *m* 1994, Sir Trevor Nunn, *qv*; 1 da (Ellie b 1991), 1 s (Jesse b 1996); *Career* actress; numerous contrib book reviews and interviews (incl: The Times, The Observer, The Guardian, Daily Mail, Daily Express); *Theatre* incl: Cabaret (Ipswich) 1985, The Boyfriend (Ipswich) 1985, Two Noble Kinsmen, The Rover and Richard II (all RSC) 1986–87 (Critics' Award for Most Promising Newcomer, nominated Olivier Award for Best Newcomer), Othello (RSC) 1989, Heartbreak House (Yvonne Arnaud Guildford and Haymarket) 1992, St Joan (Strand), Uncle Vanya (Chichester and Albery), A Street Car Named Desire (Haymarket) 1997, Blast From the Past (West Yorkshire Playhouse), Closer (Lyric) 1998, Betrayal (RNT) 1999, The Relapse (RNT) 2001, Three Sisters (Theatre Royal Bath and Southampton) 2002, Mum's the Word (Albert Theatre) 2003; *Television* incl: Deadline (BBC) 1987, The Rainbow (BBC) 1988 (Best Actress in a Series Chicago Film Festival, nominated Best Actress Royal Variety Television Awards), Relatively Speaking (BBC) 1989, Anna Lee (ITV), After The Dance (BBC), Heartbreak House, Mothertime (BBC), Othello (BBC), Blind Ambition (ITV), Big Kids; *Radio* incl: Private Lives, No Way Out, Il Cid, La Bête Humaine, When the Dead Awaken, As You Like It; *Film* incl: Nanou 1985, A Summer Story 1987 (Best Actress Evening Standard Film Awards), Erik The Viking 1988, Fellow Traveller 1989, True Colors 1990, Sandra C'est la Vie 1993, A Pin for the Butterfly 1994, Jack and Sarah 1995, Sense and Sensibility 1995, Twelfth Night 1996, Collusion 2003; *Books* The Undiscovered Road (contrib), Amazonians; *Style—* Miss Imogen Stubbs

STUBBS, John Stephen; MBE (2006); s of John Stubbs, of Warrington, and May, *née* Gibson; *b* 12 July 1965, Withington, Manchester; *Educ* Bradbury Boys Sch, North Trafford Coll; *Children* 1 s (Michael John); *Career* Paralympic archer; World Class Performance Prog UK Sport 2005–; achivements incl: IPC World Champion 2005, IPC Grand Prix Champion 2006, 2008 and 2009, Gold medal men's compound open Paralympics Beijing 2008, World Team Champion 2011, 50m world record holder, 70m Paralympic record holder; memb Grand Nat Archery Soc, memb World Archery; fabrication engr Tilghman Wheelabrator Ltd 1981–92, sales advsr Cyclone Wheelchairs Ltd 1995–2005; *Clubs* North Cheshire Bowmen, Royal Richmond Archery, Eccles Archery; *Style—* John Stubbs, Esq, MBE; ✉ 52 Oakdene Avenue, Woolston, Warrington, Cheshire WA1 4NU (☎ 07738 718050, e-mail john.stubbs2@sky.com); c/o British Paralympic Association, 40 Bernard Street, London WC1N 1ST

STUBBS, Rebecca; QC (2012); da of James Stuart Stubbs, of Barnsley, S Yorks, and Diane, *née* Rennison; *b* 29 September 1971, Barnsley, S Yorks; *Educ* Darton HS Barnsley, Downing Coll Cambridge (sr Harris scholar, Squire scholar); *m* 13 Dec 2007, Sharif Asim Shivji; 2 s (Orson Xerxes Stubbs Shivji b April 2010, Orlando Tiberius Stubbs Shivji b Aug 2011); *Career* called to the Bar: Middle Temple 1994 (Harmsworth entrance exhibitioner, Queen Mother scholar, master of the bench 2013), Supreme Court of Grenada and WI Associated States 2005; jr counsel to the Crown 2000–07; vice-chm Access to the Bar Ctee of the Bar Cncl 2007; barr rep Insolvency Court Users' Ctee; memb: Chancery Bar Assoc 1994 (memb Ctee 2013–, chm Equality and Diversity Sub-Ctee 2013–), Commercial Bar Assoc (COMBAR) 1996, Bar Cncl OCOF Working Gp 2008, Bar Standards Bd Working Gp on Alternative Business Structures 2008–09, Advocates for International Devpt, RISA 2015–; advocacy tutor Lincoln's Inn and the South Eastern Circuit; second dan black belt Shotokan karate, represented England JKA Euro Championships Bochum Germany 1997, represented GB ITU age group World Triathlon Championships Edmonton Canada 2001 and Cancun Mexico 2002; memb and level 1 qualified instructor Canadian Ski Instructors' Alliance 2008, memb and qualified instructor Swimming Teachers' Assoc 2014–; FRSA 2004; *Books* Butterworths Practical

Insolvency (contrib, 1999), Mithani on Directors Disqualification (contrib, 2002), French on Applications to Wind Up Companies (conslt ed, 2007), Butterworths Guide to the Legal Services Act 2007 (contrib, 2009); *Recreations* skiing (alpine and cross-country); *Clubs* Kandahar; *Style*— Miss Rebecca Stubbs, QC; ✉ Maitland Chambers, 7 Stone Buildings, Lincoln's Inn, London WC2A 3SZ (✆ 020 7406 1200, fax 020 7406 1300, e-mail rstubbs@maitlandchambers.com)

STUBBS, Una; da of Clarence Stubbs, of London, and Kathleen Angela Stubbs; *b* 1 May 1937; *Educ* Baylis Court Secdy Modern Sch Slough, La Roche Dancing Sch Slough; *m* 1, March 1960 (m dis), Peter Gilmor; 1 s (Jason); m 2, Oct 1969 (m dis), Nicky Henson, *qv*; 2 s (Christian, Joe); *Career* actress; *Theatre* Theatre Royal Windsor incl: A Midsummer Night's Dream 1952, Quadrille 1953, The Sun and I 1953, Goody Two Shoes 1953; other credits incl: London Palladium Revue 1954, London Royal Variety Show 1954, 1972 and 1982, Folies Bergères (Prince of Wales) 1955, Star Maker (Manchester Hippodrome) 1956, Grab Me A Gondola (Lyric) 1957, On The Brighter Side (Phoenix) 1960, Aladdin (London Palladium) 1964, A Taste of Honey and The Diary of Anne Frank (Westcliffe) 1966, A Soldier's Tale (Edinburgh Festival and The Young Vic) 1967, The Knack (Golders Green Hippodrome) 1967, Jane Eyre (Adelee Genee Theatre) 1968, Little Malcolm and His Struggle Against The Eunuchs (Young Vic) 1968, Cowardy Custard (Mermaid) 1972, Cole (Mermaid) 1974, Irma La Douce (Watford) 1975, Aladdin (Richmond) 1976, Cinderella (Bromley) 1978, Oh Mr Porter (Mermaid) 1979, Dick Whittington (Richmond) 1979, Baggage (Adelphi) 1980, Worzel Gummidge (Birmingham Rep 1981, Cambridge Theatre London 1982), The Secret Life of Cartoons (Aldwych) 1986, Bless The Bride (Sadlers Wells) 1987, It Runs in The Family (Yvonne Arnaud Theatre Guildford) 1988, Run for Your Wife (Criterion) 1988, She Stoops to Conquer (Royal Exchange) 1989, Rumours (Chichester) 1990, Days of Hope (Hampstead) 1991, An Ideal Husband (Royal Exchange Manchester) 1992, Big Night Out At Little Sands Picture Palace (Nottingham Playhouse) 1993, Peter Pan (West Yorkshire Playhouse) 1996, Philadelphia Story (Royal Exchange) 1996, Deep Blue Sea (Mercury Theatre Colchester) 1996, Twelfth Night (Sheffield Crucible), As You Like It (Sheffield Crucible and Lyric Hammersmith), Country Wife (Sheffield Crucible), Star Quality (Apollo) 2001; *Television* BBC incl: Compact, Wayne and Shuster, Boy Meets Girl, Cliff in Scandinavia, Cole, Roy Castle Show, The Rivals of Sherlock Holmes, Morecambe and Wise, The Harry Secombe Show, Happy Families, Fawlty Towers, The Dick Emery Show, It's Cliff Richard, Till Death Us Do Part, In Sickness And In Health, Morris Minar's Marvellous Motors, Tricky Business, Keeping Up Appearances, Wings, EastEnders, Sherlock, The Bleak Old Shop of Stuff; other credits incl: Cool for Cats (Rediffusion), Worzel Gummidge (Southern ITV), Worzel Gummidge Down Under (Channel 4), Give Us A Clue (Thames ITV), Woolcraft This Morning (Granada), Off the Cuff (Granada), Threads (Granada), Heartbeat (YTV), Midsomer Murders (Carlton), Worst Witch (Carlton), Casualty (Carlton); *Films* incl: Summer Holiday, 3 Hats for Lisa, Wonderful Life, Till Death Us Do Part; *Recreations* embroidery, dressmaking, cycling, water colouring; *Style*— Ms Una Stubbs

STUCHFIELD, Nicolas John (Nic); s of Clifford Roy and Ann Stuchfield; *b* 13 January 1960; *Educ* Forest Sch, Magdalen Coll Oxford (MA); *m* 28 June 1986, Jill, *née* Pendleton; 2 s (Alexander (Sandy) b 2 Feb 1992, James b 12 Aug 1996), 1 da (Lucy b 2 Sept 1993); *Career* ptnr Wedd Durlacher Mordaunt & Co 1985–86, dir BZW Securities 1988–95, chief operating offr BZW Equities 1992–95, chief operating offr and chief investment offr Global Index Investments Barclays Global Investors 1995–97, ceo Tradepoint Financial Networks plc 1997–99, md The Stuchfield Consultancy Ltd 1999–2004, chm Totem Market Valuations Ltd 2002–04, md EDX London Ltd 2003–06; London Stock Exchange plc: head of derivative products 2003–06, dir for corp devpt 2004–08; dir MTS SpA 2007–09, sr strategy advsr SIS x-clear AG 2009–15; moderator Braintree Area Churches Together 2010–12, dir (now chm) Make Jesus Known 2009–, chm Braintree Youth Project Charity 2010–13; govr Felsted Schs 2013–; memb London Stock Exchange 1983–86, fell Securities Inst 1986–2009; FRSA 1998; *Recreations* opera, walking, travel; *Style*— Nic Stuchfield, Esq; ✉ e-mail nic@stuchfield.com

STUDD, Prof John William Winston; s of Eric Dacombe Studd (d 1941), and Elsie Elizabeth, *née* Kirby (d 1995); *b* 4 March 1940; *Educ* Royal Hosp Sch Ipswich, Univ of Birmingham (MB BS, MD, DSc); *m* 7 May 1980, Dr Margaret Ann Johnson, da of Dr Frederick Johnson, of Hinton Charterhouse, Bath; 1 s (Thomas b 16 Oct 1981), 2 da (Sarah b 7 Dec 1985, Josephine b 18 Feb 1992); *Career* res fell Univ of Birmingham, lectr in obstetrics and gynaecology Univ Coll of Rhodesia 1972, conslt and sr lectr Univ of Nottingham 1974–75, subsequently conslt obstetrician and gynaecologist King's Coll Hosp and Dulwich Hosp London, currently conslt obstetrician and gynaecologist Chelsea and Westminster Hosp London and prof of gynaecology Imperial Coll London; author of papers on: labour, menopause, osteoporosis, premenstrual syndrome, post natal depression, depression in women and infertility, HIV infection in women; ed: Menopause Digest, The Diplomate; memb Editorial Bd: Jl of RSM, British Journal of Obstetrics and Gynaecology, Br Jl of Hosp Med, Int Jl of Gynaecological Endocrinology; memb Cncl and pubns offr RCOG, memb Cncl RSM, chm Nat Osteoporosis Soc, pres Section of Obstetrics and Gynaecology RSM, pres Int Soc of Reproductive Med, chm PMS and Menopause Tst, memb Hosp Conslts and Specialists Assoc; Hon DSc Univ of Birmingham 1994; memb BMA 1962, FRCOG 1982 (MRCOG 1967); *Books* Management of Labour (ed, 1985), Management of the Menopause (ed, 1988), Progress in Obstetrics and Gynaecology (volumes 1–10), Self Assessment in Obstetrics and Gynaecology, The Menopause and Hormone Replacement Therapy (1993, 2 edn 1995), Annual Progress in Reproductive Medicine (1993–94), RCOG Yearbook (1993 and 1994–95), Hysterectomy and HRT (1998), Menopause Annual (1999–2000), Vaginal Hysterectomy (2002), and other undergraduate and postgraduate textbooks; *Recreations* theatre, music, opera, history of medicine; *Style*— Prof John Studd; ✉ 27 Blomfield Road, London W9 1AA (✆ 020 7266 0058, fax 020 7266 2663, mobile 077 7477 4999, e-mail laptop@studd.co.uk); London PMS and Menopause Centre, 46 Wimpole Street, London W1G 8SD (✆ 020 7266 0105, fax 020 7224 4190, e-mail harley@studd.co.uk and lister@studd.co.uk, website www.studd.co.uk)

STUDHOLME, Sir Henry William; 3 Bt (UK 1956), of Perridge, Co Devon; DL; er s of Sir Paul Henry William Studholme, 2 Bt, DL (d 1990), and Virginia Katherine, *née* Palmer (d 1990); *b* 31 January 1958; *Educ* Eton, Trinity Hall Cambridge (MA); *m* 1 Oct 1988, (Sarah) Lucy Rosita Deans-Chrystall, o da of late Richard S Deans, of Christchurch, NZ, and late Jane R M Deans, of West Wellow, Hants; 1 da (Lorna Jane Virginia b 1 June 1990), 2 s (Joshua Henry Paul b 2 Feb 1992, Jacob William Richard Gilfred b 11 June 1993); *Heir* s, Joshua Studholme; *Career* chm SW Regnl Advsy Ctee on Forestry 2000, memb Bd SW RDA 2002– (chm 2009–12), forestry cmmr 2007– (chm 2013), dir Phaunos Timber Fund 2011– (chm 2012); FCA, CTA; *Style*— Sir Henry Studholme, Bt, DL

STUDZINSKI, John; CBE (2008); *Educ* Bowdoin Coll US (BA), Univ of Chicago (MBA); *Career* Morgan Stanley 1980–2003 (served as head European Investment Banking Div and dep chm Morgan Stanley Int), memb Gp Mgmnt Bd and co-head of investment banking HSBC 2003–07, sr md and global head Blackstone Advsy Ptnrs and memb Exec Ctee Blackstone Gp 2006–15; vice-chm Blackstone Gp 2015–; dir and memb Exec Ctee Human Rights Watch; tstee: Bowdoin Coll US, Tate Fndn, Passage Day Centre for the Homeless, Signature Theatre (USA) 2015–; chm Benjamin Franklin House 2007, memb Bd JP Getty Tst 2015–; estab Genesis Fndn 2001–; chair Emmaus Revives Lives campaign; Prince of Wales Ambassador's Award, Beacon Prize 2004, Banker of the Year UK 2007; Knight of the Order of St Gregory, Knight Cdr of St Sylvester; *Style*— John Studzinski, Esq, CBE; ✉ The Blackstone Group International Ltd, 40 Berkeley Square, London W1J 5AL

STULTIENS, (Alan) Jeffrey; s of Thomas Stultiens (d 1980), of Syresham, Northants, and Kate, *née* Whittaker (d 2000); *b* 12 September 1944; *Educ* Hutton GS, Tiffin Boys' Sch, Kingston Sch of Art, Camberwell Sch of Art and Crafts (DipAD); *m* 4 July 1992 (m dis 2016), Catherine, da of Martin Knowelden; 2 da (Ellen Alice b 1999, Isobel Kate b 2003); *Career* fine artist; lectr Sir John Cass Sch of Art City of London Poly 1967–73, sr lectr and leader Fndn Course Hertfordshire Coll of Art and Design 1983–87 (sr lectr 1974–83), visiting tutor/assessor Dip in Portraiture Heatherley Sch of Fine Art 1994–2007; Reform Club Drawing Gp 2008; first prize John Player Portrait Award Nat Portrait Gallery 1985; RP 1991 (hon sec 1993–96); *Exhibitions* John Player Portrait Award (Nat Portrait Gallery) 1984 and 1985, British Portraiture 1980–85 1985–86, Portraits for the '80s 1986, Royal Soc of Portrait Painters 1990, Women on Canvas 1991, Hunting/Observer Art Prizes 1992, The Portrait Award 1980–89 (Nat Portrait Gallery) 1992, Oriel Ynys Môn 1992, Nikkei Exhibition Tokyo 1993, Royal Coll of Pathologists 1995–96, People's Portraits 2000–01, Di Passagio Venice 2005, 400 Women 2010–11, Royal Soc of Portrait Painters (annually), Family, Familiar 2014; *Work in Collections* Nat Portrait Gallery, Merton Coll Oxford, Oriel Coll Oxford, Nat Heart and Lung Inst, Servite Houses, RNLI, Royal Med Fndn, Royal Acad of Music, Royal Coll of Pathologists, Royal Collection Windsor Castle, The Royal Soc, Royal Holloway Coll London, Clan MacLeod, Acad of Med Sciences, Royal Coll of Physicians, Girton Coll Cambridge, Trinity Coll Cambridge, The Jockey Club; *Long Term Projects* The Royal Navy in the 21st Century, Étretat Revisited; *Commissions* incl: Cardinal Basil Hume OSB OM 1987 and 1999, Sir Aaron Klug OM 2001, HM The Queen 2003, Admiral Sir James Burnell-Nugent 2008–09, Sir Mark Prescott, Bt 2014, Juan Manuel Santos (President of Colombia) 2016, numerous private cmmns; *Style*— Jeffrey Stultiens, Esq, RP; ✉ 26 St George's Close, Toddington, Bedfordshire LU5 6AT (✆ 01525 874120, e-mail jeff.stultiens@ntlworld.com)

STUNELL, Baron (Life Peer UK 2015), of Hazel Grove in the County of Greater Manchester; Rt Hon Sir (Robert) Andrew Stunell; kt (2013), OBE (1995); s of late Robert George Stunell, and late Trixie Stunell; *b* 24 November 1942; *Educ* Surbiton GS, Univ of Manchester, Liverpool Poly; *m* 29 July 1967, Gillian Mary Stunell; 2 da (Judith b 1969, Kari b 1970), 3 s (Peter b 1973, Mark b 1974, Daniel b 1979); *Career* architectural asst: various posts 1965–81, freelance 1981–85; cncllrs offr Assoc of Liberal Cncllrs 1985–88; Assoc of Lib Dem Cncllrs: political sec 1989–96, special projects offr 1996–97; cncllr: Chester City Cncl 1979–90, Cheshire CC 1981–91, Stockport MB 1994–2002; memb Assoc of CCs 1985–90 (ldr SLD Gp 1985–90); Parly candidate: Chester 1979–87, Hazel Grove 1992; MP (Lib Dem) Hazel Grove 1997–2015; Lib Dem spokesperson on energy 1997–2005, Lib Dem chief whip 2001–06, shadow spokesperson for Dept of Communities and Local Govt 2006–08, chair Local Elections Campaign Team 2008–10, Parly under-sec of state Dept for Communities and Local Govt 2010–12; sponsor of Sustainable and Secure Buildings Act 2004; *Books* Guide to Local Government Finance (1985), Success on Balanced Councils (1985), Parish Finance (1986), Success on the Council (1988), Running a Successful Council Group (1990), Budgeting For Real (1991), Open, Active and Effective (1994), Energy: Clean and Green in 2050 (1999), Cleaning up the Mess (2002); *Style*— The Lord Stunell, OBE; ✉ 84 Lyme Grove, Romiley, Stockport, Cheshire SK6 4DJ; House of Lords, London SW1A 0PW (✆ 020 7219 4130)

STURDEE, Dr David William; s of late Cdr Peter Doveton Sturdee, OBE, of Solihull, W Midlands, and Daphne, *née* Langdon; *b* 13 May 1945, Walmer, Kent; *Educ* Sherborne, St Thomas' Hosp Med Sch London (MB BS, DA), Univ of Birmingham (MD); *m* 4 Sept 1971, Elizabeth Morton, da of Dr John Morton Muir (d 1973); 1 s (Simon William b 1973), 1 da (Claire b 1975); *Career* sr registrar W Midlands rotation 1978–81, conslt obstetrician and gynaecologist Solihull 1981–2011 (past clinical dir), sr clinical lectr Univ of Birmingham 1981–2011 (res fell Dept of Obstetrics and Gynaecology 1975–77); author of many papers in jls, chapters and 4 books on hormone replacement therapy for menopausal symptoms and 2 yearbooks of obstetrics and gynaecology; chm Br Menopause Soc 1995–97, fndr memb Int Menopause Soc (sec-gen 2005–08, pres 2008–11); past chm Solihull Div BMA, hon treas Birmingham and Midlands Obstetric and Gynaecological Soc; RCOG: pubns offr and chm Pubns Editorial Ctee 1999–2002, past memb Higher Training and Sub-Specialty Bd Ctees; past ed The Diplomate, co-ed-in-chief Climacteric (Jl Int Menopause Soc) 1998–2007; Marie Curie Helper Service volunteer; FRCOG 1988; *Publications* The Effective Management of the Menopause (with DH Barlow and A Miles A, 2002), The Facts of Hormone Therapy for Menopausal Women (2003); *Recreations* singing (St Alphege choir and close harmony, CDs 'Warts and All' and 'Don't Tell the Abbot' by The Surplus Cassocks), golf, fishing; *Clubs* Copt Heath Golf; *Style*— Dr David Sturdee; ✉ Department of Obstetrics and Gynaecology, Solihull Hospital, Lode Lane, Solihull, West Midlands B91 2JL (✆ 0121 424 5390, e-mail david.sturdee@btinternet.com)

STURDY, Robert William; s of Gordon Sturdy (d 1989), and Kathleen, *née* Wells; *b* 22 June 1944; *Educ* Ashville Coll Harrogate; *m* 12 July 1969, Elizabeth Truus; 1 s (Julian), 1 da (Joanna); *Career* farmer, ptnr G E Sturdy and Son; MEP (Cons): Cambridgeshire 1994–99, Eastern England 1999–2014; dep ldr Br Cons in European Parl 1999–2001, EP (EPP-ED) co-ordinator int trade 2004–09, memb Int Trade Ctee 2004–14 (vice-chair 2009–14), subst memb Environment Ctee 1999–2009, subst memb Agric Ctee 2004–14; co-ordinator int trade ECR Gp 2009–14; co-chm Interparly WTO Cmmn; memb EU-ACP JPA; *Recreations* fishing, golf, cricket; *Style*— Robert Sturdy, Esq; ✉ website www.robertsturdymep.com

STURGEON, Dr David Alexander; s of Flt Lt Alexander Rodger Sturgeon, of Worcs, and Jean, *née* Stansfield; *b* 3 July 1947; *Educ* Hipperholme GS, Univ of Oxford, UCH (BA, MA, BM BCh); *m* 6 Dec 1975, Elizabeth, da of Eric Kurt Lederman, of London; 2 da (Kate b 28 April 1977, Natasha b 29 Aug 1979); *Career* UCH London: Leverhulme jr res fell med sch 1974–75, sr clinical lectr Dept of Mental Health 1977–86, acting head Dept of Mental Health 1981–84, tutor Faculty of Clinical Sciences 1985–87; conslt psychiatrist Camden and Islington NHS Tst and hon sr lectr UCL Hosps 1986–, conslt liaison psychiatrist UCL Hosps 1998–2008, conslt psychiatrist Student Counselling Serv UCL 2006–; author of various papers on family treatment of schizophrenia, psychophysiology of schizophrenia and psychotherapy; psychiatric advsr to: Br Assoc of Cancer United Patients (Cancer BACUP), Breast Cancer Care; hon psychiatric advsr to Brandon Centre of Counselling and Psychotherapy for Young People; fell and treas Int Coll of Psychosomatic Med; FRCPsych 1986 (MRCPsych 1976); *Books* UCH Textbook of Psychiatry (co-ed, 1990); *Recreations* writing; *Style*— Dr David Sturgeon; ✉ UCL Psychological Therapies Service, 3 Taviton St, London WC1H 0BT (✆ 07771 606416, e-mail davidalexander.sturgeon@gmail.com)

STURGEON, Nicola; MSP; da of Robert Sturgeon, of Irvine, and Joan, *née* Ferguson; *b* 19 July 1970; *Educ* Greenwood Acad Irvine, Univ of Glasgow (LLB), Dip Legal Practice; *Career* trainee slr McClure Naismith 1993–95, asst slr Bell & Craig 1995–97, assoc slr Drumchapel Law Centre 1997–99; MSP (SNP): Glasgow 1999–2011, Glasgow Southside 2011–; memb Nat Exec, dep ldr SNP and dep first min of Scotland 2007–14, cabinet sec for health and wellbeing 2007–12, cabinet sec for infrastructure, investment and cities 2012–14, ldr SNP and first min of Scotland 2014–; *Recreations* theatre, reading; *Style*— Ms Nicola Sturgeon, MSP; ✉ The Scottish Parliament, Edinburgh EH99 1SP (✆ 0131 348 5695, fax 0131 348 6475, e-mail nicola.sturgeon.msp@scottish.parliament.uk)

STURGIS, Ann Elisabeth; da of Maj Peter Sturgis (d 1986), and Rachel Sybil, *née* Borthwick (d 1998); *b* 23 October 1945; *Educ* North Foreland Lodge; *Career* estate agent; chm and md Malverns Estate Agents; dir: R H K Seelig Ltd, K A L, Moontron Ltd; *Recreations* gardening; *Style—* Miss Ann Sturgis; ✉ Garden Cottage, Dauntsey Park, Chippenham, Wiltshire SN15 4HT; Malverns Estate Agents, Malvern Court, Onslow Square, London SW7 3HU (☎ 020 7589 8122, fax 020 7589 4403, e-mail ann@malverns.co.uk)

STURLEY, Air Marshal Philip Oliver; CB (2000), MBE (1985); *Educ* St Ignatius' Coll London, Univ of Southampton, RAF Coll Cranwell, JSDC Greenwich; *m* Micheline; 1 da (Olivia b 15 Feb 1980); *Career* pilot (Phantom) 41 (F) Sqdn RAF Coningsby, pilot (Jaguar) II (AC) Sqdn RAF Laarbruch Germany, Sqdn Leader 1980, Air Staff Offr (Army) HQ 1 (Br) Corps Beilefield, Flight Cdr II (AC) Sqdn, Wing Cdr 1984, leader Strike Cmd Briefing Team RAF High Wycombe 1984–85, Cdr II AC Sqdn Germany 1987–89, memb Air Force Bd Standing Ctee Strategic Support Team MOD 1989–90, Gp Capt 1989, Dir Air Staff Briefing and Co-ordination MOD 1990–92, Cdr Tri-National Tornado Training Estab (TTTE) RAF Cottesmore 1992, Air Cdre 1993; first NATO Liaison Offr UN Force Cdr Former Yugoslavia 1993, sec NATO Mil Ctee 1994–98, Sr Air Staff Offr Strike Command and AOC 38 Gp RAF High Wycombe 1998–2000, Dep Chief Staff Ops Strike Command 2000, ACAS 2000–03, COS AIRNORTH 2003–05; pres RAF Assoc 2005–11 (currently life vice-pres), specialist advsr to House of Commons Defence Ctee 2006–13, sr military mentor Higher Command and Staff Course Shrivenham 2007–; Cabinet Office Top Mgmnt Prog; Hon Air Cdre 4624 Sqn RAuxAF 2012–; QCVSA 1980; FRAeS 1993, CCMI 2010–15; *Recreations* gliding (vice-pres RAF Gliding and Soaring Assoc, team mangr Br Gliding 2009–12), skiing, golf; *Clubs* RAF; *Style—* Air Marshal Philip Sturley, CB, MBE

STURMAN, Jim; QC (2002); s of Gp Capt Roger Sturman, of Exeter, and Anne, *née* Lomas; *b* 19 July 1958; *Educ* Bembridge Sch IOW, Univ of Reading (LLB), Cncl of Legal Educn; *m* 21 Dec 1986, Marcella Convey, da of Dr Cyrus Mineo; 3 s (Michael Edwin Mullaney b 12 Oct 1997, Jonathan James Roger b 4 Nov 1999, Mark Joseph b 22 Sept 2001); *Career* called to the Bar 1982; criminal barr 1983–; specialist criminal and sports law barr acting for the def involved in cases incl: R v Colin Stagg, R v Ian Kay, R v Bowyer and Woodgate, Shipman Inquiry; also specialist advocate in FA disciplinary cases, acted for clubs incl Chelsea FC, West Ham United FC and Tottenham Hotspur FC; memb: Bar of Gibraltar 1986, Criminal Bar Assoc, Int Bar Assoc; memb Ctee Old Bembridgians Assoc; *Style—* Jim Sturman, QC; ✉ 2 Bedford Row, London WC1R 4BU (☎ 020 7440 8888, fax 020 7242 1738, e-mail jsturman@2bedfordrow.co.uk)

STURRIDGE, Charles; s of Dr Jerome Sturridge (d 1996), and Alyson Bowman Vaughan, *née* Burke; *b* 24 June 1951; *Educ* Beaumont Coll, Stonyhurst, UC Oxford (BA); *m* 6 July 1985, Phoebe Nicholls, the actress, da of Anthony Nicholls; 3 c; *Career* director and writer; dir and chm Firstsight Films Ltd 2000–; memb BECTU; *Theatre* Hard Times (Belgrade Coventry) 1974, The Seagull (Queens) 1985, Tolomeo (Broomhill Opera) 1998; *Television* incl: World in Action (4 episodes), Coronation Street (16 episodes), Brideshead Revisited (Granada) 1981, Soft Targets (BBC) 1982, The Story Teller – A Story Short 1987, Troubles (writer only, LWT) 1987, A Foreign Field (BBC) 1993, Gullivers Travels (Channel 4) 1996, Longitude (Channel 4) 2000, Shackleton (Channel 4) 2002; *Films* Runners (debut) 1983, Aria (contrib) 1986, A Handful of Dust (co-adaptor) 1988, Where Angels Fear to Tread (co-adaptor) 1991, Fairy Tale – A True Story 1997, Ohio Impromptu (dir) 2000, Lassie 2005; *Awards* for Brideshead Revisited: 17 Awards incl BAFTA for Best Series and Best Actor (Anthony Andrews, *qv*), two Golden Globe Awards, The Grand Award (NY Film & TV Festival), Emmy for Best Supporting Actor (Laurence Olivier); for Runners: Best Film at the Karlovy-Vary Festival, Special Prize Venice Film Festival; for Gullivers Travels: Humanitas Award, Br Television Soc Team Award; 7 Emmy's incl Best Series and Best Special Effects; for Fairy Tale BAFTA Best Children's Film 1998; for Longitude 'Rockie' for Best Mini Series at BANF TV Awards; 6 further BAFTAs incl Best Series; South Bank Show Best TV Drama Award for Ohio Impromptu; for Shackleton: BAFTA Best Drama Serial, Best Costume, Emmy for Outstanding Cinematography, Outstanding Score; *Publications* The Seagull (trans with Tania Alexander, Amber Lane Press, 1983); *Clubs* Groucho; *Style—* Charles Sturridge, Esq; ✉ c/o United Agents Limited, 12–26 Lexington Street, London W1F 0LE (☎ 020 3214 0800, fax 020 3214 0801, website www.unitedagents.co.uk)

STURROCK, Philip James; MBE (2014); s of James Cars Sturrock, of Brighouse, W Yorks, and Joyce, *née* Knowles; *b* 5 October 1947; *Educ* Queen Mary's GS Walsall, Trinity Coll Oxford (MA), Manchester Business Sch (MBA); *m* 1, 5 Aug 1972 (m dis 1995), Susan, da of (William) Horace Haycock, of Walsall, W Midlands; 2 da (Anna b 23 June 1977, Jane b 3 Jan 1983), 1 s (Hugh b 5 May 1981); m 2, 8 Sept 2000, Madeleine Frances Robinson, da of Robert Francis Swift, of St Albans, Herts; *Career* md: IBIS Information Services 1972–80, Pitman Books 1980–83; gp md Routledge and Kegan Paul plc 1983–85, chm Redwood Publishing Ltd 1985–86, chm and md Cassell plc 1986–99; chm and md The Continuum International Publishing Group Ltd 1999–2006, chm Osprey Publishing Ltd 2007–08; chm PanCathay Consulting Ltd 2004–; non-exec memb Bd Industrial Devpt Advsy Bd; govr Pusey House Oxford 1975–95 (pres of govrs 1994–95), chm St Albans Int Organ Festival Soc 1983–84, chm Hatfield Phiharmonic Orch 1988–92, hon visiting prof Beijing Normal Univ 2005–10, chm of govrs Queen Mary's GS Walsall, chm Bd of Tstees United St Saviour's Charity Southwark 2008–14, chm Soc of Bookmen 2003, chm Wandle Housing Assoc 2010–14, memb Cncl and chm Finance and GP Ctee Inst of Educn Univ of London 2012–15, tstee Southwark Cathedral Devpt Tst, memb Cncl UCL 2015–; Liveryman Worshipful Co of Glaziers; FRSA; *Recreations* walking, reading, travel, music, film, theatre; *Clubs* Athenaeum; *Style—* Philip Sturrock, Esq, MBE; ✉ 62 Benbow House, 24 New Globe Walk, London SE1 9DS

STURROCK, Prof Roger Davidson; *b* 20 October 1946; *Educ* Llanelli Boys' GS, Queen Mary's Sch Basingstoke, King's Coll and Westminster Med Sch London (MB BS, AKC, LRCP, MD); *m*; 3 c; *Career* jt recipient Allessandro Robecchi International Prize in Rheumatology (Euro League Against Rheumatism) 1975, Arthritis and Rheumatism Cncl Anglo-US travelling fell to the USA 1984, currently emeritus prof of rheumatology Univ of Glasgow (former McLeod/ARC chair of rheumatology); past pres Br Soc for Rheumatology; past chair Arthritis Research Campaign; FRCPGlas 1984, FRCP 1985; *Publications* author of numerous articles in learned jls; *Style—* Prof Roger Sturrock; ✉ Centre for Rheumatic Diseases, Medicine – Division of Immunology, Infection and Inflammation, Royal Infirmary, QEB Level 3, Alexandra Parade, Glasgow G31 2ER

STURZAKER, Hugh Gerard; MBE (2016); s of George Gerard Sturzaker (d 1971), of Chandlers Ford, Hants, and Gladys Maude, *née* French (d 1990); *b* 24 June 1940; *Educ* W Buckland Sch Barnstaple, Hertford Coll Oxford (MA), Guy's Hosp Med Sch (BM BCh); *m* 30 March 1968, Ann Elizabeth, da of Ernest Philip Featherstone, of South Croydon, Surrey; 3 s (Robert b 1970, John b 1971, James b 1980), 1 da (Nicola b 1973); *Career* house physician and surgn Guy's Hosp 1966–67, jr lectr in anatomy Guy's Hosp Med Sch 1967–68, surgical registrar Guildford Hosp and Guy's Hosp 1968–73, res fell St Mark's Hosp London 1973–74, sr surgical registrar Guy's Hosp and Gt Ormond St Hosp for Children, conslt gen surgn James Paget Univ Hosps NHS Fndn Tst 1979–2005, hon sr lectr UEA and hon conslt surgn and govr James Paget Univ Hosps NHS Fndn Tst; examiner RCS(Ed); past pres: Oxford Univ Med Soc, Br Med Students' Assoc, E Anglian Surgical Club, Great Yarmouth and Waveney Div BMA; hon fell Gt Yarmouth Coll 2008; memb: Assoc of Surgns of GB and Ireland, BMA; FRCSEd 1971, FRCS 1972; *Books* James Paget University Hospital: The First 25 Years (2007), Sir James Paget: Surgeon Extraordinary and his legacies (2013); *Recreations* gardening, wine and beer making, music, travel; *Style—* Hugh Sturzaker, Esq, MBE; ✉ Hobland House, Hobland, Great Yarmouth, Norfolk NR31 9AR (☎ 01493 665287, e-mail hugh@sturzaker.plus.com)

STUTTAFORD, Dr (Irving) Thomas; OBE (1996); s of Dr William Joseph Edward Stuttaford, MC (d 1956), of Horning, Norfolk, and Mary Marjorie Dean, *née* Royden (d 1976); *b* 4 May 1931; *Educ* Gresham's, BNC Oxford, W London Hosp (MRCS, LRCP, DObstRCOG); *m* 1 June 1957, Pamela Christine (d 2013), da of Lt-Col Richard Ropner, TD (d 1975), of Aldie, Tain, Ross-shire; 3 s (Andrew b 1958, Thomas b 1961, Hugo b 1964); *Career* 2 Lt 10 Royal Hussars (PWO) 1953–55, Lt Scottish Horse TA 1955–59; jr hosp appts 1959–60, gen practice 1960–70, visiting physician BUPA 1970–96 (asst clinical dir 1979–81); clinical asst in venereology: The London Hosp 1974–93, Queen Mary's Hosp for the East End 1974–79, Moorfields Eye Hosp 1975–79; med advsr Barclays Bank 1971–87 (sr med advsr 1987–2001), sr med advsr The Rank Orgn 1980–85; private practice in occupational health 1986–2006; med columnist or med corr The Times 1981–2009, med corr The Oldie 1992–, formerly med columnist ELLE magazine and Options magazine; columnist The Oldie; med advsr: The Hunting Gp, Standard Chartered Bank, Rank Hotels and other cos; memb: Blofield and Flegg RDC 1964–66, Norwich City Cncl 1969–71; MP (Cons) Norwich S 1970–74, Parly candidate (Cons) Isle of Ely 1974 and 1979, sec Cons Health and Social Servs Ctee, Select Ctee on Sci and Technol 1970–74; memb: Cncl Res Def Soc 1970–79, Birth Control Campaign 1970–79; *Books* A Birth Control Plan for Britain (with Mr Alistair Service and Dr John Dunwoody, 1972), To Your Good Health – the Wise Drinker's Guide (1997), The Harvard Medical School Family Health Quick (med ed Br edn, 2003), What's Up Doc? Understanding Common Symptoms (2003), Stress and How to Avoid It (2004); author of chapters in: Drinking to Your Health (1989), Which Wine Guide (1991), In Your Right Mind (1999); *Recreations* living in the country, conservation of old buildings; *Clubs* Beefsteak, Athenaeum, Reform, Cavalry and Guards', Norfolk (Norwich), Garrick; *Style—* Dr Thomas Stuttaford, OBE; ✉ 36 Elm Hill, Norwich, Norfolk NR3 1HG (☎ 01603 615133)

STYLE, Vice-Adm Charles Rodney; CBE (2002); s of Lt Cdr Sir Godfrey Style, CBE, DSC, RN (d 2000), and Sigrid Elisabeth, *née* Carlberg (d 1985); *b* 15 January 1954; *Educ* Eton, Univ of Cambridge (exhibitioner, MA); *m* 31 Jan 1981, Charlotte Amanda, da of Lt Timothy Martin Woodford, RN (d 1966), and Eila Mary, *née* Stirling-Hamilton, step da of George Rudolph Wratislaw Walker; 3 da (Amanda Clare b 24 Nov 1981, Annabel Daisy b 21 Dec 1983, Elizabeth Sigrid b 2 Jan 1990); *Career* joined Royal Navy 1974, trg BRNC Dartmouth (Queen's Sword); served: Antarctic patrol ship HMS Endurance 1977–78, HMS Bacchante 1978–79, HM Yacht Britannia 1980–81, HMS Sandpiper 1981–82 (cmd), HMS Wotton 1982–83 (cmd), HMS Arethusa 1984–85; Flag Lt to C-in-C Fleet, Channel and Eastern Atlantic 1985–87, Cdr 1988, cmd frigate HMS Andromeda 1988–89, Directorate of Naval Plans MOD 1989–92, Staff Offr Ops to Cdr UK Task Gp 1992–93 (incl serv in Adriatic), Capt 1993, cmd frigate HMS Campbeltown 1993–95 (incl Armilla Task Gp cmd Gulf 1993–94), Chief Staff Offr (Ops and Trg) to Flag Offr Sea Trg (FOST) 1995–96, Cdre 1997, Princ Staff Offr to Chief of Defence Staff 1997–98, memb RCDS 1999, cmd aircraft carrier HMS Illustrious 2000–01 (incl serv off Sierra Leone and in the Arabian Sea against terrorism), Rear Admiral 2002, i/c Strategic Deployment and Precision Attack Capability MOD 2002–04, Cdr UK Maritime Force and NATO Response Force (Maritime) 2004–05, Vice-Adm 2006, DCDS (Commitments) and dir UK Mil Ops MOD 2006–07, Cmdt RCDS 2008–12; conslt and dir White Water Wave Ltd 2012–; advsr Renewal Project St Martin-in-the-Fields 2004–09; memb Advsy Panel Concordis Int 2012–; maritime advsr and ed Maritime Feedback CHIRP 2015–; tstee: Britannia Assoc 2003–09, Kids for Kids 2012–15, Queen Elizabeth Fndn 2013–, Queen Elizabeth Fndn 2013–; exec-in-residence Manchester Business Sch 2009–, memb Advsy Bd European Mentoring and Coaching Cncl (UK) 2010–12; Yr Bro Trinity House 1991, memb Hon Co of Master Mariners 2003; *Publications* In Business and Battle (lead ed and contrib, 2012); *Recreations* fishing, reading, sailing, music, paramotoring; *Clubs* Royal Yacht Sqdn (Naval memb 2004); *Style—* Vice-Adm Charles Style, CBE; ✉ e-mail charlesstyle.cs@gmail.com, website http://uk.linkedin.com/pub/charles-style/14/290/5BB

STYLE, Christopher John David; QC (2006); s of Maj David Carlyle Willoughby Style, MC, TD (d 1978), of Loweswater, Cumbria, and Dr Anne Marion, *née* Phillips; *b* 13 April 1955; *Educ* St Bees Sch Cumbria, Trinity Hall Cambridge (MA), City of London Poly; *m* 7 April 1990, Victoria Jane, *née* Miles; 3 s (George Alexander b 2 Aug 1991, Charles David b 8 Aug 1993, Peter John b 12 May 1995), 1 da (Catherine Elizabeth b 19 Dec 2000); *Career* Linklaters & Paines 1977–12: articled clerk 1977–79, slr 1979, asst slr 1979–85, ptnr 1985–12; arbitrator One Essex Court 2012–; slr advocate (Higher Cts Civil); memb London Slrs Litigation Assoc; Freeman City of London 1985, memb City of London Slrs Co; FCIArb; *Books* Documentary Evidence (6 edn, 1997); *Recreations* fell walking, rock climbing; *Style—* Mr Christopher Style, QC; ✉ Gainsborough House, 6 Gainsborough Gardens, London NW3 1BJ; One Essex Court, Temple, London EC4Y 9AR

STYLE, Montague William; OBE (2007); s of late Cdr Sir Godfrey Style, CBE, DSC, RN, and late Jill Elizabeth, *née* Caruth; *b* 9 October 1943; *Educ* Eton, Ecole des Hautes Etudes Commerciales Paris, INSEAD (MBA); *m* 18 July 1970, Susan Jennifer, da of Peter Wrightson, OBE; 1 da (Sophie Elizabeth b 20 June 1974), 1 s (Oliver Rodney b 6 May 1976); *Career* Morgan Grampian Ltd London 1965–69, The Economist Newspaper Ltd 1969–72, Pharmaceutical Div Ciba-Geigy 1973–96, Novartis 1997–98, md Style Project Partners GmbH Basel 1999–, sr exec coach I J Martin & Co Ltd Zurich 2003–; chm: Br & Cwlth Soc Mexico 1978–80, Int Sch of Basel 1982–85; pres Br-Swiss C of C 2004–06; *Recreations* pianist, walking, fly fishing; *Clubs* Rye Golf, Golf du Rhin Chalampe France; *Style—* Montague Style, Esq, OBE; ✉ 27 rue des Romains, 68480 Bettlach, France (☎ 00 33 3 89 07 50 85, mobile 00 41 79 322 57 06, e-mail montaguestyle@gmail.com)

STYLE, Rodney Hill; s of late Col (Rodney) Gerald Style, and Barbara Hill Style, of Runfold, Farnham, Surrey; *b* 25 March 1956; *Educ* Eton; *m* 24 April 1982, Georgina Eve, da of late John Kinloch Kerr of Abbottrule, of Frocester, Glos; 2 s (George b 1985, Hugo b 1985), 1 da (Elizabeth b 1989); *Career* ACA; Spicer and Pegler 1976–85, ptnr Haines Watts Chartered Accountants 1985–, dir Haines Watts Ltd (chm 2010–); Freeman City of London 1981, Liveryman Worshipful Co of Grocers 1991; ACA 1981, CTA 1983; *Recreations* tennis, hunting, shooting, skiing; *Style—* Rodney Style, Esq; ✉ Knowle Farmhouse, North Newington, Oxfordshire OX15 6AN; Haines Watts Chartered Accountants, Sterling House, 19/23 High Street, Kidlington, Oxfordshire OX5 2DH (☎ 01865 378282, fax 01865 377518)

STYLER, Trudie; da of Henry Styler, and Pauline Brassington; *b* 6 January 1954, Bromsgrove, Worcs; *m* 20 Aug 1992, Sting, *qv*; 2 s, 2 da; *Career* actress and film producer; fndr Xingu Films, co-fndr Maven Pictures; co-fndr (with Sting, *qv*) Rainforest Foundation 1989, ambass UNICEF UK; *Films* actress: Bring on the Night 1985, Mamba 1988, The Grotesque 1995 (also prodr), Me Without You 2001, Confessions of an Ugly Stepsister 2001, Cheeky 2003 (also prodr), Alpha Male 2005 (also prodr), Living Proof 2008, Paris Connections 2010; prodr: Boys from Brazil 1993, Moving the Mountain 1994, Lock Stock & Two Smoking Barrels 1998, Snatch 2000, Greenfingers 2001, The Sweatbox 2002, A Kind of Childhood 2002, A Guide to Recognizing Your Saints 2006, Moon 2009, Girl Most Likely 2012, Filth 2013, Black Nativity 2013; *Television* Poldark II 1978, The Body in the Library 1985, The Scold's Bridle 1998, Midsomer Murders 1998, Friends 2001, Empire 2004, Love Soup 2005; *Style—* Ms Trudie Styler; ✉ Maven Pictures, 35 Endell Street, London WC2H 9BA (☎ 020 7451 0600, fax 020 7451 0601)

S

STYLES, Graham Charles Trayton; *b* 16 April 1958, Farnborough, Kent; *Educ* Univ of Birmingham; *m* Rachael Jane; 2 da; *Career* diplomat; registry offr Central and Southern African Dept FCO 1977–78, registry offr Eastern European Soviet Dept FCO 1981–84, registry/communications offr Port Louis 1985–88, entry clearance offr Paris 1989–92, postings offr Personnel Mgmnt Dept FCO 1992–94, third sec UK Delgn to the OSCE Vienna 1995–98, desk offr Sierra Leone Africa Dept (Equatorial) FCO 1998–2001, UK Nat Contact Point for EU Twinning Prog FCO 2001–02, departmental report writer Directorate for Strategy and Innovation FCO 2002–04, head Mekong and Burma Team SE Asia Dept FCO 2004–05, first sec UK Mission Vienna 2006–11, ambass to Repub of Guinea 2011–14, head Kosovo Albania and Macedonia Team Western Balkans Dept FCO 2015–; *Style*— Mr Graham Styles; ✉ c/o FCO, King Charles Street, London SW1A 2AH (e-mail graham.styles@fco.gov.uk)

SUCHET, David; CBE (2011, OBE 2002); s of Jack Suchet (d 2001), and Joan, *née* Jarché (d 1992); bro of John Suchet, *qv*; *b* 2 May 1946; *Educ* Wellington, LAMDA; *m* 1976, Sheila Anne, da of William Ferris (d 1986), of Stratford-upon-Avon, Warks; 1 s (Robert b 10 May 1981), 1 da (Katherine b 21 July 1983); *Career* actor; began professional career Gateway Theatre Chester 1969; repertory theatres incl: Exeter, Worthing, Birmingham; assoc artiste RSC, memb Cncl LAMDA, govr RSC; visiting prof of theatre Univ of Nebraska 1975; FRSA; *Theatre* incl: Estragon in Waiting for Godot, John Aubrey in Brief Lives, Timon of Athens (Young Vic), This Story of Yours (Hampstead), Separation (Hampstead then Comedy Theatre), Oleanna (Royal Court then Duke of York's Theatre), Mole in Toad of Toad Hall, Sid Field in What a Performance, George in Who's Afraid of Virginia Woolf, Salieri in Amadeus (London, Los Angeles and NY), Gregor in Man and Boy (Duchess Theatre London), All My Sons (Apollo) 2010 (Best Actor in a Play What's On Stage Award 2011), Long Day's Journey Into Night (Apollo) 2012, Cardinal Benelli in The Last Confession (tour of Toronto, LA and Australia) 2014, Lady Bracknell in The Importance of Being Earnest (Vaudeville Theatre London) 2015; RSC incl: Shylock in The Merchant of Venice, Achilles in Troilus and Cressida, Bolingbroke in Richard II, Iago in Othello, Mercutio in Romeo & Juliet, Fool in King Lear, Caliban in The Tempest, Lucio in Measure for Measure; *Television* incl: Edward Teller in Oppenheimer (NNC), Freud in The Life of Freud (BBC), Blott in Blott on the Landscape (BBC), Judge O'Connor in Cause Celebre (Anglia TV), Glougauer in Once in a Lifetime (BBC), Carver in Nobody Here But Us Chickens (Channel 4), Hercule Poirot in Agatha Christie's Poirot (LWT), Joe in Separation (BBC), Verloc in The Secret Agent (BBC), Aaron in Moses (SkyTV and TNT USA), Gen Jacob in Solomon (SkyTV and TNT USA), Seesaw (LWT), John Borne in National Crime Squad, Edward Palmer in Murder in Mind, Baron Stockmar in Victoria and Albert, Augustus Melmotte in The Way We Live Now (BBC), George Carman in Get Carman, Cardinal Wolsey in Henry VIII, Richer Gilt in Going Postal, Duke of York in Richard II, In the Footsteps of St Paul 2013, In the Footsteps of St Peter 2014; *BBC Radio* incl: Ironhand, The Kreuzer Sonata, First Night Impressions, The Shout, Rosenburg in The Trenches, Debussy, Anton Chekov, The Willows in Winter, Letters from Prison, Alpha Course (radio premiere), Isaac Babel Stories, The Gorey Details; *Film* incl: Trouillfou in Hunchback of Notre Dame, Okana in Falcon and The Snowman, Beria in Red Monarch (for Channel 4), Dyer in Song for Europe, Inspector Japp in Thirteen to Dinner, Lafleur in Bigfoot & The Hendersons, Wil in When the Whales Came, Muller in A World Apart, Nagi Hassan in Executive Decision, Vlachos in Deadly Voyage, Oliver in Sunday, A Perfect Murder, RKO, Sabotage, Naji in Live from Baghdad, Thibidoux in The In Laws, Leo in Foolproof, Mr Ruskin in Effie; *Awards* nominations for Best Actor incl: Evening Standard Award for Merchant of Venice 1978, SWET Award for The Merchant of Venice 1981, BAFTA Award for Hercule Poirot 1990, 1991 and 1992, Evening Standard Awards for Timon of Athens 1991, Olivier Award for Oleanna 1994, RTA Award for What a Performance 1995; nominations for Best Supporting Actor incl: SWET Award for Once in a Lifetime 1980 and Richard II 1981, ACE Award for The Last Innocent Man 1987; other nominations incl: Actor of the Year in a New Play Award for Separation 1989, Olivier Award 1989, BAFTA Best Actor in a Supporting Role for A World Apart 1989, Olivier Award for Lady Bracknell in The Importance of Being Earnest; winner for Best Actor incl: Marseilles Film Festival for Red Monarch 1983, Brit Industry/Scientific Film Assoc Craft Award for Stress 1986, Int Emmy Award for Maxwell 2008; winner 1986 Royal TV Soc Performance Awards for Song for Europe, Freud, Blott on the Landscape; also winner Best Radio Actor Award for Kreutzer Sonata (one man show) 1979 and Variety Club Award for Best Actor for Oleanna; nominations Best Actor for Who's Afraid of Virginia Woolf incl: Evening Standard Award and Olivier Award; winner South Bank Award for Theatrical Achievement and winner Best Actor Critic's Circle Award for Who's Afraid of Virginia Woolf; winner Best Actor Variety Club 1998; Grapevine Award for Lifetime Achievement for Services to the Performing Arts, Lifetime Achievement Award RTS 2014 for 25 years of playing Hercule Poirot; for Salieri in Amadeus: nomination Best Actor Olivier Awards 1999, Tony Nomination for Best Leading Actor, Drama League Award for Outstanding Performance, Back Stage Award for Best Actor; for Melmotte in The Way We Live Now: BPG Award, RTS Award, TRIC Award, nomination BAFTA; Best Revival Olivier Awards 2013 (for Long Day's Journey into Night); *Publications* Poirot and Me (2013); author of essays in Players of Shakespeare (on Caliban, Shylock and Iago); *Recreations* photography, clarinet, ornithology; *Style*— David Suchet, Esq, CBE; ✉ c/o The Artists Partnership, 101 Finsbury Pavement, London EC2A 1RS

SUCHET, John Aleck; eldest s of Jack Suchet (d 2001), and Joan, *née* Jarché (d 1992); bro of David Suchet, CBE, *qv*; *b* 29 March 1944; *Educ* Uppingham, Univ of St Andrews (MA); *m* 1, 1968 (m dis), Moya; 3 s; m 2, 1985, Bonnie Lee; *Career* Reuters News Agency 1967–71, BBC TV News 1971–72, ITN 1972–2004 (reporter, corr, newscaster), five news 2006–07 (newscaster), presenter Going for Gold (Channel Five) 2008–09, presenter Classic FM 2010–; memb Governing Body Royal Acad of Music 2003–07; pres: Friends of the Royal Acad of Music 1998–2006, Hearing Concern 1999–2006; patron Stagetext 2003–06; hon pres Dementia UK 2010–11; TV Journalist of the Year RTS 1986, Newscaster of the Year TRIC 1996, Lifetime Achievement Award RTS 2008, Radio Personality of the Year AIB 2013, Gold Award Best Radio Personality NY Int Radio Awards 2014; Hon Dr jur Univ of Dundee 2000, Hon MA Univ of Worcester 2010; Hon FRAM 2001; *Books* TV News – The Inside Story (1989), The Last Master – Life of Beethoven (Vol 1, 1996, Vol 2, 1997, Vol 3, 1998), The Classic FM Friendly Guide to Beethoven (2006), The Treasures of Beethoven (2008), My Bonnie (2010), Beethoven, the Man Revealed (2012), The Last Waltz, the Strauss Dynasty and Vienna (2015); *Recreations* classical music, exploring the life, times and music of Beethoven; *Style*— John Suchet, Esq; ✉ c/o David Foster Management, PO Box 1805, Andover, Hampshire SP10 3ZN

SUCKLING, Prof Colin James; OBE (2006); s of late Charles Walter Suckling, CBE, FRS, of Tewin, Herts, and late Eleanor Margaret, *née* Watterson; *b* 24 March 1947, Birkenhead, Merseyside; *Educ* Quarry Bank HS, Univ of Liverpool (PhD, DSc, Leblanc medal); *m* 19 Aug 1972, Catherine Mary, da of Desmond Patrick Faulkner; 2 s (Christopher Andrew b 5 Nov 1974, Martin Charles b 23 Nov 1981), 1 da (Barbara Janet b 17 May 1977); *Career* Ciba-Geigy res fell Eidgenössische Technische Hochschule Zürich 1970–72; Univ of Strathclyde: lectr in chemistry 1972–80, Royal Soc Smith & Nephew sr res fell 1980–84, personal prof 1984–89, Freeland prof of chemistry 1989–2012, dean Faculty of Sci 1992–96, dep princ 1996–98 and 2004–05, pro-vice-princ 1998–2000, vice-princ 2000–02, research prof 2012–; public ptnr Scottish Medicines Consortium 2011–15 (chm Patient and Public Liaison Gp 2012–15); chm: Scot Advsy Ctee on Distinction Awards NHS Scot 2003–10, Lay Advsy Bd RCPSGlas 2006–09; memb: Jt Ctee on Higher Surgical Trg 2002–05, Public Liaison Ctee RCPSGlas, Bd Systems Level Integration Ltd 1997–2000, Bd of Mgmnt Bell Coll of Technol 1998–2007, Merchant's House of Glasgow 1998, Court RCPSGlas 2006–09, Cncl RCPSGlas 2006–09, Court Univ of Paisley 2007, Court Univ of W of Scotland 2007–13, Scientific Advsy Bd MGB Biopharma 2015–, THINQ Drug Discovery India 2015–; chm Bd West of Scotland Sch Symphony Orch 1996–2016, chm Harmony Music Scotland Tst 2010–16; dir Glasgow C of C 2001–03; Wolfson Research Award 1989–91, Adrien Albert lectr RSC 2009–10; hon life fell Indian Soc of Chemists and Biologists 2015; FRSC 1980, FRSE 1987, FRSA 1991, Hon FRCPSGlas 2004, Hon FRCSEd 2005; *Publications* Chemistry Through Models (1974), Enzyme Chemistry Impact and Applications (1998); author of over 200 research pubns; *Recreations* music, horn playing and conducting; *Style*— Prof Colin Suckling, OBE, FRSE; ✉ 62 North Grange Road, Bearsden, Glasgow G61 3AF (☎ 0141 942 6984); Department of Pure and Applied Chemistry, University of Strathclyde, 295 Cathedral Street, Glasgow G1 1XL (☎ 0141 548 2271, fax 0141 548 5743, e-mail c.j.suckling@strath.ac.uk)

SUDBOROUGH, Air Vice Marshal Nigel John; CB (2002), OBE (1989), JP (Leicester City, 2004); s of Alexander Sudborough (d 2003), of Northampton, and Beryl, *née* Lynes (d 2015); *b* 23 March 1948; *Educ* Oundle; *m* 24 July 1971, Anne Marie (d 2015), da of Lt-Col Kenneth C Brown (d 1994); 1 da (Emma b 31 Oct 1984), 1 s (Charles b 11 Feb 1986); *Career* OC 29 (F) Sqdn 1985–87, OC RAF Leuchars 1993–95, RCDS 1996, Higher Command and Staff Course 2000, Dep COS (Ops) HQ Strike Command 2000–02; DG Winston Churchill Meml Tst 2002–07, dir Sudborough Investments Ltd 2002, dep-chm Leics Partnership NHS Tst 2007–13, chm Mental Health Act Managers 2007–15; memb Royal Philatelic Soc; Freeman City of London; FCIPD; *Recreations* fly fishing; *Clubs* RAF; *Style*— Air Vice Marshal Nigel Sudborough, CB, OBE, JP; ✉ Knoll House, 5 London Road, Uppingham, Rutland LE15 9TJ (☎ 07940 523727)

SUFFOLK, Archdeacon of; *see:* Hunt, Ven Dr Judith Mary

SUGAR, Baron (Life Peer UK 2009), of Clapton in the London Borough of Hackney; Sir Alan Sugar; kt (2000); *b* 24 March 1947; *m*; 2 s, 1 da; *Career* Amstrad plc: fndr 1968, chm and md until 2008; chm Tottenham Hotspur plc 1991–2001; dir BETACOM 1996–; Govt enterprise tzar 2009–10; non-exec chm YouView 2011–13; appearances as chm of the bd The Apprentice (BBC2) 2005–; Hon DSc: City Univ Business Sch 1988, Brunel Univ 2005; Hon FCGI; *Style*— The Lord Sugar

SUGAR, Vivienne; *Career* chief exec City and County of Swansea 1995–2002, memb Richard Cmmn 2002–04, chair Welsh Consumer Cncl 2003–08, vice-pres Univ of Swansea 2005–, chair Consumer Focus Wales 2008–; conslt to local govt and ODPM, ind advsr for Public Appts; Welsh advsr to Joseph Rowntree Fndn (JRF) 2005–; *Style*— Ms Vivienne Sugar

SUGARMAN, Prof Philip; *Educ* MB ChB, MSc, MBA, PhD; *Career* forensic psychiatrist; conslt NHS 1994–2002, currently ceo St Andrew's Healthcare (tstee 2004–); dir: St Andrew's Property Mgmnt Co Ltd, Three Shires Hospital Ltd; tstee: RCPsych 2000–, Mental Health Provider Forum 2005–; fndr, prop and chm St Andrew's Sch 2009–; hon sr lectr KCL, visiting prof Univ of Northampton; RSM Prize 1994; FRCPsych; *Books* Firesetting and Mental Health (2012), Secure Care (2013); 140 papers; *Recreations* Alpine skiing, cydermaking, piano; *Clubs* RSM; *Style*— Prof Philip Sugarman, FRCPsych; ✉ St Andrew's Healthcare, Cliftonville, Northampton NN1 5DG (☎ 01604 616000, website www.stah.org)

SUGDEN, David Arnold; s of Thomas Sugden (d 1980), and Marjorie, *née* Jackson (d 1999); *b* 12 July 1951, Sunderland, Tyne and Wear; *Educ* Imperial Coll London (BSc); *m* Diane, *née* Arthur; 2 s (Jonathan, Mark (twins) b 17 April 1978); *Career* scholarship Rolls Royce Ltd 1969–73, teacher VSO Jamaica 1973–74, trainee accountant rising to audit sr Arthur Young McClelland Moores 1974–78, gp accountant Thomas Tillings plc 1978–79; Spear and Jackson Int plc: gp fin accountant 1979–82, gp fin dir 1982–86; Geest plc: gp fin dir 1986–89, gp chief exec 1990–96; head of value for money BBC 1997–98, chm MSB Int plc 1996–2000; non-exec dir Greencore Gp plc 2002–12; BPP Hldgs plc: non-exec dir 2004–05, dep chm 2005–06, chm 2006–09; chm Findel plc 2010–; ARCS, FCA 1978; *Clubs* Brockenhurst Manor Golf; *Style*— David Sugden, Esq

SUGDEN, Prof David Edward; s of John Cyril Gouldie Sugden (d 1963), and Patricia, *née* Backhouse (d 2016); *b* 5 March 1941; *Educ* Warwick Sch, Univ of Oxford (BA, DPhil); *m* 9 Aug 1966, Britta Valborg, da of Harald Stridsberg, of Sweden; 2 s (John Peter, Michael Edward), 1 da (Pauline Charlotta); *Career* scientific offr Br Antarctic Survey 1965–66, lectr then reader Univ of Aberdeen 1966–87; Univ of Edinburgh: prof Dept of Geography 1987–, head Sch of GeoSciences 2003–06, actg dir SAGES (Scottish Alliance for Geoscience, Environment and Society) 2006–07; visiting prof Arctic and Alpine Inst USA; pres Inst of Br Geographers 1995; memb: Royal Scot Geographical Soc, Royal Geographical Soc, Royal Soc (Edinburgh); Vega Medal Stockholm (awarded by King of Sweden) 1993, Polar Medal 2003, Seligman Crystal Int Glaciological Soc 2012; FRSE 1990; *Books* Glaciers and Landscape (with B S John, 1976), Arctic and Antarctic (1982), Geomorphology (with S Schumm and R J Chorley, 1986); *Recreations* hill walking, gardening, skiing; *Style*— Prof David Sugden, FRSE; ✉ Institute of Geography, School of Geosciences, University of Edinburgh, Drummond Street, Edinburgh EH8 9XP (e-mail david.sugden@ed.ac.uk)

SUGDEN, Prof Robert; s of Frank Gerald Sugden (d 1987), and Kathleen, *née* Buckley (d 1999); *b* 26 August 1949; *Educ* Eston GS, Univ of York (BA, DLitt), UC Cardiff (MSc); *m* 26 March 1982, Christine Margaret, da of Leslie Kenneth Upton, of Woking, Surrey; 1 s (Joe b 1984), 1 da (Jane b 1986); *Career* lectr in economics Univ of York 1971–78, reader in economics Univ of Newcastle upon Tyne 1978–85, prof of economics UEA 1985–; FBA 1996; *Books* The Principles of Practical Cost-Benefit Analysis (with A Williams, 1978), The Economics of Rights, Cooperation and Welfare (1986), Experimental Economics: Rethinking the Rules (with N Bardsley, R Cubitt, G Loomes, P Moffatt and C Starmer, 2010); *Recreations* walking, gardening; *Style*— Prof Robert Sugden, FBA; ✉ School of Economics, University of East Anglia, Norwich NR4 7TJ (☎ 01603 593423, fax 01603 250434, telex 975197, e-mail r.sugden@uea.ac.uk)

SUIRDALE, Viscount; John Michael James Hely-Hutchinson; er s and h of 8 Earl of Donoughmore; *b* 7 August 1952; *Educ* Harrow; *m* 1, 1977 (m dis 2006), Marie-Claire, da of Gerard van den Driessche (d 1985); 2 da (Hon Marie-Pierre Joanna b 1978, Hon Tatiana Louise b 1985), 1 s (Hon Richard Gregory b 1980); m 2, 28 April 2008, Nutjarin Photiruk; *Heir* s, Hon Richard Hely-Hutchinson; *Career* Bagajavion Paris 1978–89, Alfred Dunhill Ltd 1989–92, Burberry Ltd 1993–2003, Burberry Japan KK 2003–06, Lambert Howarth Gp plc 2007, Daks Simpson Gp plc 2009, Integrix Sports Gp Ltd 2010; mgmnt conslt since 2007; *Recreations* golf, skiing, fishing; *Clubs* IOD, Denham Golf, Farnham Golf; *Style*— Viscount Suirdale; ✉ 40 Guildford Road, Fleet, Hampshire GU51 3EY (suirdale@aol.com, suirdale@yahoo.com)

SULLIVAN, David; *b* 5 February 1949, Cardiff; *Educ* Queen Mary Coll London; *Career* businessman; owner: Sport Newspapers 1986–2007, Birmingham City FC 1993–2009, West Ham United FC 2009–; *Style*— David Sullivan, Esq; ✉ West Ham United FC, Boleyn Ground, Green Street, Upton Park, London E13 9AZ

SULLIVAN, Rt Hon Sir Jeremy Mirth; kt (1997), PC (2009); s of late Arthur Brian Sullivan, and Pamela Jean, *née* Kendall; *b* 17 September 1945; *Educ* Framlingham Coll, KCL (LLB, LLM); *m* 1, 1970 (m dis), Ursula Klara Marie, da of late Benno August Friederich Hildenbrock; 2 s (Richard b 1974, Geoffrey b 1976); m 2, 1993, Dr Sandra Jean Farmer, da of late Allan Stuart Fisher; 2 step s; *Career* 2 Lt Suffolk & Cambs Regt (TA) 1963–

65; called to the Bar Inner Temple 1968 (bencher 1993); lectr in law City of London Poly 1968–71, in practice Planning & Local Govt Bar 1971–97, QC 1982, recorder 1989–97, dep judge of the High Court 1993–97, judge of the High Court of Justice (Queen's Bench Div) 1997–2009, Lord Justice of Appeal 2009–15, sr pres of tbnls 2012–15, ret; attorney-gen to the Prince of Wales 1994–97; chm Tbnls Ctee Judicial Studies Bd 1999–2007, dep chm Parly Boundary Cmmn for England 2004–09, memb Parly Bar 1990–97 (hon memb 1997–); memb Cncl RTPI 1983–87, memb Exec Ctee Georgian Gp 1985–89, govr Highgate Sch 1990–2003; LAMTPI 1970, LMRTPI 1976; *Recreations* the Wotton Light Railway; *Clubs* Athenaeum; *Style*— The Rt Hon Sir Jeremy Sullivan; ✉ 50A Montpellier Spa Road, Cheltenham, Gloucestershire GL50 1UL

SULLIVAN, Michael Francis; s of Sir Richard Benjamin Magniac Sullivan, 8 Bt (d 1977), and Muriel Mary Paget Pineo (d 1988); *b* 4 April 1936; *Educ* St Andrew Coll, Clare Coll Cambridge (MA, MB BChir), St Mary's Hosp London; *m* 1, 22 Aug 1957 (m dis 1978), Inger, da of Arne Mathieson (d 1984); 1 s (Richard b 9 Jan 1961), 1 da (Nicola b 20 Aug 1965); m 2, 22 Dec 1978, Caroline Mary, da of Maj Christopher Griffin (d 1994); 1 da (Lucy b 22 Nov 1980); *Career* spinal surgn Royal Nat Orthopaedic Hosp London 1971–; visiting lectr in spinal surgery: Australia 1985, South Africa 1981, USA 1980, Canada 1982, Japan 1989, most European countries 1989–99; author of numerous articles on spinal surgery; pres European Spinal Surgns 1990–91, sec Int Lumbar Spine Surgns 1975–78; FRCS; *Recreations* cricket, sailing, shooting, golf; *Clubs* MCC, Royal Harwich Yacht, Royal Workington and Newmarket Golf; *Style*— Michael Sullivan, Esq; ✉ 12 Gloucester Crescent, London NW1 7DS (☎ 020 7485 4473); The Old Hall, Worlington, Suffolk IP28 8RX (☎ 01638 716664)

SULTOON, Jeffrey Alan; s of Maurice Sultoon, of London, and Babette, *née* Braun; *b* 8 October 1953; *Educ* Haberdashers' Aske's, St Edmund Hall Oxford; *m* 11 May 1985, Vivien Caryl, da of Peter Woodbridge, of Guildford, Surrey; 1 s (Hugh); *Career* admitted slr 1978; slr Freshfields 1978–81, ptnr Ashurst Morris Crisp (now Ashurst LLP) 1986– (slr 1981–86); past memb Company Law Ctee Law Soc; *Books* Tolley's Company Law (contrib); *Style*— Jeffrey Sultoon, Esq; ✉ Ashurst, Broadwalk House, 5 Appold Street, London EC2A 2HA (☎ 020 7638 1111, fax 020 7638 1112, e-mail jeffrey.sultoon@ashurst.com)

SUMMERFIELD, Spencer Robert; s of Robert Edward Summerfield (d 1991), and Lilian Rose Summerfield; *b* 25 February 1965, Romford, Essex; *Educ* Chigwell Sch, Gonville & Caius Coll Cambridge (MA); *m* (m dis); 1 s (Louis Robert b 29 Jan 2001), 2 da (Abigail Catherine b 13 Aug 2002, Eleanor Rose b 17 Nov 2015); *Career* Travers Smith Braithwaite (now Travers Smith): joined 1987, ptnr 1997–, head of corporate finance 2003–13, head of corporate 2013–; memb Law Soc 1989; *Publications* Tolley's Company Law (contrib); *Recreations* bodyattack, family, cinema; *Style*— Spencer Summerfield, Esq; ✉ Travers Smith, 10 Snow Hill, London EC1A 2AL (☎ 020 7295 3229, fax 020 7295 3500, e-mail spencer.summerfield@traverssmith.com)

SUMMERS, Andrew William Graham; CMG (2001); s of Basil Summers (d 1988), and Margaret, *née* Hunt; *b* 19 June 1946; *Educ* Mill Hill Sch (exhibitioner), Fitzwilliam Coll Cambridge, Harvard Business Sch (ISMP); *m* 1971, Frances, *née* Halestrap; 2 da (Sarah b 1974, Kate b 1976), 1 s (Bennet b 1979); *Career* economist CBC Bank Sydney 1968, salesman rising to brand mangr Ranks Hovis McDougall plc 1968–75, md J A Sharwood & Co 1980–85 (mktg mangr then mktg dir 1975–80), md RHM Foods Ltd 1987–90 (commercial dir 1986–87), chief exec Management Charter Initiative 1991–94, chief exec Design Council 1995–2003; chm: Brandsmiths 2003–06, Design Partners 2004–, Companies House 2007–12, Cala Social Capital 2011–; non-exec dir S Daniels plc 1991–2002, dir Ramboll Ltd 2005–11; chm: Euro Trade Ctee DTI 1986–99, RSA Migration Cmmn 2004–06, Int Advsy Bd Hong Kong Design Centre 2004–07; memb: Food from Britain Export Cncl 1982–86, BOTB 1998–99, British Trade International 1999–2003, Advsy Cncl Design Mgmnt Inst USA 1998–2003, Bd Small Business Serv 2000–07, Advsy Bd VSO 2004–06, Quality Assurance Agency for HE 2005–11, Bd UKTI Olympic Task Force 2010–12, Parly Cmmn on Future of Mgmnt and Leadership 2013–14; adjunct prof Hong Kong Poly Univ 2004–; pres OM Eton Fives Club 2004–, govr Conservatoire for Dance and Drama (chm Fin Ctee) 2005–13, chm Friends of St Mary's Barnes 2000–, chm Advsy Bd Westminster Business Sch 2010–, memb Cncl KCL (chm Audit & Compliance Ctee) 2010–, chm Barnes Music Festival 2012–, chm Design Panel UK Pavilion 2015 World Expo 2014–; Hon DLitt Univ of Westminster; FRSA 1991 (dep pres 2003–10), CCMI 1997 (chm Bd of Companions 2009–13); *Recreations* cooking, theatre, cycling; *Style*— Andrew Summers, Esq, CMG; ✉ 114 Station Road, London SW13 0NB (☎ and fax 020 8876 6719, e-mail andrew@andrewsummers.co.uk)

SUMMERS, Brian; MBE (2008); *b* 29 March 1945, West Bromwich, West Midlands; *Career* trainee then public finance accountant West Bromwich CBC 1964–73, asst county treas West Midlands CC 1975–84 (chief accountant 1973–75); Birmingham International Airport: joined as commercial dir 1984, financial dir (following company formation) 1987–90, dep md 1990–94, md 1994–2003; chair Sandwell Futures Ltd, chair/tstee The Pump (East Birmingham) Ltd; chm: Birmingham C of C Pension Tstee Co Ltd, Tourism West Midlands 2004–11; memb Cncl/Bd West Midlands Regnl Assembly 2004–10; govr Matthew Boulton Coll 2003–08; memb Cncl Birmingham C of C (memb Bd 2002–08); Hon Dr Birmingham City Univ 2006; *Recreations* West Bromwich Albion FC, golf, sport generally; *Style*— Brian Summers, Esq, MBE; ✉ e-mail summersb26@gmail.com

SUMMERS, David Lewis; OBE (2009), JP (1998); s of Maj Lewis Summers (d 1948), and Beatrice, *née* Greenaway; *b* 25 November 1941; *Educ* Mundella Sch Nottingham, St Edmund Hall Oxford (MA), Univ of Bristol, Harvard Business Sch; *m* 24 Dec 1966, Veronica Yvonne Elizabeth Summers, MBE, da of Cyril Clarence King (d 1970); 2 s (Jonathan b 1971, Benjamin b 1973); *Career* RN Lt 1963–66; Longmans 1966–69, Butterworths 1969–97 (sometime dep chm and UK chief exec), dir Royal Society of Medicine Press 1997–2003, publishing conslt 1997–, chm Wilmington plc 2005–11, former dir Reed Elsevier (UK) Ltd; ed Where to Publish in Law 1998, also contrib various chapters to professional pubns; lay memb Restrictive Practices Court 1999; memb: Competition Appeal Tbnl 2000–12, Lord Chllr's Advsy Ctee for Kent 2002–11; chm of govrs St Bede's Sch Tst Sussex 1999–2008; tstee Kraszna-Krausz Fndn 1998–2007; *Recreations* tennis, walking; *Clubs* Garrick; *Style*— David Summers, Esq, OBE, JP; ✉ Fir Tree Farm, Golford Road, Cranbrook, Kent TN17 3NW (☎ and fax 01580 715424, e-mail dl.summers@btinternet.com)

SUMMERS, Jonathan; *b* 2 October 1946; *Educ* Macleod HS Melbourne Aust, Prahan Tech Coll Melbourne; *m* 29 March 1969, Lesley; 3 c; *Career* baritone; professional debut singing title role in Rigoletto (Kent Opera under Roger Norrington, dir Jonathan Miller) 1975, ENO debut as Tonio in I Pagliacci 1976, Royal Opera House debut as Killian in Der Freischütz 1977; princ Royal Opera Co 1976–86; Order of Australia Medal 2009 *Performances* roles incl: title role in Macbeth (ENO) 1990, Figaro in Le Nozze di Figaro (Bavarian Staatsoper) 1990, Marcello in La Bohème (Covent Garden 1990, Chicago Lyric Opera 1993, Nat Theatre Munich 1993, Theâtre du Capitole Toulouse 1995), Grand Prêtre in Samson and Dalila (Covent Garden) 1991 and 1992, Balstrode in Peter Grimes (ENO) 1991, Iago in Otello (Opera Australia Sydney) 1991, Ford in Falstaff (Theâtre du Capitole Toulouse 1991 and 1995, Theâtre Municipale Lausanne 1995), Rodrigo in Don Carlos (ENO) 1992, Don Carlos in The Force of Destiny (ENO) 1992 and 1995, title role in Rigoletto (ENO and Bergen Festival) 1993, Anckarstroem in Un Ballo in Maschera (Opera Australia Melbourne) 1993, Zurga in The Pearl Fishers (ENO) 1994, De Siriex in Fedora (Covent Garden and Chicago Lyric Opera) 1994, Père Germont in La Traviata (Opera Australia Sydney) 1994, Michele in Il Tabarro (Opera Australia Sydney) 1995, title role in Nabucco (WNO 1995 and Opera Australia Melbourne 1996), Kurwenal in Tristan und Isolde (ENO) 1996, title role in Falstaff (Opera Australia Sydney) 1996, Simone Trovai in Korngold's Violanta (Opera North at BBC Proms) 1997, Amonasro in Aida (Opera North) 1997, Iago in Otello (Royal Opera Royal Festival Hall) 1997, Scarpia in Tosca (Spier Festival Cape Town) 1998, Père Germent in La Traviata (WNO & New Israeli Opera Tel Aviv) 1998, title role in Rigoletto (Opera Australia Sydney) 1998, Scarpia in Tosca (Bühnen der Stadt Cologne) 1998, Amfortas in Parsifal (ENO) 1999, Kurvenal in Tristan and Isolde (WNO) 1999, title role in Wozzeck (Opera Australia Sydney) 1999, Balstrode in Peter Grimes (ENO) 1999, title role in Rigoletto (New Israeli Opera Tel Aviv) 2000, Barnaba in La Gioconda (Opera North) 2000, title role in Simon Boccanegra (Opera Australia Sydney) 2000, title role in Wozzeck (Opera Australia Melbourne) 2000 (Opera Male Singer in a Principal Role Green Room Theatre Awards Victoria), Père Germent in La Traviata (WNO) 2001, Balstrode in Peter Grimes (Opera Australia Sydney) 2001, Die Winterreise (Sydney and Melbourne) 2001, Amfortas in Parsifal (State Opera of South Australia Adelaide) 2001 (Best Male Performer in an Opera Helpmann Awards), Pere Germont in La Traviata (New Israeli Opera Tel Aviv) 2001, Balstrode in Peter Grimes (Theatre du Capitole Toulouse) 2002, Prus in Vec Makropulos (Houston Grand Opera) 2002, Scarpia in Tosca (Buhnen der Stadt Cologne) 2002, Alfio in Cavalleria Rusticana, Tonio in I Pagliacci and Scarpia in Tosca (Opera Australia Sydney) 2002 (Best Supporting Male Performer in an Opera Helpmann Awards), Alfio in Cavalleria Rusticana and Tonio in I Pagliacci (WNO) 2003, Kurvenal in Tristan & Isolde (WNO) 2003, Iago in Otello (Opera Australia Sydney) 2003, Scarpia in Tosca (Opera Australia Melbourne) 2003, Hollander in Der Fliegender Hollander (Opera Australia Sydney) 2004, Malatesta in Francesca da Rimini, Michele in Il Tabarro and Tonio in I Pagliacci (all Opera North) 2004, Gunter in Götterdämmerung State Opera of South Australia Adelaide) 2004, Pere Germont in La Traviata and title role in Rigoletto (both WNO) 2005 Klinghoffer in The Death of Klinghoffer (Edinburgh Festival) 2005, Pere Germont in La Traviata (Israeli Opera Tel Aviv) 2005, Ezio in Attila (Chelsea Opera Group) 2006, Renato in Un Ballo in Maschera (The Israeli Opera Tel Aviv) 2006, Alfio in Cavalleria Rusticana (Hamburg Staats Oper) 2006, Tonio in I Pagliacci (Hamburg Staats Oper) 2006, title role in Rigoletto (Opera North) 2006 and 2007 (also Opera Australia Sydney 2006), The Tempest (ROH) 2007, Michele in Il Tabarro and Gianni Schicchi (Opera Australia Sydney) 2007, Wolfram in Tannhauser (Opera Australia Sydney) 2007, Geppetto in The Adventures of Pinocchio (Opera North) 2007–08, Balstrode in Peter Grimes (Opera North) 2008, Sharpless in Madam Butterfly and Barnaba in La Gioconda (Israel Opera Tel Aviv) 2008, Iago in Othello (Opera Australia Sydney and Melbourne) 2008, Alfio in Cavalleria Rusticana and Tonio in Pagliacci (Opera Australia Sydney) 2009, Phillipe the Butler in Prima Donna (Manchester Int Festival) 2009, Jack Rance in La Fanciulla Del West (West Australian Opera) 2009, Tomsky in the Queen of Spades (Opera North) 2011, Mr Redburn in Billy Budd (ENO) 2012, Forrester in Cunning Little Vixen (WNO) 2013, Don Carlos in La Forza Del Destino (Opera Australia) 2013, Le Baillie in Werther (Met Opera NY) 2014, Spencer Coyle in Owen Wingrave (Aldeburgh) 2014, Iago in Otello (ENO) 2014; concert repertoire incl: Mendelssohn Elijah, Fauré Requiem, Brahms Requiem, Elgar The Kingdom, The Apostles and The Dream of Gerontius, Orff Carmina Burana, Vaughan Williams Sea Symphony, Mahler Das Knaben Wunderhorn, Delius A Mass of Life, Berlioz L'enfance du Christ, Britten War Requiem; *Recordings* incl: Peter Grimes (Grammy Award 1979), Samson et Dalila, La Bohème (as Leoncavallo), The Bohemian Girl, Carmina Burana, Sea Symphony, Gloriana 1993; videos incl: Samson et Dalila, Der Rosenkavalier, Il Trovatore, Nabucco (with Opera Australia); *Style*— Jonathan Summers, Esq, OAM; ✉ website www.jonathansummers.co.uk

SUMMERS, Sue; *Educ* Queen's Coll London, Univ of Bristol (BA); *m* 1, 1979 (m dis 1989), Rod Allen; m 2, Philip Norman; 1 da (Jessica Rose b 22 Nov 1990); *Career* journalist and TV prodr; grad trainee Thomson Regional Newspapers, trainee reporter Reading Evening Post, TV and film corr Screen International, TV ed London Evening Standard, ed screen pages Sunday Times, asst ed (arts) London Daily News, ed 7 Days magazine Sunday Telegraph, freelance writer and broadcaster, co-md Finestripe Prodns Ltd 2005–; TV credits incl: co-prodr Child of the Death Camps: Truth or Lies, Inside Story (BBC1) 1999, co-prodr Touching the Void (winner Alexander Korda Award for Outstanding British Film BAFTA 2004), prodr Shrink Rap with Dr Pamela Connolly (More4) 2007–10 (3 series), exec prod The Day John Lennon Died (ITV) 2010, The Day Kennedy Died (ITV) 2012, The Day They Dropped the Bomb (ITV) 2015, The Day Hitler Died (ITV) 2016, Million Dollar American Princesses (with Elizabeth McGovern, Smithsonian Channel); memb: Bafta, Channel 4 Theatre Writers' Award Scheme; *Style*— Ms Sue Summers; ✉ e-mail sue@finestripe.com

SUMMERSKILL, Ben Jeffrey Peter; OBE (2009); s of Hon Michael Brynmôr Summerskill, and Florence Marion Johnston Summerskill; *b* 6 October 1961; *Educ* Sevenoaks Sch, Merton Coll Oxford (exhibitioner); *Career* asst ed The Observer 2001–03, chief exec Stonewall 2003–14, dir Criminal Justice Alliance 2014–; cmmr Equality and Human Rights Cmmn 2006–09; memb Ctee Queen's Award for Voluntary Service 2009–; *Recreations* thinking; *Style*— Ben Summerskill, Esq, OBE; ✉ Criminal Justice Alliance, Vox Studios, Durham Street, London SE11 5JH (☎ 020 3752 5709)

SUMMERTON, Edward James; s of Edward Summerton, of Dundee, and Zenna, *née* Dodds; *b* 9 February 1962; *Educ* Kirkton HS Dundee, Duncan of Jordanstone Coll of Art (BA, MA); *m* Sept 1989, Rosalie, da of Ronald Dow; 1 s (Joseph Daniel b Oct 1991), 1 da (Jasmine Sylvia Zenna b Oct 1993); *Career* lectr in drawing and painting Edinburgh Coll of Art 1990–92, lectr in fine art Duncan of Jordanstone Coll of Art 1993–; visiting artist: Univ of Calif Berkeley, Clermont Ferrand; professional memb Soc of Scottish Artists 1994, ARSA 1996; *Solo Exhibitions* Compass Gallery Glasgow, Clermont Ferrand Art Sch France, RSA Edinburgh, MacRobert Art Centre Stirling, Meffan Inst Forfar, Raw Gallery London, Bird of the Devil (ET4U Art Centre Denmark) 2006, The Rural (Edinburgh Printmakers) 2006; *Group Exhibitions* incl: Lion Rampant (Artspace San Francisco), Metropolis (RAAB Gallery Berlin), Contemporary Scottish Art (Lincoln Art Centre NY), Compass Contribution (Tramway Glasgow), New Contemporaries (Christie's London), Celtic Connections (Glasgow Royal Concert Hall), International Showcase (Limner Gallery NY), Guilding the Summer Town (Royal Scottish Acad Edinburgh) 2005, Blind Sight (Titamk Turku) 2005, Doctor Skin (Perth Museum) 2006; *Awards* Elizabeth Greenshields Award Canada 1986, artists' exchange between Scotland and France 1987, Alistair Salvesen Award 1989, RSA Latimer Award 1993 and 1994, RSA Gillies Bequest 1997; *Publications* Edward Summerton – North of Normal (catalogue, 1996), Line Controller (artist's book, 1998), Guilding the Summer Town (catalogue, 2006), Bird of the Devil (artist's book, 2006); *Recreations* getting lost; *Style*— Edward Summerton, Esq; ✉ Department of Fine Art, Duncan of Jordanstone College of Art, University of Dundee (☎ 01382 223261, fax 01382 200983)

SUMMERTON, Dr Neil William; CB (1997); s of Hila Summerton (d 1975), and Nancy Summerton (d 1975); *b* 5 April 1942; *Educ* Wellington GS, KCL (BA, PhD); *m* 1965, Pauline, *née* Webb; 2 s (Ian b 1968, Matthew b 1970); *Career* asst princ Miny of Tport 1966–69, asst sec KCL 1971–74 (PA to princ 1969–71); DOE: princ 1974–78, asst sec 1978–85, under sec Land Use Planning 1985–88, under sec Local Govt Fin Policy 1988–91, under sec Water Directorate 1991–95, dir Water and Land 1996–97; supernumerary fell Mansfield Coll Oxford 1997–2003 (now emeritus), dir Oxford Centre for the Environment, Ethics and Society 1997–2002, dir Oxford Centre for Water Research 1998–

S

2002; Partnership (UK) Ltd: exec sec 1990–97, dir 1994–, chm 1997–2014, sec 2014–; non-exec dir: Redland Bricks Ltd 1988–91, North Surrey Water Ltd 1998–2000, Folkestone & Dover Water Services Ltd 1998–2009, Three Valleys Water plc 2000–09, Veolia Water SE Ltd 2009–12, Veolia Water Central Ltd 2009–12; dir and tstee various Christian charities; *Publications* A Noble Task: Eldership and Ministry in the Local Church (revised edn 1994), Learning From the Past, Facing the Future: Essays for 'Brethren' (2011); various articles on historical, ethical, environmental and theological subjects; *Style*— Dr Neil Summerton, CB

SUMNER, Prof Ann Beatrice; da of late Tim Sumner, and Rita Sumner, of Lansdown, Bath; *b* 15 July 1960; *Educ* The Royal Sch Bath, Kingswood Sch Bath, Courtauld Inst London (BA), Newnham Coll Cambridge (PhD); *m* 1, (m dis); 2 da; m 2, 2 Jan 2009, Martin Johnson; *Career* archive asst Nat Portrait Gallery London 1984–85, asst curator Holburne of Menstrie Museum Univ of Bath 1985–88, res asst Whitworth Art Gallery Univ of Manchester 1988–89, pt/t curator Museum of Farnham 1991–92, successively keeper then research fell Dulwich Picture Gallery 1992–95, sr curator Harewood House Tst 1994–96, keeper of art Holburne of Menstrie Museum Bath 1996–2000, head of fine art Nat Museum & Gallery of Wales Cardiff 2000–07, dir Barber Inst of Fine Arts Univ of Birmingham 2007–12, dir Birmingham Museums Tst 2012, exec dir Bronte Parsonage Museum 2012–; tstee Methodist Art Collection, memb Ctee Nat Inventory of European Paintings Nat Gallery London; author of numerous art historical articles and pamphlets, regular lectr and contrib to academic seminars and confs; *Exhibition Catalogues* Gainsborough in Bath – A Bicentenary Exhibition (1988), Rembrandt's Girl at a Window (1993), Death, Passion and Politics: Van Dyck and the Digbys (jtly, 1995), Harewood Masterpieces: Watercolours by Turner, Girtin and Varley (jtly), Secret Passion for Noble Fashion: the World of the Portrait Miniature (jtly, 1999), A Classical Vision: the art of Thomas Cromek (jtly, 2000), John Brett A Pre-Raphaelite on the Shores of Wales (jtly, 2001), Thomas Jones (1742–1803): An Artist Rediscovered (jt ed, 2003), Colour and Light: 50 Impressionist Paintings at the National Museum of Wales (2005), Faces of Wales (2006), Things of Beauty (jtly, 2007), Gwen John: Mère Poussepin and the Catholic Church (2008), Court on Canvas: Tennis in Art (2011), In Front of Nature: the European Landscapes of Thomas Fearnley (jt ed, 2012), Foundations of a Collection (2012); *Recreations* tennis,theatre, cinema; *Clubs* Lansdown Lawn Tennis; *Style*— Prof Ann Sumner; ✉ The Bronte Parsonage Museum, Haworth, Keighley, West Yorkshire BD22 8DR (☎ 01535 642323, fax 01535 647131, e-mail ann.sumner@bronte.org.uk)

SUMNER, Christopher Kent; s of George Tomlinson Sumner (d 1979), and Alice Mary Bettley Sumner, *née* Brown (d 1989); *b* 28 September 1943, Liverpool; *Educ* The King's Sch Chester, Univ of Durham (BA, MA); *m* 1, 3 Aug 1967, Marjorie Prince (d 2005); 2 s (Stuart b 1970, Edward b 1974); m 2, 9 May 2015, Bernadette Marie Coates; 3 step s, 2 step da; *Career* slr; sr coroner for Merseyside (Sefton, St Helens and Knowsley districts) 1998–; chm: Social Security Appeal Tbnls 1984–2006, Disability Appeal Tbnls 1992–2006; Parly candidate (Lib) Runcorn 1970; pres Southport and Ormskirk Law Soc 1994, pres North West and North Wales Coroners' Soc 2008–10; *Recreations* golf; *Clubs* Rotary, Hillside Golf; *Style*— Christopher K Sumner, Esq; ✉ 4 Mossgiel Avenue, Ainsdale, Southport PR8 2RE (☎ 01704 573153, e-mail christopher.sumner@btinternet.com)

SUMNER, Francis Ian; s of Guy Chadwick Sumner (d 1986), and Margaret Hilliard, *née* Wilson (d 1995); *b* 25 October 1942; *Educ* Tonbridge; *m* 29 Dec 1978, Diana Harriman, da of John Ernest Newman (d 2010); 2 s (Edward John b 18 Nov 1979, Richard William b 12 May 1981), 1 da (Nicola Margaret b 6 Dec 1982); *Career* asst slr Slaughter & May 1966–72 (articled clerk 1961–66); Norton Rose: asst slr 1972–73, ptnr 1973–97, conslt 1997–98; dir: Crown Agents 1992–2011 (dep chm 1998–2011), Bankers Investment Tst plc 1997–2011; vice-pres Crown Agents Fndn Cncl 2011–; memb Cncl: City & Guilds of London Inst 1998–2016 (vice-chm 2004–09), Assessment and Qualifications Alliance 1998–2008 (vice-chm 2006–08); tstee Central Fndn Schs of London 2010–; Freeman City of London Solicitors' Co; memb: IOD, Law Soc; Hon FCGI 2003; *Recreations* golf, gardening, fishing, shooting; *Style*— Francis Sumner, Esq; ☎ 01732 462337, fax 01732 457419, e-mail francissumner@tiscali.co.uk

SUMNERS, Dr David George; s of George William Sumners, of London, and Irene Florence, *née* Kelly; *b* 23 September 1952; *Educ* William Ellis Sch, UCL (BSc, MB BS); *m* 12 June 1976, Susan Mary, da of late Thomas Arthur Bourn; 1 da (Emily Mary b 23 March 1982), 1 s (William David b 28 Feb 1985); *Career* conslt psychiatrist: Edgware Gen Hosp and Napsbury Hosp 1988–92, Grovelands Priory Hosp 1988–; dir NW Thames RHA Brain Injury Rehabilitation Unit 1988–92, med dir Barnet Healthcare NHS Tst 1992–, conslt forensic psychiatrist Kneesworth House Hosp 1992–94, conslt Brain Injury Rehabilitation Tst 1994–2014, med examiner GMC 2001–11; FRCPysch 2001 (MRCPsych 1983), FRSM; *Style*— Dr David Sumners; ✉ Crofton Medical Reports, CMR House, 425 Footscray Road, London SE9 3UL (☎ 0845 051 7777, fax 020 8331 6000)

SUMPTION, Lord; Rt Hon Jonathan Philip Chadwick Sumption; OBE, PC (2011); s of Anthony James Sumption, DSC, and Hedy, *née* Hedigan; *b* 9 December 1948; *Educ* Eton, Magdalen Coll Oxford (MA); *m* 26 June 1971, Teresa Mary, da of Jerome Bernard Whelan; 2 da (Frederique b 1979, Madeleine b 1983), 1 s (Bernard b 1981); *Career* fell Magdalen Coll Oxford 1971–75; called to the Bar Inner Temple 1975 (bencher 1990); QC 1986–2012; judge Courts of Appeal Jersey and Guernsey 1995–2012, judicial appts cmmr 2006–12, a Justice of the Supreme Court 2012–; tstee Royal Acad of Music 2002–; *Books* Pilgrimage An Image of Medieval Religion (1975), The Albigensian Crusade (1978), The Hundred Years War (vol 1 1990, vol 2 1999, vol 3 2009, vol 4 2015); *Recreations* music, history; *Clubs* Beefsteak, Garrick; *Style*— The Lord Sumption, PC; ✉ The Supreme Court of the United Kingdom, Parliament Square, London SW1P 3BD

SUNDERLAND, Adam Philip Rothwell; s of Henry Sunderland, of Doncaster, S Yorks, and Marjorie, *née* Rothwell (d 1990); *b* 13 December 1958; *Educ* Oundle, Doncaster GS, The Queen's Coll Oxford (MA); *m* Laura; 1 da (Ella), 1 s (Benjamin); *Career* Ogilvy & Mather Advertising: account exec London 1980–81, account exec NY 1981–84, account supr NY 1984–85, vice-pres/account supr NY 1985–86; vice-pres and memb Exec Ctee Saunders Lubinski and White Advertising Dallas 1986–87, vice-pres/mgmnt supr Ogilvy & Mather Advertising USA 1987–90; Woollams Moira Gaskin O'Malley: bd account dir 1990–92, client servs dir 1992–94, dep md 1994–95; managing ptnr White Door 1997–2004, md Breed Communications Ltd 2005–; *Recreations* golf, tennis, skiing, travel; *Clubs* RAC; *Style*— Adam Sunderland, Esq; ✉ Unit 4.01, Tea Building, 56 Shoreditch High Street, London E1 6JJ (☎ 020 7462 7888, fax 020 7462 7965, e-mail adam@breedcommunications.com)

SUNDERLAND, Alistair John; s of Dr Robert Slater Sunderland, and Marion, *née* Wilson; *b* 24 March 1949; *Educ* Lewis' Sch for Boys, Liverpool Poly; *m* Glenys, da of Gwylim Thomas; 2 s (Adam Thomas, Geraint John), 2 da (Sian Marion, Rhian Alice); *Career* ptnr Austin-Smith: Lord 1974–; chair Liverpool Urban Design and Conservation Advsy Panel; memb: Bd S Liverpool Regeneration, Bd Liverpool Biennial; RIBA: memb 1978–, past memb Nat Cncl, memb NW Region; *Recreations* swimming; *Clubs* Liverpool Architectural Soc (past pres), Long Lane Church; *Style*— Alistair Sunderland, Esq; ✉ Austin-Smith: Lord, Port of Liverpool Building, Pier Head, Liverpool L3 1BY

SUNDERLAND, Sir John Michael; kt (2006); s of Harry Sunderland, and Joyce Eileen, *née* Farnish; *b* 24 August 1945; *Educ* King Edward VII Lytham, Univ of St Andrews (MA); *m* Sept 1965, Jean Margaret, da of Col Alexander Grieve (d 1975); 1 da (Corianne b 1966), 3 s (Jonathan b 1969, Robin b 1972, Ben Alexander b 1978); *Career* Cadbury Schweppes plc: joined 1968, main bd dir 1993–2008, md Confectionery Stream 1993–96, chief exec 1996–2003, exec chm 2003–08; chm Merlin Entertainment Gp 2009–, chm Cambridge Educn Gp 2014–; non-exec dir: Rank Organisation 1997–2006, Barclays 2005–15; dir AFC Energy plc 2012–15; memb Advsy Bd CVC Capital Partners 2006–08; pres: Food and Drink Fedn 2002–04, Incorporated Soc of Br Advertisers (ISBA) 2002–05, CBI 2004–06 (dep pres 2007–08), Chartered Mgmnt Inst 2007–08; dir Financial Reporting Cncl 2004–11; govr Univ of Reading Cncl 2008–15, chllr Aston Univ 2011–; Hon LLD St Andrews Univ 2007, Hon DLitt Aston Univ 2011, Hon LLD Univ of Reading 2016; FRSA, FIGD, CCIMgt, assoc memb BUPA; *Style*— Sir John Sunderland; ✉ Three Barrows, Seale Road, Elstead, Surrey GU8 6LF

SUNNUCKS, John Lloyd; s of James Sunnucks, and Rosemary Ann, *née* Borradaile; *b* 4 March 1959; *Educ* Wellington, Lincoln Coll Oxford, RMA Sandhurst; *m* Lucinda Jane Frances, *née* Davies; 3 da (Isabel, Miranda, Kitty); *Career* served HM Forces 1981–87, Life Gds; City and Commercial Communications 1987–89, Brunswick Group Ltd 1989–2007 (latterly ptnr), conslt Tulchan Communications 2007–; *Clubs* Turf; *Style*— John Sunnucks, Esq

SUNNUCKS, William; s of James Horace George Sunnucks (d 2005), and Rosemary Anne, *née* Borradaile; *b* 1956; *Educ* Wellington (music scholar), Peterhouse Cambridge (MA), London Business Sch (MBA); *m* 1982, Caroline, *née* Nevill; 2 s (Charlie b 1985, Hugo b 1990), 3 da (Georgina b 1988, Katie b 1993, Annabel b 1999); *Career* Peat Marwick Mitchell 1977–82, Shell Int 1982–85, Union Square plc 1988–91, Securum Int 1992–96, English Welsh & Scottish Railway 1996–2000, Partnerships UK 2000–01, gp finance dir Capital & Regional plc 2002–08; chm Land Management Ltd; ACA 1981; *Recreations* sailing (memb Br sailing team 1990–97); *Style*— William Sunnucks, Esq; ✉ Land Management Limited, 43 Market Place, Romford RM1 3AB

SUPPERSTONE, Michael Alan; QC (1991); s of Harold Bernard Supperstone (d 1992), of London, and Muriel, *née* Weinstein (d 1978); *b* 30 March 1950; *Educ* St Paul's, Lincoln Coll Oxford (MA, BCL), Harvard Law Sch (visiting scholar); *m* 18 April 1985, Dianne, da of Abe Jaffe (d 2009); 1 s (Daniel b 1986), 1 da (Laura b 1988); *Career* called to the Bar Middle Temple 1973 (bencher 1999); recorder 1996– (asst recorder 1992–96), dep judge of the High Court 1998–; visiting lectr Nat Univ of Singapore 1981 and 1982; Administrative Law Bar Assoc: sec 1986–90, treas 1991–94, vice-chm 1994–96, chm 1997–98; fell Inst of Advanced Legal Studies 1998; *Books* Judicial Review (1992, 3 edn 2005), Halsbury's Laws of England – Administrative Law Title (4 edn, 1989 and 2001), Immigration and Asylum (1983, 1988, 1994 and 1996), Brownlie's Law of Public Order and National Security (2 edn, 1981), Local Authorities and the Human Rights Act 1998 (1999), Halbury's Laws of England Extradition Law Title (4 edn, 2000), The Freedom of Information Act 2000 (2001), Administrative Court Practice (2 edn, 2008); *Recreations* swimming, walking, reading history; *Clubs* MCC, Garrick, RAC; *Style*— Michael Supperstone, Esq, QC; ✉ 11 King's Bench Walk, Temple, London EC4Y 7EQ (☎ 020 7583 0610, fax 020 7583 9123)

SUPRAMANIAM, YB Dato Lt-Col Paul Atputhakumar Jebarajasingam; er s of late Dr James Mark Jeyasabasingam Supramaniam, PPA, Emeritus FCCP, FRCP, and late Eunice Princess Jebaranee, *née* Aiyathurai, of Jaffna; *b* 24 March 1957, Edinburgh; *Educ* Anglo-Chinese Sch Singapore, Keele Univ (BSocSci), Sidney Sussex Coll Cambridge (Wright Rogers Law scholar, LLM), Trinity Coll of Music London (ATCL, LTCL); *m* 12 Oct 1991, Margaret Rachel Vazeille, *née* Seale, niece of Sir John Seale, 5 Bt; 2 s (James Timothy Bright Aiyathuraisingam b 18 April 1993, Matthew Edward Herring Jeyathuraisingam b 1 Feb 1998); *Career* articled clerk then slr Linklaters & Paines 1984–87, slr Corp Dept Slaughter & May 1988–92, ptnr Holman Fenwick & Willan 1992–98, managing ptnr Lovells Singapore 1998–2002, sr English ptnr (Asia) Latham & Watkins 2002–07, regnl managing ptnr (Asia) Berwin Leighton Paisner 2007–10, chm Law Asia 2010–; formerly: pres Singapore UK Assoc, memb Exec Ctee Singapore Indian Devpt Assoc, judicial memb Ct of the Anglican Church of Singapore, memb Gen Synod Singapore, memb Archbishops' Advsy Bd, dir Asian Civilisations Museum Singapore, dir Save the Children Singapore, dir Singapore Lyric Opera, memb Steering Ctee Nat Art Gallery of Singapore, vice-pres Br Chamber of Commerce; currently: memb Int Ct of Arbitration for Sport Lausanne, memb Disciplinary Ctee Singapore Nat Olympic Cncl, hon legal advsr Singapore Sailing Fedn, pres Oxford and Cambridge Soc of Singapore, Endowment Ctee Singapore Symphony Orch, Indian Business Roundtable, memb Singapore Br Business Cncl, memb Advsy Bd Pinacotheque de Paris; inf offr Singapore Armed Forces 1976–79, former head Legal HQ Tradoc (Lt-Col) Singapore, memb HAC 1984; Freeman: City of London, City of London Slrs' Co; memb Law Soc 1986; Darjah Indera Makhota Pahang (Knight Companion of the Esteemed Order of Pahang Malaysia); *Recreations* opera, art, wine, classic cars, shooting, music (classical, jazz); *Clubs* HAC, Singapore Polo, Singapore Island Country, Tanglin; *Style*— YB Dato Lt-Col Paul Supramaniam, SAF; ✉ 2A Victoria Park Close, Singapore 266550; Law Asia Pte Ltd, 1 North Bridge Road #12–10, High Street Centre, Singapore 179094 (☎ 0065 633 77500, fax 0065 633 63530, e-mail paul@lawasia.com, website www.lawasia.com)

SURATGAR, David; s of Prof Lotfali Suratgar (d 1969), of Tehran, and Prof Edith Olive, *née* Hepburn (d 1985); *b* 23 October 1938; *Educ* Silcoates Sch, New Coll Oxford (MA), Columbia Univ NYC (MIA); *m* 1, 6 Aug 1962, Barbara Lita (d 1990), da of Donald Telfer Low, of Wytham Abbey, Oxford; 1 da (Roxanne Christina Noelle b 25 Dec 1964), 1 s (Karim Donald Hepburn b 4 Aug 1966); m 2, 29 Aug 1994, Wandra Edith, da of Senator Ike Smalley, of Deming, New Mexico; *Career* Legal Dept UN Secretariat 1961–62, Sullivan & Cromwell (lawyers) NYC 1963–64, legal counsel World Bank 1964–73, adjunct prof of law Georgetown 1966–73; Morgan Grenfell & Co Ltd: dir 1973–88, gp dir 1988–97, dep chm Deutsche Morgan Grenfell 1992–97; special legal counsel Bank of England 1976, special advsr European Investment Bank 1994–95; counsel Jones Day 1976–93; chm: Fortune Funds Ltd 2001–13, BMCE Bank Int plc, Masawara plc; dir: BMCE 1995–, Global Alumina Inc; chm: West India Ctee (Royal Charter) 1987–89, Advsy Bd Taylor de Jongh Inc; memb Cncl Chatham House (RIIA) 1993–2006, memb Advsy Bd XPV Capital Corp; memb: Bodleian Library Appeal 1987–2000, Bd UN Cncl on Ageing 2000–03, Bd Lead Int 2003–10, Bd Major Projects Assoc Templeton Coll Oxford, Advsy Bd Int Law Inst Washington DC, Int Advsy Bd SOAS, Bd Pictet et Cie Water Fund; Oxford Playhouse Tst 1989–2002, Garsington Opera Ltd 1989–; memb: Gray's Inn, Int Bar Assoc, Br Inst of Int and Comparative Law; *Books* Default and Rescheduling – Sovereign and Corporate Borrowers in Difficulty (1984), International Financial Law (jlty, 1980); *Recreations* opera, shooting, book collecting, theatre; *Clubs* Travellers, Brooks's, Beefsteak, Metropolitan (Washington DC); *Style*— David Suratgar, Esq; ✉ 11A Hornton Street, London W8 7NP; BMCE Bank, 26 Upper Brook Street, London W1K 7QE (☎ 020 7518 8250, fax 020 7629 0596, e-mail dsuratgar@bmce-intl.co.uk); The Great House, Burford, Oxfordshire OX18 4SN

SURFACE, Richard Charles; *b* 16 June 1948; *Educ* Univ of Minnesota, Univ of Kansas (BA), Harvard Grad Sch of Business Admin (MBA); *m* 1977, Stephanie Maria Josefa Ruth, *née* Hentschel von Gilgenheimb; 2 s, 1 da; *Career* actuarial asst National Life & Accident Insurance Co Tennessee 1970–72; corp treasy analyst Mobil Oil Corp NY 1974–77; dir of Corp Planning Northwest Industries Inc Illinois 1977–81; marketing, strategy, business devpt and gen mngr positions at American Express Co London/Frankfurt 1981–89; gen mangr Corp Devpt Sun Life 1989–91; md: Sun Life International 1991–95, Pearl Gp Ltd 1995–99, AMP (UK) Ltd; ptnr Oliver Wyman 2000–14; writer 2014–; memb Bd ABI 1998–99; *Books* The Legacy (published as Das Vermaechtnis, 2014); *Recreations* collecting antiquarian books, skiing, opera, theatre; *Clubs* RAC, Groucho; *Style*— Richard Surface

SURI, Baron (Life Peer 2014), of Ealing in the London Borough of Ealing; Ranbir Singh Suri; *Career* businessman; fndr and chm Oceanic Jewellers 1977–; fndr and chm Br Asian Cons Link, pres Cons Ethnic Diversity Cncl, gen sec Bd of Br Sikhs 1991–92; gen cmmr of income tax Wembley Div 1995–2007; memb: Bd of Visitors HM Prison Pentonville 1985–2000, Home Office Advsy Cncl on Race Relations 1988–92, Middlesex Probation Ctee 1990–91, Local Review Ctee HM Prison Pentonville 1990–93, Probation Liaison Ctee Ealing Magistrates Court 1991–93, VAT & Duties Tbnl 1993–2009, Valuation Tbnl London 1994–95, Lord Chll'rs Advsy Ctee on Gen Cmmrs of Income Tax 2003–05, London Chamber of Commerce; voluntary assoc: HM Prison Wormwood Scrubs 1982–85, Middlesex Probation Ctee 1983–85; memb Exec Ctee: Bharatiya Vidya Bhavan, Hanger Lane Residents Assoc 1989–90, Br Heart Fndn Ealing 1995–96; chm Anglo Asian Cons Assoc of Hounslow and Feltham 1978, vice-pres Shepherd's Bush Gurdwara 1980–81; advsr Khalsa Coll London 1988–89; mentor The Prince's Youth Business Tst 1997–2003, friend of Shakespeare's Globe; hon correspondent to the Br High Cmmr Kenya (Immigration Affrs) appointed by HM the Queen 1973–74; Shiromani Award (presented by vice-pres of India) 1979, Scroll of Honour (presented by PM of India) 1985; memb IoD 1991–2012; *Style*— The Lord Suri; ✉ House of Lords, London SW1A 0PW

SURMAN, Martyn Charles; s of Leslie Charles Surman (d 1970), of Brighton, and Irene Grace, *née* Rogers (d 2003); *b* 21 November 1944; *Educ* Varndean GS for Boys, Brighton Coll of Technol, Coll of Estate Mgmnt; *m* 1, 1 Oct 1966 (m dis); 2 c (David Keith, Tracey Deborah (twins) b 20 Jan 1968); m 4, 29 May 2007, Sharon Anne, *née* Meredith; *Career* trainee bldg surveyor Watney Mann Brewers 1963–69, sr architectural asst and dep to Borough Architect Architect's Dept Hove BC 1974–78 (joined 1969); PSA Services: troubleshooter Bldg Advsy Branch Croydon 1978, area design mangr Portsmouth 1984, gp planning mangr Portsmouth 1986, gp bldg surveyor 1989, acting gp mangr Portsmouth 1989, PSA dep head of profession bldg surveyors 1990, superintending bldg surveyor 1990, PSA head of profession bldg surveyors 1990–91; dir of bldg surveying PSA Specialist Services 1991–92, dir of bldg surveying servs SpS Surveying 1992–93; div dir TBV Consult Ltd 1993–94, div dir TBV Surveying 1995–96, seconded to Burrow Binnie Int Johannesburg 1996 (ldr int team for devpt of strategy policy for future maintenance of state-owned properties in South Africa), dir of mktg Schal Property Services 1996–97, ops dir Kobi Tarmac South Africa 1997–98, md Kobiprop (Pty) Ltd 1998–2002, business ops dir Nkobi Holdings (Pty) Ltd 1998–2002; Parsons Son & Basley: head Building Surveying Dept 2002–05, head Property Mgmnt Dept 2003–08, assoc ptnr 2003–10, dir Property Mgmnt Servs 2008–10, external conslt 2010–; RICS: memb Bldg Surveyors Divnl Exec 1987–91, memb Gen Cncl 1988–91, chm Health and Safety Working Gp 1989–90, memb Bldg Surveyors Divnl Cncl 1987–91, pres Bldg Surveyors Div 1990–91; memb Sussex Branch Bldg Surveyors 1991–97 (chm 1992–93); ABE: memb Gen Cncl 1994–97, memb Devpt and Monitoring Ctee 1994–97; ARMA: memb Gen Cncl 2007–10, dir ARMA Ltd 2007–10, memb Techcom 2008–10; memb numerous BSI Cmmns; author and presenter of numerous papers on bldg surveying and construction technol at nat confs seminars and BSI launch, co-author PSA tech guides; external examiner BSc Hons Building Surveying: De Montfort Univ 1993–97, Univ of Brighton 1995–2001; observer memb Sec of State's Bldg Regulations Advsy Ctee (BRAC) 1992–97, memb Buxted PC 1993–97; FRICS 1986–2012 (ARICS 1975), FIAS 1993–2009, FBEng 1993–2009, MIRPM 2007–09; *Recreations* sport, travelling, golf, theatre; *Style*— Martyn Surman, Esq; ✉ 19 Milford Court, Brighton Road, Lancing, West Sussex BN15 8RW (☎ 01903 533234, e-mail martynsurman295@btinternet.com)

SURMAN, Nancy L; *Educ* Nottingham Trent Univ (BA); *Career* theatre designer; *Productions* Birmingham Repertory Theatre: Johnny Watkins Walks on Water 1995, Bonded 1997, The Road to Hell 1997, Kaahini 1998; SNAP Theatre Co: Tom Jones 1997, Far from the Madding Crowd 1998, Maurice 1998, Rock and Roll and Barbirolli 1999, Sons and Lovers 2001, My Beautiful Launderette 2002, The Buddha of Suburbia 2004; Oxfordshire Touring Theatre Co: Don Quixote de la Mancha 1998, He Said She Said 1999, Beautiful Thing 2000; Gordon Craig Theatre Stevenage: Noel and Gertie 1999 (also nat tour), Aspects of Love 2001 (also at Octagon Theatre Yeovil), Side by Side by Sondheim 2006; Salisbury Playhouse: The Winter's Tale 2000, Rough Crossing 2000 (also at Palace Theatre Watford), The Secret Rapture 2001, The Rivals 2001, The Duchess of Malfi 2002, Barbarians 2003, Waters of the Moon 2004, To Kill a Mockingbird 2005; Jermyn St Theatre: Privates on Parade 2004, Trojan Women 2004, Much Ado About Nothing 2004; other credits incl: The Final Appearance of Miss Mamie Stuart (Torch Theatre Milford Haven), A Stinging Sea (Citizen's Theatre Glasgow) 1993, Talent (Palace Theatre Watford and Mercury Theatre Colchester) 1999, Private Lives (Octagon Theatre Bolton) 2003, Into the Woods (Trinity Coll of Music at Greenwich Theatre) 2003, Get Ken Barlow (Palace Theatre Watford) 2005, The Accrington Pals (Dukes Theatre Lancaster) 2005, Private Lives (Far East tour Br Theatre Playhouse) 2006, Dad's Army: The Lost Episodes and Dad's Army Marches On (nat tours) 2007–10, Can't Pay? Won't Pay! (Oldham Coliseum) 2008, Animal Farm (Creation Theatre Co) 2008, 'Allo 'Allo (nat tour) 2008, Dangerous Corner (New Vic Theatre Stoke-on-Trent) 2008, The Corstorphine Road Nativity (Festival Theatre Edinburgh) 2009, The Daughter in Law (New Vic Theatre Stoke-on-Trent) 2009; *Exhibitions* Costume Drawings 1988, Joseph's Dream: A Century of Civic Achievement 1989, Magic at Mottisfont 1995, Time and Space – Design for Performance 1999, 2D-3D – Designs for Theatre and Performance 2002, Collaborators – UK Design for Performance 2007; *Style*— Ms Nancy Surman; ✉ c/o Karen Baker, Associated Arts, 8 Shrewsbury Lane, London SE16 3JF (☎ 020 8856 4958)

SURR, Christopher John; s of (Frederick) Anthony Surr, of Bristol, and Mavis Barbara, *née* Hill (d 1973); *b* 19 September 1957; *Educ* St Brendan's Coll Bristol, UMIST (BSc); *m* 1989, Claire-Marie, da of Kenneth Cyril Attenborough (d 1989); 1 s (Thomas William b 1990); *Career* exec Samuel Montagu & Co 1982–85, dir Barclays de Zoete Wedd 1985–97, md Chase Manhattan Bank 1998–99, global head of mktg CreditTrade 1999–2001, vice-pres business devpt europrospectus.com 2001–05, team md Moody's Investors Service 2005–08, md Moody's Analytics 2008–10, vice-pres Morningstar 2010–11, corporate business devpt Whizz-Kidz 2011–13, corporate devpt mangr Leonard Cheshire Disability 2013–14, employer relationship mangr Leonard Cheshire Disability 2014–; fndn govr St Thomas More Sch Chelsea 2002–06, memb Fundraising Ctee Solace Women's Aid 2011–12; Freeman City of London (by redemption); Liveryman: Worshipful Co of Marketors, Worshipful Co of Basketmakers; MCIM 2001, assoc memb Inst of Fundraising 2011; *Recreations* rugby, horse racing, shooting; *Clubs* City Livery; *Style*— Christopher Surr, Esq; ✉ 4 Anderson Street, London SW3 3LU (☎ 020 7581 2576, e-mail chris.surr@hotmail.co.uk)

SURREY, Christopher Durden (Kit); s of Stephen James Surrey (d 1998), of Southampton, and Frances Vera Talbot, *née* Durden, of Newton Abbot, Devon; *b* 23 June 1946; *Educ* Tauntons GS Southampton, Southampton Art Coll, Wimbledon Sch of Art (DipAD); *m* 19 July 1969, Margaret Jillian, da of Leslie Arnold Grealey; 1 s (Thomas Hamo b 7 May 1973), 1 da (Charlotte Sarah b 18 Sept 1975); *Career* theatre designer and artist; asst designer: Citizens Theatre Glasgow 1968–69, London fringe 1970–72; designer: York Theatre Royal 1972–74, Northcott Theatre Exeter 1974–76; freelance 1976–; GB rep Int Orgn of Scenographers and Theatre Technicians E Berlin 1981 and Moscow 1982; memb Soc of Br Theatre Designers, memb Soc of Graphic Fine Art; nomination Best Designer Barclays/TMA Theatre Awards 2000, winner Best Shakespeare Prodn whatson.com 2001, nomination Best Musical Prodn Laurence Olivier Awards 2002, winner UK Sandford Drawing Prize 2002, winner Derwent Drawing Prize 2004, winner SGFA Drawing Prize 2006; *Theatre* incl: The Master Builder, Jumpers, Death of a Salesman, Toad of Toad Hall (all Theatr Clwyd), One Flew Over the Cuckoo's Nest, Shades of Brown, The Wizard of Oz, Alice in Wonderland, The Turn of the Screw, The Merchant of Venice, The Taming of the Shrew, The Last Yankee, Amadeus, The Grapes of Wrath, Richard IV (premiere), Northanger Abbey (all Northcott), Rosmersholm (Royal Exchange Manchester), Turkey Time, John Bull, The Secret Rapture (all Bristol Old Vic), Peter Grimes, The Queen of Spades (both New Sussex Opera), Troilus and Cressida (Shakespeare Theatre Washington DC) 1992, Othello, Volpone, The Servant, Divine Right (all Birmingham Rep), Blue Remembered Hills (Crucible Sheffield), Cat on a Hot Tin Roof (nat tour), Anna Karenina, Divided Loyalties (premiere), Macbeth, All at Sea (premiere, Gateway Theatre Chester), The Turn of the Screw, Bedevilled (premiere), Bouncers (Theatre Royal York), Trips (premiere, Birmingham Rep), A Midsummer Night's Dream (open-air theatre Regent's Park) 2000, Much Ado About Nothing (open-air theatre Regent's Park) 2000, Queueing for Everest (Sheffield Crucible Theatre) 2000, Love's Labour's Lost (open-air theatre Regent's Park 2001), The Real Thing (nat tour) 2001–02, Oh, What a Lovely War (open-air theatre Regent's Park) 2002, Henry IV part 1, A Midsummer Night's Dream (open-air theatre Regent's Park) 2004, Misconceptions (nat tour) 2004, The Tempest (nat tour) 2004, The Taming of the Shrew (open-air theatre Regent's Park) 2006; prodns for RSC incl: Dingo, Captain Swing, Sore Throats, A Doll's House, The Accrington Pals, Men's Beano, The Suicide, Bond's Lear, Golden Girls, The Comedy of Errors, The Merchant of Venice, Twelfth Night, Cymbeline, The Churchill Play, Playing with Trains, Much Ado About Nothing, The Bright and Bold Design; *Exhibitions* Soc of Br Theatre Designers incl: Central Sch of Art 1976, The Roundhouse 1979, Riverside Studios 1983 and 1987, RCA 1999; also exhibited at: Cleveland International Drawing Biennale 1991, 1st Malvern Open Drawing Competition 1992, Gordon Hepworth Gallery Newton St Cyres 1991, Devon & Exeter Arts Centre 1992, Coopers Gallery Bristol 1992, RA Summer Exhbn 1993 and 2002, Stansell Gallery Taunton 1994, Hawkings Gallery Salisbury 1994, Cheltenham Drawing Competition 1994, Unit 10 Gallery 1995, Taunton Drawing Competition 1995, Dillington House Somerset 1996, The Café Gallery Exeter 1998, Art Haven 2000, SW Acad of Fine Arts 2000, 2001, 2002 and 2003, Royal West of England Acad 2001 and 2003, Soc of Graphic Fine Art 2002, 2003, 2004 and 2006, The Alpine Club London 2006; *Books* Artswest (contrib 1988), British Theatre Design – The Modern Age (contrib 1989), Shakespeare in Performance (contrib, 1995), Time and Space: Design for Performance (1999); *Recreations* walking and climbing; *Clubs* Alpine; *Style*— Kit Surrey, Esq; ✉ Oak Cottage, Dunsford, Devon EX6 7DD (☎ 01647 253520)

SUSCHITZKY, (John) Peter; s of Wolfgang Suschitzky, the cinematographer, and Ilona, *née* Donath; *b* 6 April 1940; *Educ* Mountgrace Sch, Inst des Hautes Etudes Cinématographiques Paris; *m* June 1964 (m dis 1982), Johanna Roeber; 1 s (Adam b 1972), 2 da (Anya b 1969, Rebecca b 1974); m 2, July 1992, Ilona Guinsberg; *Career* dir of photography; memb: Br Soc of Cinematographers, Dirs' Guild of America; *Films* incl: Charlie Bubbles 1966, Leo The Last 1967, The Rocky Horror Picture Show 1974, The Empire Strikes Back 1978, Falling in Love 1984, Dead Ringers 1988, Where the Heart Is (Nat Soc of Film Critics Award USA for Best Cinematography) 1990, Naked Lunch 1991, The Public Eye 1991, The Vanishing 1992, M Butterfly 1993, Crash 1995, Mars Attacks 1996, The Man in the Iron Mask 1998, eXistenZ 1999, Red Planet 2000, Spider 2002, Shop Girl 2005, A History of Violence 2005, Le Concile de Pierre 2006, Eastern Promises 2007, A Dangerous Method 2011, Cosmopolis 2012, After Earth 2013; *Recreations* music, playing the transverse flute, history, cooking; *Style*— Peter Suschitzky, Esq; ✉ c/o United Agents Limited, 12–26 Lexington Street, London W1F 0LE (☎ 020 3214 0800, fax 020 3214 0801, website www.unitedagents.co.uk)

SUSMAN, Peter Joseph; QC (1997); s of Albert Leonard Susman, of London, and Sybil Rebecca, *née* Joseph; *b* 20 February 1943; *Educ* Dulwich Coll, Lincoln Coll Oxford (MA), Law Sch Univ of Chicago (JD); *m* 1, 5 June 1966 (m dis 1996), Peggy Judith Stone; 1 da (Deborah b 16 Nov 1976), 1 s (Daniel b 13 Feb 1979); m 2, 29 July 2006 (sep), Belinda Zoe Schwehr; 1 s (Gabriel b 12 Feb 1995); *Career* called to the Bar Middle Temple 1966 (bencher 2006); in practice 1967–70 and 1972– (assoc law firm NYC 1970–72), recorder 1993–2016; *Recreations* playing the clarinet, windsurfing, skiing; *Style*— Peter Susman, Esq, QC; ✉ Henderson Chambers, 2 Harcourt Buildings, Temple, London EC4Y 9DB (☎ 020 7583 9020, fax 020 7583 2686, e-mail psusman@hendersonchambers.co.uk, website www.hendersonchambers.co.uk)

SUSSKIND, Prof Richard Eric; OBE (2000); s of Dr Werner Susskind, of Glasgow, and Shirley, *née* Banks; *b* 28 March 1961; *Educ* Hutchesons' GS Glasgow, Univ of Glasgow (LLB, Dip Legal Practice), Balliol Coll Oxford (Snell exhibitioner, DPhil); *m* 11 Aug 1985, Michelle Dawn, da of Harvey Saul Latter (d 1991); 2 s (Daniel Rex b 10 Oct 1987, Jamie Ross b 28 June 1989), 1 da (Alexandra Lee b 5 Feb 1995); *Career* tutor in law Univ of Oxford 1984–86, head Expert Systems Ernst & Young 1986–89, memb Mgmnt Bd Masons 1994–97 (special advsr 1989–94); ind conslt 1997–; prof The Law Sch Univ of Strathclyde 2001 (visiting prof 1990–2001), Gresham prof of law 2000–04, emeritus prof of law Gresham Coll 2007–; visiting prof of internet studies Oxford Internet Inst Univ of Oxford 2009– (chair Advsy Bd 2011–); gen ed Int Jl of Law and IT 1992–2014 (founding ed 2014–), law columnist The Times 1999–2008; conslt Lord Woolf's inquiry into civil justice system 1995–96; expert consultee: Criminal Courts Review 2000–01, Tribunals Review 2000–01; memb Court of Appeal (Civil Div) Review Team 1996–97; chm: Advsy Panel on Crown Copyright 2003–04, Advsy Panel on Public Sector Info 2004–08, Client Advsy Bd Integreon 2011–12; memb ITAC (IT and the Courts) Ctee 1990– (co-chair 2006–), IT advsr to Lord Chief Justice 1998–, IT advsr to Jersey Legal Info Bd 1998–, memb Bd Modernising Govt Project 1999–2001, fndr memb Oxford Internet Inst Advsy Bd 2002–, memb External Advsy Bd AHRC Research Centre for Studies in Intellectual Property and Technol Law Univ of Edinburgh 2002–, memb Freedom of Information Bd 2003–05, memb Advsy Bd Lyceum Capital 2008–, memb Public Legal Educn Strategy Gp 2008–10, memb NPIA Info Systems Improvement Strategy Prog Bd 2008–09, special advsr Canadian Bar Assoc 2009–, memb Prog Bd Making Justice Work Scottish Govt 2010–13, memb Advsy Bd UCL Judicial Inst 2011–, chair ODR Advsy Gp Civil Justice Cncl 2014–, memb Pres of Queen's Bench Div's Review of Efficiency of Criminal Proceedings 2014–; George and Thomas Hutcheson Award 2001; govr Haberdashers' Aske's Schs Elstree 1998–2013, memb Balliol Coll Campaign Bd 2000–07, memb Cncl Gresham Coll 2002–04; hon prof Faculty of Laws UCL 2011–, Larry J Hoffman Greenberg Traurig Distinguished Visiting Prof in the Business of Law Univ of Miami Sch of Law 2013–14; tstee The Lokahi Fndn 2005–; Freeman City of London 1992; Worshipful Co of Info Technologists: Freeman 1992, Liveryman 1993, memb Court of Assts 1994–2003; hon memb Soc for Computers and Law 1992 (chm 1990–92, pres 2011–); hon fell Centre for Law and Computing Univ of Durham 2001, hon prof Gresham Coll 2004–10; FRSA 1992, FRSE 1997, FBCS 1997, CITP 2004; *Books* Expert Systems in Law (1987), Latent Damage Law – The Expert System (with P Capper, 1988), Essays on Law and Artificial Intelligence (1993), The Future of Law (1996), Transforming the Law (2000), Essays in Honour of Sir Brian Neill (ed, with M Saville, 2003), The Susskind Interviews: Legal Experts in Changing Times (ed, 2005), The End of Lawyers? (2008), Tomorrow's Lawyers (2013), Beyond the Professions (with D Susskind, 2015); *Recreations* running, reading, golf, cinema, skiing; *Style*— Prof Richard

S

Susskind, OBE, FRSE; ✉ 67 Aldenham Avenue, Radlett, Hertfordshire WD7 8JA (☎ 01923 469655, fax 01923 469264, e-mail richard@susskind.com)

SUTCH, Andrew Lang; s of Rev Canon Christopher Lang Sutch, of Quedgeley, Gloucestershire, and Gladys Ethelwyn, *née* Larrington; *b* 10 July 1952; *Educ* Haileybury, Oriel Coll Oxford (MA); *m* 22 May 1982, Shirley Anne, da of Gordon Alger Teichmann, of Wimbledon; 2 s (James b 12 Dec 1983, Francis b 24 Aug 1986); *Career* Lt Intelligence Corps TA 1976–86; admitted slr 1979, ptnr Stephenson Harwood 1984– (joined 1977, sr ptnr 2002–12); dir Jupiter European Opportunities Tst plc 2012, dir JP Morgan Claverhouse Investment Tst plc 2013 (chm 2015); memb Cncl RADA 2012; memb Law Soc 1979; *Recreations* theatre, running; *Style—* Andrew Sutch, Esq; ✉ Stephenson Harwood, 1 Finsbury Circus, London EC2M 7SH (☎ 020 7329 4422, fax 020 7329 7100)

SUTCLIFFE, Andrew Harold Wentworth; QC (2001); s of John Harold Vick Sutcliffe, CBE, DL, and Cecilia Mary, *née* Turton (d 1998); *b* 7 September 1960, Nairobi, Kenya; *Educ* Winchester, Worcester Coll Oxford (pres Oxford Union); *m* 17 Dec 1988, Emma Elisabeth, da of Sir Angus Stirling , *qv*; 3 da (Rose Cecilia b 18 Feb 1990, Helena Tertia Astley b 17 Oct 1993, Laura Mary b 9 June 1995), 1 s (Ralph Andrew Aeneas b 26 June 1991 d 1992); *Career* 2 Lt Royal Scots Dragoon Gds 1978–79; called to the Bar Inner Temple 1983, recorder (NE Circuit) 2000– (asst recorder 1999), dep judge of the High Court 2004; chm Great Fosters (1931) Ltd 2009–; vice-chm Fox Primary Sch Notting Hill (govr 1991–2015); memb: Exec Ctee Zebra Housing Assoc (Zebra Tst) 1985–2015 (vice-chm), Special Projects Ctee Duke of Edinburgh's Award Scheme 1986–96, Ctee Moorland Assoc 1996–2014; vice-pres Black Face Sheep Breeders Assoc, chm Kildale Agricultural Show Ctee 1988–, tstee Ralph Sutcliffe Fund for Meningitis Res 1993–98; memb Ct of Assts Fishmongers' Co 2014; *Recreations* bees, trees, swimming in the North Sea; *Clubs* MCC, Kildale Cricket (pres); *Style—* Andrew Sutcliffe, Esq, QC; ✉ Kildale Hall, Whitby, North Yorkshire YO21 2RQ; 3 Verulam Buildings, Gray's Inn, London WC1R 5NT (☎ 020 7831 8441, fax 020 7831 8479, e-mail asutcliffe@3vb.com)

SUTCLIFFE, Prof Charles Martin Sydenham; s of Gordon Edward Sutcliffe, and Florence Lillian, *née* Cole; *b* 5 January 1948; *Educ* KCS Wimbledon, Univ of Reading (BA); *Career* International Computers Ltd 1965–68, Unilever 1971–73, lectr Univ of Reading 1973–86, Northern Soc prof of accounting and fin Univ of Newcastle 1986–90, prof of finance and accounting Univ of Southampton 1990–2005, prof of finance Univ of Reading 2005–; dir Univs Superannuation Scheme Ltd 2001–07; memb Berkshire CC 1981–85; AT11 1968, MInstAM 1968, FCMA 2010 (ACMA 1985); *Books* The Dangers of Low Level Radiation (1987), Stock Index Futures (1993, 3 edn 2006), Banks and Bad Debts (1995), Management Accounting in Healthcare (1997), Developing Decision Support Systems (1997), Global Tracker Funds (1998), High-Frequency Financial Market Data (1999), Transparency and Fragmentation (2002), Distortion or Distraction: US Restrictions on EU Exchange Trading Screens (2004), Risk and Trading on London's AIM (2015), Finance and Occupational Pensions (2016); *Recreations* cycling; *Style—* Prof Charles Sutcliffe; ✉ The ICMA Centre, University of Reading, PO Box 242, Reading RG6 6BA (☎ 0118 931 8239, e-mail c.m.s.sutcliffe@rdg.ac.uk)

SUTCLIFFE, (Charles Wilfred) David; OBE (1995), DL (W Yorks 1991); s of Max Sutcliffe (d 1976), of Shipley, W Yorks, and Mary Doreen Sutcliffe (d 1977); *b* 21 June 1936; *Educ* Uppingham, Univ of Leeds (BA); *m* 6 May 1960, Hanne, da of Carl Olaf Carlsen (d 1967), of Copenhagen, Denmark; 2 s (Charles Peter David b 1961, John Mark Benson b 1963); *Career* Lt 4 Royal Tank Regt; Benson Turner Ltd: jt md 1968–, chm 1978–; chm Benson Turner (Dyers) Ltd 1976–78; dir: Bradford Microfirms Ltd 1981–88, A N Vevers Ltd 1983–2001, Bradford Breakthrough Ltd 1990–99, Bradford TEC 1991–98 (dep chm 1994); fndr chm Bradford Enterprise Agency 1983–89, pres Bradford C of C 1983–85, memb Cncl Lazards W Riding Tst 1985–93; memb High Steward's Cncl York Minster 1980–98; York Minster Fund: tstee 1987–98 and 1999–, chm of tstees 2003–09; pres Bradford Textile Soc 1987–88, chm Textiles and Clothing Regnl Innovation Strategy Bd for Yorks and Humberside 1998–2000, memb UK Textiles and Clothing Strategy Gp 1999–2001; High Sheriff Co of W Yorks 1994–95; hon fell Bradford and Ilkley Community Coll 1985; memb Co of Merchants of the Staple of England 1979 (mayor 1996–97), Freeman City of London, Liveryman Guild of Framework Knitters 1983–2005; Hon Freeman and Liveryman Worshipful Co of Clothworkers 1999 (Warden 2001–03, govr and memb Ct of Assts 2003–13); CText, FTI; *Recreations* golf, shooting, skiing, sailing, opera; *Clubs* Brooks's, Cavalry and Guards', Bradford; *Style—* David Sutcliffe, Esq, OBE, DL; ✉ Ivy House Farm, Kettlesing, Harrogate, North Yorkshire HG3 2LR (☎ 01423 770561); Dakota, The Boat Pool, Rhosneigr, Anglesey LL64 5YZ (☎ 01407 811080)

SUTCLIFFE, Gerard (Gerry); s of Henry (Harry) Sutcliffe (d 1985), of Bradford, and Margaret, *née* McCann; *b* 13 May 1953; *Educ* Cardinal Hinsley GS, Bradford Coll; *m* 14 Oct 1972, Maria, da of Eric Holgate; 3 s (Craig Anthony b 17 Aug 1973, Adrian John b 26 Aug 1975, Christopher James 14 May 1989), 1 da (Mary b 29 Dec 1982 d 1983); *Career* retail trainee Brown Muffs dept store, advtg clerk Bradford T&A, printing dept Field Printers; MP (Lab) Bradford S 1994–2015; PPS to: sec of state for Social Security 1997–98, chief sec to the Treasy 1998–99, sec of state DTI 1999–2001; Parly under sec of state for Employment Relations, Competition and Consumer Affrs; Govt whip 1999, Vice-Chamberlain of HM Household (Govt whip) 2001–06, Parly under sec of state Home Office 2006–07, min for sport and tourism 2007–10; memb Public Accounts Ctee 1996–98, chair PLP Trade Union Gp 1995–2000; Bradford Met Cncl: cncllr 1982–88 and 1990–94, dep ldr 1986–88, ldr 1992–94; chm Parly Football Team; dep sec: SOGAT 1982, GPMU (memb); *Recreations* music, sport, politics; *Style—* Gerry Sutcliffe, Esq; ✉ 76 Kirkgate, Bradford (☎ 01274 400007); House of Commons, London SW1A 0AA (☎ 020 7219 3247)

SUTCLIFFE, James Harry (Jim); *Educ* Univ of Cape Town (BSc); *m* Sharon; 2 s (Anthony, Gareth); *Career* Prudential Corporation plc: joined 1976, chief operating offr subsid Jackson National Life 1989–92, dep md Home Service Div 1992–95, main bd dir 1994–97, chief exec Prudential UK 1995–97; exec dir and dep chm Liberty International Holdings plc 1998–99, gp chief exec Old Mutual 2001–08 (chief exec Life 2000–01), chm Board for Actuarial Standards 2009–12, dir Financial Reporting Cncl 2009–15 (chm Codes and Standards Ctee 2012–15); non-exec dir: Lonmin plc, Sun Life Financial (chm 2011–), Liberty Gp; vice-chm Gunn Agri Ptnrs 2015–; FIA; *Recreations* bridge, farming; *Clubs* Pinner Hill Golf; *Style—* Jim Sutcliffe, Esq

SUTCLIFFE, Martin Rhodes; s of late John Sutcliffe, JP, DL, of Oldham, Lancs, and Hon Helen, *née* Rhodes; gs of late Lord Rhodes of Saddleworth, KG, DFC, PC, DL; *b* 21 September 1955; *Educ* Hulme GS, Univ of Sheffield (BA, DipArch); *m* 26 July 1980, Gillian Margaret, da of Arthur Price, of Rochdale, Lancs; 1 da (Hannah Sarah Rhodes b 19 April 1982), 1 s (Henry Ellis b 16 April 1987); *Career* architect; Skidmore Owings and Merrill Chicago 1977–78, Montague Assocs Derby 1980–81, Derek Latham and Assocs Derby 1981–85 (assoc 1983–85); Building Design Partnership (BDP): joined 1985, assoc 1988–90, ptnr 1990–2015, architect dir (following incorporation) 1997–2015, co dir 2002–15, head Bristol studio 2013–15, ret; registered architect 1981, RIBA 1981; *Recreations* family and home, visual and performing arts, the built and natural environment, Derbyshire well dressing; *Style—* Martin Sutcliffe, Esq; ☎ 07831 476116, e-mail martinrsutcliffe@gmail.com

SUTCLIFFE, Serena; *b* 1945; *m* David Peppercorn, MW, *qv*; *Career* translator UNESCO; author, conslt and expert on wine; dir Peppercorn and Sutcliffe 1988–91, sr dir Sotheby's London, memb European Bd and head of Int Wine Dept Sotheby's 1991–; Master of Wine 1976, chm Inst Masters of Wine 1994–95; memb Académie Internationale du Vin; Inst of Technol NY Professional Excellence Award 2002, Lifetime Achievement Award Bacchus Soc of America 2006; Chevalier dans l'Ordre des Arts et des Lettres (France), Chevalier dans l'Ordre National de la Légion d'Honneur (France); *Books* Wines of The World, Great Vineyards and Winemakers, The Wine Drinker's Handbook, A Celebration of Champagne (Decanter Book of the Year Award 1988), Bollinger (1994), The Wines of Burgundy (1995, 8 edn 2005); *Style—* Serena Sutcliffe; ✉ Sotheby's, 34–35 New Bond Street, London W1A 2AA (☎ 020 7293 5050, e-mail serena.sutcliffe@sothebys.com)

SUTCLIFFE, Thomas Dawson; *b* 12 August 1956; *Educ* Lancaster Royal GS, Emmanuel Coll Cambridge; *m* 3 c; *Career* BBC Radio: joined 1979, sometime researcher Talks and Documentaries, prodr Radio 3 and Radio 4, ed Kaleidoscope 1984–86, presenter A Good Read and Saturday Review (both BBC Radio 4); The Independent: arts ed 1986, currently columnist and assoc ed; contrib Late Review (BBC 2); winner of Peter Black Award for Broadcast Journalism 1995; *Recreations* cooking, reading, sleeping; *Style—* Thomas Sutcliffe, Esq

SUTHERELL, Maj-Gen John Christopher Blake; CB (2002), CBE (1993, OBE 1990, MBE 1982), DL (Suffolk 2006); s of Ernest John Sutherell (d 1999), and Vera Louise, *née* Blake (d 1952); *b* 23 October 1947, Chatteris, Cambs; *Educ* Staff College Camberley 1978–9, Royal College of Defence Studies 1993, Christ's Hosp, Univ of Durham (BA); *m* 1, 1979, Stephanie Glover (d 1983); m 2, 1987, Amanda Maxwell-Hudson; 1 da (Charlotte Louise b 1989); *Career* cmmnd 2 Lt Royal Anglian Regt 1968, Platoon Cdr RSO and Adj 2 Royal Anglian UK, NI and BAOR 1968–74, Troop and Sqdn Cdr 22 SAS 1974–78, Staff Coll Camberley 1979, DAA and QMG HQ DSAS 1980–82, Co Cdr 1 Royal Anglian UK and Belize 1982–84, directing staff Staff Coll Camberley 1984–87, CO 1 Royal Anglian Gibraltar, UK and NI 1987–90, Divnl Col Staff Coll 1990, cmd 8 Inf Bde NI 1990–92, RCDS 1993, DMS(A) 1994–96, Dir Special Forces 1996–99, Cmdt RMCS 1999–2002, ret 2002; Col Royal Anglian 2002–07 (Dep-Col 1997–2002), gen sec/chief exec Offrs' Assoc 2003–13; pres Royal Norfolk Regt 2001–12, cncllr Army Records Soc 2001–05, 2006–10, 2011–15 and 2016–, memb Br Cmmn for Mil Hist (BCMH) 2014–; govr Heathfield Sch 2004–06, govr Heathfield St Mary's Sch 2006–09, church warden st peter's church Yoxford 2009–; memb BCMH 2014–; cncllr Yoxford Parish cncl 2015–; *Recreations* military history, gardening, family; *Clubs* Special Forces; *Style—* Maj-Gen John Sutherell, CB, CBE, DL; ✉ 8 Herbert Crescent, London SW1X 0EZ

SUTHERLAND, Alan; *Career* chief exec Water Industry Cmmn for Scot; *Style—* Alan Sutherland, Esq; ✉ The Water Industry Commission for Scotland, Ochil House, Springkerse Business Park, Stirling FK7 7XE

SUTHERLAND, Prof Kathryn; da of Ian Donald Sutherland, and Joyce Bartaby Sutherland; *b* 7 July 1950; *Educ* Bedford Coll London (BA), Somerville Coll Oxford (DPhil); *Career* lectr in English literature Univ of Manchester 1975–93, prof of English Univ of Nottingham 1993–96; Univ of Oxford: professorial fell St Anne's Coll 1996–, reader in bibliography and textual criticism 1996–2002, prof of bibliography and textual criticism 2002–; MA (by incorporation) Univ of Oxford 1996; *Publications* Adam Smith: Interdisciplinary Essays (1995), Electronic Text: Method and Theory (1997), Jane Austen's Textual Lives: From Aeschylus to Bollywood (2005), Transferred Illusions: Digital Technology and the forms of print (2009), Jane Austen's Fiction Manuscripts: A Digital Edition (2010, www.janeausten.ac.uk); author of numerous critical edns; *Recreations* gardening, music; *Style—* Prof Kathryn Sutherland; ✉ St Anne's College, Oxford OX2 6HS (☎ 01865 274893, fax 01865 274899, e-mail kathryn.sutherland@st-annes.ox.ac.uk)

SUTHERLAND, Peter Denis William; Hon KCMG (2004), SC; s of William George Sutherland, of Dublin, and Barbara, *née* Nealon; *b* 25 April 1946; *Educ* Gonzaga Coll, UC Dublin (BCL), Hon Soc of the King's Inns; *m* 18 Sept 1971, Maruja Cabria Valcarcel, da of Paulino Cabria Garcia, of Reinosa, Spain; 2 s (Shane b 1972, Ian b 1974), 1 da (Natalia b 1979); *Career* called to the Bar: King's Inns 1968 (hon bencher), Middle Temple 1976 (bencher); attorney of NY Bar, admitted to practice before the Supreme Court of the US, practising memb Irish Bar 1968–81 (sr counsel 1980); tutor in law UC Dublin 1969–71, memb Cncl of State of Ireland and attorney-gen of Ireland 1981–1982 and 1982–84; Cmmr of EC for Competition and Relations with European Parl 1985–89; visiting fell Kennedy Sch of Govt Harvard Univ 1989, visiting prof UC Dublin 1989–93; chm Allied Irish Banks 1989–93 (non-exec dir 1995–), DG GATT 1993–95, DG World Trade Orgn 1995; British Petroleum plc: non-exec dir 1990–93 and 1995–, dep chm 1995–97, chm 1997–2009; chm Goldman Sachs International 1995–2015; chm LSE 2008–15; currently prof in practice Inst of Global Affrs (IGA) LSE; dir: Investor 1995–2005, Royal Bank of Scotland 2001–09; consultor Administration of the Patrimony of the Holy See; hon chm Trilateral Cmmn (Europe), chm Consultative Bd of the DG of the WTO 2002–04; pres: The Federal Tst, St Benet's Hall Univ of Oxford, Int Catholic Migration Cmmn (ICMC); UN special rep for migration 2006–; The David Rockefeller International Leadership Award 1998; Hon LLD: St Louis Univ 1985, NUI, Dublin City Univ, Holy Cross Univ, TCD, Open Univ, Suffolk Univ MA, Univ of Bath; Grand Cross Order of Leopold II (Belgium), Grand Cross of Civil Merit (Spain), Chevalier of the Legion d'Honneur (France), Centenary Medal (NZ), Euro Parl Gold Medal, Commandeur du Wissam (Morocco), Order of Rio Branco (Brazil), The Grand Cross of the Order of Infante Dom Henrique (Portugal), KCSG 2008, Cdr of the Royal Order of the Polar Star (Sweden) 2014; *Books* 1er Janvier 1993 – çe qui va changer en Europe (1988); *Recreations* tennis, reading; *Clubs* FitzWilliam Lawn Tennis (Dublin), Lansdowne Rugby Football, Royal Irish Yacht, Milltown Golf; *Style—* Peter Sutherland, KCMG, SC; ✉ Goldman Sachs International, Peterborough Court, 133 Fleet Street, London EC4A 2BB (☎ 020 7774 1000, fax 020 7774 4001)

SUTHERLAND, Roderick Henry (Rory); s of James Alan Sutherland, of Raglan, Monmouthshire, and late Florence Mary Sutherland; *b* 12 November 1965; *Educ* Monmouth Sch, Christ's Coll Cambridge; *m* 22 July 1989, Sophie Louisa, yr da of Sir Clive Whitmore; 2 da (Amelia Zoe Elizabeth, Henrietta Mahalia Anne (twins) b 23 July 2001); *Career* OgilvyOne: joined 1988, creative dir 1997, exec creative dir 1998–, vice-chm 2005; vice-chm Ogilvy Gp UK 2006–; memb Trg and Devpt Cncl IPA 2003–, chm IPA Creative Forum 2005–08; pres Inst of Practitioners in Advertising 2009–11; columnist: The Wiki Man The Spectator, Market Leader 2013–, Wired 2014–; hon patron Rochester Cathedral 2016, memb Bd of Goyrs Benjamin Franklin House 2013–; visiting lectr Univ of Falmouth 2014–, visiting lectr Univ of the Creative Arts 2016–; hon doctorate Brunel Univ 2012; FIPA 2007, FRSA 2008; *Books* The Wiki Man (2013), Those Things Which Have No Name (2016–17); *Recreations* reading, gadgetry, travel; *Clubs* The Walbrook, Ivy, Arts; *Style—* Roderick Sutherland, Esq; ✉ Brasted Place, Brasted, Kent TN16 1JE; Sea Containers, 18 Upper Ground, London SE1 9RQ (☎ 020 7345 3000, e-mail rory.sutherland@ogilvy.com, Twitter @rorysutherland)

SUTHERLAND, Ruth Elizabeth; da of Andrew Dodds (d 2005), and Rachael Thomas, *née* Foster; *b* 21 May 1961, Brightlingsea, Essex; *Educ* Univ of Warwick, Uni of Ulster (MSc); *m* 28 Feb 1987, Ian; 1 da (Rebecca b 17 March 1988), 2 s (Daniel b 17 Sept 1990, Benjamin b 1 Oct 1993); *Career* RGN Chelsea and Westminster Hosp 1984; health promotion mangr 1987–99, founding dir Community Devpt and Health Network 1999–2005, NI dir Rethink 2006–09, chief operating offr Alzheimers Soc 2009–11, ceo Relate 2012–14, ceo Samaritans 2015–; memb: RSA, ACEVO, NCVO; *Style—* Mrs Ruth Sutherland; ✉ Samaritans, The Upper Mill, Kingston Road, Ewell, Surrey, KT17 2AF (e-mail r.sutherland@samaritans.org, website www.samaritans.org)

SUTHERLAND, Stephen William; s of John Stuart Sutherland, of Salisbury, Wilts, and Sylvia Florence, *née* Lock; *b* 15 February 1956; *Educ* Bishop Wordsworth's GS Salisbury,

Christ Church Oxford (BA); *Career* Melody Maker: reporter/feature writer 1981–84, reviews ed 1984–86, features ed 1986–88, asst ed 1988–92, former ed Vox Magazine, ed New Musical Express 1992–2000; ed dir: New Musical Express 2000–04, IPC Ignite! 2004–; *Books* 10 Imaginary Years (with Robert James Smith, *qv* of The Cure, 1988); *Recreations* football; *Clubs* Morton's; *Style*— Steve Sutherland, Esq; ✉ IPC Ignite!, 25th Floor, King's Reach Tower, Stamford Street, London SE1 9LS (☎ 020 7261 6471, fax 020 7261 5185)

SUTHERLAND OF HOUNDWOOD, Baron (Life Peer UK 2001), of Houndwood in the Scottish Borders; Sir Stewart Ross Sutherland; KT (2002), kt (1995); s of George Arthur Caswell Sutherland (d 1974), of Aberdeen, and Ethel, *née* Masson (d 1995); *b* 25 February 1941; *Educ* Robert Gordon's Coll Aberdeen, Univ of Aberdeen (MA), Corpus Christi Coll Cambridge (MA); *m* 1 Aug 1964, Dr Sheena Sutherland (Lady Sutherland), da of John Robertson (d 1975), of Fraserburgh; 2 da (Hon Fiona Mair b 11 Dec 1966, Hon Kirsten Ann b 20 Aug 1968), 1 s (Hon Duncan Stewart b 9 March 1970); *Career* asst lectr UCNW 1965–68; Univ of Stirling: lectr 1968, sr lectr 1972, reader 1976–77; KCL: prof of history and philosophy of religion 1977–85, fell 1983, vice-princ 1981–85, princ 1985–90; vice-chllr Univ of London 1990–94, princ and vice-chllr Univ of Edinburgh 1994–2002, provost Gresham Coll 2002–08, chm Cncl Univ of London 2006– (pro-chllr 2006–08); HM chief inspector of schools HM Inspectorate 1992–94; chm YTL Education (UK) Ltd 2003–; chm: Royal Cmmn on Funding of the Long Term Care of the Elderly 1997–99, Cncl ABRSM 2006–12, House of Lords Select Ctee on Sci and Technol 2007–10; memb: C of E Bd of Educn 1980–84, UGC Arts Sub-Ctee 1983–85, City Parochial Fndn 1988–90, NW Thames HA 1992–94, Hong Kong Cncl for Academic Accreditation 1992–95, Cncl for Science and Technol 1993–2000, Humanities Research Bd 1994–95, Hong Kong UGC 1995–2004, Higher Educn Funding Cncl 1995–2002; chm: Br Acad Postgrad Studentships Ctee 1987–94, Ethiopian Gemini Tst 1987–92, CVCP Academic Standards Gp 1988–92, Cncl Royal Inst of Philosophy 1988–2006, London Conf on Overseas Students 1989–93, Ctee of Review Scottish Appeals 1994–96, Ctee of Scottish HE Princs 2000–02; vice-chm Ctee of Vice-Chllrs and Princs 1989–92; ed Religious Studies 1984–90; memb Editorial Bd: Scottish Journal of Religious Studies 1980–95, Modern Theology 1984–91; pres: Soc for the Study of Theology 1985 and 1986, Saltire Soc 2002–05, Alzheimer Scotland 2001–, David Hume Inst 2006–08; assoc fell Centre for Philosphy and Literature Univ of Warwick 1986–2010; chm Quarry Products Assoc 2002–05; memb Ct of Assts Worshipful Co of Goldsmiths 2001 (Freeman 1986, Liveryman 1991, Prime Warden 2012–13), hon memb Merchants Co Edinburgh 2007; Hon LHD: Coll of Wooster Ohio, Cwlth Univ of Virginia 1992, NYU 1996; Hon LLD: Univ of Aberdeen, Nat Univ of Ireland 1992, Univ of St Andrews 2002, McGill Univ Montreal 2003; Hon DUniv Stirling 1993; Hon DLitt: Richmond Coll 1995, Univ of Wales 1996, Univ of Glasgow 1999, Univ of Warwick 2001, Univ of London 2004, Queen Margaret UC Edinburgh 2004; Dr (hc): Uppsala Univ 1995, Univ of Edinburgh 2004; Hon DEd: Robert Gordon Univ Aberdeen 2005, Hong Kong Inst of Educn 2005 hon fell: CCC Cambridge 1989, UC Bangor 1991, Coll of Preceptors 1994, Birbeck Coll London 2003, Inst of Educn Univ of London 2004, RCGP 2005; FRSA 1986, FBA 1992, FRSE 1995 (pres 2002–05), FRCGP 2003, hon fell Faculty of Actuaries 2004, companion CIEA 2008; *Books* Atheism and Rejection of God (1977, 2 edn 1980), The Philosophical Frontiers of Christian Theology (ed with B L Hebblethwaite, 1983), God, Jesus and Belief (1984), Faith and Ambiguity (1984), The World's Religions (ed, 1988); author of numerous articles in books and learned jls; *Recreations* Tassie medallions, jazz, theatre; *Clubs* New; *Style*— The Rt Hon the Lord Sutherland of Houndwood, KT; ✉ House of Lords, London SW1A 0PW (e-mail sutherlands@parliament.uk)

SUTHERLAND SMITH, Maureen; *m* 8 Nov 1978, Alan Lewis Sutherland; 1 da (Natasha b 1980); *Career* md: BBDO PR Ltd 1972 (dir 1971), Good Relations Ltd 1973; chief exec: Good Relations Group Ltd 1975, Good Relations Group plc; chm The Communication Group plc (PR consultancy) 1985–; vice-pres Coram 2012–; Freeman City of London 2011; *Style*— Ms Maureen Sutherland Smith; ✉ The Communication Group plc, 19 Buckingham Gate, London SW1E 6LB (☎ 020 7630 1411)

SUTTIE, Dr Ian Alexander; *b* 8 June 1945; *Educ* Robert Gordon's Coll Aberdeen, Univ of Aberdeen; *m* 1 Dec 1971, Dorothy Elizabeth; 2 da (Julia b 1974, Fiona b 1976), 1 s (Martin b 1978); *Career* chm: First Subsea Ltd, IDJ Properties Ltd, Union Bridge Ltd, Densbridge Ltd, Intercity (Aberdeen) Ltd, Tano Energy Ltd, First Construction Ltd, First Tech plc, Mooring Systems Ltd, First Whisky Ltd, C&L Properties, First Scot Ltd, Nautricity Ltd, First Marine Solutions Ltd, First Integrated Services Ltd; Ernst & Young Scottish Business Services Entrepreneur 2001, Grampian Industrialist of the Year 2002, Entrepreneur of the Year Scottish Business Award 2012; Burgess of Guild City of Aberdeen; hon doctorate Univ of Aberdeen; MICAS; *Recreations* golf, curling; *Clubs* Royal Northern & Univ, Deeside Golf; *Style*— Dr Ian A Suttie; ✉ 1 Queen's Terrace, Aberdeen AB10 1XL

SUTTON, Alan John; s of William Clifford Sutton (d 1964), of Abertillery, and Emily, *née* Batten (d 1992); *b* 16 March 1936; *Educ* Hafod-Y-Dd?l GS, Bristol Univ (BSc); *m* 7 Sept 1957, Glenis, da of George Henry (d 1986), of Ebbw Vale; 1 da (Lisa Jayne b 1963 d 1998), 1 s (Andrew Jonathan b 1964); *Career* chief engr English Electric 1957–62, sales mangr Solartron 1962–69, md AB Connectors 1969–76, industrial dir Welsh Office 1976–79, exec dir Welsh Devpt Agency 1979–88, chm and chief exec Anglolink Ltd 1988–, chm A Novo DigiTec Ltd 1998–2003, chm A Novo UK Ltd 2001–05, dir A Novo Holdings Ltd 2001–05, non-exec dir A Novo SA 2003–09, chm Conforto Financial Mgmnt 2007–09 (non-exec dir 2009–10); MIET (MIEE 1962); *Recreations* golf, walking, worldwide travel; *Style*— Alan Sutton, Esq; ✉ Brockton House, Heol-y-Delyn, Lisvane, Cardiff CF14 0SR (☎ 029 2075 3194, mobile 07976 434048, e-mail alanjohnsutton@btinternet.com)

SUTTON, Andrew William; *b* 4 October 1939, Brentwood, Essex; *Educ* Brentwood Sch, Univ of Birmingham, Aston Univ; *m* 13 July 1964, Kay, da of Lionel Edge, of Birmingham; 1 da (Rebecca b 6 April 1967), 1 s (Benjamin b 21 Feb 1969); *Career* psychologist: Newport (Mon) 1965–67, Birmingham 1968–84; Univ of Birmingham: hon lectr in educnl psychology 1970–84, assoc Centre for Russian & E Euro Studies 1980–, hon res fell Dept of Psychology 1984–2004; chief exec Fndn for Conductive Educn 1986–2004; tstee Conduction 2009–, series ed Conductive Educn Press 2009–; Hon EdD Univ of Wolverhampton 2007; hon conductor Pet? Inst Budapest 1990; *Books* jtly: Home, School and Leisure in the Soviet Union (1980), Reconstructing Psychological Practice (1981), Conductive Education (1985), Mária Hári on Conductive Pedagogy (2004), András Pet? (2012), András Pet? Quotationary (2013); Last Year in Hong Kong (2011); *Recreations* gardening, garden-railways, writing, blogging; *Style*— Andrew Sutton, Esq; ✉ e-mail conductive.world@gmail.com, website www.conductive-world.info

SUTTON, Dr George Christopher; *b* 4 February 1934; *Educ* Rugby, Corpus Christi Coll Cambridge (MD, MA), UCH Med Sch London; *m* 7 Feb 1959, Angela Elizabeth, *née* Dornan-Fox; 3 da (Sarah-Jane b 1962, Caroline b 1965, Rachel b 1967); *Career* Addenbrooke's Hosp Cambridge 1962–63, med registrar St George's Hosp London 1963–67, fell in cardiology Univ of N Carolina Chapel Hill Med Sch 1965–66, sr registrar in cardiology Brompton Hosp London 1967–71, conslt cardiologist Hillingdon Hosp 1972–98, hon conslt Harefield Hosp 1972–2008, sr lectr in cardiology Nat Heart and Lung Inst Imperial Coll Sch of Med London 1972–2008, hon conslt Royal Brompton and Nat Heart and Lung Hosp London 1972–2008, distinguished research fell in cardiovascular science Nat Heart and Lung Inst Imperial Coll Sch of Med London 2008–; author of various scientific papers on cardiology; memb: Br Cardiac Soc (Cncl 1982–86), Euro Soc of Cardiology; FRCP 1977, FACC 1977; *Books* Physiological and Clinical Aspects of Cardiac Auscultation, an audio-visual programme (1967), Slide Atlas of Cardiology (1978), An Introduction to Echocardiography (1978), Clinical and Investigatory Features of Cardiac Pathology (1988), Clinical Cardiology – An Illustrated Text (1998), Heart Failure: current clinical understanding (2008); *Recreations* watching cricket, golf, music, photography; *Clubs* MCC; *Style*— Dr George Sutton

SUTTON, Prof John; s of John Sutton, and Marie, *née* Hammond; *b* 10 August 1948; *Educ* Univ Coll Dublin (BSc), Trinity Coll Dublin (MSc(Econ)), Univ of Sheffield (PhD); *m* 1974, Jean, da of Frank Drechsler; 2 da (Gillian b 4 Sept 1979, Katherine b 23 Nov 1981), 1 s (Christopher b 2 Nov 1984); *Career* lectr Univ of Sheffield 1973–77; LSE: lectr 1977–84, reader 1984–88, prof 1988–98, Sir John Hicks prof of economics 1998–; visiting prof: Univ of Tokyo 1981, Univ of Calif San Diego 1986, Harvard Univ 1998–99, Univ of Chicago Grad Sch of Business 2006; Marvin Bower fell Harvard Business Sch 1990–91, Gaston Eyskens prof Leuven Univ 1996, William Davidson visiting prof Univ of Michigan 2003; memb Advsy Cncl Access to Japanese Markets (JETRO MITI) Tokyo 1995–2003; memb Gp of Economic Analysis European Union 2002–04, memb Enterprise Policy Gp Ireland 2003–04; pres Royal Economic Soc 2004–07; Franqui medal 1992; DSc(Econ) (hc) Nat Univ of Ireland 2003, LLD (hc) Univ of Dublin 2004, Docteur ès Sciences Economiques (hc) Université de Lausanne 2004; fell Econometric Soc 1991, FBA 1996, fell European Economic Assoc 2004, foreign hon memb American Economic Assoc 2007, distinguished fell Industrial Organization Soc 2010; *Books* Protection and Industrial Policy in Europe (jtly, 1986), Sunk Costs and Market Structure (1991), Technology and Market Structure: Theory and History (1998), Marshall's Tendencies: What Can Economists Know? (2000), An Enterprise Map of Ethiopia (jtly, 2010), An Enterprise Map of Ghana (jtly, 2012), An Enterprise Map of Tanzania (jtly, 2012), Competing in Capabilities: The Globalization Process (2012); *Style*— Prof John Sutton, FBA; ✉ London School of Economics and Political Science, Houghton Street, London WC2A 2AE (☎ 020 7955 7716)

SUTTON, Karolina; da of Miroslaw Zawadzki, and Alina, *née* Rudnik; *b* 18 February 1981, Mikolow, Poland; *Educ* Girton Coll Cambridge (MA); *m* 11 July 2002, Robert Sutton; *Career* literary agent: ICM Books 2003–08, Curtis Brown 2008–; *Recreations* cinema, walking, cooking, theatre; *Style*— Ms Karolina Sutton; ✉ Curtis Brown, Haymarket House, 28–29 Haymarket, London SW1Y 4SP

SUTTON, Linda; *b* 14 December 1947; *Educ* Southend Coll of Technol, Winchester Sch of Art (BA), De Koninklijke Academie Voor Schone Kunsten Antwerp, RCA (MA); *Career* artist; *Solo Exhibitions* Galerij de Zwarte Panter Antwerp 1971, Bedford House Gallery London 1974, L'Agrifoglio Milan 1975, World's End Gallery London 1978, Ikon Gallery Birmingham 1979, Chenil Gallery London 1980, Royal Festival Hall London 1984, Stephen Bartley Gallery London 1986, Beecroft Gallery Westcliff-on-Sea (with Carel Weight, CH, CBE, RA) 1987, Jersey Arts Centre St Helier Channel Islands 1988, Christopher Hull Gallery London 1988, Beaux Arts Bath 1988, Austin/Desmond Fine Art Bloomsbury 1989, Isis Gallery Leigh-on-Sea 1993, Lamont Gallery London 1993 and 1996, Pump House Gallery Battersea Park 1994, Sutton House Hackney 1994, Chappel Galleries Essex 1995 and 2003, Bromham Mill Bedford Arts Festival 1995, Piers Feetham Gallery Fulham London 1995, 2002 and 2011, Emscote Lawn Gallery 1996, Lamont Gallery 1996, John Bloxham Fine Art London 1996, Six Chapel Row Bath 1997, Fosse Gallery Stow-on-the-Wold 1998, Stevenage Arts Centre 1999, UAC Dublin 2000, Workhouse Gallery Chelsea 2000–03, Chappel Galleries Essex 2003, Chiesa della Badia Caulonia Italy 2008, Piers Feetham 2011 and 2016; *Group Exhibitions* incl: Royal Acad Summer Exhibitions 1972–2015, British Painting 1952–77 (Royal Acad) 1977, Bath Festival 1985 and 1988, The Lefevre Gallery London 1988, Business Art Centre Islington 1991–95, Int Art Fair Olympia 1990 and 1991, Directors Choice (New Academy Gallery) 1990, Academia Italia 1990, On Line Gallery Southampton 1992–2001, Isis Gallery Leigh-on-Sea 1992, Chappel Galleries Essex 1993–2010, Fosse Galleries Stow-on-the-Wold 1992–2015, Royal Museum and Art Gallery Canterbury 1993–94, Piers Feetham Gallery 1994–2016, Russell Gallery Putney 2008–15; *Awards* prizewinner GLC Spirit of London (Royal Festival Hall) 1979, 1980 and 1981, first prize Contemporary Arts Soc 1981, prize Nat Portrait Gallery 1982, prizewinner Royal Acad Summer Exhibition 1987; *Books* illustrated: ltd edn of poems and etchings (with Brian Patten, 1996), ltd edn The Tempest (2000), Secret Language of Birds Tarot (2011), booklet of poems by Brian Patten with etchings; Metamorphoses I (2000), Metamorphoses II (2001), Metamorphoses III (2003), Opera Tarot (2016); *Recreations* opera, cooking, reading, snooker, travel; *Clubs* Chelsea Arts, Arts; *Style*— Miss Linda Sutton; ✉ 192 Battersea Bridge Road, London SW11 3AE (e-mail info@lindasutton.com, website www.lindasutton.com)

SUTTON, Prof Philip (Phil); CBE (2012); s of Percy Ronald Sutton (d 1970), and Ivy Nora, *née* Kidgell (d 1960); *b* 28 November 1953, Southampton, Hants; *Educ* Univ of Southampton (BSc, PhD); *m* 14 Sept 1974, Kim, da of Ronald Cummins; 1 s (Richard b 1977), 1 da (Victoria b 1979); *Career* Admiralty Surface Weapons Estab 1975–83, gp ldr Pre-Detector Signal Processing British Aerospace (BAe) Dynamics 1983–85; Above Water Sector DRA: head Special EO Sensors Section 1985–91, dep head then head Special Research Gp 1987–91, business mangr 1992–93, chief scientist 1994; head Battlefield and Vehicles Systems Dept Defence Evaluation and Research Agency (DERA) 1994–98; MOD: dir of corporate research 1998–2001, dir of technol devpt 2001–04, DG research and technol 2004–08, DG sci and technol strategy 2008–11; dir SSES Ltd 2011–; visiting prof: Cranfield Univ at Shrivenham 1990, Imperial Coll London 2006, UCL 2011; dir and tstee Cancer Care Soc, memb Cncl RNLI 2014; FIET 1996, FInstP 1998, FREng 2006; *Publications* author and co-author of more than 60 tech reports and papers; named inventor on 17 patents and patent applications; *Recreations* science, cycling, sailing, sub aqua diving, snowboarding, expanding limited German language skills, memb local church cncl; *Style*— Prof Phil Sutton, CBE

SUTTON, Philip John; s of Louis Sutton (d 1976), and Ann, *née* Lazarus (d 1980); *b* 20 October 1928; *Educ* Slade Sch of Fine Art UCL; *m* 11 July 1953, Heather Minifie Ellis, da of Arthur Owen Ellis Cooke; 1 s (Jacob b 11 May 1954), 3 da (Imogen b 21 Feb 1956, Saskia b 19 Jan 1958, Rebekah b 30 Sept 1960); *Career* artist; RA 1976 (ARA 1971); *Recreations* walking, swimming; *Style*— Philip Sutton, Esq, RA; ✉ 3 Cordova Gardens, Bridport, Dorset DT6 3NG (☎ 01308 421802)

SUTTON, Prof Richard; s of Dick Brasnett Sutton (d 1980), of Loddon, Norfolk, and Greta Mary, *née* Leadbeter; *b* 1 September 1940, Newport, Wales; *Educ* Gresham's, KCL, King's Coll Hosp London (MB BS), Univ of London (DSc); *m* 28 Nov 1964 (m dis 1998), (Anna) Gunilla, da of Carl-Axel Cassö (d 1976), of Stockholm, Sweden; 1 s (Edmund b 24 April 1967); m 2 30 July 2014, Jeanne-Marie Madeleine, da of Simon Francois Arrighi (d 2002), of Monte Carlo, Monaco; *Career* house offr: Plymouth Gen Hosp 1964–65, King's Coll Hosp 1965, St Stephen's Hosp 1966, London Chest Hosp 1966–67; registrar St George's Hosp 1967–68, fell in cardiology Univ of N Carolina USA 1968–69, registrar then sr registrar and temporary conslt Nat Heart Hosp 1970–76, conslt cardiologist Chelsea & Westminster (formerly Westminster Hosp) 1976–2007, conslt cardiologist Royal Brompton Hosp 1993–2007, conslt cardiologist St Mary's Hosp 2007–11; hon conslt cardiologist St Luke's Hosp for the Clergy 1980–2011, hon conslt Imperial Healthcare NHS Tst 2011–; prof of clinical cardiology Imperial Coll London 2003–11 (prof emeritus 2011–); chm Cardiology Ctee, chm Specialty Trg Ctee and dir Trg Prog Cardiology London Deanery (NW) 1992–2011; regional specialist advsr RCP 1996–2011; ed Europace 1999–2006; Govrs award American Coll of Cardiology 1979 and 1982; co fndr and former

S

pres and sec Br Pacing and Electrophysiology Gp (now British Heart Rhythm UK), memb Exec Bd Euro Heart Rhythm Assoc 2002–06, chm Euro Working Gp on Cardiac Pacing Euro Soc of Cardiology 1998–2000; Lifetime Achievement Award Heart Rhythm UK 2007, Pioneer in Cardiac Pacing and Electrophysiology Heart Rhythm Soc 2016; memb: RSM (co-fndr and first chm Section on Cardiology), Br Cardiovasc Soc, American Coll of Cardiology, American Heart Assoc, Euro Soc of Cardiology, Heart Rhythm Soc, Euro Heart Rhythm Assoc; FRCP 1982 (MRCP 1967), FHRS 2006; *Books* Pacemakers (chapter in Oxford Textbook of Medicine, 1987), Foundations of Cardiac Pacing (Pt 1 1991, Pt 2 1999); over 260 peer reviewed papers in scientific jls; *Recreations* opera, walking; *Clubs* Athenaeum, Automobile Club de Monaco, RSM; *Style—* Professor Richard Sutton; ✉ Le Beau Rivage, 9 Avenue d'Ostende, Monte Carlo, Monaco MC 98000 (☎ 00377 9330 0051, e-mail r.sutton@imperial.ac.uk)

SUTTON, Robert Hiles; s of John Ormerod Sutton, of The Old School House, Tichborne, Hants, and Margaret Patricia, *née* Buckland; *b* 19 January 1954; *Educ* Winchester, Magdalen Coll Oxford (BA); *m* 8 Aug 1981, Carola Jane (Tiggy), da of Sir Anthony Dewey, 3 Bt, of The Rag, Yeovil, Somerset; 2 s (Patrick William b 1984, Jonathan David Ormerod b 1990), 1 da (Joanna Kate b 1987); *Career* Macfarlanes Slrs: joined 1976, ptnr 1983–, sr ptnr 1999–2008; memb Law Soc; *Recreations* rackets, poker; *Clubs* Boodle's, City; *Style—* Robert Sutton, Esq

SUTTON, Timothy Patrick; s of William Arthur Sutton, of Derby, and Maria Ephigenia, *née* Macronopoulou; *b* 19 June 1958; *Educ* Queen Elizabeth's GS Ashbourne, Magdalen Coll Oxford (MA); *Career* exec chm BSMG Worldwide Europe, vice-chm BSMG Worldwide Inc, currently Weber Shandwick Europe; campaigns incl: long term repositioning prog for British Midland since 1989 (for which recipient PR Week Grand Prix 1991 and IPR Sword of Excellence 1994), defence of brewing indust against MMC recommendations 1989, campaign by independent gas cos to end British Gas plc's domestic monopoly 1993–95, advising int oil industry on the decommissioning of North Sea platforms; memb Superbrands Cncl; speaker at PR indust confs and events; memb Amnesty Int; MIPR 1992, FRSA 1996; *Recreations* flying, cinema, poetry, Derby Co FC; *Style—* Timothy Sutton, Esq; ✉ Weber Shandwick, 2 Waterhouse Square, 140 Holborn, London EC1N 2AE

SUZMAN, Dame Janet; DBE (2011); da of Saul Suzman, of Johannesburg, South Africa, and Betty, *née* Sonnenberg; *b* 9 February 1939; *Educ* Kingsmead Coll Johannesburg, Univ of the Witwatersrand (BA), LAMDA; *m* 1969 (m dis 1986), Sir Trevor Robert Nunn, *qv*; 1 s (Joshua b 1980); *Career* actress and director; performances incl: The Wars of the Roses 1964, The Relapse 1967, The Taming of the Shrew 1967, A Day in the Death of Joe Egg 1970, Nicholas and Alexandra 1971 (Acad Award nomination, Golden Globe nomination), Antony and Cleopatra 1972, Hello and Goodbye 1973 (Evening Standard Award), Three Sisters 1976 (Evening Standard Award), Hedda Gabler 1978, The Greeks 1980, The Draughtsman's Contract 1981, Vassa 1985, Mountbatten-Viceroy of India 1986, The Singing Detective 1987, Andromache 1988, A Dry White Season 1989, Another Time 1989–90, Hippolytus 1991, Nuns on the Run 1991, Leon the Pig Farmer 1992, The Sisters Rosensweig 1994–95, The Retreat From Moscow 1999, The Hollow Crown (Aust tour) 2003, Who's Life is it Anyway 2005, Coriolanus 2007 (nominated Outstanding Lead Actress in a Non-Resident Prodn Helen Hayes Awards 2008), The Dream of the Dog (Finborough Theatre) 2010, Solomon and Marion (Baxter Theatre Cape Town) 2011, (Theatre on the Square Johannesburg, Baxter Theatre Cape Town, Assembly Rooms Edinburgh and Hilton Arts Festival Natal) 2013 and (Birmingham Repertory Theatre and The Print Room London) 2014; directed: Othello (Market Theatre Johannesburg 1987, Channel 4 TV 1988), A Dream of People (RSC, The Pit) 1990, No Flies on Mr Hunter (Chelsea Centre) 1992, Death of a Salesman 1993 (Liverpool Echo Best Production Award), The Deep Blue Sea (both Theatr Clwyd) 1996, The Good Woman of Sharkville (Market Theatre Johannesburg, and UK tour) 1996, The Cherry Orchard (Birmingham Repertory Theatre) 1997 (Barclays TMA Best Director Award), The Snow Palace 1998 (UK tour, Tricycle Theatre London and Warsaw Festival 1999), The Free State (UK tour) 2000, Hamlet (Baxter Theatre Cape Town and Swan Theatre Stratford-upon-Avon) 2006, Master Harold and the Boys (LAMDA) 2009, Antony & Cleopatra (Liverpool Playhouse) 2010 and (Chichester Festival Theatre) 2012, The Marriage of Figaro (Hackney Empire, for RAM) 2015; vice-pres LAMDA Cncl 1992–, pres Shakespeare's Birthday Celebrations 2010–11; lectr Tanner Lectures BNC Oxford 1995; Pragnell Shakespeare Award 2012; Freedom of the City of London 2015; Hon MA Open Univ 1986; Hon DLitt: Univ of Warwick 1990, Univ of Leicester 1992, Queen Mary & Westfield Coll London 1997, Univ of Southampton 2002, Univ of Middlesex 2003, Kingston Univ 2006, Univ of Cape Town 2010, Univ of Buckingham 2014, Univ of Edge Hill 2015; hon doctorate Liverpool John Moores Univ 2011; hon fell Shakespeare Inst Univ of Birmingham 2010, hon fell Sch of Arts Univ of Liverpool 2010–13, life fell Shakespeare Assoc of GB 2015; *Publications* Acting with Shakespeare (1997), The Free State – A South African Response to The Cherry Orchard (2000), Commentary on Antony and Cleopatra for Applause Shakespeare Library (2001), Not Hamlet (2012); *Recreations* yacht 'Chicken Sloop'; *Style—* Dame Janet Suzman, DBE; ✉ c/o Steve Kenis & Co, 95 Barkston Gardens, London SW5 DEU (☎ 020 7434 9055, e-mail sk@sknco.com or suzcatt@waitrose.com)

SWAAB, Richard Laing; s of Jack Swaab, of London, and Zena, *née* Urquhart; *b* 7 May 1955; *Educ* KCS Wimbledon, Christ's Coll Cambridge (scholar, MA); *Career* carpenter Harvey Nichols dept store 1976–77; Lintas advtg: prodn controller 1977–79, account exec 1979–82, account dir 1982; planner Benton & Bowles 1982–83, planning ptnr Chuter Morgenthau 1983–87; planner: Ayer Barker 1987, Ogilvy & Mather 1987–90; head of planning Collett Dickenson Pearce 1990–92; WCRS: head of planning 1992–96, strategy dir 1996–98, vice-chm 1998–2001; global planning dir AMV BBDO 2001–03, head of int planning BBDO Europe 2003–04, currently dep chm BBDO EMEA; *Recreations* football, swimming, cricket, socialising; *Style—* Richard Swaab, Esq; ✉ AMV BBDO, 151 Marylebone Road, London NW1 5QE (☎ 020 3787 0767, fax 020 7616 3600, e-mail swaabr@amvbbdo.com)

SWAAB, Roger Henry; s of Cyril Henry Swaab, of Shrewsbury, and Betty Joan, *née* Moore; *b* 6 June 1944; *Educ* Brewood GS, Birmingham Sch of Arch (DipArch); *m* 18 July 1968, Elizabeth Kay, da of William Edward Smith Penlon, of Staffs; 1 s (Christian b 1973), 1 da (Beth b 1973); *Career* architect; BA Architecture Ltd 1997–, Hickton Madeley Ltd 1998–, Hickton Madeley Architects Ltd 1999–2006, dir NON Architecture.Com Ltd until 2006, dir SMC Hickton Madeley Architects Ltd until 2006, dir Cotswold Architecture 2011–; ARIBA, MCIArb; *Recreations* golf; *Style—* Roger H Swaab, Esq

SWAFFIELD, David Richard; s of Sir James Chesebrough Swaffield, CBE, DL, RD; *b* 11 November 1951; *Educ* Dulwich Coll, Downing Coll Cambridge (MA); *m* 28 March 2002, Carol, da of Roy Howard, of Chichester, W Sussex; 2 s from previous m (James b 1983, Robin b 1988); *Career* investment analysis Rowe & Pitman 1973–75, admitted slr 1979, ptnr Hill Dickinson & Co 1982–89 (slr 1979–82), dir Grayhill Ltd 1984–85; ptnr: Hill Dickinson Davis Campbell 1989–97, Hill Dickinson (Liverpool, London, Manchester, Singapore, Athens, Hong Kong and Monaco) 1997–; dir Liverpool Law Society Ltd 1991–2003 (hon sec 1997–98, vice-pres 1998–99, pres 1999–2000), mangr Liverpool & London War Risks Insurance Association Ltd 1994–98 (jt mangr 1992–94); govr Birkenhead Sch 1994–2005; dir Merseyside Youth Assoc 2010–; *Style—* David Swaffield, Esq; ✉ Cobblestones, Church Street, Malpas, Cheshire SY14 8PD; Hill Dickinson LLP, 1 St Paul's Square, Liverpool L3 9SJ (☎ 0151 600 8000, fax 0151 600 8001, e-mail david.swaffield@hilldickinson.com)

SWAIN, Ann; da of late Owen Morris, and Joan Elaine, *née* Collinson; *b* 12 September 1944; *Educ* Eggars GS Alton, Oxford Poly; *m* 1965; 1 da (Pamela Mary b 1 Feb 1973), 1 s (Martin James b 4 Dec 1975); *Career* Radiobiological Laboratory Wantage ARC 1963–65, Rutherford High Energy Laboratory Harwell SRC 1965–68, Forest Sch 1969–71, head of sci and technol Farlington Sch Horsham 1979–91, fndr Links Consultancy 1991–, md SBRC Ltd; non-exec dir S Thames Regnl Health Authy 1994–96, chm W Sussex Family Health Servs Authy 1992–96, ind memb Sussex Police Authy 1995–2007 (vice-chm 2005–07); nat pres UK Fedn of Business and Professional Women 1991–93, exec memb Women's Nat Cmmn 1991–93, exec sec Business and Professional Women International 1999–2002; chm Advsy Panel Police CRR Training 1999–2002; lay advsr to NPT 1999–2003; memb: Women's Advsy Panel RSA 1991–93, Women's Advsy Panel Opportunity 2000 1992–93; chm The 300 Group 1996–99, dir Fair Play SE 1997–; govr Tanbridge House Sch 1993–2005, chm of govrs Arunside Sch; friend WNC 1996–; MRSC; FRSA 1991; *Recreations* swimming; *Clubs* Westminster Dining; *Style—* Mrs Ann Swain; ☎ 01403 739373, fax 01403 734432, e-mail ann@horsham.co.uk

SWALE, Jessica Bronwen; da of Robin Lee Swale, and Jill Lindsey, *née* Norman; *b* 27 February 1982, Reading, Berks; *Educ* Kendrick Girls Sch Reading, Univ of Exeter (BA), Royal Central Sch of Speech and Drama (MA); *Partner* Michael Lovatt; *Career* writer (screenwriter and playwright) and director; assoc dir Out of Joint Theatre Co 2007–11, fndr and artistic dir Red Handed Theatre Co (Best Ensemble Peter Brook Empty Space Awards 2012) 2012–; patron Wokingham Theatre 2016–; winner BAFTA JJ Screenwriting Bursary 2014; *Plays* as writer: Blue Stockings (Shakespeare's Globe) 2012 (nominated Most Promising Playwright Evening Standard Award), All's Will That Ends Will (Bremen Shakespeare Co) 2013, The Secret Garden (adapter, Grosvenor Park Open Air Theatre) 2013, Thomas Tallis (Sam Wanamaker Playhouse) 2014, Sense and Sensibility (adapter, Watermill Theatre) 2014, Far From the Madding Crowd (adapter, Watermill Theatre) 2015, Nell Gwynn (Shakespeare's Globe and West End, Best New Comedy Olivier Awards 2016) 2015–16, The Mission (ArtsEd) 2016, Stig of the Dump (adapter, Grosvenor Park Open Air Theatre) 2016, The Playhouse Apprentice (Dulwich Coll/ Sam Wanamaker Playhouse) 2016; as dir: A Comedy of Errors (Marshall Islands) 2010, Bedlam (Shakespeare's Globe) 2010, The Rivals (Southwark Playhouse) 2010, The Belle's Stratagem (Southwark Playhouse) 2011 (nominated Best Director Evening Standard Award), Palace of the End (Arcola) 2011, Someone Who'll Watch Over Me (Southwark Playhouse) 2012, The Busybody (Southwark Playhouse) 2012, Winter (Theatre Newfoundland Canada) 2012, Sleuth (Watermill Theatre) 2013, School for Scandal (Park Theatre) 2013, Sense and Sensibility (Watermill Theatre) 2014, Far From the Madding Crowd (Watermill Theatre) 2015, Fallen Angels (Salisbury Playhouse) 2015; *Screenplays* Nell Gwynn 2016, Horrible Histories Movie 2016; *Books* Drama Games: For Classrooms and Workshops (2009), Drama Games: For Devising (2012), Drama Games: For Rehearsals (2015); *Style—* Miss Jessica Swale; ✉ c/o MLRep, 2nd Floor, 16 Crucifix Lane, London SE1 3JW (☎ 020 7407 9201, e-mail helen@mlrep.com, website www.mlrep.com)

SWALES, Ian Cameron; s of Harry Swales (d 1997), and Elizabeth Adamson, *née* Doig (d 1962); *b* 5 April 1953, Leeds; *Educ* Univ of Manchester (BSc); *m* 9 Sept 1972, Patricia, *née* Thew; 2 s (Christopher Ian b 8 July 1975, Richard James b 18 Jan 1978), 1 da (Kathryn Elizabeth b 12 Oct 1980); *Career* Yorks Electricity 1973–78, with ICI 1978–99, self-employed mgmnt conslt 1999–2010; MP (Lib Dem) Redcar 2010–15; chair NE Process Industries Cluster 2015–; hon life memb (for services to humanism) Br Humanist Assoc 2015; FCCA 1977, Hon FIChemE 2016; *Books* Dear Boss (2008); *Style—* Ian Swales, Esq; ✉ 39 Coast Road, Redcar, North Yorkshire TS10 3NN

SWAN, Charles; s of Grahame Swan and Rosemary *née* Richmond; *b* 9 November 1956; *Educ* Winchester (exhibitioner), Pembroke Coll Cambridge (exhibitioner, MA), Coll of Law; *m* 1989 (m dis), Marcia May Morrissy; 2 c (Julia, Tomé); *Career* articled Woodham Smith 1981–83, admitted slr 1983; slr Speechly Bircham 1983–85, ptnr The Simkins Partnership 1985–2005, Swan Turton 2005–; Hon pres Adlaw Int; memb Law Soc; Int; *Publications* Beyond the Lens (co-author), The Advertising Industry (specialist ed), Copinger and Skone James on Copyright (17 edn); *Recreations* hill walking, running; *Style—* Charles Swan, Esq; ✉ Swan Turton LLP, 68A Neal Street, Covent Garden, London WC2H 9PA (☎ 020 7520 9560, e-mail charles.swan@swanturton.com)

SWAN, Sir Conrad Marshall John Fisher; KCVO (1994, CVO 1986, LVO 1978); s of Dr Henry Swan (*né* ?wi?cicki, herb Jastrz?biec), of Vancouver Island, BC (whose f, Paul, emigrated from Poland, where the family had long been landed proprietors and from time to time represented in the Senate of pre-Partition Poland); *b* 13 May 1924; *Educ* St George's Coll Weybridge, SOAS Univ of London, Univ of Western Ontario (BA, MA), Peterhouse Cambridge (PhD); *m* 1957, Lady Hilda Susan Mary Northcote (d 1995), da of 3 Earl of Iddesleigh; 1 s, 4 da; *Career* Capt Madras Regt Indian Army 1942–47; Assumption Unv of Windsor Ontario: lectr (history) 1956–57, asst prof 1957–62; Rouge Dragon Pursuivant 1962–68, York Herald of Arms 1968–92, Registrar and Sr Herald-in-Waiting Coll of Arms 1982–92, Garter Principal King of Arms 1992–95, inspr Regtl Colours (UK) 1993–95; lectr; genealogist of Order of Bath 1972–95; consl t to the King of Jordan on orders and decorations 2003–; KStJ (genealogist of Grand Priory Order of St John 1976–95), hon genealogist Order of St Michael & St George 1989–95, Knight Principal Imperial Soc of Knights Bachelor 1995–2001; memb Ct of Assts Worshipful Co of Gunmakers (Master 1983); FSA; Knight of Honour and Devotion SMOM 1979, Cdr Royal Norwegian Order of Merit with Star 1995, Cdr Order of Merit Republic Poland 1995, Knight Cdr Lithuanian Order of the Grand Duke Gediminas 2002, Knight Grand Cross of the Most Distuinguished Order of the Nation (KGCN) (Antigua & Barbuda) 2002; *Books* Canada: Symbols of Sovereignty (1977), The Chapel of the Order of Bath (1978), Blood of the Martyrs (with Peter Drummond Murray of Mastrick, Slains Pursuivant of Arms, 1993), A King from Canada (2005); *Video* The Aboriginal in Heraldry (1996); *Recreations* music, travel; *Style—* Sir Conrad Swan, KCVO, PhD, FSA; ✉ Boxford House, Suffolk CO10 5JT (☎ 01787 210572)

SWAN, Rev Preb Ronald Frederick; s of Frederick William Swan (d 1975), of Southampton, and Doris Ann, *née* Tidridge (d 1988); *b* 30 June 1935; *Educ* Taunton's Sch Southampton, St Catharine's Coll Cambridge (MA), Coll of the Resurrection Mirfield; *m* 23 June 1973, Dr Celia Mary Phillips, *qv*, da of Percival Edmund Phillips (d 1989); 1 da (Eleanor Mary Rose b 1974), 1 s (Toby William Barnaby b 1978); *Career* RN 1954–56; curate St John the Baptist Staveley 1961–65; staff: Anglican Chaplaincy to Univ of London, St George's Bloomsbury/Christ the King Gordon Sq 1965–73, St Martin-in-the-Fields 1973–77; vicar: St Barnabas Ealing 1977–88, St Stephen Ealing 1981–88; area dean of Ealing 1984–88, vicar St Mary Harrow on the Hill 1988–98, area dean of Harrow 1990–95, preb St Paul's Cathedral 1998–, master Royal Fndn of St Katharine 1998–; memb: Diocesan Bishop's Cncl 1998–, Cncl St Paul's Cathederal 2000–; govr St Katharine and Shadwell Tst 1998–, tstee All Saints Educnl Tst 1998–; Freeman City of London 1999; *Publications* ed (St Mary's House pubns): Believing in the Church, A Fool for Christ, Advent Readings and Prayers, Travelling Hopefully; *Recreations* walking, theatre, reading, writing, travel; *Clubs* Savile, Nikaean, Zion Coll, Royal Lymington Yacht; *Style—* The Rev Preb Ronald Swan

SWANN, Graeme Peter; *b* 24 March 1979, Northampton; *m* 29 Jan 2010, Sarah; *Career* professional cricketer; Northants CCC 1998–2004, Notts CCC 2005–; England: 26 test matches, 38 one-day ints, one-day int debut v SA 2000, test debut v India 2008; ECB

Cricketer of the Year 2010; *Style*— Graeme Swann, Esq; ✉ c/o Nottinghamshire County Cricket Club, Trent Bridge, Nottingham NG2 6AG

SWANN, Kate Elizabeth; da of Ian M Prior, and Sheila Prior; *b* 21 December 1964; *Educ* Univ of Bradford (BSc); *m* 1987; 2 da; *Career* commercial exec then mktg exec Tesco plc 1986–88, brand mangr rising to gp product mangr Homepride Foods 1988–92, mktg mangr rising to gen mktg mangr CocaCola Schweppes Beverages 1992–93, gp mktg controller then mktg dir White Goods Dixons Stores Gp 1993–95, mktg dir Currys 1995–97, md Homebase 1999–2000 (mktg dir 1997–99), md Argos Ltd 2000–03, chief exec WH Smith plc 2003–13, ceo SSP 2013–; non-exec dir Babcock 2011; *Style*— Mrs Kate Swann; ✉ SSP The Food Travel Experts, 169 Euston Road, London NW1 2AE

SWANNELL, John; *b* 27 December 1946; *Career* professional photographer; began career as photographic asst Vogue Studios, former asst to David Bailey, fashion photographer (Vogue, Harpers & Queen, Tatler, Ritz newspaper); exhbns incl: several at the Nat Portrait Gallery London (which holds 80 Swannell photographs in their Permanent Collection), fashion photography since 1974 (Royal Photographic Soc Bath) July-Sept 1990; photographer of set of 26 portraits for The Prince Charles Tst 1991 (incl Sir John Gielgud, Lord King, Lord Weatherill, Harvey Goldsmith and David Hockney); other subjects photographed incl: HM The Queen and the Duke of Edinburgh (for the Golden Jubilee 2002), HM Queen Elizabeth the Queen Mother (for her 100th birthday), HRH The Princess Royal, Diana Princess of Wales with her children (private commission), King Hussein of Jordan, King Abdullah and Queen Rania, Prince and Princess Michael of Kent (for their 30th wedding anniversary) 2008, The Earl and Countess of Wessex with their children and the royal family (for the christening of their son The Viscount Severn) 2008; commissioned to photograph: Royal Family for Royal Mail stamps 2000, Tony and Cherie Blair for Christmas card 2004; portraits for book I'm Still Standing incl: Richard Attenborough, Michael Caine, Bryan Ferry, Norman Foster, Bob Hoskins, Glenda Jackson, Tom Jones, Ken Livingstone, Joanna Lumley; dir over 50 commercials since 1984 specialising in high fashion and beauty; awards incl: Gold award for Best Commercial of the Year 1984 (Boots No 7), Silver award at Cannes for Best 40 Second Commercial (Rimmel Cosmetics), Best Commercial NY 1990 (Johnsons); *Books* Fine Line (1982), Naked Landscape (1982), Twenty Years On (1996), I'm Still Standing (2002), Nudes 1978–2000 (2007); *Style*— John Swannell, Esq

SWANNELL, Robert William Ashburnham; *b* 18 November 1950; *Educ* Rugby, Inns of Ct Sch of Law; *m* Jan 1982, Patricia; 1 s, 1 da; *Career* CA 1973; KPMG 1969–73; called to the Bar Lincoln's Inn 1976; vice-chm J Henry Schroder & Co Ltd 1997–2000 (dir 1985–2000), co-chm Citigroup European Investment Bank 2002–06, vice-chm Citigroup Europe 2006–08, sr advsr Citi Europe 2009–10; chm HMV Gp 2009–11, chm Marks and Spencer 2010–; non-exec dir: British Land Co 1999–2010, 3i Gp plc 2006–10; chm Advsy Bd Shareholder Exec 2014–; chm and memb Bd Governing Body Rugby Sch 2004–14; *Style*— Robert Swannell, Esq

SWANSEA, 5 Baron (UK 1893); Sir Richard Anthony Hussey Vivian; 5 Bt (UK 1882); s of 4 Baron Swansea (d 2005), and Miriam Antoinette, *née* Caccia-Birch (d 1975); *b* 24 January 1957, Builth Wells, Powys; *Educ* Eton, Univ of Durham (BA, pres Durham Union Soc), City Univ (MBA); *m* 24 Aug 1996, Anna Clementine, *née*, Austin; 1 s (Hon James Henry Hussey Vivian b 25 June 1999), 1 da (Hon Emma Averil Mary Vivian b 8 March 2001); *Heir* s, Hon James Vivian; *Career* fin journalist 1980–98, investment research ed and supervisor 1998–2011, Guildford franchise ptnr Rosemary Bookkeeping 2013–; memb (Cons) Wandsworth BC 1994–2006 (dep mayor 2000–01); memb Cncl Newton Prep Sch Battersea 2001–12; vice-pres Morriston RFC Male Choir 2007–; Hon Alderman London Borough of Wandsworth 2006; *Publications* China's Metals and World Markets (1992); *Recreations* sudoku puzzles, croquet, horse racing; *Style*— The Lord Swansea; ✉ 48 Weyside Road, Guildford, Surrey GU1 1HX (e-mail swanseas@btinternet.com)

SWANSEA AND BRECON, Bishop of 2008–; Rt Rev John David Edward Davies; s of William Howell Davies, of Newport, Gwent, and Doiran Rallison, *née* Watkins; *b* 6 February 1953; *Educ* Bassaleg GS, Univ of Southampton (LLB), Coll of Law Chester, St Michael's Coll Llandaff, Univ of Wales Cardiff (DipTh), Univ of Wales (LLM); *m* 1986, Joanna Lucy, da of Allen Aulton, and Sylvia, *née* Hamer; 1 da (Kate Frances Lucy b 1 Aug 1988), 1 s (Christopher James Gerald b 11 July 1990); *Career* articled clerk 1975, slr 1977–82; asst curate Chepstow 1984–86, curate i/c Michaelston-y-Fedw with Rudry 1986–88, rector of Bedwas with Rudry 1988–95, vicar of Newport (Maindee) 1995–2000, dean of Brecon 2000–08; chm of tstees St David's Fndn Hospice Care 2000–03, tstee Christian Aid 2011, tstee Community Fndn for Wales 2013–15; CStJ (sub-prelate for Wales); *Recreations* music especially opera, organ and 60s and 70s pop, walking, cricket, golf, reading, entertaining; *Style*— The Rt Rev the Bishop of Swansea and Brecon; ✉ Ely Tower, Castle Square, Brecon, Powys LD3 9DJ

SWANSON, Magnus P; *b* 25 April 1958; *Educ* Univ of Edinburgh (LLB); *Career* lawyer; legal apprenticeship Steedman Ramage & Co WS Edinburgh 1980–82, foreign attorney Corp Dept Paul Weiss Rifkind Wharton & Garrison New York 1986–87; Maclay Murray & Spens Glasgow: slr 1982–86, ptnr1987–, chief exec 2003–; chm Law at Work (Hldgs) Ltd; memb: Law Soc of Scotland, Int Bar Assoc; *Publications* Aircraft Finance (co-author Scottish Chapter); *Style*— Magnus P Swanson, Esq; ✉ Maclay Murray & Spens, 151 St Vincent Street, Glasgow G2 5NJ (✆ 0141 248 5011, fax 0141 248 5819, e-mail magnus.swanson@mms.co.uk)

SWANTON, Dr (Robert) Howard; s of Robert Neil Swanton (d 1976), and Susanne, *née* Baldwin (d 2000); *b* 30 September 1944; *Educ* Monkton Combe Sch, Queens' Coll Cambridge (fndn scholar, MA, MB BChir, MD), St Thomas' Hosp Med Sch London (exhibitioner, Mead medal in med, Bristowe medal in pathology); *m* Lindsay Ann, da of Arnold Jepson, of Blackburn, Lancs; 1 s (Robert Charles b 24 Feb 1972), 1 da (Josephine Kate b 23 Jan 1975); *Career* house physician St Thomas' Hosp London 1969, house surgn St Peter's Hosp Chertsey 1970; SHO: Hammersmith Hosp 1970–71, Nat Heart Hosp 1971; med registrar Poole Hosp 1971–72, sr med registrar St Thomas' Hosp London 1975–77 (cardiac registrar 1972–74), sr registrar in cardiology Nat Heart Hosp 1977–79; conslt cardiologist: Middlesex Hosp 1979–2001, King Edward VII Hosp for Offrs 1984–, The Heart Hosp UCL Hosps 2001; Br Cardiac Soc: memb 1979–, asst sec 1986–88, sec 1988–90, pres 1998–2001; fell Euro Soc of Cardiology 1994; FRCP 1984 (MRCP 1971), FESC 1994, FACC 2005; *Books* Swanton's Cardiology (1984, 6 edn 2008), Essential Angioplasty (2012); *Recreations* music, photography; *Clubs* St Albans Medical, Arts; *Style*— Dr Howard Swanton; ✉ Kent Lodge, 10 Dover Park Drive, Roehampton, London SW15 5BG (✆ 020 8788 6920); University College Hospital, Medical Specialities Division, 3rd Floor Central, 250 Euston Road, London NW1 2PG (✆ 020 3447 5540, e-mail howard.swanton@uclh.nhs.uk); 22 Upper Wimpole Street, London W1G 6NB (✆ 020 7034 4030)

SWARBRICK, Dr Edwin Thornton; s of Richard Thornton Swarbrick, and Mary Elizabeth, *née* Cooper; *b* 29 April 1945; *Educ* Pocklington Sch, Wilbraham Acad Mass USA, St George's Med Sch London (MB BS, MD); *m* 3 March 1984, (Angela) Corinne, da of Kenneth Hamer; 2 s (Benjamin Thornton b 8 Jan 1985, Matthew Thornton b 9 Feb 1987), 1 da (Kate Hannah b 31 March 1993); *Career* house physician and surgn St George's Hosp London 1968–69, SHO Brompton Hosp 1970–71, registrar The London Hosp 1971–72, registrar St Mark's Hosp 1972–74, res fell Inst of Child Health London 1974–76, lectr in gastroenterology Bart's 1976–80, conslt physician Wolverhampton 1980–2010; hon reader in gastroenterology Univ of Wolverhampton 1995; dir of R&D Royal Wolverhampton Hosp Tst; vice-pres (endoscopy) Br Soc for Gastroenterology; chair NW Midlands CLRN Advsy Bd 2009–12, chair Medical Equestrian Assoc 2012–14; memb RSM; FRCP; *Publications* over 40 peer-reviewed publications on a range of gastroenterological and endoscopic subjects; *Recreations* equestrian sports, skiing, music, the arts; *Style*— Dr Edwin Swarbrick; ✉ Coppice Green, Shifnal, Shropshire (✆ 01952 462226, email docswarbs@hotmail.com)

SWARBRICK, Prof James; s of George Winston Swarbrick, and Edith, *née* Cooper; *b* 8 May 1934; *Educ* Sloane GS, Chelsea Coll London (BPharm, PhD, DSc); *m* 1960, Pamela Margaret Oliver; *Career* lectr Chelsea Coll 1964 (asst lectr 1962), visiting asst prof Purdue Univ 1964; Univ of Connecticut: assoc prof 1966, prof and chm Dept of Pharmaceutics 1969, asst dean 1970; dir product devpt Sterling-Winthrop Res Inst NY 1972–75, first prof of pharmaceutics Univ of Sydney 1975–76, dean Sch of Pharmacy Univ of London 1976–78, prof of pharmacy Univ of Southern Calif LA 1978–81, chm Div Pharmaceutics and prof of pharmaceutics Univ of North Carolina 1981–93, vice-pres R&D AAI Inc 1993–99; pres PharmaceuTech Inc 2001–, vice-pres Scientific Affrs aaiPharma Inc 1999–2006; visiting scientist Astra Laboratories Sweden 1971, industry conslt 1965–72, 1975–93 and 1999–, conslt Aust Dept of Health 1975–76; Food and Drug Admin: chm Generic Drugs Advsy Ctee 1995–97 (memb 1992–97), conslt 1997–; memb Ctee on Specifications Nat Formulary 1970–75, chm Jt US Pharmacopoeia Nat Formulary Panel on Disintegration 1971–75; memb: Ctee on Graduate Programs American Assoc Colls of Pharmacy 1969–71, Practice Trg Ctee Pharmaceutical Soc of NSW 1975–76, Academic Bd Univ of Sydney 1975–76, Collegiate Cncl 1976–78, Educn Ctee Royal Pharmaceutical Soc GB 1976–78, Working Pty on Pre-Registration Training 1977–78; Pharmaceutical Mfrs Assoc Fndn: memb Basic Pharmacology Advsy Ctee 1982–91, chm Pharmaceutics Advsy Ctee 1986–2007, memb Science Advsy Ctee 1986–2007; memb Editorial Bd: Jl of Biopharmaceutics and Pharmacokinetics 1973–79, Drug Devpt Communications 1974–82, Pharmaceutical Technol 1978–2008, Biopharmaceutics and Drug Disposition 1979–; series ed: Current Concepts in the Pharmaceutical Sciences, Drugs and the Pharmaceutical Sciences; fell: Acad of Pharmaceutical Sciences, Royal Pharmaceutical Society of GB 1978 (memb 1961), American Assoc of Pharmaceutical Scientists 1987; CChem, FRSC, FAAS 1966, FRIC 1970; *Publications* Physical Pharmacy (with A N Martin and A Cammarata, 2 edn, 1969, 3 edn, 1983), Encyclopedia of Pharmaceutical Technology (jt ed, 1990, 4 edn (renamed Encyclopedia of Pharmaceutical Science and Technology) 2012), Drugs and the Pharmaceutical Sciences (series ed), contrib to various pharmaceutical books and jls; *Recreations* woodwork, listening to music, golf; *Clubs* Pinehurst Country; *Style*— Prof James Swarbrick; ✉ PharmaceuTech Inc, 180 Doral Drive, Pinehurst, NC 28374, USA (✆ 00 1 910 255 3015, e-mail pharmaceutech@earthlink.net)

SWAROVSKI, Nadja; *née* Swarovski; da of Helmut Swarovski, and Danna Swarovski; *b* Munich, Germany; *Educ* St Marks Sch MA USA, Southern Methodist Univ TX USA; *m* Rupert Adams; 3 c; *Career* vice-pres of int communications and memb Exec Bd Swarovski; *Recreations* the arts, sports, fashion, charity; *Style*— Mrs Nadja Swarovski-Adams; ✉ Swarovski, 21 Sackville Street, London W1S 3DN

SWASH, Prof Michael; s of late Edwin Frank Swash, of Milford on Sea, Hants, and Kathleen, *née* Burton; *b* 29 January 1939; *Educ* Forest Sch, London Hosp Med Coll (MD), Univ of Virginia Med Sch, Case-Western Reserve Univ Ohio; *m* 22 Jan 1966, Caroline Mary, da of Edward Payne, of Box, Glos; 3 s (Jesse Edward, Thomas Henry, (Edmond) Joseph); *Career* hon conslt neurologist The Royal London Hosp (conslt neurologist 1972–2006), hon conslt neurologist St Mark's Hosp London, chief med offr Swiss Reinsurance (UK) Ltd 1985–2014, sr lectr in neuropathology The London Hosp Med Coll 1981–1994, med dir The Royal London Hosp and Assoc Community Servs NHS Tst 1991–94, dir Medhand Int AB Stockholm, dir Medical Advisory Board Best Doctors Europe; emeritus prof of neurology: Barts and The London NHS Tst, Queen Mary Sch of Med and Dentistry London 1995–2006 (now emeritus prof), hon prof of neurology Faculty of Medicine Univ of Lisbon 2007–; neurologist-adjunct Cleveland Clinic Fndn OH 1980–99; Spinoza visiting prof Univ of Amsterdam 2000 and various other visiting professorships; hon sec Section of Neurology RSM 1974–77, hon sec NETRHA Advsy Ctee for Neurology and Neurosurgery 1975–78, hon sec Assoc of Br Neurologists 1979–84; chm: Southwark and Camberwell Multiple Sclerosis Soc 1985–1999, Motor Neurone Disease Assoc 1998–2001 (tstee 1994–98), World Fedn of Neurology Research Ctee on Amyotrophic Lateral Sclerosis 1998–2005; memb Neuroscience Bd MRC 1986–91; hon memb of many British and foreign scientific socs; membre d'honneur de la Société Nationale Française de Colo-Proctologie; dir: Medland Int AB, Malvern Arts Press Ltd; memb: Trollope Soc, Anthony Powell Soc; Assoc of Br Neurologists Medallist 2010; Liveryman Worshipful Soc of Apothecaries 1989; FRCPath, FRCP 1977 (MRCP 1972), sr FRSM; *Books* incl: Clinical Neuropathology (jtly, 1982), Muscle Biopsy Pathology (jtly, 1984, 2 edn 1984), Scientific Basis of Clinical Neurology (jtly, 1985), Hierarchies in Neurology (jtly, 1989), Neurology: a concise clinical text (jtly, 1989), Clinical Neurology (2 vols, jtly, 1991), Neuromuscular Diseases (jtly, 3 edn 1995), Colour Guide: Neurology (jtly, 1997, 2 edn 2005), Outcomes in Neurology and Neurosurgery (1998), Amyotrophic Lateral Sclerosis (jtly, 2 edn 2006), Hutchison's Clinical Methods (22 edn 2008), Neurology in Focus (jtly, 2008); author of more than 500 scientific and medical research papers, founding ed Amyotrophic Lateral Sclerosis 1999–2007; *Recreations* walking, music, rowing, theatre, opera, Morgan Plus 8; *Clubs* London Rowing, Athenaeum, Rowfant (Cleveland, OH); *Style*— Prof Michael Swash; ✉ Department of Neurology, The London Independent Hospital, London E1 4NL (✆ 020 7780 2400, fax 020 7638 4043, mobile 077 6824 2335, e-mail mswash@btinternet.com)

S

SWATMAN, Philip Hilary; s of late Philip Stenning Swatman, of Parkstone, Dorset, and late Patricia, *née* Meeson; *b* 1 December 1949, Ringwood, Hants; *Educ* St Edward's Sch Oxford, ChCh Oxford (BA); *m* 1972, Rosemary, *née* Cox; 2 da (Elizabeth Harriet b 16 Aug 1978, Rowena Jane b 16 April 1984), 1 s (Richard Oliver b 14 Oct 1981); *Career* KPMG 1971–76, Nat Enterprise Bd 1976–79, N M Rothschild 1979–86 (dir 1986), Chase Property Holdings plc 1987–88; N M Rothschild: rejoined 1987, md 1996, co-head investment banking 1999–2002, vice-chm 2002–08; ptnr Cardinal Advsrs LLP; chm: Merlin Reputation Mgmnt Ltd, Raigersfield Capital Ltd; non-exec dir: Alfred McAlpine plc 2003–08, Atrium plc 2006–07, New England Seafood Int Ltd 2010–, Investec Structured Products Calculus VCT plc 2010–; FCA 1974; *Publications* The Field of Dreams (2010); *Recreations* sailing, shooting, opera, theatre, golf, fishing, fine wine, travel; *Style*— Philip Swatman, Esq; ✆ 020 8949 1360, e-mail phswatman@btconnect.com; Cardinal House, George Road, Kingston on Thames, Surrey KT2 7NU (✆ 020 8336 2712, mobile 07717 434216, e-mail pswatman@merlinpr.com)

SWAYNE, Rt Hon Sir Desmond Angus; kt (2016), PC (2011), TD, MP; s of George Joseph Swayne, and Elizabeth McAlister, *née* Gibson; *b* 20 August 1956, Berne, Switzerland; *Educ* Bedford Sch, Univ of St Andrews (MTheol); *m* 1987, Moira, *née* Teek; 3 c; *Career* schoolmaster 1981–87, systems analyst Royal Bank of Scotland 1988–97, MP (Cons) New Forest W 1997– (Parly candidate Pontypridd 1987 and West Bromwich West 1992); memb Social Security Select Ctee 1997–2001, oppn frontbench spokesman on health until 2001, oppn front bench spokesman on defence 2001–02, oppn whip 2002–04, PPS to Ldr of HM Oppn (Rt Hon Michael Howard then Rt Hon David Cameron) 2004–10, PPS to the PM 2010–12, Lord Cmmr HM Treasy (Govt Whip) 2012–13, vice-chamberlain HM Household 2013–14, min of state DFID 2014–; *Recreations* Territorial Army (Maj, Pool of Liaison Offrs and Watchkeepers Woolwich), swimming (memb Serpentine swimming club); *Clubs* Cavalry and Guards'; *Style*— The Rt Hon Sir Desmond Swayne, TD, MP; ✉ House of Commons, London SW1A 0AA (☎ 020 7219 4886)

SWAYNE, Giles Oliver Cairnes; s of Sir Ronald Swayne, MC (d 1991), and Charmian, *née* Cairnes (d 1984); *b* 30 June 1946; *Educ* Ampleforth, Trinity Coll Cambridge; *m* 1, 1972 (m dis 1983), Camilla, *née* Rumbold; 1 s (Orlando b 1974); m 2, 1984 (m dis 2002), Naa Otua, *née* Codjoe; m 3, 2002, Malu, *née* Lin; *Career* composer; studied at RAM 1968–71; dir Gonzaga Music Ltd 2002–; composer in residence Clare Coll Cambridge 2006–14; Hon ARAM 1988; *Works* Six Songs of Lust (1966), La Rivière (1966), The Kiss (1967), Sonata for String Quartet (1968), Three Shakespeare Songs (1969), Chamber Music for Strings (1970), Four Lyrical Pieces (1970), The Good-Morrow (1971), String Quartet No 1 (1971), Paraphrase (1971), Trio (1972), Canto for Guitar (1972), Canto for Piano (1973), Canto for Violin (1973), Orlando's Music (1974), Synthesis (1974), Scrapbook (1974), Canto for Clarinet (1975), Charades (1975), Duo (1975), Suite for Guitar (1976), Pentecost Music (1976), Alleluia! (1976), String Quartet No 2 (1977), A World Within (1978), Phoenix Variations (1979), CRY (1979), The Three R's (1980), Freewheeling (1980), Count-down (1981), Canto for Cello (1981), Rhythm-studies 1 and 2 (1982), Magnificat I (1982), Riff-raff (1983), A Song for Haddi (1983), Symphony for Small Orchestra (1984), Le nozze di Cherubino (1984), Naaotwà lála (1984), Missa Tiburtina (1985), Into the Light (1986), Solo (1986), godsong (1986), Nunc dimittis I (1986), O Magnum Mysterium (1986), PP (1987), Tonos (1987), Veni Creator I and II (1987), Songlines (1987), The Coming of Saskia Hawkins (1987), Harmonies of Hell (1988), The Song of Leviathan (1988), A Memory of Sky (1989), No Quiet Place (1990), No Man's Land (1990), Circle of Silence (1991), Zebra Music (1992), The Song of the Tortoise (1992), The Owl and the Pussycat I (1983), String Quartet No 3 (1993), Fiddlesticks (1994), Goodnight, Sweet Ladies (1994), Squeezy (1994), All About Henry (1995), The Tiger (1995), Communion Service in D (1995), A Convocation of Worms (1995), Two Romantic Songs (1996), The Silent Land (1996), Ophelia Drowning (1996), Tombeau (1997), Beatus Vir (1997), Mr Leary's Mechanical Maggot (1997), Chinese Whispers (1997), Petite Messe Solitaire (1997), Missa Brevissima (1997), Echo (1997), Winter Solstice Carol (1998), Groundwork (1998), Merlis Lied (1998), The Flight of the Swan (1999), HAVOC (1999), The Akond of Swat (2000), Peturbèd Spirit (2000), Canto for Flute (2000), Memory Dances (2000), The Akond of Swat (2000), Mancanza (2001), The Murder of Gonzago (2001), Bits and Bobs (2002), Epitaph and Refrain (2002), The Owl and the Pussycat II (2003), Sangre Viva (2003), Midwinter (2003), Stabat Mater (2004), Four Passiontide Motets (2004), Ave verum corpus (2004), Stations of the Cross Books I and II (2004), Magnificat II (2005), Mr Bach's Bottle-bank (2005), Four Christmas Carols (2005), Magnificat II (2005), Nunc dimittis II (2005), Bits of Mrs Bach (2005), Epithalamium (2005), Elegy for a wicked world (2005), Sonata for cello and piano (2006), Sinfonietta concertante (2006), Ten Terrible Tunes (2006), A Clare Eucharist (2006), Creepy-crawlies (2006), Two little motets (2006), There is no rose (2006), Suite for solo cello (2007), Symphony no 1 (2007), Threnody (2007), Leonardo's Dream (2008), Agnes Wisley's Chillout Fantasy (2008), Magnificat III (2008), Bagatelles for piano Book 1 (2009), The Human Heart (2009), Toil and Trouble (2009), Zig-zag (2009), The Joys of Travel (2009), String Quartet no 4 (2009), Adam Lay Ibounden (2009), O Mysteria (2009), Der Wandersmann (2010), Hubbub (2010), The Word (2010), Complaintes (2010), Dolorosa (2011), Laulu Laulülle (2011), Bagatelles Book 2 (2011), Clare Canticles (2012), Uncommon Prayers (2012), Strumming (2012), Two Little Prayers (2013), Double Act (2013), The Yonghy-Bonghy-Bo (2014), God is Gone Up (2014), Chansons Dévotes et Poissonneuses (2014), Our Orphan Souls (2014), Kaleidoscope (2015), Quackenbush The Musical (2015), Everybloom (2016); *Recordings* CRY (BBC Singers, John Poole, 1985), Magnificat (various), Choral Music of Giles Swayne (BBC Singers, Stephen Cleobury, 1997), Convocation (Nat Youth Choir, Michael Brewer), Giles Swayne Music for cello and piano (Robert Irvine, Fali Pavri, Delphian 2007), Giles Swayne Stabat Mater, The Silent Land etc (Dmitri Ensemble, Graham Ross, Naxos 2010), Stations of the Cross (Simon Nieminski, Resonus Classics 2014); *Recreations* walking, talking, thinking; *Clubs* Incorporated Soc of Musicians; *Style*— Giles Swayne; ✉ c/o Gonzaga Music Ltd, Pool House, Bockleton Road, Tenbury Wells WR15 8PW (e-mail gs@gonzagamusic.co.uk)

SWEENEY, Brian Philip; QFSM (2004); s of Philip Sweeney, and Mary, *née* Green; *b* 14 July 1961, Glasgow; *Educ* Holyrood Acad, Glasgow Caledonian Univ, Univ of Coventry (MA), IFireE (Dip); *m* 16 Oct 1994, Pamela Anne, *née* Barrat; 3 s (Alan Edward b 6 Sept 1983, Philip Anthony b 13 April 1985, Ryan Alexander b 12 Jan 1998); *Career* Strathclyde Fire & Rescue: joined 1981, leading firefighter 1983, sub offr 1986, station offr 1989, asst divnl offr 1993, divnl offr 1996, sr divnl offr 1998, asst chief offr and dir of ops 2000, dep chief offr 2003, chief offr/firemaster 2004–; Hon Dr Glasgow Caledonian Univ; Long Serv Good Conduct Medal 2000; fell: Chief Fire Offrs' Assoc, Assoc of Princ Fire Offrs 2000–; Freeman Citizen of Glasgow 2004; FIFireE, MInstD, MCGI; *Recreations* golf, reading; *Style*— Brian Sweeney, Esq, QFSM; ✉ Strathclyde Fire & Rescue, Headquarters, Bothwell Road, Hamilton, Lanarkshire ML3 0EA (☎ 01698 338240, fax 01698 338494, e-mail brian.sweeney@strathclydefire.org)

SWEENEY, Edward (Ed); CBE (2014); s of William Sweeney (d 1988), and Louise, *née* Cawley; *b* 6 August 1954; *m* 3 Jan 1987, Janet, da of Cliff Roydhouse; *Career* BIFU: research offr 1976–79, negotiating offr TSB 1979–86, national offr Scotland 1986–89, nat offr insurance 1989–91, dep gen sec 1991–96, gen sec 1996–99; gen sec UNIFI 2000–04 (jt gen sec 1999–2000), dep gen sec Amicus 2004–07, chair Acas 2007–13; visiting prof Leeds Univ Business Sch; memb: Gen Cncl TUC, Exec Ctee TUC, Bd Investors in People UK Ltd, Mgmnt Bd Employment Tbnl Serv; non-service panel memb for external interviewers for chief fire officers and chief police officers; *Recreations* sport of all kinds, reading, egyptology; *Style*— Ed Sweeney, Esq, CBE

SWEENEY, Jeremy Michael; s of Terence Ernest Michael Sweeney, and Dawn Yvonne, *née* Knight; *b* 3 June 1963; *Educ* Epsom Coll; *m* Philippa Sara, da of Maj (ret) Patrick Garway-Templeman; *Career* product devpt Wessex Medical Ltd Midhurst 1982–85, resort mangr Bladon Lines Risoul France 1986–87, crew Schooner Fleurtje Hamilton Bermuda 1987–88, with Mercury Communications 1988–89, subsequently md Ian Greer Associates public affrs conslts until 1996 (joined 1989), with A S Biss & Co 1996–2001 (dep chm), ceo JMS Resources; *Recreations* motorbikes, dogs; *Clubs* Cavalry and Guards'; *Style*— Jeremy Sweeney, Esq; ☎ 01730 829222, e-mail jeremy@jmsresources.com

SWEENEY, John Paul; s of Leonard Sweeney, and Barbara, *née* Owen; *b* 7 June 1958; *Educ* Barton Peveril GS, LSE (BSc); *m* 1985, Annie, da of Rex Patterson; 1 s (Sam b 25 November 1988), 1 da (Molly b 18 July 1992); *Career* journalist; with The Sheffield Telegraph 1981–84, freelance 1984–88, with The Observer 1989–2000, BBC 2001– (currently reporter Panorama); Journalist of the Year What the Papers Say Awards 1997, Paul Foot Award for Investigative Journalism 2005; *Publications* The Life and Evil Times of Nicolae Ceausescu (1991), Trading With the Enemy: How Britain Armed Iraq (1993), Purple Homicide: Fear and Loathing on Knutsford Heath (1997); *Recreations* poking powerful people with a stick; *Style*— John Sweeney, Esq; ✉ e-mail john.sweeney@bbc.co.uk

SWEENEY, Matthew Gerard; s of Clement Sweeney, of Co Donegal, and Josephine, *née* Lavelle; *b* 6 October 1952; *Educ* Franciscan Coll Gormanstown Co Meath, Univ Coll Dublin, Univ of Freiburg (yr abroad), Poly of N London (BA); *m* 14 Sept 1979, Rosemary, da of Benjamin Barber (d 1967); 1 da (Nico Sara b 3 Aug 1980), 1 s (Malvin Leigh b 11 April 1983); *Career* writer; writer in residence Farnham Coll 1984 and 1985, Henfield writing fell UEA 1986, events and publicity asst The Poetry Soc 1988–90, poet in residence Hereford & Worcester 1991, writer in residence The South Bank Centre 1994–95, poet in residence on internet for Chadwyck-Healey 1997–98, poet in residence Nat Library for the Blind 1999, writer in residence Univ Coll Cork 2012–13, other residencies incl Birmingham Readers & Writers Festival 1993, Salisbury Festival 1994, Aldeburgh Poetry Festival 1998; memb Aosdána 1990; gives regular readings throughout UK and abroad, has reviewed for Telegraph, Sunday Times, Observer, Times supplements and Poetry Review; featured regularly on BBC Radio; awards: Prudence Farmer Prize 1984, Cholmondeley Award 1987, Arts Cncl bursary 1992, Arts Cncl Writer's Award 1999; *Poetry* A Dream of Maps (1981), A Round House (1983), The Lame Waltzer (1985), Blue Shoes (1989), Cacti (1992), The Blue Taps (limited edn pamphlet, 1994), Emergency Kit: Poems For Strange Times (anthology, co-ed with Jo Shapcott, 1996), The Bridal Suite (1997), Penguin Modern Poets 12 (1997), Beyond Bedlam: Poems Written Out of Mental Distress (anthology, co-ed with Ken Smith, 1997), A Smell of Fish (2000), Selected Poems (2002), Sanctuary (2004), Black Moon (2007), The Night Post (2010), Horse Music (2013); for children: The Flying Spring Onion (1992), Fatso in the Red Suit (1995), Up on the Roof (2009); *Fiction* Death Comes for the Poets (jtly with John Hartley Williams, 2012); for children: The Snow Vulture (1992 and 1994), The Chinese Dressing Gown (1987); *Educational* Writing Poetry (jtly with John Hartley Williams, 1997); *Style*— Matthew Sweeney, Esq; ✉ Rogers, Coleridge & White, 20 Powis Mews, London W11 1JN (☎ 020 7221 3717)

SWEENEY, Hon Mr Justice; Sir Nigel Hamilton Sweeney; kt (2008); s of Alan Vincent Sweeney, of Dulwich, London, and Dorothy, *née* McKeer; *b* 18 March 1954, London; *Educ* Wellington, Univ of Nottingham (LLB); *m* 1, 1985, Joanna Clair, *née* Slater; 1 s (James Edward Hamilton b 21 Dec 1986), 1 da (Jessica Isabella Clair b 14 Dec 1990); m 2, 2002, Sheila Teresa, *née* Diamond; *Career* called to the Bar Middle Temple 1976 (Winston Churchill Pupillage Prize, Harmsworth scholar, bencher 1997); jr prosecuting counsel to the Crown 1987–91, first jr prosecuting counsel to the Crown 1991–92, sr prosecuting counsel to the Crown 1992–97, first sr prosecuting counsel to the Crown 1997–2000, recorder of the Crown Court 1997–, QC 2000, judge of the High Court (Queen's Bench Div) 2008–; memb: Criminal Bar Assoc 1977, Health and Safety Bar Assoc 2005; *Recreations* golf, the arts; *Clubs* Garrick, Wisley Golf; *Style*— The Hon Mr Justice Sweeney; ✉ Royal Courts of Justice, Strand, London WC2A 2LL

SWEETING, Adam Raymond Charles; s of Raymond Ernest William Sweeting (d 1966), and Vera Christine, *née* Potts (d 2012); *b* 3 January 1955; *Educ* Brentwood Sch, Univ of York (BA, MA); *Partner* Gillian Harvey; *Career* feature writer TV & Home Video magazine 1979–80, sub ed Titbits magazine 1980–81, features ed Melody Maker magazine 1984–86 (feature writer 1981–84), freelance writer 1986; currently writer on music and TV for Daily Telegraph; fndr dir Virtual Television Co (makers of Mr Rock & Roll series (Channel 4) and Pavarotti – The Last Tenor (Arena, BBC2), writer/prodr Nigel Kennedy's Polish Adventure (Imagine, BBC1) 2010), co-fndr arts website theartsdesk.com; regular contrib: The Guardian, Gramophone magazine, MotorSport magazine, British Airways Business Life; sometime contrib: Elle (UK and USA), Vogue, Q, You magazine (Mail on Sunday), Radio 4; *Books* Springsteen – Visions of America (1985), Simple Minds (1988), Cover Versions (2004); *Recreations* cricket (playing and watching), cycling, beaches, movies, opera, Formula 1, photography, learning classical guitar; *Style*— Adam Sweeting, Esq; ✉ e-mail adam.sweeting@btinternet.com

SWEETING, Prof Sir Martin Nicholas; kt (2002), OBE (1995); s of Frank Morris Sweeting (d 1994), and Dorothy May, *née* Skelton (d 2003); *b* 12 March 1951, London; *Educ* Aldenham, Univ of Surrey (BSc, PhD); *m* 1975, Christine; *Career* Marconi Space and Defence Systems 1973; Univ of Surrey: research fell 1978–81, head of research into UoSAT microsatellite system 1981–85, lectr 1981–86, prof of satellite engrg 1990, distinguished prof 2006; research dir Satellites Int Ltd 1983–84; Surrey Satellite Technol Ltd: technical dir 1985–94, md 1994–2000, ceo 2000–06, gp exec chm 2006–; chm DMCii Ltd 2006–; dir Surrey Space Centre 1996–2014 (dep dir 1990–96, chm 2014–); chm AMSAT-UK 1990–, chair Bd of Tstees Nat Space Centre Leicester 2005–, chair of tstees Radio Communications Fndn 2006–, UK Space Agency Leadership Cncl 2011–15; author of 350 pubns in jls, conferences and books; Royal Acad of Egrg Silver Medal 1995, Queen's Award for Technological Achievement 1998, UK Engrg Cncl Gold Award, Space Achievement Medal Br Interplanetary Soc, Mullard Prize Royal Soc 2000, IAA Malina Medal Space Educn 2002, Industrial Leadership Award American Astronautical Soc 2004, Queen's Award for Innovation and Enterprise 2005, Gold Medal Royal Inst of Navigation, THES Award for Innovation (for the Disaster Monitoring Constellation), Arthur Clark Lifetime Award 2008, IET Faraday Medal 2010, von Karman Award CalTech 2012, COSPAR Jeoujang Jaw Award 2014; featured in the UK's Top Ten Great Britons list 2007, Sunday Times UK's 20 most influential engineers 2014 and 2016; fell Inst Acad of Astronautics 1999; FIET, FBIS, FRAeS, MAIAA, hon memb Inst Chartered Surveyors, hon memb Inst Engrg Design, hon fell Inst Navigation, FREng 1996, FRS 2000, Hon FRAeS 2015; *Recreations* travelling, photography, amateur radio, cycling; *Style*— Prof Sir Martin Sweeting, OBE, FREng, FRS; ✉ Surrey Satellite Technology Ltd (SSTL), Tycho House, Stephenson Road, Surrey Research Park, Guildford GU2 7YE (☎ 01483 803909)

SWEETMAN, Mrs Ronald; Jennifer Joan; *see:* Dickson, Dr Jennifer

SWENSEN, Joseph; s of Anton Swensen, of Pearl River, NY, USA, and Kikue Okamoto Swensen; *b* 4 August 1960; *Educ* Juilliard Sch of Music; *Children* 3 s (David Noah b 17 Aug 1988, Jonathan Algot b 27 Sept 1996, Nicholas b 13 Oct 1999); *Career* conductor, composer, violinist, teacher; debut as violinist 1968, debut as conductor Juillard Sch 1975, violin recital debut NY 1982, London debut Sibelius Concerto with Royal Philharmonic Orch 1984; violin soloist 1984–88; performed as violinist with orchs incl: The Philharmonia, Cleveland Orch, LA Philharmonic, Pittsburgh Symphony, Bavarian and Stuttgart Radio Symphony Orchs, City of Birmingham Symphony, Bournemouth Symphony; conductor 1988–; princ conductor: Scottish Chamber Orch 1996–2005, princ conductor Malmö Opera 2007–11; conductor emeritus Scottish Chamber Orch, artistic advsr and princ guest conductor Ensemble Orchestral de Paris; princ guest conductor: Stockholm Chamber Orch 1995–, Lahti Symphony Orch Finland 1995–98, BBC Nat Orch of Wales 2000–03; conducted orchs incl: Royal Danish Symphony Orch, Stockholm Philharmonic, Finnish Radio Symphony Orch, Swedish Radio Symphony Orch (premier of composition 1995), Jerusalem Symphony, Minnesota Orch, Rochester Philharmonic, Kansas City Symphony, Bergen Philharmonic, Bournemouth Symphony, Bournemouth Sinfonietta, London Mozart Players, Helsinki Chamber Orch, Israel Chamber Orch, Aalborg Symphony, New World Symphony, Royal Liverpool Philharmonic Orch, BBC Symphony Orch, Toronto Symphony Orch, BBC Scottish Symphony Orch, City of Birmingham Symphony Orch, Hallé Orch, Ensemble Orchestral de Paris, LA Chamber Orch, Netherlands Symphony Orch, Orchestre Nationale du Capitole de Toulouse, Orquesta de la Ciudad de Granada, Orquestra Nacional do Porto; fndr/dir U-HAC (Unity Hills Arts Centers) Int; Leventritt sponsorship award 1978, Avery Fisher career award 1982; *Compositions* incl: Ghazal (for cello, orch and five female voices, premiere Helsinki Choral Orch Inkoo Finland 1993), Seven Last Words (for violin, cello, piano and percussion, premiere March 1993), Mantram (for string orch and amplified chimes, premiere Stockholm Chamber Orch Aug 1994), Elegy (for oboe and orch, premiere Finnish Radio Orch Nov 1994), Latif (for solo cello and low strings, premiere Israel Chamber Orch Dec 1994), Shizue Fantasy for Shakuhachi and String Orch (premiere Swedish Radio Orch Aug 1995), Sinfonia in B (premier Scottish Chamber Orchestra, 2007), Sinfonia-Concertante for Horn and Orch (The Fire and the Rose, premier 2008);

Style— Joseph Swensen, Esq; ✉ c/o Victoria Rowsell Artist Management Limited, 34 Addington Square, London SE5 7LB (e-mail 4management@victoriarowsell.co.uk)

SWIFT, Benjamin (Ben); *b* 5 November 1987, Rotherham, S Yorks; *Career* track and road racing cyclist; Team Sky 2010–; achievements incl: Gold medal (scratch) and 2 Silver medals (points race and madison) World Championships 2012; *Style*— Mr Ben Swift; ✉ website www.benswiftcycling.com, Twitter @swiftybswift

SWIFT, Prof Cameron Graham; s of Rev Graham Swift (d 1973), and Victoria, *née* Williamson (d 1996); *b* 5 April 1946; *Educ* Lawrence Sheriff Sch Rugby, Univ of London (MB BS), Univ of Dundee (PhD); *m* Margaret Rosemary, da of Henry K Vernon; *Career* MRC res fell in clinical pharmacology Univ of Dundee 1977–80, conslt physician Dept of Med for the elderly N Humberside 1980–84, dir of postgrad med educn N Humberside 1982–84, conslt physician and sr lectr Dept of Geriatric Med Univ of Wales Coll of Med 1984–86; prof of health care of the elderly: Univ of London 1986–2004, Univ of Kent 1986–2004 (emeritus prof 2004–); conslt physician KCH 1986–2004; sec Specialist Advsy Ctee in Geriatric Med Jt Ctee on Higher Med Trg 1992–94; visiting prof Christchurch Sch of Med NZ 1994; Br Geriatrics Soc: chm Trg Ctee 1989–91, chm Pharmacology and Therapeutics Section 1989–93, chm Scientific Ctee 1997–98, pres elect 1998–2000, pres 2000–02; memb Cncl Int Assoc of Gerontology (Europe) 1995–2002, memb Bd King's Coll/Age Concern Inst of Gerontology 1997–2004; memb: Ctee on Safety of Meds Sub-Ctee on Efficacy and Adverse Reactions) 1987–92, External Reference Gp Dept of Health National Service Framework for Older People 1999–2000, Scientific Advsy Bd Nat Osteoporosis Soc 2001–, UK Medicines Cmmn 2002–05, Scientific Advsy Ctee Assoc of Medical Research Charities 2003–07, Guideline Devpt Gps for Fall Prevention and Osteoporosis and Hip Fracture, Nat Inst for Health and Care Excellence (NICE) 2003– (chm 2009–), Br Pharmacological Soc, Br Geriatrics Soc (Founder's Medal 2011); chm Editorial Bd Age and Aging 2002–11; hon med advsr Research into Ageing 1998–2000; tstee Abbeyfield Soc 2011–, tstee Abbeyfield Research Fndn 2016–, co-convenor (Charitable Sector) UK Age Research Forum 2016–; FRCP 1988, FRCPI 1999; *Books* Clinical Pharmacology in the Elderly (ed, 1987); *Recreations* music, ornithology, hill walking, scuba diving; *Style*— Prof Cameron Swift; ✉ King's College London School of Medicine, Clinical Age Research Unit, Bessemer Road, London SE5 9PJ (☎ 020 3299 3420 (unit) or 020 8325 5816 (direct), fax 020 3299 3441, e-mail cameron.swift@kcl.ac.uk)

SWIFT, Hon Dame Caroline Jane (Lady Openshaw); DBE (2005); da of Vincent Seymour Swift (d 1979), and Amy Ruth, *née* Johnson; *b* 30 May 1955; *Educ* Lancaster Girls' GS, Univ of Durham (BA, pres Union Soc); *m* 15 Dec 1979, Charles Peter Lawford Openshaw (Hon Mr Justice Openshaw), *qv*, s of late Judge William Harrison Openshaw; 1 da (Alexandra Caroline b 17 July 1984), 1 s (William Henry b 31 Aug 1986); *Career* called to the Bar 1977 (bencher 1997), in practice Northern Circuit 1978–2005, QC 1993, recorder of the Crown Court 1995–2005 (asst recorder 1992–95), dep judge of the High Court 2000–05, leading counsel to the Shipman Inquiry 2001–05, judge of the High Court of Justice (Queen's Bench Div) 2005–15, ret; *Recreations* home and family, cooking, theatre, walking; *Style*— The Hon Dame Caroline Swift; ✉ Royal Courts of Justice, Strand, London WC2A 2LL

SWIFT, Clive Walter; s of Abram Swift, and Lillian Greenman; *b* 9 February 1936, Liverpool; *Educ* Clifton, Gonville & Caius Coll Cambridge (MA); *m* 1960 (m dis 1975), Dame Margaret Drabble, DBE, *qv*; 2 s (Adam b 31 March 1961, Joseph b 25 May 1965), 1 da (Rebecca b 10 Jan 1964); *Career* Nat Serv 1954–56; actor, author; The Actors' Centre: initiator, teacher Delivering Poems 1980–2013, currently advsr to Bd; dir: LAMDA and RADA 1970s; hon fell Liverpool John Moores Univ; Cyprus Medal; *Theatre* debut Notts Playhouse 1959, RSC original long-contract artist 1960–68; Prospect prodns 1963 and 1966, Chichester 1966, 1971 and 2000; credits incl: Man and Superman, The Young Churchill, Dear Antoine, Dirty Linen, Inadmissible Evidence, The Potsdam Quartet, Roll on Four O'Clock, Messiah, The Genius, An Enemy of the People, Othello, Mr and Mrs Nobody, An Old Man's Love, Dona Rosita, Higher Than Babel, Richard Bucket Overflows! (Cabaret) 2007–10, The Great Jowett (Balliol Coll 450th Anniversary Prodn Sheldonian Theatre Oxford) 2013; *Television* numerous single plays and series; serials incl: Dombey and Son, Dig This Rhubarb!, Waugh On Crime, South Riding, Clayhanger, The Barchester Chronicles, Churchill – The Wilderness Years, The Pickwick Papers, First Among Equals, Keeping Up Appearances (5 series), Suntrap 2015; other credits incl: Peak Practice 1998, Aristocrats 1999, Born and Bred 2001–04, The Old Guys 2009–10, Valentine's Kiss (BBC) 2014; *Radio* debut reading Fielding's Tom Jones 1962, memb BBC Radio Rep 1973; credits incl: Poor Pen 2001, The Right Time 2000–04, The Go-Between 2002, The Old Curiosity Shop 2003, Measure for Measure 2003, Insane Object of Desire 2005, The Radezky March 2005, Much Ado About Nothing 2005, Fridays When It Rains 2006, Fuente Ovejuna 2007, Mr Sponge's Sporting Tour 2008, Single Spies 2011, Political Animals (Radio 4) 2012, Strangers on a Film (Radio 4) 2012, commentator Nat Tst (Dunster Castle) 2012; *Film* incl: Catch Us If You Can, Frenzy, The National Health, Deathline, Excalibur, A Passage to India, Gaston's War, Vacuums; *Books* The Job of Acting (1976), The Performing World of the Actor (1981), All Together Now (play, co-author with Peter Buckman, 1981); numerous reviews, articles, poems for Theatre Quarterly, World Medicine, BBC World Service, part-adaptor with Michael Napier Brown and Wilma Holingbery of Anthony Trollope's An Old Mans Love 1996; *Audio Books* incl: The Moonstone, The Canterbury Tales, The History of Mr Polly, The Witch of Exmoor, The Adventures of Robin Hood; *CDs* From the Heart (own songs, 2009); *Recreations* watching cricket and soccer, playing piano, initiator of The Actors' Centre (1978), CD of own songs From the Heart (2009); *Clubs* Actors' Centre, London Library, Middlesex CC, BAFTA, Weekenders Cricket (fndr 1977); *Style*— Clive Swift, Esq; ✉ c/o Roxane Vacca Management, 61 Judd Street, London WC1H 9QT (☎ 020 7383 5971, e-mail roxane@roxanevacca.co.uk)

SWIFT, Graham Colin; s of Lionel Allan Stanley Swift, and Sheila Irene, *née* Bourne; *b* 4 May 1949; *Educ* Dulwich Coll, Queens' Coll Cambridge, Univ of York; *Career* author; *Awards* Geoffrey Faber Meml prize, Guardian Fiction prize, RSL Winifred Holtby award 1983, Booker McConnell prize nominee 1983, Premio Grinzane Cavour Italy 1987, Prix du Meilleur Livre Étranger France 1994, Booker prize 1996 (for Last Orders), James Tait Black Meml prize for fiction 1996; DLitt Univ of E Anglia, DUniv York 1998, DLitt Univ of London 2003, DLitt Univ of Sussex 2015; hon fell Queens' Coll Cambridge 2005; FRSL 1984; *Books* novels: The Sweet Shop Owner (1980), Shuttlecock (1981), Waterland (1983), Out of this World (1988), Ever After (1992), Last Orders (1996), The Light of Day (2003), Tomorrow (2007), Wish You Were Here (2011), Mothering Sunday (2016); others: Learning to Swim (short stories, 1982, reissued 1993), The Magic Wheel (anthology, ed with David Profumo, *qv*, 1986), Making an Elephant (non-fiction, 2009), England and Other Stories (short stories, 2014); *Recreations* fishing; *Style*— Graham Swift, Esq, FRSL

SWIFT, Malcolm Robin Farquhar; QC (1988); s of late Willie Swift, of Huddersfield, W Yorks, and Heather May Farquhar Swift, OBE, *née* Nield (d 1996); *b* 19 January 1948; *Educ* Colne Valley HS, KCL (LLB, AKC); *m* 1, 20 Sept 1969 (m dis 1993), (Anne) Rachael, da of Ernest Rothery Ayre, of Bolton-by-Bowland, Lancs; 2 da (Joanna b 1972, Catherine b 1975), 1 s (Daniel b 1977); m 2, 1 Aug 2003, Angela, da of Reuben Walters, of Sadberge, Co Durham; *Career* called to the Bar Gray's Inn 1970 (bencher 1998); in practice NE Circuit (ldr 1998–2002), recorder Crown Court 1987, acting grand court judge of the Cayman Islands 2013; Bar Cncl: co-opted memb Remuneration Ctee 1978–89, elected memb Public Affrs Ctee 1995–2002, elected memb Legal Servs Ctee 1998–99, elected memb Professional Standards Ctee 2000–02; *Recreations* fitness, cycling, music (formerly lead singer Count One and the TICs); *Style*— Malcolm Swift, Esq, QC; ✉ Wilberforce Chambers, 7 Bishop Lane, Kingston-upon-Hull HU1 1PA (☎ 01482 323264, fax 01482 325533); 2 Hare Court, Temple, London EC4Y 7BH (☎ 020 7353 5324, e-mail malcolmswift@2harecourt.com)

SWIFT, Rebecca Margaret; da of Clive Walter Swift, *qv*, and Margaret Drabble, CBE, *qv*; *b* 10 January 1964; *Educ* New Coll Oxford (BA), Tavistock Clinic (MA); *Career* ed Virago Press 1987–1993, fndr and dir The Literary Consultancy 1996–; tstee: The Maya Centre 2005, Writers' Centre Norwich 2005; memb Literature House Project Consortium Arts Cncl 2006; shortlisted for Kim Scott Walynn Prize 2004; Virago New Poets (1990), Letters from Margaret: The Fascinating Story of Two Babies Swapped at Birth (ed, 1992), Imagining Characters: Conversations about Women Writers – A S Byatt & Ignes Sodré (ed), Poetry in New Writing Six (1995), Spirit Child (libretto, music by J Roditi, 2000), Driftwood Magazine (2006), Staple (2008), Dickinson: Poetic Lives, a biography (2011); *Recreations* swimming, reading, art, film, theatre, opera, music; *Style*— Ms Rebecca Swift; ✉ c/o The Literary Consultancy, Free Word Centre, 60 Farringdon Road, London EC1R 3GA (☎ and fax 020 7324 2563, e-mail rebecca@literaryconsultancy.co.uk, website www.literaryconsultancy.co.uk)

SWINBURNE, Prof Richard Granville; s of William Henry Swinburne, OBE (d 1994), of Colchester, Essex, and Gladys Edith Swinburne (d 1988); *b* 26 December 1934; *Educ* Exeter Coll Oxford (MA, BPhil); *m* 1960 (sep 1985), Monica; 2 da (Caroline (Mrs David Cope) b 1961, Nicola b 1962); *Career* Fereday fell St John's Coll Oxford 1958–61, Leverhulme res fell Univ of Leeds 1961–63, lectr Univ of Hull 1963–69 (sr lectr 1969–72), visiting assoc prof of philosophy Maryland Univ 1969–70, prof of philosophy Keele Univ 1972–84, Nolloth prof of philosophy of the Christian religion Univ of Oxford 1985–2002; visiting lectureships: Wilde lectr Univ of Oxford 1975–78, Forwood lectr Univ of Liverpool 1976 and 2009, Marrett meml lectr Exeter Coll Oxford 1980, Gifford lectr Univ of Aberdeen 1982–83 and 1983–84, Edward Cadbury lectr Univ of Birmingham 1987, Wade meml lectr St Louis Univ 1990, Dotterer lectr Penn State Univ 1992, Aquinas lectr Marquette Univ 1997, Paul Holmer lectr Univ of Minnesota 2006, Lawson lectr Stetson Univ 2008, Sophia Forum lectr Azusa Pacific Univ 2013, Gilbert Ryle lectr Trent Univ Ontario 2013, Gunning lectr Univ of Edinburgh 2016, Edith Stein lectr Franciscan Univ Ohio 2016; distinguished visiting scholar Univ of Adelaide 1982, visiting prof of philosophy Syracuse Univ 1987; visiting prof: Univ of Rome 2002, Catholic Univ of Lublin 2002, Yale Univ 2003, St Louis Univ 2003; hon dr: Catholic Univ of Lublin 2015, Dimitrie Cantemir Christian Univ Bucharest 2016; FBA 1993; *Books* Space and Time (1968, 2 edn 1981), The Concept of Miracle (1971), An Introduction to Confirmation Theory (1973), The Coherence of Theism (1977, 2 edn 2016), The Existence of God (1979, 2 edn 2004), Faith and Reason (1981, 2 edn 2005), Personal Identity (with Sydney Shoemaker 1984), The Evolution of the Soul (1986, 1997), Responsibility and Atonement (1989), Revelation (1991, 2 edn 2007), The Christian God (1994), Is There a God? (1996), Providence and the Problem of Evil (1998), Epistemic Justification (2001), The Resurrection of God Incarnate (2003), Was Jesus God? (2008), Mind, Brain, and Free Will (2013); ed: The Justification of Induction (1974), Space, Time and Causality (1983), Miracles (1988), Bayes's Theorem (2002), Free Will and Modern Science (2011); *Style*— Prof Richard Swinburne, FBA; ✉ 50 Butler Close, Oxford OX2 6JG (☎ 01865 514406, e-mail richard.swinburne@oriel.ox.ac.uk, website http://users.ox.ac.uk/~orie0087/)

SWINFEN, 3 Baron (UK 1919); Roger Mynors Swinfen Eady; MBE (2016); s of 2 Baron Swinfen (d 1977), and his 1 w, Mary Aline (Mary Wesley; d 2002), da of late Col Harold Mynors Farmar, CMG, DSO; *b* 14 December 1938; *Educ* Westminster, RMA Sandhurst; *m* 24 Oct 1962, Patricia Anne, o da of Frank D Blackmore (d 1968), of Dublin; 3 da (Hon Georgina (Hon Mrs Liley) b 1964, Hon Katherine (Hon Mrs Davies) b 1966, Hon Arabella (Hon Mrs Mayo) b 1969), 1 s (Hon Charles b 8 March 1971); *Heir* s, Hon Charles Eady; *Career* Lt The Royal Scots; memb Direct Mail Services Standards Bd 1983–97; chm Parly Gp Video Enquiry Working Party 1983–85; memb: Sub-Ctee C House of Lords Euro Communities Ctee 1990–94, Sub-Ctee B House of Lords Euro Communities Ctee 2004–06 (also Sub-Ctee C 2006–10), Select Ctee on Draft Disability Bill 2004, House of Lords Hybrid Instruments Ctee 2010–, Select Ctee on the Mental Capacity Act 2013; fell Industry and Parly Tst 1983; pres SE Region Br Sports Assoc for the Disabled 1986–; patron: Disablement Income Gp 1995–, 1 in 8 Gp 1996–2004, Labrador Rescue SE 1996–, World Orthopaedic Concern 2002–, Kunde Fndn 2007–; dir: The Swinfen Charitable Tst 1998–, American Telemedicine Assoc (ATA) 2009–13; hon res fell Centre for Online Health Univ of Queensland 2001–10; JP Kent 1983–85; Liveryman Worshipful Co of Drapers; ARICS 1970–98; *Style*— The Rt Hon the Lord Swinfen, MBE; ✉ House of Lords, London SW1A 0PW

SWINNERTON-DYER; *see:* Dyer

SWINNEY, John Ramsay; MSP; s of Kenneth Swinney, of Edinburgh, and Nancy, *née* Hunter; *b* 13 April 1964; *Educ* Forrester HS Edinburgh, Univ of Edinburgh (MA); *Family* 1 da (Judith b 1994), 1 s (Stuart b 1996); m, 2003, Elizabeth M Quigley; 1 s (Matthew b 2010); *Career* research offr Scottish Coal Project 1987–88, sr mgmnt conslt Development Options 1988–92, strategic planning princ Scottish Amicable 1992–97; MP (SNP) N Tayside 1997–2001; MSP (SNP): N Tayside 1999–2011, Perthshire N 2011–; Scottish Parl: ldr of the Oppn 2000–04, convener Enterprise and Lifelong Learning Ctee 1999–2000, convenor European and External Rels Ctee 2004–05, shadow min for finance and public serv 2005–07, cabinet sec for finance and sustainable growth 2007–11, cabinet sec for finance employment and sustainable growth 2011–14, dep first min of Scotland and cabinet sec for finance, constitution and economy 2014–16, dep first min and cabinet sec for educn 2016–; SNP: nat sec 1986–92, vice-convener for publicity 1992–97, Treasy spokesman 1995–99, sr vice-convener 1998–2000, enterprise and lifelong learning spokesman 1999–2000, nat convener (pty ldr) 2000–04, finance and public service reform spokesman 2005–07; *Recreations* hill walking, cycling, running; *Style*— John Swinney, Esq, MSP; ✉ 17–19 Leslie Street, Blairgowrie PH10 6AH (☎ 01250 876576, Twitter @johnswinney); The Scottish Parliament, Edinburgh EH99 1SP (e-mail john.swinney.msp@scottish.parliament.uk, website www.johnswinneymsp.com)

SWINSON, Dr Christopher; OBE; s of Arthur Montagu Swinson, of London, and Jean, *née* Dudley; *b* 27 January 1948; *Educ* Wadham Coll Oxford (MA), Durham Univ (PhD); *m* 9 Sept 1972, Christine Margaret, da of Walter Yates Hallam (d 1973); 1 s (Timothy b 1987); *Career* mangr Price Waterhouse 1970–78; BDO Binder Hamlyn: sr mangr 1978–81, ptnr 1981–92, nat managing ptnr 1989–92; ptnr BDO Stoy Hayward 1993–2004 (sr ptnr 1997–2004); comptroller and auditor gen Jersey 2005–12; memb: Cncl ICAEW 1985–2001 (vice-pres 1996–97, dep pres 1997–98, pres 1998–99), Financial Reporting Cncl 1990–2000 (dep chm 1998–2000), Financial Reporting Review Panel 1992–98, Bd Pensions Regulator 2005–13; audit cmmr 2000–03; tstee Greenwich Fndn for the RNC 1997–2002, tstee Science Museum Gp 2008–; hon treas NCVO 1994–97; visiting prof Univ of Bournemouth 2006–; Freeman City of London 1985; memb Worshipful Co of CAs; FCA 1974; *Clubs* Athenaeum; *Style*— Dr Christopher Swinson, OBE; ✉ No Ways, Frithsden, Hemel Hempstead HP1 3DD (☎ 01442 864640, e-mail chris@swinson.co.uk)

SWINSON, Jo; *b* 5 February 1980, Glasgow; *Educ* Douglas Acad Milngavie, LSE (BSc); *Career* mktg and PR mangr Viking FM 2000–02, mktg mangr SpaceandPeople Ltd 2002–04, Scottish devpt offr UK Public Health Assoc 2004–05; MP (Lib Dem) E Dunbartonshire 2005–15 (Parly candidate (Lib Dem) Hull E 2001), shadow min for culture, media and sport 2005–06, shadow sec of state for Scotland 2006–07, shadow min for women and equalities 2007–08, shadow min for foreign affrs 2008–10, PPS to Rt Hon Vince Cable,

S

MP (as Sec of State for Business, Innovation and Skills) 2010–12, PPS to Rt Hon Nick Clegg, MP, *qqv* (as Dep PM) 2012, Parly under sec of state Dept for Business, Innovation and Skills and DCMS 2012–; memb Lib Dem Fed Exec 2002, vice-chair Lib Dem Gender Balance Task Force 2003–06, chair Lib Dem Campaign for Gender Balance 2007–08, dep ldr Scottish Lib Dems 2010–12, chair Lib Dem Policy Ctee 2012; cncllr Milngavie Community Cncl 2003–05; memb: Amnesty Int, Friends of the Earth, Unlock Democracy, New Economics Fndn; *Recreations* hiking, reading, running, ceilidh dancing; *Clubs* Amnesty Int; *Style*— Ms Jo Swinson; ✉ House of Commons, London SW1A 0AA (✆ 020 7219 8088, e-mail swinsonj@parliament.uk, website www.joswinson.org.uk); Constituency Office ✆ 0141 943 1568

SWINTON, Katherine Matilda (Tilda); *b* 5 November 1960, London; *Educ* Univ of Cambridge (BA); *Career* actress; *Theatre* RSC season 1984–85, The Tourist Guide (Almeida), Die Massnahme (Almeida), Man to Man (Traverse and Royal Court), Mozart and Salieri (Vienna, Berlin and Almeida), The Long Way Round (RNT), Cloakroom (Palais Galliera); *Television* Zastrozzi (Channel 4), Your Cheatin' Heart (BBC 1), Galápagos 2006; *Film* Caravaggio, Insel Ohne Hoffnung, The Open Universe, Aria, Friendship's Death, The Last of England, L'Ispirazione, Play Me Something, War Requiem, The Garden, The Party – Nature Morte, Edward II, Man to Man, Orlando, Wittgenstein, Blue, Female Perversions, Conceiving Ada, Love Is The Devil, War Zone, The Beach, Possible Worlds, The Deep End, Teknolust, Vanilla Sky, Adaptation, Young Adam, The Statement, Thumbsucker, Constantine, Broken Flowers, The Chronicles of Narnia: The Lion, the Witch and the Wardrobe, Michael Clayton, Burn After Reading, Julia, The Curious Case of Benjamin Button, The Limits of Control, I Am Love, The Chronicles of Narnia: The Voyage of the Dawn Treader, We Need To Talk About Kevin, Moonrise Kingdom 2012, Only Lovers Left Alive 2013, Snowpiercer 2013, The Zero Theorem 2013, The Grand Budapest Hotel 2014, Trainwreck 2015, A Bigger Splash 2016, Hail, Caesar! 2016, The Seasons in Quincy: Four Portraits of John Berger 2016; *Awards* Best Actress: Boston Film Critics, Las Vegas Film Critics, Evening Standard Br Film Awards 2009; runner-up Best Actress: NY Film Critics, Toronto Film Critics, Dallas-Fort Worth Film Critics; Best Actress nominations: Golden Globe Awards, Golden Satellite Awards, Online Film Critics, IFP Independent Spirit Awards, London Film Critics, Chicago Film Critics, Saturn Awards 2008, BAFTA 2011, European Film Awards 2011; Best Supporting Actress (for Michael Clayton): BAFTA 2008, Oscar 2008; *Style*— Ms Tilda Swinton; ✉ c/o Hamilton Hodell Ltd, 20 Golden Square, London W1F 9JL (✆ 020 7636 1221, fax 020 7636 1226)

SWIRE, Sir Adrian Christopher; kt (1982), DL (Oxon 1989); yr s of John Kidston Swire, DL (d 1983), of Hubbards Hall, Old Harlow, Essex, by his w Juliet Richenda (d 1981), da of Charles Barclay; bro of Sir John A Swire, CBE, DL, *qv*; *b* 15 February 1932; *Educ* Eton, UC Oxford (MA); *m* 1970, Lady Judith Compton, eld da of 6 Marquess of Northampton, DSO (d 1978); 2 s (Merlin, Sam), 1 da (Martha (Mrs Allfrey)); *Career* Nat Service Coldstream Gds, served RAFVR and RAuxAF (Hon Air Cdre RAuxAF 1987, AE); joined Butterfield & Swire Far East 1956; John Swire & Sons Ltd: dir 1961, dep chm 1966–87, chm 1987–97 and 2002–2004, hon pres 2005–; dir: Cathay Pacific Airways 1965–2005, Swire Pacific Ltd 1978–2008, HSBC Holdings plc 1995–2002; memb Int Advsy Cncl CITIC Beijing 1995–2005; dir: Brooke Bond Group 1972–82, NAAFI 1972–86 (dep chm 1982–85); pres Gen Cncl of Br Shipping 1980–81, chm Int Chamber of Shipping 1982–87; memb Gen Ctee Lloyd's Register 1967–99; visiting fell Nuffield Coll Oxford 1981–89 (hon fell 1998); pro-chllr Univ of Southampton 1995–2004; tstee RAF Museum 1983–91, chm RAF Benevolent Fund 1996–2001, pres Spitfire Soc 1996–2009; memb Cncl Wycombe Abbey Sch 1988–95; Elder Bro Trinity House 1990; Air League Founders Medal 2006; Liveryman: Worshipful Co of Fishmongers 1962, Hon Co of Air Pilots (formerly Guild of Air Pilots and Air Navigators) 1986; Hon DSc Cranfield Univ 1995, Hon DUniv Southampton 2002; Hon CRAeS 1991; *Clubs* White's, Brooks's, Hong Kong, Pratt's, Royal Air Squadron; *Style*— Sir Adrian Swire, DL; ✉ John Swire & Sons Ltd, Swire House, 59 Buckingham Gate, London SW1E 6AJ (✆ 020 7834 7717, fax 020 7630 0380)

SWIRE, Rt Hon Sir Hugo George William; KCMG (2016), PC (2011), MP; s of late Humphrey Swire, and Philippa Sophia, *née* Montgomerie (now Dowager Marchioness Townshend of Raynham); *b* 30 November 1959; *Educ* Eton, Univ of St Andrews, RMA Sandhurst; *m* 12 Dec 1996, Alexandra (Sasha), da of Rt Hon Sir John Nott, KCB; 2 da (Saffron, Siena); *Career* cmmnd 1 Bn Grenadier Guards 1980–83; head Devpt Office Nat Gallery 1988–92, dep dir rising to dir Sotheby's 1992–2001; Parly candidate (Scottish Cons and Unionist) Greenock & Inverclyde 1997, MP (Cons) East Devon 2001–; shadow min for the arts 2004–05, shadow min for culture 2005, shadow sec of state for culture, media and sport 2005–07, min of state for NI 2010–12, min of state FCO 2012–; non-exec dir: Photo-Me Int plc 2005–10 (chm 2008–10), Symphony Environmental Technologic plc 2008–10; FRSA 1993; *Clubs* Exmouth Cons Club (pres), Whites, Pratts, Beefsteak; *Style*— The Rt Hon Sir Hugo Swire, KCMG, MP; ✉ House of Commons, London SW1A 0AA (website www.hugoswire.org.uk)

SWIRE, Sir John Anthony; kt (1990), CBE (1977), DL (1996); er s of John Kidston Swire (d 1983); bro of Sir Adrian Swire, DL, *qv*; *b* 28 February 1927; *Educ* Eton, UC Oxford; *m* 1961, Moira Ducharne; 2 s, 1 da; *Career* served Irish Gds (UK and Palestine) 1945–48; joined Butterfield & Swire Hong Kong 1950; John Swire & Sons Ltd: dir 1955–97, chm 1966–87, hon pres 1987–97, life pres 1997; former dir: Royal Insurance Co, British Bank of the Middle East, Ocean Transport & Trading Ltd, James Finlay & Co plc, Shell Transport & Trading Co plc; memb: London Advsy Ctee Hongkong and Shanghai Banking Corp 1969–89, Euro-Asia Centre Advsy Bd 1980–91, Advsy Cncl Sch of Business Stanford Univ 1981–90; dep pro-chllr Univ of Kent at Canterbury 1993–99 (memb Cncl 1989–99); hon fell St Antony's Coll Oxford, hon fell UC Oxford; Hon DL Hong Kong Univ 1989, Hon DCL Univ of Kent at Canterbury 1995; Liveryman Worshipful Co of Fishmongers; *Style*— Sir John Swire, CBE, DL; ✉ Swire House, 59 Buckingham Gate, London SW1E 6AJ (✆ 020 7834 7717)

SWIRE, Rhoderick Martin; DL (Shropshire 2014); s of Patrick Douglas Swire, (d 1960), of Salop, and Joan Mary, *née* Allison (d 1970); *b* 27 March 1951; *Educ* Eton, Univ of Birmingham (BSc); *m* 11 June 1977, Georgina Mary, da of Christopher Ronald Thompson, of Salop; 1 s (Hugh b 1979), 2 da (Henrietta b 1981, Camilla b 1985); *Career* Peat Marwick Mitchell 1972–76; John Swire & Sons Ltd: gp accountant Hong Kong 1976–79, asst to chm Aust 1979–81, London 1981; GT Management plc: mangr unquoted investment 1981–88, main bd dir 1987–88; sr ptnr and fndr Pantheon Gp 1988–; chm Hereford Cathedral Perpetual Tst 2015; FCA 1980 (ACA 1975); *Recreations* shooting, tennis, gardening; *Clubs* Boodle's, Pratt's; *Style*— Rhoderick Swire, Esq, DL; ✉ 27 Broad Street, Ludlow, Shropshire SY8 1NJ; Pantheon Ventures Ltd, 10 Finsbury Square, London EC2A 1AF (✆ 020 3356 1800, e-mail rhoddy.swire@pantheon.com)

SWITHENBANK, Emeritus Prof Joshua (Jim); s of Joshua Swithenbank (d 1971), and Ethel Eva, *née* Forster (d 1992); *b* 19 October 1931; *Educ* Friend's Sch Wigton, Univ of Birmingham (BSc), Univ of Sheffield (PhD); *m* 29 March 1958, Margaret Elizabeth Anderson, da of Rev James Herbert Manson; 3 da (Elizabeth b 7 May 1960, Christine b 28 March 1965, Shirley Joyce b 20 May 1966), 1 s (Joshua Ross b 11 July 1962); *Career* engr Res and Devpt Dept Rolls Royce Ltd 1953–58, engr Design Dept Canadair 1958, assoc prof Mechanical Engrg McGill Univ Canada 1958–61, prof Dept of Chemical and Process Engrg Univ of Sheffield 1961–; dir Sheffield Univ Waste Incineration Centre (SUWIC) 1992–; author of over 500 articles in scientific jls and books; hon prof Univ of Leeds; fndr memb Watt Ctee on Energy Ltd 1975–, memb ACORD 1988–90, gen superintendent res Int Flame Res Fndn 1989–91; Walter Ahlström Prize Finland 2002; Hon DSc Tech Univ of Athens 1997, Hon DEng Univ of Sheffield 2003; FREng 1978, FInstE (pres 1987–88), FIChemE, FIWM; *Recreations* scuba diving, photography, travel, flying (private pilot's licence); *Clubs* British Sub Aqua (advanced diver and instr); *Style*— Emeritus Prof Jim Swithenbank, FREng; ✉ Department of Chemical and Biochemical Engineering, Sheffield University, Western Bank, Sheffield S1 4DU (✆ 0114 222 7502, fax 0114 222 7501, e-mail j.swithenbank@sheffield.ac.uk)

SYCAMORE, His Hon Judge Phillip; s of Frank Sycamore, of Lancaster, Lancs, and Evelyn Martin; *b* 9 March 1951; *Educ* Lancaster Royal GS, Univ of London (LLB); *m* 22 June 1974, Sandra, *née* Cooper; 1 da (Hannah b 1978), 2 s (Thomas b 1980, Jonathan b 1983); *Career* admitted slr 1975, recorder 1999–2001, circuit judge 2001–, Hon Recorder of Lancaster 2008–, a chamber pres 2009–, dep High Court judge 2010–; memb Criminal Compensation Appeals Panel 2000–01; ptnr in private practice 1980–2001; Law Soc: memb Cncl 1991–99, vice-pres 1996–97, pres 1997–98; govr: Lancaster Royal GS; Hon Dr of Laws: Univ of Westminster 1998, Lancaster Univ 1999; *Clubs* Royal Lytham and St Annes Golf, Athenaeum; *Style*— His Hon Judge Sycamore; ✉ c/o The Civil Justice Centre, 1 Bridge Street West, Manchester M60 9DJ

SYKES, Prof Bryan Clifford; s of Frank Sykes, and Irene, *née* Clifford; *b* 9 September 1947; *Educ* Eltham Coll, Univ of Liverpool (BSc), Univ of Bristol (PhD), Univ of Oxford (MA, DSc); *Children* 1 s (Richard b 1991); *Career* Univ of Oxford: research fell Wolfson Coll 1984–89, lectr in molecular pathology Inst of Molecular Med 1989–97, fell Governing Body Wolfson Coll 1989–, prof of human genetics 1997–, emeritus fell Wolfson Coll 2015–, emeritus prof of human genetics 2016–; chm Oxford Ancestors Ltd 2001–; *Publications* The Human Inheritance: Genes, Language and Evolution (1999), The Seven Daughters of Eve (2001), Adam's Curse (2003), Blood of the Isles (2006), DNA USA: A genetic portrait of America (2012), The Nature of the Beast (2015); also approximately 150 scientific papers; *Recreations* chess, astronomy, croquet, fly fishing; *Clubs* Athenaeum; *Style*— Prof Bryan Sykes; ✉ Wolfson College, Oxford OX2 6UD (e-mail bryan.sykes@wolfson.ox.ac.uk)

SYKES, Gerard William; s of William Joshua Sykes (d 1987), and Dorothy Lily, *née* Freeman; *b* 3 December 1944; *Educ* Sir Roger Manwoods Sandwich Kent; *m* 1974, Rosalind Mary Louise, da of S Peter Meneaugh; *Career* articled clerk Percy Gore & Co Margate, qualified chartered accountant 1966, mangr Hurdman and Cranstoun 1968–71, ptnr Thornton Baker (now Grant Thornton) 1973– (int mangr 1971–73); Freeman City of London 1977; ACA 1966; *Recreations* vintage cars, skiing; *Clubs* RAC; *Style*— Gerard Sykes, Esq; ✉ Grant Thornton, Grant Thornton House, 22 Melton Street, London NW1 2EP (✆ 020 7383 5100)

SYKES, Phillip Rodney; s of Sir Richard Adam Sykes, KCMG, MC (d 1979), and Ann Georgina, *née* Fisher; *b* 17 March 1955; *Educ* Winchester, ChCh Oxford (MA); *m* 26 June 1982, Caroline Frances Gordon, da of Michael Dawson Miller, of Scarsdale Villas, London; 2 s (Richard b 1985, Christopher b 1988), 1 da (Marina b 1991); *Career* Binder Hamlyn: joined 1976, seconded Nat West Bank plc 1985–86, ptnr 1986–94, head Insolvency and Recovery Servs 1991–94; ptnr Global Corp Fin Arthur Andersen 1994–2000; Moore Stephens: sr ptnr Restructuring and Insolvency 2000–15, head Corporate Advsy Services 2004–15; head London Restructuring Practice RSM Restructuring Advsy 2016–; ICAEW: vice-chm Investigation Ctee 1997–2003, vice-chm Insolvency Licensing Ctee 2003–09, memb Professional Standards Bd 2005–09, memb Joint Insolvency Ctee 2005–09; Assoc of Business Recovery Professionals (R3): memb Cncl 2011–, memb Gen Technical Ctee 2012–, vice-pres 2014, pres 2015–16; dist cmmr Garth South Branch Pony Club 2006–11; ACA 1986, FABRP 1998, MIPA 2000; *Recreations* riding, skiing, field sports, tennis, theatre; *Clubs* Le Beaujolais; *Style*— Phillip Sykes, Esq; ✉ RSM Restructruing Advisory LLP, 25 Farringdon Street, London EC4A 4AB (✆ 020 3201 8000, e-mail phillip.sykes@rsmuk.com)

SYKES, Sir Richard Brook; kt (1994); *b* 7 August 1942, Yorks; *Educ* Royds Hall GS Huddersfield, Paddington Tech Coll, Chelsea Coll London, Queen Elizabeth Coll London (BSc), Univ of Bristol (PhD), Univ of London (DSc); *m* Janet Mary Norman; 2 c; *Career* Glaxo Research UK 1972–77, Squibb Inst for Medical Research 1977–86; Glaxo: rejoined as dep chief exec Glaxo Group Research Ltd 1986–87, gp R&D dir Glaxo plc and chm and chief exec Glaxo Group Research Ltd 1987–93, dep chm and chief exec Glaxo plc 1993–97 (GlaxoSmithKline plc since 2000), exec chm 1997–2001, non-exec chm 2001–02; rector Imperial Coll London 2001–08, chllr Brunel Univ 2013–; chm: Merlion Pharmaceuticals Pte Ltd 2005–, Cncl for the Advancement of Science and Industry 2005–08, UK Stem Cell Fndn 2005–, Circassia Ltd 2007–12, NetScientific plc 2008–, Imperial Coll Healthcare NHS Tst 2012–, PDS Biotechnology Corp 2014–; non-exec dir: Rio Tinto plc (formerly RTZ Corporation plc) 1997–2008, Lonza 2003–12, Zeneus Holdings Ltd 2004–05, Metabometrix Ltd 2004–, Abraxis BioScience 2006–07, Eurasian Natural Resources Corp 2007–; pres: BAAS 1998–99, The R&D Soc 2002–; vice-pres: Nat Soc for Epilepsy 1995–, Br Lung Fndn 1997–; chm: Global Business Cncl on HIV/AIDS 1997–2000, Advsy Cncl to Life Scis Exec Ctee EDB Singapore 2000–, Healthcare Advsy Gp (Apax Partners Ltd) 2002–, Bioscience Leadership Cncl 2004–07; dir: Br Pharma Gp 1998–2001, Int AIDS Vaccine Initiative (IAVI) 2000–04; memb: Cncl for Science and Technol 1993–2003, Advsy Cncl Campaign for Science and Technol in the UK 1993–, Fndn for Science and Technol Cncl 1993–, Bd of Mgmnt Ct of Govrs LSHTM 1994–2003, Cncl for Industry and HE 1995–2008, Trade Policy Forum 1995–2000, Econ Devpt Bd Int Advsy Cncl 1995–, Bd of Tstees Natural History Museum 1996–2005, Advsy Gp on Competitiveness to the President of the Bd of Trade 1997–99, Bd EFPIA 1997–2000, Bd of Tstees Royal Botanic Gardens Kew 2000–05, Cncl Royal Coll of Music 2001–, Cncl RCA 2001–03, Engrg & Technol Bd 2002–05, Strategy Bd DTI 2002–04, HEFCE Bd 2002–, Int Advsy Cncl King Abdullah Univ of Science and Technol 2007–, Bd of Tstees Masdar Inst of Science and Technol 2008–, Bd of Tstees Nanyang Technological Univ Singapore 2008–; visiting prof: KCL, Univ of Bristol; author of over 100 scientific publications; Hamao Umezawa Meml Award of the Int Soc of Chemotherapy 1999; Hon DSc: Brunel Univ, Univ of Bristol, Univ of Hertfordshire, Univ of Hull, Univ of Leeds, Univ of Newcastle upon Tyne, Univ of Huddersfield, Univ of Westminster, Univ of Edinburgh, Univ of Strathclyde, Univ of Leicester, Univ of Sheffield, Univ of Warwick, Cranfield Univ, Nat Univ of Singapore 2015; Hon DUniv: Surrey, Sheffield Hallam; Hon MD Univ of Birmingham, Hon Dr in Pharmacy Univ of Madrid, Hon LLD Univ of Nottingham; hon fell: Univ of Wales Cardiff, Central Lancashire; Fleming fell Lincoln Coll Oxford; fell: KCL, Imperial Coll Sch of Med London, Imperial Coll London; assoc Inst of Med Laboratory Technologists (AIMLT); hon citizen of Singapore 2004; Hon FRCP, MInstD 1995, FRS 1997, FMedSci 1998, Hon FRPharmS 2001, FCGI 2002, FRCPath 2003, Hon FREng 2004; *Clubs* Athenaeum; *Style*— Sir Richard Sykes, FRS; ✉ Flat 11 Hale House, 34 De Vere Gardens, London W8 5QA (✆ 020 7937 0742, e-mail r.sykes@imperial.ac.uk)

SYLVESTER, Rachel; *Educ* South Hampstead HS, Somerville Coll Oxford; *m* Patrick Wintour; 2 c, 2 step-c; *Career* asst ed (politics) Daily Telegraph 1999–2008, political columnist The Times 2008–; *Style*— Ms Rachel Sylvester; ✉ The Times, News Building, 1 London Bridge Street, London SE1 9GF

SYMMONS, Prof Deborah Pauline Mary; da of late Raymond Keith Symmons, and Betty Symmons; *b* 23 March 1954; *Educ* St Bernard's Convent GS Slough, Univ of Birmingham Med Sch (MB ChB, MD); *Career* house surgn Gen Hosp Birmingham 1977–78, house physician Queen Elizabeth Hosp Birmingham 1978, SHO (communicable and tropical diseases) E Birmingham Hosp 1978–79, SHO (rheumatology and gen med) Hammersmith Hosp 1979, SHO (gen med) Selly Oak Hosp Birmingham 1979–80, registrar (gen med) Selly Oak Hosp Birmingham 1980–81, registrar (rheumatology and gen med) Guy's Hosp 1981–82, locum sr registrar Royal Sussex Co Hosp Brighton 1982–83, clinical res fell Dept of Rheumatology Univ of Birmingham 1983–85, hon sr registrar Queen Elizabeth Hosp Birmingham 1983–85, lectr Dept of Rheumatology Univ of Birmingham 1985–89 (also clinical tutor), hon sr registrar W Midlands RHA 1985–89; hon conslt rheumatologist: Manchester Royal Infirmary and Devonshire Royal Hosp Buxton 1989–94, Norwich NHS Tst 1989–, E Cheshire NHS Tst and Stepping Hill Hosp Stockport 1995–, Macclesfield Dist Gen Hosp; currently prof of rheumatology and musculoskeletal epidemiology and dep dir ARC Epidemiolgy Unit Univ of Manchester; delivered numerous lectures on rheumatology to confs and learned socs in UK and overseas; memb int ctees incl: Int League Against Rheumatism (ILAR) Ctee on Devpt of International Classification of Diseases 10 (ICD 10) to Rheumatology and Orthopedics (R&O), Bone and Joint Decade Monitor Project, Community Oriented Program for Control of Rheumatic Disease (COPCORD) prog (int advsr), EU project on indicators for musculoskeletal health; memb: Steering Ctee nat meeting on Outcome in Rheumatoid Arthritis 1987, BSR Sub-Ctee on computing 1988, BSR Educn Ctee 1989 (jr rep), BSR Heberden Ctee 1989, Arthritis Research Campaign 1992–99 (med sec); current memb: BSR Clinical Affrs Ctee, Rheumatology Specialist Working Gp (chm), RCP Rheumatology Sub-Ctee, NHS Exec Nat Specialised Definitions Working Gp, ARC Clinical Trials Sub-Ctee; memb Editorial Bd Annals of the Rheumatic Diseases; Selly Oak Hosp Jr Dr's Prize 1980, Winthrop Award for best scientific paper Midland Rheumatology Soc 1986, Stephen Whittaker Prize W Midlands Physicians 1986, Michael Mason Prize BSR 1993, Kovacs Travelling Fellowship in Rheumatology RSM 1992; memb: Assoc of Physicians of the UK and Ireland, American Coll of Rheumatology, BSR, Br Soc for Paediatric and Adolescent Rheumatology, RSM, Manchester Medical Soc, NW Rheumatology Club; MFPHM 1999, FRCP 1994 (MRCP 1980); *Publications* Autoimmunity (with W Ollier, 1992), Health Care Needs Assessment for Musculoskeletal Diseases (with C Bankhead, 1994); author of numerous book chapters, case reports, letters, research papers, invited papers and reviews, editorials and science papers; reviewer for various pubns incl: Annals of the Rheumatic Diseases, Arthritis and Rheumatism, Jl of Clinical Epidemiology, Jl of Rheumatology, Jl of Epidemiology and Community Health, Rheumatology, Scandinavian Jl of Rheumatology, The Lancet; *Style—* Prof Deborah Symmons; ✉ ARC Epidemiology Unit, University of Manchester, Stopford Building, Oxford Road, Manchester M13 9PT (☎ 0161 275 5044, fax 0161 275 5043)

SYMONDS, Dr Patrick Bruce Reith (Pat); s of John Donald Symonds (d 1997), and Irene, *née* Slaney (d 1994); *b* 11 June 1953, Bedford; *Educ* Gresham's, SE London Poly, Cranfield Univ; *m* 6 Dec 2003, Alison, *née* Holloway; 3 da (Claire, Bianca, Rachael), 2 s (Fenton, Michael); *Career* Ford Motor Co 1972–76, Hawke Racing Cars 1976–79, Royale Racing Cars 1979–81, Toleman F1 1981–85, Benetton F1 1985–2000, exec dir of engrg Renault Formula One 2000–09, conslt Neutrino Dynamics/Virgin Racing (now Marussia F1) 2009–13, chief technical offr Williams F1 team 2013–; memb MSc Motorsport Panel Cranfield Univ; columnist F1 Racing magazine; regnl chm Coutts Bank 2001–14; John Bolster Prize 2004, Sir Jackie Stewart Prize 2005, Jury of Confartigianato Motori Prize 2015; CEng, FIMechE, FRAeS; *Publications* numerous technical papers on the subject of vehicle dynamics, regular contrib of technical articles to high circulation pubns; *Recreations* motorsport, technical writing, reading and knowledge acquisition, travel; *Clubs* Br Racing Drivers; *Style—* Dr Pat Symonds; ✉ 8, Henley Court, Hernes Crescent, Oxford OX2 7PS (☎ 07703 366115, e-mail pat@neutrino-dynamics.com)

SYMONS, Christopher John Maurice; QC (1989); s of late Clifford Louis Symons, and late Pamela Constance, *née* Vos; *b* 5 February 1949; *Educ* Clifton, Univ of Kent (BA); *m* 13 July 1974, Susan Mary, da of Gordon Teichmann; 1 s (Nicholas b 1978), 1 da (Samantha b 1980); *Career* called to the Bar: Middle Temple 1972 (bencher 1998, treas 2013), Gibraltar 1985, Ireland 1988, Northern Ireland 1990, Brunei 1999; jr counsel to the Crown (common law) 1985–89, recorder 1993–2004, dep judge of High Court 1998–2015; pres Lloyd's Appeal Tbnl 2010–; int commercial arbitrator 2008–; *Recreations* hitting balls; *Clubs* Boodle's, Berkshire Golf, All England Lawn Tennis, Royal Sotogrande Golf, Valderrama Golf, Jesters; *Style—* Christopher Symons, Esq, QC; ✉ 3 Verulam Buildings, Gray's Inn, London WC1R 5NT (☎ 020 7831 8441, fax 020 7831 8479, e-mail csymons@3vb.com)

SYMONS, Mitchell Paul; s of late Alan Stanley Symons, and Louise, *née* Yager; *b* 11 February 1957; *Educ* Mill Hill Sch, LSE (LLB); *m* 1984, Penny Chorlton; 2 s (Jack b 1987, Charles b 1989); *Career* writer and broadcaster; researcher then dir BBC TV 1980–82 (progs incl Friday Night...Saturday Morning, Film 81), TV prodr 1982– (devised: Everybody's Equal 1987–, Your Number Please 1992); a princ writer British & Cwlth edns Trivial Pursuit 1985–86; regular contrib/columnist: Hello! 1988–99, Punch 1989–92, Sunday Magazine 1990–96, Evening Standard 1993–94, Daily Express, Daily Star; conslt: The Mirror 1996, Daily Mail 1996–; also contrib: New Society, The Observer, The Sun, The People, The Sunday Times, The Times, The Guardian, Sunday Express; numerous TV appearances (incl What the Papers Say), regular radio broadcaster; visiting lectr Post Graduate Media Broadcasting Course Highbury Coll Portsmouth 1996–99; If It's In the News Columnist of the Year 2002 (for Daily Express column); *Books* Forfeit! (1986), The Equation Book of Sports Crosswords (1988), The Equation Book of Movie Crosswords (1988), Journolists 1–4 (with John Koski, 1989–92), Movielists (with John Koski, 1992), Hello! Book of Crosswords (1992), Sunday Book of Crosswords (1992), The Chip & Fry Diet (with Penny Symons, 1992), Hello! Crossword Books 1, 2 and 3 (1994), The Book of Criminal Records (1994), The Man Who Short Circuited The Electric Chair (1996), Chris Tarrant's Dangly Bits (with Chris Tarrant, *qv*, 1996), The Lists Book (1997), The Celebrity Lists Book (1998), The Bill Clinton Joke Book (1998), The Celebrity Sex Lists Book (1998), National Lottery Big Draw 2000 (with David Thomas, 1999), All In (2000), The Lot (2002), That Book (2003), This Book (2004), The Other Book (2005), Why Girls Can't Throw (2005), The Sudoku Institute Book (with David Thomas, 2005), How to Avoid a Wombat's Bum (2006), How to Speak Celebrity (2006), Where Do Nudists Keep Their Hankies (2006), My Story (with Penny and Jack Symons, 2007), Don't Get Me Started (2007), Why Eating Bogeys is Good For You (2007, Blue Peter Best Book of the Year (With Facts) 2010), How Much Poo Does an Elephant Do (2008), Why Do Farts Smell Like Rotten Eggs (2009), Why You Need A Passport When You're Going To Puke (2010), Do Igloos Have Loos? (2010), That's So Gross: Animals (2011), That's So Gross: Creepy Crawlies (2011), That's So Gross: History (2011), That's So Gross: Human Body (2011), Don't Wipe Your Bum with a Hedgehog (2012), The Book of Poker Calls (with Jack Symons, 2012), Desert Island Discs: Flotsam & Jetsam (2012), The Bumper Book for the Loo (2012), Why Spacemen Can't Burp (2013), Numberland: The World in Numbers (2013), Happily Never After: Cautionary Tales (2013), Why Don't You Smell When You're Sleeping (2014), There Are Tittles in this Title (2014), The World In Numbers Calendar (2017); Forfeit! (1986), The Equation Book of Sports Crosswords (1988), The Equation Book of Movie Crosswords (1988), Journolists 1–4 (with John Koski, 1989–92), Movielists (with John Koski, 1992), Hello! Book of Crosswords (1992), Sunday Book of Crosswords (1992), The Chip & Fry Diet (with Penny Symons, 1992), Hello! Crossword Books 1, 2 and 3 (1994), The Book of Criminal Records (1994), The Man Who Short Circuited The Electric Chair (1996), Chris Tarrant's Dangly Bits (with Chris Tarrant, *qv*, 1996), The Lists Book (1997), The Celebrity Lists Book (1998), The Bill Clinton Joke Book (1998), The Celebrity Sex Lists Book (1998), National Lottery Big Draw 2000 (with David Thomas, 1999), All In (2000), The Lot (2002), That Book (2003), This Book (2004), The Other Book (2005), Why Girls Can't Throw (2005), The Sudoku Institute Book (with David Thomas, 2005), How to Avoid a Wombat's Bum (2006), How to Speak Celebrity (2006), Where Do Nudists Keep Their Hankies (2006), My Story (with Penny and Jack Symons, 2007), Don't Get Me Started (2007), Why Eating Bogeys is Good For You (2007, Blue Peter Best Book of the Year (With Facts) 2010), How Much Poo Does an Elephant Do (2008), Why Do Farts Smell Like Rotten Eggs (2009), Why You Need A Passport When You're Going To Puke (2010), Do Igloos Have Loos? (2010), That's So Gross: Animals (2011), That's So Gross: Creepy Crawlies (2011), That's So Gross: History (2011), That's So Gross: Human Body (2011), Don't Wipe Your Bum with a Hedgehog (2012), The Book of Poker Calls (with Jack Symons, 2012), Desert Island Discs: Flotsam & Jetsam (2012), The Bumper Book for the Loo (2012), Why Spacemen Can't Burp (2013), Numberland: The World in Numbers (2013), Happily Never After: Cautionary Tales (2013); *Recreations* tennis, cricket, bridge, cinema, swimming; *Clubs* Old Millhillians; *Style—* Mitchell Symons, Esq; ✉ e-mail mitchellsymons@columnist.com

SYMONS, Rex Herbert Moss; CBE (1993); s of Herbert Thomas Symons, OBE (d 1959), and Winifred May Symons (d 1999); *b* 10 May 1934; *Educ* Bournemouth Sch, Univ of Southampton (BSc, Fencing colours, pres univ theatre gp); *m* Margaret Gwendoline, da of Henry Charles Everett; 1 s (Paul Rex Charles b 1964); *Career* sales controller phenol Heavy Organic Chemicals Div ICI 1958–61; with British Drug Houses Ltd 1961–68; BDH Ltd (initially subsid of Glaxo, sold to E Merck AG 1973): mktg dir 1968–81, md 1981–89; dep chm Merck Holding Ltd (UK subsid holding co of Merck AG) 1989–91; chm: Dorset Enterprise Agency, E Dorset HA 1989–91, Bournemouth Transport Ltd 1989–2005, Dorset TEC 1991–97, Poole Hosp NHS Trust 1991–2000, CBI Health and Safety Consultative Ctee 1991–2002, Bournemouth Teaching PCT 2000–06; pres Dorset C of C and Industry 1986; memb Health and Safety Cmmn 1989–2002, memb Employment NTO 1997–2002, memb Cncl Univ of Southampton 2000– (vice-chm 2004–08), memb Better Regulation Taskforce 2002–06; govr Bournemouth and Poole Coll of Art and Design 1996–2001; FRSA, MCIM, FIMgt; *Recreations* theatre, opera, books, gardening, travel; *Style—* Rex Symons, Esq, CBE

SYMONS OF VERNHAM DEAN, Baroness (Life Peer UK 1996), of Vernham Dean in the County of Hampshire; Elizabeth Conway Symons; PC (2000); da of Ernest Vize Symons, CB (d 1990), of Richmond, and Elizabeth Megan, *née* Jenkins; *b* 14 April 1951; *Educ* Putney HS for Girls, Girton Coll Cambridge (MA); *m* 2001, Philip Alan Bassett, special advsr Strategic Communication Unit PM's Office; 1 s (James Alexander Bassett Symons b 1985); *Career* res Girton Coll Cambridge 1972–74, admin trainee DOE 1974–77, dep gen sec Inland Revenue Staff Fedn (ISRF) 1988–89 (asst sec 1977–88), gen sec Assoc of First Div Civil Servants 1989–96; sits as Labour peer in House of Lords 1996–, Parly under-sec of state FCO 1997–99, min of state MOD 1999–2001, min of state FCO 2001–05, dep ldr House of Lords 2001–05; non-exec dir British Airways plc 2005–; memb: Gen Cncl TUC 1989–96, Civil Serv Coll Advsy Cncl, Cncl Hansard Soc 1993–97, Exec Cncl Campaign for Freedom of Information, Cncl The Industrial Soc, Cncl Open Univ, Panel 2000; cmmr Equal Opportunities Cmmn, govr London Business Sch 1995–97, tstee IPPR 1994–97; hon assoc Nat Cncl of Women 1990–97, co-chm Women's Nat Commn 1997–; FRSA; *Recreations* reading, gardening, entertaining friends; *Style—* The Rt Hon Baroness Symons of Vernham Dean, PC; ✉ c/o Foreign & Commonwealth Office, King Charles Street, London SW1A 2AH

SYMS, Robert Andrew Raymond; MP; s of Raymond Clark Syms, and Mary Elizabeth, *née* Brain; *b* 15 August 1956; *Educ* Colston's Sch Bristol; *m* 1, March 1991 (m dis 1999); m 2, Feb 2000 (sep 2007), Fiona Mellersh, da of late Air Vice Marshall F R L Mellersh, CB, DFC; 1 s, 1 da; *Career* md building and plant hire co based in Chippenham Wilts 1975–; N Wilts DC: cncllr 1983–87, vice-chm and ldr majority Cons Gp 1984–87; Wiltshire CC: cncllr 1985–97, oppn spokesman 1985–90, whip 1990–93, vice-chm Fin Ctee 1990–93; MP (Cons) Poole 1997– (Parly candidate Walsall N 1992); PPS to chm Cons Pty 1999, shadow spokesman DETR 1999–2001, a vice-chm Cons Pty 2001–03, oppn whip March-Nov 2003, shadow spokesman on communities and local govt 2003–07, asst Govt whip 2012–13; memb Select Ctee: on Health 1997–2000 and 2007–, on Procedure 1998–2000, on Tport 2001–03; chm: Regulatory Reform Select Ctee 2010–12, HS2 Public Bill Ctee 2014–; fndr chm Calne Devpt Project Tst 1986–97, fndr dir N Wiltshire Enterprise Agency 1986–90; memb Wessex RHA 1988–90; *Recreations* cycling, reading, travel; *Style—* Robert Syms, Esq, MP; ✉ House of Commons, London SW1A 0AA (☎ 020 7219 4601, fax 020 7219 6867)

SYNNOTT, Hilary Nicholas Hugh; KCMG (2002, CMG 1997); s of Cdr J N N Synnott, DSC, RN, and Florence England, *née* Hillary; *b* 20 March 1945; *Educ* Beaumont Coll, BRNC Dartmouth (scholar), Peterhouse Cambridge (MA), RN Engrg Coll Manadon; *m* 28 April 1973, Anne Penelope, *née* Clarke; 1 s (decd); *Career* served RN 1962–73 (HM Submarines 1968–73); HM Dip Serv: joined 1973, UK Delgn to OECD Paris 1975–78, Br Embassy Bonn 1978–81, FCO 1981–85, head of chancery Amman 1985–89, head Western Euro Dept FCO 1989–91, head Security Co-ordination Dept FCO 1991–93, min and dep high cmmr New Delhi 1993–96, director (S and SE Asia) and subsequently (Asia-Pacific) FCO 1996–98, high cmmr to Pakistan 2000–03; Coalition Provisional Authy regnl coordinator for Southern Iraq 2003–04, consulting sr fell IISS 2004–; visiting fell Inst of Devpt Studies Univ of Sussex 1998–99; Eric Lane fell Clare Coll Cambridge 2007; tstee Impact Fndn 2004–07; hon fell Peterhouse Cambridge 2011; CEng, MIEE 1970–73; *Books* The Causes and Consequences of South Asia's Nuclear Tests (1999), Bad Days in Basra (2008), Transforming Pakistan: Ways out of Instability (2009); *Clubs* Oxford and Cambridge; *Style—* Sir Hilary Synnott, KCMG; ✉ e-mail hilsynn@aol.com

SZIRTES, Dr George Gábor Nicholas; s of László Szirtes (d 2010), and Magdalena Kardos Nussbacher (d 1975); *b* 29 November 1948; *Educ* Kingsbury Co GS, Harrow Sch of Art, Leeds Coll of Art (history of art prize, BA, travelling scholarship), Goldsmiths Coll London; *m* 11 July 1970, Clarissa, da of Rev W S Upchurch; 1 s (Thomas Andrew b 31 Dec 1973), 1 da (Helen Magdalena b 13 Jan 1976); *Career* poet and translator; pt/t teaching jobs until 1975, head of art Hitchin Girls' Sch 1975–80, dir of art and history of art St Christopher Sch Letchworth 1980–89 (pt/t 1989–92), sr lectr in poetry Norfolk Inst of Art and Design 1992–2007, reader in creative writing UEA 2007–13; memb Int PEN 1980–; Br Cncl scholar 1985 and 1989 (latter spent in Budapest), Soc of Authors travelling scholar 2002, Leverhulme research fell 2003; int writer in residence Trinity Coll Dublin 2000; chair Bd of Tstees Poetry Book Soc 2007–15, currently memb Bd of Tstees Poetry on the Underground; awarded PhD by pubn; FRSL 1982; Gold Star of the Hungarian Repub 1991; *Poetry* The Slant Door (1979), November and May (1981), Short Wave (1984), The Photographer in Winter (1986), Metro (1988), Bridge Passages (1991), Blind Field (1994), Selected Poems (1996), The Red All Over Riddle Book (for children, 1997), Portrait of My Father in an English Landscape (1998), The Budapest File (2000), An English Apocalypse (2001), Reel (2004), New and Collected Poems (2008), Shuck, Hick, Tiffey (2008), The Burning of the Books (2008), The Burning of the Books and Other Poems (2009), In the Land of Giants (for children, 2012), Bad Machine (2013), Wordless (2014), Langoustine (2014), Child Helga (2014), Uncle Zoltán (2014), Germania (2014), Notes on the Inner City (2015), 56 (with Carol Watts, 2015), Mapping the Delta (2016), How to Be a Tiger (for children, 2017); work incl in various anthologies of modern verse incl: British

Poetry Since 1945, The New Poetry, The Firebox; ed: The Collected Poems of Freda Downie (1995), The Colonnade of Teeth, Twentieth Century Hungarian Poetry (jtly with George Gömöri, also trans 1996), An Island of Sound: Hungarian Writing Before and Beyond the Iron Curtain (2004), Fire, We Say: Younger Hungarian Poets (2009); subject of Reading George Szirtes (by John Sears, 2008); *Translations* The Tragedy of Man (by Imre Madách, 1989), Through the Smoke (by István Vas, 1989), Anna Édes (by Dezső Kosztolányi, 1992), The Blood of the Walsungs (by Ottó Orbán, 1993), New Life (by Zsuzsa Rakovszky, 1994), The Adventures of Sindbad (by Gyula Krúdy, 1998), The Lost Rider (three centuries of Hungarian poetry, 1998), The Melancholy of Resistance (by László Krasznahorkai, 1999), The Night of Akhenaton: Selected Poems of Ágnes Nemes Nagy (2003), Conversation at Bolzano (by Sándor Márai, 2004), The Rebels (by Sándor Márai, 2007), Metropole (by Ferenc Karinthy, 2008), Esther's Inheritance (by Sándor Márai, 2008), The Intended (by Sándor Márai, 2009), Satantango (by László Krasznahorkai, 2012), New Order: Hungarian Poets of the Post 1989 Generation (ed, 2010); *Non-Fiction* Exercise of Power: The Art of Ana Maria Pacheco, New Writing 10 (ed with Penelope Lively, *qv*, 2001); *Awards* Geoffrey Faber Meml Prize 1980, Cholmondeley Award 1986, shortlisted Whitbread Prize 1992, shortlisted Forward Prize 2000, T S Eliot Prize for Poetry 2005, CPLE Prize for In the Land of Giants 2012; for translation: Déry Prize 1991, Gold Medal of Hungarian Republic 1991, Euro Poetry Translation Prize 1995, shortlisted Weidenfeld Prize 2000, George Cushing Prize 2002, Soc of Authors Travelling Scholarship 2002, T S Eliot Prize 2004, American PEN Translation Award 2005, Bess Hokin Prize for Poetry 2009, Best Translated Book Award (USA) for Satantango 2013, Man Booker Int Prize awarded to László Krasznahorkai, received prize as translator 2015; *Recreations* playing piano, contemporary art and music, football, table tennis, proprietor of Starwheel Press 1976–; *Style—* Dr George Szirtes, FRSL; ✉ 16 Damgate Street, Wymondham, Norfolk NR18 0BQ (✆ 01935 603533, e-mail georgeszirtes@gmail.com, website www.georgeszirtes.blogspot.co.uk); Bloodaxe Books, The Old Signal Box, Falstone, Northumberland NE48 1AB

T

TABNER, Leonard (Len); s of Arthur Leonard Tabner (d 1984), and Thelma, *née* Morten (d 2002); *b* 20 September 1946; *Educ* Victoria St Co Modern Boys South Bank Middlesbrough, Eston GS, Middlesbrough Art Coll, Bath Acad of Art (DipAD), Univ of Reading (MA); *m* 15 May 1971, Helen Lilian, da of Thomas Pitt de Paravicini, and Lillian, *née* Horrocks; 4 s (Isaac Thomas Tabner 22 April 1973, Samuel Leonard 7 Aug 1975, Reuben Frederick b 17 July 1980, Edward Arthur b 24 Jan 1983), 1 da (Kathleen Ella b 6 April 1985); *Career* artist; working on NE coast with British Steel Corp, Cleveland potash mine, Tees & Hartlepool Port Authy and Smith's Dock Shipbuilders 1976–87, offshore oil and gas industry 1987–88; cmmnd by Conoco/DOE/V&A to work in N York Moors Nat Park 1987–88, three month sea voyage to Falkland Islands and S Georgia as guest of RN 1990, two voyages on HMS Exeter N Atlantic 1992 and 1993, cmmnd by Gifu Prefectural Govt to work in the Haku-San Mountains Japan 1995; worked 1995–: Ireland, arctic Norway, Northern Alaska, Arctic Ocean, Western Isles of Scotland; painting and travelling in Japan 2005, painting in N Wales 2006–08; work in numerous public and private collections in UK and abroad; vice-pres Cleveland Wildlife Tst; *Solo Exhibitions* Middlesbrough Museum and Art Gallery 1973, Stockton Municipal Gallery 1975, Response to the Earth (N Arts Gallery Newcastle upon Tyne and Univ of Durham) 1976, Guisborough, Chapel Beck Museum and Art Gallery and touring 1977, Washington Tyne & Wear 1980, Cleveland and touring 1981, Moira Kelly Gallery London 1982, Univ of Durham 1982, 1985–86 and 1987, Oldham City Art Gallery 1985–86, Cleveland Potash Mine (Sunderland Museum and Art Gallery) 1987, Paintings and Drawings 1970–89 (Agnew's London) 1989, Cowbar Breakwater (Vanessa Devereux Gallery London) 1989, A Voyage to the South London (Broadgate) 1992, Retrospective Exhibition (Laing Art Gallery Newcastle upon Tyne) 1992 (also tour of Scotland and Ulster Museum Belfast 1993), Paintings From Recent Sea Voyages (Agnew's London) 1993, New Paintings (Agnew's London) 1995, 1996, 1997 and 1999, Myles Meehan Gallery Darlington 1998, Hatton Gallery Newcastle upon Tyne 1998, Retrospective Exhibition (North Light Gallery Huddersfield) 2001–02, Messums London 2005, 2006, 2007 and 2010, Pannett Art Gallery Whitby 2010, Retrospective Exhibition (Lemon Street Gallery Cornwall) 2013; *Two-Man Exhibitions* Redcar Blast Furnace (with Ian Macdonald) 1983–85, Smiths Dock (with Ian Macdonald, Smiths Dock and touring) 1986–87, V Fields (with Ian Macdonald, touring) 1988, Images of the Tees (with Ian Macdonald, touring) 1989, From the Land and the Sea (with Peter Prendergast, Scarborough Art Gallery and Glynn Vivian Art Gallery Swansea) 1991–92; *Group Exhibitions* numerous since 1970, incl: Artists' Parish Maps (organised by Common Ground, touring) 1986, Artists in National Parks (V&A, and touring UK and USA) 1988–89, Salute to Turner (Agnew's London) 1989, The Broad Horizon (Agnew's London) 1990, The New Patrons (Christie's London) 1992, Centenary Exhibition (Christie's London) 1994, The Power of the Sea (Royal West of England Acad) 2014; *Books* Len Tabner Drawings – Response to the Earth (1976), Smiths Dock Shipbuilders (with Ian Macdonald, 1987), Images of the Tees (with Ian Macdonald, 1989), Len Tabner – Paintings and Drawings 1970–89 (1989), Inspiration of Landscape (1989), From the Land and the Sea (with Peter Prendergast, 1991), A Voyage to the South (1992), After Japan (1998); *Recreations* building, farming/conservation; *Clubs* Royal Over-Seas League; *Style—* Len Tabner, Esq; ✉ High Boulby, Easington, Saltburn by the Sea, North Riding of Yorkshire TS13 4UT (☎ 01287 640948); c/o Thos Agnew & Sons Ltd, 43 Old Bond Street, London W1S 4BS (☎ 020 7629 6176, fax 020 7629 4359)

TABOR, Ashley; s of Michael Tabor; *Career* founder and exec pres Global Group; *Style—* Ashley Tabor, Esq; ✉ Global, 30 Leicester Square, London WC2H 7LA

TACKABERRY, John Antony; QC (1982); s of Thomas Raphael Tackaberry (d 1971), and Mary Catherine, *née* Geoghegan (d 1985); *b* 13 November 1939; *Educ* Downside, TCD, Downing Coll Cambridge (MA, LLM), Mountview Theatre Sch (Dip); *m* 1, Penelope (d 1994), da of Seth Holt (d 1971); 2 s (Christopher b 1966, Antony b 1968); m 2, Kate (d 2008), da of Mark Jones (d 2010); 1 da (Molly b 2000); *Career* lectr: Chinese Miny of Further Educn 1943–65, Poly of Central London 1965–67; called to the Bar Gray's Inn 1967, admitted Bar of Republic of Ireland 1987, California 1988; recorder of the Crown Court 1988–2005; HM Counsel NSW Aust 1990; pres: Soc of Construction Law 1983–85, European Soc of Construction Law 1985–87, Soc of Construction Arbitrators 2007–10; memb: Arbitral Panels of Los Angeles Center for Commercial Arbitration 1987–, Singapore Int Arbitration Cncl, Indian Cncl of Arbitration (panel of int arbitrators); chm CIArb 1990 (vice-pres 1988); cmmr UN Compensation Cmmn 1998–2003; chm Street UK 2004–; FCIArb, FFB; *Publications* princ ed Bernstein in Dispute Resolution, author of numerous articles;; *Recreations* good food, good wine, good company, photography; *Clubs* Athenaeum; *Style—* John Tackaberry, Esq, QC; ✉ Arbitration Chambers, 22 Willes Road, London NW 5 3DS (☎ 020 7267 2137, fax 020 7482 1018); 39 Essex Street, London WC2R 3AT (☎ 020 7832 1111, fax 020 7353 3978, e-mail john.tackaberry@39essex.com)

TAGER, Romie; QC (1995); s of Osias Tager (d 2005), and Minnie Tager (d 1974); *b* 19 July 1947, London; *Educ* Hasmonean GS Hendon, UCL (LLB, LLM); *m* 29 Aug 1971, Esther Marianne, da of Rev Leo Sichel, of Reading; 2 s (Joseph, Simon (twins) b 23 Oct 1980); *Career* called to the Bar Middle Temple 1970; practising barr specialising in commercial, professional negligence and property law; founding head Selborne Chambers 2002–15; memb Hon Socs of: Lincoln's Inn, Middle Temple, Inner Temple; memb Int Bar Assoc; chm Greenquest Gp; tstee Jewish Book Cncl; Hon PhD Bar Ilan Univ Israel; *Recreations* grandchildren, opera, theatre, travel; *Style—* Romie Tager, QC; ✉ Selborne Chambers, 10 Essex Street, London WC2R 3AA (☎ 020 7420 9500, fax 020 7420 9555, e-mail romie.tager@selbornechambers.co.uk)

TAGGART, Prof David; s of Hugh Taggart, of Coatbridge, Lanarkshire, and Agnes, *née* Graham; *b* 1 July 1958, Glasgow; *Educ* Univ of Glasgow (MB ChB, MD), Univ of Strathclyde (PhD); *Career* sr registrar Brompton Hosp London 1992–95, conslt cardiac surgn John Radcliffe Hosp Oxford 1995–, prof of cardiovascular surgery Univ of Oxford 2004–; author of over 170 peer-reviewed pubns relating to most aspects of adult cardiac surgery especially coronary revascularisation; memb: Soc of Cardiothoracic Surgns of GB and I (pres 2010–12), European Assoc for Cardio-Thoracic Surgery 1996, American Assoc for Thoracic Surgery 2005; FRCSGlas; *Recreations* snowboarding, windsurfing; *Style—* Prof David Taggart; ✉ Department of Cardiac Surgery, John Radcliffe Hospital, Oxford OX3 9DU (☎ 01865 221121, fax 01865 220244, e-mail david.taggart@orh.nhs.uk)

TAGGART, Joe; *Career* former sr chef: Balmoral Hotel Edinburgh, Amaryllis Glasgow; currently head chef Restaurant Martin Wishart Edinburgh (Michelin star 2001–); *Style—* Joe Taggart, Esq; ✉ Restaurant Martin Wishart, 54 The Shore, Leith, Edinburgh EH6 6RA

TAGGART, Michael Adrian; s of Michael Taggart (d 1985), and Susan, *née* Duffy; *b* Derry City; *Partner* Jennifer Larrissey; 1 s (Nicholas b 20 Oct 1983); *Career* co-fndr (with bro, John) and md Taggart Homes Ltd 1989–2008; *Style—* Michael Taggart, Esq

TAHIR, Dr Mustapha Mohammed; s of Mohammed Tahir (d 1969), and Sa'adatu, *née* Adamu; *b* 12 September 1960, Sokoto, Nigeria; *Educ* Govt Coll Sokoto Nigeria, Sch of Basic Studies Ahmadu Bello Univ Zaria Nigeria (regnl govt scholar), Univ of Benin Nigeria (MB BS), Royal Coll of Obstetricians and Gynaecologists London (DFRSH, Prize for original research presentation), Wessex Deanery (Joint Ctee Cert PG Trg in GP), De Monfort Law Sch Leicester (Dip Med Law & Ethics); *m* 2 July 2004, Clare Jane, *née* Murphy; 1 s (Jamal Mustapha Tahir b 25 Aug 2006); *Career* house offr then SHO rotation Univ Teaching Hosp Benin 1985–90, SHO Redruth Hosp, Royal Cornwall Hosp and Hammersmith Hosp London 1991–93, clinical research fell, lectr, clinical asst and registrar in obstetrics and gynaecology Southmead and St Michael's Hosps Bristol 1993–97, SHO Seymour Clinic and Princess Margaret Hosp Swindon 1997–99, GP registrar Old Town Surgery Swindon 1999–2000, specialist registrar Pewsey Surgery 2000–01, locum GP 2001–02, GP Riverview Park Surgery Gravesend and Shrubbery Surgery Northfleet 2003–; GP trainer Kent, Sussex and Surrey GP Deanery 2009–; memb Cncl and tstee RSM 2005–09 (London Cncl rep Finance and Exec Ctee 2005–07), GP rep for BMA Dartford, Gravesham and Swanley branch 2004–, chm BMA Bromley, Dartford, Gravesham and Medway 2008–10; elected memb Kent Local Med Ctee (LMC) 2008–; govr Dover Road Primary Sch Gravesend 2006–08; memb: GMC, BMA; FRSM, MRCOG, MRCGP; *Publications* contrib Br Jl of Obstetrics and Gynaecology 1999; *Recreations* football (Manchester United FC), travel, current affairs, medical law and ethics; *Style—* Dr Mustapha Tahir; ✉ The Swanscombe Medical Centre, Swanscombe, Kent DA10 0BF (☎ 01322 427447, fax 01474 568861); The Shrubbery Surgery, 65A Perry Street, Northfleet, Kent DA11 8RD

TAIT, Eric; MBE (Mil 1980); s of William Johnston Tait (d 1959), and Sarah, *née* Jones (d 1996); *b* 10 January 1945; *Educ* George Heriot's Sch, RMA Sandhurst, Univ of London (BSc), Univ of Cambridge (MPhil); *m* 1, 29 March 1967 (m dis 1998), Agnes Jane Boag; 1 s (Michael b 1969), 1 da (Eva b 1973); m 2, 5 Dec 1998, Stacey Jane, *née* Todd; *Career* Lt-Col RE, served Germany, Middle East, Caribbean, NI (despatches 1976); dir Euro ops Pannell Kerr Forster 1989–92, exec dir PKF International 1992–; ed-in-chief The Accountants Magazine; sec Inst of CAs of Scotland 1984–89; memb Exec Scottish Cncl for Devpt and Industry 1984–89, chm Univ of Nottingham and Trent Euro Advsy Forum 1993–98; FRSA 1997; *Recreations* hill walking, swimming, reading, writing; *Style—* Eric Tait, Esq, MBE; ✉ PKF International Ltd, Farringdon Place, 20 Farringdon Road, London EC1H 3AP (☎ 020 7065 0000, fax 020 7065 0650, e-mail eric.tait@pkf.com)

TAIT, Marion Hooper (Mrs Marion Morse); CBE (2003, OBE 1992); da of Charles Arnold Browell Tait, OBE (d 1962), of London, and Betty Maude, *née* Hooper (d 2008); *b* 7 October 1950; *Educ* Royal Acad of Dancing, Royal Ballet Sch; *m* 9 Oct 1971, David Thomas Morse, s of Thomas Walter Morse (d 1984); *Career* princ dancer with Sadler's Wells Royal Ballet (now The Birmingham Royal Ballet); ballet mistress Birmingham Royal Ballet 1995 (asst dir 2011); worked with leading choreographers and had roles created by: Sir Kenneth MacMillan, Sir Frederick Ashton, David Bintley, Christopher Bruce, Joe Layton; danced all maj classical roles; guest dancer: The Houston Ballet, Munich Ballet, Japan, Aust, Poland (Polich Ballet's Bicentennial medal of Honour); productions for: Hong Kong Ballet, Nat Ballet of Canada; nominated Olivier Award (for Romeo and Juliet) 1994, Dancer of the Year (Dance and Dancers magazine) 1994, Evening Standard Ballet Award (for outstanding performance) 1994, nominated Olivier Award for Outstanding Achievement in Dance (for Pillar of Fire) 1996; *Recreations* needlework, gardening; *Style—* Ms Marion Tait, CBE; ✉ c/o Birmingham Royal Ballet, Hippodrome Theatre, Thorp Street, Birmingham B5 4AU

TAIT, Nigel Gordon Thomas Michael; s of Leonard Horsted (d 1977), of Grove, and Teresa Tait; *b* 5 April 1963, London; *Educ* Maidstone Sch for Boys, Worthing Sixth Form Coll, Univ of Nottingham (BA), Trent Poly; *m* 1 (m dis 2005); 2 s (William James b 18 Sept 1991, Louis Frederick b 15 May 1997), 1 da (Georgia Frances b 9 July 1993 d 2011); m 2, 30 Jan 2010, Helen Louise, *née* Greene; 1 s (Hugo Thomas Michael b 30 Aug 2011); *Career* admitted slr 1988; managing ptnr Carter-Ruck 2012– (ptnr 1990–); slr-advocate; memb Law Soc ctees on privacy, defamation, pre-action protocol and 1996 Defamation Act; Carter-Ruck on Libel and Slander (contrib, 4 edn and 5 edn); *Recreations* family; *Style—* Nigel Tait, Esq; ✉ Carter-Ruck, 6 St Andrew Street, London EC4A 3AE (☎ 020 7353 5005, e-mail nigel.tait@carter-ruck.com)

TAIT, Simon John Anderson; s of William Anderson Tait (d 1973), and Alice Mary, *née* Crowther (d 2004); *b* 30 January 1948; *Educ* Hawes Down Secdy Modern Sch, Open Univ (BA); *m* 1979, Ann Sandra, da of George William Hugh Williams (d 1990); 1 s (Adam Anderson b 1988); *Career* journalist; Croydon Advertiser 1966, Brighton Evening Argus 1970, Newham Recorder 1971, Manchester Evening News 1972, writer Government Info Serv 1975, head of PR servs V&A 1980, Telegraph Sunday Magazine 1984, freelance writer 1985, The Times 1988–92, freelance 1992–; co-ed Arts Industry 2003–; pres Critics' Circle 2013–15; memb Exhbn Ctee Fedn of Br Artists 2010–; *Books* Palaces of Discovery (1989), Times Guide to Museums and Galleries (1989–90 and 1990–91), Can Museums be a Potent Force in Social and Urban Regeneration (2008), Philip Sutton: Life and Work (co-author, 2008); *Recreations* finding out; *Clubs* Garrick, Surrey CCC; *Style—* Simon Tait; ✉ 12 Derwent Grove, London SE22 8EA (☎ 020 8693 5672, mobile 07713 859218)

TALBOT, John Andrew; s of Robert Talbot and Lucy Eileen, *née* Jarvis; *b* 2 August 1949; *Educ* Queen's Sch Wisbech; *m* 1 (m dis), Susan Anne, *née* Hollingberry; 1 s (Martin b 5 March 1969 d 1998), 1 da (Helen b 28 Dec 1970); m 2, Jennifer Anne, *née* Crouch; 2 da (Hannah b 7 April 1982, Bethany b 7 Aug 1984), 1 s (George b 25 March 1991); *Career* articled clerk Larking, Larking and Whiting Wisbech 1966 (transferred to Stevenson Smart & Co Peterborough), qualified 1971, various accounting posts 1971–75, joined Spicer and Pegler Nottingham 1975 (ptnr specialising in insolvency and investigation work 1980); Arthur Andersen: ptnr establishing Corp Recovery Practice Birmingham 1983, ptnr responsible for worldwide Corp Fin Gp 1996–99 (ret); ptnr: Talbot Hughes

LLP 2001–05, Kroll Talbot Hughes 2005–09 (special advsr 2009–); chief exec Johnson Serv Gp plc 2007–, ceo Johnson Services Gp plc 2009–; chm English National Ballet 2004–; FCA 1971; *Recreations* classical dance, contemporary art, iron age history, natural history; *Style*— John Talbot, Esq; ✉ Johnson Service Group plc, Johnson House, Abbots Park, Monks Way, Preston Brook, Cheshire WA7 3GH

TALBOT, Prof Michael Owen; s of Prof Alan Talbot (d 1981), and Dr Annelise Talbot, *née* Tømmerup; *b* 4 January 1943; *Educ* Welwyn Garden City GS, Royal Coll of Music (ARCM), Clare Coll Cambridge (open scholar, BA, MusB, PhD); *m* 26 Sept 1970, Shirley Ellen Mashiane-Talbot, da of Jacob Mashiane (d 1975), of SA; 1 s (Stephen b 1975), 1 da (Natasha b 1982); *Career* Univ of Liverpool: asst lectr then lectr in music 1968–79, sr lectr in music 1979–83, reader in music 1983–86, Alsop prof of music 1986–2003, emeritus prof 2003–; memb: Royal Musical Assoc, Società Italiana di Musicologia; memb Editorial Bd: Music and Letters, Istituto Italiano Antonio Vivaldi; corresponding memb Ateneo Veneto 1986, FBA 1990; Cavaliere dell' Ordine Al Merito della Repubblica Italiana 1980; *Books* Vivaldi (1978), Vivaldi (1979), Albinoni: Leben und Werk (1980), Antonio Vivaldi: A Guide to Research (1988), Tomaso Albinoni: The Venetian Composer and His World (1990), Benedetto Vinaccesi: A Musician in Brescia and Venice in the Age of Corelli (1994), The Sacred Vocal Music of Antonio Vivaldi (1995), Venetian Music in the Age of Vivaldi (1999), The Finale in Western Instrumental Music (2001), The Chamber Cantatas of Antonio Vivaldi (2006), Vivaldi and Fugue (2009), The Vivaldi Compendium (2011); *Recreations* chess, reading novels, travel; *Style*— Prof Michael Talbot, FBA; ✉ 36 Montclair Drive, Liverpool L18 0HA (☎ 0151 722 3328); Department of Music, University of Liverpool, PO Box 147, Liverpool L69 7WW (☎ 0151 794 3095, fax 0151 794 3141, e-mail mtalbot@liv.ac.uk)

TALBOT, Patrick John; QC (1990); s of John Bentley Talbot, MC (d 2009), and Marguerite Maxwell, *née* Townley (d 1995); *b* 28 July 1946; *Educ* Charterhouse, University College Oxford (MA); *m* 1, 8 May 1976 (m dis 1999), Judith Anne, da of David Percival Urwin; 2 da (Sophie Camilla b 28 Nov 1977, Alexandra Claire Maxwell b 8 Nov 1979), 1 s (William Patrick Charles b 2 June 1983); m 2, 28 Dec 2000, Elizabeth, da of Ronald Evans; 2 s (Theodore Henry b 16 Sept 1998, Caspar Hugh b 6 May 2001); *Career* called to the Bar Lincoln's Inn 1969 (bencher 1996); in practice Chancery Bar 1970–, recorder 1997–; memb: Senate of Inns of Court and the Bar 1974–77, Cncl of Legal Educn 1977–95 (vice-chm 1992–95), Gen Cncl of the Bar 1993; a judicial chm City Disputes Panel 1997–2000, memb Premier League Disciplinary Panel 2006–; Lt Bailiff Royal Court of Guernsey 2000–, Lt Seneschal of Sark 2008–; chm Ripieno Choir 2003–07; *Recreations* watching cricket, bridge, collecting old toys, choral singing; *Clubs* MCC, Wimbledon Wanderers Cricket, E Molesey Cricket (chm 2009–); *Style*— Patrick Talbot, Esq, QC; ✉ Serle Court, 6 New Square, Lincoln's Inn, London WC2A 3QS (☎ 020 7242 6105, fax 020 7405 4004, e-mail ptalbot@serlecourt.co.uk)

TALBOT RICE, Nigel; s of Mervyn Gurney Talbot Rice (d 1979), and Eleanor Butler Adair, *née* Williamson (d 1965); *b* 14 May 1938; *Educ* Charterhouse, ChCh Oxford (MA, DipEd); *m* 20 July 1968, (Rosfrith) Joanna Sarah, da of Air-Cdr F J Manning, CB, CBE, RAF (d 1988); 4 da (Sarah (Mrs Daniel Phillips) b 24 Oct 1969, Caroline (Mrs Jonathan Bewes) b 26 Sept 1971, Rebecca (Mrs James Nash) b 2 Sept 1973, Helena b 28 Jan 1977); 1 s (Samuel b 17 March 1982); *Career* Nat Serv Coldstream Gds 1957–58; asst master Papplewick Sch Ascot 1961–64, headmaster Summer Fields Sch Oxford 1975–97 (asst master 1965–71, asst headmaster 1971–75); ptnr TR Consultancy 1997–2011; conslt English Heritage 1997–98; dir Misys Charitable Fndn 1998–2011; chm: Cancer Research Campaign Oxford Appeal 1997–99, Maclaren Tst and Maclaren Fndn 1999–2011; tstee Oxfordshire Community Fndn 2002–09; memb Cncl St Luke's Hosp Oxford (chm 2015–16); chm: Macmillan Nurses Oxford Carol Concerts 1997–2002, Dorchester Abbey Children's Hosp Christmas Concert 2006, 2008, 2010 and 2012; govr: Wychwood Sch Oxford, Hordle Walhampton Lymington, St John's Sch Northwood, Cumnor House Sch Danehill, Finton House Sch London; devpt conslt Downe House Sch 1998–2005; hon life memb Macmillan Cancer Care; memb IAPS 1971; *Books* Survey of Religion in Preparatory Schools (1965); *Recreations* golf, gardening, wine; *Style*— Nigel Talbot Rice, Esq; ✉ Yellow Wood House, Ethelred Court, Old Headington, Oxford OX3 9DA

TALBOT-PONSONBY, Nigel Edward Charles; s of Edward Fitzroy Talbot-Ponsonby (d 1996; ggs of Adm Sir Charles Talbot, KCB, who was s of Very Rev Charles Talbot, Dean of Salisbury, by Lady Elizabeth Somerset, da of 5 Duke of Beaufort; the Dean was n of 3 Baron and 1 Earl Talbot, which two dignities are now held by the Earl of Shrewsbury); *b* 24 September 1946; *Educ* Harrow; *m* 1977, Robina, da of Lt Cdr Henry Bruce, JP, DL, RN, Ret (gs of 9 Earl of Elgin and 13 of Kincardine), of London; 3 s (Henry b 1981, James b 1986, Alexander b 1987); *Career* chartered surveyor, RICS registered valuer and int hotel and leisure business conslt; fndr and past chm HLL Humberts Leisure Chartered Surveyors, non-exec dir Venture Capital Partners (VCP Advisors), dir Langrish House Hotel Ltd, conslt Bilfinger GVA Chartered Surveyors; former memb Recreation and Leisure Mgmnt Ctee RICS; FRICS; *Recreations* sailing, field sports, forestry; *Clubs* Bucks, English Speaking Union; *Style*— Nigel Talbot-Ponsonby, Esq; ✉ Langrish House, Langrish, Petersfield, Hampshire GU32 1RN (☎ 01730 263374, e-mail frontdesk@langrishhouse.co.uk); Bilfinger GVA, 65 Gresham Street, London EC2V 7NQ (☎ 08449 020304, mobile 07920 571040, e-mail ntp@gva.co.uk)

TALLIS, Prof Raymond Courtney; s of Edward Ernest Tallis, and Mary, *née* Burke; *b* 10 October 1946; *Educ* Liverpool Coll, Keble Coll Oxford (open scholar, BA, BM BCh), St Thomas' Hosp Med Sch; *m* 1972, Teresa, *née* Bonneywell; 2 s; *Career* clinical res fell Wessex Neurological Centre 1977–80, sr lectr in geriatric med Univ of Liverpool 1982–87, prof of geriatric med Univ of Manchester 1987–2006, conslt physician Salford Royal Hosps Tst 1987–2006; numerous visiting professorships; chair Healthcare Professionals for Assisted Dying; memb various med socs; numerous radio talks on topics incl: the meaning of words, the function of art, the political culture of Liverpool; Henry Cohen Gold Medal for Research into Ageing 2007, Health Watch Award for Supporting Evidence-Based Medicine 2007; Hon DLitt Univ of Hull 1997, Hon LittD Univ of Manchester 2002, Hon DSc St George's Hosp London; FRCP 1989, FMedSci 2000; *Publications* fiction: Absence (novel, 1999); various short stories; poetry: Between the zones (1985), Glints of Darkness (1989), Fathers and Sons (1993); non-fiction: Not Saussure (1988, 2 edn 1995), In Defence of Realism (1988, 2 edn 1998), The Clinical Neurology of Old Age (1988), The Explicit Animal (1991, 2 edn 1999), Brocklehurst's Textbook of Geriatric Medicine and Gerontology (jt ed, 4 edn 1992, 5 edn 1998, 6 edn 2003), Newton's Sleep (1995), Epilepsy in Elderly People (1996), Enemies of Hope (1997, 2 edn 1999), Theorrhoea and After (1998), Increasing Longevity: medical, social and political implications (1998), On the Edge of Certainty: philosophical explorations (1999), The Raymond Tallis Reader (ed by Michael Grant, 2000), A conversation with Martin Heidegger (2002), The Hand: A Philosophical Inquiry into Human Being 2003, I Am: A Philosophical Inquiry into First Person Being (2004), Hippocratic Oaths: Medicine and its Discontents (2004), Why the Mind is Not a Computer: A Pocket Lexicon of Neuromythology (2004), The Knowing Animal: A Philosophical Inquiry Into Knowledge and Truth (2005), The Enduring Significance of Parmenides: Unthinkable Thought (2007), The Kingdom of Infinite Space – A Fantastical Journey Around Your Head (2008), Hunger (2008), Michaelangelo's Finger (2010), Aping Mankind: Neuromania, Darwinitis and the Misrepresentation of Humanity (2011), In Defence of Wonder and other Philosophical Reflections (2012), Reflections of a Metaphysical Flaneur and other essays (2013), NHS SOS How the NHS Was Betrayed – and How We Can Save It (jt ed, 2013), Epimethean Imaginings: Philosophical and Other Meditations on Everyday Light (2014), Summers of Discontent: The Purpose of the Arts Today (with Julian Spalding, 2014), The Black Mirror: Fragments of an Obituary for Life (2015), The Mystery of Being Human: God, Freedom, and the NHS (2016); regular columnist Philosophy Now; author of: over 200 scientific papers and articles mainly in the field of epilepsy, stroke and the neurological rehabilitation of older people, 300 articles in philosophy and literary and cultural criticism; *Recreations* family, music, thinking, Saving the NHS from privatisation; *Clubs* 1942, Athenaeum; *Style*— Prof Raymond Tallis; ✉ 5, Valley Road, Bramhall, Stockport, Cheshire SK7 2NH (☎ 0161 439 2548, mobile 07801 834230, fax 0161 440 0434, e-mail raymond@rtallis.wanadoo.co.uk)

TALLON, David Seymour; s of Claude Reginald Tallon (d 2001), of London, and Blanche Mary, *née* Mahony (d 1984); *b* 7 October 1940; *Educ* Rugby; *Children* 3 s (Alastair James b 14 May 1966, Timothy Paul b 6 July 1967, Oliver Mark b 6 July 1967 d 1967), 4 da (Victoria Kate Rebecca b 1 March 1969, Elizabeth Jane Biddy b 16 May 1970, Sarah Georgina b 18 Oct 1994, Louise Christine b 29 May 1999); m 2, 9 April 1998, Gillian Lesley, *née* Sandford; *Career* CA 1964; Deloitte Plender Griffiths 1958–67, ptnr Dearden Harper Miller 1969, sr ptnr Dearden Farrow 1986–87; ptnr: BDO Binder Hamlyn 1987–92 (dep sr ptnr 1987–90), Sharp Parsons Tallon 1992–2002, Mercer & Hole 2002–05 (conslt 2005–); chm Children with AIDS Charity 1994–99 and 2011–14; FCA; *Books* Capital Transfer Tax Planning (2 edn 1976, 3 edn 1978), Inland Revenue Practices & Concessions (1980); *Recreations* golf; *Clubs* MCC, Hampstead CC, Old Rugbeian Golfing Society; *Style*— David Tallon, Esq; ✉ Mercer & Hole, Gloucester House, 72 London Road, St Albans, Hertfordshire AL1 1NS (e-mail davidtallon@mercerhole.co.uk)

TALMAN, Iain James Scott; s of James Maghie Talman (d 1990), and Annie Campbell, *née* Keillor (d 2009); *b* 18 July 1952, Johnstone, Renfrewshire; *Educ* Gourock HS, Greenock HS, Univ of Glasgow (LLB); *m* 1975, Sheila MacDonald, *née* Pringle; 1 s (James Scott b 1981), 1 da (Eilidh Sheila b 1983); *Career* slr; successively apprentice, asst slr and ptnr Bishop, Milne Boyd & Co (then successor firms: Bishop & Co, Bishop and Robertson Chalmers, Morison Bishop) 1974–2002, ptnr Biggart Baillie LLP and DWF Biggart Baillie 2002–14, conslt DWF LLP 2015–16, ind legal conslt 2016–; memb: Assoc of Pension Lawyers, Ind Pension Tstees Gp, Scottish Gp Pensions Mgmnt Inst, Assoc of Member-Directed Pension Schemes, Insurance and Actuarial Soc of Glasgow, Law Soc of Scotland, Royal Faculty of Procurators in Glasgow, Merchants' House of Glasgow, Old Paisley Soc (fndr), Helensburgh Heritage Tst, Alexander Thomson Soc (fndr), Innerkip Soc; *Publications* Stair Memorial Encyclopaedia (Pensions section 1995, reissues 2004 and 2013), Halliday's Conveyancing Law and Practice (2 edn, Vol 1 1996, Vol 2 1997); *Recreations* cinema, travel, saving the planet; *Clubs* Glasgow Art, Nomads (past pres); *Style*— Iain Talman, Esq; ✉ 6A Queen Street, Helensburgh, Dunbartonshire G84 9QQ (☎ 01436 679909, e-mail iain@talmans1.wanadoo.co.uk)

TALWAR, Rana Gurvirendra Singh; s of RS Talwar, and Veera Talwar; *b* 22 March 1948; *Educ* Lawrence Sch Sanawar India, St Stephen's Coll Delhi (BA); *m* 1, 1970 (m dis), Roop Som Dutt; 1 s, 1 da; m 2, 1995, Renuka Singh; 1 s; *Career* Citibank: exec trainee for int banking 1969–70, various operational, corp and institutional assignments India 1970–76, gp head Treas and Fin Insts 1976, regnl mangr E India 1977, gp head Treas and Fin Insts Gp Saudi American Bank (Citibank affiliate) Jeddah 1978–80, COS Asia Pacific Div 1981, regnl consumer business mangr Singapore, Malaysia, Indonesia, Thailand and India 1982–88, div exec Asia Pacific 1988–91, exec vice-pres and gp exec (responsible for consumer bank) Asia Pacific, ME and E Europe 1991–95, exec vice-pres Citicorp 1996–97, US and Europe rep 1996–97; Standard Chartered plc: gp exec dir 1997–98, ceo 1997–2001; chm Sabre Capital Worldwide 2002–; non-exec dir Pearson plc 2000–; govr: London Business Sch 1988–, Indian Sch of Business 1999–; *Recreations* golf, tennis, bridge, travel; *Clubs* Tanglin (Singapore), Bengal (Calcutta), Delhi Golf (New Delhi); *Style*— Rana G S Talwar, Esq

TAM, Robin Bing-Kuen; QC (2006); s of Sheung Wai Tam, and Arleta Yau-Ling, *née* Chang; *b* 1 June 1964; *Educ* The Leys Sch Cambridge, St John's Coll Cambridge, Inns of Court Sch of Law; *m* 2007, Rosemary Anger; *Career* called to the Bar Middle Temple 1986; standing prosecuting jr counsel to the Inland Revenue (SE Circuit) 1993, jr counsel to the Crown 1994–2006 (A Panel 1999–2006), QC 2006; *Publications* Asylum and Human Rights Handbook (with Anna Lotzeva, Lucy Murray and Ian Burnett, QC, *qv*, 2008); *Style*— Robin Tam, Esq, QC; ✉ Temple Garden Chambers, 1 Harcourt Buildings, Temple, London EC4Y 9DA (☎ 020 7583 1315)

TAMES, Roger; s of Albert Tames (d 1975), and Phyllis, *née* Amos; *b* 21 September 1951; *m* (m dis); 1 da (Joanne b 1979), 1 s (Ian b 1983); *Career* journalist; reporter Essex & East London Newspapers (Brentwood Argus, Dagenham Post) 1973–75, successively reporter, presenter, football commentator, sports ed and head of sport Tyne Tees Television 1976–2005, head of sports progs filmNova Sports Prodn 2005–08, dir Box to Box Media Ltd 2008–; freelance broadcaster; progs presented incl: Sportstime, Sporting Chance, Extra Time, The Back Page, Cafe Sport, Football Flashback, North East Match, Soccer Night; memb: NE Sports Bd, Variety Club of GB, Sport Newcastle; *Publications* Steve Cram: The Making of an Athlete (1990), Roker Park: The Story Video (1997); Official History of Newcastle Utd DVD; *Recreations* squash, running, golf, keeping fit – eating and drinking afterwards; *Style*— Roger Tames, Esq; ✉ Box to Box Media (e-mail roger.tames@boxtoboxmedia.com)

TAMI, Mark Richard; MP; s of Michael John Tami, of Enfield, and Patricia Tami; *b* 3 October 1962; *Educ* Enfield GS, Univ of Wales Swansea; *m* 1992, Sally, da of Arthur Richard Daniels; 2 s (Max Oscar Hugh b 3 March 1998, Oscar Joel Richard b 8 August 2000); *Career* AEEU: head of research 1992–97, head of policy 1999–2001; MP (Lab) Alyn and Deeside 2001–, memb NI Select Ctee 2001–05, former PPS to John Healey, MP, co-chair All-Pty Stem Cell Gp, oppn asst chief whip 2011–; memb: TUC Gen Cncl 1999–2001, League Against Cruel Sports; *Publications* Fabian booklet on the need for compulsory voting; *Recreations* Glamorgan CCC, Norwich City FC, fishing, antiques; *Style*— Mark Tami, Esq, MP; ✉ House of Commons, London SW1A 0AA (☎ 020 7219 8174); Constituency Office (☎ 01244 819854)

TAMLIN, Keith Maxwell; s of Sydney Thomas Tamlin (d 1946), and Madeline Isabel, *née* Prowse (d 1995); *b* 19 July 1928; *Educ* Ruthin Sch; *m* 21 June 1954, Marian, da of Thomas Roberts; 2 da (Helen Susan b 25 May 1955, Karen Michele b 26 April 1958); *Career* Nat Serv King's (Liverpool) Regt RASC 1947–49 (cmmnd 1947, served ME); slr Supreme Ct of Judicature 1954, ptnr North Kirk & Co Slrs Liverpool 1959 (joined 1954), conslt Cuff Roberts Slrs Liverpool; dir: Everton Football Club Co Ltd 1974–2004 (life vice-pres), H Samuel plc 1979–92 (and other cos within H Samuel Group incl Watches of Switzerland plc), several cos within distributive sector, various cos dealing with racehorses, publications and breeding; pres: Liverpool Jr C of C 1960, Liverpool Round Table 1965; chm Jt Ctees organising Charity Gala Performances at Liverpool Playhouse 1964–65 (to raise funds for Liverpool Central Boys' Club, Liverpool Maternity Hosp and the Br Red Cross and Women's Hosp), memb and slr Ctee Liverpool and Dist Family Servs Unit 1963–82, memb The Mail Order Traders' Assoc of GB (sec 1967, dir 1974); memb: PO Users' Nat Cncl 1970–90, Trg Ctee Distributive Indust Bd 1971–78, Mgmnt Ctee and Cncl Retail Consortium 1973–97, Cncl Advtg Assoc 1982–97, Cncl CBI 1988–92; nominated by HM Govt as a Gp 1 Employers' Rep to Econ and Social Ctee Brussels 1983–93, memb Ctee for Commerce and Distribution Euro Cmmn 1993–99; memb: Liverpool Law Soc, Law Soc (pres 1984); *Recreations* walking, swimming, watching football and professional golf; *Clubs* Athenaeum (Liverpool), East India; *Style*— Keith

Tamlin, Esq; ✉ 11 Quickswood Close, Woolton, Liverpool L25 4TT (☎ 0151 428 2088, fax 0151 428 2088)

TAMS, John Murray; s of William Murray Tams (d 1976), and Vera, *née* Stone (d 1996); *b* 16 February 1949; *m* 27 June 1992, Sally, da of Stuart Alan Ward; 1 da (Rosie b 30 Aug 1986); *Career* musician, composer and actor; early career: two seasons with Cox's Modern Amusements, hack reporter for various local newspapers Derbys, with BBC Radio Nottingham and BBC Radio Derby, lectr in popular culture WEA, freelance writer NME, Sounds and Melody Maker, involved in record production Topic Records, with E Midlands Mobile Arts theatre gp; also sometime mangr ladies underwear factory, antique dealer, maggot salesman and unrequited teacher of 9 to 13 year olds; former memb bands incl Muckram Wakes, Albion Band and Home Service; estab Rolling Stock Co choir Derbys, co-fndr and prodr No Masters co-op recording label and publisher S Yorks; winner of six BBC Radio 2 Folk Awards (incl Folk Singer of the Year 2006 and Traditional Song of the Year), winner of two Hancock Awards; Hon Dr: Sheffield Hallam Univ 2007, Derby Univ 2009; *Theatre* actor and musical dir under Bill Bryden, *qv*, NT 1977–85, prodns incl Larkrise, The World Turned Upside Down, Dispatches, The Long Voyage Home, The Iceman Cometh, Hughie, Candleford, The Crucible, Cinderella, Golden Boy, A Midsummer Night's Dream, Don Quixote, Glengarry Glen Ross and The Mysteries (and subsequent intermittent Euro tour and revival 2000), songmaker for WarHorse (nominated Sound Production Award Olivier Awards 2008); musical dir and composer: The Crucible (Birmingham/Salisbury Playhouse), Son of Man (RSC), Uncle Vanya (West End), The Three Sisters (Birmingham Rep), Of Mice and Men (Birmingham Rep); other theatre involvement incl: with United Br Artists Old Vic Theatre, RSC Aldwych Theatre, co-dir Joint Stock theatre co, TUC sponsored tour with 7:84 theatre co during 1984 miner's strike, co-creator The Ship (for Euro City of Culture Festival Glasgow 1990) and The Big Picnic, assoc dir Crucible Theatre Sheffield (incl co-dir and adaptor The Northern Mysteries), assoc dir The Building Co, actor and composer The Good Hope (NT tour); *Television and Film* script assoc, collaborator on musical score and actor (playing the part of Daniel Hagman) Sharpe series ITV; other appearances incl: Sons and Lovers, A Question of Leadership, Clapperclaw, Assembled Memories, The Raggedy Rawney, The Rainbow, God Speed Co-operation, Ill Fares the Land, Back to the Roots, Here We Go A-Wassailing, A Little Night Music, Holy City, The Rainbow, Crimestrike, The Gifted Adult, You Don't Have to Walk to Fly, Albion Market, Floodtide and Travelling Man, No Further Cause for Concern, Ruth Rendell Mysteries, Investigation, The Fool, As You Like It, Six Characters in Search of an Author, Elidor, When Saturday Comes; *Radio* for BBC Radio 4 as composer/studio prodr/ed: Sacco and Vanzetti, Pickwick Papers, Felix Hoult the Radical, HMS Ulysses, The Plutocrat, Volunteers, Daisy Miller, The Nativity, The Passion, Doomsday, Charge of the Light Brigade, From Here to Eternity; music series prodr Radio Ballads 2006 (Sony Gold Radio Award 2007); dir and adaptor WarHorse (BBC Radio 2) 2009; *Albums* Unity 2000 (Album of the Year and Song of the Year (for Harry Stone) BBC Radio 2 Folk Awards 2001), Home 2002, The Reckoning 2006 (Album of the Year and nominated Best Original Song (for Steelos) BBC Radio 2 Folk Awards); prodr Over the Hills and Far Away (album of music from the Sharpe TV series); singer, musician or prodr on over 50 albums; *Style—* John Tams, Esq; ✉ website www.johntams.co.uk

TAN, Melvyn; s of Tan Keng Hian, of Singapore, and Wong Sou Yuen; *b* 13 October 1956, Singapore; *Educ* Yehudi Menuhin Sch Surrey, Royal Coll of Music; *Career* fortepianist and harpsichord player, modern piano performer since 1997; interpreter of Baroque, classical and early Romantic works; debut Wigmore Hall 1977, played in all major UK venues; repertoire incl: Weber, Mendelssohn, Chopin; performed with orchs and ensembles incl: Acad of Ancient Music, Eng Chamber Orch, RPO, London Classical Players; US tour playing Beethoven 1985, concert series with Roger Norrington and London Classical Players 1987 and 1988; festivals in 1989 incl: The Beethoven Experience (Purchase NY, with Roger Norrington and London Classical Players), Midsummer Mozart Festival in San Francisco (also Aldeburgh, Bath, Holland and Helsinki); performed in 1990: San Francisco, toured France and Japan, Queen Elizabeth Hall; involved in bringing Beethoven's own fortepiano from Budapest to England for European tour 1992, continues to perform at most major festivals and venues around the world, involved in Singapore's burgeoning musical scene (teaching and performing) 2011–; FRCM; *Recordings* incl: Beethoven's Waldstein, Appassionato and Les Adieux sonatas, Schubert Impromptus, Beethoven Piano Concertos (with Roger Norrington and the London Classical Players), Debussy Preludes Books 1 and 2, Mozart/Beethoven Concertos (London Chamber Orch, directed from the keyboard); *Recreations* travelling to places where I don't have to do concerts; *Style—* Melvyn Tan, Esq; ✉ website www.melvyntan.com (for all contact info)

TANFIELD, Dr Amanda Susannah; *Educ* BSc, PhD; *m* 22 Nov 2003, Matthew Vernon Connolly; *Career* diplomat; MOD: joined 1988, princ Directorate of Defence Policy 1992–95, princ resources and progs (air) 1995–98; head UNSCOM and regnl proliferation Non Proliferation Dept FCO 1998–2001, head of Iraq policy ME Dept FCO 2001–03, dep head of mission and cnsllr UK Delgn OSCE Vienna 2003–07, head Drugs and Int Crime Dept FCO 2008–11, Libya Crisis Unit FCO 2011, ambass to Eritrea 2012–14; *Style—* Dr Amanda Tanfield; ✉ FCO, King Charles Street, London SW1A 2AH

TANG, Sir David; KBE (2008, OBE); *b* 2 August 1954; *Educ* Perse Sch Cambridge, Univ of London, Peking Univ, California State Univ; *Career* fndr China Club Hong Kong, Beijing and Singapore, launched China Tang at The Dorchester Hotel London and Island Tang restaurant Hong Kong, owner Pacific Cigar Co Ltd, fndr Shanghai Tang; tstee Royal Acad, chm Asia-Pacific Acquisitions Ctee Tate, advsr London Symphony Orch, advsr English Chamber Orch, pres London Bach Soc, fndr Hong Kong Cancer Fund, vice-chm European Orgn for Research and Treatment of Cancer, founding pres Hong Kong Down Syndrome Assoc, patron Hong Kong Youth Arts Fndn; Chevalier of the Ordre des Arts et des Lettres 1995; *Style—* Sir David Tang, KBE; ✉ China Tang at The Dorchester, 53 Park Lane, Mayfair, London W1K 1QA

TANKERVILLE, 10 Earl of (GB 1714); Peter Grey Bennet; also Baron Ossulston (E 1682); s of 9 Earl of Tankerville (d 1980), and Georgiana Lilian Maude, *née* Wilson (d 1998); *b* 18 October 1956; *Educ* Grace Cathedral Sch San Francisco (chorister), Oberlin Conservatory Ohio (BMus), San Francisco State Univ (MA); *Career* musician San Francisco; *Style—* The Rt Hon the Earl of Tankerville; ✉ 139 Olympia Way, San Francisco, CA 94131, USA (☎ 00 1 415 826 6639)

TANLAW, Baron (Life Peer UK 1971), of Tanlawhill in the County of Dumfries; Hon Simon Brooke Mackay; yst s of 2 Earl of Inchcape (d 1939), and Leonora Margaret Brooke (d 1996), da of HH the 3 Rajah of Sarawak (Sir Charles Vyner Brooke (d 1963)); *b* 30 March 1934; *Educ* Eton, Trinity Coll Cambridge (MA); *m* 1, 1959, Joanna Susan, o da of Maj John Henry Hirsch (d 1983); 2 da (Hon Iona Héloïse b 1960, Hon Rebecca Alexandra (Hon Mrs Ayre-Smith) b 1967), 1 s (Hon James Brooke b 1961), and 1 s decd; m 2, 1976, Rina Siew Yong, yst da of late Tiong Cha Tan, of Kuala Lumpur, Malaysia; 1 da (Hon Asia Brooke (Hon Mrs Trotter) b 1980), 1 s (Hon Brooke Brooke b 1982); *Career* sits as Ind (formerly Lib) in House of Lords; 2 Lt 12 Royal Lancers 1952–54; chm Fandstan Electric Gp Ltd, former dir Inchcape plc; pres Sarawak Assoc 1972–75, 1998–2001 and 2012; pres All-Pty Parly Astronomy and Space Environment Gp 1999–2009, chm Lighter Evenings All-Pty Gp; nat appeal chm Elizabeth FitzRoy Support for People with Learning Disabilities 1985–90; hon fell Univ of Buckingham 1981 (chllr 2011–13); Hon DUniv Buckingham 1983; Liveryman: Worshipful Co of Fishmongers, Worshipful Co of Clockmakers; FBHI 1997, FRAS 2003; *Clubs* White's, Oriental, Puffin's; *Style—* The Rt Hon the Lord Tanlaw; ✉ Tanlawhill, By Langholm, Dumfriesshire DG13 0PW

TANN, Prof Jennifer; da of Alfred John Booth, and Frances Booth, of Birmingham; *b* 25 February 1939; *Educ* Badminton Sch Bristol, Univ of Manchester (BA), Univ of Leicester (PhD); *m* 12 Oct 1963, Roger William Tann, s of Richard Henry Tann; 2 s (Edmund John b 8 March 1966, Oliver Richard b 4 June 1974); *Career* research asst Historic Towns Project Oxford 1964–66, pt/t tutor Univ of Hull 1966–69, lectr Aston Univ 1969–73, reader Aston Univ Business Sch 1973–86, dir Centre for Continuing Educn Univ of Newcastle upon Tyne 1986–89, prof of innovation studies Univ of Birmingham 1989–2008 (dean Faculty of Educn and Continuing Studies 1993–96, emerita prof 2008–), conslt Caret 1995–, dir Entrepeneurship and Innovation Centre Univ of Birmingham Business Sch 1997–2003, res dir Birmingham Business Sch 1999–2002, univ public orator 2001–07; visiting prof Dept of Economics Univ of Queensland 1985, visiting prof of mgmnt Univ of Newcastle upon Tyne 1989–94; memb Assoc for Industrial Archaeology; bishops' selection advsr; Dio of Glos: memb Bishop's Cncl, tstee Educn Cncl, memb Healing Gp, memb Synod; memb Newcomen Soc; chair Stroudwater Textile Tst; *Books* Development of the Factory (1971), Selected Papers of Boulton and Watt (1981), Children at Work (1981), Short History of the Stock Exchange Birmingham (1983), Birmingham Assay Office (1993), Wool and Water (2012), Soul Pain (2013), Matthew Boulton, Industry's Great Innovator (2013); *Recreations* reading, gardens, music, laughter; *Style—* Prof Jennifer Tann; ✉ Thanet House, High Street, Chalford, Stroud GL6 8DH (e-mail j.tann@bham.co.uk)

TANNAHILL, Dr Andrew James; s of Andrew Leckie Tannahill, of Inchinnan, Renfrewshire, and late Elizabeth Johnstone, *née* Preston; *b* 28 April 1954; *Educ* John Neilson Inst Paisley, Univ of Glasgow (MB ChB (with honours), Brunton meml prize), Univ of Edinburgh (MSc); *m* Prof Carol Elizabeth Tannahill, *née* Fyfe; *Career* lectr in pathology Univ of Glasgow and hon registrar in pathology Western Infirmary Glasgow 1981–82, registrar then sr registrar in community med Lothian Health Bd 1982–85, hon clinical tutor Univ of Edinburgh 1984–85, regional specialist in community med E Anglian RHA 1985–88, assoc lectr Univ of Cambridge 1988, sr lectr in public health med Univ of Glasgow and hon conslt in public health med Gtr Glasgow Health Bd 1988–91, chief exec Health Educn Bd for Scotland 1991–2001, hon sr lectr Univ of Dundee 1993–2001, hon fell Univ of Edinburgh 1994–2001; Univ of Glasgow: hon sr lectr 1996–2014, visiting prof 1997–2001; conslt in public health med NHS Argyll and Clyde 2001–05, interim dir of public health NHS Argyll and Clyde 2004–05, head Evidence for Action and conslt in public health med NHS Health Scotland 2005–11, non-exec bd memb NHS Educn for Scotland 2013–; FFPHM 1992 (MFCM 1985), FRCPEd 1996, FRCPGlas 1999; *Books* Health Promotion: Models and Values (1990, 2 edn 1996), Scotland's Health and Health Services (contrib, 2003); also contrib of chapters in other books; *Recreations* photography, digital imaging, painting, music, theatre, birdwatching, countryside, reading; *Style—* Dr Andrew Tannahill

TANNER, Dr Andrea Isobel; *née* Duncan; *b* 15 January 1956; *Educ* Notre Dame HS for Girls Dumbarton, Univ of Strathclyde (BA), Univ of Warwick (MA), Birkbeck Coll London (PhD), UCL (DipARM); *m* Dr John Tanner (d 2004); *Career* genealogist to Clarenceaux King of Arms at Coll of Arms 1980–95, freelance researcher; tutor in heraldry, social history, genealogy and family history for WEA, Extra Mural Dept of Birkbeck Coll, Denman Coll, Soc of Genealogists, Elderhostel Fndn; researcher offr Wellcome Tst-funded Mortality in the Metropolis Project at the Inst of Historical Research Senate House 1996–99, currently res fell Inst of Historical Research; hon archivist Gt Ormond St Hosp for Children NHS Fndn Tst 2013; founding hon sec Friends of the Public Record Office 1988–93 (vice-pres 1993–), memb Lord Chllr's Advsy Cncl on Public Records 1993–99; memb: Cncl of British Records Assoc 1996–99, Soc of Genealogists, Inst of Historical Research, Archives for London; archivist Fortnum & Mason Piccadilly; sr research fell Inst of Historical Research; delivered a variety of seminars and symposium papers in Euro, UK and USA; FSA, FSG; *Publications* Bricks and Mortals; A History of the Kensington Housing Trust (2001); in jls incl: Jl of Medical Biography, Ashmolean Jl of History of Collections, Jl of the Soc for Social History of Medicine, Hygeia Internationalis Historical Jl, The Lancet, The London Jl; *Recreations* travel, cooking, seeing my godchildren; *Style—* Dr Andrea Tanner, FSA; ✉ 81 Black Lion Lane, London W6 9BG

TANNER, Prof Brian Keith; s of Sydney Tanner (d 1979), and Gladys, *née* Godwin (d 1994); *b* 3 April 1947, Raunds, Northants; *Educ* Wellingborough GS, Balliol Coll Oxford (Kitchener scholar, MA), Oriel Coll Oxford (Robinson sr scholar, DPhil); *m* 16 Aug 1969, Ruth, *née* Simmonds; 2 s (Robert Edward b 10 Feb 1973, Thomas Matthew b 3 Feb 1975); *Career* jr research fell Linacre Coll Oxford 1971–73; Univ of Durham: univ lectr 1973–83, sr lectr 1983–86, reader 1986–90, prof 1990–, head Dept of Physics 1996–99, dean of knowledge transfer 2008–12, dean for univ enterprise 2012–; dir: Bede Scientific Instruments Ltd 1978–2000, NE Centre for Scientific Enterprise 2000–08; non-exec dir: Bede plc 2000–08, Kromek Gp plc (formerly Durham Scientific Crystals Ltd) 2008–15 (chm 2003–08), RTCNorth Ltd 2011–; chief scientific advsr NETPark Co Durham 2012–; chair Durham Economic Partnership 2012–; Queen's Award for Enterprise Promotion 2012, Gabor Medal Inst of Physics 2014; FInstP 1982, FRSA 1996; *Publications* Introduction to the Physics of Electrons in Solids (1995), X-Ray Metrology (2006); over 390 research papers in int scientific jls; *Recreations* amateur music making (organist, pianist, double bassist), walking; *Style—* Prof Brian Tanner; ✉ Department of Physics, University of Durham, South Road, Durham DH1 3LE (☎ 0191 334 3677, fax 0191 334 3211, e-mail b.k.tanner@dur.ac.uk)

TANNER, Brian Michael; CBE (1997), DL (1997); s of Gerald Evelyn Tanner (d 1964), and Mary, *née* Adamson (d 1986); *b* 15 February 1941, Scunthorpe; *Educ* Acklam Hall GS Middlesbrough, Bishops Vesey GS Sutton Coldfield, Univ of Bristol (BA); *m* 15 June 1963, June Ann, *née* Walker; 1 da (Susan Nicola b 29 July 1966), 1 s (Andrew Mark b 9 Jan 1968); *Career* trainee accountant Birmingham CBC 1962–65, gp accountant Coventry CBC 1965–68, chief accountant Teesside CBC 1968–71, asst county treas and asst chief exec Warwickshire CC 1971–75; Somerset CC: county treas 1975–90, chief exec 1990–97; dir Jupiter Int Green Investment Tst 1997–2002; advsr Assoc of CCs 1976–98, princ local authy negotiator 1985–88, pres Soc of County Treasurers 1989–90; memb Accountancy Standards Ctee 1982–84, chm Investment Mgmnt User Gp 1987–90, memb Nat Assoc of Pension Funds 1989–92, cmmr Public Works Loans Bd 1997–; chm: SW Nat Lottery Charities Bd 1997–2003, Taunton and Somerset NHS Tst 1998–2006 (non-exec dir 1997–2006), Taunton Town Partnership 1998–2003, Taunton Vision Cmmn 2003; vice-pres Taunton League of Friends 2006–; dir Somerset Trg and Enterprise Cncl 1990–97; memb: FE Funding Cncl SW Region 1996–99, Wessex Customer Servs Ctee OFWAT 1998–99; chm Wells Cathedral Cncl 2007–12 (tstee 2005–12); tstee: Central Bureau Dept of Educn and Science 1983–94, Avon and Somerset Police Community Fund 1999–2009, Somerset Crimebeat 2000–06, Somerset Community Fndn 2001–07, Somerset St Margaret's Hospice 2005–13; dir Redstone Tst 2007–10; pres Wyvern Sports and Social Club 2010–; govr: Millfield Sch 1985–99, Bridgewater Coll of FE 1994–2002, Somerset Coll 2005–12, Queens Coll Taunton 2010–; hon treas Relate 1998–2001; High Sheriff Somerset 2003–04; Freeman City of London 1990; memb CIPFA 1965; *Books* Financial Management in the 1990s (co-author, 1990); *Recreations* cricket, rugby, golf, squash, antiques, philateley; *Clubs* Sloane; *Style—* Brian Tanner, Esq; ✉ 8 Broadlands Road, Taunton, Somerset TA1 4HQ (☎ 01823 337826, e-mail btanner41@hotmail.com)

T

TANNER, Sir David Whitlock; kt (2013), CBE (2009, OBE 2003); A Douglas Tanner (d 1964), and Connie, *née* Baird (d 2010); *b* 29 December 1947, London; *Educ* Abingdon Sch, Univ of Bristol (BA), Univ of London (PGCE); *Career* teacher and rowing coach; performance dir Br Rowing 1996–, coach men's four Olympic Games 1980, coach men's coxed four Olympic Games 1988, team ldr Rowing Team GB Olympic Games 1992, 1996, 2000, 2004, 2008 and 2012; dep head Greenford HS 1986–87, headmaster Longford Community Sch 1987–96; Freeman City of London 2012, Freeman Co of Watermen and Lightermen 2013; FRSA 1992; *Recreations* theatre, classical music, sport, fine food and wine, history, keeping fit; *Clubs* Leander, London Rowing, Molesey Boat, Remenham; *Style*— Sir David Tanner, CBE; ✉ GB Rowing Team Office, 6 Lower Mall, London W6 9DJ (☎ 020 8237 6769, fax 020 8563 2265, e-mail david.tanner@gbrowingteam.org.uk)

TANNOCK, Dr Charles; MEP (Cons) London; s of Robert Tannock, and Ann, *née* England; *b* 25 September 1957; *Educ* Bradfield Coll Berks, Balliol Coll Oxford (MA), Middx Hosp Medical Sch London (MB BS); *m* 1, 1983 (m dis 1988), Rosa Maria Vega Pizarro, da of Sen Ramon Vega Hidalgo, of Santiago, Chile, and Rosa Pizarro de Vega; 1 s; m 2, 26 Oct 2007, Dr Silvia Janicinova, da of Ing Ivan Janicina and Alena Janicinova, of Bratislava, Slovakia; 2 da, 1 s; *Career* MEP (Cons) London 1999–, substitute memb Economic and Monetary Affrs Ctee of European Parl 1999–2007, substitute memb Environment, Public Health and Consumer Affrs Ctee 1999–2004, memb European Parl-Slovakia Jt Parly Ctee 1999–2004, Cons fin servs spokesman 1999–2002, assistant whip to Cons delgn 2000–02, dep chief whip to Cons delgn 2002–05, memb Foreign Affrs Human Rights and Common Security 2002–, foreign affrs spokesman 2002–; chm: European Parl-Taiwan Friendship Gp 2009, European Parl-Knights of Malta Friendship Gp 2011, European Parl Friends of Kurdistan 2014–; memb European Parl: Russia 2002–09, Ukraine 2002–, Belarus 2002–04, Moldova Delgn 2002–04, Ukraine Delgn 2004–09 (vice-pres), Human Rights Sub-Ctee 2004–; vice-pres European Parl Delgn to NATO Parly Assembly 2009–; co-ordinator ECR Gp on Foreign Affrs Ctee 2009–, cmmr for human rights Cons Pty 2011; house surgn Middlesex Hosp London and house physician Harefield Hosp Harefield 1984–85, psychiatric registrar rotation Charing Cross and Westminster Hospitals W London 1985–88, res fell Charing Cross and Westminster Hosp Med Sch 1988–90, sr registrar rotation UC/Middlesex Hosps 1990–95, conslt psychiatrist and hon sr lectr UCH and Med Sch 1995–; cncllr Royal Borough of Kensington and Chelsea 1998–2000 (former memb of Social Services and Housing Ctee); memb: Chelsea Cons Assoc 1983–, Bow Gp Cncl 1989, Foreign Affairs Forum; vice-chm Kensington Mansions Residents Assoc 1997; fndr memb Concern Against Closure of Long-Stay Mental Hospitals; honorary doctorate Yerevan State Univ Armenia 2013; Freeman City of London 2000; MRCPsych; Commendatore Order of St Maurice and St Lazarus 2000, Presidential Order of Merit of Ukraine 2006, Presidential Medal of Mkhitar Gosh Armenia 2009, Grand Official Order of San Carlos of Colombia 2010, Medal of Honour Legislative Yuan of Taiwan 2011, Presidential Order of Excellence of Georgia 2013, Order of the Brilliant Star of Taiwan (Repub of China) 2014; *Publications* Community Care – The Need for Action (1989), AIDS Dementia – A Policy Rethink (1989), A Marriage of Convenience – or Reform of the Community Charge (1991); extensive publications in medical literature; *Recreations* travel, family; *Style*— Dr Charles Tannock, MEP; ✉ 44a Southern Row, London W10 5BN (☎ 020 8962 1286, e-mail charles@charlestannock.com)

TANQUERAY, David Andrew; s of David Yeo Bartholomew Tanqueray (d 1944), and Majorie Edith, *née* Macdonald (d 2006); *b* 23 May 1939; *Educ* Rugby, Clare Coll Cambridge (MA), Univ of Calif Berkeley; *m* 20 Aug 1966, Tamsin Mary, da of Air Cdre Cyril Montague Heard; 2 da (Venetia b 1974, Tabitha b 1977), 1 s (David b 1981); *Career* conslt: Control Data Ltd 1969–84, Floating Point Systems UK Ltd 1985–91, Silicon Graphics UK Ltd 1992–2000, Cray UK Ltd 2000–10; awarded Harkness Fellowship 1966; *Recreations* music, amateur dramatics; *Style*— David Tanqueray, Esq; ✉ 27 Cheriton Avenue, Twyford, Berkshire RG10 9DB (☎ 0118 934 1544)

TANSEY, Rock Benedict; QC (1990); *Educ* Univ of Bristol (LLB, Dip Social Studies); *m* 10 Oct 1964, Wendy Jennifer Ann, *née* Carver; 3 c; *Career* called to the Bar Lincoln's Inn 1966 (bencher 2004), recorder of the Crown Court 1995–2005, memb 25 Bedford Row London (head of chambers until 2009); hon chm European Criminal Bar Assoc, chm European Criminal Bar Assoc of Defence Advocates (ECBA) 1996–2003; memb Criminal Bar Assoc; *Recreations* theatre, golf, travel; *Style*— Rock Tansey, Esq, QC; ✉ 25 Bedford Row, London WC1R 4HD (☎ 020 7067 1500, fax 020 7067 1507)

TANT, Russell Byron; s of Melvyn John Tant (d 1970), and Sadie Jacobs (d 1989); *b* 20 March 1949; *Educ* Orange Hill Co GS, UCH London (BDS, capt UCH CC); *m* 1, 1981 (m dis 1990), Elizabeth Mary Lorimer; 2 s (Radleigh Lewis Byron b 6 Oct 1983, Sebastian Charles Russell b 5 July 1985); m 2, 29 Oct 1994, Katrina Rushton; 2 da (Emilie Charlotte Maris b 3 April 1992, Mollie Briony Patricia b 11 March 1996); *Career* gen dental practice Knightsbridge 1972–76, commenced practice Harpenden Herts 1978, fully private practice Wimpole Street 1985, specialist in endodontics; pres London Dental Study Club 1983; *Recreations* cricket, golf, skiing, squash, music; *Clubs* MCC, Royal Cinque Ports Golf, Harpenden Golf; *Style*— Russell Tant, Esq

TANTAM, Prof Digby John Howard; s of Donald Harry Tantam (d 1993), and Daphne, *née* Winterbone (d 2011); *b* 15 March 1948; *Educ* St Paul's, Univ of Oxford (MA, BM BCh), Harvard Univ (MPH), Univ of London (PhD), Open Univ (BA); *m* m 1, 1 s (Robert John Geoffrey b 1978), 1 da (Grace Ruth b 1980); m 2, 1 August 1998, Emma, da of Arie Marinus van Deurzen; *Career* St George's Hosp 1974–75, Harvard Med Sch 1976–77, Maudsley Hosp 1977–83, Dept of Psychiatry Univ of Manchester 1983–90, prof of psychotherapy Univ of Warwick 1990–95, clinical prof of psychotherapy Univ of Sheffield 1995–2011 (emeritus prof 2011–); hon sr visiting research fell Univ of Cambridge 2008–16, visiting prof Middlesex Univ 2016–; dir Septimus Gp of Cos 2000–; memb Inst of Group Analysis; FRCPsych, FBPsS, fell Br Assoc of Counselling and Psychology 2007, fell UK Cncl for Psychotherapy 2008, FHEA; *Books* Making Sense of Psychiatric Cases (with M Greenberg and G Szmukler, 1986), A Mind of One's Own (1988, 2 edn 1991), Public Health Impact of Mental Disorder (with D Goldberg, 1990), College Seminars in Psychology and Social Science (with M Birchwood), Psychiatry for the Developing World (with A Duncan and L Appleby), Clinical Topics in Psychotherapy (1998), Psychotherapy and Counselling in Practice (2002), Narratives in Psychiatry (with M Greenberg, S Shergill and G Szmukler, 2002), Understanding Repeated Self-Injury (with N Huband, 2009), Can The World Afford Autistic Spectrum Disorder? (2009), Autism Spectrum Disorder through the Lifespan (2012), Emotional Well-being and Mental Health: A Guide for Counsellors and Psychotherapists (2014); *Recreations* cycling, reading, cooking, gardening, philosophy; *Style*— Prof Digby Tantam; ✉ Dilemma Consultancy, 61–63 Fortune Green Road, London NW6 1DR (☎ 020 7435 8067, e-mail digby@dilemmas.org, website www.dilemmas.org)

TAPLEY, (David) Mark; s of John Randolph Tapley (d 1972), of Stafford, and Nancy Doris Rathbone (d 1986); *b* 24 March 1946; *Educ* King Edward VI Sch Stafford, Oriel Coll Oxford (BA), London Business Sch (MBA); *m* April 1970, Judith Ann, da of Basil Wilford, of Stafford; 1 da (Charlotte Emily b June 1977), 1 s (Richard Paul b March 1979); *Career* systems engr ICL 1969–72, investment analyst and portfolio mangr JP Morgan 1974–84 (vice-pres 1982), dir of equities American Express Asset Mgmnt (later Shearson Lehman Global Asset Mgmnt and Posthorn Global Asset Mgmnt) 1984–90, and chief investment offr WestLB Asset Mgmnt (UK) Ltd 1991–2000; visiting fell Cranfield Sch of Mgmnt 2000–; regular speaker at conferences seminars and trg courses on devpts in investment mgmnt industry; chm Henderson Eurotrust plc, dir CFA Soc of UK; investment advsr Lloyd's Register; exec dir Hedge Fund Centre London Business Sch; Chartered Fin Analyst 1980; AIIMR 1976; *Books* International Portfolio Management (ed and contrib 1986); *Recreations* walking, bridge; *Style*— Mark Tapley, Esq

TAPNER, (Nicholas) Rory; s of John W Tapner, and Cherry, *née* Moreton; *b* 30 September 1959, London; *Educ* Radley, KCL (LLB); *m* 15 Oct 1988, Alex, *née* Boldero; 2 s (Freddie b 29 Oct 1990, Arthur b 14 July 2000), 2 da (Anna b 6 Sept 1992, Rosie b 16 Oct 1995); *Career* Rowe & Pitman 1983, S G Warburg 1986, global head of equity capital markets SBC 1995; UBS: global of head equity capital markets 1998, jt global head of investment banking 1999, chm and ceo Asia Pacific 2004, memb Gp Exec Bd 2006; ceo Coutts Wealth Div RBS 2010–15, chm Coutts Fndn 2014–; chm: Sanctum Wealth (India) 2016–, Intelligent Engineering 2016; chm British Ski & Snowboard 2015–; King's College London: FKC, hon treas; *Recreations* golf, skiing, collecting English clocks and watercolours; *Style*— Rory Tapner, Esq; ✉ Coutts, 440 Strand, London WC2R 0QS

TAPP, Richard; *Educ* Univ of Sheffield (LLB), Univ of Leicester (LLM), Nottingham Law Sch (MBA); *Career* trainee slr and asst slr Nat Coal Bd 1981–85, asst slr Imperial Foods Ltd 1985–86; Blue Circle Industries plc: commercial slr 1986–91, princ slr 1992–96, co sec and head of gp legal and secretariat 1996–2001; co sec and dir of legal servs Carillion plc 2001–; MCIArb, FCIS 1992, FRSA; *Style*— Richard Tapp, Esq; ✉ Carillion plc, Birch Street, Wolverhampton WV1 4HP (☎ 01902 316334, fax 01902 316340, e-mail rtapp@carillionplc.com)

TAPPER, Prof Colin Frederick Herbert; s of Herbert Frederick Tapper (d 1977), and Florence, *née* Lambard (d 1976); *b* 13 October 1934; *Educ* Bishopshalt GS, Magdalen Coll Oxford (Vinerian scholar); *m* 1 April 1961, Margaret, da of Harold White (d 1978); 1 da (Lucy b 22 Jan 1973); *Career* called to the Bar Gray's Inn 1961; lectr LSE 1959–65; Univ of Oxford: fell Magdalen Coll 1965–2002 (vice-pres 1991–92), reader in law All Souls 1979–92, univ prof of law 1992–2002, emeritus fell 2002–; visiting prof: Univ of Alabama and Univ of NY 1970, Stanford Univ 1976, Monash Univ 1984, Univ of Northern Kentucky 1986, Univ of Sydney 1989, Univ of Western Aust 1991; dir: Butterworth 1979–85, Butterworth Telepublishing 1979–90; conslt: Butterworths 1968–90, Pinsent Masons (Solicitors) 1990–2003; *Books* Computers and The Law (1973), Computer Law (1978, 4 edn 1990), Cross and Tapper on Evidence (12 edn 2010); *Recreations* reading, writing, computing; *Style*— Prof Colin Tapper; ✉ Corner Cottage, Woodstock Road, Stonesfield, Witney, Oxfordshire OX29 8QA (☎ 01993 891284); Magdalen College, Oxford OX1 4AU (☎ 01865 276055, fax 01865 276103, e-mail colin.tapper@magd.ox.ac.uk)

TAPPER, Jaimie; *b* British Columbia; *Educ* Nat Ballet Sch Canada; *Career* ballet dancer; first soloist Nat Ballet of Canada 1999 (joined 1994), princ Royal Ballet 2002– (joined 1999); Erik Bruhn Prize 1995; *Performances* with Nat Ballet of Canada incl: Giselle, Juliet, Swanilda, Odette/Odile, Aurora, Lescaut's Mistress, A Month in the Country, The Leaves Are Fading, Spring The Four Seasons (Kudelka); with Royal Ballet incl: Swanilda, Sugar Plum Fairy, Gamzatti, Nikiya, Aurora, Tatiana, Giselle, Manon, Marie Larisch, Terpsichore, Myrtha, M in Carmen, Cinderella, Chloë, L'Hiver in Les Saisons, roles in Triad, Song of the Earth, Agon, The Vertiginous Thrill of Exactitude, Symphonic Variations, Les Biches, Raymonda Act III, Gloria, The Four Temperaments, There Where She Loves; *Style*— Ms Jaimie Tapper; ✉ c/o The Royal Ballet, Royal Opera House, Covent Garden, London WC2E 9DD

TAPPIN, Andrew Brice; s of late Walter Philip Tappin, and late Daphne Mary, *née* Brice; *b* 27 January 1945; *Educ* Willington Sch, Stamford Sch, Tiffin Sch; *m* 4 Sept 1971, Barbara Jane, da of late Clive Edward Midwinter; 1 s (Rupert Clive b 22 Feb 1972), 1 da (Laura Rachel b 22 Oct 1974); *Career* chartered accountant; Annan Dexter & Co 1967–71 (articled clerk 1963–67); ptnr: Dearden Lord Annan Morrish 1972, Dearden Farrow (after merger) 1977, BDO Binder Hamlyn (after merger) 1987–94, conslt Arthur Andersen 1994–98, princ Andrew B Tappin 1999–; memb Soc of Tst and Estate Practitioners; FCA 1977 (ACA 1967); *Books* Capital Transfer Tax Planning (jtly, 1975), Financial Planning for Clients (jtly, 1979); *Recreations* France, squash, running; *Style*— Andrew Tappin, Esq; ✉ 34 Wallorton Gardens, East Sheen, London SW14 8DX (☎ 020 8287 8825, fax 020 8711 2579, e-mail andrew.tappin@blueyonder.co.uk)

TAPPIN, Michael; s of Thomas Ernest Tappin (d 2003), of Hendon, and Eileen Sarah, *née* Kitson (d 2010); *b* 22 December 1946; *Educ* Moat Mount Secdy Modern, Harrow Tech Coll, Univ of Essex, LSE, Univ of Strathclyde; *m* Oct 1971, Angela Florence, da of Douglas Murray Reed (d 2011); 1 da (Abigail Sarah b 3 September 1977), 1 s (Thomas Edward Michael b 7 Jan 1984); *Career* lectr in American politics Keele Univ 1974–94 and 1999–2010 (pt/t lectr 1994–99), ret; chm and md Hartsluz Ltd (Property and Consultancy) 2009–; MEP (Lab) Staffordshire W and Congleton 1994–99; European Parl: memb Budget Ctee 1994–99, memb Budget Control Ctee 1995–99, substitute memb Economic and Monetary Affrs Ctee 1994–99, substitute memb Delgn with US 1994–99, chm Ceramic Inter-Group 1995–99, PSE co-ordinator Budget Control Ctee 1996–99; memb: Staffordshire CC 1981–97 (chm Planning Ctee 1985–89, chm Enterprise and Econ Devpt Ctee 1989–94), Stoke-on-Trent City Cncl 2004–08 (ldr 2007–08); chm W Midlands Forum of Local Authorities 1993–94, chm South Stoke Primary Care Tst 2001–06, dep chm Staffordshire Devpt Assoc 1989–94, memb Bd N Staffs Regeneration Zone 2007–08; Stoke-on-Trent Local Strategic Partnership: chair Health Wellbeing Gp 2002–05, chair Employment Gp 2005–08, vice-chair Resources Ctee 2005–06; memb Elected Mayors Advsy Panel 2006–08 (ldr Lab Gp 2007–08), memb Stoke-on-Trent Transformation Bd 2008–10; fell Keele Univ 2010–; *Books* American Politics Today (jtly, 1981, 1985, 1989, revised edn 1991); *Recreations* walking, theatre, cinema, reading, music, guitar; *Clubs* Potters; *Style*— Michael Tappin, Esq; ✉ 63 Moorcroft Avenue, Westbury Park, Newcastle-Under-Lyme, Staffordshire ST5 4HQ (☎ and fax 01782 946117, mobile 07977 944561, e-mail michaeltappin@yahoo.com)

TAPSELL, Rt Hon Sir Peter Hannay Bailey; kt (1985), PC (2011); s of late Eustace Tapsell, and late Jessie, *née* Hannay; *b* 1 February 1930; *Educ* Tonbridge, Merton Coll Oxford (MA); *m* 1, 1963 (m dis 1971), Hon Cecilia, 3 da of 9 Baron Hawke; 1 s (decd); m 2, 1974, Gabrielle, da of late Jean Mahieu, of Normandy, France; *Career* Nat Serv Subaltern The Royal Sussex Regt Middle East 1948–50, hon life memb 6 Sqdn RAF 1971; librarian Oxford Union 1953 (rep on debating tour of USA 1954); Cons Res Dept (Social Servs and Agric) 1954–57 (PA to PM Anthony Eden 1955 Gen Election Campaign), memb London Stock Exchange 1957–90, int investment advsr to several central banks, foreign banks and trading cos; memb Business Advsy Cncl to UNO 2001–06; Parly candidate (Cons) Wednesbury by-election 1957; MP (Cons): Nottingham W 1959–64, Horncastle 1966–83, Lindsey E 1983–97, Louth and Horncastle 1997–2015; oppn front bench spokesman on: foreign and Cwlth affrs 1976–77, Treasy and econ affrs 1977–78, Father of the House of Commons 2010–15; chm Coningsby Club 1957–58, jt chm Br Caribbean Assoc 1963–64; memb: Cncl Inst for Fiscal Studies 1979–2005, Trilateral Cmmn 1979–98, Organising Ctee Zaïre River Expedition 1974–75, Ct Univ of Nottingham 1959–64, Ct Univ of Hull 1966–85; hon memb Investment Advsy Bd Brunei Govt 1976–83, Brunei Dato 1971; vice-pres Tennyson Soc 1966–2015, hon dep chm Mitsubishi Tst Oxford Fndn 1988–2014, hon fell Merton Coll Oxford 1989 (hon postmaster 1953); Back-bencher of the Year Spectator 1993, Parliamentarian of the Year Spectator 2004; *Recreations* travel, walking in mountains, reading history; *Clubs* Athenaeum, Carlton, Hurlingham, RAC; *Style*— The Rt Hon Sir Peter Tapsell; ✉ House of Commons, London SW1A 0AA (☎ 020 7219 3000)

TARENTO, Danielle Claire; da of Jacques Tarento, of Adelaide, Aust, and Julia, *née* Pullen; *b* 31 December 1972, London; *Educ* Sutton HS, Guildhall Sch of Music and Drama (BA); *Career* theatre prodr; actress 1994–2004, co-fndr Menier Chocolate Factory (jt artistic dir 2004–06); artistic dir King's Head Theatre 2008–09, freelance prodr 2009–; Peter Brook Empty Space Award for New Venue 2005, Evening Standard Milton Shulman Award for Outstanding Newcomer 2005, Whatsonstage Award for Best Off West End Production 2005, 2006, 2013 and 2014, Off West End Awards for Best New Musical and Best Prodr 2012 and Best Musical Production 2014; *Recreations* theatre, cinema, eating out; *Style*— Miss Danielle Tarento; ✉ e-mail danielle@tarento.net

TARRANT, Christopher John (Chris); OBE (2004); s of Maj B A Tarrant, MC (d 2005), and Joan Ellen, *née* Cox (d 2012); *b* 10 October 1946; *Educ* King's Sch Worcester, Univ of Birmingham (BA); *m* 1, 1977 (m dis 1982), Sheila Margaret, da of Maj Ralph Roberton (d 1982); 2 da (Helen Victoria, Jennifer Mary); *m* 2, 1991 (m dis 2008), Ingrid, da of Frederick Henry (Jimmy) Dupré de St Maur (d 1996); 1 da (Samantha Charlotte), 1 s (Toby Charles); *Career* prodr/writer/presenter of TV progs incl: ATV Today 1972, Tiswas 1974, OTT 1981, Everybody's Equal 1989, Tarrant on Television 1989–, The Main Event 1993, Lose a Million 1993, Pop Quiz 1994, Man O Man 1996, Who Wants to be a Millionaire 1998–2014, Tarrant on Top of the World: In Search of the Polar Bear 2005; presenter: Capital Radio's Breakfast Show 1987–2004, The Chris Tarrant Radio Show Smooth FM 2008–09, Colour of Money 2009, Radio 2 2010–; patron: Phoenix Centre for Handicapped Children, Children with Cancer, Lord's Taverners (pres 2009); *Awards* incl: Best On-Air Personality Int Radio Festival of NY 1987, TRIC Radio Personality of the Year 1989, Sony Radio Awards Radio Personality of the Year 1990, Variety Club of GB Independent Radio Personality of the Year 1991, Sony Radio Awards Silver Medal 1992 and 1993, Sony Radio Awards Best Breakfast Show 1995, NY World Awards Best Breakfast Show 1996, Variety Club of GB ITV Personality of the Year 1998, Broadcasting Press Guild Television Awards Best TV Performer in a Non-Acting Role 1999, Nat TV Awards Special Recognition Award 2000, TV People's Choice Award Best Game Show 2000, ITV Lifetime Achievement Award 2000, Nat TV Awards Best Game Show 2000, 2001, 2002, 2003 and 2005, GQ Magazine Light Entertainment Show of the Year 2000, TV Quick Light Entertainment Show of the Year 2000, Disney Channel Kids' Award Best Children's TV Show 2000, Sony Radio Industry Gold Award 2001, Radio Acad Lifetime Achievement Award 2002, Commercial Radio Lifetime Achievement Award 2013; *Books* Ken's Furry Friends (1986), Fishfriar's Hall Revisited (1987), Ready Steady Go (1990), Rebel Rebel (1991), Tarrant Off the Record (1997), Netty Nutters (1999), Tarrant on Millionaires (1999), Millionaire Moments (2002), Tarrant on Top of the World: In Search of the Polar Bear (2005), Dad's War (2014); *Recreations* fishing, cricket; *Clubs* White Swan Piscatorials, Red Spinners, The Nth Degree, Ivy; *Style*— Chris Tarrant, Esq, OBE; ✉ c/o Paul Vaughan, PV Media Ltd, County House, St Mary's Street, Worcester WR1 1HB (☎ 01905 616100, fax 01905 610709, e-mail md@pvmedia.co.uk)

TATCHELL, Peter Gary; s of Gordon Basil Tatchell, of Melbourne, Aust, and Mardi Aileen Nitscke, *née* Rhodes; *b* 25 January 1952, Melbourne, Aust; *Educ* Mount Waverley HS Melbourne, West London Coll (Dip), Poly of N London (BSc); *Career* human rights campaigner, co-organiser of LGBT human rights gp OutRage! 1990–2012, freelance journalist and author; sec Christians for Peace 1970–71, exec Vietnam Moratorium Campaign 1971, activist Gay Liberation Front 1971–73, chair Rockingham Estate Tenants' Assoc 1980–81, sec Southwark and Bermondsey Lab Party 1980–85, co-ordinator UK AIDS Vigil Orgn 1987–89, co-organiser Green & Socialists Confs 1987–89, activist ACT UP London 1989–91; Parly candidate (Lab) Bermondsey (by-election) 1983, London Assembly candidate (Ind Green Left) 2000; memb: Republic 2002–, Green Party 2004–; human rights spokesperson Green Party 2007–15; dir Peter Tatchell Fndn 2011–; Campaigner of the Year Observer Ethical Award 2009, Southwark Blue Plaque 2010, Irwin Prize Secularist of the Year 2012, Lifetime Achievement Nat Diversity Award 2012, Attitude Awards Icon Award for Outstanding Achievement 2012, Lifetime Achievement Award Out in the City & G3 Awards 2013; Hon DLitt Univ of Sussex 2010, Hon LLD London S Bank Univ 2011, Hon Dr of Law De Montfort Univ 2014; Hon Fellowship Goldsmiths Coll Univ of London 2014; The Battle for Bermondsey (1983), Democratic Defence: A Non-Nuclear Alternative (1985), AIDS: A Guide to Survival (1986, 3 edn 1990), Europe in the Pink: Lesbian & Gay Equality in the New Europe (1992), Safer Sexy: The Guide to Gay Sex Safely (1994), We Don't Want to March Straight: Masculinity, Queers & the Military (1995); contrib: Nuclear-Free Defence (1983), Into the Twenty-First Century (1988), Getting There: Steps to a Green Society (1990), Anti-Gay (1996), The Penguin Book of Twentieth Century Protest (1998), Teenage Sex: What Should Schools Teach Children? (2002), The Hate Debate: Should Hate be Punished as a Crime? (2002), Sex & Politics in South Africa (2005), Second Thoughts on the Family (2008), 50 Voices of Disbelief – Why We Are Atheists (2009), Good Company – Ideas on Modern Republicanism (2009), The Meaning of Matrimony – Debating Same-Sex Marriage (2013), The Alphabet Club Anthology Book (2016); *Recreations* mountain hiking, surfing, art and design, ambushing tyrants and torturers; *Clubs* Heaven; *Style*— Peter Tatchell; ✉ Peter Tatchell Foundation, Studio 5, Disney Place House, 14 Marshalsea Road, London SE1 1HL (☎ 020 3397 2190, e-mail peter@petertatchellfoundation.org, website www.petertatchell.net, Twitter @petertatchell)

TATE, Catherine; *Educ* Central Sch of Speech and Drama; *Career* actor and writer; *Theatre* incl: All My Sons (Oxford Theatre Co), The Princes Play (NT), The Way of the World (NT), Catherine Tate Show (Soho Theatre London and Pleasance Theatre Edinburgh), A Servant to Two Masters (RSC, West End and world tour), Some Girl(s) (Gielgud Theatre), The Exonerated (Lyric Hammersmith), Under the Blue Sky (Duke of York), Season's Greetings (NT), Much Ado About Nothing (Wyndham's Theatre), Assassins (Menier Chocolate Factory), The Vote (Donmar Warehouse); *Television* incl: Big Train (BBC), Wild West (BBC), The Catherine Tate Show (BBC), The Bad Mother's Handbook (ITV), Dr Who (BBC), Nan's Christmas Carol (BBC), Catherine Tate's Nan (BBC), The Office: An American Workplace (NBC), Big School (BBC); *Film* incl: Love and Other Disasters, Starter for Ten, Scenes of a Sexual Nature, 66, Mrs Ratcliffe's Revolution, Gulliver's Travels, SuperBob, Nativity 3; *Style*— Ms Catherine Tate; ✉ c/o Dawn Sedgwick Management, 3 Goodwins Court, London WC2N 4LL (☎ 020 7240 0404, fax 020 7240 0415, e-mail office@dawnsedgwickmanagement.com)

TATE, David Read; s of Maurice Tate, of Penarth, S Glamorgan, and Florence, *née* Read; *b* 10 February 1955; *Educ* Penarth GS, Jesus Coll Oxford (MA), UCL (MSc), INSEAD Paris (AMP); *m* Karen Patricia, *née* Rogers; 1 da (Francesca Claire Sian), 1 s (Matthew James Rhys); *Career* Deloitte Haskins & Sells CAs 1977–83 (Mgmnt Consultancy Div 1980–83), Barclays de Zoete Wedd Ltd 1983–90 (dir 1987–90), dir Corporate Fin Div West Merchant Bank Ltd 1990–98, exec dir and head of princ investments WestLB Panmure Ltd 1998–2004, ptnr Nova Capital Gp 2004–06, fndr and managing ptnr Tempo Capital Ptnrs LLP 2006–11, managing ptnr Draper Esprit Secondaries LLP 2012–; FCA 1992 (ACA 1980), FRSA; *Recreations* golf, hill walking, opera, music; *Clubs* Royal Porthcawl Golf, Royal Blackheath Golf, Oxford and Cambridge; *Style*— David R Tate, Esq; ✉ Draper Esprit Secondaries LLP, 23 Hanover Square, London W1S 1JB (☎ 020 3102 4718, e-mail david.tate@draperesprit-secondaries.com)

TATE, Dr Jeffrey Philip; CBE (1990); s of Cyril Henry Tate, of Odiham, Hants, and Ivy Ellen, *née* Naylor; *b* 28 April 1943; *Educ* Farnham GS, Christ's Coll Cambridge (MA, MB BChir), St Thomas' Hosp London; *Career* trained as doctor of med St Thomas' Hosp London 1961–67, left medicine to join London Opera Centre 1969, joined Covent Garden staff 1970, assisted conductors incl Kempe, Krips, Solti, Davies and Kleiber 1973–77; later assisted: Boulez (Bayreuth Ring) 1976–81, Sir John Pritchard (Cologne Opera) 1977; conducted Gothenburg Opera Sweden 1978–80; NY Met Opera debut USA 1979, Covent Garden debut 1982, Salzburg Festival debut 1985; princ conductor English Chamber Orch 1985–; princ guest conductor: French Nat Radio Orch 1989–, Royal Opera House Covent Garden 1991–94 (princ conductor 1986–91), Orchestra Nazionale di RAI Italia 1998–; music dir Rotterdam Philharmonic Orch 1991–94, chief conductor Minnesota Orch Summer Festival 1997–; pres: Assoc for Spina Bifida and Hydrocephalus, Music Space; patron Br Lung Fndn, tstee Firebird Tst; hon fell Christ's Coll Cambridge 1989, hon fell St Thomas' and Guy's Hosp Med Sch 1994; Hon DMus Univ of Leicester 1993; Officier de l'Ordre des Arts et des Lettres (France) 1990, Chev Ordre Nationale de la Légion d'Honneur 1999; *Recreations* reading, looking at the world going by, a bit of gastronomy; *Style*— Dr Jeffrey Tate, CBE; ✉ c/o English Chamber Orchestra, 2 Coningsby Road, London W5 4HR (☎ 020 8840 6565, fax 020 8567 7198)

TATE, (William) John; s of William Kenneth Tate (d 1961), and Dorothy, *née* Pinfold (d 2012); *b* 12 June 1951; *Educ* Eastcliffe GS Newcastle upon Tyne, KCL (LLB), Inns of Court Sch of Law; *m* 1976, Helen Elizabeth, da of late Alfred Quick; 1 s (Nicholas b 1981), 1 da (Sarah b 1982); *Career* called to the bar Gray's Inn 1974, in practice 1974–76, Flt Lt Legal Dept RAF 1976–78, Slr's Office HM Customs & Excise 1978–88, asst dir Serious Fraud Office 1988–96, dep Parly Cmmr for administration and legal advsr 1996–99, slr to Bloody Sunday Inquiry 1999–2003, dir of legal services Independent Police Complaints Cmmn 2003–09, ret; non-exec dir: NHS Kingston PCT 2007–10, First Community Health and Care CIC 2011–12; non-exec chair Your Healthcare CIC 2010–14, ret; lay Cncl memb Gen Social Care Cncl 2009–12, chair of specialist schs NHS London Deanery 2010–14; memb Hon Soc of Gray's Inn 1974; *Books* Current Law (delegated legislation ed, 1975–95); *Recreations* rowing, music, modern history, gardening; *Clubs* RAF; *Style*— John Tate, Esq

TATE, Dr (Edward) Nicholas; CBE (2001); s of Joseph Edwin Tate (d 2015), and Eva Elsie, *née* Hopkinson (d 1987); *b* 18 December 1943; *Educ* Huddersfield New Coll, Balliol Coll Oxford (MA), Univ of Liverpool (MA, PhD), Univ of Bristol (PGCE); *m* 1973, Nadya, *née* Grove; 2 da (Emily Sarah b 1974, Harriet Louisa b 1976), 1 s (Oliver Lucian b 1985); *Career* asst master De La Salle Coll Sheffield 1966–71, lectr City of Birmingham Coll of Educn 1972–74, sr lectr Moray House Coll of Educn Edinburgh (joined as lectr) 1974–88, professional offr Nat Curriculum Cncl 1989–91, asst chief exec Sch Examinations and Assessment Cncl 1991–93, chief exec Sch Curriculum and Assessment Authy 1994–97 (asst chief exec 1993–94), chief exec Qualifications and Curriculum Authy 1997–2000, headmaster Winchester Coll 2000–03, DG The Int Sch of Geneva 2003–11, chm Int Educn Systems 2011–13; memb: Bd Int Schs Assoc 2005–10, Bd of Govrs Int Baccalaureate 2009–15, Haut Conseil de l'evaluation de l'école (France) 2000–05; tstee Nat Tst 1996–99, tstee Richmond The American Int Univ in London 2008–; Hon DCL Univ of Huddersfield 1998; *Books* Pizarro and the Incas (1982), Modern World History (1988), People and Events in the Modern World (1988), A History of the Modern World (1994), What is Education For? (2015); *Clubs* Reform; *Style*— Dr Nicholas Tate, CBE; ✉ e-mail nick@nicholastate.com

TATEOSSIAN, Robert; *Educ* Wharton Sch, Univ of Pennsylvania (BA, BSc); *Career* jewellery designer; with Investment Banking Div Merrill Lynch Int 1985–90; prop Tateossian Ltd 1990–; British Export Fashion Award 1995 and 2000; *Style*— Robert Tateossian, Esq; ✉ Suite 3, Fulham Business Exchange, The Boulevard, Imperial Wharf, London SW6 2TL (☎ 020 7384 8300, fax 020 7384 8333, mobile 07768 698635, e-mail robert@tateossian.com)

TATHAM, Amanda Jane; da of Christopher Tatham, MW, of Winchester, Hants, and Regine, *née* Legge; *b* 13 March 1953; *Educ* St Paul's Girls' Sch, London Coll of Printing (BA), Sivananda Yoga Teachers' Training Cert, Centre for Psycotherapy and Counselling Educn Fndn Course (CCPE) and CCPE Y1 Dip; *m* 1997 (sep), Rupert Wollheim; 2 s (Oscar b 1994, Otto b 1998); *Career* graphic designer asst to Alan Fletcher Pentagram Design 1975–79, fndr Amanda Tatham Design Ltd 1979–84, fndr ptnr Lambton Place Design 1984–87, co-fndr and ptnr Tatham Pearce Ltd 1987–96, fndr Tatham Design Ltd 1996, fndr dir Designer Breakfasts 2006; graphic design (corp and brand identities, packaging, brochures, websites and annual reports) for clients incl: Barclays, Cushman & Wakefield Inc, Inst of Masters of Wine, Lloyds Bank, Next, PricewaterhouseCoopers, Royal Mail, Summerdown Pure Mint; Communication Arts Award for Design Excellence, Spicer & Oppenheim Effective Finance Communications Award, Stock Exchange & Chartered Accountants' Annual Award for Smaller Companies' Published Accounts, Business Link for London selected best design project, nomination D&AD Pencil Award for Royal Mail Magic! stamps; memb: Design Business Assoc (Cncl of Mgmnt 1988–90), D&AD 1978; fndr Nadayoga 2015, teacher Sivananda Yoga Centre London; memb Complementary Therapists Assoc 2015; FCSD 1986–2015 (memb Cncl 1990–93 and 2003–04), FRSA 1992; *Recreations* yoga and meditation, nature, vegetarian food; *Style*— Ms Amanda Tatham; ✉ 4 Phillimore Gardens, London W3 9AY (e-mail amanda@tathamdesign.co.uk and amanda@nadayoga.co.uk, website www.tathamdesign.co.uk and www.designerbreakfasts.net)

TATTERSALL, Geoffrey Frank; QC (1992); s of late Frank Tattersall, of Ashton-under-Lyne, and Margaret, *née* Hassall; *b* 22 September 1947; *Educ* Manchester Grammar, ChCh Oxford (exhibitioner, MA), Lincoln's Inn (Tancred studentship in common law); *m* 7 Aug 1971, Hazel, da of late Harold Shaw, and late Alice Shaw; 1 s (Mark b 13 Sept 1976), 2 da (Victoria Louise b 5 April 1979, Hannah Jayne b 12 Nov 1984); *Career* called to the Bar Lincoln's Inn 1970 (bencher 1997), in practice N Circuit 1970–, recorder 1989–, judge of appeal Isle of Man 1997–, dep judge of the High Court 2003–; called to the Bar NSW 1992, sc 1995; lay chm Bolton Deanery Synod 1993–2002, chm House of Laity and vice-pres Manchester Diocesan Synod 1994–2003, memb Gen Synod 1995– (chm Standing Orders Ctee 1999–, memb Legislative Ctee 2010–, memb Panel of Chm 2011–16), hon lay canon Manchester Cathedral 2003, chllr Dio of Carlisle 2003–, dep chllr Dio of Durham 2003–05, chllr Dio of Manchester 2004–, dep vicar-gen Dio of Sodor and Man 2004–08, 2011 and 2014–15, vicar-gen Dio of Sodor and Man 2015–; chm: Disciplinary Tbnls under Clergy Discipline Measure 2006–, Revision Ctees for draft C of E Marriage Measure 2006–07, Revision Ctee for draft C of E Ecclesiastical Offices Measure 2007–08, draft Convocations (Elections to Upper House (amendment)), Clergy Representation Rules (amendment) and Church Representation Rules (amendment) Resolution 2014, draft Safeguarding and Clergy Discipline Measure 2015, draft Mission and Pastoral etc (amendment) Measure 2016; memb Steering Ctee for draft C of E Bishops and Priests (Consecration and Ordination of Women) Measure 2009–12; external reviewer of decisions of Dir of Fair Access 2005–13; parish clerk St George-in-the-East 2008–; memb Worshipful Co of Parish Clerks 2009; *Recreations* family, music, travel; *Clubs* Nobody's Friends; *Style*— Geoffrey Tattersall, QC; ✉ 12 Byrom Street, Manchester M3 4PP (☎ 0161 829 2100); 5 Essex Court, Temple, London EC4Y 9AH (☎ 020 7410 2000)

TATTERSALL, Rev John Hartley; s of Robert Herman Tattersall (d 1958), of Conwy, Gwynedd, and Jean, *née* Stevens (d 1995); *b* 5 April 1952; *Educ* Shrewsbury, Christ's Coll Cambridge (MA); *m* 8 Sept 1984, Madeleine Virginia, da of Robert Edward Hugh Coles, of Caversham, Berks; 2 s (Robert b 1985, Luke 1987), 1 da (Clare b 1990); *Career* ptnr PricewaterhouseCoopers (formerly Coopers & Lybrand before merger) 1985–2009 (joined 1975), dir Bradford & Bingley plc 2010– (chm 2016–); chm Risk and Regulation Ctee ICAEW Financial Services Faculty 2007–09; memb: Banking Sub-Ctee ICAEW 1989–

2007, Capital Ctee Securities and Futures Authy 1993–2001, Prudential Sourcebook Advsy Gp FSA 2000–06, Bd Gibraltar Financial Services Cmmn 2009–15 (chm 2014–15), Ind Cmmn on the Equitable Life Payments Scheme 2010–11, CEO Advsy Ctee The Children's Soc 2015–; dir: London City Ballet Trust Ltd 1987–96 (dep chm 1995–96), English Touring Opera Ltd 1998–2010, South East Inst for Theological Educn 2004– (treas 2010–), R Raphael & Sons plc 2009–16, UK Asset Resolution Ltd 2010– (chm 2016–), NRAM Ltd 2010– (chm 2016–), CCLA Investment Mgmnt Ltd 2011–, UBS Ltd 2011– (chm 2016–); chm and dir: Retail Charity Bonds plc 2014–, RC Bond Holdings Ltd 2014–; advsy govr St Augustine's Priory Ealing 1995–2002, tstee Swalcliffe Park Sch 2011–, chm Oxford Diocesan Bd of Finance 2014–; memb Ct Royal Fndn of St Katharine 2009– (treas 2010–12, chm 2012–); ordained: deacon 2007, priest 2008; asst curate Wykeham Benefice Oxon 2007–; Liveryman Worshipful Co of Int Bankers 2006; FCA 1989 (ACA 1978); *Books* Towards a Welfare World (jtly, 1973), The Investment Business – Compliance with the Rules (1990), Current Issues in Auditing (contrib, 1997), A Practitioner's Guide to FSA Regulation of Banking (ed, 2002 and 2006), A Practitioner's Guide to the Basel Accord (ed, 2005), Towards a Framework for Financial Stability (contrib, 2009); *Recreations* walking, opera, ballet; *Clubs* Athenaeum; *Style—* The Rev John Tattersall; ✉ 3 St Ann's Villas, Holland Park, London W11 4RU (☎ 020 7603 1053, e-mail jhtatters@aol.com)

TATTERSFIELD, Dr Brian; s of Norman Tattersfield (d 1959), and Marian, *née* Rogers; *b* 12 April 1936; *Educ* Heckmondwike GS, Batley Sch of Art (NDD), RCA (ARCA); *m* 20 April 1963, (Elizabeth) Mary Tindall, da of Richard Newton Wakelin (d 1964), of Richmond, Surrey; 2 da (Jane Charlotte Wakelin b 1964, Emma Louisa Wakelin b 1972); *Career* art dir Young and Rubicam Ltd 1962–63, designer Fletcher Forbes Gill 1963, co-fndr, ptnr and creative head Minale Tattersfield 1964–95, ret; visiting lectr RCA 1978, visiting prof in design Univ of Brighton 1988–; design awards incl: Typomundus Canada 1964, creativity on paper NY 1966, Silver award D&AD 1968 (1970 and 1974–84), Gold award Art Dir Club NY 1975, Poster award Warsaw Biennale 1969, Br Poster Design award 1970, Liderman Gold award for graphic design Madrid 1983, Civic Tst award 1985, D&AD president's award for outstanding contrib to Br design 1987; exhibitions: MOMA NY 1978, London Design Centre 1981, Glasgow Design Centre 1981, MOMA Milan 1983, Cultural Centre of Madrid 1985, Axis Gallery Tokyo 1988; various articles in Br and int jls; memb D&AD; Hon PhD Anglia Poly Univ, Hon DSc Univ of Huddersfield; hon fell RCA, FCSD, FRSA; *Style—* Prof Brian Tattersfield; ✉ Sarisberie Cottage, The Street, West Clandon, Surrey GU4 7ST (☎ 01483 222908); 178 High Street, Aldeburgh, Suffolk IP15 5AQ (☎ 01728 452240)

TATTON-BROWN, Duncan; *b* 15 March 1965; *Educ* Kings Coll Cambridge (MA); *m* ; 3 c; *Career* RN 1984–87; fin analyst Rank Xerox (UK) Ltd 1987–90, gp corp finance Financial Analyst Gp 1990–92, various fin and commercial roles Burton Gp plc 1996–97, fin dir Virgin Entertainment Gp 1998–2000, fin dir virgin.com 2000; Kingfisher plc: fin dir B&Q plc 2001–03, gp fin dir 2004–, ceo int 2008–; chief fin offr Fitness First Gp 2010–; non-exec dir Rentokil Initial plc 2005–; ACMA 1990; *Style—* Duncan Tatton-Brown, Esq; ✉ Fitness First Group, 58 Fleets Lane, Poole, Dorset BH15 3BT

TAUNTON, Archdeacon of; *see:* Reed, Ven John Peter Cyril

TAUSIG, Peter; s of Dr Walter Charles Tausig (d 1969), and Judith, *née* Morris (d 1995); *b* 15 August 1943; *Educ* Battersea GS, UCL (BSc); *m* 28 June 1987 (m dis 1997); 2 da (Eva Lily Ibolya b 3 April 1988, Katja Francesca b 30 Dec 1990); *Career* economist: Aust Bureau of Census and Statistics 1965–69, CBI 1969, Bank of London and S America 1970–74, International Marine Banking Co 1974–76, S G Warburg/Warburg Securities 1976–88 (dir 1983); exec dir UBS Phillips & Drew 1989–91; dir: Crédit Lyonnais Securities and Crédit Lyonnais Capital Markets 1992–95, Whittingdale Ltd 1996–99; chm Research Ethics Ctee Royal Marsden Hosp 1999–2004, chm Thames Valley Research Ethics Ctee 2004–07 (vice-chm 2002–03); chm: Kateva Mgmnt 1992–, Ladbroke Square Montessori Sch 1992–, Annemount Sch 1993–96; dir Hampstead Theatre 2010–; tstee: St Botolphs Project 1999–2004, Heath Hands 2000–, Br Czech Slovak Assoc 2000–02, Heath and Hampstead Soc 2005–; *Recreations* theatre, literature, music, walking, skiing, travel; *Clubs* Groucho, Oriental; *Style—* Peter Tausig, Esq; ✉ 11 Downshire Hill, Hampstead, London NW3 1NR (☎ 020 7435 7099, e-mail peter_tausig@hotmail.com)

TAUSSIG, Andrew John; s of Leo Taussig, and Magda, *née* Szücs; *Educ* Winchester (scholar), Magdalen Coll Oxford (MA), Harvard Univ (PhD); *m* 1971, Maggie Celia, *née* Whines; 2 da, 1 s; *Career* prodr of various BBC progs incl Talk-In with Sir Robin Day and David Dimbleby 1973–79, special asst to dir news and current affairs BBC 1979–80, dep ed Nationwide prog BBC 1980–81, chief asst TV current affairs BBC 1981–86, controller European services and head of Europe region BBC World Service 1988–96, dir foreign language services BBC World Service 1996–2000; research associate Centre for Socio-Legal Studies Univ of Oxford 2001–, conslt to Br Cncl for World Summit on the Information Soc; memb Cncl Chatham House (RIIA) 2002–05, networking memb Cwlth Prog for Technol Mgmnt (CPTM), tstee Voice of the Listener and Viewer (VLV), tstee Int Inst of Communications; *Publications* author of articles in various jls incl Commonwealth Broadcaster, Intermedia (International Institute of Communications), Historical Jl of Film, Radio and Television and Media Asia; *Recreations* photography, antique browsing, travelling; *Clubs* Le Beaujolais; *Style—* Andrew Taussig

TAVERNE, Baron (Life Peer UK 1996), of Pimlico in the City of Westminster; Dick Taverne; QC (1965); s of Dr Nicolaas Jacobus Marie Taverne (d 1966), and Louise Victoria, *née* Koch (d 1961); *b* 18 October 1928, Pladjoe, Sumatra; *Educ* Charterhouse, Balliol Coll Oxford; *m* 6 Aug 1955, Janice, da of late Dr Robert Samuel Fleming Hennessey; 2 da (Hon Suzanna b 1960, Hon Caroline b 1963); *Career* called to the Bar 1954; MP (Lab) Lincoln 1962–72: Parly sec Home Office 1966–68, min of state Treasy 1968–69, fin sec 1969–70, resigned Labour Party 1972; re-elected Independent Social Democrat MP Lincoln 1973–74; first dir Inst for Fiscal Studies 1971 (chm 1979–83), chm Public Policy Centre 1984–87, Br memb Spierenburg Ctee to examine working of Euro Cmmn 1979; PRIMA Europe: dir 1987–98, chm 1991–94, pres 1994–98; chm AXA Equity & Law Life Assurance Society plc 1998–2001 (dir 1972–97), dir BOC Group plc 1975–95; chm: OLIM Convertible Trust 1989–99, Alcohol and Drug Abuse Prevention and Treatment Ltd 1996–2008, Sense About Science 2002–12; Parly Science Communicator of the Year 2006; hon fell Mansfield Coll Oxford 1997; *Books* The Future of the Left (1974), The March of Unreason – Science, Democracy and the New Fundamentalism (2005), Against the Tide, Politics and Beyond (2014); *Recreations* sailing; *Style—* The Lord Taverne; ✉ 25 Tufton Court, Tufton Street, London SW1P 3QH (☎ 020 7233 2409)

TAVERNOR, Prof Robert; *b* 19 December 1954, Worcester; *Educ* Chatham House GS Ramsgate, Harvey GS Folkestone, South Bank Poly (BA), PCL (DipArch), Br Sch at Rome (scholar in architecture), St John's Coll Cambridge (PhD); *m* Denise Alexandra, *née* Mackie; 2 da (Joanna b 1984, Faye b 1985), 1 s (James b 1989); *Career* architect; assoc architect Cambridge Design Architects 1983–85, dir Richard Reid Architects 1985–86, founding ptnr Alberti Gp 1988–94, founding dir Design Gp Bath Architects 1990–92; pt/t lectr PCL 1980–82, coll tutor Univ of Cambridge 1980–87 (pt/t lectr 1982–87), lectr in architecture Univ of Bath 1987–92, initiator Centre for Advanced Studies in Architecture Univ of Bath 1991–92, Forbes prof of architecture Univ of Edinburgh 1992–95, prof of architecture Univ of Bath 1995–2005 (head of dept 2003–05), prof of architecture and urban design and dir Cities Prog LSE 2005–10 (emeritus prof of architecture and urban design 2011–); visiting prof Center for Medieval and Renaissance Studies UCLA 1998–99, EU visiting scholar Texas A&M Univ 2002, visiting prof of architecture and urbanism Univ of São Paulo 2004; memb Editorial Bd Architectural Res Quarterly 1994–97 and 1999–; dissertations examiner RIBA 1986–97; awards incl Bath Environmental Award 1992 and 1993; RIBA 1984, ARIAS 1994–96, FRSA 1994; *Publications* L B Alberti On the Art of Building in Ten Books (with J Rykwert and N Leach, 1991), Palladio and Palladianism (1991), Edinburgh (ed, 1995), Andrea Palladio The Four Books on Architecture (ed with R Schofield, 1997, The Architecture Review Architectural Publication of the Year 1997, The Architects' Jl Architectural Publication of the Year 1998), On Alberti and the Art of Building (1998, The Architects' Jl Architectural Publication of the Year 1999), Body and Building: the changing relation of body and architecture (ed with G Dodds, 2002), Smoot's Ear: the measure of humanity (2007), Vitruvius, On Architecture (intro with trans, by R Schofield, 2009); other publications incl: chapters in 14 books, 1 dictionary entry, 15 essays in refereed jls, 17 essays in professional jls, 35 book reviews; *Style—* Prof Robert Tavernor; ✉ Tavernor Consultancy, Southcot House, 37 Lyncombe Hill, Bath BA2 4PQ (☎ 01225 466723, e-mail robert@tavernorconsultancy.co.uk)

TAYAR, Dr René Benedict; s of Oscar Tayar, of Sliema, Malta, and Violet, *née* Riccardi; *b* 3 October 1945; *Educ* St Aloysius' Coll Malta, Royal Univ of Malta (MD); *m* 25 Jan 1971, Margaret Rose, da of Louis Francis Tortell, of Sliema, Malta; 1 s (Benjamin b 8 Sept 1978); *Career* sr registrar in radiology Bristol Royal Infirmary 1977–81 (registrar in radiology 1974–77); conslt radiologist: St Helier Hosp Carshalton 1981–2010, Nelson Hosp Raynes Park 1981–2010, Parkside Hosp Wimbledon 1984–, St Helier Hosp NHS Tst (also sec Med Staff Ctee), Atkinson Morley Imaging Centre Wimbledon 1992–96, St Anthony's Hosp N Cheam 1995–, Royal Hosp for Neurodisability Putney 2008–12; lead radiologist Epsom and St Helier NHS Tst 2009–10; hon sr lectr St George's Hosp Med Sch 1988–2010; fndr memb: Sir Harry Secombe Scanner Appeal, Secombe Magnet Appeal; hon sec Magnetic Resonance Radiologists Assoc 1998–2003; FRCR; *Publications* several pubns in peer reviewed medical journals and presentations to learned societies and colleges; *Recreations* tennis, music, literature; *Clubs* RAC, Pall Mall; *Style—* Dr René Tayar; ✉ 45 Epsom Lane South, Tadworth, Surrey KT20 5TA (☎ 01737 813582)

TAYLOR, Alexander; s of Stephan Taylor, and Lesley, *née* Thorburn; *b* 3 October 1975, Bishop Auckland, Co Durham; *Educ* Nottingham Trent Univ (BA); *m* 3 Aug 2002, Phillippa, *née* Oakley Hill; 1 s (Wilf Alexander b 12 June 2005), 2 da (Clara Marie b 19 Feb 2008, Audrey Ren Lucy b 24 April 2011); *Career* industrial designer Alexander Taylor Ltd; Fold lamp incl perm collection MOMA NY and Chicago Art Inst; visiting lectr: Royal Coll of Art London, Ecal Switzerland; Young Designer of the Year Elle Decoration Magazine 2005, Designers of the Future (with Established & Sons) Design Basel/Miami 2006, Chicago Athenaeum Museum Good Design Award (for Butterfly table Zanotta); *Publications* 21 Designers for Twenty-first Century Britain (contrib); *Style—* Alexander Taylor, Esq; ✉ Unit 210, 3rd Floor, 122–150 Hackney Road, London E2 7QS (☎ 07990 971202, e-mail info@alexandertaylor.com, website www.alexandertaylor.com)

TAYLOR, Alexandra; da of Kenneth Taylor, and Maureen, *née* Bell; *b* 17 February 1959; *Educ* Blaydon Comp, Newcastle upon Tyne Sch of Art (HND, DipAD); *Career* art dir: BBD&O advtg 1981–83, Saatchi & Saatchi 1983–89; sr art dir, gp head and bd dir WCRS 1989; Saatchi & Saatchi: rejoined as gp head and bd dir 1989, head of art 1992–, creative dir 1996–; dir Paul Weiland Film Co/Weiden & Kennedy 2001, creative dir Publics Ad 2002, appeared in Campaign The A List 2004, freelance art dir 2008; D&AD: memb Exec Ctee 1998–, joined Bespoke prog with Art of Art Direction master classes 2008; *Awards* 195 entries in D&AD, 7 Silver Pencil Awards D&AD, 9 nominations D&AD, 6 Gold ADCE, 2 Gold and 17 Silver Campaign Big Awards, 1 Gold Creative Circle, 2 Gold and 3 Silver Cannes, Best Overall TV Ad Cannes 1992, 6 Silver BTA, ITV Award 1992, presented with the D&AD President's Award for outstanding creative contribution to advertising (first female winner) 2014; *Clubs* Groucho; *Style—* Alexandra Taylor; ☎ 07919 217834

TAYLOR, Prof Andrew; *b* North Wales; *Educ* Bartlett Sch of Architecture (BSc), Dip Arch RIBA; *Career* architect; MacCormac Jamieson Pritchard, ptnr Patel Taylor Architects 1989–; tutor Bartlett Sch of Architecture, prof Welsh Sch of Architecture Univ of Cardiff 2003–; Civic Tst assessor 1997–99, RIBA Awards assessor, external examiner Univ of Cardiff; memb CABE Enabling Panel; *Competitions* incl: Sainsbury's supermarket 1987, sheltered accomodation Clywd Wales 1989, the city and the river Antwerp Belgium 1990, Choral and Music Centre Rhondda Heritage Park Wales 1990, Europan II Châteauroux France 1991, Peckham London 1991, Ayr Citadel 1993, Europan III Pierre-Bénite France 1994, Thames Barrier Park London 1995, Footbridge Balmaha Scotland 1996, Portland College Nottinghamshire 1998; *Awards* Royal Acad Summer Exhibition Non-Members Award 1988, RIBA Architecture Award (for Arts Centre Wales) 1992, Geoffrey Gribble Conservation Award (for PACE Counselling Centre London) 1995, Glass and Glazing Award (for PACE Counselling Centre London) 1995, Saltire Geddes Planning Award (for Ayr Citadel Scotland) 1995, shortlisted Young Architect of the Year 1997, 4 RIBA Architecture Awards (for Thames Barrier Park, Benslow Music Sch, Peace Park Pavilion and Apartment Battersea) 2001; *Style—* Prof Andrew Taylor; ✉ Patel Taylor Architects, 53 Rawstorne Street, London EC1V 7NQ (☎ 020 7278 2323, fax 020 7278 6242, e-mail pta@pateltaylor.co.uk)

TAYLOR, Andrew David; s of Vernon Taylor (d 2006), and Elizabeth, *née* McGhie (d 1995); *b* 6 March 1952, Leicester; *Educ* Magdalen Coll Sch Oxford, Lincoln Coll Oxford (MA, Hockey blue); *m* 10 Dec 1977, Alison Jane; 1 s (Henry Guy Jonathan b 11 March 1982), 2 da (Julia Poppy b 15 April 1984, Lucy Caroline b 24 Sept 1986); *Career* admitted slr 1980; Richards Butler: joined as articled clerk 1977, ptnr 1983–, chm 2000–05; sec and treas Br Maritime Law Assoc; *Publications* Voyage Charters (4 edn 2014); *Recreations* skiing, hiking, opera, wine; *Clubs* Travellers, City Law, Vincent's (Oxford); *Style—* Andrew Taylor, Esq; ✉ Reed Smith LLP, The Broadgate Tower, 20 Primrose Street, London EC2A 2RS (☎ 020 7247 6555, e-mail adtaylor@reedsmith.com)

TAYLOR, Andrew John (Andy); s of Thomas Sowler Taylor (d 1986), of Newcastle-upon-Tyne, and Sarah, *née* McGinley (d 1986); *b* 23 February 1950, Newcastle upon Tyne; *Educ* Rutherford GS Newcastle, Trinity Coll Cambridge (MA); *m* 23 Sept 1985, Elizabeth, *née* Robertson; 2 da (Claire Madderson Sarah b 2 Aug 1985, Louise Frances Anne b 11 Oct 1986); *Career* fndr Sanctuary Gp 1976 (ceo until 2006), currently ceo Phantom Music Mgmnt Ltd and chm Concept Venues Ltd; Music Week Strat award for lifetime contrib to the music industry; FCA 1976, FRSA; *Recreations* wine, fell walking, travel, horse racing; *Clubs* Soho House, The George; *Style—* Andy Taylor, Esq; ✉ Phantom Music Management Ltd, Bridle House, 36 Bridle Lane, London W1F 9BZ (e-mail andy.taylor@phantom-music.com)

TAYLOR, Andrew John Robert; s of Rev Arthur John Taylor, of Monmouth, and Hilda Mary, *née* Haines; *b* 14 October 1951; *Educ* The King's Sch Ely, Woodbridge Sch, Emmanuel Coll Cambridge (BA), UCL (MA); *m* 8 Sept 1979, Caroline Jane, da of Ian George Silverwood; 1 da (Sarah Jessica b 9 June 1986), 1 s (William John Alexander b 6 March 1989); *Career* writer; various jobs ranging from boatbuilding to teaching 1973–76, freelance sub ed for London publishers 1975–84, library asst then asst librarian London Borough of Brent 1976–81, self-employed writer 1981–; ed The Author (jl of Soc of Authors) 2004–06; memb: Soc of Authors, Crime Writers' Assoc, Asociación Internacional de Escritores Policiácos; *Awards* John Creasey Meml Award Crime Writers' Assoc 1982 and Edgar nomination from Mystery Writers of America (for Caroline Minuscule), Our Fathers' Lies shortlisted for Gold Dagger of Crime Writers Assoc 1985, Snapshot shortlisted for NatWest Children's Book of the Year award 1989, Ellis Peters

Historical Dagger of Crime Writers' Assoc 2001 (for The Office of the Dead) and 2003 (for The American Boy), Cartier Diamond Dagger of Crime Writers' Assoc 2009 (for sustained excellence in crime writing), Martin Beck Award (Sweden, for Bleeding Heart Square), Historical Dagger of Crime Writers' Assoc (for The Scent of Death) 2013; *Books* for children incl: Hairline Cracks (1988), Private Nose (1989), Snapshot (1989), Double Exposure (1990), Negative Image (1992), The Invader (1994); for adults incl: Caroline Minuscule (1982), Waiting for the End of the World (1984), Our Fathers' Lies (1985), An Old School Tie (1986), Freelance Death (1987), The Second Midnight (1988), Blacklist (1988), Blood Relation (1990), Toyshop (1990), The Raven on the Water (1991), The Sleeping Policeman (1992), The Barred Window (1993), Odd Man Out (1993), An Air That Kills (1994), The Mortal Sickness (1995), The Four Last Things (1997), The Lover of the Grave (1997), The Judgement of Strangers (1998), The Suffocating Night (1998), The Office of the Dead (2000), Where Roses Fade (2000), Death's Own Door (2001), Requiem for an Angel (2002), The American Boy (2003), Call the Dying (2004), A Stain on the Silence (2006), Naked to the Hangman (2006), Bleeding Heart Square (2008), The Anatomy of Ghosts (2010), Broken Voices (2012), The Scent of Death (2013), The Leper House (2014), The Silent Boy (2014), The Scratch (2014), The Ashes of London (2016), The Writing House (2016), Fireside Gothic (forthcoming, 2016); *Clubs* Detection; *Style*— Andrew Taylor, Esq; ✉ website www.andrew-taylor.co.uk; c/o Greene & Heaton, 37 Goldhawk Road, London W12 8QQ (☎ 020 8749 0315, e-mail info@greeneheaton.co.uk)

TAYLOR, Bernard Irvin; s of Albert Ernest Taylor (d 1965), of Swindon, Wilts, and Edna Marion, *née* Tanner; *b* 2 October 1934; *Educ* Swindon Sch of Art, Chelsea Sch of Art (Chelsea Dip, Nat Dip Design), Univ of Birmingham (BA, Art Teacher's Dip); *Career* author and playwright; teacher and book illustrator London 1960–63, teacher and painter of portraits and landscapes, actor New York 1963–70, writer and actor UK 1970–; memb: Actors' Equity, Soc of Authors; *Plays* Daughter of the Apachés (1973), Mice on the First Floor (1974, Thames TV most promising playwright award 1974), Maggie it's Me! (1975); *Novels* The Godsend (1976, translated into 17 languages and filmed), Sweetheart Sweetheart (1977), The Reaping (1980), The Moorstone Sickness (1982), The Kindness of Strangers (1986), Madeleine (1987), Mother's Boys (1988, also made into a film), Saddle the Wind (as Kate Irvine, 1989), Charmed Life (1991), Evil Intent (1994), Since Ruby (1999), So Long at the Fair (as Jess Foley, 2001), Too Close to the Sun (as Jess Foley, 2002), Saddle the Wind (as Jess Foley, 2003), Wait for the Dawn (as Jess Foley, 2005), No Wings to Fly (as Jess Foley, 2006), Kiss It Better (2011), The Comeback (2016); *Non-Fiction* Cruelly Murdered (1979), Perfect Murder (with Stephen Knight, 1987, Crime Writers' Assoc Gold Dagger award), Murder at the Priory (with Kate Clarke, 1988), There Must Be Evil (2015); has also published numerous short stories; *Style*— Bernard Taylor, Esq; ✉ c/o A M Heath & Co Ltd, 6 Warwick Court, London WC1R 5DJ (☎ 020 7242 2811)

TAYLOR, Bernard John; DL (Oxon 2011); s of John Taylor (d 1962), and Evelyn Frances Taylor (d 1995); *b* 2 November 1956; *Educ* Cheltenham Coll, St John's Coll Oxford (scholar, MA); *m* 16 June 1984, Sarah Jane, da of John Paskin Taylor, of Paris; 1 s (Henry Bernard Charles b 22 Sept 1992); *Career* dir Med Div Smiths Industries plc 1983–85 (business planning and acquisitions 1979–82); exec dir: Baring Bros & Co Ltd 1985–94 (mangr and asst dir Corp Fin Dept), Robert Fleming & Co Ltd 1994– (dep chm and chief exec), Robert Fleming Holdings Ltd 1995– (jt chief exec investment banking 1998–2000), Chase Manhattan 2000 (vice-chm EMEA), JP Morgan plc 2001–06 (vice-chm 2001–06); chm and chief exec Braveheart Financial Servs Ltd 2006–, chief exec Evercore Ptnrs Ltd 2007–12 (currently non-exec chm), vice-chm Evercore Ptnrs Inc 2007–; non-exec dir: New Focus Healthcare 1986–90, ISIS Innovation Ltd 1997–2013 (chm 2001–13), Oxford Investments plc 2002–12, Ti Automotive plc (dep chm) 2001–2007, Texture Restaurants Ltd 2007–, Oxford Sciences Innovation plc 2015–; Univ of Oxford: memb Cncl until 2012, chm Audit and Scrutiny Ctee 2006–12, memb Nominations Ctee 2007–10, chm Remuneration Ctee 2007–12, memb Finance Ctee 2011–, dep steward 2012–, memb Bd Medical Scis Div 2012–, memb Physical and Life Sciences Bd 2014–; memb Devpt Ctee Royal Opera House 2003–11; Royal Cmmn for 1851: cmmr 2005–, chm Finance Ctee 2006–12, chm 2012–; Royal Soc: memb Investment Ctee 2010–13, chm Advsy Bd 2012–, chm Audit Ctee 2013–16; Garsington Opera: memb Advsy Bd 2005–07, tstee 2007–, memb Relocation Ctee 2010–11, chm 2012–; dir Oxfordshire County Agricultural Assoc 2000–09 (chm Thame Show 2003), chm Rycote Park Farms 2000–, patron Oxford Historic Churches Tst (chm Jubilee Appeal), chm Ashmolean Museum 2011–; dir ERA Fndn 2010–; LRPS (memb 1971), FRSC (memb 1972), CSci, CChem; hon fell St John's Coll Oxford (chm Remuneration Ctee 2010–14); *Books* Photosensitive Film Formation on Copper (I) (1974), Photosensitive Film Formation on Copper (II) (1976), Oxidation of Alcohols to Carbonyl Compounds, Synthesis (1979); *Recreations* photography, gardening, wine; *Clubs* Oxford and Cambridge, Brooks's, Whites, No. 5 Hertford Street; *Style*— Bernard Taylor, Esq, DL

TAYLOR, Prof Brent William; s of Robert Ernest Taylor (d 1971), and Norma Gertrude, *née* Collett (d 2008); *b* 21 November 1941; *Educ* Christchurch Boys' HS, Univ of Otago (MB ChB), Univ of Bristol (PhD); *m* 17 Jan 1970, Moira Elizabeth, da of Thomas Richard Hall (d 1983), of Palmerston North, NZ; 1 s (Samuel b 1973), 1 da (Katherine b 1975); *Career* jr med posts Christchurch NZ 1967–71, res and trg posts Great Ormond Street and Inst of Child Health London 1971–74, sr lectr in paediatrics Christchurch NZ 1975–81, conslt sr lectr in social paediatrics and epidemiology Univ of Bristol and visiting paediatrician and epidemiologist Riyadh Al Kharj Hosp prog 1981–84, conslt sr lectr in child health St Mary's Hosp Med Sch London 1985–88, prof of community child health Royal Free and Univ Coll Med Sch UCL 1988–2008, prof of community child health emeritus Inst of Child Health UCL 2008–; FRACP 1981 (MRACP 1970), FRCP 1985 (MRCP 1971), FRCPCH 1997; *Recreations* opera, walking, London, scepticism; *Style*— Prof Brent Taylor; ✉ 42 Oakley Road, London N1 3LS (☎ 020 7354 8442, e-mail brent.taylor@mac.com); General and Adolescent Paediatric Unit, Institute of Child Health, University College London, Guilford Street, London WC1N 1EH (☎ 020 7354 8442, e-mail brent.taylor@ucl.ac.uk)

TAYLOR, Charles Spencer; s of Leonard Taylor (d 1991), and Phyllis Rose, *née* Emerson (d 1982); *b* 18 January 1952; *Educ* William Fletcher Sch Bognor Regis, Univ of Hull (LLB); *m* 7 Sept 1973 (m dis 2009), Elizabeth Mary (Liz), da of Ernest Richard Stephens; 2 s (Leo John Julius b 5 June 1987, Jack Michael Marius b 10 Feb 1990); *Career* called to the Bar Middle Temple 1974, in practice SE Circuit; Parl candidate (Lab) Arundel and S Downs 2001; memb Hon Soc of the Middle Temple 1969; *Recreations* gardening; *Style*— Charles Taylor, Esq; ✉ 12 North Pallant, Chichester, West Sussex PO19 1TQ (☎ 01243 784538)

TAYLOR, Prof Christopher Malcolm; *b* 15 January 1943; *Educ* KCL (William Siemens prize, Engrg Centenary prize, Jelf medal, BSc Eng), Univ of Leeds (MSc, PhD, DEng); *Career* res engr Lubrication Labs English Electric Co Ltd Whetstone 1967–68; Univ of Leeds: sr engr Industrial Unit of Tribology 1968–71, lectr in mechanical engrg 1971–80, sr lectr in mechanical engrg 1980–86, reader in tribology Dept of Mechanical Engrg 1986–90, dir Inst of Tribology 1987–2001, prof of tribology Dept of Mechanical Engrg 1990–2001, head Dept of Mechanical Engrg 1992–96, dean Faculty of Engrg 1996–97, pro-vice-chllr 1997–2001; vice-chllr Univ of Bradford 2001–07; conf organizer and jt ed Proceedings series of Leeds-Lyon Symposia on Tribology 1974–2000, ed Proceedings Inst of Mechanical Engrs 1993–2002; referee EPSRC and NSF res grants and reports 1986–2001; sr res assoc Nat Res Cncl of America at NASA Res Center Cleveland OH 1976–77; author of numerous articles in scientific jls and pubns; Tribology Silver Medal 1992, IMechE Tribology Gp Donald Julius Groen Prize 1993; CEng, FIMechE (vice-pres 1997–2003, pres 2003–04), CEng, FREng 1995, FCGI 1999; *Style*— Emeritus Prof Christopher Taylor, FREng

TAYLOR, Dr Christopher Michael; s of Harry Taylor (d 1983), and Margaret Elizabeth, *née* Leigh; *b* 27 July 1952; *Educ* Hutton GS, Christ's Coll Cambridge (MA), King's Coll Hosp Med Sch Univ of London (MB BChir); *m* 4 Nov 1978, Soopamah, da of Arnasalon Munisami (d 1991), of Mauritius; 1 da (Rachel Kevina b 1980), 2 s (Michael Khrishnen b 1983, Andrew James Silven b 1987); *Career* conslt psychiatrist Leeds Partnerships Fndn Teaching NHS Tst 1986– (area mangr Gen Psychiatry 1991–95); FRCPsych; *Style*— Dr Christopher Taylor; ✉ Newsam Centre, Seacroft Hospital, York Road, Leeds LS14 6WB (☎ 01133 056434)

TAYLOR, (Samantha) Claire; MBE (2010); da of Fred Roger Taylor, and Barbara, *née* McDonald; *b* 25 September 1975, Amersham, Bucks; *Educ* Queen's Coll Oxford (BA); *Career* cricketer; with Berkshire WCCC; England: Test debut v India 1999, memb Ashes-winning side 2005 and 2008, memb touring squad Aust and NZ 2008, memb World Cup-winning sides One Day Int and Twenty20 2009; Vodafone Player of Year 2008 and 2009, ICC Player of the Year 2009, Wisden Cricketer of the Year 2009; IT systems mangr Procter and Gamble 1998–2001, mgmnt conslt SUMS Consulting 2006–; *Style*— Miss Claire Taylor, MBE; ✉ The England and Wales Cricket Board, Lord's Cricket Ground, London NW8 8QZ (☎ 020 7432 1200)

TAYLOR, Sir Cyril Julian Hebden; GBE (2004), kt (1989); s of Rev Cyril Eustace Taylor (d 1935), and Marjory Victoria, *née* Hebden (d 1994); *b* 14 May 1935; *Educ* St Marylebone GS London, Roundhay Sch Leeds, Trinity Hall Cambridge (MA), Harvard Business Sch (MBA); *m* 5 June 1965, June Judith (Judy), da of Earl Denman (d 1970); 1 da (Kirsten Livia Hebden b 1970); *Career* Nat Serv 1954–56 (cmmn with E Surrey Regt seconded to 3 Bn King's African Rifles in Kenya during Mau Mau emergency); brand mangr Procter & Gamble Cincinnati OH 1961–64; fndr chm AIFS Inc 1964– (cos incl American Inst for Foreign Study, Camp America, Au Pair in America, American Cncl for Int Studies, AIFS (Aust), AIFS Germany); chllr Richmond The American Int Univ London; chair Specialist Schools and Academies Tst 1987–2007, advsr to ten secretaries of state for educn and skills 1987–2007; Parly candidate (Cons): Huddersfield E Feb 1974, Keighley Oct 1974; Gtr London Cncl for Ruislip Northwood: memb 1977–86, chm Profession and Gen Servs Ctee 1978–81, oppn spokesman for tport, policy and resources 1981–86, dep ldr of the oppn 1983–86; memb Bd of Dirs Centre for Policy Studies 1984–98; pres: Ruislip Northwood Cons Assoc 1986–97, Harvard Business Sch Club of London 1990–93; vice-pres Alumni Cncl Harvard Business Sch 1994–96; chm: Br Friends of Harvard Business Sch, Lexham Gdns Residents' Assoc; memb Prince's Charities Cncl 2009–12; High Sheriff Gtr London 1996–97; Hon PhD: New England 1991, Richmond Coll 1997, Open Univ 2001, Brunel Univ 2005; FRSA; *Books and Pamphlets* The Guide to Study Abroad (with Prof John Garraty and Lily von Klemperer), Peace has its Price (1972), No More Tick (1974), The Elected Member's Guide to Reducing Public Expenditure (1980), A Realistic Plan for London Transport (1982), Reforming London's Government (1984), Qualgoes Just Grow (1985), London Preserv'd (1985), Bringing Accountability Back to Local Government (1985), Employment Examined: The Right Approach to More Jobs (1986), Raising Educational Standards (1990), The Future of Britain's Universities (jtly, 1996), Value Added and Educational Outcomes of Specialist Schools (jtly, 1999, 2000, 2001, 2002, 2003, 2004, 2005 and 2006), Excellence in Education: The Making of Great Schools (with Conor Ryan, 2005), Who Will Champion our Vulnerable Children? (2006), Education, Education, Education: 10 Years On (with Tony Blair and Liz Reid, 2007), A Good School For Every Child (2009), Sir Cyril – My Life as a Social Entrepreneur (autobiography, 2013); *Recreations* keen swimmer and gardener; *Clubs* Chelsea Arts, Hurlingham, Carlton, Harvard (New York), Racquet and Tennis (New York); *Style*— Sir Cyril Taylor, GBE; ✉ 1 Lexham Walk, London W8 5JD (☎ 020 7370 2082); American Institute for Foreign Study, 37 Queen's Gate, London SW7 5HR (☎ 020 7581 7391, fax 020 7581 7388, e-mail ctaylor@aifs.co.uk)

TAYLOR, David John; s of late John Robert George Taylor, of Norwich, and Elizabeth Anne Castell, *née* Spalding; *b* 22 August 1960; *Educ* King Edward VI Sch Norwich, St John's Coll Oxford (BA); *m* 22 June 1990, Rachel Elizabeth, da of late Richard Paul Hore; 3 s (Felix John Richard b 29 Oct 1992, Benjamin Anthony Castell b 17 Jan 1996, Leo David Alexander b 13 April 2000); *Career* writer; contrib various papers incl: Independent on Sunday, TLS, The Spectator, Private Eye, The Guardian, Wall Street Journal, The Tablet; FRSL 1997; *Books* Great Eastern Land (novel, 1986), A Vain Conceit: British Fiction in the 1980s (1989), Other People: Portraits From the Nineties (with Marcus Berkmann, 1990), Real Life (novel, 1992), After The War: The Novel and England Since 1945 (1993), W M Thackeray: A Shabby Genteel Story and other writings (ed, 1993), W M Thackeray: The Newcomes (ed, 1994), English Settlement (novel, 1996, Grinzane Cavour Prize Italy 1999), George Gissing: New Grub Street (ed, 1997), After Bathing at Baxter's (stories, 1997), Trespass (novel, 1998), Thackeray (biography, 1999), The Comedy Man (novel, 2001), Orwell: The Life (2003, Whitbread Biography Prize 2003), Kept (novel, 2006), On the Corinthian Spirit: The Decline of Amateurism in Sport (2006), Bright Young People: The rise and fall of a generation 1918–1940 (2007), Ask Alice (novel, 2009), At the Chime of a City Clock (novel, 2010), Derby Day (novel, 2011), Secondhand Daylight (novel, 2012), What You Didn't Miss: A Book of Literary Parodies (2012), The Windsor Faction (novel, 2013, Sidewise Award for Alternate History), George Orwell: Nineteen Eighty-Four, The Annotated Edition (ed, 2013), From the Heart (novella, 2014), Wrote For Luck (stories, 2015), George Gissing: The Whirlpool (ed, 2015), The Prose Factory: Literary Life in England since 1918 (2016), The New Book of Snobs (2016); *Recreations* reading, following Norwich City FC; *Style*— D J Taylor, Esq, FRSL; ✉ c/o Curtis Brown, Haymarket House, 28–29 Haymarket, London SW1Y 4SP (☎ 020 7393 4400, website www.curtisbrown.co.uk)

TAYLOR, David Paul; *b* 5 August 1956, London; *Educ* Shooters Hill GS for Boys; *Career* head of real estate Berwin Leighton Paisner LLp 1980–2000, Herbert Smith LLP 2000–04, jt global ldr and EMEA gp head Real Estate Practice Gp DLA Piper 2004–11, currently sr conslt Pinsent Masons; *Style*— David Taylor, Esq; ✉ Pinsent Mason, 30 Crown Place, London EC2A 4ES (☎ 020 7418 7000, mobile 07770 942097, e-mail david.taylor@pinsentmasons.com)

TAYLOR, David William; s of Brig Harry William Taylor, of Croydon, Surrey, and Eva Wade, *née* Day; *b* 10 July 1945; *Educ* Bancroft's Sch (Draper's Co Sch Leaving Award), Worcester Coll Oxford (Open Exhibitioner in Classics, MA), Inst of Educn Univ of London (PGCE distinction, Story-Miller Prize); *m* 1972, Pamela Linda, da of Edward John Taylor, of Coventry; 1 s (Alexander David Nicholas b 11 April 1979), 1 da (Penelope Caroline Louise b 13 May 1983); *Career* Watford Boys' GS: asst classics teacher 1968–73, head of classics 1973–78; chief examiner A Level classics Univ of London 1975–78; HMI Schools: appointed 1978, district inspector Barnet and Newcastle 1978–86, staff inspector secondary and classics 1986–92; OFSTED: programme mangr 1992–93, head of strategic planning and resources 1993–96, head of teacher educn and training 1996–99, dir of inspection 1999–2004; educnl conslt 2004–, Office of the Schs Adjudicator 2005–08; School Teacher Fellowship Merton Coll Oxford 1978; seconded to Touche Ross Mgmnt Conslts 1991; memb: Jt Assoc of Classical Teachers (JACT) 1968– (exec sec 1976–78, conslt sec 2005–08), London Assoc of Classical Teachers (LACT) 1968– (ed 1970–73, hon treas 1973–76); memb Nat Tst; Freeman Guild of Educators 2003– (Master 2008–

T

09); *Publications* Cicero and Rome (1973), Work in Ancient Greece and Rome (1975), Acting and the Stage (1978), Roman Society (1980), The Greek and Roman Stage (1999), Classical Literature and Society (ed, 2007–); numerous articles in books and professional jls; *Recreations* classical music (especially choral), chess, literature (especially classical), cricket, rookie golf, theatre, travel; *Clubs* Athenaeum, Nizels Golf; *Style*— David Taylor, Esq

TAYLOR, Prof David William; s of Leslie David Taylor (d 1973), of Erith, Kent, and Doris Evelyn, *née* Jarvis; *b* 23 February 1949; *Educ* Picardy Secdy Modern Sch for Boys Erith, Bromley Tech Coll, Univ of Southampton (BSc), Univ of Cambridge (PhD); *m* Susan Miriam, da of Donald Robert Baggett; *Career* lab technician Wellcome Labs for Tropical Med The Wellcome Fndn Beckenham 1967–70, undergraduate Univ of Southampton 1970–73, postgraduate Univ of Cambridge 1973–77, Nat Acad of Sci (USA) postdoctoral fell Nat Naval Med Center Bethesda Maryland 1977–79; Dept of Pathology Univ of Cambridge: research assoc 1979–82, sr research assoc 1982–86, lectr in parasitology 1986–94; Univ of Edinburgh: prof of tropical animal health 1994–, dir Centre for Tropical Veterinary Med 1994–2001, convenor of African studies 1996–2001, Centre for Infectious Diseases 2003–; dep DG Int Livestock Research Inst Kenya 2000–02; *Recreations* bird watching, painting, cooking, gardening, living in France, DIY; *Style*— Prof David W Taylor; ✉ Centre for Infectious Diseases, College of Medicine and Veterinary Medicine, Ashworth Laboratories, University of Edinburgh, Edinburgh EH9 3JT (☎ 0131 650 7996, e-mail david.w.taylor@ed.ac.uk)

TAYLOR, David Wilson; CBE (2007); s of Eric Taylor, and Sybil Taylor; *b* 9 May 1950; *Educ* Galashiels Acad, Univ of Dundee (DipArch, Dip Urban and Regnl Planning); *m* 1980, Brenda Elizabeth Birchall; 2 s; *Career* research and journalism 1979–81, advsr on regnl policy to John Prescott, MP (now Rt Hon the Lord Prescott (Life Peer), *qv*) 1981– 83; Lancs Enterprises Ltd: dep md 1983–85, md 1985–89; AMEC plc: md AMEC Regeneration 1989–92, md AMEC Devpts 1992–93; chief exec English Partnerships 1993–96, gp chief exec Lancs Enterprises (subsequently Enterprise plc) 1996–2000, chm David Taylor Partnerships Ltd 2000–; non-exec chm: Angela Campbell Gp 1996–98, Vektor Ltd 1996–2004, Era Ltd 1997–2005, Hull Citybuild Ltd 2003–, Elevate East Lancs 2003–, Silvertown Quays Ltd 2003–10, BL-Canada Quays Ltd 2005–, Parking Eye Ltd 2005–, Professional Devpt TV Ltd 2005–, Venture Extreme Ltd 2006–; dir: INWARD 1996–99, Preston North End plc 1996– (also dep chm), Energy 10 Ltd 2009–, Rockpools Ltd 2010–; non-exec dir: John Maunders Gp plc 1996–98, Central Lancs Devpt Agency 1997–2001, United Waste Services 1997–2000, Mancester Cwlth Games Ltd 1999–2003, London and Southern Ltd 2000–05, UK Regeneration Ltd 2004–06; special advsr to dep PM 1997–98; chm NW Film Cmmn 1996–2001, dir Olympic Delivery Authy 2006–12; chm Phoenix Tst 1997–2001, tstee Prince's Fndn 2000–03; hon fell Univ of Central Lancs 1996; FRSA 2006; *Recreations* football (British and American), rugby (union and league); *Clubs* RAC, Royal Cwlth Soc; *Style*— David Taylor, Esq, CBE; ✉ DTP Ltd, 88 Fishergate Hill, Preston PR1 8JD

TAYLOR, HE Duncan John Rushworth; CBE (2002); s of late Sir Jock Taylor, and Molly, Lady Taylor; *b* 17 October 1958, New Malden, Surrey; *Educ* Univ of Cambridge (MA); *m* 1981, Marie-Béatrice (Bébé) Terpougoff; 2 s, 3 da; *Career* diplomat; entered HM Dip Serv 1982, asst desk offr West African Dept FCO 1982–83, third later second sec Havana 1983–87; FCO: head Japan Section Far Eastern Dept 1987–89, Personnel Ops Dept 1989– 90, head Personnel Mgmnt Review Implementation Task Force 1990–91; head Commercial Section Budapest 1992–96, on loan as dir Latin American affrs Rolls Royce 1996–97, head Consular Div FCO 1997–2000, dep consul-gen (press and public affrs) and dep head of post NY 2000–05, high cmmr to Barbados and Eastern Caribbean States 2005–09, govr Cayman Islands 2010–13, ambass to Mexico 2013–; *Style*— HE Mr Duncan Taylor, CBE; ✉ 035013, BFPO 5531 HA4 6EP

TAYLOR, Prof Eric Andrew; s of Dr Jack Andrew Taylor, of Bruton, Somerset, and Grace, *née* Longley; *b* 22 December 1944; *Educ* Clifton (scholar), Univ of Cambridge (MA, MB BChir, Dean meml prize), Harvard Univ, Middx Hosp Med Sch (med and psychiatry prizes); *m* Dr Anne Patricia Roberts (d 2000); 2 s (Thomas b 1976, Paul b 1980); *Career* hon conslt child and adolescent psychiatry Bethlem Royal Hosp, Maudsley Hosp and KCH 1978–; prof of developmental neuropsychiatry Univ of London 1993– (reader 1987– 93), emeritus prof Inst of Psychiatry KCL (prof of child and adolescent psychiatry 1998– 2008); non-exec dir S London and Maudsley NHS Fndn Tst 2007–11; ed: Jl of Child Psychology and Psychiatry 1983–95, European Child and Adolescent Psychiatry 2003– 10; memb scientific staff MRC 1990–2000; memb Cncl Assoc of Child Psychology and Psychiatry 1983–95, sub-dean RCPsych 1996–2000, chair Assoc for Child and Adolescent Mental Health 2010–13; Ruane Prize NARSAD 2009, Heinrich Hoffman Medal World Fedn of ADHD 2011; FRCP 1986, FMedSci 2000, Hon FRCPsych 2012 (FRCPsych 1988); *Books* The Overactive Child: Clinics in Developmental Medicine No 97 (1986), The Hyperactive Child: A Parent's Guide (1986), The Epidemiology of Childhood Hyperactivity (1991), Child and Adolescent Psychiatry: Modern Approaches (ed jtly, 1993, latest edn 2013), People with Hyperactivity (2008), Disruptive Mood (2015); *Clubs* RSM, Athenaeum; *Style*— Prof Eric Taylor

TAYLOR, Fraser Haxton; *b* 20 February 1960; *Educ* Glasgow Sch of Art (BA), RCA (MA); *Career* artist; fndr memb The Cloth (commercial design studio producing textiles and fashion collections) 1981–87, painting, exhibiting and lecturing in Britain, Europe, USA and the Far East 1987–2001; instr drawing and print on fabric: Glasgow Sch of Art 1984–2001, Edinburgh Coll of Art 1985–2001, Central St Martins Coll of Art and Design 1987–2001, RCA 1992–95, C&G Sch of Art 1997–2001; visiting artist Dept of Fiber and Material Studies Sch of the Art Inst of Chicago 2001–03 (adjunct assoc prof 2003–); resident artist: Aurobora Press San Francisco 2002 and 2003, Mahon and Band Press Melbourne 2005; visiting critic: Univ of Illinois at Chicago 2002, Northern Illinois Univ De Kalb 2003; external examiner Liverpool John Moores University 1991–95; curator: 100% Cotton (Gallery X Sch of the Art Inst of Chicago) 2003, Alternative Constructions (Booster and Seven Chicago) 2004, Again & Again (Open End Gallery Chicago) 2006; Lloyds Young Printmakers Prize 1984; *Solo Exhibitions* incl: The Obscure Objects of Desire (Thumb Gall London) 1985, True to Form (Thumb Gall London) 1987, Land Marks (Jill George Gall London) 1989, Fraser Taylor (Gallery Boards Paris) 1993, Pillar to Post (MacKintosh Museum Glasgow Sch of Art) 1998, Drawing Installation (Gall Aoyama Tokyo) 1998, Even as a Blur (Jill George Gall London) 1998, Out of Place (Tim Olsen Gall Sydney) 1999, Placed Apart (Jill George Gall London) 2000, All So Slippery (Edinburgh Coll of Art) 2000, West Coast Scotland (Gall Aoyama Tokyo) 2000, Paintings (Thomas McCormick Gallery Chicago) 2001, Dialogues Develop, British Art Now (Spica Museum Tokyo) 2001, Between Sundays (Tim Olsen Gallery Sydney) 2001, Amusements: Monotypes (Aurobora Press San Francisco) 2002, Occupation (Thomas McCormick Gallery Chicago) 2003, Edges (Spica Museum Tokyo) 2003, Contours (Aurobora Press San Francisco) 2003, The Assembled Line (Contemporary Art Workshop Chicago) 2004, From Chicago, Paintings and Prints (Jill George Gallery London) 2004, Graft (mn gallery Chicago) 2004, Cul de sac (Bucket Rider Gallery Chicago) 2005, Constraints (Tim Olsen Gallery Sydney) 2005, Reverse Transcriptase (Hyde Park Art Center In The Loop Gallery Chicago) 2006; *Group Exhibitions* incl Beneath the Cloth (RCA London) 1982, The Music Show (Thumb Gall London) 1983, Beneath the Cloth (Oliver and Pink London) 1984, The Cloth (Compass Gall Glasgow) 1985, Human Figure (Royal Acad of Art London) 1986, Two by Eight (Thumb Gall London) 1987, Friends and Contemporaries (John Jones Gall London) 1991, Big Works (Fine Art Consultancy London) 1993, One Hundred Years of

Design (RCA London) 1996, Artists of Fame and Promise (Beaux Art Cork Street London) 1997, British Art Now 1998 (Axis Gall Tokyo) 1998, Four Scots (Australian Gall Melbourne) 1999, 2x2 (Tim Olsen Gallery Sydney) 2000, British Art Now (The Music Room London) 2001, Summer Suites (Aurobora Press San Francisco) 2002, Kitchen Sink (Thomas McCormick Gallery Chicago) 2002, Triplex (Sybaris Gallery Michigan) 2003, Evanston Biennial (Evanston Arts Center Illinois) 2004, Exquisite Corpse (Bowdoin College Museum of Art Brunswick) 2004, Black and White (Linda Ross Contemporary Art Projects Michigan) 2004, The Monoprint Show (Jill George Gallery London) 2005, Ukrainian Inst of Modern Art Chicago 2005, Flattened (Evanston Arts Center Illinois) 2006, flowers (de de ce Melbourne) 2006, Optica (Video Art Festival Gojon) 2006; works featured in art fairs incl: Glasgow Art Fair 1996, 1997, 1998 and 1999, Madrid Art Fair 1990, Int Contemporary Air Fair Los Angeles 1986, 1987, 1988 and 1989, Bath Contemporary Art Fair 1984, 1985, 1986, 1987, 1989 and 1990, San Francisco Art Fair 1999 and 2000, Chicago Art Fair 2000; work in public collection at V&A and Art Inst of Chicago; *Style*— Fraser Taylor, Esq; ✉ website www.frasertaylor.com

TAYLOR, Prof Fredric William; s of William Taylor (d 1996), of Amble, Northumberland, and Ena Lloyd, *née* Burns (d 1993); *b* 24 September 1944; *Educ* Duke's Sch, Univ of Liverpool (BSc), Univ of Oxford (DPhil); *m* 28 June 1970, Doris Jean, da of Iver Buer; *Career* sr scientist Jet Propulsion Laboratory Caltech 1970–79; Univ of Oxford: fell Jesus Coll 1979–, head Dept of Atmospheric, Oceanic and Planetary Physics 1979–2000, Halley prof of physics 2000–11, emeritus prof 2011–; medal for exceptional scientific achievement Nat Aeronautics and Space Admin 1981, Rank prize for opto-electronics 1989, special award Worshipful Co of Scientific Instrument Makers 1990; FRMS (vice-pres), FRAS, FRSA; *Books* Cambridge Atlas of the Planets (1982, 3 edn 2001), Remote Sensing of Atmospheres (1984), Titan: The Earthlike Moon (2000), non-LTE in the Atmosphere (2001), Elementary Climate Physics (2006), Titan: Exploring an Earthlike World (2008), the Scientific Exploration of Mars (2009), Planetary Atmospheres (2010), Radiation and Climate (2011), The Scientific Exploration of Venus (2014), Exploring the Planets: A Memoir (2016); *Recreations* walking, gardening, history, literature, theatre, sport, gastronomy, railways, poker; *Clubs* Meteorological, Astronomical; *Style*— Prof Fredric Taylor; ✉ Department of Atmospheric, Oceanic and Planetary Physics, Clarendon Laboratory, Parks Road, Oxford OX1 3PU

TAYLOR, Dr George Browne; s of late John Taylor, and Doreen, *née* Browne; *b* 11 May 1949; *Educ* St Aidan's Sch Sunderland, Univ of Newcastle upon Tyne Med Sch (MB BS, EdD); *m* Penelope Rose Anne, *née* Stanford; 2 da (Sarah b 2 Dec 1972, Ruth b 4 May 1979), 2 s (Matthew b 15 Dec 1975, James b 13 Nov 1981); *Career* princ in gen practice Guide Post Northumberland 1976–2001; assoc regnl advsr in gen practice Univ of Newcastle upon Tyne 1986–97, dep dir gen practice Univ of Newcastle upon Tyne 1997– 2001; dir of postgrad GP educn and assoc dean Univ of Leeds 2001–; RCGP: memb Examination Bd 1982–89, memb Cncl 1992–94 and 1996–97, chm Quality Network 1995– 97; visitor Jt Ctee on Postgrad Trg in Gen Practice 1990–; fndr Northumberland Young Practitioner Educnl Gp 1977; Nuffield visiting scholar Fiji Sch of Med 1970, RCGP visiting scholar The Netherlands 1984; FRCGP 1986 (MRCGP 1976); *Recreations* family, travel, France, wine; *Style*— Dr George Taylor

TAYLOR, Gordon; OBE (2008); s of Alec Taylor (d 1980), of Ashton under Lyne, Lancs, and Mary, *née* Walsh; *b* 28 December 1944; *Educ* Ashton under Lyne GS, Bolton Tech Coll, Univ of London (BSc Econ); *m* 27 July 1968, Catharine Margaret, da of Frederick Johnston, of Bury, Lancs; 2 s (Simon Mark b 1970, Jonathan Peter b 1973); *Career* professional footballer: Bolton Wanderers 1960–70, Birmingham City 1970–76, Blackburn Rovers 1976–78, Vancouver Whitecaps (N American Soccer League) 1977, Bury 1978– 80; sec and chief exec PFA 1981– (chm 1978–80), pres Int Body FIF-PRO 1994–2004 (hon pres 2004–); Hon MA Loughborough Univ 1986, Hon DArt De Montfort Univ 1998; *Recreations* theatre, music, reading, watching sport; *Style*— Gordon Taylor, Esq, OBE; ✉ Professional Footballers Association, 20 Oxford Court, Bishopsgate, Manchester M2 3WQ (☎ 0161 236 0575, fax 0161 228 7229)

TAYLOR, Helen Sian; da of Stephen Colin Taylor, of Winchester, Hants, and Elizabeth Anne, *née* Biddle; *b* 4 July 1970, Brighton, E Sussex; *Educ* St Anne's Convent Sch Southampton, Peter Symonds Sixth Form Coll Winchester, Victoria Univ of Manchester (BA, BArch); *Partner* Tim Altmann; 1 da (Sophie Elizabeth b 6 Feb 2007), 1 s (Rufus William b 7 May 2010); *Career* architect; sr architect then assoc Architecture PLB 2004– 11, assoc dir Capita Symonds 2012–13, assoc Bam Design 2013–14, practice dir Scott Brownrigg 2014–; memb RIBA Cncl 2002–08 and 2015– (hon sec 2005–07), fndr memb and co-chair Architects for Change RIBA Equality and Diversity Forum 2000–10, convenor RIBA Schs Forum 2008–10, chair RIBA Inclusive Design Ctee 2008–10, dep chair CIC Green Contruction Panel 2014–; RIBA 1999, FRSA; RIBA Employment Policy (2004), RIBA Access and Inclusion Policy (2005), RIBA Good Practice Guide: Employment (foreword, 2006); *Recreations* painting and drawing, cycling, reading detective novels; *Style*— Ms Helen Taylor; ✉ Scott Brownrigg, 77 Endell Street, London WC2H 9DZ (☎ 020 7240 7766, e-mail h.taylor@scottbrownrigg.com, website www.scottbrownrigg.com)

TAYLOR, Sir Hugh Henderson; KCB (2009, CB 2000); s of Leslie Henderson Taylor (d 1982), and Alison, *née* Brown (d 2013); *b* 22 March 1950; *Educ* Brentwood Sch, Emmanuel Coll Cambridge (BA); *m* 13 May 1989, Diane Heather, da of Idwal George Bacon; 2 da (Alice Joy b 25 Sept 1991, Madeleine Louise b 6 May 1993); *Career* Home Office: joined 1972, private sec to Min of State 1976–77, Radio Regulatory Dept 1977–81, princ Criminal Policy Dept 1981–83, princ private sec to Home Sec 1983–85, asst sec 1984, head Parole and Lifer Div 1985–88; seconded to Cabinet Office 1988–91, head Personnel Div Prison Service 1992–93, under sec Home Office 1993–96, seconded as head Civil Service Employer Gp Cabinet Office (OPS) 1993–96 (also dir Top Mgmnt Prog 1994–96), dir of services Prison Service 1996–97; Dept of Health: dir of HR NHS Exec 1998–2001, DG (external and corporate affrs, corporate affrs, then departmental mgmnt) 2001–06, perm sec 2006–10; chair: Guy's and St Thomas's NHS Fndn Tst, Nat Skills Acad for Health; tstee: Macmillan Cancer Support, Nuffield Tst, Cicely Saunders Int; chair James Allen's Girls Sch; *Recreations* reading, watching cricket, rugby and football, music and opera, visiting galleries; *Style*— Sir Hugh Taylor, KCB

TAYLOR, Hugh Matthew; OBE (2009); s of Derek Taylor, of Hampstead, London, and Diane, *née* Milman; *b* 3 March 1965, London; *Educ* Hasmonean GS Hendon, Middx Business Sch (BA), CIM (Dip), Pennsylvania State Univ (MSc); *m* 2 Jan 1994, Katie, *née* Baum; 1 da (Ellie b 12 Jan 1997), 3 s (Josh b 17 Oct 1998, Sam b 22 Oct 2001, Joe b 11 Oct 2003); *Career* mktg mangr Norfolk Capital Hotels 1989–90, mktg dir Radisson Edwardian Hotels 1990–92, mktg dir Ramada Jarvis Hotels 1992–2001; Hilton Hotels UK: vice-pres mktg 2001–04, regnl vice-pres 2004–07; chief exec Hilmar Hotel Mgmnt 2008–10, chief exec Michels and Taylor (London) Ltd 2010–; chm: Hotel Mktg Assoc 1995–98, Hilton in the Community Fndn, VisitEngland 2003–09; dir VisitBritain 2003–09; 15 hotel mktg awards 1998–2004, Caterer and Hotelkeeper (Catey) Award 1996 and 2004; memb Hotel and Catering Int Mgmnt Assoc 1997, fell Tourism Soc 1998, FCIM 1998; *Publications* Hotel and Catering Advertising (1999); *Recreations* tennis, theatre; *Style*— Hugh Taylor, Esq, OBE; ✉ 5 Amberden Avenue, London N3 3BJ (☎ 020 8343 4392); Michels and Taylor LLP, Suite 3, Caspian House, The Waterfront, Elstree Road, Elstree WD6 3BS (☎ 020 8905 2500, e-mail hugh.taylor@michelsandtaylor.com)

TAYLOR, Prof Irving; s of Samuel Taylor (d 1992), and Fay, *née* Valcovitch; *b* 7 January 1945; *Educ* Roundhay Sch Leeds, Univ of Sheffield Med Sch (MB ChB, MD, ChM); *m* 31

Aug 1969, Berenice Penelope, da of Dr Henry Brunner, of Slough; 3 da (Justine Samantha b 20 Oct 1971, Tamara Zoe b 5 June 1973, Gabrielle Rivka b 31 Aug 1983); *Career* sr registrar surgery Sheffield 1973–77 (registrar surgery 1971–73, res registrar 1973), sr lectr in surgery Liverpool 1977–81, prof of surgery and head Dept of Surgery Univ of Southampton 1981–93; UCL: head Dept of Surgery and chm Bd of Surgery 1993–, vice-dean and dir of clinical studies 2003–06, vice-dean professional affairs 2006–; case examiner GMC 2003; Hunterian prof RCS 1981, Jacksonian prof RCS 1996, Stanford Cade lectr RCS 2000, Bradshaw lectr RCS 2012; ed sec Assoc of Surgns 1987, ed-in-chief Euro Jl of Surgical Oncology, ed Annals RCS 2004–09; pres: Surgical Research Soc 2005–07 (sec 1985–87), Br Assoc Surgical Oncology, European Soc of Surgical Oncology (ESSO) 2006–08; chm MRC Colorectal Working Party, memb Cncl RCS 2004–, sec Assoc of Profs of Surgery 1988; FRCS 1972, memb RSM 1982, memb ILT 2002, FMedSci; *Books* Complications of Surgery of Lower Gastrointestinal Tract (1985), Progress in Surgery 1 (1985), Progress in Surgery 2 (1987), Progress in Surgery 3 (1989), Benign Breast Disease (1989), Recent Advances in Surgery 14–22 (1990 and annually 1992–2015), Fast Facts in Colorectal Cancer (2000, 3 edn 2010); *Recreations* swimming, bridge, theatre, golf, travel; *Style—* Prof Irving Taylor; ✉ Department of Surgery, University College London, 74 Huntley Street, London WC1E 6AU (☎ 020 7679 6490, e-mail irving.taylor@ucl.ac.uk)

TAYLOR, Sheriff Principal James Alastair; s of Alastair Robert Taylor (d 1983), of Nairn, and Margaret Robertson Fraser; *b* 21 February 1951; *Educ* Nairn Acad, Univ of Aberdeen (BSc, LLB); *m* 1 Nov 1980, Lesley Doig Macleod; 2 s (Andrew James b May 1983, Robbie Macleod b June 1985); *Career* apprentice to Brander & Cruickshank and Lefevre & Co Aberdeen 1975–77, asst then ptnr A C Morrison & Richards Aberdeen 1978–86; McGrigor Donald: joined 1987, ptnr 1988–98, head Litigation Dept 1992–98; slr advocate (practising in Court of Session) 1993–98; appointed all Scotland floating sheriff based in the Sheriffdom of Lothian & Borders 1998–99, sheriff of Glasgow and Strathkelvin 1999–2005, sheriff princ of Glasgow and Strathkelvin 2005–11; chm Disciplinary Bd Inst of Chartered Accountants in Scotland 2001–, memb Bd Civil Courts Review 2007–10, chm Review of the Expenses and Funding of Civil Litigation in Scotland 2011–13; dir Lodging House Mission 2002–12, sec Nairn United Reform Church 2015–; visiting prof of law Univ of Strathclyde 2007–13; Hon LLD Univ of Glasgow 2013; *Publications* International Intellectual Property Litigation (contrib), Sentencing Practice (contrib), Macphail, Sheriff Court Practice (contrib 3 edn); *Recreations* golf, jazz, food and wine; *Clubs* Royal Aberdeen Golf, Nairn Golf, Nairn Dunbar Golf; *Style—* Sheriff Principal James Taylor; ✉ Tyninghame, Albert Street, Nairn IV12 4HQ (☎ 01667 451676, e-mail jtaylor210@btinternet.com)

TAYLOR, John Edward; CBE (2013); s of Thomas Taylor (d 1962), and Margaret, *née* Renwick; *b* 14 November 1949, Chester-le-Street, Co Durham; *Educ* Chester-le-Street GS, Univ of Durham (BA); *Career* grad trainee Littlewoods Mail Order Stores Wolverhampton 1971–72, exec offr Dept of Employment 1972–75, dep to Ops Mangr ACAS 1975–77 (also sec trade union side), policy analyst Dept of Employment 1977–79, private sec to Min of State for Employment 1979–80; Manpower Servs Cmmn: personnel mangr 1980–83, branch head Strategy Branch Trg Div 1983–84; regnl mangr Employment Serv Midlands 1984–86, head Overseas Lab Unit Dept of Employment 1986–88, actg chief exec, dep chief exec and dir of ops Rural Devpt Cmmn 1988–95; chief exec: Devpt Bd for Rural Wales 1995–98, TEC SE Wales 1998–2001, ACAS 2001–13, ret; visiting prof in employment rels Univ of Glamorgan 2002–12 (memb Business Sch Mgmnt Bd 1999–2001); chm Modis UK Ltd 1999–2001; chair Workers' Educnl Assoc 2013–16, chair Careers Service Wales 2013–; memb: Industrial Rels Ctee Cabinet Office 2001–05, NHS Partnership Forum 2001–13, Bd Learning and Skills Devpt Agency 2004–06, Bd Govt Skills Cncl 2004–09, Bd Quality Improvement Agency 2006–08, Steering Bd Employment Tbnl System 2006–10 (memb Task Force 2001–06, memb Nat User Gp 2002–); memb consortium of rural TEC 1990–95, dir Powys TEC 1996–98, dir TEC S E Wales 1998–2001, memb Cncl Welsh TECs 1998–2001, memb Equal Opportunities Gp TEC Nat Cncl 1999–2001, chm Welsh TEC Equal Opportunities Forum 1999–2001; memb: EU Experts Gp on Mobility of Lab 1986–88, UK Tourism Task Force 1991–92, Rural Action for England 1993–95 (sometime chm), Mid-Wales Partnership 1995–98, N Wales Economic Forum 1996–98, SW Wales Economic Forum 1997–98, SE Wales Economic Forum 1998–2001, Wales New Deal Task Force 1998–2001, Youth Enterprise Mgmnt Bd 1998–2001, Youth Task Gp Nat Assembly for Wales 1999–2001, Objective 3 Monitoring Ctee (Wales) 2000–01, Llanwern Task Force (Corus Steel Closure Prog) 2000–01, Port Talbot Task Force (Tata Steel closure); dir Wales European Centre Brussels 1999–2001; Olympics Legacy advsr to Rio de Janeiro; dir Mgmnt Bd Ystrad Mynach Coll 2000–01, govr Univ of W London (formerly Thames Valley Univ) 2005– (dep chair of govrs 2010–14); German Marshall Fellowship scholar to USA 1986; Hon DLit Univ of W London 2014; MInstD 1997, CCMI 2003, memb Inst of Assoc Mgmnt 2006; *Recreations* cricket, travel, real ale; *Clubs* Durham CCC, Sunderland AFC; *Style—* John Taylor, Esq, CBE; ✉ Careers Wales, Tyglyn Unit 4 Brecon Court, William Brown Close, Llantarnam Park, Cwmbran NP44 3AB (☎ 07900 406994, e-mail jtaylor49@btinternet.com)

TAYLOR, Dr John Hilton; s of Charles Ronald Taylor, of St Helens, Merseyside, and Brenda, *née* Hilton; *b* 7 May 1958; *Educ* Grange Park Secdy Sch St Helens, Cowley Boys Sch St Helens, Univ of Birmingham (BA, PhD); *m* 24 Sept 1988, Rhona Margaret, da of James Henry Minshull; 1 da (Katherine Sarah Minshull b 29 Aug 1991), 1 s (James Nicholas Minshull b 26 Oct 1994); *Career* Egyptologist; memb Egypt Exploration Soc expedition to Amarna 1981; lectr in Egyptology: Workers Educnl Assoc 1981 and 1985–86, Dept of Extramural Studies Univ of Birmingham 1985–87; curator Dept of Ancient Egypt and Sudan British Museum 1988–; specialist conslt to Gold of the Pharaohs exhbn City Art Centre Edinburgh 1987–88, exhbn organiser Howard Carter – Before Tutankhamun Br Museum 1992–93, exhbn organiser Mummy: The Inside Story Br Museum 2004–05, exhibition curator Journey through the Afterlife: Ancient Egyptian Book of the Dead Br Museum 2010–11, exhibition curator Ancient Lives: New Discoveries Br Museum 2014–15; memb Univ of Cambridge Theban Mission to Luxor 1999–2000; memb Ctee Egypt Exploration Soc 1988–91, 1993–95, 1997–2000 and 2004–06 (hon librarian 1993–98), memb Ctee Assoc for the Study of Travel in Egypt and the Near East 2004–10; reviews ed Jl of Egyptian Archaeology 1993–2005, ed Egyptian Archaeology 1994–96; memb Cncl Soc for Libyan Studies 1997–2005; hon fell Inst for Advanced Research in the Humanities Univ of Birmingham 1987–89; *Books* Egyptian Coffins (1989), Egypt and Nubia (1991), Howard Carter – Before Tutankhamun (with Nicholas Reeves, 1992), Unwrapping a Mummy (1995), Death and the Afterlife in Ancient Egypt (2001), The Theban Necropolis: Past, Present and Future (jt ed with Nigel Strudwick, 2003), Mummy: The Inside Story (2004), Mummies: Death and the Afterlife in Ancient Egypt – Treasures from the British Museum (with Nigel Strudwick, 2005), Journey through the Afterlife: Ancient Egyptian Book of the Dead (jt ed, 2010), Egyptian Mummies (2010), Spells for Eternity (2010), Ancient Lives: New Discoveries (with Daniel Antoine, 2014); *Recreations* genealogy, English literature, music; *Style—* Dr John H Taylor; ✉ Department of Ancient Egypt and Sudan, The British Museum, Great Russell Street, London WC1B 3DG (☎ 020 7323 8330, e-mail jtaylor@britishmuseum.org)

TAYLOR, John Leonard; s of Leonard William Taylor, and Kathleen, *née* Markey; *b* 21 June 1957; *Educ* St Peter's Sch Southbourne; *m* Moyra; 1 da (Verity b 5 Sept 1989), 1 s (Sean b 22 Jan 1992); *Career* media planner/buyer Allen Brady & Marsh Ltd 1975–78; FCB Advertising Ltd: media mangr 1978–86, media dir 1986–90, dep md 1990–92; md Optimedia UK 1992–96, dir of int ops Optimedia International Ltd 1999–2001 (dir Euro ops 1996–2001), chief operating offr Optimedia Worldwide 2001–, dir strategic resources and client service ZenithOptimedia Gp 2002–, global chm ZenithOptimedia 2009; *Recreations* triathlon, motorcycling, golf, skiing; *Style—* John Taylor, Esq

TAYLOR, Sir John Michael; kt (2004), OBE (1994); s of Eric John Taylor (d 1979), and Dorothy Irene, *née* Spring (d 2000); *b* 15 February 1943; *Educ* King Edward's Sch Birmingham, Emmanuel Coll Cambridge (MA, PhD); *m* 14 Aug 1965, Judith, *née* Moyle; 4 c; *Career* UK Govt 1969–84: supt Computer Applications Div RSRE Malvern 1979–81, head of Command Systems Div Admiralty Surface Weapons Estab 1981–82, head of Command Control and Communications Dept Admiralty Res Estab 1982–84; dir: Info Systems Laboratory Hewlett-Packard Laboratories 1984–86, Bristol Res Centre 1986–90, Hewlett-Packard Laboratories Europe 1990–98 (memb Bd of Dirs Hewlett Packard Ltd 1992–98); DG Research Cncls DTI 1999–2003, chm Roke Manor Research 2004–10; non-exec dir Rolls Royce 2005–07; visiting prof Univ of Oxford 2003–10; pres IEE (UK) 1998–99, memb Cncl Royal Acad of Engrg 2004–07, chair Web Science Tst 2009–14; hon fell Emmanuel Coll Cambridge 2000–; FREng 1986, FRS 1998, FIEE, FBCS, FInstP; *Recreations* family, music, theatre, photography, sailing; *Style—* Sir John M Taylor, OBE, FRS, FREng

TAYLOR, John Russell; s of Arthur Russell Taylor (d 1966), of Dover, Kent, and Kathleen Mary, *née* Picker (d 1991); *b* 19 June 1935; *Educ* Dover GS, Jesus Coll Cambridge (MA), Courtauld Inst of Art London; *Partner* Ying Yeung Li (civil partner, 2006); *Career* The Times: sub ed Educnl Supplement 1959–60, ed asst Literary Supplement 1960–62, film critic 1962–73, American cultural corr 1972–78, art critic 1978–2005; prof Cinema Div Univ of Southern Calif 1972–78, ed Films and Filming 1983–90; memb: Critics' Circle 1962, Private Libraries Assoc 1967 (pres 1986–88), Assoc Art Historians 1985; AICA 1978; *Books* incl: Anger and After (1962), Cinema Eye Cinema Ear (1964), The Art Nouveau Book in Britain (1966), The Rise and Fall of the Well-Made Play (1967), The Art Dealers (1969), The Hollywood Musical (1971), The Second Wave (1971), Graham Greene on Film (ed 1972), Directors and Directions (1975), Hitch (1978), Impressionism (1981), Strangers in Paradise (1983), Alec Guinness (1984), Edward Wolfe (1986), Orson Welles (1986), Bernard Meninsky (1990), Impressionist Dreams (1990), Ricardo Cinalli (1992), Muriel Pemberton (1993), Igor Mitoraj (1994), Claude Monet (1995), Michael Parkes: The Stone Lithographs (1996), Bill Jacklin (1997), The Sun is God (1999), Peter Coker (2002), Philip Sutton Printmaker (2005), Adrian Henry (2005), The Art of Michael Parkes (2006), Roboz (2006), Donald McGill (2006), The Painter's Quarry (2006), Carl Laubin (2007), The Glamour of the Gods (2008), Philip Sutton (2008), Exactitude (2009), Kurt Jackson (2010), Face to Face (2011), Philip Hicks (2013), High Relief (2016), Robert Barnes Man of Mysteries (2016); *Recreations* buying books, talking to strange dogs; *Style—* Mr John Russell Taylor

TAYLOR, Jonathan Francis; CBE (2005); s of Sir Reginald William Taylor (d 1971), of Great Haseley, Oxon, and Lady (Sarah) Ruth, *née* Tyson (d 1993); *b* 12 August 1935; *Educ* Winchester, CCC Oxford (MA); *m* 8 April 1965, (Anthea) Gail, da of Robert Vergette Proctor (d 1985), of Sheffield, S Yorks; 3 s (Luke b 1968, Matthew b 1970, James b 1972); *Career* Nat Serv 2 Lt KAR 1954–56; Booker plc: joined 1959, chm Agric Div 1976–80, dir 1980, chief exec 1984–93, chm 1993–98, chm Booker Prize Mgmnt Ctee 1996–2001, chm Booker Prize Fndn 2001–15 (pres 2016–); non-exec dir: Tate & Lyle plc 1988–99, MEPC plc 1992–2000, The Equitable Life Assurance Society 1995–2000; chm Ellis & Everard 1993–2000; pres IBEC Inc (USA) 1980–84; Arbor Acres Farm Inc USA 1991–98, Winrock Int (USA) 1991–2001; dir and past chm Fndn for the Devpt of Polish Agric 1991–2002; chm: Governing Body SOAS Univ of London 1999–2005 (govr 1988–2005), Paintings in Hospitals 1996–2006, Caine Prize for African Writing 1999–, Marshall Cmmn 2000–07, Int Prize for Arabic Fiction 2005–13; memb Advsy Cncl UNIDO 1986–93, curator Bodleian Library 1989–98; govr: RAC Cirencester 1995–2010, Int Inst for the Environment & Devpt, Cwlth Inst 1998–2005; hon fell CCC Oxford, hon fell SOAS Univ of London 2010–; CIMgt 1984, FRSA 1990; *Recreations* travel, collecting watercolours, reading; *Clubs* Brooks's; *Style—* Jonathan Taylor, Esq, CBE; ✉ 48 Edwardes Square, Kensington, London W8 6HH (e-mail jonathan@jftaylor.com)

TAYLOR, Jonathan Jeremy Kirwan; s of Sir Charles Stuart Taylor, TD, DL; *b* 12 October 1943, London; *Educ* Eton, St Edmund Hall Oxford (MA); *m* 1966 (sep 1999), Victoria Mary Caroline, da of Hon John Francis McLaren (d 1953); 4 da (Arabella b 1969, Lucinda b 1972, Caroline b 1976, Katherine b 1979); partner, Dominique Vulliamy; 1 da (Coco b 1999); *Career* called to the Bar Middle Temple 1968; dir Baring Asset 1989–97 (formerly Baring Int Investment Mgmnt Ltd) and other Baring Investment Gp Cos; chm: Dragon Partners Ltd, Schroder Japan Growth Fund plc; md Onyx Country Estates Ltd; dir Greater China Fund Inc; *Recreations* skiing (Br Olympic Team 1964), golf, tennis, boating; *Clubs* White's, Hong Kong; *Style—* Jonathan Taylor, Esq; ✉ Rynehill House, Kingham, Oxfordshire OX7 6UL (e-mail jonathan.taylor@dragonpartners.co.uk)

TAYLOR, Jonathan McLeod Grigor; s of John Grigor Taylor, and Dorothy Jean, *née* McLeod; *b* 5 March 1955, London; *Educ* Bedales, New Coll Oxford (BA); *m* 1984, Stella, *née* Schimmel; 1 s (James b 1991), 1 da (Venetia b 1995); *Career* HM Treasy 1977–98, cnsllr economics and finance UK Permanent Representation to EU 1994–98, dir macroeconomic policy and int fin HM Treasy 1998–2002, head of public policy UBS AG 2002–05, DG London Investment Banking Assoc (LIBA) 2005–; chm Jt Money Laundering Steering Gp 2009–; *Style—* Jonathan Taylor, Esq; ✉ London Investment Banking Association, 6 Frederick's Place, London EC2R 8BT

TAYLOR, Eur Ing Kenneth; JP (1983); s of Kenneth Warburton Taylor (d 1989) and Kathleen, *née* Dilworth (d 2007); *b* 26 January 1941, Great Harwood, Lancs; *Educ* Accrington Tech Sch, Burnley Coll (HNC), Openshaw Coll (IHVE); *m* 10 June 1960, Jean, da of Dr Staff (d 1956); 1 s (John b 1961), 1 da (Jeanette b 1962); *Career* design engr Burnley Co Borough 1963–71, princ Taylor Marren and Haslam (consltg engrs) 1971–85, chief building serv engr Oldham Met Borough 1985–88, chm Taylor Associates Ltd (consltg forensic engrs) 1988–; expert witness; many pubns in professional jls on legal matters; past chm CIBSE North West; memb Adjudication Soc; Freeman City of London 1999, Liveryman Worshipful Co of Plumbers; CEng, Eur Ing, MAE, FCIBSE, FIPlantE, FSOE, RP, FCIPHE, FRSA, FCMI, memb American Soc of Heating, Refrigerating and Air-Conditioning Engrs (MASHRAE); *Books* A Practical Guide for the Expert Witness, Plant Engineers Reference Book (jt author); *Recreations* music, lectures on building services and health and safety matters; *Clubs* Foreign Travel; *Style—* Eur Ing Kenneth Taylor; ✉ 71 Beaufort Avenue, Bispham, Blackpool, Lancashire FY2 9AG (☎ 01253 596308); Taylor Associates Ltd (fax 01253 596818, e-mail forensic.engineer@tiscali.co.uk, website www.kentaylor.org.uk)

TAYLOR, Prof Kenneth MacDonald (Ken); s of Hugh Baird Taylor (d 1996), of Crail, Fife, and Mary, *née* MacDonald (d 1978); *b* 20 October 1947; *Educ* Jordanhill Coll Sch Glasgow, Univ of Glasgow (MB ChB, MD); *m* 14 May 1971, Christine Elizabeth (d 2010), da of John Buchanan (d 1986), of Ullapool, Ross-shire; 1 s (Iain b 1972), 1 da (Kirstin b 1975); *Career* Hall fell in surgery Western Infirmary Glasgow 1971–72, sr lectr in cardiac surgery Royal Infirmary Glasgow 1980–83 (lectr 1974–79); Imperial Coll Sch of Med at Hammersmith Hosp (Royal Postgrad Med Sch until merger 1997): Br Heart Fndn prof of cardiac surgery 1983–2007 (emeritus prof of cardiac surgery 2007–), vice-chm Cardiovascular and Respiratory Div 1997–2007, memb Principals' Advsy Gp 1997–2002, clinical dir Cardiac Servs Hammersmith Hosp 2003–07, pres Friends of Hammersmith Hosp 2007–; memb: Assoc of Profs of Surgery, Specialist Advsy Ctee in Cardiothoracic

T

Surgery (chm 1992–95), Dept of Health Working Pty on Waiting Times for Coronary Artery Disease 1994–95, Nat Serv Frameworks Reference Panel for Coronary Heart Disease Dept of Health 1998–2002; chm: Database Ctee Euro Assoc for Cardiac Surgery 1994–2002, UK Central Cardiac Audit Steering Ctee 1995–2002; pres Soc of Perfusionists GB and Ireland 1989–94 (hon memb 1997); dir Sch of Perfusion Sciences, govr Drayton Manor HS London 1989–94; tstee: Garfield Weston Tst, European Bd of Cardiovascular Perfusion; memb Editorial Bd: Annals of Thoracic Surgery 1990–2000, Jl of Cardiothoracic and Vascular Anaesthesia 1993–, Jl of Heart Valve Disease 1992–; Br Heart Fndn: memb Cncl 2000–10, memb Exec Ctee 2000–06, tstee 2006–10; hon memb American Acad of Cardiovascular Perfusion; memb: Surgical Res Soc 1977, Soc of Cardiothoracic Surgns of GB and Ireland 1979, British Cardiac Soc 1983, Soc of Thoracic Surgns of America 1986 (memb Database Ctee 1998–), Euro Assoc for Cardiothoracic Surgery 1988 (emeritus fell 2008–), American Assoc for Thoracic Surgery 1989 (honored guest 1998, hon memb 1998); hon alumnus Dept of Cardiovascular and Thoracic Surgery Cleveland Clinic USA; FRCS, FRCSGlas, FESC, fell European Bd of Thoracic and Cardiovascular Surgeons (FETCS); Books Pulsatile Perfusion (1982), Handbook of Intensive Care (1984), Perfusion (ed, 1984–2007), Cardiopulmonary Bypass – Principles and Management (1986), Principles of Surgical Research (1989, 2 edn 1995), Cardiac Surgery and the Brain (1992); numerous scientific jl publications in cardiac surgery; Recreations family, church, music; Style— Prof Ken Taylor; ✉ 129 Argyle Road, Ealing, London W13 0DB (e-mail k.m.taylor@imperial.ac.uk)

TAYLOR, Prof Laurence John (Laurie); s of Stanley Douglas Taylor, and Winifred Agnes, née Cooper; Educ St Mary's Coll Liverpool, Rose Bruford Coll, Birkbeck Univ of London (BA), Univ of Leicester (MA); m 1; 1 s (Matthew b 5 Dec 1960); m 2, 16 Dec 1988 (m dis 2009), Catherine, da of Harold Francis Mahoney; Career librarian Liverpool City Cncl 1952–54, salesman British Enka Ltd 1954–57, actor Theatre Workshop Stratford 1960–61, teacher Forest Hill Comp 1961–64; Univ of York: lectr 1965–70, sr lectr 1970–73, reader 1973–75, prof 1975–94; visiting prof: Birkbeck Coll London 1994–, Univ of Westminster 2004–; presenter In Confidence (Sky Arts) 2010; various radio appearances incl: Stop the Week, Speaking as an Expert, The Afternoon Shift, Thinking Allowed, Room for Improvement; Hon DLitt Univ of Nottingham 1992, Hon DPhil Univ of Central England 1993, Hon DLitt Univ of Leicester 2004; fell Birkbeck Coll London; Books Psychological Survival (1972), Escape Attempts (1976), In The Underworld (1984), Professor Lapping Sends His Apologies (1986), The Tuesday Afternoon Time Immemorial Committee (1989), Escape Attempts Revisited (1992), Laurie Taylor's Guide to Higher Education (1994), What are Children For? (2002); Recreations football, jazz; Clubs Groucho; Style— Prof Laurie Taylor; ✉ e-mail lolsoc@dircon.co.uk

TAYLOR, Leon; s of Roy Taylor, and Sue Taylor; b 2 November 1977; Career diver; achievements incl: Bronze medal 10m platform Cwlth Games 1998, Bronze medal 10m synchronised European Championships 1999, fourth place 10m synchronised Olympic Games Sydney 2000, Silver medal 10m platform Cwlth Games 2002, Silver medal 10m synchronised Olympic Games 2004, Bronze medal 10m synchronised World Championships 2005; Style— Leon Taylor, Esq

TAYLOR, Margaret Cecilia (Maggie); da of John Marcus Kisch (d 1992), of Dunsfold, Surrey, and Gillian May, née Poyser; b 31 March 1955; Educ Godolphin Sch, St Hilda's Coll Oxford (BA); m 30 June 1984, Lee Taylor, s of Edward Thomas Taylor; 1 da (Chloë May b 9 March 1992), 1 s (Henry Thomas b 1 July 1994); Career research exec Br Market Research Bureau 1978–80, sr research exec Market Behaviour Ltd 1980–83; Saatchi & Saatchi Advertising: account planner 1983–87, bd dir 1987–90, divnl planning dir 1990; fndr planning ptnr Cowan Kemsley Taylor 1990–97, dir RPM3 (following merger with Butler Lutos Sutton Wilkinson) 1997–2003, fndr dir Kisch Taylor Consulting 2003–; dir Project Tst 1999–; memb: Market Research Soc 1978–, Assoc of Qualitative Research Practitioners 1982, Account Planning Gp 1983–, Women in Advertising and Communication London 1997–; vol Samaritans 2007–; MIPA 1990; Recreations skiing, amateur dramatics (memb Cranbourne Amateur Dramatic Soc); Style— Mrs Maggie Taylor; ✉ The Old Fox, Winkfield Row, Berkshire RG42 6NG

TAYLOR, Margie; CBE; b Edinburgh, Scotland; Educ Univ of Edinburgh (BDS, MSc), MBA, FDSRCSEd, FDSRCPS (Glasg), FFPH, FFGDP; Career chief administrative dental offr Fife Health Bd 1988–94, conslt in dental public health NHS Lanarkshire 1994–2007, chief dental offr Scottish Govt 2007–; FDSRCSE, FDSRCPS, FFGDP; Style— Ms Margie Taylor, CBE; ✉ Scottish Government Health and Social Care Directorate, St Andrew's House, Edinburgh EH1 3DG

TAYLOR, Mark Christopher; s of Joseph Norman Taylor, and June Taylor; b 24 November 1958; Educ Loughborough GS, Univ of Birmingham (BA), Leeds Poly (Dip Hotel Mgmnt); m (m dis); 2 s (Jack b 1990, Liam b 1994), 1 da (Eleanor b 1991); Career hotel mangr Norfolk Capital Hotels 1981–84; chm: Network of Euro Museum Organisations 1998–2001, Campaign for Learning Through Museums 1998–2003, Tourism Heritage Export 2003–05; dir Museums Assoc 1989–2014 (conf mangr 1984–89), memb Bd Nat Campaign for the Arts 1999–2008; memb Bd: Bedfordshire Music Tst 2002–, Bedfordshire Museum Tst 2002–15, Culture Unlimited 2008–12, Harpur Tst 2016–; tstee Campaign for Museums 2004–08; Interim CEO VocalEyes 2014–15, CE Soc of Homeopaths 2015–; Recreations sport, film, food; Style— Mark Taylor, Esq; ✉ e-mail taylors.bedford@ntlworld.com

TAYLOR, Mark R F; b 6 December 1943; Educ Oriel Coll Oxford (MA), Univ of Manchester (NHS UK Admin Trg Scheme), Canadian Coll of Health Serv Execs (Certified Health Exec); m; Career lectr/tutor Dip Course in Health Servs Admin Aston Univ Birmingham 1968–70, admin The Aga Khan Hosp Kenya 1971–74 (asst admin 1970), conslt Peat Marwick & Partners Canada 1974–79, exec sec The Aga Khan Fndn Kenya 1979–81, princ Woods Gordon (Ernst & Young) Management Consultants Canada 1981–84, sr vice-pres Toronto Western Hosp Canada 1984–86, chief exec Cromwell Hosp London 1987–89, pres Addiction Research Fndn Toronto 1989–94; chief exec: Royal Devon & Exeter Healthcare NHS Tst 1994–96, Royal Brompton Hosp NHS Tst 1996–98, Royal Brompton and Harefield NHS Tst 1998–2003; chm Devon Partnership NHS Tst 2009–13; non-exec dir NICE 2003–09 (vice-chm 2005–09), assoc Healthcare Cmmn 2003–09; memb Bd Ind Hosps Assoc 1988–89, fndr memb Bd Crossmatch Health Personnel Agency Ltd 1988–89, chm Toronto Academic Health Scis Cncl 1990–94, hon vice-pres Int Cncl on Alcohol and Addictions 1991– (chair Fin Panel 1992–97), dir CORDA (Heart charity) 1998–2003; govr Univ of Plymouth 2005–09, stee St Loye's Fndn 2014–, tstee Community Care Tst SW 2015–, vice-chari St Loye's Fndn and Community Care Tst SW 2016–; contrib various learned jls and other pubns; Recreations sailing, travel; Clubs Royal Dart Yacht; Style— Mark R F Taylor, Esq; ☎ 07768 751355, e-mail mrft@btopenworld.com

TAYLOR, Prof Sir Martin John; kt (2009); s of John Maurice Taylor, of Leicester, and Sheila Mary Barbara, née Camacho; b 18 February 1952; Educ Wyggeston GS, Pembroke Coll Oxford (MA), KCL (PhD); m 1 Dec 1973, Sharon Lynn, da of Harold Marlow; 2 da (Rebecca b 28 July 1977, Deborah b 9 May 1979), 2 s (Andrew b 19 March 1981, James b 3 July 1983); Career res asst KCL 1976–77, jr lectr Univ of Oxford 1977–78, lectr QMC London 1978–81, professeur associé Besançon 1979–80, fell Trinity Coll Cambridge 1981–85, chair in pure mathematics UMIST (now Univ of Manchester) 1985–; London Mathematical Soc: memb Cncl, jr Whitehead prize 1982, Adams prize 1983, pres 1998–2000, Fröhlich lectr 2003; Royal Soc: Leverhulme sr res fell 1991–92, memb Cncl 2000–01, Wolfson Research Merit Award holder 2002–, vice-pres and physical sec 2004–09; chm Bramhall Cncl of Churches; Warden Merton Coll Oxford 2010, hon fell Pembroke

Coll Oxford 2012; Hon DSc Univ of Leicester 2006, Hon DSc Univ of Bordeaux 2009; FRS 1996, EPSRC sr fell 1999– (memb Cncl 2004–09); Books Classgroups of Group Rings (1983), Elliptic Functions and Rings of Integers (with P Cassou-Noguès), Algebraic Number Theory (with A Fröhlich), L-functions and Arithmetic (with J Coates), Group Rings and Class Groups (with K Roggenkamp), Elliptic Functions and Rings of Integers (with P Cassou-Noguès); Style— Prof Sir Martin Taylor, FRS; ✉ Merton College, Oxford OX1 4JD (☎ 01865 276352, e-mail wardens@merton.ox.ac.uk)

TAYLOR, Baron (Life Peer UK 2010), of Truro in the County of Cornwall; Matthew Owen John Taylor; s of Kenneth Heywood (Ken) Taylor, and Gillian Dorothea, née Black; bro of Vikki Heywood, qv; b 3 January 1963; Educ St Paul's, Tremorvah Sch, Treliske Sch, Univ Coll Sch, Lady Margaret Hall Oxford (BA); m 2007, Victoria Sophie Garner; 3 s; Career pres Oxford Univ Students' Union 1985–86, econ research asst Parly Lib Pty 1986–87 (attached to late David Penhaligon, MP for Truro); MP (Lib until 1988, then Lib Dem): Truro (March by-election) 1987–97, Truro and St Austell 1997–2010; Lib Dem Parly spokesman on: energy 1987–88, local govt, housing and tport 1988–89, trade and industry 1989–90, educn 1990–92, Citizens' Charter and youth issues 1992–94, the environment 1994–99, Lib Dem shadow chllr 1999–2003, chm Lib Dem Parly Party 2003–05, Lib Dem shadow for Cabinet Office and social exclusion 2006–07, special advsr to the govt on sustainable rural communities (land use and planning) 2007–08 (author Living Working Countryside report 2008); chm: Lib Dem Communications Ctee 1989–92, Lib Dem Campaigns & Communications Ctee 1992–94, Government Review of Planning Practice Guidance 2013–14; chm Nat Housing Fedn 2010–, fndr chair The Rural Coalition 2009–12; owner dir Taylor & Garner Ltd 2009–; non-exec dir: South West Water Ltd 2010–, Mayfield Market Towns Ltd 2013–, Bridgehall Real Estate Ltd 2013–; pres Nat Assoc of Local Cncls (NALC) 2015–; visiting prof of planning Plymouth Univ 2015–; Publications Living Working Countryside (2008), The Rural Challenge (2010), Planning Practice Guidance Review (2013), Garden Villages (2015); Style— The Lord Taylor of Goss Moor; ✉ House of Lords, London SW1A 0PW

TAYLOR, Michael Paul Gordon; s of Gordon Taylor, and Stella, née Marsh; b 2 March 1949; Educ Altrincham GS, St John's Coll Cambridge; Career ptnr Norton Rose 1979–2009 (based in Milan office 2000–08), ptnr Gowlings 2010–; Freeman City of London Slrs Co; memb: Int Bar Assoc, Law Soc, MInstEn; Recreations sport, theatre, reading; Clubs RAC; Style— Michael Taylor, Esq

TAYLOR, Air Cdre Neil Ernest; s of William Ernest Taylor (d 1999), of Sheffield, and Marjorie, née Needes (d 1999); b 6 December 1947; Educ Central Tech Sch Sheffield, Univ of Sheffield (BSc), Univ of Cambridge (MA); m 14 Feb 1976, Angela, da of Bernard Hirst; 3 s (Andrew James b 7 Dec 1976, Richard Jeremy b 17 May 1979, Mark Nicholas b 14 Dec 1982); Career cmmnd RAF Coll Cranwell 1971; pilot trg 1971–73, pilot (Lightning, Phantom) 1974–81, Flt Cdr 111 Sqdn and 23 Sqdn 1981–84, personnel offr 1984–85, attended JSDC 1985–86, staff offr MOD 1986–88, OC 23 Sqdn 1988–91, dir of Def Studies (RAF) 1991–94, CO RAF Akrotiri 1994–96, dep dir MOD 1997, sr air advsr HQ Bosnia-Herzegovina 1997–98, dir of personnel RAF 1998–99, asst COS Ops NATO HQ AIRCENT 1999–2000, COS Reaction Force Air Staff Kalkar Germany 2000–01; fell Hughes Hall Cambridge 2002–15 (life fell 2016–); vice-pres Royal Soc of St George (Westminster branch); memb RAF Oxford and Cambridge Soc; Books Soviet Forces in Transition (1992), The Gulf War and Some Lessons Learned (1992), The Role of Air Power in Crisis Management (1993), AP3000 Air Power Doctrine (1993), A Short History of the Royal Air Force (1994); Recreations private pilot, golf, computing, gardening, carpentry; Clubs RAF; Style— Air Commodore N E Taylor; ✉ Hughes Hall, Cambridge CB1 2EW

TAYLOR, Neil Frederick; b 25 May 1951; Educ Batley GS, Univ of Sheffield (BA, Dip Architecture); Career architect; ptnr FaulknerBrowns; commissions incl: The Dome Doncaster, Civic Offices Chester-le-Street, Claremont Sports Hall, Blackburn Leisure Pool, Perth Waters, Leeds Pedestrianisation; contrib various publications incl: Architects Jl, Architects Review, Domus, Design, Beven Wohnen, Architekt, Architecture d'Aujourd'hui, Sunday Times, Financial Times, Guardian, Telegraph, Economist, Building Design; Summer Exhibition RA (rep UK World Expo Brisbane 1988); Awards incl: Civic Tst, RIBA, Europa Nostra, IAKS, Structural Steel, Financial Times; visiting prof Univ of Newcastle 1992–, external examiner Liverpool John Moores Univ (previously for Univ of Newcastle), visiting critic Univ of Sheffield; memb: Urban Design Gp, Validation Ctee Liverpool John Moores Univ, RIBA Visiting Bd of Educn, Higher Educn Funding Cncl Validation Bd, ARCUK; RIBA, MIMgt; Recreations involved in local education, architectural history, social evolution of history, football, cricket, riding; Style— Neil Taylor, Esq

TAYLOR, Nicholas (Nick); Educ Univ of Oxford, INSEAD; Career Waterman Partnership: joined 1982, assoc dir 1987–94, dir 1994, jt md 2000, chm Waterman Structures 2005, chief exec Waterman Gp plc 2007– (memb Bd 2003–); MICE 1986; Style— Nick Taylor, Esq; ✉ Waterman Group plc, Pickfords Wharf, Clink Street, London SE1 9DG

TAYLOR, (John) Patrick Enfield; s of Arthur Hugh Enfield Taylor, RNVR (d 1983), and Monica Soames, née Cooke (d 2003); b 3 April 1948; Educ Eton; m 1972, Heather Diana, da of Col Roger Barratt (d 2004); 3 da (Melissa b 1976, Pippa b 1980, Hermione b 1983), 1 s (Rupert b 1979); Career ptnr Coopers & Lybrand 1980–86 (qualified 1972), fin dir Langdale Group plc 1986–88, dir of fin and business devpt Capital Radio plc 1989–96, chief exec GWR Group plc 2001–03 (non-exec dir 1994–96, dep chief exec and fin dir 1996–2001), chm Nonstop Adventure Ltd, non-exec dir Future plc 2001–11, chm Centaur Media plc 2009– (non-exec dir 2004–09), chm Skiplex Ltd 2011–; FCA; Recreations tennis, sailing, skiing, walking; Clubs Boodles, Muthaiga (Nairobi); Style— Patrick Taylor, Esq; ✉ e-mail patrick@nonstopadventure.com

TAYLOR, Prof Peter; s of Peter Taylor (d 1980), and Margaret Alice, née Tedman (d 2003); b 21 November 1944, Tring, Herts; Educ Henry Mellish GS Nottingham, Univ of Liverpool (BA, PhD); m 30 Oct 1965, Enid; 1 s (Carl Richard b 8 June 1966), 1 da (Clare Elizabeth b 6 Dec 1969); Career lectr rising to prof of political geography Univ of Newcastle upon Tyne 1970–96, prof of geography Loughborough Univ 1995–2010 (co-dir Globalization and World Cities (GaWC) research network), prof of human geography Northumbria Univ 2010–15 (emeritus prof 2015–); founding ed: Political Geography 1982–98, Review of Int Political Economy 1992–97; author of more than 400 pubns; Hon Dr: Univ of Oulu 2006, Univ of Ghent 2008; AcSS 2001, FBA 2004; Publications The Political Geography of the Twentieth Century (ed, 1992), Political Geography: World-Economy, Nation-State, Locality (1993, 6 edn (with C Flint) 2011), Geographies of Global Change: Remapping the World in the Late Twentieth Century (jt ed, 1995), World Cities in a World-System (jt ed, 1995), The Way the Modern World Works: World Hegemony to World Impasse (1996), Open the Social Sciences (Gulbenkian Cmmn, 1996), Modernities: A Geohistorical Interpretation (1999), The American Century: Consensus and Coercion in the Projection of American Power (jt ed, 1999), World City Network: A Global Urban Analysis (2004), Cities in Globalization (jt ed, 2006), The Globalization of Advertizing (jtly, 2010, Global Urban Analysis: A Survey of Cities in Globalization (jt ed, 2010), International Handbook of Cities and Globalization (jt ed, 2011), Extraordinary Cities: Millennia of Moral Syndromes, World-Systems and City/State Relations (2013); also author of numerous book contribs, jl papers, reports and reviews; Style— Prof Peter Taylor; ✉ 33 Percy Park, Tynemouth NE30 4JZ (☎ 0191 259 1113, e-mail crogfam@yahoo.com); School of Built and Natural Environment, Northumbria University, Ellison Place, Newcastle upon Tyne NE1 8ST

TAYLOR, Philip (Phil); OBE (2011); s of Alexander Taylor (d 1989), and Veronica, *née* Walsh (d 2001); *b* 21 January 1953, Macclesfield; *Educ* All Hallows RC Sch Macclesfield; *m* 5 Jan 1990, Lesley Ann Jenkins; 1 da (Nina Louise b 29 March 1982), 1 s (Alexander James b 5 May 1984); *Career* joined HM Prison Serv 1978; prison offr HMDC Kirklevington and HMP Frankland 1978–88, sr offr HMP Stafford 1989–91 (prison offr 1988–89), princ offr PSC Wakefield and HM Young Offenders Inst Brinsford 1991–93, govr HMP Sudbury, HMP Drake Hall and HMP Birmingham 1993–2000, dep govr HMP Gartree 2000–03, govr HMP Swansea 2003, govr HMP Bullingdon 2006, sr govr HMP Wormwood Scrubs, ret from prison service 2013; currently: conslt Int Centre for Prison Studies, memb Awarding Panel Butler Tst, tstee Prison Advice and Care Tst (PACT), project dir Jt European Social Fund and Nat Offender Mgmnt Service Project, non-exec dir Pact Futures 2014–; *Recreations* hot air ballooning, Formula One motor racing, walking, swimming with dolphins, spending time with my grandchildren; *Style—* Phil Taylor, Esq, OBE; ✉ e-mail philandles@btopenworld.com

TAYLOR, (Louis) Philip Chetwynd; s of Philip Hugh Taylor (d 2000), and Mable Doreen, *née* Bladen (d 1986); *b* 9 October 1950; *Educ* Malvern Coll; *m* 22 May 1976, Odette, da of Thomas Demajo (d 2014); 2 da (Ruth Doreen Theresa b 21 Nov 1980, Harriet Charlotte Christina b 6 May 1984); *Career* PricewaterhouseCoopers (formerly Price Waterhouse before merger): London 1970–75, Johannesburg 1975–78, ptnr 1985, sr ptnr 1993–2007; chm Hawksford Int Ltd 2011–; dir: Royal Bank of Scotland Int Ltd 2012, City Merchants High Yield Tst Ltd 2012–, St John's Wood Square Ltd 2012–, JP Morgan Global Convertibles Income Tst Ltd 2013–; regional chm Coutts Channel Islands 2012–; chm Jersey Branch IoD 1990–93, memb Accounting and Actuarial Discipline Bd 2011–12, memb Conduct Ctee and Case Management Ctees Financial Reporting Cncl 2012–15; cmmr Jersey Financial Services Cmmn 2009–12; dir Jersey Int Business Sch 2009–; chm Jersey Coll for Girls 2000–13; FCA (ACA 1973); *Recreations* cricket, gardening; *Clubs* United (St Helier); *Style—* Philip Taylor, Esq; ✉ Pont Marquet Farm, La Rue du Pont Marquet, St Brelade, Jersey JE3 8DS (✆ 01534 744584, e-mail lpc.taylor@gmail.com)

TAYLOR, Raymond Barry (Ray); s of John Gordon Taylor, of Potters Bar, Herts, and Jean Mary, *née* Hasloch; *b* 26 July 1958; *Educ* Chancellor's Sch; *m* 1982, Sally Patricia, da of Donald Robert Roser; 2 s (Barry b 8 April 1987, Josh b 6 Jan 1992); *Career* set up mktg communications business in 1979 (TPS, renamed Revolution 1995) incorporating Revolution Interactive Ltd (new media based solutions), Revolution Ltd (brand interaction and mktg communications), Revolution Interactive (new media based mktg communications), Revolution Environments (interior design, retail and leisure), Revolution Marketing Logistics Ltd (data capture and fulfilment) and Inc Ltd (print based solutions) 1998–2000, chm Transmission Gp Ltd 2001– (following sale of Revolution to china.com and formation of new gp), chm Co-Incidence Ltd 2003; *Recreations* skiing, sailing, classic cars, family; *Style—* Mr Ray Taylor; ✉ Transmission Group Ltd, RML Suite, Rawmec Business Park, Plumpton Road, Hoddesdon, Hertfordshire EN11 0EE (✆ 01992 801953, e-mail ray.taylor@transmissiongroup.com)

TAYLOR, Dr Richard Thomas; MBE (2014); s of Thomas Taylor (d 1962), of Lancs, and Mabel, *née* Hickley (d 1992); *b* 7 July 1934; *Educ* The Leys Sch Cambridge, Clare Coll Cambridge (BA), Westminster Hosp (BChir, MB); *m* 1, 1962 (m dis 1986), Ann, da of John Brett; 2 da (Sally b 1 Oct 1964, Caroline b 3 March 1967), 1 s (Stephen b 25 Oct 1968); m 2, 1990, Christine, da of William Miller; 1 da (Georgina b 3 March 1993); *Career* house physician Westminster Hosp 1959, house surgeon Kingston Hosp 1960, house physician London Chest Hosp 1960–61; RAF: gen duties MO 1961–63, SMO Christmas Island 1963, MO RAF Hosp Halton 1963–64; St Stephen's Hosp: sr house physician 1964–65, med registrar 1965–66; Westminster Hosp: med registrar 1966–67, sr med registrar 1967–72; conslt in gen med with special interest in rheumatology Kidderminster Gen Hosp and The Droitwich Centre for Rheumatic Diseases 1972–95; hon clinical tutor Charing Cross and Westminster Med Sch 1985, examiner Birmingham Med Sch 1986–87; chm: Hosp Med Staff Ctee 1975–77 and 1986–90, Kidderminster Hosp League of Friends 1996–2001 (staff rep 1975–90), Cancer Resource Centre Appeal 1997–98, Save Kidderminster Hosp Campaign Ctee 1997–2000, Health Concern 2000–; memb: BMA, Kidderminster Dist Med Ctee 1974–78, Kidderminster DHA 1982–86, Exec Ctee W Midlands Physicians' Assoc 1983–85, Kidderminster Community Health Cncl 1997–98; pres: Kidderminster Med Soc 1993, Kidderminster Civic Soc, Leukaemia Care; MP (IKHHC) Wyre Forest 2001–10, memb Health Select Ctee 2001–10; memb: RSPB, Worcs Wildlife Tst, RHS, Nat Tst, English Heritage, Inst of Advanced Motorists, Severn Valley Railway; FRCP 1979 (MRCP 1965); *Recreations* family, wildlife, 1950s and 60s cars, Victorian watercolours; *Clubs* RSM; *Style—* Dr Richard Taylor, MBE; ✉ 11 Church Walk, Kidderminster, Worcestershire DY11 6XY (✆ 01562 60010)

TAYLOR, (Andrew) Robert; s of Harry Taylor, of Longborough, Glos, and Phyllis, *née* Waring (d 1993); *b* 6 February 1968, Dover, Kent; *Educ* Calday Grange GS West Kirby, Hatfield Coll Durham (BA), Univ of Cambridge (PGCE); *m* 16 July 1994, Sarah, *née* Walliker; 2 s (Andrew b 7 Jan 2001, Edward b 4 April 2004), 1 da (Laura b 14 April 2007); *Career* Wellington Coll 1992–2003 (housemaster 1997–2003), headmaster Ashdown House Prep Sch 2003–09, registrar Harrow Sch 2009–14, headmaster Cargilfield Prep Sch 2014–; *Recreations* cricket, running, mountains; *Style—* Robert Taylor, Esq; ✉ Cargilfield School, 45 Gamekeeper's Road, Edinburgh EH4 6HU

TAYLOR, Prof Robert Henry; s of Robert Earl Taylor (d 1985), and Mabel, *née* Warren (d 1995); *b* 15 March 1943; *Educ* Greenville HS Ohio, Ohio Univ (BA), Antioch Coll (MA), Cornell Univ NY (PhD); *m* 1, 1967 (m dis 1999), Joan, da of Edwin Lutton; 1 da (Emily Sara b 1969), 1 s (Edwin Daniel b 1970); m 2, 2000, Ingrid G M Porteous; *Career* social studies teacher Cardozo HS Washington 1965–67, instructor in political science Wilberforce Univ Ohio 1967–69, lectr in govt Univ of Sydney 1974–79; SOAS, Univ of London 1980–96: successively lectr, sr lectr then prof of politics, pro-dir 1992–96; Univ of Buckingham: vice-chllr 1997–2000, visiting prof 2007–; conslt on Asian affrs 2001–, chm Br Acad S E Asian Studies Ctee 2001–09, visiting sr research fell Inst of Southeast Asian Studies Singapore 2003–17 (visiting professorial fell 2012–14), memb editorial Bd Asian Affrs, visiting prof City Univ of Hong Kong 2010–12; lay memb Asylum and Immigration Tbnl 2003–11; *Books* In Search of Southeast Asia (1985), Marxism and Resistance in Burma (1985), The State in Burma (1987), The Politics of Elections in Southeast Asia (1996), Burma: Political Economy under Military Rule (2001), Ideas of Freedom in Asia and Africa (2002), The Emergence of Modern Southeast Asia (2005), Myanmar: Beyond Politics to Societal Imperatives (2005), Dr Maung Maung: Gentleman, Scholar, Patriot (2008), The State in Myanmar (2009), General Ne Win: A Political Biography (2015), The Armed Forces in Myanmar Politics: A Terminating Role? (2015), Can Myanmar's NLD Government Cut the Gordian Knot of Ethnicity and Territory? (2016); *Recreations* London, music, wine, fiction; *Clubs* Travellers; *Style—* Prof Robert Taylor; ✆ 020 8361 4002, e-mail d.r.tinhla@gmail.com

TAYLOR, Roger Meddows; s of Michael Meddows Taylor, and Winifred Taylor; *b* 26 July 1949; *Educ* Truro Sch, London Hosp Med Coll, N London Poly (BSc); *m*; 2 s (Felix Luther, Rufus Tiger), 3 da (Rory Eleanor, Tigerlily, Lola Daisy May); *Career* drummer, vocalist and songwriter; co-fndr: Smile 1968, Queen 1970– (with Freddie Mercury (d 1991), Brian May, John Deacon, *qv*), The Cross 1987–; Queen albums: Queen (1973, platinum), Queen II (1974, platinum), Sheer Heart Attack (1974, platinum), A Night at the Opera (1975, platinum), A Day at the Races (1976, platinum), News of the World (1977, platinum), Jazz (1978, gold), Live Killers (1979, gold), The Game (1980, platinum), Flash Gordon Original Soundtrack (1980, gold), Greatest Hits (1981, 12 times platinum), Hot Space (1982, gold), The Works (1984, double platinum), A Kind of Magic (1986, double platinum), Live Magic (1986, platinum), The Miracle (1989, platinum), Queen at the Beeb (1989), Innuendo (1991, platinum), Greatest Hits Two (1991, 8 times platinum), Made in Heaven (1995, 4 times platinum); The Cross albums: Shove It (1988), Mad Bad and Dangerous to Know (1990), Blue Rock (1991); other albums: Gettin' Smile (earlier recordings of Smile, 1982), Fun In Space (solo, 1981), Strange Frontier (solo, 1984), Happiness (solo, 1994); number 1 singles: Bohemian Rhapsody 1975 and 1991 (with days of Our Lives), Under Pressure 1981, Innuendo 1991, Somebody to Love (with George Michael), electric fire (solo 1998); produced 1st hit by Jimmy Nail (Love Don't Live Here Any More); numerous tours worldwide, performed at Live Aid Concert Wembley Stadium 1985; voted Best Band of the Eighties ITV/TV Times 1990, Br Phonographic Indust award for Outstanding Contribution to Br Music 1990, Rock and Roll Hall of Fame 2001; Chevalier de l'Ordre des Arts et des Lettres (France) 1997; *Recreations* cars, travel, reading, renovating, working, boating, skiing; *Style—* Roger Taylor, Esq

TAYLOR, Roger Miles Whitworth; s of Richard Taylor (d 1965), of Stafford, and Joan Elizabeth, *née* Whitworth; *b* 18 May 1944; *Educ* Repton, Univ of Birmingham (LLB); *m* 1, 26 July 1969 (m dis 2003), Georgina Lucy, da of Francis Tonks (d 1973), of Sark, CI; 2 s (Richard Francis Miles b 1971, Matthew William Roger b 1976), 2 da (Sarah Elizabeth May, Lucy Emily Jane (twins) b 1981); m 2, 19 July 2003, Gabriele Eva, da of Tadeusz Sauter (d 1999), of Wernigerode, Germany; *Career* admitted slr 1968; asst slr: Staffordshire CC 1968–69, Cheshire CC 1969–71; asst co clerk Lincs parts of Lindsey 1971–73, dep co sec Northants CC 1971–73, town clerk and chief exec City of Manchester 1985–88 (dep town clerk 1979–85), chief exec Birmingham City Cncl and sec W Midlands Jt Ctee 1988–94, dir Local Govt Newchurch and Company Strategic Mgmnt Conslts 1994–2000 (chm 1998–2000), md JSS Pinnacle Consulting 2000–, gp dir Pinnacle-psq 2000–04; memb Farrand Ctee on Conveyancing 1983–84, clerk Gtr Manchester Passenger Tport Authy 1986–88; dir Birmingham Training and Enterprise Cncl 1990–93, chm Ofwat Central CSC 2000–02, memb Bd Standards Bd for England 2001–; Mancunian of the Year Manchester Jr C of C 1988; *Recreations* sailing, walking; *Style—* Roger Taylor, Esq

TAYLOR, Hon Mrs Sarah Lovell; *née* Rippon; 2 da of Baron Rippon of Hexham, PC, QC (Life Peer, d 1997); *b* 10 February 1950; *Educ* Sherborne Sch for Girls Dorset, St Paul's Girls' Sch London, St Anne's Coll Oxford (MA); *m* 1978 (m dis 1988), Michael Taylor; 2 s (James Geoffrey Bethune b 1979, Alexander Edward Yorke b 1982); *Career* admitted slr 1978; called to the NY Bar 1980; Theodore Goddard Solicitors 1974–77, Nixon Hargraves Devans & Doyle NY (Lawyers) 1980–84; dir: Robert Fraser Group Ltd 1986–91, Robert Fraser & Partners Ltd and subsid 1986–91; subsequently ptnr Penningtons and ptnr Woodroffes, currently conslt to Pettman Smith (Knightsbridge); dir: Savoy Asset Mgmnt plc, Jubilee Investment Tst plc; *Style—* The Hon Mrs Sarah Taylor; ✉ 10 Quarrendon Street, London SW6 3SU (✆ 020 7736 7843)

TAYLOR, Rev Dr Simon Wheldon; QC (2003); s of Thomas Henry Taylor, of London, and Enid, *née* Wheldon; *b* 4 July 1962, Whitechapel, London; *Educ* Highgate Sch London, Trinity Coll Cambridge (MA), Inns of Court Sch of Law, London Hosp Med Coll (MB, BChir); *m* 24 Nov 1990, Elizabeth Lawes, *née* Paine; 1 s, 2 da; *Career* barr; house offr London Hosp and Mile End Hosp 1987–88; tenant: 6 Pump Court 1989–98 (pupillage 1988–89), Cloisters 1998–; recorder 2002–; ordained: deacon 2012, priest 2013–; part time curate St Philip Tunbridge Wells 2012–; *Style—* The Rev Dr Simon Taylor, QC; ✉ Cloisters, 1 Pump Court, Temple, London EC4Y 7AA (✆ 020 7827 4000, e-mail st@cloisters.com)

TAYLOR, Prof Stephen John Charles; s of Bernard Taylor (d 2013), and Margaret Armstrong, of Surrey; *b* 11 October 1960, Windsor, Berks; *Educ* Peterhouse Coll Cambridge (BA), Jesus Coll Cambridge (PhD); *m* 1988, Sarah Brewer; 2 da (Beatrice b 1990, Octavia b 1995); *Career* research fell Inst of Historical Research 1985–86, research fell Jesus Coll Cambridge 1986–88, lectr, reader and prof Univ of Reading 1988–2012, prof in the history of early modern England Durham Univ 2012– (currently head History Dept); hon academic ed Royal Historical Soc, gen ed C of E Record Soc; FRHistS; *Publications* The Church of England c. 1689 – c. 1833 (1993), Tory and Whig (1997), The Entring Book of Roger Morrice IV: 1687–89 (2007), National Prayers. Special Worship Since the Reformation (2013), The Nature of the English Revolution Revisited (2013); *Style—* Prof Stephen Taylor; ✉ Department of History, Durham University, 43 North Bailey, Durham DH1 3EX (✆ 0191 3341060, e-mail s.j.c.taylor@durham.ac.uk)

TAYLOR, Timothy; *m* 18 July 1992, Lady Helen Marina Lucy, *née* Windsor (*see* Royal Family section); *Career* fndr Timothy Taylor Gallery 1996–; *Style—* Timothy Taylor, Esq; ✉ Timothy Taylor Gallery, 15 Carlos Place, London W1K 2EX (✆ 020 7409 3344, fax 020 7409 1316, e-mail mail@timothytaylorgallery.com)

TAYLOR, Tot; *b* Cambridge; *Career* composer, writer and curator; co-dir (with Virginia Damtsa, *qv*) Riflemaker Gallery 2003–; composer of film soundtracks and music for the Nat Theatre; *Books* The Story of John Nightly (novel, 2011); *Style—* Tot Taylor, Esq; ✉ Riflemaker, 79 Beak Street, Regent Street, London W1F 9SU

TAYLOR, Wendy Ann (Mrs Bruce Robertson); CBE (1988); da of Edward Philip Taylor (d 2008), and Lilian Maude, *née* Wright (d 2003); *b* 29 July 1945; *Educ* St Martin's Sch of Art (LDAD); *m* 1982, Bruce Robertson, s of Maurice Robertson; 1 s (Matthew Thomas b 1984); *Career* sculptor; examiner Univ of London 1982–83, memb Ct RCA 1982–, memb Cncl Morley Coll 1985–88, conslt New Town Cmmn Basildon (formerly Basildon Devpt Corp) 1985–88, specialist advsr Fine Art Bd CNAA 1985–93 (memb 1980–85, memb Ctee for Art Design 1987–91), memb Royal Fine Art Cmmn 1981–99, design conslt London Borough of Barking and Dagenham 1989–93 and 1997–2003; memb London Docklands Design Advsy Bd 1989–98; tstee LAMA 1993–2010; memb PCFC 1989–90; fell Queen Mary & Westfield Coll London 1993; FZS 1989, FRBS 1994, FRSA 2004; *Major Commissions* The Travellers (London) 1969, Gazebo (edn of 4 London, NY, Oxford, Suffolk) 1970–72, Triad (Oxford) 1971, Timepiece (London) 1973, Calthae (Leics) 1977, Octo (Milton Keynes) 1979, Counterpoise (Birmingham) 1980, Compass Bowl (Basildon) 1980, Sentinel (Reigate) 1982, Bronze Relief (Canterbury) 1981, Equatorial Sundial (Bletchley(1982, Essence (Milton Keynes) 1982, Opus (Morley Coll London) 1983, Gazebo (Golder's Hill Park London) 1983, Network (London) 1984, Geo I and Geo II (Stratford-upon-Avon) 1985, Landscape and Tree of the Wood (Fenhurst Surrey) 1986, Pharos Peel Park (East Kilbride) 1986, Ceres (Fenhurst Surrey) 1986, Nexus (Corby Northants) 1986, Globe Sundial (Swansea Maritime Quarter) 1987, Spirit of Enterprise (Isle of Dogs London) 1987, Silver Fountain (Guildford Surrey) 1988, The Whirlies (East Kilbride) 1988, Pilot Kites (Norwich Airport) 1988, Fire Flow (Hamilton Scotland) 1988, Armillary Sundial (Basildon Essex) 1989, Pharos II (East Kilbride) 1989, Phoenix (East Kilbride) 1990, Globe Sundial (London Zoological Gardens), Continuum (Guildford), Sundial (Sheffield) 1991, Anchorage (Salford Quays Manchester), Square Piece (Plano Illinois USA), Wyvern Leicestershire 1992, Railings (Univ of Sheffield) 1993, Stained Glass Window (St George's Church Sheffield) 1994, Jester (Emmanuel Coll Cambridge) 1994, Jester II (NY) 1994, Challenge (Stockley Park Middlesex), Equilibrium (London) 1995, Spirit Vann (Surrey), Rope Circle (London) 1997, Spirit of Barrow (Cumbria) 1997, Waves (London) 1998, Dancer (Chelsea and Westminster Hosp) 1999, Dung Beetles (Millennium Conservation Bldg Zoological Soc London) 1999, Mariners Astrolabe (Brunswick Quay London) 1999, Globe View (Blackfriars London) 2000, Millennium Fountain (New River Loop Chase Gardens Enfield) 2000, Tortoises With Triangle and Time (Holland Park London) 2000, Voyager (Cinnibar Wharf London) 2001, Three Reclining Rope Figures (GlaxoSmithKline Middx) 2001, Conqueror (GlaxoSmithKline Middx) 2001, Through the

T

Loop (Pacific Place Hong Kong) 2002, Around the Square (Pacific Place Hong Kong) 2002, Chain Piece (Warren OH 2002), Knowledge (QMC London) 2003, Acorn Wall Relief (Brunswick Wharf London) 2003, Anchor Iron (Anchor Iron Wharf Greenwich) 2004, Feather Piece (Capital East London) 2005, Gravesham Heritage 2006, Silver Fountain II (Bryn Mawr Pennsylvania), Square Chain Piece (Hillside Bartlesville Oklahoma) 2007, Meml to the Civilians of E London WWII 1939–1945 (Hermitage Meml Garden Wapping London) 2007, Spirit I (Capital West Royal Docks London) 2007–08, Hares (A2 pedestrian bridges Gravesham) 2008, Unity (Unison Centre London) 2011, Swirl (Atrium Building Park Road London) 2013; *Awards* Walter Neurath 1964, Pratt 1965, Sainsbury 1966, Arts Cncl 1977, Duais Na Riochta (Kingdom prize), Gold medal Repub of Ireland 1977, winner silk screen Barcham Green Print Competition 1978, Civic Tst Partnership Award Chase Green Enfield 2002, Building of the Year Award Architectural Sculpture 2004; *Recreations* gardening; *Style*— Ms Wendy Taylor, CBE; ✉ 73 Bow Road, Bow, London E3 2AN (✆ 020 8981 2037, e-mail wendytaylorsculptor@gmail.com, website www.wendytaylorsculpture.co.uk)

TAYLOR, William Gibson (Bill); s of John Taylor (d 1983), and Brenda Louise, *née* Gibson; *b* 27 January 1957; *Educ* Rushcliffe Comp Sch Nottingham, Univ of Sheffield (RIBA Nat Students prize, MA, Dip Architecture); *m* 1982, Denise, da of George Roper; 2 s (Robert John Gibson b 1987, Andrew George Gibson b 1989); *Career* worked with Mervyn Awon (architect) on Central Bank of Barbados 1979–80; ptnr Michael Hopkins and Partners 1988– (architect 1982–88); external examiner: Univ of Nottingham, Sheffield Hallam Univ; visiting tutor Queen's Univ Belfast; memb: Br Cncl of Offices, RIBA Sustainable Futures Ctee, Pan European Tensinet Working Gp into Membrane Architecture, Olympic Design Review Panel CABE 2006–; RIBA (assessor), FRSA; *Style*— Bill Taylor, Esq; ✉ Hopkins Architects, 27 Broadley Terrace, London NW1 6LG (✆ 020 7724 1751, fax 020 7723 0932, e-mail bill.t@hopkins.co.uk)

TAYLOR, William James; QC (Scot 1986), QC (1998); s of Cecil Taylor (d 1997), of Inverness, and Ellen, *née* Daubney; *b* 13 September 1944; *Educ* Robert Gordon's Coll, Univ of Aberdeen (MA, LLB, pres Aberdeen Univ Union, vice-pres Scottish Union of Students); *Career* admitted Faculty of Advocates 1971, standing jr DHSS 1978–79, standing jr counsel FCO 1979–86, called to the Bar Inner Temple 1990, first person to hold rank QC in Scot and Eng; memb Criminal Injuries Compensation Bd 1997–2000; temp sheriff 1997–99, memb Scot Criminal Cases Review Cmmn 1998–2004; cncllr (Lab) Edinburgh Corporation 1973–75, cncllr (Lab) Lothian Regnl Cncl 1974–82; arbitrator Motor Insurers Bureau; pt/t Sheriff 2003–; chm Scottish Opera 2004–08; FRSA; *Recreations* music, theatre, restoring a garden, cooking, Scottish mountains, sailing; *Clubs* Royal Highland Yacht; *Style*— William Taylor, Esq, QC; ✉ Parliament House, Parliament Square, Edinburgh EH1 1RF (✆ 0131 226 2881, fax 0131 225 3642, e-mail qc@wjt.org.uk); 9 Carmelite Street, London EC4Y 0DR (✆ 020 7936 6300)

TAYLOR BRADFORD, Barbara; *see:* Bradford, Barbara Taylor

TAYLOR OF BLACKBURN, Baron (Life Peer UK 1978), of Blackburn in the County of Lancaster; Thomas Taylor; CBE (1974, OBE 1969), JP (Blackburn 1960), DL (Lancs 1994); s of James Taylor; *b* 10 June 1929; *Educ* Blakey Moor Higher Grade Sch; *m* 1950, Kathleen, da of John Edward Nurton; 1 s (Hon Paul Nurton b 1953); *Career* memb Blackburn Town Cncl 1954–76 (ldr, and chm Policy and Resources Ctee 1972–76), dep pro-chllr Lancaster Univ 1972–95 (elected life memb Ct), chm Govt Ctee of Enquiry into Mgmnt and Govt of Schs, non-exec dir Grove Ltd 1997– (chm), past chm Juvenile Bench; non-exec dir AES Drax Ltd 2001–04; conslt: BAE Systems plc 1994–, Initial Electronic Security Systems Ltd; advsr: Electronic Data Systems Ltd 1992–, AES Electric Ltd 1999–, Experian 1999–, United Utilities plc 2000–; pres: Free Church Cncl 1962–68, Mill Hill Community Centre Blackburn, Friends of Blackburn Museum and Art Gallery, Assoc of Lancastrians London; patron: Lancashire Wildlife Tst, Friends of Real Lancashire 1999–, Outreach Schools, Holidays for Carers 2000–, Alzheimers Soc (Blackburn, Darwen, Hyndburn and Ribble valley Branch); former memb: Norweb Bd, Select Ctee on Sci and Technol, Cwlth Parly Assoc; Hon LLD Lancaster Univ 1996; Freeman: City of London, Borough of Blackburn; FRGS 1994; *Style*— The Rt Hon the Lord Taylor of Blackburn, CBE, DL

TAYLOR OF BOLTON, Baroness (Life Peer UK 2005), of Bolton in the County of Greater Manchester; (Winifred) Ann Taylor; PC (1997); *b* 2 July 1947; *Educ* Bolton Sch, Univ of Bradford, Univ of Sheffield; *m*; 1 s (b 1982), 1 da (b 1983); *Career* MP (Lab) Bolton W Oct 1974–83 (also contested Feb 1974), Parly candidate Bolton NE 1983, MP (Lab) Dewsbury 1987–2005; PPS to: Sec of State for Defence 1976–77, Sec of State DES 1975–76; Govt whip 1977–79; oppn front bench spokesman: on educn 1979–81, on housing 1981–83, on home affrs 1987–88; memb Shadow Cabinet 1990–97; chief oppn spokesman: on environmental protection 1988–92, on educn 1992–94; shadow chllr of Duchy of Lancaster 1994–95; shadow ldr House of Commons 1994–97, Pres of the Cncl and Ldr of the House of Commons 1997–98, Parly sec to the Treasy (Govt chief whip) 1998–2001, Parly under sec of state for defence equipment and support 2007–10; memb Select Ctee on Standards in Public Life (Nolan Select Ctee) 1995, memb Standards and Privileges Ctee 1995–97; chair Select Ctee on Modernisation 1997–98, Intelligence and Security Ctee 2001; dep chair Independent Football Cmmn 2002–; memb Jt Ctee on Parly Privilege 1997–99; former teacher, tutor Open Univ; *Books* Political Action (with Jim Firth, 1978), Choosing Our Future (1992); *Style*— The Rt Hon the Lady Taylor of Bolton, PC

TAYLOR OF HOLBEACH, Baron (Life Peer UK 2006), of South Holland in the County of Lincolnshire; John Derek Taylor; CBE (1992), PC (2014); s of Percy Otto Taylor (d 2000), and Ethel, *née* Brocklehurst (d 2011); *b* 12 November 1943, Holbeach, Lincs; *Educ* St Felix Sch Felixstowe, Bedford Sch; *m* 18 April 1968, Julia Aileen, *née* Cunnington; 2 s (Hon Giles Edward Augustus b 15 Feb 1972, Hon Adam Edwin John b 3 May 1975); *Career* dir Taylors Bulbs of Spalding 1968–2010, chm Springfields Horticultural Soc 2000–09 (dir 1991–2010), chm EC Working Pty on European Bulb Industry 1982, chm Bulb Sub-Ctee NFU 1982–87; govr: Glasshouse Crops Research Inst 1984–88, Inst of Horticultural Research 1987–90; memb: Horticultural Devpt Cncl 1986–91, Min of Agriculture's Regnl Panel (Eastern Region) 1990–92 and (East Midlands Region) 1992–96, Taylor Review Science Agriculture and Horticulture 2010; sits as Cons in House of Lords 2006–, oppn whip and spokesman on environment, work and pensions, and Wales 2006–07, shadow min for DEFRA and oppn whip for work and pensions 2007–10, Lord in waiting to HM The Queen and govt whip House of Lords 2010–11, princ govt spokesman for Cabinet Office and spokesman in energy and climate change and work and pensions 2010–11, parly under sec of state DEFRA 2011–12, parly under sec of state Home Office 2012–14, Govt chief whip; Cons Pty: memb Exec Ctee E Midlands Cncl 1966–98, memb Bd of Finance 1985–89, memb Bd of Mgmnt 1996–98 and 2000–03, pres Nat Union of Cons Assoc and chm Pty Conf 1997–98, dep pty chm 2000–03, chm Nat Cons Convention 2000–03, chair Conservatives Abroad 2001–08, chm Candidates Ctee 2002–05, chm Cons Agents Superannuation Fund 2006–10; Parly candidate (Cons): Chesterfield (gen election) 1974, Nottingham (European Parl election) 1979; tstee Brogdale Horticultural Tst 1998–2005; chm Holbeach and Elloe Hosp Charitable Tst 1989–2006 (patron 2006–); pres: Lincs Agricultural Soc 2012–13, East of England Agricultural Soc 2014; memb: Lincoln Diocesan Bd of Finance 1995–2001 (memb Assets Ctee 1995–2001 and 2003–11), Lincoln Diocesan Synod 1997–2001; Liveryman: Worshipful Co of Farmers 2009, Worshipful Co of Gardeners 2010; Captain Honourable Corps of Gentlemen at Arms 2014–; Chevalier La Confrérie des Chevaliers du Tastevin 2013; FRSA 1994, ARAgS 2012, CHort 2015 (FCIHort 2014, MIHort 2012); *Publications* Taylor's Bulb Book (ed,

1994); *Recreations* English landscape and vernacular buildings, travel (particularly in France), literature, arts, music; *Clubs* Farmers'; *Style*— The Rt Hon the Lord Taylor of Holbeach, CBE; ✉ House of Lords, London SW1A 0PW (✆ 020 7219 3000, e-mail angela2@taylors-bulbs.com)

TAYLOR-JOHNSON, Sam; OBE (2011); *b* 4 March 1967, London; *Educ* Goldsmiths Coll London; *m* 1, 1997 (m dis 2008), Jay Jopling , *qv*; 2 da (Angelica b April 1997, Jessie b 2007); *m* 2, 2012, Aaron Taylor-Johnson; 2 da (Wylda Rae b July 2010, Romy Hero b Jan 2012); *Career* artist and film dir; Illy Cafe Prize Most Promising Young Artist Venice Biennale 1997, nominated Turner Prize 1998; *Solo Exhibitions* incl: Matthew Marks Gallery NY 2000, Espacio Uno Madrid 2000, Centrum Sztuki Wspólczesnej Zamek Ujazdowski Warsaw 2000, Photographies et films (Centre Nationale de la Photographie Paris) 2001, Kunstlerverein Malkasten Düsseldorf 2001, Mute (White Cube London) 2001, Shiseido Tokyo 2002, Films and Photographs (Stedelijk Museum Amsterdam) 2002, Hayward Gallery London 2002, Musée d'Art Contemporain de Montréal Quebec 2002, Bawag Fndn Vienna 2003, David (Nat Portrait Gallery London) 2004, Strings (Edinburgh Coll of Art) 2004, Sorrow, Suspension, Ascension (Matthew Marks Gall NY) 2004, New Work (White Cube) 2004, Ascension (Donald Young Gallery Chicago) 2004, Sam Taylor-Wood (State Russian Museum St Petersburg and Museum Contemporary Art Moscow) 2004, Sex and Death and A Few Trees (Galleria Lorcan O'Neill Rome) 2005; *Group Exhibitions* incl: Fourth Wall: Turner on the Thames (Public Arts Devpt Tst South Bank London) 2000, Sincerely Yours. British Art from the 90's (Astrup Fearnely MOMA Oslo) 2000, Making Time: Considering Time as a Material in Contemporary Video & Film (Palm Beach Inst of Contemporary Art) 2000, Out There (White Cube 2 London) 2000, Media City Seoul 2000, Nurture and Desire (in aid of Breakthrough Breast Cancer, Hayward Gallery London) 2000, Contemporary Film and Video (Moderna Museet Stockholm) 2000, Beautiful Productions: Art to Play, art to wear, art to own (Whitechapel Art Gallery London) 2001, A Baroque Party – Moments of Theatrum Mundi in Contemporary Art (Kunsthalle Vienna) 2001, The Body of Art (Valencia Biennial) 2001, Idea Festival Video in the City (Centrum Hedendaagse Kunst Maastrict) 2001, 6 Biennale d'Art Contemporain de Lyon (Musée d'Art Contemporain de Lyon) 2001, Intimacy (Paco des Artes São Paulo) 2002, The Rowan Collection Contemporary British & Irish Art (Irish MOMA Dublin) 2002, Landscape (Saatchi Gallery London) 2002, Embracing the Present: The UBS PaineWebber Art Collection (Portland Art Museum) 2002, Animal, Vegetable, Mineral (Israel Museum Jerusalem) 2002, Social Strategies, Redefining Social Realism (Univ Art Museum Univ of Calif) 2003, Revelation: Representations of Christ in Photography (Israel Museum Jerusalem and Int House of Photography Hamburg) 2003, A Bigger Splash: British Art from Tate 1960–2003 (Pavilhão Lucas Nogueira Garcez São Paulo) 2003, Make Life Beautiful! The Dandy in Photography (Brighton Museum and Art Gallery) 2003, A Century of Artists' Film in Britain (Tate Britain London) 2003, Something More Than Five Revolutionary Seconds (Fondazione Davide Halevim Milan) 2003, Ideal and Reality. A History of the Nude form Neoclassicism to the Present Day (Galleria d'Arte Moderna Bologna) 2004, Contemporary Photography Collection (Fundacion Telefonica Madrid) 2004, Symbolic Space & Repetition (Hudson Valley Centre for Contemporary Art NY) 2004, Other Times British Contemporary Art (City Art Gallery Prague) 2004, Secrets of the 90's (Museum voor Moderne Kunst Arnhem) 2004, Unframed (Standpoint Gallery London) 2004, Some Versions of Light (The Telephone Repeater Station Brompton-on-Swale) 2004, Uproar of Emotions (Museum für Photographie Braunschweig) 2004, The Charged Image (Joseloff Gallery Connecticut) 2004, Hors d'Oeuvre (Cap Musee d'Art Contemporain de Bordeaux) 2004, Canterbury Festival 2004, Perspectives @ 25 (Museum of Contemporary Art Houston) 2004, Masters of Illusion: 150 Years of Trompe 'Oeil in America (Kresge Art Museum MI), The Stuff of Life (City Museum and Art Gallery Bristol and Laing Gallery Newcastle) 2005, Coleccion de Fotografia Contemporanea de Telefonica (MARCO Vigo) 2005, Edvard Munch and the Art of Today (Museum am Ostwall Dortmund) 2005, Between Art and Life (MOMA San Francisco) 2005, Mother and Child (Salvatore Ferragamo NY) 2005, (My Private) Heroes (MARTA Herfod) 2005, Painting on Photography: Photography on Painting (Museum of Contemporary Photography Chicago) 2005, Body: New Art from the UK (Vancouver Art Gallery) 2005, Chronos (CeSAC Caraglio) 2005, Bidibidobidiboo (Turin) 2005; *Works in Collections* incl: New Orleans Museum, Royal Museum of Fine Arts Copenhagen, San Francisco MOMA, Tate Gallery London, Nat Portrait Gallery London, Israel Museum Jerusalem, Fondacio 'La Caixa' Barcelona, Saatchi Collection London, British Cncl London, Samsung Museum, The Robert Shiffler Collection Greenville, Bangkok Museum of Contemporary Art; *Film* Love You More (short film, 2008), Nowhere Boy 2009, Fifty Shades of Grey 2015; *Books* Unhinged (1996), Contact (2001), Crying Men (2004); *Style*— Ms Sam Taylor-Johnson, OBE; ✉ White Cube, 144 152 Bermondsey Street, London SE1 3TQ (✆ 020 7930 5373, fax 020 7749 7480)

TAYTON, Her Hon Judge Lynn Margaret; QC (2006); *Career* called to the Bar 1981; barr 36 Bedford Row 1995–2011, circuit judge (Midland Circuit) 2011–; *Style*— Her Hon Judge Tayton, QC; ✉ c/o Northampton Combined Court, 85/87 Ladyâs Lane, Northampton NN1 3HQ

TCHENGUIZ, Robert; *Career* fndr and co-chm (with bro, Vincent Tchenguiz) Rotch Property Gp Ltd; *Style*— Robert Tchenguiz, Esq; ✉ R20 Ltd, Leconfield House, Curzon Street, London W1J 5JA (✆ 020 7550 3860, e-mail sara@rotch.com)

TE KANAWA, Dame Kiri Jeanette; DBE (1982, OBE 1973), ONZ (1995), AC; da of late Thomas Te Kanawa, of Auckland, NZ, and late Elanor Te Kanawa; *b* 6 March 1944, Gisborne, NZ; *Educ* St Mary's Coll Auckland, London Opera Centre; *Children* 1 s, 1 da; *Career* opera singer; studied singing under Dame Sister Mary Leo 1959–65 and Vera Rózsa; has sung major roles at: ROH, Met Opera (NY), Paris Opera, San Francisco Opera, Sydney Opera, Cologne Opera, La Scala (Milan); sang at Royal Wedding of HRH Prince of Wales to Lady Diana Spencer 1981; appeared on 2000 Today from Gisborne on 1 January 2000; sang at Queen's Jubilee Concert Buckingham Palace 2002, appeared on Downton Abbey 2013; Hon LLD: Univ of Dundee, Warwick 1989; Hon DMus: Univ of Durham 1982, Univ of Oxford 1983, Univ of Cambridge 1997, Univ of Nottingham 1992, Univ of Waikato 1995, Univ of Sunderland 2003, Univ of Bath 2005; *Publications* Land of the Long White Cloud (1989), Opera for Lovers (1997); *Style*— Dame Kiri Te Kanawa, DBE, ONZ, AC

TEAGUE, His Hon Judge (Edward) Thomas Henry; QC (2000); s of Harry John Teague, and Anne Elizabeth, *née* Hunt; *b* 21 May 1954, Weymouth, Dorset; *Educ* St Francis Xavier's Coll Liverpool, Christ's Coll Cambridge (MA); *m* 8 Aug 1980, Helen Mary, da of Daniel Matthew Howard (d 1974); 2 s (Michael b 1983, Dominic b 1985); *Career* called to the Bar Inner Temple 1977; in practice Wales & Chester Circuit 1978–2006, in practice Western Circuit 2002–06, recorder 1997–2006 (asst recorder 1993–97), circuit judge 2006–, hon memb Northern Circuit 2007–; legal assessor GMC 2002–06; chm Chester Bar Ctee 2004–06; author of various astronomical papers; FRAS; *Style*— His Hon Judge Teague, QC; ✉ Queen Elizabeth II Law Courts, Derby Square, Liverpool L21XA

TEALE, Polly; da of Richard Teale, of Sheffield, and Mary, *née* Willis; *b* 2 December 1962, E Grinstead, W Sussex; *Educ* High Storrs Sch Sheffield, Univ of Manchester (BA); *m* 19 May 2005, Ian Rickson; 1 da (Eden b 2 Aug 2000); *Career* writer and director; jt artistic dir Shared Experience Theatre Co; as writer plays incl: After Mrs Rochester (winner Best Director Evening Standard Award and Best Production Time Out Award), Brontë, Mine; *Style*— Ms Polly Teale; ✉ Julia Tyrell Management, 57 Greenham Road, London N10 1LN

TEARE, (Eleanor) Christine; da of James Ralph Teare (d 1990), of the Isle of Man, and Kathleen Mona, *née* Duggan; *b* IOM; *Educ* Castle Rushen HS IOM, Royal Acad of Music (two scholarships from Countess of Munster Fndn, DipRAM); *Career* soprano; princ soprano WNO 1985–89, freelance 1989–; roles with WNO incl: Donna Anna in Don Giovanni (debut) 1982, Die Kaiserin in Die Frau ohne Schatten, Amelia in Un Ballo in Maschera, Countess Almaviva in The Marriage of Figaro, Ortlinde and Helmwig in Die Walküre; other opera roles incl: Donna Anna (Opera North) 1986, First Lady in The Magic Flute (ENO) 1986, Helmwig in Die Walküre (ROH debut) 1988 (also Ortlinde, Helmwig and Third Norn in full Ring Cycle 1991), Berta in The Barber of Seville (ENO) 1992, title role in Turandot (ROH) 1996, Flower Maiden in Parsifal (ENO), Donna Anna in Don Giovanni (Opera North), Brünnhilde in Das Ringchen (Pocket Opera Nuremburg), Die Kaiserin in Die Frau Ohne Schatten (Augsburg), Tosca (Augsburg), title role in Elektra (Hagen Opera Dortmund) 2006; concert performances incl: Elgar's The Kingdom, Verdi's Requiem, Haydn's Creation and Schoenberg's Gurrelieder, Marietta in Korngold's Die Tote Stadt (Queen Elizabeth Hall London); ARCM, FTCL, Hon ARAM; *Recreations* theatre, golf, Manx history and culture; *Style*— Miss Christine Teare; ✉ website www.christinetearesoprano.co.uk

TEARE, His Hon Jonathan James; s of Prof Donald Teare (d 1979), and Kathleen Agnes Teare; *b* 13 December 1946; *Educ* Rugby, Middle Temple; *m* 1972, Nicola Jill, da of Lt Col Peter Spittall; 2 da (Caroline Clare b 20 December 1974, Joanna Hazel b 6 June 1977); *Career* HAC 1965–69, RRF (TA) 1970–72; called to the Bar Middle Temple 1970; in practice Midland & Oxford Circuit 1971–98, asst recorder 1985–90, recorder 1990–98, circuit judge (Midland & Oxford Circuit) 1998–2014, presiding sr judge Sovereign Base Areas Cyprus 2007–14 (dep sr judge 2001–07); memb Mental Health Review Tbnl 2002–; tstee Egalitarian Tst 2014–; Freeman City of London 1981, Liveryman Worshipful Soc of Apothecaries 1980; *Recreations* travel, shooting, wine, kitchen garden; *Style*— His Hon Jonathan Teare

TEARE, Hon Mr Justice; Sir Nigel John Martin; kt (2006); s of Eric John Teare (d 1980), and Mary Rackham, *née* Faragher (d 1985); *b* 8 January 1952; *Educ* King William's Coll Castletown IOM, St Peter's Coll Oxford (MA); *m* 16 Aug 1975, (Elizabeth) Jane, da of Alan James Pentecost, of Nottingham; 2 s (Roland b 1981, David b 1984), 1 da (Charlotte b 1982); *Career* called to the Bar Lincoln's Inn 1974, jr counsel to treasy in Admty matters 1989–91, QC 1991, recorder 1997–2006 (asst recorder 1993–97), actg deemster IOM High Ct 1998–2006, judge of the High Court of Justice (Queen's Bench Div) 2006– (dep judge High Court 2002); presiding judge Western Circuit 2015–; memb Panel Lloyd's Salvage Arbitrators 1994–2000; arbitrator Lloyd's Salvage Appeal 2000–06; hon fell St Peter's Coll Oxford 2010; *Recreations* collecting Manx paintings, golf; *Clubs* RAC; *Style*— The Hon Mr Justice Teare; ✉ c/o Royal Courts of Justice, Strand, London WC2A 2LL

TEASDALE, Anthony Laurence; s of John S Teasdale (d 2009), and Pauline, *née* Tomlinson (d 1983); *b* 4 June 1957; *Educ* Slough GS, Balliol Coll Oxford (MA), Nuffield Coll Oxford (MPhil); *m* 2001, Jacqueline Louise Philips; *Career* lectr in politics CCC and Magdalen Coll Oxford 1980–82; policy advsr European Democratic Gp in European Parl Brussels 1982–86, asst to DG for Econ and Fin Affrs EC Cncl of Mins Brussels 1986–88; special advsr to: Sec of State for Foreign and Cwlth Affrs 1988–89, Dep PM, Lord Pres of the Cncl and Ldr of House of Commons 1989–90, Chllr of the Exchequer 1996–97; research fell Nuffield Coll Oxford 1992–93; head London Office EPP Gp in European Parl 1993–95 and 1997–2002, head of policy strategy EPP Gp in European Parl Brussels 2002–07; Office of the Pres of the European Parl: head of strategy 2007–12, dep COS 2009–12; European Parl administration: dir EU internal policies 2012–13, DG EP Research Service 2013–; visiting fell European Inst LSE 2011–; *Books* The Penguin Companion to European Union (jtly, 2012); *Recreations* music, reading, cinema, travel; *Style*— Anthony Teasdale, Esq; ✉ European Parliament, Rue Wiertz, Brussels B-1047 (☎ 00 322 284 1678, e-mail anthony.teasdale@ep.europa.eu)

TEATHER, Sarah; *b* 1 June 1974; *Educ* Univ of Cambridge; *Career* former health and social policy advsr Macmillan Cancer Relief; cncllr (Lib Dem) Islington BC 2002–03; MP (Lib Dem) (by-election): Brent East 2003–2010, Brent Central 2010–15 (Parly candidate (Lib Dem) Finchley and Golders Green 2001); Lib Dem spokesperson: on health 2003–04, for London 2004–05, for community and local govt 2005–06, for educn 2006–07, for business and enterprise 2007–08, for housing 2008–10; min of state for children and families 2010–12; *Style*— Sarah Teather; ✉ House of Commons, London SW1A 0AA (e-mail teathers@parliament.uk, website www.sarahteather.org.uk)

TEBBIT, Sir Kevin Reginald; KCB (2002), CMG (1997); *b* 1946; *Educ* Cambridgeshire HS for Boys, St John's Coll Cambridge (sr history scholar); *m*; 2 c; *Career* joined MOD 1969, asst private sec to Sec of State MOD 1972, on secondment HM Dip Serv as first sec UK delegation to NATO Brussels 1979–82; HM Dip Serv: with E Euro and Soviet Dept FCO then head of Chancery Turkey 1982–87, dir of Cabinet to NATO Sec-Gen 1987–88, politico-military cnsllr Washington 1988–91, head Econ Relations Dept subsequently dir of resources and chief inspr FCO 1992–97; dep under sec of state for def and intelligence 1997–98, memb Jt Intelligence Ctee 1997–98, dir GCHQ 1998, perm under sec of state MOD 1998–2005; strategic conslt and co dir 2006–; non-exec dir Smiths Gp plc 2006–, chm Finmeccanica UK 2007–12, sr advsr J C Bamford Excavators Ltd 2007–; visiting prof Queen Mary Coll London 2006–; chm Lifeboat Fund 2004–; *Recreations* music, classical archaeology, walking, West Ham United FC; *Style*— Sir Kevin Tebbit, KCB, CMG

TEBBIT, Baron (Life Peer UK 1992), of Chingford in the London Borough of Waltham Forest; Norman Beresford Tebbit; CH (1987), PC (1981); 2 s of Leonard Albert and Edith Tebbit, of Enfield, Middx; *b* 29 March 1931, Enfield, Middx; *Educ* Edmonton Co GS; *m* 1956, Margaret Elizabeth, da of Stanley Daines, of Chatteris; 2 s (Hon John Beresford b 1958, Hon William Mark b 1965), 1 da (Hon Alison Mary b 1960); *Career* RAF 1949–51, RAuxAF 1952–55; journalist 1947–49, in publishing and advertising 1951–53, airline pilot 1953–70 (memb BALPA and former lay official); MP (Cons): Epping 1970–74, Chingford 1974–92; formerly: memb Select Ctee Science and Technol, chm Cons Aviation Ctee, vice-chm and sec Cons Housing and Construction Ctee, sec New Town MPs; PPS to Min of State for Employment 1972–73, Parly under sec of state for trade 1979–81, min of state for industry 1981, sec of state for employment 1981–83, sec of state for trade and industry 1983–85, chllr of Duchy of Lancaster 1985–87, chm Cons Pty 1985–87; political commentator BSkyB television 1989–97; columnist: The Sun 1995–97, Mail on Sunday 1997–2001; blogger Daily Telegraph 2010–; dir: BET plc 1987–96, BT plc 1987–96, Sears plc 1987–99, JCB Excavators Ltd 1987–91, The Spectator (1828) Ltd 1989–2004; Liveryman Honourable Co of Air Pilots; CRAeS; *Books* Upwardly Mobile, An Autobiography (1988), Unfinished Business (1991), The Game Cook (2009), Ben's Story (2014); *Style*— The Rt Hon Lord Tebbit, CH, PC; ✉ c/o Julia Dunnicliffe, House of Lords, London SW1A 0PW (e-mail dunnicliffejm@parliament.uk)

TEDDER, 3 Baron (UK 1946); Robin John Tedder; s of 2 Baron Tedder (d 1994), and Peggy Eileen, *née* Growcott; *b* 6 April 1955; *m* 1, 1977, Jennifer Peggy (d 1978), da of John Mangan, of Christchurch, NZ; m 2, 1980, (Rita) Aristea, yr da of John Frangidis, of Sydney, Aust; 2 s (Hon Benjamin John b 1985, Hon Christopher Arthur b 1986), 1 da (Hon Jacqueline Christina b 1988); *Heir* s, Hon Benjamin Tedder; *Career* merchant banker and investor; dir of various cos; *Recreations* sailing, golf; *Clubs* Royal Sydney Yacht Squadron, Royal & Ancient Golf (St Andrews), The Australian Golf; *Style*— The Rt Hon the Lord Tedder

TEDDY, Prof Peter Julian; s of Francis Gerald Teddy, of Te Awamutu, NZ, and Beryl Dorothy Fogg; *b* 2 November 1944; *Educ* Rhyl GS, Univ of Wales (BSc), Univ of Oxford (MA, DPhil, BM BCh); *m* 1, 1 June 1974 (m dis 1988), Fiona Margaret, da of late Richard Edward Millard, CBE, JP; 2 s (Alexander Francis b 1982, William Peter b 1986); m 2, 1989, Rosalee Margaret Elliott; 1 s (Timothy James Elliott b 1990); *Career* former conslt neurosurgeon and clinical dir Dept of Neurological Surgery Radcliffe Infirmary Oxford, conslt neurosurgeon Nat Spinal Injuries Centre, Dept of Spinal Neurosurgery Univ of Oxford, Stoke Mandeville Hosp, currently prof and conslt neurosurgeon Dept of Neurosurgery Royal Melbourne Hospital Parkville Victoria; former clinical dir Oxford Neuroscience Directorate; St Peter's Coll Oxford: sr res fell 1983, emeritus fell; clinical sr lectr (formerly dir of clinical studies) Univ of Oxford Med Sch, examiner Surgical Neurology Intercollegiate Bd; formerly asst ed Br Jl of Neurosurgery; memb: Soc Br Neurological Surgeons, World Fedn Neurosurgery/American Assoc Neurological Surgery, Neurosurgical Soc Australasia, Soc of Univ Neurosurgeons; FRCS, FRACS, fell Faculty of Pain Medicine, Australian and NZ Coll of Anaesthetists; *Recreations* sailing, volcanology, foreign travel; *Style*— Prof Peter Teddy

TEE, Harry Leonard; CBE (2008); s of William Stephen Tee, of Kilsyth, N Lanarkshire, and Janet Tee (d 2004); *b* 14 October 1945, Kilsyth, N Lanarkshire; *Educ* BSc; *m* Jane Elizabeth, *née* Thorpe; *Career* ITT 1972–78, Schlumberger 1978–87, exec dir Graseby plc 1987–90; Dialight plc (formerly Roxboro Gp): fndr 1990, chief exec 1990–2005, chm 2005–; chm: Scientific Digital Imaging plc, Piezotag Ltd; chm Electronics Leadership Cncl, dir SEMTA; Master Worshipful Co of Scientific Instrument Makers; FIET, fell Royal Instn, FRSA, CCMI; *Recreations* fly fishing, golf, garden design; *Clubs* Caledonian, Country Clubs UK; *Style*— Harry Tee, Esq, CBE; ✉ Dialight plc, Exning Road, Newmarket, Suffolk, England, CB8 0AX

TELLER, Juergen; *b* Erlangen, Germany; *Educ* Bayerische Staatslehranstalt für Photographie Munich; *Career* photographer; campaigns incl: Anna Molinari, Blumarine, Miu Miu, Comme des Garçons, Helmut Lang, Hugo Boss, Katharine Hamnett, Strenesse, Jigsaw, Yves Saint Laurent, Alberto Biani and Alessandro Dell' Aqua, Zucca, Marc Jacobs, Stüssy, Shisedo, Louis Vuitton, Amex, Italian Telecom, Ungaro, Marc Jacobs Perfume; editorial incl: The Face, ID, Arena, Arena Hommes Plus, Vogues Hommes Int, Vogue (French, Italian, Br, American, Aust), Dazed & Confused, French Glamour, Interview, Details, Suddeustche Zeitung magazine, AbeSea, Per Lui, Marie Claire (Germany), Vibe, Six Magazine, Stern, O3 Tokyo Calling, Jo's Magazine, Visionaire, W magazine, Index, Purple, Liberation, Self Service; record covers: Björk, Elton John, Elastica, Simply Red, Hole, Cocteau Twins, A R Kane, Sinead O'Connor, Everything but the Girl, Scritti Politti, Stereo MCs, PM Dawn, Terry Hall, Herbert Gronemeyer, Babaa Maal, Richie Rich, Neneh Cherry, Soul II Soul, Texas, Supergrass, Terranova, New Order; film projects incl: Calvin Klein Eternity commercial 1996 and 2001, Marc Jacobs (short film) CDFA awards, Can I Own Myself (short film starring Kate Moss) 1998, Go-Sees (short film) 2001; *Solo Exhibitions*: Br Cncl RCA 1990, Festival de la Monde (Deauville 1990, Budapest 1991, Barcelona 1992 (Canon Photographer of the Year), Monaco 1993 (solo exhbn winner Photographer of the Year), Paris 1995, Biarritz 1996), Parco (Tokyo) 1992, Positive View (Saatchi Gallery) 1995, Fashion Exposures 1992–95, exhbn for HIV charity NY Acad of Art, 1 Telford Road London 1996, Der Verborgene Brecht Ein Berliner Stadtrundgang (Cubitt Gallery London and Scalo Gallery Zurich) 1998, The Photographers Gallery (London) 1998, Go-Sees (Pitti Imagine Discovery Gallery Florence) 1999, 90 x 60 x 90 (Museo Jacobo Borges Caracas) 2000, Remake Berlin (Fotomuseum Winterthur, Switzerland) 2000, Lehmann Maupin Gallery (NY) 2000 and 2003, Century Cities (Tate Modern London) 2001, Märchenstüberl (Modern Art London) 2001, Munich Fotomuseum 2002, Folkswang Museum 2002; *Group Exhibitions* Tempo Magazine (Hamburg), 2-Kiss (Paris), Jam (Barbican London) 1996, Biennale di Firenze (Florence) 1996, Mayday communities/communication (The Photographers' Gall London) 1999, Living in the Real World (Museum Dhondt-dhaenens Belgium) 2000; *Books* Juergen Teller (1996), Der Vergorgone Brecht, Ein Berliner Stadtrundgang (1997), Go-Sees (1999), Tracht (2001), More (2001); *Style*— Juergen Teller, Esq

TEMIRKANOV, Yuri; *Career* conductor; artistic dir and chief conductor Kirov Opera until 1988, music dir and princ conductor St Petersburg Philharmonic Orch 1988–, princ conductor Royal Philharmonic Orch 1978–98, princ guest conductor Danish Nat Radio Symphony 1997–2008, conductor laureate Royal Philharmonic Orch 1998–; music dir Baltimore Symphony Orch 2000–06, music dir Teatro Regio di Parma 2009–13; other orchs conducted incl: Berlin Philharmonic, Vienna Philharmonic, Dresden Staatskapelle, Orchestre National de France, Royal Concertgebouw Orch, all major American orchs; recording contract with BMG/RCA 1988–2002; *Style*— Yuri Temirkanov, Esq; ✉ c/o Nicholas Mathias, IMG Artists Europe, The Light Box, 111 Power Road, London W4 5PY (☎ 020 8233 5800, fax 020 8233 5801)

TEMKIN, Prof Jennifer (Mrs Graham Zellick); da of late Michael Temkin, of London, and late Minnie, *née* Levy; *b* 6 June 1948; *Educ* South Hampstead HS for Girls, LSE, Univ of London (LLB, LLM, LLD), Inns of Court Sch of Law; *m* 18 Sept 1975, Prof Graham John Zellick, s of Reginald H Zellick, of Windsor, Berks; 1 s (Adam b 1977), 1 da (Lara b 1980); *Career* called to the Bar Middle Temple 1971 (bencher 2009), lectr in law LSE 1971–89, visiting prof of law Univ of Toronto 1978–79, prof of law and dean Sch of Law Univ of Buckingham 1989–92, prof of law Univ of Sussex 1992–2012 (dir Centre for Legal Studies 1994–97, emeritus prof 2012–), prof of law City Univ London 2012–; memb: Editorial Advsy Gp Howard Jl of Criminal Justice 1984–, Scrutiny Ctee on Draft Criminal Code Old Bailey 1985–86, Editorial Bd Jl of Criminal Law 1986–2005, Home Sec's Advsy Gp on Use of Video Recordings in Criminal Proceedings (Pigot Ctee) 1988–89, Ctee of Heads Univ Law Schs 1989–92 and 1994–97, Nat Children's Home Ctee on Children who Abuse other Children 1990–92, External Reference Gp Home Office Sex Offences Review 1999–2000, Ctee of Experts on the Treatment of Sex Offenders in Penal Instns and the Community Cncl of Europe 2003–05, Expert Gp on Rape and Sexual Assault Victims of Violence and Abuse Prevention Prog Dept of Health 2005–07, Nat DNA Database Ethics Gp 2014–; govr S Hampstead HS for Girls 1991–99; FRSA 1989, FAcSS 2009; *Books* Rape and the Legal Process (1987, 2 edn 2002), Rape and Criminal Justice (1995), Sexual Assault and the Justice Gap: A Question of Attitude (jtly, 2008); *Style*— Prof Jennifer Temkin; ✉ The City Law School, City University London, Northampton Square, London EC1V 0HB (e-mail jennifer.temkin.1@city.ac.uk)

TEMPERLEY, Alice; MBE (2011); *b* 1975; *Educ* Central St Martin's Coll of Art, RCA (MA); *m* 2002, Lars von Bennigsen; *Career* fashion designer; launched Temperley London (own label) 2000, concessions worldwide and store NY; official stylist BAFTAs 2005; *Awards* English Print Designer of the Year Indigo Paris 1999, Elle Young Designer of the Year Elle Style Awards 2004, Walpole British Designer of the Year Walpole British Excellence Awards 2004, Most Prominent Designer (in their twenties) American Vogue 2005, Designer of the Year Glamour 2005; *Style*— Ms Alice Temperley, MBE; ✉ Temperley London, 6–10 Colville Mews, Lonsdale Road, London W11 2DA (☎ 020 7229 7957, fax 020 7243 6538)

TEMPERLEY, Prof Howard Reed; s of Fred Temperley (d 1972), and Eva May Temperley (d 1965); *b* 16 November 1932, Sunderland; *Educ* Royal GS Newcastle upon Tyne, Magdalen Coll Oxford, Yale Univ; *m* 1, 1957 (m dis 1966), Jane Mary, da of William Flambert (d 1993); 1 da (Alison b 1962); m 2, 1966, Rachel Stephanie (d 1990), da of Rowley S Hooper (d 1951); 1 da (Rebecca b 1969), 1 s (Nicholas b 1971); m 3, 1998, Mary Kathryn, da of Lemuel Powe (d 1990); *Career* Nat Serv 2 Lt Armoured Corps 1951–53;

T

asst lectr UCW Aberystwyth 1960–61, lectr Univ of Manchester 1961–67; UEA: sr lectr 1967–81, prof 1981–97, emeritus prof 1997–; chm Br Assoc for American Studies 1986–89; *Books* British Antislavery 1833–1870 (1972), Lieut Colonel Joseph Gubbins's New Brunswick Journals of 1811 and 1813 (ed, 1980), Introduction to American Studies (ed jtly, 1981, 3 edn 1998), White Dreams, Black Africa: The Antislavery Expedition to the Niger 1841 to 1842 (1991), Britain and America since Independence (2002), How It Was: Memories of Growing Up in the 1930s, '40s and '50s (2010), There Were Dinosaurs Everywhere: A Rhyming Romp Through Dinosaur History (2012); *Recreations* graphic art, children's verse; *Clubs* Norfolk; *Style—* Prof Howard Temperley; ✉ The Oaks, Gurney Lane, Cringleford, Norfolk NR4 7SB (☎ 01603 528023, e-mail h.temperley@uea.ac.uk, website www.howardtemperley.com)

TEMPEST, Kate; *b* 22 December 1985; *Career* poet, rapper and playwright; works incl: Everything Speaks in its Own Way (poetry), Wasted (theatre), Brand New Ancients (theatre, Battersea Arts Centre) 2012, Everybody Down (album) 2014, The Bricks that Built the Houses (novel) 2016, Let Them Eat Chaos (album) 2016; *Style—* Ms Kate Tempest; ✉ c/o Toby Donnelly, ATC Management, 166 Camden Street, London NW1 9PT (☎ 020 7580 7773, Twitter @KateTempest)

TEMPEST-MOGG, Dr Brenden Dayne; s of Alan Reginald Mogg, JP (NSW), Capt RAAF (d 1994), and Ethyl Mavis Tempest-Hay (d 2000); *b* 10 April 1945, Sydney; *Educ* The Scots Coll Sydney, Univ of NSW (BA), Univ of Essex (MA), Hertford Coll Oxford (MLitt), George Washington Univ Washington DC (EdD), Aust Inst of Professional Counsellors (Dip Counselling); *m* 27 May 1984 (m dis 1990), Galina, da of Ivan Mikhailovich Kobzev (d 1995), of Frunze, Russia; 1 da (Gloria Dela Hay b 27 Feb 1987); *Career* pres: Warnborough Coll UK 1973–, Warnborough Univ Ireland 1997–2006, Warnborough Coll Ireland 2006–, Warnborough Publishing 2010–; visiting overseas lectr 1976–; psychotherapist and clinical counsellor 1995–; conslt on int educn 1988–, conslt on accreditation and quality assurance 1990–, advsr distance learning 1995–, ceo Dr Brenden Educn Solutions 2015–; chm Warnborough Univ Alliance 2008–; memb: Oxford Business Alumni Said Business Sch Univ of Oxford, Oxford Educn Soc, Dept of Educn Oxford, Oxford Law Soc, Assoc of Int Educators, Oxford Union; JP (NSW) 1967–2005; MInstD 1997–2008; FRSA 1994; *Books* ed A Life in Colourful Word (by E M Tempest-Mogg); *Recreations* travel, polo, reading, poetry; *Clubs* Cirencester Park Polo; *Style—* Dr Brenden D Tempest-Mogg; ✉ e-mail president@warnborough.ac.uk, website http://uk.linkedin.com/pub/dr-brenden-d-tepest-mogg/5/827/6b2)

TEMPLE, Anthony Dominic Afamado; QC; s of Sir Rawden John Afamado Temple, CBE, QC (d 2000), and Margaret, *née* Gunson (d 1980); bro of Victor Bevis Afoumado Temple, QC, *qv*; *b* 21 September 1945; *Educ* Haileybury and ISC, Worcester Coll Oxford (MA); *m* 28 May 1983, Susan Elizabeth, da of Ernst Bodansky (d 1990), of Broadbridge Heath, W Sussex; 2 da (Jessica Elizabeth b 11 Dec 1985, Alexandra Louise b 21 Aug 1988); *Career* called to the Bar Inner Temple 1968; Crown Law Office Western Australia 1968–69; in practice UK 1970–2015, recorder of the Crown Court 1989–2006 (asst recorder 1982), dep judge of the High Court 1995–2010; chm Modern Pentathlon Assoc of GB 2004–, memb Bd European Confederation of Modern Pentathlon 2012–; *Recreations* modern pentathlon, travel; *Style—* Anthony Temple, QC; ✉ 15 Lansdowne Walk, London W11 3AH (e-mail atemple@anthonytemple.com)

TEMPLE, Prof Sir John Graham; kt (2003); s of Joseph Henry Temple (d 2000), and Norah, *née* Selby (d 1987); *b* 14 March 1942; *Educ* William Hulme's GS Manchester, Univ of Liverpool (MB ChB, ChM); *m* 11 April 1966, (Margaret) Jillian Leighton, da of Robert Leighton Hartley (d 1966), of Wigan; 2 s (Robert b 27 Oct 1967, Christopher b 5 July 1972), 1 da (Caroline b 29 Dec 1969); *Career* prof of surgery Univ of Birmingham, conslt surgn Queen Elizabeth Hosp Birmingham 1979–2000; postgrad dean Univ of Birmingham 1991–2000, chair conf of post grad medical deans (COPMed); regnl advsr in surgery RCS England 1990–94, special advsr to CMO (Calman Training) 1995–2000, chm Specialist Trg Authy Med Royal Colls 2000–07 (memb 1996–2000), chm Research Cncl and tstee Healing Fndn 2003–; Hon Col 202 Field Hosp (V) 2004–09; memb Cncl Univ of Warwick 2004–15; memb: BMA 1965, Assoc of Surgns of GB 1974; Hon DSc Univ of Bristol 2014; FMedSci, FRCSEd (memb Cncl 1995–, pres 2000–03), Hon FRCS (previously FRCS), FRCSGlas, FRCPEd, FRCP, FACS, FHKCS, Hon FRCGP, Hon FRCSI, Hon FFAEM, FRCA, FFICM 2014; *Recreations* skiing, sailing; *Style—* Prof Sir John Temple; ✉ Wharncliffe, 24 Westfield Road, Edgbaston, Birmingham B15 3QG (☎ 0121 454 2445, e-mail jgtemple@compuserve.com)

TEMPLE, Magnus Alexander; *Career* freelance documentary dir; co-fndr Firefly 2004 (renamed Dragonfly, sold 2007), co-fndr and jt chief exec Garden Productions 2010– (sold to ITV 2013); exec prodr: The Family (BAFTA nominated), One Born Every Minute (Best Factual Series BAFTA), 24 Hours in A&E (Best Documentary Series RTS Award), Inside Claridge's, Keeping Britain Alive: The NHS in a Day (BAFTA nominated); *Style—* Magnus Temple, Esq; ✉ The Garden Productions, 1 America Street, London SE1 0NE (☎ 020 7261 1252, e-mail magnus.temple@thegardenproductions.tv, website www.thegardenproductions.tv)

TEMPLE, Martin John; CBE (2005); s of John Douglas Temple (d 1982), and Kathleen, *née* Cook; *b* 30 August 1949, Scarborough; *Educ* Bridlington Sch, Univ of Hull (BSc), Newcastle Poly (DipM), INSEAD (AMP); *m* Aug 1972, Lesley, da of James Leonard Imeson; 1 da (Sarah Elizabeth b 7 April 1977), 1 s (Paul James b 11 Feb 1979); *Career* various positions BSC Consett 1970–79, gen mangr British Steel Corp Refractories Gp 1979–85, works dir G R Stein Refractories 1985–87, dir of sales and marketing British Stainless Steel 1987–92; Avesta Sheffield: dir of mktg and sales 1992–95, vice-pres Sales and Distribution Div 1995–98; Engineering Employers Fedn (EEF): DG 1999–2016, chm 2008–16; gp chm 600 Gp plc 2007–11; chm CEEMET until 2009; memb: Bd Women in Science and Engrg (WISE) until 2007 (also former chm), Engrg Technol Bd (ETB) until 2008, Supervisory Bd Sci, Engrg, Technol and Maths Network (SETNET) until 2007, Bd Sci Engrg Manufacturing Technological Alliance (SEMTA) until 2009, Bd Nat Metals Technol Centre (NAMTEC) until 2009, Bd (Business Gp) BERR, Bd Design Cncl 2009–16 (currently chm); chm Govt Business Support Simplification Prog 2008–11, chair Health and Safety Exec 2016–; dir Vestry Ct Ltd 1999–2014; memb Cncl Univ of Warwick 2011–16 (chm Warwick Business Sch 2014–16 (memb Bd 2011–16)), memb Bd Sheffield Teaching Hosp Tst 2013–, memb Bd The Great Exhibition of the North; Freeman Worshipful Co of Cutlers; Hon DSc Univ of Hull 2011, hon doctorate Sheffield Hallam Univ 2014; Hon FFOM 2008; *Recreations* rugby, music, countryside, current affairs; *Style—* Martin Temple, Esq, CBE; ✉ Churchfield House, Church Lane, Old Ravenfield, Rotherham, South Yorkshire S65 4NG

TEMPLE, Nicholas John (Nick); s of Leonard Temple (d 1990), and Lilly Irene, *née* Thornton; *b* 2 October 1947; *Educ* Kings Sch Gloucester; *Family* 1 s (Alexander James b 10 Jan 1975), 2 da (Charlotte Elizabeth b 22 July 1977, Rosanna Louise b 12 July 1980); m, 14 Oct 2004, Lucinda, *née* Westmacott; *Career* IBM: joined as systems engr 1965, conslt on R&D 1981, estab banking industry products lab Germany 1983, vice-pres Systems and Product Mgmnt IBM Europe 1985–87, ceo IBM Central Europe, ceo IBM UK Ltd 1991–95, chm IBMUK Ltd 1995–96; mgmnt conslt 1996–; ceo Armature 1997–99; chm: Retail Business Solutions 2001–07, Blick plc 2002–04, FoxIT 2002–10, Hotelscene 2008–12, Capula Ltd 2007–09; non-exec dir: Electrocomponents plc 1997–2007, Datacash plc 2000–10, Datatec plc, 4Imprint Gp plc 2003–12, intela Ltd 2008–13; chm Business in the Community 1993–98; *Recreations* rowing, opera, cooking; *Clubs* Henley Royal Regatta, Glyndebourne; *Style—* Nick Temple, Esq; ✉ 10 Markham Square, London SW3 4UY (☎ 020 77581 2181, fax 020 7584 0644, e-mail mail@nicktemple.co.uk)

TEMPLE, Nina Claire; da of Landon Royce Temple, and Barbara Joan Temple; *b* 21 April 1956; *Educ* Imperial Coll London (BSc); *Children* 1 da (Rebecca 1986), 1 s (Oliver b 1988); *Career* nat sec Communist Pty GB 1990– and led transformation into Democratic Left; co-ordinator Democratic Left 1991–2000; helped found: Unions 21, Make Votes Count; *Recreations* rambling, swimming, gardening, movies; *Style—* Ms Nina Temple

TEMPLE, Richard; s of Maurice Victor Temple, and Margaret Temple; *b* 4 September 1962, Stourton, Staffs; *Educ* The Kings Sch Worcester, Univ of Keele (BA), Chester Coll of Law, Univ of Birmingham (LLM); *m* 17 April 1999, Camilla; 1 s, 2 da; *Career* admitted slr 1989; articled clerk then assoc Lovell White Durrant 1987–95, sr assoc Ashurst Morris Crisp 1996–97; ptnr: CMS Cameron McKenna 1997–2004, Hogan & Hartson 2005–07, Osborne Clarke 2007–09, Field Fisher Waterhouse 2009–10, McCarthy Tetrault 2011–; memb: Law Soc 1989, Int Bar Assoc 1996; The World Bank Water Sanitation Toolkit (1997 and 2006); *Recreations* tennis, running, Japanese art; *Style—* Richard M Temple, Esq; ✉ McCarthy Tetrault, 125 Old Broad Street, London EC2N 1AR (☎ 020 7786 5706, e-mail rtemple@mccarthy.ca)

TEMPLE, Victor Bevis Afoumado; QC (1993); s of Sir Rawden Temple, QC, CBE (d 2000), and Margaret, *née* Gunson (d 1980); bro of Anthony Dominic Afamado Temple, QC, *qv*; *b* 23 February 1941; *Educ* Shrewsbury, Inns of Court Sch of Law; *m* 1974, Richenda, *née* Penn-Bull; 2 s (Benjamin, Samuel); *Career* mktg exec: S H Benson 1960–63, J Lyons 1964–65, Beecham Group 1965–68, Alcan Aluminium 1968; called to the Bar Inner Temple 1971 (bencher 1996), sr prosecuting counsel to the Crown 1991–93 (jr prosecuting counsel 1985–91), recorder 1989–; DTI inspr into National Westminster Bank 1992, a chm Police Discipline Appeals Tbnls 1993; *Recreations* rowing, carpentry; *Clubs* Thames Rowing (pres 2009); *Style—* Victor Temple, Esq, QC; ✉ 21 College Hill, London EC4R 2RP (☎ 020 7583 0410)

TEMPLE-MORRIS, Baron (Life Peer UK 2001), of Llandaff in the County of South Glamorgan and of Leominster in the County of Herefordshire; Peter Temple-Morris; s of His Honour Sir Owen Temple-Morris (d 1985), and Vera, *née* Thompson (d 1986); *b* 12 February 1938; *Educ* Malvern Coll, St Catharine's Coll Cambridge; *m* 1964, Taheré, er da of H E Senator Khozeimé Alam, of Teheran; 2 s, 2 da; *Career* called to the Bar Inner Temple 1962, admitted slr 1989; Hampstead Cons Political Centre 1971–73, second prosecuting counsel Inland Revenue SE Circuit 1971–74; MP (Cons until Nov 1997, Ind One-Nation Cons 1997–98, Lab 1998–2001) Leominster Feb 1974–2001, PPS to Sec of State for Tport 1979; memb: Commons Select Ctee on Foreign Affrs 1987–90, Delegated Powers and Regulatory Reform Ctee House of Lords 2002–06, Lord Chllr's Advsy Ctee on Nat Records and Archives Kew, Sub Ctee E (Justice and Institutions) House of Lords European Ctee 2010–13; chm: Br-Iranian Parly Gp 1983–2005, Br-Netherlands Parly Gp 1988–2001 (sec or treas 2001–14), Br-Spanish Parly Gp 1992–2001 (treas 2001–05), All-Pty Southern Africa Gp 1992–94, South Africa Gp 1994–95 (vice-chm 1995–2001); vice-chm: Cons Parly Foreign Affrs Ctee 1982–90, Cons Parly NI Ctee 1990–92, Cons European Affrs Ctee 1990–97; chm Br Gp Inter-Parly Union 1982–85 (exec 1976–96), first Br co-chm Br-Irish Inter-Parly Body 1990–97 (memb 1997–2005), vice-chm GB-Russia Centre 1992–97, memb Exec Commonwealth Parly Assoc (UK Branch) 1993–98 (vice-chm 1994–95), vice-pres UN Assoc Cncl; pres Iran Soc 1995–2010, pres Br-Iranian Business Assoc 1995–2005, chm Br-Iranian C of C 2002–04; conslt slr Moon Beever 2001–14; chm Exec and vice-chm Soc of Cons Lawyers 1995–97 (memb Exec 1968–71 and 1990–95); memb Cncl Malvern Coll 1977–2002, memb Academic Cncl Wilton Park (FCO) 1990–97, pres St Catharine's Coll Cambridge Soc 2003–04; Liveryman Worshipful Co of Basketmakers; Chief Steward City of Hereford 2009–; Chevalier du Tastevin (Château de Clos de Vougeot), Jurade de St Emilion, Knight Cdr of the Order of Orange Nassau (Netherlands) 2007; *Publications* Across the Floor (2015); *Recreations* films, books, wine, food, travel; *Clubs* Cardiff and County, Reform (memb Ctee 2007–10); *Style—* The Rt Hon the Lord Temple-Morris; ✉ House of Lords, London SW1A 0PW (☎ 020 7219 4181, e-mail templemorrisp@parliament.uk)

TEMPLE-RICHARDS, Charles Leofric Thomas; s of Lt Cdr Leofric Douglas Temple-Richards, RN, of Stibbard, Norfolk (d 1999), and Geraldine Beatrice, *née* Cook; *b* 21 September 1955, Havant, Hants; *Educ* Eton, Magdalene Coll Cambridge; *m* 1986, Virginia Jane, *née* Scott; 2 da (Cornelia b 23 Sept 1989, Juliana b 16 Nov 1991), 1 s (Alec b 30 March 1995); *Career* chartered surveyor Carter Jonas 1977–79; stockbroker: Scrimgeour Kemp-Gee 1979–86, James Capel (later HSBC) 1986–2001, Barratt & Cooke 2001–; MRICS, FCSI; *Recreations* shooting, fishing, the countryside, skiing; *Clubs* Millennium, Allsorts; *Style—* C L T Temple-Richards, Esq; ✉ Sennowe Park, Guist, Norfolk NR20 5PB; Barratt & Cooke, 5 Opie Street, Norwich NR1 3DW (☎ 01603 624236, e-mail charlietr@barrattandcooke.co.uk)

TEMPLETON, Prof (Alexander) Allan; CBE (2009); s of Richard Templeton (d 1968), and Minnie, *née* Whitfield (d 2001); *b* 28 June 1946; *Educ* Aberdeen GS, Univ of Aberdeen (MB ChB, MD); *m* 17 Dec 1980, Gillian Constance, da of Geoffrey William John Penney (d 2002), of Eastbourne; 3 s (Richard b 1981, Robert b 1983, Peter b 1987), 1 da (Katherine b 1985); *Career* lectr then sr lectr Univ of Edinburgh 1976–85, regius prof of obstetrics and gynaecology Univ of Aberdeen 1985–2007; pres RCOG 2004–2007; author of various pubns on human infertility and gynaecological endocrinology; FRCOG 1987 (MRCOG 1974), FMedSci 2002, FRCPEd 2005, FRCP 2006, FACOG 2007; *Books* The Early Days of Pregnancy (1987), Reproduction and the Law (1990), Infertility (1992), The Prevention of Pelvic Infection (1996), Evidence-Based Fertility Treatment (1998); *Recreations* mountaineering and life in Wester Ross; *Style—* Prof Allan Templeton, CBE, MD, FRCOG, FRCP, FMedSci; ✉ Oak Tree Cottage, Leacnasaide, Gairloch IV21 2AP (☎ 01445 741354, e-mail allan.templeton@abdn.ac.uk)

TEMPLETON, Suzannah Clare (Suzie); da of Ian George Templeton, of Dunbridge, Hants, and Roberta Lambie Mansell, *née* Dearborn; *b* 2 August 1967; *Educ* UCL (BSc), Surrey Inst of Art and Design (BA), RCA (MA); *Children* 1 da (Briar Rose Stoces b 8 July 2009); *Career* writer, dir and animator; Hon DLitt Univ of Portsmouth 2008; *Films* Stanley (1999), Inside (2000), Dog (2001), Peter and the Wolf (2006); 42 int film awards incl: McLaren Award 2001, BAFTA 2002, Hiroshima Prize 2002, Br Animation Award 2002, Utrecht Grand Prix 2002, Siena Grand Prix 2002, Melbourne Best Overall Film 2002, Tampere Best Animation 2003, Pulcinella Award 2007, Golden Rose 2007, Annecy Grand Prix 2007, Br Animation Award 2008, Acad Award 2008; *Style—* Ms Suzie Templeton

TENCH, Les; *b* 18 April 1945, St Helens, Merseyside; *Educ* Univ of Nottingham (BSc); *Career* md Twyfords Bathrooms 1976–85, md Steetley Building Products 1985–92, md CRH UK 1992–98, dir Shepherd Building Group 1994–2004, md CRH Europe Building Products 1998–2002, chm SIG plc 2004–; dir Staffs Trg and Enterprise Cncl 1994–97, memb Bd Learning and Skills Cncl 2001–03; govr tertiary colls 1994–97; *Recreations* walking, trekking, visiting unusual places, photography, theatre, music; *Style—* Les Tench, Esq; ✉ SIG plc, Hillsborough Works, Langsett Road, Sheffield S6 2LW (☎ 0114 285 6300)

TENNANT, David; s of Alexander McDonald, of Paisley, Strathclyde, and E Helen McDonald; *b* 18 April 1971, Bathgate, Lothian; *Educ* RSAMD; *m* Georgia Moffett; 1 da (Olive b 2011), 1 adopted s (Tyler); *Career* actor; acted with the 7:84 Theatre Company; *Theatre* incl: Touchstone in As You Like It (RSC) 1996, Romeo in Romeo and Juliet (RSC) 2000, Antipholus of Syracuse in Comedy of Errors (RSC) 2000, Jeff in The Lobby Hero (Donmar Warhouse and New Ambassadors) 2002 (nominated Best Actor Laurence Olivier Theatre Awards 2003), title role in Hamlet (RSC) 2008, Much Ado About Nothing

(Wyndham's Theatre) 2011; *Television* incl: Casanova in Casanova 2005, Secret Smile 2005, The Chatterley Affair 2006, The Romantics 2006, The Doctor in Doctor Who 2005–10 (Outstanding Drama Performance Nat TV Awards 2008), Einstein and Eddington 2008, title role in Hamlet 2009, Single Father 2010, Twenty Twelve 2011–12, True Love 2012; *Films* incl: Bright Young Things 2003, Harry Potter and the Goblet of Fire 2005, Glorious 39 2009, St Trinian's 2: The Legend of Fritton's Gold 2009, How to Train Your Dragon 2010, United 2011, The Decoy Bride 2011, Fright Night 2011, The Pirates! In an Adventure with Scientists! 2012; *Style*— David Tennant; ✉ c/o ICM, Oxford House, 76 Oxford Street, London W1N 0AX (☎ 020 7636 6565, fax 020 7323 0101)

TENNANT, Hon Emma Christina; da of late 2 Baron Glenconner by his 2 w; *b* 20 October 1937; *Educ* St Paul's Girls' Sch; *m* 1, 1957 (m dis 1962), Sebastian Yorke, s of Henry Yorke and Hon Mrs (Adelaide) Yorke, da of 2 Baron Biddulph; m 2, 1963 (m dis), Christopher Booker, *qv*; m 3, 1968 (m dis 1973), Alexander Cockburn; m 4, 2008, Timothy Owens; *Career* novelist; founder ed literary newspaper Bananas; Hon DLitt Univ of Aberdeen 1996; FRSL; *Books* The Bad Sister (1979, reprinted 1999), Wild Nights (1979), The House of Hospitalities (1983), Sisters and Strangers (1989), Frankenstein's Baby (BBC film), Faustine (1992), ABC of Writing (1992), Tess (1993), Pemberley (1994), An Unequal Marriage (1994), Elinor and Marianne (1995), Emma in Love (1996), Strangers: A Family Romance (1998), Girlitude (1999), Burnt Diaries (1999), The Ballad of Sylvia and Ted (2001), A House in Corfu (2001), Felony: a private history of The Aspern Papers (2002), Balmoral (jtly, as Isabel Vane, 2004), Heathcliff's Tale (2005), The Harp Lesson (2005), Confessions of a Sugar Mummy (2007), The Autobiography of The Queen (2007), Seized (2008), Waiting for Princess Margaret (2009); *Recreations* exploring, walking in Dorset; *Style*— The Hon Mrs Timothy Owens, known professionally as Emma Tennant; ✉ c/o Jonathan Cape, Random House, 20 Vauxhall Bridge Road, London SW1V 2SA

TENNANT, Mark Edward; s of Sir Iain Tennant, KT, JP, and the Lady Margaret Tennant; *b* 9 May 1947; *Educ* Eton; *m* 16 Oct 1971, Hermione Rosamond, da of Lt-Col Maurice Howe, OBE; 2 da (Miranda Rosamond Hermione b 15 June 1974, Clementina Margaret Georgina b 21 Nov 1977), 1 s (Edward Iain b 12 May 1983); *Career* vol serv Ockenden Venture India 1965–66, Capt Scots Gds 1966–73; Hambros Bank Ltd: trainee 1973–74, mangr Banking Control Dept 1973–76, mangr International Fixed Interest Dept 1976–81, md Hambro Pacific Ltd Hong Kong 1981–83; dir Fidelity International Ltd 1983–86, chm Bell Laurie White & Co Ltd 1986–91, chm Hill Samuel Unit Trust Managers Ltd and dir Hill Samuel Investment Services Group Ltd 1986–91, md Chase Global Securities Services (Scotland) 1991–95, chief fin offr Chase Global Securities, Chase Manhattan plc 1995–96, sr vice-pres Global Fund Services ChaseManhattan Bank (subsequently JP Morgan Chase) 1996–2004, sr advsr JP Morgan Securities 2004–, chm IBE Consulting 2004–16, chm (formerly dir) F&C Private Equity plc 2004–; non-exec dir Quality Street Ltd 1993–95; dir: Scotland International 1994–95, JP Morgan Tstees Ltd 1999–2004, Grameen Scotland 2013–; chm The Money Portal plc 2005–08; memb Int Advsy Bd T Rowe Price Global Investment Servs 2004–, chm Centrica Pension Fund 2016–; head of youth leadership St John Ambulance 1973–83, cncllr Surrey Heath DC 1977–79, treas Scottish Cons Pty 1991–94; tstee Royal Hospital Chelsea 2004–; Party candidate (Cons) Dunfermline E 1992, European Parly candidate (Cons) Highlands and Islands 1994; offr Royal Company of Archers 2004–; FRSA 1996; *Recreations* golf, field sports, Scottish music, politics, opera, playing the bagpipes; *Clubs* Boodle's, Pratt's, Swinley Forest Golf, Hong Kong, Sheko (Hong Kong); *Style*— Mark Tennant, Esq, FRSA; ✉ Innes House, Elgin, Moray IV30 8NG (☎ 01343 842410, e-mail mark@inneshouse.co.uk); JP Morgan plc, 25 Bank St, London E14 5JP

TENNANT OF BALFLUIG, Mark Iain; Baron of Balfluig (cr 1650); s of Maj John Tennant, TD, KStJ (d 1967), of Wittersham, Kent, and Hon Antonia Mary Roby Benson (later Viscountess Radcliffe; d 1982), da of 1 Baron Charnwood; *b* 4 December 1932; *Educ* Eton, New Coll Oxford (MA); *m* 11 Dec 1965, Lady Harriot Pleydell-Bouverie, da of 7 Earl of Radnor, KG, KCVO, JP, DL (d 1968); 1 da (Sophia Roby b 1967), 1 s (Lysander Philip Roby b 1968); *Career* Lt The Rifle Bde (SRO); called to the Bar Inner Temple 1958 (bencher 1984); recorder of the Crown Court 1987, Master of the Supreme Court (Queen's Bench Div) 1988–2005; restored Balfluig Castle (dated 1556) in 1967 being the first to obtain a grant from the Historic Buildings Council for Scotland for a building neither inhabited nor habitable; chm Royal Orchestral Soc (formerly Royal Orchestral Soc for Amateur Musicians) 1989–2009 (pres 2009); *Recreations* music, architecture, books, shooting; *Clubs* Brooks's; *Style*— Mark Tennant of Balfluig; ✉ 30 Abbey Gardens, London NW8 9AT (☎ 020 7624 3200); Balfluig Castle, Alford, Aberdeenshire AB33 8EJ

TEPER, Carl Wolf; s of Joseph Elliot Teper, and Pauline, *née* Mercado (d 1992); *b* 15 June 1955; *Educ* Aylestone Sch, Univ of Warwick (LLB), Cncl of Legal Educn; *Career* called to the Bar Middle Temple 1980; pupillage in chambers of Lord Boston of Faversham, QC 1980–81, head of chambers 1 Gray's Inn Sq 1990– (dep head 1988–90), acting stipendiary magistrate 1999–2000, dep dist judge 2000–, parking and traffic adjudicator 2001–; Cncl of Legal Educn: assessor and examiner 1987–97, memb Bd of Examiners 1990–97, memb Bd of Studies 1992–97; memb Bd of Examiners Inns of Court Sch of Law 1997–2000; external examiner: Coll of Law 1997–2001, BPP Law Sch 2003–06; pt/t chm Employment Tbnls 1992–2006, memb Social Security Appeal Tbnl 1992–93; memb: Middle Temple 1977, Gray's Inn 1988; *Recreations* running, studying the Talmud, philanthropy; *Style*— Carl Teper, Esq; ✉ carl.teper@gmail.com

TER HAAR, Rev Roger Eduard Lound; QC (1992); s of Dr Dirk ter Haar (d 2002), and Christine Janet ter Haar (d 2005); *b* 14 June 1952; *Educ* Felsted, Magdalen Coll Oxford (BA); *m* 10 Sept 1977 (m dis 2012), Sarah Anne, da of Peter Leyshon Martyn; 2 s (James b 1978, Harry b 1983), 1 da (Camilla b 1980); m 2, Jan 2014, Charlotte Mary Elizabeth Barney, *née* Raeburn, da of Ashley Raeburn, CBE; *Career* called to the Bar Inner Temple 1974 (bencher 1992), called to the Bar of Gibraltar 1984, called to the Irish Bar 1997; appointed recorder and dep High Court judge 2003; ordained: deacon 2006, priest 2007; curate Holy Trinity Bramley 2006–07, asst priest St Peter's Hascombe and St Mary and All Saints Dunsfold 2007–13; Construction Insurance and UK Construction Contracts (jt ed, 2 edn 2008), Remedies in Construction Law (jtly, 2010); *Recreations* gardening, golf; *Clubs* Brooks's, Garrick; *Style*— Rev Roger ter Haar, QC; ✉ Crown Office Chambers, Temple, London EC4Y 7HJ (☎ 020 7797 8100, fax 020 7797 8101)

TERERA, Giles; s of Giles Terera (d 1977), and Valda, *née* Tudor (d 2007); *b* 14 December 1976, London; *Educ* Mountview Theatre Sch; *Career* actor; *Theatre* Generations of the Dead (Young Vic), Six Degrees of Separation (Sheffield Crucible), The Tempest (RSC), Darker Face of the Earth (RNT), Honk! (RNT), Candide (RNT), Troilus and Cressida (RNT), Up On The Roof (Chichester Festival Theatre), You Don't Kiss (Stratford Circus), Rent (Prince of Wales Theatre), 125th Street (Shaftesbury Theatre), Jailhouse Rock (Theatre Royal Plymouth and Piccadilly Theatre), Ratpack (Strand Theatre and int tour), Avenue Q (Noel Coward Theatre, Best Ensemble Whatsonstage Award 2007), Playboy of the Western World (Abbey Theatre Dublin), The Hour We Knew Nothing of Each Other (RNT), Don't You Leave Me Here (West Yorkshire Playhouse), Death & The Kings Horseman (RNT), Hamlet (RNT), The Tempest (Theatre Royal Haymarket); *Television* Horrible Histories 2009–10; *Film* London Boulevard; dir and prodr Muse of Fire; *Style*— Mr Giles Terera; ✉ c/o Simon Beresford, Dalzell and Beresford, 26 Astwood Mews, London SW7 4DE

TERFEL, Bryn; CBE (2003); *né* Bryn Terfel Jones; s of Hefin Jones, of Garndolbenmaen, Gwynedd, and Nesta, *née* Jones; *b* 9 November 1965, Pwllheli; *Educ* Ysgol Dyffryn Nantlle Gwynedd, Guildhall Sch of Music and Drama (Kathleen Ferrier scholar, Gold Award); *m* 22 August 1987, Lesley, da of George Winston Halliday; 3 s (Morgan, Tomos, Deio Siôn); *Career* bass baritone; pres: Nat Youth Choir of Wales, Festival of Wales, Welsh Nursery Schs, Bardsey Island Tst, Bella Cora Ladies Choir, Int Performers' Aid Tst, Shelter Cymru; vice-pres: Cymru A'r Byd, Llangollen Int Eisteddfod, Cymdeithas Owain Glyndwr; patron: Mid Wales Opera, Taunton Choral Soc, Hope House, Cor Meibion Hart, Criccieth Memorial Hall, Aylestone Sch Music Plus Fund, Royal Town of Caernarfon Chamber of Trade and Indust, Ysbyty Gwynedd Kidney Patients Assoc, NW Wales Chambers of Trade and Industry, Usher Hall Appeal, ATSAIN Music Therapy Tst, Bobath Wales; ambass Prince's Tst; hon fell: Univ of Wales Aberystwyth, Welsh Coll of Music and Drama, Univ of Wales Bangor; Hon Dr Univ of Glamorgan, Hon DMus Univ of Wales Cardiff; white robe Gorsedd Eisteddfod Genedlaethol Frenhinol Cymru; *Roles* incl: Guglielmo in Cosi Fan Tutte (WNO) 1990, Figaro in Le Nozze di Figaro (WNO) 1990, Sprecher in Die Zauberflöte (La Monnaie de Brussels) 1991, Figaro in Figaro's Wedding (ENO) 1991, Figaro in Le Nozze di Figaro (Santa Fe) 1991, Spirit Messenger in Die Frau ohne Schatten (Salzburg Easter Festival) 1992, Masetto in Don Giovanni (Covent Garden) 1992, Jochanaan in Salome (Salzburg Festival) 1992 and 1993, Donner in Das Rheingold (Lyric Opera of Chicago) 1993, Ford in Falstaff (WNO) 1993, Figaro in Le Nozze di Figaro (Châtelet, Paris and Lisbon) 1993, 4 male roles in Les Côntes d'Hoffman (Vienna State Opera) 1994, Leporello in Don Giovanni (Salzburg Festival) 1994, 1995 and 1996, Figaro in Le Nozze di Figaro (Metropolitan Opera NY) 1994, Figaro in Le Nozze di Figaro (Covent Garden) 1994, Balstrode in Peter Grimes (Covent Garden) 1995, Leporello in Don Giovanni (Metropolitan Opera and Lyric Opera of Chicago) 1995, Figaro in Le Nozze di Figaro (Salzburg Festival) 1995, Jochanaan in Salome (Covent Garden) 1995, Nick Shadow in The Rake's Progress (WNO) 1996, Sharpless in Madame Butterfly (New Japan Philharmonic) 1996, 4 male roles in Les Côntes d'Hoffmann (Vienna State Opera) 1996 and 1997, title role in Don Giovanni (Hanover, Köln and London concert performances) 1996, Jochanaan in Salome (Lyric Opera Chicago) 1996, Leporello in Don Giovanni (Ferrara Musica) 1997, Balstrode in Peter Grimes (Vienna State Opera) 1997, Figaro in Le Nozze di Figaro (La Scala Milan and San Francisco) 1997, Wolfram in Tannhäuser (Metropolitan Opera NY) 1997, Figaro in Le Nozze di Figaro (Lyric Opera Chicago, Metropolitan Opera NY and La Scala Milan) 1998, Jochanaan in Salome (Bayerische Staatsoper) 1998, Scarpia in Tosca (Netherlands Opera) 1998, Falstaff in Falstaff (Australian Opera, Chicago Lyric Opera, Royal Opera Covent Garden) 1999, title role in Don Giovanni (Opera National de Paris) 1999, Leporello in Don Giovanni (Vienna State Opera) 1999, Jochanaan in Salome (Vienna State Opera) 1999, 4 male roles in Les Contes d'Hoffmann (Met Opera NY) 2000, Nick Shadow in The Rakes Progress (San Francisco Opera) 2000, Don Giovanni in Don Giovanni (Metropolitan Opera House NY) 2000, Falstaff in Falstaff (Bayerische Staatsoper Munich and Salzburg Festival) 2001, Jochanaan in Salome (Vienna Staatsoper) 2001, Don Giovanni in Don Giovanni (Vienna Staatsoper) 2001, Figaro in Le Nozze di Figaro (Munich Festival) 2001, Dulcamara in L'Elisir d'Amore (Netherlands Opera) 2001, Don Giovanni in Don Giovanni (ROH) 2002, Falstaff in Falstaff (Met Opera NY and BayerischeStaatsoper) 2002, 4 male roles in Les Cantes d'Hoffmann (Opera Nationale de Paris) 2002, Sweeney Todd in Sweeney Todd (Lyric Opera of Chicago) 2002, Jochanaan in Salome (Vienna Staatsoper) 2003, Falstaff in Falstaff (Covent Garden and Vienna Staatsoper) 2003, Jochanaan in Salome (Metropolitan Opera) 2004, Méphistophélès in Faust (Covent Garden) 2004, Don Giovanni in Don Giovanni (Lyric Opera of Chicago) 2004, Wotan in Das Rheingold (Covent Garden) 2004 and 2005, Wotan in Die Walküre (Covent Garden) 2005, Falstaff in Falstaff (Houson, LA and Metropolitan Opera) 2005, Holländer Der Fliegende Holländer (WNO) 2006, Scarpia in Tosca (ROH) 2006, Sweeney Todd in Sweeney Todd (Royal Festival Hall) 2007, Figaro in Le nozze di Figaro (Met Opera) 2007, Gianni Schicchi in Gianni Schicchi (ROH) 2007, Falstaff in Falstaff (Vienna Staatsoper) 2007, Don Giovanni in Don Giovanni (Vienna Staatsoper) 2007, Falstaff in Falstaff (WNO) 2008; *Recordings* on Decca, Deutsche Grammophon, L'Oiseau-Lyre, Archiv, Sony Classical, Philips, RCA, Chandos, Hyperion, EMI Classics, BMG Classics, Sain; *Awards* Lieder Prize Cardiff Singer of the World 1989, first winner Br Critics Circle Award (for most outstanding contribution to musical life in GB) 1992, Gramophone Magazine Young Singer of the Year 1992, Newcomer of the Year Int Classic Music Award 1993, Caecilia Prize (for recording of Vagabond) 1995, Gramophone Award (for recording of An die Musik) 1995, Grammy Award for Best Classical Vocal Performance (for recording of opera arias) 1996, People's Award Gramophone Awards (for recording of Vagabond) 1996, Britannia Record Club Members Award (for Something Wonderful) 1997, Best Singer 1998–99 Lyric Season Gran Teatre del Liceu Barcelona, Artist of the Year BBC Music Magazine 1999, John Edwards Meml Award 2000, Best Opera Recording Grammy Award for The Rake's Progress (Deutsche Grammophon) 2000, Male Artist of the Year Classical Brit Award 2000, Prix Caecilia (for recording of Wagner Arias with Claudio Abbado) 2003, Album of the Year (for Bryn) Classical Brit Awards 2004, Male Artist of the Year Classical Brit Awards 2004 and 2005, Grammy Award for Best Classical Crossover Album (for Simple Gifts) 2007, Shakespeare Prize Alfred Toepfer Fndn Hamburg 2006, Queen's Medal for Music 2006, Grammy Award for Best Opera Recording (for Metropolitan Opera's recording of Richard Wagner's Der Ring Des Nibelungen) 2013; *Recreations* golf, supporting Manchester United, collecting Fob watches, collecting wine; *Style*— Bryn Terfel, Esq, CBE; ✉ c/o Harlequin Agency Ltd, 5th Floor, Gloworks, Porth Teigr, Cardiff CF10 4GA (☎ 029 2075 0821, e-mail carys.davies@harlequin-agency.co.uk or doreen@harlequin-agency.co.uk, website www.harlequin-agency.co.uk, Twitter @HarlequinA_M)

TERRAS, (Christopher) Richard; s of Frederick Richard Terras (d 1976), and Katherine Joan, *née* Anning (d 1998); *b* 17 October 1937; *Educ* Uppingham, UC Oxford (MA); *m* 1, 27 Oct 1962 (m dis 2003), Janet Esther May (d 2010), da of Leslie Harold Sydney Baxter (d 1980); 3 da (Clare b 1964, Penelope b 1968, Joanna b 1971), 1 s (Nicholas b 1965); m 2, 11 Nov 2005, Barbara, da of Leslie Bury (d 2004); *Career* chartered accountant; ptnr: Swanwick Terras & Co 1963–65, Abbott & Son 1963–65, Arthur Andersen 1971–99; UK nat tax dir 1989–99, tax practice dir 15 European and other countries; treas Univ of Manchester 1999–2004; chm NW Kidney Research Assoc 1992–2006; *Recreations* cricket (played for Cheshire, represented Univ of Oxford); *Clubs* Free Foresters, MCC, Cheshire CCC, Cheshire Gentlemen, Northern Nomads, Vincent's (Oxford), Forty, St James's (Manchester); *Style*— Richard Terras, Esq; ✉ 21 St Hilary's Park, Alderley Edge, Cheshire SK9 7DA (☎ 01625 583832)

TERRINGTON, 6 Baron (UK 1918) Christopher Richard James Woodhouse; s of 5 Baron Terrington, DSO, OBE, FRSL (d 2001), and Lady Davidema (Davina) Katharine Cynthia Mary Millicent, *née* Bulwer-Lytton (d 1995), da of 2 Earl of Lytton, KG, GCSI, GCIE, PC (d 1947); *b* 20 September 1946, Knebworth, Herts; *Educ* Winchester, Guy's Hosp Med Sch London (MB BS); *m* 27 Feb 1975, Hon Anna Margaret Philipps, da of late Baron Milford; 1 s (Hon Jack b 7 Dec 1978), 1 da (Hon Constance b 1 Jan 1982); *Heir* s, Hon Jack Woodhouse; *Career* Inst of Urology UCL: sr lectr 1981–97, reader in urology 1997–2005, prof of adolescent urology 2005–11, emeritus prof 2011–; visiting prof: Univ of Pennsylvania Med Sch 2001, Harvard Univ Med Sch 2001; conslt urologist: Royal Marsden Hosp 1981–2014, St George's Hosp 1985–95; hon conslt urologist: St Peter's Hosp 1981–2006, Gt Ormond St Hosp for Children 1981–2011, UC Hosp London 2006–11; chm Br Jl of Urology Int 1999–2010, numerous pubns in learned jls; corresponding memb American Urological Assoc 1985, hon memb Urological Soc of Aust 1999, corresponding memb American Assoc of Genito-Urinary Surgns 2003, hon memb German Urological Soc 2004; Liveryman Worshipful Soc of Apothecaries; FRSM 1981,

T

FRCS 1975, FEBU 1993; *Books* Physiological Basis of Medicine-Urology and Nephrology (1987), Long Term Paediatric Urology (1991), Management of Urological Emergencies (2004), Adolescent Urology and Long-term Outcomes (2015); *Recreations* skiing, stalking; *Clubs* Leander; *Style*— Prof the Rt Hon the Lord Terrington; ✉ Chelsea Urology, Lister House, Chelsea Bridge Road, London SW1W 8RH (e-mail info@chelseaurology.com)

TERRINGTON, Derek Humphrey; s of late Douglas Jack, of Newmarket, Suffolk, and late Jean Mary, *née* Humphrey; *b* 25 January 1949; *Educ* Sea Point Boys' HS, Univ of Cape Town (MA); *m* 15 July 1978, Jennifer Mary, da of late Leslie Vernon Jones; 1 da (Sarah b 29 Sept 1984), 1 s (William b 18 Nov 1996); *Career* assoc ptnr Grieveson Grant 1984, exec dir Phillips & Drew 1991 (asst dir 1987, dir 1988), dir Kleinwort Benson Securities 1991–96, dir and head of equity research Teather & Greenwood 1996–98, media analyst AXA Investment Managers 1998–2000, media analyst Credit Lyonnais Securities 2000–02, head of pan-European media research Commerzbank Securities 2003–04, sr analyst Blue Oak Capital 2005–08, ind equity research conslt 2009–12, Hardman & Co 2013–; tstee Hampton Fuel Allotment Charity 2013–; AIIMR, FRSA; *Style*— Derek Terrington, Esq; ✉ 46 Wensleydale Road, Hampton, Middlesex TW12 2LT (e-mail dterrington@gmail.com)

TERRY; *see also:* Imbert-Terry

TERRY, Air Marshal Sir Colin George; KBE (1998, OBE 1984), CB (1995); s of George Albert Terry, of Shropshire, and Edna Joan, *née* Purslow; *b* 8 August 1943; *Educ* Bridgnorth GS, RAF Colls Henlow and Cranwell, Imperial Coll London (BSc(Eng), ACGI, hockey colours); *m* 12 March 1966, Gillian, da of late Conrad Glendore Grindley; 2 s (Sarn Conrad b 22 May 1969, Leon Alexander b 24 Jan 1974), 1 da (Adrienne Miya b 24 Nov 1976); *Career* tech cadet RAF Tech Coll Henlow 1961, cmmnd engrg offr 1962, various engrg and instructing appts at tport, trg and fighter stations 1962–69, trg as serv pilot 1969–71, promoted Sqdn Ldr 1971, aircraft project offr Royal Navy Belfast 1971–74, sr engrg offr RAF Phantom sqdns Germany 1974–77, engrg authy for Vulcan, Victor and VC10 propulsion systems HQ Strike Cmd 1977–79, attended RAF Staff Coll Bracknell 1979, promoted Wing Cdr 1979, CO Engrg Wing RAF Coltishall (Jaguars and Sea Kings) 1979–81, engrg authy Lightnings and Phantoms HQ Strike Cmd 1981–82, sr RAF engr and OC Engrg Wing RAF Stanley Falkland Is 1982, promoted Gp Capt 1984, engrg authy Cmd Staff, OC RAF Abingdon (Jaguars, Hawks and Buccaneers), RCDS 1989, promoted Air Cdre 1989, Dir of Support Mgmnt 1989–93, promoted Air Vice-Marshal 1993, DG Support Mgmnt (RAF) 1993–95, COS and Dep C-in-C Logistics Cmd 1995–97, Chief Engr (RAF) 1996–99, promoted Air Marshal 1997, Air Force Bd Memb as Air Memb for Logistics and AOC-in-C Logistics Cmd 1997–99, ret 1999; gp md Inflite Engrg Services Ltd 1999–2001, non-exec chm Meggitt plc 2004– (non-exec dir 2003–); Fg offr RAFVR(T) 1999–; RAeS: memb Cncl 1999–, chm Learned Soc 2003–, pres 2005–; memb Senate Engrg Cncl 1999–2002, chm UK Engrg Cncl, bd memb Engrg & Technology Bd, dir ETB 2002–05; UK advsr to: Aermacchi 2002–, SNECMA 2003–; memb Ctee Queen's Award for Enterprise 2002–, pres CGCA 2002–04; Cdre RAF Sailing Assoc 1994–99, pres Assoc Services Yacht Clubs 1997–99; Freeman City of London; Liveryman Worshipful Co of Engrgs 2004; CEng, FRAeS, FRSA, FILog, FCGI, FREng; *Recreations* sailing, flying, skiing, cooking, music; *Clubs* RAF; *Style*— Air Marshal Sir Colin Terry, KBE, CB; ✉ 6AEF RAF Benson, Wallingford, Oxfordshire OX10 6AA

TERRY, (Robert) Jeffrey; s of Robert James Terry (d 1996), of Stockport, and Emily, *née* Davison (d 1975); *b* 10 September 1952; *Educ* William Hulme's GS Manchester, King's Coll London (LLB), City Univ (MA (Business Law)); *m* 15 July 1978, Susan Jane, da of Reginald Trevor Kingston Gregory (d 1997), of Bath; 2 da (Sarah Louise b 7 Aug 1983, Anna May Emily b 7 May 1987); *Career* called to the Bar Lincoln's Inn 1976, community lawyer Southend CAB 1976–78; in private practice: London 1978–, Manchester 1989– (chm 8 King St Chambers Business Gp); memb: Northern Circuit Commercial Bar Assoc (fndr memb), Northern Chancery Bar Assoc, Professional Negligence Assoc, American Bar Assoc; CEDR accredited mediator; FCIArb 1997, fell Soc for Advanced Legal Studies 1998; *Recreations* walking, photography, reading, smallholding husbandry; *Style*— Jeffrey Terry, Esq

TERRY, John George; *b* 7 December 1980, Barking, London; *m* 2007, Toni Poole; 2 c (George John, Summer Rose (twins) b 18 May 2006); *Career* professional footballer; Chelsea FC: joined as apprentice, first team debut 1998, capt 2004–, winners FA Cup 2000, 2007 and 2009 (finalists 2002), winners FA Premiership 2005 and 2006 (runners-up 2004 and 2007), League Cup 2005 and 2007, finalists UEFA Champions League 2008, Europa League 2013; England: over 60 caps, 6 goals, debut v Serbia and Montenegro 2003, capt 2006–10 and 2011–12 (capt Under 21s 2001–02), memb squad European Championships 2004 and World Cup 2006 and 2010, ret 2012; PFA Footballer of the Year 2005; *Style*— Mr John Terry; ✉ c/o Chelsea Football Club, Fulham Road, London SW6 1HS

TERRY, (John) Quinlan; CBE (2015); s of Philip John Terry (d 1990), and Phyllis May Whiteman (d 1998); *b* 24 July 1937; *Educ* Bryanston, Architectural Assoc; *m* 9 Sept 1961, Christina Marie-Therese, da of Joachin Tadeusz de Ruttié (d 1968); 4 da (Elizabeth b 1964, Anna b 1965, Martha b 1979, Sophia b 1982), 1 s (Francis Nathanael b 1969); *Career* architect in private practice; works incl: new infirmary Royal Hosp Chelsea, office, retail and housing devpt at 264–267 Tottenham Court Road, Richmond Riverside, 22 Baker Street, Dufours Place Soho, Regent Street Cambridge, Colonial Williamsburg VA, country houses in the classical style in England, Germany and America, new Howard Bldg Downing Coll Cambridge, new Brentwood Cathedral, six villas in Regent's Park for the Crown Estate Cmmrs, new library and new theatre Downing Coll, restoration of St Helen's Bishopsgate, restoration of the three state rooms No 10 Downing St; memb Royal Fine Art Cmmn 1994–98; FRIBA 1962; *Recreations* the Pauline Epistles; *Style*— Quinlan Terry, Esq, CBE; ✉ Quinlan & Francis Terry, Old Exchange, High Street, Dedham, Colchester CO7 6HA (☎ 01206 323186, website www.qftarchitects.com)

TESFAYE, Prof Solomon; s of Ato Tesfaye Ashebir, of Ethiopia, and Weizero Mihret Tsegue; *b* 21 December 1958, Ethiopia; *Educ* Sevenoaks Sch, Univ of Bristol Med Sch (MB ChB, MD); *m* 12 Jan 2003, Sophia Mekuria; 2 c (Aida, Samuel); *Career* sr med registrar 1993–96, conslt physician and diabetologist Royal Hallamshire Hosp Sheffield 1997–, currently prof of diabetic medicine Univ of Sheffield; fndr Neuropathic Foot Ulcer Clinic; former assoc ed Diabetologia, author of numerous articles in learned jls incl The Lancet and New England Jl of Med, cmmr on diabetes in Sub-Saharan Africa (SSA) The Lancet 2015–17; profiled in The Lanet 2014; chm Neurodiab 2006–09; memb: DH/MRC Diabetes Advsy Gp, Cardiovascular Advsy Gp Medicines and Healthcare Products Regulatory Agency, Advsy Cncl Neuropathy Tst, Bd Quantitative Sensory Testing Soc, Diabetes UK, American Diabetic Assoc, European Diabetic Neuropathy Study Gp, DPFS Panel MRC 2015–; North of England Neurological Assoc Prize 1994, Camillo Golgi Prize for Outstanding Research in Diabetes European Assoc for the Study of Diabetes 2014; fndr Sheffield Health Action Resource for Ethiopia (SHARE); FRCP 2001 (MRCP 1988); *Publications* Diabetic Neuropathy (jt ed, 2009); *Recreations* table tennis, Impressionist painting, travelling, music; *Style*— Prof Solomon Tesfaye; ✉ Royal Hallamshire Hospital, Glossop Road, Sheffield S10 2JF (e-mail solomon.tesfaye@sth.nhs.uk)

TESORIERE, Ambassador (Harcourt) Andrew Pretorius; HM Operations Service Medal Afghanistan 2008, NATO Service medal Afghanistan 2008; s of Maj Pieter Ivan Tesoriere, and Joyce Margaret, *née* Baxter; *b* 2 November 1950; *Educ* NC Pangbourne, BRNC Dartmouth, UC Wales Aberystwyth (BSc), Ecole Nationale d'Admininistration Paris; *m* 1987, Dr Alma Gloria Vasquez; *Career* RNR 1964–68, offr RN 1969–73; HM Dip Serv: joined FCO 1974, Persian language trg SOAS Univ of London and Iran 1975, oriental sec Kabul 1976–79, third sec Nairobi 1979–81, second sec Abidjan (also accredited to Niamey and Ouagadougou) 1981–84, FCO 1985–87, first sec and head of Chancery then chargé d'affaires Damascus 1987–91, first sec FCO 1991–94, head of field ops UN Office for the Co-ordination of Humanitarian Affrs (OCHA) Afghanistan 1994–95, ambass to Albania 1996–98, on secondment as actg head of mission and sr political advsr UN Special Mission to Afghanistan 1998–2000, chargé d'affaires Kabul 2001–02, ambass to Latvia 2002–05, OSCE electoral advsr for Afghan elections 2004 and 2005, ambass to Algeria 2005–07, sr policy advsr to ISAF Cdr S Afghanistan 2007–08, FCO secondment as OSCE ambass to Kyrgyzstan 2008–12 (chm Bd of Tstees OSCE Acad 2008–12); ambass and head EU Assistance Mission to Moldova and Ukraine (EUBAM) 2015–; FRGS 1993; *Publications* Afghanistan: From Relief to Self-reliance (jtly, 1995), Afghanistan at Close Quarters (jtly, 2000), Mediation and Quiet Diplomacy in the Field (2010), HMG cross-Govt study on conflict and stability in Central Asia including Afghan dimension (2012), HMG triennial review of Westminster Foundation for Democracy (2014); *Recreations* travel, sport, foreign languages, art, countryside, Afghan society; *Style*— Ambassador H A P Tesoriere

TETLOW, Stephen; *Career* chief exec Vehicle and Operator Servs Agency; *Style*— Stephen Tetlow, Esq; ✉ Vehicle and Operator Services Agency, Berkeley House, Croydon Street, Bristol BS5 0DA

TEWSON, Jane; CBE (1999); da of Dr Tim Tewson, of Oxford, and Dr Blue Johnston; *b* 9 January 1958; *Educ* Headington Sch Oxford, Lord William's Sch Thame; *m* 16 May 1992, Dr Charles Lane; 2 s (Charlie, Sam); *Career* project co-ordinator MENCAP 1979–83, fndr and chief exec Charity Projects and Comic Relief 1984–96, fndr PilotLight 1996–99, fndr Timebank 1999, dir PilotLight Australia 2000, dir St James Ethics Centre; tstee Reichstein Fndn; *Recreations* travel, walking, gardening, reading; *Style*— Ms Jane Tewson, CBE; ✉ 35 Cressy Street, Malvern 3144, Melbourne, Australia

THACKARA, John Alexander; s of Alexander Daniel Thackara, of Bath, and Eleanor Hazel, *née* Miller; *b* 6 August 1951; *Educ* Marlborough, Univ of Kent (BA), Univ of Wales (Dip Journalism); *m* 1, 20 April 1989, Hilary Mary, da of late Bowyer Arnold, DFC; 1 da (Kate Eleanor b 1989); m 2, Kristi, da of A C M van Riet; *Career* commissioning ed Granada Publishing 1975–79, managing ed NSW Univ Press 1979–80, ed Design Magazine 1981–85, freelance design critic 1985–87, fndr and dir Design Analysis Int 1987, dir of research RCA 1989–92, dir Netherlands Design Inst 1993–99, currently dir Doors of Perception, prog dir Designs of the Time 2006–08; former chm European Design Industry Summit (EDIS); former memb Virtual Platform (advising Dutch Govt), memb Standing Cmmn on Design, memb various expert gps advising EC on innovation policy; memb Advsy Bd: Design Impact (India), Pecha Kucha Fndn (Japan), Pixelache Festival (Finland); fell Musashino Univ 2009; fell Young Fndn 2009–, sr fell RCA 2011; FRSA 1987; *Books* incl: New British Design (1987), Design after Modernism (1988), Lost in Space: A Traveller's Tale (1995), In the Bubble: Designing In A Complex World (2005); *Recreations* writing; *Style*— John Thackara, Esq; ✉ Doors of Perception, 17 Grand Rue, 34190 Ganges, France (e-mail john@doorsofperception.com, website www.doorsofperception.com); website www.thackara.com

THACKER, David Thomas; s of Thomas Richard Thacker, and Alice May, *née* Beaumont; *b* 21 December 1950, Higham Ferrers; *Educ* Wellingborough GS, Univ of York (BA, MA); *m* Margot Elizabeth, *née* Leicester; 3 s (Thomas David b 1984, William Charles b 1986, Edward Arthur b 1989), 1 da (Elizabeth Grace b 1992); *Career* theatre director; York Theatre Royal: asst stage mangr, dep stage mangr then stage mangr 1974–75, asst dir 1975–76; Chester Gateway Theatre: Arts Cncl asst dir 1976–77, assoc dir 1977–78; Duke's Playhouse Lancaster: Arts Cncl assoc dir 1978–79, dir 1980–84; dir Young Vic 1984–93; dir in residence RSC 1993–95; artistic dir Octagon Theatre Bolton 2009–15 (assoc artistic dir 2015–); prof of theatre Univ of Bolton 2015; tstee: Hoghton Tower Shakespeare Centre, Shakespeare Nat Tst, Haringey Med Tst; govr Tetherdown Primary Sch; *Theatre* over 150 prodns incl: sixteen plays by William Shakespeare, ten plays by Arthur Miller, seven plays by Samuel Beckett, three plays by Henrik Ibsen, three plays by Eugene O'Neil, Ghosts (Young Vic and West End, London Fringe Award for Best Dir and Olivier Award nomination for Outstanding Achievement 1987), Who's Afraid of Virginia Woolf? (Young Vic, London Fringe Award for Best Prodn 1987), A Touch of the Poet (Young Vic and West End), An Enemy of the People (Young Vic and West End, Olivier Award nomination for Best Dir 1989), The Last Yankee (Young Vic and West End) 1993, Broken Glass (RNT and West End, Olivier Award Play of the Year) 1994, A View From The Bridge (West End) 1994, Death of a Salesman (RNT) 1996; RSC prodns incl: Pericles (Olivier Award Best Dir and Best Revival of a Play 1991), The Two Gentlemen of Verona (also West End), As You Like It, The Merchant of Venice, Julius Caesar, Coriolanus, The Tempest; *Television* over 30 prodns incl: A Doll's House (BAFTA Best Single Drama nomination), Measure for Measure, Death of a Salesman, Broken Glass, The Scold's Bridle, Silent Witness, Waking the Dead, Faith, Murder in Mind, Dalziel and Pascoe; Channel 4 prodns incl Lock Stock; ITV prodns incl: Kavanagh QC, The Vice, Grafters, Foyle's War, The Mayor of Casterbridge, Faith; *Recreations* sport, politics, film, reading, family; *Style*— David Thacker; ✉ 84 Ferme Park Road, London N8 9SD (☎ 020 8444 8436, e-mail davidtthacker@sky.com)

THANE, Sarah Ann; CBE (2003), JP (W Suffolk 2005); da of John Arnold Cecil Thane (d 1972), and Winifred Blanche, *née* Wayne (d 2000); *b* 21 September 1951, Birmingham; *Educ* Sutton Coldfield GS for Girls, County HS Stourbridge, City of Birmingham Poly (Dip); *m* 30 March 1996, Peter Robert Wenban; 3 step s, 2 step da; *Career* ITC: dir of public affrs 1990–96, dir of progs and cable 1996–2001, dir of progs and advtg 2001–03; advsr content and standards Ofcom 2003–05; pt/t advsr to: BBC Govrs 2005–06, BBC Tst 2007–08; chm RTS 2000–02 (vice-chm 1998–2000); non-exec dir Films of Record 2005–08; cmmr Nat Lottery Cmmn 2005–13; govr Teachers TV 2008–10; dep chm West Suffolk Bench 2012–14; chair Suffolk Craft Soc 2014–; Hon DUniv Birmingham City Univ 2010; FRTS 1994; *Publications* Exploratory Review of the System of Regulating Child Performances (for DCSF and DCMS, 2010); *Recreations* music, visual arts, cooking, gardening, time with friends and family; *Clubs* Reform; *Style*— Ms Sarah Thane, CBE, JP

THANKI, Bankim; QC (2003); s of B D Thanki (d 2004), and Vijayalaxmi Thanki; *b* 19 April 1964; *Educ* Owen's Sch, Balliol Coll Oxford (MA); *m* 21 June 1988, Catherine Jane Margaret (d 2015), da of James Spotswood (d 2006), and Sheila Spotswood (d 2011); 3 s (Alexander Anand b 15 July 1993, Daniel Rohan b 5 May 1995, Joseph Dev b 26 Dec 2003), 1 da (Olivia Priya b 22 Oct 1998); *Career* called to the Bar Middle Temple 1988 (Harmsworth scholar 1988, bencher 2008); memb Fountain Court Chambers 1989–; memb Commercial Bar Assoc; *Publications* Carriage by Air (co-author, 2000), Commercial Court Procedure (jt ed, 2001), Law of Bank Payments (contrib, 2004, 4 edn 2010), Law of Priviledge (ed, 2006, 2 edn 2011); *Recreations* Manchester United FC; *Clubs* RAC, Athenaeum; *Style*— Bankim Thanki, Esq, QC; ✉ Fountain Court, Temple, London EC4Y 9DH (☎ 020 7583 3335, fax 020 7353 0329)

THATCHER, Anthony Neville; s of Edwin Neville Thatcher (d 1978), and Elsie May, *née* Webster; *b* 10 September 1939; *Educ* Sir John Lawes Sch Harpenden, Univ of Manchester (MSc); *m* 20 Oct 1968, Sally Margaret, da of Henry Joseph Clark, of Norfolk; *Career* Ultra Electronics 1967–77, md Dowty Electronics Controls Ltd 1978–82, gp chief exec Dowty Group plc 1986–91 (md Electronics Div 1982–86, memb Bd 1983), vice-chm Thyssen Bornemisza Group SAM Monaco 1991–98; memb: Electronics and Avionics Requirements Bd of DTI 1981–85, Cncl Electronics Engrg Assoc 1983–91 (pres 1986), Cncl Soc of Br Aerospace Cos 1986–91, RARDE Mgmnt Bd (industrial) 1986–91, Engrg

Mkts Advsy Ctee DTI 1988–90, Mgmnt Bd Engrg Employers Fedn 1988–91 (vice-pres 1990), Innovation Advsy Bd DTI 1988–91, Bd SW Electricity Bd 1989–91, Engrg Cncl 1989–91; memb Cncl Cheltenham Ladies' Coll 1989–91; Liveryman and tstee Worshipful Co of Glass Sellers; CEng, FIMechE; *Recreations* art, jazz piano, opera, fishing, gardening, bird watching; *Clubs* Athenaeum, Carlton, George Town (Washington DC), RAF; *Style*— Anthony Thatcher, Esq; ✉ The Athenaeum, 107 Pall Mall, London SW1Y 5ER

THEAKSTON, Jamie; *b* 21 December 1970, Sussex; *Educ* BA; *m* 2007, Sophie; 2 s (Sidney b 11 April 2008, Kit b 29 Sept 2009); *Career* presenter, broadcaster and actor; *Radio* started as radio travel news reader 1993, former presenter GLR and Radio FiveLive (shows incl Saturday Sports Show, Sportscall, Friday Night on 5, Jamie Theakston's Cricket Show, Radio 5 Sport), presenter BBC Radio 1 1999–2002 (shows incl The Sunday Lunch, The Jamie Theakston Show, One Big Sunday), presenter breakfast show Heart 106.2 2005–; *Television* as presenter incl: The O-Zone (BBC 2), Live And Kicking (with Zoe Ball, *qv*, BBC 1) 1996–99, Top Of The Pops (BBC 1) 1999–2002, Holiday (BBC 1), A Question of Pop (BBC 1), The Priory (Channel 4), Beg Borrow or Steal (BBC 2), With A Little Help From My Friends (ITV), The Games (Channel 4), People's Quiz (BBC 1), UK Music Hall of Fame (Channel 4), The Oscars (Sky1/Sky Movies), The Search (Channel 4), Holiday: You Call The Shots (BBC 1), Sport Relief (BBC 1), Wish You Were Here (ITV), Glastonbury, The Eclipse (BBC 1), Queen's Jubilee Concert (BBC 1), Natural Born Losers (BBC 1), The Millennium (BBC 1), Pick n Mix (UK Play), Comic Relief (BBC 1), Landmarks (BBC 2), Aqua (BBC 2), Not a Lot of People Know That (BBC 1), Children In Need (BBC 1), The Brits (BBC 1), 100 Greatest Kids Shows (Channel 4), Behind the Music (VH1), Traffic Cops (BBC 1), Car Wars (BBC 1), Richest Kids (ITV), Bitesize (BBC 2), The Grammys (BBC 2), The Simpsons Quiz (Channel 4), 50 Years, 50 Records (ITV), Top of the Pops Awards (BBC 1), All Star Golf (Sky 1), Sky Cops (BBC 1), This Morning (ITV), The One Show (BBC 1), Forbidden History (BBC), Britain's Best Brain (Channel 5), The People's Quiz (BBC 1), Concert for Diana (BBC 1), The Olympic Torch Concert (BBC 1), Have I Got News For You (BBC 1); as actor incl: Murder in Mind (BBC 1), Mad About Alice (BBC 1), Linda Green (ITV), Agatha Christie (ITV), Rock Profile (BBC 2), Drive (BBC 1), Afternoon Plays (BBC 1), Miss Marple: Body in the Library (ITV), Taggart, Bob Martin (ITV), Little Britain (BBC 3); *Theatre* Art (Whitehall), Home & Beauty (Lyric), Marat/Sade (Playhouse), Murder in the Cathedral (Spitalfields); *Recreations* sport, theatre; *Style*— Jamie Theakston; ✉ c/o Richard Thompson, M&C Saatchi Merlin, 36 Golden Square, London W1F 9EE (☎ 020 7259 1460)

THEOBALD, Prof Michael Francis; s of George Charles Theobald (d 1994), and Elise Dorothy, *née* Baker (d 2012); *b* 1 September 1946; *Educ* KCL, Univ of Manchester (BSc, MA, PhD); *m* 26 Oct 1972, Pauline Florence, da of Capt Christopher Herbert Harman (d 1989), of St Leonards, nr Ringwood; 1 s (Jonathan Harman b 3 Sept 1978), 1 da (Sarah Pauline b 5 June 1981); *Career* chartered accountant; Price Waterhouse & Co: London 1968–72, Buenos Aires 1972–74; Univ of Manchester 1974–85; prof Univ of Birmingham 1985–2010 (sometime head Dept of Accounting and Finance and dir of research Birmingham Business Sch, emeritus prof 2011–); visiting prof: La Trobe Univ Melbourne, NYU, Northwestern Univ, IDEA Buenos Aires; former chm: Market Analytical Techniques, Mifranthe and Associates; chm: Int Exams Ctee Certified Int Investment Analysts, LACFA; memb: Trg and Qualifications Cmmn Euro Fedn of Financial Analysts' Socs, various ctees UK Soc of Investment Professionals; conslt to the ESRC and Accounting Standards Bd; dir Euro Capital Markets Inst; dir LAPRO, tstee and memb Research Advsy Bd Chartered Financial Analysts Research Fndn USA, dep chm of tstees Ralph Hope Meml Fund; memb Fin Instruments Task Force; expert witness; academic advsr European Fedn of Financial Analysts' Socs; memb Editorial Bd: Jl of Banking and Finance, Br Accounting Review, Jl of Business Finance and Accounting, Quarterly Int Jl of Finance, Jl of Derivative Accounting, Jl of Corporate Finance; fell UK Soc of Investment Professionals 2000, FCA 1972; *Publications* Research Method and Methodology (co-author); articles published in: Jl of Finance, Jl of Financial Economics, Jl of Financial and Quantitive Analysis, Jl of Banking and Finance, Jl of Portfolio Mgmnt, Jl of Futures Markets, Jl of Derivatives, Jl of Financial Markets; *Recreations* sport, literature, travel, music, theatre, fine wine and dining; *Style*— Prof Michael Theobald; ✉ e-mail m.f.theobald@bham.ac.uk

THEROUX, Louis; s of Paul Theroux, and Anne Castle; *b* 20 May 1970, Singapore; *Educ* Westminster, Magdalen Coll Oxford; *m* Nancy Strang; 2 s (Albert b 14 Feb 2006, Frederick b 4 Feb 2008); *Career* presenter and journalist; early career as journalist on San Jose Metro and Spy magazine; Richard Dimbleby Award BAFTA 2000 and 2001; memb BAFTA; *Television* incl: TV Nation 1994–95, Weird Weekends 1998–2000, When Louis Met... 2000–02, Louis and the Brothel 2003, Louis, Martin & Michael 2003, Louis and the Nazis 2003, Gambling in Las Vegas 2006, The Most Hated Family in America 2007, Under the Knife 2007, Behind Bars 2008, African Hunting Holiday 2008, Law and Disorder 2008, A Place for Paedophiles 2009 (Best Presenter RTS Award 2010), Louis Theroux: Savile 2016; *Books* The Call of the Weird: Travels in American Subcultures (2005); *Style*— Louis Theroux, Esq; ✉ c/o Capel & Land Ltd, 29 Wardour Street, London W1D 6PS (☎ 020 7734 2414, fax 020 7734 8101)

THETFORD, Bishop of 2009–; Rt Rev Dr Alan Winton; *Educ* Chislehurst and Sidcup GS, Lincoln Theological Coll, Univ of Sheffield (PhD); *m* 1982, Pippa; 2 da (Sarah b 1986, Natasha b 1988); *Career* ordained 1991; team rector Welwyn Team Miny Dio of St Albans 1999–2009; *Style*— The Rt Rev the Bishop of Thetford; ✉ The Red House, 53 Norwich Road, Stoke Holy Cross, Norwich NR14 8AB

THEWLIS, David; s of Alec Raymond Wheeler, of Blackpool, and Maureen, *née* Thewlis; *b* 20 March 1963; *Educ* Highfield HS Blackpool, St Anne's Coll of FE, Guildhall Sch of Music and Drama; *m* 10 April 1992 (m dis 1993), Sara Jocelyn, da of Paul Sugarman; 1 da (Gracie Ellen Mary b 9 July 2005), with Anna Friel, *qv*; *Career* actor; *Theatre* incl: Buddy Holly at the Regal (Greenwich), Ice Cream (Royal Court), Lady and the Clarinet (Netherbow Edinburgh, winner Fringe First, also at King's Head Islington), The Sea (NT); *Television* incl: Dandelion Dead, Valentine Park, Road, Singing Detective, Bit of a Do, Skullduggery, Journey to Knock (Best Actor Rheims Film Festival 1992), Filipina Dreamgirls, Frank Stubbs Promotes, Prime Suspect 3, Endgame (Beckett on Film series), Hamilton Mattress, Dinotopia; *Films* incl: Short and Curlies, Vroom, Resurrected, Afraid of the Dark, Life is Sweet, Damage, The Trial, Naked (Best Actor Cannes Film Festival 1993), Black Beauty, The Island of Dr Moreau, Divorcing Jack, Besieged, Whatever Happened to Harold Smith?, Gangster No1, Goodbye Charlie Bright, Cheeky, Timeline, Harry Potter and the Prisoner of Azkaban, Kingdom of Heaven, The New World, Basic Instinct 2, The Omen, The Inner Life of Martin Frost, Harry Potter and the Order of the Phoenix, The Boy in the Striped Pyjamas, Harry Potter and the Half-Blood Prince, Mr Nice, Harry Potter and the Deathly Hallows: Part 1, London Boulevard, Harry Potter and the Deathly Hallows: Part 2, War Horse, The Lady, Anonymous, Red 2, The Zero Theorem, The Fifth Estate; *Books* The Late Hector Kipling (2007); *Recreations* painting; *Style*— David Thewlis, Esq

THEWLIS, Sarah Anne; *née* Bennett; da of Geoffrey Frank Bennett (d 1996), of Enysford, Kent, and Mollie, *née* Bates; *b* 12 May 1958, Dartford, Kent; *Educ* Dartford GS for Girls, Univ of Hull (BA), Relate Cert in Marital and Couple Counselling, Univ of Glasgow (MML); *m* 1983, Rev Canon Dr John Charles Thewlis, s of Dennis Jones Thewlis; *Career* Marks & Spencer plc 1979–91: personnel mangr Marble Arch branch 1984–85, category mangr for store asst personnel mangrs 1985–88, divnl personnel controller for distribution centres 1989–91; dep sec Royal Coll of Physicians 1991–94, co sec and gen mangr Royal Coll of Gen Practitioners 1994–2002, chief exec and registrar Nursing and Midwifery Cncl 2002–08; Gundersen Partners (formerly GBR Search): princ conslt 2009–, London mangr 2010; md Thewlis Graham Assocs 2010–; chair of Assoc Exec Recruiteres 2014–; temp conslt in Oman WHO 2006; memb: The Bishop's Equal Opportunities Ctee 2001–, Archbishop's Cncl Ctee on deployment, remuneration and conditions of service 2006–11, Home Office Ethics Gp for the Nat DNA Database 2007–15, Audit Ctee RCGP 2010–14; memb Bd Recruitment and Employment Confederation 2013–, memb Bd Int Women's Forum 2014–16, chair Mulberry Center 2016–; lay memb Employment Tbnl Panel 1999–2008; non-exec memb Phoenix Futures 2007– (vice-chair 2012–); govr Queen Anne's Caversham 2012– (chair Personnel Ctee 2014–); Liveryman Worshipful Co of Needlemakers 2010; FCIPD 1998 (MIPD 1991), FRSA 2001, Hon FRCGP 2002; *Recreations* horses, cats, people, current affairs; *Style*— Sarah Thewlis; ✉ The Rectory, 2 Talbot Road, Carshalton, Surrey SM5 3BS (☎ 020 8647 2366, e-mail sat@thewlis.org.uk); Thewlis Graham Associates, Portland House, Bressenden Place, London SW1E 5RS (☎ 020 7850 4781, e-mail sat@thewlisgraham.com)

THEXTON, Susan Elizabeth Lee; da of John W Thexton, and Dorothy Topham, *née* Lee; *b* 13 September 1960, Newcastle upon Tyne; *Educ* London Coll of Printing (BA); *m* 1 Oct 1994, Peter Worlock; 1 da (Amy b 5 May 1999); *Career* UK sales mangr Software Div Letraset UK Ltd 1984–89, gen mangr Adobe Northern Europe 1989–94, vice-pres Macromedia EMEA 1994–2004, ptnr Thexton Worlock Ltd 2004–05, md ITN Source 2005–08, vice-pres EMEA Datawatch Inc 2008–11, sr vice-pres EMEA Brightcove 2011–; memb Cncl and TV Ctee BAFTA; tstee and non-exec dir NESTA Futurelab; Middx Univ: Hon DSc Sch of Computer Sci 2008, hon visiting prof; FRSA; *Recreations* gardening, drinking good red wine, reading avidly; *Style*— Ms Susan Thexton; ✉ 157 Park Road, Chiswick, London W4 3EX

THIAM, Tidjane Cheick; s of Amadou Thiam, and Marietou Sow; *b* 29 July 1962, Côte d'Ivoire; *Educ* École Polytechnique de Paris, École Nationale Superieure des Mines de Paris, INSEAD (MBA); 1991, Annette April Anthony; 2 s; *Career* internat conslt in Paris, NY and Europe McKinsey & Co 1986–89, on sabbatical Young Professionals Prog World Bank Washington DC 1989–90, assoc dir Financial Services Practice Paris 1991–94, ceo Nat Bureau for Tech Studies and Devpt Côte d'Ivoire 1994–98 (chm 1998–99), ptnr McKinsey & Co Paris 2000–02; Aviva plc: gp strategy and devpt dir 2002–06, md Aviva Int 2006, ceo Aviva Europe 2006–07; Prudential plc: gp chief fin offr 2008–09, gp chief exec 2009–15; chief exec Credit Suisse 2015–; non-exec dir Arkema 2006–09; memb: Africa Progress Panel 2007–, Cncl ODI 2011–, Int Business Cncl, Wef, PM's Business Advsy Gp 2012–, European Fin Round Table 2013–, UK ASEAN Business Cncl; chm: UKTI Strategic Advsy Gp, G20 High Level Panel for Infrastructure Investment 2011–, Assoc of Br Insurers 2012–14; Br business ambass UKTI 2014–; Grand Prix de L'Economie Les Echos 2013; Chevalier of the Legion d'Honneur 2011; *Style*— Mr Tidjane Thiam; ✉ Credit Suisse, One Cabot Square, London E144QJ

THIAN, Bob; s of Clifford Peter Thian, of Jersey, and Frances Elizabeth, *née* Stafford-Bird (d 1980); *b* 1 August 1943, South Africa; *Educ* Oundle, Univ of Geneva; *m* 24 Oct 1964, Liselotte, da of Wilhelm Von Borges; 2 da (Stefanie, Samantha); *Career* called to the Bar Gray's Inn; legal advsr Glaxo Gp Ltd 1968–69, project devpt exec Glaxo-Allenburys Export Ltd 1968–72, md Glaxo Farmaceutica Lda 1972–80, business devpt dir (Europe) Abbott International 1980–82, regnl dir (Europe) Abbott Laboratories 1982–87, vice-pres international ops Pharmaceutical Div Novo Industri A/S 1987–89, gp chief exec North West Water Gp plc 1990–93, fndr and chief exec Renex Ltd 1993–, gp chief exec The Stationery Office Gp 1996–99; chm: IMO Gp Ltd 1999–2000, Tactica Solutions Ltd 1999–2001, Orion Gp Ltd 2001–04, Astron Gp Ltd 2001–05, Whatman plc 2002–08, Southern Water Ltd 2003–07, Cardpoint plc 2006–08, Equiniti Ltd 2007–09; dep chm Lansen Pharmaceutical Hldgs Ltd (Hong Kong) 2010–11; dir: Celltech Gp plc (now Celltech plc) 1992–99, Medeval Ltd 1995–98; memb Mgmnt Advsy Bd TowerBrook Capital Ptnrs (UK) LLP 2010–; *Recreations* golf; *Clubs* Chantilly Golf (France), Monaco Golf, Monte-Carlo Golf, Black Diamond Golf (Florida); *Style*— Bob Thian, Esq; ✉ e-mail bob.thian@renex.net

THIMBLEBY, Prof Harold William; s of Peter Thimbleby, of Rugby, Warks, and Angela Marion, *née* Hodson; *b* 19 July 1955; *Educ* Rugby, Univ of London (BSc, MSc, PhD); *m* 16 Feb 1980, Prudence Mary (Prue), da of Rev Capt Arundel Charles Barker, of Matlock, Derbys; 3 s (William, Samuel, Isaac), 1 da (Jemima); *Career* lectr in computer sci: Queen Mary Coll 1980–82, Univ of York 1982–88; prof of info technol Univ of Stirling (in Dept of Computing 1988–93, Dept of Psychology 1993–94); Univ of Middx: prof of computing research 1994–2001, dir of research 1995–2000; dir Interaction Centre and prof of interaction UCL 2001–05, 28th Gresham prof of geometry Gresham Coll 2001–, prof of computing science Univ of Swansea 2005–; co-inventor of Liveware (technique for exploiting computer viruses) 1989; Br Computer Soc Wilkes Medal 1987, Toshiba Year of Invention Award; Freeman: City of London, Worshipful Co of Information Technologists; CEng, FIET, Hon FRSA, FRCPEd, Hon FRCP, FLSW; *Books* author of over 500 pubns incl: Formal Methods In Human-Computer Interaction (ed with M D Harrison, 1989), User Interface Design (1990), Hyperprogramming (with G F Coulouris, 1993), Press On (2007); *Recreations* hill walking, woodwork, electronics; *Style*— Prof Harold Thimbleby; ✉ Swansea University, Swansea SA2 8PP (e-mail harold@thimbleby.net)

THIRLWALL, Prof Anthony Philip; s of Isaac Thirlwall (d 1960), and Ivy, *née* Ticehurst (d 1988); *b* 21 April 1941; *Educ* Clark Univ USA (MA), Univ of Leeds (BA, PhD); *m* 1, 26 March 1966 (m dis), Gianna, da of Bruno Paoletti (d 1985); 2 s (Lawrence b 1967, Adrian b and d 1975), 1 da (Alexandra 1974); m 2, Dr Penelope Pacheco Lopez; 1 s (Oliver b 26 Dec 2010); *Career* asst lectr in economics Univ of Leeds 1964; Univ of Kent: lectr in economics 1966, prof of applied economics 1976–2004, emeritus prof 2004–; visiting prof and lectr at several overseas univs; econ advsr Dept of Employment 1968–70; conslt: Pacific Islands Devpt Prog 1989–90 and 1996, African Devpt Bank 1993–94 and 1999, Asian Devpt Bank 2003, UN Conf on Trade and Devpt (UNCTAD) 2005–; memb Editorial Bd: Jl of Post Keynesian Economics, African Devpt Review; memb Action Aid; memb Royal Economic Soc; *Books* Economics of Development (1972, 9 edn 2011), Inflation, Saving and Growth in Developing Economies (1974), Regional Growth and Unemployment in the United Kingdom (with R Dixon, 1975), Financing Economic Development (1976), Keynes and International Monetary Relations (ed, 1976), Keynes and Laissez Faire (ed, 1978), Keynes and the Bloomsbury Group (ed with D Crabtree, 1980), Balance of Payments Theory and the United Kingdom Experience (1980, 4 edn 1991), Keynes as a Policy Adviser (ed, 1982), Keynes and Economic Development (ed, 1987), Nicholas Kaldor (1987), Collected Essays of Nicholas Kaldor Volume 9 (ed with F Targetti, 1989), The Essential Kaldor (ed with F Targetti, 1989), European Factor Mobility: Trends and Consequences (ed with I Gordon, 1989), Deindustrialisation (with S Bazen, 1989, 3 edn 1997), The Performance and Prospects of the Pacific Island Economies in the World Economy (1991), Keynes and the Role of the State (ed, 1993), Economic Growth and the Balance of Payments Constraint (with J McCombie, 1994), The Economics of Growth and Development: Selected Essays of A P Thirlwall Vol 1 (1995), Macroeconomic Issues from a Keynesian Perspective: Selected Essays of A P Thirlwall Vol 2 (1997), Economic Dynamics, Trade and Growth: Essays on Harrodian Themes (ed with G Rampa and L Stella, 1998), The Euro and Regional Divergence in Europe (2000), The Nature of Economic Growth: An Alternative Framework for Understanding the Performance of Nations (2002), Trade, the Balance

T

of Payments and Exchange Rate Policy in Developing Countries (2003), Essays on Balance of Payments Constrained Growth: Theory and Evidence (with J McCombie, 2004), Trade Liberalisation and The Poverty of Nations (with P Pacheco-Lopez, 2008), Economic Growth in an Open Developing Economy: the Role of Structure and Demand (2013), Essays on Keynesian and Kaldorian Economics (2015); *Recreations* growing geraniums, athletics, tennis, travel; *Clubs* Royal Over-Seas League; *Style*— Prof Anthony Thirlwall; ✉ 14 Moorfield, Canterbury, Kent (☎ 01227 769904); Keynes College, University of Kent, Canterbury, Kent (☎ 01227 827414, e-mail a.p.thirlwall@kent.ac.uk, website www.kent.ac.uk/economics/staff/profiles/tony-thirlwall.html)

THISELTON, Prof Rev Canon Anthony Charles; s of Eric Charles Thiselton (d 1979), of Woking, Surrey, and Hilda Winifred, *née* Kevan (d 1969); *b* 13 July 1937, Woking, Surrey; *Educ* City of London Sch, KCL (BD, MTh), Univ of Sheffield (PhD), Univ of Durham (DD); *m* 21 Sept 1963, Rosemary Stella, da of Ernest Walter Harman (d 1979), of Eastbourne, E Sussex; 2 s (Stephen b 1964, Martin b 1969), 1 da (Linda b 1966); *Career* curate Holy Trinity Sydenham 1960–63, chaplain Tyndale Hall Bristol 1963–67, recognised teacher in theology Univ of Bristol 1965–70, sr tutor Tyndale Hall 1967–70, lectr in biblical studies Univ of Sheffield 1970–79 (sr lectr 1979–85), visiting prof and fell Calvin Coll Grand Rapids 1982–83; princ: St John's Coll Nottingham 1985–88, St John's Coll Durham 1988–92 (hon prof in theology 1992); prof of Christian theology and emeritus in residence Dept of Theology Univ of Nottingham 2001– (prof of Christian theology and head of Dept of Theology 1992–2001); canon theologian: Leicester Cathedral 1995–2007, Southwell Minster 2000–07; canon emeritus 2007–; emeritus prof of Christian theology Chester Coll; memb: C of E Doctrine Cmmn 1976–91 and 1996– (vice-chm 1987–91 and 1996–97), C of E Faith and Order Advsy Gp 1971–81 and 1986–91, CNAA Ctee for Arts and Humanities 1983–87, CNAA Ctee for Humanities 1987–90, Revised Catechism Working Pty 1988–89, C of E Initial Ministerial Educn Ctee 1990–92, Cncl Lincoln Theological Coll 1992–97, Cncl of St John's Nottingham 1992–2001, Human Fertilisation and Embryology Authy 1995–98, Crown Appointments Cmmn of C of E 1998–2007, C of E Theological Training Ctee 1999–2007, Clergy Discipline (Doctrine) Gp 1999–2004, Studiorum Novi Testamenti Societas, Soc for the Study of Theology, American Acad of Religion; Gen Synod C of E: rep northern univs 1995–2000, rep Dio of Southwell 2000–05; conslt Women in the Episcopate House of Bishops Working Pty 2001–05; memb Editorial Bd: Biblical Interpretation (Leiden) 1992–02, Lund Lectures Chicago 1997, Int Jl of Systematic Theology 1998–2008, Expository Times (Edinburgh) 2003–; memb: Steering Gp and Revision Ctee C of E Daily Lectionary 2004, Task Gp Theological Educn in the Anglican Communion 2004–; examining chaplain to: Bishop of Sheffield 1976–80, Bishop of Leicester 1979–86 and 1993–2000, Bishop of Southwell 2001–; pres Soc for the Study of Theology 1998–2000; Br Acad Research Award 1995–96; hon fell St John's Coll Durham, FKC, FBA; *Books* Language, Liturgy and Meaning (1975), The Two Horizons: New Testament Hermeneutics and Philosophical Description (1980, trans into Korean 1990, reprinted 1993), The Responsibility of Hermeneutics (jtly, 1985), New Horizons in Hermeneutics (1992), Interpreting God and the Post-Modern Self (1995), The Promise of Hermeneutics (jtly, 1999), 1 Corinthians: A Commentary in the Greek Text (2000), Concise Encyclopedia of Philosophy of Religion (2002), Thiselton on Hermeneutics: Collected Writings (2006), Reading Luke: Interpretation, Reflection and Formation (jt ed, 2006), The Hermeneutics of Doctrine (2007), Hermeneutics (2009), The Living Paul (2009), Commentary on 1 and 2 Thessalonians (2010), Life after Death (American title) or The Last Things (British title, 2012), The Holy Spirit – In Biblical Teaching, Through the Centuries, and Today (2013), A Lifetime in the Church and the University (2015), The Thisleton Companion to Christian Theology (2015), The SPCK Companion to Theology and Hermeneutics (2015), Systematic Theology (2015), Discovering Romans: Content, Interpretation, Reception (2016), A Shorter Guide to the Holy Spirit (2016), An Approach to the Philosophy of Religion (forthcoming, 2016–17); contrib: Believing in the Church, We Believe in God, Their Lord and Ours, The Bible the Reformation and the Church, Jesus of Nazareth: Lord and Christ; Cambridge Companion to Biblical Interpretation; six books translated into Korean and one in Russian; *Recreations* organ, music, opera, Cavalier King Charles dog; *Style*— Prof the Rev Canon Anthony C Thiselton; ✉ 390 High Road, Chilwell, Nottingham NG9 5EG (☎ 01159 176391, email thiselton@ntlworld.com)

THISTLETHWAYTE, (John) Robin; JP; s of Lt Cdr Thomas Thistlethwayte, RNVR (d 1956), of Old Bursledon, Hants, and Hon Eileen Gwladys (d 1955), *née* Berry, eld da of 1 and last Baron Buckland; *b* 8 December 1935; *Educ* Bradfield Coll, RAC Cirencester; *m* 22 Jan 1964, Mary Katharine, da of Lt-Gen Sir (Arthur) Edward Grasett, KBE, CB, DSO, MC, of Adderbury, Oxon; 2 s (Mark b 1964, Hugo b 1967), 1 da (Sophia (Mrs Alexander Davies) b 1972); *Career* chartered surveyor; ptnr Savills 1961–86, conslt to Savills plc 1986–96; dir Porchester Equity Ltd; mayor of Chipping Norton 1964 and 1965; chm: Chipping Norton Petty Sessional Div 1984 and 1985, N Oxfordshire and Chipping Norton PSD 1989–91; FRICS; *Recreations* shooting, travel; *Clubs* Boodle's, St James's; *Style*— J Robin Thistlethwayte, Esq; ✉ Sorbrook Manor, Adderbury, Oxfordshire OX17 3EG (☎ 01295 810203); The Estate Office, Southwick, Fareham, Hampshire PO17 6EA

THODAY, Jon; *Career* co-fndr and jt md Avalon Entertainment Ltd 1989–; *Style*— Jon Thoday, Esq; ✉ Avalon Entertainment Ltd, 4a Exmoor Street, London W10 6BD

THOM, (James) Stuart; s of James Robert Thom (d 1981), and Constance Daphne, *née* La Frenais (d 1979); *b* 20 July 1942, Kebwick, Cumbria; *Educ* George Watson's Coll Edinburgh, Edinburgh University (MA, LLB), Manchester Business Sch (DipBA); *Children* 1 da (Lucy b 23 Aug 1977), 1 s (Alexander b 19 Jan 1980); *Career* sr mangr Booker plc 1978–83, Lonrho Exports, first sec (commercial) Br Embassy Moscow 1985–88, dir Business Devpt CIS Russia Ernst & Young 1988–96; Wandsworth borough cncllr 2006–, mayor of Wandsworth 2014–15; chair GB-Russia Soc, tstee Wandsworth Museum, govr South Thames Coll; *Recreations* gardening, reading, skiing, tennis, travel; *Clubs* Caledonian, Carlton; *Style*— Councillor Stuart Thom, Esq; ✉ 49 Goulden House, Bullen Street, London SW11 3HG (☎ 020 7924 2081, e-mail sthom@rsmi.freeserve.co.uk); Town Hall, Wandsworth High Street, London SW18 2PU (☎ 020 8871 6044, e-mail sthom@wandsworth.gov.uk)

THOMAS, Dr Adrian Mark Kynaston; s of Prof Peter Kynaston Thomas (d 2008), of London, and Mary Truscott Cox (d 1977); *b* 1 April 1954; *Educ* Christ Coll Finchley, UCL, UCHMS (MB BS, BSc); *m* 8 July 1978 (m diss 2015), Susan Margaret, da of Arthur Oliver Viney, of Amersham, Bucks; 2 s (Gareth Kynaston b 1985, Owen Matthew Truscott b 7 July 1990), 1 da (Charlotte Mary Truscott b 1988); *Career* sr registrar Hammersmith Hosp 1981–87; conslt radiologist Bromley Hosps NHS Trust Hosp and Sloane Hosp 1987–; chm Bromley Div BMA 1995–96 and 1998–99; chm Br Soc for the History of Radiology (formerly Radiology History and Heritage Charitable Tst) 2005–; memb: BMA 1976, RSM 1981 (pres Radiology Section 1999–2000), Br Inst of Radiology 1981 (hon sec 1999–2005, hon librarian 2005–); pres Br Soc for the History of Medicine (2011–13); chm The Int Soc for the History of Radiology (2011–); hon prof Univ of Buenos Aires 2009–; Christian Med Fellowship 1989; FRCR 1984 (MRCR 1982), FRCP 1996, FBIR (2007); *Books* Self Assessment in Radiology and Imaging: Nuclear Medicine (jt ed, 1989), The Invisible Light, 100 Years of Medical Radiology (jt ed, 1995), Classic Papers in Modern Diagnostic Radiology (jt ed, 2004), The History of Radiology (2013); *Recreations* history of radiology and allied sciences; *Clubs* Osler (hon sec 2004–, pres 2009–11); *Style*— Dr Adrian Thomas

THOMAS, Adrian Peter; OBE (1995); s of George Lynn Thomas (d 1998), of Holland-on-Sea, Essex, and Glady Ella Grace, *née* Webster (d 1992); *b* 19 February 1945; *Educ* Forest Sch, Wadham Coll Oxford (MA), SOAS Univ of London (MA); *m* 1977, Robyn Alycon, da of Prof J Laurence Malcolm (d 2001); 1 da (Clare Sally b 1978), 2 s (Hugh Robert, Neil Malcolm (twins) b 1980); *Career* VSO teacher Ihungo Sedy Sch Tanzania 1967–68, various jobs in market res and accountancy 1969–70; British Council: asst rep Sierra Leone 1970–73, regnl offr N Africa 1973–75, Overseas Educnl Appointments Dept 1975–77, Univ of London 1977–78, regnl dir Isfahan 1978–80, asst and dep dir Tech Co-operation Trg Dept 1980–84, regnl rep E Malaysia 1984–88, dep dir Nigeria 1988–91, dir Sudan 1991–95, dir E India 1995–99; sec RAS 2000–03, exec sec Linnean Soc 2004–07; memb: Amnesty Int, Friends of the Earth; Hon PhD Univ of Gezira Sudan 1995; *Recreations* running, hill walking, history, poetry, natural history; *Style*— Mr Adrian Thomas, OBE; ✉ 30 Warner Road, Crouch End, London N8 7HD (☎ 020 8348 4897, e-mail adrianpthomas@btinternet.com)

THOMAS, Prof Adrian Tregerthen; s of Rev Owen George Thomas, of Cardiff, and Jean Tregerthen, *née* Short; *b* 11 June 1947; *Educ* Kingswood Sch Bath, Univ of Nottingham (BMus), UC Cardiff (MA), Conservatory of Music Kraków Poland; *Career* Queen's Univ Belfast: lectr in music 1972–82, sr lectr 1982–85, Hamilton Harty prof of music 1985–90 and 1993–96; head of music BBC Radio 3 1990–93, prof of music Univ of Wales Cardiff 1996–2010 (emeritus prof 2010–), chair of music Gresham Coll 2003–06 (emeritus prof 2006–); conductor Br première Lutoslawski's Trois Poèmes d'Henri Michaux 1969, medal Polish Composers' Union for outstanding servs to contemporary Polish music 1989, Order of Merit for Polish Culture 1996, Medal Lutoslawski Soc Warsw 2005, Gold Medal Polish Gloria Artis Award 2013; chm Music Ctee Arts Cncl of NI 1986–90, chm BBC Central Music Advsy Ctee 1987–89, memb BBC Gen Advsy Cncl 1988–90; memb Royal Musical Assoc, memb Br Acad of Composers and Songwriters; *Compositions* Intrada (orchestra, 1981), Elegy (violin and piano, 1983), Rau (string octet, 1985), Black Rainbow (a cappella choir, BBC cmmn, 1989); *Books* Gra?yna Bacewicz: Chamber and Orchestral Music (1985), Górecki (1997), Polish Music since Szymanowski (2005, Polish translation 2016); *Recreations* hill walking, poetry, Oriental arts; *Style*— Prof Adrian Thomas; ✉ e-mail adrianthomasmusic@me.com, website www.onpolishmusic.com)

THOMAS, Sir (John) Alan; kt (1993); s of late Idris Thomas, of Langland, Swansea, and Ellen Constance, *née* Noakes; *b* 4 January 1943; *Educ* Dynevor Sch Swansea, Univ of Nottingham (Richard Thomas & Baldwins Industrial scholar, BSc); *m* 1966, Angela, da of Kathleen Taylor; 2 s (Andrew James b 1971, Alexander Michael b 1974); *Career* chief exec Data Logic Ltd 1973–85, pres and ceo Raytheon Europe 1985–89, vice-pres Raytheon Co (US), dir various Raytheon subsid cos 1978–89, seconded to MOD as head of Def Export Servs Orgn 1989–94; chm: Micro Quoted Growth Trust plc 1997–2001, Chelverton Asset Mgmnt Ltd 1997–2005, Three Valleys Water plc 2000–10, Hyder Consltg plc 2002–14, Global Design Technologies LLC 2006–08; dir: PowerGen plc 1996–99, Radstone Technology plc 2004–06; sr industrial advsr to DG OFWAT 1997–2000; memb: Defence Industries Cncl 1990–94, Engrg Cncl 1994–96; pres Computing Servs & Software Assoc 1980–81; dir Centre for Policy Studies 1996–2003; visiting prof Univ of Westminster 1982, chm Ct of Govrs Univ of Westminster 1999–2005 (govr 1989–2005, dep chm 1995–98); dir London Welsh RFC 1997–2008; Hon DSc; Liveryman Co of Info Technologists 1988–; CEng, FIEE, FCMA (1st prizewinner); *Recreations* music, sport; *Clubs* Athenaeum; *Style*— Sir Alan Thomas

THOMAS, Alun; WS; s of Gordon Eric Thomas, of Aust, and Pauline Susan, *née* Hooper; *b* 4 March 1958, Henley; *Educ* George Heriots Edinburgh, Univ of Edinburgh (LLB); *m* 11 Sept 1992, K P Thomas, *née* Philip; 1 s (Lloyd Rhys b 2 July 1995); *Career* admitted slr 1983; ptnr J+F Anderson Strathern (now Anderson Strathern) 1990– (currently head Employment Unit and Educn Gp); accredited specialist in employment law Law Soc of Scotland 1996, 2001, 2006 and 2011–, CEDR and Scottish Mediation Network registered mediator; memb Ctee Scottish Discrimination Law Assoc; memb: Employment Lawyers Assoc, Law Soc of Scotland; FRSA; *Style*— Mr Alun Thomas; ✉ Anderson Strathern, 1 Rutland Court, Edinburgh EH3 8EY (☎ 0131 625 7245, fax 0131 625 8018, e-mail alun.thomas@andersonstrathern.co.uk)

THOMAS, Andrew Gerald; *b* 19 July 1942; *Educ* Rydal Sch Colwyn Bay; *m* Lesley; 1 da (Helen b 13 May 1967), 1 s (Julian b 3 July 1969); *Career* former chm Greenalls Group plc; currently chm Moors Andrew Thomas Private Clients Ltd; chm: Greenalls Pension Tst Ltd, Randalls Ltd, Summerseat Hldgs Ltd; non-exec dir Playtech plc; memb Inst of Taxation, memb ICA; *Recreations* theatre, football; *Style*— Andrew Thomas, Esq

THOMAS, Anthony Charles (Tony); s of Charles Derek Thomas (d 1990), and Rosina Miriam, *née* Dukes; *b* 27 May 1952; *Educ* Leamington Coll Leamington Spa, Univ of Manchester (LLB); *m* June 1976, Penelope Bebbington; 2 s (Oliver b 7 Sept 1981, Nicholas b 9 Jan 1987), 1 da (Rebecca b 12 Sept 1983); *Career* Clyde & Co: joined as articled clerk 1974, slr 1976–, ptnr 1980–, currently head Shipping Dept; memb Law Soc; *Recreations* squash, tennis, cricket, rugby (now as spectator), theatre, motor cars; *Clubs* Guildford & Godalming Rugby (vice-pres); *Style*— Tony Thomas, Esq; ✉ Clyde & Co, 51 Eastcheap, London EC3M 1JP (☎ 020 7623 1244, fax 020 7623 5427, mobile 07831 866839, e-mail tony.thomas@clydeco.com)

THOMAS, Christopher (Chris); s of Neofitos Theophilou, of London, and Mary, *née* Mouzouris; *b* 1 September 1963; *Educ* Highgate Wood Sch London; *Career* bd dir MJP Carat Int 1989–92 (joined as trainee media exec 1980), bd dir MCW Ltd 1992–97, managing ptnr IAG 1997–2000, md Ergonomy Ltd 2000–03, chief operating offr Million-2-1 Ltd 2003–04, dir IMPAQ Gp 2005–08, dir Sports Fusion 2008–; dir Int Advertising Assoc (UK Chapter) 1985–92 (joined 1981); accredited mediator London Sch of Psychotherapy 2005; FRGS 1992; *Recreations* cooking, tennis, Arsenal FC; *Style*— Chris Thomas, Esq; ✉ Sports Fusion,10 Hatton Place, London EC1N 8RU (☎ 020 7242 0105, fax 020 7242 6200, e-mail chris.thomas@sportsfusion.eu)

THOMAS, Christopher Peter (Chris); s of Cecil Stevens Thomas, and Ruth Ela, *née* Roberts; *b* 13 January 1947; *Educ* Latymer Upper Sch, Royal Acad of Music (jr exhibitioner); *m* (m dis); 1 da (Carla b 22 Nov 1971), 1 s (Jan Stevens b 29 Sept 1970); 1 s (Michael James b 15 May 1988), 1 da (Mia b 1 Feb 1991) by another relationship; *Career* pop music producer; credits incl: Climax Blues Band (Climax Chicago Blues Band, The Climax Blues Band Plays On, A Lot of Bottle, Tightly Knit), Nirvana (Dedicated to Markos III), Procol Harum (Home, Broken Barricades, Live with The Edmonton Symphony Orchestra, Grand Hotel, Exotic Birds and Fruit), Mick Abrahams Band (Mick Abrahams Band, At Last), Christopher Milk (Some People Will Drink Anything), John Cale (Paris 1919), Roxy Music (For Your Pleasure, Stranded, Siren, Viva Roxy Music), Badfinger (Ass, Badfinger, Wish You Were Here), Sadistic Mika Band (Black Ship, Hot! Menu), Kokomo (Kokomo), Bryan Ferry (Let's Stick Together), Krazy Kat (China Seas), Eno (Here Comes The Warm Jets), The Sex Pistols (Never Mind the Bollocks, Filthy Lucre Live), Frankie Miller (Full House), Chris Spedding (Hurt), Tom Robinson Band (Power in the Darkness), Wings (Back to The Egg), The Pretenders (Pretenders, Pretenders II, Learning to Crawl), Pete Townshend (Empty Glass, All The Best Cowboys Have Chinese Eyes, White City), Elton John (The Fox, Jump Up, Too Low For Zero, Breaking Hearts, Reg Strikes Back, Sleeping With the Past, The One, tracks on The Lion King soundtrack album, Live Like Horses (with Luciano Pavarotti), The Big Picture), INXS (Listen Like Thieves, Kick, X), Dave Stewart & The Spiritual Cowboys, Shakespear's Sister (Goodbye Cruel World (prodr), Stay (co-prodr)), Miss World debut album, Marcella Detroit (Jewel), Bryan Adams, Sting and Rod Stewart (All for Love), Pulp (Different Class, This is Hardcore), Paul McCartney

(Run Devil Run), Hoggboy, David Gilmour (On an Island), Razorlight (Razorlight), Mystery Jets (Serotonin), State of Shock (Queen and Michael Jackson); mixing credits incl: Pink Floyd (Dark Side of the Moon, The Division Bell (jtly)), Roxy Music (Country Life), Ronnie Lane (One for the Road); 40 albums produced went silver, gold, platinum; winner: Rolling Stone Critics' Award 1980, Best Single Prodr Billboards 1988, Best Prodr BRIT Awards 1990, Gold Badge Br Acad of Songwriters and Composers 2005; fell Assoc of Professional Recording Services; Hon ARAM; *Recreations* travelling, meeting people; *Style—* Chris Thomas; ✉ c/o Geoff Travis, Rough Trade (☎ 020 8960 9888)

THOMAS, Dr Christopher Sydney; QC (1989); s of John Raymond Thomas (d 1982), and Daphne May, *née* Thomas; *b* 17 March 1950; *Educ* King's Sch Worcester, Univ of Kent at Canterbury (BA), Faculté International de Droit Comparé (Diplome de Droit Comparé), KCL (PhD); *m* 26 May 1979, Patricia Jane, da of Leslie Heath (d 1994), of Gillingham, Kent; 1 s (Alexander), 1 da (Felicity); *Career* called to the Bar Lincoln's Inn 1973 (Hardwick and Jenkins scholarships); recorder 2000; counsel, arbitrator and adjudicator in building and civil engrg disputes UK and overseas; CEDR accredited mediator 1999; FCIArb 1994; *Publications* Legal Obligations in Contruction (contrib, 1992), Contemporary Issues in Construction Law (contrib, 1997), Construction Law: Looking to the Future (contrib, 1998), Understanding the New FIDIC Red Book (intro, 2006); papers in the published proceedings of the 11th and 12th annual conferences of the Centre of Construction Law and Management; *Recreations* farming, boating; *Style—* Dr Christopher Thomas, QC; ✉ Keating Chambers, 15 Essex Street, London WC2R 3AA (☎ 020 7544 2600, fax 020 7544 2700)

THOMAS, David; *Career* chm: McKay Securities Gp plc 2007– (non-exec dir 2005–), Exterity Ltd; fndr dir Jarvis Hotels Ltd; FCA; *Style—* David Thomas, Esq; ✉ McKay Securities plc, 20 Greyfriars Road, Reading, Berkshire RG1 1NL

THOMAS, David; s of Harold Bushell Thomas (decd), of Bebington, Wirral, and Margaret, *née* Browne (decd); *b* 7 November 1945; *Educ* St Anselm's Coll Birkenhead, Univ of Liverpool (LLB); *m* 1 (m dis); 1 da (Rachel Elenore b 27 Aug 1974), 3 s (Mark Aidan b 10 July 1976, James Matthew, Neil William (twins) b 28 Feb 1980); m 2, Jane Bibby; *Career* F S Moore & Price Birkenhead: slr 1969–71, ptnr 1971–85, managing ptnr 1984–85; managing ptnr: Lees Moore & Price Birkenhead 1985–88, Lees Lloyd Whitley Liverpool 1988–93; chm Lees Lloyd Whitley Liverpool and London 1993–96; Banking Ombudsman 1997–2001; Fin Ombudsman Serv: Princ Ombudsman (Banking and Loans) 1999–2004, Princ Ombudsman and corp dir 2004–09, Chief Ombudsman 2009–10, strategy conslt 2010–14; Scottish Public Serv Ombudsman: memb Audit Advsy Ctee 2007–11, ind service delivery complaint reviewer 2011–14; conslt on financial consumer protection World Bank 2011–; memb Ctee Int Network of Financial Services Ombudsman Schemes 2009–14; pres Liverpool Law Soc 1987–88; Law Soc: memb Cncl 1987–96, chm Specialisation Ctee 1989–92, Practice Devpt Ctee 1992–95, Quality Standards Working Party 1995–96, Research Sub-Ctee 1991–96; memb: Accountancy and Actuarial Discipline Bd Financial Reporting Cncl 2001–09, Ctee City of London Law Soc 2004–09, Cncl Queen Mary Univ of London 2006–14, Bd Office of Legal Complaints 2009–15, Ct City of London Solicitors' Co 2009–11, Regulatory Bd Assoc of Chartered Certified Accountants, Policy Advsy Bd Which? 2015–; chm Bd Channel Islands Financial Ombudsman 2014–; *Publications* author of two World Bank reports on financial ombudsmen (with Francis Frizon); *Recreations* theatre, modern history, walking; *Clubs* Royal Over-Seas League; *Style—* David Thomas, Esq; ✉ e-mail david_thomas@hotmail.co.uk

THOMAS, David; QC (2002); s of Lloyd Thomas (d 2002), and Kathleen, *née* Meanwell; *b* 20 December 1958, Godalming, Surrey; *Educ* Midhurst GS, Wadham Coll Oxford; *m* 1987, Victoria, *née* Cochrane; 1 s (Frederick Roland Charles b 1 Aug 1994), 1 da (Cecily Mary Augusta b 17 Aug 2000); *Career* called to the Bar 1982, called to the Bar Gibraltar 1996; practising barr, currently memb Keating Chambers; accredited mediator 2003; treas Oman Br Lawyers Assoc 2010–; Keating on Construction Contracts (contrib, 8 edn), Construction Law International (regular contrib); *Recreations* family, gardening; *Clubs* MCC; *Style—* David Thomas, Esq, QC; ✉ c/o Paul Cooklin, Keating Chambers, 15 Essex Street, London WC2R 3AU (☎ 020 7544 2600, fax 020 7544 2700, e-mail pcooklin@keatingchambers.com)

THOMAS, David Gavin; s of Cecil Goring Thomas (d 1974), of Penarth, and Vera Winifred, *née* Wilson (d 1998); *b* 30 January 1943; *Educ* Wycliffe Coll; *m* 14 Aug 1971, Jane Annette, da of John Edward Verdon (d 1984); 2 da (Joanna Louise b 10 April 1975, Laura Anne b 6 July 1979), 1 s (William David b 24 Dec 1976); *Career* qualified CA Peat Marwick Mitchell 1966–68 (articled clerk 1960–66), fin accountant GKN (S Wales) Ltd 1972–73 (mgmnt accountant 1968–72), chief accountant Nova Jersey Knit Ltd 1973–74; Golley Slater & Partners Ltd: co sec 1974–75, fin dir 1976–87, gp fin dir 1987–; FCA; *Recreations* golf, sailing, bridge; *Clubs* Cardiff and County, Glamorganshire Golf, Penarth Yacht, Royal Porthcawl Golf; *Style—* David G Thomas, Esq; ✉ 20 Clinton Road, Penarth, Vale of Glamorgan CF64 3JD (☎ 029 2070 5677); Golley Slater Group, Wharton Place, Wharton Street, Cardiff CF10 1GS (☎ 029 2038 8621, fax 029 2023 8729)

THOMAS, David Glyndor Treharne; s of Dr John Glyndor Treharne Thomas, MC (Capt RAMC, d 1955), of Cambridge, and Ellen, *née* Geldart (d 1970); *b* 14 May 1941; *Educ* Perse Sch Cambridge, Gonville & Caius Coll Cambridge (MA, MB BChir); *m* 29 Dec 1970, Hazel Agnes Christina, da of William John Cockburn (d 1977), of Paisley; 1 s (William b 1972); *Career* St Mary's Hosp London: house surgn 1966, asst lectr in anatomy 1967–68, SHO in neurology 1969, casualty offr 1969; Royal Postgrad Med Sch Hammersmith Hosp London: SHO in surgery 1970, registrar in cardio-thoracic surgery 1970–71; Inst of Neurological Scis Southern Gen Hosp Glasgow: registrar, sr registrar and lectr in neurosurgery 1972–76; conslt neurosurgn Nat Hosp for Neurology and Neurosurgery and Northwick Park Hosp Harrow 1976–2006, prof of neurosurgery Inst of Neurology 1992–2006 (sr lectr 1976–92), conslt neurosurgn St Mary's Hosp London 1994–2006; numerous invited lectures and visiting professorships worldwide; chm EORTC Experimental Neuro-Oncology Gp 1986–88; memb: Med Acad Staff Ctee BMA 1981–82, Jt Hosp Med Servs Ctee 1981–82; pres Euro Soc for Stereotactic and Functional Neurosurgery, vice-pres European Assoc of Neurosurgical Socs 1991–95, vice-pres World Fedn of Neurosurgical Socs 2001–05 (parliamentarian 2009–); Freeman City of London 1969, Liveryman Worshipful Soc of Apothecaries 1971; MRCS 1966, FRCSEd 1972, FRCPG 1985, FRCP 1994 (MRCP 1970), FRCSEng 1998; *Books* Brain Tumours: Scientific Basis, Clinical Investigation and Current Therapy (ed with D I Graham, 1980), Biology of Brain Tumour (ed with M D Walker, 1986), Neuro-oncology: Primary Brain Tumours (ed, 1989), Stereotactic and Image Directed Surgery of Brain Tumours (ed, 1993), Handbook of Stereotaxy Using the CRW Apparatus (ed with M F Pell, 1994); *Recreations* military and naval history; *Clubs* Athenaeum, RSM; *Style—* Prof David Thomas; ✉ 106 Globe Wharf, 205 Rotherhithe Street, London SE16 5XX; The National Hospital, Box 147, Queen Square, London WC1N 3BG (☎ 020 3448 8993, fax 020 3448 8816, e-mail roseann.mccrea@uclh.nhs.uk)

THOMAS, Prof David John (Dafydd); s of Jack Lloyd Thomas (d 1997), of Fulmer, Bucks; *b* 7 December 1943, Cwmgors, Glamorgan; *Educ* Alleyn's Sch Dulwich, Clare Coll Cambridge (MA, MB BChir), Univ of Birmingham Med Sch (Arthur Thompson scholar, MD); *m* 1966, Celia Margaret, da of Sir Charles Barratt (d 1971), of Kenilworth, Warwicks; 3 da (Dr Rachel b 25 Jan 1970, Eleanor b 13 July 1980, Dr Laura b 3 Feb 1983), 2 s (Dr Charles Lloyd b 18 Aug 1971, George Llewellyn b 26 Jan 1973); *Career* neurological registrar then sr registrar Queen Elizabeth Hosp and Midland Centre for Neurology and Neurosurgery 1972–76, MRC research fell Inst of Neurology and St Thomas' Hosp 1976–78 (Queen Square prize), conslt neurologist and head of dept St Mary's Hosp 1978–2006 and E Berkshire Hosps 1978–2000, sr lectr in neurology and hon conslt neurologist Inst of Neurology and Nat Hosps for Neurology and Neurosurgery 1980–2006, prof of stroke medicine Imperial Coll Faculty of Medicine 2005–06, prof emeritus of clinical neuroscience Imperial Coll 2006–; former chm Special Advsy Ctee on Neurology to Royal Colls, princ neurological investigator MRC Asymptomatic Carotid Surgery Trial 1994–2008; govr Nat Soc for Epilepsy; memb Cncl Stroke Assoc 1992–2007; tstee: Assoc of Br Neurologists 2004–07, Stroke Cncl (American Heart Assoc) 1991, Euro Stroke Cncl 1994, Int Affrs Ctee 1997; FRCP 1985 (MRCP 1972), FRSM; *Books* Strokes and their Prevention (1988), Neurology, What Shall I Do? (1989, 2 edn 1997), The Eye in Systemic Disease (1990); *Recreations* photography, reading; *Style—* Prof Dafydd Thomas; ✉ 14 Queen Court, Queen Square, London WC1N 3BB (e-mail dafydd.thomas@imperial.ac.uk)

THOMAS, Sir David John Godfrey; 12 Bt (E 1694), of Wenvoe, Glamorganshire; s of Sir Michael Thomas, 11 Bt (d 2003); *b* 11 June 1961; *Educ* Harrow; *m* 21 Dec 2004, Nicola Jane Lusty; *Career* dir; *Recreations* squash (Eng int), tennis; *Clubs* Hurlingham, MCC, Jesters, Escorts; *Style—* Sir David Thomas, Bt; ✉ 1 Waters Edge, Eternit Walk, London SW6 6QU (☎ 020 7381 4078)

THOMAS, Prof David Stephen Garfield; s of Frederick Garfield Thomas, of Dover, Kent, and Ruth Muriel, *née* Hopper; *b* 2 October 1958, Dover, Kent; *Educ* Dover GS for Boys, Hertford Coll Oxford (Henry Oliver Becket Meml Prize, BA), Univ of Oxford (PGCE, MA, DPhil); *m* 1, 11 April 1987, Helen Elizabeth Martin (d 1990); 2, 21 March 1992, Lucy Marie Heath; 2 da (Mair Lucy b 23 Nov 1994, Alice Clara 2 March 1998); *Career* Dept of Geography Univ of Sheffield: lectr 1984–95, prof 1995–2004, dir Sheffield Centre for Int Drylands Research 1995; prof of geography Univ of Oxford 2004– (head of dept 2008–), fell Hertford Coll Oxford 2004–; hon prof Univ of Cape Town 2006–, hon prof Univ of the Witswatersrand 2013–; vice-pres RGS 2000–04 and 2013–, pres British Geomorphological Research Gp 2001–02; Dorothy Hodgkin Award BAAS 1994, Geological Soc of America Farouk El-Baz Award 2011; FRGS 1997; *Books* incl: Arid Zone Geomorphology (1987, 3 edn 2010), The Kalahari Environment (1991), World Atlas of Desertification (1992, 2 edn 1997), Desertification: Exploding the Myth (1994), Dictionary of Physical Geography (2002, 4 edn 2015); *Recreations* running (half marathons), cycling, travel; *Style—* Prof David Thomas; ✉ School of Geography and Environment, Oxford University Centre for the Environment, South Parks Road, Oxford OX1 3QY (☎ 01865 275844, fax 01865 285073, e-mail david.thomas@ouce.ox.ac.uk); Hertford College, Catte Street, Oxford OX1 3BW (Twitter @KalahariDave)

THOMAS, Prof Edward John; s of John Henry Thomas (d 1958), of Plymouth, Devon, and Lily Elizabeth Jane Thomas; *b* 25 November 1937; *Educ* Devonport HS, Keble Coll Oxford (MA), Univ of London (MSc), Univ of Manchester (PhD); *m* 12 Sept 1964, Erica Jean, da of Eric Distin (d 1977), of Salcombe, Devon; 1 da (Katherine Grace b 1965), 1 s (Gerard William b 1969); *Career* research scientist GEC plc 1962–64, lectr Univ of Manchester 1964–68; Univ of Bristol: staff tutor 1968–80, sr lectr 1980–81, prof of adult educn 1981–92, prof of continuing educn 1992–2003 (emeritus prof 2003–), sometime dir of continuing educn; sec gen Euro Univs Continuing Educn Network 1991–2000; life memb Univs Assoc for Continuing Educn 2000; tstee Friends of WNO 2005–12; FRSA 1983; *Books* Type II Superconductivity (1969), From Quarks to Quasars (1977), Lifelong Learning in a Changing Continent (ed, 2003), Adults in Higher Education (ed, 2004); *Recreations* reading, writing, eating, drinking, talking; *Style—* Prof Edward Thomas; ✉ Graduate School of Education, University of Bristol, Bristol BS8 1HH (☎ 0117 373 8700, e-mail e.j.thomas@bristol.ac.uk)

THOMAS, Prof Sir Eric Jackson; kt (2013); s of late Eric Jackson Thomas, and late Mary Margaret, *née* Murray; *b* 24 March 1953, Hartlepool, Co Durham; *Educ* Ampleforth, Univ of Newcastle upon Tyne (MB BS, MD); *m* 26 Oct 1976, Narell Marie, *née* Rennard; 1 da (Rachel Frances b 6 Jan 1985), 1 s (David Alexander b 11 June 1986); *Career* lectr in obstetrics and gynaecology Univ of Sheffield 1985–87, sr lectr in obstetrics and gynaecology Univ of Newcastle upon Tyne 1987–90; Univ of Southampton: prof of obstetrics and gynaecology 1991–2001, research co-ordinator Sch of Med 1992–95, head Sch of Med 1995–98, dean Faculty of Med, Health and Biological Sciences 1998–2000; vice-chllr Univ of Bristol 2001–15; exec sec Cncl of Heads of Med Schs and Deans of UK Faculties 1999–2000; conslt obstetrician and gynaecologist: Newcastle Gen Hosp 1987–2000, Southampton Univ Hosps Tst 1991–2001; non-exec dir Southampton Univ Hosps Tst 1997–2000; meds cmmr 2002–03; RCOG: convenor of scientific meetings 1992–95, memb Cncl 1995–2001, chm Scientific Advsy Ctee 1998–2000, tstee 2013–; chm: Strategy Bd SW HE RDA 2002–04, DfES Taskforce on Voluntary Giving in HE 2003, Worldwide Univ Network (WUN) 2003–07, Tstees ERIC 2006–12, Bd CASE Europe 2010–13 (memb 2007–13); memb: Bd SW RDA 2003–08, SW Regnl Sports Bd 2003–07, Cncl for Industry and HE 2003–15 (tstee 2005–15), Univs UK 2006–15 (chm Research Policy Ctee 2006–11, chm Eng and NI Cncl 2009–11, vice-pres 2009–11, pres 2011–13), Global Advsy Bd Chicago Booth Sch of Business 2006–15; dir UCAS 2005–09; pres Bristol Cwlth Soc 2002–14; chm Westport 2006–11; cmmr Marshall Aid Cmmn 2010–13; tstee: Nat Centre for Univs and Business 2013–15, IntoUniversity 2013–; Hon LLD Univ of Bristol 2004, hon fell Univ of Bristol 2015, hon DCL Univ of Newcastle upon Tyne 2016; Hon DSc: Univ of Southampton 2006, Univ of Teesside 2008, Univ of West of England 2010, Univ of S Wales 2016; DL Bristol 2007–15; FRSA 1998, FMedSci 1998, FRCOG 2001 (MRCOG 1983), FRCP 2004; *Recreations* golf, Newcastle United; *Clubs* Athenaeum; *Style—* Prof Sir Eric Thomas; ✉ Abbey Farmhouse, Oakley Road, Mottisfort, Romsey, Hampshire, SO51 0LQ

THOMAS, Gareth; MP; *Career* teacher 1992–95, cncllr London Borough of Harrow 1990–97 (spokesperson Health and Social Services 1990–97, chief whip 1996–97), MP (Lab) Harrow W 1997–; PPS to Rt Hon Charles Clarke, MP until 2003, Parly under sec of state DFID 2003–08, Parly under-sec of state for trade policy and consumer affrs Dept for Business, Enterprise and Regulatory Reform 2007–08, min of state DFID 2008–10, min of state Dept for Business, Enterprise and Regulatory Reform 2008–09; chm: Parly Renewables and Sustainable Energy Gp, Co-op Pty; chair All-Pty Olympic Ctee 2003, memb Environment Audit Select Ctee 1997–99; *Recreations* canoeing, Welsh rugby union, running; *Style—* Gareth Thomas, Esq, MP; ✉ House of Commons, London SW1A 0AA (☎ 020 7219 3000)

THOMAS, Dr Gareth; s of late Rev Evan George Thomas, and late Nina Mary, *née* Clargo; step s of late Olwen Elizabeth, *née* Jones; *b* 3 November 1945; *Educ* Merchant Taylors', Imperial Coll London, St Mary's Hosp Med Sch (MB BS), Univ of London (MD), Univ of Wales (LLM); *m* 20 Sept 1969, Alison Muir, da of late David Muir Kelly, of Haile, Cumbria; 3 s (Mark b 1971, Robert b 1973, James b 1976), 2 da (Anna b 1980, Abigail b 1982); *Career* obstetrician and gynaecologist; house physician St Mary's Hosp London 1969; resident med offr: Queen Charlotte's Hosp London 1970–71, Samaritan Hosp London 1971–72; lectr and hon registrar UCL 1972–75, hon lectr Univ of Oxford 1975–77, sr registrar Oxfordshire RHA 1975–79, conslt Ipswich and East Suffolk 1979–2006, clinical dir Dept of Gynaecological and Maternity Servs 1991–97, chm Med Staff Ctee The Ipswich Hosp 1997–99, dep med dir Ipswich Hosp NHS Tst 1999–2004; pres Medico-Legal Soc 1998–99, pres East Anglia Obstetrics & Gynaecology Soc 2000–03; chm Ethics Ctee RCOG 1998–2001: memb Professional Standards Ctee 2004–07; Law Soc expert; FRCOG 1987; *Recreations* sailing, landscaping, walking, grandparenting; *Clubs* Royal Soc of Medicine, Waldringfield Sailing; *Style—* Dr Gareth Thomas; ✉ Riverdale, Deben Lane, Waldringfield, Suffolk IP12 4QN (☎ 01473 811745)

T

THOMAS, Dr Geoffrey Price; s of Richard Lewis Thomas (d 1983), and Aerona, *née* Price (d 1969); *b* 3 July 1941, Maesteg, Glamorgan; *Educ* Maesteg GS, Univ Coll of Swansea (BSc), Churchill Coll Cambridge (PhD); *m* 1965, Judith Vaughan, da of Arsul John Williams; 2 da (Susannah Judith *b* 1965, Rachel Louise *b* 1967); *Career* res assoc Cavendish Laboratory 1966–67, staff tutor Univ Coll of Swansea 1967–78; Univ of Oxford: dep dir Dept for External Studies 1978–86, dir Dept for Continuing Educn 1986–2007, founding pres Kellogg Coll Oxford 1990–2007 (pres emeritus and hon fell 2007–); memb Higher Educn Funding Cncl for Wales 2000–08; visiting scholar: Smithsonian Inst, Harvard Univ, Univ of Washington, Univ of Calif Berkeley, Northern Illinois Univ, Univ of Georgia; govr Univ of Glamorgan 2009–11, dir Merthyr Tydfil Coll 2009–11, chair Univ of Wales Trinity St David 2010–14; patron David Mather Fndn 2012; aelod Gorsedd Beirdd Ynys Prydain 2014; hon fell Linacre Coll Oxford 1990– (fell 1978–90), sr fell Univ of Georgia 2003–, hon fell Trinity Univ Coll Carmarthen 2007–, Paul Harris fell Rotary Int 2007–, hon fell Swansea Met Univ 2009; Hon DSc Univ of Wales Trinity St David 2014; FLSW 2014; *Books* The Nuclear Arms Race (jt ed with C F Barnaby, 1982), Science and Sporting Performance (jt ed with B Davies, 1982), University Continuing Education 1981–2006 (jt ed with B Jones and R Moseley, 2010); *Style*— Dr Geoffrey Thomas; ✉ Kellogg College, Oxford OX2 6PN (✆ 01865 741758, e-mail ggpptt@gmail.com)

THOMAS, Geraint; MBE (2009); *b* 25 May 1986, Cardiff; *Career* cyclist; currently memb Team Sky, completed Tour de France 2007; achievements incl: Silver medal European Jr Points Championship 2004, Gold medal scratch race Jr World Track Championships 2004, Gold medal team pursuit and Silver medal scratch race European Under 23 Championships 2006, Bronze medal points race Cwlth Games 2006, overall winner Flech du Sud (road race) 2006, Gold medal team pursuit World Track Championships 2007 and 2008 (Silver medal 2006), Gold medal team pursuit Olympic Games Beijing 2008, world champion men's team pursuit and Silver medal men's madison Track World Championships 2012, Gold medal team pursuit Olympic Games London 2012, Gold Medal Commonwealth Games Road Race 2014, Bronze Medal Commonwealth Games Time-Trial 2014; *Style*— Geraint Thomas, Esq, MBE; ✉ website www.geraintthomas.com, Twitter @geraintthomas86

THOMAS, Harvey; CBE (1990); s of Col John Humphrey Kenneth Thomas (d 1984), of Leamington Spa, and Olga Rosina, *née* Noake (d 2001); *b* 10 April 1939; *Educ* Westminster, Univ of Minnesota, Univ of Hawaii, Northwestern Coll Minnesota; *m* 22 Dec 1978, Marlies, da of Erich Kram, of Wölmersen, Germany; 2 da (Leah Elisabeth *b* 1984, Lani Christine *b* 1986); *Career* Billy Graham Evangelistic Assoc 1960–75, int PR conslt 1976–, dir presentation and promotion Cons Party 1985–91, field dir PM's Election Tour 1983 and 1987, dir The London Cremation Co 1984–, dir CAMEO Ltd, chm Trans World Radio (UK); chm Cremation Soc of GB 2009–, memb Oakwood Baptist Church N London; fell Chartered Inst of Journalists; FCIPR, FRSA; *Books* In the Face of Fear (1985), Making an Impact (1989), If They Haven't Heard It, You Haven't Said It! (1995); *Recreations* family, travel, trains; *Clubs* IOD; *Style*— Harvey Thomas, Esq, CBE; ✉ 23 The Service Road, Potters Bar, Hertfordshire EN6 1QA (✆ 01707 649910, e-mail harvey@hthomas.net)

THOMAS, Prof Hilary; da of John Dewi Thomas, of Barnet, Herts, and Maureen Edith, *née* Thomas; *b* 12 November 1959, London; *Educ* Bishop's Hatfield Girls' Sch, New Hall Cambridge (MA), UCH London (MB BS), Univ of London (PhD); *Children* 2 da (Isobel Angharad Thomas *b* 18 Feb 1990, Phoebe Clara Thomas *b* 13 Feb 1993); *Career* SHO: in cardiology Middx Hosp 1986, in med Hammersmith Hosp 1986–87, in neurology Royal Free Hosp 1987; registrar in clinical oncology Hammersmith Hosp 1987–90, clinical res fell ICRF 1990–94, sr lectr in clinical oncology Hammersmith Hosp 1994–98, prof of oncology Univ of Surrey 1998–, lead clinician Macmillan Cancer Network (Surrey, W Sussex, Hants) 2001–04, med dir Royal Surrey County Hosp 2004–07, gp medical dir Care UK 2007–09; KPMG LLP: assoc ptnr 2009–11, ptnr 2011–, chief med advsr 2014–; leadership assoc Kings Fund 2008–10; vice-chm Breakthrough Breast Cancer 2008–15, tstee Breast Cancer Now 2015–; memb GMC 1994–2003; FRCP 1999 (MRCP 1987), FRCR 1991; *Books* Fight Cancer (with Karol Sikora, 1989), Cancer: A Positive Approach (with Karol Sikora, 1995); *Clubs* Bloomsbury; *Style*— Prof Hilary Thomas; ✉ KPMG LLP, 15 Canada Square, London E14 5GL

THOMAS, Prof Emeritus Howard Christopher; s of Harold Thomas (d 1986), and Hilda, *née* Pickering (d 1980); *b* 31 July 1945; *Educ* Thornbury GS, Univ of Newcastle upon Tyne (BSc, MB BS, Phillipson prize in med), Univ of Glasgow (PhD); *m* 31 May 1975, Dilys, da of John Andrew Ferguson (d 1979); 2 s (Robin James *b* 4 Oct 1978, Oliver *b* 11 July 1992), 1 da (Lucy *b* 18 Feb 1980); *Career* lectr in immunology Univ of Glasgow 1971–74; Royal Free Hosp Med Sch London: lectr in med 1974–78, sr Wellcome fell in clinical sci 1978–83, reader in med 1983–84, prof of med 1984–87; prof and chm of med St Mary's Hosp Med Sch/Imperial Coll Sch of Med Univ of London 1987–97, conslt physician and hepatologist St Mary's Hosp 1987–2011, dep head Div of Med Imperial Coll Sch of Med 1997–2002, dean (clinical) Faculty of Med Imperial Coll Sch of Med 2001–04, head of hepatology and gastroenterology Division of Medicine Imperial Coll London 2002–11, emeritus prof Faculty of Medicine Imperial Coll London 2011–; chm and non-exec dir Riotech Pharmaceuticals Ltd 2004–; chm: Dept of Health Advsy Gp on Hepatitis 1999–2009 (memb 1989–99), Dept of Health Steering Gp on Hepatitis C Strategy 2001–03, NW Thames Hepatology Clinical Network 2004–06, Pan-London Hepatitis Commissioning Gp 2004–06; pres: Br Assoc for Study of Liver 1996–98, Euro Soc for Study of Liver 1997; memb: Dept of Health Advsy Panel for Infected Health Care Workers 1994–2000, Cncl and Exec Ctee RCP 2001–04, Cncl Br Soc of Gastroenterology 2002–05, Nominations Ctee RCP 2002–09, Australian Ctee to review Nat Hepatitis C Strategy 2002, Nat Expert Panel on New and Emerging Infections 2003–10, Advsy Bd German Network of Competence in Med (Viral Hepatitis) 'Hep-Net' 2003–06, Hepatitis Bd Health Protection Agency 2005–07, Hepatitis C Action Planc Co-ordinating Gp Health Protection Scotland 2006–08, Int Advsy Bd Univ of Mauritius Med Sch 2008, Hepatitis B and C Public Policy Assoc 2009–, Infra Structure Gp Nat Liver Plan 2010–11; vice-pres Br Liver Tst 2000– (memb Med Advsy Ctee 1990–96); chm Bd of Tstees Liver Res Tst 1988–, chm Cross Cutting Gp (Viral Hepatitis) Nat Liver Plan 2010–11, chm NICE Hepatitis B Clinical Prog Devpt Gp 2011–14, co-chair Hepatitis B and C European Policy Gp 2015–; tstee: Hepatitis B Fndn 2007–, Caxton Tst 2011–, Skipton Tst 2012–; ed Jl of Viral Hepatitis 1993–2014; Humphry Davy Rolleston lectr RCP 1986, Cohen lectr Israel 1988, Bushell lectr Aust Soc of Gastroenterology 1990, Hans Popper lectr (SA) 1996, Inaugural Ralph Wright lectr Univ of Southampton 1999, Sheila Sherlock lectr British Soc of Gastroenterology 2005; hon pres European Assoc for the Study of the Liver 2017; British Soc of Gastroenterology Res Medal 1984, Hans Popper Int Prize for Distinction in Hepatology 1989, Ivanovsky Medal of Russian Acad of Med Sciences 1997, Lifetime Achievement Award European Soc for the Study of the Liver 2010, Lifetime Recognition Award Br Soc for the Study of the Liver 2010, Kowsar Award Iran 2011, Imperial College Medal 2014; fell Acad of Medical Sciences 1999–; FRCP, FRCPS, FRCPath, FMedSci; *Books* Clinical Gastrointestinal Immunology (1979), Recent Advances in Hepatology (jt ed Vol 1 1983, Vol 2 1986), Viral Hepatitis (ed, 1993, 1997, 2004, 2013); author of various publications on hepatology incl: Induction of Tolerance to a Soluble Protein Antigen by Oral Adminstration (Immunology, 1974), Mutation Preventing Formation of Hepatitis B e Antigen in Chronic Hepatitis B (Lancet, 1989), Health Benefits of Antiviral Therapy for Mild Hepatitis C (Health Technology Assessment, 2006), Genome-wide Association

Study Identifies Loci Influencing Liver Enqymes (Nature Genetics, 2011), Guidelines for the Diagnosis and Treatment of Cholangiocarcinoma: An Update (2012), Diagnosis and Management of Chronic Hepatitis B in Children Young People and Adults: Summary of NICE Guidance (BMJ, 2013); *Recreations* boating, golf, gardening; *Clubs* Athenaeum; *Style*— Prof Emeritus Howard Thomas; ✉ Department of Medicine, Imperial College School of Medicine at St Mary's Hospital, Praed Street, London W2 1PG (✆ 020 7886 6454, e-mail h.thomas@ic.ac.uk)

THOMAS, Hugh; *see:* Thomas of Swynnerton, Baron

THOMAS, Huw George; s of Thomas (Tommy) Thomas, and Phyllis Owen, *née* Lewis; *b* 17 June 1944, Fishguard, Pembrokeshire; *Educ* St Michael's Llanelli, Haverfordwest GS, Birmingham Sch of Architecture (BSc, Dip Arch), Architectural Assoc London (AADip); *m* 1, 1969 (m dis), Priscilla Beatrice, *née* Thomas; 1 s (Nathan Richard 12 March 1975), 2 da (Rebecca Alice Iowri *b* 27 July 1977, Angharad Bethan *b* 18 Feb 1979); *m* 2, 2002, Sarah Louise, da of Bruce Parker, *qv*; 2 s (Milo Conrad, Felix George (twins) *b* 12 Aug 2003), 1 da (Daisy Ann *b* 9 Feb 2006); *Career* architect Bank of Uganda 1969–70, sr princ architect Hants CC 1973–80, co-fndr Stevenson and Thomas 1980–1994, fndr Huw Thomas Architects 1994 (specialises in re-use of redundant buildings, incl redeveloping Peninsula Barracks Winchester); hon life memb SAVE Britain's Heritage, hon life memb SAVE Jersey's Heritage, specialist conservation advsr to the Defence Estate, memb Test Valley Architects Advsy Panel; RIBA, RICS and CLA awards for numerous building designs; author of articles for newspapers, magazines and architectural jnls, contrib to TV and radio progs; hon life memb Friends of Winchester Cathedral; RIBA 1971; *Recreations* watercolour painting, history, playstations; *Clubs* The Exchange (Winchester); *Style*— Huw Thomas, Esq; ✉ Madoc House, Southgate Street, Winchester SO23 9EB; Huw Thomas Architects, Madoc House, Southgate Street, Winchester SO23 9EB (✆ 01962 856169, fax 01962 877752, e-mail mail@huwthomasarchitects.co.uk, website www.huwthomasarchitects.co.uk)

THOMAS, Prof Hywel Rhys; s of Howard Lionel Thomas (d 1976), and Elizabeth Sybil Thomas (d 2007); *b* 20 April 1951, Llandovery, Carmarthenshire; *Educ* UC Swansea (BSc, PhD), Imperial Coll London (MSc, DIC); *m* Dr Aleksandra Koj; 3 c from previous m (Elizabeth Rose *b* 21 Feb 1978, Anna Mary *b* 26 Oct 1979, Matthew Rhys *b* 12 March 1982); *Career* asst resident engr Scott, Wilson, Kirkpatrick and Partners 1976–78 (grad engr 1973–76), sr research asst UC Swansea 1978–80; Cardiff Univ: lectr in civil engrg 1980–90, sr lectr 1990–92, reader 1992–95, prof of civil engrg 1995–, dir Geoenvironmental Research Centre 1996–, head Div of Civil Engrg 2002, head Sch of Engrg 2002–10, dep pro-vice-chllr (innovation and engagement) 2007–10, pro-vice-chllr (engagement and internationalisation) 2010–12, pro-vice-chllr (internationalisation and engagement) 2012–15, pro-vice-chllr (research, innovation and enterprise) 2013–; CEng 1977, FICE 2000 (MICE 1977), FGS 2001, FREng 2003, FLSW 2011, FRS 2012, MAE 2012; *Publications* author of 100 articles in learned jls; *Style*— Prof Hywel R Thomas; ✉ 34 Chandlers Way, Penarth, Vale of Glamorgan CF64 1SP; Cardiff University, Main Building Room 0.46, Park Place, Cardiff CF10 3AT (✆ 029 2087 0650, fax 029 2087 0689, mobile 07788 106499, e-mail thomashr@cardiff.ac.uk)

THOMAS, Ian Mitchell; OBE (1998); s of John Bythell Thomas (d 1977), of Connah's Quay, Clwyd, and Gladys Ethel, *née* Miller (d 1994); *b* 17 May 1933; *Educ* Liverpool Coll, Selwyn Coll Cambridge (MA); *m* 1, 1960 (m dis 1976), Jenifer Diana, da of Dr George Fletcher Morris (d 1999), of Coggeshall, Essex; 2 s (James *b* 1961, Mark *b* 1965), 2 da (Emma *b* 1963, Victoria *b* 1969); *m* 2, 1977 (m dis 1998), Diana Lesley Kathryn, wid of Nicholas Thorne (d 1976); *Career* Nat Serv 4 KORR 1952–54 (2 Lt 1953), PA to COS Br Cwlth Forces Korea 1953, Capt The Liverpool Scottish Queen's Own Cameron Highlanders TA; asst md Hobson Bates and Partners 1965 (dir 1963), jt md Cavenham Foods Ltd 1965–67, md Fabbri and Partners Ltd 1968–70, chm and md Culpeper Ltd 1972–2003, dir Emmetts of Peasenhall 2000–; cncllr (cons) Islington Cncl 1968–70; vice-pres Herb Soc 1986–87 (memb Cncl 1978–87); pres Old Lerpoolian Soc 1997–99; chm Kent Film Fndn 2011–; *Books* Culpeper's Book of Birth (1985), How to Grow Herbs (1988), Culpeper Herbal Notebook (1991); *Recreations* walking Teddy, sailing, skiing, gardening, golf; *Clubs* Royal Temple Yacht, Oxford and Cambridge; *Style*— Ian Thomas, Esq, OBE; ✉ 12 Nelson Crescent, Ramsgate, Kent CT11 9JF (✆ 01843 599745, e-mail ianmthomas@aol.com)

THOMAS, James Robert Graham; s of Cyril John Thomas (d 1987), and Hilary Allcroft, *née* Palins (d 1976); *b* 19 March 1934, Fulham, London; *Educ* Whitgift Sch, UCL (state scholar, Bartlett exhibitioner, BA (Arch)), Univ of Westminster (DipTP); *m* 24 Aug 1963, Anne Margaret, da of Thomas Arthur Pawsey (d 1982); 2 da (Joanna Susan (Mrs Weedon) *b* 1965, Catherine Sara (Mrs Flett) *b* 1966), 1 s (James William Pawsey *b* 1968); *Career* architect and town planner; asst architect: with Sir Basil Spence 1957, with Jorn Utzon 1960, with Sir Denys Lasdun 1964–66; dep gp ldr GLC 1966–68, gp planner London Borough of Lewisham 1968–70, princ architect-planner GLC 1972–79 (dep surveyor of historic buildings 1970–72), dep city architect and planning offr City of London 1979–81, dir of devpt London Borough of Tower Hamlets 1981–85, dir of planning and transportation City of Westminster 1985–87, princ Rothermel Thomas 1987–2003, conslt Howard Sharp & Ptnrs 2003–05; memb Structural Advsy Gp Athenaeum 1993–96; pres Soc of Architects Cities of London and Westminster 1986–88; RIBA: vice-pres 1995–97, memb Policy Mgmnt Bd 1995–98, memb Cncl, hon librarian, chm Library Bd; ARCUK: former memb Cncl, memb Bd of Architectural Educn, memb Discipline Ctee; memb: Ctee Soc of Chief Architects in Local Authy 1979–81, Assoc of London Borough Architects 1979–87, Assoc of London Borough Planning Offrs 1979–87, Met Planning Offrs Soc 1979–87, Assoc of London Borough Engrs and Surveyors 1985–, Exec Ctee City Heritage Soc; memb Southwark Diocesan Advsy Ctee for the Care of Churches 1970–73; Royal Acad exhibitor 1986 and 1990; Freeman City of London 1979, fndr memb and Liveryman Worshipful Co of Chartered Architects (Master 1987–88), Liveryman Worshipful Co of Fan Makers (Master 2004); FRIBA 1968, FRTPI 1974; *Books* Battle of the Styles (1974), Salisbury Cathedral Close: Conservation and Management (1990); *Recreations* theatre, reading, walking, family, wine; *Clubs* Middlesex CCC, City Livery; *Style*— James R G Thomas, Esq; ✉ Brook Cottage, 22A Lower Camden, Chislehurst, Kent BR7 5HX (✆ 020 8467 3662)

THOMAS, Jeremy Jack; CBE (2009); s of Maj Ralph Thomas, MC (d 2001), and Joy Eveleyn, *née* Spanjer; *b* 26 July 1949; *Educ* Millfield; *m* 1, (m dis 1977), Claudia Frolich; 1 da (Jessica Emily); *m* 2, 1982, Vivien Patricia, da of Adolph Coughman; 2 s (Jack Felix, Joshua Kit); *Career* film producer; BFI: chm 1992–97, life fell; former pres jury: Tokyo Film Festival, San Sebastian Film Festival, Berlin Film Festival; served on jury Cannes Film Festival 1987; *Film* credits incl: Mad Dog Morgan 1976, The Shout 1977, The Great Rock 'n' Roll Swindle 1979, Bad Timing 1979, Eureka 1982, Merry Christmas Mr Lawrence 1982, The Hit 1983, Insignificance 1984, The Last Emperor (winner of nine Academy Awards incl Best Picture) 1988, Everybody Wins 1989, The Sheltering Sky 1990, Let Him Have It (exec prodr) 1991, Naked Lunch 1991, Little Buddha 1993, Victory (exec prodr) 1994, Stealing Beauty 1995, Crash 1995, Blood and Wine 1996, The Ogre (exec prodr) 1996, The Brave (exec prodr) 1996, All The Little Animals (dir) 1998, The Cup (exec prodr) 1999, Gohatto (exec prodr) 2000, Brother 2000, Sexy Beast 2001, Rabbit-Proof Fence (exec prodr) 2002, Triumph of Love (exec prodr) 2002, Young Adam 2003, The Dreamers 2003, Travellers and Magicians (exec prodr) 2003, Promised Land Hotel (exec prodr) 2004, Dreaming Lhasa (exec prodr) 2004, Heimat 3 (exec prodr) 2004, Don't Come Knocking (exec prodr) 2004, Tideland 2004, Fast Food Nation 2005, Glastonbury (exec prodr) 2005, Mister Lonely (exec prodr) 2006, Joe Strummer: The Future is Unwritten (exec prodr) 2007, Franklyn 2008, The Palermo Shooting (exec prodr) 2007, Creation 2009, Essential Killing (exec prodr) 2010, Thirteen Assassins (exec prodr) 2010, Pina (exec prodr) 2011, Hari-Kiri: Death of a Samurai 2011, A Dangerous Method 2011, Kon-Tiki 2012, Only Lovers Left Alive 2013, Don Hemingway 2014, High Rise 2015, Tale of Tales 2015; *Awards* Best Picture Acad Award (for The Last Emperor) 1987, Michael Balcon BAFTA Award for Contribution to Br Cinema 1991, Evening Standard Lifetime Achievement in Cinema Award 1992, Screen Int Prize for World Cinema Achievement European Film Awards 2006; *Style*— Jeremy Thomas, CBE; ✉ The Recorded Picture Co, 24 Hanway Street, London W1T 1UH (☎ 020 7636 2251, fax 020 7636 2261, e-mail rpc@recordedpicture.com)

THOMAS, Jessica D E; *see:* Mann, Jessica D E

THOMAS, Julian Paul; s of Ronald Norman Thomas, and Sylvia Elsie, *née* Goddard; *b* 30 December 1966, Redbridge; *Educ* Bancroft's Sch, KCL (BSc), Queen's Coll Cambridge (PGCE), Univ of Hull (MBA); *m* 21 July 2001, Julia Helen, *née* Wade; 2 s (George b 31 Jan 2002, Christian b 1 April 2003); *Career* maths teacher Forest Sch 1995–97, head of year St Dunstan's Coll 1997–2000, dir of studies The Portsmouth GS 2000–03, second master Hampton Sch 2003–07, headmaster Caterham Sch 2007–15, master Wellington Coll 2015–; tstee Wellington Coll Multi-Academy Tst, tstee Crowthorne C of E Primary Sch; FRSA 2007; *Books* Foundation Maths for Teachers (1998), Intermediate Maths 2 (1998), GCSE Maths in a Year (1999), Formula One Maths B1 (2001), Formula One Maths B2 (2001); *Recreations* walking, running, climbing; *Clubs* Hawks' (Cambridge), East India; *Style*— Julian Thomas, Esq

THOMAS, Kathrin (Kate); CVO (2002), JP, DL (Mid Glamorgan 1989); *née* Evans; da of Dillwyn Evans (d 1974), and Dorothy Nelle, *née* Bullock (d 2000); *b* 20 May 1944; *Educ* Cheltenham Ladies' Coll, Sorbonne; *m* 21 Jan 1967, Edward Vaughan Thomas (d 2006), s of Edward Thomas; 2 s (Richard Edward b 7 Feb 1969, Robert Dillwyn b 12 Jan 1971); *Career* dir Penywaun Farms Ltd Nelson Mid Glamorgan; Prince's Tst: chm S Wales 1988–95, chm Prince's Tst Cymru and memb Advsy Cncl 1996–2001; chm: Mid Glamorgan FHSA 1990–94, Mid Glamorgan HA 1994–96, Bro Taf HA 1996–2000; pres Royal Welsh Agricultural Soc 2009; Hon Col 203 (W) Field Hosp (V) 1998–2006 (hon patron 2008–); High Sheriff of Mid Glamorgan 1986–87, HM Lord-Lt Mid Glamorgan 2003–; DStJ; *Recreations* reading, grandchildren; *Clubs* Army and Navy; *Style*— Mrs Kate Thomas; ✉ Clerk to the Lieutenancy, 14 de Londres Close, Porthcawl CF36 3JE

THOMAS, His Hon Judge Keith Garfield; s of (William Geoffrey) Howard Thomas, of Cardiff, and (Dorothy) Shirley Thomas; *b* 10 August 1955; *Educ* Mill Hill Sch, Bristol Poly (LLB), Inns of Court Law Sch; *m* 5 July 2003, Melinda Jane, *née* Vaughan; *Career* called to the Bar Gray's Inn 1977; asst provincial stipendiary magistrate 1995–97, asst recorder 1996–2000, recorder 2000–04, circuit judge 2004–, resident judge Swansea Crown Court 2011–, hon recorder of the City & County of Swansea 2011–; vice-chm Glamorgan Wanderers RFC 1999–2008; *Style*— His Hon Judge Keith Thomas; ✉ Swansea Crown Court, The Law Courts, St Helen's Road, Swansea SA1 4PF (☎ 01792 637000, fax 01792 637049, e-mail hhjudge.thomas2@hmcourts-service.gsi.gov.uk)

THOMAS, Sir Keith Vivian; kt (1988); s of Vivian Jones Thomas (d 1987), and Hilda Janet Eirene, *née* Davies (d 1979); *b* 2 January 1933, Wick, Glamorgan; *Educ* Barry Co GS, Balliol Coll Oxford (MA, hon fell 1984); *m* 16 Aug 1961, Valerie June, da of Eric Charles Little, of Beaconsfield, Bucks; 1 da (Emily b 1963), 1 s (Edmund b 1965); *Career* fell: All Souls Coll Oxford 1955–57 and 2001–15 (hon fell 2015), St John's Coll Oxford 1957–86 (hon fell 1986); prof of modern history Univ of Oxford 1986 (reader 1978–85), pres CCC Oxford 1986–2000 (hon fell 2000), pro-vice-chllr Univ of Oxford 1988–2000; delg OUP 1980–2000; memb: ESRC 1985–90, Reviewing Ctee on Export of Works of Art 1990–93, Royal Cmmn on Historical MSS 1992–2002; tstee: Nat Gallery 1991–98, Br Museum 1999–2008; chm: Br Library Advsy Ctee for Arts, Humanities and Social Sciences 1997–2002, Supervisory Ctee Oxford Dictionary of National Biography 1992–2004, Advsy Cncl Warburg Inst Univ of London 2000–08; Norton Medlicott Medal Historical Assoc 2003, Lifetime Achievement Award All-Pty Parly Gp on Archives and History 2015; Hon DLitt: Univ of Kent 1983, Univ of Wales 1987, Univ of Hull 1995, Univ of Leicester 1996, Univ of Sussex 1996, Univ of Warwick 1998, Univ of London 2006; Hon LLD Williams Coll Mass 1988, Oglethorpe Univ Georgia 1996; Hon LittD: Univ of Sheffield 1992, Univ of Cambridge 1995, Columbia Univ 2011; Hon DPhil Uppsala Univ 2014; hon fell Univ of Wales Cardiff 1995, hon fell Warburg Inst Univ of London 2008; foreign hon memb American Acad of Arts and Sci 1983, hon memb Japan Acad 2009; FRHistS 1970 (jt literary dir 1970–74, memb Cncl 1975–78, vice-pres 1980–84, hon vice-pres 2001–), FBA 1979 (memb Cncl 1985–88, pres 1993–97), memb Academia Europaea 1993 (tstee 1997–2002), founding FLSW 2010; Cavaliere Ufficiale Ordine al Merito della Repubblica Italiana 1991; *Books* Religion and the Decline of Magic (1971), Puritans and Revolutionaries (ed with Donald Pennington, 1978), Man and the Natural World (1983), The Oxford Book of Work (ed, 1999), Roy Jenkins: A Retrospective (ed with Andrew Adonis, 2004), The Ends of Life (2009), The Wolfson History Prize 1972–2012: An Informal History (2012); also author of articles and reviews in books, learned jls and literary periodicals; *Recreations* looking for secondhand bookshops; *Clubs* Athenaeum; *Style*— Sir Keith Thomas, FBA; ✉ The Broad Gate, Broad Street, Ludlow, Shropshire SY8 1NJ; All Souls College, Oxford OX1 4AL (e-mail keith.thomas@all-souls.ox.ac.uk)

THOMAS, Kristian; *b* 14 February 1989; *Career* gymnast; achievements incl: Bronze medal (team) Cwlth Games 2006, Silver medal (team) European Championships 2010, Bronze medal (floor) World Championships 2010, Gold medal (team) World Championships 2012, Bronze medal (team) Olympic Games 2012; *Style*— Mr Kristian Thomas

THOMAS, Dr Leslie; QC (2014); *b* 29 April 1965, London; *Educ* Kingston Univ (LLB); *Career* called to the Bar Inner Temple 1988, called to the Cwlth of Dominica Bar 2003 called to the Antigua and Barbuda Bar 2007; practising barr specialising in human rights and civil rights torts against the police and inquests, memb Garden Court Chambers 1989–; former lectr: Univ of Westminster, Kingston Univ; former chm Mgmnt Ctee Central London Law Centre; Legal Aid Barr of the Year Legal Aid Practitioners Assoc Award 2012; memb: INQUEST Lawyers, Standards in Public Life Ctee London Borough of Lewisham; Hon LLD Kingston Univ 2013; *Publications* INQUESTS: A Practitioner's Guide (co-author, 3 edn 2014); *Recreations* tenor saxophone, jazz music, languages and linguistics, Russian; *Style*— Dr Leslie Thomas, QC; ✉ Garden Court Chambers Ltd, 57–60 Lincoln's Inn Fields, London WC2A 3LS (☎ 020 7993 7600, e-mail lesliet@gclaw.co.uk, website www.gclaw.co.uk)

THOMAS, Leslie John; OBE (2005); s of David James Thomas, MN (ka 1943), and Dorothy Hilda Court Thomas (d 1943); *b* 22 March 1931; *Educ* Dr Barnardo's Kingston upon Thames, Kingston Tech Sch; *m* 1, 1956 (m dis 1970), Maureen, da of Charles Crane; 2 s (Mark, Gareth), 1 da (Lois); m 2, Nov 1971, Diana Miles; 1 s (Matthew); *Career* Nat Serv Singapore, Malaya 1949–51; journalist 1951–63: Exchange Telegraph 1955–57, London Evening News 1957–63; many radio and TV appearances; vice-pres Barnardo's 1998; Hon MA Univ of Wales 1995, Hon DLitt Univ of Nottingham 1998; *Television Plays and Documentaries* incl: Great British Isles (Channel 4 series, also presented) 1989, The Last Detective (adapted from Dangerous Davies novels, ITV) 2003, 2004 and 2005; *Novels* The Virgin Soldiers (1966), Orange Wednesday (1967), The Love Beach (1968), Come to the War (1969), His Lordship (1970), Onward Virgin Soldiers (1971), Arthur McCann and All His Women (1972), The Man with Power (1973), Tropic of Ruislip (1974), Stand Up Virgin Soldiers (1975), Dangerous Davies (1976), Bare Nell (1977), Ormerod's Landing (1978), That Old Gang of Mine (1979), The Magic Army (1981), The Dearest and the Best (1984), The Adventures of Goodnight and Loving (1986), Dangerous in Love (1987), Orders for New York (1989), The Loves and Journeys of Revolving Jones (1991), Arrivals and Departures (1992), Dangerous By Moonlight (1993), Running Away (1994), Kensington Heights (1995), Chloe's Song (1997), Dangerous Davies and the Lonely Heart (1998), Other Times (1999), Waiting for the Day (2003), Dover Beach (2005), Soldiers and Lovers (2007); *Non-Fiction* Some Lovely Islands (1968), The Hidden Places of Britain (1981), A World of Islands (1983), Almost Heaven – Talk from a Cathedral (2010); *Autobiographies* This Time Next Week (1964), In My Wildest Dreams (1984, revised edn 2006); *Recreations* cricket, music, antiques, stamp collecting; *Clubs* MCC, Lord's Taverners, Saints and Sinners; *Style*— Leslie Thomas, Esq, OBE

THOMAS, Prof Lyn Carey; s of William Carey Thomas (d 1994), and Eunice, *née* Morgan (d 1968); *b* 10 August 1946; *Educ* The Lewis Sch Pengam, Jesus Coll Oxford (Dip Mathematics, MA, DPhil); *m* 30 July 1970, Margery Wynn, da of Frederick James Bright; 2 s (Matthew James Carey b 22 June 1974, Stephen Daniel Adam b 10 April 1980), 1 da (Elizabeth Angharad b 29 Sept 1976); *Career* Pilcher sr res fell Dept of Mathematics UC Swansea 1973–74 (res fell 1971–73), lectr then sr lectr in decision theory Univ of Manchester 1974–85, prof of mgmnt sci Univ of Edinburgh 1985–2000, prof of mgmnt sci Univ of Southampton 2000–; NRC sr res assoc Naval Postgrad Sch Montery 1982–83; adjunct prof Monash Univ Melbourne and Edith Cowan Univ Perth; memb: Operational Res Soc 1974 (pres 1994 and 1995, Goodeve Medal 1999 and 2011, Beale Medal 2008), Informs 1979, Edinburgh Mathematical Soc 1985; FIMA 1989, FRSE 1991, FOR 2005; *Books* Games, Theory and Applications (1984, 2 edn 2004), Operational Research Techniques (1986), Credit Scoring and Credit Control (1992), Credit Scoring and its Applications (2002), Readings in Credit Scoring (2004), Consumer Credit Models (2009); *Recreations* reading, walking, rugby; *Style*— Prof Lyn Thomas, FRSE; ✉ School of Management, University of Southampton, Highfield, Southampton SO17 1BJ (e-mail l.thomas@soton.ac.uk)

THOMAS, Lynda; *Career* Macmillan Cancer Support: head of media 2001–07, dir of external affrs 2007–11, dir of fundraising 2011–14, interim chief exec 2014–15, chief exec 2015–; *Style*— Ms Lynda Thomas; ✉ Macmillan Cancer Support, 89 Albert Embankment, London SE1 7UQ

THOMAS, Mark David; *b* 1 March 1967; *Career* trained Fleet Street news agency 1985–88, news reporter The People 1988–94, news reporter then chief reporter News of the World 1994–97, features ed then asst ed Daily Mirror 1997–2001, dep ed Sunday Mirror 2001–03, ed The People 2003–; *Style*— Mark Thomas, Esq; ✉ The People, One Canada Square, London E14 5AP (☎ 020 7293 3614, fax 020 7293 3887, e-mail m.thomas@mgn.co.uk)

THOMAS, Dr Martyn Rhys; *Educ* Bart's Med Coll, King's Coll Hosp Univ of London (MD); *Career* trg in interventional cardiology KCH 1988– (currently also dir of cardiac servs); nat and int trainer in coronary angioplasty, introduced radiation therapy to UK 1998; pres Br Cardiovascular Intervention Soc (BCIS), expert to NICE 1999 and 2005; FRCP 2000 (MRCP 1985); *Recreations* season ticket holder at Crystal Palace FC; *Style*— Dr Martyn Thomas; ✉ King's College Hospital, Denmark Hill, London SE5 9RS (☎ 020 7346 3748, fax 020 7346 3489)

THOMAS, Michael David; CMG (1985), QC (1973); s of D Cardigan Thomas and Kathleen Thomas; *b* 8 September 1933; *Educ* Chigwell Sch Essex, LSE; *m* 1, 1958 (m dis 1978), Jane Lena Mary, eldest da of late Francis Neate; 2 s, 2 da; m 2, 1981 (m dis 1986), Mrs Gabrielle Blakemore; m 3, 1988, Baroness Dunn, DBE (Life Peer), *qv*; *Career* called to the Bar Middle Temple 1955 (bencher 1982); jr counsel to Treasury in admiralty matters 1966–73, wreck cmmr and salvage arbitrator Lloyd's 1974–83, attorney-gen Hong Kong 1983–88; memb of Exec and Legislative Cncls Hong Kong 1983–88; *Recreations* tennis, travel, art history; *Clubs* Garrick, Queen's Lawn Tennis, Hong Kong; *Style*— Michael Thomas, Esq, CMG, QC; ✉ Essex Court Chambers, 24 Lincoln's Inn Fields, London WC2A 3ED (☎ 020 7813 8000, fax 020 7813 8080)

THOMAS, Michael Graham; s of Graham Gerard Thomas, and Dulcie Elizabeth Thomas; *b* 6 January 1960, Porthcawl, S Wales; *Educ* Hornchurch GS, Swayne Sch Rayleigh, SE Essex Sixth Form Coll, Middx Hosp Med Sch (BSc, MB BS, Thomas Yates Prize in Anatomy, ICI Prize in Neuropharmacology), Univ of London (MS); *Career* house surgn Middx Hosp London 1984–85, house physician Orsett Hosp 1984–85; SHO: orthopaedics and traumatology Royal Nat Orthopaedic Hosp Stanmore 1985–86, A&E Edgware Hosp 1986, orthopaedics and traumatology Central Middx Hosp London 1986, gen surgery and renal transplantation Southmead Hosp Bristol 1986–88, Hepatopancreatobiliary Unit Hammersmith Hosp London 1988; surgical registrar KCH London 1988–89, res fell and hon clinical registrar Royal Postgrad Med Sch and St Mark's Hosp London 1989–90; surgical registrar: Hammersmith Hosp 1990–92, Ashford Hosp Middx 1992–93; surgical registrar and locum sr registrar Hammersmith Hosp 1993; lectr in surgery and hon sr surgical registrar: Broadgreen Hosp Liverpool 1993–94, Royal Liverpool Univ Hosp 1994–95; sr lectr and conslt Univ of Bristol 1995–2001, conslt colorectal surgn Bristol Royal Infirmary 1995–; visiting prof Chennai India 2001, visiting lectr All Indian Med Centre New Delhi 2001, Shri Prakash lectr DR N R Res and Digestive Disease Educnl Tst Chennai India 2000; visitor: Nat Cancer Centre Hosp Tokyo 1996, Mt Sinai Hosp NY 1999, Mayo Clinic Rochester, Minneapolis and St Paul's MN 2001; referee: Br Jl of Surgery, Br Jl of Cancer, Res Bd RCS, NW NHS Exec R&D; hon dr Somerset RFU; memb: Surgical Res Soc, Br Soc of Gastroenterology (memb SW Div), Assoc of Surgns, Assoc of Coloproctologists, SW Surgns, Nat Clinical Trials Ctee; admitted Royal Ct of Examiners England; Arris and Gale lectureship RCS 1993 (delivered at Hammersmith Hosp 1994), Ethicon travelling fellowship RCS 1996, res scholarship Fndn for the Promotion of Cancer Research Japan 1996, Continuing Med Educn fellowship RCS(Ed) 1998–2001, travelling fell American Assoc of Colorectal Surgns/Assoc of Coloproctologists GB and I 2001–02; FRCS 1989, FRCSEd 1989, FRCS (Gen) 1996; *Publications* author of numerous articles, abstracts and book reviews published in learned jls; *Recreations* rugby, football, cricket, athletics, swimming, tennis, chess, drama; *Clubs* Birkenhead Park RFC (sometime hon sec), Yatton RFC, Law Soc RFC; *Style*— Michael Thomas, Esq; ✉ 45 Sydenham Hill, Cotham, Bristol BS6 5SL (☎ 0117 962 9549, e-mail mgtbristol@aol.com); Department of Surgery, Level 4, Bristol Royal Infirmary, Marlborough Street, Bristol (☎ 0117 928 3066, mobile 07876 597388)

THOMAS, Col Michael John Glyn; s of Glyn Pritchard Thomas (d 1985), and Mary, *née* Moseley (d 1987); *b* 14 February 1938, Flintshire; *Educ* Haileybury and ISC, Univ of Cambridge (MA, MB BChir), Bart's; *m* 23 May 1969, (Sheelagh) Jane, da of Harold Thorpe (d 1979); 1 da (Fleur b 1970); *Career* RMO 2 Bn Para Regt 1964–67, trainee in pathology BMH Singapore 1967–71; specialist in pathology: Colchester MH 1971–74, Singapore 1974–76; sr specialist in pathology and 2 i/c Army Blood Supply Depot (ABSD) 1977–82, exchange fell Walter Reed Army Medical Centre Washington DC 1982–83, offr i/c Leishman Lab 1984–87, CO ABSD 1987–94; private conslt in transfusion medicine and clinical dir The Blood Care Foundation 1995–; memb BMA: Cncl 1973–74 and 1977–82, Central Ethical Ctee 1976–82 (chm 1977–82), Armed Forces Ctee 1971–82 and 1988–93, Jr Membs Forum 1971–78 (chm 1974), Bd of Sci and Educn 1987–93, Rep Body 1972–82 and 1987–93, Expert Ctee on AIDS 1986–, EEC Ctee 1989–93; fell BMA 1995; expert witness on gene mapping ESC, jt patent holder of new method of freezing blood together with special bag in which it is frozen; memb: Br Blood Transfusion Soc 1987 (fndr chm Autologous Transfusion Special Interest Group 1992–98, sec 1998–, memb Cncl 1998–2001), Inst of Medical Ethics 1987, Int Soc of Blood Transfusion 1988 (pres Int Congress

T

2004), Euro Sch of Transfusion Med (faculty memb) 1993 (faculty memb Slovenia 1997, Italy 1998), American Assoc of Blood Banks 1997, Int Soc of Travel Med 2002, Br Travel Health Assoc 2003; DTM&H 1965, LMSSA 1982, FRCPEd 1997; *Books* co-author: Control of Infection (1989), Nuclear Attack, Ethics and Casualty Selection (1988), Handbook of Medical Ethics (1979 and subsequent edns); Our Genetic Future, Medicine Betrayed, A Code of Practice for the Safe Use and Disposal of Sharps – Dictionary of Medical Ethics (contrib), AIDS and Human Rights a UK Perspective (contrib), Wylie and Churchill Davidson's A Practice of Anaesthesia (contrib chapter on Autologous Transfusion), Cryopreservation and Freeze-Drying Protocols (contrib chapter on Cryopreservation of Human Red Blood Cells), Transfusion in Europe (contrib), A Manual for Blood Conservation (contrib chapter on History of Blood Transfusion); *Recreations* DIY, photography, philately; *Clubs* Tanglin (Singapore); *Style*— Dr Michael J G Thomas; ✉ 8 Aveley Way, Maldon, Essex CM9 6YQ (✆ 01621 851144, e-mail michaelgj.thomas2@btinternet.com)

THOMAS, Michael Stuart (Mike); s of late Arthur Edward Thomas, and late Mona, *née* Parker; *b* 24 May 1944; *Educ* Latymer Upper Sch, King's Sch Macclesfield, Univ of Liverpool (BA); *m* 31 July 1976, Maureen Theresa, da of late Denis Kelly; 1 s by previous m (Paul b 1973); *Career* pres Liverpool Univ Guild of Undergrads 1965–66 (memb Nat Exec NUS 1966–68), head Research Dept Co-op Pty 1966–68, sr research assoc Policy Studies Inst 1968–73, dir The Volunteer Centre 1973–74, MP (Lab and Co-op 1974–81, SDP 1981–83) Newcastle upon Tyne East 1974–83 (Parly candidate: (Lab) Hertfordshire East 1970, (SDP) Newcastle upon Tyne East 1983 and Exeter 1987); PPS to Rt Hon Roy Hattersley MP 1974–76, memb House of Commons Select Ctee on Nationalised Industries 1975–79, chm PLP Trade Gp 1979–81, SDP spokesman on Health and Social Security 1981–83; SDP: memb Policy Ctee 1981–83 and 1984–90, memb Nat Ctee 1981–90, chm Orgn Ctee 1981–88, chm Fin Ctee 1988–89; mgmnt conslt 1978–; dir: Dewe Rogerson Ltd 1984–88, BR Western Region 1985–92, Corporate Communications Strategy 1988–2004, Education 2000 1991–94, Lopex plc 1998–99, Metal Bulletin plc 1998–2002; chm: Burnaby Communications and Information Services Ltd 1978–2005, Media Audits Ltd 1990–2001, Fotorama Ltd 1995–2000, Atalink Ltd 1998–2001, SMFI Ltd 2000–12, Music Choice Europe plc 2000–05, 422 Ltd 2001–02, WAA Ltd 2003–08, H K Wentworth Ltd 2005–08, UTarget plc 2007–08, Finance South East 2008–10, AdIQ Ltd 2008–11, VRL Financial News Publishing 2011–12; trg conslt Inspirational Devpt Gp 2009–; chm: Industrial Engrg Plastics Gp 2015–, PlasRecycle Ltd 2015–; site moderator www.charter2010.co.uk 2010; fndr Parliament's weekly jl The House Magazine 1976, ed The BBC Guide to Parliament 1979 and 1983, author of various articles, reviews and pamphlets; mentor Finance South East 2014–; *Publications* Reform and Reformers (with Peter Urbach, 2014); various pubns for PEP (now Policy Studies Inst); *Recreations* collecting election pottery and medals, gardening, walking, countryside, music, opera, theatre, fine arts and architecture; *Clubs* Reform; *Style*— Mike Thomas, Esq; ✉ c/o Reform Club, 104, Pall Mall, London SW1Y 5EW (e-mail mikethomas77@virginmedia.com)

THOMAS, Michael Tilson; s of Ted Thomas, and Roberta Thomas; *b* 21 December 1944; *Educ* Univ of Southern Calif; *Career* conductor, pianist and composer; studied under Ingolf Dahl, John Crown and Alice Ehlers; music dir Young Musicians' Fndn Debut Orch 1963, pianist and conductor Monday Evening Concerts LA 1963–68, asst conductor then principal guest conductor Boston Symphony Orch 1969–74, conductor NY Philharmonic Young People's Concerts 1971–77, music dir Buffalo Philharmonic 1971–79, princ guest conductor LA Philharmonic 1981–85, princ conductor Great Woods Music Festival 1985–88, fndr and artistic dir New World Symphony (trg orch for young musicians USA) 1988–, Pacific Music Festival Sapporo Japan 1990–, princ guest conductor LSO 1995– (princ conductor 1988–95), music dir San Francisco Symphony Orch 1995–; American Music Center Award 2000; recordings incl: Copland orchestral works 1986, Tchaikovsky, Liszt and Rachmaninov Piano Concertos 1986, Mahler Symphony No 3 1987, Kurt Weill Seven Deadly Sins and Little Threepenny Opera 1987, Ravel orchestral works 1988, John McLaughlin Guitar Concerto 1988, Prokofiev Piano Concertos Nos 1 and 2 1988, Steve Reich The Four Sections 1988, Brahms Serenades 1989, Haydn Variations 1989, Tchaikovsky Swan Lake 1990, Janácek Glagolitic Mass 1990, Debussy orchestral works 1991, Tavener Dance Lament of the Repentent Thief 1991, Ives Three Places in New England 1992, Bernstein On the Town 1992, Strauss Lieder 1993, Schumann and Grieg Piano Concertos 1993, Shostakovich Concertos Nos 1 and 2 1993, Bartók Violin Concerto No 2 1993, Copland Quiet City and Emily Dickinson Songs 1994, Barber orchestral works 1994, Villa-Lobos (with New World Symphony Orch, for BMG) 1996, Stravinsky 1996 (with LSO), Copland and Stravinsky 1996, New World Jazz 1998 (with New World Symphony Orch), Mahler Symphony No 7 1999 (with LSO), Stravinsky ballets (Persephone, Firebird, Rite of Spring) 1999 (for San Francisco Symphony Orch, winner of 3 Grammy awards), Mahler Symphony No 6 (with San Fransisco Orch) 2001, Ives Symphony No 4 1999; television: Discovery concerts with LSO (BBC), On the Town 1993 (winner of Gramophone Award for Best Musical Recording), Concerto! (with Dudley Moore, Channel 4/BMG 1993); festivals/tours with LSO (Barbican): Shell LSO UK Tour 1986, The Gershwin Years 1987, The Flight of the Firebird 1989, Steve Reich Series 1989, Childhood 1991, Takemitsu Festival 1991, The Mahler Festival 1994 and 1995, Salzburg Summer Festival 1988 and 1991, USA and Japan 1989, 1991, 1992, Canary Islands 1989, Pacific Music Festival Sapporo Japan 1990, Israel 1991, Salzburg Whitsun Festival 1991 and 1995, USA and several Euro visits 1992, Austria, Germany and USA 1993, Italy and Spain 1994, Japan and Austria 1995 and 1997, Germany 1997, 2001 and 2002; with New World Symphony Orch: Lincoln Center USA 1996, US tour 1997, tour in Monaco 1995; with San Francisco Symphony Orch: 1996 US tour incl American Music Festival, Volkert-Cmmn (world premiere), Adams-Lollapalooza and Penderecki-Violin Concerto no 2 (US premieres), 1997 US tour incl Schubert/Henze-Erlkonig (US premiere), tour in Netherlands, Belgium, France, Germany and Austria 1996, tour in Japan and Hong Kong 1997, tour in Europe 2002 and 2003; opera (with LSO): Rimsky-Korsakov Mlada 1989, L'Enfant et Les Sortilèges 1991, Bernstein On the Town 1992, La Bohème 1994; Robin Holloway Concerto No 3 (world première) 1996; *Awards* Koussevitzky Prize Tanglewood 1968, Ditson Award 1994, Conductor of the Year USA 1994, 3 Grammy awards for Stravinsky ballets with BMG 1999, Grammy Award for Mahler Symphony No 6 2003, Grammy Award for Mahler Symphony No 3 2004; *Style*— Michael Tilson Thomas, Esq

THOMAS, Neil Philip; s of Simon David Thomas (d 2002), of Stanmore, Middx, and Jessie, *née* Blagborough; *b* 29 April 1950; *Educ* Stowe (scholar), Univ of London (BSc), Middlesex Hosp Med Sch (MB BS); *m* 1, 25 Jan 1974, Mary Josephine Christian (d 1977), da of A V M Patrick Joseph O'Connor, CB, OBE; 1 da (Joanna b 19 June 1977); m 2, 29 April 1979, Julia Vera (d 2012), da of J J Ashken (d 2003); 1 s (James b 17 March 1981), 1 da (Gemma b 15 Oct 1982); m 3, 4 Sep 2013, Barbara Diane, da of A Plough Jr (d 2008); *Career* late sr registrar in orthopaedics: Royal Nat Orthopaedic Hosp, UCH and the Westminster Hosp; conslt orthopaedic surgn N Hampshire Hosp Hampshire Clinic and Wessex Knee Unit (emeritus conlst N Hampshire Hosp 2011–); instigator of arthroscopic knee courses RCS 1995; memb ACL Study Gp 2002–; pres: Br Assoc of Surgery of the Knee (BASK) 2002–04 (sec 1993–96, chm BASK and Nat Blood Service Allograft Working Gp), European Soc of Knee and Arthroscopic Surgery 2004–06 (vice-pres 2000–04); memb Int Knee Soc; memb Editorial Bd: The Knee 1998–, Knee Surgery Sports Traumatology Arthroscopy Jl (KSSTA) 2000– (chm Bd of Tstees 2007–); Jl of Bone and Joint Surgery: assoc ed 2001–, memb Editorial Bd 1998–2002, chm Website Ctee 2000–10, memb Cncl 2003–, sec 2006–07, treas 2007–10, chm Cncl 2010–; visiting prof Perugia Univ 2005, chm Nomination Ctee European Soc of Sports, Knee Surgery and Arthroscopy 2006–08 (life memb 2010–); travelling fell European Soc of Sports, Knee Surgery and Arthroscopy (ESSKA)/American Orthopaedic Soc for Sports Med (AOSSM) 2005; Fitton Prize for Orthopaedics 1974, Sir Herbert Seddon Prize and Medal 1986, President's Medal Br Assoc of Surgery of the Knee 1985–86, Best Paper Award ESSKA Basel 1986, Silver Merit Award NHS 2007, Best Paper Award KSSTA Jl 2013/14, Alwin Jager Best Video Award ESSKA Congress Amsterdam 2014; fell Br Orthopaedic Assoc (memb Cncl 1999–2001 and 2010–13); FRCS 1978, FRSM; Clinical Challenges in Orthopaedics: The Knee (co-ed, 2000); author various original articles, book chapters and videos on knee surgery; *Recreations* shooting, horticulture, wine, ornithology; *Clubs* Athenaeum; *Style*— Neil Thomas, Esq; ✉ The Parsonage, Itchen Stoke, Alresford, Hampshire SO24 0QU(✆ 01962 760233); The Hampshire Clinic, Basing Road, Basingstoke, Hampshire RG24 7AL (✆ 01256 819222, e-mail neilthomas@wessexknee.co.uk)

THOMAS, (Robert) Neville; QC (1975); s of Robert Derfel Thomas (d 1983), of Clwyd, and Enid Anne, *née* Edwards (d 1990); *b* 31 March 1936; *Educ* Ruthin Sch, Univ of Oxford (MA, BCL); *m* 28 March 1970, Jennifer Anne, da of Philip Henry Akerman Brownrigg, CMG, DSO, OBE, TD (d 1998); 1 s (Gerran b 19 March 1973), 1 da (Meriel b 21 Aug 1975); *Career* Lt Intelligence Corps 1955–57; called to the Bar Inner Temple 1962 (bencher 1985); recorder of the Crown Court 1975–82, head of chambers; *Recreations* fishing, walking, gardening; *Style*— Neville Thomas, Esq, QC; ✉ Milford Hall, Milford, Newtown, Powys SY16 3HT; 3 Verulam Buildings, Gray's Inn, London WC1R 5NT (✆ 020 7831 8441, fax 020 7831 8479, e-mail clerks@verulam.co.uk)

THOMAS, Nick; s of Douglas William Thomas (d 1979), and Mona Ellen, *née* Duckworth (d 1993); *b* 16 December 1959, Dorset; *Educ* Scarborough Boys' HS, Graham Sch Scarborough; *m* 2 March 1985, Sandra Jane, *née* Finnigan; 2 da (Verity Jane b 23 Jan 1987, Christie Jayne b 19 Dec 1991); *Career* fndr and prop Nick Thomas Entertainment Ltd 1981–85, co-fndr and jt md Pentagon Prodns & Mgmnt Ltd 1985–86, fndr and ceo Nick Thomas Enterprises Ltd 1987–93, fndr and ceo Artiste Mgmnt Gp Ltd (AMG) 1993–99, fndr and chair Qdos Entertainment Ltd 1999–; memb UK Theatre 1993–; charities vice-pres Royal Variety Charity, fundraiser Great Ormond St Hosp, memb Heroes' Welcome supporting Armed Forces; *Recreations* theatre, entertainment memorabilia, motor cars, restaurants, travel; *Clubs* Arts, Groucho, Ivy, London; *Style*— Nick Thomas, Esq; ✉ Qdos Entertainment, Qdos House, Queen Margarets Road, Scarborough, North Yorkshire YO11 2YH (e-mail nthomas@qdosentertainment.co.uk, website www.qdosentertainment.com, Twitter @QdosNick)

THOMAS, (James) Nigel; s of Charles Walter Thomas (d 1956), of Bradford, W Yorks, and Kathleen, *née* Lister; *b* 11 May 1944; *Educ* Bradford GS, St Edmund Hall Oxford (MA), Univ of Oxford Med Sch (BM BCh); *m* 1 April 1968, Gerda, da of Gustav Oelgeklaus (d 1967), of Lengerich, Westphalia; 2 da ((Julia Elizabeth) Kirsten b 22 Sept 1970, (Heide Alicia) Katrin b 28 Aug 1972), 1 s ((Charles Walter) Christian b 31 May 1978); *Career* conslt ENT specialist Groote Schuur Hosp Cape Town SA 1974–76, first asst Radcliffe Infirmary Oxford 1976–79; conslt ENT surgn: KCH London 1979, Guy's and St Thomas' Hosp; George Herbert Hunt fellowship Univ of Oxford 1978; memb Camberwell HA 1987–92; pres Osler House Club 1967–68; FRCS 1972; *Books* Mawson's Diseases of the Ear (contrib, 1988); *Recreations* rugby, squash, music; *Style*— Nigel Thomas, Esq

THOMAS, Prof Noel L'Estrange; s of Richard Gratton Thomas (d 1971), of Sale, Manchester, and Gladys L'Estrange (d 1978); *b* 5 December 1929; *Educ* Sale Co GS for Boys, Univ of Manchester (BA), Univ of Liverpool (MA), Univ of Salford (PhD); *m* 20 Feb 1954, Norma, da of Robert Brown (d 1950), of Manchester; 2 da (Katharine b 1962, Ruth b 1965); *Career* asst Das erste Bundesrealgymnasium Graz 1951–52; asst master: Holt HS for Boys Liverpool 1953–59, Canon Slade GS Bolton 1959–64; Univ of Salford Sch of Modern Languages: lectr in German 1964–73, sr lectr 1973–83, prof 1983–, chm 1984–89; visiting lectr Pädagogische Hochschule Erfurt 1993–94; dir Services for Export and Language; *Books* Modern Prose Passages for Translation into German (with G Weischedel, 1968), Modern German Prose Passages (with G Weischedel, 1972), The Narrative Works of Günter Grass – a critical interpretation (1983), Interpreting as a Language Teaching Technique (ed with Richard Towell, 1985), Grass: Die Blechtrommel (1985), Grass: Katz und Maus (1992); *Recreations* fell walking, choral singing; *Style*— Prof Noel Thomas; ✉ 4 Forest Way, Bromley Cross, Bolton, Lancashire BL7 9YE (✆ 01204 591682)

THOMAS, Patricia Eileen (Pat); OBE (2003); da of Ieuan Gwynn Thomas (d 1989), and Lovice Eileen, *née* Phillips (d 1998); *b* 3 June 1949; *Educ* St Joseph's Convent Reading, St Hugh's Coll Oxford (MA); *Career* admitted slr 1974; slr specialising in planning and environmental law; early career as planning slr with GLC and London Borough of Southwark; ptnr: Denton Hall Wilde Sapte (formerly Denton Hall & Burgin) 1982–88, SJ Berwin & Co 1988–2006; princ Pat Thomas Planning Law 2006–12; advsr ATLAS; former chm Planning and Environmental Law Ctee Law Soc, former chm Environmental Law Ctee Int Bar Assoc; memb Planning and Environmental Law Ctee Law Soc; hon solicitor and sec Royal Town Planning Inst; tstee and vice-chm Town and Country Planning Assoc; tstee: Mausolea and Monuments Tst, ACOUK, Hestercombe Gardens Tst, Hermitage River Projects; memb City of London Slrs' Co; *Books* Surveyors Factbook (contrib), Planning Factbook (ed and contrib); *Recreations* architecture, fly fishing, travel; *Style*— Miss Pat Thomas, OBE; ✉ 68 Brook Drive, London, SE11 4TS (e-mail pat@pthomasplanninglaw.com)

THOMAS, His Hon Judge Patrick Anthony; QC (1999); s of Basil Thomas (d 1965), and Marjorie, *née* Tait (d 1977); *b* 30 October 1948; *Educ* Rugby, Lincoln Coll Oxford (BA); *m* 1978, Sheila, da of Reg Jones; 2 da (Victoria b 1980, Rebecca b 1982); *Career* called to the Bar Grays Inn 1973 (bencher 2005), recorder 1992–2008, circuit judge 2008–; *Recreations* reading, theatre, walking, France; *Style*— His Hon Judge Patrick Thomas, QC; ✉ Queen Elizabeth II Law Courts, 1 Newton Street, Birmingham B4 7NA

THOMAS, Rear Adm Paul Anthony Moseley; CB (1998); s of late Glyn Pritchard Thomas, and late Mary Thomas, *née* Moseley; *b* 1944, Rhyl, Clwyd; *Educ* Haileybury and ISC; *m* 1972, Rosalyn Patricia, da of John Edgar Lee; 2 da (Briony b 1974, Charlotte b 1982), 1 s (Daniel b 1976); *Career* joined RN 1963, Asst Marine Engr Offr HMS Renown 1971–74, Desk Offr Reactor Design Section 1974–77, Sr Engr Offr HMS Revenge 1977–81, Asst Marine Engr Offr Flag Officer Submarines 1980–81, Staff Offr Shore Support 1981–82, asst dir Nuclear Safety 1982–84, Naval Supt Vulcan Naval Reactor Test Estab Dounreay 1984–87, chm Naval Nuclear Tech Safety Panel 1987–90, dir Nuclear Propulsion 1990–94, Capt RNEC Manadon 1994–95, Chief Strategic Systems Exec MOD (Procurement Exec) 1995–98, ret Rear Adm; dir Strategic Devpt AEA Technology Nuclear Engineering 2000–01, dir Environment, Health, Safety and Quality BNFL 2001–08; non-exec dir: RSSB Ltd 2005–15 (chm 2008–15), NNB Gen Co 2011–, Magnox Ltd 2013; pres The Nuclear Inst 2008–10, chm The Hazards Forum 2009, chm The Process Safety Forum 2010, hon fell Safety and Reliability Soc 2012; Queen's Commendation for Brave Conduct 1980; FREng, MCGI, FIMechE, FCGI, hon fell Nuclear Inst; Legion of Merit (US) 1998; *Recreations* cycling, ballooning, walking, anything mechanical; *Style*— Rear Adm Paul Thomas, CB, FREng; ✉ Byway, Chapel Lane Box, Corsham, Wiltshire SN13 8NU (✆ 01225 743134, mobile 07710 864762, e-mail paul.a.thomas@btconnect.com)

THOMAS, Prof Peter David Garner; s of David Thomas (d 1967), and Doris, *née* Davies (d 1965); *b* 1 May 1930; *Educ* St Bees Sch Cumberland, Univ Coll of N Wales (BA, MA), UCL (PhD); *m* 1963 (m dis 1992), Sheila; 2 s (Alan b 1963, Michael b 1965, d 1983), 1 da (Sally b 1970); *Career* lectr Univ of Glasgow 1959–65 (asst lectr 1956–59); UCW: lectr 1965–68, sr lectr 1968–71, reader 1971–75, prof 1976–97, prof emeritus 1997–; chm: Dyfed LTA 1981–2002, Aberystwyth Lib Democrats 1988–98; awarded Soc of Cincinnati Book Prize 1992, Lib Dem Harriet Smith Award 2008; FRHistS 1971; *Books* The House of Commons in the Eighteenth Century (1971), British Politics and the Stamp Act Crisis (1975), Lord North (1976), The American Revolution (1986), The Townshend Duties Crisis (1987), Tea Party to Independence (1991), Revolution in America – Britain and the Colonies 1763–76 (1992), John Wilkes: A Friend to Liberty (1996), Politics in Eighteenth Century Wales (1997), George III: King and Politicians 1760–1770 (2002); *Recreations* lawn tennis, bridge; *Clubs* Aberystwyth Tennis (pres 2010–); *Style*— Prof Peter Thomas; ✉ 16 Pen-y-Craig, Aberystwyth, Ceredigion SY23 2JA (☎ 01970 612053)

THOMAS, (Hywel) Rhodri Glyn; AM; s of Thomas Glyn Thomas (d 1973), and Eleanor, *née* Roberts; *b* 11 April 1953; *Educ* Ysgol Morgan Llwyd Wrexham; UCW Aberystwyth (BA), UCW Bangor (BD), UCW Lampeter (MTh); *m* 1975, Marian Gwenfair Thomas; 1 da (Lisa Mererid Glyn b 1982), 2 s (Deian Iorweth Glyn b 1985, Rolant Elidir Glyn b 1988); *Career* minister of religion St Clears area 1978–89 and 1992–; md Cwmni'r Gannwyll Cyf (TV prodn co) 1989–95, Welsh spokesman Forum of Private Business 1992–99, memb Nat Assembly for Wales (Plaid Cymru) Carmarthen East & Dinefwr 1999–; dir 'Sgript' Cyf 1992–, shadow spokesman for Agric and Rural Devpt 1999–2000, memb Euro Affairs Ctee 2000–, spokesman for Plaid Cymru on Sustainable Devpt 2001–, chair SW Wales Regnl Ctee 2001–02, shadow min Agric and Rural Affrs 2002–03, shadow min for Health and Social Services 2003–; Nat Assembly for Wales: chair Agric and Rural Devpt Ctee 2000, chair Culture Ctee 2000–; dep business mangr 2001–; London Marathon 1996 and 2000, memb NSPCC; *Recreations* walking, reading, watching sport; *Style*— Rhodri Glyn Thomas, AM; ✉ Talar Wen, 37 Wind Street, Ammanford, Carmarthenshire SA18 3DN (☎ 01269 597677, fax 01269 591334, e-mail rhodri.thomas@wales.gov.uk)

THOMAS, Richard James; CBE (2009); s of late Daniel Lewis Thomas, JP, of Southend-on-Sea, Essex, and late Norah Mary, *née* James; *b* 18 June 1949; *Educ* Bishop's Stortford Coll, Univ of Southampton (LLB), Coll of Law Guildford; *m* 18 May 1974, Julia Delicia Thomas, da of late Dr Edward Granville Woodchurch Clarke, MC, of Shurlock Row, Berks; 2 s (Andrew b 1977, Christopher b 1983), 1 da (Gemma b 1979); *Career* articled clerk and asst slr Freshfields 1971–74, slr CAB Legal Serv 1974–79, legal offr and head of resources gp Nat Consumer Cncl 1979–86, dir Consumer Affairs Office of Fair Trading 1986–92, dir Public Policy Clifford Chance 1992–2002, Info Cmmr 2002–09, chm Admin Justice and Tbnls Cncl 2009–13; author of reports, articles and broadcasts on a range of legal, consumer and info issues; visiting prof Univ of Northumbria 2007–13; tstee W London Fair Housing Gp 1976–79; memb: Mgmnt Ctee Gtr London CAB Serv 1977–79, Lord Chllr's Advsy Ctee on Civil Justice Review 1985–88, Mgmnt Ctee Royal Courts of Justice CAB 1992–98, Cncl Banking Ombudsman Scheme 1992–2001, Advsy Ctee Oftel 1995–99, Advtg Advsy Ctee ITC 1996–2002, Direct Mktg Authy 1997–2002, Bd Fin Ombudsman Serv 1999–2002, Cncl Consumers Assoc 2008–13 (dep chm 2009–13), Bd Whitehall and Industry Gp 2008–14, Ctee on Standards in Public Life 2012–; global stategy advsr Centre for Information Policy Leadership Hunton & Williams 2009–; Int Privacy Leadership Award Int Assoc of Privacy Professionals 2008; Hon LLD Univ of Southampton 2007; memb Law Soc; *Recreations* family, maintenance of home and garden, travel, sailing; *Style*— Richard Thomas, Esq, CBE; ✉ 36 Park Lane, Reigate, Surrey RH2 8JX

THOMAS, Rt Rev Roderick Charles Howell (Rod); *see:* Maidstone, Bishop of

THOMAS, His Honour Judge Roger; QC (2000); s of Donald Thomas (d 1980), of Halifax, Yorks, and Jessie, *née* Attwood (d 2002); *b* 18 August 1954, Halifax, Yorks; *Educ* Worksop Coll Notts, Univ of Hull, Inns of Court Sch of Law; *m* 1 Aug 1981, Vanessa, *née* Van Limburg Stirum; 1 s (George Charles b 3 Feb 1983), 2 da (Laura Jessie b 17 July 1985, Isobel Julia b 16 July 1988); *Career* called to the Bar Inner Temple 1976; practising barr and memb of chambers Broadway House Bradford 1976–2004, circuit judge (Northern and North Eastern Circuits) 2004– (Liverpool Crown Court 2004–05, Manchester Crown Court 2005–12, Bradford Crown Court 2012– (also Hon Recorder of Bradford)); memb Cncl of Circuit Judges; Parly candidate (Lib) Brighouse and Spenborough 1979; *Recreations* sport (playing and watching), cycling; *Style*— His Hon Judge Roger Thomas, QC; ✉ Bradford Crown Court, Exchange Square, Drake Street, Bradford BD1 1JA

THOMAS, Roger Geraint; OBE (1997), DL (S Glamorgan 2013); s of Geraint Phillips Thomas (d 1989), and Doreen Augusta, *née* Cooke (d 1975); *b* 22 July 1945, Cardiff; *Educ* Penarth Co Sch, Leighton Park Sch Reading, Univ of Birmingham (LLB); *m* 23 Oct 1971, Rhian Elisabeth Kenyon, da of Erith Kenyon Thomas (d 1975), of Cardigan; *Career* ptnr Eversheds (formerly Phillips & Buck slrs) 1969–2000 (conslt 2000–06), judge Provincial Court Church of Wales 2006–; memb: Ct Nat Museum of Wales 1983–2002 (memb Cncl 1985–2002, vice-pres 2000–02), Welsh Cncl CBI 1987–97, 1998–2004 and 2005–11, Cncl CBI 1991–97, Gen Advsy Cncl BBC 1992–95, Bd Wales Millenium Centre 1996–98; dep chm Business in Focus Ltd 1998–2014; vice-chm Techniquest Cardiff 1986–2010; dir Welsh National Opera Ltd 2000–10; business partnership advsr Nat Assembly for Wales 1999–2002, memb Ministerial Advsy Gp Welsh Assembly Govt Dept for Educn and Skills 2008–14, memb Welsh Assembly Govt Review of HE in Wales 2008–09; memb Cncl Univ of Cardiff 2000–02, chm and pro-chllr Univ of Glamorgan 2002–08 (govr 1994–2008, dep chm 2001–02), dir Univs and Colls Employers Assoc 2004–08, chair HE Funding Cncl for Wales 2008–14; chm Penarth Headland Link 2016–; memb Law Soc 1969–; High Sheriff South Glamorgan 2011–12; Hon DUniv Glamorgan 2008; CCMI 1996 (chm Cardiff Branch 1988–90, Branch pres 2001–03); FRSA 2000; OStJ 2003; *Recreations* hill walking and music; *Clubs* Cardiff and County, Penarth Yacht, Glamorganshire Golf; *Style*— Roger G Thomas, Esq, OBE, DL; ✉ e-mail rgt@rgtpenarth.co.uk

THOMAS, Roger Lloyd; QC (1994); s of David Eyron Thomas, CBE, of Cardiff, and Mary Lloyd James; *b* 7 February 1947; *Educ* Cathays HS Cardiff, UCW Aberystwyth (LLB); *m* 10 Aug 1974, Susan Nicola, da of Stuart Ernest Orchard; 1 s (Adam Nicholas Lloyd b 22 Nov 1978), 1 da (Kirsty Nicola Claire b 15 Jan 1981); *Career* called to the Bar Gray's Inn 1969; recorder of the Crown Court 1987–; specialises in criminal law; memb Criminal Bar Assoc; *Recreations* tennis, music, reading; *Clubs* Cardiff Lawn Tennis; *Style*— Roger Thomas, Esq, QC; ✉ 9 Park Place, Cardiff CF1 3DP (☎ 029 2038 2731, fax 029 2022 2542); 4 King's Bench Walk, Second Floor, Temple, London EC4Y 7DL (☎ 020 7822 7000, fax 0870 429 2781)

THOMAS, Simon; *b* 3 February 1960; *Educ* Plymouth Coll of Art & Design (fndn course), Ravensbourne Coll of Art & Design (BA), RCA (MA); *Career* sculptor; asst to: John Maine for Arena on S Bank London 1983–84, Philip King on Docklands Sculpture Project Canary Wharf 1984, pt/t research fell and artist in residence Physics Dept Univ of Bristol 1995, artist in residence Sch of Maths Univ of Bristol 2002–03, research into the geometric structure of soap bubble foam Dept of Mathematics Univ of Portsmouth 2005–06; Kemijarvi Int Wood Carving Symposium Kemijarvi Finnish Lapland 1987, Peterborough festival of carving 1988, lecture tour Finnish Lapland centering on Art and Soc Symposium Sarestoniemi Art Museum (for Lappish Summer Univ) 1989, 'Tir Saile' Sculpture Symposium Co Mayo 1993, Rachana Int Sculpture Symposium Lebanon 1995, Third Annual Sculpture Symposium Barichara Santander Columbia 1996, Sixth Int Sculpture Symposium Maalot Galilee Israel 1997; Madame Tussauds Award 1988, WBRL funded research project 'Order in Space' Hewlett Packard BRIMS Research Labs Bristol 1997, Morris Singer Casting Prize 1999, winner Gateway to Cornwall/New Celtic Cross competition 2000–01; *Solo Exhibitions* Albermarle Gallery London 1989, Order in Space (Hewlett Packard Research Labs Bristol) 1997–98; *Group Exhibitions* incl: Sculptors of Fame and Promise (Chichester Cathedral) 1988, New Milestones (Dorchester Co Musem) 1988, Concept 88 – Reality 89 (Univ of Essex) 1989, Dartmoor (Plymouth City Art Gallery) 1989, Trees Woods and the Green Man (Craft Cncl Gallery and tour) 1989, Art at Your Fingertips (St Mary Tradescant Museum of Garden History Lambeth) 1990, London Art Fair 1991, 20th C Art Fair (RCA) 1991, British Art Fair (RCA) 1992, Out of Italy (Eagle Gallery London) 1992, Touch (Milton Keynes Exhbn Centre) 1994, Cabinet Pieces (Jason Rhodes Gallery London) 1995, Sculptors of Fame and Promise (Beaux Arts Bath) 1998, inaugural exhbn Spike Island Studio Complex Bristol 1998; *Commissions* New Milestones (Common Ground on Coastal Walk Durdle Moor Dorset) 1985, Three Large Wood Carvings (London Wildlife Tst) 1986, Burning Bush (Louisville Kentucky USA) 1990, Belhus Pole (Essex) 1991, Dryad (Rhinefield House) 1991, two large stone carvings (Louise Steinman Von Hess Museum Penn USA) 1993, three large wood carvings for Leicester Square model farm Norfolk 1994, Hypercone (2m steel sculpture for Nat Tst Gardens Antony House Torpoint Cornwall) 1997, Hypercone 15/15/17 (highly polished 1.2m stainless steel for Hewlett Packard Research Labs Bristol) 1998, Stretching a Point (26m installation for Physics Dept Univ of Bristol) 1998, Inst of Physics Publishing Co (limited edn print) 1999, Small Words (sculpture commemorating Paul Dirac at Expolre Bristol Harbourside) 2000, Tree of Life (tribute to all POWs St Wyllow Lanteglos by Fowey Cornwall) 2002, tribute sculpture to David Green (Gardens of Bristol Sch of Maths) 2003, Spores (collaboration with City Engrg for pirvate coll of Robert Davies) 2003, Star Dust (installation Westbury on Trym Methodist Church) 2004; *Style*— Simon Thomas, Esq; ✉ website simonthomas-sculpture.com

THOMAS, Simon; AM; *b* 1964; *Educ* UCW Aberystwyth (BA), Coll of Librarianship Aberystwyth (Dip Librarianship); *m* Gwen; 1 da, 1 s; *Career* asst curator Nat Library of Wales Aberystwyth 1986–92, policy and res offr Taff-Ely BC 1992–94; Wales Cncl for Voluntary Action 1994–2000: Welsh language devpt offr, anti-poverty devpt offr, mangr Jigso; dir of policy and res Plaid Cymru Nat Exec 1995–98, memb Plaid Cymru Nat Assembly Policy Gp 1997–99, memb Plaid Cymru Policy Forum, policy co-ordinator for the Environment; press mangr (Plaid Cymru) Euro Parl campaign SE Wales 1994, campaign mangr (Plaid Cymru) Gen Election campaign Pontypridd 1997; cncllr Ceredigion CC 1999–2000; MP (Plaid Cymru) Ceredigion 2000–05 (by-election); vice-chair Parly Environment Gp; memb: Environmental Audit Ctee, All-Pty Gp on Volunteering, Parly Catering Ctee, Standards and Privileges Select Ctee; served on standing ctee: Children Leaving Care Bill, Office of Communications Bill; sec All-Pty Wales Campaign against the Poll Tax; vice-chm PRASEG (Parly Renewal Energy Gp); memb Nat Assembly for Wales (Plaid Cymru) Mid and W Wales 2011–; vice-chair: GLOBE (Global Legislators for the Environment), Ct of Govrs Nat Library of Wales, Ct Univ of Wales; fndr memb and sec Radio Ceredigion; *Publications* O'n gwirfodd/As good as our words; Plaid Cymru manifestos: Co Cncls (1992), Unitary Authorities (1995), General Election (1997); National Assembly manifesto (with Cynog Dafis, 1999); numerous articles in Welsh and English language jls; *Recreations* cycling, family life; *Style*— Simon Thomas, Esq, AM; ✉ Constituency Office, Ty Bres, Bres Road, Llanelli, Carmarthenshire SA15 1UA (☎ 01554 774393, e-mail simon.thomas@wales.gov.uk, website www.simonthomas.plaidcymru.org, Twitter @simonthomasac); National Assembly for Wales, Cardiff Bay, Cardiff CF99 1NA

THOMAS, Dr Trevor Anthony; s of Arthur William Thomas (d 1981), and Gladys Mary Gwendoline, *née* Hulin (d 1986); *b* 16 March 1939; *Educ* Bristol GS, Univ of St Andrews (MB ChB); *m* 10 July 1965, Yvonne Louise Mary, da of Percy Charles Branch (d 1946); 1 s (Jeremy Simon b 1969); *Career* sr conslt anaesthetist St Michaels Hospital 1975–2002, chm Anaesthesia Div United Bristol Hosp 1977–80 (conslt anaesthetist 1972), South Western regnl assessor in anaesthesia for Confidential Enquiries into Maternal Deaths 1978–2000, central assessor in anaesthesia to the Confidential Enquiry into Maternal Deaths 2000–02, hon clinical sr lectr Univ of Bristol 1980–, chm Hosp Med Ctee Bristol and Weston Health Dist 1988–90 (chm Med Audit Ctee 1991–94), special tstee United Bristol Hosps 1992–99, tstee and cncl of management memb St Peter's Hospice 1996–2011, med vice-chm Regnl Distinction Awards Ctee 1991–93, dep chm Part 1 Examination for Fellowship of the Royal Coll of Anaesthetists 1991–96 (examiner 1985–96), vice-chm SW Regnl Hosp Med Advsy Ctee 1991–93 (memb 1989–93), emeritus conslt United Bristol Healthcare NHS Tst 2002–; ed Anaesthesia Points West 1976–80; pres: Obstetric Anaesthetists Assoc 1996–99, Soc of Anaesthetists of the South Western Region 1996–97 (hon sec 1985–88); hon sec: Obstetric Anaesthetists Assoc 1981–84 (memb Ctee 1979–81 and 1994–96), Section of Anaesthetics RSM 1993–95 (memb Cncl 1989–96); chm Obstetric Anaesthesia and Analgesia Sub-Ctee World Fedn of Socs of Anaesthesiology 1992–96 (memb Ctee 1988–92); FFARCS 1969, FRCA 1989; *Books* Principles and Practice of Obstetric Anaesthesia and Analgesia (with A Holdcroft, 1999); chapters in: Prescribing in Pregnancy (ed Gordon M Stirrat and Linda Beeley in Clinics in Obstetrics and Gynaecology, 1986), Problems in Obstetric Anaesthesia (ed B M Morgan, 1987), Cardiopulmonary Resuscitation (ed P J F Baskett, 1989), Controversies in Obstetric Anaesthesia 1 & 2 (ed B M Morgan, 1990 and 1992), Handbook of Obstetric Analgesia and Anaesthesia (ed Graham H McMorland and Gertie F Marx, 1992), International Practice of Anaesthesia (ed C Prys-Roberts and B R Brown, 1996), Pain Relief and Anaesthesia in Obstetrics (ed Andre van Zundert and Gerard W Ostheimer, 1996), Clinical Problems in Obstetric Anaesthesia (ed Ian F Russell and Gordon Lyons, 1997), Textbook of Obstetric Anaesthesia (ed David Birnbach, Stephen Gatt and Sanjay Datta, 2000), Regional Analgesia in Obstetrics, A Millennium Update (ed Felicity Reynolds, 2000); *Recreations* Tai Chi, genealogy, swimming, music, theatre, Spain; *Style*— Dr Trevor A Thomas; ✉ 14 Cleeve Lawns, Downend, Bristol BS16 6HJ (☎ 0117 956 7620)

THOMAS, Vivian William Piers; s of John Thomas, and Leonora, *née* Digby-Smith; *b* 28 January 1958, Edgware, London; *Educ* Univ Coll Sch Hampstead, St Luke's Coll Univ of Exeter (BEd, Rugby, Football and Tennis colours), Open Univ (MA); *m* 2 Aug 1993, Rowena, *née* Mears; *Career* dir of sport Univ Coll Sch London 1987–94, Escuela Campo Alegre Caracas 1994–96, head of maths and dep head Arnold House Sch London 1997–2001, headmaster Keble Prep Sch London 2001–06, headmaster Arnold House Sch London 2006–; memb IAPS 2001; *Recreations* tennis, golf, skiing, reading, chess, 20th century history, animal welfare; *Style*— Vivian Thomas, Esq; ✉ Arnold House School, 1 Loudon Road, St John's Wood, London NW8 0LH (☎ 020 8266 4840, e-mail office@arnoldhouse.co.uk)

THOMAS, William Ernest Ghinn; s of Kenneth Dawson Thomas (d 1998), and Monica Isobel, *née* Markham (d 2011); *b* 13 February 1948, London; *Educ* Dulwich Coll, KCL (BSc), St George's Hosp Med Sch London (MB BS); *m* 30 June 1973, Grace Violet, da of Alfred Henry Samways (d 1979), of London; 3 da (Nicola b 1974, Jacqueline b 1979, Hannah b 1983), 2 s (Christopher b 1977, Benjamin b 1985); *Career* Hunterian prof RCS 1987 (Arris and Gale lectr 1982, Bernard Sunley fell 1977), tutor in surgical skills 1995–2003, Moynihan fell Assoc of Surgns 1982, conslt surgn and clinical dir Royal Hallamshire Hosp Sheffield 1986–2010, conslt surgn emeritus Sheffield Teaching Hosps

T

NHS Fndn Tst 2010–; dean Acad of Int Soc of Surgery 2011–; exec ed Current Practice in Surgery 1988–97; memb Editorial Bd: Hospital Update, Surgery; memb Ct of Examiners RCS 1992–2000, memb Intercollegiate Court of Examiners, pres Surgical Section RSM 2000; RCS: memb Cncl 2003–13, dir of int activities 2003–08, chm of educn 2003–08, vice-pres 2008–10; memb: BMA 1974, BSG 1980, SRS 1981, Assoc of Surgns 1986; memb Gideons Int 1972– (nat pres 1987–90, vice-pres 1994–96, nat pres 1996–99, int treas 2007–10, int vice-pres 2010–13, int pres 2013–16); Royal Humane Soc Award for Bravery 1974, Dr of the Year Award 1985, European Soc Prize for Surgical Res 1981, Med Mangr of the Year Award 1995; FRCS 1976, MS 1980; *Books* Preparation and Revision for the FRCS (1986), Self-assessment Exercises in Surgery (1986), Nuclear Medicine: Applications to Surgery (1988), Colour Guide to Surgical Pathology (1992), Preparation and Revision for the MRCS and AFRCS (1999 and 2004), Symptoms and Signs of Surgical Disease (2005), Investigation and Management of Surgical Disease (2010), Fundamentals of Surgery (2016); *Recreations* skiing, photography, oil painting; *Style—* William Thomas, Esq; ✉ Ash Lodge, 65 Whirlow Park Road, Whirlow, Sheffield S11 9NN (☎ 0114 262 0852, e-mail wegthomas@btinternet.com, website www.wegthomas.com)

THOMAS, Prof (Meurig) Wynn; OBE (2007); s of William John Thomas (d 1962), and Tydfil, *née* Rees (d 1983); *b* 12 September 1944; *Educ* Gowerton Boys' GS (major state scholar, prize for best arts A-Levels), UC Swansea (Coll scholar, E A Williams jr and sr prizes, major state studentship, BA); *m* 20 Sept 1975, Karen Elizabeth, da of W A Manahan; 1 da (Elin Manahan b 26 Aug 1977); *Career* UC Swansea/Swansea Univ: asst lectr 1966–69, lectr in English 1969–88, sr lectr 1988–94, prof of English 1994–, Emyr Humphreys prof of Welsh writing in English 2009–, dir Centre for Research into the English Literature and Language of Wales 1998–2008; visiting prof: Harvard Univ 1991–92 (Harvard Summer Sch 1989), Univ of Tübingen 1994–95; Obermann fell Center for Advanced Studies Univ of Iowa 1992; presenter arts progs (BBC Radio Cymru) 1985–88; chm Welsh Books Cncl 2004–, chm English Grants Ctee Welsh Books Cncl 2004–16; vice-chm: Yr Academi Gymreig (Welsh Acad, Welsh language section) 1996–97 (memb 1986–, acting chm 1997–98), Friends of Welsh Books Cncl 1996–2005; sec Univ of Wales Assoc for the Study of Welsh Writing in English 1983–96; memb: Welsh Arts Cncl and chm Literature Ctee 1985–91, Br Library Advsy Ctee for the Arts Humanities and Social Sciences 2000–02, Wales Arts Review 2006; tst memb UK Year of Literature; chm Univ of Wales Press 1998–2004; memb Bd Seren Books 1992–2003, memb Editorial Bd Walt Whitman Quarterly Review, assoc ed Welsh Writing in English: a Yearbook of Critical Essays 1995–2007; nominator The Arts Fndn 1993, adjudicator David Cohen Prize 1996–97; executor of unpublished work to late R S Thomas 2000–07; hon memb Nat Eisteddfod Gorsedd of Bards 2000; hon fell Coleg Cymraeg Cenedlaethol 2012; FBA 1996, FEA 2005, FLSW 2010 (vice-pres 2010–); *Books* Morgan Llwyd (1984), The Lunar Light of Whitman's Poetry (1987), Llyfr y Tri Aderyn (ed, 1988), A Toy Epic (ed, 1989), Emyr Humphreys (1989), R S Thomas: Y Cawr Awenydd (ed, 1990), Morgan Llwyd: ei gyfeillion a'i gyfnod (1991, Welsh Arts Cncl prize, Vernam Hull Meml prize, Ellis Griffith Meml prize), Wrenching Times: Whitman's Civil War Poetry (ed, 1991), Internal Difference: literature in twentieth-century Wales (1992), The Page's Drift: R S Thomas at Eighty (ed, 1993), Walt Whitman, Dail Glaswellt (trans, 1995), DiFfinio Dwy Lenyddiaeth Cymru (ed, 1995), Walt Whitman and the World (ed British Isles Section, 1996), Annotated Bibliography of English Studies (ed Welsh Studies Section, 1996), John Ormond (1997), Corresponding Cultures: studies in relations between the two literatures of Wales (1999), Gweld Sêr: Cymru a Chanrif America (ed, 2001), Emyr Humphreys, Conversations and Reflections (ed, 2002), Kitchener Davies (2002), Detholion o waith Kitchener Davies (co-ed, 2002), R S Thomas, Residues (ed, 2002), Welsh Writing in English (ed, 2003), Transatlantic Connections: Whitman US-UK (2005), Welsh Time (ed, 2009), In the Shadow of the Pulpit: Literature and Nonconfirmist Wales (2010), R S Thomas: Serial Obsessive (2013), The Nations of Wales, 1890–1914 (2016); also author of numerous book chapters and articles in learned jls; *Recreations* reading, music, sport (couch-potato style); *Style—* Prof M Wynn Thomas, OBE, FBA, FLSW; ✉ Department of English, Swansea University, Singleton Park, Swansea SA2 8PP (☎ 01792 295306, fax 01792 295761, e-mail m.w.thomas@swansea.ac.uk)

THOMAS OF CWMGIEDD, Baron, of Cwmgiedd in the County of Powys; Rt Hon Sir (Roger) John Laugharne Thomas; kt (1996), PC (2003); s of Roger Edward Laugharne Thomas (d 1970), of Cwmgiedd, Ystradgynlais, and Dinah Agnes, *née* Jones (d 1994); *b* 22 October 1947; *Educ* Rugby, Trinity Hall Cambridge (BA), Univ of Chicago Law Sch (JD); *m* 6 Jan 1973, Elizabeth Ann, da of Stephen James Buchanan (d 1984), of Ohio, USA; 1 s (David b 1978), 1 da (Alison b 1980); *Career* teaching asst Mayo Coll India 1965–66; called to the Bar Gray's Inn 1969 (bencher 1992); QC 1984, QC Eastern Caribbean Supreme Court 1986, recorder of the Crown Court 1987–96, judge of the High Court of Justice (Queen's Bench Div Commercial Court) 1996–2003, a presiding judge Wales & Chester Circuit 1998–2001, judge i/c Commercial Court 2002–03, a Lord Justice of Appeal 2003–13, sr presiding judge for England and Wales 2003–06, pres Queen's Bench Div 2011–13 (vice-pres 2008–11, dep head of criminal justice 2008–13), Lord Chief Justice of England and Wales 2013–; pres European Network for the Cncls of the Judiciary 2008–10; DTI inspr Mirror Group Newspapers plc 1992–2001; cwlth fell Univ of Chicago Law Sch 1969–70, faculty fell Univ of Southampton 1990, Lord Morris of Borth-y-Gest lectr Univ of Wales 2000, fell Aberstwyth Univ 2002–, fell Swansea Univ 2003–, hon fell Trinity Hall Cambridge 2004, fell Cardiff Univ 2005; Hon LLD: Univ of S Wales 2003, Univ of West of England 2007, Univ of Wales 2011, Cardiff Met Univ 2015; fell Univ of Bangor 2008–; FLSW 2015; *Publications* author of articles and papers on commercial law, devolution in Wales, the Welsh courts and the constitutional position of the judiciary; *Recreations* gardens, travel, walking; *Style—* The Rt Hon the Lord Thomas of Cwmgiedd; ✉ Royal Courts of Justice, Strand, London WC2A 2LL

THOMAS OF GRESFORD, Baron (Life Peer UK 1996), of Gresford in the County Borough of Wrexham; (Donald) Martin Thomas; OBE (1982), QC (1979); s of Hywel Thomas (d 1961), of Wrexham, and Olwen, *née* Jones; *b* 13 March 1937; *Educ* Grove Park GS Wrexham, Peterhouse Cambridge (MA, LLB); *m* 1, 22 July 1961, Nan (d 2000), da of John Kerr, of Fauldhouse, W Lothian; 1 da (Hon Claire b 15 July 1964), 3 s (Hon Andrew b 18 Oct 1965, Hon Gavin b 9 April 1969, Hon Jamie b 18 March 1975); *m* 2, 21 Oct 2005, Baroness Walmsley (Life Peer), *qv*; *Career* admitted slr 1961, lectr 1966–68; called to the Bar Gray's Inn 1967 (bencher 1989); jr counsel Wales & Chester Circuit 1968–79, recorder of the Crown Court 1976–2002, dep judge of the High Court 1985–; memb Criminal Injuries Compensation Bd 1985–93; chm Marcher Sound Ltd (ind local radio for N Wales and Chester) 1992–2000 (vice-chm 1985–92); pres: Welsh Lib Pty 1978 (chm 1969–71), Welsh Lib Dems 1993–97; Parly candidate (Lib): W Flint 1964, 1968 and 1970, Wrexham 1974, 1979, 1983 and 1987; pres: London Welsh Chorale, Sirenien Singers, Friends of Wrexham Maelor Hosp; hon fell Peterhouse Cambridge; *Recreations* rugby football, rowing, fishing, music making; *Clubs* Reform; *Style—* The Rt Hon Lord Thomas of Gresford, OBE, QC; ✉ Glasfryn, Gresford LL12 8RG (☎ 01978 852205); Goldsmith Chambers, Goldsmith Building, Temple, London EC4Y 7BL (☎ 020 7353 6802, fax 020 7583 5255, e-mail thomasm@parliament.uk)

THOMAS OF MACCLESFIELD, Baron (Life Peer UK 1997), of Prestbury in the County of Cheshire; Terence James (Terry) Thomas; CBE (1997); s of William Emrys (d 1993), of Carmarthen, Dyfed, and Mildred Evelyn Thomas (d 2000), of Ammanford, Dyfed; *b* 19 October 1937; *Educ* Queen Elizabeth 1 GS Carmarthen, Univ of Bath Sch of Mgmnt (Postgrad Dip), INSEAD (Advanced Mgmnt Prog); *m* 27 July 1963, Lynda, da of William John Stevens (d 1994); 3 s (Hon Justin b 12 July 1965, Hon Neil b 2 May 1967, Hon Brendan b 9 Jan 1969); *Career* banker; various positions rising to mangr National Provincial Bank then National Westminster Bank, seconded as research mangr then national sales mangr Joint Credit Card Co (Access) 1971–73; Co-operative Bank plc: joined as mktg mangr 1973, subsequently asst gen mangr, jt gen mangr then dir of gp devpt, md 1988–97; former pres Int Co-operative Banking Assoc, former memb Cncl Chartered Inst of Bankers (chief examiner in Mktg of Financial Servs 1983–85); visiting prof Univ of Stirling 1988–91; chm: Venture Technic (Cheshire) Ltd 1984–2000, North West Media Tst Ltd 1998–99, NW Devpt Agency 1998–2002; former chm: NW Partnership, NW Business Leadership Team Ltd, Vector Investments, East Manchester Partnership; former non-exec dir: Stanley Leisure plc, English Partnerships (Central) 1998–99, Cmmn for the New Towns 1998–99; former memb Bd of Tstees: Campaign to Promote the Univ of Salford (CAMPUS), UNICEF; author of various articles in banking and financial jls, has addressed various financial seminars and conventions on banking issues; hon fell Univ of Central Lancashire 2000; Hon DLitt Univ of Salford 1996, Hon Dr Manchester Metropolitan Univ 1998, Hon DUniv Manchester 1999, Hon DUniv UMIST 1999; Mancunian of the Year 1998; FCIB, CIMgt, FRSA 1992; *Publications* An Inclusive Community with Integrity (2008); *Style—* The Rt Hon Lord Thomas of Macclesfield, CBE; ✉ 51 Willowmead Drive, Prestbury, Cheshire SK10 4DD (☎ 01625 266594 or 01625 828092, mobile 07815 887325)

THOMAS OF SWYNNERTON, Baron (Life Peer UK 1981), of Notting Hill in Greater London; Hugh Swynnerton Thomas; s of Hugh Whitelegge Thomas, CMG (d 1960; s of Rev T W Thomas and sometime of the Colonial Serv, sec for Native Affairs in the Gold Gold Coast; chief commissioner Ashanti 1932 and UK rep to League of Nations *re* Togoland Mandate Report 1931 and 1934), and Margery Angelo Augusta, *née* Swynnerton; *b* 21 October 1931; *Educ* Sherborne, Queens' Coll Cambridge (maj scholar, MA); *m* 1962, Hon Vanessa Mary Jebb, da of 1 Baron Gladwyn (d 1996); 2 s (Hon Charles Iñigo Gladwyn b 1962, Hon (Henry) Isambard Tobias b 1964), 1 da (Hon Isabella Pandora (Mrs Georgios Varouxakis) b 1966); *Career* sits as cross-bencher in House of Lords; historian; with Foreign Office 1954–57, sec to UK Delgn to UN Disarmament Sub-Ctee 1955–56, lectr RMA Sandhurst 1957, prof of history Univ of Reading 1966–76, visiting prof Sch of Hispanic American Studies Seville 2000; chm Centre for Policy Studies 1979–91; King Juan Carlos I prof of Spanish civilisation NYU 1995–96, univ prof Boston Univ 1996; co pres Hispano-British Tertulias 1987–93; Somerset Maugham Prize 1962, Arts Cncl Prize for History (first Nat Book Awards) 1980, Rafael Calvo Serer Prize 2008, Nonino Prize 2009, Boccacio Prize 2009, Joaquin Romero Murube Prize Seville 2013; hon fell Queens' Coll Cambridge 2008; Knight Grand Cross Order of Isabel la Católica (Spain) 2001 (Cdr 1987), Order of the Aztec Eagle (Mexico) 1995, Cdr Ordre des Arts et des Lettres (France) 2008, Grand Cross Order of Alfonso el Sabio (Spain) 2014; *Publications* as Hugh Thomas: The World's Game (1957), The Spanish Civil War (1961, revised edn 1977, revised and illustrated edn Spain 1979), The Suez Affair (1967), Cuba, or the Pursuit of Freedom (1971), The Selected Writings of José Antonio Primo de Rivera (ed, 1972), Goya and the Third of May 1808 (1972), Europe, the Radical Challenge (1973), John Strachey (1973), The Cuban Revolution (1977), An Unfinished History of the World (1979, revised edn 1989, published in the US as A History of the World 1979), The Case for the Round Reading Room (1983), Havannah (novel, 1984), Armed Truce (1986), A Traveller's Companion to Madrid (1988), Klara (novel, 1988), The Conquest of Mexico (1993, US title Conquest 1994), The Slave Trade (1997), Who's Who of the Conquistadors (2000), Rivers of Gold (2003), Barreiros: Motor of Spain (2007), Letter from Asturias (2007), Beaumarchais in Seville (2007), The Golden Empire (2010), World Without End: the Spanish Empire (2014), Max Mazin, a hero of our time (2017); *Clubs* Athenaeum, Beefsteak; *Style—* The Rt Hon Lord Thomas of Swynnerton; ✉ House of Lords, London SW1A 0PW

THOMAS OF WALLISWOOD, Baroness (Life Peer UK 1994), of Dorking in the County of Surrey; Susan Petronella Thomas; OBE (1989), DL (Surrey 1996); da of John Arrow, and Ebba Fordham, *née* Roll; *b* 20 December 1935; *Educ* Univ of Oxford; *m* 1958, David Churchill Thomas, CMG, o s of late David Bernard Thomas; 1 s, 2 da; *Career* Parly candidate (Lib Dem) Mole Valley 1983 and 1987, Euro Parly candidate Surrey constituency 1994, Lib Dem frontbench spokesperson on tport 1994–2001, Lib Dem frontbench spokesperson on women 2001–06, Lib Dem frontbench spokesperson on women and equality 2007–; memb EU Sub-Ctee Law and Instns 2001–05, memb Lords EU Select Ctee 2005–07, chm EU Sub-Ctee (Social Policy and Consumer Affrs) 2005–07; former pres Women Lib Dems; Surrey CC: memb 1985–97, served on various ctees, vice-chair Cncl and chair Highways and Tport Ctee 1993–96, chair of CC 1996–97; Surrey CC rep ACC, Airports Policy Consortium and SERPLAN until 1997; former memb E Surrey Community Health Cncl, non-exec dir E Surrey Hosp and Community Healthcare Tst 1993–97, memb Surrey Probation Ctee 1997–2001, memb Surrey Probation Bd 2001–; *Recreations* gardening, reading, ballet, theatre, travel; *Style—* The Rt Hon Baroness Thomas of Walliswood, OBE, DL; ✉ Hidden House, 15 Guilden Road, Chichester, West Sussex PO19 7LA (e-mail dchurchillthomas@aol.com)

THOMAS OF WINCHESTER, Baroness (Life Peer UK 2006), of Winchester in the County of Hampshire; Celia Marjorie Thomas; MBE (1985); da of David Leslie Roberts Thomas (d 1973), of Winchester, and Marjorie, *née* Best (d 1983); *b* 14 October 1945, Winchester, Hants; *Educ* St Swithun's Sch Winchester; *Career* administrator Winchester Diocesan Bd of Finance 1964–66, fundraiser Winchester Cathedral 1966–67, administrator Pilgrims' Sch Winchester 1967–72, administrator Christ Church Cathedral Sch Oxford 1972–74, Office of Rt Hon Jeremy Thorpe MP 1975–76, head Lib Dem Whips office House of Lords 1977–2006; memb Procedure Ctee 2007–10, memb chm Delegated Powers and Regulatory Reform Ctee 2010–15, memb Select Ctee on Equality Act and Disability Ctee 2015–16; chair Keynes Forum (formerly Lib Summer Sch) 2001–, pres Winchester Lib Dems, vice-pres Lloyd George Soc; patron Winchester Churches Nightshelter, patron Avonbrook Projects Abroad, vice-pres and tstee Muscular Dystrophy Campaign, patron Thrive, patron Pinotage Youth Devpt Acad SA; *Recreations* music, gardening, theatre; *Clubs* 2 Brydges Place; *Style—* The Baroness Thomas of Winchester, MBE; ✉ House of Lords, London SW1A 0PW (☎ 020 7219 3586)

THOMAS-SYMONDS, Nick; MP; s of Jeffrey Symonds, and Pamela, *née* Thomas; *b* 26 May 1980, Panteg, Torfaen; *Educ* St Alban's RC HS Pontypool, St Edmund Hall Oxford (MA); *m* 17 June 2006, Rebecca, *née* Nelson; 2 da (Matilda b 22 July 2009, Florence b 15 April 2012); *Career* practising barr 2004–15; sec Torfaen Constituency Lab Pty 2009–15, MP (Lab) Torfaen 2015–; tutor/lectr in politics St Edmund Hall Oxford 2002–15; govr St Alban's RC HS 2007–15; FRHistS (2012); *Books* Attlee: A Life in Politics (2010), Nye: The Political Life of Aneurin Bevan (2014); *Recreations* reading, football fan; *Style—* Nick Thomas-Symonds, Esq, MP; ✉ 73 Upper Trosnant Street, Pontypool, Torfaen NP4 8AU (Twitter @NickTorfaenMP)

THOMASON, (Kenneth) Roy; OBE (1986); s of Thomas Roger Thomason (d 1989), and Constance Dora, *née* Wilcox (d 1998); *b* 14 December 1944; *Educ* Cheney Sch Oxford, Univ of London (LLB); *m* 6 Sept 1969, Christine Ann, da of William Richard Parsons (d 1985); 2 s (Richard b 1972, Edward b 1974); 2 da (Julia b 1978, Emily b 1981); *Career* admitted slr 1969, sr ptnr Horden & George Bournemouth 1979–91; MP (Cons) Bromsgrove 1992–97, Cons ldr Environment Select Ctee 1994–97; vice-chm Cons Environment Ctee 1992–97, jt chm All Pty Export Gp 1995–97; Cons Pty: constituency chm Bournemouth West 1981–82, chm Wessex Area Local Govt Advsy Ctee 1981–83, memb Nat Local Govt Advsy Ctee 1981–97 (vice-chm 1989–91), memb Nat Union Exec 1989–91; ldr Bournemouth BC 1974–82 (memb 1970–92, hon alderman 1993); Assoc of Dist Cncls: memb Cncl 1979–91, Cons gp ldr 1981–87, chm Housing and Environmental Health Ctee 1983–87, chm 1987–91; chm: Charminster Estates Ltd and other property cos 1998–, London Strategic Housing 2002–06 (dir 2001–06); fell Industry and Parly Tst; Bailiff Bromsgrove Court Leet 2012–13 (Reeve 2011–12, Ealdorman of the Court 2013–); FRSA; *Recreations* family, reading, architectural history, local church and village activities; *Style—* Roy Thomason, Esq, OBE; ✉ Charminster Estates Ltd, 120 High Northgate, Darlington DL1 1UR (☎ 01325 357040)

THOMLINSON, Nick; *Educ* Stowe Sch, Univ of Oxford (MA); *Career* md Knight Frank Kan & Baillieu (Hong Kong) 1984–86, global head Knight Frank Residential 2000–04, sr ptnr Knight Frank LLP 2004–13, ret; FRICS; *Style—* Nick Thomlinson, Esq

THOMPSELL, Nicholas Peter; s of Peter John Thompsell, and Renate, *née* Dietz; *b* 27 September 1959, Warks; *Educ* Bablake Sch, KCL (LLB), Coll of Law Chester; *m* 6 Sept 1986, Amanda Ann Bence, *née* Giddins; 2 da (Emma Ann Sophie b 13 Sept 1987, Camilla Ann Lucy b 22 Sept 1989); *Career* admitted slr 1985; slr Slaughter and May 1985–92 (trainee slr 1983–85); Field Fisher Waterhouse LLP: slr 1992–93, ptnr 1993–2009, sr ptnr 2009–; tstee London Suzuki Gp; memb: London Solicitors' Co, Rail Study Assoc, Assoc of Partnership Practitioners, Law Soc 1985; AKC; *Publications* Encyclopedia of Professional Partnerships (sub-ed), Working with Technology (contrib); *Recreations* theatre, museums; *Style—* Nicholas Thompsell, Esq; ✉ Field Fisher Waterhouse LLP, 35 Vine Street, London EC3N 2AA (☎ 020 7861 4292, e-mail nicholas.thompsell@ffw.com, website www.ffw.com)

THOMPSON, Adrian Richard; s of Harold Albert Thompson, of London, and Daphne Yvonne, *née* Shrimpton (d 1990); *b* 28 July 1954; *Educ* Wandsworth Sch, Guildhall Sch of Music & Drama; *m* 30 July 1977, Judith Mary, da of John William Panes (decd); 2 s (George Harold Gwilym b 16 Oct 1982, Samuel John b 17 June 1985); *Career* tenor; opera performances incl: title role Peter Grimes, Skuratov in The House Of The Dead (Oper Frankfurt), Canio I Pagliacci (Oper Frankfurt), Monostatos in Die Zauberflöte (ROH), Arv in Nielson's Maskarade (ROH), Valzacchi in Der Rosenkavalier (ROH), Florestan in Fidelio (WNO), Albert Gregor in The Makropoulos Case (Opera Zuid), Erik in Der Fliegende Holländer (Opera Zuid), Laca in Jenufa (Opera Zuid), the title role Janacek's The Diary of One who Disappeared (Brussels and Aix-en-Provence Festivals), Zivny in Janacek's Osud (Garsington Opera), Midas in Die Liebe Der Danae (Garsington Opera), Grigory in Boris Godunov (Brighton Festival), Bacchus in Ariadne Auf Naxos (Barbican); other performances incl: Lutoslawski's Paroles Tisées (London Sinfonietta), Janacek's Glagolitic Mass (Hallé Orch), Elgar's Dream of Gerontius (Czech Philharmonic Orch); repertoire incl: Beethoven 9th Symphony, Verdi Requiem and Mahler Das Lied von der Erde, Bach St John and St Matthew Passions; performed with: Glyndebourne Festival Opera, ENO, Scottish Opera, Opera du Rhin, Badisches Staatstheater, Karlsruhe, Oper de Stadt Köln, Staatstheater Stuttgart, Staatstheater Darmstadt, Théâtre des Champs Elysées, New Israeli Opera, Netherlands Opera, LSO, London Philharmonic, The Philharmonia, London Mozart Players, Eng Chamber Orch, BBC Symphony Orch, Northern Sinfonia, RTE Symphonia Orch; *Recreations* walking, trams, touring; *Style—* Adrian Thompson, Esq

THOMPSON, Amanda J; OBE (2012); *b* 1962, London; *m* 2004, Stephen Thompson; *Career* fndr and pres Stageworks Worldwide Prodns 1980–; Pleasure Beach Blackpool: dep md 2000–04, md 2004–; dir: Big Blue Hotel, Grand Theatre Blackpool; dir Int Assoc of Amusement Parks and Attractions; Dir of the Year Michael Elliott Tst Award 2002, Lancs Excellence in Tourism Skills Commitment to Industry Award 2007, Blackpool Tourism Special Recognition Award 2009; *Style—* Mrs Amanda Thompson, OBE; ✉ Pleasure Beach, Ocean Boulevard 525, Promenade, Blackpool, Lancashire FY4 1EZ

THOMPSON, Bruce Kevin; s of Keith Thompson, of Cheltenham, Glos, and Kathleen, *née* Reeves; *b* Bath; *Educ* Newcastle HS, New Coll Oxford; *m* 23 Oct 1993, Fabienne, *née* Goddet; 2 da (Séverine b 13 Feb 1995, Aurélie b 19 June 1997); *Career* head of classics Cheltenham Coll 1986–94, dep rector Dollar Acad 1994–2000, headmaster Strathallan Sch 2000–; schs rep Scottish Rugby Cncl, dir New Park Tst, memb HMC 2000– (memb Sports Ctee); chair Scottish Div 2010; *Recreations* indoor rowing, weight training, literature, cycling; *Clubs* Leander; *Style—* Bruce Thompson, Esq; ✉ Coventrees, Forgandenny, Perth PH2 9HP (☎ and fax 01738 815002); Strathallan School, Forgandenny, Perth PH2 9EG (☎ 01738 815000, fax 01738 815001, e-mail headmaster@strathallan.co.uk)

THOMPSON, Dr Catriona; da of John MacIntosh (d 1938), and Kate Ann, *née* Mackinnon (d 1975); *b* 29 May 1937; *Educ* Portree HS Isle of Skye, Univ of Edinburgh (MB ChB); *m* 16 July 1964, Douglas Theophilus Thompson, s of George Batchin Thompson, MBE (d 1958); 2 s (Hal b 1 Sept 1968, Andrew b 20 Jan 1975); *Career* hon lectr Dept of Anaesthetics Univ of Zimbabwe 1972–76; conslt anaesthetist: Harare Central Hosp Zimbabwe 1967–77, Parirenyatwa Gp of Hosps Harare Zimbabwe 1970–82, Ayrshire and Arran Health Bd Crosshouse Hosp 1988–2002; first nat pres Zimbabwe Assoc of Univ Women 1980–82, pres Glasgow Assoc of Women Graduates 1995–98, memb Br Fedn of Women Graduates 1986–2006, pre convener Membership Ctee Int Fedn of Univ Women 1989–92, pres Edinburgh Assoc of Women Graduates 2005–08, chm Presidents Fund Edinburgh Assoc of Univ Women 2005–08 and 2013– (tstee 2009–), first pres Scottish Fedn of Univ Women 2006–09; procedural advsr: 79 and 80 Cncls 25 Conf of Int Fedn of Univ Women Japan 1995, 81 Cncl of Int Fedn of Univ Women Geneva 1997; constitutional and procedural advsr: Int Fedn Univ Women 1999–2005, Socttish Fedn of Univ Women 2010–; co-ordinator International Relations for Br Fedn of Women Graduates 1999–2005; chm Scottish Standing Ctee 1997–98; memb: NW Regnl Pain Soc 1986–93, North British Pain Assoc 1993–; FFARCS 1970; *Recreations* golf, badminton, walking, bridge; *Style—* Dr Catriona Thompson; ✉ 101/2 Greenbank Drive, Edinburgh EH10 5GB (e-mail catrionatho@googlemail.com)

THOMPSON, Prof Christopher; s of Derek Thompson, of Lincoln, and Frances Margaret, *née* Anthony (d 2005); *b* 23 September 1952, Lincoln; *Educ* UCL (MB, BS, BSc), Inst of Psychiatry (MD, MPhil); *m* 15 May 1976, Cecilia, *née* Robertson; 3 da (Juliette b 1983, Helen b 1985, Alice b 1987); *Career* psychiatry trainee Maudsley Hosp 1978–81, res fell Wellcome Tst 1981–84, sr lectr Charing Cross Hosp 1984–88, prof Univ of Southampton 1988–2004 (head of medical sch 2000–04), CMO Priory Gp 2004–; memb: Cncl UCL, Bd Depression Alliance; RCPsych: Gold medal 1983, registrar 1993–97, vice-pres 1997–99; fndr and past pres Int Soc for Affective Disorders; author of seven books and 100 res papers in peer reviewed jls; FRCPsych 1981, Hon FRCP 1995, Hon MRCGP 1997; *Recreations* classical guitar, wine; *Style—* Prof Chris Thompson; ✉ e-mail christhompson@priorygroup.com

THOMPSON, Lt-Col Sir Christopher Peile; 6 Bt (UK 1890), of Park Gate, Guiseley, Yorks; s of Lt-Col Sir Peile Thompson, OBE, 5 Bt (d 1985), and his wife, Barbara Johnson (d 1993), da of late Horace Johnson Rampling; *b* 21 December 1944, Chester, Cheshire; *Educ* Marlborough, RMA Sandhurst, Staff Coll; *m* 1, 1969 (m dis 1997), Anna Elizabeth, da of late Maj Arthur George Callander, of Avebury, Wilts; 1 da (Alexandra Lucy (Mrs Lucy Portman) b 1973), 1 s (Peile Richard b 1975); m 2, 2001, Penelope, Viscountess Portman, *née* Allin, wid of 9 Viscount Portman (d 1999); *Heir* s, Peile Thompson; *Career* 11 Hussars (PAO), then Royal Hussars (PWO), cmmnd 1965, CO Royal Hussars 1985–87, ret 1990; private sec to HRH Prince Michael of Kent 1990–92 (equerry 1989–); dir: The Hyde Park Appeal 1991–96, Nuclear Decommissioning Ltd 1994–2000 (non-exec chm 1995–2000), Logical Security Limited 1996–98, Falcon Security Control (Overseas) Ltd 2000–04, Nuclear Decommissioning Servs Ltd 2007 (non-exec chm 2007–11, non-exec dir 2011–14); memb Standing Cncl of the Baronetage 2001–10; patron: Earth 2000 1997–2000, Tusk Tst; *Recreations* fishing, golf, reading, travel; *Clubs* Cavalry and Guards', Mill Reef (Antigua); *Style—* Sir Christopher Thompson, Bt

THOMPSON, Sir Clive Malcolm; kt (1996); *b* 4 April 1943; *Educ* Clifton, Univ of Birmingham (BSc); *Career* formerly exec Royal Dutch Shell Group, Boots Co plc and Cadbury Schweppes plc; Rentokil Initial plc (formerly Rentokil Gp plc): gp chief exec 1982–2003, non-exec chm 2003–04; non-exec dir: Caradon plc 1986–96, Wellcome plc 1993–95, Seeboard plc 1995–96, BAT Industries plc 1995–98, J Sainsbury plc 1995–2001; non-exec chm European Home Retail plc 2000–06, chm Storm Financial Ltd 2003–, chm Bars London Ltd 2003–, dep chm Strategic Equity Capital plc 2005–; memb Advsy Bd: CVC Capital Ptnrs 2003–06, SVQ (formerly SVG and GVO) Public Equity Funds 2003–; pres CBI 1998–2000 (dep pres 1997–98 and 2000–01), vice-pres CIM, dep chm Financial Reporting Cncl 1999–2001, memb Ctee on Corp Governance 1996–98; Hon DSc Univ of Birmingham 1999; *Style—* Sir Clive Thompson

THOMPSON, Damian Mark; s of Leonard Gilbert Thompson (d 1985), and Pamela Mary, *née* Benbow; *b* 24 January 1962; *Educ* Presentation Coll Reading, Mansfield Coll Oxford (MA), LSE (PhD); *Career* reporter The Reading Chronicle 1984–88; religious affairs correspondent The Daily Telegraph 1991–95, currently ed-in-chief The Catholic Herald; author of reviews and articles in: Daily Telegraph, Sunday Telegraph, The Times, The Spectator; *Books* The End of Time: Faith and Fear in the Shadow of the Millennium (1996, 1999); *Recreations* playing the piano; *Clubs* Athenaeum; *Style—* Damian Thompson, Esq; ✉ 19 Moorhouse Road, London W2 5DH (☎ 020 7229 1948)

THOMPSON, David; s of Bernard Thompson, of Castleford, W Yorks, and Violet, *née* Laidler; *b* 28 October 1944, Durham; *Educ* King's Sch Pontefract; *m* 24 Oct 1970, Glenys, da of Harry Colley, of Badsworth, W Yorks; 2 s (Anthony David b 24 Aug 1972, Richard Martin b 17 Feb 1976); *Career* John Gordon Walton CAs until 1975, conslt Buckle Barton 2007–08 (ptnr 1978–81, sr ptnr 1981–2007), conslt Montpelier Professional (Leeds) Ltd 2008–; fin dir: European Concert Orchestra Ltd 1991– (also co sec), Campbells Leisure (Bradford) Ltd 1996–2001, Claudia Media Mgmnt Ltd 2008–14, Environmental Quality Intelligence Ltd (formerly Environmental Quality Squared Ltd) 2008–, Sirius Mktg Ltd 2011–12; chm: Omnis Associates Ltd 1986–95, DT Financial Consultants Ltd 1986–, Buckle Barton Pensioneer Trustees Ltd 1988–97; dir: Wellington 1 Ltd (formerly Tong Garden Centre Ltd) 2001–, Dermatology.co.uk Ltd 2004–05, Trilogy Records Ltd 2006–11 (also co sec), Marshall Minerals Ltd 2006–15 (also co sec), Great Northern Solutions Ltd 2007–14 (also co sec), Xperience GB Ltd 2007–09, Mr Yorkshire Ltd 2007– (also co sec), Cable-Talk Communications Ltd 2007–10 (also co sec), Yorkshire Fndn 2007–11, Planet Yorkshire Ltd 2007–09, Conections Ltd 2008–, Conectivity Ltd 2008–09, Smartskill Ltd 2008–10 (also co sec), Clearpath Ltd 2008–14 (also co sec), Aquados Ltd 2011–16 (co sec 2006–07), WTJ Insurance Brokers Ltd 2011–, WTJ Hldgs Ltd 2011–, WTJ Marine Ltd 2011–, Beechholme Mgmnt Ltd 2011–, Enpac Ltd 2011–, Badsworth Estates Ltd 2013–, Berks Windwood Ltd 2013–, Olmak Future Ltd 2013–, HKU Hldgs Ltd 2013–, EastZEast Ltd 2014–15, Stockton Hldgs Ltd 2016–, Tasty Sweets & Snacks Ltd 2016–, Teaco Ltd 2016–; co sec: Anthony Thompson (Trumpet) Ltd 1998–, Goodprofit Ltd 2005–, Vision Chemicals Ltd 2005–, Jack Burton Enterprises Ltd 2006–08; Bradford City AFC Ltd: fin dir 1986–2001, vice-chm 1990–2001, hon life vice-pres 2001–; memb Advsy Bd Salvation Army (Yorks Div) 1998–; hon fell Leeds Coll of Music (govr 1998–2006, chm of govrs 2000–06), dir Leeds Professional Coll 2011; FCA 1979 (ACA 1969); *Recreations* football, most sports; *Style—* David Thompson, Esq, FCA; ✉ Stone Lea, Badsworth Court, Badsworth, Pontefract, West Yorkshire WF9 1NW (☎ 01977 645467, e-mail dt25@aol.com); Montpelier Professional (Leeds) Ltd, Sanderson House, Station Road, Horsforth, Leeds LS18 5NT (☎ 0113 258 8216, fax 0113 239 0270, mobile 07836 265365, e-mail dthompson@montpeliergroup.com); Environmental Quality Intelligence Ltd (e-mail dt@eqi-group.com, website www.eqi-group.com)

THOMPSON, David Anthony Roland; *Career* The Boots Company plc: joined 1966, fin dir Retail Div 1980–89, gp fin controller 1989–90, gp fin dir 1990–2002, jt gp md and fin dir 1997–2000, dep chief exec and fin dir 2000–02; memb Bd: Cadbury Schweppes plc 1998–2008, Nottingham Building Society 2002–14 (chm 2004–14), Reach Learning Disability Ltd 2000– (chm 2003–); FCA; *Style—* David Thompson, Esq; ✉ The Court, Back Lane, Cropwell Butler, Nottingham NG12 3AD (☎ 0115 933 4605)

THOMPSON, David George (Dave); s of John Thompson (d 1998), and Doreen, *née* Grant (d 1971); *b* 20 September 1949, Lossiemouth, Moray; *Educ* Lossiemouth HS, Inverness Coll (HNC), Dept of Trade Cert, Dip Consumer Affrs; *m* 1969, Veronica Marion, *née* McLeod; 3 da (Tracy b 1969, Sarah b 1975, Eilidh b 1978), 1 s (Christopher b 1971); *Career* trading standards offr Banff Moray and Nairn CC 1971–73, asst chief trading standards offr Ross and Cromarty CC 1973–75, chief trading standards offr Comhairle nan Eilean Siar 1975–83; Highland Cncl: dep dir of trading standards 1983–86, dir of trading standards 1986–95, dir of protective services 1995–2001; MSP (SNP): Highlands and Islands 2007–11 (Scottish Parly candidate Ross, Skye and Inverness W and list 2003, UK Parly candidate Inverness, Nairn, Badenoch and Strathspey 2005), Skye, Lochaber and Badenoch 2011–16; various posts incl constituency assoc convener SNP 1965–; various posts NALGO and UNISON 1967–92, memb MPO / GMB 1992–2008 (chm Highland branch 1994–2001, life memb GMB 2001–), memb Kinmylies Church of Scot 2006, memb An Comunn Gàidhealach, memb Inverness Credit Union, memb Cooperative Gp; memb Trading Standards Inst 1971– (vice-pres 2009–); convener Christians for Independence 2009–, tstee Nat Prayer Breakfast Scotland 2011–, memb Scottish Bible Soc 2012–; *Recreations* DIY, golf, hill walking; *Style—* Dave Thompson, Esq; ✉ website www.dauvit.scot, Twitter @davyt49

THOMPSON, David Marcus; *Educ* Univ of Cambridge; *Career* documentary prodr Open University Productions 1975, prodr Everyman and Shadowlands (winner BAFTA and Emmy awards) 1979; BBC: creator and exec prodr Screenplay series, exec prodr single drama (incl Woman in White and A Rather English Marriage), head of films and single drama 1997–2008; estab Origin Pictures (in film and TV prodn co) 2008 (prodns incl Freefall); films for cinema and TV incl: Perfect Strangers, The Lost Prince, Conspiracy, Mrs Brown, The Gathering Storm, Out of Control, Ratcatcher, Tomorrow La Scala!, Captives, Face, Billy Elliot, Dirty Pretty Things, In This World, Morvern Callar, I Capture the Castle, The Mother, Iris, The Heart of Me, Sylvia, Last Resort, The Life and Death of Peter Sellers, Code 46, The Mighty Celt, Mrs Henderson Presents, Red Dust, Millions, My Summer of Love, Stage Beauty, Sweet Sixteen, In This World, Bullet Boy, The History Boys, Red Road, Starter for 10, Miss Potter, Notes on a Scandal, Eastern Promises, The Other Boleyn Girl, The Duchess, Revolutionary Road, In the Loop, Bright Star, Fish Tank, An Education, The Men Who Stare a Goats, Creation, The Awakening, Mandela: Long Walk to Freedom; *Awards* 3 BAFTAS, Primetime Emmy, Golden Globe Awards, Int Emmy, Monte Carlo Nymphe D'Or, Prix Europa, Prix Futura, Euro Television Programme of the Year, RTS Awards, Gold Medal New York Film and TV Festival, Evening Standard Br Film Award, Banff Festival Best Drama; *Style—* David M Thompson, Esq; ✉ Origin Pictures Ltd, 23 Denmark Street, London WC2H 8NH

THOMPSON, Derek Paul; s of Stanley Moorhouse Thompson (d 1985), and Lilian, *née* Forster; *b* 31 July 1950; *Educ* Fyling Hall, Guisborough GS; *m* 1996, Julie; 2 s from previous m (Alexander McLaren b 5 June 1982, James Gordon b 5 Nov 1984), 1 da (India Elizabeth b 14 Dec 1997), 1 s (Hugo Stanley Peter b 16 July 2002); *Career* horce-racing

T

commentator and presenter; BBC Radio Sport 1972–81, ITV Sport 1981–85, Channel 4 Racing 1985–; racecourse commentator UK and Dubai Racing Club; *Recreations* tennis, golf, jogging; *Style*— Derek Thompson, Esq; ✉ Channel Four Racing, Teddington Studios, Teddington, Middlesex TW11 9NT (☎ 020 8781 2770, fax 020 8781 2762)

THOMPSON, Dame (Ila) Dianne; DBE (2015, CBE 2006); da of Ronald Wood, of Thornhill Lees, W Yorks, and Joan, *née* Pinder (d 1985); *b* 31 December 1950; *Educ* Batley Girls' GS, Manchester Poly (Univ of London external BA), Inst of Mktg (sr exec dip); *m* 9 Aug 1972 (m dis 1992), Roger Paul Thompson, s of William Thompson; 1 da (Joanna Rachel b 29 Aug 1984); *Career* product and gp product mangr Cooperative Wholesale Soc 1972–74, export and UK mktg mangr ICI Paints Div 1974–79, md Thompson Maud Jones (Advertising) Ltd 1981–86, mktg dir Sterling Roncraft 1986–88, md Sandvik Saws and Tools Ltd 1988–92, dir of mktg Woolworths plc 1992–94, mktg dir Signet Group plc (formerly Ratners) 1994–97, chief exec Camelot Gp plc 2000– (commercial ops dir 1997–1999); non-exec chair RadioCentre 2009–; non-exec dir: RAC Gp plc 2002–05, Wyevale Garden Centres 2005, Domino's Pizza 2006 10; dir London First 2008–11; sr lectr in strategic planning and marketing Manchester Poly 1979–86, sr conslt Business and Technol Centre 1985–86; pres CIM 2000–04, pres MRS 2014–; tstee Born Free 2007–12; chair Advsy Bd Aston Univ Business Sch 2008–10, chllr Manchester Met Univ 2011–; memb: Mktg Gp, Women's Advtg Club of London, Cncm ISBA 1998–2006, Cncl ASA 2001–04, Bd DTI Gp 2002–04, Press Complaints Cmmn 2003–08, President's Ctee CBI 2004–07; Veuve Clicquot Business Woman of the Year 2000, Marketer of the Year 2001, Gold Medal CMI 2006, European Women of Achievement Award for Business 2006, Yorks Woman of the Year 2007, Lifetime Achievement Award Marketing Soc 2014; Companion Inst of Mgmnt 2002; Liveryman Worshipful Co of Marketors; Hon DBA Manchester Metropolitan Univ, Hon DCL Univ of Huddersfield, Hon DLitt Middlesex Univ, Hon DLitt Westminter Univ, Hon DLitt Oxford Brookes Univ, Hon DSc Cranfield Univ, Hon DSc Aston Univ; fell Mktg Soc 2001; FCIM 2000, FRSA 2000, FCAM 2003; *Recreations* theatre, entertaining, dining out, travel, reading; *Style*— Dame Dianne Thompson, DBE; ✉ Camelot Group plc, Tolpits Lane, Watford, Hertfordshire WD18 9RN (☎ 01923 425000)

THOMPSON, Dr Dorothy Joan; da of Frank William Walbank, and Mary Woodward, *née* Fox (d 1987); *b* 31 May 1939; *Educ* Birkenhead High Sch GPDST, Girton Coll Cambridge (William Menzies exhibitioner in classics, Thérèse Montefiore and Alfred Zimmern prizes, MA, PhD), Univ of Bristol (CertEd), Br Sch of Archaeology Athens; *m* 1 (m dis 1979), Michael Hewson Crawford; m 2, 1982, John Alexander Thompson; *Career* Henry Carrington and Bentham Dumont Koe studentship Univ of Cambridge 1962–64; Girton Coll Cambridge: Eugénie Strong research fell and lectr in classics 1965–68, official fell and lectr in classics and history 1968–2006, grad tutor (arts) 1971–81 and 1995–96, sr tutor 1981–92, dir of studies in classics 1983–2006, life fell 2006–; lectr in classics Clare Coll Cambridge 1973–2006 (bye fell 2006–), Isaac Newton Tst lectr in classics Univ of Cambridge 1992–2005; visiting memb Inst for Advanced Study Princeton (Fulbright Travel award and scholarship, Volkswagenstiftung award) 1982–83; Princeton Univ: visiting prof Dept of Classics 1986, visiting sr fell Cncl of the Humanities and Old Dominion fell 1986; Josephus Daniels fell Research Triangle Fndn Nat Humanities Center NC 1993–94; major res fell Leverhulme Tst 2002–04; pres Assoc Internationale de Papyrologues 2001–07 (hon pres 2007–); memb: Classical Assoc 1961, Hellenic Soc 1963, Fondation Égyptologique Reine Elisabeth Bruxelles 1964, Roman Soc 1977, American Soc of Papyrologists; Br Cncl and Flemish Nationaal Fonds voor Wetenschappelijk Onderzoek award (jtly) 1993–94; Hon DLitt Univ of Liverpool 2013; FBA 1996; *Books* Kerkeosiris: an Egyptian village in the Ptolemaic period (1971), Studies on Ptolemaic Memphis (jtly, 1980), Memphis under the Ptolemies (1988, 2 edn 2012, James H Breasted prize American Historical Assoc 1989), Counting the People in Hellenistic Egypt (jtly, 2006), The Ptolemies, the Sea and the Nile (jtly, 2013); also author of numerous book chapters and articles in learned jls; *Recreations* reading, walking; *Style*— Dr Dorothy J Thompson, FBA; ✉ Girton College, Cambridge CB3 0JG (☎ 01223 354588, fax 01223 338896, e-mail djt17@cam.ac.uk)

THOMPSON, Emma; *b* 15 April 1959, London; *Career* actress; *Television* incl: Alfresco 1983, The Young Ones 1984, Assaulted Nuts 1985, Tutti Frutti 1987, Fortunes Of War 1987, The Winslow Boy 1988, Thompson 1988, Cheers 1992, Ellen 1997, The Song of Lunch 2010, Playhouse Presents 2012; *Films* incl: The Tall Guy 1989, Look Back in Anger 1989, Henry V 1989, Dead Again 1991, Impromptu 1991, Howards End 1992, Peter's Friends 1992, The Remains of the Day 1993, Much Ado About Nothing 1993, In the Name of the Father 1993, Junior 1994, My Father the Hero 1994, The Blue Boy 1994, Carrington 1995, Sense and Sensibility 1995, Hospital! 1997, The Winter Guest 1997, Primary Colors 1998, Judas Kiss 1998, Maybe Baby 2000, Wit 2001, Love Actually 2003, Harry Potter and the Prisoner of Azkaban 2004, Nanny McPhee 2005 (also writer), Stranger Than Fiction 2006, Harry Potter and the Order of the Phoenix 2007, Brideshead Revisited 2008, Last Chance Harvey 2008, An Education 2009, The Boat That Rocked 2009, Nanny McPhee and the Big Bang 2010 (also writer), Harry Potter and the Deathly Hallows: Part II 2011, Voyage of Time 2012, Men In Black III 2012, Brave 2012, Beautiful Creatures 2013, Saving Mr Banks 2013, Love Punch 2013, Effie Gray 2014 (also writer); *Style*— Ms Emma Thompson; ✉ Hamilton Hodell, 20 Golden Square, London W1F 9JL

THOMPSON, Estelle Margaret; *b* 8 June 1960, West Bromwich; *Educ* Sheffield City Poly (BA), RCA (MA); *m* 6 Oct 1999, Dennis de Caires; 1 da (Odile Eileen Denise de Caires); *Career* artist; pt/t lectr: St Martin's Sch of Art, Christie's Fine Art Course, Ruskin Sch of Art, RCA, Slade Sch of Fine Art; sr research fell De Montfort Univ 1995–99, prof and head Sch of Media, Arts and Design Glynd?r Univ 2001–14; *Solo Exhibitions* incl: Purdy Hicks Gallery 1989, 1991, 1993, 1996, 1998, 1999, 2001, 2003, 2006 and 2009, Purdy Hicks Gallery London touring to Winchester Gallery Winchester Sch of Art, Towner Art Gallery Eastbourne and Darlington Arts Centre 1993, Galerie Helmut Pabst Frankfurt 1996 and 1999, Abbot Hall Art Gallery Kendal 1997, Usher Gallery Lincoln 1998, Mead Gallery Warwick 1998, South Hill Park Bracknell 1998, NY Print Fair 1998, Angel Row Gallery Nottingham, The New Art Gallery Walsall 2001, Wetterling Gallery Stockholm 2004, Oriel Sycharth Gallery Wrexham 2014; *Group Exhibitions* incl: Prospects (Towner Art Gallery Eastbourne) 1993, Critics' Choice: New Br Art (Christie's London) 1993, BDO Binder Hamlyn Art Collection London 1993, Moving into View: Recent British Painting (Royal Festival Hall London touring to Darlington Arts Centre, Chapter Cardiff, Oriel Gallery Mold, Newlyn Orion Gallery Penzance, Univ of Northumbria Newcastle upon Tyne, Drumcroon Arts Centre Wigan, Harrogate Museum and Art Gallery and Victoria Art Gallery Bath) 1993–96, Castlefield Gallery 10th Anniversary (Whitworth Art Gallery Univ of Manchester) 1994, Six British Painters (Galerie Helmut Pabst Frankfurt), Cabinet Paintings (Jason Rhodes Gallery London) 1995, A Question of Scale (Winchester Gallery Arnolfini Bristol) 1995 Artists who studied with Peter de Francia (Camden Arts Centre London) 1997, Shadow of Life (Art97 London) 1997, The Printshow (Flowers Graphics and Purdy Hicks Gallery) 1997, Etchings from Hope (Sufferance Press Marlborough Graphics) 1998, New York Publishers' Fair (Brooke Alexander Edns NY) 1998, History (Ferens Art Gallery Hull, Fruitmarket Gallery Edinburgh, Cartwright Hall Bradford, Orleans House Twickenham, Towner Art Gallery Eastbourne, York City Art Gallery and Laing Art Gallery Newcastle-upon-Tyne) 1998–99, Recent Graphic Work (Purdy Hicks Gallery) 1999, Blue: borrowed and new (The New Art Gallery Walsall) 2000, Einmal Leiwand, Einwand Papier (Galerie Helmut Pabst Frankfurt) 2000, British Abstract Painting (Flowers East London, Rosenburg & Kaufman Fine Art NY) 2001, Felim Egan, Estelle Thompson (Rosenburg & Kaufman Fine Art NY) 2001, European Contemporary Artists (Jane Deering Gallery Gloucester) 2002, Ols & Co London 2002, Three from the Royal Coll of Art London (Suffolk Univ Boston) 2003, Drawing Two Hundred (The Drawing Room London) 2005, 2007 and 2009, Multiple Choice (Fermynwoods Contemporary Art Kettering) 2006, KIAF (Seoul S Korea) 2006, London Original Print Fair (Royal Acad of Arts London) 2006, Drawing Breath (Wimbledon Sch of Art London, NAS Galleries Sydney and Royal West of England Acad Bristol) 2006–07, Print Basel (Basel) 2007, Tipping Point (Purdy Hicks Gallery London) 2008, L'apres moderne (Projet Midi Brussels) 2008, Voice and Nothing More (Slade Research Centre London) 2009, Calligrams (Eagle Gallery London) 2010, Drawing 2011 Biennial Fundraiser (Drawing Room Tannery Arts London) 2011, A is not equal to A (Quare London) 2011, Maquettes (Furnished Space London) 2011, Back and Forth (B55 Gallery Budapest) 2012, Double Vision (Lion X Lamb) 2012, Abbot Hall at Fifty (Abbot Hall Art Gallery) 2012, Colour As Material Finnish Academy of Fine Arts Helsinki 2013, Rogue Project Space Manchester 2013, Head to Head (Standpoint London) 2014, Small is Beautiful XXI, Who's Afraid of Red Yellow & Blue (Flowers Gallery London) 2014, Theory & Practice of the Small Painting (Equator Art Projects Singapore) 2014, Do You Believe In Angels? (Equator Art Projects Mo Space Manila), Jerwood 20 Years (Jerwood Gallery Hastings) 2014, H-Project Space Bangkok, Transition Gallery London 2014, In Light of the Monochrome (Dye House Gallery Bradford) 2015, Kaleidoscope Eyes (Austen Forum London) 2015, Equivalence (Asa Briggs Hall London) 2015, Carbon Meets Silicon (OSG Wrexham) 2015; *Collections* Arts Cncl, Br Cncl, Br Museum, Towner Art Gallery Sussex, The Contemporary Art Soc, County NatWest, Credit Suisse First Boston, Reed International, Unilever plc, Coopers & Lybrand, De Beers Consolidated Mines Ltd, Pearl Assurance, New Hall Cambridge, Oldham Art Gallery Greater Manchester, Univ of Warwick, De Montfort Univ Leicester, Glyndwr Univ, Said Business Sch Univ of Oxford, Chelsea & Westminster Hosp, Ferens Art Gallery Hull, Deutsche Bank, Economist Gp, Reynolds Porter Chamberlain, TI Group plc, New York Public Library, Br Midland, Goldman Sachs, Pearson plc New York, The New Art Gallery Walsall; *Commissions* Quaglino's Restaurant 1989, Milton Keynes Theatre 1999, Glyndwr Univ 2008, S Bristol Community Hosp 2008–09, Orchard Park Primary Healthcare Centre Hull 2009, Creative Industries Glyndwr Univ 2010–11; *Awards* Royal Over-Seas League Travel Award 1988, Prudential awards for the arts/Arts Cncl special award 1990; *Books* Estelle Thompson (2002), Painting Today (2009); *Recreations* cinema, cricket, opera, reading, travel; *Style*— Prof Estelle Thompson; ✉ 62 Ladbroke Grove, London W11 2PB (☎ 07500 005188)

THOMPSON, Prof George Edward; OBE (2000); s of John Henry Thompson (d 1994), of Liverpool, and Elsie May, *née* Serridge (d 1983); *b* 7 March 1946; *Educ* Alsop High Sch Liverpool, Univ of Nottingham (BSc, PhD); *m* 1971, Marilyn Judith, da of Norman Lucas Wright; 1 s (James Robert b 18 Sept 1975), 1 da (Sarah Louise b 6 April 1979); *Career* postdoctoral res assoc Univ of Nottingham 1970–73, section ldr rising to princ scientist Howson-Algraphy Leeds 1973–78, UMIST (now Univ of Manchester): successively lectr, sr lectr and reader 1978–90, prof of corrosion science and engrg 1990–2015 (emeritus prof 2015–); author of over 1000 pubns in int jls and confs; Beilby Medal 1987, T P Hoar Award 1997, selected to class of fells of the Electrochemical Soc 1998, U R Evans Award 2000, Sainte-Claire Deville Medal 2001, Jim Kape Meml Medal 2001, 2002 and 2006, Cavallero Medal 2006, Corrosion Sci Award RSC 2008, Highly Cited Author 2008, Kilburn and Williams Medal of the Univ of Manchester 2009, Platinum Medal IOM3 2010; Hon DSc Victoria Univ of Manchester 1998, Dr (hc) Universidad de Santiago de Chile 2014; FIMF, FICorrST, FIMMM, FREng; *Recreations* gardening, football, travel; *Style*— Prof George Thompson, OBE; ✉ Corrosion and Protection Centre, School of Materials, University of Manchester, PO Box 88, Manchester M13 9PL (☎ 0161 306 4859, fax 0161 306 4865, e-mail george.thompson@manchester.ac.uk)

THOMPSON, Prof Gilbert Richard; s of Lt-Col Richard Louis Thompson (d 1976), and Violet Mary, *née* Harrison (d 1955); *b* 20 November 1932; *Educ* Downside, St Thomas' Hosp Med Sch (MB BS), Univ of London (MD), Imperial Coll London (DSc); *m* 14 June 1958, Sheila Jacqueline Mary, da of Melchior Deurvorst (d 1977); 2 da (Anna b 1959, Jennifer b 1977), 2 s (Mark b 1961, Philip b 1971); *Career* Lt RAMC Royal Army Med Coll Millbank 1957–58; Capt RAMC mil hosp: Accra Ghana 1959–61, Millbank 1961–63; registrar and sr registrar in med Hammersmith Hosp 1963–66, research fell Harvard Med Sch and Mass Gen Hosp Boston 1966–67, lectr in med Royal Postgrad Med Sch and conslt physician Hammersmith Hosp 1967–72, asst prof Baylor Coll of Med and Methodist Hosp Houston 1972–73, sr lectr in med Royal Postgrad Med Sch 1972–74, conslt MRC Lipid Metabolism Unit Hammersmith Hosp 1975–83, visiting prof Royal Victoria Hosp Montreal 1981–82, conslt MRC Lipoprotein Team Hammersmith Hosp 1984–98, currently emeritus prof of clinical lipidology Imperial Coll Faculty of Med Hammersmith Hosp; former chm Br Atherosclerosis Soc, former chm Br Hyperlipidaemia Assoc; FRCP 1973 (MRCP); *Books* A Handbook of Hyperlipidaemia (1989, 2 edn 1994), Coronary Risk Factors and their Detection (1992), Hammersmith Marathon (1999), Dyslipidaemia in Clinical Practice (2002, 2 edn 2006), From Bugbrooke to Brompton (2008), The Cholesterol Controversy (2008), Nobel Prizes That Changed Medicine (2012), Pioneers of Medicine Without A Nobel Prize (2014); *Recreations* hill walking, fly fishing; *Clubs* Flyfishers; *Style*— Prof Gilbert Thompson; ✉ Metabolic Medicine, Imperial College Faculty of Medicine, Hammersmith Hospital, Du Cane Road, London W12 0NN (☎ and fax 020 8994 6143, e-mail g.thompson@imperial.ac.uk)

THOMPSON, Guy Charles Wallace; s of Cdr John Lionel Wallace Thompson (d 1987), and Patricia June, *née* Etchells (d 1997); *b* 23 November 1952, Londonderry; *Educ* Sutton Valence, Univ of Newcastle upon Tyne (BA, BArch); *m* 2 Aug 1975 (m dis 2003), Gillian Edna, da of P R Brown; 1 da (Amy Charlotte b 21 Nov 1982), 1 s (Joel Henry Xavier b 31 Dec 1991); *Career* architectural asst PSA Edinburgh 1974–75, design conslt Planning Dept Tyne & Wear Cncl (Highways and Environmental Works Team Section) 1977; Norman & Dawbarn: architectural asst 1977, assoc 1983, ptnr/dir 1988–2005, md 1994–99, chief exec 1999–2005; projects incl: operating theatres RAF Hosp Ely 1978, Mil Works Force accommodation Chilwell 1984, Southwood Business Park Farnborough, Consulate and Cultural Centre Queensgate Kensington, Wembley Community Care Centre; dir Capita Norman and Dawbarn 2005–06, head of architecture housing and sustainability The Concrete Centre 2006–; ed Concrete Quarterly 2006–; RIBA: chm W Surrey Branch 1994–96, regnl lottery advsr 1996–98, chm SE Regn 1998–2000 (vice-chm 1995–97), memb Nat Cncl 1998–2004, dir RIBA Enterprises 2002–05, memb Housing Gp 2007–09; chm Construction Industry Cncl SE region 2002–03; dir The Wren Insurance Association Ltd 1990–2005; dir and vice-pres Thames Valley C of C and Industry 1995–96; pres: Guildford and Dist C of C 1995–97, Surrey C of C 1997–99; dir Surrey Business Link 1997–99, chm Surrey Economic Partnership 2006–10; govr St Nicholas C of E Infant Sch 1997–2005; memb ARCUK 1978, ARIBA 1978, Ordre des Architectes 1993–2007; *Awards* Northern Brick Fedn Design Award 1977, competition winner Hawth Centre for the Performing Arts 1986, Civic Design Award Best Office Building 1991, Downlands Prize The Church 1999, NHS Best Primary Care Premises Devpt Wembley Centre for Health and Care 2000, Downlands Prize Southfields Community Learning Centre 2001; *Publications* Concrete Quarterly; *Recreations* wine, walking, architecture; *Clubs* Reform; *Style*— Guy Thompson, Esq; ✉ The Bumpers, Seale Lane, Puttenham, Surrey GU3 1AX (☎ 01483 810696); The Concrete Centre, Gillingham House, 38–44 Gillingham Street, London SW1V 1HU (☎ 020 7963 8000)

THOMPSON, Prof (John) Jeffrey; CBE (1989); s of John Thompson (d 1968), of Southport, Lancs, and Elsie May, *née* Wright (d 2005); *b* 13 July 1938; *Educ* King George V Sch Southport, St John's Coll Cambridge (MA), Balliol Coll Oxford (MA), Hatfield Poly (PhD); *m* 6 April 1963, Kathleen Audrey, da of Francis Arthur Gough (d 1989), of Southport, Lancs; 3 da (Karen b 1965, Alison b 1966, Lynda 1971); *Career* schoolmaster Blundell's Sch 1961–65, head of chemistry Watford GS 1965–69, lectr KCL 1968–69, Shell fell UCL 1969–70, lectr and tutor Dept of Educnl Studies Univ of Oxford 1970–79, lectr in chemistry Keble Coll Oxford 1970–76, emeritus prof of educn Univ of Bath (prof of educn 1979–2005, pro-vice-chllr 1986–89); chm Examining Bd Int Bacc 1984–89, dep chm Sch Examinations and Assessment Cncl 1988–92, vice-pres and gen sec BAASc 1984–91 (chm Cncl 1991–96, vice-pres 1996–99); dir for int educn Int Bacc Organisation (IBO) 2000–02, academic dir IBO 2002–03, head of Int Bacc Research Unit 2000–05, chair Int Primary Curriculum Advsy Bd 2004–, dir United World Colls Int Bd 2006–; dep chm Examinations Appeals Bd DfEE 1999–2002, chm EAB 2002–; chm Assoc for Sci Educn 1981; memb: Cncl Wildfowl and Wetlands Tst, Royal Soc Educn Ctee, Assoc for Sci Educn, Nat Cmmn for Educn, English Nat Bd for Nursing Midwifery and Health Visiting 1993–2002; tstee Bath Royal Literary and Scientific Inst 1992–2001, chair of tstees Alliance for Int Educn 2002–08 and 2011–; Outstanding Contribution to Int Educn Award European Cncl of Int Schs 2005, Lifetime Contribution to Int Educn Award Int Schs Assoc Geneva 2006, Lifetime Achievement Award Global Education Forum Dubai 2016; Hon DLitt Univ of Hertfordshire 2000, Hon EdD Univ of Bath 2014; Freeman City of London 1992, Liveryman Worshipful Co of Goldsmiths 1992; hon memb: Assoc for Science Educn, Br Assoc for Advancement of Science (BAASc); FRSC, FRSA 1984, hon fell BAASc 2006; *Books* An Introduction to Chemical Energetics (1967), Study of Chemistry Programmes (1972), Modern Physical Chemistry (1982), A Foundation Course in Chemistry (1982), Dimensions of Science (ed, 1986), The Chemistry Dimension (1987), International Education: Principles and Practice (ed 1998), International Schools and International Education (ed, 2000), International Education in Practice (ed, 2002), Handbook of Research in International Education (ed, 2007, 2 edn 2015), International Schools: Growth and Influence (jtly, 2008), Taking the MYP Forward (ed, 2011), Taking the DP Forward (ed, 2011), Taking the IPC Forward (ed, 2012), Continuity in International Education (ed, 2013), MYP: New Directions (ed, 2016), International Schools: current issues and future prospects (ed, 2016), Sage Library of Educational Thought and Practice: International Education (3 vols, ed, 2016); *Recreations* N country art and music, collecting sugar wrappers and tongs, 4 granddaughters and 2 grandsons; *Style—* Prof Jeffrey Thompson, CBE; ✉ Department of Education, University of Bath, Claverton Down, Bath BA2 7AY

THOMPSON, Jeremy Gordon; s of Gordon Alfred Thompson, and Edna Betty, *née* Illman; *b* 23 September 1947, Kent; *Educ* Sevenoaks Sch, King's Sch Worcester; *m* 1, 1970 (m dis 1980), Nichola Wood; 2 s (James Spencer b 1971, Adam Redvers b 1972); m 2, 1986, Lynn Patricia Bowland; *Career* TV news presenter and foreign affairs correspondent; reporter: Cambridge Evening News 1967–71, BBC Radio Sheffield 1971–74, Look North (BBC TV Leeds) 1974–77; N of England corr BBC TV News 1977–82; ITN: chief sports corr 1982–86, Asia corr based in Hong Kong 1987–90, corr covering Gulf War and Yugoslavia 1990–91, Africa corr 1991–93; Sky Television: Sky News sr Africa corr 1993–95, Sky News US corr 1995–98, presenter Sky News at Five 1998–; sports stories: Olympic Games LA 1984, Seoul 1988, Atlanta 1996 and Beijing 2008, England cricket tours to Aust, W Indies, India and Pakistan, football World Cup Spain 1982, rugby World Cup South Africa 1995, numerous other sporting events; major news stories: Yorkshire Ripper hunt and trial, assassination of Indira Gandhi 1984, Bhopal tragedy India 1984, student political uprising Tiananmen Square China 1989, democracy riots in South Korea, Benazir Bhutto's first election in Pakistan, child labour scandal in India, Sri Lankan civil war, Phillipine and Fiji coups, Vietnamese pull out from Cambodia, famine in Somalia, end of apartheid and election of President Nelson Mandela in South Africa, genocide in Rwanda, civil wars in Sudan, Mozambique and Angola, O J Simpson trial, 5 US presidential elections including Barack Obama's historic election and inauguration, the Lewinsky scandal, 1999 Kosovo campaign, 9/11 terror attacks in the USA, Soham murders 2002, Iraq war 2003, Madrid train bombings, Asian tsunami 2004, death of Pope John Paul II 2005, London bombings 2005, Israel/Lebanon war 2006, the Arab Spring 2011, Lybia regime overthrow, Syria civil conflict, death of Nelson Mandela 2013, Oscar Pistorius trial South Africa 2014, Charlie Hebdo terror attack Paris (anchor for Sky) 2015; memb: NUJ, Cricket Writers Club 1982–, Rugby Writers Club 1982–, Hong Kong Foreign Correspondents Assoc; winner Outstanding Coverage of a Single Breaking News Story EMMY for report on Bisho massacre South Africa 1992 (first News EMMY won by a British network), Gold Award for Best Corr NY TV Festival 1994 and 1995, RTS News Event Award for Kosovo liberation day 1999–2000, RTS News Channel of the Year Award 2001/02, BAFTA News Award for coverage of Sept 11 attacks 2001/02, RTS News Event Award for coverage of Soham murder case 2002/03, BAFTA News Award for coverage of Soham murders 2002/03, RTS News Channel Award for coverage of Iraq War 2003, TRIC Digital/Satellite TV Personality of the Year 2004, RTS TV News Presenter of the Year 2005, Int Emmy for Pakistan: Terror's Frontline report 2010; appeared (as TV news reporter) in films: Volcano, Hearts & Minds, Incendiary, Chromophobia, St Trinian's, Shaun of the Dead, The Bourne Ultimatum, The Bourne Legacy; TV dramas incl: Spooks, The Grid; Mandela documentary Miracle Rising 2013; *Recreations* cricket, golf, swimming, walking, safaris, watching rugby and cricket, four grandchildren; *Clubs* Harlequins RFC, Surrey CCC, Hampton Court Palace Golf, Los Arqueros Golf (Spain); *Style—* Jeremy Thompson, Esq; ☎ (work) 020 7705 3000, e-mail jeremy.thompson@bskyb.com, website http://skynews.skypressoffice.co.uk/biographies/news-presenters/jeremy-thompson

THOMPSON, Jeremy Sinclair; s of late Norman Sinclair Thompson, CBE, of Burton Bradstock, Dorset, and Peggy, *née* Sivil; *b* 6 April 1954; *Educ* Durham Sch, Keble Coll Oxford (MA); *m* 12 June 1982, Lucy Jane Thompson, da of Peter Joseph Wagner (d 1983); 2 da (Victoria b 1986, Poppy b 1989), 1 s (Samuel b 1995); *Career* Peat Marwick Mitchell 1976–80, dir accounting servs Air Florida Europe Ltd 1980–82, conslt Coopers & Lybrand Associates 1982–84; md: Sinclair Thompson Associates 1985–86, Tranwood Earl & Co Ltd 1986–91; dir: Tranwood plc 1987–91, Filofax Group plc 1990–92; gp md Vaile Sinclair Ltd 1991–97, md Contessa Investments Ltd 1998–, chm Futures Training 2001–10; ACA 1980; *Recreations* rowing, sailing, flying, vintage cars; *Clubs* Leander, Royal Ocean Racing, VSCC, Bentley Drivers; *Style—* Jeremy Thompson, Esq; ✉ Milton Manor, Milton Abbas, Dorset DT11 0AZ (☎ 01258 880857, e-mail jeremysthompson@aol.com)

THOMPSON, Sir (Thomas d'Eyncourt) John; 6 Bt (UK 1806), of Hartsbourne Manor, Hertfordshire; s of Sir Lionel Tennyson Thompson, 5 Bt (d 1999); *b* 22 December 1956; *Educ* Eton, King's Coll London; *m* 2002, Tanya, da of Michael Willcocks, of Chideock, Dorset; 2 da (Arabella Grace b 22 May 2004, Sofia Ellinor b 3 May 2009), 1 s (Thomas Boulden Cameron b 31 Jan 2006); *Career* assoc Folkard & Hayward 1984–90, assoc King Sturge 1991–95, dir Weatherall Green & Smith Madrid 1995–97, dir King Sturge Madrid 1997–2006, dir Rockspring Iberia Madrid 2006–; professional associate RICS; *Clubs* East India; *Style—* Sir John Thompson, Bt; ✉ Covarrubias 3, 1D, 28010 Madrid, Spain (☎ 0034 91 4482253, fax 0034 91 4468474)

THOMPSON, John Michael Anthony; s of George Edward Thompson (d 1982), and Joan, *née* Smith (d 2010); *b* 3 February 1941, Bae Colwyn, Conwy; *Educ* William Hulme's GS Manchester, Univ of Manchester (BA, MA); *m* 24 July 1965, Alison Sara, da of Walter Bowers, of Cheadle Hulme, Gtr Manchester; 2 da (Hannah Jane b 19 March 1973, Harriet Mary b 13 Feb 1976); *Career* res asst Whitworth Art Gallery 1964–66, keeper Rutherston Collection Manchester City Art Gallery 1966–68; dir: NW Museum and Gallery Serv 1968–70, Arts and Museums Bradford 1970–75, Tyne & Wear Co Museums and Galleries 1975–86, Tyne & Wear Jt Museums Serv 1986–91; museums and heritage conslt 1991–; dir: Museums and Galleries Consultancy 1992–95, Jarrow 700AD Ltd 1993–2007; assoc dir Barker Langham Consultancy 2008–13; fndr memb and hon sec Gp of Dirs of Museums in Br Isles, pres Museums North 1990–91; advsr Assoc of Met Authorities 1983–91; chm Gosforth Adult Educn Assoc 1993–2005, tech advsr Heritage Lottery Fund 1996–2000, external verifier for Museums Trg Inst 1996–99, external verifier for QFI (Qualifications for Industry) 1999–2006, advsr UNESCO 2001–05, professional reviewer Museums Assoc 2004–, learning and access expert advsr Heritage Lottery Fund 2004–13, chair Friends of Shipley Art Gallery 2009–14; conslt Prince Research Consultants 1993–2007; memb: Standards Steering Ctee Museums Trg Inst 1990–93 (chair Curatorship Gp 1990–93), Ctee Tyne and Wear Building Preservation Tst 2008–, various ctees Newcastle Quaker Meeting; govr Gosforth HS 1993–2013; FMA 1977 (AMA 1970), MICM 1994; *Books* Manual of Curatorship, A Guide to Museum Practice (1984, new edn 1992); *Recreations* running, travel, music, visiting exhibitions, classical guitar; *Style—* John Thompson, Esq; ✉ 21 Linden Road, Gosforth, Newcastle upon Tyne NE3 4EY (☎ and fax 0191 284 2797, e-mail jma_thompson@hotmail.com)

THOMPSON, (Charles Arthur) Jonathan; s of William Arthur Lisle Thompson, of Liverpool and Anglesey, and Margaret Elizabeth; *b* 27 May 1954; *Educ* Liverpool Coll, Blackpool Coll (HND); *m* 4 Oct 1986, Caroline Jane, da of John Albert Howard; 2 da (Elizabeth Jane b 3 March 1989, Emily Louise b 25 Sept 1990); *Career* Historic House Hotels 1983–2016, ret (gen mangr Bodysgallen Hall 1983–88, dir and gen mangr Hartwell House 1989–2016, ret); currently philanthropic hospitality advsr; past memb Overseas Mktg Intelligence Ctee; chm Thames and Chilterns Div BHA; memb: Hotel Catering and Institutional Mgmnt Assoc, Restaurateurs Assoc of GB, Confrèrie des Chevalliers de Tastevin; Master Innholder 1990–; AA Red Stars 1983–, RAC Blue Ribbons 1988, Hotel of the Year Andrew Hayer's Hideaway Report 1985–87 and 1992, Welsh Tourist Bd award for services to tourism 1986–, Queen's award for export achievement 1987, Good Hotel Guide César award for outstanding restoration and first class hotel mgmnt 1988–, Good Food Guide Buckinghamshire County Restaurant of the Year 1989, Which? Hotel Guide Buckinghamshire County Hotel of the Year 1996; FIH; *Recreations* history, astronomy, British churches, linen lunches, sport; *Style—* Jonathan Thompson, Esq; ✉ Awelfor, Ffordd Llechi, Rhosneigr, Isle of Anglesey, Gwynedd LL64 5JY (☎ 01407 810289, e-mail cajt13@icloud.com)

THOMPSON, Prof Kevin (Kit); OBE (2011); Baron of Glenelg (matriculation Lord Lyon 2011); *Educ* GRSM, MA, PhD; *m* Dr Patricia A Thompson; *Career* former princ: Birmingham Conservatoire, Dartington Coll; dir Hong Kong Acad for Performing Arts 2004–12, master (dir do colegio and prof expecialmente recrutado) UC Universidade de Macau 2012–; chm EXCEL Co Ltd 2004–12; bd dir Assoc Culturelle Le French May; patron: Royal Overseas League, Royal W of England Acad 2012–; former chm: Pilot Theatre Co, York Theatre Royal 2012–; hon doctorate Univ of Plymouth 2008; Sir Winston Churchill fell 1992; FRCM, Hon FTCL, Hon FBC, FRSA, FTCL, FRSE 2012, ARMCM; Officier de l'Ordre des Arts et des Lettres 2012; *Clubs* Hong Kong; *Style—* Prof Kit Thompson, OBE; ✉ Director do Colegio, Universidade de Macau, Hengqin, Macao SAR (☎ 00 853 8822 9260, e-mail kitthompson@umac.mo, website www.mcmc.rc.umac.mo)

THOMPSON, Mark; s of Owen Edgar Thompson (d 1997), and Barbara Adele, *née* Lister (d 2014); *b* 12 April 1957; *Educ* Radley, Univ of Birmingham; *Partner* Anthony Ward, *qv* (civil partnership); *Career* set and costume designer; *Theatre* rep incl: Worcester, Exeter, Sheffield, Leeds; for Royal Manchester Exchange credits incl: Jumpers, The Country Wife, Mumbo Jumbo (also Hammersmith Lyric), The School for Scandal; for Almeida credits incl: Volpone, Betrayal, Party Time, Butterfly Kiss; for RSC credits incl: Measure for Measure, The Wizard of Oz, Much Ado About Nothing, The Comedy of Errors, Hamlet; for NT credits incl: The Wind in the Willows, The Madness of George III, Arcadia (also Haymarket West End, Lincoln Centre New York), Pericles, What the Butler Saw, The Day I Stood Still, Henry IV part 1 and 2, Once in a Lifetime, The Alchemist, The Rose Tattoo, England People Very Nice, Three Days in the Country 2015; for Royal Court credits incl: Six Degrees of Separation (also Comedy Theatre), Hysteria (also Mark Taper Forum LA), The Kitchen, WildEast, The Woman Before, Piano/Forte, Birthday 2012; other credits incl: Owners (Old Vic), Good (Brussels), The Scarlet Pimpernel (Chichester and Her Majesty's), Cabaret (Strand), The Sneeze (Aldwych), Ivanov, Much Ado About Nothing (both Strand), A Little Night Music (Piccadilly), Shadowlands (Queen's and Broadway), Joseph and the Amazing Technicolor Dreamcoat (Palladium and Canadian/Aust/USA tours), Insignificance, Company (both Donmar Warehouse and Albery), Art (Wyndhams), The Unexpected Man (RSC and NYC), Doctor Dolittle (Hammersmith Apollo), The Lady in the Van (Queen's), The Blue Room (Donmar Warehouse and New York), Mamma Mia! (Prince Edward, Broadway and Australian, US, Canadian and World tours), Blast! (Hammersmith Apollo and Broadway), Bombay Dreams (Apollo Victoria and Broadway), Twelfth Night (Donmar Warehouse and BAM, costumes only), Uncle Vanya (Donmar Warehouse and BAM, costumes only), And Then There Were None (Gielgud), Kean (Apollo), God of Carnage (Gielgud and Broadway), The Female of the Species (Vandeville), Funny Girl (Chichester), Fastest Clock in the Universe (Hampstead Theatre), Rope (Almeida), London Assurance (Nat Theatre), Charlie and the Chocolate Factory (Theatre Royal Drury Lane), A Raisin in the Sun (Broadway) 2014, Welcome Home Captain Fox (Donmar Warehouse) 2016; *Opera* credits incl: Carmen (L'Opera Comique), Falstaff (Scottish Opera), Peter Grimes (Opera North), Ariadne Auf Naxos (Salzburg), Il Viaggio A Reims (ROH), Hänsel and Gretel (Sydney Opera House), The Two Widows (ENO), Queen of Spades (Met, New York), Montag Aus Licht (costume only, La Scala, Milan), Macbeth (Met Opera), Mikado (Chicago Opera); *Ballet* Don Quixote (Royal Ballet); *Films* costumes for The Madness of King George; *Awards* for Wind in the Willows: Olivier Award 1991, Plays and Players Award 1991, Critics' Circle Award 1991; other awards incl: Olivier Award for Set Design and Costume Design for Joseph and the Amazing Technicolor Dreamcoat and The Comedy of Errors 1992, Olivier Award for Set Design for Hysteria 1994, Critics' Circle Award for The Kitchen 1995, Best Costume Design Olivier Award 2014 (for Charlie and the Chocolate Factory); *Style—* Mark Thompson

THOMPSON, Mark John Thompson; s of Duncan John Thompson Thompson (d 1986), of Preston, and Sydney Columba, *née* Corduff (d 2002); *b* 31 July 1957; *Educ* Stonyhurst (scholar), Merton Coll Oxford (postmaster, MA, Violet Vaughan Morgan English prize, ed Isis); *m* 20 Sept 1987, Jane Emilie, da of Prof Baruch Samuel Blumberg, former master Balliol Coll Oxford; 2 s, 1 da; *Career* BBC: joined as res asst trainee 1979, researcher Everyman and Nationwide 1979–80, asst prodr Nationwide 1980–82, prodr Breakfast Time 1982–84, output ed London Plus 1984–85, output ed Newsnight 1985–87, ed Nine O'Clock News 1988–90, ed Panorama 1990–92, head of Features Dept 1992–94, head of Factual Progs 1994–96, controller of BBC2 1996–98, dir of national and regnl broadcasting 1998–2000, dir of television 2000–02; chief exec Channel Four Television Corp 2002–04, DG BBC 2004–12, chief exec and pres New York Times 2012–; visiting fell Nuffield Coll Oxford 2005, hon fell Merton Coll Oxford 2006, fell Univ of Central

T

Lancs; chair Edinburgh Int TV Festival 1996; Monte Carlo TV Festival Golden Nymph Award for Panorama film Drowning in Blood 1991, RTS Home Current Affrs Award for Panorama film The Max Factor 1992; memb Advsy Bd Reuters Inst; patron Art Room; hon doctorate: Univ of Exeter, Edge Hill Univ, Univ of Salford; FRTS 1998, FRSA 2000, fell RIBA; *Recreations* walking, cooking; *Clubs* Reform; *Style—* Mark Thompson, Esq

THOMPSON, Martin William; s of John William Thompson (d 1968); *b* 8 May 1946; *Educ* Deacons Sch Peterborough, Goldsmiths' Sch of Art (DipAD); *m* 1972, Lynda Mia Minka, da of Sir John Peel; 3 s (Ansel b 7 Feb 1977, Robbie b 5 Jan 1980, Murray b 24 July 1982); *Career* photographer; asst to John S Clarke 1969–72, freelance 1972–74, carpenter and gen builder 1974–78, advtg photography 1978–; currently co-prop All Your Prey Ltd; campaigns incl: Volvo, Sainsbury's, Benson & Hedges, Sherwoods, COI; winner 4 Campaign Silver Awards; *Recreations* sailing, keeping a small flock of sheep; *Clubs* Haven Ports, Cruising Assoc; *Style—* Martin Thompson, Esq

THOMPSON, Dr (Ian) McKim; s of John William Thompson (d 1976), of Solihull, and Dr Elizabeth Maria, *née* Williams (d 1998); *b* 19 August 1938; *Educ* Epsom Coll, Univ of Birmingham (MB ChB); *m* 8 Sept 1962 (m dis 1988), Dr (Veronica) Jane, da of John Dent Richards (d 1987), of Fladbury; 2 s (David b 1966, Peter b 1969), 1 da (Suzanne b 1972); *Career* lectr in pathology Univ of Birmingham 1964–67, conslt forensic pathologist to HM Coroner City of Birmingham 1966–97, dep sec BMA 1969–96, memb GMC 1979–95, lectr Dept of Adult Educn Keele Univ 1985–2000, vice-pres BMA 1998–, pres Birmingham Med Inst 2003–10 (fell 2010), fndr memb AMEC, chm Retired Membs Forum BMA 2009–11 (vice-chm 2007–09); pres Sands Cox Soc Univ of Birmingham 2006; hon memb Collegiate Med Coll of Spain 1975, memb Royal Medical Fndn 1998–2009 (life govr 2009–), pres Russell Newbery Register 2011–; pres Dudley Canal Tst 2014–; Richard Bird Medal Inland Waterway Assoc 2008; BMA 1961 (life memb 2011), FRSM 1988–98; *Books* The Hospital Gazetteer (ed, 1972), BMA Handbook for Trainee Doctors in General Practice (ed 1985), BMA Handbook for Hospital Junior Doctors (ed, 1985); *Recreations* inland waterways, rambling; *Style—* Dr McKim Thompson; ✉ Canal Cottage, Hinksford Lane, Kingswinford DY6 0BH

THOMPSON, Michael; s of Eric Thompson, of Menston, W Yorks, and Mary, *née* Shuttleworth; *b* 18 June 1954; *Educ* Bradford GS, Trinity Coll Cambridge (MA); *Children* 2 s (Christopher, Luke), 1 da (Bethany); *Career* RAF Reservist 1973–76; Freshfields: articled clerk 1977–79, asst slr 1979–85, ptnr Corporate Tax Dept 1985–2005, conslt 2005–10; ptnr Vinson & Elkins 2010–; memb UK Oil Industry Tax Ctee; Freeman City of London Slrs' Co 1987; memb Law Soc; *Recreations* cycling, motorcycling, fell walking; *Style—* Michael Thompson, Esq; ✉ Vinson & Elkins RLLP, CityPoint, 33rd Floor, One Ropemaker Street, London EC2Y 9UE (☎ 020 7065 6000, e-mail mthompson@velaw.com)

THOMPSON, (John) Michael Strutt; s of John Thompson (d 1951), of Weald, Kent, and Donnie Agnes Beatrice, *née* Strutt (d 1979); *b* 14 December 1931; *Educ* Felsted; *m* 24 Oct 1959, Fiona Mary, da of Wing Cdr Malcolm Glassford Begg, MC (d 1969), of Alresford, Hants; 1 s (Marcus Peter Strutt b 1961), 1 da (Julia Mariette (Mrs Gallagher) b 1963); *Career* Nat Serv 2 Lt cmmnd Rifle Bde 1956–58; res sub agent RH & RW Clutton Hursley Estate Hants 1958–65, agent and sec Ernest Cook Tst Fairford Glos 1965–73, chief agent Fitzwilliam Estates Milton Park Peterborough Cambs 1974–97, sec Earl Fitzwilliam Charitable Tst 1997–2007; gen cmmr Income Tax Peterborough 1981–2006; pres: local Cons branch 1981–97, Land Agency and Agric Div RICS 1985–86; chm Landowners' Gp 1987–91; pres: Cambs CLA 1994–96, Longhorn Cattle Soc 1998–2000; FRICS 1956, FAAV 1986; *Recreations* fishing, shooting, golf; *Clubs* Farmers; *Style—* Michael Thompson, Esq; ✉ Top House, Thorpe Langton, Market Harborough, Leicestershire LE16 7TS (☎ 01858 545342)

THOMPSON, Sir Michael Warwick; kt (1991); s of Kelvin Warwick Thompson (d 1985), and Madeleine, *née* Walford; *b* 1 June 1931; *Educ* Rydal Sch, Univ of Liverpool (BSc, DSc, Oliver Lodge prizewinner); *m* 1, 1954, Sybil Noreen (d 2000), da of John Rosser Spooner (d 1959); 2 s (Andrew Warwick b 5 Dec 1957, Dr Paul Warwick Thompson, *qv*, b 9 Aug 1959); m 2, Jennifer Ann, da of C Douglas Mitchell; *Career* res scientist AERE Harwell 1953–65, prof of experimental physics Univ of Sussex 1965–80 (pro-vice-chllr 1972–78), vice-chllr UEA 1980–86, vice-chllr and princ Univ of Birmingham 1987–96 (emeritus prof of physics 1996–); tstee Barber Inst of Fine Art 1987–2007; non-exec dir: Alliance & Leicester Building Society (which became Alliance & Leicester plc) 1979–2000 (dep chm 1995–99), Cobuild Ltd 1987–96, W Midlands RHA 1990–96 (memb 1987–90, dep chm 1995–96); Inst of Physics C V Boys prizewinner 1972; memb: E Sussex Educn Ctee 1973–78, E Sussex AHA 1973–80, Physics Ctee SRC 1972–79 (sometime chm), Cncl Ctee of Vice-Chllrs and Princs 1989–93 and 1994–96, Cncl Assoc of Commonwealth Univs 1990–95, Cncl Queen Mary & Westfield Coll London 1996–2000; chm Ctee for Academic Research Collaboration Br Cncl 1988–97; tstee Bart's Med Coll 1998–2000; pres: Bodmin Decorative and Fine Arts Soc 2000–11, Fowey River Assoc 2001–07; chm Fowey Harbour Statutory Consultation Gp 2010–13; hon fell Univ of Sussex 2012; Hon LLD Univ of Birmingham 1997, Hon DSc Univ of Sussex 1998; FInstP 1964; Grosserverdienst Kreuz (German Federal Republic) 1997; *Publications* Defects and Radiation Damage in Metals (1969); author of one book, several edited works and numerous papers in sci jls; scientific interests incl radiation damage and atomic collisions in solids, nuclear power, its civil applications and energy policy; *Recreations* the Arts, sailing, fly fishing, gardening, walking; *Clubs* Athenaeum, Royal Fowey Yacht; *Style—* Sir Michael Thompson; ✉ Readymoney Cottage, 3 Tower Park, Fowey, Cornwall PL23 1JD (☎ 01726 833420)

THOMPSON, Sir Nicholas Annesley Marler; 2 Bt (UK 1963), of Reculver, Co Kent; s of Sir Richard Hilton Marler Thompson, 1 Bt (d 1999); *b* 19 March 1947; *Educ* King's Sch Canterbury, Univ of Kent at Canterbury (BA); *m* 1982, Venetia Catherine, yr da of John Horace Broke Heathcote, of Conington House, nr Peterborough; 3 s (Simon William b 1985, Charles Frederick b 1986, David Jonathan b 1990), 1 da (Emma Louise b 1991); *Heir* s, Simon Thompson; *Career* admitted slr 1973, sr lawyer CMS Cameron McKenna LLP 1997–2008; memb Westminster City Cncl 1978–86, dep Lord Mayor of Westminster 1983–84; Parly candidate (Cons) Newham South 1983; memb: Exec Ctee Standing Cncl of the Baronetage 2003–12 and 2014– (chm 2016–), Political Ctee Carlton Club 2008–, Ctee United and Cecil Club 2008–; *Recreations* foreign travel, walking, theatre, reading, cycling, visiting historic houses and gardens, museums and galleries; *Clubs* Carlton (memb Gen Ctee 2011–14 and 2015–); *Style—* Sir Nicholas Thompson, Bt

THOMPSON, Owen; MP; *b* Glasgow; *Educ* Edinburgh Napier Univ (BA); *Career* MP (SNP) Midlothian 2015–; *Style—* Owen Thompson, MP; ✉ House of Commons, London SW1A 0AA

THOMPSON, Paul; *see:* Warwick Thompson, Dr Paul

THOMPSON, Sir Paul Anthony; 2 Bt (UK 1963), of Walton-on-the-Hill, City of Liverpool; s of Sir Kenneth Pugh Thompson, 1 Bt (d 1984), MP (Cons) for Walton Liverpool 1950–64, Asst PMG 1957–59, and Nanne, Lady Thompson, JP (d 1994), *née* Broome; *b* 6 October 1939; *m* 1971, Pauline Dorothy, da of Robert Orrell Spencer, of Tippett House, Smithills, Bolton, Lancs; 2 s (Richard, David), 2 da (Karena, Nicola); *Heir* s, Richard Thompson; *Career* co dir; *Style—* Sir Paul Thompson, Bt; ✉ Woodlands Farmhouse, Ruff Lane, Ormskirk, Lancashire L39 4UL

THOMPSON, Paul Hungerford; s of Dr A H Thompson (d 1974), and B D Thompson (d 1972); *b* 26 March 1954, London; *m* 1979, Jacqueline; 2 s; *Career* ptnr Bircham Dyson Bell (and predecessor firms) 1982–; *Books* Parliaments and Assemblies of the United Kingdom (1999); *Style—* Paul Thompson, Esq; ✉ Bircham Dyson Bell, 50 Broadway, London SW1H 0DY (☎ 020 7783 3438, fax 020 7233 1351, e-mail paulthompson@bdb-law.co.uk)

THOMPSON, Prof Paul Richard; *b* 1935; *Educ* Bishop's Stortford Coll, CCC Oxford, The Queen's Coll Oxford (MA, DPhil); *m* 1, Thea, *née* Vigne; 1 s (Stephen), 1 da (Sarah); m 2, Natasha Burchardt; 1 da (Esther); m 3, Elaine Bauer; *Career* jr research fell The Queen's Coll Oxford 1961–64; Univ of Essex: lectr in sociology 1964–69, sr lectr 1969–71, reader 1971–88, research prof of social history 1988–2008, currently emeritus prof of sociology; sr research fell Nuffield Coll Oxford 1968–89, visiting prof of art history Johns Hopkins Univ 1972, Hoffman Wood prof of architecture Univ of Leeds 1977–78, Benjamin Meaker prof Univ of Bristol 1987; dir: Nat Life Story Collection 1987–96, Qualidata 1994–2001; sr research fell Inst of Community Studies 2002–; ed: Victorian Soc Conf Reports 1965–67, Oral History 1970–, Life Stories 1985–89, Int Yearbook of Oral History and Life Stories 1992–96, Memory and Narrative 1996–2002; Hon DLitt Univ of Aberdeen, Univ of Sussex, Univ of Essex; *Books* History of English Architecture (jtly, 1965, 2 edn 1979), The Work of William Morris (1967, new edns 1977 and 1991), Socialists Liberal and Labour: The Struggle for London 1880–1914 (1967), William Butterfield (1971), The Edwardians: The Remaking of British Society (1975, new edn 1992), Living the Fishing (1983), The Voice of the Past: Oral History (3 edn, 2000), I Don't Feel Old (1990), The Myths We Live By (jtly, 1990), The Nineties: Personal Recollections of the 20th Century (1993), Listening for a Change: Oral Testimony and Development (jtly, 1993), Between Generations: Family Models, Myths and Memories (jtly, 1993), City Lives (with Cathy Courtney, 1996), Pathways to Social Class (jtly, 1997), Growing Up in Step Families (jtly, 1997), Narrative and Genre (jtly, 1998), On Living through Soviet Russia (jtly, 2004), Sea-change: Wivenhoe Remembered (2006), Jamaican Hands Across the Atlantic (with Elaine Bauer, 2006); *Recreations* cycling, drawing, music, friendship, travel; *Style—* Prof Paul Thompson; ✉ 154 Clark Street, London E1 3HD (☎ 020 7790 9556, e-mail paulth_wivenhoe@yahoo.co.uk)

THOMPSON, Peter John Stuart (Nimble); s of late Douglas Stuart Thompson, and Irene Agnes, *née* Laird, OBE; *b* 28 September 1946; *Educ* Rossall Sch, Univ of Leeds (LLB); *m* 18 July 1970, Morven Mary, da of late Guy Hanscomb; 2 s (Angus Iain Stuart b 1973 d 1988, Archibald Fergus Stuart b 1992), 1 da (Siona Catherine Stuart b 1975); *Career* admitted slr 1971; Eversheds: ptnr 1973–99, managing ptnr 1989–94, sr ptnr Leeds and Manchester 1994–99, dep chm 1995–98; chm: N G Bailey Gp Ltd 2000–13, TEP Electrical Distributors Ltd; non-exec dir: S Lyles plc 1994–99, Rushbond plc, Skipton Building Soc (dep chm 2013–16) and other companies; chm of govrs Leeds Metropolitan Univ 2000–06, govr Giggleswick Sch 1999–16 (vice-chm 2001–07); chm of tstees EUREKA! museum for children 2003–07, tstee Yorkshire Children's Hosp Fund until 2010; chm IoD Yorkshire Region 2005–09, non-exec dir IoD 2008– (dep chm 2012–); former chm: Royal Armouries Business Partnership, CIArb NE Branch; memb Law Soc; Hon Dr of Laws Leeds Met Univ; MCIArb, FInstD; *Recreations* fishing, walking and talking; *Clubs* RAC; *Style—* Nimble Thompson, Esq; ✉ The Grange, Kirkby Malzeard, Ripon, North Yorkshire HG4 3RY (☎ 01765 658398, e-mail nimble@nimble.entadsl.com)

THOMPSON, Phil; *Career* Auberge du Lac Welwyn: joined 2002, exec chef 2005– (Michelin star 2009–); *Style—* Phil Thompson, Esq

THOMPSON, Rhodri; QC (2002); s of Ralph Thompson (d 1989), and Dilys, *née* Hughes; *b* 5 May 1960, Farnborough, Kent; *Educ* Eastbourne Coll, UC Oxford (MA, BPhil), City Univ (Dip Law); *m* 5 Aug 1989, Paula, *née* Donaghy; 2 da (Oonagh b 17 Oct 1993, Fionnuala b 27 Nov 1999), 1 s (Patrick b 24 Oct 1995); *Career* called to the Bar Middle Temple 1989; practising barr, memb Monckton Chambers 1990–2000, memb Matrix 2000– (chair Mgmnt Ctee 2004–06); jt chair Jt Working Party Bars and Law Societies of the UK; memb: Bar European Gp, UK Assoc for European Law; Single Market for Pharmaceuticals (1994), EC Law of Competition (contrib, 4–7 edns); *Recreations* music, tennis, golf, walking; *Style—* Rhodri Thompson, Esq, QC; ✉ Matrix, Griffin Building, Gray's Inn, London WC1R 5LN (☎ 020 7611 9316, fax 020 7404 3448, e-mail rhodrithompson@matrixlaw.co.uk)

THOMPSON, Richard Henry; s of Lt-Col Richard Louis Thompson (d 1976), and Violet Mary, *née* Harrison (d 1955); *b* 6 August 1936, London; *Educ* Downside, St Catharine's Coll Cambridge (county major scholarship, MA); *m* 14 July 1962, Cynthia Joan, da of Col Nicholas Hurst, MC; 2 da (Emma Catharine b 16 April 1963, Lucinda Mary b 20 Aug 1966); *Career* Nat Serv cmmnd RE 1954–56; qualified with Sir Alexander Gibb & Partners 1959–63, exec dir P E Consulting Group Ltd 1964–75, chief exec New Court & Partners Ltd 1976–77; co-fndr and chm: Thompson Clive & Partners Ltd 1978–, Pantheon Hldgs 1988–96, Solon Ventures Ltd 2005–; CEng, MICE 1963, FIMC 1975; *Publications* Real Venture Capital – Building International Businesses (2008); *Recreations* literature, music, fishing, tennis, golf; *Clubs* Brooks's, Hawks' (Cambridge), Lansdowne, Queen's; *Style—* Richard Thompson, Esq; ✉ Solon Ventures Ltd, 24 Old Bond Street, London W1S 4AW (☎ 020 7535 4910, fax 020 7493 9172)

THOMPSON, Sir Richard Paul Hepworth; KCVO (2003); s of Stanley Henry Thompson (d 1966), and Winifred Lillian Collier (d 2002); *b* 14 April 1940; *Educ* Epsom Coll, Univ of Oxford (MA, DM), St Thomas's Hosp Med Sch; *m* 1974, Eleanor Mary, da of Timothy Noel Joseph Hughes (d 1979); *Career* conslt physician: St Thomas' Hosp 1972–2005, King Edward VII Hosp for Offrs 1982–2005; physician: to the Royal Household 1982–93, to HM The Queen 1993–2005; examiner: in med Soc of Apothecaries 1976–80, Faculty of Dental Surgery RCS 1980–87; govr Guy's Hosp Med Sch 1980–82; memb: Mgmnt Ctee Inst of Psychiatry 1981–95, Mgmnt Ctee King Edward VII's Fund for London 1985–89 and 1992–96, Cncl Royal Med Fndn of Epsom Coll 2003–10; vice-chm Cncl Br Heart Fndn 2001–06, pres RCP 2010–14 (treas 2003–10); tstee: Thrive 2001–10 (patron 2010–), Henry Smith Charity 2007–14; patron The Grange; hon fell Worcester Coll Oxford 2008; Liveryman Worshipful Soc of Apothecaries; FRCP; *Publications* An Introduction to Physical Signs (1980), Lecture Notes on the Liver (1985), chapters and pubns in scientific jls; *Recreations* gardening; *Clubs* RSM, Hurlingham, Queen's; *Style—* Sir Richard Thompson, KCVO; ✉ 36 Dealtry Road, London SW15 6NL (☎ 020 8789 3839, e-mail richard@rpht.co.uk)

THOMPSON, Richard William; s of Eric Thompson, and Barbara, *née* Ballentyne; *b* 25 October 1966, Sutton, Surrey; *Educ* Cheam HS; *m* 4 Nov 2005, Danielle, *née* Hayward; 2 da (Holly Rose b 6 Feb 2007, Chloe May b 14 July 2011), 1 s (Luke William b 12 Nov 2008); *Career* sales mangr Copyright Computer Supplies 1982–86, fndr and chm First Stop Computer Gp 1986–96, fndr and chm EMS Ltd 1995–2003 (chief operating offr following sale to Mosaic Gp plc), fndr and chm M&C Saatchi Merlin Ltd 2003–; chm: MAMA Gp plc 2013–15, TwoFour Gp 2013–, Surrey CCC, Kennington Oval Ltd, Oval Event Ltd; non-exec dir English Cricket Bd; chm Debrett's People of Today; NatWest Bank Young Entrepreneur Award 1990, IBM Dealer of the Year 1994, Mktg Agency of the Year 1998; FInstSMM 1988; *Recreations* cricket, cycling, golf; *Clubs* RAC, Soho House (memb Ctee), Ivy, Arts, Mark's; *Style—* Richard Thompson, Esq; ✉ M&C Saatchi Merlin Ltd, 36 Golden Square, London W1F 9EE (☎ 020 7259 1460, e-mail richard.thompson@mcsaatchimerlin.com, website www.mcsaatchimerlin.com)

THOMPSON, Robert; s of Peter J F Thompson-Smith, and Carol, *née* Rymer; *b* 24 May 1982, Bedford; *Educ* Sharnbrook Upper Sch, Thames Valley Univ (Student of the Year); *m* Diana Claire, *née* Gould; *Career* chef; Chimneys Restaurant Bawtry S Yorks, Winteringham Fields Lincs 2001–07, Waldo's Restaurant Cliveden House Hotel Taplow

2007–08, chef patron Robert Thompson at The Hambrough IOW 2008–13 (featured in Top 10 Chef-owned Hotels in the World The Times Top 50 Things To Do in the World), The Pond Café Isle of Wight (7/10 Good Food Guide 2009 (37th in country)); Craft Guild Young Chef of the Year 2004, Acorn Award 2006, Michelin Star 2006–, 3 AA Rosettes; *Recreations* fishing, eating out; *Style*— Robert Thompson, Esq

THOMPSON, (Peter) Robin; s of Robert Leslie Thompson (d 1967), of Bristol, and Ellen Mabel, *née* Gibbons (d 1966); *b* 30 September 1941; *Educ* Farmor's Sch, Hinckley Sch; *m* 27 March 1965, Pauline Ann, da of Frederick Box; 2 s (Julian Guy b 25 July 1967, Dominic Giles b 23 Jan 1971); *Career* chief reporter Wiltshire and Gloucestershire Standard 1963 (joined 1958), sr journalist Bristol Evening Post 1967–73 (acted as corr for most nat media, subsequently specialised in Glos region), first PR offr Reading BC 1973–78 (work incl promotion of the Hexagon Centre), PR mangr to six cos under Vickers Ltd 1978–80, sr practitioner design consultancy 1980–81, founding ptnr Contact Marketing Services (now Earl & Thompson Marketing Ltd) 1981 (chm and jt md until 1996), dep chm The Marketing Services Group plc 1996–97, md Thompson and Wilson Communications 1997, currently mktg conslt; formerly memb SW Regnl Cncl CBI, chm Glos Prince's Tst (presented with commemorative certificate by HRH The Prince of Wales in appreciation of work for the Prince's Tst and volunteers), chm Glos Crimestoppers 1995, dir Business Link Advsy Bd, Pied Piper Appeal for Children's Hosps (children's room named Robin Thompson Room in new Pied Piper funded children's hosp), Cirencester AFC, Rotary co-ordinator Glos Emergencies Steering Gp 2008, memb Police Panel 2009, chm Cirencester Neighbourhood Panel 2010, chm Oak and Furrows Wildlife Rescue Centre 2016; Glos business ambass 2013; CIPR 1979, memb PRCA 1989; *Recreations* theatre, travel, sport, my work, Corinium Probus Club, my family and friends, cinema, music, reading, walking; *Clubs* Nailsworth Rotary; *Style*— Robin Thompson, Esq; ✉ 8 Morestall Drive, Cirencester, Gloucestershire GL7 1TF (☎ 01285 641573, mobile 07966 495908, e-mail robin@pollybox.co.uk)

THOMPSON, Simon Robert; s of Robert Sydney Thompson, and Patricia Thompson; *b* 16 June 1959; *Educ* Manchester Grammar, University Coll Oxford (MA); *m* 5 April 1986, Anne Fiona, *née* Graham-Bryce; *Career* Lloyds Bank International 1981–85, NM Rothschild & Sons Ltd 1985–94, dir SG Warburg & Co Ltd 1994–95, Minorco SA 1995–99; Anglo American plc: ceo Zinc 1999–2001, ceo Base Matals 2003–04, chm Exploration 2003–07, chm Tarmac 2004–07, exec dir 2005–07; non-exec dir: AngloGold Ashanti Ltd 2004–07, UC Rusal 2007–, Sandvik AB 2008–, Newmont Mining Corporation 2008–, Amec plc 2009; *Recreations* mountaineering; *Clubs* Athenaeum, Alpine Club; *Style*— Simon Thompson, Esq

THOMPSON, Sophie; da of Eric Norman Thompson, and Phyllida Law; *Educ* Camden Sch for Girls, Bristol Old Vic Theatre Sch; *Career* actress; *Theatre* Bristol Old Vic: Perdita in The Winter's Tale, Dulgrett and Ange in Top Girls, Chorus in The Bacchae, Violet in The Merry Gentlemen, Lavinia in Androcles and the Lion, In Times Like These, The Fourth of July; Renaissance Theatre Co: Margaret in Much Ado About Nothing, Celia in As You Like It, Ophelia in Hamlet; RSC: Rosalind in As You Like It, Helena in All's Well That Ends Well, Marcie Banks in Wildest Dreams; other credits incl: The Daughter in The Real Thing (Strand Theatre London), Lika in The Promise (Latchmere Theatre London), Dog in The Garden Girls (Bush Theatre London), Rita in A Prayer for Wings, The Daughter in Laburnum Grove (Palace Theatre Watford), The Maid in A Month in the Country (Cambridge Theatre Co), Laurel in The Chalk Garden (Chichester Festival Theatre), Juliet in Romeo and Juliet (NT Studio), Amy in Company (Albery Theatre London), Baker's Wife in Into the Woods (Donmar Warehouse London), A Period of Adjustment (Palace Theatre Watford), The Schoolmistress (Royal Exchange Theatre Manchester), A Midsummer Night's Dream (NT Studio), Tess in The Female of the Species (West End), Bev/Kathy in Clybourne Park (Royal Ct and West End), Mrs Hardcastle in She Stoops to Conquer (NT); *Television* BBC: Clare in Nelson's Column, Gillian Player in A Message to Posterity, A Traveller in Time, The Crucible; other credits incl: Aggie in The Master Blackmailer (Granada), Val in The Complete Guide to Relationships (Kudos Prodns/Carlton), Secret Orchards (Granada), Blind Men (LWT), Mrs Perks in The Railway Children (Carlton), Stella in Eastenders, A Room with a View, A Harlot's Progess, Penny in Love Life (ITV), Inside Number Nine (BBC), The Day We Sang (BBC), Celebrity Masterchef (Shine TV) 2014; *Film* credits incl: Mission Girl in The Missionary, Francesca in 21, Lydia in Four Weddings and a Funeral, Mary Musgrave in Persuasion, Miss Bates in Emma, Rose in Dancing at Lughnasa, Moxie in Relative Values, Dorothy in Gosford Park; *Awards* Clarence Derwent Award 1996 (for Company), Best Actress in a Musical Olivier Awards 1999 (for Into the Woods); nominated: Best Supporting Actress Olivier Awards 1994 (for Wildest Dreams), Best Supporting Actress in a Musical Olivier Awards 1996 (for Company), Best Supporting Actress London Film Critics' Circle Awards 2001 (for Relative Values), Best Bitch Inside Soap Awards 2007 (for Eastenders), Best Actress Olivier Awards 2011 (for Clybourne Park); *Style*— Ms Sophie Thompson; ✉ c/o Independent (☎ 020 7636 6565)

THOMPSON, Steven; QC (2015); *Career* called to the Bar 1996; *Style*— Steven Thompson, Esq, QC; ✉ XXIV Old Buildings, Lincoln's Inn, London WC2A 3UP

THOMPSON, Suki Frances Allison; da of Barry Bunker, of Wales, and Alison Harris, *née* Hayman; *b* 7 March 1967, Wimbledon, London; *Educ* Truro HS, St Austell Coll, Univ of Leeds (BA), Kingston Business Sch; *Children* 2 c (Jazmyn b 14 Jan 1998, Sam b 13 Oct 1999); *Career* various communications and advtg agencies incl TBWA, FCA and Rapp Collins 1991–95, md Kendall Tarrant Hong Kong 1996–97; md and fndr: Club Spirit (Bunker Gin) 1998–2000, Haystack Gp 2001–08, Dystercatchers 2009; bd chm Mktg Soc; memb Women in Advtg and Communications London (WACL); *Recreations* triathlons, theatre, cooking, shopping, my children; *Style*— Mrs Suki Thompson; ✉ 3rd Floor, Berkshire House, 168–173 High Holborn, London WC1V 7AA

THOMSON, Sir Adam McClure; KCMG (2014, CMG 2009); s of Sir John Thomson, GCMG, and Elizabeth, *née* McClure (d 1988); *Educ* Trinity Coll Cambridge (MA), Harvard Univ (MPP); *m* 1984, Fariba, *née* Shirazi; *Career* FCO: joined 1978, postings in London, Moscow, UK Delegation to NATO Brussels, Washington DC and New Delhi, ambass and dep perm rep UK Mission to UN NY 2002–06, dir South Asia and Afghanistan 2006–09, high cmmr to Pakistan 2010–14; *Clubs* Athenaeum; *Style*— Sir Adam Thomson, KCMG; ✉ FCO, King Charles Street, London SW1A 2AH

THOMSON, Alan Matthew; s of George Kerr Thomson (d 1991), and Jean Lees, *née* Gemmell, of Renfrewshire; *b* 6 September 1946, Lennoxtown, E Dunbartonshire; *Educ* Eastwood HS Renfrewshire (capt Scottish Schs football team), Univ of Glasgow (MA); *m* 1, 8 Aug 1973, Linda Mary, da of Peter Hamilton, of W Lothian; 2 da (Jennifer b 5 March 1976, Victoria b 27 June 1987), 2 s (Paul b 26 Sept 1977, Richard b 2 Aug 1983); m 2, 22 Dec 2005, Angela Manuello; *Career* professional footballer Glasgow Rangers FC 1962–66, trainee chartered accountant Fleming and Wilson Glasgow 1967–70, auditor Arthur Andersen & Co Glasgow 1970–71, audit mangr Price Waterhouse Paris 1971–75; Rockwell International: fin dir Paris 1975–78, treasy mangr Pittsburgh 1978–79, fin dir UK 1979–82; chief fin offr Raychem Ltd Swindon 1982–84, fin controller Courtaulds Textiles plc 1984–87, fin dir Courtaulds Coatings 1987–92, gp fin dir The Rugby Group plc 1992–95, gp fin dir Smiths Group plc 1995–2006; chm: Bodycote plc 2007–, Hays plc 2010–, HSBC Bank plc 2013–14, Polypipe plc 2014–15, Oxford Instruments plc 2016–; non-exec dir/sr ind dir Johnson Matthey 2002–11, non-exec dir: Alstom SA 2007–, HSBC plc 2013/14; MICAS 1970 (pres 2010–11); *Recreations* golf, opera, football; *Clubs* Copt Heath Golf, Caledonian; *Style*— Mr Alan Thomson

THOMSON, Alexander James (Alex); s of Archie Thomson, and Marjorie Thomson; *Educ* Cranbourne Comp Basingstoke, Queen Mary's Coll Basingstoke, UC Oxford (BA), Univ of Cardiff (Dip Journalism); *m* 2008, Sarah Spiller; 2 s (George, Henry (twins) b 2000); *Career* with BBC TV Cardiff 1984, trainee BBC London 1985–86, reporter Spotlight BBC TV Belfast 1986–88, reporter Channel 4 News 1988–98, presenter and chief corr Channel 4 News 1998–; external examiner Cardiff Journalism Sch Univ of Wales 2005; RTS Awards 1990, 1994, 1998 and 2010, BAFTA Award 1996, BAFTA Award 2004, series of awards for int war reporting NY Festival and Monte Carlo Festival; hon fell UC Falmouth Sch of Journalism 2006; *Books* Ram Ram India (1985), Smokescreen: The Media and the Gulf War (1991); *Recreations* surfing, natural history, Newcastle United FC; *Style*— Alex Thomson

THOMSON, Prof Andrew James; OBE (2008); s of Andrew Henderson Thomson (d 1997), of Shoreham-by-Sea, W Sussex, and Eva Frances Annie Thomson (d 1979); *b* Steyning, Sussex; *Educ* Steyning GS, Wadham Coll Oxford (state scholar, BA), Univ of Oxford (DPhil, MA); *m* Anne, da of Jack Marsden; 2 s (Mark Andrew b 29 May 1967, Neil Henderson b 25 March 1969); *Career* research asst prof Dept of Biophysics Michigan State Univ 1965–67; Sch of Chemical Sciences (later Sch of Chemical Sciences and Pharmacy then Sch of Chemistry) UEA: sr demonstrator 1967–68, lectr 1968–77, sr lectr 1977–83, reader 1983–84, head Inorganic Chemistry Sector 1984–93, prof of chemistry 1985–2007, dean 2002–04; dean Faculty of Science UEA 2004–07, emeritus prof of chemistry and biology 2008–; jt dir UK Centre for Metallobiology 1988–2008; Silver Medal for analytical spectroscopy RSC 1991, Hugo Müller lectr RSC 1997, Interdisciplinary Award RSC 2002, Chatt lectr RSC 2003; author of over 300 original papers in jls; hon fell Wadham Coll Oxford 2011; memb: British Biophysical Soc, Biochemical Soc; FRS 1993, fell Royal Soc of Medicine 2007, FRSC; *Recreations* hill walking, ballroom dancing, choral singing; *Style*— Prof Andrew Thomson, OBE, FRS; ✉ 12 Armitage Close, Cringleford, Norwich NR4 6XZ (☎ 01603 504623); School of Chemistry, University of East Anglia, Norwich NR4 7TJ (e-mail a.thomson@uea.ac.uk)

THOMSON, (Hon) Caroline A M; da of Lord Thomson of Monifieth, KT, PC, DL, FRSE (Life Peer), and Grace, *née* Jenkins; *b* 15 May 1954; *Educ* Mary Datchelor Girls' Sch Camberwell London, Univ of York (BA); *m* 1, 12 Nov 1977 (m dis 1981), Ian Campbell Bradley; m 2, 30 July 1983, Lord Liddle, *qv*; 1 s (Andrew b 29 Oct 1989); *Career* BBC: trainee BBC News 1975–77, parly reporter 1977–78, sr prodr various radio and TV progs incl Analysis and Panorama 1978–82, dir Policy and Legal 2000–05, dir Strategy and Distribution 2005–06, chief operating offr 2006–12; political asst to Rt Hon Roy Jenkins MP 1982–83; Channel 4 TV: commissioning ed 1984–90, head of corp affrs 1990–95; BBC World Service: dir of strategy and corp affairs 1995–96, dep md 1996–98, dep chief exec 1998–2000; pres Prix Italia 2005–08 (hon pres 2008–); dir Edinburgh Film Festival 1994–95, chm World Service Tst 1998–2001, dep chair Nat Gallery, chair Digital UK; exec dir English Nat Ballet 2013–16; non-exec dir: The Pensions Regulator 2005–09, CN Gp 2012–, NHS Trust Devpt Authy 2013–16, Vitec plc 2015–, Shareholder Exec 2015–16, UKGI 2016–, NHSI 2016–, London First 2016–; tstee: Tullie House Museum 2010–, English Nat Ballet 2016–; Hon DUniv Univ of York 2013, hon fell Univ of Cumbria 2015; memb: fell RTS 2007, BAFTA 1988; *Recreations* domesticity, singing, Italian; *Style*— Miss Caroline Thomson

THOMSON, Charles Grant; s of William Eddie Spalding Thomson (d 2000), of Bearsden, Glasgow, and Helen Donaldson, *née* Campbell (d 1994); *b* 23 September 1948; *Educ* Jordanhill Coll Sch, Univ of Glasgow (BSc); *m* 11 July 1970, Pamela Anne, da of Frederick Simpson Mackay (d 1987), of Bearsden, Glasgow; 1 da (Susan b 1975), 1 s (Richard b 1979); *Career* Scottish Mutual Assurance plc (t/o by Abbey National plc 1992): joined 1969, actuary 1990, dir and dep chief exec Scottish Mutual Group 1992–94, dir and actuary Abbey National Life plc 1993–95, dir and actuary Scottish Mutual Assurance plc 1994–95; dir and appointed actuary Scottish Widows Fund and Life Assurance Society 1997–2000 (exec bd dir 1995–2000), dir and actuary Direct Line Life 1997–99, dir and actuary Tesco Personal Finance Life 1998–2000, dir, dep chief exec and actuary Scottish Widows plc 2000, chief exec Equitable Life 2001–; Faculty of Actuaries: memb Cncl 1983–86, 1989–92 and 1997–2000, chm Faculty Examinations Bd 1989–92 (memb 1982–92, sec 1985–89); chm Life Bd of Faculty and Inst of Actuaries 1998–2000; FFA 1973; *Recreations* golf, travel, fine wine; *Clubs* Glasgow Golf, Windyhill Golf, Caledonian; *Style*— Charles Thomson, Esq; ✉ London House, Aldersgate Street, London

THOMSON, Sir (Frederick Douglas) David; 3 Bt (UK 1929), of Glendarroch, Co Midlothian; s of Sir (James) Douglas Wishart, 2 Bt (d 1972), and Bettina, er da of late Lt Cdr David William Shafto Douglas, RN; *b* 14 February 1940; *Educ* Eton, UC Oxford (BA); *m* 1, 1967 (m dis 1994), Caroline Anne, da of late Maj Timothy Stuart Lewis, Royal Scots Greys; 2 s, 1 da; m 2, 2003 Hilary Claire, da of late Sidney Paul Youldon, MC; *Heir* s, Simon Thomson; *Career* dir: Ben Line Steamers Ltd 1964–89, Britannia Steamship Insurance Assoc Ltd 1965–2008, Through Transport Mutual Insurance Assoc Ltd 1973–2013; chm: S A Meacock & Co Ltd 1996–, The Investment Co plc 2005–; memb Queen's Body Guard for Scotland (Royal Co of Archers); *Clubs* Boodle's; *Style*— Sir David Thomson, Bt; ✉ Holylee, Walkerburn, Peeblesshire EH43 6BD (☎ 07831 355691, e-mail sirdthomson@holylee.go-plus.net)

THOMSON, Elizabeth Mary (Liz); da of Frederick William Charles Thomson (d 2015), and Catherine Edna, *née* Fardell (d 1999); *b* 12 September 1957; *Educ* East Barnet Sch, Univ of Liverpool (BA); *Career* publishing asst Arabian Publications 1980, music ed Music Sales and Omnibus 1980–82, freelance ed 1983; Publishing News: editorial asst rising to feature writer 1984–97, assoc ed 1998–2003, ed 2003–08; ed Books 1995–2003, founding ed BookBrunch.co.uk 2008; frequent broadcaster in Britain and abroad; visiting fell Open Univ Sixties Res Gp 1999–2002; tstee Desmond Elliott Literary Prize, fndr and tstee Square Roots Prodns (charity celebrating Anglo-American folk music heritage) 2015; memb: The Book Soc (formerly Soc of Bookmen), Soc of Authors, NUJ; *Publications* Conclusions on the Wall: New Essays on Bob Dylan (1980), Folk Songs and Dances of England (1982), Folk Songs and Dances of Scotland (1982), The Lennon Companion (co-ed, 1987 and 2004), The Dylan Companion (co-ed, 1990, revised edn 2001), The Bowie Companion (co-ed, 1993), No Direction Home: The Life and Music of Bob Dylan (ed, revised edn 2011), Chickenshed: An Awfully Big Adventure (2013); book contrib: Turning On: Rock in the Late Sixties (1985), Whitaker's Almanack (1996), The New Grove Dictionary of Music & Musicians (revised edn, 2001); newspaper and magazine contrib: The Times, Sunday Telegraph, The Independent, The Listener, Books & Bookmen, New Statesman, Bulletin, Chic (literary ed 1993–94), Classical Music, Mojo, Guardian, Washington Post; *Recreations* music, travel, photography; *Style*— Ms Elizabeth Thomson; ✉ Birchwood Mansions, 133 Fortis Green Road, London N10 3LX (e-mail elizabethmthomson@googlemail.com)

THOMSON, Gordon; s of John Thomson, and Kate Beveridge; *b* 13 January 1972, Falkirk; *Educ* St Katherine's Sch Bristol, Univ of Glasgow (MA); *m* 12 Sept 2003, Lydia, *née* Chambers; 1 s (Charlie b 1 Feb 1999), 2 da (Grace b 19 Oct 2000, Ava b 24 June 2004); *Career* contributing ed Goal 1997–98, freelance writer 1997–99, asst prodr Sky Sports News 1999; Maxim (UK): commisioning ed 1999–2000, sr ed 2000–02; dep ed Observer Sport Monthly 2002–04, latterly ed Time Out; shortlisted New Ed of the Year BSME Awards 2005; *Books* The Man in Black (1998); *Recreations* cooking, eating out, squash, cinema, music, golf, exploring London with family, the arts; *Clubs* Groucho, Scotch Malt Whisky Soc; *Style*— Gordon Thomson, Esq

T

THOMSON, Ian; s of John Murray Thomson (d 2002), and Ingrid, *née* Haugas; *b* 24 June 1961, London; *Educ* Dulwich Coll, Univ of Cambridge (MA); *m* 1991, Laura, da of Dr John Fleminger, and Dr Ruth Jackson; *Career* freelance writer and journalist 1983–; RSL W H Heinemann Award 2003, RSL Ondaatje Prize 2010, Dolman Prize 2010; affiliate London Haiti Support Gp, Royal Literary Fund fell UCL 2009–11; FRSL 2004; *Books* Southern Italy (1989), Bonjour Blanc: A Journey Through Haiti (1990), Primo Levi: A Life (2002), The Dead Yard: Tales of Modern Jamaica (2009); *Clubs* The Academy; *Style—* Ian Thomson, Esq; ✉ c/o United Agents Ltd, 12–26 Lexington Street, London W1F 0LE (☎ 020 3214 0800, fax 020 3214 0801)

THOMSON, Dr James Phillips Spalding; s of Dr James Laing Spalding Thomson, MB, ChB, MRCGP, and Peggy Marion, *née* Phillips; *b* 2 October 1939, Bournemouth, Dorset; *Educ* Haileybury and ISC, Middx Hosp Med Sch London (MB BS, LRCP, DObstRCOG, MS); *m* 1968, Dr Anne Katharine Thomson, MRCP, da of Richard Derek Richards, FRCS; 1 s (James Richards Phillips b 2 Feb 1971), 3 da (Rebecca Jane Katharine b 21 Aug 1973, Sally Anne Charlotte b 9 Feb 1979, Georgina Mary Caroline b 22 Jan 1985); *Career* jr med and surgical appts: Kettering Gen Hosp 1962, Middx Hosp 1963, 1968, 1969 and 1971–74, Cheltenham Gen Hosp 1966–67, Central Middx Hosp 1970, St Mark's Hosp 1970–71; demonstrator Dept of Anatomy Middx Hosp Med Sch 1964–66, pt/t hon conslt surgn St John's Hosp for Diseases of the Skin 1973–75; conslt surgn: St Mark's Hosp 1974–99 (clinical dir 1990–97, now emeritus conslt surgn), Royal Northern Hosp 1975–77, Hackney and Homerton Hosps 1977–90, Central Middlesex Hosp 1999; hon conslt surgn St Luke's Hosp for the Clergy 1976–99 (vice-chm Cncl 1992–2003, vice-pres 2016–), hon conslt surgn St Mary's Hosp 1982–99; civil conslt in surgery RAF 1984–99 (now hon conslt surgn), civilian conslt in colorectal surgery RN 1986–99 (now emeritus conslt in surgery), hon conslt advsr in surgery Ileostomy Assoc of GB and Ireland 1986–99, hon sr lectr in surgery Bart's Med Coll 1977–94, hon sr clinical lectr in surgery Imperial Coll Sch of Med 1994–99; chm Notarial Advsy Bd 2008–10; memb RCS Ct of Examiners, examiner in surgery at Univs of Cambridge, Liverpool and London; convenor: Gatherings for Holders of Lambeth Degrees 1990–2007, Gathering of Masters of Historic Almshouses 2003–11; administrator The Priory Church of St Bartholomew the Great W Smithfield 2000–02, master Sutton's Hosp in Charterhouse 2001–12; Liveryman: Worshipful Soc of Apothecaries, Worshipful Co of Barbers, Worshipful Co of Merchant Taylors 2014–, chm UK Appeal Ctee Anglican Centre in Rome 2013–; memb: Travelling Surgical Soc (sec 1982–90, pres 1999–2002), Surgical Research Soc, Br Soc of Gastroenterology (memb Ctee Surgical Section 1986–88), Assoc of Coloproctology of GB and Ireland (sec 1989–90), NE Thames Metropolitan Surgical Soc, BMA, Med Soc for the Study of Venereal Disease, RN Med Club, Military Surgical Soc; associate memb Br Assoc of Clinical Anatomists; Section of Coloproctology RSM: memb Cncl 1983–96, vice-pres 1986–88 and 1990–94, hon sec 1988–90, pres 1994–95, Frederick Salmon Medal 1996; pres: Friends of St Mark's Hosp 2005–, Haileybury Soc 2006–07; tstee: Rev Dr George Richards Charity 2001–11, Medical Coll of St Bartholomew's Hosp Tst 2002–11, St Andrew's (Holborn) Fndn 2003–11; govr: Corporation of the Sons of the Clergy 1985–, Tancreds Charities 2001–11; DM (Lambeth) 1987; fell Queen Mary Univ of London 2006–; fell Assoc of Surgns of GB and Ireland (memb Cncl 1983–86), fell Hunterian Soc (memb Cncl 1994–97, pres-elect 2000–01, pres 2001–02), patron and fell Burgon Soc 2003– (pres 2011–); memb Order of Our Lady of Walsingham 2010–; FRCS 1969 (MRCS 1962); *Books* Colorectal Disease – An Introduction for Surgeons and Physicians (jtly, 1981), Frontiers in Colorectal Disease (jtly, 1986), Updates in Coloproctology (jtly, 1992), Familial Adenomatous Polyposis (jtly, 1994); A Kalendar of Holy Days approved for use in the Diocese of London (ed, 2012), The Story of Salvation: Lambeth Palace Chapel Stained Glass Windows – A Guide (with Lyndall Hacker, 2014); also author of pubns and chapter contribs to books mainly on colon and rectal surgery; *Recreations* church history and music, railways and canals, heraldry; *Clubs* Athenaeum, RSM; *Style—* Dr James P S Thomson, DM, MS, FRCS; ✉ Gallery House, 13 New Street, Holt, Norfolk NR25 6JJ (☎ 01263 711214, mobile 07550 079522, e-mail jamespsthomson@aol.com); 15 Nelson Terrace, London N1 8DG (☎ 020 7253 1052)

THOMSON, John K; s of Sir Ian Thomson, KBE, CMG (d 2008), and Nancy, *née* Kearsley (d 1988); *b* 17 February 1950; *Educ* St Kentigern Coll Auckland, Edinburgh Acad, Univ of Strathclyde (BA), Univ of Oxford (Dip Econ Devpt); *m* July 1973, Lorna, da of Allan White; 1 s (Alastair b Aug 1991); *Career* research economist South Pacific Bureau for Economic Co-operation Fiji 1973–75, research offr Scottish Cncl (Devpt and Industry) Edinburgh 1976–80, analyst Scottish Investment Trust Edinburgh 1980–82; Standard Life: investment mangr 1982–94, asst gen mangr (Devpt) 1994–96, chief investment mangr 1996–97; md Stewart Ivory 1998–2000, md Ailsa Capital Mgmnt 2001–03, chm/ceo RIA Capital Markets 2004–10 (dir 2010–), chm Ohmedics 2009–, dir TT Club 2010–; MSI 1993, FCSI 2005; *Recreations* scuba diving, walking, cycling; *Style—* John K Thomson

THOMSON, Brig Dr John Reid; QVRM (2003), TD (1988), DL (Edinburgh 2008); s of Alexander Patrick Thomson (d 2001), and Helen, *née* Reid (d 2011); *b* 17 August 1953; *Educ* Dalry HS Ayrshire, RMA Sandhurst, Univ of Southampton (BA), Strathclyde Grad Business Sch (MBA), CIM (DipM), Inst of Direct Mktg (Dip Direct Mktg), Aberdeen Business Sch Robert Gordon Univ (PhD); *Career* cmmnd RA 1973; HM Armed Forces (Army) 1971–76, TA 1976– (dep inspr gen 2000–03); accountant then fin dir then md London 1979–86, business devpt dir Edinburgh 1987–91, dir of open learning (MBA prog) and sr lectr in marketing Napier Univ Business Sch 1991–, non-exec dir Imumed International Germany 2000–02, chm S Edinburgh Amenities Gp 2012–; int mgmnt conslt; completed major projects in: Switzerland, Belarus, Germany, UK; ADC to HM The Queen 1997–2003; dir Scottish Bd Chartered Inst of Mktg 2013–; conslt and friend Hopetoun House Preservation Tst, supporter and friend RA Heritage Appeal, past chm and memb Scottish Vol Offrs' Charity Ball Ctee; chm: City of Edinburgh Artillery Offrs Assoc 2000–05, Nat Artillery Assoc 2003–14, Scottish Artillery Historical Soc 2005–; Hon Col Glasgow & Strathclyde Univs OTC 1998–2008, Hon Col Cmdt Royal Regt of Artillery 2001–12, Hon Col 105 Regt RA (Volunteers) 2004–13; Freeman City of London 1985; MILT 2001, FCIM 2007, FHEA 2007; *Recreations* equestrian, tennis, swimming, walking, gardening, arts; *Clubs* Royal Scots (Edinburgh); *Style—* Dr John R Thomson, QVRM, TD, DL; ✉ Napier University Business School, Craiglockhart Campus, Edinburgh EH14 1DJ (☎ 0131 455 4406, fax 0131 455 4540, e-mail jo.thomson@napier.ac.uk)

THOMSON, Prof Joseph McGeachy; s of James Thomson, of Campbeltown, and Catherine Morrans, *née* McGeachy; *b* 6 May 1948; *Educ* Keil Sch Dumbarton, Univ of Edinburgh (LLB); *m* 1999, Annie Iverson; *Career* lectr: Univ of Birmingham 1970–74, KCL 1974–84; prof of law Univ of Strathclyde 1984–90, regius prof of law Univ of Glasgow 1991–2005; Scottish law cmmr 2000–09, dep gen ed Stair Meml Encyclopaedia of the Laws of Scotland 1985–96, ed Juridical Review 2009; Hon Sheriff Campbeltown; FRSE 1996, FRSA 1996, Hon FSALS 2001; *Books* Contract Law in Scotland (with Hector L McQueen, 2000, 4 edn 2016), Delictual Liability (5 edn, 2014), Scots Private Law (2006), Family Law in Scotland (7 edn, 2014); *Recreations* bridge, food and wine; *Style—* Prof Joseph Thomson, FRSE; ✉ Askomel End, Low Askomil, Campbeltown, Argyll PA28 6EP (☎ 01586 554930, e-mail joseph.m.thomson@btinternet.com)

THOMSON, Malcolm George; QC (Scot 1987); s of George Robert Thomson, OBE (d 1987), and Daphne Ethel, *née* Daniels (d 2011); *b* 6 April 1950; *Educ* The Edinburgh Acad, Univ of Edinburgh (LLB); *m* 1, 18 March 1978 (m dis 2001), Susan Gordon, da of Gordon Aitken (d 1997); 2 da (Victoria b 1982, Jacqueline b 1989); m 2, 27 March 2008, Maybel, da of Dr Hugh Hutton (d 1996); *Career* advocate at the Scottish Bar 1974, barr Lincoln's Inn 1991; standing jr counsel 1982–87: Dept of Agriculture and Fisheries for Scotland, The Forestry Cmmn Scotland; temp judge Court of Session Scotland 2002–; Scottish case ed Current Law 1977–96, ed Scots Law Times Reports 1989–2003, chm NHS Tbnl (Scotland) 1995–2005, memb Scottish Legal Aid Bd 1998–2006; *Recreations* sailing, skiing; *Clubs* New (Edinburgh); *Style—* Malcolm Thomson, Esq, QC; ✉ 12 Succoth Avenue, Edinburgh EH12 6BT (☎ 0131 337 4911); Advocates Library, Parliament House, Edinburgh EH1 1RF (☎ 0131 226 5071)

THOMSON, Mark C A; *Career* nat coordinator Nicaragua Solidarity Campaign London & Nicaragua 1982–84, community educn offr Tower Hamlets Int Solidarity London 1984–88, Latin America and Caribbean programme offr World Univ Service Geneva and Latin America 1988–91, inter-governmental organisations coordinator Amnesty Int 1991–92, dep dir Int Service for Human Rights Geneva 1992–2001, sec-gen Assoc for Prevention of Torture Geneva 2001–; *Style—* Mark C A Thomson, Esq

THOMSON, Neil Alexander; s of Alexander and Irene Thomson; *b* 17 May 1959; *Educ* Aberdeen HS, Aberdeen Coll of Commerce (Scot HND), Middlesex Business Sch (MBA); *m* 29 June 1985, Karen Ann, da of George McGregor; 1 da (Cassia b 3 June 1991); *Career* CA 1983; roles at PPHN, Courtalds Coatings, PA Consulting, and Deloittes Haskins & Sells, chief operating offr St Lukes Communications Ltd 1995–; dir Job Ownership Ltd; ACMA 1985, MBIM 1987; *Recreations* running half marathons, fitness training, chess; *Style—* Neil Thomson, Esq; ✉ St Lukes Communications Ltd, 22 Dukes Road, London WC1H 9AD (☎ 020 7380 8888, fax 020 7380 8899)

THOMSON, Prof Neil Campbell; s of late Prof Adam Simpson Turnbull Thomson, of Ayr, and late Margaret Campbell, *née* Templeton; *b* 3 April 1948, Kilmarnock, Scotland; *Educ* Spiers Sch Beith, Univ of Glasgow (MB ChB, MD); *m* 16 Aug 1973, Lorna Jean, da of late William Sim Walker Fraser, of Perth; 2 s (David Fraser b 10 July 1976, Andrew Campbell b 8 May 1978), 1 da (Jennifer Lorna b 22 May 1985); *Career* jr hosp doctor Glasgow Teaching Hosps 1972–80, res fell McMaster Univ Ontario Canada 1980–81, conslt physician Western Infirmary Glasgow 1982–2011, hon prof Univ of Glasgow 1996–2001, prof of respiratory med Univ of Glasgow 2001–11 (emeritus prof 2011–); chm Res Ctees: Br Lung Fndn, The Nat Asthma Campaign; memb: Advsy Bd MRC, Ctee on the Safety of Med 1999–2001; memb: Assoc of Physicians (memb Exec 2003–06), Br Thoracic Soc (former hon sec), American Thoracic Soc, Scot Soc of Physicians, Br Soc for Allergy and Clinical Immunology; FRCP, FERS 2014; *Books* Handbook of Clinical Allergy (1990), Asthma: Basic Mechanisms and Clinical Management (1988, 3 edn 1998), Manual of Asthma Management (1995, 2 edn 2001), Asthma and COPD: Basic Mechanisms and Clinical Management (2002, 2 edn 2009); published over 200 scientific articles and chapters on airway diseases; *Recreations* reading, gardening, walking; *Style—* Prof Neil Thomson; ✉ Institute of Infection, Immunity and Inflammation, University of Glasgow and Respiritory Medicine, Gartnavel General Hospital, Glasgow G12 0YN (☎ 0141 211 0095, fax 0141 211 3464, e-mail neil.thomson@glasgow.ac.uk)

THOMSON, Dr Wendy; CBE (2005); da of Shirley Basil Thomson (d 1970), and Grace, *née* Frazer (d 2008); *b* 28 October 1953, Montreal, Quebec, Canada; *Educ* Verdun HS, McGill Univ Montreal (Dip Collegial Studies, Batchelor of Social Work, Master of Social Work), Univ of Bristol (PhD); *Children* 1 adopted da (Mia b 14 Oct 2001), 2 step s (Samuel Dorne b 11 Feb 1983, Jack Dorne b 12 Feb 1985); *Career* exec dir Head and Hands Community Clinic (Montreal) 1977–80, exec dir West Island Association for the Intellectually Handicapped (Quebec) 1981–82, sr prog offr GLC 1985–86, sr prog offr London Strategic Policy Unit (LSPU) 1986–87, dep chief exec London Borough of Islington 1987–93, chief exec Turning Point 1993–96, chief exec London Borough of Newham 1996–99, dir of inspection Audit Cmmn 1999–2001, DG OPSR 2001–05, prof of social policy McGill Univ Montreal 2005–, dir Sch of Social Work McGill Univ 2005–14, chief exec Norfolk County Council 2014–; DG Cabinet Office 2001–05; cmmr Ontario Cmmn to Promote Sustainable Child Welfare 2009–12, chair Expert Gp on Health Care Financing in Quebec 2012–14; int expert Advsy Gp African Cmmn for Local Govt Improvement 2011–; research affiliations incl: Centre for Interuniversity Research and Analysis of Organizations 2010–, McGill Centre for Research on Children and Families 2006–; memb Cncl UEA 2014–; YWCA Woman of Distinction in the Field of Education 2014–; *Books* incl: Bureaucracy and Community (contrib, 1990), Citizen's Rights in a Modern Welfare System (contrib, 1992), Management for Quality in Local Government (contrib, 1992), Fitness for Purpose: Shaping New Patterns for Organisations and Management (co-author, 1993), Future Directions for In-Care Services in a Sustainable Child Welfare System (2010), Towards Sustainable Child Welfare (2010), Jurisdictional Comparisons of Child Welfare System Design (2010), Reducing Administrative Burden in Child Welfare (2010), A New Approach to Funding Child Welfare in Ontario (2011), Aboriginal Child Welfare in Ontario: A Discussion Paper (2011), Realizing a Sustainable Child Welfare System in Ontario (2012), Clarifying the Scope of Child Welfare Services (2012), A New Approach to Accountability and System Management (2012), Exploring the Intersection of Culture and Education in Nunavik (co-author, 2012), Evidence-based Management in Child Welfare: Researchers and Decision-makers Working Hand in Hand (co-author, 2012), Money to Follow the Patienr (2014); author of working papers for govts of Ontario and Quebec on child welfare and healthcare, also contrib to various other publications and author numerous conf papers; *Recreations* single parenting, tennis, skiing; *Clubs* Montreal Athletics Assoc, Monkland Tennis; *Style—* Dr Wendy Thomson, CBE; ✉ Chief Executive, Norfolk County Council, Martineau Lane, Norwich NR1 3DA

THORBEK, Erik; s of Kai Birch (d 1988), and Dr Agro Grete Thorbek; *b* 10 January 1941; *Educ* Billum Coll Denmark; *m* 1, 6 April 1963 (m dis 2008), Susan Margaret, da of Sidney Gair (d 1977); 2 s (Alexander b 1964, Nikolas b 1973), 2 da (Francesca b 1966, Natasha b 1975); m 2, 27 June 2011, Liubov, da of Prof Valery Varvarov, of Moscow; *Career* chm and chief exec H & T Walker Ltd 1963–; *Recreations* fine dining, travel, sailing, skiing, golf, horse racing, shooting; *Clubs* Turf, Helford River Sailing, Marks, Harry's Bar, Annabel's; *Style—* Erik Thorbek

THORBURN, Andrew; s of James Beresford Thorburn (d 1972), and Marjorie Clara Thorburn (d 1987); *b* 20 March 1934, Buckhurst Hill, Essex; *Educ* Bridport GS, Univ of Southampton (BSc); *m* 1957, Margaret Anne, da of Reginald Crack (d 1964); 1 s (Edward), 2 da (Jenny, Anna); *Career* dir Notts/Derbys Sub-Regnl Study 1968–70, county planning offr of E Sussex 1973–83, chief exec English Tourist Bd 1983–85, head of tourism and leisure Grant Thornton 1986–90, princ Thorburns (leisure planning consultancy) 1990–; chm :Bow Street Partners Ltd 1999–2005, Ringstall Ltd 2011–; pres Royal Town Planning Inst 1982; memb: Int Soc of City and Regnl Planners, Town and Country Planning Assoc; fell Tourism Soc; FRTPI; *Books* Planning Villages (1971), The Missing Museum (2006); *Recreations* sailing; *Style—* Andrew Thorburn, Esq; ☎ 07941 070729

THORLEY, Simon Joe; QC (1989); s of Sir Gerald Bowers Thorley, TD (d 1988), and Beryl Preston, *née* Rhodes (d 2011) (who m 2, Sir David Lancaster Nicolson (d 1996)); *b* 22 May 1950; *Educ* Rugby, Keble Coll Oxford (MA); *m* 7 May 1983, Jane Elizabeth (d 2007), da of Frank Cockcroft, of Saltburn by Sea, Cleveland; 2 s (Matthew b 1984, Nicholas b 1985), 1 da (Francesca b 1988); *Career* called to the Bar Inner Temple 1972 (bencher 1999, reader 2012, treas 2013); barr specialising in patent matters 1972–2014; arbitrator 2014–; appointed to hear Trade Mark Appeals 1996–2003, dep chm Copyright Tbnl 1997–2006, dep judge of the High Court 1998–2014, int judge of the Int Commercial Court of Singapore 2015–; chm Intellectual Property Bar Assoc (formerly Patent Bar Assoc) 1995–99, memb Bar Cncl 1995–99; tstee: Addenbrooke's Charitable Tst 2015–,

The Medical Coll of St Bartholomew's Hospital Tst 2015–; *Books* Terrell on Patents (jt ed, 13, 14, 15 and 16 edn); *Recreations* family, shooting, opera; *Style—* Simon Thorley, Esq, QC; ✉ Brick Court Chambers, 7–8 Essex Street, London WC2R 3LD (☎ 020 7379 3550, fax 020 7520 3558)

THORN, Jeremy Gordon; s of James Douglas Thorn (d 1999), of Appleton, Cheshire, and Daphne Elizabeth, *née* Robinson; *Educ* Mill Hill Sch, Univ of Leeds (BSc), European Coll of Marketing (Dip), Cranfield Sch of Mgmnt, London Business Sch, Oxford Psychologists; *m* 24 July 1971 (m dis 1997), Eilis Anne, da of Christopher Maurice Coffey, of Street, Somerset; 4 da (Jessica b 1977, Rachel b 1982, Alicen b 1984, Stephanie b 1987); *Career* dir of sales and mktg: Baugh & Weedon Ltd 1978–81, Bradley & Foster Ltd 1981–83, Spear & Jackson Ltd 1984–86, British Ropes Ltd 1986–89, Bridon Fishing Ltd 1989–93; chm Bristol Wire Rope Ltd 1988–93, md Bridon Ropes Ltd 1989–93; Bridon Ropes Ltd awarded Investor in People Award 1992 and 1993, Design Award 1993, Prince Michael of Kent Award for Road Safety 1993, Queen's Award for Technol 1993; chm Fedn of Wire Rope Manufacturers of GB 1989–92, UK spokesman Euro Wire Rope Info Serv 1986–93; chm: QED Consltg 1998–2007 (md 1993–98), Thorn Hinton Ltd 1998–2007 (dir 1993–98), LightWork Design Ltd 2000–06, Navis Works Ltd 2002–06, Office Works Ltd 2003–06, Machine Works Ltd 2003–06; dir: Barnsley/Doncaster TEC (dep chm) 1989–93, Quantum Generation Ltd 1993–95, Spawforth Planning and Urban Regeneration Ltd 2004–09, Elektron Tech Plc 2010–12, Z-Tech Process Control Ltd 2010–12; pres Doncaster Branch Inst of Mgmnt 1989–2009, chm Judging Panel Nat Trg Awards 1998–2000 (memb 1993–98); CEng, MIM, CCMI, FRSA; *Books* How to Negotiate Better Deals (1989, 3 edn 2009), The First Time Sales Manager (1990, 2 edn 2009), Developing Your Career in Management (1992), Effective Presentations (2000), Pricing Strategy (2001), Recruitment Practice (2002); *Recreations* music (church organist), sport (former chm W Midlands Region Amateur Fencing Assoc, sometime fencing team capt Univ of Leeds, Warks, W Midlands and Yorks, former Warks épée and sabre champion and W Midlands and Yorks sabre champion); *Style—* Jeremy Thorn, Esq; ✉ e-mail jeremy@jeremythorn.co.uk, website www.jeremythorn.co.uk

THORNBERRY, Emily; MP; da of late Cedric Thornberry, and Sallie, *née* Bone; *b* 27 July 1960, London; *Educ* Univ of Kent at Canterbury; *m* Christopher Nugee, QC, *qv*; 3 c; *Career* called to the Bar Grays Inn 1983; memb Tooks Court 1985–; MP (Lab) Islington S and Finsbury 2005–, shadow AG 2011–14, shadow min for employment 2015–16, shadow foreign sec and shadow sec of state for leaving the EU 2016–; memb Health Select Ctee 2015; *Style—* Ms Emily Thornberry, MP; ✉ House of Commons, London SW1A 0AA

THORNBERY, Hugh; CBE (2016); s of Keith Thornbery (d 2014), and Jeanne, *née* Sorton (d 1996); *b* 14 February 1955, Woking, Surrey; *Educ* CQSW, MBA; *Children* 2 da (Hannah b 13 Nov 1980, Emma b 29 April 1982); *Career* Wolverhampton BC 1977–93, Rainer Fndn 1993–97, Action for Children 1997–2012, dir of business devpt then chief exec Adoption UK 2012–; chair of tstees Chance UK; *Recreations* music, opera, reading, cycling, travel, walking; *Style—* Hugh Thornbery, Esq, CBE; ✉ Twitter @HThornbery

THORNE, Clive Duncan; s of late Desmond Clive Thorne, of East Dean, E Sussex, and May, *née* Davey; *b* 21 January 1952; *Educ* Eastbourne GS, Trinity Hall Cambridge (MA); *m* 1, 11 Oct 1975 (m dis 1982), Catherine Sykes; m 2, 12 July 1986, Alison Mary Healy, da of Cdr Michael Healy, MBE, of Beaulieu sur Mer, France; *Career* articled clerk Clifford-Turner 1975–77; admitted slr England 1977, slr Hong Kong 1984, barr and slr Victoria Aust 1985; ptnr Denton Hall (later Denton Wilde Sapte) 1987–2004, ptnr Arnold and Porter London office 2004–10, ptnr Reynolds Porter Chamberlain 2010–14, currently ptnr Wedlake Bell; memb: Arbitrators Panel Patents County Court, World Intellectual Property Orgn (WIPO), domain name disputes panel and arbitrators panel, Working Gp on High Court Intellectual Property Protocol; ICC arbitrator; author of numerous articles on intellectual property incl Euro Intellectual Property Review and other jls; associate: Chartered Inst of Trade Mark Agents, Chartered Inst of Patent Agents; memb: Law Soc, AIPPI, Int Bar Assoc (sec and treas Technol Ctee); fndr memb and chm: The Intellectual Property Lawyers Orgn (TIPLO), Computer Law Gp; tstee HMS Victory Preservation Tst, memb Devpt Bd Nat Museum of the Royal Navy; Advanced Mediation Cert WIPO; Liveryman Worshipful Co of Arbitrators; FCIArb; *Books* Sony Guide to Home Taping (contrib, 1983), Intellectual Property – The New Law (1989), User's Guide to Copyright (jtly, 2006), Users Guide to Design Law (jtly, 2010), International Design Protection (consulting ed, 2012), Intellectual Property in Electronics and Software (jtly, 2013); *Recreations* English music, opera, reading, walking, flute playing, marine art; *Style—* Clive Thorne, Esq; ✉ Wedlake Bell, 52 Bedford Row, London WC1R 4LR (☎ 02073 953000, e-mail cthorne@wedlakebell.com)

THORNE, Lesley Karen; da of Lt-Col James Shaw, of Hereford, and Catherine, *née* Barrie; *b* 19 November 1973, Rinteln, Germany; *Educ* Royal Sch Bath, Univ of Warwick (BA); *m* 17 July 2004, Matthew David Jon Thorne; 1 s (Luke David James); *Career* PA to md Fourth Estate 1996–97, editorial asst to Publisher Hamish Hamilton then editorial dir Viking 1997–99, asst to md rising to agent Aitken Alexander Associates Ltd (formerly Gillon Aitken Associates) 1999– (currently managing literary client list and handling film and TV); *Recreations* film, music, walking, literature; *Style—* Mrs Lesley Thorne; ✉ Aitken Alexander Associates Ltd, 18–21 Cavaye Place, London SW10 9PT (☎ 020 7373 8672, fax 020 7373 6002, e-mail lesley@aitkenalexander.co.uk)

THORNE, Matthew Wadman John; s of Robin Horton John Thorne, CMG, OBE (d 2004), of Old Heathfield, E Sussex, and Joan Helen, *née* Wadman (d 2000); *b* 27 June 1952; *Educ* Dragon Sch, King's Sch Canterbury, Trinity Coll Oxford (MA); *m* 1978, (Sheila) Leigh, da of Col Hon Robert George Hugh Phillimore, OBE (d 1984), 3 s of 2 Baron Phillimore, MC, DL; 2 da (Aelene b 17 June 1981, Marini b 4 Aug 1992), 3 s (Robin b 15 Feb 1983, Andrew b 27 Feb 1986, Edward b 16 July 1989); *Career* Price Waterhouse 1975–78, County Natwest 1978–83, Beazer plc 1983–91 (dir 1984–91); dir Ricardo International plc 1991–92, gp fin dir McCarthy & Stone plc 1993–2007, chm Pegasus Retirement Homes plc 2007–08; non-exec dir: BM Group plc 1991–93, UMECO plc 1992–2002, Bournemouth Univ 1996–2002, Bankers Investment Tst 2008–, Custodian REIT plc 2014–; advsr Consensus Business Gp 2007–; memb Advsy Bd and Panel Greenwich Hosp 2012–; memb Cncl Cheltenham Ladies Coll 2005–14; FCA 1978; *Style—* Matthew Thorne, Esq; ✉ The Mount, Bannerdown Road, Batheaston, Bath BA1 8EG

THORNE, Prof Michael Philip; CBE (2016); *b* 19 October 1951, Chelmsford, Essex; *Educ* QMC London (BSc), Univ of Birmingham (PhD); *m* 1975, Val, *née* Swift (d 2011); 3 s (Jonathan Mark b 1976, William James b 1987, Edward Alexander 1994); *Career* lectr: SE Derbyshire Coll 1973–75, UCL 1978–79, UC Cardiff 1979–88; head Sch of Computing Univ of Sunderland 1989–93, pro-vice-chllr Univ of Sunderland 1993–97, vice-princ Napier Univ 1998–2001, vice-chllr Univ of E London 2001–07, vice-chllr Anglia Ruskin Univ 2007–16; chair Advsy Cncl on Libraries 2008–10; memb Bd: London Thames Gateway Urban Devpt Corp 2004–07, Learning and Skills Network 2006–11; non-exec dir Scottish Univ for Industry, chair Open Learning Fndn, former chair Lead Scotland; memb Bd: Northern Sinfonia, Northern Jr Philharmonic, Broadway Theatre 2006–07; tstee Sir John Cass Fndn 2009–; FIMA, FBCS, FRSA; *Publications* author and co-author of 11 books and numerous academic papers, articles and radio and TV progs; *Recreations* music (bassoon and conducting), theatre, hill walking, reading funding council circulars; *Clubs* Reform; *Style—* Prof Michael Thorne, CBE

THORNE, Peter Geoffrey; s of Ernest Geoffrey Thorne (d 1976), of Duncliffe, Saunton, N Devon, and Edwina Mary, *née* Wilkinson; *b* 2 June 1948; *Educ* Clifton; *m* Jane Frances, da of John David Henson, MC, OBE; 1 s (Benjamin David Geoffrey b 11 July 1981), 1 da (Lucy Frances Alice b 18 Jan 1984); *Career* articles Messrs Sargent & Probert Slrs of Exeter 1965–70, admitted slr 1971 (Sir George Fowler prize for best qualifier from Devon); Norton Rose (formerly Norton Rose Botterell & Roche): joined 1971, specialist in asset fin (particularly ship and aircraft), ptnr 1977–, Hong Kong office 1981–83; memb: City of London Slrs Co, Law Soc, Int Bar Assoc, RAeS, GAPAN; *Recreations* flying, fishing, philately, skiing; *Style—* Peter Thorne, Esq

THORNE, Rosemary Prudence; da of Arnold Rex Bishop, of Clevedon, Avon, and Brenda Prudence, *née* Withers; *b* 12 February 1952; *Educ* Univ of Warwick (BSc); *Career* accountant BOC 1974–77, chief accountant Mothercare 1977–82, gp financial controller Habitat Mothercare 1982–85, gp financial controller Storehouse 1986, finance dir and co sec Harrods Ltd (House of Fraser plc) 1986–90, gp financial controller Grand Metropolitan 1990–92, gp finance dir J Sainsbury 1992–99, gp finance dir Bradford & Bingley 2000–06, gp finance dir Ladbrokes 2006–07; non-exec dir: Royal Mail Hldgs 1998–2004, Cadbury Schweppes 2004–07, Santander UK 2006–15, Virgin Radio 2007–08, Smurfit Kappa Gp 2008–, Solvay 2014–, First Global Tst Bank 2015–; hon memb Hundred Gp of Fin Dirs (memb 1992–2007), memb Financial Reporting Cncl 1998–2007, Financial Reporting Review Panel 1996–2006; memb Cncl: Univ of Warwick 2001–07, RCA 2006–09; FCMA, CGMA, FCT, CCMI; *Style—* Miss Rosemary P Thorne

THORNEWILL, Fiona Susan; MBE (2006); da of Ralph Cowling, of Upton, Notts, and Jean Cowling; *b* 10 July 1966, Upton, Notts; *Educ* Rodney Sch Kirklington; *m* 26 May 1996, Mike Thornewill, s of Peter Leslie Graham Thornewill (d 1983); *Career* explorer; first Br female to: walk to Geographic S Pole 2000, walk to Geographic N Pole 2001 (first female to walk to both geographic poles), walk solo and unsupported to Geographic S Pole 2004 (also fastest person to do so: 41 days and 8 hours); formerly prop of ladies gym, currently recruitment conslt Harpers; pt/t polar guide; motivational speaker; supporter: NSPCC, Macmillan Cancer Care; Pride of Britain Award 2000, RADAR Award for Human Achievement 2001, European Woman of the Year 2004; *Recreations* running, cycling, sailing, the great outdoors, socialising; *Style—* Mrs Fiona Thornewill, MBE; ✉ Bluebell Barn, Thurgarton, Nottinghamshire NG14 7FW (☎ 07979 538772, e-mail fiona@polarchallenge.org)

THORNHILL, Dr John Joseph; OBE (2016), JP (1983); s of Walter Thornhill (d 1980), and Anne Margaret, *née* Dunphy (d 1993); *b* 1 July 1945, Liverpool; *Educ* St Francis Xaviers Coll Liverpool, Univ of Hull (BA), Univ of Edinburgh (DipEd), Manchester Met Univ (Grad Dip), Univ of Wales Aberystwyth (MPhil), Manchester Met Univ (LLD); *Career* Madras Coll St Andrews: teacher of classics 1968–70, head of classics 1970–72; dir of studies Notre Dame HS Liverpool 1972–78, curriculum devpt offr ICT Liverpool Poly 1978–82, sr lectr ICT Liverpool Hope Univ 1982–85, teacher advsr Liverpool Educn Authy 1985–94, dir of ICT Calderstones Sch 1994–97, inspector OFSTED 1997–; conslt Dept for Educn 2007–; called to the Bar Middle Temple 2002; chm Magistrates' Assoc 2008–11; judicial memb European Network of Cncls for Judiciary 2009–15, Judicial Appointments cmmr 2012–14; chm Nat Mock Trials Competition 2013–15, pres Nat Cncl of Ind Monitoring Bds 2013, professional conslt to Steering Gp EuroJustice Forum – Restorative Justice 2013–, conslt to Max Plank Inst on Legal Pluralism; nat ldr of governance Dept of Educn 2014–; chm of govrs Sudley Jr Sch, chm of govrs All Saints Catholic High Sch Kirkby; Hon LLD Manchester Met Univ 2013; FRSA; *Publications* Micro Computing in Sport and Education (jtly, 1982), Analysis of Practical Skills (1985); *Recreations* former professional referee football/rugby league, int athletics official, skiing, listening to classical music, Scottish/Irish culture and country dancing, spending time with sister Monica, niece Lucy and their families; *Clubs* Army & Navy, Athenaeum (Liverpool); *Style—* Dr John Thornhill, OBE, JP; ✉ Independent Monitoring Board, Ministry of Justice, 9th Floor, Post Point 9.51, THe Tower, 102 Petty France, London SW1H 9AJ (☎ 020 3334 5076, e-mail president.nc@imb.cjsm.net)

THORNHILL, Richard John; s of Richard Norwood Thornhill, and Eleanor Louise, *née* Hoey; *b* 13 November 1954; *Educ* Malvern, St John's Coll Oxford (MA); *m* 30 Aug 1980, Nicola, da of Peter John Dyke, of Derby; 3 s (Hugo b 1989, Frederick b 1992, Rafe b 1997); *Career* admitted slr 1979, admitted slr of the Supreme Court Hong Kong 1982; Slaughter and May: articled clerk 1977–79, asst slr Hong Kong Office 1982–84, ptnr 1986–2013, sr ptnr Slaughter and May Hong Kong 1991–2013; chm LME Clear Ltd; *Recreations* walking, theatre, opera; *Style—* Richard Thornhill, Esq

THORNTON, Andrew Robert; *b* 28 October 1972, North Tees; *Educ* Barnard Castle Sch Co Durham; *m* 16 Sept 2015, Yvonne, *née* Dennis; 1 s (Harry b 6 May 2014); *Career* national hunt jockey; several winners incl: The Ritz Club Chase 1996, The Pertemps King George VI 1997, The Tote Cheltenham Gold Cup 1998, Royal and Sun Alliance Novice Hurdle 1998, The Sun King of the Punters' Tolworth Hurdle 1998, The Racing Post Trophy 1998, The Betterware Cup Steeplechase 1998, The Emblem Chase 1998; other races incl: Pertemps Christmas Hurdle 1998, Prix la Barka 1999, Rehearsal Chase 1999, Agfa Chase 1999, Rehearsal Chase Chepstow 1999, 2002 and 2003, Scottish Grand National 2001, Hennessey Cognac Gold Cup 2002, Badger Beer Chase 2002 and 2003, Edward Mamner Grade 2 Chase 2003, EBF Mares Hurdle Final 2004, Noel Novice Chase 2004 and 2005, The Reynoldstown Chase 2005, Dipper Novices Chase 2006, Cotswold Chase 2006, The Great Yorkshire Chase 2006 and 2007, Coral Welsh Grand National 2007, Vodka Red Square Gold Cup 2008, Victor Chandler Chase Ascot 2011 and 2012; winner Lester Award Jockey Assoc of GB 1996 and 1997, Jump Ride of the Year on Kingscliff 2003 and on Miko de Beauchene 2007; tstee Injured Jockeys Fund; *Recreations* football, golf, cricket; *Style—* Andrew Thornton, Esq; ✉ Village Farm House, Rainton, North Yorkshire YO7 3PX (☎ 07831 102 065, e-mail andrewthornton72@btinternet.com, website andrewthornton.net)

THORNTON, His Hon Anthony Christopher Lawrence; QC (1988); s of Maj Richard Thornton (d 1983), and Margery Alice Clerk, CBE (d 1993); *b* 18 August 1947, London; *Educ* Eton, Keble Coll Oxford (MA, BCL); *m* 1, 18 Feb 1983 (m dis), Lyn Christine, da of Laurence Thurlby, of Cambridge; 1 s (Matthew James b 12 June 1983); m 2, 24 June 2006, Dawn Elisabeth Collins; *Career* called to the Bar Middle Temple 1970 (bencher 1992); recorder 1992–94 (asst recorder 1988–92), circuit judge 1994–2015, official referee 1994–98, judge of Technol and Construction Court 1998–2015, dep High Court judge Administrative Court and Queen's Bench Div 2005–15; memb Gen Cncl of the Bar 1988–94 (treas 1990–92, chm Professional Standards Ctee 1992–93); Freeman City of London 1976, memb Ct of Assts Worshipful Co of Leathersellers 1996 (2nd Warden 2014–15, Master 2015–16); MIArb 1987; *Books* Halsbury's Laws Vol 4: Building Contracts (jt ed and contrib, 1972, reissue 1992), Construction Law Review (jt ed), Burns – The Expert Witness (contrib, 1989); *Recreations* opera, football, legal history, Orkney; *Clubs* S Rolandsay Golf; *Style—* His Hon Anthony Thornton, QC

THORNTON, Baroness (Life Peer UK 1998), of Manningham in the County of West Yorkshire; (Dorothea) Glenys Thornton; da of Peter Thornton, and Jean, *née* Furness; *b* 16 October 1952; *Educ* Thornton Secdy Sch Bradford, LSE (BSc(Econ)); *m* Feb 1977, John Carr, s of Henry Carr; 1 s (Hon George Carr b 4 Aug 1986) 1 da (Hon Ruby Carr b 10 March 1988); *Career* nat organiser Gingerbread 1976–78, projects dir Inst of Community Studies 1979–81, political sec Royal Arsenal Co-op Soc 1981–86, public and political affrs advsr CWS 1986–92, gen sec Fabian Soc 1993–94 (dir of devpt 1994–96); dir Emily's List 1993–; chm Gtr London Lab Pty 1986–91, min Govt Whips Office 2008–; chair Social Enterprise Coalition 2001–; govr LSE 2002–; FRSA; *Recreations* canoeing, hill walking, Star Trek; *Style—* The Rt Hon the Baroness Thornton; ✉ House

T

of Lords, London SW1A 0PW (✆ 020 7219 8502, fax 020 7263 0157, e-mail thorntong@parliament.uk)

THORNTON, James Michael (Jim); s of Dr Michael Thornton, of Audlem, Cheshire, and Margaret, *née* Hastie; *b* 19 January 1963, Nantwich, Cheshire; *Educ* Malvern Coll, Royal Holloway Coll Univ of London (BA), Watford Coll; *m* 2 Sept 1989, Melanie, *née* Hoare; 1 da (Ellerie b 19 Jan 1994), 1 s (Oliver b 7 May 1996); *Career* advtg agency copywriter: JWT (J Walter Thompson) 1986–95, GGT 1995–97; copywriter/creative dir TBWA 1997–99, creative dir Mother 1999–2003, exec creative dir Leo Burnett Ltd 2003–07, dir Lord Plumpton Ltd (advtg and mktg consultancy) 2007–; gardening corr Marmalade Magazine 2003–04; memb D&AD 1997; *Recreations* being a dad; *Clubs* Stoke City London Supporters, Sussex CCC, Century, Hurst House; *Style—* Jim Thornton, Esq; ✉ Lord Plumpton Limited, Little Hackmans, Plumpton Lane, Plumpton, Lewes, East Sussex BN7 3AJ (✆ 01273 891866, e-mail jim@lordplumpton.com)

THORNTON, HE James Sebastian; s of Edward Alfred Thornton (d 1984), and Mary Thornton Howard, *née* Maries; *Educ* Lincoln Coll Oxford (BA); *m* Anne; 2 da (Helena b 2002, Julia b 2006); *Career* diplomat; non-nuclear energy desk offr Environment, Science and Energy Dept FCO 1990–91, second sec political/economic/commercial Algiers 1992–94, N Africa desk offr Nr East and N Africa Dept FCO 1994–95, Perm Under Sec's Dept FCO 1995–96, head War Crimes Section UN Dept FCO 1997–99, head Political Sectin Mexico City 2000–03, dep head of mission Abidjan 2003–04, dep head Sudan Unit FCO/Dept for Int Devpt 2005–07, dep head of mission UK Delgn to the OECD 2007–11, high cmmr to Zambia 2012–15, Br ambass to Bolivia 2016–; *Style—* HE Mr James Thornton; ✉ c/o FCO, King Charles Street, London SW1A 2AH (e-mail james.thornton@fco.gov.uk, website www.fco.gov.uk)

THORNTON, Prof Dame Janet Maureen; DBE (2012, CBE 2000); da of James Stanley McLoughlin, of Dorset, and Kathleen, *née* Barlow; *b* 23 May 1949; *Educ* Univ of Nottingham (BSc), KCL and Nat Inst for Med Research (PhD); *m* 25 July 1970, Alan David Thornton, s of David Thornton; 1 s (Alexander b 29 Oct 1975), 1 da (Hazel b 7 Dec 1977); *Career* research asst Lab of Molecular Biophysics Univ of Oxford 1973–78; tutor Open Univ 1976–83; research scientist Molecular Pharmacology Nat Inst for Med Research 1978; Birkbeck Coll London: SERC advanced fell Crystallography Dept 1979–83, lectr 1983–89, sr lectr 1989–90, head Jt Research Sch in Biomolecular Sciences 1996–, Bernal chair Crystallography Dept 1996–, dir BBSRC Centre for Structural Biology 1998–2001; prof of biomolecular structure UCL 1990–2001, dir European Bioinformatics Inst 2001–, fell Churchill Coll Cambridge 2002–; Wellcome visiting prof Rutgers State Univ 1995; chm BBSRC Bioinformatics Ctee 1995–98, chm Br Biophysical Soc 1995–98; memb: SERC Biochemistry/Biophysics Sub-Ctee for grant peer review 1989–92, Protein and Peptide Research Gp Ctee Biochemical Soc 1989–92, Ctee Br Biophysical Soc 1992–94, Advsy Bd Brookhaven Protein Structure Databank 1992–, MRC Molecular and Cellular Med Bd B 1993–97, Chemicals and Pharmaceuticals Directorate BBSRC 1994–97, BBSRC Strategy Bd 1999–, EPSRC Life Sciences Peer Review Coll 1999–, Cncl Protein Soc 1999–; memb Editorial Bd: Protein Engineering, Current Opinion in Structural Biology, Structure, Folding and Design, Molecular Recognition, Jl of Molecular Biology; memb Scientific Advsy Bd Oxford Molecular Ltd 1990–97; conslt Euro Bioinformatics Inst; Ronald Tress Prize for Research 1986, Pfizer Academic Award for Excellence in Research 1991, Federation of European Biochemical Societies lectr 1993, Han Neurath Award Protein Soc 2000–, ISCB Sr Scientist Accomplishment Award 2005, Premio Citta di Firenze sulle Scienze Moelcari 2007, Dorothy Crowfoot Hodgkin Award 2009; hon DSc: Univ of Leeds 2007, Univ of St Andrews 2007, UCL 2007, Univ of Kent 2008; hon degree Bergen Univ Norway 2008, hon DTech Brunel Univ 2008; foreign assoc memb Nat Acad of Scientists USA; FRS 1999; *Publications* author of 200 papers in scientific and learned jls; *Recreations* reading, music, walking, gardens; *Style—* Prof Dame Janet Thornton, DBE, FRS; ✉ European Bioinformatics Institute, The Wellcome Trust Genome Campus, Cambridge CB10 1SD (✆ 01223 494648, fax 01223 494000, e-mail thornton@ebi.ac.uk)

THORNTON, Kate Louise; da of Dennis Thornton, and Sandra, *née* Parker; *b* 7 February 1973; *Children* 1 s (Ben b 2008); *Career* television and radio presenter; feature writer/entertainment columnist Daily Mirror and Sunday Mirror 1993–95, ed Smash Hits 1995–96, contributing ed Marie Claire 1997–2003, writer Sunday Times 1997–2004; guest and documentary presenter Radio 2 2002–; television incl: presenter Top of the Pops 1998–99, entertainment reporter This Morning (ITV) 1998–2000, The Ideal Home Show 2001–02, Holiday (BBC 1) 2001–03, Holiday – You Call the Shots (BBC 1) 2001–03, Pop Idol Extra (ITV 2) 2001–03, co-presenter Loose Women (ITV) 2009–; *Recreations* music; *Style—* Ms Kate Thornton

THORNTON, Prof (Robert) Kelsey Rought; s of Harold Thornton (d 1975), and Mildred, *née* Brooks (d 1995); *b* 12 August 1938, Huddersfield, Yorks; *Educ* Burnley GS, Univ of Manchester (BA, MA, PhD); *m* 1, 3 Aug 1961 (m dis 1976), Sarah Elizabeth Ann, da of Hendri Griffiths; 2 s (Jason b 1965, Ben b 1968); m 2, 22 Sept 1989 (m dis 2003), Eileen Valerie, da of Maurice Davison; 1 da (Amy b 1979), 1 s (Thomas b 1982); m 3, 28 Feb 2004, Hilary Marchant, da of Francis Thompson; *Career* Univ of Newcastle upon Tyne: lectr 1965–75, sr lectr 1975–84, prof 1984–89, visiting prof 2001–; prof Sch of Eng Univ of Birmingham 1989–2000 (head of Sch 1989–96); chm John Clare Soc 1987–90; pres Friends of the Dymock Poets; FRSA; *Books* incl: John Clare: The Midsummer Cushion (1978), John Clare: The Rural Muse (1982), The Decadent Dilemma (1983), Gerard Manley Hopkins: The Poems (1973), All My Eyes See: The Visual World of Gerard Manley Hopkins (1975), Ivor Gurney Collected Letters (1991), Ivor Gurney: Best Poems and the Book of Five Makings (1995), Poetry of the 1890s (1997), Ivor Gurney: 80 Poems or So (1997), Ernest Dowson: Collected Shorter Fiction (2003), Ernest Dowson: Collected Poems (2003), Random Rhymes (2009), Self-Portrait of My Father and Other Poems (2011), Adlestrophes (2012), Joseph Skipsey (2012), Correspondence of Gerard Manley Hopkins (2 vols, 2013, Morton Cohen Prize Modern Language Assoc of America 2015), Ivor Gurney: Poems of War (2014); ed jls: The Ivor Gurney Soc Jl (1995–), 28 vols in the series Decadents, Symbolists, Anti-Decadents (1993–96); *Recreations* water colour painting, book collecting; *Clubs* Pen and Palette; *Style—* Prof Kelsey Thornton; ✉ 2 Rectory Terrace, Gosforth, Newcastle upon Tyne NE3 1XY (✆ 0191 284 3083, e-mail rkrthornton@btinternet.com)

THORNTON, Kevin Nicholas; s of Edmond Thornton (d 2005), and Rita, *née* Landy; *b* 26 April 1958, Cashel, Co Tipperary, Ireland; *Educ* Christian Bros Sch Cashel, Regnl Tech Coll Galway, Nat Coll of Art and Design (Dip), Dublin Inst of Technol Coll of Catering; *m* Muriel, *née* O'Connor; 2 s (Edward, Conor); *Career* chef and restaurateur; jr chef positions Galway, London, Switzerland, Dublin, and Toronto 1974–87, sous chef Marcel's Bistro Toronto 1985, chef sausiere Shelbourne Hotel Dublin 1986, chef de partie Restaurant Paul Bocuse Lyon 1987 (3 Michelin Stars), sous chef Shelbourne Hotel Dublin 1988, chef de cuisine Adare Manor Co Limerick 1989; chef and prop: The Wine Epergne Dublin 1990, Thornton's Restaurant Dublin 1994– (2 Michelin Stars 2001 (Michelin Star 1995), 4 AA Rosettes 2000 (3 Rosettes 1998); Restaurant of the Year: Egon Ronay 1996, Jameson Good Food Guide 1997 and 2003, AA Good Food Guide 2000, Food and Wine Magazine 2001); lectr Coll of Catering Dublin 1992; 2 Gold medals and Silver medal Chef Ireland 1991 (Silver and Bronze medals 1989), Hotelympia Silver medal 1992 (Bronze medal 1990), Bocuse D'Or 1992, Gilbeys Gold medal 1996; Chef of the Year: Egon Ronay 1995, Wedgwood 1997, Food and Wine Magazine 2001 (runner-up 2003 and 2004); *Publications* Food for Life; *Style—* Kevin Thornton, Esq; ✉ Thornton's Restaurant, 128 St Stephens Green, Dublin 2, Ireland (✆ 00 353 1 478 7008, fax 00 353 1 478 7009, e-mail thorntonsrestaurant@eircom.net, website www.thorntonsrestaurant.com)

THORNTON, Sir (George) Malcolm; kt (1992); s of George Edmund Thornton by his w Ethel; *b* 3 April 1939; *Educ* Wallasey GS, Liverpool Nautical Coll; *m* 1, 1962; 1 s; m 2, 1972, Sue Banton (d 1989); m 3, 1990, Rosemary, *née* Hewitt; *Career* former River Mersey pilot; memb: Wallasey County Borough Cncl 1965–74, Wirral Metropolitan Cncl 1973–79 (ldr 1974–77); chm Merseyside Dists Liaison Ctee 1975–77; vice-pres: Assoc of Met Authorities, Burnham Ctee 1978–79; chm: AMA Educn Ctee 1978–79, Cncl of Local Educn Authorities 1978–79; MP (Cons): Liverpool Garston 1979–83, Crosby 1983–97; PPS to Rt Hon Patrick Jenkin: as Industry Sec 1981–83, as Environment Sec 1983–84; memb Select Ctee on: Environment 1979–81, Educn and Employment 1985–97 (chm 1988–97); sec: Cons Parly Shipping and Shipbuilding Ctee 1979–81, Cons Parly Educn Ctee; chm: Broadskill Ltd (formerly Intuition Gp Ltd) 2002–08, Value Based Solutions 2006–; non-exec dir: Stack Computer Solutions Ltd 2001–, HB Villages Ltd 2011–; chm: Bd of Tstees Mersey Mission To Seafarers 2002–09, Birmingham Local Educn Partnership 2009–13; co-chm Liverpool Seafarers Centre 2008–10; tstee Enquire Learning Tst 2013–; pro-chllr and chm Bd Liverpool John Moores Univ 2007–13 (memb Bd 2001–13, chm Audit Ctee 2003–07); fell Industry and Parliament Tst, hon ambass fell Liverpool John Moores Univ; Hon Col 156 (NW) Tport Regt the Royal Logistic Corps (V) 2000–05, Hon DEd De Montfort Univ; FRSA; *Recreations* golf, home entertaining, word games; *Clubs* Heswall Golf; *Style—* Sir Malcolm Thornton, FRSA; ✉ Meadow Brook, 79 Barnston Road, Heswall, Wirral CH60 1UE

THORNTON, Margaret Barbara; da of Cyril Arthur Wales (d 1983), and Anna Margaret Wales, MBE, *née* Chang; *b* 28 January 1940; *Educ* Burgess Hill PNEU Sussex, Mary Wray Secretarial Coll Sussex; *m* 1972, Adrian Heber Thornton, s of Nigel Heber Thornton, Croix de Guerre (d 1941); 2 da (Emily Harriet b 1973, Rebecca Louise b 1980), 1 s (Jasper Hamilton b 1975); *Career* dir and gallery owner Redfern Gallery; artists represented: Sarah Armstrong-Jones, Frank Avray Wilson, Elizabeth Butterworth, Paul Emsley, Paul Feiler, Annabel Gault, William Gear, RA, Danny Markey, Brendan Neiland, RA, Bryan Organ, Patrick Procktor, David Tindle, RA, Paul Wunderlich; *Recreations* visiting galleries, museums and antique markets; *Style—* Mrs Margaret Thornton; ✉ The Redfern Gallery, 20 Cork Street, London W1 (✆ 020 7734 1732, 020 7734 0578, e-mail art@redfern-gallery.com, website www.redfern-gallery.com)

THORNTON, Peter Anthony; s of Robert Thornton (d 1990), and Freda, *née* Willey (d 2000); *b* 8 May 1944, Yorks; *Educ* Bradford GS, Univ of Manchester (BSc); *m* 1, 1969 (m dis 1987); 2 da (Victoria Jane b 1973, Charlotte Sarah b 1974), 1 s (James William b 1976); m 2, 1997, Susan, da of Herbert Harris, of Maidstone, Kent; *Career* chartered surveyor and engineer; chm Greycoat Real Estate LLP; Liveryman Worshipful Co of Chartered Surveyors; FRICS, FICE; *Recreations* tennis, water skiing, cars; *Clubs* Riverside; *Style—* Peter Thornton, Esq; ✉ Van Buren Cottage, Queen's Ride, Barnes Common, London SW13 0JF (✆ 020 8788 1969); Greycoat Real Estate LLP, 9 Savoy Street, London WC2E 7EG (✆ 020 7379 1000, fax 020 7379 8708, mobile 07768 152584, e-mail pthornton@greycoat.co.uk)

THORNTON, His Hon Judge Peter Ribblesdale; QC (1992); s of Robert Ribblesdale Thornton, of Winterborne Whitechurch, Dorset, and Ruth Eleanor, *née* Tuckson; *b* 17 October 1946; *Educ* Clifton, St John's Coll Cambridge (BA); *m* 13 June 1981, Susan Margaret, da of Maneck Ardeshir Dalal; 1 s (Daniel Richard Dalal b 14 July 1990), 1 da (Amy Christina Dalal b 30 June 1992); *Career* called to the Bar Middle Temple 1969 (bencher 2001); recorder 1997–2007 (asst recorder 1994–97), dep judge of the High Court 2003–, sr circuit judge (South Eastern Circuit) 2007–16, chief coroner of England and Wales 2012–16; jt head Doughty Street Chambers 2005–07 (fndr memb, dep head 1990–2005); chm: NCCL 1981–83, Civil Liberties Tst 1991–95; *Books* Public Order Law (1987), Decade of Decline: Civil Liberties in the Thatcher Years (1989), The Penguin Civil Liberty Guide (co-ed, 1989), Archbold: Criminal Pleading, Evidence and Practice (contrib ed, 1992–), The Law of Public Order and Protest (jtly, 2010); *Style—* His Hon Judge Peter Thornton, QC; ✉ Central Criminal Court, Old Bailey, London EC4M 7EH

THORNTON, Sara Joanne; CBE (2011), QPM (2006); *Career* Thames Valley Police: asst chief constable special ops 2000–03, dep chief constable 2003–06, acting chief constable 2006–07, chief constable 2007–15; vice-pres ACPO 2011–15, chair Nat Police Chiefs' Cncl (NPCC) 2015–; *Style—* Ms Sara Thornton, CBE, QPM; ✉ National Police Chiefs' Council, 1st Floor, 10 Victoria Street, London SW1H 0NN

THORNTON, Stephen; CBE (2002); s of Harry Thornton, and Alice, *née* Ainsworth; *b* 23 January 1954; *Educ* Paston Sch North Walsham, Univ of Manchester (BA); *m* Lorraine; 2 c; *Career* joined NHS nat grad mgmnt trg prog 1979, subsequently held various NHS operational mgmnt appts running servs for mental health, learning disability, community health servs and health promotion, exec dir E Anglian RHA (incl period of secondment to Dept of Health) then chief exec Cambridge and Huntingdon HA until 1997, chief exec NHS Confedn 1997–2001, chief exec The Health Fndn 2002–; cmmr Healthcare Cmmn 2003–06, non-exec dir Monitor (ind regulator of NHS fndn tsts) 2006–, expert memb Nat Quality Bd 2009–; writer and regular speaker on health and health serv issues in UK and abroad; dir Christian Blind Mission (UK) 2002–05, memb Cncl Open Univ 2002–06; FRSM, Hon FRCP 2010; *Clubs* Commonwealth; *Style—* Stephen Thornton, Esq, CBE; ✉ The Health Foundation, 90 Long Acre, London WC2E 9RA (✆ 020 7257 8000, fax 020 7257 8001, e-mail stephen.thornton@health.org.uk)

THORNTON, Victoria; OBE (2012); *Educ* Birkbeck London (MA); *Career* dir RIBA Architecture Centre 1991–98, fndr dir Open-City 1992–, architecture conslt Br Cncl 1998–2000; memb Bd: Irish Architecture Fndn 2005–, Green Sky Thinking Sounding 2012–; memb Advsy Bd Spacehive, dir Architecture & Built Environment Centres Network 2013–; expert advsr: Bartlett 2050 Leadership Prog 2013–, Farrell Review for Architecture Policy 2013–; Hon MA London Met Univ; hon fell RIBA 2003; *Style—* Ms Victoria Thornton, OBE; ✉ Open-City, 18 Ensign Street, London E1 8JD (website www.open-city.org.uk)

THOROLD, Sir (Anthony) Oliver; 16 Bt (E 1642); s of Sir Anthony Thorold, 15 Bt, OBE, DSC (d 1999); *b* 15 April 1945; *Educ* Winchester, Lincoln Coll Oxford; *m* 1977, Prof Genevra Richardson, *qv*, da of John L Richardson (d 2002), of Broadshaw, W Lothian; 1 s (Henry b 1981), 1 da (Lydia b 1985); *Heir* s, Henry Lowry; *Career* barr Inner Temple 1971; *Style—* Sir Oliver Thorold, Bt

THORP, Jeremy Walter; CMG (2001); s of Walter Thorp (d 1977), of Dublin, and Dorothy Bliss (d 1989); *b* 12 December 1941; *Educ* King Edward VII Sch Sheffield, CCC Oxford (MA); *m* 15 Sept 1973, Estela Maria, da of Alberto Lessa (d 1968), of Montevideo, Uruguay; *Career* HM Treasy 1963–78: asst private sec to Sec of State for Econ Affrs 1967–69, financial attaché HM Embassy Washington 1971–73; FCO: joined 1978, first sec head of Chancery and consul-gen Lima 1982–86, dep head of mission Dublin 1988–92, head Res and Fin Dept FCO 1993–97; with Unilever plc 1997–98; ambass to Colombia 1998–2001 (ret), dir Br Bankers' Assoc 2002–06, sec Jt Money Laundering Steering Gp 2002–06; memb Advsy Cncl Inst Briefing and Conf Centre Farnham Castle 2002–06; tstee Children Change Colombia (formerly Children of the Andes) 2002–15, memb Bd Br-Colombian C of C 2002–, chm Anglo-Colombian Soc 2006–10 (memb Exec Ctee 2002–); *Recreations* music, walking, travel, reading, modern Irish history, looking at paintings, Germany, Latin America; *Style—* Jeremy Thorp, Esq, CMG; ✉ 9 Coutts Crescent, St Albans Road, London NW5 1RF (e-mail jeremy@thorp31.plus.com)

THORPE; *see also:* Gardner-Thorpe

THORPE, Adam Naylor; s of Bernard Naylor Thorpe, and Sheila Grace, *née* Greenlees (d 2003); *b* 5 December 1956; *Educ* Marlborough, Magdalen Coll Oxford (BA); *m* 23 Nov 1985, Joanna Louise Wistreich; 2 s (Joshua, Sacha), 1 da (Anastasia); *Career* co fndr Equinox Travelling Theatre 1980, drama and mime teacher City and E London Coll Stepney 1983–87, lectr in English PCL 1987–90, poetry critic The Observer 1989–95, currently book critic The Guardian; author and poet; winner: Eric Gregory award 1985, second prize Nat Poetry Competition 1986; *Poetry* Mornings in the Baltic (1988, shortlisted Whitbread Prize for Poetry 1988), Meeting Montaigne (1990), From the Neanderthal (1999), Nine Lessons from the Dark (2003), Birds with a Broken Wing (2007); *Novels* Ulverton (1992, Winifred Holtby Prize for best regnl novel), Still (1995), Pieces of Light (1998), Nineteen Twenty-One (2001), No Telling (2003), The Rules of Perspective (2005), Between Each Breath (2007); *Plays* The Fen Story (Monday play Radio 4, 1991), Offa's Daughter (Sunday play Radio 3, 1993), Couch Grass and Ribbon (stage play, 1996), Devastated Areas (Saturday play Radio 4, 2006); *Short Story Collections* Shifts (2000), Is This The Way You Said? (2006); *Recreations* walking, swimming, music, theatre; *Style—* Adam Thorpe

THORPE, Prof Alan John; OBE (2016); s of Jack Fielding Thorpe (d 1987), and Dorothy Kathleen, *née* Davey (d 2003); *b* 15 July 1952, Newcastle upon Tyne; *Educ* Univ of Warwick (BSc), Imperial Coll London (PhD); *m* 17 February 1979, Helen Elizabeth, *née* Edgar; 1 da (Alison Mary b 16 May 1980), 1 s (David Leslie b 16 Dec 1982); *Career* postdoctoral research asst Imperial Coll London 1976–81, scientist Met Office 1981–82, lectr, reader then prof of meteorology Univ of Reading 1982–99, dir Hadley Centre Met Office 1999–2001, dir NERC Centres of Atmospheric Science 2001–05, chief exec NERC 2005–; visiting prof Univ of Reading; author of over 100 papers in peer-reviewed jls; L F Richardson Prize 1976, RMS Buchan Prize 1992; *Recreations* art history and appreciation; *Style—* Prof Alan Thorpe, OBE; ✉ Natural Environment Research Council, Polaris House, North Star Avenue, Swindon SN2 1EU (e-mail hqpo@nerc.ac.uk)

THORPE, Amelia Jane; da of Robert Barrie Thorpe, of Boxford, Suffolk, and Margaret, *née* Davenport; *b* 1 July 1961; *Educ* Beaconsfield HS, Goldsmiths Coll London (BA); *m* 23 Dec 1991, Adam Russell, s of Peter Caton Russell; 2 da (Evelina b 28 March 1994, Edie b 4 May 1996); *Career* publishing dir Merehurst Ltd 1983–89, md Ebury Press (responsible for Ebury Press, Vermilion, Rider, Fodor's) and memb Exec Mgmnt Ctee Random House Gp 1989–2002, publishing, editorial conslt and design writer 2002–; FRSA; *Recreations* food and wine, art and antiques; *Style—* Ms Amelia Thorpe; ✉ 4 Lyndhurst Square, London SE15 5AR (☎ 020 7703 1026, e-mail ameliathorpe@hotmail.com)

THORPE, David Allan; s of Albert David Thorpe (d 1979), of Upton-upon-Severn, Worcs, and Gertrude Kathleen, *née* Wilkins; *b* 7 August 1949, Stourport-on-Severn, Worcs; *Educ* Hanley Castle GS Worcs; *m* 1, 1971 (m dis 1989), Maureen June Adams; m 2, 22 March 2003, Sheila, *née* York; 2 da (Karen Julie, Andrea Louise); *Career* early career as accountant in local govt Worcs, Essex and London (latterly asst treas London Borugh of Havering), subsequently in sales and mktg Honeywell; EDS: joined 1994 (i/c developing govt business), ceo UK 1995, chief operating offr EMEA 1996, pres European business until 2003; currently chm: Radius Ltd, Arena Racing Company Ltd, JLA Ltd; former non-exec dir: Torex plc, Staffware plc, Anite plc (interim ceo 2003), iSoft plc, VT Gp plc, Interserve plc; former non-exec chm: Tunstall Hldgs Ltd, Morgan Chambers plc, Arena Leisure plc, SHL Ltd, CAS Services Ltd, Innovation Gp plc, Lumesse Ltd, Teufel GmbH, BHA Ltd; chm Racecourse Assoc 2004–09, dir BHB, dir Horserace Betting Levy Bd; Liveryman Worshipful Co of Info Technologists; IPFA 1971; *Recreations* horses (breeding and racing), wine and food; *Clubs* RAC; *Style—* David Thorpe, Esq; ☎ 07790 491000, e-mail david@bobblefarm.co.uk, Twitter @davidathorpe

THORPE, Geoffrey Digby; s of late Gordon Digby Thorpe, and Agnes Joyce Saville, *née* Haines; *b* 24 September 1949; *Educ* Windsor GS for Boys, Architectural Assoc Sch of Architecture (AA Dip); *m* 29 Sept 1973, Jane Florence, da of late James Hay McElwee, of Havant, Hampshire; 1 da (Holly b 1980); *Career* indust gp architect; Milton Keynes Devpt Corp 1974–78, asst co architect East Sussex 1978–80, chm Thorpe Architecture Ltd 1980–, princ Thorpe Architecture 1993–2006, princ Thorpe Wheatley Ltd 2006–; chm Prospace Ltd; memb Br Cncl for Offices; RIBA 1975; memb: ARCUK 1975, AA; *Recreations* fly and game fishing, boating; *Style—* Geoffrey Thorpe, Esq; ✉ Thorpe Wheatley Ltd, Sparks Yard, Tarrant Street, Arundel, West Sussex BN18 9SB (☎ 01903 883500, fax 01903 882188, e-mail geoff@twarch.co.uk, website www.thorpewheatley.com)

THORPE, Rt Hon Sir Mathew Alexander; kt (1988); yr s of late Michael Alexander Thorpe, of Petworth, W Sussex, and Dorothea Margaret, *née* Lambert; *b* 30 July 1938; *Educ* Stowe, Balliol Coll Oxford; *m* 1, 30 Dec 1966, Lavinia Hermione, da of Maj Robert James Buxton (d 1968); 3 s (Gervase b 1967 d 2008, Alexander b 1969, Marcus b 1971); m 2, 3 Aug 1989, Mrs Carola Millar; *Career* called to the Bar Inner Temple 1961 (bencher 1985); QC 1980, recorder of the Crown Court 1982, judge of the High Court of Justice (Family Div) 1988–95, a Lord Justice of Appeal 1995–2013, head of International Family Justice 2005–13; *Style—* The Rt Hon Sir Mathew Thorpe

THREADGOLD, Andrew Richard; s of Stanley Dennis Threadgold, of Brentwood, Essex, and late Phyllis Ethel, *née* Marsh; *b* 8 February 1944; *Educ* Brentwood Sch, Univ of Nottingham (BA), Univ of Melbourne (PhD); *m* 1, 1966 (m dis), Rosalind; 2 s (Richard b 1967, Matthew b 1971); m 2, 1994, Deirdre; 1 da (Zoe b 1995); *Career* mangr econ info Int Wool Secretariat 1971–74, advsr Econ Div Bank of England 1974–84, on secondment chief economist Postel Investment Management Ltd 1984–86, head fin supervision Gen Div Bank of England 1986–87, chief exec and dir securities investment Postel Investment Management Ltd 1987–93, with AMP 1993–98 (latterly chief investment offr); non-exec dir: Equitable Life 2001–, Inflexion 2004–; *Style—* Andrew Threadgold, Esq

THRIFT, Prof Sir Nigel John; kt (2015), DL (West Midlands 2014); s of Leonard John Thrift (d 1997), and Joyce Mary, *née* Wakeley; *b* 12 October 1949, Bath; *Educ* Nailsea Sch, UCW Aberystwyth (BA), Univ of Bristol (PhD, DSc); *m* 6 May 1978, Lynda Jean Thrift; 2 da (Victoria Caroline Jane b 29 April 1979, Jessica Abigail b 26 May 1982); *Career* research offr Martin Centre for Architectural and Urban Studies Univ of Cambridge 1975–76, research fell Dept of Geography Univ of Leeds 1976–78, sr research fell Dept of Human Geography ANU 1981–83 (research fell 1979–81); Dept of Geography St David's UC Lampeter: lectr 1984–86, Univ of Wales reader 1986–87; Univ of Bristol: lectr then reader Dept of Geography 1987–90, prof Sch of Geographical Sciences 1990–2003 (head of sch 1995–99), emeritus prof 2003–, chair Univ Research Ctee 2001–03; head Div of Life and Environmental Sciences and prof Sch of Geography Univ of Oxford 2004–05, student ChCh Oxford, pro-vice-chllr (research) Univ of Oxford 2005–06 (visiting prof 2006–), vice-chllr Univ of Warwick 2006–16; exec dir Schwarzman Scholars 2016–; hon memb of faculty Dept of Geography UCLA 1984, hon memb of faculty Geographical Inst ETH Zürich 1987, hon research scholar Sch of Earth Sciences Macquarie Univ Sydney 1989, visiting prof Grad Sch of Architecure and Urban Planning UCLA 1992, fell Netherlands Inst of Advanced Study Wassenaar 1993, guest prof Institut für Geographie Univ of Vienna 1998, fell Swedish Collegium for Advanced Study in the Social Sciences Uppsala 1999, distinguished visiting prof Nat Univ of Singapore 2002; chair Research Assessment Exercise 2008 Main Panel H HEFCE 2005–07, chair Ind Cmmn on HE 2012–, chair IPPR Cmmn on the Future of HE; memb: Research Assessment Exercise 2001 Panel for Geography HEFCE 1999–2001, Geography Panel Leverhulme Prize Fellowship 2000–06, Research Priorities Bd ESRC 2001–05, Bd Higher Educn Statistics Agency 2008–, American Cncl of Educn Blue Ribbon Panel on Global Engagement 2010–11, Bd Coventry and Warks Local Enterprise Partnership 2010–, Nat Curriculum Review Advsy Panel 2012–, Govt Bd European Inst of Innovation and Technol; tstee: Cncl for Industry and HE 2011–, Liverpool Sch of Tropical Medicine, Higher Educn Policy Inst 2015–, Univ Devpt Fndn Sacramento 2015–; cmmr FCO Marshall Fund 2010–; ed: Environment and Planning A; author, co-author, ed or co-ed of 37 books and 200 papers in jls and edited collections, memb 10 editorial bds; RGS Heath Award 1988, RSGS Newbigin Prize 1998, Univ of Helsinki Medal 1999, RGS Victoria Medal 2003, Distinguished Scholarship Honours Assoc of American Geographers 2007, Scottish Geographical Medal RSGS 2009; MA (by incorporation) Univ of Oxford 2004, Hon LLD Univ of Bristol 2010, Hon LLD Monash Univ Melbourne 2013; AcSS 2000, FBA 2003; *Clubs* Reform; *Style—* Prof Sir Nigel Thrift, DL; ✉ Schwarzman Scholars, 641 Lexington Avenue, New York NY10 022 (☎ 001 212 314 8753, e-mail nigel.thrift@schwarzmanscholars.org)

THUBRON, Colin Gerald Dryden; CBE (2007); s of Brig Gerald Ernest Thubron, DSO, OBE (d 1992), of Piltdown, E Sussex, and Evelyn Kate Mary, *née* Dryden (d 2007); *b* 14 June 1939; *Educ* Eton; *m* 2011, Margreta de Grazia; *Career* on editorial staff: Hutchinson & Co 1959–62, Macmillan Co NY 1964–65; freelance film-maker 1962–64; author; RSGS Mungo Park Medal 2000, RSAA Lawrence of Arabia Memorial Medal 2000, RGS Ness Award 2011, International Prize Spanish Geographical Soc 2014; Hon DLitt Univ of Warwick; FRSL 1969 (vice-pres 2003–09, pres 2010–); *Books* Mirror to Damascus (1967), The Hills of Adonis (1968), Jerusalem (1969), Journey Into Cyprus (1975), The God in the Mountain (1977), Emperor (1978), Among the Russians (1983), A Cruel Madness (1984, Silver Pen Award), Behind the Wall (1987, Hawthornden Prize, Thomas Cook Award), Falling (1989), Turning Back the Sun (1991), The Lost Heart of Asia (1994), Distance (1996), In Siberia (1999, Prix Bouvier), To the Last City (2002), Shadow of the Silk Road (2006), To a Mountain in Tibet (2011); *Style—* Colin Thubron, Esq, CBE, FRSL; ✉ 28 Upper Addison Gardens, London W14 8AJ

THURLEY, Dr Simon John; CBE (2011); s of late Thomas Manley Thurley, and Rachel, *née* House; *b* 29 August 1962; *Educ* Kimbolton Sch, Bedford Coll London (BA), Courtauld Inst (MA, PhD); *m* 2008, Dr Anna Keay; 1 s (b 2008 (twin)), 1 da (b 2008 (twin)); *Career* inspector of ancient monuments Crown Bldgs and Monuments Gp English Heritage 1981–89, curator of the Historic Royal Palaces 1989–97, dir Museum of London 1997–2002, chief exec English Heritage 2002–14, chief exec Historic England 2014; sr research fell Inst of Historical Research 2014–; visiting prof of the built environment Gresham Coll 2008–; tstee Canal and River Tst 2012–, memb Bd Br Library 2015–; tstee Andrew Lloyd Webber Fndn 2015–; hon fell Royal Holloway Univ of London 2003; FSA, FRHS, Hon RIBA, Hon RICS; *Publications* The Royal Palaces of Tudor England – Architecture and Court Life 1460–1547 (1993), Whitehall Palace – An Architectural History (1999), Hampton Court – An Architectural and Social History (2003), Lost Buildings of Britain (2004), Somerset House – Palace of England's Queens (2008), Men From the Ministry (2013), The Building of England (2013); contrib many volumes, magazines and jls; *Style—* Dr Simon Thurley, CBE; ✉ website www.simonthurley.com

THURLOW, Dr Alexander Cresswell; s of Maurice Cresswell Thurlow (d 1940), and Despina Alexandra, *née* Evangelinou; *b* 13 April 1940; *Educ* Brighton Hove E Sussex GS, St Mary's Hosp Med Sch (MB BS); *m* 29 June 1963, Joanna, da of Stefan Woycicki, of Wilts; 2 da (Susan Kristina b 1965, Jane b 1966); *Career* sr registrar in anaesthesia St Thomas' Hosp and Hosp For Sick Children 1969–72; conslt anaesthetist: St George's Hosp 1972–, Royal Dental Hosp 1972–82; asst prof of anaesthesia Stanford Univ 1975–76, tutor and lectr in anaesthesia Royal Coll of Anaesthetists 1977–2000; chm Southern Soc of Anaesthetists, memb Assoc of Anaesthetists, memb Assoc of Dental Anaesthetists; memb BMA, FRCA 1968; *Books* contrib: Clinics In Anaesthesiology (1983), Anaesthesia and Sedation in Dentistry (1983), A Practice of Anaesthesia (1984); *Recreations* swimming, travel, opera, theatre; *Style—* Dr Alexander Thurlow; ✉ Department of Anaesthesia, St George's Hospital, Blackshaw Road, London SW17 0QT (☎ 020 8672 1255)

THURLOW, Prof David George; OBE (1987); s of Frederick Charles Thurlow (d 1986), of Bury St Edmunds, Suffolk, and Audrey Isabel Mary, *née* Farrow; *b* 31 March 1939; *Educ* King Edward VI Sch Bury St Edmunds, Dept of Architecture Cambridge Coll of Art, Sch of Architecture Canterbury Coll of Art, Univ of Cambridge (MA); *m* 19 Dec 1959, Pamela Ann, da of Percy Adolphous Rumbelow; 3 da (Suzanne Elizabeth, Jane Ann, Emma Louise); *Career* architect; fndr ptnr: Cambridge Design Group 1970, Cambridge Design Architects 1975, Design Group Cambridge 1988, Thurlow, Carnell & Curtis 1991, David Thurlow Partnership 2002; Faculty of Architecture Univ of Cambridge 1970–77, Sch of Architecture Univ of Nottingham 1991–96, emeritus prof of architecture South Bank Univ 1998– (head Architecture Div 1996–97), dir MA in architectural design Univ of Bath 2001–05; exhibitor Royal Acad Summer Exhibition 1983–; awards incl: RIBA Award 1976, 1984, 1986 and 1990, Civic Tst Award 1978 and 1986, DOE Housing Award 1985; assessor: RIBA Awards 1979, 1984, 1986 and 1990, Civic Tst Awards 1979–97; fndr memb: Granta Housing Soc, Cambridge Forum for the Construction Industry 1981 (chm 1985–86); memb PSA Design Panel 1987–89; pres Assoc of Conslt Architects (ACA) 1991–93, Surveyors Club 2004; ARIBA 1965; *Recreations* cricket, golf, food; *Clubs* MCC; *Style—* Prof David Thurlow, OBE

THURSBY-PELHAM, Douglas Thomas Harvey; s of late Col Donald Hervey Thursby-Pelham, and Chantal Jeanne Marie Anne, *née* Walsh de Serrant; *b* 27 September 1956; *Educ* Wellington, KCL (BA); *m* 9 Aug 1986, Zoë Anne, da of late David Stanley Joseph Moseley; 2 da (Alexandra Anne b 10 Aug 1988, Victoria Alice b 26 July 1993), 1 s (Charles David Harvey b 13 Dec 1989); *Career* Londsdale Advertising Ltd: grad trainee 1979–81, account exec 1981–83, account mangr 1983–84; account dir Allen Brady and Marsh Ltd 1985–86 (joined 1984), bd dir BMP DDB Needham (formerly known as Reeves Robertshaw Needham then DDB Needham Worldwide) 1988–89 (joined 1986), client servs dir Publicis Ltd 1994–97 (gp account dir 1990–94), md Clark and Taylor 1997–98, account md Young & Rubicam EMEA 1998–2007, md Innocean Worldwide Europe 2008–09, ptnr Vinculum Fund Mgmnt 2010–; IPA Advertising Effectiveness Award 1992, Advtg and Mktg Effectiveness Award New York Festival 1995; *Clubs* MCC; *Style—* Douglas Thursby-Pelham, Esq; ✉ Littledean, Bramdean, Alresford, Hampshire SO24 0JU (☎ 01962 771358, e-mail dthursbypelham@aol.com)

THURSO, 3 Viscount (UK 1952); Sir John Archibald Sinclair; 6 Bt (GB 1786), PC; s of 2 Viscount Thurso (d 1995), and Margaret Beaumont, *née* Robertson; *b* 10 September 1953; *Educ* Eton, Westminster Tech Coll; *m* 12 June 1976, Marion Ticknor, da of Louis D Sage, of Connecticut, USA, and Constance Cluett Ward (d 2012); 1 da (Hon Louisa Ticknor Beaumont b 15 March 1980), 2 s (Hon James Alexander Robin b 14 Jan 1984, Hon George Henry MacDonald b 29 Oct 1989); *Heir* s, Hon James Sinclair, yr of Ulbster; *Career* mgmnt trainee Savoy Hotel plc 1972–77, reception mangr Claridge's 1978–81, gen mangr Hotel Lancaster Paris (part of the Savoy Gp) 1981–85, dir SA Lancaster 1982–85, vice-chm Prestige Hotels 1984–89, fndr gen mangr Cliveden Bucks for Blakeney Hotels 1985–92; dir Cliveden House Ltd 1987–94, chief exec Granfel Holdings Ltd 1992–95; md Fitness and Leisure Holdings Ltd 1995–2001; non-exec chm: Thurso Fisheries Ltd, Sinclair Family Trust Ltd, Int Wine and Spirit Competition 1999–; non-exec dir: Savoy Hotel plc 1993–98, Walker Greenbank 1997–99, Millennium & Copthorne plc 2002–09; sat as Lib Dem in House of Lords 1995–99; MP (Lib Dem) Caithness, Sutherland & Easter Ross 2001–15; spokesman for Scottish affrs 2001–06, spokesman for transport 2003–05; chm: Game Conservancy Bucks 1990–92, Clubs Panel BHA 1992–95, Scrabster Harbour Tst

T

1996–2001, Walker Greenbank 1999–2002; patron: HCIMA 1997–2003, Inst of Mgmnt Services 1998–; pres: Licensed Victuallers Schs 1996–97, Acad of Food and Wine Service 1998–; Hon DBA Oxford Brookes Univ 2004; Freeman City of London 1991; FHCIMA 1991, FInstD 1997, Master Innholder 1991 (chm 1995–97); *Recreations* fishing, shooting, food, wine; *Clubs* New (Edinburgh), Brooks's; *Style*— The Rt Hon the Viscount Thurso, PC; ✉ Thurso East Mains, Thurso, Caithness KW14 8HW

THURSTON, Julian Paul; s of Ronald Thurston, of Dunstable, Beds, and Eileen Joyce Thurston, *née* Salmon; *b* 11 May 1955; *Educ* Bedford Sch, Merton Coll Oxford (MA), Coll of Law London; *m* 11 July 1981, Julia Sarah, da of Thomas George Kerslake (d 1966); 1 da (Sarah b 1987), 1 s (Thomas b 1989); *Career* admitted slr 1979; ptnr: CMS Cameron McKenna (formerly McKenna & Co) 1986–99 (latterly head Technology Gp and Commercial Practice Gp), Arnold & Porter 1999–2003, Morrison & Foerster LLP 2003–; non-exec dir Cancer Research Campaign Technology (then Cancer Research Ventures) 1988–2002; *Style*— Julian Thurston, Esq

THWAITE, Ann Barbara; da of A J Harrop (d 1963), and Hilda Mary, *née* Valentine (d 1990); *b* 4 October 1932, London; *Educ* Marsden Sch Wellington NZ, Queen Elizabeth Girls' GS Barnet, St Hilda's Coll Oxford (MA, DLitt); *m* 4 Aug 1955, Anthony Thwaite, OBE, FRSL, *qv*; 4 da (Emily b 1957, Caroline b 1959, Lucy b 1961, Alice b 1965); *Career* writer; occasional reviewer: TLS 1963–85, The Guardian, TES, Washington Post, Daily Telegraph, Times; visiting prof Tokyo Joshi Daigaku 1985–86 and 2005, Helen Stubbs lectr Toronto Public Library 1991, Ezra Jack Keats lectr Univ of Southern Mississippi 1992; govr: St Mary's Middle Sch Long Stratton 1990–2002, Hapton VC Primary Sch 1994–2006; vice-pres Tennyson Soc; Churchill fell 1993, Gladys Krieble Delmas fell British Library 1998, hon fell Univ of Surrey 2001; Hon DLitt UEA 2007; FRSL; *Books* children's books incl: The Camelthorn Papers (1969), Allsorts 1–7 (ed, 1968–75), Tracks (1978), Allsorts of Poems (ed, 1978), The Ashton Affair (1995), The Horse at Hilly Fields (1996); other publications: Waiting for the Party: The Life of Frances Hodgson Burnett (1974, reissued 1994 and (as Beyond the Secret Garden) 2007), My Oxford (ed, 1977), Edmund Gosse: A Literary Landscape (1984, Duff Cooper Meml Award 1985, reissued 2007), A A Milne: His Life (1990, Whitbread Biography Prize 1990, reissued 2006), Portraits from Life: Essays by Edmund Gosse (ed, 1991), The Brilliant Career of Winnie-the-Pooh (1992), Emily Tennyson, the Poet's Wife (1996), Glimpses of the Wonderful: the life of Philip Henry Gosse (2002), Passageways: The Story of a New Zealand Family (2009), Running in the Corridors: Seven Stories (2014); *Recreations* other people's lives, punting on the Tas; *Clubs* Soc of Authors, Royal Over-Seas League, Children's Books History Soc; *Style*— Ann Thwaite; ✉ The Mill House, Low Tharston, Norfolk NR15 2YN (✆ 01508 489569); c/o Curtis Brown, 28/29 Haymarket, London SW1Y 4SP (✆ 020 7396 6600)

THWAITE, Anthony Simon; OBE (1990); s of Hartley Thwaite, JP (d 1978), and Alice Evelyn, *née* Mallinson (d 1998); *b* 23 June 1930; *Educ* Kingswood Sch, ChCh Oxford (MA); *m* 4 Aug 1955, Ann Barbara Thwaite, *qv*, da of Angus John Harrop (d 1963), of NZ and London; 4 da (Emily b 1957, Caroline b 1959, Lucy b 1961, Alice b 1965); *Career* Nat Serv Sgt Instr Rifle Bde and RAEC 1949–51; lectr English lit Univ of Tokyo 1955–57, prodr BBC radio 1957–62, literary ed The Listener 1962–65, asst prof English Univ of Libya Benghazi 1965–67, literary ed New Statesman 1968–72, co-ed Encounter 1973–85, Japan Fndn fell 1985–86, dir André Deutsch Ltd 1986–92 (editorial conslt 1992–95), writer in residence Vanderbilt Univ Nashville USA 1992; Richard Hillary Meml Prize 1968, Cholmondeley Award for Poetry 1983, chm of judges Booker Prize 1986; former memb: Ctee of Mgmnt Soc of Authors, Lit Panel Arts Cncl of GB, Lit Advsy Ctee Br Cncl, Cncl RSL; current memb: Soc of Authors, Soc for Post-Medieval Archaeology, Medieval Pottery Research Gp, Soc for Libyan Studies, Philip Larkin Soc (pres); former memb Ctee RLF; hon lay canon Norwich Cathedral 2005; Hon LittD: Univ of Hull 1989, UEA 2007; FRSL 1978, FSA 2000; *Books* incl Poems 1953–83 (1984), Six Centuries of Verse (1984), Poetry Today (1985, revised edn 1996), Letter From Tokyo (1987), Philip Larkin: Collected Poems (ed, 1988, 2 edn 2003), Poems 1953–88 (1989), Philip Larkin: Selected Letters 1940–1985 (ed, 1992), The Dust of the World (1994), Selected Poems 1956–96 (1997), Penguin Book of Japanese Verse (co-ed revised edn, 1998, 2 edn 2009), Anthony Thwaite in Conversation with Peter Dale and Ian Hamilton (1999), A Different Country (2000), Philip Larkin, Further Requirements (ed, 2001), A Move in the Weather (2003), The Ruins of Time (ed, 2006), Collected Poems (2007), Poet to Poet: John Skelton (2008), Philip Larkin: Letters to Monica (ed, 2010), Late Poems (2010), Going Out (2015); *Recreations* archaeology, antiquarian beachcombing, pottery; *Style*— Anthony Thwaite; ✉ The Mill House, Low Tharston, Norfolk NR15 2YN (✆ 01508 489569)

THWAITES, George Stanley; s of Ronald Thwaites, and Judith, *née* Myers; *b* 25 September 1973, London; *Educ* Hampton Sch, Univ of Bristol (BA); *m* 25 Aug 2002, Eleanor Lucy, *née* Wood; 1 s (Louis Aaron b 17 July 2004), 1 da (Audrey Indigo b 6 Sep 2006); *Career* Daily Telegraph: various roles 1996–98, asst features ed 1998–2000; Mail on Sunday: dep ed Review 2000–06, ed Review 2006–11; fndr Clearwood Communications 2011–; *Recreations* family, music, tennis; *Style*— George Thwaites, Esq; ✆ 07884 117534, e-mail george@clearwoodcommunications.com

THWAITES, Ronald; QC (1987); s of Stanley Thwaites, of Stockton-on-Tees, and Aviva, *née* Cohen; *b* 21 January 1946; *Educ* Richard Hind Secdy Tech Sch Stockton, Grangefield GS Stockton, Kingston Coll of Technol (LLB); *m* 7 Aug 1972, Judith Adelaide Foley, da of late Barry Baron Myers; 3 s (George b 1973, David b 1976, Harry b 1981), 1 da (Stephanie b 1980); *Career* called to the Bar Gray's Inn 1970 (ad eundem Inner Temple 1981); head of chambers Ely Place Chambers 2000–10; *Recreations* lighting bonfires; *Style*— Ronald Thwaites, Esq, QC; ✉ Ely Place Chambers, 30 Ely Place, Holborn Circus, London EC1N 6TD (✆ 020 7400 9600, fax 020 7400 9630)

TIBBUTT, Dr David Arthur; s of Sidney Arthur William Tibbutt (d 1955), of Wadhurst, E Sussex, and Dorothy Ellen, *née* Lay (d 1994); *b* 8 March 1941; *Educ* The Skinners' GS Tunbridge Wells, St Peter's Coll Oxford (MA, BM BCh, DM); *m* 26 Nov 1966, Jane, da of Air Vice-Marshal Sir George David Harvey, KBE, CB, DFC (d 1969), of Over Worton, Oxon; 2 s (Mark David b 1968, William George b 1970); *Career* jr hosp doctor United Oxford Hosp 1968–76; Worcester Royal Infirmary NHS Tst: conslt physician 1976–98, clinical dir for med 1994–96; coordinator and advsr for continuing medical educn Miny of Health of Republic of Uganda and Tropical Health and Educn Tst 1998–2004, visiting conslt physician to Kitovu Hosp Masaka Uganda 2003–10, visiting physician Kirambi Health Centre Rwanda 2007–12; visiting lectr and external examiner Makerere Univ Med Sch Kampala Uganda 1965–97, post grad clinical tutor (Worcester Dist) 1987–92, RCP tutor for Worcester Dist 1987–93; ed Charles Hastings Postgraduate Jl 1991–98, pres Worcester Dist Br Heart Fndn 1984–98, tstee Worcestershire Hosp Charitable Tst 1987–, ed Uganda Continuing Medical Education Newsletter 1998–2011, memb Editorial Bd South Sudan Medical Jl 2009–; memb Bd Worcester Citizens' Advice Bureau 2001–15, chm Worcester Cons Assoc Policy Forum 2002–04, memb Worcester Dist Community Health Cncl 2001–03, memb Patient and Public Involvement in Health Forum Worcester Acute Hosp Tst 2003–06, memb Sounding Bd Worcs Royal Hosp NHS Tst 2011– (memb Shadow Cncl of Govrs 2010–11); cncllr Worcester City Cncl 2004–14 (memb Cabinet 2006–11, Mayor 2011–12); chm Worcester City Cncl Adentan Municipal Assembly (Ghana) Local Economic Devpt Prog Cwlth Local Govt Forum 2010–13, chm Worcester Conservative Assoc 2013–; tstee: Worcester Municipal Charities 2003–15, Worcester Racial Equality Cncl 2004–11; memb: BMA 1968, W Midlands Physicians Assoc 1976, Br Cardiac Soc 1993; FRCP 1983 (MRCP 1971), FRSM 1992–98; *Books* Pulmonary Embolism: Current Therapeutic Concepts (1977); author of various pubns on thromboembolic disease and medicine in the Tropics 1974–; *Recreations* watercolour painting, gardening, philately; *Clubs* Worcs Oxford Univ Soc (past chm); *Style*— Dr David Tibbutt; ✉ Kitovu, 8, Stuart Rise, Red Hill Lane, Worcester WR5 2QQ (✆ and fax 01905 355451, e-mail david@tibbutt.co.uk)

TICEHURST, His Hon Judge David Keith; s of Frederick John Ticehurst, of Bryher, Isles of Scilly, and Barbara Elisabeth, *née* Hyde; *b* 1 May 1950; *Educ* Taunton's Sch Southampton, Keynsham GS Bristol, Kingston Poly (BA); *m* 25 March 1972, Gillian, da of Reginald Colston Shepherd, and Daphne, *née* Sapey; *Career* articled clerk Lawrence & Co Bristol 1972–74, admitted slr 1975, Lawrence & Co Bristol 1975–78, Osborne Clarke 1978–98 (ptnr Osborne Clarke 1980–98), asst recorder 1991–94, recorder 1994–98, circuit judge (Western Circuit) 1998–, resident judge Taunton Crown Court 2013–; Higher Court advocate (all proceedings) 1994; lectr in law and broadcast journalism UWE 1990–94; memb Law Soc 1975, fndr memb Employment Lawyers Assoc (SW region rep); govr Sidcot Sch 1999–2007, tstee Fly2help 2007–13, patron Lighthouse Charity Weston Super Mare 2013–; *Recreations* cricket, watching rugby, painting, reading; *Clubs* Gloucestershire CCC (life memb), Bristol RFC, Winscombe RFC (vice-pres), Old Herpesians CC (pres); *Style*— His Hon Judge Ticehurst; ✉ Taunton Crown Court, Shire Hall, Taunton TA1 4EU

TICKELL, Dame Clare; DBE (2010); *b* May 1958, London; *Educ* Univ of Bristol (CQSW); *m* 15 March 1987, Edward Andres; 2 s (Finn b 20 March 1989, Luke b 14 March 1991); *Career* asst warden Avon Probation Service 1982–84, dep dir Centrepoint 1986–89, dir Riverpoint 1989–1992; chief exec: Phoenix House 1991–97, Stonham Housing Assoc 1997–2004, Action for Children (formerly NCH) 2004–13, Hanover Housing Assoc 2014–; memb Mgmnt Bd Information Cmmn 2003–10, cmmr 2020 Public Services Tst 2010; memb Bd Guinness Tst 2010–14, chair CVLS Honours Ctee 2012–, chair Help the Hospices Cmmn into End of Life Care 2011–13; Third Sector Most Admired Chief Exec 2008; Hon LLD Univ of Bristol 2012, Hon DUniv Bishop Grosseteste 2013; FCGI, FRSA; *Publications* Tickell Review of the Early Years Fndn Stage (2011); *Recreations* swimming, reading, art, cycling; *Style*— Dame Clare Tickell, DBE; ✉ e-mail clare.tickell@hanover.org.uk, Twitter @ClareTickell

TICKELL, Sir Crispin Charles Cervantes; GCMG (1989), KCVO (1983, MVO 1958); s of Jerrard Tickell (d 1966), and Renée Oriana, *née* Haynes (d 1992); *b* 25 August 1930; *Educ* Westminster (King's scholar), ChCh Oxford (Hinchliffe and hon scholar, Gladstone Meml exhibitioner, MA); *m* 1, 1954 (m dis 1976), Chloë, da of Sir James Gunn, RA; 2 s, 1 da; m 2, 1977, Penelope Thorne Thorne, da of Dr Vernon Thorne Thorne; *Career* Coldstream Gds 1952–54; joined British Dip Serv 1954, served FO 1954–55, The Hague 1955–58, Mexico 1958–61, FO Planning Staff 1961–64, Paris 1964–70; private sec to Mins responsible for British entry into Euro Community 1970–72, head Western Orgns Dept FCO 1972–75, fell Center for Int Affairs Harvard Univ 1975–76, chef de cabinet to Pres of Cmmn of Euro Community 1977–81, visiting fell All Souls Coll Oxford 1981, British ambass to Mexico 1981–83, dep under sec of state (Economic) FCO 1983–84, permanent sec Overseas Devpt Admin 1984–87, British permanent rep to UN 1987–90; warden Green Coll Oxford 1990–97, dir Green Coll Centre for Environmental Policy and Understanding 1992–2006, dir Policy Foresight Prog James Martin Inst for Science and Civilisation 2006–08, dir Policy Foresight Prog James Martin 21st Century Sch Univ of Oxford 2008–11; dir BOC Fndn for the Environment 1990–2003; non-exec dir: IBM UK Hldgs Ltd 1990–95 (memb Advsy Bd 1995–2000), Govett Mexican Horizons Investment Co Ltd 1992–96, Govett American Smaller Cos Tst 1996–98, Govett Enhanced Income Investment Tst 1999–2004; chm: Climate Inst Washington DC 1990–2002 and 2012–, Int Inst for Environment and Devpt 1990–94, Earthwatch Europe 1991–97, Advsy Ctee Darwin Initiative for the Survival of Species 1992–99, St Andrews/Conoco Phillips Prize for the Environment 2000–14; pres: Royal Geographical Soc 1990–93 (Patron's Medal 2000), Marine Biological Assoc 1990–2001, Nat Soc for Clean Air 1997–99, Gaia Soc 1998–2001, Tree Aid 2007–14; tstee: Natural History Museum 1992–2001, WWF (UK) 1993–99, Royal Botanic Garden Edinburgh 1997–2001, Thomson Reuters Fndn 2000–, Fndn for the Future 2007–; convenor of the Govt Panel on Sustainable Devpt 1994–2000, memb Task Force on Urban Regeneration 1998–99, memb Task Force on Potentially Hazardous Near Earth Objects 2000; sr visiting fell Harvard Univ Center for the Environment 2002–03; chllr Univ of Kent 1996–2006; advsr-at-large to the pres Arizona State Univ 2004–; minor planet named No 5971 Tickell 2006; Hon LLD: Univ of Massachusetts USA 1990, Univ of Birmingham 1991, Univ of Bristol 1991, Univ of Kent at Canterbury 1996, Univ of Nottingham 2003; Hon DUniv Stirling 1990; Hon DSc: UEA 1990, Univ of Sussex 1991, Cranfield Univ 1992, Loughborough Univ 1995, Sheffield Hallam Univ 1996, Univ of East London 1998, Univ of Exeter 1999, Univ of Hull 2001; Hon DLitt: PCL (now Univ of Westminster) 1990, Univ of Plymouth 2001, Univ of St Andrews 2002, Univ of Southampton 2002, Oxford Brookes Univ 2002, Univ du Littoral Cote d'Opale 2002, Univ Juarez Autonoma de Tabasco 2011; hon fell: Westminster Sch 1993, St Edmund's Coll Cambridge 1995, Green Coll Oxford 1997, Royal Instn of GB 2002, Soc for the Environment 2013; Hon FRIBA 2000; hon memb: Academia Mexicana de Derecho Internacional 1983, Orden Academica de Derecho, de la Cultura, y de la Paz 1989; Offr Order of Orange Nassau (Netherlands) 1958, Order of Mali 1979, Order of the Aztec Eagle with sash (Mexico) 1994, Chinese Govt Friendship Award 2004; *Books* The Evacuees (contrib, 1968), Life After Death (1976), Climatic Change and World Affairs (Harvard Univ 1977, Pergamon 1978, jt revised edn 1986), The United Kingdom-The United Nations (1990), Sustaining Earth (1990), Science for the Earth (contrib, 1995), The Changing World (contrib, 1996), Mary Anning of Lyme Regis (1996), Remaking the Landscape (contrib, 2002), Managing the Earth (contrib, 2002), Johannesburg Summit 2002 (contrib, 2002), Roy Jenkins: A Retrospective (contrib, 2004), Great Natural Historians (contrib, 2007), Sudden and Disruptive Climate Change (contrib, 2008), Making the Difference (contrib, 2011); *Recreations* climatology, palaeohistory, art (especially pre Columbian); *Clubs* Brooks's, Garrick; *Style*— Sir Crispin Tickell, GCMG, KCVO; ✉ Ablington Old Barn, Ablington, Cirencester, Gloucestershire GL7 5NU (website www.crispintickell.org/com/net)

TICKLE, Geraldine Ellen; da of Michael Casey (d 1994), and Johanna, *née* Abbott (d 1996); *b* 11 February 1951, Bromley, Kent; *Educ* Holy Trinity Convent, KCL (LLB), Cncl of Legal Educn; *m* 8 Nov 1980 (m dis); 2 da (Victoria Alexandra b 9 Dec 1982, Olivia Catherine b 10 Dec 1986); m 2, 21 July 2013, Guy Leigh (d 2015); *Career* called to the Bar Gray's Inn 1973, admitted slr 1982; pupil then tenant barr's chambers London 1973–76, HM Customs and Excise Legal Office 1976–83, Wragge and Co Solicitors 1984–95 (joined as legal researcher, later commercial lawyer then competition ptnr), ptnr Martineau Johnson 1995–2008; vice-chm Competition Law Assoc 2003–09 (chm Working Party on Competition Law), past vice-pres Ligue International du Droit de la Concurrence, past memb Advsy Ctee Inst of European Law Birmingham Univ; memb Soc of Authors 2011; *Publications* Kaleidoscope Lives (ebook, 2011); contrib to numerous pubns incl Remedies for Breach of EC Law, International Intellectual Property Law, Structuring International Contracts, European Community Law, Antitrust Between EC Law and National Law; articles for periodicals including PFI Intelligence, Utility Week and Motor Law; *Recreations* boating, travel, reading, cinema, theatre, skiing; *Style*— Mrs Geraldine Tickle; ✉ e-mail geraldine.tickle@gmail.com

TIDBALL, Paul William; s of Trevor James Tidball, of Rhiwbina, Cardiff, and Brenda, *née* Cross; *b* 14 April 1950, Cardiff; *Educ* Cardiff HS; *m* 20 Dec 1972, Jean, *née* Munro; 1 s

(Matthew b 19 Nov 1974), 1 da (Jessica b 2 Aug 1977); *Career* trainee and mgmnt positions with nat cos 1970–76, joined HM Prison Serv as asst govr 1976, asst govr HM Borstal Hewell Grange Redditch 1976–80, asst govr HMP Cardiff 1980–88, dep govr HMP Featherstone Wolverhampton 1988–91, Prison Serv Trg and Devpt Gp 1991–97 (latterly head of activities and servs trg); govr HMP Drake Hall Staffs 1997–2003, govr HMP Cardiff 2003–06; pres Prison Govrs Assoc 2006–10; memb Lib Dem Parly Home Affrs Justice and Equality Ctee 2010–13; assoc St Georges House Windsor Castle; FRSA; *Recreations* travel, Wales tourism, music, concert goer, theatre (supporter Menier Chocolate Factory), comedy (supporter Edinburgh Festival Fringe), conservation (memb Woodland Tst), outdoor pursuits, historic tport (Severn Valley Railway), rugby (memb WRU Supporters Club), cooking with pears and entertaining, CAMRA life memb; *Style*— Paul Tidball, Esq; ✉ e-mail jean.munro@yahoo.co.uk

TIDE-FRATER, Susanne; *b* Germany; *Educ* Sorbonne, Institut Français de la Mode Paris; *Career* early career with German Mktg Inst and Peclers Paris; head Design Mgmnt Dept and head int rels Institut Français de la Mode; Selfridges: joined creative dept 1996, head creative direction 2002–04; creative dir Harrods 2004–06, brand conslt 2006–; fashion dir 19 Entertainment 2008–, brand and strategy dir Farfetch.com 2010–; memb Advsy Bd Centre of Fashion Enterprise 2007–, dir Venture Bd Whitechapel Art Gallery 2008–, memb Selection Ctee Br Fashion Cncl Newgen 2008–; *Style*— Ms Susanne Tide-Frater; ✉ 154 Cholmley Gardens, London NW6 1AD

TIDMARSH, Sir James Napier; KCVO, MBE (1989), JP (1977); yr s of late Edward and Madeline Tidmarsh; *b* 15 September 1932; *Educ* Taunton Sch; *m* Virginia, yr da of Robin and Audrey Warren; 2 s (Mark b 1969, Toby b 1971); *Career* Nat Serv cmmnd 1 Bn DCLI 1952–54, TA 4/5 Som LI 1955–60; factory mangr/dir/md in footwear industry UK and Australasia 1955–72; md Dycem Ltd 1972–96, fndr dir GWR Radio plc 1985–89, dir Bristol Chamber of Commerce and Initiative 1992–2015, dir Learning Partnership West 1995–99, chm SouthWest One 2008–11; pres Avon and Bristol Fedn of Clubs for Young People 1994–98 (chm 1982–94), vice-chm Nat Assoc Prison Visitors 1966–69, memb Cncl Univ of Bristol 1994–2000; memb Cook Soc; patron: Young Bristol 1999–, Avon Youth Assoc 2000–16, Bristol District Merchant Navy Assoc 2005–, West Country branch Britain-Australia Soc 2008; tstee Br Empire and Cwlth Museum 2003–14, patron, pres and memb of many local and regnl charitable tsts; memb Soc of Merchant Venturers (Master 1994–95); pro-chancellor Univ of Bristol 2007–14; High Sheriff Avon 1995–96, HM Lord-Lt County and City of Bristol 1996–2007; Hon Col RMR SW England 1998–2005; Hon LLD: Univ of Bristol 2002, UWE 2003; FRSA 2000; KStJ 1997; *Clubs* Army and Navy, Saintsbury, Clifton (Bristol); *Style*— Sir James Tidmarsh, KCVO, MBE; ✉ 8 Prince's Buildings, Clifton, Bristol BS8 4LB (☎ 0117 973 0462, fax 0117 970 6649)

TIDY, William Edward (Bill); MBE (2001); *b* 9 October 1933; *m* 1960, Rosa; 2 s (Nick (decd), Robert), 1 da (Sylvia); *Career* Mil Serv RE 1952–56, worked within advtg agency 1956–57, professional cartoonist 1957–; cartoon strips incl: Chelm of Tryg (Punch) 1966–67, The Cloggies (Private Eye) 1967–81, (The Listener) 1985–86, Doctor Whittle (General Practitioner) 1970–2001, Grimbledon Down (New Scientist) 1970–94, The Fosdyke Saga (The Daily Mirror) 1971–85, Kegbuster (What's Brewing) 1976–, The Sporting Spagthorpes (Titbits) 1976–79, Intergalactic Mirror (The Mirror Group) 1979–81, The Last Chip Shop (Private Eye) 1981–85, The Crudgingtons (Today) 1986–87, Billy Bucket (Private Eye) 1988–89, Savage Sports (The Mail On Sunday) 1988–89, God's Own County (Yorkshire Post) 1989–90, String King (Punch) 1996–97; TV presenter: Weekend (Granada), Three Days Last Summer (BBC 2), Tidy Up Walsall (BBC 1), Tidy Up Naples (BBC 2), It's My City (BBC 1), Draw Me (BBC 2); numerous radio and TV guest appearances incl This Is Your Life 1975; radio presenter Tidy Answers (BBC Radio 4); after-dinner speaker for numerous orgns incl pub cos; designer of stage sets and costumes; produces range of greetings and christmas cards; Granada TV's What The Papers Say Cartoonist of the Year 1974, The Soc of Strip Illustrators Award 1980; *Publications* playwright: The Great Eric Ackroyd Disaster (Oldham Coliseum), The Cloggies (Theatre Clwyd), The Fosdyke Saga (Bush Theatre and Arts Cncl tour); writer and illustrator: Laugh with Bill Tidy, Tidy's World, The Fosdyke Saga (15 vols), The World's Worst Golf Club, Robbie And The Blobbies, A Day At Cringemound School, The Incredible Bed, Draw Me 387 Baked Beans, Save Daring Waring with a Pencil?, Is There Any News of the Iceberg? (autobiography, 1995), Kegbuster Remembers (1997), The Tidy Book of Quotations (1998), Disgraceful Archaeology (with Dr Paul Bahn, 1999); illustrator: The Exploding Present (by John Wells), Napoleon's Retreat From Wigan (by Mike Harding), The Book of Heroic Failures (by Stephen Pile), Everbody's Doing It (by Max Hodes), Fisherman's Friend (with Derrick Geer), Rosa Tidy's Pasta Book (by Rosa Tidy), Fine Glances (by Mike Seabrook), Golfing Anthology (by Mike Seabrook), Food For All The Family (by Magnus Pike), Service Banking (by Michael Hanson), F U C Smith The Greatest Cricketer of Them All; *Recreations* supporting Everton FC, cultivating peas and beans, watching ships and aircraft, playing cricket, looking after various dependants, furry friends and masses of goldfish; *Clubs* Cartoonists' Club of GB, Lord's Taverners, Armed Forces Benevolent Fund; *Style*— Bill Tidy, Esq, MBE; ✉ Terry Meadow Farm, Boylestone, Derbyshire DE6 5AB (☎ 01335 330343, fax 01335 330 858, e-mail bill@billtidy.com, website www.broadband.co.uk/billtidy)

TIFFIN, Simon; *Career* journalist; early career chief sub ed and sports ed GQ, ed GQ Active 1998–2001 (dep ed 1996–98), dep ed Harpers & Queen 2001–03, ed Esquire 2003–06, publisher Standpoint 2008; Ed of the Year (Men's Magazines) BSME Awards 2003; *Style*— Simon Tiffin, Esq

TIGHE, Anthony Rodger; s of Brian Anthony Michael Tighe, of Bickerstaffe, Lancs, and Paula Angela, *née* Capper; *b* 9 March 1951, Liverpool; *Educ* St Edward's Coll Liverpool, Univ of Greenwich; *m* 1991 (m dis), Rachel Suzanne, *née* Pearson; 2 c; *Career* with Berger Paints 1972–74, in family business 1974–76; Wilsons Brewery Manchester: sales force 1976–78, area sales mangr 1978–80, sales promotion mangr 1980–82, PR mangr 1982–83; head of PR Grand Metropolitan Brewing North 1983–84; fndr chief exec Greenwood Tighe Public Relations (now part of Havas Gp) 1984–93; fndr chm Mere Communication Gp (now part of BJL Gp) 1993–2013; chm Lake Design (UK) Ltd 1998–, non-exec dir Tameside Acute NHS Tst 1993–98, non-exec dir Sale Sharks Rugby Club 2011; chm Everton Collection Charitable Tst 2005–08; first winner Chartered Inst of PR Sword of Excellence for product relations 1984; MIPR 1984, FCIPR 2009; *Recreations* golf, Everton FC; *Clubs* Mere Golf and Country (capt 2003–, chm 2008–10), RAC, Knutsford Golf; *Style*— Anthony Tighe, Esq; ✉ Lake Design Ltd, Campaign House, 8 Cecil Road, Hale, Cheshire WA15 9PA (☎ 0161 926 9898, e-mail tony@lakemail.co.uk)

TILBIAN, Lorna Mona; da of Berdge A Tilbian (d 1979), and Mayda B, *née* Ouzounian (d 2009); *b* Nicosia, Cyprus; *Educ* Cheltenham Ladies' Coll, Univ of Southampton; *m* 1992 (m dis 1999); *Career* Sheppards 1984–88, S G Warburg 1988–95, Panmure Gordon 1995–2001, exec dir Numis Corp plc 2001–, non-exec dir ProVen VCT plc 2013–; non-exec dir Jupiter UK Growth Investment Tst 2001–; *Clubs* Addison; *Style*— Ms Lorna Tilbian; ✉ Numis Corporation, 10 Paternoster Square, London EC4M 7LT (☎ 020 7260 1000, e-mail l.tilbian@numiscorp.com)

TILBURY, Charlotte; da of Lance Clive Rupert Tilbury, and Patricia Mary Dodd; *b* 10 February 1973, Kensington, London; *Educ* Glauca Rossi Sch of Makeup London; *m* 2006, Charles Forbes; 1 s (Flynn); *Career* make-up artist; has worked with Mario Testino, Kate Moss, Gisele Bündchen, Vogue, Vanity Fair, LOVE, V Magazine, British, French and American Vogue and Interview Magazine; portfolio incl fashion shows and campaigns such as Michael Kors, Donna Karan, Buberry, Yves Saint Laurent, Miu Miu, Prada, Versace, Calvin Klein and Louis Vuitton; launched make-up collection 2013; *Style*— Ms Charlotte Tilbury; ✉ website www.charlottetilbury.com, Twitter @ctilburymakeup

TILEY, Timothy Francis Thornhill; s of Rev George Edward Tiley (d 1985), and Cecilia Frances Mystica Thornhill (d 1982); descended from ancient family of Thornhill, of Thornhill in Yorks, which can trace continuous line of descent from saxon theign Eisulf de Thornhill (1080–1165), membs of the family of Jordan de Thornhill (s of Eisulf) are portrayed in a group of the most famous of the 13th century miracle windows in the Trinity chapel of Canterbury Cathedral; *b* 6 June 1949; *Educ* Malvern Coll, St Peter's Coll Oxford (MA); *m* 12 Oct 1990, Margaret Reid; *Career* fndr and md Tim Tiley Ltd (publishers of philosophical and religious prints) 1978–; co-fndr of Brass Rubbing Centres: Oxford 1973, Bristol 1974, Stratford-upon-Avon 1974, London 1975, Edinburgh 1976, Bath 1976, Glastonbury 1977, Washington DC 1977; FInstD 1992; *Recreations* singing, reading, travelling, historical studies; *Style*— Timothy Tiley, Esq; ✉ 12 Salisbury Road, Redland, Bristol BS6 7AW (☎ 0117 942 3397, e-mail tim@timtiley.com)

TILL, Prof Jeremy William; s of Barry Till (d 2013), and Shirley, *née* Phillipson (d 1991); *b* 5 April 1957; *Educ* Univ of Cambridge (MA), Poly of Central London (DipArch), Middlesex Univ (MA); *Partner* Prof Sarah Wigglesworth; *Career* architect and academic; architect Alex Gordon Partnership 1984–87, architect David Gibson Architects 1987–88, Peter Currie Architects 1988–93, ptnr Sarah Wigglesworth Architects 1993–; sr lectr Kingston Poly Sch of Architecture 1986–92, Univ of Pennsylvania Philadelphia 1991, Bartlett Sch of Architecture UCL 1991–98: lectr 1992–93, sub-dean of faculty and faculty tutor 1993–96, sr lectr in architecture 1996–98; prof of architecture and head of sch Univ of Sheffield Sch of Architecture 1999–2008, dean of architecture and the built environment Univ of Westminster 2008–12, head Central St Martins and pro-vice-chllr Univ of Arts London 2012–; RIBA: memb 1995, memb Educn and Professional Devpt Bd 1996–98, chm review gp 1997, memb Educn Strategy Ctee 1998–2001, chair RIBA Awards Gp 2004–06; UK entry: Venice Architecture Biennale 2006, Shenzhen Biennale 2013; tstee New Economics Fndn 2015–; *Awards* incl: Bannister Fletcher Prize for dissertation 1983, Fulbright Arts Fell 1990, EAAE Biennial Award for Architectural Writing 1995, Civic Tst Award 2002, RIBA Sustainability Award 2004, RIBA Architecture Award 2004, RIBA President's Award for Research 2007, 2009 and 2011; *Publications* The Everyday and Architecture (with Sarah Wigglesworth, 1998), Architecture and Participation (2005), Flexible Houseing (with Tatjana Schneider, 2007), Architecture Depends (2009), Spatial Agency (with Nishat Awan and Tatjana Schneider, 2011), Design of Scarcity (2014); numerous book chapters, jl articles and published conf papers on architecture and urban devpt; *Recreations* growing, cooking and eating food; *Style*— Professor Jeremy Till; ✉ Central St Martins, Granary Building, 1 Granary Building, King's Cross, London N1C 4AA (website www.jeremytill.net)

TILL, Stewart; CBE (2000); *b* 24 April 1951; *Career* early career in advtg: Leo Burnett, Saatchi & Saatchi; TV project mangr and mktg dir WEA Records 1979–83, regnl dir for N Europe and vice-pres CBS/Fox Video 1983, dep md Sky TV 1988–90, head of movies BSkyB 1990–92, with PolyGram Filmed Entertainment 1992–99 (latterly pres), pres Universal Pictures International 1999–2000, pres Signpost Films 2000–02, chm and ceo United International Pictures 2002–; co-chair Film Policy Review Gp DCMS 1997–99, chm Film Cncl 2004– (dep chm 1999–2004), vice-chm Skillset; tstee Nat Film and TV Sch Fndn; govr Dulwich Coll; *Style*— Stewart Till, Esq, CBE

TILLEY, Andrew Raymond; s of Raymond Hugh Tilley, of Tettenhall, Wolverhampton, and Carrie, *née* Lucas; *b* 22 September 1956; *Educ* Regis Comp Tettenhall, Univ of Southampton (BSc, PhD); *m* 16 Nov 1990, Olwen Mary, da of James Anthony Rice, of Rugeley, Staffs; 1 da (Grace Elizabeth b 27 June 1995); 2 c from prev m (Laura Anne b 18 Sept 1983, Mark Thomas b 14 Aug 1985); *Career* water quality controller Essex Water Co 1978–79, postgrad res 1979–82; Boase Massimi Pollitt advtg: joined as trainee media planner 1982, assoc dir 1984–86, bd dir 1986–89, md BMP Solutions in Media (subsid) 1987–89; Delaney Fletcher Slaymaker Delaney & Bozell (formerly Delaney Fletcher Delaney): media planning dir 1989, exec media dir 1989–91, dep md 1991; Zenith Media: dir of strategic planning 1991–94, dep md 1994–95, md 1995–97; fndr managing ptnr Unity independent communications consultancy 1997–2003, founding ptnr The Ingram Partnership 2003–07, prop Unity 2007–13, chief strategy offr Talon 2013–; chm Media Circle 1995–99; dir Prince's Tst 2001–10; MIPA 1990; *Recreations* football, cricket, photography, horse racing, collecting old maps; *Style*— Andrew Tilley, Esq

TILLMAN, Harold Peter; CBE (2010); s of late Jack Tillman, of London, and late Frances, *née* Cornbloom; *b* 15 October 1945, London; *Educ* Balham Co GS, Pitman's Coll, London Coll of Fashion; *m* 15 June 1969, Stephanie, *née* Ogus; 1 s (Mitchell b 2 Aug 1975), 1 da (Meredith b 9 March 1982); *Career* fndr and md Lincroft Kilgour plc 1966–74, vice-chm Sumrie Clothes plc 1980–83; chm: Honorbilt Group plc 1986–90, BMB Group 1999–2004, Jaeger 2003–11; prop and chm First Restaurant Gp 2008; chm of alumni Univ of Arts London 2007, chm Br Fashion Cncl 2008–13, chm Fashion Matters London Coll of Fashion; tstee V&A 2011; hon prof Univ of the Arts London 2008; Freeman of the City of London 2014; *Recreations* gym, tennis, golf, physical training; *Clubs* Annabel's, Arts, Café Royal; *Style*— Harold Tillman, Esq, CBE; ✉ 37 Sheldon Avenue, Highgate, London N6 4JP (e-mail harold@haroldtillman.com)

TILLMANN, Prof Ulrike Luise; da of Ewald Tillmann, and Marie-Luise Tillmann; *Educ* Gymnasium Georgianum Vreden, Brandeis Univ (BA summa cum laude, Volleyball blue letter), Stanford Univ (MA, PhD), Bonn Univ; *Career* SERC res asst Univ of Cambridge 1990–92, jr res fell Clare Hall Cambridge 1990–92; Univ of Oxford: fell and tutor in mathematics Merton Coll 1992–, univ lectr in mathematics 1992–, titular prof 2000–; visiting prof: Trondheim Univ 2001, Münster Univ 2003 and 2008; EPSRC Advanced Fellowship 1997–2003; conference organiser: Br Topology Meeting 1997, New Developments in K-Theory (Quillen's 60th) 2001, Topology, Geometry and Quantum Field Theory (Segal's 60th) 2002, AIM hot topics 2005, Moduli spaces Bonn 2008; invited speaker: Br Mathematical Colloquium 2000 and 2002, Int Congress of Mathematics 2002; delivered numerous conference talks; ed Topology 2002–06, founding ed Jl of Topology 2007–; memb Editorial Bd: Oxford QJM 2000–, Algebraic and Geometric Topology 2000–, London Mathematical Soc jls 2004–07; memb: EPSRC Coll 1997–, Scientific Advsy Bd Courant Research Center Göttingen 2007–, Prog Ctee ICMS Edinburgh 2005–10; Whitehead Prize London Mathematical Soc 2004, Chaire de la Vallée Poussin 2006–07, L M S Cartwright lectr 2006, Bessel Prize Humboldt Fndn 2008; FRS 2008; *Publications* author of book reviews and numerous papers in mathematical jls; *Recreations* singing; *Style*— Prof Ulrike Tillmann, FRS; ✉ Mathematical Institute, 24–29 St Giles, Oxford OX1 3LB

TILLYARD, Stella; da of Stephen Tillyard, and Margot Tillyard; *b* 16 January 1957; *Educ* St Anne's Coll Oxford (BA), Harvard Univ (Knox fell), Linacre Coll Oxford (Domus student, PhD); *m* Prof John Brewer; 2 c (Grace b 1987, Fox b 1995); *Career* lectr Harvard Univ and UCLA until 1992; sometime writer: New York Times, The Times, The Guardian, Esquire, Traveller; contrib radio and TV progs; author of numerous articles and reviews; memb Soc of Authors; *Awards* Nicolaus Pevsner Prize 1987, History Today Book of the Year 1994, Fawcett Prize 1995; *Books* The Impact of Modernism (1987), Aristocrats: Caroline, Emily, Louisa & Sarah Lennox (1994), Citizen Lord: Edward Fitzgerald 1763–98 (shortlisted Whitbread Biography Award 1997), A Royal Affair (2006); *Recreations* swimming, architecture, reading, sleep; *Clubs* YMCA, Tropos (Florence); *Style*— Miss Stella Tillyard

T

TILLYER, William; *b* 25 September 1938; *Educ* Middlesbrough Coll of Art, Slade Sch of Fine Art, Atelier 17 Paris; *Career* artist and lectr; Central Sch of Art 1964–70, Bath Acad of Art 1964–72, Watford Sch of Art 1970–73, Goldsmiths Coll London 1975–76, Loughborough Sch of Art 1975–76; visiting prof Rhode Island Sch of Brown Univ 1975–76; visiting lectr: Reading Coll of Art 1975–76, St Martin's Sch of Art 1980; artist in residence: Univ of Melbourne 1981–82, David and Sarah Kowitz Program Bedford Hills NY 2001, Cill Rialaig Project Co Kerry 2001; City of Cadiz residency 2006; Hon Dr of Arts Teesside Univ; *Solo Exhibitions* incl: Arnolfini Gallery Bristol 1970–73, Serpentine Gallery 1971, Galerie Theodor Hoss Stuttgart 1974, Museum of Contemporary Art Utrecht 1975, ICA 1975, Sunderland Arts Centre 1975–79, Melbourne Univ Gallery 1982, Jan Turner Gallery LA 1987, Smith Anderson Gallery Calif 1989, Bernard Jacobson Gallery 1989, 1991 and 1993, Wildenstein & Co 1991 and 1994, Adelson Galleries NY 1993, Andre Emmerich Gallery NY 1994, Galerie Miya Tokyo 1995, The Fluxion Paintings (Bernard Jacobson Gallery) 1996, William Tillyer 1956–1996 (The Cleveland Gallery Middlesbrough 1996 and Whitworth Art Gallery Manchester 1997), Bernard Jacobson Gallery 1999 and 2000, Annandale Galleries Sydney Aust 1996, Annandale Galleries 2002, Bernard Jacobson London and NY 2002, The Encounter Works (Bernard Jacobson Gallery) 2002, In the South (works on paper, Bernard Jacobson Gallery) 2003, The Farrago Constructs (Bernard Jacobson Gallery) 2004, Five Larger Paintings 1990–2003 (Eton Coll) 2004, The Revisionist Wire Works (Bernard Jacobson Gallery) 2006, The Cadiz Caprices (Jacobson Howard Gallery NY) 2008, William Tillyer Season – four months celebrating 40 years of collaboration (Bernard Jacobson Gallery London) 2010, Survey Show (Annandale Galleries Sydney) 2010, Mima Against Nature catelogue essay John Yau 2013, Platform A Gallery Middlesbrough 2013, Haven (Nat Park Gallery Danby N Yorks) 2013, New Work (Bernard Jacobson Gallery) 2013, Retrospective Middlesborough Inst of Modern Art 2013–14; *Group Exhibitions* incl: Young Contemporaries (ICA) 1959 and 1961, Forty Christmas Trees (Arnolfini Gallery) 1972, Recent Acquisitions (V&A) 1973, Le Jeune Gravure Contemporaine (Musée d'Art Madame Paris) 1974, British Painting 1952–77 (RA, New Dehli, touring) 1977, British Art since 1960 (Kunsthalle, Lund Univ) 1979, Eight British Artists (Bernard Jacobson Gallery NY) 1980, Four British Artists (Jan Turner Gallery LA) 1988, Cleveland Gallery 1994, Jerwood Painting Prize 1998, New Acquisitions (UCL Art Collections) 2006; *Work in Collections* V&A, Arts Cncl of GB, The Br Cncl, Tate, Manchester City Art Gallery, Univ of Reading, MOMA NY, Brooklyn Art Museum NY, Boston Museum of Art, Fort Worth Art Museum TX, Northern Arts Assoc, Museum of Contemporary Art Friedrickstad, Museum of Art Lód?, Museum of Contemporary Art Utrecht, Westminster Bank London, Bank of America, Univ of Melbourne, Federal Savings Bank LA, The Art Gallery of Western Aust, Broadgate Collection London, Cleveland Gallery, Whitworth Gallery Manchester; stained glass cmmn for Arts and Crafts Church Northumberland 2007, worked with master glassblower on Sunderland Sky Dishes Nat Glass Centre Sunderland 2013; *Publications* Hardware: Variations on a theme of encounter (catalogue essay, 2002); subject of: William Tillyer: Against the Grain (monograph by Prof Norbert Lynton, 2000), The Cadiz Caprices (essay by John Yau, 2008), William Tillyer Watercolours (essay by John Yau), New Paintings – Clouds (essay by Ben Wiedel-Kaufmann), William Tillyer: Against Nature (by John Yau, 2013); *Style*— William Tillyer, Esq, FRSA; ✉ Bernard Jacobson Gallery, 28 Duke Street St James's, London SW1Y 6AG (☎ 020 7734 3431, e-mail william@tillyer.com, website www.tillyer.com or www.jacobsongallery.com)

TILSON, Jake; s of Joe Tilson, *qv*, of Wilts, and Jos, *née* Morton; *b* 14 February 1958; *Educ* Holland Park Sch, Chippenham GS, Chelsea Sch of Art (BA), Royal Coll of Art (MA); *m* Jennifer Elizabeth Lee, *qv*, da of Ernest McLean Bovelle Lee; 1 da (Hannah Lee Tilson b 26 May 1995); *Career* artist; lectr in communication design RCA 1987–2000, lectr Painting Dept Ruskin Sch of Art Oxford; Erna Plachte artist in residence The Laboratory Ruskin Sch of Drawing and Fine Art 1994–96; ed and publisher: Cipher magazine 1979–81, Atlas magazine 1985–; designer Jake Tilson Studio, clients incl Haworth Tompkins, Paul Smith, Stephen Farthing, Robert Wilson, Ortigia and Fontshop International; creator website www.thecooker.com 1994 and www.jaketilson.com; tstee Oxford Symposium on Food and Cookery; *Solo Exhibitions* Xerographies 1977–83 (Galerie J et J Donguy Paris) 1983, Excavator-Barcelona-Excavator (Nigel Greenwood Gallery) 1986, One World (Warehouse London & Liverpool) 1987, Collages 1986–89 (Stylt Göteborg Sweden) 1989, How Far is an Hour (Nigel Greenwood Gallery) 1989, How Far is an Hour (Galleria Cavallino Venice Italy) 1990, The Terminator Line (Nigel Greenwood Gallery) 1990, The Terminator Line Outtakes (Printed Matter at Dia, NY) 1991, Investigations in Cities 1977–97 (retrospective exhibition, Museo Internacional de Electrografia Cuenca Spain) 1997; *Group Exhibitions* Northern Young Contemporaries (Whitworth Gallery Manchester) 1977, Ecritures (Fondation National des Arts Graphiques et Plastiques Paris) 1980, Ars Machina (La Maison de la Culture de Rennes) 1982, Paris Bienale 1982, New Media 2 (Malmö Konsthall Sweden) 1984, Copyart Biennale Barcelona 1985, Br Art & Design (Vienna) 1986, Artist as Publisher (Crafts Cncl) 1986, Rencontres Autour de la Revue Luna-Park (Centre Georges Pompidou) 1987, Br Artists' Books (Centre for the Book Arts NY) 1987, Art in Production (Manchester City Art Gallery) 1988 and 1989, Exhibition Road – 150 Years (RCA) 1988, Atlas 3 (Nigel Greenwood Gallery) 1988, Echtzeit (Kasseler Kunstverein) 1988, Paper (Amics Tokyo) 1988, Self Image (Design Museum) 1991, Langu(im)age (Nigel Greenwood Gallery) 1992, John Moores Exhbn Liverpool 1992, John Moores 18 Liverpool 1993, Whitechapel Open London 1994, tidsvag Göteborg 1994, Artists Books Tate Gallery 1995, Airport (The Photographers Gallery) 1997, European Echoes (Goteborg) 1998, Eye Was A Child (Saatchi Gallery) 1998, La Biennale De Montréal 1998, Sound (Refusalon San Francisco) 1998, Not There (Rena Bransten Gallery San Francisco) 1999, Net Conditions (ZKM) 1999, Art Journeaux (Kassel Kunstverein) 2000, The Year Dot, Black Box (Aspex Gallery) 2000, Over The Ocean (Roda Sten) 2000, Independence (South London Gallery) 2003, Ways of Saying (Loman Street Studio) 2003, A Net of Eels (Wapping Project and Babylon Gallery Ely) 2009; *Film, Video and Audio* Jour et Nuit (Atlas Films, 1989), Jeff and Jake Get Married (Atlas Films, 1990), Put the Message in the Box (World Party, Ensign Records, 1990), Thankyou World (World Party, Ensign Records, 1991), Outtakes (Atlas Films, 1991), Dry Signals (Atlas Films, 1992), Gate 23 (Atlas audio, 1993), Foundsounds CD (Atlas, 1994), City Picture Fiction (Atlas Audio, 1996), Vulture Reality (Atlas Films, 1999), Hannah Sleeps (Atlas Audio, 1999), Hungerford Bridge (Atlas Audio, 1999), Market Forces (Jake Tilson Studio) 2009; *Awards* London Arts Assoc Literature grant 1980, Art Cncl Arts Publishing subsidy 1981, Unilever prize 1983, Major Travelling scholarship RCA 1983, first prize Royal Over-Seas League Exhibition 1988, nominated Andre Simon Award 2007; *Books* artists' books incl: Light and Dark (1979), Exposure (1980), 8 Views of Paris (1980), The V Agents (1980), Excavator-Barcelona-Excavador (1986), Breakfast Special (1989), The Terminator Line (1991), 3 Found Fonts (2003), Independence Lunch (2003), A Tale of 12 Kitchens (2006), In At The Deep End – Cooking Fish Venice to Tokyo (2011), Cooking Christmas 1 (2014), Cooking Christmas 2 (2015); *Style*— Jake Tilson, Esq; ✉ 16 Talfourd Road, London SE15 5NY (websites ww.jaketilson.com. www.thecooker.com and www.areaatlas.com)

TILSON, Joseph Charles (Joe); s of Frederick Arthur Edward Tilson (d 1973), and Ethel Stapeley Louise, *née* Saunders (d 1982); *b* 24 August 1928, London; *Educ* Brixton Sch of Building, St Martin's Sch of Art, RCA, Br Acad Rome; *m* 2 Aug 1956, Joslyn, da of Alistair Morton (d 1963); 1 s (Jake, *qv*, b 1958), 2 da (Anna Jesse b 1959, Sophy Jane b 1965); *Career* RAF 1946–49; painter, sculptor, printmaker; worked in Italy and Spain 1955–57; visiting lectr 1962–63: Slade Sch of Art, King's Coll London, Univ of Durham; teacher Sch of Visual Arts NY 1966, visiting lectr Staatliche Hochschule für Bildende Künste Hamburg 1971–72; memb Arts Panel and Cncl 1966–71; exhbns incl Venice Biennale 1964; work at: Marlborough Gallery 1966, Waddington Galleries; retrospective exhbns: Boymans Van Beuningen Museum Rotterdam 1973, Vancouver Art Gallery 1979, Volterra 1983, Palazzo Pubblico Siena 1995, Sackler Galleries Royal Acad of Arts 2002; Biennale prizes Kraków 1974 and Ljubljana 1985, subject of TV films 1963, 1968 and 1974; memb Accademia Nazionale di San Luca Rome; ARCA 1955, RA 1991 (ARA 1985); *Recreations* planting trees, music, reading; *Style*— Joe Tilson, Esq, RA; ✉ c/o Alan Cristea Gallery, 31 Cork Street, London W1X 2NU (☎ 020 7439 1866, fax 020 7734 1549, e-mail info@alancristea.com, website www.alancristea.com); Marlborough Fine Art (London) Ltd, 6 Albemarle Street, London W1S 4BY (☎ 020 7629 5161, fax 020 7629 6338, e-mail mfa@marlboroughfineart.com. website www.marlboroughfineart.com)

TILT, Sir (Robin) Richard; kt (1999); s of Francis Arthur Tilt (d 1988), of Malvern, Worcs, and Mary Elizabeth, *née* Ashworth; *b* 11 March 1944; *Educ* King's Sch Worcester, Univ of Nottingham (BA), Open Univ (Dip); *m* 22 Oct 1966, Kate, da of Thomas Henry and Mabel Busby; 2 s (Jonathan Richard b 12 Nov 1967, Matthew Edward b 3 Jan 1970), 1 da (Rachel Gwynedd b 20 June 1974); *Career* with HM Prison Service; asst govr HM Borstal Wellingborough 1968–71, tutor Prison Serv Staff Coll Wakefield 1971–74, govr HM Borstal Pollington 1974–75; dep govr: HM Prison Ranby 1975–78, HM Prison Gartree 1978–80; govr HM Prison Bedford 1980–82, head Manpower Section HQ 1982–84, govr HM Prison Gartree 1984–88, dep regnl dir Midlands 1988–89, head of industrial rels HQ 1989–92, head of fin Police Dept 1992–94; Prison Serv: dir of servs 1994, dir of security 1994–95, DG 1995–99; cmmr Social Fund 2000–; chm Leics, Northants and Rutland SHA 2002–06; memb Sentencing Advsy Panel 1999–2002, chm Social Security Advy Ctee 2004–; Churchill fell 1991; *Recreations* theatre, reading, walking; *Style*— Sir Richard Tilt; ✉ Internet Watch Foundation, Discovery House, Vision Park, Chivers Way, Histon, Cambridge CB24 9ZR

TIMBERS, Brig Kenneth Alan; s of Capt Arthur Robert Timbers (d 1942), and Nancy Gwendoline, *née* Smith (d 1985); *b* 11 July 1935; *Educ* Harvey GS Folkestone, RMA Sandhurst; *m* 21 Sept 1957, (Ursula) Bridget, da of Canon Eric Arthur Newman (d 1970); 1 da (Tricia b 1959), 2 s (Stephen b 1961, Michael b 1962); *Career* cmmnd RA 1956, gunnery staff course 1963–64, army staff course 1966–68, promoted Maj 1967, Lt-Col 1974, cmd 47 Field Regt RA 1976–78, GSO1 (W) HQ DRA 1978–81, promoted Col 1981, project mangr 155mm Systems 1981–85, promoted Brig 1985, dir Quality Assurance 1985–88, ret 1988; history sec RA Instn 1988–99, ret 1999; chm: RA Hist Tst 2001–06, RA Hist Soc 2001–13, Friends Nat Army Museum 2002–08; dir RA Museums Ltd 2001–06, dep chm Friends of RA Museum 2001–; conslt on history of artillery; *Publications* The Royal Artillery in Woolwich – A Celebration (conslt ed, 2008), The Royal Arsenal, Woolwich (ed, 2011); *Recreations* fine arts, photography, travel; *Clubs* Army and Navy; *Style*— Brig K A Timbers; ✉ 32 Strongbow Road, Eltham, London SE9 1DT (☎ 020 8850 8397, e-mail ken.timbers@ntlworld.com)

TIMMER, Damien; *Educ* Univ of Oxford; *Career* head of drama ITV Prodns 2002–07 (credits incl: Housewife 49, Lewis, Ballet Shoes, Casanova), fndr and jt md Mammoth 2007– (credits incl: Lost in Austen, Endeavour, Parade's End); *Style*— Damien Timmer, Esq; ✉ Mammoth Screen, Third Floor, 142–144 New Cavendish Street, London W1W 6YF

TIMMINS, Col Sir John Bradford; KCVO (2002), OBE (1973), TD (1968 and bar 1974), JP (1987); s of Capt John James Timmins (d 1972); *b* 23 June 1932; *Educ* Dudley GS, Aston Univ (MSc); *m* 1956, Jean, *née* Edwards; 5 s, 1 da; *Career* Col TA; ADC to HM The Queen 1975–80; Cdr 75 Engr Regt 1971–73, Dep Cdr 30 Engr Brigade 1973–75; Hon Col: 75 Engr Regt 1980–90, Manchester & Salford UOTC 1990–98, Gtr Manchester ACF 1991–2007; former civil engr and chartered builder, chm Warburton Properties Ltd 1973–, NW regnl pres Nat Fedn of Building Trades Employers 1974–75; HM Lord-Lt Gtr Manchester 1987–2007 (High Sheriff 1986–87); vice-pres TA&VRA for NW England and IOM 1987–2007 (pres 1994–99); co pres Order of St John 1988–2007, pres Royal Soc of St George Gtr Manchester 1988–2007 (fell 2009), pres Gtr Manchester Army Benevolent Fund 1990–2010, pres SSAFA Gtr Manchester 1992–2012; Hon DSc Univ of Salford 1990, Hon LLD Univ of Manchester 2001; Hon RNCM 1994; KStJ 1988; *Recreations* gardening; *Clubs* Army and Navy, Manchester Literary and Philosophical; *Style*— Col Sir John Timmins, KCVO, OBE, TD

TIMMS, Rt Hon Stephen Creswell; PC (2006), MP; s of Ronald James Timms (d 1991), and Margaret Joyce, *née* Johnson; *b* 29 July 1955; *Educ* Farnborough GS, Emmanuel Coll Cambridge (exhibitioner, sr scholar, MA, MPhil); *m* 26 July 1986, Hui-Leng, da of C C Lim (d 2009); *Career* conslt Logica Ltd 1978–86, mangr telecommunications reports Ovum Ltd 1994 (princ conslt 1986–94); MP (Lab): Newham NE 1994–97, East Ham 1997–; memb Treasy Select Ctee 1995–97, PPS to Min of State for Employment 1997–98 and to Sec of State for NI 1998, Parly under sec DSS 1998–99, min of state DSS 1999, fin sec to the Treasy 1999–2001, min of state for school standards 2001–02, min of state for e-commerce, communications and competitiveness 2002–03, min of state for energy, e-commerce and postal services 2003–04, financial sec to HM Treasy 2004–05, min of state for pensions DWP 2005–06, chief sec to the Treasy 2006–07, min of state Dept for Business, Enterprise and Regulatory Reform 2007–08, min of state for employment and welfare reform DWP 2008, financial sec to HM Treasy 2008–10, min for digital Britain 2009–10, shadow min for employment 2010–; Lab Pty vice-chm for faith gps 2007–, chair All Pty Parly Gp on Faith and Soc 2011–; sec: Little Ilford branch Lab Pty 1979–81, Newham NE CLP 1981–84; London Borough of Newham: cncllr 1984–97, chm Planning Ctee 1987–90, ldr 1990–94; memb: E London Business Alliance Newham Area Bd 1990–2005, Stratford Devpt Partnership Bd 1992–94; hon pres Telecommunications Users' Assoc 1995–98; chm Christian Socialist Movement 2012– (vice-chm 1996–98), chm of tstees Traidcraft Fndn 2012– (tstee 2011–), vice-pres Tear Fund 2013–; memb: Ramblers' Assoc, Plaistow Christian Fellowship; Hon DEd Univ of E London 2002; *Books* Broadband Communications: The Commercial Impact (with Richard Kee, 1986), ISDN: Customer Premises Equipment (with Richard Kee, 1988), Broadband Communications: Market Strategies (with Iain Stevenson, 1992); *Recreations* walking and cycling; *Style*— The Rt Hon Stephen Timms, MP; ✉ House of Commons, London SW1A 0AA (☎ 020 7219 4000, e-mail stephen@stephentimms.org.uk, website www.stephentimms.org.uk)

TIMOTHY, Christopher Hugh; s of Eifion Andrew Comber Timothy (d 1990), and Gwladys Marian, *née* Hailstone (d 2007); *b* 14 October 1940; *Educ* Priory GS, Central Sch of Speech and Drama (John Gielgud scholar, Laurence Olivier Award); *m* 1; 4 s (Simon Jon, Nicholas Eifion, Robin James, David), 2 da (Tabitha Jane, Kate Elizabeth); m 2; 1 da (Grace Jane); *Career* actor; various radio plays and voice-overs for both radio and TV; *Theatre* weekly rep Worthing, 3 years with NT; roles incl: MP in Chips with Everything (NY), Petruchio in Taming of the Shrew (Farnham), Brian in A Day in the Death of Joe Egg (Haymarket Leicester), Fanny in Charlie's Aunt (Theatre Royal Plymouth), Rassendyl and The King in The Prisoner of Zenda (Bromley and Chichester), Trofimov in The Cherry Orchard (Chichester), Henry in Quartermaine's Terms 2008, Childcatcher in Chitty Chitty Bang Bang, Dial M For Murder (UK tour) 2014, Mrs Warren's Profession (Everyman Theatre Cheltenham) 2015; West End incl: Chesney Allen in Underneath the Arches, Hibbert in Journey's End, Bernard in Happy Birthday, Rosencrantz in Rosencrantz and Guildenstern Are Dead, Walter Plinge in The Actor's Nightmare, Clive in See How They Run, Dangerous Corner; nat tours incl: The Cure For Love, The Real Thing, Moment of

Weakness, Confusions, Darling Buds of May, Barbara Taylor-Bradford's Dangerous To Know, Mindgame, Heroes 2006, Hay Fever 2007; various pantomime roles incl Robinson Crusoe (also prodr/dir, Theatre Royal Brighton) 1990–91; *Television* James Herriot in All Creatures Great and Small (series, BBC), Murder Must Advertise (Lord Peter Wimsey series, BBC), Julius Caesar, Much Ado About Nothing, Twelfth Night, Ladykillers, Galton and Simpson Playhouse, The Ronnie Barker Playhouse, Murder Most English (Flaxborough Chronicles), The Moon Shines Bright on Charlie Chaplin, Take Three Girls, Take Three Women, The Fenn Street Gang, Z-Cars, The Liver Birds, Return of the Saint, Doctors (also dir) 2000–06, Casualty 2004; other appearances incl: Celebrity Squares, Give Us a Clue, The Two Ronnies, Call My Bluff; also dir of several episodes of Doctors and Glasgow Dreams; *Films* Othello, Here We Go Round The Mulberry Bush, The Virgin Soldiers, Alfred the Great, The Mind of Mr Soames, Spring and Port Wine, Up the Chastity Belt; co-produced and presented James Herriot's Yorkshire...the film (1993); *Awards* Outstanding Male Personality of the Year Screenwriters' Guild 1978, BBC Personality of the Year Variety Club of GB (jtly) 1979; *Style*— Christopher Timothy, Esq; ✉ c/o Phil Beldfield, Belfield and Ward, 80 St Martins Lane, London

TIMPSON, (Anthony) Edward; MP; s of (William) John Anthony Timpson, CBE, *qv*, and Alexandra Winkfield Timpson, MBE, *née* Dodd; *b* 26 December 1973, Knutsford, Cheshire; *Educ* Uppingham, Hatfield Coll Durham (BA); *m* 29 June 2002, Julia Helen, *née* Still; 1 s (Sam Edward Claude b 11 Feb 2004), 2 da (Elizabeth Winkfield b 7 Nov 2005, Lydia Frances b 29 Feb 2008); *Career* called to the Bar 1998, in practice as family law barr Cheshire 1999–2008; MP (Cons) Crewe and Nantwich 2008–, PPS to Rt Hon Theresa May, MP, *qv* 2010–12, Parly under sec of state for children and families 2012–15, min of state for children and families 2015–; *Recreations* football (watching and playing), cricket, travel; *Style*— Edward Timpson, Esq, MP; ✉ House of Commons, London SW1A 0AA

TIMPSON, James; OBE (2011); *m* Roisin; 3 c (Bede, Patrick, Niamh); *Career* chief exec Timpson; HRH Prince of Wales ambass for responsible business in the NW, chair Prison Reform Tst; Albert Medal RSA 2015; *Style*— James Timpson, Esq, OBE; ✉ Timpson House, Claverton Road, Roundthorn Industrial Estate, Manchester M23 9TT

TIMPSON, (William) John Anthony; CBE (2004); s of Anthony Timpson (d 1998), and Hilda, *née* Smith (d 1997); *b* 24 March 1943, Altrincham, Cheshire; *Educ* Oundle, Univ of Nottingham (BA); *m* 3 Feb 1968, Alexandra, *née* Dodd (d 2016); *Career* Timpson: joined 1960–, md 1975, chm and chief exec 1985, chm 2010; tstee Uppingham Sch; *Books* Ask John (2014), High Street Heroes (2015); Dear James (2002), How to be a Great Boss (2002), Cobbled Together (2003), How to Play Golf Quickly (2005), Upside Down Managment (2010); *Recreations* golf, tennis, real tennis, writing; *Clubs* Manchester Tennis & Racquets, Delamere Forest Golf; *Style*— John Timpson, Esq, CBE; ✉ Sandymere, Cotebrook, Tarporley, Cheshire CW6 9EH; Timpson Limited, Timpson House, Claverton Road, Wythenshawe, Manchester M23 9TT (☎ 0161 946 6225, fax 0161 946 6201)

TIMSON, Mrs Rodney; Penelope Anne Constance; *see:* Keith, Penelope Anne Constance

TINDALL, Gillian Elizabeth; da of D H Tindall; *b* 4 May 1938; *Educ* Univ of Oxford (MA); *m* 1963, Richard G Lansdown; 1 s; *Career* novelist, biographer, and historian; freelance journalist; occasional articles and reviews for: The Observer, The Guardian, New Statesman, New Society, London Evening Standard, The Times, Encounter, Sunday Times, The Independent, Daily Telegraph, New York Times; occasional broadcaster BBC, plays for Radio 4; JP Inner London Area 1980–98; FRSL; Chevalier de l'Ordre des Arts et des Lettres (France) 2001; *Books* novels: No Name in the Street (1959), The Water and the Sound (1961), The Edge of the Paper (1963), The Youngest (1967), Someone Else (1969, 2 edn 1975), Fly Away Home (1971, Somerset Maugham Award 1972), The Traveller and His Child (1975), The Intruder (1979), Looking Forward (1983), To the City (1987), Give Them All My Love (1989), Spirit Weddings (1992); short stories: Dances of Death (1973), The China Egg and Other Stories (1981), Journey of a Lifetime (1990); biography: The Born Exile: George Gissing (1974); other non-fiction: A Handbook on Witchcraft (1965), The Fields Beneath (1977, 5 edn 2010), City of Gold: the biography of Bombay (1981, 3 edn 2010), Rosamond Lehmann: an appreciation (1985), Architecture of the British Empire (contrib, 1986), Countries of the Mind: the meaning of place to writers (1991), Célestine: Voices from a French Village (1995, Franco-British Soc Award), The Journey of Martin Nadaud (1999), The Man Who Drew London: Wenceslaus Hollar in reality and imagination (2002), The House by the Thames (2006), Footprints in Paris (2009), Three Houses, Many Lives (2012), The Tunnel Through Time: a New Route for an Old London Journey (2016); *Recreations* keeping house, foreign travel; *Clubs* Royal Over-Seas League; *Style*— Ms Gillian Tindall, FRSL; ✉ c/o Curtis Brown Ltd, 4th Floor, Haymarket House, 28–29 Haymarket, London SW1Y 4SP (☎ 020 7393 4400, fax 020 7393 4401)

TINDALL, Justin Matthew Robert; s of David Tindall, of Pewsey, Wilts, and Brenda May, *née* Randall; *b* 17 August 1965, Taplow, Berks; *Educ* Stubbington House Ascot, Seaford Coll Sussex, Goldsmiths Coll Univ of London (BA); *m* Susan McKellar Cameron; 2 da (Misty May b 27 Sept 1998, Ava Rose b 17 April 2011), 1 s (Baxter Fife b 26 Sept 2013); *Career* art dir SMI Advertising 1991–96, art dir FCA! 1996–99; BMPDDB London: joined 1999, creative dir and head of art 2004–06, memb Exec Bd 2005–06; creative ptnr Red Brick Road 2006–10, gp exec creative dir Leo Burnett London 2010–; *Awards* incl: 5 Awards for outstanding excellence D&AD, 3 Gold, 1 Silver and 1 Bronze Lions Cannes Awards, 2 Grand Clios, 7 Gold, 5 Silver and and 3 Bronze Clio Awards, 5 Gold, 3 Silver and 2 Bronze at The One Show, 4 British Television Awards, 4 Gold Eurobest Awards, 1 Gold London International Awards, 2 Gold Epica Awards, 2 Gold, 4 Silver CIMTIG Awards, 1 Gold and 9 Sivler Campaign Poster Awards, 2 Gold, 4 Silver and 1 Bronze Campaign Press Awards, 3 Gold, 10 Silver amd 3 Bronze Creative Circle Awards; *Recreations* tennis, golf, painting; *Clubs* Royal Automobile, Quo Vadis, Arts; *Style*— Justin Tindall, Esq; ✉ Leo Burnett London, Warwick Building, Kensington Village, Avonmore Road, London W14 8HQ (☎ 020 7751 1800, e-mail justin.tindall@leoburnett.co.uk)

TINDALL, Michael James (Mike); MBE (2004); *b* 18 October 1978, Wharfedale; *Educ* Queen Elizabeth GS Wakefield; *m* 30 July 2011, Zara Phillips (*see Royal Family section*); 1 da (Mia Grace b 17 Jan 2014); *Career* rugby union player (centre); clubs: Bath until 2005, Gloucester 2005–; England: 62 caps, debut v Ireland 2000, winners Six Nations Championship 2000, 2001 and 2003 (Grand Slam 2003), ranked no 1 team in world 2003, winners World Cup Aust 2003; *Style*— Mike Tindall, Esq, MBE

TINDLE, David; s of Ernest Edwin Cook (d 1975), and Dorothy, *née* Smith (who m 2, 1946, William Tindle, and d 1974); assumed surname of Tindle 1946; *b* 29 April 1932; *Educ* Coventry Secdy Modern Sch, Coventry Sch of Art; *Career* artist; visiting tutor many art schs 1956–, tutor RCA 1972–83; Ruskin Master of Drawing and Fine Art Oxford 1985–87 (MA 1985); many one man exhibitions incl: Piccadilly Gallery 1954–83, Coventry City Art Gallery 1957, Galerie du Tours San Francisco 1964, Northern Art Gallery 1972, Fischer Fine Art 1985, 1989 and 1992, Gallery XX Hamburg 1974, 1977, 1980 and 1985, St Edmund Hall Oxford 1994, Redfern Gallery 1994, 1996, 2000, 2001, 2003, 2005, 2007, 2009, 2014 and 2016, Redfern Gallery work from 1987–97, Huddersfield City Art Gallery; represented in exhibitions: Royal Acad 1954, 1968, 1970 and 1972– (annually), Salon de la Jeune Peinture (Paris) 1967, Internationale Biennale of Realist Art (Bologna) 1967, Eros in Albion – Six English Painters (Florence) 1989; work represented at: The Tate Gallery, The Arts Cncl, Chantrey Bequest DOE, London Museum, De Beers Collection, Royal Acad, Nat Portrait Gallery, Ashmolean Museum Oxford, Govt Art Collection; designed stage set for Tchaikovsky's Iolanta (Aldeburgh Festival) 1988; Johnson Wax Award Royal Acad 1983; hon fell St Edmund Hall Oxford 1988; ARA 1973, RA 1979, FRCA 1981, Hon FRCA 1983; *Style*— David Tindle, Esq, RA; ✉ c/o The Redfern Gallery Ltd, 20 Cork Street, London W1S 3HL (☎ 020 7734 1732, e-mail art@redferngallery.com)

TINDLE, Sir Ray Stanley; kt (1994), CBE (1987, OBE 1974), DL (Surrey); s of John Robert Tindle (d 1975), and Maud, *née* Bilney (d 1952); *b* 8 October 1926; *Educ* Torquay GS, Strand Sch; *m* 8 Oct 1949, Beryl Julia, da of David Charles Ellis (d 1968); 1 s (Owen Charles b 1956); *Career* Capt Devonshire Regt 1944–47, served Far East; chm: Farnham Castle Newspapers Ltd 1969–, Tindle Newspapers Ltd, Farnham Herald, Cornish Times, Cornish & Devon Post, Mid Devon Advertiser, Tenby Observer, Cambrian News, 166 other titles, and 3 radio stations; memb MMC Newspaper Panel 1987–93; fndr Tindle Enterprise Centres for the Unemployed 1984, treas Newspaper Soc 1988–2002 (pres 1971–72), memb Cncl Cwlth Press Union, vice-pres Newspaper Press Fund; life patron Small Business Bureau 1995; chm Project Planning Sub Ctee Univ of Surrey 1964–69; memb Ct of Assts Worshipful Co of Stationers and Newspaper Makers (Master 1985–86); Hon Dr Letters Univ of Buckingham, Hon Dr Univ of Surrey 2008; FCIS, FCIArb, FCIJ; *Style*— Sir Ray Tindle, CBE, DL; ✉ Tindle Newspapers Ltd, The Old Court House, Farnham, Surrey GU9 7PT (☎ 01252 735667, fax 01252 734007)

TINER, John Ivan; CBE (2008); s of Kenneth Ivan Tiner, of Surrey, and Joan, *née* Benham; *b* 25 February 1957, Guildford, Surrey; *Educ* St Peter's Sch Guildford, Kingston Univ (accountancy fndn course); *m* 1978, Geraldine Marion Alison, da of James Henry Kassell; 2 s (Mark Andrew James b 1981, Matthew Paul Ivan b 1984), 1 da (Annabelle Elizabeth Mary b 1987); *Career* chartered accountant Tansley Witt (merged with Arthur Andersen) 1976–79; Arthur Andersen: joined 1979, mangr 1982, ptnr 1988–2001, head of fin markets 1993–99, managing ptnr UK Financial Markets 1995–99, managing ptnr Worldwide Financial Service Industry 1997–2001, managing ptnr UK Business Consulting 1998–2001; FSA: md Consumer, Investment and Insurance Directorate 2001–03, chief exec 2003–07; non-exec dir New Star Asset Mgmnt Gp plc 2008–; ldr: Bank of England review of UK Banking Supervision 1996, Govt's review of corporate governance of the NAO 2007–08; non-exec dir Lucida plc, dir Financial Skills Cncl; tstee Br Urological Fndn; ACA 1980; *Books* Accounting for Treasury Products (jtly, 1988, 2 edn 1991); *Recreations* tennis, golf, sailing; *Clubs* Mosimann's; *Style*— John Tiner, Esq, CBE

TINKER, Prof Anthea Margaret; CBE (2000); *née* Collins; da of James Collins (d 1991), and Margaret, *née* Herring (d 1999); *b* 24 October 1932; *Educ* Convent of Our Lady of Compassion Olton, Univ of Birmingham (BCom, William Morton meml prize), City Univ London (PhD); *m* 29 Dec 1956, Rev Prebendary Eric Tinker, OBE (d 2011), s of Frank Stanley Tinker (d 1923); 2 s (Jonathan Hugh b 27 March 1959, Andrew Michael b 14 May 1960), 1 da (Rachel Mary b 4 May 1964); *Career* asst then buyer Boxfoldia Ltd Birmingham 1953–54, HM inspr of factories 1954–58; pt/t lectr and res: Univ of Birmingham and Birmingham Sch of Planning 1958–65, Dept of Extra Mural Studies Univ of London and other London colls 1965–75 (full time res Royal Cmmn on Local Govt 1967); res fell City Univ London 1975–77, sr then princ res offr DOE 1977–88, dir Age Concern Inst of Gerontology KCL 1988–98, prof of social gerontology Univ of London 1988–, visiting Tower res fell Victoria Univ of Wellington NZ 2001; memb C of E Synod Working Pty on Ageing 1987–90, govr Centre for Policy on Ageing 1988–94, conslt OECD Paris 1989–94 and 2000, memb Joseph Rowntree Fndn Inquiry into the Costs of Continuing Care 1994–96, expert Euro Union 1991–, conslt WHO 2003–04; chair and memb various nat advsy ctees on ageing, scientific advsr to various Govt Depts; chm Research Ethics Ctee KCL 2001–11; vice-pres Section Gerontology/Geriatrics RSM 2000–02 (pres 1998–2000); FKC 1998, founding AcSS 1999; memb: Social Res Assoc, Social Policy Assoc, Assoc for Educnl Gerontology, Royal Soc of Arts, Br Assoc, Cncl Int Soc of Gerontechnology 1999–2003 and 2010–; FRSM, fell Br Soc of Gerontology 2008; *Books* The Non-Specialist Graduate in Industry (1954), The Inner London Education Authority (1968), Housing the Elderly: How Successful are Granny Annexes? (1976), Housing the Elderly near Relatives: Moving and Other Options (1980), Women in Housing: Access and Influence (with Marion Brion, 1980), Elderly People in Modern Society (1981, 2 edn 1984, 3 edn 1992, 4 edn 1997), Families in Flats (with Judith Littlewood, 1981), Staying at Home: Helping Elderly People (1984), The Telecommunication Needs of Disabled and Elderly People (1989), An Evaluation of Very Sheltered Housing (1989), A Review of Research on Falls Among Elderly People (jtly, 1990), Falls and Elderly People: a Study of Current Professional Practice in England and Innovations Abroad (jtly, 1991), Medication in Sheltered Housing (jtly, 1992), Caring: The Importance of Third Age Carers (jtly, 1992), Life after Sixty – A Profile of Britain's Older Population (jtly, 1992), Homes and Travel: Local Life in the Third Age (jtly, 1992), The Information Needs of Elderly People (jtly, 1993), Loneliness in Old Age (ed, 1993), The Care of Frail Elderly People in the UK (jtly, 1994), Difficult to Let Sheltered Housing (jtly, 1995), Getting Around After Sixty (jtly, 1996), Alternative Models of Care for Older People: Research Vol 2 Royal Cmmn on Long Term Care (jtly, 1999), Home Ownership in Old Age: financial benefit or burden? (jtly, 1999), To Have and to Hold: the bond between older people and the homes they own (jtly, 1999), Eighty-five not out (jtly, 2001), University Research Ethics Committees: The role, remit and conduct (jtly, 2004), Facts and Misunderstandings about Pensions and Retirement Ages (jtly, 2005), Improving the Provision of Information about Assistive Technology (jtly, 2005), UK Study of Abuse and Neglect of Older People: Prevalence Survey Report (jtly, 2007), Remodelling Sheltered Housing and Residential Care Homes to Extra Care Housing (jtly, 2007), Grandparenting in Europe (jtly, 2010), Grandparenting in Europe: Family Policy and grandparents' role in providing childcare (jtly, 2013), The Long Term Care Revolution (jtly, 2013), The Long Term Care Revolution: a case study of the Netherlands (2013), An Age-Friendly City – How Far Has London Come? (jtly, 2015); over 300 book chapters and jl articles; *Recreations* social policy, family, houses; *Clubs* Royal Soc of Medicine; *Style*— Prof Anthea Tinker, CBE; ✉ 35 Theberton Street, Islington, London N1 0QY (☎ 020 7359 4750); Institute of Gerontology, King's College London, Strand, London WC2R 2LS (☎ 020 7848 2747, e-mail anthea.tinker@kcl.ac.uk)

TINNISWOOD, Peter; s of late Maurice Tinniswood, of Oxford, and Anne, *née* Matchett; *b* 30 May 1951; *Educ* Charterhouse, Magdalen Coll Oxford (MA, PGCE), INSEAD (MBA); *m* 1975, Catharina, *née* Oeschger; *Career* asst master: Repton Sch 1974–76, Marlborough Coll 1976–80; sec-gen Franco-Br C of C and Indust 1981–83; asst master, head of Dept and housemaster Marlborough Coll 1983–91, master Magdalen Coll Sch Oxford 1991–98, head master Lancing Coll 1998–2005; tstee: Cambridge Business Studies Project Tst 1991–2001, Choir Schools' Assoc Bursary Tst 1994–98; govr: Dorset House Sch 2000–06, Mowden Sch 2002–05, St Paul's Sch São Paulo 2007–; *Publications* Marketing Decisions (1981), Marketing and Production Decisions (1991); *Style*— Peter Tinniswood, Esq; ✉ Samvara, Les Girvaysses, 81170 Noailles, France

TINSON, Dame Susan (Sue); DBE (1990); *Career* Independent Television News (ITN): joined as trainee 1964, sr ed News at Ten 1982, assoc ed 1989–2001, dir of external rels 2001–03; media advsr to ITN and ITV plc; non-exec dir: Freeserve 1999–2001, Yorkshire Building Soc 1999–2006, Chime Communications plc 2001–07, St Ives plc 2004–08, ITV London 2004–07; tstee Nat Heritage Lottery Fund 1995–2000; cmmr Cwlth War Graves Cmmn 1999–2004; memb Int Press Inst; FRSA, FRTS 1996; *Style*— Dame Sue Tinson, DBE

T

TIPPING, Luke; *Career* exec chef dir Simpsons Birmingham (Michelin star); prof of culinary arts Univ Coll Birmingham 2010–; *Style—* Luke Tipping, Esq; ✉ Simpsons Restaurant, 20 Highfield Road, Edgbaston, Birmingham B15 3DU

TIPTAFT, David Howard Palmer; CBE (1992), JP (1972); s of C Paxman Tiptaft, MC, JP (d 1984), of Wentworth, S Yorks, and Irene, *née* Palmer (d 1968); *b* 6 January 1938; *Educ* Shrewsbury; *m* 1 June 1963, Jennifer Cherry, da of Gerald Richard Millward (d 1967); 2 da (Elgiva b 10 March 1964, Genovefa b 20 Dec 1966), 2 s (Justyn b 30 Sept 1965, Quintin b 19 June 1970); *Career* qualified CA 1962, Arthur Young 1961–64, princ Tiptaft Smith & Co 1966–; chm Don Valley Cons Assoc 1964–75, treas Rother Valley Cons Assoc 1976–83, chm Wentworth Cons Assoc 1983–92, chm Yorks Area Conservatives 1993–96 (treas 1988–93), chm S Yorks Area Conservatives 2006–11; treas Yorks Gardens Tst; FCA 1973; *Recreations* opera, Wagner, conversation and debate, chess; *Style—* David Tiptaft, Esq, CBE; ✉ Old Village Hall, Blyth, Worksop, Nottinghamshire S81 8EW (☎ 01909 591920); Tiptaft Smith and Co, Marchman House, 3A West Street, Mexborough, South Yorkshire (☎ 01709 582991, e-mail tiptaft@aol.com, website www.tiptaft.co.uk)

TIRAMANI, Jennifer Jane (Jenny); da of Fredo Paulo Tiramani, and Barbara Doreen, *née* King; *Educ* Dartford GS for Girls, Central Sch of Art and Design, Trent Poly; *Career* theatre designer and dress historian; designer 7:84 England and 7:84 Scotland theatre cos 1978–84, assoc designer Theatre Royal Stratford E 1980–97, designer Renaissance Theatre Co 1988–90; Shakespeare's Globe: assoc designer 1997–2002 (designs incl: Hamlet 2000, Twelfth Night 2002), dir of theatre design 2003–05 (designs incl The Tempest 2005); dress advsr and contrib to Searching for Shakespeare exhbn Nat Portrait Gallery 2006; West End prodns incl: Steaming (Comedy Theatre) 1981, The Big Life (Apollo Theatre) 2005, Twelfth Night and Richard III (Apollo Theatre) 2012; designs for opera incl: Orlando (Opera Lille) 2010, La Clemenza di Tito (Aix-en-Provence Festival) 2011 (costumes), Anna Bolena (Met Opera NY) 2011 (costumes); princ Sch of Historical Dress 2012–; visiting prof Sch of Art and Design Nottingham Trent Univ 2008–11; Laurence Olivier Award for Costume Design (for Twelfth Night) 2003, Sam Wanamaker Award for contribution to Shakespeare (co-recipient with Mark Rylance and Claire van Kampen) 2007, Best Costume Design of A Play Tony Awards (for Twelfth Night in NY) 2014; *Publications* Janet Arnold and the Globe Wardrobe: Handmade Clothes for Shakespeare's Actors (in Costume (vol 34), 2000), The Sanders Portrait (in Costume (vol 39), 2005), Exploring Early Modern Stage and Costume Design in Shakespeare's Globe: A Theatrical Experiment (2008), Patterns of Fashion 4: The Cut and Construction of Linen Shirts, Smocks, Neckwear, Headwear and Accessories for Men and Women 1540–1660 (jtly, 2008), Seventeenth Century Women's Dress Patterns Book One (2011), Seventeenth Century Women's Dress Patterns Book Two (2012); *Style—* Ms Jenny Tiramani; ✉ The School of Historical Dress, 52 Lambeth Road, London SE1 7PP (e-mail jtiramani@theschoolofhistoricaldress.org.uk); agent Sam Lambourne, Performing Arts (e-mail sam@performing-arts.co.uk)

TISHLER, Gillian; da of Harry Tishler, of Ponteland, Northumberland, and Joyce, *née* Andrews; *b* 27 March 1958; *Educ* St Anne's Coll Oxford (BA); *m* 8 June 1991, Richard Wood; *Career* fast stream trainee rising to private sec to jr min MAFF 1979–87, Parly offr rising to head of public affrs RNIB 1987–93, chief exec YWCA of GB 1993–; *Style—* Ms Gillian Tishler; ✉ YWCA (England & Wales), Clarendon House, 52 Cornmarket Street, Oxford OX1 3EJ (☎ 01865 304209)

TITCHMARSH, Alan Fred; MBE (2000), VMH (2004), DL (Hants 2001); s of Alan Titchmarsh (d 1986), of Ilkley, W Yorks, and Bessie, *née* Hardisty (d 2002); *b* 2 May 1949; *Educ* Shipley Art and Tech Inst, Hertfordshire Coll of Agriculture and Horticulture (Nat Cert Horticulture), Royal Botanic Gardens Kew (Dip Horticulture, Sir Joseph Hooker Prize, Keith Jones Cup for public speaking); *m* 1975, Alison Margaret, da of Geoffrey Herbert Needs; 2 da (Polly Alexandra b 1980, Camilla Rose b 1982); *Career* freelance writer, presenter, interviewer and broadcaster 1979–; apprentice gardener Parks Dept Ilkley Urban District Cncl 1964–68, staff training supervisor Royal Botanic Gardens Kew 1972–74, asst ed Gardening Books Hamlyn Publishing Group 1974–76, dep ed Amateur Gardening magazine 1978–79 (asst ed 1976–78); gardening corr: Woman's Own 1982–85, Daily Mail 1986–99, Radio Times 1996–2001 and 2004–08, Daily Express and Sunday Express 1999–, Country Life 2011–; gardening ed Homes and Gardens 1985–89; columnist Sunday Telegraph 2013–; pres: Gardening for Disabled Tst 1989–, Telephones for the Blind 1993–, Plant Heritage (NCCPG) 2010–; vice-pres: Wessex Cancer Tst 1988–, Butterfly Conservation 2000–, RHS 2009–; patron Rainbow Tst 1993–, vice-patron Jubilee Sailing Tst 1999–2012; tstee: Nat Maritime Museum 2005–09, Garden Museum 2009–; chllr Univ of Winchester 2015–; ambass: Prince's Tst, Prince's Countryside Fund; cmmr Royal Hosp Chelsea 2010–16; High Sheriff IOW 2008–09; Freeman City of London 1989, Liveryman Worshipful Co of Gardeners 1989; Hon DSc Univ of Bradford 1999; Hon DUniv: Essex 1999, Leeds Met Univ 2004, Winchester 2007; FIHort, FCGI 2000, Hon FSE 2014; *Radio* BBC Radio progs: You and Yours 1975–82, Down to Earth 1982–89, A House In A Garden 1987–91, Radio 2 Arts Prog 1990–97, Melodies for You 2007–, Classic FM 2012–; *Television* presenter BBC TV progs: Nationwide (gardening expert) 1980–83, Breakfast Time (gardening expert) 1983–86, The Chelsea Flower Show 1983–97 and 2001–13, Open Air 1986–87, Daytime Live 1987–90, Grow Biz Quiz 1989, Songs of Praise 1989–94, More Than Meets The Eye 1990, Scene Today 1990, Pebble Mill 1991–96, Titchmarsh's Travels 1991, Titchmarsh On Song 1992, Sweet Inspiration 1993–94, Gardeners' World 1996–2002, Ground Force 1997–2002, Ask the Family 1999; presenter: Down by the River (Meridian) 1994–95, Relative Knowledge (Meridian) 1997, How to be a Gardener 2002–03, The Royal Gardeners 2003, BBC Proms 2004–07, British Isles: A Natural History 2004, 20th Century Roadshow 2005, The Gardener's Year 2005, Britain's Best (UKTV) 2007, The Great British Village Show 2007, Saving Planet Earth 2007, The Nature of Britain 2007, The Alan Titchmarsh Show (ITV) 2007–14, All the Queen's Horses (ITV) 2009, The Seasons (ITV) 2010, All The Queen's Men (ITV) 2010, Alan Titchmarsh's Garden Secrets 2010, Prince Philip at 90 (ITV) 2011, Love Your Garden (ITV) 2011–, Prince Charles: A Royal Restoration (ITV) 2012, Elizabeth: Queen, Wife, Mother (ITV) 2012, All The Queen's Horses: A Diamond Jubilee Special (ITV) 2012, The Queen's Garden 2014, Britain's Best Back Gardens 2015, Capability Found 2015, Masterpiece 2016, The Queen's 90th Birthday Celebration 2016; *Awards* Gardening Writer of the Year 1980 and 1983, Royal Horticultural Soc's Gold Medal Chelsea Flower Show 1985, Yorkshireman of the Year 1997 and 2007, Variety Club of Great Britain TV Personality of the Year 1999 (for the Ground Force team), Special Award Inst of Horticulture 2004, Special Award TRIC 2004, Lifetime Achievement Award Garden Media Guild 2004; *Books* incl: Gardening Under Cover (1979), Climbers and Wall Plants (1980), Gardening Techniques (1981), The Allotment Gardener's Handbook (1982), The Rock Gardener's Handbook (1983), Supergardener (1983), Alan Titchmarsh's Avant-Gardening (1984 and 1994), Daytime Live Gardening Book (1990), The English River (1993), Alan Titchmarsh's Favourite Gardens (1995), Mr MacGregor (novel, 1998), Alan Titchmarsh's Complete Book of Gardening (1999), Ground Force Weekend Workbook (conslt ed, 1999), The Last Lighthouse Keeper (novel, 1999), Animal Instincts (novel, 2000), Only Dad (novel, 2001), How to be a Gardener: The Basics (2002), Trowel and Error (2002), How to be a Gardener: Secrets of Success (2003), The Royal Gardeners (2003), Rosie (novel, 2004), British Isles: A Natural History (2004), Fill My Stocking (anthology, 2005), The Gardener's Year (2005), Love and Dr Devon (novel, 2006), Nobbut a Lad (2006), England Our England (2007), The Nature of Britain (2007), The Kitchen Gardener (2008), Folly (novel, 2008), Knave of Spades (memoir, 2009), Alan Titchmarsh's How to Garden: Lawns, Containers, Gardening in Shade, Garden Design, Vegetables and Herbs, Pruning (2009), Growing Fruit, Greenhouse Gardening, Climbers and Wall Shrubs, Perennial Garden Plants, Flowering Shrubs (2010), When I Was a Nipper (memoir, 2010), Wildlife Gardening, Growing Roses, Growing Bulbs, Pests and Problems (2011), The Complete Countryman (2011), The Haunting (novel, 2011), Elizabeth: Her Life, Our Times (2012), My Secret Garden (2012), Love Your Garden (2012), Bring Me Home (novel, 2014), The Queen's Houses (2014), Mr Gandy's Grand Tour (novel, 2016); *Recreations* boating; *Clubs* Lord's Taverners, RAC, Athenaeum; *Style—* Alan Titchmarsh, Esq, MBE, VMH, DL; ✉ c/o Arlington Enterprises, 1–3 Charlotte Street, London W1T 1RD (☎ 020 7580 0702)

TITCOMB, Hugh Harrison; s of Francis William Titcomb, of Newbury, and Margaret Ann, *née* Bright; *b* 21 December 1959, Newbury, Berks; *Educ* Christ's Hosp, Univ of Warwick (BA); *m* 10 Sept 1994, Karen Jane, *née* Basson; 1 s (Christopher b 5 Feb 1997), 1 da (Anna b 25 Feb 1999); *Career* dir Robert Fleming 1994–2002, md Bank of New York 2002–03, ceo Ansbacher Gp 2003–09, ceo Principal Investment Mgmnt Gp 2009–12, head of private banking Brown Shipley 2014–; chm and non-exec dir Harpenden Building Soc 2008–; FCIB 2003; *Style—* Hugh Titcomb, Esq; ✉ e-mail hugh@thetitcombs.co.uk

TITE, Prof Michael Stanley; s of Arthur Robert Tite (d 1985), and Evelyn Francis Violet, *née* Endersby (d 1971); *b* 9 November 1938; *Educ* Trinity Sch of John Whitgift Croydon, ChCh Oxford (exhibitioner, MA, DPhil); *m* 10 June 1967, Virgina Byng, da of Rear Adm Gambier John Byng Noel, CB (d 1995), of Haslemere, Surrey; 2 da (Sarah Beatrice b 1970, Alice Evelyn Byng b 1972); *Career* ICI res fell Univ of Leeds 1964–67, lectr Univ of Essex 1967–75, keeper Res Lab British Museum 1975–89, Edward Hall prof of archaeological science Univ of Oxford 1989–2004 (emeritus prof 2004–), fell Linacre Coll Oxford 1989–2004 (emeritus fell 2004–); fell Int Inst for Conservation (FIIC) 1990–2004; FSA 1977; *Books* Methods of Physical Examination in Archaeology (1972), Production Technology of Faience and Related Vitreous Materials (jtly, 2008); *Recreations* walking, gardening, travel; *Clubs* Oxford and Cambridge; *Style—* Prof Michael Tite, FSA; ✉ Research Laboratory for Archaeology and the History of Art, Dyson Perrins Building, South Parks Road, Oxford OX1 3QY

TITE, Nicholas William Spencer (Nick); s of William Timpson Tite (d 1970), and Stephanie Frances, *née* Spencer; *b* 29 July 1950; *Educ* Wellingborough Sch, Northampton Sch of Art (travelling scholar), Winchester Sch of Art (DipAD, first year painting prize); *Career* Studio Prints Queen's Crescent London 1974–76, etching technician Central Sch of Art 1976–78, Editions Alecto (working on Tom Phillips's Dante's Inferno) 1978, creation of Talfourd Press (prodn controller Tom Phillips's Dante's Inferno) 1980–83, ed RA Magazine 1983–2001, head of publishing operations RA Publications 2007– (ed dir 1998–2006); responsible for exhibitions in Friends' Room at Royal Acad incl: Ghika, Bryan Kneale, Carel Weight, S W Hayter, Leonard McComb, RAs Through the Lens, Etchings by Academicians 1985–98; *Recreations* tennis; *Style—* Nick Tite, Esq; ✉ RA Publications, Royal Academy Enterprises, Royal Academy of Arts, Burlington House, London W1J 0BD (☎ 020 7300 5659, fax 020 7300 5881, e-mail nick.tite@royalacademy.org.uk)

TITLEY, Gary; s of late Wilfred James Titley, and Joyce Lillian Titley; *b* 19 January 1950; *Educ* Univ of York (BA, PGCE); *m* 1975, Maria (Charo) Rosario; 1 s (Adam), 1 da (Samantha); *Career* various positions until 1973 incl: bus conductor, delivery driver, postman, security guard, labourer and barman; TEFL Bilbao 1973–75, history teacher Earls High Sch Halesowen 1976–84; campaign mangr to Terry Pitt, MEP (and later John Bird, MEP) 1983–89; Parly candidate (Lab): Bromsgrove 1983, Dudley W 1987; memb Bolton W CLP; memb W Midlands CC 1981–86: vice-chm Econ Devpt Ctee 1981–84, vice-chm Consumer Servs Ctee 1984–86; MEP (Lab): Greater Manchester W 1989–99, NW England 1999–2009; leader EP Labour Gp 2002–; former memb: Environment, REX, Econ and Monetary, and Tport Ctees; pres Jt Parly Ctee with: Finland 1991–93, European Economic Area 1993–94 (vice-pres 1994–97), Slovenia 1997–; vice-pres delgn to Czech, Slovak and Slovenian Parliaments 1994–97; pres EP Jt Parly Ctee with Lithuania; rapporteur on: Finland's accession to EU, Future of the Euro Defence Industries; dir W Midlands Enterprise Bd 1982–89, vice-chair Euro Parly Delgn for Rels with Czech Republic, rapportuer on Finland's accession to EU 1995; chm: W Midlands Co-op Finance Co 1982–89, Black Country Co-op Development Agency 1982–88; Cdr Order of the White Rose of Finland, Austrian Gold Cross, Order of Lithuanian Grand Duke Gediminas; *Recreations* family, reading, sport; *Style—* Gary Titley, Esq

TITTERINGTON, David Michael; s of Geoffrey Bridge Titterington, of Beverley, E Yorks, and Claire Elizabeth, *née* Parsons; *b* 10 January 1958; *Educ* Northern Sch of Music, Pembroke Coll Oxford (organ scholar, MA), Conservatoire Rueil-Malmaison Paris; *Career* organist; debut Royal Festival Hall 1986; concert and concerto performances at major festivals and venues worldwide incl: Bicentennial Festival of Sydney 1988 and festivals of Hong Kong, New Zealand, Istanbul, Schleswig-Holstein, Cheltenham, Adelaide and Israel; BBC Proms debut 1990; orchestras played with incl: BBC Symphony, BBC Scottish Symphony, Bournemouth Sinfonietta, English Sinfonia, Berlin Symphony, Lahti Symphony; has given masterclasses internationally; numerous recordings made incl complete works of César Franck (for BBC), also recorded for Hyperion Records, Multisonic and ASV; world premiere performances incl: Petr Eben's Job 1986, Naji Hakim's Rubaiyat 1990, Diana Burrell's Arched Forms with Bells (Proms cmmn) 1990, Henze Symphony No 9 (BBC Proms) 2000, Stephen Montague's Toccare Incandescent (Southbank Centre cmmn, Royal Festival Hall) 2004, Giles Swayne's 14 Stations of the Cross (25th Cambridge Festival cmmn, King's Coll Cambridge), Sally Beamish's Chaconne (Southbank Centre cmmn, Royal Festival Hall and USA premiere, Symphony Hall San Francisco) 2016; organ conslt: Pembroke Coll Oxford 1995, Chapel Royal HM Tower of London 2000, St Catherine's Coll Cambridge 2002, Sidney Sussex Coll Cambridge 2007–, Canterbury Cathedral 2007–, KCL 2016–; organ curator St John's Smith Square 2012–; artistic dir: Euro Organ Festival 1992, St Albans Int Organ Festival 2007–; Royal Acad of Music: prof of organ 1990–, head of organ studies 1996–; visiting prof Ferenc Liszt Acad Budapest 1997–; gen ed organ repertoire series United Music Publishers London 1987–97; Ian Fleming award 1983, French Government Scholarship 1983–84, Arts Council Bursary 1984, Premier Prix 1984, Prix d'Excellence 1985 (Rueil-Malmaison Conservatoire, Paris); memb: Royal Soc of Musicians of GB 1996; elected to SCR Pembroke Coll Oxford 1999; hon fell Univ of Bolton 1992, hon prof and Hon DMus Liszt Ferenc Univ Budapest 2000, Hon DUniv Huddersfield 2010; Hon ARAM 1994 (Hon RAM 2008), Hon FRCO 1999; *Recreations* silence, being by the sea; *Clubs* Travellers, Nobleman and Gentlemen's Catch; *Style—* David Titterington, Esq; ✉ c/o Royal Academy of Music, Marylebone Road, London NW1 5HT (☎ 020 7873 7339, fax 020 7873 7439, e-mail d.titterington@ram.ac.uk)

TITTERRELL, Andrew James (Andy); s of Charles Titterrell, and Carol Titterrell; *b* 10 January 1981, Dartford, Kent; *Educ* Sevenoaks Sch, Hugh Christie Technol Coll; *m* 17 July 2005, Delyth; *Career* rugby union player (hooker); clubs: Saracens, Waterloo, Sale Sharks 2001–07, Gloucester 2007–09 (winners Parker Pen Shield 2002, European Challenge Cup 2005), Leeds Carnegie 2009–; England: 5 caps, debut v NZ 2004; memb British and Irish Lions touring squad NZ 2005; strength and conditioning coach; *Recreations* qualified personal trainer, accredited strength and conditioner; *Style—* Mr Andy Titterrell

TOALSTER, John Raymond; s of Chief Petty Offr John Edward Toalster, RNVR (ka 1944), and Adeline Enid, *née* Smith; *b* 12 March 1941; *Educ* Kingston HS Hull N Humberside, LSE (BSc); *m* 21 Sept 1963, Christine Anne, da of Edward Percy Paget (d 1970); 1 s

(Quentin Simon Edward b 1966), 2 da (Rachel Jane b 1969, Bethan Claire b 1981); *Career* lectr in economics Univ of Sierra Leone 1964–67, corp planner Mobil Oil 1967–69, sr analyst (oils) stockbroking 1970–77, corporate fin mangr Kuwait International Investment Co 1977–81, energy specialist stockbroking 1982–90; dir: Hoare Govett 1982–90, Security Pacific, Société General Strauss Turnbull 1990–, Fig Tree Real Estate Ltd, Toalster Properties Ltd; FInstPet 1988; private circulation to clients; *Recreations* swimming, sailing, badminton; *Style*— John Toalster, Esq; ✉ Fig St Farm, Sevenoaks, Kent (☎ 01732 453357); Société General Strauss Turnbull, Exchange House, Primrose Street, London EC2A (☎ 020 7638 5699, fax 020 7588 1437)

TOBIAS, Prof Jeffrey Stewart; s of Gerald Joseph Tobias, of Bournemouth, Dorset, and Sylvia, *née* Pearlberg; *b* 4 December 1946; *Educ* Hendon GS, Gonville& Caius Coll Cambridge (MA, MD), Bart's Med Coll; *m* 1, 16 Nov 1973, Dr Gabriela Jill Jaecker (d 2008), da of Hans Jaecker, of Crowborough, E Sussex; 1 da (Katharine Deborah b 1978), 2 s (Benjamin Alexander b 1980, Max William Solomon b 1983); m 2, Dr Susan Jacqueline Kiernan, da of Dr Wolfgang Kiernan, of Edinburgh; *Career* SHO Bart's, UCH and Hammersmith Hosp 1972–73, fell in med (oncology) Harvard Med Sch 1974–75, sr registrar Royal Marsden Hosp and Inst of Cancer Research 1976–80, conslt clinical oncology UCH and Middlesex Hosps London 1981–2015, clinical dir Meyerstein Inst of Oncology 1992–97, prof of cancer med UCL Med Sch 2002–; hon sec Br Oncological Assoc 1985–90, chm UK Co-ordinating Ctee for Cancer Research Head and Neck Working Pty 1989–, pres Assoc of Head and Neck Oncologists of Great Britain 1995–97; memb: MRC Working Pty in Gynaecological and Brain Tumors, Cancer Research Campaign Working Pty in Breast Cancer (chm New Studies Sub-Gp), Cncl Royal Coll of Radiologists 1991–95; chair Cancer Research Campaign Educn Ctee; tstee and memb Cancer Research UK; Cncl fell American Soc for Therapeutic Radiology; FRCP, FRCR; *Publications* Primary Management of Breast Cancer (1985), Cancer and its Management (with R L Souhami, 1986, 7 edn 2014), Cancer – A Colour Atlas (1990), Cancer: What Every Patient Needs to Know (1995), Current Radiation Oncology Vols 1 – 3 (1994–98), Breast Cancer: New Horizons in Research and Treatment (2000), Informed Consent in Medical Research (with L Doyal, 2001); author of original articles in med jls, features and editorials in BMJ and The Lancet; *Recreations* music, writing, theatre, cycling, walking; *Clubs* Garrick, Les Six; *Style*— Prof Jeffrey Tobias; ✉ 4 Canonbury Place, London N1 2NQ (☎ 07814 702063); Department of Oncology, University College Hospital, London NW1 2EB (☎ 020 3447 9088, fax 020 3447 9055, e-mail j.tobias@uclh.org)

TOBIN, Michael; OBE (2014); *b* London; *m* Shalina; 2 da (Eloise and Rose), 1 s (Nelson); *Career* apprenticeship in electronic and electrical engineering (awarded HND), electronics engineer Rockwell Gp 1980–86, md Goupil Computers Ltd 1986–90, int business devpt dir Int Computer Gp 1990–94, European sales dir and gen manager Tricord Systems Inc 1994–96, int business devpt dir GlobalServe SA 1996–98, gen manager ICL Fujitsu Services 1998–2000, md Fujitsu Corp 2000–02; TelecityGroup (formerly Redbus Interhouse): sales and mktg dir 2002–03, ceo 2003–; non-exec dir: Think London 2003–11, Pacnet 2012–, PeoplePerHour.Com 2013–; chm Friends of The Loomba Tst 2005–, memb Bd Byte Night 2007–, ceo Sleepout Charity Action for Children 2007–; memb: Princes Tst Technology Leadership Panel 2009–, Ctee Make A Wish Fndn 2010–, Princes Tst Internet & Medial Panel 2010–, Ctee Great Ormond Street Hosp 2011–14; Business Turnaround of the Year London Business Awards 2005, Technology CEO of the Year PWC 2007, Outstanding Ldr in Data Centres Data Centre Europe 2007 and 2008, techMARK Achievement of the Year Award 2008, LCCI Business Growth Co of the Year 2008 and 2009, IPO of the Year UK Innovations Awards 2008, Ernst & Young Entrepreneur of the Year (London regnl winner) 2009, 2010 and 2011, techMARK Personality of the Year 2009, Industry Ldr of the Year Datacentre Dynamics Datacentre Award 2009, Business Person of the Year Award London Chamber of Commerce 2009 and 2010, Lifetime Achievement Award for Contrib to the Data Centre Industry Data Centre Europe Awards 2011, Third Sector Business Charity Champion 2013; *Books* Forget Strategy Get Results (2014); *Style*— Michael Tobin, Esq, OBE; ✉ TelecityGroup, 4th Floor, 2 Harbour Exchange Square, London E14 9GE

TOD, Alison Jane; da of Robin Tod, of Abergavenny, and Jacqueline Rendall, *née* Davies; *b* 24 September 1963; *Educ* St David's Ursuline Convent Brecon, Alsager Coll, Univ of Lampeter (BA); *Partner* Neil Thomas; *Career* fashion designer; designs for: Kangol, Harpers & Queen A list for Millinery, London Fashion Week; exhibited at: V&A, Museum of Hatting; shows: Hay-on-Wye (for pres Bill Clinton), Clothes Show Live; Welsh Designer of the Year (fashion and accessories) 1995 and 1996; memb Br Hat Guild; memb: NSPCC (Full Stop Campaign), Cancer Research Campaign, Soroptomists, Save the Children, Stroke Assoc, Lady Taverners, Variety Club of GB, Br Heart Fndn, NHS Tst St David's Fndn, Carers' Assoc (Prince's Royal Tst for Carers); *Recreations* art galleries, travel, collecting antiques, horses, charity work; *Style*— Miss Alison Tod; ✉ Hatherleigh Place, Merthyr Link Road, Abergavenny, Monmouthshire NP7 7RL (☎ 01873 855923, fax 01873 856891)

TODD, Dr (William Taylor) Andrew; s of James McArthur Todd, of Edinburgh, and Jean Morley, *née* Smith; *b* 14 July 1953; *Educ* George Heriot's Sch, Univ of Edinburgh (BSc, MB ChB); *m* 1 July 1978, Morag Jennifer, da of Trevor John Ransley, of Edinburgh; 3 da (Jennifer b 1980, Rachel b 1983, Anna b 1987); *Career* Royal Infirmary Edinburgh: res house offr 1977, SHO in med 1978, registrar 1979–82; sr registrar City Hosp Edinburgh 1984 (registrar 1979–81); visiting lectr Univ of Zimbabwe 1983, conslt physician Monklands Hosp 1985–; chair: Speciality Advsy Ctee (infectious diseases/tropical med), jt ctee on higher med training; elder Church of Scotland; trg and manpower co-ordinator Cncl Br Infection Soc 1997–2002; consortium head west region deanery Foundation; FRCPE, FRCPG; *Publications* Principles and Practice of Medicine (contrib to infection/tropical med section); *Recreations* curling, hill walking; *Style*— Dr Andrew Todd; ✉ 17 Crosshill Drive, Rutherglen, Glasgow G73 3QT (☎ 0141 647 7288, e-mail wtat@ntlworld.com); Infectious Diseases Unit, Monklands Hospital NHS Trust, Airdrie, Lanarkshire ML6 0JS (☎ 01236 746120)

TODD, (HE) Damian Roderic (Ric); s of late George Todd, and Annette Todd; *b* 29 August 1959; *Educ* Lawrence Sherriff GS Rugby, Worcester Coll Oxford; *Career* joined HM Dip Serv 1980; FCO 1980–81, third later second sec Pretoria and Cape Town 1981–84, FCO 1984–87, consul and first sec Prague 1987–89, FCO 1989–91, first sec (economic) Bonn 1991–95, on secondment HM Treasy 1995–97, FCO 1997–98, on secondment HM Treasy 1998–2001, head EU Co-ordination and Strategy (EUCS), ambass to Slovakia 2001–04, finance dir FCO 2004–07, ambass to Poland 2007–11, govr Turks and Caicos Islands 2011–14, high cmmr to Cyprus 2014–; *Recreations* history, family life, looking at buildings; *Style*— Mr D R Todd; ✉ c/o Foreign & Commonwealth Office (Nicosia), King Charles Street, London SW1A 2AH (☎ 020 7270 3000)

TODD, Daphne Jane; OBE (2002); da of Frank Todd (d 1976), and Annie Mary, *née* Lord (d 2009); *b* 27 March 1947; *Educ* Simon Langton GS for Girls Canterbury, Slade Sch of Fine Art (DFA, Higher Dip Fine Art); *m* 31 Aug 1984, Lt-Col (Patrick Robert) Terence Driscoll; 1 da (Mary Jane b 12 Nov 1977); *Career* artist specialising in portraits incl: HRH the Prince of Wales (Official Tour Artist with TRH the Prince of Wales and Duchess of Cornwall to Tanzania and S. Africa 2011), Dr Stephen Spurr, the Rt Rev Graeme Knowels, HRH the Grand Duke of Luxembourg, Lord Adrian, Dame Janet Baker, Spike Milligan, Sir Neil Cossons, Baron Klingspor, Sir Kirby and Lady Laing, Christopher Ondaatje, Dame Anne Mueller, Lord Sainsbury of Preston Candover, Lord Sharman, Sir Tom Stoppard, Lord Ashburton, Lord Deedes, Lord Tugendhat, Lord Fellowes, Lord Armstrong of Ilminster, Lord and Lady Tebbit, Lord Bledisloe, Viscount Mackintosh, Peter Scott, CBE, Bill Packer, Brig Peter Madsen, Lady Armstrong, Lord Fellowes, Sir Peter Gwynne Jones, Viscount Gage, Dame Marilyn Strathern; exhibitions incl retrospective exhibition Morley Gallery 1989, solo exhbns: Messum Gall 2001, 2004, 2008 and 2015, Mall Galleries 2012; work in numerous collections incl: Royal Acad (Chantrey Bequest), Regtl HQ Irish Guards, London, Cambridge, Oxford, Wales and De Montfort Univs, Royal Holloway Museum and Art Gallery, Bishop's Palace Hereford, BMA, Instn of Civil Engrs, Ondaatje Hall, Nat Portrait Gallery, Science Museum, Royal Collection Windsor, People's Portraits Girton Coll Cambridge, St James' Church Piccadilly, Chapter House St Paul's Cathedral; television incl: In Your Face 2005, Big Painting Challenge (BBC 1) 2015, ; dir of studies Heatherley Sch of Art 1980–86; govr: Thomas Heatherley Educnl Tst 1986–2014, Fedn of Br Artists 1994–2000; pres Royal Soc of Portrait Painters 1994–2000 (hon sec 1990–91); memb Honours Ctee Friends of the Canterbury Museums 2011 hon memb Soc of Women Artists 1995; David Murray Award for Landscape Painting 1971, Br Inst Award for Figurative Painting 1972, second prize John Player Portrait Award Nat Portrait Gallery 1983, first prize Oil Painting of the Year Hunting Group Nat Art Prize Competition 1984, GLC Prize 1984, Ondaatje Prize for Portraiture 2001, RP Gold Medal 2001, First Prize BP Portrait Award NPG 2010; Hon Dr of Arts De Montfort Univ 1998, Hon Dr of Arts Univ of Kent 2014; ambass for East Sussex 2004; Freeman: City of London 1997, Worshipful Co of Painter-Stainers 1997 (Hon Liveryman 2004); NEAC 1984, RP 1985, FRSA; *Clubs* Arts, Chelsea Arts, Athenaeum; *Style*— Miss Daphne Todd, OBE; ✉ Salters Green Farm, Mayfield, East Sussex TN20 6NP (☎ and fax 01892 852472, e-mail daphne.todd@btinternet.com, website www.daphnetodd.com)

TODD, Michael Alan; QC (1997); s of Charles Edward Alan Todd, and Betty, *née* Bromwich (d 1997); *Educ* Kenilworth GS, Keele Univ (BA); *m* 1976, Deborah, da of Harold Thomas Collett (decd); *Career* called to the Bar Lincoln's Inn 1977 (bencher); jr counsel to the Crown (Chancery) 1992–97, head Erskine Chambers 2010–; chm Chancery Bar Assoc 2008–10, chm of the Bar 2012 (vice-chm 2011); LLD (hc) Keele Univ 2015; *Recreations* equestrianism; *Style*— Michael Todd, Esq, QC; ✉ Erskine Chambers, 33 Chancery Lane, London WC2A 3EN (☎ 020 7242 5532, fax 020 7831 0125)

TODD, Roland C W; *Career* slr; articled clerk Slaughter and May 1984–86, asst slr Slaughter and May 1986–90; Simpson Curtis Slrs: asst slr 1990–91, assoc 1991–93, ptnr 1993–94; ptnr Garretts Slrs 1994–2000, ptnr DLA Slrs 2000–04, co sec and legal counsel Cattles Ltd 2004–; *Style*— Roland Todd, Esq; ✉ Cattles Ltd, c/o Welcome Financial Services, Mere Way, Ruddington Fields Business Park, Ruddington, Nottingham NG11 6NZ

TODOLÍ, Vicente; *b* 31 May 1958, Valencia, Spain; *Career* Valencia Inst for Modern Art: chief curator 1986–88, artistic dir 1989–96; founding dir Museum of Contemporary Art Fundação De Serralves Porto 1996–2003, dir Tate Modern 2003–10; curator of numerous Tate Modern exhbns incl: Sigmar Polke 2004, Robert Frank 2005; curator of numerous Museu Serralves exhbns incl: James Lee Byars, Franz West, Gary Hill, Hamish Fulton, Lothar Baumgarten, Roni Horn, Claes Oldenburg, Coosje van Bruggen, Richard Hamilton/Dieter Roth, Francis Bacon; *Style*— Vicente Todoli, Esq; ✉ Tate Modern, Bankside, London SE1 9TG (☎ 0207 401 5223, e-mail jennifer.bailey@tate.org.uk)

TOFT, Dr Anthony Douglas; CBE (1995), LVO (2010); s of William Vincent Toft (d 1982), and Anne, *née* Laing (d 2001); *b* 29 October 1944, Perth, Scotland; *Educ* Perth Acad, Univ of Edinburgh (BSc, MB ChB, MD); *m* 23 July 1968, Maureen Margaret, da of John Darling (d 1986); 1 s (Neil b 1970), 1 da (Gillian b 1972); *Career* conslt physician gen med and endocrinology Royal Infirmary Edinburgh 1978–2009, chief MO Aegon UK 1982–2015; Royal Coll of Physicians of Edinburgh: memb Cncl 1985–88, vice-pres 1990–91, pres 1991–94; memb Assoc of Physicians of GB and I 1984, chm Scottish Royal Colleges 1992–94, vice-chm UK Conf of Med Royal Colleges 1993–94, chm Jt Ctee on Higher Med Trg 1994–96, memb Health Advsy Appts Ctee 1994–2000; memb GMC 1996–2003; physician to HM The Queen in Scotland 1996–2009; chm Professional and Linguistic Assessments Bd (PLAB) 2000–06, pres Br Thyroid Assoc 1996–99; FRCPEd 1980, FRCP 1992, FRCPGlas 1993, FRCPI 1993, FRCSEd ad hominem 1994; Hon: FCPS (Pakistan) 1990, FRACP 1993, FACP 1993, FRCP (Canada) 1994, FRCGP 1994, FCPS (Bangladesh) 1994, FFPM 1994, MAM (Malaysia) 1994, FAM (Singapore) 1994, FFAEM 1997; *Books* Diagnosis and Management of Endocrine Diseases (1982); *Recreations* golf, gardening, collecting contemporary Scottish art; *Style*— Dr Anthony Toft, CBE, LVO; ✉ 41 Hermitage Gardens, Edinburgh EH10 6AZ (☎ 0131 447 2221); Spire Murrayfield Hospital, Edinburgh EH12 6UD (☎ 0131 316 2530)

TOKSVIG, Sandi Birgitte; OBE (2014); da of Claus Bertel Toksvig (d 1988), and Julie Anne, *née* Brett, of Surrey; *b* 3 May 1958; *Educ* Mamaroneck HS NY, Tormead Sch Guildford, Girton Coll Cambridge (MA, Therese Montefiore Meml Award); *Career* actress, comedienne and writer; Channel 4 Political Humourist of the Year 2007, Radio Broadcaster of the Year Broadcast Press Guild 2007; *Theatre* Nottingham Rep 1980–81, New Shakespeare Co (Open Air Theatre Regents Park) 1981, with The Comedy Store Players 1987–93; plays incl: The Pocket Dream (co-writer with Elly Brewer, Nottingham Playhouse then Albery Theatre) 1991–92, Big Night Out At The Little Sands Picture Palace (writer, Nottingham Playhouse) 1993, Big Night Out At The Little Palace Theatre (co-writer, Palace Theatre Watford) 2002, Cinderella (Old Vic) 2007–08, Bully Boy (writer) 2011; *Television* incl: Number 73 (co-writer) 1982–87, Toksvig (co-writer), Whose Line Is It Anyway?, Behind The Headlines, The Big One (co-writer), Sindy Hits Thirty, The Talking Show, Call My Bluff, Island Race (co-writer), Great Journeys, What the Dickens (Sky Arts) 2008; *Radio* reg contrib to Loose Ends (BBC Radio 4), Pick of the Week (BBC Radio 4) 1993, presenter Sound Company (BBC Radio 4) 1995, host Darling You Were Marvellous (BBC Radio 4) 1996, presenter Excess Baggage (BBC Radio 4) 2002–, presenter The Sandi Toksvig Show (LBC) 2003, chair The News Quiz (Radio 4) 2006–15, reg on I'm Sorry I Haven't A Clue; also co-writer: Kin of the Castle, Cat's Whiskers; *Film* Paris By Night, Sweet Nothings; *Books* Island Race: Improbable Voyage Round the Coast of Britain (with John McCarthy, 1996), Supersaver Mouse (1998), Suspersaver Mouse to the Rescue (1999), Unusual Boy (1996), Whistling for the Elephants (1999), The Troublesome Tooth Fairy (2000), Flying Under Bridges (2001), The Gladys Society (2002), The Travels of Lady Bulldog Burton (2002), Hitler's Canary (2005), Melted into Air, Girls Are Best (2008), Valentine Grey (2012); *Recreations* skiing, arboreal activities; *Clubs* 2 Brydges Place, Univ Women's, Ivy; *Style*— Ms Sandi Toksvig, OBE; ✉ c/o United Agents Ltd, 12–26 Lexington Street, London W1F 0LE (☎ 020 3214 0800, fax 020 3214 0801, website www.unitedagents.co.uk)

TOLAND, Prof John Francis; s of Joseph Toland (d 1986), and Catherine, *née* McGarvey (d 2001); *b* 28 April 1949; *Educ* St Columb's Coll Derry, Queen's Univ Belfast (BSc), Univ of Sussex (MSc, DPhil); *m* 2 July 1977, Susan, *née* Beck; *Career* Battelle Advanced Studies Centre 1973, Fluid Mechanics Research Inst Univ of Essex 1973–79, lectr UCL 1979–82, prof Univ of Bath 1982–2011, dir Int Centre for Mathematical Sciences Edinburgh 2002–10, N M Rothschild & Sons prof of mathematical sciences and dir Isaac Newton Inst for Mathematical Sciences Univ of Cambridge 2011–16; memb: London Mathematical Soc (pres 2005–07), Edinburgh Mathematical Soc; Sr Berwick Prize London Mathematical Soc 2000; hon prof of mathematics: Univ of Edinburgh, Heriot-Watt Univ; hon fell UCL 2008, fell St John's Coll Cambridge 2011; Royal Soc Sylvester Medal 2012; Hon DSc: Queen's Univ Belfast 2000, Univ of Edinburgh 2007, Heriot-Watt Univ 2007, Univ of Essex 2009, Univ of Bath 2016, Univ of Sussex 2017; FRS 1999, FRSE 2003; *Books*

T

Analytic Theory of Global Bifircation (with B Buffoni, 2003); *Recreations* dogs, horses; *Style*— Prof John Toland; ✉ 15 Lansdown Park, Bath BA1 5TG (☎ 01225 330996, e-mail jft26@newton.ac.uk)

TOLHURST, Kelly Jane; MP; da of Morris Tolhurst, and Christine Tolhurst; *b* 23 August 1978, Gillingham; *Career* MP (Cons) Rochester and Strood 2015–; *Style*— Miss Kelly Tolhurst, MP; ✉ House of Commons, London SW1A 0AA (☎ 020 7219 5387, e-mail kelly.tolhurst.mp@parliament.uk, website www.kelly4rochesterandstrood.com, Twitter @KellyTolhurst)

TOLLEMACHE, Sir Lyonel Humphry John; 7 Bt (GB 1793), JP (Leics), DL (Leics); s of Maj-Gen Sir Humphry Thomas Tollemache 6 Bt, CB, CBE, DL (d 1990), and Nora Priscilla, *née* Taylor (d 1990); *b* 10 July 1931; *Educ* Uppingham, RAC Cirencester; *m* 6 Feb 1960, Mary Joscelyne, da of Col William Henry Whitbread, TD; 2 da (Katheryne Mary b 1960, Henrietta Joscelyne (Mrs David Chubb) b 1970), 2 s (Lyonel Thomas b 23 Jan 1963 d 1996, Richard John b 4 May 1966); *Heir* s, Richard Tollemache, JP; *Career* cmmnd Coldstream Gds, Maj; High Sheriff Leics 1978–79, cncllr Melton RDC/BC 1969–87 (Mayor 1976–77), cncllr Leics CC 1985–97; Liveryman Worshipful Co of Grocers; FRICS; *Style*— Sir Lyonel Tollemache, Bt, JP, DL; ✉ The Old Vicarage, Buckminster, Grantham NG33 5RT (☎ 01476 860349)

TOLLEMACHE, Hon Michael David Douglas; s of 4 Baron Tollemache (d 1975); *b* 23 August 1944; *Educ* Eton, Trinity Coll Cambridge (MA); *m* 1, 5 Feb 1969 (m dis 2000), Thérèsa, da of Peter Bowring; 2 s (twins), 1 da; m 2, 15 Feb 2002, Clare, da of David Lawman; *Career* dir: Michael Tollemache Ltd 1967–2000, Artemis SA 1985–93, Partridge Fine Arts plc 1997–2000, Nevill Keating Tollemache Ltd 2002–07; chm Soc of London Art Dealers 1995–98, vice-pres Confédération Internationale des Négociants en Oeuvres d'Art 2000–; *Clubs* White's; *Style*— The Hon Michael Tollemache; ✉ Michael Tollemache Fine Art, 43 Duke Street, St James's, London SW1Y 6DD

TOLLEMACHE, 5 Baron (UK 1876); Timothy John Edward Tollemache; KCVO (2015); s of 4 Baron Tollemache, MC, DL (d 1975); *b* 13 December 1939; *Educ* Eton; *m* 1970, Alexandra Dorothy Jean, da of Col Hugo Meynell, MC, JP, DL (d 1960); 1 da (Hon Selina b 1973), 2 s (Hon Edward b 1976, Hon James b 1980); *Heir* s, Hon Edward Tollemache; *Career* cmmnd Coldstream Gds 1959–62; farmer and landowner; HM Lord-Lt Suffolk 2003–14 (DL 1984, Vice Lord-Lt 1994–2003); pres: Suffolk Assoc of Local Cncls 1978–96, Friends of Ipswich Museums 1980–96, Suffolk Family History Soc 1988–2003, Suffolk Agric Assoc 1988, Ipswich and District CAB 1998–2003, Suffolk Scout Cncl 2003–14, St John Cncl for Suffolk 2003–14, Music for Country Churches (Suffolk) 2003–14, Army Benevolent Fund (Suffolk) 2003–14, Royal Life Saving Soc (Suffolk) 2003–14, Friends of Suffolk Record Office 2003–14, Britain-Australia Society (Suffolk) 2003–14, Suffolk Reserve Forces and Cadet Assoc 2003–14, E Anglia Reserve Forces and Cadet Assoc 2008–14, Ipswich Sch Music Sch Appeal 2011–14; chm: HHA (E Anglia) 1979–83, Cncl St John (Suffolk) 1982–89, St Edmundsbury Cathedral Appeal 1986–90, Suffolk Branch CLA 1990–93, Suffolk Historic Churches Tst 1996–2003, Lord Chllr's Advsy Ctee on JPs 2003; vice-pres: Cheshire BRCS 1980–2014, Suffolk Preservation Soc; patron: Suffolk Accident Rescue Services 1983–2014, E Suffolk Assoc for the Blind 1992–2006, Suffolk Preservation Soc 2003–14, NSPCC (Suffolk) 2003–14, BRCS (Suffolk) 2003–14, Disability Care Enterprise 2003–11, Debenham Bowls Club 2003–14, Suffolk Historic Churches Tst 2003–14, Gainsborough's House Museum 2003–14, Magistrates Assoc (Suffolk) 2003–14, Friends of St Edmundsbury Cathedral 2003–14, Suffolk Wildlife Tst 2003–14, Suffolk Acre 2003–14, Help the Aged (Suffolk) 2003–14, SSAFA – Forces Help (Suffolk) 2003– (pres 1996–2003), East Anglia Children's Hospice 2005–14, St Matthew's Housing 2005–14, St Nicholas Hospice Bury St Edmunds 2006–14, Friends of Royal Hosp Sch 2006–14, Suffolk Community Fndn 2006–14, E Anglian Air Ambulance 2006–14, Royal Watercolour Soc E Anglia 2006–14, Suffolk Heraldry Soc 2011–14, Guildhall Project Bury St Edmunds 2011–14; govr Framlingham Coll; KStJ 2004 (CStJ 1988); *Clubs* White's, Pratt's, Special Forces; *Style*— The Lord Tollemache, KCVO; ✉ Endeavour House, Russell Road, Ipswich, Suffolk IP1 2BX

TOLLEY, David Anthony; s of Frank Stanley Tolley, of Sale, Cheshire, and Elizabeth, *née* Dean; *Educ* Manchester Grammar, King's Coll Hosp Med Sch (MB BS); *m* 4 July 1970, Judith Anne, da of Wing Cdr Dennis Martin Finn, DFC (d 1983), of Salisbury, Wilts; 3 s (Nicholas, Christopher, Jeremy), 1 da (Felicity Jane); *Career* conslt urological surgeon: Royal Infirmary Edinburgh 1980–91, Western Gen Hosp 1991–; dir the Scottish Lithotriptor Centre Western Gen Hosp Edinburgh 1991–; prog dir East of Scotland Trg Prog in Urology 1996–2001; ed Surgeons News 2006–09; memb: Urological Cancer Working Pty MRC 1983–94, Editorial Bd Br Jl of Urology 1994–99, Jt Ctee on Higher Surgical Trg in Urology 1995–2001, Editorial Ctee Jl of Endourology, Cncl RCSEd 2000– (hon treas 2006–09, pres 2009–), Jt Intercollegiate Examination Bd Urology 2000– (examiner 1995–2000), Bd European Soc for Urotechnology, Bd Minimal Access Therapy Trg Unit Scotland, various ctees Br Assoc of Urological Surgns (also memb Cncl), various ctees Royal Coll of Surgns Edinburgh, Cncl RCS Edinburgh, Cncl Br Assoc Urological Surgns (BAUS); pres: Br Soc of Endourology 1995–98, European Intrarenal Surgery Soc 2003–04; chm: Specialty Advsy Bd in Urology RCS(Ed) 1997–2002, Section of Endourology BAUS, Urology Specialist Trg Ctee East of Scotland; chm Quincentenary Executive RCSEd; ed BAUS Today 2000–01; FRCS 1974, FRCSEd 1983, FRCPEd 2006, FDSRCSE (ad hom) 2008; *Recreations* golf, countryside, music; *Clubs* New (Edinburgh), Luffness New Golf; *Style*— David Tolley, Esq; ✉ Murrayfield Hospital, Corstorphine Road, Edinburgh (☎ 0131 334 0363)

TOLMAN, Jeffery Alexander Spencer; *b* 1950; *Educ* St Clement Danes GS, Univ of Wales Sch of Int Politics; *Career* product mangr Birds Eye Foods (Unilever) 1971–73, account exec Ogilvy & Mather 1973–74; McCann Erickson 1974–79: account supervisor, account dir, assoc dir then dir; fndr ptnr Grandfield Rork Collins 1979–85; Saatchi & Saatchi Advertising: gp account dir 1985–86, dep chm 1987–91, chief exec (strategy) 1987–91, non-exec dep chm 1991–93; Tolman Cunard Ltd: chm (strategy and corp communication specialists) 1992–2004, advsr and thought leader on contemporary strategy, sustainability and stakeholder engagement 2004–; non-exec dep chm Forward Publishing 1991–97, non-exec dir RAC Holdings Ltd 1995–99, memb Euro Advsy Bd Masai SA 2000–02, operating ptnr Duke St Capital 2008–12, non-exec dir Oasis Healthcare Ltd 2008–12, non-exec dir H H Global 2012–; hon prof Warwick Business Sch 2008–; alumnus British-American Project; Liveryman Worshipful Co of Coachmakers and Coach Harness Makers; *Recreations* walking, eating, drinking, politics; *Clubs* RAC, RNIYC; *Style*— Jeffery Tolman, Esq; ✉ e-mail tolman@dukestreet.com

TOLSTOY-MILOSLAVSKY, Count Nikolai Dmitrievich; s of (Count) Dimitry Tolstoy-Miloslavsky, QC (d 1997), and his 1 w, Frieda Mary, *née* Wicksteed; *b* 23 June 1935; *Educ* Wellington, TCD (MA); *m* 1971, Georgina Katherine, da of Maj Peter Brown, of Radlett, Herts; 3 da (Alexandra b 1973, Anastasia b 1975, Xenia b 1980), 1 s (Dmitri b 1978); *Heir* s, (Count) Dmitri Tolstoy-Miloslavsky; *Career* author, historian, biographer; has appeared on numerous TV and radio progs and delivered lectures at univs and int academic confs worldwide; Int Freedom Award US Industrial Cncl Educnl Fndn 1987; appointed Terek Cossack Host 1993; chllr Monarchist League, hon memb Russian Heraldry Soc; life memb: Royal Martyr Church Union, Forty-Five Assoc; memb: Roman Soc, Int Arthurian Soc; vice-pres Royal Stuart Soc; Adele Mellen Prize 2008; FRSL; *Books* The Founding of Evil Hold School (1968), Night of The Long Knives (1972), Victims of Yalta (1978), The Half-Mad Lord (biography of Thomas Pitt, 1978), Stalin's Secret War (1981), The Tolstoys – Twenty-Four Generations of Russian History (1983), The Quest for Merlin (1985), The Minister and the Massacres (1986), States, Countries, Provinces (1986), The Coming of the King – The First Book of Merlin (1988), Patrick O'Brian: The Making of the Novelist (2004), The Oldest British Prose Literature: The Compilation of the Four Branches of the Mabinogi (2009), The Mysteries of Stonehenge: Myth and Ritual at the Sacred Centre (2016); author of numerous articles and reviews on Celtic studies in learned jls; *Recreations* second-hand and academic bookshops, walking; *Clubs* Cavalry & Guards, Sublime Society of Beef Steaks; *Style*— Count Tolstoy-Miloslavsky; ✉ Court Close, Southmoor, Abingdon, Berkshire OX13 5HS (☎ 01865 820186)

TOLVAS-VINCENT, Christina Elisabeth; *née* Tolvas; da of Ilpo Tolvas, of Turku, Finland, and Riitta, *née* Haahdenniemi; *b* 7 September 1964, Turku, Finland; *Educ* Katedralskolan i Åbo Finland, Univ of Turku (LLM); *m* 10 Aug 1991, Dr Jonathan David Vincent; *Career* memb Finnish Bar 1994, admitted slr Eng and Wales 1995; reporter Radio Åboland Finnish Broadcasting Co 1988–90, lectr and acting grad asst in business law Univ of Tampere 1988–90; Hepherd Winstanley & Pugh: paralegal 1991–95, slr then sr slr 1995–97, ptnr 1997; ptnr Bond Pearce (now Bond Dickinson LLP following merger 2013) 1998– (currently local head of employment team); author of numerous articles on employment law issues; hon consul of Finland 2011 (Hants, Dorset and W Sussex); memb: Law Soc, European Employment Lawyers' Assoc, Employment Lawyers Assoc, Finnish Bar Assoc; *Recreations* classical music (formerly harpsichordist, pianist, clarinetist and singer, now mainly listener), travel, languages; *Style*— Ms Christina Tolvas-Vincent; ✉ Bond Dickinson LLP, Oceana House, 39–49 Commercial Road, Southampton SO15 1GA (☎ 0345 415 0000, fax 0345 415 8200, e-mail christina.tolvas-vincent@bonddickinson.com)

TOM, Peter William Gregory; CBE (2006); s of late John Gregory Tom, and Barbara, *née* Lambden (d 2009); *b* 26 July 1940; *Educ* Hinckley GS; *m* 1; 1 s (John b 1966 (decd)), 2 da (Saffron b 1972, Layla b 1975); m 2, April 2002, Kay, *née* Shires; 1 s (Joseph b 2004), 1 da (Georgia b 2008); *Career* joined Bardon Hill Quarries Ltd 1956, chief exec Bardon Gp plc until 1997, non-exec chm Aggregate Industries Ltd 2006–08 (chief exec 1997–2005), chm Breedon Aggregates Ltd; chm Leicester Football Club plc (Leicester Tigers rugby club); dir Leaf Clean Energy; former dir England Rugby Ltd; Hon DTech De Montfort Univ; CIMgt; *Recreations* tennis, theatre, cycling; *Style*— Peter W G Tom, Esq, CBE; ✉ Leicester Tigers, Aylestone Road, Leicester LE2 7TR (☎ 01162 171302, e-mail linda.lawrence@rise-rocks.com)

TOMALIN, Claire; da of Emile Delavenay (d 2003), and Muriel Emily, *née* Herbert (d 1984); *b* 20 June 1933; *Educ* Lycée Français de Londres, Girls GS Hitchin, Dartington Hall Sch, Newnham Coll Cambridge (MA); *m* 1, 17 Sept 1955, Nicholas Osborne Tomalin (d 1973), s of Miles Ridley Tomalin (d 1983); 3 da (Josephine Sarah b 1956, Susanna Lucy b 1958 d 1980, Emily Claire Elizabeth b 1961), 2 s (Daniel b and d 1960, Thomas Nicholas Ronald b 1970); m 2, 5 June 1993, Michael Frayn, *qv*; *Career* writer; publishers ed, reader, journalist 1953–67; literary ed: New Statesman 1974–78 (dep literary ed 1968–70), Sunday Times 1980–86; vice-pres English PEN and Soc of Authors 1999, vice-pres Royal Literary Fund 2000– (tstee 1975–99, registrar 1984–2000); memb: Mgmnt Ctee Soc of Authors 1996–99 (memb London Library Ctee 1997–2000), Advsy Ctee for the Arts, Humanities and Social Sciences British Library 1997–2002, Cncl Royal Soc of Literature 1997–2000; tstee Nat Portrait Gallery 1992–2002; fell Wordsworth Tst 2003– (tstee 2001–03); Samuel Pepys Award 2003, Rose Mary Crawshay Prize 2003, Sky South Bank Award in Literature 2012; hon fell: Lucy Cavendish Coll Cambridge 2003, Newnham Coll Cambridge 2003; Hon LittD: UEA 2005, Univ of Birmingham 2005, Univ of Greenwich 2006, Univ of Cambridge 2007, Open Univ 2008, Goldsmiths Coll London 2009, Univ of Roehampton 2011, Univ of Portsmouth 2012; FRSL 1974, memb American Philosophical Soc 2012; *Books* Life and Death of Mary Wollstonecraft (1974, reissued 1993), Shelley and His World (1980), Katherine Mansfield: A Secret Life (1987), The Invisible Woman: The Story of Nelly Ternan and Charles Dickens (1990), Mrs Jordan's Profession (1994), Jane Austen: A Life (1997), Maurice (ed, 1998), Several Strangers (1999), Samuel Pepys: The Unequalled Self (2002, Whitbread Book of the Year 2002), Thomas Hardy: The Time-torn Man (2006), Selected Poems of Thomas Hardy (ed, 2006), Selected Poems of Milton (ed, 2008), Selected Poems of Keats (ed, 2009); *Plays* The Winter Wife (1991), Charles Dickens: A Life (2011); *Style*— Mrs Claire Tomalin, FRSL; ✉ c/o David Godwin, 55 Monmouth Street, London WC2H 9DG

TOMBS, Sebastian; s of David Martineau Tombs (d 1986), and Jane Burns, *née* Parley (d 2000); *b* 11 October 1949; *Educ* Bryanston, Corpus Christi Coll Cambridge (choral exhibitioner, DipArch); *m* Eva, da of Leo Heirman (d 1983); 2 s (Michael b 1985, Leonardo b 1988), 1 da (Rowena b 1987); *Career* on staff in architectural/planning office N Philadelphia USA 1972–73 (yr practical trg from CCC Cambridge), RMJM Partnership Edinburgh 1975–76, Roland Wedgwood Associates Edinburgh 1976–77, Fountainbridge Housing Assoc 1977–78, area architect Housing Corp 1978–81, private sector work Housing Dept Edinburgh DC 1981–86, sec and treas RIAS 1995–2005 (dep sec and dir of practice 1986–94), chief exec Architecture and Design Scotland 2005–09; chm: Edinburgh Gp Anthroposophical Soc 1986–89, Scottish Ecological Design Assoc (co-fndr) 1994–97, Assoc of Planning Suprs (co-fndr) 1995–97; co-chair Anthroposophical Soc in GB 2011–13; memb City of Edinburgh's Lord Provost's Cmmn on Sustainable Devpt 1997–98; Parly candidate (Scot Lib Dem) Edinburgh N and Leith: Scot 1999 and 2003, UK 2001; Parly candidate (Scot Lib Dem) Kilmarnock and Loudoun 2010; ARCUK 1977, FRIAS 1990 (ARIAS 1978), RIBA 1994, MCIArb 2002 (ACIArb 1991); *Publications* Tracing the Past, Chasing the Future (2000); *Recreations* self-building new home, designing cartograms, sketching, reverse cycling, composing songs and doggerel; *Style*— Sebastian Tombs, Esq; ☎ 01631 760128, e-mail sebastiantombs99@yahoo.co.uk

TOMISON, Maureen; da of Andrew Learmonth Tomison (d 1954), and Maureen, *née* Miskimmin; *b* 31 May 1941; *Educ* Univ of St Andrews, London Guildhall Univ (MA), Eng Gardening Sch (class prize); *m* 1, 1970 (m dis 1983), Maurice Trowbridge (decd); 1 s (Andrew b 30 Sept 1971); m 2, 1994, Lt Cdr David Sandford, RN; *Career* with Bristol Evening Post 1963–65, with The Sun 1965–68 (first female political corr for a nat newspaper), with Daily Sketch 1968–71; political advsr State of the Nation Granada TV; Parly candidate (Cons): Dundee W Feb 1974, Norwich S Oct 1974; advsr Cons front bench Yes to Europe Vote 1975; Parly candidate (Lab) Folkestone & Hythe 2005; ceo and fndr Politics Europe, ceo and fndr Decision Makers (int political and PR consultancy), ceo EMU ConsltS; corp communications dir IOD, public affrs dir Hill and Knowlton 1982–84, corporate communications dir Sea Containers 1984–87, sec-gen EFPA 1988–95 (pan European mfrg gp); chair UK Women of Europe 1999–, life memb European Movement (exec), chair E Kent European Movement, Labour Movement for Europe, fell Br Assoc of Women Entrepreneurs, MIPR; FCMI; *Awards* honoured by Women of Scot 1988 and 1992, European Business Woman of Achievement 1991, Best Political Campaign PR Week 1991 (runner-up 1992), nomination UK Women of Europe 1991 and 1992; *Books* English Sickness (1971), Thatcherism: A Fundamental Departure (1983); *Recreations* skiing, gardening, music, water sports, singing Gaelic songs, history, fencing, bridge; *Clubs* Ski Club of GB, Cwlth Soc; *Style*— Ms Maureen Tomison; ✉ Elinlegh Court, Stone Street, Stelling Minnis, Kent CT4 6DF; Politics Europe (e-mail mtomison@politicseurope.com)

TOMKINS, Prof Peter Maurice; s of Rowland Maurice Tomkins, of Leeds, W Yorks, and Gwendoline Mary, *née* Dunkley; *b* Leeds; *Educ* Leeds Modern Sch, Univ of Bradford (BTech), Univ of Leeds (PhD); *m* 14 May 1988 (m dis 2009), Rosemary Anne, da of John Gale Harrison, of Stockport, Cheshire; 1 da (Amber Lauren b 17 Oct 1990), 1 s (Sebastian

Rowan Matt b 19 August 2004); *Career* R&D scientist Albright & Wilson plc 1963–64, univ demonstrator then fell Univ of Leeds 1964–67, dept mangr (mfrg, R&D devpt, brands) Mars Confectionery Ltd 1967–69, mangr then princ conslt Arthur Young & Co 1969–71, vice-pres and gen mangr Encyclopaedia Britannica International Ltd 1971–73, chief exec and dir D M Management Consultants Ltd (strategic relationship mktg consultancy) 1973–; NE chair Grallo.com 2014–; memb Advsy Bd Cass Business Sch 2004–; author of mgmnt and mktg articles in various jls; memb Lloyd's 1978–; memb: Bd BDMA 1979–91, Cncl Inst of Mgmnt Conslts 1986–98 (pres 1995–96), Companions and Nominations Bds CMI 2009–15; tstee Int Cncl of Mgmnt Consulting Insts (ICMCI) 1995–2000, global tstee ICMCI 2013–; vice-chm Bd of Tstees Chartered Inst of Mktg 2001–08; pres European Mktg Confedn 2003–08; chm Community Industry Bd (Nat Assoc of Youth Clubs) 1975–78, vice-pres UK Youth 1982– (former dep chm), fndr tstee CAF Cert 1984–93, tstee Bd Volunteer Centre UK 1992–96, chm and tstee National Confederation of Parent Teacher Assocs 1997–2005; chm Schoolympics Ltd 2006–; memb SW Thames RHA 1986–90, non-exec dir Bath Royal United Hosp NHS Tst 2006–10, sr govr Cncl of Govrs Kingston NHS Fndn Tst 2012–; Freeman City of London; Liveryman Worshipful Co of Marketors 1996–; memb RSC 1968, CChem 1970, CCMI (FIMgt 1972), FInstD 1980, FIMC 1982, memb DMA 1992 (fndr memb), FCIM 1992, FIDM 1994, chartered marketer 1998, CSci 2004, CMgr 2012; *Recreations* squash, skiing, jogging, charity work; *Clubs* IOD; *Style*— Prof Peter Tomkins; ☎ 020 7499 8030, mobile 07802 484789, e-mail pmt@dmmc.co.uk, website www.dmmc.co.uk

TOMKINSON, Matthew; s of Roy Tomkinson, of Manchester, and Linda, *née* Williams; *b* 25 June 1975, Stockport, Gtr Manchester; *Educ* Altrincham GS for Boys, Univ of Central England (BA); *Partner* Alexandra Coxon; *Career* head chef The Goose Britwell Salome until 2008 (Michelin star), chef The Terrace Montague Arms Beaulieu 2008– (Michelin star 2009–); Roux Scholar 2005; *Recreations* cooking, cycling, reading; *Style*— Matthew Tomkinson, Esq; ✉ The Terrace, The Montagu Arms Hotel, Beaulieu, New Forest, Hampshire SO42 7ZL (☎ 01590 612324, e-mail chef@montaguarmshotel.co.uk, website www.montaguarmshotel.co.uk, Twitter @mtomkinsonchef)

TOMLIN, Rt Rev Dr Graham; *see:* Kensington, Bishop of

TOMLINSON, Prof Geoffrey Railton; OBE (2011); *b* Whitehave, Cumbria; *Career* prof of engrg dynamics and pro-vice-chllr for research Univ of Sheffield until 2009 (joined as head Dept of Mechanical Engrg 1995), currently int advsr Advanced Manufacturing Inst; fell RAeS, FREng, FIMechE, CEng; *Publications* 4 books, 170 publns; *Recreations* golf, skiing; *Style*— Prof Geoffrey Tomlinson, OBE, FREng; ✉ Department of Mechanical Engineering, University of Sheffield, Mappin Street, Sheffield S1 3JD

TOMLINSON, Baron (Life Peer UK 1998), of Walsall in the County of West Midlands; John Edward Tomlinson; *Career* MP (Lab) Meriden 1974–79, PPS to PM Harold Wilson 1975–76, Parly under sec of state FCO 1976–79; MEP (Lab/Co-op) Birmingham W 1984–99; memb Parly Assembly: Cncl of Europe, WEU; House of Lords rep Convention on the Future of Europe, memb EU Select Ctee and Home Affrs Sub-Ctee; memb: Cncl Britain in Europe, UK Delgn to Parly Assembly Cncl of Europe 2005–; pres of tstees Industry and Parliament Tst until 2007; pres Br Flouridation Soc until 2011; chm Assoc of Ind HE Providers until 2012, chm Advsy Bd London Sch of Commerce, memb Bd Anglia Ruskin Univ 2008–14 (vice-chm 2009–10, chm 2010–), chm Assoc of Business Execs 2011–14; Hon LLD Univ of Birmingham; fell Univ of Wales Inst Cardiff; *Style*— The Lord Tomlinson; ✉ House of Lords, London SW1A 0PW

TOMLINSON, Sir John Rowland; kt (2005), CBE (1997); s of Rowland Tomlinson (d 1994), and Ellen, *née* Greenwood (d 1969); *b* 22 September 1946; *Educ* Accrington GS, Univ of Manchester (BSc), Royal Manchester Coll of Music; *m* 9 Aug 1969, Moya, *née* Joel; 2 da (Abigail 27 Aug 1971, Ellen Tamasine 15 Feb 1973), 1 s (Joseph b 3 March 1976); *Career* operatic bass; princ: Glyndebourne Festival 1971–74, ENO 1974–80; also roles with: Royal Opera, Opera North, Scottish Opera; major roles incl: Boris in Boris Godunov (ENO Manchester) 1982, Don Basilio in Il Barbiere di Seville (Covent Garden) 1985, Moses in Moses (ENO) 1986, Fiesco in Simone Boccanegra (ENO) 1988, Wotan/The Wanderer in The Ring (Bayreuth) 1988–98, Wanderer in Siegfried (Bologna) 1990, Mefistofeles in Faust (Santiago, Chile) 1990, Attila in Attila (Opera North) 1990, Filippo II in Don Carlos (Opera North) 1992, Konig Marke in Tristan & Isolde (Bayreuth Festival) 1993, Mefistofeles in Damnation de Faust (La Fenice Venice) 1993, Hans Sachs in Die Meistersinger (Covent Garden) 1993 and 1997, Gurnemanz in Parsifal (Staatsoper Berlin) 1992–94, Claggart in Billy Budd (Covent Garden) 1995, Hans Sachs in Die Meistersinger (Staatsoper Berlin) 1995, Kingfisher in Midsummer Marriage (Covent Garden) 1996, Bluebeard in Bluebeard's Castle (Berlin Philharmonic) 1996, 4 Villains in Tales of Hoffman (ENO) 1998, Moses in Moses and Aron (NY Met) 1999, Golaud in Pelleas and Melisande (Glyndebourne Festival) 1999, Mefistofeles in Faust (Staatsoper Munich) 2000, Hagen in Gotterdammerung (Bayreuth Festival) 2000, Baron Ochs in Rosenkavalier (Staatsoper Dresden) 2000, Borromeo in Palestrina (Covent Garden) 2001, Gurnemanz in Parsifal (NY Met) 2001, Wotan/Wanderer in The Ring (Munich) 2003, title role in Boris Godunov (Covent Garden) 2003, title role in Flying Dutchman (Bayreuth Festival) 2003–04, Balstrode in Peter Grimes (Salzburg Festival) 2005, Wanderer in Siegfried (Covent Garden) 2005, Fiesco in Simone Boccanegra (Hamburg) 2006, Hagen in Götterdämmerung (Covent Garden) 2006; numerous appearances at international venues incl: ROH Covent Garden (debut 1976), Paris Opera, Berlin, Vienna, Amsterdam, Geneva, NY, Tokyo, Salzburg, Lisbon, Madrid, Santiago, Milan, Bologna, Florence, Copenhagen, Stuttgart, Bayreuth, Dresden, Munich, Bordeaux, Avignon, Aix-en-Provence, Orange, San Diego, Pittsburgh, Chicago, Vancouver and San Francisco; awards incl Royal Philharmonic Soc singing award 1991 and 1998, Wagner Soc Reginald Goodall Award 1996, South Bank Show Award 1998, Evening Standard Opera Award 1998; Hon FRNCM 1996, Hon DMus: Univ of Sussex 1997, Univ of Manchester 1998, Univ of Birmingham 2004, Univ of Nottingham 2004; *Recreations* tennis; *Style*— Sir John Tomlinson, CBE; ✉ c/o Music International, 13 Ardilaun Road, Highbury, London N5 2QR (☎ 020 7359 5183)

TOMLINSON, Michael James; MP; s of Howard Tomlinson, and Heather, *née* Morcumb; *b* 1 October 1977, Wokingham; *m* 2000, Frances Tomlinson-Mynors, *née* Mynors; 1 s, 2 da; *Career* called to the Bar (Middle Temple) 2002; MP (Cons) Mid Dorset and N Poole 2015–; Queen Mother's Scholar Middle Temple 2001; *Recreations* reading, going to the beach with my family, sport; *Clubs* Hamworthy Cricket, Poole Hockey; *Style*— Michael Tomlinson, Esq, MP; ✉ House of Commons, London SW1A 0AA (e-mail michael.tomlinson.mp@parliament.uk, Twitter @Michael4MDNP)

TOMLINSON, Sir Michael John; kt (2005), CBE (1997); s of Jack Tomlinson (d 1993), of Rotherham, S Yorks, and Edith, *née* Cresswell (d 1988); *b* 17 October 1942; *Educ* Oakwood Tech HS Rotherham, Bournemouth Sch, Univ of Durham (BSc), Univ of Nottingham (PGCE); *m* 17 July 1965, Maureen Janet, da of Wilfred Ernest Tupling; 1 s (Philip John b 3 Jan 1968), 1 da (Jane Louise 23 March 1970); *Career* chemistry teacher Henry Mellish GS Nottingham 1965–69, head of chemistry Ashby-de-la-Zouch GS 1969–78, seconded to ICI Ltd 1977, chief inspr of schs HM Inspectorate of Schs 1989–92 (joined 1978), dir of inspection OFSTED 1995–2000 (dep dir 1992–94), HM's chief inspr of schs OFSTED 2000–02, chair tst bd responsible for Hackney Educn Services 2002–07, chief advsr for London schs 2008–09; dir Nat Science Year 2002–03, pres Assoc for Science Educn 2005, chair Quality and Standards Ctee City and Guilds; chair Govt's working gp on 14–19 reform 2003–04; non-exec dir: RM plc 2004–13, Piscari Ltd 2008–10; chair Bd Myscience 2008–16; tstee: Comino Fndn 2002–11, Industrial Tst 2003–07, Business Dynamics 2004–07, Trident 2005–07, Farming and Countryside Educn Tst, Baker-

---

Dearing Tst 2010–, Oxford Tst 2010–14; memb Educn Advsy Ctee London Symphony Orch 2007–14, pres Royal Agricultural Soc of England 2010–12; Educational cmmnr for Birmingham 2014–; author of various pubns for BP Ltd 1974–78; govr: Univ of Herts 2004–09, Merchant Taylors' Sch; chair of govrs RSA Acad; Hon Dr Univs of: Wolverhampton 2004, Middx 2005, East Anglia 2005, Northumbria 2005, Nottingham Trent 2005, De Montfort 2005, Leicester 2006, Durham 2007, Manchester Met 2008, Warwick 2011, York 2012, Bucks New Univ 2012, Birmingham City Univ 2016; Chemical Soc Educn Bronze Medal 1975; Queen's Silver Jubilee Medal 1977; hon fell City and Guilds 2009; Freeman City of London 2013, Liveryman Merchant Taylors' Co 2014 (Freeman 2013); FRSA (hon life fell 2006); *Books* New Movements in the Study and Teaching of Chemistry (1975), Organic Chemistry: A Problem-Solving Approach (1977), Mechanisms in Organic Chemistry: Case Studies (1978), 14–18: A New Vision for Secondary Education (2012); *Recreations* gardening, fishing, reading, food and drink; *Style*— Sir Michael Tomlinson, CBE; ✉ Brooksby, Mayhall Lane, Chesham Bois, Amersham, Buckinghamshire HP6 5NR (☎ 01494 726967, fax 01494 727338)

TOMLINSON, Prof Richard Allan; s of James Edward Tomlinson (d 1963), and Dorothea Mary, *née* Grellier (d 1983); *b* 25 April 1932; *Educ* King Edward's Sch Birmingham, St John's Coll Cambridge (MA); *m* 14 Dec 1957, Heather Margaret (d 2009), da of Ernest Fraser Murphy (d 1965); 3 s (Nicholas John b 1959, Peter Brian b 1962, Edward James b 1965), 1 da (Penelope Ann b 1961); *Career* asst Dept of Greek Univ of Edinburgh 1957–58; Univ of Birmingham: asst lectr 1958–61, lectr 1961–69, sr lectr 1969–71, prof of ancient history and archaeology 1971–95; vice-pres Br Sch at Athens 2001– (dir 1995–96); memb: Victorian Soc, Hellenic Soc; FSA; *Books* Argos and the Argolid (1972), Greek Sanctuaries (1976), Epidauros (1980), Greek Architecture (1989), The Athens of Alma Tadema (1991), From Mycenae to Constantinople (1992), Greek and Roman Architecture (1994), A gazetteer of the Cyrene Necropolis (jtly, 2009); *Recreations* walking; *Style*— Prof Richard Tomlinson, FSA; ✉ c/o Institute of Archaeology and Antiquity, University of Birmingham, Birmingham B15 2TT (☎ 0121 414 5497, fax 0121 414 3595)

TOMLINSON, Prof Sally; *b* 22 August 1936; *Educ* Macclesfield HS, Univ of Liverpool (BA), Univ of Birmingham (MSocSci), Univ of Warwick (PhD); *m* Sqdn Ldr Brian Joseph Tomlinson (RAF ret); 2 da, 1 s; *Career* lectr and sr lectr W Midlands Coll of Educn 1969–73, sr res fell Univ of Warwick 1974–77, prof of educn Lancaster Univ 1984–91 (lectr and sr lectr 1978–84), prof of educn UC Swansea 1991–92; Goldsmiths Coll London: Goldsmith prof of policy and mgmnt in educn 1992–98 (emeritus prof 1998–), dean Faculty of Educn 1993–95, pro-warden 1994–97; sr research fell Dept of Educnl Studies Univ of Oxford 1998–, visiting prof Univ of Wolverhampton 2008–11; sr assoc memb St Antony's Coll Oxford 1984–85; memb: Univ Cncl for Educn of Teachers 1984–2000, Cmmn of the Future of Multi-ethnic Britain 1998–2000, Ct Univ of Bradford 2001–04, Cncl Univ of Gloucestershire 2001–09; Leverhulme emeritus fell 2009–11, assoc fell Dept of Sociology Univ of Warwick 2014–17; chair of tstees Africa Educn Tst 2005–09 (tstee 1992–2012); res assoc IPPR 1990–92; *Books* Colonial Immigrants in a British City – A Class Analysis (with John Rex, 1979), Education Subnormality – A Study in Decision Making (1981), Special Education: Policy Practices and Social Issues (jt ed, 1981), A Sociology of Special Education (1982), Ethnic Minorites in British Schools: A Review of the Literature 1960–1982 (1983), Home and School in Multicultural Britain (1984), Special Education and Social Interests (ed with Len Barton, 1984), Affirmative Action and Positive Policies in the Education of Ethnic Minorities (ed with Abraham Yogev, 1989), The School Effect: A Study of Multi-Racial Comprehensives (with David Smith, 1989), Multi-Cultural Education in White Schools (1990), The Assessment of Special Educational Needs: Whose Problem? (with David Galloway and Derrick Armstrong, 1994), Educational Reform and its Consequences (1994), Ethnic Relations and Schooling (ed with Maurice Craft, 1995), Education 14–19: Critical perspectives (1997), School Effectiveness for Whom? (ed with Slee R and Weiner G, 1998), Hackney Downs: The School that Dared to Fight (with M O'Connor, E Hales, and J Davis, 1999), Education in a Post-Welfare Society (2001, 2 edn 2005), Selection Isn't Working (with T Edwards, 2002), Race and Education: Politics and Policy in Britain (2008), Social Inclusion and Higher Education (with T Basit, 2012), Low Attainers in a Global Knowledge Economy (2013), The Politics of Race, Class and Special Education: The Selected Works of Sally Tomlinson (2014); *Style*— Prof Sally Tomlinson; ✉ Department of Education, University of Oxford, 15 Norham Gardens, Oxford OX2 6PY (☎ 01865 274024)

TOMLINSON, Prof Stephen; CBE (2007); s of Frank Tomlinson, of Bolton, Lancs, and Elsie, *née* Towler; *b* 20 December 1944; *Educ* Hayward GS Bolton, Univ of Sheffield (MB ChB, MD); *m* 14 Oct 1970, Christine Margaret, da of George Hope, of Sheffield, S Yorks; 2 da (Rebecca b 1974, Sarah b 1977); *Career* Wellcome Tst sr lectr 1980–85 (sr res fell 1977–80), reader in med Univ of Sheffield 1982–85; Univ of Manchester Med Sch: prof of med 1985–2001, dean Med Sch and Faculty of Med 1993–97, dean Faculty of Med Dentistry and Nursing 1997–99, vice-chllr Univ of Wales Coll of Med 2001–2004, provost Cardiff Univ 2004–10 (emeritus prof of medicine 2010–); author of pubns on mechanisms of hormone action, and intracellular signalling and orgn of health care in diabetes; exec sec Cncl Heads of Med Schs & Faculties of Med in the UK 1997–99; chm Assoc of Clinical Profs of Med 1996–99 (sec 1994–96); chm Fedn Assoc of Clinical Profs 1997–2000, pres Assoc of Physicians of GB and I 2002–03 (sec 1988–93, treas 1993–98); chm: R&D Ctee Velindre NHS Tst 2002–12, Wales Advsy Ctee 2003–07, Quality Assurance Agency for HE (QAA), Tropical Health and Educn Tst 2007–10, Vale for Africa 2009–14, Wales for Africa Healthlinks Network 2012–14 (vice-chm 2010–12); chm ASH Wales 2007–13; memb: JMAC Review RAE 2002, HEFCE Steering Gp on PG Research Trg 2002, Bd Velindre NHS Tst 2002–12 (also chm Research and Devpt Ctee), Bd QAA 2003–07 (also chm Wales Advsy Ctee), MRC Task Force on the Future of the Nat Inst for Med Research 2004, MRC Evaluation Ctee 2006, Panel Ind Review of MMC (Tooke Inquiry) 2006, Advsy Bd UK Research Integrity Office (UKRIO) 2007–12, Health and Educn Nat Strategic Exchange (Dept of Health/ HEFCE) Review of Med and Dental Sch Intakes 2012, UK Health Advsy Ctee 2012–15, Cncl and Univ Ethics Ctee Univ of Exeter 2013–, HE Funding Cncl Wales 2013–15 (also memb Research, Innovation and Engagement Ctee); memb and dep chm Biological Standards Ctee Cardiff Univ, pres and vice-pres Cardiff Scientific Soc 2006–09; Hon DSc Univ of Sheffield 2012; FRCP, FMedSci; *Books* Mechanisms of Disease (jt ed, 2 edn 2008); *Recreations* arts, health and well-being, history of medicine, international health; *Clubs* Medical Pilgrims (hon sec 1995–2012); *Style*— Prof Stephen Tomlinson, CBE; ✉ Ty Gwyn, St Andrews Major, Dinas Powys CF64 4HD (☎ 029 2051 2041)

TOMLINSON, Rt Hon Lord Justice; Rt Hon Sir Stephen Miles Tomlinson; kt (2000), PC (2010); s of Capt Enoch Tomlinson, and Mary Marjorie Cecelia, *née* Miles; *b* 29 March 1952; *Educ* King's Sch Worcester, Worcester Coll Oxford (MA); *m* 15 March 1980, Joanna Kathleen, da of Ian Joseph Greig; 1 s, 1 da; *Career* called to the Bar Inner Temple 1974 (bencher 1990), QC 1988, judge of the High Court of Justice (Queen's Bench Div) 2000–10, Lord Justice of Appeal 2010–; memb of governing body Shrewsbury Sch 2003–; *Recreations* cricket, gardening, walking, family; *Clubs* Garrick, MCC; *Style*— The Rt Hon Lord Justice Tomlinson; ✉ Royal Courts of Justice, Strand, London WC2A 2LL

TOMS, Michael Rodney (Mike); JP; s of Walter Toms (d 2005), of Hebden Bridge, W Yorks, and Anne Brown (d 1957); *b* 1 July 1953, Stoke-on-Trent, Staffs; *Educ* Rotherham GS, UC Durham (BA), Univ of Nottingham (MA); *m* 26 June 1976, Jane Rosemary, *née* Moss; 2 da (Natalie b 15 Oct 1981, Hannah b 11 March 1985), 1 s (Matthew b 17 Nov 1989); *Career* various positions Br Airports Authy 1978–87; BAA plc: various sr positions incl chief economist and strategy dir 1987–2002, memb Bd and gp planning dir 2002–06; chair NIE plc 2007–11; dir: Birmingham Airport Hldgs, Oxera Consulting, Bellway plc, J Murphy and Sons Ltd; memb Governing Bd Airports Cncl Int (ACI) 2002–06; MRTPI 1978, MRICS 1980, FRAeS 2001; *Style*— Mike Toms, Esq, JP

TOMS, Dr Rhinedd Margaret; da of David Peregrine Jones (d 1983), of Llanelli, Carmarthenshire, and Margaret Edith, *née* Davies (d 1996); *b* 18 June 1942; *Educ* Howells Sch Denbigh, Girton Coll Cambridge (MA), Westminster Med Sch (MB BChir); *m* 19 Oct 1968, Brian Frank Toms (d 1985), s of Harold Frank Toms (d 1989), of Rushden, Northants; 1 da (Eleanor b 1969), 1 s (David b 1971); *Career* clinical MO London Borough of Southwark 1968–71, SMO Lambeth Lewisham and Southwark AHA 1973–75, trg posts in psychiatry 1976–84, conslt psychiatrist NE Essex Mental Health Tst 1984–2005; hon conslt St Luke's Hosp for the Clergy 1990–2004, clinical tutor in psychiatry Br Postgrad Med Fedn 1988–92, Tst med advsr 1993–96; second opinion appointed dr Mental Health Act Cmmn (now part of Care Quality Cmmn) 1987–2014; *Recreations* gardening, music, craft, choral singing; *Style*— Dr Rhinedd Toms; ✉ 33 Bunyan Close, Thorpe St Andrew, Norwich NR7 0UZ (☎ 01603 432945)

TONBRIDGE, Bishop of 2002–; Rt Rev Dr Brian Colin Castle; s of Ernest Castle, and Sarah, *née* Shepherd; *b* 7 September 1949; *Educ* Wilson's GS London, UCL (BA), Univ of Oxford (MA), Grad Sch of Ecumenical Studies Bossey Switzerland (Cert Ecumenical Studies), Univ of Birmingham (PhD), Cuddesdon Theol Coll; *m* Jane; 1 s (Jamie), 2 da (Sarah, Bethan); *Career* social worker Lambeth 1972–74, teacher Lesotho (through USPG) 1974; ordained: deacon 1977, priest 1978; curate St Nicholas' Sutton 1977, curate St Peter's Limpsfield 1977–81, priest-in-charge Chingola, Chililabombwe and Solwezi Northern Zambia (through USPG) 1981–84 (also lay trg offr, memb Diocesan and Provincial Synod, memb Bishop's Cncl), tutor Grad Sch Ecumenical Inst Bossey Switzerland 1984–85, vicar of North Petherton and Northmoor Green 1985–92, vice-princ and dir of pastoral studies Ripon Coll Cuddesdon 1992–2001 (actg princ 1993 and 1996), hon canon Rochester Cathedral 2002–; Archbishop's advsr in alternative spiritualities and new religious movements; Univ of Oxford: memb Faculty of Theology, examiner (BTh and MTh), chair of examiners for MTh, chm Supervisory Ctee for BTh and MTh, memb Faculty of Theology Ctee preparing for Dept of Educn Teaching Quality Assessment; PhD examiner Univ of Birmingham, external examiner (BTh) Univ of Wolverhampton 1999–2004; memb: Steering Gp Oxford Partnership for Theol Educn and Trg, Miny Ctee Dio of Oxford, Faith and Order Cmmn 2010–; co-chair Mission Theology Advsy Gp (Sub-Ctee of Archbishops' Cncl Bd of Mission and Public Affrs); delivered various lectures and talks, conducted ordination retreats, invited preacher Boston Univ; *Publications* Hymns: The making and shaping of a theology for the whole people of God (1990), Sing a New Song to the Lord (1994), Unofficial God? Voices from Beyond the Walls (2004), Reconciling One and All – God's Gift to the World (2008), Reconciliation – The Journey of a Lifetime (2014); various articles and book reviews published in Christian jls; *Recreations* music, fly fishing, cross-country skiing, photography; *Style*— The Rt Rev the Bishop of Tonbridge; ✉ Bishop's Lodge, 48 St Botolph's Road, Sevenoaks, Kent TN13 3AG (☎ 01732 456070, fax 01732 741449, e-mail bishop.tonbridge@rochester.anglican.org)

TONEY, Terence (Terry); s of Norman Toney, of Bradford, Yorks, and Margaret, *née* Taglione; *b* 23 August 1952, Bradford, W Yorks; *Educ* Cardinal Hinsley GS Bradford, KCL (BA), Inst of Educn London (CertEd), Univ of Lancaster (MA); *m* 14 May 1977, Young Hae, *née* Kim; 1 s (James Alexander b 17 May 1983); *Career* English teacher in Sweden, Germany and Japan 1975–76, posts in English language mgmnt Br Cncl Japan, London, Colombia and Brazil 1983–94, dir Br Cncl offices Korea and Japan 1994–2002, memb Sr Mgmnt Team (Exec Bd) Br Cncl London 2002–06, regnl dir SE Europe Br Cncl Vienna 2006–09, head of business transformation Br Cncl London 2009–2011, regnl dir E Asia Br Cncl Singapore 2011–15, currently head Business Devpt, Educn and Society Br Cncl London; memb: Bd of Tstees English sch Bogotá Colombia 1999–2002, Bd of Tstees The Tokyo Br Sch 2002–06, Bd TESOL Int Res Fndn; *Recreations* reading, travel, swimming, skiing, walking; *Style*— Terry Toney, Esq; ✉ British Council, 10 Spring Gardens, London SW1A 2BN

TONG, Chee Hwee; s of Hong Hoe Tong, of Ipoh, Malaysia, and Ah Looi Chong; *b* 28 May 1963; *Educ* Sungei Pari HS Malaysia; *m* 26 March 1996, Sow Fun Ho; 2 s (Kah Yin Tong b 13 Feb 1999, Kah Weng Tong b 9 Oct 2000); *Career* trained Happy Valley Restaurant Singapore 1982–84, third fryer chef Happy Valley Restaurant Malaysia 1985–87, third fryer chef Carlton Hotel Singapore 1988–89, second fryer chef Sheraton Towers Singapore 1989–95, first fryer chef Marriott Hotel Singapore 1995–96, sr fryer chef Ritz Carlton Singapore 1996–2001, head chef Hakkasan London 2001– (1 Michelin Star 2003–, Oriental Restaurant of the Year 2003 Carlton Restaurant Awards); *Recreations* cooking, sports (swimming, playing badminton, etc); *Style*— Mr Tong Chee Hwee; ✉ Hakkasan, 8 Hanway Place, London W1P 9DH (☎ 020 7927 7000, fax 020 7907 1889)

TONG, Peter (Pete); MBE (2014); *b* 30 July 1960, Kent; *Educ* King's Sch Rochester; *Career* DJ and music prodr; Blues & Soul Magazine: staff writer 1979–80, features ed 1980–83; A&R mangr London Records 1983; presenter: Invicta Radio 1984–87, Capital Radio 1988–91, BBC Radio 1 1991– (currently host Pete Tong Friday Night Show and Essential Mix); resident DJ Pure Pacha nightclub Ibiza 2003–07, DJ Wonderland @ Eden Ibiza 2008–; *Style*— Pete Tong, Esq, MBE; ✉ BBC Radio 1, Yalding House, 152–156 Great Portland Street, London W1N 6DJ

TONGE, Baroness (Life Peer UK 2005), of Kew in the London Borough of Richmond upon Thames; Dr Jennifer Louise (Jenny) Tonge; da of Sidney Smith (d 1958), of W Midlands, and Violet Louise, *née* Williams (d 1991); *b* 19 February 1941; *Educ* Dudley Girls' HS, UCL, UCH (MB BS); *m* 1964, Dr Keith Angus Tonge (d 2013), s of Kenneth Gordon Tonge; 2 s (Hon David b 1968, Hon Richard b 1976), 1 da (Mary b 1970 d 2004); *Career* sr family planning doctor 1974–97, sr med offr Women's Servs Ealing HA 1983–88, mangr Community Health Servs West London Healthcare Tst 1992–97; MP (Lib Dem) Richmond Park 1997–2005 (Parly candidate Richmond and Barnes 1992); int devpt spokesperson for Lib Dems 1997–2003; memb Select Ctee on Int Devpt 1997–99; memb Lib Dem Federal Policy Ctee, chair Lib Dem Health Panel 1992–97; chair Richmond and Barnes Lib Assoc 1978–80 (chair Social Servs Ctee 1983–87), memb London Borough of Richmond upon Thames Cncl (Kew Ward) 1981–90; chair of govrs Waldegrave Sch 1988–92; fell Royal Soc for Public Health 1996, Hon FFSRH 1999, Hon FRCOG 2015; *Style*— The Rt Hon the Lady Tonge

TONGUE, Carole; da of Walter Archer Tongue, of Lausanne, Switzerland, and Muriel Esther, *née* Lambert; *b* 14 October 1955; *Educ* Brentwood Co HS, Loughborough Univ of Technol (BA); *m* 28 Dec 1990, Chris Pond, MP, *qv*; 1 da (Eleanore Christabel b 20 Dec 1992); *Career* asst ed Laboratory Practice 1977–78, courier for Sunsites Ltd in France 1978–79, Robert Schumann scholarship for res in social affrs Euro Parliament 1979–80, sec and admin asst in Socialist Gp Secretariat of Euro Parliament 1980–84; MEP (Lab) London East 1984–99; spokesperson on media/culture policy for Pty of the Gp of Euro Socialists Euro Parliament (memb Youth, Media and Culture Ctee, substitute memb Social Affairs Ctee); ptnr CSPH Int 2010–; chair UK Coalition for Cultural Diversity 2005–, chair European Coalitions for Cultural Diversity 2015–; vice-chair Couper Collection 2001–; sr visiting fell Dept of Euro Studies Loughborough Univ, visiting prof Univ of the Arts 2005–15; hon doctorate Univ of Lincoln 2005; memb: BECTU, Fabian Soc; FRSA; *Recreations* piano, cello, tennis, squash, riding, cinema, theatre, opera; *Style*— Ms Carole Tongue

TONKING, His Hon (Russel) Simon William Ferguson; DL; s of Lt-Col John Wilson Tonking, MBE, TD (d 1992), and Mary Oldham Tonking, *née* Ferguson (d 1971); *b* 25 March 1952, Amersham, Bucks; *Educ* The King's Sch Canterbury, Emmanuel Coll Cambridge (MA); *m* 10 July 1976, (Sylvia) Mithra, da of Colin Ian McIntyre; 1 da (Flora b 1984), 1 s (William b 1988); *Career* called to the Bar Inner Temple 1975 (bencher 2011); recorder 1994–97 (asst recorder 1991–94); circuit judge: Midland & Oxford Circuit 1997–2001, Midland Circuit 2001–; resident judge Stafford Combined Court 2006–15, ret, hon recorder Stafford 2008–15; memb Criminal Ctee Judicial Studies Bd 2005–08, jt course dir Criminal Induction Judicial Coll 2008–13; steward Lichfield Cathedral (head steward 1984–86, pres 2003–04), dep chllr Dio of Southwell 1997–2005, chm Lichfield Cathedral Cncl 2009–; Hon DUniv Staffs 2009; *Publications* The Bench Book Companion (jtly, 2015), The Crown Court Compendium (jtly, 2016); *Style*— His Hon Simon Tonking; ✉ Stafford Combined Court Centre, Victoria Square, Stafford ST16 2QQ (☎ 01785 610730)

TONRY, Prof Michael; *b* 7 June 1945, Martinsburg, WV; *Educ* Univ of N Carolina Chapel Hill (AB), Yale Law Sch (LLB); *Career* in private practice Sonnenschein Carlin & Nath Chicago 1970–71, research assoc Center for Studies in Criminal Justice Univ of Chicago 1971–73, lectr in law Faculty of Law Univ of Birmingham 1973–74, in private practice Dechert Price & Rhoads Philadelphia 1974–76, prof of law Univ of Maryland Sch of Law 1976–83, private solo law practice Castine ME 1983–90, Sonosky prof of law and public policy Univ of Minnesota 1990–, dir Inst of Criminology and prof of law and public policy Univ of Cambridge 1999–2004; sr research fell Netherlands Inst for the Study of Crime and Law Enforcement Leiden 2003–; visiting prof: Univ of Leiden 1996–98, Max-Planck Inst for Int and Comparative Criminal Law 1998–99, Univ of Lausanne 2001–; visiting fell All Souls Coll Oxford 1994–95; dir MacArthur Fndn/US Dept of Justice Prog on Human Devpt and Criminal Behavior 1986–90, scientific memb Max-Planck Gesellschaft 2013–; ed: Crime and Justice – A Review of Research 1977–, The Castine Patriot 1987–90 (also publisher), Overcrowded Times 1989–2000, Studies in Crime and Public Policy 1992–, Readers in Crime and Justice 1993–; Humboldt-Stiftung Forschungspreisesträger 1997–2002; *Publications* Research on Sentencing: The Search for Reform (co-ed and contrib, 1983), Reform and Punishment – Essays on Criminal Sentencing (co-ed, 1983), Hypnotically Refreshed Testimony: Enhanced Memory or Tampering with the Evidence? (jtly, 1985), Communities and Crime (co-ed, 1986), The Sentencing Commission – Guidelines for Criminal Sanctions (jtly, 1987), Sentencing Reform Impacts (1987), Prediction and Classification (co-ed, 1987), Managing Appeals in Federal Courts (jtly, 1988), Family Violence (co-ed, 1989), Drugs and Crime (co-ed, 1990), Between Prison and Probation – Intermediate Punishments in a Rational Sentencing System (jtly, 1990), Human Development and Criminal Behaviour (jtly, 1991), Modern Policing (co-ed, 1992), Beyond the Law: Crime in Complex Organizations (co-ed, 1993), Intermediate Sanctions in Overcrowded Times (co-ed, 1995), Building a Safer Society (co-ed, 1995), Malign Neglect – Race, Crime, and Punishment in America (1995), Sentencing Matters (1996), Sentencing Reform in Overcrowded Times – A Comparative Perspective (co-ed, 1997), Ethnicity, Crime, and Immigration – Comparative and Cross-national Perspectives (ed, 1997), Intermediate Sanctions in Sentencing Guidelines (1997), Youth Violence (co-ed, 1998), The Handbook of Crime and Punishment (ed, 1998), Prisons (co-ed, 1999), Sentencing and Sanctions in Western Countries (co-ed, 2001), Penal Reform in Overcrowded Times (ed, 2001), Reform and Punishment: The Future of Sentencing (co-ed, 2002), Ideology, Crime and Criminal Justice: A Symposium in Honour of Sir Leon Radinowicz (co-ed, 2002), Youth Crime and Youth Justice: Comparative and Cross-national Perspectives (co-ed, 2003), Confronting Crime: Crime Control under New Labour (ed, 2003), Cross-national Studies of Crime and Justice (co-ed, 2003), Thinking about Crime: Sense and Sensibility in American Penal Culture (2004), Punishment and Politics: Evidence and Emulation in the Making of English Crime Control Policy (2004), Crime and Punishment in Western Countries 1980–99 (jt ed, 2006), Crime and Justice in the Netherlands (jt ed, 2007), Crime, Punishment, and Politics in Comparative Perspective (2007), The Oxford Handbook of Crime and Public Policy (ed, 2009), Thinking about Punishment: Penal Policy across Space, Time and Discipline (2009), Punishing Race: A Continuing American Dilemma (2011), The Oxford Handbook of Crime and Criminal Justice (ed, 2011), Retributivism Has a Past. Has It a Future? (ed, 2011), Crime and Justice in Scandinavia (co-ed, 2011), Why Punish? How Much? (ed, 2011), Prosecutors and Politics: A Comparative Perspective (ed, 2012), Crime and Justice in America, 1975–2025 (ed, 2013), The Oxford Handbook of Ethnicity, Crime and Immigration (co-ed, 2013); author of numerous articles in learned jls; *Style*— Prof Michael Tonry; ✉ e-mail tonry001@umn.edu

TOOBY, Michael Bowen; s of Leslie and Jill Tooby, of Long Itchington, Warks; *b* 20 December 1956; *Educ* King Henry VIII Sch Coventry, Magdalene Coll Cambridge; *Career* asst curator Kettles Yard Cambridge 1978–80, exhbns organiser Third Eye Centre Glasgow 1980–84, keeper Mappin Art Gallery Sheffield 1984–92, curator Tate Gallery St Ives 1992–2000, dir Nat Museum and Gall Cardiff 2000–06, dir progs and learning Amgueddfa Cymru/Nat Museums Wales 2006–11; chm Engage (Nat Orgn for Gallery and Visual Arts Educators) 1999–2004, memb Stabilisation Advsy Panel Arts Cncl of England 1999–2004, memb Museums and Galleries Ctee AHRC 2005–, visiting prof in contemporary curatorial practice Univ of Glamorgan; *Style*— Michael Tooby, Esq

TOOKEY, Christopher David; s of Alan Oliver Tookey, and Winifreda, *née* Marsh; *b* 9 April 1950; *Educ* Tonbridge, Exeter Coll Oxford (MA, ed Isis, pres Oxford Union); *m* 2 Sept 1989, Frances Anne, da of Henry Robert Heasman; 1 s (Daniel b 12 April 1991); *Career* writer, broadcaster, director, producer and composer of musicals; prodns incl: Hard Times 1973, Room with a Revue 1974, Retrogrim's Progress 1974, Hanky Park 1975, Dick Whittington 1975 and 1976, An Evening with Noel and Gertie 1975 and 1976, The Resurrection of the British Musical 1977, Him 'n' Her 1979, Ladies and Jurgen 1980, Hard Times – The Musical 1998 and 2000; asst theatre dir Belgrade Theatre Co 1973–74, Haymarket and Phoenix Theatre Leicester 1974–75, TV prodr and dir Associated Television 1975–82, weekend ed and assoc features ed TV-am 1982–83, freelance TV dir 1983–89; credits incl: Revolver, After Dark, Network 7, various rock videos; as freelance journalist: Books and Bookmen 1983–86, film critic Sunday Telegraph 1989–92 (freelance feature writer 1986, TV critic 1987–89), TV critic and feature writer Daily Telegraph 1986–93, film critic, feature writer and occasional theatre critic Daily Mail 1993–, theatre critic Mail on Sunday 1993; also freelance journalist for Prospect, Applause, The Sunday Times, The Observer, The European, The Literary Review, Drama, and National Review (US); freelance broadcaster 1989– (progs incl Sky News, The Arts Prog (BBC Radio 2), What the Papers Say (BBC 2), Book Choice (Channel 4), Meridian (BBC), First Edition (BSB), Open House (Channel 5), presenter Back Row and The Film Programme (BBC Radio 4)); presenter ALFS Awards Ceremony (London Film Critics) 1994–99; chm Film Critics' Circle 1994–98; *Publications* The Critics' Film Guide (1994), Tookey's Movie Guide (internet pubn, 2002–); *Style*— Christopher Tookey, Esq; ✉ 53 Thornhill Road, London N1 1JT (☎ 020 7697 4737)

TOOLEY, Dr Peter John Hocart; s of Dr Patrick Hocart Tooley (d 1991), of Guernsey, and Brenda Margaret, *née* Williams (d 1939); *b* 28 February 1939, St Helen's, Lancs; *Educ* Elizabeth Coll Guernsey, St George's Sch Harpenden, Univ of London, London Hosp Med Coll (MRCS, LRCP, MB BS, MRCGP, DObst RCOG, DMJ), Dip of the Faculty of Family Planning (DFFP), LLM; *m* 1, 1966 (m dis 1983), Elizabeth Monica, da of Percy Roche (d 1991), of Twyford, Berks; 2 da (Lucy b 1967, Josephine b 1971), 1 s (Patrick b 1969); *m* 2, 1987, Diana Edith, *née* Sturdy; *Career* sr ptnr gen med practice Twyford 1974–90 (princ 1966, trainer 1977–81), asst dep coroner Borough of Reading 1984–89; Janssen-Cilag Ltd (formerly Janssen Pharmaceutical Ltd): med conslt gen practice affrs 1986–90, sr med advsr 1990–93, head of med affrs 1993–98, med dir Ireland 1996–98; med dir Daiichi Sankyo UK Ltd (formerly Sankyo Pharma UK Ltd) 1998–, med dir Alliance Pharmaceuticals 1998–2007, conslt medical dir A Menarini Pharma UK SRL 2006–; conslt pharmaceutical physician 1998–; MO: Oxfordshire RFU 1970–97, Henley RFC 1970–97, Marks & Spencer plc Reading 1980–90, Wasps RFC 1993–98; memb: Berks Local Med Ctee 1978–86, Reading Pathological Soc, memb Bolam Soc 1995– (hon sec); chm Reading Med Club 1980–83 and 1987–90 (fndr memb), vice-chm Polehampton Charities 1986–90 (tstee 1975); Freeman City of London, Liveryman Worshipful Soc of Apothecaries 1965 (memb Livery Cmmn 1994–2005, chm 2002–04, asst 2008–11, Jr Warden 2011–12, Sr Warden 2012–13, Master 2013–14); memb: BMA, Br Acad of Forensic Sciences, Br Assoc of Pharmaceutical Physicians, Faculty of Pharmaceutical Medicine (MFPM); FRSM; *Recreations* rugby football, gardening, Guernsey and family history; *Clubs* Royal Channel Islands Yacht, Guernsey RUFC; *Style*— Dr Peter Tooley; ✉ Les Mielles, Les Mielles Road, Vale, Guernsey GY3 5AZ (☎ 01481 242607, fax 01481 242505, e-mail peter@pjtpharma.co.uk)

TOOP, Prof David; s of Leslie John Toop, of Waltham Cross, Herts, and Doris Ada May, *née* Purver; *b* 5 May 1949; *Educ* Broxbourne GS, Hornsey Coll of Art, Watford Coll of Art; *m* 1, 30 May 1987, Kimberley (d 1995), da of Les Leston; 1 da (Juliette Angelica b 13 Feb 1990); m 2, 11 Oct 2003 (m dis 2016), Eileen, da of John Peters; *Career* musician, author, curator; played with Paul Burwell 1970–80, gave three illustrated music talks BBC Radio 3 1971–75, recorded three pieces for The Obscure Label 1975, launched record label Quartz 1978, recorded with Flying Lizards 1979, publisher and co-ed Collusion magazine 1981–83, pop music critic The Sunday Times 1986–88, monthly music columnist and feature writer The Face 1984–96, music critic The Times 1988–96; contrib to Arena, Wire, GQ, Bookforum, NY Times, Gramophone, Times Higher Education, and various books; composed soundtrack to Lisbon Expo Acqua Matrix night show spectacular 1998; curator Sonic Boom sound art exhbn (Hayward Gallery) 2000, sound curator Radical Fashion exbhn (V&A) 2001, curator Not Necessarily English Music (2 CD compliation for Leonardo Music JI/MIT Press), composed and performed Siren Space Thames Festival 2002; sound installations: Tokyo ICC 2000, Bruges WAV Festival 2002, Charles Fort Kinsale 2005, Beijing Zhongshan Park 2005, Beijing Capital Museum 2006, Stourhead Garden 2006, Stavanger 2008, Nat Gallery 2009–10, Armitt Museum Ambleside 2012, Star-Shaped Biscuit (opera, performed at Snape Maltings) 2012; curator Playing John Cage (Arnolfini Bristol) 2006, curator Blow Up (Fiat Time House) 2010; London Coll of Communication: visiting research fell and visiting lectr Sch of Media 2000–05, AHRC research fell in creative and performing arts 2004–07, sr research fell 2007–; visiting prof Univ of the Arts London 2005–13, visiting prof Leeds Coll of Music 2012–; prof of audio culture and improvisation Univ of the Arts London 2013– (chair 2013–); dir Unknown Devices: the Laptop Orchestra; memb: Electronic Music Fndn, Japanese Garden Soc, Takemitsu Soc; *Recordings* Buried Dreams (with Max Eastley) 1994, Screen Ceremonies (solo album) 1995, Pink Noir (solo album) 1996, Spirit World (solo album) 1997, Museum of Fruit (solo album) 1999, Hot Pants Idol (solo album) 1999, Needle in the Groove (with Jeff Noon) 2000, 37th Floor at Sunset (solo album) 2000, Black Chamber (solo album) 2003, Doll Creature (with Max Eastley) 2004, Sound Body (solo album) 2007, Mondo Black Chamber (solo album) 2014, Lost Shadow: In Defence of the Soul (field recordings) 2015, Life On the Inside (solo album) 2016, Entities Inertias Faint Beings (solo album) 2016; *Books* The Rap Attack (1984), The Rap Attack 2 (1991), Ocean of Sound (1995), Exotica (1999), Rap Attack 3 (1999), Haunted Weather (2004), Sinister Resonance (2010), Into the Maelstrom (2016); *Style*— Prof David Toop; ✉ website www.davidtoopblog.com

TOPE, Baron (Life Peer UK 1994), of Sutton in the London Borough of Sutton; Graham Norman; CBE (1991); s of Leslie Norman Tope (d 1983), of Sutton, and Winifred Sophia, *née* Merrick (d 1972); *b* 30 November 1943, Plymouth; *Educ* Whitgift Sch; *m* 22 July 1972, Margaret, da of Frank East; 2 s (Hon Andrew b 3 July 1974, Hon David b 21 June 1976); *Career* with Unilever Group 1961–69, insurance mangr Air Products Ltd 1970–72, MP (Lib) Sutton and Cheam 1972–74, dep gen sec Voluntary Action Camden 1975–90; London Borough of Sutton: cncllr (Lib/Lib Dem) 1974–2014, ldr 1986–99, cncl spokesman on libraries and heritage, community safety and economic devpt 1999–2006, cncl spokesman on community safety, leisure and libraries 2006–12, vice-chair Environment and Neighbourhoods Ctee 2012–14; EU Ctee of the Regions: UK memb 1994–2014, ldr ELDR (Lib) Gp 1996–2002, Bureau memb 1996–2014; chair Constitutional Affairs Cmmn 2002–04 (vice-chair 2004–06); pres London Lib Dems 1991–2000; London Assembly (GLA): memb (Lib Dem) 2000–08, ldr Lib gp, chair Fin Ctee on Met Police Authy 2000–08, memb Mayor of London's Advsy Cabinet 2000–04; Assoc of London Govt: Lib Dem ldr 1997–2000, Lib Dem Int and Euro spokesman 1997–2000; House of Lords: Lib Dem spokesperson on educn 1994–2000, asst Lib Dem whip 1999–2000, Lib Dem communities and local govt spokesperson 2008–10, Lib Dem London Parly spokesperson 2015–; co-chair Lib Dem Communities and Local Govt Parly Ctee 2010–15, chair Libraries All Pty Parly Gp 2014–15, vice-chair Sudan All Pty Parly Gp 2016–; chair Local Govt Gp for Europe 2005–, vice-pres Local Govt Assoc 2013–; pres Sutton Branch Save the Children 2006–, chair London Borough of Sutton WWI Commemoration Forum 2014–; Hon Freeman London Borough of Sutton 2014; *Books* Liberals and the Community (1974), A Life in Politics (2011); *Recreations* politics, history, reading, walking, gardening; *Clubs* Whitgiftian Assoc (pres 2016); *Style*— The Rt Hon the Lord Tope, CBE; ✉ House of Lords, London SW1A 0PW (☎ 020 7219 3098, e-mail topeg@parliament.uk)

TOPOLSKI, Daniel; s of Feliks Topolski (d 1989), the artist, of London, and Marion Everall Topolski (d 1985); *b* 4 June 1945; *Educ* French Lycée London, Westminster, New Coll Oxford; *m* Susan Gilmore, da of James Gilbert; 2 da (Emma Sheridan b 30 Jan 1987, Tamsin Lucy Gilbert b 17 Nov 1990), 1 s (Lucien Sinclair Feliks b 21 May 1997); *Career* asst prodr BBC TV 1969–73; writer on travel and sport, TV and radio commentator, journalist, photographer, motivational speaker; memb: London Rowing Club 1964–, Leander Club 1965–; Henley Royal Regatta: competitor 1962–93, winner 1969–70 and 1976–77, Henley Steward 1991–; major championships incl: second place lightweight coxless fours World Championships (Nottingham) 1975, Gold medal lightweight eights World Championships (Amsterdam) 1977; participant Oxford v Cambridge Boat Race 1967 (winner) and 1968, chief coach to Oxford Univ for Boat Race 1973–87 (won 12, longest ever Oxford winning sequence (10), 3 course records 1974, 1976 and 1984), Oxford Boat Race coaching conslt 1995–; coach: Nat Women's Rowing Squad 1978–80, Women's VIII Olympic Games Moscow 1980, Men's Pair Olympic Games LA 1984; expdns: Brazil 1964, Iran 1973; winner Travel Radio Prog of Year Award 1994; tstee Topolski Century museum charity; Churchill fell; hon fell New Coll Oxford 2013; *Books* Muzungu: One Man's Africa (1976), Travels with My Father: South America (1983), Boat Race: The Oxford Revival (1985), True Blue: The Oxford Boat Race Mutiny (1989, sports book of the year, filmed 1996), Henley the Regatta (1989); *Style*— Daniel Topolski, Esq; ✉ 69 Randolph Avenue, London W9 1DW (☎ 020 7289 8939, fax 020 7266 1884, e-mail dtopo35410@aol.com)

TORA, Brian Roberto; adopted s of Ernest Carlo Tora (d 2005), and Betty Lilian, *née* Squires (d 1971); *b* 21 September 1945; *Educ* Bancroft's Sch; *m* 1, 4 July 1975 (m dis 1988), Jennifer, da of (Julius) Dennis Israel Blanckensee (d 1951); 2 s (Matthew b 26 Dec 1977, Thomas b 5 June 1979); m 2, 20 Oct 1989, Elizabeth Mary, *née* Edgecombe; *Career* Grieveson Grant 1963–74, investment mangr Singer & Friedlander 1974–79, investment dir van Cutsem & Assocs 1979–82, investment dir Touche Remnant Fin Mgmnt 1982–85, head of retail mktg James Capel & Co 1985–91; Gerrard Investment Mgmnt Ltd (formerly Greig Middleton): mktg dir 1991–98, head of asset mgmnt 1998–2000, head Intermediary Div 2002–05, investment communications dir 2005–06; princ The Tora Partnership 2007–; regular broadcaster, columnist in Fund Strategy, Money Marketing and others; chartered FCSI; *Publications* The Second Financial Services Revolution (1995); contrib articles on investment to several jls; *Recreations* bridge, reading, food and wine, travel; *Style*— Brian Tora, Esq; ✉ Enniskillen Lodge, Little Waldingfield, Suffolk CO10 0SU (☎ 01787 247783)

TORDOFF, Baron (Life Peer UK 1981), of Knutsford in the County of Cheshire; Geoffrey Johnson Tordoff; s of late Stanley Acomb Tordoff, of Marple, Cheshire; *b* 11 October 1928; *Educ* Manchester Grammar, Univ of Manchester; *m* 1953, Mary Patricia (d 2013), da of Thomas Swarbrick, of Leeds; 3 da (Hon Mary Catherine b 1954, Hon Frances Jane b 1956, Hon Paula Mary b 1960), 2 s (Hon Nicholas Gregory b 1958, Hon Mark Edmund b 1962); *Career* contested (Lib) Northwich 1964, Knutsford 1966 and 1970; Lib Party: chm Assembly Ctee 1974–76, memb Nat Exec 1975–84, chm 1976–79, pres 1983–84, chm Campaigns and Elections Ctee 1980 and 1981; House of Lords: dep Lib chief whip 1983–84, Lib chief whip 1984–88, Lib Dem chief whip 1988–94, a dep speaker 1994–, princ dep chm of ctees 1994–2001, chm Select Ctee on the European Communities 1994–2001, chm of ctees 2001–02; memb PCC 1995–2002; extra Lord in Waiting 2004–; *Clubs* National Liberal; *Style*— The Rt Hon the Lord Tordoff; ✉ House of Lords, London SW1A 0PW

TORODE, John; s of Douglas Torode, and Anne, *née* Foley (d 1970); *b* 23 July 1965, Melbourne; *Educ* St Bedes Coll Melbourne; *m* 8 Sept 2007, Jessica Ruth, *née* Thomas; 1 s (Jonah b 14 March 2004), 1 da (Loulou b 17 Aug 2006); 2 s from a previous relationship (Marcel b 8 June 1995, Casper b 10 May 1997); *Career* Pont de la Tour 1992, sous chef Quaglinos Conran Gp 1992, head chef Mezzo Soho 1995, prop Smiths of Smithfield 2000–, prop The Luxe Spitalfields 2009–; co-presenter Masterchef (formerly Masterchef Goes Large, BBC) 2005–; James Beard Award 1998; pres RASE; *Books* Mezzo Cook Book (1995), Relax It's Only Food (1998), Torode's Thai Trek (1999), John Torode's Beef and Other Bovine Matters (2008), John Torode's Chicken and Other Birds (2009); *Recreations* cooking, cycling, swimming, fine wine; *Style*— John Torode, Esq; ✉ Smiths of Smithfield, 67–77 Charterhouse Street, London EC1M 6HJ (☎ 020 7236 7666, fax 020 7236 0488, e-mail lucy@smithsofsmithfield.co.uk)

TORRANCE, (David) Andrew; s of James Torrance (d 2005), and Gladys, *née* Riley (d 1995); *b* 18 May 1953; *Educ* Merchant Taylors' Sch Crosby, Emmanuel Coll Cambridge (MA), London Business Sch (MSc); *m* 30 Dec 1983, Ann Lesley, da of George Tasker (d 1972), of Bebington, Wirral; 1 da (Lucy b 1984), 1 s (James b 1987); *Career* The Boston Consulting Group Ltd 1976–92, chm and chief exec ITT London & Edinburgh Insurance Group 1995–98 (joined 1992), ceo Allianz Insurance plc 2003–13 (joined 1999, non-exec dir 2015–), ceo Fireman's Fund Insurance Co 2013–15; chm The Motor Insurance Repair Research Centre (Thatcham) 2000–05, chm Climatewise 2008–11; dir Pool Reinsurance Co Ltd 2010–13, non-exec dir Novae Gp plc 2016–; memb Worshipful Co of Insurers; *Recreations* cars, tennis, food, wine; *Style*— Andrew Torrance, Esq; ✉ 117 Lansdowne Road, London W11 2LF (☎ 020 7727 9019, mobile 07803 512714, e-mail andrew18.torrance@gmail.com)

TORRANCE, David; MSP; *b* 13 March 1961, Kirkcaldy, Fife; *Educ* Balwearie HS Kirkcaldy, Adam Smith Coll Kirkcaldy (HND); *Career* cncllr Fife Cncl 1995–2012, MSP (SNP) Kirkcaldy 2011–; *Recreations* Scouts; *Style*— David Torrance, Esq, MSP; ✉ M5.15, The Scottish Parliament, Edinburgh EH99 1SP (☎ 0131 348 6892 (parliament), 01592 200349 (constituency office), e-mail david.torrance.msp@scottish.parliament.uk, website www.scottish.parliament.uk/David-Torrance-MSP)

TORRINGTON, 11 Viscount (GB 1721); Sir Timothy Howard St George Byng; 11 Bt (GB 1715); Baron Byng of Southill (GB 1721); s of Hon George Byng, RN (d on active service 1944, himself s of 10 Viscount, whom present Viscount suc 1961), and Anne Yvonne Bostock, *née* Wood; *b* 13 July 1943; *Educ* Harrow, St Edmund Hall Oxford (BA); *m* 1973, Susan Honor, da of Michael George Thomas Webster, of Dummer, Hants; 3 da (Hon Henrietta Rose b 1977, Hon Georgina Isabel b 1980, Hon Malaika Anne b 13 April 1982); *Heir* kinsman, Colin Cranmer-Byng; *Career* md Anvil Petroleum plc 1975–85, exec dir Flextech plc 1988–93, md Heritage Oil Corp (Canada) 1995–2000, dir Lansdowne Oil & Gas plc; chm Sub-Ctee F House of Lords Select Ctee on European Community 1984–87; *Recreations* travel and field sports; *Clubs* White's, Pratt's, Muthaiga (Nairobi); *Style*— The Rt Hon the Viscount Torrington

TOSSWILL, (Timothy Maurice) Stephen; s of Timothy Dymond Tosswill (d 1991), and Sigrid, *née* Bohn (d 1985); *b* 28 April 1949; *Educ* Rugby, St Paul's, Univ of London (LLB, LLM); *Career* criminal lawyer, admitted slr 1976; princ Tosswill & Co 1985– (ptnr 1976–85), author of articles in legal periodicals; *Recreations* masterly inactivity; *Style*—Stephen Tosswill, Esq; ✉ 260 Brixton Hill, London SW2 1HP (☎ 020 8674 9494, fax 020 8671 8987, e-mail tmst@criminallaw.co.uk)

TOUHIG, Baron (Life Peer UK 2010), of Islwyn and of Glansychan in the County of Gwent; Rt Hon (James) Donnelly (Don) Touhig; PC (2006); s of Michael Touhig (d 1982), and Agnes Catherine, *née* Corten; *b* 5 December 1947; *Educ* St Francis Sch, E Monmouth Coll; *m* 21 Sept 1968, Jennifer, da of Clifford Hughes (d 2014); 2 s (Matthew b 24 Jan 1972, James b 19 April 1978), 2 da (Charlotte b 3 May 1975, Katie b 27 Sept 1983); *Career* apprentice radio and TV engr, journalist then ed; gen mangr newspaper gp, business devpt gp and printing company; MP (Lab) Islwyn 1995–2010; PPS to Chllr of the Exchequer 1997–99, govt whip 1999–2001, Parly under sec of state Wales Office 2001–05, Parly under sec MOD 2005–06, oppn spokesman on defence 2015; memb Select Ctee for: Welsh Affrs 1996–97, Public Accounts 2006; memb Leadership Campaign Team (responsible for devolution campaign in Wales) 1996–97; memb Lab Pty Departmental Ctee for: Home Affrs 1997–2001, Trade and Industry 1997–2001, Treasury 1997–2001, Health 1997–2001; chm Select Ctee on Members' Allowances 2009, memb Speakers Ctee on Independent Parly Standards Authy 2009; hon sec Welsh Regnl Gp of Lab MPs 1995–99; memb Co-operative Pty, chair Co-operative Parly Gp 1999 and 2009; memb Mensa; Freeman City of London 2013; KSS 1991; *Recreations* reading, cooking for family and friends; *Style*— The Lord Touhig, PC; ✉ House of Lords, London SW1A 0PW (e-mail touhigjd@parliament.uk)

TOULSON, Lady; Elizabeth; CBE (1999), DL (2010); da of Henry Bertram Chrimes (d 1997), and Suzanne Corbett-Lowe (d 2000); *b* 10 November 1948; *Educ* Univ of Liverpool (LLB), Univ of Cambridge (Dip Comparative Law); *m* April 1973, Lord Toulson, *qv*, s of Stanley Kilsha Toulson; 2 da (Susanna Jane b 4 Feb 1975, Rachel Elizabeth b 26 Feb 1977), 2 s (Henry Alexander b 4 Nov 1979, Thomas Grenfell b 8 April 1984); *Career* called to the Bar 1974; WRVS: tstee 1981, vice-chair 1989–93, chm 1993–99; govr: Charterhouse 1998–2016 (ret), Sutton's Hosp Charterhouse 2004–07; dir Queen Elizabeth Fndn for the Disabled 1999–2006; chm: Children's Soc 2001–, Nykia-Vwaza Tst 2004, Time for Families 2006, Guildford Cathedral Cncl 2011, lay canon Guildford Cathedral 2013–; pres St John Ambulance 2010; High Sheriff Surrey 2009–10; FRSA 2006; *Recreations* skiing, tennis, walking, swimming, classical music; *Style*— Lady Toulson, CBE, DL; ✉ Billhurst Farm, White Hart Lane, Wood Street Green, Surrey GU3 3DZ (☎ 01483 235246, fax 01483

T

235347, mobile 07977 489256, e-mail elizabeth@toulsonfamily.co.uk); 201 Rowan House, 2 Greycoat Street, London SW1P 2QD (☎ 020 7630 5325)

TOULSON, Lord; Rt Hon Sir Roger Grenfell Toulson; kt (1996), PC (2007); s of Stanley Kilsha Toulson (d 1992), of Redhill, Surrey, and Lilian Mary Toulson (d 1985); *b* 23 September 1946; *Educ* Mill Hill Sch, Jesus Coll Cambridge (MA, LLB); *m* 28 April 1973, Elizabeth (Lady Toulson, CBE), *qv*, da of Henry Bertram Chrimes (d 1997), of Wirral, Merseyside; 2 da (Susanna b 1975, Rachel b 1977), 2 s (Henry b 1979, Thomas b 1984); *Career* called to the Bar Inner Temple 1969 (bencher 1995); QC 1986, recorder of the Crown Court 1987–96, judge of the High Court of Justice (Queen's Bench Div) 1996–2007, presiding judge Western Circuit 1997–2002, a Lord Justice of Appeal 2007–13, a Justice of the Supreme Court 2013–; chm Law Cmmn 2002–06, memb Judicial Appts Cmmn 2007–12; Hon LLD: UWE 2002, Univ of Bradford 2008; *Books* Confidentiality (with C M Phipps, 1996, 3 edn 2012); *Recreations* skiing, tennis, gardening; *Style*— The Lord Toulson, PC; ✉ The Supreme Court of the United Kingdom, Parliament Square, London SW1P 3BD

TOVEY, Russell; *b* 14 November 1981, Essex; *Educ* Shenfield HS; *Career* actor; *Theatre* incl: Howard Katz (Cottesloe Theatre and RNT) 2001, Henry V (RNT) 2003, His Girl Friday (RNT) 2003, His Dark Materials (RNT) 2003–04, The History Boys (Lyttelton Theatre, RNT, Lyric Theatre Hong Kong Acad of Performing Arts, St James Wellington, Sydney Theatre and Broadhurst Theatre Broadway) 2004–06, A Respectable Wedding (Young Vic London) 2007, The Sea (Theatre Royal Haymarket) 2008; *Television* incl: Rob Brydon's Annually Retentive (BBC 3) 2007, Gavin and Stacey (BBC 3) 2007–09, Doctor Who (BBC 1) 2007 and 2010, Being Human (BBC 3) 2008–12, Little Dorritt (BBC 1) 2008, Him & Her 2010–13 (Best Comedy Performance RTS Award 2012), Sherlock 2012, The Job Lot 2013, What Remains 2013, Looking 2014; *Film* The Pirates! In an Adventure with Scientists! 2012; *Style*— Russell Tovey, Esq; ✉ c/o Independent Talent Group, 40 Whitfield Street, London W1T 2RH (Twitter @russelltovey)

TOWERS, John; CBE (1995); *b* 30 March 1948; *Educ* Durham Johnston Sch, Univ of Bradford (BTech(MechEng)); *m* Bethanie, *née* Williams; 1 da (Laura b 23 Sept 1980), 1 s (Michael b 30 Aug 1982); *Career* gen mangr Perkins Engines Ltd Peterborough 1985–86 (joined 1970), vice-pres Varity Corporation Ltd Toronto (formerly Massey-Ferguson, parent co of Perkins Engines) 1986–87, md Massey-Ferguson Tractors Ltd Coventry 1987–88; Rover Group: dir of mfrg and acting md Land Rover Ltd Solihull 1988–89, dir of product devpt Rover Group Ltd Coventry 1989–91, md product supply 1991–92, gp md 1992–94, chief exec 1994–96; chief exec Concentric plc 1996–, fndr dir HatWel Ltd (mgmnt conslts) 1996–, chm Serck Heat Transfer Group 1998–2000, chm MG Rover Group 2000–05; non-exec dir: Honda UK Ltd 1989–94, Midland Bank plc 1994–96, B Elliott plc 1996–98; memb Design Cncl; FIMechE, CEng, FIIM, FREng 1992; *Recreations* golf, squash, tennis, music; *Style*— John Towers, Esq, CBE, FREng

TOWERS, Jonathan Henry Nicholson; s of John Richard Hugh Towers, of Lund House, Harrogate, N Yorks, and Gwyneth Helen Marshall, *née* Nicholson; *b* 5 April 1939; *Educ* Radley, Clare Coll Cambridge (MA); *m* 29 Sept 1979, Vanessa Catherine, da of Francis John Milward, of Barlow Woodseats Hall, Derbys; 2 s (Edward b 1982, Harry b 1988); *Career* ptnr Grays slrs York 1967–98, sole practitioner 1998–2008; under sheriff Yorks and Hallamshire 1987–2014, hon treas Under Sheriffs' Assoc 1991– (hon sec 2008–), hon sec Sheriffs' Millennium 1992–94, attorney The Company of Merchants of the Staple of England 1995–; hon treas The Shrievalty Assoc 2002–06 (hon sec 1995–2001, memb Cncl 2001–04); hon sec Nat Crimebeat 1997–2001 and 2004–12 (hon treas 2005–12), past chm York Area Appeals Ctee for Mental Health; memb Law Soc 1966; pres The Yorkshire Law Soc 1996–97; *Recreations* golf, shooting, walking, reading, skiing; *Clubs* Leander; *Style*— Jonathan Towers, Esq; ✉ West House, Nun Monkton, York YO26 8ER (☎ 01423 330643, e-mail jonathantowers@btinternet.com)

TOWILL, Prof Denis Royston; *b* 28 April 1933; *Educ* Univ of Bristol (BSc), Univ of Birmingham (MSc, DSc); *m* 27 March 1961, Christine Ann Forrester; 1 da (Rachel b 22 Dec 1962), 2 s (Jonathan b 2 Dec 1964, Edwin b 17 May 1970); *Career* engr; dynamic analyst Br Aerospace Weston/Filton 1957–59, conslt Norris Consultants Bristol 1959–62; subsequently: sr lectr RMCS Shrivenham, prof and head of dept UWIST Cardiff (reader 1966–69, prof 1970–87); prof and head Sch of Electrical, Electronic and Systems Engrg Univ of Wales Coll of Cardiff 1988–92, Univ of Wales Lucas research prof 1992, research prof Cardiff Business Sch 2000–; memb Exec Cmmn to oversee formation of Cardiff Univ 1987–88; served on various SERC, Technol Foresight, IFAC and Royal Acad of Engrg ctees, memb IEE Cncl (chm IEE Mgmnt and Design Bd 1990–91); distinguished overseas scientist fell of Eta Kapa Nu 1978; Clerk Maxwell Langham Thompson and McMichael premiums IERE, Lord Hirst premium IEE; MIProdE 1964, FIEE 1972, FREng 1988; *Books* Transfer Function Techniques for Control Engineers (1970), Coefficient Plane Models for Control System Analysis and Design (1981), Systems Approach to AMT Deployment (1993); *Recreations* music, sport; *Clubs* Glamorgan CC, Radyr CC (vice-pres); *Style*— Prof Denis R Towill, FREng; ✉ Logistics Systems Dynamics Group, Cardiff Business School, Cardiff University, Aberconway Building, Colum Drive Cardiff CF10 3EU (☎ 029 2087 6083, fax 029 2087 4301)

TOWLER, Peter Jeremy Hamilton; s of Stuart Hamilton-Towler, MBE (d 2002), and Betty Irene, *née* Hardwidge; *b* 21 March 1952; *Educ* Peter Symonds Sch (now Peter Symonds Coll) Winchester, Clare Coll Cambridge (MA); *m* 15 Sept 1979, Dr Martha Crellin, da of Norman Langdon-Down (d 1991), of Shepperton-on-Thames, Middx; 1 s, 1 da; *Career* called to the Bar Middle Temple 1974 (Harmsworth scholar); recorder (Western Circuit) 1997–; memb: Western Circuit 1976– (memb Circuit and Wine Ctee 1990–96), Planning and Environment Bar Assoc 1988–; legal examiner Diocese of Winchester 1994–2006; fndr memb and chm Ampfield Conservation Tst 1988–92 (pres 1992–99); chm Stroud Sch Assoc 1993–95, vice-pres Hants CCC 2012– (memb Ctee 1999–2012, tstee 2012–), chm Rose Bowl Appeal 2001–02, chm Howzat Appeal 2003–05; Freeman City of London 1982, Liveryman Worshipful Co of Weavers 1982; FCIArb 1994 (ACIArb 1984); *Recreations* cricket, reading, conservation, gardening; *Clubs* MCC, Hants CCC; *Style*— Peter Towler, Esq; ✉ 12 College Place, Fauvelle Buildings, Southampton SO15 2FE

TOWNEND, Richard Frank Stuart; s of Col H Stuart Townend (d 2002), and Beatrice May, *née* Lord; *b* 15 July 1942; *Educ* Westminster, Univ of Lausanne, Royal Coll of Music, Academie d'Orgue Romainmôtier Switzerland; *m* 1970, Janet Elaine, da of James Gibson; 2 s (William b 19 Jan 1974, Edmund b 4 March 1977); *Career* organist; resident recitalist St Margaret Lothbury, specialising in Renaissance and Baroque repertoire; given recitals throughout Europe incl Int Organ Festival Switzerland (first English musician so invited), numerous broadcasts and recordings; headmaster and owner Hill House Int Junior Sch 2002–; sometime visiting lectr Int Organ Acad St Vith Belgium, Fachakademie für Evangelische Kirchenmusik Bayreuth Germany; fell Lancashire Sch of Music, fell Guild of Musicians and Singers, hon fell Acad of St Cecilia; memb Royal Soc of Musicians; Master Worshipful Co of Parish Clerks 2007–08; *Clubs* Savage, National, Garrick; *Style*— Richard Townend, Esq; ✉ Hill House, 17 Hans Place, London SW1X 0EP (☎ 020 7584 1331, e-mail r.townend@btconnect.com)

TOWNSEND, (John) Anthony Victor; s of John Richard Christopher Townsend (d 1996), of Kintbury, Berks, and Carla Hillerns, *née* Lehmann (d 1990); *b* 24 January 1948, London; *Educ* Harrow, Selwyn Coll Cambridge (MA); *m* 16 April 1971, Carolyn Ann, da of Sir Walter Salomon (d 1987); 1 s (Christopher b 26 Feb 1974), 1 da (Alexandra b 26 Feb 1976); *Career* with Brown Shipley & Co Ltd bankers 1969–74, Rea Brothers Ltd bankers 1974–78, John Townsend & Co (Hldgs) Ltd 1979–87, Finsbury Asset Management Ltd (investment banking) 1988–98; chm: British and American Investment Tst plc, F & C Global Smaller Cos plc, Finsbury Growth & Income Tst plc, Miton Global Opportunities Tst plc; chm Assoc of Investment Tst Cos 2001–03; chm of govrs Cranleigh Sch, chm of tstees Harrow Mission; chm Gresham House plc; Past Master Worshipful Co of Pattenmakers; FRSA; *Recreations* shooting, skiing; *Clubs* City of London, RAC, Brooks's; *Style*— Anthony Townsend, Esq; ✉ The Coach House, Winterfold, Barhatch Lane, Cranleigh, Surrey GU6 7NH (☎ 01483 271366); 22 Donne Place, London SW3 2NH (☎ 020 7589 9856, fax 020 7589 2144, e-mail anthonytownsend@dsl.pipex.com)

TOWNSEND, Christopher James (Chris); s of Michael Townsend, of Cheltenham, and Gillian Townsend, *née* Wickson; *b* 1 December 1972, Wokingham; *Educ* Dean Close Sch, Brasenose Coll Oxford (BA); *m* 21 Oct 2000, Melanie, *née* Teige; 1 s (David b 3 Sept 2001), 1 da (Lydia b 1 Dec 2003); *Career* housemaster Dean Close, housemaster and head of boarding Stowe Sch until 2010, dep head Felsted Sch 2010–15, head Felsted Sch 2015–; memb HMC 2015; *Recreations* cricket, reading, running; *Clubs* East India, MCC; *Style*— Chris Townsend, Esq; ✉ Felsted School, Felsted, Essex CM6 3LL

TOWNSEND, Brig Ian Glen; CBE (2005); s of Kenneth Townsend, of Leamington Spa, Warks, and Irene Dorothy, *née* Singleton; *b* 7 February 1941; *Educ* Dulwich Coll, RMA Sandhurst, Staff Coll; *m* 1, 19 Sept 1964 (m dis 1988), Loraine Jean, da of William A H Birnie (d 1978), of USA; 2 da (Lucie, Helen (twins) b 1966); *m* 2, 17 Feb 1989, Susan Natalie, da of Cdr Frank A L Heron-Watson (d 1990), of Scotland; 2 step s (Anthony b 1965, Ben b 1969); *Career* regtl and staff appts in UK, Germany, NI, Belgium 1961–91 incl: mil asst to UK Mil Rep NATO HQ 1979–81, CO 27 Field Regt RA 1981–83, Col operational requirements MOD 1983–86, Cdr artillery 1 Armd Div 1986–88, ACOS (Trg) HQ UKLF 1988–91, ret 1991; dir mktg and sales VSEL 1991–93, md Townsend Associates 1993–96, DG Royal Br Legion 1996–2006; dir: Legion Enterprise Ltd 1999–2001, 7 Armd Div Meml Ltd 2000–08, Nat Meml Arboretum 2003–08, NMA Enterprise 2003–07; chm Confedn Serv and Ex-Service Orgns 2002–03, chm World Veterans Fedn Europe 2002–10, vice-pres World Veterans' Fedn 2006–, tstee Armed Forces Meml Tst 2003–14; dir Tidworth Coll 1999–2001, govr Salisbury Coll 2001–03; World Veterans' Fedn Gold Medal 2016; Freeman City of London 1999; CCMI (FIMgt 1988), FRSA 2006; *Recreations* gardening, golf, painting, music, wine; *Clubs* Army and Navy; *Style*— Brig Ian Townsend, CBE; ✉ Airleywight, Stapleford, Wiltshire SP3 4LJ

TOWNSEND, Jonathan Richard Arthur; s of David Charles Humphrey Townsend (d 1997), and Honor Stobart, *née* Hancock (d 1967); *b* 30 November 1942; *Educ* Winchester, CCC Oxford (BA); *m* Sarah Elizabeth, da of Cdr Gordon Chalmers Fortin, RN, of Lavenham, Suffolk; 2 da (Honor Sarah b 2 Sept 1968, Louise Rosamond b 12 March 1971); *Career* prodn mangr DRG plc 1961–62 and 1965–68; ptnr: Laing and Cruickshank 1972–73 (joined 1968), de Zoete and Bevan 1973–86; md Barclays de Zoete Securities 1986–90, dir i/c business devpt Kleinwort Benson 1990–93, vice-chm ABN AMRO Hoare Govett Corporate Finance Ltd 1993–98, ind conslt 1998–2003, dir John East and Partners 2004–08, ind conslt 2008–11 and 2012–, chm Beaufont Int 2011–12; FSI; *Recreations* my girls, Italy, opera, shooting, bridge, cricket, horse racing; *Clubs* IZ, Free Foresters, Butterflies, Durham CC, Suffolk CC, Wils CC, Brooks's, MCC, Vincent's (Oxford), IOD; *Style*— Jonathan Townsend, Esq; ✉ The Old Post Office, 6 High Street, Lavenham, Suffolk CO10 9PR (☎ 01449 736953, e-mail jrat@btopenworld.com)

TOWNSEND, Lady Juliet Margaret; LVO (1981); *née* Smith; da of 2 Earl of Birkenhead, TD (d 1975); *b* 9 September 1941; *Educ* Westonbirt Sch, Somerville Coll Oxford; *m* 1970, John Richard Townsend, s of Lt-Col Clarence Henry Southgate Townsend, OBE, MC, TD, MRCVS (d 1953); 3 da; *Career* lady-in-waiting to HRH The Princess Margaret, Countess of Snowdon 1965–71, extra lady-in-waiting 1971–2002; High Sheriff of Northamptonshire 1991–92, HM Lord-Lt Northamptonshire 1998–2014 (DL 1990); *Style*— The Lady Juliet Townsend, LVO; ✉ Newbottle Manor, Banbury, Oxfordshire OX17 3DD (☎ 01295 811295)

TOWNSEND, Michael; s of Edgar Maurice Townsend (d 1985), and Agnes, *née* Pearson (d 1988); *b* 10 June 1941; *Educ* Harrogate GS, Sidney Sussex Coll Cambridge (minor scholar, MA); *m* 1966, Gillian Maryska, da of Wilfred Dorrien Wickson (d 1992); 3 s (Alistair John b 3 Sept 1970, Christopher James b 1 Dec 1972, Jonathan Mark b 13 Nov 1975); *Career* articled clerk Blackburns Robson Coates CAs (now Robson Rhodes) Leeds 1963–69, various posts rising to fin controller Sperry Gyroscope Ltd Bracknell 1969–75, fin controller Plessey Radar Ltd 1975–79, gp fin controller Smiths Industries plc 1988–90 (fin controller Smiths Industries Aerospace Defence Systems 1979–88); Rolls-Royce plc: gp fin controller 1990–91, fin dir 1991–99; non-exec chm Spirax-Sarco Engineering plc 2005–09 (non-exec dir 1997–2009); non-exec dir Northern Electric plc 1992–97; sec Irish Setter Assoc England 1995–2001, chm of tstees Kennel Club Charitable Tst 2002–16 (tstee 1998–2014, memb Gen Ctee 2002–16); FCA 1976 (ACA 1966); *Recreations* cricket, all ball games, dogs (especially Irish Setters), canals; *Clubs* Kennel, MCC; *Style*— Michael Townsend, Esq; ✉ Hawthorns, Oakley Road, Cheltenham, Gloucestershire GL52 6NZ (☎ 01242 521872, e-mail townsend@waitrose.com)

TOWNSEND, Peter Sandham; s of William Henry Townsend (d 1960), and Emma May, *née* Keys; *b* 19 November 1948, Grantham, Lincs; *Educ* King's Sch Grantham; *m* 1975, Judith Ann, *née* Hirst; 2 s (Richard b 1977, Andrew b 1980), 1 da (Lucy b 1983); *Career* Duncan & Toplis 1967– 2014 (currently chm), Castlegate Financial Mgmnt 1996– (currently chm), Springfield Park Properties 1996–; formerly regnl cncllr CBI; tstee King's Sch Tst; Freeman City of London; FCA; *Recreations* squash, tennis, gardening; *Clubs* East India; *Style*— Peter Townsend, Esq, FCA; ✉ Castlegate Financial Management Ltd, 8 Castlegate, Grantham, Lincolnshire NG31 6SE (☎ 01476 591022, e-mail petert@casfin.co.uk)

TOWNSEND, Dr Ralph Douglas; s of Harry Douglas Townsend, of Perth, Aust, and Neila Margaret, *née* McPherson; *b* 13 December 1951, Perth, Aust; *Educ* Scotch Coll Aust, Univ of Western Aust (Cwlth scholar, BA), Univ of Kent (MA), Keble Coll Oxford (sr scholar, DPhil); *m* 25 Aug 1973, Cathryn Julie, *née* Arnold; 1 da (Elspeth Mary b 24 March 1983), 1 s (Francis Harry b 12 Dec 1984); *Career* asst master Dover Coll 1975–77, asst master Abingdon Sch 1977–78, warden St Gregory's House Oxford 1978–82, research fell and dean of degrees Lincoln Coll Oxford 1982–85, asst master and head of Eng Eton Coll 1985–89, headmaster Sydney GS 1989–99, headmaster Oundle Sch 1999–2005, headmaster Winchester Coll 2005–16; sr advsr China Educn Research Fndn; author of books and articles on church history, Christian spirituality and education, gen ed Studies in Early Australian History and Letters 1995–99, ed World Leading Sch Assoc Record; govr of numerous ind schs, dir of 2 Acad Bds; Hon Liveryman Grocers' Co 2005; Knight Equestrian Order of the Holy Sepulchre of Jerusalem 2011; *Recreations* music, reading, fell walking; *Clubs* Savile; *Style*— Dr Ralph Townsend; ✉ The Savile Club, 69 Brook Street, London W1K 4ER (e-mail wiccamical@msn.com)

TOWNSHEND, Prof Alan; s of Dr Stanley Charles Townshend (d 2000), of Ammanford, Carms, and Betsy, *née* Roberts (d 2001); *b* 20 June 1939, Clydach, Swansea; *Educ* Pontadawe GS, Univ of Birmingham (BSc, PhD, DSc), Univ of Hull (BA); *m* 11 Aug 1962, Enid, da of Harold Horton (d 1990), of South Kirkby, W Yorks; 3 s (Robert Michael b 1966, Peter Charles b 1967, Gareth Richard b 1970); *Career* lectr in chemistry Univ of Birmingham 1964–80; Univ of Hull: sr lectr then reader in analytical chemistry 1980–84, prof 1984–2004, dean Sch of Chemistry 1989–92 and 1997, dir Inst for Chemistry in Industry 1993–96 and 1999–2004, dep dean Faculty of Sci and the Environment 1997–2000, dep dean Faculty of Sci 2000–01, emeritus prof 2004–; ed Analytica Chimica Acta 1981–2006, ed-in-chief Analytical Chemistry Research 2014–; Royal Soc of Chemistry

Silver medal 1975 (Gold medal 1991), AnalaR Gold medal 1987, Geoff Wilson medal Deakin Univ Aust 2003; Theophilus Redwood lectr 1988; memb Analytical Div Ctee Int Union of Pure and Applied Chemistry 1991–95, pres Analytical Div Royal Soc of Chemistry 1996–98; CChem, FRSC 1978; *Books* Inorganic Reaction Chemistry: Systematic Chemical Separation (1980), Inorganic Reaction Chemistry: Reactions of the Elements and their Compounds Part A: Alkali Metals to Nitrogen (1981), Inorganic Reaction Chemistry: Reactions of the Elements and their Compounds Part B: Osmium to Zirconium (1981), Dictionary of Analytical Reagents (1993), Flame Chemiluminescence Analysis by Molecular Emission Cavity Detection (1994), Encyclopedia of Analytical Science (10 vols, ed-in-chief, 1995, 2 edn 2004), Analytica Chimica Acta (sr ed until 2009), Flow Analysis with Spectrophotometric and Luminometric Detection (2012); *Recreations* food and wine, archaeology, gardening; *Style*— Prof Alan Townshend; ✉ Department of Chemistry, University of Hull, Hull HU6 7RX (✆ 01482 465418, fax 01482 470225)

TOWNSHEND, Hon Charlotte Anne; DL (Dorset 1999); *née* Monckton; da of 9 Viscount Galway (d 1971), and Lady Teresa Agnew, *née* Fox-Strangways (d 1989); *b* 16 April 1955, London; *m* 1, 1983 (m dis 1987), Guy Martin James Morrison; 1 s (Simon George Strangways b 1984); m 2, 1995, James Reginald Townshend; 1 da (Melissa Susan Charlotte b 1996); *Career* High Sheriff Dorset 2005–06; *Style*— The Hon Mrs Townshend; ✉ Melbury House, Melbury Sampford, Dorchester, Dorset DT2 0LF (✆ 01935 83231, fax 01935 83959, e-mail melbury.house@ilchester-estates.co.uk)

TOWNSHEND, Peter Dennis Blandford (Pete); s of Cliff Townshend; *b* 19 May 1945; *Educ* Acton Co GS, Ealing Art Coll; *m* 1968 (m dis 2009), Karen Astley; 1s, 2 da; *Career* musician; memb: The Detours 1961–63, The High Numbers (released single I'm The Face 1964) 1963–64, The Who 1964–89, solo 1979–; albums with The Who: My Generation (1965, reached UK no 5), A Quick one (1966, UK no 4), The Who Sell Out (1968, UK no 13), Tommy (1969, UK no 2, Broadway musical 1993, winner 5 Tony awards, revived London 1996), Live At Leeds (live, 1970, UK no 3), Who's Next (1971, UK no 1), Meaty Beaty Big And Bouncy (compilation, 1971, UK no 9), Quadrophenia (1973, UK no 2), Odds And Sods (compilation, 1974, UK no 10), Tommy (soundtrack, 1975, UK no 14), The Who By Numbers (1975, UK no 7), The Story Of The Who (compilation, 1976, UK no 2), Who Are You? (1978, UK no 6), The Kids Are Alright (compilation, 1979, UK no 26), Quadrophenia (soundtrack, 1979, UK no 23), Face Dances (1981, UK no 2), It's Hard (1982, UK no 11), Who's Last (1984, UK no 48), Who's Better, Who's Best (1988, UK no 10), Joined Together (1990), 30 Years of Maximum R&B (1994); solo albums: Who Came First (1972, UK no 30), Rough Mix (with Ronnie Lane, 1977, UK no 44), Empty Glass (1980, UK no 11), All The Best Cowboys Have Chinese Eyes (1982, UK no 32), Scoop (1983), White City (1985, UK no 70), Scoop II (1987), The Iron Man (1989, London musical at Young Vic 1993), Psychoderelict (1993), Best of Pete Townshend (1996); appearances at festivals incl: National Jazz and Blues Festival 1965, 1966 and 1969, Monterey Pop Festival 1967, Rock at the Oval 1972, Farewell Tour 1982–83, Live Aid Wembley 1985, Who Reunion Tour 1989; films incl: Tommy, Quadrophenia, The Kids Are Alright; publisher; owner Eel Pie Recording Ltd 1972–; fndr: Eel Pie (bookshops and publishing) 1972–83, Meher Baba Oceanic (UK archival library) 1976–81; ed Faber & Faber 1983–; *Awards* Ivor Novello Award for Contribution to Br Music 1982, Br Phonographic Industry Award 1983, BRIT Lifetime Achievement Award 1983, BRIT Award for Contribution to Br Music 1988, Living Legend Award Int Rock Awards 1991, Tony Award for Tommy score 1993, Grammy Award for Tommy 1993, Dora Mavor Moore Award for Tommy in Toronto 1994, Olivier Award for Tommy in London 1997, Q Award for Lifetime Achievement 1997, Ivor Novello Lifetime Achievement Award 2001, BMI President's Award 2002, PRS & BMI Awards for CSI, CSI Miami and CSI NY, Silver Clef 30th Anniversary Award for The Who 2005, VH1 Rock Honors 2008, Kennedy Center Honor 2008, Classic Rock Award 2011, TEC Fndn Les Paul Award 2012; hon doctorate Univ of West London 2010; *Books* Horses Neck (1985), Who I Am (2012); *Recreations* sailing; *Style*— Pete Townshend, Esq; ✉ Trinifold Management, 12 Oval Road, Camden, London NW1 7DH (website www.thewho.com)

TOWNSLEY, Barry Stephen; CBE (2004); s of Dr William Townsley; *b* 14 October 1946; *Educ* Hasmonean GS; *m* 3 Nov 1975, Hon Laura Helen, da of Baron Wolfson of Marylebone (Life Peer); 3 da (Alexandra Jane Wolfson b 3 May 1977, Georgina Kate Wolfson b 20 May 1979, Isabella Edith Wolfson b 22 June 1994), 1 s (Charles Ralph Wolfson b 2 June 1984); *Career* W Greenwell & Co 1964–69; dir Astaire & Co 1969–76; fndr and sr ptnr Townsley & Co 1976–99, chm Insinger Townsley 1999–2004, dir Bank Insinger de Beaufort plc 1999–2004, chm Hobart Capital Markets LLP; pres Weizmann Inst Fndn, fndr memb and princ sponsor Stockley Acad; vice-chm and tstee Serpentine Gallery London, patron Trinity Hospice 2009– (tstee 2006–09), chm of patrons Sheffield Inst Fndn for Motor Neurone Disease 2006–13, dir William J Clinton Fndn Insamlingsstiftelse 2010–; tstee Alzheimer Research UK; *Recreations* contemporary art, golf; *Style*— Barry Townsley, Esq, CBE; ✉ Hobart Capital Markets LLP, 8–10 Grosvenor Gardens, London SW1W 0DH (e-mail barry.townsley@hobartcapital.com)

TOY, Carol Margaret (Maggie); da of Dr Mark Toy, and Patricia Beryl Toy; *Educ* Marple Hall Co HS Cheshire, Portsmouth Poly (BA, Postgrad Dip); partner Tim Forster; 2 s (Hector Cavanagh Forster-Toy b 8 Oct 2002, Arthur Cavanagh Forster-Toy b 7 Dec 2004); *Career* architectural asst Moxham Clark Partnership Manchester 1982, architectural asst Derek Arend Associates London 1986–87; asst Academy Editions 1988; Academy Gp Ltd: house ed Architectural Design Magazine 1989–92 (ed 1993–2002), commissioning and managing ed 1993–97, sr publishing ed of Architecture 1997–2003; dir and fndr The Toy Factory 2007–; delivered numerous lectures and chaired architecture debates; exhibitions curated incl: Theory and Experimentation 1991, Architecture on the Horizon 1996; co-fndr Magpip; *Publications* Deconstruction: A Pocket Guide (jtly, 1990), Free Spirit in Architecture (jtly, 1992), Los Angeles (1994), Educating Architects (jt ed, 1995), Building Sights (jt ed, 1995), Practically Minimal (2000), The Architect (2001); author of articles and reviews in architecture journals; *Recreations* designing and sewing wedding, bridesmaid and ball dresses, opera, music, theatre, cinema, cycling, swimming; *Style*— Ms Maggie Toy; ✉ 60 Torbay Road, London NW6 7DZ (mobile 07803 906146, e-mail maggietoy@tiscali.co.uk); The Toy Factory (website www.thetoyfactory.org.uk)

TOYE, Bryan Edward; JP; s of Herbert Graham Donovan Toye (d 1969), and Marion Alberta, *née* Montignani (d 1999); *b* 17 March 1938; *Educ* St Andrews, Eastbourne, Stowe; *m* 8 Oct 1982, Fiona Ann, da of Gordon Henry James Hogg, of Wellington, NZ; 3 s (Charles Edward Graham b 16 Dec 1983, Frederick Gordon Bryan b 6 Jan 1988, Christopher James Guy b 15 Sept 1997), 1 da (Elisabeth Fiona Ann b 27 July 1985); *Career* joined Toye & Co 1956, dir Toye Kenning & Spencer 1962–, dir Toye & Co 1966, chm Toye and Co plc and 23 assoc subsid cos 1969–, dep chm Futurama Sign Gp Ltd 1992–96; memb Cncl DMA 2003–09, memb Cncl ADS 2009–10, memb ADS Defence Sector Bd 2010–, vice-chm ADS Commercial Legal Gp 2009–, memb ADS Small Co Ctee 2010–; chm Clothing Interest Gp (CLING) 2009–; memb Cncl NCPCC London 1966–69; chm Greater London Playing Fields Assoc 1988–90, memb Cncl London Playing Fields Soc 1990–92; memb Ctee King George's Fund for Sailor's Policy and Resources 1990–92; tstee: Queen Elizabeth Scholarship Tst (also founder memb) 1990–96, NED Trehaven Tst Ltd 1990–97, Britain-Australia Bicentennial Tst until 2007, Black Country Museum (London Gp) 1991–97, British Red Cross (London Branch, dep chm then vice-pres); memb stewards enclosure Henley Royal Regatta 1968–, assoc memb Leander Club 1968–, memb Wasps Rugby Club 1938– (vice-pres 1969–, chm Exec Ctee 1995–97), memb Wentworth Golf Club 1970–84; govr (and dep chm then vice-pres): King Edward's Sch Witley 1988–93, Bridewell Royal Hosp 1989–96, Christ's Hosp 1989–96, City of London Freemen's Sch 1993–96; hon memb Ct of Assts Hon Artillery Co 1983–96, Hon Col 55 Ordnance Co ROAC (V) 1988–93, Hon Col 124 Havering Petroleum Sqdn (V) RLC 1994–2000; Hon Ordnance Offr Tower of London 1994–2008; memb Territorial Aux & Vol Reserve Assoc for Greater London 1992–99, memb City of London Territorial Aux & Vol Reserve Assoc 1992–99; NED HR (Navy) 1999–2005; memb: City of London Royal Soc of St George 1981–, Ct RCA 1983–86, Huguenot Soc 1985–, Ctee Old Stoic Soc 1985–92, Advsy Bd House of Windsor Collection Ltd 1994–95, memb Nat Huguenot Centre Appeal Advsy Bd 2012–; pres Royal Warrant Holders Assoc 1991–92 (memb Cncl 1982–, Hon Auditor 1998–); memb Lloyd's 1985–91; Alderman The Ward of Lime St 1983–97, pres City Livery Club 1988–89, life memb RAC 1968–; memb Ct of Assts: Worshipful Co of Gold & Silver Wyre Drawers (Master 1984), Worshipful Co of Broderers (Master 1996–97), Guild of Freemen of the City of London 1981 (memb Ct 1990–97); Prime Warden Worshipful Co of Goldsmiths 2004–05 (Liveryman 1985, Warden 2001–); memb Chartered Inst of Purchasing and Supply 1974–; FInstD 1966, FIMgt 1983, FRSA 1985; OStJ 1980; *Recreations* rugby, cricket, squash, shooting, swimming, tennis, gardening, classical music, entertaining; *Clubs* Leander, RAC, Middx Co RFC, Wasps RFC (tstee and vice-pres, chm Exec Ctee 1992–93), British-American Armed Forces Dining, MCC, Broadway Cricket (vice-pres); *Style*— Bryan Toye, Esq, JP; ✉ Toye & Co plc, Regalia House, Newtown Road, Bedworth, Warwickshire CV12 8QR (✆ 024 7684 8800, fax 024 7664 3018, e-mail bryan.toye@toye.com, website www.toye.com)

TOYE, Prof John Francis Joseph; s of John Redmond Toye (d 1997), and Adele, *née* Francis (d 1972); *b* 7 October 1942; *Educ* Christ's Coll Finchley, Jesus Coll Cambridge (MA), Harvard Univ, SOAS Univ of London (MSc, PhD); *m* 18 March 1967, Janet, da of late Richard Henry Reason, of Harrow, London; 1 s (Richard b 1973), 1 da (Eleanor b 1970); *Career* asst princ HM Treasy 1965–68, res fell SOAS London 1970–72, fell (later tutor) Wolfson Coll Cambridge 1972–80 (asst dir of devpt studies 1977–80); dir: Commodities Research Unit Ltd 1980–82, Centre for Devpt Studies UC Swansea 1982–87, Inst of Devpt Studies Univ of Sussex (dir and professorial fell) 1987–97, UN Conf on Trade and Devpt Geneva 1998–2000; visiting prof Univ of Oxford 2000–03, chair Advsy Cncl Oxford Dept of Int Devpt 2010–; memb: Wandsworth Community Rels Cncl 1968–72, Cambridge Cncl of Community Rels 1972–80, W Glamorgan Equal Opportunities Gp 1983–87; pres Devpt Studies Assoc of GB and I 1994–96; *Books* Taxation and Economic Development (1978), Trade and Poor Countries (1979), Public Expenditure and Indian Development Policy (1981), Dilemmas of Development (1987), Does Aid Work in India? (1990), Aid and Power (1991), Keynes on Population (2000), The UN and Global Political Economy (2004), UNCTAD at 50: A Short History (2014); *Recreations* music, walking, theatre; *Style*— Prof John Toye; ✉ 31 Riverside Road, Oxford OX2 0HT

TOYNBEE, Polly; da of Philip Toynbee (d 1981), and Anne Barbara Denise, *née* Powell (d 2004); *b* 27 December 1946; *Educ* Badminton Sch Bristol, Holland Park Comprehensive, St Anne's Coll Oxford (John Gamble scholar); *m* 28 Dec 1970, Peter George James Jenkins (d 1992), s of Kenneth E Jenkins, of Norfolk; 2 da (Millicent (Milly) b 5 Dec 1971, Flora b 17 Dec 1975), 1 s (Nathaniel b 10 Jan 1985), 1 step da (Amy b 29 Oct 1964); *Career* journalist; reporter The Observer 1968–71, ed The Washington Monthly USA 1971–72, feature writer The Observer 1972–77, columnist The Guardian 1977–88, social affrs ed BBC 1988–95, assoc ed and columnist The Independent 1995–97, political and social commentator The Guardian 1997–; dir Political Quarterly; pres Social Policy Assoc 2005–08, vice-pres Br Humanist Assoc 2012– (pres 2008–12); Catherine Pakenham Award for Journalism 1975, Columnist of the Year British Press Awards 1986 and 1997, Writer of the Year (Consumer Mags) PPA Awards 1997, George Orwell Prize 1997, Columnist of the Year Nat Press Awards 2006; memb NUJ; Parly candidate (SDP) Lewisham E 1983–; chair Brighton Dome and Festival 2006–; *Books* Leftovers (1966), A Working Life (1972), Hospital (1979), The Way We Live Now (1981), Lost Children (1985), Did Things Get Better? (with David Walker, 2001), Hard Work: Life in Low Pay Britain (2003), Better of Worse? Has Labour Delivered? (with David Walker, 2005), Unjust Rewards (with David Walker, 2008), The Verdict – Did Labour Change Britain? (with David Walker, 2010), Dogma and Disarray – Cameron at Half-Time (with Davd Walker, 2012), Cameron's Coup – How the Tories Took Britain to the Brink (with David Walker, 2015); *Recreations* children, grandchildren; *Style*— Ms Polly Toynbee; ✉ The Guardian, Kings Place, 90 York Way, London N1 9GU (✆ 020 3353 2000)

TOYNBEE, Simon Victor; yst s of Ralph Victor Toynbee (d 1970), and Bridget, *née* Monins (d 2005); *b* 30 January 1944; *Educ* Winchester; *m* 12 Aug 1967, Antoinette Mary (d 2003), da of John Walter Devonshire (d 2006); 3 da (Georgina b 1969, Elizabeth (Mrs Anthony Lang) b 1971, Susannah b 1980); *Career* 2 Lt The RB 1963–65; Jessel Toynbee and Co Ltd 1966–72, Singer and Friedlander Ltd 1973–82 (dir Investment Dept 1977–82), Henderson Administration Ltd 1982–90 (dir 1986–90), investment dir Mercury Fund Managers Ltd 1990–92, investment mangr PPP 1992–94, sr investment mangr Majedie Investments plc 1995–99; dir Majedie Investment Trust Mgmnt Ltd 1995–99, exec chm Progressive Value Mgmnt Ltd 1999–2007, dir Progressive Asset Mgmnt Ltd 1999–, md Progressive European Markets 2013–; memb Cncl Winchester Coll Soc; *Recreations* gardening, golf, walking; *Clubs* The Rifles, MCC, Boodle's, Rye Golf; *Style*— S V Toynbee, Esq; ✉ Old Tong Farm, Brenchley, Kent TN12 7HT (✆ 01892 723552); Progressive Asset Management Ltd, 145–157 St John Street, London EC1V 4RU (✆ 020 7566 5551)

TOYNE SEWELL, Maj-Gen Timothy Patrick; DL (Greater London); s of Brig Edgar Patrick Sewell, CBE (d 1956), and Elizabeth Cecily Mease, *née* Toyne, MBE; *b* 7 July 1941; *Educ* Bedford Sch, RMA Sandhurst; *m* 7 Aug 1965, Jennifer, *née* Lunt; 1 s (Patrick b 1967), 1 da (Melanie b 1969); *Career* cmmnd KOSB 1961; served: Aden, Malaysia, BAOR, NI; Staff Coll 1973, CO 1 KOSB 1981–83, COS HQ British Forces Falkland Island 1983–84, Cdr 19 Inf Bde 1985–87, RCDS 1988, Cdr BMATT Zimbabwe 1989–91, Cmdt RMA Sandhurst 1991–94, head Recruiting Implementation Team 1994–95; dir Goodenough Coll 1995–2006, chair Int Bd United World Colls 2006–13; non-exec Catalyst Investment Gp 2007–12; govr Haileybury Sch 1994–2008, govr Lambrook Haileybury Sch 2003–08 (chm 2003–08), memb Cncl Queen Mary & Westfield Coll London, memb Bd UWC Dilijan 2013–, chm Bd Seeb Sch Oman 2013–, memb Bd Trichord Abrahamic Fndn Poland 2014–; tstee: Bill Marshall Tst, Med Coll of St Bartholomew's Hosp Tst 1996–2005; Col KOSB 1996–2001; pres Army Tennis & Rackets Assoc 1994–2001; chm: Benjamin Britten Int Violin Competition 2003–10, Kyiv Festival 2003–10; Freeman City of London 2006; *Recreations* music, tennis, golf, fishing; *Clubs* Royal Over-Seas League (memb Cncl 2002–09); *Style*— Maj-Gen T P Toyne Sewell, DL

TOZZI, Keith; s of Edward Thomas Tozzi (d 1995), and Winifred, *née* Killick (d 2005); *b* 23 February 1949; *Educ* Dartford GS, City Univ (BSc), Univ of Kent (MA), Harvard Business Sch (ISMP); *m* (m dis); 1 da (Sarah b 24 Aug 1975), 2 s (Matthew b 23 Nov 1977, Alexander b 7 Sept 1998); m 2, 14 Dec 2013, Fiona Ann Begley; 1 da; *Career* div dir Southern Water 1988–92, gp tech dir Southern Water plc 1992–96, chief exec British Standards Institution 1996–2000, gp chief exec Swan Gp plc 2000–03, non-exec dir Legal & General UK Select Investment Tst plc 2000–03, non-exec chm RSVP.com 2000–, non-exec dir Seal Analytical Ltd 2004–08, non-exec chm Inspicio plc 2005–08, chm Concateno plc 2006–10, chm Kane Insurance Gp 2011–14, non-exec dir Ingemino Ltd 2011–14, dir The Body Detectives 2014–; chm: National Joint Utilities Gp 1993–96, IOD (Sussex) 1995–97; Liveryman Worshipful Co of Water Conservators; FICE 1975, FIWEM 1976, CIMgt

T

1979, FRSA 2002; *Recreations* classic cars, gardening; *Style*— Keith Tozzi, Esq; ✉ The Top House, Chalfont Heights, Gerrards Cross, Buckinghamshire SL9 9TD (☎ 01753 889497, e-mail keithtozzi@aol.com)

TOZZI, Nigel Kenneth; QC (2001); s of Ronald Kenneth Tozzi (d 2001), and Doreen Elsie Florence, *née* Baddams (d 2002); *b* 31 August 1957; *Educ* Hitchin Boys' GS, Univ of Exeter (LLB), Cncl of Legal Educ; *m* 7 May 1983, Sara Louise Clare, da of Derek Charles Cornish; 2 s (Adam Thomas Edward b 15 Feb 1987, Matthew Charles William b 4 Oct 1990), 1 da (Alice Kathleen Clare b 24 Oct 1988); *Career* called to the Bar Gray's Inn 1980 (Holt scholar); memb: Commercial Bar Assoc, Professional Negligence Bar Assoc, Bar Insurance Law Assoc, London Common Law and Bar Assoc, Justice; *Recreations* playing hockey, watching cricket, theatre, walking my dogs; *Clubs* Sevenoaks Hockey, MCC; *Style*— Nigel Tozzi, Esq, QC; ✉ 4 Pump Court, Temple, London EC4Y 7AN (☎ 020 7842 5555, fax 020 7583 2036, e-mail ntozzi@4pumpcourt.com)

TRACE, Anthony John; QC (1998); s of Commander Peter Trace, RD (and bar), RNR (d 1981), and Anne, *née* Allison-Beer (d 2010); *b* 23 October 1958; *Educ* Uppingham, Magdalene Coll Cambridge (MA, Bundy Scholarship, Master's Reading Prize); *m* 1986, Caroline Tessa, da of His Hon Anthony Durrant; 4 c (Charlotte, Oliver (twins) b 13 May 1988, Hugo b 18 April 1991, Rupert b 27 July 1993); *Career* called to the Bar Lincoln's Inn 1981 (bencher 2006), winner Crowther Advocacy Shield 1981, jt winner Observer Mace Debating competition 1981; memb: Chancery Bar Assoc 1982– (hon sec 1997–2001, vice-chm 2001–04), COMBAR 1997–, ACTAPS 1997–, Insolvency Lawyers Assoc 1997–, R3 1997–, Commercial Fraud Lawyers Assoc 2010–, Restructuring and Insolvency Specialists Assoc 2015–; Silk of the Year (Commercial Litigation) Legal 500 UK Awards 2013, Banking Barrister of the Year UK Finance Monthly Awards 2016, Commercial Litigation Barrister of the Year England Global Law Experts Awards 2016; fndr memb: Campaign for Real Gin 1978–, Friends of Turkey 2006, CRAFT Salcombe 2013; memb: St Luke's (Kew) Parochial Church Cncl 1987–90 and 1996–97, St Luke's House Ctee 1988–89, Queen's Sch (Kew) PTA 1996–97, Grand Order Soc for the Protection of the English Language 2014–; tstee Uppingham Sch 1999–2014, churchwarden St Helen's Church Saddington 2009–; Freeman City of London, Liveryman Worshipful Co of Musicians; *Publications* Butterworths European Law Service Company Law (contrib, 1992), dep managing ed Receivers, Administrators and Liquidators Quarterly 1993–2002, Butterworths Practical Insolvency (contrib, 1999); *Recreations* stalking, shooting, fishing, the Turf, music, messing about in boats, socialising with friends; *Clubs* Pitt (Cambridge), Athenaeum, Garrick, Beefsteak; *Style*— Anthony Trace, Esq, QC; ✉ Maitland Chambers, 7 Stone Buildings, Lincoln's Inn, London WC2A 3SZ (☎ 020 7406 1200, fax 020 7406 1300, e-mail clerks@maitlandchambers.com)

TRACEY, Craig Paul; MP; s of Edward Tracey, and Joyce, *née* Alderson; *b* 21 August 1974, Durham; *Educ* Framwellgate Moor Comprehensive Sch Durham; *m* 25 Sept 2014, Karen, *née* Mercer; *Career* prop and fndr Dunelm Insurance Brokers 1996–2015; MP (Cons) Warks N 2015–; *Style*— Craig Tracey, Esq, MP; ✉ House of Commons, London SW1A 0AA

TRACEY, Eric Frank; s of late Allan Lewis Tracey, of Auckland, NZ, and late Marcelle Frances, *née* Petrie; *b* 3 July 1948; *Educ* Mount Albert GS Auckland, Univ of Auckland (BCom, MCom); *m* 16 May 1970, Patricia, da of late G S (Bill) Gamble, of Hatch End, Middx; *Career* Inland Revenue NZ 1965, lectr Univ of Auckland 1970–72, with Touche Ross (now Deloitte LLP) London 1973–2004 (ptnr 1980–2004), actg finance dir Amey 2002–03, finance dir Wembley plc 2005; ptnr GO Investment Ptnrs LLP 2011–; sr ind dir: Chloride Gp 2005–10, Findel 2009–; non-exec dir: NEC 2008–15, Burtons Hldgs 2009–13; columnist (bi-monthly) Financial Director magazine 2010–12; ind dir Goodenough Coll 2005–14 (vice-chair 2014–), memb Cncl Stroke Assoc 2010–, chair UK Friends of Auckland Univ 2012–, tstee The Christchurch Earthquake Fund UK 2011–14 (vice-chm 2015–); acting bursar King's Coll Cambridge 2004; UK New Zealander of the Year NZ Soc 2014; Master Worshipful Co of World Traders 2003–04; FCA 1975 (ACA 1970), ACIS 1972; *Recreations* walking, rugby, cricket, cooking, creative gardening, opera; *Clubs* MCC, Fonthill Park Cricket; *Style*— Eric Tracey, Esq

TRACEY, Prof Ian Graham; DL (Merseyside 2015); s of William Tracey (d 1994), and Helene Mignon, *née* Harris (d 2001); *b* 27 May 1955; *Educ* Highfield Sch, Trinity Coll of Music, St Katharine's Coll Liverpool (PGCE); *Career* organist and master of the choristers Liverpool Cathedral 1980–2007 (organist titulaire 2008–); prof, fell and organist Liverpool John Moores Univ (formerly Liverpool Poly) 1988–; chorus master Royal Liverpool Philharmonic Soc 1985–, organist City of Liverpool (formerly conslt organist) 1986–; pres Inc Assoc of Organists 2001–03; memb: Jospice Int, Cambridge Soc of Musicians, Int Contemporary Music Awards; Award for Classical Music NW Arts 1994; Hon DMus Univ of Liverpool 2006; FTCL 1976, FRSA 1988, Hon FRCO 2002, FRSCM 2008, FGCM 2009; *Recreations* cookery, fine wines, canal boating, fell walking; *Clubs* Artists' (Liverpool); *Style*— Prof Ian Tracey, DL; ✉ Mornington House, Mornington Terrace, Upper Duke Street, Liverpool L1 9DY (☎ and fax 0151 708 8471, website www.iantracey.com)

TRACEY, Richard Patrick; JP (1977); s of P H (Dick) Tracey (d 1959), and Hilda, *née* Timms (d 1998); *b* 8 February 1943; *Educ* King Edward VI GS Stratford-upon-Avon, Univ of Birmingham (LLB); *m* Katharine R, da of John Gardner (d 1969); 1 s (Simon b 1974), 3 da (Nicola b 1976, Emma b 1980, Polly b 1982); *Career* ldr writer Daily Express 1964–66, presenter of current affrs programmes BBC Radio and TV 1966–78, documentaries BBC 1974–76; dep chm Gtr London Cons Pty 1981–83; MP (Cons) Surbiton 1983–97, Parly under sec of state for Environment and min for Sport 1985–87; memb: Select Ctee on Televising the House of Commons 1988–91, Ctee of Selection 1992–94, Public Accounts Ctee 1994–97; Cons London election coordinator 1989–93, chm London Cons MPs 1990–97; strategic marketing and media conslt 1997–2008, memb Exec Ctee Assoc of Former MPs 2007–, memb London Assembly (Cons) Merton and Wandsworth 2008–16, London Mayor's ambass for river transport 2009–16; vice-chm Special Olympics UK 1989–93, chair ProActive South London Sport England 2006–08, memb Met Police Authy 2008–10, memb and vice-chm London Fire and Emergency Planning Authy 2010–12, chm London Waste and Recycling Bd 2012–16; memb IAM 1993; fell Industry and Parliament Tst 1985; Freeman City of London 1984, memb Co of Watermen and Lightermen; *Books* The World of Motor Sport (with R Hudson-Evans), Hickstead - The First Twelve Years (with M Clayton); *Recreations* boating, riding, wildlife conservation; *Style*— Richard Tracey, JP; ☎ 07884 366739, e-mail rdicktracey@msn.com

TRAFFORD, Hon Mark Russell; QC (2015); s of The Lord Trafford of Falmer (d 1989), and Helen, Lady Trafford (*née* Chalk); *m* 2 Sept 1995, Brigitte Anne, *née* Howe; 2 da (Jessica b 15 Feb 1990, Katherine b 1 March 1999 (twin)), 2 s (Luc b 1 March 1999 (twin), Joseph b 14 Aug 2000); *Career* called to the Bar Lincoln's Inn (Megarry scholar) 1992; *Style*— The Hon Mark Trafford, QC; ✉ 23 Essex Street, London WC2R 3AA

TRAHAR, Anthony John; s of Thomas Walter Trahar, and Thelma, *née* Ashmead-Bartlett; *b* 1 June 1949; *Educ* St John's Coll Johannesburg, Univ of the Witwatersrand (BCom); *m* Patricia Jane; 1 s (Andrew), 1 da (Frances); *Career* CA (SA) 1973; Anglo American Corp of SA Ltd: mgmnt trainee 1974, PA to chm 1976–77; exec chm Mondi Paper Co 1989–2002, exec dir Anglo American Corp 1991, chm Mondi Europe 1993–2003, chm Ford South Africa 1996–2000, chm AECI Ltd 1999–2001, chm Anglo Forest Products 1999–2003, chm Anglo Industrial Minerals (Tarmac) 1999–2004, ceo Anglo American plc 2000–07, fndr and chm Bartlett Resources 2007–; mining conslt Barclays Capital 2007–13, advsr Macquarie Capital 2013–; PhD (hc) Univ of Pretoria; Knight Cdr Gold Cross with Star (Austria); *Recreations* trout fishing, shooting, classic cars, music; *Clubs* RAC; *Style*— Tony Trahar, Esq

TRAILL, Sir Alan; GBE (1984), QSO (1990); s of George Traill, and Margaret Eleanor, *née* Matthews; *b* 7 May 1935; *Educ* St Andrew's Sch Eastbourne, Charterhouse, Jesus Coll Cambridge (MA); *m* 1964, Sarah Jane, *née* Hutt; 1 s (Philip); *Career* dir Morice Tozer & Beck 1960–73; chm: Traill Attenborough Ltd 1973–81, Lyon Holdings 1981–86; dir: Lyon Traill Attenborough (Lloyd's Brokers) 1981–86, PWS Holdings 1986–87, Aegis Insurance Brokers 1987–89, Medex Assistance (Europe) plc 1993–98; md: Colburn Traill Ltd 1989–96, Colburn French & Keen Ltd 1994–96; div dir: First City Insurance Brokers 1996–2000, Pathfinder Team Consulting Ltd 1996–; dir Int Disputes Resolution Centre Ltd 1999–2014; dir Monetary Authy Cayman Is 2003–06; currently an Arbitrator & Expert Witness; memb: Lloyd's 1964–89, Ct of Common Cncl City of London 1970–2005, London Ct of Int Arbitration 1981–86; memb Cncl Br Insurance Brokers' Assoc 1978–79 (chm Reinsurance Brokers' Ctee 1978), hon memb ARIAS (UK) 1998–; Alderman Langbourn Ward 1975–2005, Sheriff 1982–83, Lord Mayor of London 1984–85; vice-pres City Arts Tst 2008 (dir 1980–2008), govr Christ's Hosp Fndn 2003– (almoner 1980–2003); vice-pres King Edward's Sch Witley 2003–05, govr St Paul's Cathedral Choir Sch Fndn 1987–95, chm govr Yehudi Menhuin Sch 2000–11 (vice pres 2011–), patron Lord Mayor Treloar Coll 2002–; tstee RSC 1982–2004, memb Advsy Bd and Educn Ctee London Symphony Orchestra 1996–, tstee Ann Driver Tst 1998–2014; chllr City Univ 1984–85 (Hon DMus 1984); chm: UK-NZ 1990 Ctee, Link Fndn; Livery memb Worshipful Co of Cutlers (Master 1979–80), memb Ct Worshipful Co of Musicians (Master 1999–2000); *Recreations* DIY, music and opera, assisting education; *Style*— Sir Alan Traill, GBE, QSO; ✉ Wheelers Farm, Thursley, Surrey GU8 6QE (☎ 01252 703271, mobile 07714 328204, e-mail atraill.granary@btinternet.com)

TRAINOR, Prof Sir Richard Hughes; KBE (2010); s of late William Richard Trainor, and Sarah Frances, *née* Hughes; *b* 31 December 1948; *Educ* Calvert Hall HS, Brown Univ (BA), Princeton Univ (MA), Merton Coll Oxford (MA), Nuffield Coll Oxford (DPhil); *m* 28 June 1980, Dr Marguerite Wright Dupree, da of Prof A Hunter Dupree; 1 s (Richard Hunter b 1987), 1 da (Marguerite Sarah b 1992); *Career* jr research fell Wolfson Coll Oxford 1977–79, lectr Balliol Coll Oxford 1978–79; Univ of Glasgow: lectr in economic history 1979–89, sr lectr in economic and social history 1989–95, prof of social history 1995–2000, dir Design and Implementation of Software in History Project 1985–89, co-dir Computers in Teaching Initiative Centre for History, Archaeology and Art History 1989–99, dean Faculty of Social Sciences 1992–96, vice-princ 1996–2000; vice-chllr and prof of social history Univ of Greenwich 2000–04, princ and prof of social history KCL 2004–14, rector Exeter Coll Oxford 2014–; pres: Glasgow and West of Scotland Branch Historical Assoc 1991–93, Universities UK 2007–09 (memb Bd 2002–05 and 2009–10, treas 2006–07, co-chair UK/US Study Gp 2008–09); memb: Jt Information Systems Ctee 2001–05, HEFCE Quality Assurance, Learning and Teaching Ctee 2003–06, London Higher Steering Ctee Bd 2003–06, US/UK Fulbright Cmmn 2003–09 (patron 2010–), HE Acad Bd 2004–07, Leadership, Governance and Mgmnt Ctee HEFCE 2006–07, Cncl AHRC 2006–11, Cncl Univ of Oxford 2015–; convenor: Steering Gp Learning and Teaching Support Network 2000–04, Steering Gp UUK/DfES Review of Student Servs 2002, Steering Gp Nat Teaching Fellowship Scheme 2005–07; chair Advsy Cncl Inst of Historical Research 2004–09, hon sec Econ History Soc 1998–2004 (pres 2013–); chair London Met Network 2002–06, memb Exec Ctee then Membership Ctee The Pilgrims 2004–10; govr: Henley Mgmnt Coll 2003–05, St Paul's Sch 2012–14, Royal Acad of Music 2013–, Museum of London 2014–; Hon DCL Univ of Kent 2009, Hon DHL Rosalind Franklin Univ of Medicine and Science 2012, Hon DUniv Univ of Glasgow 2014; hon fell: Trinity Coll of Music 2003, Merton Coll Oxford 2004, Inst of Historical Research 2009; FRHistS 1990, FRSA 1995, FAcSS 2001; *Books* Historians, Computers and Data: Applications in Research and Teaching (ed with E Mawdsley et al, 1991), Towards an International Curriculum for History and Computing (ed with D Spaeth et al, 1992), The Teaching of Historical Computing: An International Framework (ed with D Spaeth et al, 1993), Black Country Elites: The Exercise of Authority in an Industrialised Area 1830–1900 (1993), Urban Governance: Britain and Beyond Since 1750 (ed with R Morris, 2000), University, City and State: The University of Glasgow since 1870 (with M Moss and J F Munro, 2000); also author of numerous articles in books and jls; *Recreations* parenting, observing politics, tennis; *Clubs* Athenaeum; *Style*— Prof Sir Richard Trainor, KBE; ✉ Rector's Office, Exeter College, Oxford OX1 3DP (☎ 01865 279605, fax 01865 279645)

TRANTER, Jane; da of Donald Tranter, and Joan, *née* Gay; *b* 17 March 1963; *Educ* Kingswood Sch Bath, King's Coll London (BA English Lit); *m* David Attwood; *Career* asst floor mangr BBC 1986–88, script ed Casualty BBC Drama Dept 1988, script ed BBC Films Dept 1989–92 (TV credits incl award-winning Alive and Kicking, The Last Romantics, The Kremlin Farewell and Bad Girl, feature films credits The Hour of the Pig and Sarafina); Carlton TV: commissioning ed Drama 1992–93, head of drama 1993–95; exec prodr Carlton UK Productions 1995–97, re-joined BBC as exec prodr Films and Single Drama 1997–98, series exec prodr BBC 1 Drama Serials and Single Films 1998–2000, controller Drama Commissioning BBC 2000–06, controller BBC Fiction 2006–09, head BBC Worldwide Prodns 2009–, head Adjacent Prodns 2012–; memb Lab Pty; Special Award BAFTA 2009; *Style*— Ms Jane Tranter

TRAPP, Deirdre; *b* Ipswich, Suffolk; *Educ* St Hilda's Coll Oxford; *m* Roger; 3 da; *Career* slr; specialises in EU and UK competition law; ptnr Freshfields Bruckhaus Deringer 1995– (co-head Antitrust, Competition and Trade Gp 2000–06, global client ptnr 2009–12); *Style*— Mrs Deirdre Trapp; ✉ Freshfields Bruckhaus Deringer, 65 Fleet Street, London EC4Y 1HS (e-mail deirdre.trapp@freshfields.com)

TRAVERS, Prof David; QC (2010); s of George Bowes Travers (d 1966), and Gertrude Colbert, *née* Churnside (d 2015); *b* 19 March 1957; *Educ* Spennymoor Secdy Sch, Regents Coll London, KCL (LLB, AKC, LLM), Inns of Court Sch of Law; *m* 13 Oct 1984, Sheila Mary, da of Martin Killoran, CBE, QFSM; 2 da (Rosamond Mary b 11 Oct 1988, Jennifer Claire b 15 April 1991), 1 s (James David b 28 July 1992); *Career* called to the Bar Middle Temple 1981 (Harmsworth scholar), memb Northern Circuit 1982–88 (memb Exec Northern Circuit 1985–87), in practice Midland & Oxford Circuit 1988–, accredited mediator 2000; legal advsr: Professional Conduct Ctee GMC 2002–12, Medical Practitioners Tbnl Service 2012–, Professional Conduct Ctee General Dental Cncl; pt/t lectr Accountancy Tuition Centre Manchester and Liverpool 1982–83, occasional lectr Dept of Mgmnt Scis UMIST 1986–87, occasional libel reader Express newspapers 1987–88, occasional tutor Dept of Biomedical Sci and Biomedical Ethics Univ of Birmingham 1995–96, visiting prof Business Accountability and Responsibility Centre Newport Business Sch 2011–13, visiting prof Univ of S Wales 2013–; lectr at professional conferences; after dinner speaker; exec ed King's Counsel 1979 (ed 1978); Royal Inst sci scholar 1975, memb Delegacy Governing Body KCL 1977–78, sabbatical pres KCL Union of Students 1979–80 (hon life memb 1980), pres Middle Temple Students' Assoc 1980–81; participant Warwick Int Workshop on Corporate Control and Accountability 1991; memb: Hon Soc of the Middle Temple 1978, Bar Cncl 1995–2000, Birmingham Law Soc IT Ctee 1995–97, Law Reform Ctee Bar Cncl 1996–98, Bar Services & IT Ctee Bar Cncl 1996–99, Planning and Environment Bar Assoc, UK Enviromental Law Assoc, Food Law Gp, Int Bar Assoc, Health and Safety Lawyers Assoc; hon fell Soc of Food Hygiene and Technol 2012; *Publications* Planning Law and Practice (jtly, 2013), Planning Enforcement (jtly, 2015); also various articles on regulatory law and corp governance issues; *Recreations* family, language, music, running; *Clubs* Chaîne des Rôtisseurs;

Style— Prof David Travers, QC; ✉ 6 Pump Court, Temple, London EC4Y 7AR (☎ 020 7797 8400, fax 020 7797 8401, e-mail davidtravers@6pumpcourt.co.uk, website www.6pumpcourt.co.uk/barrister/david-travers-qc)

TRAVERS, Harry Anthony; s of Sidney Travers, and Marice, *née* Berger; *b* 7 November 1963, Manchester; *Educ* Manchester Grammar, St Edmund Hall Oxford (open scholar, BCL, MA); *m* 1 Sept 2002 (m dis), Miriam Farbey; 3 s (William Nicholas Louis b 11 Jan 2004, Alexander Nico, Oliver Jackson b 21 April 2014 (twins)); *Career* called to the Bar Middle Temple 1990; admitted slr 1990; specialises in law relating to white collar crime; Berwin Leighton 1987–91, BCL Burton Copeland 1991– (ptnr 1995–); placed in Chambers 100 2013; memb: Fraud Lawyers Assoc, Int Bar Assoc; *Recreations* golf, Manchester United FC, music, jazz; *Style*— Harry Travers, Esq; ✉ BCL Burton Copeland, 51 Lincoln's Inn Fields, London WC2A 3LZ (☎ 020 7430 2277, fax 020 7430 1101, e-mail htravers@bcl.com)

TRAVERSE-HEALY, Kevin Timothy; DL (2001); s of Prof Tim Traverse-Healy, OBE, *qv*, and Joan, *née* Thompson; *b* 30 November 1949, Bishop's Stortford, Herts; *Educ* Xaverian Coll Brighton, Redrice Coll, Lewes Tech Coll, Coll of Law London, Univ of Leicester (MA); *m* 12 Jan 1974, Sarah-Jane (Sally), *née* Magill; 1 da (Alexia Claire b 9 Aug 1979), 1 s (James Timothy Brendan b 16 May 1983); *Career* articled clerk Duchin & Co and Berwin & Co 1969–72; exhibitions offr (later PR exec) British Oxygen Co and PR exec BOC International (Southern Africa) 1972–76, dir Traverse-Healy Ltd 1976–92, fndr md Traverse-Healy & Regester Ltd 1980–87, md Charles Barker Traverse-Healy Ltd 1987–91, chief exec (ops) Charles Barker Ltd 1991–92 (chm 2013–), md Centre for Public Affairs Studies 1992–2005, ind mgmnt conslt 1992–; advsr National Commercial Bank of Saudi Arabia 1995–96; dir e.g. Ltd 1996–98, conslt Communication Skills Europe Ltd 1998–2005; ptnr Traverse-Healy Consult 1996–, ptnr Equal Dentsu Aegis Media 2012–14; strategic conslt COI 2006–12, conslt Miny of Social Affrs Estonia 2015–; assoc trainer Capita Civil Service Learning 2012–; dir Rainbow Rovers Ltd (charity) 1989–98; advsr ACFA 1998–2005 (ed Army Cadet magazine), Lt Col ACF 1998–2012 (ret TA as Maj 2012); chm Astrolabe Communications Ltd 2002–06 and 2012–, memb Vice-Pres's Steering Gp on Communications Strategy European Cmmn 2004–06, memb European Evaluation Soc; vice-patron Atlantic Cncl of the UK 2003–04; visiting prof Univ of Lugano 1998–, contrib course author Univ of Leicester 2012, visiting lectr Govt of Estonia Communication Acad 2014–; lectr and contrib to various PR handbooks; first recipient CERP (Centre European de Relations Publique) medal for contrib to European PR 1985; tstee IPR Benevolent Fund 1995–2000, tstee Transglobe Expedition Tst, memb Inland Waterways Assoc (IWA), live govr RNLI; memb Honours and Awards Ctee Greater London Lieutenancy 2016–; FCIPR (pres 1985), FRSA; *Publications* Strategic Public Relations (contrib, 1985 and 1995), Payback and Return on Marketing Investments (ROMI) in the Public Sector (co-author, 2009), Evaluating the Financial Impact of Public Sector Marketing Communication (co-author, 2010), Convergence – time to embrace communication interdependence (2013), Measuring Both Halves – measurement and evaluation of government communication in the context of channel shift (jtly, 2014), Social media guidance for civil servants (2015), Social License to Operate: Positioning and the Communication Professional (jtly, 2016); *Recreations* communication, canals, countryside; *Clubs* London Flotilla, Club of Venice; *Style*— Kevin Traverse-Healy, Esq, DL; ✉ Traverse-Healy Consult, 51 Cardigan Steet, London SE11 5PF (☎ 07778 021720, e-mail traversehealy@btinternet.com)

TRAVIS, (Ernest Raymond) Anthony; s of Ernest Raymond Travis (d 1988), and Constance Mary, *née* Edwards (d 2015); *b* 18 May 1943; *Educ* Harrow; *m* 1, 1967 (m dis 1977), Hon Rosemary Gail, da of Baron Pritchard (d 1995), of Haddon; 1 s (Matthew James b 9 Dec 1976); m 2, 1978, Jean Heather, da of John MacDonald (d 1983); m 3, 1987, Peta Jane, da of Sir Peter Foster; *Career* called to the Bar Inner Temple 1965; Travis Perkins plc: dir 1966–2001, chm and chief exec 1981–1999, exec chm 1999–2001; chm Anglia Maltings (Holding) Ltd 2005–09; chm of tstees Constance Travis Charitable Tst 1988–, tstee ESCP Europe Business Sch 2002– (chm 2007–), govr Royal Acad of Music 2006–, dir Assoc Bd Royal Schs of Music 2007–; dir Northampton Saints plc 2000–06; Hon FRAM 2009; *Recreations* opera, theatre, tennis, rugby union; *Style*— Anthony Travis, Esq; ✉ 86 Drayton Gardens, London SW10 9SB (e-mail travisfamily86@mac.com)

TRAVIS, John Anthony; s of Leonard Kirkbride Travis (d 2000), of Brighton, E Sussex, and Elsie, *née* Rainey (d 1961); *b* 18 August 1945, Brighton; *Educ* Brighton Sch of Music & Drama, Doris Isaacs Sch of Dancing, Royal Ballet Sch, Univ of Manchester (Dip); *Career* dancer Covent Garden Opera Ballet; London Festival Ballet (English Nat Ballet): dancer then leading soloist 1966–77, created London Festival Ballet Archive 1979, prog presenter and head Educn Dept 1980–87; on secondment to study at V&A 1977, studied at Lincoln Centre NY 1978; teaching: annually at Nat Festivals of Youth Dance classes and repertoire at all levels, at community centres, theatres, schs; five Brazilian Cities 1982 and first Summer Sch in Dominica 1990; teacher of classical ballet and coordinator for all performances and projects Northern Sch of Contemporary Dance Leeds 1989–95; guest teacher Northern Ballet Sch Manchester 1985–88; lectr on history of dance; artistic co-ordinator Dance Advance 1988–89 (touring mangr for China visit 1989), dir of 3 Youth Dance Spectaculars for Greater London Arts and Opening Gala of Northern Sch of Contemporary Dance 1988; dir: Bd Phoenix Dance Co 1985–93, British Ballet Organization 1995; patron: East London Regnl Dance Cncl, Harehills Dance Umbrella; memb: Exec Ctee Nat Organization for Dance and Mime (Dance UK) 1984–89, Cncl of Mgmnt Br Ballet Orgn 1991–95, Bd Northern Ballet Theatre (chm Educn Ctee) 1990–93, Bd Dance UK 1998–, Bd Mark Baldwin Dance Co 1999–2002; memb Dance Panel: SE Arts 1982–87, Eastern Arts 1983–87, Gtr London Arts Assocs 1980–86, Laurence Olivier Awards (Dance Panel) 1998–99; tstee: Dancers Resettlement Fund 1989–93, Dance Teachers' Benevolent Fnd 1995–2015, Cncl for Dance Educn and Trg 1995–99 and 2002–10; patron Ind Ballet Wales 2006–; *Style*— John Travis, Esq; ✉ 3 Nassau Lodge, Nassau Road, Barnes, London SW13 9QD (☎ 07736 596359, e-mail johntravis1945@outlook.com)

TRAYHURN, Prof Paul; s of William George Trayhurn (d 1975), and Eileen Ella, *née* Morphew (d 1986); *b* 6 May 1948; *Educ* Colyton GS, Univ of Reading (BSc), Univ of Oxford (DPhil, DSc); *m* 12 July 1969, Deborah Hartland, *née* Gigg; 3 s (Theo William b 24 Dec 1977, Hanno Edmund b 9 March 1983, Felix Timothy b 13 May 1985), 1 da (Venetia Harriet b 24 Aug 1980); *Career* NATO Euro res fell Centre de Neurochimie CNRS 1972–73, post-doctoral fell Univ of Oxford 1973–75, MRC scientific staff Dunn Nutrition Laboratory 1975–86, prof and heritage scholar Nutrition and Metabolism Res Gp Univ of Alberta 1986–88; head Div of Biochemical Sciences Rowett Research Inst 1988–2000 (asst dir Academic Affrs 1997–2000), prof of nutritional biology Univ of Oslo Norway 2000–01, prof of nutritional biology Univ of Liverpool 2001–09 (emeritus prof 2009–), dean of research Univ of Buckingham 2011–14, prof of obesity Univ of Highlands & Islands 2012–14, distinguished scientist fell and prof of biology King Saud Univ 2014–15; hon prof: Depts of Biomedical Sciences and Molecular and Cell Biology Univ of Aberdeen 1992–2000, Univ of Buckingham 2009–, Univ of Sydney 2010–16 (Evelyn Williams visiting prof 1992), Univ of the Highlands and Islands 2016–; chm: Scientific Ctee 8th Euro Congress on Obesity (Dublin), Exec Cncl Korean Collaboration Centre for Biotechnology and the Biological Sciences 1995–2000, BBSRC Agri-Food Directorate Ctee 1997–99, MRC Advsy Bd 1997–2003, Awards Ctee Int Assoc for the Study of Obesity 1998–, MRC Population and Systems Medicine Bd 2008–12, Scientific Ctee 12th Int Congress on Obesity (Kuala Lumpur); chair Int Scientific Ctee and exec memb World Obesity Fedn 2014–16; ed-in-chief Br Jl of Nutrition 1999–2005; author of over 400 scientific pubns; Wasserman Award European Assoc for the Study of Obesity 2008; memb: Biochemical Soc 1970, Nutrition Soc 1975 (chm Scottish section 1993–95, tstee 2013–16); FRSE 1997, FRSM 2011, FRSB 2014; *Recreations* listening to classical music, bemoaning the decline of universities and the culture of science; *Style*— Prof Paul Trayhurn, FRSE

TREACY, Rt Hon Lord Justice; Sir Colman Maurice Treacy; kt (2002), PC (2012); s of Dr Maurice Colman Treacy, and Mary Teresa, *née* Frisby; *b* 28 July 1949; *Educ* Stonyhurst, Jesus Coll Cambridge (open scholar, MA); *m* 1 (m dis); 1 s, 1 da; m 2, 2002, Jane Ann, da of Edwin Hooper and Maureen Hooper; 1 step da; *Career* called to the Bar Middle Temple 1971 (bencher 1999); in practice Midland & Oxford Circuit, QC 1990, recorder of the Crown Court 1991–2002, head of chambers 1994–2000, asst boundary cmmr 2000–02, judge of the High Court (Queen's Bench Div) 2002–12, presiding judge Midland Circuit 2006–09, a Lord Justice of the Court of Appeal 2012–; memb: Mental Health Review Tbnl 1999–2002, Warwickshire Criminal Justice Strategy Ctee 2000–02, Sentencing Cncl for England and Wales 2010– (chair 2013–); tstee Lively Minds 2014–; hon fell Jesus Coll Cambridge 2014; *Style*— The Rt Hon the Lord Justice Treacy; ✉ Royal Courts of Justice, Strand, London WC2A 2LL (☎ 020 7947 6000)

TREACY, Philip Anthony; OBE; s of James Vincent Treacy (d 1978), and Katie Agnes Treacy (d 1993); *b* 26 May 1967; *Educ* St Cuan's Coll Castle Blakeney Co Galway, Regional Tech Coll Galway, Nat Coll of Art and Design Dublin (BA), RCA (MDes); *Career* milliner; estab Philip Treacy Ltd 1990; hat designer to fashion houses incl: Karl Lagerfeld at Chanel (Paris), Gianni Versace (Milan), Valentino (Rome), Rifat Ozbek (London), Givenchy (Paris), Alexander McQueen (London); design dir for interiors G W County Galway (Monogram's Hotel) 2005, luxury sports wear range for Umbro 2006; Accessory Designer of the Year (British Fashion Awards) 1991, 1992, 1993, 1996 and 1997, Haute Couture Paris 2000, 2001 and 2003, Moet&Chandon Award for Outstanding Contrib to Fashion 2001, Design of the Year China Fashion Awards 2004; Hon Dr NUI, Hon Dr RCA; *Style*— Philip Treacy, Esq, OBE; ✉ 1 Havelock Terrace, London SW8 4AS (☎ 020 7738 8080, website www.philiptreacy.co.uk)

TREANOR, Frances Mary Elizabeth; da of George Francis Treanor (d 1978), of London, and Biddy, *née* Maunsell (d 1964); *Educ* Convent of the Sacred Heart HS for Girls Hammersmith, Goldsmiths Coll London (NDD), Hornsey Coll of Art (ATC); *m* 1, 9 Oct 1965 (m dis 1969), Francis John Elliott, s of Aubrey Elliott (d 1988), of Wales; 1 da (Lizzie Taylor b 1966); m 2, 30 Oct 1969 (m dis 1982), (Thomas) Anthony Taylor, s of Thomas Taylor (d 1984), of Cornwall; *Career* artist; ILEA teacher DES 1966, pt/t teacher of art ILEA 1967–87, sessional lectr in art and design at American Coll in London 1979–87; vice-chm Blackheath Art Soc 1974, memb Steering Gp Greenwich Lone Parent Project 1984, memb Ctee Women in Docklands 2004, first artist-in-residence Royal Park Greenwich 2005–06; memb Consumer Research Focus Gp 2013; vol Environment Champions Scheme 2013; memb Cncl Pastel Soc, FBA 1982 and 1986; Freedom of the City of London 2015; *Commissions* Volvo purchase 1987, Govt purchase Art of Govt Scheme Derry's Gift 1987, Govt print purchase Inland Revenue and Custom & Excise 1988, set design OUDS prodn of Shakespeare's As You Like It summer tour Japan, USA and England 1988, 3i Commercial Property 1988, Capital & Counties 1988, Dean Witter International 1989, Woolwich 1989, Japan Development Bank 1990, Bruce McGaw Graphics NY 1990, NBJ Brokers (Insurance) 1991, Collyer-Bristow (Solicitors) purchase 1992, UNICEF 1992, Camden Graphics 1993, Broomfield Hosp Mid-Essex NHS Tst Arts Project 2001, Granville Domus (Susan Williams Memorial Fund) 2006, Embassy of Ireland in London 2009, Dr Weinberg Vice-Chllr Kingston Univ 2011; *Exhibitions* Greenwich and Docklands Festival 1996, University of Central England 1997, Century Gallery Datchet 1997, Chelsea Town Hall Gall 1994, Alexandra Palace 1994, Bonham's Salerooms 1994, The Second CBI Art Initiative Receptions 1994, Woodlands Art Open 1995, Marks and Spencer (c/o Coram Gall) 1995, Alrsford Gall 1995, AIM Show NEC Birmingham 1995, Making a Mark Mall Galleries 1995, Contemporary Art Group 1996, House and Garden Show Olympia 1996–99, Gallery at Architecture Ltd Greenwich (solo) 1997–99, Royal West of England Acad 1997, Artifex Flora and Erotica 1998, Innocent Fine Art Bristol 1998, Woodlands' Open Exhibition 1999, Great Wyrley HS 1999, The Pastel Society 2000, English Heritage Rangers House 2000, St Alfege Church 2000, Greenwich and Docklands 2000; *Awards* L'Artiste Assoifée 1975, George Rowney Pastel 1982, Frank Herring Award for Merit 1984, Willi Hoffman-Guth Award 1988, nominated Governing Bd of Eds American Biographical Inst Woman of the Year 2006; *Books and Publications* Pastel Painting Techniques (with Guy Roddon, 1987), The Medici Society (1987), Choosing & Mixing Colours (with J Galton, 1988), Drawing With Colour (with J Martin, 1990), Women Artists Diary (contrib, 1988), Pastel Masterclass (contrib, ed by Judy Martin, 1993), Vibrant Flower Painting (1995); contrib to The Artist, Artists' and Illustrators' Magazine and various other pubns; *Recreations* TV, conversation, antique markets, gardening; *Clubs* London Press, Soc of Women Writers and Journalists, Aldersgate Ward; *Style*— Miss Frances Treanor; ✉ 121 Royal Hill, Greenwich, London SE10 8SS (☎ 020 8692 3239, e-mail francestreanor@btinternet.com, website www.francestreanor.com)

TREASURE, Prof Tom; s of Wilfrid Samuel Treasure, of Cheltenham, Glos, and Rita, *née* Luanaig (d 1991); *b* 12 August 1947; *Educ* St Boniface's Coll Plymouth, Guy's Hosp Med Sch Univ of London (MB BS, MRCS, LRCP, MS, MD); *m* 25 June 1977, Prof Janet Linda Treasure, da of Peter Burden; 1 s (Samuel Wilfrid b 17 Dec 1981), 1 da (Jean Dorothy b 6 Nov 1983); *Career* surgical trg Addenbrooke's Hosp, Hammersmith Hosp, Charing Cross Hosp, St Thomas' Hosp and Kent & Canterbury Hosp 1972–77, specialist trg The London Chest Hosp, The Brompton Hosp and Univ of Alabama 1978–81; res trg: Anatomy Dept Univ of Newcastle upon Tyne 1971–72, Sherrington Sch of Physiology St Thomas' Hosp Med Sch 1976–77, Dept of Surgery Univ of Alabama 1981; Middlesex Hosp and UCL (London) 1982–90, St George's Hosp London 1990–2001, prof of cardiothoracic surgery Thoracic Unit Guy's Hosp London 2001–07, Clinical Operational Research Unit Dept of Mathematics UCL 2007–; chair: Nat Confidential Enquiry into Patient Outcome and Death, Guideline Devpt Gp NICE; memb Ed Advsy Bd BMJ; Hunterian prof RCS 1983; memb: Cncl Br Cardiac Soc 1986–90, Specialist Advsy Ctee in Cardiothoracic Surgery RCS 1989–96, Cncl Euro Assoc of Cardiothoracic Surgery 1989–92, Br Cardiac Soc, Br Assoc of Clinical Anatomists, BMA, Br Thoracic Soc, European Assoc for Cardiothoracic Surgery (former pres, chair Thoracic Ctee), MRS, RSM (memb Cncl 1996), Soc of Thoracic and Cardiovascular Surgns of GB and I, Surgical Res Soc; FRCS 1975, fell Fellowship of Postgrad Med 1991; *Books* A Pocket Examiner in Surgery (with J M A Northover, 1984), Belcher's Thoracic Surgical Management (5 edn with M F Sturridge, 1985), Current Surgical Practice Vol 5 (ed with J Hadfield and M Hobsley, 1990), Current Surgical Practice Vols 6 & 7 (ed with M Hobsley and A Johnson, 1993), Disorders of the Cardiovascular System (with David Patterson, 1994); *Style*— Prof Tom Treasure; ✉ Clinical Operational Research Unit, Department of Mathematics, University College London, 4 Taviton Street, London WC1E 6BT

TREBILCOCK, Peter James; s of James Charles Trebilcock, of Chorley, and Joan, *née* Craig; *b* 19 June 1957; *Educ* Liverpool Poly (BA Arch, DipArch, Sch of Architecture Prize for Architecture); *m* 7 Jan 1989, Elizabeth Ann, da of Robert Alfred Stanton; 2 s (Aaron Robert James b 15 Sept 1996, Joel Peter b 14 April 1999); *Career* architect; Austin-Smith Lord Warrington 1983–85, assoc Building Design Partnership Preston and Manchester offices 1989–96 (joined 1985), head of architecture AMEC Group Ltd 2000–07 (joined

T

1996), dir for design and building information modelling champion Balfour Beatty Construction Northern Ltd 2007–, dir of design Balfour Beatty Major Projects 2013–, prog dir Design and Building Information Modelling Balfour Beatty Construction Services UK 2013–; conslt architect to Steel Construction Inst and British Steel 1990–2003; pres N Lancs Soc of Architects 1995–97; RIBA: memb Nat Cncl 1997–2003, chm NW Regn 1998–2000, vice-pres membership 2001–03, memb Holdings Bd 2001–03, chair Professional Services Bd 2003; author of several publications; designer of projects across the UK and in Germany, Kuwait and China; regular conference speaker on sustainability and building information modelling; judge Young Architect of the Year Awards 1998 and 1999; jt first prize RIBA/British Gas Energy Mgmnt Competition (hosp design) 1982, Charles Reynolds bursary Concrete Soc 1983, finalist Apple Computers/Designers Jl Design Competition 1990, first prize Cynamid European Architectural Competition 1981 (teenage bedroom design), two RIBA Awards 2006, Civic Tst Award 2006; RIBA 1985, MaPS 1995; *Publications* incl: Optimising Costs of Steel Construction through Value Engineering (2000), Architectural Design in Steel (jtly, 2003), Designing Better Buildings (contrib, 2003); regular contrib to the construction press on building information modelling; *Recreations* travel, writing, church activities (The Church of Jesus Christ of Latter-day Saints); *Style—* Peter Trebilcock, Esq; ✉ Balfour Beatty Construction Services, 5 Churchill Place, Canary Wharf, London E14 5HU (☎ 020 3810 2243, peter.trebilcock@balfourbeatty.com, website www.balfourbeatty.com)

TREDINNICK, David; MP; s of Stephen Victor Tredinnick (d 1995) and Evelyn Mabel, *née* Wates; *b* 19 January 1950; *Educ* Eton, Mons Offr Cadet Sch, Grad Business Sch Univ of Cape Town (MBA), St John's Coll Oxford (MLitt); *m* 7 July 1983 (m dis 2008), Rebecca, da of Roland Shott; 1 da (Sophie b 22 Feb 1987), 1 s (Thomas b 6 July 1989); *Career* Grenadier Gds 1968–71; sales and mktg computer industry 1976–79; MP (Cons) Bosworth 1987–, jt sec Cons Backbench Defence and Foreign Affrs Ctees 1990, PPS to Rt Hon Sir Wyn Roberts as min of state for Wales 1990–94; chm: Anglo-East Euro Trading Co, Br Atlantic Gp of Young Politicians 1989–91, Future of Europe Tst 1991–95, Ukraine Business Agency 1992–97; chm: Jt Ctee on Statutory Instruments 1997–2005, Select Ctee on Statutory Instruments 1997–2005, Parly Gp for Integrated and Complementary Health Care 2006– (treas 1989–, co-chm 2002–06); memb Health Select Ctee 2010–15, memb Science and Technol Ctee 2013–15; co-chm Br Meml Garden Tst UK Ltd 2003–05; *Recreations* golf, skiing, windsurfing, tennis; *Style—* David Tredinnick, Esq, MP; ✉ House of Commons, London SW1A 0AA (☎ 020 7219 4514, e-mail davidtredinnickmp@parliament.uk)

TREDINNICK, Dr Noël Harwood; s of Harold James Tredinnick (d 2003), of Beckenham, Kent, and Nola Frewin, *née* Harwood; *b* 9 March 1949, Camberwell, London; *Educ* St Olave's GS for Boys, Southwark Cathedral, Guildhall Sch of Music and Drama, Inst of Educn Univ of London (PGCE); *m* 3 July 1976, Fiona Jean, da of James Malcolm Couper-Johnston, of Beckenham, Kent; 1 da (Isabel Jane b 1983), 1 s (James Alexander Johnston b 24 Aug 1994); *Career* school master Langley Park Sch for Boys Beckenham 1971–75, prof and lectr Guildhall Sch 1975–, organist and dir of music All Souls Church Langham Place London 1972–, artistic dir Langham Arts 1987–, prof of conducting Guildhall Sch of Music 1993–; composer, orchestrator and conductor: Beckenham Chorale 1971–72, All Souls Orch 1972–, BBC Concert Orch 1985–89, BBC Radio Orch 1988–90; musical dir: BBC Radio (Religious Dept), Songs of Praise BBC TV; writer and broadcaster radio series; fndr and conductor Prom Praise, conductor Palm Beach Opera Orch 1994–95, musical dir Billy Graham Mission Toronto 1995 and Ottawa 1998, conductor Sofia Symphony Orch 2008, conductor Northern Sinfonia 2009, conductor Scottish Chamber Orch 2012; vice-chm Jubilate Hymns Ltd; numerous recordings and performances incl Cliff Richard, Mary O'Hara, Harry Secombe, Lesley Garrett, Ben Heppner and Amy Grant; dir music for HM Queen Elizabeth II St James's Palace 1996, Balmoral 2000 and Golden Jubilee celebrations 2002; memb Archbishop's Cmmn on Church Music; Hon DMus (Lambeth) 2002; FRSCM 2009; *Publications* New Songs of Praise Books 1–5 (music ed), Carol Praise; *Recreations* theatre, architecture, country walking; *Clubs* ACG; *Style—* Dr Noël Tredinnick; ✉ 2 All Souls Place, London W1B 3DA (☎ 020 7935 7246, fax 020 7935 7486, e-mail noel.tredinnick@allsouls.org, website www.allsoulsorchestra.com)

TREDRE, Roger Ford; s of Dr Alec Ford Tredre, and Angela Joyce, *née* Morris; *b* 9 March 1962; *Educ* Epsom Coll, Sidney Sussex Coll Cambridge (scholar, MA), Univ of the Arts London (PGCE); *m* Aug 2004, Jennifer Chen, *née* Feier Chen; 1 da (Olivia Chen b 20 Jan 2005), 1 s (Nicholas Ford b 10 May 2006); *Career* journalist; staff writer The Bulletin Brussels 1984–86, dep ed Fashion Weekly 1989 (news ed 1987–88), fashion and design corr The Independent 1989–93, news and features writer The Observer 1993–97, arts corr The Observer 1997–99, ed-in-chief Worth Global Style Network 1999–2006, ed view-network.com 2009–10, sr vice-pres stylus.com 2010–13, news ed PantoneView.com 2013–15; assoc lectr Fashion MA Central St Martins Sch of Art & Design (now Central St Martins) 1999–2014, fashion journalism pathway ldr Fashion Communication MA Central St Martins 2014–; *Publications* The Great Fashion Designers (jtly, 2009); *Recreations* Dartmoor walking, visiting Provence; *Style—* Roger Tredre, Esq; ✉ 40 Upham Park Road, London W4 1PG (e-mail rtredre@gmail.com)

TREDWELL, Paul Philippe; s of Ronald Jean Tredwell, of Dudley, W Midlands, and Rita May, *née* Pugh; *b* 23 February 1956; *Educ* Queen Mary's GS, Queens' Coll Cambridge (MA, LLB); *m* 31 Oct 1987, Melanie Barbara Alice, da of Robin Stuart Brown; 1 da (Rosanna Elise b 4 Nov 1989), 1 s (Rory Luc b 11 Nov 1992); *Career* account mangr Young & Rubicam advtg 1980–83 (joined as graduate trainee 1979); Abbott Mead Vickers BBDO Ltd: joined 1983, account dir 1984–93, bd dir 1987–93; client gp dir Euro RSCG Ltd (now Euro RSCG Wnek Gosper) 1993–96, client servs dir Leagas Delaney Partnership 1998–99 (bd account dir 1996–97), dir Saatchi & Saatchi 1999–; memb Mktg Soc, MIPA; *Recreations* Rugby Union, golf; *Style—* Paul Tredwell, Esq; ✉ Saatchi & Saatchi, 80 Charlotte Street, London W1A 1AQ (☎ 020 7462 7010, e-mail paul.tredwell@saatchi.co.uk)

TREES, Baron (Life Peer UK 2012), of The Ross in Perth and Kinross; Prof Alexander John (Sandy) Trees; *b* 12 June 1946; *Educ* Univ of Edinburgh (BVMS, PhD); *m* 1970, Frances Ann, *née* McAnally; 1 da (Katherine Lucy b 15 Oct 1977); *Career* research Univ of Edinburgh expdn to Kenya 1969–70, asst in gen vet practice Derby 1970–71, research assoc Centre for Tropical Vet Med (CTVM) Univ of Edinburgh 1971, memb CTVM/Vom Collaboration Project Nat Inst for Vet Research Vom Nigeria 1974–76; Elanco Products Co Rome: vet advsr for ME 1977–79, vet advsr ME, Turkey and Africa 1979–80, head Animal Science ME and Africa 1980; Faculty of Vet Science Univ of Liverpool: appointed lectr Dept of Vet Parasitology 1980 (tenure granted 1983), head Dept of Vet Parasitology 1992–2001, prof of vet parasitology (personal chair) 1994–2011, dean 2001–08, emeritus prof 2011–; Liverpool Sch of Tropical Med: head Parasite and Vector Biology Div 1994–97, memb Cncl 1995–2004; MRC visiting sr scientist MRC Lab Bo Sierra Leone 1984–88, visiting prof Univ of Glasgow 2012–; memb Vet Med Interest Gp Wellcome Tst 1998–2003; memb Editorial Bd: Research in Vet Science 1991–2001, Trends in Parasitology (formerly Parasitology Today) 1992–2007; memb Exec Ctee World Assoc for the Advancement of Veterinary Parasitology 2007–, chair Moredun Research Inst 2011–; veterinary ed-in-chief Veterinary Record and In Practice (BMJ Pubns) 2011–; author of numerous book chapters, reviews, articles and other contribs to learned jls, invited speaker at confs and symposia worldwide; Assoc of Vet Teachers and Research Workers (AVTRW): memb 1980–, jr vice-pres 1995–96, memb Cncl 1995–2001, pres 1996–97, Selborne Medal for vet research 2005; memb: Br Soc of Parasitology 1980–, BVA 1980– (chair Educn Gp and memb Vet Policy Gp 1997–2001), Royal Soc of Tropical Med and Hygiene 1986– (memb Cncl and Medals Ctee 1997–2000); Birrel-Grey Travelling Scholarship Univ of Edinburgh 1971, Cwlth Fndn Fellowship 1982, founding diplomate European Vet Parasitology Coll (DipEVPC) 2003, BVA Wooldridge lecture and Medal 2009, McCall lecture Univ of Glasgow 2010, Amoroso Award Br Small Animals Vet Assoc 2011; DVetMed (hc) Royal Veterinary Coll Univ of London 2012, hon DVMS Univ of Glasgow 2016; MRCVS 1969 (memb Cncl and Educn Ctee 2000–15, vice-pres 2008–09, pres 2009–10, sr vice-pres 2010–11, chair Science Advsy Panel 2013–), hon FRSE 2016; *Style—* The Lord Trees; ✉ House of Lords, London SW1A 0PW

TREFETHEN, Prof Lloyd N; *b* 30 August 1955; *Educ* Phillips Exeter Acad, Harvard Univ (AB), Stanford Univ (MS, PhD); *m* (m dis); 2 c; *Career* NSF post-doctoral fell and adjunct asst prof Courant Inst of Mathematical Scis New York Univ 1982–84, assoc prof of applied mathematics MIT 1987–91 (asst prof 1984–87), prof of computer sci Cornell Univ 1994–97 (assoc prof 1991–93), prof of numerical analysis Univ of Oxford 1997–; ed: SIAM Jl on Numerical Analysis 1984–99, Numerische Mathematik 1988–99, SIAM Review 1989–2007, Calcolo 1998–; assoc ed: Jl of Computational and Applied Mathematics 1987–2012, Japan Jl of Industrial and Applied Mathematics 1991–96; FRS 2005, memb Nat Acad of Engrg USA 2007; *Books* Numerical Conformal Mapping (ed, 1986), Finite Difference and Spectral Methods for Ordinary and Partial Differential Equations (1996), Numerical Linear Algebra (with David Bau, 1997), Spectral Methods in MATLAB (2000), Schwarz-Christoffel Mapping (with Tobin Driscoll, 2002), Spectra and Pseudospectra (with Mark Embree, 2005), Trefethen's Index Cards (2011); also author of numerous articles in learned jls; *Style—* Prof Lloyd Trefethen; ✉ Balliol College, Oxford OX1 3BJ (☎ 01865 273886, fax 01865 273839, e-mail trefethen@maths.ox.ac.uk)

TREFGARNE, 2 Baron (UK 1947); David Garro Trefgarne; PC (1989); s of 1 Baron Trefgarne (d 1960), and Elizabeth (who m 2, 1962 (m dis 1966), Cdr Anthony Tosswill Courtney, OBE (d 1988); and 3, 1971, Hugh Cecil Howat Ker (d 1987); d 2007), da of late Charles Edward Churchill, of Ashton Keynes, Wilts; *b* 31 March 1941; *Educ* Haileybury, Princeton Univ; *m* 1968, Rosalie, er da of Baron Lane of Horsell (Life Peer), *qv*; 2 s (Hon George b 1970, Hon Justin b 1973), 1 da (Hon Rebecca b 1976); *Heir* s, Hon George Trefgarne; *Career* oppn whip House of Lords 1977–79, a Lord in Waiting (govt whip) 1979–81; under sec of state: Dept of Trade 1981, FCO 1981–82, DHSS 1982–83, MOD (for armed forces) 1983–85; min of state for def support 1985–86, min of state for def procurement 1986–89, min for trade DTI 1989–90; elected memb of the House of Lords 1999–; dir and conslt various cos; non-exec dir Siebe plc 1991–98; pres: Mech and Metal Trades Confedn 1990–2005, Popular Flying Assoc 1992–2003, British Assoc of Aviation Consultants 1995–; hon pres: Instn of Incorporated Engrs 2003–06, Welding Inst 2006–08; dep pres Instn of Engrg and Technol 2006–07; chm: Engrg & Marine Trg Authy (now Science, Engrg and Mfrg Technologies Alliance (SEMTA)) 1994–2006, Brooklands Museum Tst 2002–14; life govr Haileybury 1992–, govr Guildford Sch of Acting 1992–2000, tstee Mary Rose Tst 1994–2000; Royal Aero Club Bronze medal (jtly) for flight from UK to Aust and back in light aircraft 1963; Hon Dr Staffordshire Univ 2004, hon fell Univ of Central Lancashire 2004; Hon FIIE; *Recreations* flying, photography; *Clubs* RAF; *Style—* The Rt Hon the Lord Trefgarne, PC; ✉ House of Lords, London SW1A 0PW

TREFGARNE, Hon Trevor Garro; 2 s of 1 Baron Trefgarne (d 1960), and Elizabeth, *née* Churchill (d 2007); *b* 18 January 1944; *Educ* Cheltenham Coll, Cranfield Sch of Mgmnt; *m* 1, 1967 (m dis 1979), Diana Elizabeth, da of late Michael Gibb, of Taynton, Oxon, by his w Ursula; 2 s (Rupert b 1972, Oliver b 1974), 1 da (Susannah b 1976); m 2, 1979, Caroline France, da of Michael Gosschalk, of Monte Carlo; 1 s (Mark b 1982), 1 da (Camilla b 1988); *Career* dir Pentos plc 1972–75, chm Nesco Investments plc 1976–87; dir: Templeton Emerging Markets Investment Trust plc 1989–2002, EFG plc 1992–94, Templeton Central & Eastern European Investment Co 1996–98, Global Yatirim Holding AS 2002–09, Franklin Templeton Investment Funds 2002–, Gartmore High Income Tst plc 1999–2007; chm: Recovery Tst plc 2001–08, Enterprise Insurance Co Ltd Ghana; *Style—* The Hon Trevor Trefgarne; ✉ Enterprise Group Limited, PO Box 50, 11 High Street, Accra, Ghana

TREGELLES, Janine Lesley; da of Arthur Sales, and Iris, *née* Skilton; *b* 2 March 1962, Warlingham, Surrey; *m* 28 May 2010, Howard Andrew Sinclair; 2 da (Anna Southern b 10 Oct 1990, Esther Southern b 26 Jan 1996); *Career* devpt dir New Era Housing 1984–97; Mencap: joined 1997, dir of personal support 2002–13, chief exec 2013–; *Recreations* cinema, reading, walking; *Style—* Mrs Janine Tregelles; ✉ Mencap, 123 Golden Lane, London EC1Y 0RT

TREGGIARI, Prof Susan Mary; *née* Franklin; da of Walter Howard Franklin (d 1987), of Great Rissington, Glos, and Elizabeth Mary, *née* Washbourn; *b* 11 March 1940, Moreton-in-Marsh, Glos; *Educ* Cheltenham Ladies' Coll (scholar), Lady Margaret Hall Oxford (scholar, MA), Univ of Oxford (BLitt, DLitt); *m* 1964, Arnaldo Treggiari; 2 da (Joanna b 1965, Silvia b 1967); *Career* pt/t lectr Goldsmiths Coll London 1965–66, lectr North-Western Poly London 1966–69; Dept of Classical Studies Univ of Ottawa: asst prof 1970–71, assoc prof 1971–79, prof 1979–84, chm 1981–82; Stanford Univ: prof Dept of Classics 1982–2001 (chm 1987–90, 1992–93), Anne T and Robert M Bass prof Sch of Humanities and Sciences 1992–2001; memb Sub-Faculty of Ancient History Univ of Oxford 2001–; visiting prof: Sweet Briar Coll VA 1969–70, Dept of Classics and History Yale Univ 1993–94; visiting fell: BNC Oxford 1976–77, All Souls Coll Oxford 1995–96; jt ed Classical News and Views/Echos du monde classique 1974–81 (actg ed 1973–74), gen ed (jtly) Clarendon Ancient History Series 1994–, co-ed Ancient History Bulletin 1996–2003; memb Editorial Bd: Phoenix 1972 and 1975–78, Florilegium 1979–98; pres: Assoc of Ancient Historians 1981–84, American Philological Assoc 1997; Charles J Goodwin Award of Merit American Philological Assoc 1993, John Simon Guggenheim Meml Fndn Fellowship 1995–96; fell American Acad of Arts and Sciences 1995, hon fell Lady Margaret Hall Oxford 2011; *Books* Roman Freedmen during the Late Republic (1969, reissued 2000), Cicero's Cilician Letters (1973, 2 edn 1997), Roman Marriage (1991), Roman Social History (2002), Terentia, Tullia and Publilia (2007); *Style—* Prof Susan Treggiari

TREGLOWN, Prof Jeremy Dickinson; s of late Rev Geoffrey Leonard Treglown, MBE, Hon CF, of Cheltenham, Glos, and late Beryl Miriam Treglown; *b* 24 May 1946; *Educ* Bristol GS, St Peter's Coll Saltley, St Peter's Coll Oxford (MA, BLitt), UCL (PhD); *m* 1, 1970 (m dis 1982), Rona Mary Bower; 1 s, 2 da; m 2, 1984, Holly Mary Belinda Eley, *née* Urquhart (d 2010); m 3, 2013, Maria Alvarez; 1 da by Jennifer Lewis; *Career* lectr in English Lincoln Coll Oxford 1973–76, lectr UCL 1976–79, ed TLS 1982–90 (asst ed 1980–82), prof of English Univ of Warwick 1993– (chair Dept of English and Comparative Literature Studies 1995–98); contrib to jls incl: FT, TLS, New Yorker; visiting fell All Souls Coll Oxford 1986, Mellon visiting assoc Caltech, fell Huntington Library San Marino 1988, Ferris prof Princeton Univ 1992, Jackson Brothers fell Beinecke Library Yale Univ 1999, Leverhulme res fell 2001–03, Mellon fell Humanities Res Center Univ of Texas Austin 2002, Margaret and Herman Sokol fell Center for Scholars and Writers NY Public Library 2002–03, fell in history Bogliasco Fndn 2011, fell Rockefeller Fndn Bellagio 2011; hon res fell UCL 1991–; chm of judges: Booker Prize 1991, Whitbread Book of the Year Award 1997; FRSL 1989 (memb Cncl); *Publications* The Letters of John Wilmot, Earl of Rochester (ed, 1980), Spirit of Wit: Reconsiderations of Rochester (ed, 1982), The Lantern-Bearers: Essays by Robert Louis Stevenson (ed, 1988), Roald Dahl: A Biography (1994), Grub Street and the Ivory Tower: Literary Journalism and Literary Scholarship from

Fielding to the Internet (ed with Bridget Bennett, 1998), Romancing: The Life and Work of Henry Green (2000), V S Prichett: A Working Life (2004), Essential Stories by V S Pritchett (ed, 2005), The Complete Short Stories of Roald Dahl (ed, 2006), Franco's Crypt: Spanish Culture and Memory since 1936 (2013); *Style—* Prof Jeremy Treglown; ✉ Department of English and Comparative Literary Studies, University of Warwick, Coventry CV4 7AL

TREGONING, Christopher William Courtenay; 3 and yst s of Lt-Col John Langford Tregoning, MBE, TD (d 1976), of Inkpen, Newbury, and Sioned Georgina Courtenay, *née* Strick (d 1994); bro of Julian George Tregoning, *qv*; *b* 15 June 1948; *Educ* Harrow, Fitzwilliam Coll Cambridge (MA); *m* 15 Sept 1973, Antonia Isabella Mary, da of Maj John Albert Miles Critchley-Salmonson, of Great Barton, Suffolk; 3 s (Harry John William b 28 Jan 1976, Daniel Christopher Leonard b 30 Dec 1977, Thomas Anthony Cecil b 26 Jan 1982); *Career* Thomson McLintock & Co 1970–74, Barclays Bank Ltd 1974–79, dep md Den Norske Bank plc (formerly Nordic Bank plc) 1986–2008 (joined 1979); dir: DNB NOR Asset Mngmnt Ltd 2008–10, Canaccord Genuity Ltd 2008–, Roebuck Capital Ltd 2009–11, DNB UK Ltd 2015–; tstee Nat Horseracing Museum 2009– FCA 1974; *Recreations* field sports, racing, sporting paintings, country house architecture; *Style—* Christopher Tregoning, Esq

TREGONING, Julian George; 2 s of Lt-Col John Langford Tregoning, MBE, TD (d 1976), and Sioned Georgina Courtenay, *née* Strick (d 1994); bro of Christopher William Courtenay Tregoning, *qv*; *b* 24 October 1946; *Educ* Harrow, BRNC Dartmouth; *m* Tessa Jane, da of Cdr Norman Lanyon, DSC* (d 1982); 2 s (Oliver b 1973, Guy b 1975); *Career* RN 1965–68; dir: Save & Prosper Group Ltd 1985–95 (joined 1968), Robert Fleming & Co Ltd 1995–98, BNY Mellon 2000–12, Montanaro Asset Mgmnt Ltd 2008–; dep chm Univ of London Pension Scheme 1999–; chm Assoc of Unit Tst and Investment Funds 1993–95 (int rep 1993–99), pres Fédération Européene des Fonds et Sociétés d'Investissement 1997–98; treas Royal UK Beneficent Assoc (Rukba) 1990–2003, tstee City of London Club (chm 2000–03); memb Ct of Assts Worshipful Co of Grocers (Master 2001–02); govr Oundle Sch (chm 2010–); MSI; *Recreations* messing about in boats, opera, watercolours, wine; *Clubs* Boodle's (memb Gen Ctee), City of London, MCC, St Moritz Tobogganing; *Style—* Julian Tregoning, Esq

TREGONING, Marcus Philip Norris; s of Peter Norris Tregoning, MC, and Anne Katherine, *née* Fitzgeorge-Parker; *b* 31 July 1959, Birmingham; *m* 7 March 1998, Arabella Julia, *née* Wright; 2 s (George b 11 Sept 1998, Peter b 29 Sept 2003), 2 da (Jessica b 23 Oct 1999, Alice b 4 Aug 2004); *Career* racehorse trainer; formerly asst trainer to Major W R Hern, trainer Kingwood House Stables 1998–2013, trainer Whitsbury Manor Stables 2013–; horses trained incl Sir Percy (winner Epsom Derby 2006); Flat Trainer of the Year Horserace Writers and Photographers Assoc 2006; *Recreations* shooting, fishing; *Style—* Marcus Tregoning, Esq; ✉ Whitsbury Manor Stables, Whitsbury, Hampshire SP6 3QQ (☎ 01725 518889, e-mail info@marcustregoningracing.co.uk, website www.marcustregoningracing.co.uk)

TREHEARNE, Ian Richard; s of Edward Brian Geoffrey Trehearne, of Keyhaven, Hants, and Mary Violet, *née* Blake; *b* 17 May 1950, Birmingham; *Educ* Felsted, Univ of Durham (BA); *m* 1975, Madeleine Elizabeth, *née* Epstein; 1 da (Ghislaine Florence b 1984); *Career* slr; called to the Bar 1980; local govt (Newham, Islington, Westminster, Camden) 1972–84; ptnr Berwin Leighton Paisner 1988– (joined 1985); memb Planning Ctee Br Cncl of Offices; supporter Planning Aid Tst; MRTPI; *Recreations* sailing, theatre, books; *Style—* Ian Trehearne, Esq; ✉ 20 New End Square, London NW3 1LN (☎ 020 7435 6310, fax 020 7794 8816); Berwin Leighton Paisner, Adelaide House, London Bridge, London EC4R 9HA (☎ 020 7760 4259, fax 020 7760 1111, e-mail ian.trehearne@blplaw.com)

TREITEL, Prof Sir Guenter Heinz; kt (1997), QC (1983); s of Theodor Treitel (d 1973), and Hanna, *née* Levy (d 1951); *b* 26 October 1928; *Educ* Kilburn GS, Magdalen Coll Oxford (MA, BCL, DCL); *m* 1 Jan 1957, Phyllis Margaret, da of Ronald Cook (d 1990); 2 s (Richard James b 1958, Henry Marcus b 1960); *Career* called to the Bar Gray's Inn 1952, hon bencher 1982; asst lectr LSE 1951–53; Univ of Oxford: lectr Univ Coll 1953–54, fell Magdalen Coll 1954–79 (emeritus fell 1979), All Souls reader in Eng law 1964–79, Vinerian prof of Eng law 1979–96 (emeritus prof 1996), fell All Souls Coll 1979–96 (emeritus fell 1996); visiting lectr/prof 1963–2003 Univs of: Chicago, Houston, Southern Methodist, Virginia, Santa Clara, W Aust; visiting scholar Ernst von Caemmerer Stiftung 1990; tstee Br Museum 1983–98, memb Cncl Nat Tst 1984–93; FBA 1977; *Books* The Law of Contract (1962, 11 edn 2003), An Outline of the Law of Contract (1975, 6 edn 2004), Remedies for Breach of Contract, A Comparative Account (1988), Unmöglichkeit, 'Impracticability' und 'Frustration' im anglo-amerikanischen Recht (1991), Frustration and Force Majeure (1994, 3 edn 2014), Some Landmarks of Twentieth Century Contract Law (2002, Chinese trans 2010); jt ed: Benjamin's Sale of Goods (1974, 9 edn 2014), Chitty on Contracts (23–32 edns 1968–2015), Dicey (& Morris) Conflict of Laws (7 edn 1958, 8 edn 1967), English Private Law (2000, 2 edn 07), Carver on Bills of Lading (2001, 3 edn 2011); *Recreations* reading, music; *Style—* Prof Sir Guenter Treitel, QC, FBA; ✉ All Souls College, Oxford OX1 4AL (☎ 01865 279379, fax 01865 279299)

TRELAWNY, (James Edward) Petroc; s of Richard Trelawny, and Jennifer, *née* Blackwood; *b* 27 May 1971; *Educ* Helston Sch Cornwall; *Career* radio broadcaster; Classic FM 1992–94, London News Radio 1994–97, co-presenter (with Victoria Derbyshire) breakfast show BBC GMR 1997, BBC Radio 3 1998–; regular television presenter of classical music progs BBC 2, BBC 4 and Sky Arts; contrib: The Spectator, Irish Times, Catholic Herald, BBC Music Magazine; tstee Br Friends of Zimbabwe Acad of Music, pres Lennox Berkeley Soc, pres Luton Music; *Recreations* travel, music, literary affairs; *Style—* Petroc Trelawny, Esq; ✉ c/o Noel Gay Artists, 19 Denmark Street, London WC2H 8NA (Twitter @petroctrelawny)

TREMAIN, Rose; CBE (2007); da of Keith Nicholas Thomson, and Viola Mabel, *née* Dudley; *b* 2 August 1943; *Educ* Sorbonne, UEA (BA); *m* 1, 7 May 1971 (m dis 1976), Jon Tremain; 1 da (Eleanor Rachel b 16 July 1972); m 2, 2 Aug 1982 (m dis 1991), Jonathan Dudley; *Career* author; chllr UEA 2013; FRSL 1983; *Awards* Dylan Thomas Prize 1984, Giles Cooper Award 1985, Angel Prize 1985 and 1989, Sunday Express Book of the Year Award 1989, James Tait Black Meml Prize 1992, Prix Femina Étranger 1994, Whitbread Novel Prize 1999, Orange Prize for Fiction 2008, Good Housekeeping Fiction Prize 2008; *Books* Sadler's Birthday (1975), Letter to Sister Benedicta (1978), The Cupboard (1980), The Colonel's Daughter (1982), The Swimming Pool Season (1984), The Garden of The Villa Mollini (1986), Restoration (1989), Sacred Country (1992), Evangelista's Fan (1994), Collected Short Stories (1996), The Way I Found Her (1997), Music and Silence (1999), The Colour (2003), The Darkness of Wallis Simpson (2005), The Road Home (2007), Trespass (2010), Merivel: A Man of His Time (2012), The American Lover (2015), The Gustav Sonata (2016); *Recreations* gardening, yoga; *Style—* Ms Rose Tremain, CBE; ✉ 2 High House, South Avenue, Thorpe St Andrew, Norwich NR7 0EZ

TRENCHARD, 3 Viscount (UK 1936); Sir Hugh Trenchard; 3 Bt (UK 1919); also Baron Trenchard (UK 1930); DL (Herts 2008); s of 2 Viscount Trenchard, MC (d 1987), and Patricia (d 2016), da of Adm Sir Sidney Bailey, KBE, CB, DSO; *b* 12 March 1951, London; *Educ* Eton, Trinity Coll Cambridge; *m* 1975, Fiona Elizabeth, da of 2 Baron Margadale, TD, DL (d 2003); 2 s (Hon Alexander Thomas b 1978, Hon William James b 1986), 2 da (Hon Katherine Clare b 1980, Hon Laura Mary b 1987); *Heir* s, Hon Alexander Trenchard; *Career* Kleinwort Benson Ltd 1973–96 (chief rep in Japan 1980–85, dir 1986–96); Kleinwort Benson International Inc: gen mangr Tokyo 1985–88, pres 1988–95, dep chm 1995–96; rep in Japan of Kleinwort Benson Group plc 1993–95; dir: Dover Japan Inc 1985–87, ACP Holdings Ltd 1990–94, Robert Fleming & Co Ltd 1996–98, Robert Fleming International Ltd 1998–2000, Berkeley Technology Ltd 1999–2011, Westhall Capital Ltd 2001–03, Dryden Wealth Mgmnt Ltd 2004–05, Stratton Street PCC Ltd 2006– (chm 2009–), Bache Global Series SICAV 2007–14, UK Koyu Corporation Ltd 2009–, Lotte Chemical UK Ltd 2010–; chm The Dejima Fund Ltd 2001–09, sr advsr Prudential Financial Inc 2002–08, md Mizuho Int plc 2007–12, conslt and sr advsr Mizuho Bank Ltd 2013–14, conslt Simon Robertson Assocs LLP (formerly Robertson Robey Assocs LLP) 2013–, sr external advsr Rolls-Royce Power Engrg plc 2014–15, sr advsr Optum Health Socs UK Ltd 2014–, sr advsr Adamas Asset Mgmnt (Hong Kong) Ltd 2014–; DG European Fund and Asset Mgmnt Assoc 2006; European Business Community in Japan: chm Securities Ctee 1993–95, vice-chm Cncl 1995; dir: Japan Securities Dealers Assoc 1994–95, Bond Underwriters Assoc of Japan 1994–95; memb: Japan Assoc of Corp Execs 1987–95, Cncl Japan Soc 1992–93 and 1995–2004 (vice-chm 1996–2000, jt chm 2000–04); hon treas House of Lords All-Pty Defence Study Gp 1992–93, vice-chm Br-Japanese Parly Gp 1997–99 and 2004–, memb Jt Ctee on Fin Servs and Markets 1999, elected hereditary peer House of Lords 2004–; pres NE Herts Cons Assoc 2001–; Capt 4 Royal Green Jackets TA 1973–80, Hon Air Cdre 600 (City of London) Sqdn RAuxAF 2006–, chm RAF Benevolent Fund 2006–13 (memb Cncl 1991–2003, dep chm 2014–); Lt City of London 2014; Order of the Rising Sun Gold and Silver Star Japan 2014; *Clubs* Brooks's, Cavalry and Guards, Pratt's, Tokyo; *Style—* The Rt Hon the Viscount Trenchard, DL; ✉ Standon Lordship, Ware, Hertfordshire SG11 1PR (☎ 01920 823785, e-mail trenchardh@aol.com)

TRENOUTH, Dr Michael John; s of John Trenouth, of Grange-over-Sands, and Marjorie Trenouth; *b* 2 June 1946; *Educ* Friend's Sch Lancaster, Univ of Manchester (BSc, BDS, MDS, PhD, DOrth, DDO, FDS, RCPS); *Career* Manchester Dental Hosp: house offr 1971–72, lectr in oral surgery 1972–75, lectr in dental anatomy and hon registrar orthodontics 1975–78, lectr in orthodontics and hon sr registrar orthodontics 1978–85; conslt orthodontist Preston Royal Hosp 1985–2008, dental post graduate tutor Lancaster, Preston, Chorley and Blackpool Dists 1991–98; treas Manchester and Region Orthodontic Study Gp 1980–85; chm NW Regnl Ctee Hosp Dental Servs 2003–06 (hon sec 1996–2003); author of over 60 pubns in scientific jls, mainly on craniofacial growth and Twin block functional orthodontic appliance and dental history; Pierre Fauchard Award American Biographical Inst 2011, Best Scientific Paper Award Jl of Orthodontics 2013; life memb: Manch Med Soc, RSM, RCPSGlas; *Recreations* skiing, sailing, fell walking, ice skating; *Style—* Dr Michael Trenouth; ✉ Royal Preston Hospital, Sharoe Green Lane, Preston PR2 9HT (☎ 01772 522597, e-mail michaeltrenouth@hotmail.co.uk)

TRESCOTHICK, Marcus Edward; MBE (2006); *b* 25 December 1975, Keynsham, Somerset; *m* Hayley; 1 da (Ellie Louise b 2005); *Career* professional cricketer; with Somerset CCC 1993–; England: 76 test matches, 123 one-day ints, test debut v West Indies 2000, one day int debut v Zimbabwe 2000, memb team touring Pakistan and Sri Lanka 2000–01, Zimbabwe, India and NZ 2001–02 (capt one-day int v Zimbabwe 2001), Bangladesh and Sri Lanka 2003, West Indies 2004, South Africa 2004–05 and Pakistan 2005; *Style—* Marcus Trescothick, Esq, MBE; ✉ c/o Somerset CCC, The County Ground, Taunton, Somerset TA1 1JT

TREUHERZ, Julian Benjamin; s of late Werner Treuherz (d 1999), and Irmgard, *née* Amberg (d 2001); *b* 12 March 1947; *Educ* Manchester Grammar, ChCh Oxford (MA), UEA (MA); *Partner* Peter de Figueiredo (civil partnership 2005); *Career* Manchester City Art Gallery: trainee 1971, asst keeper of fine art 1972, keeper of fine art 1974; keeper of art galleries National Museums Liverpool 1989–2007; memb: Museums Assoc 1971, Victorian Soc 1971 (hon sec Manchester Group 1972–79, chm Manchester Group 1980–83); memb Ctee: NACF Merseyside Gp 1991–2007, Whitworth Art Gallery 1993–2005, Burlington Magazine Consultative 2003–; tstee Lakeland Arts Tst 1997–2010; Hon LLD Univ of Liverpool 2009; *Publications* Pre-Raphaelite Paintings from the Manchester City Art Gallery (1981), Hard Times – Social Realism in Victorian Art (1987), Country Houses of Cheshire (jtly with Peter de Figueiredo, 1988), Victorian Painting (1993), Dante Gabriel Rossetti (jtly, 2003), The Railway: Art in the Age of Steam (jtly, 2008), Ford Madox Brown: Pre-Raphaelite Pioneer (2011), 111 Places in Liverpool That You Shouldn't Miss (with Peter de Figueiredo, 2016); various articles in art-historical jls; *Recreations* playing the piano, cooking, opera; *Style—* Dr Julian Treuherz, Esq; ✉ 1 Ingestre Road, Oxton, Wirral CH43 5TZ

TREVAIL, Charles; s of Donald Charles Trevail (d 1986), and Lois Mary, *née* Rowse (d 2003); *b* 22 August 1960; *Educ* Plymouth Coll, Univ of Durham (BA), Postgrad Dip Mktg; *m* 1995, Imelda Primrose; 2 da (Florence Lois Kate b 15 Sept 1996, Martha Elizabeth b 8 May 1999); *Career* formerly: various mktg posts LDDC and Acco Rexel, business conslt Strategy International; Sampson Tyrrell Enterprise (Enterprise Identity Group t/a Enterprise IG since 1998): account dir 1988–91, bd dir 1991–95, md 1995–99; ceo FutureBrand (brand consultancy of Interpublic) 1999–2003, memb Bd McCann Europe, fndr Promise Corp plc (business consultancy) 2004; reg speaker at confs on branding and commentator in media, occasional advsr to New Labour on strategy; memb Marketing Soc; FRSA; *Recreations* football, tennis, sailing, hill walking, bird watching, politics, family; *Style—* Charles Trevail, Esq

TREVELYAN, Ann-Marie; MP; da of Leonard Beaton (d 1971), and Katherine Beaton; *Educ* St Paul's Girls Sch, Oxford Poly; *m* 1998, John Trevelyan; 1 s (James), 1 da (Emily); *Career* CA; MP (Cons) Berwick-upon-Tweed 2015–; *Recreations* gardening, tennis, walking; *Style—* Mrs Anne-Marie Trevelyan, MP; ✉ House of Commons, London SW1A 0AA (Twitter @annietrev)

TREVELYAN KEE, Hon Mrs (Catherine Mary); OBE (1977); da of Baron Trevelyan (Life Peer, d 1985), and Violet Margaret, *née* Bartholomew; *b* 1943; *Educ* St Mary's Sch Calne, Univ of St Andrews; *m* 10 Dec 1990, Robert Kee; *Career* exec dir New York City Cultural Cncl and Cultural Cncl Fndn 1969–73, admin Windsor Festival 1974–76, dep sec-gen London Celebrations Ctee for the Queen's Silver Jubilee 1976–77, exhbn organiser 1978–80, Carlton Cleeve Ltd, md The Burlington Magazine 1980–2012, dir The Burlington Magazine Fndn Inc 1986–2012; govr Int Students House Univ of London until 1997; tstee: Public Catalogue Fndn 2006–09 and 2011–, Nat Gallery Tst 2008–, Thistle Tst 2008–; *Style—* The Hon Mrs Trevelyan Kee, OBE

T

TREVERTON-JONES, Ronald; s of Dennis Ford Treverton-Jones (d 1950), of Newport, Gwent, and Alison Joy Bielski, *née* Morris-Prosser (d 2014); *b* 1 August 1949; *Educ* Malvern Coll, Univ of Wales Swansea (BSc); *m* 1, 31 July 1970 (m dis 1985), Margaret Jean, da of Donald John Purser, of Northfield, Birmingham; 2 s (Peter b 1976, Michael b 1978); m 2, 17 Oct 1987, Jacqueline Diane, da of James Leslie Beckingham Welch (d 1974), of Quinton, Birmingham; *Career* grad trainee National Westminster Bank 1970–72, trainee N Lea Barham & Brooks 1972–74, sr ptnr Harris Allday 1992–2006 (ptnr 1976–), md EFG Harris Allday 2006–12 (chm 2012–), dir EFG Private Bank Ltd 2006–14; vice-chm The Bow Group London 1979–80, chm Birmingham Bow Group 1979–80; chm Birmingham Stock Exchange Assoc 1995–99; memb Stock Exchange 1975; *Books* Financing our Cities (with Edwina Currie and Peter McGauley, 1976), Right Wheel – A Conservative Policy for the Motor Industry (1977); *Recreations* country pursuits, woodland management, travel, Caribbean development; *Style—* Ronald Treverton-Jones, Esq; ✉ Ravenhill Court, Lulsley, Knightwick, Worcestershire WR6 5QW (☎ 01886 821242); EFG Harris Allday, 33 Great Charles Street, Birmingham B3 3JN (☎ 0121 214 2221, fax 0121 236 2587, e-mail ronald.treverton-jones@efgha.com)

TREVES, Vanni Emanuele; CBE (2012); s of Giuliano Treves (ka 1944), and Marianna, *née* Baer; *b* 3 November 1940; *Educ* St Paul's (fndn scholar), Univ of Oxford (MA), Univ of

Illinois (res fell, Fulbright scholar, LLM); *m* 7 Jan 1971, Angela Veronica, da of Lt-Gen Sir Richard Fyffe, DSO, OBE, MC (d 1971); 2 s (Alexander b 1973, William b 1975), 1 da (Louise b 1983); *Career* slr; ptnr Macfarlanes Slrs 1970–2002 (sr ptnr 1987–99); dir: Oceonics Group plc 1984–95, Saatchi & Saatchi Co plc 1987–90, Fiskars Ltd 1989–2008, Amplifon 2000–12; chm: BBA Group plc 1989–2001, McKechnie plc 1991–2000, Dennis Group plc 1996–99, Channel Four Television Corporation 1998–2003, Equitable Life Assurance Society 2001–09, Intertek Group plc 2001–11, Korn/Ferry International UK 2004–; dir Homerton Univ Hosp NHS Tst 2012–; sr advsr Oliver Wyman 2007–09; chm: London Business Sch 1998–2006, Nat Coll for Sch Leadership 2004–12; tstee: J Paul Getty Jr Charitable Tst, 29th May 1961 Charitable Tst, Prisoners Educn Tst, Fledgeling Equity and Bond Funds (chm 1992–2000); govr: Coll of Law 1999–2006, Sadler's Wells Fndn 1999–2008; vice-pres London Fedn of Clubs for Young People, fell NSPCC, fell St Paul's Cathedral; slr to the Royal Acad of Arts; hon fell London Business Sch; Knight of the Star of Italy 2014; *Recreations* walking, eating, watercolours, clocks; *Clubs* Boodle's; *Style*— Vanni Treves, Esq, CBE

TREVETT, Peter George; QC (1992); s of George Albert Trevett (d 1995), of Surbiton, Surrey, and Janet, *née* Ayling (d 1992); *b* 25 November 1947; *Educ* Kingston GS, Queens' Coll Cambridge (MA, LLM); *m* 8 July 1972, Vera Lucia; 2 s (Thomas b 1973, Philip b 1978), 1 da (Jessica b 1982); *Career* called to the Bar Lincoln's Inn 1971 (bencher), practising revenue barr 1973–; author of various articles in professional jls; *Recreations* golf, collecting succulent plants, gardening, book collecting, reading; *Style*— Peter Trevett, Esq, QC; ✉ 11 New Square, Lincoln's Inn, London WC2A 3QB (✆ 020 7242 4017, fax 020 7831 2391)

TREVITT, William James Piper; OBE (2012); s of William John Maskell Trevitt, of Hereford, and Jane Valerie, *née* Piper; *b* 8 April 1969; *Educ* Royal Ballet Schs; *m* 9 Aug 1992, Rebecca, *née* Holmes; 3 s (Joseph Zebulon b 15 April 1994, Zachary George b 25 Aug 1996, Elijah Ben b 4 April 2002); *Career* Royal Ballet: joined 1987, first artist 1989–90, soloist 1990–93, first soloist 1993–94, princ 1994–99; fndr memb K Ballet; perfs incl: Siegfried in Swan Lake, Solor in La Bayadère, Count Albrecht in Giselle, the Prince in Cinderella, the Prince in Sleeping Beauty, Colas in La Fille Ma Gardee, Oberon in The Dream, the Rake in The Rake's Progress, lead in Push Comes to Shove, Mr Jeremy Fisher in Tales of Beatrix Potter, Mercutio in Romeo and Juliet, Lescaut in Manon, the Friend in The Judas Tree, Mr Wordly Wise in Mr Worldly Wise, leading man in Ballet Imperial; other perfs incl: Agon, Stravinsky Violin Concerto (Aria I), Symphony in C (Third Movement), Duo concertant, La Ronde, Herman Schmerman; co-founded George Piper Dances with Michael Nunn , *qv*; perfs with George Piper Dances incl: Steptext, Sigue, Truly great thing, Critical Mass, Torsion, other mens wives, Approximate Sonata I, V, Mesmerics, restaged Halleloo, choreographed Tangoid and Moments of Plastic Jubilation; also with Michael Nunn: co-filmed and co-directed Ballet Boyz and Ballet Boyz II – The Next Step (Channel 4), presented 4Dance (Channel 4) 2003 and 2004, created Critic's Choice ***** (featuring Matthew Bourne, *qv*, Michael Clark, Akram Khan, *qv*, Russell Maliphant, *qv* and Christopher Wheeldon) 2004, Broken Fall (commissioned by Russell Malipahnt, premiered ROH) 2004, dir and choreographer of Naked (premiered at Sadler's Wells) 2005; *Awards* nominated South Bank Show Dance Award 2001 and 2003, nomination (for Memerics) Best New Dance Production Laurence Olivier Award 2004, winner (for Broken Fall) Best New Dance Production Laurence Olivier Award 2004; *Recreations* photography, cinema; *Style*— William Trevitt, Esq, OBE; ✉ George Piper Dances, Sadler's Wells, Rosebery Avenue, London EC1R 4TN (✆ 020 7863 8238, e-mail william@gpdances.com)

TREVOR, William; Hon KBE (2002, Hon CBE 1977); *b* 24 May 1928; *Educ* St Columba's Coll Dublin, Trinity Coll Dublin; *m* 1952, Jane, da of C N Ryan; 2 s; *Career* writer; Allied Irish Banks' Prize 1976, Hudson Review Prize 1990, David Cohen Prize 1999, Ireland Fund Literary Prize 2005; Hon DLitt: Univ of Exeter 1984, Trinity Coll Dublin 1986, Queen's Univ Belfast 1989, Nat Univ of Ireland Cork 1990; memb Irish Acad of Letters; CLit 1994; *Books* The Old Boys (1964, Hawthornden Prize), The Boarding House (1965), The Love Department (1966), The Day We Got Drunk on Cake (1967), Mrs Eckdorf in O'Neill's Hotel (1969), Miss Gomez and the Brethren (1971), The Ballroom of Romance (1972), Elizabeth Alone (1973), Angels at the Ritz (1975, Royal Soc of Literature Award), The Children of Dynmouth (1976, Whitbread Award), Lovers of Their Time (1978), The Distant Past (1979), Other People's Worlds (1980), Beyond the Pale (1981), Fools of Fortune (1983, Whitbread Award), A Writer's Ireland (1984), The News from Ireland (1986), Nights at the Alexandra (1987), The Silence in the Garden (1989, Yorkshire Post Book of the Year), Family Sins (1990), Two Lives (1991), Juliet's Story (1991), Collected Stories (1992), Excursions in the Real World (1993), Felicia's Journey (1994, Sunday Express Book of the Year, Whitbread Book of the Year), After Rain (1996), Death in Summer (1998), The Hill Bachelors (2000, Macmillan/PEN Award, Irish Times Literature Prize), The Story of Lucy Gault (2002, Listowel Prize for Irish Fiction), Love and Summer (2009); *Style*— William Trevor, KBE

TREWAVAS, Prof Anthony James; s of Clifford John Trewavas (d 1986), of Penzance, Cornwall, and Phyllis Mary, *née* Timms (d 1993); *b* 17 June 1939; *Educ* Roan GS, UCL (BSc, PhD); *m* 29 Aug 1963, Valerie, da of Ivor John Leng; 2 da (Seren Angharad b 6 Jan 1969, Eira Siobhan b 14 Feb 1970), 1 s (Joseph Jonathan Christopher b 16 July 1979); *Career* postdoctoral fell UEA; prof of plant biochemistry Univ of Edinburgh 1990– (lectr 1970–84, reader 1984–90); visiting prof: Michigan State Univ 1973, Nat Acad of Sciences Poland 1979, Univ of Illinois 1980, Univ of Alberta 1983, Univ of Calif Davis 1985, Univ of Bonn 1987, Univ of N Carolina 1988, Nat Univ of Mexico 1989, Univ of Milan 1996; memb Editorial Bd Plant Physiology 1989–; elected memb American Soc of Plant Physiologists 1999, memb Academia Europaea 2002; FRSE 1993, FRS 1999; *Publications* Plasticity in Plants (with D E Jennings, 1985), Molecular and Cellular Aspects of Calcium in Plant Development (1986), Plant Behaviour and Intelligence (2014); 250 scientific papers; *Recreations* music, reading, bonsai growing; *Style*— Prof Anthony Trewavas, FRS, FRSE, AcadEurop; ✉ Old Schoolhouse, Croft Street, Penicuik, Midlothian EH26 9DH (✆ 01968 673372); Institute of Molecular Plant Science, King's Buildings, University of Edinburgh, Edinburgh EH9 3JH (✆ 0131 650 5328, fax 0131 651 3331, e-mail trewavas@ed.ac.uk)

TREWBY, John Allan; CB (1999); s of late Vice Adm Sir Allan Trewby, KCB, of Henley-on-Thames, Oxon, and Lady Sandra Trewby, *née* Stedham; *b* 17 September 1945; *Educ* Marlborough, Trinity Coll Cambridge (MA); *m* 1971, Belinda Mary, *née* Boving; 3 c (Penny b 1973, Alexander b 1975, Alice b 1984); *Career* RN: joined 1963, memb Jt Serv Expdn to the Sahara Desert 1969, Cdr HMS Collingwood 1979, weapon engrg offr HMS Illustrious (Falklands War) 1982, Capt 1984, Cdre Clyde Submarine Base 1992–94, Rear Adm 1994, chief exec Naval Bases and Supply Agency 1996–99, chief naval engr offr 1997–99; naval advsr BAE Systems 1999–2007, defence conslt 2007–; chm: ITT Defence Ltd, ITT Defence España 2010–; govr West Hill Park Sch 1998–2010, special cmmr Duke of York's Royal Military Sch Dover 1999–2010, chm Southampton Univ Hosps Tst 2007–; Liveryman Worshipful Co of Engrs 2000, Freeman City of London 2000; MInstD, FIEE 1985, FREng 1999; *Recreations* golf, tennis, skiing; *Clubs* Army and Navy; *Style*— Rear Adm John Trewby, CB, FREng; ✉ Defence Advisers Ltd, Old Sheet House, 34 London Road, Petersfield, Hampshire GU31 4BE (✆ 01730 265606, e-mail john.trewby@defenceadvisers.com)

TREWIN, Ion Courtenay Gill; s of John Courtenay Trewin, OBE (d 1990), the theatre critic and author, and Wendy Elizabeth, *née* Monk (d 2000); *b* 13 July 1943; *Educ* Highgate

Sch; *m* 7 Aug 1965, Susan Harriet, da of Walter Harry Merry (d 1953), of Highgate, London; 1 s (Simon, *qv*, b 1966), 1 da (Maria b 1971); *Career* reporter: The Independent & South Devon Times Plymouth 1960–63, The Sunday Telegraph 1963–67; The Times: ed staff 1967–79, ed The Times Diary 1969–72, literary ed 1972–79; ed Drama Magazine 1979–81; publisher: Hodder & Stoughton 1979–92 (sr ed 1979–85, editorial dir 1985–91, publishing dir 1991–92), Orion Publishing Gp 1992–2006 (publishing dir Weidenfeld & Nicolson imprint 1992–96, dir 1994–2006, md Weidenfeld & Nicolson div 1996–2002, ed-in-chief 2001–06); chm: Library Ctee Highgate Literary and Scientific Inst 1974–90, Soc of Bookmen 1986–88, Cheltenham Festival of Literature 1997–2007; chm of judges Booker Prize for Fiction 1974; memb: Lit Panel Arts Cncl of GB 1975–78, Arts and Library Ctee MCC 1988–98, Advsy Ctee Man Booker Prize (formerly Booker Prize) 1989–; literary dir Man Booker prizes 2006– (formerly administrator); special prof Univ of Nottingham 2007–; author of introductions to new edns of classic thrillers (for Leslie Charteris, Sapper and Dornford Yates); *Books* Journalism (1975), Norfolk Cottage (1977), Alan Clark's Diaries: Into Politics (ed, 2000), Alan Clark's The Last Diaries (ed, 2002), The Hugo Young papers: Thirty Years of British Politics – Off the Record (ed, 2008, Channel 4 Political Book of the Year Award 2009), Alan Clark: the Biography (2009), Alan Clark: A Life In His Own Words, the Edited Diaries 1972–1999 (2010); *Recreations* indulging grandsons, watching cricket, gossip, gardening; *Clubs* Garrick (memb Gen Ctee 2007–10), MCC; *Style*— Ion Trewin, Esq; ✉ South Wing, Snettisham House, Snettisham, King's Lynn, Norfolk PE31 6RZ (e-mail itrewin@aol.com)

TREWIN, Simon Courtenay; s of Ion Trewin , *qv*, and Susan Harriet, *née* Merry; *b* 24 May 1966, London; *Educ* Highgate Sch, Univ of Kent at Canterbury (BA); *m* 1992, Helen Adie; 1s (Jack Courtenay b 1993); *Career* as memb Equity: Chichester Festival Theatre 1984–85, Birmingham Rep 1985–86, various West End theatres via Duncan Weldon Ltd 1985–93; literary agent Sheil Land Associates 1993–99; PFD (formerly Peters, Fraser and Dunlop Ltd): dep head Literary Dept 1999–2006, dir 2006–07, jt head Literary Dept 2006–07; United Agents: dir 2008–12, jt head Literary Dept 2008–10, head Literary Dept 2010–12; currently ptnr and head UK Literary Dept William Morris Endeavor Entertainment LLC; visiting prof Southampton Solent Univ 2010–11; sec Assoc of Authors' Agents 2001–04; tstee Salisbury Playhouse 2011–15, tstee Cncl of Mgmnt Arvon Fndn 2012–; *Publications* Rock and Pop Elevens (jtly, 2004), Live8: The Official Book (jtly, 2005), The Encyclopaedia of Guilty Pleasures (jtly, 2006), Shopping While Drunk (jtly, 2007). When Cockshut Meets Sandy Balls (2008); *Recreations* collecting work by emerging artists, theatre, live music; *Clubs* Old Cholmelians, The Hospital, Soho House, Ivy, Hon; *Style*— Simon Trewin, Esq; ✉ WME (William Morris Endeavor Entertainment LLC) (e-mail sct@wmeentertainment.com, website www.wmeauthors.co.uk and www.wma.com)

TRIBE, Elisabeth Jane; da of Michael Tribe, and Wendie, *née* Farley; *Educ* N London Collegiate Sch, Emmanuel Coll Cambridge (MA); *m* Martin Gammon; 1 s (Oscar), 1 da (Lydia); *Career* successively sec, editorial asst, jr ed and commissioning ed Routledge 1987–93, sr commissioning ed then publisher Hodder & Stoughton 1993–96, ed dir rising to dir schools publishing Hodder Headline 1996–, md Schs Div Hodder Educn 2007–; former chair WHSmith Link-Up Charities Tst, former govr S Camden Community Sch; *Recreations* gardening, reading, walking, cycling; *Style*— Mrs Elisabeth Tribe; ✉ Hodder Education, 338 Euston Road, London NW1 3BH (✆ 020 7873 6287, e-mail elisabeth.tribe@hodder.co.uk)

TRIBE, John Edward; s of George Edward Tribe (d 1996), and Gwendoline, *née* Morton (d 2011); *b* 24 March 1946, March, Cambs; *Educ* Oundle, Univ of Reading (BSc); *Career* dir family farming businesses 1969–97; dir Marcam & MDS Supplies Ltd 1978–2004, chm United Farmers Trading Agency 1990–95 (dir 1989–95); first chm March and Chatteris Trg Gp 1978–80; chm: March Branch NFU 1985–86, Cambs Area Trg Ctee Agric Trg Bd (ATB) 1987–90, Fenland Crime Prevention Panel 1988–89, Cambs Co NFU 1990; E of England Agric Soc: chm Safety Ctee 1990–93, memb Cncl 1990–2016, memb Fin Ctee 1998–2003, chm Dog Show Ctee 1999–2002, chm Flower Show Ctee 2003–11; memb: Bd ATB W Anglia (LATB9) 1990–93, Corp Cambs Coll of Agric and Horticulture until merger 1998; dir Cambs TEC (Central and Southern Cambs Trg and Enterprise Cncl) 1990–97, first chm Consortium of Rural TEC's 1991–97; *Recreations* shooting, classic cars, wine, historic buildings, travel; *Style*— John Edward Tribe, Esq; ✉ Brampton Hall, Brampton, Beccles, Suffolk NR34 8DS; (e-mail jetribe@btinternet.com)

TRICKETT, Jon; MP; s of Laurence Thomas Trickett, of Leeds, and Rose Trickett; *b* 2 July 1950; *Educ* Univ of Hull (BA), Univ of Leeds (MA); *m* 1994, Sarah, da of Thomas Balfour, of Carlisle; 1 s (Daniel Paul b 1975), 1 da (Emma Rachel b 1975); *Career* leader Leeds City Cncl 1989–96 (cncllr 1984–96); MP (Lab) Hemsworth 1996–, PPS to Min Without Portfolio 1997–98, PPS to Sec of State DTI 1998–99, shadow sec of state for communities and local govt & shadow sec for the constitutional convention 2015–; *Recreations* cycling; *Style*— Jon Trickett, Esq, MP; ✉ House of Commons, London SW1A 0AA (✆ 020 7219 5074)

TRICKETT, Lynn; *née* Fishman; da of Dr Jack Fishman, of London, and Eileen, *née* Slonims; *b* 19 May 1945, Sutton, Surrey; *Educ* St Martin in the Fields HS for Girls, Chelsea Sch of Art; *m* 8 March 1968, Terence Wilden Trickett; 1 s (Alexander Wilden b 9 Aug 1973), 2 da (Polly Kate b 4 Nov 1977, Rosey Anna b 22 Dec 1983); *Career* designer: Planning Unit 1966–67, Wiggins Teape 1967–69, FFS Advertising Agency NY 1969–70; fndr ptnr Trickett & Webb 1971–2003, Trickett Associates 2003–; work exhibited and published throughout the world, winner of numerous awards in Europe, Asia and USA; regular jury memb D&AD and RSA Bursaries and other European and American design competitions, external examiner various BA and MA graphic design courses, memb Graphic Design Ctee CNAA 1986–87, past memb Cncl Chartered Soc of Designers; tstee and memb Br Design and Art Direction Exec Ctee 2001–04; chm Nat Graphic Design & Print Awards 1990, chm and co fndr Donside Student Awards, chm Loerie Design Awards SA 2003, chm Consort Royal Student Awards 2004–05, foreman Graphics Jury D&AD Awards 2004, chm Howard Smith Paper Student Awards 2006–07, jury memb D&AD 50th Anniversary Awards 2012; lectures given on graphic design and stamp design in Europe, USA and Australia; FCSD, FRSA; *Publications* contrib to and featured in numerous books on graphic design incl: A Smile in the Mind, The Graphics Book, International Women in Design, Graphic Design and Designers, Who's Who in Graphic Design, Media Careers/Design First Choice, A Smile in the Mind 2; *Recreations* Russian avant garde art, British art of the 1930s-1950s, British poster design; *Style*— Mrs Lynn Trickett; ✉ 9 Hamilton Terrace, London NW8 9RE (✆ 020 7286 5209, e-mail lynntrick@mac.com)

TRIESMAN, Baron (Life Peer UK 2004), of Tottenham in the London Borough of Haringey; David Maxim Triesman; s of Michael Triesman (d 1992), of London, and Rita, *née* Lubran (d 1986); *b* 30 October 1943; *Educ* Stationers' Company's Sch London, Univ of Essex (BA, MA), King's Coll Cambridge; *m* 2004, Lucy, da of Ben Hooberman, and Ellen Hooberman; 1 da (Anna); *Career* research offr in addictions Inst of Psychiatry Univ of London 1970–74, seconded to ASTMS 1974–75, sr lectr and co-ordinator of postgrad research in social sciences South Bank Poly (now London South Bank Univ) 1975–84, dep gen sec Nat Assoc of Teachers in Further and Higher Educn 1984–93, gen sec Assoc of Univ Teachers 1993–2001; gen sec Lab Pty 2001–03, Lord in Waiting 2004–, Govt whip 2004–05, Parly under sec of state FCO 2005–07, Parly under sec of state Dept for Innovation, Univs and Skills 2007–08, shadow business min 2010–11, shadow FCO min 2011–14; memb EU External Affrs Sub-Ctee 2015–; memb European Leadership Network 2014–; chm FA 2008–10, memb Bd Wembley Nat Stadium Ltd 2008–10, patron

Tottenham Hotspurs Fndn 2007–, tstee The Football Fndn 2008–10, chm FIFA England World Cup Bid 2008–10; chm Triesman Assocs 2012–; non-exec chm: Mortgage Credit Corp (UBS) 1980–2000, Victoria Management Ltd 1999–2001; chm Templewood Student Investment Ltd 2012–13; chm Bd of Advsrs Templewood Merchant Bank 2010–13, memb Bd Augur Buckler 2010–13, non-exec memb Bd Havin Bank Ltd 2013–, memb Bd One Ocean Ltd 2015–; dir: Salamanca Gp 2013–, Funding Affordable Homes 2013–, FAH Housing Assoc 2015–; chm: Usecolour Fndn 2001, Bd Chester Collection of Art 2012–13, The Design Cmmn 2015–; chm Teacher's Panel Burnham FHE Ctee 1980–84; memb: Kensington, Chelsea and Westminster AHA 1976–82, Univ Entrance and Schs Examinations Bd for social science 1980–84, Home Office Consultative Ctee on Prison Educn 1980–83, Gtr London Manpower Bd (additional memb GLC) 1981–86, TUC Public Servs Ctee 1984–1990, Highgate Literary and Scientific Inst 1990, Independent Review of Higher Educn (Bett Ctee) 1998–99, Panel on Public Appts DTI 1997–2001, HEFCE Standing Ctee on Business and the Community 1999–2001, Br North American Ctee 1999–2015, Public Management Fndn 2000–01, Cncl Ruskin Coll Oxford 2000–02, Better Regulation Task Force (Cabinet Office) 2000–02, Public Service Productivity Panel (HM Treasy) 2000–02, Charles Rennie MacKintosh Soc, Bd Affordable Homes Investment Fund 2013–, Bd of Govrs Haringey, Enfield & NE London Coll 2016–; jt chm All-Pty Gp on St Lucia 2013–, vice-chm All-Pty Gp on Chinese in the UK 2013–; visiting prof in social economics S Lawrence Univ 1977, visiting scholar in economics Wolfson Coll Cambridge 2000–, sr visiting fell Univ of Warwick 2003–, visiting fell in govt LSE 2004–; hon fell Univ of Northampton; Hon LLD London South Bank Univ 2009, Hon DUniv Essex 2010; FSS 1984, FRSA 1992; *Books* The Medical and Non-Medical Use of Drugs (1970), Football Mania (with G Vinai, 1972), Football in London (1985), College Administration (1988), Managing Change (1991), Can Unions Survive? (1999), approx 50 academic papers on epidemiology, addiction and economics; *Recreations* family, football (memb Tottenham youth team 1961–63), walking, fine art and print collecting, blues guitar; *Clubs* Tottenham Hotspur Supporters', Middlesex CCC; *Style—* The Lord Triesman

TRIGG, Prof Roger Hugh; s of Rev Ivor Trigg, of Taunton, Somerset, and Muriel Grace, *née* Collins; *b* 14 August 1941; *Educ* Bristol GS, New Coll Oxford (MA, DPhil); *m* 12 July 1972, Julia, da of Wilfred Gibbs, of Taunton, Somerset; 1 s (Nicholas b 10 May 1973 d 1990), 1 da (Alison b 26 Jan 1977); *Career* Univ of Warwick: lectr 1966–74, sr lectr 1974–78, reader 1978–87, chm Dept of Philosophy 1984–91 and 1994–95, founding dir Centre for Res in Philosophy and Literature 1985–91, prof of philosophy 1987–2007, emeritus prof 2007–; interim dir Ian Ramsey Centre Univ of Oxford 2006–07 (sr research fell 2007–), academic dir Centre for Study of Religion in Public Life Kellogg Coll Oxford 2009–12 (sr research fell 2010–12), assoc scholar Religious Freedom Project Berkley Center Georgetown Univ 2011–14, research assoc Dept of Constitutional Law and Philosophy of Law Univ of the Free State SA 2012–15; visiting fell: St Cross Coll Oxford 1986–87, 1991–92 and 2006–10, Harris Manchester Coll Oxford 1996; Stanton lectr in philosophy of religion Univ of Cambridge 1997; visiting fell Center of Theol Inquiry Princeton 2002; pres: British Soc for the Philosophy of Religion 1993–96, Mind Assoc 1997–98, European Soc for the Philosophy of Religion 2008–10; chm Nat Ctee for Philosophy 1998–2003, founding chm Br Philosophical Assoc 2003–04; JP Warks 1981–91; *Books* Pain and Emotion (1970), Reason and Commitment (1973), Reality at Risk (1980, revised edn 1989), The Shaping of Man (1982), Understanding Social Science (1985, 2 edn 2000), Ideas of Human Nature (1988, 2 edn 1999), Rationality and Science (1993), Rationality and Religion (1998), Philosophy Matters (2001), Morality Matters (2004), Religion in Public Life (2007), Equality, Freedom and Religion (2012), Religous Diversity (2014), The Roots of Religion (ed, with Justin Barrett, 2014) Beyond Matter (2015); *Style—* Prof Roger Trigg; ✉ St Cross College, Oxford OX1 3LZ (☎ 01865 278490, e-mail roger.trigg@theology.ox.ac.uk)

TRIGGER, His Hon Ian James Campbell; s of Lt Walter James Trigger (d 1961), and Mary Elizabeth, *née* Roberts (d 1984); *b* 16 November 1943; *Educ* Ruthin Sch, UCW Aberystwyth (LLB), Downing Coll Cambridge (MA, LLM); *m* 28 Aug 1971, Jennifer Ann, da of Harry Colin Downs (d 1986); 2 s (Ieuan Mungo Campbell b 12 Oct 1973, Simon Huw Campbell b 21 April 1977); *Career* lectr in law UWIST 1967–70; called to the Bar Inner Temple 1970 (major scholar 1968); in practice Northern Circuit 1970–93, asst recorder 1986–90, recorder 1990–93, circuit judge (Northern Circuit) 1993–2014, ret; pres Mental Health Review Tbnl 1995–; pt/t chm: Social Security Appeal Tbnl 1983–93, Med Appeal Tbnl 1989–93, Disability Appeal Tbnl 1992–93, Immigration Appeal Tbnl 1998–2005; immigration judge 2005–07; churchwarden: St Saviour's Oxton 1986–88, St Garmon's Llanarmon-yn-Iâl 2005–07; licensed lay reader Church in Wales 2005–, judge Provincial Court Church in Wales 2005–, chm St Asaph Diocesan Conf 2005–07; chair Standards Ctee Denbighshire CC 2012–; *Recreations* preserving the countryside from the ravages of greed and the Church from mediocrity; *Style—* His Hon Ian Trigger; ✉ Queen Elizabeth II Law Courts, Derby Square, Liverpool L2 1XA (☎ 0151 473 7373)

TRIGGS HODGE, Andrew; MBE (2009); s of Peter Triggs Hodge, and Liv Triggs Hodge; *b* 3 March 1979; *Educ* Upper Wharfedale Sch Skipton, South Craven Sch Keighley, Staffs Univ (BSc), Univ of Oxford (MSc); *Career* rower; joined Molesey Boat Club 2000; winner (pair) GB Trials 2004, 2005 and 2006; memb winning Oxford crew Oxford and Cambridge Boat Race 2005, Gold medal (coxless fours) World Championships 2005 and 2006 (Bronze medal (eights) 2003), Gold medal (coxless fours) Olympic Games Beijing 2008, Silver medal (coxless pair) World Championships 2009, 2010 and 2011, Gold medal (coxless fours) Olympic Games 2012; BOA Athletes of the Year (jtly, as memb coxless fours); *Style—* Andrew Triggs Hodge, Esq, MBE; ☎ 07887 775991

TRIMBLE, Baron (Life Peer UK 2006), of Lisnagarvey in the County of Antrim; (William) David Trimble; PC (1998); s of William Trimble (d 1968), and Ivy, *née* Jack; *b* 15 October 1944; *Educ* Bangor GS, Queen's Univ Belfast (LLB); *m* 1978, Daphne Elizabeth, da of Gerald Montgomery Orr (d 1981); 2 s (Richard David b 1982, Nicholas James b 1986), 2 da (Victoria Claire b 1984, Sarah Elizabeth b 1992); *Career* called to the Bar of NI 1969; sr lectr Faculty of Law Queen's Univ Belfast 1977–90 (lectr 1968–77), ed NI Law Reports 1975–90; MP (UUP) Upper Bann 1990–2005, MLA (UUP) Upper Bann 1998–2007; ldr UUP 1995–2005; elected NI Forum 1996–98, first min NI Assembly 1998–2002; winner Nobel Peace Prize 1998, Parliamentarian of the Year Zurich/Spectator Parly Awards 2001; *Books* Housing Law in Northern Ireland (co-author, 1984), Human Rights and Responsibilities in Britain and Ireland (contrib, 1986), To Raise Up a New Northern Ireland (2001); *Recreations* music, opera, history, reading; *Style—* The Rt Hon the Lord Trimble, PC; ✉ House of Lords, London SW1A 0PW

TRIMBLE, Jonathan Wesley; s of Oliver Trimble (d 1996), and Sylvia, *née* Curran; *b* 26 June 1975, Kenton, London; *Educ* Reeds Sch Surrey (scholarship), Royal Holloway London (BA); *m* 17 Dec 2005, Zoe, *née* Dando; 1 s (Zachary Ellis b 14 Nov 2012); *Career* grad trainee RKCR/Y&R 1998–2007, head of account mgmnt DDB London 2007–09, gp dir Fallon London 2009–11, ceo 18 Feet & Rising 2011–; 2 Silver D&AD Awards 2004; memb agency IPA; *Recreations* cinema, music; *Style—* Jonathan Trimble, Esq; ✉ 18 Feet & Rising, Threeways House, 40–44 Clipstone Street, London W1W 5DW (website www.18feet.com, Twitter @18feetandrising)

TRIMBLE, Rob; *Career* chief exec Bromley-by-Bow Centre 2002–; Seiff Award for Outstanding Leadership Business in the Community 2008; *Style—* Rob Trimble, Esq; ✉ Bromley by Bow Centre, St Leonard's Street, Bromley by Bow, London E3 3BT

TRINICK, Prof Anthony Graham Kyle (Tony); s of Alexander Leslie Trinick (d 1983), and Jean Edna Kyle, *née* Ferrier (d 1983); *b* 26 October 1943; *Educ* St Dunstan's Coll Catford, Borough Poly London (ONC, Dip H&V Engrg, HNC); *m* 1, 1967, Clare Elisabeth (d 2005), da of Dr Paul Freeman; 2 s (Mark David Kyle b 21 Sept 1973, Andrew Timothy Kyle b 5 April 1977); m 2, 2007, Carol Ann Wright; *Career* G N Haden & Sons Ltd: apprentice 1962–66, engr 1966–73, design mangr Lloyds Computer Centre 1973–77, project mangr Haden International 1977–81, project dir Torness NPS 1981–84, project dir Aldermaston AWRE 90 Building 1984–87, HQ dir 1987–91, dir Haden Young Ltd 1987–92, dir Haden Building Services Ltd and Haden International Ltd 1992–95; princ TriTone Partnership 1995–, visiting prof Dept of Architecture and Building Technol Univ of Nottingham 1995–98; devpt dir: Fox Linton Assoc (interior design and architecture) 1996–, Panel-Built Environment HEFCE RAE 2001 1999–2002; special prof Sch of the Built Environment Univ of Nottingham 2000–; memb: American Soc for Heating, Refrigeration and AC Engrs 1970–2000, Assoc of Project Mangrs 1979; Freeman City of London, Liveryman Worshipful Co of Fan Makers; CEng 1990; MCIA 1996; FCIBSE 1989 (MCIBSE 1966), FREng 1994; *Recreations* sailing, swimming, walking, bee keeping (memb Kent Beekeepers' Assoc); *Clubs* IOD, Castle Baynard Ward (chm 2010, planted centenary tree at St Paul's Cathedral 2010); *Style—* Prof Tony Trinick, FREng; ✉ TriTone Partnership, 5 Little Thrift, Petts Wood, Orpington, Kent BR5 1NQ (☎ and fax 01689 820838, e-mail tonytrinick@trinick.com)

TRINICK, (George) Marcus Arthur; QC (2010); s of George Edward Michael Trinick, OBE, DL (d 1994), and Maud Elizabeth Lyon, *née* Hutchinson (d 1998); *b* 11 June 1952, Surrey; *Educ* Haileybury and ISC, Queen's Univ Belfast (BA); *m* 1, 3 Nov 1978 (m dis); 1 s (John Michael Robert b 11 Dec 1980), 1 da (Loveday Jessica Mary b 4 Oct 1983); m 2, 2009, Geraldine; *Career* admitted slr 1983 (rights of audience in higher courts 2007); slr specialising in energy, planning and environmental law; ptnr: Coodes 1985–90 (joined 1983), Bond Pearce 1990–2008 (trainee then slr 1979–83, rejoined 1990), Eversheds 2008–; memb Bd Br Wind Energy Assoc (now RenewableUK), memb American and European Wind Energy Assocs, memb Scottish Renewables; runner-up Ptnr of the Year The Lawyer magazine 2004; memb Law Soc 1983, legal memb RTPI 2003; *Books* From The Great War to the Holy Land – The Odyssey of Lieutenant George Trinick (2014); *Recreations* walking, travel, reading, Roman history, cricket, writing; *Clubs* Lobsters Cricket, Trevithick Soc, Nat Tst, Rockbourne Wine; *Style—* Marcus Trinick, Esq, QC; ✉ Eversheds LLP, 1 Callaghan Square, Cardiff CF1 (☎ 01725 551198, mobile 07747 118762, e-mail marcustrinick@eversheds.com)

TRIPP, Rt Rev Howard George; s of Basil Tripp (d 1981), and Alice, *née* Haslett (d 1985); *b* 3 July 1927, Croydon; *Educ* John Fisher Sch Purley, St John's Seminary Wonersh; *Career* asst priest: St Mary Blackheath 1953–56, E Sheen 1956–62; diocesan covenant organiser 1958–68, asst fin sec 1962–68, parish priest E Sheen 1965–71, sec Southwark Catholic Childrens' Soc 1971–80, auxiliary bishop in Southwark 1980–2004, titular bishop of Newport 1980–; *Recreations* reading; *Style—* The Rt Rev Howard Tripp; ✉ 35 St Catherine's Close, London SW20 9NL (☎ 020 8542 4886, e-mail howardtripp@outlook.com)

TRIPPIER, Sir David; kt (1992), RD, JP (Rochdale 1975), DL (Lancashire 1994); s of Maj Austin Wilkinson Trippier, MC (d 1993), of Norden, Rochdale, Greater Manchester, and Mary Trippier (d 1974); *b* 15 May 1946; *Educ* Bury GS; *m* 1975, Ruth Worthington, barr; 3 s; *Career* cmmnd Offr Royal Marines Reserve 1968; MP (Cons): Rossendale 1979–83, Rossendale and Darwen 1983–92; PPS to Kenneth Clarke as min of state for health DHSS 1982–83; Parly under sec of state: for trade and industry 1983–85, Dept of Employment 1985–87, Dept of the Environment 1987–89; min of state DOE 1989–92; sec Cons Parly Def Ctee 1980–82; ldr Cons Gp Rochdale Cncl 1974–76 (cncllr 1969–78); nat vice-chm Assoc of Cons Clubs 1980, dep chm Cons Pty May-Dec 1990; chm: W H Ireland Ltd Stockbrokers, Sir David Trippier & Associates Ltd; dir Granada TV Ltd; govr Manchester GS 1993–2004; fndr: Rossendale Enterprise Trust, Rossendale Groundwork Trust; pres: Manchester Chamber of Commerce and Industry 1999–2000, Royal Lancs Agric Soc 1999–2000; Hon Col Royal Marines Reserve Merseyside 1996–; High Sheriff Lancs 1997–98; memb Stock Exchange 1968; FRSA 2006; Lend me Your Ears (autobiography, 1999); *Style—* Sir David Trippier, RD, JP, DL

TRITTON, (Robert) Guy Henton; s of Alan George Tritton, of Great Leighs, Essex, and Elizabeth Clare Throckmorton, of Coughton Court, Alcester; *b* 18 November 1963; *Educ* Eton, Univ of Durham (BSc); *m* 30 Aug 1995, Ursula Jane, da of Carl Pycraft; 1 da (Lara Ursula b 6 Sept 1996), 2 s (Luke Charles Henton b 16 Oct 1998, Jocelyn Raphael Malet b 5 April 2002); *Career* barrister; called to the Bar Inner Temple 1987, Pegasus scholar 1990; practising in intellectual property; chm Rhino Ark (UK); *Books* Intellectual Property in Europe (1996, 3 edn 2007); *Recreations* piano playing, shooting, windsurfing, music; *Style—* Guy Tritton, Esq; ✉ Hogarth Chambers, 5 New Square, London WC2A 3RJ (☎ 020 7404 0404, fax 020 7404 0505, e-mail guy.tritton@btinternet.com)

TROLLOPE, Andrew David Hedderwick; QC (1991); s of Arthur George Cecil Trollope, of Overton, Hants, and Rosemary, *née* Hodson; *b* 6 November 1948; *Educ* Charterhouse, Univ of Nancy; *m* 1978, Anne Forbes; 2 s (Harvey Evelyn b 16 Jan 1980, Francis Henry b 2 Nov 1981); *Career* called to the Bar Inner Temple 1971 (bencher 2002); recorder of the Crown Court 1989– (asst recorder 1984), head of chambers; memb: Criminal Bar Assoc Ctee 1991–2002, SE Circuit Ctee 1990–93, 1994–97, 2006–09 and 2013–; chm: N London Bar Mess 1998–2001, Int Rels Ctee Bar Cncl 2002–08, Advsy Cncl Br Inst of Int and Comparative Law; dir St Julian's Estates Ltd; fell Soc of Advanced Legal Studies (FSALS) 1998; *Recreations* opera, jazz, travel, tennis, sailing, gardening; *Clubs* Garrick, Hurlingham; *Style—* Andrew Trollope, Esq, QC; ✉ 187 Fleet Street, London EC4A 2AT (☎ 020 7430 7430, fax 020 7430 7431, e-mail chambers@187fleetstreet.com)

TROLLOPE, Joanna; OBE (1996); da of Arthur George Cecil Trollope, of Overton, Hampshire, and Rosemary, *née* Hodson; *b* 9 December 1943; *Educ* Reigate Co Sch For Girls, St Hugh's Coll Oxford (MA); *m* 1, 14 May 1966 (m dis 1984), David Roger William Potter, *qv*, s of William Edward Potter, of Durweston, Dorset; 2 da (Louise (Mrs Paul Ansdell) b 15 Jan 1969, Antonia (Mrs Jonathan Prentice) b 23 Oct 1971); m 2, 12 April 1985 (m dis 1999), Ian Bayley Curteis, *qv*, s of John Richard Jones, of Lydd, Romney Marsh; *Career* writer; Info Res Dept FO 1965–67, English teacher in various schs, feature writer Harpers and Queen, freelance work for maj newspapers; chair Dept of Nat Heritage Advsy Ctee on Nat Reading Initiative 1996–97, memb Govt Ctee for Nat Year of Reading 1997–, memb Advsy Bd Costa Awards (judge 2002, chair 2007), judge Melissa Nathan Award 2005–11, chair Orange Prize 2012, judge Sunday Times Short Story Award, memb Advsy Body for Seighart Report on E-Lending for Libraries DCMS 2012 and 2013, chair Sunday Times EFG Short Story Award 2013; fndr and co-tstee Joanna Trollope Charitable Tst; pres March Fndn, ambass Meningitis Tst, ambass RNIB (especially Talking Books), ambass Children's Reading Fund for Nat Literary Tst 2012, ambass Chess in Schools and Communities 2013–, tstee Nat Literacy Tst 2013–, tstee Royal Literary Fund 2016–; memb Campaign Bd St Hugh's Coll Oxford 1996–; memb: Soc of Authors (memb Cncl), Trollope Soc, Romantic Novelists' Assoc, West Country Writers' Assoc, Int PEN; chair Nat Portrait Gallery Fund Raising Gala 2009; patron: Mulberry Bush Sch Standlake, Dementia UK, Gloucs Community Fndn 1998–2008, Chawton House Library 2015–; DL Gloucs 2002–08; *Books* Parson Harding's Daughter (Historical Novel of the Year, 1980), The Taverners' Place (1986), Britannia's Daughters (non-fiction, 1983), The Choir (1988), A Village Affair (1989), A Passionate Man (1990), The Rector's Wife (1991), The Men and the Girls (1992), A Spanish Lover (1993), The

T

Best of Friends (1995), A Country Habit – An Anthology (ed and introduction, 1993), Next of Kin (1996), Other People's Children (1998), Marrying the Mistress (2001), Girl From the South (2002), Brother and Sister (2004), The Book Boy (2006), Second Honeymoon (2006), Friday Nights (2008), The Other Family (2010), Daughters in Law (2011), The Soldier's Wife (2012), Sense and Sensibility (2013), Balancing Act (2014); under pseudonym Caroline Harvey: Legacy of Love (1992), A Second Legacy (1993), A Castle in Italy (1993), Parson Harding's Daughter (reissue, Corgi, 1995), The Steps of the Sun (1996), The Brass Dolphin (1997); *Style—* Miss Joanna Trollope, OBE; ✉ c/o United Agents, 12–26 Lexington Street, London W1F 0LE (☎ 020 3214 0800, fax 020 3214 0801, e-mail joanna@joannatrollope.com, website www.joannatrollope.com)

TROMANS, Christopher John; s of Percy Tromans (d 1979), and Phyllis Eileen, *née* Berryman (d 1991); *b* 25 November 1942; *Educ* Truro Sch, St Edmund Hall Oxford (MA); *m* 31 May 1969, Gillian, da of John Delbridge Roberts (d 1966); 1 da (Sarah b 1970), 1 s (Andrew b 1972); *Career* admitted slr 1968; ptnr: Sitwell Money and Murdoch Truro 1971–79, Murdoch Tromans and Hoskin Truro and Redruth 1979–88, Murdoch Tromans Truro 1988–92; NP 1970; memb No 4 SW Legal Aid Area Ctee and Appeals Panel 1982–92, dep High Court and County Court registrar Western Circuit 1987–90, dep district judge 1991–92, jt district judge Plymouth District Registry of High Court and Plymouth County Court 1992–2012, nominated care district judge 1996–2008, district bench sec Western Circuit 1999–2009, Judicial Studies Bd trg judge 2001–12; Univ of Plymouth: visiting lectr 1995–2012, consIt law degree course validation 2001; govr Truro Sch 1975–2005 (dep chm 1978–91), memb Cncl Coll of St Mark and St John Plymouth (now Univ of St Mark and St John) 2001–09, govr Kelly Coll 2007–14, fndn govr Tavistock Church Schs' Fedn 2016–; memb Devonshire Assoc; Nordom Prize, Easterbrook Prize; memb Law Soc 1965; hon memb Western Circuit 1992–2012; ACIArb 1978, FRSA 1990; *Recreations* country life, travel, military history; *Clubs* East India, West Devon (Tavistock); *Style—* Christopher Tromans, Esq; ✉ Chynowen, Manor Close, Tavistock PL19 0PN (e-mail christromans@yahoo.com)

TROMANS, Stephen; QC (2009); *Career* called to the Bar 1999; lectr Univ of Cambridge 1981–87, ptnr Hewitson, Becke & Shaw Cambridge 1987–90, ptnr and head of environmental law Simmons & Simmons 1990–99, currently jt head of chambers 39 Essex St; chm Environmental Law Fndn 2011–; memb Editorial Bd Jl of Environmental Law, Oil and Gas Law; memb Cncl English Nature 1995–2001; CEDR accredited mediator; Environment and Planning Silk of the Year Chambers Bar Award 2012; hon fell Chartered Instn of Waste Mgmnt; *Style—* Stephen Tromans, Esq, QC; ✉ 39 Essex Street, London WC2R 3AT

TROMPETER, Dr Richard Simon; s of Nysen Trompeter, and Betty, *née* Rubin; *b* 27 January 1946; *Educ* Orange Hill Co GS for Boys London, Guy's Hosp Med Sch (MB BS, ed Guy's Hosp Gazette 1969–70); *m* 26 March 1978, Barbara Ann, da of Ervin Blum; 2 da (Sara b 1973, Rebecca b 1986), 2 s (Alexander b 1979, Nicholas b 1981); *Career* house surgn Guy's Hosp and house physician St Mary Abbots Hosp 1970–71; SHO 1971–74: Renal Unit Royal Free Hosp, paediatrics Guy's Hosp and The London Hosp, neonatal paediatrics John Radcliffe Hosp, Gt Ormond St Hosp; registrar Hosp for Sick Children Gt Ormond St 1975–77, research fell Dept of Immunology Inst of Child Health 1977–78, hon sr registrar and lectr in paediatrics Guy's Hosp Med Sch 1979–84, sr lectr in paediatrics Royal Free Hosp Sch of Med 1984–87, conslt paediatric nephrologist The Royal Free Hosp 1986–89 (Sch of Med: hon sr lectr, memb Academic Staff Assoc 1984–87, memb Educn Cncl 1984–89, memb Sch Cncl 1986–87, memb Library Ctee 1988–89); Hosp for Sick Children Great Ormond St: conslt paediatric nephrologist 1986–89, princ appt 1989–2009, clinical dir Medical Unit and Urology Directorate 1991–97, clinical dir Int and Private Patient Directorate 1997–2000, memb Clinical Ethics Forum 1995–2000, chm BMA Local Negotiating Ctee 1996–97, chm Clinical Ethics Ctee 2000–05, currently hon conslt paediatrician and paediatric nephrologist Int & Private Patient Centre; currently hon conslt nephrologist Centre for Nephrology Royal Free Hosp; hon reader in paediatric nephrology UCL 2006–; memb Advsy Bd Novartis Pharmaceuticals UK Ltd 2000–05; memb Editorial Bd: Paediatric Transplantation 2000–14, Paediatric Nephrology 2004–; examiner (MRCP) RCP 1996–2000, sr examiner (MRCPCH) RCPCH 2004–09; memb RCP Standing Ctee of Membs 1976–78, jr staff rep Br Paediatric Assoc Cncl 1982–83, clinical rep Conf of Med Academic Reps 1982–83, govr ILEA Royal Free Hosp Sch 1985–89, memb Bd of Studies in Med Univ of London 1986–89, chm Div of Child Health Hampstead Authy 1987–89 (memb Div of Physicians 1984–89, memb Exec Ctee 1988–89), memb Exec Ctee and Cncl Renal Assoc 1989–93, sec Assoc of Paediatricians N Thames (East) 1995–97, memb Finance Ctee RCPCH 1998–2002, memb Clinical Ethics Ctee Br Transplantation Soc 2003–05, cncllr Int Paediatric Transplant Assoc 2005–07, treas Br Assoc for Paediatric Nephrology 2006–09, memb Ethics Ctee European Renal Assoc – European Dialysis and Transplant Assoc (ERA-EDTA) 2010–15, pres Int Pediatric Transplant Assoc 2011–13 (treas and sec 2006–09, pres elect 2009–11), memb Educn Ctee RSM 2012–; memb Cncl Norwood Children and Families Tst 2007–15, chair of tstees Kids Kidney Research 2008–, tstee Assoc of Medical Registered Charities 2012–; FRCP 1989 (MRCP 1973), FRCPCH 1997; *Publications* Hemolytic Uremic Syndrome and Thrombotic Thrombocytopenic Purpura (jt ed, 1992); *Recreations* literature, theatre; *Style—* Dr Richard Trompeter; ✉ International and Private Patient Centre, Great Ormond Street Hospital for Children NHS Trust, Great Ormond Street, London WC1 3JH (☎ 020 7762 6943, fax 020 7829 8635, e-mail richard.trompeter@gosh.nhs.uk, website www.privatepaediatricnephrology.co.uk)

TROTMAN, Andrew Frederick; s of Campbell Grant Trotman (d 2009), and Audrey, *née* Simpson (d 1974); *b* 9 December 1954; *Educ* Alleyne's GS Stevenage, Balliol Coll Oxford (MA, PGCE, Greyhounds XV Rugby, Coll 1st VIII Rowing); *m* 1980, Mary Rosalind, da of Dr Phillip Spencer (d 1961), and Joan, *née* Vickers (d 2005); 1 da (Eleanor Mary b 1989), 1 s (Jack William Andrew b 1991); *Career* asst master Radley Coll 1978–84, housemaster Abingdon Sch 1984–90, dep rector Edinburgh Acad 1991–95, head master St Peter's Sch York 1995–2004, Warden St Edward's Sch Oxford 2004–11, acting headmaster Repton Sch 2012, dir Aspirance Leadership Services 2013; memb HMC; JP City of York 1997–2003; *Recreations* music, rowing, walking, bagpiping; *Style—* Andrew Trotman, Esq; ✉ The Grey House, Ilmington, Shipston-on-Stour, Warwickshire CV36 4LE

TROTT, Laura; OBE (2013); *b* 24 April 1992, Cheshunt, Herts; *Career* track cyclist; achievements incl: Gold medal (team pursuit) European Championships 2010, 2 Gold medals (team pursuit and omnium) European Championships 2011, Gold medal (team pursuit) World Championships 2011, 2 Gold medals (team pursuit and omnium) World Championships 2012, 2 Gold medals (team pursuit and omnium) Olympic Games 2012, 2 Gold medals (team pursuit and omnium) Olympic Games 2016; *Style—* Ms Laura Trott, OBE; ✉ c/o Rocket Sports Management, 1 Blythe Road, London, W14 0HG, UK; website www.lauratrott.co.uk

TROTT, Philip David Anthony; s of Sqdn Ldr Sydney Harold Trott (d 1985), of Fareham, and Ruth, *née* Neubauer (d 2001); *b* 5 June 1952; *Educ* Oxford Poly, UCL (LLB); *Partner* Kate Edwards; *Career* admitted slr 1979; Dale Parkinson & Co 1977–78; Lawford & Co: articles 1978–79, asst slr 1979–82, ptnr 1982–89; ptnr: Thomson Snell & Passmore 1989–92, Bates Wells & Braithwaite 1992–; lectr and speaker at various legal conferences and seminars; hon legal advsr Holborn Cross CAB 1979–96, advsr to Art Law 1983–84, joint chm Sub-Ctee Immigration Law Practitioners' Assoc (ILPA) 1988– (chm 1986–88, memb Exec 1984–90, 1994–95 and 2001–02); memb: memb Advsy Panel to Office of Immigration Servs Cmmr 2001–06, Editorial Bd Lexis Nexis PSL on Immigration 2012–; occasional author of legal articles on immigration and employment law, occasional speaker on immigration issues on radio and TV; lectr UWE; memb: Law Soc, Industrial Law Soc 1978–89, Employment Lawyers' Assoc 1993, American Immigration Lawyers' Assoc 1993–; *Publications* Immigration & International Employment Law (ed, 1999–2001), McDonald's Immigration Law and Practice (chapter author, 7 edn), Jackson's Immigration Law and Practice (chapter author, 3 edn), Lexis PSL Immigration (contrib, 2012–); *Recreations* sailing, swimming, hill walking, flying, travel, VW campervan owner; *Clubs* Lensbury, House of St Barnabas, VW Campervan Owners; *Style—* Philip Trott, Esq; ✉ Bates Wells & Braithwaite, 10 Queen Street Place, London EC4R 1BE (☎ 020 7551 7777, fax 020 7551 7800, e-mail p.trott@bwbllp.com)

TROTTER, Maj Alexander Richard; CVO (2013); s of Maj H R Trotter (d 1962), and Rona M, *née* Murray; *b* 20 February 1939; *Educ* Eton, City of London Tech Coll; *m* 1 June 1970, Julia Henrietta, da of Sir Peter McClintock Greenwell, 3 Bt (d 1979); 3 s (Henry b 1972, Edward b 1973, Rupert b 1977); *Career* served Royal Scots Greys 1958–68, mangr Charterhall Estate and Farm 1969, chm Meadowhead Ltd (formerly Mortonhall Park Ltd) 1973–, memb Cncl Scot Landowners' Fedn 1975–2004 (convener 1982–85, vice-pres 1986–96, pres 1996–2001), dir Timber Growers GB Ltd 1977–82, vice-chm Border Grain Ltd 1984–2003; memb Berwickshire CC 1969–75 (chm Roads Ctee 1974–75), memb Dept of Agric Working Party on the Agric Holding (Scotland) Legislation 1981–82, chm Scottish Ctee of Nature Conservancy Cncl 1985–90, memb UK Ctee for Euro Year of the Environment 1986–88; Ensign Royal Co; chm Thirlestane Castle Tst 1996–2007; DL Berwicks 1987, HM Lord-Lt Berwicks 2000–14; FRSA 1987; OStJ 2005; *Recreations* skiing, country sports, golf; *Clubs* Turf, New (Edinburgh), Pratt's; *Style—* Maj Alexander Trotter, CVO; ✉ Whinkerstones Farm, Duns, Berwickshire TD11 3RE (☎ 01890 840635, office 01890 840301, fax 01890 840651, e-mail alex@charterhall.net)

TROTTER, Andrew James; s of Geoffrey Trotter (d 1999), and Mella, *née* Sanger; *b* 5 August 1954, London; *Educ* Lancing Coll (scholar), Merton Coll Oxford (MA, exhibitioner); *m* 21 Dec 1985, Jilly, *née* Edge; 1 da (Sarah b 5 Oct 1987), 1 s (Luke b 29 May 1989); *Career* admitted slr 1981; grad trainee Surrey CC 1975–77, Withers 1978–83, Norton Rose 1983–85, ptnr Donne Mileham and Haddock 1987–97 (joined 1985), ptnr and head of corporate Shadbolt LLP 1997–2010, ptnr Clyde & Co LLP 2010–; memb Law Soc 1981; *Recreations* golf, football, tennis, travel; *Style—* Andrew Trotter, Esq; ✉ Clyde & Co LLP, 1 Stoke Road, Guildford, Surrey GU1 4HW (☎ 020 7876 5000, e-mail andrew.trotter@clydeco.com)

TROTTER, Prof David; *b* 25 July 1951, London; *Career* King Edward VII prof of English Univ of Cambridge, fell Gonville & Caius Coll Cambridge; FBA 2004; *Publications* The Making of the Reader: Language and Subjectivity in Modern American, English and Irish Poetry (1984), Circulation: Defoe, Dickens and the Economics of the Novel (1988), The English Novel in History 1895–1920 (1994), Edwardian Fiction: An Oxford Companion (jtly, 1997), Cooking with Mud: The Idea of Mess in Nineteenth-Century Art and Fiction (2000), Paranoid Modernism: Literary Experiment, Psychosis, and the Professionalization of English Society (2001), Cinema and Modernism (2007), The Uses of Phobia: Essays on Literature and Film (2010), Literature in the First Media Age: Britain between the Wars (2013); *Style—* Prof David Trotter; ✉ Gonville & Caius College, Trinity Street, Cambridge CB2 1TA; Faculty of English, 9 West Road, Cambridge CB3 9DP

TROTTER, Dame Janet Olive; DBE (2001, OBE 1991), DL (Glos 2006); da of Anthony George Trotter, of Canterbury, and Joyce Edith, *née* Patrick; *b* 29 October 1943; *Educ* Tech HS for Girls Maidstone, Derby Diocesan Coll of Educn, Univ of London (BD, MA), Brunel Univ (MSc); *Career* teacher: Hythe Secdy Sch Kent 1965–67, Chartham Secdy Sch Kent 1967–69, Rochester GS for Girls 1969–73; lectr: King Alfred's Coll of HE Winchester 1973–85, St Martin's Coll of HE Lancaster 1985–86; dir Univ of Glos (formerly Cheltenham and Gloucester Coll of HE) 1986–2006; memb: HE Funding Cncl 1992–96, Teacher Trg Agency 1994–99; memb and chair Gloucester Health 1993–96, chair S and West NHS Exec 1996–2001, chair Glos Hosps NHS Fndn Tst 2006–; contrib to various pubns on religious educn and curriculum devpt; involvement with various church orgns incl Fndn for Church Leadership, chair Winston's Wish (charity for bereaved children); hon fell King Alfred's Coll 1999, hon fell Canterbury Christchurch UC 2001; Hon DTech PECS Univ Hungary, Hon LLD Univ of Bristol; Hon DEd: UWE 2001, Brunel Univ 2004, Univ of Leicester 2006; CCMI 2002; *Recreations* walking, cycling and music; *Style—* Dame Janet Trotter, DBE, DL; ✉ Gloucestershire Hospitals NHS Foundation Trust, 1 College Lawn, Cheltenham GL53 7AG

TROTTER, John Geoffrey; *b* 13 July 1951; *Educ* Lancing, Worcester Coll Oxford (Open exhibitioner, BA), Coll of Law London; *Career* Hogan Lovells: qualified in 1977, based New York 1980–82, ptnr London 1983–2010, latterly conslt; chm Insurance Ctee Int Bar Assoc 2002–04; memb: Law Soc, London Slrs' Litigation Assoc, City of London Law Soc; FCIArb; *Books* Liability of Lawyers and Indemnity Insurance (co-ed); *Recreations* golf, tennis, ornithology, theatre, gardening; *Clubs* Roehampton; *Style—* J G Trotter, Esq

TROTTER, Sir Neville Guthrie; kt (1997), JP (Newcastle upon Tyne 1973), DL (Tyne & Wear 1997); s of Capt Alexander Trotter (d 1941), and Elizabeth, *née* Guthrie (d 1992); *b* 27 January 1932; *Educ* Shrewsbury, Univ of Durham (BCom); *m* 1983, Caroline, da of Capt John Darley Farrow, OBE, RN (d 1999), and Oona, *née* Hall (d 2008); 1 da (Sophie b 1985); *Career* RAF (short serv cmmn) 1955–58; CA, ptnr Thornton Baker & Co 1962–74, conslt Grant Thornton 1974–2005; MP (Cons) Tynemouth 1974–97 (stood down); former memb: Select Ctees on Tport and Defence, Trade & Industry Sub-Ctee of Expenditure Ctee, House of Commons Armed Forces Parly Scheme (RAF) 1990–91, Parly Defence Study Gp; chm All Party Gp for Prevention of Solvent Abuse; memb Advsy Bd Northern Defence Industries Ltd (forme pres); memb Cncl NE C of C 1998–2014; vice-pres: Soc of Maritime Industries 1996– (former Parly conslt), Soc for Prevention of Solvent Abuse 1996–; chm British American C of C in the North East of England 1999–2014; regnl ambass of the NE in N America (appointed by UKTI and One NorthEast) 2008–11; Cons Parly Ctees: sec Military Aviation Ctee 1976–79, chm Shipping and Shipbuilding Ctee 1979–85 and 1994–97 (vice-chm 1976–79), sec Industry Ctee 1981–83, sec Tport Ctee 1983–84; former Parly conslt to: British Transport Police Federation, Bowrings plc, Go Ahead Gp; former dir: MidAmerican Energy Holdings Co (parent co of Northern Electric plc), Wm Baird plc, Darchem Ltd, Romag plc; private bills passed on Consumer Safety, Licensing Law, Intoxicating Substances Supply (Glue Sniffing); memb: Newcastle City Cncl 1963–74 (Alderman 1970–74, chm Fin Ctee, Traffic, Highways and Tport Ctee, Theatre Ctee), Cncl European Atlantic Gp 1997–; formerly: memb Tyne & Wear Met Cncl, memb CAA Airline Users Ctee, vice-chm Northumberland Police Authy; pres: Northern Area Cons Pty 1996–2003, Tyneside branch Royal Marines Assoc 2001–; former memb: Northern Econ Planning Cncl, Tyne Improvement Cmmn, Tyneside Passenger Tport Authy, Industrial Relations Tbnl; currently memb: UK Defence Forum, UK Atlantic Cncl, US Naval Inst, RUSI (former memb Cncl), Air League, Railway Studies Assoc, NE Reserve Forces and Cadets Assoc 1997–, US Navy League, US Air Force Assoc, Assoc of the US Army; Hon Col: Royal Marines Reserve 1998–2003, Durham Army Cadet Force 2003–05; pres T S Dauntless Gosforth Sea Cadets 2006–; High Sheriff Co of Tyne & Wear 2004–05; memb Cncl: High Sheriff's Assoc of England and Wales 2005–11, Liveryman Worshipful Co of Chartered Accountants; memb Hon Co of Air Pilots (formerly Guild of Airline Pilots and Navigators) 2006–; FCA, FRAeS, FCIT; *Recreations* aviation, military history, gardening, fell walking, defence, study of foreign affrs; *Clubs* RAF, Northern Counties, Newcastle upon Tyne; *Style*— Sir Neville Trotter, DL, FCA, FRAeS, FCIT; ✉ Northern Counties Club, Hood Street, Newcastle upon Tyne NE1 6LH

TROTTER, Thomas Andrew; s of His Hon Richard Stanley Trotter (d 1974), of Heswall, Merseyside, and Ruth Elizabeth, *née* Pierce (d 1982); *b* 4 April 1957; *Educ* Malvern Coll, RCM, Univ of Cambridge (MA); *Career* concert organist; scholar RCM 1974; organ scholar: St George's Chapel Windsor 1975–76, King's Coll Cambridge 1976–79; organist: St Margaret's Church Westminster 1982–, to the City of Birmingham 1983–; debut Royal Festival Hall 1980, Prom Royal Albert Hall 1986, Mozart's Fantasia in F minor (BBC Proms) 1997; festival performances in UK and Europe; tours to: USA, Aust, and the Far East; recording artist for Decca 1989–; first prize winner: Bach Prize, St Albans Int Organ Competition 1979, Prix de Virtuosité, Conservatoire Rueil-Malmaison Paris 1981, Franz Liszt Grand Prix du Disque 1995; Instrumental Award Royal Philharmonic Soc 2002; Int performer of the Year Award, NYC Chapter of the American Guild of Organists 2012, Medal for Achievements in Organ Playing RCO 2016; Hon Dr Univ of Central Eng 2003, Hon DMus Univ of Birmingham 2006; ARCM, FRCO; *Style*— Thomas Trotter, Esq; ✉ c/o Symphony Hall, Broad Street, Birmingham B1 2EA (☎ 0121 200 2000)

TROTTER, Timothy Hugh Southcombe; s of Antony Stuart Trotter (d 1976), of Brandsby, N Yorks, and Marie Louise, *née* Brook; *b* 7 January 1959; *Educ* Wellington, Thames Valley Univ (BA, capt of Tennis, capt of Rugby); *m* 31 May 1986, Caroline, da of Peter Edney Brewer; 2 s (Alexander Antony Stuart b 16 May 1989, Oliver Peter Hugh b 3 Sept 1991); *Career* ptnr and dep md Hill Murray Ltd 1985–91, fndr and chm Ludgate Communications Ltd 1991–98; Ludgate Group Ltd: md 1991–98, chm 1997–98; dep chm Weber PR Worldwide 1997–98, chm Trotter & Co 1998–, chm Glenfern 2005–; FIPR 1998 (MIPR 1986), FCIM 2005 (MCIM 1984), FInstD 2006 (MInstD 1993); *Recreations* tennis, skiing, shooting, backgammon, equestrianism, theatre; *Clubs* City of London, Queen's, Harlequins RFC, RAC; *Style*— Timothy Trotter, Esq; ✉ Glenfern, 2nd Floor, 77 Queen Victoria Street, London EC4V 4AY

TROUBRIDGE, Sir Thomas Richard; 7 Bt (GB 1799); s of Sir Peter Troubridge, 6 Bt (d 1988), and Hon Venetia (now Hon Mrs (Derick) Forbes), da of 1 Baron Weeks; *b* 23 January 1955; *Educ* Eton, Univ Coll Durham; *m* 1984, Hon Rosemary Douglas-Pennant, da of 6 Baron Penrhyn, DSO, MBE (d 2003); 1 da (Emily Rose b 1987), 2 s (Edward Peter b 1989, Nicholas Douglas St Vincent b 1993); *Heir* s, Edward Troubridge; *Career* former ptnr PricewaterhouseCoopers (formerly Price Waterhouse before merger), ret 2015; FCA; *Recreations* sailing ('Spreadeagle'), skiing; *Clubs* Hurlingham, Itchenor Sailing, White's; *Style*— Sir Thomas Troubridge, Bt; ✉ 96 Napier Court, Ranelagh Gardens, London SW6 3XA; PricewaterhouseCoopers, 1 Embankment Place, London WC2N 6RH

TROULLIDES, Andrew John (Andy); s of Joannis Panayis Troullides, of London, and Mirianthi, *née* Stylianou; *b* 1 September 1957; *Educ* Archbishop Tenison's GS London; *m* Sept 1991, Clare Jane, da of Richard E Little; 2 da (Lydia b 29 July 1993, Celia b 20 Dec 1999), 1 s (William b 21 Aug 1995); *Career* Ulster TV 1974–77, Anglia TV 1978–79, J Walter Thompson 1979–82, dir Lowe Howard-Spink 1982–90, media dir Burkitt Weinreich Bryant 1990–93, md MediaCom UK Ltd (part of WPP Group) 1994–99 (gen mangr 1993–94), jt gp md MediaCom TMB (part of WPP Group) 1999, md Optimad Media Systems 1999–2006, chief media officer Independent Media Distribution plc 2007–, chief media officer IMD Media 2011–; advsr GCI Film 2011–; fndr chm Blandford St Soc; MIPA 1993; *Style*— Andy Troullides, Esq

TROUP, (John) Edward Astley; s of Vice Adm Sir Anthony Troup, KCB, DSC, and Lady Cordelia Mary; *b* 26 January 1955; *Educ* Oundle, CCC Oxford (MA, MSc); *m* 16 Dec 1978, Siriol Jane, da of Lt-Col John Samuel Martin, OBE; 3 s (Lawrence b 18 May 1985, Madoc b 19 May 1989, Galen b 23 Feb 1991), 1 da (Mabyn b 9 April 1987); *Career* admitted slr 1981; ptnr Simmons & Simmons 1984–95, special advsr (on tax matters) HM Treasy 1995–97, head of tax strategy Simmons & Simmons 1997–2004, dir of business and indirect tax HM Treasy 2004–10, DG tax and welfare HM Treasy 2010–12, second perm set and tax assurance cmmr HMRC 2012–16, exec chm HMRC 2016–; Freeman: Worshipful Co of Grocers, City of London 1980; CTA; *Recreations* cinema, cycling, bird-watching, Beethoven; *Style*— Edward Troup, Esq; ✉ HM Revenue and Customs, 2/74 100 Parliament Street, London SW1A 2BQ (☎ 03000 586231)

TROUP, Prof Malcolm; s of William John Troup (d 1971), of Toronto, and Wendela Mary, *née* Seymour Conway (d 1960); *b* 22 February 1930; *Educ* Royal Conservatory of Music Toronto (ARCT), Saarlandisches Konservatorium, Univ of York (DPhil Mus), Guildhall Sch of Music and Drama (FGSM); *m* 24 Feb 1962, Carmen Lamarca-Bello Subercaseaux, da of Arturo Lamarca-Bello (d 1963), of Paris, Santiago and San Francisco; 1 da (Wendela (Mrs Christopher Lumley) b 1963); *Career* concert pianist 1954–70; toured worldwide; int festivals incl: Prague, Berlin, York, Belfast, Montreal Expo, CBC Toronto, Halifax, Cwlth Arts Festival London; played with leading orchestras incl: LSO, Hallé, Berliner-Sinfonie, Hamburg, Bucharest, Warsaw, Oslo Philharmonic, Bergen Harmonien, Toronto, Winnipeg, São Paulo, Lima, Santiago; first performances of important modern works, numerous recordings; dir of music Guildhall Sch of Music and Drama 1970–75, prof of music and head of dept City Univ London 1975–93, emeritus, founder and visiting prof 1995; visiting prof Universidad Catolica de Chile Santiago 2010; judge: CBC Nat Talent Competition, Eckhard-Grammaté Piano Competition, Young Musicians of the Year, Chopin Competition of Aust 1988, 1st Dvorák Int Piano Competition 1997, Int Piano Competition Rome 1997, 1st EPTA Int Piano Competition Zagreb 1999, Reykjavik 2000, Cyprus 2001 and Rome 2002, 1st Claudio Arrau Int Piano Competition Santiago and Chillan 2003, Gina Bachauer Int Piano Competition Salt Lake City 2006 and Prague 2009, Int Israeli Music Competition, Int Ernest Bloch Music Competition 2009–; vice-pres Oxford Int Piano Festival, vice-pres World Piano Competition, fndr and vice-pres Asociación Latinoamericana de Profesores de Piano (ALAPP/Chile), vice-pres Music Therapy Charity Tst, vice-pres Euro Piano Teachers Assoc, chm Beethoven Piano Soc of Europe, tstee Jewish Music Inst; ed Piano Journal 1987–; external examiner: KCL, Univ of York, Keele Univ; music advsr: Royal Netherlands Govt, Br Cncl, Canada Cncl, Leverhulme Tst; Cwlth medal 1955, Harriet Cohen Int award, Medal of the American Liszt Soc 1998; Freeman City of London 1971, Liveryman Worshipful Co of Musicians 1973 (memb Ct of Assts 1991–, Sr Warden 1997–98, Master 1998–99); memb RSM 1988; hon prof Univ of Chile 1966, Hon LLD Meml Univ of Newfoundland 1985, Hon DMus City Univ London 1995; FRSA 1986; *Books* Serial Strawinsky in 20th Century Music, Orchestral Music of the 1950s and 1960s in The Messiaen Companion (1994), 'The Piano' in Science & Psychology of Music Performance (jtly, 2002); author of various articles in: Composer, Music and Musicians, Music Teacher, Piano Journal, Revista Universitaria de Chile; *Style*— Prof Emeritus Malcolm Troup; ✉ 86–88 Lexham Gardens, Kensington, London W8 5JB

TROWELL, Dr Joan Mary; da of Gordon Watson Trowell (d 1984), and Vera, *née* Kilham (d 1969); *b* 2 January 1941; *Educ* Walthamstow Hall Sevenoaks, Royal Free Hosp Med Sch London (MB BS); *m* 31 Oct 1970, John Percy Perry (d 1985), s of Percy Perry (d 1964); 1 s (Mark b 1972), 1 da (Helen b 1974); *Career* house physician London: Royal Free Hosp 1964, Royal Northern Hosp 1965, Brompton Hosp 1967, Hammersmith Hosp 1969; med registrar: Addenbrooke's Hosp Cambridge 1968, Hammersmith Hosp 1969; res fell Nuffield Dept of Clinical Med Oxford 1971, emeritus fell Nuffield Dept Clinical Med 2007, hon conslt physician John Radcliffe Hosp Oxford 1981, dep dir of Clinical Studies Oxford 1995–98; exec of Oxon Cncl for Alcohol and Drug Use; Med Cncl on Alcoholism: dep chm, regnl and univ rep, memb Educn Ctee and memb Nat Exec Ctee 1998–2008; memb and vice-chm Bd of Visitors Oxford Prison 1987–96, memb Ind Monitoring Bd (formerly Bd of Visitors) HM Prison Grendon & Springhill 1996–2013; memb local review ctee Parole Bd; Med Women's Fedn: pres Oxford Region 1991–93, memb Nat Cncl 1993–99, memb Nat Exec Ctee 1994–99, nat vice-pres 1997–98, pres 1998–99; GMC: memb (representing Univs of Oxford and Cambridge) 1998–2003, memb Educn Ctee 1999–2003, elected memb 2005–08, chm Fitness to Practise Ctee 2003–06; memb: BMA (pres Oxford Div 1992–93), Info Standards Bd NHS Nat Prog for IT 2003–08; chm of tstees Royal Medical Benevolent Fund 2007–13; Hon MA Univ of Oxford 1971; FRCP 1987; *Books* Topics in Gastroenterology (1975), Oxford Textbook of Medicine (contrib, 1986), Oxford Textbook of Pathology (contrib, 1991), Medical Woman (ed, 1999–2001); *Clubs* Reform, Oxford and Cambridge; *Style*— Dr Joan Trowell; ✉ 18 Ashford Close, Woodstock OX20 1FF; Nuffield Department of Medicine, John Radcliffe Hospital, Headington, Oxford OX3 9DU (e-mail joan.trowell@ndm.ox.ac.uk)

TROWELL, Stephen Mark; QC (2015); s of Peter Trowell, and Judith, *née* Bailey; *b* 5 October 1967; *Educ* Keble Coll Oxford (MA), Wolfson Coll Oxford (DPhil); *m* 2 Aug 1997, Leila, *née* Habib; 2 s (Alexander b 14 Nov 2000, Henry b 10 Dec 2006), 1 da (Susannah b 25 Dec 2002); *Career* called to the Bar 1995; memb Family Law Bar Assoc; *Style*— Stephen Trowell, Esq, QC; ✉ 1 Hare Court, Temple, London EC4Y 7BE

TROWER, William Spencer Philip; QC (2001); s of late Anthony Gosselin Trower, of Stanstead Bury, Herts, and Catherine Joan, *née* Kellett; *b* 28 December 1959; *Educ* Eton, ChCh Oxford (MA), City Univ (Dip Law); *m* 30 Aug 1986, Mary Louise, da of Gerard Nicolas Pyemont Chastel de Boinville; 4 da (Emily Katherine b 18 Aug 1987, Alice Charlotte b 29 Jan 1989, Lucy Harriet b 14 May 1992, Rosanna Mary b 20 Dec 1993); *Career* called to the Bar 1983; bencher Lincoln's Inn 2009; dep High Court judge (Chancery) 2007; memb Insolvency Rules Ctee 2001–11; *Books* Corporate Administrations and Rescue Procedures (jtly, 1994, 2 edn 2004), Montgomery and Ormerod on Fraud (contrib, 2008), Parry on Transaction Avoidance in Insolvencies (consulting ed, 2011), O'Dea on Schemes of Arrangement (consulting ed, 2012); *Clubs* Garrick; *Style*— William Trower, Esq, QC; ✉ Walkern Bury Farm, Bassus Green, Stevenage, Hertfordshire SG2 7JH; 3–4 South Square, Gray's Inn, London WC1R 5HP (☎ 020 7696 9900, fax 020 7696 9911, e-mail williamtrower@southsquare.com)

TROWSDALE, Prof John; s of Roy R Trowsdale, and Doris, *née* Graham; *b* 8 February 1949, Hull; *Educ* Beverley GS, Univ of Birmingham (BSc, PhD); *m* 1971, Susan Price; 3 c (Sam A b 1975, Jodie L b 1977, Alice R Z b 1989); *Career* Euro fell Biochemical Soc France 1973–75, research fell Scripps Clinic and Research Fndn La Jolla Calif 1975–78, SRC research fell Univ of Oxford 1978–79; ICRF London: fell 1979–82, research scientist 1982–85, sr scientist 1986–90, princ scientist 1990–97; prof of immunology Univ of Cambridge 1997–; FMedSci 2000; *Publications* author of articles in scientific jls; *Recreations* music, art; *Style*— Prof John Trowsdale; ✉ Immunology Division, Department of Pathology, Tennis Court Road, Cambridge CB2 1QP (☎ 01223 330248, fax 01223 333875)

TRUDGILL, Prof Peter John; s of John Trudgill (d 1986), of Norwich, and Hettie Jean, *née* Gooch; *b* 7 November 1943; *Educ* City of Norwich Sch, King's Coll Cambridge (MA), Univ of Edinburgh (MA, PhD); *m* 15 Feb 1980, Jean Marie, da of Wade F Hannah; *Career* successively lectr, reader then prof Univ of Reading 1970–86, reader then prof Univ of Essex 1986–92, prof of English language and linguistics Univ of Lausanne Switzerland 1993–98, prof of English linguistics Univ of Fribourg Switzerland 1998–; Dr (hc) Uppsala Univ Sweden 1995, Dr (hc): UEA 2002, La Trobe Aust; fell Norwegian Acad of Arts and Sciences 1995, fell Norwegian Acad of Sciences and Letters 1996, FBA 1989; *Books* academic: The Social differentiation of English in Norwich (1974), Sociolinguistics: an introduction (1974, reprinted 17 times, 3 edn 1995), Accent dialect and the school (1975), Sociolinguistic patterns in British English (ed, 1978), English accents and dialects: an introduction to social and regional varieties of British English (with A Hughes, 1979, 3 edn 1996), Dialectology (with J K Chambers, 1980), International English: a guide to varieties of Standard English (with J Hannah, 1982), On dialect: social and geographical perspectives (1982), Language in the British Isles (ed, 1984), Applied sociolinguistics (ed, 1984), A grammar of English dialect (with V Edwards and B Weltens, 1984), Dialects in contact (1986), Dialects of England (1990), Bad language (with L G Andersson, 1990), English dialects: Studies in grammatical variation (ed with J K Chambers, 1991), Introducing language and society (1992), Dialects (1994), Language Myths (ed with L Bauer, 1998), New-dialect Formation (2004), Investigations in Sociohistorical Linguistics: stories of colonisation and contact (2010), Sociolinguistic typology: social determinants of linguistic structure and complexity (2011); non academic: Coping with America: A beginners guide to the USA (1982, shortlisted Thomas Cook Travel Book Prize 1983, 2 edn 1985), In Sfakia: passing time in the wilds of Crete (2008); *Style*— Prof Peter J Trudgill, FBA; ✉ School of Language, Linguistics and Translation Studies, University of East Anglia, Norwich NR4 7TJ (e-mail peter.trudgill@unifr.ch)

TRUE, Baron (Life Peer UK 2010), of East Sheen in the County of Surrey; Nicholas Edward True; CBE (1992); s of Edward Thomas True (d 1991), and Kathleen Louise (d 2013); *b* 31 July 1951; *Educ* Nottingham HS, Peterhouse Cambridge (MA); *m* 7 July 1979, Anne-Marie Elena Kathleen Blanco, da of Robin Adrian Hood (d 1993); 2 s (James Alexios Edward b 26 Aug 1981, Thomas-Leo Richard b 30 May 1984), 1 da (Sophia Miriam Marie-Louise Blanco b 10 Aug 1992); *Career* memb Cons Res Dept 1976–82, PA to Lord Whitelaw 1978–82, special advsr to Sec of State DHSS 1982–86, dir of Public Policy Unit Ltd 1986–90, dep head Prime Minister's Policy Unit 1990–95, ministerial nominee English Sports Cncl 1996–97, special advsr PM's Office 1997, private sec to Ldr of the Oppn House of Lords 1997–2010; cncllr Richmond-upon-Thames 1986–90, 1998– (dep ldr 2002–06, ldr of the oppn 2006–10, ldr 2010–); tstee: Sir Harold Hood's Charitable Tst 1996–, Richmond Civic Endowment Tst 2006–10; chm Orleans House Tst 2010–; *Recreations* books, cricket, Italy, Byzantium; *Clubs* Brooks's, Travellers, Beefsteak; *Style*— The Lord True, CBE; ✉ 114 Palewell Park, London SW14 8JH (☎ 020 8876 9628, fax 020 8876 3096, e-mail truen@parliament.uk); London Borough of Richmond upon Thames, York House, York Street, Twickenham, Middlesex (☎ 020 8487 5001, e-mail cllr.lordtrue@richmond.gov.uk)

TRUEMAN, Paul; *Educ* Univ of Abertay (BSc); *Career* gp mktg dir UK & I LG Electronics until 2011, head of mktg UK & I MasterCard 2011–; *Style*— Paul Trueman, Esq; ✉ MasterCard, 10 Upper Bank Street, Canary Wharf, London E14 5NP

TRULUCK, (Maj-Gen) Ashley Ernest George; CB (2001), CBE (1997); s of Maj George William Truluck, RA (d 2012), of Ely, Cambs, and Elizabeth, *née* Kitchener (d 1986); *b* 7 December 1947; *Educ* RMA Sandhurst, Open Univ (BA), Staff Coll Camberley, RMCS Shrivenham, RCDS; *m* 21 Feb 1976, Jennifer Jane, *née* Bell; 1 da (Cherry Louise b 25 July 1981), 1 s (Laurence James George b 13 March 1985); *Career* regtl duty Bde of Gurkhas 1970–74, ADC to Cdr Land Forces Far East 1974–75, communications offr Gds Armd Bde 1976–77, staff offr MOD 1980–81, Sqdn Cdr BAOR UK 1982–84, memb Directing Staff RMCS Shrivenham 1984–86, Regtl Cdr BAOR 1986–88, Col Army Staff Duties 1989–90, cdr Royal Sch of Signals and Blandford Garrison 1991–92, Brig Gen Staff UK Land Command 1994–96, dir Attack Helicopter 1997–98, ACOS SHAPE 1998–2000; Col Cmdt Royal Corps of Signals 2001–07, chm Royal Signals Trustee Ltd 2003–14; chm Defence Housing Review 2000, chief exec London Magistrates Courts 2001–03, chm London Criminal Justice Bd 2002–03, md Ashley Truluck Associates Ltd 2003–, nat project dir Fire and Rescue Servs Communications Project 2005–10, strategic advsr IBM (i2) 2010–14, managing conslt The Cultural Experience Ltd 2012–, chm/md Chalke

T

Valley Community Hub Ltd 2013–, chm Soc for Army Historic Research; Adm Royal Signals Yacht Club 2003–12; FIoD; *Recreations* offshore sailing, hill walking, country pursuits, military history, the arts, family; *Clubs* Army and Navy, Int Assoc of Cape Horners; *Style*— Ashley Truluck, CB, CBE; ✉ e-mail atruluck@broadchalke.net

TRUMAN, Crispin Marshall; s of Anthony Barratt Truman (d 1975), and Jill Estelle, *née* Marshall; *b* 7 February 1964, Manchester; *Educ* Ashton Park Comp Bristol, St Peter's Coll Oxford (BA, MSc); *m* June 1996, Maria Luise, *née* Mehlstaeubl; 3 s (Lukas b 2 Dec 1996, Leon b 3 Feb 2000, Valentin b 25 Feb 2003); *Career* social worker Family Housing Assoc 1991–93; Revolving Doors Agency: devpt worker 1993–97, chief exec 1997–2003; chief exec Churches Conservation Tst 2003–; chair: London Cycling Campaign 1998–2004, European Religious Heritage Network 2010–; tstee: Rethink 2004–09, Building Exploratory 2006–, Heritage Alliance 2009–; memb ACEVO 1997; chair of govrs Stoke Newington Sch and Sixth Form 2015–; *Style*— Crispin Truman, Esq; ✉ The Churches Conservation Trust, Society Building, 8 All Saints Street, London N1 9RL (✆ 020 7841 0402, e-mail ctruman@thecct.org.uk)

TRUMPINGTON, Baroness (Life Peer UK 1980), of Sandwich in the County of Kent; Dame Jean Alys Barker; DCVO (2005), PC (1992); da of late Maj Arthur Edward Campbell-Harris, MC, and Doris Marie, *née* Robson; *b* 23 October 1922; *Educ* privately in England and France; *m* 1954, William Alan Barker (d 1988); 1 s (Hon Adam Campbell Barker, *qv* b 1955); *Career* sits as Cons peer in House of Lords; Cons cncllr Cambridge City Cncl Trumpington Ward 1963–73 (Mayor of Cambridge 1971–72, Dep Mayor 1972–73), Cons co cncllr Cambs Trumpington Ward 1973–75, hon cncllr City of Cambridge 1975–; JP: Cambridge 1972–75, S Westminster 1976–82; UK delegate to UN Status of Women Cmmn 1979–81; Baroness in Waiting to HM The Queen 1983–85; Parly under-sec of state: DHSS 1985–87, MAFF 1987–89; min of state MAFF 1989–92; Baroness in Waiting 1992–97, Extra Baroness in Waiting to HM The Queen 1998–; hon fell Lucy Cavendish Coll Cambridge 1980, Hon FRCPath, Hon ARCVS; Officier de l'Ordre Nationale du Mérite; *Recreations* bridge, racing, antique hunting; *Style*— The Rt Hon the Baroness Trumpington, DCVO, PC; ✉ House of Lords, London SW1A 0PW

TRUSCOTT, Baron (Life Peer UK 2004), of St James's in the City of Westminster; Peter Derek Truscott; s of late Derek Truscott, of Newton Abbot, Devon; *b* 20 March 1959; *Educ* Newton Abbot GS, Exeter Coll Oxford (MA, DPhil); *m* 1991, Svetlana, da of late Col Prof Nicolai Chernicov, of St Petersburg, Russia; *Career* memb Colchester BC 1988–92, MEP (Lab) Herts 1994–99, Lab Pty spokesman on Foreign Affrs and Defence 1997–99; vice-pres Ctee on Security and Disarmament 1994–99; departmental liaison peer MOD 2004–05, Parly under-sec of state for energy and govt spokesman Dept of Trade and Industry 2006–07; memb: TGWU 1986–2009, Co-op Pty 1987–2009, Foreign Affrs Ctee 1994–99, Foreign Affrs, Def and Devpt Sub-Ctee House of Lords Full Select Ctee 2005–09; assoc fell: IPPR 2000– (visiting research fell 1999–2000), RUSI 2005–; *Books* Russia First (1997), European Defence (2000), Kursk (2002), Putin's Progress (2004), The Ascendancy of Political Risk Management (2006), European Energy Security (2009); *Style*— The Lord Truscott

TRUSS, Rt Hon Elizabeth Mary; PC (2014), MP; *b* 26 July 1975; *Educ* Merton Coll Oxford; *Career* MP (Cons) Norfolk SW 2010–, Parly under sec of state for educn and childcare 2012–14, sec of state for environment, food and rural affrs 2014–16, Lord Chllr and sec of state for justice 2016–; *Style*— The Rt Hon Elizabeth Truss, MP; ✉ House of Commons, London SW1A 0AA (website www.elizabethtruss.com)

TRUSS, Lynne; da of Ernest Edward Truss (d 1991), and Joan Dorothy, *née* Sellar; *b* 31 May 1955, Kingston upon Thames; *Educ* Tiffin Girls' GS Kingston upon Thames (Gamble Prize), UCL (BA, Morley Medal Award, George Smith Prize, Rosa Morrison scholar); *Career* dep literary ed Times Higher Education Supplement 1978–1986, literary ed The Listener 1986–90, columnist, critic and sportswriter The Times 1991–2000, columnist SAGA magazine 2010–; many plays, series, comedies and talks for BBC Radio; Columnist of the Year 1996; memb Soc of Authors 2005, FRSL 2005; With One Lousy Free Packet of Seed (1994), Making the Cat Laugh (1995), Tennyson's Gift (1996), Going Loco (1999), Tennyson and his Circle (1999), Eats, Shoots and Leaves (2003, Book of the Year Br Book Awards 2004), Talk to the Hand (2005), Get Her Off the Pitch (2009), Cat Out Of Hell (2014); *Recreations* theatre, travel; *Clubs* Groucho; *Style*— Lynne Truss; ✉ c/o Anthony Goff, David Higham Associates Ltd, 5–8 Lower John Street, London W1F 9HA (✆ 020 7434 5900, e-mail gavin@lynnetruss.com); website www.lynnetruss.com

TRUST, Howard Bailey; *b* 6 October 1954; *Educ* Gonville & Caius Coll Cambridge (MA); *m* (m dis); 4 c; *Career* slr: Lovell, White & King London 1980–85, Morgan Grenfell & Co Ltd London 1985–87; co sec Morgan Grenfell plc London 1987–89, gp legal dir Barclays de Zoete Wedd Holdings Ltd London 1989–95, gp gen counsel and sec Barclays plc 1995–2003, currently gen counsel Schroders; memb: Law Soc, City of London Slrs' Co; *Clubs* Oxford & Cambridge; *Style*— Howard Trust, Esq; ✉ Schroders plc, 31 Gresham Street, London EC2V 7QA (✆ 020 7658 6444, e-mail howard.trust@schroders.com)

TRYE, Anna March; DL (Warks 2011); da of Alexander Innes (d 1985), and Mary, *née* Christopher (d 2008); *b* 1 April 1944, Birmingham; *Educ* Edgbaston HS Birmingham, Brilliamont Coll (Cert, Dip); *m* 26 June 1965, Christopher Peter Trye; 4 da (Penelope, Caroline b 4 Nov 1967 (twins), Patricia b 4 April 1973, Jennifer-Jane b 12 May 1974); *Career* Cruse-Bereavement Care: cnsllr 1986–, chm 1995–98, dep chm and supervisor 1998–; parent govr Warwick Prep Sch 1980–85, church warden and worship ldr St James Old Milverton, pres Warks Carers Service 2013–; tstee: Myton Hospice 2007–, Crimebeat, Mayday Tst 2009–; visitor Elizabeth Finn Charity; JP 1986–2005, High Sheriff Warks 2008–09; memb: Br Assoc for Counselling and Psychotherapy 1999, Wives Fellowship, NADFAS; *Recreations* skiing, walking, reading, theatre, ballet, opera; *Clubs* Leamington Spa Tennis; *Style*— Mrs Anna Trye, DL; ✉ 59 Northumberland Road, Leamington Spa, Warwickshire CV32 6HF (✆ 01926 421010)

TUBBS, Andrew; *Career* admitted slr 1983; Shoosmiths: joined Commercial Property Dept 1986, ptnr 1989, head Financial Institutions Div 1994, chm 2002–15, dir of quality and risk 2006–15; ptnr Real Estate Practice Gp; *Style*— Andrew Tubbs, Esq; ✉ Shoosmiths, 6th Floor, 2 Colmore Square, 38 Colmore Circus Queensway, Birmingham B4 6SH

TUCK, (Anne) Victoria (Vicky); *Educ* Univ of Kent (BA), Inst of Educn Univ of London (PGCE), Univ de Lille et de Paris (Dip Supérieur de Droit et de Français des Affaires), South Bank Univ (MA); *Career* teacher Putney HS 1976–81, head of modern languages Bromley HS 1981–86, lectr Inst of Educn Univ of London 1991–94, dep head City of London Sch for Girls 1994–96, princ Cheltenham Ladies' Coll 1996–2011, DG Int Sch of Geneva 2011–; external examiner KCL until 1999; pres GSA 2008, vice-chair ISC 2009–10 (chair Educn Ctee 2009–10); MIL 1999; *Style*— Mrs Vicky Tuck; ✉ Le Manoir, Ecole Internationale de Genève, 62 route de Chêne, CH 1208 Genève (✆ 0041 22 787 2400, fax 0041 22 787 2410, e-mail vicky.tuck@ecolint.ch)

TUCKER, Alistair John James; s of James Charles Henry Tucker (d 1982), and Mary Hannah, *née* Featherstonehaugh (d 1975); *b* 17 February 1936; *Educ* Southend HS, Keble Coll Oxford (MA); *m* 2 Sept 1967, Deirdre Ann Forster (d 2014), da of George Moore; 1 s (Alistair b 1976), 1 da (Hannah b 1972); *Career* Subaltern The Green Howards 1958–60; exec dir within Transport Holding Co 1967–70, md Alistair Tucker Halcrow and Assoc 1970–91, dir Air Tport Practice Price Waterhouse Management Consultants 1991–95, princ Alistair Tucker Associates 1995–; special advsr UK House of Commons Tport Ctee 1992–97; visiting prof Univ of Surrey 1987–93; MCIT 1972, MRAeS 1980; *Recreations*

walking, travel, archaeology; *Clubs* Athenaeum; *Style*— Alistair Tucker, Esq; ✉ 50 Primrose Gardens, London NW3 4TP (✆ 020 7586 0027, e-mail alistairtucker@gmail.com)

TUCKER, Derek Alan; s of Gwynne Tucker (d 1989), and Sheila Elizabeth, *née* Lynch (d 2003); *b* 31 October 1953; *Educ* Quarry Bank GS Liverpool, Municipal GS Wolverhampton; *m* 1 (m dis 1991); 1 s (Paul), 1 da (Elizabeth); *m* 2, 8 June 2000, Marilyn Lyla Sclater; *Career* journalist; Express & Star 1972–92: trainee reporter, reporter, chief reporter, news ed, news ed and dep ed; ed Press & Journal Aberdeen 1992–; memb Press Complaints Ctee 1996–98 and 2006–08, chm Eds' Ctee Scottish Daily Newspaper Soc 2003–05, memb Code of Practice Ctee 2002–05; former offr RAF (volunteer reserve) 1988–94; hon dr (hc) Univ of Aberdeen 2007; *Recreations* golf, travel, any sport not involving horses; *Clubs* Royal Northern & Univ; *Style*— Derek Tucker, Esq; ✉ Aberdeen Journals, Lang Stracht, Mastrick, Aberdeen AB15 6DF (✆ 01224 343300, fax 01224 344114, e-mail pj.editor@ajl.co.uk)

TUCKER, John Channon; s of John Basil Laurence Tucker, and Ursula Thackeray, *née* Hill (d 2001); *b* 31 July 1958, Brisbane, Aust; *Educ* South Aust Inst of Technol (BA), Univ of Adelaide (LLB); *m* 24 Sept 1983, Madeleine Jane Penn, *née* Boucaut; 3 s (Samuel b 30 Jan 1985, Joshua b 19 Sept 1986, Michael b 8 Feb 1989), 1 da (Rebecca b 2 Aug 1992); *Career* barr and slr S Aust 1980, admitted slr Eng and Wales 1988; ptnr Finlaysons Adelaide 1984–89, ptnr Linklaters London 1990–2016 (global head of banking 1999–2007, global head of finance and projects 2007–11, managing ptnr Americas 2007–10); dir London First, tstee Asthma UK, govr The Study Prep Sch for Girls Wimbledon; memb: Devpt Ctee Shakespeare's Globe, Glyndebourne Festival Soc; memb Law Soc 1988; assoc Aust Soc of Certified Practising Accountants 1984; *Recreations* sailing, golf, tennis, opera, music, gardening; *Clubs* Adelaide, RORC, Hurlingham, MCC, Surrey CCC, Wimbledon Park Golf, Glyndebourne; *Style*— John Tucker, Esq; ✆ 07973 506967, e-mail john@jctucker.co.uk

TUCKER, Her Hon Judge Katherine Jane Greening; *Career* called to the Bar 1993; fee-paid employment judge 2004–09, salaried employment judge 2009–14, circuit judge (Midland Circuit) 2014–; *Style*— Her Hon Judge Tucker; ✉ c/o Birmingham Civil Justice Centre, 33 Bull Street, Birmingham, West Midlands B4 6DS

TUCKER, (John) Keith; s of Reginald John Tucker (d 1976), and Nancy, *née* Harker (d 1993); *b* 24 March 1945; *Educ* Haberdashers' Aske's, Charing Cross Hosp Med Sch (MB BS); *m* 4 Oct 1975, Jill Margaret, da of Dr Thomas Oliphant McKane (d 1972), of Greater Easton, Essex; 3 s (Timothy b 1977, Alexander b 1979, Ian b 1981); *Career* house surgn Charing Cross Hosp 1969, registrar Addenbrooke's Hosp Cambridge 1971–73, sr registrar St Bartholomew's Higher Orthopaedic Training Scheme 1973–77, conslt orthopaedic surgn Norfolk and Norwich Hosp 1977–2012, conslt orthopaedic surgeon Spire Hosp Norwich 1992–; hon clinical tutor in med Univ of Cambridge; author of numerous articles on hip replacement and other orthopaedic subjects, co-designer of Hip Replacements System 1982–; external examiner in surgery Univ of Cambridge 1994–97; chm Orthopaedic Data Evaluation Panel Nat Inst for Clinical Excellence (NICE); chair Beyond Compliance Advsy Gp 2012–; memb: The Br Hip Soc (hon sec 1998–2005, vice-pres 2005, pres 2007–08), Br Orthopaedic Assoc (memb Cncl 1993–96), BMA, National Joint Registry Steering Ctee 2007–; FRCS (MRCS), LRCP; *Recreations* family; *Style*— Keith Tucker, Esq; ✉ 77 Newmarket Road, Norwich (✆ 01603 614016, fax 01603 766469)

TUCKER, Sir Paul M W; kt (2014); s of B W Tucker, and late H M Tucker, *née* Lloyd; *b* 24 March 1958; *Educ* Codsall HS, Trinity Coll Cambridge (MA); *m* Sophie Dierick; *Career* Bank of England working on monetary policy, financial stability, markets and bank supervision 1980–2013; roles incl: corp financier (seconded) at merchant bank 1980–87, advsr (seconded) to Hong Kong Securities Review Ctee Hong Kong Govt 1987–88, private sec to Govr 1989–92, memb Monetary Policy Ctee 2002–13, dep govr and memb Ct 2009–13, memb Financial Policy Ctee 2011–13, memb Prudential Regulation Authy Bd 2013–; memb G20 Financial Advsy Bd 2009–13, memb Bd of Bank for Int Settlements 2009–13; govr Ditchley Fndn; sr fell Harvard Kennedy Sch and Harvard Business Sch 2013/14, visiting fell Nuffield College Oxford, Int Advsy Ctee Judge Business Sch Cambridge; *Clubs* Athenaeum; *Style*— Sir Paul M W Tucker; ✉ Bank of England, Threadneedle Street, London EC2R 8AH (✆ 020 7601 4444)

TUCKER, Sir Richard Howard; kt (1985); s of His Hon Judge Howard Archibald Tucker (d 1963), and Margaret Minton, *née* Thacker (d 1976); *b* 9 July 1930, Walsall, W Midlands; *Educ* Shrewsbury, The Queen's Coll Oxford (MA); *m* 1, 1958 (m dis 1974), Paula Mary Bennett Frost; 1 s (Stephen), 2 da (Anneli, Gemma); *m* 2, 1975, Wendy Kate Standbrook (d 1988); *m* 3, 16 Sept 1989, Mrs Jacqueline S R Thomson, wid of William Thomson; *Career* called to the Bar Lincoln's Inn 1954 (bencher 1979, treas 2002); QC 1972, recorder 1972–85, judge of the High Court of Justice (Queen's Bench Div) 1985–2000, presiding judge Midland & Oxford Circuit 1986–90; memb: Employment Appeal Tbnl 1986–2000, Parole Bd 1996–2003 (vice-chm 1998–2000); cmmr Royal Court of Jersey 2003–10, memb Cmmn of Enquiry Grand Cayman 2008; qualified mediator 2004–; hon fell The Queen's Coll Oxford 1992; *Recreations* gardening, wood turning, model railways; *Clubs* Garrick, Bean (Birmingham); *Style*— Sir Richard Tucker; ✉ Treasury Office, Lincoln's Inn, London WC2A 3TL

TUCKER, Dr Sam Michael; s of Harry Tucker (d 1970), and Ray Tucker (d 1982); *b* 15 October 1926; *Educ* Benoni HS, Univ of the Witwatersrand (MB BCh); *m* 13 Dec 1953, Barbara Helen, da of M Kaplan; 1 da (Dana b 1956), 2 s (Mark b 1957, Trevor b 1962); *Career* conslt paediatrician Hillingdon Hosp Uxbridge and 152 Harley St London, clinical tutor and examiner RCP; memb Hillingdon Dist HA, chm Med Advsy Ctee Portland Hosp 1987–88; assoc prof Brunel Univ Uxbridge 1988–; RSM: pres Section of Paediatrics 1987–88 and 2005–06, memb Cncl 1996, sr hon treas 2000–; tstee: Child Bunns Tst, Friends of Russian Children; *Recreations* football, golf; *Style*— Dr Sam Tucker; ✉ 65 Uphill Road, Mill Hill, London NW7 4PT (✆ 020 8959 0500, e-mail sammtucker@btinternet.com)

TUCKEY, Andrew Marmaduke Lane; s of Henry Lane Tuckey (d 1982), and Aileen Rosemary, *née* Newsom-Davis; *b* 28 August 1943; *Educ* Plumtree Sch Zimbabwe; *m* 24 June 1967 (m dis 1998), Margaret Louise, da of Dr Clive Barnes (d 1979); 1 s (Jonathan b 1970), 2 da (Clara b 1972, Anna b 1982); *m* 2, 27 August 1998, Tracy Elisabeth, da of Stanley Long (d 2012); 2 da (Eleanor b 1999, Florence b 2002); *Career* chm Baring Bros & Co Ltd and dir various Baring subsids 1968–95, conslt ING Barings 1995–96; sr advsr: Donaldson Lufkin & Jenrette 1996–2000, Credit Suisse First Boston 2000–01, Bridgewell 2001–07, Landsbanki Securities 2007–08; Quayle Munro: dep chm 2008–10, chm 2010–12, sr advsr 2012–; *Recreations* music, theatre; *Clubs* White's; *Style*— Andrew Tuckey, Esq; ✉ Quayle Munro Limited, 22 Berners Street, London W1T 3LP

TUCKEY, Rt Hon Sir Simon Lane; kt (1992), PC (1998); s of Henry Lane Tuckey (d 1982), and Aileen Rosemary, *née* Newsom-Davis (d 2014); *b* 17 October 1941; *Educ* Plumtree Sch Zimbabwe; *m* 1964, Jennifer Rosemary, da of Sir Charles Edgar Matthews Hardie (d 1998); 1 s (Bill Tuckey, *qv*, b 1966), 2 da (Camilla (Mrs Richard Parsons) b 1965, Kate b 1970); *Career* called to the Bar Lincoln's Inn 1964, QC 1981, recorder of the Crown Court 1984, judge of the High Court of Justice (Queen's Bench Division) 1992–98, presiding judge Western Circuit 1995–97, judge i/c Commercial List 1997–98, a Lord Justice of Appeal 1998–2009, arbitrator 20 Essex St 2009–, justice of appeal Gibraltar 2010–12, ret; chm Review Panel Fin Reporting Cncl 1990, co-chm Civil and Family Ctee Judicial Studies Bd 1993–95; *Recreations* sailing, tennis; *Style*— The Rt Hon Sir Simon Tuckey; ✉ 20 Essex Street, London WC2 3AL

TUCKEY, William Matthew Lane (Bill); s of Sir Simon Tuckey (Rt Hon Lord Justice Tuckey), *qv*, and Jennifer, *née* Hardie; *b* 18 May 1966, London; *Educ* Westminster; *m* 1997, Diane, *née* Kerridge; 1 da (Mia b 27 March 1997), 2 s (Alexander b 22 July 1999, Charles b 23 May 2004); *Career* DJ Kiss FM 1984–98, co-fndr Touch Magazine 1990 (sold 1999), foreign news ed New Nation 1996–98, chief sub-ed The Independent Magazine 1999–2002, asst features ed The Independent 2002–04, dep ed Independent on Sunday Review 2004–07, ed The New Review Independent on Sunday 2007–; *Recreations* books, wine, music, family; *Style*— Bill Tuckey, Esq; ✉ The New Review, The Independent on Sunday, Independent House, 191 Marsh Wall, London E14 9RS (☎ 020 7005 2000, e-mail b.tuckey@independent.co.uk)

TUCKNOTT, John Anthony; MBE; s of late Eric Arthur Tucknott, and late Ethel, *née* Holland; *b* 2 January 1958, Bournemouth; *Educ* KCL (MA); *m* Riitta-Leena Lehtinen; 1 s; *Career* diplomat; clerical offr Communications Operations Dept FCO 1977–78, clerical offr Office of the Lord Privy Seal FCO 1978–80, archivist Rome 1980–82, asst mgmnt offr Cairo 1982–85, asst desk offr N America Dept FCO 1986–87, desk offr W Africa Dept FCO 1987–88, dep head of mission Beirut 1988–93, head of section Security Policy Dept FCO 1993–95, first sec UK Mission to the UN NY 1995–98, dep head Non-Proliferation Dept FCO 1998–2000, UK coordinator for war crime issues FCO 2000–01, dir trade and investment devpt Stockholm and consul-gen Gothenberg 2002–05, sr directing staff Royal Coll of Defence Studies London 2005–07, dep head of mission Baghdad 2007–09, dir Global Investment Conference London 2010 UKTI 2009–10, ambass to Nepal 2010–13, dep high cmmr to Pakistan 2013–; UKTI dir for Pakistan 2013–, UK trade champion for Pakistan 2013–; *Clubs* Sind; *Style*— Mr John Tucknott, MBE; ✉ email: john.tucknott@fco.gov.uk

TUDOR, Dr (Fiona) Philippa; da of (James) Brian Tudor, and late Rosaleen, *née* O'Connor; *b* 15 February 1958, Shrewsbury; *Educ* Sch of Saints Mary and Anne Abbots Bromley, Somerville Coll Oxford (MA, DPhil); *m* 30 Sept 1989, David Beamish, *qv*; 1 da (Amelia May Tudor Beamish b 31 May 1994); *Career* House of Lords: clerk 1982, sr clerk 1986, chief clerk 1993, Clerk of Private Bills 1997–2001; head Parly and Constitutional Div Scotland Office 2001–03, head of HR House of Lords 2003–07, finance dir House of Lords 2007–11, clerk of ctees House of Lords 2011–; author of biography of Isobel Holst and articles on history and parliamentary procedure; FCIPD, DipCG; *Recreations* historical research, classical music, walking; *Style*— Dr Philippa Tudor; ✉ Committee Office, House of Lords, London SW1A 0PW

TUDOR JOHN, William (Bill); DL (Herts 2006); s of Tudor John (d 2001), of Castle House, Llantrisant, Mid Glamorgan, and Gwen, *née* Griffiths (d 1969); *b* 26 April 1944; *Educ* Cowbridge Sch, Downing Coll Cambridge; *m* 1, 25 Feb 1967, Jane (d 2007), da of Peter Clark (d 2006), of Cowbridge, Mid Glam; 3 da (Rebecca (Mrs Ben le Fleming) b 1971, Katherine (Mrs Alexander Turner) b 1974, Elizabeth (Mrs Nicholas Atkinson) b 1980); m 2, 11 April 2014, Joanna, da of Joseph Clayton (d 1988), of Stevenage, Herts; *Career* Allen & Overy: articled clerk 1967–69, asst slr 1969–70; banker Orion Bank Ltd 1970–72; Allen & Overy: ptnr 1972–2001, managing ptnr 1992–94, sr ptnr 1994–2000; md and chm Euro Commitment Ctee Lehman Brothers 2000–08, md and sr advsr Nomura Int 2008–12; non-exec chm: Suttons Seeds Ltd 1978–93, Horticultural and Botanical Holdings Ltd 1985–93, The Portman Building Soc 2006–07 (non-exec dir 2001–07); non-exec dir: Woolwich plc 2000, Nat Film and Television Sch 2000–, Sun Bank plc 2001–03, Grainger plc 2005–11; dep chm Nationwide Building Soc 2007–11; vice-chm Financial Markets Law Ctee 2002–09 (memb 1996–2009); chm Advsy Cncl Oxford Univ Law Fndn 1998–2003; memb Devpt Bd: Univ of Oxford 1999–, Nat Museum of Wales 2006–; memb: Ct Univ of Herts 2006–, Advsy Bd Welsh Nat Opera 2012–; chm Wales in London 2001–06; appeal steward Br Boxing Bd of Control 1980–; tstee St Albans Abbey Building Tst 2005–; assoc fell Downing Coll Cambridge 1986–92 and 1997–; Freeman City of London, memb City of London Slrs' Co 1972, Liveryman Worshipful Co of Gunmakers 1994; memb: Law Soc 1969, Int Bar Assoc 1976; High Sheriff Herts 2006–07; *Recreations* shooting, rugby football, reading, music; *Clubs* Justinians, Cardiff and County; *Style*— Bill Tudor John, Esq, DL; ✉ Willian Bury, Willian, Hertfordshire SG6 2AF (☎ 01462 683532, e-mail tjwillian@btinternet.com)

TUDOR-CRAIG, Dr Pamela (Pamela, Lady Wedgwood); da of Herbert Wynn Reeves (d 1972), and Madeleine Marian, *née* Brows; *b* 26 June 1928, London; *Educ* Courtauld Inst (BA, PhD); *m* 1, 1956, (Algernon) James Riccarton Tudor-Craig, FSA (d 1969), o s of Maj Sir Algernon Tudor Tudor-Craig, KBE, FSA (d 1943); 1 da (Elizabeth Jocelyn b 1960); m 2, 1982, as his 2 w, Sir John Hamilton Wedgwood, 2 Bt, TD (d 1989); *Career* art historian; prof of art history: Univ of Evansville at Harlaxton Coll 1979–89 (fndr Annual Int Symposium on Inter-disciplinary Eng Medieval Studies 1984), Grinnell London 1990–95; speaker in confs at Poitiers, Regensburg and Landegg; lecture tours of America: Kalamazoo, Smithsonian and Nat Gallery Washington, Harvard Univ, Metropolitan Museum NY (twice), Univ Museum in Philadelphia, Stanford Univ; TV work incl: Richard III with Barlow and Watt 1976, Light of Experience 1976, Round Table at Winchester (Horizon) 1977, Richard III for Timewatch 1983, The Trial of Richard III for ITV (nominated as programme of the year) 1984, The Secret Life of Paintings BBC2 1986; many radio progs; memb ctee to advise on conservation: West Front at Wells Cathedral 1973–85, Exeter Cathedral 1979–86; chm and vice-chm Paintings Ctee Cncl for the Care of Churches 1975–96; memb: DAC St Edmundsbury and Ipswich 1966–69, DAC London 1970–73, Cathedrals Advsy Cmmn for Eng 1976–91, Architectural Advsy Panel Westminster Abbey 1979–98, Ctee Fabric Southwell Minster 1984–2001, Ctee Fabric Lincoln Cathedral 1986–92, Ctee Fabric Peterborough Cathedral 1987–96, Cncl Soc of Antiquaries 1989–92, Cultural Affrs Ctee ESU 1990–2000; fndr Cambridgeshire Historic Churches Tst 1982; chm Friends of Sussex Historic Churches 2002–10; judge of History Today annual History Prize 1993–98; FSA 1957 (medal for services to its aims and objects 2014), memb Br Archaeological Assoc; *Publications* incl: Richard III (1973), The Secret Life of Paintings (with Richard Foster, 1986), New Bell's Cathedral Guide to Westminster Abbey (jtly, 1986), Old St Paul's (2004), Harlaxton Symposium Volumes; author of numerous articles, contrib to Arts Page of Church Times, History Today and Resurgence; author with colleagues of catalogue of pictures belonging to the Soc of Antiquaries (2015); *Recreations* wildlife, dogs and cats, music, opera, reading, friendship, travel, walking; *Style*— Dr Pamela Tudor-Craig, FSA; ✉ 9 St Anne's Crescent, Lewes, East Sussex BN7 1SB (☎ 01273 479564)

TUDOR-WILLIAMS, Dr Robert; s of David Tudor-Williams, LDS RCS (d 1990), and Nanette *née* Llewellin (d 2010); *b* 4 November 1945; *Educ* Haverfordwest GS, Guy's Hosp (BDS, LDS, RCS); *m* 1971, Margaret Ann, da of Alfred Hector Morris (d 1998); 2 s (Laurence b 6 April 1973, Dylan b 8 April 1974), 1 da (Rebecca b 16 Jan 1979); *Career* asst house surgn Guy's Hosp 1970, house surgn KCH 1970–71, sr hosp dental offr Eastman Dental Hosp 1972, gen practice in City and West End 1970–72, princ of gp practice Fulham 1972–80, clinical asst in oral surgery Charing Cross Hosp 1974–87; in private practice: Esher 1980–2010, Harley St 1988–2005; special interests: cosmetic and restorative dentistry, headaches, migraines and disorders of the TMJ 1988–; lectr Hammersmith and W London Coll: to dental surgery assts 1977–88, to med secs 1978–87; lectr and course dir to dental surgery assts BDA 1988–94; LBC's radio dentist 1989–96; memb Panel of Examiners: RCS(Ed) 1988–2011, Examining Bd for Dental Surgery Assts 1982–94; external examiner RCS 1991–93; memb: BDA 1970–2009 (chm Kingston and Dist Section 1983–84), Ealing Hammersmith and Hounslow LDC 1975–90, Br Soc of Periodontology 1985–2009, L D Pankey Assoc 1985–2010, Br Dental Migraine Study Gp 1985–, Br Soc of Gen Dental Surgery 1986–2009, Br Dental Health Fndn 1988–2010, Fédération Dentaire Internationale (FDI) 1990–2010, Faculty of Gen Dental Practice UK 1992–2005, American Equilibration Soc 1996–, Assoc of Broadcasting Doctors and Dentists 1995–, Exec Ctee Central London Private Practitioners' Forum; Freeman City of London 1997; Liveryman: Worshipful Soc of Apothecaries, Worshipful Co of Blacksmiths; MGDS RCSEd 1986, FRSM 1986; *Recreations* sailing, gardening, theatre, swimming, cycling, shooting, fishing; *Clubs* IOD, Esher 41; *Style*— Dr Robert Tudor-Williams; ✉ The Birches, 50 Grove Way, Esher, Surrey KT10 8HL (☎ 020 8398 0108, e-mail roberttudorwilliams@hotmail.co.uk)

TUFFREY, Michael William (Mike); *b* 30 September 1959; *Educ* Douai Sch Woolhampton, Univ of Durham (BA); *m*; 1 s, 2 da; *Career* accountant KPMG London 1981–84, research and parly offr Lib/SDP Whips Office House of Lords 1984–87, memb GLC/ILEA for Vauxhall 1985–86, dir of Fin and Admin Action Resource Centre London 1987–90, community affrs conslt Prima Europe London 1990–97, elected memb Lambeth Cncl 1990–2002 (Lib Dem ldr 1990–98, de facto jt cncl ldr 1994–98), dir The Corporate Citizenship Co London mgmnt consultancy 1997– (ed Corporate Citizenship Briefing 1991–); GLA: memb London Assembly (Lib Dem) London (list) 2002–12, ldr Lib Dem Gp 2006–10, memb Budget Ctee, memb Environment Ctee, memb London Fire and Emergency Planning Authy 2002–08 and 2010–12; memb Assoc of London Govt Ldrs Ctee; Lambeth rep AMA and LGA; memb bd various regenerative initiatives incl: Brixton Challenge, Business Link London, London Devpt Partnership, Cross River Partnership, Central London Partnership, South Bank Partnership; memb: Lib Dem Pty (formerly Lib Pty) 1978–, Friends of the Earth, Amnesty Int; parish memb St Mary's Clapham; assoc ICAEW; *Recreations* licensed radio amateur (G8LHQ); *Style*— Mike Tuffrey, Esq; ✉ 50 Lynette Avenue, London SW4 9HD (☎ 020 8673 1684, e-mail mike.tuffrey@gmail.com)

TUGENDHAT, Baron (Life Peer UK 1993), of Widdington in the County of Essex; Sir Christopher Samuel Tugendhat; kt (1990); er s of Dr Georg Tugendhat (d 1973), of London, and Máire, *née* Littledale (d 1994); bro of Sir Michael George Tugendhat, QC (Hon Mr Justice Tugendhat), *qv*; *b* 23 February 1937; *Educ* Ampleforth, Gonville & Caius Coll Cambridge; *m* 1967, Julia Lissant, da of Kenneth D Dobson, of Keston, Kent; 2 s (Hon James Walter b 1971, Hon Angus George Harry b 1974); *Career* leader and feature writer Financial Times 1960–70; MP (Cons): Cities of London and Westminster 1970–74, City of London and Westminster South 1974–76; Br EEC cmmr (responsible for budget, fin control, personnel and admin) 1977–81, vice-pres Cmmn of Euro Communities (responsible for budget, fin control, fin insts and taxation) 1981–85; chm: CAA 1986–91, Royal Inst of Int Affrs Chatham House 1986–95, Abbey National plc 1991–2002, Blue Circle Industries plc 1996–2001; non-exec chm European Advsy Bd Lehman Brothers Europe 2002–07; dep chm Nat Westminster Bank 1990–91 (dir 1985–91); non-exec dir: The BOC Group plc 1985–96, Commercial Union Assurance Co plc 1988–91, LWT (Holdings) plc 1991–94, Eurotunnel plc 1991–2003, Rio Tinto plc (formerly RTZ Corporation plc) 1997–2004; chllr Univ of Bath 1998–; chair Imperial Coll Healthcare NHS Tst 2007–; hon fell Gonville & Caius Coll Cambridge 1998; Hon LLD Univ of Bath 1998, Hon DLitt UMIST 2002; *Publications* books incl: Oil: The Biggest Business (1968), The Multinationals (1971), Making Sense of Europe (1986), Options for British Foreign Policy in the 1990's (with William Wallace, 1988); pamphlets incl: Britain, Europe and the Third World (1976), Conservatives in Europe (1979), Is Reform Possible? (1981); *Recreations* conversation, reading, being with my family; *Clubs* Athenaeum; *Style*— The Rt Hon Lord Tugendhat; ✉ 35 Westbourne Park Road, London W2 5QD

TUGHAN, John; QC (2015); *b* Belfast; *Educ* Campbell Coll Belfast, Univ of Liverpool (LLB); *Career* called to the Bar 1991; memb Family Law Bar Assoc; *Style*— John Tughan, Esq, QC; ✉ 4 Paper Buildings, Temple, London EC4Y 7EX

TUITE, Sir Christopher Hugh; 14 Bt (I 1622), of Sonnagh, Westmeath; s of Sir Dennis George Harmsworth Tuite, 13 Bt, MBE (d 1981, descended from the Sir Richard de Tuite or Tuitt, who was one of Strongbow's followers in his invasion of Ireland in 1172); *b* 3 November 1949; *Educ* Wellington, Univ of Liverpool (BSc), Univ of Bristol (PhD); *m* 1976, Deborah Ann, da of A E Martz, of Punxutawny, USA; 2 s (Thomas Livingstone b 1977, Jonathan Christopher Hannington b 1981); *Heir* s, Thomas Tuite; *Career* res offr The Wildfowl Tst 1978–81; pres Spirutec Inc (Arizona) 1982–86, controller Nature Conservancy Washington DC 1987–99, controller Int Fund for Animal Welfare 1999– (latterly dir wildlife and habitat protection); *Style*— Sir Christopher Tuite, Bt

TULLO, Carol Anne; *née* Dodgson; da of late Edward Alan Dodgson, and late Patricia, *née* Masterson; *b* 9 January 1956, Liverpool; *Educ* Holly Lodge, Univ of Hull (LLB), Inns of Court Sch of Law, City Univ; *m* 5 May 1979, Robin Brownrigg Tullo, s of James Francis Swanzy Tullo, of London; 1 da (Alice Sophia b 1986), 1 s (Luke Edward Swanzy b 1991); *Career* called to the Bar Inner Temple 1977; dir Stevens 1985–96, publishing dir Sweet & Maxwell Ltd 1988–96, dir ESC Publishing Ltd 1990–96, dir Legal Information Resources Ltd 1994–96, publishing conslt 1996–97, controller HM's Stationery Office, Queen's Printer and Govt Printer for NI 1997–, Queen's Printer for Scotland 1999–, dir Office of Public Sector Information 2005–, dir Nat Archives 2006–; chm Law Publishers' Exec Publishers' Assoc 1995–2004; memb Bd Cncl of Academic and Professional Publishers 1995–2004, memb External Advsy Panel Centre for IT Leadership Cass Business Sch 2009–; Bd memb jt ctee on legal deposit 2013–; hon visiting prof Dept of Information Science City Univ 2000–; Liveryman Hon Soc of Stationers and Newspaper Makers 2014–; *Style*— Mrs Carol Tullo; ✉ The National Archives, Kew, Richmond, Surrey TW9 4DU (☎ 020 8392 5387, e-mail carol.tullo@nationalarchives.gsi.gov.uk)

TULLOCH, Alastair Robert Clifford; s of James Richard Moore Tulloch (d 1998), and Heather Netta (d 1989); *b* 1 October 1955; *Educ* St Andrew's Coll, Magdalen Coll Oxford; *m* 15 Aug 1987, Hilary, da of Rev Alasdair Macdonell, of St Mary's Haddington, Scotland; 1 da (Emma Heather b 1988), 4 s (Robin b and d 1989, Hugh Gordon b 1991, Iain Alastair, Angus James (twins) b 1992); *Career* asst slr: Lovell White and King 1980–82 (articled 1978–80), McNeil and Co Dubai 1982–84, Clifford Turner 1984–86; ptnr: Frere Cholmeley Bischoff 1987–98, Eversheds (following merger) 1998; sole princ Tulloch & Co 1999– (ptnr 2009); memb Law Soc; *Recreations* DIY, skiing, sailing, hill walking; *Style*— Alastair Tulloch, Esq

TULLOCH, Clive William; s of Ewan William Tulloch (d 2001), of Richmond, Surrey, and Sylvia Phoebe, *née* Mott; *b* 21 June 1948; *Educ* Winchester; *m* Tessa Celia Geraldine, da of Prof Harry Frederick Trewman; 1 da (Caroline Sylvia Geraldine b 2 Dec 1982), 1 s (James Harry William b 23 Aug 1985); *Career* Coopers & Lybrand 1967–79, ptnr Morison Stoneham & Co 1980–81 (joined 1979), PricewaterhouseCoopers (formerly Coopers & Lybrand before merger 1998) 1981–2006 (ptnr 1983–2006, ptnr responsible for risk mgmnt in UK HR consulting practice 1997–2006 and tax practice 2001–06); chief exec Free Representation Unit 2006–11; memb ICAEW Working Pty on Practice Assurance for Tax 2002; London C of C: chm Taxation Ctee 1994–97 (memb 1987–2001), memb Cncl 1994–2001; memb Advice Quality Standard Mgmnt Ctee Advice Services Allance 2012–; tstee: Tax Advsrs' Benevolent Fund 2000–10, Tax Advsrs' Charitable Tst 2000–10, TaxAid UK 2001–04, Tax Volunteers (Tax Help for Older People) 2009– (chm 2013–), CILEx Pro Bono Tst 2012–15; govr St Nicholas Primary Sch Chislehurst 1989–95; hon treas The Bach Choir 1997–2006; tstee Carducci Music Tst 2009– (chm 2013–); Liveryman Worshipful Co of Tax Advsrs (memb Ct of Assts 1998–, Master 2004–05); FCA 1976 (ACA 1971), CTA (fell) (FTII 1994); *Books* The CCH Company Car Tax Guide 1999–2000 (jt author and princ ed (and on previous edns)), Car or Cash? (2 edn), Employee Share Schemes in Practice; *Recreations* choral singing, walking; *Clubs* Lansdowne, RSA,

T

Aldrich Catch; *Style*— Clive W Tulloch, Esq; ✉ Lamorna, Sleeper's Hill, Winchester, Hampshire SO22 4NB

TULLOCH, Iain William Patrick; s of Maj William Alexander Tulloch, (d 1988), of Monkton, Ayrshire, and Margaret Edith Phyllis, *née* Farquhar (d 1968); *b* 12 December 1940; *Educ* Rugby, Brown Univ USA; *m* 5 Oct 1967, Charmian Mary, da of Michael Anthony Callender, of Alton, Hants; 1 da (Leesa b 1969), 1 s (Gillen b 1971); *Career* Lt Ayrshire Yeomanry 1966; qualified CA 1966; exec dir: Murray Johnstone Ltd 1987–98, Murray Ventures 1992–98; non-exec dir: American Opportunity Trust 1989–, Galtres Foods Ltd (chm 1998–2001) until 2001, IFC Group 1990–92, Mining (Scotland) Ltd 1995–2000, Murray VCT plc 1995–, Ward Packaging Ltd 1994–2000; current appointments: Msele Nedventures 2000–, chm Swiss Technol Venture Capital Fund 2000–; memb Cncl Br Venture Capital Assoc 1988–94; *Recreations* royal tennis, squash, golf, gardening; *Clubs* Prestwick Golf, Western; *Style*— Iain Tulloch, Esq; ✉ Swallow Ha', Symington, Ayrshire KA1 5PN

TULLY, David John; s of William Scarth Carlisle Tully, CBE (d 1987), and Patience Treby, *née* Betts (d 2005); *b* 13 March 1942; *Educ* Twyford, Sherborne; *m* 7 May 1965, Susan Patricia, da of (James) Geoffrey Arnott; 1 s (James Herbert b 1967), 2 da (Louise Patience b 1969, Clare Jane b 1972); *Career* slr; sr ptnr Addleshaw Goddard (formerly Addleshaw Sons & Latham Manchester) 1994–97 (ptnr 1969–99); chm Joseph Holt Ltd 2000–14, non-exec dir Cheshire Building Society 2000–07; chm CRH Charitable Tst, vice-chm Booths Charities; former chm: Manchester Young Slrs, Nat Young Slrs, Cransley Sch; former pres Manchester Law Soc; govr Manchester GS; *Recreations* shooting, fishing; *Clubs* St James's (Manchester, former chm and pres), Manchester Tennis and Racquets; *Style*— David Tully, Esq; ✉ The Cherries, 5 Greenside Drive, Hale, Altrincham, Cheshire WA14 3HX (☎ 0161 928 3029)

TULLY, Marcello; s of Guilherme Edward Tully (d 2005); *b* 20 June 1969, Maceio, Brazil; *Career* head chef Home Rouxl 1990, head chef Kinloch Lodge Isle of Skye 2007– (3 AA Rosettes, Michelin star); *Style*— Mr Marcello Tully; ✉ Kinloch Lodge, Sleat, Isle of Skye IV43 8QY (Twitter @marcello_tully)

TULLY, Sir (William) Mark; KBE (2002, OBE 1985); s of late William Scarth Carlisle Tully, CBE, and Patience Treby, *née* Betts; *b* 24 October 1935; *Educ* New Sch Darjeeling India, Twyford Sch Winchester, Marlborough, Trinity Hall Cambridge (MA); *m* 13 Aug 1960, (Frances) Margaret, da of late Frank Howard Butler; 2 da (Sarah b 1961, Emma b 1963), 2 s (Sam b 1965, Patrick b 1967); *Career* Nat Serv 2 Lt 1 Royal Dragoons 1954–56; regnl dir Abbeyfield Soc for housing old people 1960–64; BBC: Personnel Dept 1964–65, asst then acting rep BBC Delhi 1965–69, Hindi prog organiser External Servs London 1969–70, chief talks writer External Servs 1970–71, chief Delhi Bureau 1972–93, S Asia corr 1993–94 (resigned from the BBC); currently freelance journalist and broadcaster, presenter Something Understood (Unique Broadcasting Ltd for BBC Radio 4) 1995–; hon fell Trinity Hall Cambridge 1994; Hon DUniv Bradford 1992, Hon DLitt Univ of Strathclyde 1997, Hon Dr Richmond Univ in London 1999, Hon DUniv Central England 2002, Hon Dr Univ of York 2008, Hon Dr Open Univ 2009, hon doctorate Queen's Univ Belfast; *Awards* Dimbleby Award BAFTA 1984, Radio and Critics Broadcasting Press Guild Radio Award 1984, Sony Award for Radio Documentary 1994; *Books* Amritsar Mrs Gandhi's Last Battle (with Satish Jacob, 1985), Raj to Rajiv (with Zareer Masani, 1988), No Fullstops in India (Viking, 1991), The Heart of India (Viking, 1995), The Lives of Jesus (BBC, 1996), India in Slow Motion (2002), India's Unending Journey (2007), India The Road Ahead (2011); *Recreations* reading, fishing, bird watching; *Clubs* Oriental, Press and Gymkhana (Delhi), Bengal (Kolkata); *Style*— Sir Mark Tully, KBE; ✉ B26 Nizamuddin West, Delhi 110013, India (☎ 00 91 11 4103 3839, e-mail marktullydelhi@gmail.com)

TUNBRIDGE, Dr (William) Michael Gregg; s of Sir Ronald Ernest Tunbridge, OBE (d 1984), of Leeds, and Dorothy, *née* Gregg (d 1999); *b* 13 June 1940; *Educ* Kingswood Sch Bath, Queens' Coll Cambridge (MA, MD), UCH; *m* 28 Aug 1965, Felicity Katherine Edith, da of Arthur Myers Parrish (d 1987), of Bangor; 2 da (Clare b 1968, Anne b 1970); *Career* conslt physician Newcastle Gen Hosp 1977–94, sr lectr in med Univ of Newcastle upon Tyne until 1994, dir of postgrad med educn and trg Univ of Oxford and Region 1994–2003, conslt physician Oxford Radcliffe Hosps NHS Tst 1994–2005, emeritus physician Nuffield Dept of Medicine 2005–; professorial fell Wadham Coll Oxford 1994–2003 (emeritus fell 2003–); memb: Diabetes UK, Br Thyroid Assoc, Soc for Endocrinology; FRCP 1979; *Publications* Thyroid Disease: the Facts (with Mark Vanderpump, 4 edn, 2008); *Recreations* walking, golf; *Clubs* Athenaeum; *Style*— Dr Michael Tunbridge; ✉ Millstone, Ranmoor Lane, Hathersage, Hope Valley, Derbyshire S32 1BW (☎ 01433 650765, e-mail tunbridgemf@btinternet.com)

TUNNACLIFFE, Paul Derek; *b* 13 April 1962; *Career* co sec: Hanson plc 1997–2008 (asst sec 1987–97), Diageo plc 2008–; FCIS 1993; *Style*— Paul Tunnacliffe, Esq; ✉ Diageo plc, Lakeside Drive, Park Royal, London NW10 7HQ

TUNNICLIFFE, Benjamin Rafe (Ben); s of Rafe Tunnicliffe (d 2001), and Anne, *née* Sheath; *b* 4 January 1971, Bournemouth, Dorset; *Educ* St Peter's RC Sch Bournemouth, Lansdowne Coll of FE Dorset (Dip); *m* 1999, Kinga Teresa, *née* Magiera; 2 s (Oliver b 20 Nov 2005, Alexander b 24 Feb 2010); *Career* restaurateur; L'Aubergade France 1988, Chewton Glen Hants 1989, sous chef rising to head chef at numerous prominent hotels and restaurants 1989–2000, chef prop The Abbey Restaurant Cornwall 2000–08 (Michelin Star), head chef The Scarlet Hotel Mawgan Porth 2009–; lectr Camborne Catering Coll 2005; *Recreations* surfing, golf, mountain biking; *Style*— Ben Tunnicliffe, Esq; ✉ The Scarlet Hotel, Mawgan Porth, Cornwall TR8 4DQ (e-mail ben.tunnicliffe@scarlethotel.co.uk, website www.scarlethotel.co.uk)

TUNNICLIFFE, Baron (Life Peer UK 2004), of Bracknell in the County of Berkshire; Denis Tunnicliffe; CBE (1993); *b* 17 January 1943; *Educ* Henry Cavendish Sch Derby, UCL (State scholar, BSc), Coll of Air Trg Hamble; *m* 1968, Susan, *née* Dale; 2 s (Hon Alan Dale b 29 Sept 1971, Hon Richard Dale b 1 March 1973); *Career* British Airways: co-pilot VC10 then B747 1966–72, various personnel and industrial rels roles BOAC (latterly Overseas Div BA) 1972–77, head of planning Flight Ops 1977–80, controller of fuel 1980–82, gen mangr Caribbean 1982, head of consultancy servs 1982–83, sr gen mangr Market Centres 1983–84, dir of marketplace performance 1984–86; chief exec Aviation Div International Leisure Group 1986–88, md London Underground Ltd 1988–98, chief exec London Transport 1998–2000 (memb Bd 1993–2000); non-exec chm: UKAEA 2002–04, Rail Safety and Standards Bd 2003–08; non exec memb Bd Def Logistics Orgn 2006–07, non-exec memb Bd Def Equipment and Support 2007–08; cncllr: New Windsor BC 1971–75, Berks CC 1974–77, Bracknell DC 1979–83; Lord in Waiting (govt whip) 2008–; *Recreations* boating, church, flying; *Clubs* RAF, RAC; *Style*— The Rt Hon the Lord Tunnicliffe, CBE; ✉ House of Lords, London SW1A 0PW

TUNNICLIFFE, Michael John (Mike); s of Brian Tunnicliffe, of London, and Dorothy Anne Baxendale, *née* Richardson; *b* 19 January 1961; *Educ* Bramhall HS; *m* 24 Aug 1990, Elaine Clare, *née* Jackson; 1 da (Ava Talullah Grace b 14 Jan 1994), 1 s (Milo Oscar Jack b 17 Jan 1997); *Career* advtg sales exec Link House Publications 1979–80, advtg sales mangr Burke House Periodicals 1980–81, media exec, media mangr then dep gp dir Saatchi and Saatchi Advertising 1981–83, media mangr Leagas Delaney Partnership 1983–84, media mangr, assoc dir then dir HDM: Horner Collis and Kirvan 1984–90; CIA Group plc: dir CIA Media UK 1990, dep md CIA Media UK 1993, dir CIA UK Holdings 1994–97, md CIA Medianetwork UK 1994–97, dir CIA Medianetwork Europe Holdings 1995–97; Interpublic Gp: md Western International Media 1998–2000, exec vice-pres Initiative Media 2000–05, chief strategic offr Initiative North America 2005–06, global client and network devpt dir Initiative 2006–07, fndr and pres Tuna Music LLC and Strategic Action Station Inc 2007–; IPA Advertising Effectiveness Award 1988; memb: Media Circle 1981, Mktg Soc 1994; *Recreations* sailing, golf, tennis; *Clubs* RAC; *Style*— Mike Tunnicliffe, Esq

TUOHY, Denis John; s of John Vincent Tuohy (d 1976), of Scariff, Co Clare, and Anne Mary, *née* Doody; *b* 2 April 1937; *Educ* Clongowes Wood Coll Ireland, Queen's Univ Belfast (BA, Blayney exhibition prize, Peel prize, debating medal); *m* 1, 1960 (m dis 1988), Eleanor Moya, da of Felix Charles McCann; 2 s (Mark b 12 June 1962, Christopher b 3 April 1964), 2 da (Eleanor b 14 July 1969, Catherine b 21 Oct 1974); m 2, 1998 (m dis 2007), Elizabeth Moran; *Career* TV reporter, presenter and writer and radio presenter: BBC NI 1960–64 (also actor), Late Night Line Up (BBC 2) 1964–67, 24 Hours (BBC 1) 1967–71 (also prodr), Man Alive (BBC 2) 1971–72, Panorama (BBC 1) 1974–75, This Week (Thames) 1972–74 and 1986–92, TV Eye (Thames) 1979–86, People and Politics (Thames) 1973, Midweek (BBC 1) 1974, Tonight (BBC 1) 1975–79, Reporting London (Thames) 1981–82, The Garden Party (BBC 1) 1990–91, Central Weekend (Central) 1993, Classic FM 1993, Something Understood (BBC Radio 4) 1995–, The Jimmy Young Programme (BBC Radio 2) 1996, The World Tonight (BBC Radio 4) 2001, The Sunday Show (RTE Radio 1) 2003, A Living Word (RTE Radio 1) 2003, The Midnight Court (RTE TV) 2003; prodr Southern Eye (BBC South) 1993, newscaster ITN 1994–2001; many documentaries as presenter, writer and narrator incl: Lord of the Rings (BBC 1) 1974, A Life of O'Reilly (BBC 1) 1974, Mr Truman Why Did You Drop the Second Bomb? (BBC 1) 1975, Do You Know Where Jimmy Carter Lives? (BBC 1) 1977, To Us a Child (Thames, UNICEF) 1986, The Blitz (Thames) 1990, The Longest Walk (BBC 2) 1994, Secret History: Dad's Army (Channel 4) 1998, Secret History: The Real Saatchi Brothers Masters of Illusion (Channel 4) 1999, The Law and the Lunatic (BBC 1) 1999, Vets on the Wild Side (Discovery) 1999–2001, Cards of Identity (RTE Radio 1) 2002, prodr and presenter The Troubles I've Seen (UTV) 2008, writer and narrator UTV at 50 (UTV) 2009, reporter Belfast Blitz Anniversary (UTV) 2011, presenter The Troubles I've Seen (UTV) 2012, 2014 and 2015, narrator Thatcher's Ireland (UTV) 2013; actor: Fair City (RTE TV), The Clinic (RTE TV) 2003, Fallout (RTE TV) 2006, The Tempest (Cork Midsummer Festival) 2006, Killinaskully (RTE TV) 2007–08, Strength and Honour (film, 2007), Scapegoat (BBC NI) 2009, Betrayal of Trust (BBC NI) 2011; Eisenhower travelling fellowship (survey of public TV in USA) 1967; contrib: Irish Times, Sunday Independent, Belfast Telegraph, The Tablet, The Independent, New Statesman, The Scotsman, The Irish News, British Poetry Review; memb NUJ 1970–; *Publications* Wide-eyed in Medialand (memoirs, 2005); *Recreations* watching rugby and cricket, theatre, cinema, walking; *Clubs* London Irish RFC; *Style*— Denis Tuohy, Esq; ✉ 16 Aurora na Mara, Shore Road, Rostrevor, Co Down BT34 3UP (☎ 02841 739945)

TURCAN, Henry Watson; s of Henry Hutchison Turcan, TD (d 1977), of Newburgh, Fife, and Lilias Cheyne (d 1975); *b* 22 August 1941; *Educ* Rugby, Trinity Coll Oxford (MA); *m* 18 April 1969, Jane, da of Arthur Woodman Blair, WS, of Dunbar, E Lothian; 1 da (Chloë b 1972), 1 s (Henry b 1974); *Career* called to the Bar Inner Temple 1965 (bencher 1992); legal assessor Gen Optical Cncl 1982–2002, recorder of the Crown Court 1985–2013, special adjudicator immigration appeals 1998–2005, immigration judge 2005–11; *Recreations* shooting, fishing, golf; *Clubs* Royal and Ancient Golf (St Andrews), Hon Co of Edinburgh Golfers (Muirfield), New (Edinburgh); *Style*— Henry Turcan, Esq; ✉ 49A Elm Park Gardens, London SW10 9PA

TURCAN, Robert Cheyne; s of H H Turcan (d 1977), of Lindores, Fife, and Lilias, *née* Cheyne (d 1975); *b* 28 May 1947; *Educ* Rugby, Trinity Coll Oxford, Univ of Edinburgh; *m* 1974, Elizabeth Catherine, da of John Carslake, DL, of Preston Bagot, Warwicks; 2 s, 2 da; *Career* apprentice Shepherd & Wedderburn 1970–72; Dundas & Wilson: joined 1973, ptnr 1973–97, head of Private Client Dept 1989–97; jt sr ptnr Turcan Connell (slrs and asset mangrs) 1997–2013; jt master Fife Foxhounds 1994–2009; *Recreations* gardening, fishing, walking, stalking; *Clubs* New (Edinburgh), Royal & Ancient Golf; *Style*— Robert Turcan, Esq; ✉ Lindores House, Cupar, Fife (☎ 01337 840369); Turcan Connell WS, Princes Exchange, 1 Earl Grey Street, Edinburgh EH13 9EE (☎ 0131 228 8111, fax 0131 228 8118)

TURLEY, Anna; MP; *Career* MP (Lab Co-op) Redcar 2015–; *Style*— Ms Anna Turley, MP; ✉ House of Commons, London SW1A 0AA

TURNAGE, Mark-Anthony; CBE (2015); *b* 10 June 1960; *Educ* Royal Coll of Music, Tanglewood USA (Mendelssohn scholar); *Career* composer; studied with Oliver Knussen, John Lambert, Gunther Schuller, Hans Werner Henze; composer in assoc CBSO 1989–93, composer in assoc ENO 1995–2000, assoc composer BBC Symphony Orch 2000–; artistic conslt Contemporary Opera Studio, composer in residence at Winnipeg New Music Festival and Avanti Summer Sounds 1998, composer in residence Cheltenham Festival 1999; subject of retrospective South Bank Centre 1998; *Compositions* orchestral works incl: Night Dances 1981, Three Screaming Popes 1989, Momentum 1991, Drowned Out 1993, Your Rockaby 1993, Dispelling the Fears (2 trumpets and orch, cmmnd by Philharmonia Orch) 1995, Four-Horned Fandango (CBSO) 1995–96, Silent Cities (cmmnd by Tokyo Philharmonic Orch for UK 98 Japan Festival) 1999, Another Set To (BBC Symphony Orch) 2000, Dark Crossing 2001, Etudes and Elegies 2001–02; voice and ensemble: Lament for a Hanging Man 1983, Greek Suite 1989, Some Days 1989, Twice Through the Heart (Aldeburgh) 1997; various ensembles: On All Fours 1985, Release 1987, Three Farewells 1990, This Silence 1993, Blood on the Floor (cmmnd by Ensemble Modern) 1994, Bass Inventions (Dave Holland/Asko) 2001; other compositions incl: Sarabande (soprano saxophone and piano) 1985, Greek (2 Act opera, cmmnd by Munich Biennale, televised 1990) 1988, Kai (solo cello and ensemble) 1990, Sleep On (cello and piano) 1992, Two Elegies Framing a Shout (soprano saxophone and piano) 1994, The Silver Tassie (opera, cmmnd by ENO, televised) 2000; *Recordings* labels: EMI Classical, Universal, NMC Recordings, Black Box; *Awards* winner Yorkshire Arts Young Composers' Competition (Entranced) 1982, Munich Biennale Prize for Best Score and Best Libretto 1988, RPS/Charles Heidsieck Music Award for best television prog (Greek) 1990, South Bank Show Award (The Silver Tassie) 2000, Olivier Award for Outstanding Achievement in Opera (The Silver Tassie) 2001; recording of Your Rockaby with Night Dances and Dispelling the Fears nominated for 1997 Mercury Music Prize; *Style*— Mark-Anthony Turnage, Esq, CBE

TURNBERG, Baron (Life Peer UK 2000), of Cheadle in the County of Cheshire; Prof Sir Leslie Arnold; kt (1994); s of Hyman Turnberg (d 1985), and Dora, *née* Bloomfield (d 2006); *b* 22 March 1934; *Educ* Stand GS, Univ of Manchester (MB ChB, MD); *m* 30 Jan 1968, Edna, da of Berthold Barme (d 1981); 1 s (Daniel b 1970 d 2007), 1 da (Helen b 1971); *Career* lectr Royal Free Hosp 1966–67, research fell Univ of Texas Dallas 1967–68, prof of med Univ of Manchester 1973–97 (sr lectr 1968–73, dean of Faculty of Med 1986–89); pres: RCP 1992–97, Assoc of Physicians of GB 1996, Medical Protection Soc (MPS) 1997–2007, Med Cncl on Alcoholism 1998–2002, Br Soc of Gastroenterology 1999–2000; chm: Conf of Med Royal Colls 1994–96, Specialist Trg Authority of Medical Royal Colls 1996–98, Bd of Public Health Laboratory Service (PHLS) 1997–2002, Bd of Health Quality Serv 1999–2004, UK Forum on Genetics and Insurance 1999–2002, National Centre for the Replacement, Refinement and Reduction of Animals in Research 2004–07, Medical Advsy Bd Nations Healthcare 2005–07; vice-pres Acad of Med Sci 1998–2004; scientific advsr Assoc of Medical Research Charities (AMRC) 1997–; former memb: GMC, Med Advsy Ctee of Ctee of Vice-Chllrs and Principals, MRC; currently memb: Br Soc of

Gastroenterology, Assoc of Physicians of GB, Select Ctee on Science and Technology House of Lords 2001–05, Bd Renovo plc 2006–11; tstee: Hadassah UK 1996–2012, Wolfson Fndn 1997–, Foulkes Fndn 2000–16, DIPEX 2004–10, Ovarian Cancer Action 2006–; Hon DSc: Univ of Salford 1997, Univ of Manchester 1998, Univ of London 2000; FRCP 1973, FRCPS 1995, FRCPEd 1996, FRCOG 1996, FRCOphth 1997, FRCS 1997, FRCPsych 1997, FMedSci 1998; *Books* Intestinal Transport (1981), Electrolyte and Water Transport Across Gastro-Intestinal Epithelia (1982), Clinical Gastroenterology (1989), Forks in the Road (2014); *Recreations* reading, chinese ceramics, walking, painting; *Style*— The Rt Hon the Lord Turnberg; ✉ House of Lords, London SW1A 0PW

TURNBULL, (Charles Colin) Andrew; s of Charles Elliot Turnbull, of Ilkley, W Yorks, and Vera Mavis, *née* Clarke; *b* 10 May 1950; *Educ* Leeds GS, Coll of Estate Management Univ of Reading, Univ of Liverpool (BA Econ), Univ of Birmingham (MSc); *m* 31 July 1976, Una Jane, da of Arnold Raymond Humphrey; 3 da (Hannah Elizabeth b 24 Sept 1981, Holly Katherine b 13 March 1984, Lydia Helen b 13 June 1988); *Career* British Airways: joined 1973, cargo marketing offr 1974, passenger traffic forecasts offr 1975, sr forecasts offr 1977–78; project work in: Ecuador, Venezuela, USA, Ghana, Ivory Coast, Sudan, SA, Saudi Arabia, Abu Dhabi, Dubai; Poulter plc: joined as res mangr 1979, head of res 1981, dir of res and planning 1983, ptnr 1985, dep md 1992–98; independent market res conslt 1998–; awarded Communications, Advertising and Marketing Dip 1979, Kelliher Cup (Communications Advertising and Marketing Fndn) for paper on int advtg 1979; memb: Market Res Soc 1980, Account Planning Group 1989, Mktg Soc 1995; *Recreations* sailing, tennis, music, three daughters; *Style*— Andrew Turnbull, Esq; ✉ Low Rigg, 15 Clifton Road, Ben Rhydding, Ilkley, West Yorkshire LS29 8TU (☎ 01943 609367)

TURNBULL, Baron (Life Peer UK 2005), of Enfield in the London Borough of Enfield Andrew Turnbull; KCB (1998, CB 1990), CVO (1992); s of Anthony Turnbull, and Mary, *née* Williams; *b* 21 January 1945; *Educ* Enfield GS, Christ's Coll Cambridge (BA); *m* 1967, Diane Elizabeth, da of Roland Clarke, and Elizabeth Clarke; 2 s (Adam b 1974, Benet b 1977); *Career* economist Govt of Zambia 1968–70; HM Treasy: joined 1970, seconded to IMF Washington 1976–78, asst sec 1978–83, under sec 1985–88; private sec of econ affrs to the PM 1983–85, princ private sec to the PM 1988–92; HM Treasy: dep sec of public fin 1992–93, second perm sec of public expenditure 1993–94; perm sec: DOE 1994–97, DETR 1997–98, HM Treasy 1998–2002; Sec to the Cabinet and Head of the Home Civil Service 2002–05; sr advsr Booz & Co 2006–10, chm BH Global Ltd 2008–12; non-exec dir: British Land 2006–, Prudential 2006–15, Frontier Economics 2006–15; vice-patron Disabled Sailing Assoc, chm Zambia Orphans of AIDS 2007–, chm of govrs Dulwich Coll 2009–15; *Recreations* walking, opera, golf, sailing; *Style*— Lord Turnbull, KCB, CVO

TURNBULL, John Neil; s of John Smith Turnbull (d 1941), of South Shields, and Kathleen Bernadette Higgins; *b* 13 February 1940; *Educ* St Cuthbert GS Newcastle upon Tyne, King's Coll Durham (BSc); *m* 1966, Aloysia, *née* Lindemann; 2 s (John Michael b 13 Oct 1968, David Stephen b 11 Dec 1970); *Career* British Petroleum: technologist BP Research Centre 1961–64, commissioning engr BP refinery Dinslaken W Germany 1964–66, project ldr BP Res Centre 1966–70, commissioning engr BP Chemicals Baglan Bay W Glamorgan 1970–74, prodn control mangr BP Baglan Bay 1974–76, tech devpt mangr BP Baglan Bay 1976–77, asst works mangr BP Baglan Bay 1977–79, gen mangr polyethylene BP Chemicals Geneva 1979–84, dir polymers BP Chemicals London 1984–86, dir technol petrochemicals and polymers BP Chemicals London 1986–89, dep chief exec nitrogen/nitriles BP Chemicals America 1989–91, dep chief exec mfrg technol BP Chemicals London 1991–93, ret; conslt 1994–, dir International Forum Stowe Vermont USA 1995–2001; FIChemE, FREng 1992, FRSA 2006; *Recreations* music, reading, theatre, travel; *Style*— John Turnbull, Esq, FREng, FRSA; ✉ Mulberry House, Vineyard Drive, Bourne End, Buckinghamshire SL8 5PD (☎ 01628 850768, e-mail jayentee@btinternet.com)

TURNBULL, Mark; *Educ* Marlborough Coll, Univ of Liverpool, Univ of London (MA); *m* Ruth Turnbull; 3 c; *Career* Sevenoaks Sch: geography teacher, head of dept, housemaster, head of boarding; formerly dep head Eastbourne Coll, hm Giggleswick Sch 2014–; *Clubs* MCC, East India; *Style*— Mark Turnbull, Esq; ✉ Giggleswick School Settle, North Yorkshire, BD24 0DE (☎ 01729 893005, e-mail enquiries@giggleswick.org.uk)

TURNBULL, Peter John; s of John Colin Turnbull, of Rotherham, S Yorks, and Patricia, *née* O'Brien; *b* 23 October 1950; *Educ* Oakwood Secdy Modern Sch Rotherham, Richmond Coll of FE, Cambs Coll of Arts & Technol (BA), Univ of Huddersfield (MA), UC Cardiff (CQSW); *Career* offr Regnl Cncl Public Serv of Strathclyde 1978–92, Leeds City Cncl 1992–95; crime writer 1981–; *Books* Deep and Crisp and Even (1981), Dead Knock (1982), Fair Friday (1983), Big Money (1983), The Claws of the Gryphon (1986), Two Way Cut (1988), Condition Purple (1989), The Justice Game (1990), And Did Murder Him (1991), Long Day Monday (1992), The Killing Floor (1994), The Killer Who Never Was (1996), Embracing Skeletons (1996), The Man With No Face (1998), Death Trap (2000), The Return (2001), Perils and Dangers (2001), Dark Secrets (2002), Reality Checkpoint (2004), Chill Factor (2005), The Trophy Wife (2005), Sweet Humphrey (2005), False Knight (2006), Fire Burn (2007), Chelsea Smile (2007), Once a Biker (2007), Turning Point (2008), Informed Consent (2009), Improving the Silence (2009), Aftermath (2010), Deep Cover (2011), The Altered Case (2012), The Garden Party (2012), Gift Wrapped (2013), Denial of Murder (2014), In Vino Veritas (2015), A Dreadful Past (2016); *Recreations* relaxing in the company of good friends; *Style*— Peter Turnbull, Esq; ✉ c/o United Agents, 12–26 Lexington Street, London W1F 0LE (☎ 020 3214 0800, fax 020 3214 0801, website www.unitedagents.co.uk)

TURNBULL, Rev Dr Richard Duncan; s of Alan Turnbull, of Doncaster, Yorks, and Kathleen, *née* Ormston (d 1978); *b* 17 October 1960, Manchester; *Educ* Moseley GS, Normanton HS W Yorks, Univ of Reading (BA), St John's Coll Univ of Durham (BA, PhD), Univ of Oxford (MA); *m* Caroline, *née* Andrew; 3 da (Sarah b 7 May 1989, Kathryn b 12 Jan 1992, Rebecca b 4 Nov 1996), 1 s (Matthew b 2 Dec 1993); *Career* CA 1985; trainee rising to mangr Ernst & Young 1987–90; curate Highfield 1994–97, vicar Chineham 1998–2005 (also memb various Dio of Winchester ctees incl chm House of Clergy and memb Standing Ctee Bishops Cncl 2000–05), princ Wycliffe Hall Oxford 2005–12, dir Centre for Enterprise, Markets and Ethics 2012–; C of E appts incl: memb Gen Synod 1995–2005 (chm Business Ctee 2004–05), memb Inter-Diocesan Finance Forum 1997–2005, chm Clergy Stipends Review 1999–2001, memb Archbishops' Cncl 2003–05 (memb Finance Ctee 1997–2005); advsr on ethical investment Ecclesiastical Insurance Gp 2002–; author of articles in academic jls and on the subject of evangelicals and the ecumenical movement; chair of govrs Portswood Primary Sch Southampton 1995–97; *Publications* Anglican and Evangelical? (2007), Shaftesbury – the Great Reformer (2010), Reviving the Heart (2012), A Passionate Faith (2012); *Recreations* reading, walking, family, friends, real tennis; *Style*— The Rev Dr Richard Turnbull; ✉ Centre for Enterprise, Markets and Ethics, 1st Floor, 31 Beaumont Street, Oxford OX1 2NP (☎ 01865 513453, e-mail richard.turnbull@theceme.org)

TURNBULL, Steven Michael; s of Philip Peveril Turnbull (d 1987), of Rock, Cornwall, and Dorothy June Turnbull; *b* 24 October 1952; *Educ* Monkton Combe Sch, UC Oxford (BA); *m* 22 Sept 1985, Mary Ann, da of David M Colyer, of Cheltenham, Glos; 1 s (Matthew b 11 July 1987), 1 da (Clare b 21 Aug 1988); *Career* Linklaters: joined 1975, slr 1978, joined Corporate Dept, ptnr 1985; memb Law Soc, memb City of London Slrs' Co; *Recreations* golf, tennis, family; *Clubs* Oxford and Cambridge Golfing Soc, Royal Wimbledon Golf; *Style*— Steven Turnbull, Esq

TURNER, Amédée Edward; QC (1976); s of Frederick William Turner (d 1945), and Ruth Hempson (d 1970); mother's side Huguenot Swiss; *b* 26 March 1929; *Educ* ChCh Oxford; *m* 1960, Deborah Dudley, da of Dr Philip Owen; 1 s, 1 da; *Career* called to the Bar Inner Temple 1954; in practice Patent Bar 1954–57, assoc Kenyon & Kenyon patent attorneys NY 1957–60, in practice London 1960–2008; Parly candidate (Cons) Norwich N gen elections 1964, 1966 and 1970; MEP (EDG 1979–92, EPP 1992–94): Suffolk and Harwich 1979–84, Suffolk and SE Cambs 1984–94; vice-chm Legal Ctee 1979–84; memb: Econ and Monetary Ctee 1979–84, ACP Jt Assembly 1979–94, Tport Ctee 1981–84, Energy and Technol Ctee 1983–89; chief whip European Democratic Gp 1989–92, chm Ctee on Int Affrs and Civil Rights 1992–94; hon sec Middle East Gp Cons Cwlth Cncl 1954–57, 1960 and 1979, hon memb European Parl 1994–, memb Exec Ctee European League for Economic Co-operation 1996–2002; sr counsel to: Oppenheimer, Wolff & Donnelly (US lawyers) 1994–2002, APCO Europe (Brussels) 1995–99, Worldspace Ltd 1999–2001; assisted Macedonian Parl to play fuller part in political system and its rules of procedure 2001–02; memb Advsy Cncl Anglican Observer UN 2002–06, organiser and author of report of Anglican, Episcopalian and Muslim discussions on attitudes of lay Muslims to democracy, human rights and rule of law throughout USA and Britain 2005–06, Muslim Grassroots in the West Discuss Democracy (speaking tours involving 120 events in US, Britain, Continental Europe, Canada and Turkey; study extended to Italy, Germany, France and Spain) 2011–12; *Publications* The Law of Trade Secrets (1962, supplement 1968), The Law of the New European Patent (1979), Manual for the Macedonian Parliament (2002), Muslim Grassroots in the West Discuss Democracy Report 2007–08, Everything that is Actually in the Qur'an Described by a Non-Muslim Westerner for Non-Muslim Readers Including the Most Telling Quotations (published online 2014), Addendum to Qu'ran Paper: Every Instruction or Comment About Killing Human Beings...with Special Reference to the ISIS Beheadings (pub online 2014), A Qur'an Paper (Google, 2016); author of over 40 European Parly reports, reports on patent litigation for the European Cmmn 2003 and 2006, and numerous Cons Pty study papers on defence, oil and Middle East; *Recreations* Westleton garden design, painting; *Clubs* Coningsby, Twenty; *Style*— Amédée Turner, Esq, QC; ✉ Penthouse 7, Bickenhall Mansions, Bickenhall Street, London W1U 6BS (☎ 020 7935 2949, fax 020 7935 2950, e-mail amedee.turner@btinternet.com); The Barn, Westleton, Saxmundham, Suffolk; La Combe de la Boissière, St Maximin, Uzès, France; 15 La Bastide d'Uzès, Chemin de l'Escallete, 30700 Uzès, France

TURNER, Andrew Charles; s of Ralph Turner (d 2008), of Leeds; *b* 1956; *Educ* Leeds GS, Christ's Coll Cambridge (MA); *m* 1982, Janice Helen, da of Albert Charles Minker; 3 s (Nicholas b 1987, William, Jonathan (twins) b 1990); *Career* PricewaterhouseCoopers (formerly Coopers & Lybrand): London office 1977–85 and 1988–2003, Tokyo office 1985–88, audit and consulting ptnr 1990–2003, ptnr-in-charge Banking and Capital Markets Regulatory Consulting Gp 1999–2003, seconded as head of gp regulatory risk to Royal Bank of Scotland Gp 2002–03; compliance dir Abbey (formerly Abbey National) 2003–05, gp compliance offr Zurich Financial Servs 2006–07, compliance dir Northern Rock plc 2009–11, head of compliance RBS Corp Banking 2012–13, fndr and dir Conduct Risk Consulting 2013–; FCA 1990 (ACA 1980); *Recreations* genealogy, photography, Jimi Hendrix (music and memorabilia); *Style*— Andy Turner; ✉ e-mail aturner447@aol.com

TURNER, Andrew John; MP; s of Eustace Albert Turner (d 2001), and Joyce Mary, *née* Lowe (d 1994); *b* 24 October 1953; *Educ* Rugby, Keble Coll Oxford (MA), Univ of Birmingham, Henley Mgmnt Centre; *Career* teacher Lord Williams's Sch Oxon 1978–84, educn desk then trade and indust desk Cons Res Dept 1984–86, special advsr to sec of state for Social Servs 1986–87, dir Grant Maintained Schs Fndn 1988–97, educn conslt 1997–2001, head of Minerva project GDST 1999–2000, head of educn policy and resources London Borough of Southwark 2000–01, MP (Cons) Isle of Wight 2001– (Parly candidate: Hackney S and Shoreditch 1992, Isle of Wight 1997; Euro Parl candidate Birmingham E 1994); memb: Educn and Skills Select Ctee, Exec 1922 Ctee 2001–03, 2007–12 and 2014–, Political & Constitutional Reform Select Ctee 2010–15, Panel of Chairs 2010–, Public Administration Ctee 2013–, European Scrutiny Ctee 2015–; a vice-chm (campaigning) Cons Pty 2003–05, shadow min for charities 2005–06; memb Oxford City Cncl 1979–96; Sheriff Oxford 1994–95; FRSA; *Recreations* walking, countryside, avoiding gardening; *Style*— Andrew Turner, Esq, MP; ✉ House of Commons, London SW1A 0AA (e-mail mail@islandmp.org)

TURNER, Brian James; CBE (2002); s of late Lawrence Turner, of Morley, Leeds, and late Lily, *née* Riley; *b* 7 May 1946; *Educ* Morley GS, Leeds Coll of Food Technol, Borough Poly, Ealing Hotel Sch; *m* Denise, da of Alan Parker, of Rothwell, W Yorks; 2 s (Simeon James b 18 Nov 1974, Benjamin Jon b 5 July 1977); *Career* chef/restaurateur; Simpsons on the Strand London 1964–66, Savoy Hotel London 1966–69, Beau-Rivage Palace Lausanne-Ouchy Switzerland 1969–70, Claridges Hotel London 1970–71, Capital Hotel London 1971–86, Turners of Walton Street London 1986–2001, ptnr Foxtrot Oscar restaurant chain 2001–03, opened Brian Turner Restaurant Crowne Plaza Hotel NEC Birmingham 2002 (closed 2005), opened Brian Turner Mayfair 2003 (closed 2008), opened Turner's Grill Copthorne Hotel Slough 2005 (closed 2008), opened Turner's Grill Copthorne Hotel Birmingham 2006 (closed 2008); pres Royal Acad of Culinary Arts (formerly Acad of Culinary Arts) 2004– (chm 1993–2004); hon prof Thames Valley Univ 2001; Good Food Guide Special Award 1996, Caterer & Hotelkeeper Catey Chef of the Year 1997, Craft Guild of Chefs Special Award 1997, Wedgwood Award 1997, Nestle Toque d'Or 2003, Caterer & Hotelkeeper Special Award 2004, Ambassadorial Award Yorks Life Food & Drink Award 2004, Awards for Excellence Springboard Special Award 2004, Lifetime Achievement Award Yorks TV Award 2005, Br Hospitality Award 2006, Nat Assoc of Catering Butchers Award for Outstanding Contrib to the Br Food Industry 2007, Hon Apprenticeship Award Apprenticeship Ambassadors Network 2009; hon doctorate Leeds Met Univ 2006, hon doctorate Sheffield Hallam Univ 2008; FHCIMA 1988 (MHCIMA 1980–88), FCGI 2005, FRSA 2006; *Books* Ready Steady Cook (with Antony Worrall-Thompson, 1996), Brian Turner: A Yorkshire Lad (2000), Brian Turner's Favourite British Recipes (2003), Great British Grub (2009), A Taste of Summer (2011); *Style*— Brian Turner, Esq, CBE; ✉ 212 Central Meat Markets, London EC1A 9LH (☎ 020 7248 1005, fax 020 7248 1006, e-mail turnerrest@aol.com, website www.brianturner.co.uk)

TURNER, Prof Bryan Stanley; s of Stanley William Turner (d 1974), and Sophia, *née* Brooks (d 1995); *b* 14 January 1945; *Educ* George Dixon GS Birmingham, Univ of Leeds (BA, PhD), Univ of Cambridge (MA); *m* Hoa Kim Nguyen; *Career* lectr Univ of Aberdeen 1969–82, prof Flinders Univ Adelaide Aust 1982–86, prof Univ of Utrecht Netherlands 1986–89, prof Univ of Essex 1989–92, prof Deakin Univ Aust 1992–98, prof Univ of Cambridge 1998–2005, professorial fell Fitzwilliam Coll Cambridge 2002–05, prof Nat Univ of Singapore 2005–08, professorial fell Australian Catholic Univ 2013; presidential prof of sociology Grad Center City Univ of NY 2010, Max Planck guest prof Potsdam Univ Germany 2016–; Max Planck Award 2015; memb: Br Sociological Assoc 1970–, Aust Acad of Social Sciences 1987–, American Sociological Assoc 1990–; involved with Ismaili Inst London; Hon DLitt Flinders Univ Aust, Hon LittD Univ of Cambridge 2009; FRSA 2002; *Publications* Cambridge Dictionary of Sociology (2006), Vulnerability and Human Rights (2006), Pragmatism in European Social Theory (jt ed, 2007), Rights and Virtues (2008), Globalization East and West (jtly, 2010), Religion and Modern Society (2011), The Religious and the Political (2013), The Future of Singapore: Population,

T

society and the nature of the state (with Kamaludeen Mohamed Nasir, 2014), L'antivieillissement. Vieillir à l'ère des nouvelles biotechnologies (with Alex Dumas, 2016); *Recreations* gardening, travel, collecting books; *Style*— Prof Bryan S Turner; ✉ The Graduate Center, 365 Fifth Avenue, New York, NY 10016–4309, USA

TURNER, Dr Christian Philip Hollier; CMG (2012); *Educ* DPhil; *m* Claire; 1 s, 1 da; *Career* diplomat; sec Better Regulation Task Force 1998–99, sec Economics and Domestic Ctees of Cabinet 1999–2000, private sec to Min of State Cabinet Office 2001–02, Prime Minister's Strategy Unit 2002–03, first sec Br Embassy Washington 2003–06, dep head of mission designate Tehran 2006–07, private sec to PM 2007, cabinet offr and dep dir ME, N Africa and N America Overseas and Defence Secretariat 2007–08, dep dir ME and N Africa FCO 2008–09, dir ME and N Africa FCO 2009–12, high cmmr to Kenya 2012–15, DG ME and Africa 2016–; *Style*— Dr Christian Turner, CMG; ✉ c/o FCO, King Charles Street, London SW1A 2AH

TURNER, Daniel Robert (Dan); s of Robert Edward Turner, and Margaret Anne Turner; *b* 11 January 1967, Kings Langley, Herts, *Educ* Watford GS, Univ of Bristol (BSc), London Business Sch (MBA); *m* 1995, Samantha Jane, *née* Hunt; *Career* sr engr Halliburton Energy Servs US, Africa and ME 1989–94, business devpt dir XL Technol Ltd 1996–2000, md Dynamid Ltd 2000–01; chief technol offr and chief operating offr ByBox Hldgs Ltd 2001–14; DG Logibag SAS France 2005–; treas Bledlow Pre-Sch 1998–2000, memb Bledlow Village Hall Ctee 1998–2000; Meritorious Award for Engrg Achievement Offshore Technol Conf (jtly) 1999, numerous Tech Track awards; memb: Bledlow Village Hall Ctee 1998–2000, Soc of Petroleum Engrs 1998; *Recreations* skiing, diving, cycling, walking; *Style*— Dan Turner, Esq; ✉ e-mail dan.turner@bybox.com

TURNER, David Andrew; QC (1991); s of James Turner (d 1986), and Phyllis, *née* Molyneux (d 2006); *b* 6 March 1947; *Educ* King George V Sch Southport, Queens' Coll Cambridge (MA, LLM); *m* 18 March 1978, Mary Christine (d 2012) , da of Eric Herbert Moffatt, of Douglas, IOM; 2 s (James b 1981, Charles b 1982), 1 da (Helen b 1984); *Career* called to the Bar Gray's Inn 1971 (bencher 2001); recorder of the Crown Court 1990–, panel deemster IOM 2008–; dep high bailiff Isle of Man 2013; *Recreations* music; *Style*— David Turner, QC; ✉ Exchange Chambers, Pearl Assurance House, Derby Square, Liverpool L2 9XX (☎ 0151 236 7747)

TURNER, His Hon Judge David George Patrick; QC (2000); s of George Patrick Turner (d 1988), of Londonderry, and Elsie Bamford, *née* McClure; *b* 11 July 1954; *Educ* Foyle Coll Londonderry, KCL (LLB, AKC), Coll of Law London; *m* 4 March 1978, Jean Patricia, da of Gerald William Hewett (d 2010); 2 s (Robert b 7 Oct 1980, Richard b 30 Oct 1982); *Career* called to the Bar Gray's Inn 1976 (bencher 2015); in practice South Eastern Circuit 1976–2004, recorder 2000–04 (asst recorder 1997–2000), circuit judge (South Eastern Circuit) 2004–; chllr Dio of Chester 1998–, dep chllr Dio of Liverpool 2001–02, dep chllr Dio of London 2002–; lay reader All Souls' Langham Place (churchwarden 1983–2006), memb Legal Advsy Cmmn C of E 2006–10, a chm Clergy Discipline Tbnls 2007–; tstee: Langham Partnership, St Paul's Tst (Portman Square) 1987–2010, London Lectures Tst; memb: Ecclesiastical Law Soc, Ecclesiastical Judges Assoc, Patron's Circle Sir John Soane's Museum 2008–14; pres Foyle Coll Former Pupils' Assoc 2016–17; *Recreations* reading, family; *Style*— His Hon Judge David Turner, QC; ✉ c/o The Crown Court, New Street, Chelmsford, Essex CM1 1EL (☎ 0245 603000, fax 01245 603011); e-mail dgptqc@hotmail.com

TURNER, Prof Denys Alan; s of Alan, and Barbara Turner; *Educ* Mount St Mary's Coll Spinkhill, UC Dublin (BA, MA), Univ of Oxford (DPhil); *Career* UC Dublin: coll lectr in philosophy 1967–74, univ lectr in philosophy 1974–76; Univ of Bristol: lectr in the philosophy of religion 1977–89, sr lectr 1989–95; H G Wood prof of theology Univ of Birmingham 1995–99, Norris-Hulse prof of divinity Univ of Cambridge 1999– (fell Peterhouse); Exec Ctee Catholic Inst for Int Rels: 1982–86, chm 1986–94; memb: Catholic Theological Assoc of GB 1986–, Eckhart Soc 1989–, Editorial Bd Reviews in Religion and Theology; chm Newman Fellowships Tst 1989–96, tstee St Mary's Hospice Birmingham 1996–99; *Books* The Philosophy of Karl Marx (1969), Marxism and Christianity (1983), Eros and Allegory (1995), The Darkness of God (1995), Faith Seeking (2002); *Recreations* classical music from Dufay to Debussy, digging; *Style*— Prof Denys Turner; ✉ Faculty of Divinity, University of Cambridge, West Road, Cambridge CB3 9BS (☎ 01223 763020, e-mail dat25@cam.ac.uk)

TURNER, Derek; CBE (2003); *b* 8 May 1953, Surbiton, Surrey; *Educ* Hinchley Wood Co Secdy Sch, Univ of Sheffield (BEng); *m* (m dis); 1 da, 1 step s; *Career* asst engr Herts CC 1974–80, professional offr Transportation and Devpt Dept GLC 1980–82, princ engr Directorate of Technical and Contract Servs London Borough of Hackney 1982–85, gp planner Highways Planning and Transportation Planning Dept London Borough of Islington 1985–86, dep borough engr Technical Servs Dept London Borough of Wandsworth 1988–90 (asst borough engr 1986–88), borough engr and surveyor Technical Servs Directorate London Borough of Haringey 1990–91, traffic dir for London 1991–2000 (prog dir London Bus Initiative 1999–2000, established Red Routes and bus lane enforcement cameras), md Street Mgmnt Transport for London 2000–03 (devised, designed and implemented Central London Congestion Charging, created London Traffic Control Centre and responsible for pedestrianisation of Trafalgar Square London), princ Derek Turner Consltg Ltd 2003–04, dir Colin Buchan and Partners 2004–05, nat traffic dir for motorways and trunk roads in England Highways Agency 2005– (memb Bd Highways Agency 2005–); non-exec dir Infocell Hldgs Limited 2003–05; visiting prof in civil and environmental engrg UCL 2003–; chm Transport Bd ICE 1999–2000; former memb: London Area Traffic Survey Steering Gp, Assoc of London Authorities/London Boroughs Assoc Transport Jt Working Party, London Transportation Study Steering Gp, Assoc of London Borough Engrs and Surveyors (gp chm 1991), Transport for London Implementation Gp, London Bus Initiative (chm Strategy Gp), Road Pricing Working Party, Millennium Access Co-ordination Gp, London Bus Priority Steering Gp, Urban Traffic Mgmnt and Control (UTMC) Steering Gp, Traffic Control Systems Unit (TCSU) Mgmnt Liaison Ctee; former chair: World Squares for All Steering Gp, London Sustainable Distribution Partnership; currently: memb Degree Prog Advsy Panel UCL, memb Road Capacity and Congestion Charging Forum; author of conf papers and int lectures on traffic and highway engrg, transportation policy and mgmnt, gives professional evidence to Transport Select Ctee House of Commons; Bus Industry Innovation Award for Bus Lane Enforcement Cameras 1998, AA Award 2000, Transport Planner of the Year Transportation Planning Soc 2003, European Transport Planner of the Year 2003; CEng, memb Inst of Municipal Engrs 1979, MCMI 1985, FIHT 1991 (MIHT 1978), FICE 1991 (MICE 1980), FCILT 1995, FRSA, FILT, FREng 2005; *Style*— Derek Turner, Esq, CBE

TURNER, Frank; s of Frank Turner (d 1977), of Earby, Lancs, and Marion, *née* Robinson (d 2005); *b* 7 June 1943; *Educ* Keighley Tech Coll, Univ of Salford (BSc), Columbia Univ Business Sch NY (long distance running trophy); *m* 1967, Byrnece, da of Jack Crawshaw; 1 da (Suzanne Nicola b 5 Feb 1972), 1 s (Julian Mark b 4 July 1977); *Career* Rolls-Royce Ltd: apprentice 1960, grad apprentice 1963–67, machine tool devpt engr 1967–69, tech asst and prog mangr RB211 1969–72, fin controller Rolls Royce 1971 Ltd Barnoldswick 1972–73, prodn products mangr Barnoldswick 1973–75, product centre mangr Derby 1975–78, gen mangr prodn 1978–80, dir mfrg 1980–83, dir mfrg engrg 1983–85, dir industrial and marine Ansty 1985–87, chm Cooper Rolls Inc 1985–87, dir Civil Engines Rolls-Royce plc 1987–92, dir International Aero Engines AG 1987–92, memb Bd Rolls-Royce Inc 1987–90, appointed to Main Bd Rolls-Royce plc 1988, chm Sawley Packaging

Co 1990–92; md Aerospace Lucas Industries plc 1992–96, chief exec BM Aviation Services Ltd 1996–2000; dir: British Midland plc 1997–2000, British Regional Airlines Holdings Ltd 1997–98; non-exec dir: ASW plc 1995–2002, Wagon Industrial Holdings plc 1996–2002, AeroInventory plc 2000–05 (chm), Material Logistics plc 2000–04, Mott MacDonald 2000–05; chm: Potenza Gp Ltd 2000–, Mettis Gp Ltd 2001–03, SRTechnics Holding 2002–06, Symmetry Medical Inc 2006–09, GCAT (Global & Commerical Aviation Training) Ltd 2006–08, Westfield Sports Cars Ltd 2006–, GTM Cars Ltd 2007–, Oxford Aviation Acad Ltd 2008–12, Hardy Transaction Mgmnt 2013–; prof Univ of Warwick 1993–; pres: IProdE (now IET (Inst of Engrg and Technol)) 1986, BAAS 1993–94, Aviation Trg Assoc 1994–98, Int Fedn of Airworthiness 2006–; memb Cncl: RAeS 1998–2004, British Aerospace Cos 1998–2000; Mensforth Gold Medal IProdE (for contrib to Br mfrg technol) 1985, James Clayton Award IMechE (for contrib to design, devpt and mfr of aero gas turbines); FREng 1986, FIEE 1986, FIMechE 1986–2009, FRAeS 1989, FInstD 2000–09; *Recreations* family, sailing, running, windsurfing, keep fit, music; *Clubs* South Carnarvon Yacht; *Style*— Frank Turner, Esq, FREng; ✉ Potenza Enterprises Ltd, 46 Main Street, Kings Newton, Derbyshire DE73 8BX (☎ 01332 862179, e-mail f.turner@ potenzaenterprises.com)

TURNER, Prof Grenville; s of Arnold Turner (d 1999), and Florence Turner (d 2009); *b* 1 November 1936, Todmorden, Yorks; *Educ* Todmorden GS, St John's Coll Cambridge (MA), Balliol Coll Oxford (DPhil); *m* 8 April 1961, Kathleen, da of William Morris (d 1986), of Rochdale; 1 s (Patrick b 1968), 1 da (Charlotte b 1966); *Career* asst prof Univ of Calif Berkeley 1962–64, res assoc Caltech 1970–71, prof of physics Univ of Sheffield 1980–88 (lectr 1964–74, sr lectr 1974–79, reader 1979–80), prof of isotope geochemistry Univ of Manchester 1988–2002 (research prof 2002–12, prof emeritus 2012–), visiting assoc in geochemistry Caltech 2013; memb Ctees: SERC, Br Nat Space Centre, PPARC; Rumford Medal Royal Soc 1996, Leonard Medal Meteoritical Soc 1999, Urey Medal European Assoc of Geochemistry 2002, Gold Medal Royal Astronomical Soc 2004; Hon Citizen Todmorden 2013; fell Geochemical Soc and European Assoc of Geochemistry 1996, fell Meteoritical Soc 1980, fell American Geophysical Union 1998; FRS 1980 (memb Cncl 1990–92); *Recreations* photography, walking, theatre; *Style*— Prof Grenville Turner, FRS; ✉ 42 Edgehill Road, Sheffield S7 1SP; School of Earth, Atmosphere and Environmental Sciences, The University of Manchester M13 9PL (☎ 0161 275 0401, fax 0161 275 3947, e-mail grenville.turner@manchester.ac.uk)

TURNER, James; QC (1998); s of James Gordon Melville Turner, GC (d 1967), and Peggy Pamela, *née* Masters; *b* 23 November 1952; *Educ* Robertsbridge Secndy Modern Sch, Bexhill GS, Univ of Hull (LLB); *m* 7 July 1979 (m dis), Sheila, da of John Barclay Green, OBE, of Woking, Surrey (d 1994); 3 s (George b 27 Jan 1981, Roderick b 1 Nov 1986, Felix b 31 Jan 1991), 2 da (Phoebe b 23 Nov 1983, Poppy b 11 Nov 1992); *Career* called to the Bar Inner Temple 1976 (bencher 2006), memb Supplementary Panel of Treasy Counsel (common law) 1995–98; memb: Criminal Bar Assoc, Family Law Bar Assoc, Administrative Law Bar Assoc, Howard League for Penal Reform, Justice; *Publications* Archbold's Criminal Pleading, Evidence & Practice (jt ed); *Recreations* eating, reading, cinema, soul music, theatre; *Style*— James Turner, Esq, QC; ✉ 1 King's Bench Walk, London EC4Y 7DR (☎ 020 7936 1500, fax 020 7936 1590, e-mail jturner@1kbw.co.uk)

TURNER, James Alan; s of Dr David Charles Turner, and Elizabeth Abbott, *née* Eglington; *b* 16 July 1971, London; *Educ* Loughborough Univ (BA), Univ of Middx (CPE), Nottingham Trent Univ (LPC); *Partner* Wendy Rainbow; *Career* admitted slr; trainee Wilson Browne 1995–97, assoc slr Criminal Law Dept Toller Hales & Collcutt 1997–2000, ptnr Tuckers Slrs' 2000–; memb: Law Soc, Criminal Law Slrs' Assoc, Peer Review Panel; *Recreations* motorbikes, guitars, poker; *Style*— James Turner, Esq; ✉ Tuckers Solicitors, 210 Corporation Street, Birmingham B4 6QB (☎ 0121 236 4324, fax 0121 236 4364, e-mail turnerj@tuckerssolicitors.com)

TURNER, Sqdn Ldr Jim; *b* 27 February 1973; *Educ* Kings Sch Canterbury; *m* Karen; 2 s (Aidan, Finlay); *Career* joined RAF 1991, Jaguar pilot based at RAF Coltishall, selected as RAF Jaguar display pilot 2004; Red Arrows: Red 5, Synchro 2 and Synchro ldr 2005–07, Red 1 and team ldr 2012–14; *Style*— Squadron Leader Jim Turner; ✉ c/o PR Office, The Red Arrows, Royal Air Force Scampton, Lincoln LN1 2ST

TURNER, Prof John Richard George; s of George Hugh Turner (d 1983), of Liverpool, and Elsie Ellen, *née* Booth (d 2002); *b* 11 September 1940; *Educ* Quarry Bank HS Liverpool, Univ of Liverpool (BSc), Univ of Oxford (DPhil, DSc); *m* 3 April 1967, Sandra Fordyce, da of Alexander Thomson Millar (d 1994), of Dundee; 1 s (Richard b 1970), 1 da (Lois b 1977); *Career* research asst NY Zoological Soc Trinidad and Tobago 1964, lectr in biology Univ of York 1965–72, assoc prof of biology Stony Brook Campus NY State Univ 1971–77, princ scientific offr Rothamsted Experimental Station Harpenden 1977–78; Univ of Leeds: lectr in genetics 1978–81, reader in evolutionary genetics 1981–87, prof of evolutionary genetics 1987–2000, research prof 2000–03, hon fell 2003–09, hon visiting fell (biology) 2009–, hon visiting fell (French) 2012–; memb: Race and Intelligence Ctee Genetics Soc of America 1976, Animal Procedures Ctee Home Office 1997–2000; memb Editorial Bd: Heredity, Evolution, Entomologist, Evolutionary Ecology; Scott Holland lectr KCL 1989; various radio and TV appearances, trans broadcast BBC Radio 3 2013; fndr memb Conservation Soc, jt sec Cncl for Academic Autonomy; memb: Lepidopterists' Soc, Yorkshire Wildlife Tst, Yorkshire Naturalists Union, Br Dragonfly Soc, Plantlife, American Soc of Naturalists 1971; reading/recital Clothworkers' Hall Leeds 2010; Liverpool Biological Soc Prize 1961, Edward Forbes Prize Univ of Liverpool 1962; FRES 1962, FRSA 1993; *Publications* incl: Rimbaud translations in Poetry and Audience (1989), translations of Verlaine, Prudhomme and Dante (commendations Times Stephen Spender Prize 2005, 2009, 2011, 2012 and jt 3rd 2013), translation of Seven Tricky Verlaines (first prize John Dryden Translation Competition Br Comparative Literature Assoc 2008/09, Comparative Critical Studies 2010, PNReview 2010); poetry (Litro, 2010); author of over 100 papers in scientific jls and book reviews for Spectator, TLS and NY Times; contrib to books on: evolution, ecology, behaviour, genetics, butterflies, biogeography, history of science; *Recreations* opera, swimming, collecting things, wildlife, drawing, spoonerising; *Style*— Prof John Turner; ✉ Faculty of Biological Sciences, University of Leeds, Leeds LS2 9JT (☎ 0113 343 2828, fax 0113 343 2835, e-mail j.r.g.turner@leeds.ac.uk)

TURNER, Jon; QC (2006); *Educ* Univ of Cambridge (MA), Harvard Univ (LLM); *Career* called to the Bar 1988; *Style*— Jon Turner, Esq, QC; ✉ Monckton Chambers, 1 & 2 Raymond Buildings, Grays Inn, London WC1R 5NR

TURNER, Jon Lys; s of Edward Turner (d 1976), and Anne, *née* Telfer; *b* 1 May 1959; *Educ* Felsted, Newport Art Sch (BA), RCA (MA); *Career* prop Jon Lys Turner Ltd 1984–88, divnl dir (retail) Fitch RS 1988–90, gp creative head Imagination Ltd 1990–94, head of global design The Body Shop International plc 1994–2000, exec creative dir Enterprise IG WPP Gp 2000–02, creative dir Boots plc 2002–, fndr Jon Lys Turner Archive and Collection 2012; *Books* The Visitors' Book: In Francis Bacon's Shadow: The Lives of Richard Chopping and Denis Wirth-Miller (2016); *Style*— Jon Turner, Esq; ☎ 0115 959 5109, e-mail jon.turner@boots.co.uk; c/o Clare Conville, Conville & Walsh, 5th Floor, Haymarket House, 28–29 Haymarket, London SW1Y 4SP

TURNER, Jonathan David Chattyn; s of Maxwell Turner, and Naomi, *née* Myers; *b* 13 May 1958, Stourbridge; *Educ* Rugby, Corpus Christi Coll Cambridge (BA, MA), Université Libre de Bruxelles (Lic Sp Dr Eur), Queen Mary Coll London; *m* 23 Nov 1986, Caroline Frances Esther, da of Lawrence Sam Berman, CB; 2 s (Jacob b 1988, Gabriel b 1992), 1 da (Camilla b 1990); *Career* called to the Bar Gray's Inn 1982, pupillage in chambers of

Leonard Hoffmann QC, Robin Jacob QC and Alastair Wilson QC 1982–83, in private practice as barr specialising in intellectual property and competition law 1983–95 and 1997–, head of IP and IT law Coopers and Lybrand 1995–97; dir Authors' Licensing and Collecting Soc 2011–, dir Copyright Licensing Agency 2013–15; chair UK Lawyers for Israel 2011–; domain name panelist World Intellectual Property Orgn and Czech Arbitration Court; *Books* Halsbury's Laws of England, EC Competition Law (1986), European Patent Office Reports (1986–1995), Forms and Agreements on Intellectual Property and International Licensing (1979–89), Law of the European Communities, Competition Law (1986–2010), Countdown to 2000 – A Guide to the Legal Issues (1998), European Patent Infringement Cases (1999), Domain Names – A Practical Guide (2002), Intellectual Property and EU Competition Law (2010, 2015); *Recreations* walking, theatre, music; *Style—* Jonathan D C Turner, Esq; ✉ Three Stone, 3 Stone Buildings, Lincoln's Inn, London WC2A 3XL (☎ 020 7831 4445, e-mail mail@jonathanturner.com, website www.jonathanturner.com)

TURNER, Karl; MP; *b* Kingston upon Hull, E Riding of Yorks; *Educ* Univ of Hull; *Career* barr; MP (Lab) Hull E 2010–; *Style—* Karl Turner, Esq, MP; ✉ House of Commons, London SW1A 0AA

TURNER, Emeritus Prof Kenneth John; s of Graham Leslie Turner (d 1970), of Glasgow, and Christina McInnes, *née* Fraser; *b* 21 February 1949; *Educ* Hutchesons Boys' GS, Univ of Glasgow (BSc), Univ of Edinburgh (PhD); *m* 15 Sept 1973, Elizabeth Mary Christina, da of Rev William James Hutton, of Glasgow; 2 s (Duncan b 1979, Robin b 1981); *Career* data communications conslt 1980–86, prof of computing sci Univ of Stirling 1986–; memb: Int Fedn for Info Processing; *Books* Formal Description Techniques (ed, 1988), Using Formal Description Techniques (ed, 1993), Service Provision (ed, 2004), Advances in Home Care Technologies (ed, 2012); *Recreations* choral activities, handicrafts, sailing; *Style—* Emeritus Prof Kenneth Turner; ✉ Department of Computing Science and Mathematics, University of Stirling, Stirling FK9 4LA (☎ 01786 467000, fax 01786 464551, e-mail kjt@cs.stir.ac.uk)

TURNER, HE (Robert) Leigh; CMG (2014); s of Prof John Derfel Turner (d 2013), of Gatley, Cheshire, and Dr Susan Broady Turner, *née* Hovey; *b* 13 March 1958, Nantwich, Cheshire; *Educ* Downing Coll Cambridge (BA); *m* Pamela Major; 1 s, 1 da; *Career* Dept of Transport 1979, Property Servs Agency 1980, Dept of Environment 1981, HM Treasy 1982, 2 sec (chancery) Vienna 1984–87, 1 sec (economic) Moscow 1992–95, dep head then head Hong Kong Dept FCO 1995–98, cnsllr (EU/economic) Bonn then Berlin 1998–2002, dir of overseas territories FCO 2006–08, ambass to Ukraine 2008–12, HM consul gen Istanbul and DG UK Trade and Investment Turkey, South Caucasus and Central Asia 2012–16, ambass to Austria and UK perm rep to UN in Vienna 2016–; *Recreations* writing, walking, Lundy Island; *Style—* HE Mr Leigh Turner, CMG; ✉ Twitter @leighturnerfco; FCO (Vienna), King Charles Street, London SW1A 2AH (e-mail leigh.turner@fco.gov.uk)

TURNER, Mark; *b* 1961, Hampstead, London; *Educ* Rossall Sch Lancs, Univ of Oxford (MA), RMA Sandhurst, Univ of Cambridge; *Career* Oundle Sch: asst master 1987–88, head of geography and master in charge of hockey 1988–90, housemaster 1990–95; headmaster Kelly Coll 1995, subsequently headmaster Abingdon Sch until 2010, headmaster Shrewsbury Sch 2010–; sch inspector 1998–; Tatler Headmaster of the Year 2009; *Style—* Mark Turner, Esq; ✉ Shrewsbury School, The Schools, Shrewsbury SY3 7BA (☎ 01743 280525, e-mail hm@shrewsbury.org.uk)

TURNER, Hon Mr Justice Mark George; QC (1998); s of Jeffrey Farrar Turner, of Kendal, Cumbria, and Joyce, *née* Barkas; *b* 27 August 1959, Kendal, Cumbria; *Educ* Sedbergh, The Queen's Coll Oxford (BA); *m* 23 Jan 1988, Caroline Sophia, da of George Haydn Bullock, of Richmond, Surrey; 3 da (Alice Elizabeth b 29 Oct 1989, Fiona Maud b 6 June 1991, Lydia Sophia b 20 May 1993); *Career* called to the Bar Gray's Inn 1981 (bencher), tenant Deans Ct Chambers Manchester 1982–2013, called to the Bar Northern Circuit 1982, recorder 2000–13 (asst recorder 1998–2000); dep High Court judge 2007–13, High Court judge 2013–, presiding judge Northern Circuit 2013–; *Publications* Occupational Asthma, Mucous Membrane Disease-Industrial Diseases Litigation (2003), Occupational Stress (2006); *Recreations* classical music, history, general knowledge quizzes; *Clubs* Mastermind (semi finalist 1988); *Style—* The Hon Mr Justice Turner; ✉ Royal Courts of Justice, Strand, London WC2A 2LL

TURNER, Martin Paul; s of Fredrick William Harold Turner, of Llanfoist, Gwent, and Magaret Mary, *née* Downey; *b* 28 February 1951; *Educ* Tredegar GS, Harvard Business Sch; *m* 8 Aug 1970, Elizabeth Jane, da of Haydn Hedworth Houlding; 2 da (Kathryn Louise b 17 Aug 1976, Carys Elizabeth b 1 Nov 1987), 2 s (David Martyn b 15 Jan 1980, Peter John b 17 Aug 1990); *Career* finance trainee N Monmouthshire Health Authy 1969, chief internal auditor Hosp Mgmnt Ctee 1974; Gwent Health Authy: asst treas 1976–77, finance offr 1977–81, sr asst treas 1981–, dep treas 1982–86, gen mangr Community Servs 1986–90, gen mangr (Hosp Servs) 1990–92; chief exec: Gwent Healthcare NHS Tst (formerly Glan Hafren NHS Tst) 1993–99, Gwent Healthcare NHS Tst, Adelaide Health Service Australia 2009–11; int mgmnt conslt (health) 2011–; dep pres ACCA 2013; FCCA, FCIM, CIHM; *Recreations* golf, travel, gardening; *Style—* Martin Turner, Esq; ✉ Maescoed, Bettws Newydd, Usk, Gwent NP15 1EQ (☎ 01873 880841); Gwent Healthcare NHS Trust, Grange House, Llanfrechfa Grange, Cwmbran, Torfaen NP44 8YN (☎ 01633 623483, mobile 07860 338899, fax 01633 623817)

TURNER, Michael John; s of Gerald Mortimer Turner, of Ashtead, Surrey, and Joyce Isobel Marguerite, *née* Healy; *b* 12 June 1951; *Educ* Eton; *m* 17 July 1982, Diana Mary St Clair, da of David Michael St Clair Weir; 4 s (Fred b 1985, Munchie b 1987, Harry b 1989, Tom b 1992); *Career* Fuller Smith & Turner plc: dir 1985–, md 1992–2002, chief exec 2002–13, chm 2007–; chm George Gale and Co Ltd 2006–; Master Worshipful Co of Vintners 2011–12, Liveryman Worshipful Co of Brewers; FCA; *Recreations* skiing, shooting, golf, tennis, motor racing, travel; *Clubs* Aldeburgh Golf, Eton Vikings, Berkshire Golf, Hurlingham; *Style—* Michael Turner, Esq; ✉ 5 Bowerdean Street, London SW6 3TN; Fuller Smith & Turner plc, Griffin Brewery, Chiswick, London W4 2QB

TURNER, Michael John; s of Geoffrey Maurice Turner (d 1993), and Peggy Patricia Dora, *née* Brookes; *b* 8 February 1950; *Educ* King Edward VI Sch Southampton; *m* 7 July 1975, Kazue, da of Goro Shimada; 2 da (Anna-Marie Namie b 2 Jan 1977, Louisa-Jane Kei b 4 March 1981); *Career* articled clerk Hamilton and Rowland CA's Southampton 1968–72; Touche Ross (now Deloitte & Touche): joined 1972, ptnr 1979–, ptnr i/c Japanese Business 1983, gp ptnr Audit Dept London 1984–94, ptnr Chinese Business 1992–94, ptnr i/c Korea Desk 1998–2000, ptnr i/c Company Secretarial Div; Deloitte Touche Tohmatsu: dep chm European Japanese Exec, chm Finance Ctee; govr Hampton Sch; FCA 1980 (ACA 1972); *Recreations* golf, hockey, tennis; *Clubs* Teddington Hockey (vice-pres), Burhill Golf; *Style—* Michael Turner, Esq; ✉ Miyabi, 92 Burwood Road, Walton on Thames, Surrey KT12 4AP (☎ 01932 223679, fax 01932 223679); Deloitte & Touche, Hill House, 1 Little New Street, London EC4A 3TR (☎ 020 7303 3552, fax 020 7583 8517)

TURNER, Michael John (Mike); CBE (1999); s of Thomas Albert Turner, of Stockport, Cheshire, and Hilda, *née* Pendlebury; *b* 5 August 1948; *Educ* Didsbury Tech HS Manchester, Manchester Poly (BA); *m* 1, 1972 (m dis 1984), Rosalind, *née* Thomas; 2 s (Andrew Richard b 14 Sept 1976, Nicholas James b 5 July 1978); m 2, 1985, Jean Crotty; 2 step da (Johanna Crotty (Mrs Clement) b 17 Jan 1969, Victoria Crotty (Mrs Morley) b 25 May 1971); *Career* BAE Systems plc (and predecessor cos): contracts officer Hawker Siddeley Aviation Manchester 1970 (undergrad apprentice 1966–70), contracts mangr (military) Manchester Div British Aerospace Aircraft Gp 1978–80, admin mangr 1980–81, exec dir admin 1981–82, divnl admin dir 1982–84 (concurrently ldr Advanced Turboprop Project), divnl dir and gen mangr Kingston 1984–86, dir and gen mangr Weybridge, Kingston and Dunsfold 1986–87, dir of mktg and product support Mil Aircraft Div 1987–88, exec vice-pres defence mktg 1988–92, chm and md British Aerospace Regional Aircraft Ltd and chm Jetstream Aircraft 1992–94, chm British Aerospace Airbus Ltd 1994, main bd dir 1994–2008, gp md British Aerospace plc 1997–98, exec dir 1998–99, chief operating officer 1999–2002, chief exec 2002–08; non-exec chm Babcock Int Gp plc 2008–, non-exec chm GKN plc 2012; Bd dir Lazard 2006–; chair Def Industries Cncl (DIC); pres: Soc of Br Aerospace Cos 1996 (vice-pres 1995–96), AeroSpace and Defence Industries Assoc of Europe (ASD) 2003–04; jt chm Aerospace Innovation and Growth Team; Br Inst of Mgmnt Young Mangr of the Year 1973; Hon Dr Manchester Met Univ 2006, Hon DSc Cranfield Univ 2007, Hon DSc Loughborough Univ 2007; ACIS 1973, FRAeS 1991; *Recreations* golf, cricket, rugby, Manchester United; *Style—* Mike Turner, Esq, CBE; ✉ Babcock International Group plc, 33 Wigmore Street, London W1U 1QX (☎ 020 7355 5300, website www.babcockinternational.com)

TURNER, Dr Michael Skinner; s of Sir Michael William Turner, CBE (d 1980), of London, and Lady Wendy, *née* Stranack (d 1999); *b* Hong Kong; *Educ* Marlborough, St Thomas' Hosp (MB BS, MRCS, LRCP), Washington USA (MD); *Children* 3 da (Lucinda b 6 Dec 1974, Camilla b 3 July 1980, Alexia b 29 Jan 1984); *Career* chief med advsr: Br Ski and Snowboard Fedn 1973–99, Br Horseracing Authy 1992–2013; dir of med services Br Olympic Assoc 1992–94; med advsr 1980–97: Texaco, P&O, Vickers, Barclays de Zoete Wedd, ANZ/Grindlays Bank, Hongkong & Shanghai Banking Group, Hoare Govett; Br team doctor Winter Olympics: Calgary 1988, Albertville 1992, Lillehammer 1994; memb Med Ctee Int Ski Fedn 1989–99; currently: chief med advsr Lawn Tennis Assoc, med dir Int Concussion and Head Injury Research Fndn, memb Sports Science and Medicine Cmmn Int Tennis Fedn; memb Editorial Bd Br Jl of Sports Med; Desborough Award for Services to Olympic Sport 1994, Sir Robert Atkins Award for Services to Sports Medicine 2006, Carl Aarvold Award for Int Achievement 2015; Freeman City of London 1971, Liveryman Worshipful Co of Skinners; fell Faculty of Sport and Exercise Medicine; *Publications* articles in peer-review jls on concussion, injuries in horse racing and stress fractures in tennis; *Recreations* skiing, tennis, watersports; *Style—* Dr Michael Turner; ✉ 9 Harley Street, London W1G 9QY (e-mail miketurnerlondon@aol.com)

TURNER, Michelle Karen (Mich); MBE (2010); *née* Clark; da of Ralph Andrew Clark, of Devon, and Celia Mary, *née* Hill; *b* 17 February 1970, Totnes, Devon; *Educ* King Edward VI Coll Devon, Univ of Surrey (BSc); *m* 15 Nov 1997, Phillip Martin Turner; 2 s (Marlow James b 10 Nov 2002, George Charles b 9 Oct 2006); *Career* mangr Realfood Store London 1992–95, bakery and patisserie buyer Harvey Nichols London 1996–99, dir and fndr Little Venice Cake Co Ltd 1999–; television appearances incl: Couture Wedding Cakes 2010, judge Britain's Best Bakery (ITV1) 2012 and 2013; public face of Scottish Baker of the Year 2013, 2014, 2015 and 2016; involvement with Tommy's The Baby Charity; Harpers Bazaar and Chanel Entrepreneur of the Year 2006, Best Wedding Cake Supplier Wrapit Industry Awards 2008, Walpole Luxury Brands of Tomorrow 2009, Retail and Consumerism First Woman Awards 2009; *Books* Spectacular Cakes (2005, Best Dessert Book World Cookbook Awards 2006), Wedding Bible (contrib, 2006), Fantastic Party Cakes (2007), Couture Wedding Cakes (2009), Mich Turner's Cake Masterclass (2011, Best Book for Food Professionals World Cookbook Awards 2012), Mich Turner's Cake School (2014); *Style—* Mrs Mich Turner, MBE; ✉ Little Venice Cake Company Ltd, 11–14 Grafton Street, Mayfair London W1S 4EW (☎ 07940 559875, e-mail mich@lvcc.co.uk, website www.lvcc.co.uk); c/o Limelight Management, 10 Filmer Mews, 75 Filmer Road, London SW6 7JF (☎ 020 7384 9950)

TURNER, Nicola Mary (Niki); da of Alan John Turner, and Mary Frances, *née* Sawbridge; *b* 7 September 1967, Guildford, Surrey; *Educ* Wadhurst Coll, Reigate Sch of Art, Central St Martins Coll of Art (BA); *m* Alfred Theodore Coles; 2 da (Iona Evelyn b 31 March 2003, Iris Rose b 13 May 2008), 1 s (Arthur Neill b 21 April 2005); *Career* set and costume designer; art dir Inside Out (film); McColl Arts Fndn Travel Bursary 1990; *Productions* Oxford Stage Co: A Midsummer Night's Dream, Johnny Blue, The Comic Mysteries; Derby Playhouse: The Glass Menagerie, Grapevine, Lips Together Teeth Apart, Extremities, Danny Bouncing, Watching the Sand from the Sea; W Yorks Playhouse: Spend Spend Spend, The World Goes 'Round, Pilgermann, The Snow Queen; Salisbury Playhouse: Wallflowering, The Rover, The Banished Cavaliers, The Crucible; Eastern Angles tour: A Bad Case of Love, Inheritance, Boats; Mercury Theatre Colchester: Romeo and Juliet, A View From the Bridge, Shirley Valentine, Grounded, The Aspern Papers; Gate Theatre Notting Hill: The False Servant, Talking Tongues, The Gentleman from Olmedo (costumes); RSC: As You Like It (co-designer), Oroonoko, Brixton Stories, The Island Princess; other credits incl: Things Fall Apart (Royal Court and W Yorks Playhouse, also US and UK tour), Henceforward (New Victoria Stoke), Maddie (West End and Salisbury Playhouse), Adam Bede (Derby Playhouse and York Theatre Royal), Time and the Conways (Salisbury Playhouse and Mercury Theatre Colchester), The Beatification of Area Boy (W Yorks Playhouse, Brooklyn Acad and Euro tour), The Winslow Boy (Birmingham Rep and W Yorks Playhouse), Artemisia (mixed media project for Turtle Key Prodns), Our Boys (Derby Playhouse and Donmar Warehouse), Carmen (Regency Opera tour and Holland Park Opera), Great Expectations (Derby Playhouse and Philadelphia), La Traviata (English Touring Opera), Tender (Birmingham Rep and Hampstead Theatre), Further than the Furthest Thing (RNT, Tricycle Theatre, Tron Theatre and Traverse Theatre, Fringe First Award Edinburgh Festival), The External (Theatre Royal Bath and Greenwich Theatre touring co-prodn), Soul Train (Turnstyle No 1 tour), Speaking in Tongues (Hampstead Theatre and Derby Playhouse), L'Amore Industrioso (Holland Park Opera), Junk (Oxford Stage Co and Den Nationale Scene Norway), Othello (New Victoria Stoke), On the Piste (Tivoli Theatre Dublin), A Passage to India (Shared Experience), Gone to Earh (Shared Experience), Embryonic Dreams (Edinburgh Festival), Yerma (Edinburgh Festival), Sarka (Garsington Opera), Osud (Garsington Opera), Rusalka (Opera North and Sydney Opera House, Green Room Award for Best Design, Helpmann Award for Best Opera), Cherevichki (Garsington Opera), A Midsummer Night's Dream (ROH), Rigoletto (Den Jeyske Opera), Rakes Progress (Garsington Opera), La Traviata (Den Jyske Opera), A Streetcar Named Desire (Scottish Ballet); *Recreations* walking, gardening, house restoration, visiting exhibitions (especially contemporary and installation art); *Style—* Niki Turner; ✉ c/o Clare Vidal Hall, 57 Carthew Road, London W6 0DU (☎ 020 8741 7647, fax 020 8741 9459)

TURNER, Prof Raymond; s of Mrs Winifred Howe; *b* 28 April 1947; *Career* prof of logic and computation Univ of Essex 1985– (lectr 1973–85, dean Grad Sch 1999–); Sloan fell in cognitive sci Univ of Mass 1982 (sr res fell 1986 and 1989), visiting prof Univ of Rochester NY 1982, visiting fell Centre for Study of Language and Information Stanford Univ Calif 1984 (conslt in sci 1982), visiting prof Univ of Texas Austin 1987; *Books* Logics for Artificial Intelligence (1984), Truth and Modality for Knowledge Representation (1990), Constructive Foundations for Functional Languages (1991), Computable Models (2009); *Style—* Prof Raymond Turner; ✉ Department of Computer Science, University of Essex, Colchester, Essex CO4 3SQ (e-mail turnr@essex.ac.uk, website http://essex.academia.edu/RaymondTurner)

TURNER, Richard Keith; OBE (2007); s of Richard Louis Turner, and Queenie Kate Turner; *b* 2 October 1944, London; *Educ* E Barnet GS, Univ of Leeds (BSc), Univ of Bradford (MSc); *m* 1968, Jenny Georgina, *née* Whitehead; 2 s (Richard b 1969, Simon b 1969), 1

T

da (Salie b 1972); *Career* grad engr Herts CC 1965–67, sr engr Leeds CC 1967–73; Freight Transport Assoc: highways and traffic advsr 1973–83, dir of planning 1983–95, dep DG 1995–2000, ceo 2001–07; memb: Cmmn for Integrated Transport 2004–10, Planning Ctee London Thames Gateway Devpt Corp 2007–12; CEng 1972, MICE 1972, FIHT 1980, FILT 1993; *Recreations* big DIY, cycling, swimming; *Style*— Richard K Turner, Esq, OBE; ✉ e-mail turner@t-44.co.uk

TURNER, Richard Timmis; CMG (2002), OBE (1978); s of Dr John Richard Timmis Turner (d 2003), and Alison Elizabeth, *née* Bythell (d 2003); *b* 17 August 1942; *Educ* Shrewsbury, Univ of Manchester (BA); *m* 11 Sept 1982, Margaret Rose Mary, da of Dr Ivor Corbett (d 1982); 2 da (Catherine b 1983, Rebecca b 1985); *Career* joined Rolls-Royce Ltd 1965, commercial mangr Rolls-Royce Inc NY 1971–74, mktg exec civil engines Rolls-Royce Ltd 1977, commercial dir civil engines Rolls-Royce plc 1986–88, dir STC plc 1989–91 (gp mktg dir 1988–91), dir Rolls-Royce plc 1992–2002 (re-joined as gp mktg dir 1991); non-exec dir: Corus Gp plc 1994–2004, Senior plc 1996–2004; memb: Cncl Soc of Br Aerospace Companies 1992–2002 (pres 1994–95), Bd Br Trade Int 1999–2003 (chm Business Advsy Panel 1999–2003), Bd Nat Campaign for the Arts 2006–15 (chair 2011), Bd Bath Festivals 2009–; MInstD, FRAeS; *Recreations* opera, music, rugby; *Clubs* Athenaeum; *Style*— Richard Turner, Esq, CMG, OBE; ✉ 6 Widcombe Terrace, Bath BA2 6AJ (☎ and fax 01225 338583, mobile 07770 442333, e-mail richardturner45@yahoo.co.uk)

TURNER, Roger Burton; s of late Jack Burton Turner, and late Jean, *née* Trevor; *b* 28 July 1947; *Educ* Hawes Down Co Secdy Sch, KCL (BD, MTh), Inst of Educn Univ of London (PGCE), Univ of Kent (MA), Inns of Court Sch of Law, Coll of Law, Birkbeck Coll London (Dip); *m* 13 April 1998, Jennifer, da of late Dr Harry Bound, of Guernsey; *Career* asst master Ashford GS 1972–77, lectr in New Testament studies La Sainte Union Coll of Higher Educn Southampton 1977–80, called to the Bar Gray's Inn 1982, in practice SE Circuit 1983–99, admitted slr 1999, slr-advocate (all higher courts) 1999, conslt Wainwright Cummins 1999–2000, conslt Foreman Young 2000–03, conslt Dalton Holmes Gray 2003–, conslt Family Law Dept Lawrence & Co 2011–16, conslt Gary Jacobs & Co 2016–; memb Law Soc's Adult and Children Panel 2013; visiting research fell Inst of Historical Research Univ of London 1995–96; art critic Guernsey Press and Star 2005–09; contrib: New Dictionary of National Biography (articles on Jacobites and eighteenth century lawyers); contrib symposium The Earl of Burlington and His Politics 1995; pres W London Law Soc 2003–04; memb Catholic Writers' Guild; *Publications* Manchester and the '45: a study of Jacobitism in context (1996), Chaplains in the Household of Lord Burlington 1715–53, in Lord Burlington – The Man and His Politics: Questions of Loyalty (1998); author of various exhbn reviews; *Recreations* looking at buildings, visiting art galleries, philosophy, Classical Greek; *Clubs* Lansdowne, E India, English Speaking Union; *Style*— Roger Turner, Esq; ✉ 26 Evesham Road, London N11 2RN (☎ 020 8368 1430, e-mail roger.turner47@googlemail.com)

TURNER LAING, Sophie; da of Graham Turner Laing (d 2007), and Gilly Drummond, *qv*, *née* Clark; *b* 7 September 1960; *m* 30 May 1987, Carlo Comninos, s of Michael Comninos; 1 s (Alexander b 5 March 1989), 1 da (Marina b 14 Oct 1992); *Career* broadcaster; events co-ordinator Variety Club of GB 1979–80, asst to md K M Campbell Pty Melbourne 1980–82, sales dir Henson Int Television 1982–89, jt fndr, dep md and bd dir HIT Entertainment plc 1989–95, vice-pres broadcasting Flextech Television 1995–98, controller Prog Acquisition BBC Broadcasting 1998–2003, dir Film Channels and Acquisitions BSkyB 2003–04, dep md Sky Networks 2004, md Content BSkyB 2007–14, chief exec Endemol Shine Gp 2015–; non-exec dir Debenhams plc 2009–15; vice-pres TV BAFTA until 2015, govr Nat Film and Television Sch 2004–16; *Clubs* Variety, Mark's, Soho House, Bafta, 30 Club; *Style*— Ms Sophie Turner Laing; ✉ Endemol UK, Shepherd's Building Central, Charecroft Way, London W14 0EE (☎ 020 8222 4990, e-mail sophie.turner.laing@endemolshinegroup.com)

TURNER OF ECCHINSWELL, Baron (Life Peer UK 2005), of Ecchinswell in the County of Hampshire; (Jonathan) Adair Turner; s of Geoffrey Vincent Turner, and Kathleen Margaret, *née* Broadhurst (d 1977); *Educ* Hutchesons' GS Glasgow, Glenalmond Sch, Gonville & Caius Coll Cambridge (scholar, MA, chm Cambridge Univ Cons Assoc, pres Cambridge Union); *m* 4 May 1985, Orna Ni Chionna; 2 da (Eleanor Catherine b 18 Nov 1988, Julia Christine b 1 Sept 1991); *Career* Corp Planning Dept BP 1979, Chase Manhattan Bank NA 1979–82; McKinsey & Co (strategic consltts): joined 1982, princ (ptnr) 1988, dir (sr ptnr) 1994; DG CBI 1995–99; vice-chm Merrill Lynch Europe 2000–06; non-exec dir: United Business Media plc 2000–08, Netscalibur Ltd 2000–01, Siemens plc 2006–08, Standard Chartered plc 2006–08, OakNorth 2015–; ind advsr HM Govt's Forward Strategy Unit 2001–02; chm: Ind Pensions Cmmn 2002–06, Low Pay Cmmn 2003–06, Financial Servs Authy 2008–13, Inst for New Economic Thinking 2013–; chair: ESRC 2007–08 (memb 2003–07), Ctee on Climate Change 2008–12, Energy Transitions Cmmn 2016–; tstee British Museum 2012–; visiting prof: LSE, Cass Business Sch, City Univ, Int Center for Islamic Finance (INCEIF) Kuala Lumpur; sr fell Centre for Financial Studies Frankfurt 2015–, visiting fell People's Bank of China Sch of Finance Beijing Univ 2015–; hon degree City Univ; *Books* Just Capital: The Liberal Economy (2001), Economics After the Crisis (2012), Between Debt and the Devil (2015); *Recreations* theatre, opera, skiing; *Style*— The Lord Turner of Ecchinswell

TURNOR, Richard William Corbet; s of Maj Anthony Richard Turnor, CBE, DL, and Joyce Winnifred, *née* Osborn; *b* 15 March 1956; *Educ* Maidwell Hall Sch, Eton, Keble Coll Oxford (BA); *m* 31 Dec 1985, Louisa Mary, da of Andrew Garden Duff Forbes; 1 s (William Michael Francis b 1988), 2 da (Elizabeth Beatrice b 1990, Rosalind Mary b 1993); *Career* admitted slr 1980; Allen & Overy: joined 1979, ptnr 1985–2009, memb Private Client Dept and Commercial Tst and Partnerships Gp until 2009; fndr Maurice Turnor Gardner LLP 2009; chm Assoc of Partnership Practitioners 2001–04, memb Law Soc Regulations Review Working Pty 1999–2003; tstee Royal Marsden Cancer Campaign 2002–08, dir Royal Marsden NHS Fndn Tst 2009–, tstee Royal Marsden Cancer Charity 2012–; memb Law Soc 1981; *Recreations* conservation, growing trees, field sports, skiing; *Style*— Richard Turnor, Esq; ✉ Maurice Turnor Gardner LLP, 15th Floor, Milton House, Milton Street, London EC2Y 9BH (☎ 020 7456 8610, fax 020 7456 8620, website www.mauriceturnorgardner.com)

TURPIN, Adrian Brian; *Educ* Merton Coll Oxford; *m* Pru Rowlandson; 1 da (Holly b 30 Dec 2010), 1 s (Arthur b 9 Aug 2013); *Career* assoc ed Sunday Review Magazine The Independent 2001–02, ed Ecosse Sunday Times 2002–04, dir Wigtown Book Festival 2007–; *Style*— Adrian Turpin, Esq; ✉ Wigtown Book Festival, County Buildings, Wigtown, Dumfries & Galloway DG8 9JH

TURVEY, Timothy John (Tim); JP (2008); s of Raymond Hilton Turvey, of Oxford (d 1995), and Mary, *née* Drown (d 2014); *b* 13 October 1947, London; *Educ* Monkton Combe Sch Bath, UC Cardiff (BSc), Univ of Bath (DipEd); *m* 1 May 1993, Dr Janet Hilary Webster; 1 s (James Christopher Corke-Webster b 18 May 1987); *Career* asst master The Edinburgh Acad 1970–75, head of biology and dir of studies Monkton Combe Sch 1975–90; The Hulme GS Oldham: dep head 1990–95, headmaster 1995–2000; headmaster The King's Sch Chester 2000–07, freelance educnl conslt and schs' inspr 2007–; chief examiner Assessment and Qualifications Alliance, conslt ed Longmans, chm Ind Schs Cncl Teacher Induction Panel; memb: Common Entrance Sci Panel, Cncl SHA (chm NW area), Ctee HMC, Gen Assembly Univ of Manchester; CBiol 1978, FIBiol 1993 (MIBiol 1978), FLS 1984; Gas Exchange and Transport in Plants (ed, 1985), Biology Study Guide I (ed, 1985), Biology Teachers' Guide I (ed, 1985), Inheritance (1986), GCSE Dual Award Balanced Science (1988), Nuffield Co-ordinated Sciences: Biology (ed, 1988), Nuffield Co-ordinated Sciences: Teachers' Guide (contrib, 1988), Biology Course Guide (ed, 1994), Biology Projects and Investigations (ed, 1994), Biology Foundation Unit (ed, 1994), The Entitlement Curriculum in Independent Schools (1995); *Recreations* theatre, cooking; *Clubs* Cheshire Pitt, Leander; *Style*— Tim Turvey, Esq; ✉ 5 Plowley Close, Didsbury, Manchester M20 2DB (☎ 07771 801054, e-mail timturvey@btinternet.com)

TURZYNSKI, Gregory Michael Stefan (Greg); s of Leon Dominik Turzynski, of Piltdown, E Sussex, and Olivia Lilian, *née* Ball (d 2002); *b* 16 June 1959; *Educ* St Mary's RC Sch, St Ignatius Coll, Bedford Coll London (BSc); *m* 25 June 1993, Kim, da of Sidney Burgess; *Career* Young & Rubicam advtg: joined 1982, gp buying mangr 1986–90, broadcast dir 1990–92, dep media dir 1992–94, media dir 1994–96; md Optimedia 2002–03 (managing ptnr 1996–2002), fndr Experience 2003–; *Style*— Greg Turzynski, Esq

TUSA, Sir John; kt (2003); s of John Tusa, OBE (d 1994), and Lydia, *née* Sklenarova (d 1997); *b* 2 March 1936, Zlín, Czechoslovakia; *Educ* Gresham's, Trinity Coll Cambridge (BA); *m* 1960, Ann Hilary, da of Stanley Dowson, of Lancs; 2 s (Sash, Francis); *Career* BBC: presenter Newsnight (BBC 2) 1980–86, presenter Timewatch (BBC 2) 1982–84, md BBC World Service 1986–92, presenter One O'Clock News 1993–95; md Barbican Centre 1995–2007, chm Univ of the Arts London 2007–13; pres Wolfson Coll Cambridge 1993; chm Advsy Ctee Govt Art Collection until 2003, a vice-chm London Int String Quartet Competition 1995–2011, chm V&A 2007, chm Clore Leadership Prog 2009–14, hon chm theartsdesk.com 2010–13, co-chm European Union Youth Orchestra 2014–, chm Br Architecture Tst Bd (BATB) RIBA 2014–; memb Bd: English National Opera 1996–2003, Design Museum 1998–2000; tstee: Nat Portrait Gallery 1988–2000, Br Museum 2000–09 (dep chm 2004–09), Somerset House 2004–06, Turquoise Mountain Tst 2006–, New Deal of the Mind 2009–12; former tstee: Thomson Fndn, Wigmore Hall Tst (chm 1999–2011); RTS Journalist of the Year 1984, BAFTA Richard Dimbleby Award 1984, Harvey Lee Award BPG Radio Awards 1991, RTS Presenter of the Year 1995; hon memb Royal Acad of Music and the Guildhall Sch of Music and Drama 1999; Freeman City of London 1997; Hon LLD Univ of London 1993, Hon DUniv Heriot-Watt 1994, Hon DLitt City Univ 1997, Hon DUniv Essex 2006, Hon DUniv Kingston 2007, Hon DUniv Kent 2008, Hon Dr Univ of the Arts London 2014; Hon ISM 2001, Hon FRIBA 2001, hon fell Royal Acad 2011; Knight First Class Order of the White Rose of Finland 1997; *Books* The Nuremberg Trial (co-author with Ann Tusa, 1984), The Berlin Blockade (co-author with Ann Tusa, 1988), Conversations with the World (1990), A World in Your Ear (1992), Art Matters: Reflecting on Culture (1999), On Creativity – Interviews Exploring the Process (2003), The Janus Aspect: Artists in the Twenty-First Century (2005), Engaged with the Arts – Writings from the Frontline (2007), Pain in the Arts (2014); *Recreations* tennis, opera, listening; *Style*— Sir John Tusa; ✉ 16 Canonbury Place, London N1 2NN (☎ 020 7704 2451)

TUSHINGHAM, Rita; da of John Tushingham, of Liverpool, and Enid Ellen, *née* Lott; *b* 14 March 1942; *Educ* La Sagesse Convent Liverpool; *m* 1, 1 Dec 1962 (m dis 1976), Terence William Bicknell; 2 da (Dodonna b 1 May 1964, Aisha b 16 June 1971); m 2, 27 Aug 1981 (m dis 1996), Ousama Rawi, s of Najib El-Rawi, of Geneva, Switzerland; *Career* actress; began career Liverpool Repertory Theatre 1958; hon fell Liverpool John Moores Univ 2009, hon assoc London Film Sch 2011; *Television* incl: Bread 1988, Dante and Beatrice in Liverpool 1989, Sunday Pursuit 1990, Dieter Gütt ein Journalist 1991, The Stretford Wives 2002, New Tricks 2005, Miss Marple – The Sittaford Mystery 2005, Angel Cake 2006, Bedlam 2010, In The Flesh (BBC) 2014, 50th anniversary documentary for Hard Day's Night (voiceover) 2014, Neil Gaiman's Likely Stories (Sky Arts) 2016; *Radio* Patty and Chip's with Scrap's 1997, Margo Beyond the Box 2003; *Film* A Taste of Honey (first film) 1961, The Girl with Green Eyes 1965, The Knack 1965, Doctor Zhivago 1966, The Trap 1967, The Guru 1968, Bedsitting Room 1969, A Judgement in Stone 1986, Resurrected 1988, Hard Days Hard Nights 1989, Paper Marriage 1991, The Rapture of Deceit 1991, Desert Lunch 1992, Hamburg Poison (for TV) 1992, An Awfully Big Adventure 1994, The Boy From Mercury 1995, Under the Skin 1996, A Night with Joan (for TV) 1997, Swing 1998, Out of Depth 1998, Home Ground 2000, Shadow Play (for TV) 2001, Being Julia 2003, Loneliness and the Modern Pentathalon 2004, Puffball 2006, The Hideout 2006, Broken Lines 2007, Telstar 2007, The Calling 2007, Come Here Today 2007, One of the Things that Makes Me Doubt 2010, Sea Monsters 2010, Outside Bet 2011, The Wee Man 2013; *Awards* incl: Cannes Film Festival Award for Best Actress, New York Film Critics' Award, Golden Globe Award (for A Taste of Honey); Variety Club of GB Best Actress Award (for The Girl with Green Eyes), Mexican Film Festival Award for Best Actress (for The Knack); *Recreations* incl: care and protection of animals, cooking, painting, gardening; *Style*— Miss Rita Tushingham; ✉ c/o Michele Milburn, Milburn Browning Associates, The Old Truman Brewery, 91 Brick Lane, London E1 6QL (☎ 020 3582 9370, e-mail michele@milburnbrowning.com)

TUTSSEL, Glenn Gifford; s of J H Tutssel, of Barry, Glamorgan, and C I Tutssel (d 1992); *b* 2 May 1951; *Educ* Barry Boys Comp, W of England Coll of Art, London Coll of Printing (BA); *m* 1976, Jane Alison, da of P Bowles; 1 da (Lauren May b 1982), 1 s (Leon Paul b 1988); *Career* designer/dir Lock Pettersen 1974–84; creative dir Michael Peters plc 1984–92, Tutssels 1993– (estab holding co The Brand Union with Lambie-Nairn & Co 1997); external examiner: Univ of Dundee 1990–95, Univ of Plymouth 1995–; memb Exec Ctee D&AD; D&AD Silver Awards 1984, 1987, 1990 and 2001, Communication Arts Awards (USA) 1981, 1984, 1985, 1990, 1991, 1992, 1996 and 1998, Clio Awards (USA) 1988, 1989, 1990 and 1997, Br Design Effectiveness Awards (for brands and literature) 1995, Gold Studio Awards (Canada) 1989 and 1990 and Silver Studio Awards 1990 and 1991; memb: Sportsman's Assoc, Nat Small-Bore Rifle Assoc, Br Western Soc, Nat Bit Spur and Saddle Collectors' Assoc (USA), Royal Mail Stamp Advsy Ctee; *Recreations* formerly judo (First Dan aged 16); *Clubs* Teddington Cricket, Ham and Petersham Rifle; *Style*— Glenn Tutssel, Esq

TUTSSEL, Mark Christopher; s of Stanley Ernest Tutssel, of Barry, S Wales; *Educ* Barry Boys' Comp Sch, Cardiff Coll of Art & Design (DipAD, Harrison Cowley advtg fell); *m* Julie Elizabeth, da of Dennis James Cripps; 1 s (Lewis James); *Career* jr art dir Saatchi & Saatchi advtg 1980, art dir MWK/Aspect 1981–85; Leo Burnett Ltd: art dir 1986–89, creative gp head 1989–91, assoc creative dir 1992–93, bd creative dir 1994–98, jt exec creative dir 1998–2002, vice-chm/dep chief creative offr Leo Burnett USA 2002–05, vice-chm and dep chief creative offr Leo Burnett Worldwide 2005–06, chief creative offr Leo Burnett Worldwide 2006–, creative chm Publicis Communications 2016–; pres Cannes 2008, 2010, 2013 and 2016; memb: Creative Cncl Facebook, One Show Creative Bd, P12 Exec Ctee Publicis Groupe; winner various advtg industry awards incl: 7 Cannes Grand Prix, 3 Cannes Titanium Lions, 2 Cannes Glass Lions, 480 Cannes Lions, 2 D&AD Black Pencils, 1 D&AD White Pencil, The British Television Grand Prix, three times inducted into the Clio Hall of Fame; MSIAD 1980, FRSA; *Books* Humankind (jtly); *Recreations* modern art, sport (former Welsh schoolboys champion football and basketball), music, my son; *Clubs* Design and Art Direction, New York One Club, Soho House, Royal Soc of Arts; *Style*— Mark Tutssel, Esq; ✉ e-mail mark.tutssel@leoburnett.com

TUTT, Leo Edward; s of Leo Edward Tutt (d 1975), of Sydney, Aust, and Dorothy, *née* McAdam (d 1988); *b* 6 April 1938; *Educ* Knox GS NSW; *m* 26 May 1961, Heather Elphinstone, da of Charles Walter Coombe (d 1965), of Sydney, Aust; 2 s (Leo, James), 1 da (Katherine); *Career* chartered accountant in public practice 1966–73; chm Tutt Bryant Ltd 1973–96 (jt md 1973–74), dir and chief exec Escor Ltd 1974–78, chm and chief exec Bowater Industries Aust 1974–96, dir and chief exec Aust and Far East Rexam plc (formerly Bowater plc) 1978–96; non-exec dep chm Bundaberg Sugar Company Ltd

(Aust Listed Co) 1984–91, non-exec dir Friends Provident Life Office 1987–93; dir: State Rail Authy NSW 1989–94, Metway Bank Ltd (Aust Listed Co) 1992–96, Suncorp-Metway Ltd 2007–; chm: MIM Holdings Ltd (Aust Listed Co) 1991–2003, Detroit Diesel-Allison Aust Pty Ltd 1996–2001, Promina Gp Ltd 1996–2007, Pirelli Cables Aust Ltd 1999–2005, Internet Travel Gp Ltd 2001–02, Crane Gp Ltd (Aust Listed Co) 2001–; dir Aust Graduate Sch of Business 1999–2004; hon fell Univ of Sydney 1996; FCA 1966, FAIM 1966, FCPA 1994, FAICD 2001; *Recreations* sailing, golf; *Clubs* American, Avondale Golf, Elanora Country, Royal Motor Yacht, Royal Prince Alfred Yacht, Royal Sydney Yacht Squadron, Union, Univ and Schs (Sydney); *Style—* Leo Tutt, Esq; ✉ Sedlescombe, 58 Prince Alfred Parade, Newport, NSW 2106, Australia (☎ 00 61 2 9979 5744, e-mail leo.tutt@crane.com.au)

TWEED, Jill (Mrs Hicks); da of late Maj Jack Robert Lowrie Tweed, and Kathleen Janie, *née* Freeth; *b* 7 December 1935; *Educ* Slade Sch of Art (BA); *m* Philip Lionel Sholto Hicks, s of Brig P Hicks; 1 da (Nicola b 1960), 1 s (David b 1971); *Career* sculptor; solo and gp exhibitions incl: Royal Acad 1979, Poole-Willis Gallery NYC 1984, Barbican Centre 1990, Flowers East Gallery 1991, Bruton Street Gallery London 1997–, Messum's London 2004–; cmmns incl: HM Queen Elizabeth Queen Mother 1980, HRH Prince Charles and Lady Diana Spencer 1981, HE The Governor of Guernsey, Hampshire Sculpture Tst 1991, Adm Lord Fieldhouse Falklands Gardens Gosport 1992, public sculpture Cirencester 1997; 4m bronze purchased by Hants CC for Caen Normandy (D-Day Remembrance) 1994, other work incl 3m high bronze (The Railwayman) Eastleigh 1995, 3m high bronze (The Bargeman) Sittingbourne Kent 1996, public sculpture (The Maltmaker) Ware Herts 1998, public sculpture (War Meml) for Eastleigh Hants 2000; FRBS, FRSA; *Recreations* horse riding; *Style—* Ms Jill Tweed; ✉ e-mail jill.tweed@zen.co.uk, website www.jilltweed.com

TWEED, (David) John; s of William Tweed (d 1989), and Margaret, *née* Gittus (d 1984); *b* 14 December 1946; *Educ* The King's Sch Chester, Univ of Manchester (BA, BArch); *m* 26 April 1980, Helen Elspeth Hamilton, da of Dr Frank Hamilton-Leckie, MC, TD, of Monklands, Uddingston, Glasgow; 2 da (Hilary b 1986, Anna b 1994); *Career* currently ptnr Tweed Nuttall Warburton chartered architects Chester (founded as John Tweed Assocs); cmmns incl: masterplanning phase 1 Old Port of Chester Regeneration Programme, major housing schemes for Wainhomes, Crosby Homes, Taylor Woodrow Devpts and Bellway Homes, Scout HQ Chester (Civic Award) 2000; RIBA: memb Cncl NW Region 1983–87 and 1994–98, memb NW Educn Cee 1987–, chm NW Practice Ctee 1994–98; chm Mgmnt Ctee Architects Benevolent Soc Claverton Ct Chester 1985–89, pres Cheshire Soc of Architects 1985–86, memb Cncl The Architects Benevolent Soc 1986–; chm: Chester Historic Bldgs Preservation Tst 1991–92, Chester Sustainable Environmental Educn Network 1997–; memb Cheshire West and Chester Cncl Design Review Panel 2014–; tstee Chester Civic Tst 2000–; RIBA 1974, ACIArb 1983, FRSA 1995; *Publications* Vision 2050 – A Sustainable Future for Cheshire West and Chester (jtly, 2009); *Recreations* family, rowing, sailing, gardening, boatbuilding; *Clubs* Royal Chester Rowing; *Style—* John Tweed, Esq; ✉ Ivy House, Hob Hill, Tilston, Malpas, Cheshire SY14 7DU (☎ 01829 250301); Duncraig House, Salen, Argyll PH36 4JN; Tweed Nuttall Warburton, Chartered Architects, Chapel House, City Road, Chester CH1 3AE (☎ 01244 310388, fax 01244 325643, e-mail john.tweed@tnw-architecture.co.uk)

TWEED, Paul; s of William Park Tweed (d 2003), and Mary Elizabeth, *née* Loudon (d 2004); *b* 6 June 1955, Belfast; *m* 11 July 2003, Selena Mary, *née* Kerins; 2 s (Conor Duncan b 22 March 1983, Oliver Maximillian b 22 Aug 2006), 2 da (Shannon Julia b 9 March 1987, Emily Lena Elizabeth b 17 Jan 2008); *Career* admitted slr: NI, England and Wales, Repub of Ireland; registered foreign legal conslt State Bar of Calif; slr specialising in defamation and defence litigation; sr ptnr Johnsons Slrs; clients incl: Liam Neeson, Britney Spears, Jennifer Lopez, Nicholas Cage, Louis Walsh, Vanessa Redgrave, Chris de Burgh, Patrick Kielty, Justin Timberlake and The Corrs; acted in the case B J Eastwood v Barry McGuigan resulting in highest libel award in Northern Irish legal history (£450,000); memb: Law Soc of NI 1978, Law Soc of England and Wales 1992, Law Soc of Ireland 1999; *Recreations* running, tennis, squash, boxing; *Style—* Paul Tweed, Esq; ✉ Johnsons, Johnson House, 50–56 Wellington Place, Belfast BT1 6GF (☎ 028 9024 0183, fax 028 9023 3266, e-mail paul.tweed@johnsonslaw.co.uk)

TWEEDIE, Prof Sir David Philip; kt (1994); s of Adrian Ian Tweedie, of Doncaster, and Marie Patricia, *née* Phillips; *b* 7 July 1944; *Educ* Grangemouth HS, Univ of Edinburgh (BCom, PhD); *m* 6 June 1970, Janice Christine, da of George Haddow Brown; 2 s (Ross Steven b 10 June 1976, Mark David b 25 May 1977); *Career* apprentice Mann Judd Gordon & Co Chartered Accountants Glasgow 1969–72, CA 1972; Univ of Edinburgh: lectr Dept of Accounting and Business Methods 1973–78, dir of studies 1973–75, assoc dean Faculty of Social Scis 1975–78; tech dir Inst of Chartered Accountants of Scotland 1978–81, nat res ptnr KMG Thomson McLintock 1982–87, nat tech ptnr KPMG Peat Marwick McLintock 1987–90; chm: Accounting Standards Bd 1990–2000 (ex officio memb Fin Reporting Cncl), Urgent Issues Task Force 1990–2000, Int Accounting Standards Bd 2001–11, Standards Advsy Cncl 2001–05, Int Valuation Standards Cncl 2012–; Lancaster Univ: visiting prof of accounting Int Centre for Res in Accounting (ICRA) 1978–88, tstee ICRA 1982–93, dep chm Bd of Tstees ICRA 1986–93; visiting prof of accounting Dept of Economics Univ of Bristol 1988–2000, visiting prof of accounting Mgmnt Sch Univ Edinburgh 2000–; memb Cncl ICAEW 1989–91 (memb Auditing Res Fndn 1988–90), chm CCAB Auditing Practices Ctee 1989–90 (vice-chm 1986–88, memb 1985–90), UK and Irish rep Int Auditing Practices Ctee 1983–88, UK and Irish rep International Accounting Standards Ctee 1995–2000; chm Leuchie House 2011–; pres ICAS 2012–13; awarded ICAEW Founding Societies Centenary Award 1997, CIMA Award 1998, IFAC Int Gold Service Award 2011, memb Accounting Hall of Fame 2013; Freeman City of London 2014; Hon DSc(Econ) Univ of Hull 1993, Hon DSc(SocSci) Univ of Edinburgh 2001; Hon LLD: Lancaster Univ 1993, Univ of Exeter 1997, Univ of Dundee 1998; Hon DLitt Heriot-Watt Univ 1996; Hon DBA: Napier Univ 1999, Oxford Brookes Univ 2004, Univ of Lincoln 2012; Hon FIA 2000, FRSE 2001, Hon FSIP 2004, Hon FCCA 2005, Hon CPA (Australia) 2012; *Books* The Private Shareholder and The Corporate Report (with T A Lee, 1977), Financial Reporting Inflation and The Capital Maintenance Concept (1979), The Institutional Investor and Financial Information (with T A Lee, 1981), The Debate on Inflation Accounting (with G Whittington, 1984); *Style—* Prof Sir David Tweedie; ✉ ICAS, CA House, 21 Haymarket Yard, Edinburgh EH12 5BH (☎ 0131 347 0100)

TWEEDY, Colin David; LVO (2003), OBE (2000); s of Clifford Harry Tweedy, of Abbotsbury, Dorset (d 2014), and Kitty Audrey, *née* Matthews (d 2010); *b* 26 October 1953; *Educ* City of Bath Boys' Sch, St Catherine's Coll Oxford (MA); *m* 2015, Campbell Guthrie Gray (civil partnership 2008); *Career* mangr Thorndike Theatre Leatherhead 1976–78, corp fin offr Guinness Mahon 1978–80, asst dir Streets Financial PR 1980–83, chief exec Arts & Business (Assoc for Business Sponsorship of the Arts (ABSA)) 1983–2012 (vice-pres 2012–), chief exec The Building Centre 2012–, chief exec The Built Environment Tst 2015–; chm Comité Européen pour le Rapprochement de l'Economie et de la Culture (CEREC); memb: UK Nat Ctee Euro Cinema and TV Year 1988–89, Cncl Japan Festival 1991, Cncl for Charitable Support, Global Advsy Bd of the Mariinsky Theatre under the patronage of The Prince of Wales, Cncl NMSO (Nat Musicians Symphony Orch), Design Cncl Sounding Board 2013–; memb Advsy Panel Costa (formerly Whitbread) Book Awards; judge: PR Week Awards, Art & Work Awards 2002; tstee: The Ideas Fndn, Serpentine Gallery, Next Generation Fndn; dir: Covent Garden Int Festival 1995–2001, Headlong Theatre (formerly Oxford Stage Co), Mariinsky Theatre Tst, Prince's Fndn for Children and the Arts, Arts Interlink 2012–; former dir Crusaid; selector Discerning Eye 2000 exhibition; Hollis Sponsorship Personality of the Year 2003; govr Univ of the Creative Arts 2009–; Freeman City of London 1978; CCMI 2002, FRSA; *Books* A Celebration of Ten Years' Business Sponsorship of the Arts (1987); *Recreations* the arts in general, opera, theatre and contemporary art in particular, food, Italy and travel; *Clubs* Groucho; *Style—* Colin Tweedy, Esq, LVO, OBE; ✉ The Building Centre, 26 Store Street, London WC1E 7BT (e-mail ctweedy@buildingcentre.co.uk, website www.buildingcentre.co.uk)

TWEMLOW, William Antony (Tony); s of Richard Lawrence Twemlow (d 1994), of West Kirby, Wirral, and Sylvia Doreen Twemlow (d 1991); *b* 2 December 1943; *Educ* Calday Grange GS, Downing Coll Cambridge (MA); *m* 12 Oct 1968, Margaret, da of William Thompson Scollay (d 1979); 2 s (Roy William b 15 Dec 1971, James Antony b 28 Sept 1982), 1 da (Laura Jane b 6 July 1973); *Career* Cuff Roberts: articled clerk 1965–68, asst slr 1968–71, managing ptnr 1986–93; currently legal dir Hill Dickinson; licensed insolvency practitioner 1987; chm: Liverpool Young Slrs Gp 1969–70, Young Slrs Gp Law Soc 1978–79, Liverpool Bd of Legal Studies 1988–91; dir Slrs' Benevolent Assoc 1980–91, memb: Law Soc 1968, Liverpool Law Soc 1968, Remuneration and Practice Devpt Ctee Law Soc 1980–92, Insolvency Lawyers Assoc 1989, Insolvency Practitioners Assoc 1990; pres Liverpool Law Soc 1994–95; memb Royal Liverpool Philharmonic Choir 1965–94, dep vice-chm Royal Liverpool Philharmonic Soc 1988–91 (memb Bd 1986–93); dir Hoylake Cottage Hosp Tst Ltd 1989–92; *Recreations* music, tennis; *Style—* Tony Twemlow, Esq

TWIGG, Derek; MP; *b* 9 July 1959; *Educ* Bankfield Sch Widnes, Halton Coll of FE; *Career* former civil servant until 1996; MP (Lab) Halton 1997–; PPS to: min of state for Energy and Euro Competitiveness 1999–2001, Rt Hon Stephen Byers, MP, *qv*, 2001–02; asst Govt whip 2002–04, Parly under sec of state DfES 2004–05, Parly under-sec of state Dept of Tport 2005–06, Parly under-sec of state and min for veterans MOD 2006–08; chm Halton Constituency Lab Pty 1985–96, chm NW Gp of Labour MPs 1999–2000; memb Public Accounts Ctee 1998–99; cnCllr Cheshire CC 1981–85; Halton BC: cnCllr 1983–97, chm housing 1987–93, chm fin 1993–96; *Recreations* various sporting activities, hill walking, reading military history; *Style—* Derek Twigg, Esq, MP; ✉ House of Commons, London SW1A 0AA (☎ 020 7219 3000, e-mail twiggd@parliament.uk)

TWIGG, Stephen; MP; *b* 25 December 1966; *Educ* Southgate Sch, Balliol Coll Oxford (BA, pres NUS 1990–92); *Career* Amnesty Int, NCVO, research asst to Margaret Hodge, MP, lobbyist Rowland Gp, gen sec Fabian Soc until 1997; MP (Lab): Enfield Southgate 1997–2005, Liverpool W Derby 2010–; Parly sec Privy Cncl Office 2001–02, Parly under sec of state DfES 2002–04, min of state for schs 2004–05, shadow sec of state for educn 2011–; dir Foreign Policy Centre 2005–10; special projects dir Aegis Tst; chair: Progress, Young People Now Fndn; memb: Amicus, Holocaust Educnl Tst; tstee Workers Educn Assoc; cnCllr Islington BC 1992–97 (chief whip 1994–96, dep ldr 1996); govr Jubilee Primary Sch; *Style—* Stephen Twigg, Esq, MP

TWIGGER, Terry; *b* 21 November 1949; *Educ* Univ of Bristol (BSc); *m*; 2 da; *Career* early career with: Deloitte & Touche, Lucas Aerospace (latterly finance dir); Meggitt plc: dir of finance 1993–95, gp finance dir 1995–2001, memb Bd 1995–, chief exec 2001–; dir: ADS, Filtrona plc; FCA, MRAeS; *Recreations* shooting, fishing, walking, reading; *Style—* Terry Twigger, Esq; ✉ Meggitt plc, Atlantic House, Aviation Park West, Bournemouth International Airport, Christchurch, Dorset BH23 6EW (☎ 01202 597571)

TWIGGY; *see:* Lawson, Lesley

TWINCH, Richard William; s of Richard Herbert Twinch, of Whitchurch, Salop, and Roma Bayliss, *née* Silver; *b* 29 October 1950; *Educ* Wellington, Clare Coll Cambridge (MA), AA Sch of Architecture (AADipl); *m* Hazel Cecilia, da of James Herbert Merrison (d 1987); 1 s (Oliver b 1975), 2 da (Jemila b 1977, Anna b 1981); *Career* architect and special technol conslt; lectr and tutor Prince of Wales's Inst of Architecture 1992–95, lectr in architecture Oxford Brookes Univ 1996–2000; author of tech software for architects incl: Condensation Control 1981–92, Heat Loss Performance 1983–91; dir: Richard Twinch Design, Chisholme Inst Beshara Sch of Esoteric Educn 1985–2001; commentator to Beshara Magazine 1986–90, lectr and conslt in CAD; MA external examiner Visual and Traditional Arts Unit RCA 1990 and 1991; computer columnist to Building Design magazine 1985–96, author of numerous articles on CAD in architectural press, papers incl Thermal Insulation and Condensation and Building Materials (1988); sign conslt Crowne Plaza Hotel Heathrow 1998; external examiner to Prince's Fndn 2000–01, expert validation assessor Univ of Wales 2000–; projects incl house extensions and conversions in Oxford; finalist Downland Prize 1999; RIBA; *Recreations* listening to music, walking, tennis; *Style—* Richard Twinch, Esq; ✉ 7 Hill Top Road, Oxford OX4 1PB (☎ 01865 202108, e-mail twinch@community.co.uk, website www.twinchdesign.co.uk)

TWINING, Prof William Lawrence; Hon QC (2002); s of Baron Twining (Life Peer, d 1967); *b* 22 September 1934, Kampala; *Educ* Charterhouse, BNC Oxford (DCL), Chicago Univ (JD); *m* 1957, Penelope Elizabeth, da of Richard Wall Morris; 1 s, 1 da; *Career* prof of jurisprudence Queen's Univ Belfast 1965–72, prof of law Univ of Warwick 1972–82, Quain prof of jurisprudence UCL 1983–96 (research prof of law 1996–2004, Quain prof of jurisprudence emeritus 2004–); pres Soc of Public Teachers of Law 1978–79, chm Cwlth Legal Educn Assoc 1983–93; Hon LLD: Victoria Univ BC Canada 1980, Univ of Edinburgh 1994, Queen's Univ Belfast 1999, Southampton Inst 2000, York Univ Toronto 2002, Univ of Windsor Ontario 2009, Coll of Law 2011; FBA 1997, foreign hon memb American Acad of Arts and Sciences 2007, FAcSS 2013; *Books* Karl Llewellyn and the Realist Movement (1973, 2 edn 2012), How to do Things with Rules (jtly, 5 edn 2010), Theories of Evidence – Bentham & Wigmore (1985), Rethinking Evidence (1990, 2 edn 2006), Analysis of Evidence (jtly, 1991, 2 edn 2005), Legal Records in the Commonwealth (jtly), Blackstone's Tower: The English Law School (1994), Law in Context: Enlarging a Discipline (1997), Globalisation and Legal Theory (2000), The Great Juristic Bazaar (2002), Evidence and Inference in History and Law (jt ed, 2003), General Jurisprudence (2009), Human Rights: Southern Voices (ed, 2009), Globalisation and Legal Scholarship (2011), Legal Fictions in Theory and Practice (2015); *Style—* Prof William Twining, QC; ✉ 10 Mill Lane, Iffley, Oxford OX4 4EJ

T

TWINN, Dr Ian David; s of David Twinn (d 2005), of Cambridge, and Gwynneth Irene, *née* Ellis; *b* 26 April 1950, Cambridge; *Educ* Netherhall Secdy Modern Sch Cambridge, Cambridge GS, UCW Aberystwyth (BA), Univ of Reading (PhD); *m* 28 July 1973, Frances Elizabeth, da of Godfrey Nall Holtby (d 1988); 2 s (David b 1983, John b 1986); *Career* sr lectr in town planning Poly of the South Bank 1975–83; MP (Cons) Edmonton 1983–97, dir of public affrs ISBA 1998–, MEP (Cons) London 2003–04 (Euro Parly candidate 1999, 2004 and 2009); PPS to: Rt Hon Sir Peter Morrison 1985–90, David Trippier as Min of State DOE 1990–92, Sir John Cope as Paymaster-Gen at the Treasy 1992–94; regnl chm Cons Pty in London 2014–; currently vice-chm Br-Caribbean Assoc; Freeman City of London 1981; FRGS (MIBG 1972), FRSA 1989; Cdr Order of Honour (Greece) 2000; *Recreations* antique furniture restoration, collecting second-hand books, bookcase building; *Clubs* RAC; *Style—* Dr Ian Twinn; ✉ 85 Calton Avenue, London SE21 7DF (☎ 020 8299 4210, e-mail twinn@aflex.net)

TWIST, Stephen John; s of late James Twist, of Darlington, Co Durham, and Kathleen Twist; *b* 26 September 1950; *Educ* Queen Elizabeth GS Darlington, Univ of Liverpool (LLB), Inns of Court Sch of Law London; *m* 4 May 1990, Ann, *née* Stockburn; 1 s (Miles Henry b 16 March 1993); *Career* called to the Bar Middle Temple 1979; in practice: London 1979–88, York 1988–; memb: Hon Soc of Middle Temple, North Eastern Circuit,

Public Access Bar Assoc; specialist in family law; advsr to constabularies and public authorities on admin law, professional standards, ethics, human rights and firearms; public sector arbitrator and mediator; sometime broadcaster on deafness issues and the law BBC and Channel 4; registered and panel mediator CEDR (former memb Public Sector Working Party); FCIArb 2000; *Publications* ADR Management and Resolution of Complaints in Relation to Police Disputes and Misconduct (1999), A Guide for Panels under the Police (Conduct) Regulations (2008); *Recreations* early music, environmental conservation, Argentine tango; *Style—* Stephen Twist, Esq; ✉ Dere Stret Barristers, 14 Toft Green, York YO1 6JY (☎ 01904 620048, e-mail twist.stephen@gmail.com, website www.derestreet.co.uk); 33 Broad Chare, Newcastle upon Tyne NE1 3DQ (☎ 0844 335 1551)

TWISTON DAVIES, David James; s of Mervyn Peter Twiston Davies (d 2002), of Somerset, and Isabel Anne, *née* Fox (d 2002), of Montreal, Canada; *b* 23 March 1945; *Educ* Downside; *m* 10 June 1970, Margaret Anne (Rita), da of Francis Gerard Montgomery (d 1978); 3 s (Benedict, James, Huw), 1 da (Bess); *Career* journalist; East Anglian Daily Times 1966–68, Winnipeg Free Press 1968–70; The Daily Telegraph: news sub ed 1970–77, asst literary ed 1977–86, dep obituaries ed 1986–87, letters ed 1987–88, ed Peterborough column 1988–89, letters ed 1989–2001, chief obituary writer 2001–10; memb Jacobite Studies Tst; Freeman City of London; *Books* Canada from Afar: The Daily Telegraph Book of Canadian Obituaries (ed, 1996), The Daily Telegraph Book of Letters (ed, 1998), The Daily Telegraph Book of Military Obituaries (ed, 2003), The Daily Telegraph Book of Naval Obituaries (ed, 2004), The Daily Telegraph Military Obituaries Book Two (2006), The Daily Telegraph Book of Imperial and Commonwealth Obituaries (ed, 2009), The Daily Telegraph Military Obituaries Book Three (2015); *Recreations* defending the reputation of the British Empire; *Clubs* Travellers; *Style—* David Twiston Davies, Esq; ✉ Courtlands, Courtenay Close, Sutton Courtenay, Abingdon OX14 4AU (☎ 01235 848871, e-mail david.twiston-davies@telegraph.co.uk)

TWIVY, Paul Christopher Barstow; s of Dr Samuel Barstow Twivy (d 2004), of Dunstable, Beds, and Sheila, *née* Webster (d 1993); *b* 19 October 1958; *Educ* Haberdashers' Aske's, Magdalen Coll Oxford (BA); *m* 1, 31 July 1982 (m dis), Martha Mary Ball; 2 s (Samuel b 1985, Joshua b 1988); m 2, 27 Oct 1991, Gabrielle Ruth Guz; 1 s (Max b 1994), 2 da (Eve b 1995, Clara b 1999); *Career* bd dir Hedger Mitchell Stark 1982–83, md Still Price Court Twivy D'Souza Lintas 1985–92, dep chm J Walter Thompson 1992–93, gp chief exec Bates Dorland 1994–96; mktg advsr: BBC 1997–99, New Millennium Experience Co 1997; chm Circus Communications Ltd 1998–2002, chief strategic planning offr McCann-Erickson 2002, dir Twivy Consultancy Ltd 2002–; ceo and co-fndr The Big Lunch 2008–10, fndr and ceo Big Soc Network 2010, ceo and fndr Your Square Mile 2010–; mktg advsr Cutty Sark 2011–; non-exec dir: The Partners, We Are What We Do; advsr Comic Relief, memb PM's Cncl on Social Action; author, spokesman for advtg industry; business ldr Mktg Soc; FIPA 2012, FRSA; *Books* Change the World for a Fiver; *Recreations* freelance comedy writer, playwright, poetry, reading, skiing, tennis, badminton, music (guitar and piano), novelist; *Clubs* Oxford Union, Groucho; *Style—* Paul Twivy, Esq; ✉ 46 Pattison Road, London NW2 2HJ (☎ and fax 020 7794 1610, mobile 07767 345630, e-mail paul.twivy@btconnect.com)

TWOMLOW, His Hon Judge Richard William; *b* 19 November 1953, Loughborough; *Educ* Whitchurch HS Cardiff, Trinity Coll Cambridge; *Career* called to the Bar Gray's Inn 1976; asst recorder 1998, recorder 2000, circuit judge Wales Circuit 2011–; *Style—* His Hon Judge Twomlow

TWYMAN, Prof Michael Loton; s of Lawrence Alfred Twyman (d 1980), and Gladys Mary, *née* Williams (d 2001); *b* 15 July 1934; *Educ* Sir George Monoux GS, Univ of Reading (BA, PhD), Trinity Coll Cambridge; *m* 31 July 1958, Pauline Mary, da of Edward Frank Andrews; 2 s (Jeremy James b 9 Oct 1960, Daniel John Soulby b 9 Oct 1966), 1 da (Nicola Clare b 25 Jan 1963); *Career* Univ of Reading: asst lectr in typography and graphic art 1959–62, lectr 1962–71, sr lectr in typography & graphic communication 1971–76, prof and head Dept of Typography & Graphic Communication 1976–98, dir Centre for Ephemera Studies 1993–, prof emeritus 1998–; visiting fell Mellon Center for British Art Yale 1981; chm: ICOGRADA (Int Cncl of Graphic Design Assocs) Working Gp on Graphic Design History 1984–88, Curatorium Int Inst for Information Design Vienna 1989–2002; Assoc Typographique Internationale: chm Ctee for Educn in Letterforms 1974–77, chm Res and Educn Ctee 1991–95, memb Bd of Dirs 1994–99; Printing Historical Soc: memb Ctee 1964–, asst ed Jl 1969–84, chm 1991–2004, vice-pres 2004–; memb Graphic Design Panel Nat Cncl for Diplomas in Art & Design 1971–74; Cncl for Nat Academic Awards: memb Ctee of Art & Design 1978–81, vice-chm Graphic Design Bd 1972–80, memb Sub-Ctee for Res Degrees 1978–83; tstee: Fndn for Ephemera Studies (pres 1999–2010), Printing Heritage Tst (chm 1999–); Samuel Pepys Medal for Outstanding Contribution to Ephemera Studies 1983, American Printing History Assoc Individual Award for Distinguished Achievement 2007, Sir Misha Black Medal for distinguished services to design education 2014, Ewell L Newman Award American Historical Print Collector's Soc 2015; Hon DLitt Univ of Reading 2008; *Books* John Soulby, printer, Ulverston (1966), Lithography 1800–1850: the techniques of drawing on stone in England and France and their application in works of topography (1970), Printing 1770–1970: an illustrated history of its development and uses in England (1970, reprinted 1998), A Directory of London Lithographic Printers 1800–1850 (1976), Henry Bankes's Treatise on Lithography (1976), The Landscape Alphabet (1986), Early Lithographed Books (1990), Early Lithographed Music (1996), The British Library Guide to Printing: History and Techniques (1998), The Encyclopedia of Ephemera (ed and completed, 2000, reprinted 2001), Breaking the Mould: The First Hundred Years of Lithography (2001), L'Imprimerie: Histoire et Techniques (2007), Barnett Freedman: The graphic art (contrib, 2006), Images en couleur: Godefroy Engelmann, Charles Hullmandel et les débuts de la chromolithographie (2007), The Cambridge History of the Book in Britain Vol 5 1695–1830 and Vol 6 1830–1914 (contrib, 2009), Edward Lear the Landscape Artist (contrib, 2009), Art for All: British Posters for Transport (contrib, 2010), Philadelphia on Stone (contrib, 2012), A History of Chromolithography: Printed Colour for All (2013), The Plates of The Herefordshire Pomona (in The Herefordshire Pomona, 2014); numerous articles in professional jls; *Style—* Prof Michael Twyman; ✉ Department of Typography & Graphic Communication, The University of Reading, 2 Earley Gate, Whiteknights, Reading, Berkshire RG6 6AU (☎ 0118 931 8081, e-mail lithomn@totalise.co.uk)

TYDEMAN, John Peter; OBE (2003); s of George Alfred Tydeman (d 1960), of Cheshunt, Herts, and Gladys Florence Beatrice, *née* Brown (d 1982); *b* 30 March 1936; *Educ* Hertford GS, Trinity Coll Cambridge (MA); *Career* 2 Lt 1 Singapore Regt RA 1954–56, served Malaya; drama director; head of drama radio BBC 1986–94 (radio drama prodr 1960–79, asst head radio drama 1979–86); awarded: Prix Italia 1970, Prix Futura 1979 and 1983, Broadcasting Press Guild Award for outstanding radio prodn 1983, Sony Special Award for Servs to Radio 1994, Radio Acad Life Achievement Award 2010; stage prodns incl: Objections to Sex and Violence (Royal Court) 1975, The Bells of Hell (Garrick Theatre) 1977, Falstaff (Fortune Theatre) 1984, Night Must Fall (Haymarket) 1996; *Recreations* swimming, foreign places, theatre; *Clubs* Garrick; *Style—* John Tydeman, Esq, OBE; ✉ Bay Tree Cottage, 28, The Street, North Lopham, Diss, Norfolk IP22 2NB (☎ 01379 687339, e-mail jt@tydlyn.demon.co.uk)

TYE, Alan Peter; *b* 18 September 1933; *Educ* Regent St Poly Sch of Architecture (DipArch); *m* 1, 1960; 1 da (Helen Elna b 1962), 1 s (Martin Anders b 1964); m 2, 1966, Anita Birgitta Goethe-Tye; 1 da (Madeleine b 1967), 2 s (Nicolas b 1969, Kevin b 1973); *Career* Arne Jacobsen Copenhagen 1960, Alan Tye Design 1962–; visiting tutor RCA 1978–83 (external assessor 1987–), guest prof Royal Acad of Fine Arts Copenhagen 1996; inaugural RDI lecture LA 1998; memb Selection Ctee Cncl of Industrial Design 1967, Civic Tst Award assessor 1968 and 1969, fndr Healthy Industrial Design process 1977, specialist advsr on ind design CNAA 1980, London regnl assessor RIBA 1981, RSA Bursary judge 1983–2003, chm Product Liability Seminar CSD 1987, awards assessor RIBA 1988, external assessor RCA degrees 1989, chm RSA New for Old EEC Bursary 1993–2003, external examiner Guildhall Univ MA Design for Disability 2000; founder memb Product Innovation in Architecture Soc of RIBA 1999; RIBA 1959, RDI 1986; *Awards* Int Design Prize Rome 1962, Cncl of Ind Design Award 1965, 1966 and 1981, Br Aluminium Design Award 1966, first prize GAI Award 1969, Observer (London) Design Award 1969, Ringling Museum of Art (Fla) Award 1969, Gold Medal Graphic Design 1970, first prize GAI Award Int Bldg Exhibition 1971, British Aluminium Eros Trophy 1973, 4 awards for design excellence Aust 1973, commendation for architecture 1977, Inst of Business Designers Int Award (NY) 1982, Int Bldg Exhibits top design award 1983 (1985), ROSCOE Design Award NY 1988, finalist Prince Philip Designer of the Year Award 1993 and 1999, RIBA Regnl Design Award 1995; RDI 1986, hon fell Royal Coll of Arts; *Recreations* tai chi, aikido; *Style—* Alan Tye, Esq; ✉ The Red House, Great West Plantation, Tring, Hertfordshire HP23 6DA (☎ 01442 823325, fax 01442 827723)

TYERS, Anthony Gordon; s of Arthur Tyers, of Sunbury on Thames, Surrey, and Marion Joan, *née* Cheal; *b* 14 September 1944; *Educ* Hampton Sch, Charing Cross Hosp Univ of London (MB BS); *m* 7 Oct 1983, Renée Constance Barbara, da of Frits De Waard, of Waalre, Netherlands; 2 s (Jonathan b 30 July 1986, Richard b 30 April 1989), 2 da (Johanna b 19 May 1991, Rebecca b 9 Nov 1993); *Career* registrar Univ Coll Hosp London 1973–76, sr registrar Moorfields Eye Hosp 1978–81, fell Massachusetts Eye and Ear Infirmary Boston USA 1981–82, fell Academic Medical Centre Amsterdam 1982, sr registrar Moorfields Eye Hosp and Middx Hosp London 1982–86; conslt ophthalmic surgn: Salisbury Gen Hosps 1986–, Moorfields Eye Hosp 1997–99; visiting conslt St John Eye Hosp Jerusalem 1995–; former pres Br Oculo-Plastic Surgery Soc, former pres European Soc of Ophthalmic Plastic and Reconstructive Surgery; chm Salisbury Hosps Fndn; memb: BMA, RSM, Southern Ophthalmological Soc; FRCS(Eng) 1974, FRCSEd 1980, FRCOphth 1989; *Books* Basic Clinical Ophthalmology (contrib, 1984), Colour Atlas of Ophthalmic Plastic Surgery (jtly, 1994, 3 edn 2007), Eyetext.net (contrib, 2000), Plastic and Orbital Surgery (contrib, 2001), Maxillo-Facial Trauma and Esthetic Reconstruction (contrib, 2002, 2 edn 2012), Ophthalmic Surgery Principles and Practice (contrib, 2012); over 40 papers in peer-reviewed jls; *Recreations* sailing, skiing, music; *Style—* Anthony Tyers, Esq; ✉ Salisbury District Hospital, Salisbury SP2 8BJ (☎ 01722 336262, fax 01722 425155, website www.anthonytyers.net); New Hall Hospital, Salisbury SP5 4EY (☎ 01722 439680, fax 01722 410143)

TYLDESLEY, Clive; *b* Radcliffe, Lancs; *Educ* Kirkham GS, Univ of Nottingham; *m* 5 July 2013, Susan; *Career* sports commentator; Radio Trent 1975–77, Radio City 1977–88, Granada TV 1988–92 (memb ITV World Cup commentary team 1990), BBC TV Sport 1992–96, sr football commentator ITV Network Sport 1996–; columnist Daily Telegraph 2000–08; Sony Radio Sports Commentator of the Year 1985, RTS Sports Commentator of the Year 1998, 2000, 2002 and 2005; *Style—* Mr C Tyldesley; ✉ ITV Sport, 15th Floor, London Television Centre, Upper Ground, London SE1 9LT

TYLER, Antony Nigel (Tony); s of Maj-Gen Sir Leslie Tyler, KBE, CB (d 1992), and Sheila, *née* Field (d 2003); *b* 27 April 1955, Moascar, Egypt; *Educ* Worth Sch, Brasenose Coll Oxford (BA); *Children* 2 s (Andrew b 1981, Robert b 1983), 1 da (Florence b 1990); *Career* joined Swire Gp 1977; Cathay Pacific Airways: joined 1978, dir of serv delivery 1994–96, dir of corp devpt 1996–2004, chief operating offr 2005–07, chief exec 2007–; chm Dragonair; chm Int Air Tport Assoc (IATA); memb Bd Asian Youth Orch; *Recreations* tennis, hiking, rock and folk guitar; *Clubs* Hong Kong Country, Hong Kong, RAC, Foreign Correspondents'; *Style—* Tony Tyler, Esq; ✉ Cathay Pacific Airways Limited, 8 Scenic Road, Hong Kong International Airport, Hong Kong (☎ 00 852 2747 5051)

TYLER, Dr Chris; s of John Tyler, and Val Tyler; *b* 29 May 1978; *Educ* Univ of Durham, Univ of Cambridge (PhD); *m* 2011, Josie Cluer; *Career* Sense Bbout Science 2005–07, science advsr House of Commons Science and Technol Select Ctee 2007–10, exec dir Centre for Science and Policy Univ of Cambridge 2010–12, dir Parly Office of Science and Technol (POST) 2012–; memb Bd Campaign for Science and Engrg; *Recreations* music, basketball, walking; *Style—* Dr Chris Tyler; ✉ Parliamentary Office of Science and Technology, 7 Millbank, London SW1P 3JA (Twitter @cptyler)

TYLER, Colin Andrew; *b* Sep 1968; *Educ* Sidney Sussex Coll Cambridge; *Career* OC&C Strategy Consultants: sr ptnr 1995–, head Technology, Media and Telecoms Practice and memb Int Exec Ctee 2012–; ptnr Regis McKenna Inc (Silicon Valley) 1997–2002; named in Debrett's 500 most influential people 2014, 2015 and 2016 for his role in shaping Britain's technol and media landscape; *Style—* Colin Tyler, Esq; ✉ OC&C Strategy Consultants, 6 New Street Square, London EC4A 3AT

TYLER, David; s of Ronald Julian Meek, of Stoke-on-Trent, and Ruth Hannah, *née* Sewell, of Wembley; *b* 24 June 1961; *Educ* Haberdashers' Aske's, Clare Coll Cambridge (fndn scholar, MA); *Children* 2 s, 2 da; *Career* prodr; toured UK, Edinburgh Festival and Australia with Cambridge Footlights (prodns incl Hawaiian Cheese Party, Feeling the Benefit and Get Your Coat Dear, We're Leaving) 1983–85; stand-up comedian and writer (Week Ending and News Huddlines) 1985; prodr/dir 1986– BBC Radio 4: Radio Active, Week Ending, Cabaret Upstairs, The Big Fun Show, Dial M for Pizza, Hey Rrradio, Unnatural Acts, At Home With the Hardys, Live on Arrival, The Woody Allen Reader, Jeremy Hardy Speaks to the Nation, King Stupid, The Very World of Milton Jones, The House of Milton Jones, Crown Jewels, The 99p Challenge, Giles Wemmbley-Hogg Goes Off, Deep Trouble, Armando Iannucci's Charm Offensive, Cabin Pressure, Another Case of Milton Jones, Bigipedia, The Genuine Particle, Jo Caulfield Won't Shut Up, The 3rd Degree Series, My First Planet, Strap In – It's Clever Peter! Kevin Eldon Will See You Now series, The Brig Society, Thanks A Lot Milton Jones, The Castle, Shush!, The Lentil Sorters, John Finnemore's Double Acts; prodr: Spitting Image series 6 and 7, The Sound of Maggie (ITV) 1989, The Paul and Pauline Calf Audio Experience, The Tony Ferrino Phenomenon, Introducing Tony Ferrino – Who and Why?, A Quest (BBC) 1995–96, Up Yer News (BSB) 1990, And Now in Colour, It's A Mad World World World World, The Paul Calf Video Diary, The Imaginatively-Titled Punt & Dennis Show, Three Fights Two Weddings and a Funeral, Angus Deayton's End of the Year Show, Paul Merton – The Series, Dead at Thirty, Absolutely, Cows, tlc, Gash, The Strategic Humour Initiative, The Comic Side of 7 Days, Music Hall Meltdown, Giles Wemmbley-Hogg Goes Off... To Glastonbury, Saturday Live Again! 2007, For One Night Only 2008, Milton Jones Live Universe Tour: Part 1 – Earth, Milton Jones – On The Road, Milton Jones – Lion Whisperer; formed Pozzitive TV (with prodr/dir Geoff Posner) 1993–; exec prodr: The Marriage of Figaro (BBC) 1994, dinnerladies (BBC1); prodr/writer: Coogan's Run, The Big Snog 1995 (Channel 4); series prodr The Jack Docherty Show (Channel 5) 1997, co-dir The Man Who Thinks He's It (national and West End tour); author of articles in The Independent and The Guardian and regular contrib to New Moon and Nexus magazines; memb: Equity 1984, Labour Party; *Awards* BAFTA Best Comedy Award for Three Fights Two Weddings and a Funeral 1994, Crystal Award Winner Golden Prague Int Television Festival for The Marriage of Figaro 1994, Sony (Bronze) Award for Jeremy Hardy Speaks to the Nation series 2 1995, Silver Rose of Montreux for The Tony Ferrino Phenomenon 1996, Sony (Bronze) Award for Crown Jewels 1996, Sony (Bronze) Award for The Very World of Milton Jones 2000, Sony (Silver) Award for The 99p Challenge 2004, Sony (Bronze) Award for Armando Iannucci's Charm Offensive 2006, Sony (Silver) Award for Giles Wemmbley Hogg Gent Zum Fussball Weltmeisterschaft Weg 2006, Best British Radio Sitcom comedy.co.uk for Another Case of Milton Jones 2010, Sony (Silver) Award for Another Case of Milton Jones 2011, Writer's Guild Award 2011, 2012 and 2013 for Cabin Pressure and 2014 for The Brig Society and Cabin Pressure, Best Entertainment Producer Radio Academy Production Award 2013, Best Regularly Scheduled Comedy Programme (Bronze) New York Int Radio Prog Awards for Cabin Pressure 2014; *Recreations* spotting dumped cars in Crouch End; *Clubs* The British Interplanetary Society; *Style*— David Tyler, Esq; ✉ c/o Pozzitive Television, 1st Floor, 41 Goodge Street, London W1T 2PY (✆ 020 7255 1112, fax 020 7255 1116, e-mail david@pozzitive.co.uk)

TYLER, David; s of Alan Tyler, and Jill Tyler; *b* 23 January 1953; *Educ* Rendcomb Coll, Trinity Hall Cambridge (MA); *m* 1977 (m dis 2011), Sharon Lantin; 1 da, 1 s; *Career* Unilever plc 1974–86, County Natwest Ltd 1986–89, fin dir Christie's Int plc 1989–96, fin dir GUS plc 1997–2007; chm: 3i Quoted Private Equity Ltd 2007–09, Logica plc 2007–12, J Sainsbury plc 2009–, Hammerson plc 2013–, Domestic & General Ltd; non-exec dir: Burberry Gp plc 2002–15, Experian plc 2006–12, Reckitt Benckiser Gp plc 2007–09; chm Hampstead Theatre 2012–; FCMA 1983, MCT 1991; *Recreations* barn life in Sussex, family, friends, current affairs, theatre, listening to music, washing up; *Style*— David Tyler, Esq; ✉ J Sainsbury plc, 33 Holborn, London EC1N 2HT

TYLER, Ian Paul; s of Ray Lindley Tyler (d 2002), and Peggy May, *née* Boreham; *b* 7 July 1960, Wells, Somerset; *Educ* Ringwood Comp Sch, Univ of Birmingham (BCom); *m* 25 June 1983, Janet Lynn, *née* Kempson; 2 da (Amy Rebecca b 6 Oct 1993, Lucy Charlotte b 17 Nov 1995); *Career* Arthur Anderson & Co 1982–88, gp treas and financial comptroller Storehouse plc 1988–91, gp financial comptroller Hanson plc 1991–93, finance dir Arc Ltd 1993–96; Balfour Beatty plc: finance dir 1996–2002, chief operating offr 2002–04, chief exec 2005–; non-exec dir Cable & Wireless Communications plc; pres Construction Industry Charity for the Homeless (CRASH); CA 1985; *Recreations* flying, fitness; *Style*— Ian Tyler, Esq; ✉ Balfour Beatty plc, 130 Wilton Road, London SW1V 1LQ (✆ 020 7216 6825, e-mail ian.tyler@balfourbeatty.com)

TYLER, Leonard Charles; s of Sydney James Tyler, and Elsie May, *née* Reeve; *b* 14 November 1951; *Educ* Southend HS, Jesus Coll Oxford (open exhibitioner, MA), City Univ (MSc); *m* 22 Sept 1984, Ann Wyn, da of William Evans; 1 s (Thomas Huw b 11 Oct 1985), 1 da (Catrin Victoria b 13 Feb 1987); *Career* DOE 1975–78; British Council: asst rep Malaysia 1978–81, asst rep Sudan 1981–84, regnl offr S E Asia 1984–86, trg City Univ 1986–87, Information Technology Gp 1987–93, dir Nordic Countries Copenhagen 1993–98; chief exec RCPCH 1998–2009; author 2007–; vice-chair Crime Writers Assoc 2013, chair Crime Writers Assoc 2015; Hon FRCPCH 2010; *Novels* The Herring Seller's Apprentice (2007), A Very Persistent Illusion (2009), Ten Little Herrings (2009), The Herring in the Library (2010, Best Comic Crime Novel Last Laugh Award 2010), Herring on the Nile (2011), Crooked Herring (2014, Best Comic Crime Novel Last Laugh Award 2014), A Cruel Necessity (2014), Masterpiece of Corruption (2016), Cat Among the Herrings (2016), The Plague Road (2016); *Recreations* hill walking, reading, crosswords, memb Mensa; *Clubs* Detection; *Style*— Leonard Tyler, Esq; ✉ DHH Literary Agency Ltd, 23–25 Cecil Court, London WC2N 4EZ ((✆ 02078 367376, e-mail enquiries@dhhliteraryagency.com, website www.lctyler.com);

TYLER, Prof Nicholas (Nick); CBE (2011); *b* 3 September 1954, Harrow, Middx; *Educ* Univ Coll Sch London, Poly of Central London (MSc), UCL (PhD); *Career* Chadwick prof of civil engrg UCL; tstee Engineers Without Borders; ARCM 1975, FICE 2004, FRSA 2010, FREng 2014; *Publications* Accessibility and the Bus System (2002, 2 edn Accessibility and the Bus System: Transforming the World 2015); *Recreations* music; *Style*— Prof Nick Tyler, CBE, FREng; ✉ 206, Chadwick Building, University College London, Gower Street, London WC1E 6BT (e-mail n.tyler@ucl.ac.uk)

TYLER, Baron (Life Peer UK 2005), of Linkinhorne in the County of Cornwall; Paul Archer Tyler; CBE (1985), PC (2014); s of Oliver Walter Tyler (d 1957), and (Ursula) Grace Gibbons, *née* May (d 2001); *b* 29 October 1941; *Educ* Sherborne, Exeter Coll Oxford (MA); *m* 27 June 1970, Nicola Mary (Nicky), da of Michael Warren Ingram, OBE, of South Cerney, Glos; 1 da (Hon Sophie Grace Auriol b 1972), 1 s (Hon Dominick Michael Archer b 1975); *Career* dep dir then dir of public affrs RIBA 1966–73, regnl organiser and bd memb Shelter 1975–76, md Courier Newspaper Group 1976–81, dir then sr conslt Good Relations Ltd 1982–92, dir Western Approaches PR Ltd 1987–2000; MP: (Lib) Bodmin Feb-Oct 1974, (Lib Dem) N Cornwall 1992–2005; Lib Dem shadow ldr House of Commons 1997–2005; Lib Dem chief whip 1997–2001; Lib Dem Parly spokesman on: agriculture and rural affrs 1992–97, food 1997–2000; shadow min for constitutional affrs House of Lords; memb Jt Ctee on House of Lords Reform 2002–03; memb Select Ctee: on Procedure 1992–97, on Parly Privilege 1997–99, on Modernisation of House of Commons 1997–2005; memb: Jt Ctee on Lords/Commons Conventions 2006–08, Jt Ctee on Draft House of Lords Reform Bill 2011–12, Trade Union Political Funds and Political Party Funding Select Ctee 2016; chm All-Pty Coastal Gp 1992–97, chm All-Pty Organophosphate Gp 1992–2005, treas All-Pty Tourism Gp 1992–97, hon sec All-Pty Water Gp 1992–97; cncllr Devon CC 1964–70, memb Devon and Cornwall Police Authy 1965–70, vice-chm Dartmoor Nat Park 1965–70; vice-pres: Br Resorts Assoc, YHA; DL Cornwall 2006–10; MIPR 1987; *Publications* Power to the Provinces (1968), A New Deal for Rural Britain (1978), Country Lives, Country Landscapes (1996), Britain's Democratic Deficit (2003), House of Lords Reform: Breaking the Deadlock (2005), Beating the Retreat: The Government's Flight from Constitutional Reform (jtly, 2008), Constitutional Renewal Bill (2009), Lords Reform: A Guide for MPs (jtly, 2012), Funding Democracy: Breaking the Deadlock (jtly, 2013), Who Decides? (with Norman Thelwell, 2014), Political Parties (Funding and Expenditure) Bill 2016; *Recreations* sailing, walking, Cornish ancestry; *Style*— The Rt Hon Lord Tyler, CBE, PC; ✉ House of Lords, London SW1A 0PW (website www.paultyler.libdems.org)

TYLER, Richard Herbert (Dick); s of Peter Anthony Tyler, of Winchcombe, Glos, and Barbara Margaret, *née* Wilson; *b* 19 February 1959, Cheltenham, Glos; *Educ* Cheltenham GS, Fitzwilliam Coll Cambridge (MA); *Career* McKenna & Co Slrs: articled clerk 1983–85, asst slr 1985–92, ptnr 1992–97; CMS Cameron McKenna: ptnr 1997–2000, managing ptnr 2000–08, sr ptnr 2011–; exec ptnr CMS Legal Services EEIG 2008–11; memb: Law Soc, City of London Slrs' Co; chm London Legacy 2020 Culture Bd 2006– (chm 2008–); pres Old Patesians Rugby Football Club 2006–; *Style*— Dick Tyler, Esq; ✉ CMS Cameron McKenna LLP, Mitre House, 160 Aldersgate Street, London EC1A 4DD (✆ 020 7367 3000, e-mail dick.tyler@cws-cmck.com)

TYLER OF ENFIELD, Baroness (Life Peer UK 2011), of Enfield in the London Borough of Enfield; Claire Tyler; *b* 4 June 1957; *Educ* Latymer GS, Univ of Southampton (BSc), South Bank Poly (postgrad dip); *Career* GLC/ILEA 1978–88, mgmnt posts Dept for Employment 1988–92, divnl mangr DfES 1992–97, head Connexions Unit 1998–2000, chief exec Connexions Nat Unit 2000–02, dir Social Exclusion Unit Cabinet Office then Office of the Dep PM subsequently Dept for Communities and Local Govt 2002–06, dir Vulnerable Children Gp DfES 2006–07, ceo Relate 2007–12 (vice-pres 2012–), pres Nat Children's Bureau 2012–; vice-chair: Assoc Parly Gp for Parents and Families, All Pty Parly Gp on Carers, All Pty Parly Gp on Strengthening Relationships; co-chair All Pty Parly Gp on Wellbeing Economics, co-chair All Pty Parly Gp on Social Mobility; chair Lib Dem Policy Gp Balanced Working Life, vice pres Liberal Int GB, co-chair Growing Giving Parly Inquiry, memb Lords Select Ctee on Social Mobility 2015–16, chair Lords Select Ctee on Financial Exclusion 2016–17; chair Values-based Child and Adolescent Mental Health System Cmmn, chair Children and Family Court Advsy and Support Service 2012–, chair Making Every Adult Matter coalition of charities 2013–; memb Poverty and Disadvantage Ctee Joseph Rowntree Fndn 2002–06; *Style*— The Baroness Tyler of Enfield; ✉ House of Lords, London SW1A 0PW

TYNAN, Bill; s of James Tynan, and Mary Tynan; *b* 18 August 1940, Glasgow; *Educ* St Mungo's Acad, Stow Coll; *m* 11 July 1964, Elizabeth, *née* Mathieson; 3 da (Caroline b 1965, Pauline b 1967, Angela b 1976); *Career* trade union official, memb numerous ctees AEU; joined Lab Pty 1969, MP (Lab) Hamilton S 1999–2005 (by-election), pt/t researcher for John Robertson, MP 2005–15; currently special advsr to All Pty Parly Nuclear Energy Gp; political interests incl Europe and NI, employment law, social security, int devpt, equal opportunities and social inclusion; successfully piloted private members' bill on firework legislation through House of Lords and House of Commons 2002/03; dir: Lanarkshire Voluntary Sector (SoLVE) 2006–, Trade Unions for Safe Nuclear Energy (TUSNE) 2007–; memb Bd Vaslan 2011–; *Recreations* golf, gardening, DIY, watching football, lawn bowls; *Clubs* Colville Park Golf, Low Waters Bowling; *Style*— Bill Tynan, Esq; ✉ 6 East Scott Terrace, Hamilton ML3 6LL (✆ and fax 01698 421660)

TYRE, Hon Lord Colin Jack; CBE (2010), QC (1998); s of James Tyre, of Dunoon, Argyll (d 1993), and Lilias, *née* Kincaid; *b* 17 April 1956, Dunoon, Argyll; *Educ* Dunoon GS, Univ of Edinburgh (LLB, Lord Pres Cooper Mem Scholarship Prize), Univ of Aix-Marseille (Dip); *m* 18 Sept 1982, Elaine, *née* Carlin (d 2010); 2 da (Kirsty b 8 Aug 1986, Catriona b 1 Jan 1989), 1 s (Euan b 18 May 1992); *Career* called to Scottish Bar 1987; apprentice Shepherd and Wedderburn 1977–79, lectr in law Univ of Edinburgh 1980–83, tax ed CCH Editions Ltd 1983–86, advocate 1987–2010, pt/t cmmr Scottish Law Cmmn 2003–09, senator Coll of Justice 2010–; pres Cncl of Bars and Law Socs of Europe 2007 (head UK delgn 2004); memb Faculty of Advocates 1987; chm Bd of Govrs Fettes Coll Edinburgh 2012–; Grand Decoration of Honour (Austria) 2009; CCH Inheritance Tax Reporter (1984), Tax for Litigation Lawyers (co-author, 2000), contrib to Stair Mem Encyclopedia (contrib, 1986–); *Recreations* mountain walking, golf, orienteering, popular music; *Style*— The Hon Lord Tyre; ✉ Supreme Courts, Parliament House, 11 Parliament Square, Edinburgh EH1 1RQ (✆ 0131 225 2595, fax 0131 240 6711)

TYRER, His Hon Christopher John Meese; DL (2008); s of late Jack Meese Tyrer, of Rhiwbina, Cardiff, and Margaret Joan, *née* Wyatt; *b* 22 May 1944; *Educ* Wellington, Univ of Bristol (LLB); *m* 9 Feb 1974, (Monica) Jane Tyrer, JP, da of late Peter Beckett; 1 da (Rebecca b 1979), 1 s (David b 1981); *Career* called to the Bar Inner Temple 1968; dep judiciary 1979 (dep judge 1979–82), asst recorder 1982–83, recorder 1983–89, circuit judge (SE Circuit) 1989–2011, designated family judge Bucks 1990–97, inner London 1998–2005, resident judge Aylesbury Crown Court 2005–11, hon recorder Aylesbury 2010–11; vice-chm St John's Sch Lacey Green 1989–90 (govr 1984–92), chm Speen Sch 1989–90 and 1995–96 (govr 1984–96), memb Bucks Assoc of Govrs of Primary Schs 1989–90 (chm High Wycombe Div 1989–90), govr The Misbourne Sch 1993–2007 (vice-chm 1995–2000, chm 2000–07), patron Bucks New Univ Student Law Soc 2002–11, chair New Leaf Project 2011–, vice patron OASIS 2014–; chm English Baroque Choir 1998–99; hon doctorate Bucks New Univ 2010; *Recreations* music, reading, photography, growing things, supporting Wycombe Wanderers FC; *Style*— His Hon Christopher Tyrer, DL; ✉ Randalls Cottage, Loosley Row, Princes Risborough, Aylesbury, Buckinghamshire HP27 0NU (✆ 01844 344650)

TYRIE, Rt Hon Andrew; PC (2015), MP; *Educ* Felsted, Trinity Coll Oxford (MA), Coll of Europe Bruges, Wolfson Coll Cambridge (MPhil); *Career* with British Petroleum at Group Head Office; full time advsr to Rt Hon Nigel Lawson, MP and then Rt Hon John Major, MP as Chllrs of the Exchequer 1986–90; contested Houghton and Washington 1992; former sr economist EBRD; MP (Cons) Chichester 1997–, shadow financial sec 2003–04, shadow paymaster gen 2004–05; chm Parly Cmmn on Banking Standards 2012–13; memb: House of Commons Select Ctee on Public Admin 1997–2001, Public Accounts Cmmn 1997– (chm 2011), Treasy Select Ctee 2001–03 and 2009– (chm 2010–), Exec Ctee of 1922 Ctee 2005–06, Justice Ctee (formerly Constitutional Affrs Select Ctee) 2005–10, Jt Ctee on Draft Constitutional Renewal Bill 2008, Reform of the House of Commons Select Ctee 2009–10, Jt Ctee on Tax Law Rewrite Bills 2009–10 (chm 2010), Liaison Ctee 2010–; Woodrow Wilson Scholar 1990, fell Nuffield Coll Oxford 1990–91; Backbencher of the Year Spectator Award 2000 and 2009, Select Ctee Chm of the Year Spectator Award 2011; *Publications* The Prospects for Public Spending (1996), Sense on EMU (1998), Reforming the Lords: A Conservative Approach (1998), Leviathan at Large: The New Regulator for the Financial Markets (jtly, 2000), Mr Blair's Poodle: An Agenda for Reviving the House of Commons (2000), Back from the Brink (2001), Statism by Stealth: New Labour, new collectivism (jtly, 2002), Axis of Anarchy: Britain, America and the New World Order after Iraq (2003), Pruning the Politicians: The Case for a Smaller House of Commons (2004), Mr Blair's Poodle Goes to War: The House of Commons, Congress and Iraq (2004), The Conservative Party's proposals for the funding of political parties (2006), One Nation Again (2006), An Elected Second Chamber: A Conservative View (jtly, 2009), Extraordinary Rendition: Closing the Gap (jtly, 2009), After the Age of Abundance (2011), The IMF and the Euro Zone (2012), Neither Just nor Secure: The Justice and Security Bill (jtly, 2013, UK Publication of the Year Prospect Magazine), Voice and Veto: Answering the West Lothian Question (2015), The Poodle Bites Back: Select Committees and the Revival of Parliament (2015); *Clubs* RAC, Garrick, MCC; *Style*— The Rt Hon Andrew Tyrie, MP; ✉ House of Commons, London SW1A 0AA

TYRRELL, Prof Robert James; *b* 6 June 1951; *Educ* Univ of Oxford (MA), LSE (MSc); *Career* chm and chief exec The Henley Centre 1986–96, non-exec dir New Solutions Ltd 1997–2000, non-exec devpt ptnr Cognosis strategic consultancy 1998–2000, chm RISC Futures Paris 1999–2000, chm Sociovision UK 2001–06, Euro chm Global Futures Forum 2001–06, non-exec dir Trajectory 2010–; memb: Advsy Cncl Demos 1993–2001 (tstee 2001–03, chm 2003–06), Cncl Cons Pty Policy Forum 1999–2001, Advsy Cncl BUPA 2007–; visiting prof City Univ Business Sch 1994–2000; presenter Radio 4 Analysis Prog 1997–2007; *Style*— Prof Robert Tyrrell

TYRWHITT, Sir Reginald Thomas Newman; 3 Bt (UK 1919), of Terschelling, and of Oxford, DL (2014); s of Adm Sir St John Reginald Joseph Tyrwhitt, 2 Bt, KCB, DSO, DSC (d 1961), and Nancy Veronica (d 2010), da of Charles Newman Gilbey (gn of Sir Walter Gilbey, 1 Bt); gs of 1 Bt Adm of the Fleet Sir Reginald York Tyrwhitt, GCB, DSO; Sir St John's gf's gf, Richard, was 3 s of Capt John Tyrwhitt, RN (d 1812), of Netherclay House, Somerset, by his w Katherine (paternal gda of Lady Susan Clinton, da of 6 Earl of Lincoln (a dignity now subsumed in the Duchy of Newcastle); Richard's er bro was (Sir) Thomas, *née* Tyrwhitt, who assumed (1790) the name of Jones (although subsequent holders of the Btcy appear to have been known as Tyrwhitt) and was cr a Bt 1808; Sir Thomas's ggs, Sir Raymond Tyrwhitt, 4 Bt, inherited his mother's Barony of Berners; John Tyrwhitt of Netherclay was seventh in descent from Marmaduke Tyrwhitt, yr s of Sir William Tyrwhitt, of Kettilby; *b* 21 February 1947; *Educ* Downside; *m* 1, 1972 (m dis 1980, annulled 1984), Sheila Gail, da of late William Alistair Crawford Nicoll, of Liphook, Hants; m 2, 1984, Charlotte, o da of Capt Angus Jeremy Christopher Hildyard, DL, RA (d 1995); 1 s (Robert St John Hildyard b 1987), 1 da (Letitia Mary Hildyard b 1988); *Heir* s, Robert Tyrwhitt; *Career* served Royal Artillery 1966–69; subsequent career with cos associated with UK paper industry; *Recreations* drawing, fishing, shooting; *Style*— Sir Reginald Tyrwhitt, Bt, DL

T

TYZACK, His Hon David Ian Heslop; QC (1999); s of Ernest Rudolf Tyzack, MBE (d 1973), and Joan Mary, *née* Palmer (d 1993); *b* 21 March 1946; *Educ* Allhallows Sch, St Catharine's Coll Cambridge (MA); *m* 27 Jan 1973, Elizabeth Anne, da of Maj Henry Frank Cubitt, TD (d 1991); 1 da (Anna b 6 April 1981), 1 s (William b 12 June 1983); *Career* called to the Bar Inner Temple 1970, in practice Western Circuit, head of chambers 1988–2000, asst recorder of the Crown Court 1995–2000, recorder 2000, dep judge of High Court of Justice 2000–, circuit judge (Western Circuit) 2000–14, judge of the ct of protection 2007–, bencher Inner Temple 2007–; chm Devon & Cornwall Branch Family Law Barristers' Assoc, memb The Hon Soc of the Inner Temple 1970; *Books* Essential Family Practice (2000); *Recreations* gardening, walking, skiing, church; *Clubs* Devon and Exeter Inst; *Style*— His Hon David Tyzack, QC; ✉ Magdalen Chambers, Victory House, Dean Clarke Gardens, Southernay East, Exeter EX2 4AA

U

UCHIDA, Dame Mitsuko; DBE (2009); da of Fujio Uchida, of Tokyo, Japan, and Yasuko Uchida; *b* 20 December 1948; *Educ* Hochschule für Musik und Davstellende Kunst Vienna; *Career* pianist; artist in residence Cleveland Orch 2002–, co-dir (with Richard Goode) Marlboro Music Festival; has played with most major int orchs (repertoire ranges from Mozart to Schönberg, Méssiaen and Birtwistle); gave US première of Harrison Birtwistle's piano concerto Antiphonies with Los Angeles Philharmonic Orch and Pierre Boulez; opened Harrods Int Piano Series commemorating 150th anniversary of Chopin's death at Royal Festival Hall 2000; performed Mitsuko Uchida: Vienna Revisited series Carnegie Hall 2003; *Recordings* incl: complete Mozart piano sonatas, all Mozart piano concertos, Debussy 12 Études, R Schumann Carnaval, Beethoven piano concerto series, all Schubert sonatas and impromptus, Schoenberg Piano Concerto, Beethoven Piano Sonatas 101, 106, 109, 110 and 111; *Awards* first prize Int Beethoven Competition Vienna, second prize Int Chopin Competition Warsaw; numerous record prizes incl: The Gramophone Award 1989, Edison prize (Holland), Gramophone Award 2001, Royal Philharmonic Soc Instrumentalist Award 2004, Grammy Award 2010; *Recreations* music; *Style*— Dame Mitsuko Uchida, DBE; ✉ c/o Victoria Rowsell Artist Management, 34 Addington Square, London SE5 7LB (☎ and fax 020 7701 3219, e-mail ch@victoriarowsell.co.uk)

UDDIN, Baroness (Life Peer UK 1998), of Bethnal Green in the London Borough of Tower Hamlets; Manzila Pola Uddin; *née* Khan; da of late M Khan, and Hasma Khan; *b* 17 July 1959, Rajshahi, Bangladesh; *Educ* Plashet GS, Univ of N London; *m* 1976, Komar Uddin; 4 s (Hon Shamim b 1978, Hon Sabid b 1980, Hon Shareef b 1986, Hon Shakeeb b 1997), 1 da (Hon Tasneem b 1992); *Career* mangr Women's Projects 1982–88, successsively social worker, mangr and mgmnt conslt London Borough of Newham Social Services 1992–2000, project mangr Addaction 2008–; cncllr Shadwell Ward London Borough of Tower Hamlets Cncl 1990–98 (dep ldr Lab Gp 1993–94, dep ldr Cncl 1994–95); chair Govt Taskforce on BAME Women 2008–09; memb: Lords European Community Ctee, All-Pty Children, Women and Disablement Gp, Inter-Parly Union, Cwlth Parly Assoc; *Style*— The Baroness Uddin; ✉ House of Lords, London SW1A 0PW (☎ 020 7219 8506, e-mail uddinm@parliament.uk)

UDDIN, Dr Wali Tasar; MBE (1995), JP (1984); *b* 17 April 1952, Moulvibazar, Bangladesh; *Educ* Moulvibazar Govt HS, Putney Coll (HNC); *m* 1975, Syeda; 2 s (Shahan, Ahsan), 3 da (Hafiza, Suhaly, Ruhaly); *Career* chm and chief exec Universal Koba Corp Ltd and Britannia Spice Scot Ltd 2000–, also conslt The Verandah and Lancers Brassiere; estab Travel Link Worldwide Ltd (pres 2013–), chm and chief exec Frontline Int Air Services UK Ltd 1997–; conslt in restaurant and travel trade sectors; chm: Ornate Arcade (BD) Ltd, Holly Sylhet Holding Ltd 2012–, Dhaka Hldgs; hon consul-gen of Bangladesh in Scot 1993–98 and 2002–, chief co-ordinator Indian Earthquake Disaster Appeal Fund Scot 2001, chief co-ordinator Bangladesh Flood Victim Appeal Fund Scot, chm Bangladesh-Br C of C, founding dir Edinburgh Mela (Asian Festival) Ltd, fndr and chm Bangladesh Samity (Assoc) Edinburgh; co-ordinator Expo Bangladesh 2005, pres European-Bangladesh Fedn of Commerce and Industry, sr advsr Vision Bangladesh (project of BRAC UK); chm: Cwlth Soc Edinburgh, Bangladeshi Cncl in Scot, Scot Bangladeshi Int Humanitarian Tst, Bangla Scot Fndn, Ethnic Enterprise Centre Edinburgh; dir Edinburgh C of C 2002–; patron: Bangladesh Cyclone Disaster Appeal Fund, Royal Hosp for Sick Children Edinburgh, Scot Sch of Asian Cuisine Fife Coll, Bangladesh Inst of Journalism and Electronic Media (BIJEM); dir: Sylhet Women's Med Coll and Hosp 2005, Al-Ameen Dental Coll and Hosp; advsr Atish Dipankar Univ of Science and Technol 2004; chm Advsy Bd Univ of E London Business Sch 2004–; patron Lion Children's Hosp Sylhet 1997; tstee: Bangladesh Female Acad 2004, Shahajalal Mosque Edinburgh; memb Edinburgh Merchant Co, bd memb Cncl for Foreign C of C and Industries; exec memb Royal Cwlth Soc Edinburgh, life memb London Bangla Press Club 2013, pres European Bangladesh Fedn of Commerce and Industry (EBFCI); brand ambass and advsr Solace Global UK; Young Scot Award Int Jr C of C 1992, Lifetime Achievement Award Asian Jewel Awards 2006, listed Lloyds TSB Asian Power 100 2005; DBA (hc) Queen Margaret UC 2000, Hon DLitt Heriot-Watt Univ 2007, Hon DUniv Edinburgh Napier Univ 2007; MInstD, MCMI, FInstSMM; *Publications* Wali Uddin Blessed Son of Two Nations; *Recreations* supporting Heart of Midlothian FC and the Bangladesh cricket team, football, family, working with the televisual media (ethnic, national and international); *Clubs* Rotary Int, Edinburgh Rotary; *Style*— Dr Wali Tasar Uddin, MBE; ✉ Universal Koba Corporation Ltd, Britannia Spice Restaurant, 150 Commercial Street, Ocean Drive, Leith, Edinburgh EH6 6LB (☎ 07894 910099, e-mail drwalidba@gmail.com, website www.britanniaspice.co.uk); Frontline International Air Services Ltd, 22 Chalton Street, London NW1 1JH

UDEN, Martin David; *Educ* Univ of London (LLB); *m* Fiona; 2 s; *Career* diplomat; called to the Bar 1977; 3 sec FCO 1977–78, 2 sec Seoul 1978–81, 2 then 1 sec FCO 1981–86, 1 sec Bonn 1986–90, 1 sec FCO 1990–94, cnsllr (political) and consul-gen Seoul 1994–97, cnsllr (trade/econ) Ottawa 1997–2001, dir int InvestUK 2001–03, consul-gen San Francisco 2003–07, ambass to Repub of Korea 2008–11; *Style*— Mr Martin Uden; ✉ c/o FCO, King Charles Street, London SW1A 2AH

UFF, Prof John Francis; CBE (2002), QC (1983); s of Frederick Uff (d 1981), and Eva Uff (d 1969); *b* 30 January 1942; *Educ* Stratton Sch, KCL (BSc, PhD); *m* 29 July 1967, Diana Muriel, da of Prof Ronald Graveson, CBE; 2 s (Alexander John b 1973, Christopher Edward b 1975), 1 da (Leonora Meriel b 1977); *Career* civil engr 1966–70, called to the Bar 1970, practised in chambers of Donald Keating QC, head of chambers 1992–97; bencher of Gray's Inn 1993 (vice-treas 2010, treas 2011), recorder of Crown Court 1998–2005; appointed arbitrator in many UK and foreign commercial disputes (mostly engrg and construction), chm Ind Cmmn of Inquiry into Yorkshire Water 1996, chm Public Inquiry into Southall rail accident 1997, jt chm Public Inquiry into Train Protection Systems 1999, chm Cmmn of Enquiry into Public Construction Sector Trinidad & Tobago 2008–10; dir Centre of Construction Law and Mgmnt KCL 1987–99, Nash prof of engrg law Univ of London 1991–2003, emeritus prof of engrg law 2003–; memb Bd of Tstees Engrg Cncl 2012–; Inst of Civil Engrgs Gold Medal 2002; Master Worshipful Co of Arbitrators 2014–15; FKC 1997; FICE 1982, FCIArb 1982, FREng 1995; *Books* ICE Arbitration Practice (1985), Construction Contract Policy (1989), International and ICC Arbitration (1991), Legal Obligations in Construction (1992), Keating on Building Contracts (contrib, 2012), Chitty on Contracts (contrib, 2012), Construction Law (11 edn 2012, 12 edn 2016), Keating on Construction Contracts (contrib, 2016); *Recreations* fiddling with violins, painting, walking; *Clubs* Athenaeum; *Style*— Prof John Uff, CBE, QC, FREng; ✉ 15 Essex Street, Outer Temple, London WC2R 3AU (☎ 020 7544 2600); Pale Farm, Chipperfield Hertfordshire WD4 9BH

UFLAND, Richard Mark; s of Bertram Ufland, and Shirley, *née* Gross; *b* 4 May 1957; *Educ* St Paul's Sch, Downing Coll Cambridge (MA); *m* 20 Oct 1985, Jane Camilla, da of Louis Rapaport; 2 s (James b 1987, William b 1990), 1 da (Olivia b 1994); *Career* ptnr: Stephenson Harwood 1986–98, Hogan Lovells (formerly Lovells) 1998–; Freeman: City of London, Worshipful Co of Slrs of the City of London; memb Law Soc (former chair Company Law Ctee); *Recreations* opera, bridge, theatre, skiing; *Style*— Richard Ufland, Esq; ✉ Hogan Lovells, Atlantic House, Holborn Viaduct, London EC1A 2FG (☎ 020 7296 2000, fax 020 7296 2001, e-mail richard.ufland@hoganlovells.com)

ULIJASZEK, Prof Stanley; *b* 3 July 1954; *Educ* Victoria Univ of Manchester (BSc), Queen Elizabeth College Univ of London (MSc), KCL (PhD); *m* Pauline; 2 s (Michael, Peter), 1 da (Alexandra); *Career* Univ of Cambridge: memb Faculty of Biology 1986–2005, asst lectr, univ lectr then research assoc Dept of Biological Anthropology 1986–97, MA (by incorporation) 1990, memb CCC 1994–99; assoc prof and head Dept of Nutrition Curtin Sch of Public Health Aust 1997–99; Univ of Oxford: MA (by incorporation) 1999, univ lectr Inst of Biological Anthropology 1999–2001, univ lectr Inst of Social and Cultural Anthropology 2001–04, sr research assoc Oxford Inst of Ageing 2002–, sr research assoc Centre for Devpt Studies Queen Elizabeth House 2003–, prof of human ecology Inst of Social and Cultural Anthropology 2004– (head 2012–), fell St Cross Coll (vice-master 2010–); Japan Soc for the Promotion of Science fell and visiting prof Univ of Tokyo 1994, visiting assoc prof Univ of Pennsylvania 1994, research assoc PNG Inst of Medical Research 2001, visiting fell ANU 2004, 2005 and 2009, fell Univ of Melbourne 2005– (visiting fell 2002, 2004 and 2005), visiting prof Univ of Adelaide 2008–; ed Jl of Comparative Human Biology (Homo) 2002–, assoc ed Economics and Human Biology 2003–04; memb Editorial Bd: Jl of Biosocial Science 1991– (book review ed 1996–), Anthropologischer Anzeiger 1997–, Annals of Human Biology 1998–2004, American Jl of Human Biology 2003–08; author of numerous articles in peer-reviewed jls and chapters in books; foreign co-op researcher Kagoshima Univ Research Center for the Pacific Islands 1993–, UK rep Int Assoc of Human Biologists 1994–97, memb Review Panel Wenner-Gren Fndn for Anthropological Research 2005–08; memb: Soc for the Study of Human Biology 1983– (memb Ctee 1989–99 and 2000–09 prog sec 1991–96 and 2002–06), Nutrition Soc 1986–, Int Cmmn on the Anthropology of Food 1987–2007 (cmmr Asia-Pacific region 1997–2003), Biosocial Soc 1988– (memb Ctee 1990–99 and 2000–04, treas 1992–96), Human Biology Assoc USA 1990–, American Assoc of Physical Anthropologists 1991–, Australasian Soc for Human Biology 1993– (memb Ctee 1998–99), European Anthropological Assoc 1994– (memb Cncl 1995–98), American Anthropology Assoc 1994–, American Soc for Nutritional Sciences 1997–2007, NY Acad of Science 1997–, Int Union of Anthropological and Ethnological Sciences 1998–; *Books* Nutritional Anthropology: Prospects and Perspectives (jtly, 1993), Seasonality and Human Ecology (jt ed, 1993), Anthropometry: the Individual and the Population (jt ed, 1994, 2 edn 2005), Health Intervention in Less Developed Nations (ed, 1995), Human Energetics in Biological Anthropology (1995, 2 edn 2005), Long-term Consequences of Early Environment: Growth, Development and the Lifespan Developmental Perspective (jt ed, 1996), Human Adaptability, Past, Present, and Future (jt ed, 1997), Cambridge Encyclopedia of Human Growth and Development (jt ed, 1998), Urbanism, Health and Human Biology in Industrialised Countries (jt ed, 1999), Population, Reproduction and Fertility in Melanesia (ed, 2006), Health Change in the Asia-Pacific Region (jt ed, 2007), Holistic Anthropology (jt ed, 2007), Human Variation from Laboratory to the Field (jt ed, 2010), Insecurity, Inequality and Obesity (jt ed, 2012), Evolving Human Nutrition (jtly, 2012); *Recreations* cycling, swimming, painting; *Style*— Prof Stanley Ulijaszek; ✉ Institute of Social and Cultural Anthropology, 51 Banbury Road, Oxford OX2 6PF

ULLATHORNE, Peter Lindley; JP (SW London 1994); s of Philip Stanley Ullathorne (d 1990), and Mary Lindley, *née* Burland (d 1996); *b* 6 August 1948, Chesterfield, Derbys; *Educ* Chesterfield GS, AA Sch of Architecture (AADipl); *m* 7 Dec 2015, Ian Laing Robertson (civil partnership converted); *Career* architect; Richard Rogers Partnership 1971–74, Louis De Soissons Partnership 1974–77, GMW Partnership 1977–80, YRM Architects 1980–83, DEGW Architects 1983–86, md First Architecture Group plc 1986–89, gp dir McColl Gp Ltd 1989–91, dir Chanin Hartland Ullathorne 1991–94, vice-pres Gensler and Associates/Architects 1994–2002, vice-pres HOK International 2002–04, dir Navigant Consulting Inc 2004–08, currently princ Ullathorne Consultancy; RIBA client advsr, memb RIBA Professional Conduct Panel 2014, examiner Architectural Assoc 2014, CABE built environment expert (BEE) Design Cncl 2015; memb Assoc Parly Design Gp; visiting prof Univ of Cincinnati 1985; Freeman City of London 1990; memb AA 1971, RIBA 1974, FRSA 1989, AIA 1995, FRSH 1997; *Publications* Aqua Gp Guide to Procurement, Tendering and Contract Administration (contrib, 2013), Being an Effective Construction Client (2015); *Recreations* reading, architecture, music, opera, seaside life; *Clubs* Reform; *Style*— Peter Lindley Ullathorne, Esq; ✉ 136 Somerset Road, Wimbledon, London SW19 5HP (☎ 020 8879 1208, e-mail peteru136@aol.com, website www.ullathorne.com)

ULLMAN, Tracey; da of Anthony John Ullman (d 1966), and Dorin, *née* Cleaver; *b* 30 December 1959; *Educ* The Italia Conti Stage Sch Brixton; *m* 27 Dec 1983, Allan McKeown, *qv*; 1 da (Mabel Ellen b 2 April 1986), 1 s (John Albert Victor b 6 Aug 1991); *Career* comedy actress and singer; *Dancer* Gigi (Theatre des Westerns Berlin) 1976, Second Generation (Blackpool and Liverpool) 1977; musicals: Elvis (Astoria) 1978, Oh Boy (Astoria) 1978, Rocky Horror Show (Comedy Theatre) 1979; *Theatre* Talent (Everyman Liverpool) 1980, Dracula (Young Vic) 1980, Four in a Million (Royal Court) 1981, She Stoops to Conquer (Lyric Hammersmith) 1982, The Taming of the Shrew (NY Shakespeare Festival Broadway) 1990, The Big Love (one woman show) 1991; *Television* incl: Three of a Kind 1981–83, A Kick up the Eighties 1981 and 1983, The Young Visitors 1984, Girls on Top 1985, The Tracey Ullman Show 1987–90, Tracey Takes On 1996, Ally McBeal 1998–99, Visible Panty Lines 2001; *Film* Plenty 1984, I Love You to Death 1989, Panic 2000, Small Time Crooks 2000, C-Scam 2000, A Dirty Shame 2004; *Recordings* various top ten singles 1981–84, You Broke my Heart in Seventeen Places (album, Gold record); *Awards* Most Promising New Actress London Theatre Critics Award 1981, Best Light Entertainment Performance BAFTA 1983, five American comedy awards 1988–90, Best Female Comedy Performance Golden Globe Awards USA 1988; Emmy Awards (USA): Best Variety Show TV 1989, Best Writing 1990, Best Performance in a Variety Music or Comedy Show 1990, 1994 and 1997; *Recreations* hiking, riding, finding unspoilt areas of the earth and being quiet; *Style*— Miss Tracey Ullman

ULLSTEIN, Augustus Rupert Patrick Anthony; QC (1992); s of Frederick Charles Leopold Ullstein (d 1988), of Chiswick, London, and Patricia, *née* Guinness (d 2002); *b* 21 March 1947; *Educ* Bradfield, LSE (LLB); *m* 12 Sept 1970, Pamela Margaret, da of Claude Wells (d 1974), of Woodford, Essex; 2 da (Elizabeth b 1 June 1977, Caroline b 28 Oct 1978), 2 s (William b 3 July 1980, George b 29 April 1983); *Career* called to the Bar Inner Temple 1970; dep registrar Family Div 1987, recorder 1999– (asst recorder 1994–99); memb Cncl Acad of Experts 1995–; dir Saxon Radio 1980–87; Freeman City of London 1982, Worshipful Co of Bowyers 2002–09; *Books* The Law of Restrictive Trade Practices and Monopolies (second supplement to second edn, 1973), Matrimonial and Domestic Injunctions (1982), Compensation for Personal Injury in English, German and Italian Law (with Sir Basil Markesinis, QC); *Recreations* after dinner speaking, my children; *Style*— Augustus Ullstein, Esq, QC; ✉ 39 Essex Chambers, 81 Chancery Lane, London WC2A 1DD

ULLSWATER, 2 Viscount (UK 1921); Nicholas James Christopher Lowther; LVO (2002), PC (1994); s of Lt John Arthur Lowther, MVO, RNVR (d 1942); suc ggf, 1 Viscount Ullswater, GCB (s of late Hon William Lowther, bro of late 3 Earl of Lonsdale), 1949; *b* 9 January 1942; *Educ* Eton, Trinity Coll Cambridge; *m* 1967, Susan, da of late James Howard Weatherby, by his w Mary (4 da of Sir Hereward Wake, 13 Bt, CB, CMG, DSO, JP, DL); 2 da (Hon Emma (Hon Mrs Stewart-Smith) b 1968, Hon Clare (Hon Mrs Flawn-Thomas) b 1970), 2 s (Hon Benjamin b 1975, Hon Edward b 8 Oct 1981); *Heir* s, Hon Benjamin Lowther; *Career* Capt Royal Wessex Yeo TAVR 1973–78; a Lord in Waiting 1989–90; Parly under-sec of state Dept of Employment 1990–93, Capt HM Body Guard of Hon Corps of Gentlemen at Arms (Chief Govt Whip) 1993–94, min of state DOE 1994–95; private sec to HRH The Princess Margaret, Countess of Snowdon 1998–2002; elected to House of Lords 2003; *Style*— The Rt Hon the Viscount Ullswater, LVO, PC; ✉ Whiteacres, Cross Lane, Brancaster, King's Lynn, Norfolk PE31 8AE (☎ 01485 210488)

UNDERHILL, Prof John Richard; s of Edward James William Underhill, of Havant, Hants, and Kathleen Ivy, *née* Thorn; *b* 5 January 1961, Portsmouth; *Educ* Portsmouth GS, Univ of Bristol (BSc), Univ of Wales (PhD); *m* 25 Sept 1985, Rosemary Anne, *née* Gigg; 1 da (Laura Kathleen Anne b 5 Oct 1993), 1 s (Matthew Robert Edward b 31 March 1995); *Career* exploration geoscientist Shell International 1985–89, prof of stratigraphy Grant Inst of Earth Science Univ of Edinburgh 1989–, assoc prof Dept of Petroleum Engrg Heriot-Watt Univ; memb All Pty Parly Gp for Earth Sciences 2003–; memb Cncl Geological Soc of London; Distinguished Lectr Award European Assoc of Petroleum Geoscientists Meeting Berlin 1989 and Paris 1992, Pres's Award Geological Soc 1990, Matson Award for Excellence in Presentation American Association of Petroleum Geologists Annual Meeting Calgary 1992, American Association of Petroleum Geologists Distinguished Lectr US and Canada tour 1998–99, Wollaston Fund Geological Soc 2000; AAPG 1984, FGS 1984, FRSE 2004; *Recreations* squash, football refereeing, running; *Style*— Prof John Underhill; ✉ Grant Institute of Earth Sciences, School of Geosciences, University of Edinburgh, The King's Buildings, West Mains Road, Edinburgh EH9 3JW (☎ 0131 650 1000, fax 0131 668 3184, e-mail jru@glg.ed.ac.uk)

UNDERHILL, Rt Hon Lord Justice; Sir Nicholas Edward Underhill; kt (2006), PC (2013); s of Michael Thomas Ben Underhill (d 1987), and Rosalie Jean Beaumont, *née* Kinloch (d 2010); *b* 12 May 1952; *Educ* Winchester, New Coll Oxford (MA); *m* 1987, Nina Charlotte Margarete, *née* Grunfeld; 2 s (b 1987 and 1998), 2 da (b 1990 and 1992); *Career* called to the Bar Gray's Inn 1976 (bencher 2000); QC 1992, recorder of the Crown Court 1994–2006, judge of the High Court of Justice (Queen's Bench Div) 2006–13 (dep judge1998–2006), a Lord Justice of Appeal 2013–; judge Employment Appeal Tbnl 2000–03 and 2006–13; Attorney-Gen to HRH The Prince of Wales 1998–2006; chair Bar Pro Bono Unit 2002–05, pres Employment Appeal Tbnl 2009–11; tstee St John's Smith Square 1996–2014 (chair 2010–13), tstee London Library 2008–12 (vice-chair 2011–12); hon fell New Coll Oxford 2015; *Books* The Lord Chancellor (1976); *Style*— The Rt Hon the Lord Justice Underhill; ✉ Royal Courts of Justice, Strand, London WC2A 2LL

UNDERHILL, Nicholas Peter; s of Kenneth Underhill, and Evelyn Ellen, *née* Barnard; *b* 15 January 1955; *Educ* William Ellis Sch; *m* 28 July 1973, Julie Ann Evelyn, da of Wilfred Augustus Michael Chard, of London; 4 s (Matthew, James, Julian, Oliver), 1 da (Lyndsey); *Career* property advtg mangr Evening Standard 1974–75, ptnr Druce & Co 1978–81, equity ptnr Hampton & Sons 1986–87, md Hamptons (estate agents) 1988–89, chm Underhill Group of Companies 1989–92; dir: Keith Cardale Groves 1992–96, Hamptons International 1996–98, Stirling Ackroyd Hong Kong and Dublin 1998–2003; md Stirling Ackroyd 1998–2003; currently: md City and Mayfair Properties, dir and head of int residential devpt Chesterton Humberts; chm Mayfair Media Marketing 1998–2002; memb Land Inst; *Recreations* shooting, rugby, skiing, opera, real tennis; *Clubs* Carlton, MCC, Saracens RFC, Lord's Taverners, Annabel's; *Style*— Nicholas Underhill, Esq; ✉ e-mail nick.underhill@chestertonhumberts.com

UNDERHILL, (Christopher) William Youard; s of Christopher James Avery Underhill, and Frances Mary Underhill; *Educ* LSE (LLB); *m* 1999, Maxine Louise Harrison; *Career* slr; Slaughter and May: joined 1981, ptnr 1990–; memb Law Soc, memb City of London Solicitors' Co; *Style*— William Underhill, Esq; ✉ Slaughter and May, One Bunhill Row, London EC1Y 8YY (☎ 020 7090 3060, e-mail william.underhill@slaughterandmay.com)

UNDERWOOD, Ashley Grenville; QC (2001); s of Dennis William Underwood (d 1995), and Brenda Stephenson, *née* Witts; *b* 28 December 1953, Kent; *Educ* LSE (LLB); *m* 28 Aug 1982, Heather, *née* Legget; 1 da (Sally Davina b 22 July 1986); *Career* called to the Bar Gray's Inn 1976 (master); head of chambers 2 Field Court 1999–2006, now memb Cornerstone Barristers 2–3 Gray's Inn Square; leading counsel: Robert Hamill Inquiry, Azelle Rodney Inquiry, Mark Duggan Inquest; *Publications* Hill and Redman (ed); *Recreations* sailing, classic cars; *Clubs* Sloane; *Style*— Ashley Underwood, Esq, QC; ✉ Cornerstone Barristers, 2–3 Gray's Inn Square, London WC1R 5JH (☎ 020 7242 4986, e-mail ashleyu@cornerstonebarristers.com)

UNDERWOOD, Prof Geoffrey; s of Stanley Underwood (d 1978), of Hull, E Yorks, and Marjorie, *née* Hulme (d 2003); *b* 16 May 1947, Hull, E Yorks; *Educ* Kelvin Hall Hull, Bedford Coll London (BSc), Univ of Sheffield (PhD); *m* 1 Aug 1969, Jean Dianne Marina, *née* Strange; *Career* Univ of Nottingham: lectr in psychology 1972–86, sr lectr in psychology 1986–88, reader in cognitive psychology 1988–90, prof of cognitive psychology 1990–, head Sch of Psychology 1998–2001; asst prof of psychology Univ of Waterloo Canada 1974–75; ed Br Jl of Psychology 2000–05; Hon DSc Univ of London 1995; FBPsS 1994, FRSA 2002; *Books* Computers and Learning (with Jean Underwood, 1990), Eye Guidance in Reading and Scene Perception (ed, 1998), Oxford Guide to the Mind (ed, 2001); *Recreations* skiing, mountain walking, supporting Hull City FC; *Style*— Prof Geoffrey Underwood; ✉ School of Psychology, University of Nottingham, University Park, Nottingham NG7 2RD (☎ 0115 951 5313, fax 0115 951 5311, e-mail geoff.underwood@nottingham.ac.uk)

UNDERWOOD, Grahame John Taylor; s of Wing Cdr Shirley Taylor Underwood, OBE (d 2011), and Joyce Mary, *née* Smith; *b* 1 July 1944, Kirby Muxloe, Leics; *Educ* Ashby de la Zouch GS, Poly of N London (DipArch); *m* 4 May 1968, Christine Elva, da of Sqdn Ldr Cecil Reginald Long, MBE, DSM (d 1972); 2 s (Christopher Taylor b 1971, Toby Grahame b 1972), 1 da (Lucy Jane b 1974); *Career* Watkins Gray International: architect and planner 1969–72, assoc 1972–83, ptnr and dir 1983–, gp chm 2003–07; dir: Watkins Gray Peter Jones 1983–90, Watkins Gray International Ltd 1983–2007, Watkins Gray Ho & Partners 1989–2000, WGI Interiors Ltd 1997–2007, WGI Sports and Leisure Ltd 1997–2007, WGI Education Ltd 1998–2000, WGI Housing Ltd 1999–2002, WGI Leeds Ltd 1999–2007, GGA WatkinsGray Ltd 2001–07, WGI Halliday Meecham Ltd 2003–07, Wren Insurance Assoc Ltd 2003–06; memb Watkins Gray International LLP 2002–07 (conslt 2007–); princ designs incl: Royal Masonic Hosp, Nat Heart and Chest Hosps London and Baghdad, Dammam and Unayzah Hosps Saudi Arabia, Bromley Hosp, Orpington Hosp, Ekaterinburg Cardiology Hosp and Oncology Hosp, Togliatti Maternity Hosp, Belfast Children's Hosp (design competition winner), Altnagelvin Hosp, Joyce Green Hosp, health planning for govts of Syria and Indonesia, Kwong Wah Hosp Hong Kong, Mater Infirmorum Belfast (design competition winner), Downpatrick Community Hosp (design competition winner), Ambulatory Care Centre Birmingham, Sha Tin Dementia Centre Hong Kong, E Kent Hosps Master Plan, Peterborough Hosps Master Plan, Dundonald Hosp Belfast, St George's Hosp London, Cork Univ Hosp, Kent Cardiac Centre, master plan Antrim Hosp, Craigavon Hosp, Ulster Hosp, Shropshire Community Care, Enniskillen and Omagh Hosps, Northampton Mental Health Hosp, 3 Shires Community Hosp Prog, ExtraCare housing prog Salops, luxury housing Brisbane, Jersey General Hosp, Overdale Hosp Jersey; fndr memb Care Health Planning; memb NHS Design Review Panel 2007–, design champion Salops CC, design champion States of Jersey 2013–; chair Mental Health Assessment Panel Maidstone 2012, memb Advsy Ctee Mid Kent Coll 2012, ldr Kent Young Entrepreneurs' Challenge 2012 and 2013, business mentor Kent Young Entrepreneurs 2016–; chm Edgbaston Round Table 1984, dir Kent Gliding Club (chm 1998–2003 and 2013–); fndr and ceo GU Consulting Ltd 2013–; Liveryman Honourable Co of Air Pilots 2014 (formerly Guild of Air Pilots and Air Navigators (Freeman 1993, Liveryman 2006)); RIBA 1973, MRIN 1996; *Books* Architects Jl Handbook of Ironmongery (1979), The Security of Buildings (1984); author of numerous tech articles; *Recreations* flying, gliding, riding, travel, art, design, creative writing, history; *Clubs* RAF; *Style*— Grahame Underwood, Esq; ☎ 01622 631734, e-mail gu@gjtu.com, website www.gjtu.com

UNDERWOOD, Prof Ian; s of Robert Underwood, of Airdrie, and Mary, *née* O'Connor; *b* 24 June 1959, Airdrie; *Educ* Univ of Glasgow (BSc), Univ of Strathclyde (MSc), Univ of Edinburgh (PhD); *m* 11 Sept 2002, Muriel June; 1 da (Victoria Joy), 1 s (James Robert); *Career* Univ of Edinburgh: lectr 1989, reader 1999, prof 2005; Microemissive Displays Ltd: co-fndr 1999, dir of product devpt 2001, dir of strategic mktg 2003; design authy for the world's smallest colour TV screen Guinness Book of Records 2004; Fulbright fell 1991; Ben Sturgeon Award Soc for Information Display 1999, Ernst & Young Emerging Entrepreneur of the Year 2003, Gannochy Prize for Innovation RSE 2004; memb Soc of Information Display; MIEEE, FRSE 2004; *Style*— Prof Ian Underwood; ✉ Scottish Microelectronics Centre, West Mains Road, Edinburgh EH9 3BU

UNDERWOOD, Kerry; s of Ernest Albert Underwood, of Harrow, Middlesex, and Jeanie, *née* Barr; *b* 4 June 1956, South Ruislip, London; *Educ* Trent Poly, Coll of Law; *Career* admitted slr 1981; ptnr Tilley Underwood 1986–90, sr ptnr Underwoods Slrs 1991–, sr ptnr Underwoods South Africa; judge Employment Tbnls 1993–2000; conslt LexisNexis, conslt to various Cwlth countries; chief exec Law Abroad plc; involved with: Toynbee Hall (vol memb legal advice team), Lord Taverners charity; lectr, writer, blogger and broadcaster; columnist: Litigation Funding, Claims Magazine, New Law Jl, Slrs Jl, Law Soc Civil Justice Section Newsletter; cncllr (Lab) London Borough of Harrow 1978–82, Parly candidate (Lab) Worthing 1979; qualified cricket umpire; KStJ; *Books* No Win, No Fee, No Worries (1998, revised edn 2000), Fixed Costs (2004, 2 edn 2006), Insurance Disputes, Kerry on... Qualified One-Way Costs Shifting, Section 57 and Set-Off (2016), Selected Writings: Vol 1 (2016), My Dad and Other Writings (2016), Kerry on... Fixed Costs, Portals and Small Claims; *Recreations* cricket, football, travelling, photography, literature, gardening, Elvis Presley, T S Eliot; *Clubs* Queen's Park Rangers FC, Lord's Taverners, Bovingdon CC, Hemel Hempstead Town FC (sponsors), Hemel Stags Rugby League Club (sponsors); *Style*— Kerry Underwood, Esq; ✉ Underwoods Solicitors, 79 Marlowes, Hemel Hempstead HP1 1LF (☎ 01442 430900, e-mail kerry.underwood@lawabroad.co.uk, blog http://kerryunderwood.wordpress.com, Twitter @kerry_underwood)

UNDERWOOD, Susan Lois; OBE; da of John Ayton Underwood, of St Andrews, and Sheila Lois, *née* Rankin; *b* 6 August 1956; *Educ* Kilgraston Sch, Allhallows Sch, Univ of St Andrews (MA), Univ of Leicester (grad cert mus studies), TEFL; *Children* 1 da (Mitya Susan Underwood b 16 July 1983), 1 s (Callum John Underwood b 17 June 1987); *Career* res supvr Yorkshire & Humberside Museums Cncl 1981–82, volunteer Yorkshire Museum of Farming 1982–83, curator Nat Railway Museum York 1983–84, keeper of local history Scunthorpe Museum and Art Gall 1985–88, dir NE Museums 1990–2001 (dep dir 1988–90), chief exec NE Museums Libraries and Archives Cncl 2001–05, dir Sharjah Museums Dept UAE 2005–; pres Museums North 1992–93; chair: Social History Curators Gp 1990–91, East End Carers (Newcastle) 1996–97; Bd memb: Northern Centre for Contemporary Art 1990–92, Northern Arts 1992–98, Live Theatre Co Ltd 1992–97; memb Nat Tst Regnl Ctee 1996–2003; memb Cncl Univ of Newcastle 1998–; tstee Baltic Flour Mills Visual Arts Tst 1998–2004; cmmr English Heritage 1997–2004; examiner Mus Assoc dip 1990–92, external examiner Museum Studies Univ of Leicester 1998–; FMA 1993 (AMA 1985); *Recreations* walking, tennis, the arts, spending time with my children; *Clubs* St Rules Golf (St Andrews); *Style*— Miss Susan Underwood, OBE

UNMACK, Timothy Stuart Brooke; s of Randall Carter Unmack (d 1978), and Anne Roberta, *née* Stuart (d 1972); *b* 5 August 1937; *Educ* Radley, Christ Church Oxford (MA); *m* 21 May 1966, Eleanor Gillian, da of George Aidan Drury Tait (d 1970); 2 s (Guy Douglas b 13 March 1975, Neil Alexander b 29 July 1977); *Career* Nat Serv RN; admitted slr 1965, sr ptnr Beaumont and Son 1987–97 (ptnr 1968–97), Shadbolt & Co: conslt 1998–2000, ptnr 2000–04; conslt Clyde & Co 2004–13; chm Central Asia and Transcaucasia Law Assoc; memb Int Law Assoc's Ctee on Legal Aspects of Air Traffic Control, memb Trade Terms Working Pty of Int C of C 1976; dir HealthProm; former chm Royal Philanthropic Soc Redhill; memb Worshipful Co of Barbers; memb: Law Soc 1965, Royal Soc for Asian Affairs 1987, fell Royal Aeronautical Soc 2004; *Books* Civil Aviation: Standards and Liabilities; *Recreations* sailing, languages; *Clubs* Oxford and Cambridge; *Style*— Timothy Unmack, Esq; ✉ 43 Pilgrims Way, Reigate, Surrey RH2 9LG

UNSWORTH, Prof Anthony; s of James Unsworth (d 1984), and Annie, *née* Halliwell (d 2000); *b* 7 February 1945; *Educ* Worsley Coll, Warrington Tech Coll, Univ of Salford (BSc Mechanical Engrg (1st class)), Univ of Leeds (MSc, Samuel Denison Prize, PhD, DEng); *m* 22 Dec 1967, Jill, da of late Kenneth Chetwood; *Career* apprentice David Brown Corp 1961, research engr David Brown Gear Industries 1967–69, ARC lectr in bioengineering Univ of Leeds 1971–76 (ARC research fell 1969–71); Durham Univ: lectr 1976–79, sr lectr 1979–83 (visiting research scientist Mechanical and Aerospace Engrg Cornell Univ NY 1981), reader 1983–89, memb Senate 1984–87, 1990–94 and 1996–2006, prof of engrg 1989– (now emeritus prof), chm Sch of Engrg and Applied Sci 1989–94 and 2000–2006, dir Centre for Biomedical Engrg 1989–2012, memb Cncl 1993–2003, dean of science 1994–2000, dir of research Faculty of Science 2006–10, also memb or chm numerous univ ctees; memb Ctee Engrg in Med Gp IMechE 1984– (chm 1989–92), memb HEFCE Res Assessment Panels for Engrg (RAE2001 and RAE2008) Output Assessor for REF2014 (Gen Engrg), memb Ctee ACTION Research 1989–95 (chm Bioengineering

Advsy Panel 1992–95); memb Bd of Govrs Univ of Teesside (formerly Poly) 1986–2000, dir ACTION (charity) 1992–95, memb S Durham HA 1993–96; chm: S Durham Research Ethics Ctee 1993–96, Northern Regnl Research Ethics Ctee 1995–96; memb Editorial Bd: Jl of Orthopaedic Rheumatology 1987–98, Current Orthopaedics 1988–98; ed Engrg in Med Newsletter IMechE 1988–90, ed Proceedings of Instn of Mech Engrs Part H Engrg in Med 1993– (memb Editorial Bd 1988–); scientific referee for papers submitted to various learned jls; author of over 320 publications; deliverer of over 150 lectures to learned socs (incl 60 overseas); Tribology Silver Medal IMechE 1972, Donald Julius Groen Prize IMechE 1991, James Clayton Prize IMechE 1999, James Alfred Ewing Medal ICE 2005, Int Soc for Technol in Arthroplasty Lifetime Achievement Award 2011; hon life memb Int Soc for Technol in Arthroplasty 2013; FIMechE 1984 (MIMechE 1972, vice-pres 2008–11), FREng 1996, FICE 2003–12; *Recreations* singing operetta and sacred music; *Style—* Prof Anthony Unsworth, FREng; ✉ School of Engineering, University of Durham, South Road, Durham DH1 3LE (☎ 0191 334 2521, e-mail tony.unsworth@durham.ac.uk)

UNSWORTH, Michael Anthony; s of Lt Cdr John Geoffrey Unsworth, MBE, of Hayling Island, Hants, and Joan Rhyllis, *née* Clemes; *b* 29 October 1949; *Educ* St John's Coll Southsea, Enfield Coll of Technol (BA); *m* 1 Dec 1973, Masa, da of Prof Zitomir Lozica, of Orebic, Croatia; 2 da (Tania Elizabeth b 10 Oct 1978, Tessa Joanna b 27 June 1981); *Career* res analyst Grieveson Grant & Co 1972–79; Scott Goff Hancock & Co: sr oil analyst 1979–81, ptnr 1981–86, co merged with Smith Bros to form Smith New Court plc 1986, dir i/c energy res 1986–95, dir i/c res 1989–95, Bd dir 1991–95, md Capital Markets 1994–95; dep chief exec Smith New Court Far East Ltd 1995, head of research Asia Pacific Region Merrill Lynch 1995–98, co-ceo Merrill Lynch Phatra Securities Co 1998–2000; pres Supervisory Bd Jadran Capital dd; dir: Smart City People (Thailand) Recruitment Co Ltd, Clipper Hldgs Ltd, dwp Gp; *Recreations* sailing, opera, theatre; *Clubs* Royal Bangkok Sports, British Bangkok, Little Ship, J K Labud; *Style—* Michael Unsworth, Esq

UNSWORTH, Dr Philip Francis; s of Stephen Unsworth (d 1959), of Manchester, and Teresa *née* McElin (d 1997); *b* 18 September 1947; *Educ* St Bede's Coll, Univ of Manchester (BSc, MB ChB); *Career* house surgn and physician Manchester Royal Inf 1971–72; lectr: Middlesex Hosp 1972–75, St Thomas' Hosp 1975–76; microbiologist Colindale 1977–79; undergraduate clinical tutor Tameside Hosp 1980–2003; conslt microbiologist: Tameside and Glossop DHA 1979–94, Tameside and Glossop Acute Services NHS Tst 1994–2008, Tameside Hosp NHS Fndn Tst 2008–; hon clinical lectr in Med Microbiology Manchester Med Sch 1999–; memb: Hospital Infection Soc 1981–, Br Infection Assoc, Br Soc of Antimicrobial Chemotherapy; FRCPath 1989 (MRCPath 1978); *Recreations* reading, sports, walking, music, languages; *Style—* Dr Philip Unsworth; ✉ Department of Microbiology, Tameside Hospital NHS Foundation Trust, Ashton-under-Lyne, Lancashire OL6 9RW (☎ 0161 922 6500, fax 0161 922 4414, e-mail philip.unsworth@tgh.nhs.uk)

UNWIN, Sir (James) Brian; KCB (1990); s of Reginald Unwin (d 1975), and Winifred Annie, *née* Walthall (d 1989); *b* 21 September 1935; *Educ* Chesterfield Sch, New Coll Oxford (MA), Yale Univ (MA); *m* 5 May 1964, Diana Susan, da of Sir David Aubrey Scott, GCMG; 3 s (Michael Alexander, Christopher James, Nicholas Edward); *Career* Nat Serv 2 Lt (Sherwood Foresters) 1953–55, HM Civil Serv: asst princ CRO 1960, private sec to High Cmmr Fedn of Rhodesia and Nyasaland 1961–64, first sec Accra 1964–65, FCO 1965–68, HM Treasy 1968–85 (private sec to chief sec 1970–72, asst sec 1972, under sec 1976, seconded to Cabinet Office 1981–83, dep sec 1983–85), UK dir European Investment Bank 1983–85, dep sec Cabinet Office 1985–87, chm of the Bd HM Customs & Excise 1987–93, pres European Investment Bank 1993–99 (hon pres 2000–), govr European Bank for Reconstruction and Development 1993–99, chm Supervisory Bd European Investment Fund 1994–99; chm Asset Trust Housing Ltd 2003–12, chm Asset Trust Housing Assoc 2012–14; memb: Bd of Dirs ENO 1993–94 and 2000–08 (hon sec 1987–93), Bd Centre d'Etudes Prospectives (CEPROS) 1996–2000, Bd Fondation Pierre Werner Luxembourg 1998–2000, Bd of Dirs Dexia 2000–10, Cncl Federal Tst for Educn and Research 2003–; chm: Civil Serv Sports Cncl 1989–93, Customs Co-operation Cncl 1991–92; pres European Centre for Nature Conservation (ECNC) 2001–13 (hon pres 2014–); chm European Task Force on Banking and Biodiversity 2003–09; hon fell New Coll Oxford 1997, pres New Coll Soc 2004–08; CIMgt 1988; Médaille d'Or Fondation du Mérite Européen 1995, Grand Offr L'Ordre de la Couronne (Belgium) 2001, Grand Croix de l'Ordre Grand Ducal de la Couronne de Chêne (Luxembourg) 2001, Cdr Order of Ouissam Aloui (Morocco) 1998; *Publications* Terrible Exile: The Last Days of Napoleon on St Helena (2010, shortlisted Fndn Napoléon History Prize), Financial Regulation: Britain's Next European Challenge (jtly, 2010), A Tale in Two Cities: Fanny Burney and Adèle, Comtesse de Boigne (2014); *Recreations* bird watching, opera, Wellingtoniana, Trollope; *Clubs* Reform; *Style—* Sir Brian Unwin, KCB; ✉ c/o Reform Club, 104 Pall Mall, London SW1Y 5EW

UNWIN, (Eric) Geoffrey (Geoff); s of Maurice Doughty Unwin, and Olive Milburn, *née* Watson; *b* 9 August 1942; *Educ* Heaton GS Newcastle upon Tyne, Kings Coll Durham (BSc); *m* 1 July 1967, Margaret Bronia, *née* Element; 1 s (b 1 May 1973), 1 da (b 25 April 1975); *Career* with Cadbury 1963–68; Hoskyns Group plc (computer servs gp): joined John Hoskyns & Co 1968, md Hoskyns Systems Development 1978, dir Hoskyns Group plc 1982–93, md 1984–88 (incl Stock Exchange flotation 1986), exec chm 1988–93; chief operating offr Cap Gemini Sogeti 1993–2000, ceo Cap Gemini Ernst & Young 2000–02, memb Bd Cap Gemini Gp (formerly Cap Gemini Ernst & Young) 2000–02 (non-voting memb 2002–12); non-exec dir United News & Media plc 1995–2002, chm United Business Media 2002–07; chm: Trigenix Ltd (formerly 3G Lab) until 2002, Halma plc 2003–13 (dep chm 2002), Liberata plc 2003–11, Omnibus Systems Ltd 2005–10, The Cloud Networks Ltd 2005–06, Taptu Ltd 2007–12, ReD 2011–, OpenCloud 2011–, Xchanging plc 2012–, Tryzens Hldgs Ltd 2014–; non-exec dir Towry Hldgs Ltd 2014–; pres UK Computing Servs Assoc 1987–88, memb Info Technol Advsy Bd 1988–91; Freeman City of London 1987, fndr memb and Liveryman Worshipful Co of Information Technologists 1987; CIMgt 1987 (memb Bd of Companions 1990–93); *Recreations* golf, skiing, the Arts, theatre, gardening, riding; *Clubs* RAC, Hendon Golf, Hunstanton Golf, Royal North West Norfolk Golf, Morfontaine Golf (France); *Style—* Geoff Unwin, Esq; ✉ e-mail geoff.unwin@gunwin.co.uk

UNWIN, Julia; CBE (2006, OBE 2000); da of P W Unwin, and Monica Unwin; *b* 6 July 1956; *Educ* Univ of Liverpool (BA), Open Univ (Dip Effective Mgmnt), LSE (MSc); *Partner* Patrick Kelly; 2 da; *Career* health and social services field worker Liverpool Cncl for Voluntary Service 1978–80, community liaison offr Social Services Dept London Borough of Southwark 1980–82, head Voluntary Sector Liaison Team Gr London Cncl 1982–86, dir Homeless Network 1986–92, memb Bd Housing Corp 1992–2002 (chair Investment Ctee 1992–2001), cmmr Charity Commission 1998–2003, dep chair Food Standards Agency 2003–; freelance conslt work 1993–: sr assoc and chair Cmmn of Inquiry into Care Market Kings Fund, ind advsr Natwest Gp Charitable Tst 1995–2000, policy advsr Baring Fndn and Nat Lottery Charities Bd, and memb Cabinet Office Peer Reviews of Govt Depts; ind adjudicator Audit Cmmn 2001–04; DTI: ind memb Mgmnt Bd Fair Markets Gp 2002–, memb Audit Ctee 2002–; memb: Bd QUEST 1999–2002, Ctee of Reference and Ethical Investment Ctee Friends Provident 2000– (chair 2004–), Bd Nat Consumer Cncl 2001–; chair Refugee Cncl 1995–98, tstee Public Mgmnt Fndn 1997–2001, memb Public Interest Gen Cncl Office for Public Mgmnt 2003–; *Publications* Who Pays for Core Costs? (1999), The Grant Making Tango (2004); *Style—* Ms Julia Unwin, CBE; ✉ Food Standards Agency, Aviation House, 125 Kingsway, London WC2B 6NH

UNWIN, Vicky; da of Thomas Michael Unwin, of Milverton, Somerset, and Sheila Margaret Findlay Mills; *b* 3 November 1957; *Educ* Wycombe Abbey, Oxford HS, Girton Coll Cambridge (BA); *m* 18 June 1983, Ross Brett Cattell, s of Dr William Ross Cattell, of London; 1 s (Thomas William b 21 Jan 1988), 1 da (Louise Ann b 7 Dec 1989 d 2011); *Career* dir Heinemann Educnl Boleswa 1987–93, publishing dir Heinemann Educnl Books 1987–90 (graduate traineeship 1979–80), md Heinemann International Literature and Textbooks 1990–93, ptnr Specialist Advsy Gp on Africa 1993–96, mangr Telegraph Books 1996–97, dir of Enterprises Telegraph Gp Ltd 1997–99, md PRNewswire Europe 1999–2003, md World Publications Ltd 2003–05, chief exec Third Millennium Information Ltd 2005, media dir Aga Khan Fund for Econ Devpt 2006–08, chm Art First Ltd; film critic and travel writer; memb Caine Prize Cncl 2011–; sec Int Charity Assoc for Teaching Caribbean and African Literature 1984–87; ambass Angelus Fndn; *Recreations* skiing, walking, riding, gardening, reading, diving, visual and performing arts; *Clubs* Hospital, 2 Brydges Place; *Style—* Ms Vicky Unwin; ✉ 4 Parkhill Road, London NW3 2YN (☎ 020 7424 9423, e-mail vickyunwin@blueyonder.co.uk, websites www.vickygoestravelling.com, www.vickyatthemovies.net, www.healthylivingwithcancer.com)

UPPAL, Paul Singh; *b* Birmingham; *Educ* Univ of Warwick; *Career* MP (Cons) Wolverhampton SW 2010–15; *Style—* Paul Uppal, Esq; ✉ House of Commons, London SW1A 0AA

UPSHON, Laurence Marshall (Laurie); s of Lt-Col Hector Llewellyn Marshall Upshon (d 1957), and Hilda Winifred, *née* Southgate; *b* 21 June 1950; *Educ* St Peter's Sch Merrow; *m* 18 July 1970, Heide Maria, da of Gustav Hawlin, of Salzburg, Austria; 1 da (Claire b 1976), 2 s (Rupert b 1977, Robin b 1979); *Career* asst gp ed Stratford Express Gp 1974–76, Southern TV 1976–87 (features ed 1980); TVS Television: exec prodr news and current affairs 1982–84 (sr prodr 1981), ed Coast to Coast 1984–85; controller of news and operations ITV Central (formerly Carlton Broadcasting Central Region) 1995– (ed Central News 1985, controller of news Central Television 1989–95); fndr chm Media Archive for Central England; training conslt Thomson Fndn; dir: Central Independent Television, Digital Media Centre Univ of Central England, Upshon Media Ltd 2005–; life vice-pres Newspaper Press Fund 1999–, chm Journalists' Charity 2013–14; memb RTNDA(US); FRTS 1997; *Recreations* sport (cricket), painting, reading, music; *Style—* Laurie Upshon, Esq

UPTON, Prof Graham; DL (Oxfordshire 2014); s of late William Upton, of Sydney, Aust, and Edna May, *née* Groves; *b* 30 April 1944; *Educ* Univ of Sydney (MA, DipEd), Univ of NSW (MEd), Univ of Wales (PhD); *m* 1 (m dis 1984), Jennifer Ann; 1 s (Stuart Ingham b 10 Jan 1969), 1 da (Sonja Cape b 13 March 1970); m 2, Elizabeth Mary Hayward, da of Jack Speed; 1 s (James Llewellyn b 20 Dec 1986), 1 da (Hermione Catherine b 19 Jan 1988); *Career* schoolteacher NSW 1966–71, lectr in special educn Leeds Poly 1972–74; UC Cardiff 1974–88: lectr, sr lectr, reader, head Dept of Educn, dean Faculty of Educn; pro-vice-chllr Univ of Birmingham 1993–97 (prof of educn and head Sch of Educn 1988–93), vice-chllr Oxford Brookes Univ 1997–2007; conslt Miny of Educn Brunei Darussalam 2007–10; interim vice-chllr Univ of Cumbria 2010–11, interim vice-chllr Glynd?r University 2015–16; chair Oxfordshire Community Partnership 2002–07, chair Experience Oxfordshire 2013–; memb Cncl Headington Sch Oxford 1999–2007, pres Oxford Playhouse 2009–15 (memb Bd 2001–09, chair 2005–09); chair Oxford Expressions Technol, memb Bd of Govrs UWE, hon fell Univ of Cumbria 2012; Sheriff Oxon County 2012–13, High Sheriff Oxon County 2013–14; Hon DUniv Oxford Brookes; FBPsS 1996, FRSA 1999, AcSS 2000; *Books* Physical & Creative Activities for the Mentally Handicapped (1979), Educating Children with Behaviour Problems (1983), Staff Training and Special Education Needs (1991), Special Educational Needs (1992), Emotional and Behavioural Difficulties (1994), Voice of the Child (1996), Effective Schooling for Pupils with Emotional and Behavioural Difficulties (1998); *Recreations* long distance cycling, theatre; *Style—* Prof Graham Upton, DL; ✉ e-mail grahamupton@hotmail.co.uk

UPTON, Paul David; s of John Clement and Deidre Joy Upton, of Bexleyheath; *b* 19 August 1960; *Educ* Bexley & Erith Tech HS for Boys, Univ of Sussex (BA); *m* 1986, Esther Helen Eva, da of Eric Slade; 3 s (Samuel b 1987, Alexander b 1989, William b 1995); *Career* Lloyd's underwriter; marine underwriter Cigna Re (UK) Co Ltd 1983–87; former reinsurance underwriter and active underwriter Kingsmead Underwriting Agency Ltd (formerly Claremount Underwriting Agency Ltd), former active underwriter Advent Syndicate 780; underwriter marine and energy Endurance Worldwide Insurance Ltd 2004–; ACII 1995; *Recreations* most sports, classical music, Chelsea FC; *Style—* Paul Upton, Esq

URBAN, Mark; s of Harry Urban, and Josephine Urban; *b* 1961, London; *Educ* KCS Wimbledon, LSE; *m* 1993; 1 s, 2 da; *Career* asst prodr BBC 1983–86, def corr The Independent 1986–90, reporter Newsnight (BBC) 1990–93, ME corr BBC 1993–94, dip ed Newsnight (BBC) 1995–; tstee Royal Armouries 2012–; *Publications* Soviet Land Power (1983), War in Afghanistan (1987), Big Boys' Rules (1992), UK Eyes Alpha (1996), The Illegal (1996), The Linguist (1998), The Man Who Broke Napoleon's Codes (2001), Rifles: Six Years with Wellington's Legendary Sharpshooters (2003), Generals: Ten British Commanders Who Shaped the World (2005), Fusiliers: Eight Years with the Redcoats in America (2007), Task Force Black: The Explosive True Story of the Special Forces War in Iraq (2010), The Tank War, the Men, the Machines and the Long Road to Victory (2013); *Style—* Mark Urban, Esq; ✉ Newsnight, Zone D3, New Broadcasting House, London W1A 1AA

URBAN, Stuart; s of Dr Garri Urban, of Caracas, Venezuela, and Josephine Maureen, *née* Johnson; *b* 11 September 1958; *Educ* KCS Wimbledon, Balliol Coll Oxford (exhibitioner, MA); *m* 12 July 1987, Dr Dana Beanov, da of Ilija Beanov; 1 da (Leah Jessie Rebecca b 13 Sept 1988), 1 s (David Alexander b 2 March 1991); *Career* writer and director; made two as teenager (The Virus of War 1972 and Spaghetti Special 1974) since preserved in Nat Film Archive; professional debut as dir Pocketful of Dreams (BBC Playhouse) 1981; dir of series incl: Bergerac, The Bill, Our Friends in the North; writer and dir An Ungentlemanly Act (BBC); writer Deadly Voyage (HBO/BBC) 1996, writer/prodr/dir Preaching to the Perverted (feature film) 1997, writer/prod/dir/co-writer (with Harold Pinter) Against the War (BBC) 1999, writer/prod/dir Revelation (feature film) 2001, writer/prod/dir Tovarisch I Am Not Dead (doc feature) 2007 (Lancia Award Italy, Silver Medal NY Festivals, nomination Br Ind Film Awards, shortlist Grierson Award), writer/prod/dir May I Kill U? (feature film, Melies D'Argent 2013); writer/exec prod The Secret (miniseries) ITV starring James Nesbitt 2016; *Awards* BAFTA Award for Best Single Drama 1992, Gold Plaques (best TV movie, best direction) and Silver Plaque (screenplay) Chicago Film Festival 1992, BAFTA Award for Best Drama Serial and RTS Best Drama Serial (Our Friends in the North) 1996, Monte Carlo Silver Nymph for Best Screen Play (Deadly Voyage) 1997; *Publications* Hors de Combat Vol II (contrib); *Recreations* snow and water skiing; *Clubs* Annabel's, Tramp; *Style—* Stuart Urban, Esq; ✉ c/o Conrad Williams, Blake Friedman Literary Agency, First Floor, Selous House, 5–12 Mandela Street, London NW1 0DU; website www.tovarisch.net

URE, James (Midge); OBE (2005); *b* 10 October 1953; *Career* singer, songwriter, prodr and video dir; with bands: Slik (number one single Forever and Ever 1976), The Rich Kids, Thin Lizzy (for USA tour 1979), Visage (Visage and Anvil albums), Ultravox 1979–86; albums with Ultravox: Vienna 1980, Rage in Eden 1981, Quartet 1982, Lament 1984, The

Collection 1984, U Vox 1986, If I Was – The Very Best of Ultravox 1993; solo albums: The Gift 1985, Answers 1988, Pure 1991; co-writer and prodr Band Aid's Do They Know It's Christmas? 1984 (UK's biggest selling single); composer film music: Max Headroom (C4), Turnaround (Major Film Prodns), Playboy Late Night Theme (Playboy Channel); has produced records and directed videos for various other artists; tstee Band Aid; musical dir: Prince's Tst 1986–88 and 2010, Nelson Mandela Concert 1988; *Style*— Midge Ure, Esq, OBE

URE, Jean Ann; da of William Ure (d 1969), of Croydon, and Vera Primrose, *née* Belsen (d 1988); *b* 1 January 1944; *Educ* Croydon HS, Webber-Douglas Acad of Dramatic Art; *m* 12 Aug 1967, Leonard Gregory; *Career* writer; memb Soc of Authors; Redbridge Book Award 2004; *Books* incl: Dance for Two (children's book, publ while at sch), See You Thursday (1980), A Proper Little Nooryeff (1981), Plague 99 (1989, Lancs Book Award 1990), Skinny Melon and Me (1996), Becky Bananas (1997), Whistle and I'll Come (1997, Stockton Children's Book Award), Just 16 (1999), Fruit and Nutcase (1999), Secret Life of Sally Tomato (2000), Shrinking Violet (2002), Bad Alice (2003), Secret Meeting (2004), Is Anybody There? (2004), Sugar and Spice (2005), Star Crazy Me (2008), Fortune Cookie (2009), Love and Kisses (2009); *Recreations* animals, walking, reading, music; *Style*— Ms Jean Ure; ⊠ 88 Southbridge Road, Croydon CR0 1AF (☎ 020 8760 9818, fax 020 8688 6565, e-mail jean.ure@btopenworld.com); c/o Caroline Sheldon Literary Agency, 71 Hillgate Place, London W8 7SS (☎ 020 7727 9102)

UREN, Sir (John) Michael Leal; kt (2016), OBE (1999); s of Arthur Claude Uren (d 1977), of Rickmansworth, Herts, and Doris May, *née* Leal (d 1983); *b* 1 September 1923; *Educ* Sherborne, Imperial Coll London (BSc, ACGI); *m* 26 Nov 1955, Serena Anne, da of Edward Raymond Peal, of Salisbury; 2 s (David Richard b 1960, (Robert) Mark b 1962); *Career* RN 1943–46; cmmnd Sub-Lt RNVR, air engr offr Fleet Air Arm; chartered civil engr: Sir Alexander Gibb & Partners Persia 1946–51, sr engr The Cementation Co Scot 1951–53, Holland & Hannen and Cubitts NZ 1953–55, Industrial Complex for Pressed Steel Co Swindon 1955–56, British European Airways Base Heathrow 1956–58, Dowsett Engineering Construction Ltd (dir 1958, md 1961); fndr and developer Civil and Marine Ltd 1955 (played a major part in devpt of UK offshore marine aggregates indust and pioneered devpt of blast furnace slag as a special cement to enhance the durability of concrete, whilst reducing emission of carbon dioxide gases by over 90% compared with standard cement prodn, thereby saving over 2.5 million tonnes of CO2 per annum, in the interest of global warming; fndr Michael Uren Fndn 2006 (over £55m since donated to its chosen charities, focusing on the UK Armed Forces, Gurkhas in Nepal, advanced medical research and wildlife, including endangered species and preservation of the rainforest); former chm: Civil and Marine (Holdings) Ltd, Civil and Marine Slag Cement Ltd, The Appleby Group Ltd, Calumite Ltd, Calumite sro (Czech Repub), Civil and Marine Inc (USA); pres Cementitious Slag Makers Assoc, memb Cncl Quarry Products Assoc 1993–2003; vice-pres Royal London Soc for the Blind (memb Cncl 1974–94, chm 1981–94), vice-pres Chatham Historical Dockyard Tst 2016–; govr King Edward VII Hosp Sister Agnes 2007–; Freeman City of London 1958, Master Worshipful Co of Cordwainers 1990–91 (Liveryman 1958–); CEng, MICE, MIStructE, MCIWEM, FRICS; *Recreations* 15th and 16th century timber framed buildings, country pursuits, farming; *Clubs* Naval, Naval and Military, Royal Fusiliers Officers Mess Tower of London (hon life memb), Brigade of Gurkhas Assoc (hon life memb); *Style*— Sir Michael Uren, OBE; ⊠ Priory Farm, Appledore Road, Tenterden, Kent TN30 7DD (☎ 01580 765779)

URQUHART, Linda Hamilton; OBE (2012), WS (1985); da of Douglas Hamilton Urquhart (d 2009), and Ina Allan, *née* Priest (d 1991); *b* 21 September 1959, Edinburgh; *Educ* James Gillespie's HS Edinburgh, Univ of Edinburgh (LLB, DipLP); *m* 20 Aug 1988, David Spencer Burns; 2 da (Isla b 2 July 1991, Joanna b 20 March 1994); *Career* trainee slr Steedman Ramage & Co WS 1981–83; Morton Fraser: slr 1983–85, ptnr 1985–2012, chief exec 1999–2011, chm 2011–; chm CBI Scotland 2009–11, memb Edinburgh Business Forum 2010–, memb Bd CBI 2011–, memb Bd Scottish Enterprise 2011–16, chm Investors in People Scotland 2011–; memb Bd Adam Bank 2012–, non-exec dir Edinburgh Airport Ltd 2013–; co-ed Greens Property Law Bulletin; ambass Girl Guiding UK, tstee Royal Scottish Acad Fndn 2013, tstee Marie Curie Cancer Care 2014–, co-chair Fair Work Convention 2015–; The Insider Elite Readers' Award 2003, Assoc of Scottish Business Women Outstanding Contribution to Business Award 2009, Action for Children Scotland's Woman of Influence 2015; *Recreations* skiing, sailing, walking, golfing, singing; *Clubs* Royal Highland Yacht; *Style*— Miss Linda H Urquhart, OBE, WS

URQUHART, Peter William; s of Maj-Gen Ronald Walton Urquhart, CB, DSO, DL (d 1968), of Tibberton, Glos, and Jean Margaret, *née* Moir; *b* 10 July 1944; *Educ* Bedford Sch,

Pembroke Coll Cambridge (MA); *m* 1 May 1976 (m dis 1998), Hon Anne Serena, da of Baron Griffiths, MC, PC (Life Peer), of Kensington, London; 3 da (Katherine b 1978, Flora b 1981, Serena b 1984), 1 s (James b 1980); *Career* RMA Sandhurst 1963–64, Lt RE 1964–69; stockbroker: James Capel 1969–75, Gilbert Elliot 1975–76, Sheppards & Chase 1976–79, Mercury Asset Management (formerly Warburg Investment Management) 1981–96 (dir 1984–96); non-exec dir Phase Eight 1996–2002, dir Little London Hldgs 2007–11; tstee: Henry Smith charity 1996–2006, Urquhart Charitable Tst 2007–; FSI 1992; *Recreations* field sports, horses, golf, gardening; *Style*— Peter Urquhart, Esq; ⊠ Fisherton de la Mere House, Warminster, Wiltshire BA12 0PZ

URSELL, Bruce Anthony; s of Stuart Ursell (d 2005), and Nancy, *née* Fallowes (d 2009); *b* 28 August 1942, Ripley, Derbys; *Educ* William Ellis Sch Highgate; *m* 19 Feb 1966, Anne Carole, da of John Pitt (d 1970); 1 s (Piers John b 1971), 2 da (Philippa Anne b 1972, Virginia Anne b 1974); *Career* chief exec: Guinness Mahon & Co Ltd 1984–87 (dir 1974–84), British & Commonwealth Merchant Bank plc 1987–90; chm Lockton Developments plc 1985–95; dir: Surrey Broadcasting (USA) 1986–93, British & Commonwealth Holdings plc 1987–90, Oppenheimer Fund Management (USA) 1989–90, Standard Bank London Ltd 2000–07 (conslt 1998), Heathcote Property plc 2008–10; chm Standard Master Funds (Ireland) 2000–14; chm North of England Zoological Soc (Chester Zoo) 2016– (tstee 2010–16); *Recreations* theatre, cinema, reading, mountain walking; *Clubs* East India; *Style*— Bruce Ursell; ⊠ Oak House, 1 The Crescent, Hartford, Cheshire (☎ 01606 781219, mobile 07785 995096, e-mail bu2000@hotmail.co.uk)

USBORNE, (Thomas) Peter; MBE (2011); s of Thomas George Usborne (d 1993), and Gerda, *née* Just (d 1989); *b* 18 August 1937; *Educ* Summerfields Sch, Eton, Balliol Coll Oxford, INSEAD (MBA); *m* 1, 30 Oct 1964 (m dis), Cornelie, da of Alfred Tücking, of Munich; 1 s (Martin b 3 May 1973), 1 da (Nicola b 12 Dec 1969); m 2, 20 Sep 2013, Wendy Browning; *Career* 2 Lt Rifle Brigade, seconded VI KAR 1956–58; co-fndr and md Private Eye Magazine 1962–65, sr scientist Metra Sigma Martech Management Consultancy, publishing dir Macdonald Educational 1968–73, fndr and md Usborne Publishing Ltd; *Recreations* flying, sailing, France; *Clubs* Garrick, Groucho; *Style*— Peter Usborne, Esq, MBE; ⊠ Usborne Publishing Limited, Usborne House, 83–85 Saffron Hill, London EC1N 8RT (☎ 020 7430 2800)

USHERWOOD, Nicholas John; s of Stephen Dean Usherwood (d 2000), and Hazel, *née* Weston (d 1968); *b* 4 June 1943; *Educ* Westminster, Courtauld Inst of Art London (BA); *m* 1, 1979 (m dis 1990), Henrietta Mahaffy; 1 s (Theodore Patrick John b 1981), 1 da (Constance Hazel Kate b 1985); m 2, 1991, Jilly Szaybo; *Career* lectr in art history Portsmouth and Wimbledon Colls of Art 1965–68, res under Sir Nikolaus Pevsner on Pelican history of Art 1966–68; Royal Acad of Arts: admin Turner Bicentenary Exhibition 1974), exhibitions sec 1974–77; dep keeper i/c exhibitions and PR British Museum 1977–78; freelance writer, critic, lectr and exhibition organiser and curator 1978–; curator and cataloguer of exhibitions incl: David Inshaw (Brighton Gallery and Museum) 1978, Algernon Newton RA (Sheffield and Royal Acad of Arts) 1980, The Ruralists (Arnolfini Bristol and Camden Arts Centre) 1981, Tristram Hillier (Bradford and Royal Acad of Arts) 1983, Julian Trevelyan (Watermans Art Centre) 1985, Peter Blake – Commercial Art (Watermans Art Centre Brentford) 1986, Alfred Munnings 1878–1959 (Manchester City Art Galleries) 1986, Mass Observation (Watermans Art Centre Brentford) 1987, Richard Eurich War Paintings (Imperial War Museum) 1991, Sir Sidney Nolan 75th Birthday Retrospective (Terrace Gallery Harewood House) 1992, Richard Eurich Retrospective (Southampton Art Gallery) 1994, Sir Sidney Nolan (Agnews, London) 1997, Julian Trevelyan Retrospective (Royal Coll of Art) 1998, Feliks Topolski Collections 2001–02, Joash Woodrow Retrospective 2005, Discerning Eye 2005, Leonard McComb (Agnew's) 2006, Norman Adams Retrospective (Univ Art Gallery Newcastle-upon-Tyne) 2007; exhibitions organized: Athena Art Awards 1985–88, Images of Paradise 1989, New Generation (Bonhams London) 1990, Painting Today (Bonhams London) 1991, 1992 and 1993, Endangered Spaces (CPRE/Christies) 1996; regular contrib to: Daily Telegraph, The Guardian, Galleries (features ed 1998–); regular lectr at regnl art schs; Picker fell and critic in residence Kingston Poly (now Kingston Univ) 1990–91 and 1992–93, tstee Evelyn Williams Tst 1995–, tstee Mall Galleries 2012–; memb: CNAA 1976–78, Int Assoc of Art Critics (sec Br section 1995–99, pres Br Section 2000–02); Chevalier Order of Leopold II of Belgium 1972; *Publications* Norman Adams (2007), Evelyn Williams (2008), Sonia Lawson (2014); *Recreations* maps (new), music, poetry, new places (town and country), cricket, talking to painters; *Style*— Nicholas Usherwood, Esq; ⊠ Flat 1, Ditchingham House, Norwich Road, Bungay, Suffolk NR35 2JP (☎ 01986 896335)

V

VADERA, Baroness (Life Peer UK 2007), of Holland Park in the Royal Borough of Kensington and Chelsea; Rt Hon Shriti Vadera; PC (2009); *Career* Parly under-sec of state: Dept for Int Devpt 2007–08, Dept for Business, Enterprise and Regulatory Reform and Cabinet Office 2008–09, sr advsr to the G20 Presidency 2009–10; non-exec dir: AstraZeneca 2011–, BHP Billiton 2011–; chm Santander UK 2015; *Style—* The Rt Hon the Baroness Vadera; ✉ House of Lords, London SW1A 0PW

VADGAMA, Prof Pankaj; s of Maganlal Premji Vadgama (d 1963), and Champaben, *née* Gajjar; *b* 16 February 1948; *Educ* King's Sch Harrow, Orange Hill GS, Univ of Newcastle upon Tyne (MB BS, BSc, PhD); *m* 1977, Dixa, da of Mohanlal Bakrania; 2 da (Reena b 10 March 1978, Preeya b 1 May 1988), 1 s (Rooshin b 2 Nov 1979); *Career* house physician Newcastle Gen Hosp 1971–72, demonstrator in histopathology 1972, sr registrar in clinical biochemistry Royal Victoria Infirmary Newcastle 1977–78 (registrar 1973–77), MRC trg fell Univ of Newcastle upon Tyne 1978–81, sr registrar in clinical biochemistry Newcastle Gen Hosp 1981–83; Univ of Newcastle upon Tyne: princ res assoc 1983–87, dir of Biosensor Gp 1987–88; Univ of Manchester: prof of clinical biochemistry 1988–2000, head Dept of Med Hope Hosp 1992–98 (hon chemical pathologist 1988–2000), memb of staff Manchester Materials Science Centre 1999–2000; currently dir Interdisciplinary Research Centre in Biomedical Materials Queen Mary Univ of London, past hon conslt chemical pathologist and head of service Royal London Hosp, memb: Med Engrg & Sensors Ctee EPSRC 1987–92, Molecular Sensors Ctee LINK/EPSRC 1989–96, Project Mgmnt Gp EC Concerted Action on In Vivo Sensors 1988–96, MEDLINK 1995–, EPSRC Med Engrg Coll 1994–; memb Editorial Bd: Physiological Measurement, Analyst 1990–2003, Medical Engineering and Physics; sec UK Heads of Academic Depts of Clinical Biochemistry 1992–96; IEE Engineering Sci and Educn Jl Prize 1994, Sandoz lectr Br Geriatrics Soc 1989, invited lectr to numerous other meetings and confs; invited organiser of scientific meetings for: Br Biophysical Soc, IEE, Assoc of Clinical Biochemists, American Chemical Soc, etc; awarded over £5m of grants for research into biosensors since 1989; memb Assoc of Clinical Biochemists 1988; FRCPath 1989, FRSC 1996, CPhys, FInstP 2000, fell Inst Mining Minerals and Materials, CSci, FSB; *Publications* author of numerous original articles and reviews in scientific jls on biosensors; *Recreations* reading, walking; *Style—* Prof Pankaj Vadgama; ✉ 16 Wellfields Loughton, Essex IG10 1NX; IRC in Biomedical Materials, Queen Mary, University of London, Mile End Road, London EN4 4NS (☎ 020 7882 5151, e-mail p.vadgama@qmul.ac.uk)

VAIZEY, Rt Hon Edward Henry Butler (Ed); PC (2016), MP; s of John Ernest Vaizey (Baron Vaizey (Life Peer), d 1984), and Marina Alandra Vaizey (Lady Vaizey), *qv*; *b* 5 June 1968; *Educ* St Paul's, Merton Coll Oxford (MA), City Univ (Dip), Inns of Court Sch of Law; *m* 2005, Alexandra Mary Jane Holland; 1 s (b 2006), 1 da (b 2008); *Career* called to the Bar Middle Temple 1993; desk offr Cons Research Dept 1989–91, practising barr 1993–96, dir Public Policy Unit 1996–97, dir Politics Int 1997–98, dir Consolidated Communications 1998–2003, chief speech writer to Ldr of the Oppn 2004, MP (Cons) Wantage 2005– (Parly candidate (Cons) Bristol E 1997); shadow min for the arts 2006–10, Parly under-sec of state for culture, communications and creative industries 2010–14, min of state for culture and the digital economy 2014–; memb Consumer Credit Bill Standing Ctee 2005, Modernisation Select Ctee 2005, Environmental Audit Select Ctee 2006, numerous All Pty Gps; dep chm Cons Globalisation and Global Poverty Policy Gp 2006; non-exec dir Edexcel Ltd 2007–10; tstee Trident Tst, vice-chm Home Farm Tst; pres Didcot Town FC 2005–; vice-pres Nat Churches Tst; patron: Friends of St Mary's Church Buckland, Hansard Soc; memb Bd Bush Theatre London 2008–10; *Publications* ed Blue Books series: A Blue Tomorrow (jtly, 2001), The Blue Book on Transport (jtly, 2002), The Blue Book on Health (2002); *Recreations* riding, watching Chelsea FC and Didcot Town FC; *Clubs* Soho House; *Style—* The Rt Hon Ed Vaizey, MP; ✉ House of Commons, London SW1A 0AA (☎ 020 7219 6350, e-mail vaizeye@parliament.uk)

VAIZEY, Lady; Marina; CBE (2009); o da of late Lyman Stansky, of New York, USA, and late Ruth Stansky; *b* 16 January 1938; *Educ* Brearley Sch New York, Putney Sch Vermont, Radcliffe Coll Harvard Univ (BA), Girton Coll Cambridge (MA); *m* 1961, Baron Vaizey (Life Peer, d 1984); 1 da (Hon Polly (Hon Mrs McAndrew) b 1962), 2 s (Hon Thomas b 1964, Hon Edward, *qv* b 1968); *Career* author, broadcaster, exhibition organiser, lecturer, ctee memb; art critic: Financial Times 1970–74, Sunday Times 1974–92; dance critic Now! 1979–81; ed Nat Art Collections Fund Publications 1991–94, conslt Nat Art Collections Fund 1994–98; memb: Govt Art Ctee DOE 1975–81, Cncl Br Museum Soc 1977–84, Visual Arts Advsy Ctee Br Cncl 1987–2004, Art Working Gp Nat Curriculum DES 1990–91, Advsy Ctee (Spoliation) Nat Museum Directors' Cncl 1999–, Governance Forum Museums Assoc 2003–09; govr Camberwell College of Arts and Crafts 1971–82, tstee: Arts Cncl 1975–79, Nat Museums and Galleries on Merseyside 1986–2001, Crafts Cncl 1988–94, Geffrye Museum London 1990–2010, Imperial War Museum 1991–2003, South Bank Centre 1993–2003, 20th Century Soc 1995–98, London Open House 1996–2008, Int Rescue Ctee UK 1998–2007, Nat Army Museum 2001–08, Contemporary Applied Arts 2014–; memb Cncl: Friends of the V&A 2001–13 (chm 2007–13), Friends of the Nat Army Museum 2002–06, Friends of the Imperial War Museum 2003–; judge Turner Prize 1997; tstee The Musical Brain 2010–; *Books* 100 Masterpieces of Art (1979), Andrew Wyeth (1980), The Artist as Photographer (1982), Peter Blake (1985), Christo (1990), Christiane Kubrick (1990), Picasso's Ladies (1998), Sutton Taylor (1999), Felim Egan (1999), Great Women Collectors (1999), Art: The Critics' Choice (ed, 1999), Magdalene Odundo (2001), The British Museum Smile (2002), Colin Rose (2003), Wendy Ramshaw (2004), Andrew Logan (2008), Rooms of Dreams (2012), Lucian Freud (2012), Tracey Emin (2012), Photography and Art (2013), Between Dream and Nightmare (2014), Through the Lens, essays on photography (2015); contrib reviews: V and A, Despatches, Burlington, The Art Newspaper, www.theartsdesk.com, The Tablet, Art Quarterly 2009–; *Recreations* arts, travel; *Clubs* Athenaeum; *Style—* The Lady Vaizey, CBE; ✉ 41 Brackley Road, Chiswick, London W4 2HW (☎ 020 8994 7994, e-mail marinavaizey@virginmedia.com)

VAJDA, Christopher Stephen; QC (1997); *b* 6 July 1955; *Educ* Winchester, CCC Cambridge, Institut D'Etudes Européens, Université Libre de Bruxelles; *Career* called to the Bar Gray's Inn 1979 (bencher), called to the Bar Northern Ireland 1996; memb Supplementary Panel of Treasury Counsel 1993–97, arbitrator Sports Dispute Resolution Panel; *Publications* Bellamy & Child's European Community Law of Competition (contrib), Competition Litigation in the UK (contrib); *Recreations* architecture, opera, tennis, theatre; *Clubs* RAC; *Style—* Christopher Vajda, Esq, QC; ✉ Monckton Chambers, 1 Raymond Buildings, Gray's Inn, London WC1R 5WR (☎ 020 7405 7211, fax 405 2084, webiste www.monckton.com)

VALDINGER, Jan Robin; s of late Maj Stefan Valdinger-Vajda, MC, and Peggy, *née* Chadwick; *b* 28 September 1945; *Educ* Univ of Newcastle upon Tyne (LLB), Acad of Exec Coaching; *m* 28 Sept 1974 (m dis), Rosemary Jane, da of late Brendan O'Conor Donelan; 1 s (Stefan b 1975), 2 da (Anna b 1977, Juliet b 1980); *Career* slr Clifford Turner & Co 1970–74, corp fin exec Morgan Grenfell & Co 1974–79; Standard Chartered Merchant Bank Ltd: chief exec Merchant Banking Div India 1979–83, md Hong Kong 1983–87, dir Advsy Servs London 1987–91; dir of corp servs TI Group plc 1991–92, chief-exec PPF Investment Company 1996–2003, exec coach and managing ptnr Change Partnership for Czech and Slovak Republics;; *Clubs* Hong Kong, Hong Kong Jockey, Karlstejn Golf; *Style—* Jan Valdinger, Esq; ✉ Change Partnership, Trneny Ujezd 53, 267 18 Karlstejn, Czech Republic (☎ 00 420 311 329898, e-mail valdinger@changepartnership.cz, website www.changepartnership.cz)

VALE, Prof (John) Allister; s of John Richard Vale (d 1994), of Grappenhall, Cheshire, and Ellen, *née* Warburton (d 2004); *b* 13 June 1944; *Educ* Co GS Altrincham, Guy's Hosp London (MB BS, MD); *m* 4 Sept 1971, Elizabeth Margaret Hastings, da of Brig Leonard Walter Jubb (d 1979), of Chislehurst, Kent; 2 da (Fiona b 1974, Katherine b 1975); *Career* conslt clinical pharmacologist and dir Nat Poisons Info Service (Birmingham Unit) and W Midlands Poisons Unit City Hosp Birmingham, Sch of Biosciences and Coll of Medical and Dental Sciences Univ of Birmingham, dir Centre for Chemical Incidents 1996–99; censor RCP 2002–04; chm MRCP(UK) Part 1 Examining Bd 1995–2003 (sec 1982–95), chm MRCP(UK) Policy Ctee 2002–03 (sec 1994–2002), med dir MRCP(UK) Examination and Central Office 2003–06, chm MRCP(UK) Mgmnt Bd 2003–06, chm MOD Research Ethics Ctee 2006–; examiner: RCP (MRCP(UK) and AFOM), Univ of Birmingham (med and toxicology), Univ of London (clinical pharmacology); conslt to: DOH, DOT, DOE, MOD, CEC, WHO/IPCS; chm W Midlands Advsy Ctee on Chemical Incidents 1990–99; ed-in-chief Toxicological Reviews 2003–06, reviews ed Clinical Toxicology 2008– (dep ed 2001–04); memb Editorial Bd: Medicine (chm 2003–15), Drugs; memb: W Birmingham HA 1985–90, Poisons Bd Home Office 1985–99; Euro Assoc of Poisons Centres and Clinical Toxicologists (EAPCCT): pres 1992–98, memb Scientific Ctee 1992–2008 (chm 1992–2000), pres Soc of Toxicology Clinical and Translational Specialty Section 2013–14; President's Medal RCP 2006, Career Achievement Award American Acad of Toxicology 2008; pres Br Toxicology Soc 2004–06 (memb Exec 1997–2008); FRSM, FRCP 1984, fell American Acad of Clinical Toxicology 1988 (tstee 1991–97), FFOM (by distinction) 1992, FRCPEd 1994, FRCPGlas 1997, fell Br Toxicology Soc 2006, Hon FRCPS Glas 2007, fell Br Pharmacological Soc 2012, fell European Assoc of Poisons Centres and Clinical Toxicologists 2014; *Books* Poisoning – Diagnosis and Treatment (with T J Meredith, 1979), A Concise Guide to the Management of Poisoning (with T J Meredith, 1981), Our National Life (ed, 1998), Oxford Desk Reference: Toxicology (with D N Bateman, R D Jefferson, S H L Thomas and J P Thompson, 2014); *Recreations* reading, travel, photography; *Clubs* National; *Style—* Prof Allister Vale; ✉ National Poisons Information Service (Birmingham Unit), City Hospital, Birmingham B18 7QH (☎ 0121 507 4123, fax 0121 507 5580, e-mail allistervale@npis.org)

VALENTINE, Baroness (Life Peer UK 2005), of Putney, in the London Borough of Wandsworth; Josephine Clare (Jo) Valentine; da of late Michael Valentine, and Shirley, *née* Hall; *b* 8 December 1958, Putney, London; *Educ* St Paul's Girls' Sch, Univ of Oxford; *m* 30 Aug 1990, Simon Acland; 2 da (Hon Eloise Anne b 22 Oct 1991, Hon Isabel Agnes b 6 Nov 1993); *Career* corp finance mangr Barings plc 1981–88, ceo The Blackburn Partnership 1988–90, head of corp finance and planning BOC Gp plc 1990–95, ceo Central London Partnership 1995–97; London First: chief operating offr 1997–2003, ceo 2003–; bd memb: HS2 2014–, UCL 2014–; cmmr Nat Lottery 2001–05; tstee Teach First 2005–08, tstee Peabody 2012–; hon fell St Hugh's Coll Oxford; hon degree Univ of Roehampton; *Recreations* bridge, travel, piano; *Style—* The Lady Valentine; ✉ London First, 4th Floor, Middlesex House, 34–42 Cleveland Street London W1T 4JE (☎ 020 7665 1500, fax 020 7665 1501, e-mail jvalentine@londonfirst.co.uk)

VALIOS, Nicholas Paul; QC (1991); *b* 5 May 1943; *Educ* Stonyhurst; *m* 2 Sept 1967, Cynthia Valerie; 1 da (Natalie b 6 Aug 1969), 1 s (Mark b 11 Sept 1973); *Career* called to the Bar Inner Temple 1964; recorder of the Crown Court 1986– (asst recorder 1981); *Recreations* windsurfing, scuba diving, computing; *Style—* Nicholas Valios, Esq, QC; ✉ 4 Breams Buildings, Temple, London EC4A 1HP

VALLANCE, Air Vice Marshal Andrew George Buchanan; CB (2003), OBE (1987); s of George Charles Buchanan Vallance, and Dorothy Mabel, *née* Wootton; *Educ* RAF Coll Cranwell, Queens' Coll Cambridge (MPhil); *m* 1972, Katherine Ray, *née* Fox; 1 da (Sophie Clare b 25 Nov 1974), 1 s (Marcus Gregory Buchanan b 21 Aug 1979); *Career* cmmnd RAF 1969, sqdn pilot 9, 617 and 27 Sqdns, Flight Cdr 50 Sqdn 1977–79, RAF Staff Coll 1980, personal staff offr to Air Memb for Personnel 1981, OC 55 Sqdn 1982–84, personal staff offr to Chief of Air Staff 1984–87, dir Defence Studies 1988–90, chief Mil Co-operation SHAPE 1991–93, OC RAF Wyton 1993–95, dep dir Nuclear Policy MOD 1995, chief Special Weapons Br SHAPE 1996–98, COS Reaction Forces Air Staff NATO 1998–2000, COS and Dep C-in-C RAF Personnel and Trg Command 2000, Exec Asst to COS (EACOS) Cmd Structure Implementation Supreme HQ Allied Powers Europe (SHAPE) 2001–04, sec Def Press and Broadcasting Advsy Ctee 2005–; chm Servcies Sound and Vision Corp 2008–; memb IISS 1988, MRUSI 1988, FRAeS 1999; *Books* Air Power (1989), RAF Air Power Doctrine (1990), The Air Weapon (1995); *Recreations* miltary history, classical music, structural gardening, strategic studies; *Clubs* RAF; *Style—* Air Vice Marshal Andrew Vallance, CB, OBE; ✉ Defence and Security Media Advisory Committee, Main Building, Whitehall, London SW1A 2HB (☎ 020 7218 2206, fax 020 7218 5857, e-mail andrew.vallance935@mod.uk or secretary@dsma.uk)

VALLANCE, Charles Alexander Bester; s of Julian Vallance, of Follifoot, N Yorks, and Sylvia, *née* Wright; *b* 23 September 1964; *Educ* Sedbergh, Univ of Nottingham (MA); *m* 31 Jan 1993, Irina, da of late Mikhail Corcashvilli; *Career* advtg exec: BWBC, BBH, WCRS; founding ptnr VCCP 2002–; major clients incl: O2, easyJet, comparethemarket.com, Hiscox, Molson Coors; awards incl: Boxbuster's CC Cafeteria Award 1996, VCCP Fndrs' Day Flask 2003, 2004, 2005, 2006, 2008 and 2010; *Recreations* very amateurish cricket, golf and riding; *Clubs* The Academy, Moortown Golf (Yorks), Boxbusters' CC (Soho), London County CC, MCC; *Style—* Charles Vallance, Esq; ✉ VCCP, Greencoat House, Francis Street, London SW1P 1DH

VALLANCE, Dr Elizabeth Mary (Lady Vallance of Tummel); JP (Inner London); da of William Henderson McGonnigill, and Hon Jean, da of 1 Baron Kirkwood of Bearsden; *b* 8 April 1945; *Educ* Univ of St Andrews (MA), LSE (MSc), Univ of London (PhD), London Business Sch; *m* 5 Aug 1967, Baron Vallance of Tummel (Life Peer), *qv*; 1 da (Hon Rachel Emma Jane (Hon Mrs William Densham) b 1972), 1 s (Hon Edmund William Thomas b 1975); *Career* Queen Mary University of London: univ lectr, reader in politics 1968–84, head Dept of Political Studies 1985–88, visiting prof 1990–97, hon fell 1997; dir: HMV Group 1990–97, Norwich Union plc 1995–2000, Charter Pan-European Tst plc 1998–2002, CGNU plc 2000–02, Aviva plc 2002–06, Charter European Tst plc 2002–12, Medical Protection Society 2005–13; chm: St George's Healthcare NHS Tst 1993–99, Inst of Education Univ of London 2000–09, NHS Advsy Ctee on Distinction Awards 2000–03, Advsy Ctee on Clinical Excellence Awards 2003–05, ICAN 2007–15, Centre for Mental Health 2010, CEDR 2010, Nat Autism Project 2014; vice-chm Health Fndn 2000–08, memb Ctee on Standards in Public Life 2004–11, memb PCC Appointments Cmmn; fndr and chm Me Too 1999; govr LSE 2015, chm of govrs Sutton Valence Sch 2016; Sloan fell London Business Sch 1989, hon fell Inst of Educn Univ of London 2010, hon fell Coll of Teachers 2010; author; Hon DCL Univ of Kent 2013; High Sheriff Gtr London 2008–09; FRSA 1990, FCGI 2004; *Books* The State, Society and Self-Destruction (1975), Women in the House (1979), Women of Europe (1985), Member of Parliament (jtly, 1987, 2 edn 1990), Business Ethics in a New Europe (jtly, 1992), Business Ethics at Work (1995); *Style—* Dr Elizabeth Vallance; ✉ Centre for Mental Health, 134–138 Borough High Street, London SE1 1LB

VALLANCE, Philip Ian Fergus; QC (1989); s of Aylmer Vallance (d 1955), and Helen, *née* Gosse (d 1952); *b* 20 December 1943; *Educ* Bryanston, New Coll Oxford (scholar, BA); *m* 23 June 1973, Wendy Lee, da of J D Alston, CBE, of Diss, Norfolk; 1 s (Henry b 6 Dec 1979), 1 da (Lucy b 10 April 1981); *Career* called to the Bar Inner Temple 1968; *Clubs* Travellers; *Style—* Philip Vallance, Esq, QC; ✉ Berrymans Lace Mawer, Salisbury House, London Wall, London EC2M 5QN (☎ 020 7638 2811)

VALLANCE OF TUMMEL, Baron (Life Peer UK 2004), of Tummel in Perth and Kinross; Sir Iain David Thomas Vallance; kt (1994); s of Edmund Thomas Vallance, CBE, ERD; *b* 20 May 1943; *Educ* Edinburgh Acad, Dulwich Coll, Glasgow Acad, BNC Oxford (BA), London Business Sch (MSc); *m* 5 Aug 1967, Dr Elizabeth Mary Vallance, JP, *qv*; 1 da (Hon Rachel Emma Jane b 1972), 1 s (Hon Edmund William Thomas b 1975); *Career* joined GPO 1966; British Telecommunications (BT) plc: dir (following separation from GPO) 1981–2001, chief of operations 1985–86, chief exec 1986–95, chm 1987–2001, pres emeritus 2001–02; chm: Nations Healthcare Ltd 2005–07, Amsphere Ltd 2006–; non-exec vice-chm Royal Bank of Scotland Group plc 1994–2005 (dir 1993–2005); memb: Bd of Dirs Mobil Corp 1996–99, Supervisory Bd Siemens AG 2003–13, European Advsy Cncl Rothschild Group 2003–09, Allianz Int Advsy Bd; pres CBI 2000–02 (memb Pres's Ctee 1988–2008); chm: European Services Forum 2003–08, RSAMD (now RCS) 2006–; dep chm FRC 2001–02; memb: Euro Advsy Ctee NYSE (chm 2000–02), Int Advsy Bd Br-American C of C 1991–2002, Pres's Ctee and Advsy Cncl Business in the Community 1998–2002, Bd Scottish Enterprise 1998–2001, House of Lords Economic Affrs Ctee 2005–10 (chm 2008–10), EU Sub-Ctee A 2010–15, Science and Technol Ctee 2015–; vice-pres Princess Royal Tst for Carers 1999–2012 (chm 1991–98); Freeman City of London 1985, Liveryman Worshipful Co of Wheelwrights 1986; Hon DSc: Univ of Ulster 1992, Napier Univ 1994, City Univ 1996; Hon DTech: Loughborough Univ of Technol 1992, Robert Gordon Univ 1994; Hon DBA Kingston Univ 1993, Hon DEng Heriot-Watt Univ 1995; fell London Business Sch 1989, hon govr Glasgow Acad 1993–, patron Loughborough Univ 1996–, hon fell BNC Oxford 1997; FCIBS 2002; *Recreations* walking, playing the piano, listening to music; *Style—* The Lord Vallance of Tummel

VALLANCE-OWEN, Dr Andrew John; MBE (2014); s of Prof John Vallance-Owen (d 2011), and Renée, *née* Thornton; *b* 5 September 1951, London; *Educ* Epsom Coll Surrey, Univ of Birmingham Med Sch (MB ChB), Open Univ (MBA); *m* 1977, Frances Mary, da of Albert William Glover (d 1990); 2 s (Anthony Ian b 20 April 1983, Simon Huw b 10 Sept 1985), 1 da (Nicola Louise b 4 July 1988); *Career* surgical trg: Newcastle upon Tyne 1977–80 and 1981–83, Melbourne Aust 1980; BMA: provincial sec N of England 1983–85, Scottish sec 1986–89, head of central servs, int affrs and policy devpt London 1989–94, sec BMA charitable tsts 1989–94; Bupa: med dir Bupa Health Servs 1994–95, group med dir 1995–2012, dep chm Bupa Fndn 1998–2012; non-exec dir: Health Dialog Servs Corp Boston USA 1997–2006 and 2008–11, Outcome Technologies Ltd 2002–08; cmmr: Office of Health Economics Cmmn on NHS Productivity and Performance 2007–08, Local Govt Assoc Health Cmmn 2008; chm UKTI Healthcare Business Gp 2011–13, specialist med advsr Healthcare UK UKTI, chm Dept of Health Patient Reported Outcomes Stakeholder Gp 2009–13, chm Dr Foster Ethics Ctee 2011–14, chm SW Academic Health Science Network 2013–15, chm Private Healthcare Information Network, sr non-exec dir Royal Brompton and Harefield NHS Fndn Tst, chm Ethics Advsy Panel Medicover Private Health Care Bd (Poland); chm Cncl Royal Medical Fndn of Epsom Coll, chm govr Epsom Coll, dep chm govr Epsom Coll Malaysia, chm Univ of Birmingham Guild of Students Tstee Bd 2011–13; fndn govr and chm Fund-raising Appeal Ctee The Latymer Sch Edmonton 1994–2009, govr Queenswood Sch Herts 2001–14, tstee Coll of Medicine 2013–15, tstee Barrett's Oesophagus Campaign; Freeman City of London, Liveryman Worshipful Soc of Apothecaries; Hon DUniv Birmingham 2012; memb BMA 1976; FRSCEd 1982, FRSM 1989, FRSA 1992; *Publications* Medical Audit and Accountability (co-ed, 1992), The Health Debate Live: 45 Interviews for 'Leading for Health' (1992); *Recreations* music, sailing, gardening, photography, family; *Style—* Dr Andrew Vallance-Owen, MBE; ✉ 13 Lancaster Avenue, Hadley Wood, Hertfordshire EN4 0EP (☎ 020 8440 9503, mobile 07836 750252, e-mail vallanca1@gmail.com)

VALLO, (Maria) Ambra; da of Gianni Vallo, of Naples, Italy, and Lucia Acquaviva; *b* Naples, Italy; *Educ* Royal Ballet Sch of Flanders Antwerp; *Career* ballet dancer; former soloist Royal Ballet of Walloons and Royal Ballet of Flanders, with Eng Nat Ballet 1993–96 (latterly sr soloist), with Birmingham Royal Ballet 1996– (princ 2001–); repertory incl: Giselle in Giselle, Juliet in Romeo and Juliet, Odette/Odile in Swan Lake, Aurora in The Sleeping Beauty, Sugar Plum Fairy in The Nutcracker, Swanhilda in Coppélia, Kitri in Don Quixote, Lise in La Fille Mal Gardée, Lead Girl in Etude, Young Girl in The Two Pigeons, Polka and Girl in Solitaire, Bathsheba in Far from the Madding Crowd, Isabella in Edward II, Guinevere in Arthur, Roxane in Cyrano, Belle and wild girl in Beauty and the Beast, Annunciation in The Protecting Veil, Maggie, Vicky and Salvation Army in Hobson's Choice, Lover Girl in Carmina Burana, Titania and Desdemona in The Shakespeare Suite, Spring in The Seasons, princ in Powder, Calliope Rag in Elite Syncopations, La Capricciosa in Lady and the Fool, Sanguine Variation in The Four Temperaments, Graduation Ball, Voices of Spring, The Walk to the Paradise Garden, Symphonic Variations, Serenade, Symphony in Three Movements, Concerto Barocco, Tarantella, Square Dance, Violin Conerto No 2 Mouvement, Tchaikovsky pas de deux Apollo, princ girl 2nd movement in Western Symphony, Chorus, Dance House, In the Upper Room, That's Life in Sinatra Songs, Five Tangos, Spring Waters, ballerina in Petruska; first prize Luxembourg Int Grand Prix, Gold medal Rieti Int Competition, Silver medal Houlgate France, Most Talented Up-and-Coming Dancer Positano Critics Circle Award 1991, Best Female Dancer Danza & Danza Critics Circle Award 2004, Best Performance Positano Critics Circle Award 2002; *Recreations* engine-free hang gliding, travel, country walking, cinema, reading; *Style—* Miss Ambra Vallo

VALNER, Nicholas Edmund; *b* 14 September 1953; *Educ* Stonyhurst, Univ of Oxford (MA); *m*; 3 c; *Career* Frere Cholmeley Bischoff: articled clerk (admitted 1979), ptnr 1985–98, head of Media; ptnr Eversheds (following merger) 1998– (head of Int Arbitration and London Commercial Litigation); chair numerous confs on arbitration law Inst of Arbitrators, frequent speaker IBA, Inst of Civil and Comparative Law and American Bar Assoc; memb: IBA, London Slrs' Litigation Assoc; ACIArb; *Style—* Nicholas Valner, Esq; ✉ Eversheds, 1 Wood Street, London EC2V 7WS (☎ 020 7919 4500, fax 020 7919 4919)

van COMMENÉE, Charles; s of Otto van Commenée, of Amsterdam, Netherlands, and Ineke Smit; *b* 22 June 1958, Amsterdam, Netherlands; *Educ* Univ of Amsterdam for Applied Sciences; *Career* club coach at five track and field clubs in The Netherlands 1977–96, coach Netherlands nat track and field team 1987 and 1992–2000, coach to several Olympic medallists and World Championship medallists of various nationalities 1992–2004, technical dir UK Athletics 2000–04, performance dir Netherlands Olympic Ctee 2004–08, chef de mission Netherlands Olympic Team Beijing 2008, head coach Br Athletics 2008–12, public speaker on coaching and high performance culture 2013–; Mussabini Medal 2000; *Style—* Mr Charles van Commenée; ✉ e-mail charles@charlesvancommenee.com; British Athletics, Alexander Stadium, Perry Barr, Birmingham B42 2BE

van de VEN, Prof Johan Jacob (Hans); s of Henricus Marius Gerardus Johannes van de Ven, and Reinera Johanna Liduina, *née* Jonker Roelants; *b* 10 January 1958, The Hague, Netherlands; *Educ* Leiden Univ (BA), Harvard Univ (PhD); *m* 16 July 1983, Susan Elizabeth, *née* Kerr; 3 s (Johan Malcolm, Derek Marius (twins) b 10 Oct 1991, Willem Andrew b 8 Nov 1997); *Career* Faculty of Oriental Studies Univ of Cambridge: lectr 1988, sr lectr 2000, reader 2002, prof 2004; chm Ivonne van de Ven Fndn; Philip Lilienthal Prize 1991; Br Acad research reader 1996–98; memb: Assoc of Asian Studies, European Assoc of Asian Studies; FBA 2013; *Publications* From Friend to Comrade: The Founding of the Chinese Communist Party (1991), War and Nationalism in China (2001), The Battle for China (2012), Breaking with the Past (2014); *Recreations* tennis, camping, sailing; *Style—* Prof Hans van de Ven; ✉ Faculty of Asian and Middle Eastern Studies, University of Cambridge, Sidgwick Avenue, Cambridge CB3 9DA (☎ 01223 338331, e-mail jjv10@cam.ac.uk)

VAN DE WALLE, Leslie; s of Philippe Van de Walle, of Paris, France, and Luce, *née* Beaubien; *b* 27 March 1956; *m* 22 June 1982, Domitille; 2 da (Stephanie b 1 May 1984, Philippine b 17 July 1986); *Career* product mangr Danone France 1980–84; Cadbury Schweppes plc: md France 1984–1990 and 1992–93, md Benelux 1990–92, md Iberia 1993–94; United Biscuits plc: md European Snacks 1994–96, chief exec European Snacks and Biscuits 1996–98, chief exec McVities Gp 1998–99, gp chief exec 1999–2002; successively pres Shell S America and Africa Shell Int, pres Shell Europe Oil Products then exec vice-pres global retail Royal Dutch Shell 2001–07, chief exec Rexam plc 2007–09; non-exec chm Robert Walters plc 2012–, non-exec dir Aegis Gp plc 2003–; memb: Golf Mgmnt Bd, Food and Drink Fedn, Food and Drink Assoc; *Recreations* golf, movies, reading, tourism; *Clubs* Foxhills Golf, Chantilly Golf, Chairman's; *Style—* Leslie Van de Walle, Esq

van den ASSUM, HE Laetitia; *b* 18 September 1950; *Educ* Univ of Amsterdam, Columbia Univ NY (LLM); *Career* Dutch diplomat; legal advsr Netherlands Orgn for Devpt Cooperation The Hague 1975–77, various positions related to UN affrs, population and gender Miny of Foreign Affrs The Hague 1977–87, rep of UNICEF for Tanzania and Sechelles Dar es Salaam 1988–92, dir for int orgns The Hague 1992–95, ambass to Thailand, Cambodia, Laos and Burma 1995–2000, ambass to SA, Lesotho and Swaziland 2000–04, special advsr to UNAIDS Geneva 2005–06, ambass to Kenya, Seychelles and Somalia 2006–11, ambass to Mexico and Belize 2011–12, ambass to the Ct of St James's 2012–15; *Style—* HE Ms Laetitia van den Assum; ✉ e-mail lon@minbuza.nl or laetitia.assum@minbuza.nl

VAN DER BIJL, His Hon Judge Nigel Charles; s of late Nicholas Alexander Christian Van der Bijl, and Mollie Van der Bijl; *b* 28 April 1948; *Educ* Trinity Coll Dublin (BA, LLB); *m* 1974, Loba, *née* Nassiri; 1 s, 1 da; *Career* called to the Bar Inner Temple 1973; co sec Int Div Beecham Pharmaceutical 1973–74, legal mangr Shahpur Chemical Co Ltd and Nat Iranian Oil Co Tehran 1974–77, barr in private practice 1977–2001, recorder 1996–2001, circuit judge (SE Circuit) 2001–, hon recorder City of Canterbury 2004–; friend Br Sch of Athens 1996–; *Recreations* cycling; *Clubs* Bar Cycling (pres); *Style—* His Hon Judge Van der Bijl; ✉ c/o The Law Courts, Chaucer Road, Canterbury, Kent CT1 1ZA

van ELTEN, Thorsten; s of Heinrich van Elten, and Elisabeth, *née* Riddermann; *b* 2 August 1967, Germany; *Career* designer; formerly with Christopher Farr and SCP, fndr Thorsten van Elten manufacturing and retail business 2002– (furniture, accessories and lighting designs launched at 100% Design, Milan Furniture Fair and Pulse); UK agent and distributor for int companies incl roomsafari, Trico, Richard Hutten, Goods, Interior Tools, Details, Czech Mania, Artificial, Kaether & Weise, Decorum and Derin; *Style—* Thorsten van Elten, Esq; ✉ 295 Euston Road, London NW1 3AD (☎ 020 7739 7237, fax 020 7613 1123, e-mail info@thorstenvanelten.com, website www.thorstenvanelten.com)

van GASS, Jaco-Albert; s of Deon van Gass, of Pretoria, S Africa, and Aloma, *née* Kritzinger; *b* 20 August 1986, Middelburg, S Africa; *Career* paratrooper Parachute Regt 2007–09; Walking With The Wounded 2010–12: successfully trekked unsupported to the Geographical North Pole, summited Gran Paradiso Italian Alps (4061m), summited Manaslu Nepal (8164m, 8th highest peak in the world), summited Lobuche Nepal (6119m), Everest summit attempt camp 3 South Col (7470m), a major participant in events raising over £1.5m for charity, conducted Alpine and Arctic trg for various expeditions in France, Italy and Norway; other achievements incl: represented Br Army in downhill Alpine ski racing with the Combined Services Disabled Ski Team (CSDST) 2010 and 2011, successful world record trek unsupported to Geographical North Pole 2011 (Harry's Arctic Heroes), record holder for first disabled South African to summit Mt Manaslu (8164m, 8th highest peak in the world) 2011, successfully completed Safaricom marathon Kenya, Marine Corps marathon (with 35lb Bergen) Washington DC and NY marathon raising thousands of pounds in aid of charity, completed UK Ironman 2012, successful summit of Mt McKinley (20320 feet) 2013 (became one of 25 out of 1000 climbers to climb from 14000 feet all the way to the summit in one day); Olympic torchbearer 2012; memb GB Paralympic Cycling Team Rio 2016; memb Advsy Bd Endeavour Fund lead by Fndn of Prince William and Prince Harry 2012; Sun Milly Award 2012; *Style—* Jaco van Gass, Esq

VAN GELDER, Daniel; *Career* surveyor CB Richard Ellis 1993–95, dir Devpt Securities plc 1995–2003, co-fndr Exemplar Properties 2003–, co-owner Prestige Yachting 2012–; chm City and Westminster Property Assocs 2013–16; FRICS 1994; *Style—* Daniel Van Gelder, Esq; ✉ Exemplar Properties, Kent House, Market Place Bar, 14–17 Market Place, London W1W 8AJ

VAN GELDER, Peter Samuel; s of Joseph van Gelder (d 1988), and Sylvia, *née* Cornberg (d 2013); *b* 12 August 1953; *Educ* Westmount HS Montreal, Aston Univ (BSc), UC Cardiff (Postgrad Dip Journalism); *m* Mary-Jane, da of Hugh Campbell Drummond; 1 s (Joseph Robert b 22 Jan 1989), 1 da (Katharine Elizabeth b 12 Feb 1992); *Career* news asst BBC Wales Cardiff 1977–78, news prodr and political corr BBC Radio Leeds 1978–81, asst prodr Newsnight BBC TV London 1981–82; TV-am: asst prodr Michael Parkinson Show

1982–84, news reporter 1984–86, prodr Good Morning Britain 1986–88, ed Children's Progs 1988–89, asst managing ed 1989–91, managing ed 1991–93; md Teletext Ltd 1993–97, md British Interactive Broadcasting 1997–98, princ and md Informed Sources 1999–2002, dir Westminster Forum Projects (Westminster Media Forum, Westminster eForum, Westminster Food and Nutrition Forum, Westminster Health Forum, Westminster Educn and HE Forums, Westminster Energy, Environment and Transport Forum, Westminster Legal Policy Forum, Policy Forum for Wales, Scotland Policy Conferences, Policy Forum for NI) 2002–; *Books* Offscreen Onscreen (1991); *Recreations* music, writing, pinball; *Style*— Peter van Gelder, Esq

van HEYNINGEN, Prof Veronica; CBE (2010); da of Laszlo Daniel (d 1973), and Anne, *née* Eisler (d 2008); *b* 12 November 1946, Hungary; *Educ* Humphrey Perkins Sch, Girton Coll Cambridge (MA), Northwestern Univ IL (MS), Lady Margaret Hall Oxford (DPhil); *m* 1968, Simon van Heyningen, s of William E van Heyningen; 1 s (Paul b 5 July 1975), 1 da (Eleanor b 25 Dec 1976); *Career* Beit Memorial fell: Oxford Genetics Laboratory 1973–74, MRC Mammalian Genome Unit Edinburgh 1974–76; MRC Human Genetics Unit Edinburgh: MRC postdoctoral scientist 1977–81, appt of unlimited tenure 1981–86, appt to sr scientist grade 1986–91, special appt grade 1991–2012, head Medical and Developmental Genetics Section 1992–2010; Howard Hughes Int Research Scholar 1993–98; hon treas Genetical Society 1994–98; Human Genome Organisation (HUGO): memb, memb Human Genome Mapping Committee 1994, chm 1996; pres European Soc of Human Genetics 2003, pres Genetics Soc 2009–12; memb: Human Genetics Cmmn 2000–05, European Molecular Biology Organisation 2002–; memb Editorial Bd: British Journal of Cancer 1990–97, Human Molecular Genetics 1996–2003, PLOS Genetics 2005–15; hon prof Inst of Ophthalmology UCL 2012–, hon prof and visiting scientist Univ of Edinburgh 2013–; tstee National Museums of Scotland 1993–2000, patron Aniridia Network UK, chair Muscular Dystrophy Campaign Grant Ctee; pres Galton Inst 2014–; hon prof Faculty of Medicine Univ of Edinburgh 1995, FRSE 1997, FMedSci 1999, FRS 2007; *Publications* author of over 200 articles in learned jls; *Recreations* museums, theatre, travel, cooking; *Style*— Prof Veronica van Heyningen, CBE; ✉ e-mail veronica.vanheyningen@igmm.ed.ac.uk or vvanheyningen@gmail.com, website https://iris.ucl.ac.uk/iris/browse/profile?upi=VVANH41

VAN ORDEN, Brig Geoffrey Charles; MBE (1973), MEP (Cons) Eastern England; s of late Thomas Van Orden, and Mary Van Orden; *b* 10 April 1945; *Educ* Sandown Sch, Mons Officer Cadet Sch, Univ of Sussex (BA), Indian Defence Services Staff Coll; *m* 1974, Frances; 3 da; *Career* cmmnd Intelligence Corps 1964, operational service in Borneo, NI etc, directing staff Führungs Akademie der Bundeswehr Hamburg 1985–88, COS and ACOS G2 Berlin (Br Sector) 1988–90, Assessment Staff Cabinet Office 1990, res assoc IISS and service fell Dept of War Studies KCL 1990–91, head Int Military Staff Secretariat NATO HQ 1991–94, transferred to Reg Res 1994; sr official EC Directorate-General External Relations 1995–99; MEP (Cons) Eastern England 1999–, Cons spokesman on def, memb Foreign Affrs, Human Rights and Def Ctee European Parl (vice-chm 2001–06), chm delgn to India, memb delgns to NATO and to Turkey, Parly rapporteur on Bulgaria; vice-chm Euro Conservatives and Reformists Group (ECR) 2009–; memb: IISS 1991–, Friends of the Union 1997–, Countryside Alliance 1999–, Bow Gp 1999–, BASC 2014–; fndr memb: Anglo-German Officers Assoc 1991–, Friends of India, Friends of Turkey; chm Friends of Sri Lanka, chm Euro-India Chamber of Commerce; founding pres New Direction – Fndn for European Reform; Freeman: City of London 1991, Worshipful Co of Painter-Stainers 1991; FIMgt 1993; *Publications* various articles on foreign and security policy issues; *Clubs* Army and Navy; *Style*— Geoffrey Van Orden, Esq, MBE, MEP; ✉ 88 Rectory Lane, Chelmsford, Essex CM1 1RF (☎ 0032 2 284 7332, fax 0032 2 284 9332, e-mail geoffrey.vanorden@europarl.europa.eu)

VAN OUTEN, Denise; *b* 1974, Basildon, Essex; *m* 2009 (sep), Lee Mead; 1 da (Betsy b 2010); *Career* television personality and actress; *Theatre* Chicago (London) 2001–02 and (Broadway) 2002, Tell Me On A Sunday (Gielgud Theatre) 2003, Rent (London) 2007, Legally Blonde: The Musical (Savoy) 2010–11; *Television* appearances incl: Crossbow 1986, Kappatoo 1990, Operation Good Guys 1997, The Young Person's Guide to Becoming a Rock Star 1998, Jack and the Beanstalk 1998; presenter: The Big Breakfast 1995–99 and 2000–01, Something for the Weekend 1999, Prickly Heat 2000, The Race 2006, Who Dares Sings 2008; panelist Any Dream Will Do 2008; narrator The Only Way Is Essex 2010–; starred in Babes in the Wood 1998; *Film* appearances incl: Tube Tales 1999, Love Honour And Obey 2000, Run For Your Wife 2012; *Radio* co-presenter Capital Breakfast (Capital FM) 2008–09, presenter Magic FM 2013–; *Style*— Ms Denise Van Outen

VAN REENEN, Prof John; s of L Van Reenen and A Van Reenen, *née* Williams; *b* 26 December 1965, Carlisle; *Educ* Queens Coll Cambridge (Joshua King Prize, BA), LSE (MSc), UCL (PhD); *m* 20 May 2001, Sarah Chambers; *Career* research fell Inst for Fiscal Studies 1992–99, prof Dept of Economics UCL 1994–2003, currently dir Centre for Economic Performance and prof Dept of Economics LSE; visiting prof Dept of Economics Univ of California 1998–99; policy advsr on educn, enterprise and tax 10 Downing St 1999–2000, sr policy advsr to Sec of State for Health 2000–01, advsr to Chief Economist of DG Competition EC 2003–, academic assoc HM Treasy 2003–; memb Editorial Bd: Review of Economic Studies 1997–2003, European Economic Review 1999–2003, Jl of Industrial Economics 1999– (assoc ed 1996–), Editorial Policy 2000–03; author of numerous articles in learned jls incl American Economic Review, Br Jl of Industrial Relations and Quarterly Jl of Economics; ptnr Lexecon Ltd 2001–02; Jahnsson Award 2009, EIB Prize for Excellence in Economics 2014; memb: Econometric Soc, American Economic Assoc; FBA; *Books* Investing for Propserity (2013); *Clubs* Blacks; *Style*— Prof John Van Reenen; ✉ Centre for Economic Performance, London School of Economics, Houghton Street, London WC2A 2AE (☎ 020 7955 6976, e-mail j.vanreenen@lse.ac.uk)

van RIJSBERGEN, Prof Cornelis Joost; s of Jacob Adam van Rijsbergen (d 1987), and Gerritdina, *née* Verheij; *b* 17 October 1943; *Educ* Univ of W Aust (BSc), Univ of Cambridge (PhD); *m* 22 May 1965, Juliet Hilary, da of Ernest Arthur Clement Gundry, of Perth, Aust; 1 da (Nicola b 1973); *Career* tutor in mathematics Univ of W Aust 1966–68, lectr Monash Univ 1973–75, Royal Soc res fell Univ of Cambridge 1975–79 (sr res offr King's Coll 1969–72); prof of computer sci: Univ Coll Dublin 1980–86, Univ of Glasgow 1986–; ed-in-chief The Computer Jl 1993–2000; Tony Kent Strix Award 2004, Gerald Salton Award ACM SIGIR 2006; Fell BCS 1971, FRSE 1994, FREng 2004, FACM 2004; *Books* Information Retrieval (2 edn, 1979), The Geometry of Information Retrieval (2004); *Recreations* swimming, cinema, travel, fiction; *Style*— Prof Cornelis van Rijsbergen, FRSE; ✉ 14 Park Parade, Cambridge CB5 8AL (☎ 01223 360318); School of Computing Science, University of Glasgow, Glasgow G12 8QQ (☎ 0141 330 4463, fax 0141 330 4913, e-mail rijsbergen@acm.org)

van WALSUM, Joeske; s of Hans van Walsum, of Amsterdam, Holland, and Lies, *née* Schuurman-Stekhoven; *b* 26 May 1949; *Educ* Robert Gordon's Coll Aberdeen, RCM London; *m* 10 July 1969 (m dis 2002), Elizabeth Ann, da of Ronald Charles Marsh; 2 da (Georgiana b 27 Feb 1976, Abigail b 16 Dec 1977); m 2, 17 April 2003, Rachel, da of Mark Bostock; 1 s (Hans b 12 March 2008); *Career* freelance musician and flute teacher 1971–74, chm Van Walsum Management (int mangrs of conductors, composers, musicians, singers and orchs and promoters of concert series and tours) 1975–2008, chm Maestro Arts (music and visual arts conslts) 2011–; chm Br Assoc of Concert Agents 1989–92; organiser and chm Musicians for Armenia benefit concert 1988; *Recreations* white water canoeing, long distance walking, roller blading, cycling; *Style*— Joeske van Walsum, Esq

VANE PERCY, Christopher David; s of Kenneth Vane Percy (d 1998), and Jean Farquharson; *b* 15 March 1945; *Educ* Bedford Sch; *m* 17 May 1973, Lady Linda Denise Grosvenor, da of 5 Baron Ebury, DSO (d 1957); 1 s (Maximilian Egerton b 1979), 2 da (Grace Dorothy Denise b 1981, Tryce Mary Susanne b 1991); *Career* interior designer; pres Int Interior Design Assoc (London chapter), chm, heritage and evironment dir and past pres Br Inst of Interior Design (formerly Br Interior Designers Assoc; vice-chm 2012–13); memb Exec Cncl Historic Houses Assoc (regnl chm East Anglia), memb Ctee Historic Environment Forum East of England, vice-pres Cambs and Peterborough Branch CPRE 2012–; Br Inst of Interior Design Award of Merit 2007; patron Cambridge Gardens Tst, tstee Moggerhanger House Preservation Tst 2013–; memb Godmanchester Town Cncl 1985–, mayor of Godmanchester 2012–13; Garrick Club David Garrick Medal 2010; *Books* The Glass of Lalique – A Collector's Guide (1977); *Style*— Christopher Vane Percy, Esq; ✉ Island Hall, Godmanchester, Cambridgeshire PE29 2BA (☎ 01480 459676); CVP Designs Ltd, The Old Dairy, 7 Hewer Street, London W10 6DU (☎ 020 8960 9026, fax 020 8969 3589, e-mail cvp@cvpdesigns.com)

VANEZIS, Prof Peter Savvas; OBE (2001); s of Savvas Vanezis, and Efrosini Vanezis; *b* 11 December 1947, Nicosia, Cyprus; *Educ* Univ of Bristol (MB ChB, MD), Univ of London (PhD); *m* Maria; 2 c (Andrew, Frosini); *Career* Univ of Glasgow: regius prof of forensic med and science 1993–2003, dir Human Identification Centre 1994–2003, visiting prof 2003–; DG Centre for Int Forensic Assistance 2001–03, chief forensic med offr and head of Dept of Forensic Medical Scis Forensic Sci Serv London 2003–06, dir Cameron Forensic Medical Sciences Barts and London Sch of Medicine and Dentistry Univ of London 2006–, CMO iGene (London) Ltd 2013–15; conslt in forensic medicine Govt of Malaysia 2010–; visiting prof: South Bank Univ 2001–, Univ of Hong Kong 2004–, Univ of Leicester; dir and founding fell Acad of Forensic Medial Sciences 2010, UCL 2015–; advsr in forensic medicine to Int Ctee of the Red Cross, sr conslt in forensic medicine to the Armed Forces 1992–2010; ed-in-chief Med Sci Law; FRCPath 1990, FRCPGlas 1998, FFFLM 2006, FFSSoc; *Publications* Pathology of Neck Injury (1989), Suspicious Death – Scene Investigation (1996); over 100 pubns in books and peer reviewed jls; *Recreations* reading, music, golf, painting; *Style*— Prof Peter Vanezis, OBE; ✉ Cameron Forensic Medical Sciences, William Harvey Research Institute, Barts and the London, Charterhouse Square, London EC1M 6BQ (☎ 020 7882 3401, e-mail p.vanezis@qmul.ac.uk or vanezis@btinternet.com, website www.qmul.ac.uk)

VANN JONES, Prof John; s of John Jones (d 1975), and Elizabeth, *née* Kelly; *b* 8 May 1945; *Educ* Hyndland Sch Glasgow, Univ of Glasgow (MB ChB, PhD); *m* 23 Sept 1970, Anne Margaret, da of Andrew Abercrombie, of Glasgow; 2 s (Richard John, Simon Andrew), 2 da (Kerstin Anne, Caroline Patricia); *Career* lectr in cardiology Univ of Glasgow 1972–77 (res fell 1969–72), MRC travelling fell Univ of Gothenburg 1975–76, reader in cardiovascular med Univ of Oxford 1980–81 (lectr 1977–80), conslt cardiologist Bristol 1981–; memb: Br Cardiac Soc, Br Hypertension Soc; hon prof Univ of Bristol 1993; FRCP 1987; *Books* Scientific Foundations of Cardiology (1983), Outline of Cardiology (1983 and 1992), Essential Medicine (1993 and 1998); *Recreations* golf, table tennis, swimming; *Clubs* Bristol Clifton Golf, Saunton Golf; *Style*— Prof John Vann Jones; ✉ Park House, Chew Lane, Chew Magna BS40 8QA (☎ 01275 332164); Cardiology Department, Royal Infirmary, Bristol BS2 8HW (☎ 0117 923 0000)

VANNER, Michael John; s of Walter Geoffrey Vanner (d 1933), of Winkfield, Berks, and Doris Ellen, *née* Hall (d 1977); *b* 6 December 1932; *Educ* Blundell's, Sidney Sussex Coll Cambridge (MA); *m* 1 July 1961, Myra, da of William John Sharpe (d 1982), of Fetcham, Surrey; 2 s (Luke b 1967, Guy b 1970); *Career* res engr Electrical Res Assoc 1955–64, chief devpt engr BICC Construction Co Ltd 1964–75, engrg conslt Balfour Beatty Power Construction Ltd 1981–86 (engrg mangr 1975–81), princ Construction and Material Servs (int consulting) 1986–, princ engr Ewbank Preece Ltd 1989–92, transmission engr AMEC Power Ltd 1992–94, OHL engr Merz & McLellan 1994–2007; chm IEE PG Power Cables and Overhead Lines 1988–91, chm BSI PEL/11 Overhead Lines 1991–2009, chm CIGRE SC22–07 Overhead Lines 1995–2002; CEng, FIEE 1994 (MIEE 1984), CPhys, MInstP 1962, MBGS 1961; *Books* The Structure of Soil and A Critical Review of The Mechanisms of Soil Moisture Retention And Migration (1961); *Recreations* walking, sailing; *Style*— Michael Vanner, Esq; ✉ Construction and Material Services, 11 West Avenue, Redhill, Surrey RH1 5BA (☎ 01737 762729)

VANSTONE, Hugh; s of J R B Vanstone, of Exeter, and M L Vanstone; *b* 8 August 1965; *Educ* Exeter Sch; *Partner* George Stiles, composer, *qv*; *Career* lighting designer; trained Northcott Theatre Exeter 1980–86, conslt Imagination 1986–, freelance 1989–, assoc to Andrew Bridge, *qv* (lighting designer) 1989–94; has worked extensively for UK's national theatre and opera companies on over 160 productions worldwide; memb Assoc of Lighting Designers 1983–; *Theatre* recent credits incl: Strictly Ballroom (directed by Baz Luhrmann Sydney), Matilda (London and NY), Ghost (London, NY, Korea, USA and UK tours), Andrew Lloyd Webber's prodn of The Wizard of Oz (West End, Toronto and USA tour), Tanz Der Vampire (dir Roman Polanski), I'll Eat You: A Chat with Sue Mengers (starring Bette Midler, Broadway), La Bête (with Mark Rylance, David Hyde Pierce and Joanna Lumley, West End and Broadway), A Steady Rain (with Hugh Jackman and Daniel Craig, Broadway); *Opera* credits incl: Macbeth (ROH), The Rake's Progress (WNO), La Bohème, Dialogues of the Carmelites (ENO), Die Fledermaus (Scottish Opera), Carmen (Opera North), The Bartered Bride (Glyndebourne); *Ballet* Alice in Wonderland (English Nat Ballet), Don Quixote (choreographed by Carlos Acosta, Royal Ballet London); *Awards* Olivier Award for Best Lighting Designer 1999 and 2001, Best Visual Presentation Lighting Design Nat Broadway Theatre Awards 2002; *Clubs* Soho House (international); *Style*— Hugh Vanstone, Esq; ✉ website www.hughvanstone.com; c/o Judy Daish, Judy Daish Associates, 2 St Charles Place, London W10 6EG (☎ 020 8964 8811, e-mail judy@judydaish.com)

VARA, Shailesh Lakhman; MP; s of Lakhman Arjan Vara, and Savita, *née* Gadher; *b* 4 September 1960, Uganda; *Educ* Aylebury GS, Brunel Univ (LLB); *m* 2002, Beverley, *née* Fear; 2 s; *Career* slr; articled Richards Butler 1988–90, Crossman Block 1991–92, Payne Hicks Beach 1992–93, CMS Cameron McKenna 1994–2001; vice-chm Cons Pty 2001–05; MP (Cons) Cambridgeshire NW 2005– (Parly candidate (Cons): Birmingham Ladywood 1997, Northampton S 2001), shadow dep ldr House of Commons 2006–10, asst Govt whip 2010–12; memb Select Ctee on: Environment, Food and Rural Affrs 2005–06, Finance and Services 2011–13, Administration 2010–11; vice-chm Exec Ctee Soc of Cons Lawyers 2006–09 (treas 2001–04), chm Cons Parly Friends of India 2008–10, vice-chm Cons China Parly Gp 2009–10; vice-pres Huntingdonshire CCC 2007–; hon fell Brunel Univ 2010; Asian Jewel Award 2004; *Recreations* travel, cricket, Tae Kwon Do; *Style*— Shailesh Vara, Esq, MP; ✉ House of Commons, London SW1A 0AA (☎ 020 7219 3000, e-mail varas@parliament.uk, website www.shaileshvara.com)

VARCOE, (Christopher) Stephen; s of Philip William Varcoe, OBE (d 1980), and Mary Northwood Varcoe (d 2004); *b* 19 May 1949; *Educ* King's Sch Canterbury, King's Coll Cambridge (MA), Guildhall Sch of Music, Univ of York (PhD); *m* 22 April 1972, Melinda, da of William Arthur Davies; 2 da, 3 s; *Career* baritone; freelance concert and opera singer 1970–; Calouste Gulbenkian Fndn Fellowship 1977; prof Royal Coll of Music 2003–; fell Murray Edwards Coll Cambridge 2009–10; *Publications* Cambridge Companion to Singing (contrib), Sing English Song, New Percy Grainger Companion

V

(contrib); *Recreations* building, painting, gardening; *Style*— Stephen Varcoe, Esq; ✉ website www.stephenvarcoe.co.uk

VARDY, Prof Alan Edward; s of John Moreton Vardy (d 1990), and Margaret, *née* Thompson (d 2009); *b* 6 November 1945, Sheffield, S Yorks; *Educ* High Storrs GS Sheffield, Univ of Leeds (BSc, PhD, DEng, Heseldin Graduation Prize, Yorks Union of Insts Prize), Univ of Dundee (DSc); *m* 5 Oct 1991, Susan Janet, *née* Upstone; 2 s (Hamish b 1970, Malcolm b 1972), 1 da (Jennifer b 1971); *Career* lectr Univ of Leeds 1972–75 (research offr 1971–72), Royal Soc Warren research fell Univ of Cambridge 1975–79; Univ of Dundee: prof of civil engrg 1979–95, dep princ and vice-princ 1988–89 (dep princ 1985–88), pt/t research prof in civil engrg 1995–; dir Dundee Tunnel Research 1995–; chm and ed of ten int confs; founder memb Tport Sector Panel Technology Foresight, tstee Dundee Univ Students' Assoc (DUSA) 1989–2007; memb: Int Assoc for Hydraulic Research 1991; FRSA 1982, FICE 1989 (MICE 1975), FASCE 1995 (MASCE 1980), FRSE 2002, FHEA 2007, FREng 2007; *Publications* Fluid Principles (1990); author of 190 jl papers and refereed conf papers; *Recreations* wine, walking, wife, DIY; *Style*— Prof Alan Vardy; ✉ Dundee Tunnel Research, Kirkton, Abernyte, Perthshire PH14 9SS (☎ 01828 686241)

VARLEY, John Christian; OBE (2016), TD (1991, and bar 1997); s of Maurice Varley, of Northallerton, N Yorks, and Audrey, *née* Whitfield; *b* 5 October 1960, Leeds, W Yorks; *Educ* Univ of Leeds (BA), McGill Univ Montreal (MBA); *m* 25 Aug 1995, Rebecca, *née* Warner; 2 da (Helena b 1 Nov 1997, Rosanna b 10 May 2000), 1 s (Thomas b 10 July 2002); *Career* mktg exec Dunlop Holdings 1982–84, asst product mangr Gestetner Int 1984–86; Br Telecom: mktg mangr IDD 1986–90, mangr IDD Strategy Products & Services Div 1990–92, mangr Int Telephony Products & Services Div 1992–95, sr customer and field ops mangr Networks and Systems Div Scotland South 1995–98, gen mangr customer serv Corporate Clients 1998, prog dir AT&T/BT Global Venture 1998–99, dir Project Heritage 1999–2000; ceo Clinton Devon Estates 2000–; chm: Rural Ctee Estates Business Gp 2008–15, Environment Agency Pension Fund 2012–15; memb Bd: Countryside Agency 2002–06 (chm Audit and Risk Mgmnt Ctee 2003–06), Cmmn for Rural Communities 2006–09 (chm Audit and Risk Ctee 2006–09, memb Panel Uplands Inquiry 2009–10), Environment Agency 2009–; dir SW Chamber of Rural Enterprise 2003–11; memb: SW Sustainable Food and Farming Steering Gp 2002–05, SW Regnl Assembly 2003–05, Govt's Digital Inclusion Panel 2003–04, SW Regnl Forestry Framework Steering Gp 2004–12, Rural Enterprise Panel Nat Tst 2005–, Govt's Anerobic Digestion Task Gp 2009, Govt's Wildlife Network Review Panel 2009–10, Govt's Forestry Advsy Panel 2011–12, Govt's Nature Improvement Area Selection Panel 2011–12, Bd Natural England 2015–; chm of tstees David Arnold-Forster Tst 2003–, tstee E Devon Pebblebed Heaths Conservation Tst 2006–, memb Royal Agricultural Soc of England Practice with Science Gp 2009–13; Offr Cadet Leeds Univ OTC 1978, cmmnd 2 Lt 1980; Herts & Beds Yeomanry: Lt 1982–87, Capt (also Capt RHQ 100 Field Regt RA) 1987–93, Maj and Batty Cdr 1993–96; Maj and Dep Pres Territorial Cmmns Bd Scotland 1996–2000, RARO 2000–; FCIM, FRAgS; *Publications* Jl of the Royal Agricultural Soc of England (contrib, 2008); *Recreations* theatre, horse riding, outdoor pursuits; *Clubs* Cavalry & Guards, Farmers; *Style*— John Varley, Esq, OBE, TD; ✉ Clinton Devon Estates, Rolle Estate Office, Bicton Arena, East Budleigh, Devon EX9 7BL (☎ 01395 441141, e-mail john.varley@clintondevon.com, website www.clintondevon.com)

VARLEY, John Silvester; *b* 1 April 1956; *Educ* Downside, Oriel Coll Oxford (MA), Coll of Law; *m* 1981, Carolyn Thorn, da of Sir Richard Thorn Pease, Bt, *qv*; 1 da (Emma b 1989), 1 s (George b 1994); *Career* slr Commercial Law Dept Frere Cholmeley Slrs 1979–82, asst dir Corporate Fin Dept Barclays Merchant Bank (renamed latterly as Barclays De Zoete Wedd (BZW)) 1982–89, md BZW Asia 1989–91, dep chief exec BZW Global Equities Div 1991–94, dir Odey Asset Mgmnt 1994–95, chm BZW Asset Mgmnt 1995–96, chm BZW Property Investment Mgmnt 1995–96, chm BZW Investment Mgmnt 1995–96, dir Barclays Private Bank 1995–2000, dir Barclays Global Investors 1995–2000, memb Gp Exec Ctee Barclays 1996–2010, chm Barclays Asset Mgmnt Gp 1996–98, dir Barclays and Barclays Bank plc 1998–2010, chief exec Barclays Retail Financial Services 1998–2000, gp fin dir Barclays 2000–03, gp chief exec Barclays 2004–10; non-exec dir: AstraZeneca plc 2006– BlackRock 2009–, Rio Tinto plc 2011–; pres Business Disability Forum, chm Business Action on Homelessness; chm Marie Curie Cancer Care; *Recreations* fishing; *Clubs* Brooks's, White's; *Style*— John Varley, Esq

VARLEY, Rosemary Margaret (Rosie); OBE (2007); da of Ratcliffe Bowen Wright (d 1998), and Dr Margaret Bowen Wright, *née* Davies Williams; *b* 22 December 1951; *Educ* New Hall Chelmsford, St Mary's Coll Durham (BA), Univ of Manchester (MA); *m* 1976, Andrew Iain Varley (d 2005), s of William Thomas Varley; 1 s (Hugo Benedict Tancred George b 23 Oct 1980), 1 da (Beatrice Mary Annunciata b 24 Oct 1984); *Career* Univ of Manchester: research asst Health Servs Mgmnt Unit 1977–80, lectr in social admin 1980–81, lectr in health servs mgmnt 1981–83 (concurrently tutor to the NHS Nat Admin Trg Scheme); ind sch mgmnt Moreton Hall 1983–93, memb W Suffolk HA 1984–92 (vice-chm 1988–92), memb NHS Nat Trg Authy 1989–91, chm Mid Anglia Community Health NHS Tst 1992–97; regnl chm: NHS Exec Anglia and Oxford 1997–98, NHS Exec Eastern Regn 1999–2001; non-exec dir W Suffolk Hosps NHS Tst 2011–; regnl cmmr NHS Appts Cmmn 2001–06, public appointments assessor Office of the Commissioner for Public Appointments 2012–; chm: Gen Optical Cncl 1999–2009, Skills for Health Eastern Region 2006–, Public Guardian Bd 2007–, Gen Social Care Cncl 2008–; lay memb: Mental Health Review Tbnl 1995–, Ind Tbnl Serv (Disability Benefit Panel) 1997–; memb Cncl for Healthcare Regulatory Excellence 2001–08 (acting chair 2006–08), chair Appointments Ctee Gen Dental Cncl 2015–; govr Priory Sch Bury St Edmunds 2007–15, govr St Benedict's RC Upper Sch 2012–; Freeman City of London 2005; Liveryman Worshipful Co of Spectacle Makers 2006; Hon DUniv: East Anglia 2009, Essex 2009; FRSM, hon fell Coll of Optometrists 2009; *Recreations* walking, bridge, all things Italian, family; *Clubs* Royal Soc of Medicine; *Style*— Mrs Rosie Varley, OBE; ✉ e-mail rosievarley@btinternet.com

VARMA, Moni; s of Pooran Chand Varma, and Chanan Devi Varma; *b* 21 January 1949, Ludhiana, India; *m* Shobha, *née* Sharma; 1 da (Priya b 24 June 1983), 1 s (Rajiv b 18 Sept 1985); *Career* early career as salesman printing firm Malawi, fndr then md steel co (bought out by President of Malawi 1971), worked in steel industry UK 1980, fndr Veetee Rice 1986; hon consul for Malawi; *Recreations* golf, cricket; *Clubs* Reform; *Style*— Moni Varma, Esq; ✉ Aston House, 23 Russell Road, Moor Park, Northwood, Middlesex HA6 2LP (☎ 01923 822352, fax 01923 824843); Veetee Rice Ltd, Veetee House, 21 Neptune Close, Medway City Estate, Rochester, Kent ME2 4LT (☎ 01634 292819, fax 01634 717792, e-mail moni@veetee.com)

VARNEY, Sir David Robert; kt (2006); s of Robert Kitchener Frederick Varney, and Winifred Gwendolen, *née* Williams; *b* 11 May 1946, London; *Educ* Brockley Co GS, Univ of Surrey (BSc), Manchester Business Sch (MBA); *m* 31 July 1971, Dr Patricia Ann, *née* Billingham; 1 s (Justin Sinclair b 12 June 1975), 1 da (Meredith Louise b 25 Feb 1978); *Career* personnel asst Shell Refining Co 1968; Shell Co of Aust: strategic planning mangr 1974, islands mangr 1974–77; euro prods trading mangr Shell Int Petroleum Maatschapi (SIPM) 1977–79, business devpt dir Shell Coal 1979–83, chief exec Svenska Shell 1987–90, head of mktg Branding and Product Devpt Dept Shell Int Petroleum Co (SIPCO) 1990–92, md Downstream Oil Shell UK 1992–95, dir Oil Products SIPCO Europe 1996, chief exec BG plc 1996–2000, chm mmO2 plc 2001–04, exec chm HM Revenue and Customs 2004–06, sr advsr on transformational govt strategy to Chllr of the Exchequer 2006–07, non-exec dir HM Treasy 2004–07, non-exec dir Civil Serv Steering Bd 2006–09, PM's advsr on public service transformation 2007–09, chm Packt Publishing Ltd 2012–; non-exec dir Cable and Wireless plc 1999–2000; pres UK Petroleum Industry Assoc 1993–94, pres Inst of Petroleum 1994–96, vice-pres Combined Heat and Power Assoc 1996–2000, memb Bd of Oil & Gas Projects and Supplies Office (OSO) 1996–99, chm Business in the Community 2002–04, pres Inst for Employment Studies 2003–07; memb: President's Cncl CBI 1997–2000 and 2001–04, Food and Farming Cmmn 2001–02, Advsy Cncl Nat Consumer's Assoc 2002–07, Cncl Royal Soc of Med 2003–05, Advsy Cncl Doughty Centre 2008–; chm Stroke Assoc 2013–, chm Citizens Advice Bureau 2015–; Alumnus of the Year Univ of Manchester 2005; memb Cncl Univ of Surrey 1994–2002, pro-chllr Univ of Surrey 2016–; Hon DTechMet Univ 2006, Hon LLD Univ of Bath 2006, Hon DUniv Surrey 2007; CIMgt (pres 2005–06), CIGE, FRSM, FInstE; *Recreations* opera, rugby, formula one motor racing, sailing; *Clubs* Royal Soc of Med, Athenaeum; *Style*— Sir David Varney; ✉ 5 College Road, Dulwich, London SE21 7BQ (e-mail david@varney.uk.com)

VARNISH, Peter; OBE (1982); s of John Varnish (d 1985), and Hilary Ilma Ada, *née* Godfrey (d 1982); *b* 30 May 1947, Leamington Spa; *Educ* Warwick Sch, UCNW (BSc); *m* 10 Aug 1968, Shirley Anne, da of George Bertram Bendelow; 2 s (Jason b 7 March 1973, David b 8 May 1975); *Career* SERL: memb Res Gp on High Power Lasers 1968–70, memb Res Gp on High Power Travelling Wave Tubes 1970–72; head Electron Bombarded Semiconductor Res RSRE 1972–75, scientific advsr to MOD British Embassy Washington 1975–79; MOD: UK electronic warfare co-ordinator ARE Portsdown 1979–81, head Antenna Section and offr i/c ARE Funtington 1981–84, head Radar Div ARE Portsdown 1984, head Signature Control Div ARE Funtington 1984–89, head Electronic Warfare and Weapons Dept ARE 1989–90, dir Above Water Warfare ARE 1990, Business Sector dir Above Water Systems DRA 1991–92, RCDS 1992, dir Strategic Defence Initiative Participation Office 1993, dir Science Ballistic Missile Defence 1994–95; dir Business Devpt Defence Evaluation and Research Agency (DERA), dir of Technol (DERA) 2000–01; chief exec: S3T Ltd 2001–06, Consols Ltd 2006–08; chm: Definition Int Ltd 2002–09, Wrightson Gp 2003–11, AeroGB 2010–; dir: Closed Solutions Ltd 2002–16, CMB Technol 2003–05, CMB Inc 2003–, CMBIE Ltd 2003–04, Sparks Technol Ltd 2003–05, Geopolitical Solutions Ltd 2004–, Table 27 Ltd 2004–08, QTEL Europe plc 2005–06, BlueStar Capital 2008–13, Instantlabs Inc 2008–10, WPM Ltd 2008–11, Trango Ltd 2009–11, Halcyon LLP 2010–12, Tridex Ltd 2010–11, Deep Secure 2011, Blueknot 2012–14, Worldwide Water Ltd 2014–, Cambridge Global UK Ltd 2015–, ITC Gp 2015–; advsr to: Alchemie Ltd, Evesham Ltd, Radiation Watch Ltd, Rolatube Ltd, Strategic Communications Laboratory Ltd, PegasusBridge Fund Mgmnt, Alegro Capital Ltd, FBM Babcock 2004–08, Aerospace Resources Ltd 2006–15, Lockheed Martin Inc 2009, Risk Engrg Sofia 2012–14; defence advsr to Cons Pty shadow min for defence procurement, technology advsr D Gp London 2001–, sr military advsr to Northrop-Grumman 2009–14, security advsr Broadcast Networks Ltd; sr advsr: Portsmouth Aviation 2012, Cambridge Global Capital LLP 2013–, Tayrona LLP 2014–; chm: Stealth Conf 1988 and 2002, Military Microwaves 1990–97, Asia DEF EX, IDEX 1995–99, 2001, 2003 and 2005, IMDEX-ASIA 1997–99, Gulf Def Conference Abu Dhabi 2001, 2003 and 2005, Int Geopolitical Solutions Ltd 2001–04, Air Launched Weapons 2002–03 and 2005, Stealth 2003–2005, Interoperability 2003–04 and 2005, Aviation Repair and Maintenance 2004–05, Homeland Defence and Asymmetric Warfare 2004–05, Homeland Defence Symposium Dubai 2005, Global Security Singapore 2007 (vice-chm 2005), Technol Transfer and Offset GOCA NY 2006, Technol for C-Terrorism City Forum 2006, ID Cards and Terrorism City Forum 2007, Gulf Defence Conf Abu Dhabi 2009, Seeing in the Night Bisley 2009, Critical Nat Infrastructure London 2010, Smart Security Washington 2010, IFSEC Judging Panel 2011; lectr Higher Staff Course Bracknell 2000; memb: Sensors Ctee Defence Scientific Advsy Cncl, Stealth Working Pty Defence Scientific Advsy Cncl, Jt MOD Industry Liaison Ctee of Guided Weapons, MOD Faraday Initiative 2005–, Mgmnt Bd ARE, Cncl ERA Ltd, Advsy Ctee Dept of Electrical and Electronics Engrg Univ of Surrey, Faraday Initiative, Faculty Duke Univ USA 2013, Advsy Bd Cambridge Global Capital LLC 2014–, Royal Navy SeaMore Appeal Ctee 2014–; author of numerous scientific and defence papers and patents; TV appearances on Discovery channel and Horizon; Liveryman Worshipful Co of Coachmakers and Coach Harness Makers, Freeman City of London; memb Assoc of Electronic Warfare 1978–, SMIEEE 1976, CEng 1988, FIET (FIEE 1988), MIMgt 1989, FREng 1995 (memb Sainsbury Award Ctee), FRSA 1997; *Publications* numerous learned papers on radar, counter-terrorism, activity-based intelligence, stealth and engineering design to withstand threats; *Recreations* watching rugby football, being a grandfather, hill walking, cyber security, photography, classical music; *Clubs* Army and Navy, Brooks's, Savage; *Style*— Peter Varnish, Esq, OBE, FREng; ✉ Four Corners, 1 Greatfield Way, Rowlands Castle, Hampshire PO9 6AG (☎ 023 9241 2440, mobile 078469 140542, e-mail peter.varnish@btinternet.com); Maurice Crocker, Station House, North Street, Havant PO9 1QU (☎ 023 9248 4356, fax 023 9249 8163)

VARVILL, Michael; s of Robert Varvill, DSC (d 2003), of West Wittering, W Sussex, and Rachel, *née* Millar (d 2014); *b* 21 October 1950, Calabar, Nigeria; *Educ* Gordonstoun, Schule Schloss Salem Germany, Univ of London (LLB), Coll of Law; *m* 16 March 2015, Yoko, *née* Harada; *Children* 2 s (Wilfrid Halfdan b 28 Aug 1982, John Fitzadam b 11 April 1987), 1 da (Celia Anemone b 29 June 1984); *Career* admitted slr 1974; ptnr: Lane & Partners LLP (subsequently Bird & Bird LLP following merger in 2008) 1981–2011 (asst slr 1974–81), Wender, Murase & White (latterly Marks & Murase) NY 1984–97, ptnr HGF Ltd and HGF Law LLP 2011–15; Freeman City of York; memb Law Soc, memb Inst of Trade Mark Attorneys (MITMA), MCIArb; *Recreations* sport, the arts; *Clubs* Royal Thames Yacht; *Style*— Michael Varvill, Esq; ✉ The Mill House, Fittleworth, West Sussex RH20 1EP (☎ 020 7776 5100, fax 020 7776 5101)

VAUGHAN, Prof David John; s of Samuel John Vaughan (d 1982), of Newport, Gwent, and Esther Ruby, *née* Edwards (d 1984); *b* 10 April 1946; *Educ* Newport HS, UCL (BSc), Imperial Coll London (MSc), UC Oxford (DPhil, DSc); *m* 1, 31 Dec 1971 (m dis 1993), Heather Elizabeth, da of Alan Marat Ross (d 1979); 1 s (Emlyn James b 1979); m 2, 14 July 2007, Jane Mary, da of Ronald Barrett (d 1992); *Career* res assoc Dept Earth and Planetary Sci MIT 1971–74, reader mineralogy Aston Univ 1979–88 (lectr geological scis 1974–79), visiting prof Virginia Poly Inst and State Univ 1980, prof mineralogy Univ of Manchester 1988–; pres: Mineralogical Soc (GB & Ireland) 1988–89, European Mineralogical Union 2000–04, Mineralogical Soc of America 2014; RSC Award in Geochemistry 2005, Schlumberger Medal Mineralogical Soc 2006; FIMM 1984, fell Mineralogical Soc of America, fell Geochemical Soc; *Books* Mineral Chemistry of Metal Sulfides (with J Craig, 1978), Ore Microscopy and Ore Petrography (with J Craig, 1981), Resources of The Earth (with J Craig and B Skinner, 1988), Sulfide Mineralogy and Geochemistry (2006); *Recreations* painting, walking, music; *Style*— Prof David Vaughan; ✉ c/o School of Earth, Atmospheric and Environmental Sciences, University of Manchester, Manchester M13 9PL (☎ 01298 79169, e-mail david.vaughan@manchester.ac.uk)

VAUGHAN, Johnny; *b* 1966; *Educ* Uppingham; *Career* formerly employed as: grill chef, jewel courier, sales asst, video shop mangr; launched Two's A Crowd Theatre Co 1984; TV presenter of shows incl: Moviewatch (Channel Four) 1994, Here's Johnny (Channel 4) 1997, The Big Breakfast (Channel Four) 1997–2001, The Johnny Vaughan Film Show (Channel 4) 1999, My Kind of Town 2005, Space Cadets (Channel 4) 2005; other TV incl:

Orrible (writer and actor, BBC) 2001, Top Buzzer (writer, MTV and five) 2004; radio presenter: Fighting Talk (BBC Radio 5 Live) 2003, breakfast show (Capital) 2003–11, Absolute Radio 2012; *Awards* Best Entertainer TV Quick 1998, GQ Man of the Year 1998, TRIC Best TV Entertainer on Independent TV, Sun Best TV Entertainer 1998, Loaded Magazine Best TV Presenter, GQ Magazine Best TV Presenter 1999, RTS Best Presenter Award 1999–2000, runner-up Richard Dimbleby BAFTA for best news features presenter 2000, Creative Freedom Award for Best Entertainer, Butlins Favourite Entertainer 2000 (hon Red Coat), Sony Silver Award for Best Radio Personality 2008; *Style*— Johnny Vaughan, Esq; ✉ c/o Duncan Heath,Independent Talent Group 40 Whitfield Street, London W1T 2RH (✆ 020 7636 6565, fax 020 7323 0101)

VAUGHAN, Michael Paul; OBE (2006); *b* 29 October 1974, Manchester; *Career* former professional cricketer with Yorkshire CCC; England: 82 test matches (highest test score 197 v India 2002), 86 one-day ints, 2 Twenty20 appearances, capt 2003–08 (ret as one-day capt 2007, 26 Test match wins as capt (the England record), toured with under-19 team, capt England A team 1998–99, test debut v South Africa 1999–2000; ret 2009; sport commentator BBC, columnist The Telegraph; Professional Cricketers' Association Player of the Year 2002; Freeman City of Sheffield 2005; *Style*— Michael Vaughan, Esq, OBE

VAUGHAN, Peter; QPM (2013), DL (Mid Glamorgan 2013); *s* of Cyril Vaughan, and June Vaughan; *b* 7 September 1962; *Educ* Univ of Wales, Univ of Cambridge; *m* Suzanne; 1 s (Scott), 1 da (Danielle); *Career* joined S Wales Police1984, Asst Chief Constable Wilts Police 2003–07; S Wales Police: Dep Chief Constable 2007–09, Chief Constable 2010; v-pres NPCC; chair Strategic Policing Requirement; chm Jt Emergency Services Gp Wales, vice-pres ACPO, chair Acquisitive Crime Portfolio ACPO 2010–13, chair Strategic Nat User Gp, chair All Wales Criminal Justice Bd 2012–; memb Prince's Tst Cymru, memb Professional Ctee; ind tstee St John's Cymru 2014–; hon fell Cardiff Univ 2014–, Hon Dr South Wales Univ 2015; CCMI; CStJ (2016, OStJ 2013); *Recreations* fitness, surfing, holidays, family; *Style*— Mr Peter Vaughan, QPM, DL; ✉ South Wales Police Headquarters, Bridgend CF31 3SU

VAUGHAN, Dr Roger; *s* of late Benjamin Frederick Vaughan, and late Marjorie, *née* Wallace; *b* 14 June 1944; *Educ* Manchester Grammar, Univ of Newcastle upon Tyne (BSc, PhD); *m* 1; 3 s (Adam John b 1973, Benjamin Nicholas Gray b 1974, Thomas Peter b 1976), 2 da (Ellen Kate b 1979, Anna Cecilia b 1980); *m* 2, Valerie; 2 step s (James Maxwell Phillpott b 1973, Jonathan Peter Phillpott b 1975 d 1998); *Career* student apprentice Vickers Group 1962, shipbuilding devpt engr Swan Hunter Shipbuilders Ltd 1970–71, md A & P Appledore Ltd (joined 1971), dir Performance Improvement and Productivity Br Shipbuilders 1981–86, dir Swan Hunter Ltd, chm and chief exec Swan Hunter Shipbuilders Ltd until 1993, conslt 1993–95, chief exec Sch of Mgmnt Univ of Newcastle upon Tyne 1995–99 (visiting prof 2000–01 and 2005–10); non-exec dir Newcastle City Health NHS Tst 1996–2001; dir Northern Sinfonia Concert Soc Ltd 1996–2002; chm: Safinah Ltd 1998–, Three Rivers Learning Tst Ltd 2011– (chm 2011–14); pres Shipbuilders and Shiprepairers Assoc 1991–93; memb Nat Curriculum Council (NCC) 1992–93; Shipbuilding Gold Medal NE Coast Inst of Engrs and Shipbuilders 1969; FRINA (MRINA 1963), FREng 1990, FRSA 1993–2009; *Publications* Managing Complex Projects (with N Alderman, C Ivory, and I McLoughlin, 2014); *Recreations* music, theatre, ballet, opera, sailing, walking, reading; *Style*— Dr Roger Vaughan, FREng; ✉ Correslaw, Netherwitton, Morpeth, Northumberland NE61 4NW (✆ and fax 01670 772686, e-mail roger.vaughan@correslaw.co.uk)

VAUX OF HARROWDEN, 11 Baron (E 1523); Anthony William Gilbey; *s* of 10 Baron (d 2002), by his 1 cous Maureen Gilbey; *b* 25 May 1940; *Educ* Ampleforth; *m* 4 July 1964, Beverley, o da of Charles Alexander Walton, of Cooden, E Sussex; 2 s (Hon Richard b 1965, Hon Philip b 1967), 2 da (Hon Victoria b 1969, Hon Elizabeth b 1989); *Heir* s, Hon Richard Gilbey; *Career* accountant, farmer; Liveryman Worshipful Co of Vintners; *Recreations* walking, fishing, shooting; *Style*— The Rt Hon the Lord Vaux of Harrowden; ✉ Rusko, Gatehouse of Fleet, Kirkcudbrightshire

VAVALIDIS, Barbara Joan; *see:* Donoghue, Barbara Joan

VAVER, Prof David; *s* of Ladislav Vaver (d 1996), and Pola, *née* Komito (d 2003); *b* 28 March 1946; *Educ* Univ of Auckland (BA, LLB), Univ of Chicago (JD), Univ of Oxford (MA); *m* 30 Nov 1978, Maxine, *née* McClenaghan; 1 s (Daniel Alexander b 1 Sept 1986), 1 da (Amy Louise b 25 Feb 1990); *Career* called to the Bar NZ 1970; visiting asst prof of law Univ of Br Columbia 1971–72, lectr rising to sr lectr in law Univ of Auckland 1972–78, assoc prof of law Univ of Br Columbia 1978–85, prof Osgoode Hall Law Sch York Univ Toronto 1985–98 (prof of intellectual property law 2009–), prof of intellectual property and IT law Univ of Oxford 1998–2007 (emeritus prof 2008–), dir Oxford Intellectual Property Research Centre 1998–2007, emeritus fell St Peter's Coll Oxford; memb Royal Soc Working Gp on Intellectual Property 2001–03, memb Intellectual Property Advsy Ctee 2001–05; ed Intellectual Property Jl 1984–98 and 2009–; INTA/Pattishall Medal for Teaching of Trade Marks 2012; academic memb Intellectual Property Inst of Canada 1986, assoc memb Chartered Inst of Patent Agents 1999; *Publications* Intellectual Property Law (1997, 2 edn 2011), Copyright Law (2000), Intellectual Property Rights: Critical Concepts in Law (5 vols, 2006); numerous articles in UK and int legal periodicals; *Recreations* music, art, reading; *Style*— Prof David Vaver; ✆ 01865 862400, e-mail dv_ip@yahoo.com

VAZ, Rt Hon (Nigel) Keith Anthony Standish; PC (2006), MP; *s* of late Tony Vaz, and Merlyn Verona Rosemary, *née* Pereira; bro of Valerie Vaz, MP, *qv*; *b* 26 November 1956, Aden, Yemen; *Educ* Latymer Upper Sch, Gonville & Caius Coll Cambridge (MA); *m* 3 April 1993, Maria Fernandes; 1 s (Luke Swraj b 2 March 1995), 1 da (Anjali Olga Verona b 4 April 1997); *Career* slr Richmond upon Thames Cncl 1982, sr slr London Borough of Islington 1982–85, slr Highfields & Belgrave Law Centre Leicester 1985–87; called to the Bar 1990; contested Euro elections: Richmond & Barnes 1983, Surrey West 1984; MP (Lab) Leicester E 1987–; memb: Home Affrs Select Ctee 1987–92 (chm 2007–), Constitutional Affrs Select Ctee 2003–07; memb Standing Ctees on: Immigration Bill 1987–88, Legal Aid Bill 1988, Children Bill 1989, Football Spectators Bill 1989, NHS and Community Care Bill 1989–90, Cts and Legal Servs 1990–, Armed Forces Bill 1991; chm: Lab Party Race Action Gp 1983–, Unison Gp 1990–99, Lab Pty Regnl Exec 1994–96; chair: Parly Nupe Gp, All-Pty Parly Footwear and Leather Industry Gp; jt vice-chair Lab Pty Dept Ctee for Int Devpt 1997–2000, memb Lab Pty Dept Ctee for Home Affrs 1997–2001, chm Ethnic Minority Taskforce 2006–, memb Nat Exec Ctee 2007–; treas All-Pty Race and Community Gp 2003–, chair All-Pty Yemen Gp; treas Tribune Gp (vice-chair 1992); sec: Legal Servs Campaign, Indo-Br Parly Gp, Lab Educn Gp, Parly Lab Party Wool and Textiles Gp; co-ordinator BCCI Parly Gp 1991–, shadow jr min for environment (with responsibilities for inner city and local govt) 1992–94, shadow min for planning and regeneration 1994–97, PPS to the Attorney Gen 1997–99, Parly sec Lord Chancellor's Department 1999, min for Europe 1999–2001; memb Exec Ctee Inter-Parly Union; vice-chair Br Cncl 1998–99; EU ambass for the year of intercultural dialogue 2008; pres: Thurnby Lodge Boys Club 1987–1997, Leicester and S Leicestershire RSPCA 1988–2000, Hillcroft Football Club 1988–2000, Leicester & South Leicestershire RSPCA 1988, India Devpt Gp (UK) 1992–, Nat Orgn of Asian Businesses; govr: Hamilton Community Coll Leicester 1987–91, St Patrick's Sch Leicester 1985–89, Regent Coll 1998; patron: Ginger Bread 1990–99, Leicester Rowing Club 1992–99, Asian Business Club 1998–99; columnist: Tribune, Catholic Herald; memb Nat Advsy Bd Crime Concern; memb: UNISON, Lab Party; memb Clothing and Footwear Inst 1988, memb Bd Br Cncl 1999; *Style*— The Rt Hon Keith Vaz, MP; ✉ 144 Uppingham Road, Leicester (✆ 0116 212 2028, fax 0116 2122121); House of Commons, London SW1A 0AA

VAZ, Valerie Carol Marian; MP; da of Anthony Xavier Vaz (d 1970), and Merlyn Verona, *née* Pereira (d 2003); sis of Rt Hon Keith Vaz, MP, *qv*; *b* 7 December 1954, Aden, Yemen; *Educ* Twickenham County GS, Bedford Coll Univ of London (BSc), Sidney Sussex Coll Cambridge, Coll of Law; *m* 11 July 1992, Paul Townsend; 1 da; *Career* admitted slr 1984; articled clerk Herbert Smith, local govt slr 1986–92, estab Townsend Vaz Slrs 1992–2001, Govt legal serv Treasy Slrs Dept and Miny of Justice 2001–10, memb Health Select Ctee 2010–, memb Regulatory Reform Ctee 2010–, vice-chair Parly Lab Party 2010–; cncllr Ealing Borough Cncl 1986–90 (dep ldr 1988–89), MP (Lab) Walsall S 2010–; Parly candidate Twickenham 1987, European candidate E Midlands 1999; dep district judge Midland & Oxford Circuit 1996–2000; memb Lay Advsy Panel Coll of Optometrists 2007; presenter and interviewer Network East (BBC) 1987; regular contrib articles in pubns; memb: Lab Pty, Law Soc, Assoc of Women Slrs, Equity, Nat Tst, Premier Friend of Kew Gardens; *Recreations* music (playing piano), gardening, tennis; *Style*— Ms Valerie Vaz, MP; ✉ House of Commons, London SW1A 0AA

VEEDER, Van Vechten (Johnny); QC (1986); *s* of John Van Vechten Veeder (d 1976), and Helen, *née* Townley; *b* 14 December 1948; *Educ* Neuilly Paris, Clifton, Jesus Coll Cambridge (MA); *Career* called to the Bar Inner Temple 1971; *Publications* The ICCA National Report on England (1988 and 1996), The Final Report on the Independent Inquiry into the Capital Market activities of the London Borough of Hammersmith and Fulham (with Barratt and Reddington, 1991); *Recreations* sailing, reading, travelling; *Clubs* Aldeburgh Yacht, Orford Sailing, Little Ship, Garrick; *Style*— V V Veeder, Esq, QC; ✉ Essex Court Chambers, 24 Lincoln's Inn Fields, London WC2A 3ED (✆ 020 7813 8000, fax 020 7813 8080)

VELJANOVSKI, Dr Cento; *s* of Gavril Veljanovski, of Macedonia, and Margaret, *née* Wagenaar; *b* 19 February 1953; *Educ* Monash Univ (BEc, MEc), Univ of Oxford (DPhil); *m* 1990, Annabel, da of Col William Fazakerley, of Sherborne, Dorset; 1 da (Lydia Rose b 17 Oct 1992), 1 s (Tomas Cento b 6 July 1995); *Career* jr res fell Wolfson Coll Oxford 1978–84, visiting prof Univ of Toronto 1980–81, lectr UCL 1984–87, res and ed dir Inst of Econ Affairs 1987–91; dir Lexecon Ltd 1990–94, non-exec dir Flextech plc 1993–95, managing ptnr Case Associates 1996–; econ advsr Republic of Macedonia 1991–94; memb: Int Bar Assoc, CIArb, IOD, Competition Law Assoc; Freeman City of London, Liveryman Worshipful Co of Glass Sellers; *Books* Selling the State – Privatisation in Britain (1987), Privatisation and Competition (1989), Freedom in Broadcasting (1989), The Media in Britain Today (1990), Regulators and the Market (1991), Pay TV in Australia (1999), The Economics of Law (2006), Economic Principles of Law (2007); *Recreations* rowing, art, television, walking; *Clubs* Oxford and Cambridge, Chelsea Arts, Annabel's, Commonwealth; *Style*— Dr Cento Veljanovski

VELMANS, Marianne H; da of Loet A Velmans, of Sheffield, MA, and Edith, *née* van Hessen; *b* 5 July 1950; *Educ* Int Sch of Geneva, Univ of Sussex (BA); *m* Paul A Sidey; 1 s (Jack b 18 Oct 1984), 1 da (Saskia b 23 April 1990); *Career* Penguin Books 1973–80, head of London office Doubleday & Co Inc 1980–87, publishing dir Doubleday (Transworld Publishers Ltd) 1987–; *Books* Working Mother – A Practical Handbook (with Sarah Litvinoff, 1987, revised edn 1993); *Style*— Ms Marianne Velmans; ✉ Doubleday, 61–63 Uxbridge Road, London W5 5SA (✆ 020 8579 2652, fax 020 8579 5479, e-mail m.velmans@transworld-publishers.co.uk)

VENABLES, Robert; QC (1990); *s* of Walter Edwin Venables, MM, of Wath upon Dearne, Rotherham, and Mildred Daisy Robson, *née* Taylor; *b* 1 October 1947; *Educ* Wath upon Dearne Co GS, Merton Coll Oxford (MA), LSE (LLM); *Career* lectr: Merton Coll Oxford 1972–75, UCL 1973–75; Univ of Oxford: official fell and tutor in jurisprudence St Edmund Hall 1975–80 (fell by special election 1992), CUF lectr; called to the Bar Middle Temple 1973 (bencher 1999), in practice 1976–; chm Revenue Bar Assoc 2001–; conslt g ed The Offshore Tax Planning Review, The Personal Tax Planning Review and The Corporate Tax Review, chm Advsy Editorial Bd The Charity Law and Practice Review; treas CRUSAID 1991–96 (pres Cncl 1996–2000, memb Cncl 1996–), dir Yves Guihannec Fndn 1992–, tstee Temple Music Tst 2001–; FTII 1983 (memb Cncl 1999–); *Books* Inheritance Tax Planning (3 edn, 1996), Tax Planning Through Trusts (1990), National Insurance Contribution Planning (1990), Tax Planning and Fundraising for Charities (2 edn, 1994, 3 edn, 2001), Non-Resident Trusts (7 edn, 1998, 8 edn, 2001); *Recreations* music making; *Clubs* Travellers; *Style*— Robert Venables, Esq, QC; ✉ 61 Harrington Gardens, London SW7 4JZ

VENKITARAMAN, Prof Ashok; *Educ* Christian Medical Coll Vellore India (MB, BS, Kutumbiah Gold Medal in Medicine, Carman Prize in Surgery, Chandy Gold Medal for Clinical Studies), UCL (PhD), Univ of Cambridge (MA); *m* Dr Rajini, da of Col PV Ramana; *Career* house physician Christian Medical Coll Hosp Vellore India 1983–84, fell Lady Tata Meml Tst UCL & Charing Cross & Westminster Med Sch 1985–88; MRC Laboratory of Molecular Biology Cambridge: fell Beit Meml Tst 1988–91, memb Scientic Staff 1991–98; Ursula Zoellner prof of cancer research Sch of Clinical Medicine Univ of Cambridge 1998–; dir MRC Cancer Unit 2010–; memb EMBO European Acad 2004; professorial fell Pembroke Coll Cambridge, emeritus fell New Hall Cambridge; FMedSci; *Publications* numerous articles in scientific and medical jls; *Style*— Prof Ashok Venkitaraman; ✉ Hutchison/MRC Research Centre, University of Cambridge, Hills Road, Cambridge CB2 2XZ (✆ 01223 336901, fax 01223 763374)

VENNING, Philip Duncombe Riley; OBE (2003); *s* of Roger Riley Venning, MBE (d 1953), and Rosemary Stella Cenzi, *née* Mann; *b* 24 March 1947; *Educ* Sherborne, Principia Coll IL, Trinity Hall Cambridge (MA); *m* 4 April 1987, Elizabeth Frances Ann, da of late Michael Anthony Robelou Powers; 2 da (Laura Rosemary Ann b 28 May 1993, Grace Merlyn Frances b 14 July 1995); *Career* journalist Times Educnl Supplement 1970–81 (asst ed 1978), freelance writer 1981–84, sec Soc for the Protection of Ancient Buildings 1984–2012; memb: Westminster Abbey Fabric Cmmn 1998–, Cncl Nat Tst 1992–2001, Expert Panel Heritage Lottery Fund 2005–11, East of England Ctee Heritage Lottery Fund 2013–; tstee: Nat Churches Tst (formerly Historic Churches Preservation Tst) 1995–2005 (vice-pres 2006–08), Heritage Link 2002–03; contrib to books and publns on educn and historic building conservation; Queen Mother Meml Medal for contribution to craftsmanship 2011; FSA 1989, FRSA 1990; *Recreations* visiting old buildings, book collecting; *Style*— Philip Venning, Esq, OBE, FSA; ✉ Wyke House, Mill Lane, Docking, Norfolk PE31 8NX

VENTERS, Ewan; *s* of Alexander Venters, and Josephine, *née* Durkin; *b* 24 August 1972, Dumferline; *Educ* St Serf's Edinburgh; *m* 10 Oct 1998, Jane, *née* Houghton; 2 da (Charlotte b 16 Jan 2010, Sophia b 28 Sept 2012); *Career* Sainsbury's Supermarkets Ltd: mgmnt trainee/dept mangr fresh produce 1989–91, new store logistics controller 1991–92, PA to Northern Regnl Dir 1992–94; PA to Gp Dep Chm J Sainsbury plc 1994–97, food buyer Sainsbury's Supermarkets Ltd 1997–99, buying controller Brake Bros 1999–2001, commercial dir Brake Bros 2001–03, sales operations dir Brakes 2003, UK nat account dir Brakes 2003–04, md Brakes White Tablecloth Business 2005, exec dir for food, restaurants and online business Selfridges 2005–12, chief exec Fortnum & Mason plc 2012–; *Recreations* food, cooking and restaurants, theatre, cinema, tennis, skiing, art, travel; *Style*— Ewan Venters, Esq; ✉ Fortnum & Mason plc, 181 Piccadilly, London W1A 1ER (Twitter @ewanventers)

VENTRESS, Peter; *b* 3 December 1960; *Educ* Univ of Oxford (MA), MBA; *Career* chief exec Corporate Express NV 2007–08, pres Staples Int 2008–09, chief exec Berendsen plc 2009–; *Style*— Peter Ventress, Esq; ✉ Berendsen plc, 4 Grosvenor Place, London SW1X 7DL

VENTRY, 8 Baron (I 1800); Sir Andrew Wesley Daubeny de Moleyns; 8 Bt (1797); assumed by deed poll 1966 the surname of Daubeny de Moleyns; s (by 2nd w) of Hon Francis Alexander Innys Eveleigh-Ross-de-Moleyns (d 1964), s of 6 Baron Ventry, and his 2 w Joan (later Mrs Nigel Springett; d 1993), eldest da of Harold Wesley, of Surrey; suc uncle, 7 Baron, 1987; *b* 28 May 1943; *Educ* Aldenham; *m* 1, 20 Feb 1963 (m dis 1979), Nelly Edouard Renée, da of Abel Chaumillon, of Loma de los Riseos, Villa Angel, Torremolinos, Malaga, Spain; 2 da (Hon Elizabeth-Ann b 1964, Hon Brigitte b 1967), 1 s (Hon Francis b 1865); m 2, 1983, Jill Rosemary, da of Cecil Walter Oram; 1 da (Hon Lisa b 1985); *Heir* s, Hon Francis Daubeny de Moleyns; *Career* farmer 1961–, in electronics 1986–; dir: Burgie Lodge Farms Ltd 1970–, C & R Briggs Commercials 1986–87, Glenscott Motor Controls Inc 1987–88 (vice-pres), Glenscott Motor Controls Inc 1988–94 (pres); European mktg mangr Unico Int 1994–; *Recreations* travel, photography, sailing, skiing; *Style*— The Rt Hon the Lord Ventry

VENUGOPAL, Dr Sriramashetty; OBE; s of Satyanarayan Sriramashetty (d 1962), and Manikyamma, *née* Akkenapalli; *b* 14 May 1933, Nalgonda, India; *Educ* Osmania Med Coll Hyderabad (BSc, MB BS), Madras Univ (DMRD); *m* 22 May 1960, Subhadra (Meena), da of Raja Bahadur Sita Ramachander Rao (d 1949); 1 da (Anu b 1962), 1 s (Arun b 1964); *Career* med posts Osmania Hosp, state med servs Hyderabad Singareni Collieries 1959–65, registrar in radiology Selly Oak Hosp Birmingham 1965–66, registrar in chest med Springfield Hosp Grimsby 1966–67, princ in gen practice Aston Birmingham 1967–2001, hosp practitioner in psychiatry All Saints Hosp Birmingham 1972–96; contrib jls on medico-political subjects; fndr memb and chm Link House Cncl 1975–92, memb Local Review Ctee for Winson Green Prison 1981–83, fndr memb Osmania Grad Med Assoc in UK 1984–; memb: W Birmingham HA 1984–89, Working Gp DHSS 1984–89 (Local Med Ctee 1975–2001, Dist Med Ctee 1978–93), GMC 1984–99, Birmingham Community Liaison Advsy Ctee 1985; vice-chm: Hyderabad Charitable Tst 1985, Birmingham Div BMA 1980 (chm 1985–86); Overseas Doctors' Assoc: fndr memb 1975–, dep treas 1975–81, nat vice-chm 1981–87, chm info and advsy serv 1981–99, nat chm 1987–93, nat pres 1993–99; since retirement involved with Rotary charity work, aided Tsunami affected fishermen families at Cuddalore India, coordinator annual eye camps in India (enabled over 1000 eye operations); FRSM 1986, FRIPHH 1988, FRCGP 1997 (MRCGP 1990), MFPHM 1998; *Recreations* medical politics, music, gardening; *Clubs* Aston Rotary (former pres, elected Paul Harris fell); *Style*— Dr Sriramashetty Venugopal, OBE; ✉ 24 Melville Road, Edgbaston, Birmingham B16 9JT (☎ 0121 454 1725, e-mail s_venugopal@msn.com)

VENVILLE, Malcolm Frank; s of Barry Venville (d 1978), of Birmingham, and Catherine Louise, *née* May; *b* 5 September 1962; *Educ* Lighthall Comp, Solihull Tech Coll, Poly of Central London (BA); *Career* engrg apprenticeship British Leyland 1980–81, Art and Design foundation course Solihull Tech Coll 1981–83, photographic asst 1987–90, freelance photographer 1990–; film dir: 44 Inch Chest 2009, Henry's Crime 2010; *Awards* Creative Circle Advtg Awards: bronze Most Promising Beginner for Photography 1992, silver Most Promising Beginner for Direction 1993, various gold and silvers; Assoc of Photographers: 3 merits and 1 silver Tenth Awards 1993, 2 silvers and 1 merit Eleventh Awards 1994, 1 merit 1995; 1 silver and inclusions D&AD; *Style*— Malcolm Venville, Esq

VERE HODGE, Dr (Richard) Anthony; s of Rev Preb Francis Vere Hodge, and Eleanor Mary, *née* Connor; *b* 27 December 1943; *Educ* Radley, Trinity Coll Dublin (BA), Worcester Coll Oxford (DPhil); *m*; 1 s, 2 da; *Career* joined Beecham Pharmaceuticals (then SmithKline Beecham Pharmaceuticals, now GlaxoSmithKline) 1969, worked on Interferon Inducers then Human Interferon (project mangr 1974–76), transferred to Antiviral Chemotherapy Project (which discovered Penciclovir 1983, and Famiclovir 1985); princ author of first publication with named antiherpesvirus compounds Famciclovir and Penciclovir (1989) and other articles on subject; seconded to Worldwide Strategic Product Devpt SmithKline Beecham 1993, assoc dir Anti-infectives Section 1995–96; dir Vere Hodge Antivirals Ltd 1996–, conslt Pharmasset Inc 2000–05; reviews ed Antiviral Chemistry and Chemotherapy (AVCC) 2005–08; memb: The Chromotographic Soc 1989, Int Soc for Antiviral Research 1990 (memb Pubn Ctee 2006–, hon sec 2008–14, chair 2014–), American Soc for Microbiology 1997; MRSC 1968; *Publications* Integration of Pharmaceutical Discovery and Development: Case Studies (1998, contrib a chapter), Antiviral Agents vol 1 Encyclopedia of Virology (2008, contrib a chapter), General Mechanisms of Antiviral Resistance, Genetics and Evolution of Infectious Diseases (with Hugh J Field, ed Michel Tibayrenc, 2011, contrib a chapter), Antiviral Agents for Herpes Simplex Virus (with Hugh J Field, Advanced Pharmacology 2013, contrib a chapter); reviews: Telbivudine/Torcitabine – Current Opinion in Investigational Drugs (2004), Recent Developments in Anti-Herpesvirus Drugs (with Hugh J Field, 2013); *Recreations* bell ringing, gardening, hill walking; *Style*— Dr Anthony Vere Hodge

VEREKER, Sir John Michael Medlicott; KCB (1999, CB 1992); s of Cdr Charles William Medlicott Vereker (d 1995), and Marjorie Hughes, *née* Whatley (d 1984); *b* 9 August 1944; *Educ* Marlborough, Keele Univ (BA); *m* 7 Nov 1971, Judith, da of Hobart and Alice Rowen, of Washington, DC; 1 da (Jennifer b 1973), 1 s (Andrew b 1975); *Career* asst princ: ODM 1967–69, World Bank Washington 1970–72; princ ODM 1972, private sec to successive Mins at ODM, asst sec 1978, PM's Office 1980–83, under sec FCO ODA 1983–88 (princ fin offr 1986–88), dep sec (teachers) DES 1988, dep sec (further and higher educn and science) DES 1988–94, permanent sec ODA 1994–97, permanent sec Dept for Int Devpt 1997–2002, govr and C-in-C Bermuda 2002–07; chm Student Loans Co Ltd 1989–91; ind dir: XL Gp plc, MWH Global; *Style*— Sir John Vereker, KCB

VEREKER, Rupert David Peregrine Medlicott; s of John Stanley Herbert Medlicott Vereker, and Valerie Ann Virginia, *née* Threlfall; *b* 31 July 1957; *Educ* Radley, Univ of Bradford (BA); *m* 9 Aug 1986, Philippa Janet, da of Geoffrey Stocks; 2 s (Frederick James Herbert Medlicott b 30 June 1990, Jack Rupert William Medlicott b 30 Jan 1992); *Career* advertising exec; Benton & Bowles (now DMB & B) 1980–85 (graduate trainee then account mangr), Doyle Dane Bernbach (now BMP DDB Needham) 1985–87 (account mangr then dir), md BV Gp plc 1987–2003, md Sonic Network 2004–; *Style*— Rupert Vereker, Esq

VEREY, Sir David John; kt (2015), CBE (2004); s of Michael John Verey (d 2000), and Sylvia Mary, *née* Wilson; cous of (Henry) Nicholas Verey (d 1996); *b* 8 December 1950; *Educ* Eton, Trinity Coll Cambridge (MA); *m* 1, 1974 (m dis 1990), Luise, *née* Jaschke; 2 s, 1 da; m 2, 1990, Emma Katharine Broadhead, da of Sir Christophor Laidlaw, *qv*; *Career* Lazard Brothers & Co: joined 1972, dir 1983–2001, dep chief exec 1985–90, chief exec 1990–2000, chm 1992–2001; dep gp chm Cazenove Gp plc 2001–02, chm The Blackstone Gp UK 2004– (special advsr 2003); non-exec dir: Pearson plc 1996–2000, Daily Mail and General Trust plc 2004–; sr advsr Lazard & Co ltd 2010–; Lead non-exec Dir DCMS 2010–; chm Art Collections Fund 2004–, Sofina SA 2014, The Art Fund 2004–14, Govt art collection advsy BD 2013–, chm of tstees Tate Gallery 1999–2004 (tstee 1992–2004), N fell Eton Coll 1997–, hon fell St Hugh's Coll Oxford; tstee Br Cncl 2014–; *Recreations* stalking, bridge, gardening, travel; *Style*— Sir David Verey, CBE

VERITY, Dr Christopher Michael; s of Rev Harry William Verity (d 1988), of Cambridge, and Gladys, *née* Banks; *b* 18 February 1946; *Educ* Merchant Taylors' Sch Crosby, Leeds GS, Keble Coll Oxford (MA, BM BCh), St Thomas' Hosp Med Sch; *m* 5 May 1984, Dorothy Bowes (Kelly), da of Clifford Claud Jupp, of Br Columbia; *Career* MO Save The Children Fund Phnom Penh Cambodia 1974, med registrar St Thomas' Hosp 1974–75, house physician Hosp For Sick Children Gt Ormond St 1977, fell Dept of Paediatric Neurology Univ of Br Columbia Canada 1980–81, lectr Dept of Child Health Bristol Royal Hosp For Sick Children 1982–85, conslt paediatric neurologist Addenbrooke's Hosp Cambridge 1985–, assoc lectr Univ of Cambridge Med Sch 1985–, princ investigator PIND Research Gp Addenbrooke's Hosp Cambridge 1997–; chair: MacKeith Meetings Ctee 1992–97, Br Paediatric Surveillance Unit Exec Ctee 1995–2001, Nat Clinical Co-ordinating Gp Children's Epilepsy Surgery Service 2012–; vice-pres RCPCH 2003–08; memb Ctee Br Branch International League against Epilepsy 1996–2003, med advsr Roald Dahl Fndn 1997–; chair Editorial Bd Mac Keith Press 2009–; memb Br Paediatric Neurology Assoc; FRCP 1990, FRCPCH 1997; *Publications* author of papers on: the Polle syndrome, follow up after cerebral hemispherectomy, hereditary sensory neuropathies, febrile convulsions in a nat cohort, variant Creutzfeldt-Jakob disease in UK children, swine 'flu vaccination and narcolepsy, Guillain-Barre syndrome in children; *Recreations* skiing, golf, painting; *Style*— Dr Christopher Verity; ✉ PIND Research Group, Box 267, Addenbrooke's Hospital, Hills Road, Cambridge CB2 0QQ (☎ 01223 216299, fax 01223 586508, e-mail christopher.verity@addenbrookes.nhs.uk)

VERJEE, Baron (Life Peer UK 2013), of Portobello in the Royal Borough of Kensington and Chelsea; Rumi Verjee; CBE (2009); *Educ* Downing Coll Cambridge; *Career* chm Thomas Goode & Co; Wilkins fell Cambridge 2003; *Style*— The Lord Verjee, CBE; ✉ The Rumi Foundation, 19 South Audley Street, London W1K 2BN

VERMA, Baroness (Life Peer 2006), of Leicester in the County of Leicestershire; Sandip Verma; da of late Shivcharan Singh Rana; *b* 30 June 1959, India; *Educ* De Montfort Univ; *m* 1977, Ashok Kumar Verma; 1 da (Tamanna b 9 May 1979), 1 s (Tarun b 9 March 1982); *Career* business woman since age 19; Parly candidate 2001 and 2005, appointed to House of Lords 2006, promoted to Cons front benches as whip for educn and health 2006; currently: min for int devpt; patron on several orgns and charities; recipient of numerous awards and nominations; *Recreations* walking, reading, travelling; *Style*— The Rt Hon the Lady Verma; ✉ 28 Knighton Road, Leicester LE2 3HH (☎ 0116 270 1686); House of Lords, London SW1A 0PW (e-mail vermas@parliament.uk)

VERNON, Annie; *b* 1 September 1982, Truro, Cornwall; *Educ* Univ of Cambridge; *Career* rower; debut GB sr squad 2005; achievements incl: Bronze medal pair World Rowing U23 Championships 2004, Gold medal quadruple sculls World Rowing Championships 2007, Silver medal quadruple sculls Olympic Games Beijing 2008, Silver and Bronze medals quadruple sculls World Cup Series 2011; *Clubs* Marlow Rowing; *Style*— Ms Annie Vernon

VERNON, 11 Baron (GB 1762); Anthony William Vernon-Harcourt; s of Col William Ronald Denis Vernon-Harcourt, OBE (d 1999), and Nancy Everil, *née* Leatham; suc kinsman, 10 Baron Vernon, 2000; *b* 29 October 1939, Richmond, N Yorks; *Educ* Eton, Magdalene Coll Cambridge (MA); *m* 3 Dec 1966, Cherry Stanhope, *née* Corbin; 1 da (Hon Charlotte Lucy (Hon Mrs Kaye) b 1968), 3 s (Hon Simon Anthony b 1969, Hon Edward William b 1973, Hon Oliver Thomas b 1977); *Heir* s, Hon Simon Vernon-Harcourt; *Career* fndr and chm Monks Partnership 1980–2002, dir PricewaterhouseCoopers 2000–02; ed Charterhouse Top Management Remuneration 1978–88; sometime memb: IPM, IOD; *Publications* incl: Executive and All-Employee Share Schemes (1981), Company Car Policy Guide (1981–87), Boardroom Pay and Incentives in Growth Companies (1984), Performance Related Bonuses for Senior Management (1989), Archibald Sturrock: Pioneer Locomotive Engineer (2007), Yorkshire Engine Sheffield's Locomotive Manufacturer (2008), L F Vernon-Harcort Civil Engineer (2012); *Recreations* cycling, railway history, gardening; *Style*— The Rt Hon the Lord Vernon

VERNON, Dr Clare Christine; da of Stephen Vernon, 12 Willows Ave, Lytham St Annes, Lancashire, and Mary, *née* Dewhirst; *b* 23 October 1951; *Educ* Queen Mary Sch Lytham, Girton Coll Cambridge (MA, MB BChir), Bart's; *m* 17 July 1976 (m dis 1988), George, s of Herbert Evans (d 1984); *Career* registrar in radiotherapy: Royal Free Hosp 1979, Middx Hosp 1982; sr registrar in radiotherapy Mount Vernon Hosp 1984, conslt clinical oncologist Hammersmith Hosp 1986–; prof in radiation oncology Hong Kong, Alexandria and Lahore; memb: BMA 1976, GMC 1976, 1951 Club 1986; FRCR 1984, MPS 1989; *Recreations* sports, music, archaeology; *Clubs* 1951; *Style*— Dr Clare C Vernon; ✉ 18 Brookfield Avenue, Ealing, London W5 1LA (☎ 020 8997 1786, e-mail clarecvernon@hotmail.co.uk)

VERNON, Diana Charlotte; da of Roderick W P Vernon, of Chobham, Surrey, and Jennifer F F, *née* Tyrrell; *b* 30 April 1961; *Educ* St Michael's Burton Park, St Mary's Coll Durham (BA), KCL (PGCE); *Career* editorial asst John Wiley & Sons Ltd 1982–84, account exec Business Image PR 1984–85, Grayling PR 1985–87, Thorn EMI plc 1987–89, LIG plc 1989–93; Downe House Sch Newbury 1994–2000; headmistress: Woldingham Sch Caterham 2000–07, City of London Sch for Girls 2007–; govr: Lilian Baylis Sch London 1985–2002, Flexlands Sch Chobham 1994–2004, Princes Mead Sch Winchester 1999–2001, Conifers Sch Midhurst 2003–06, Stoke Brunswick East Grinstead 2003–06, Cumnor House Danehill 2003–05, St Christopher's Hampstead 2003–, Notting Hill Prep Sch 2008–; *Recreations* theatre, travel, cookery, swimming; *Style*— Miss Diana Vernon

VERNON, Prof Stephen Andrew; s of Alan Vernon (d 1979), of Alderley Edge, Cheshire, and Phyllis Mary Vernon (d 2014); *b* 10 February 1955; *Educ* King's Sch Macclesfield, Univ of Bristol Med Sch (MB ChB), Univ of Nottingham (DM); *m* 1 Sept 1985, Alison Elizabeth Mary, da of Claude Walton (d 1990), of Mansfield, Notts; 1 da (Olivia Katherine b 2 Dec 1989), 1 s (Simon Alexander Alan b 5 Feb 1992); *Career* house physician Bristol Royal Infirmary 1978–79, house surgn Frenchay Hosp Bristol 1979, demonstrator and lectr in anatomy Bristol Med Sch 1979–80, SHO and registrar in ophthalmology Bristol Eye Hosp 1980–83, sr registrar Oxford Eye Hosp 1983–86, sr lectr and founding head Academic Unit of Ophthalmology Univ of Nottingham and hon conslt ophthalmologist Nottingham HA 1986–94, conslt ophthalmologist Univ Hosp NHS Tst Nottingham 1994–2015, special prof of ophthalmology Univ of Nottingham 2008–15; dir Vernon Eyecare Ltd 2014–; author of academic pubns on ophthalmic epidemiology, diabetic retinopathy and glaucoma detection and mgmnt; memb: Euro Glaucoma Soc, Midlands Ophthalmic Soc (treas 1992–99, pres 2000–01), UK and Eire Glaucoma (memb Cncl 2000–05, chm 2005–); FRCS 1982, FRCOphth 1989 (vice-pres 2016–), Hon FCOptom 2009; *Books* Ophthalmology (1988), Passing Postgraduate Examinations in Ophthalmology (1992), Differential diagnosis in Ophthalmology (1998); *Recreations* golf, skiing, music and drama; *Style*— Prof Stephen A Vernon; ✉ The BMI Park Hospital, Sherwood Lodge Drive, Arnold, Nottingham NG5 8RX (e-mail profsavernon@doctors.org.uk)

VERRILL, John Rothwell; s of Dr Peter John Verrill, of Aldeburgh, and Christine Mary, *née* Rothwell; *b* 25 March 1954; *Educ* Univ Coll Sch, UCL (LLB); *m* 1980; 4 s; m 2, 23 Dec 2002, Louise Verrill, *qv*; *Career* admitted slr 1981; Lawrence Graham: asst slr 1982–86, ptnr 1986–, head of Corp Recovery Gp; Licensed Insolvency Practitioner 1990–; Freeman Worshipful Co of Slrs 1988; memb: Law Soc, City of Westminster Law Soc, Int Bar Assoc (UK Energy Lawyers Gp), Insolvency Practitioners Assoc, Cncl and pres Assoc of Business Recovery Professionals, R3; memb Insolvency Lawyers Assoc, dir INSOL Int; *Books* Butterworth's Insolvency Meetings Manual (1995); *Recreations* rowing, shooting, opera; *Clubs* Leander, Travellers; *Style*— John Verrill, Esq; ✉ Lawrence Graham, 190 Strand, London WC2R 1JN (☎ 020 7379 0000, fax 020 7379 6854, e-mail john.verrill@lg-legal.com)

VERRILL, Louise; da of Geoffrey Gay, of Amesbury, Wilts, and Ann, *née* Rickman; *b* 29 March 1955, London; *Educ* Benenden, UWE (DipLP); *m* 23 Dec 2002, John Verrill, *qv*; 1

da (Catherine Elisabeth Fox b 15 Dec 1981), 1 s (William Marcus St Vigor Fox b 17 Aug 1984), 4 step s; *Career* admitted slr 1997; slr specialising in insolvency and corporate restructuring; ptnr and head of London Business Support and Restructuring team Addleshaw Goddard; memb Exec Ctee INSOL Europe 2004–, co-chm G36 INSOL Int 2004–07 (tech chair Int European Regnl Conf Prague 2004); memb: Ctee Int Bar Assoc, Investigation Ctee ICAEW 2001–04; former ed Eurofenix, memb Editorial Bd INSOL World, author of articles for legal and accountancy press; pres: Insolvency Practitioners Assoc 2005–06, Insolvency Lawyers Assoc 2007–; memb: American Bankruptcy Inst, Assoc of Business Recovery Professionals, Assoc of Partnership of Practitioners Law Soc; licensed insolvency practitioner; *Recreations* gardening, tennis, skiing, sailing, shooting; *Style*— Mrs Louise Verrill

VERTUE, Beryl; CBE (2016, OBE 2000); *Career* chm and prodr Hartswood Films Ltd; chm PACT 1999–2001; credits incl: Men Behaving Badly (six series and two Christmas specials, BBC, exec conslt US version), Wonderful You (ITV), Is it Legal? (three series), In Love With Elizabeth (documentary, BBC1), Officers and Gentlemen (documentary, BBC2), The Red Baron (documentary, BBC2), Border Café (BBC1), The War behind the Wire (BBC2), The Savages (BBC1), Coupling (four series, BBC2), Carrie and Barry (two series, BBC1), Fear, Stress and Anger (BBC2), Jekyll (BBC1), Sherlock (BBC1); BAFTA Award for Outstanding Creative Contribution to Television 2004, RTS Lifetime Achievement Award 2012; FRTS; *Style*— Ms Beryl Vertue, CBE; ✉ Hartswood Films Ltd, Twickenham Studios, The Barons, St Margarets, Twickenham, Middlesex TW1 2AW (☎ 020 8607 8736, fax 020 8607 8744)

VESSEY, Prof Martin Paterson; CBE (1994); s of Sydney James Vessey (d 1988), of Mill Hill, London, and Catherine, *née* Thomson (d 2000); *b* 22 July 1936; *Educ* UCS Hampstead, UCL, UCH Med Sch (MD, MA Oxon); *m* 21 May 1959, Anne, da of Prof Benjamin Stanley Platt, CMG (d 1969); 2 s (Rupert b 1964, Ben b 1967), 1 da (Alice b 1970); *Career* prof of public health Univ of Oxford 1974–2000, fell St Cross Coll Oxford 1974–; memb: Oxford Preservation Tst, Nat Tst, Campaign to Protect Rural England, BMA, Soc for Social Med; author of 3 books and over 400 scientific papers; FFPH (FFCM 1972), FRCP 1979, FRCGP 1983, FRCOG 1989, FRS 1991, FFFP 1994, FMedSci 1998; *Recreations* fine arts, motoring, Victorian engineering, conservation; *Style*— Prof Martin Vessey, CBE, FRS; ✉ Clifden Cottage, Burford Road, Fulbrook, Oxfordshire OX18 4BL (☎ 01993 824985); Nuffield Department of Population Health, University of Oxford, Old Road Campus, Headington, Oxford OX3 7LF (e-mail martin.vessey@dph.ox.ac.uk)

VESTEY, 3 Baron (UK 1922); Sir Samuel George Armstrong Vestey; 3 Bt (UK 1913), KCVO (2009), DL (Glos 1982); s of Capt the Hon William Howarth Vestey, Scots Gds (ka Italy 1944, only s of 2 Baron Vestey), and Pamela, da of George Nesbitt Armstrong, s of Charles Nesbitt Frederick Armstrong and Dame Nellie Melba, GBE, the opera singer; suc gf 1954; *b* 19 March 1941; *Educ* Eton; *m* 1, 1970 (m dis 1981), Kathryn Mary, da of John Eccles, of Moor Park, Herts; 2 da (Hon Saffron Alexandra (Hon Mrs Foster) b 1971, Hon Flora Grace (Hon Mrs Hall) b 1978); m 2, 1981, Celia Elizabeth, yr da of Maj (Hubert) Guy Broughton Knight, MC (d 1993), of Lockinge, Oxon, and Hester, sis of Countess (w of 6 Earl) Clanwilliam; 2 s (Hon William Guy b 1983, Hon Arthur George b 1985), 1 da (Hon Mary Henrietta b 1992); *Heir* s, Hon William Vestey (page of honour to HM The Queen 1995–98); *Career* Lt Scots Gds 1960–63; chm Vestey Group plc and associated cos; pres: London Meat Trade and Drovers' Benevolent Assoc 1973, Inst of Meat 1978–83, Royal Bath & W of England Soc 1994, Br Horse Soc 1994–95; chm: Steeplechase Co Cheltenham 1990–2011, Meat Trg Cncl 1992–95, Royal Agricultural Soc of the Cwlth; Master of the Horse 1999–; Liveryman Worshipful Co of Butchers; patron of one living; patron Gloucestershire CCC 1999–2012; Queen's Golden Jubilee Medal 2002, Queen's Diamond Jubilee Medal 2012; GCStJ, Lord Prior of the Order of St John 1991–2001; *Clubs* White's, Jockey (Newmarket), Melbourne (Melbourne), I Zingari; *Style*— The Rt Hon the Lord Vestey, KCVO, DL; ✉ Stowell Park, Northleach, Gloucestershire GL54 3LE (☎ 01285 720308, fax 01285 720360)

VETTRIANO, Jack; OBE (2003); *b* 1951, Fife; *Career* artist; *Solo Exhibitions* incl: Lovers and Other Strangers (Portland Gall London and Kirkcaldy Museum & Art Gall Fife) 2000, Affairs of the Heart (Portland Gall London) 2004, Love, Surrender and Devotion (Portland Gall London and Kirkcaldy Museum & Art Gall Fife) 2006; also in Edinburgh, London, Hong Kong, NY and Johnannesburg; *Group Exhibitions* incl: Royal Scottish Acad Annual Exhbn 1989, Royal Acad Summer Exhbn 1990, Int 20th Century Arts Fair (The Armory NY) 1999, artLONDON 2002; work in permanent collection of Kirkcaldy Art Gall; Hon DLitt Univ of St Andrews 2003; *Books* subject of: Fallen Angels: Paintings by Jack Vettriano (ed W Gordon Smith, 1999), Lovers and Other Strangers: Paintings by Jack Vettriano (ed Anthony Quinn, 2002), Jack Vettriano (Anthony Quinn, 2004); *Style*— Jack Vettriano, Esq, OBE; ✉ c/o Karen Swan, 12 Braehead House, Victoria Road, Kirkcaldy, Fife KY1 2SD

VICARI, Andrew; s of Cavaliere Vittorio Vicari, and Italia, *née* Bertani; *b* 20 April 1938, Port Talbot, W Glamorgan; *Educ* Neath GS for Boys, Slade Sch of Fine Art London; *Career* artist; official painter: king and govt of Saudi Arabia, Interpol, Compagnie Republicaine de Securite (CRS); European Parl and Cncl of Europe Beaux Arts Prize 1995; world patron Millennium Tst, hon memb European Hotel Mangrs Assoc; Hon Col US 6 Cavalry, hon memb Rotary Int; pres Carwyn James Rugby Sch Wales, hon vice-pres Neath Male Voice Choir; Freeman City of London 2002, memb Guild of Freemen of the City of London, memb Worshipful Co of Firefighters, Liveryman of Wales; FZS; Brig d'Honneur CRS (France), Brig d'Honneur de la Police Nationale (France), Commanduer Confrerie des Chevaliers des Tastevins (France), Chevalier Order of Merit (Monaco); *Major Exhibitions* incl: New Burlington Galleries London 1955, Redfern Gallery London 1956, Obelisk Gallery London 1956, Exhibitions Grand Palais des Champs Elysées Societe des Artists Français Paris 1957, RBA Galleries London 1957, United Soc of Artists 1957, Grand Palais des Champs Elysées Paris 1959, Faces in Wales (Temple of Peace Civic Centre Cardiff) 1960, The Last Supper (Foyle's Art Gallery London) 1960, Thomson House Cardiff 1960, Vicari Exhibition of Paintings and Drawings (Leicester Sq London) 1961 (in aid of ICRF), Kalamazoo Museum of Art MI 1962, Columbus Museum of Art OH 1963, Harrison Library NY 1963, Contemporary Art Soc of GB Vicari Retrospective (UC Wales) 1963, Bath Festival 1964, Circolo Della Stampa Rome 1965, The Virgin and the Gypsy (London Screenplays) 1970, Archer Gallery London 1972, Madden Galleries London 1973, Galerie Vendome Beirut 1974, The Triumph of the Bedouin (King Faisal Conf Centre Riyadh) 1974–78, Romantic Realism of Vicari (8th Int Art Fair Basle) 1977, Chevy Chase Art Center Washington DC 1978, Salle Empire Hotel de Paris Monte Carlo 1981, Galerie du Carlton Cannes 1981, The Majesty of King Faisal (King Faisal Fndn Riyadh) 1984, Petit Palais MOMA Geneva 1984, Les Vigonades de la Concorde (Hotel de Crillon Paris) 1988, Interpol World HQ Lyons 1989, Siege Credit Lyonnais Bank Lyons 1989, The Majesty of King Fahd (Rashid Engrg Museum Riyadh) 1989, Palais Amerique-Latin Monaco 1991, La Guerre du Golfe (Les Invalides Paris) 1991, Hotel Meurice Paris 1991, CRS Versailles 1994, Palais des Beaux Arts Beijing 1995, Governor's Palace St Petersburg 1995, La Vigonade des Motards de la Police Nationale (Miny of the Interior Paris) 2000, The Vicari Collection of Paintings and Drawings Produced in the Kingdom of Saudi Arabia 1998–2001 (Royal Suite Riyadh Intercontinental Hotel) 2001, An Essex Celebration of Constable & Gainsborough (10 landscapes) 2003, Parable of Majesty & Reconciliation (retrospective, Abu Dhabi and The Palace One & Only Royal Mirage Dubai) 2005, 4 Caravaggios and 1 Vicari (Sardinia, Malta and Minorca) 2006, portraits of iconic figures of the 20th Century (Dubai Community Theatre and Arts Centre) 2006, The Enigma: A Retrospective Exhibition of Paintings and Drawings 1956–2006 (Grosvenor House Dubai) 2006; *Commissions* incl: The Children of Tymorfa four panels for Glamorgan Educn Authy 1956, Cyclorama: Harlequins, Colombines & Children for Nat Eisteddfod Llandudno 1964, Bath Festival Exhibition 1964, The Vigonade of the Millennium Stadium mural for S dressing room (to remove notorious jinx) Millennium Stadium Cardiff 2002, Triptych of Sir Alex Ferguson 2003 for Manchester United Carrington Training Ground 2003, Retrospective Vicari Exhibition for the Cultural Fndn of Abu Dhabi 2005, Iconic Portraits of the 20th Century Vicari Exhibition for the opening of Dubai Community Theatre and Arts Centre, The San Guines of Andrew Vicari (Chateau Saint Martin, Venice, Cote d'Azur); *Work in Collections* incl: Dallas Museum of Fine Arts, Nat Library of Wales, Museum of Tel Aviv, Contemporary Arts Soc of GB, Tate Gallery, Columbus Museum of Fine Arts, Pezzo Pozzoli Museum Milan, Petit Palais MOMA Geneva, David Lloyd Kreeger Collection Washington DC, IBM Collection Armonk, Palais Princier Monaco, Musée des Timbres et Monnaie Monaco, Hermitage Museum St Petersburg, King Faisal Conf Centre Riyadh, Chinese Miny of Culture Beijing, King Faisal Fndn Museum Riyadh, Rashid Engrg Museum Riyadh, Collection National Library of Riyadh, Credit Lyonnais Bank Lyons and Paris, Tournament Identity for Celtic Manor Wales Open Golf Championship 2007, series of landscape paintings as official artist to the Ryder Cup Course at Celtic Manor 2007; *Publications* Triumph of the Bedouin (1978), Ghazi A Al Ghosaibi: From the Orient and the Desert (illustrations, 1984), The Mystery of Memory: The Truth is Not Enough (vol 1 of autobiography, 2007); *Recreations* cinema, squash, food and wine; *Clubs* MCC, East India and Public Schools, Cardiff and County, Bristol Channel Yacht; *Style*— Maitre Andrew Vicari; ✉ e-mail a.vicari@andrew-vicari.com, website www.andrew-vicari.com; c/o Daniel Curzi (manager) e-mail daniel.curzi@wanadoo.fr

VICK, Graham; CBE (2009); *b* 30 December 1953; *Career* artistic dir Brimingham Opera Co, dir of prodns Glyndebourne Festival Opera; hon prof of music Univ of Birmingham; Chevalier de l'Ordre des Arts et des Lettres (France); *Style*— Graham Vick, Esq, CBE; ✉ c/o Ingpen & Williams Ltd, 7 St George's Court, 131 Putney Bridge Road, London SW15 2PA (☎ 020 8874 3222, fax 020 8877 3113)

VICK, Laurence; s of Alfred Spencer Vick (d 1996), and Patricia Mae, *née* Eyles (d 1987); *b* 14 December 1952, Birmingham; *Educ* King Edward VI Camp Hill Sch Birmingham, Lanchester Poly Coventry (LLB), Coll of Law Guildford; *m* 11 March 1983, Josie, *née* Gale; 3 s (Andrew b 2 April 1985, Alex 10 April 1989, Harry 19 Dec 1992), 1 da (Hannah b 8 Oct 1987); *Career* admitted slr 1981, chartered insur practitioner 1999; slr specialising in clinical negligence; ptnr: Haxby Jarvis Coventry 1981–91, Brindley Twist Tafft and James Coventry 1991–94, Tozers Exeter 1994–99, Michelmores Exeter 1999–; memb Law Soc 1981; lead slr Bristol Heart Children Action Gp at Bristol Heart Inquiry); assoc Chartered Insur Inst; *Recreations* family, guitar, garden, Aston Villa FC; *Style*— Laurence Vick, Esq; ✉ Michelmores Solicitors, Pynes Hill, Exeter EX2 5WR (☎ 01392 688688, fax 01392 360563, e-mail laurence.vick@michelmores.com, Twitter @LaurenceVick)

VICKERMAN, Prof Roger William; s of William Vickerman (d 1965), and Gertrude Ethel, *née* Passingham (d 1996); *b* 31 August 1947; *Educ* Clare Coll Cambridge (MA), Univ of Sussex (DPhil); *m* 1973, Christine Ann, *née* Wragg; 2 s (Stephen Roger b 10 Nov 1979, Thomas John b 15 March 1986), 2 da (Jennifer Ann b 10 Nov 1979, Karen Elizabeth b 21 June 1984); *Career* jr res fell in tport economics Univ of Sussex 1972, lectr in economics Univ of Hull 1972–76; Univ of Kent at Canterbury: lectr in economics 1977–79, sr lectr in economics 1979–87, dir Channel Tunnel Res Unit 1986–93, prof of regnl and tport economics 1989–98, dir Centre for Euro Regnl and Tport Economics 1993–, head Dept of Economics 1993–99 and 2005–09, Jean Monnet prof of Euro economics 1998–, dean Brussels Sch of Int Studies 2009–14, dean for Europe 2014–; visiting res scholar Universität Münster Germany 1980, visiting assoc prof Dept of Economics Univ of Guelph Ontario Canada 1984, visiting prof Inst for Tport Studies Univ of Sydney Australia 1999, visiting prof Central European Univ Budapest 2002–05; memb Standing Advsy Ctee on Trunk Road Assessment DETR 1996–99; memb Ed Bd: Regional Studies, Papers in Regional Science, les Cahiers Scientifiques du Transport, Transport Policy (ed-in-chief 2010–); churchwarden St Cosmus and St Damian in the Blean (2005–11); Hon Dr Univ Marburg 2002; FRSA 1989, FCILT 1996, AcSS 2001; *Publications* The Economics of Leisure and Recreation (1975), Spatial Economic Behaviour (1980), Urban Economies – Analysis and Policy (1984), The Channel Tunnel: Public Policy, Regional Development and European Integration (with I M Holliday and G Marcou, 1991), Infrastructure and Regional Development (ed, 1991), The Single European Market: Prospects for Economic Integration (1992), Le Tunnel Sous La Manche: Entre Etats et Marché (ed, 1992), Convergence and Divergence among European Regions (ed, 1995), The Econometrics of Major Transport Infrastructures (ed, 1997), Transport Infrastructure (ed, 2002), Principles of Transport Economics (2004), Growth and Economic Development: Essays in Honour of AP Thirlwall (ed, 2006), Handbook of Transport Economics (ed, 2011), Recent Developments in the Economics of Transport (ed, 2012); also 91 chapters in edited books and 73 articles in learned jls; *Recreations* music, travel and transport, photography; *Style*— Professor Roger Vickerman; ✉ School of Economics, Keynes College, University of Kent, Canterbury, Kent CT2 7NP (☎ 01227 823495, e-mail r.w.vickerman@kent.ac.uk)

VICKERS, Hugo Ralph; DL (Berks, 2010); s of Ralph Cecil Vickers, MC (d 1992), and Dulcie, *née* Metcalf (d 1992); nephew of Baroness Vickers, DBE (d 1994); *b* 12 November 1951; *Educ* Eton, Strasbourg Univ; *m* 23 Sept 1995 (m dis 2014), Elizabeth Anne Blyth, yr da of Michael Vickers (d 2007), of Montfailloc, France; 2 s (Arthur Hugo Blyth b 12 March 1999, George Henry Edward b 1 Feb 2001), 1 da (Alice Elizabeth Margaret (twin) b 1 Feb 2001); *Career* author, reviewer, broadcaster, lectr; worked with London Celebrations Ctee for Queen's Silver Jubilee 1977, admin Great Children's Pty 1979; literary executor to the late Sir Charles Johnston and the late Sir Cecil Beaton; lay steward St George's Chapel Windsor Castle 1970– (capt 2014–); Golo Mann Distinguished lectr Claremont McKenna Coll US 2007; historical advsr The King's Speech (film) 2010; chm Jubilee Walkway Tst 2002–12 (tstee 2000–12); memb: Prince of Wales's Royal Parks Tree Appeal 1987–2003, Cncl of Windsor Festival 1999–, Cncl of Friends of St George's 2001–04 and 2005–11; chm Outdoor Tst 2012–, tstee Age Unlimited 2010–, patron Me2 Club 2013–; Liveryman Worshipful Co of Musicians; *Books* We Want The Queen (1977), Gladys, Duchess of Marlborough (1979, reissued 1987), Debrett's Book of the Royal Wedding (1981), Cocktails and Laughter (ed, 1983), Cecil Beaton – The Authorised Biography (1985, reissued 1986, 1993, 2002 and 2003), Vivien Leigh (1988, reissued 1990), Royal Orders (1994), Loving Garbo (1994, reissued 1995), The Private World of the Duke and Duchess of Windsor (1995), The Kiss: The Story of an Obsession (1996, reissued 1997, Stern Silver Pen Award for Non-Fiction 1997), Alice, Princess Andrew of Greece (2000, reissued 2001), The Unexpurgated Beaton (ed, 2002), Beaton in the Sixties (ed, 2003), Alexis: The Memoirs of the Baron de Redé (ed, 2005), Elizabeth, The Queen Mother (2005), The Rich Spoils of Time (ed, 2006), Horses and Husbands (ed, 2007), St George's Chapel, Windsor Castle (2008), Behind Closed Doors (2011), A Walk for the Queen (2012), Coronation (2013), Jeffrey (ed, 2014), Cecil Beaton – Portraits & Profiles (ed, 2014); *Recreations* photography, reading, music, walking, travel; *Clubs* Beefsteak; *Style*— Hugo Vickers, Esq, DL; ✉ 62 Lexham Gardens, London W8 5JA (e-mail hugovickers@wyeford.co.uk, website www.hugovickers.co.uk); The Manor House, East Chisenbury, Pewsey, Wiltshire SN9 6AQ

VICKERS, Jeffrey; MBE (2011); s of Edward Vickers (d 1984), and Rose, *née* Soloman (d 2001); *b* 3 June 1937; *Educ* Harold Co Sch Stratford; *m* 1 (m dis 1982), Angela Vickers; 1 da (Joanne b 1 May 1965), 1 s (Andrew b 11 Feb 1967); m 2, 22 July 1982, Barbara, da of James Ebury Clair May, DSM, RN (d 1986); *Career* chm: DPM Gp of Cos 1959–, Chromacopy 1979– (name changed to C2 Media, fndr and ptnr Chromacopy of America 1979–), Genix Imaging Ltd; Prince of Wales Award for Industrial Innovation and Prodn, Avery and Owen Award RPS Int Print Exhbn 2008, Fenton Medal Royal Photographic Soc; licentiate Master Photographers' Assoc (LMPA) 2004; ambass Royal Photographic Soc; ambass Manchester Museum of Football 66 Celebrations; FInstD 1983, Hon FRPS 1997; *Recreations* photography, sailing, swimming, classical music and opera; *Clubs* Hurlingham; *Style*— Jeffrey Vickers, Esq, MBE

VICKERS, Prof Sir John Stuart; kt (2005); s of Aubrey and Kay Vickers, of Eastbourne, E Sussex; *b* 7 July 1958; *Educ* Eastbourne GS, Oriel Coll Oxford (BA), Univ of Oxford (MPhil, DPhil); *m* 1991, Maureen Emily, da of David and Dorothy Freed; 1 s (James Alexander b 19 Oct 1994), 2 da (Zoë Elizabeth, Hannah Rose (twins) b 26 Nov 1996); *Career* fin analyst Shell UK 1979–81; Univ of Oxford: fell All Souls Coll 1979–84 and 1991–2008, Roy Harrod fell in the economics of business and public policy Nuffield Coll 1984–90, Drummond prof of political economy 1991–2008, Warden All Souls Coll 2008–; exec dir and chief economist Bank of England and memb Monetary Policy Ctee 1998–2000; OFT: DG 2000–03, chm 2003–05; chm Ind Cmmn on Banking 2010–11; visiting scholar Princeton Univ 1988, visiting lectr Harvard Univ 1989 and 1990, visiting prof London Business Sch 1996; pres: Inst for Fiscal Studies 2003–07, Royal Economic Soc 2007–10; delg Oxford Univ Press 2006–; Rhodes tstee 2006–11; Hon DLitt UEA 2001; hon fell Oriel Coll Oxford 2005; FBA 1998 (President's Medal 2012), fell Econometric Soc 1998; *Books* Privatization – An Economic Analysis (with George Yarrow, 1988), Regulatory Reform (with Mark Armstrong and Simon Cowan, 1994); author of articles on industrial orgn, regulation and competition in jls; *Style*— Prof Sir John Vickers, FBA; ✉ All Souls College, Oxford OX1 4AL (☎ 01865 279379, fax 01865 279299)

VICKERS, Martin John; MP; *b* 13 September 1950, Lincs; *Educ* Grimsby Coll, Univ of Lincoln; *m* Ann; 1 da; *Career* MP (Cons) Cleethorpes 2010–; *Style*— Martin Vickers, Esq, MP; ✉ House of Commons, London SW1A 0AA

VICKERS, Prof Michael; *Educ* UCNW Bangor (BA), CCC Cambridge (Dip Classical Archaeology), Univ of Wales (DLitt); *Career* asst lectr in ancient history and classical archaeology UC Dublin 1966–69, lectr in archaeology Univ of Libya Benghazi 1969–70; Ashmolean Museum Oxford: asst keeper 1971–88, tenure 1976, actg keeper 1987, 1992, 1996, 2000–01 and 2002, sr asst keeper 1988–2010; sr research fell Jesus Coll Oxford 1996–2010 (garden master 2001–08, dean of degrees 2002–, emeritus fell 2010–), prof of archaeology Univ of Oxford 2002–10 (reader 1996–2002, emeritus prof of archaeology 2010–) visiting prof: Scuola di Specializzazione in Archeologia Università di Catania 2002, Dept of Classics Univ of Boulder Colorado 2003 and 2013, Tbilisi State Univ 2012, Batumi State Univ 2014–; visiting lectr Univ of Texas at Austin 1979–80; visiting memb: UC Cambridge 1970–71, Inst for Advanced Study Princeton 1976, Inst for Advanced Studies Hebrew Univ of Jerusalem 1993; George Tait Meml lectr Eton Coll 1987, Kress lectr Archaeological Inst of America 2002–03; corresponding memb German Archaeological Inst 1978, hon memb Vani Expdn Centre for Archaeological Studies Georgian Acad of Sciences 1995, chm Friends of Academic Research in Georgia 2005–10, corresponding memb Archaeological Inst of America 2010; Hon DUniv Batumi State Georgia 2008; FSA 1978, FRSA 1993; *Books* The Roman World (1977, 2 edn 1989), Hellas (with K Branigan, 1980), Artful Crafts: Ancient Greek Silverware and Pottery (with David Gill, 1994), Pericles on Stage: Political Comedy in Aristophanes' Early Plays (1997), Pichvnari 1: Results of Excavations Conducted by the Joint British-Georgian Expedition 1998–2002 (with Amiran Kakhidze, 2004), Sophocles and Alcibiades: Athenian Politics in Ancient Greek Literature (2008), Aristophanes and Alcibiades: Echoes of Contemporary History in Athenian Comedy (2015); *Style*— Prof Michael Vickers; ✉ Jesus College, Oxford OX1 3DW (e-mail michael.vickers@jesus.ox.ac.uk)

VICKERS, Paul Andrew; s of John Frederick Vickers, of Chislehurst, Kent, and Daphne Rosemary, *née* Reed; *b* 20 January 1960; *Educ* Alleyn's Sch Dulwich, Univ of Southampton (LLB); *m* 21 May 1988, Eileen Anne, da of John Danial MacDonald; *Career* called to the Bar Inner Temple 1983, in practice 1983–86, legal mangr London Daily News 1986–87; TV-am plc: co lawyer 1987–88, co sec 1988, exec dir 1991, asst md 1992–93; dir Independent Music Radio Ltd (Virgin Radio Ltd) 1992–93, sec and gp legal dir Mirror Group Newspapers plc 1992–94, exec dir Mirror Group plc 1994–99, sec and gp legal dir Trinity Mirror plc 1999–; *Recreations* food, wine, reading, films; *Style*— Paul Vickers, Esq; ✉ Trinity Mirror plc, One Canada Square, Canary Wharf, London E14 5AP (☎ 020 7293 3358)

VICKERY, Benedict Simon; s of late Alan Vane Vickery, of Baylham, Suffolk, and Heather Felicity Ann Vickery; *b* 23 June 1959; *Educ* Univ of Bristol (BA), Univ of Sheffield (BArch); *m* 24 April 1996, Susan Marjorie, *née* Hoyal; 1 da (Sophie Rebecca Hoyal); *Career* architect; Frederick Gibberd Coombes & Partners 1984–88, YRM Architects 1988–93; Populous (formerly HOK Sport): joined 1993, work on Stadium Australia 1996–98, managing architect Wembley Stadium 1998–2007, currently sr princ; memb: ARB 1985, RIBA 1985, RIAI 2007; *Style*— Benedict Vickery, Esq; ✉ Populous, 14 Blades Court, Deodar Road, Putney, London SW15 2NU (☎ 020 8874 7666, fax 020 8874 7470)

VICKERY, Philip; s of Robert Edmund Vickery, of Densole, Kent, and Theresa Mary, *née* Billington; *b* 2 May 1961; *Educ* St Edmund's RC Secdy Sch Dover, S Kent Coll of Technol Folkestone; *m* 1, 25 Aug 1990 (m dis), Sarah Ann, da of William Brian Lock; m 2, 24 May 2000, Fern Britton, *qv*; 1 da, 2 step s, 1 step da; *Career* apprentice chef Burlington Hotel Folkestone 1978–79; chef: Michael's Nook Country House Hotel Grasmere 1979–84, Gravetye Manor East Grinstead 1985–86 and 1987–88, Restaurant 74 Winchen Canterbury 1986–87, Mount Somerset Country House Hotel Taunton 1989–90, Castle Hotel 1990–99 (company dir until 2000, shareholder); awards for Castle Hotel: Michelin star, Egon Ronay star, Egon Ronay Dessert Chef of the Year 1995, four out of five Good Food Guide 1996 and 1997, eight out of ten Good Food Guide 1998, West Country Restaurant of the Year 1998, Egon Ronay Chef of the Year 1998, AA Restaurant Guide 2000 four rosettes 1996–99; memb Académie Culinaire de France 1992; former memb Int Squad Amateur Judo Assoc; *Books* Just Food (1999), The Proof of the Pudding (2003), Britain: The Cookbook (2007); *Style*— Philip Vickery, Esq; ✉ c/o John Rush, Lacey Associates, Lacey Farm, Low Street, Sloley, Norfolk NR12 8HD (☎ 01692 538032, website www.vickery.tv)

VICTOR, Ed; CBE (2016); s of Jack Victor (d 1987), of Los Angeles, CA, and Lydia Victor (d 2000); *b* 9 September 1939; *Educ* Dartmouth Coll NH (BA), Pembroke Coll Cambridge (MLitt); *m* 1, 1963, Michelene Dinah, da of Avram Samuels (d 1985); 2 s (Adam b 1964, Ivan b 1966); m 2, 1980, Carol Ryan, da of Clifton Boggs (d 1992), of San Diego, CA; 1 s (Ryan b 1984); *Career* editorial dir: Weidenfeld & Nicolson 1965–67, Jonathan Cape Ltd 1967–70; sr ed Alfred A Knopf Inc NY 1971–72, dir John Farquharson Ltd 1973–77, chm and md Ed Victor Ltd 1977–; *Books* The Obvious Diet (2001); *Recreations* opera, golf, travel; *Clubs* Garrick; *Style*— Ed Victor, Esq, CBE; ✉ 10 Cambridge Gate, Regents Park, London NW1 4JX (☎ 020 7224 3030); Ed Victor Ltd, 6 Bayley Street, Bedford Square, London WC1B 3HB (☎ 020 7304 4100, fax 020 7304 4111, e-mail ed@edvictor.com)

VIDLER, Andria; da of Trevor Vidler, and Carol Vidler; *b* 12 May 1966; *Educ* Tunbridge Wells Girls' GS, Sevenoaks Sch, Cambridge Poly (BA), Univ of Bradford (MBA); *m* 20 April 1996, Adrian Gibb; 2 da (Tabitha, Imogen); *Career* grad mgmnt trainee Coats Viyella 1987–90, business dir Still Price Lintas 1992–94 (business mangr 1990–92), mktg mangr BBC Radio 5 Live 1994–96, head mktg BBC News 1996–98, head mktg and business devpt BBC Sport 1998–2001 (temporarily overseeing mktg and communications BBC Radio and Music Div), md Capital Radio and Capital Gold 2001–02, md Capital FM Network 2002–03, md Magic FM 2005–09, chief exec EMI 2009–13, chief exec Centaur Media 2013–; dir Capital Charities Ltd, memb Mktg Soc; *Recreations* swimming, theatre; *Style*— Mrs Andria Vidler

VIGGERS, Sir Peter John; kt (2008); s of John Sidney Viggers (d 1969), of Gosport, Hants; *b* 13 March 1938; *Educ* Alverstoke Sch, Portsmouth GS, Trinity Hall Cambridge (MA); *m* 1968, Jennifer Mary, da of Dr R B McMillan (d 1975); 1 da, 2 s; *Career* RAF pilot 1956–58, TA 1963–70; co slr Chrysler (UK) Ltd 1968–70; dir: Edward Bates & Sons Ltd 1970–75, Richardson Smith Ltd (chm), Gough Hotels Ltd and other cos 1970–76, Premier Consolidated Oilfields Ltd 1973–86, Sweetheart International Ltd 1982–86, Nynex Group of Cos 1991–95, Tracer Petroleum Corporation 1996–98; MP (Cons) Gosport 1974–2010, PPS to Slr Gen 1979–83, delegate to N Atlantic Assembly 1980–86 and 1992–2010 (vice-chm Political Ctee 1995–2000, chm 2000–05), PPS to Chief Sec to Treasy 1983–85, Parly under sec of state for NI (indust min) 1986–89, chm British-Japanese Parly Gp 1992–99 (vice-chm 2000–10); memb Select Ctee on: Membs' Interests 1991–93, Defence 1992–97 (vice-chm 2000–05), Treasy 2005–10; underwriting memb of Lloyd's 1973–2002 (memb Cncl 1992–96), chm tstees Lloyd's Pension Fund 1996–2010; life vice-pres RNLI 2008– (memb Nat Ctee 1980–2008, vice-pres 1990–2008); *Books* Vigorous Times (2014); *Recreations* Opera, walking, reading, Burgundy; *Clubs* Boodle's; *Style*— Sir Peter Viggers; ✉ 30 Smith Square, London SW1P 3HF

VIKANDER, Alicia Amanda; *b* 3 October 1988; *Career* producer, actress and dancer; *Films* incl: Darkness of Truth 2007, The Rain 2007, My Name is Love 2008, Susans längtan 2009, Pure 2010, Jeu de chiennes 2011, The Crown Jewels 2011, A Royal Affair 2012, Anna Karenina 2012, Hotel 2013, The Fifth Estate 2013, Testament of Youth 2014, Son of a Gun 2014, Seventh Son 2014, Ex Machina 2015, Ingred Bergman: In Her Own Words 2015, The Man from U.N.C.L.E. 2015, Burnt 2015, The Danish Girl 2015 (Best Supporting Actress Critics' Choice Movie Award 2016, Outstanding Performance by a Female Actor in a Supporting Role Screen Actors Guild Awards 2016, Best Supporting Actress Academy Awards 2016), Jason Bourne 2016, The Light Between Oceans 2016, Tulip Fever 2016, Euphoria 2016, Submergence 2016; *Style*— Ms Alicia Vikander

VILLAGE, Peter Malcolm; QC (2002); s of Malcolm Rowland Village (d 1987), and Margaret Village; *b* 3 February 1961; *Educ* Repton, Univ of Leeds (LLB), Inns of Court Sch of Law; *m* 28 March 1992, Alison Helen, da of Herbert Wallis; 1 s (Thomas b 2 March 1993), 2 da (Alice, Emily (twins) b 21 June 1994); *Career* called to the Bar: Inner Temple 1983 (bencher 2011), NI 1997; specialist in planning and compulsory purchase; memb: Planning and Environmental Law Bar Assoc, Compulsory Purchase Assoc; govr Repton Sch 1998–; *Recreations* shooting, fly fishing, skiing, walking the dog; *Clubs* Brooks's; *Style*— Peter Village, Esq, QC; ✉ 39 Essex Street, London WC2R 3AT (☎ 020 7832 1111, e-mail peter.village@39essex.com)

VILLAR, Richard Neville; s of George Roger Villar, DSC, RN, and Diana Mary, *née* Thomas; *b* 24 April 1953; *Educ* Marlborough, St Thomas' Hosp Medical Sch (BSc, MB BS), Univ of Cambridge (MA), Univ of Southampton (MS); *m* 4 June 1983, (Barbara) Louise Bell, da of Patrick George Arthur Ross Lobban; 2 s (Ruairidh b 1985, Angus b 1988), 1 da (Felicity b 1995); *Career* RAMC 1979–84; conslt Addenbrooke's Hosp Cambridge 1988–2004 (sr registrar 1985–88), clinical dir Cambridge Hip and Knee Unit; memb World Orthopaedic Concern; memb: Euro Hip Soc, Br Assoc for Surgery of the Knee; Lord of the Manor of: Twineham Benfield, Eltisley, Guilden Morden; FBOA 1989, FRCS; *Recreations* fell running, mountaineering, cross country skiing; *Style*— Richard Villar, Esq; ✉ Spire Cambridge Lea Hospital (☎ 01223 266900, e-mail rvillar@uk-consultants.co.uk)

VILLAS-BOAS, Manuel de Magalhães e Menezes; s of Augusto de Magalhães e Menezes Villas-Boas, and Maria Luisa, *née* Ribeiro de Sá Ramos Chaves Bessone Basto; *b* 29 May 1945; *Educ* Economics Inst Lisbon Univ (BA); *m* 20 April 1985, Christine Marie Françoise, da of Michael Julien Gudefin, Chev Legion d'Honneur, of Greenwich, Connecticut, USA; 2 s (António b 1986, Alexandre b 1990); *Career* asst mangr Banco Espírito Santo e Comercial de Lisboa Lisbon 1972–76, sr mangr Manufacturers Hanover Ltd London 1976–79; exec dir 1979–83: The Royal Bank of Canada, Orion Royal Bank Ltd London; sr vice-pres and London rep Espírito Santo International Holding London 1983–2008; dir: Espírito Santo Financial Gp SA 1990–2008, Banco Espírito Santo e Comercial de Lisboa Lisbon 1992–2008, Banco Espírito Santo de Investimento 1992–2008, ret; FRGS; Knight of Honour and Devotion Sovereign and Military Order of Malta, Knight Cdr Order of Infante D Henrique; *Books* Os Magalhães (1998), João Jacinto de Magalhães, um Empreendedor Científico na Europa do Século XVIII (2000); *Recreations* art, music, sport, history; *Clubs* Turf (Lisbon), Malta Union (Sliema Malta); *Style*— Manuel de Magalhães e Menezes Villas-Boas, Esq; ✉ 1862 Vjal Portomaso, Paceville, Saint Julian, STJ 4016, Malta (☎ 00 356 9916 0128 or 00 351 91 559 5373

VILLIERS, Jane Hyde; da of John Hyde Villiers, and Ursule Louise, *née* Collins; *Educ* West Heath Sch, Coaching Inn Southover Manor Lewis; *m* Jeremy Thomas; *Career* self-employed in fashion industry 1980–89, literary agent Sheil Land 1989–94, ptnr and md Sayle Screen 1994; prodr My Little Eye (Working Title feature film) 2001, exec prodr Before The Rains 2006, exec prodr Young@Heart 2007; *Recreations* travelling, swimming, cinema; *Style*— Ms Jane Villiers; ✉ Sayle Screen Ltd, 11 Jubilee Place, London SW3 3TD (☎ 020 7823 3883, e-mail jane@saylescreen.com)

VILLIERS, Rt Hon Theresa; PC (2010), MP; da of George Villiers (d 2013), and Virginia, *née* Threlfall; *b* 5 March 1968; *Educ* Sarum Hall Sch, Francis Holland Sch, Univ of Bristol (LLB), Jesus Coll Oxford (BCL), Inns of Court Sch of Law; *m* June 1999 (m dis 2006), Sean Wilken; *Career* barr Lincoln's Inn 1993–95, lectr in law KCL 1995–99; MEP (Cons) London 1999–2005, Cons dep chm European Parl 2001–03; MP (Cons) Chipping Barnet 2005–, shadow chief sec to the Treasy 2005–07, shadow sec of state for tport 2007–10, min of state for tport 2010–12, sec of state for NI 2012–; House of Commons: memb Select Ctee on Environmental Audit 2005–, vice-chair All-Pty Israel Gp 2005–; Freeman City of London; *Publications* Waiver, Variation and Estoppel (co-author with Sean Wilken), European Tax Harmonisation: the impending threat; author of various legal texts; *Style*— The Rt Hon Theresa Villiers, MP; ✉ House of Commons, London SW1A 0AA

VINCE, Dr Frank Peter; s of Dr Rupert James Vince (d 1987), of Doncaster, and Olive Myra Vince (d 1985); *b* 19 June 1937; *Educ* Doncaster GS, Sidney Sussex Coll Cambridge (BA), The London Hosp Med Sch (MB BChir); *m* 7 Jan 1967, Sheila, da of Dr Laurence Cleveland Martin (d 1981), of Cambridge; 1 da (Joanna b 1968), 1 s (Richard James Martin b 1970); *Career* med registrar Addenbrooke's Hosp Cambridge 1964–66, lectr and sr registrar The London Hosp Whitechapel 1967–71 (house offr 1962–63), conslt physician Coventry Hosp 1971–2002, chief med offr Friends Life (previously Axa Equity and Law Insurance Soc) 1982–, sr lectr in postgrad med Univ of Warwick 1985–1997; various pubns in med jls on subjects of diabetes, endocrinology and problems of growth and development; pres Assurance Medical Soc 2005–07; former tstee Home Farm Tst (chm 1997–2000), former co-opted memb Coventry City Cncl; former memb Coventry HA; memb: Coventry Educn Authy 1981–90, Cncl Assurance Medical and Underwriting Soc; memb Worshipful Co of Worsted Weavers of Coventry; FRSM, FRCP 1979; *Recreations* music; *Style—* Dr Frank Vince; ✉ 42 Kenilworth Road, Coventry CV3 6PG (☎ 024 7641 0347, e-mail shvince@globalnet.co.uk)

VINCENT, Prof Angela Carmen; *née* Molony; da of Sir Joseph Molony, KCVO, QC (d 1978), and Carmen, *née* Dent (d 2003); *b* 30 September 1942, Woking, Surrey; *Educ* St Mary's Convent Ascot, Westminster Hospital Medical Sch (MB, BS), UCL (MSc); *m* 1967, Philip Vincent; 2 da (Prof Antonia (Tonia) Vincent (Mrs Hilary Davan Wetton) b 24 May 1968, Dr Katherine Sleeman (Mrs James Sleeman) b 22 July 1974), 2 s (Patrick b 27 May 1970, Bruno b 29 March 1979); *Career* UCL: research asst 1969–72, research assoc 1972–77; research fell and hon sr lectr Royal Free Hospital Sch of Medicine 1977–88; Univ of Oxford: research fell 1988–92, univ lectr in clinical neuroimmunology 1992–98, prof of neuroimmunology 1998–, head Dept of Clinical Neurology 2005–08; emeritus fell Somerville Coll Oxford 2008– (Janet Vaughan lectr in biomedical sciences 1998, fell 1992–2008); visiting prof of neuroimmunology Univ of Liverpool 2000–03, visiting prof and Moskovitz lectr London Ontario 2003, hon prof UCL 2008–; memb: Steering Ctee Medical Gp Amnesty Int (Br Section) 1990–98, Assoc of Br Neurologists 1994– (ABN Medal 2009), Int Soc for Neuroimmunology (vice-pres 1996–2001, pres 2001–04), American Neurological Assoc 1997 (hon fell 2011), Br Soc for Immunology (chair Neuroimmunology Gp 1998–2000), Scientific Ctee Patrick Berthoud Tst 1998– (chair 2006–09), Scientific Bd European Sch of Neuroimmunology 1999–; Guarantor of Brain 1999– (memb Bd of Mgmnt 2003–14), Myasthenia Gravis Fndn of America (Scientific Programme Ctee 2000–03), Soc for Neuroscience 2002–, MRC Neurosciences and Mental Health Bd 2004–08; Dr (hc) Bergen Norway 2004, MRCS, LRCP, FRCPath 1997 (MRCPath 1991), FMedSci 2003, FRCP, FRS 2011; *Publications* Neuromuscular Transmission: Basic and Applied Aspects (ed with Dennis Wray, 1990), Autoantibodies in Neurological Diseases (ed with G Martino, 2001), Clinical Neuroimmunology (ed with J Antel, G Birnbaum and H-P Hartung, 2006), Inflammatory and Autoimmune Disorders of the Nervous System in Children (ed with R Dale, 2010); more than 350 peer reviewed publications, over 50 chapters and reviews; *Recreations* tennis, opera particularly Wagner, children and grandchildren; *Style—* Prof Angela Vincent; ✉ Taverners, Woodeaton, Oxford OX3 9TH; Neuroimmunology Group, Level 6 West Wing, John Radcliffe Hospital, Oxford OX3 9DU (☎ 01865 234630, fax 01865 222402)

VINCENT, Ernest Herbert; OBE (2012); s of Ernest Herbert Vincent, and Martha Vincent; *b* 20 April 1948, Cheltenham, Glos; *Educ* Kings Sch Gloucester; *m* Diana Margaret, *née* Turnbull; *Career* gen mangr Nat Exhibition Centre Birmingham 1980–86, dir and dep gen mangr Hong Kong Convention and Exhibition Centre 1986–90, gen mangr Queen Sirikit Nat Convention Centre Bangkok 1990–92, dir Taipei Dist World Trade Centre 1993–96, gen mangr Nat Trade Centre Toronto 1999–2003, chief exec Queen Elizabeth II Conference Centre 2003–13, ret; non-exec memb Bd Central Hall Westminster 2012–; *Recreations* tennis, walking, reading, current affairs, volunteering; *Style—* Ernest Vincent, OBE; ✉ e-mail ernestvincent@me.com

VINCENT, Rev Dr John James; s of David Vincent (d 1976), and Ethel Beatrice, *née* Gadd (d 2001); *b* 29 December 1929; *Educ* Manchester Grammar, Richmond Coll London (BD), Drew Univ (STM), Univ of Basel (DTheol); *m* 4 Dec 1958, Grace Johnston, da of Rev Wilfred Stafford; 2 s (Christopher b 1961, James b 1966), 1 da (Faith b 1964); *Career* Sgt RAMC 1947–49; min Manchester and Salford Mission 1956–62; supt min: Rochdale Mission 1962–69, Sheffield Inner City Ecumenical Mission 1970–97; dir Urban Theol Unit Sheffield 1970–97 (dir emeritus 1997–), supervisor Doctoral Prog in Contextual, Urban and Liberation Theologies Univ of Sheffield 1993–, Univ of Birmingham 2003–; visiting prof of theol: Univ of Boston Autumn 1969, NY Theol Seminary Spring 1970; visiting prof of theol Drew Univ NJ 1977; chm NW CND 1957–65; founding memb and leader Ashram Community Tst 1967–, chm Urban Mission Training Assoc of GB 1976–77 and 1984–91, memb Cncl Christian Orgns for Social, Political and Economic Change 1981–89, exec Assoc Centres of Adult Theol Educn 1984–90, memb Studiorum Novi Testamenti Societas 1961–, pres Methodist Church GB 1989–90, hon lectr Biblical Studies Dept Univ of Sheffield 1990–, co-ordinator British Liberation Theology Institute 1990–, hon lectr Theol Dept Univ of Birmingham 2003–; Centenary Achievement Award Univ of Sheffield 2005; fell St Deiniol's Library 2003; memb Partnership Bd Burngreave New Deal for Communities 2001–11; *Books* Christ in a Nuclear World (1962), Christ and Methodism (1965), Secular Christ (1968), The Race Race (1970), The Jesus Thing (1973), Alternative Church (1976), Starting All Over Again (1981), OK, Let's be Methodists (1984), Radical Jesus (1986, revised edn 2004), Britain in the 90's (1989), Discipleship in the 90's (1991), Liberation Theology UK (ed, 1995), Gospel From the City (ed, 1997), The Cities: A Methodist Report (jtly 1997), Liberation Spirituality (ed, 1999), Hope from the City (2000), Bible and Practice (ed, 2001), Journey: Explorations into Discipleship (2001), Faithfulness in the City (ed, 2003), Methodist and Radical (jt ed, 2004), Mark: Gospel of Action (ed, 2006), Primitive Christianity (ed, 2007), Biblical Challenges: The City (with J W Rogerson, 2009), A Lifestyle of Sharing (2009), The Drama of Mark (with M D Hooker, 2010), Stilling the Storm (ed, 2011), British Liberation Theology: For Church and Nation (ed, 2012), Acts in Practice (ed, 2012), Christ in the City: The Dynamics of Christ in Urban Theological Practice (2013), Methodism Unbound: Christ and Methodism for the 21st Century (2015), The Farewell Discourses in Practice (ed, 2015); *Recreations* writing, jogging; *Style—* The Rev Dr John Vincent; ✉ 178 Abbeyfield Road, Sheffield, S4 7AY (☎ 0114 243 6688); Urban Theology Unit, 210 Abbeyfield Road, Sheffield S4 7AZ (☎ and fax 0114 243 5342, e-mail john@utu-sheffield.demon.co.uk)

VINCENT, Sir William Percy Maxwell; 3 Bt (UK 1936), of Watton, Co Norfolk; s of Sir Lacey Vincent, 2 Bt (d 1963), and Helen, Lady Vincent (d 2000); *b* 1 February 1945; *Educ* Eton, New York Inst of Finance; *m* 1976, Christine Margaret, da of Rev Edward Gibson Walton (d 1989), of Petersfield, Hants; 3 s; *Heir* s, Edward Vincent; *Career* late 2 Lt Irish Gds, served Malaya; dir Save & Prosper Investment Management 1980–85, Touche Remnant & Co 1985, md and investment dir Touche Remnant Co 1986, dir Société Générale Touche Remnant 1989–92, dir M & G (North America) Ltd 1992–95, md Cambridge Associates (UK) Ltd 1995–2015, currently memb investment ctees for 5 family offices; *Recreations* sailing, skiing; *Clubs* Household Div Yacht; *Style—* Sir William Vincent, Bt; ✉ Battlegreen, Green Lane, Hambledon, Hampshire PO7 4TB

VINCENT OF COLESHILL, Baron (Life Peer UK 1996), of Shrivenham in the County of Oxfordshire; Field Marshal the Lord Richard Frederick Vincent; GBE (1990), KCB (1984), DSO (1972); s of Frederick Vincent (d 1992), and late Frances Elizabeth, *née* Coleshill; *b* 23 August 1931, Norwood Green, Middlesex; *Educ* Aldenham, RMC of Sci Shrivenham; *m* 1955, Jean Paterson, da of late Kenneth Stewart; 1 da (Amanda Jane b 29 May 1959), 1 s (Mark Andrew Frederick b 3 Sept 1960) (and 1 s decd); *Career* Cmdt RMC of Sci 1980–83, Master Gen of the Ordnance MOD 1983–87, Chief of the Def Staff 1991–92 (Vice-Chief 1987–91), chm Mil Ctee NATO 1993–96; Col Cmdt: REME 1983–87, RA 1983–2000; Hon Col: 100 (Yeo) Field Regt RA (Volunteers) TA 1982–91, 12 Air Def Regt 1985–91; Master Gunner St James's Park 1996–2001; chm: Hunting Engineering Ltd 1998–2001 (dir 1996–1998), Hunting-BRAE Ltd 1998–2003 (dir1997–98), Hunting Defence Ltd 1996–2003; pres Defence Manufacturers Assoc 2000–05 (vice-pres 1996–2000); dir: Vickers Defence Systems Ltd 1996–2002, INSYS Ltd 2002–05; non-exec dir Royal Artillery Museums Ltd 1996–2000, memb Cmmn on Britain and Europe (RIIA) 1996–; Kermit Roosevelt lectr USA 1988, visiting fell Aust Coll of Def and Strategic Studies 1995–99; pres: Combined Servs Winter Sports Assoc 1983–90, Army Skiing Assoc 1983–87, Cncl of Univ Military Educn Ctees 1999–2006; chm Cranfield Tst 1999–2011; memb Ct Cranfield Inst of Technol 1981–83, govr Aldenham Sch 1987–, chm of Govrs Imperial Coll of Sci, Technology and Med 1996–2004 (govr 1995), memb Ct Univ of Greenwich 1997–2001, chllr Cranfield Univ 1998–2010; patron: INSPIRE Charity Fndn 1997–, Nat Serv Veterans Assoc 2007–; fell Imperial Coll London 1995, fell City and Guilds of London Inst 1999, sr fell Cranfield Univ 2011–; Jordanian Order of Merit (First Class), USA Legion of Merit (Degree of Cdr); Freeman: City of London (memb Guild of Freemen), Worshipful Co of Wheelwrights 1997; Hon DSc Cranfield 1985; FIMechE 1990, FRAeS 1990, FCGI 1991; *Recreations* establishing a second career, seven grandchildren; *Clubs* Army and Navy, Cavalry and Guards; *Style—* Field Marshal The Lord Vincent of Coleshill, GBE, KCB, DSO; ✉ House of Lords, London SW1A 0PW

VINCENZI, Penny; da of Stanley George Hannaford (d 1985), of New Milton, Hants, and Mary Blanche, *née* Hawkey (d 1987); *b* 10 April 1939; *Educ* Notting Hill and Ealing HS; *m* 27 May 1960, Paul Robert Vincenzi, s of Dr Julius Vincenzi (d 1996), of Earls Colne, Essex; 4 da (Polly b 1963, Sophie b 1965, Emily b 1975, Claudia b 1979); *Career* freelance journalist and author; formerly first fashion ed Nova Magazine; *Books* The Complete Liar (1979), There's One Born Every Minute (1985), Old Sins (1989), Wicked Pleasures (1992), An Outrageous Affair (1993), Another Woman (1994), Forbidden Places (1995), The Dilemma (1996), Windfall (1997), Almost a Crime (1999), No Angel (2000), Something Dangerous (2001), Into Temptation (2002), Sheer Abandon (2005), An Absolute Scandal (2007), The Best of Times (2009); *Recreations* family life, talking, eating and drinking; *Style—* Mrs Penny Vincenzi; ✉ c/o Headline Publishing, 338 Euston Road, London NW1 3BH

VINCZE, Ernest Anthony; *b* 1942; *Career* director of photography; started in the field of documentaries; past head of dept Cinematography Nat Film Sch; features and TV series incl: Mystic Masseur, The Dance, Macbeth, Sea of Souls, Shooting the Past, A Very British Coup, A Woman of Substance, Kennedy, Roseland, The Camomile Lawn, Jeeves and Wooster, Nightmare Years, A Perfect Hero, Heavy Weather, Stone Scissors Paper, Scrubbers, Shanghai Surprise, Winstanley, Biggles; *Documentary Awards* incl: Flaherty Award, Prix Italia, Golden Gate San Francisco, BAFTA; *Awards* nominated Br Acad Award for Best Cinematography 1984 and 1989, winner Emmy (for A Very British Coup) 1988, winner Best Cinematography Festival Internacional de Cinema de Troia (for The Dance) 1999; memb BSC, fell Moving Image Soc, memb Cncl BAFTA; *Style—* Ernie Vincze, BSC

VINE, Barbara; *see:* Rendell of Babergh, Baroness

VINE, Deirdre Ann; da of Paul Ashley Lawrence Vine, of Pulborough, W Sussex; *Educ* UCL (BA); *Career* ed-in-chief Womans Journal 1988–99, editorial conslt and writer 1999–, launch ed (with Eve Pollard, *qv*) Aura; memb: Br Guild of Travel Writers 1978, BSME 1986, Women in Journalism 1996, PEN 2001; *Books* Boulogne (1983), Paris and Ile De France (1992); *Recreations* opera, theatre, cinema, reading, tennis; *Clubs* Oxford and Cambridge; *Style—* Ms Deirdre Vine; ✉ e-mail deirdrevine@gmail.com

VINE, Dennis; s of Harold Edward Vine (d 1966), of Ealing, London, and Mary Maud Vine (then Nicholls, d 2004); *b* 24 April 1937; *Educ* Penyrenglyn Treherbert, Drayton Manor GS Ealing, Regent St Poly (now Univ of Westminster); *m* 12 June 1965, Anne, da of H S Hawley; 1 s (Richard Edward b 9 March 1967), 1 da (Joanna b 6 March 1969); *Career* surveyor; Ealing BC 1954, Westminster City Cncl 1960; Vigers Chartered Surveyors (now GVA): joined 1962, ptnr responsible for building surveying 1969, jt sr ptnr 1983, sr ptnr 1990, ptnr of new merged practice 1991–98, conslt GVA; RICS: memb 1962–, pres Building Surveyors Div 1987–88; memb Bd Br Home & Hosp for Incurables (BHHI); tstee and memb Bd Royal Masonic Benevolent Inst (RMBI); Freeman City of London 1987, Liveryman Worshipful Co of London Surveyors 1987; hon fell Coll of Estate Mgmnt 1997; FRICS 1971; *Recreations* tennis, golf; *Clubs* RAC, West Surrey Golf; *Style—* Dennis Vine, Esq; ✉ GVA, 65 Gresham Street, London EC2 7NQ (☎ 020 7911 2131, fax 020 7911 2426, e-mail dzv@gva.co.uk, mobile 07836 773049, home ☎ and fax 01483 422200)

VINE, Jeremy Guy; s of Dr Guy Vine, of Cheam, Surrey, and Diana, *née* Tillett; bro of Tim Vine, *qv*; *b* 17 May 1965; *Educ* Epsom Coll, Univ of Durham (BA); *m* 14 Sept 2002, Rachel Katherine; 2 da (Martha b 16 March 2004, Anna b 12 Dec 2006); *Career* journalist; reporter Coventy Evening Telegraph 1986–87; BBC: news trainee 1987–89, reporter Today prog 1989–93, lobby corr 1993–97, Africa corr 1997–2000; presenter: Newsnight 1999–2002, The Politics Show (BBC 1) 2003–05, Jeremy Vine Show (Radio 2) 2003–, Election graphics 2006–, Panorama (BBC 1) 2007–10, Points of View (BBC 1) 2008–; Stendhal Award for European coverage 1995, Amnesty International Radio Award for Sierra Leone reports 1999, Monte Carlo Silver Nymph for exposé on South African Police 1999, Speech Broadcaster of the Year Sony Awards 2005 and 2010 (Silver Award 2006 and 2012), Interview of the Year Sony Award 2010; *Clubs* Soho House, Reform, Chelsea FC; *Style—* Jeremy Vine, Esq; ✉ Radio 2, BBC Western House, London W1W 7NY (☎ 020 7765 0858, e-mail jeremy.vine@bbc.co.uk)

VINE, John; CBE (2007), QPM (2002); *Educ* North Staffs Poly (BA), Univ of Abertay (MSc); *Career* joined W Yorks Police 1981, uniform patrol and community constable then sargeant Bradford and Leeds, selected for special course Police Staff Coll Bramshill, patrol sargeant Halifax 1985–87, Toller Lane and Manningham Sub Divs Bradford: 1987–90, Chief Constable's staff offr in rank of Chief Inspr 1990–92, Supt 1992–95; strategic command course 1995, Asst Chief Constable Lancashire Constabulary 1996–2000 (ops, personnel and training, latterly corp devpt), Chief Constable Tayside Police 2000–08, currently Ind Chief Inspr of Borders and Immigration; responsible for policing arrangements for G8 World Ldrs Summit 2005; ACPO Scotland: pres 2003–04, chm Road Policing Business Area and Operational Policing Business Area; ind chief inspector Borders and Immigration 2008–; Hon DBA Univ of Abertay Dundee 2009; FCIPD; *Clubs* Caledonian; *Style—* John Vine, Esq, CBE, QPM

VINE, Brig (Martin) Spencer; OBE (1995); s of Francis Vine; *b* 29 March 1953; *Educ* King Edward's Sch Bath, RMA Sandhurst, Army Staff Coll Camberley; *m* 10 May 1975, Miranda Frances, *née* King; 1 da (Pippa b 20 May 1981), 1 s (Charlie b 19 July 1983); *Career* regtl duty 1 Glosters 1973–89, chief instr RMA Sandhurst 1990–92, CO 1 Glosters 1992–94 (last CO of Regt), Cdr Battle Gp Trg Unit 1994–95, Dep Cdr Br Forces Former Yugoslavia 1995–96, US Army War Coll 1996–97, Asst Mil Attaché Br Embassy Washington DC 1997–2000, COS HQ Infantry 2000–02, Dep Cdr London District 2002–05, Cdr Multinational Force (NW) Bosnia 2005, def advsr to Br High Cmmr Islamabad 2005–07; chief operating offr IIC Ptnrs Exec Search 2008–12, Personal Advisor 2013–; Rifles County Col Herefordshire 2014–; int fell US Army War Coll; memb Friends of the Regts of Gloucestershire Regt Museum; Meritorious Service Medal USA 2000; *Recreations* field sports; *Clubs* Herefordshire Officers Club; *Style—* Brig M S Vine, OBE; ✉ Regimental Office, The Rifles, Custom House, 31 Commercial Road, Gloucester GL1 2HE

VINE, Timothy Mark (Tim); s of Dr Guy Vine, of Cheam, Surrey, and Diana, *née* Tillett; bro of Jeremy Vine, *qv*; *b* 4 March 1967; *Educ* Epsom Coll; *Career* comedian; stand-up incl: The Tim Vine Fiasco 1995, The Tim Vine Shambles, Current Puns 2006, Tim Vine: Live in Concrete 2007, Punslinger 2008, The Joke-amotive 2010; television appearances incl: The Sketch Show (also writer), Not Going Out (as actor), Live at the Apollo; Best Newcomer Perrier Award 1995; *DVDs* Live (2005), Live – So I Said To This Bloke... (2008), Punslinger Live (2010), The Joke-amotive Live (2011); *Style—* Mr Tim Vine; ✉ c/o Tim Payne (e-mail tim@timpayne.tv, website www.timvine.com)

VINE-LOTT, Anthony Keith; s of Keith Miles Vine-Lott, of Hyde, Cheshire, and Jessie, *née* Meadowcroft; *b* 24 October 1947; *Educ* King Edward VI Macclesfield, Hallam Univ Sheffield; *m* 1, 13 Dec 1969 (m dis 1980), Barbara Elaine; 1 da (Anne Marie Elizabeth b

V

4 Jan 1974); m 2, 18 June 1982 (m dis 1998), Dr Ailsa Vine-Lott; m 3, 10 July 1999, Catherine Rosemary Reid (Kate) Avery, *qv*; *Heir* Ethan Bowler; *Career* engrg scholarship Wimpey UK Ltd 1966–70, mktg mangr UK computer software co's 1970–76, md Surlodge Ltd 1976–78, field servs mangr Honeywell Network Information Systems Ltd (taken over by General Electric USA) 1978–81, mktg servs dir WANG UK Ltd 1981–86, chm The Cleaver Co; md Barclays Stockbrokers Ltd 1988–96, dir Barclays Financial Services Ltd 1993–96, chm Barclays Bank Trust Co Ltd 1995–96, chm Barclays Insurance Services Co Ltd 1995–96; head Fin Servs and Business Transformation Consultancy Robson Rhodes CA 1997–2000; DG Tax Incentivised Savings Assoc (formerly PEP and ISA Managers Assoc) 2000–14, dir Jt Money Laundering Steering Gp 2000–14, chm Nat Skills Acad for Financial Servs until 2012; ret; Lord of the Manor of Beckett; FCIM 1990, FRSA 1991, FCISI 2006; *Recreations* yachting, gardening, golf; *Clubs* RAC; *Style—* Anthony Vine-Lott, Esq; ✉ Broom House, Crabtree Lane, Headley, Epsom, Surrey KT18 6PS (☎ 01372 374728, e-mail Tony.vinelott@btinternet.com)

VINES, Prof David Anthony; s of Robert Godfrey Vines, and Vera Frances Vines; *b* 8 May 1949; *Educ* Scotch Coll Melbourne, Univ of Melbourne (BA), Univ of Cambridge (MA, PhD); *m* 1, 1979, Susannah Lucy Robinson (m dis 1992); 3 s; m 2, 1995, Jane Elizabeth Bingham; 2 step s; *Career* Univ of Cambridge: fell Pembroke Coll 1976–85, research offr and sr research offr Dept of Applied Economics 1979–85; research fell Centre for Economic Policy Research London 1985–, Adam Smith prof of political economy Univ of Glasgow 1985–92, adjunct prof of economics Research Sch of Pacific and Asian Studes ANU 1991–; Univ of Oxford: fell and tutor in economics Balliol Coll 1992–, reader in economics 1997–2000, prof of economics 2000–; memb Bd: Channel 4 Television 1987–92, Glasgow Devpt Agency 1990–92; economic conslt to Sec of State for Scotland 1987–92, conslt IMF 1988 and 1989; memb ESRC: Economic Affairs Ctee 1985–87, Research Progs Bd 1992–93; dir Research Prog on Global Economic Instns 1994–2000, memb Academic Panel HM Treasy 1986–1995, memb Cncl Royal Economic Soc 1988–92; memb Bd: Analysys 1989–2002, Scot Early Music Consort 1990–; cmmr BFI Enquiry into the Future of the BBC 1992; *Publications* Stagflation Vol II: Demand Management (jtly, 1983), Macroeconomic Interactions Between North and South (jtly, 1988), Macroeconomic Policy: inflation, weath and the exchange rate (jtly, 1989), Deregulation and the Future of Commercial Television (jtly, 1989), Information, Strategy, and Public Policy (jtly, 1991), North South and International Macroeconomic Policy (jtly, 1995), Europe, East Asia and APEC (jtly, 1998), The Asian Financial Crises (jtly, 1999), The World Bank: structure and policies (jtly, 2000), The IMF and its Critics: Reform of Global Financial Architecture (jtly, 2004); papers on international macroeconomics and macroeconomic policy in professional jls; *Recreations* hill walking, music; *Style—* Prof David Vines; ✉ Balliol College, Oxford OX1 3BJ (☎ 01865 271067, fax 01865 271094, e-mail david.vines@economics.ox.ac.uk)

VINK; *see:* de Vink

VINNEY, Prof John; *Educ* Univ of the West of England (BEng, PhD, PGCE); *Career* lectr Coventry Univ 1991–92; Univ of the West of England: sr lectr 1992–99, princ lectr of mechancial and aeronautical engrg 1999–2001, head Faculty of Computing, Engrg and Mathematical Sciences 2001–03, assoc dean Faculty of Computing, Engrg and Mathematical Sciences 2003–05, dean Faculty of Computing, Engrg and Mathematical Sciences 2005–06; Bournemouth Univ: dean Sch of Design, Engrg and Computing 2006–08, pro-vice-chllr (resources) 2008–09, pro-vice-chllr (educn and professional practice) 2009–10, vice-chllr 2010–; FIMechE, FHEA; *Style—* Prof John Vinney; ✉ Bournemouth University, Fern Barrow, Talbot Campus, Poole, Dorset BH12 5BB

VIÑOLY, Rafael; *b* 1944, Uruguay; *Career* fndr Rafael Viñoly Architects PC 1983– (projects incl: Univ of Chicago Grad Sch of Business 2004, Bronx County Hall of Justice 2006, Cleveland Museum of Art 2008, Brooklyn Children's Museum 2008, Battersea Power Station Master Plan (currently in design)); FAIA 1993, memb Japan Inst of Architects, int fell RIBA 2006; *Style—* Rafael Viñoly, Esq; ✉ Rafael Viñoly Architects PC, 2–4 Exmoor Street, London W10 6BD

VINSON, Baron (Life Peer UK 1985), of Roddam Dene in the County of Northumberland; Nigel Vinson; LVO (1979), DL (1990); s of Ronald Vinson (d 1976), of Wateringbury, Kent, and his 2 w, Bettina Myra Olivia (d 1966), da of Dr Gerald Southwell-Sander; *b* 27 January 1931; *Educ* RNC Pangbourne; *m* 10 June 1972, Yvonne Ann, da of Dr John Olaf Collin, of Forest Row, E Sussex; 3 da (Hon Bettina Claire (Mrs Witheridge) b 1974, Hon Rowena Ann (Mrs Cowen) b 1977, Hon Antonia Charlotte (Mrs Bennett) b 1979); *Career* Lt Queen's Royal Regt 1949–51; fndn donor Martin Mere Wildfowl Tst; fndr Plastic Coatings Ltd (chm 1952–72); dir: Sugar Bd 1968–75, British Airports Authority 1973–80, Centre for Policy Studies 1974–80; dep chm: Electra Investment Trust 1975–98, Barclays Bank UK 1982–88; memb Cncl King George V Jubilee Tst 1974–78, hon dir Queen's Silver Jubilee Tst 1974–78: dep chm CBI Smaller Firms Cncl 1979–84, chm: Cncl for Small Industries in Rural Areas 1980–82, Newcastle Technol Centre 1985–88, Rural Devpt Cmmn 1980–90, Bd of Tstees Inst of Econ Affrs 1989–96 (memb 1971–, chm 1987–95, life vice-pres 1996–); Industrial Participation Assoc: chm 1971–78, pres 1979–90; pres NE Civic Tst 1996–2000, chm Prince's Tst NE Region 1997–2000; tstee: St George's House Windsor Castle 1990–96, CIVITAS 2004–, Chillingham Wild Cattle Assoc 2009; gave village green to parish of Holburn Northumberland 2007; FIMgt, FRSA; *Books* Personal and Portable Pensions for All (1985), Take Upon Retiring (1997), Making Things Happen: The Life and Original Thinking of Nigel Vinson (2015); *Recreations* horses, objets d'art, crafts, farming; *Clubs* Boodle's, Pratt's; *Style—* The Rt Hon Lord Vinson, LVO, DL

VINTER, Graham David; s of Alan James Vinter (d 1993), and Lilian Ann Esther, *née* Brown (d 1985); *b* 4 March 1956; *Educ* Chichester HS for Boys, BNC Oxford (BA), Ludwig-Maximilians-Universität Munich; *m* 22 Sept 1990, Anne Elizabeth, da of Alec Baldock; 1 da (Rebecca Jane Alexandra b 28 July 1991), 2 s (William Oliver James b 9 Sept 1993, Edward Thomas Adam b 19 Oct 1997); *Career* Allen & Overy: articled clerk 1980–82, assoc 1982–88, ptnr 1988–2007, head Projects Gp 1996–2007; gen counsel BG Gp plc 2007–15 (conslt 2015–); chair GC100 2014 and 2015; memb Law Soc 1980; cncllr Mole Valley DC 1998–2000; *Books* Project Finance: A Legal Guide (1994, 4 edn 2013); *Recreations* tennis, golf, skiing, chess; *Clubs* RAC; *Style—* Graham Vinter, Esq

VINTON, Alfred Merton; *b* 1938, Argentina; *Educ* Choate Sch CT, Harvard Univ (BA); *m* Anna (-Maria) Vinton, *qv*; 1 da (Isabel Anousha b 3 Dec 1985), 1 s (George Oliver b 21 Oct 1987); *Career* J P Morgan: dir Banco Frances del Rio de la Plata Argentina 1968–73, responsible for Latin American business 1973–77, gen mangr Saudi International Bank London 1977–80, sr vice-pres and gen mangr Morgan Guaranty's London Branch 1980–86, vice-chm Morgan Guaranty Ltd and chm Morgan Guaranty Sterling Securities Ltd London 1986–87; chief operating offr N M Rothschild & Sons Ltd 1988–92; ceo Entreprises Quilmes SA and Three Cities Holdings Ltd 1992–94; chm Electra Partners Ltd 1995–2009; non-exec dir: Dinamia 2003–, Sand Aire Investments plc 1995–15, Sagitta Investment Advisers Ltd 1996–2001, Unipart Gp 1998–2014, Amerindo Internet Fund plc 2000–06, Dinamia 2003–, GP Investments Ltd 2006–, Hochschild Mining plc 2009–13, European Goldfields Ltd 2010–12; chm Lambert Howarth Gp plc 2000–07; chm American Banks Assoc of London 1984–85; memb Exec Ctee BBA 1984–85; chm American Museum in Bath 1993–; *Style—* Alfred Vinton, Esq; ✉ Stoke Albany House, Stoke Albany, Market Harborough, Leicestershire LE16 8PT (☎ 01858 535227, fax 01858 535482, e-mail fred@vinton-uk.com)

VINTON, Anna (-Maria); da of Charles Dugan-Chapman, and Mary Elizabeth Chapman; *b* 17 November 1947; *Educ* Chatelard Sch Les Avants Switzerland, Guildhall Sch of Music and Drama; *m* 1 (m dis), Anthony Greatrex Hawser; m 2, Alfred Merton Vinton, *qv*; 1 da (Isabel Anusha b 3 Dec 1985), 1 s (George Oliver b 21 Oct 1987); *Career* theatre agent: Cochrane Theatrical Agency 1967–68, Norma Skemp Agency 1969–70; private property co 1970–72; fndr and mangr: The Reject Linenshop Beauchamp Place London 1972, The Reject Shops plc 1973 (jt chm 1973–94); chm: Saxon Foods Ltd 1997–2001, Rap Ltd 1997–2003, Rap Spiderweb Ltd 2003–, Wilton Antiques Ltd 2002–; dir: Prepco Ltd 1998–2000, Printing Hldgs Co Ltd 2000–; non-exec dir: Cadbury Schweppes plc 1991–97, Courtaulds Textiles plc 1992–98, Thomas Jourdan plc 1996–97, WEW Group 1997–99, Remploy Ltd 2000–06, Bibendum Wine Ltd 2002–16; tstee: Marie Curie Fndn (patron Leics), Winged Fellowship Tst (now Vitalise) 1998–2009; memb: School Teachers' Review Body 1992–96, Covent Garden Market Authy 1992–98, FE Funding Cncl 1999–2001, Royal Parks Advsy Bd 1999–2002; *Recreations* skiing, riding, gardening, theatre, reading; *Style—* Mrs Anna Vinton; ✉ Stoke Albany House, Market Harborough, Leicestershire LE16 8PT; Pelham Cottage, 24 Pelham Street, London SW7 2NG

VIRGILS, Katherine Ruth; da of Russell Virgils, of San Marcos, Texas, and Shirley, *née* Koppen; *b* 28 August 1954; *Educ* Brighton Art Coll, Ravensbourne Art Coll (BA), RCA (MA); *m* 1989, Peter Raymond Camp, s of Maurice Raymond Camp; 2 s (Louis Elliot Virgils Camp b 4 July 1990, Maurice Emil Linwell Camp b 28 Sept 1995); *Career* artist; design dir: Katherine Khadi, Cloth of the Day, clothconfidential; memb: Royal Coll of Art Soc 1982, Crafts Cncl 1983, Ranthamhore Soc 1989, Tibet Soc 1991; FRGS 1991; *Solo Exhibitions* Head Faces Elevations (Camden Arts Centre) 1983, Spirit Syntax Structure (Thumb Gallery London) 1986, Moguls Myths Minatures (Thumb Gallery) 1988, Ruth Segel Gallery NY 1988, Tales of Tigers and Temples (Jill George Gallery London) 1989, The Latitude of Ruins (Jill George Gallery) 1995, Echoes of Pilgrimage (The Orangery Holland Park) 2001; *Group Exhibitions* V&A 1981, Hayward Annual London 1982, LA Int Art Fair 1987–90; important works in the collections of: Contemporary Art Soc, Sainsbury Collection, Crafts Cncl Collection, Merrill Lynch, Calvin Klein, Glaxo Export HQ, IBM, BR, Herbert Smith, Lloyds Bank HQ (Cannons Marsh Bristol), Prudential Insurance Co, Harlech TV, Honeywell, Sir Terence Conran, Mitsui, Royal Caribbean, Private Residence of the Ruling Family of the Gulf States; *Awards*: Crafts Cncl grant 1982, Oxford Arts Cncl award 1984, Sainsbury prize (Chelsea Fair) 1985; *Books* The Latitude of Ruins (1992); *Recreations* travel in India, Mayan architecture and ruins; *Style—* Ms Katherine Virgils; ✉ The Bowling Hall, 346 Kennington Road, London SE11 4LD (☎ 020 7840 0454, mobile 07833 582689, e-mail kvirgils@ymail.com (personal) or katherinekhadi@ymail.com (work), website www.katherinevirgils.com, blog http://clothconfidential.wordpress.com)

VIRK, Manjinder; da of Harbhajan Singh, of Coventry, Warks, and Jasvir Kang; *b* Coventry, Warks; *Educ* De Montfort Univ (BA); *m* 1 July 2006, Neil Biswas; 1 da (Lyla Virk Biswas b 6 Dec 2009), 1 s (Robhin Biswas b 30 Dec 2013); *Career* actress and playwright; writer-in-residence Red Ladder Theatre Co 2002; one of Screen International's Stars of Tomorrow 2007; nominated: Asian Woman of Achievement Award 2008, Asian Woman Award (Entertainment) 2008, Best Actress and Newcomer Br Ind Film Awards 2010, Best Newcomber London Film Festival Award 2010; *Television* Trial by Jury, Doctors, Swiss Toni, The Bill, Ready When You Are Mr McGill, Green Wing, Child of Mine, Ghost Squad, Bradford Riots (channel 4) 2005–06 (nominated Best Drama South Bank Awards and Grierson Award), Britz (channel 4) 2006–07 (Best Drama Serial RTS Award, Best Drama Serial BAFTA, nominated Int Emmy 2008), Runaway (BBC) 2009, Monroe (ITV) 2011, Hunted (BBC) 2012, JAMILLAH (as writer, CBeebies/ Kindle) 2014, Ameera Khatun in Call the Midwife (BBC), regular Marianna Morton in Ordinary Lies (BBC), regular pathologist Kam Karimore in Midsomer Murders (ITV); *Theatre* as actor: The Magic Storybook (Unicorn Theatre), The Millennium Mysteries (Belgrade Theatre), Princess Talia in Sleeping Beauty (London Bubble Theatre), Hermia in A Midsummer Night's Dream (Belgrade Theatre Coventry), Wintersun (Leicester Haymarket), Workers Writes (Royal Court Theatre), Going Public (Red Room/Tricycle Theatre), Chumpa Chumelli in Unsuitable Girls (Lyric Hammersmith/ Pilot Theatre Co) 2002, Come Out Eli!, Juliet in Bill Shakespeare's Italian Job (Gilded Balloon Edinburgh), writer and performer Autobiography of a Face (one woman show Lyric Hammersmith and Nat tour), Shabnam in Shabnam (Lyric Hammersmith), Free Outgoing (Royal Court Theatre) 2007; as writer: Glow (nat tour and published in Theatre Centre Plays for Young People: An Anthology of Plays Vol 1) 2003; *Radio* as writer: Tonight I Write (BBC Radio 4) 2003; *Film* Cross My Heart, Two Minutes, Orange People, World of Wrestling, The Blue Tower (winner Raindance Film Festival 2008), writer and dir Forgive 2009 (short film), Lost Paradise 2010 (short film), The Arbor 2010, writer, dir and actor Out of Darkness 2013 (short film, premiered at BFI London Film Festival, winner Best Film and Best Drama Aesthetica Film Festival), writer Phoebe in History's Future 2015; *Style—* Ms Manjinder Virk; ✉ website www.manjindervirk.com; c/o Michael Symons, Hamilton Hodell, 5th Floor, 66–68 Margaret Street, London W1W 8SR (☎ 020 7636 1221, fax 020 7636 1226, e-mail info@hamiltonhodell.co.uk); writing agent Frances Arnold, Rochelle Stevens & Co, 2 Terrett's Place, Islington, London N1 1QZ (☎ 020 7359 3900, e-mail frances@rochellestevens.com)

VITEZ, Charles Oscar; s of Samuel Thomas Vitez (d 1972), and Suzanne Vitez; *b* 24 October 1948, Budapest, Hungary; *Educ* Westminster City Sch; *Career* CA 1972, ptnr KPMG 1987–93 (joined as taxation specialist 1973), ptnr Charles Vitez & Co 1993–; *Books* Taxation of UK Life Assurance Business (1986), Taxation of Unit Trusts (1994), MacLeod & Levitt, Taxation of Insurance Business (contrib, 1999); *Style—* Mr Charles Vitez; ✉ 37 Preston Road, Wembley, Middlesex HA9 8JZ (☎ 020 8904 5996, fax 020 8908 3207, e-mail vitez@btinternet.com)

VITMAYER, Janet; CBE (2011); *Career* head of research and curation Imperial War Museum 1976–82, dir Livesey Museum for Children 1982–92, head of educn and public servs Horniman Tst 1993–98, dir Horniman Museum and Gardens 1999–; *Style—* Ms Janet Vitmayer, CBE; ✉ The Horniman Museum & Gardens, 100 London Road, Forest Hill, London SE23 3PQ

VIVIAN, 7 Baron (UK 1841), of Glynn, and of Truro, Co Cornwall; Sir Charles Crespigny Hussey Vivian; 7 Bt (UK 1828); s of 6 Baron Vivian (d 2004), and Catherine Joyce, *née* Hope (now Countess of Mexborough); *b* 20 December 1966, Durham; *Educ* Milton Abbey; *Career* Henderson Administration 1987–92, Club Mediterrane 1992–96, Citigate Dewe Rogerson 1996–2002, founding dir Pelham PR 2004–09, currently md and ptnr Geopolitical Bell Pottinger; *Recreations* waterskiing, rugby, cricket, shooting, theatre, travel; *Clubs* White's, Greenhouse; *Style—* The Rt Hon the Lord Vivian; ✉ 28 Walpole Street, London SW3 4QS (☎ 020 7823 4561, mobile 07977 297903, e-mail cvivian@bellpottinger.com)

VOAK, Jonathan Russell Saunders; s of Capt Allan Frederick Voak, of St Brelade, Jersey, and Annette Mary, *née* Langlois; *b* 25 October 1960; *Educ* Victoria Coll Jersey, Leicester Poly (now De Montfort Univ) (BA); *m* 1 (m dis 1994); m 2, 1995, Colette Louise, *née* Townsend; 2 da (Bethany Lillie Rose b 10 March 1997, Bella Summer Céleste b 27 July 1998), 2 s (Joshua Jacques Louis b 21 Nov 2000, Benjamin Jean Pierre b 16 July 2003); *Career* curatorial asst to dir of V&A (Sir Roy Strong) 1984–87 (museum asst Metalwork Dept 1983–84), curator Apsley House Wellington Museum 1987–95 (also curator Ham House and Osterley Park House 1989–90); dir: Hunt Museum 1996, Atelier Ltd 1997–; conslt The Osborne Gp 1998–99; publications ed V&A Museum Report of the Bd of

Tstees 1983–86 and 1986–89; co-ed: (with Sir Hugh Casson) V&A Album Gold Edition 1987, John Le Capelain exhbn catalogue Jersey 1988; contrib: Wellington in Spain exhbn catalogue Madrid 1988, Baixella da Victoria – Portugal's Gift of Silver to the Duke of Wellington 1992, London – World City exhbn catalogue Essen 1992; co-author and ed Apsley House, The Wellington Collection at Apsley House, Wellington Museum 1995, ed Atelier Ltd Catalogues 1997–, author of numerous articles; Eighth Wellington lectr Univ of Southampton 1996; memb: BADA, LAPADA, CINOA (Int Assoc of Art and Antique Dealers), La Société Jersiaise (memb Exec Ctee), Attingham Soc; tstee: Jersey Heritage Tst, Chantrey Tst; chef tenant Du Fief De La Reine Grouville; *Recreations* motor racing, painting, sailing; *Style—* Jonathan Voak, Esq; ✉ Atelier Ltd, Le Bourg Farm, Le Grand Bourg, Grouville, Jersey JE3 9UY (☎ 01534 855728, e-mail art@atelierlimited.com)

VOGENAUER, Prof Stefan; s of Dieter Vogenauer, of Eutin, Germany, and Brigitte Maria, *née* Franz; *b* 4 August 1968, Eutin, Germany; *Educ* Kiel Univ, Univ of Paris, Trinity Coll Oxford (MJur, Clifford Chance prize, Herbert Hart prize); *m* 3 May 1997, Jutta; 2 s (Johannes Benedikt, David Nikolaus), 1 da (Veronika Elisabeth); *Career* research asst Law Faculty Regensburg, research fell Max Planck Inst for Comparative Law and Private Int Law, pt/t lectr Bucerius Law Sch, qualified as German Rechtsanwalt, fell BNC Oxford 2003–15, prof of comparative law Univ of Oxford 2003–15, dir Oxford Inst for European and Comparative Law 2004–15, dir Max Planck Inst for European Legal History Frankfurt 2015–; scientific memb Max Planck Soc 2014–; Die Auslegung von Gesetzen in England und auf dem Kontinent (2001), Ius Commune Casebook for the Common Law of Europe: Cases, Material and Text on Contract Law (2 edn, 2010), Commentary on the UNIDROIT Principles of International Commercial Contracts (2 edn, 2015); *Style—* Prof Stefan Vogenauer; ✉ Max Planck Institute for European Legal History, Hansaallee 41, D60323 Frankfurt (e-mail vogenauer@rg.mpg.de)

VOGT, (Susan) Harriet; da of Richard Vogt, of Washington DC, and Joan, *née* Davis; *b* 31 July 1954; *Educ* Sidwell Friends Sch Washington DC, Westonbirt Sch, Univ of Sussex (BAPsych); *Partner* common law husband, Philip Gallagher; 2 s (Matthew Patrick Pierce Gallagher b 20 March 1991, James Conor Osmond Gallagher b 18 March 1993); *Career* dir of planning Ayer Advertising 1985–91 (dir 1984–91), corp cnsllr and strategist 1992–93, dir Portman Communications 1993–, dir Techmedia 1997–2001, ptnr Two Brains Brand Planning and Qualitative Res; *Recreations* consuming books, films, clothes, Italian food and culture; *Style—* Ms Harriet Vogt; ✉ East Grange, Steeple Aston, Oxfordshire OX25 4SR

VOLTERRA, Robert Gustavo; s of Vito Volterra, of Toronto, Canada, and Gail, *née* Gnaedinger; *b* 20 September 1964, Toronto, Canada; *Educ* Univ of Western Ontario (Lt-Govr of Ontario scholar, BA), York Univ Toronto (LLB), Trinity Hall Cambridge (Cwlth scholar, LLM); *Career* barr and slr Upper Canada, slr advocate Eng and Wales; slr specialising in public int law and int dispute resolution; slr with law practice of Prof Sir Elihu Lauterpacht, CBE, QC, *qv*, 1994–96, head Public Int Law Gp Freshfields Bruckhaus Deringer 1996–2001, ptnr and head Public Int Law Gp Herbert Smith 2001–05, ptnr Latham & Watkins LLP 2005–11 (also global chair Int Dispute Resolution Practice and head Public Int Law Gp), estab Volterra Fietta 2011–; Faculty of Law Osgoode Hall Law Sch York Univ Toronto 1992–94, research fell Research Centre for Int Law Univ of Cambridge 1994–96, Faculty of Law Univ de Paris X 1996–99, Geopolitics and Boundaries Research Centre Univ of London 1998–, visiting prof Faculty of Law UCL 2000–; jt sec Br branch Int Law Assoc, memb Latin American Arbitration Ctee Int C of C, memb Expert Panel for States UNCTAD Prog on Dispute Settlement in Int Trade, Investment and Intellectual Property, memb Mgmnt Bd Forum on Int Investment Law Br Inst of Int and Comparative Law, legal expert Legal Advsy Task Force Energy Charter Secretariat; First Class Order of Bahrain 2001; *Style—* Robert G Volterra; ✉ Volterra Fietta, 1 Fitzroy Square, London W1T 5HE (☎ 020 7380 3898, fax 020 7387 7433, e-mail robert.volterra@volterrafietta.com, website www.volterrafietta.com)

von DOHNÁNYI, Christoph; *b* Berlin; *Educ* Munich Acad of Music (Richard Strauss Prize), Florida State Univ; *Career* conductor and repetiteur Frankfurt Opera 1953, gen music dir Lübeck, chief conductor Westdeutsche Rundfunk Sinfonie Orchester Cologne, gen music dir and opera dir Frankfurt Opera, intendant and chief conductor Hamburg Opera, music dir Cleveland Orch 1984–2002 (music dir designate 1982, music dir laureate 2002); Philharmonia Orch: princ guest conductor 1994–97, princ conductor 1997–2008, hon conductor for life 2008–; chief conductor NDR Symphony Orch Hamburg 2004–; guest conductor: ROH Covent Garden, La Scala Milan, Met Opera NY, Lyric Opera Chicago, Zurich Opera, Vienna State Opera, Berlin Philharmonic, Vienna Philharmonic, Israel Philharmonic, Orchestre de Paris, Royal Concertgebouw Orch, NY Philharmonic, Pittsburgh Symphony Orch, Philadelphia Orch, Chicago Symphony Orch, Boston Symphony Orch; recordings with Cleveland Orch incl: complete symphonies of Beethoven, Brahms and Schumann, symphonies by Bruckner, Dvořák, Mahler, Mozart, Schubert and Tchaikovsky, works by Adams, Bartók, Berlioz, Birtwistle, Busoni, Ives, Ravel, Richard Strauss, Varèse and Webern; prodns with Vienna Philharmonic incl: Der Rosenkavalier, Salome, Cosi fan Tutte, Erwartung, Duke Bluebeard's Castle, Die Zauberflöte, Ariadne auf Naxos, Die Bassariden, Baal; prodns with Philharmonia Orch incl: Die Frau ohne Schatten, Moses und Aron, Oedipus Rex, Hänsel und Gretel, Die Schweigsame Frau, Arabella (all at Chatelet Theatre Paris), Edinburgh Festival 2002, BBC Proms 2002, Luzern Festival 2002; *Style—* Christoph von Dohnányi, Esq

von HIPPEL, Dr Karin; *Educ* Yale Univ (BA), Univ of Oxford (MA), LSE (PhD); *Career* project mangr The Somalia Project LSE 1995, conslt on governance EC Somalia Unit 1997, political advsr to rep of the Secretary Gen UN Political Office for Somalia (UNPOS) 1998–99, civil affrs offr UN Interim Administration Mission in Kosovo 2000, sr research fell Centre for Defence Studies KCL 2001–05, dir and co-dir Post-Conflict Reconstruction Project Center for Strategic and International Studies (CSIS) 2005–10, sr advsr Bureau for Counterterrorism Dept of State 2010–11, dep asst secretary for overseas operations Bureau of Conflict and Stabilisation Operations Dept of State 2011–14, chief of staff Special Presidential Envoy for the Global Coalition to Counter ISIL 2014–15, DG RUSI 2015–; *Style—* Dr Karin von Hippel

VON MALLINCKRODT, George W; Hon KBE (1997); s of Arnold Wilhelm von Mallinckrodt, and Valentine, *née* von Joest; *b* 19 August 1930; *Educ* Salem; *m* 31 July 1958, Charmaine, da of Helmut Schroder; 2 da (Claire b 11 Aug 1960, Sophie b 8 Aug 1967), 2 s (Philip b 26 Dec 1962, Edward b 29 June 1969); *Career* merchant banker; Schroders: joined 1954, dir Schroders plc 1977–2008, exec chm Schroders plc 1984–95, pres 1995–; dir: Allianz of America Inc NY 1978–84, Nat Mutual Life Assoc of Australasia 1987–90, Siemens plc 1989–98; memb World Economic Forum 1970– (chm Cncl 1995–97), chm Br Invisibles 1995–98; advsr: McGraw-Hill Inc 1986–89, Bain & Co 1997–2005; memb: Br N American Ctee (BNAC) 1988–2013, Chllr's Ct of Benefactors Univ of Oxford 1990–, Dean's Cncl John F Kennedy Sch of Govt Univ of Harvard 2005–; pres: German YMCA London 1962–, German Chamber of Industry & Commerce UK 1992–95 (vice-pres 1995–); memb: INSEAD Circle of Patrons 1995, Advsy Bd Inst of Business Ethics 1998–, Advsy Ctee on Finance St George's Coll Windsor 2003–; tstee Christian Responsibility in Public Affrs 1994–, patron Three Faiths Forum 2005–; Annual Sternberg Interfaith Award 2005; Hon DCL Bishop's Univ Quebec 1994, Hon LLD Washington Univ St Louis 2011; Freeman City of London 2004; FRSA, CIMgt; Cross of the Order of Merit FRG 1986, Offr's Cross of the Order of Merit FRG 1990, Cdr's Cross of the Order of Merit FRG 2001, KCSG 2012; *Style—* George W von Mallinckrodt, KBE; ✉ Schroders plc, 31 Gresham Street, London EC2V 7QA

von SIMSON, Piers; s of Prof Werner von Simson (d 1996), of Freiburg, Germany, and Kathleen Aimee, *née* Turner (d 1996); bro of David von Simson, *qv*; *b* 23 September 1946; *Educ* Lancing, New Coll Oxford (BA), Univ of Calif Berkeley (LLM); *m* 1, 6 Aug 1977, Lindsay, da of late Prof E J H Corner; 2 da (Cara Isabel Camilla b 15 June 1978, Isabel Victoria b 17 April 1982), 1 s (James Francis Louis b 16 April 1983); m 2, 17 April 1996, Sarah, da of David Phillips, of Prisk, S Glamorgan; 3 s (Thomas Maximilian b 25 July 1996, Felix, Charles (twins) b 22 Aug 1997), 1 da (Florence Lily b 17 Dec 2001); *Career* called to the Bar Middle Temple 1969, dir S G Warburg & Co Ltd 1979–95 (joined 1972), dir S G Warburg Group plc 1989–95, md SBC Warburg 1995–96, dir Soditic Ltd 1996–; *Recreations* opera, books, sailing, winter sports; *Style—* Piers von Simson, Esq; ✉ Soditic Ltd, Wellington House, 125 Strand, London WC2R 0AP (☎ 020 7872 7000, fax 020 7872 7102)

VOORSANGER, Jessica; *Educ* Parson Sch of Design, Brooklyn Museum Art Sch, Tyler Sch of Art Temple Univ, Rhode Is Sch of Design (BFA), Goldsmiths Coll London (MA); *Career* artist; fndr (with Bob Smith, *qv*) Leytonstone Centre for Contemporary Art; *Solo Exhibitions* Romance Novels (Freud's Bar London) 1991, Travel Tips (Travellers Bookshop London) 1991, Birthday Party (Peter Doig's Studio London) 1994, Baby Shower (Camden Arts Centre) 1995, Star Sightings (Modern Culture NY) 1996, The Retrieval Series: Bob Geldof (Modern Culture Project Space NY) 1996, Let's Go Rangers (Modern Culture Project Space NY) 1997, Art Stars (Anthony Wilkinson Gallery London), 1998, Stinky Village (Virgin Megastore London) 1999, Bono & Sting Wouldn't Be Anything Without: Jessica Voorsanger's The David's (The International 3 Manchester) 2001; *Group Exhibitions* Sex Salon (Epoche Gallery NY) 1990, China June 6 1989 (PS1) 1990, The Capsule (Tower Bridge Piazza) 1991, Bingo Bongo (Tower Bridge Piazza) 1992, Relative Values (Smith Art Gallery & Museum Stirling) 1993, The Pet Show (63 Union St London) 1993, Blood Brothers: Jessica Voorsanger meets David & Shaun Cassidy (installation, Nosepaint Performance Art Gp) 1993, Fete Worse than Death (Hoxton Square London) 1994, Something's Wrong (The Tannery London) 1994, Candyman II (Unit 7 Bermondsey London) 1994, The Curator's Egg (Anthony Reynolds Gallery London) 1994, Sarah Staton's Supastore (Laure Genillard Gallery London) 1994, Art Unlimited: Multiples of the 1960s and 1990s from the Arts Cncl Collection (Glasgow Contemporary Arts and Royal Festival Hall) 1994–95, Hit & Run (1–4) (various venues incl Miny of Sound London) 1994–95, Miniatures (The Agency London) 1995, Dad (Gasworks London) 1995, Life of its Own (Zivot Sam O Sobe) (Br Cncl Window Gallery Prague) 1995, Lost Property (W-139 Amsterdam and Great Western Studios London) 1995, Supastore (Middlesbrough) 1995, Imprint 93 (City Racing Gallery London) 1995, The Hanging Picnic (Factual Nonsense in Hoxton Square London) 1995, 10 Years of Student Exhibitions (Economist Plaza London) 1995, Gang Warfare (London & McKinney Contemporary Arts Dallas) 1995, Cocaine Orgasm (Bank Space @ Burbage House London) 1995, My Darling Cicciolina (Last Orders London) 1995, Glass Shelf Show (ICA) 1995–97, Kiss This (Focal Point Gallery Southend-on-Sea) 1996, Yer Self is Steam (85 Charlotte St London) 1996, Gol'96 (Sam's Salon London) 1996, Live/Life (Musee d'Arte Moderne de la cite de Paris) 1996, BANK TV, Video Myths (Dog Gallery London) 1996, Club Shiop (Sam's Salon London) 1996, 100 Per Cent Love (Coin Copy Store London) 1996, It's A Stitch Up! (Dog Gallery London) 1997, Big Blue (Coin Copy Store London and tour) 1997, Imprint 93 (Norwich Gallery) 1997, Posture: An Assessment of Figuration (David Klein Gallery Birmingham MI) 1997, The Meltdown Festival (Royal Festival Hall) 1997, Double Life (Waiting Room Univ of Wolverhampton and Art Coll Wolverhampton) 1997, BANK TABLOID (ICA London) 1997, Networking (Arts Cncl touring exhbn) 1997–99, Date With an Artist (NGCA Sunderland) 1998, Again Again (Galerie Carbone & Alberto Peola Arte Contemporanae Turin) 1998, Fame (Firstdraft Sydney) 1998, Global Housewarming (1st Floor Gallery Melbourne) 1998, Host (Tramway Glasgow) 1998, Cloth-Bound (Laure Genillard Gallery London) 1998, Show Me the Money 1 (8 Duke Mews London) 1998, Channel 3 (Team Gallery NY) 1998, Feeringbury VIII Cultivated (Feeringbury Manor Essex) 1998, Show Me The Money 3 (8 Duke Mews London) 1998, Vauxhall Gardens (Norwich Gallery) 1998, home1 (home London) 1998, My Eye Hurts (Thread Waxing Space NY and Green Room Manchester) 1999, 48 Hours (The Tablet London) 1999, Reciprocity (The Sun & Dove London) 1999, Cab Gallery London 1999 (exhibited on the inside and outside of a London taxi), MuSEUM MAgOgO (Glasgow Project Space) 1999, Liverpool Biennial 1999–, Tectonic (La Panderia Mexico City) 2000, Crush (Hoax London) 2000, Drawing of Lots (The Gallery Univ of Central Lancashire) 2000, Combi (Stavanger Norway) 2000, Playmaker (Galerie Paula Boettcher Berlin) 2000, Family Art Project (with Bob Smith, SITE Kunstverein Dusseldorf) 2000, Realm of the Senses (with Bob Smith, Turku Art Museum) 2000, In the City (Modern Culture at the Gershwin Hotel NY) 2000, Then there is no mountain, then there is (Generator Dundee) 2001, Porta-Project (Goldsmiths Coll London) 2001, Century City (Tate Modern London) 2001, Ecole de Bob Smith & David Burrows (Trade Apartment London) 2001, CRYlawn (Goldman Tevis Gallery LA) 2001, Record Collection (VTO Gallery London), Sally Barker Gallery at 291 Gallery London 2001, Teeth & Trousers (Cell Project Space Ideal House London) 2001, Across the Pond (The Practice Space LA) 2001; *Style—* Ms Jessica Voorsanger; ✉ 49 Rhodesia Road, Leytonstone, London, E11 4DF

VORA, Dr Jiten; *b* 3 April 1954; *Educ* St John's Coll Cambridge (Humphry Davy exhbn, scholarship and studentship, coll prize, Rolleston travel exhbn, Wright prize, MA, MB BChir, MD); *m* Cerys; 2 s; *Career* house surgn New Addenbrooke's Hosp Cambridge 1979, house physician Ipswich Hosp 1979–80, SHO Leicester Hosps 1980–82, registrar Leicester Royal Infirmary 1982–84, res fell Dept of Med Univ of Wales Coll of Med 1984–87, lectr and hon sr registrar in med, gen med, diabetes and endocrinology Univ of Wales Coll of Med 1987–91, Fulbright sr res scholar and visiting prof Dept of Med (Div of Nephrology and Hypertension) Oregon Health Sciences Univ 1991–93, conslt physician Royal Liverpool Univ Hosp and hon sr lectr Univ of Liverpool 1993–, examiner Univ of Liverpool; regular lectr at univs and learned socs; pres Local Charter Br Diabetic Assoc; chm Diabetes Working Sub-Gp Dist Med Advsy Ctee (also Royal Liverpool Univ Hosp rep); organiser: WHO Multi City Action Plan in Diabetes, Regnl HA Study Day – Diabetes and Renal Disease, Nat/Int Meeting – Renal Disease in Type II Diabetes; regnl co-ordinator and organiser Soc for Endocrinology; Royal Liverpool Univ Hosp rep Regnl Med Ctee Speciality Sub-Ctee for Diabetes and Endocrinology; memb: S Sefton HA Diabetes Advsy Gp, Liverpool Diabetes Register/Shared Care Gp, Diabetes UK Strategic Review Gp, S Sefton Diabetes Register Working Gp, Regnl Diabetes Care Devpt Panel, Regnl Diabetes Services Accreditation Panel, Advsy Panel Med Devices Agency, Working Party RC Opthalmologists (memb Guidelines Gp for treatment of diabetic retinopathy), NHS R&D Screening Ctee (Sub-Gp on Diabetic Retinopathy), Renal and Retinopathy Gps Nat Service Framework – Diabetes; assoc ed Diabetic Med (jl of Br Diabetic Assoc); memb: Med Res Soc, RSM, Soc of Endocrinology, Diabetes UK, Euro Assoc for the Study of Diabetes, Euro Diabetic Nephropathy Study Gp, Nat Kidney Fndn, Br Hypertension Soc; FRCP 1996 (MRCP 1981); *Publications* author of numerous articles published in learned jls and papers presented to learned societies; regular reviewer for jls incl: Diabetes, Diabetes Care, Diabetologia, Diabetic Medicine, J Diab Complications, BMJ, New England Jl of Medicine, The Lancet, Nutrition; *Recreations* cooking, cricket, squash, skiing, mountain cycling, golf; *Style—* Dr Jiten Vora; ✉ Royal

Liverpool University Hospital, Prescot Street, Liverpool L7 8XP (☎ 0151 706 3470, fax 0151 706 5871, e-mail jiten.vora@rlbuh-tr.nwest.nhs.uk)

VORDERMAN, Carol Jean; MBE (2000); *b* 24 December 1960; *Educ* Ysgol Mair Rhyl, Blessed Edward Jones HS Rhyl, Sidney Sussex Coll Cambridge (MA); *Family* 1 da (Katie), 1 s (Cameron); *Career* broadcaster and author; civil engr Sir Alfred McAlpine 1981; columnist: Daily Telegraph 1996–98, Daily Mirror 1998–2004; memb DTI Task Force Action into Engrg 1995; tstee Nat Endowment for Science, Technology and the Arts (NESTA) 1998–2001; memb Home Office Internet Task Force 2001–02; fndr The Maths Factor 2010 (online maths sch www.themathsfactor.com); patron: Express Link Up, CLAPA (Cleft Lip and Palate Assoc); hon fell Univ of Wales (Bangor), Hon MA Univ of Bath, Hon D Univ Leeds Metropolitan Univ; Assoc MICE; FRSA; *Television* progs incl: Countdown (first woman to appear on Channel 4) 1982–2008, World Chess Championship Kasparov v Short (Channel 4) 1993, educn corr GMTV 1993–94, Tomorrow's World (BBC1) 1994–95, Computers Don't Bite (BBC 2) 1997, National Lottery Live (BBC 1) 1997, Carol Vorderman's Better Homes (ITV) 1999–2003, Find a Fortune (ITV) 1999–2000, Star Lives 1999–2000, Pride of Britain Awards Ceremony 2000–, Britain's Brainiest (ITV) 2001–02, anchor presenter Loose Women (ITV1) 2011–, Food Glorious Food (ITV1) 2013; host various confs and awards ceremonies; *Books* incl: How Mathematics Works (1996), Carol Vorderman's Guide to the Internet (1998, 2 edn 2001), Maths Made Easy (1999), Science Made Easy (2000), English Made Easy (2000), Carol Vorderman's Detox For Life (with Ko Chohan, 2001), Carol Vorderman's Summer Detox (2003), Carol Vorderman's Detox Recipes (2004), How To Do Sudoku (2005), Super Brain (2007), It All Counts (autobiography, 2010), Help Your Kids with English (2013), Maths Made Easy Extra Tests (2013); *Style*— Carol Vorderman; ✉ c/o John Miles Organisation, Cadbury Camp Lane, Clapton-in-Gordano, Bristol BS20 9SB (☎ 01275 854675, fax 01275 810186)

VOREMBERG, Rhoderick Peter Grosvenor (Rhoddy); s of late Dato' Rudolf Peter Voremberg, DKDS, PJK, and Rosella, *née* Bartelot; *b* 19 November 1954, Trowbridge, Wilts; *Educ* Cumnor House Sch Sussex, Rugby, Magdalene Coll Cambridge (MA); *m* 15 March 1980, Susan Mary, *née* Burnet; 2 da (Jessica b 14 March 1983, Fuchsia b 30 Nov 1987), 1 s (Rupert b 17 April 1985); *Career* slr; articled clerk then asst slr Burges Salmon Bristol 1978–82, Wilsons Salisbury 1982–2010 (sr ptnr 2003–06), ptnr Farrer & Co 2010–; Tax Ctee Estates Business Gp 2009–, Tax and Political Ctee Historic Houses Assoc 2010–; tstee: Stanley Picker Tst 1998–, Wilts Community Fndn 1998–2006, Salisbury Almshouse and Welfare Charities 1999–2010, Roche Court Education Tst 2005–; chm Salisbury Arts Centre 2006–13, chm Heritage Gp of Professional Advsrs 2013–; memb Cncl RCM 2011–; memb Soc of Tst and Estate Practitioners 1991 (chm Investment Ctee 2016–); *Recreations* amateur silversmith, match rifle shooting (capt English Eight 1996–2001), fly-fishing, books, typography, fine art; *Clubs* Hawks' (Cambridge), English Eight (Bisley), Athenaeum, Flyfishers'; *Style*— R P G Voremberg, Esq; ✉ Farrer & Co, 66 Lincoln's Inn Fields, London WC2A 3LH (☎ 020 3375 7000, fax 020 3375 7917, e-mail rhoddy.voremberg@farrer.co.uk)

VOS, Rt Hon Lord Justice; Sir Geoffrey Charles Vos; kt (2009), PC (2013), QC (1993); s of Bernard Vos (d 1974), and Pamela Celeste Rose, *née* Heilbuth (d 2011); *b* 22 April 1955; *Educ* UCS, Gonville & Caius Coll Cambridge (MA); *m* 31 March 1984, Vivien Mary, da of Albert Edward Dowdeswell (d 1982), of Birmingham; 1 da (Charlotte b 1985), 2 step da (Maria b 1965, Louise b 1965), 1 step s (Carl b 1973); *Career* called to the Bar Inner Temple 1977, bencher Lincoln's Inn; judge Courts of Appeal of Jersey and Guernsey 2005–09, judge Court of Appeal of Cayman Islands 2008–09, High Court judge 2009–13, a Lord Justice of Appeal 2013–; chm: Chancery Bar Assoc 1999–2001 (hon sec 1994–97, vice-chm 1997–99), Bar Cncl 2007 (vice-chm 2006, chm Fees Collection Ctee 1995–2004,

chm Professional Standards Ctee 2004–06 (vice-chm 2001–03)); memb Alan Milburn's Panel on Fair Access to the Profession 2009; ex officio memb Gen Cncl of the Bar 1999–2001 and 2004–07; pres of european network of cncls for the judiciary 2015–; chm of tstees Social Mobility Fndn 2008–11, tstee Slynn Fndn 2009–, chm European Ctee Judges' Cncl 2012–; hon fell Gonville & Caius Coll Cambridge 2015; *Recreations* farming, wine, photography; *Clubs* Oxford and Cambridge, Worcs Golf; *Style*— The Rt Hon the Lord Justice Vos; ✉ Royal Courts of Justice, London WC2A 2LL

VOSS, Prof Christopher Arnold; s of Dr H J Voss, of Cottingham, Northants, and Matthew, *née* Arnold (d 1989); *b* 23 December 1942, Enfield; *Educ* Bedford Sch, Imperial Coll London (BSc), London Business Sch (MSc, PhD); *m* 14 Dec 1977, Carolyn Jill, da of Sir Richard Kingsland, DFC, (of Canberra, Aust; 1 da (Georgina b 1978), 1 s (Barnaby b 1981); *Career* mangr Stuarts & Lloyds Ltd 1960–67, conslt Harbridge House Europe 1970–75, visiting prof Univ of Western Ontario 1975–77, lectr London Business Sch 1977–84, Alan Edward Higgs prof of mfrg strategy and policy Univ of Warwick 1984–90; dep dean London Business Sch 1999–2002, prof of operation mgmnt Warwick Business Sch 2012–, emeritus prof of operations mgmnt London Business Sch 2010–; distinguished scholar Acad of Mgmnt 2008; dir European Case Clearing House 2002–08; chm European Ops Mgmnt Assoc 1989–2001; MBICS 1971, FRSA 1989, fell Br Acad of Mgmnt 1995, FIMechE 2001, fell Prodn and Ops Mgmnt Soc 2005, fell Decision Science Inst 2005; *Books* Operation Management in Service Industries and the Public Sector (1985), Just-In-Time Management (1988), Performance Measurement in Service Industries (1992), Manufacturing Strategy – Process and Content (1992), Made in Europe (1994), International Manufacturing Strategies (1998), Innovation in Experiential Services (2007), Service Research Priorities in a Rapidly Changing Context (2015); *Recreations* skiing, violin, book collecting; *Style*— Prof Christopher Voss; ✉ London Business School, Sussex Place, Regents Park, London NW1 4SA (☎ 020 7000 8812, fax 020 7000 7001)

VRANCH, Dr Richard Leslie; s of Leslie William Frank Vranch (d 1991), of Somerset, and Rea Helen Vranch (d 2005); *b* 29 June 1959; *Educ* Bristol GS, Trinity Hall Cambridge (MA, PhD); *m* 2008, Lauren Ann Bishop; *Career* actor, writer and former musician; writing incl: films for NatWest, Boots, AA, Harper Collins, Ryman and the Sheik (play for Tamasha Theatre Co) 2002, articles, comedy sketches, feature film script Sole Representation 1999; Plessey res fell St John's Coll Oxford 1984–85; guest speaker Big Science (Royal Instn) 2013; *Theatre* work incl: Aftertaste (with Tony Slattery, *qv*) 1981–, The Comedy Store Players 1986–, English Teaching Theatre (tour to Europe, ME and Mexico) 1988–94, Secret Policeman's Biggest Ball (Cambridge Theatre) 1990, Hysteria 2 and Hysteria 3 1991, Clive in The Dead Set 1992, Paul Merton Show (London Palladium) 1994, Lifegame (West Yorkshire Playhouse), Mexico (one-man show) 1999, YarnBards 2004–, Paul Merton's Impro Chums 2004–, Paul Merton Out of My Mind (Vaudeville Theatre) 2013; *Television* appearances incl: Whose Line Is It Anyway? (Channel 4) 1988–97, The Secret Policeman's Biggest Ball 1990, Jackanory (BBC) 1993 and 1994, The Music Game (Channel 4) 1993, Cue the Music 1994–96, Beat That Einstein (Channel 4) 1994, Paul Merton at the Palladium (BBC) 1994, Mind Games (BBC) 2005, Celebrity Weakest Link (BBC) 2005; various animations and voice overs; writer Smack the Pony 1999–2002; *Radio* for BBC Radio 4 incl: The Hot Club 1989, Wordly Wise 1997, Cross Questioned 1997, Just a Minute 1999, Puzzle Panel 2005, Loose-Ends 2010; Jammin (BBC Radio 2, team capt) 2001–04; *Film* Balloon Seller in The Suicidal Dog; *Publications* Defects in Irradiated MOS Structures (PhD thesis); 'Spin-dependent and localisation effects at Si/SiO2 device interfaces' in Semi-conductor Science and Technol, vol 4, 1999; Cartoons in Punch, Maxim (with Lucy Lee-Allen), The Spectator; *Recreations* travel in Europe and Latin America; *Style*— Richard Vranch; ✉ c/o Sue Terry Voices (☎ 020 7434 2040)

W

WAAGE, Prof Jeffrey King; OBE (2007); s of Prof Karl Mensch Waage, of Connecticut, USA, and Elizabeth, *née* King; *b* 15 March 1953; *Educ* Hopkins GS, Princeton Univ (AB, Phi Beta Kappa), Imperial Coll London (Marshall fell, PhD, DIC); *m* 18 March 1983, Cynthia, da of Dr Charles Day Masters (m dis); 1 da (Hannah b 23 Nov 1984), 3 s (Alexander b 26 Sept 1986, Nicholas b 29 March 1989, Theodore b 27 Feb 1994); *Career* postdoctoral work in entomology Univ of Texas Austin 1978, lectr in insect ecology Imperial Coll London 1978–86, dir Int Inst of Biological Control 1992–98 (joined as chief research offr 1986, subsequently dep dir), chief exec CABI Bioscience 1998–2001, head Dept of Agric Sciences Imperial Coll London 2001, currently dir London Int Devpt Centre; pres Int Orgn of Biological Control 1996–2000, chair Global Invasive Species Prog 2000–03; has worked extensively in tropical America, Africa and Asia on aspects of ecology and pest mgmnt since 1975; memb: Br Ecological Soc 1978, Royal Entomological Soc of London 1978, Entomological Soc of America 1980; MIBiol 2001; *Recreations* walking; *Style*— Prof Jeffrey Waage, OBE

WACE, Rupert; s of Rodney Sant Wace, and Heather Mary Wace; *Educ* Marlborough; *m* Emma Chichester Clark; 3 s (Timothy, Oliver, Arthur); *Career* formerly with: Sotheby's London, Christie's; prop Rupert Wace Ancient Art Ltd 1988–; supporter: KIDS, Br Museum, Chelsea Physic Gdn; memb: BADA 1999, IADAA 1995, ADA 1989; *Books* Celtic Sculpture (1989), Egyptian, Greek and Roman Antiquities (1991), Pharoah's Creatures: Animals from Ancient Egypt (2004), Eternal Woman: The Female Form in Antiquity (2005), In Our Own Image – Gods & Mortals in Ancient Art (2008), A Collector's Menagerie – Animal Sculpture from the Ancient World (2010); *Recreations* salmon fishing, tennis, horse racing, travel, cinema, cricket, music; *Clubs* Dover Street Arts; *Style*— Rupert Wace, Esq; ✉ Rupert Wace Ancient Art, 19 Crown Passage, St James's, London SW1Y 6PP (☎ 020 7495 1623, fax 020 7495 8495, e-mail rupert@rupertwace.co.uk)

WADDELL, Bruce; s of Ken Waddell, and Christina Ann Waddell; *b* 18 March 1959, Bo'ness, W Lothian; *m* 15 Oct 1994, Cathy, *née* Cullis; 1 s (Daniel b 24 Dec 1995); *Career* with Johnston Newspapers 1977–87, sub ed then chief sub ed Scottish Sun 1987–90, dep ed Sunday Scot 1990–91, mktg and sales exec Murray Int 1991–93, dep ed Scottish Sun 1993–98, ed Scottish Sun 1998–2003, ed Daily Record 2003–09, ed-in-chief Scottish Daily Record and Sunday Mail Ltd 2009–; memb: Newspaper Press Fund, Scottish Daily Newspaper Soc; *Recreations* football, classic cars, cinema, golf; *Style*— Bruce Waddell, Esq; ✉ Daily Record, One Central Quay, Glasgow G3 8DA (☎ 0141 309 3000, fax 0141 309 3340)

WADDELL, Heather; yr da of Robert (Roy) Waddell (d 1980), of Hughenden, Glasgow, and Maureen, *née* Buchanan, MBE (d 2006); *b* 1950; *Educ* Westbourne Sch Glasgow, St Leonard's Sch St Andrews, Univ of St Andrews (MA), Byam Shaw Sch of Art London (Dip Fine Art, Leverhulme bursary), Univ of the Arts, Univ of London (CertEd); *Partner* 1974–78, Roger Wilson (d 1999), Australian artist; *Career* author, art critic, artist, photographer and publisher; lectr in English and gen studies Paddington Coll London 1978, researcher Int Artists Exchange Prog in Aust and NZ (Gulbenkian award 1979), admin Int Artists' Exchange Prog ACME Gallery London 1978–80, London corr Vie des Arts 1979–89, Central Bureau for Educational Visits and Exchanges grant to set up art sch exchange links in Belgium and Holland 1980, fndr and md Art Guide Publications Ltd 1980–87 (art guides to London, NY, Paris, Berlin, Amsterdam, Madrid, Glasgow, Aust and UK), publisher Art Guides imprint A&C Black 1987–90, arts ed élan arts magazine The European 1990–91, visual arts ed Time Out Publications 1989–93, lectr in art history American Univ Summer Sch Paris 1995; freelance art critic: The Evening Standard 1974, The Artist 1974–75, TES 1977, The Glasgow Herald 1994– (London art critic 1980–84), Artnews USA 1986, New Art International Paris 1986, Artline UK 1985–92, The Independent 1988–89, Independent on Sunday 1993, visual arts ed Chic magazine 1994–98, The Times 1996 and 2010–, BBC World Servs 1998, ITV News 2000, BBC TV World News 2013– (freelance art expert); co-organiser New Scottish Prints Exhbn as part of Britain Salutes NY (toured USA) 1983, conslt Int Contemporary Art Fair London 1984–90, organiser Henri Goetz Exhibition London 1986, chm of judges The Art Show 1994; judge: Bernard Denvir AICA Art Critics' Prize 1994, 2003 and 2006, Royal Over-Seas League Open 1998, Art for the Millennium Guernsey 2000; artist and photographer: Battersea Arts Centre 1979, 5 + 1 Aust photos exhibition NSW House Art Gallery London 1980, Morley Gallery (IAA exhbn) 1984), Art Guides (London and Glasgow), Blue Guides (London and Paris), The Independent, The European, Time Out Publications, National Portrait Gallery London (20 photographs Photographic Collection); 27 Holland Park Avenue Ltd: company dir 1987–2012, company sec 1992–2012; Int Assoc of Art Critics (AICA): memb 1980–, memb Exec Ctee 1982–97 and 2001–06, treas 1984–86, PR 1990–97, created AICA UK archives (now in Tate archives) 2004–, organiser BD AICA Award 1995, 2003 and 2006; mentor to St Andrews Univ arts students 2003–; memb: Exec Ctee Int Assoc of Artists 1978–84, Soc of Young Publishers 1980–86, Ind Publishers' Guild 1980–89 and 2002–, Map and Guide Book Ctee and Art Book Publishers' Ctee Publishers' Assoc 1983–87, Soc of Authors 2003–, Association Internationale Des Critiques d'Art; *Books* author of: London Art and Artists Guide (1979, 12 edn 2016), The London Art World 1979–99 (2000), The Artists' Directory (1981, 3 edn 1989), Henri Goetz: 50 Years of Painting (1986), Art Snakes and London Ladders (forthcoming); contrib: London Encyclopaedia (1983, 1990 and 2008), L'Ecosse: pierre, vent et lumière (1988), Blue Guide to Spain (1988), Londres (Editions Autrement Paris, 1997 and 2000); visual arts section in Time Out: London Guide, New York Guide, Visitor's Guide, Shopping Guide 1987–92; British Figurative Art 1980–92: Paintings of Hope and Despair (1992); artist catalogues/statements: Kenneth Lauder, Victoria Achache, Natasha Kissell and Peter Harrap, Denis Clarke, Peter Griffin and Mim Hain; *Recreations* travel, swimming, cycling, contemporary literature and films, enjoying life; *Clubs* Royal Over-Seas League (hon memb), Serpentine Swimming, Ladbroke Square Gardens; *Style*— Heather Waddell; ✉ e-mail hwlondon@btinternet.com, websites www.hwlondonartandartistsguide.co.uk, www.londonartandartistsguide.co.uk

WADDELL, Martin; s of Martin Mayne Waddell, and Alice, *née* Duffell; *b* 10 April 1941, Belfast; *Educ* Eaton House Sch London, St Clement Danes Sch London, Down HS Downpatrick; *m* Dec 1969, Rosaleen Margaret, da of Thomas Arthur Carragher; 3 s (Thomas Mayne (Tom) b 1970, David Martin b 1972, Peter Matthew b 1975); *Career* writer (also writes as Catherine Sefton) 1966–; former work experience incls bookselling and junk-stalling; The Hans Christian Andersen Award 2004; memb: Soc of Authors, Irish Writers' Union, Children's Literature Assoc of Ireland; *Books include* Starry Night (The Other Award, runner-up Guardian Young Fiction Award), Can't You Sleep Little Bear (Smarties Prize, Sheffield Book Award, Prix de Critiques de Livres pour Enfants de la Communauté Française de Belgique, Prix Verselle), The Park in the Dark (Emil/Kurt Maschler Award), The Hidden House (Emil/Kurt Maschler Award short list), Rosie's Babies (Best Book for Babies Award), Squeak-a-Lot, Grandma's Bill (runner-up Bisto Book of the Year Award, Acorn Award short list), Farmer Duck (Smarties Prize, Emil/Kurt Maschler Award short list), Owl Babies; *Style*— Martin Waddell, Esq; ✉ c/o David Higham Associates, 5–8 Lower John Street, Golden Square, London W1R 4HA (☎ 020 7437 7888, fax 020 7437 1072)

WADDINGTON, Baron (Life Peer UK 1990), of Read in the County of Lancashire; Sir David Charles Waddington; GCVO (1994), PC (1987), QC (1971), DL (Lancashire 1991); s of late Charles Waddington, JP, of Read, Lancs, and Minnie Hughan Waddington; *b* 2 August 1929, Burnley, Lancs; *Educ* Sedbergh, Hertford Coll Oxford; *m* 1958, Gillian Rosemary, da of Alan Green, CBE, of Sabden, Lancs; 3 s (Hon James Charles b 1960, Hon Matthew David b 1962, Hon Alistair Paul b 1965), 2 da (Hon Jennifer Rosemary b 1965, Hon Victoria Jane b 1971); *Career* 2 Lt 12 Royal Lancers 1951–53; called to the Bar Gray's Inn 1951, recorder of the Crown Court 1972; former dir: J J Broadley Ltd, J and J Roberts Ltd, Wolstenholme Rink Ltd; Parly candidate (Cons): Farnworth 1955, Nelson and Colne 1964, Heywood and Royton 1966; MP (Cons): Nelson and Colne 1968–74, Clitheroe March 1979–83, Ribble Valley 1983–90; Lord Cmmr of the Treasy 1979–81, Parly under sec employment 1981–83, min of state Home Office 1983–87, govt chief whip 1987–89, home sec 1989–90; Lord Privy Seal and Leader of the House of Lords 1990–92, govr and C-in-C Bermuda 1992–1997; *Style*— The Rt Hon Lord Waddington, GCVO, PC, QC, DL; ✉ Old Bailiffs, South Cheriton, Templecombe, Somerset BA8 0BH

WADDINGTON, Prof David James; s of Eric James Waddington (d 1958), and Marjorie Edith, *née* Harding (d 1995); *b* 27 May 1932; *Educ* Marlborough, Imperial Coll London (BSc, ARCS, DIC, PhD); *m* 17 Aug 1957, Isobel, da of Ernest Hesketh (d 1994); 2 s (Matthew b 1963, Rupert b 1964), 1 da (Jessica b 1970); *Career* head Sci Dept Wellington Coll 1961–64 (teacher 1956–64); York Univ 1965–: prof of chemical educn 1978–2000, head dept 1983–92, pro-vice-chllr 1985–91, emeritus prof 2000–; visiting prof Univ of Kiel 2000–; pres Educn Div Royal Soc Chem 1981–83, chm Ctee Teaching Chemistry Int Union Pure and Applied Chem 1981–85, sec Ctee Teaching Sci Int Cncl Sci Unions 1985–89 (chm 1989–94); hon prof Mendeleev Univ of Chemical Technology Moscow; Nyholm medal Royal Soc Chem 1985, Brasted Award American Chem Soc 1988, ACS-CEI Award American Chemical Soc 2012; Liveryman Worshipful Co of Salters 2001; Brazilian Grand Cross National Order of Merit 1997; *Books* Kinetics and Mechanism: Case Studies (1977), Modern Organic Chemistry (1985), Chemistry, The Salters' Approach (1989), Salters' Advanced Chemistry (1994, new edn 2000); ed: Teaching School Chemistry (1984), Chemistry in Action (1987), Education Industry and Technology (1987), Bringing Chemistry to Life (1992), Science for Understanding Tomorrow's World: Global Change (1994), Global Environmental Change: Science Education and Training (1995), Partners in Chemical Education (1996), Salters' Higher Chemistry (1999), Evaluation as a Tool for Improving Science Education (2005), Context Based Learning of Science (2005), Standards in Science Education (2007), The Essential Chemical Industry (2010), The Essential Chemical Industry (online, 2013, revised 2015); *Recreations* golf; *Style*— Prof David Waddington; ✉ Department of Chemistry, University of York, Heslington, York YO10 5DD (☎ 01904 322523, e-mail djw1@york.ac.uk)

WADDINGTON, Hon James; QC (2015); s of David Waddington, and Gillian, *née* Green, of South Cheriton, Wincanton; *b* 12 October 1960, Preston; *Educ* Radley, Univ of Exeter (LLB); *m* Anne Mannion; 1 da (Lucy b 12 June 1992), 1 s (Harry b 16 July 1994); *Career* called to the Bar (Gray's Inn) 1983, recorder 2004–; memb: south Eastern Circuit 1984, Criminal Bar Assoc 1985; *Recreations* cinema, cricket, reading, travel, theatre, art; *Clubs* Travellers; *Style*— The Hon James Waddington, QC; ✉ 5A Shepherd Market, London W1J 7PD; 9–12 Bell Yard, London WC2A 2JR (☎ 020 7400 1800, e-mail j.waddington@912by.com)

WADDINGTON, Prof (Peter Anthony) James (Jim); s of James William Harker Waddington (d 1980), and Patricia Ann, *née* Nil; *b* 6 March 1947; *Educ* Moseley Road Sch of Art, Matthew Boulton Tech Coll, Univ of London (external BSc), Univ of Leeds (MA, PhD); *m* 1968, Diane Anita, da of George Atherley; 1 s (Daniel Bevan b 15 Nov 1978), 1 da (Claire Shelley b 9 April 1980); *Career* Univ of Leeds: SSRC studentship 1969–70, res offr/fell Dept of Adult Educn 1970–74, lectr in sociology 1974–76; Univ of Reading: lectr in sociology 1976–92, reader in police studies 1992–95, prof of sociology 1995–99, prof of political sociology 1999–2006; prof of social policy and dir History and Governance Research Inst Univ of Wolverhampton 2006–; *Books* The Training of Prison Governors (1983), Arming an Unarmed Police (1988), The Strong Arm of the Law (1991), Calling the Police (1993), Liberty and Order (1995), Policing Citizens (1999), Violent Workplace (2006), What is Policing? (2010); *Recreations* walking; *Style*— Prof Jim Waddington; ✉ School of Law, Social Sciences and Communications, University of Wolverhampton, Wulfruna Street, Wolverhampton WV1 1SB (☎ 01902 321000, e-mail paj.waddington@wlv.ac.uk)

WADDINGTON, Susan (Sue); *Educ* Blyth GS Norwich, Univ of Leicester (BA, MEd); *Career* early career as community project ldr and lectr in social policy; asst dir of educn: Derbys CC 1988–90, Birmingham CC 1990–94; MEP (Lab) Leicestershire and S Lincolnshire 1994–99, European devpt offr Nat Inst of Continuing Educn 2000–; memb (Lab) Leics CC 1973–91 and 2003–; Parly candidate Leics NW 1987, European Parly candidate E Midlands 1999; vice-pres European Assoc for the Educn of Adults 2001; *Style*— Ms Sue Waddington

WADDON, Rik; *b* 27 February 1977; *Career* Paralympic cyclist; achievements incl: 3 Gold medals (road time trial, 1km time trial and 3km pursuit) Para-Cycling European Championships 2001, Gold medal (team sprint) and 2 Silver medals (1km time trial and flying 200 time trial) Paralympic World Cup 2005, Gold medal (team sprint) Track World CP Championships 2005, Gold medal (team sprint) Para-Cycling European Track Championships 2005, Silver medal (1km time trial) Paralympic World Cup 2006, Gold medal (team sprint) Paralympic World Cup 2007, Gold medal (team sprint) and Silver medal (men's 1km time trial) Para-Cycling World Championships 2007, Silver medal

W

(1km time trial) and Bronze medal (team sprint) Paralympic World Cup 2008, Silver medal (men's 1km time trial) Paralympic Games 2008, 2 Silver medals (1km time trial and pursuit) Para-Cycling World Championships 2009, Silver medal (kilo) and Bronze medal (individual pursuit) Para-Cycling Track World Championships 2011, Silver medal (team sprint) Paralympic Games 2012; *Style*— Mr Rik Waddon; ✉ Facebook /rikwaddon, Twitter @riks_world

WADE, Dr John Philip Huddart; s of Dr Edward Geoffrey Wade (d 1999), of Cheadle Hulme, Cheshire, and Mary Ward Pickering, *née* Huddart; *b* 19 April 1950; *Educ* Cheadle Hulme Sch, Univ of Cambridge (BA), Manchester Med Sch (MB BChir), Univ of Cambridge (MD); *m* 26 April 1976, Charlotte, da of Dr Elozor Leslie Feinmann (d 1983) and Sylvia Feinmann (d 1989); 1 da (Jessica Alice Feinmann), 1 s (Charles Louis Feinmann); *Career* registrar St Thomas' Hosp 1978, sr registrar Nat Hosp for Nervous Disease London and St Bartholomew's Hosp 1984–85, res fell Cerebrovascular Disease Univ of Western Ontario 1985–86, currently conslt neurologist Charing Cross Hosp and conslt neurologist Wexham Park Hosp Slough; present research interests incl: role of functional neuroimaging in neurology, early diagnosis of dementia, evaluation of individual patients with severe extracranial occlusive vascular disease; memb Assoc Br Neurologists 1986, fell Stroke Cncl American Heart Assoc 1988, FRCP 1992; *Publications* papers incl: Reactivity of the cerebral circulation in patients with occlusive carotid disease (with M M Brown, R W Ross Russell and C Bishop, 1986), CBF and vasoreactivity in patients with arteriovenous malformations (with J K Farrar and V C Hachinski, 1987); various invited chapters in books; abstract papers incl: Cerebral blood flow in subjects with high oxygen affinity haemoglobin at Euro Conf of Haemorheology London (with T C Pearson), Impact of contra lateral ICA stenosis on outcome of symptomatic ICA occlusion at Associates of Br Neurologists Glasgow (with V Hachinski and H J M Barnett, 1989); *Recreations* sailing; *Style*— Dr John Wade; ✉ 11 Gardnor Road, Hampstead, London NW3 (☎ 020 7431 2900); Department of Neurosciences, Charing Cross Hospital, Fulham Palace Road, London W6 (☎ 020 8846 1303, fax 020 8846 1187)

WADE, Keith Martin; *Educ* Bosworth Coll Desford, LSE (BSc, MSc); *Career* res offr Centre for Economic Forecasting London Business Sch 1984–88; Schroders: joined 1988, UK economist 1988–91, chief economist 1992–; memb Addenbrookes Investment Ctee 2006–; tstee ACT 2011; memb Soc of Business Economists; *Books* Macroeconomics (co-author, 1995); *Recreations* cricket, golf; *Style*— Keith Wade, Esq; ✉ Schroders plc, 31 Gresham Street, London EC2V 7AS (☎ 020 7658 6000)

WADE, Laura; *b* 16 October 1977, Bedford; *Educ* Lady Manners Sch Bakewell, Univ of Bristol; *Career* playwright; plays: Colder Than Here (Soho Theatre) 2005, Breathing Corpses (Royal Court) 2005, Other Hands (Royal Court) 2006, Catch (Royal Court) 2006, Posh (Royal Court) 2010 and (Duke of York Theatre) 2012, Kreutzer vs. Kreutzer (Sydney Opera House and Australian Tour) 2010 and (Globe Theatre) 2015; films: The Riot Club 2014; tstee Belarus Free Theatre; Most Promising Playwright Critics' Choice Theatre Award 2005, George Devine Award 2006; *Recreations* birdwatching; *Style*— Ms Laura Wade; ✉ c/o Knight Hall Agency Ltd, Lower Ground Floor, 7 Mallow Street, London EC1Y 8RQ

WADE, Martyn John; OBE (2015); s of Albert R Wade (d 1979), of Birmingham, and Nancy Joan, *née* Exon (d 1980); *b* 24 March 1955, Birmingham; *Educ* King Edward IV Five Ways GS Birmingham, Newcastle Poly (BA), Univ of Wales Aberystwyth (MLib); *m* 1978, Anne Rosemary, *née* Patterson; *Career* trainee librarian Northumberland CC 1976–78, branch librarian Sunderland MBC 1978–81, branch librarian and librarian in charge Sutton LBC 1981–87, librarian Northumberland CC 1987–91, area librarian Leicestershire CC 1991–93, area library offr Cambridgeshire CC 1994–99, head of libraries, info and learning Glasgow City Cncl 1999–2002, nat librarian and chief exec Nat Library of Scotland 2002–14, ret; chair Chartered Inst of Library and Information Professionals 2014–, chair Ctee for Freedom of Access to Information and Freedom of Expression Int Fedn of Library Assocs and Insts; chair of govrs Mortification of Innerpeffray; visiting prof Robert Gordons Univ 2011–; memb Heritage Lottery Fund Ctee for Scotland 2016–; MCLIP 1978, FRSA 2006; *Recreations* motorcycling, reading, the arts, cooking; *Clubs* Scottish Motorcycle; *Style*— Martyn Wade, Esq, OBE; ✉ e-mail m.wade@nls.uk

WADE, Michael John; s of Peter Wade (d 2005), and Lorna A M Harris (d 2016); *b* 22 May 1954; *Educ* Royal Russell, N Staffs Coll; *m* 1997, Dr Caroline Sarah Dashwood, da of Sir Francis Dashwood, Bt (d 2000); 1 s (Alexander Francis Neville b 1 Jan 1998); *Career* fndr and chm Holman Wade Ltd 1980–93, dir Horace Clarkson plc 1986–93, fndr and chief exec Rostrum Gp Ltd 2000–; memb Lloyd's 1980–, memb Cncl and Ctee Lloyd's 1987–92, chm Lloyd's Community Prog 1988–94, memb Lloyd's Taskforce 1991, fndr Corporate Lloyd's Membership Ltd 1993, chief exec CLM Insurance Fund plc (appointed dep chm on merger with SVB Holdings plc 1999); chm: Opera Interludes Ltd 1990–, Bowood Holdings Ltd 2005–08; dir: Rostrum Gp Ltd 2000–09, Optex Gp Ltd (formerly Paterson Martin Ltd) 2006 (chm 2008–11, Optex Gp acquired by Besso Insurance Gp Ltd); exec chm Besso Insurance Gp Ltd 2011–12; non-exec dir BRIT Holdings plc 2002–03; treas Cons Pty 2000– (memb Economic Competitiveness Policy Gp 2006–), chm Cons Friends of Pakistan 2012–15, Crown rep for insurance Cabinet Office 2013–15, sr advsr to the Cabinet Office 2015–; tstee Salisbury Cathedral Girl Choristers' Tst 2003–, chm London Festival Opera 2007–; *Publications* Essential Ingredients for Integration (2013); *Recreations* music, shooting, flying, architectural restoration; *Clubs* Brooks's; *Style*— Michael J Wade, Esq; ✉ Trafalgar Park, nr Salisbury, Wiltshire SP5 3QR (website www.trafalgarpark.com); 87 Vincent Square, London SW1P 2PQ (☎ 020 7821 0675, e-mail michaeljwade@hotmail.com)

WADE, Mike; s of James Edward Wade, and May, *née* Wakefield; *b* 1949, Redcar, Yorks; *Educ* Royal Liberty GS, Coll for Distributive Trades (HNC); *m* Penny Helen; 3 c by previous m (Elizabeth, Jennifer, Christopher); *Career* grad trainee Unilever, mktg dir Ciba-Giegy Consumer Products, ptnr Owen Wade Delmonte, md Chetwyn Haddons, md Index Advtg, ceo FCA! Ltd, dir of strategy Publicis UK; fndr Quoll Strategic Solutions; lectr IPA and Inst of Mktg; MIPA 1971, MMRS 1985; *Publications* Wolfe (Tamla Motown album, 1969), Dear God (1979), Hole in my Pocket (2014); *Recreations* music, photography, nature, travel, literature; *Style*— Mike Wade, Esq; ✉ Publicis, 82 Baker Street, London W1U 6AE (☎ 020 7935 4426, mobile 07831 289239, e-mail mike.wade@publicis.co.uk)

WADE, Nicholas James; s of William John Wade, and Sarah Ellen, *née* Ostick; *b* 27 March 1942; *Educ* Queen Elizabeth's GS Mansfield, Univ of Edinburgh (BSc), Monash Univ (PhD); *m* 1965, Christine, *née* Whetton; 2 da (Rebecca Jane b 1971, Helena Kate b 1972); *Career* postdoctoral fell Max Planck Inst for Behavioural Physiology Seewiesen Germany 1969–70; Univ of Dundee Dept of Psychology: lectr 1970–78, reader 1978–91, prof of visual psychology 1991–2009, emeritus prof of psychology 2009–; memb Experimental Psychology Soc 1974; FRSE 1997; *Publications* The Art and Science of Visual Illusions (1982), Brewster and Wheatstone on Vision (1983), Visual Allusions: Pictures of Perception (1990), Visual Perception: An Introduction (1991, new edn 2013), Psychologists in Word and Image (1995), A Natural History of Vision (1998), Purkinje's Vision: The Dawning of Neuroscience (2001), Destined for Distinguished Oblivion: The Scientific Vision of William Charles Wells 1757–1817 (2003), Perception and Illusion: Historical Perspectives (2005), The Moving Tablet of the Eye: The Origins of Modern Eye Movement Research (2005), Insegne Ambigue Percorsi Obliqui tra Storia, Scienza e Arte, de Galileo a Magritte (2007), Circles: Science, Sense and Symbol (2007), Giuseppe Moruzzi, Ritratti de uni scienziato, Portraits of a Scientist (2010), Galileo's Visions: Piercing the Spheres of the Heavens by Eye and Mind (2014), Art and Illusionists (2016); *Recreations* golf, cycling, hill walking; *Clubs* Scotscraig Golf, New Golf (St Andrews), The Newport; *Style*— Prof Nicholas Wade, FRSE; ✉ Psychology, University of Dundee, Dundee DD1 4HN (☎ 01382 384616, e-mail n.j.wade@dundee.ac.uk)

WADE, Richard Samuel Marlar; s of Neil Wade, of Mayfield, East Sussex, and Jane, *née* Marlar; *b* 28 February 1968, Brighton, Sussex; *Educ* Brighton Coll, Univ of Birmingham (LLB), Coll of Law; *m* 6 Aug 1994, Denise, *née* Jones; 2 da (Kira Josephine b 17 Feb 2004, Juliet Clare b 22 July 2006); *Career* trainee slr then slr Dentons (formerly Wilde Sapte) 1992–97; Blake Morgan: slr 1997–2000, ptnr 2000–, head of construction 2004–; memb: Law Soc 1994, Soc of Construction Law (Oxford regnl coordinator), TeCSA (Technology and Construction Court Slrs Assoc) 1999; *Recreations* sport, music (contemporary and classical), travel, wine; *Clubs* Primary, Wooden Spoon Soc, MCC (assoc); *Style*— Richard Wade, Esq; ✉ Blake Morgan, Seacourt Tower, West Way, Oxford OX2 0FB (☎ 01865 254244, fax 01865 243167, e-mail richard.wade@blakemorgan.co.uk)

WADE OF CHORLTON, Baron (Life Peer UK 1990), of Chester in the County of Cheshire; Sir (William) Oulton Wade; kt (1982), JP; s of Samuel Norman Wade, of Chester, and Joan Ferris, *née* Wild; *b* 24 December 1932; *Educ* Birkenhead Sch, Queen's Univ Belfast; *m* 1959, Gillian Margaret, da of Desmond Leete, of Buxton; 1 s (Hon Christopher James Oulton b 1961), 1 da (Hon Alexandra Jane b 1964); *Career* farmer and cheesemaker; dir MITON Gp plc 2003– (chm 2012–), chm Rocktron Ltd 2003–14; dir Rising Stars Growth Fund Ltd 2001–14; former memb Cheshire CC, chm City of Chester Cons Assoc 1973–76, jt hon treas Cons Pty 1982–90; chm: English Cheese Export Cncl 1982–84, Rural Economy Gp, Chester Heritage Tst, Historic Cheshire Churches Preservation Tst 1992–2012; chm Children's Safety Educn Fndn 2004–13; Freeman City of London, Liveryman Worshipful Co of Farmers; *Clubs* Chester City, Portico Library (Manchester); *Style*— The Rt Hon Lord Wade of Chorlton; ✉ Chorlton House, 1 Rectory Close, Farndon, Chester CH3 6PS (☎ 01829 270747)

WADHAM, John; s of Ernest George Wadham (d 1997), and Unity Winifred, *née* Errington (d 2003); *b* 24 January 1952, Croydon, Surrey; *Educ* Stanley Tech Sch London, LSE (BSc), Univ of Surrey (MSc, Cert), Coll of Law; *m* Christine Buccella; *Career* admitted slr 1989; social worker London Borough of Richmond 1975–77, legal advsr Wandsworth Law Centres 1976–86; Liberty: legal advsr 1990–95, dir 1995–2003; dep chair IPCC 2003–07, gen counsel Equality and Human Rights Cmmn 2007–13, exec dir Interights (Centre for the Legal Protection of Human Rights) 2013–14, chair UK Nat Preventive Mechanism 2016–; memb Editorial Bd European Human Rights Law Review; hon lectr: Law Sch and Scarman Centre Univ of Leicester, Univ of Auckland; associate Doughty Street Chambers; visiting fell Univ of Bristol, visiting sr research fell KCL 2014; memb: Liberty, Amnesty Int, Soc of Lab Lawyers, Law Soc (memb Human Rights Ctee 2015); *Publications* Blackstone's Guide to the Identity Cards Act (2006), Blackstone's Guide to the Equality Act 2010 (2010, 3 edn 2016), Blackstone's Guide to the Human Rights Act (6 edn 2011, 7 edn 2015), Blackstone's Guide to the Freedom of Information Act (5 edn 2013); *Recreations* flying (private pilot); *Style*— John Wadham; ✉ Doughty Street Chambers, 53–54 Doughty St, London WC1N 2LS (☎ 02074 041313, e-mail johngeorgewadham@gmail.com)

WADHAM, Julian Neil Rohan; s of Rohan Nicholas Wadham, and Juliana, *née* Macdonald Walker; *b* 7 August 1958; *Educ* Ampleforth, Central Sch of Speech and Drama; *Career* actor; *Theatre* RNT incl: This House, Much Ado About Nothing, Tartuffe, Once in a While The Odd Thing Happens, The Changeling, Mountain Language, The Madness of King George III, The Winter's Tale; Royal Court incl: That Face, Falkland Sound, The Recruiting Officer, Our Country's Good, Serious Money; other credits incl: Another Country (Queen's and Trafalgar Studios), Our Country's Good (Garrick), When We Are Married (Whitehall), A Letter of Resignation (Comedy), Plenty (Albery), The Good Samaritan (Hampstead), The Prince of Homburg (Donmar Warehouse), A Midsummer Night's Dream (Rose Theatre Kingston), The Tempest (Theatre Royal Haymarket); *Television* Silk, Father Brown, Ghostboat, Egypt, Justice in Wonderland, Middlemarch, Goodbye Cruel World, Blind Justice, The Guest, After The War, Bright Eyes, Baal, The Gentle Touch, Me and My Girl, Hot Metal, Chancer, Bergerac, Poirot, Casualty, Growing Pains, Between the Lines, Stay Lucky, Full Stretch, The Wingless Bird, Lucan – The Trial, A Dance to the Music of Time, Gypsy Woman, A Touch of Frost, Wallis and Edward, Sherlock Holmes, The Government Inspector, Tom Brown's Schooldays, The Alan Clarke Diaries, Island at War, Christopher Wren, Foyle's War, Lewis, Midsomer Murders, My Boy Jack, Downton Abbey, A Casual Vacancy, The Outcast, Outlander, Tokyo Trial; *Film* Goya's Ghosts, Maurice, Mountbatten – The Last Viceroy, The Madness of King George, The Secret Agent, The English Patient, Keep the Aspidistra Flying, High Heels and Low Lifes, Exorcist – The Beginning, A Different Loyalty, Wah Wah, Outpost, Legacy, Fake Identity, The Iron Lady, Cheerful Weather for the Wedding, Warhorse, Scapegoat, Queen and Country, The Riot Club, Now Is Good, The 9th Life of Louis Drax, Churchill; *Style*— Julian Wadham; ✉ c/o Gilly Sanguinetti, The Artist's Partnership, 101 Finsbury Pavement, London EC2A 1RS (☎ 020 7439 1456, fax 020 7734 6530, e-mail gilly@theartistspartnership.co.uk)

WADHAMS, Prof Peter; s of Frank Cecil Wadhams (d 1971), and Winifred Grace, *née* Smith (d 2001); *b* 14 May 1948, Little Thurrock, Essex; *Educ* Palmer's Sch Grays, Churchill Coll Cambridge (coll scholar, MA), Scott Polar Res Inst Univ of Cambridge (PhD), Univ of Cambridge (ScD); *m* 11 Oct 1980, Maria Pia, da of Renato Casarini, of Milan, Italy; *Career* research scientist Bedford Inst of Oceanography Dartmouth NS (participant in Hudson-70, first expedition to circumnavigate Americas) 1969–70, postdoctoral fell Inst of Ocean Sciences Victoria BC 1974–75; Scott Polar Research Inst Univ of Cambridge: research assoc 1976–81, asst dir of research 1981–88, dir 1988–92, reader in Polar studies 1992–2001, prof of ocean physics 2001–02; prof of ocean physics Dept of Applied Maths and Theoretical Physics (DAMTP) Univ of Cambridge 2002–15 (emeritus prof 2015–), sr fell Scottish Assoc for Marine Science Dunstaffnage Marine Lab Oban 2003–04; sr res fell Churchill Coll Cambridge 1983–93; visiting prof of arctic marine science US Naval Postgrad Sch Monterey CA 1980–81, Green scholar Scripps Inst of Oceanography La Jolla CA 1987–88, Walker-Ames prof Univ of Washington Seattle 1987–88, visiting prof Nat Inst of Polar Research Tokyo 1995 and 1996–97, professeur associé Université Pierre et Marie Curie Paris 2005 and 2007–09; co-ordinator: Int Prog for Antarctic Buoys, World Climate Research Prog; UK delg Arctic Ocean Sciences Bd, pres Cmmn for Sea Ice IAPSO; memb: Scientific Ctee European Environment Agency, SCAR Gp of Specialists on Climate Change, Working Gp on Global Change Int Arctic Science Ctee; awarded: W S Bruce Prize (Royal Soc of Edinburgh) 1977, Polar Medal 1987, Italgas Prize for Environmental Sciences (Italy) 1990; fell Clare Hall Cambridge 2013; memb: Int Glaciological Soc 1970, American Geophysical Union 1976, Challenger Soc 1983, Remote Sensing Soc 1984; fell: Arctic Inst of N America 1983, Explorers' Club 1998; FRGS 1989, memb Finnish Acad of Sci and Letters 2006; *Books* Ice Technology for Polar Operations (co-ed, 1990), Advances in Ice Technology (co-ed, 1992), Marine, Offshore and Ice Technology (co-ed, 1994), The Arctic and Environmental Change (co-ed, 1996), The Freshwater Budget of the Arctic Circle (co-ed, 2000), Ice in the Ocean (2000), Arctic Sea Ice Thickness: Past, Present and Future (co-ed, 2007), Planet Earth We Have a Problem – Feedback Dynamics and the Acceleration of Climate Change (co-author, 2007), The Great Ocean of Truth (2009), A Farewell to Ice (2016); *Recreations* painting, sailing, maritime history; *Clubs* Explorers (NY), Rotary; *Style*— Prof Peter

Wadhams; ☎ 01223 576433; Department of Applied Mathematics and Theoretical Physics (DAMTP), University of Cambridge, Centre for Mathematical Sciences, Wilberforce Road, Cambridge CB3 0WA (☎ 01223 760372, mobile 07748 032371, fax 01223 760493, e-mail p.wadhams@damtp.cam.ac.uk)

WADHWANI, Dr Sushil; CBE (2002); *b* 7 December 1959; *Educ* LSE (BSc, MSc, PhD); *Career* economist; reader/lectr LSE 1984–91, dir Equity Strategy Goldman Sachs Int 1991–95, dir of res Tudor Proprietary Trading 1995–99, ptnr Caxton Associates; external memb Monetary Policy Ctee 1999–2002; fund mangr Keynes QS Fund; visiting prof: City Univ Business Sch, LSE (also govr); *Style*— Dr Sushil Wadhwani, CBE; ✉ Wadhwani Asset Management LLP, 40 Berkeley Square, London W1J 5AL (☎ 020 7663 3400, fax 020 7663 3410, e-mail sushilw@waniasset.com)

WADIA, Nina; da of Minoo Wadia, and Homai Wadia; *Educ* Island Sch Hong Kong, London Theatre Sch (Dip classical acting); *Career* comedienne and actress; supporter of numerous charities; *Theatre* credits incl: Romeo and Juliet (Theatre Royal, Stratford East), Macbeth (Globe Theatre), Alice in Wonderland, Vagina Monologues (West End); *Television* credits incl: Goodness Gracious Me (nomination Int Emmy Awards), Sita Gita (nomination Best Performance by a TV Actress Emma Awards), New Tricks, Waking the Dead, All About Me (shortlist Golden Rose Award 2004), Murder In Mind, Perfect World, Chambers, White Teeth, The Barftas, The Vicar of Dibley, Kiss Me Kate, The Stangerers, Holby City, The Bill, Casualty, Gandhi vs Gandhi, Freedom's Daughter, EastEnders; *Film* credits incl: Code 46, Sixth Happiness, Such a Long Journey, Flight, Cup & Lip, Gran, Shooting Cupid, Delivering Mina, Four; *Radio credits* incl: The Tempest (BBC Radio 3), The Taming of the Shrew (BBC Radio 3), Westway (BBC World Serv); *Awards* Greatest Achievement by an Actress Soc for the Black Arts in Br 1994, Sony award 1997 and 1998, Br Comedy award 1998, Into Leadership Diversity award 2000, Cmmn for Racial Equality (CRE) award 2000 and 2001, Comic Heritage award 2000, Woman of Achievement Cosmopolitan Magazine 2000, BBC Asia 2001, Women in Film and Television, Asian Women of Achievement; *Recreations* sports, interior design, cooking, my husband; *Style*— Ms Nina Wadia; ✉ c/o Independent Talent, 40 Whitfield Street, London W1T 2RH

WADLEY, Veronica; da of Neville John Wadley, and Anne Hawise Colleton, *née* Bowring; *b* 28 February 1952; *Educ* Francis Holland Sch London, Benenden; *m* 1 June 1985, Tom Bower, s of George Bower; 1 da (Sophie b 18 April 1986), 1 s (Alexander b 4 Oct 1990); *Career* journalist; Condé Nast Publications 1971–74, Sunday Telegraph Magazine 1978–81, Mail on Sunday 1982–86; Daily Telegraph: features ed 1986–89, asst ed 1989–94, dep ed 1994–95; Daily Mail: assoc ed 1995–98, dep ed 1998–2002; ed Evening Standard 2002–09; ind dir Times Newspapers Hldgs Gp 2011–, non-exec dir Berkeley Gp 2012–; sr advsr to the Mayor of London 2012–16; memb Nat Cncl and chair Arts Cncl London 2010–, govr Yehudi Menuhin Sch 2012–, chm Mayor's Music Fund 2014–; FRSA; *Recreations* London's theatres, galleries and concert halls, swimming, cooking for family and friends, skiing; *Style*— Miss Veronica Wadley; ✉ c/o Arts Council England, 21 Bloomsbury Street, London WC1B 3HF

WADSWORTH, Brian; s of George and Betty Wadsworth; *b* 18 January 1952; *Educ* Univ of Br Columbia (BA); *m* 1987, Anne Jacqueline; *Career* princ BA, BAA, NBC privatisations 1986–89, sec BA plc 1989–91, sec Br Oxygen plc 1995; Dept of Tport: dir of finance 1995–97, dir Logistics and Maritime Tport 1999–2007, dir Strategic Roads, Planning and Nat Networks 2007–08, transport and public affrs conslt 2008–; chm: Consultative Shipping Gp 1999–2007, European Maritime Safety Agency 2003–09; dir Road Ahead Gp 2011–; advsr on railway restructuring and privatisation World Bank; memb Glyndebourne Festival Soc; Liveryman Worshipful Co of Carmen (Master 2009–10), Liveryman Worshipful Co of Plumbers (Upper Warden 2015–16), Freeman City of London 1997, FRIN, FCILT; *Books* Best Methods of Railway Restructuring and Privatisation (contrib, 1995), Moving On: Fairer Motoring Taxes and Investment for Growth and Jobs (2011), Funding Our Roads: A Better Way (2015); *Recreations* travel, opera, sailing, classic cars; *Clubs* United Wards, Castle Baynard Ward, Phyllis Court; *Style*— Brian Wadsworth, Esq

WADSWORTH, David Grant; s of Fred Wadsworth (d 1960), and Lona, *née* Booth (d 1970); *b* 30 December 1944; *Educ* Hipperholme GS, Oriel Coll Oxford (MA), Univ of Newcastle upon Tyne (MPhil); *m* Marcia Armour, *née* Lyles; 1 step s (Robert James b 1980), 1 step da (Susanne Jane b 1984); *Career* teacher Glos and Blackpool 1966–73, admin posts Educn Dept Leeds City Cncl 1973–85, dep dir of educn Northumberland 1985–89, chief educn offr Beds 1989–96, chief exec Service Children's Educn 1997–; memb: Yorks CCC and RFU, Cambridge Univ RUFC, Army RFU; Hon DEd De Montfort Univ 1996; Chevalier de l'Ordre des Palmes Académiques 1992, Cavaliere dell'Ordine Al Merito della Repubblica Italiana 1994; *Recreations* rugby and cricket (passively), epicurean delights; *Clubs* Oxford and Cambridge; *Style*— David G Wadsworth, Esq; ✉ HQ SCE, BFPO 40

WADSWORTH, Roger Leonard; s of Leonard Wadsworth (d 1985), and Irene Nellie, *née* Hughes (d 2001); *b* 2 May 1950; *Educ* Hurstpierpoint Coll, Kingston Poly (BA); *m* 1988, Sandra Anne, da of R A Carney, of Barry County, MO; *Career* chm and md Wadsworth Holdings Ltd 1979–; chm: Blazepoint Ltd 2000, Wadsworth Rugged Systems Ltd 2003; fndr and sec Knoydart Deer Mgmnt Gp 1988–93, nat tstee dir and vice-chm British Deer Soc 2002–; *Recreations* wildlife management, game and habitat conservation, stalking, shooting, Lusitano horses; *Clubs* Outrigger, Honolulu, RAC, Home House, Outrigger (Honolulu); *Style*— Roger Wadsworth, Esq

WAGNER, Erica; da of Arthur Malcolm Wagner, of NYC, and Ellen Franklin Wagner; *Educ* The Brearley Sch NYC, St Paul's Girls' Sch, CCC Cambridge (BA), UEA (MA); *m* Francis Jonathan Gilbert, s of Peter Gilbert; 1 s (Theodore Malcolm); *Career* journalist; freelance ed, researcher and book reviewer 1992–95; The Times: asst to literary ed 1995–96, literary ed 1996–2013; contrib New Statesman, consulting literary ed Harper's Bazaar; judge Man Booker Prize 2002 and 2014; *Books* Gravity: Stories (1997), Ariel's Gift: Ted Hughes, Sylvia Plath and the Story of Birthday Letters (2000), Seizure (novel, 2007), First Light: A Celebration of Alan Garner (2016); *Recreations* family life, stories, walking, bridges; *Style*— Ms Erica Wagner; ✉ websites www.antonyharwood.com, www.ericawagner.co.uk

WAGNER, Roger Henry Melchior; s of Sir Anthony Richard Wagner, KCB, KCVO (d 1995), and Dame Gillian Wagner, DBE, *qv*; *b* 28 February 1957; *Educ* Eton, Lincoln Coll Oxford (open scholar, MA), Royal Acad Schs; *m* 24 Oct 1998, Anne, da of Dr Towy Myrddin-Evans; *Career* artist; *Solo Exhibitions* incl: Anthony Mould Ltd 1985, 1988, 1995, 1999, 2000, 2004 and 2013, 42nd Aldeburgh Festival 1989, Ashmolean Museum Oxford 1994 (retrospective), Out of the Whirlwind: illustrations to the Book of Job (Bartlemas Chapel Oxford) 1995, touring exhbn to Ely Cathedral, Norwich Cathedral, St Edmundsbury Cathedral, Southwark Cathedral, Wells Cathedral, Chester Cathedral, The Chapel Royal Brighton, Mirfield Abbey and the Ark-T Centre 1997–2004, The Prince's Fndn 2001, Lady Margaret Hall Oxford 2004, Phillip Mould Historical Portraits 2006, Montgomery Town Hall 2008, St Giles Church Oxford 2010, Ashmolean Museum 2010; *Group Exhibitions* incl: New Icons (Mead Gallery Univ of Warwick, The Royal Albert Museum Exeter and The Usher Gallery Lincoln) 1989–90, Images of Christ (Albermarle Gallery) 1991, Images of Christ (Northampton Museum and Art Gallery and St Paul's Cathedral) 1993, Europe: Art et Passages (Paris) 1999, The Light of the World (Edinburgh City Art Gallery) 1999–2000, The Salutation (Oxford) 2000, Blake's Heaven (Scholar Fine Art) 2000, Roads to Damascus (Eton Coll) 2002, Thomas Gibson Fine Art 2002, St Paul's Cathedral 2004, Art-T Centre 2004, Loughborough Univ 2004, The Queen's Coll Oxford 2006, 2007, 2009, 2010, 2011, 2014 and 2016, William Blake's House 2007, Exeter Coll 2008, Insights into British Art Today Regensburg 2011, The Ocean in a Tree Snape Maltings 2012; *Publications* Fire Sonnets (1984), In a Strange Land (1988), The Book of Praises Book One (1994), A Silent Voice (1996), Out of the Whirlwind (1997), The Book of Praises Book Two (2008), The Book of Praises Book Three (2013), The Penultimate Curiosity (with Andrew Briggs, 2016); *Clubs* Reynolds; *Style*— Roger Wagner, Esq; ✉ e-mail rhmwagner@aol.com, website www.rogerwagner.co.uk; c/o Anthony Mould Ltd, 21 Bruton Street, London W1J 6QD

WAHHAB, Iqbal; OBE (2010); s of S A Wahhab, and Razia Begum; *b* 22 August 1963, Bangladesh; *Educ* LSE; *Career* fndr Tandoori Magazine 1994, owner Cinnamon Club 2001–04, owner Roast 2005–; FRSA; *Books* The Cinnamon Club Cookbook (co-author, 2003); *Style*— Iqbal Wahhab, Esq, OBE; ✉ Roast, The Floral Hall, Stoney Street, London SE1 1TL (e-mail iqbal@roast-restaurant.com, Twitter @IqbalWahhab)

WAINE, Peter Edward; s of Dr Theodore Edward Waine, of Bilton, Warks, and Mary Florence, *née* Goodson; *b* 27 June 1949; *Educ* Bilton Grange, Worksop Coll, Univ of Bradford (BSc); *m* 21 June 1973, Stefanie Dale, da of Philip Albert Snow, OBE, JP, of Angmering, W Sussex, and niece of late Baron Snow of Leicester, CBE (C P Snow, the author); 1 da (Philippa Wigmore b 21 May 1981); *Career* personnel mangr: GEC 1970–74, Cape Industries 1974–79, Coopers & Lybrand 1979–83; dir: CBI 1983–88, Blue Arrow 1988–90, W R Royle & Sons (non-exec) 1988–96, SSK Ltd 1994–98; co-fndr Hanson Green 1990–; non-exec chm: Corecare Ltd 1990–92, Arkley House Finance Ltd 1990–92, The Sales Training Co 1994–97; chm: WildWiki Ltd 2011–, Liquid Claims UK 2012; non-exec dir Quarto Gp 1998–2013; nat chm Campaign to Protect Rural England; visiting fell Bradford Business Sch 1994; nat vice-chm The Bow Group 1972 (chm Birmingham Gp 1971); cncllr Rugby DC 1973–77, Parly candidate (Cons) Nottingham North 1979; non-exec dir: East Herts Dist Health Authy 1990–92, East Herts Tst 1994–96; memb Int Cricket Cncl 1994–2005; judge Contrarian Prize 2012–; tstee Royal Opera House 1999–2001; formerly: memb Current Affairs Ctee ESU, chm Brogdale Tst 2001–06, chm The Tree Cncl, Welwyn Garden City Soc, memb Cncl European Business Sch; visiting prof: Cass Business Sch London 2004–11, Warwick Business Sch until 2011; Freeman: City of London 1978, Worshipful Co of Carmen, Worshipful Co of Gardeners (memb Ct); FIMgt (former memb Cncl); *Publications* Spring Cleaning Britain (1974), Withering Heights (1976), The Independent Board Director (with Dr David Clutterbuck, 1993), Takeover (with Mike Walker, 2000, trans 5 languages), The Board Game (2002), Under A Passing Sky (poetry, 2011); weekly columnist under pseudonym for London newspaper (1984–87); *Recreations* gardening, walking, tennis; *Clubs* MCC, Savile, Housman Soc; *Style*— Peter Waine, Esq; ✉ Hanson Green, 110 Park Street, London W1K 6NX (☎ 020 7493 0837, fax 020 7355 1436)

WAINSCOAT, Prof James Stephen; s of Arnold John Wainscoat (d 2004), and Mary Hilda, *née* Bateman (d 1989); *b* 7 May 1949; *Educ* Holme Valley GS, Univ of Liverpool (MB ChB), Univ of Birmingham (MSc); *m* 14 Aug 1971, Beverly Susan, da of Walter Hannah (d 1987); 1 s (Luke), 2 da (Emma, Nancy); *Career* conslt haematologist Oxford Radcliffe Hosp 1985–2011, ret; prof Univ of Oxford 1998– (sr lectr 1986–98), hon dir Molecular Haematology Unit Leukaemia Res Fund Univ of Oxford 1988–2011; FRCP 1991 (MRCP 1976), FRCPath 1992 (MRCPath 1980); *Recreations* music, sport; *Style*— Prof James Wainscoat; ✉ Department of Haematology, Oxford Radcliffe Hospital, Headington, Oxford OX3 9DU (☎ 01865 220330)

WAINWRIGHT, Dr (Anthony) Christopher; yr s of Robert Everard Wainwright, CMG (d 1990), of Shaftesbury, Dorset, and Bridget Doris, *née* Alan-Williams (d 2001); *b* 25 October 1943; *Educ* Marlborough, St Thomas' Hosp Univ of London (MB BS); *m* 6 Sept 1968, Ursula, da of Ernest Herbert Jeans (d 1977), 1 s (James b 1972 d 1998), 1 da (Sophie b 1975); *Career* sr registrar Univ Hosp Wales 1971–72, lectr in anaesthesia Univ of Bristol 1972–75, conslt anaesthetist Univ of Southampton Hosps and hon clinical teacher Univ of Southampton 1975–2006; memb RSM; co fndr Wig and Scalpel Soc, former chm Copythorne Parish Cncl, memb New Forest Advsy Bd ((formerly New Forest Advsy Ctee) Nat Tst; FRCA 1971; *Books* chapters in Lee's Synopsis of Anaesthesia, Anaesthesia Review 4 and Co2 Lasers in Otolaryngology; author of papers on ophthalmic anaesthesia; *Recreations* horses, music, medieval architecture; *Style*— Dr Christopher Wainwright; ✉ Ashton Cottage, Kewlake Lane, Cadnam, Southampton SO40 2NT

WAINWRIGHT, Faith Helen; MBE (2012); da of Cdr Brian Hebden Wainwright, OBE, RN, and Anne Vera, *née* Temple; *b* 25 May 1962, Dunfermline, Fife; *Educ* Queen Anne's Caversham, St Edmund Hall Oxford (BA); *m* 2 July 1988, Kieran J Glynn, s of Brian J Glynn; 1 s (Brian b 17 July 1993), 2 da (Finola, Eleanor (twins) b 9 Aug 1995); *Career* structural engr; Arup: joined 1983, dir 1998–; memb Extreme Events Mitigation Task Force 2001–; non-exec dir Knowledge Transfer Network Ltd 2015–; vice-chair Jt Bd of Moderators 2004–10; memb: Standing Ctee on Structural Safety 2001–07, Cncl IStructE 2003–06, Ctee for Safety in Tall Buildings, Advsy Cncl Br Library 2004–10, Cncl Royal Acad of Engrg 2010–13; juror: BBC Design Awards 1996, OASYS Design Awards 2001; dean Arup Univ 2011–13; hon fell St Edmund Hall Oxford 2015; Hon DEng Univ of Bath 2014; MIOD, FIStructE 2003 (MIStructE 1987), FREng 2003, FICE 2003; *Projects* incl: ITN London, Lycée Albert Camus Frejus, Western Morning News Plymouth, American Air Museum Duxford, Tate Modern London, Hong Kong and Shanghai Banking Corp HQ Canary Wharf London, London Bridge Tower; *Recreations* sailing, theatre; *Style*— Ms Faith Wainwright, MBE, FREng; ✉ Arup, 13 Fitzroy Street, London W1T 4BQ (☎ 020 7755 2051, e-mail faith.wainwright@arup.com, Twitter @FaithWainwright)

WAINWRIGHT, Geoffrey John; MBE; s of Frederick Wainwright, and Dorothy, *née* Worton; *b* 19 September 1937; *Educ* Pembroke Docks Sch, Univ of Wales, Univ of London; *m* 23 Dec 1977, Judith; 2 da (Rhiannon b 1961, Sarah b 1963), 1 s (Nicholas b 1966); *Career* prof of environmental archaeology Univ of Baroda India 1961–63, princ inspector of ancient monuments DOE 1980–89 (inspector 1963–80), chief archaeologist English Heritage 1989–99, fndr Bluestone Partnership 1999; visiting prof: Univ of Southampton 1991–, Inst of Archaeology UCL 1995–2005; Soc of Antiquaries: dir 1984–90, vice-pres 1997–2001, treas 2001–07, pres 2007–10; vice-chm Royal Cmmn on Ancient Monuments (Wales) 1987–2002, pres Prehistoric Soc 1981–85, pres Cambrian Archeological Assoc 2002–03, chm Bd of Dirs Wessex Archaeology 2004–10, memb Cncl Cambria Archaeology 2004–, pres Pembrokeshire Historical Soc 2008–; hon memb European Archaeology Cncl 2000–; hon MCIFA; fell Univ of Wales Coll of Cardiff 1985, hon fell Univ of Wales Lampeter 1996; FSA, FRSA, FLSW; *Books* Coygan Camp (1967), Stone Age in India (1967), Durrington Walls (1971), Mount Pleasant (1979), Gussage All Saints (1979), The Henge Monuments (1989), Balksbury Camp Hampshire (1995); *Recreations* rugby, food and drink, walking; *Style*— Geoffrey Wainwright, Esq, MBE, FSA; ✉ March Pres, Pontfaen, Fishguard, Pembrokeshire SA65 9TT (☎ 01348 881423, fax 01348 881370, e-mail geoff@bluestone.eu.com)

WAINWRIGHT, Michael John; s of H Anthony Wainwright, and Jean Warren; *b* 9 November 1957, West Kirby, Wirral; *Educ* Shrewsbury Sch, Univ of Exeter; *m* 31 Aug 1990, Annie, *née* Williams; 1 da (Honour b 9 Nov 1995 (twin)), 1 s (Geordie b 9 Nov 1995 (twin)); *Career* qualified CA 1983; Peat Marwick Mitchell 1979–84, md Boodles (formerly Boodle & Dunthorne) 1984–; tstee Rainbow Tst Children's Charity; memb ICA; *Recreations* gardening, golf, horse racing, walking, wine, Liverpool FC, shooting; *Style*— Michael Wainwright, Esq; ✉ Goodchilds Hill, Stratfield Saye, Reading RG7 2DR

W

(☏ 07971 061294, e-mail mjw@boodles.com); Boodles, 178 New Bond Street, London W1S 4RH

WAINWRIGHT, Rob; *b* Carmarthen, Wales; *Educ* LSE (BSc); *Career* head UK Liaison Bureau Europol 2000–03, dir int Nat Criminal Intelligence Service 2003–06, chief Int Dept UK Serious Organised Crime Agency 2006–09, dir Europol 2009–; *Style—* Mr Rob Wainwright; ✉ Europol, PO Box 908 50, 2509 LW The Hague, The Netherlands

WAINWRIGHT, Sally Anne; da of Harry Wainwright (d 2001), and Dorothy Wainwright; *b* 19 November 1963, Huddersfield, W Yorks; *Educ* Sowerby Bridge GS, Univ of York (BA); *m* 22 Dec 1990, Austin Sherlaw-Johnson; 2 s (George Sherlaw-Johnson b 16 Feb 1997, Felix Sherlaw-Johnson b 1 June 1999); *Career* writer and director; progs incl: At Home with the Braithwaites 2000, Sparkhouse 2002, The Canterbury Tales: The Wife of Bath 2003, Jane Hall 2005, ShakespeaRe-Told: The Taming of the Shrew 2005, The Amazing Mrs Pritchard 2006, Bonkers 2007, Unforgiven 2009, Scott & Bailey 2011–, Last Tango in Halifax 2012–13 (Best Drama Series BAFTA 2013, Best Writer BAFTA 2013), Happy Valley 2014 (Best Drama Series BAFTA 2015, Best Writer BAFTA 2015, Edgar Allan Poe Award 2015); *Style—* Ms Sally Wainwright; ✉ c/o Bethan Evans, The Agency (London) Ltd, 24 Pottery Lane, Holland Park, London W11 4LZ

WAITE, Charlie; s of Air Cdre R N Waite (d 1974), and Jessamy, *née* Lowenthal (d 2001); *b* 18 February 1949; *Educ* Salisbury Coll of Art; *m* 1974, Jessica, *née* Benton; 1 da (Ella Bahama b 8 Oct 1975); *Career* landscape photographic artist; early career in Br theatre and TV; over 250 lectures on landscape photography in UK; Hon FBIPP 2000, FRPS 2014; *Exhibitions* incl: London (five times), Tokyo (twice), Centre for Photographic Art Carmel CA 1999, Broadway NY 2002, OXO Gallery London 2002, 2003 and 2004; *Publications* National Trust Book of Long Walks (1982), Long Walks in France (1983), Landscape in Britain (1983), David Steel's Border Country (1984), English Country Towns (1984), The Loire (1985), Provence (1985), Languedoc (1985), Dordogne (1985), Villages in France (1986), Tuscany (1987), The Rhine (1987), Landscape in France (1988), Scottish Islands (1989), Charlie Waite's Venice (1989), Charlie Waite's Italian Landscapes (1990), Andalusia (1991), Lombardy (1991), Charlie Waite's Spanish Landscapes (1992), The Making of Landscape Photographs (1992), Seeing Landscapes (1999), In My Mind's Eye (2003), Landscape: The Story of Fifty Favourite Photgraphs (2005), Arc and Line (2012); *Recreations* looking at river banks and the sky, listening to birdsong and buffooning with twin girl grandchildren; *Style—* Charlie Waite, Esq; ✉ PO Box 1558, Gillingham, Dorset SP8 5RE (☏ 01747 824727, e-mail charlie@charliewaite.com, website www.charliewaite.com)

WAITE, (Winston Anthony) John; s of John Clifford Waite (d 1989), of Gawsworth, Cheshire, and Margaret Ada, *née* Van Schuyk-Smith; *b* 26 February 1951; *Educ* Wilmslow GS, Univ of Manchester (BA); *m* 13 July 1984, Cate Anne Valerie, da of Stuart-Campbell, of Islington, London; 2 s (Gulliver b 1994, Diggory b 1996), 2 da (Flossie b 1990, Jessica b 1991); *Career* BBC: graduate trainee 1973–76, TV and radio presenter 1976–; radio progs incl: Face the Facts (formerly, BBC Radio 4), You and Yours (BBC Radio 4); TV progs incl: On the Line (BBC 2), Wildlife Showcase (BBC 2); *Recreations* music, reading, wine; *Style—* John Waite, Esq; ✉ BBC Radio 4, Broadcasting House, London W1A 1AA

WAITE, Jonathan Gilbert Stokes; QC (2002); s of Capt Henry David Stokes Waite, RN (d 2005), and Joan Winifred, *née* Paull (d 2012); *b* 15 February 1956; *Educ* Sherborne, Trinity Coll Cambridge (MA); *Career* called to the Bar Inner Temple 1978; in practice in common law SE Circuit 1979–; hon sec Bar Golfing Soc 1987–93; *Recreations* golf, bridge, wine, skiing, SW France; *Clubs* Woking Golf, Aldeburgh Golf, Rye Golf, Royal St George's Golf; *Style—* Jonathan Waite, Esq, QC; ✉ 76 Forthbridge Road, Battersea, London SW11 5NY (☏ 020 7228 4488); Fauret, 82100 Bouloc, Tarn-et-Garonne, France (☏ 0033 0563 326056); Crown Office Chambers, 2 Crown Office Row, Temple, London EC4Y 7HJ (☏ 020 7797 8100, fax 020 7797 8101, e-mail waite@crownofficechambers.com)

WAKE-WALKER, David Christopher; s of Capt Christopher Baldwin Hughes Wake-Walker, RN (d 1998), and Lady Anne, da of 7 Earl Spencer; 1 cous to Diana, Princess of Wales (d 1997); *b* 11 March 1947; *Educ* Winchester, Univ of St Andrews (MA); *m* 1979, Jennifer Rosemary, only da of Capt Patrick Vaulkhard (d 1995); 2 s (Frederic b 1981, Nicholas b 1985); *Career* dir Kleinwort Benson Ltd 1981–1995 (joined 1969), md Kleinwort Benson (Hong Kong) Ltd 1983–86, dir Kleinwort Benson Gp plc 1990–95, dir Dentons Hldgs Ltd 2004–, dir President Energy PLC 2006–15, chm Delsol Ltd 2001–; chm Orwell Park Sch 1997–2011, memb Accounting and Finance Forum Univ of Greenwich 2008–11; ACIB 1972; *Clubs* Wanderers, Hong Kong, Shek O Country; *Style—* David Wake-Walker Esq; ✉ 82 Royal Hill, London SE10 8RT (☏ 020 8691 4666); 7 Trebeck Street, London W1J 7LU (☏ 020 7409 7233, fax 020 7408 0783, e-mail david@wake-walker.com)

WAKEFIELD, Bishop of 2015–; Rt Rev Anthony William (Tony) Robinson; *b* 25 April 1956; *Educ* Bedford Modern Sch, Salisbury and Wells Theol Coll; *Career* asst curate St Paul Tottenham 1982–85, team rector Resurrection Leicester 1989–97 (team vicar 1985–89), rural dean Christianity North Leicester 1992–97, hon canon Leicester Cathedral 1994–97, archdeacon of Pontefract 1997–2003, bishop of Pontefract 2002–15; *Style—* The Rt Rev the Bishop of Wakefield; ✉ Pontefract House, 181a Manygates Lane, Wakefield WF2 7DR (☏ 01924 250781, e-mail bishop.tony@westyorkshiredales.anglican.org)

WAKEFIELD, Sir (Edward) Humphry Tyrrell; 2 Bt (UK 1962), of Kendal, Co Westmorland; s of Sir Edward Birkbeck Wakefield, 1 Bt, CIE (d 1969, himself yr bro of 1 Baron Wakefield of Kendal); *b* 11 July 1936; *Educ* Gordonstoun, Trinity Coll Cambridge (MA); *m* 1, 1960 (m dis 1964), Priscilla, da of (Oliver) Robin Bagot; m 2, 1966 (m dis 1971), Hon Elizabeth Sophia Sidney, da of 1 Viscount De L'Isle, VC, KG, GCMG, GCVO, PC; 1 s; m 3, 1974, Hon Katherine Mary Alice Baring, da of 1 Baron Howick of Glendale, KG, GCMG, KCVO (d 1973); 1 s (and 1 s decd), 1 da; *Heir* s, Capt Maximilian Wakefield, Royal Hussars (PWO); *Career* Capt 10 Royal Hussars, acting ADC to Maj-Gen the Lord Thurloe; fndr Stately Homes Collection, exec vice-pres Mallett America Ltd 1970–75, former dir Mallett & Son (Antiques) Ltd; chm: Tyrrell & Moore Ltd 1975–91, Sir Humphry Wakefield & Partners Ltd; former dir Spoleto Festival, dir Tree of Life Fndn (UK charity), memb Standing Cncl of the Baronetage; pres: Northumberland Mountain Rescue Services, Avison Tst, Tibetan Spaniel Assoc; patron: Actors Centre (North), Medicine and Chernobyl, Shadow Dance, Gilbert White Fndn, Widerness Fndn (formerly chm), etc; memb: Soc of the Dilettante, Surtees Soc, etc; tstee Chillingham Wild Cattle Assoc, Waterbird Project, etc; joined membs of NZ Everest Expedition on their first ascent of Mt Wakefield NZ 1992 (and subsequently on Everest Expedition), memb Mt Vaughan Antarctic Expedition 1994; fell Pierrepont Morgan Library USA; Lord of the Manor Chillingham and Sedgwick; FRGS; Freedom of Kansas City, hon citizen Cities of Houston and New Orleans, Hon Col Louisiana; Hereditary Diwan of Naba State Punjab India; *Publications* author of numerous articles on antique furniture and architecture; *Clubs* Harlequins RFC (hon life memb), Beefsteak, Cavalry and Guards', Turf, Scott Polar (life memb); *Style—* Sir Humphry Wakefield, Bt; ✉ Chillingham Castle, Chillingham, Northumberland

WAKEHAM, Baron (Life Peer UK 1992), of Maldon in the County of Essex; John Wakeham; PC (1983), JP (Inner London 1972), DL (Hants 1997); s of Maj Walter John Wakeham (d 1965), of Godalming, Surrey; *b* 22 June 1932; *Educ* Charterhouse; *m* 1, 1965, Anne Roberta (k 1984), da of late Harold Edwin Bailey; 2 adopted s (Hon Jonathan Martin b 1972, Hon Benedict Ian b 1975); m 2, 1985, Alison Bridget, MBE, DL, da of Ven Edwin James Greenfield Ward, LVO; 1 s (Hon David Robert b 1987); *Career* CA; contested (Cons): Coventry East 1966, Putney Wandsworth 1970; MP (Cons): Maldon 1974–83, Colchester S and Maldon 1983–92; asst Govt whip 1979–81, a Lord Cmmr to the Treasy (Govt whip) 1981, under sec of state for Industry 1981–82, min of state Treasy 1982–83, Parly sec to the Treasy and chief whip 1983–87, Lord Privy Seal 1987–88, Lord Pres of the Cncl 1988–89, ldr of the House of Commons 1987–89, sec of state for Energy 1989–92, responsible for devpt of presentation of Govt policies 1990–92, Lord Privy Seal and ldr of the House of Lords 1992–94; chair Royal Cmmn on the reform of the House of Lords 1999; chm: PCC 1995–2002, British Horseracing Bd 1996–98 (memb 1995); chllr Brunel Univ 1997–2012; tstee HMS Warrior 1860 1997–2015; pres GamCare 1997–2002; chm Alexandra Rose Day 1998–2010; govr: Sutton's Hosp Charterhouse 1992–, St Swithun's Sch 1994–2002; *Recreations* sailing, racing, reading; *Clubs* Buck's, Carlton (chm 1992–98), Garrick, Royal Yacht Squadron; *Style—* The Rt Hon Lord Wakeham, PC, DL, FCA; ✉ House of Lords, London SW1A 0PW (☏ 020 8767 6931)

WAKEHAM, Sir William Arnot; kt (2009); s of Stanley William Wakeham (d 1969), of Bristol, and Winifred Gladys, *née* Crocker (d 1946); *b* 25 September 1944; *Educ* Bristol Cathedral Sch, Univ of Exeter (BSc, PhD, DSc); *m* 1, 1969 (m dis 1978), Christina Marjorie, da of Kenneth Stone, of Weymouth, Dorset; 1 s (Leigh b 1974); m 2, 23 Dec 1978, Sylvia Frances Tolley; 2 s (Russell Jon b 1983, Nicholas Ashley b 1986); *Career* research assoc Brown Univ USA 1969–71; Imperial Coll London: lectr dept of chemical engrg 1971–79, reader in chemical physics of fluids 1979–85, prof of chemical physics 1985–2001, head Dept of Chemical Engrg 1988–96, pro-rector (research) 1996, pro-rector (resources) 1999, dep rector 1997–2001; vice-chllr Univ of Southampton 2001–09; visiting prof: Instituto Superior Tecnico Lisbon 2008–, Imperial Coll London, Univ of Exeter; chair Exeter Science Park ltd 2009–; memb: SEEDA 2004–09, EPSRC 2005–11; sr vice-pres Royal Acad of Engrg 2011–15, pres IChemE 2011; dir ILIKA plc; memb: Rank Prizes Tst, SE Physics Network (chair 2009–); tstee Royal Anniversary Tst 2010–; Touloukian medal American Soc of Mechanical Engrs, Rossini lectr, Ared Cezairliyan lectr; Hon DSc: Lisbon Univ, Univ of Exeter, Loughborough Univ 2010, Univ of Southampton, Universidade Nova de Lisboa 2012, Univ of Portsmouth 2013; Hon DEd Southampton Solent Univ; CEng, CPhys; FIChemE, FInstP, FIEE, FCGI, FIC, FREng 1997; *Books* Intermolecular Forces: Their Origin and Determination (1981), The Forces Between Molecules (1986), The Transport Properties of Fluids (1989), International Thermodynamic Tables of the Fluid State: Vol 10 – Ethylene (1989), Measurement of the Transport Properties of Fluids (1991), Status and Future Developments in the Study of Transport Properties (1992), Measurement of the Thermodynamic Properties of Single Phases (2003), Engaging Philanthropy for University Research (2008), Review of UK Physics (2008), Financial Sustainability and Efficiency in Full Economic Costing of Research in UK Higher Education Institutions (2010), Commonly Asked Question in Thermodynamics (2011), Experimental Thermodynamics Vol IX (2014), Wakeham Review of STEM Degree Provision and Graduate Employability (2016); *Recreations* power boating, gardening; *Clubs* Athenaeum; *Style—* Sir William Wakeham, FREng; ✉ Beacon Down, Rewe, Exeter EX5 4DX (☏ 01392 861390, e-mail w.a.wakeham@soton.ac.uk)

WAKELEY, Amanda Jane; OBE (2010); da of Sir John Cecil Nicholson Wakeley, 2 Bt, *qv*; *b* 15 September 1962; *Educ* Cheltenham Ladies' Coll; *Career* fashion designer; early career experience working in fashion indust NY 1983–85, in business working for private cmmns 1987–90, fndr Amanda Wakeley lifestyle luxury brand 1990; collections sold in England, Europe, USA, Far East and Middle East, opened flagship shop Chelsea Sept 1993; co-chair Fashion Targets Breast Cancer 1996– (raised over £14m); winner Glamour category British Fashion Awards 1992, 1993 and 1996; *Recreations* water-skiing, snow-skiing, driving, travel, photography; *Style—* Miss Amanda Wakeley, OBE

WAKELIN, Dr (Alexander) Peter; s of Richard Langford Wakelin (d 1987), and Rosemary Margaret, *née* Culley (d 1998); *b* 13 February 1962, Swansea; *Educ* Olchfa Comp Sch Swansea, Swansea Coll of Art, Keble Coll Oxford (BA, proxime accessit Henry Oliver Beckitt Dissertation Prize), Ironbridge Gorge Museum/Univ of Birmingham (MSocSci), Wolverhampton Poly (PhD); *partner* Clive Hicks-Jenkins; *Career* Wolverhampton Poly: res asst Sch of Humanities and Cultural Studies 1984–88, dir and ESRC named res fell Portbooks Prog Faculty of Arts Wolverhampton Poly 1988–90; inspr of ancient monuments and historic bldgs Cadw 1990–2003, head Regeneration Unit Communities Directorate Welsh Assembly Govt 2003–05, sec Royal Cmmn on the Ancient and Hist Monuments of Wales 2005–13, dir of collections and research Amgueddfa Cymru-National Museum Wales 2013–15, freelance writer and curator 2015–; memb: Cncl Assoc for Industrial Archaeology 1986–95, UK Ctee Assoc for History and Computing 1987–90; Cncl for British Archaeology: memb Res and Conservation Ctee 1995–2000, memb Pubns Ctee 2000–; ed Industrial Archaeology News 1988–95, memb Editorial Bd Industrial Archaeology Review 1995–; Contemporary Art Soc for Wales: memb Exec Ctee 1998–, purchaser 2002; advsr Wakelin Award Glynn Vivian Art Gallery Swansea 1999–, memb Advsy Bd Planet: The Welsh Internationalist 2004–07, memb Arts and Humanities Research Cncl Peer Review Coll, memb Advsy Bd Centre for Advanced Welsh and Celtic Studies 2014–; hon fell Univ of Wales Sch of Art Aberystwyth 2004–, hon fell Univ of Swansea 2008–; FSA 2002, hon memb Royal Soc of Architects in Wales 2012; incl: The Encyclopaedia of Industrial Archaeology (contrib, 1992), The Gloucester Coastal Port Books 1575–1765: A summary (co-author, 1995, database on CD-ROM 1998), Collieries of Wales: Engineering and Architecture (co-author, 1995), Creating an Art Community: 50 Years of the Welsh Group (1999), Glenys Cour: Paintings and Works on Paper 1980–2003 (co-author, 2003), An Art-Accustomed Eye: John Gibbs and Art Appreciation in Wales 1945–1996 (2004), A Guide to Blaenavon Ironworks and World Heritage Site (2006, 2 edn 2011), The Painter's Quarry: The Art of Peter Prendergast (co-author, 2006), Hidden Histories: Discovering the Heritage of Wales (co-author, 2008), The Book of Ystwyth: Six Poets on the Art of Clive Hicks-Jenkins (ed, 2011); author of articles in jls and newspapers and chapters in books incl New Dictionary of National Biography, Industrial Archaeology Review, Archaeologica Cambrensis, The Local Historian, Landscape History, Design History, Art Review, The Guardian and Heritage in Wales, Worktown: The Drawings of Falcon Hildred (2012), War Underground: Memoirs of a Bevin Boy in the S Wales Coalfield (2013), Pontcysylte Aqueduct and Canal World Heritage Site (2015), Romancing Wales: Romanticism in the Welsh Landscape since 1770 (2016); *Style—* Dr Peter Wakelin; ✉ Ty Isaf, Llanilar, Aberystwyth SY23 4NP (☏ 029 2057 3205)

WAKEMAN, Prof Richard John; s of late Ronald Wakeman, and Kathleen, *née* Smith, of Exmouth, Devon; *b* 15 April 1948; *Educ* King Edward VI GS Bury St Edmunds, UMIST (BSc, MSc, PhD); *m* 24 July 1971, Patricia Joan, da of Jack Morris; 2 s (Simon Richard b 24 June 1976, Mark Andrew b 4 April 1979); *Career* Lennig Chemicals Ltd: chemical engr 1970, conslt engr 1972–; research asst UMIST 1972–73; Univ of Exeter: lectr 1973–86, reader in particle technol 1986–90, prof of process engrg 1990–95; Loughborough Univ: prof of chemical engrg 1995–2008 (assoc dean of engrg 1997–2000), head of chemical engrg 2000–08, emeritus prof 2008–; visiting engr Univ of Calif Berkeley 1980, visiting prof Univ of Pardubice 2004–, visiting fell Univ of Mumbai 2008–09, visiting prof Univ of Chun Yuan 2008–; Filtration Soc: memb Cncl 1982–89 and 2000–, chm 1987–89, tstee 1989–, hon sec 2000–; chm Working Party European Fedn of Chemical Engrs 1996–2006 (memb 1984–2006); exec ed The Transactions of the Institution of Chemical Engrs 1999–2008; non-exec dir: The Filtration Society Ltd 1983–89 and 2000–, Exeter Enterprises Ltd 1987–90; author of over 450 research articles, patents and books/book contribs 1971–; Suttle Award Filtration Soc 1971, Moulton Medal IChemE 1991 and 1995 (Jr Moulton Medal 1978), Gold Medal Filtration Soc 1993, 2003 and 2005, Chemical Weekly Award Indian Inst of Chemical Engrs 2004;

CEng 1977, FIChemE 1989 (MIChemE 1977, Arnold Greene Medal 2008), Eur Ing 1989, FREng 1996, CSci 2004; *Recreations* philately, antiquities, industrial archaeology; *Style—* Prof Richard Wakeman, FREng; ✉ e-mail richard@richardwakeham.co.uk, website www.richardwakeman.co.uk

WALCOTT, Theodore (Theo); *b* 16 March 1989, London; *Career* professional footballer; clubs: Southampton 2004–06, Arsenal 2006–; England: 36 caps, 5 goals, debut v Hungary 2006 (youngest player to represent England), memb squad World Cup 2006; *Style—* Theo Walcott, Esq; ✉ c/o Arsenal FC, Arsenal Stadium, Highbury, London N5 1BU

WALD, Prof Sir Nicholas John; kt (2008); s of Adolf Max Wald (d 2007), of London, and Frieda Shatsow (d 1986); *b* 31 May 1944; *Educ* Owen's Sch, UCH (MB BS), Univ of London (DSc); *m* 2 Jan 1966, Nancy Evelyn, *née* Miller; 1 da (Karen b 1966), 3 s (David b 1968, Richard b 1971, Jonathan b 1977); *Career* MRC Epidemiology and Med Care Unit 1971– (memb sci staff), ICRF Cancer Epidemiology and Clinical Trials Unit Oxford 1972–83, prof and head of Centre for Environmental and Preventive Med Bart's 1983– (dir Wolfson Inst of Preventive Medicine 1992–95 and 1997–); ed-in-chief Jl of Medical Screening (inaugural ed) 1994–; hon dir Cancer Research Campaign Screening Gp 1986–2000, hon conslt East London & City and Oxford RHA's; Advsy Cncl on Sci and Technol: memb Med Res and Health Ctee 1991–92; MRC: memb Steering Ctee of the MRC Study on Multivitamins and Neural-Tube Defects 1982–92, chm Smoking Review Working Gp 1986–90, chm Study Monitoring Ctee of the MRC Randomised Clinical Trial of Colo-Rectal Cancer Screening 1986–, chm Steering Ctee for Multicentre Aneurysm Screening Study 1997–; Dept of Health: memb Advsy Ctee on Breast Cancer Screening 1986–99, memb Ind Sci Ctee on Smoking and Health 1983–91, Central Research and Devpt Ctee 1991–96, memb Chief Medical Offr's Health of the Nation Working Gp 1991–97, memb Chief Medical Offr's Advsy Gp on Folate Supplementation in the Prevention of Neural Tube Defects 1991–92, memb Scientific Ctee on Tobacco and Health 1993–2002, memb Advsy Ctee on Cervical Screening 1996–99, memb Medicines and Healthcare Products Regulatory Agency Expert Advsy Panel 1996–, Population Screening Panel 1993–1998, Ctee on Med Aspects of Food and Nutrition Policy, Working Gp of Nutritional Status of Population, Folic Acid Subgroup 1996–2000, Ctee Nat Screening, Antenatal Subgroup 1997, HPV/LBC Pilots Steering Gp 2000–03, Advsy Gp for the Evaluation of UK Colorectal Cancer Screening Pilot 2000–03; Royal Coll of Physicians: memb Ctee on Ethical Issues in Medicine 1988–, memb Sub-Ctee on Ethical Issues in Clinical Genetics 1988–91, memb Special Advsy Gp to Med Info Technol Ctee 1984–94; NE Thames RHA: memb Clinical Genetics Advsy Sub-Ctee 1984–1992, memb Dist Res Ethics Ctee 1990–95, memb Cncl Coronary Prevention Gp 1993–94; memb: Action on Smoking and Health Res Ctee 1982–91, Wellcome Trust Physiology and Pharmacology Panel 1995–2000, Nuclear Test Veterans Advsy Gp Nat Radiological Bd 2000–04, Faculty of Public Health Info Sub-Ctee 2001–05, Lung Cancer Gp Nat Cancer Res Network 2001–05, WHO Working Gp on Methodologies of Non-Communicable Disease Screening 2001–, Bd of Dirs Int Soc of Prenatal Diagnosis; Nat Ctee for Clinical Lab Standards (NCCLS), Sub-Ctee on Maternal Serum Screening 2001–; memb Editorial Bd: Prenatal Diagnosis, Philosophical Transactions of the Royal Soc Biological Sciences 2008–; FFPH 1982, FRCP 1986, FRCOG 1992, FMedSci 1998, CBiol, FIBiol 2000, FRS 2004; *Awards* William Julius Mickle Fellowship 1990, Kennedy Fndn Int Award in Scientific Research 2000, US Public Health Service and Centers for Disease Control Award (jtly with Richard Smithells) 2002, RCP Lord Rayner Lecture 2009, RSM Jephcott Lecture and Medal 2011, Hamdan Award for Medical Research Excellence 2012, RCP Croonian Lecture 2015; *Books* Alpha-Fetoprotein Screening – The Current Issues (ed with J E Haddow, 1981), Antenatal and Neonatal Screening (ed, 1984, 2 edn (ed with I Leck) 2000), Interpretation of Negative Epidemiological Evidence for Carcinogenicity (ed with R Doll, 1985), The Epidemiological Approach (1985, 4 edn 2004), UK Smoking Statistics (jt ed, 1988 and 1991), Nicotine Smoking and the Low Tar Programme (ed with P Froggatt, 1989), Smoking and Hormone Related Disorders (ed with J Baron, 1990), Passive Smoking: A Health Hazard (jt ed, 1991), International Smoking Statistics (co-author, 1994); *Recreations* boating, economics; *Clubs* Athenaeum; *Style—* Prof Sir Nicholas Wald; ✉ Centre for Environmental and Preventive Medicine, Wolfson Institute of Preventive Medicine, Bart's and The London School of Medicine and Dentistry, Queen Mary University of London, Charterhouse Square, London EC1M 6BQ (☎ 020 7882 6269, fax 020 7882 6270, e-mail n.j.wald@qmul.ac.uk)

WALDEGRAVE, Lady (Linda Margaret) Caroline; OBE (2000); da of Maj Richard Burrows, of Tunbridge Wells, Kent, and Molly, *née* Hollins; *b* 14 August 1952; *Educ* Convent of the Sacred Heart Woldingham, Cordon Bleu Sch of Cookery, Univ of Roehampton (postgrad dip); *m* 1977, Baron Waldegrave of North Hill, PC (Life Peer), *qv*, s of 12 Earl Waldegrave, KG, GCVO, TD (d 1995); 3 da (Katharine Mary b 15 Sept 1980, Elizabeth Laura b 27 Oct 1983, Harriet Horatia b 28 Jan 1988), 1 s (James Victor b 12 Dec 1984); *Career* joined Leith's Catering as jr cook 1972; proprietor: Leiths Sch of Food and Wine 1994–2008 (estab with Prue Leith 1975), Barley Mow Dorset St 2012–, Dudwell Sch 2013–; dir Waldegrave Farms Ltd 1994–; memb Health Educn Authy 1985–88; pres Portobello Tst 1987–2000; advsr Nat Life Story Collection; *Books* Leith's Cookery School (with Prue Leith, 1985), The Healthy Gourmet (1986), Sainsbury's Low Fat Gourmet (1987), Leith's Cookery Bible (with Prue Leith, 1991), Leith's Complete Christmas (jtly, 1992), Leith's Fish Bible (jtly, 1995), Leith's Easy Dinner Parties (jtly, 1995), Leith's Healthy Eating (jtly, 1996); *Recreations* tennis, bridge, skiing; *Style—* Lady Waldegrave, OBE; ✉ Provost's Lodge, Eton College, Windsor SL4 6DH (☎ 01753 671335, e-mail c.waldegrave@etoncollege.org.uk)

WALDEGRAVE OF NORTH HILL, Baron (Life Peer UK 1999), of Chewton Mendip in the County of Somerset; William Arthur Waldegrave; PC (1990); 2 s of 12 Earl Waldegrave, KG, GCVO, TD (d 1995), and Mary Hermione, *née* Grenfell (d Nov 1995); *b* 15 August 1946; *Educ* Eton, CCC Oxford, Harvard Univ; *m* 1977, (Linda Margaret) Caroline (Lady Waldegrave, OBE, *qv*), da of Maj Richard Burrows, of Tunbridge Wells, Kent; 3 da (Hon Katharine Mary b 15 Sept 1980, Hon Elizabeth Laura b 27 Oct 1983, Hon Harriet Horatia b 28 Jan 1988), 1 s (Hon James Victor b 12 Dec 1984); *Career* fell All Souls Oxford 1971; CPRS 1971–73, on political staff 10 Downing St 1973–74, head Political Office of Rt Hon Edward Heath (as ldr of the oppn) 1974–75; with GEC Ltd 1975–81, memb IBA Advsy Cncl 1980; MP (Cons) Bristol W 1979–97, jt vice-chm Fin Ctee to Sept 1981, under sec of state DES (for Higher Educn) 1981–83, chm Ctee for Local Authy Higher Educn 1982–83, under sec of state DOE 1983–85, min of state DOE 1985, min of state FCO 1988, sec of state for Health 1990–92, Chancellor of the Duchy of Lancaster (with responsibility for the Citizen's Charter and Sci) 1992–94, min for agriculture fisheries and food 1994–95, chief sec to the Treasy 1995–97; pres Parly and Sci Ctee 2001; md Corp Fin Dresdner Kleinwort Wasserstein 1998–2003; vice-chm Investment Banking Div UBS 2003–09; provost Eton Coll 2009–; chm Biotech Growth Tst (formerly Finsbury Life Sciences Investment Tst) 2012–16 (also dir); dir: Bristol & West plc, Henry Sotheran Ltd 1998–2015 (chm 2007–15), Waldegrave Farms Ltd; chm Advsy Ctee Royal Mint 2011–; tstee: Rhodes Tst 1992– (chm 2002–11), Beit Memorial Fellowships for Med Res; chm Nat Museum of Sci and Indust 2002–10, chm of tstees Bristol Cathedral Tst; JP Inner London 1975–79; *Books* The Binding of Leviathan – Conservatism and the Future (1977), Changing Gear – What the Government Should Do Next (pamphlet, co-author, 1981), A Different Kind of Weather (memoir, 2015), various other pamphlets; *Clubs* Beefsteak, Pratt's, White's, Leander; *Style—* The Lord Waldegrave of North Hill, PC

WALDEN, Celia Isobel; da of George Walden, CMG, of W London, the former MP for Buckingham, and Sarah, *née* Hunt; *b* 8 December 1975, Paris; *Educ* Univ of Cambridge (BA); *m* 24 June 2010, Piers Morgan, *qv*; 1 da (b Nov 2011); *Career* rights exec Yale Univ Press Publishers 2000–02, reporter Night and Day magazine The Mail on Sunday 2002–05, columnist, feature writer and interviewer The Daily Telegraph 2005– (incl ed Spy column); motoring columnist GQ Magazine, interviewer Glamour Magazine; *Books* Harm's Way (novel, 2008), Babysitting George (2011); *Recreations* writing, tennis, cinema, motoring; *Style—* Miss Celia Walden; ✉ Ed Victor Ltd, 6 Bayley Street, Bedford Square, London WC1B 3HE (☎ 020 7304 4100, fax 020 7304 4111)

WALDEN, David Peter; CBE (2013); s of Gerald Isaac Walden, of Newcastle upon Tyne, and Shirley Betty, *née* Rothfield (d 1981); *b* 23 September 1954; *Educ* Royal GS Newcastle upon Tyne, St John's Coll Oxford (BA, Gibbs Prize for modern history); *m* 1981, Janet Rosamund, da of Harry Day, MBE; 1 s (Jonathan Paul b 2 Aug 1985), 1 da (Rachel Sarah b 23 Nov 1987); *Career* DHSS: admin trainee 1977, princ Nurses' Pay 1982–85, private sec to dep chm NHS Mgmnt Bd 1985–86, asst sec Doctors' Pay and Conditions 1989–90, on secondment as personnel dir Poole Hosp NHS Tst 1991–93, head Community Care Branch Dept of Health 1993–96, under sec and head Health Promotion Div Dept of Health 1996–99, head Social Care Policy Dept of Health 1999–2001, seconded as exec dir of health servs devpt Anchor Tst 2001–03, transition dir Ind Regulator of NHS Fndn Tsts 2003–04, dir of strategy Cmmn for Social Care 2004–09, dir of adult servs Social Care Inst for Excellence 2009–; *Style—* David Walden, Esq, CBE; ✉ Social Care Institute for Excellence, Fifth Floor, 2–4 Cockspur Street, London SW1Y 5BH (☎ 020 7024 7668, mobile 07789 653522)

WALDEN, Will; *Career* reporter/prodr ITN 1997–2000; BBC News: sports news prodr and North of England prodr 2000–02, sr political prodr 10 O'Clock News 2002–03, dep bureau ed North America 2003–06, dep ed UK News 2009, Westminster news ed 2006–12, dir of communications and external affairs and chief spokesman for Boris Johnson, MP, Mayor of London 2012–; *Style—* Will Walden, Esq; ✉ Greater London Authority, City Hall, The Queen's Walk, More London, London SE1 2AA

WALDIE, Ian Michael; s of George Alistair (Ted) Waldie, of Queensland, Aust, and Dulcie Michel, *née* Clark; *b* 21 January 1970; *Educ* Burnside HS Nambour Aust, Queensland Coll of Art Brisbane Aust (Assoc Dip of Arts in Applied Photography); *Career* news photographer; cadet photographer The Sunshine Coast Daily (Maroochydore Queensland) 1988–89, photographer The Brisbane Courier Mail (Brisbane Queensland) 1989–92, freelance photographer Scotland 1992–93 (working for The Herald, The Scotsman, The Daily Record, The Sunday Mail, Take-A-Break and Rex Features), stringer photographer (covering Scotland for the Reuters UK and int serv) Reuters Ltd 1993–96, staff photographer Reuter UK Pictures (based London) 1996–2002, sr photographer EMEA Getty Images 2002–; notable assignments since 1993 incl: numerous royal visits and functions, state visits by John Major, Mikhail Gorbachov, Nelson Mandela, Paul Keating, The Dalai Lama, Mother Theresa, the PM of Finland and The King and Queen of Norway, Scottish Cup Finals 1993 and 1994, Rugby Five Nations Tournament 1992, 1993, 1994 and 1995, Scottish Open Golf Championships 1993, 1994 and 1995, Alfred Dunhill Cup Golf Championships 1993, 1994 and 1995, Cons Pty Conf 1994 and 1995, Lab Pty Conf 1995 and 1997, Rugby World Cup South Africa 1995, World Championships in Athletics 1995 and 1997, conflict in NI over Protestant marching season in Portadown, Belfast, Londonderry, Inniskillen and Bellaghy 1997, Boris Yeltsin and Bill Clinton summit meeting in Helsinki 1997, followed Tony Blair on campaign bus in run-up to the general election 1997, Wimbledon Championships 1997, Br Open Golf Championships 1997, funeral of Diana, Princess of Wales 1997, Scottish Devolution vote and count 1997, HM The Queen's Golden Wedding Anniversary 1997, Sharjah Champions Trophy UAE 1997, Peace Referendum in Ireland 1998, World Cup Football France 1998, Omagh bombing in NI 1998, Lab Pty Conf 1998, Euro Cup Winners Cup Final (Chelsea v Stuttgart) 1998, FA Cup Final (Arsenal v Newcastle) 1998, England Cricket Tour Australia 1998–99, Cricket World Cup 1999, Wimbledon Tennis Championships 1999, Royal Wedding of Prince Edward and Sophie Rhys Jones 1999; memb: Australian Journalists Assoc (AJA) 1988–93, NUJ 1992; *Awards* Best Sports Picture (Scottish Sports Photography Awards) 1994, Best News Picture (Scottish Airports Press Photography Awards) 1994, Photographer of the Year, Young Photographer of the Year and Best News Photographer of the Year (Br Picture Eds Guild) 1994, Nikon UK Press Photographer of the Year 1997, Fujifilm Photographer of the Year 2002, British Press Photographer of the Year 2002, Guinness Best Black and White Photographer of the Year (Picture Editor's Awards) 2003; *Recreations* surfing (in Australia), music (ex-drummer), squash, rally driving, various other sports; *Style—* Ian Waldie, Esq

WALDMAN, Guido; s of Milton Waldman, and Marguerite, *née* David; *Educ* Downside (exhibitioner), BNC Oxford (open scholarship, BA); *m* Lalage; 2 da (Nicola, Zoë Axelle); *Career* subsid rights manager, ed, dir The Bodley Head 1958–88, contracts dir The Bodley Head and Jonathan Cape 1985–88; The Harvill Press: ed 1988–2000, editorial dir and head of contracts 1995–2000; Weidenfeld (translation) Prize 1998; *Books* A Fogazzaro: A House Divided (trans, 1963), The Penguin Book of Italian Short Stories (ed, 1969), L Ariosto: Orlando Furioso (trans, 1974), I Went to School One Morning (1978), The Late Flowering of Captain Latham (1979), G Greene and M F Allain: The Other Man (trans, 1983), G Boccaccio: The Decameron (trans, 1993), A Baricco: Silk (trans, 1997) La Fontaine: Forbidden Fruit (trans, 1998), J Echenoz: Lake (trans, 1998), La Fontaine: The Complete Tales in Verse (trans, 2000), Publishing Agreements (contrib, 3 edn), J Echenoz: I'm Off (trans, 2001), A Buzzi: The Perfect Egg (trans, 2005), R Alajmo: Palermo (trans, 2010); *Recreations* piano, Spanish guitar, cartoon-drawing, translating; *Style—* Guido Waldman, Esq; ✉ 9 Elia Street, London N1 8DE (☎ 020 7837 9656, fax 020 7837 9677)

WALDMAN, Simon; *b* 26 January 1966; *Educ* Liverpool Coll Liverpool, Univ of Bristol (BA); *Career* journalist; reporter Shoe & Leather News 1988–89, reporter Drapers Record 1989, dep ed Media Week 1990–93, freelance journalist 1993–96; The Guardian: joined 1996, head of Guardian Unlimited (award-winning network of websites) 1999–2010, dir of digital publishing 2001–10, memb bd Guardian Newspapers Ltd 2001–06, gp dir of digital strategy and devpt Guardian Media Gp 2006–10; gp product dir LOVEFiLM 2010–; *Style—* Simon Waldman, Esq

WALDMANN, Dr Carl; s of Leon Waldmann (d 1970), and Rene, *née* Schafer; bro of Prof Herman Waldmann, *qv*; *b* 25 March 1951; *Educ* Forest Sch, Sidney Sussex Coll Cambridge (BA), London Hosp (MA, MB BChir, DA); *m* 27 July 1980 (m dis 1988), Judith; 3 da (Anna b 1981, Mia b 2004, Felicity b 2006); *Career* Flt-Lt Unit MO RAF Brize Norton 1977–78, Sqdn Ldr 1981–82, sr specialist anaesthetics RAF Ely 1980–82 (specialist 1978–80); sr registrar in intensive care Whipps Cross Hosp 1982–83; sr registrar in anaesthetics: London Hosp 1984–85 (houseman 1975–76, sr house offr in anaesthetics 1976–77, lectr in anaesthetics 1983–84), Great Ormond St Hosp 1985–86; conslt in anaesthetics and dir of intensive care Royal Berks and Battle Hosps Reading 1986–; European dip in Intensive Care Med 1993; ed Care of the Critically Ill 2000– (dep ed 1997); Intensive Care Soc: elected to Cncl 1998, ed jl 1999, treas 2003, pres 2007, hon memb 2013; memb European Soc of Intensive Care Medicine 1993 (chm Technol Assessment Section 2002, UK rep 2012–15); FFARCS 1980, FICM 2011 (vice-dean 2014); *Books* Pocket Consultant Intensive Care (1985), Respiration: The Breath of Life (1985), Hazards and Complications of Anaesthesia (1987), Kaufman, Anaesthesia Reviews, Intensive Care Manual, Intensive Care Aftercare, Oxford Desk Reference Critical Care

W

(2008), Law & Ethics in Intensive Care (2010), SAQs for FRCA (2011); *Recreations* fencing, squash, skiing, water-skiing, club dr for Leyton Orient FC; *Clubs* Hanover Int (Reading), Berkshire Raquets; *Style—* Dr Carl Waldmann; ✉ 2 Dewe Lane, Burghfield, Reading RG30 3SU (☎ 0118 957 6381, e-mail cswald@aol.com); Intensive Therapy Unit, Royal Berkshire Hospital, Reading (☎ 0118 322 7250, fax 0118 322 7250)

WALDMANN, Prof Herman; s of Leon Waldmann (d 1970), and Rene, *née* Schafer; bro of Dr Carl Waldmann, *qv*, and David Waldmann; *b* 27 February 1945; *Educ* Sir George Monoux GS Walthamstow, Sidney Sussex Coll Cambridge (exhibitioner, hon scholar, MA, PhD), London Hosp Med Sch (open scholar, MB BChir, Hutchinson prize for clinical res); *m* 1971, Judith Ruth; *Career* house physician and surgeon London Hosp 1969–70, MRC jr res fell 1970–73; Dept of Pathology Univ of Cambridge: demonstrator 1973–76, lectr 1975–76, reader in therapeutic immunology 1985, Kay Kendall prof of therapeutic immunology 1989–94; King's Coll Cambridge: res fell 1973–78, side tutor 1975–76, fell 1985–94; prof of pathology Sir William Dunn Sch of Pathology Univ of Oxford 1994–2012 (emeritus prof 2012–), fell Lincoln Coll Oxford 1994–; visiting scientist with Dr C Milstein Laboratory of Molecular Biology Cambridge 1978–79, SHO Dept of Med Royal Postgrad Med Sch London 1982, Eleanor Roosevelt fell Stanford Univ 1987; memb Advsy Ctee MRC Cell Bd 1986–91; invited speaker at numerous symposia in the areas of immunology, haematology and transplantation; Graham Bull prize RCP 1989–90; hon ScD Univ of Cambridge 2008; hon fell: Queen Mary & Westfield Coll London 1996, Sidney Sussex Coll Cambridge 2008, Kings Coll Cambridge 2009; founding fell Acad of Med Sci; FRCPath (MRCPath), FRS 1990, FRCP 2010 (MRCP); *Publications* author of numerous articles in learned jls; *Recreations* family, friends, food, travel, music, tinnitus, walking in a straight line; *Style—* Prof Herman Waldmann, FRS; ✉ 4 Apsley Road, Oxford OX2 7QY; Sir William Dunn School of Pathology, South Parks Road, Oxford OX1 3RE (☎ 01865 275500)

WALDRON, Graham; *Career* chm Headlam Gp plc 1991–99 and 2006–; *Style—* Graham Waldron, Esq; ✉ Headlam plc, PO Box 1, Gorsey Lane, Coleshill, Birmingham B46 1LW

WALDUCK, (Hugh) Richard; OBE (2001), JP (Middx, Haringey 1974–2003, City of London 2003–11), DL (Herts 2000); s of Hugh Stanley Walduck (d 1975), and Enid Rosalind (Wendy) Walduck, of Melbourne, Australia; *b* 21 November 1941; *Educ* Harrow, St Catharine's Coll Cambridge (MA); *m* 1, 1969 (m dis 1980); 2 s (Alexander b 1971, Nicholas b 1972), 2 step s (Richard b 1966, Simon b 1968), 1 step da (Nicola b 1971); m 2, 1981, Susan Marion Sherwood; *Career* dir and sec Imperial London Hotels Ltd 1964–; county pres St John Ambulance Herts 1990–2005; pres Royal Br Legion N Mymms 1998–; memb: Action on Addiction Cncl 1993–2000, Ct Univ of Herts; dir Nat Crimebeat 1998–, vice-pres Herts Community Fndn 2000; tstee: Br Humane Assoc 2001–08, Royal Engrs Museum Fndn; patron: St Alban's Cathedral, Isabel Hospice, HAPAS, Herts Agric Soc, Caribbean Women's Standing Conference, Herts Action on Disability; memb Cncl Shrievalty Assoc 1999–2001; signatory to Leadership Challenge for Racial Equality 1999; Chapter Gen Order of St John 1990–99, Chapter Priory of England Order of St John 2002–03; hon life memb Soc of the Golden Keys; High Sheriff Herts 1997; Liveryman Worshipful Co of Basketmakers 1968 (Prime Warden 2007), Alderman of the City of London (Ward of Tower) 2003–07; Hon DLitt Univ of Herts 2001; KStJ 2000 (OStJ 1989, CStJ 1997); *Recreations* heritage; *Clubs* City Livery, United Guilds, Royal Soc of St George, Pilgrims, Cooks, Tower Ward; *Style—* Richard Walduck, Esq, OBE, DL; ✉ c/o Director's Office, Imperial Hotel, Russell Square, London WC1B 5BB

WALES, Anthony Edward; s of Albert Edward Wales, of Collingham, Nottinghamshire, and Kathleen May, *née* Rosenthal; *b* 20 December 1955; *Educ* Stamford Sch, Worcester Coll Oxford (MA); *m* 1 Sept 1984, Lynda, da of Leonard Page (d 1987); 2 s (Edward b 1987, Thomas b 1989), 1 da (Victoria b 1993); *Career* slr; ptnr Turner Kenneth Brown 1986–94 (joined 1979), gen counsel The Economist Newspaper Ltd 1994–2001, sr vice-pres and gen counsel AOL Europe 2002–07, sr vice-pres and gen counsel AOL Int 2007–09, dir of legal affrs and co sec Br Standards Instn 2010–; visiting research fell Oxford Internet Inst 2009–; memb: Law Soc 1981, Law Soc Hong Kong 1986; *Style—* Anthony Wales, Esq

WALES, Archbishop of 2003–; Most Rev Dr Barry Cennydd Morgan; s of Rhys Haydn Morgan (d 1983), and Mary Gwyneth, *née* Davies (d 1988); *b* 31 January 1947; *Educ* UCL (BA), Selwyn Coll Cambridge (MA), Westcott House Cambridge (Powis exhibitioner), Univ of Wales (PhD); *m* Aug 1969, Hilary Patricia (d 2016), da of Ieuan Lewis; 1 s (Jonathan Rhodri b 19 July 1975), 1 da (Lucy Rachel Angharad b 4 Feb 1977); *Career* ordained (Llandaff): deacon 1972, priest 1973, bishop 1993; curate St Andrew's Major Dinas Powis 1972–75, chaplain Bryn-y-Don Community Sch 1972–75, chaplain and lectr St Michael's Coll Llandaff 1975–77, lectr UC Cardiff 1975–77, warden Church Hostel Bangor, Anglican chaplain and lectr in theol UCNW 1977–84, ed Welsh Churchman 1975–82; examining chaplain: to Archbishop of Wales 1978–82, to Bishop of Bangor 1983; in-serv trg offr 1979–84, warden of ordinands Dio of Bangor 1982–84, canon of Bangor Cathedral 1983–84, rector Rectorial Parish of Wrexham 1984–86, archdeacon of Merioneth and rector of Criccieth 1986–93, bishop of Bangor 1993–99, bishop of Llandaff 1999–2003; chm: Archbishop's Doctrinal Cmmn 1983–93 (memb 1982, chm 1990–93), Div of Stewardship Provincial Bd of Mission 1988–94; vice-pres Bible Soc 1999, vice-pres Nat Soc 2003 (vice-chm 1999); memb: Central Ctee World Cncl of Churches 1996–2006, Primates Standing Ctee 2003–11; pres Welsh Centre for Int Affrs 2004–10; pro-chllr Univ of Wales 2006; hon fell: Bangor Univ, Cardiff Univ, Univ of Wales Lampeter, Cardiff Metropolitan Univ, Univ of Swansea 2009, Trinity Univ of Carmarthen 2009; Hon DLitt Cardiff Metropolitan Univ; FLSW 2013; *Publications* O Ddydd i Ddydd, Pwyllgor Darlleniadau Beiblaidd Cyngor Eglwysi Cymru (1980), History of the Church Hostel and Anglican Chaplaincy at University College of North Wales Bangor (1986), Concepts of Mission and Ministry in Anglican University Chaplaincy Work (1988), Strangely Orthodox: R S Thomas and his Poetry of Faith (2006); *Recreations* golf; *Style—* The Most Rev Dr the Archbishop of Wales; ✉ Llys Esgob, The Cathedral Green, Llandaff, Cardiff CF5 2YE (☎ 029 2056 2400, fax 029 2056 8410, e-mail archbishop@churchinwales.org.uk)

WALES, Gordon; *Career* dir of operational support Scottish Ct Service; *Style—* Gordon Wales, Esq; ✉ Scottish Court Service, Hayweight House, 23 Lauriston Street, Edinburgh EH3 9DQ

WALES, Gregory John; s of A J Wales, of Guildford, Surrey, and B Wales, *née* Read; *b* 17 May 1949; *Educ* RGS Guildford, London Univ (BSc, MA); *m* 1, 1972 (m dis), Jennifer Hilary Brown; 2 s (Nicholas b 1978, Andrew b 1981); m 2, 2013, Gabrielle M B Twigg; *Career* CA 1974; sr lectr City 1976–79, mgmnt conslt 1976–80, mangr Arthur Andersen & Co 1980–82, ptnr Coombes Wales Quinnell 1982–90; dir: Sherbourne Fndn, Triarius Fndn; sr conslt CeEx Inc (strategic consultancy); pres Action Sociale pour la RDC; Freeman City of London; FCA 1976; *Books* The Incompetent Ape (as Lewis Richards); *Recreations* cricket, squash, real tennis; *Style—* G J Wales; ✉ PO Box 859, Water Mill, New York 11976, USA

WALES, Jimmy Donal; *b* 7 August 1966, Huntsville, AL; *Educ* Randolph HS AL, Auburn Univ, Univ of Alabama; *m* Kate Garvey; *Career* fndr Wikipedia 2001–, chm Wikimedia Fdn 2003–06, pres Wikia Inc 2004–, chm emeritus Wikimedia Fndn 2006–; Pioneer Award EFF 2006, Business Process Award The Economist 2008; *Style—* Jimmy Wales, Esq; ✉ Wikimedia UK, 4th Floor, Development House, 56–64 Leonard Street, London EC2A 4LT

WALEY-COHEN, Robert Bernard; 2 s of Sir Bernard Waley-Cohen, 1 Bt (d 1991), and Hon Joyce (Hon Lady Waley Cohen, JP, d 2013), da of 1 Baron Nathan (d 1963); *b* 10 November 1948; *Educ* Eton; *m* 1975, Hon Felicity Ann, da of 3 Viscount Bearsted, TD, DL (d 1986); 3 s (Marcus Richard b 1977, Sam Bernard b 1982, Thomas Andrew b 1984 d 2004), 1 da (Jessica Suzanna b 1979); *Career* exec Christie's 1969–81 (gen mangr USA 1970–73); fndr chm and ceo Alliance Imaging Inc 1983–88, fndr and chief exec Alliance Medical Ltd 1989–2006 (dep chm 2006–10); steward Jockey Club 1995–2000; chm: Point-to-Point Authy 2005–11, Pony Racing Authy 2007–09, NH Ctee Thoroughbred Breeders Assoc 2010–15, Cheltenham Racecourse 2011– (dir 1986); memb Cncl Countryside Alliance 1998–2002, memb Cncl Nat Tst 2001–10; tstee: Countryside Fndn for Educn 1997–2001, Animal Health Tst 2007–10, Place 2 Be 2007–10; High Sheriff Warks 2012–13; *Recreations* the arts, conservation, racing (racehorses include: Rustle, The Dragon Master, Katarino, Makounji, Libertine, Long Run, Rajdhani Express); *Clubs* Jockey, Boodles, Turf; *Style—* Robert Waley-Cohen, Esq; ✉ e-mail rwc@uptonviva.com

WALEY-COHEN, Sir Stephen Harry; 2 Bt (UK 1961), of Honeymead, Co Somerset; s of Sir Bernard Nathaniel Waley-Cohen, 1 Bt (d 1991), and Hon Lady Waley-Cohen (d 2013); *b* 22 June 1946; *Educ* Eton, Magdalene Coll Cambridge (MA); *m* 1, 1972 (m dis 1986), Pamela Elizabeth, yr da of J E Doniger, of Knutsford, Cheshire; 2 s (Lionel Robert b 7 Aug 1974, Jack David b 7 Sept 1979), 1 da (Harriet Ann b 20 June 1976); m 2, 1986, Josephine Burnett, yr da of Duncan M Spencer, of Bedford, New York; 2 da (Tamsin Alice b 4 April 1986, Freya Charlotte b 20 Feb 1989); *Heir* s, Lionel Waley-Cohen; *Career* fin journalist Daily Mail 1968–73, ed Money Mail Handbook 1972–74, dir and publisher Euromoney Publications Ltd 1969–83, chief exec Maybox Group plc (theatre and cinema owners and managers) 1984–89; dir Publishing Holdings plc 1986–88, chm Willis Faber & Dumas (Agencies) Ltd 1992–99 (dir 1988), dir St Martin's Theatre Ltd 1989–, md Victoria Palace 1989–2014; chm: Thorndike Holdings ltd 1989–1998, Policy Portfolio plc 1993–98, First Call Group plc 1996–98, Portsmouth & Sunderland Newspaper plc 1998–99 (dir 1994–98); dir: Stewart Wrightson Members Agency Ltd 1987–98, Exeter Preferred Capital Investment Trust plc 1992–2003, Savoy Theatre Ltd 1996–98, Ambassadors Theatre 2007–; md: Mousetrap Productions Ltd 1994–, Vaudeville Theatre 1996–2001, Savoy Theatre Management Ltd 1997–2005; advsy dir Theatres Mutual Insurance Co 1995–2004; chm RADA 2007– (memb Cncl 2004–); memb Fin Ctee UCL 1984–89, chm JCA Charitable Fndn (formerly Jewish Colonisation Assoc) 1992– (memb Cncl 1984–), memb Soc of London Theatres 1984– (memb Bd 1993–2012, pres 2002–05), chm Exec Ctee Br American Project for the Successor Generation 1989–92, chm Garrick Charitable Tst 2008– (tstee 2003–), chm Combined Theatrical Charities 2010–, memb Ctee Wormwood Scrubs Charitable Tst 2016–, vice-pres Exmoor Soc 2016–; tstee: Badgworthy Land Tst 1982–, The Theatres Tst 1998–2004, Royal Theatrical Fund 2010–; govr Wellesley House Sch 1972–97; Parly candidate (Cons) Manchester 1974; Liveryman Worshipful Co of Clothworkers; Hon PhD Ben-Gurion Univ Israel; *Clubs* Garrick; *Style—* Sir Stephen Waley-Cohen, Bt; ✉ 1 Wallingford Avenue, London W10 6QA

WALFORD, Dr Diana Marion; CBE (2002); *née* Norton; da of late Lt-Col Joseph Norton, of Beckenham, and Thelma, *née* Nurick; *b* 26 February 1944; *Educ* Calder HS for Girls Liverpool, Univ of Liverpool (George Holt scholarship, BSc, MB ChB, MD, George Holt medal, J Hill Abram prize), Univ of London (MSc, N and S Devi prize); *m* 9 Dec 1970, Arthur David Walford, s of Wing Cdr Adolph A Walford (decd), of Bushey Heath, Herts; 1 da (Sally b 8 Aug 1972), 1 s (Alexander b 5 May 1982); *Career* house surgn Liverpool Royal Infirmary March-Aug 1969 (house physician 1968–69); SHO: St Mary's Hosp 1969–70, Northwick Park Hosp 1970–71; sr registrar rotation 1972–75, N London Blood Transfusion Centre MRC res fell and hon sr registrar Clinical Res Centre Northwick Park Hosp 1975–76, hon conslt haematologist Central Middx Hosp 1977–87; Dept of Health: sr med offr Medicines Div 1976–79, princ med offr Sci Servs Equipment Building Div 1979–83, sr princ med offr and under sec Med Manpower and Educn Div 1983–86, sabbatical LSHTM 1986–87, sr princ med offr and under sec Int Health Microbiology of Food and Water and Communicable Disease Div 1987–89, dep chief med offr and med dir NHS Mgmnt Exec 1989–92, dir Public Health Laboratory Service 1993–2002, princ Mansfield Coll Oxford 2002–11, pro-vice-chllr Univ of Oxford 2010–11, pro-chllr and chair Bd of Tstees Regent's Univ London 2015–; contrib to various med books and jls; govr Ditchley Fndn 2001–, tstee Sue Ryder Care 2008–, dep chm Cncl London Sch of Hygiene and Tropical Medicine 2010–, non-exec dir UCLH NHS Fndn Tst 2011–; memb State Honours Ctee 2010–; MA (by incorporation) Univ of Oxford 2002; FRSM 1972, FRCPath 1986 (MRCPath 1974), FRCP 1990 (MRCP 1972), FFPHM 1994 (MFPHM 1989), FRSA 2002; *Style—* Dr Diana Walford, CBE; ✉ UCLH NHS Foundation Trust, Trust Headquarters, 2nd Floor Central, 250 Euston Road, London NW1 2PG (e-mail diana.walford@mansfield.ox.ac.uk)

WALFORD, Prof Geoffrey; *b* 30 April 1949, London; *Educ* Univ of Kent (BSc, PhD), Open Univ (BA, MSc, MBA), Univ of Oxford (PGCE, MA, MPhil, DLitt), Univ of London (MA); *Career* SSRC conversion fell St John's Coll Oxford 1976–78; Aston Univ: lectr in sociology of educn 1979–83, lectr in educn policy and mgmnt 1983–90, sr lectr in sociology and educn policy 1990–94; Univ of Oxford: fell Green Coll 1995–2008, lectr in educnl studies 1995–97, reader in educn policy 1997–2000, prof of educn policy 2000–, jr proctor 2001–02, fell Green Templeton Coll 2008–; series ed Studies in Educnl Ethnography 1997–2008, jt ed Br Jl of Educnl Studies 1999–2002 (memb Editorial Bd 1998–2002), ed Oxford Review of Educn 2004–10 (memb Editorial Bd 2001–), dep ed Ethnography and Educn 2005–; memb Editorial Bd: Jl of Educn Policy 1995–, Br Educnl Research Jl 1996–99 and 2004–10, Int Jl of Research and Method in Educn 2004–10, Diaspora, Indigenous and Minority Educn 2005–12; author of more than 100 academic articles and book chapters; *Books* Life in Public Schools (1986), Restructuring Universities: Politics and Power in the Management of Change (1987), Privatization and Privilege in Education (1990), City Technology College (jtly, 1991), Doing Educational Research (ed, 1991), Choice and Equity in Education (1994), Researching the Powerful in Education (ed, 1994), Educational Politics: Pressure Groups and Faith-Based Schools (1995), Affirming the Comprehensive Ideal (jt ed, 1997), Doing Research About Education (ed, 1998), Policy, Politics and Education: Sponsored Grant-Maintained Schools and Religious Diversity (2000), Doing Qualitative Educational Research (2001), Private Schooling: Tradition and Diversity (2005), Markets and Equity in Education (2006), How to do Educational Ethnography (2008), Blair's Educational Legacy (2010), Privatisation, Education and Social Justice (ed, 2016); *Recreations* reading, travel, walking; *Style—* Prof Geoffrey Walford; ✉ Department of Education, University of Oxford, 15 Norham Gardens, Oxford OX2 6PY (☎ 01865 274141, e-mail geoffrey.walford@education.ox.ac.uk)

WALFORD, His Hon John de Guise; s of Edward Wynn Walford (d 1989), and Dorothy Ann, *née* Bouchier (d 2010); *b* 23 February 1948; *Educ* Sedbergh, Queens' Coll Cambridge (MA); *m* 30 July 1977, Pamela Elizabeth, da of Dr Peter Russell; 1 da (Caroline Louise b 6 May 1978), 1 s (Charles de Guise b 17 Sept 1979); *Career* called to the Bar Middle Temple 1971, in practice NE Circuit 1974–93, recorder of the Crown Court 1989–93 (asst recorder 1985–89), standing counsel (Criminal) DSS NE Circuit 1991–93, circuit judge (NE Circuit) 1993–2015; chllr Diocese of Bradford 1999–2015; *Recreations* cricket, tennis, opera, watching Middlesbrough FC; *Clubs* Hawks' (Cambridge), Free Foresters CC; *Style—* His Hon John Walford

WALKER; *see also:* Forestier-Walker

WALKER, Adam Christopher; s of Terence Jolley, and Sheila, *née* Baron; *b* 26 September 1967, Leicester; *Educ* Uppingham (top entrance scholar), Univ of Newcastle (BA); *m* 3

Nov 1995, Yvonne, *née* Leckie; 3 s (Sebastian Charles b 31 May 1997, Frederick Alexander b 18 May 1999, Samuel Joseph b 18 Sept 2004), 1 da (Eloise Rose b 18 Dec 2006); *Career* corp fin mangr Touche Ross & Co 1989–94, assoc dir corp fin NatWest Markets 1994–98, dir Arthur Andersen 1998–2000, jt md GorillaPark 2000–01, gp fin dir Nat Express Gp plc 2003– (head of corp devpt 2001–03), fin dir Informa plc 2008–13, gp fin dir GKN plc 2014–; ACA 1992; *Recreations* cricket, rugby, opera, theatre; *Style*— Adam Walker, Esq; ✉ GKN plc, Ipsley House, Ipsley Church Lane, Redditch B98 0TL (e-mail adam.walker@gkn.com)

WALKER, Alan Edward; s of Ben Walker, of Fort Worth, TX, and Hilda, *née* Roberts (d 2002); *b* 13 November 1965, Bury, Lancs; *Educ* Bury GS, Magdalene Coll Cambridge (BA, Norah Dias Prize, scholar (hc), LLM), Guildford Law Sch; *Career* slr; Addleshaw Booth & Co 1989–2000; ptnr: Cobbetts LLP 2000–13, DWF LLP 2013–; memb: Property Litigation Assoc, Law Soc, Dilapidations Forum; *Style*— Alan Walker, Esq; ✉ DWF LLP, 1 Scott Place, 2 Hardman Street, Manchester M3 3AA (☎ 0161 838 0464, e-mail alan.walker@dwf.co.uk)

WALKER, Prof Andrew Charles; s of Maurice Frederick Walker, of Harrow, Middx, and Margaret Florence, *née* Rust; *b* 24 June 1948, Wembley, London; *Educ* Kingsbury County GS, Univ of Essex (BA, MSc, PhD); *m* 2 April 1972, Margaret Elizabeth, da of Arthur Mortimer, of Heckmondwike, W Yorks; 2 c (Edmund, Abigail (twins) b 1978); *Career* Nat Res Cncl of Canada postdoctoral fell Ottawa Canada 1972–74, Sci Res Cncl fell Dept of Physics Univ of Essex 1974–75, sr scientific offr UK AEA Culham Laboratory 1975–83; Heriot-Watt Univ: lectr in physics 1983–85, reader then prof of physics 1985–88, chair of modern optics 1988–, dir of postgrad studies 1998–2001, dep princ (resources) 2001–06, vice princ 2006–10, sr dep princ 2010–13, prof emeritus 2013–; sec and treas Carnegie Tst for the Univs of Scotland 2013–; memb Ctee: Quantum Electronics Gp Inst of Physics 1979–85 (hon sec 1982–85), Scottish Branch Inst of Physics 1985–88; memb: SERC/DTI Advance Devices and Materials Ctee 1992–94; chm Scottish Branch Inst of Physics 1993–95 (vice-chm 1991–93, past chm 1995–97); dir: Terahertz Photonics Ltd 1998–2000 (chm of Bd), Edinburgh Business Sch 2001–, Technology Ventures Scotland 2002–05, SeeByte Ltd 2008–13, Heriot-Watt Univ Malaysia Sdn Bhd 2011–13 (ceo 2011–12); tstee: RSE Scotland Fndn 2003–05 (chm 2004–05), Scottish Bldg Fedn Edinburgh and Dist Charitable Tst; author of over 200 scientific articles and letters in the field of optoelectronics; FInstP 1987, FRSE 1994 (memb Cncl and sec for meetings 1998–2001, vice-pres 2001–04, fellowship sec 2005–08); *Recreations* music (piano), sailing; *Clubs* Cramond Boat, Commodore; *Style*— Prof Andrew Walker, FRSE; ✉ Carnegie Trust for the Universities of Scotland, Andrew Carnegie House, Pittencrieff Street, Dunfermline, Fife KY12 8AW

WALKER, (Hon) Anna; CB (2003); *née* Butterworth; er da of Baron Butterworth, CBE (Life Peer, d 2003); *b* 5 May 1951; *Educ* Oxford HS, Benenden, Bryn Mawr Coll USA (ESU scholarship), Lady Margaret Hall Oxford (MA); *m* 1983, Timothy Edward Hanson Walker, *qv*, s of Harris Walker; 3 da (Sophie (adopted) b 1975, Beth b 1984, Polly b 1986); *Career* Br Cncl 1972–73, CBI 1973–74; HM Civil Serv: ME Div DTI 1975–76, Post and Telecommunications Div DTI 1976–77, private sec to Sec of State for Industry 1977–78, princ Shipping Policy Div DTI 1979–83, princ Fin Div DTI 1983–84, interdepartmental review of budgetary control 1985–86, Cabinet Office 1986–87, Personnel Div 1987–88, asst sec Competition Policy Div DTI 1988–91, dir of competition Office of Telecommunications (Oftel) 1991–94, dep DG Oftel 1994–97, dep DG Energy DTI 1998, DG Energy DTI 1998–2001, DG (land use and rural affrs) DEFRA 2001–03, chief exec Healthcare Cmmn 2004–09, chm Office of Rail and Road 2009–15; memb Bd Consumer Focus 2008–11, chair Ind Review of Household Water and Sewerage Charging 2008–09, chair Young Epilepsy 2009–, memb Bd Welsh Water 2011–, memb Cncl Which? 2013–; *Recreations* travel, cycling, family; *Style*— Mrs Anna Walker, CB; ✉ Office of Rail Regulation, One Kemble Street, London WC2B 4AN (☎ 020 7282 3696, e-mail anna@aebwalker.com)

WALKER, Charles; OBE (2015), MP; *Educ* Univ of Oregon; *m* Fiona; 2 s (Alistair, James), 1 da (Charlotte); *Career* former dir Blue Arrow; cncllr Wandsworth BC 2002–06; MP (Cons) Broxbourne 2005– (Parly candidate (Cons) Ealing N 2001); *Style*— Charles Walker, Esq, OBE, MP; ✉ House of Commons, London SW1A 0AA (☎ 020 7219 3000)

WALKER, David; s of Francis Allen Walker (d 1994), of Tibshelf, Derbys, and Dorothy, *née* Buck; *b* 23 October 1947; *Educ* Tupton Hall GS, Hertford Coll Oxford (BA, 4 times Soccer blue, capt Univ XI); *m* 1972, Elizabeth Grace, *née* Creswell; 2 s (Simon David, Mark Jonathan (twins) b 17 Aug 1975), 1 da (Kathryn Elizabeth b 25 Feb 1978); *Career* graduate trainee Marley Buildings Ltd 1970–72; E J Arnold & Son Ltd: area mangr 1972–74, product mangr 1974–77, merchandise mangr 1977–79, divnl dir 1979–84; Lex Volvo (subsid of Lex Service plc): gen mangr 1984–86, ops dir 1987–89, divnl dir 1990–94; md Hyundai Car (UK) Ltd (now subsid of RAC plc) 1994–; MCIM; *Recreations* walking, cycling; *Style*— David Walker, Esq; ✉ Hyundai Car (UK) Ltd, St Johns Court, Easton Street, High Wycombe, Buckinghamshire HP11 1JX (☎ 01494 428600, fax 01494 428699)

WALKER, David; s of John Walker, and Irene, *née* Connor; *b* 8 November 1950; *Educ* Corby GS, St Catharine's Coll Cambridge (scholarship, Figgis Prize, sr scholarship, MA), Univ of Sussex/Ecole Pratique des Hautes Etudes (MA); *m* 9 Feb 1974 (m dis 1997), Karen; 1 s (Michael b 7 Dec 1982); *Career* sr reporter Times Higher Educn Supplement 1973–77, Harkness fell, congressional fell and visiting scholar Graduate Sch of Public Policy Univ of Calif Berkeley 1977–79, journalist Britain section The Economist 1979–81, local govt corr and ldr writer The Times 1981–86, chief ldr writer London Daily News 1987, public admin corr The Times 1987–90, chief ldr writer The Independent 1996–98, writer and section ed The Guardian 1998–2004, ed Guardian Public magazine 2004–08 (contrib ed 2010–); md communications and public reporting Audit Cmmn 2008–10, dir getstats Royal Statistical Soc 2011–13, head of policy Acad of Social Sciences 2014–16; presenter Analysis (BBC Radio) 1988–; non-exec dir Places for People Gp 1999–2003; memb Cncl ESRC 2007–13, memb Ethics and Governance Cncl UK Biobank 2014–; non-exec dir and dep chair CNLW Tst 2011–; tstee: National Centre for Social Res 2002–09, Nuffield Tst 2007–09; tstee Franco-Br Cncl (Br Section) 2007–; hon memb CIPFA; hon dr Univ of Aberdeen 2015; *Books* Media Made in California (1981), Municipal Empire (1983), Sources Close to the Prime Minister (1984), The Times Guide to the State (1995), Public Relations in Local Government (1997); with Polly Toynbee: Did Things Get Better (2001), Better or Worse (2005), Unjust Rewards (2008), The Verdict (2010), Dogma and Disarray: Cameron at Half Time (2012), Cameron's Coup (2015), Exaggerated Claims? The ESRC 50 years on (2016); *Recreations* tennis, clarinet, running; *Clubs* Reform; *Style*— David Walker, Esq; ✉ 2 Eton College Road, London NW3 2BS (e-mail davidwlkr0@gmail.com, Twitter @exauditor77)

WALKER, Sir David Alan; kt (1991); *b* 31 December 1939; *Educ* Chesterfield Sch, Queens' Coll Cambridge (MA); *m* 20 April 1963, Isobel, *née* Cooper; 2 da (Elspeth b 4 June 1966, Penelope b 12 April 1970), 1 s (Jonathan b 29 Jan 1968); *Career* HM Treasy: joined 1961, private sec to Jt Perm Sec 1964–66, seconded Staff IMF Washington 1970–73, asst sec 1973–77; Bank of England: chief advsr then chief Econ Intelligence Dept, asst dir 1980, exec dir fin and indust 1982–88; chm: ohnson Matthey Bankers Ltd (later Minories Finance Ltd) 1985–88, Securities and Investments Bd 1988–1992, The Agricultural Mortgage Corp plc 1993–94; exec chm Morgan Stanley Group (Europe) plc (latterly Morgan Stanley Dean Witter (Europe) Ltd) 1994–2006 (sr advsr 2006–), chm Barclays plc 2012–15, chm Winton Capital 2015–; dep chm Lloyds Bank plc 1992–94, dir Morgan Stanley Inc 1994–97, exec chm Morgan Stanley International Inc 1995–2001 (currently sr adviser); chm RVC Europe Ltd; non-exec dir: Bank of England until 1993, National Power plc 1993–94, British Invisibles 1993–, Reuters Holdings plc 1994–2000, Legal & General 2002– (vice-chm 2004–); chm Financial Markets Gp LSE 1987–94, pt/t memb Bd CEGB 1987–89, nominated memb Cncl Lloyd's 1988–92; chm Exec Ctee Int Orgn of Securities Cmmns 1990–92; govr: Henley Mgmnt Coll 1993–99, LSE 1993–95; memb and treas Gp of Thirty 1993–; co-chm Cambridge Univ 800th Anniversary Campaign 2005–; hon fell Queens' Coll Cambridge, Hon LLD Univ of Exeter 2002; *Recreations* music, long-distance walking; *Clubs* Reform; *Style*— Sir David Walker

WALKER, Air Marshal Sir David Allan; KCVO (2011, MVO 1992), OBE (1995); s of Allan Walker (d 1999), and late Audrey, *née* Brothwell; *b* 14 July 1956; *Educ* City of London Sch, Univ of Bradford (RAF cadet, BSc), RAF Coll; *m* 1983, Jane Alison, *née* Calder; *Career* equerry to HM The Queen 1989–92, loan serv South Africa 1994, Cmd RAF Halton 1997–98, dir Corp Communications RAF 1998–2002, dir Personnel and Trg Policy RAF 2002–03, AOC RAF Trg Gp and chief exec Trg Gp Defence Agency 2003–04, Master HM Household 2005–, Extra Equerry to HM The Queen 2005; vice-patron Royal Int Air Tatoo, hon pres London Wing ATC 2012; MCIPD; *Recreations* walking dogs, keeping fit(ish), old cars, shooting, military history; *Clubs* Army and Navy, RAF, Royal Over-Seas League; *Style*— Air Marshal Sir David Walker, KCVO, OBE; ✉ Buckingham Palace, London SW1A 1AA

WALKER, Rt Rev David Stuart; *see:* Manchester, Bishop of

WALKER, Rt Rev Dominic Edward William Murray; DL (2014); *b* 28 June 1948; *Educ* Plymouth Coll, KCL (AKC), Heythrop Coll London (MA), Univ of Wales (LLM); *Career* ordained priest 1972, chaplain to the Bishop of Southwark 1973–76, rector of Newington 1976–85, rural dean of Southwark and Newington 1980–85, team rector and rural dean of Brighton 1985–97, canon and prebendary of Chichester Cathedral 1985–97, bishop of Reading 1997–2003, bishop of Monmouth 2003–13, ret; hon asst bishop Diocese of Swansea and Brecon 2013–; memb Oratory of the Good Shepherd (father supr 1990–96); vice-pres RSPCA 2001–, pres Anglican Soc for the Welfare of Animals 2008; govr: Univ of Wales Newport 2003–10, St Michael's Coll Llandaff 2003–13; Hon DLitt Univ of Brighton; OGS; *Publications* The Ministry of Deliverance (1997); *Style*— The Rt Rev Dominic Walker, OGS, DL; ✉ 2 St Vincent's Drive, Monmouth NP25 5DS (☎ 01600 772151, e-mail dwalker@ogs.net)

WALKER, Dorothy (Lady Lauriston); da of John Walker (d 1982), and Dorothy, *née* Reid (d 2008); *b* 18 July 1957; *Educ* Montrose Acad, Inst of Archaeology Univ of London (BA); *m* 1985, William Newlands of Lauriston, *qv*; *Career* conslt Comshare 1981–87, mktg mangr Digital Equipment Corp 1987–94, ed-in-chief Boston Morgan London 1994–2001, dir 1994–2001 & 2015–; writer; columnist Times Educational Supplement; contrib: The Times, Sunday Times, Mail on Sunday, Evening Standard, Daily Telegraph, The Guardian, The Independent, The Scotsman, Saga Magazine; Technology Writer of the Year BT Technology Awards 1997; first runner-up Miss United Kingdom 1977; hon sec Convention of the Baronage of Scotland 1998–2004; govr Sons and Friends of the Clergy; memb Incorporation of Wrights in Glasgow (Master Court, Deacon's Key 2013–14, Collector 2014–15, Deacon 2016–17), memb Hatfield Guild of Coll Youths, Freeman City of London, Liveryman Worshipful Co of Basketmakers, memb Guild of Freemen City of London; memb Soc of Authors; FSA Scot; *Books* Education in the Digital Age (1998); *Clubs* Bluebird, City Livery, Western (Glasgow); *Style*— Lady Lauriston; ✉ Suite 45, 405 Kings Road, London SW10 0BB (☎ 020 7351 6468); Lauriston Castle, St Cyrus, Kincardineshire DD10 0DJ (☎ 01674 850488, e-mail mail@dorothywalker.com, website www.writeabetterbid.com)

WALKER, Canon Dr Ian Robert; s of Robert Douglas Walker, and Rhoda Walker; *Educ* Bankers' Inst of Australasia (ABIA), Melbourne Theol Coll (LTh), Univ of Bristol (BA), Univ of Wales Swansea (PhD); *Career* head of religious studies Badminton Sch 1977–79, tutor Univ of Wales Swansea 1978, head of religious studies Dulwich Coll 1979–86, headmaster King's Sch Rochester 1986–2012; dir Quintillion 2012–; memb HMC 1986–2012; lay canon and memb Chapter Rochester Cathedral 1998–2008; Freeman City of London, Liveryman Worshipful Soc of Apothecaries; FCP 1988, FRSA 1992; Knight Grand Cross Order of St George (Hungary) 2004; *Publications* Plato's Euthyphro (1984), Christ in the Community (1990), Classroom Classics (1991), Faith and Belief: A Philosophical Approach (1994); numerous academic articles on philosophy; *Recreations* writing, oil painting, cricket, Egyptology; *Clubs* Athenaeum; *Style*— Canon Dr Ian Walker; ✉ e-mail ian.kerriewalker@gmail.com

WALKER, Prof Isobel Deda; da of Dr Thomas Alfred Christie, of Auchterarder, Perthshire, and Edith Anderson, *née* Young; *b* 4 October 1944; *Educ* Jordanhill Coll Sch Glasgow, Univ of Glasgow (MB, ChB, MD); *m* 13 April 1966, Dr Colin Alexander Walker; 2 s (Jason b 1969, Lewis b 1975), 3 da (Nicola b 1972, Emily b 1979, Abigail b 1982); *Career* conslt haematologist Glasgow Royal Infirmary 1978–, hon prof Univ of Glasgow 2003–; dir UK Nat External Quality Assurance Scheme (NEQAS) in Blood Coagulation 2005–; pres Br Soc for Haematology 1999–2000, pres Scottish Haematology Soc 2002–, chair Scottish Regnl Cncl RCPath 2004–; FRCPath 1984, FRCPEd 1985; *Recreations* French language, needlework, opera; *Style*— Prof Isobel Walker; ✉ Department of Haematology, Glasgow Royal Infirmary, Castle Street, Glasgow G40 1SF (☎ 0141 552 5692, fax 0141 211 4919)

WALKER, James Michael; s of Alan Walker, and Pamela, *née* Senior; *b* 24 May 1965; *Educ* Allerton Grange Sch Leeds, LSE (BSc(Econ)); *m* 11 Sept 1992, Siân, *née* Salt; 1 s (George Hubert b 1994), 1 da (Olivia Grace b 1997); *Career* dir of media consultancy Henley Centre 1995–97, jt md J Walter Thompson & Co London 1997–98, worldwide chm ATG MindShare 1998–, fndr Edge Marketing 1999–2003, chm Brand Science 1999–2003; Accenture: EMEA md Accenture Marketing Sciences (AMS) 2003, ptnr 2003, pres Int Accenture Marketing Sciences 2008; md MOFILM 2010–11, sr ptnr Prophet 2011–; *Style*— James Walker, Esq; ✉ The Smithy, Plough Lane, Chester CH3 7BA

WALKER, Janet Sheila; da of David Walker, of Chew Magna, Bristol, and Sheila, *née* Rapps; *b* 21 April 1953; *Educ* Keynsham GS, Somerville Coll Oxford (MA), L'Institut des Hautes Études Internationales Univ of Nice; *Career* Price Waterhouse 1976–80 (qualified FCA), chief accountant Handmade Films 1980–81, cost controller Channel 4 1981–82, head of prog fin Thames TV 1982–84, London Films and Limehouse 1984–87, fin dir British Screen Finance 1987–88, dep dir of fin Channel 4 1988–94 (concurrently UK rep EURIMAGES film funding orgn), fin controller for regnl broadcasting BBC 1994–96, fin dir Granada Media Group 1996–98, dir of fin and business affrs Channel 4 1998–2003, commercial and fin dir Ascot Racecourse 2003–10; bursar Eton Coll 2011–; non-exec dir: Pizza Express plc 1999–2003, Design Council 2006–10, Henderson High Income Trust plc 2007–, Royal Holloway Coll 2009–10, BAFTA 2013–2015; *Style*— Miss Janet Walker; ✉ Eton College, Windsor SL4 6DJ (☎ 01753 370540)

WALKER, Janey P W; da of Brig Harry Walker (d 1968), and Patsy, *née* Iuel-Brockdorff; *b* 10 April 1958; *Educ* Brechin HS, Benenden Sch, Univ of York (BA), Univ of Chicago Illinois (Benton fell); *m* 26 July 1997, Hamish Mykura; 2 da (twins b 2000); *Career* prodr: BBC News and Current Affrs 1982–87, The Late Show BBC TV 1989–91, Edge WNET New York City 1991–92; BBC New York 1992–95, series ed Wired World Wall to Wall TV 1995–96, commissioning ed arts and music Channel Four Television Corp 1996–99, managing ed commissioning Channel Four Television Corp 1999–2010 (also head of educn 2006–10); memb Ofcom Content Bd 2011–; *Recreations* visual arts, modern fiction, walking; *Style*— Ms Janey Walker; ✉ e-mail walker.jenny@gmail.com

W

WALKER, Jeremy; s of Raymond St John (Henry) Walker (d 1980), and Mary, *née* Dudley; *b* 12 July 1949; *Educ* Brentwood Sch, Univ of Birmingham (BA, Barber Prize for local history); *m* 1968, June, da of Robert Lockhart; 2 s (Patrick b 1968, Toby b 1974), 1 da (Tamsin b 1969); *Career* civil servant; admin trainee Dept of Employment 1971–73, private sec to chm MSC 1974–76, princ Health & Safety Executive 1976–77, Economic Secretariat Cabinet Office 1977–79, princ Employment Service MSC 1979–82, asst sec Australian Dept of Employment & Indust Rels Canberra 1982–84, regnl employment mangr for Yorks & Humberside MSC 1984–86, head of community progs and new job trg scheme MSC 1986–88, regnl dir Yorks & Humberside Dept of Employment 1988–94 (ldr Leeds/Bradford City Action Team 1990–94), regnl dir Govt Office for Yorkshire and the Humber 1994–99, chief exec North Yorks CC 1999–2005, public policy conslt 2005–; chm Yorks Regnl Flood Defence Ctee 2005–09, chair Regnl Advsy Ctee for Yorks and Humber Forestry Cmmn 2007–13, memb Bd Environment Agency 2009–15, chair Slowing the Flow Partnership 2009–, chair N Yorks Timber Freight Partnership 2011–, chair Yorks and Humber Climate Change Partnership 2013–16, memb N Yorks Moors Nat Park Authy 2013–; *Recreations* gardening, walking; *Style*— Jeremy Walker, Esq

WALKER, Johnnie (né Peter Waters Dingley); MBE (2006); *b* 30 March 1945, Solihull, W Midlands; *Educ* Solihull Sch, Gloucester Tech Coll; *m* 1, 1971 (m dis), Frances; 1 s (Sam), 1 da (Beth); m 2, 2002, Tiggy; *Career* radio disk jockey; early career with Swingin Radio England and Radio Caroline; BBC Radio 1: Saturday show 1969–70, weekday morning show 1970–71, weekday early afternoon show 1971–76, The Saturday Sequence 1987–88 and 1991–95; BBC GLR 1988–91, The AM Alternative (BBC Radio 5) 1991–94; BBC Radio 2: joined 1997, Drivetime 1999–2006, Sunday show 2006–, Pirate Johnnie Walker 2009–; Sony Gold Award 2004; *Books* Johnnie Walker - The Autobiography (2007); *Recreations* photography, motor cycling, walking; *Clubs* Union; *Style*— Johnnie Walker, Esq, MBE; ✉ BBC Radio 2, Western House, 99 Great Portland Street, London W1W 7NY

WALKER, Malcolm Conrad; CBE (1995); s of Willie Walker (d 1960), and Ethel Mary, *née* Ellam (d 1987); *b* 11 February 1946, Huddersfield, W Yorks; *Educ* Mirfield GS; *m* 4 Oct 1969, (Nest) Rhianydd, da of Benjamin Jones (d 1976); 3 c; *Career* trainee mangr F W Woolworth & Co 1964–71, jt fndr and exec chm Iceland Frozen Foods plc 1970–2001, fndr Cooltrader 2001, chief exec Iceland Foods Ltd 2005–; chm Individual Restaurant Co 2011–; *Recreations* skiing, family, home; *Style*— Malcolm Walker, Esq, CBE; ✉ Iceland Foods Ltd, Second Avenue, Deeside Industrial Park, Deeside, Flintshire CH5 2NW

WALKER, Prof Martin; *Educ* Univ of Newcastle upon Tyne (BA, PhD); *m* Carolyn Emma Walker; *Career* reader in accounting and finance LSE, prof of accounting and business computing Univ of Dundee; Univ of Manchester: prof of finance and accounting 1989–, head of accounting and finance 1990–94, dean Faculty of Social Sciences and Law 2000–03; jt ed Jl of Business Finance and Accounting; *Books* Information and Capital Markets (with Norman Strong, 1987); *Style*— Prof Martin Walker; ✉ Manchester Business School, The University of Manchester, Booth Street West, Manchester M15 6PB

WALKER, Matthew Benedict (Matt); MBE (2009); s of late Alan Walker, of Stockport, Cheshire, and Anne, *née* Durward; *b* 25 April 1978, Stockport, Cheshire; *Educ* Univ of Manchester (MA); *m* 2013, Rachel Walker; 1 da (Grace Alana); *Career* Paralympic swimmer; achievements incl: 2 Silver medals (50m freestyle and 100m freestyle) European Championships 1997, Bronze medal 100m breaststroke European Championships 1997, Gold medal 50m freestyle World Championships 1998, Bronze medal 100m breaststroke World Championships 1998, Gold medal 4x100m freestyle Paralympics Sydney 2000, Athens 2004 and Beijing 2008, Silver medal 50m freestyle Paralympics Sydney 2000 and Athens 2004, Bronze medal 100m breaststroke Paralympics Sydney 2000, Silver medal 100m freestyle Paralympics Athens 2004, Gold medal 4x50m freestyle Paralympic World Cup 2006, Bronze medal 50m freestyle Cwlth Games Melbourne 2006, Gold medal 3x100m freestyle IPC World Championships Durban 2006, 2 Bronze medals (50m freestyle and 100m freestyle) IPC World Championships Durban 2006, Gold medal 50m freestyle Paralympic World Cup 2007, Bronze medal 50m freestyle Paralympic World Cup 2008, 2 Silver medals (50m freestyle and 50m butterfly) Paralympics Beijing 2008, 2 Bronze medals (100m freestyle and 200m individual medley) Paralympics Beijing 2008, Silver medal 50m freestyle Paralympic World Cup 2009, Bronze medal 100m freestyle Paralympic World Cup 2009, 4 Gold medals (50m freestyle, 100m freestyle, 50m butterfly and freestyle relay) IPC European Swimming Championships Reykjavik 2009, Silver medal 200m individual medley IPC European Swimming Championships Reykjavik 2009, Gold medal 50m freestyle IPC World Swimming Championships Rio de Janeiro 2009, Silver medal 100m freestyle IPC World Swimming Championships Rio de Janeiro 2009, 2 Bronze medals (100m individual medley and freestyle relay) IPC World Swimming Championships Rio de Janeiro 2009, Gold medal 50m freestyle European Championships 2011, Bronze medal 50m freestyle Paralympic Games 2012, Gold Medal 50m freestyle IPC World Championships Montreal 2013; swimming coach Marple Swimming Club 2001 (head coach 2009), head coach Paddles Disability Swimming Club Leek, head coach Matt Walker Disability Swimming Academy; ambass for CP Sport and Diane Modahl Sports Fndn; Stockport Young Sports Person of the Year 1997, Cerebral Palsy Swimmer of the Year 1998, 2005 and 2009, BT Five Nations Challenge Trophy 2000, Stockport Sports Personality of the Year 2000, BBC Sports Personality Team of the Year 2000, John Wilkinson Swimming Trophy 2000 and 2006, Imagine FM Local Hero Award 2004, Splash Award Male Disability Swimmer of the Year 2006, John Wright Trophy for Outstanding Service in Cheshire County 2008, 2009 and 2010, Swimmer of the Year COMAST (City of Manchester Swimming Team) 2013–14; ldr Cub Scouts; *Style*— Matt Walker, Esq, MBE; ✉ c/o Marple Swimming Club, Stockport, Cheshire SK6 6AA

WALKER, Dr Michael John; s of Stephen Thomas Walker, of Mount Bures, Suffolk, and Sheila, *née* Ereaut; *b* 24 November 1955, Colchester, Essex; *Educ* Colchester Royal GS, CCC Cambridge (BA, PhD, Manners scholarship), Univ of Cambridge (PGCE, coll award); *m* 1, 1977 (m dis 2005), Rita Carpenter; 1 s (David Alexander b 5 July 1985), 2 da (Sarah Frances b 29 March 1987, Anna Bridget Grace b 13 May 1995); m 2, 2007 (m dis 2014), Corinne Anne Francis; *Career* visiting lectr Birmingham-Southern Coll AL 1977–78, supervisor Univ of Cambridge 1978–82; Dulwich Coll: asst history master 1982–86, housemaster 1983–86; head history Gresham's Sch 1986–89; King Edward VI GS Chelmsford: sr teacher 1989–92, second dep head 1992–94, first dep head 1994–99, headmaster 1999–2008, headmaster Felsted Sch 2008–; memb: SHA 2002–, HMC 2008–; fndr and memb Steering Gp Consortium for Sch Improvement in Essex, chm Consortium of Selective Schs in Essex 2003–04 (vice-chair 2000–03), memb Nat Leading Edge Steering Gp 2003–04, lead memb Nat Heads' Gp Innovation Unit DfES 2005–07, Next Practice project Higher Level Teaching Skills 2006, Core Gp memb UK ARIA project on assessment 2007–08, memb Bd London Academies and Enterprise Tst 2012– (memb Curriculum Advsy Gp 2012–); vice-pres Helen Rollason Cancer Care Tst, memb Bd Tom Clark Appeal (Teenage Cancer Tst); memb Old Chelmsfordians Assoc, memb European Round Square Heads' Conference 2010–, tstee Friends of the Round Square 2012–, dir European Region Round Square 2013–, memb Strategic Planning Ctee Round Square World Bd 2013; govr Sutton Valence Sch 2012–, govr Petchey Acad 2012–; visiting fell (Michaelmas term) Fitzwilliam Coll Univ of Cambridge 2014; FRSA 2006; *Recreations* art, design, set design, reading, walking, photography, painting, squash, tennis; *Clubs* Essex; *Style*— Dr Michael Walker; ✉ Felsted School, Felsted, Essex CM6 3LL (☎ 01371 822600, fax 01371 822607, e-mail info@felsted.org)

WALKER, Nigel Keith; DL (S Glamorgan 2003); s of Frank George Walker, and Joyce Merle, *née* Foster; *b* 15 June 1963; *Educ* Rumney HS, Open Univ, Univ of Glamorgan; *m* Mary; 3 da (Rebecca b Aug 1993, Eleanor b March 1995, Abigail b 18 Dec 1997); *Career* former athlete and rugby player; with Cardiff Athletics Club; honours at 110m hurdles: UK champion 1983, AAA champion 1984, semi-finalist Olympic Games LA 1984, Bronze medal Euro Indoor Championships France and World Indoor Championships USA 1987; 26 UK int appearances 1983–92 (jr int 1980–82); ret from athletics 1992; debut for Cardiff RFC 1992, debut for Wales 1993 v Ireland; ret from rugby 1998; civil servant 1982–93, devpt offr Sports Cncl for Wales 1993–97, fitness conslt Cardiff RFC 1996–97; presenter: HTV 1996–2000, Channel Four Athletics 1998–99, commentator Eurosport 1999–2001; player devpt mangr Welsh Rugby Union 2000–01; BBC Wales: head of sport 2001–08, head of change and internal communications 2009–10; nat dir English Inst of Sport 2010–; memb Bd UK Sport 2006–10, memb Bd Cwlth Games Eng 2015–; *Recreations* DIY, journalism; *Style*— Nigel Walker, Esq, DL; ✉ Ground Floor, 21 Bloomsbury Street, London WC1B 3HF

WALKER, Dr Paul Crawford; s of Dr Joseph Viccars Walker, KHS (d 1986), of Northants, and Mary Tilley, *née* Crawford (d 1984); *b* 9 December 1940; *Educ* Queen Elizabeth GS Darlington, Downing Coll Cambridge (MA, MB BChir); *m* 1962, Barbara Georgina, da of Albert Edward Bliss, of Cambs; 3 da (Kate, Victoria, Caroline); *Career* Capt RAMC(V) 1975–78; regnl med offr NE Thames RHA 1977–85, gen mangr Frenchay HA 1985–88, hon conslt in community med Bristol and Weston HA 1988–89, dir public health Norwich HA 1989–93, dir Centre for Health Policy Res UEA 1990–93, sr lectr Univ of Wales Coll of Med 1993–1994; dir Independent Public Health 1993–, dir of public health Powys Local Health Bd 2003–05, dir of public health Ceredigion Local Health Bd 2004–05; chm CAER Consortium 1985–89; memb: Exec Ctee Gtr London Alcohol Advsy Service 1978–85, Mgmnt Ctee Kings Fund Centre 1980–84, NHS Computer Policy Ctee 1984–85, Advsy Cncl on Misuse of Drugs 1984–87, Bristol and District Community Health Cncl 1996–99, Avon Probation Ctee 1997–99, Avon and Somerset Police Authy 1998–99; Essex Cmmn for the Peace 1980–85, Avon Cmmn for the Peace 1985–89 and 1995–2006; vice-chm Professional Advsy Gp NHSTA 1987–88, pres Socialist Health Assoc 2003–08 (vice-pres 1999–2003), chm Welsh Food Alliance 1998–2000, chm Welsh Public Health Assoc 2004– (sec 1998–2004), tstee UK Public Health Assoc 2004–, memb Bristol Link 2006–, memb Yeovil and District Fndn Tst 2006–; Powys Alliance for Health 1999–2003, Ceredigon Local Health Gp 2001–03; chm Transform Drug Policy Fndn 2007– (hon treas 2007), dir and tstee Lles Cymru Wellbeing Wales 2010–; jt ed Health Matters; hon sr lectr LSHTM 1983–85, visiting prof QMC London 1985, hon sr lectr UEA 1990–93; visiting fell: UWE 1999–2004, Univ of Glamorgan 2004–09; cncllr City and Co of Bristol 1995–99; *Publications* From Public Health to Wellbeing: The new driver for policy and action (2011); *Recreations* railway history, anthropology, music (particularly singing); *Clubs* RSM; *Style*— Dr Paul Walker; ✉ e-mail paulcrawfordwalker@googlemail.com

WALKER, Paul Mackenzie; s of David Gordon Mackenzie Walker (d 2001), and Jean Mackenzie Walker (d 2006); *b* 26 August 1960; *Educ* The High Sch Glasgow, Univ of Glasgow (MA), Strathclyde Graduate Business Sch (MBA), Univ of Northumbria (LLB, BVC, LLM); *m* 2006, Alison Johnston, da of Alistair Lindsay, of Dalry and Balmaclellan; 1 da (Emily b 2007); *Career* civil servant 1977–81; researcher House of Commons 1986–87; special advsr Corp Policy Dept Cumbria County Cncl 1987–92; asst regnl dir (Scotland and N England) CBI 1993–96, exec search conslt 1996–98; dir gen Fertiliser Manufacturer's Assoc 1998–2000; portfolio of writing, lecturing, consulting and mediation work 2000–; called to the Bar Lincoln's Inn 2004; CEDR accredited mediator 2006; Parly candidate (Scottish Cons & Unionist) gen elections of 1983 and 1987; memb Royal Naval Reserve 1997–2011, vol business mentor for Prince's Scottish Youth Business Tst 2001–11, memb Valuation Appeals Ctee for Fife; Elder Church of Scotland 1993–; FRSA, MCIArb; *Recreations* skiing, sailing (cruising), walking; *Clubs* Farmers'; *Style*— Paul M Walker, Esq; ✉ The Glebe, Collessie, Fife KY15 7RQ

WALKER, Richard John; OBE; s of George Walker (decd), and Gwendolen, *née* Clarke (decd); *b* 1952, Reading, Berks; *Educ* Woolverstone Hall Ipswich, Guildford Coll, St Peter's Coll Oxford (MA), Univ of Manchester (Dip, PGCE); *m* 1978, Lauren Michaela; 1 da (Rowan Frances b 1979), 1 s (William George Arthur b 1986); *Career* English teacher: Spain 1976–77 and 1980–81, Kuwait 1977–78; lectr Univ of Manchester 1979–80, sr lectr Coll of St Mark and St John 1989–92; Br Cncl: advsr to Thai govt 1983–85, dep dir literature Arts Dept 1985–87, asst dir of arts, culture and English Lagos Nigeria 1987–89, first sec (cultural) New Delhi India 1994–98, dir São Paulo Brazil 1998–2000, regnl dir East Asia 2000–05, dir Cyprus 2005–07, dir Greece 2007–, dir EU operations Brussels 2011–, dep regnl dir EU 2015–; Language for Literature, A Curious Child; reviews, articles in THES and Literary Review, radio drama and monologues on BBC Radio 3, 4 and World Service; *Recreations* travel, other cultures, arts especially literature, visual arts, history, sport: tennis, walking, football, cricket, rugby; *Clubs* Manchester United FC; *Style*— Richard Walker, Esq, OBE

WALKER, Hon Robin Caspar; MP; s of Lord Walker of Worcester, MBE, PC (Life Peer 1992, d 2010), and Tessa Joan, *née* Pout; *b* 12 April 1978; *Educ* St Paul's, Balliol Coll Oxford; *m* 9 April 2011, Charlotte Clementine, *née* Keenan; *Career* Property Map Ltd 2000–01, exec search I-Search Ltd 2001–03, Finsbury Gp Ltd 2003–10 (ptnr 2009); MP (Cons) Worcester 2010–; *Clubs* Carlton; *Style*— The Hon Robin Walker, MP; ✉ House of Commons, London SW1A 0AA (website www.walker4worcester.com)

WALKER, Sir Rodney Myerscough; kt (1996); s of Norman Walker (d 1943), of Wakefield, W Yorks, and Lucy, *née* Kitchen (d 1987); *b* 10 April 1943, Wakefield, W Yorks; *Educ* Thornes House GS Wakefield; *m* 16 March 1974, Anne Margaret, da of Walter Aspinall (d 1972), of Leeds; 2 s (Alexander b 1976, Timothy b 1977); *Career* currently controlling shareholder Myerscough Holdings Ltd; chm: The Rugby Football League 1993–2002, UK Sports Cncl 1997–2003, Wembley National Stadium Tst 2000–02, Empire Interactive plc 2000–06, Donington Park Estates 2000–05, Manchester 2002 Commonwealth Games until 2001, Leicester City plc until 2002, Goals Soccer Centres plc 2002–13, Spice Holdings plc 2002–08, Titanic Exhibitions 2003–04, World Snooker 2003–09, Healthcare Communications plc 2004–06, Archial Gp plc 2004–10, Skin Health Spa plc 2005–06, Lightsong Media Ltd 2009–, Brand Cellar Ltd 2011–13, Sports Pathways Ltd 2011–; chair 2014 Tour de France Grand Depart Delivery Ctee 2013–14, chair TdFHub 2014 Ltd 2014; former chm and pres Wakefield Round Table; pres: Wakefield Theatre Tst, Yorks Cancer Research 2002–, The Myerscough Charitable Tst 2003–, Amateur Athletics Assoc 2004–11; vice-chm NSPCC Full Stop Appeal 1998–2008, vice-pres Hospital Heartbeat Appeal 2004–12; tstee: St Oswald Charitable Tst, The Rowland St Oswald (1984) Charitable Tst, The Clarke Hall Farm Tst Ltd; first Wakefield Lifetime Achievement Award 2007, Yorkshire Man of the Year 2008; Freeman City of Wakefield 2012; Hon DUniv: Univ of Bradford, Univ of Huddersfield; *Recreations* charity work; *Clubs* IOD; *Style*— Sir Rodney Walker; ✉ Tower House, Bond Street, Wakefield, West Yorkshire WF1 2QP (☎ 01924 374349, fax 01924 374358, mobile 07802 252281, e-mail mail@sirrodneywalker.uk.com)

WALKER, Sarah Elizabeth Royle (Mrs R G Allum); CBE (1991); da of Alan Royle Walker, and Elizabeth Brownrigg; *b* 11 March 1943, Cheltenham, Glos; *Educ* Pate's GS for Girls Cheltenham, RCM; *m* 1972, Graham Allum; *Career* mezzo-soprano; maj appearances in Br, America, Aust, NZ, Europe; operatic debuts incl: Coronation of Poppea (Kent Opera 1969, San Francisco Opera 1981), La Calisto (Glyndebourne 1970), Les Troyens (Scottish Opera 1972, Wienstaatsoper 1980), princ mezzo-soprano ENO 1972–77, Die Meistersinger

(Chicago Lyric Opera 1977), Werther (Covent Gdn 1979), Giulio Caesare (Le Grand The?tre Metro Opera 1986), Mrs Sedley in Peter Grimes (La Scala Milan 2000); numerous recordings and videos incl title role in Britten's Gloriana; Prince Consort prof of singing RCM 1993–, prof Vocal Faculty RAM 2009–; vocal performance conslt GSMD 1999–; pres Cheltenham Bach Choir 1986–; FRCM 1987, LRAM, FGSM 2000, Hon RAM 2015; *Recreations* interior design, encouraging husband with gardening; *Clubs* Univ Women's; *Style*— Miss Sarah Walker, CBE; ✉ Cheffings, Witheridge, Tiverton, Devon EX16 8QD (✆ 01884 860132, e-mail megamezzo@sarahwalker.com, website www.sarahwalker.com and www.soundcloud.com/sarah-walker-1)

WALKER, Simon Edward John; s of Louis Charles Vivian Walker (d 1997), of London, and Joan Wallace, *née* Keith (d 1979); *b* 28 May 1953, South Africa; *Educ* South African Coll Sch Cape Town, Balliol Coll Oxford (pres Oxford Union); *m* Mary Virginia Strang; 1 s (Jeremy b 26 Oct 1985), 1 da (Gini b 3 June 1992); *Career* TV journalist NZ 1975–79, professional journalism fell Stanford Univ 1979–80, dir of communications/dir Parly Oppn Research Unit NZ 1980–84, concurrently presenter Fair Go (TVNZ); dir: Communicor Public Relations Wellington NZ 1984–89, NZ Centre for Independent Studies 1987–89; Hill & Knowlton: dep head of public affrs London 1989–90, dir of Euro public affrs and md Brussels 1990–94; ptnr Brunswick Group Ltd 1994–98 (special advsr to the PM No 10 Policy Unit 1996–97), dir of communications British Airways plc 1998–2003, seconded as communications sec to HM The Queen 2000–02, dir of corporate mktg and communications then advsr to the CEO and Chm Reuters plc 2003–07, ceo British Private Equity and Venture Capital Assoc 2007–11, DG IOD 2011–; chm Global Network of Directors' Insts 2016–; dir Comair Ltd (SA) 2000–01, chm Adamant Ventures 2011–15, non-exec dir Seven Dials PR 2012–15; memb: NZ Broadcasting Tbnl 1987–88, Better Regulations Cmmn 2006–08, Speaker's Advsy Cncl on Public Engagement House of Commons; tstee: NZ-UK Link Fndn 2003–09, Reuters Fndn, Jamestown UK Fndn; govr Westminster Fndn for Democracy 2015–; Hon DBA UWE 2015, Hon LLD Univ of Warwick 2016; PR Professional of the Year 2002; *Books* Rogernomics: Economic Reform in New Zealand 1984–1989 (ed, 1989); *Recreations* reading, politics, music, gardening; *Clubs* Athenaeum; *Style*— Simon Walker, Esq; ✉ 86 Brook Green, London W6 7BD (✆ 020 7602 3883, e-mail simon.walker@communicormedia.com); Institute of Directors, 116 Pall Mall, London SW1Y 5ED (✆ 020 7839 1233, e-mail simon.walker@iod.com)

WALKER, Simon Jeremy; s of Alan William Walker, of Oxon, and Shirley Ann Lillian, *née* Fremel; *b* 2 April 1967, London; *Educ* Abingdon Sch, Trent Poly (BA); *m* 11 Aug 1990, Frances Mary, da of William Godfrey Townsend; 1 da (Daisy Megan b 28 Dec 1996), 1 s (Benjamin John William b 13 May 1998); *Career* photographer; freelanced for various Br newspapers and magazines 1988–89, The Independent 1989, Sunday Telegraph 1990 (joined 1989), Sunday Express 1990–91, Sunday Times 1991; The Times: freelance 1993–95, joined staff 1995, news picture ed 2004–10; fndr and ceo Glopho Ltd 2010–14, media conslt 2014–; contrib Gamma Press Agency 1991–; dir Hall & Ptnrs 2015–; David Hodge/Observer Young Photojournalist of the Year 1987, Nikon Press Photographer of the Month July 1989, runner-up Most Promising Newcomer Category Br Press Photographer of the Year Awards 1990 (commended 1989), highly commended Nikon Royal Photographer of the Year 1998; FRSA 2002; *Books* Para – Inside the Parachute Regiment (1993); *Recreations* tennis, walking the dogs; *Clubs* Chelsea Arts; *Style*— Simon Walker, Esq; ✉ 8 Fairlawn Grove, London W4 5EH (✆ 020 8995 9029, e-mail simonwalker@me.com)

WALKER, Tim Philip Buchanan; s of W L B Walker, and Claudine Ella, *née* Mawby; *b* 23 June 1963, Oxford; *Educ* Millfield; *Career* journalist; Evening Echo Bournemouth 1983–85, Evening Argus Brighton 1985–87, diary ed The Observer 1987–90, diary ed The European 1990–93, assoc ed Tatler 1993–94, Daily Mail 1994–2002 (dep diary ed 1998–2002, Mail on Sunday); Sunday Telegraph: diary ed 2002–14, theatre critic 2005–14; diary ed Daily Telegraph 2008–14, ed-at-large Tempus Magazine 2015–; freelance presenter: LBC London 1989–94, Channel 4 2000, Sky 2002–11, BBC 2002–, ITN 2002–05; Young Journalist of the Year Br Press Awards 1987; cameo appearances in Top Hat (Aldwych Theatre) 2013 and Spamalot (Playhouse) 2014 (in the role of God); *Books* Norma – A Biography (1993); *Recreations* theatre, travelling; *Clubs* Garrick; *Style*— Tim Walker, Esq; ✉ Twitter @thattimwalker

WALKER, Timothy Alexander; AM (2000); s of Keith James Walker (d 2014), of Launceston, Tasmania, and Elaine, *née* Edwards (d 2002); *b* 23 November 1954, Hobart, Tasmania; *Educ* Riverside HS, Launceston Matriculation Coll, Univ of Tasmania (BA, Dip Ed, AMusA), Univ of New England (Dip Fin Mgmnt); *Career* teacher The Don Coll 1978–81, concerts mangr Canberra Sch of Music Aust Nat Univ 1981–87, public progs mangr Nat Film and Sound Archive 1987, gen mangr Aust Chamber Orchestra 1989–99 (marketing and devpt mangr 1987–89); ceo World Orchestras 1999–2003, chief exec and artistic dir LPO 2003–; involved with: Henry Wood Hall Tst, Rachmaninoff Fndn 2013; memb: Int Soc for the Performing Arts 1989, Royal Philharmonic Soc 2003; HonRCM 2014; *Clubs* Athenaeum; *Style*— Timothy Walker, Esq, AM; ✉ London Philharmonic Orchestra, 89 Albert Embankment, London SE1 7TP (✆ 020 7840 4218)

WALKER, Timothy Edward Hanson; CB (1998); s of Harris and Elizabeth Walker; *b* 27 July 1945; *Educ* Tonbridge, Brasenose Coll Oxford (MA, DPhil); *m* 1, 1969, Judith, *née* Mann (d 1976); 1 da; m 2, 1983, Anna Walker, CB, *qv*, *née* Butterworth; 2 da; *Career* res fell UC Oxford and exhibitioner of Royal Cmmn of 1851 Oxford and Paris 1969–71; Harkness fell: Commonwealth Fund of New York 1971, Univ of Virginia 1971, Northwestern Univ 1972; strategic planner GLC 1974–77, princ DTI 1977–83, Sloan fell London Business Sch 1983; DTI: asst sec 1983–85, head of Policy Planning Unit 1985–86, princ private sec to Secs of State for Trade and Industry 1986–87, under sec and dir Inf Engrg Directorate/dir Alvey Prog 1987–89, head of Atomic Energy Div 1989–95; dep sec and DG Immigration and Nationality Dept Home Office 1995–98, dep chm and cmmr HM Customs and Excise 1998–2000, DG Health and Safety Exec 2000–05; exec dir Financial Reporting Cncl 2008–12; non-exec dir: ICI Chemicals and Polymers Ltd 1988–89, Govt Div UKAEA 1994–95 (govr IAEA (UK) 1989–94), Inland Revenue 1998–2000, London Strategic Health Authy 2006–09; Third Church Estates Cmmr 2006–12; chm Accountants and Actuaries Disciplinary Bd 2008–12; memb: Cncl Inst of Employment Studies 2001–05, Science and Technol Ctee Int Risk Governance Cncl 2004–12, Audit Ctee St John of Jerusalem Eye Hosp 2013–; hon vice-pres Inst of Occupational Safety and Health 2002–05, chm Assembly of Donors EBRD Nuclear Safety Account 1993–95; memb Cncl Univ of Warwick 2000–06; tstee: Prostate Cancer Charity 2006–13, De Morgan Fndn 2006–12, Drinkaware 2014–; Hon DSc Cranfield Univ 2003, hon fell Warwick Mfrg Gp 2005; FRSA 2000, CEng 2003, FInstP 2003, FIET 2004; *Publications* If You Can Read You Can Cook, Twixt the Commons; pubns in scientific jls; *Recreations* African tribal art, gardening, cookery; *Style*— Timothy Walker, Esq

WALKER OF ALDRINGHAM, Baron (Life Peer UK 2006), of Aldringham in the County of Suffolk; Gen Sir Michael John Dawson Walker; GCB (2000, KCB 1995), CMG (1997), CBE (1990, OBE 1982), DL (Gtr London 2007); s of William Hampden Dawson Walker; *b* 7 July 1944; *Educ* Milton Sch Bulawayo, Woodhouse Grove Sch Yorks, RMA Sandhurst; *m* 1973, Victoria Margaret, da of late Maj-Gen Michael Walter Holme, CBE, MC; 2 s (Hon Alexander James Dawson b 1978, Hon Harry Thomas Dawson b 1980 (twin)), 1 da (Hon Alice Rose Victoria b 1980 (twin)); *Career* commissioned Royal Anglian Regt 1966, Staff Coll 1976–77, CO 1 Royal Aglian Regt 1985–87, Cdr 20 Armoured Bde 1987–89, COS 1 (Br) Corps 1989–91, GOC NE District and Cd 2 Inf Div 1991–92, GOC Eastern District 1992, Asst Chief of Gen Staff Min of Defence 1992–94, Cdr Allied Command Europe Rapid Reaction Corps 1994–97, Cdr Land Component Peace Implementation Force Bosnia 1995–96, C-in-C Land Command 1997–2000, CGS 2000–03, Chief of Defence Staff 2003–06; Col Commandant Queen's Div 1991–2000, Army Air Corps 1994–2004, Col Royal Anglian Regt 1997–2002; govr Royal Hosp Chelsea 2006–; Hon DLL UEA, Hon DSc Univ of Cranfield; *Clubs* Army and Navy, Sloane, Queen's; *Style*— Gen the Lord Walker of Aldringham, GCB, CMG, CBE, DL; ✉ Royal Hospital Chelsea, London SW3 4SR

WALKINGTON, Alexander Stuart Burnett (Sandy); s of Capt Ian Alexander Greet Walkington (d 2012), and Shelagh Winnifred Mary Mackenzie, *née* Munro (d 1994); *b* 5 December 1953, Dingwall, Scotland; *Educ* Cheltenham Coll (scholar), Trinity Hall Cambridge (Dr Cooper law student, MA), Coll of Law London, Tulane Univ New Orleans; *m* 1988, Francesca Mary, da of Francis Weal; 2 s (Edward Alexander Alban b 1 Nov 1988, Thomas Francis Pageant b 12 Oct 1990), 1 da (Dora Clementine Bianca b 25 Dec 1995); *Career* called to the Bar Gray's Inn 1976 (Gerald Moody scholar); Tulane Univ 1977–78, Parly asst to Emlyn Hooson, QC, MP (subsequently Baron Hooson, QC (Life Peer)) 1978–79, head of research Parly Lib Pty 1979–81, various positions rising to mangr of external affrs Texaco Ltd 1981–91, mangr of int PR Texaco Inc NY 1991–92, dir of public affrs BT Group plc 1992–2005, dir general election communications Lib Dem Pty 2005, dir gp public affrs Transport for London 2005–06, public policy advsr and professional speaker 2006–; memb Advsy Bd Editorial Intelligence 2006–10; memb Nat Cncl CBI 1998–2002; Parly candidate (Lib/SDP Alliance) St Albans 1983 and 1987, memb St Albans City Cncl 1984–91, Lib Dem Parly candidate St Albans 2010 and 2015, memb Herts CC 2013–; tstee St Albans Bereavement Network, patron WombTwin; fell Industry and Parliament Tst; MIPR, FRSA; *Recreations* family, walking, studying architecture; *Style*— Sandy Walkington, Esq; ✉ 6 Hobbs Hill, Welwyn, Hertfordshire AL6 9DS

WALKLEY, Geoffrey; s of Alexander Joseph Charles Walkley (d 1993), and Vera Cecilia Walkley (d 2002); *b* 25 July 1944; *Educ* East Ham GS for Boys, Univs of Durham and Newcastle (LLB); *m* 18 Jan 1969, Barbara Eunice, da of Ernest Dunstan; 1 s (Richard Andrew b 21 Dec 1970 d 2006), 1 da (Sarah Elizabeth b 29 April 1973); *Career* admitted slr 1968; Bartlett & Gluckstein: articled 1966–68, asst slr 1968–71, ptnr 1971–78; ptnr Bartlett & Gluckstein Crawley & De Reya (later Bartletts, De Reya) 1978–88, ptnr Nabarro Nathanson 1988–93, ptnr Penningtons 1993–2004 (conslt 2004–09); memb: Law Soc, Slrs' Benevolent Assoc, RYA, RHS; assoc memb RSC; *Publications* Negotiating Technical Assistance Agreements (1995); *Recreations* sailing, books, gardening, carpentry; *Clubs* Maylandsea Bay Sailing (Cdre and hon treas); *Style*— Geoffrey Walkley, Esq; ✉ 3 Dalewood Close, Emerson Park, Hornchurch, Essex RM11 3PJ (✆ 01708 459092, e-mail walkleyg@dircon.co.uk)

WALKLING, (Anthony) Kim; s of William Charles Walkling (d 1989), and Vida Karina, *née* Beare; *b* 27 September 1957; *Educ* Sutton HS Plymouth, UCL (LLB); *m* 20 Sept 1986, (Margaret Caroline) Deirdre, *née* Moore, da of Samuel James Moore (d 2007), of Purley, Surrey; 1 s ((James) Christopher Charles b 1990), 1 da (Katherine Sophie Olivia b 1994); *Career* articled clerk Slaughter and May 1980–82, asst slr Watson, Farley & Williams 1982–87; ptnr: SJ Berwin & Co 1987–92, Theodore Goddard 1992–97, Simmons & Simmons 1998–2012; private aviation and defence conslt; memb: Law Soc 1982, European Air Law Assoc 1989; *Recreations* photography, music, good food and wine, travel; *Clubs* Probus Guildford; *Style*— Kim Walkling, Esq; ✉ Pine Court, Mill Road, Tadworth, Surrey KT20 7TE (e-mail kimwalkling@gmail.com)

WALL, Elizabeth; *see:* Sclater Wall, Madeleine Elizabeth Ramsden

WALL, Geoffrey; s of Frank Wall, and Gwyneth, *née* Chadwick; *b* 1950, Cheshire; *Educ* Wallasey GS, Univ of Sussex (BA), Sorbonne, St Edmund Hall Oxford (BPhil); *Children* 1 da (Gianna b 1983), 3 s (Malachi b 1986, Thomas b 1989, Christopher b 1991); *Career* Univ of York: lectr 1975–97, sr lectr 1997–, reader 2002–; ed Cambridge Quarterly 1998–; freelance journalist and travel writer; literary biographer; Leverhulme Research Fellowship 2007–08; memb: Greenpeace, Amnesty Int; *Books* Flaubert: A Life (2001, shortlisted Whitbread Award for Biography), The Enlightened Physician (2013); *Recreations* cycling, walking the moors, going to Paris; *Style*— Geoffrey Wall; ✉ c/o David Higham Associates, 5–8 Lower John Street, Golden Square, London W1R 4HA (website www.davidhigham.co.uk/html/Clients/Geoffrey_Wall); e-mail gw2@york.ac.uk, website www.york.ac.uk/depts/engl/staff/academic/wall

WALL, Dr Jasper V; s of Philip Errington Wall (d 1973), and Lilian Margaret, *née* Blackburn (d 1980); *b* 15 January 1942; *Educ* Vankleek Hill Collegiate Inst, Queen's Univ at Kingston (BSc), Univ of Toronto (MSc), Australian Nat Univ (PhD); *m* 1969, Jennifer Anne, da of Prof Stanley D Lash (d 1994), and Ruth Lash (d 1992); 1 da (Kristina b 1965), 1 s (Matthew b 1976); *Career* res sci Australian Nat Radio Astronomy Observatory Parkes NSW 1970–74, RAS Leverhulme Fell Cavendish Lab 1974–75, Royal Soc Jaffé Donation Fell Cavendish Lab 1975–79, head Astrophysics and Astrometry Div Royal Greenwich Observatory 1979–87, offr-in-charge Isaac Newton Gp of Telescopes La Palma Canary Islands 1987–90; Royal Greenwich Observatory: head Technol Div 1990–91, head Astronomy Div and dep dir 1991–93, head Royal Greenwich Observatory and head Astronomy Div Royal Observatories 1993–95, dir Royal Greenwich Observatory 1995–98; visiting reader Univ of Sussex 1980–90, visiting prof Dept of Astrophysics Univ of Oxford 1998–, adjunct prof Dept of Physics and Astronomy Univ of British Columbia 2003–; chm Editorial Bd Astronomy & Geophysics 1999–2002; FRAS 1975 (memb Cncl 1992–96, vice-pres 1996), FRSA 1998–2012; *Publications* Modern Technology and its Influence on Astronomy (ed with A Boksenberg, 1986), Optics in Astronomy (1993), The Universe at High Redshifts (with A Aragón-Salamanca and N Tanvir, 1997), Practical Statistics for Astronomers (with C Jenkins, 2003, 2 edn 2012); author of 200 papers in professional jls; *Recreations* skiing, music; *Style*— Dr J V Wall; ✉ e-mail jvw@phas.ubc.ca

WALL, Jonathan; *Career* BBC Radio 5 Live: dep controller and commissioning ed 2008–13, controller 2013–; *Style*— Jonathan Wall, Esq; ✉ BBC Radio 5 Live, Quay House, MediaCityUK, Salford M50 2QH

WALL, Malcolm Robert; s of Maj Gen Robert P W Wall, of Essex, and Patricia, *née* O'Brien, of York; *b* 24 July 1956; *Educ* Allhallows Sch Dorset, Univ of Kent (BA); *m* Elizabeth; 3 da (Emma b 4 Aug 1985, Josephine b 10 March 1987, Rebecca b 28 June 1991); *Career* sales exec Southern Television 1978–80, sales exec rising to sales dir Anglia Television Ltd 1980–87, sales and mktg dir Granada Television 1988–92, dep ceo Meridian Broadcasting 1992–94, md Anglia Television Ltd 1994–96; dep dir United Broadcasting & Entertainment Ltd 1996–98, md of HTV Group 1997–99, chief exec United Broadcasting and Entertainment Ltd 1999–2000, ceo United Business Media plc 2001–05, chief exec Content Div Virgin Media 2006–09, chief exec Abu Dhabi Media 2011–12; non-exec dir: Five, Creston plc 2007–, ITE Gp plc; chm Harlequin FC Ltd 1997–2000; *Clubs* Harlequin FC, MCC, RAC; *Style*— Malcolm Wall, Esq

WALL, Michael Charles; s of James Wall, and Joan Margaret Wall; *Educ* Trinity Sch of John Whitgift, Univ of Sussex (UAU rugby, tennis capt); *Career* bd dir Simons Palmer, ptnr and fndr Fallon Ltd (managing ptnr London until 2004) pres int ops Fallon Worldwide 2004–09, global chief exec Lowe and Ptnrs 2009–; MIPA 2000; *Recreations* tennis, golf; *Clubs* Brocket Hall Golf; *Style*— Michael Wall, Esq

WALLACE, Prof (William) Angus; s of Dr William Bethune Wallace (d 1981), of Dundee, Scotland, and Dr Frances Barret, *née* Early (d 1992); *b* 31 October 1948; *Educ* Dundee HS, Univ of St Andrews (MB ChB); *m* 2 Jan 1971, Jacqueline Vera Studley, da of Dr George William Eglinton Studley (d 1995), of East Finchley, London; 1 da (Suzanne b

W

1973), 2 s (Malcolm b 1975, Andrew b 1979); *Career* jr house offr Dundee Royal Infirmary and Maryfield Hosp 1972–73, demonstrator in anatomy Univ of Nottingham 1973–74; SHO: Nottingham 1974–75, Derby 1975; basic surgical trg registrar Newcastle and Gateshead Hosps 1975–77, orthopaedic registrar Nottingham Hosps 1978–81, res fell MRC 1979, lectr in orthopaedic surgery Univ of Nottingham 1981–84, visiting res fell Toronto W Hosp Canada 1983, sr lectr in orthopaedic surgery Univ of Manchester 1984–85, med dir North Western Orthotic Unit and med advsr Dept of Orthopaedic Mechanics Univ of Salford 1984–85, prof of orthopaedic and accident surgery Univ of Nottingham 1985–, med dir MSc Course in Sports Med Univ of Nottingham 1995–2001, chm Inter Collegiate Specialty Bd in Trauma and Orthopaedic Surgery 2002–05; RCSEd: memb Cncl 1990–2000 and 2005–07 (vice-pres 1997–2000), dean Faculty of Med Informatics 2000–05, chair Specialty Advsy Ctee in Trauma and Orthopaedic Surgery 2008–09, memb Policy Bd 2013–14; dir of professional affrs (E Midlands) RCS 2014–17; pres: Br Orthopaedics Sports Trauma Assoc 1997–99, Br Elbow and Shoulder Soc 2001–03; chm: Clinical Curriculum Ctee Nottingham Med Sch 1992–95, Nat Osteoporosis Soc 1996–98, Nat Sports Medicine Inst of the UK 1999–2003; memb Int Bd for Shoulder Surgery 1992–2019, co-chair Research Gp Health Technologies (Faraday) and Knowledge Transfer Network 2002–, memb Exec Ctee European Soc for Surgery of the Shoulder and Elbow 2003–06, vice-pres CP Sport (England and Wales) 2004–, memb Cncl Faculty of Sport and Exercise Medicine UK 2006– (chair Excellence Awards Ctee 2013–14); tstee AA Motoring Tst 2003–07, memb Cncl Inst of Advanced Motorists 2011–16; pres Disabilities Living Centre Nottingham 2001–; Sir Walter Mercer Gold Medal RCSEd 1985, Weigelt-Wallace Award for Med Care 1995; hon fell Hong Kong Coll of Orthopaedic Surgeons 2011, hon fell Magyar Ortopéd Társaság 2011; memb RSM; FRCSEd 1977, FRCSEd (orthopaedic) 1985, FRCS 1997, Fndn FFSEM 2006; *Publications* Shoulder Arthroscopy (1992), Management of Disasters and their Aftermath (1994), Joint Replacement of the Shoulder and Elbow (1998), A Handbook of Sports Medicine (1999); numerous articles in learned jls on osteoporosis, shoulder surgery, sports medicine and biomechanics; *Recreations* narrowboat cruising, jogging, woodwork; *Style*— Prof W Angus Wallace; ✉ University Hospital, Queen's Medical Centre, Nottingham NG7 2UH (☎ 0115 823 1121, fax 0115 823 1118, e-mail angus.wallace@rcsed.ac.uk)

WALLACE, Brian Godman; s of James Alexander Gaul Wallace, and Phyllis May, *née* Godman; *b* 1 March 1954; *Educ* Royal High Sch Edinburgh, Univ of St Andrews (MA); *Children* 1 da (Fiona b 11 March 1984), 1 s (Callum James b 27 April 1986); *Career* mangr Price Waterhouse CAs Dubai 1980–82 (asst mangr London 1976–80); Schlumberger: chief accountant Dubai 1982–84, European financial controller London 1984–85, Middle E financial controller Dubai 1985–87, Eastern Hemisphere finance dir Paris 1987–89; gp financial controller APV plc London 1989–91, gp finance dir Geest plc 1991–95, gp financial dir Hilton Group plc 1995–2006 (dep gp chief exec 2000–06), finance dir Ladbrokes plc 2007–; non-exec dir: Hays plc 2001–, Scottish & Newcastle plc 2006–; ACA; *Recreations* golf, tennis, theatre; *Style*— Brian Wallace, Esq

WALLACE, Lt-Gen Sir Christopher Brooke Quentin; KBE (1997, OBE 1983, MBE 1978), DL (Hants 2004); s of late Major Robert Quentin Wallace, and late Diana Pamela Wallace, *née* Galtrey; *b* 3 January 1943; *Educ* Shrewsbury, RMA Sandhurst; *m* 6 Dec 1969, Delicia Margaret Agnes, da of Gerald Curtis; 1 s (Wyndham b 4 July 1971), 1 da (Suzannah b 16 Feb 1974); *Career* cmmnd 1962, CO 3 Bn Royal Green Jackets 1983–85, Cdr 7 Armd Bde 1986–88, dir Public Relations (Army) 1989–90, Cdr 3 Armd Div 1990–93, Cmdt Staff Coll Camberley 1993–94, team ldr Permanent Joint HQ Implementation 1994–96, Chief of Jt Ops Perm Jt HQ (UK) 1996–99, ret Army 1999; Cmdt RCDS 2001–04; memb Cncl RUSI 1996–2000; rep Col Cmdt: Royal Green Jackets 1995–98, Light Div 1998–99; pres Army Golf Assoc 1995–2000; chm Royal Green Jackets Museum Tstees 1999–2015, dep chm Imperial War Museum 2006–08 (tstee 1999–08); *Books* A Brief History of The King's Royal Rifle Corps, 1755–1965 (2005), Focus on Courage: The 59 Victoria Crosses of The Royal Green Jackets (2006), Rifles and Kukris: Delhi 1857 (2007); *Recreations* military history; *Clubs* Army and Navy; *Style*— Lt-Gen Sir Christopher Wallace, KBE, DL; ✉ c/o RHQ The Rifles, Peninsula Barracks, Winchester, Hampshire SO23 8TS

WALLACE, Daniel Frederick (Danny); *b* 16 November 1976, Dundee; *Educ* Univ of Westminster; *Career* writer and presenter; patron Build Africa; PPA Columnist of the Year 2011; *Television* incl: creator and presenter How to Start Your Own Country (BBC 2) 2005, presenter Test The Nation (BBC 1) 2006; *Radio* prodr The Mighty Boosh (BBC Radio 4), creator and prodr Ross Noble Goes Global (BBC Radio 4), presenter Saturday morning show XFM London 2008, presenter weekday breakfast show XFM London 2011– (Gold Best Use of Branded Content, Silver Best Live Event Coverage and Bronze Best Competition Sony Radio Acad Awards 2012, Funniest Radio Show LAFTA 2012); *Books* Join Me (2003), Random Acts of Kindness: 365 Ways to Make the World a Nicer Place (2004), Yes Man (2005), Danny Wallace and the Centre of the Universe (2006), Friends Like These (2008), Awkward Situations for Men (2010), More Awkward Situations for Men (2011), Charlotte Street (2012); *Style*— Mr Danny Wallace; ✉ website www.dannywallace.com, Twitter @dannywallace; c/o James Grant Group Ltd, 94 Strand On The Green, Chiswick, London W4 3NN

WALLACE, Prof Sir David James; kt (2004), CBE (1996); s of Robert Elder Wallace, and Jane McConnell, *née* Elliot; *b* 7 October 1945; *Educ* Hawick HS, Univ of Edinburgh (BSc, PhD); *m* 1970, Elizabeth Anne Yeats; 1 da; *Career* Harkness fell Dept of Physics Princeton Univ 1970–72, reader Dept of Physics Univ of Southampton 1978–79 (lectr 1972–78), Tait prof of mathematical physics Univ of Edinburgh 1979–93 (head of physics 1984–87), vice-chllr Loughborough Univ 1994–2006, master Churchill Coll Cambridge 2006–14, dir Isaac Newton Inst for Mathematical Sciences and J N M Rothschild & Sons prof of mathematical sciences Univ of Cambridge 2006–11; dir: Edinburgh Concurrent Supercomputer 1987–89, Edinburgh Parallel Computing Centre 1990–93; author of pubns in research and review jls in various areas of theoretical physics and computing; memb Cncl and chm Science Bd SERC 1990–94 (chm Physics Ctee 1987–90), memb Cncl and chm Tech Opportunities Panel EPSRC 1994–98, pres Physics Section Br Assoc for the Advancement of Science 1994; Office of Science and Technol: memb Link and TCS Bds 1995–2001, chm TCS quinquennial review 2001, chm e-Science Steering Ctee 2001–06; memb numerous panels in science, info and communication technols European Cmmn, memb European Science and Technol Assembly 1997–98; memb Scottish Higher Educn Funding Cncl 1993–97, chm CVCP/SCOP Task Force on Sport in Higher Educn 1995–97, chm Value for Money Steering Ctee HEFCE 1997–2003; non-exec dir: Scottish Life Assurance Co 1999–2001, Taylor & Francis Gp plc 2000–04; pres Inst of Physics 2002–04, vice-pres and treas Royal Soc 2002–07, vice-pres Royal Soc of Edinburgh 2013–; DL Leics 2001–06; Maxwell Medal Inst of Physics 1980; memb Ct Univ of St Andrews 2014–; Hon DEng Heriot-Watt Univ 2002; Hon DSc Univs of: Edinburgh 2003, Leicester 2005, Loughborough 2006, Southampton 2006, East Anglia 2009; CIMgt 2001; FRS 1986, FRSE 1982, FInstP 1991, FREng 1998, hon FIMA 2009; *Recreations* exercise, eating well, mycophagy; *Clubs* New (Edinburgh); *Style*— Prof Sir David Wallace, CBE, FRS, FREng; ✉ website www.chu.cam.ac.uk/people/view/david-wallace

WALLACE, Dame Helen Sarah; DBE (2011), CMG (2000); da of Edward Rushworth (d 1975), of Bradford, and Joyce, *née* Robinson (d 2002); *b* 25 June 1946; *Educ* Univ of Oxford (MA), Coll of Europe Bruges (Dip European Studies), Univ of Manchester (PhD); *m* 24 Aug 1968, Baron Wallace of Saltaire (Life Peer) , *qv*, s of William Edward Wallace (d 1995); 1 da (Hon Harriet Katharine b 1 Sept 1977), 1 s (Hon Edward William Joseph b 5 May 1981); *Career* admin offr Dept of Extra-Mural Studies Univ of Manchester 1968–69, res assoc Dept of Govt Univ of Manchester 1972–73, lectr UMIST 1974–78, lectr and sr lectr Civil Service Coll 1978–85, on secondment Planning Staff FCO 1979–80, sr res fell and dir W European Prog RIIA 1985–92, prof of contemporary European studies and dir then co-dir Sussex European Inst Univ of Sussex 1992–2001, prog dir One Europe or Several? Prog ESRC 1998–2001, dir Robert Schuman Centre Euro Univ Inst Florence 2001–06, foreign sec Br Acad 2011–15; visiting prof Coll of Europe 1976–2001, centennial then emeritus prof European Inst LSE 2007–13; hon Jean Monnet chair of contemporary Euro studies 1997; hon degree: Univ of Aston, Loughborough Univ, Univ of Sussex, Sciences-Po Paris; FBA 2000; Chevalier dans l'Ordre National du Mérite 1996; *Publications* Interlocking Dimensions of European Integration (2001), Policy-Making in the European Union (with Mark Pollack and Alasdair Young, 7 edn 2015); author of numerous books, essays and articles in learned jls; *Style*— Dame Helen Wallace, DBE, CMG, FBA

WALLACE, Jessie; da of James Wallace, of Blackmore, Essex, and Annette, *née* Leach; *b* 25 September 1971, Enfield, London; *Educ* Coll of NE London, The Poor Sch London; *Children* 1 da (Tallulah Lilac b 2004); *Career* actress; patron The Music Hall Guild of GB and America; *Television* incl: Kat Moon in EastEnders (BBC 1) 2000–05 and 2010– (Best Newcomer Br Soap Award 2001, Most Popular Newcomer Nat Television Award 2001, Best Newcomer Inside Soap Award 2001, Best Newcomer TV Quick and Choice Award 2001, Best Soap Actress TV Quck and Choice Award 2003, Most Popular Actress Nat Television Award 2003, Best Couple Inside Soap Award (with Shane Ritchie) 2004, Best Actress Br Soap Award 2007, Best Actress Inside Soap Award 2011), A Class Apart (BBC 1), The Dinner Party, Miss Marie Lloyd – Queen of The Music Hall (BBC 4), Wild at Heart (ITV 1) 2008, The Road to Coronation Street 2010 (nomination Best Supporting Actress BAFTA 2011); *Theatre* incl: Rent (West End) 2007–08, Haunted (Arts Theatre) 2008, Stepping Out (nat tour); *Style*— Ms Jessie Wallace; ✉ c/o Creative Artists Management, 4th Floor, 111 Shoreditch High Street, London E1 6JN

WALLACE, John Williamson; CBE (2011, OBE 1995); s of Christopher Kidd Wallace, of Glenrothes, Fife, and Ann Drummond, *née* Allan; *b* 14 April 1949; *Educ* Buckhaven HS, King's Coll Cambridge (MA); *m* 3 July 1971, Elizabeth Jane, da of Prof Ronald Max Hartwell, of Oxford; 2 s (Cosmo b 1979, Esme b 1982); *Career* asst princ trumpet LSO 1974–76, princ trumpet Philharmonia 1976–95, artistic dir brass RAM 1992–2001, princ RSAMD 2002–; performed obligato trumpet at Royal Wedding 1981, performed first performance Malcolm Arnold Concerto 1982, Sir Peter Maxwell Davies trumpet concerto Hiroshima 1988, Tim Souster Trumpet Concerto 1988, Robert Saxton, Dominic Muldowney, James Macmillan Trumpet Concerto 1993, Sir Peter Maxwell Davies Trumpet Quintet 1999; trumpet duets: Prime Number (1990), Odd Number (1991), Even Number (1991); soloist Last Night of the Proms 1996; formed Wallace Collection Brass Ensemble 1986 (19 solo and gp recordings); hon memb RCM 1982, FRAM, FRSAMD, FRNCM; *Books* First Book of Trumpet Solos (1985), Second Book of Trumpet Solos (1985), The Cambridge Companion to Brass Instruments (co-ed); *Style*— John Wallace, Esq, CBE

WALLACE, Keith; *Educ* Mill Hill Sch, KCL (Postgrad Cert); *Career* admitted slr 1971; ptnr Bird & Bird 1972–84, clerk Richard Cloudesley's Charity 1976–2012, ed Pension Lawyer 1984–99, ptnr and now conslt Reed Smith (formerly Reed Smith Richards Butler) 1985–; memb Takeover Panel 1994; chm: Maldon Unit Trust Managers Ltd 1987–2000, Independent Pension Trustee Ltd 1990–2000, Wiggins Teape Pension Scheme 2001–07, London Endowed Charities Forum 2002–12, Beaufort Trust Corporation Ltd (dir 1985–); ed/commentator (Pensions) Television Educn Network 1992–98; vice-pres Holborn Law Soc 1983–84; memb: Ctee Assoc Pension Lawyers 1984–89, NAPF Investment Ctee 1991–96, Cncl Occupational Pensions Advsy Serv (now TPAS) 1992–2007, Editorial Bd Trust Quarterly Review 2013–; tstee Wishbone Tst 2000–03, Cncl The Assoc of Corporate Tstees (TACT, pres 2015–), memb English Chamber Choir 1993–2000, cancellarius English Chantry Choir 2002–; fell TPAS 2012; *Books* Tomorrow's Lawyers: Computers and Legal Training (1981), Trust Deed and Rules Checklist (1993), Banking Litigation (1999, 3 edn 2011); *Style*— Keith Wallace, Esq, FPAS; ✉ Reed Smith, Broadgate Tower, Primrose Street, London EC2A 2RS (☎ 020 3116 3624, fax 020 3116 3999)

WALLACE, Marjorie Shiona (Countess Skarbek); CBE (2008, MBE); da of William Wallace (d 1975), and Doris Gertrude, *née* Tulloch (d 1989); *b* 10 January 1945, Kenya; *Educ* Rodean Sch Johannesburg, Parsons Mead, UCL (BA); *m* Count Andrzej Skarbek; 3 s (Sacha b 29 May 1972, Stefan b 2 March 1976, Justin Maximillian b 3 October 1979), 1 da (Sophia Augusta b 23 January 1984); *Career* writer and researcher Frost Programme ITV 1966–69, reporter and film dir Nationwide and Midweek BBC 1969–72; Sunday Times: reporter Insight team 1972–89, social services corr 1974–89, sr feature writer; conslt Earth Year 2050 TVS 1983–84, fndr SANE 1986– (chief exec 1989–), fndr Prince of Wales Int Centre for SANE Research Oxford 2003–; awards: Campaigning Journalist of the Year Br Press Awards 1982 and 1986, John Pringle Meml Award 1986, Oddfellow Prize Book Tst 1987, Snowdon Special Award 1988, Medical Journalist of the Year 1988, Evian Health Award 1991 and 1995, European Woman of Achievement 1992, Br Neuroscience Public Voice Award 2003, shortlisted Lifetime Achievement Award UK Charity Awards 2002 and Beacon Awards 2003, Int Pioneer and Diversity Award 2005; research fell Nuffield Coll Oxford 1989–91; regular lectr and tv/radio guest; memb: Mgmnt Advsy Ctee Inst of Psychiatry 1989–2002 (memb Advsy Ctee 2003–), Ethical Research Ctee Inst of Psychiatry 1991–2002, BUPA 1997–, National Disability Cncl 1998–2002; chm Friends of the Open Air Theatre Ctee 1991–, patron Hay Literary Festival 2002; fell Univ of London; Hon DSc City Univ 2001; Hon FRCPsych 1997; *Publications* On Giant's Shoulders (1976), Suffer the Children, the Thalidomide Campaign (co-author, 1978), The Superpoison (1979), The Silent Twins (1986), Campaign and Be Damned (1991); screenplays: On Giant's Shoulders (1978, Int Emmy), The Silent Twins (1986); documentaries: Whose Mind Is It? (BBC, 1988), Circles of Madness (BBC, 1994); *Recreations* poetry, opera, piano, Victorian ballads, dining out, friends; *Clubs* Groucho, Athenaeum; *Style*— Marjorie Wallace, CBE; ✉ 26 Bisham Gardens, London N6 6DD; SANE, 1st Floor, Cityside House, 40 Alder Street, London E1 1EE (☎ 020 7375 1002, fax 020 7375 2162)

WALLACE, Richard; *b* 11 June 1961; *Career* US ed Daily Mirror 2002–03, dep ed Sunday Mirror 2003–04, ed Daily Mirror 2004–12; *Clubs* Savile; *Style*— Richard Wallace, Esq

WALLACE, (Wellesley) Theodore Octavius; s of Dr Caleb Paul Wallace (d 1981), of Whitecroft, West Clandon, Surrey, and Dr Lucy Elizabeth Rainsford, *née* Pigott (d 1968); *b* 10 April 1938; *Educ* Charterhouse, Christ Church Oxford (MA); *m* 23 Jan 1988, Maria Amelia, o da of Sir Ian George Abercromby, 10 Bt (d 2003); 1 s (James Abercromby Octavius b 18 Jan 1989), 1 da (Lucy Mary Diana b 4 Nov 1991); *Career* 2 Lt RA 1958, Lt Surrey Yeomanry TA 1959; called to the Bar Inner Temple 1963 (Duke of Edinburgh Scholarship); memb Lloyd's; govr Inner London Schs 1966–86, chm Chelsea Cons Assoc 1981–84, chm VAT and Duties Tribunal 1992–2009 (pt/t chm 1989–92), special cmmr 1999–2009 (dep special cmmr 1992–99), judge Upper Tbnl Tax and Chancery Chamber 2009–12; hon sec Taxation Sub-Ctee Soc of Cons Lawyers 1975–92; Cons candidate: Pontypool Feb 1974, South Battersea Oct 1974 and May 1979; *Recreations* tennis, racing, skiing, golf; *Clubs* Army and Navy; *Style*— Theodore Wallace, Esq; ✉ Whitecroft, West Clandon, Surrey GU4 7TD (☎ 01483 222574); 46 Belleville Road, London SW11 6QT (☎ 020 7228 7740)

WALLACE, Vivien Rosemary Lumsdaine; da of late Capt James Edward Lumsdaine Wallace, and late Gwynne Wallace, *née* Jones; *b* 11 February 1944; *Educ* St Martin's Sch Solihull,

Emma Willard Troy NY (ESU scholarship), Arts Cncl of GB bursary; *m* 1, 2 Sept 1964, Anthony Thomas Etridge; m 2, 27 June 1981, Terence Francis Frank Coleman, *qv*; 1 da (Eliza b 1983), 1 s (Jack b 1984); *Career* press offr London Festival Ballet 1969–71, first ever press offr Royal Ballet Covent Garden 1972–74, chief press offr National Theatre 1975–77; Granada Television International: NY mangr 1979, head of sales 1981, dir of sales 1983, chief exec 1987–92; md Lippin-Wallace (television mktg co based London and LA) 1993–96, head of public affairs National Theatre 1996–2003, devpt dir Old Vic Theatre Co 2005– (mktg dir 2004–05); dir: Granada Television Ltd 1987–92, Nat Assoc of TV Production Execs USA 1988–92; chm TBA Films and Television Hamburg 1989–92; FRSA; *Style*— Miss Vivien Wallace

WALLACE OF SALTAIRE, Baron (Life Peer UK 1995), of Shipley in the County of West Yorkshire; Rt Hon William John Lawrence Wallace; PC (2012); s of William Edward Wallace, and Mary Agnes, *née* Tricks; *b* 12 March 1941; *Educ* Westminster Abbey Choir Sch, St Edward's Sch Oxford, King's Coll Cambridge (BA), Cornell Univ (PhD); *m* 25 Aug 1968, Helen Sarah, da of Edward Rushworth (d 1975); 1 da (Hon Harriet Katherine b 1 Sept 1977), 1 s (Hon Edward William Joseph b 1981); *Career* lectr in govt Univ of Manchester 1966–77, dir of studies RIIA 1978–90, Hallstein fell St Antony's Coll Oxford 1990–95, prof of int relations LSE 1999–2005 (currently emeritus prof, reader in int relations 1995–99); visiting prof of int studies Central European Univ 1994–97; memb various Lib Pty and SDP Lib Alliance Nat Ctees 1973–88; Parly candidate Lib Pty: Huddersfield West 1970, Manchester Moss Side 1974, Shipley 1983 and 1987; Lib Dem spokesman on foreign affairs House of Lords, memb Euro Union Ctee House of Lords 1996–2001, dep ldr Lib Dem Gp House of Lords 2005–10, govt whip and spokesman on foreign policy and defence 2010–12, spokesman on foreign policy and Cabinet Office 2012–; *Books* The Transformation of Western Europe (1990), The Foreign Policy Process in Britain (1976), Policy Making in the European Community (1983, 5 edn 2005), Regional Integration: the West European Experience (1994); *Style*— The Rt Hon the Lord Wallace of Saltaire; ✉ House of Lords, London SW1A 0PW

WALLACE OF TANKERNESS, Baron (Life Peer 2007), of Tankerness; James Robert; PC (2000), QC (Scot 1997); s of John Fergus Thomson Wallace, of Annan, Dumfriesshire, and Grace Hannah, *née* Maxwell; *b* 25 August 1954, Annan, Dumfriesshire; *Educ* Annan Acad, Downing Coll Cambridge (MA), Univ of Edinburgh (LLB); *m* 9 July 1983, Rosemary Janet, da of late William Grant Paton Fraser, OBE, TD, of Milngavie, Glasgow; 2 da (Helen b 1985, Clare b 1987); *Career* admitted Faculty of Advocates 1979; memb Scottish Lib Pty Nat Exec 1976–85 (vice-chm 1982–85), ldr Scottish Lib Dems 1992–2005; MP (Lib until 1988, subsequently Lib Dem) Orkney and Shetland 1983–2001 (Parly candidate (Lib) Dumfries 1979, Euro Parly candidate (Lib) S Scotland 1979); Lib Parly spokesman on defence and dep whip 1985–87, Alliance election spokesman on tport 1987, Lib chief whip and defence spokesman 1987, Lib Dem chief whip 1988–92; Lib Dem spokesman: on employment and fisheries 1988–92, on Scotland 1992, on maritime affairs and fishing 1992–97; Advocate Gen for Scotland 2010–15; ldr Lib Dem Peers and dep ldr House of Lords 2013–15; MSP Orkney (Lib Dem) 1999–2007; Scottish Exec: dep first minister 1999–2005 (acting first min 2000 and 2001), min for Justice 1999–2003, min for Enterprise and Lifelong Learning 2003–05; memb Cmmn on Scottish Devolution 2008–09; chm Relationships Scotland 2008–10, Advocate General for Scotland 2010–15; memb Bd St Magnus Int Festival Ltd 2007–14, dep ldr House of Lords 2013–15, Leader of Lib Dem Peers 2013–; hon prof Inst of Petroleum Engrg Heriot-Watt Univ 2007–10, hon bencher Lincoln's Inn 2012; Hon DLitt Heriot-Watt Univ 2007, Hon DUniv Open 2009, Hon Dr Univ of Edinburgh 2009; Elder of Church of Scotland; *Recreations* music, reading, golf, travel; *Clubs* Caledonian, Scottish Liberal; *Style*— Lord Wallace of Tankerness, QC; ✉ Northwood House, Tankerness, Orkney KW17 2QS (☎ 01856 861383); House of Lords, London SW1A 0PW (e-mail wallacej@parliament.uk)

WALLACE-HADRILL, Prof Andrew Frederic; OBE (2004); s of John Michael Wallace-Hadrill (d 1985), of Oxford, and Anne, *née* Wakefield; *b* 29 July 1951; *Educ* Rugby (scholar), CCC Oxford (Charles Oldham scholar, Hertford and da Paravicini scholar, Craven and Ireland scholar, BA), St John's Coll Oxford (sr scholar, DPhil); *m* 31 July 1975, Josephine Claire, da of John Temple Forbes Braddock; 1 da (Sophie Margaret Anne b 22 Sept 1980), 1 s (Michael Sutherland b 9 June 1984); *Career* fell and dir of studies in classics Magdalene Coll Cambridge 1976–83, jt lectr in classics Jesus Coll Cambridge 1979–83, lectr in ancient history Univ of Leicester 1983–87, prof of classics Univ of Reading 1987–2009, dir British Sch at Rome 1995–2009, master Sidney Sussex Coll Cambridge 2009–13 (emeritus fell 2016–), dir of research Faculty of Classics Univ of Cambridge 2012–; ed Jl of Roman Studies 1990–95; memb Soc for the Promotion of Roman Studies 1973–; dir Herculaneum Conservation Project 2001–16, dir Impact of the Ancient City Project 2016–; Hon DLitt Univ of Reading 2015; FSA 1998, FBA 2010; *Books* Suetonius: the scholar and his Caesars (1983), Ammianus Marcellinus – The Later Roman Empire AD 354–378 (1986), Patronage in Ancient Society (ed, 1989), City and Country in the Ancient World (jt ed, 1991), Augustan Rome (1993), Houses and Society in Pompeii and Herculaneum (1994), Domestic Space in the Roman World: Pompeii and Beyond (jt ed, 1997), The British School at Rome: One Hundred Years (2001), Rome's Cultural Revolution (2008), Herculaneum: Past and Future (2011); *Style*— Prof Andrew Wallace-Hadrill, OBE, FBA; ✉ Rowan House, Cambridge Road, Madingley, Cambridgeshire CB23 8AH

WALLER, Guy de Warrenne; s of Desmond de Warrenne (d 1978), and Angela Mary, *née* Wright; *b* 10 February 1950; *Educ* Hurstpierpoint Coll, Worcester Coll Oxford (MA), Wolfson Coll Oxford (MSc); *m* 30 Aug 1980, Hilary Ann, da of Rt Rev D J Farmbrough; 4 c (Becky b 11 Nov 1982, Lottie b 27 May 1984, Lucy b 13 April 1988, Jocelyn b 4 Dec 1989); *Career* Radley Coll: asst master 1974–93, head of chemistry 1982–88, housemaster 1988–93, master i/c hockey 1975–78, coach 1st XV backs 1979–86, master i/c cricket 1983–92; headmaster Lord Wandsworth Coll 1993–97, headmaster Cranleigh Sch 1997–2014 (ret); FRSA 1993; *Publications* Thinking Chemistry (1980), Advancing Chemistry (1982), Condensed Chemistry (1985), Teach Yourself GCSE Chemistry (1987); *Recreations* music, sport (two hockey blues, and a cricket blue), chess, family, British motorcycles; *Clubs* MCC, Free Foresters, Vincent's (Oxford), Ladykillers; *Style*— Guy Waller, Esq; ✉ The Old Dairy House, Thames Street, Charlbury, Oxon OX7 3QL

WALLER, Jane Ashton; da of Charles Ashton Waller, of Bucks, and Barbara Mary *née* Batt; *b* 19 May 1944; *Educ* Ladymede Sch Little Kimble, Croham Hurst Sch Croydon, Hornsey Art Sch (BA), Royal Coll of Art (MA); *m* 11 June 1983, Michael Hugh Vaughan-Rees, s of Lyle Vaughan-Rees (d 1962); *Career* since 1982: exhibited ceramics and life-drawings in London and many other parts of the country also in Kuwait, collections in London, LA, Chicago and Miami; work is sold at Bonhams and Sothebys, exhibits ceramics, life-drawings and drawings of Dancers in Movement from a box at Covent Garden Ballet Dress Rehearsals; author of articles in Ceramic Review and hand-blown glass in la revue de la Céramique et du Verre; started successful one woman campaign to save the Oxo Tower on the South Bank; involved in Coin St Orgn; added huge collection of patterns and women's magazines 1920–1960 to help inaugurate Nat Collection of Knitting Winchester Art Coll Library 2008; *Books* A Stitch in Time (jtly, 1972, 2 edn 2008), Some Things for the Children (1974), A Man's Book (1977), The Thirties Family Knitting Book (1981), The Man's Knitting Book (1984), Women in Wartime (jt 1987), Women in Uniform (jt 1989), Handbuilt Ceramics (1990), Blitz (jtly 1990), Colour in Clay (1998), The Human Form in Clay (2001), Knitting Fashions of the 1940s (2006), A Stitch in Time Vol 2 (2011), Below the Green Pond (2013), Under Buckingham Palace (2013), Saving the Dinosaurs (2013, 2 edn 2014), The Egyptian Princess (2013), Weather Or Not (forthcoming), Me Jane – A 1950s Childhood (forthcoming); *For Children* Below the Green Pond (1982), Saving the Dinosaurs (1994), The Sludge-Gulpers (1997); *Recreations* reading, gardening, knitting, writing, conservation, cooking, ceramics, tennis, music, walking in the country; *Style*— Ms Jane Waller; ✉ e-mail janewaller@metronet.co.uk, websites www.janewaller.co.uk and www.michaelvr.com

WALLER, Jonathan Neil; s of Douglas Victor Waller (d 2007), and Kristine Daphne Desmond Rieley (d 1982); *b* 16 April 1956; *Educ* Cherry Orchard HS Northampton, Northampton GS, Nene Coll Northampton, Coventry (Lanchester) Poly, Chelsea Sch of Art (BA, MA); *Career* artist; painting fellowship S Glamorgan Inst of HE Cardiff 1985–86, full time artist London 1987–; pt/t sr lectr Coventry Univ; grants incl: Welsh Arts Cncl 1986, British Cncl 1990; first prize Midland View 3 1984, Mark Rothko Meml Tst travelling scholarship to USA 1988; *Solo Exhibitions* Paton Gallery London 1986 and 1988, Flowers East London 1990, 1992, 1993 and 1994, Doncaster Museum and Art Gallery 1994, New End Gallery London 1997, New End Gallery London 1998, Axiom Centre for the Arts Cheltenham, Transcriptions (Art at Glebe House Leamington Spa) 2000, Lanchester Gallery Coventry 2003, Jonathan Waller's True Adventures (Nat Maritime Museum Cornwall Falmouth) 2005, Jonathan Waller's True Adventures (Arlington Gallery London) 2006, Drawings and Sculpture (Herbert Cafe Coventry) 2007–08; *Group Exhibitions* New Contemporaries (ICA) 1984, Midland View 3 (Nottingham and tour) 1984, Four New Painters (Paton Gallery) 1986, Royal Over-Seas League London 1986, London Glasgow New York (Met Museum NY) 1988, The New British Painting (Cincinnati and tour) 1988, Pacesetters (City Art Gallery Peterborough) 1988, The Thatcher Years: An Artistic Retrospective (Flowers East) 1989, Confrontation: Three British Artists (Joy Emery Gallery Detroit) 1989, Angela Flowers Gallery 1990 Barbican 1989, Flowers at Moos (Gallery Moos NY) 1990, This Sporting Life (Flowers East) 1990, Kunst Europa (Badischer Kunstverein Karlsruhe) 1991, Nudes (Waterman's Arts Centre Brentford) 1991, Artists Choice (Flowers East) 1992, Human Form (Parnham House) 1992, Heads (Royal Museum and Art Gallery Canterbury) 1993, But Big is Better... (Flowers East) 1993, New Figurative Painting (Salander-O'Reilly Galleries/Fred Hoffman Beverly Hills) 1993, By Underground to Kew (London Transport Museum and Kew Gardens Gallery) 1994, Six Gallery Artists (Angela Flowers Gallery) 1994, After Redoute (Flowers East) 1994, Twenty-fifth Anniversary (Flowers East) 1995, The Discerning Eye (Mall Galleries London) 1995, Naked (Flowers East) 1997, Angela Flowers Gallery 1997, Taboo (New End Gallery) 1997, Provocative Prints (New End Gallery) 1998, Cheltenham Open Drawing Exhibition 1998, Cheltenham & Gloucester College of HE, Künstlerwerkstalt Banhof Westend Berlin, Univ of Lincolnshire and Humberside 1998–99, Modern Portraits: Expressions of Intimacy (Golden Gate Univ San Francisco) 1998, Love Religion Explosives (St Margaret's Church Norwich) 1999, Small is Beautiful (Flowers East) 1999, The Comfort of Strangers (Waterman's Art Centre Brentford) 1999, Drawing Parallels (Lanchester Gallery Coventry) 2000, Small is Beautiful (Flowers East) 2002, Sun and Moon (Falmouth Art Gallery) 2004, We can work it out (Three Colts Gallery London) 2004, Paintings from the Nineties (Flowers Central London) 2005, The Circus Show (Three Colts Gallery London) 2005, Through the Looking Glass (Three Colts Gallery London) 2006, Ctrl, Alt, Delete (Lanchester Gallery Coventry) 2006), The Great Exhibition Room (Arlington Gallery London) 2006–07, Black and White (The Herbert Coventry) 2007, Re/Cognition (The Herbert Coventry) 2008, A Gothic Story (Shoreditch Town Hall Basement London) 2008, Jerwood Drawing Prize 2008 (Jerwood Space, London and tour) 2008, Drawing Breath (Lugar do Desentio, Fundaçáo Julio Resende Porto) 2008, Small is Beautiful (Flowers London) 2008; *Commissions* poster for London Underground on subject of Kew Gardens 1994, two paintings for Terminal 3 Heathrow Airport on subject of London parks 1995; work in the collections of: Metropolitan Museum NY, Contemporary Art Soc, Unilever plc, Dept of the Environment, Bankers Trust, Readers Digest London and NY, London Underground, Br Airports Authy, Tate Gallery, Basildon Hosp; *Style*— Jonathan Waller, Esq; ✉ 35 Campbell Road, Walthamstow, London E17 6RR (☎ 020 8509 0537, e-mail j.waller@coventry.ac.uk)

WALLER, Rt Hon Sir (George) Mark; kt (1989), PC (1996); s of The Rt Hon Sir George Stanley Waller, OBE (d 1999) (a former Lord Justice of Appeal), and Hon Lady Elizabeth Margery Waller, *née* Hacking (d 2008); *b* 13 October 1940; *Educ* Oundle, Univ of Durham (LLB); *m* 1967, Rachel Elizabeth, da of His Hon Christopher Beaumont, MBE (d 2002), of Boroughbridge, N Yorks; 3 s (Charles b 1968 d 1997, Richard b 1969, Philip b 1973); *Career* called to the Bar Gray's Inn 1964 (treas 2009), QC 1979, recorder of the Crown Court 1986–89, judge of the High Court of Justice (Queen's Bench Div) 1989–96, presiding judge (NE Circuit) 1992–95, judge i/c Commercial List 1995–96, a Lord Justice of Appeal 1996–2010, chm Judicial Studies Bd 1999–2003, pres Cncl of the Inns of Ct 2003–06, vice-pres Court of Appeal (Civil Div) 2006–10, intelligence services cmmr 2011–; *Recreations* tennis, golf; *Clubs* Garrick, MCC, Huntercombe; *Style*— The Rt Hon Sir Mark Waller; ✉ Serle Court, 6 New Square, Lincoln's Inn, London WC2A 3QS

WALLER, Rev Dr Ralph; *b* 11 December 1945; *Educ* John Leggot GS Scunthorpe, Univ of Oxford (MA), Richmond Coll Divinity Sch Univ of London (BD, Westcott New Testament Greek Prize, Hodson Smith Church History Prize), Univ of Nottingham (MTh), Univ of London (PhD); *m* 28 Dec 1968, Carol, *née* Roberts; 1 da (Elizabeth b 24 June 1983); *Career* VSO teacher and house master Shri Shivajh Mil Sch Poona India 1967–68; teacher Riddings Comp Sch Scunthorpe 1968; student Richmond Coll Divinity Sch Univ of London 1969–72; Methodist min Melton Mowbray Circuit 1972–75 (ordained 1975); min of Elvet Methodist Church Durham City and Methodist chaplain Univ of Durham 1975–81; chaplain St Mary's Coll and St Aidan's Coll Durham 1979–81; chaplain Westminster Coll Oxford (also tutor in theology and res tutor) 1981–88; princ Harris Manchester Coll Oxford 1988–, chm Theology Faculty Univ of Oxford 1995–97, pro vice-chllr Univ of Oxford 2010– (memb Hebdomadal Cncl 1997–2000), dir Fndn for the Study of Christianity and Soc 1990–98, dir Farmington Inst 2001–; Alfred North Whitehead distinguished visiting lectr Univ of Redlands CA 1992, Judge Russell distinguished visiting lectr on mgmnt Menlo Coll CA; select preacher Univ of Oxford 1992, 1997 and 2006; individual winner Templeton UK Award 1993; govr: St Mary's Coll Durham 1979–81, Kingswood Sch 1994–2006, Rydal Sch 2002–07, Cumberland Lodge 2008–, Alleyn's Sch 2012–; memb: Dr Barnardo's Adoption Ctee 1979–81, Mary Humphrey Churchill Tst 1993–2005; chm Joan Crewdson Tst; Hon DLitt Menlo Coll CA 1995, Hon DLitt Ball State Univ IN 1997, Hon DTheol Uppsala Univ 1999, Hon DH St Olaf Coll MN 2001, Hon DD Hartwick Coll NY 2003, Hon DHL Christopher Newport Univ 2005, Hon DH Univ of Indianapolis 2006, Hon DD Univ of Wales Trinity Saint David; *Publications* Truth, Liberty and Religion (contrib, 1986), Grace and Freedom (contrib, 1988), Studies in Church History (contrib to vol 25, 1988), Christian Spirituality (1999), John Wesley: A Personal Portrait (2003), Joy of Heaven (2003); *Recreations* walking, swimming, cycling; *Clubs* United Oxford and Cambridge; *Style*— The Rev Dr Ralph Waller; ✉ Harris Manchester College, Oxford OX1 3TD (☎ 01865 271007, e-mail ralph.waller@hmc.ox.ac.uk)

WALLER, His Hon Judge Stephen Philip; s of Ronald Waller, and Susannah Waller; *b* 2 January 1950; *Educ* Mill Hill Sch, UCL (LLB); *m* 1, 1972 (m dis), Anne Brooksbank; 1 s, 1 da; m 2, 1986, Jennifer Welch; 1 da; *Career* called to the Bar Inner Temple 1972; circuit judge (SE Circuit) 1996–; *Recreations* music; *Style*— His Hon Judge Waller; ✉ c/o Croydon Crown Court, Altyre Road, Croydon CR9 5AB

W

WALLERSTEINER, Dr Anthony Kurt; *b* 7 August 1963; *Educ* King's Sch Canterbury (scholar), Trinity Coll Cambridge (MA, open scholar, Crawford travelling scholar), Univ of Kent (PhD); *m* 1994, Valerie Anne, *née* MacDougall-Jones; 2 da (Isabella b 22 April 1995, Imogen b 12 July 1996), 1 s (Caspar b 1 June 1999); *Career* asst master: Bancroft Sch Woodford Green 1986, Sherborne 1986–89, St Paul's Sch 1989–92; Tonbridge Sch: head of history 1992–2000, housemaster 1999–2003; headmaster Stowe Sch 2003–; govr: Ashfold Sch 2004–, Winchester House Sch 2004–, Summerfields Prep Sch 2006–, Maidwell Hall 2008–, Buckingham Sch 2009–10; contrib various reviews for Burlington Magazine; memb: HMC 2003–, Cncl Tate St Ives 2005–09; Children in Crisis: tstee 2013–, chm 2016–; Terre Verte: the paintings of Alan Rankle (1998), The Head Speaks (contrib, 2008), Cradles of Success (contrib, 2012); *Recreations* Cornish art, music, trials biking, supporting West Ham United; *Clubs* East India, Lansdowne; *Style*— Dr Anthony Wallersteiner; ✉ Kinloss, Stowe, Buckingham MK18 5EH (☎ 01280 818240, fax 01280 818182); Stowe School, Buckingham MK18 5EH (☎ 01280 818000, fax 01280 818181, e-mail awallersteiner@stowe.co.uk)

WALLEY, Joan Lorraine; da of Arthur Simeon Walley (d 1968), and Mary Emma, *née* Pass (d 1991); *b* 23 January 1949; *Educ* Biddulph GS, Univ of Hull (BA), Univ Coll of Swansea (Dip); *m* 2 Aug 1980, Jan Ostrowski, s of Adam Ostrowski; 2 s; *Career* local govt offr NACRO, memb Lambeth Cncl 1982–86, MP (Lab) Stoke-on-Trent N 1987–2015; oppn front bench spokesman on: environment 1988–90, transport 1990–95; memb: Environment Audit Ctee, All-Pty Parly Football Ctee, All-Pty Parly Street Lighting Gp, Chm's Panel 2008–; pres Stoke on Trent Primary Sch Sports Assoc; vice-pres: Inst of Environmental Health Offrs, SERA; *Recreations* swimming, walking, music, German language; *Style*— Joan Walley; ✉ House of Commons, London SW1A 0AA (☎ 020 7219 4524, fax 020 7219 2397, e-mail walleyj@parliament.uk); constituency office: Unit 5, Burslem Enterprise Centre, Moorland Road, Burslem, Stoke-on-Trent ST6 1JN (☎ 01782 577900, fax 01782 836462, website www.joanwalleymp.org.uk)

WALLIAMS, David; s of Peter Williams (d 2007), and Kathleen Williams; surname changed upon joining Equity; *b* 20 August 1971; *Educ* Reigate GS, Univ of Bristol; *m* 16 May 2010, Lara Stone, the model; 1 s (Alfred b 2013); *Career* comedian, actor, writer; acted with Nat Youth Theatre; *Theatre* incl: Sir Bernard Chumley and Friends (Edinburgh Festival) 1995, 1996 and 1997, Little Britain Tour 2005–07, No Man's Land (Gate Theatre Dublin and Duke of York's Theatre London) 2008, A Midsummer Night's Dream (Noël Coward Theatre) 2013; *Television* incl: Rock Profile 1999–2000, Sir Bernard's Stately Homes 1999, Attachments 2000 and 2001, Spaced 2001, Randall and Hopkirk (Deceased) 2002, Little Britain 2003, 2004, 2005 and 2006, Hustle 2003, Cruise of the Gods 2003, Agatha Christie's Miss Marple: The Body in the Library 2004, Waking the Dead 2004, French and Saunders 2005, Stoned 2006, A Cock and Bull Story 2006, Virgin Territory 2007, Capturing Mary 2007, Hotel Babylon 2007, Little Britain USA 2007–08, Frankie Howerd: Rather You Than Me 2008, Come Fly With Me 2011, Wall of Fame 2011, Dr Who 2011, judge Britain's Got Talent 2012–14, Mr Stink 2012, Gangsta Granny 2013, Big School 2013–14; *Radio* incl Little Britain (BBC Radio 4) 2001 and 2002; *Film* Stardust 2007, Run Fat Boy Run 2007, The Chronicles of Narnia: Prince Caspian 2008, Marmaduke 2010, Dinner for Schmucks 2010, Great Expectations 2012, The Look of Love 2013, Justin and the Knights of Valour 2013, Pudsey the Dog: The Movie 2014; *Awards* for Little Britain: Silver Sony Radio Acad Award 2003, Gold Best Comedy Spoken Word Publisher Awards 2004, Best Comedy Performance and Best Entertainment RTS Awards 2004, Best Comedy Nat TV Awards 2004, 2005 and 2006, Best Comedy South Bank Show Awards 2005, Best Comedy Broadcast Magazine Awards 2005, Best TV Show NME Awards 2005, Best Comedy TRIC Awards 2005, Best Comedy Golden Rose TV Awards 2006, Best Comedy Int Emmy 2006; British Comedy Awards: Best Newcomer 2003, People's Choice Award 2004, Best Comedy Actor (jtly with Matt Lucas) 2004, Best Br Comedy 2004, Best TV Comedy 2005, Ronnie Barker Writer's Award 2005; BAFTA Awards: Best Comedy Series 2004 and 2005, Best Comedy Performance 2005; for swimming the English Channel: Sports Personality of the Year Special Award 2006, Special Recognition Nat TV Awards 2006, Inspiration Award Pride of Britain 2006, Landmark Achievement Award Nat TV Award 2012; *Books* The Boy in the Dress (2008), Mr Stink (2009), Billionaire Boy (2010), Gangsta Granny (2011), Ratburger (2012), Camp David (autobiography, 2012), Demon Dentist (2013), Awful Auntie (2014); *Style*— David Walliams; ✉ c/o Troika Talent, 10a Christina Street, London EC2A 4PA (☎ 020 7336 7868)

WALLINGER, John David Arnold; s of Sir Geoffrey Arnold Wallinger, GBE, KCMG (d 1979), and Diana, *née* Peel Nelson (d 1986); *b* 1 May 1940; *Educ* Winchester, Clare Coll Cambridge (BA); *m* 16 Feb 1966, Rosamund Elizabeth, da of Jack Philip Albert Gavin Clifford Wolff, MBE; *Career* ptnr: Panmure Gordon & Co 1972–75, Rowe & Pitman 1975–86; dir S G Warburg Securities 1986–95, vice-chm S G Warburg International 1994–95; exec dir SBC Warburg Dillon Read (UBS Warburg) 1995–98; dir: Spring Pond Farming 1998, Jupiter European Opportunities Tst plc 2000–, JEOT Securities Ltd 2001–, Attica Int Portfolio Ltd 2003–; chm: General & Oriental Holdings 1999–2001, Attica Inst Multi-Manager plc 2000–, Attica 360 Funds plc, Zebedee European Fund Ltd 2001–, Zebedee Capital Int Ltd 2001–, Greenfield Ventures Ltd 2001–03, Kingsbridge Capital Ltd 2002–, Kingsbridge Capital Advsrs Ltd 2003–; conslt: UBS AG 1998–, TSI, IMRS; *Recreations* golf, fishing, racing; *Clubs* White's, Swinley Forest Golf, New Zealand Golf, Holyport Tennis, Le Cercle de Deauville, Jockey; *Style*— John Wallinger, Esq

WALLIS, Diana Paulette; MEP; *b* 28 June 1954; *Career* slr in private practice 1983–99; MEP (Lib Dem) Yorks and the Humber 1999–; European Parl: vice-pres 2007–, ldr Lib Dem European Parly Pty 2001–04 and 2006–07, memb Legal Affrs Ctee (European Lib Dem spokesperson), memb Petitions Ctee, pres delgn to Iceland, Norway and Switzerland EEA Jt Parly Ctee 2004–07 (first vice-pres of delgn 1999–2004); cncllr Humberside Cncl 1994–95, dep ldr E Riding Unitary Cncl 1995–99, memb Regnl Assembly Ldr's Gp 1995–99; pt/t lectr in European business law Univ of Hull 1995–99; pres Inst of Translation and Interpreting 2002–; memb Law Soc (and EU Ctee 2002–), Campaign for Yorks; *Clubs* National Liberal; *Style*— Ms Diana Wallis, MEP

WALLIS, Prof Kenneth Frank; s of Leslie Wallis (d 1982), of Wath upon Dearne, S Yorks, and Vera Daisy, *née* Stone (d 1993); *b* 26 March 1938; *Educ* Wath upon Dearne GS, Univ of Manchester (BSc, MScTech), Stanford Univ (PhD); *m* 26 July 1963, Margaret Sheila, da of William Harold Campbell (d 2003), of Churchill, Somerset; *Career* lectr and reader LSE 1966–77, professor of econometrics Univ of Warwick 1977–2001 (emeritus prof 2001–), dir ESRC Macroeconomic Modelling Bureau 1983–99; exec memb NUS 1961–63; memb Cncl: RSS 1972–76, Royal Econ Soc 1989–94, Econometric Soc 1995–97, Br Acad 2002–05; chm HM Treasy Acad Panel 1987–91 (memb 1980–2001), memb Nat Statistics Methodology Advsy Ctee 2001–11; Hon DUniv Groningen 1999, fell Econometric Soc 1975, FBA 1994, fell Int Inst of Forecasters 2003; *Books* Introductory Econometrics (1972, 1981), Topics in Applied Econometrics (1973, 1979), Models of the UK Economy 1–4 (1984–87), Econometrics and Quantitative Economics (ed with D F Hendry, 1984), Macroeconometric Modelling (1994), Time Series Analysis and Macroeconometric Modelling (1995), Advances in Economics and Econometrics, vols I-III (ed with D M Kreps, 1997); *Recreations* travel, music, gardening, swimming; *Style*— Prof Kenneth F Wallis, FBA; ✉ Department of Economics, University of Warwick, Coventry CV4 7AL (☎ 024 7652 3055, fax 024 7652 3032, e-mail k.f.wallis@warwick.ac.uk)

WALLOP, Harry; *Educ* Univ of Oxford; m; 4 c; *Career* ed MTN Week 1998–2001, writer Investors Chronicle 2001–04; Daily Telegraph: business corr 2004–07, consumer affrs ed 2007–11, retail ed 2011–12, feature writer 2012–; presenter: Dispatches, Superscrimpers, Food: What Goes in Your Basket, Something for Nothing, Shop Secrets; Consumer Journalist of the Year London Press Club 2008; *Publications* Consumed: How Shopping Fed the Class System (2013); *Style*— Harry Wallop, Esq; ✉ Daily Telegraph, 111 Buckingham Palace Road, London SW1W 0DT

WALLS, (William) Alan; s of Harold Walls, of Sedgefield, Co Durham, and Marjorie, *née* Orton; *b* 18 September 1956; *Educ* Trinity Hall Cambridge (MA); *m* 29 July 1978, Julie, da of John Brown; 2 s (Thomas William b 4 Sept 1985, Adam Edward b 11 Feb 1991), 1 da (Rachel Hannah Louise b 8 June 1987); *Career* slr; Linklaters: articled 1979–81, slr 1981–87, ptnr 1987–2014, conslt 2014–, licensed insolvency practitioner 1990–; memb: Int Bar Assoc, London Slrs Litigation Assoc, City of London Slrs Co 1987, Law Soc; *Recreations* walking, sailing; *Style*— Alan Walls, Esq; ✉ Linklaters, One Silk Street, London EC2Y 8HQ (☎ 020 7456 2000, fax 020 7456 2222, e-mail awalls@linklaters.com)

WALLWORK, John; CBE (2012), DL (2008); s of Thomas Wallwork, and Vera, *née* Reid; *b* 8 July 1946; *Educ* Accrington GS, Univ of Edinburgh (BSc, MB ChB); *m* 1973, Elizabeth (Ann), da of John Selwyn Medley (d 1988), of New Plymouth, NZ; 2 da (Sarah b 18 April 1977, Alice b 9 May 1989), 1 s (Nicholas b 25 March 1982); *Career* surgical registrar Royal Infirmary Edinburgh 1975–76; sr registrar: Royal Infirmary Glasgow 1978–79, Bart's 1979–81, Adelaide Hosp 1977–78; chief res in cardiovascular and cardiac transplant surgery Stanford Univ 1980–81, prof of cardiothoracic surgery Papworth Hosp Cambs until 2011, ret, currently chm Bd of Dirs Papworth Hosp NHS Fndn Tst; memb: Br Transplant Soc, Cardiac Soc, Int Soc for Heart and Lung Transplantation, Scot Thoracic Soc, Soc of Thoracic and Cardiovascular Surgns of GB and Ireland, Euro Assoc for Cardio-Thoracic Surgery, Transplant Soc, Euro Soc for Organ Transplantation; past pres Int Soc for Heart and Lung Transplants, pres Red Cross Cambs 2005; Lister Professorship RCSEd 1985–86, hon chair in cardiothoracic surgery Univ of Cambridge 2002; Hon MA Univ of Cambridge 1986; fellowships ad eundem: FRCS 1992, FRCPEd 1999, FRCP 2001; FRCSEd, FMedSci 2002; *Books* Heart Disease: What it is and How it is Treated (1987), Heart and Heart-Lung Transplantation (1989); *Clubs* Garrick; *Style*— John Wallwork, Esq, CBE, DL; ✉ Papworth Hospital, Papworth Everards, Cambridgeshire CB23 3RE (☎ 01480 364573, fax 01480 831281, e-mail john.wallwork@papworth.nhs.uk)

WALMSLEY, Andrew; *Educ* Kingston Univ (MBA); *m*; 1 s, 1 da; *Career* TV buyer BMP 1988, co-fndr BMP Interaction (now Tribal DDB) 1995, head of digital media Bartle Bogle Hegarty 1997, co-fndr (with Charlie Dobres, *qv*) i-level 1998–2010 (chief operating offr 1998–2007, dep chm 2007–10); first chm Digital Mktg Gp (now part of IPA); Queen's Award for Enterprise 2007; *Style*— Andrew Walmsley, Esq

WALMSLEY, Claire; *née* Slavin; da of John Patrick Slavin (d 1971), and (Margaret) Mabel, *née* Reader; *b* 6 May 1944; *Educ* Convent of the Holy Child Jesus Blackpool, Royal Coll of Music London; *m* 1964 (m dis 1982), Christopher Roberts Walmsley (d 1995); 2 da (Frances b 18 Nov 1964, Jennie b 13 April 1968), 1 s (Alexis b 14 April 1971); *Career* broadcaster, TV prodr and documentary film maker; BBC 1976–90, md Boxclever Productions Ltd 1990–, media conslt and communication coach 2000–; memb: BAFTA, RTS, IOD, Forum; FRSA; *Books* Assertiveness – The Right to be You (1991), Letting Go (1993); *Recreations* theatre, scuba diving, travel, sailing, exploring Scotland, family; *Style*— Mrs Claire Walmsley; ✉ e-mail claire@clairewalmsley.co.uk

WALMSLEY, Prof Ian Alexander; s of Richard Melville Walmsley, and Hazel Florence, *née* Wilkinson; *b* 13 January 1960, Hyde, Cheshire; *Educ* Imperial Coll London (BSc), Univ of Rochester (PhD); *m* 17 May 1986, Katherine Frances Pardee; 2 s (Alexander Pardee Walmsley b 22 May 1992, Nathaniel Pearre Walmsley b 27 Feb 1994), 1 da (Penelope Clair Walmsley b 25 April 1997); *Career* postdoctoral research assoc Cornell Univ 1986–87; Inst of Optics Univ of Rochester: asst prof 1988–93, assoc prof 1994–97, prof 1998–2002, interim dir 2000–01, adjunct prof 2002–06; visiting prof Universität Ulm Germany 1995; Univ of Oxford: prof 2001–05, head Sub-Dept of Atomic and Laser Physics 2002–09, Hooke prof of experimental physics 2005–, pro-vice-chllr (research) 2009–11, pro-vice-chllr (research, academic services and univ collections) 2011–; sr visiting fell Princeton Univ 2002–08; memb: Optics Express Implementation Ctee 1997, NRC Visiting Ctee for JILA 2000–02, Inst of Physics QEP Gp Ctee 2005–07, EPSRC Technical Opportunities Panel 2006–10, EPSRC Physics Strategic Advsy Team 2006–07, QIPC '06 Program Ctee, IQEC '07 Sub-Ctee (chair); topical ed Jl of the Optical Soc of America B 1999–2005; advsy ed: Jl of Physics B 1999–2004, Jl of Modern Optics 2000–; memb Convocation Univ of London; hon degree Université Libre de Bruxelles 2008; fell Optical Soc of America 1997 (dir at large 2006–), fell American Physical Soc 2000, FInstP 2004, FRS 2012; *Awards* National Science Fndn Presidential Young Investigator Award 1990, Sch of Engineering and Applied Science Undergraduate Teaching Award 1995, Goergen Award for Undergraduate Teaching 1999, Leibinger Innovationspreis 2006, Wolfson-Royal Soc Research Merit Award 2007, American Physical Soc Outstanding Referee 2008, American Physical Soc J F Keithley Award 2011, Inst of Physics Young Prize and Medal 2011; Ultrafast Optics IV (jt ed, 2004), Proceedings of the Conference on Coherence and Quantum Optics (jt ed, 2004); numerous articles in scientific jls; *Style*— Prof Ian Walmsley; ✉ Department of Physics, University of Oxford, Clarendon Laboratory, Parks Road, Oxford OX1 3PU (☎ 01865 272 205, fax 01865 272 375, e-mail walmsley@physics.ox.ac.uk)

WALMSLEY, Baroness (Life Peer UK 2000), of West Derby in the County of Merseyside; Joan Margaret Walmsley; *née* Watson; da of Leo John Watson, and Monica *née* Nolan; *b* 12 April 1943, Liverpool; *Educ* Notre Dame HS Liverpool, Univ of Liverpool (BSc), Manchester Metropolitan Univ (PGCE); *m* 21 Oct 2005, Baron Thomas of Gresford, OBE, QC (Life Peer), *qv*; *Career* cytologist Christie Hosp Manchester 1966–67, teacher Buxton Coll 1979–86, PR conslt Intercommunication 1987–89, PR conslt Hill & Knowlton UK Ltd 1989–95, prop JWPR and Walmsley Jones Communications 1995–2003; memb Bd Botanic Gardens Conservation Int (chm 2004–13); patron: SKCV Childrens Tst, Helena Kennedy Tst, Infant Tst, Family Planning Assoc; NSPCC and UNICEF Parly ambass; *Recreations* music, theatre, gardening; *Clubs* Reform; *Style*— The Rt Hon the Lady Walmsley; ✉ House of Lords, London SW1A 0PW (☎ 020 7219 6047, fax 020 7219 8602, e-mail walmsleyj@parliament.uk)

WALMSLEY, Nigel Norman; s of Norman Walmsley (d 1996), and Ida Walmsley (d 2008); *b* 26 January 1942; *Educ* William Hulme Sch Manchester, Univ of Oxford (BA); *m* Jane, author and broadcaster; 1 da (Katie b 8 Sept 1977); *Career* asst sec Dept of Industry 1975–77, dir of mktg Post Office 1979–82, md Capital Radio Gp 1982–91; Carlton Communications plc: exec dir 1991–2001, chm Carlton TV 1994–2001 (chief exec 1991–94); ptnr DLJ European Media Credit Suisse 2006–09; chm: GMTV 2000–2001, Tourism South East 2002–09, BARB 2002–13; non-exec dir: Energis plc 1997–2002, Ambassador Theatre Gp 2000–04, De Vere Gp plc 2001–06, Eagle Rock Entertainment 2002–14 (chm 2002–07); vice-chm Advtg Assoc 1992–2003; dir: London Ambulance Service Tst 2010–11, ATVOD 2010–; dep chm: ASA 2004–10, Passenger Focus 2005–13, Postwatch 2006–08; former chm: GLAA, Ind Radio Industry Res Ctee, Wren Orch of London; govr South Bank Centre; *Recreations* theatre, walking; *Clubs* City of London; *Style*— Nigel Walmsley, Esq; ✉ Authority for Television on Demand, 27 Sheen Street, Windsor, Berkshire SL4 1BN

WALMSLEY, Dr Thomas (Tom); s of late Prof Robert Walmsley, of St Andrews, Fife; *b* 15 August 1946; *Educ* Fettes, Univ of Dundee (MB ChB), Univ of Edinburgh (DPM); *m* 1,

1973 (m dis 1981), Jane Walsh, of Edinburgh; 1 da (Anna); m 2, 1981, Linda Hardwick, of Arbroath, Scotland (d 2003); 2 s (William George, Christopher Robert (Kit)); m 3, 2004, Sally Westaway, of Port Elizabeth, SA; *Career* lectr in psychiatry Univ of Edinburgh 1975–77, conslt psychiatrist Royal Edinburgh Hosp 1977–81, conslt psychiatrist Wessex RHA 1981–2010; regnl advsr in psychiatry 1998–2003; visiting prof Univ of Kuwait 1994; MRCPsych 1974, FRCPsych 1997; *Recreations* reading, walking, maps; *Style—* Dr Tom Walmsley; ✉ Russell Place, Trampers Lane, North Boarhunt, Hampshire PO17 6DQ; Osborn Centre, Fareham, Hampshire PO16 7ES (☎ 01329 288331)

WALPOLE, HE Hon Alice Louise; er da of 10 Baron Walpole, JP, *qv*, and Judith Chaplin, OBE, MP (d 1993); *b* 1 September 1963; *Educ* Norwich HS, New Hall Cambridge; *m* 1990 (m dis 2010), Dr Angel Cesar Carro Castrillo; 3 da (Hester Nancy, Beatrice Maud b 1990 (twins), Isobel Clemency b 1993), 3 s (Inigo Robert b 1996, Ralph Horatio, Edmund Gabriel b 1999 (twins)); *Career* diplomat; desk offr Eastern European Dept FCO 1985–86, conference support offr UK Mission to the UN NY 1986–87, desk offr Info Dept FCO 1987, third sec devpt UK Rep to the EC Brussels 1987–90, second sec political Dar es Salaam 1991–94, desk offr Policy Planning Staff FCO 1994–96, head Peacekeeping Unit UN Dept FCO 1996–98, first sec European defence UK Del to NATO 1998–2000, first sec European defence UK Rep to EU 2000–01, first sec environment UK Mission NY 2001–06, dep head Stabilisation Unit 2006–08, dep head Corporate Communications Gp FCO 2008–09, consul-gen Basra 2009–11, ambass to Luxembourg 2011–16, ambass to Mali and non-resident ambass to Niger 2016–; *Recreations* sewing, gardening; *Style—* HE the Hon Alice Walpole; ✉ British Embassy, Cite du Niger II, Bamako, Mali (☎ 00 223 44 97 69 13)

WALPOLE, Lee; s of John Walpole, and Carole Walpole; *b* 25 May 1980, Exeter; *m* Hayley Walpole; *Career* sound editor and re-recording mixer; memb Television Acad, memb BAFTA; *Television* incl: State of Play 2003, William and Mary 2004–05, Primeval 2007–08, Generation Kill 2008 (Outstanding Sound Editing for a Miniseries, Movie or a Special Primetime Emmy 2009), The Prisoner 2009, Strike Back 2010–15, Silk 2011, Mad Dogs 2012, Peaky Blinders 2013, Esiotrot 2014, Klondike (MPSE Golden Reel winner) 2014, Halo: Nightfall (MPSE Golden Reel winner) 2014, War and Peace 2016, The Crown 2016; *Film* incl: Run Fatboy Run 2007, The Damned United 2009, Glorious 39 2009, The King's Speech 2010, Les Misérables 2012 (Sound BAFTA 2013, Film Sound Ed of the Year UK Screen Conch Award 2012, IPA Satellite Award 2013), The Imitation Game 2014, The Woman in Black: Angel of Death 2015, London Has Fallen 2016; *Style—* Lee Walpole, Esq; ✉ Boom Post, 27–29 Berwick Street, London W1F 8RQ (☎ 020 7478 8600, e-mail leew@boompost.co.uk, website www.boompost.co.uk)

WALPOLE, 10 Baron (GB 1723); Robert Horatio Walpole; JP (Norfolk); also 8 Baron Walpole of Wolterton (GB 1756); patron of 6 livings; s of 9 Baron Walpole, TD (d 1989); *b* 8 December 1938; *Educ* Eton, King's Coll Cambridge (MA, Dip Agric); *m* 1, 30 June 1962 (m dis 1979), (Sybil) Judith (d 1993), yr da of late Theodore Thomas Schofield, of Harpenden, Herts; 2 da (Hon Alice Louise b 1 Sept 1963, Hon Emma Judith b 10 Oct 1964), 2 s (Hon Jonathan Robert Hugh b Nov 16 1967, Hon Benedict Thomas Orford b 1 June 1969); m 2, 1980, Laurel Celia, o da of Sidney Tom Ball (d 2004), of Swindon, Wilts; 2 s (Hon Roger Horatio Calibut b 1980, Hon Henry William b 1982), 1 da (Hon Grace Mary b 1986); *Heir* s, Hon Jonathan Walpole; *Career* sits as crossbencher in House of Lords (elected 1999); memb: Agric Sub-Ctee of Select Ctee on European Communities 1991–94, Environment Sub-Ctee of Select Ctee on European Communities 1995–99, Select Ctee on Euro Communities 1996–99, EU Sub-Ctee Environment Agriculture and Consumer Protection 2001–03, EU Sub-Ctee Energy, Industry and Tport 2003–06, Ecclesiastical Ctee; chm All Pty London Gp House of Lords 2013; hon fell St Mary's UC Strawberry Hill; *Style—* The Rt Hon the Lord Walpole; ✉ Mannington Hall, Norwich, Norfolk NR11 7BB

WALPORT, Prof Sir Mark Jeremy; kt (2009); *b* 25 January 1953; *Educ* St Paul's, Clare Coll Cambridge (MA, MB BChir, Harrison-Watson student, PhD), Middx Hosp Med Sch; *m*; 4 c; *Career* jr hosp appts Middx, Hammersmith, Guy's and Brompton Hosps 1977–82, MRC trg fell MRC Centre Cambridge and hon sr registrar Addenbrooke's Hosp Cambridge 1982–85 (dir of studies in pathology Clare Coll Cambridge 1984–85); Royal Postgrad Med Sch Hammersmith Hosp: head Rheumatology Unit Dept of Med 1985–97, sr lectr in rheumatology 1985–90, reader in rheumatological med 1990–91, prof of med 1991–97, vice-dean (research) 1994–97; dir R&D Hammersmith Hosps Tst 1994–98, prof of med and chm Div of Med Imperial Coll Sch of Med Hammersmith Hosp (following merger) 1997–2003, dir The Wellcome Tst 2003–13 (govr 2000–03); chief scientific advsr to HM Govt and head Govt Office of Science 2013–; fell Imperial Coll 2006, hon distinguished prof of medicine Imperial Coll London 2013–; Br Soc for Rheumatology: memb Cncl 1989–95, memb Heberden Ctee 1990–95 (chm 1993–95); memb: Scientific Co-ordinating Ctee Arthritis and Rheumatism Cncl 1992–99, Working Ctee on Ethics of Xenotransplantation Nuffield Bioethics Cncl 1995–96, Molecular and Cell Panel Wellcome Tst 1995–2002 (chm 1998–2002), Health Ctee Br Cncl 1998–2002, Cncl for Science and Technol 2004–; fndr fell, memb Cncl and registrar Acad of Med Sciences 1998–2003; asst ed Br Jl of Rheumatology 1981–86, advsy ed Arthritis and Rheumatism 1996–2001, series ed Br Medical Bulletin 1998–2003, ed-in-chief Clinical and Experimental Immunology 1998–2000; memb Assoc of Physicians 1990, hon memb American Assoc of Physicians 2001; Roche Rheumatology Prize 1991, Graham Bull Prize in Clinical Sci RCP 1996; Philip Ellman Lecture RCP 1995; Hon DSc: Univ of Sheffield 2006, KCL 2007, Univ of Aberdeen 2010, Univ of Leicester 2012, Univ of Glasgow 2013, Cranfield Univ 2013, Keele Univ 2013; Hon DUniv York 2012, Hon DCL Newcastle Univ 2013; hon fell Clare Coll Cambridge 2012; FRCP 1990, FRCPath 1997, FMedSci 1998, FRS 2011, Hon FRSM 2012; *Books* Clinical Aspects of Immunology (jt ed, 5 edn 1993), Immunobiology (jtly, 6 edn 2005); author of numerous scientific papers; *Clubs* Athenaeum; *Style—* Prof Sir Mark Walport; ✉ Government Office for Science, 1 Victoria Street, London SW1H 0ET (☎ 020 7215 1032)

WALSH, Amanda (Mrs Brian Stewart); da of David Joseph Walsh, of Thurlestone, S Devon, and Eileen Julia Frances Walsh; *b* 27 November 1955; *Educ* St Mary's Convent Worcester, Kingston Univ (BA); *m* 28 Sept 1989, Brian Stewart; 1 step da (Sophie b 25 Sept 1982); *Career* sales and mktg exec Tek Translation Ltd 1978–80, account exec Wasey Campbell Ewald Advertising 1980–83; WCRS: joined 1984, bd dir 1987–89, client servs and new business dir 1990–93, md 1993–95; ptnr and ceo Walsh Trott Chick Smith 1995–2003, European ceo United Gp (formerly Red Cell Network) 2004–06, ceo Lowe London 2006–; memb Bd UK Film Cncl 2006–; pres Women's Advertising and Communications Club London 2002, memb Mktg Soc 1991; tstee Brain and Spine Fndn; MIPA (memb Bd 1993–2003); *Style—* Ms Amanda Walsh

WALSH, Andrew; *Career* dir of investigations and corporate servs Public Services Ombudsman for Wales; *Style—* Andrew Walsh, Esq; ✉ Public Services Ombudsman for Wales, 1 Ffordd yr Hen Gae, Pencoed CF35 5LJ

WALSH, Barbara Ann; da of late James Walsh, and late Audrey Walsh, MBE, JP; *b* 1 March 1955, Manchester; *Educ* Manchester HS, Univ of Birmingham (BSc); *m* 1; 1 da (Emma Jane b 29 Oct 1981), 1 s (James Nicholas b 26 Aug 1984); m 2, Peter Charles Wozencroft; 2 s (William George b 23 Dec 1996, Daniel Charles b 9 Nov 1999); *Career* gen mangr Hillingdon HA 1985–88, chief exec Riverside Mental Health NHS Tst 1988–93, chief exec Community Health Sheffield NHS Tst 1993–2001, chief exec S Yorks Workforce Confedn 2001–05; dir Homestart Sheffield; vice-chair Governing Body Netherthorpe Primary Sch 2010–11, chair Governing Body King Edward VII Secdy Sch (formerly vice-chair), chair S Yorks Housing Assoc; foster parent; MHSM 1981; *Recreations* family, walking, cooking, reading; *Style—* Ms Barbara Walsh; ☎ 07494 570116, e-mail ms.barbara.walsh@gmail.com

WALSH, Campbell; s of Isaac Walsh, of Stirling, Scotland, and Shelagh, *née* Campbell; *b* 26 November 1977, Glasgow; *Educ* Univ of Nottingham (MSc); *Career* canoeist; K1 slalom: Silver medal Olympic Games Athens 2004, champion World Cup 2004, European champion 2008; BBC E Midlands Sportsman of the Year 2004; *Clubs* CR Cats Canoe; *Style—* Campbell Walsh, Esq; ✉ c/o British Canoe Union HQ, 18 Market Place, Bingham, Nottingham NG13 8AP

WALSH, Colin Stephen; *b* 26 January 1955; *Educ* Portsmouth GS, ChCh Oxford (MA); *Career* asst organist Salisbury Cathedral 1978–85, organist and master of the music St Albans Cathedral 1985–88, organist and master of the choristers Lincoln Cathedral 1988–, organist laureate 2003–; has given many organ recitals in UK and overseas: French organ music from Salisbury 1985, French organ music from St Albans 1987, Great European Organ Series Lincoln Cathedral 1989, Vierne 24 Pieces en Style Libre 1991, English organ music 1992, Vierne Symphonies 2 and 3 1993, Popular Organ Music 1993, 1898!, Two Willis Organs 1998, French organ music from Lincoln 2004, Widor Symphonies 5&6 2007, Frank: Organ Works 2008, Colin Walsh and the organ of Lincoln Cathedral (recorded on DVD) 2009; Hon DMus Univ of Lincoln 2013; ARCM 1972, FRCO 1977; *Recreations* walking, dining out, travel, theatre, steam trains; *Style—* Colin Walsh, Esq; ✉ Lincoln Cathedral, 12 Minster Yard, Lincoln LN2 1PJ (☎ 01522 561646, e-mail colinwalsh1@btinternet.com)

WALSH, John Henry Martin; s of Martin Walsh (d 1986), of Galway, Eire, and Anne, *née* Durkin (d 1998); *b* 24 October 1953; *Educ* Wimbledon Coll, Exeter Coll Oxford (BA), Univ Coll Dublin (MA); *m* Angie O'Rourke; 2 da (Sophie Matilda Hart-Walsh b 11 Aug 1987, Clementine Hart-Walsh b 5 July 1995), 1 s (Max Henry Thomas Hart-Walsh b 30 Aug 1991); *Career* journalist 1978–; Advtg Dept The Tablet, Gollancz publishers 1977–78, assoc ed The Director Magazine 1978–82; lit ed then features and lit ed Evening Standard 1986–88, lit ed and feature writer The Sunday Times 1988–93, ed Independent Magazine 1993–95; The Independent: lit ed 1995–96, feature writer 1996–, asst ed (features) 1998–2013; freelance feature writer and reviewer for various newspapers and magazines incl: The Times, Time Out, Tatler, Harpers, Q, Mojo, Word, New Yorker; broadcaster: Books and Company (Radio 4), The Write Stuff (Radio 4); script ed Book Choice (Channel 4) 1995–; dir Cheltenham Literary Festival 1997 and 1998; pres Authors' Club 2008–; *Books* Growing Up Catholic (1989), The Falling Angels: An Irish Romance (1999), Are You Talking To Me?: A Life Through the Movies (2003), Sunday at the Cross Bones (2007); *Recreations* drinking, talking, music; *Clubs* Groucho, National Liberal; *Style—* John Walsh, Esq; ✉ 4 Westbourne Park Villas, London W2 5EA

WALSH, (Michael) Louis; *b* 5 August 1952, Kiltimagh, Co Mayo, Ireland; *Career* mangr of pop artists incl: Boyzone, Ronan Keating, Samantha Mumba, Westlife, Girls Aloud, G4, Shayne Ward; *Television* judge: Popstars: Ireland 2001, Popstars: The Rivals (ITV) 2002, You're A Star (RTÉ 1) 2003–04, The X Factor (ITV) 2004–; *Style—* Louis Walsh, Esq; ✉ Louis Walsh Management, 24 Courtney House, Appian Way, Dublin 6, Ireland

WALSH, His Hon Judge Martin Fraser; s of Nicholas Joseph Walsh, of Kilkenny, Ireland, and Maureen, *née* McGlone; *b* 7 January 1955, Upminster, Gtr London; *Educ* St Bede's Coll Manchester, Univ of Manchester (LLB), Coll of Law Chester; *Children* 1 da (Dr Anna Siobhán b 27 May 1990); *Career* admitted slr 1979, called to the Bar Gray's Inn 1990; Messrs Cyril Morris & Arkwright Slrs Bolton: articled 1977–79, ptnr 1980–90; Peel Court Chambers 1990–2008, recorder 2001, Lincoln House Chambers 2008–09, circuit judge (Midland Circuit) 2009–; *Style—* His Hon Judge Martin Walsh; ✉ Wolverhampton Combined Court Centre, Pipers Row, Wolverhampton WV1 3LQ (☎ 01902 481000)

WALSH, Michael Jeffrey; s of Kenneth Francis Walsh, of Alford, Lincs, and Edith, *née* Hudson; *b* 1 October 1949; *Educ* Hulme GS Oldham, Univ of Durham; *m* Sally, da of Rev Ronald Forbes Shaw; 1 s, 1 da; *Career* advertising exec; Young & Rubicam: grad trainee 1972, account exec 1972–74, account mangr 1974–78, account dir 1978–80, bd dir 1980, new business dir 1981–82, memb UK Exec Ctee; Ogilvy & Mather: dir Bd and mgmnt supervisor 1983–84, head of account mgmnt 1984–85, dir of client service 1985–86, md 1986–89, elected to Worldwide Bd 1989, chm 1989–90, UK gp chm 1990–99, ceo EMEA 1994–; tstee British Red Cross 1994–2004 (vice-chm 1994–2000, then hon vice-chm), worldwide tstee WWF 1996–99, chm UK Disaster Emergency Ctee 2005–; chm Alkrington Young Conservatives 1966–67; *Recreations* collecting Victorian and Edwardian children's books, antiques, tennis, sailing, golf; *Clubs* RAC, Hunstanton Golf, Highgate Golf, Marks, Annabel's, Royal West Norfolk Golf; *Style—* Michael Walsh, Esq; ✉ Ogilvy & Mather, 10 Cabot Square, Canary Wharf, London E14 4QB (☎ 020 7345 3000)

WALSH, Michael Ravell; s of Lt-Col John Mainwaring Walsh, MC, RA (d 2007), and Dr Wendy Felicitée Walsh, *née* Storey (d 2014); *b* 1949, Singapore; *Educ* Wellington (exhibitioner), Trinity Coll Dublin, Clare Coll Cambridge (exhibitioner, MA); *m* 1975, Nei Rotee Katarina Tekee; 2 da (Sophia Mamaua Annabelle (Mrs Blackmore) b 1979, Cordelia Kabobo Wendy b 1986), 1 s (Philip Edgar Tekee Prendergast b 1980); *Career* econ advsr Govt of Gilbert and Ellice Islands 1971–76, FCO 1976–78, dir planning and info servs Crown Agents 1978–86; various posts: PA Consulting Gp 1986–95, SchlumbergerSema 1995–2001, Xansa plc 2001–03; fndr MAANA Ltd 2003–09 (md 2005–09), dir TERIKI Ltd 2009–15; hon consul Republic of Kiribati; memb Cncl Pacific Islands Soc of the UK and Ireland (chm 2002–08); Liveryman Worshipful Co of Mgmnt Conslts; *Publications* A Guide to Programme Management; *Recreations* gardening, country pursuits, traditional Irish, Scottish and Appalachian music; *Style—* Michael Walsh, Esq; ✉ Kiribati Consulate, The Great House, Llanddewi Rhydderch, Monmouthshire NP7 9UY (☎ 01873 840375, e-mail mravellwalsh@btopenworld.com)

WALSH, (Mary) Noelle (Mrs Heslam); da of late Thomas Walsh, and Mary Kate, *née* Ferguson; *b* 26 December 1954; *Educ* UEA (BA); *m* 15 Oct 1988, David Howard Heslam, s of late Capt James William Heslam; 1 da (Ciara b 15 Aug 1989), 1 s (Calum b 17 May 1991); *Career* news ed Cosmopolitan Magazine 1979–85, ed Good Housekeeping Magazine 1987–91 (dep ed 1985–87), journalist Daily Telegraph 1991–92, dir The Value for Money Co Ltd 1992–, dir websites www.gooddealdirectory.co.uk, www.gooddealhouse.com and www.ukgrandsales.co.uk; *Books* Hot Lips – The Ultimate Kiss and Tell Guide (1985), Ragtime to Wartime – The Best of Good Housekeeping 1922–1939 (1986), The Home Front – The Best of Good Housekeeping 1939–1945 (1987), Good Housekeeping – The Christmas Book (1988), Food Glorious Food – Eating and Drinking with Good Housekeeping 1922–42 (1990), Things My Mother Should Have Told Me – The Best of Good Housekeeping 1922–40 (1991), Childhood Memories – Growing Up with Good Housekeeping 1922–1942 (1991), The Good Deal Directory (annually 1994–2005), The Home Shopping Handbook (1994), Baby on a Budget (1995), Wonderful Weddings (1996), Factory Shopping and Sightseeing Guide (1996), The Good Mail Order Guide (1996); *Recreations* bargain hunting, antiques, sailing; *Style—* Miss Noelle Walsh; ✉ Cottage by the Church, Filkins, Lechlade, Gloucestershire GL7 3JG (☎ 01367 860017, fax 01367 860177, e-mail nheslam@aol.com)

WALSH, Paul S; *Educ* Royton & Compton Sch Oldham, Manchester Poly; *Career* Grand Metropolitan: joined 1982, finance dir Brewing Div 1986, subsequently with InterContinental Hotels, chief exec Pillsbury 1992–99; Diageo plc 2000– (chief operating offr 2000, ceo 2000–13); non-exec dir Federal Express Corp, non-exec memb Bd Unilever plc 2009–; lead non-exec dir Dept for Energy and Climate Change 2011–13; chm Scotch

W

Whisky Assoc 2008–11 (memb Cncl 2001–, vice-chm 2006–08); memb Bd of Tstees The Prince of Wales Int Business Leaders Forum, memb PM's Business Advsy Gp 2010–12; *Style—* Mr Paul S Walsh; ✉ Diageo plc, Lakeside Drive, Park Royal, London NW10 7HQ

WALSH, Stephen John; s of C A Walsh, LLM, of Winchester, Hants, and E B Walsh, *née* Boardman; *b* 14 September 1945; *Educ* Lancing, Coll of Law Guildford, Royal Coll of Art (MA); *m* 22 Feb 1975, Georgina Elizabeth, da of George William Stott; 3 da (Jessica Anne Elizabeth b 18 Oct 1980, Antonia Sarah Georgina b 29 May 1982, Clarissa Rachel Emily b 20 Jan 1989); *Career* articled clerk to Messrs Arnold Cooper and Tompkins Slrs 1965–67, designer Apple Corps (The Beatles co) 1967–68, postgrad student RCA 1969–72, pt/t creative dir Scenses Art Gallery London 1972–73, design conslt DI Design and Development Consultants Inc 1974–78, regnl dir (Middle East) Fitch & Co 1978–82, md Fitch (International) Ltd 1982–84, fndr and chief exec Crighton Ltd 1984–90, md Crighton McColl 1990–92, dir Business Design Group McColl 1992–95, dir Hanseatica Project Design and Development 1995–2003; dir ARC Airport Retail Consultants 1999–; dir ARCH 1995–; FCSD; *Recreations* sailing, skiing, drawing, travelling; *Clubs* Durban Country (Natal), Dubai Offshore Sailing, Capital (Dubai); *Style—* Stephen Walsh, Esq; ✉ 64 Cranbury Road, London SW6 2NJ (☎ 020 7736 8991, e-mail sw@hanseat.demon.co.uk)

WALSHAM, Prof Geoff; s of Harry Walsham (d 1976), and Charlotte, *née* Wood (d 2006); *b* 10 June 1946, Manchester; *Educ* Manchester Grammar, Univ of Oxford (MA), Univ of Warwick (MSc), Univ of Cambridge (LittD); *m* 7 March 1970, Alison, *née* Evans; 1 da (Jenny b 17 Oct 1973), 3 s (Peter b 16 Jan 1976, Matthew b 18 July 1978, Thomas b 22 Feb 1980); *Career* lectr in mathematics Mindanao State Univ Philippines 1966–67, operational res analyst BP Chemicals Int London 1968–72, lectr in operational res Univ of Nairobi 1972–75, lectr in mgmnt studies Engineering Dept Univ of Cambridge 1975–94, prof of info mgmnt Lancaster Univ 1994–96; Univ of Cambridge: assoc dir of exec educn Judge Inst of Mgmnt Studies 1996–98, res prof of mgmnt studies 1998–2001, prof of mgmnt studies (info systems) Judge Business Sch 2001–10 (emeritus prof of mgmnt studies 2010–); *Publications* Interpreting Information Systems in Organizations (1993), Making a World of Difference: Information Technology in a Global Context (2001); author of over 100 other pubns; *Recreations* mountain walking, travel, gardening, reading; *Style—* Prof Geoff Walsham; ✉ Judge Business School, University of Cambridge, Trumpington Street, Cambridge CB2 1AG (☎ 01223 339606, e-mail g.walsham@jbs.cam.ac.uk, website www.jbs.cam.ac.uk/faculty-research/fellows-associates-a-z/geoff-walsham/

WALSOM, Roger Benham; *b* March 1953; *Educ* Brighton Hove and Sussex GS, Univ of Southampton (LLB), Coll of Law; *m* 1984, Susan, *née* Pitcairn; 1 s (Patrick b July 1989), 1 da (Louise b Feb 1993 d 2011); *Career* admitted slr 1980; Excess Insurance 1970–74, Slaughter and May 1978–83, Ashurst LLP 1983–2005 (ptnr 1988–2005, conslt 2005–08); non-exec dir: The Pensions Regulator 2004–08, St James's Place plc 2005–, Invesco Income Growth Tst 2006–, Miller Insurance Broking Gp 2009–; chm of two private companies; memb Law Soc; Insurance M&A: Structuring Complex Transactions (contrib, 1999), The Financial Services and Markets Act 2000: A Practical Legal Guide (contrib, 2001), C Shares and S Shares: a different class of share (1997); *Recreations* reading, writing, walking, music; *Style—* Roger Walsom, Esq; ✉ Invesco Income Growth Trust plc, 125 London Wall, London EC2Y 5AS

WALTER, Dame Harriet Mary; DBE (2011, CBE 2000); da of Roderick Walter (d 1996), of London, and Xandra Carandini, *née* Lee (later Lady de Trafford; d 2002); *b* 24 September 1950; *Educ* Cranborne Chase Sch, LAMDA; *m* 2011, Guy Paul; *Career* actress; debut Duke's Playhouse Lancaster 1974; nat tours 1975–78 with: 7:84, Joint Stock, Paines Plough; assoc artist RSC 1987, RSC Govr and hon assoc artist 2015; memb: Amnesty Int, Friends of the Earth, PEN; Hon DLitt Univ of Birmingham 2001; *Theatre* Royal Court Theatre 1980–81 incl: Cloud Nine, The Seagull, Ophelia in Hamlet; RSC incl: Helena in All's Well That Ends Well (Broadway 1983), The Castle 1985 (Olivier Award nomination), Twelfth Night, The Duchess of Malfi, Macbeth 1999–2000, Much Ado About Nothing 2002, Antony and Cleopatra 2006–07; RNT incl: Dinner (also at Wyndhams), Life x 3 (also at Old Vic, Olivier Award nomination), Arcadia, The Children's Hour, Women Beware Women 2010; other work incl: Three Birds Alighting on a Field (Royal Court and Manhattan Theatre Club NY), Old Times (Wyndhams), Hedda Gabler (Chichester Festival Theatre), Ivanov (Almeida), The Late Middle Classes (Watford), The Royal Family (Theatre Royal Haymarket), Us and Them (Hampstead), Mary Stuart (Donmar Warehouse and Apollo Theatre) 2005 and (Broadway) 2009, Brutus in all-female Julius Caesar (Donmar Warehouse) 2012–13 and (St Anne's Warehouse NY) 2013, title role in Henry IV (Donmar 2014 and St Anne's Warehouse NY 2015), title role in Boa (Trafalgar Studios 2015), Linda Loman in Death of a Salesman (RSC Stratford and Noel Coward) 2015; *Television* incl: The Imitation Game, Harriet Vane in the Lord Peter Wimsey Mysteries, The Price, The Men's Room, Ashenden, Unfinished Business, Dance to the Music of Time, George Eliot: A Scandalous Life, Ballet Shoes 2008, Little Dorrit 2008, A Short Stay in Switzerland 2009, Law and Order 2009–13, Downton Abbey 2013–15, London Spy 2015, The Crown 2016, Black Sails (Season 4) 2016, Call the Midwife (Season 6) 2016; *Film* incl: Turtle Diary 1985, The Good Father 1985, Milou en Mai 1990, Sense and Sensibility 1995, The Governess 1998, Bedrooms and Hallways 1998, Onegin 1999, Villa des Roses 2002 (Br Ind Film Award nomination), Bright Young Things 2003, Chromophobia 2005, Babel 2006, Atonement 2007, The Young Victoria 2009, The Wedding Video 2011, Suite Francaise 2014, Man Up 2015, Mindhorn 2016, The Sense of an Ending 2017, Denial 2017; *Awards* Olivier Award (for The Three Sisters, Twelfth Night and A Question of Geography) 1988, Sony Radio Award 1988 and 1992, Evening Standard Award (for Mary Stuart) 2005, Pragnell Shakespeare Award 2007, nominated Tony Award (for Mary Stuart) 2009; *Books* Other People's Shoes (1999), Macbeth (Actors on Shakespeare series, 2002), Facing It (2011), Brutus and Other Heroines (2016); contributions to other books incl: Clamorous Voices – Shakespeare's Women Today (1988), Players of Shakespeare Vol 3 (1993), Mothers: Reflections by Daughters (1995), Living With Shakespeare (2013); *Style—* Dame Harriet Walter, DBE; ✉ c/o Tavistock Wood Management Ltd, 45 Conduit Street, London W1S 2YN (☎ 020 7494 4767)

WALTER, Jeremy Canning (Jerry); s of Richard Walter, OBE, and Beryl, *née* Pugh; *b* 22 August 1948; *Educ* King's Sch Canterbury, Sidney Sussex Coll Cambridge (MA, LLB); *m* 1, 24 Aug 1973 (m dis 1985), Judith Jane, da of Dr Denton Rowlands, of Tamworth, Staffs (d 1987); 2 da (Emma b 1976, Alison b 1979); m 2, 17 Oct 1992, Dawna Beth, da of Sidney Rosenberg (d 1965), of Lawrence, Mass, USA; *Career* Ellis Piers & Young Jackson 1971–73, admitted slr 1973; Simmons & Simmons: asst slr 1973–76, ptnr 1976–, head Corp Dept 1996– (also responsibility for activities in Middle East), head Energy Gp 1998–; conslt ed (Company Law) Jl of Soc for Advanced Legal Studies 1998–; memb: Law Soc, Exec Ctee Br Polish Legal Assoc 1992–, Int Bar Assoc (Arab Regnl Forum Cncl 1998– (vice-chair 2000–03), East-West Forum), American Bar Assoc (Int Law and Practice Section), Int C of C Fin Servs Cmmn, The Securities Inst, Soc of Advanced Legal Studies, Ctee of City of London Law Soc 1999–; Freeman City of London Slrs Co; *Recreations* sport, travel; *Clubs* MCC; *Style—* Jerry Walter, Esq; ✉ Simmons & Simmons, CityPoint, One Ropemaker Street, London EC2Y 9SS (☎ 020 7628 2020, fax 020 7628 2070)

WALTER, Michael; s of Leonard Walter (d 1990), and Anne, *née* Rue; *b* 6 May 1956; *Educ* The King's Sch Chester, Christ's Coll Cambridge (MA); *m* 27 Nov 1982, Joan Margaret, da of Arthur Colin Hubbard (d 1978); 1 da (Helen Margaret b 1984), 1 s (Matthew Michael b 1987); *Career* admitted slr 1981 (England and Wales, Hong Kong); Stephenson Harwood: articled clerk 1979–81, asst slr 1981–86, ptnr 1986–97; Herbert Smith Freehills: ptnr 1997–2015, global head of corporate practice 2005–10, managing ptnr SE Asia region 2012–14; memb: Law Soc, Law Soc of Hong Kong, Law Soc of Singapore; Freeman: City of London 1987, Worshipful Co of Slrs 1987; *Recreations* orienteering, trekking, sailing, reading, music, skiing, photography, scuba diving; *Clubs* Royal Hong Kong Yacht, Royal Hong Kong Jockey, Hong Kong FC, Singapore Cricket, Harlequins RFC, Oriental; *Style—* Michael Walter, Esq; ✉ 82 Grange Road, #19–04 The Colonnade, Singapore 249587 (e-mail mwalter@btinternet.com and michael.walter.singapore@gmail.com)

WALTER, Natasha; da of late Nicolas Walter, and Ruth Walter; *b* 20 January 1967; *Educ* N London Collegiate Sch, St John's Coll Cambridge, Harvard Univ; *Children* 1 da (Clara Lattimer Walter b 16 Dec 2000), 1 s (Arthur Grey Lattimer Walter b 27 Jan 2009); *Career* writer and human rights activist; jr teaching fell Harvard Univ 1989, dep literary ed The Independent 1993–94; currently contrib: Newsnight Review (BBC 2), Front Row (BBC Radio 4), The Guardian, The Observer, The Independent; fndr and dir Women for Refugee Women; Humanitas visiting prof in women's rights Univ of Cambridge 2015; *Books* The New Feminism (1998), On the Move: Feminism for a new generation (ed, 1999), Living Dolls: The Return of Sexism (2010); *Style—* Ms Natasha Walter; ✉ c/o Anna Webber, United Agents, 12–26 Lexington Street, London W1F 0LE (☎ 020 3214 0876, e-mail awebber@unitedagents.co.uk)

WALTER, Robert John; s of Richard Walter (d 2001), of Warminster, Wilts, and Irene Walter (d 2012); *b* 30 May 1948; *Educ* Warminster, Aston Univ (BSc, DLitt); *m* 28 Aug 1970, Sally (d 1995); 1 da (Elizabeth b 1974), 2 s (Charles b 1976, Alexander b 1977); *Career* former investment banker and farmer; dir: FW Holst (Europe) Ltd 1984–86, TV-UK Ltd 1988, Silver Apex Films Ltd 2003–06; vice-pres Aubrey G Lanston & Co Inc 1986–97; visiting lectr Univ of Westminster; farmer in West Country; MP (Cons) N Dorset 1997–2015 (Parly candidate (Cons) Bedwellty 1979); oppn front bench spokesman on constitutional affairs (Wales) 1999–2001; memb: Health Select Ctee 1997–99, Int Devpt Select Ctee 2001–03, European Scrutiny Ctee 1998–99, Treasury Select Ctee 2003–05; memb Exec 1922 Ctee 2002–05; vice-chm: All-Pty Gp on Lupus, Free Trade Gp, Human Rights Gp 2003–, Prison Health Gp 2005–; treas: Br-Japanese Parly Gp 1997–, Br-Caribbean Parly Gp 1997–, All-Pty Gp on Charities 1997–; chm: Aston Univ Cons Assoc 1967–69, W Wilts Young Cons 1972–75, Euro Democrat Forum 1979–84, Foreign Affrs Forum 1985–87, Cons Gp for Europe 1992–95 (vice-chm 1984–86, dep chm 1989–92), Positive European Gp of Cons MPs and Peers; memb: Assembly of WEU 2001– (chm Defence Ctee, pres Federated Gp of Christian Democrats and European Democrats, pres 2008–11), Parly Assembly of the Cncl of Europe 2002– (chm Media Sub-ctee, ldr UK Delgn 2010–, vice-pres 2011–); vice-chm Br Irish Parly Assembly 2010–, chm Br Gp Inter Parly Union 2010–14, chm European Democrat Gp 2011–14, vice-pres Inter-Parly Union 2014–; chm Bd of Govrs Tachbrook Sch 1980–2000; Vice Cdre House of Commons Yacht Club 2006– (hon sec 1998–99, Rear Cdre 2001); Freeman City of London 1983, Liveryman Worshipful Co of Needlemakers 1983; AMIIMR, MSI; *Recreations* sailing, shooting; *Clubs* Blandford Constitutional; *Style—* Robert Walter, Esq; ✉ House of Commons, London SW1A 0AA (☎ 020 7219 6981, e-mail bobwaltertemp@yahoo.co.uk, website www.bobwaltermp.com)

WALTERS, Chris; *b* 16 May 1969, London; *Educ* LSE (BSc), Birkbeck Coll, Univ of London (MSc), London Business Sch (PhD, scholar); *Career* London Business Sch: lectr in economics 1992–99, economic conslt 1999–2003; economic advsr Competition Cmmn 2003–07; OFT: joined as asst dir (economics) OFT 2007, dir of economics Goods and Consumer Gp until 2013, chief economist 2013–; memb Bd Govt Economic Service 2013–; *Recreations* watching football, particularly Arsenal; *Style—* Chris Walters, Esq; ✉ Office of the Chief Economist, Office of Fair Trading, Fleetbank House, 2–6 Salisbury Square, London EC4Y 8JX

WALTERS, Cynthia Sue (Cindy); da of Bert Walters (d 2014), and Jane Walters, of Perth, Australia; *Educ* Univ of Natal Durban (BArch), UCL (MPhil); *m* April 1991, Jan Blekkingh; 2 da (Anna b 18 Feb 1997, Eve b 3 Aug 2002); *Career* Foster + Partners 1990–94, founding ptnr and dir Walters & Cohen Architects 1994–; AJ Woman Architect of the Year Award 2012, Civic Trust Award 2010 (for Gallery of Botanical Art Kew Gardens), RIBA Nat Award 2016 (for Regent High School London); *Recreations* cinema, music, opera, reading, travel, walking, climbing, mountaineering; *Style—* Ms Cindy Walters; ✉ Walters & Cohen Architects, 2 Wilkin Street, London NW5 3NL (☎ 020 7428 9751, e-mail cindy@waltersandcohen.com)

WALTERS, His Hon Judge Geraint Wyn; s of Thomas Eifion Walters, of Glanyrafon, Rhyd-y-fro, Pontardawe, Swansea, W Glamorgan, and Dilys, *née* Deer; *b* 31 December 1957, Glanamman, Carmarthenshire; *Educ* Ysgol Gyfun Ystalyfera, Univ Coll of Wales Aberystwyth (LLB, Calcott Pryce Mooting Award 1978, pres Aberystwyth Law Students 1979), Inns of Court Sch of Law; *m* 26 May 1986, Kathryn Ann Walters, da of John Jenkins; 3 da (Lowri Angharad b 1 May 1987, Catrin Wyn b 1 Jan 1989, Heledd Medi b 3 Sept 1992); *Career* called to the Bar Gray's Inn 1981, junior Wales and Chester Circuit 1998, head Angel Chambers Swansea 2000–15, recorder 2001, circuit judge (Wales Circuit) 2015–; cmmr Boundary Cmmn for Wales 2001–15; former hon sec and chm Guild for the Promotion of Welsh Music; *Recreations* gardening, music, opera, travel, walking; *Style—* His Hon Judge Walters

WALTERS, Humphrey; s of John Henry Walters (d 2000), and Janet, *née* McIntyre (d 2005); *b* 18 February 1942, Poona, India; *m* Susan, *née* Gully; 1 da (Claudia), 1 s (Mark); *Career* freelance Newsweek Magazine 1968–72, freelance Stars & Stripes 1968–72, ceo MaST 1972–1996, formerly MIT, fndr Humphrey Walters Associates; visiting fell of inspirational leadership Henley Mgmnt Coll; memb Bd RNLI, memb Bd Juvenile Diabetes Research Fndn; *Books* Global Challenge, The Little Book of Inspiration, The Little Book of Winning, The Little Book of Nutrition; *Recreations* cricket, gardening, golf, motorsport, sailing (sailed around the world), shooting, walking, running marathons; *Clubs* MCC, Royal Yacht Squadron, St George's Hill Golf; *Style—* Humphrey Walters, Esq; ✉ 3 Oxford Gate, London W6 7DA; Crown House, 71 Hammersmith Road, London W14 8TH (☎ 0870 1149149, mobile 07778 599009, e-mail humphrey@humphreywalters.com, website www.humphreywalters.com)

WALTERS, John Latimer; QC (1997); s of John Paton Walters (d 1993), and Charlotte Alison, *née* Cunningham (d 1984); *b* 15 September 1948; *Educ* Rugby, Balliol Coll Oxford (MA); *m* 2, 1990, Caroline Elizabeth, *née* Byles; 2 da (Isolde, Susanna), 1 step s (Alexander Bain); *Career* chartered accountant: Arthur Andersen & Co 1970–73, Josolyne Layton-Bennett & Co 1973–75, Peat Marwick Mitchell & Co 1975–76; legal career: called to the Bar Middle Temple 1977, in practice Gray's Inn 1978–; dep special cmmr and pt/t chm of VAT and Duties Tbnl 2002–; local preacher in Methodist Church (Diss Circuit); FCA 1974, ATII 1974; *Books* VAT and Property (with David Goy, QC, 1989, 2 edn 1993); *Recreations* gardening, genealogy, painting, tapestry; *Style—* John Walters, QC; ✉ Gray's Inn Tax Chambers, Gray's Inn, London WC1R 5JA (☎ 020 7242 2642, fax 020 7831 9017, e-mail jw@taxbar.com)

WALTERS, Julie; CBE (2008, OBE 1999); *b* 22 February 1950; *Career* actress; Outstanding Achievement South Bank Award 2013; *Theatre* incl: seasons at Everyman Theatre Liverpool and Bristol Old Vic, Educating Rita (RSC Warehouse and Piccadilly Theatre), Having a Ball (Lyric), Jumpers (Royal Exchange), Fool for Love (NT and Lyric), When I was a Girl I Used to Scream and Shout (Whitehall), Frankie and Johnnie, Serafina in

The Rose Tattoo (dir Sir Peter Hall), All My Sons (NT, Olivier Award for Best Actress), Acorn Antiques the Musical (Theatre Royal Haymarket), The Last of the Haussmans (NT); *Television* incl: The Birthday Party, Secret Diary of Adrian Mole, Victoria Wood – As Seen on TV (BAFTA nomination), Boys From the Blackstuff (BAFTA nomination), She'll Be Wearing Pink Pyjamas, Say Something Happened (by Alan Bennett, BAFTA nomination), Intensive Care (by Alan Bennett), Talking Heads (by Alan Bennett), GBH (by Alan Bleasdale), Julie Walters & Friends (TV special Christmas 1991, 2 BAFTA nominations), Wide Eyed and Legless (Screen One, BBC, BAFTA nomination), Bambino Mio (Screen One), Pat and Margaret (Screen One), Jake's Progress (by Alan Bleasdale, Channel 4), Little Red Riding Hood and the Wolf (by Roald Dahl, BBC), Bathtime (short film, BBC), Brazen Hussies (BBC Screen Two film), Melissa (BBC), Green Card, Dinner Ladies (with Victoria Wood, BBC), Jack and the Beanstalk, My Beautiful Son (ITV, BAFTA Award for Best Actress), Murder (BAFTA Award for Best Actress), The Wife of Bath (BAFTA Award for Best Actress), The Return (Broadcasting Press Guild TV Awards Best Actress), Ahead of the Class, Ruby in the Smoke (BBC), Mary Whitehouse, A Short Stay in Switzerland (Best Actress Int Emmy Award), Mo (Best Actress BAFTA Television Award 2010, Best Actress Int Emmy Award 2011), The Jury, Henry IV Parts I and II, Henry V, Indian Summers 2015; *Film* incl: Rita in Educating Rita (Oscar nominee, BAFTA Award, Golden Globe Award), Buster, Personal Services (BAFTA nomination), Joe Orton's mother in Prick Up Your Ears, Killing Dad, Steppin' Out (Variety Club Award, BAFTA nomination) Just Like a Woman, Clothes in the Wardrobe, Sister My Sister, Intimate Relations, Girls' Night, Titanic Town, Billy Elliot (BAFTA Award, Oscar nomination), Harry Potter and the Philosopher's Stone, Before You Go, Harry Potter and the Chamber of Secrets, Calendar Girls, Harry Potter and the Prisoner of Azkaban, Mickybo and Me, Wah-Wah, Driving Lessons, Becoming Jane, Harry Potter and the Order of the Phoenix, Mamma Mia, Harry Potter and the Deathly Hallows: Part 1, Harry Potter and the Deathly Hallows: Part 2, Effie, One Chance, Harry Hill The Movie, Brave, Paddington, Brooklyn; *Books* Maggie's Tree (novel, 2006), That's Another Story (autobiography, 2008); *Style—* Ms Julie Walters, CBE; ✉ c/o Independent Talent Group Ltd, 40 Whitfield Street, London W1T 2RH (☎ 020 7636 6565, fax 020 7323 0101)

WALTERS, Prof Kenneth; *b* 14 September 1934; *Educ* Dynevor GS Swansea, UC Swansea (state scholar, BSc, MSc, PhD), Univ of Wales (DSc); *m*; 3 c; *Career* res assoc Brown Univ RI and asst prof San Diego State Coll CA 1959–60; Univ of Wales Aberystwyth: lectr in applied mathematics 1960–65, sr lectr 1965–70, reader 1970–73, prof 1973–; pres Br Soc of Rheology 1974–76, pres European Soc of Rheology 1996–2000, chm Int Ctee on Rheology 2000–04; memb Editorial Bd: Rheologica Acta 1972–2008, Jl of Rheology 1988–2002; exec ed Jl of Non-Newtonian Fluid Mechanics 1975–2001; Gold Medal Br Soc of Rheology 1984, Weissenberg Award European Soc of Rheology 2002; Hon Dr: Université Joseph Fourier Grenoble 1998, Univ of Strathclyde 2011, Univ of Aberystwyth 2016; hon fell Univ Coll Swansea 1992, foreign memb Nat Acad of Engrg USA 1995, memb Int Acad of Engrg 2014; FRS 1991, founding FLSW 2010; *Books* Rheometry (1975), Rheometry: Industrial Applications (ed, 1980), Numerical Simulation of non-Newtonian Flow (with M J Crochet and A R Davies, 1984), An Introduction to Rheology (with H A Barnes and J F Hutton, 1989), Rheological Phenomena in Focus (with D V Boger, 1993), Rheology: An Historical Perspective (with R I Tanner, 1998), The Way it Was (2003), More Personal Stories from New Testament Times (2012); *Style—* Prof Kenneth Walters, FRS; ✉ Institute of Mathematics, Physics and Computer Science, University of Aberystwyth, Ceredigion SY23 3BZ (☎ 01970 622750, e-mail kew@aber.ac.uk)

WALTERS, Minette Caroline Mary; da of Samuel Henry Doddington Jebb (d 1960), and Minette Colleen Helen, *née* Paul; *b* 26 September 1949; *Educ* Godolphin Sch Salisbury, Univ of Durham (BA); *m* 1978, Alexander Hamilton Walters, s of Dr F J H Walters; 2 s (Roland Francis Samuel b 13 Dec 1979, Philip Gladwyn Hamilton b 12 Jan 1982); *Career* sub ed then ed IPC Magazines 1972–76, freelance writer 1976–; prison visitor; Hon DLitt: Bournemouth Univ, Southampton Solent Univ; *Books* The Ice House (1992, Crime Writers' Assoc John Creasey Award), The Sculptress (1993, Edgar Allen Poe Award, Macavity Award), The Scold's Bridle (1994, Crime Writers' Assoc Gold Dagger Award), The Dark Room (1995), The Echo (1997), The Breaker (1998), The Shape of Snakes (2000, Pelle Rosenkrantz Award Denmark), Acid Row (2001), Fox Evil (2002, Crime Writers' Assoc Gold Dagger Award), Disordered Minds (2003), The Tinder Box (2004), The Devil's Feather (2005), Chickenfeed (2006), The Chameleon's Shadow (2007), A Dreadful Murder (2013), The Cellar (2015); *Recreations* DIY, books, Radio 4, Scrabble, films, TV, walking, farming, cookery, theatre, crossword puzzles; *Style—* Mrs Minette Walters; ✉ c/o Gregory & Company, 3 Barb Mews, London W6 7PA (☎ 020 7610 4676, fax 020 7610 4686)

WALTERS, Philip; MBE (2010); s of Moss Walters (decd), and Eileen Walters (decd); *b* 15 March 1954, London; *Educ* Highgate Sch, Keble Coll Oxford (BA); *m* Jennie, *née* Spurgeon; 2 s (Patrick b 22 July 1987, Nicholas b 12 Nov 1989); *Career* Hodder: joined 1976, md Hodder Educn 1997–2006, ceo 2006–09; chm: Rising Stars 2009–14, GL Educn Gp 2012–16, Book Source 2014–, Centre for Agriculture and Bioscience Int (CABI) 2015–; non-exec dir NelsonCroom 2010–; former chair Educnl Publishers Cncl, assoc Inst of Ideas 2006–, dir Publishers Licensing Soc 2006–11; tstee: Book Aid Int 2000–11 (chair 2011–14), Yale Univ Press (London) 2010–13; memb Advsy Bd Investcorp (Europe); Liveryman Worshipful Co of Stationers 2011–; *Recreations* golf, film, watching Spurs, watching England and Middlesex play cricket; *Clubs* Middlesex County Cricket; *Style—* Philip Walters, Esq, MBE; ✉ 31 Half Moon Lane, Herne Hill, London SE24 9JX (☎ 020 7274 6242, mobile 07778 709534)

WALTERS, Rhodri Havard; CB (2014); s of late Havard Walters, and Veigan Walters; *b* 28 February 1950; *Educ* Cyfarthfa Castle GS Merthyr Tydfil, Jesus Coll Oxford (exhibitioner, MA, DPhil); *Career* clerk Parliament Office House of Lords 1975–2014 (ret), seconded to Cabinet Office as private sec to Ldr of the House and Govt Chief Whip 1986–89, Civil Service Nuffield and Leverhulme travelling fell (attached to US Congress) 1989–90, establishment offr (clerk to Fin, Staff and Refreshment Sub-ctees) House of Lords 1993–2000, clerk of public bills 2000–02, clerk of ctees 2002–07, clerk of the Overseas Office 2002–14, reading clerk and head of corporate services 2007–14; sec Ecclesiastical Ctee 2000–03, clerk Jt Ctee on the Draft House of Lords Reform Bill 2011–12; *Publications* How Parliament Works (1987, 7 edn 2015), 'The House of Lords' in the British Constitution in the Twentieth Century (2003); various articles in Economic History Review, Welsh History Review and The Table; *Recreations* rowing, gardening, skiing, church music; *Clubs* Garrick; *Style—* Rhodri Walters, Esq, CB; ✉ 40 Cleveland Gardens, London SW13 0AG (☎ 020 8878 7494, e-mail rhwalters@blueyonder.co.uk)

WALTERS, Robert; *Career* Touche Ross 1975–78, Michael Page Int plc 1978–84, ceo and fndr Robert Walters plc 1985–; *Style—* Robert Walters, Esq; ✉ Robert Walters plc, 11 Slingsby Place, St Martin's Courtyard, London WC2E 9AB

WALTERSON, Inga Ruth; da of Francis Sinclair Walterson (d 2008), of W Burrafirth, Shetland, and Mary Olive, *née* Bowie; *b* 27 May 1964; *Educ* Univ of Aberdeen (MA); *m* Ian James Douglas Anderson, s of John Robertson Anderson (d 1987), of Lerwick, Shetland, and Ella, *née* Morrison (d 1986); 2 s (Bo Ellis b 1998, Finn Erik b 2002); *Career* md Shetland Islands Broadcasting Company Ltd; *Style—* Ms Inga Walterson; ✉ Shetland Islands Broadcasting Company Ltd, Market Street, Lerwick, Shetland ZE1 0JN (☎ 01595 695299, fax 01595 695696, e-mail info@sibc.co.uk)

WALTHER, Robert Philippe; s of Prof David Philippe Walther (d 1973), and Barbara, *née* Brook; *b* 31 July 1943; *Educ* Charterhouse, ChCh Oxford (MA); *m* 21 June 1969, Anne, da of Lionel Wigglesworth, of Woldingham, Surrey; 1 da (Julie Clare b 1973), 1 s (Luke b 1978); *Career* Clerical Medical Investment Group: joined 1965, dep investment mangr 1972, investment mangr 1976, asst gen mangr (investments) 1980, dir 1985–2001, gp chief exec 1994–2001; memb Exec Ctee Halifax plc 1999–2001; chm: Fleming Claverhouse 1997–2005, Fidelity European Values 2001–2011 (dir 1995–2011), Investment Ctee Assoc of Br Insurers; dir: Nationwide Building Soc 2002–12 (dep chm 2006–12), BUPA 2004–09, ret; AIIMR 1969, FIA 1970; *Recreations* fishing, golf, bridge, sailing; *Style—* Robert Walther, Esq; ✉ Ashwell's Barn, Chesham Lane, Chalfont St Giles, Buckinghamshire HP8 4AS (☎ 01494 875575, fax 01494 876518, e-mail rob_walther@hotmail.com)

WALTON, Alastair Henry; s of Sir Raymond Henry Walton (d 1988), of Wimbledon, London, and Helen Alexandra, *née* Dingwall; *b* 26 August 1954; *Educ* Winchester, Balliol Coll Oxford (BA); *m* 28 July 1984, Hon Mary Synolda, *née* Butler, da of 28 Baron Dunboyne (d 2004), of Chelsea, London; 4 da (Alexandra Mary b 1985, Christina Frances b 1986, Stephanie Katherine b 1988, Florence Lucy b 1992); *Career* called to the Bar Lincoln's Inn 1977 (Isaac Wolfson scholar), in practice 1978–2016; *Recreations* lawn tennis; *Style—* Alastair Walton, Esq; ✉ 26 Paradise Walk, Chelsea, London SW3 4JL (☎ 020 7376 5304)

WALTON, Dr Bryan; s of Henry Walton (d 1985), and Helen, *née* Pincus (d 1989); *b* 29 August 1943, London; *Educ* City of London Sch, London Hosp Med Coll (MB BS); *m* 1, 7 July 1968 (m dis), (Sarah) Ruth, da of Philip Levitan (d 1989); 1 da (Anna b 1973), 1 s (Jonathan b 1976); m 2, 9 Nov 2002, Heather Teresa, da of Eric Ball; *Career* conslt anaesthetist London Hosp 1974–95, advsr in anaesthesia Princess Grace Hosp London 1984– (advsr in intensive care 1984–2008); memb: Med Prof Soc, Assoc of Anaesthetists 1972, Anaesthetic Res Soc 1980, Hunterian Soc 1985, Chelsea Clinical Soc 1989; FRCA; *Books* chapters: Adverse Reactions to Anaesthetic Drugs (1981), Scientific Foundations of Anaesthesia (3 edn 1982, 4 edn 1990), Hazards and Complications of Anaesthesia (1987, 2 edn 1993), Medicine in the Practice of Anaesthesia (1989); many pubns on anaesthesia and the liver, and anaesthesia and immunology; *Recreations* classical music; *Style—* Dr Bryan Walton; ✉ Foxmeadow Cottage, Grove Lane, Chesham, Buckinghamshire HP5 3QQ (☎ 01494 259066)

WALTON, Christopher Henry; MBE; s of Frank Pearson Walton (d 1966), of Eastbourne, E Sussex, and Marion Ada Beasley (d 1989); *b* 20 June 1930; *Educ* Stockport GS, Gonville & Caius Coll Cambridge (MA); *m* 25 April 1959, Judith Vivien, da of Ernest Leslie Philp (d 1950), of Alexandria, Egypt; *Career* 2 Lt Lancs Fus 1949–51, Capt Royal Fus TA 1951–59; Cwlth Devpt Corp 1954–65, initiator and dir Kenya Tea Devpt Authy 1959–65; exec and dir: Kyle Products Ltd Gp 1965–67, Eastern Produce Ltd Gp 1967–69; div chief Projects Dept Eastern and Western Africa World Bank Washington 1969–87; Wolfson Coll Oxford: bursar 1987–95, emeritus fell 1995–; fin advsr Oxford Union Soc 1995–2000, hon sec Oxford Literary and Debating Soc 1996–2010; on Cons Party Candidates List 1966–69, dep chm Cons Party Overseas Devpt Ctee 1967–68; govr: Pusey House Oxford 1990–2004 (vice-pres 2004–), Stowe Sch 1992–2005; chm Oxfordshire Historic Churches Tst 1999–2008 (pres 2009–14); *Recreations* ecclesiastical architecture, conservative politics, rowing; *Clubs* Oriental, Leander; *Style—* Christopher Walton, Esq, MBE; ✉ The Corner House, Foxcombe Lane, Boars Hill, Oxford OX1 5DH (☎ 01865 735179, e-mail chris.walton@wolfson.ox.ac.uk)

WALTON, Field Laurence Joseph; s of Joseph Field Horace Walton (d 1982), and Marie Joan, *née* Lennard (d 1984); *b* 17 April 1940; *Educ* Loughborough Univ (BTech, MSc, played rugby for Eng Univs 1st XV); *m* 26 May 1965, Susan Thompstone, da of Basil Rowe; 1 da (Virginia Mary Spencer b 15 Dec 1966), 1 s (Francis Joseph Field b 1 Feb 1968); *Career* electrical apprentice then project engr Hawker Siddeley 1958–67, project mangr John Laing plc 1968–70, planning mangr Plessey plc 1970–71, engrg analyst Cazenove & Co 1971–74, engrg analyst Quilter Hilton Goodison 1974–77, investment mangr Electra Funds and md Temple Bar Fund Managers 1977–85, md Guinness Mahon Fund Managers 1985–89, chm Guinness Mahon Asset Managers 1989–92; chm: Eleco Holdings plc 1983–97 (ind dir 1997), Henry Cooke Group plc 1993–95, Biofuels Corp plc 2003–06, Edgerley Power Ltd 2010–; independent dir: Temple Bar Investment Trust 1983–2010, Martin International Holdings plc 1994–2004, Romney, Hythe & Dymchurch Railway plc 1995–; dir: MacArthur & Co Ltd 1997–2007 (assoc 1995–97), Rocktron Ltd 1998–2004, Peter Peregrinus Ltd 1998–2005, Hazid Technologies Ltd 2008–, Harrods Gp Tstees Ltd 2000–09 (chm 2009–); memb Enterprise Bd Loughborough Univ 2007–11; Freeman: City of London, Worshipful Co of Glass Sellers; CEng, FIET; *Recreations* golf; *Clubs* Leicester FC, Beaconsfield Golf, Rye Golf; *Style—* Field Walton, Esq; ✉ Christow Cottage, Seer Green Lane, Jordans, Buckinghamshire HP9 2ST (☎ 01494 874971, mobile 07774 770494, e-mail fieldwalton@supanet.com)

WALTON, Prof John Christopher; s of W G C Walton, and R M Walton, *née* Wheeler; *b* 4 December 1941, St Albans, Herts; *Educ* Watford GS for Boys, Univ of Sheffield (BSc, DSc), St Andrews Univ (PhD); *m* 28 July 1971, Jane, *née* Lehman; 1 s (Christopher), 1 da (Emma); *Career* asst lectr Univ of Dundee 1966–69; St Andrews Univ: lectr 1969–80, sr lectr 1980–86, reader 1986–96, prof of reactive chemistry 1997–2007, research prof of chemistry 2007–; chm Electron Spin Resonance Gp RSC 2001–04; memb Seventh-day Adventist Church; RSC Silver medal and Award for organic reaction mechanisms 1994; CChem 1991, FRSC 1991, FRSE 1995; Free Radical Chemistry (1974), Radicals (1979); author of over 290 articles and reviews in sci jls; *Recreations* origins science, fitness classes; *Style—* Prof John Walton; ✉ University of St Andrews, School of Chemistry, North Haugh, St Andrews, Fife KY16 9ST (☎ 01334 463864, fax 01334 463808, e-mail jcw@st-and.ac.uk)

WALTON, Richard William; s of Anthony Walton, and Valerie, *née* Hall, of Wembury, Devon; *b* 30 June 1965, Plymouth; *Educ* Plymouth Coll, Univ of Portsmouth (BSc), LSE (MSc); *m* Jill, *née* Grieves; 2 da (Jasmine b 10 Aug 1995, Ella b 6 Aug 1997), 1 s (Joshua b 29 March 1999); *Career* Metropolitan Police: dep borough cdr 2006–08, borough cdr 2007–10, staff offr to the cmmr of police 2009–11, cdr and head Counter Terrorism Command 2011–16; dir Counter Terrorism Global Ltd 2016–; sr assoc fell RUSI 2016–; chm The Educational Frontier Tst (TEFT); registered ind security conslt (RISC), memb Assoc of Security Conslts (ASC); *Recreations* skiing, travel, walking; *Style—* Richard Walton, Esq; ✉ Suite 707, 8 Shepherd Market, Mayfair, London W1J 7JY (e-mail enquiries@counterterrorism.global, website www.counterterrorism.global)

WANAMAKER, Zoë; CBE (2001); da of Sam Wanamaker, CBE (d 1993), and Charlotte Holland (d 1997); *Educ* King Alfred Sch, Sidcot Sch, Hornsey Coll of Art, Central Sch of Speech and Drama; *m* 7 Nov 1994, Gawn Grainger; *Career* actress; tstee and hon pres Globe Theatre; vice-pres Dignity in Dying; Hon DLitt: Southbank Univ 1995, Richmond American Int Univ 1999; hon doctorate Univ of E Anglia 2012; *Theatre* Manchester 69 Co incl: A Midsummer Night's Dream 1970, Guys and Dolls 1972; Edinburgh Lyceum Theatre incl: The Cherry Orchard 1971 (also at the Stables Theatre Club 1970), Dick Whittington 1971–72; Young Vic 1974 incl: Tom Thumb, Much Ado About Nothing; Nottingham Playhouse 1975–76 incl: A Streetcar Named Desire, Pygmalion, The Beggar's Opera, Trumpets and Drums; Piccadilly Theatre incl: Wild Oats 1977, Once in a Lifetime 1979–80 (RSC 1978–79, SWET Award 1979); RSC Stratford and London 1976– incl: The Devil's Disciple, Wild Oats (also West End), Ivanov, The Taming of the Shrew, Captain Swing, Piaf (also West End and Broadway, Tony nomination 1981), A Comedy of Errors, Twelfth Night and The Time of Your Life 1983–85 (all Olivier Award nominations), Mother Courage (Drama Award 1985), Othello (Olivier Award nomination 1989); NT incl: The Importance of Being Earnest 1982–83, The Bay at Nice and Wrecked

W

Eggs 1986–87, Mrs Klein (also West End, Olivier Award nomination) 1988–89, The Crucible 1990–91 (Olivier Award nomination), Battle Royal 1999–2000; other credits incl: Twelfth Night (Leeds Playhouse 1971, Cambridge Theatre Co 1973–74), Cabaret (Farnham) 1974, Kiss Me Kate (Oxford Playhouse) 1974, The Taming of the Shrew (New Shakespeare Co Round House) 1975, Loot (Manhattan Theatre Club, Music Box Theatre Broadway, Tony nomination 1986), Made in Bangkok (Mark Taper Forum LA) 1988, The Last Yankee (Young Vic (Olivier Award nomination)) 1993, Dead Funny (Hampstead and West End (Variety Club Best Actress Award)) 1994, The Glass Menagerie (Donmar and Comedy (Olivier Award nomination for Best Actress 1996)) 1995, Sylvia (Apollo) 1996, Electra (Chichester Festival and Donmar (Olivier Award for Best Actress 1998, Variety Club Award for Best Actress 1998)) 1997, The Old Neighbourhood (Royal Court) 1998, Electra (McCarter Theatre Princeton, Barrymore Theatre Broadway (Tony nomination Best Actress 1999)) 1998, Boston Marriage (Donmar Warehouse and New Ambassadors (Olivier Award nomination Best Actress 2002)) 2001, His Girl Friday (RNT) 2003, Awake & Sing! (Belasco Theatre NY) 2006 (NY City Drama Desk Award for Outstanding Ensemble Performance, Calloway Award, nomination Tony Award for Best Performance), The Rose Tattoo (RNT) 2007, Much Ado About Nothing (RNT) 2007–08, All My Sons (Apollo) 2010 (Best Actress in a Play What's On Stage Award 2011), The Cherry Orchard (RNT) 2011, Passion Play (Duke of York's) 2013, Stevie (Chichester Festival Theatre) 2014 and (Hampstead Theatre) 2015, Zorba (City Center NY) 2015; *Television* Sally For Keeps 1970, The Eagle Has Landed 1972, Between the Wars 1973, The Silver Mask 1973, Lorna and Ted 1973, The Confederacy of Wives 1974, The Village Hall 1975, Danton's Death 1977, Beaux Strategem 1977, The Devil's Crown 1978–79, Strike 1981, Baal 1981, All the World's A Stage 1982, Richard III 1982, Enemies of the State 1982, Edge of Darkness 1985, Paradise Postponed 1985, Poor Little Rich Girl 1987, Once in a Lifetime 1987, The Dog it was that Died 1988, Ball Trap on the Côte Sauvage 1989, Othello 1989, Prime Suspect (BAFTA nomination) 1990, Love Hurts (BAFTA nomination) 1991, 1992 and 1993, Dance to the Music of Time 1997, Gormenghast 1999, David Copperfield (BBC) 1999, Adrian Mole, The Cappuccino Years 2000, My Family (BBC series) 2002–10 (2 BAFTA nominations, Best Actress Rose d'Or 2005), Marple: A Murder is Announced 2004, Dr Who: The End of the World 2005, Johnny and the Bomb (BBC) 2005, A Waste of Shame (BBC) 2005, Poirot: Cards on the Table 2006, Dr Who: New Earth (BBC) 2006, Poirot: Mrs McGinty's Dead 2008, Poirot: The Third Girl 2008, Who Do You Think You Are? 2009, Poirot: A Halloween Party 2009, An Innocent Abroad (BBC4) 2013, Poirot: Elephants Can Remember 2013, Poirot: Dead Man's Folly 2013, Mr Selfridge 3 2014; as narrator: Testimony Films, Veterans – 'Last Survivors of the Great War' (BBC) 1998 (Gold Hugo Award); *Radio* incl: The Golden Bowl, Plenty 1979, Bay at Nice 1987, A February Morning 1990, Carol (book reading) 1990, Such Rotten Luck 1991 (series I & II 1989); *Films* incl: Inside the Third Reich 1982, The Raggedy Rawney 1987, Wilde (BAFTA nomination) 1997, Swept From The Sea, Harry Potter and the Philosopher's Stone 2001, Five Children and It 2004, It's a Wonderful Afterlife 2009, My Week With Marilyn 2011, The Man 2012; TV films: The Blackheath Poisonings (Central) 1991, Memento Mori (BBC) 1991, Countess Alice (BBC) 1991, The English Wife 1994, The Widowing of Mrs Holroyd (BBC) 1995, Leprechauns (Hallmark) 1999; *Computer Games* voice of Theresa in Fable 2, 3 and 4; *Style—* Ms Zoë Wanamaker, CBE; ✉ c/o Conway van Gelder Ltd, 3rd Floor, 8–12 Broadwick Street, London W1F 8HW (☎ 020 7287 0077, fax 020 7287 1940); PA: Vanessa Green (e-mail vgreen@dsl.pipex.com)

WANLESS, Peter; CB (2007); s of Thomas Wanless, and Pam Wanless; *b* 1964, Chippenham, Wilts; *Educ* Sheldon Sch Chippenham, Univ of Leeds; *m* Beccy; 1 s (Bertie); *Career* HM Treasy 1988–2008, sr civil servant Dept for Educn 1998–2008, ceo Big Lottery Fund 2008–13, ceo NSPCC 2013–; *Recreations* cricket (Somerset); *Clubs* MCC; *Style—* Peter Wanless, Esq, CB; ✉ NSPCC, Weston House, 42 Curtain Road, London EC2A 3NH

WAPLES, John Charles; s of Brian Waples (d 1994), and Judy, *née* Higgins; *b* 13 September 1960, Epping, Essex; *Educ* Haileybury, Nene Coll (BA); *m* 25 Nov 1989, Tracey, *née* Lloyd; 2 s (William b 2 July 1991, Charles b 18 Feb 1994); *Career* Bishop's Stortford and Harlow Gazette 1983, Estates Times 1988; Sunday Times: business reporter 1994–98, dep city ed 1998–2000, dep business ed 2000–05, business ed 2005–10, sr md and UK head of strategic communications FTI Consulting 2010–; UK head of strategic communications FTI Consulting 2013; runner-up Fin Journalist of the Year British Press Awards 2000, Best Corporate Fin Submission Business Journalist of the Year Awards 2000, Best Insur Article Jardine Lloyd Thompson Award 2003; Jaguar: Selling the Legend (2004); *Recreations* golf, sailing, tennis, reading, fine wines; *Clubs* Royal Corinthian Yacht, Bishop's Stortford Lawn Tennis; *Style—* John Waples, Esq; ✉ Oakley, Albury, Hertfordshire SG11 2LG (☎ 01279 771021, e-mail jcwaples@yahoo.com); FTI Consulting, Holborn Gate, 26 Southampton Buildings, London WC2A 1PB

WAPSHOTT, Nicholas Henry; s of Raymond Gibson Wapshott (d 1995), of Hereford, and Olivia Beryl, *née* Darch (d 1970); *b* 13 January 1952; *Educ* Rendcomb Coll, Univ of York; *m* Louise Nicholson, da of (Royden) Joseph Nicholson; 2 s (William Henry Joseph Nicholson b 5 Aug 1988, Oliver Evelyn Samuel Nicholson b 4 July 1990); *Career* journalist, broadcaster and author; The Scotsman 1973–76, The Times 1976–83, political ed The Observer 1988–92 (features ed 1983–88), ed The Times Magazine (formerly The Saturday Review) 1992–97, ed Saturday Times 1997–2001, N American corr The Times 2001–05, nat and foreign ed NY Sun 2006–08, sr ed The Daily Beast 2008–09, editorial conslt oprah.com 2009–10, columnist Reuters 2011–14, columnist New Statesman 2012–, int ed Newsweek 2013–15, opinion ed Newsweek 2015–; Liveryman Worshipful Co of Leathersellers; *Books* Peter O'Toole (1982), Thatcher (with George Brock, 1983), The Man Between: A Biography of Carol Reed (1990), Rex Harrison (1991), Older: A Biography of George Michael (with Tim Wapshott, 1998), Ronald Reagan and Margaret Thatcher: A Political Marriage (2007), Keynes Hayek: The clash that defined modern economics (2011), The Sphinx: Franklin Roosevelt, the Isolationists and the Road to World War II (2014); *Recreations* watching films, travelling, elephants; *Clubs* Garrick, Century Assoc NY; *Style—* Nicholas Wapshott, Esq; ✉ c/o Raphael Sagalyn, The Sagalyn Agency, 4922 Fairmont Avenue, Suite 200, Bethesda, Maryland, MD 20814, USA (☎ 00 1 301 718 6440, e-mail query@sagalyn.com)

WARBURG, (Christina) Clare Barham; da of Dr (Alan) Barham Carter (d 1995), of Weybridge, Surrey, and Mollie Christina, *née* Sanders (d 1995); *Educ* St Michael's Sch, Université de Poitiers; *m* 1, 8 June 1968 (m dis 1975), Andrew Oscar Warburg, s of late Brig Thomas Raphael Warburg, CBE, of Maidstone, Kent; 2 s (Mark b 9 Jan 1971, Daniel b 2 Dec 1972); m 2, 28 Feb 1983 (m dis 1987) Peter Brian Adie; m 3, 13 May 1995, Dr Stuart St Pierre Slatter; *Career* paper conservator and watercolour restorer; fine art dealer 1975–: Kensington Park Galleries 1975–78, freelance 1978–; memb: Kensington Ctee Save The Children Fund, Avenues Youth Project Ctee; *Recreations* gardening, antiques, photography; *Style—* Mrs Clare Warburg; ✉ Tarrant Abbey, near Blandford, Dorset DT11 9HU

WARBURTON, David; s of Harold Warburton, (d 1988), of Shipley, W Yorks, and Ada, *née* Sinfield (d 1960); *b* 10 January 1942; *Educ* St Walburgas Sch Shipley, Cottingley Manor Sch Bingley, Coleg Harlech; *m* 15 Oct 1966, Carole Anne Susan, da of Frank Tomney (d 1984), of Rickmansworth, Herts, and former MP for Hammersmith; 2 da (Sara Anne b 25 Sept 1968, Caroline Susan b 28 July 1970); *Career* GMWU educn offr 1965–67 (regnl offr 1967–73), nat industrial offr GMBATU 1973–90, sr nat offr GMB and APEX 1990–95; vice-pres Int Fedn Chemical and Energy Workers 1986–92, sec UK Chemical Unions Cncl 1978–85, chm TUC Gen Purpose Ctee 1984–95; memb: NEDC 1973–86, Cwlth Devpt Corp 1979–87, MOD Industrial Cncl 1988–91, Civil Air Tport Nat Jt Cncl 1992–95, Industrial Tbnl 1995–, Construction Task Force 1997–98, Employment Tbnls 1998–; dir Friends of the Speaker 1996–2002; sec Friends of Palestine 1983–; memb: Upper Wharfedale Museum Soc 1978–, Yorkshire Soc 1983–, Assoc for Int Cancer Research 1989–, Amnesty Int 1990–, Crazy Horses Investment Tst; ed People First! 2002–; memb Chorleywood PC 2002–06; *Books* Pharmaceuticals for the People (1973), Drug Industry (1975), UK Chemicals: The Way Forward (1977), Economic Detente (1980), The Case for Voters Tax Credits (1983), Forward Labour (1985), Facts Figures and Damned Statistics (1987), Breakthrough in Legal Aid (1998); contrib numerous articles to leading jls; *Recreations* hill climbing, music, 1930–50 film memorabilia; *Clubs* Victoria (Westminster); *Style—* David Warburton, Esq; ✉ 47 Hill Rise, Chorleywood, Rickmansworth, Hertfordshire WD3 7NY (☎ 01923 778726)

WARBURTON, Jonathan; *m* Kim; 1 da (Charlotte), 3 s (Harry (twin), Jack (twin), Angus); *Career* Warburtons: nat account mangr then sales dir then mktg dir, subsequently commercial dir then jt md, chm 2001–; non-exec dir Samworth Bros Ltd 1997–; hon doctorate Univ of Manchester 2003; *Style—* Jonathan Warburton, Esq; ✉ Warburtons Ltd, Back o'th Bank House, Hereford Street, Bolton BL1 8HJ

WARBURTON, Ross; MBE (2004); *Educ* Oriel Coll Oxford; *Children* 1 s (Jimmy), 1 da (Ellen); *Career* Warburtons: joined 1985, exec chm 1991–2001, currently exec dir; chm: Richmond Foods plc 2001–06, Uniq plc 2007–09; pres Food and Drink Federation 2008–10, chm Inst for Family Business (IFB) 2011–; dir OnSide; *Style—* Ross Warburton, Esq, MBE; ✉ Warburtons Ltd, Back o'th'Bank House, Hereford Street, Bolton BL1 8HJ

WARBY, Sarah; *Educ* Univ of Oxford (MEng); *Career* UK mktg dir Heineken until 2012, mktg dir Sainsbury's 2012–; mentor Mktg Acad; non-exec dir Sainsbury's Bank 2014–; Mktg Soc Mktg Ldr of the Year 2013; fell Mktg Soc; *Style—* Ms Sarah Warby; ✉ Sainsbury's Supermarkets Ltd, 33 Holborn, London EC1N 2HT

WARCHUS, Matthew; *b* 24 October 1966; *Educ* Univ of Bristol (BA Music and Drama, special commendation for practical work in drama); *Career* director; dir Nat Youth Theatre of GB 1989 and 1990, Bristol Old Vic 1991, asst dir RSC 1991–92, assoc dir W Yorkshire Playhouse 1993; also freelance dir, artistic dir The Old Vic 2015; *Theatre* for RSC (as dir) incl: Henry V 1995, The Devil is an Ass (The Swan & Pit) 1995, Hamlet 1997, The Unexpected Man 1998; for West Yorkshire Playhouse: Life is A Dream (nominated TMA Best Dir), Who's Afraid of Virginia Woolf, Fiddler on the Roof 1992, The Plough and the Stars, Much Ado About Nothing 1993, Death of a Salesman, Betrayal, True West 1994, Peter Pan 1995; other prodns incl: The Life of Stuff (Donmar), True West (Donmar) 1994, Volpone (RNT) 1995, Art (Wyndhams) 1996, The Unexpected Man (Duchess) 1998, Life x3 (RNT, The Old Vic) 2001–01, Our House (Cambridge) 2002, Tell Me On A Sunday (Gielgud) 2003, Lord of the Rings (Toronto, Drury Lane) 2006–07, Speed-the-Plow, The Norman Conquests (The Old Vic, Broadway) 2008–09, God of Carnage (Gielgud, Broadway) 2008–09, Boeing Boeing (Comedy Theatre) 2008, La Bête (Comedy Theatre and Broadway) 2010, Matilda The Musical (RSC, Cambridge Theatre, Broadway, Australi Tour, US Tour) 2010– (Best Dir Olivier Award 2012), Ghost The Musical (Manchester, Piccadilly Theatre, UK Tour, US Tour, Int Tour) 2011–; *Film* Simpatico 1999, Pride 2014; *Opera* Troilus and Cressidi (Opera North), The Rake's Progress (WNO), Falstaff (Opera North and ENO); *Awards* Shakespeare's Globe Award for Most Promising Newcomer 1994, The Sydney Edward's Award for Best Director (for Volpone and Henry V) 1995, Evening Standard Award for Best Dir (for Volpone and Henry V); Olivier Award nomination for Best Director (for Volpone, Henry V, Art and Hamlet) 1996, Olivier Award for Best Director (Matilda The Musical) 2012; *Style—* Matthew Warchus, Esq

WARD, Dr Adam Anthony; s of Dennis Harold Ward (d 2003), and Margaret Maud, *née* Record (d 2005); *b* 15 June 1947; *Educ* Tonbridge, Springhill Sch, King's Coll London, Westminster Med Sch Univ of London (MB BS), LSHTM (MSc), Hotel Dieu Univ of Paris (DipOrthMed); *Career* clinician, lectr and broadcaster; ed Broadway Magazine 1970, registrar London Sch of Hygiene and Tropical Medicine, lectr and hon sr registrar (epidemiology) Westminster Med Sch 1978–79, physician Dept of Orthopaedic Med Hotel Dieu Paris 1982–83, dir Dept of Musculoskeletal Medicine Royal London Hosp for Integrated Medicine 1983–2011, specialist Hospitals Div UCL Hosps NHS Tst; conslt orthopaedic and musculoskeletal physician and specialist in integrative med; past memb Bd: British Inst of Musculoskeletal Med, Faculty of Homoeopathy London, British Med Acupuncture Soc; memb Editorial Bd Acupuncture in Medicine jl; past examiner Soc of Apothecaries London; author of clinical papers and specialist book chapters; MRCGP; *Recreations* walking and relaxing; *Style—* Dr Adam A Ward; ✉ 41 Frankfield Rise, Tunbridge Wells, Kent TN2 5LF (☎ 01892 525799)

WARD, Anthony John; s of John George Ward (d 1995), and Joyce Finlay, *née* Ford; *b* 23 September 1962, Winchester, Hants; *Educ* Downside, SSEES Univ of London (BA), Coll of Law; *m* 1 July 1991, Hilary Jane; 2 s (Henry b 17 Sept 1992, Archie b 23 Sept 1996), 2 da (Kate b 25 March 1994, Charlotte b 8 Sept 2000); *Career* slr; ptnr: Ashurst Morris Crisp 1996–98, Shearman & Sterling 1998–; *Style—* Anthony Ward, Esq; ✉ Shearman & Sterling LLP, Broadgate West, 9 Appold Street, London EC2A 2AP (☎ 020 7655 5959)

WARD, Anthony Robert; s of Stanley Roy Ward, of Worcestershire, and Jeanette, *née* Mantle; *b* 6 January 1957; *Educ* Wrekin Coll, Wimbledon Sch of Art (BA); *Partner* Mark Thompson, *qv*, theatre designer; *Career* set and costume designer; worked extensively in rep incl: Royal Exchange Manchester, Bristol Old Vic, Derby Playhouse, Haymarket Theatre Leicester, Nottingham Playhouse, Theatre Royal Plymouth, Theatre Royal York; *Theatre* for RSC incl: A Midsummer Night's Dream, King Lear, The Tempest, Artists & Admirers, The Winter's Tale, The Alchemist, The Virtuoso, Troilus & Cressida, Cymbeline, Twelfth Night, The Lion, The Witch and the Wardrobe, The Secret Garden; for RNT incl: Sweet Bird of Youth, Napoli Milionaria, The Way of the World, La Grande Magia, John Gabriel Borkman, Othello, The Invention of Love, Oklahoma! (Lyceum Theatre and Broadway), Remember This, The Royal Hunt of the Sun, Twelfth Night, Rocket to the Moon, The Captain of Kopenick, My Fair Lady (also Theatre Royal); other credits incl: Chitty Chitty Bang Bang (London Palladium and Broadway), Oliver! (London Palladium and nat tour), The Magic Flute (Glyndebourne), Gypsy (Broadway), The Rehearsal, A Hard Heart, Dona Rosita, The Novice (all Almeida), Assassins, Nine, To The Green Fields Beyond, Uncle Vanya, Tweflth Night (all Donmar Warehouse), Burning Issues (Hampstead Theatre), The Royal Family (Theatre Royal), Breakfast at Tiffany's (Theatre Royal), Mary Stuart (Donmar Warehouse and Apollo Theatre), The Night of the Iguana (Lyric Theatre), The Royal Hunt of the Sun (NT); *Opera* for Opera North incl: La Bohème, Yolande, The Nutcracker, L'Étoile, Gloriana (also ROH), Peter Grimes, Carousel; other credits incl: The Makropulos Case (Metropolitan Opera, NY), Tosca (De Vlaamse Opera, Antwerp), Manon Lescaut (Opera de Paris, Bastille & De Vlaamse Opera), Macbeth (Bastille), Dialogues of the Carmelites (ENO and WNO), Il Ritorno d'Ulisse (Aix-en-Provence Festival), Alcina (Vienna State Opera); *Ballet* The Nutcracker (Adventures in Motion Pictures, Sadlers Wells), Masquerade, Les Rendezvous, Dance Variations (all Royal Ballet), The Nutcracker (Royal Danish Ballet); *Film* A Midsummer Night's Dream (RSC prodn, dir Adrian Noble, *qv*), Gloriana – A Film (BBC); *Awards* Olivier Award nominations incl: Best Costume & Set Design (for A Winter's Tale) 1994, Best Set Design (for Sweet Bird of Youth and The Tempest) 1995, Best Set Design (for A Midsummer Night's Dream, La Grande Magia and The Way of the World) 1996; Tony Award nomination for Scenic Design (for A Midsummer Night's Dream) 1995–96, Best Costume & Set Design My Fair Lady 2002, Best Set Design Chitty Chitty Bang Bang

2003; winner Olivier Award Best Costume Design (for A Midsummer Night's Dream, La Grande Magia and The Way of the World) 1996, winner Olivier Award Best Set Design (for Oklahoma!) 1999, winner OBIE for set design (for Uncle Vanya) 2002–03, winner Best Costume Design of a Play Tony Award (for Mary Stuart) 2009; *Style*— Anthony Ward, Esq; ✉ c/o agent, Harriet Cruickshank, 97 Old South Lambeth Road, London SW8 1XU (📞 020 7735 2933, fax 020 7820 1081, website www.anthonywarddesign.com)

WARD, Christopher John; s of late John Stanley Ward, and Jacqueline Law Hume, *née* Costin (d 1996); *b* 25 August 1942; *Educ* Royal Masonic Sch Bushey, KCS Wimbledon; *m* 1 (m dis 1987); 2 da (Sadie b 13 Aug 1973, Martha b 6 April 1976), 1 s (William b 18 April 1979); *m* 2, 1991, Nonie Niesewand; *Career* reporter: Driffield Times 1959, Newcastle Evening Chronicle 1960–63; reporter, columnist and sub-ed Daily Mirror 1963– 76, asst ed Daily and Sunday Mirror 1976–81, ed Daily Express 1981–83, jt fndr Redwood London 1983– (formerly Redwood Publishing Ltd, chm 1983–2014); non-exec dir Acorn Group plc (formerly Acorn Computer Group plc) 1983–99, chm Redwood Custom Communications Toronto 2007–09, dir College Valley Estates Northumberland 2008–; cruise ship lectr 2012–; tstee: WWF 1994–2000, WWF Int 2002–08; chm WWF-UK 2002– 08, memb Farne Islands Advsy Ctee 2007–; Mark Boxer Award BSME 1995; *Books* How to Complain (1974), Our Cheque is in the Post (1980), And The Band Played On (2011); *Recreations* photography, shooting, rearing bantam hens; *Clubs* Garrick; *Style*— Christopher Ward, Esq; ✉ Glenburn Hall, Jedburgh, Roxburghshire TD8 6QB (📞 01835 865801, e-mail cj.ward@btinternet.com); Redwood London, Bankside 3, 90 Southwark Street, London SE1 0SW (📞 020 3787 0881)

WARD, Clive Richard; s of William Herbert Ward (d 1982), and Muriel, *née* Wright; *b* 30 July 1945; *Educ* Sevenoaks Sch, Univ of Cambridge (MA); *m* 9 Sept 1972, Catherine Angela, da of Lt Cdr Godfrey Joseph Hines (d 1999), of Droxford, Hants; 3 da (Joanna b 1975, Diana b 1977, Emily b 1979); *Career* CA 1971, asst sec Take Over Panel 1975–77, ptnr Ernst and Young 1979–90 (head corp fin London 1987), corp devpt dir Shandwick plc 1990–91, dir The Capita Group plc 1992–94, ptnr Ernst & Young 1994–2006, dir EY Trustees Ltd 2006–; treas Victim Support 2002–10; Worshipful Co of Barbers 1985, Worshipful Co of Tobacco Pipe Makers and Tobacco Blenders 1975; FCA 1979; *Books* Guide to Company Flotation (1989); *Recreations* golf, fishing, music, gardening; *Clubs* RAC; *Style*— Clive Ward, Esq; ✉ Market Heath House, Brenchley, Tonbridge, Kent TN12 7PA (📞 01892 722172); Ernst & Young LLP, 1 More London Place, London SE1 2AF (e-mail cward5@uk.ey.com)

WARD, David; s of Kenneth Arthur Ward (d 1992), and Eileen, *née* Onn; *b* 24 June 1953; *Educ* Boston GS, Univ of Bradford (MBA, MPhil), Univ of Leicester (MSc), Chartered Inst of Public Fin and Accountancy; *m* 14 Sept 1974, Jacqueline Ann, *née* Dodd; 2 s (Joseph b 2 Sept 1983, Samuel b 27 May 1987); *Career* Lincs CC 1971–79, Leeds Met Univ 1985–2010; cncllr Bradford DC 1984–2010, MP (Lib Dem) Bradford East 2010–15; *Recreations* football, reading, running; *Clubs* Idle Working Mens; *Style*— David Ward, Esq; ✉ Constituency Office, 458 Killinghall Road, Bradford BD2 4SL (📞 01274 403973); House of Commons, London SW1A 0AA

WARD, David; *Educ* Univ of London (BA); *Career* head of communications UN Children's Fund until 1988, chief policy advsr to late Rt Hon John Smith, QC, MP 1988–94, currently DG FIA Fndn (DG European Bureau Brussels 1996–2001); exec sec Cmmn for Global Road Safety, memb Exec Bd World Bank's Global Road Safety Facility; *Style*— David Ward, Esq; ✉ FIA Foundation for Automobile and Society, 60 Trafalgar Square, London WC2N 5DS

WARD, Dr David; s of Ernest Ward, and Hilda Grace Ward; *b* 25 March 1947, Rochester, Kent; *Educ* Old Swinford Hosp, Guy's Hosp (BSc, MB BS, Gowland Hopkins Prize), Univ of London MD; *Career* trained in cardiology St Bart's, conslt St George's Hosp 1986–; special interest in electrophysiology; memb: Br Cardiac Soc 1981, Apothecaries Soc 1985, Piano Player Gp; Freeman City of London 1983; FACC 1981, FRCP 1989; *Publications* Clinical Electrophysiology of the Heart (1987); over 200 articles and papers on cardiology; *Recreations* music, walking, squash; *Clubs* RSM; *Style*— Dr David E Ward

WARD, HE David; *Educ* Magdalene Coll Cambridge (MA); *Career* diplomat; asst desk offr EU Dept (External) FCO 1992–93, Japanese language trg 1994–95, second sec (political) Tokyo 1995–98, head Instn Section Common Foreign and Security Policy Dept FCO 1998–2001, dep head of mission Kathmandu 2002–05, dep counsellor (political) Beijing 2006–09, sr strategy advsr Policy Unit FCO 2010–11, dep head of mission Tripoli 2011– 12, dep head of mission Provincial Reconstruction Team Lashkar Gah 2013–14, ambass to Eritrea 2014–16, high cmmr to the Solomon Islands, Vanuatu and Nauru; *Recreations* music, skiing, reading; *Style*— HE Mr David Ward; ✉ c/o FCO (Honiara), King Charles Street, London SW1A 2AH

WARD, David James; s of Leslie Edward Ward, of Egham, Surrey, and Margaret, *née* Cook; *b* 1 May 1946; *Educ* Manor Croft Sch Egham, Brookland Tech Coll, Richmond Coll of Technol; *m* 10 April 1971, Glenora Ann, da of late Robert Gordon Tott; 2 da (Joanna Louise b 1 March 1980, Sarah Michele b 30 July 1982); *Career* freelance photographer 1978–; press photographer, work published in various magazines papers and books, photographer of Royalty, show business people and actors, specialist in portraiture; winner of many merits and awards incl: Press Photographer of the Year, Kodak Photographer of the Year, Panorama Photographer of the Year, Kodak Gold Award for Portrait Photography 1993, UK Portrait Photographer of the Year 1996; BIPP Press Photographer of the Year 1997; Br Photographers' Assoc 1990; FBIPP 1994; *Books* Wonderful World Series (1985); *Recreations* jogging, squash, cycling; *Clubs* Roundtable (Egham); *Style*— David Ward, Esq; ✉ Latchets, Harpesford Avenue, Virginia Water, Surrey GU25 4RE (📞 01344 843421); The Studio, Latchets, Harpesford Avenue, Virginia Water, Surrey GU25 4RE (📞 01344 843421)

WARD, Graham Norman Charles; CBE (2004); s of Ronald Charles Edward Ward (d 1999), and Hazel Winnifred, *née* Ellis (d 2002); *b* 9 May 1952; *Educ* Dulwich Coll, Jesus Coll Oxford (MA, Boxing blue); *m* 1, 1975 (m dis 1981), Ingrid Imogen Sylvia, da of Hubert Edward Philip Peter Baden-Powell (d 1994); 2 s (Peter Ronald Norman b 15 June 1978, Andrew Charles Richard b 16 Sept 1980); *m* 2, 1993, Ann, da of Joseph Mistri (d 2009); 1 s (Alexander Christopher Edward b 14 Feb 1996); *Career* PricewaterhouseCoopers (formerly Price Waterhouse before merger): articled clerk 1974–77, personal tech asst to chm Account Standards Ctee 1978–79, seconded to HM Treasy 1985, ptnr 1986–2010, dir Electricity Services Europe 1990–94, dir Business Devpt 1993–94, chm World Utilities Gp 1994–96, dep chm World Energy Gp 1996–98, World Utilities ldr Global Energy and Mining Gp 1998–2000, sr ptnr Global Energy and Utilities Gp 2000–14; chief cmmr Ind Cmmn for Aid Impact 2010–15; dir Civil Aviation Authy 2013–; chm: Young Chartered Accountants Gp 1980–81, London Soc of Chartered Accountants 1989–90 (memb Ctee 1983–91), Chartered Accountants in the Community 1996–2002, Consultative Ctee of Accountancy Bodies 2000–01, Power Sector Advsy Gp UK Trade & Investment 2001– 04; membership sec Pensions Res Accountants Gp 1985–90; memb: Cncl Soc of Pension Conslts 1988–90, Cncl ICAEW 1991–2003 (vice-pres 1998–99, dep pres 1999–2000, pres 2000–01), Ctee Br Energy Assoc 1997–2004 (vice-chm 1998–2001, chm 2001–04), Takeover Panel 2000–01, Financial Reporting Cncl 2000–07 (dep chm 2000–01), Bd Int Fedn of Accountants 2000–06 (pres 2004–06), Auditing Practices Bd 2001–04 (vice-chm 2003–04), Bd UK-Indian Business Cncl (formerly Indo British Partnership Network) 2005–13 (vice-chm 2008–13), Financial Servs Sector Advsy Bd UK Trade & Investment 2006–10; auditor of the Duchy of Cornwall 2001–10; vice-chair World Energy Cncl 2008– 14 (hon offr 2014–); pres: Jesus Coll Assoc 1990–91, Chartered Accountants Students'

Soc of London 1992–96 (vice-pres 1987–92); vice-pres Univ of Oxford Amateur Boxing Club 1990–, Soc of Cons Accountants 1992–2001, Epilepsy Research UK (formerly Epilepsy Research Fndn) 1997–2015; govt: Goodenough Coll 2004–, Dulwich Coll 2008–; hon financial advsr St Paul's Cathedral 2008–; Freeman: City of London 1994, Worshipful Co of Chartered Accountants 1994 (memb Ct of Assts 1997, Jr Warden 2007–08, Sr Warden 2008–09, Master 2009–10); FCA 1983 (ACA 1977), CIGEM, FEI, FRSA; *Books* The Work of a Pension Scheme Actuary (1987), Pensions: Your Way Through The Maze (1988), A Practitioner's Guide to Audit Regulation in the UK (conslt ed, 2004), The Handbook of International Corporate Governance (contrib, 2009); *Recreations* boxing, rugby, opera, ballet; *Clubs* Carlton, Vincent's (Oxford); *Style*— Graham Ward, Esq, CBE; ✉ Civil Aviation Authority, CAA House, 45–59 Kingsway, London WC2B 6TE (📞 020 7435 6757, website www.caa.co.uk)

WARD, Ian; s of Alan Ward (d 1990), of Washington, Tyne and Wear and Ann, *née* Anderson; *b* 12 May 1959, Newcastle upon Tyne; *Educ* Washington Sch, Univ of Durham (BA); *m* 5 April 1991, Andrea Helen, *née* Wilson; 2 da (Antonia b 20 June 1994, Emilia b 4 June 1997); *Career* slr; ptnr: Eversheds 1989–97 (joined as articled clerk 1981), Dickinson Dees 1997–; memb Law Soc; *Recreations* travel, skiing; *Style*— Ian Ward, Esq; ✉ Bond Dickinson, 1 Trinity Gardens, Broad Chare, Newcastle upon Tyne (📞 0191 279 9244, fax 0191 230 8920, e-mail ian.ward@bonddickinson.com)

WARD, Prof Ian Macmillan; *b* 9 April 1928; *Educ* Royal GS Newcastle upon Tyne, Magdalen Coll Oxford (MA, DPhil); *m* 1960, Margaret, *née* Linley; 3 c; *Career* tech offr Fibres Div ICI Ltd Harrogate 1954–61, res assoc Div of Applied Mathematics Brown Univ USA 1961–62, head Basic Physics Section ICI Fibres 1962–66 (ICI res assoc 1965– 66), sr lectr in physics of materials H H Wills Physics Laboratory Univ of Bristol 1966– 70; Univ of Leeds: prof of physics 1970–94, chm of dept 1975–78 and 1987–89, Cavendish prof 1987–94, dir Interdisciplinary Res Centre in Polymer Sci and Technol 1989–94, research prof 1994–14; emeritus prof 2014–; Staudinger Durer Prize ETH Zurich 2013; visiting prof Univ of Bradford 2008–; chm: Br Polymer Physics Gp Inst of Physics 1971– 75 (sec 1967–71), Macromolecular Physics Section Euro Physical Soc 1976–81; pres Br Soc of Rheology 1984–86; memb Advsy Bd Jl of Macromolecular Science (Physics) 1966–, jt ed Solid State Science Series Cambridge Univ Press 1966–, ed Polymer 1974–2002; memb Editorial Bd: Jl of Materials Science 1974–, Plastics and Rubber Processing and Applications 1981–, Jl of Applied Polymer Science 1989–; A A Griffiths Silver Medal Inst of Materials 1982, S G Smith Meml Medal Textile Inst 1984, Swinburne Medal Inst of Materials 1988, Charles Vernon Boys Medal and Prize Inst of Physics 1993, Glazebrook Medal Inst of Physics 2004, Netlon Medal Inst of Materials 2004, Staudinger-Durrer Prize ETH 2013; hon degree Univ of Bradford 1993; FRS 1983, FInstP, FIM; *Publications* Mechanical Properties of Solid Polymers (1971, 3 edn with J Sweeney 2013), Structure and Properties of Oriented Polymers (ed, 1975, 2 edn 1997), Ultra High Modulus Polymers (ed jtly, 1979), Advances in Oriented Polymers – 1 (ed, 1982), Advances in Oriented Polymers – 2 (1987), An Introduction to the Mechanical Properties of Solid Polymers (with D W Hadley, 1993, 2 edn with J Sweeney, 2004), Solid Phase Processing of Polymers (ed jtly, 2000), Mechanical Properties of Solid Polymers (3rd edn with J Sweeney, 2013); around 700 papers in polymer science; *Style*— Prof Ian M Ward, FRS; ✉ School of Physics and Astronomy, University of Leeds, Leeds LS2 9JT

WARD, (William) Ian Roy; s of William Gerald Roy Ward (d 1977), of St Leonards-on-Sea, and Ellinor Ward, *née* Ostergaard (d 1964); *b* 17 September 1936; *Educ* Bembridge Sch, Thames Nautical Trg Coll HMS Worcester; *m* 21 Nov 1964, Vivienne, da of George Edward Garton Watson (d 1971), of Cape Town, South Africa; 2 da (Michele b 4 Sept 1967, Alison b 31 Aug 1975), 1 s (Duncan b 30 Sept 1969); *Career* Lt RNR until 1965; Merchant Navy 1954–58 and 1962–64, called to the Bar 1962, Admiralty Chambers 1964– 75, ptnr (specialising in shipping) Lovell White Durrant 1976–95, conslt Holman Fenwick & Willam 1996–2000, p/t immigration judge 1999–2008; vice-chm Sailors' Soc; Freeman Worshipful Co of Solicitors; memb Law Soc 1976, FCIArb 1972; *Recreations* sailing, walking; *Clubs* East India; *Style*— Ian Ward, Esq; ✉ 67 The Avenue, Kew, Richmond, Surrey TW9 2AH (📞 020 8940 0260); Castle Hill, Newport, Pembrokeshire SA42 0QD (📞 01239 820263)

WARD, Sir John MacQueen; kt (2003), CBE (1995); s of Marcus Waddie Ward (d 1963), of Edinburgh, and Catherine, *née* MacQueen (d 1996); *b* 1 August 1940; *Educ* Edinburgh Acad, Fettes; *m* Barbara MacIntosh; 3 da (Marsali, Mhairi, Morag); 1 s (Marcus); *Career* IBM: plant controller 1966–75, dir of info systems Euro 1975–79, manufacturing controller 1979–81, dir Havant Manufacturing Plant 1982–90 (first Br Quality Award, Wills Faber Award, two Queen's Awards for export and technol), dir UK Govt and Public Serv Business 1991–95, res dir Scotand & N England 1991–97; chm 1990–94: Scottish Electronics Forum, Quality Scotland Fndn, Advsy Scottish Cncl for Educn and Trg Targets, CBI; chm: Euro Assets Tst 1995–2015, Scottish Homes 1996–2002, Scottish Post Office Bd 1997–2001, Scottish Qualification Authy 2000–04, Scottish Enterprise 2004–09; non-exec chm: Macfarlane Gp plc 1995–2003 (chm 1998–2003), Dunfermline Bldg Soc 2002–07; memb: Sec of State's Scottish Econ Cncl 1990–94, Sec of State's Scottish Business Forum 1998–99; chm of govrs Queen Margaret UC 2000–04; tsee Nat Museums of Scotland until 2013; visiting prof Heriot-Watt Univ; Hon DSc Napier Univ, Hon DBA Univ of Strathclyde, Hon DL Glasgow Caledonian Univ, Hon DUniv Heriot-Watt; hon fell SCOTVEC; MICAS, FIET, FRSA, FRSE; *Recreations* walking, DIY, reading; *Clubs* New (Edinburgh), Bruntsfield Links Golf; *Style*— Sir John Ward, CBE

WARD, (Christopher) John William; s of Gp Capt Thomas Maxfield Ward, CBE, DFC (d 1969), and Peggy, *née* Field (d 2004); *b* 21 June 1942; *Educ* CCC Oxford (BA Lit Hum), Univ of E Anglia (DipEcon); *m* 1, 1971 (m dis 1988), Diane, *née* Lelliott; *m* 2, 2008, Susan Corby; *Career* Bank of England 1965–74; gen sec: Bank of England Staff Organisation 1974–80, Assoc First Div of Civil Servants 1980–88; head of devpt Opera North 1988– 94, dir of corp affairs West Yorkshire Playhouse 1994–97, dir of devpt ENO 1997–2002, dir of devpt Crafts Cncl 2003–04, devpt advsr Welsh Nat Opera 2003–; *Style*— John Ward, Esq; ✉ Welsh National Opera, Wales Millennium Centre, Cardiff Bay, Cardiff CF10 5AL (📞 029 2063 5042)

WARD, Rev Prof (John Stephen) Keith; s of John Ward (d 1983), of Hexham, Northumberland, and Evelyn, *née* Simpson; *b* 22 August 1938; *Educ* Hexham GS, Univ of Wales (BA), Linacre Coll Oxford (BLitt, DD), Trinity Hall Cambridge (MA, DD); *m* 21 June 1963, Marian, da of Albert Trotman (d 1942), of Ystrad Rhondda, S Wales; 1 s (Alun James b 1968), 1 da (Fiona Caroline b 1966); *Career* lectr in logic Univ of Glasgow 1964–69, lectr in philosophy Univ of St Andrews 1969–71, lectr in philosophy of religion King's Coll London 1971–76, ordained priest C of E 1972, fell and dean Trinity Hall Cambridge 1976–83, F D Maurice prof of moral and social theology Univ of London 1983–86, prof of history and philosophy of religion King's Coll London 1986–91, regius prof of divinity Univ of Oxford and canon of Christ Church 1991–2003, prof of divinity Gresham Coll London 2004–08, professorial research fell Heythrop Coll London 2009–; pres World Congress of Faiths, memb Cncl Royal Inst of Philosophy; FBA 2002; *Books* Kant's View of Ethics (1972), The Concept of God (1974), Rational Theology and the Creativity of God (1982), The Living God (1984), Images of Eternity (1987), Divine Action (1990), A Vision to Pursue (1991), Religion and Revelation (1994), Religion and Creation (1996), God Chance and Necessity (1996), Religion and Human Nature (1998), God Faith and the New Millennium (1998), Religion and Community (2000), A Short Introduction to Christianity (2000), God: A Guide for the Perplexed (2002), The Case for Religion (2004), What the Bible Really Teaches (2004), The Big Questions in Science and Religion

(2008), The God Conclusion (2009), The Word of God? (2010), More than Matter? (2010), The Philosopher and the Gospels (2011), Morality, Autonomy, and God (2013); *Recreations* music, walking; *Style*— The Rev Prof Keith Ward; ✉ 39 Coopers Lane, Abingdon OX14 5GU (website www.keithward.org)

WARD, Dr Keith Douglas; s of Thomas Derek Ward, of Malvern, Worcs, and Doreen, *née* Johnson; *b* 1955, Birmingham; *Educ* Univ of Cambridge (MA), Univ of Birmingham (PhD); *m* 1978, Hilary Janet, da of Frederick Stubbs; *Career* research scientist on radar RSRE Malvern 1977–95, dir T W Research Ltd (radar systems) 1995–2008, tech dir Igence Ltd 2008–; winner: Electronics Letters Premium IEE 1980, Mountbatten Prize 1990; MIEEE (USA) 1989, FIEE 1996 (MIEE 1989), FREng 1997; *Books* Sea Clutter: Scattering, the K Distribution and Radar Performance; author of over 100 papers and reports; *Recreations* travel, walking, photography, music, gardening, DIY; *Style*— Dr Keith Ward, FREng; ✉ T W Research Ltd, Harcourt Barn, Harcourt Road, Malvern, Worcestershire WR14 4DW (☎ 01684 563882, e-mail keith.ward@ieee.org, website www.igence.com)

WARD, Maxwell Colin Bernard; s of Maj Bernard Maxwell Ward, LVO (d 1991), and Margaret Sunniva, *née* Neven-Spence (d 1962); *b* 22 August 1949; *Educ* Harrow, St Catharine's Coll Cambridge (MA); *m* 17 April 1982, Sarah, da of Lt-Col Peter William Marsham, MBE (d 1970); 2 da (Laura Sunniva b 2 April 1984, Antonia Hersey b 27 Sept 1993), 2 s (Charles Bernard Maxwell b 27 Feb 1986, Frederick Peter Neven b 15 Feb 1989); *Career* ptnr Baillie Gifford & Co 1975–2000 (investment trainee 1971–74); dir: Scottish Equitable Life Assurance Society 1988–94, Scottish Equitable plc 1995–98, Aegon UK plc 1999–2010, Foreign & Colonial Investment Tst plc 2000–11, Edinburgh Investment Tst 2011–; md The Independent Investment Tst plc 2000–; chm: Dunedin Income Growth Investment Tst plc 2001–06, Aegon Asset Mgmnt UK 2010–11; memb General Cncl The King's Fund 1998–; *Recreations* tennis, squash, bridge, country pursuits, golf; *Clubs* New (Edinburgh), Cavalry and Guards; *Style*— Maxwell Ward, Esq; ✉ Stobshiel House, Humbie, East Lothian EH36 5PD (☎ 01875 833646); The Independent Investment Trust, 17 Dublin Street, Edinburgh EH1 3PG (☎ 0131 558 9434)

WARD, Michael James; s of Arthur Ward (d 2010), and Edna, *née* Morris (d 2012); *b* 5 January 1959, Wolverhampton; *Educ* Univ of Birmingham (LLB); *m* 13 July 1991, Julie, *née* Finnigan; 2 da (Charlotte b 15 April 1992, Francesca b 30 Oct 2001), 1 s (Jamie b 6 Aug 1994); *Career* admitted slr 1984; ceo Gateley plc; former pres Birmingham Chamber of Commerce and Industry, former pres and treas Birmingham Law Soc; former chm: Young Slrs Gp, Trainee Slrs Gp; memb Law Soc; *Clubs* Edgbaston Golf; *Style*— Michael Ward, Esq; ✉ Gateley plc, One Eleven Edmund Street, Birmingham B3 2HJ (☎ 0121 234 0030, e-mail michael.ward@gateleyplc.com)

WARD, (Charles John) Nicholas; *b* 1 August 1941; *Educ* Charterhouse, INSEAD (MBA); *m* 1967, Deirdre Veronica, *née* Shaw; 2 da; *Career* now ret; early career spanned several cos engaged in textiles, venture capital, overseas trading, retail, distribution, healthcare, leisure and property sectors, since 1990s chm or non-exec dir of numerous cos in retail, textile, healthcare, tport, stockbroking and fund mgmnt, coal mining, student accommodation, agric, environmental and online direct mktg sectors; chm: Ryan Group Ltd 1995–2004, ADAS Holdings Ltd 1998–2007, UPP Projects Ltd 2006–07, Interactive Prospect Targeting Hldgs plc 2008–10; dep chm Albert E Sharp Hldgs 1996–98; conslt to Deutsche Bank and Bank Austria 1995–2014, conslt to 3i 1998–2007, special advsr to Swiss Re 2008–09; ind memb Steering Bd Insolvency Service (agency of DTI) 2004–06, public memb Network Rail Ltd 2011–13; non-exec dir: Anglia & Oxford RHA 1990–96, D1 Oils plc 2010; chm NHS Supplies Authy 1995–98; chm Govt advsy gps on volunteering: Make a Difference Team 1994–96, Volunteering Partnership 1995–96, Volunteering Partnership Forum for England 1996–97; pres Independent Custody Visiting Assoc (formerly Nat Assoc for Lay Visiting) 1996–2006 (chm 1992–96), chm Lay Visiting Charitable Tst 1995–; chm: The British Liver Tst 1999–2004, CORGI Tst 2005, Sulgrave Manor Tst 2011–13; memb Devpt Cncl City of London Sch for Girls 2003–07; Parly candidate (Cons) Liverpool Edge Hill by-election and gen election 1979, candidate (independent) opposing HS2 Westminster N gen election 2015; fell Inst for Turnaround Professionals 2001–11 (dir 2001–03), distinguished fell INSEAD 2014; Liveryman Worshipful Co of Tylers and Bricklayers (Master 1991–92); FCA 1964; *Clubs* RSM; *Style*— Nicholas Ward, Esq; ✉ Bacon House, Greatworth, Banbury, Oxfordshire OX17 2DX (☎ 01295 712732); Flat 12, 77 Warwick Square, London SW1V 2AR (☎ 020 7834 9175, mobile 07774 184762, e-mail nicholasward@variouscompanies.co.uk)

WARD, Peter Terry; *b* 8 October 1945; *m*; 1 da, 1 s; *Career* Standard-Triumph Motor Co: service liaison offr 1967–69, area mangr field service engrg and parts 1969–71, parts sales supervisor 1971–72, seconded to British Leyland France 1972, parts sales mangr Jaguar Rover Triumph Ltd (following gp reorganisation) 1973–75; Unipart Ltd: commercial mangr 1975–76, mangr distributor devpt 1976–77, sales dir 1977–79; dir parts ops Talbot Motor Co (and md subsid Motaquip Ltd) 1979–83; Rolls-Royce Motor Cars Ltd: dir sales and mktg 1983–84, md Sales and Mktg Div 1984–86, md 1986, md and chief exec 1987, chief exec Rolls-Royce Motors Holdings Ltd 1990, exec dir Vickers plc (parent co of Rolls-Royce) 1991–95, chm and chief exec Rolls-Royce Motor Cars Ltd 1991–94 (chm only 1995, resigned Feb), md ops Vickers plc 1993–94; former chm and chief exec Cunard Line and exec dir Trafalgar House plc (taken over by Kvaerner ASA 1996), exec chm TG21 plc (formerly TOAD Gp plc) 2002– (non-exec chm 2001–02), chm Raymarine plc 2005–10; non-exec dir Bridon plc 1994–, dir European Advsy Bd Harley-Davidson Inc; pres Soc of Motor Manufacturers and Traders 1994–95 (also chm SMMT Int Trade Ctee), bd memb Association des Constructeurs European d'Automobiles, chm Crewe Economic Devpt Exec, vice-pres Motor and Allied Trades Benevolent Fund (BEN); Liveryman Worshipful Co of Coachmakers & Coach Harness Makers; *Style*— Peter Ward, Esq

WARD, Philip; s of Albert Edwin Ward, of Doncaster, and Mildred, *née* Elsey; *Educ* Haberdashers' Aske's Sch Hampstead, Perugia, Coimbra, MECAS (Lebanon); *m* 4 April 1964, Audrey Joan, da of Lawrence Monk, and Ellen Monk, of Newport, Essex; 2 da (Carolyn b 1966, Angela b 1968); *Career* coordinator Library Servs Libya 1963–71, Unesco expert Library Servs and Documentation Egypt 1973, Unesco dir of Nat Library Serv Indonesia 1973–74, professional writer 1974–; fndr Private Libraries Assoc 1956–, FRGS, FRSA, ALA; *Books* The Oxford Companion to Spanish Literature (1978), A Dictionary of Common Fallacies (2 vols, 1978–80), A Lifetime's Reading (1982), Contemporary Designer Bookbinders (1995); novels: Forgotten Games (1984), The Comfort of Women (2002); poetry: Impostors and their Imitators (1978), Lost Songs (1981), His Enamel Mug (2003); plays: Garrity (1970); travel books incl: Japanese Capitals (1985), Travels in Oman (1986), Finnish Cities (1987), Polish Cities (1988), Bulgaria (1989), Wight Magic (1990), South India (1991), Western India (1991), Bulgarian Voices: Letting the People Speak (1992), Sofia (1993), Bahrain: a Travel Guide (1993), Gujarat, Daman, Diu: a Travel Guide (1994); *Recreations* meditative basketball (following the teachings of Hirohide Ogawa) and reading; *Style*— Philip Ward, Esq

WARD, Rear Adm Rees Graham John; CB (2002); s of John Walter Ward, and Helen Burt, *née* Foggo; *b* 1 October 1949, Malta; *Educ* Dunfermline HS, Plympton GS, Queens' Coll Cambridge (MA), Cranfield Univ (MSc 1981, MSc 2001); *Career* served HMS Russel 1972–73 (Queen's Sword 1972), served HMS Brighton 1977–79, Seawolf Project MOD PE 1981–83, promoted Cdr 1983, served HMS Ark Royal 1984–87, mil asst to Controller of the Navy 1988–89, promoted Capt 1990, asst dir Surface Weapons DOR (Sea) 1990–92, mil asst to Chief of Defence Procurement 1992–94, memb Cncl RUSI 1994–98, promoted Cdre 1995, DOR (Sea) 1995–97, promoted Rear Adm 1999, Asst Chief of Defence Staff (Operational Requirements) 1999, Capability Mangr (Strategic Deployment) 1999–2002, chief exec Defence Communication Services Agency 2002–07, DG Defence Manufacturers Assoc 2007–09; ceo ADS Gp Ltd 2009–12, md Eversfield Advisors Ltd 2013–; non-exec dir Amethyst Risk Mgmnt Ltd 2010–16, sr advsr KBR 2013–; represented GB and Scotland at athletics and cross-country running 1972–77; FIEE 1997, CRAeS 2007; *Publications* Allies in Conflict – European Defence Industry (paper, 1998); *Recreations* reading, mountain bike riding; *Clubs* Hawks' (Cambridge), IOD, Army & Navy; *Style*— Rear Adm Rees Ward, CB; ✉ e-mail: rees.ward@eversfieldadv.com

WARD, Dr Richard Churchill; s of Alan Ward (d 2004), and Margaret Ward (d 1999); *b* 1957, Sunninghill, Berks; *Educ* Wellington Coll, Univ of Exeter; *m* 2 Oct 1990, Carol, *née* Cole; 2 s (Christopher (Kit) b 1992, Sebastian b 2003); *Career* scientist SERC 1982–88, sr mangr BP Research 1988–91, head of business devpt BP Oil Trading Int 1991–94, head of mktg Tradition Financial Services 1994–95; Int Petroleum Exchange: dir product devpt and research 1995–96, exec vice-pres 1996–99, chief exec 1999–2005, vice-chm 2005–06; chief exec Lloyd's of London 2006–13; non-exec dir Partnership Assurance Gp plc 2013–, non-exec chm Brit plc 2014–, exec chm Cunningham Lindsey Gp Inc 2014–; MRI, FRSA; *Recreations* dinghy sailing, skiing, tennis; *Style*— Dr Richard Ward; ✉ Brit plc, 55 Bishopsgate, London EC2N 3AS (☎ 020 7098 6988, e-mail richard.ward@britinsurance.com)

WARD, Prof Richard Samuel; s of Walter John Ward (d 1986), and Eileen, *née* Phillips; *b* 6 September 1951, South Africa; *Educ* Rhodes Univ SA (BSc, MSc), Univ of Oxford (DPhil); *m* 30 June 1991, Rebecca Nora, *née* Barlow; 1 s (Michael James b 15 Feb 1993), 1 da (Susanna Naomi b 18 June 1997); *Career* jr research fell Merton Coll Oxford 1977–79, lectr and fell TCD 1979–82; Univ of Durham: lectr 1983–, prof 1991–; Jr Whitehead Prize London Mathematical Soc 1989; FRS 2005; *Publications* Twistor Geometry and Field Theory (jtly, 1990); *Recreations* family, music, reading; *Style*— Prof Richard Ward; ✉ Department of Mathematical Sciences, University of Durham, South Road, Durham DH1 3LE (☎ 0191 334 3118, e-mail richard.ward@durham.ac.uk)

WARD, Simon Charles Vivian; s of Maj Vivian Horrocks Ward (d 1998), and Leila Penelope, *née* Every (d 2007); *b* 23 March 1942; *Educ* Shrewsbury, Trinity Coll Cambridge (MA); *m* 18 Sept 1965, Jillian, da of Thomas Roycroft East (d 1980), of Dublin; 3 da (Victoria Penelope Jane (Mrs Matthew Doull) b 1969, Antonia Lisa (Mrs Charles Crawshay), Lucinda Fiona (The Hon Mrs Nicholas Napier) (twins) b 1971); *Career* trainee stockbroker Govett Sons & Co 1963–65; ptnrs' asst: Hedderwick Hunt Cox and Co 1965–67, Hedderwick Borthwick and Co 1967–70; ptnr Montagu Loebl Stanley and Co 1972–86; dir: Fleming Montagu Stanley Ltd 1986–89, Fleming Private Asset Management Ltd 1989–2000; chm: Fleming Private Fund Management Ltd 1989 (dir 1975–2000), The Conduit Mead Company Ltd 2003– (dir 2001–); *Recreations* skiing, tennis, shooting, gardening, opera, ballet; *Clubs* Boodle's; *Style*— Simon Ward, Esq; ✉ Thorpe House, Hall Street, Long Melford, Suffolk CO10 9HZ (☎ 01787 319707, office 01787 319707, e-mail dowerhouse@talk21.com)

WARD, Tony; OBE (1998); *Educ* Univ of Leeds (BSc); *Career* various personnel positions Grand Metropolitan plc until 1992, dir of human resources Kingfisher plc 1992–97; BAA: gp human resources 1997–99, gp services dir 1999–2007; non-exec dir SThree plc, non-exec dir OCS Gp Ltd; memb Bd Which? Ltd; dep chair Cmmn for Racial Equality 1993–95 (cmmr 1990–95); memb CBI Employment Ctee 1995–2004, dep chair Consumer's Assoc; FIPD, FRSA; *Recreations* golf, Manchester United, cycling; *Clubs* Lambourne; *Style*— Tony Ward, Esq, OBE

WARD THOMPSON, Prof Catharine Joan; da of Peter Michaeljohn Ward, of Croxley Green, Herts, and Janet Mary, *née* Bruce (*see* Debrett's Peerage, Bruce, Bt cr 1628); *b* 5 December 1952, Headington, Oxon; *Educ* Holy Cross Convent Chalfont St Peter, Rickmansworth GS, Univ of Southampton (BSc), Univ of Edinburgh (DipLA, PhD); *m* 30 Dec 1983, Henry Swift Thompson, s of Henry Swift Thompson (d 2004), of Grass Valley, CA, and Hancock Point, ME, USA; 2 da (Emma b 27 Sept 1985, Joanna b 19 Sept 1991), 1 s (James b 21 Nov 1987); *Career* landscape asst Justice and Webb Landscape Architects Vancouver BC Canada 1974–75, landscape architect and sr landscape architect W J Cairns & Ptnrs 1976–81, princ LDS Assocs Landscape Architects and Landscape Scientists 1986–90; Edinburgh Coll of Art: lectr 1981–88, head Dept of Landscape Architecture 1989–2000, prof 1999–2011, dir of research Environmental Studies 2000–02, research prof of landscape architecture 2002–11; prof Univ of Edinburgh 2011– (hon prof 2007–10); dir OPENspace Research Centre 2001–; visiting research scholar Univ of Pennsylvania, Harvard 1994–95, hon prof Univ of Exeter Med Sch 2016–19; landscape advsr Forestry Cmmn 1998–2009; memb: Amnesty International, World Devpt Movement; FLI, Chartered Landscape Architect (Design); FRSA; *Books* Open Space: People Space (jt ed, 2007), Innovative Approaches to Researching Landscape and Health (jt ed, 2010); *Recreations* dance, choreography, theatre; *Style*— Prof Catharine Ward Thompson; ✉ 11 Douglas Crescent, Edinburgh EH12 5BB; Hancock Point, Maine 04640, USA; OPENspace Research Centre, University of Edinburgh, 74 Lauriston Place, Edinburgh EH3 9DF (☎ 0131 651 5827, e-mail c.ward-thompson@ed.ac.uk)

WARD-SMITH, Richard James; s of Derrick William Smith, of Stevenage, Herts, and Patricia, *née* Cheek; *b* 10 October 1964; *Educ* Alleyne's Boys' Sch, Stevenage Coll of Art & Design (DATEC), Berkshire Coll of Art & Design (BTEC); *m* 6 Sept 1986, Sally Josephine, da of Edward Terrence Fisher (d 1982); 1 da (Elizanell Jessica Ellen b 5 Sept 1988), 2 s (Oscar Arthur Edward James b 26 June 1991, Moses Blue Edward James b 14 Oct 1995); *Career* designer; freelance designer 1985–86; KB Design: designer 1987–89, sr designer 1989–90, sr designer Pentagram Design Ltd 1990–92; assoc dir Crescent Lodge Design Ltd 1994–97 (sr designer 1992–94); Communication Arts America Award of Excellence 1988, Int Logo and Trademark Assoc NYC Award of Excellence 1989, Art Directors' Club Award of Merit 1992; work featured in numerous jls and annuals; *Recreations* native American tradition, alternative life style, cinema, travel; *Style*— Richard Fisher-Smith, Esq

WARDELL, Gareth Lodwig; s of John Thomas Wardell, and Jenny Ceridwen Wardell; *b* 29 November 1944; *Educ* Gwendraeth GS, LSE (BSc, MSc); *m* 1967, Jennifer Dawn Evans; 1 s (Alistair); *Career* former teacher, princ lectr in geography Trinity Coll Carmarthen 1997–2000 (sr lectr in geography 1973–82); election agent then research asst to Dr Roger Thomas as MP for Carmarthen 1979–82, MP (Lab) Gower 1982–97, chm Select Ctee on Welsh Affrs 1984–97; dir The Industry Tst; non-exec dir Milford Docks Co 2003–07; memb: Bd Environment Agency 1997–2004, Forestry Cmmn 1999–2006, Cmmn for Wales; planning and environmental conslt 2006–; lay memb GMC 1995–2008 (memb 1994); FRGS, hon fell Inst for Waste Mgmnt 2001; *Recreations* swimming, cross-country running; *Style*— Gareth Wardell, Esq; ✉ 67 Elder Grove, Carmarthen, Dyfed SA31 2LH

WARDLE, Anthony Peter; s of Peter John Wardle, of Minehead, Somerset, and Caroline Mina Gertrude, *née* Salter; *b* 9 August 1948; *Educ* Hertford GS, Thames Nautical Training Coll, Univ of Southampton Sch of Navigation; *m* 24 June 1972, Susan Margaret, *née* Lewis; 2 da (Jessica Ann b 3 June 1979, Eleanor Katherine b 18 June 1981); *Career* navigating apprenticeship Peninsular & Oriental Steam Navigation Co 1966–69, mktg consultancy 1970–, Mann Wardle Group Ltd (acquired by Saatchi & Saatchi plc 1987), chm Saatchi & Saatchi subsids 1987–93, ptnr Wardle & Associates 1991–2012, dir Paragon Art 2012–; *Recreations* shooting, fishing, scribbling; *Style*— Anthony Wardle, Esq

WARDLE, Peter; s of late Alec Wardle, and Patricia, *née* Haker; *b* 3 July 1962; *Educ* Emanuel Sch, Merton Coll Oxford (BA); *m* 19 Feb 2005, Jo Gray; *Career* private sec to Min for Higher Educn and Sci Dept of Educn and Sci 1987–90; Inland Revenue: admin trainee 1985–87, princ 1990–94, asst dir 1994–98, dir of strategy and planning 1998–2000; dir of corporate servs Cabinet Office 2000–03, chief exec Electoral Cmmn 2004–15; non-exec dir Basildon & Thurrock Univ Hosps NHS Fndn Tst 2004–12 (vice-chm 2007–10); memb Gp Audit Ctee Circle Anglia Housing Gp 2008–; advsr: Venice Cmmn Cncl of Europe 2015–, Cambridge Conference on Electoral Democracy 2015–; external rep Qualifications Bd Assoc of Electoral Administrators 2016–; FRSA; *Recreations* music, fell-walking, cycling; *Clubs* Essex Roads Cycling; *Style*— Peter Wardle, Esq

WARDROPE, James (Jim); CBE (2009); s of James Wardrope, of Bathgate, W Lothian, and Elizabeth Wilson, *née* Young (d 1989); *b* 14 March 1954; *Educ* Bathgate Acad, Univ of Edinburgh (BSc, MB ChB), Univ of Sheffield (MD); *m* 31 March 1978, Diana Jane, da of Bruce Stuart Fothergill, of Sheffield; 1 s (Alistair b 1988), 1 da (Katie b 1986); *Career* registrar and res registrar Leeds Gen Infirmary 1982–85, sr registrar Royal Hallamshire Hosp Sheffield 1985–87, conslt in accident and emergency med Northern Gen Hosp Sheffield 1987–2014; FRCS (Edin) 1982, FRCS 1982, FFAEM 1994 (treas 1998–2004, pres 2005–08); *Books* The Management of Wounds and Burns (2 edn, with J A Edhouse, OUP, 1999), Musculo Skeletal Medicine (with B English, OUP, 1997), ABC of Common Soft Tissue Disorders (with F Morris and P Hattam, 2016); *Recreations* cycling, running, gardening; *Style*— Jim Wardrope, Esq, CBE; ☎ 07890 493119, e-mail jimwardrope@hotmail.com

WAREHAM, Dr Campbell; s of Charles Howard Wareham, of Wellington, NZ, and Susan Mary, *née* Evans; *b* 27 February 1971, Wellington, NZ; *Educ* St Patrick's Coll Silverstream NZ, Univ of Westminster (BSc), Nat Sch of Podiatry (dip), NZ Coll of Podiatric Surgery (post-grad dip), Univ of Ulster (doctorate); *m* 16 April 1994, Alison Mary, *née* Feltwell; 2 s (Adam Stephen b 9 Jan 1998, Charles Richard b 5 Sept 2000); *Career* Durham Sch of Podiatric Med: staff podiatrist 1994–96, clinical asst (surgery) 1996–2000, sr lectr 2000–03; conslt podiatric surgn Camden PCT 2004–06, conslt podiatric surgn Dept of Podiatric Surgery Suffolk PCT 2006–; Allied Health Professions rep for Nat Patient Safety Agency; visiting sr lectr School of Podiatric Medicine Univ of East London; author of articles, pubns and lectures in podiatric surgery; memb NZ Coll of Podiatric Surgery 1994, fell Coll of Podiatrists UK (Surgery) 2000, FRSM 2008; *Recreations* sailing, fencing; *Style*— Dr Campbell Wareham; ✉ Nuffield House Hospital, Foxhall Road, Ipswich IP4 5SW

WAREING, Kierston Faye; da of Alan Peter Wareing, and Lyn Carol, *née* Bailey; *b* Romford, Essex; *Educ* St Bernard's Convent HS for Girls Essex, Havering Coll (Dip); *Career* actress; slr's clerk High Courts 2006; memb Equity 2003; *Television* Wire in the Blood 2007, Trial and Retribution 2008, The Take (Sky) 2009; *Film* It's a Free World 2007 (nominated: Best Actress and Best Newcomer Br Ind Feature Film Awards 2007, Best Actress BAFTA TV Awards 2008), Rise of the Footsoldier 2007, Fish Tank 2009; *Style*— Miss Kierston Wareing; ✉ c/o Elaine Murphy Associates, Suite 1, 50 High Street, London E11 2RJ (☎ 020 8989 4122, fax 020 8989 1400)

WAREING, Marcus; *b* 1970, Southport, Lancs; *Career* chef-restaurateur; chef 1986–93 incl: Savoy hotel, Le Gavroche, The Point NY, Grand Hotel Amsterdam and Gravetye Manor W Sussex; sous chef Aubergine 1993–95, worked with Daniel Boulud NY and Guy Savoy Paris 1995, head chef L'Oranger London 1996–98 (Michelin star 1997 and 1998); chef-patron Pétrus 1999–2008 (two Michelin stars), Savoy Grill 2003–07 (Michelin star), Marcus (2 Michelin stars) 2007–; *Style*— Mr Marcus Wareing; ✉ Marcus, The Berkeley, Wilton House, 87 Knightsbridge, London SW1X 7RB

WARENIUS, Prof Hilmar Meek; s of Tor Adolph Warenius (d 1971), and Ruby Gwendoline, *née* Meek; *b* 12 January 1942, Penzance, Cornwall; *Educ* Penzance GS, Downing Coll Cambridge (MA, PhD), Middlesex Hosp Med Sch London (MB BChir (Cantab), DMRT); *m* 19 Aug 1972, Rosamund Jean Talbot, da of Leopold Edward Hill (d 1957); 1 s (Christopher b 1976), 2 da (Eleanor b 1979, Fleur b 1985); *Career* sr house offr Royal Marsden Hosp 1970–71, registrar in radiotherapy Middlesex Hosp 1972–74; first asst to Prof Mitchell at Addenbrooke's Hosp Cambridge 1974–75, MRC clinical res fell Univ of Cambridge 1975–79, first asst to Mr William Ross Univ of Newcastle and Newcastle Gen Hosp 1979–80, conslt in radiotherapy and oncology in Newcastle 1980–82, CRC prof of radiation oncology Univ of Liverpool 1982–90, MRC hon clinical coordinator Fast Neutron Studies 1982–89, prof and dir Oncology Res Unit Dept of Med Univ of Liverpool 1990–2006, currently visiting prof Anticancer Drug Devpt Sch of Chemistry Univ of Southampton; former fndr chief med offr and dir of R&D Theryte Ltd, currently ceo HilRos Ltd, co-fndr Pronec Ltd 2015–; visiting prof and hon conslt Dept of Clinical Oncology Hammersmith Hosp London 1995–97; Cardiff Univ accredited expert witness 2005; FRCR, FRCP; *Recreations* swimming, guitar, choral society, cooking, building a scale model of HMS Belfast from mahogony; *Style*— Prof Hilmar Warenius; ✉ 14 Delavor Road, Heswall, Wirral, Merseyside (☎ 0151 342 3034, e-mail hilmarwarenius@outlook.com)

WARHAM, Mark Francis; s of Joseph Warham, of Leeds, and Eileen, *née* Northover; *b* 2 January 1962, Leeds; *Educ* St Thomas Aquinas GS Leeds, St Catherine's Coll Oxford (BA); *m* 12 Feb 2000, Olivia, *née* Dagtoglou; 3 da (Eleanor, Francesca (twins) b 5 July 2002, Anna b 23 April 2004); *Career* investment controller 3i 1982–86, J Henry Schroder & Co Ltd 1986–2000 (dir 1995); Morgan Stanley & Co Ltd: md 2000–07 (seconded as DG Takeover Panel 2005–07), vice-chm Europe 2008–09, chm UK investment banking 2008–09; Barclays: md and co-head European M&A 2009–13, vice-chm investment banking and head EMEA M&A 2013–14; exec vice-chm Rothschild 2014–; Mergers and Acquisitions: Guide to Principles and Practice (ed, 1998–99); *Recreations* mountaineering, ornithology, photography; *Clubs* Alpine, Brooks's; *Style*— Mark Warham, Esq; ✉ Rothschild, New Court, St Swithin's Lane, London EC4N 8AL

WARING, Prof Michael John; s of Frederick Waring (d 1998), and Kathleen Waring (d 1999); *b* 8 November 1939, Lancaster; *Educ* Friends' Sch Lancaster, Downing Coll Cambridge (MA), Univ of Cambridge (PhD, ScD); *m* 1973 (m dis 1979), A J Milner; 1 s (Christian Stephen Milner b 7 March 1974); *Career* fell Dept of Terrestrial Magnetism (DTM) Carnegie Instn of Washington 1964–65; Univ of Cambridge: demonstrator in biochemistry 1965–67, lectr in pharmacology 1967–90, reader in chemotherapy 1990–99, prof of chemotherapy 1999–; fell and lectr in biochemistry Jesus Coll Cambridge 1965– (sometime tutor, dir of studies in biological sciences and med, librarian and steward, chm Wine Ctee, sr treas and tstee Boat Club); hon visiting conslt Cancer Research Laboratory Auckland 1975–; visiting prof: H C Ørsted Inst Copenhagen 1983, Université du Québec Montreal 1985, Institut Pasteur Paris 1989, Université de Paris 1991, Univ of Texas at Austin 1998, Caltech 2003 and 2005 (visiting scientist 1992, visiting assoc in chemistry 1999); memb: Biochemical Soc 1965–, Br Pharmacological Soc 1968–, Cambridge Centre for Molecular Recognition 1995–; memb advsy panels for orgns incl: Human Frontier Science Prog, Danish Nat Research Fndn, Australian Research Cncl, US Nat Science Fndn, NZ MRC, Auckland Med Research Fndn, Minority Biomedical Research Support Prog NIH, Israel Science Fndn, Health Research Bd of Ireland, Restore Burns and Reconstructive Surgery Research Tst, Institut National de la Santé et de la Recherche Médicale (INSERM); conslt Center for Molecular Med and Drug Devpt Karachi; organiser for int meetings, plenary and guest lectr at symposia and confs worldwide; series ed Cancer Biology & Medicine Kluwer Academic Publishers; memb Editorial Bd: Biochemical Jl 1974, Antimicrobial Agents & Chemotherapy 1978–91, Molecular Pharmacology 1979–98, Oncology Research 1984–, Jl of Molecular Recognition 1987– (ed 1991–98), Biochimica et Biophysica Acta 1996–2004, Current Medicinal Chemistry – Anti Cancer Agents 2000–, The Open Cancer Jl 2007–, Drug Design, Devpt and Therapy 2007–; Br Cncl exchange fell Consejo Superior de Investigaciones Cientificas (CSIC) Spain 1975 and 1978, EMBO res fell Madrid 1977, Royal Soc exchange fell Spain 1979 and 1982, Royal soc exchange fell Poland 1984; Rex Williamson lectr Deakin Univ Geelong 1999; memb Monumental Brass Soc 1965–, memb Cambridge Philosophical Soc 1967–; memb Bd of Govrs: Witan Hall Reading 2002, Sevenoaks Sch 2005; fell Int Union Against Cancer 1977, membre correspondant Muséum National d'Histoire Naturelle Paris 1995; Freeman of the City of London; FRSC 2006; *Publications* European Brasses (jtly, 1967), The Molecular Basis of Antibiotic Action (jtly, 1972, 2 edn 1981), Molecular Aspects of Anti-Cancer Drug Action (jt ed, 1983), Biology of Carcinogenesis (jt ed, 1987), The Science of Cancer Treatment (jt ed, 1990), The Search for New Anti-Cancer Drugs (jt ed, 1991), Molecular Aspects of Anticancer Drug-DNA Interactions (jt ed, vol 1 1993, vol 2 1994), The Genetics of Cancer (jt ed, 1995), Methods in Enzymology, vol 340: Drug-Nucleic Acid Interactions (jt ed, 2001), Topics in Current Chemistry, vol 253: DNA Binders and Related Subjects (jt ed, 2005), Sequence-Specific DNA Binding Agents (2006); also author of 313 pubns in learned jls; *Recreations* music (organ, choral), monumental brasses, aviation; *Style*— Prof Michael Waring; ☎ 00 64 2 1045 2910; Jesus College, Cambridge CB5 8BL (☎ 01223 339441); Department of Pharmacology, University of Cambridge, Tennis Court Road, Cambridge CB2 1PD (e-mail mjw11@cam.ac.uk)

WARK, Kirsty; *b* 3 February 1955, Dumfries, Scotland; *Educ* Univ of Edinburgh; *m* Alan Clements; 1 s, 1 da; *Career* BBC Radio 1976–83: researcher, prodr (Good Morning Scotland, Order Order, World at One); BBC TV 1983–; fndr ptnr Wark Clements & Co (later IWC Media) 1990–2005, dir Black Pepper Media Ltd; presenter: Breakfast Time (BBC) 1986–90, General Election Night 1987, 1992, 1997 and 2001 (BBC TV), The Late Show 1990–93 (BBC TV), One Foot in the Past 1993–2000 (BBC TV), Newsnight 1993– (BBC TV), Newsnight Review (BBC TV) 1993–2009, Scottish Referendum 1997 (BBC TV), Turning into Children 1998– (BBC Radio), Vote '99 – Scotland Decides (BBC TV), Rough Justice (BBC TV) 1999–, Restless Nation (BBC TV), The Kirsty Wark Show 1999–2001 (BBC TV), Building a Nation (BBC TV), Lives Less Ordinary 2002 (BBC TV) and 2003 (BBC Scotland), Scottish Parliamentary Elections 2003 (BBC Scotland), Tales from Europe (BBC TV) 2004, 2005 and 2006, The Book Quiz (BBC 4) 2008 and 2009, The Samuel Johnson Prize for Non-Fiction (BBC 4) 2008–, A Question of Genius (BBC 2) 2009 and 2010, The Review Show (BBC TV) 2010–, The Home Movie Roadshow (BBC 2) 2010, The Man Who Collected the World: William Burrell (BBC TV) 2013, Iain Banks: Raw Spirit (BBC TV) 2013, Kirsty Wark meets Donna Tartt: A Review Show Special (BBC 4) 2013, Blurred Lines: The New Battle of the Sexes (BBC 2) 2014, Would I Lie to You (BBC) 2014, Scotland's Art Revolution: The Maverick Generation (BBC) 2014, The Summer Exhibition: BBC Arts at the Royal Academy (BBC) 2014 and 2015, Edinburgh Extra (BBC) 2014, General Election 2015 (BBC) 2015, Our World: Kidnapped for a Decade (BBC) 2015, Manchester International Festival (BBC) 2015, BBC TV Proms 2015 and 2016; appearances in: Only an Excuse (BBC Scotland) 2015, The TV That Made Me (BBC 1) 2016; cameo appearances in: The Amazing Mrs Pritchard (BBC 1) 2006, Dr Who (BBC TV) 2007, The IT Crowd (Channel 4) 2007, Spooks (BBC TV) 2009, Beyond the Pole 2009, Party Animals (BBC TV) 2009, Absolutely Fabulous the Movie 2016; patron Maggie's Centres, ambass Prince's Tst; Journalist of the Year BAFTA Scotland 1993, Best TV Presenter BAFTA Scotland 1997, Glenfiddich and Scotland on Sunday Scot of the Year 1998, Outstanding Contribution to Broadcasting BAFTA 2013; Hon FRIBA; *Books* The Legacy of Elizabeth Pringle (2014); *Recreations* family, tennis, swimming, cooking, beachcombing, architecture, reading, music; *Style*— Ms Kirsty Wark; ✉ Black Pepper Media Limited (e-mail info@blackpeppermedia.com, website www.blackpeppermedia.com)

WARKENTIN, Juliet; da of John and Germaine Warkentin, of Toronto, Canada; *b* 10 May 1961; *Educ* Univ of Toronto (BA); *m* (m dis), Andrew Lamb; *Career* former ed: Toronto Life Fashion, Drapers Record, Marie Claire; md Mktg and Internet Devpt Arcadia Gp plc; formerly: ptnr The Fourth Room, editorial dir Redwood Gp, content dir WGSN, chief creative offr Stylistpick; currently content and brand strategy conslt; Canadian Nat Magazine Award 1989, Business and Professional Magazine Editor of the Year PPA Awards 1995; FRSA; *Style*— Ms Juliet Warkentin

WARLAND, Philip John; s of Ernest Alfred Henry Warland (d 1998), and Winifred Mary Warland (d 1991); *Educ* KCS; *m* 1 (m dis); 3 s (David b 1972, Richard b 1973, John b 1978); m 2, 2003, Sheila Anne Nicoll; *Career* head Info Div Bank of England 1985–89, gp personnel resources mangr Standard Chartered Bank 1989–90, DG Assoc of Unit Tsts and Investment Funds 1991–2001, advsr Euro regulatory consulting PricewaterhouseCoopers 2001–06, Halsey Consulting 2006–09, head of public policy Fidelity Int 2009–; chm Oasis Charitable Tst 1986–2006; *Recreations* golf, cricket, walking; *Style*— Philip Warland, Esq; ✉ Fidelity International Ltd, 25 Cannon Street, London EC4M 5TA

WARMAN, Alister Seager; s of Mark Warman, and Zillah Warman; *Educ* Harrow, Courtauld Inst of Art London; *Career* lectr Poly of Newcastle upon Tyne 1970–74, Art Dept Arts Cncl of GB 1975–85, dir Serpentine Gallery London 1985–91, princ Byam Shaw Sch of Art Central St Martins Coll of Art and Design Univ of the Arts London 1991–; *Style*— Alister Warman, Esq; ✉ Byam Shaw School of Art, 2 Elthorne Road, London N19 4AG (☎ 020 7281 4111, fax 020 7281 1632)

WARMAN, Matt; MP; *b* 1981; *m* Rachel; *Career* consumer technol ed Telegraph 2008–13, technol ed (head of technol) Telegraph 2013–15; MP (Cons) Boston and Skegness 2015–; *Style*— Matt Warman, Esq, MP; ✉ House of Commons, London SW1A 0AA (e-mail matt.warman.mp@parliament.uk, Twitter @MattWarman)

WARMINGTON, Neil; s of Terrence Clifford Warmington, and Rita Mary, *née* Lankester; *Educ* Boswells Sch Chelmsford, Braintree Coll of FE, Maidstone Coll of Art (BA), Motley Theatre Design Sch (MA); *Career* artist and designer; *Theatre* set and costume designs: I Put a Spell On You (Leicester Haymarket), Coriolanus (Tramway Glasgow), Arsenic & Old Lace (Royal Lyceum Edinburgh), Initmate Exchanges (Duke's Playhouse Lancaster), Merlin (Part 2) (Royal Lyceum Edinburgh), Comedians (Royal Lyceum Edinburgh), Fiddler on the Roof (West Yorkshire Playhouse), Life is a Dream (West Yorkshire Playhouse), Merlin (Tankred Däcrst) (Royal Lyceum Edinburgh), Much Ado About Nothing (Liverpool Everyman Theatre), Waiting for Godot (Liverpool Everyman Theatre), The Life of Stuff (Donmar Warehouse London), Blithe Spirit (York Theatre Royal), Henry V (RSC), Troilus and Cressida (Grand Theatre Leeds and ROH), Desire Under the Elms (Shared Experience Theatre and Tricycle Theatre London), Angels in America (7:84 Theatre Co), The Tempest (Contact Theatre Manchester), Women Laughing (Watford Palace and Duke of York's Theatre), Passing Places (Traverse Theatre Edinburgh), Dissent (Traverse Theatre), The Duchess of Malfi (Bath Theatre Royal), The Glass Menagerie (Royal Lyceum Edinburgh), Glasgow 1999 Year of Architecture launch (Scottish Exhibition and Conference Centre (SECC)), Jane Eyre (Shared Experience Theatre and Young Vic), Don Juan (English Touring Theatre), Family (Traverse Theatre), The Taming of the Shrew (English Touring Theatre), Riddance (Paines Plough), The Drowned World (Paines Plough), The Straits (Paines Plough and tour to NY), Splendour (Paines Plough and Traverse Theatre), The Marriage of Figaro (Garsington Opera Festival), Prada (Milan), Solemn Mass for a Full Moon (Barbican and Traverse Theatre), King of the Fields (Traverse Theatre), Love's Labour

Lost (English Touring Theatre), Gagarin's Way (Traverse Theatre, RNT, West End and NY), Wiping My Mother's Arse (Traverse Theatre), Woyzeck (Royal Lyceum Edinburgh), Ghosts (English Touring Theatre), King Lear (Old Vic/English Touring Theatre), Helmet (Traverse Theatre and Paines Plough), Slab Boys Trilogy (Traverse Theatre), Playhouse Creatures (West Yorkshire Playhouse), Dumbstruck (Dundee Rep), Scenes from an Execution (Dundee Rep, nominee Best Design and Best Prodn Ctitic's Awards for Theatre in Scotland), Lie of the Mind (Dundee Rep), Knives in Hens (Tag), The Birthday Party (Tag); *Solo Exhibitions* Hutcheson Hall Glasgow, GFT Glasgow, Swanston Street Studios Glasgow, Donmar Warehouse London, King Street Gallery Glasgow, 23 Edinburgh Billboards Glasgow Year of Architecture, The Connecticut Gallery USA; *Group Exhibitions* Leicester Haymarket, Almeida Theatre London, Theatre Museum London, Coventry Gallery London, Leith Open Edinburgh, Pacesetters (Peterborough Art Gallery), RNT, CCA Glasgow, Sandra Drew Gallery Canterbury, John Moores Liverpool, Serpentine Gallery London; *Awards* Linbury Prize for Stage Design, 3 awards for Best Design TMA, 5 Edinburgh Fringe Festival awards, Sir Alfred Munnings Florence Prize for Painting, Noel Machin Painting Prize; *Recreations* galleries, theatre, chess; *Style—* Neil Warmington, Esq; ✉ c/o Michael McCoy, Independent Talent, Oxford House, 76 Oxford Street, London W1D 1BS (☎ 020 7636 6565, e-mail michael_mccoy@icmlondon.co.uk)

WARNE, Penelope; *Career* senior partner, chair of board and head of energy CMS London; *Style—* Ms Penelope Warne; ✉ CMS, Cannon Place, 78 Cannon Street, London EC4N 6AF

WARNER, Alan; s of Frank Warner (d 1996), of Oban, Argyll, and Patsy, *née* Bowman (d 2000); *b* 5 August 1964; *Educ* Oban HS, Ealing Coll of HE (BA), Univ of Glasgow (MPhil); *m* 6 Aug 1996, Hollie Cleak; *Career* novelist; FRSL 2013; *Novels* Morvern Callar (1995, Somerset Maugham Award, shortlisted Whitbread First Book Award, shortlisted IMPAC, film 2002), These Demented Lands (1997, Encore Award), The Sopranos (1998, Saltire Scottish Book of the Year Award), The Man Who Walks (2002, nominated Saltire Scottish Book of the Year Award), The Worms Can Carry Me to Heaven (2006), The Stars in the Bright Sky (2010, longlisted Man Booker Prize 2010), The Deadman's Pedal (2012, nominated Saltire Scottish Book of the Year 2012, winner James Tait Black Prize 2013), Their Lips Talk of Mischief (2014); *Recreations* searching for that innocent hobby; *Clubs* Tesco Club Card; *Style—* Alan Warner

WARNER, Deborah; CBE (2006); da of Roger Harold Metford Warner, of Oxon, and Ruth Ernestine, *née* Hurcombe; *b* 12 May 1959; *Educ* Sidcot Sch, St Clare's Coll, Central Sch of Speech and Drama London; *Career* artistic dir Kick Theatre Co 1980–86, res dir RSC 1987–89, assoc dir RNT 1990–98, assoc dir Abbey Theatre Dublin 2000–04; Officier de l'Ordre des Arts et des Lettres (France) 2000 (Chevalier 1992); *Productions* Kick Theatre Co: The Good Person of Szechwan 1980, Woyzeck 1981 and 1982, The Tempest 1983, Measure for Measure 1984, King Lear 1985, Coriolanus 1986; RSC: Titus Andronicus (Best Dir Olivier Awards, Best Dir Evening Standard Awards 1989) 1987, King John 1988, Electra 1988 and 1990; RNT: The Good Person of Sichuan 1989, King Lear 1990, Richard II 1995–96, The PowerBook 2002–03, Happy Days 2007–08 (also Paris, Madrid Festival, Kennedy Center Washington, BAM, Holland Festival and Epidavros Greece), Mother Courage 2009; other credits incl: Hedda Gabler 1991 (Abbey Theatre Dublin and Playhouse Theatre London, Best Director and Best Prodn Olivier Awards 1992 (TV version 1992)), Wozzeck (Opera North) 1993 and 1996, Coriolan (Salzburg Festival) 1993–94, Footfalls (The Garrick) 1994, Don Giovanni (Glyndebourne Festival Opera and Channel 4) 1994 and 1995, The Waste Land (Fitzroy Prodns) 1995–99, The St Pancras Project and The Tower Project (LIFT Festival) 1995 and 1999, Une Maison de Poupée (Odéon, Paris) 1997, Honegger's Joan of Arc at the Stake (BBC Proms) 1997, The Turn of the Screw (ROH, Evening Standard and South Bank Awards 1998) 1997 and 2001, Bobigny 1998, The Diary of One Who Vanished (ENO/Bobigny/NT and New York) 1999, The Angel Project (Perth Int Art Festival) 2001 (Lincoln Center Festival) 2003, Medea (Abbey Theatre Dublin, Queens Theatre London) 2000–01 (BAM/USA tour and Broadway) 2002–03, St John Passion (ENO) 2000 and 2003, Fidelio (Glyndebourne Festival Opera) 2001 and 2006, The Rape of Lucretia (Munich) 2004, Julius Caesar (Barbican, Chaillot Paris, Madrid and Luxembourg) 2005, Dido and Aeneas (Vienna) 2006 and (Paris l'Opera Comique) 2008 and (Holland Festival) 2009, Fidelio (Glyndebourne) 2006, La Voix Humanire (Opera North) 2006, Death in Venice (ENO) 2007, Le Monnaie (Brussels) 2008 and (La Scala) 2011, The School for Scandal (Barbican and Holland Festival) 2011; *Film* The Last September 1999; *Recreations* travelling; *Style—* Ms Deborah Warner, CBE; ✉ c/o Leah Schmidt, The Agency, 24 Pottery Lane, Holland Park, London W11 4LZ (☎ 020 7727 1346, fax 020 7727 9037)

WARNER, Edmond William (Ed); OBE (2012); s of William John Warner, of Shepperton, Middlesex, and Kathleen Elizabeth, *née* Rooke-Matthews (d 2007); *b* 17 August 1963, Farnborough, Kent; *Educ* St Olave's GS Orpington, Worcester Coll Oxford (BA); *m* 1988, Katharine Louise, *née* Wright; 2 da (Eleanor b 1994, Clemency b 1995); *Career* GT Mgmnt 1985–87, UBS Phillips and Drew 1987–89, Thornton Mgmnt 1989–91, Baring Securities 1991–93, Dresdner Kleinwort Benson 1993–97, NatWest Markets, BT Alex Brown 1997–99, Old Mutual 1999–2003, chief exec IFX Gp 2003–06, chm UK Athletics 2007–; chm: LMAX, Standard Life European Private Equity Tst; non-exec dir: Clarksons, SafeCharge Int Gp; chm and non-exec dir: Blackrock Commodities Income Investment Tst, Grant Thornton UK LLP; *Recreations* running with the Fittleworth Flyers; *Style—* Ed Warner, Esq, OBE; ✉ UKA, Athletics House, Alexander Stadium, Walsall Road, Perry Barr, Birmingham B42 2BE

WARNER, Dr Francis Robert Le Plastrier; s of Canon Hugh Compton Warner (d 1955), vicar of Epsom, Surrey, and Nancy Le Plastrier, *née* Owen (d 1992); *b* 21 October 1937; *Educ* Christ's Hosp, London Coll of Music, St Catharine's Coll Cambridge (choral exhibitioner, MA), Univ of Oxford (MA, DLitt); *m* 1, 1958 (m dis 1972), Mary, *née* Hall; 2 da (Georgina b 1962, Lucy b 1967); m 2, 1983, Penelope Anne, da of John Hugh Davis, of Blagdon, nr Bristol; 1 da (Miranda b 1985), 1 s (Benedict b 1988); *Career* poet and dramatist; Univ of Cambridge: supervisor in English St Catharine's Coll 1959–65, staff tutor in English, memb Bd of Extramural Studies 1963–65, hon fell (residential) St Catharine's Coll 1999–; Univ of Oxford: Lord White fell in English literature and sr English tutor St Peter's Coll 1965–99, fell librarian 1966–76, univ lectr 1966–99, dean of degrees 1984–2006, vice-master 1987–89, pro-proctor 1989–90, 1996–97 and 1999–2000, emeritus fell St Peter's Coll 1999–; conductor Honegger's King David in King's Coll Chapel 1958 (Landmark CD issued 2003); Messing Int Award (USA) for Distinguished Contribs to Literature 1972, Silver Medal Benemerenti of the Constantinian Order of St George (Italy) 1990, elected academico correspondente estrangeiro Portuguese Academia de Letras e Artes 1993; memb Southern Arts Drama Panel Arts Cncl of GB 1976–80 (chm 1978–79 and 1979–80); Hon DMus William Jewell Coll USA 2012; *Poetry* Perennia (1962), Early Poems (1964), Experimental Sonnets (1965), Madrigals (1967), The Poetry of Francis Warner (USA, 1970), Lucca Quartet (1975), Morning Vespers (1980), Spring Harvest (1981), Epithalamium (1983), Collected Poems 1960–84 (1985), Nightingales: Poems 1985–96 (1997), Cambridge (2001), Oxford (2002), By the Cam and the Isis (2005), Blitz Requiem (music by David Goode, St Paul's Cathedral London, 2013), Six Anthems (music by David Goode, 2014); *Plays* Maquettes, a trilogy of one-act plays (1972); Requiem: Pt 1 Lying Figures (1972), Pt 2 Killing Time (1976), Pt 3 Meeting Ends (1974); A Conception of Love (1978), Light Shadows (1980), Moving Reflections (1983), Living Creation (1985), Healing Nature: The Athens of Pericles (1988), Byzantium (1990), Virgil and Caesar (1993), Agora: an Epic (1994), King Francis 1st (1995), Goethe's Weimar (1997), Rembrandt's Mirror (1999); *Prose Editor* Eleven Poems by Edmund Blunden (1965), Garland (1968), Studies in the Arts (1968), Beauty for Ashes – Selected Prose (2012, 2 edn 2013); *Recreations* grandchildren, cathedral music, travel; *Clubs* Athenaeum; *Style—* Dr Francis Warner; ✉ St Peter's College, Oxford OX1 2DL (☎ 01865 278 900); St Catharine's College, Cambridge CB2 1RL (☎ 01223 338300)

WARNER, James Royston; s of Peter John Warner, of Broadway, Worcs, and Joan Emily May, *née* Hodge; *b* 27 August 1948; *Educ* Prince Henry's GS Evesham, Gonville & Caius Coll Cambridge (MA); *m* 23 May 1992, Melissa, da of Ronald Brooks, of Tollerton; 1 da (Chloe Jane Brooks-Warner b 15 July 1985); *Career* industrial engr British Leyland 1970–73; Mars Ltd: mgmnt servs mangr 1973–75, distribution mangr 1975–78, materials and purchasing mangr 1978–80, factory mangr 1980–82; PricewaterhouseCoopers (formerly Coopers & Lybrand before merger): conslt 1982–85, ptnr 1985–, practice ldr Manufacturing and Logistics (Europe) 1990 (head (UK) 1988), worldwide ldr Supply Chain Management Practice 1993; fell: Inst of Logistics, Br Inst of Operations Mgmnt; *Recreations* music, walking on Dartmoor, cooking, spending time with my family; *Style—* James Warner, Esq; ✉ mobile 07802 201741, e-mail james.r.warner@uk.pwcglobal.com

WARNER, Jeremy; s of Jonathan Warner, and Marigold, *née* Brayshaw; *b* 23 September 1955; *Educ* Magdalen Coll Sch Oxford, UCL; *m* 17 May 1988, Henrietta, *née* Franklin; 1 s (Sam b 17 Dec 1987), 2 da (Florence b 17 July 1992, Emma b 22 June 2000); *Career* reporter The Scotsman 1978–82; The Times: business reporter 1982–84, business corr 1984–86; The Independent: business corr 1986–88, assoc business ed 1988–92, city ed (The Independent on Sunday) 1992–94, business and city ed 1994–2009, asst ed Daily Telegraph 2009–; tstee The Independent pension scheme; *Awards* Br Press Award Specialist Writer of the Year 1992, Wincott Award Fin Journalist of the Year 1993, Wincott Award Fin Jl of the Year 1997 and 2005, Special Guild of Br Newspaper Eds Award for outstanding contribution in defense of the freedom of the press 1997; *Recreations* walking, running; *Style—* Jeremy Warner, Esq; ✉ Daily Telegraph, 111 Buckingham Palace Road, London SW1W 0DT (☎ 07710 613962, e-mail jeremy.warner@telegraph.co.uk)

WARNER, Prof John Oliver; OBE (2013); s of Henry Paul Warner (d 1992), and Ursula, *née* Troplowitz, of London; *b* 19 July 1945, Birmingham; *Educ* The Lawrence Sheriff Sch Rugby, Univ of Sheffield Med Sch (MB ChB, MD, DCH, Pleasance prize in paediatrics); *m* 1990, Dr Jill Amanda Warner, da of Maurice Halliday; 2 da (Olivia b 26 May 1991, Abigail b 21 Aug 1994); *Career* jr hosp posts Sheffield 1968–72; Hosp for Sick Children Great Ormond St: registrar 1972–74, res fell 1974–77, sr registrar 1977–80; conslt paediatric chest physician Royal Brompton Nat Heart and Lung Hosp (jt hosp and acad appt with Nat Heart and Lung Inst) 1980, subsequently sr lectr then reader in paediatrics Univ of London until 1990, prof of child health Univ of Southampton 1990–2006, prof of paediatrics Imperial Coll London (also head Dept of Paediatrics until 2015); ed-in-chief Paediatric Allergy and Immunology 1998–2010; hon prof Univ of Cape Town; memb: Br Soc for Allergy and Clinical Immunology 1979 (former sec and chm Paediatric Sub-Ctee), Br Thoracic Soc 1983, American Thoracic Soc 1992, Euro Respiratory Soc 1991 (head of Paediatric Assembly 1993–97), Advsy Ctee for Novel Foods and Processes FSA 1998–2012; pres Academic Paediatric Assoc (GB and NI); fndr chm Cystic Fibrosis Holiday Fund Charity 1986–90; BSACI William Frankland Award for Services to Allergy 2005, Lifetime Achievement Award European Respiratory Soc 2009, Pepys lectr BSACI 2011, Harry Morrow-Brown lectr BSACI 2015; FRCP 1986, FRCPCH 1997, FMedSci 1999, fell European Respiratory Soc (ERS) 2015; *Publications* Childhood Asthma: a guide for parents and children (with S J Goldsworthy, 1981, 1982 and 1983), Scoliosis: Prevention (proceedings of Phillips Zorab symposium, 1983), British Medical Bulletin (scientific ed, 1992), A Colour Atlas of Paediatric Allergy (with W F Jackson, 1994), Textbook of Pediatric Asthma: An international perspective (jt ed, 2001); also author of over 400 published scientific papers; *Recreations* cricket, horse riding; *Clubs* MCC; *Style—* Prof John Warner, OBE; ✉ Navaho, Hurdle Way, Compton, Winchester SO21 2AN; Department of Paediatrics, Imperial College, St Mary's Campus, Wright-Fleming Institute, Norfolk Place, London W2 1PG (☎ 020 7594 3990, e-mail j.o.warner@imperial.ac.uk)

WARNER, Prof Dame Marina Sarah; DBE (2015, CBE 2008); da of Col Esmond Pelham Warner, TD (d 1982), and Emilia, *née* Terzulli (d 2008); *b* 9 November 1946; *Educ* Lady Margaret Hall Oxford (MA); *m* 1, 31 Jan 1972 (m dis 1980), (Hon) William Hartley Hume Shawcross, *qv*, s of Baron Shawcross (Life Peer, d 2003); 1 s (Conrad Hartley Pelham b 1977); m 2, 16 Dec 1981 (m dis 1998), John Piers Dewe Mathews, s of Denys Cosmo Dewe Mathews (d 1986), of London; m 3, 20 Dec 2015, Graeme Segal, FRS; *Career* writer; Getty Scholar Getty Center for the History of Art and the Humanities 1987–88, Tinbergen prof Erasmus Univ Rotterdam 1991, Reith lectr 1994; visiting prof: Queen Mary & Westfield Coll London 1994–2008, Univ of Ulster 1994–95, Mellon prof of history of art Univ of Pittsburgh 1997, Univ of St Andrews, Stanford Univ 2000, Royal Coll of Art 2008–12; distinguished visiting prof Queen Mary Univ of London 2008–11; prof Dept of Literature, Film and Theatre Studies Univ of Essex 2004–14, prof of English and Creative Writing Birkbeck Coll Univ of London 2014–; Whitney J Oates fell Princeton Univ 1996, fell commoner Trinity Coll Cambridge 1998, hon research fell Birkbeck Coll London 1999, hon fell Lady Margaret Hall Oxford 2000, hon fell Mansfield Coll Oxford and St Cross Coll Oxford 2013, fell All Souls Coll Oxford 2014–16, Weidenfeld Humanities Prof Univ of Oxford 2016; Clarendon lectr Univ of Oxford 2001, Tanner lectr Yale Univ 1999, Robb lectr Auckland NZ 2004, Presidential lectr Stanford 2008; memb Cncl Br Sch at Rome 2008–16; memb: Exec Ctee Charter 88 1993–97, Advsy Bd Royal Mint to 1993, Ctee London Library 1996–2000, Advsy Cncl Br Library 1997–99, Arts Cncl Literature Panel 1997–2000, Friends of Bodleian Library 2011–; pres Br Comparative Literature Assoc 2010–16; tstee Artangel 1999–2004, vice-pres Nat Cncl for One Parent Families/Gingerbread 2002– (memb Mgmnt Ctee 1992–2000), patron Hosking Houses Tst, patron Reprieve 2009–, tstee Nat Portrait Gallery 2009–16; contrib: Times Literary Supplement, Washington Post Book World, London Review of Books, Independent, Independent on Sunday, New York Times Book Review, Times Higher Educn Supplement; chair of judges Man Booker Int Prize 2015; Aby-Warburg Prize 2004, Nat Book Critics Circle Award (Criticism) 2012, Truman Capote Award for Literary Criticism 2013, Sheikh Zayed Book Award for Arab Culture in Non-Arabic Languages 2013; Hon DLitt: Univ of Exeter 1995, Sheffield Hallam Univ 1995, Univ of York 1997, Univ of North London 1997, Univ of St Andrews 1998, Tavistock Inst Univ of East London 1999, Royal Coll of Art London 2004, Univ of Kent 2005, Univ of Oxford 2006, Univ of Leicester 2006, KCL 2009; FRSL 1985, FBA 2005; Chevalier de l'Ordre des Arts et des Lettres (France) 2004, Commendatore della Stella della Solidarietà (Italy) 2005; *Books* The Dragon Empress (1972), Alone of All Her Sex: The Myth and the Cult of the Virgin Mary (1976), Queen Victoria's Sketchbook (1980), Joan of Arc: The Image of Female Heroism (1981), Monuments and Maidens: The Allegory of the Female Form (1985), Into the Dangerous World: Childhood and its Costs (1991), L'Atalante (1993), Managing Monsters: Six Myths of Our Time (Reith lectures, 1994), Wonder Tales (ed, 1994), From the Beast to the Blonde: On Fairy Tales and Their Tellers (1994), The Inner Eye (catalogue, 1996), Donkey Business Donkey Work: Magic and Metamorphoses in Contemporary Opera (1996), No Go the Bogeyman: Scaring, Lulling and Making Mock (1998), Collected Poems by Sall Purcell (preface, 2002), Fantastic Metamorphoses, Other Worlds (Clarendon lectures, 2002), Phantasmagoria (2006), Eyes, Lies and Illusions (exhbn catalogue, 2006), Stranger

Magic: Charmed States & the Arabian Nights (2012), The Symbol Gives Rise to Thought: Essays on Art (2012), Once Upon a Time: A Short History of Fairy Tale (2014), Fly Away Home (2015); fiction: In A Dark Wood (1977), The Skating Party (1983), The Lost Father (1988), Indigo (1992), The Mermaids in the Basement (short stories, 1993), The Leto Bundle (2001), Murderers I Have Known (short stories, 2002), Signs and Wonders: Essays on Literature (2003); children's books: The Impossible Day (1981), The Impossible Night (1981), The Impossible Bath (1982), The Impossible Rocket (1982), The Wobbly Tooth (1984); juvenile: The Crack in the Teacup (1979); libretti: The Queen of Sheba's Legs (1994), In the House of Crossed Desires (1996); *Recreations* travel, looking at pictures; *Style*— Prof Dame Marina Warner, DBE; ✉ c/o Rogers, Coleridge and White, 20 Powis Mews, London W11 1JN (☎ 020 7221 3717, website www.marinawarner.com)

WARNER, Baron (Life Peer UK 1998), of Brockley in the London Borough of Lewisham; Norman Reginald Warner; PC (2006); s of Albert Henry Edwin Warner, and Laura Edith, *née* Bennett; *b* 8 September 1940; *Educ* Dulwich Coll, Univ of Calif Berkley (MA, Harkness fell), Nuffield Coll Oxford (Gwilym Gibbon fell); *m* 1 (m dis 1981), Anne Lesley; 1 s (Hon Andrew Simon b 1967), 1 da (Hon Justine Emma b 1969); m 2, Suzanne Elizabeth; 1 s (Hon Joel James Stephen b 1981); *Career* DHSS: various posts concerned with NHS 1960–74, princ private sec to Sec of State for Social Services 1974–76, asst sec Supplementary Benefit 1976–79, asst sec Operational Planning 1979–81, regnl controller Wales and SW Region 1981–83, under sec Supplementary Benefit and Housing Benefit 1984–85; dir Social Services Kent County Cncl 1985–91, chm City and E London Family Services Authy 1991–94, md Warner Consultancy and Training Services 1991–97, chm National Inquiry into Children's Homes 1992, memb Local Govt Cmmn 1995–96, sr policy advsr to Home Sec 1997–98; memb: Science and Technol Ctee House of Lords 2008–12, Govt's Cmmn on the Funding of Care and Support 2010–11, Adoption Legislation Ctee House of Lords 2012, Jt Select Ctee on Care Bill 2012–13, Jt Select Ctee on Draft Modern Slavery Bill 2013–14, House of Lords Select Ctee on NHS Sustainability 2016–17; Parly under sec of state (Lords) Dept of Health 2003–05, min of state (NHS reform) Dept of Health 2005–06; sr research fell in European social welfare and chm European Inst of Social Services Univ of Kent, cmmr for children's social care Birmingham City Cncl 2014–15; chm: The Residential Forum 1993–97, Royal Philanthropic Soc 1993–98 (vice-chm 1998–99), Youth Justice Bd for England and Wales 1998–2003, London Sports Bd 2003, Provider Devpt Agency NHS London 2007–09; former chm NCVO; tstee Leonard Cheshire Fndn and MacIntyre Care 1994–97, former memb Assoc of Dirs of Social Services, children's cmmr Birmingham City Cncl 2014–; *Recreations* walking, sport, reading, cinema, theatre, art, travel; *Style*— The Rt Hon the Lord Warner

WARNER, Peter Mark; s of late Dr Marcel Mark Warner, of Weybridge, Surrey, and late Birthe Johanna Warner; *b* 21 June 1959; *Educ* Woking County GS, Kingston Poly Business Sch (BA); *m* Carolyn Frances, *née* Rice; 3 da (Charlotte Emily (Lottie) b 30 Nov 1997, Abigail Leah (Abbie) b 11 April 2000, Henrietta Eve Warner b 7 Jan 2003); *Career* account exec Tim Arnold and Associates (sales promotion agency) 1981–83, client services dir IMP Ltd 1989–93 (joined as account exec 1983), ptnr HHCL and Partners 1993–2015; entrepreneur; *Recreations* gardening, fell walking, rare breed sheep, motorcycling, canal restoration; *Clubs* Goodwood Road Racing; *Style*— P Warner, Esq; ✉ Rodgate, Rodgate Lane, Haslemere, Surrey GU27 2EW (☎ 01428 707124, e-mail peterwarner@rodgate.com)

WARNER, Sir Philip Courtenay Thomas; 4 Bt (UK 1910), of Brettenham, Suffolk; s of Sir (Edward Courtenay) Henry Warner, 3 Bt (d 2011), and Jocelyn Mary Beevor (d 2014); *b* 3 April 1951; *Educ* Eton; *m* 1982, Penelope Anne, yr da of John Lack Elmer (d 1973); 1 s, 4 da; *Heir* s; *Career* barr; chm Warner Estate Hldgs plc 1993–2013 (memb Bd 1979–2013); dir of private cos; *Recreations* fishing; *Style*— Sir Philip Warner, Bt

WARNER, Simon Metford; s of Roger Harold Metford Warner, of Burford, Oxford, and Ruth Ernestine, *née* Hurcombe; *b* 12 January 1951; *Educ* Downs Sch Colwall, Leighton Park Sch Reading, Churchill Coll Cambridge (MA), Univ of Bristol; *m* 1974, Judith, da of Capt W Adams; 1 s (Leo b 1980); *Career* photographer, video artist and ind researcher 1975–; touring exhbn Airedale – a Changing Landscape (Bradford Museums) 1998, video installation Follow a Shadow (Impressions Gallery York) 2003, video A Guide to Yorkshire Rivers (Cartwright Hall Art Gallery Bradford) 2003, High Tide (touring exhbn) 2004, video installation Leaving Home (Brontë Parsonage Museum Haworth) 2005, Alchemy (touring exhbn) 2006–07, performance Lavater – The Shadow of History 2006–07, exhibition Walking Out (Huddersfield Art Gallery) 2009, public art project Seven Streams (Bradford) 2010, environmental art project Confluence (N Devon Biosphere Reserve) 2011–12, exhibition Ways to the Stone House (Pennine Prospects, Bronte Parsonage Museum) 2012, group survey Art in Yorkshire – from Turner to Hockney (Mercer Art Gallery, Harrogate) 2014, exhibition Image, Instinct and Imagination – Landscape as Sign Language (with Jay Appleton, RGS London) 2014, mixed media dance project 50 Steps (venues along Pennine Way) 2015, video installation North & South (Harewood House) 2016; co-dir Whitestone Arts Company 2003; NESTA research fell 2006–08; nomination Northern Art Prize 2011; *Publications* Pennine Landscapes (with J Warner, 1978), Discovering West Yorkshire 1999, The Brontës at Haworth (with Ann Dinsdale, 2006); contribs incl: National Trail Guides to the Pennine Way and Peddars Way, Country Life, Telegraph Magazine, Radio Times; *Recreations* cycling, theatre, walking, contemporary art; *Clubs* Magic Lantern Soc; *Style*— Simon Warner, Esq; ✉ Whitestone Farm, Stanbury, Keighley, West Yorkshire BD22 0JW (☎ 01535 644644, e-mail photos@simonwarner.co.uk, website www.simonwarner.co.uk)

WARNER, Val; da of Alister Alfred Warner (d 1987), and Ivy Miriam Warner, *née* Robins (d 1985); *b* 15 January 1946, Middx; *Educ* Harrow County Sch for Girls, Somerville Coll Oxford (BA); *Career* pt/t teacher 1968–71, freelance proof-reader and copy ed 1971–77, writer in residence Univ of Swansea 1977–78, writer in residence Univ of Dundee 1979–81, freelance writer 1981–; memb Writers in Prison Ctee English PEN 1998–2011; Gregory Award for Poetry 1975; FRSL 1999; *Publications* poetry: These Yellow Photos (1971), Under the Penthouse (1973), Before Lunch (1986), Tooting Idyll (1998); The Centenary Corbière (trans, 1975, reissued 2003), The Collected Poems and Prose of Charlotte Mew (ed, 1981), The Collected Poems and Selected Prose of Charlotte Mew (ed, 1997, reissued 2003); *Recreations* reading, walking; *Clubs* PEN; *Style*— Ms Val Warner; ✉ 7 Rushmore Road, London E5 0ET (☎ 020 8985 3942, e-mail valwarner@etce.freeserve.co.uk)

WARNICK, Marilyn Karen; da of Edward Stephen Warnick, of State College, PA, and Mary Kozel Warnick; *b* 20 June 1948; *Educ* Pennsylvania State Univ (BA, MA); *Career* ed Quartet Books 1978–80, mangr NY office Quartet Books 1980–85, sr ed Penguin 1986–88, publishing dir Telegraph Books 1988–96, commissioning ed (features) Daily Mail 1996–97, features ed Good Housekeeping 1997–99, books ed Mail on Sunday 1999–; memb Women in Journalism; *Recreations* travel, opera, gardening, family; *Clubs* The Academy, Biographer's; *Style*— Ms Marilyn Warnick; ✉ 56 The Avenue, London NW6 7NP; The Mail on Sunday, Northcliffe House, 2 Derry Street, London W8 5TS (☎ 020 3615 3255, mobile 07720 412145, e-mail marilyn.warnick@mailonsunday.co.uk)

WARNOCK, Hon Felix Geoffrey; er s of Sir Geoffrey Warnock (d 1995), and Baroness Warnock (Life Peer), *qv*; *b* 18 January 1952; *Educ* Winchester, Royal Coll of Music (ARCM); *m* 27 Aug 1975, Juliet, da of Arthur Robert Lehwalder, of Seattle, Washington, USA; 1 s (Daniel Arthur Richard b 1985), 2 da (Eleanor Denise b 1982 d 2013, Polly Patricia b 1986); *Career* bassoonist: Acad of St Martin-in-the-Fields 1975–89, Albion Ensemble 1980–92, Acad of Ancient Music 1981–89; prof of bassoon Trinity Coll of Music 1985–90; gen mangr Orchestra of the Age of Enlightenment 1989–94, dir of early music RAM 1993–95, gen mangr The English Concert 1995–2011; chm Dr John Radcliffe Tst 2003–; *Recreations* bridge, golf; *Style*— The Hon Felix Warnock; ✉ 5 Kingsbridge Road, London W10 6PU

WARNOCK, Baroness (Life Peer UK 1985), of Weeke in the City of Winchester; Dame (Helen) Mary Warnock; DBE (1984); da of Archibald Edward Wilson (d 1924), of Winchester, and Ethel Mary (d 1952), eldest da of Sir Felix Otto Schuster, 1 Bt; *b* 14 April 1924; *Educ* St Swithun's Sch Winchester, Lady Margaret Hall Oxford (MA, BPhil); *m* 1949, Sir Geoffrey Warnock (d 1995), s of James Warnock, OBE, MD (d 1953), of Leeds; 2 s (Hon Felix Geoffrey, *qv*, b 1952, Hon James Marcus Alexander b 1953), 3 da (Hon Kathleen (Kitty) b 1950, Hon Stephana (Fanny) (Hon Mrs Branson) b 1956 d 2008, Hon (Grizel) Maria (Hon Mrs Henriques) b 1961); *Career* fell and tutor in philosophy St Hugh's Coll Oxford 1949–66, headmistress Oxford HS 1966–72; former memb SSRC, chm Ctee of Enquiry into Human Fertilisation, former memb IBA; chm: Advsy Ctee on Animal Experiments, Ctee of Enquiry into Education of Handicapped; chair Planning Aid Tst; memb Royal Cmmn on Environmental Pollution 1979–85; Albert Medallist RSA; Talbot Res fell LMH until 1976, FCP; mistress Girton Coll Cambridge 1985–91 (life fell); hon degrees: Open Univ, Essex, Melbourne, Bath, Exeter, Manchester, Glasgow, York, Warwick, Liverpool, London, St Andrews, Ulster; hon fell: St Hugh's Coll Oxford, Lady Margaret Hall Oxford, Hertford Coll Oxford; Hon FBA, Hon FRCP, hon fell Acad of Medical Sciences; *Books* Ethics Since 1900, Existentialism, Imagination, Schools of Thought, What Must We Teach? (with T Devlin), Education: A Way Forward, Memory, A Common Policy for Education, The Uses of Philosophy, Imagination and Time, Women Philosophers, An Intelligent Person's Guide to Ethics, A Memoir: People and Places, Making Babies, Nature and Mortality: A Philosopher in Public Life, Easeful Death (with Elizabeth Macdonald), Dishonest to God: How to Keep Religion out of Politics; *Recreations* gardening, music; *Style*— The Lady Warnock, DBE; ✉ 101 Moremead Road, London SE6 3LR

WARNOCK, His Hon Judge (Alastair) Robert Lyon; s of Alexander Nelson Lyon Warnock (d 2001), and Anobel Forest Lyon, *née* Henderson (d 1974); *b* 23 July 1953; *Educ* Sedbergh, UEA (BA); *m* 20 March 1993, Sally Mary, *née* Tomkinson; *Career* called to the Bar Lincoln's Inn 1977 (Tancred scholar); pupillage with Her Hon Judge Downey 1977–78, practising barr specialising in common law Northern Circuit 1977–2003 (memb Chambers of His Hon Judge D Forster Liverpool), recorder 2000–03 (asst recorder 1993–2000), circuit judge 2003–, sr judge Sovereign Base Area Admin Cyprus 2012, review judge Office for Judicial Complaints; pres SW Lancs Magistrates Assoc 2006–12; memb Merseyside Probation Tst 2013–; former pres Royal Liverpool Golf Club Village Play; vice-pres Artisan's Golf Assoc; *Recreations* golf, wine, travel; *Clubs* Royal Liverpool Golf, Artists' (Liverpool), Bar Golf Soc; *Style*— His Hon Judge Warnock; ✉ QE II Law Courts, Derby Square, Liverpool L2 1XA (☎ 0151 473 7373, fax 0151 258 1587, e-mail robert.warnock@aol.co.uk)

WARNOCK-SMITH, Shân; QC (2002); da of Thomas John Davies (d 1983), and Denise Dorothy, *née* Newman (d 2003); *b* 13 September 1948, Portsmouth; *Educ* Westlake HS Auckland, Portsmouth HS, KCL (LLB, LLM); *Partner* Andrew de la Rosa; 1 s (Henry John b 25 Oct 1983), 1 da (Harriet Shân b 5 Sept 1985); *Career* called to the Bar 1979; practising barr Chancery Bar 1979–, memb Cayman Islands Bar 2010–; emeritus bencher Lincoln's Inn; tstee Eric Anker-Petersen Charity 2004–; author of numerous articles in professional jls; memb: Soc of Trust and Estate Practitioners, Assoc of Contentious Trust and Probate Specialists, Chancery Bar Assoc; academician Int Acad of Trust and Estate Law; *Recreations* Chicago, travel, interior design, architecture; *Style*— Mrs Shân Warnock-Smith, QC; ✉ International Chancery and Trust Chambers, George Town, Grand Cayman, Cayman Islands (☎ 001 345 926 5211, e-mail sws@ictchambers.com)

WARRELL, Prof David Alan; s of Alan Theophilus Warrell, ISO, of Abingdon, and late Mildred Emma, *née* Hunt; *b* 6 October 1939, Singapore; *Educ* Portsmouth GS, ChCh Oxford (MA, DM, BCh, DSc), St Thomas' Hosp Med Sch London; *m* 11 Oct 1975, Mary Jean, da of George Prentice, of London; 2 da (Helen b 1981, Clare b 1985); *Career* lectr and conslt physician Royal Postgrad Med Sch London 1974–75, conslt physician Radcliffe Infirmary Oxford 1975–79, fell St Cross Coll Oxford 1977–2006 (hon fell 2007–), hon conslt physician Oxfordshire HA 1979–2007, founding dir Wellcome-Mahidol Univ Oxford Tropical Med Prog Bangkok 1979–86, hon clinical dir Alistair Reid Venom Res Unit Liverpool Sch of Tropical Med 1983–2009; Univ of Oxford: prof of tropical med and infectious diseases 1987–2006 (emeritus prof of tropical med 2006–), dir Centre for Tropical Med 1987–2001 (founding dir emeritus 2001–), head Nuffield Department of Clinical Med 2002–04; visiting prof Faculty of Tropical Med Mahidol Univ Bangkok 1997–2006, princ fell Aust Venom Res Unit Univ of Melbourne 1998–, profesor honorario Universidad Nacional Mayor de San Marcos Lima 2005–, adjunct prof Xi'an Univ Medical Sch 2009–, visiting prof Capital Medical Univ Beijing 2011–; chm AIDS Therapeutic Trials Ctees MRC 1987–93, chm MRC China UK Research Ethics Ctee 2007–09; hon conslt in malariology to the Army 1989–, hon med advsr RGS 1994– (also memb Cncl), memb FCO Pro Bono Medical Panel 2002–, sr advsr in tropical medicine MRC 2001–07, hon med advsr Earth Watch Int 2008–, int advsr Australian DFAT-GPFD Myanmar Snakebite Project Univ of Adelaide 2015–; pres Br Venom Gp 1992–, pres Int Fedn for Tropical Med 1996–2000, pres Royal Soc of Tropical Med and Hygiene 1997–99; WHO: conslt on malaria, rabies and snake bites, memb Steering Ctee for Chemotherapy of Malaria 1986–91, memb Expert Advsy Panel on Malaria 1989–; tstee Tropical Health and Educn Tst 1988–2004, patron Cambodia Tst 1991–2003, delegate OUP 1999–2006, hon memb Instituto de Medicina Tropical Alexander von Humboldt Universidad Peruana Cayetano Heredia Lima 2010–; Chalmer's Medal Royal Soc 1981, Ambuj Nath Bose Prize RCP 1994, Harveian orator RCP 2001, Busk Medal RGS 2003, Guthrie Medal RAMC 2004, Mary Kingsley Centenary Medal Liverpool Sch of Tropical Med 2005, Lloyd-Roberts lectr RSM 2008, Osler Meml Medal Univ of Oxford 2010, Int Soc on Toxinology Redi Award 2012; hon fell: Ceylon Coll of Physicians, Australasian Coll of Tropical Med, Australasian Soc for Infectious Diseases, Assoc of Physicians of GB and I, American Soc of Tropical Med and Hygiene (ASTMH), Royal Coll of Physicians Thailand, W African Coll of Physicians; FRCP (int dir (Hans Sloane fell) 2012–16), MRCS, FRCPEd, FZS 1967 (Hon Conservation FZS 2009), FRGS 1989, FMedSci 1998, hon fell Coll of Physicians and Surgeons India; Companion Order of the White Elephant (Thailand) 2004; *Books* Rabies – The Facts (1986), Oxford Textbook of Medicine (1987, 5 edn 2010), Essential Malariology (1993, 4 edn 2002), Expedition Medicine (1998, 2 edn 2002), Concise Oxford Textbook of Medicine (2000), Oxford Handbook of Expedition and Wilderness Medicine (2008, 2 edn 2015), Venomous Bites by Non-Venomous Snakes (2011), Oxford Textbook of Medicine: Infection (2012); *Recreations* music, hill walking, natural history, book collecting; *Clubs* RSM; *Style*— Prof David Warrell; ✉ Nuffield Department of Clinical Medicine, University of Oxford; John Radcliffe Hospital, Headington, Oxford OX3 9DU (☎ 01865 234664, fax 01865 760683, e-mail david.warrell@ndm.ox.ac.uk)

WARREN, Prof Graham Barry; s of Charles Graham Thomas Warren (d 2009), and Joyce Thelma, *née* Roberts (d 2006); *b* 25 February 1948; *Educ* Willesden Co GS, Pembroke Coll Cambridge (MA, PhD); *m* 18 June 1966, Philippa Mary Adeline, da of Alexander Edward Temple-Cole (d 1981), of Shoreham, Kent; 4 da (Joanna b 5 Nov 1966, Eleanor b 20 Aug 1969, Katya b 13 Nov 1979, Alexandra b 7 Dec 1980); *Career* MRC jr res fell

Nat Inst for Med Res London 1972–74, res fell Gonville & Caius Coll Cambridge and Stothert res fell of the Royal Soc Biochemistry Dept Univ of Cambridge 1975–77, sr scientist Euro Molecular Biology Lab Heidelberg W Germany (formerly gp ldr) 1977–85, prof and head of Dept of Biochemistry Univ of Dundee 1985–88, princ scientist Imperial Cancer Res Fund 1988–99, prof of cell biology Yale Univ Med Sch until 2006, scientific dir Max F Perutz Labs Vienna 2007–; memb: EMBO, Austrian Acad of Sciences 2011; FRS; *Style*— Prof Graham Warren, FRS; ✉ Max F Perutz Laboratories, Dr Bohr-Gosse 9, A-1030 Vienna, Austria (☎ 00 43 664 60277 24001, e-mail graham.warren@mfpl.ac.at)

WARREN, John Anthony; *b* 11 June 1953; *Educ* Tiffin Sch, Univ of Bristol (BSc); *m* 1975, Anna; 2 s; *Career* Ernst & Young 1974–81; United Biscuits (Holdings) plc: chief accountant rising to fin dir UK, Int Sr Mgmnt Programme Harvard Business Sch 1990, gp fin dir (main bd) 1990–2000, chief exec Asia Pacific 1995–96; gp fin dir WH Smith plc 2000–05; non-exec dir: Rexam plc 1994–2003, RAC plc 2003–05, Rank Gp 2005–, Arla Foods UK plc 2006–07, Bovis Homes Group plc 2006–, Spectris plc 2006–, BPP Holdings plc 2006–, Uniq plc 2007–; ACA 1977; *Style*— John Warren, Esq

WARREN, Prof Lynda May; da of Leonard Warren (d 2011), and Peggy, *née* Tatnell (d 1984); *b* 26 April 1950, Croydon; *Educ* Croydon HS for Girls, Univ of London (BSc, PhD), Croydon Coll (LLB), Univ of Wales Cardiff (MSc); *m* 1, 3 June 1973 (m dis), Christopher Tydeman; m 2, 19 July 1986, Barry Thomas; 1 s (Marc b 26 July 1986); *Career* postgrad res asst Univ of London 1975–81, sr lectr in biology Poly of Central London 1981–84, lectr in biology Goldsmiths' Coll London 1984–87, lectr then sr lectr in law Univ of Wales Cardiff 1987–95, prof of environmental law Univ of Wales Aberystwyth 1996–2003; memb: Countryside Cncl for Wales 1992–2003, Radioactive Waste Mgmnt Advsy Ctee 1994–2004, Bd Environment Agency 2000–06, Ctee on Radioactive Waste Mgmnt 2003–, Royal Cmmn on Environmental Pollution 2005–11, Jt Nature Conservation Ctee 2006–12 (dep chair 2008–12), DEFRA Science Advsy Cncl 2011–16, Bd Natural Resources Wales 2012–15; chair Salmon and Freshwater Fisheries Review Gp 1998–2000; ind environmental advsr Dwr Cymru Welsh Water 2012–13; ed: Environmental Law Review, Law, Science and Policy; author of over 100 scientific and legal papers; tstee: WWF-UK 2002–04, W & SW Wales Wildlife Tst 2004–15 (chair 2009–15), Assoc of River Tsts 2004–08, Field Studies Cncl 2005–09; Churchill Fell 2007 (sec Welsh Assoc of Churchill Fells); FRSB 1990; *Recreations* travel especially in the Middle East, fashion; *Style*— Prof Lynda Warren; ✉ Ynys Einion, Eglwys Fach, Machynlleth SY20 8SX (☎ 01654 781344, e-mail lm.warren@btopenworld.com)

WARREN, Marc; *b* 20 March 1967, Northampton; *Career* actor; *Television* incl: Band of Brothers (HBO) 2001, Reversals 2003, Hustle (BBC 1) 2004–07 and 2012, Terry Pratchett's Hogfather (Sky 1) 2006, Dracula 2006, Ballet Shoes 2007, Messiah: The Rapture 2008, Mutual Friends 2008, Do Elephants Pray? 2009, Worried About the Boy 2010, Without You 2011, Mad Dogs 2011–12, The Good Wife 2012; *Film* Wanted 2008; *Theatre* Cool Hand Luke (Aldwych Theatre) 2011; *Style*— Marc Warren, Esq; ✉ c/o Ken McReddie Associates, 11 Connaught Place, London W2 2ET

WARREN, Martin Hugh; s of Frederick Michael Warren, of Devon, and Anne, *née* Phillips; *b* 12 February 1961, Bideford, Devon; *Educ* Univ of Bristol (LLB, Sweet and Maxwell Prize); *m* (sep); 2 da (Katie, Sarah), 1 s (Thomas); *Career* admitted slr 1985; slr specialising in employment law; articled Osborne Clarke; Eversheds: joined 1985, asst slr 1985–86, assoc 1986–89, ptnr 1989–, currently head of labor law, head of dept 2004–06, head of HR practice gp 2006–; employment advsr CBI; memb Law Soc 1985; *Recreations* diving, cycling, walking; *Clubs* Reform; *Style*— Martin Warren, Esq; ✉ Eversheds LLP, 1 Callaghan Square, Cardiff CF10 5BT (☎ 029 2047 7570, fax 029 2046 4347, e-mail martinwarren@eversheds.com)

WARREN, Michael Christopher; s of Joseph Henry Warren (d 1971), and Helen, *née* Ashworth (d 1946); *b* 30 December 1944; *Educ* Palmers Sch for Boys Thurrock, Central Sch of Speech and Drama; *m* 1, 1969 (m dis 1978), Kathleen Mary, *née* Reindorp; m 2, 1992 Lindsay Kathlyn, da of William Heathcote Roberts; 1 da (Rebecca Roberts-Warren b 19 Aug 1983); *Career* journalist Essex and Thurrock Gazette 1963–65, various theatre work (incl 69 Theatre Co Manchester) 1969–71, res exec and assoc dir Research Services Ltd 1971–81, head of Survey Unit Consumers' Assoc 1981–86, dir of res COI 1986–93, DG Market Research Soc 1993–97 (memb Professional Standards Ctee 1988–91, memb Educn Ctee 1992–93), assoc dir Market Research Solutions Ltd 1997–98, research conslt/author 1998– (incl work with Surrey Social and Market Research Ltd, Univ of Surrey); memb Research Resource Bd ESRC 1994–98; visiting prof Sch of Human Sciences Univ of Surrey 2000–06; exec ed Int Jl of Market Res 2000–05; author of various articles on research techniques and mgmnt; dir Acad of Social Sciences 2002–04, fndr memb Social Research Assoc, memb Market Research Soc 1975–2010, FRSA 1995–2009; *Recreations* jazz, cricket, theatre, rugby, competitive model aviation; *Clubs* Ronnie Scott's, Harlequins; *Style*— Michael Warren, Esq; ✉ 30 Cole Park Road, Twickenham, Middlesex TW1 1HS (☎ 020 8891 3130, e-mail michael.c.warren@btinternet.com)

WARREN, Hon Mr Justice; Sir Nicholas Roger Warren; kt (2005); s of Roger Warren (d 1991), and Muriel, *née* Reeves (d 1998); *b* 20 May 1949, Guildford; *Educ* Bryanston, UC Oxford (scholar, BA); *m* 1, 1978 (m dis 1989); 2 s, 1 da; m 2, 1994; *Career* called to the Bar Middle Temple 1972 (Astbury scholar); QC 1993, recorder 1999–2005 (asst recorder 1995–99), judge of the High Court of Justice (Chancery Div) 2005– (dep judge of the High Court 1999–2005), pres Tax and Chancery Chamber Upper Tbnl 2009–15; chm Chancery Bar Assoc 2001–03; *Recreations* music, sailing; *Style*— The Hon Mr Justice Warren; ✉ Royal Courts of Justice, 7 Rolls Building, Fetter Lane, London EC4A 1NL

WARREN, Prof Peter Michael; s of Arthur George Warren (d 1947), and Alison Joan, *née* White (d 1942); *b* 23 June 1938; *Educ* Sandbach Sch, Llandovery Coll, UCNW Bangor (BA), CCC Cambridge (MA, PhD); *m* 18 June 1966, Elizabeth Margaret, da of Percy Halliday, of Beaconsfield, Bucks; 1 da (Diktynna b 1979), 1 s (Damian b 1984); *Career* reader in Aegean archaeology Univ of Birmingham 1976 (lectr 1972–74, sr lectr 1974–76); Univ of Bristol: prof of ancient history and classical archaeology 1977–2001 (emeritus prof 2001–), dean Faculty of Arts 1988–90, pro-vice-chllr 1991–95, fell 1995–96, sr res fell 2001–; visiting prof Univ of Minnesota 1981, Geddes-Harrower prof of Greek art and archaeology Univ of Aberdeen 1986–87, Félix Neubergh lectr Univ of Göteborg 1986, foreign fell Onassis Fndn Greece 2007; pres: Wotton-under-Edge Historical Soc 1986–90, Bristol Anglo-Hellenic Cultural Soc 1987–98, Birmingham and Midlands Branch Classical Assoc 1996–97, Bristol and Glos Archaeological Soc 2000–01 (memb Cncl 1977–, vice-chm 1980–81, chm 1981–83, vice-pres 1989–93); Br Sch Athens: chm Managing Ctee 1979–83 (memb 1973–77, 1978–79, 1986–90 and 1994–98), memb Cncl 1999–2003, acting chm 2000, chm 2003–04, vice-pres 2005–; hon sec Friends of the British Sch Athens 2011–; memb Cncl Soc for the Promotion of Hellenic Studies 1978–81, memb Italian Nat Research Cncl Review Panel 2009; Distinguished Service Award Inst for Aegean Prehistory 2015; hon fell Historical, Folklore and Archaeological Soc of Crete 1980, hon fell Archaeological Soc of Athens 1987, corresponding fell Soc for Cretan Historical Studies 1992, corresponding memb Austrian Acad of Scis 1997; Dr (hc) Univ of Athens 2000; FSA 1973, FBA 1997; *Books* Minoan Stone Vases (1969), Myrtos An Early Bronze Age Settlement in Crete (1972), The Aegean Civilizations (1975 and 1989), Minoan Religion as Ritual Action (1988), Aegean Bronze Age Chronology (with V Hankey, 1989), The Early Minoan Tombs of Lebena, Southern Crete (with St Alexiou, 2004), Ardtornish House, The Architectural Marbles and Granite (2012), Knossos, A Middle Minoan III Building in Bougadha Metochi (with G Rethemiotakis, 2014); *Recreations* Manchester United, history of Mediterranean botany, growing Cistaceae (national collection), Mediterranean coloured marble; *Style*— Prof Peter Warren, FSA, FBA; ✉ Claremont House, 5 Merlin Haven, Wotton-under-Edge, Gloucestershire GL12 7BA (☎ 01453 842 290); Department of Archaeology and Anthropology, University of Bristol, 43 Woodland Road, Bristol BS8 1UU (☎ 0117 954 6084/954 6060)

WARREN, Rebecca; *b* 21 March 1965; *Educ* Goldsmiths Coll (BA), Chelsea Coll of Art (MA); *Career* sculptor; prof of painting and sculpture Kunstakademie Düsseldorf; nominated Turner Prize 2006; RA 2014; *Solo Exhibitions* incl: Galerie Max Hetzler Berlin 2007, Matthew Marks Gallery New York 2007 and 2009, Serpentine Gallery 2009, The Renaissance Society Univ of Chicago 2010, The Art Inst of Chicago 2010, Maureen Paley London 2011, Galerie Max Hetzler Berlin 2012, Museum Dhondt Dhaenens Ghent 2012, Kunstverein München e. V Munich 2013, Dallas Museum of Art 2016; *Public Commissions* incl: Pas de Deux (Plaza Monument) Eagle Family Plaza Dallas Museum of Art 2016; *Style*— Ms Rebecca Warren; ✉ c/o Maureen Paley, 21 Herald Street, London E2 6JT

WARREN, Dr Roderic Ellis; s of Ronald Thomas Warren (d 1970), of Tadworth, Surrey, and Mabel Elsie Warren; *b* 24 October 1948; *Educ* Whitgift Sch Croydon, Gonville & Caius Coll Cambridge (MA, MB BChir), Westminster Hosp Med Sch; *m* 6 Sept 1976, Pamela Rose, da of Frederick John Taft (d 1976), of Canterbury; 1 s (Charles), 2 da (Elizabeth, Eleanor); *Career* conslt microbiologist Addenbrooke's Hosp 1976–93, dir Public Health Laboratory Royal Shrewsbury Hosp 1993–95 and 2001–10, conslt microbiologist Shrewsbury and Telford Hosp NHS Tst 2003–; gp dir Public Health Laboratory Service Midlands 1995–2002; hon sr lectr Univ of Birmingham 1993–2010; FRCPath 1989; *Recreations* occasional; *Style*— Dr Roderic Warren; ✉ Microbiology Laboratory, Royal Shrewsbury Hospital, Mytton Oak Road, Shrewsbury SY3 8XQ (☎ 01743 261161)

WARREN-GASH, Haydon; s of Alexis Patrick Warren-Gash (d 1997), and Cynthia June, *née* Phillips (d 2013); *b* 1949, Kenya; *Educ* Marlborough, Sidney Sussex Coll Cambridge (MA); *m* 1973, Caroline, *née* Leather; 1 s (Alexander b 1975), 1 da (Vanessa b 1977); *Career* HM Dip Serv 1971–2008: Latin American Desk FCO 1971–72, Turkish language student Univ of London 1972–73, third sec Ankara 1973–77, second then first sec Political Section Madrid 1977–81, staff Perm Under Sec's Dept rising to private sec to Min of State (Sir Cranley Onslow then Sir Richard Luce) FCO 1981–85, first sec Commercial Section Paris 1985–89, dep head Southern Euro Dept FCO 1989–91, dep high cmmr Nairobi 1991–94, head Southern Euro Dept FCO 1994–97, ambass to the Ivory Coast (concurrently accredited to Liberia, Burkina Faso and Niger) 1997–2001, ambass to Morocco 2002–05 (concurrently accredited to Mauritania), ambass to Colombia 2005–08, chm Br and Colombian C of C 2013–; dir FoRo Consulting 2010–, chm Veventis Consulting, dir NewCo; *Recreations* travel, politics, current affairs, the arts, opera, food and wine, nature and wildlife; *Clubs* Muthaiga; *Style*— Haydon Warren-Gash, Esq

WARRINGTON, Bishop of 2009–; Rt Rev Richard Finn Blackburn; s of William Brow Blackburn (d 1987), of Leeds, and Ingeborg, *née* Lerche-Thomsen (d 1991); *b* 22 January 1952; *Educ* Eastborne Coll, St John's Coll Durham (BA), Univ of Hull (MA), Westcott House Theol Coll Cambridge; *m* 1980, Helen Claire, da of Edward Davies; 3 da (Charlotte b 23 Oct 1982, Emma b 25 Sept 1984, Isabelle b 18 July 1988), 1 s (Robert b 27 Sept 1986); *Career* NatWest Bank 1976–81, curate St Dunstan and All Saints Stepney 1983–87, priest-in-charge St John's Isleworth 1987–92, vicar of Mosborough 1992–99, rural dean of Attercliffe 1996–99, hon canon Sheffield Cathedral 1998–99, archdeacon of Sheffield and Rotherham 1999–2009, residentiary canon Sheffield Cathedral 1999–2005 (acting dean 2003), dignitary in convocation 2000–05, chair Churches Regnl Cmmn for Yorks and the Humber 2005–07, vice-chair Church of England Pensions Bd 2006–09; memb Sch Cncl: Worksop Coll 2001–09, Ranby Hall Sch 2001–09; *Recreations* music, gardening, walking, rowing; *Clubs* Parrs Priory Rowing; *Style*— The Rt Rev the Bishop of Warrington; ✉ St James House, 20 St James Road, Liverpool L1 7BY (☎ 0151 705 2140, e-mail bishopofwarrington@liverpool.anglican.org)

WARRY, Dr Peter Thomas; s of Vivian Warry (d 2010), and Pamela, *née* Lane (d 2007); *b* 31 August 1949; *Educ* Clifton, Merton Coll Oxford (open exhbn, MA), Univ of London (LLB), Univ of Reading (PhD); *m* 1981, Rosemary Olive, *née* Furbank; 1 da (Sarah b 1987); *Career* various positions 1968–79: MoD, Electricity Cncl, British Leyland; md Self-Changing Gears Ltd 1979–82, gp md Aerospace Engineering plc 1982–84, special advsr and dep head PM's Policy Unit 1984–86, dir of planning and business devpt Plessey Telecoms 1986–87, dir and chm Building Products Div Norcros plc 1988–94, bd dir British Energy plc 1996–98; chief exec Nuclear Electric 1995–98; chm: Victrex plc 1999–2008, BSS Gp plc 2004–10 (non-exec dir 1999–2003), Kier Gp plc 2004–07 (non-exec dir 1998–2003), Morrison Utility Services Gp Ltd 2008–13, Mutual Energy Ltd (formerly Northern Ireland Energy Hldgs Ltd) 2008–13, Apollo Gp Hldgs Ltd 2009–12, Keepmoat Gp Ltd 2012–14, Royal Mint 2012–, Cobalt Health 2014–; non-exec dir: Heatherwood and Wexham Park Hospitals Tst 1992–95, PTS Gp plc 1995–99, Office of the Rail Regulator 1999–2003, Thames Water Utilities Ltd 2001–05, River and Mercantile Gp plc 2014–; chm Economic Impact Gp Office of Sci and Innovation 2006; industrial prof Univ of Warwick 1993–, visiting research fell in archaeology Univ of Reading 2011–; chm: PPARC 2001–07, STFC 2007–09, AGR and PWR Liabilities Review Dept of Energy and Climate Change 2015; memb Cncl Royal Acad of Engrg 2007–10; memb Cncl Univ of Reading 2006–11 (treas 2009–11), tstee Oxford Archaeology 2009–; hon fell Merton Coll Oxford 2007; CEng, FCMA 1983, FIET 1995, FIMechE 1995, FREng 2006, FRSA 2008, FSA 2013; *Publications* A New Direction for the Post Office (1991), Efficiency in Price-Control Reviews (2000), Tegulae: Manufacture, Typology and Use in Roman Britain (2006); *Recreations* archaeology, walking, tennis; *Style*— Dr Peter Warry, FREng, FSA; ✉ e-mail pwarry@btinternet.com

WARSHAW, Justin Alexander Edward; QC (2015); s of Clive Warshaw, and Michèle, *née* Steiner, of Nassau, Bahamas; *b* London; *Educ* ChCh Oxford; *m* 2001, Stephanie, *née* Marshall; 2 da (Ursula b 2005, Lauren b 2007); *Career* called to the Bar 1995; *Clubs* MCC, North Hatley (Quebec); *Style*— Justin Warshaw, Esq, QC; ✉ 1 Hare Court, Temple, London EC4Y 7BE

WARSI, Baroness (Life Peer UK 2007), of Dewsbury in the County of West Yorkshire; Sayeeda Hussain Warsi; PC (2010); *b* 28 March 1971, Dewsbury, W Yorks; *Educ* Birkdale HS, Dewsbury Coll, Univ of Leeds (LLB), York Coll of Law; *Career* trainee slr with CPS and Immigration Dept Home Office, subsequently slr Whitfield Hallam Goodall Slrs, then estab George Warsi Slrs; Parly candidate (Cons) 2005, shadow min for community cohesion and social action 2007–10, chm Cons Pty 2010–12, sr Foreign Office minister and min for faith and communities 2012–14; *Style*— The Rt Hon the Baroness Warsi; ✉ House of Lords, London SW1A 0PW

WARWICK, Archdeacon of; *see:* Paget-Wilkes, Ven Michael Jocelyn James

WARWICK OF UNDERCLIFFE, Baroness (Life Peer UK 1999), of Undercliffe in the County of West Yorkshire; Diana Warwick; *b* 16 July 1945; *Educ* Univ of London (BA); *m* 1969, Sean Terence Bowes Young; *Career* tech asst NUT 1969–72, asst sec Civil and Public Servs Assoc 1972–83, gen sec Assoc of Univ Teachers 1983–92, first chief exec Westminster Fndn for Democracy (all-pty advsy gp for newly democratised countries) 1992–95, chief exec Universities UK (formerly Ctee of Vice-Chllrs and Principals) 1995–2009, chair Human Tissue Authy 2009–2014; chair Nat Housing Fedn 2015–; non-exec dir Pension Protection Fund 2011–, non-exec dir USS Ltd 200–09, Lattice plc 2000–03; chm Tstees Ctee VSO 1994–2004 (life vice pres 2004–), chm Tstees Int House 2006–;

memb: Bd British Cncl 1985–95, Employment Appeals Tbnl 1987–99, Exec Bd Industrial Soc 1987–93, Gen Cncl TUC 1989–92, Ctee on Standards in Public Life 1995–99, Technol Foresight Steering Gp 1998–2004; govr Cwlth Inst 1988–95; memb Cncl: UCL 2009–, Nottingham Trent Univ 2013–; Hon DLitt Univ of Bradford, Hon Dr Open Univ, Hon DSc Univ of London, Hon DPhil London Met Univ, Hon DEd Brunel Univ; *Style*— Baroness Warwick of Undercliffe; ✉ House of Lords, London SW1A 0PW

WARWICK THOMPSON, Dr Paul; s of Prof Sir Michael Warwick Thompson, *qv*, and Sybil, *née* Spooner; *b* 9 August 1959; *Educ* Bryanston, Univ of Bristol (BA), UEA (MA, PhD); *m* 1985, Adline, da of Max Finlay; 1 da (Roberta Beatrice b 1987), 1 s (Oscar Leo b 1990); *Career* scriptwriter/researcher The Design Cncl London 1987–88; Design Museum London: curator contemporary design 1988–90, curator 1990–92, curatorial dir 1992–94, dir 1994–2001; dir Smithsonian Cooper-Hewitt Nat Design Museum NY 2001–09, rector and vice-provost RCA 2009–; chair Advsy Bd Fabrica Spl Italy 2012–14; tstee V&A; memb Bd of Visitors Ashmolean Museum Univ of Oxford; adjunct prof Inst of Global Health Innovation Imperial Coll; FRSA; *Books* Review 1 New Design (1989), Review 2 New Design (1990); *Style*— Dr Paul Warwick Thompson; ✉ Royal College of Art, Kensington Gore, London SW7 2EU (✆ 020 7590 4101, fax 020 7590 4100, e-mail paul.thompson@rca.ac.uk, website www.rca.ac.uk)

WASHINGTON, Joan; *Educ* Central Sch of Speech and Drama (distinction), Univ London (distinction); *m* 1 Nov 1986, Richard E Grant *qv*; 1 da (Olivia b 4 Jan 1989); *Career* accent/dialogue coach; began career teaching in remand homes, comprehensive schs, RCN; taught over 320 accents, has taught regularly at RADA and Central; *Theatre* West End prodns incl: Anything Goes, Orpheus Descending (Broadway), Crazy for You, City of Angels, She Loves Me, Sunset Boulevard, Whistle Down the Wind, The Iceman Cometh, Plenty, The King and I, Calico, Suddenly Last Summer, The Goat or Who is Sylvia?, Death of a Salesman, Guys and Dolls, Evita, Glengarry Glen Ross, The Children's Hour; RNT: Guys and Dolls, Beggar's Opera, Brighton Beach Memoirs, A View from the Bridge, Cat on a Hot Tin Roof, The Shaughraun, The Crucible, After the Fall, Pygmalion, Carousel, Sweeney Todd, Angels in America, The Children's Hour, Sweet Bird of Youth, Broken Glass, Guys and Dolls, Oklahoma, Our Lady of Sligo, EdMOND, Mourning Becomes Electra, The Dark Materials, Once in a Lifetime, The Reporter; RSC: The Merchant of Venice, The Jew of Malta, Across Oka, Great Expectations; Royal Court: Rat in the Skull, The Edward Bond Season, Serious Money, The Queen and I, The Weir, A Really Classy Affair, A Dublin Carol; *Television* incl: The Singing Detective, Lorna Doone, Old Times, Top Girls, Roots, Suddenly Last Summer, Middlemarch, Scarlett, Our Friends from the North, Tom Jones, The Russian Bride, Daniel Deronda, May 33rd, Jane Eyre; *Films* incl: Yentl, The Bounty, Greystoke, Plenty, Prick up your Ears, A World Apart, The Trial, Damage, Second Best, Carrington, Jane Eyre, Jude, French Kiss, Fierce Creatures, The Borrowers, 101 Dalmations, My Life So Far, Eugene Onegin, 102 Dalmations, Captain Corelli's Mandolin, Charlotte Gray, In My Country, Stage Beauty, Goal, Wah-Wah, River Queen, Breaking and Entering, Notes on a Scandal, A Mighty Heart, Miss Pettigrew Lives for a Day, Churchill: The War Years, Green Zone, the Debt, London Boulevard, Coriolanus, Bel Ami, Safe House, Great Expectations, The Invisible Woman, Miss Julie, Trespass Against Us, Cinderella, Alone in Berlin, The History of Love, Love and Friendship, The Zookeeper's Wife; *Animations* The Miracle Maker, The Canterbury Tales; *Broadcasts* How the Edwardians Spoke (BBC4); *Style*— Ms Joan Washington

WASINONDH, HE Kitti; *b* 23 November 1951; *Educ* Chulalongkorn Univ Bangkok, Nat Inst of Devpt Admin Bangkok (MPA); *m* 1980, Nutchanart; *Career* Thai diplomat; attaché then third sec Southeast Asia Div Dept of Political Affrs Miny of Foreign Affrs 1978–79, third sec then second sec Belgrade 1982–85; Dept of Economic Affrs: second sec then first sec chief of GAAT Section Div of Int Economic Affrs 1986–87, seconded to Royal Thai Army 1988–90, chief of secretariat then chief Div of Economic Rels 1991; min cnsllr Brussels 1993, dir Commerce and Industry Div Dept of Assoc of SE Asian Nations Affrs 1997, dep DG Dept of Info 1998, dep DG Dept of East Asian Affrs 1999, consul-gen Sydney 2000, DG Dept of Assoc of SE Asian Nations Affairs 2002, DG Dept of Info 2006, ambass extraordinary and plenipotentiary to the Court of St James's 2007–; Knight Grand Cordon (Special Class) of the Most Noble Order of the Crown of Thailand 2005, Knight Grand Cordon of the Exalted Order of the White Elephant 2010; *Style*— HE Mr Kitti Wasinondh; ✉ Royal Thai Embassy, 29–30 Queen's Gate, London SW7 5JB (✆ 020 7589 2944, fax 020 7823 9695, e-mail thaiembassy.info@btconnect.com)

WASON, (Robert) Graham; s of Cathcart Roland Wason, and Margaret Ogilvie, *née* Lamb; gs of Rear Adm Cathcart Romer Wason, CMG, CIE (d 1941), ggs of Rt Hon Eugene Wason, MP (Liberal MP and Chm Scottish Liberal Party) and Allen Douglas Graham (fndr of children's charity ICAN), gggs of P R Wason, MP for Ipswich, Promoter of Reform Bill 1832 and co-fndr of Reform Club; *b* 6 January 1951, Cossington, Somerset; *Educ* Alleyne's GS Stevenage, Univ of Surrey (BSc); *m* Malgorzata Barbara Kucharska; 1 s (Roland Tomek); *Career* ptnr Deloitte Conslting 1983–98, md Greenwich Gateway 1998–99; co-fndr All Being Well Ltd 1999–; formerly in tourism and hotels ops in Europe and Africa and 'Holiday Which?'; dir The Tourism Soc 1997–2008 (vice-chm 1997–99, chm 1999–2004); vice-pres of Strategy and Devpt World Travel and Tourism Cncl 1999–2003; chm Tourism Leisure Sports and Recreation Ctee Br Conslts Bureau until 1995; memb Advsy Bd: Sch of Mgmnt Univ of Surrey, Inst of Tourism Guiding; chm Cut Tourism VAT Campaign for Reduced VAT for Tourism 2011–; owner-guardian Cossington Park, owner Les Alpes d'Azur (France); fell Tourism Soc; FRSA; *Publications* The Luxury Country House Hotel Survey (1987), The European Incentive Travel Survey (1993), European Golf Facilities (1995), Tourism Taxation: Striking a Fair Deal (1999), Corporate Social Leadership in Travel and Tourism (2002); *Recreations* tennis, travel, cultural exchange and Making a Difference missions; *Style*— R Graham Wason, Esq; ✉ Cossington Park, Bridgwater, Somerset TA7 8LH (✆ 07977 040579, e-mail gw@rgwason.com and rgwason@gmail.com, websites www.rgwason.com, www.allbeingwell.com, www.cuttourismvat.co.uk, www.cossingtonpark.com and www.lesalpesdazur.com)

WASS, Alexandra (Sasha); QC (2000); da of Sir Douglas Wass, GCB, and Dr Milica Pavicic; *b* 19 February 1958; *Educ* Wimbledon HS, Univ of Liverpool; *m* 31 May 1986, Nigel Ronald Adrian Hall; 1 s (Adam Edward b 19 Nov 1986), 1 da (Harriet Grace b 25 Feb 1989); *Career* called to the Bar: Gray's Inn 1981 (bencher 2003), Gibraltar 2008; asst recorder 1997–2000, recorder (SE Circuit) 2000–; Criminal Bar Assoc: memb Ctee 1992–, treas 1997–2000, dir of educn 2002–; *Style*— Miss Sasha Wass, QC; ✉ 6KBW, 21 College Hill, London EC4R 2RP

WASS, Prof John Andrew Hall; s of Samuel Hall Wass (d 1970), and June Mary Vaudine, *née* Blaikie (d 1992); *b* 14 August 1947; *Educ* Rugby, Guy's Hosp Med Sch London (MB BS, MD); *m* 1, 1970 (m dis 1997), Valerie *née* Vincent; 1 da (Katherine b 1974), 1 s (Samuel b 1979); m 2, 1998, Sally Smith; *Career* registrar: KCH London 1973–74, Guy's Hosp London 1974–75; sub-dean of Med Coll and prof of clinical endocrinology Bart's London 1989–95 (univ lectr 1976–81, sr lectr 1982–85, reader 1985–89), conslt in endocrinology Churchill Hosp Oxford 1995–2012, emeritus prof of endocrinology Univ of Oxford 1998–; advsr to Cancer-BACUP 1985–, med dir Bart's City Life Saver 1993–; Linacre fell RCP 1994–98; ed Clinical Endocrinology jl 1991–94; vice-chm Ctee of Mgmnt Royal Med Benevolent Fund 1990–94 (memb 1982–94 and 1996–2000); pres: Euro Fedn of Endocrine Socs 2001–03 (memb Exec Ctee 1994–2001, vice-pres 1998–2001), Endocrine Section RSM 1997–98 (sec 1988–92); chm Soc for Endocrinology 2005–09 (sec 2002–05); sec: Assoc of Clinical Profs Univ of London 1993–95, Clinical Endocrinology Tst 1996–2005; memb Exec Ctee Int Soc of Endocrinology 1996–2000; admissions tutor fell Green Coll Oxford 2001–03; co-fndr The Pituitary Fndn 1994 (tstee 1999–2006); chm Bart's Choral Soc 1992–95; govr Purcell Sch 2000–12; memb: American Endocrine Soc, Assoc of Physicians; Freeman City of London 1983, Liveryman Worshipful Co of Barbers; fell Green Coll Oxford (MA) 1995; FRSM, FRCP 1986 (MRCP 1973, academic vice-pres 2012–15); *Publications* Clinical Endocrine Oncology (ed, 1997, 2 edn 2008), Oxford Textbook of Endocrinology (ed, 2002, 2 edn 2012), Oxford Handbook of Endocrinology(2002, 3 edn 2014); also author of articles and chapters on: acromegaly, pituitary tumours, growth hormone, adrenal disease, osteoporosis; *Recreations* music, theatre, wine, Scotland; *Clubs* Garrick; *Style*— Prof John Wass; ✉ Holmby House, Sibford Ferris, Banbury, Oxfordshire OX15 5RG (✆ 01295 780589); Department of Endocrinology, Churchill Hospital, Old Road, Headington, Oxford OX3 7LE (✆ 01844 358031, e-mail john.wass@nhs.net)

WASTELL, David John; s of Ian Wastell, of London, and Audrey, *née* Overton; *b* 3 January 1957; *Educ* Latymer Sch Edmonton, New Coll Oxford (MA); *Partner* Fiona Turner; 3 da (Kirsty b 27 Dec 1993, Catriona b 7 June 1996, Eilidh b 2 May 1998); *Career* Tavistock Times and Sunday Independent (Mirror Group Newspapers Grad Trainee Scheme) 1979–81, feature writer Scottish Daily Record 1981–86; Sunday Telegraph: reporter/feature writer 1986–88, political corr 1988–92, political ed 1992–98, Washington corr 1998–2002, dep foreign ed 2002–05, foreign ed 2005–; *Recreations* mountaineering, walking, sailing, skiing; *Style*— David Wastell, Esq

WATERHOUSE, Norman; s of Norman Waterhouse, and Jean Gardner Hamilton Reid; *b* 13 October 1954; *Educ* Salesian Coll Farnborough, Univ of Birmingham Med Sch (MB ChB); *m* Elizabeth Clare; 2 da (Suki, Imogen); *Career* plastic surgn trg: Frenchay Hosp Bristol, Hospital Tondu Bordeaux, South Australian Craniofacial Unit Adelaide, Mount Vernon Hosp Northwood, Tokyo Metropolitan Hosp; former conslt in plastic and reconstructive surgery: St Bart's Hosp and The London Hosp Whitechapel 1989–91, Charing Cross Hosp, St Mary's Hosp Paddington, Westminster Hosp; currently conslt in craniofacial, aesthetic and reconstructive plastic surgery Chelsea & Westminster Hosp; pres Royal Soc of Med (plastic surgery section); memb European Craniofacial Soc; FRCS 1982, FRCSEd 1982, FRCS (plastic surgery) 1988; *Recreations* rock climbing, mountaineering, Wado-ryu karate (2nd Dan); *Style*— Norman Waterhouse, Esq; ✉ 55 Harley Street, London W1N 1DD (✆ 020 7636 4073, fax 020 7636 6417, e-mail wtrhouse@globalnet.co.uk)

WATERLOW, Sir Christopher Rupert; 5 Bt (UK 1873), of London; s of (Peter) Rupert Waterlow (d 1969), of Knightsbridge, London, and Jill Elizabeth, *née* Gourlay (d 1961); gs of Sir Philip Alexander Waterlow, 4 Bt (d 1973), and 3 cous twice removed of Sir Thomas Waterlow, 3 Bt, CBE, of Harrow Weald; *b* 12 August 1959, London; *Educ* Stonyhurst, Ravensbourne Coll of Design & Communication; *m* 23 May 2009, Shirley Patricia, *née* Anderson; *Heir* kinsman, Antony Waterlow; *Career* camera supervisor (formerly sr lighting cameraman) QVC The Shopping Channel; memb: Stonyhurst Assoc, Berchman Soc, Guild of Television Cameramen; fell Inst of Videography; *Publications* Videoskills: The Core Competences of Videography (jtly, 2008), The House of Waterlow – A Printer's Tale (2012); *Recreations* music, good food; *Style*— Sir Christopher Waterlow, Bt

WATERMAN, Clive Adrian; s of Harvey Waterman (d 1967), of Hendon, London, and Hannah, *née* Spector (d 1995); *b* 13 August 1949; *Educ* Haberdashers' Aske's Sch Elstree, London Hosp Med Coll (BDS), Royal Dental Hosp of London (MSc); *Career* clinical asst London Hosp 1973–75 (house surgn 1973), registrar Eastman Dental Hosp 1976–77, pt/t clinical asst Guy's Hosp 1977–84, gen and specialist practice 1977–, pt/t lectr King's Coll 1985–2002, specialist in periodontics 1998–; chm GP Section Br Soc of Periodontology 1990–94, asst sec BSP 1994–95; memb: Kingston and Richmond Local Dental Ctee 1988–, Cncl BSP 1990–95, memb BDA Scientific Programme Sub-Ctee 1990–; *Recreations* cricket, skiing, squash, wine, dining; *Clubs* Riverside, Reform, MCC; *Style*— Clive Waterman, Esq; ✉ 4 Elm Grove Road, Barnes, London SW13 0BT (✆ 020 8878 8986, fax 020 8878 9755, e-mail clive@c4gum.co.uk)

WATERMAN, Howard John; *b* 23 May 1953; *Educ* Univ of Southampton (LLB), Coll of Law; *m* 1 Nov 1981, Sharon; 1 da (Lauren b 1 Sept 1988), 1 s (Craig b 13 Dec 1992); *Career* admitted slr 1977; ptnr Cameron Markby Hewitt 1984–94, ptnr Sidley Austin 1994–; memb Law Soc 1977; *Recreations* chess, bridge, sports; *Style*— Howard Waterman, Esq; ✉ The Folly, 2 Newgate Street Village, Hertfordshire SG13 8RA (✆ 01707 875338); Sidley Austin (✆ 020 7360 3600, e-mail hwaterman@sidley.com)

WATERMAN, Peter Alan (Pete); OBE (2005); s of John Edward Waterman (d 2002), of Coventry, and Stella, *née* Lord (d 1978); *b* 15 January 1947; *Educ* Frederick Bird Secdy Modern Coventry; *m* 1, 1970, Elizabeth Reynolds; 1 s (Paul Andrew b 1972 d 2005); m 2, 1980, Julie Reeves; 1 s (Peter Alan b 1981); m 3, 1991, Denise Gyngell; 2 da (Toni Tuesday b 1990, Charlie Ella b 1991); *Career* record producer; former disc jockey at local pubs and Mecca dancehall, former Arts and Repertoire man for various record cos; formed Loose Ends Productions with Peter Collins working with artists incl Musical Youth and Nick Kershaw until 1983, fndr ptnr Stock Aitken Waterman (with Mike Stock and Matt Aitken) 1984–93; has won numerous Silver, Gold and Platinum Discs since 1985 for writing and/or producing artists incl: Princess, Hazell Dean, Dead or Alive, Bananarama, Mel and Kim, Sinitta, Rick Astley, Kylie Minogue, Brother Beyond, Jason Donovan, Donna Summer, Sonia, Big Fun, Cliff Richard, Westlife, Steps; involved with charity work incl SAW Goes to the Albert (Royal Marsden Hosp) and records: Let it Be (Ferry Aid), The Harder I Try (Young Variety Club of GB), Help (Comic Relief), Lets All Chant, I Haven't Stopped Dancing Yet and Use It Up and Wear It Out (Help a London Child), Ferry 'Cross the Mersey (Mersey Aid), Do They Know It's Christmas? (Ethiopia Famine Appeal), You've Got a Friend (Childline), Especially For You (Children In Need), Thank Abba for the Music (Brits School); judge: Pop Idol (ITV) 2001 and 2003, Popstars: The Rivals (ITV) 2002; ldr of consortium that purchased the first passenger part of BR to be privatised 1993; Hon DBA Coventry Univ 2001, Hon DMus Univ of Liverpool 2004; *Awards* BPI Best British Producers 1988; Music Week Top Producers for: Singles (1st) and Albums (3rd) 1987, Singles (1st) and Albums (1st) 1988 and 1989; Ivor Novello awards (UK): Songwriters of the Year 1987, 1988 and 1989, Writers of Most Performed Works 1987, 1988 and 1989; BMI awards (USA) Writers of Most Performed Works 1987, 1988 and 1989, Jasrac awards (Japan) and Cash awards (Hong Kong) Writers of Most Performed Foreign Works 1989, Music Week Award for Outstanding Achievement in the Music Industry 1999; *Books* I Wish I Was Me (autobiography, 2001); *Recreations* steam railways, model railways; *Style*— Pete Waterman, Esq, OBE; ✉ www.pwl-empire.com

WATERMAN, Prof Peter George; s of George Leonard Waterman (d 1992), and Queenie Rose Waterman (d 1988); *b* 28 April 1946; *Educ* Judd GS Tonbridge, Univ of London (BPharm, DSc), Univ of Strathclyde (PhD); *m* 1968, Margaret, da of Carl Humble; *Career* Univ of Strathclyde: asst lectr 1969–72, lectr 1972–83, sr lectr 1983, reader 1983–87, personal prof 1987, prof of phytochemistry Dept of Pharmaceutical Sciences 1990; dir Centre for Phytochemistry Southern Cross Univ NSW 1999–2003, currently emeritus prof of phytochemistry; formerly dir of natural products prog Strathclyde Inst for Drug Research 1991–99; sr res Nat Museums of Kenya 1983–85; founding ceo Australian Phytochemicals Ltd, formerly dir BioProspect Ltd; consltt: Forestry Res Inst of Malaysia, Western Australian Herbarium, Australian Nat Herbarium, ODA; Tate and Lyle award

W

Phytochemical Soc of Europe 1983; author of 6 books and numerous papers in scientific jls; former ed-in-chief Biochemical Systematics and Ecology; Hon Dr Université de Franche-Comte 1994; memb: Phytochemical Soc of Europe, American Soc for Pharmacognosy, Linnean Soc, Int Soc for Chemical Ecology; FRSE 1991; *Recreations* ornithology, conservation of rainforest remnants; *Style—* Prof Peter G Waterman, FRSE; ✉ Centre for Phytochemistry and Pharmacology, Southern Cross University, PO Box 157, Lismore, NSW 2480, Australia (☎ 61 2 6622 3211, fax 61 2 6622 3459)

WATERS, Brian Richard Anthony; s of late Montague Waters, QC, of London, and late Jessica Freedman; *b* 27 March 1944; *Educ* City of London Sch, St John's Coll Cambridge (MA), Univ of Cambridge (DipArch), PCL (DipTP); *m* 1 Nov 1974, Myriam Leiva, da of José Ramon Leiva Alvarez, of Bogotá, Colombia; *Career* chartered architect and town planner; princ The Boisot Waters Cohen Partnership (design); dir Land Research Unit Ltd; pres Cities of London and Westminster Soc of Architects 1980–82, vice-pres RIBA 1988–89 and 1991–92 (memb Cncl 1987–92); chm London Planning Devpt Forum 1990–, chm Nat Architecture Conf London 1991, vice-pres (professions) Nat Planning Forum 2010– (chm 2011–), chm APEC Forum Cambridge Univ Land Soc 2014–; memb Cncl Assoc of Consultant Architects 1997– (vice-pres 2003–06 and 2015–, pres 2007–11); jt publishing ed Planning in London (Int Building Press Magazine of the Year 2007); town planning corr Architects' Jl 1997–, ed Architectural Journalist of the Year commendation 1979, 1982, 1984 and 1986; pres John Carpenter Club (Old Citizens' Assoc) 2004–05; Best Personal Contribution London Planning Awards 2007 (highly commended); Freeman: City of London, Co of Chartered Architects (memb Ct 1991–, Master 2002); RIBA, MRTPI, FRSA; *Books* author of books, articles and reviews for various architectural pubns, Inst Economic Affairs and CPC; *Recreations* tennis, dressage, painting (exhbn of work at Leighton House 2002), pots, growing lavender in Cataluña; *Clubs* RAC, Hurlingham; *Style—* Brian R A Waters, Esq; ☎ 020 8948 2387, e-mail brian@bwcp.co.uk, website www.bwcp.co.uk

WATERS, Brian Wallace; s of Stanley Wallace Waters (d 1993), of Harpenden, Herts, and Kathleen, *née* Thake (d 2002); *b* 24 November 1936; *Educ* City of London Sch, Harvard Business Sch; *m* 1 April 1961, Gillian, da of Herbert William Harris (d 1976); 4 s (Andrew b 1963, James b 1965, Richard b 1967, Mark b 1975); *Career* Ernst & Young: ptnr 1968, exec vice-chm (Europe) 1979–82, chm (Europe) 1982–85, managing ptnr East Anglia 1985–92, managing ptnr Ernst & Young Birmingham 1992–96, managing ptnr Midlands and E Anglia Region 1992–97; chm London Soc of Chartered Accountants 1976–77, memb Cncl ICAEW 1983–87, memb Exec Ctee Union Européennes des Experts Comptables 1983–87; memb Horserace Betting Levy Appeal Tbnl 1986–2008, tstee and charity sec The Evelyn Tst 1997–2011, public interest memb of Ctees of Personal Investment Authy and Financial Services Authy 1998–2001; MFH United Hunt Co Cork 1998–2007; Worshipful Co of Drapers; FCA 1960, FCMA 1962; *Recreations* cricket, hunting, horse racing, fishing; *Clubs* MCC, Lord's Taverners; *Style—* Brian Waters, Esq; ✉ The Chequers, Preston, Hitchin, Hertfordshire SG4 7TY

WATERS, Donald Henry; OBE (1994); s of Henry Lethbridge Waters (d 1978), of Edinburgh, and Jean Manson, *née* Baxter (d 1987); *b* 17 December 1937, Edinburgh; *Educ* George Watson's Coll Edinburgh, Inverness Royal Acad; *m* 5 May 1962, June Leslie, da of Andrew Hutchison (d 1984), of Forres, Moray; 2 da (Jennifer Dawn b 1963, Gillian Claire b 1966), 1 s (Andrew Henry Lethbridge b 1969); *Career* Grampian Television plc: dir 1979–97, chief exec 1987–97, dep chm 1993–97; dir: John M Henderson Ltd 1972–75, Glenburnie Properties Ltd 1976–97 (chm 1993–97), Scottish Television and Grampian Sales Ltd (STAGS) 1980–98, Blenheim Travel Ltd 1981–91, Moray Firth Radio Ltd 1982–97, Independent Television Publications Ltd 1987–90, Cablevision Scotland plc 1987–91, Central Scotland Radio Ltd Scot FM 1994–96 (chm 1995–96), GRT Bus Group plc (now Firstgroup plc) 1994–95, British Linen Bank Group Ltd 1995–99, Scottish Media Group plc 1997–2005, Digital 3 and 4 Ltd 1997–98, James Johnston & Co of Elgin Ltd 1999–2016 (dep chm), Aberdeen Asset Mgmnt plc 2000–11 (sr non-exec dir 2004–11); memb: Ct British Linen Bank Ltd 1994–98, Consignia Advsy Bd for Scotland (formerly Scottish Post Office Bd) 1996–2003, North of Scotland Bd Bank of Scotland 1999–2001; visiting prof of film and media studies Univ of Stirling 1991, memb Cncl Cinema and Television Benevolent Fund 1986–99, chm Celtic Film and TV Assoc 1994–96 (tstee Scotland 1990–97), memb Independent Television Association Ltd 1994–97; chm Police Dependent Tst Grampian Region 1991–96, dir Aberdeen Royal Hosps NHS Tst 1996–99 (chm New Aberdeen Royal Children's Hosp Project Steering Gp), jt chm Grampian Cancer Macmillan 1999–2004; memb: RTS 1988–, BAFTA UK 1980 (Scottish vice-chm 1992–97), Cncl SATRO, CBI Scotland Cncl 1994–2001, Grampian Initiative, Grampian and Islands Family Tst (GIFT) 1988–2006; govr Univ of Aberdeen 1998–99; a Burgess of Guild Aberdeen 1979– (assessor 1998–2001); MICAS 1961, FRSA 1990; *Recreations* gardening, travel, hill walking; *Clubs* Royal Northern and Univ Aberdeen (past chm); *Style—* Donald Waters, Esq, OBE, CA; ✉ Balquhidder, 141 North Deeside Road, Milltimber, Aberdeen AB13 0JS (☎ 01224 867131, e-mail donaldwaters@btinternet.com)

WATERS, Malcolm Ian; QC (1997); s of Ian Power Waters (d 2003), of Purley, Surrey, and Yvonne, *née* Mosley (d 2004); *b* 11 October 1953; *Educ* Whitgift Sch, St Catherine's Coll Oxford (BA, BCL); *m* 2002, Setsu Sato; *Career* called to the Bar Lincoln's Inn 1977; memb: Chancery Bar Assoc 1978, Professional Negligence Bar Assoc 1992; *Publications* Wurtzburg and Mills Building Society Law (jtly, 15 edn, 1989 and annual looseleaf updates to 2014), The Building Societies Act 1986 (jtly, 1987), The Law of Investor Protection (jtly, 3 edn, 2003), Halsbury's Laws of England Vol 19 (1): Friendly Societies (conslt ed, 4 edn, 2007); contrib: Standard Conditions of Sale (1 to 5 edn), Standard Commercial Property Conditions (1 and 2 edns), Halsbury's Laws of England Vol 50: Financial Services and Institutions (conslt ed, 5 edn, 2008), Retail Mortgages: Law, Regulation and Procedure (jtly, 2013), Halsbury's Laws of England Vol 48: Financial Institutions (conslt ed, 5 edn, 2015); *Recreations* music; *Style—* Malcolm Waters, Esq, QC; ✉ Radcliffe Chambers, 11 New Square, Lincoln's Inn, London WC2A 3QB (☎ 020 7831 0081, fax 020 7405 2560, e-mail mwaters@radcliffechambers.com)

WATERS, Sarah; *b* 1966, Pembrokeshire; *Educ* Univ of Kent, Lancaster Univ, Univ of London; *Career* writer; former assoc lectr Open Univ; *Publications*Tipping the Velvet (1998, TV adaptation 2002, Betty Trask Award 1999, Library Jl's Best Book of the Year 1999, Mail on Sunday/John Llewellyn Rhys Prize 1999, NY Times Notable Book of the Year Award 1999, Lambda Literary Award for Fiction 2000), Affinity (1999, TV adaptation 2011, American Library Assoc GLBT Roundtable Book Award 2000, Ferro-Grumley Award for Lesbian and Gay Fiction 2000, Somerset Maugham Award 2000, Sunday Times Young Writer of the Year Award 2000, shortlist Lambda Literary Award for Fiction 2000, shortlist Mail on Sunday/John Llewellyn Rhys Prize 2000), Fingersmith (2002, TV adaptation 2005, British Book Awards Author of the Year 2002, Crime Writers' Assoc Ellis Peters Historical Dagger 2002, shortlist Man Booker Prize for Fiction 2002, shortlist Orange Prize for Fiction 2002), The Night Watch (2006, TV adaptation 2011, shortlist Man Booker Prize for Fiction 2006, shortlist Orange Prize for Fiction 2006), The Little Stranger (2009, shortlist Man Booker Prize for Fiction 2009), The Paying Guests (2014, shortlisted Baileys Women's Prize for Fiction 2015); *Style—* Ms Sarah Waters; ✉ c/o Judith Murray, Greene & Heaton, 37 Goldhawk Road, London W12 8QQ (☎ 020 8749 0315, fax 020 8749 0318)

WATERSON, Prof Michael John (Mike); s of late Geoffrey Waterson, and Christine Mary Waterson, of Leamington Spa, Warks; *b* 29 July 1950, Meriden, Warks; *Educ* Bude GS, Univ of Warwick (BA, PhD), LSE (MSc); *m* 1972, Sally Ann, *née* Davis; 1 s (Thomas Philip b 16 Nov 1984), 1 da (Alice Jane b 11 July 1989); *Career* Univ of Newcastle upon Tyne: lectr in economics 1974–86, reader in economics 1986–88; visiting lectr in economics Univ of Sydney 1987–88, prof of economics Univ of Reading 1988–91, prof of economics Univ of Warwick 1991–; visiting prof Univ of Rome Tor Vergata 2013–14; research assoc ZEW Mannheim Germany 2013–; chm Utilities Appeal Panel Guernsey 2002–07, memb Competition Cmmn 2005–14, specialist advsr Sub-Ctee B House of Lords Select Ctee 2005–06, memb Scientific Advsy Bd DIW Berlin, memb Economist Reference Gp Cooperation and Competition Panel for NHS-Funded Servs, ind chair Parly Review of Secondary Ticketing 2015–16; FRSA 1989; Economic Theory of the Industry (1984), Regulation of the Firm and Natural Monopoly (1988), Buyer Power and Competition in European Food Retailing (jtly, 2002); *Recreations* walking, travel, playing musical instruments; *Style—* Prof Mike Waterson; ✉ Department of Economics, University of Warwick, Coventry CV4 7AL (☎ 024 7652 3427, fax 024 7652 3032, e-mail michael.waterson@warwick.ac.uk)

WATERSTONE, Timothy John Stuart; s of Malcolm Stuart Waterstone, MBE (d 1977), of Maresfield, E Sussex, and Sylvia Catherine, *née* Sawday (d 1967); *b* 30 May 1939; *Educ* Tonbridge, St Catharine's Coll Cambridge (MA); *m* 1, Oct 1962 (m dis 1971), Patricia Harcourt-Poole; 2 s (Richard b 1963, Martin b 1965), 1 da (Sylvie b 1969); m 2, Oct 1972 (m dis 1990), Clare Perkins; 2 da (Amanda b 1975, Maya b 1977), 1 s (Oliver b 1980); m 3, Feb 1991, Mary Rose Alison; 2 da (Lucy Rose b 1992, Daisy Alison b 1994); *Career* Carritt Moran & Co Calcutta 1962–64, Allied Breweries plc 1965–73, W H Smith Group plc 1973–81, fndr chm and chief exec Waterstone & Co 1982–93; fndr chm HMV Media Gp plc (merged business of Waterstone's, Dillons and HMV) 1998–2001; fndr and chm Chelsea Stores Ltd (incl Daisy & Tom, and Early Learning Centre 2004) 1996–; chm Priory Investments Ltd 1990–95, dep chm Sinclair-Stevenson Publishers Ltd 1989–92; memb Bd: Futurestart (BT Venture Capital Fund) 1992–, Hill Samuel UK Emerging Cos Investment Tst plc 1996–2001, Yale Univ Press 1992–, Virago Publishers 1995–96; chm DTI Working Gp on Smaller Quoted Companies and Private Investors 1999; tstee International House 1986–92, memb Ctee Booker Prize 1986–93; chm: Princes Youth Business Tst Awards 1990, Shelter 25th Anniversary Appeal 1991–92, London Int Festival of Theatre 1990–92, The Elgar Fndn 1992–98, KCL Library Bd 1999–2002; co-fndr Bookaid 1992; dir: The Academy of Ancient Music 1990–95, The London Philharmonic Orchestra 1990–97; memb: Bd Downing Classic VCT 1998–2003, National Gallery Co 1996–2003; *Fiction* Lilley & Chase (1994), An Imperfect Marriage (1995), A Passage of Lives (1996); *Non-Fiction* Swimming Against The Stream (2006); *Recreations* being with Rosie Alison; *Clubs* Garrick; *Style—* Timothy Waterstone, Esq

WATERTON-ANDERSON, David Alexander Richard; s of John (Jack) Anderson (d 1985), of Kinneddar, and Alice, *née* Waterton (d 2000); *b* 16 May 1944, Hazlewood Castle, Yorks; *Educ* Univ of Leeds (BA), Univ of Dundee (Cert); *m* 29 Sept 1989, Elizabeth, *née* MacLauchlan; *Career* De La Rue/Security Express Ltd 1966–70, Rank Organisation 1970–80, 3M Health Care 1981–94, various business interests 1994–; webmaster to the Assoc of Papal Orders in GB; Baron Baillie to the Baron of Myrton; memb Armigerous Cncl Clan Anderson; guest piper 1 Bn Scots Guards; St John Ambulance Service Medal 1979, Int Emergency Service Medal, Volunteer Medical Service Medal; Grand Bailiwick of Scotland; Companion Order of Malta 1992, Order of Malta Lourdes Medal 1994, Jerusalem Cross of Honour 1997, KSG 2006, Order of Malta Meritori Melitensi Silver Medal 2012, Knight Offr Cross 2013, Offr Order of St Lazarus of Jerusalem 2015 (webmaster); *Publications* Tartan As Armorial Ensign (1966), Anderson Heraldry (1994), Heraldry at Gilling Castle (2004–); author/presenter of a series of fourteen nostalgia videos on Scottish cities, towns and districts; *Recreations* music, heraldry, genealogy; *Style—* David A R Waterton-Anderson, KSG; ✉ Stapleton Lodge, High Street, Carlton-Juxta-Snaith, North Yorkshire DN14 9LU (☎ 01405 860165, e-mail watertonanderson@gmail.com)

WATES, Andrew Trace Allan; OBE (2013), DL (Surrey 2006); s of Sir Ronald Wallace Wates (d 1986), and Lady Phyllis Mary, *née* Trace (d 2006); *b* 16 November 1940; *Educ* Oundle, Emmanuel Coll Cambridge (BA); *m* 19 June 1965, Sarah Mary de Burgh Wates, *née* McCartney; 5 s (Timothy Andrew de Burgh b 3 June 1966, Jonathan Giles Macartney b 16 June 1967, Richard James Alexander b 1 Feb 1971, Simon David Sam b 17 March 1975, William Ronald James b 11 April 1977 (decd)); *Career* joined Wates Gp 1964, dir sales and mktg Wates Construction 1972–73, chm Wates Leisure 1973, chm Wates Gp 2000–06, chm Wates Family Holdings 2006–08; chm: United Racecourses 1996–2003, Leisure & Media VCT 2002–, Gambado Ltd 2004–; dir Jockey Club Racecourses (formerly Racecourse Holdings Trust) 1994–2008; dir: Inst for Family Business 2004–10, International Family Business Network 2004–; patron and tstee various Surrey charities; pro-chllr Univ of Surrey 2016–; FNAEA; *Recreations* horse racing, golf, shooting, fishing; *Clubs* White's, Turf; *Style—* Andrew Wates, Esq, OBE, DL; ✉ Henfold House, Beare Green, Surrey RH5 4RW (☎ 01306 631324, fax 01306 631794); Wates Group Limited, Wates House, Station Approach, Leatherhead, Surrey KT22 7SW (☎ 01372 861051, fax 01372 861053, e-mail andrew.wates@wates.co.uk)

WATKIN, Prof David John; s of Thomas Charles Watkin (d 2006), and Vera Mary, *née* Saunders (d 1996); *b* 7 April 1941; *Educ* Farnham GS, Trinity Hall Cambridge (MA, PhD, LittD); *Career* Univ of Cambridge: fell Peterhouse 1970–, lectr in history of art 1972–, head Dept of History of Art 1989–92 and 2006–07, prof of history of architecture 2001– (reader 1993); memb: Historic Bldgs Advsy Ctee, Historic Bldgs and Monuments Cmmn 1980–95, vice-chm Georgian Gp; Hon Dr of Arts De Montfort Univ 1996; Hon FRIBA 2001; FSA 1979; *Books* Thomas Hope 1769–1831 and The Neo-Classical Idea (1968), The Life and Work of CR Cockerell RA (1974), Morality and Architecture (1977), English Architecture: A Concise History (1979, 2 edn 2000), The Rise of Architectural History (1980), Neo-Classical and Nineteenth Century Architecture (with Robin Middleton, 1980), Athenian Stuart: Pioneer of the Greek Revival (1982), The English Vision: The Picturesque in Architecture, Landscape and Garden Design (1982), A History of Western Architecture (1986, 5 edn 2011), German Architecture and the Classical Ideal: 1740–1840 (with Tilman Mellinghoff, 1987), Sir John Soane: Enlightenment Thought and the Royal Academy Lectures (1996), The Age of Wilkins: The Architecture of Improvement (2000), Sir John Soane: The Royal Academy Lectures (2000), Morality and Architecture Revisited (2001), Alfred Gilbey: A Memoir by Some Friends (ed, 2001), John Simpson: The Queen's Gallery Buckingham Palace and other Works (with Richard John, 2002), The Architect King: George III and the Culture of the Enlightenment (2004), Radical Classicism: The Architecture of Quinlan Terry (2006), Thomas Hope: Regency Designer (ed and contrib, 2008), The Roman Forum (2009), The Classical Country House: From the Archives of Country Life (2010), Giacomo Vignola, Canon of the Five Orders of Architecture (intro, 2011), The Art of Classical Details: Theory, Design and Craftsmanship (contrib, 2012), Moggerhanger Park Bedfordshire (contrib, 2013), John Nash: Architect of the Picturesque (contrib, 2013), Classical Interiors: Historical and Contemporary (contrib, 2013), William Kent: Designing Georgian Britain (contrib, 2013), The Architectural Capriccio: Memory, Fantasy and Invention (contrib, 2014), Lady Ursula d'Abo, The Memoirs (ed, 2014), The Practice of Classical Architecture: Quinlan and Francis Terry 2005–15 (2015), The Architecture of John Simpson: The Timeless Language of Classicism (2016); *Clubs* Brooks's, Beefsteak; *Style—* Prof David Watkin; ✉ St Margaret's Place, King's Lynn PE30 5DL; Peterhouse, Cambridge CB2 1RD

WATKINS, Anna; MBE (2013); *née* Bebington; *b* 13 February 1983, Leek, Staffs; *Educ* Westwood HS Leek, Newnham Coll Cambridge; *m* Sept 2009, Dr Oliver Watkins; *Career*

rower; achievements incl: Gold medal fours World Rowing Under 23s Championships 2004, Bronze medal pairs World Rowing Under 23s Championships 2005, Bronze medal double sculls World Rowing Championships 2007, Bronze medal double sculls Olympic Games Beijing 2008, Silver medal double sculls World Rowing Championships 2009, Gold medal double sculls World Rowing Championships 2010, Gold medal double sculls Olympic Games 2012; World Rowing Female Crew of the Year 2010; *Clubs* Leander; *Style*— Mrs Anna Watkins, MBE

WATKINS, Prof Hugh Christian; *b* 7 June 1959; *Educ* Gresham's, St Bartholomew's Med Coll London (BSc, MB BS, Brackenbury and Bourne prize in gen med), Univ of London (PhD, MD), Univ of Oxford (MA); *Career* house physician Professorial Med Unit St Bartholomew's Hosp London 1984–85, SHO John Radcliffe Hosp Oxford 1985–87, registrar in gen med and cardiology Thomas' Hosp London 1988–89; Harvard Med Sch: research fell in med 1990–94, instr in med 1994–95, asst prof of med 1995–96; concurrently: assoc physician Brigham and Women's Hosp Boston 1994–96, hon sr lectr Dept of Cardiological Scis St George's Hosp Med Sch London 1995 (lectr 1990–94); Field Marshal Alexander prof of cardiovascular med (head Dept of Cardiovascular Med) Univ of Oxford 1996–, professorial fell Exeter Coll Oxford 1996–2015, hon conslt in cardiology and gen med John Radcliffe Hosp Oxford 1996–, Radcliffe prof of medicine and head Radcliffe Dept of Medicine Univ of Oxford 2016–, professorial fell Merton Coll Oxford 2016–; sr investigator NIHR 2009; Young Research Worker Prize Br Cardiac Soc 1992, Goulstonian lectr RCP 1998, Graham Bull Prize RCP 2003, Paul Dudley White Lecture American Heart Assoc 2011; FMedSci 1999, fell American Heart Assoc (FAHA) 2001, FRCP; *Style*— Prof Hugh C Watkins; ✉ Radcliffe Department of Medicine, Level 6, West Wing, John Radcliffe Hospital, Oxford OX3 9DU (e-mail hugh.watkins@rdm.ox.ac.uk)

WATKINS, Jacob Saul (Jake); *s* of Melvin Watkins, and Eileen, *née* Collington; *b* 30 March 1971, Southampton, Hants; *Educ* Belmore Sch Southampton, St Mary's Coll Southampton; *Career* restaurateur; apprenticeship with Jean-Christophe Novelli 1988–89, experience in a number of top London restaurants 1990–96, head chef Holbeck Ghyll Lake District 1996–98, chef prop Restaurant JSW 2000– (Michelin Star 2004–, 2 Stars Harden's Guide, 6/10 Good Food Guide); *Recreations* wine, fishing; *Style*— Jake Watkins, Esq; ✉ Restaurant JSW, 20 Dragon Street, Petersfield, Hampshire GU31 4JJ (☎ 01730 262030, e-mail jsw.restaurant@btconnect.com, website www.jswrestaurant.com)

WATKINS, Paul Alan; *s* of John Llewellyn Watkins (d 1984), and Patricia Frances, *née* Story (d 2009); *b* 5 February 1946, Abergavenny, Monmouthshire; *Educ* King Henry VIII GS Abergavenny, Univ of Manchester Sch of Architecture (BA, BArch); *Partner* Maureen Anne Betts; 1 da (Rebecca Josephine b 30 Oct 1974); *Career* Tripe & Wakeham Partnership 1972–74; Sheppard Robson (architects, planners and interior designers) London: joined 1974, assoc 1979–88, ptnr 1988–2006, conslt 2006–11; projects incl: Royal Mint Court London EC3 (offices, residential and community use) 1985–90, 103 Wigmore St London W1 (major office refurbishment) 1993–96, 1 Silk St London EC2 (major HQ office renovation) 1994–96, 1 St James's Sq London SW1 (HQ office redevelopment) 1995–98, 70 Grosvenor Sq London W1 (HQ office redevelopment) 1997–99, 10 Aldermanbury London EC2 (HQ Office redevelopment) 1997–2000, 95 Queen Victoria St London EC4 (office and leisure redevelopment) 2000–03, One Hanover Square London W1 (retail, office and residential redevelopment) 2002–04, 77 Grosvenor St London W1 (office redevelopment) 2004–06, Abford House London SW1 2004–10, Abbey Mill House Reading (office and residential redevelopment) 2006–09; chm City of London Conservation Area Advsy Ctee 2011–14 (vice-chm 2014–); RIBA 1974; *Recreations* walking, swimming, tennis; *Style*— Paul Watkins, Esq; ☎ 020 7722 4792, e-mail paul-watkins@tiscali.co.uk

WATKINS, Richard Valentine; *b* 23 September 1950; *Educ* Wellington, Loughborough Univ of Technol (BSc); *m* 1978 (m dis 2007), Charlotte, *née* de Laszlo; 2 s, 1 da; *Career* Phillips & Drew Inc 1972–77, mangr and overseas rep Kleinwort Benson 1977–83, md Phillips & Drew Inc (NY) 1983–86, pres Hoare Govett Inc (NY) 1986–88, chm Burns Fry Hoare Govett Inc (NY) 1988, exec dir J Henry Schroder Wagg & Co Ltd 1988–92, former chief exec Schroder Securities Ltd and dir of related cos in SE Asia, Japan, Korea, Switzerland; fndr dir and chief exec BBV LatInvest Securities and dir related cos 1992–98, dir LatInvest Holdings 1992–2000, chm Deutsche Latin American Companies Tst plc 1999–2004, fndr dir and chief exec Liability Solutions 1999–; *Recreations* skiing; *Style*— Richard Watkins, Esq; ✉ 7 Chesham Mews, London SW1X 8HS (☎ 020 7235 2434)

WATKINS, Dr Stephen John; *s* of Norman Watkins (d 1975), and Lois Watkins (d 1995); *b* 2 July 1950, Nelson, Lancs; *Educ* Nelson GS, Univ of Manchester (Haworth maj entrance scholar, BSc, MB ChB, MSc); *m* 2 Nov 1985, Elizabeth Watkins; *Career* hosp dr trg Manchester and Macclesfield 1974–79, gen medical practitioner Macclesfield 1979, public health trg posts Blackburn, Salford, Manchester and Oldham 1979–84, specialist in community medicine Oldham 1984–90, dir of public health for Stockport 1990–, lectr in public health and epidemiology Univ of Manchester 1991–; lead dir of public health Gtr Manchester: transport and land planning 2002–, research 2004–08, cancer 2005–06, work and enterprise 2006–, mental well-being 2008–13, clinical reference gp for hosp reconfiguration 2013–15; lead dir of public health NW Region: sustainable devpt 2007–13, community cohesion (jtly) 2007–11; pres Medical Practitioners' Union 1988–98; BMA: memb Cncl 1991–, dir 1991–2015, chm Public Health Ctee 1992–98; chm Transport and Health Study Gp 1993–, Manchester Medical Soc 1996– (pres Public Health Forum 2004–05); dep chair UK Cncl of Caldicott Guardians 2005–09, chm Prog for Popular Participation in Parliament; James Preston Meml Award 2000; FFPH 1993 (MFPH 1984), MILT 2002, hon fell Faculty of Sexual and Reproductive Healthcare 2004; *Publications* Medical Manpower and Career Structure (1980), Medicine and Labour: The Politics of a Profession (1987), Health on the Move (ed, 1991), Conviction by Mathematical Error (2000), A Country City (2001), Health on the Move 2 (ed, 2011); Annual Public Health Reports of Stockport (1991–2009); author of papers on unemployment and health, work and health, and economic policy and health in WHO and other pubns 1984–94 and on transport and health in various pubns 2011–; *Recreations* rambling, railway enthusiast; *Style*— Dr Stephen Watkins; ✉ Stockport MBC, Fred Perry House, Stockport SK1 3XE (☎ 0161 474 2450, e-mail stephen.watkins1@nhs.net)

WATKINSON, Dame Angela; DBE (2013), MP; *b* 18 November 1941; *Educ* Wanstead Co HS, Anglia Poly Univ; *m* (m dis); 1 s, 2 da; *Career* early career in banking, former local govt offr; former cncllr (Cons): Havering BC, Essex CC; MP (Cons): Upminster 2001–10, Hornchurch and Upminster 2010–; oppn whip 2002–04, shadow min for educn 2004–05, shadow min for local govt affrs and communities 2005–10, lord cmmr (whip) 2010–12; treas All Pty Sweden Gp 2002, treas All Pty Isle of Man Gp 2004, memb Ctee on Standards in Public Life 2012–; memb UK Cncl of Europe 2005–06, memb Cncl of Europe 2012–15; former chm Upminster Cons Assoc (Emerson Park Branch); memb EDG Gp; Freeman City of London 2003; *Clubs* Carlton; *Style*— Dame Angela Watkinson, DBE, MP; ✉ House of Commons, London SW1A 0AA

WATKINSON, David Robert; *s* of late Robert Douglas Watkinson, of Woking, Surrey, and Muriel Winifred, *née* Reeves; *b* 6 October 1947; *Educ* Woking GS for Boys, Clare Coll Cambridge (MA, LLB); *Partner* Suzanne Eve Tarlin; 1 da (Eva Rose b 1 July 1980); *Career* called to the Bar Middle Temple 1972; fndr memb chambers Wellington St London 1974–88 (committed to working in social welfare areas of law), memb Garden Court Chambers 1988–2013 (jt head of chambers 2011–12)ret 2013, door tenant Garden Court Chambers 2013–; specialist in housing law and law relating to gypsies/travellers

including planning, ret from legal practice 2013; memb: Exec Ctee Family Squatting Advsy Service 1972–75, N Islington Law Centre 1974–78; memb and legal advsr to campaign against criminal trespass laws 1974–78, occasional legal advsr Advsy Serv to Squatters 1975–2012, concerned with publicity for campaign of limitation of rights of defence in W Germany late 1970s, campaigned to extend grant of Legal Aid in particular to Magistrates' Courts 1979–80, memb Stop the Criminal Trespass Law Campaign 1983–84, teacher of housing law Univ of Warwick 1984 and occasional expert witness/course ldr 1997–2004, observer on behalf of Haldane Soc for Socialist Lawyers and Agric Allied Workers Branch TGWU at trial of agric day labourers in Spain 1986, lectures on legal aspects of housing South Bank Poly and other instns 1988, assoc dir Nat Housing Law Serv 1991–93, memb Legal and Parly Ctee SQUASH (Squatters Action for Secure Homes) 1993–94; vice-chm Housing Law Practitioners Assoc 1994–2000 (memb Exec Ctee 1994–2012), chair Housing and Land Ctee Civil Justice Cncl 2000–03 (memb 2000–11); exec memb Ctee Admin Law Bar Assoc 1999–2006, memb Civil Justice Cncl (appointed by Lord Chllr) 2000–02; occasional lectr Local Govt Gp Law Soc 1995, 1997, 1998 and 1999; training course leader Administrative Law Bar Assoc 1996, course leader and advsr Legal Servs Cmmn 2000–08, Planning Aid 2007 and 2008; accredited mediator 2008 (continues to practise as mediator from Gordon Court Chambers); author of reviews and articles on housing 1974– (Legal Action, Roof, Law Soc's Gazette, Haldane Soc Bulletin, All England Legal Opinion, Solicitor's Jl, From the Lawyers Collective Mumbai, Travellers Advice Team (TAT) bulletin); former memb Haldane Soc Socialist Lawyers Legal Action Gp (vice-pres 2014–); memb: Admin Law Bar Assoc prev, Housing Law Practitioners' Assoc prev, Nicaragua Solidarity Campaign prev; Barr of the Year Award Legal Aid Practitioners Gp 2005; *Books* Law in a Housing Crisis (contrib, 1975), NCCL Civil Rights Guide (1978), Squatting – The Real Story (1980), Critical Lawyers Handbook (1992); Squatting Trespass and Civil Liberties (jtly, 1976), Gypsy and Traveller Law (jtly, 2004, 3 edn 2016); *Recreations* travel, theatre, cinema, ethnic music, history, archaeology, fiction, swimming; *Style*— David Watkinson, Esq; ✉ Garden Chambers, 57–60 Lincoln's Inn Fields, London WC2A 3LJ (☎ 020 7993 7600, fax 020 7993 7700, e-mail davidw@gclaw.co.uk, website www.gardencourtchambers.co.uk)

WATKINSON, Douglas Arthur; *s* of Raymond Arthur Watkinson (d 1947), and Joan Lilian, *née* Crawley (d 1972); *b* 5 July 1945; *Educ* Haberdashers' Aske's, East Fifteen Acting Sch; *m* 20 June 1972, Lesley Moira, da of Stanley Thompson; 2 da (Fenella Laurie b 31 May 1978, Ailsa Morag b 2 Nov 1983), 2 s (Callum Neil b 21 Aug 1979, Duncan Clyde b 23 Feb 1981); *Career* freelance writer; began as actor, script ed BBC 1972–75, freelance writer 1975–; contrib to TV series/serials incl: Z Cars, The Brothers, Owen MD, Duchess of Duke Street, Spy Trap, Onedin Line, Juliet Bravo, The Bill, Boon, Maybury, Lovejoy, Poirot, Anna Lee, Midsomer Murders, Kavanagh, QC, Heartbeat; sole writer of series: For Maddie With Love, Strange True Stories, The New Statesman, Forever Green, Land of Promise; stage plays: Let's Do It My Way, The Dragon's Tail, Caesar and Me, The Wall; author of the Nathan Hawk crime novels: Haggard Hawk, Easy Prey, Scattered Remains, Evil Turn; memb Writers' Guild; *Recreations* travel, bonsai, reading; *Clubs* National Liberal; *Style*— Douglas Watkinson, Esq; ✉ c/o David Higham Associates, 5–8 Lower John Street, Golden Square, London W1F 9HA (☎ 01296 748270, mobile 07718 090782, e-mail authordaw@gmail.com, website www.douglaswatkinson.com, Twitter @DAWatkinson)

WATNEY, (John) Adrian; *s* of Maj John Douglas Watney, RA (d 1983), and Barbara Ann, *née* Smith (d 2001); *b* 3 October 1943, Woking, Surrey; *Educ* Sherborne; *m* 9 Sept 1967, Angela Winifred, da of Dudley Partridge (d 1982); 3 da (Katherine b 1970, Sarah b 1972, Victoria b 1976), 1 s (Christopher b 1981); *Career* admitted slr 1968; former ptnr Pinsent Masons Solicitors; dir Longacre Estates Ltd; chm: Porteo Ltd, Kleinwort Benson Bank; chm Advsy Bd, tstee and chm Classical Roadshow; former tstee and chm: Alzheimer's Research UK (currently hon fell), Medical Coll of St Bart's; hon memb Faculty of Divinity Univ of Cambridge; hon fell QMC London; former memb Law Soc; Freeman: City of London, Merchant Adventureres of York 1990–; Liveryman Worshipful Co Mercers (memb Ct 1986–, Master 1990–91); *Recreations* golf, cricket, rugby, opera, shooting; *Clubs* Home House, Royal and Ancient Golf (St Andrews), MCC, Rye Golf, Walton Heath Golf, Hon Co of Edinburgh Golfers, Arts; *Style*— Adrian Watney, Esq; ✉ 131 Clifford's Inn, Fetter Lane, London EC4 1BY (☎ 07860 872550)

WATSON; *see also*: Inglefield-Watson, Milne-Watson"

WATSON, Adrian Keith; *s* of Keith Watson, and Stella, *née* Crippin; *b* 20 November 1952, Birmingham; *Educ* Dudley GS, Univ of Sheffield (BA); *m* 24 Sept 1977, Joanna, *née* Round; 1 s (James b 11 June 1985); *Career* slr; ptnr: Rigbey Loose & Mills 1979–82 (joined 1976), Pinsent & Co 1983–86 (joined 1982), Anthony Collins Slrs 1986–95, Garrett & Co 1995–99, DLA 1999–2005, DWF LLP (formerly Cobbetts) 2005–14; conslt Veale Wasbrough Vizards LLP 2015–; past chm Midlands Bd Investment Property Forum 2008; memb Law Soc 1978; released music album Hostage to Fortune 2006; *Recreations* music (piano, singing), golf, skiing; *Clubs* Stourbridge Golf; *Style*— Adrian Watson, Esq; ✉ Veale Wasbrough Vizards LLP, Three Brindleyplace, Birmingham B1 2JB (☎ 0121 227 3709, e-mail awatson@vwv.co.uk)

WATSON, Alan Carlos; *s* of William Carlos Watson (d 1990), and Doris May, *née* Putwain; *b* 26 October 1940; *Educ* Willesden Tech Coll (HNC); *m* 12 Sept 1964, Sandra Mary, da of John Bruce Garner; 1 s (Ashley b 8 April 1966), 1 da (Martine b 11 Dec 1968); *Career* student apprentice Matthew Hall Mechanical Services Ltd, ptnr Building Design Partnership 1988– (joined 1972); expert witness for House of Commons Select Ctee Channel Tunnel Hybrid Bill; FCIWEM; *Recreations* golf; *Style*— Alan Watson, Esq; ✉ 17 Silver Close, Harrow, Middlesex HA3 6JT

WATSON, Prof Alan Rees; *Educ* Univ of Edinburgh Med Sch (BSc, MB ChB); *Career* surgical house offr Princess Margaret Hosp Nassau Bahamas 1973, med house offr Eastern Gen Hosp Edinburgh 1974, neonatal house offr Elsie Inglis Maternity Hosp Edinburgh 1974–75, SHO in paediatrics Royal Hosp for Sick Children Edinburgh 1975, SHO in gen med Eastern Gen Hosp Edinburgh 1975–76, locum GP Muswellbrook NSW and Deputising Serv Sydney Aust 1976, locum casualty offr Lyell McEwin Hosp Adelaide S Aust 1976, registrar in paediatrics King Edward VIII Hosp Durban SA 1977, locum lectr/conslt Dept of Child Health Univ of Natal Durban SA 1978, tutor in child health Univ of Manchester (hon registrar) 1979, lectr in child health Royal Manchester Children's Hosp Univ of Manchester (hon sr registrar) 1979–82, clinical fell (subspeciality res) in paediatric nephrology Hosp for Sick Children Toronto 1982–83, staff nephrologist and asst prof Hosp for Sick Children Toronto and Univ of Toronto Canada 1983–85, conslt paediatric nephrologist and unit dir Children and Young People's Kidney Unit City Hosp NHS Tst Nottingham 1985–2010; Univ of Nottingham: special sr lectr Div of Child Health Sch of Human Devpt 1999–2005, special prof of paediatric nephrology 2005–10, emeritus prof of paediatric nephrology 2010–; inaugural chm City Hosp Ethics of Clinical Practice Ctee 1994–2004, chair UK Clinical Ethics Network 2003–09; fndr and organiser: Trent and Anglia Paediatric Nephro-urology Gp 1994–, Trent Paediatric Nephrology Gp 1999–2010, Trent and Anglia Paediatric Haemofiltration Gp 2000–; fndr and gp co-ordinator Euro Paediatric Peritoneal Working Gp 1999–; advsr: Nat Kidney Res Fund Helpline 2000–10, Nat Kidney Fund 2003–10; memb Scientific Ctee Int Soc for Peritoneal Dialysis Montreal 2001, memb Cncl European Soc of Paediatric Nephrology 2003–06 (chm Scientific Ctee 2006); memb: Manchester Paediatric Club 1980–83, Br Paediatric Assoc 1980–99, Assoc for Paediatric Educn in Europe 1981–83, Paediatric Res Soc 1981–99, American Soc of Nephrology 1983–2010, Int Soc of Nephrology 1984–2015,

Int Paediatric Nephrology Assoc 1984– (memb Cncl 2007–), Br Assoc of Paediatric Nephrology 1985–, Renal Assoc UK 1986–, Euro Soc of Paediatric Nephrology 1986–2015, Int Soc for Peritoneal Dialysis 1986–2010, Nottingham Medico-Chirurgical Soc 1986–, Nottingham Medico-Legal Soc 1988–92, Int Soc of Nutrition and Metabolism in Renal Disease 1992–2010; B Merit Award NHS 1998; Licentiate Med Cncl of Canada 1983; MRCP 1976, FRCPEd 1988, FRCPCH 1997; *Publications* 215 papers and 32 chapters in books; *Style*— Prof Alan R Watson; ✉ Children's Renal and Urology Unit E17, QMC Campus, Nottingham University Hospitals, Derby Road, Nottingham NG7 2UH (☎ 0115 970 9420, e-mail alan.watson@nuh.nhs.uk)

WATSON, Alastair Alexander Linton; LVO (2011); s of Maj-Gen Andrew Linton Watson, CB, and Mary Elizabeth, *née* Rigby; *b* 15 February 1953, Wüppertal, Germany; *Educ* Eagle House Sandhurst Camberley, Wellington Coll, New Coll Oxford (MA), Staff Coll Camberley, RMCS Shrivenham (CGIA); *m* 28 Sept 1980, Selina, *née* Mather; 2 da (Sophia, Alice), 1 s (Harry); *Career* Black Watch Br Army 1975–91 (Maj), sales dir then central ops dir Fired Earth plc and Fired Earth Ltd 1991–2003, private sec to HRH The Duke of York 2003–12, dir and conslt 2012–: Alastair Watson Assocs, Orlop Assocs; dir D Gp 2013–; memb Bd Arab Br C of C 2014–; *Recreations* country pursuits, choral music, First World War battlefields; *Clubs* Pitt, Vincent's (Oxford), Farmers; *Style*— Alastair Watson, Esq, LVO; ✉ Grove Farm House, Cold Aston, Cheltenham, Gloucestershire GL54 3BJ (e-mail aalwatson@hotmail.com)

WATSON, Prof (George) Alistair; s of George Arthur Watson (d 1972), and Grace Ann, *née* MacDonald (d 2006); *b* 30 September 1942, Aberfeldy, Perth and Kinross; *Educ* Breadalbane Acad, Univ of Edinburgh (BSc, MSc), Australian Nat Univ (PhD); *m* 6 April 1971, (Margaret) Hilary, da of Robert Whitton Mackay (d 1971); 1 da (Kirsty b 1989); *Career* Univ of Dundee: lectr 1970–82, sr lectr 1982–84, reader 1984–88, prof 1988–2007, head Dept of Mathematics and Computer Sci 1992–97, head Dept of Mathematics 1997–98 and 2004–06, prof emeritus 2008–; FIMA 1972; FRSE 1996; *Books* Computational Methods for Matrix Eigenproblems (with A R Gourlay, 1973), Approximation Theory and Numerical Methods (1980); *Recreations* opera, photography, gardening; *Style*— Prof Alistair Watson, FRSE; ✉ Westercraig, 8 Dundee Road, Broughty Ferry, Dundee DD5 1LY (☎ 01382 730204, e-mail craigievar@btinternet.com); Division of Mathematics, University of Dundee, Dundee DD1 4HN (☎ 01382 344472, e-mail gawatson@maths.dundee.ac.uk)

WATSON, Dr (Nicholas) Andrew; s of Phillip Charles Watson, of Brundall, Norfolk, and Venetia Madeline Le Poer, *née* Wyon; *b* 25 August 1952; *Educ* Boston GS, Univ of Nottingham Med Sch (BMedSci, MB BS, DCH); *m* 18 Nov 1977, Elaine Alma, da of late Jack Attack; 1 da (Helen Ruth b 5 Jan 1983), 1 s (Edward Phillip b 29 Oct 1984); *Career* jr house offr Derby Royal Infirmary and Nottingham City Hosp 1975–76; SHO in Depts of: Geriatric Med City Hosp 1976–77, Med City Hosp 1977, Traumatology Queens Med Centre 1978, Paediatrics Queen's Med Centre 1978–79; postgrad traineeship in gen practice Nottingham 1977–78 and 1979, princ in gen practice Keyworth 1979–82, specialist in orthopaedic med 1982–; lectr in USA and UK with Soc of Orthopaedic Med 1982–; author of numerous published papers letters and articles on orthopaedic med; pres Soc of Orthopaedic Med 1992–2001 (elected to Cncl 1982, chm 1988–92); MRCGP 1979, fell Soc of Orthopaedic Med 1982 (memb 1981); *Recreations* music (has played piano, viola, mandolin and crumhorn), plays jazz guitar in a jazz band; *Style*— Dr Andrew Watson; ✉ 10 Golf Course Road, Stanton on the Wolds, Nottinghamshire NG12 5BH (☎ 0115 937 3603)

WATSON, Prof Andrew James; s of Leslie John Watson (d 1996), of Steyning, W Sussex, and Ena Florence, *née* Bence (d 2000); *b* 30 November 1952, Worthing, W Sussex; *Educ* Steyning GS, Imperial Coll London (BSc), Univ of Reading (PhD); *m* 1978, Jacqueline Elizabeth, *née* Pughe; 2 s (Adam Richard b 1982, James Geraint Robert b 1985); *Career* research scientist: Dept of Atmosphere, Ocean and Space Sciences Univ of Michigan 1978–81, Marine Biological Assoc 1981–88, Plymouth Marine Lab 1989–95; prof of environmental science UEA 1996–; author of numerous papers and articles in scientific jls; memb Challenger Soc for Marine Science 1994; Nansen medallist European Geosciences Union 2004; FRS 2003; *Style*— Prof Andrew Watson; ✉ School of Environmental Sciences, University of East Anglia, Norwich NR4 7TJ (☎ 01603 592560, e-mail a.watson@uea.ac.uk)

WATSON, Andrew Stewart; s of Leslie Donald Watson, of Malvern, Worcs, and Joan Beatrice, *née* Everton; *b* 29 March 1950; *Educ* King's Sch Worcester, St John's Coll Oxford; *m* 11 Dec 1976, Lea Karin, da of Eino Arvid Nordberg (d 1963); *Career* admitted slr 1975; Thomson Snell and Passmore: articled clerk 1973, ptnr 1981, head Litigation Dept 1986; memb Law Soc (memb specialist clinic negligence panel); *Recreations* running, reading, music, cooking; *Style*— Andrew Watson, Esq; ✉ 3 Lonsdale Gardens, Tunbridge Wells, Kent TN1 1NX (☎ 01892 510000, fax 01892 549884)

WATSON, Dr Anthony; CBE (2009); s of Lt Cdr Andrew Patrick Watson, RNR, and Harriet, *née* Hewardine (d 1981); *b* 2 April 1945; *Educ* Campbell Coll Belfast, Queen's Univ Belfast (BSc); *m* 29 July 1972, Heather Jane, da of Lt Cdr Wilfred Norman Dye, RNR (d 1988); 2 s (Edward b 1975, Tom b 1976), 1 da (Tilly b 1980); *Career* called to the Bar Lincoln's Inn 1976 (bencher 2002); dir: Touche Remnant & Co 1978–85, Touche Remnant Hldgs 1978–85; chief investment offr Citibank NA 1985–90, chm Citifunds Ltd 1985–90, chm Citicare Ltd 1985–90; AMP Asset Management plc: dir int investment 1991–95, md 1996–98; Hermes Pensions Mgmnt: chief investment offr 1998–2001, chief exec 2002–06; chm: Asian Infrastructure Fund Ltd 1999–2010 (dir 1994–), MEPC Ltd 2004–06 (dir 2000–06), Marks & Spencer Pension Tst 2006–11; dir: Cathay Holdings Ltd 1992–96, Virgin Direct Financial Services Ltd 1996–98, Innisfree plc 1997–98, Edinburgh Fund Managers plc 2001–02, Botts & Co Holding Ltd 2001–03, Securities Inst 2001–06, Investment Mgmnt Assoc Ltd 2002–05, Hermes Equity Ownership Services Ltd 2005–07, Vodafone Gp plc 2006–, Witan Investment Trust plc 2006– (sr ind dir 2009–), Hammerson Gp plc 2006– (sr ind dir 2009–), Lloyds Banking Gp plc 2009– (sr ind dir 2012–); chm Strategic Investment Bd for NI 2003–09; memb: Fin Reporting Cncl 2004–07, Advsy Cncl Norges Bank Investment Mgmnt 2007–, Bd Shareholder Exec 2008–14, Advsy Cncl Assoc of Corporate Treasurers 2008–; dir Fndn Bd Queen's Univ Belfast 2002–14; played for London Irish RFC first XV 1967–68; Freeman City of London 2008, Liveryman Leathersellers' Co 2008 (Master 2014/15); Hon DSc (Econ) Queen's Univ Belfast 2012; ASIP 1971, Hon FCSI 2006; *Recreations* golf, skiing, rugby, reading; *Clubs* RAC, MCC, Royal St Davids Golf; *Style*— Dr Anthony Watson, CBE

WATSON, Anthony Gerard (Tony); s of George Maurice Watson, JP, of Market Deeping, Lincs, and Anne, *née* McDonnell; *b* 28 May 1955; *Educ* St John Fisher Peterborough, North Staffs Poly (BA); *m* 1, 17 Sept 1982, Susan Ann, da of Malcolm Gutteridge, of Stockton on Tees; 2 s (Samuel John b 3 Sept 1983, Tom b 10 Jan 1985), 1 da (Emily Anne b 7 Feb 1987); m 2, 1994, Sylvie Helen, *née* Pask; 1 s (Daniel James b 6 Sept 1993), 1 da (Sabrina Helen b 23 April 1997); *Career* reporter Stamford Mercury 1978–79, news ed Evening Despatch Darlington 1983–84 (reporter 1979–81), reporter Yorkshire Post 1984–86, researcher World in Action Granada TV 1986–88, ed Yorkshire Post 1989–2003 (dep ed 1988–89); Press Assoc: head of business devpt 2003–04, editorial dir 2004–07, ed-in-chief and dir 2007–, md 2008–; awarded Br Press Awards 1986 and 1987, YTV Journalist of the Year 1986; memb Bd Soc of Eds; *Style*— Tony Watson, Esq

WATSON, Antony Edward Douglas; QC (1986); s of William Edward Watson, of Hanchurch, Staffs, and Margaret Douglas; *b* 6 March 1945; *Educ* Sedbergh, Sidney Sussex Coll Cambridge (MA); *m* 15 Sept 1972, Gillian Mary, da of Alfred John Bevan-Arthur, of Bramishall, Staffs; 2 da (Edwina b 1978, Willa b 1981); *Career* called to the Bar Inner Temple 1968; specialising in Intellectual Property Law; head of chambers 2004–; dep chm Copy Right Tbnl 1994–98; *Recreations* country pursuits, wine, opera; *Style*— Antony Watson, Esq, QC; ✉ 3 New Square, Lincoln's Inn, London WC2A 3RS (☎ 020 7405 1111)

WATSON, Arthur James; s of David Lyall Watson, of Aberdeen, and Nance Harding, *née* Nicol; *b* 24 June 1951; *Educ* Aberdeen GS, Grays Sch of Art Aberdeen (Dip Art); *m* 1, 1972 (m dis 1980), Jennifer Moncrieff Sutherland; m 2, 1981 (m dis 1989), Joyce Winifred Cairns; *Career* sculptor and artist; fndr and dir Peacock Printmakers 1974–95; Duncan of Jordanstone Coll of Art & Design (DJCAD): visting lectr 1988–95, course dir MFA 1995–, head Graduate Studies in Fine Art 2000–03; tstee RSA Fndn 2012–; maj works incl: sculptures Sea Sign, Northern Light at Peterhead Power Station Boddam 1986, Across The Sea at the Venice Biennale 1990, A New Light Univ of Aberdeen 1991; recordings incl: Beware of the Aberdonian (1976), The Fighting Scot (1991); PRSA 2012–; *Style*— Arthur Watson, Esq, PRSA, HRA, HRHA; ✉ Sculpture Corridor, Level 5, Matthew Building, DJCAD, 13 Perth Road, Dundee DD1 4HT

WATSON, Charles Basil Lucas; s of Capt Basil Watson, RN, of Hampshire, and Heather, *née* McMullen; *Educ* Sherborne, KCL (BA); *m* Fiona, da of Alan Mitchell; 1 s (Jack b 4 June 1992), 1 da (Rosie b 4 Feb 1996); *Career* communications conslt Good Relations Group 1983–87, investor rels conslt Valin Pollen Group 1987–89, transatlantic sailing expdn to Orinoco Delta (on sabbatical) 1989–90 (Royal Cruising Club Exploration Award), chief exec Financial Dynamics 2001–10 (global chm 2011–), led MBO of Fin Dynamics Int 2003, led process resulting in acquisition of FD by FTI Consulting 2006 (left 2010); chm Karma Communications Gp 2011–14, currently chm Teneo Int;, govr Bedales Sch, tstee Haller Fndn; *Recreations* skiing, fishing, sailing, modern history, ski mountaineering; *Clubs* Royal Cruising; *Style*— Charles Watson, Esq; ✉ Teneo International, 20 Balderton Street, 3rd Floor, London W1K 6TL

WATSON, Christopher Ian (Chris); s of Philip James Watson, of Weybridge, Surrey, and Freda Ethel, *née* Duerre; *b* 2 May 1957, Swansea; *Educ* Marlborough (scholar), New Coll Oxford (MA); *m* 1, 1984; 1 da (Emma Charlotte Duerre b 15 May 1990), 1 s (Alexander Sebastien Luesby b 1 Dec 1992); m 2, 11 Dec 1999, Elizabeth Ann, *née* Green; 1 s (Toby Philip Lowell b 25 Jan 2003), 2 da (Nina Islay Emily, Lucy Eireann Ruth b 10 Sept 2004); *Career* admitted slr Eng and Wales 1981, avocat Paris Bar 1993; ptnr: Simmons and Simmons 1988–99 (trainee slr 1981–83, asst slr 1983–88), Allen and Overy LLP 2000–05, Dechert LLP 2006–08, CMS Cameron McKenna LLP 2008–; chm Communications Law Ctee Int Bar Assoc 2011 and 2012, memb Cncl Int Bar Assoc 2014–; memb Law Soc 1983; Royal Pilier La Confrérie des Piliers Chablisiens; *Recreations* flyfishing, cricket, books, wine, music; *Clubs* Lowtonian Soc, Order of the Knights of the Round Table, Flyfishers, MCC, Brooks's; *Style*— Chris Watson, Esq; ✉ CMS-CMCK, 160 Aldersgate Street, London EC1A 4DD (☎ 020 7367 3701, fax 020 7367 2000, e-mail chris.watson@cms-cmck.com)

WATSON, Christopher John; s of Allan John Watson (d 1965), of Uxbridge, and Dorothy C, *née* Perry (d 2005); *b* 21 June 1940; *Educ* Leighton Park Sch Reading, Univ of Bristol (BA); *m* 20 July 1963, Mary, da of Andrew Warden Vincent (d 1986), of Hereford; 1 da (Clare b 1967), 2 s (Angus b 1969, Peter b 1972); *Career* KCL 1962–63, Northumberland CC 1963–65, Univ of Sussex 1966–68, res offr Scottish Devpt Dept 1968–72; Centre for Urban and Regional Studies Univ of Birmingham: res fell 1972–79, lectr 1979–83, sr lectr 1983–2002, dir of int affrs 1984–94, head of dept 1988–93, hon sr lectr 2002–; dir The Japan Centre Univ of Birmingham 1994–2002; regnl co-ordinator (Midlands) Japan 2001, project dir (W Midlands) W Midlands-Shizuoka Prefecture Link 2003–10; memb Bd of Mgmnt Mercian Housing Assoc Ltd 1984–2006 (chm 1999–2005), memb Bd FRC Gp 2002–, co sec Housing Vision 2007–; *Publications* Housing in Clydeside 1970 (with J B Cullingworth, 1971), Housing Policy and the Housing System (with Alan Murie and Pat Niner, 1975), Housing and the New Welfare State: Perspectives from East Asia and Europe (with Richard Groves and Alan Murie, 2007), Renewing Europe's Housing (with Richard Turkington, 2015), contrib to various books and jls; *Recreations* music, travel; *Style*— Christopher Watson, Esq; ✉ Housing and Communities Research School of Social Policy, University of Birmingham, Birmingham B15 2TT

WATSON, His Hon Judge (Anthony) Dennis; QC (2009); *Career* called to the Bar 1985; recorder 2002, circuit judge (Northern Circuit) 2012–; *Style*— His Hon Judge Dennis Watson, QC; ✉ Liverpool Crown Court, The Queen Elizabeth II Law Courts, Derby Square, Liverpool L2 1XA

WATSON, Prof Elaine Denise; da of Alexander Watson (d 1987), and Isabella, *née* Petticrew (d 2016); *b* 8 September 1955, Ayrshire; *Educ* Univ of Glasgow (BVMS, MVM), Univ of Bristol (PhD), Univ of Edinburgh (DSc), European Coll of Animal Reproduction (Dip); *m* 9 Sept 1989, Christopher Clarke; 1 s (Marcus b 13 Sept 1996); *Career* res offr MAFF Cattle Breeding Centre Sheffield 1979–82, vet res offr ARC Inst for Res on Animal Disease 1982–84, res assoc Univ of Bristol Sch of Veterinary Science 1984–87, asst prof of equine reproduction Univ of Pennsylvania 1987–91; Royal (Dick) Sch of Veterinary Studies: sr lectr 1991–95, reader 1995–99, prof of veterinary reproduction 1999–2012, dean 2003–11; dean Ross Univ Sch of Veterinary Medicine 2012–15; hon prof Univ of Edinburgh 2012–; pres European Coll of Animal Reproduction; memb: Scientific Advsy Ctee, Scot Agricultural Coll, Cncl RCVS, Leadership Cncl DeVry Educn Gp 2013–15; Richard Hartley Clinical Prize Equine Veterinary Jl 1988; FRCVS 1990; *Books* Equine Medicine, Surgery and Reproduction (jtly, 1997); contrib: The Equine Manual (1995), Diagnostic Techniques in Equine Medicine (1997), Self Assessment Colour Review of Equine Internal Medicine (1997), Equine Practice 3 (1998); *Recreations* cycling, walking, horse riding, travel, theatre, films; *Clubs* Caledonian, Farmers; *Style*— Prof Elaine Watson; ✉ e-mail elaine.watson111@btinternet.com

WATSON, Emily Margaret; OBE (2015); *b* 14 January 1967, Islington; *Educ* Univ of Bristol (BA); *m* 1995, Jack Waters; 1 da (Juliet b 2005), 1 s (Dylan b 2008); *Career* actress; hon MA Univ of Bristol 2003; *Theatre* incl: various work with RSC 1993, The Children's Hour (RNT) 1994, Uncle Vanya/Twelfth Night (Brooklyn Acad of Music) 2003 and (Donmar Warehouse) 2004; *Television* incl: A Summer Day's Dream 1994, The Mill on the Floss 1997, The Memory Keeper's Daughter 2008, Appropriate Adult 2011 (Best Actor (Female) RTS Award 2012, Best Actress BAFTA 2012), The Politician's Husband 2013, Song for Jenny 2015, Marilyn 2015, The Dresser 2015, Apple Tree Yard (BBC) 2015; *Film* incl: Breaking the Waves 1996 (nomination Acad Award 1996, nomination Golden Globe Award 1996, nomination BAFTA 1996, Best Actress Bodil Award 1996, European Film Award 1996, Evening Standard Br Film Award 1996, Ft Lauderdale Int Film Festival Award 1996, Best Newcomer Irish Film & TV Awards 1996, New Generation Award LA Film Critics Assoc Award 1996, Nat Soc of Film Critics Award USA 1996, NY Film Critics Circle Award 1996), Metroland 1997, The Boxer 1997, Hilary and Jackie 1998 (nomination Acad Award 1998, nomination BAFTA 1998, nomination Golden Globe 1998, nomination Screen Actors Guild Award 1998), Cradle Will Rock 1999, Angela's Ashes 1999 (nomination BAFTA 1999, Irish Film & TV Award 1999), Trixie 2000, The Luzhin Defence 2000 (Br Ind Film Award 2000), Gosford Park 2001, Punch-Drunk Love 2002 (Best Female Supporting Performance Toronto Film Critics Assoc Award 2002), Red Dragon 2002 (Best Supporting Actress Irish Film & TV Award 2002), Equilibrium 2002, The Life and Death of Peter Sellers 2004 (nomination Golden Globe 2004), The Proposition 2005, Wah-Wah 2005, Corpse Bride 2005 (voice), Separate Lies 2005, Miss Potter 2006, The Water Horse 2007, Fireflies in the Garden 2008,

Synecdoche, New York 2008, Cold Souls 2009, Within The Whirlwind 2009, Cemetery Junction 2010, Oranges and Sunshine 2010, War Horse 2011, Anna Karenina 2012, Some Girl(s) 2013, Molly Moon 2013, Belle 2013, The Book Thief 2013, Little Boy 2014, Theory of Everything 2014, Everest 2014, Girls' Night Out 2014, Testament of Youth 2015; *Style*— Ms Emily Watson, OBE; ✉ c/o Independent Talent Group, 40 Whitfield Street, London W1T 2RH

WATSON, Graham Forgie; s of George William Forgie Watson (d 1982), and Margaret Kinlay, *née* Hogg (d 1983); *b* 14 January 1958; *Educ* George Heriot's Sch Edinburgh, Univ of Edinburgh (LLB); *m* 3 May 1983, (Elspeth) Margaret, da of Alexander Brewster (d 1983); 2 da (Rebecca b 1989, Sally b 1991); *Career* CA 1982; KPMG 1979–83, dir Noble Grossart Ltd 1984–91, md The Carnegie Partnership Ltd 1991–93, ptnr Deloitte & Touche 1994–2003, md MacFarlane Gray Corp Finance 2004–07, dir Winning Scotland Fndn 2005–09; dir N Lanarkshire Leisure Tst 2006–16, dir Positive Leadership Ltd 2009–; chm Scottish Health Innovations Ltd 2015–; memb Cncl Law Soc of Scotland 2014–; memb Ct Heriot-Watt Univ 2015–; FRSA; *Recreations* golf, squash, skiing; *Clubs* New (Edinburgh), Golf House Club Elie, St Andrews Golf; *Style*— Graham F Watson, Esq; ✉ Positive Leadership Limited, 2 Glencairn Crescent, Edinburgh EH12 5BS (☎ 07774 883103, website www.positiveleadership.co.uk, Twitter @posleadership)

WATSON, Sir Graham Robert; kt (2011); s of Gordon Graham Watson (d 1991), and Stephanie, *née* Revill-Johnson (d 2008); *b* 23 March 1956; *Educ* City of Bath Boys' Sch, Heriot-Watt Univ (BA); *m* 5 Sept 1987, Dr Rita Giannini, da of Dr Mario Giannini; 1 da (Frederica b 26 Jan 1992), 1 s (Gregory b 27 April 1995); *Career* freelance interpreter and translator 1979–80, administrator Paisley Coll of Technology (now Paisley Univ) 1980–83, head private office ldr Lib Pty (Rt Hon David Steel, MP (now Lord Steel of Aikwood)) 1983–87, sr press offr TSB Gp plc 1987–88; HSBC Holdings plc: sr public affairs mangr 1993–94 (public affairs mangr 1988–93, seconded to EBRD 1991); MEP: Somerset and N Devon 1994–99, SW England 1999–2014; currently md Bagehot Ltd; ldr Euro Lib Dem MEPs 2002–09, ldr Alliance of Liberals and Democrats for Europe Pty 2011–15; fndr memb Euro Community's Youth Forum 1980, gen sec Int Fedn of Liberal and Radical Youth 1979–81 (vice-pres 1977–79), memb Governing Bd Euro Youth Centre 1980–82, chm Euro Parl Ctee on Justice and Home Affairs 1999–2001, ldr UK Lib Dem Pty Euro Parl 1999–2001; MIL, MIPR; *Books* The Liberals in the North-South Dialogue (ed, 1980), To the Power of Ten (ed, 2000), Liberalism and Globalisation (ed, 2001), Liberal Language (2003), EU've Got Mail (2004), Liberal Democracy and Globalisation (2006), Liberalism: Something to shout about (2006), The Power of Speech (2006), Building a Liberal Europe (2010), Letters from Europe (2012), Continental Drift (2014); *Recreations* sailing, choir singing, writing; *Clubs* Cercle Royal Gaulois; *Style*— Sir Graham Watson; ✉ Bagehot's Foundry, Beard's Yard, Langport, Somerset TA10 9PS (website www.grahamwatson.eu, Twitter @sirgrahamwatson)

WATSON, Her Hon Judge Hilary Jane; *Career* circuit judge (Midland Circuit) 2008–; *Style*— Her Hon Judge Hilary Watson; ✉ c/o Midland Circuit Office, Priory Courts, 33 Bull Street, Birmingham B4 6DW

WATSON, Ian; *b* 20 April 1943, St Albans; *Educ* Tynemouth Sch, Balliol Coll Oxford (scholar, BA); *m* 1 Sept 1962, Judith, *née* Jackson (d 2001); 1 da (Jessica b 1973); m 2, 17 Jan 2013, Cristina Macia; *Career* author; Eng and French lit res Oxford 1963–65 (res degree 1965), lectr in lit UC Dar es Salaam Tanzania 1965–67, lectr in Eng lit Tokyo Univ of Educn 1967–70 (pt/t Keio Univ Tokyo and Japan Women's Univ), lectr then sr lectr in complementary studies Sch of History of Art Birmingham Poly and course teacher in sci fiction and futures studies 1970–76; memb Cncl Sci Fiction Fndn London 1974–91; features ed Foundation – The Review of Science Fiction 1974–91 (reg contrib sci fiction criticism), Euro ed SFWA Bulletin 1983–; memb Towcester and Dist Lab Pty 1980–, CND 1980–; CC candidate (Lab): Helmdon Div Northamptonshire 1981, Towcester Div Northamptonshire 1984, Middleton Cheney Div Northamptonshire 1989; *Books* incl: Japan – A Cat's Eye View (1969), The Embedding (1973, Prix Apollo 1975, Premios Zikkurath for best foreign novel in Spanish trans 1978), The Jonah Kit (1975, Br Sci Fiction Orbit award 1976, Br Sci Fiction Assoc award 1977), The Martian Inca (1977), Japan Tomorrow (1977), Alien Embassy (1977), Miracle Visitors (1978), The Very Slow Time Machine – Science Fiction Stories (1979, finalist World Sci Fiction Achievement (Hugo) award), God's World (1979), The Gardens of Delight (1980), Under Heaven's Bridge (with Michael Bishop, 1981), Deathhunter – Pictures at an Exhibition (ed, 1981), Sunstroke and Other Stories (1982), Chekhov's Journey (1983), Changes (ed, 1983), The Book of the River (1984), Converts (1984), The Book of the Stars (1984), The Book of Being (1985), The Book of Ian Watson (1985), Slow Birds and Other Stories (1985), Afterlives (ed, 1986), Queenmagic Kingmagic (1986), Evil Water and Other Stories (1987), The Power (1987), The Fire Worm (1988), Whores of Babylon (1988), Meat (1988), Salvage Rites and Other Stories (1989), The Flies of Memory (1990), Inquisitor (1990), Stalin's Teardrops (1991), Space Marine (1993), Lucky's Harvest: the first book of Mana (1993), The Coming of Vertumnus and other stories (1994), The Fallen Moon: the second book of Mana (1994), Harlequin (1994), Chaos Child (1995), Hard Questions (1996), Oracle (1997), The Lexicographer's Love Song (2001), The Great Escape (2002), Mockymen (2003), The Butterflies of Memory (2006), The Beloved of My Beloved (with Roberto Quaglia, 2009), Orgasmachine (2010), Saving for a Sunny Day (2012), The Waters of Destiny (with Andy West, 2012), The Best of Ian Watson (2013), The Uncollected Ian Watson (2013); screen credit for screen story for Steven Spielberg's AI Artificial Intelligence 2001; *Style*— Mr Ian Watson; ✉ Avda de la Constitución 15, 4 Derecha, 33208 Gijón, Spain (e-mail jonahkit@gmail.com, website www.ianwatson.info)

WATSON, Jenny; *Career* former dir Global Ptnrs and Assocs; chair Equal Opportunities Cmmn 2005–07 (cmmr 1999–2007, dep chair 2000–05), chair Electoral Cmmn 2009–; chair Ind Complaints Panel Portman Gp 2013–; former dep chair: Ctee on Radioactive Waste Mgmnt, Banking Code Standards Bd; tstee Money Advice Tst 2008–; *Style*— Ms Jenny Watson

WATSON, John Grenville Bernard; OBE (1998); s of Norman Victor Watson (d 1969), of Leeds, and Ruby Ernestine, *née* Hawker (d 1962); *b* 21 February 1943; *Educ* Bootham Sch York, Coll of Law; *m* 12 June 1965, Deanna, da of Jack Wood (d 1970), of Sheffield; 1 s (Alexander b 1973), 2 da (Melinda b 1975, Sophie b 1975); *Career* asst slr Hepworth & Chadwick 1967–69, mgmnt trainee John Waddingtons Ltd 1969–73, md Waddingtons Games Ltd 1976–79 (mktg dir 1973–76), dir Main Bd John Waddingtons plc 1979–89; MP (Cons): Skipton 1979–83, Skipton and Ripon 1983–87; PPS 1981–86; dir Goddard Kay Rogers (Northern) Ltd 1989–93; memb Leeds Devpt Corp 1988–93, chief exec Bradford City Challenge Ltd 1992–97, chm Heritage Lottery Fund for Yorkshire 2005–12, chm Partnership Investment Finance Ltd, chm Nymet Ltd 2015–; non-exec dir Yorkshire Building Society 1995–2004; chm Bradford Community NHS Tst 1996–2002; memb N Yorks CC 2005–13 (dep ldr 2009–); nat chm Young Cons 1970–72, chm Cons Candidates Assoc 1975–79, pres Br Youth Cncl 1979–83, Freeman City of London, memb Ct of Assts Worshipful Co of the Makers of Playing Cards; memb Law Soc; *Books* Home from Home (1973), Changing Gear (contrib, 1982), View From The Terrace (contrib, 1986); *Recreations* walking, bungee jumping, travel; *Style*— John Watson, Esq, OBE; ✉ Evergreen Cottage, Main Street, Kirk Deighton, Wetherby LS22 4DZ (☎ 01937 588273, e-mail johnwatson@bigfastweb.net)

WATSON, (Joseph) John Henderson; s of Charles Henderson Watson, and Elsie Mary Watson; *Educ* Univ of Leeds; *Career* project engr ICI 1962–67, prodn and tech mangr DIO Factory 1967–72, personnel and industrial rels mangr Boots Gp 1972–85, personnel dir Boots Pharmaceuticals 1985–91, md Boots Contract Manufacturing 1991–2001, gp bd dir Boots Co plc 1996–2001; chm: Boots Pensions Ltd, Boots Charitable Tst; currently chm Nottingham Development Enterprise; govr Nottingham Trent Univ; FIMechE, FIPD; *Recreations* bridge, golf, political issues; *Style*— John Watson, Esq

WATSON, John Michael (Mike); s of (George) Ian Watson, and Caroline Murray, *née* Gilchrist; *Educ* Clifton, CCC Cambridge; *m* 1997, Liz, *née* Andrews; 3 c from previous m; *Career* various roles rising to tech dir Europe Honeywell Inc 1968–82, dir mktg and tech strategy ICL plc 1982–88, md BICC Technologies Ltd (part of BICC Gp plc) 1988–91, non-exec chm Signal Processors Ltd 1992–94, non-exec dir OSI Gp plc 1992–95, dir business devpt OASiS Gp plc 1992–94, exec dir mktg and sales AEA Technology plc 1994–98, chief exec Tertio Ltd 1998–99, chm NWP Communications Ltd 2001–04, regnl chm Vistage Int Ltd 2002–09, chm FWL Technologies Ltd 2002–04; non-exec dir: Spectrum Interactive plc 2005–09, Zamano plc 2006–12, chm Wychwood Wild Garden 2009–; lead lecturer IEE Faraday Lecture 1986–87, presented BCS-sponsored lecture RSA 1990; Liveryman Worshipful Co of Information Technologists; memb Br Computer Soc; FRSA, FIEE, FREng (past memb Cncl); *Recreations* skiing, golf, gardening, theatre; *Style*— Mike Watson, Esq; ✉ Bank House, High Street, Shipton-under-Wychwood, Oxfordshire OX7 6BA (☎ 07860 681843, e-mail jmichaelwatson@compuserve.com)

WATSON, Joyce; AM; da of William Roberts, and Jean, *née* Rennie; *b* 2 May 1955, Lanarkshire; *Educ* Cardigan Comp, Pembrokeshire Coll, Univ of Wales Swansea (BSc); *m* 1986, Colin Watson; 2 da (Heather (Mrs Snow) b 1972, Fiona (Mrs Openshaw) b 1974), 1 s (William b 1986); *Career* self employed retail and hospitality trade 1980–2002, mangr Women's Voice 2002–07; AM (Lab) Mid and West Wales 2007–; memb: Finance Ctee, Communities and Culture Ctee, Equality Ctee, Subordinate Legislation Ctee; vice-chair Looked After Children Working Gp, chair Domiciliary Care LCO Ctee, chair Cross Pty Gp on Trafficking of Women and Children; former cncllr Pembrokeshire Cncl (ldr opposition 1999–2005); memb: Unite, Bevan Fndn, Fawcett Soc; chair Garth Youth Project, former memb Bd MEWN (Minority Ethnic Women's Network) Cymru, former memb Ct of Govrs Univ of Wales, fndr memb Wales Gender Budget Gp, former memb Dyfed Powys Police Authy; *Publications* Not Bad for a Woman (2002); *Recreations* coastal path walking with dog, reading, bird watching, family meals; *Clubs* Soroptimists; *Style*— Mrs Joyce Watson, AM; ✉ National Assembly for Wales, Cardiff Bay, Cardiff CF99 0NA (☎ 029 20 898972, fax 029 20 898419, e-mail joyce.watson@wales.gov.uk)

WATSON, Mark Andrew; *b* 13 February 1980, Bristol; *Educ* Bristol GS, Queen's Coll Cambridge; *m* Emily Watson-Howes; 1 c; *Career* comedian; stand-up incl: Mark Watson's Overambitious 24-Hour Show 2004, 50 Years Before Death And The Awful Prospect Of Eternity 2005, 2005 Years in 2005 Minutes 2005, I'm Worried That I'm Starting To Hate Almost Everyone In The World 2006, Mark Watson's Seemingly Impossible 36-Hour Circuit Of The World 2006, Can I Briefly Talk To You About The Point Of Life? 2007, All The Thoughts I've Had Since I Was Born 2008, Mark Watson's Earth Summit 2011, The Mark Watson Edit 2011; television appearances incl: host We Need Answers (BBC 4) 2009, host Mark Watson Kicks Off (ITV 4) 2010, team capt The Mad Bad Ad Show (Channel 4) 2012, Mock the Week, guest host Never Mind the Buzzcocks 2009, Have I Got News For You, Would I Lie To You?, Argumental, Michael McIntyre's Comedy Roadshow, Live at the Apollo, Dave's One Night Stand; *Books* Bullet Points (2004), A Light-Hearted Look At Murder (2007), Crap at the Environment (2008), Eleven (2010); Bullet Points (2004), A Light-Hearted Look At Murder (2007), Crap at the Environment (2008), Eleven (2010); *DVD* Mark Watson Live (2011); *Style*— Mr Mark Watson

WATSON, Dr Michael Leonard; OBE (2012); s of Col Edgar Stewart Watson, OBE, of Bridlington and Dorothy, *née* Mansfield; *b* 29 March 1949, Bridlington, Yorks; *Educ* Merchiston Castle Sch Edinburgh, Univ of Edinburgh (BSc, MB ChB, MD); *m* 1, 27 March 1971, Penelope Ann, da of William H A Bartlett, of Elvanfoot; 1 da (Fiona Jane b 15 Oct 1976), 1 s (James Stuart Michael b 31 Jan 1979); m 2, 6 Sept 1992, Marion, da of R T Emond, of London; 2 da (Harriet Lucy b 8 Dec 1996, Gemma Gertrude b 21 Dec 1998); *Career* travelling fell MRC 1981–82, conslt physician Royal Infirmary Edinburgh 1984–2009, head of Med Services Royal Infirmary Edinburgh 1996–2001; med dir NHS Educn Scotland 2005–12, ret from NHS 2012; FRCPEd 1986; *Recreations* mountaineering, sailing; *Clubs* Scottish Mountaineering; *Style*— Dr Michael L Watson, OBE; ✉ 44 Ann Street, Edinburgh EH4 1PJ (☎ 0131 332 2205)

WATSON, Mike; *see:* Rt Hon Lord Watson of Invergowrie

WATSON, Peter Frank Patrick; s of Frank Patrick Watson (d 1963), of Birmingham, and Lilian Ethel, *née* Hopwood (d 1993); *b* 23 April 1943; *Educ* Cheltenham GS, Univ of Durham (Psychology prize), Univ of London, Univ of Rome; *m* 1 (m dis), Nichola Theodas; m 2 (m dis), Lesley Rowlatt; *Career* intern Tavistock Clinic 1966–68; dep ed New Society 1968–71, Sunday Times 1971–81, The Times 1981–83, The Observer 1985–2001, Sunday Times 2001–07; research assoc McDonald Inst for Archaeological Research Univ of Cambridge 1997–2007; regular contrib New York Times; Italian Govt music scholarship 1964, US Govt bursary 1970, Crime Writers of Britain Gold Dagger 1982, SAFE Beacon Award 2006; memb: PEN 1988, Br Psychological Soc; *Books* War on the Mind: the Military Uses and Abuses of Psychology (1973), Twins (1980), The Caravaggio Conspiracy (1982), Wisdom & Strength: the Biography of a Renaissance Masterpiece (1990), From Manet to Manhattan: the Rise of the Modern Art Market (1992), Nureyev: a Biography (1994), The Death of Hitler (with Ada Petrova, 1995), Sotheby's: Inside Story (1997), A Terrible Beauty: the People and Ideas that Shaped the Modern Mind (2000), Ideas: A History from Fire to Freud (2005), The Medici Conspiracy: Organized Crime, Looted Antiquities, Rogue Museums (with Cecilia Todeschini, 2006), The German Genius: Europe and Third Renaissance, the Second Scientific Revolution and the Twentieth Century (2009), The Great Divide: Nature and Human Nature in the Old World and the New (2012), The Age of Nothing (UK, The Age of Atheists US, 2014), Convergence: The Deepest Idea in the Universe (2016); author of 9 novels, 2 under the pen name of Mackenzie Ford; books translated into 25 languages; *Recreations* opera, cricket, fishing; *Clubs* Garrick; *Style*— Peter Watson, Esq

WATSON, Prof (John) Richard; s of Reginald Joseph Watson, and Alice Mabel, *née* Tennant; *b* 15 June 1934; *Educ* Magdalen Coll Oxford (MA, Matthew Arnold Meml Prize), Univ of Glasgow (PhD); *m* 21 July 1962, Pauline Elizabeth, *née* Roberts; 1 s (David James b 1966), 2 da (Elizabeth Emma b 1968, Rachel Clare b 1971); *Career* 2 Lt RA 1953–55; lectr: Univ of Glasgow 1962–66, Univ of Leicester 1966–78; Univ of Durham: prof of English 1978–99, public orator 1989–99, emeritus prof 1999–; select preacher Univ of Cambridge 2010; gen ed Dictionary of Hymnology Research Project 2001– (co-ed 2012, published online since 2013 at www.hymnology.co.uk); memb Archbishops' Cmmn on Church Music 1988–92, chm Modern Humanities Research Assoc 1990–99; pres Int Assoc of Univ Profs of English 1995–98, pres Charles Lamb Soc 2003–12, vice-pres Charles Wesley Soc 1994–2003; hon fell Harris Manchester Coll Oxford 2010–, fell Royal Sch of Church Music 2014–; *Books* Wordsworth's Vital Soul (1982), Everyman's Book of Victorian Verse (ed, 1982), English Poetry of the Romantic Period 1789–1830 (1985), The Poetry of Gerard Manley Hopkins (1987), Companion to Hymns and Psalms (with K Trickett, 1988), A Handbook to English Romanticism (with J Raimond, 1992), The English Hymn (1997), An Annotated Anthology of Hymns (2002), Romanticism and War (2003), Awake My Soul (2004); articles on Romantic and Victorian literature and Philip Larkin; *Recreations* playing the piano, bookbinding, cycling; *Style*— Prof Richard Watson; ✉ Stoneyhurst, 27 Albert Street, Durham DH1 4RL (☎ 0191 384 5716);

University of Durham, English Department, Hallgarth House, 77 Hallgarth Street, Durham DH1 3AY (e-mail j.r.watson@durham.ac.uk)

WATSON, Prof Sir Robert Tony; kt (2012), CMG; *b* 21 March 1948; *Educ* Beal GS for Boys Ilford, Queen Mary Coll London (BSc, PhD); *Career* postdoctoral research scientist: Univ of Calif Berkeley 1973–74, Univ of Maryland 1974–76; Jet Propulsion Lab Pasadena: sr scientist 1976–78, memb Technical Staff 1978–80, research scientist 1980–87; NASA: branch chief Upper Atmospheric Research and Tropospheric Chemistry Progs Earth Science and Applications Div 1987–90, dir Process Studies Prog Office 1990–93, dir Science Div and chief scientist Office of Mission to Planet Earth 1993; Office of Science and Technol Policy White House: conslt 1993, assoc dir for environment 1993–96; World Bank: sr advsr for environment Environment Div 1996–97, dir Environment Dept 1997–99, chief scientist 2000–07, dir for environmentally and socially sustainable devpt 2000–03, sr advsr for environmentally and socially sustainable devpt 2003–06, sr advsr for sustainable devpt 2006–07; chief scientific advsr Defra 2007–, prof and strategic dir Tyndall Centre Univ of E Anglia 2007–; NASA Exceptional Service Medal 1983, NASA Public Service Gp Achievement Award 1986 and 1989, NASA OSSA Edelson Award 1987, NASA Gp Achievement Award 1989 and 1993, NASA Distinguished Service Medal 1989, American Geophysical Union's Edward A Flinn III Award 1991, NASA Cooperative External Achievement Award 1992, Nat Acad of Sciences Award for Scientific Reviewing 1992, American Meteorological Soc Special Award 1993, Climate Inst Scientific Achievement Award 1993, American Assoc for hte Advancement of Sci Award for Scientific Freedom and Responsibility 1993, US Environmental Protection Agency Award for Scientific Understanding of the Ozone Layer 1994, UNEP Award for Protection of the Ozone Layer 1995, US Environmental Protection Agency Climate Protection Award 2000, Global Green Award for Int Environmental Leadership 2003, UN Environment Prog/World Meteorological Orgn Vienna Convention Award 2005, American Assoc for the Advancement of Sci Int Scientific Cooperation Award 2008, Ashai Glass Fndn Blue Planet Prize 2010; Hon DSc: UMIST 2003, Univ of E Anglia 2003, Cranfield Univ 2009; fell Queen Mary Coll London 2010; FRS 2011; *Publications* 40 refereed jl pubns, 60 refereed nat and int scientific assessments and reviews, 4 key World Bank pubns and 3 book chapters; *Style—* Prof Sir Robert Watson, CMG, FRS; ✉ Defra, Nobel House, 17 Smith Square, London SW1P 3JR (☎ 020 7238 1645, fax 020 7238 1504, e-mail robert.watson@defra.gsi.gov.uk)

WATSON, Rod; *Career* dir of corporate communications Dept for Business, Enterprise and Regulatory Reform; *Style—* Rod Watson, Esq; ✉ Department for Business, Enterprise and Regulatory Reform, 1 Victoria Street, London SW1H 0ET

WATSON, Sheila; da of Ron Watson (d 2000), of Sunderland, and Sheila Watson; *b* 21 December 1965; *Educ* Univ of Oxford (BA), Univ of London (MSc); *m* Andrew Trigg; 3 s (George b 23 June 1998, Tom b 11 Dec 2001, Jack b 17 April 2004); *Career* res offr Inst for Fiscal Studies 1988–90, econ advsr to Rt Hon Margaret Beckett, MP, *qv*, 1990–94, dep dir and conslt economist Centre for Local Econ Strategies 1994–97, special advsr to Pres of the Bd of Trade 1997–2001, special advsr to Leader of the House 1998–2001, special advsr to sec of state for Environment, Food and Rural Affrs 2001–06, latterly sr special advsr to Foreign Sec, currently dir of environment FIA Fndn; *Publications* Economic Policy and the division of income within the family (1990), Modelling the effects of prescription charge rises (in Fiscal Studies, 1990), What should count as public expenditure? (in Public Expenditure, ed D Corry, 1997), The Role of Development Trusts (1997), The consequences of the abolition of the Inner London Education Authority (in Fiscal Studies, 1988); *Style—* Ms Sheila Watson; ✉ FIA Foundation, 60 Trafalgar Square, London WC2N 5DS (☎ 020 7930 3882, e-mail s.watson@fiafoundation.org, website www.fiafoundation.org)

WATSON, Ven Sheila; *b* 1953; *Educ* Edinburgh Theological Coll, CCC Oxford, Univ of St Andrews (MA, MPhil); *Career* ordained: deaconess 1979, deacon 1987, priest 1994; Bridge of Allan St Andrews Diocese 1979–80, Alloa 1979–80, Monkseaton St Mary Newcastle Diocese 1980–84, adult educn offr London Diocese 1984–87, hon curate Chelsea St Luke and Christ Church 1987–96, selection sec ABM 1992–93, sr selection sec ABM 1993–96, advsr on CME Salisbury Diocese 1997–2002, dir Miny 1998–2002, canon and prebendary Salisbury Cathedral 2000–02, archdeacon of Buckingham 2002–07, archdeacon of Canterbury and canon residentiary of Canterbury Cathedral 2007–; *Style—* The Ven the Archdeacon of Canterbury; ✉ 29 The Precincts, Canterbury, Kent CT1 2EP (☎ 01227 865238)

WATSON, Sheila Mary; da of Joseph Herbert Watson, OBE, MC (d 1990), and Evelyn Ada, *née* Patching (d 1993); *b* 8 March 1931; *Educ* The Warren Worthing, King's Coll London, Univ of Bordeaux (BA); *m* 1, 2 Sept 1961 (m dis), Neil Francis Elliot Blackmore, s of late William Blackmore, MD; 2 da (Karen Anne b 30 May 1964, Laura b 10 Sept 1967); m 2, 15 April 1972, David Hugh Arthur Christie-Murray; *Career* dir David Higham Associates (authors' agents) 1955–71, dir and sec Bolt & Watson Ltd 1971–83, currently chair Watson Little Ltd (md 1983–2003); *Recreations* reading, walking; *Style—* Ms Sheila Watson; ✉ 48 Greenhill, Prince Arthur Road, Hampstead, London NW3 5UA (☎ 020 7431 7383); Watson Little Ltd (☎ 020 7388 7529, e-mail sw@watsonlittle.com)

WATSON, Shirley; *née* Johnson; da of Andrew Johnson, of Hexham, Northumberland, and Adella, *née* Cowen; *b* 24 May 1955; *Educ* Queen Elizabeth GS, Univ of Bradford (BSc); *m* 22 Sept 1979, David Alan Watson, s of Harold Roy Watson (d 1971); *Career* articled clerk rising to asst mangr Ernst & Young CAs 1984–88, mgmnt accountant rising to fin dir Marketing Solutions Ltd 1988–89, UK fin controller Boase Massimi Pollitt advtg agency 1988–89, fin dir BMP DDB 1989–2014, ret; currently conslt; ACA 1981, MIPA 1990; *Style—* Mrs Shirley Watson; ✉ 68 Games Road, Ludgrove Hall, Barnet EN4 9HT (☎ 020 8441 7169); DDB UK Ltd, 12 Bishop's Bridge Road, London W2 6AA (☎ 020 7258 4856, fax 020 7723 9846)

WATSON, Simon John; s of John Charles Watson, of Reigate, Surrey, and Lorna Kathleen, *née* Whitehouse; *b* 13 May 1958; *Educ* Maidstone GS, St Catherine's Coll Oxford (MA); *Career* admitted slr 1983; ptnr Simmons & Simmons 1988– (articled clerk 1981–83, asst slr 1983–88); memb Law Soc; *Recreations* opera, bridge; *Style—* Simon Watson, Esq; ✉ City Point, One Ropemaker Street, London EC2Y 9SS (☎ 020 7628 2020, fax 020 7628 2070)

WATSON, Prof Stephen Roger; s of John Cole Watson, MBE (d 1987), and Marguerite Freda Rose, *née* Seagrief (d 2007); *b* 29 August 1943; *Educ* UCS Hampstead, Emmanuel Coll Cambridge (MA, MMath, PhD); *m* 26 July 1969, Rosemary Victoria, da of Rt Rev Cyril James Tucker, CBE (d 1992), of Cambridge; 1 s (Oliver b 5 Feb 1972), 1 da (Emily b 18 Feb 1975); *Career* planning asst Shell International Petroleum Co 1970–71; Univ of Cambridge: fell Emmanuel Coll 1971– (res fell 1968–70), lectr Engrg Dept 1971–86, Peat Marwick prof of mgmnt studies 1986–94, dir Judge Inst of Mgmnt Studies 1990–94; dean Management Sch Lancaster Univ 1994–2001, princ Henley Management Coll 2001–05; dir: Cambridge Decision Analysts 1984–94, Environmental Resources Management 1989–95; *Books* Decision Synthesis (with D M Buede, 1988); *Recreations* overseas development, singing; *Style—* Prof Stephen Watson; ✉ 33 De Freville Avenue, Cambridge CB4 1HW (☎ 01223 319527, e-mail srw12@cam.ac.uk)

WATSON, Tom; MP; *b* 1967; *Educ* King Charles I Sch Kidderminster; *Career* dep gen election co-ordinator Lab Pty until 1997, political offr AEEU 1997–2001; MP (Lab) West Bromwich E 2001–, PPS to Rt Hon Dawn Primarolo MP 2003–04, asst govt whip 2004–05, lord cmmr to HM Treasy 2005–06, Parly under sec of state MOD 2006, Parly sec Cabinet Office 2008–10, Lab Pty dep chair 2011–, Lab Pty campaign co-ordinator 2011–13, dep ldr Lab Pty 2015–; *Style—* Tom Watson, Esq, MP; ✉ House of Commons, London SW1A 0AA

WATSON OF INVERGOWRIE, Baron (Life Peer UK 1997), of Invergowrie in Perth and Kinross; Michael Goodall (Mike) Watson; s of Clarke Carter Watson (d 1995), and Agnes Hope, *née* Goodall (d 1991); *b* 1 May 1949; *Educ* Dundee HS, Heriot-Watt Univ (BA); *Career* devpt offr and tutor Mid-Derbyshire Workers Educnl Assoc 1974–77, trade union official ASTMS (now Amicus) 1977–89 (divnl offr 1977–87, regnl offr 1987–89), MP (Lab) Glasgow Central (by-election) 1989–97; memb: Select Ctee on Parly Cmmr for Admin 1990–95, Public Accounts Ctee 1995–97, Leadership Campaign Team (with responsibility for foreign affairs) 1995–97; chm PLP Ctee on Overseas Devpt Aid 1991–97, sec PLP Trade Union Gp 1990–97; dir P S Communication Consultants Ltd 1997–99; MSP (Lab) Glasgow Cathcart 1999–2005; min for tourism, culture and sport 2001–03; memb Exec Ctee Lab Pty Scot Cncl 1987–90; *Books* Rags to Riches – The Official History of Dundee United Football Club (1985), Year Zero: An Inside View of the Scottish Parliament (2001); *Recreations* cycling, watching Dundee United FC, reading; *Style—* The Lord Watson of Invergowrie; ✉ House of Lords, London SW1A 0PW (☎ 020 7219 8731, e-mail watsonm@parliament.uk)

WATSON OF RICHMOND, Baron (Life Peer UK 1999), of Richmond in the London Borough of Richmond upon Thames; Alan John Watson; CBE (1985); s of Rev John William Watson (d 1980), of Bognor Regis, and Edna Mary, *née* Peters (d 1985); *b* 3 February 1941; *Educ* Kingswood Sch Bath, Jesus Coll Cambridge (MA); *m* 1965, Karen, da of Hartwig Lederer (d 1966), of Frankfurt-on-Main; 2 s (Hon Stephen b 1966, Hon Martin b 1968); *Career* history scholar and res asst to regius prof of modern history Cambridge 1962–64; broadcaster; presenter The Money Programme (BBC 2) and Panorama (BBC 1) 1964–76, head of radio & TV EEC Cmmn 1976–80; presenter: You and 92 (BBC 1) 1990, The Germans (Channel 4) 1992, Key Witness (BBC Radio 4) 1996; chief exec Charles Barker City Ltd 1980–83, dep chm Sterling PR Ltd 1985–86; chm: City and Corporate Counsel Ltd 1987–93, Corporate Vision Ltd 1989–98, Threadneedle Publishing Gp plc 1989–94, CTN Communications (Corporate Television Networks) Ltd 1992–, Burson-Marsteller Europe 1996–2007 (chm Burson-Marsteller UK 1994–96), Coca-Cola European Advsy Bd 2004–06, Raisin Social Ltd 2005–, Bd Havas Media UK 2008–; visiting fell Louvainium Business Sch Brussels 1990–94, Erasmus visiting prof Catholic Univ of Louvain 1990–, hon prof German Studies Univ of Birmingham 1997–, memb Bd GB Studies Centre Humboldt Univ Berlin 1999–, visiting fell Oriel Coll Oxford 2003–; pres Lib Pty 1984–85, vice-chm European Movement 1995–2001, pres European Atlantic Movement 2006–; memb: House of Lords Select Ctee on the EU 2000–04 and 2006–10, Exec Bd UNICEF 1985–92, Exec Jesus Coll Cambridge Soc 1987–94, Bd Prince of Wales Int Business Leaders' Forum 1996–2005, BT Bd Community and Charities Ctee 1996–2004, Advsy Cncl Centre for Politics Univ of Virginia; chm: Royal Television Soc 1992–94, British-German Assoc 1992– (chm 1992–2000, pres 2001), Royal Acad Devpt Bd 1999–2001, Cncl of Cwlth Socs 2003–, Br-German Koenigswinter Conf 2004–10, Br Accreditation Cncl 2007–11; pres: Heathrow Assoc for the Control of Aircraft Noise 1991–95, Franco-Br Soc 2012–; chm: Bd of Govrs Westminster Coll Oxford 1988–94, Richmond Theatre Appeal 1990–91, Father Thames Tst 1998–, Cambridge Univ Chemistry Advsy Bd 2000–, The Cambridge Fndn 2005–; govr: Kingswood Sch 1984–90, ESU 1993– (dep chm 1995–99, chm 2000, int chm 2002–06, int chm emeritus 2006–, vice-pres 2012–); tstee Richmond Univ; patron European Movement 2008–; Churchill Medal 2005; Hon Doctorate St Lawrence Univ 1992, Hon Doctorate Moldova Univ 2007, Hon Doctorate Richmond American Int Univ 2008, Hon Doctorate Spiru Hatet Univ Burcharest 2009, Hon Doctorate Tirana Univ 2010, Hon Doctorate Bucharest Univ 2011; hon prof of int studies Univ of St Petersburg 2003–, hon fell Jesus Coll Cambridge 2004, hon prof Korea Univ 2004, High Steward Univ of Cambridge 2010–; Int Award Manila Univ 2005; FRTS 1992, FIPR 1999, FIVCA 2000; German Order of Merit 1995 (Grand Cross 2002), Grand Cross Romanian Order of Merit 2004, Cwlth of Virginia Cert of Public Recognition 2007, German Order of the Knights Grand Cross 2007; *Books* Europe at Risk (1974), The Germans (1992, 1994 and 1995), Jamestown: The Voyage of English (2007), The Queen and the USA (2012); *Recreations* travel, wines, boating; *Clubs* Brooks's, RAC, Kennel, Beefsteak; *Style—* The Rt Hon the Lord Watson of Richmond, CBE; ✉ Cholmondeley House, 3 Cholmondeley Walk, Richmond, Surrey; Somerset Lodge, Nunney, Somerset

WATSON-GANDY OF MYRTON, Professor Mark; s of James Alastair Christian Campbell Watson-Gandy, and Barbara Jadwiga Theresa, *née* Madry; *b* 8 November 1967; *Educ* Dr Challoner's GS, Univ of Essex (LLB), Inns of Court Sch of Law; *m* 1997, Emanuella Johanna Christina, *née* Giavarra; 1 s (James Campbell Alexander b 2002), 1 da (Isabella Sophia Vere b 2010); *Career* called to the Bar Inner Temple 1990; practising barr, one of the prosecuting counsel to the DTI 1999–2002, jr counsel to the Crown 2000–12; called to the Bar Eastern Caribbean Supreme Court (Br Virgin Islands) 2013; legal advsr Genesis Initiative 2010–; visiting prof Univ of Westminster 1999–, special lectr Cass Business Sch 2007–; chm Ctee of Tstees Inst of Heraldic and Genealogical Studies 2004–09, tstee and dir Apostleship of the Sea 2009–; head of professional standards and hon fell Inst of Certified Bookkeepers 1997; chm Mental Health First Aid England (2014–); Rector's Medal Univ of Trnava 2014; memb Ct Univ of Essex 2015–; memb Guild of Freemen; Freeman City of London 1995, Liveryman Worshipful Co of Scrivener's 1996 (memb Ct of Assistants 2012); CF, fell Assoc of Business Recovery Professionals (BRPA), assoc Inst of Fin Accountants, assoc Assoc of Int Accountants; KM 2002, KSG 2007, Knight Constantinian Order of St George 2007, Cross Order pro Merito Melitensi 2014; *Publications* books incl: Beyond the Peradventure, Thomson Tax Guide (co-ed), Watson-Gandy on Accountants (1990, 2 edn 2008), Watson-Gandy on Corporate Insolvency Practice (2010), Watson-Gandy on Personal Insolvency Practice (2012), Butterworths Corporate Law Service (co-ed), International Trends of Criminal Compliance (UK contrib, 2015); jls incl: Justice of the Peace (local govt ed, 1993–99), Family Court Reporter (asst ed, 1993–99), Litigation (ed, 1994–98), European Current Law (contributing ed, 1998–2000); *Style—* Professor Mark Watson-Gandy; ✉ Three Stone Chambers, 3 Stone Buildings, Lincoln's Inn, London WC2A 3XL (☎ 020 7242 4937, e-mail mwg@threestone.law, website www.threestone.law)

WATT; *see also:* Harvie-Watt

WATT, Alison; OBE (2008); da of James Watt, and Annie (Nancy), *née* Sinclair; *b* 11 December 1965; *Educ* Glasgow Sch of Art (postgrad studies, painting prize, Armour prize for painting); *Career* artist; associate artist National Gallery London 2006–; *Solo Exhibitions* One Woman Show (The Scottish Gallery, London) 1990, One Woman Show – Contemporary Art Season (Kelvingrove Art Gallery and Museum Glasgow) 1990, Flowers East Gallery London 1993 and 1995, Charles Belloc Lowndes Fine Art Chicago 1996, Monotypes (Flowers East Gallery London) 1997, Fold (The Fruitmarket Gallery Edinburgh) 1997, Aberdeen Art Gallery 1998, Leeds Metropolitan Univ Gallery 1998, Scottish Nat Gallery of Modern Art Edinburgh 2000, Dulwich Picture Gallery London 2001, Still (installation, Old St Paul's Church Edinburgh) 2004, Dark Light (Ingleby Gallery Edinburgh) 2007, Pier Art Centre Orkney 2007, Nat Gallery 2008, Hiding in Full View (Ingleby Gallery Edinburgh), GENERATION (Scottish Nat Gallery of Modern Art) 2014, Paintings 1986–2014 (Perth Museum & Art Gallery) 2014, Reality (Sainsbury Centre Norwich) 2014, The Sun Never Knew How Wonderful It Was (Parafin London) 2016; *Group Exhibitions* incl: British Inst Fund (Royal Acad of Arts London) 1986, Nat Portrait Competition (Nat Portrait Gallery London) 1987, Six Women Artists (Scottish Gallery Edinburgh) 1988, London Opening (Scottish Gallery London) 1989, Royal Scottish

Portrait Award (Royal Scottish Acad Edinburgh) 1989, The Compass Contribution (Tramway Glasgow) 1990, Scottish Art in the 20th Century (Royal West of England Acad Bristol) 1991, The Portrait Award (Nat Portrait Gallery London) 1992, Plymouth City Museum & Art Gallery 1992, LA Art Fair 1992, Art '93 London 1993, Decouvertes (Paris Art Fair) 1993, Fred Hoffman Gallery LA 1993, Inner Visions (Flowers East Gallery London) 1994, The Twenty Fifth Anniversary Exhibition (Flowers East at London Fields) 1995, The Power of Images (Martin Gropius Bau Berlin) 1996, Four British Painters (John McEnroe Gallery NY) 1996, Bad Blood (Glasgow Print Studio) 1996, Paintings (Mendenhall Gallery Pasadena) 1996, Treasures For Everyone (Nat Art Collections Fund Christie's London) 1997, Von Kopf Bis Fuss (Ursula Buckle Stiftung Kraichtal) 1997, Body Politic (Wolverhampton Art Gallery) 1997, Londres, Glasgow (Galerie Rachlin Lemarie Paris) 1998, Human Figure (Gallerie de Belle Feuille Montreal) 1999, Narcissus (Nat Portrait Gallery London) 2001, Fold (City Art Gallery Leicester) 2002, Jerwood Painting Prize Exhbn (Jerwood Space London) 2003, Picturing Women (Bryn Mawr Coll Philadelphia) 2004, Strands City Art Gallery Edinburgh 2006, Divided Selves (Fleming Collection London) 2006, The Naked Portrait (Compton Verney Warks) 2007, Autoiatratto (Uffizi Gallery Florence) 2010, Standing Room Only (Flowers East London) 2010, Autoportraits (Musée des Beaux Arts Lyon) 2016, Facing the World: from Rembrandt to Ai Weiwei (Scottish National Portrait Gall Edinburgh) 2016; *Commissions* HRH Queen Elizabeth The Queen Mother (Nat Portrait Gallery London), Kelvingrove Art Gallery and Museum Glasgow, The Observer, EMI Records, News Scotland Ltd, Mirror Gp Newspapers, Collins Publishers, Wallspace London 2010, Uffizi Gallery Florence, Scottish Opera, numerous private cmmns; *Works in Collections* Nat Portrait Gallery, Glasgow Art Gallery and Museum, BBC, Robert Fleming Holdings Ltd London, Robert and Susan Kasen Summer NY, Aberdeen Art Gallery, National Westminster Bank plc, McMaster Univ Art Gallery, The Freud Museum London, Ferens Art Gallery Hull, Christie's Corporate Art Collection, Scottish Nat Gallery of Modern Art, Deutsche Bank, Southampton City Art Gallery, Scottish Parliament, Uffizi Gallery Florence, Br Cncl, Scottish Nat Portrait Gallery, Gallery of Modern Art Glasgow, Artemis London, Kirkcaldy Museum and Art Gallery, Hunterian Museum Glasgow, Scottish Opera, Perth Museum and Art Gallery; *Awards* first prize for painting Br Inst Fund (Royal Acad of Arts) 1986, winner John Player Portrait Award (Nat Portrait Gallery) 1987, Elizabeth Greenshields Fndn Award Montreal Canada 1989, special commendation Morrison Scottish Portrait Award (Royal Scottish Acad) 1989, The Lord Provost's Prize 1993, Artist's Award Scottish Arts Cncl 1996, shortlisted Jerwood Painting Prize 2003, Creative Scotland Award 2004, ACE Award for Art in a Religious Space 2005; *Books* The Sun Never Knew How Wonderful It Was (2016); *Publications* Fold (1997), Shift (2000), Still (2004), Phantom (2008), Hiding in Full View (2011); *Style—* Ms Alison Watt, OBE; ✉ c/o Parafin, 18 Woodstock Street, London W1C 2AL

WATT, Prof Graham Charles Murray; s of Alan Crombie Robertson Watt (d 1989), of Skene, Aberdeenshire, and Helen, *née* Hughes; *b* 3 January 1952; *Educ* Aberdeen GS, Univ of Aberdeen (BMedBiol, MB ChB, MD, Cardno prize in anatomy, McWillie prize in biochemistry and physiology, Durno prize and Lizard medal in anatomy, Munday and Venn prize, Watt prize in social med); *m* 29 Dec 1983, Elizabeth Anne, da of John Munro; 2 da (Nuala Catherine Morley b 12 Dec 1984, Vari Helen Munro b 29 May 1986); *Career* med house officer City Hosp Aberdeen 1976–77, surgical house officer Gilbert Bain Hosp Lerwick 1977, registrar in histopathology and morbid anatomy Leicester General Hosp 1977–78, surgical house officer in general med Aberdeen Hosps 1978–80, registrar in geriatric med Dept of Health Care of the Elderly Sherwood Hosp Nottingham 1980, res registrar MRC Epidemiology and Med Care unit Northwick Park Hosp 1980–82, paediatric vocational trainee in general practice Ladywell Med Centre and Sch of Community Paediatrics Univ of Edinburgh 1982–83, head MONICA Project Centre and res fell Dept of General Practice Univ of Glasgow 1983–86, hon lectr Cardiovascular Epidemiology Unit Univ of Dundee 1983–86, trainee GP Townhead Health Centre Glasgow 1986, trainee in community med Greater Glasgow Health Bd 1986–87, sr med offr Chief Scientist Office Scottish Home and Health Dept 1987–89, prof of general practice Univ of Glasgow 1994– (sr lectr in public health 1990–94); currently hon conslt in public health med Greater Glasgow Health Bd; memb: BMA, Soc of Social Med, Assoc of Univ Depts of General Practice; MRCP 1979, MRCGP 1986, FRCPGlas 1991, FFPHM 1994 (MFPHM 1987), FMedSci 2000; *Publications* author of numerous research pubns and invited scientific presentations on epidemiology of cardiorespiratory disease in families, inequalities in health, environmental health and health servs research; *Clubs* Kettle; *Style—* Prof Graham Watt; ✉ University Department of General Practice, 1 Horselethill Road, Glasgow G12 9LX (✆ 0141 330 8345, fax 0141 330 8331)

WATT, Iain Alasdair; s of Dr Andrew Watt (d 1999), of Edinburgh, and Margaret Fawns, *née* Brown (d 1967); *Educ* Edinburgh Acad, Univ of Hull (BSc); *m* 30 June 1971, Lynne Neilson, da of Harold Livingston (d 1984), of Kirkcaldy; 3 s (Nicholas b 15 Feb 1973, Christopher Nial b 25 April 1975, Oliver Noel b 10 July 1980), 1 da (Gemma Stephanie Margaret b 12 April 1985); *Career* joined Bank of Scotland Gp 1964, dir British Linen Bank Ltd (subsid) 1986–, former chief exec Edinburgh Fund Managers Gp plc; dir other cos incl Edinburgh Dragon Trust Ltd 2014–; bd tstee Nat Museums Scotland Ltd 2015–, tstee Nat Museums Scotland Charitable Tst Ltd 2104–; memb Cncl Queens Nursing Inst in Scotland; FCIB; *Recreations* tennis, golf; *Clubs* Golf House Elie, Bruntsfield Golf, N Berwick Golf, Mid Ocean Bermuda, Aberdour Tennis; *Style—* I A Watt, Esq; ✉ Sycamore Bank, North Queensferry, Fife (✆ 01383 413645)

WATT, John Gillies McArthur; QC (Scot 1992); s of Peter Julius Watt (d 1978), and Nancy, *née* McArthur (d 1998); *b* 14 October 1949; *Educ* Clydebank HS, Univ of Glasgow, Univ of Edinburgh (LLB); *m* 1 (m dis 1988), Catherine, yr da of Robert Russell, of Toronto; 2 da (Rowan b 5 Nov 1976, Harriet b 27 Dec 1979); m 2, Nov 1988, Susan, o da of Dr Tom C Sparks Jr, of Ardmore, Oklahoma and Breckenridge, Colorado; *Career* law apprentice Messrs Mackenzie Roberton Glasgow, admitted slr 1974, ptnr Stewart & Bennett, Argyll 1975–78, admitted Faculty of Advocates 1979, advocate depute 1989, temp sheriff 1991, called to the English Bar Middle Temple 1992; memb Incorporation of Coopers of Glasgow 1976–; *Recreations* shooting, sailing, skiing, opera, golf; *Clubs* Lansdowne, Royal Western Yacht (Glasgow), Dornick Hills Country Club; *Style—* John Watt, Esq, QC; ✉ 301 Country Club Road, Ardmore, OK 73401–1125, USA (✆ 00 1 580 490 2494, e-mail jgmwatt1@cableone.net)

WATT, Laurence Johnstone (Laurie); s of Alexander D J Watt (d 1991), and Rosalind Chris, *née* Valentine; *b* 30 March 1946, London; *Educ* Tonbridge Sch; *m* 13 Sept 1975 (m dis 2002), Lyndal Joan; 2 s (Alexander b 1977, Theo b 1980); *Partner* Gwendolyn Parkin; *Career* admitted slr Hong Kong 1978, admitted barr and slr Supreme Ct of Victoria Aust 1983; Cole and Cole: articled clerk 1964–70, admitted slr 1970; Charles Russell LLP: joined 1972, ptnr 1974, sr ptnr 1998–2006, sr counsel 2006–; int sec ALFA International; dir and memb Bd and Advsy Cncl London Philharmonic Orch Ltd, dir London Philharmonic Trading Ltd; memb: Law Soc, Legal Advsy Bd Wesleyan Assurance Soc, Royal Philharmonic Soc (Hon Slr), Int Bar Assoc; chair Exec Ctee and treas Cwlth Lawyers Assoc; former chair Schubert Ensemble Tst; tstee: Assoc of Br Orchestras Tst (also chair), Awards for Young Musicians; *Publications* various articles on musico-legal and musical subjects; *Recreations* music (performing and listening), photography, popular science, reading; *Clubs* Garrick; *Style—* Laurie Watt, Esq; ✉ c/o Charles Russell Speechlys, 5 Fleet Place, London EC4M 7RD (✆ 020 7203 5000, mobile 07831 633088, e-mail laurie.watt@crsblaw.com.co.uk)

WATT, Peter; s of David Thomas Watt (d 2007), and Sandra, *née* Booth; *b* 20 July 1969, York; *Educ* Bournemouth Univ (RGN); *m* 31 December 2003, Vilma Paola, *née* Espinoza; 1 s (Benjamin Daniel b 7 July 1991), 4 da (Ivanna Nicole Bermudez b 30 March 1994, Anya Marie b 24 Jan 1995, Ruby Eveline b 14 Sept 2007, Gabriella Elisa b 10 March 2008); *Career* RGN 1992–96; Lab Party 1992– (gen sec 2006–07), chief exec The Campaign Co 2008–09, chief exec Counsel and Care 2011, dir of child protection advice and awareness NSPCC 2011–; political commentator and blogger; *Publications* Inside Out (2010); *Style—* Peter Watt, Esq; ✉ e-mail watt-p@sky.com

WATTERS, James Andrew Donaldson; s of Andrew James Watters (d 2003), of Dumfriesshire, and Elsa Donaldson, *née* Broatch (d 2016); *b* 16 March 1948; *Educ* KCS Wimbledon, Pembroke Coll Oxford (BA); *m* 1, 21 July 1973 (m dis), Lesley Jane Aves, da of Cyril Joseph Churchman (d 1963); 2 s (Alexander b 4 March 1978, Rupert b 11 June 1980), 1 da (Flora b 16 May 1985); m 2, 22 Sept 2012, Nina Kellgren; *Career* admitted slr 1972, articled clerk and slr Stephenson Harwood 1970–75, slr Norton Rose 1976–79, sr legal advsr 3i plc 1980–82; ptnr: Goodwille & Co 1982–85, Stephenson Harwood 1985–92, Watson Farley & Williams 1992–2013; dir Donaldson/Watters Ltd 2013–; Freeman City of London; memb Law Soc 1972; *Publications* Palmer on Bailment (contrib); *Recreations* music; *Clubs* Groucho; *Style—* James Watters, Esq; ✉ 137 Hertford Road, London N1 4LR

WATTIS, Prof John Philip; s of Philip William Wattis (d 2007), and (Elizabeth) Joan, *née* Nickson; *b* 4 February 1949; *Educ* St Joseph's Coll Blackpool, Univ of Liverpool Med Sch (MB ChB); *m* 12 July 1969, Florence Elizabeth (Libby), da of David John Roberts (d 1980); 2 s (Mark b 1980, Peter b 1985), 2 da (Sharon b 1982, Ruth b 1988); *Career* house offr The Royal Infirmary Liverpool 1972–73, med supt Amudat Mission Hosp Uganda 1973–75, registrar in psychiatry John Conolly Hosp Birmingham 1975–78, lectr in health care of the elderly Univ of Nottingham 1978–81, sr lectr and conslt in old age psychiatry St James's Univ Hosp Leeds 1986–2000 (conslt 1981–86); Leeds Community and Mental Health NHS Trust: med dir 1995–99, assoc dir R&D 1999–2000; visiting prof in psychiatry of old age Univ of Huddersfield 2000–, conslt in psychiatry of old age and actg R&D dir Calderdale and Huddersfield NHS Tst 2001–02, conslt in psychiatry of old age and assoc med dir SW Yorks NHS Tst 2002–05; Section for Psychiatry of Old Age RCPsych (past chm, hon sec and public educn offr), chm Gen and Old Age Psychiatry Specialty Advsy Ctee RCPsych 1997–2001; memb Dementia Gp Christian Cncl on Ageing (past chm); former chm and fndr Leeds Branch Alzheimer's Disease Soc; FRCPsych 1991 (MRCPsych 1978); *Books* Psychological Assessment of Old People (ed with I Hindmarsh, 1988), Confusion in Old Age (1989), Practical Management of Affective Disorders in Old Age (ed with S Curran, 2008), Practical Management and Leadership for Doctors (with S Curran, 2011), Practical Management of Dementia: A Multidisciplinary Approach (ed with S Curran, 2011), Practical Psychiatry of Old Age (5 edn with S Curran, 2013); *Recreations* cycling, walking; *Style—* Prof John Wattis; ✉ Harold Wilson Building, University of Huddersfield, Queensgate, Huddersfield HD1 3DH (✆ 01484 343451, e-mail j.wattis@hud.ac.uk or johnwattis@aol.com)

WATTS, Prof Cedric Thomas; s of Thomas Henry Watts (d 1964), of Cheltenham, Glos, and Mary Adelaide, *née* Cheshire (d 1965); *b* 19 February 1937; *Educ* Cheltenham GS, Pembroke Coll Cambridge (BA, MA, PhD); *m* 3 Jan 1963, Judith Edna Mary (d 2007), da of Charles Edward Hill (d 1974); 2 da (Linda b 1964 d 1985, Sarah b 1972), 1 s (William b 1967); *Career* Nat Serv RN 1956–58; asst lectr Cambs Coll of Arts and Technol 1964–65, Univ of Sussex: lectr 1965–79, reader 1979–83, prof English and American Sch 1983–2011, emeritus prof of English 2011–; *Books* Conrad's Heart of Darkness: A Critical and Contextual Discussion (1977), Cunninghame Graham: A Critical Biography (jtly, 1979), A Preface to Conrad (1982), R B Cunninghame Graham (1983), The Deceptive Text (1984), A Preface to Keats (1985), William Shakespeare: Measure for Measure (1986), Hamlet (1988), Joseph Conrad: A Literary Life (1989), Literature and Money (1990), Joseph Conrad: Nostromo (1990), Romeo and Juliet (1991), Thomas Hardy: Jude the Obscure (1992), Joseph Conrad (1994), A Preface to Greene (1997), Henry V, War Criminal? and Other Shakespeare Puzzles (jtly, 2000), Joseph Conrad: The Secret Agent (2007), Thomas Hardy: Tess of the d'Urbervilles (2007), Thomas Hardy's Tess of the d'Urbervilles (jtly, 2012), Final Exam: A Novel (as Peter Green, 2013), Shakespeare Puzzles (2014), Fantastic Finds (2014), The Connell Guide to Shakespeare's Second Tetralogy (2014), Shakespeare's 'Julius Caesar': A Critical Introduction (2015); *Style—* Prof Cedric Watts; ✉ University of Sussex, Brighton, East Sussex BN1 9QN (✆ 01273 606755, e-mail c.t.watts@sussex.ac.uk)

WATTS, Charles Robert (Charlie); *b* 2 June 1941; *m* 14 Oct 1964, Shirley Anne, *née* Shepherd; 1 da; *Career* drummer; joined Rolling Stones 1963; signed recording contracts with: Impact Records/Decca 1963, London Records/Decca 1965, Rolling Stones Records, CBS 1983, Virgin 1992; albums with Rolling Stones: The Rolling Stones (1964, reached UK no 1), The Rolling Stones No 2 (1965, no 1), Out of Our Heads (1965, UK no 2), Aftermath (1966, UK no 1), Big Hits (High Tide and Green Grass) (compilation, 1966, UK no 4), got LIVE if you want it! (live, 1967), Between The Buttons (1967, UK no 3), Flowers (US compilation, 1967, US no 3), Their Satanic Majesties Request (1967, UK no 3), Beggars Banquet (1968, UK no 3), Through The Past Darkly (Big Hits Volume 2) (compilation, 1969, UK no 2), Let It Bleed (1969, UK no 1), Get Yer Ya-Ya's Out! (live, 1970, UK no 1), Stone Age (compilation, 1971, UK no 4), Sticky Fingers (1971, UK no 1), Hot Rocks 1964–71 (US compilation, 1972, US no 9), Goats Head Soup (1973, UK no 1), It's Only Rock'N'Roll (1874, UK no 2), Made In The Shade (compilation, 1975, UK no 14), Rolled Gold – The Very Best of The Rolling Stones (compilation, 1975, UK no 7), Black and Blue (1976, UK no 2), Love You Live (live, 1977, UK no 3), Some Girls (1978, UK no 2), Emotional Rescue (1980, UK no 1), Tattoo You (1981, UK no 2), Still Life (American Concert 1981) (live, 1981, UK no 4), Undercover (1983, UK no 3), Rewind 1971–84 (compilation, 1984, UK no 23), Dirty Work (1986, UK, no 4), Steel Wheels (1989, UK no 2), Flashpoint (live, 1991, UK no 6), Voodoo Lounge (1994, UK no 1), Bridges to Babylon (1997, UK no 6), Forty Licks (2002); has toured with The Charlie Watts Orchestra 1985–86; solo albums: Charlie Watts Orchestra – Live at Fulham Town Hall 1986, From One Charlie (with book Ode to a High Flying Bird) 1992, A Tribute to Charlie Parker 1992, Warm & Tender 1993, From One Charlie 1995, Long Ago & Far Away 1996; concert films: Sympathy For The Devil (dir Jean Luc Godard) 1969, Gimme Shelter 1970, Ladies and Gentleman, The Rolling Stones 1977, Let's Spend The Night Together (dir Hal Ashby) 1983, Flashpoint (film of 1990 Steel Wheels Tour) 1991; *Books* Ode To A High Flying Bird (1965); *Recreations* jazz; *Style—* Charlie Watts, Esq; ✉ c/o Munro Sounds, 5 Church Row, Wandsworth Plain, London SW18 1ES

WATTS, Prof Colin; s of George Watts (d 1982), and Kathleen Mary, *née* Downing; *b* 28 April 1953, London; *Educ* The Friends Sch Saffron Walden, Univ of Bristol (BSc), Univ of Sussex (DPhil); *m* 21 Dec 1979, Susan Mary, *née* Light; 2 da (Helen Mary b 12 Sept 1981, Emily Rose b 14 Sept 1984), 1 s (Simon James b 26 Feb 1989); *Career* EMBO fell UCLA 1980–82, Beit meml fell MRC Lab of Molecular Biology Cambridge 1982–85; Univ of Dundee: lectr 1992–98, reader 1992–98, prof of immunobiology 1998–; E de Rotschild & Y Mayent fell Inst Curie Paris 1999; contrib to various scientific jls; memb: Basel Inst for Immunology 1991, European Molecular Biology Orgn 1996; Tenovus Scotland Margaret Maclellan Prize 2000, Descartes Prize EU 2002; FRSE 1999, FRS 2005, FMedSci 2009; *Recreations* music, cities, armchair sport; *Style—* Prof Colin Watts; ✉ Wellcome Trust Biocentre, School of Life Sciences, University of Dundee DD1 5EH (✆ 01382 384233, fax 01382 385783, e-mail c.watts@dundee.ac.uk)

W

WATTS, Baron (Life Peer UK 2015), of Ravenhead in the County of Merseyside; David Leonard (Dave) Watts; s of late Leonard Watts, and late Sarah, née Rowe; b 26 August 1951; Educ Seel Road Secdy Sch; m 1972, Charmaine Avril (d 2005), da of O P Davies; 2 s (Paul, David); Career full time cncllr 1989–92, regnl organiser Lab Pty 1991–92; researcher to: Angela Eagle, MP, qv, 1992–93, The Rt Hon Lord Evans of Parkside, qv, 1993–97; MP (Lab) St Helens N 1997–2015; PPS to: Rt Hon John Spellar, qv, Rt Hon John Prescott, qv, 2003–05; Govt whip 2005–; memb Foreign Affs Advsy Ctee 2010, memb EU Home Affrs Ctee House of Lords; sometime UK pres Euro Gp of Industrial Regions; chm St Helens FE Coll; vice-chm AMA; Style— The Lord Watts; ✉ House of Commons, London SW1A 0AA (✆ 020 7219 3000); constituency office: Ann Ward House, 1 Milk Street, St Helens, Merseyside WA10 1PX (✆ 020 7219 6325)

WATTS, Edward (Ted); s of Edward Samuel Window Watts (d 1975), of Hornchurch, Essex, and Louise, née Coffey (d 2000); b 19 March 1940; Educ East Ham GS for Boys, SW Essex Tech Coll; m 18 June 1960, Iris Josephine, da of Edward John Frost, MBE; 2 s (Mark Edward b 3 March 1963, Paul Jonathan b 27 June 1968), and 1 da decd; Career Cotton Ballard & Blow Architects 1959–62, E Wookey & Co General Practice Surveyors 1962–64, chief surveyor Ian Fraser & Assoc (Architects & Town Planners) 1964–66, team leader Housing Devpt Br GLC 1966–67, fndr Edward Watts & Co 1967–99 (now Watts plc); dir: RICS Journals Ltd 1982–88 (chm 1986–88), People Need Homes plc 1991–96, Avilla Developments Ltd 1999–2013; non-exec dir: WSP Group 1993–2002, Thamesmead Town 1994–2000; fndr chm Hyde Housing Assoc 1967–70 (memb until 1985), chm: Empty Homes Agency 1997–2002, Tilfen Ltd 1999–2002, Blackheath Preservation Tst 2001–09 (dir 2000–09), Cedar Rydal Ltd; memb: Gen Cncl RICS 1982–95 (pres 1991–92), ARCUK 1991–97, Urban Villages Group 1992–96, Ministerial Advsy Bd PACE 1995–2000, Home Office Steering Gp on strategy for Central London accommodation 1995–97; Freeman City of London; Hon DSc South Bank Univ 1992; FRICS 1971 (ARICS 1962); Recreations sailing, cruising; Clubs Royal Cruising, Lymington Town Sailing, Royal Lymington Yacht, Cruising Assoc; Style— Ted Watts, Esq; ✉ Flexford Farm, South Sway Lane, Sway, Lymington, Hampshire SO41 6DP (✆ 01590 681053, e-mail ted.watts@flexfordfarm.co.uk)

WATTS, (Edward) Jonathan; s of Albert Edward Watts (d 1972), of Blackpool, and Joan Mary Watts (d 1972); b 5 December 1954, Blackpool, Lancs; Educ Arnold GS Blackpool, Univ of Hertfordshire; m 10 Aug 1996, Lisa Mary, née Gernon; Career sales and mktg mangr Control Dataset Ltd 1977–82, gen mangr Control Data UK Data Services 1982–84, md Datapoint Corp (NZ) Ltd 1984–87, gp mktg and business devpt dir Sintrom plc 1987–90, gp md BellSouth Europe/Air Call Communications Ltd 1990–94, md NB3/Dolphin Telecommunications 1994–97, md COLT Telecommunications 1998–2002; non-exec dir Alliance & Leicester plc 2000–08, pres Geo Networks Ltd 2004–14, currently chm CORTEX plc; Recreations golf, property renovation, travel, public speaking; Style— Jonathan Watts

WATTS, Kevan Vincent; s of late Spencer Frederick Watts, and late Olive Mary Watts; b 27 December 1950, Folkestone, Kent; Educ Kent Coll Canterbury, Univ of Oxford (BA, Philosophy prize, BPhil); m Prudence Mary, née Lloyd Vine; 2 da (Lucinda, Elizabeth), 1 s (Henry); Career with HM Treasy 1974–81; Merrill Lynch: joined 1981, subsequently various roles in corp finance and M&A NY and London offices until 1993, head of investment banking EMEA 1993–97, sr vice-pres Merrill Lynch & Co Inc 1997–2009, exec chm Asia Pacific region 1997–2000, co-head of global investment banking 2000–02, chm EMEA and Pacific Rim 2002–04, chm int 2004–07, pres India 2008–10, chm UK-ASEAN Business Cncl; vice-chm global banking HSBC, advsr Huawei Technologies, dir Tottenham Hotspur FC, advsr Corsair Capital; Recreations horse racing, golf, farming; Clubs Boodles, London Capital; Style— Kevan Watts, Esq; ✉ e-mail kvwatts@btinternet.com or kevan.watts@hsbc.com

WATTS, Mela Lesley Jane; CBE (2008); da of Edward Watts (d 2008), and Pamela, née Burke; b 12 September 1963, Chalfont St Peter, Bucks; Educ Dr Challoners HS Bucks, Portsmouth Poly (BSc); Career Dept for Educn and Science (now Dept for Educn): joined 1986, posts incl estab Funding Agency for Schs, private sec to Min of Sport, estab Nursery Voucher Scheme, bill mangr Special Educational Needs and Disability Act 2002, Curriculum Div, princ private sec to Sec of State 2004–08, dir sch performance and reform 2008–10, dir of free schs 2010–; Recreations wine tasting, walking; Style— Ms Mela Watts, CBE; ✉ Department for Education, Sanctuary Buildings, Great Smith Street, London SW1P 3BT (✆ 020 7783 8421, e-mail mela.watts@education.gsi.gov.uk)

WATTS, Dr Richard Arthur; s of Richard W E Watts, FRCP, and Joan E M Lambert, FRCOG; Educ Highgate Sch London, Hertford Coll Oxford (MA, DM); Career conslt rheumatologist Ipswich Hosp NHS Tst 1994–, sr lectr UEA 2005–; visiting prof Univ Campus Suffolk 2011; ed Rheumatology 2002–08; memb Assoc of Physicians of the UK and Ireland 2005; fell American Coll of Rheumatology 1990, fell Br Soc of Rheumatology 1995 (tstee 2009–12), FRCP 1999; Publications Autoimmune Rheumatic Diseases (jtly, 2 edn, 1999), Oxford Desk Reference Rheumatology (jtly, 2009), Oxford Textbook of Rheumatology (jtly, 2013); author of numerous academic papers relating to rheumatology; Recreations skiing, gardening, Central Asian travel; Style— Dr Richard Watts; ✉ Ipswich Hospital NHS Trust, Heath Road, Ipswich IP5 5PD (✆ 01473 702362, fax 01473 702039, e-mail richard.watts@ipswichhospital.nhs.uk)

WATTS, Timothy; DL (West Midlands, 2005); s of late Walter Watts, and Constance, née Daniels (d 1998); b 30 September 1948, Birmingham; m 6 Aug 2004, June, née Hunt; 2 da (Amy b 25 May 1980, Fay b 9 July 1983); Career Pertemps Gp of Cos: joined Pertemps family business 1970, early career Wolverhampton office, employment conslt in commercial and tech divs, became Pertemps Recruitment Partnership 1994, resigned as chm 2002, lifetime pres Pertemps Network Gp (encompassing over 120 individual cos) 2002–; ambass Advantage West Midlands 2005, former memb W Midlands Cncl CBI, founding sponsor Tomorrow's Company; vice-pres Spinal Injuries Assoc 2005–; lifetime pres Birmingham and Black Country Community Fndn; memb Beta Gamma Sigma Soc Aston Univ 2006–; Daily Telegraph/British Telecom Award for Customer Service 1995, Business of the Year (Pertemps) 1997, Businessman of the Year 1997, Master Entrepreneur of the Year Central England 2002, Best Family Business Coutts Prize 2005, Most Influential Ldrs in the European Staffing Industry 2014, inducted into Recruitment International Hall of Fame 2014, included in Sunday Times Top 100 Companies (Pertemps); High Sheriff W Midlands 2014–15; Hon DSc: Aston Univ 2007, Birmingham City Univ 2009; fell Inst of Employment Conslts; Style— Timothy Watts, Esq, DL; ✉ P Investments Ltd, Meriden Hall, Main Road, Meriden CV7 7PT (✆ 01676 525000, fax 01676 525109, e-mail tim.watts@pertemps.co.uk)

WATTS-ROBERTSON, John; s of Joseph Watts-Robertson, of Warwickshire, and Romaine, née Howell; b 3 May 1957; Educ Alcester GS, West Bromwich Coll of Commerce and Technol, London Coll of Printing (NCTJ proficiency certificate); m 3 May 1980, Susan Margaret, née Field; 1 da (Sarah Louise b 24 May 1984); Career photographer: Stratford-upon-Avon Herald 1974–75, Wellingborough News Echo 1975–77, Northants Evening Telegraph 1977–93; freelance photographer: The Guardian 1993– (part time 1989–93), The Sunday Telegraph 1993– (part time 1992–93); Awards News Photographer of the Year E Midlands Allied Press 1985 and 1986, Press Photographer of the Year UK Press Gazette 1989, British Regnl Press Photographer of the Year 1989, News Photographer of the Year Birmingham Press Club 1989, winner Ilford Nat Photo of the Month Aug 1991, winner (Features) Ilford Nat Awards 1991; ARPS; Recreations cinema, theatre, reading, swimming, ice skating; Style— John Watts-Robertson, Esq; ✉ 1 Nansen Close,

Rothwell, Kettering, Northamptonshire NN14 6TZ (✆ 078 5093 1219, e-mail jr.photos@freeuk.com); Picture Desk, The Guardian, Kings Place, 90 York Way, London N1 9GU

WAUGH, Andrew Peter; QC (1998); Educ Brighton Coll, City Univ London (BSc, Dip Law); Career called to the Bar 1982; practising barr specialising in intellectual property law; currently memb of chambers Three New Square; memb: Intellectual Property Bar Assoc, Chancery Bar Assoc, Int Assoc for the Protection of Intellectual Property (AIPPI); Style— Andrew Waugh, Esq, QC; ✉ Three New Square, Lincoln's Inn, London WC2A 3RS

WAUGH, Prof Michael Anthony; s of Anthony Lawrence Waugh, of Richmond, Surrey, and Nancy Genevieve, née Vernon; b 19 September 1943; Educ St George's Coll Weybridge, Charing Cross Hosp Med Sch London (MB BS); Partner Stuart Long (civil partnership 2006); Career conslt physician genito-urinary medicine Gen Infirmary Leeds 1975–2004, pt/t secondment Aids Unit Dept of Health 1992–93; pres Med Soc for Study of Venereal Diseases 1989–91 (hon sec 1981–89); Int Union Against Sexually Transmitted Infections: sec gen 1984–95, pres 1995–99, sr cnsllr 2001; founding dep ed Int Jl of STD and Aids 1993; memb Editorial Bd: Skin Med 2002–, Community Dermatology 2005–14, Acta Dermatovenerologica Croatica 2005; prof Marconi Univ Rome 2013–; observer Venereology and Dermatovenereology Specialists Ctee Union of Euro Med Specialists 1984–92; hon sr lectr Univ of Leeds 1985–2004 (Soc of Apothecaries lectr in history of med 1984–2000); hon librarian, offr and memb Cncl RSM 1995–99; extra memb of Cncl RSM 1999–2001; corresponding memb Austrian Soc for Dermatology and Venereology 1990, conslt Thai Training Insts Postgrad Course on STDs 2000–, memb Bd European Acad of Dermatology and Venereology 1994–2000 (hon life memb 2001, sec Ethics Cmmn 2004, chm 2009–13), conslt advsr Dept of Disease Control Thailand 2006; Lifetime Achievement Award International Union Against Sexually Transmitted Infections 2005, Distinguished Serv Award European Acad of Dermatology and Venereology 2006, Cert of Appreciation Int League of Dermatological Socs 2007; fell The Netherlands Soc for Dermatology and Venereology 1996, hon fell Hungarian STD Soc 2000, hon memb Deutsche STD Gesellschaft 2005, hon sub-dean RSM (Northern and Yorkshire branch) 2005–10, hon memb Slovakian Derm-Ven Soc 2006, hon memb Romanian Derm-Ven Soc 2007, hon fell Sri Lanka Coll of Venereologists 2010; Liveryman Worshipful Soc of Apothecaries 1970; DHMSA 1970, Dip Venereology 1974; fell Australasian Coll of Sexual Health Physicians 1996, fndn fell Australasian Chapter of Sexual Health Medicine (FAChSHM) 2004; FRCPI 1994 (MRCPI 1993), FRCP 1995; Books Sexually Transmitted Diseases (contrib, 2 edn, 1990), History of Sexually Transmitted Diseases (1990), Sex, Disease and Society (jt ed, 1997), Oxford Illustrated Companion to Medicine (venereology section, 2001), Dictionary of National Biography (contrib 3 sections, 2004), Sexual Health Medicine (Male Homosexuality and Bisexuality) (2005), Imported Skin Diseases (Sexually Transmitted Infections) (2006, 2 edn 2013), Emergency Dermatology (contrib, 2010), Manual of Gender Dermatology (contrib, 2011), History of Sexually Transmitted Infections (foreword, ed Gerd Gross & Stephen Trying, 2011); Recreations gardening, travelling, philately (FRPSL); Style— Professor Michael Waugh; ✉ Wellfield House, 151 Roker Lane, Pudsey, Leeds LS28 9ND (✆ 0113 256 5255, e-mail mike@mawpud.fsnet.co.uk)

WAUGH, Simon John; s of Peter Waugh (d 2001), and Christine Waugh (d 2008); b 24 April 1958, London; Educ Sevenoaks Sch; m 11 March 2000, Refilwe, da of Arthur Maimane; 2 da (Amy b 4 Feb 1989, Ella b 22 July 2001), 4 s (Peter b 24 Oct 1990, Stuart, Matthew (twins) b 5 Feb 1992, Zachary b 23 March 2003); Career UK sales and mktg dir American Express 1976–88, commercial dir Lloyds Bank Insurance 1988–93, md Saga 1993–97; Centrica plc: gp mktg dir 1997–2004, md Centrica Financial Servs 1997–2002, dep md British Gas 2002–04; chm AWD Chase De Vere 2005–08, non-exec dir: Johnston Press 2003–07, CMC Markets plc, My Drive Solutions 2011–; ceo Nat Apprenticeship Service/Skills 2008–12; chm Southern Health Fndn Tst 2012–, chm The Compliance Consortium (TCC) 2012–; dep chm Sparks Children's Charity, tstee and dir Help the Aged; hon life fell: Mktg Soc, DMA; Recreations sport (rugby, football, golf), politics, reading; Clubs Worplesdon Golf; Style— Simon Waugh, Esq; ✉ AWD Chase De Vere, 10 Paternoster Square, London EC4M 7DY (✆ 020 7029 9451, fax 020 7236 8341, e-mail simon.waugh@awdplc.com)

WAUGH, Lady Teresa Lorraine; da of 6 Earl of Onslow, KBE, MC, TD (d 1971); sis of 7 Earl of Onslow, qv; b 1940; m 1961, Auberon Waugh (d 2001); 2 s, 2 da; Career translator and novelist; Books Painting Water (1984), Waterloo Waterloo (1986), An Intolerable Burden (1988), Song at Twilight (1989), Sylvia's Lot (1994), The Gossips (1995), A Friend Like Harvey (1999), The House (2002); Style— Lady Teresa Waugh

WAVERLEY, 3 Viscount (UK 1952); John Desmond Forbes Anderson; o s of 2 Viscount Waverley (d 1990), and Lorna Myrtle Ann, née Ledgerwood; b 31 October 1949; Educ Malvern; Heir s, Hon Forbes Anderson; Career elected hereditary peer House of Lords 1999–; advsr CCC Gp; memb RIIA; Grand Cross Order of San Carlos (Colombia) 1998, Jubilee Medal (Kazakhstan) 2002; Recreations golf, walking; Clubs Rye Golf; Style— The Rt Hon the Viscount Waverley; ✉ House of Lords, London SW1A 0PW

WAX, Ruby; da of Edward Wax, and Berta, née Goldmann; b 19 April 1953; Educ Evanston Township HS, Univ of Denver, Univ of Calif Berkeley, RSAMD (Gold Medal in acting); m 16 May 1988, Edward Richard Morison Bye; 1 s (Maximillian b 11 Nov 1988), 2 da (Madeline b 10 Dec 1990, Marina b 5 Nov 1993); Career actor and comedienne; Performer of the Year British Comedy Awards 1993; Theatre Crucible Theatre 1976, Royal Shakespeare Co 1978–82, Wax Acts (one woman show, UK tour and West End) 1992, Stressed (one woman show, UK, Aust and NZ tour) 2000, Sane New World (St James Theatre) 2015; Television Not The Nine O'Clock News (writer) 1983, Girls On Top 1984–85, Don't Miss Wax 1985–87, Hit and Run 1988–89, Full Wax 1989–94, Ruby Wax Meets... 1996–98, Ruby 1997–99 and 2000, Ruby's American Pie 1999–2000, Hot Wax 2001, Life with Ruby 2002, Commercial Breakdown 2002, Ruby Wax with... 2003; documentaries incl: Miami Memoirs 1987, East Meets Wax 1988, Ruby Takes a Trip 1992; Publications How Do You Want Me? (autobiography, 2002), Sane New World – Taming the Mind (2013), A Mindfulness Guide for the FRAZZLED (2016); Style— Miss Ruby Wax; ✉ c/o PFD, Drury House, 34–43 Russell Street, London WC2B 5HA (✆ 020 7344 1000, fax 020 7836 9523, e-mail info@pfd.co.uk)

WAXMAN, Prof Jonathan; s of David Waxman, and Shirley, née Friedman; b 31 October 1951; Educ Haberdashers' Aske's, UCL (BSc, MB BS, MD); Children 1 da (Thea Millie b 22 Dec 1993), 1 s (Frederick Merlin b 24 April 1996); Career trained in med UCH London, registrar in med St Mary's Hosp London 1979–81, sr registrar in oncology Bart's 1981–86, conslt oncologist Hammersmith Hospital 1986–; fndr and life pres Prostate Cancer UK; FRCP; Books The New Endocrinology of Cancer (jtly, 1988), The Molecular Biology of Cancer (jtly, 1989), Urological Oncology (jtly, 1992), Interleukin II (jtly, 1992), Molecular Endocrinology of Cancer (1996), Cancer Chemotherapy Treatment Protocols (1998), Cancer and the Law (1999), The Prostate Cancer Book (2001), Treatment Options in Urological Oncology (2001), Lecture Notes in Oncology (2006), Lecture Notes in Oncology (2015), The Elephant in the Room (fiction, 2011), MacLeod's Introduction to Medicine (fiction, 2013), Big Prick (fiction, 2014); Recreations Yodelling; Clubs Butlin's Beaver; Style— Prof Jonathan Waxman; ✉ Department of Oncology, Hammersmith Hospital, Imperial College, Du Cane Road, London W12 0NN (✆ 020 8383 4651, fax 020 8383 4653)

WAY, Adam Gerald Richmond (Bertie); s of Col A G Way, MC; b 29 February 1952; Educ Eton; m Susanna, née, Nicholas; Career short serv cmmn Grenadier Gds 1972–75; dir i/c gp business devpt Chime Communications plc (formerly Lowe Bell Communications Ltd) 1991– (joined 1986); non-exec chm The Blomfield Group (exec search and recruitment conslts); memb Cncl WellBeing (health research charity for women and babies), chm Starlight Fndn; *Recreations* country pursuits; *Style*— A G R Way, Esq; ✉ Chime Communications plc, 14 Curzon Street, London W1Y 8LP (☎ 020 7861 8543, fax 020 7861 8520)

WAY, Andrew Mark; s of Maxwell Andrew Way (d 1975), and Jane Kathleen, *née* Palliser (d 2013); *b* 27 February 1959, Bournemouth, Dorset; *Educ* Bournemouth Sch, Bristol Sch of Nursing (SRN), Thomas Guy Sch of Nursing (RMN), Charles West Sch of Nursing (RSCN), City Univ (BSc), Keele Univ (MBA); *Career* gen mangr St George's Hosp Tooting 1992–95, gen mangr and chief operating offr Hammersmith Hosps NHS Tst 1995–2002, chief exec Heatherwood & Wrexham Hosps NHS Tst 2002–05, chief exec Royal Free Hampstead NHS Tst 2005–09, chief exec Alfred Health Melbourne 2009–; *Recreations* swimming, skiing, travel, bridge; *Style*— Andrew Way, Esq; ✉ Alfred Health, Commercial Road, Melbourne 3181, Australia (e-mail andrew.way@alfred.org.au)

WAY, Patrick Edward; QC (2013); s of John Francis Way (d 1996), of Solihull, and Margaret Helen Laura, *née* Ewins (d 2000); *b* 6 February 1954; *Educ* Solihull Sch, Univ of Leeds (BA); *m* 10 June 1978, Judith Anne, da of late Dr Peter Orchard Williams, CBE; 3 s (Oliver Christopher Patrick b 16 Dec 1983, Frederick William Patrick b 6 Feb 1987, Dominic Hugo Patrick b 29 Nov 1988); *Career* admitted slr 1979, asst slr Lawrence Graham 1979–82, tax ptnr Nabarro Nathanson 1985–87 (asst 1982–85), ptnr and head of Corp Tax Dept Gouldens 1987–94, called to the Bar Lincoln's Inn 1994, tax barr Gray's Inn 1994–; memb Attorney Gen's B Panel as Jr Counsel to the Crown 2010–13; QC 2013; founding ed Trusts and Estates 1985, tax ed The BES Magazine 1986; memb: Revenue Bar Assoc, Chancery Bar Assoc; dir Richmond (Rugby) FC Ltd; *Books* Death and Taxes (1985), Maximising Opportunities under the BES (1986), The BES and Assured Tenancies – The New Rules (1988), Tax Advice for Company Transactions (ed and contrib, 1992), The Enterprise Investment Scheme (1994), Joint Ventures (ed and contrib, 1994), Tolley's Tax Planning (contrib, 2012–13); *Recreations* rugby, contemporary art; *Clubs* Travellers; *Style*— Patrick Way, Esq, QC; ✉ Field Court Tax Chambers, 3 Field Court, Gray's Inn, London WC1R 5EP(☎ 020 3693 3700, e-mail pw@fieldtax.com)

WAYNE, Prof Richard Peer; s of Arthur W Wayne, and Stella B, *née* Lloyd; *b* 5 December 1938; *Educ* Worthing HS, Trinity Coll Cambridge (open scholar, sr scholar, research scholar, MA, PhD, Mathison prize), Univ of Oxford (MA); *m* 6 April 1963, Brenda, da of Richard Tapp; 1 da (Carol Elisabeth b 17 Aug 1969), 1 s (Andrew Richard b 30 April 1971); *Career* res asst Univ of Liverpool 1963–65, dept demonstrator Physical Chemistry Lab Univ of Oxford 1965; ChCh Oxford: elected tutor and coll lectr 1965, elected official student 1966, elected Dr Lee's reader in chemistry 1973, tutor for graduates 1988–92; Univ of Oxford: appointed lectr 1967, chm Sub-Faculty of Chemistry 1986–88 (sec 1978–79), dir of graduate studies physical sciences 1988–90, chm Faculty Bd of Physical Sciences 1990–92 (vice-chm 1988–90), memb Ctee to review Robert Hooke Inst 1990–91, memb advsy ctee on Encaenia hon degrees 1991–94, chm co-ordinating ctee for first year course in physical sciences 1991–92, memb Telecommunications Ctee 1993–2000, examiner in natural sciences, doctoral examiner and res supervisor, prof of chemistry 1996–, student emeritus ChCh 2006, prof emeritus Univ of Oxford 2006; visiting prof of photochemistry Univ of Calif Riverside 1968–69, visiting sr scientist Nat Bureau of Standards Washington DC 1973, visiting sr scientist Centre de Recherches en Physique de l'Environnement Orléans 1975–76, conseiller scientifique Centre National d'Etudes des Télécommunications 1976–80, guest scientist Universität Wuppertal 1984 and 1986, visiting scientist UCLA, professeur invité Université de Bordeaux 1993, visiting prof and prof honorario Univ of Córdoba Argentina 1996, hon prof Univ of Copenhagen 2008; memb: Ctee on the Meteorological Effects of Stratospheric Aircraft (COMESA), Working Gp (ii) Br Nat Ctee for Solar Terrestrial Physics, Atmospheric Neutral Chemistry Study Gp of Middle Atmospheric Prog, Co-ordinating Ctee for Res in Atmospheric Chemistry (CCRAC), Science Panel on Stratospheric Ozone Cmmn of Euro Communities, Mgmnt Panel Atmospheric Chemistry Initiative Science and Engrg Res Cncl, EUROTRAC Applications Project 1993–, Electoral Bd Chair of Atmospheric Physics Univ of Stockholm 1994–95, Scientific Steering Gp Lab Studies in Atmospheric Chemistry NERC 1995, Electoral Bd Chair of Atmospheric Chemistry Univ of Copenhagen 1999, Conseil de l'École Doctorale Sciences et Technologie Université d'Orléans 2000–11; conseillor scientifique l'Institut Français du Pétrole 1991–2006, co-opted memb LACTOZ Steering Ctee 1994, memb local organising ctee XVIIth Int Photochemistry Conf 1994–95; ed-in-chief Jl of Photochemistry (now Jl of Photochemistry and Photobiology) 1972–2006, memb Comité Éditorial Revue de l'Institut Français du Pétrole 1996–2008; doctoral examiner Univ of Cambridge and numerous univs in UK, France Germany, Ireland, Sweden; external examiner: Univ of Plymouth 2000–04, UC Dublin 2009–11; lectures and addresses incl: BAAS 1986, plenary lectr autumn meeting RSC 1993, Bedson lectr Univ of Newcastle 1991, Iddles Millennium lectr Univ of New Hampshire 2000, Irvine lectr Univ of St Andrews 2002; invited guest lectr: CNRS Orléans 2007, Manchester 2008, Bayreuth 2010; public lecture RSC London 2010; RSC award for Reaction Kinetics 2000; Dr (hc) Univ Castilla-La Mancha Spain 2002; FRSC 2005; *Publications* Photochemistry (1970), Chemistry of Atmospheres (1985, 3 edn 2000), Principles and Applications of Photochemistry (1988), The Nitrate Radical: Physics, Chemistry and the Atmosphere (sr exec ed, 1991), Chemical Instrumentation (1994), Halogen Oxides: Radicals, Sources and Reservoirs in the Laboratory and in the Atmosphere (sr exec ed, 1995), Photochemistry (with C E Wayne, 1996), Atmospheric Chemistry (with A M Holloway, 2010); author of over 275 research papers, reviews and chapters in books in fields of reaction kinetics, photochemistry, and atmospheric chemistry; *Style*— Prof Richard Wayne; ✉ Physical and Theoretical Chemistry Laboratory, South Parks Road, Oxford OX1 3QZ (☎ 01865 275434, fax 01865 275410, e-mail richard.wayne@chem.ox.ac.uk)

WEAIRE, Prof Denis Lawrence; *b* 17 October 1942; *Educ* Belfast Royal Acad, Clare Coll Cambridge (BA), Univ of Calif Berkeley, Univ of Chicago, Univ of Cambridge (PhD); *Career* res fell Harvard Univ 1969–70, J W Gibbs instr Yale Univ 1970–72 (asst prof 1972–73, assoc prof 1973–74), sr lectr Heriot-Watt Univ 1974–77 (reader 1977–79, prof 1979), prof of experimental physics UC Dublin 1980–84 (head of dept 1983–84 and 2003–05), Erasmus Smith's prof of natural and experimental philosophy Trinity Coll Dublin 1984– (head of dept 1984–89, fell 1987–, dean of sci 1989–92); ed-in-chief Jl of Physics 1994–97, pres Euro Physical Soc 1997–99 (vice-pres 1996–97 and 1999–2000), chm Solid State Physics Sub-Ctee Inst of Physics 1981–84 (memb 1979–81); sec/treas Euro Assoc of Deans of Sci 1990–92, dir Magnetic Solutions Ltd 1994–; vice-pres Royal Irish Acad 2001–02; memb: Advsy Ctee Inst for Amorphous Studies Michigan USA 1983–, Irish Nat Ctee for Physics (Royal Irish Acad) 1984–, MRS Euro Ctee 1984–86, Jt Res Centre EEC Scientific Cncl 1985–88, Advsy Bd Physics Bulletin 1985–88, Bd DIAS Sch of Cosmic Studies 1985–90, Editorial Bd Jl of Physics 1986–88 (hon ed 1994–98), EEC Evaluation Panel on Non-Nuclear Energies 1985–86, Royal Irish Acad delegate Cncl of the Euro Physical Soc 1986–88, Royal Irish Acad/RDS Ctee on Historic Scientific Instruments 1986, Semiconductors and Insulators Section Ctee EPS 1988–94, Ed Panel Modern Physics B World Scientific Co 1988–92, Royal Irish Acad Ctee on History and Philosophy of Sci 1987–, Editorial Advsy Bd Forma 1988–, Cncl Royal Irish Acad 1989–93 and 2000–, Advsy Ctee Hitachi Res Ireland 1989–94, Bd of Birr Sci and Heritage Tst 1990–99, Ed Advsy Ctee Materials Res Bulletin 1991–95, CODAS 1993–, Physics Panel EC Human Capital and Mobility Prog 1992–94; vice-pres Academia Europaea 2003– (memb 1998–, memb Cncl 1999–2002); EPS Cecil Powell Medal 2002, Cunnigham Medal Royal Irish Acad 2005; Dr (hc) Tech Univ of Lisbon 2001; FRS 1999; *Books* Introduction to Physical Mathematics (with P G Harper, 1985), The Physics of Foams (with S Hutzler, 1999), The Pursuit of Perfect Packing (with T Aste, 2000); Tetrahedrally Bonded Amorphous Semi-conductors (ed with S Kirkpatrick and M H Brodsky, 1974), The Recursion Method (ed with D Pettifor, 1985), Solid State Science – Past, Present and Predicted (ed with C Windsor, 1987), Tradition and Reform: Science and Engineering in Ireland 1800–1930 (ed with N McMillan, J R Nudds, S P McKenna Lawlor, 1988), Epioptics (ed with J F McGilp and C Patterson, 1995), The Kelvin Problem (ed, 1997); *Style*— Prof Denis Weaire, FRS; ✉ Physics Department, Trinity College, Dublin, Ireland (☎ 3531 608 1055, fax 3531 671 1759, e-mail dweaire@tcd.ie)

WEALE, Prof Albert Peter; CBE (2013); s of Albert Cecil Weale (d 1978), of Brighton, and Elizabeth Margaret, *née* Granger (d 1975); *b* 30 May 1950; *Educ* Varndean GS for Boys Brighton, Clare Coll Cambridge (MA, PhD); *m* 1, 17 Sept 1976 (m dis 1987), Jane, *née* Leresche; m 2, 28 Jan 1994, Jan, *née* Harris; *Career* Sir James Knott res fell Dept of Politics Univ of Newcastle upon Tyne 1974–76, lectr in politics 1976–85, asst dir Inst for Res in the Social Sciences Univ of York 1982–85, prof of politics UEA 1985–92, prof of govt Univ of Essex 1992–2009, prof of political theory and public policy UCL 2010–15 (emeritus prof 2015–); ESRC professorial fell 2009–12; chm: Nuffield Cncl of Bioethics Working Party on Ethics of Xenotransplantation 1996, Grants Ctee The King's Fund 1996–2001, Nuffield Cncl on Bioethics 2008–12 (memb 1998–2004); co-ed Br Jl of Political Science 1992–2009; vice-pres British Acad 2008–12; FRSA 1993, FBA 1998; *Books* Equality and Social Policy (1978), Political Theory and Social Policy (1983), Lone Mothers, Paid Work and Social Security (co-author, 1984), Cost and Choice in Health Care (ed, 1989), Controlling Pollution in the Round (co-author, 1991), Innovation and Environmental Risk (co-ed, 1991), The New Politics of Pollution (1992), Environmental Standards in the European Union in an Interdisciplinary Framework (co-ed, 1995), Citizenship, Democracy and Justice in the New Europe (co-ed, 1997), Political Theory and the European Union (co ed, 1998), Democracy (1999, 2 edn 2007), Environmental Governance in Europe (co-authored 2000), Risk, Democratic Citizenship and Public Policy (ed, 2002), Democratic Citizenship and the European Union (2005), Democratic Politics and Party Competition (co-ed, 2006), Democratic Justice and the Social Contract (2013); *Recreations* walking, music, company of friends, visual arts; *Style*— Prof Albert Weale, CBE, FBA; ✉ Department of Political Science, School of Public Policy, University College London, 29/31 Tavistock Square, London WC1H 9QU (☎ 020 7679 4993, e-mail a.weale@ucl.ac.uk)

WEALE, Dr Martin Robert; CBE (1999); s of the late Prof Robert Weale, and Betty Weale; *b* 4 December 1955, Barnet; *Educ* Highgate Sch, Clare Coll Cambridge (BA), Univ of Cambridge (ScD); *Career* ODI fell Nat Statistical Office Malawi 1977–79, research offr Dept of Applied Economics Cambridge 1979–87, lectr Faculty of Economics and Politics Univ of Cambridge 1987–95, dir NIESR 1995–2010 (sr research fell 2010–), prof of economics Queen Mary Univ of London 2011–; memb: HM Treasy Ind Panel of Economic Forecasting Advsrs 1996–97, Statistics Cmmn 2000–08, Bd of Actuarial Standards 2006–10; external memb Monetary Policy Ctee 2010–; treas Alzheimer's Research Tst 1992–2008; Hon DSc City Univ 2007; hon fell Inst of Actuaries 2001; *Books* British Banking (1986), Macroeconomic Policy – Inflation, Wealth and the Exchange Rate (1989), Reconciliation of National Income and Expenditure (1995); *Clubs* Athenaeum; *Style*— Dr Martin Weale, CBE; ✉ National Institute of Economic and Social Research, 2 Dean Trench Street, London SW1P 3HE (☎ 020 7222 7665, e-mail mweale@niesr.ac.uk)

WEALE, Timothy Donald; TD, DL (Hampshire 2012); s of Donald Jones Weale (d 1971), and Freda Jessy, *née* Gardiner (d 1991); *b* 10 April 1951; *Educ* Magdalen Coll Sch Oxford, Coll of Estate Mgmnt Reading; *m* 12 Oct 1974, Pamela Anne, da of Gerard Gordon Moore (d 1972); 1 s (Edward b 21 April 1981), 1 da (Alice b 15 April 1983); *Career* TA, ret; Wessex Regt (Rifle Vols) 1979–86, Inns of Ct and City Yeomanry (ICCY) 1986–94 (tstee 1995–); vice-pres Royal Yeomanry (ICCY) Band 1992–; ptnr Pearsons 1984–86, dir Prudential Property Services 1986–89, ptnr Healey and Baker (now Cushman & Wakefield) 1989–2012, ceo Healey and Baker Al Bourj Dubai UAE 2001–02, ceo Cushman & Wakefield, Healey & Baker Gulf Operations 2002–04, ptnr C&W Capital Markets Gp UK 2004–12 (conslt 2012–); dir Ribbongate Ltd 2012–; chm Cncl Order of St John Hants; advsy memb BYFC 1985–95; tstee: Army Cadet Force Assoc 2010, Yeomanry Benevolent Fund 2012; Freeman City of London 1996; FRICS, FRGS; *Recreations* sailing, skiing, vintage cars, gardening, field sports, music, antiques, design; *Clubs* Cavalry and Guards', Leander, Select Soc of Auctioneers; *Style*— Timothy Weale, Esq, TD, DL, FRICS, FRGS; ✉ Test Cottage, Longparish, Andover, Hampshire SP11 6PZ (☎ 01264 720362 or 07834 825197); C&W 43–45 Portman Square, London W1A 3BG (☎ 020 7152 5583)

WEARING, Gillian; OBE (2011); *b* 1963; *Educ* Chelsea Sch of Art (BTech), Goldsmiths Coll London (BA); *Career* artist; subject of profile South Bank Show (LWT) 1998, guest ed Documents sur L'art 1996; tstee Tate 2000–; BT Young Contemporaries 1993, Turner Prize 1997, Phaidon Press Award 1999; RA 2011; *Solo Exhibitions* City Racing London 1993, Maureen Paley Interim Art London 1994, 1996, 1997 and 1999, Valentina Moncada Br Cncl Rome 1996, Br Cncl Prague 1996, Le Consortium Dijon 1996, Wish You Were Here (Amsterdam) 1996, Emi Fontana Milan 1997, Bloom Gallery Amsterdam 1997, Kunsthaus Zurich 1997, 10–16 Chisenhale Gallery London 1997, Kunstler Wiener Secession Vienna 1997, Jay Gorney Modern Art NY 1997, Galerie Drantmann Brussels 1997, Centre d'Art Contemporain Geneva 1998, Gallery Koyanagi Tokyo 1998, Maureen Paley Interim Art London 1999 and 2003, Serpentine Gallery 2000, Gorney, Bravin & Lee NY 2000, Regen Projects LA 2000, Angel Row Gallery Nottingham 2001, Unspoken (Kunstverein München) 2001, Museo do Chiado Portugal 2001, Sous Influence (Musée d'Art Moderne de la Ville de Paris) 2001, la Caixa (Madrid) 2001, Centro Galego de Arte Contemporánea (Santiago Spain) 2001, Trilogy (Vancouver Art Gallery) 2002, Mass Observation (MCA Chicago and tour) 2002, Kunsthaus Glarus Switzerland 2002, Album (Maureen Paley Interim Art London and Gorney Bravin & Lee NY) 2003 and (Regen Projects LA) 2004, Kiasma/Museum of Contemporary Art Helsinki 2004, Frans Hals Museum Haarlem 2004, Snapshot (Bloomberg Space London) 2005, Family History (Maureen Paley London) 2006, Living Proof (Australian Centre for Contemporary Art Melbourne) 2006, Elsewhere? (Galleria Emi Fontana Milan) 2007, Family Monument (Galleria Civica di Arte Contemporanea Trento) 2007, Regen Projects (LA) 2008, Confessions: Portraits, Videos (Musée Rodin Paris) 2009, People (Tanya Bonakdar Gallery NY) 2011, Whitechapel Gallery, touring to K20, Kunstsammlung Nordrhein-Westfalen, Dusseldorf and Museum Brandhorst Munich 2012, Museum Brandhorst Munich 2013, Maureen Paley London 2014; *Collections* Arts Cncl of GB, Br Cncl London, Contemporary Art Soc London, Govt Art Collection GB, Irish MOMA, Kunsthaus Zurich, Peter & Eileen Norton Family Fndn LA, Saatchi Collection, Simmons & Simmons London, Southampton City Cncl, South London Gallery, Südwest LB Stuttgart, Tate Gallery; *Style*— Ms Gillian Wearing, OBE; ✉ c/o Maureen Paley, 21 Herald Street, London E2 6JT (☎ 020 7729 4112, fax 020 7729 4113)

WEATHERALL, Vice Adm Sir James Lamb (Jim); KCVO (2001), KBE (1989), DL (Hants 2004); s of Lt Cdr Alwyne Thomas Hirst Weatherall, RNR (d 1939), and Olive Catherine Joan, *née* Cuthbert (d 1977); *b* 28 February 1936, Renfrewshire; *Educ* Gordonstoun; *m* 12 May 1962, Jean Stewart, *née* Macpherson, da of 1 Baron Drumalbyn, KBE, PC; 2 s (Niall b 1967, Ian b 1976), 3 da (Sarah b 1968, Annie b 1974, Elizabeth b 1976); *Career* cadet BRNC Dartmouth, HMS Triumph 1954, midshipman HMS Albion 1955–56; Sub Lt: HMS

W

Scotsman 1956, HM Yacht Britannia 1958; Lt: HMS Lagos 1959–60, HMS Wizard 1960–61, Long Navigation Course 1961–62, HMS Houghton 1962–64, HMS Tartar 1964, HMS Eastbourne 1965–66; Lt Cdr Advanced Navigation Course 1966, HMS Soberton 1966–67 (i/c), HMS London 1968–70; Lt Cdr/Cdr HMS Ulster 1970–72 (i/c); Cdr: MOD 1972–74, HMS Tartar 1975–76 (i/c), Cdr Sea Trg 1976–77, HMS Ark Royal 1978; Capt: Nato Def Coll 1979, MOD-Naval Plans 1979–81, HMS Andromeda (i/c), and 8 Frigate Sqdn 1982–84 (incl Falklands), RN Presentation Team 1984–85, HMS Ark Royal (i/c) 1985–87; ADC HM The Queen 1986–87; Rear Adm Staff of Supreme Allied Cdr Europe 1987–89; Vice Adm Dep Supreme Allied Cdr Atlantic 1989–91, HM Marshal of the Diplomatic Corps 1992–01, extra equerry to HM The Queen 2001–, HM Lt for the City of London 2001–; chm: Sea Cadet Assoc 1992–98, Sea Cadet Cncl 1992–98 (vice-pres 2009–), Lord Mayor of London's Charity 1997–98; patron Marwell Wildlife (tstee 1992–2003, chm 1999–2007); pres Int Social Service (UK) 1996–2001; tstee and warden Box Hill Sch 2003– (govr 1992–2003, chm 1993–2003), warden Gordonstoun Sch 2004–11 (govr 1993–2003, chm 1996–2003); fell WWF (UK) (tstee 2001–07); Sea Cadet Medal 1998; Freeman City of London 1985, Liveryman Worshipful Co of Shipwrights 1985 (memb Ct of Assts 1989, Prime Warden 2001–02), Younger Brother Trinity House 1986; *Recreations* fishing, stamp collecting; *Clubs* RN of 1765 and 1785; *Style—* Vice Adm Sir James Weatherall, KCVO, KBE, DL; ✉ Craig House, Bishop's Waltham, Southampton SO32 1FS (☎ 01489 892483)

WEATHERILL, (Hon) Bernard Richard; QC (1996); s of Baron Weatherill, PC, DL (Life Peer) (d 2007), and Lyn, *née* Eatwell; *b* 20 May 1951; *Educ* Malvern, Principia Coll Illinois (int scholar), Univ of Kent (BA); *m* 1, 1977 (m dis 2001), Sally Maxwell, da of late John Ronald Fisher; 1 da (Julia Rosemary b 12 April 1982), 1 s (Thomas Bernard b 3 March 1984); m 2, 2005, Clare, da of late Peter W de B Forsyth; *Career* called to the Bar Middle Temple 1974 (bencher 2002); asst recorder 1998–2000, recorder 2000–; memb Gen Cncl of the Bar 1990–92 and 1993–95; memb: Chancery Bar Assoc, Professional Negligence Bar Assoc, Assoc of Contentious Tst and Probate Specialists (ACTAPS), Property Bar Assoc; chm Bar Services Co Ltd 2001–08, non-exec dir: A Cohen & Co plc 1989–2000, Croydon Business Ventures Ltd 2009–; memb Cncl Tennis and Rackets Assoc 2010–, memb Cncl Justice 2010–; ACIArb 1997, mediator 2002; *Recreations* wine, lawn tennis, real tennis, bridge, golf, avoiding gardening, cultivating friendships; *Clubs* All England Lawn Tennis and Croquet, Hurlingham, Royal Tennis Court, Jesters, Royal Wimbledon Golf, Lucifer Golfing Soc, Holyport Real Tennis; *Style—* Bernard Weatherill, QC; ✉ Enterprise Chambers, 9 Old Square, Lincoln's Inn, London WC2A 3SR (☎ 020 7405 9471, fax 020 7242 1447)

WEATHERILL, Prof Stephen Robson; *b* 21 March 1961; *Educ* Queens' Coll Cambridge (MA), Univ of Edinburgh (MSc); *Career* research asst Brunel Univ 1985, lectr Univ of Reading 1986–87, lectr Univ of Manchester 1987–90; Univ of Nottingham: lectr 1990–93, reader 1993–95, prof of European law 1995–97; Jacques Delors prof of European law Univ of Oxford 1998–; *Style—* Prof Stephen Weatherill; ✉ Somerville College, Oxford OX2 6HD (☎ 01865 270600, fax 01865 270620, e-mail stephen.weatherill@law.ox.ac.uk)

WEATHERLEY, Michael Richard (Mike); *b* 1957, Clevedon, Somerset; *Educ* London South Bank Univ (BA); *m* (m dis); 2 s, 1 da; *Career* fin dir and part owner Cash Bases 1994–2000, fin controller Pete Waterman Gp 2000–05, vice-pres of finance and administration (Europe) Motion Picture Licensing Co 2007–10; MP (Cons) Hove 2010–15; writer of intellectual property reviews on search engines and 'follow the money' topics, intellectual property advsr to the PM 2013–14; for Cash Bases: Queen's Award for Enterprise 1997 and 1998, Sussex Co of the Year Award 1999; fell CIMA, MCIM; *Publications* reports for the PM: Search Engines (2014), Follow The Money (2014), IP Education and Awareness (2014), Internet Service Providers (2015); *Recreations* heavy rock and metal music; *Style—* Mike Weatherley, Esq; ✉ House of Commons, London SW1A 0AA (websites www.mikeweatherley.com, www.rockthehousehoc.com, www.filmthehouse.com)

WEATHERUP, Hon Mr Justice; Sir Ronald Eccles Weatherup; kt (2001); s of Rev Samuel Weatherup (d 1953), and Meta, *née* Reaney; *Educ* Methodist Coll Belfast, Queen's Univ Belfast; *m* Muriel, *née* Stewart; 1 s (Colin), 2 da (Clare, Diane); *Career* called to the Bar NI 1971, QC (NI) 1993, judge of the High Court of Justice in NI 2001–; *Style—* The Hon Mr Justice Weatherup; ✉ c/o Royal Courts of Justice, Chichester Street, Belfast BT1 3JF

WEAVER, Barrie Keith; s of James Richard Weaver (d 1977), of Corton, Norfolk, and Theresa, *née* Cooper; *b* 10 December 1946; *Educ* Wallington Sch, Central Sch of Art (BA); *m* 15 Nov 1996, Angela Wendy, da of Stephen Douglas Hawksley, of Davenham, Cheshire; 1 da (Honor Georgina May b 28 June 2003); *Career* designer: Conran Assocs 1971–73, Pentagram Design 1973–76; fndr Roberts Weaver Design 1977, chm Weaver Associates 1990–98, dir Weaver Design Ltd 1999–, fndr Engenius.i 2013; cmmns incl: TI Group 1978–80, British Telecom 1982–84, Herman Miller, STC 1984–85, Applied Materials USA 1985–87, Plessey 1985–87, Nixdorf 1986–88, Hitachi, Matsushita Japan 1988–89, Qualcast, Nissan Japan 1990–91, LG, Samsung Korea 1991–92, BICC 1991–92, Airbus 1992, Stiga 1992, Whirlpool 1993, Universal Pictures, Mizuno Japan 1994, British Telecom 1995, Braun Germany 1996, Medison Korea 1996, Ransomes UK 1996, Antonov Ukraine 1997–98, Netas Turkey, Tunstall UK 1998–99, Subaru Japan 2001–02, nxt audio 2003; recipient: four Br Design Awards, Industrie Form Germany 1988 and 1996, Prince Philip Award, Designer of the Year 1990, Good Design Award Norway 1993, Design Innovations Award Germany 1994 and 1995; judge Sony Design Bursaries 1998–2002; memb Design Cncl 1989–95; FRSA 1984, FCSD 1982; *Recreations* antiques, paintings, gardening, looking at buildings; *Clubs* Lansdowne; *Style—* Barrie Weaver, Esq; ✉ 7 Park Street, Bath BA1 2TB (e-mail barrie@weaver.co.uk, website www.weaver.co.uk or www.engineeringanimage.com); Le Moutier, Aubry le Panthou, 61120, France (☎ 0033 02 33 35 99 99)

WEAVER, (Christopher) Giles Herron; s of Lt-Col John Frederick Herron Weaver (d 1993), and Ursula Priscilla Marie Gabrielle, *née* Horlick (d 1997); *b* 4 April 1946; *Educ* Eton, London Business Sch (MSc); *m* 30 July 1974, Rosamund Betty, da of Lionel Mayhew (d 1992), of Alton, Hants; 2 da (Flora b 1975, Johanna b 1983), 2 s (Freddy b 1977, Jack b 1986); *Career* CA; articles with Arthur Young 1966–71; asst to chm: Jessel Securities 1973–75, Berry Wiggins 1975–76; i/c pension funds Ivory and Sime plc 1976–86, md pensions mgmnt Prudential Portfolio Mangrs 1986–90; Murray Johnstone Ltd: investment dir 1990–93, md 1993–99, chm 1999–2000; former chm: Murray Emerging Growth and Income Tst plc, Helical Bar plc; dir: James Finlay Ltd, EP Global Tst plc; prop Greywalls Hotel Gullane 1976–; former chm Historic Houses Assoc in Scotland, former dep chm of tstees Nat Galleries of Scotland; FCA 1977 (ACA 1970); *Recreations* skiing, golf, tennis, stalking, bridge; *Clubs* New (Edinburgh), Boodle's, HCEG (Muirfield), Hurlingham, Denham; *Style—* Giles Weaver, Esq; ✉ Hill Fort House, Drem, East Lothian EH39 5AZ (e-mail gilesweaver@hillforthouse.co.uk); 47 Glebe Place, London SW3 5JE (mobile 07774 896471)

WEAVER, (Richard) Irving; s of John Weaver (d 1991), and Joyce, *née* Roebuck (d 1997); *b* 15 March 1949, Doncaster, Yorks; *Educ* Mexborough GS, Sheffield Poly; *m* 5 July 1972, Dorothy, *née* Crowcroft; 2 s (Andrew Richard b 24 Aug 1973, Simon Daniel b 20 Dec 1977), 1 da (Helen Jayne b 14 Nov 1975); *Career* Strata Homes Ltd (formerly Weaver Building Gp Ltd (founded by gf, Oscar Weaver)): surveyor 1968, md 1978, chm 1989–, majority shareholder; majority shareholder Strata Construction Ltd 2005–; Entrepreneur of the Year IOD Yorks region 2005; *Clubs* sailing, golf, theatre, travel; *Style—* Irving Weaver, Esq; ✉ Strata, Quay Point, Lakeside, Doncaster DN4 5PL (☎ 01302 308508, website www.stratahomes.co.uk)

WEAVER, Karl; s of Max and Enid Weaver; *b* 21 July 1972; *Educ* Woodbridge HS, Bancroft's Sch, Queen Mary & Westfield Coll London (BSc, MSc); *m* 3 May 1997, Fiona *née* Harvey; 1 s (Luke), 1 da (Esther); *Career* analyst OHerlihy Associates Ltd 1994–95, sr conslt The Henley Centre London 1995–99, managing ptnr Advanced Techniques Gp (ATG) Worldwide MindShare 1999–2003, dir D2D Ltd 2003–12, ceo Data2Decisions 2012–16, chief growth offr Dentsu Aegis Network; Freeman City of London (by redemption); Liveryman Worshipful Co of Marketors; *Recreations* trumpet playing, motorsport, music; *Style—* Karl Weaver; ☎ 07960 991741, e-mail karl.weaver@data2decisions.com

WEAVER, Prof Lawrence Trevelyan; s of Sir Toby Weaver, CB (d 2001), and Marjorie (Lady Weaver, d 2003), da of Rt Hon Sir Charles Trevelyan, 3 Bt (d 1958); *b* 13 October 1948; *Educ* Clifton, CCC Cambridge (exhibitioner, MA, MB BChir), DObstRCOG, DCH (London), Univ of Cambridge (MD, Lionel Whitby medal), Univ of Glasgow (DSc); *m* Camilla, *née* Simmons; 1 s, 1 da; *Career* MRC Dunn Nutrition Lab and Dept of Paediatrics Addenbrooke's Hosp Cambridge 1984–86, Fulbright travel scholar Harvard Med Sch and Massachusetts Gen Hosp Boston 1987–88, MRC Scientific Staff Dunn Nutrition Lab and conslt paediatrician Addenbrooke's Hosp and Univ of Cambridge 1988–94, conslt paediatrician Royal Hosp for Sick Children Yorkshill Glasgow 1994–2011, Samson Gemmell prof of child health Univ of Glasgow 1996–2011 (reader in human nutrition 1994–96); FRSA, FRCPCH, FRCP, FRCPGlas; *Recreations* being outdoors; *Style—* Prof Lawrence Weaver; ✉ Centre for the History of Medicine, Lilybank House, University of Glasgow, Glasgow G12 8RT (e-mail lawrence.weaver@glasgow.ac.uk)

WEBB, Prof Sir Adrian Leonard; kt (2000); s of Leonard Webb, of Melksham, Wilts, and Rosina, *née* Staines; *b* 19 July 1943; *Educ* St Julian's HS Newport Gwent, Univ of Birmingham (BSocSci), LSE (MSc), Loughborough Univ (DLitt); *m* 1, (m dis); 2 s (Rhicert b 20 April 1967, Geraint b 17 July 1971); m 2, 1996, Monjulee, da of Dass, of Kuala Lumpur, Malaysia; *Career* lectr LSE 1966–74, res dir Personal Social Servs Cncl 1974–76; Loughborough Univ: prof of social policy 1976–93, dir Centre for Res in Social Policy 1982–91, dep-vice-chllr 1988–93; vice-chllr Univ of Glamorgan 1993–2005; chm: Bd of Govrs Volunteer Centre 1978–84, Ctee on Workforce Planning and Trg in Social Servs 1987–88, Dept of Health Task Force on Nursing Research 1992–93, Heads of HE in Wales 2000–03, Pontypridd and Rhondda NHS Tst 2005–08, Enquiry into FE Wales 2006–07, Wales Employment and Skills Bd 2008–12, Enquiry into HE in NE Wales 2012–13; memb: DHSS Res Liaison Gps 1975–90 (sci advsr Chief Scientist's Departmental Res Ctee DHSS 1987–90), Sociology and Social Admin Ctee SSRC 1976–80, Cncl on Tbnls 1985–91, Eng Nat Bd on Nursing Midwifery and Health Visiting 1988–93, CBI Cncl Wales 1993–98, Dearing Ctee of Enquiry on Higher Educn 1996–97, Public Servs Productivity Panel HM Treasy 2000–06, Administrative Justice and Tbnls Cncl 2008– (also chair Wales 2013–), Big Lottery Fund UK 2012– (also chair Wales Ctee 2012– and non-exec dir UK Bd); non-exec dir: Nat Cncl Education and Learning Wales (ELWa) 2001–06, Nat Assembly for Wales 2003–08, Bd Wales Govt 2012–, E Glamorgan NHS Tst; chair Public Policy Inst Wales 2013–; advsr on social policy and social work: Univ Funding Cncl 1989–92, Leics DHA 1992–93, NHS Wales R&D Forum 1993–96; vice-pres Leics Regnl Cncl Guideposts Tst Ltd 1988–93; chm Social Admin Assoc 1977–80; memb: Social Policy Assoc, Br Sociological Assoc, Political Studies Assoc; FRSA 1987, FCGI 2011; *Books* numerous articles and books on social policy incl (jtly): Change Choice and Conflict in Social Policy (1975), Planning Need and Scarcity – Essays on the Personal Social Services (1986), The Economic Approach to Social Policy (1986), Social Work Social Care and Social Planning (1987), Joint Approaches to Social Policy – Rationality and Practice (1988); *Recreations* walking, painting (water colour), ornithology; *Style—* Prof Sir Adrian Webb

WEBB, Dr Andrew Roy; s of Michael Edward John Webb, of Oundle, Northants, and Carol Janice, *née* Finlay; *b* 6 February 1958, Croydon; *Educ* Sponne Sch Towcester, Northampton GS, WNSM (MB, BCh), Univ of Wales (MD); *m* 27 March 1999, Suzanne Elizabeth, *née* Gunn; 5 s (Matthew James Andrew b 25 Feb 1983, Adam Mark Richard b 5 Jan 1985, Tomas Michael Roy b 12 Nov 2002, James Robert Dylan b 31 Aug 2004, Alexander Samuel Ieuan b 12 Dec 2006); *Career* UCL Hosps NHS Fndn Tst: conslt physician in intensive care medicine 1990–2009, clinical dir intensive care services 1992–2001, clinical dir cardiac services 1997–2001, med dir clinical services 2001–06, med dir Acute Hosp 2006–09, vice-pres of medicine Fraser Health Authy (BC, Canada) 2009–15; clinical prof Univ of BC 2009–, prof Simon Fraser Univ 2014–, sr medical advsr Min of Health (BC, Canada) 2015–; Intensive Care Soc: memb Cncl 1997–2003, hon treas 2000–03, memb Higher Awards Ctee 2004–09, hon memb 2010–; chm All Wales Critical Care Devpt Ctee 2001–09; asst ed and memb Editorial Bd Intensive Care Medicine jl 1990–95 (memb Editorial Advsy Bd 1995–2003), section ed for health technol assessment Jl of Critical Care 2001–09, memb Editorial Bd Perioperative Medicine jl 2011–; FRCP 1997 (MRCP 1984); Critical Care Algorithms (jtly, 1991), Medical Emergencies Algorithms (jtly, 1994), The Oxford Handbook of Critical Care (jtly, 1997, 3 edn 2009), The Oxford Textbook of Critical Care (jtly, 1999, 2 edn 2015), The Oxford American Handbook of Critical Care (jtly, 2008); numerous book chapters and articles; *Style—* Dr Andrew Webb; ✉ 200–1333 West Broadway, Vancouver, BC V6H 4C6, Canada (☎ 001 604 714 2290)

WEBB, Prof Brian James; s of Frederick William Webb (d 1972), and Esther, *née* Foxall; *b* 15 January 1945; *Educ* Brookfield Sch Liverpool, Liverpool Coll of Art, Canterbury Coll of Art (DipAD); *m* 1969, Gail Elizabeth, da of George Henderson Barker (d 1986); 1 da (Holly Katharine b 4 Feb 1976), 1 s (James William Robin b 4 Jan 1980); *Career* asst graphic designer Michael Tucker Assocs 1967–69, graphic designer Derek Forsyth Partnership 1969–71; designer and dir: Trickett & Webb Ltd 1971–2003, Webb & Webb 2003–; visiting prof Univ of the Arts London 1999–, hon fell Univ of the Creative Arts 2005, visiting lectr numerous colls in UK, USA and Asia; work has been exhibited and published throughout the world; contrib Penrose Annual, Best of British Packaging, Best of British Corporate Identity and other jls; winner of numerous awards D&AD, Donside and Nat Calendar Awards for work on clients incl: Thames TV, Midland Bank, Royal Mail; pres CSD 2003–06 (memb Cncl 1980–87 and 1989–, chm Graphics Gp 1980–85), memb Exec Ctee D & AD 1987–89; memb juries: D&AD 1975–, Design Bursary RSA 1980–; external assessor CNAA UK; Master Artworkers Guild 2008; fell UC of the Creative Arts 2004; memb D&AD 1972, FCSD 1972, FRSA 1980, FSTD 1994; *Publications* For Shop Use Only – Eric Ravilious, Curwen and Dent stock blocks and devices (1994), Submarine Dream – Eric Ravilious, lithography (1996–7), Austerity to Affluence – British Art and Design 1945–62 (graphic design and typhography section, 1997), A thousand years, a thousand words – a celebration of the Royal Millennium Stamp Project (2000), Design: Edward Bawden and Eric Ravilious (2005), Design: Paul Nash and John Nash (2006), Design: E McKnight Kauffer (2007), Design: Harold Curwen and Oliver Simon (2008), London Transport Posters: A Century of Art and Design (2008), Design: David Gentleman (2009), Design: Peter Blake (2010), Design: FHK Henrion (2011), Design: Lovat Fraser (2012), Edward Bawden's London (2012), Design: John Piper (2013), Design: Abram Games (2013), Design: Enid Marx (2014), Edward Bawden's Kew Gardens (2014); *Recreations* walking, working; *Style—* Prof Brian Webb; ✉ Webb & Webb Design Limited, Studio 505, The Pill Box, 115 Coventry Road, London E2 6GG (☎ 020 7739 7895)

WEBB, Bryan Wyndham; s of Bernard Webb (d 1979), of Crumlin, Wales, and Elsie May Skillen, *née* Smith; *b* 6 August 1960; *Educ* Greenfield Secdy Sch Newbridge Gwent; *m* 2, Susan; 1 s (Christopher b 23 Jan 1985); *Career* chef; The Crown Whitebrook Gwent 1976–78, The Drangway Swansea 1978–83, Kirroughtree Hotel Newton Stewart Scotland

1983–85, Café Rouge (not chain) London 1985–87, Hilaire Restaurant London 1987–2002, proprietor and head chef Tyddyn Llan 2002– (Michelin star); *Style*— Bryan Webb, Esq; ✉ Tyddyn Llan, Llandrillo, Nr Corwen, Denbighshire LL21 0ST

WEBB, Prof Colin; s of Sidney Joseph Webb (d 1985), and Stella Taylor, *née* Botten (d 1976); *b* 11 October 1954; *Educ* Leominster GS, Aston Univ (BSc, PhD); *m* 14 April 1984, Ann Elizabeth, da of Charles Edward Kelly; 1 s (Richard Hereford b 11 Oct 1985), 1 da (Kate Elizabeth b 24 April 1989); *Career* Univ of Manchester (formerly UMIST): research assoc 1979–83, lectr in chem engrg 1983–91, sr lectr chem engrg 1991–94, Satake prof of grain process engrg 1994–, head Dept of Chemical Engrg 2000–04, assoc dean 2004–05, head Sch of Chemical Engrg and Analytical Science 2005–07; examiner Inst of Brewing 1997–2002; ed-in-chief The Biochemical Engineering Journal 1998–; fell Int Acad of Food Science and Technol 1999; FIChemE 1992 (vice-pres 2012–15); *Publications* Process Engineering Aspects of Immobilised Cell Systems (1986), Plant and Animal Cells: Process Possibilities (1987), Studies in Viable Cell Immobilisation (1996), Cereals: Novel Uses and Processes (1997), Comprehensive Biotechnology Vol 2: Engineering Fundamentals (2 edn, 2011), Food Industry Wastes: Assessment and Recuperation of Commodities (2013); also more than 270 publications in learned jls in the area of biochemical engrg; *Recreations* cycling, walking; *Style*— Prof Colin Webb; ✉ University of Manchester, School of Chemical Engineering and Analytical Science, C77, The Mill, Oxford Road, Manchester M13 9PL (☎ 01613 064370, e-mail colin.webb@manchester.ac.uk)

WEBB, Prof Colin Edward; MBE (2000); s of Alfred Edward Webb (d 1985), and Doris, *née* Collins (d 1966); *b* 9 December 1937, Erith, Kent; *Educ* Erith GS, Univ of Nottingham (Ford (Dagenham) Trust scholar, BSc), Univ of Oxford (DPhil, Prize in Waverley Gold Medal Competition for Scientific Essay); *m* 1, 6 June 1964, Pamela Mabel Cooper (d 1992), da of Maj Wilfred Alan Cooper White (d 1984); 2 da (Susan Patricia (Mrs S Steel) b 17 March 1967, Julie Diane (Mrs T Pottle) b 28 August 1970); m 2, 25 July 1995, Margaret Helen Marshall, da of Gordon Dewar (d 1968); *Career* memb tech staff Bell Telephone Labs Murray Hill NJ 1964–68; Clarendon Lab Univ of Oxford: AEI res fell in physics 1968–71, lectr 1971–90, reader in physics 1990–92, prof of laser physics 1992–2002; Jesus Coll Oxford: official tutorial fell 1973–88, sr res fell in physics 1988–2005, emeritus fell 2005–; visiting prof Dept of Physics Univ of Salford 1988–2004, visiting prof dept of mechanical engr Cranfield Univ 1999–2004; chm and fndr Oxford Lasers Ltd 1977–2014 (non-exec dir 2015–); govr Launceston Coll 2013–; Achievement Award of Worshipful Company of Scientific Instrument Makers 1986, Queen's Award for Export 1987, Queen's Award for Technol 1989 and 1991), Clifford Patterson Lecture & Medal Royal Soc 1998; Optical Soc of America: memb 1960–88, fell 1988–, dir-at-large 1991–94; pres UK Consortium for Photonics and Optics (UKCPO) 1998–2002; FInstP 1985 (memb 1968–85, Duddell Medal and Prize 1985, Glazebrook Medal and Prize 2001), FRS 1992; *Publications* Handbook of Laser Technology and Applications (ed-in-chief, 2004), Laser Physics (jtly, 2010); over 100 papers in scientific jls and numerous chapters in books; *Recreations* music, photography, travel, reading; *Clubs* Royal Society; *Style*— Prof Colin Webb, MBE, FRS; ✉ Oxford Lasers Ltd, Unit 8, Moorbrook Park, Didcot, Oxfordshire OX11 7HP (☎ 01235 810088, fax 01235 810060); Department of Atomic and Laser Physics, University of Oxford, The Clarendon Laboratory, Parks Road, Oxford OX1 3PU (☎ 01865 272254, fax 01865 272375, e-mail c.webb1@physics.ox.ac.uk, website www.jesus.ox.ac.uk/fellows-and-staff/fellows/professor-colin-webb)

WEBB, Prof David John; s of Alfred William Owen Webb, of London, and Edna May, *née* Parish; *b* 1 September 1953, Greenwich, London; *Educ* Dulwich Coll (Kent scholar), The Royal London Hosp (MB BS, MD), Univ of Edinburgh (DSc); *m* 1, 23 June 1984 (m dis 2007), Dr Margaret Jane Cullen, da of Dr Archibald Skinnider Cullen; 3 s (David Matthew b 29 July 1992, Matthew Owen Cullen b 28 Aug 1995, Mark Ewen b 11 May 1999); m 2, 2009, Dr Louise Eleanor Bath, da of Dr Desmond Sackville Gwyn Bath; *Career* MRC clinical research fell MRC Blood Pressure Unit Glasgow 1982–85, lectr in clinical pharmacology Dept of Pharmacology and Clinical Pharmacology St George's Hosp Med Sch London 1985–89; Univ of Edinburgh: sr lectr Dept of Med and dir Clinical Research Centre 1990–95, Christison prof of therapeutics and clinical pharmacology Clinical Pharmacology Unit and Research Centre 1995–, head Dept of Med Western Gen Hosp 1997–98, head Dept Med Sciences 1998–2001, ldr Wellcome Tst Cardiovascular Initiative 1997–2001, ldr Wellcome Tst Clinical Research Facility Educn Prog 1998–, head Centre for Cardiovascular Science 2000–04; hon conslt physician Lothian Univ Hospitals NHS Tst Edinburgh 1990–; hon tstee and jt research dir High Blood Pressure Fndn 1991–2011; chm: Lothian Area Drug and Therapeutics Ctee 1998–2005, Coll Ctee on Clinical Pharmacology and Therapeutics, RCP 1999–2000, RCP(Ed) Symposium Ctee 1999–2008; chair: Scottish Exec's New Drugs Ctee 2001–04, Project Grants Ctee Br Heart Fndn 2004–09, Profs and Heads CPT 2004, Scottish Medicines Consortium 2004–08; dep ldr Medical Research Cncl Scottish Clinical Pharmacology and Pathology 3 (MRC SCP3) 2010; dir Wellcome Tst Scottish Translational Medicine and Therapeutics Initiative 2008, non-exec dir Medicines and Healthcare Products Regulatory Agency 2013–; hon pres European Assoc for Clinical Pharmacology and Therapeutics 2009–; vice-pres RCPEd 2006–09; memb: MRS 1982, Scottish Soc for Experimental Med 1982 (memb Cncl 1994–97), Br Hypertension Soc 1985 (memb Exec Ctee 1991–94), Euro Soc of Hypertension 1987, Int Soc of Hypertension 1988, Scottish Cardiac Soc 1992, Faculty of Pharmaceutical Med RCP UK 1992, Research Defence Soc 1992, American Heart Assoc 1994, Euro Network of Therapeutics Teachers (assoc) 1994, Assoc of Physicians of GB and I 1994, Scottish Soc of Physicians 1995 (pres 2010), Assoc of Clinical Profs of Med 1996, Soc for Meds Research 1996, Advsy Bd MRC 1997–98, Wellcome Tst Physiology & Pharmacology Panel 1997–2000, Scottish Exec's Scottish Medical and Scientific Advsy Ctee 2001; Br Pharmacological Soc: memb 1988, memb Exec 1994–96, hon sec, dir and tstee 1996–99, memb Cncl and dir 2004–, vice-pres (meetings) 2011–14, pres-elect 2015–; Biennial SmithKline Beecham Fndn Prize for Research Br Pharmacological Soc 1994, Lilly Biennial Prize and Gold Medal for Research in Clinical Pharmacology Br Pharmacological Soc 2003; memb Scottish Malt Whisky Soc; FRCP, FRSE, FESC, FFPM, FMedSci, fell Br Pharmacological Soc (pres 2016/17), fell Br Hypertension Soc 2014, vice-chair Clinical Section Int Union of Pharmacologists and Clinical Pharmacologists; *Books* The Molecular Biology and Pharmacology of the Endothelins (Molecular Biology Intelligence Unit Monograph Series, with G A Gray, 1995), The Endothelium in Hypertension (ed with P J T Vallance, 1996), Vascular Endothelium in Human Physiology and Pathophysiology (ed with P J T Vallance, 1999), The Year in Therapeutics Vol 1 (2005); *Recreations* summer and winter mountaineering, scuba diving, opera, bridge, chess, ski touring; *Clubs* Scottish Mountaineering; *Style*— Prof David Webb; ✉ 75 Great King Street, Edinburgh EH3 6RN (☎ 0131 556 7145); Clinical Pharmacology Unit, Centre for Cardiovascular Science, Queen's Medical Research Institute, Room E3.22, 47 Little France Crescent, Edinburgh EH16 4TJ (e-mail d.j.webb@ed.ac.uk)

WEBB, Iain Andrew; s of Eric Webb, of York, and Oris, *née* Dyson; *b* 30 March 1959; *Educ* Scalby Secdy Sch Scarborough, Joseph Rowntree Secdy Sch York, Rambert Sch of Ballet London, The Royal Ballet Sch London; *m* 30 July 1982, Margaret, da of Ettore Barbieri; 1 s (Jason Alexander b 29 July 1987); *Career* Sadlers Well's Royal Ballet (now The Birmingham Royal Ballet) 1979–89; princ roles: Oberon in Ashton's The Dream, The Young Man in Ashton's The Two Pigeons, Franz in Wright's Coppélia, Colas and Alain in Ashton's La Fille mal Gardée, Prince Siegfried and Benno in Wright's Swan Lake, Pas de Quatre in Nureyev's Raymonda Act III, Blue Bird and Pas de Quatre in Wright's Sleeping Beauty, The Poet in Les Sylphides; Balanchine's The Prodigal Son, Van Manen's 5 Tango's, Kay in Bintley's The Snow Queen; created roles in: Bintley's Polonia, Night Moves, Choros The Swan of Tuonela, Flowers of the Forest; performed Petrushka 1988/89 season; joined The Royal Ballet at Covent Garden 1989; debut as the King of the South in MacMillan's The Prince of the Pagodes, Mercury in Bintley's The Plants, danced in first performances of Balanchine's Violin Concerts and Page's Bloodline, Alain in Ashton's La Fille mal Gardée, guest appearances in Spain and SA 1989 and 1992, received sponsorship to study with Royal Danish Ballet March 1992, prog organiser and conslt for the Celebration of Classical Dance evening Harrogate Festival 1992; 1992–93 season: Bottom in The Dream, Mrs Tiggywinkle and Alexander Bland Pig in The Tales of Beatrix Potter, the small ugly sister (Ashton's Role) in Ashton's Cinderella, Sancho Panza in Mikhail Barysnikov's Don Quixote and the Pas de Quatra in MacMillan's Gloria; 1993–94 season: The Doctor in MacMillan's Different Drummer, Gallison in Anthony Dowell's Sleeping Beauty; prod and dir Patrick Armand and Friends Gala for 1993 Harrogate Int Festival, co-prodr an evening with principals and soloists of the Stuttgart Ballet 1994, prodr gala performance for the 150th anniversary of the Shaftesbury Homes at the Banqueting House 1994; co-dir The Dance Agency 1993–, fndr Dance Cares 1994, memb Bd of Dirs Adventures in Motion Pictures 1994, asst dir K Ballet Japan 2003–, tutor London Studio Centre; *Recreations* history of ballet, collecting ballet memorabilia, music, photography; *Style*— Iain Webb, Esq

WEBB, Justin Oliver; s of Charles Webb (d 1983), and Gloria, *née* Crocombe (d 2006); *b* 3 January 1961; *Educ* Friends' Sch Sidcot, LSE (BSc(Econ)); *m* 30 Aug 1996, Sarah Louise, da of Charles G A Gordon; 3 c (Martha Sarah, Samuel Oliver (twins) b 28 March 2000, Clara Jayne b 1 Feb 2004); *Career* BBC: news trainee 1984–86, reporter BBC Radio Ulster 1986–87, reporter Today prog Radio 4 1987–88, news reporter and foreign affrs corr BBC Radio and Television 1988–93 (assignments incl: Gulf War, Russia, USA, Middle E, India, Western and Eastern Europe, South Africa, Bosnia), full-time presenter Breakfast News 1994–99 (occasional presenter 1993–94), Europe corr 1999–2002, chief Washington corr 2002–07, North America ed 2007–09, presenter Today Programme (BBC Radio 4) 2009–; *Style*— Justin Webb, Esq; ✉ Today Programme, BBC Radio 4, Room G630, Stage 6, Television Centre, Wood Lane, London W12 7RJ

WEBB, Richard; s of Lt-Col Richard Webb (d 1988), and Iris Webb (d 1996); *b* 26 July 1943; *Educ* Marlborough; *m* 25 Feb 1992, Gillian Blane, *née* Jenkins; *Career* Condé Nast Publications Ltd 1966–70, dir Michael Joseph Ltd publishers London 1970–74; co-fndr and md: Webb & Bower (Publishers) Ltd 1975–99, Richard Webb, Publisher 2000–; *Clubs* Royal Dart Yacht; *Style*— Richard Webb, Esq; ✉ Driftwood Quay, Warfleet, Dartmouth, Devon TQ6 9BZ (☎ 01803 835525, e-mail mail@richardwebb.co.uk, website www.dartmouthbooks.co.uk)

WEBB, Robert Stopford; QC (1988); s of R V B Webb, MC, of Styal, Cheshire, and Isabella Raine, *née* Hinks; *b* 4 October 1948; *Educ* Wycliffe Coll, Univ of Exeter (LLB); *m* 1 April 1975, Angela Mary, da of Bernard Bruce Freshwater (d 1978); 2 s (Alfred b 1978, William b 1980); *Career* called to the Bar: Inner Temple 1971 (bencher 1998), Lincoln's Inn 1996; head of chambers 5 Bell Yard 1988–98, recorder 1993–98; general counsel Br Airways 1998–2009, general counsel Rolls-Royce 2012–; chm Air Law Ctee Royal Aeronautical Soc 1988–92, chm Int Practice Ctee Bar Cncl, memb Bd Int Acad of Trial Lawyers; dir London Stock Exchange 2001–15; dir Holdingham Gp Ltd (formerly Hakluyt) 2005–, non-exec dir BBC 2007–12, chm BBC Worldwide 2009–12, chm Autonomy Corporation plc 2009–12, dir Argent Gp 2009–12, chm Sciemus Ltd 2010–11, chm Dark Trace Ltd 2014–; tstee Migratory Salmon Fndn 1997–, fell Unicef 2006–11, tstee Comic Relief 2011–; FRAeS; *Recreations* golf, conservation; *Clubs* Reform, Brook's, Soho House, RAC, Royal Wimbledon Golf, Royal Lytham St Anne's Golf, Prestbury Golf, Hampstead Golf; *Style*— Robert Webb, Esq, QC

WEBB, Sarah; OBE (2009, MBE 2005); *b* 13 January 1977, Ashford, Middx; *Career* yachtswoman; early career in Laser Radial class, subsequently 470 class 2000 (Silver medal Br Olympic trials 2000), J24 class 2001, IOD class 2002, J22 class 2002, Yngling class 2003– (sailing with: Sarah Ayton and Shirley Robertson 2003–05, Sarah Ayton and Pippa Wilson 2006–); achievements in Yngling class incl: Bronze medal SPA Olympic Class Regatta Holland 2003, Gold medal Pre-Olympics Athens 2003, Gold medal Olympic Games Athens 2004, Gold medal Hyeres 2004 (Silver medal 2005), Gold medal Spa Regatta 2005, Bronze medal Skandia Sail for Gold Regatta 2006, Silver medal Rolex Miami OCR 2007, Gold medal Breitling Holland Regatta 2007 (Silver medal 2006), Gold medal ISAF World Championships 2007, Gold medal Olympic Test Event Qingdao 2007, Gold medal ISAF World Championships 2008, Gold medal European Championships 2008, Gold medal Olympic Games Beijing 2008; Yachting Journalists Assoc Young Yachtsman of the Year 1996, Yachting Journalists Assoc Yachtsman of the Year 2004 and 2008; *Style*— Ms Sarah Webb, OBE; ✉ c/o Merlin Elite Ltd, Hammersmith Studios, 55 Yeldham Road, London W6 8JF (☎ 020 8834 8900, e-mail richard.thompson@merlinelite.co.uk, website www.sarahwebbconsulting.com, Twitter @iamsarahgosling)

WEBB, Steven; *Career* economist Inst of Fiscal Studies 1986–95, prof of social policy Univ of Bath 1995–97; MP (Lib Dem) Northavon 1997–2015; Lib Dem: shadow min for work and pensions 1999–2005, shadow min for health 2005–07, chair Lib Dem Manifesto 2006–07, shadow min for the environment, food and rural affrs 2007–08, shadow min for energy and climate change 2008–09, shadow min for work and pensions 2009–10, min of state for pensions 2010–; *Style*— Steve Webb; ✉ House of Commons, London SW1A 0AA (☎ 020 7219 3000)

WEBB, Prof William; s of Christopher Webb, of Woking, Surrey, and Genebeth, *née* Mooring; *b* 4 May 1967, Hersham, Surrey; *Educ* Univ of Southampton (BEng, PhD), Southampton Univ Mgmnt Sch (MBA); *m* 17 June 1995, Alison, *née* Porter; 2 da (Katherine b 17 Dec 1997, Hannah b 23 Feb 2001); *Career* engr; Multiple Access Communications Ltd 1989–93 (dir 1992–93), Smith System Engrg Ltd 1993–97 (head of spectrum mgmnt 1995–97), head of wireless local loop div Netcom Conslts 1997–98, Motorola 1998–2001 (dir of corp strategy 2000–01), mgmnt conslt in wireless technol practice PA Consulting 2001–03, head of R&D and sr technologist Ofcom 2003–11, chief technol offr Neul Ltd 2011–, ceo Weightless SIG 2012–; visiting prof: Centre for Communications Systems Research (CCSR) Univ of Surrey 2003–, De Montfort Univ 2007–11, Univ of Southampton 2014–, TCD 2014–; memb Judging Panel Wall St Jl Innovation Awards 2002–; Hon DSc Univ of Southampton 2015, Hon DTech Anglia Ruskin Univ 2015; vice-pres IEE 2004–06, pres IET 2014–15 (vice-pres 2009–12, dep pres 2013–14); CEng 1992, FIEEE 2008 (SMIEEE 1995), FIEE 2001, FREng 2005; *Publications* Modern Quadrature Amplitude Modulation (1994, 2 edn 2004), Introduction to Wireless Local Loop (1998, 2 edn 2000), Understanding Cellular Radio (1998), The Complete Wireless Communications Professional (1999), Single and Multi-Carrier QAM (2000), The Future of Wireless Communications (2001), Wireless Communications: The Future (2007), Essentials of Modern Spectrum Management (2007), Being Mobile (2010), Understanding Weightless (2012), Dynamic White Space (2013), Using Spectrum (2015); *Recreations* cycling, music, reading; *Style*— Prof William Webb; ✉ e-mail wwebb@theiet.org; Hawksmead, Moat Lane, Melbourn, Herts SG8 6EH

WEBBER, John Anthony; s of Walter James Webber (d 1972), of Birmingham; *Educ* Birmingham Secdy Sch, Birmingham Coll of Food and Domestic Arts (City & Guilds), Westminster Coll of Food London (City & Guilds); *m* 5 Aug 1987, Caroline Isobel, da of Ian Jackson, of Appin, Argyll; 1 s (Nigel John b 10 Feb 1989), 2 da (Chloe Caroline b 4 Jan 1992, Abigail Louise b 14 Feb 1995); *Career* chef; first commis chef rising to chef de partie Park Lane Hotel Piccadilly 1969–73; Dorchester Hotel Park Lane: second commis chef 1973–75, first commis chef 1975–76, chef de partie 1976–79, sous chef 1979–80; head chef: Gidleigh Park Hotel Chagford 1980–85 (Michelin rosette 1982), Clivedon 1985–88; exec chef 'Kinnaird' Kinnaird Estate 1988–98 (Michelin rosette 1992, 4/5 Good Food Guide 1996), culinary dir Drambuie Scottish Chefs National Cookery Centre 1998–, culinary dir Nairns Cook Sch 2000–, dir Umami Culinaire 2008; Cert of Merit (Salon Culinaire de Londres) 1976, Silver Medal (City of Truro Festival of Culinary Arts) 1980, Gold Medal (Torquay Gastronomic Festival) 1981; Master Craftsman Craft Guild of Chefs, Master Chef Master Chefs Inst; *Recreations* fishing, eating out, music; *Style*— John Webber, Esq; ✉ Sonas, 22 Vennacher Avenue, Callander, Stirlingshire FK17 8JQ (☎ and fax 01877 339552)

WEBER, Prof Richard Robert; s of Richard Robert Weber (d 1988), and Elizabeth, *née* Bray; *b* 25 February 1953, London; *Educ* Walnut Hills HS, Solihull Sch, Downing Coll Cambridge (MA, Mayhew Prize, PhD); *Career* Univ of Cambridge: research fell Queens' Coll 1977–78, tutor and dir of studies in mathematics, manufacturing engrg and management studies Queens' Coll 1978–92, lectr Dept of Engrg 1984–92 (asst lectr 1978–84), reader in management science 1992–94, Churchill prof of mathematics for operational research Dept of Pure Mathematics and Mathematical Statistics 1994–, vice-pres Queens' Coll 1996–2007; memb: Operational Research Soc, INFORMS; FRSS; *Recreations* hiking, fitness training, travel; *Style*— Prof Richard Weber; ✉ Queens' College, Cambridge CB3 9ET (☎ 01223 335570); Department of Pure Mathematics and Mathematical Statistics, Statistical Laboratory, University of Cambridge, Wilberforce Road, Cambridge CB3 0WB (☎ 01223 337944, fax 01223 337956, e-mail rrwl@cam.ac.uk)

WEBSTER, Prof Alec; s of Richard Webster (d 1979), and Gladys, *née* Hargreaves (d 1997); *b* 5 June 1950, Accrington, Lancs; *Educ* Accrington GS, Keele Univ (BA), UCL (MSc), Univ of Leicester (PGCE), Univ of Nottingham (PhD), Univ of Bristol (MPhil); *m* 1, 1972 (m dis 1987), Anne Isobel, da of Jack Hindmoor; 3 s (Joseph b 26 Nov 1977, Rick b 1 Dec 1979, Robin b 10 Aug 1987), 1 da (Elizabeth b 26 March 1982); m 2, 1995, Valerie Joy, da of Dennis Crome; *Career* teacher 1973–76, educnl psychologist ILEA 1976–77, educnl psychologist Bucks LEA 1977–80, sr specialist educnl psychologist for language and hearing-impaired children Berks LEA 1980–86, sr educnl psychologist Clwyd LEA 1986–88, memb Advsy Team Clwyd LEA 1988–90, area sr educnl psychologist Avon LEA 1990–92 (mangr Bristol Psychology Serv team); Univ of Bristol: lectr Grad Sch of Educn and dir Centre for Literacy Studies 1993–96, reader in educn 1997, co-ordinator Centre for Psychology and Language Studies 1997–99, dir Professional Trg in Educnl Psychology 1998, co-ordinator Centre for Applied Educnl Psychology 1999, co-ordinator EdD in educnl psychology 1999, prof of educnl psychology 2000–06, prof emeritus in educnl psychology 2006–; secondment as lectr in special educn then research fell Bulmershe Coll of FE 1984–86; visiting lectr: Univ of Reading, Bracknell Coll of HE, UCL, Univ of Southampton, Univ of Birmingham, Med Sch Univ of Cambridge, Inst of Educn Univ of London, Univ of Manchester, Univ of Sheffield; conslt psychologist Mary Hare Sch for the Deaf 1980–86, memb Deafness Research Gp Univ of Nottingham 1985–91, memb Policy Review Forum Royal Coll of Speech and Language Therapists 1995–; memb Editorial Bd: Br Jl of Special Educn 1988–91, Br Jl of the Assoc of Teachers of the Deaf 1995–, Deafness and Educn Int 1997–, Educnl and Child Psychology 2000–02; delivered numerous addresses and conf presentations; FBPsS 1988, CPsychol 1992; *Publications* The Hearing-Impaired Child in the Ordinary School (jtly, 1984), Deafness, Development and Literacy (1986), Children with Speech and Language Difficulties (jtly, 1987), Children with Hearing Difficulties (jtly, 1989), Profiles of the Hearing-Impaired (jtly, 1990), Profiles of the Language-Impaired (jtly, 1991), Start-Right Profile: A Good Start to School (jtly, 1991), The Essential Evaluation Toolkit (1991), Literacy and Hearing-Impaired Children: A Distance Learning Course for Teachers (1991), School Marketing (jtly, 1992), Profiles of Development: Planning for Individual Progress within the National Curriculum (jtly, 1992), Supporting Learning: Hearing-Impairment (jtly, 1993), Managing Change through a Consortium: An Evaluation of TVEI (jtly, 1994), Supporting Learning in the Primary School: Meeting Individual Needs under the new Code of Practice (jtly, 1994), Managing the Literacy Curriculum: How Schools can become Communities of Readers and Writers (jtly, 1995), Supporting Learning in the Secondary School: Raising Individual Achievement under the New Code of Practice volume 1 – Management and Co-ordination (jtly, 1995), Supporting Learning in the Secondary School: Meeting Individual Needs under the New Code of Practice volume 2 – Issues for Practitioners (jtly, 1995), Behaviour Education: Teaching Positive Behaviour in the Primary School (jtly, 1996), Raising Achievement in Hearing-Impaired Pupils (jtly, 1997), Children with Visual Impairments: Social Interaction, Language and Learning (jtly, 1998, shortlisted 1999 Book of the Year Award Nat Assoc of Special Educnl Needs/TES), Addressing the Literacy Needs of Offenders under Probation Supervision (jtly, 1998), Supporting Learning in the Early Years (jtly 1998); ed of numerous books and jls, author of book contribs and papers in refereed academic and professional jls; *Recreations* playing cello and violin, drawing and painting; *Style*— Prof Alec Webster; ✉ Graduate School of Education, University of Bristol, 35 Berkeley Square, Bristol BS8 1JA (☎ 01856 850798, e-mail alec.webster@bris.ac.uk)

WEBSTER, Alistair Stevenson; QC (1995); s of His Hon Ian Webster (d 2002), of Rochdale, Lancs, and Margaret, *née* Sharples; *b* 28 April 1953; *Educ* Hulme GS Oldham, BNC Oxford (BA); *m* 4 June 1977, Barbara Anne, da of Dr Donald Longbottom (d 1961); 2 da (Elizabeth b 1982, Alexandra b 1985); *Career* called to the Bar Middle Temple 1976 (bencher 2004); hon sec Northern Circuit 1988–93, recorder 1996– (asst recorder 1992); memb Gen Cncl of the Bar 1994–95; memb Legal and Judicial Ctees Lancs and Gtr Manchester Local Criminal Justice Bds; *Recreations* skiing, cricket, tennis; *Clubs* Rochdale Racquets; *Style*— Alistair Webster, Esq, QC; ✉ 33 Chancery Lane, London WC2A 1EN (e-mail websterqc@aol.com)

WEBSTER, David Gordon Comyn; s of Alfred Edward Comyn Webster (d 1998), and Meryl Mary, *née* Clutterbuck (d 1970); *b* 11 February 1945; *Educ* Glasgow Acad, Univ of Glasgow (LLB); *m* 12 Feb 1972, (Pamela) Gail, da of Dr Dennis Frank Runnicles, of Sevenoaks, Kent; 3 s (Michael Gordon Comyn b 25 Sept 1974, Nicholas Gordon Comyn b 9 Jan 1978, Jonathan Hugo Comyn b 27 Feb 1983); *Career* Lt RNR, ret 1970; admitted slr 1968, corp fin Samuel Montagu & Co 1969–72, Wm Brandts 1972–73, fin dir Oriel Foods Ltd 1973–76; Safeway plc (formerly Argyll Group plc): co-fndr, fndr dir 1977–2004, fin dir 1977–89, exec dep chm 1989–97, exec chm 1997–2004; chm: Makinson Cowell Ltd 2004–13, InterContinental Hotels Gp plc 2004–12 (non-exec dir 2003); non-exec dir: Reed International plc 1992–2002, Reed Elsevier plc 1993–2002 (non-exec chm 1998–99), Elsevier NV 1993–2002; dir: Temple Bar Investment Tst plc 2009–, Amadeus IT Hldg SA 2010–; memb Bd Amadeus IT SA 2010–; pres Inst of Grocery Distribution 2001–02; memb: Nat Employers' Liaison Ctee 1992–2002, Corp Advsy Gp Tate Gallery 1997–2004, Appeals Ctee Panel on Takeovers and Mergers 2007–; tstee Nat Life Story Collection 2005–15; *Recreations* military history, gardening, family; *Style*— David Webster, Esq; ✉ e-mail dgcwebster@gmail.com

WEBSTER, Evelyn; *Career* IPC Media: joined as grad trainee 1992, rising to publisher IPC Inspire, md IPC Inspire 2003–04, memb Bd 2003–11, md IPC Connect 2004–09, chief exec 2009–11; exec vice pres Lifestyle Gp Time Inc 2011–; *Style*— Ms Evelyn Webster

WEBSTER, Rev Prof John Bainbridge; *b* 20 June 1955; *Educ* Clare Coll Cambridge (MA, PhD); *Career* Stephenson fell Univ of Sheffield 1981–82, tutor in systematic theology St John's Coll Durham 1982–86, prof of systematic theology Wycliffe Coll Univ of Toronto 1986–96, Lady Margaret prof of divinity Univ of Oxford and canon of Christ Church Oxford 1996–2003; Univ of Aberdeen: prof of systematic theology 2003–, prof of divinity 2013–; FRSE 2005; *Books* Eberhard Jüngel (1986), The Possibilities of Theology (1994), Barth's Ethics of Reconciliation (1995), Barth's Moral Theology (1998), Theology after Liberalism (ed, 2000), The Cambridge Companion to Karl Barth (ed, 2000), Barth (2000), Word and Church (2001), Holiness (2002), Holy Scripture (2002), Confessing God (2005), Barth's Earlier Theology (2005), The Oxford Handbook of Systematic Theology (ed, 2007), The Domain of the Word (2012), God Without Measure (2012); also author of various articles in learned jls; *Style*— The Rev Prof John Webster; ✉ St Mary's College, The School of Divinity, University of St Andrews, South Street, St Andrews KY16 9JU (e-mail jbw5@st-andrews.ac.uk)

WEBSTER, John Vernon; s of Dr (Francis) Vernon Webster, CBE, of Maidenhead, Berks, and Jill Mary, *née* Archer; *b* 27 May 1961, Maidenhead, Berks; *Educ* Maidenhead GS (now Desborough Sch), Univ of Manchester (LLB), Coll of Law London; *m* 9 Aug 1986, Karen Ann, *née* Campbell-Trotter; 1 da (Eleanor Charlotte b 14 May 2003); *Career* slr Blandy & Blandy 1985–88 (articled clerk 1983–85); Veale Wasbrough Vizards Slrs: slr 1988–94, ptnr 1994–, head Personal Injury Dept (now branded Augustines Injury Law) 1996–; memb Glos Courts Bd 2004–10, SW regnl coordinator Assoc of Personal Injury Lawyers (APIL) 2003–06, accredited memb Personal Injury Panel Law Soc 1995–, chm Bristol Civil Courts Ctee 1998–; memb: Law Soc 1985–, Bristol Law Soc (memb Cncl 1998–2005); fell Assoc of Personal Injury Lawyers 2000; APIL Personal Injury: Law, Practice and Precedents (2006); *Recreations* skiing, football, walking, travel, family, athletics; *Style*— John Webster, Esq; ✉ Augustines Injury Law, St Augustines Yard, Orchard Lane, Bristol BS1 5DE (☎ 0117 314 5400, fax 0117 314 5405, e-mail jwebster@vwv.co.uk)

WEBSTER, Michael Gordon Comyn; *b* 25 September 1974; *Educ* Radley Coll, Oxford Brookes Univ (BA); *m* Victoria; 1 da (Isabelle b 24 March 2011), 1 s (Toby b 28 Nov 2012); *Career* researcher House of Commons 1997, account dir Brunswick Gp 1999, founding dir Gorkana 2003–, dir Gorkana Gp Ltd 2010–13, dir Telum Media 2013–; *Clubs* HAC, Naval & Military; *Style*— Michael Webster, Esq; ✉ Telum Media Ltd Pte, 19 Cecil Street, Singapore 04970

WEBSTER, Prof Nigel Robert; s of Derek Stanley Webster, of Walsall, and Sheila Margaret Flora, *née* Squire; *b* 14 June 1953; *Educ* Univ of Leeds (BSc, MB ChB, PhD); *m* 1, 2 July 1977 (m dis 2013), Diana Christina Shirley, da of Brian Robert Galt Hutchinson, of York, 2 da (Lorna Elizabeth b 1984, Lucy Anne b 1987), 1 s (Oliver James b 1986); m 2, Helen Frances, *née* Galley; *Career* memb Scientific Staff Div of Anaesthesia MRC Clinical Res Centre 1986–88, conslt in anaesthesia, dir of transplant anaesthesia and co-dir of intensive care St James' Univ Hosp Leeds 1988–94, prof Dept of Anaesthesia and Intensive Care Univ of Aberdeen and hon conslt Aberdeen Royal Infirmary 1994–; memb: Intensive Care Soc, Euro Soc of Intensive Care Med, Soc for Free Radical Res, Elgar Soc; FFARCS, FRCP; *Books* Research Techniques in Anaesthesia (1988), Intensive Care: Developments and controversies (1992); *Recreations* flying, music, gardening; *Style*— Prof Nigel Webster; ✉ Aberdeen Royal Infirmary, Forester Hill, Aberdeen AB25 2ZD (☎ 01224 681818, e-mail n.r.webster@abdn.ac.uk)

WEBSTER, Paul; *b* 19 September 1952; *Career* co-dir Osiris Film London 1979–81, fndr Palace Pictures 1982–88, launched Working Title Film LA 1990–92, head of prodn Miramax Films 1995–97 (responsible for films incl The English Patient, Welcome to Sarajevo, Wings of the Dove), chief exec Film Four Ltd 1998–2002, head Kudos Pictures 2004–11; prodr: The Tall Guy 1988, Drop Dead Fred 1990, Bob Roberts 1992 (exec prodr), Romeo Is Bleeding 1993, Little Oddessa 1994 (Silver Lion Venice Film Festival), The Pallbearer 1995, Gridlock'd 1996, The Yards 1998, Buffalo Soldiers 2001, The Warrior 2001, Dog Eat Dog 2001, Charlotte Gray 2001, Miranda 2002, Once Upon a Time in the Midlands 2002, It's All About Love 2003, The Priniciples of Lust 2003, The Actors 2003, To Kill a King 2003, The Motorcycle Diaries 2004, Atonement 2008 (Best Film BAFTA 2008), Eastern Promises 2007, Miss Pettigrew Lives for a Day 2008 (exec prodr), Brighton Rock 2010, Salmon Fishing in the Yemen 2011, Anna Karenina 2012, Hummingbird 2013, Locke 2013; memb: BAFTA Cncl, BAFTA Film Cncl; *Style*— Paul Webster, Esq

WEBSTER, Prof (John) Paul Garrett; s of Leonard Garrett Webster (d 1976), and Dorothy Agnes, *née* White (d 1991); *b* 16 July 1942, Ripon, N Yorks; *Educ* The Leys Sch Cambridge, Univ of Reading (BSc), Univ of London (Dip Farm Business Admin, PhD); *m* 1972, Amanda Jane, *née* Hetigin; 1 s (Michael Garrett b 1974), 1 da (Lucy Jean b 1977); *Career* Dept of Agric Sciences Imperial Coll London (merged with Wye Coll 2000): joined 1965, prof of agric business mgmnt 1991–2005, emeritus prof 2005–; lectr in rural economy Makere Univ Uganda 1970–71, Drapers' Co lectr Univ of New England Armidale Aust 1974, visiting prof Lincoln Univ NZ 1999–2000; economist Engrg Dept Int Rice Research Inst Philippines 1980–81; pres Agric Economics Soc 1999–2000 (chm Exec Ctee 1991–96), chm Educn Ctee Int of Agric Mgmnt 1991–95, ind memb Advsy Ctee on Pesticides MAFF 1992–99; tstee Frank Parkinson Agricultural Tst 2005–; author of various book contribs and papers in learned jls; Hon Freeman Worshipful Co of Farmers 2000; fell Royal Agric Socs 2002; FBIM 1980, FRSA 1987, FIAgrM 1996; *Recreations* masters swimming (ASA ranked, French Open Masters Champion 100m freestyle 70+ age group); *Clubs* City of Canterbury Swimming, Entente Provencal Manosque Natation (France), Farmers, Ashford; *Style*— Prof Paul Webster; ✉ 25 Chequers Park, Wye, Kent TN25 5BB

WEBSTER, Richard Joseph; s of Peter Joseph Webster, of Dulwich, London; *b* 7 July 1953; *Educ* Dulwich HS, Harvard Business Sch; *m* 1980, Patricia Catherine, da of Gerald Stanley Edwards, of East Grinstead, W Sussex; 1 da (Victoria Catherine b Sept 1983), 1 s (James Joseph b April 1985); *Career* insurance underwriting with Brit Insurance; *Recreations* family, golf, watching rugby; *Clubs* City of London, Annabel's; *Style*— Richard J Webster, Esq; ✉ Brit Global Specialty, The Leadenhall Building, 122 Leadenhall Street London EC3V 4AB (☎ 020 3857 0331, e-mail richard.webster@britinsurance.com)

WEBSTER, Stephen; MBE; *b* 13 August 1959, Dartford, Kent; *Educ* Medway Coll of Design; *Career* jewellery designer; fndr Stephen Webster Ltd 1998, dir Garrard 2008–; curator Br Film Cncl Rock Vault 2012; memb Nat Assoc of Goldsmiths; special ambass Malaria No More; UK Nat Jewellery Awards: Designer of the Year 1997, 1998 and 2006, Luxury Jeweller 2000, 2001, 2003 and 2005, Diamond Jeweller 2004, Brand of the Year 2008, Andrea Palladio Award for Best Int Jewellery Designer VicenzaORA 2013; Liveryman City of London 2009; hon degree Kent Inst of Art & Design; *Style*— Stephen Webster, Esq, MBE; ✉ Stephen Webster Ltd 93 Mount Street, London W1K 2SY (☎ 0845 539 1840, fax 0845 539 1849, e-mail info@stephenwebster.com)

WEBSTER, Sue; da of Ray and Linda Webster; *b* 1967; *Educ* Leicester Poly, Nottingham Poly (BA); *Career* artist; collaborator with Tim Noble, *qv*; residency Dean Clough Halifax 1989–92; *Two-Person Exhibitions* British Rubbish (Independent Art Space London) 1996, Home Chance (Rivington St London) 1997, Vague Us (Habitat London) 1998, WOW (Modern Art London) 1998, The New Barbarians (Chisenhale Gallery London) 1999, I Love You (Deitch Projects NY) 2000, British Wildlife (Modern Art London) 2000, Masters of the Universe (Deste Fndn, Athens) 2000, Instant Gratification (Gagosian Gallery Beverly Hills) 2001, Ghastly Arrangements (Milton Keynes Gallery) 2002, Black Magic (MW Projects London) 2002, Real Life is Rubbish (Statements at Art Basel Miami) 2002, PS1/MoMA (Long Island City NY) 2003, Modern Art is Dead (Modern Art London) 2004, Noble & Webster (MFA Boston) 2004, The New Barbarians (CAC Málaga) 2005, The

Joy of Sex (Kukje Gallery Seoul) 2005, The Glory Hole (Bortolami Dayan NY) 2005; *Group Exhibitions* incl: Lift (Brick Lane London) 1993, Hijack (NY London and Berlin) 1994, Fete Worse Than Death (Hoxton Square London) 1994, Absolut Art (RCA London) 1994, Self Storage (Artangel London) 1995, Hanging Picnic (Hoxton Sq London) 1995, Fools Rain (ICA London) 1996, Turning the Tables (Chisenhale Gallery London) 1997, Livestock Market (London) 1997, Sex and the British (Galerie Thaddaeus Ropac Salzburg and Paris) 2000, Man-Body in Art from 1950 to 2000 (ARKEN Copenhagen) 2000, Apocalypse (Royal Acad of Art London) 2000, Tattoo Show (Modern Art London) 2001, Form Follows Fiction (Castello di Rivoli Turin) 2001, Casino 2001 (SMAK Ghent) 2002, 2001 A Space Oddity (A22 Projects London) 2001, Shortcuts (Nicosia Municipal Arts Centre Cyprus) 2001, Art Crazy Nation (Milton Keynes Gallery) 2002, State of Play (Serpentine Gallery London) 2004, New Blood (Saatchi Gallery London) 2004, Monument To Now (Dakis Joannou Collection Athens) 2004, Masquerade (MCA Sydney) 2006; *Recreations* DJing; *Clubs* Colony Room; *Style—* Miss Sue Webster; ✉ e-mail info@modernartinc.com

WEDDLE, Stephen Norman; s of Norman Harold Weddle, of Sutton Coldfield, W Midlands, and Irene, *née* Furniss; *b* 1 January 1950; *Educ* Fairfax High Sch Sutton Coldfield, NE London Poly (BSc), Bedford Coll London; *m* July 1977 (m dis 1980), Brigid, da of late Edward Couch; *Career* grad trainee journalist Birmingham Post and Mail 1972–75, reporter BBC Radio Stoke-on-Trent 1975–76; BBC TV: prodr Cool It 1985–90, ed Daytime Live 1987–90, ed Daytime UK 1990–91, ed Pebble Mill 1991–94 (researcher, dir and prodr 1976), ed Special Projects 1994–2001; dir Invisible Inc (prodn co) 2001–12; RTS Best Original TV Achievement Award 1987, Variety Clubs International Media Award 1993, RTS Midland Centre Award; *Books* It Starts With a Kiss (2014); *Recreations* supporting Tottenham Hotspur FC, cinema, travel, reading novels, running, writing; *Style—* Stephen Weddle, Esq; ✉ 60 Clarence Road, Four Oaks, Sutton Coldfield B74 4AR (☎ 0121 308 0993, e-mail stevewed@hotmail.com)

WEDGWOOD, Antony John Wedgwood; 5 Baron (UK 1942); s of Dr John Wedgwood, CBE (d 2007), and Margaret Webb Mason (d 1995); *b* 31 January 1944; *Educ* Marlborough, Trinity Coll Cambridge (MA); *m* 18 July 1970, Angela Margaret Mary, da of Dr E D Page; 2 da (Elizabeth b 15 July 1975, Caroline b 7 July 1981), 1 s (Tom b 20 April 1978); *Heir* s, Josiah Thomas Antony Wedgwood; *Career* Peat Marwick Mitchell & Co (now KPMG): articled 1966 (qualified 1969), ptnr 1981–2001; memb: various professional ctees and working parties Auditing Practices Bd, ICAEW, Br Bankers' Assoc, Financial Reporting Review Panel 2001–07; tstee and treas Historic Churches Preservation Tst 2002–08, tstee Nat Churches Tst 2007–12; FCA (ACA 1969); *Publications* A Guide to the Financial Services Act 1986 (jtly 1986), author of numerous articles on accounting and banking; *Recreations* reading, old cars and wirelesses, travel; *Clubs* Athenaeum; *Style—* The Rt Hon the Lord Wedgwood; ✉ 10 Milner Place, London N1 1TN (☎ 020 7607 2954)

WEDGWOOD, Pamela, Lady; *see:* Tudor-Craig, Dr Pamela

WEDLAKE, William John; s of late William John Wedlake, of South Zeal, Devon, and Patricia Mary, *née* Hunt; *b* 24 April 1956, W Wyke, Devon; *Educ* Okehampton GS, Exeter Coll of Educn, Univ of Warwick (BSc); *m* 4 July 1987, Elizabeth Kessick, da of late Brian Kessick Bowes; 3 s (Joshua William b 2 May 1989, James Henry b 29 Aug 1990, George Oliver b 5 December 1999), 1 da (Sophie Elizabeth b 16 April 1992); *Career* CA; formerly with: Arthur Andersen Bristol, Price Waterhouse USA and London; fin dir Schroders 1987–93, fin dir Guardian Insurance (Guardian Royal Exchange) 1993–96, chief fin offr Terra Nova (Bermuda) Hldgs 1996–2000; NextPharma Technologies Hldg Ltd: chief fin offr 2000–02, ceo 2002–11; Wedlake Consulting Ltd 2012–; pres Piramal Pharma Solutions 2013–; FCA; *Recreations* horse riding, walking, motor racing; *Style—* William J Wedlake, Esq; ✉ Wedlake Consulting Ltd, Furlongs, Franks Field, Peaslake, Guildford GU5 9SR (☎ 01306 730245, e-mail wedlake@msn.com)

WEEDON, Matt; *b* 25 March 1975, Aylesbury, Bucks; *Career* head chef: Seaham Hall Durham 2003–04, L'Ortolan Restaurant Reading 2004–06 (Michelin star), Glenapp Castle Ayrshire 2006–08 (Michelin star), exec chef Lords of the Manor Glos 2008– (Michelin star 2009–); *Style—* Matt Weedon, Esq; ✉ The Lords of the Manor, Upper Slaughter, Gloucestershire GL54 2JD (☎ 01451 820243, e-mail chef@lordsofthemanor.com, website www.lordsofthemanor.com)

WEEDS, Dr John Ian; s of Mike Weeds, of Rudgwick, W Sussex, and Barbara, *née* Denyer; *b* 21 October 1962, Horsham, W Sussex; *Educ* Collyers Sch Horsham, Collyer's Sixth Form Coll Horsham, Pembroke Coll Cambridge (MA), Univ of Durham (PGCE), Univ of Nottingham (MPhil), Nat Coll for Sch Leadership, Univ of Roehampton (EdD); *m* 18 Aug 1990, Sarah, *née* Turner; 3 s (Tom b 15 May 1993, Henry b 21 Aug 1994, Jamie b 27 Aug 1997); *Career* teacher Hampton Sch Middx 1987–90, teacher Bolton Sch Boy's Div 1990–93, head Classics Dept and housemaster Bedford Sch 1993–2000, dep head Slough GS 2000–06, princ Reading Sch Berks 2006–12, headmaster Cranbrook Sch 2012–; memb GCE Subject Criteria Review Gp Qualifications and Curriculum Authy (QCA) 2005–, chair Examination Review Gp Jt Assoc of Classical Teachers (JACT) 2005–; author articles on teaching classics; *Recreations* travel literature, literary criticism and philosophy, snooker, running, guitar; *Clubs* Friends of Mount Athos, London Wasps RUFC; *Style—* Dr John Weeds; ✉ Cranbrook School, Waterloo Road, Cranbrook, Kent TN17 3JD (☎ 01580 711801, mobile 07501 221229, e-mail the_weeds@btinternet.com or weedsj@cranbrook.kent.sch.uk)

WEEKS, Romilly; *b* 15 December 1972; *Educ* Univ of Edinburgh (MA); *m* 9 July 2011, Nick Green; 1 da (Saskia Green b 2 Dec 2008), 1 s (Dashiell Green b 6 Oct 2010); *Career* ITV News: royal corr and newscaster 2006–09, news corr 2009–12, political corr 2012–; *Style—* Ms Romilly Weeks; ✉ c/o Knight Ayton Management, 35 Great James Street, London WC1N 3HB (☎ 020 7831 4400, e-mail info@knightayton.co.uk, Twitter @RomillyWeeks)

WEEKS, Wilfred John Thomas (Wilf); OBE (2006); s of William Weeks, of Launceston, Cornwall, and Kathleen, *née* Penhale; *b* 8 February 1948; *Educ* Shebbear Coll, KCL (BD); *m* 10 June 1981, Anne Veronica, da of late Arnold Harrison; 3 s (Orlando b 8 Aug 1983, Matthew b 20 May 1985, Caspar b 10 Jan 1988); *Career* youth and community offr/educn offr and sec Fedn of Cons Students 1974–76, head of the private office of Rt Hon Sir Edward Heath 1976–80, fndr chm GJW Government Relations 1980–2000, chm European Public Affrs Weber Shandwick 2002–10, chm British Future 2011–13 (tstee 2013–); chm Friends of the Tate Gallery 1990–99, memb Cncl Tate Britain 1999–2002, chm Bd of Tstees Dulwich Picture Gallery 2000–06, chm Heritage Educn Tst 2005–08, non-exec dir Helical Bar 2005–12, chm Spitalfields Festival 2006–08, chm Devpt Bd Charterhouse 2014; tstee: LAMDA 2000–10 (chm Devpt Bd 2002–06), Tst for London 2007–, Buccleuch Living Heritage Tst 2011–, PACT Prison and Advice Care Tst 2011, Resource for London 2011, Edward Heath Charitable Fndn 2012–14 (chm 2013–14); tstee and chm Devpt Bd Gainsborough House Museum 2014–; hon treas Hansard Soc 1999–2007; Goodman Award 2004; *Recreations* gardening; *Clubs* Garrick; *Style—* Wilf Weeks, Esq, OBE; ✉ 25 Gauden Road, London SW4 6LR (☎ 020 7622 0532)

WEERERATNE, (Rufina) Aswini; QC (2015); da of Rienzie Weereratne, of Colombo, Sri Lanka, and Elaine Weereratne (d 2001); *b* 6 June 1963, Colombo, Sri Lanka; *Educ* Ursuline Sch Wimbledon, Sussex Univ (BSc), City Univ London (DipLaw), SOAS (LLM); *m* 5 Dec 1997, David Pallister; 1 s (Sam b 21 June 1999); *Career* called to the Bar (Gray's Inn) 1986, barr Russell Jones and Walker Slrs (now Slater Gordon LLP) 1988–91, barr in ind practice Chambers of Geoffrey Robertson QC Doughty Street Chambers 1991–; *Style—* Ms Aswini Weereratne, QC; ✉ Doughty Street Chambers, 53–54 Doughty Street, London WC1N 2LS (☎ 020 7404 1313, e-mail s.wilkins@doughtystreet.co.uk, website www.doughtystreet.co.uk)

WEETMAN, Prof Anthony Peter; s of Kenneth Weetman (d 1991), and Evelyn, *née* Healer; *b* 29 April 1953; *Educ* Univ of Newcastle upon Tyne Med Sch (BMedSci, MB, MD, DSc); *m* 20 Feb 1982, Sheila Lois, da of John Seymour Thompson, OBE, (d 1985); 1 s (James b 1986), 1 da (Chloe b 1989); *Career* MRC trg fell 1981–83, MRC travelling fell 1984–85, Wellcome sr res fell 1985–89, lectr in med Univ of Cambridge and hon conslt physician Addenbrooke's Hosp 1989–91; Univ of Sheffield: prof of med 1991–, dean Medical Sch 1991–2008, pro-vice-chllr for med 2008–15; hon conslt physician Northern General Hosp 1991–; chair Medical Schs Cncl 2009–13, chair UK Healthcare Educn Advsy Ctee (UKHEAC) 2011–15; Goulstonian lectr RCP 1991, Merck Prize European Thyroid Assoc 2002, Bradshaw lectr RCP 2006, Clinical Endocrinology Tst lectr 2006, Pitt-Rivers lectr 2010, Jacobeus Prize Novo Nordisk Fndn 2012, Paul Starr Award American Thyroid Assoc 2013; FRCP 1990 (MRCP 1979), FMedSci 1998, FRCPEd 2004, FAcadMEd 2012; *Publications* author of original papers on thyroid disease and autoimmunity; *Recreations* fell walking; *Style—* Prof Anthony Weetman; ✉ Faculty of Medicine, Dentistry and Health, Barber House, 387 Glossop Road, Sheffield S10 2HQ (☎ 0114 222 8712, fax 0114 222 8756, e-mail a.p.weetman@sheffield.ac.uk)

WEGENEK, Robert Jan; s of Boleslaw Wegenek, of Wolverhampton, and Celina, *née* Nowakowska; *b* 12 August 1966, Wolverhampton; *Educ* Wolverhampton GS, St Aidan's Coll Durham (BA), Coll of Law Chester; *m* 28 Sept 2002, Suzi, *née* Sherlock; 2 s (Alek Leo b 27 April 2004, Boris Adam b 16 Sept 2008), 2 da (Molly Izabela b 4 Jan 2006, Anastasia Clementine b 30 May 2014); *Career* admitted slr 1991; ptnr: Edge Ellison 1998–2000 (nat head of commercial servs 1999–2000), Hammonds 2000–10 (head of London office 2006–09), Squire Patton Boggs UK LLP 2011–; trg princ Law Soc 2001; memb Law Soc 1991; E-Commerce: A Guide to the Law of Electronic Business (ed-in-chief, 2002), Vertäge in der Werbebranche (2007); *Recreations* mountain biking, football, horse racing, cooking; *Style—* Robert Wegenek, Esq; ✉ Squire Patton Boggs, 7 Devonshire Square, Cutlers Gardens, London EC2M 4YM (☎ 0870 839 1534, fax 0870 458 2926, e-mail robert.wegenek@squirepb.com)

WEGG-PROSSER, Benjamin Charles; *b* 11 June 1974, London; *Educ* Univ of Sheffield (BA); *m* Yulia, *née* Khabibullina; *Career* publisher Society Guardian The Guardian Newspaper 2000–05, dir of strategic communications PM's Office 2005–07, co-fndr and dir of corporate devpt SUP Media 2007–10, currently co-fndr (with Rt Hon the Lord Mandelson, *qv*) and managing ptnr Global Counsel; *Style—* Benjamin Wegg-Prosser, Esq; ✉ Global Counsel, 5 Welbeck Street, London W1G 9YQ (☎ 020 3667 6500, website www.global-counsel.co.uk)

WEI, Baron (Life Peer UK 2010), of Shoreditch in the London Borough of Hackney; Nathanael Ming-Yan (Nat) Wei; *b* 19 January 1977; *Educ* Jesus Coll Oxford; *m* Cynthia; 2 c; *Career* co-fndr Teach First 2002, fndr Shaftesbury Partnership 2006, joined Absolute Return for Kids 2006, govt advsr Big Society 2010–; *Style—* The Lord Wei; ✉ House of Lords, London SW1A 0PW

WEIL, Prof Daniel; s of late Dr Alfredo Leopoldo Weil, and Mina, *née* Rosenbaum; *b* 7 September 1953; *Educ* Universidad Nacional de Buenos Aires (Arquitecto FAU UMBA), RCA (MA); *Career* industrial designer and lectr; unit master Dip Sch Architectural Assoc 1983–86, external examiner MA design Glasgow Sch of Art 1987–90; visiting lectr: RCA, Middx Poly, Kingston Poly, Sch of Architecture Univ of Milan, Bezalel Sch of Art Jerusalem; md Parenthesis Ltd 1982–90, fndr and ptnr Weil and Taylor (design consultancy for major clients) 1985–91, ptnr Pentagram design conslts 1992–, prof of industrial design RCA; exhibitions incl: Memphis Milan 1982, 100 Designers Trienale of Milan 1983, Design Since 1945 (Philadelphia Museum of Art) 1983, Heavy Box (Architectural Assoc) 1985, Contemporary Landscape (MOMA Kyoto) 1985, British Design (Kunstmuseum Vienna) 1986, Inspiration (Tokyo, Paris, Milan) 1988, Metropolis (ICA London) 1988, The Plastic Age (V&A) 1990; work in public collections incl The Bag Radio (MOMA NY); memb Design Sub-Ctee D&AD, juror BBC Design Awards 1990; sr fell RCA 2002; FCSD 1989; *Style—* Prof Daniel Weil; ✉ Pentagram Design Ltd, 11 Needham Road, London W11 2RP (☎ 020 7229 3477)

WEIL, Peter Leo John; s of Robert Weil of Berlin, Germany, and Renate Scheyer; *b* 7 September 1951; *Educ* Methodist Coll Belfast, Queens' Coll Cambridge (BA); *Career* researcher Granada TV 1973–77 (Granada Reports, World in Action); BBC: prodr BBC TV Current Affairs 1977–84 (Nationwide, Newsnight, Panorama), head of Youth Progs BBC NI 1984–86 (actg dep head of progs 1986), ed Open Air BBC NW 1986–88, exec prodr Wogan 1988–89, head of topical features 1989–90, head of network TV BBC North 1990–92; head of progs Barraclough Carey North Productions 1992–98, exec news ed London News Network 1998; Discovery Networks Europe: vice-pres (content) Discovery UK until 2003, gen mangr and sr vice-pres Animal Planet Int 2003–07, dir prodn and digital channels Media Tst and Community Channel 2007–09, ceo CTVC 2009–; exec prodr: People's Parliament, The Other Side of Midnight, First Edition; *Recreations* cinema, walking, good food; *Style—* Peter Weil, Esq

WEINBERG, Sir Mark Aubrey; kt (1987); s of Philip Weinberg (d 1933); *b* 9 August 1931, Durban, South Africa; *Educ* King Edward's Johannesburg, Univ of the Witwatersrand, LSE; *m* 1980, Anouska (Anouska Hempel, the fashion designer), da of Albert Geissler (d 1980); *Career* md Abbey Life Assurance 1961–70, chm Allied Dunbar Assurance 1971–90, dir BAT Industries 1985–89, dep chm Securities Investment Bd 1986–90; chm: J Rothschild Assurance plc 1991–2002, St James's Place Capital 1991–2004 (currently pres), Life Assurance Holding Corp 1995–2003, Pension Insurance Corp 2006–; sr advsr Stanford Assocs 2011–; jt chm The Per Cent Club 1985–97, chm Stock Exchange Ctee on Private Share Ownership 1995–, tstee Tate Gallery 1985–92; *Books* Take-overs and Mergers (5 edn, 1989); *Recreations* bridge; *Clubs* Portland, RAC, Army and Navy; *Style—* Sir Mark Weinberg; ✉ St James's Place, Spencer House, 27 St James's Place, London SW1A 1NR (☎ 020 7514 1960)

WEIR, Arabella; da of Sir Michael Weir, KCMG (d 2006), and Alison, *née* Walker; *b* 1957, San Francisco CA; *Career* comedienne, actress, writer; columnist The Guardian 2001–04; *Television* incl: The Corner House 1987, Les Girls 1988, The All New Alexei Sayle Show (also writer) 1994, The Fast Show (also writer) 1994–2003, Ted & Ralph 1998, My Summer with Des 1998, She's Gotta Have It (presenter) 1998, The Creatives 1998, Posh Nosh (also writer) 2003; appearances incl: Loose Women 2004, Grumpy Old Women 2006; *Film* incl Shooting Fish 1997; *Radio* Smelling of Roses (BBC Radio 4) 2000–03; *Books* Does My Bum Look Big in This? (1997), Onwards and Upwards (1999), Stupid Cupid (2002); *Style—* Ms Arabella Weir; ✉ c/o Roxane Vacca Management, 73 Beak Street, London W1F 9SR (☎ 020 7734 8085, fax 020 7734 8086)

WEIR, Hon Lord; David Bruce; s of James Douglas Weir (d 1981), of Argyll, and Kathleen Maxwell, *née* Auld (d 1975); *b* 19 December 1931; *Educ* The Leys Sch Cambridge, Univ of Glasgow (MA, LLB); *m* 1964, Katharine Lindsay, da of Hon Lord Cameron (decd); 3 s (Donald b 1965, Robert b 1967, John b 1971); *Career* admitted to Faculty of Advocates 1959, QC (Scot) 1971, advocate depute 1979–82, senator of the Coll of Justice in Scotland 1985–97; justice Ct of Appeal Repub of Botswana 2000–02; chm: Med Appeal Tbnl 1972–77, Pension Appeals Tbnl for Scotland 1978–84 (pres 1984–85), NHS Tbnl Scotland 1983–85; memb: Criminal Injuries Compensation Bd 1974–79 and 1984–85, The Parole Bd for Scotland 1988–91; govr Fettes Coll 1986–95 (chm 1989–95), vice-chm S Knapdale Community Cncl 1997–2005, memb Bd Scottish Int Piano Competition 1997–2007; memb

Cncl RYA 2005–08; hon sheriff North Strathclyde at Campbeltown; *Recreations* sailing (Tryad), music; *Clubs* New (Edinburgh), Royal Cruising, Royal Highland Yacht; *Style*— The Hon Lord Weir

WEIR, Fiona; *Career* sr atmosphere and climate change campaigner and acting campaigns dir Friends of the Earth 1988–95, dir of campaigns Amnesty Int UK 1995–2000, head of public affrs Which? (Consumers Assoc) 2000–02, dir of policy and communications Save the Children 2002–07, ceo Gingerbread 2008–; *Style*— Ms Fiona Weir; ✉ Gingerbread, 520 Highgate Studios, 53–79 Highgate Road, London NW5 1TL

WEIR, Dame Gillian Constance; DBE (1996, CBE 1989); da of Cecil Alexander Weir (d 1941), of Martinborough, NZ, and Clarice Mildred Foy, *née* Bignell (d 1965); *b* 17 January 1941, Martinborough, New Zealand; *Educ* Wanganui Girls Coll, Royal Coll of Music; *m* 1, 1967 (m dis 1971), Clive Rowland Webster; m 2, 1972, Lawrence Irving Phelps (d 1999), s of Herbert Spencer Phelps (d 1979), of Somerville, MA; *Career* int concert organist 1965–; concerto appearances incl: all leading Br orchs, Boston Symphony Orch, Seattle Symphony Orch, Aust ABC Orchs, Euro orchs (incl Vienna Philharmonic); regular performer at int festivals incl: Edinburgh, Bath, Flanders, Proms, Aldeburgh; performed in major int concert halls and cathedrals incl: Royal Albert Hall, Royal Festival Hall, Sydney Opera House, Disney Hall, Leipzig Gewandhaus, Salzburg Mozarteum, Lincoln Center, Kennedy Center; frequent nat and int radio and TV appearances (incl own 6 part series The King of Instruments (BBC), 60 Minutes documentary on life/career and ITV's South Bank Show), adjudicator int competitions, artist in residence at major univs, lectures and master classes held internationally; Prince Consort prof Royal Coll of Music 1999–, distinguished visiting lectr Peabody Inst of Music Baltimore 2005–12; recordings for: Priory, Virgin Classics, Argo, Chandos, Koss Classics, Decca, Collins Classics (Complete Works of Olivier Messiaen released 1994 (rereleased on Priory 2002), Complete Works of César Franck released 1997), Priory, Linn; prizes incl: St Albans Int Organ Competition 1964, Countess Munster Award 1965, Int Performer of the Year American Guild of Organists NY USA 1981, Musician of the Year Int Music Guide 1982, Turnovsky Fndn Award 1985, Silver Medal Albert Schweitzer Assoc 1998, Evening Standard Award for Outstanding Solo Performance 1998, Lifetime Achievement Award NZ Soc (later Link Soc) London 2005; subject of South Bank Show documentary 2000; first woman pres: Incorporated Assoc of Organists 1981–83, Royal Coll of Organists 1994–96; pres: Incorporated Soc of Musicians 1992–93, Soloists' Ensemble 1997–; co-opted to Cncl Royal Philharmonic Soc 1995–2001 (elected memb); tstee Eric Thompson Tst; memb Royal Soc of Musicians of GB 1996–; patron: Oundle Int Festival, Friends of Young Artists' Platform, Cirencester Early Music Festival; Hon Freeman Worshipful Co of Musicians 2015; Hon DMus: Univ of Victoria Wellington NZ 1983, Univ of Hull 1999, Univ of Exeter 2001, Univ of Leicester 2003, Univ of Aberdeen 2004, Univ of London 2009, Durham Univ 2012; Hon DLitt Univ of Huddersfield 1997, Hon DUniv Central England 2001; hon fell Hatfield Coll Durham Univ 2014; hon memb RAM, Hon FRCO 1975, hon fell Royal Canadian Coll of Organists 1983, hon bencher Middle Temple 2012; Hon FRCM 2000; *Publications* Grove's International Dictionary of Music and Musicians (contrib), The Messiaen Companion (contrib); frequent contrib to professional jls; *Recreations* theatre; *Style*— Dame Gillian Weir, DBE; ✉ website www.gillianweir.com

WEIR, Dr Hugh William Lindsay; s of Maj Terence John Collison Weir (d 1958), and Rosamund Suzanne, *née* Gibson (d 2001); *b* 29 August 1934; *Educ* Ireland and abroad, DLitt; *m* 1973, Hon Grania Rachel O'Brien, da of 16 Baron Inchiquin (d 1968); *Career* teacher, illustrator, journalist, historian, environmentalist, lecturer, broadcaster, author and publisher; Royal Norfolk Regt (Far East, ME) 1952–56; actor memb Norfolk Players Hong Kong 1956, actor memb Ashton Prodns Cork 1959; md: Weir Machinery Ltd 1965–75, Ballinakella Press, Bell'Acards; fndr memb Assoc for teachers of Foreign Students in Ireland, dir Cappaghbeg Language Centre 1971–73; memb Nat Cncl CARE; Irish Heritage Historian 1980–, lectr Inst of Irish Studies; fndr and pres Young Environmentalist Fedn; pres: Clare Young Environmentalists 1980–, N America Irish Media Campaign 1982; vice-pres Clare Archeological and Historical Soc until 2014, Nat Monuments advsr Clare Co Cncl 1995–2000, chm Clare Heritage Forum 2003–07; memb Editorial Ctee The Other Clare 1996–97, environment corr The Clare Champion 1977–2011; regular contrib: Church of Ireland Gazette, Catholic Twin Circle 1982–84; Oidhreacht Award 1990 for journalism and environmental promotion; diocesan lay preacher Limerick and Killaloe 1974–2011; memb: Killaloe Diocesan Synod 1970–99, Gen Synod Church of Ireland 1974–99 (memb Standing Ctee 1980–86), Church of Ireland Representative Body 1980–89, Cncl of Reference Christian Trg Inst 1999–2000 and 2004– (dir 2000–04); dir Hunt Museums Tst 2000–11; dir Post Polio Syndrome Gp Ireland 2006–10; FRGS; *Books* Hall Craig, Words on an Irish House (1978), O'Brien – People and Places (1984), Houses of Clare (1986), Ireland – A Thousand Kings (1988), Ennis, 750 Facts (1990), Trapa – An Adventure in Spanish and English (1990), O'Connor – People and Places (1994), CYE: A Social, Educational and Environmental Exercise (1999), One of Our Own – Memoirs of Change (2001), Brian Boru – High King of Ireland, 941–1014 (2003), Keels, Wheels and Wings: Travels by Mode (2011), Traumas; Transylvanian and Others (2016); *Recreations* writing, art, angling, travel; *Style*— Dr Hugh Weir; ✉ Ballinakella Lodge, Whitegate, Co Clare, V94 T956, Ireland (☎ 00 353 61 927030, e-mail hughwlweir@hotmail.com)

WEIR, Michael Fraser (Mike); MP; *b* 24 March 1957; *Educ* Arbroath HS, Univ of Aberdeen (LLB); *Career* slr 1981–2001; MP (SNP) Angus 2001–; dean Soc of Procurators and Slrs in Angus 2001; memb SNP; *Style*— Mike Weir, Esq, MP; ✉ 16 Brothock Bridge, Arbroath, Angus DD11 1NG (☎ 01241 874522, e-mail mike.weir.mp@parliament.uk)

WEIR, Peter James; MLA; s of late James Weir, and Margaret, *née* Maxwell; *b* 21 November 1968; *Educ* Bangor GS, Queen's Univ Belfast (MSocSci, LLB); *Career* barr-at-law NI Bar 1992–98, lectr in constitutional and admin law Univ of Ulster Jordanstown 1993, public rep 1996–; memb NI Forum (N Down) 1996–98, memb UUP Talks Team 1996–98, vice-chm Forum Educn Ctee 1997–98; MLA (DUP) N Down 1998–; memb NI Assembly: Standing Orders Ctee 1998–99, Finance and Personnel Ctee 1998–2010 and 2012–15, Environment Ctee 2007–15, Business Ctee 2007–15, Justice Ctee 2011–12; vice-chm Employment and Learning Ctee 2010–11, chief whip (DUP) 2010–16, chair Assembly Educn Ctee 2015–16, min for educn NI 2016–; cncllr N Down 2005–; vice-pres NI Local Govt Assoc 2006–10; former chm: Queen's UU, UU Students Orgn, Ulster Young Unionist Cncl; memb: Orange Order and Royal Black Preceptory, Hamilton Road Presbyterian Church, 3rd Bangor Boys' Bde 1974–87, Senate Queen's Univ Belfast, Cncl for Legal Educn, SE Educn and Library Bd 2005–10, NI Police Bd 2006–; ed Ulster Review 1998–2000; *Publications* The Anglo Irish Agreement – Three Years On (co-author, 1998), Unionism, National Parties and Ulster (co-author, 1991), UUP Submission on Electoral Reform (1997); *Recreations* football, cricket, history, books, music; *Style*— Peter Weir, Esq, MLA; ✉ Northern Ireland Assembly, Parliament Buildings, Stormont Estate, Belfast BT4 3XX

WEIR, Sarah Jane St Clair; OBE (2011); da of David Michael St Clair Weir (d 2009), and Marion Baldwin Cox, *née* Miller, of Suffolk; *b* 9 October 1958, Edinburgh; *Educ* St Agnes and St Michael's Convent East Grinstead, Birkbeck Coll London (BA); *Partner* Dr Louise Mary Hide (civil partnership 21 Feb 2006); *Career* md Aldgate Gp Brokers 1992–94 (joined 1979), asst Purdy Hicks Gallery London 1994–95; dep DG Arts & Business 1995–97, fundraising dir Royal Acad of Arts 1997–2001, exec dir Almeida Theatre 2001–03, exec dir Arts Cncl London 2003–07, head of arts and cultural strategy Olympic Delivery Authy 2008–11, dir of arts and culture Olympic Park Legacy Co 2011–12, ceo The Legacy List 2012–13, ceo Waddesdon Manor 2013–; tstee Alzheimer's Soc 2013–; First Women Award For Public Service CBI 2013; fell Birkbeck Coll London 2013; FRSA 2003; *Publications* Cultural Leadership Programme: A Cultural Reader (2010); *Recreations* the arts, walking, reading, contemplating; *Style*— Ms Sarah Weir, OBE; ✉ Waddesdon Manor, Nr Aylesbury, Bucks HP18 0JH (☎ 01296 653333, e-mail sarah.weir@waddesdon.org.uk, www.waddesdon.org.uk)

WEIR, 3 Viscount (UK 1938); William Kenneth James Weir; also Baron Weir (UK 1918); s of 2 Viscount Weir, CBE (d 1975), of Montgreenan, Kilwinning, Ayrshire, and his 1 w, Lucette Isabel, *née* Crowdy (d 1972); *b* 9 November 1933; *Educ* Eton, Trinity Coll Cambridge (BA); *m* 1, 1964 (m dis 1972), Diana Lucy, da of late Peter Lewis MacDougall of Ottawa, Canada; 1 s (Hon James William Hartland b 6 June 1965), 1 da (Hon Lorna Elizabeth b 17 May 1967); m 2, 6 Nov 1976 (m dis), Mrs Jacqueline Mary Marr, da of late Baron Louis de Chollet, of Fribourg, Switzerland; m 3, 24 Nov 1989, Marina, da of late Marc Sevastopoulo; 1 s (Hon Andrew Alexander Marc b 1989); *Heir* s, Hon James Weir; *Career* Nat Serv with RN 1955–57; chm: Great Northern Investment Trust Ltd 1975–82, Weir Group plc 1983–98 (vice-chm 1981–83, chm and chief exec 1972–81, chm 1983–99); co-chm RIT and Northern plc 1982–83, vice-chm St James's Place Capital plc; dir: British Steel Corporation 1972–76, Balfour Beatty plc (formerly BICC plc) 1977– (chm 1996–2003), Br Bank of the Middle East 1977–79, Canadian Pacific Ltd 1989–2001, CP Ships (chm 2001–04), L F Rothschild Unterberg Towbin 1983–85; memb: Ct of Bank of England 1972–84, Scottish Econ Cncl 1972–84, Engrg Industries Cncl 1975–80, London Advsy Ctee of Hongkong and Shanghai Banking Corp 1980–92; chm: Engrg Design Res Centre 1988–91, Patrons of Nat Galleries of Scotland 1984–94, Major British Exporters 1994–99, British Water 1998–2000; pres BEAMA 1988–89 and 1993–95; Hon DEng Univ of Glasgow 1993; FIBF 1984, MIES 1985, FRSA 1987, Hon FREng 1993; *Recreations* golf, shooting; *Clubs* White's; *Style*— The Rt Hon the Viscount Weir; ✉ Rodinghead, Mauchline, Ayrshire KA5 5TR (☎ 01563 884233)

WEISMAN, Malcolm; OBE (1997); s of David Weisman (d 1969), and Jeanie Pearl Weisman (d 1980); *Educ* Parmiter's Sch, Harrogate GS, London School of Economics, St Catherine's Coll Oxford (MA); *m* 1958, Rosalie, da of Dr A A Spiro (d 1963), of St John's Wood; 2 s (Brian b 1959, Daniel b 1963); *Career* Jewish chaplain RAF 1956, hon chaplain Univ of Oxford 1971–, sr chaplain HM Forces 1972–, sec-gen Allied Air Forces Chiefs of Chaplains Ctee 1980–92 (hon pres 1993), sec Former Chiefs of Air Forces Chaplains Assoc 1994; called to the Bar Middle Temple 1961, asst cmmr Parly Boundaries 1976–88, dep circuit judge 1976–80, recorder of the Crown Court 1980, head of chambers 1982–90, special immigration adjudicator 1998, memb Bar Disciplinary Tbnl; chm various HM Prisons; memb: MOD Advsy Ctee on Mil Chaplaincy, Cabinet of Chief Rabbi of Cwlth, Nat Exec Cncl of Christians and Jews (also tstee), Three Faiths Forum Working Pty; ed Menorah magazine 1970; vice-pres and religious advsr Cwlth Jewish Cncl, religious advsr to small Jewish communities and Hillel cnsllr to Oxford and New Univs; memb Cts of Univs of East Anglia, Sussex, Kent, Lancaster, Essex and Warwick; memb SCR Univs of Kent, East Anglia and Lancaster; fell Univ of Essex Centre for Study of Theol; govr and tstee Parmiter's Sch, former govr Carmel Coll and Selly Oak Coll of Christian Jewish Relations; tstee: Multi-Faith and Int Multi-Faith Chaplaincy Centre Univ of Derby, Jewish Music Heritage Tst; patron Jewish Nat Fund; hon chaplain to Lord Mayor of Westminster 1992–93, chaplain to Mayor of Barnett 1994–95, chaplain to Mayor of Redbridge 2005–06, chaplain to Mayor of Montgomery 2006–07, chaplain US Forces UK 2010; Blackstone Pupillage Award 1961, Man of the Year Award 1980, Chief Rabbi's Award for Excellence 1993, USA Mil Chaplaincy Award for Outstanding Serv 1998, Gold Medal Int Cncl of Christians and Jews 2002, United Synagogue Rabbinic Cncl Award for Work and Leadership 2005, Peterborough Inter-Faith Award 2008, Special Award Canadian Defence Forces 2008, Peterborough Inter Faith Award 2011, 2013, 2014, 2015 and 2016; hon fell Univ of Lancaster 2006; *Recreations* reading, walking, doing nothing; *Style*— Malcolm Weisman, Esq, OBE; ☎ 020 8459 4372; 1 Gray's Inn Square, London WC1R 5AA (☎ 020 7405 0001, fax 020 7405 0002)

WEISS, Prof Bernard Lawson; s of Joseph Joshua Weiss, and Frances Sonia, *née* Lawson; *b* 9 July 1948, Newcastle upon Tyne; *Educ* Univ of Newcastle upon Tyne (BSc, PhD, DEng), Univ of Surrey (DSc); *m* 12 Dec 1982, Sheila Margaret, *née* Hermiston; 1 s (Oliver Joseph b 23 Sept 1987), 1 da (Jessica Anne b 18 May 1989); *Career* Univ of Newcastle upon Tyne: SRC ad hominem postdoctoral research fell 1975–76, Wolfson Fndn research fell 1977; SRC research fell UCL 1977–79; Univ of Surrey: lectr 1979–86, sr lectr 1986–93, reader 1993–96, prof of microelectronics 1996–, head Sch of Electronics and Physical Sciences 2001 (dep head 1996–2001), pro-vice-chllr 2005–; visiting scholar Univ of Berkeley California 1980; visiting prof: Univ of Cincinnati 1991, Technische Hochschule Darmstadt Germany 1994–95, Univ of Michigan Ann Arbor 2000; hon prof Univ of Hong Kong 1996–2000 (reader 1994–96, William Mong visiting research fell 1997); non-exec dir Surrey Satellite Technol 2003–05; memb Governing Body Frensham Heights Sch Surrey 2002–08, memb Governing Body St Mary's Univ Coll 2005–; 150th Anniversary Medal Warsaw Univ of Technol 1993, Achievement Medal IEE 2004; Leadership Fndn fell 2006; FIEE 1989, FInstP 1994, FREng 2005; over 125 articles in professional jls and 50 in published conference proceedings; *Recreations* walking, cycling, collecting antique maps; *Style*— Prof Bernard Weiss

WEISS, Prof Nigel Oscar; s of Oscar Weiss (d 1994), and Ursula Mary, *née* Kisch (d 1998); *b* 16 December 1936; *Educ* Hilton Coll South Africa, Rugby, Clare Coll Cambridge (MA, PhD, ScD); *m* 29 June 1968, Judith Elizabeth, da of Brig Ronald Martin, OBE, MC; 2 da (Catherine Anne b 4 Oct 1970, Naomi Alison b 1 Nov 1982), 1 s (Timothy Francis b 5 March 1973); *Career* research assoc UKAEA Culham Lab 1962–65; Univ of Cambridge: lectr Dept of Applied Mathematics and Theoretical Physics 1965–79, fell Clare Coll 1965, dir of studies in mathematics Clare Coll 1966–79, tutor for grad students Clare Coll 1970–73, reader in astrophysics 1979–87, prof of mathematical astrophysics 1987–2004 (prof emeritus 2004–), chm Cncl Sch of Physical Sciences 1993–98; visiting prof: Sch of Mathematical Sciences Queen Mary & Westfield Coll London 1986–96, Dept of Applied Mathematics Univ of Leeds 2001–07; pres RAS 2000–02 (Gold Medal 2007); sr fell SERC 1987–92; FRS 1992; *Books* Sunspots and Starspots (jtly, 2008), Magnetoconvection (jtly, 2014); *Publications* papers on astrophysics, fluid mechanics and nonlinear dynamics; *Recreations* travel; *Style*— Prof Nigel Weiss, FRS; ✉ 10 Lansdowne Road, Cambridge CB3 0EU (☎ 01223 355032); Department of Applied Mathematics and Theoretical Physics, University of Cambridge, Wilberforce Road, Cambridge CB3 0WA (☎ 01223 337910, fax 01223 765900)

WEISS, Prof Robert Anthony (Robin); s of Hans Weiss, and Stefanie, *née* Löwinsohn; *b* 20 February 1940; *Educ* UCL (BSc, PhD); *m* 1 Aug 1964, Margaret Rose D'Costa; 2 da (Rachel Mary b 1966, Helen Anne b 1968); *Career* lectr in embryology UCL 1964–70, Eleanor Roosevelt Int Cancer Research fell Univ of Washington Seattle 1970–71, visiting assoc prof of microbiology Univ of Southern Calif 1971–72, staff scientist Imperial Cancer Research Fund Labs 1972–80, prof of viral oncology Inst of Cancer Research 1980–98 (dir 1980–89, dir of research 1990–96); Gustav Stern Award in Virology 1973, Beijerinck Prize Royal Netherlands Acad of Arts and Scis 2001; Hon DM Uppsala Univ 2003, Hon DsC Inst of Cancer Research Univ of London 2008; FRCPath 1985, Hon FRCP 1998, FRS 1997, FMedSci 1998, foreign assoc US Nat Acad of Scis 2013; *Books* RNA Tumor Viruses (1982, 2 edn 1985), HIV and The New Viruses (1999), Infections and Human Cancer (1999); author of various articles on virology, cell biology and genetics; *Recreations* music, natural history; *Style*— Prof Robin Weiss, FRS; ✉ Division of Infection and Immunity,

Cruciform Building, University College London, Gower Street, London WC1E 6BT (☎ 020 3108 2137, e-mail r.weiss@ucl.ac.uk)

WEISZ, Rachel; *Career* actress; *Theatre* The Courtesans (NT Studio), Design for Living (Gielgud Theatre), Suddenly Last Summer (Donmar Warehouse), The Shape of Things (Almeida and NY), A Streetcar Named Desire (Donmar Warehouse) 2009 (Best Actress Evening Standard Theatre Award 2009, Best Actress Critics' Circle Theatre Award 2010, Best Actress Laurence Olivier Award 2010); *Television* Inspector Morse 1987, Scarlet and Black 1993, My Summer with Des 1998; *Film* Seventeen 1994, Stealing Beauty 1996, Chain Reaction 1996, Swept from the Sea 1997, Going All the Way 1997, The Land Girls 1998, I Want You 1998, The Mummy 1999, Sunshine 1999, Enemy at the Gates 2001, The Mummy Returns 2001, Beautiful Creatures 2001, About a Boy 2001, The Shape of Things 2002, Confidence 2002, The Runaway Jury 2003, Marlowe 2003, Envy 2004, The Constant Gardener 2005 (Best Supporting Actress Golden Globe Awards, Screen Actors Guild Awards and Academy Awards, Best British Actress London Film Critics' Circle Awards), Constantine 2005, Eragon 2006 (voice), Fred Claus 2007, My Blueberry Nights 2007, Definitely Maybe 2008, The Brothers Bloom 2008, Agora 2009, The Lovely Bones 2009, The Whistleblower 2010, Deep Blue Sea 2011, 360 2011, Dream House 2011, The Bourne Legacy 2012, Oz the Great and Powerful 2013; *Style—* Ms Rachel Weisz; ✉ c/o Independent Talent Group, 40 Whitfield Street, London W1T 2RH (☎ 020 7636 6565, fax 020 7323 0101)

WEITZENHOFFER, Max; s of Aaron Weitzenhoffer (d 1960), and Clara Rosenthal (d 2000); *b* 30 October 1939, Oklahoma City; *Educ* Univ of Oklahoma (BA); *m* Ayako, *née* Takahashi; 1 s (Owen Weitzenhoffer), 1 da (Nikki Weitzenhoffer); *Career* pres Weitzenhoffer Prodns 1976–, co-owner (with Nica Burns, OBE, *qv*) and chm Nimax Theatres Ltd (comprising 6 West End theatres) 2005–; memb: SOLT, League of American Theatres; Tony Award 1977 and 1991, Olivier Award 2000 and 2013; hon doctorate Univ of Oklahoma; *Clubs* Century Assoc NYC; *Style—* Mr Max Weitzenhoffer; ✉ 1100 Chenrystone Cir, Norman, Oklahoma, OK 73072, USA; Nimax Theatres Ltd, 11 Maiden Lane, London WC2E 7NA

WELBURN, Paul; *b* Scarborough, N Yorks; *Educ* Scalby Sch Scarborough, Yorks Coast Coll Scarborough; *Career* formerly: 30 St Mary Axe, Rhodes in the Square, private chef to Partouche family Cannes Princess Sany, Star Inn Harome, head chef Rhodes W1 (Michelin star and 3 AA Rosettes); head chef Searcys (opening several sites in Britain) until 2015, head chef Leconfield Restaurant 2015–; representing NE of England in Great British Menu (BBC 2) 2014; *Recreations* golf, squash; *Style—* Paul Welburn, Esq; ✉ The Leconfield Restaurant, New Street, Petworth, West Sussex GU28 0AS

WELBY, Most Rev and Rt Hon Justin Portal; *see:* Canterbury, Archbishop of

WELCH, Brig Anthony Cleland; OBE (2003); s of Brian Desmond Joseph Welch (d 1989), of Te Aroha, NZ, and Valerie Isabelle Boxall, *née* Davison; *b* 15 September 1945, Hamilton, NZ; *Educ* Prior Park Coll Bath, St John's Coll Southsea, Univ of Portsmouth (MA, MSc, PhD), RMCS, Staff Coll Camberley, Higher Command and Staff Coll; *m* 1, 1971 (m dis), Victoria, *née* Mathews; 1 s (Simon Alexander Cleland b 31 Aug 1974), 1 da (Alexandra Victoria Cleland b 3 Nov 1977); m 2, 6 May 1983, Pamela Jane, *née* Darnell; *Career* tech sales mangr Rediffusion TV (Hong Kong) Ltd 1964–68, 2 Lt rising to Brig British Army 1969–93, chief of policy planning and coordination and COS to Special Rep of the Sec-Gen for the former Yugoslavia 1993–94, gen mangr Allmakes Projects Ltd Oxford 1994–95, head EU monitor mission in Albania/Serbia and Montenegro 1995–96, coordinator Orgn for Security and Co-operation in Europe (OSCE) Balkan States 1996–98, conflict and security advsr DFID 1998–2000, UN regnl admin Northern Kosovo 2000–01, dir Dyncorp Int (Europe) 2001–05, coordinator internal security sector review of Kosovo UNDP 2006, researcher and lectr Centre for Security Secotr Mgmnt Cranfield Univ 2009, advsr Multi-Lateral Orgns UK Govt Stabilisation Unit 2015–, advsr Sovereign Global UK 2015–; special advsr to Lord Chidgey on int devpt and foreign policy in Africa, security and justice in MENA advsr Security and Justice Gp Govt Stabilisation Unit; European Parl candidate (Lib Dem) SW 2004, cncllr Havant BC 2002–07; dir Marine Gate Mgmnt Co 2014–; govr S Downs Coll Portsmouth; tstee: Centre for S Eastern European Studies Sofia, Vencorp Private Equity Ptnrs Geneva; memb New Zealand Armed Forces Law Assoc, memb panel of experts Univ of Leicester, memb Bd of Experts 1325 Policy Gp Stockholm; FInstD (MInstD 1992); Ten Years On: The British Army in the Falklands War (contrib, 1992), Mapping the Security Environment: Understanding the perceptions of local communities, peace support operations and assistance agencies (jtly, 2005), The Security Dimensions of EU Enlargement: Wider Europe, Weaker Europe? (jtly, 2007), Security Sector Reform and the Paradoxical Tension Between Local Ownership and Gender Equality (with E Gordon and E Roos, 2015); author of academic papers on security issues; *Recreations* horse racing, golf, sailing, shooting; *Clubs* Army and Navy, Auckland Racing, Knysna Golf, Bramley Shooting Syndicate; *Style—* Brig Anthony Cleland Welch, OBE; ✉ Institute of Directors, 116 Pall Mall, London SW1Y 5ED

WELCH, Prof Janet Mary (Jan); MBE (2006); da of Patrick Palles Lorne Elphinstone Welch, of Farnham, Surrey, and Ann Courtenay, *née* Edmonds; *b* 11 June 1955; *Educ* Farnham Girls' GS, Farnborough Tech Coll, St Thomas' Hosp Med Sch London (entrance scholar, Tite scholar, BSc, MB BS); *m* 1989, Gary Richards, s of Jack Richards; 1 da (Fabia Rosamund b 2 Oct 1990), 1 s (Toby Lorne b 8 June 1993); *Career* house physician then SHO in microbiology St Thomas' Hosp London 1981, registrar in infectious diseases London 1983, sr registrar in genitourinary med St Thomas' Hosp London 1987–90 (in virology 1984–87); KCH: conslt in HIV/genitourinary med 1990–, dir of postgrad med educn 1998–2005; prof of postgrad medical educn KCL 2016–; dir South Thames Fndn Sch 2005–; fndr and clinical dir Haven Sexual Assault Referral Centre Camberwell 2000–14; FRCP, FFFLM, FAcadMEd, Hon FRCOG; *Books* Looking After People with Late HIV Disease (1990), ABC of Domestic and Sexual Violence (ed Susan Bewley and Jan Welch 2014); *Recreations* gardening, skiing; *Clubs* Island Sailing; *Style—* Professor Jan Welch, MBE; ✉ e-mail jan.welch@kcl.ac.uk

WELCH, Sir John Reader; 2 Bt (UK 1957), of Chard, Co Somerset; s of Sir Cullum Welch, 1 Bt, OBE, MC (d 1980); *b* 26 July 1933; *Educ* Marlborough Coll, Hertford Coll Oxford (MA); *m* 25 Sept 1962, Margaret Kerry, o da of Kenneth Victor Douglass (d 1996); 1 s, 2 da; *Heir* s, James Douglass Cullum Welch; *Career* Nat Serv 2nd Lt Royal Signals 1952–54 (Gen Servs Medal with Canal Zone Clasp), capt Middx Yeo (TA) 1954–62; admitted slr 1960; ptnr: Bell Brodrick & Gray 1961–71, Wedlake Bell 1972–96; chm: John Fairfax (UK) Ltd 1977–90, London Homes for the Elderly 1981–90; registrar Archdeaconry of London 1964–99, memb Court of Common Cncl (City of London) 1975–86 and chm Planning and Communications Ctee 1981–1982; govr: City of London Sch for Girls 1977–82, Haberdashers' Aske's Schs Elstree 1981–85 and 1990–91; Sr Grand Warden United Grand Lodge of England 1998–2000; pres Freemasons' Grand Charity 1985–95; pres City Livery Club 1986–87 (hon slr 1983–90), chm Walbrook Ward Club 1978–79; Clerk Worshipful Co of Furniture Makers 1963–66, Liveryman and Past Master Emeritus Worshipful Co of Haberdashers (Master 1990–91), Freeman and Past Master Emeritus Worshipful Co of Parish Clerks (Master 1967–68); FRSA 1991; CStJ 1981; *Clubs* Hurlingham; *Style—* Sir John Welch, Bt; ✉ 28 Rivermead Court, Ranelagh Gardens, London SW6 3RU (☎ 020 7736 2775)

WELCH, Melvin Dennis (Mel); s of Robert Charles Welch (d 1991), of Watford, Herts, and Rose Elizabeth, *née* Oakley (d 1993); *b* 21 November 1946; *Educ* Bushey GS, Univ of Sussex (BSc, MSc); *m* 18 Sept 1971, Susan Jane, da of Arthur Jeffcoatt (d 1976), of Coventry, Warks; 1 s (Timothy b 1972), 1 da (Josephine b 1974); *Career* sec: English Basketball Assoc 1970–91, Br and Irish Basketball Fedn 1970–2003, Cwlth Basketball Fedn 1978–91; co-ordinator Carnegie Nat Sports Devpt Centre 1991–2005, sec Fed of Yorkshire Sport 1991–2011, memb Yorkshire Sports Bd 2000–03; memb: Eligibility Ctee Int Basketball Fedn 1984–2002, Olympic Review Ctee Sports Cncl 1985–86; Br Inst of Sports Admin: fndr memb 1979, memb Exec Ctee 1985–2002, vice-chm 1992–94 and 1998–2001, chm 1994–1998, fell 1995–2004, vice-pres 2001–04; Sports Aid Fndn: memb UK Grants Ctee 1986–1996, chm Eng Grants Ctee 1996–2003, govr and memb Exec Ctee Sports Aid Fndn 1996–2003; dir Eng Fedn of Disability Sport Operating Co 2001–09; coaching review panel Sports Cncl 1989–91; dir: Basketball Publishing Ltd 1986–91, Basketball Marketing Ltd 1986–87, EBBA Outdoor Basketball Initiative 1997–2013 (chm 1999–2013), Weltech Solutions Ltd 1998–2013, dir Nidderdale Plus Partnership Ltd 2009–14; chm Sport Nidderdale 2009–; sec Leeds Sports Fedn 2002–08 (vice-pres 2008–), treas European Assoc for Sport Mgmnt 2002–08, treas Dacre & Hartwith Playing Fields Assoc 2012–, tstee Scarborough 95 Sports Tst 2016–; life vice-pres: English Basketball Assoc 1991, Cwlth Basketball Fedn 2002–06; tstee Darley Playing Fields Assoc 2009–2014; memb Management Ctee Darley Memorial Hall 2012–; *Books* EBBA Yearbook (1971–91), Intersport Basketball (1981), Encyclopaedia Britannica Book of Year (contrib, 1985–90), Getting Things Done (1992), Raising Money (1992), Running Meetings (1992), Running a Club (1992), Looking after the Money (1992), Getting It Right (1994), Making Your Point (1994), Making A Match (1994), Towards Gender Equality in Sports Management (1999), Fair Play in Yorkshire Sport (1999), A Level Playing Field – an exemplary action plan for Local Authorities for the provision of a sports development programme for black and other ethnic minorities (jtly, 2000), For the Love of the Sport (2000), Part of the Game? – an examination of racism in grass roots football (jtly, 2000), Show Me the Money (2002), Understanding Leisure & Sport (contrib, 2001), Racial Equality in Football: A Survey (jtly, 2004); *Recreations* tennis, golf, walking; *Clubs* Roundhay Tennis, Dacre Tennis, Sand Moor Golf; *Style—* Mel Welch, Esq; ✉ Green Acres, Sheepcote Lane, Darley, North Yorkshire (e-mail mwelch@sportnidderdale.org)

WELDON, Duncan Clark; s of Clarence Weldon (d 1980), of Southport, and Margaret Mary Andrew (d 2006); *b* 19 March 1941; *Educ* King George V GS Southport; *m* 1 (m dis 1971), Helen Shapiro; m 2, 9 July 1974, Janet, da of Walter Mahoney (d 1982); 1 da (Lucy Jane b Oct 1977); m 3, 3 Aug 2005, Ann Sidney; *Career* theatrical producer, formerly photographer; co-fndr Triumph Theatre Productions Ltd 1970; dir: Duncan C Weldon Productions Ltd, Triumph Proscenium Productions Ltd, Malvern Festival Theatre Trust Ltd; artistic dir Chichester Festival Theatre 1995–97; co-fndr Triumph Entertainment Ltd 2000; first stage prodn A Funny Kind of Evening (with David Kossoff, Theatre Royal Bath) 1965, first London prodn Tons of Money (Mayfair) 1968, presentations also in Europe, Aust, Russia, Canada and Hong Kong; *Theatre Productions* has presented over 200 in London incl in 1970: When We Are Married; in 1971: The Chalk Garden, Big Bad Mouse, The Wizard of Oz; in 1972: Lord Arthur Savile's Crime, Bunny, The Wizard of Oz; in 1973: Mother Adam, Grease, The King and I; in 1974: Dead Easy; in 1975: The Case in Question, Hedda Gabler (RSC), Dad's Army, Betzi, On Approval; in 1976: 13 Rue de l'Amour, A Bedful of Foreigners, Three Sisters, Fringe Benefits, The Seagull, The Circle; in 1977: Separate Tables, Stevie, Hedda Gabler, On Approval, The Good Woman of Setzuan, Rosmersholm, Laburnham Grove, The Apple Cart; in 1978: Waters of the Moon, Kings and Clowns, The Travelling Music Show, A Family, Look After Lulu, The Millionairess; in 1979: The Crucifer of Blood; in 1980: Reflections, Rattle of a Simple Man, The Last of Mrs Cheyney, Early Days (RNT); in 1981: Virginia, Overheard, Dave Allen, Worzel Gummidge; in 1982: Murder in Mind, Hobson's Choice, A Coat of Varnish, Captain Brassbound's Conversion, Design For Living, Uncle Vanya, Key for Two, The Rules of the Game, Man and Superman; in 1983: The School for Scandal, Dash, Heartbreak House, Call Me Madam, Romantic Comedy, Liza Minnelli, Beethoven's Tenth (also Broadway), Edmund Kean (also Broadway), Fiddler on the Roof, A Patriot for Me (also LA), Cowardice, Great and Small, The Cherry Orchard, Dial M for Murder, Dear Anyone, The Sleeping Prince, The School for Scandal, Hi-De-Hi!; in 1984: Hello Dolly!, The Aspern Papers, Strange Interlude (also Broadway), Serjeant Musgrave's Dance, Aren't We All? (also Broadway), American Buffalo, The Way of the World, Extremities; in 1985: The Wind in the Willows, The Lonely Road, The Caine Mutiny Court-Martial, Other Places, Old Times (also in LA), The Corn is Green, Waste (RSC), Strippers, Guys and Dolls (RNT), Sweet Bird of Youth, Interpreters, Fatal Attraction, The Scarlet Pimpernel; in 1986: The Applecart, Across from the Garden of Allah, Antony and Cleopatra, The Taming of the Shrew, Circe & Bravo, Annie Get Your Gun, Long Day's Journey into Night, Rookery Nook, Breaking the Code (also Broadway), Mr and Mrs Nobody; in 1987: A Piece of My Mind, Court in the Act!, Canaries Sometimes Sing, Kiss Me Kate (RSC), Melon, Portraits, Groucho – A Life in Review, A Man for all Seasons, You Never Can Tell, Babes in the Wood; in 1988: A Touch of the Poet, The Deep Blue Sea, The Admirable Crichton, The Secret of Sherlock Holmes, A Walk in the Woods, Orpheus Descending (also Broadway), Richard II; in 1989: Richard III, The Royal Baccarat Scandal, Ivanov, Much Ado About Nothing, The Merchant of Venice (also Broadway), Frankie & Johnny, Veterans Day, Another Time, The Baker's Wife, London Assurance; in 1990: Salome (RNT), Bent (RNT), An Evening with Peter Ustinov, The Wild Duck, Henry IV, Kean, Love Letters, Time and the Conways; in 1991: The Homecoming, The Philanthropist, The Caretaker, Becket, Tovarich, The Cabinet Minister; in 1992: Talking Heads, Heartbreak House, Hamlet, A Woman of No Importance (RSC), Lost in Yonkers, Trelawny of the Wells, Cyrano de Bergerac; in 1993: Macbeth (RSC), Relative Values, Two Gentlemen of Verona (RSC); in 1994: Travesties (RSC), A Month in the Country (also Broadway), The Clandestine Marriage, Peer Gynt, Rope, An Evening with Peter Ustinov, Arcadia (RNT), Home, Saint Joan, Lady Windermere's Fan, The Rivals; in 1995: Dangerous Corner, Cell Mates, The Duchess of Malfi, Taking Sides (also Broadway), Old Times, Communicating Doors, Hobson's Choice, The Hothouse; in 1996: Uncle Vanya, When We Are Married, Talking Heads, The Cherry Orchard (RSC); in 1997: Live & Kidding, The Herbal Bed (RSC), Life Support, A Letter of Resignation, Electra (also Broadway), The Magistrate; in 1998: Rent, New Edna – The Spectacle; in 1999: Richard III (RSC), The Prisoner of Second Avenue, Hay Fever, Love letters, The Importance of Being Earnest, Collected Stories; in 2000: Enigmatic Variations (also Los Angeles), Napoleon, God Only Knows, The Importance of Being Earnest (extensive tour); in 2001: The Importance of Being Earnest (Savoy Theatre London), Peggy Sue Got Married, Private Lives (also Broadway); in 2002: My One and Only, The Hollow Crown (RSC, Aust and NZ); in 2003: The Tempest, Coriolanus (RSC), The Merry Wives of Windsor (RSC), The Master Builder, Thoroughly Modern Millie; in 2004: Rattle of a Simple Man, Suddenly Last Summer, Blithe Spirit; in 2005: The Birthday Party, The Philadelphia Story, As You Desire Me; in 2007: The Last Confession, Macbeth (also Broadway), Nicholas Nickleby; in 2009: Waiting for Godot, Taking Sides, Collaboration; in 2010: Private Lives (also Broadway), When We Are Married, Blithe Spirit; in 2011: Pygmalion, Rosencrantz and Guildenstern Are Dead, The Tempest, The Lion in the Winter; other Broadway prodns incl: Brief Lives 1974, Wild Honey (NT) 1986, Blithe Spirit and Pygmalion 1987; *Television Productions* co-prodr (with Carlton TV) Into the Blue (by Robert Goddard and starring John Thaw) 1997; *Style—* Duncan C Weldon, Esq

WELDON, Fay; CBE (2001); *née* Franklin Birkinshaw; da of Dr Frank Birkinshaw (d 1947), and Margaret, *née* Jepson; *b* 22 September 1931, Alvechurch, Worcs; *Educ* Christ Church

W

Girls' HS NZ, South Hampstead HS, Univ of St Andrews (MA); *m* 1; 1 s (Nicholas b 1954); m 2, June 1961 (m dis 1994), Ron Weldon; 3 s (Daniel b 1963, Thomas b 1970, Samuel b 1977); m 3, 1995, Nicolas Fox; *Career* screen writer, playwright, novelist, critic, essayist; chm of judges Booker McConnell Prize 1983; prof of creative writing Brunel Univ 2006–12, currently prof of creative writing Bath Spa Univ; memb: Soc of Authors, Writers' Guild (US); Hon DLitt: Univ of Bath 1989, Univ of St Andrews 1992, Univ of Birmingham 2001, Univ of Connecticut 2007; FRSL 1986, FRSA; *Books* The Fat Woman's Joke (1967), Down Among the Women (1971), Female Friends (1975), Remember Me (1976), Little Sisters (1978), Praxis (1978, Booker Prize nomination), Puffball (1980), Watching Me Watching You (1981), The President's Child (1982), Life and Loves of a She Devil (1984, televised 1986), Letters to Alice-on First Reading Jane Austen (1984), Polaris and Other Stories (1985), Rebecca West (1985), The Shrapnel Academy (1986), Heart of the Country (1987, televised 1987), The Hearts and Lives of Men (1987), The Rules of Life (1987), Leader of the Band (1988), The Cloning of Joanna May (1989), Darcy's Utopia (1990), Growing Rich (1990, televised 1990), Moon Over Minneapolis or Why She Couldn't Stay (1991), Life Force (1992), Affliction (1994), Splitting (1995), Wicked Women (1995), Worst Fears (1996), Big Women (1998), Hard Time To Be a Father (1998), Godless in Eden (1999), Rhode Island Blues (2000), The Bulgari Connection (2001), Auto-Da-Fay (autobiography, 2002), Nothing to Wear Nowhere to Hide (short stories, 2002), Mantrapped (2004), She May Not Leave (2005), What Makes Women Happy (2006), The Spa Decameron (2007), The Stepmother's Diary (2008), Chalcot Crescent (2009), Kehua (2010), Habits of the House (2012), Long Live the King (2013), The New Countess (2013), The Ted Dreams (ebook novella, 2014) Mischief (2015), Before the War (2016); children's books: Wolf the Mechanical Dog (1988), Party Puddle (1989), Nobody Likes Me (1999); *Style—* Fay Weldon, CBE, FRSL; ✉ website www.fayweldon.co.uk; c/o Georgina Capel, Capel and Land, 29 Wardour Street, London W1V 3HB (☎ 020 7734 2414, e-mail georgina@capelland.co.uk)

WELDON, Tom; s of Patrick Weldon, and Pamela, *née* Grant; *Educ* Westminster, St John's Coll Oxford (BA); *Career* ed Macmillan Publishers 1985–88, editorial dir William Heinemann 1989–96, publishing dir Penguin 1997–; *Recreations* racing, movies, skiing, travel; *Clubs* Charlie Chester's Casino; *Style—* Tom Weldon, Esq; ✉ Penguin Books, 80 Strand, London WC2R 0RL (☎ 020 7010 3280, e-mail tom.weldon@penguin.co.uk)

WELEMINSKY, Judy Ruth; da of Dr Anton Weleminsky, of Manchester, and Gerda, *née* Loewenstamm; *b* 25 October 1950; *Educ* Pontefract & Dist Girls' HS, Roundhay HS, Univ of Birmingham (BSc), Lancaster Univ (MA); *m* Robert J A Smith; 2 da (Emma Jane Weleminsky-Smith b 6 Feb 1991, Alice Rose Weleminsky-Smith b 13 Feb 1993); *Career* personnel and training offr Lowfield (S & D) Ltd 1973–75, community rels offr Lambeth Cncl for Community Rels 1975–78, equal opportunities offr Wandsworth BC 1978–80, employment devpt offr Nat Assoc for Care and Resettlement of Offenders (NACRO) 1980–82; chief exec: Nat Fed of Community Orgns 1982–85, Nat Schizophrenia Fellowship 1985–90, NCVO 1991–94; mgmnt conslt 1994–2005, assoc Volprof 1994–96, ptnr Mentoring Directors 1995–97, sr assoc Compass Partnership 1994–2005, chief exec Mental Health Providers Forum 2005–11, interim chief exec Three Wings Tst 2012; assoc mentor Clutterbuck Schneider & Palmer 1996–99; tstee: Cosmopolitan Devpt Tst 1997–2000, Makaton Vocabulary Devpt Project 1998–2012; public speaker; co-ordinator: Chiswick & Kew Jewish Gp 1997–2004, Kew Giving Circle 1998–; dir Venture Community Assoc 2005; memb: Bd Children and Families Ct Advsy and Support Service (CAFCASS) 2001–04, Cncl Gen Social Care Cncl 2001–04, ACEVO; co sec Wimbledon and District Synagogue 2011–13 (tstee 2011–14), chair Univ of Roehampton Jewish Resources Centre 2012–, fndr Pro Israel, Pro Palestine, Pro Peace 2014; tstee Renaissance Pubns 2015–; FRSA 1992; *Recreations* family, friends and food; *Style—* Ms Judy Weleminsky; ✉ e-mail judywele@blueyonder.co.uk

WELFARE, Jonathan William; s of Kenneth William Welfare (d 1966), and (Dorothy) Patience Athole, *née* Ross; *b* 21 October 1944; *Educ* Bradfield Coll, Emmanuel Coll Cambridge (MA, Boxing Blue); *m* 6 Sept 1969, Deborah Louise, da of James D'Arcy Nesbitt, of West Kirby, Cheshire; 3 da (Harriet b 1973, Laura b 1975, Amy b 1979), 1 s (Oliver b 1987); *Career* economist Drivers Jonas and Co 1966–68, conslt Sir Colin Buchanan and Ptnrs 1968–70, economist and corp planning mangr Milton Keynes Devpt Corp 1970–74, chief economist and dep chief exec S Yorks Met CC 1974–84, dir The Landmark Tst 1984–86; dir (co-fndr) The Oxford Ventures Gp 1986–90; dir: Granite TV Ltd 1988–2002, Oxford Innovation Ltd 1988–98; md Venture Link Investors Ltd 1990–95, chief exec Bristol 2000 1995–96, mgmnt conslt 1996–98; chief exec: Elizabeth Finn Care (estab as Distressed Gentlefolks Aid Assoc 1897, charity), Elizabeth Finn Trading Ltd, Elizabeth Finn Homes Ltd 1998–2010; chm The Nominet Tst 2008–12, chm Gingerbread 2014–; fndr Turn2Us 2007 (dir 2007–10), fndr UK's first virtual museum 2008; tstee: The Oxford Tst 1985–2005 and 2011 (chm 1985–95), The Northmoor Tst 1986–99 (chm 1986–95); memb Bd English Community Care Assoc 2000–10;tstee The Town and Manor of Hungerford and the Liberty of Sanden Fee 2016–; Care Innovator of the Year 2007; Freeman City of London, Freeman Worshipful Co of Info Technologists; FRSA; *Books* Sources of EEC Funding for Local Authorities (1977); *Recreations* family, cricket, fishing, gardening; *Clubs* Hawks' (Cambridge); *Style—* Jonathan Welfare, Esq; ✉ The Garden House, c/o 34 High Street, Hungerford RG17 0NF (☎ 01488 684228)

WELFARE, Simon Piers; s of Kenneth William Welfare (d 1966), of Stradbroke, Suffolk, and Dorothy Patience, *née* Ross; *b* 21 November 1946; *Educ* Harrow, Magdalen Coll Oxford; *m* 3 Aug 1968, Lady Mary Katharine Welfare, da of Marquess of Aberdeen and Temair, CBE (d 1974), of Haddo House, Aberdeenshire; 2 da (Hannah b 30 Sept 1969, Alice b 6 Sept 1971 d Feb 2004), 1 s (Toby b 29 March 1973); *Career* broadcaster and writer Yorkshire TV Ltd 1968–81, freelance prodr 1982–, md Granite Film and TV Prodns 1989–; *Books* Arthur C Clarke's Mysterious World (with A C Clarke and John Fairley, 1980), Arthur C Clarke's World of Strange Powers (with A C Clarke and J Fairley, 1984), Great Honeymoon Disasters (1986), Arthur C Clarke's Chronicles of the Strange & Mysterious (with A C Clarke and J Fairley, 1987), Red Empire (with Gwyneth Hughes, 1990), The Cabinet of Curiosities (with J Fairley, 1991), Days of Majesty (with Alastair Bruce, 1993), Arthur C Clarke's A-Z of Mysteries (with J Fairley, 1993); *Recreations* collecting arcane knowledge, flying, objecting to wind turbines; *Style—* Simon Welfare, Esq; ✉ 1 Wester Coull Cottages, Tarland, Aboyne AB34 4YS (☎ 01339 880175)

WELLDON, Dr Estela Valentina; da of Gildo D'Accurzio (d 1983), and Julia, *née* Barbadillo (d 1957); *b* 3 November 1936; *Educ* Universidad de Cuyo Argentina (MD), Menninger Sch of Psychiatry USA, Univ of London; *m* Ronald Michael Charles Welldon (d 1970); 1 s (Daniel Alexis b 2 Feb 1970); *Career* psychiatrist Henderson Hosp 1964; Portman Clinic London: conslt psychiatrist 1975–, clinic tutor 1987–92; private practice 44 Harley Street; specialist in the application of gp analysis to social and sexual deviancy, pioneer in teaching of forensic psychotherapy, fndr in forensic psychotherapy Univ of London; pres Int Assoc for Forensic Psychotherapy 1991–95 (hon pres 1995–); organisational conslt 1997–, conslt 1997–; assessor British Jl of Psychiatry, expert on female crime and sexual deviation Panel of Specialists RCPsych, Br corr and memb Editorial Bd Argentinian Jl of Gp Psychotherapy; currently sr lectr: Dept of Psychiatry Sassari Univ Sardinia, Dept of Psychology Univ of Bologna Italy; Visitante Distinguido Univ and City of Cuzco Peru 1989; memb: Gp Analytic Soc 1968, Br Assoc of Psychotherapists 1972, Inst for Study and Prevention of Delinquency, American Gp Psychotherapy Assoc, Int Assoc of Gp Psychotherapy, Inst of Gp Analysis; fndr memb Bd of Dirs Int Acad of Law and Mental Health, memb Bd of Dirs Int Assoc of Gp Psychotherapy, hon memb Soc of Couple Psychoanalytic Psychotherapists Tavistock Clinic, hon memb American Psychoanalytic Assoc 2013; Hon DSc Oxford Brookes Univ 1997; memb Soc of Authors; FRCPsych 1987 (MRCPysch 1973); *Books* Mother, Madonna, Whore (1988), A Practical Guide to Forensic Psychotherapy (1996), Sadomasochism (2002), Playing with Dynamite (2011); *Recreations* opera, theatre, swimming; *Clubs* Groucho; *Style—* Dr Estela Welldon; ✉ 44 Harley Street, London W1G 9PS (mobile 07932 715757, e-mail estelawelldon@me.com)

WELLER, Prof Malcolm Philip Isadore; s of Solomon George Weller (d 1958), and Esther, *née* Black; *b* 29 May 1935; *Educ* Perse Sch Cambridge, Univ of Cambridge (MA, prize winner, capt coll athletics team), Univ of Newcastle upon Tyne (MB BS, scholarship and prize winner), Br Cncl travel award; *m* 8 May 1966, (Celia) Davina, da of Solomon Reisler (d 1973); 2 s (Ben b 19 Aug 1969, Adrian b 17 Dec 1970); *Career* psychiatrist; emeritus conslt Barnet Enfield and Haringey NHS Mental Health Tst, hon research prof Middlesex Univ; formerly lectr and first asst Charing Cross Hosp Sch of Med; visiting fell Fitzwilliam Coll Cambridge 1994–95; pubns incl over 150 chapters, papers and editorials on psychiatric and medico-legal subjects, 5 books, ed in chief Baillìere's Clinical Psychiatry series; Univ of London: co-opted memb Bd of Studies in Psychology and Higher Degrees Sub-Ctee, memb Examination Ctee; external examiner Univs of Manchester and Singapore (RCPsych rep), prize adjudicator RSM 2005–11 (also memb Exec Ctee and Cncl Psychiatry Section); rep to NICE (currently exec Ctee Neuopsychiatric and Academic Faculties and Clinical Excellence Award advsr); chm: CONCERN 1994–99, London Regnl Psychiatric Ctee 1995–, Haringey Div of Psychiatry 1992–94, Joint London Chairmen Working Gp, Jt Thames Psychiatric Chairmen and Exec Ctee; former vice-chm London Regnl Ctee for Hosp Med Servs; cmmr Mental Health Act; former organiser Newcastle Music Festival, former co-opted memb Mgmnt Ctee Laing Art Gallery; former local cncllr, former chm of govrs Gosforth Middle Sch, memb NY Acad of Sciences; memb Central Ctee BMA; memb Cncl RSM, emeritus memb AAAS, memb Br Neuropsychiatry Assoc, fndr memb Br Assoc of Psychopharmacology, int fell American Psychiatric Assoc, emeritus memb American Assoc for the Advancement of Science, invited FRSA; FBPsS (chartered psychologist, memb Neuropsychiatry Section) 1986, FCINP 1987 (hon lifetime achievement fell 2009), FRCPsych 1987, FRSA; *Books* Scientific Basis of Psychiatry (1983 and 1992), International Perspectives in Schizophrenia (1990), MCQs on the Basic Sciences (1992), Dimensions of Community Care (1993), Progress in Clinical Psychiatry (1996); Baillìere's Clinical Psychiatry Series (ed in chief, 11 vols); *Recreations* history of art, music; *Clubs* RSM; *Style—* Prof Malcolm Weller; ✉ 30 Arkwright Road, Hampstead, London NW3 6BH (☎ 020 7794 5804, fax 020 7431 1589, e-mail office@malcolmweller.com)

WELLER, Sara; CBE (2015); *b* 1 August 1961; *Educ* Weymouth GS, New Coll Oxford (Beresford Hope scholar, MA, Badminton blue); *Career* Mars Confectionery UK: mktg grad trainee 1983–85, grad recruitment mangr Mars Gp UK 1986–87, personnel mangr Sales Div 1987–88, mktg mangr 1989–94, mktg controller UK and Europe 1994–96, consumer devpt dir Europe 1996; Abbey National plc: customer mktg dir 1996–98, retail mktg dir 1998–99; Sainsbury's Supermarkets Ltd: mktg dir 2000–2001, asst md 2001–03, memb Gp Bd 2002–04, dep md 2003–04; md Argos Ltd 2004–; non-exec dir Mitchells & Butlers plc 2003–; *Recreations* golf (irregular), natural history/evolution/philosophy, cooking, home improvements, children; *Style—* Mrs Sara Weller, CBE

WELLER, Timothy Grainger; *b* 6 January 1961, London; *Educ* Blundell's, Cardiff Univ (BSc); *m* 3 Dec 1989, Jacqueline, *née* Mathiesen; 1 da (Emily), 2 s (Harry, George); *Career* VNI Business Pubns 1982–87, Centaur Communications 1987–94 (dir 1989–94), md Reuters Publishing 1994, fndr and gp chief exec Incisive Media 2000–; chm PPA Business and Professional 2005–08; chm and non-exec dir: RDF Media 2005–10, InternetQ 2013–, Trustpilot 2013–, Merimedia 2014–; non-exec chm Polestar 2009–11; memb Shadow Cabinet New Enterprise Cncl; PPA Publisher of the Year 1997 and 1998, Ernst and Young Entrepreneur of the Year London 2001, Marcus Morris Award 2005; *Recreations* cricket, shooting, skiing; *Style—* Tim Weller, Esq; ✉ Incisive Media, Haymarket House, 28–29 Haymarket, London SW1Y 4RX

WELLINGS, Prof Paul William; CBE (2012); s of William Wellings (d 1979), and Beryl, *née* Roscoe (d 1981); *b* 1 November 1953, Nottingham; *Educ* Royal GS Lancaster, KCL (BSc), Univ of Durham (MSc), UEA (PhD); *m* 22 Dec 1990, Annette Frances Schmidt; *Career* NERC research fell UEA 1980–81, research scientist CSIRO Entomology Canberra 1981–95, chief of div CSIRO Entomology Canberra 1995–97, first asst sec Dept of Industry, Science and Resources Aust govt 1997–99, dep chief exec CSIRO Canberra 1999–2002, vice-chllr Lancaster Univ 2002–11, vice-chllr Wollongong Univ NSW 2012–; chair 1994 Gp 2009–11; memb Bd: Aust Nuclear Science and Technol Orgn 1997–99, Aust Centre for Int Agric Research 1999–2002, Cumbria Rural Regeneration Co 2002–06, HEFCE 2006–11, Universities UK 2006–11, Bundanon Tst 2015–; memb: Advsy Ctee New Colombo Plan Canberra 2013–, NSW Int Educn Advsy Bd 2014–, Advsy Cncl ARC 2014–; DL Lancs 2009–11; Hon DSc Lancaster Univ 2014; fell Aust Inst of Co Dirs (FAICD), FRSA; *Publications* numerous papers in population ecology and insect pest mgmnt; *Recreations* cricket, fell walking; *Style—* Prof Paul Wellings, CBE; ✉ Vice-Chancellor's Office, Wollongong University, NSW 2522, Australia (☎ 0061 2 4221 3909, fax 0061 2 4226 5810, e-mail paul_wellings@uow.edu.au)

WELLINGTON, 9 Duke of (UK 1814); (Arthur) Charles Valerian Wellesley; OBE (1999), DL (Hampshire 1999); s of 8 Duke of Wellington, KG, LVO, OBE, MC (d 2014); *b* 19 August 1945; *Educ* Eton, ChCh Oxford; *m* 3 Feb 1977, Antonia (pres Guinness Tst), da of HRH Prince Frederick von Preussen (d 1966, s of HIH Crown Prince Wilhelm, s and h of Kaiser Wilhelm II), and Lady Brigid Ness; 2 s (Arthur Gerald, Marquess of Douro b 31 Jan 1978, Lord Frederick Charles b 30 Sept 1992), 3 da (Lady Honor Montagu b 25 Oct 1979, Lady Mary Luise b 16 Dec 1986, Lady Charlotte Santo Domingo b 8 Oct 1990); *Heir* s, Marquess of Douro; *Career* chm: Dunhill Holdings plc 1991–93 (dep chm 1990–91), Framlington Group plc 1994–2006, Vendôme Luxury Group plc 1993–99, Sun Life & Provincial plc 1995–2000; dep chm: Thames Valley Broadcasting 1975–84, Deltec Panamerica SA 1985–89, Guinness Mahon Holdings plc 1988–91; dir: Transatlantic Holdings plc 1983–95, Sun Life Corporation plc 1988–96, GAM Worldwide Inc, Eucalyptus Pulp Mills 1979–88, Compagnie Financière Richemont 2000–, Sanofi-Aventis 2002–14, Pernod Ricard 2003–11, RIT Capital Partners 2010–; MEP (Cons) Surrey West 1979–89, Parly candidate Islington N (Cons) 1974; cmmr English Heritage 2003–07; chm King's Coll London 2007–; High Steward Winchester Cathedral 2013–; *Style—* His Grace the Duke of Wellington, OBE, DL; ✉ Richemont Holdings plc, 15 Hill Street, London W1J 5QT (☎ 020 7838 8502); Stratfield Saye House, Hampshire RG7 2BZ; Apsley House, Piccadilly, London W1J 7NT

WELLS, (William Arthur) Andrew; TD (1984); s of Sir John Wells, DL, MP Maidstone 1959–87; *b* 14 June 1949; *Educ* Eton, Univ of Leicester (MA); *m* 19 Oct 1974, Tessa Margaret, da of Lt-Col Jocelyn Eustace Gurney, DSO, MC*, DL (d 1973), of Tacolneston Hall, and Sprowston, Norfolk; 2 s (Maj William b 1980, Maj Frederick b 1982), 1 da (Augusta (Mrs Robert Macdougall) b 1984); *Career* TA: cmmnd Wessex Yeo (Royal Glos Hussars) 1971, visiting lectr Jr Div Staff Coll 1978–79, Maj Royal Green Jackets 1981–90; publishing 1969–81; property mgmnt: Minories Hldgs Ltd and Watermen's Co 1981–91, Leeds Castle Kent 1992–2003; curatorial conslt Leeds Castle 2003–14, expert adviser Nat Heritage Memorial Fund 2004–14; tstee Chevening Estate 1992–2002, chm SE Region Historic Houses Assoc 1997–2001; pres: Maidstone Mencap, St John Ambulance Tunbridge Wells and Tonbridge; tstee: Kent Gardens Tst, Safer Kent for

Kent People's Tst; author of several historic building guidebooks; High Sheriff Kent 2005–06; Hon Freeman Watermen's Co 1991; SBStJ 2011; *Recreations* architectural and art history, country pursuits, gardening; *Clubs* City Livery, Rifles Officers; *Style*— Andrew Wells, Esq, TD; ✉ Mere House, Mereworth, Maidstone, Kent ME18 5NB (website www.mere-house.co.uk)

WELLS, Boyan Stewart; s of Gordon Tebbutt Wells, of Bristol, and Vera, *née* Stanisic; *b* 3 June 1956; *Educ* Colston's Sch Bristol, Wadham Coll Oxford (MA, Hockey blue); *m* 11 Aug 1984, Alison Jayne, da of Michael Albert Good, of Bristol; 3 da (Holly Catharine b 8 May 1987, Elena Rose b 2 Dec 1988, Laura Elizabeth b 9 Dec 1994); *Career* ptnr Allen & Overy LLP 1987– (joined 1979); Freeman: City of London, Worshipful Co of Slrs 1987; memb Law Soc; *Recreations* golf, cinema; *Clubs* Richmond Hockey, Dulwich Golf; *Style*— Boyan Wells, Esq; ✉ Allen & Overy, One Bishops Square, London E1 6AD (☎ 020 3088 0000, fax 020 3088 0088)

WELLS, Dr Cecilia; OBE (1996); *Educ* Open Univ (BSc), Centre for Personal Construct Psychology (Dip), Royal Holloway Univ of London (PhD); *Career* various HR roles British Leyland 1972–81, UK recruitment and staff devpt mangr Manpower plc 1981–88, ind conslt in trg and HR mgmnt 1988–98, fndr dir Ionann Mgmnt Conslts Ltd 1998–99, dir and co-prop Astar Mgmnt Conslts Ltd 1999–; memb: Parole Bd for England and Wales 1988–94, Race Rels Advsy Gp DfEE 1990–96, Equal Opportunities Cmmn 1990–96, Ethnic Minorities Ctee Judicial Studies Bd 1992–96, Cncl ACAS 1992–2000 (actg chair 2000), Employee Rels Advsy Panel DTI 2001–, Bd Office of the Ind Adjudicator for HE 2005–11, Bd Office of the Parly and Health Serv Ombudsman 2005–09; ind assessor for public appts 2000–; arbitrator ACAS; vice-chair Centrepoint 1993–2007, chair Regnl Advsy Cncl BBC SE 1995–98, non-exec dir then vice-chair Bedford and Shires Community and Care Tst 1995–99; *Style*— Dr Cecilia Wells, OBE; ✉ Astar Management Consultants Ltd, PO Box 6927, London W1A 6FB (☎ 020 7224 0771, e-mail ceciliawells@astarltd.co.uk)

WELLS, Prof David Arthur; s of Arthur William Wells (d 1993), of Lancing, West Sussex, and Rosina Elizabeth, *née* Jones (d 1986); *b* 26 April 1941; *Educ* Christ's Hosp, Gonville & Caius Coll Cambridge (MA, PhD); *Career* lectr in German: Univ of Southampton 1966–69, Bedford Coll London 1969–74; prof of German: The Queen's Univ of Belfast 1974–87, Birkbeck Coll London 1987–2006; hon treas Modern Humanities Res Assoc 2001–09 (hon sec 1969–2001); Int Fedn for Modern Languages and Literatures: sec-gen 1981–2005, pres 2005–08; FRSA 1985; *Books* The Vorau Moses and Balaam (1970), The Wild Man from the Epic of Gilgamesh to Hartmann von Ave's Iwein (1975), A Complete Concordance to the Vorauer Bücher Moses (1976), The Years Work in Modern Language Studies (jt ed, 1976–2005), The Central Franconian Rhyming Bible (2004); *Recreations* travel; *Style*— Prof David Wells

WELLS, David Patrick Casey; s of late Frank Wells, and Bridget Theresa, *née* Casey; *b* 24 November 1950; *Educ* St Joseph's Coll Blackpool, QMC London (LLB); *m* 28 Dec 1991, Michele Jane; 2 da (Holly, Hannah), 1 s (Samuel); *Career* admitted slr 1976; slr Herbert Smith 1976–81; ptnr: Reynolds Porter Chamberlain 1981–88, Titmuss Sainer & Webb (now Decherts) 1988–96, DAC Beachcroft LLP (formerly Beachcroft Stanleys then Beachcroft Wansbroughs then Beachcroft LLP) 1996–; memb Law Soc; *Recreations* rugby (Blackheath), swimming, reading and family; *Style*— David Wells, Esq; ✉ DAC Beachcroft LLP, 100 Fetter Lane, London EC4A 1BN

WELLS, Dean of; *see:* Clarke, Very Rev John Martin

WELLS, Graham Holland; s of Edmund Holland Wells, RD (d 1974), and Pamela Doris, *née* Siddall (d 2013); *b* 28 May 1959; *Educ* Shrewsbury, BNC Oxford (MA); *m* 21 Jan 1984, Dr Susan Margaret, da of James Edgar Riley Tompkin (d 2000); 1 s (Adam Holland b 22 Aug 1990), 1 da (Victoria Susan b 23 Oct 1992); *Career* called to the Bar Middle Temple 1982; mediator 2007, recorder 2009; memb: Professional Negligence Bar Assoc (PNBA), Northern Circuit Medico-Legal Assoc, Acad of Experts; *Recreations* skiing, hill walking, kayaking; *Style*— Graham H Wells, Esq; ✉ Oriel Chambers, 14 Water Street, Liverpool, Merseyside L2 8TD (☎ 0151 236 7191, fax 0151 227 5909, e-mail graham.wells@orielchambers.co.uk)

WELLS, James Henry (Jim); MLA; s of Samuel Henry Wells, of Lurgan, Co Armagh, and Doreen, *née* Campbell; *b* 27 April 1957; *Educ* Lurgan Coll, Queen's Univ Belfast (BA Dip Town and Country Planning); *m* 26 July 1983, Grace, da of Sydney Wallace; 2 da, 1 s; *Career* memb NI Assembly 1982–86; asst regnl public affrs mangr Nat Tst 1989–98; MLA (DUP) S Down 1998–; sec DUP Assembly Gp; *Recreations* hill walking, bird watching; *Style*— Jim Wells, Esq, MLA; ✉ Parliament Buildings, Stormont, Belfast BT4 3XX (☎ 02890 521110, mobile 07856 235144, e-mail jimwells6@gmail.com)

WELLS, Prof John Christopher; s of Rev Philip Cuthbert Wells (d 1974), of Walton-on-Trent, and Winifred May, *née* Peaker (d 1997); *b* 11 March 1939; *Educ* St John's Sch Leatherhead, Trinity Coll Cambridge (BA), UCL (MA, PhD); *Partner* Gabriel Parsons (civil partnership 2006); *Career* UCL: asst lectr in phonetics 1962–65, lectr 1965–82, reader 1982–88, prof 1988–2006, emeritus prof 2006–; former pres World Esperanto Assoc, pres Esperanto Assoc of GB 2004–13, former pres Int Phonetic Assoc, pres Spelling Soc 2003–13; FBA 1996; *Books* Teach Yourself Concise Esperanto Dictionary (1969, reissued as English-Esperanto-English Dictionary 2010), Practical Phonetics (1971), Jamaican Pronunciation in London (1973), Accents of English (1982), Longman Pronunciation Dictionary (1990, 3 edn 2008), English Intonation: An Introduction (2006), Sounds Interesting (2014), Sounds Fascinating (2016); *Style*— Prof J C Wells, FBA; ✉ Department of Phonetics & Linguistics, University College, Gower Street, London WC1E 6BT (☎ 020 8542 0302, e-mail j.wells@ucl.ac.uk, website www.phon.ucl.ac.uk/home/wells)

WELLS, Prof Michael; s of John Thomas Wells (d 1975), of Cannock, Staffs, and Lily, *née* Ellis; *b* 7 August 1952; *Educ* Pool Hayes Sch Willenhall, Univ of Manchester (BSc, MB ChB, MD); *m* 1, 21 Dec 1974 (m dis 1992), Jane Cecilia, da of John Parker Gill, of Gosforth, Cumbria; 1 s (James b 1980), 1 da (Rosemary b 1982); m 2, 27 May 1994, Lynne Margaret Austerberry, da of Raymond George Walker, of Blythe Bridge, Staffs; *Career* lectr in pathology Univ of Bristol 1978–79, sr lectr in pathology Univ of Leeds 1988–93 (lectr 1980–88); hon conslt United Leeds Teaching Hosps NHS Trust 1983–93; clinical sub dean: Leeds West Univ of Leeds Sch of Med 1988–91, St James's Univ Hosp 1994–96; hon conslt pathologist St James's Univ Hosp Leeds 1993–96, ptnr Roundhay Pathologists (BUPA Hosp) Leeds 1993–96, ptnr govr Chesterfield Royal Hosp NHS Fndn Tst 2008–; prof of gynaecological pathology: Univ of Leeds 1993–96, Univ of Sheffield 1997–2014, ret (dir of studies phase 3A 2006–09, emeritus prof 2014–); dir of int affrs Faculty of Medicine, Dentistry and Health Univ of Sheffield 2013–14; hon conslt histopathologist Sheffield Teaching Hosps 1997–, pt/t conslt histopathologist Leeds Teaching Hosps NHS Tst 2015–; external examiner in pathology Univ of Manchester 1995–99, external examiner in pathology Univ of Cambridge 2000 and 2002, external examiner in histopathology Trinity Coll Dublin Sch of Medicine 2008–11, external examiner in pathology Univ of Medical Sciences & Technol Khartoum 2014; conslt and memb Med Advsy Bd PathLore Ltd 2001–10 (dir (gynaecological pathology) 2001–06); memb: Assoc of Clinical Pathologists Speciality Ctee on Histopathology 1989–93, Part 1 MCQ Sub-Ctee RCOG 1989–95, Cncl Br Gynaecological Cancer Soc 1990–92 (pres 1994–97), Editorial Advsy Bd Placenta 1990–95, Kliofem Steering Ctee Novo Nordisk Pharmaceuticals Ltd 1990–2000, Exec Ctee Int Soc of Gynecological Pathologists 1991–94 (pres 2003–05), Sub-Ctee for the Co-ordination of Research into Gynaecological Cancer of the UK Co-ordinating Ctee on Cancer Research 1991–98, Jt RCOG/Wellbeing Research Advsy Ctee 1996–98, Exec Ctee European Soc of Pathology 2004– (pres 2009–11), Gynaecological Visiting Soc of GB and I 2005–, Panel of Examiners in Histopathology RCPath, Scientific Ctee European Congress of Pathology London 2014, Bd of Dirs Int Collaboration on Cancer Reporting 2014–; memb Editorial Bd: Int Jl of Gynecological Pathology 1993–2011 (assoc ed 1998–2003), Jl of Pathology 1998–2002, Virchows Archiv 2002–11, Gynecol Oncol 2005–07; ed Histopathology 2003–11, assoc ed Papillomavirus Report 1990–93; hon sec Br Div of the Int Acad of Pathology 1988–93 (pres 2012–14), meetings sec Pathological Soc of GB and I 1996–2000 (gen sec 2000–03); FRCPath 1995 (MRCPath 1983, memb Cncl 1998–2001 and 2008–11, chm Specialty Advsy Ctee on Histopathology 2008–, vice-pres 2011–14), FRCOG (ad eundem) 2004; *Publications* Haines and Taylor Obstetrical and Gynaecological Pathology (asst ed, 4 edn, 1995; co-ed, 5 edn, 2003); author/co-author of approx 230 chapters, review articles and original papers, numerous invited lectures nationally and internationally incl 2 George Cunningham Lecture Br Div of the Int Acad of Pathology Glasgow (2007); *Recreations* reading, singing, skiing, gardening; *Clubs* Athenaeum; *Style*— Prof Michael Wells; ✉ The Barn, West End Farm, Stainburn, Otley, West Yorkshire LS21 2QW (☎ 0113 203 7581, mobile 07791 192548, e-mail m.wells@sheffield.ac.uk)

WELLS, Michael Frederick; OBE (2013); s of Frederick William Wells (d1983), of Chislehurst, Kent, and Victoria, *née* Priddis (d 1942); *b* 2 August 1938, Chislehurst, Kent; *Educ* Chislehurst and Sidcup Co GS, South Devon Technical Coll; *m* 28 July 1966, (Margaret) Ann, *née* Stephens; 2 s (Ian Michael b 25 April 1967, Neil Stephen b 11 June 1968); *Career* Nat Serv RAF (Kai Tak, Hong Kong) 1957–59; admin asst Royal Festival Hall 1959–63, asst mangr then mangr Mayfair Hotel Durban SA 1966–68, hotel mgmnt North Trust Hotels Edinburgh 1968–71, dir and gen mangr Coral Island Hotel Co Bermuda 1971–74, gen mangr and dir North British Trust Hotels 1974–79; M F Wells (Hotels) Ltd: dir and shareholder 1979–, chm 2004–; fell Inst of Hotel Keeping and Catering 1966; Walking from Lochs and Glens Hotels (2005), Ardgartan Hotel and its Surroundings (2013); *Recreations* hill walking, cycling, garden railways; *Style*— Michael Wells, Esq, OBE; ✉ M F Wells (Hotels) Ltd, School Road, Gartocharn, Dunbartonshire G83 8RW (☎ 01389 713713, fax 01389 713700, e-mail enquiries@lochsandglens.com, website www.lochsandglens.com)

WELLS, Prof Peter Neil Temple; CBE (2009); s of Sydney Parker Temple Wells (d 1976), and Elizabeth Beryl Wells (d 1987); *b* 19 May 1936, Bristol; *Educ* Clifton, Aston Univ (BSc), Univ of Bristol (MSc, PhD, DSc); *m* 15 Oct 1960, Valerie Elizabeth, da of Charles Edward Johnson (d 1982), of Burnham-on-Sea, Somerset; 3 s (Andrew b 1963, Alexander b 1965, Thomas b 1970), 1 da (Lucy b 1966); *Career* res asst United Bristol Hosps 1960–71, prof of med physics Welsh Nat Sch of Med (now Cardiff Univ) 1972–74, area physicist Avon AHA (teaching) 1975–82; chief physicist: Bristol and Weston HA 1982–91, United Bristol Healthcare NHS Tst 1991–2001; Univ of Bristol: hon prof in clinical radiology 1986–2000, hon dir Centre for Physics and Engrg Res in Med 1996–2000, prof of physics and engrg in med 2000–01, emeritus prof of physics and engrg in med 2001–; distinguished research prof Cardiff Univ 2004–; over 300 pubns mainly on med applications of ultrasonics, ed-in-chief Ultrasound in Med and Biology 1992–2006; former pres: Br Inst of Radiology, Br Med Ultrasound Soc, Instn of Physics and Engrg in Med; vice-pres World Fedn for Ultrasound in Med and Biology; Duddell Medal and Prise Inst of Physics 2006, Sir Frank Whittle Medal Royal Acad of Engrg 2014, MAE 2014; Royal Medal Royal Soc 2013; Hon DTech Univ of Lund, Hon MD Erasmus Univ, Hon DSc Aston Univ; FInstP 1970, FIET (FIEE 1978), FREng 1983, Hon FRCR 1987, Hon FIPEM 1988, FRS 2003, FMedSci 2005, FLSW 2010; *Books* Physical Principles of Ultrasonic Diagnosis (1969), Ultrasonics in Clinical Diagnosis (1972, 3 edn 1983), Biomedical Ultrasonics (1977), Computers in Ultrasonic Diagnostics (1977), New Techniques and Instrumentation in Ultrasonography (1980), Scientific Basis of Medical Imaging (1982), Emerging Technologies in Surgery (1984), Clinical Applications of Doppler Ultrasound (1988, 2 edn 1995), Advances in Ultrasound Imaging and Instrumentation (1993), The Perception of Visual Information (1993, 2 edn 1997), The Invisible Light (1995); *Recreations* cooking; *Style*— Prof Peter Wells, CBE, FRS, FREng, FMedSci, FLSW, MAE; ✉ School of Engineering, Cardiff University, Queen's Buildings, The Parade, Cardiff CF24 3AA (☎ 029 2087 4154, e-mail wellspn@cardiff.ac.uk)

WELLS, Prof Sir Stanley William; kt (2016), CBE (2007); s of Stanley Cecil Wells, MBE (d 1952), of Hull, and Doris, *née* Atkinson (d 1986); *b* 21 May 1930; *Educ* Kingston HS Hull, UCL (BA), The Shakespeare Inst Univ of Birmingham (PhD); *m* 23 April 1975, Susan Hill, CBE, *qv*; 3 da (Jessica b 1977, Imogen b and d 1984, Clemency b 1985); *Career* Nat Serv RAF 1951 (invalided out); Shakespeare Inst: fell 1962–77, lectr 1962, sr lectr 1971, reader 1973–77, hon fell 1979–88 and 1998–; prof of Shakespeare studies and dir Shakespeare Inst Univ of Birmingham 1988–97 (emeritus prof 1997–); conslt in Eng Wroxton Coll 1964–80, head of Shakespeare Dept OUP 1978–88, sr research fell Balliol Coll Oxford 1980–88, fell UCL 1994; dir Royal Shakespeare Theatre Summer Sch 1971–99, pres Shakespeare Club of Stratford-upon-Avon 1972–73; chm Int Shakespeare Assoc 1991–2000; memb: Exec Ctee Shakespeare's Birthplace 1976–78 and 1988– (tstee 1975–81 and 1984–, dep chm 1990, chm 1991–); Royal Shakespeare Co: govr 1974–, memb Exec Ctee 1976–2003, chm Membership Ctee 1991–2001, chm Collections Ctee 1991–2000, vice-chm Bd of Govrs 1991–2003, hon govr emeritus 2003–; guest lectr at Br and overseas univs, Br Acad Annual Shakespeare lectr 1987, Br Cncl Melchiori lecture Rome 1991; govr King Edward VI GS for Boys 1973–77; assoc ed New Penguin Shakespeare 1967– (gen ed 2004–), gen ed Oxford Shakespeare 1978–, ed Shakespeare Survey 1980–99; author of contribs to: Shakespeare Survey, Shakespeare Quarterly, Shakespeare Jahrbuch, Theatre Notebook, Stratford-upon-Avon Studies, TLS, and others; memb: Soc for Theatre Research 1963–, Cncl Malone Soc 1967–90, tstee Rose Theatre 1991–, dir Globe Theatre Tst 1990– (tstee 1998–2003); pres Birmingham and Midland Inst 2008–09; Walford Prize (for sustained contribs to bibliography) Library Assoc 1994; Hon DLitt: Furman Univ 1976, Univ of Hull 2005, Univ of Durham 2005, Univ of Warwick 2008; Hon DPhil: University of Munich 1999, Univ of Craiova 2008, Univ of Marburg 2010; *Books* Thomas Nashe, Selected Writings (ed, 1964), A Midsummer Night's Dream (ed, 1967), Richard II (ed, 1969), Shakespeare, A Reading Guide (1969 and 1970), Literature and Drama (1970, reprinted 2004), The Comedy of Errors (ed, 1972), Shakespeare (ed 1973, 2 edn 1990), English Drama Excluding Shakespeare (ed, 1975), Royal Shakespeare (1977 and 1978), Nineteenth Century Burlesques (compiled in 5 vols, 1977, reprinted 2004), Shakespeare: An Illustrated Dictionary (1978 and 1985), Shakespeare: The Writer and his Work (1978), Thomas Dekker, The Shoemaker's Holiday (ed with RL Smallwood, 1979), Modernizing Shakespeare's Spelling, with Three Studies in the Text of Henry V (with Gary Taylor, 1979), Re-editing Shakespeare for the Modern Reader (1984), Shakespeare's Sonnets (ed, 1985), The Complete Oxford Shakespeare (ed with Gary Taylor *et al*, 1986), The Cambridge Companion to Shakespeare Studies (ed, 1986), William Shakespeare: A Textual Companion (with Gary Taylor *et al*, 1987), An Oxford Anthology of Shakespeare (1987), Shakespeare: A Dramatic Life (1994), Shakespeare and the Moving Image (ed, with E A Davies, 1994), Twelfth Night (ed with Roger Warren, 1994), Shakespeare in the Theatre: An Anthology of Criticism (ed, 1997), The Oxford Dictionary of Shakespeare (1998), King Lear (ed, 2000), The Cambridge Companion to Shakespeare (ed, with Margreta da Grazia, 2001, 2 edn 2010), The Oxford Companion to Shakespeare (ed, with Michael Dobson, 2001), Shakespeare: For All Time (2002), Looking for Sex in Shakespeare (2004), Shakespeare's Sonnets (with Paul Edmondson, 2004), Shakespeare & Co (2006), Is It True What They Say About Shakespeare? (2007), Coffee with

W

Shakespeare (with Paul Edmondson, 2008), Shakespeare, Sex – and Love (2010), Great Shakespeare Actors (2015), William Shakespeare: A Very Short Introduction (2015); *Recreations* music, theatre, travel; *Style*— Prof Sir Stanley Wells, CBE; ✉ 9 New St., Stratford upon Avon, Warwickshire CV376BX (☎ 07760 336533); The Shakespeare Centre, Stratford upon Avon, Warwickshire (☎ 01789 201828, e-mail stanley.wells@shakespeare.org.uk, website www.stanleywells.co.uk)

WELLS, Sir William Henry Weston; kt (1997); s of Sir Henry Wells, CBE (d 1970), and Rosemary Halliday, *née* Whitchurch (d 1977); *b* 3 May 1940; *Educ* Radley, Magdalene Coll Cambridge (BA); *m* 1 Jan 1966, Penelope Jean, da of Col R B Broadbent (d 1979); 3 s (Rupert d 1969, George b 1971, Henry b 1972); *Career* pres Chesterton International plc 1998–2005 (ptnr 1965–88, chm 1984–98); chm: Land and House Property Group 1977 (dir 1972–76), Frincon Holdings Ltd 1977–87, ADL plc 2006–, CMG Ltd 2007–16 (dir 2016–), Ashley House plc 2007–13, Pure Sports Medicine Ltd 2007–, Restore plc 2009–15, Health and Surgical Hldgs plc 2010–14, SUSSD Ltd 2010–14, Libra Holdco Ltd 2011–14, The Practice plc 2013–, Facilities First LLP 2013–; dir: London Life Association 1984–89, Pearl Group Ltd 1994–2005, AMP (UK) plc 1994–2003, Norwich & Peterborough Building Society 1994–2003, NFC plc 1996–2000, AMP (UK) Holdings 1997–2003, NPI Ltd 1999–2005, Nat Provident Life Ltd 1999–2005, Exel plc 2000–05, HHG plc 2003–05, SQW Gp 2006–14, Dods plc 2010–, HC One plc 2011–, Skyfall Ltd 2014–; pres Royal Free Hosp Retirement Fellowship 1994–; chm: Special Tstees of the Royal Free Hosps 1979–2001, Hampstead HA 1982–90, Royal Free Hampstead NHS Tst 1990–94, South Thames NHS Exec 1996–99, NHS Appts Cmmn 2001–07, Commercial Advsy Bd Dept of Health 2003–07, Guys and St Thomas' Charity 2009–; regnl chm: S Thames RHA 1994–96, S E NHS Exec 1999–2001; memb Bd of Govrs: Royal Free Hosp 1968–74, Camden and Islington AHA 1974–82; memb Cncl: Royal Free Hosp Sch of Med 1977–91, NHS Tst Fedn 1991–93 (vice-chm 1992–93), UMDS of Guy's and St Thomas' Hosps 1994–98, St George's Hosp Med Sch 1994–98, KCL 1998–2001, City Univ 1999–2000, Priory of England and the Islands 2000–02; Univ of Surrey: memb Cncl 1998 vice-chm Cncl 1999–2000, chm Cncl 2001–06, pro-chllr 2008–; memb Delagacy King's Coll Sch of Med and Dentistry 1994–98, memb Kings Fund Cncl and Mgmnt Ctee 1995–; tstee Nat Museum of Science and Industry 2003–10; vice-pres Royal Coll of Nursing 2005– (hon treas 1988–2005), vice-pres Accord 2006–, hon treas Nat Assoc Hosp and Community Friends 1992–2003; FRICS; Hon FRCP 2002; *Recreations* family, philately, gardening; *Clubs* Boodle's; *Style*— Sir William Wells

WELLWOOD, James McKinney; s of James Wellwood (d 1967), of Belfast, and Violet Armstrong McKinney (d 1978); *b* 18 December 1940, Belfast; *Educ* Fettes, Univ of Cambridge, St Thomas' Hosp Med Sch London; *m* 1, 8 March 1975, Frances Alexandria Ruth, da of Stephen Howard, of Herts; m 2, 24 July 1982, Anne Margaret, da of Sydney Jones Samuel, of Llanelli, Wales; 1 s (James b 1984), 1 da (Laura b 1988); *Career* conslt surgn Whipps Cross Hosp Leytonstone London 1979–2010 (hon conlst surgeon 2010–), hon sr lectr Med Coll of St Bartholomew Smithfield London 1979–2010, clinical tutor Waltham Forest Dist 1983–91, clinical dir of surgery Whipps Cross Hosp 1991–2000; full-time medical expert 2011–; Br delg European Soc of Surgical Oncology 1986–90, hon overseas sec Br Assoc of Surgical Oncology 1986–91 (hon sec 1982–86); memb: Educn Advsy Ctee Assoc of Surgns of GB and Ireland 1987–90, Waltham Forest DHA 1983–90, UK Cncl Assoc of Endoscopic Surgns of GB and I 1994–99; Fulbright scholar 1976; hon fell Friends Med Centre Med Research, Training and Science Organisation India 1996–; Queen's Commendation for Brave Conduct 1971; Liveryman Worshipful Soc of Apothecaries; *Publications* Computer Diagnosis of Abdominal Pain (1989), The Management of Patients with Major Injuries (1990), Laparoscopic Cholecystectomy (1991); *Recreations* skiing, shooting, travel; *Clubs* Athenaeum, Royal Soc of Medicine; *Style*— James Wellwood, Esq; ✉ 50 Clifton Hill, St John's Wood, London NW8 0QG (☎ 020 7625 5697)

WELSH, Prof (James Anthony) Dominic; s of James Welsh (d 1967), of Port Talbot, and Teresa, *née* O'Callaghan (d 1996); *b* 29 August 1938, Port Talbot; *Educ* Bishop Gore Sch Swansea, Merton Coll Oxford (exhibitioner, MA, DPhil), Carnegie Mellon Univ PA (Fulbright scholar); *m* 1965, Bridget Elizabeth, da of Very Rev John Francis Pratt; 3 s (James Justin Siderfin b 16 June 1967, Simon David Patrick b 19 Nov 1969, John Francis b 3 Oct 1971 d 1990); *Career* research Bell Telephone Labs Murray Hill NJ 1961; Univ of Oxford: lectr Mathematical Inst 1966–90 (jr lectr 1963–66), tutor in mathematics Merton Coll 1966–90, fell Merton Coll 1966–2005 (emeritus fell 2005–), chm Faculty of Mathematics 1976–78, chm Faculty Bd of Mathematics 1984–86, ad hominem reader in mathematical scis 1990–92, ad hominem prof of mathematics 1992–2005, chm of mathematics 1996–2001; research visitor Univ of Michigan 1968, visiting prof Univ of Waterloo 1969, visiting prof Univ of Calgary 1974, John von Neumann prof Univ of Bonn 1990–91, visiting Oxford fell Univ of Canterbury NZ 2005, research visitor CRM Barcelona 2006–07; chm Br Combinatorial Soc 1983–87, memb London Mathematical Soc 1964 (memb Cncl 1972–76); Hon DMath Univ of Waterloo 2006; *Books* Matroid Theory (1976), Probability; an Introduction (with G R Grimmett, 1986, 2 edn 2014), Codes and Cryptography (1988), Complexity: Knots Colourings and Counting (1993), Complexity and Cryptology: An Introduction (with J Talbot, 2006); *Recreations* most sports, art, walking; *Style*— Prof Dominic J A Welsh; ✉ Merton College, Oxford OX1 4JD (☎ 01865 276310)

WELSH, John Christopher; s of Thomas A Welsh, and Mary, *née* Croker, of Cumbria; *b* 29 March 1962; *Educ* William Ellis Sch, Ulverston Victoria HS, Sedbergh Coll, Univ of Durham; *Partner* Nicholas Yiannarakis (civil partnership); *Career* draughtsman Brian Clouston & Ptnrs 1984–87, asst ed Designers' Jl 1987–89, buildings ed Building Design 1990–93 (features writer 1989–90); ed: RIBA Jl 1993–99, Property Week 1999–2003, Travel Trade Gazette 2003–07; digital dir UBM Live 2007–; memb: Editorial and Public Affrs Ctee PPA, Educn and Training Ctee ITT; *Books* Rick Mather's Zen Restaurants (1992), Massimiliano Fuksas (1994), Modern house (1995), Cees Dam (2000); *Style*— John Welsh, Esq; ✉ UBM Live, 7th Floor, Ludgate House, 245 Blackfriars Road, London SE1 9UY (☎ 020 7921 8012)

WEN, Eric Lewis; s of Adam Kung Wen, of California, and Mimi, *née* Seetoo; *b* 18 May 1953; *Educ* Dalton Sch, Columbia Univ (BA), Yale Univ (MPhil), Churchill Coll Cambridge (res award); *Family* 2 da (Lily Havala b 5 Nov 1990, Florence Lydia b 26 May 1993); m 30 Dec 1999, Rachel Stadlen; 1 s (Tovi Daniel b 14 March 2003); *Career* lectr in music: Yale Univ 1977–78, Guildhall Sch of Music and Drama 1978–84, Goldsmiths Coll London 1980–84, Mannes Coll of Music 1984–86, Curtis Inst of Music 1999– (chm of Musical Studies 2002–); ed: The Strad 1986–89, The Musical Times 1988–90; md Biddulph Recordings and Publishing 1990–99; *Books* Schenker Studies (contrib, 1990), Trends in Schenkerian Research (contrib, 1990), The Cambridge Companion to the Violin (contrib, 1992), Giuseppe Guarneri del Gesù (contrib, 1998), Schenker Studies 2 (contrib, 1999), Structure and Meaning in Tonal Music (contrib, 2006), Essays from 3rd Schenker Symposium (contrib, 2006); *Publications* The Heifetz Collection (ed, 1995), The Fritz Kreisler Collection (ed, 1990, 1996, 1999, 2005), The Joseph Szigeti Collection (ed, 2000), Hebrew Melodies (ed, 2001), Masterpieces for Violin (ed, 2005), Masterworks for Violin (ed, 2006); *Recreations* chess, cookery, film, card magic; *Style*— Eric Wen, Esq; ✉ 34 St George Street, Hanover Square, London W1R 0ND (☎ 020 7491 8621, fax 020 7495 1428)

WENGER, Arsène; *b* 22 October 1949; *Educ* Strasbourg Univ; *Career* footballer and coach; player: Mutzig, Mulhouse, Strasbourg (French League Champions 1979); mangr: AS Nancy 1984–87, AS Monaco 1987–94 (French League Champions 1988, winners French Cup 1991), Grampus 8 Japan 1995–96 (Emperor's Cup winners 1995, Super Cup winners 1996), Arsenal FC 1996– (winners FA Premier League 1998, 2002 and 2004 (record for remaining unbeaten during season), FA Cup 1998, 2002, 2003 and 2005 (finalists 2001), finalists UEFA Champions League 2006); Manager of the Year: France 1988, England 1998, 2002 and 2004; *Style*— Arsène Wenger, Esq; ✉ c/o Arsenal FC, Highbury House, 75 Drayton Park, London N5 1BU (☎ 020 7704 4000, website www.arsenal.com)

WENSLEY, Prof (John) Robin Clifton; s of Maj George Leonard Wensley (d 1998), and Jeanette Marion, *née* Robbins, of Cambridge; *b* 26 October 1944; *Educ* Perse Sch Cambridge, Univ of Cambridge (BA), London Business Sch (MSc, PhD); *m* 19 Dec 1970, Susan Patricia, da of Kenneth Royden Horner (d 1975), and Irene Lucy Horner; 2 da (Helen Rebecca b 1973, Ruth Elizabeth b 1975), 1 s (Benjamin Royden b 1978); *Career* brand mangr Rank Hovis McDougall 1966–69 (former PA), consltTube Investments Ltd 1971–73, asst dir of Studies Ashridge Coll 1973–74, sr lectr London Business Sch 1974–85 (former lectr); Warwick Business Sch: prof of strategic mgmnt and mktg 1985–2012, chm 1989–94, chm Faculty of Social Studies 1997–99, dep dean 2001–04, emeritus prof of policy and mktg 2012–; dir Advanced Inst of Mgmnt Research 2004–12; sometime visiting prof: UCLA, Univ of Florida; chm Cncl Tavistock Inst of Human Relations 1998–2004 (memb 1992–2004); jt chair Assoc of Business Schs 1993–94; memb: UK Foresight Panel for the Construction Industry 1996–98, Built Environment and Transport Panel 1999–2001, Cncl ESRC 2001–04 (memb Research Grants Bd 1993–96); *Books* Marketing Strategy: Planning, Implementation and Control (1986), Readings in Marketing Strategy (1989), Interface of Marketing and Strategy (1990), Rethinking Marketing (1998), Handbook of Marketing (2002), Effective Management in Practice (2013); *Recreations* DIY, walking, recreational cycling; *Style*— Prof Robin Wensley; ✉ 147 Leam Terrace, Leamington Spa CV31 1DF (☎ 01926 425022, e-mail robin.wensley@warwick.ac.uk)

WENTWORTH, Richard; CBE (2011); *b* 1947, Samoa; *Educ* Hornsey Coll of Art London, RCA (MA); *Career* artist/sculptor; worked with Henry Moore 1967, teacher Goldsmiths Coll London 1971–88, latterly worked and lived NYC; Ruskin master of drawing Univ of Oxford 2002–; author of numerous articles, essays and lectures; Mark Rothko Meml award 1974; *Solo Exhibitions* Greewich Theatre Gallery London 1972, Various Drawings Greewich Theatre Gallery 1973, Istalment Artnet London 1975, Felicity Samuel Gallery London 1975, La Sala Vincon Barcelona 1975–76, Lisson Gallery London 1984, Galerie 't Venster Rotterdam 1984, Galeri Lang Malmo 1986, Riverside Studios London 1987, Galerie Paul Andriesse Amsterdam 1987, Wolff Gallery NY 1987, 1988 and 1989, Sala Parpallo Valencia (travelled to Metronom Barcelona) 1988, Lisson Gallery 1989, Quint Krichman Projects San Diego 1990, Gallerie Franz Paludetto Turin 1991, Mark Quint Gallery San Diego 1991, Kohji Ogura Gallery Nagoya 1992, Tapko – The Place Copenhagen 1992, Serpentine Gallery London; *Group Exhibitions* incl: Young Comtemporaries RCA 1970, Whitechapel Open 1977, 1980, 1983 and 1992, The Sculpture Show Hayward and Serpentine Galleries 1983, The British Show Art Gallery of NSW and touring Aust 1985, Out of Line Walker Art Gallery Liverpool 1986, Modern Art? It's a Joke Cleveland Gallery Middlesbrough 1986, Richard Wentworth – Art and Language – Scott Burton Lisson Gallery in Forum Zurich Int Art Fair 1986, Fire and Metal Goldsmiths' Gallery London 1988, Starlit Waters – British Sculpture – an International Art 1968–86 Tate Gallery Liverpool 1988, New Urban Landscape World Fin Center NY 1988, British Sculpture 1960–88 Museum Van Hedendaagse Kunst Antwerp 1989, Biennale of Sydney 1990, Glasgow's Great British Art Exhibition McLellan Galleries Glasgow 1990, Janice Tchalenko with Richard Wentworth – Works in Clay Crafts Cncl Shop at V&A 1990, Kunst – Europa travelling Germany 1991, The Kitchen Show St Gallen Switzerland 1991, Objects for the Ideal Home – the Legacy of Pop Art Serpentine Gallery 1991, Oh! Cet Echo! Centre Cultural Suisse Paris 1992, Material culture: the object in British art of the 1980s and 90s (Hayward Gallery) 1997; *Style*— Richard Wentworth, Esq, CBE

WENTWORTH-STANLEY, (David) Michael; s of Geoffrey David Wentworth-Stanley (d 2005), and Bridget, *née* Pease; *b* 29 February 1952; *Educ* Eton; *m* 7 Oct 1975, Jane, da of Col Tom Hall, CVO, OBE; 3 da (Laura b 12 Dec 1978, Emma b 28 May 1981, Harriet b 7 Aug 1985); *Career* chartered accountant 1974; Cazenove Inc NY 1981–83, md Cazenove & Co 2001–05 (joined 1975, ptnr 1982–2001), md J P Morgan Cazenove 2005–; memb Bd SFA 1995–2001; FCA 1979 (ACA 1974); *Recreations* countryside, gardening, skiing; *Clubs* White's, MCC; *Style*— Michael Wentworth-Stanley, Esq; ✉ 41 Old Church Street, London SW3 5BS (☎ 020 7352 3419); J P Morgan Cazenove, 25 Bank Street, Canary Wharf, London E14 5JP

WENTZELL, Pamela; da of Herbert Thomas Moran, of London, and Teresa McDaid, *née* Conway; *b* 3 February 1950; *Educ* Pitman's Sch Ealing, Marlborough Coll London, Université Catholique de l'Ouest France, Southampton Univ; *m* 18 Oct 1969, Christopher John, s of Charles John Wentzell, of Gurnard, IOW; *Career* md: JP Communicators Ltd (PR consultancy) 1980–2001, Business Expo Ltd 1997–; chm: Southampton Publicity Assoc 1985–86, Wessex Branch IPR 1997–98; MIPR 1980, FInstD 1989, FCIPR 2000; *Recreations* theatre-going, classical music, learning languages; *Style*— Mrs Pamela Wentzell; ✉ 15 Erisey Terrace, Falmouth, Cornwall TR11 2AP (☎ 01326 210412, e-mail pamela.wentzell@googlemail.com)

WERNICK, David; *b* 3 April 1957, Essex; *Educ* Univ of London (BSc); *m* 10 Oct 1988, Lucy; 2 s (Jonathan b 23 Jan 1990, Alexander b 9 May 1992); *Career* former local cncllr (also chm of constituency), chief exec Wernick Gp 1993–; *Recreations* skiing, reading, travelling; *Clubs* Skibo Castle; *Style*— David Wernick, Esq; ✉ Wernick Group, Molineux House, Russell Gardens, Wickford, Essex SS11 8BL (☎ 01268 735544, e-mail david.wernick@wernickwickford.co.uk, website www.wernick.co.uk)

WERNICK, Jane M; CBE (2015); da of Irving Wernick, and Doreen Wernick; *b* 21 April 1954; *Educ* Haberdashers' Aske's Sch for Girls, Univ of Southampton; *Career* structural engr; engr Ove Arup & Ptnrs London 1976–79, project engr Birdair Structures Inc NY 1980–81; Ove Arup & Ptnrs: assoc London 1982–86 (projects incl Terminal Building Stansted Airport), princ-in-charge LA 1986–88 (projects incl Cerritos Community Arts Centre), assoc dir London 1989–98 (projects incl: The Millennium Wheel, footbridge for CODA Atlanta, renovation of the fly tower of Opéra Garnier Paris, Lille TGV station); dir Jane Wernick Assocs Ltd 1998–2015 (projects incl: Xstrata Treetop Walkway Kew, The Young Vic, Living Architecture houses, Oundle SciTec, Royal Soc of Chemistry, Maggie's Centre Fife, RSPB Rainham and Aveley marshes, bridges and teaching node, Two St James, Goodwood Educn Centre, Cystal Palace Park, Singing Ringing Tree Burnley, The Lightbox Woking, Cremorne Boating Yard Kensington, Potters' Fields Kiosks); dir engineersHRW incorporating Jane Wernick Assocs 2015– (projects incl: Tara Arts Theatre, Boathouse 4 Portsmouth); built environment expert Design Cncl Cabe; memb: Cncl Architectural Assoc, Design Review Panel Design South East, Camden Design Review Panel; former Royal Acad of Engrs visiting prof of design Univ of Southampton; FREng, Hon FRIBA, FRSA, CEng, FIStructE, FICE; *Books* Building Happiness, architecture to make you smile (ed); *Recreations* singing, playing baroque oboe, gardening, travel; *Style*— Ms Jane Wernick, CBE; ✉ Jane Wernick Associates, Unit 10d, Printing House Yard, Hackney Road, London E2 7PR (☎ 020 7749 1066, fax 020 7749 1067, website www.wernick.eu.com)

WERTENBAKER, Timberlake; da of Charles Christian Wertenbaker, of Ciboure, France, and Lael Luttrell Tucker Wertenbaker; *m* 30 June 1991, John Man; 1 da (Dushka Sophia Christiana Wertenbaker-Man b 15 April 1992); *Career* playwright; resident writer: Shared Experience 1983, Royal Court 1984–85; Leverhulme artist in residence Freud Museum 2011–12; dir English Stage Co 1992–98, artistic dir Natural Perspective Theatre Co 2007–;

memb Advsy Bd RADA 2008–; visiting prof Georgetown Univ 2005–06, Unesco city of literature prof of creative writing UEA 2012, chair in playwriting UEA 2013–; Guggenheim Award 2004; memb: PEN, RSL, Nat Acad of Writing; Hon Dr Open Univ 2002; FRSL 2000 (memb Cncl 2011–); *Awards* Evening Standard Most Promising Playwright 1988, Olivier Award 1988, Eileen Anderson Central TV Drama Award 1989, Susan Smith Blackburn Prize 1992, London Critics' Circle Award 1992, Writers' Guild Award 1992; *Plays* incl: New Anatomies (1981), The Grace of Mary Traverse (1985), Our Country's Good (1988), The Love of the Nightingale (1988), Three Birds Alighting on a Field (1991), The Break of Day (1995), After Darwin (1999), Dianeira (1999), The Ash Girl (2000), Credible Witness (2001), The H File (2003), Galileo's Daughter (2004), Scenes of Seduction (2005), Divine Intervention (2006), Jenufa (adaptation of Gabriela Preissova, 2007), Arden City (2008), Hippolytus (Temple Theatre and Riverside Studios, 2009), Phèdre (Stratford and Ontario, 2009 and ACT San Francisco, 2010) The Line (Arcola, 2009), Elektra (trans, The Getty LA, 2010 and ACT San Francisco, 2012), Britannicus (trans, Wilton's Music Hall) 2011, The Memory of Gold (2011), The Princess' Salon (Queen Elizabeth Hall, 2012), Our Ajax (Southwark Playhouse) 2013, The Ant and the Cicada (RSC Stratford-upon-Avon) 2014, Jefferson's Garden (Watford Palace) 2015 (Writers' Guild of GB Award 2016), My Father, Odysseus (Unicorn Theatre) 2016; *Opera* The Love of the Nightingale (Sydney Opera House, 2011); *Radio* adaptations incl: Ismail Kadare's The H File 2003, A S Byatt's Possession 2012, Tolstoy's War and Peace 2015, Elena Ferrante's My Brilliant Friend 2016; *Publications* Sophocles: Oedipus Tyrannos; Oedipus at Kolonos; Antigone (trans, 1992), Timberlake Wertenbaker Plays 1 (1996), Timberlake Wertenbaker Plays 2 (2002), Euripides' Hecuba (trans), False Admissions, Successful Strategies, La Dispute: Three Plays by Marivaux (trans), Our Ajax (2013), The Ant and the Cicada (2014), Jefferson's Garden (2015), My Father, Odysseus (2016); *Recreations* mountains; *Style*— Miss Timberlake Wertenbaker; ✉ c/o Leah Schmidt, The Agency, 24 Pottery Lane, Holland Park, London W11 4LZ (☎ 020 7727 1346)

WESKER, Sir Arnold; kt (2006); s of Joseph Wesker (d 1959), and Leah, *née* Perlmutter (d 1976); *b* 24 May 1932; *Educ* Upton House Central Sch Hackney; *m* 1958, Doreen Cecile, da of Edwin Bicker, of Norfolk; 2 s (Daniel, Lindsay Joe), 2 da (Tanya Jo, Elsa Sarah); *Career* playwright and director; Nat Serv RAF 1950–52 (material gathered for later play Chips with Everything); various positions Norfolk 1952–54 (incl seed sorter, farm labourer and kitchen porter), trained pastry cook London and Paris 1954–56; awarded Arts Cncl grant 1958 and Writers' Bursary 1996; artistic dir Centre Fortytwo 1961–70, chm Br Centre of Int Theatre Inst 1978–82, pres Int Playwrights' Ctee 1979–83; awarded Last Frontier Lifetime Achievement Award for Distinguished Service in the Theatre 1999; Hon DLitt UEA 1989, hon fell Queen Mary & Westfield Coll London 1995, Hon Dr of Humane Letters Denison Univ of Ohio 1997; FRSL; *Stage Plays* The Kitchen (1957), Chicken Soup with Barley (1958), Roots (1959), I'm Talking About Jerusalem (1960), Chips with Everything (1962), The Four Seasons (1965), Their Very Own and Golden City (Marzotto Prize, 1966), The Old Ones (1970), The Friends (1970), The Journalists (1972), The Wedding Feast (1974), Shylock (1976), Love Letters on Blue Paper (stories 1974, play 1976), One More Ride on the Merry-Go-Round (1978), Fatlips (book 1978, play as Tamak – Island of Lethargy (later renamed Voices in the Wind) 1980), Caritas (1980, wrote libretto for Caritas opera cmmnd by Huddersfield Festival of Contemporary Music 1988), Sullied Hand (1981), Anne Wobbler (1982), Four Portraits – of Mothers (1982), Yarsdale (1983), Cinders (1983), Whatever Happened to Betty Lemon (1986), When God Wanted a Son (1986), Badenheim 1939 (1987), Shoeshine & Little Old Lady (1987), Lady Othello (1987), Beorhtel's Hill (1988), The Mistress (1988), Three Women Talking (1990), Letter To A Daughter (1990), Blood Libel (1991), Wild Spring (1992), Circles of Perception (1996), Denial (1997), Break My Heart (1997), Groupie (2001), Longitude (2002), Letter to Myself (for 13-year-old actress, 2004); *Radio and Television Plays* Menace (1971), Breakfast (1981), Bluey (radio play 1984, stage play 1993), Thieves in the Night (4 part adaptation of Arthur Koestler's novel, 1984–85), Phoenix Phoenix Burning Bright (TV play 1992, stageplay 2006), Barabbas (2000), Groupie (radio play 2001, stageplay 2003), Shylock (radio adaptation, 2005), The Rocking Horse (BBC World Serv cmmn, 2007, adapted for stage as The Rocking Horse Kid 2008); *Film Scripts* The Wesker Trilogy (1979), Lady Othello (1980), Homage to Catalonia (1991), Maudie (film version of Lessing's novel Diary of a Good Neighbour 1995), The Kitchen (2005); *Stories, Collections* Six Sundays in January (1971), Love Letters on Blue Paper (1974), Said The Old Man to The Young Man (1978), The King's Daughters (erotic stories) 1998; *Essays* Fears of Fragmentation (1971), Words – as definitions of experience (1976), Distinctions (1985), Wesker on Theatre (2010); *Other writings* Say Goodbye You May Never See Them Again (text for book on John Allin's naive paintings of the East End, 1974), Fatlips (story for young people, 1978), Journey into Journalism (diary of two months researching The Sunday Times, 1977), A Mini-Biography (1988), As Much As I Dare (autobiography, 1994), The BIRTH of Shylock and the DEATH of Zero Mostel (1997), When I Was Your Age (for young people, 2001), Grief (libretto for one-woman opera, 2003), Honey (novel, 2005), All Things Tire of Themselves (poetry, 2008), Wester's Monolgues; *Stage Dir* The Four Seasons (Havana) 1968, The Friends (Stockholm and London) 1970, The Old Ones (Munich) 1973, Their Very Own and Golden City (Aahus) 1974, Love Letters on Blue Paper (Nat Theatre 1978 and Oslo 1980), The Entertainer (Theatr Clwyd) 1983, Annie Wobbler (Birmingham and London) 1984, Yarsdale (RSC Actor's Festival Stratford) 1985, Yarsdale and Whatever Happened to Betty Lemon (London) 1987, Shylock (workshop prodn, London) 1989, The Merry Wives of Windsor (Oslo) 1989–90, The Kitchen (Univ of Wisconsin USA) 1990, The Mistress (Rome) 1991, The Wedding Feast (Denison Univ of Ohio USA), Letter to a Daughter (music by Benjamin Till Edinburgh Festival) 1998; *Style*— Sir Arnold Wesker, FRSL; ✉ Hay-on-Wye, Hereford HR3 5RJ (☎ 0149 820473, fax 0149 821005, e-mail wesker@compuserve.com, website www.arnoldwesker.com); c/o National Westminster Bank plc, 298 Seven Sisters Road, London N4 2AF

WESSELY, Prof Sir Simon; kt (2013); s of Rudolph Wessely, of Prague, Czech Repub, and Wendy Anne Cecilia Wessely; *b* 23 December 1956; *Educ* King Edward VII Sch Sheffield, Lamar Sr HS Houston TX, Trinity Hall Cambridge (MA, BM BCh), UC Oxford (MSc, MD); *m* 2 Jan 1988, Prof Clare Gerada, MBE, *qv*; 2 s (Alexander b 5 Feb 1990, Benjamin b 24 Aug 1992); *Career* medical rotation Newcastle 1982–84, psychiatric trg Maudsley Hosp 1984–88, sr lectr GKT 1991, chair and head Dept of Psychological Medicine and vice dean Inst of Psychiatry KCL 1994, sr investigator Nat Inst of Health 2008, pres RCPsych 2014–; hon civilian advsr in psychiatry Br Army Med Servs 2001, chair NATO Advsy Ctee on Social and Psychological Consequences of Terrorism 2002–, memb Def Scientific Advsy Cncl 2008; memb MRC, Wellcome and NIHR panels 1998–2013; FRCP 1993 (MRCP 1984), FRCPsych 2000 (MRCPsych 1988), FMedSci 2002, FKC 2012; *Publications* Chronic Fatigue and its Symptoms (1999), Clinical Trials in Psychiatry (2003), From Shellshock to PTSD; over 750 academic pubns on chronic fatigue, psychiatry, epidemiology, military health, history and gen hosp psychiatry; numerous public activities, incl radio and TV broadcasts, newspaper articles, literary and science festivals and others; *Recreations* skiing, cycling, Russian history, journalism, arguing in wine bars, watching Chelsea FC; *Style*— Prof Sir Simon Wessely; ✉ Department of Psychological Medicine, Institute of Psychiatry, Denmark Hill, London SE5 8AF (e-mail simon.wessely@kcl.ac.uk)

WESSON, Jane Louise; *b* 26 February 1953; *Educ* Wolverhampton Girls' HS, Univ of Kent at Canterbury (BA, Anthony London prize); *Career* Lancaster Coll of Law 1975–76, articled clerk Pothecary & Barratt London 1976–78, slr Hepworth & Chadwick (now Eversheds) Leeds 1978–89; chm Harrogate Healthcare NHS Tst 1993–2000; chm Nat Clinical Assessment Authy 2000–02, chm Cncl for Healthcare Regulatory Excellence 2003–07; a chm Child Support Appeal Tbnls 1992–99; memb Bd: Northern Counties Housing Assoc 1993–96, Anchor Tst 2003–09, Nuffield Health 2005–14; accredited assessor Office of the Cmmr for Public Appointments 2000–12; memb Bd Age UK 2009–12; *Recreations* sailing, singing, gardening; *Style*— Mrs Jane L Wesson

WEST, Prof Anthony Roy (Tony); s of Percy Frederick West (d 1976), and Winifred Audrey, *née* Baker (d 1993); *b* 21 January 1947; *Educ* Harvey GS Folkestone, Univ Coll Swansea (BSc), Univ of Aberdeen (PhD, DSc); *m* 1972, Sheena, da of Stanley Cruickshank; 1 s (Graeme Michael b 12 April 1976), 1 da (Isla Morven b 4 March 1978); *Career* Univ of Aberdeen: lectr 1971–84, sr lectr 1984–86, reader 1986–89, prof 1989–99; prof Univ of Sheffield 1999– (head Dept Engineering Materials 1999–2007); visiting prof: Nat Univ of Mexico 1976–77 and 1984, Univ of Stockholm 1986, Osaka Nat Research Inst 1989, Moscow State Univ 1992, Tokyo Inst of Technology 1993, Universiti Pertanian Malaysia 1994, Universidad de Barcelona 1996, Universidad Nacional del Sur Argentina 1997, Universidad Carlos III de Madrid 2008–09; chm Materials Chemistry Forum RSC 1993–2002; founding ed Jl of Materials Chemistry RSC 1990; memb Functional Materials Coll EPSRC 1996–, pres Inorganic Chemistry Div IUPAC 2004–08; Blackwell Prize Univ of Aberdeen 1986, Solid State Chemistry Prize RSC 1996, Epsilon de Oro Award Spanish Soc of Ceramics and Glass 2007, Griffiths Medal and Prize IMMM 2008, Goodenough Award in Materials Chemistry RSC 2013; CChem, CPhys, FRSC, FInstP, FIM, FRSE 1997; *Books* Solid State Chemistry and Its Applications (1984, 2 edn, student edn 2014); also author of over 450 research papers in learned jls; *Recreations* athletics, gardening, Spanish and Latin American interests; *Style*— Prof Tony West, FRSE; ✉ University of Sheffield, Department of Materials Science and Engineering, Sir Robert Hadfield Building, Mappin Street, Sheffield S1 3JD (☎ 0114 222 5501, fax 0114 222 5943, e-mail a.r.west@sheffield.ac.uk)

WEST, Catherine; MP; *Career* MP (Lab) Hornsey and Wood Green 2015–; *Style*— Ms Catherine West, MP; ✉ House of Commons, London SW1A 0AA

WEST, Guy; s of Keith Edward West, and Diana Mary, *née* Humphreys; *Educ* Wellingborough Sch for Boys; *m* 2 April 2004, Fiona Mairi, *née* Main; 1 da (Jet Diana Velvet b 12 July 2004); *Career* shoe designer, estab Jeffery-West 1987; curator Life and Sole exhbn Northampton Footwear Museum; patron: Northampton Footwear Museum, Cordwainers, Nene Univ Coll, Leicester De Montfort Univ; Best Men's Fashion Footwear UK Footwear Awards 1999 and 2000, FHM Best Men's Footwear Award 2000–01, Best Men's Footwear/Fashion Retailer London Lifestyle Award 2010; memb Northampton Shoemakers 1992–, memb Br Footwear Fedn 1995–; *Recreations* UK U16 water ski squad, UK underwater hockey, local cricket and squash teams; *Clubs* Blacks; *Style*— Guy West, Esq; ✉ 16 Piccadilly Arcade, London SW1Y 6NH (☎ 020 7499 3360, fax 020 7499 3340)

WEST, James Glynn; *b* 21 April 1947; *Educ* Eton; *m* 1969, Pippa, *née* Mackay Miller; 1 s (Alexander b 1973), 1 da (Charlotte b 1975); *Career* md Globe Investment Trust plc 1987–90 (joined 1973), md Lazard Bros & Co Ltd and chief exec Lazard Asset Management Ltd 1990–94; currently chm: Canaccord Genuity Ltd, New City High Yield Fund Ltd, Associated Br Foods Pension Fund Ltd; currently non-exec dir: Aberdeen Smaller Companies High Yield Tst plc, British Assets Trust plc, UK Select Tst Ltd; FCA; *Recreations* golf, oil painting; *Clubs* City; *Style*— James West, Esq; ✉ Orchard House, Eastling, Faversham, Kent ME13 0AZ (☎ 01795 890432, fax 01795 890353)

WEST, Dr (A) Joshua (Josh); s of Geoffrey Brian West, of Santa Fe NM, and Jacqueline Jean, *née* Boggs; *b* 25 March 1977, Santa Fe, USA; *Educ* Santa Fe Prep Sch, Yale Univ (BA), Univ of Cambridge (MPhil, PhD); *Career* rower; achievements incl: memb Univ of Cambridge Boat Race crew 1999, 2000, 2001 and 2002, winner eights World Cup 2001, Silver medal coxless fours World Championships 2002 and 2003, Bronze medal eights World Championships 2007, Silver medal eights Olympic Games Beijing 2008; Anglo-Jewish Sports Personality of the Year 2001; research fell in geochemistry Univ of Oxford 2006–, Zinsmeyer early career chair in geochemistry Univ of S Calif 2010–; *Recreations* travelling, walking, cooking, reading, geology; *Clubs* Leander, Hawks' (Cambridge); *Style*— Dr Josh West

WEST, Martin; s of Alan West, of Bolton, Lancs, and Janet Elizabeth, *née* Carlton; *b* 14 January 1969; *Educ* Bury GS, St Catharine's Coll Cambridge (MA, Master's Sizar), Royal Acad of Music (scholar, Dip Advanced Studies), St Petersburg Conservatory of Music; *Career* conductor; music dir Cambridge Philharmonic Soc 1998–2005, princ conductor English Nat Ballet 2004–07 (resident conductor 1997–2004), music dir and princ conductor San Francisco Ballet 2005–; guest conductor Pimlico Opera Br tours 1997, 1998 and 2001; guest work with: Royal Liverpool Philharmonic Orch, Hallé Orch, London Concert Orch, Holland Sinfonia, NY City Ballet, Houston Ballet, Symphony Orch; ARAM; *Recordings* Nutcracker Complete, Russian Masterpieces, Mozart Piano Concerti, Nutcracker (DVD), Opus Arte; *Recreations* cookery, cricket, swimming, cosmology; *Clubs* Flying Ducksmen CC; *Style*— Martin West, Esq; ✉ e-mail martin.west@virgin.net; San Francisco Ballet, 455 Franklin Street, San Francisco, CA 94102, USA (☎ 00 1 415 861 5600, e-mail mwest@sfballet.org); agent: Robert Gilder (☎ 020 7580 7758)

WEST, Robert John; s of Clifford Lennard West (d 1997), of Maidenhead, Berks, and Joan, *née* Naylor (d 1983); *b* 1 January 1952; *Educ* Maidenhead GS, Clare Coll Cambridge (MA); *m* 13 June 1987, Elisabeth, da of Sydney and Joyce Hynd; 2 s (David Robert b 29 May 1988, Andrew James b 5 Jan 1990); 1 da (Annabel b 22 Nov 1991); *Career* asst slr Freshfields 1977–82 (articled clerk 1975–77), ptnr Baker & McKenzie 1985– (asst slr 1982–85); former chm Assoc of Pension Lawyers, former dir Pensions Advsy Serv, memb Law Soc; *Books* Butterworths Law for Accountants; *Recreations* football, tennis, golf, cricket, running; *Style*— Robert West, Esq; ✉ Baker & McKenzie, 100 New Bridge Street, London EC4V 6JA (☎ 020 7919 1000, e-mail robert.west@bakermckenzie.com)

WEST, Samuel Alexander Joseph; *b* 19 June 1966; *Educ* Alleyn's Sch Dulwich, Lady Margaret Hall Oxford (BA); *Partner* Laura Wade, *qv*; 1 da (b 2014); *Career* actor and dir; artistic dir Sheffield Theatre 2005–07; memb: Cncl Equity 1996–2000 and 2008–14, Bd Bristol Old Vic; assoc artist RSC; chair Nat Campaign for the Arts; *Theatre* as actor: Les Parents Terribles 1988, A Life in the Theatre 1989, Hidden Laughter 1990, Henry IV Pts I & II 1996, Dr Faustus, The Master and Margerita (Chichester) 2004, Much Ado About Nothing (Crucible Sheffield) 2005, A Number (Crucible Sheffield) 2007, Betrayal (Donmar Warehouse) 2007, The Family Reunion (Donmar Warehouse) 2008, ENRON (Chichester, Royal Court and Noel Coward Theatre) 2009–10, Uncle Vanya (also dir, Vaudeville Theatre) 2012; for RNT: The Sea 1991, Arcadia 1993, Antony and Cleopatra 1998, A Number (Menier) 2010 and (Cape Town) 2011; for RSC: Richard II 2000, Hamlet 2001; as dir: The Lady's Not for Burning 2002, Les Liaisons Dangereuses 2003, Cosi fan Tutte 2003, Three Women and a Piano Tuner 2004, Insignificance 2005, The Romans in Britain 2006, The Clean House 2006, As You Like It (Crucible Sheffield and RSC) 2007, Dealer's Choice (Menier and Trafalgar Studios) 2007–08, Waste (Almeida) 2008, Close The Coalhouse Door (Northern Stage and tour) 2012, After Electra (Plymouth and Tricycle) 2015; *Television* incl: Frankie and Johnnie 1985, Prince Caspian and The Voyage Of The Dawn Treader 1989, Stanley and the Women 1991, Voices in the Garden 1992, As Time Goes By 1992, Open Fire 1994, Zoya 1995, The Vacillations of Poppy Carew 1995, Heavy Weather 1995, Strangers 1996, Over Here 1996, The Ripper 1997, Hornblower 1999, Longitude 2000, Waking the Dead 2002, Cambridge Spies 2003, Margaret Thatcher: The Long Walk to Finchley 2008, New Tricks 2008,

Desperate Romantics 2009, Murder on the Orient Express 2010, Any Human Heart 2010, Law and Order 2011, Eternal Law 2012, Mr Selfridge (2 series, 2013–15), Fleming: The Man Who Would be Bond 2014, Jonathan Strange & Mr Norrell 2015; *Film* incl: Reunion 1989, Howards End 1992, Archipel 1992, A Feast At Midnight 1994, A Breed Of Heroes 1994, Carrington 1995, Persuasion 1995, Jane Eyre 1995, Stiff Upper Lips 1998, Rupert's Land 1998, The Dance of Shiva 1998, Notting Hill 1999, Complicity 2000, Pandemonium 2000, Iris 2001, Van Helsing 2003, Kingdom in Twilight 2004, Schweitzer 2009, Hyde Park on Hudson 2012, The Riot Club (2014), Suffragette (2015); *Radio* as dir incl: Money (BBC Radio 3 2011), Close the Coalhouse Door (BBC Radio 4 2012); *Recreations* birding, travelling, poker, cricket, supporting AFC Wimbledon, growing chillies; *Clubs* Groucho, Century; *Style*— Samuel West; ✉ c/o United Agents Ltd, 12–26 Lexington Street, London W1F 0LE (☎ 020 3214 0800, fax 020 3214 0801, website www.unitedagents.co.uk)

WEST, Dr Stephen Craig; s of Joseph West, and Louise West; *b* 11 April 1952; *Educ* Univ of Newcastle upon Tyne (BSc, PhD); *m* 1, (m dis) Mina; m 2, Svetlana Khoronenkova; *Career* post-doctoral res assoc: Univ of Newcastle 1977–78, Dept of Molecular Biophysics and Biochemistry and Therapeutic Radiology Yale Univ 1978–83; res scientist ICRF 1983–85, sr scientist ICRF 1985–89, princ scientist Cancer Research UK 1989–2015, sr gp ldr Francis Crick Inst 2015–; prof Dept of Biochemistry UCL 1997–; chm Sectional Ctee 7 Royal Soc 1996–98 (memb 1995–98); memb: Molecular Biology and Genetics Grants Ctee 1991–94, SERC, Hooke Ctee Royal Soc 1995–97; assoc ed Genes to Cells 1996–98; memb Ed Bd: Nucleic Acids Research 1995–97, EMBO Jl 1996–98 (memb Advsy Ed Bd 1999–), EMBO Reports 2000–; memb Genetics Soc; memb EMBO 1994; Swiss Bridge Prize for Cancer Research 2001 and 2009, Jeantet Prize for Medicine 2007, Novartis Prize Biochemical Soc 2008, GlaxoSmithKline Prize Royal Soc 2010, Genetics Soc Medal 2012; FRS 1995, FMedSci 1999, foreign assoc Nat Acad of Sciences (USA) 2016; *Publications* DNA Repair and Recombination (with T Lindahl, 1995), Philosophical Transactions of the Royal Soc of London (ed, 1995), Mechanisms of Homologuous Recombination (contrib, 1999); also author of more than 240 scientific papers and articles; *Style*— Dr Stephen West, FRS; ✉ Francis Crick Institute, Clare Hall Laboratories, South Mimms, Hertfordshire EN6 3LD (☎ 01707 625868, fax 01707 625801, e-mail stephen.west@crick.ac.uk)

WEST, Prof Steven George; *b* 27 March 1961, Luton; *Educ* BSc; *m* 3 Sept 2000, Samantha, *née* Watson; 5 c (Emma, Rebecca, Bethany, George, Alex); *Career* podiatrist and podiatric surgn 1982–; lectr then sr lectr 1984–90: Chelsea Sch of Chiropody and Podiatric Med, London Foot Hosp, Univ of Westminster; developed research interests Dept of Bioengineering KCL and Roehampton Limb Fitting Centre, assoc dean and head Dept of Podiatry Univ of Huddersfield 1990–95 (dean Sch of Health and Behavioural Sciences 1992–95); UWE: joined 1995, dean Faculty of Health and Social Care and prof of health and social care, pro-vice-chllr 2005, dep vice-chllr 2006, actg vice-chllr 2007, pres and vice-chllr 2008–; chair W of England Academic Health Science Network; regnl chair (SW) CBI, pres Bristol Chamber of Commerce and Initiative; Hon LLD Univ of Bristol, Hon DEd Taylor's Univ Kuala Lumpur Malaysia 2016; memb: Soc of Chiropodists and Podiatrists, RSM, RSA; fell Coll of Podiatric Med; *Recreations* motorsport, scuba diving; *Style*— Prof Steven West; ✉ University of the West of England, Frenchay Campus, Coldharbour Lane, Bristol BS16 1QY (☎ 01173 282201, e-mail steven.west@uwe.ac.uk, website www.uwe.ac.uk)

WEST, Timothy Lancaster; CBE (1984); s of (Harry) Lockwood West (d 1989), actor, and Olive Carleton-Crowe; *b* 20 October 1934; *Educ* John Lyon Sch Harrow, Regent St Poly; *m* 1, 1956 (m dis), Jacqueline Boyer; 1 da; m 2, 1963, Prunella Scales, *qv*; 2 s; *Career* actor and director; pres: LAMDA, Soc of Theatre Research; Hon DUniv Bradford; Hon DLitt: UWE, UEA, Hull, London; Hon LLD Univ of Westminster; FRSA; *Theatre* West End debut in Caught Napping (Piccadilly Theatre) 1959; other performances incl: Gentle Jack, The Trigon, The Italian Girl, Abelard and Heloise, Exiles, The Constant Couple, Laughter, The Homecoming, Beecham, Master Class, The War at Home, When We Are Married, The Sneeze, Long Day's Journey into Night, It's Ralph, Twelve Angry Men, The Old Country, The Collection, A Number, King Lear (Dublin), Willy Loman in Death of a Salesman (Theatr Clwyd), Iago in Othello (Nottingham), Sir Anthony Absolute in The Rivals (Chichester), Galileo (Birmingham), Mail Order Bride and Getting On (West Yorkshire Playhouse); with RSC 1962–66 (London and Stratford season 1964–66) incl: debut in Nil Carborundum and Afore Night Come (Arts Theatre) 1962, Hedda Gabler (tour Aust, Canada and USA), Coriolanus; with Prospect Theatre Co 1966–82: King Lear, Prospero in The Tempest, Claudius in Hamlet, Enobarbus in Antony and Cleopatra, Shylock in The Merchant of Venice, Bolingbroke in Richard II, Mortimer in Edward II, Shpigelsky in A Month in the Country, Emerson in A Room with a View; with Bristol Old Vic Co incl: Trelawny, Falstaff in Henry IV (both parts), Sartorius in Widowers' Houses, Solness in The Master Builder, Lord Ogleby in The Clandestine Marriage, Vanya in Uncle Vanya; other credits incl: Falstaff in Henry IV (parts I & II, Old Vic) 1997, Gloucester in King Lear (RNT) 1997, The Birthday Party 1999, The External 2001, Luther (RNT) 2002, Lear (Old Vic) 2003, Galileo 2006, The Old Country 2006, Coriolanus 2007, The Winslow Boy 2009, The Handyman 2012; *Television* incl: Edward VII, Horatio Bottomley, Hard Times, Crime and Punishment, Churchill and the Generals, Brass, The Last Bastion, The Monocled Mutineer, A Very Peculiar Practice, The Good Doctor Bodkin Adams, What the Butler Saw, Harry's Kingdom, The Sealed Train, When We Are Married, Breakthrough at Reykjavik, Strife, A Shadow on the Sun, The Contractor, Blore, MP, Beecham, Survival of the Fittest, Why Lockerbie?, Framed, Smokescreen, Eleven Men Against Eleven, Cuts, Rebecca, King Lear, Murder in Mind, Bedtime, New Tricks, Bleak House, Exile, Inside Number 9, Coronation Street; *Film* incl: Twisted Nerve, Nicholas and Alexandra, The Day of the Jackal, Oliver Twist, Hedda, Joseph Andrews, The Devil's Advocate, Agatha, Masada, The Thirty Nine Steps, Rough Cut, Cry Freedom, Ever After, Joan of Arc, Iris, Beyond Borders; *Publications* A Moment Towards the End of the Play (2000); *Recreations* listening to music, travelling, inland waterways; *Clubs* Garrick, Groucho; *Style*— Timothy West, CBE; ✉ c/o Gavin Barker Associates, 2D Wimpole Street, London W1M 7AA (☎ 020 7499 4777, fax 020 7499 3777)

WEST OF SPITHEAD, Baron (Life Peer UK 2007), of Seaview in the County of Isle of Wight; Adm Sir Alan William John West; GCB (2004, KCB 2000), DSC (1982), PC (2010), ADC (2003); s of Mr W H West, and Mrs J M A West, *née* Bliss; *b* 21 April 1948; *Educ* Windsor GS, Clydebank HS, BRNC Dartmouth; *m* Rosemary, *née* Childs; 3 c; *Career* CO HMS Yarnton 1973, princ warfare offr 1977 (thereafter specialist appts on HMS Juno, HMS Ambuscade and HMS Norfolk), Cdr 1980, CO HMS Ardent 1980–82 (took ship to Falkland Islands where sunk in successful retaking of islands), Directorate of Naval Plans MOD 1982–84, Capt 1984, Asst Dir of Naval Staff Duties 1985–86, CO HMS Bristol and Capt Dartmouth Trg Sqdn 1987–88, led study on future employment of women in RN 1988, head Maritime Intelligence Directorate 1989–92, RCDS 1992, Higher Command and Staff Course 1993, Cdre 1993, Dir of Naval Staff Duties 1993–94, Rear Adm 1994, Naval Sec and DG Naval Manning 1994–96, COMUKTG/CASWSF (Commander United Kingdom Task Gp/Commander Anti-Submarine Warfare Striking Force) 1996–97, Vice Adm 1997, Chief Defence Intelligence 1997–2000, Adm 2000, C-in-C FLEET and EASTLANT and Cdr Allied Naval Forces North 2000–02, First Sea Lord and CNS 2002–06; inspired and led RN Trafalgar 200 celebrations; chm Quinetic DAB 2006–07; min for security Home Office 2007–10; chllr Southampton Solent Univ; pres: Ardent Assoc, Falkland Islands Chapel Tst, Merchant Navy Medal Fund, Ship Recognition Corps (SRC), Merchant Naval Assoc; patron: St Annes Limehouse, Docklands Sinfonica; Master Mariner, Yr Brother Trinity House, Knight President Knights of the Round Table; Freeman Worshipful Co of Watermen and Lightermen; *Books* The Oxford Handbook of War (maritime section); *Recreations* maritime history, boating; *Clubs* Royal Yacht Squadron, Naval, Destroyer, Anchorite, Pilgrims, RN Club of 1765/85, Pepys, RNSA, Sr Barbara Assoc, Britannia Assoc, Woodroffe, BAFDC, Royal Naval Club Mayfair; *Style*— Adm the Rt Hon the Lord West of Spithead, GCB, DSC; ✉ Southampton Solent University, East Park Terrace, Southampton, Hampshire SO14 0YN (e-mail admirallordwest@gmail.com)

WEST-KNIGHTS, Laurence James; QC (2000); s of Maj Jan James West West-Knights (d 1990), and Amy Winifred, *née* Gott (d 1999); *b* 30 July 1954, Windlesham, Surrey; *Educ* Perse Sch Cambridge, Hampton Sch, Emmanuel Coll Cambridge (MA); *m* (m dis 2010), Joanne Anita Florence, *née* Ecob; 2 da (Imogen Amy b 26 Aug 1992, Honor Victoria b 17 Oct 2001), 1 s (Frederick Hugh Merriman b 11 March 1994); *Career* seaman offr London Div RNR 1981–94 (Lt Cdr); called to the Bar Gray's Inn 1977 (bencher 2003), practising barr 1978–, asst recorder 1994–99, recorder 1999–, QC 2000, head Hailsham Chambers Commercial Gp; memb Bar NI, chm Hailsham Chambers Pupillage Ctee 2002–10; Soc for Computers and Law: memb Cncl 1995–96, vice-chm 1996–2001, chm 2001–02; memb Cncl Incorporated Cncl of Law Reporting 1996–2004, vice-chm London Common Law and Commercial Bar Assoc 2015–; chm IT Industry Enquiry into Govt Contracts 2000; fndr memb and tstee Br and Irish Legal Information Inst (BAILII) 2000–02; memb: Editorial Bd Judicial Studies Bd Jl 1996–2003, ITAC Civil Litigation Working Pty 1997–2003; memb PCC Christ Church Turnham Green Chiswick 1997–2001 (lay chm 1998–2001); FCIArb 1993; *Publications* Jordan's Civil Court Service (contrib, 1999–); *Recreations* scuba diving, cricket, shooting (winner Kennet Shoot Trophy 2003), motorcycling, my children, sailing; *Clubs* MCC, Bar Yacht, RNVR Yacht, Cambridge Univ Motorcycle; *Style*— L J West-Knights, Esq, QC; ✉ Hailsham Chambers, 4 Paper Buildings, Temple, London EC4Y 7EX (☎ 020 7643 5000, fax 020 7353 5778, e-mail laurie.west-knightsqc@hailshamchambers.com, website www.west-knights.com)

WESTABY, Mark; s of Donald Westaby, of Winterton, S Humberside, and Patricia, *née* Morwood; *b* 26 June 1955; *Educ* Frederic Gough, Brunel Univ (BSc); *m* Sarah Frances Elizabeth, *née* Cox; 1 da (Sofia Elizabeth Olga); *Career* Ove Arup & partners and Res Dept British Gas 1979–81; former PRO: John Drewry Associates, HPS Ltd 1983–84, Countrywide Communications (London) 1984–90 (latterly dir, work on Tandem Computers responsible for PR Indust Best Consultancy award 1987); Kinnear Ltd management conslts in communication 1990–93; dir rising to jt md Portfolio Communications Ltd 1993–; chm Business & Technol Gp PR Consultants Assoc (chm elect 1989–91); *Recreations* all sports, music, reading, travel; *Style*— Mark Westaby, Esq; ✉ Spectrum Insight, 85–90 Paul Street, London EC2A 4NE

WESTBROOK, Michael John David (Mike); OBE (1988); s of Philip Beckford Westbrook (d 1981), of Devon, and Vera Agnes, *née* Butler (d 1995); *b* 21 March 1936; *Educ* Kelly Coll Tavistock Plymouth Coll of Art (NDD), Hornsey Coll of Art (ATD); *m* 1; 1 s (Anthony Guy b 9 April 1964), 1 da (Joanna Maria b 14 June 1966); m 2, 23 Sept 1976, Katherine Jane (Kate), da of Prof Alec Naraway Duckham, CBE (d 1988); *Career* composer, pianist and bandleader; formed first band at Plymouth Art Sch 1958; moved to London 1962 and has since led a succession of gps incl: The Mike Westbrook Brass Band (with Phil Minton) 1973–, The Mike Westbrook Orchestra 1974–, The Westbrook Trio (with Kate Westbrook and Chris Biscoe) 1982–; toured in Britain, Europe, Australia, Canada, NY, Singapore and Hong Kong, written cmmnd works for festivals in GB and Europe; composed music for theatre, opera, dance, radio, TV and films and made numerous recordings incl: Marching Song (1967), Metropolis (1969), Tyger (Nat Theatre musical with Adrian Mitchell, 1971), Citadel/Room 315 (1974), The Westbrook Blake (1980), On Dukes Birthday (1984), Big Band Rossini (1987), Off Abbey Road (1988), Bean Rows and Blues Shots (saxophone concerto, 1991), The Orchestra of Smith's Academy (1998), Glad Day (1999); TV scores incl Caught on a Train (1980), cinema score Moulin Rouge (1990); concert works with Kate Westbrook incorporating Euro poetry and folk song: The Cortège (1979), London Bridge is Broken Down (1987); music theatre pieces incl: Mama Chicago (1978), Westbrook Rossini (1984), The Ass (1985), Pier Rides (1986), Quichotte (1989); other works incl: Good Friday 1663 (an opera for TV, with libretto by Helen Simpson), Coming Through Slaughter (with Michael Morris, based on novel by Michael Ondaatje), Measure for Measure (1992), Blues for Terenzi (1995), Bar Utopia (big band cabaret, lyrics by Helen Simpson) 1995, Stage Set 1996, Love Or Infatuation (duo with Kate Westbrook) 1997, Jago (opera, libretto by Kate Westbrook) 2000; current projects and recordings incl Platterback (lyrics by Kate Westbrook with ensemble Westbrook & Co), Chanson Irresponsable (lyrics by Kate Westbrook, for New Westbrook Orch), Classical Blues (for BBC Concert Orch), L'Ascenseur/The Lift (with Kate Westbrook and Chris Biscoe, for Westbrook Trio), Turner in Uri (libretto by Kate Westbrook) for Alpentöne Switzerland 2003, Art Wolf (text by Kate Westbrook) for Aargauer Kunsthaus Switzerland 2003, The Nijinska Chamber (Kate Westbrook album) 2005, The Waxeywork Show 2006 and English Soup – The Battle of the Classic Trifle 2008 (texts Kate Westbrook) for The Village Band, Cape Gloss, Mathilda's Story (one-woman opera, libretto by Kate Westbrook) 2007, Fine n' Yellow (lyrics Kate Westbrook) 2009, Allsorts (Kate Westbrook and Mike Westbrook duo) 2009, The Serpent Hit 2011 (with Kate Westbrook, for voice, saxophone quartet and percussion), Three into Wonderfull (trio album with Kate Westbrook and Chris Biscoe) 2012, Five Voyages (text Kate Westbrook) 2012, Glad Day Live (William Blake settings DVD and CD) 2014, A Bigger Show 2015 (The Bigger Orchestra with Kate Westbrook and the 22-piece big band), Paintbox Jane – Raoul Duffy paints a portrait 2016 (libretto by Kate Westbrook, performed by Company Westbrook); Hon DMus Univ of Plymouth 2004; *subject of* The Music of Mike Westbrook by Gary Bayley (PhD thesis); *Recreations* walking by the sea; *Clubs* Chelsea Arts, Vout-O-Reenees (London); *Style*— Mike Westbrook, Esq, OBE; ✉ e-mail admin@westbrookjazz.co.uk

WESTBROOK, Prof Roy; *Educ* Univ of Leicester, London Business Sch; *m* 1981, Rosemary Cooper; 2 s; *Career* civil servant 1971–80, research offr and conslt 1980–84, appointed to post in ops mgmnt London Business Sch 1984 (appointed assoc dean Sloan Prog 1995), prof of ops mgmnt and dep dean Saïd Business Sch Univ of Oxford 2009– (formerly MBA course dir); vice-princ, fell and tutor in mgmnt studies St Hugh's Coll Oxford; *Books* incl: Opera: A History (with Christopher Headington and Terry Barfoot, 1987), Understanding Supply Chains: Concepts, Critiques and Futures (ed with Steve New, 2004); *Recreations* classical music, literature, theatre, sports; *Style*— Prof Roy Westbrook; ✉ St Hugh's College, Oxford OX2 6LE; Saïd Business School, Park End Street, Oxford OX1 1HP

WESTBURY, Prof David Rex; OBE (2001); s of Harold Joseph Westbury (d 1966), of Rubery, Worcs, and Kathleen, *née* Hedderley (d 1996); *b* 24 June 1942; *Educ* Bromsgrove Co HS, ChCh Oxford (MA, BSc, BM BCh, DM); *m* 19 Feb 1966, Pauline, da of James Robinson (d 1988), of Darlington, Co Durham; 1 s (Paul b 1969), 1 da (Claire b 1971); *Career* Univ of Birmingham: lectr 1968–74, sr lectr 1974–82, reader 1982–86, exec dean Med Faculty 1984–92, prof 1987–, vice-princ 1992–2002; ind conslt 2002–08; dir: Birmingham Research and Development Ltd 1993–2002, S Birmingham Mental Health NHS Tst 1994–99, Univ Hosp Birmingham NHS Tst 1999–2007; chm Jt Costing and Pricing Steering Gp for HE 1997–2005; chm UM Assoc Ltd 2003–07, chm UM Services Ltd 2003–07, dir UM Assoc (Special Risks) Ltd 2005–07; memb Physiological Soc 1968; FRSA; *Recreations* food and wine, hill walking, golf, amateur radio communications; *Style*— Prof David Westbury, OBE; ✉ Rose Cottage, Cruise Hill, Ham Green, Feckenham, Worcestershire B97 5UA; University of Birmingham, Edgbaston, Birmingham B15 2TT

WESTBURY, Paul Stephen; CBE (2013); s of Prof David Rex Westbury, OBE, of Worcs, and Pauline, *née* Robinson; *b* 11 November 1969, Birmingham; *Educ* King Edward's Sch Birmingham, Jesus Coll Cambridge (exhbn, scholar, Baker Prize for Engrg, MA); *m* ; 1 da; *Career* engr; Buro Happold: joined 1991, ptnr and dir 2000–14, md Europe 2008–10, ceo 2010–14; gp technical dir Laing O'Rourke 2014–; MacRobert Award for Innovation Royal Acad of Engrg 1999, Silver Medal Royal Acad of Engrg 2008, Gold Medal IStructE 2012; CEng 1996, FICE 2002, FREng 2003, FIStructE 2004, FRSA 2008; *Publications* author of tech papers in scientific jls and for conferences; *Recreations* design, architecture, technology, skiing, rugby; *Style*— Paul Westbury, Esq, CBE; ✉ Laing O'Rourke, Anchor Boulevard, Admirals Park, Kent DA2 6SN (e-mail pwestbury@laingorourke.com)

WESTLAKE, Darren; *Career* md ID Telecommunications Ltd 2000–05, product mangr Kingston Communications 2007–09, product mangr KCOM 2009–10, ceo Crowdcube Ltd 2010–; *Style*— Darren Westlake, Esq; ✉ Crowdcube, The Innovation Centre, University of Exeter, Rennes Drive, Exeter EX4 4RN

WESTLEY, Stuart Alker; s of Arthur Bancroft Westley (d 1949), and Gladys, *née* Alker (d 1998); *b* 21 March 1947; *Educ* Lancaster Royal GS, CCC Oxford (MA, Cricket blue); *m* 1979, Mary Louise, *née* Weston; 1 da (Sarah Elizabeth b 9 April 1987); *Career* headmaster; former professional cricketer Gloucestershire CCC 1969–72; asst master King Edward VII Sch Lytham (winters only) 1969–72, housemaster/dir of studies Framlingham Coll 1973–84, dep head Bristol Cathedral Sch 1984–89, princ King William's Coll IOM 1989–96, master of Haileybury 1996–2009, gen sec Assoc of Governing Bodies of Ind Schs 2009–; memb: ASCL 1984, HMC 1989; chm of govrs of two prep schools and one sr school; *Recreations* golf and other sports, architecture, gardening, choral and orchestral music, France; *Clubs* East India; *Style*— Stuart Westley, Esq; ✉ Holly Hall, Church Street, Old Welwyn, Hertfordshire AL6 9LN

WESTMACOTT, Sir Peter John; GCMG (2016, KCMG 2003, CMG 2000), LVO (1993); s of late Preb Ian Westmacott, of Bristol, and Rosemary Patricia Spencer, *née* Watney; *b* 23 December 1950; *Educ* Taunton Sch, New Coll Oxford (MA); *m* 1, 1972, Angela, *née* Lugg; 2 s (Oliver b 1975, Rupert b 1979), 1 da (Laura b 1977); m 2, 2001, Susan Nemazee; *Career* joined HM Dip Serv 1972, third then second sec Tehran 1974–78, with EC 1978–80, first sec Paris 1980–84, PR sec to min of state 1984–97, head of Chancery Ankara 1987–90, dep private sec to HRH The Prince of Wales 1990–93, political cnsllr Washington DC 1993–97, dir Americas FCO 1997–2000, dep under-sec of state FCO 2000–01, ambass to Turkey 2002–06, ambass to France 2007–12, ambass to USA 2012–16; hon fell New Coll Oxford 2012; FRSA 1991; *Recreations* tennis, skiing, travel; *Style*— Sir Peter Westmacott, GCMG, LVO; ✉ e-mail pjwestmacott@gmail.com

WESTMINSTER, Dean of; *see:* Hall, Very Rev John Robert

WESTMINSTER, Very Rev John Robert Hall; s of Ronald John Hall, FCIB, FCIS (d 2006), and Katie Margaret Brock, *née* Walker (d 1998); *b* 13 March 1949; *Educ* St Dunstan's Coll Catford, Univ of Durham (BA), Cuddesdon Theological Coll Oxford; *Career* asst curate St John the Divine Church Kennington 1975–78, priest-in-charge All Saints' Wimbledon 1978–84, vicar St Peter's Streatham 1984–92, diocesan dir of educn Blackburn 1992–98, canon residentiary Blackburn Cathedral 1994–98, gen sec Church of England Bd of Educn 1998–2002, gen sec Nat Soc for Promoting Religious Educn 1998–2006, chief educn offr Church of England 2002–06, hon curate St Alban's S Norwood 2003–06, dean Most Honourable Order of the Bath 2006–, dean of Westminster 2006–; officiated at the wedding of Prince William of Wales and Catherine Middleton 2011; pro-chllr Roehampton Univ 2011–; chair of govrs: Westminster Sch, Westminster Abbey Choir Sch 2006–, Harris Westminster Sixth Form 2014–; companion St Dunstan's Educational Fndn 2014; Hon DD Roehampton Univ 2007, Hon DTheol Univ of Chester 2008, Hon DLitt Univ of Westminster 2014, Hon DLitt Univ of Hull 2016; hon fell: Canterbury Christ Church Univ 2007, St Chad's Coll Durham 2009, Coll of Teachers 2009, Univ of Wales Trinity St David's 2015; Hon Liveryman Worshipful Co of Educators 2015; FRSA, FSA 2014; *Publications* Queen Elizabeth II and Her Church: Royal Service at Westminster Abbey (2012); *Clubs* Athenaeum, Royal Overseas League (vice-pres), Beefsteak; *Style*— The Very Rev the Dean of Westminster; ✉ Westminster Abbey, The Deanery, London SW1P 3PA (e-mail dean@westminster-abbey.org, website www.westminster-abbey.org, Twitter @deanwestminster)

WESTMINSTER, Archbishop of Westminster (RC) 2009–; His Eminence the Cardinal Vincent Gerard Nichols; s of Henry Joseph Nichols, and Mary Nichols, *née* Russell; *b* 8 November 1945; *Educ* St Mary's Coll Crosby, Gregorian Univ Rome (STL, PhL), Univ of Manchester (MA), Loyola Univ Chicago (MEd); *Career* chaplain St John Rigby VI Form Coll Wigan 1972–77, priest in the inner city of Liverpool 1978–81, dir of Upholland Northern Inst (with responsibility for the in-service training of clergy and for adult Christian educn 1981–84); advsr Cardinal Hume and Archbishop Worlock at the Int Synods of Bishops 1980, 1983, 1987 and 1991, gen sec Bishops' Conf of England and Wales 1984–92, Catholic bishop in North London 1992–2000, archbishop of Birmingham 2000–09; del: Synod of Bishops 1994, Synod of European Bishops 1999; pres Catholic Bishops' Conf of England and Wales, memb Congregation for Bishops 2013–, memb Coll of Cardinals 2014–; chllr St Mary's Univ Twickenham 2014–; *Publications* Promise of Future Glory: Reflections on the Mass (1997), Missioners: Priests and people today (2007), St John Fisher, Bishop and Theologian in Reformation and Controversy (2011); *Style*— His Eminence the Cardinal Archbishop of Westminster; ✉ Archbishop's House, Ambrosden Avenue, Westminster, London SW1P 1QJ (☎ 020 7798 9033, fax 020 7798 9077, website www.rcdow.org.uk)

WESTMORLAND, 16 Earl of (E 1624); Anthony David Francis Henry Fane; also Baron Burghersh (E 1624); s of 15 Earl of Westmorland, GCVO, DL (d 1993), and Barbara Jane (d 2009), da of Lt-Col Sir Roland Lewis Findlay, 3 and last Bt (d 1979); *b* 1 August 1951; *Educ* Eton, Spain; *m* 1985, Mrs Caroline E Fairey, da of Keon Hughes, and former w of Charles Fairey; 1 da (Lady Daisy Caroline b 18 Jan 1989); *Heir* bro, Hon Harry Fane; *Career* dir: Phillips Auctioneers 1994–2002, Bonhams Auctioneers 2002–03, Watson Westmorland Ltd (Ind Art Advisers) 2003–; memb Orbitex Arctic Ocean Research Project Expedition to North Pole 1990; life pres St Moritz Sporting Club; FRGS; *Recreations* countryside pursuits, DIY; *Clubs* Turf; *Style*— The Rt Hon the Earl of Westmorland; ✉ 50 Cornwall Gardens, London SW7 4AD

WESTMORLAND, Archdeacon of; *see:* Howe, Ven George Alexander

WESTON, Adrian Robert; MBE (2016); s of Harold Gibbons Weston (d 1987), of Leicester, and Alwyne Gabrielle, *née* Appelbee; *b* 7 June 1935; *Educ* Ratcliffe Coll, The Queen's Coll Oxford (MA); *m* 29 Sept 1963, Bridget Ann (d 2014), da of William Henry Smith (d 1964), of Leicester; 1 da (Alexandra b 1967), 1 s (Thomas b 1968); *Career* admitted slr 1961; ptnr Harvey Ingram Slrs 1963–98, ret 1999; dir: Everards Brewery Ltd 1984–; capt Leics Co Hockey Assoc 1965–66; vice-pres: The Hockey Assoc 1979– (chm 1972–78), Leics CCC; memb Cncl Univ of Leicester 1999–2008; Hon LLD Univ of Leicester (distinguished hon fell 2014); *Recreations* golf, reading, history; *Clubs* Leicestershire Golf, RAF; *Style*— Adrian R Weston, Esq, MBE; ✉ 27 Main Street, Smeeton Westerby, Leicester LE8 0QJ

WESTON, Alannah; *Career* contributing ed Telegraph Magazine 1994–98, press offr Burberry 1998–2000, creative dir Windsor Florida 2001–04, creative dir Selfridges 2004–; dir: Wittington Investments Canada, Brown Thomas Ireland, Holt Renfrew Canada, Zephyr Projects 2003–04; tstee: Reta Lila Howard Fndn and Reta Lila Weston Tst 1998– (chm of tstees 2011–14), Blue Marine Fndn 2012–, Selfridges Fndn 2016–; *Style*— Ms Alannah Weston; ✉ Selfridges & Co, 400 Oxford Street, London W1A 1AB

WESTON, Christopher John; s of Eric Tudor Weston, of Plaxtol, Kent, and Evelyn, *née* Snell; *b* 3 March 1937; *Educ* Lancing; *m* 12 July 1969, Josephine Annabel, da of Dr Moir; 1 da (Annabel b 1973); *Career* RAF 1955–57; life pres Phillips Son & Neale 1998– (chm and chief exec 1972–98); dir: Foreign & Colonial Pacific Investment plc 1984–99, Hodder Headline plc 1986–99 (non-exec chm 1997–99), Foreign & Colonial Enterprise Trust plc 1987–99; chm and ceo Plaxbury Gp 1998–; vice-pres QUIT 2004– (Nat Soc of Non Smokers, chm 1993–2002); Freeman: City of London; FRSA; *Recreations* theatre, music; *Clubs* Oriental; *Style*— Christopher Weston, Esq; ✉ 5 Hillside Close, Carlton Hill, London NW8 0EF (☎ 020 7624 4780, fax 020 7372 5042, e-mail plaxbury@gmail.com)

WESTON, (Willard Gordon) Galen; OC (1990); s of W Garfield Weston (d 1978), of Toronto, Canada and London, and Reta Lila Howard (d 1967); yr bro of Garry Weston, DL (d 2002); *b* 29 October 1940; *Educ* Univ of Western Ontario (BA); *m* 1966, Hilary Mary Frayne; 2 c; *Career* chm and pres George Weston Ltd; exec chm: Loblaw Companies Ltd, Selfridges, Brown Thomas (Ireland), Holt, Renfrew & Co Ltd; dir: Associated Br Foods plc (UK), Fortnum & Mason plc (UK); life memb: Art Gallery of Ontario, Royal Ontario Museum; Hon LLD Univ of Western Ontario; Cdr OStJ 1997; *Recreations* outdoor sports, comtemporary arts; *Clubs* White's, Sunningdale Golf, Badminton & Racquet (Toronto), Toronto Golf, York (Toronto), Windsor (Florida), Brooks (NY), Rosedale Golf, Deepdale (NY); *Style*— W Galen Weston, OC; ✉ George Weston Ltd, 22 St Clair Avenue East, Toronto M4T 2S7, Canada (☎ 00 1 416 922 2500, fax 00 1 416 922 6401)

WESTON, George Garfield; s of Garfield Howard Weston (d 2002), and Mary Ruth, *née* Kippenberger; *b* 4 March 1964, Sydney, Aust; *Educ* Westminster, New Coll Oxford (MA), Harvard Business Sch (MBA); *m* 20 Jan 1996, Katharine Mary, *née* Acland; 1 da (Sally b 8 Sept 1999), 3 s (Gregory b 27 March 2001, Garfield b 4 April 2002, Gulliver b 15 July 2004); *Career* gen mangr Weston Milling Aust 1988–90, md Westmill Foods Ltd UK 1992–98, ceo Allied Bakeries 1999–2003, ceo George Weston Foods Ltd Aust 2003–05 (chm 2004), ceo Associated British Foods plc 2005–; *Style*— George Weston, Esq; ✉ Associated British Foods plc, 10 Grosvenor Street, London W1K 4QY (☎ 020 7399 6511, fax 020 7399 6588, e-mail caroline.priestley@abfoods.com)

WESTON, John Pix; CBE (1993); *b* 16 August 1951; *Educ* Kings Sch Worcester, Trinity Hall Cambridge (MA); *Children* 1 s, 1 da; *Career* BAE Systems (formerly British Aircraft Corp then British Aerospace plc): apprentice engr 1970, seconded to MOD 1982–84, dir Al-Yamamah prog, md Military Aircraft Div 1990–92, chm BAE defence 1991–96, appointed exec dir 1993, group md 1996–98, chief exec 1998–2002; chm: Spirent plc 2002–06, Acra Controls Ltd 2003–11, Inbis plc 2004–05, iSoft Group 2005–07, MBAerospace 2007–, AWS Ltd 2008–13, Accesso plc 2011–, Torotrak plc 2011–, Fibrecore plc 2012–; lifetime vice-pres RUSI; Freeman City of London; FREng, FRAeS, FRSA; Commander Order of the Pole Star (Sweden) 2000; *Recreations* skiing, photography, mountain walking; *Style*— John Weston, Esq, CBE, FREng, FRAeS

WESTON, Martin Wynell Lee; s of Quentin V L Weston, OBE, and Jill, *née* Gamon; *b* 29 July 1952; *Educ* Sevenoaks Sch, Univ of Oxford (MA), Coll of Law; *m* 24 Aug 1984, Fidelity Anne, da Colin Simpson; 4 c; *Career* called to the Bar 1976, practising barr 1977–78; commercial lawyer Cwlth Devpt Corp 1978–82, corp fin dept Lazard Brothers 1982–83, established co now known as Weald Group Ltd 1984; hon consul for the Republic of Nauru; *Recreations* sports incl: running, swimming, tennis, football, walking; *Clubs* Vincent's (Oxford), St Julian's (Sevenoaks); *Style*— Martin Weston, Esq; ✉ Weald Group Limited, Romshed Courtyard, Underriver, Sevenoaks, Kent TN15 0SD (☎ 01732 743125, fax 01732 746062, e-mail grp@weald.co.uk, website www.wealdgroup.com)

WESTROPP, Anthony Henry (Harry); s of Col Lionel Henry Mountefort Westropp (d 1991), and Muriel Constance Lilian, *née* Jorgensen; *b* 22 December 1944; *Educ* Sherborne, KCL; *m* 1, 7 Dec 1977 (m dis 1991), Zoë Rosaleen, da of (Charles) Douglas Neville Walker, of Paris; m 2, 6 May 1993, Hon Victoria Monica Watson, da of 3 Baron Manton; 1 da (Marina b 1993); *Career* with Lazard Bros & Co Ltd 1967–72, dir of subsidiaries Trafalgar House Gp 1972–75, md private gp of cos 1975–81; gp md: Bardsey plc 1981–90, The Beckenham Gp plc 1990–91; chm: MCD UK Ltd 1994–97, Britton Gp plc 1992–95, Abacus Gp plc 1994–2009, Norbain plc 1996–99, Upperpoint Ltd 1999–2006, Belvoir Fruit Farms Ltd 2002–, Scyron Ltd 2008–09, Dataset Communications Ltd 2012–; non-exec dir: Portman Building Soc 1982–2003, Agrivert Ltd 1990–2015, Nickerson Gp Rothwell Ltd 1991–2006, Marling Industries plc 1994–97, The Throgmorton Tst plc 2003–15; Freeman Co of Cutlers (Sheffield) 1982; *Recreations* rural pursuits, skiing; *Clubs* Boodle's; *Style*— Harry Westropp, Esq; ✉ Goadby Hall, Melton Mowbray, Leicestershire LE14 4LN (☎ 01664 464202)

WESTROPP, George Victor; s of Edward L Westropp (d 1962), of Epsom, Surrey, and Mary Breward, *née* Hughes (d 1973); *b* 2 November 1943; *Educ* Bedford Sch; *m* 1, 12 Jan 1972 (m dis 1973), Alexander Jeanne, da of Joseph Steinberg; m 2, 9 May 1977 (m dis 1988), Christine June, da of Alan Ashley; 2 s (Edward b 1980, Kit b 1982); m 3, 31 May 2003, Helen Elizabeth Elliott, da of Dr Peter H Cooper; *Career* reporter City Press 1961–63, city reporter Sunday Express 1963, fin journalist Evening Standard 1963–68, asst city ed Extel 1968–69; dir Shareholder Relations Ltd 1969–73, fin PR exec PPR International Ltd 1974–76, md Hemingway Public Relations Ltd 1977–79, nat dir of communications Touche Ross (now Deloitte) 1979–2000 (ptnr 1985–2000); dir: RHS Special Events Ltd 2002–12, Herpetosure Ltd 2005–13, Three Shires Ltd 2009–13; vice-chm Salmon & Trout Conservation 2004–; MCIPR, FRSA; *Books* The Lake Vyrnwy Fishing Book (1979), Lake Vyrnwy – The Story of a Sporting Hotel (1992), The Westropp Family 1250–2000 (1999), The Gallowglass (2014); *Recreations* salmon and trout fishing, gardening; *Clubs* London Press (chm 1990–99); *Style*— George Westropp, Esq; ✉ Mistlethrush Barn, Thame Road, Longwick, Buckinghamshire HP27 9SW (☎ 01844 345526 mobile 07774 412480, e-mail george.westropp@btconnect.com)

WESTROPP, Helen Elizabeth; *née* Elliott Cooper; da of Dr Peter Henry Cooper (d 1991), and Hilary Tasker *née* Stock; *b* 1 June 1961, Cheshire; *Educ* Cranbrook Sch, Lancaster Univ (BA); *m* 31 May 2003, George Victor Westropp, s of late Edward L Westropp, of Fleet Street, London; *Career* market analyst Institut Proscop 1984–85, privatisation research exec Dewe Rogerson 1986, account dir and assoc dir Hill Murray Fin PR 1986–89, dir Landor Associates Europe 1990–97, owner and principal Delphi Marques 1998–2011, corp business dir Coley Porter Bell 2011–15, commercial dir Sutton Young 2016–; memb London Ctee RNID 1989–91, advsr RNID Poolmead campaign 1991, chair and memb Bd Oxfordshire Community Devpt Assoc 1999–2003, graduate Common Purpose 2003, memb Cncl RSA 2004–11, memb Ctee E Midlands RSA, friend of the Royal Acad; memb: London Oriana Choir 1986–90, Action Aid, Br Heart Fndn, Simon Community, Salmon and Trout Assoc, Countryside Alliance, RHS, Royal Nat Rose Soc; FRSA; *Books* The Westropp Family 1250–2000 (with G V Westropp, 2000); *Recreations* fishing, shooting, gardening, music, travel; *Style*— Mrs George Westropp; ✉ Mistlethrush Barn, Thame Road, Longwick, Buckinghamshire HP27 9SW (e-mail helen.westropp@btconnect.com or helen@suttonyoung.com)

WESTWELL, Dr Alan Reynolds; OBE (1996); s of Stanley Westwell (d 1980), of Liverpool, and Margaret, *née* Reynolds (d 1962); *b* 11 April 1940; *Educ* Old Swan Coll, Liverpool Poly (ACT Hons), Univ of Salford (MSc), Keele Univ (PhD); *m* 30 Oct 1967, (Elizabeth) Aileen, da of John Birrell (d 1975), of Fife, Scotland; 1 da (Julie b 1970), 2 s (Stephen, Colin (twins) b 1972); *Career* asst works mangr (previously engrg apprentice and tech

W

asst) Liverpool City Tport Dept 1956–67; chief engr: Southport Corp Tport Dept 1967–69, Coventry Corp Tport Dept 1969–72, Glasgow Corp Tport Dept 1972–74; dir of public tport Tayside Regnl Cncl 1974–79, DG Strathclyde Passenger Tport Exec 1979–86, chm and md Strathclyde Buses Ltd 1986–90; chief exec and md: Greater Manchester Buses Ltd 1990–93, Greater Manchester Buses (North) Ltd 1993–97, Dublin Buses Ltd 1997–2005; public tport professional advsr Convention of Scottish Local Authorities (COSLA) 1975–85; pres: Scottish Cncl of Confedn of Br Road Passenger Tport 1982–83 (vice-pres 1981–82), Bus and Coach Cncl 1989–90 (vice-pres 1985–88, sr vice-pres 1988–89); chm Scottish Centre Automobile Div IMechE 1982–84, memb Parly Road Tport Ctee 1986–97, memb Cncl CIT UK 1986–89 (chm Scottish Centre 1983–84); Int Public Tport Union (UITP, based Brussels): memb Int Met Railway Ctee, memb Exec Mgmnt Ctee 1992–, chm Br Membership 1993–98, vice-pres 1997, memb EU Ctee (formerly European Action Ctee), memb Tport and Urban Life Cmmn (formerly Public Tport and Urban Planning Cmmn); CEng, MIMechE, MIET, FCIT; *Recreations* swimming, music, reading; *Clubs* Altrincham Probus (chm 2012–13); *Style*— Dr Alan Westwell, OBE; ✉ 6 Amberley Drive, Hale Barns, Cheshire WA15 0DT (☎ 0161 980 3551)

WESTWOOD, Lee John; OBE (2011); *b* 24 April 1973, Worksop, Notts; *m* Jan 1999, Laurae, *née* Coltart; 1 s (Samuel Bevan b 2001), 1 da (Poppy Grace b 2004); *Career* golfer; professional debut 1993; tournaments won: Volvo Scandinavian Masters 1996 and 2000, Sumitomo Visa Taiheiyo Masters 1996, 1997 and 1998, Malaysian Open 1997 and 2014, Volvo Masters Andalucia 1997, Australian Open 1997, Dunlop Phoenix Tournament 1998, Freeport-McDermott Classic 1998, Deutsche Bank SAP Open 1998 and 2000, English Open 1998, Loch Lomond Invitation 1998, Belgacom Open 1998 and 2000, Macau Open 1999, TNT Dutch Open 1999, Smurfit European Open 1999 and 2000, Canon European Masters 1999, Dimension Data Pro Am SA 2000, Compaq European Grand Prix 2000, Cisco World Match Play Championship 2000, BMW International Open 2003, Dunhill Links Championship 2003, Nelson Mandela Invitational 2003, Valle Romano Open de Andalucia 2007, Quinn Direct British Masters 2007, Portugal Masters 2009, Dubai World Championship 2009, St Jude Classic 2010, Nedbank Golf Challenge 2010 and 2011, Indonesian Masters 2011, 2012 and 2015, Ballantine's Championship 2011, Thailand Golf Championship 2011 and 2014, Nordea Masters (previously Volvo Scandinavian Masters) 2012; memb: England team Alfred Dunhill Cup 1996, 1997, 1998 and 1999, European team Ryder Cup 1997 (winners), 1999, 2002 (winners), 2004 (winners), 2006 (winners), 2008, 2010 (winners), 2012 (winners), 2014 (winners), GB & Ireland team Seve Trophy 2000, 2002 (winners) and 2003 (winners), European team Royal Trophy 2007 (winners); fndr Lee Westwood Acad 2009; European Tour Golfer of the Year 1998, 2000 and 2009, European Tour Order of Merit 2000 and 2009; Hon DSc Nottingham Trent Univ 2007; *Style*— Mr Lee Westwood, OBE; ✉ c/o International Sports Management, Cherrytree Farm, Cherrytree Lane, Rostherne, Cheshire WA14 3RZ

WESTWOOD, Hon Nigel Alistair; DL (Tyne and Wear 2011); yr s of 2 Baron Westwood, JP (d 1991), and Marjorie, *née* Bonwick; *b* 1950; *Educ* Fettes; *m* 1977, Joan Elizabeth, yr da of Reginald Ibison, CBE; 2 s (David Alistair b 1983, Peter Robert b 1986); *Career* chartered surveyor; dir: Universal Building Soc 2000–06, Newcastle Building Soc 2006–11; High Sheriff Tyne & Wear 2007–08; hon Norwegian consul, chllr Consular Corps Newcastle-upon-Tyne (pres 1991–92 and 2008–09), chm Assoc Norwegian Consuls in Br Isles, I and Gibraltar 1999–2001, pres Hebburn and Sunderland Sea Cadets; Knight First Class Royal Norwegian Order of Merit 1995; FRICS; *Recreations* tennis, skiing, Lake District; *Clubs* Den Norske; *Style*— The Hon Nigel Westwood, DL; ✉ 7 Fernville Road, Gosforth, Newcastle-upon-Tyne NE3 4HT

WESTWOOD, Tim; *Career* DJ; radio DJ: LWR (pirate), Kiss FM (pirate, former co-owner), Capital FM 1987–94, BBC Radio 1 1994–2013, BBC Radio 1Xtra 2009–11, Capital Xtra; also club DJ in venues across UK and European summer clubbing resorts; TV presenter: N Sign (ITV Night Network) 1990–92, Westwood Presents (UK Play) 2000, Westwood TV (Channel U) 2004–, Pimp my Ride UK (MTV) 2005–08, Westwood's Trick It Out 2006, Flava 2010–11, Bad Meaning Good TV documentary; magazine journalist: Westwood column Max Power 2004–, ed 33Hz 2004–; columnist The Sun 2004–; patron: Radio Feltham YOI, Body and Soul Teen Spirit, Nordoff Robins Dance Charity, Sonic DB, Willow Fndn, Hepatitus C Tst; memb: Radio Acad, Equity, Big Dawg Pitbulls (NYC); *Albums* Westwood the Album Volume 1 (Silver) 2001, Westwood Volume 2 (Gold) 2001, Westwood Volume 3 (Gold) 2002, Westwood Platinum Edition (Platinum) 2003, Westwood The Jump Off (Gold) 2004, Westwood The Takeover (Gold) 2004, Westwood The Big Dawg (Gold) 2004, Westwood The Invasion (Gold) 2005, Westwood Heat (Gold) 2005, Westwood – Ride with the Big Dawg 2006, Westwood – The Greatest 2006, Westwood – The Big Dawg Is Back 2010; *DVD* The Takeover 2004, Westwood Raw 2005; *Awards* Sony Awards: Best Specialist Music Prog 1990, 1991 and 1999, Best Music Broadcaster 1996 and 2000 (nominated 2001 and 2003), nomination Best Music Programme 2001, nomination Best Specialist 2005 and 2007, Silver Best Entertainment Prog 2011, Best Community Radio Programming 2013; Hip Hop Connection Magazine Best Radio DJ 1992, 1993, 1994, 1995, 1996, 1997, 1998, 1999, 2000, 2001, 2002, 2003, 2004, 2005 and 2006; Best Radio Show Muzik Magazine Awards 1999, Best UK Radio DJ MOBO Awards 2000, 2003, 2005, 2007 and 2008, Best Hip Hop DJ Pacha Awards 2003, Best R'n'B and Hip Hop DJ Sidewinder Awards 2003 and 2004, Radio Acad John Peel Award for Outstanding Contrib to Music 2010, Radio Acad Hall of Fame Outstanding Contrib to Music 2011, European DJ of the Year Global Spin Award 2012; voted no 1 rap DJ by the readers of Hip Hop Connection magazine for 14 successive years; *Style*— Tim Westwood; ✉ c/o Helen Galibardy (☎ 020 7935 7902, e-mail helen@timwestwood.com, website www.timwestwood.com)

WESTWOOD, Vivienne Isabel; DBE (2006, OBE 1992); *née* Swire; *b* 8 April 1941; *Career* fashion designer; a series of influential avant garde collections showcased at World's End 430 King's Road (formerly named Let it Rock, Too Fast to Live Too Young to Die, Sex, Seditionaries) 1971–82, opened Vivienne Westwood shop at 6 Davies St London 1990, flagship shop at 44 Conduit St London, head office Milan, stores worldwide; Gold Label collections show in Paris every season; other collections launched incl: Vivienne Westwood Man (Milan) 1996, Red Label (NY) 2000, Anglomania collections every season; fragrance launched Boudoir 1998; launched manifesto at Wallace Collection 2007; Vivienne Westwood 36 years in fashion exhbn (V&A) 2004 and (worldwide tour) 2005–; contrib to exhbns: Radical Fashion (V&A) 2001, Men in Skirts (V&A) 2002, Tiaras (V&A) 2002; prof of fashion: Vienna Acad of Applied Arts 1989–91, Berlin Hochschule 1993–; hon sr fell RCA 1992; British Designer of the Year Br Fashion Cncl 1990 and 1991, Queen's Award for Export 1998; subject of Moët & Chandon Fashion Tribute (V&A) 1998, Moët & Chandon Red Carpet Dresser 2006; trustee Civil Liberties Tst 2007, patron Reprieve 2011; Hon Dr: RCA 2008, Heriot Watt Univ 2008; Hon FKC 2008; *Style*— Dame Vivienne Westwood, DBE; ✉ Vivienne Westwood Ltd, Westwood Studios, 9–15 Elcho Street, Battersea, London SW11 4AU (☎ 020 7924 4747)

WETHERED, (James) Adam Lawrence; *b* 2 April 1953; *Educ* Eton, Christ's Coll Cambridge (BA, LLB); *m* Dr Diana Wethered; 5 c; *Career* called to the Bar Inner Temple 1975; J P Morgan: 1976–2000, chief exec J P Morgan Securities Ltd 1991–97, head of Asset Mgmnt Servs, Institutional and Private Clients Europe and JP Morgan Investment Mgmnt Inc 1998–2000; co-fndr Lord North Street Ltd Private Investment Office 2000, sold to Sandaire Ltd 2014, currently vice-chm Sandaire Investment Office; dir Centre for Social Justice; *Recreations* sailing, skiing, riding, shooting, walking; *Clubs* White's, Pratt's, Garrick; *Style*— Adam Wethered, Esq; ✉ e-mail adam.wethered@sandaire.com

WETHERELL, Gordon Geoffrey; CMG (2011); s of late Geoffrey Wetherell, of Addis Ababa, Ethiopia, and late Georgette Maria, *née* Matkovitch; *b* 11 November 1948, Addis Ababa; *Educ* Bradfield, New Coll Oxford (MA), Univ of Chicago (MA); *m* 11 July 1981, Rosemary Anne, da of late Cdr Terence Macrae Myles, RN, ret; 4 da (Christine b 1982, Stephanie b 1985, Emily b 1987, Alexandra b 1989); *Career* W African Dept FCO (concurrently third sec/vice-consul Chad) 1973–74, third then second sec E Berlin 1974–77; first sec: Arms Control and Disarmament Dept FCO 1977, UK delegation to comprehensive test ban negotiations Geneva 1977–80, New Delhi 1980–83, NATO Desk Defence Dept FCO 1983–85; secondment to HM Treasy 1986–87, asst head Euro Communities Dept (External) FCO 1987–88, cnsllr and dep head of mission Warsaw 1988–92, cnsllr Bonn 1992–94, head Personnel Servs Dept FCO 1994–97, ambass to Ethiopia 1997–2000 (concurrently non-resident ambass to Eritrea and Djibouti), ambass to Luxembourg 2000–04, high cmmr to Ghana 2004–07 (concurrently non-resident ambass to Togo, Niger, Burkina Faso, Cote d'Ivoire), govr Turks and Caicos Islands 2008–11; *Recreations* tennis, travel, reading, Manchester United FC; *Clubs* Oxford and Cambridge; *Style*— Mr Gordon Wetherell, CMG

WETZEL, Dave; s of Fred Wetzel (d 1982), and Ivy, *née* Donaldson (d 1981); *b* 9 October 1942, Isleworth, Middx; *Educ* Spring Grove GS Isleworth, Henry George Sch of Social Sci, Southall Coll, Ealing Coll, Kingston Coll; *m* 14 Feb 1973, Heather Jacqueline, da of Edmond John Allman (d 1976), of Staines; 2 da (Emma b 9 Dec 1968, Chantel b 1 Jan 1974); *Career* student engr Wilkinson Sword 1959–62, bus conductor, driver and inspr London Transport 1962–69, Lab cncllr London Borough of Hounslow 1964–68, branch mangr Initial Servs 1969–70, pilot roster offr BEA/BA 1970–74, political organiser London Co-op 1974–81, convenor Trade Union and Co-op Esperanto Gp 1975–81, ed Civil Aviation News 1978–81, Lab memb GLC, chair Transport Ctee GLC 1981–86, unemployed then minicab driver 1986, cncllr London Borough of Hounslow 1986–94 (chair of planning 1986–87, ldr 1987–91), ptnr antique shop 1994–99, vice-chair Transport for London 2000–08 (chair London Buses 2000–01, chair Safety, Health and Environment Ctee 2004–08), ceo Transforming Communities 2008–; pres: London Univ Transport Studies Soc 1991–92, W London Peace Cncl 1982–94, Lab Land Campaign 1983–; chair Professional Land Reform Gp, chair Tport Trading Ltd 2000–01; gen sec Int Union for Land Value Taxation 2010–12 (pres 2013–15); int lectr on land value taxation and tport; memb: UNITE, Green Party, Socialist Environmental Resources Assoc; dir DaRT (charity) 1989–94; author of various articles on land reform, congestion charging and transport funding; FCILT, FRSA 2002–08; *Recreations* lectures on land value taxation, Esperanto, travel; *Style*— Dave Wetzel; ✉ 40 Adelaide Terrace, Great West Road, Brentford, Middlesex TW8 9PQ (☎ 020 8568 9004, e-mail dave.c.wetzel@gmail.com)

WEYMAN, Anne Judith; OBE (2000); da of Joseph Stanley Weyman, and Rose, *née* Hellinger; *b* 1 February 1943; *Educ* Tollington GS, Univ of Bristol (BSc), LSE (BSc); *Career* head of fin and admin Int Secretariat Amnesty Int 1977–86 (est charity 1985), dir and non-exec chair Pinter Publishers Ltd 1974–95; Nat Children's Bureau: info and public affrs dir, co sec 1986–96; chief exec fpa (Family Planning Assoc London) 1996–, non-exec chair Family Planning Sales Ltd 1996–2002, non-exec dir Islington Primary Care Tst 2002–; estab: Sex Educn Forum 1987, Drug Educn Forum 1995; co-fndr: Forum on AIDS and Children 1992, Children's Play Cncl 1990; pres Sex Educn Forum 1996– (fndr 1987, chair 1987–96), chair of Nat Child Care Campaign and the Day Care Tst 1986–87, fndr memb Campaign for Res into Human Reproduction 1984–90, memb Nat Joint Ctee of Working Women's Orgns 1979–84, hon sec Socialist Health Assoc 1977–84, sec Cncl for Disabled Children 1986–96; tstee: Children's Rights Office 1991–99, Pharmacy Health Care Scheme 1996–2001; memb: Mgmnt Ctee of Nat Children's Play and Recreation Unit 1990–94, Personal Social and Health Educn Advsy Gp 1998–2001, The Sexual Health Strategy Gp 1999–2000, Women's Nat Cmmn Steering Gp 1999–2003, The Ind Advsy Gp on Teenage Pregnancy 2000–; co vice-chair Independent Advsy Gp on Sexual Health 2003–; govr of schs in Westminster and Islington 1970s-90s; memb: NE Dist of Kensington, Chelsea and Westminster CHC 1974–78, NW Thames Regnl HA 1978–80; cncllr Westminster City Cncl 1978–82; Hon LLD Univ of Bristol 2005; FCA 1968; A Sociological View of Large Groups (with Earl Hopper, in Large Groups (ed Lionel Kreeger) 1975, Modern British Society: A Bibliography (with J Westergaard and Paul Wiles, 1977), Social Behaviour Assesment Schedule (with S Platt and S R Hirsch, *qv*, 1983), Finding and Running Premises (with J Unell, 1985), Starting and Running a Voluntary Group (with S Capper and J Unell, 1989), Individual Choices, Collective Responsibility: Sexual Health, a Public Health Issue (with Maria Duggan, 1999), Sexual and Reproductive Health and Rights in the UK: 5 Years on from Cairo (with Marge Berer and Amy Kapczynski, 1999), Handbook of Sexual Health in Primary Care (with Toni Belfield, Yvonne Carter, *qv*, Philippa Matthews and Catti Moss, 2006); contrib to numerous jls 1972–; *Recreations* gardening (garden open under the Nat Gardens Scheme), theatre, music and opera; *Style*— Ms Anne Weyman, OBE; ✉ fpa, 50 Featherstone Street, London EC1Y 8QU (☎ 020 7608 5240, e-mail anne-w@fpa.org.uk)

WHALEN, Sir Geoffrey Henry; kt (1995), CBE (1989); s of Henry Charles Whalen (d 1981), and Mabel Elizabeth Whalen (d 1965); *b* 8 January 1936; *Educ* East Ham GS, Magdalen Coll Oxford (MA); *m* 1961, Elizabeth Charlotte, da of Dr Eric Waud, of Helperby, N Yorks; 3 da (Catherine b 1963, Anna b 1965, Georgina b 1975), 2 s (Thomas b 1967, Henry b 1977); *Career* personnel dir Leyland Cars British Leyland 1975–78; Peugeot Motor Co PLC: asst md 1981–84, md 1984–95, dep chm 1990–95, non-exec dep chm 1995–2003; currently div Camden Ventures Ltd; former dir: Robins and Day Ltd, Talbot Ireland Ltd, Proptal UK Ltd, Motaquip Ltd, Sunbeam-Talbot Ltd, T & N plc, Lombard North Central plc, Hall Engineering (Holdings) plc, Camden Motors Ltd, Coventry Building Society, Federal Mogul Corp; pres Soc of Motor Manufacturers & Traders 1988–90 and 1993–94 (dep pres 1997–98); govr Coventry Univ (formerly Poly) 1989–95; Hon DBA; Hon FCGI, CIMgt, FIMI; Chevalier de la Legion d'Honneur 1990; *Recreations* cricket, golf; *Style*— Sir Geoffrey Whalen, CBE; ✉ 8 Park Crescent, Abingdon, Oxfordshire (☎ and fax 01235 523917)

WHALEY, Prof Joachim; *b* Dulwich; *Educ* Christ's Coll Cambridge (BA), Univ of Cambridge (PhD, LittD); *Career* fell Gonville & Caius Coll Cambridge, prof of German History and Thought Univ of Cambridge; FBA, FRHistS; *Books* Mirrors of Mortality: Studies in the Social History of Death (ed, 1981), Religious Toleration and Social Change in Hamburg 1529–1819 (1985), German and the Holy Roman Empire, 1493–1806 (2 vols, 2012); *Clubs* Athenaeum, Lansdowne; *Style*— Prof Joachim Whaley, FBA; ✉ Gonville & Caius College, Cambridge CB2 1TA

WHALLEY, Andrew David; s of Donald Allan Whalley (d 1998), and Marjorie, *née* Craven; *b* 27 February 1962; *Educ* Dollar Acad, Mackintosh Sch of Architecture Glasgow Sch of Art and Univ of Glasgow (BArch), AA Sch of Architecture (AADipl); *m* 1986, Fiona, da of Andrew Biggim Douglas Galbraith; 2 da (Catriona Grace b 1993, Morven Sylvia Jane b 1996); *Career* architect; Grimshaw Architects LLP (formerly Nicholas Grimshaw & Partners Ltd): dir 1986–2007, ptnr 2007–, managing ptnr Grimshaw NY, princ Grimshaw Industrial Design LLC, dep chm 2011–; work incl numerous tport, arts and public bldgs, and commercial and technol projects; projects incl: redevelopment of Paddington Station London, Fundación Caixa Galicia Art Gallery A Coruña Spain, The Eden Project Cornwall, Donald Danforth Plant Science Center St Louis MO USA, Miami Intermodal Center FL USA, Grimshaw Architects PC USA, Experimental Media and Performing Arts Centre Troy NY, Queens Museum of Art Expansion NY, Earthpark Iowa, Fulton Street Transit Center NY, Museum of Steel Monterrey Mexico, Southern Cross Station

Melbourne Aust, Miami Museum of Science FL, Univ of NY 20 Year Masterplan; projects in partnership with Galbraith Whalley: house in Scotland utilising new glazing technol, house in London utilising low energy systems; exhibitions: Product & Process (RIBA) 1987, Structure, Space & Skin (RIBA) 1993, Through the Mac (Glasgow and Brazil) 1997; visiting lectr Dept of Industrial Design and Design Innovation Unit RCA 1989–92, tutor AA London 1993–95, visiting tutor Bartlett Sch of Architecture 1995–2003; lectr at home and abroad incl: Royal Acad London 1996, Mackintosh Sch of Architecture 1997, Art and Architecture Fndn 1998, Ruth and Norman Moore visiting prof Washington Univ MO USA; memb Cncl Architectural Assoc; Otis AJ Architecture Competition commendation 1985, Glasgow Eurodrome commendation 1988, RIBA Award for Architecture (Scotland) 1990, Eric Lyon Housing Award commendation 1992; RIBA 1990; registered architect: UK ARB 1990, USA State of Missouri 1998; memb AIA, memb RIBA; FRSA; *Publications* The Architecture of Eden (with Hugh Pearman), Blue – an innovative response to issues of global concern (ed, bi-annual); author of papers on steel frame construction (especially the use of steel in Waterloo terminal for British Steel) 1992–95, tech articles on interactive structures published in New Scientist, Sunday Times and the design press, sustainability columnist Architecture Magazine (USA) and RIBA Jl; *Recreations* architecture, photography, skiing; *Clubs* Chelsea Arts, The Norwood; *Style—* Andrew Whalley, Esq; ✉ Grimshaw Architects PC – New York Office, 637W 27th Street, New York, NY 10001, USA (☎ 001 646 293 3600)

WHARTON, James Stephen; MP; *b* 16 February 1984; *Educ* Univ of Durham, Coll of Law York; *Career* slr; MP (Cons) Stockton S 2010–; *Style—* James Wharton, Esq, MP; ✉ Stockton Conservatives, DTV Business Centre, Orde Wingate Way, Stockton On Tees TS19 0GD (☎ 01642 636235, e-mail james@jameswharton.co.uk); House of Commons, London SW1A 0AA

WHARTON, Rt Rev (John) Martin; CBE (2011); s of John Wharton, of Dalton-in-Furness, Cumbria, and Marjorie Elizabeth, *née* Skinner (d 1962); *b* 6 August 1944; *Educ* Ulverston GS, Univ of Durham (BA), Univ of Oxford (MA); *m* 29 Aug 1970, Marlene Olive; 1 da (Joanna Helen b 17 Nov 1972), 2 s (Andrew Benjamin b 1 March 1974, Mark Richard b 6 March 1978); *Career* Martins Bank Ltd 1960–64; ordained: deacon 1972, priest 1973; curate: St Peter Spring Hill Birmingham 1972–75, St John the Baptist Croydon 1975–77; dir of pastoral studies Ripon Coll Cuddesdon 1977–83, curate All Saints Cuddesdon 1979–83, sec Bd of Min and Trg Dio of Bradford 1983–92, residentiary canon Bradford Cathedral 1992, area bishop of Kingston 1992–97, bishop of Newcastle 1997–2014; memb House of Lords 2002–14; *Books* Knowing Me, Knowing You (with Malcolm Goldsmith, 1993); *Recreations* sport; *Clubs* Lancs CCC; *Style—* The Rt Rev Martin Wharton

WHARTON, Rt Rev (John) Martin; CBE (2011); *see:* Newcastle, Bishop of

WHATELY, Julian Richard; s of Gerald Arthur Whately, OBE (d 1985), and Nina Abigail Whately, *née* Finlayson (d 1994); *b* 10 August 1949; *Educ* Eton, Univ of Bristol (BA); *m* 1973, Clare Magdalen Hallett; 3 s (Richard Marcus b 11 March 1977, Hugo Thomas b 4 May 1979, Benjamin William b 26 Sept 1980); *Career* admitted slr 1974; sr ptnr Lee and Pembertons 2000–2007, ptnr Rooper & Whately 2009–; dir Rathbone Tst Co Ltd 2009–; tstee Herbert and Peter Blagrave Charitable Tst; *Recreations* hill walking, fishing, ski touring, tennis; *Clubs* Boodle's, The Kandahar; *Style—* Julian Whately, Esq; ✉ The Manor House, Holybourne, Alton, Hampshire GU34 4HD

WHATELY, Kevin; s of Richard Whately (d 1968), of Humshaugh, Northumberland, and Mary, *née* Pickering; *b* 6 February 1951; *Educ* Humshaugh Sch, Barnard Castle Sch, Central Sch of Speech and Drama; *m* 30 April 1984, Madelaine, da of Jack Newton (d 1983); 1 da (Catherine Mary b 13 April 1983), 1 s (Kieran John Richard b 12 Oct 1984); *Career* actor; memb Northumberland and Durham County Cross Country Running Team 1968; vice-pres NCH; ambass: Prince's Tst, Alzheimer's Soc, City of Newcastle upon Tyne, City of Sunderland; capt Variety Club Golf Soc 2013; Hon Dr Univ of Northumberland; *Theatre* incl: Prince Hal in Henry IV Part 1 (Newcastle) 1981, Andy in Accounts (Edinburgh and London) 1982, title role in Billy Liar (nat tour) 1983, John Proctor in The Crucible (Leicester) 1989, Daines in Our Own Kind (Bush) 1991, Twelve Angry Men (Comedy) 1996, Snake In The Grass (Peter Hall Co, Old Vic) 1997, How I Learned to Drive (Donmar) 1998, Gypsy (Chichester) 2014; *Opera* Judas in The Peoples Passion (BBC); *Television* incl: Kevin in Coronation Street (Granada) 1981, Bob in The Dig (BBC) 1981, Adams in Shackleton (BBC) 1982, Neville in Auf Wiedersehen Pet (Central) 1982–84, Sgt Lewis in Inspector Morse (Central) 1985–2000, Steve in B & B (Thames) 1992, Jack Kerruish in Peak Practice (Central) 1993–95, Trip Trap (BBC) 1995, Gobble 1996, Jimmy Griffin in The Broker's Man 1997–98, Pure Wickedness (BBC) 1998, What Katy Did (Tetra) 1999, Plain Jane (Carlton) 2001, Nightmare Neighbour (BBC) 2001, Hurst in Promoted to Glory 2003, The Legend of the Tamworth Two 2003, Belonging 2004, Dad (BBC) 2005, Footprints in the Snow (ITV) 2005, Lewis (ITV) 2005–15, New Tricks (BBC) 2006, Who Gets the Dog? (BBC) 2007, The Children (ITV) 2008, Who Do You Think You Are? (BBC) 2008, Joe Maddison's War (ITV) 2009, George Gently 2012; *Film* Return of the Soldier, Hardy in The English Patient (Miramax) 1996, Paranoid 1999, Purely Belter 2000, Silent Cry 2001; *Awards* incl: Pye Comedy Performance of the Year Award 1983, Variety Club Northern Personality of the Year 1990; *Recreations* looking over the next horizon, charity golf events; *Style—* Kevin Whately, Esq; ✉ c/o Belinda Wright, CDA, 167–69 Kensington High Street, London W8 6SH (☎ 020 7937 2749)

WHATLEY, Prof Christopher Allan (Chris); OBE (2015); s of Herbert Allan Whatley, of Nantwich, Cheshire, and Evelyn Stanley, *née* Whitfield (d 1977); *b* 29 May 1948; *Educ* Bearsden Acad, Clydebank Coll, Univ of Strathclyde (BA, PhD); *m* 1, 1975, Lilian, *née* Beattie; 1 da (Eilidh b 1977), 1 s (Neil Allan b 1979); m 2, 1997, Patricia Elizabeth, *née* Kelleher; *Career* lectr Univ of Dundee 1979–88, lectr in Scottish history Univ of St Andrews 1988–92; Univ of Dundee: sr lectr then reader 1994–97, head of history 1995–2002, prof of Scottish history 1997–, dean Faculty of Arts and Social Sciences 2002–06, vice-princ and head Coll of Arts and Social Sciences 2006–14; chair Scottish Historical Review Tst 2001–06; FRHistS 1988 (memb Cncl 2008–12), FRSE 2003; *Books* incl: The Scottish Salt Industry, 1570–1850 (1987), The Manufacture of Scottish History (ed, 1992), The Life and Times of Dundee (1992), The Industrial Revolution in Scotland (1997), Scottish Society, 1707–1830: Beyond Jacobitism, Towards Industrialisation (2000), Bought and Sold for English Gold? Explaining the Union of 1707 (2001), The Scots and the Union (2006, Saltire Soc History Book of the Year 2007), A History of Everyday Life in Scotland 1600–1800 (ed, 2010), The Scots and the Union: Then and Now (2014), Immortal Memory: Burns and the Scottish People (2016); *Recreations* music, walking; *Clubs* New Club Edinburgh; *Style—* Prof Chris Whatley, OBE; ✉ School of Humanities, University of Dundee, Dundee DD1 4HN (☎ 07972 229750, e-mail c.a.whatley@dundee.ac.uk)

WHATMORE, Andrew; s of late Charles Sydney Whatmore, and late Monica Mabel, *née* Tucker; *b* 18 June 1946, Surbiton, Surrey; *Educ* The Skinners' Sch Tunbridge Wells, Woolwich Poly, Univ of London (BSc(Eng)); *m* 17 Dec 1983, Elizabeth, da of late James Stewart Morrison Sim, and late Isobel McLuckie, *née* Russell, of Dollar, Clackmannanshire; 1 s (Charles Stewart b 1984), 1 da (Kathryn Elizabeth b 1985); *Career* resident engr: (EAEC) Kenya 1980, Roughton and Ptnrs Al Ain UAE 1981; chief engr Taylor Woodrow Int Ghana 1983, agent Christiani & Nielsen S Wales 1987, dep chief engr Geoffrey Osborne Chichester 1988, sr planning engr Edmund Nuttall Kilsyth Glasgow 1989, chief engr Skye Crossing Miller-Dywidag 1992, regnl chief engr Birse Construction Northampton 1994, chief engr Mid Orient Technical Services 1995, planner Balfour Beatty Kingston Bridge Glasgow 1996 and Edinburgh and Lyon 1998, bid mangr Edinburgh 2003, civil engr Scottish and Southern 2007, planning mangr Scotland Carillion 2008, engrg mangr Bilfinger Berger UK 2008, ind consulting engr West Netherton Engrg Services Ltd 2011, currently with Briggs Marine & Environmental Services; CEng, MICE; *Recreations* riding, tennis, walking, beach-combing, curling, gardening, photography; *Style—* Mr Andrew Whatmore; ✉ West Netherton Farm, Milnathort, Kinross-shire KY13 0SB (☎ 01577 865018, mobile 07876 137984, e-mail andrew.whatmore@btinternet.com)

WHEATCROFT, Baroness (Life Peer UK 2010), of Blackheath in the London Borough of Greenwich; Patience Jane Wheatcroft; *b* 28 September 1951; *Educ* QEGS Tamworth, Coll of Technol Chesterfield, Univ of Birmingham (LLB); *m* 1976, Anthony Salter; 2 s (Kelhem b 1981, Sebastian b 1986), 1 da (Lucy b 1982); *Career* journalist; London Chamber of Commerce 1972–73, reporter/news ed Estates Times 1973–76, city reporter Daily Mail 1976–77, city reporter Sunday Times 1977–79, Prufrock The Sunday Times 1979–82, fin ed Working Woman 1982–83, dep city ed The Times 1982–84, ed Retail Week 1988–94, profile writer Daily Telegraph 1990–95, dep city ed Mail on Sunday 1995–97, city and business ed The Times 1997–2006, ed Sunday Telegraph 2006–07; non-exec dir: St James's Place plc 2012–, Fiat SpA 2012–; memb: UK-India Round Table, Advsy Bd BOA; tstee Br Museum; *Recreations* opera, skiing; *Style—* The Baroness Wheatcroft

WHEATER, Prof Howard Simon; s of late Claude Wheater, and late Marjorie Wheater; *b* 24 June 1949; *Educ* Nottingham HS, Univ of Cambridge (MA), Univ of Bristol (PhD); *m* 1, 1970 (m dis 2004), Elisabeth; 2 s; m 2, 2007 (m dis 2010), Prof Valerie Isham; m 3, 2010, Prof Patricia Gober; *Career* grad apprentice Aero Engine Division Rolls-Royce Ltd 1967–1972, research asst Dept of Civil Engrg Univ of Bristol 1972–78; Dept of Civil and Environmental Engrg Imperial Coll London: lectr 1978–87, sr lectr 1987–90, reader 1990–93, prof of hydrology 1993–; Canada excellence research chair in water security Univ of Saskatchewan Canada 2010–, distinguished research fell and emeritus prof of hydrology Imperial Coll London 2010–; head Environmental and Water Resource Engrg, chm Centre for Environmental Control and Waste Mgmnt, memb Int Ct of Arbitration Concerning the Indus Waters Treaty 2010–, memb Int Court of Arbitration for the Indus Waters Treaty The Hague 2010–13, memb Provincial Environmental Monitoring Panel Alberta Environment 2011, chair Cncl Canadian Academies Expert Panel on Sustainable Mgmnt of Water in the Agricultural Landscapes of Canada 2011–13; co-chair UNESCO GWADI Prog 2002–, vice-chair World Climate Research Prog GEWEX Project 2009–13; scientific advsr to Repub of Argentina with respect to environmental impacts of proposed industrial devpts on Uruguay water quality at the Int Courts of Justice The Hague 2006–10; pres British Hydrological Soc 1999–2001, life memb Int Water Acad Oslo; memb and chair various nat and int advsy panels and ctees incl: UK Govt-MAFF, DEFRA, Environment Agency, NERC, UNESCO; conslt: Flood Study Northern Oman 1981, Yucca Mountain nuclear waste repository NV USA 2003–; counsel and advocate Republic of Hungary Int Court of Justice GNBS Danube barrage system 1993–1997; Prince Sultan bin Abdulaziz Int Water Prize 2006; CEng, FREng, FICE; 200 refereed papers and 7 books; *Recreations* sailing (dinghy racing and yacht cruising), music (orchestral trumpet player); *Style—* Prof Howard Wheater; ✉ Department of Civil and Environmental Engineering, Imperial College London SW7 2BU (☎ 020 7594 6066, fax 020 7594 1511, e-mail h.wheater@imperial.ac.uk); Canada Execellence Research Chair, University of Saskatchewan, National Hydrology Research Centre, 11 Innovation Boulevard, Saskatoon S7N 3H5, Canada (☎ 001 306 966 1990, e-mail howard.wheater@usask.ca)

WHEATLEY, Alan Edward; s of Edward Wheatley (d 1991), and Margaret Rosina Turner; *b* 23 May 1938; *Educ* Ilford GS; *m* 30 June 1962, Marion Frances, da of John Douglas Wilson (d 1968), and Maud Fletcher; 1 da (Susan b 1966), 2 s (Michael b 1968, Jonathan b 1974); *Career* Price Waterhouse 1960–92 (sr ptnr London Office 1985–92); chm: 3i Group plc 1992–93, Foreign & Colonial Special Utilities Investment Trust plc 1993–2003, New Court Financial Services Ltd 1996–99, IntaMission, Unigro Ltd 2002–05, AKJ Inc 2002–, Utilico Investmetn Tst plc 2003–07, Burlington Chase LLP 2009–; non-exec dep chm: Cable & Wireless plc 1984–85 (govt dir 1981–84), Ashtead Group plc 1994–2003; vice-chm Carlton Capital Ptnrs 2005–09; non-exec dir: EBS Investments Ltd (Bank of England subsid) 1977–90, British Steel plc 1984–94, Babcock International Group plc 1993–, Legal & General Group plc 1993–2002, Forte plc 1993–96, NM Rothschild & Sons Ltd 1993–99; dir Industrial Devpt Advsy Bd 1985–92; tstee V&A Museum 1996–99, tstee dir V&A Enterprises Ltd 1996–2000; FCA; *Recreations* golf, music, bridge; *Clubs* Wildernesse Golf; *Style—* Alan E Wheatley, Esq; ☎ 01732 779350

WHEATLEY, Hon Rt Lord John Francis; PC (2007); s of Baron Wheatley, PC (Life Peer, d 1988), and Agnes Mary, da of Samuel Nichol; *b* 9 May 1941; *Educ* Mount St Mary's Coll, Univ of Edinburgh (BL); *m* 1970, Bronwen Catherine, da of Alastair Fraser, of Dollar; 2 s; *Career* called to the Bar Scot 1966; advocate depute 1974–78, QC (Scot) 1992, Sheriff of Perthshire and Kinross-shire 1980–1998, Sheriff Principal Tayside, Central and Fife 1998–2000, senator Coll of Justice 2000–10; chm Judicial Studies Ctee 2002–06; *Recreations* gardening, music; *Style—* The Rt Hon Lord Wheatley; ✉ Braefoot Farmhouse, Fossoway, Kinross-shire (☎ 0157 74 212); Parliament House, Parliament Square, Edinburgh EH1 1RF

WHEATLEY, Martin; s of Arthur James Wheatley (d 1992), of London, and Jean Florence, *née* French; *b* 11 December 1958; *Educ* St Edward's Sch, Univ of York (BA), City Univ (MBA); *m*; 4 c; *Career* London Stock Exchange: joined 1985, responsible for introduction of SETS electronic order book 1997, memb Bd 1998–2004, dep chief exec 2001–05; Securities and Futures Cmmn Hong Kong: chm 2005–06, ceo 2006–11; md Consumer and Markets Business Unit FSA 2011, currently chief exec Financial Conduct Authy; chm FTSE Int; IPFA 1985; *Recreations* cycling, golf, cabinet making; *Style—* Martin Wheatley, Esq

WHEATLEY, Rt Rev Peter William; er s of late William Nobes Wheatley, and late Muriel, *née* Ounsted; *b* 7 September 1947; *Educ* Ipswich Sch, The Queen's Coll Oxford (MA), Pembroke Coll Cambridge (MA), Coll of the Resurrection Mirfield, Ripon Hall Oxford; *Career* ordained deacon 1973, priest 1974; asst curate All Saints Fulham 1973–78; vicar: Holy Cross with St Jude and St Peter St Pancras 1978–82, St James W Hampstead 1982–95; priest i/c: All Souls Hampstead and St Mary Kilburn 1982–90, St Mary with All Souls Kilburn 1990–95; dir of post ordination trg (Edmonton Episcopal Area) 1985–94, area dean of N Camden (Hampstead) 1988–93; archdeacon of Hampstead 1995–99, bishop of Edmonton 1999–2014, currently hon asst bishop Dios of London, Southwark and Chichester; *Style—* The Rt Rev Peter Wheatley; ✉ 47 Sedlescombe Road, St Leonards-on-Sea, East Sussex TN38 0TB (☎ 01424 424814, e-mail peter.wheatley@outlook.com)

WHEELER, Adrian Christopher de Vaux Cathcart; s of Paul Murray Wheeler, and Lucinda Mary de Vaux Cathcart Mure, *née* McKerrell, of St Germans, Cornwall; *b* 5 November 1949; *Educ* Dulwich Coll, Clare Coll Cambridge (open exhibitioner, MA); *m* 1997, Katerina Koudelova; 1 s (Thomas b 10 Dec 1999), 1 da (Anna-Katerina b 2 May 2004); *Career* dir Brian Dowling Ltd 1974–76 (exec 1971–74), md Sterling Public Relations 1976–87, chief exec GCI Group London 1998–99 (md 1994–98), chief exec GCI UK 1999–2006, chm GCI Europe 2001–06; non-exec dir Firefly Communications Ltd; chm PRCA 1998–2000; dir British-American Business, memb Vice-Chllr's Communications Advsy Panel Univ of Cambridge, dir Speakers' Corner Tst; memb Ct of Assts Guild of PR Practitioners 2000–; memb Mktg Soc, FCIPR 1998 (memb 1972); *Recreations* skiing, sailing, tennis; *Clubs* Royal Ocean Racing, Egypt Exploration Soc; *Style—* Adrian Wheeler, Esq

W

WHEELER, Colin; s of Stanley Arthur Thomas Wheeler (d 1978), and Lilian Mary, *née* Covey (d 1985); *b* 23 February 1938; *Educ* Farnham GS, Farnham Sch of Art, Royal Acad Schs London; *m* 1962, Jacqueline Anne Garelli Buchanan, da of Neville R Buchanan; 3 da (Andrée b 1963, Jacqueline b 1966, Vivien b 1968); *Career* cartoonist; asst lectr Bolton Coll of Art then High Wycombe Coll of Art 1961–63 then various pt/t teaching appts London, first published cartoon Times Educnl Supplement c 1963; freelance contrib of cartoons, illustrations and occasional writing to Daily Telegraph and other national broadsheet press, Private Eye, New Statesman, TES and The Teacher until 1986, front page cartoonist, illustrator and writer The Independent 1986–98; currently freelance cartoonist especially to The Spectator, Private Eye, The Oldie and TES; *Books* A Thousand Lines (1979), Off the Record (1980); *Recreations* painting and drawing, the protection of old buildings and the encouragement of good modern architecture; *Style—* Colin Wheeler, Esq; ✉ e-mail colin.wheeler@cartoonist.fsbusiness.co.uk

WHEELER, Heather Kay; MP; *m* Bob; 1 da; *Career* insurance broker Lloyd's 1977–87; cncllr Wandsworth BC 1982–86, cncllr S Derbys DC 1995–2011 (ldr 2007–10); MP (Cons) S Derbys 2010–; PPS to Attorney Gen 2014–15, PPS to Sec of State for Culture, Media and Sport; ACII; *Style—* Mrs Heather Wheeler, MP; ✉ House of Commons, London SW1A 0AA

WHEELER, Rt Hon Sir John Daniel; kt (1990), PC (1993), JP (Inner London 1978), DL (Gtr London 1989, rep DL Merton 1997); s of late Frederick Harry Wheeler, and Constance Elsie, *née* Foreman; *b* 1 May 1940; *Educ* County Sch Suffolk, Staff Coll Wakefield; *m* 1967, Laura Margaret Langley; 1 s, 1 da; *Career* former asst prison govr; MP (Cons): Paddington 1979–83, Westminster N 1983–97; min of state for NI 1993–97; memb: Home Office Standing Ctee on Crime Prevention 1977–85 (chm Sub-Ctee on Mobile Crime 1983–84), Home Affrs Select Ctee 1980–92 (chm 1987–92, chm Sub-Ctee on Race Rels and Immigration 1980–87), Home Office Steering Ctee on Crime Prevention 1985–93; chm: Residential Burglary Working Gp 1986–87, All-Pty Penal Affairs Gp 1986–93 (vice-chm 1979–86), Cons Gtr London Area Membs' Ctee 1983–90 (jt sec 1979–83), Policy Gp for London 1988–93, Br-Pakistan Parly Gp 1988–93; vice-chm: Cons Urban Affrs and New Towns Ctee 1980–83, Cons Home Affrs Ctee 1987–93 (jt sec 1980–87); non-exec dir of various cos 1976–93 and 1997–; chm Serv Authorities for the Nat Criminal Intelligence Serv and Nat Crime Squad 1997–2002, chm UK Govt's Review of Airport Security 2002–03, head Aust Govt's Review into Airport Security and Policing 2005, dep chm UK Border Security Advsy Ctee 2007–08; Order of St John: memb Cncl 1990–, memb Chapter-Gen 1995–99, registrar 1997–99, sub-chllr 1999–2002, memb Priory Chapter for Eng 1999–2008, chllr and tstee 2002–08; tstee: Butler Tst 1997–2000, The Police Fndn 2004–; chm The Traveller's Club 2014–; KStJ 1997 (Offr Bro 1991, CStJ 1992); Hilal-i-Quaid-i-Azam (knight) of Pakistan 1991; *Style—* The Rt Hon Sir John Wheeler, JP, DL; ✉ PO Box 890, London SW1P 1XW

WHEELER, Michael (Mike); CBE (2015); *b* 1 November 1951; *Educ* Haileybury, Univ of Liverpool; *m* 1977, Linda May; 1 da (Sarah b 1984), 2 s (Andrew b 1986, Charles b 1990); *Career* mangr Peat Marwick Mitchell 1973–81, vice-pres Bank of America 1982–84, ptnr KPMG 1985–2005 (head Financial Advsy Servs 2001–05); non-exec dir Citadel Securities; conslt Glitnir; non-exec dir Mgmnt Bd Dept of Health 2006–14; chm Audit Ctee Dubai Hldg; non-exec Sunseeker Int'l; *Books* International Insolvency Procedures (1997); *Recreations* mountaineering, rugby, skiing; *Clubs* RAC, MCC, Royal Geographic, Chatham House; *Style—* Mike Wheeler, Esq, CBE

WHEELER, Prof Michael David; s of David Mortimer Wheeler, and Hilda Lois Stansfield, *née* Eke; *b* 1 September 1947; *Educ* St Albans Sch, Magdalene Coll Cambridge (scholar, MA), UCL (PhD); *m* 1970 (m dis 2009), Vivienne Rees; 1 s (Joshua b 1973), 2 da (Charlotte, Emily (twins) b 1975); *Career* Quain student (lectr) Univ of London 1972–73; Lancaster Univ: lectr in English 1973–85, sr lectr 1985–90, prof of English literature 1990–99; prof of English literature Univ of Southampton 1999–2001 (visiting prof 2001–); dir: Ruskin Prog (interdisciplinary res gp) 1990–99, Ruskin Collection Project 1990–99, Chawton House Library Hampshire 1999–2001; visiting lectr USA, Canada, Denmark, India, Iraq, Japan, Poland, Yugoslavia, Switzerland, Italy, Turkey, Aust, Germany, France and Norway 1975–; NADFAS lectr 2006–15; exhibition Reading the Book of Books, then and now: The King James Bible 1611–2011 (Winchester Cathedral) 2011; pres Ruskin Soc 2008–12 (chm 2002–07); tstee Gladstone's Library Hawarden 1994– (chm 2015–), chm Murray Bequest to Birkbeck Coll 1994–; lay canon and memb Chapter Winchester Cathedral 2005–08; Companion Guild of St George 1992–; *Publications* The Art of Allusion in Victorian Fiction (1979), English Fiction of the Victorian Period 1830–1890 (1985, 2 edn 1994), Death and the Future Life in Victorian Literature and Theology (1990, winner US Conf on Christianity and Literature award, 1991–92, abridged as Heaven, Hell and the Victorians 1994), The Lamp of Memory: Ruskin, Tradition and Architecture (co-ed, 1992), Ruskin and Environment: The Storm-Cloud of the Nineteenth Century (ed, 1995), Ruskin's God (1999), The Kindest Cut of All: On the Making of Gravestones in the Kindersley Workshop (jtly, 2005), The Old Enemies: Catholic and Protestant in Nineteenth Century English Culture (2006), St John and the Victorians (2012); Longman Literature in English Series (jt gen ed, 35 vols), Time and Tide: Ruskin Studies 1996 (ed, 1996), Works of John Ruskin (CD-ROM; manuscript ed, 2002), The Athenaeum and the Making of Modern Britain (forthcoming); *Recreations* walking, gardening; *Clubs* Athenaeum; *Style—* Prof Michael Wheeler; ✉ 1 Amport Park Mews, Amport, Andover, Hampshire SP11 8BS (☎ 01264 771394, e-mail m-wheeler@live.co.uk)

WHEELER, Nick; s of John Wheeler, and Geraldine, *née* Jones (d 1970); *b* 20 January 1965, Ludlow; *Educ* Eton, Univ of Bristol; *m* 2 Sept 1995, Chrissie Rucker, MBE, *qv*; 1 s (Tom b 1996), 3 da (Ella b 1998, India b 2000, Bea b 2004); *Career* strategic conslt Bain & Co 1987–89, fndr and chm Charles Tyrwhitt 1989–; *Books* Male Order (2008); *Style—* Nick Wheeler, Esq; ✉ Charles Tyrwhitt, Cottons Centre, Cottons Lane, London SE1 2QG (☎ 0844 482 4000, fax 020 8735 1066)

WHEELER, Oliver; s of Christopher Wheeler, of Surrey, and Margaret Wheeler; *b* 13 November 1969; *Educ* Magdalen Coll Sch Oxford; *m* 16 Dec 2006, Tina Hobley, *qv*; 1 da (Olivia Kitty Alice b 18 April 2008), 1 s (Orson Henry Attwood b 1 March 2010); *Career* apprenticeship under Baron Bell (Life Peer), *qv*, Chime Communications 1993–95, bd dir Freud Communications 1995–; *Recreations* competitor UK Nat Sports Cars, drummer with rock band Westbourne Circus; *Clubs* Aspinall's, Soho House, British Racing and Sports Car; *Style—* Oliver Wheeler, Esq; ✉ Freud Communications, 55 Newman Street, London W1T 3EB (☎ 020 3003 6412, fax 020 3003 6303, e-mail oliver@freud.com)

WHEELER, Gen Sir Roger Neil; GCB (1997, KCB 1993), CBE (1984); s of late Maj-Gen T N S Wheeler, CB, CBE; *b* 16 December 1941; *Educ* All Hallows Sch Devon, Hertford Coll Oxford (MA); *m* 1980, Felicity Hares; 3 s and 1 da from prev m; *Career* early Army serv Borneo and ME 1964–70, Bde Maj Cyprus Emergency 1974, memb Lord Carver's Staff Rhodesia talks 1977, Bn Cmd Belize, Gibraltar, Berlin and Canada 1979–82, COS Falklands Is Jun-Dec 1982, Bde Cmd BAOR 1985–86, Dir Army Plans 1987–89, Cdr 1st Armoured Div BAOR 1989–90, ACGS MOD 1990–92, GOC and Dir of Mil Ops NI 1993–96, C-in-C Land Cmd 1996–97, Chief of the Gen Staff 1997–2000; ADC Gen to HM The Queen 1996–2000, Col The Royal Irish Regt 1996–2001, Col Cmdt Intelligence Corps 1996–2001; constable HM Tower of London 2001–09; non-exec dir Thales Group 2001–14, chm Thales UK Air Defence 2003–14; non-exec dir Serious Organised Crime Agency 2006–09; pres: Army RFU 1995–2000, Army Rifle Assoc 1995–2000, Combat Stress, Ex-Services' Mental Welfare Soc, Forces Pension Soc; vice-pres Sandes Homes; chm Tank Museum Bovington; patron Police Fndn; tstee: Historic Royal Palaces, Royal Armouries 2001–09; Liveryman Worshipful Co of Painter-Stainers (Master 2011); hon fell Hertford Coll Oxford; FRGS; *Recreations* fly fishing, cricket, shooting, ornithology; *Clubs* Army and Navy, Beefsteak, Stragglers of Asia CC, NIRFCC; *Style—* Gen Sir Roger Wheeler, GCB, CBE

WHEELER, Sara Diane; da of John Wheeler, and Diane, *née* Vernon; *Educ* Redland HS Bristol, BNC Oxford (exhibitioner, BA); *Career* writer; contrib ed Literary Review 2009–; writer and presenter Captain Scott's Men (series, BBC Radio 4) 2012; memb Cncl RSL 2001–05; tstee London Library 2005–09 and 2014–, tstee Sibs 2009–; Hawthornden fell 2010; FRSL 1999; *Books* Evia: An Island Apart (1992), Travels in a Thin Country: a Journey through Chile (1994), Terra Incognita: Travels in Antarctica (1996), Cherry: A Biography of Apsley Cherry-Garrard (2001), Too Close to the Sun: A Life of Denys Finch Hatton (2006), The Magnetic North: Notes from the Arctic Circle (2009, Best Adventure Travel Book Banff Mountain Festival, 2011), Access All Areas: Selected Writings 1990–2010 (2011), O My America!: Second Acts in a New World (2013); *Clubs* Academy; *Style—* Ms Sara Wheeler; ✉ Aitken Alexander, 18–21 Cavaye Place, London SW10 9PT (☎ 020 7373 8672, fax 020 7373 6002, e-mail reception@aitkenalexander.co.uk)

WHEELER, (John) Stuart; adopted s of Alexander Hamilton Wheeler (d 1942), and Betty Lydia, *née* Gibbons (d 1990); *b* 30 January 1935, London; *Educ* Eton, ChCh Oxford; *m* 14 July 1979, Teresa Anne, *née* Codrington; 3 da (Sarah Rose b 9 July 1980, Jacqetta Lydia b 16 Oct 1981, Charlotte Mary b 24 Jan 1985); *Career* Nat Serv 2 Lt Welsh Guards 1953–55; called to the Bar Inner Temple 1959, barr 1959–62; mangr Investment Dept J H Vavasseur 1968–73, First Nat Fin Corp 1973; IG Group (formerly IG Index): fndr 1974, chief exec 1974–2002, chm 1985–2003; one time biggest donor to Cons Pty but expelled 2009 for supporting UKIP, formed Trust Pty 2010, contested Bexhill and Battle, treas UKIP 2011–14; Coronation Medal 1953; *Publications* A Crisis of Trust (2010); *Recreations* bridge, poker, tennis, theatre; *Clubs* Portland, White's, Naval; *Style—* Stuart Wheeler, Esq; ✉ Chilham Castle, Chilham, Kent CT4 8DB (☎ 01227 733100, e-mail stuartwheeler@chilham-castle.co.uk)

WHEELER-BOOTH, Sir Michael Addison John; KCB (1994); s of Addison James Wheeler, and Mary Angela Wheeler-Booth, *née* Blakeney-Booth; *b* 25 February 1934; *Educ* Leighton Park Sch Berks, Magdalen Coll Oxford (MA); *m* 1982, Emily Frances Smith , *qv*; 2 da (Kate b 1985, Charlotte b 1987), 1 s (Alfred James b 1990); *Career* Nat Serv Midshipman (Sp) RNVR 1952–54; clerk House of Lords 1960, private sec to Ldr of House of Lords and Govt Chief Whip 1965, seconded as jt sec Inter Party Conf on House of Lords Reform 1967, clerk of the Journals 1970, chief clerk Overseas and Euro Office 1972, princ clerk 1978, reading clerk House of Lords 1983–88, clerk asst of the Parliaments 1988–90, Clerk of the Parliaments 1991–97; Magdalen Coll Oxford: visiting fell 1997–98, special lectr in politics 1998–2009; Waynflete lectr 1998; chm Study of Parliament Group 1982–84 (pres 2004–09), tstee History of Parliament Tst 1991–97, tstee Industry and Parliament Tst 1994–97, cmmr Standing Orders Cmmn for Nat Assembly of Wales 1998–99; memb: Royal Cmmn on Reform of House of Lords 1999–2000, Fabian Cmmn on the Future of the Monarchy 2002–03, Richard Cmmn on Powers and Electoral Methods of the Nat Assembly of Wales 2002–04; chm Ind Panel on Salaries, Pensions and Allowances for Welsh Assembly Members 2007–08; govr Magdalen Coll Sch Oxford 2001–10 (chm Fin and Gen Purposes Ctee 2004–09); hon fell Magdalen Coll Oxford 2004; *Publications* Griffith & Ryle on Parliament (contrib, chapter on the House of Lords, 2 edn 2003), Halsbury's Laws of England (vol 34) on Parliament (jt ed), contrib to Parly jls; *Recreations* reading, ruins, paintings, opera, bucolic; *Clubs* Brooks's, Garrick; *Style—* Sir Michael Wheeler-Booth, KCB; ✉ Northfields, Sandford St Martin, Chipping Norton, Oxfordshire OX7 7AG (☎ 01608 683632, e-mail wbsmith@btinternet.com)

WHEEN, Francis James Baird; s of James Francis Thorneycroft Wheen, and Patricia Winifred, *née* Ward; *b* 22 January 1957; *Educ* Copthorne Sch Sussex, Harrow, Royal Holloway Coll London (BA); *partner* Julia Jones; 2 s (Bertie, Archie); *Career* journalist; editorial asst The Guardian 1974–75, staff writer New Statesman 1978–84, news ed New Socialist 1983–84, contributing ed Tatler 1985, diarist The Independent 1986–87, contributing ed Sunday Correspondent Magazine 1989–90, diarist Independent on Sunday 1990–91, regular contrib Private Eye 1987–, contributing ed Vanity Fair 1992–93; columnist: Observer 1993–95, Esquire 1993–98, Guardian 1994–2001; freelance work for numerous pubns incl: The Times, Daily Mirror, London Evening Standard, Sunday Telegraph, Los Angeles Times, The Nation (NY), The New Yorker, Literary Review; was for several years regular presenter of News-Stand (BBC Radio) and What The Papers Say (Granada TV); regular panellist The News Quiz (BBC Radio) 1991–; Columnist of the Year What The Paper Say Awards 1997; hon fell Royal Holloway Coll London 2008; *Books* The Sixties (1982), World View 1982 (1982), Television: A History (1985), The Battle For London (1985), Tom Driberg: His Life And Indiscretions (1990), The Chatto Book of Cats (1993), Lord Gnome's Literary Companion (1994), The Vintage Book of Cats (ed, 1996), Karl Marx (1999), Hoo-Hahs and Passing Frenzies (2002), Who Was Dr Charlotte Bach? (2002), How Mumbo-Jumbo Conquered the World (2004), Marx's Das Kapital: A Biography (2006), Strange Days Indeed (2009); *Clubs* MCC, Essex CCC, High Roding CC; *Style—* Francis Wheen; ✉ Sokens, Green Street, Pleshey, Chelmsford, Essex CM3 1HT (☎ 01245 231566)

WHELAN, Prof Michael John; s of William Whelan, ISM (d 1978), of Aldershot, Hants, and Ellen, *née* Pound (d 1972); *b* 2 November 1931; *Educ* Farnborough GS, Gonville & Caius Coll Cambridge (MA, PhD); *Career* Univ of Cambridge: demonstrator in physics 1961–65, asst dir of res in physics 1965–66; fell Gonville & Caius Coll Cambridge 1958–66; Univ of Oxford: reader in physical examination of materials 1966–92, prof of microscopy of materials 1992–97 (emeritus prof 1997–); fell Linacre Coll Oxford 1968–97 (emeritus fell 1997–); hon prof Univ of Sci and Technol Beijing 1995; Hughes Medal of Royal Soc 1988, Distinguished Scientist Award Microscopy Soc of America 1998, Gjønnes Medal of Int Union of Crystallography 2011; hon fell: Royal Microscopical Soc 2001, Japanese Soc of Microscopy 2003, Microscopy Soc of America 2009; FRS 1976, FInstP 1976; *Books* Electron Microscopy of Thin Crystals (co-author), Worked Examples in Dislocations, High-Energy Electron Diffraction and Microscopy (co-author); *Recreations* gardening, tinkering, Japanese language; *Style—* Prof M J Whelan, FRS; ✉ 18 Salford Road, Old Marston, Oxford OX3 0RX (☎ and fax 01865 244556); Department of Materials, Oxford University, Parks Road, Oxford OX1 3PH (☎ 01865 273742, fax 01865 283333, email michael.whelan@materials.ox.ac.uk)

WHELAN, Paul David; s of Don Whelan, of NZ, and Beris, *née* Pashby; *b* 29 September 1966; *Educ* Wellington Conservatoire, Royal Northern Coll of Music (Marianne Mathy scholar); *Career* bass-baritone; studied with Flora Edwards, Patrick McGuigan, Robert Alderson and David Harper; *Concerts* conducted by: Sir Simon Rattle, Gary Bertini, Kent Nagano, Richard Hickox, Sir Yehudi Menuhin, Paolo Olmi, Sir David Willcocks, Sir Charles Farncombe; performed with: LSO, City of Birmingham Symphony Orch, Hallé Orch, BBC Philharmonic Orch, BBC Symphony Orch, City of London Sinfonia, London Sinfonietta, English Chamber Orch, RIAS Berlin Chamber Choir, Budapest Symphony Orch; venues incl: Wigmore Hall, St David's Hall Cardiff, Blackheath Concert Halls, Cheltenham Festival, Nello Santi, Valery Gergiev, Marcus Creed; *Opera* incl: title role in The Doctor of Myddfai (debut for WNO), Figaro in The Marriage of Figaro (Scottish Opera), Shaklovity in Khovanshchina (ENO), Marcello in La Bohème (Glyndebourne Touring Opera and Bavarian State Opera) 1997, Flint in Billy Budd (Geneva Opera), Schaunard in La Bohème (Netherlands Opera, Stuggart Opera, Royal Opera House,

Metropolitan Opera NY), Guglielmo in Cosi fan Tutte (Dublin Grand Opera), Masetto in Don Giovanni (Bordeaux), Demetrius in A Midsummer Night's Dream (Australian Opera), title role in Don Giovanni (Australian Opera) 1997, title role in Eugene Onegin (Australian Opera) 1997, Ned Keene in Peter Grimes (Metropolitan Opera) 1997, The Count in Marriage of Figaro (Santiago)1998 (also Sydney Opera House 2004), Silvio in I Pagliacci (Nantes) 1998, Guglielmo in Cosi fan Tutte (New Israeli Opera) 1999, Marcello (Bavarian State Opera and Bastille Opera Paris) 1998, Tarquinius in Rape of Lucretia (Nantes) 1999, Belcore in Elisir D'Amore (New Israeli Opera) 1999, Apollo in Alceste (Netherlands Opera) 1999, Count in Marriage of Figaro (Scottish Opera) 1999–2000, Jesus in St John Passion (ENO) 2000, Escamillo in Carmen (WNO) 2000, Oliver in Cappriccio (Opera Australia) 2000, La Damnation de Faust (BBC Philharmonic) 2001, Villians in Tales of Hoffman (New Zealand) 2001, Christus in St Mathew Passion (CBSO) 2001, Richard Blackford's Voices of Exile (premiere), A Midsummer Night's Dream (Pittsburgh Opera) 2003, Gurrelieder (Bolshoi Theatre Moscow) 2003, Des Knaben Wunderhorn (BBS SSO) 2003, The Apostles (BBC Philharmonic) 2003, The Prodigal Child (premiere, Michael Williams Opera NZ) 2003, Argante in Rinaldo (Bavarian State Opera) 2004, Don Giovanni (Lithuania National Opera) 2004; *Recordings* A Midsummer Night's Dream (with LSO under Sir Colin Davis), Kurt Weill's Silbersee (under Markus Stenz), Le Rossignol (with LPO, under Robert Craft), Elegy (songs with piano), Cecil Coles' Fra Giacomo, Edgor Bainton's English Idyll; *Awards* Webster Booth-Esso Award, Brigitte Fassbaender Award for Lieder, Lieder Prize Cardiff Singer of the World 1993; scholarships incl: Wolfson Fndn, Countess of Munster Musical Tst, Peter Moores Fndn; *Recreations* tennis, hiking, skiing; *Style*— Paul Whelan, Esq

WHELAN, Ronnie; da of John Connolly, and Josephine Connolly; *b* 9 June 1952; *Educ* St Martin's Sch for Girls, London Coll of Printing; *m* June 1982, Dennis Whelan (d 1992); 3 step da; *Career* ed asst Stitchcraft 1973–75, sr designer Ideal Home 1975–81, dep art dir Options 1981–83, dep ed and art dir Woman's World 1983–90 (runner-up PPA Designer of the Year for Art Direction 1985), freelance designer 1990–91, art dir Hello! 1991–2001, freelance designer (incl dep ed Asian Art newspaper) 2001–03, ed Hello! 2003–07, ed Int Special Edns Hello 2007–08, freelance 2008, ed The Essential Kitchen Bathroom Bedroom magazine 2009–11, freelance consulting ed incl Hello! Queen's Diamond Jubilee Special 2012; *Recreations* travel, music, restaurants, architecture, exhibitions; *Style*— Ronnie Whelan; ✉ veronicawhelan@btinternet.com

WHELDON, Susan Lynne (Sue); da of Derek Wheldon (d 1963), of Silsoe, Beds, and Joan Mary, *née* Neville; *b* 5 October 1951; *Educ* Bedford HS, Royal Masonic Sch for Girls, Univ of Liverpool (BA), Architectural Assoc (grad study year); *Career* architect and interior designer; set designer BBC 1974–75, freelance architectural design 1975–79 (incl work with Alaverdian Architectural Assocs Teheran 1976–77), in own practice Sue Wheldon Architectural Design 1980–95 (specialising in designs for the leisure and retail industries and for architectural applications of corp identity and brand devpt), retail design dir Design House Consultants Ltd 1995–97, md BDG McColl Branded Environments 1997–2001, fndr Brand Architects International Consulting Consortium 2002–, dir Douglas Wallace Architects and Designers 2003–09; hon memb Bd Lamda Alpha International (Land Economic Forum); memb: RIBA, Franco-Br Union of Architects; FRSA; *Recreations* travel (Spain, Italy, India and Africa particularly), tennis, swimming, snorkelling, walking in the countryside, chess, 20th Century painting, music, reading travel books, visiting restaurants, shops and hotels; *Style*— Ms Sue Wheldon; ✉ 6 Bridstow Place, London W2 5AE (e-mail suewheldon@brandarchitects.gb.com)

WHEWAY, (Jonathan) Scott; s of Barry Wheway (d 1999), and Cynthia Gill (d 1995); *b* 26 August 1966, Sheffield; *Educ* Rowlinson Comp Sch Sheffield; *m* 23 Sept 2000, Amanda; *Career* various mgmnt appts Tesco stores 1984–2003, ceo Tesco Japan 2003–04, retail dir Boots plc (latterly Alliance Boots plc) 2005–07; memb Bd Br Retail Consortium; ind non-exec dir Aviva plc 2007–; ceo Bestbuy Europe 2009–; *Style*— Scott Wheway, Esq

WHICHER, Dr John Templeman; s of Leonard Sydney Whicher, of Piddinghoe, E Sussex, and Ethel Adelaid, *née* Orton; *b* 31 July 1945; *Educ* Sherborne, Univ of Cambridge (MA, MB BChir), Westminster Hosp Med Sch, Univ of London (MSc); *m* 1 (m dis 1982), Alba Heather Phyllida Leighton Crawford; 1 da (Emma b 1973), 1 s (Hugo b 1975); m 2, 17 Sept 1982, Jennefer Whitney, da of Dr Arthur Benson Unwin, of London; 2 da (Alexandra b 1986, Charlotte b 1989); *Career* dep dir Protein Reference Unit Westminster Hosp 1975–78, conslt chem pathologist Bristol Royal Infirmary 1978–87; Univ of Leeds: prof of chem pathology 1987–91, prof of molecular pathology 1991–96; former chm Scientific Ctee Assoc of Clinical Biochemists, former conslt advsr to Chief MD DHSS, chm Ctee on Plasma Proteins Int Fedn of Clinical Chemistry 1990–2000; former visiting prof in Lab Med Univ of Leeds; WHO Expert Advsy Panel on Health Lab Servs 1996–2003; Editorial Bd Clinical Chem Lab Med 1996–2004; dir and co sec Lyttondale Associates Ltd; FRCPath, FGS; *Books* Immunochemistry in Clinical Laboratory Medicine (jointly, 1978), A Short Textbook of Chemical Pathology (jointly, 1989), The Biochemistry of Inflammation (jointly, 1990); *Publications* author of numerous pubns on the geology of Dorset; *Recreations* aviation, conchology, geology, natural history; *Clubs* Geological Soc, Geologists Assoc, Br Shell Collectors, Wessex Cephalopod; *Style*— Dr John Whicher; ✉ Higher Marsh Farm, Marsh Lane, Henstridge, Templecombe, Somerset BA8 0TQ (☎ 01963 363715, e-mail john@whicher.plus.com)

WHILE, Prof Alison Elizabeth; da of Harold Arthur Armstrong While, MBE, TD (d 1983), and Janet Bell Symington Clark; *b* 24 July 1953; *Educ* Wycombe Abbey, Univ of Southampton (BSc), Poly of the South Bank (MSc), Univ of London (PhD), St Thomas' Hosp (RGN), Univ of Southampton (RHV); *m* Philip Allan Gore-Randall; 2 s (William b 1986, Edward b 1987); *Career* health visitor N Kensington 1977–80, Chelsea Coll London: lectr 1980–89, sr lectr 1989–92; prof of community nursing KCL 1992–2014 (emeritus prof 2014–); non-exec dir Audley Care; visiting prof: TCD, Second Military Medical Univ China; memb: Royal Coll of Nursing 1977, Community Practitioners' and Health Visitors' Assoc 1977; conslt ed Br Jl of Community Nursing; Freeman City of London 1979, Liveryman Worshipful Co of Farriers 1979; FRSM 2007, fell Queen's Nursing Inst 2008; *Books* Research in Preventive Community Nursing Care (1986), Health in the Inner City (1989), Caring for Children (1991); numerous papers in academic and professional jls; *Recreations* tennis, good food, travel, The Cotswolds; *Style*— Prof Alison While; ✉ e-mail alison.while@kcl.ac.uk

WHILEY, Johanne (Jo); *b* 4 July 1965, Northampton; *Career* radio DJ and television presenter; formerly: presenter WPFM (BBC Radio 4), prodr and presenter The Indie Show (BSB), music prodr The Word (Channel 4); BBC Radio 1: co-presenter The Evening Session 1993–97 (with Steve Lamacq, co-host Sound City live music festivals and Phoenix Festival), presenter lunchtime slot 1997–2001, presenter mid-morning slot 2001–09, presenter weekend slot 2009–11; BBC Radio 2 2011–; presenter Jo Whiley Show (Channel 4); *Recreations* music, swimming, wakeboarding, snowboarding, windsurfing, volleyball, partying, Jack Daniels; *Style*— Ms Jo Whiley; ✉ BBC Radio 2, Western House, 99 Great Portland Street, London W1W 7NY (e-mail jo.whiley@bbc.co.uk)

WHISHAW, Anthony Popham Law; s of Robert Whishaw, and Joyce Evelyn Mary, *née* Wheeler (d 1996); *b* 22 May 1930; *Educ* Tonbridge (Higher Cert), Chelsea Sch of Art, RCA (travelling scholarship, drawing prize); *m* 1957, Jean Gibson; 2 da (Phoebe, Zoe); *Career* artist; RA 1989 (ARA 1980), ARCA, RWA 1992 (Hon RWA 2003); *Collections* incl: Arts Cncl GB, Coventry Art Gallery, Euro Parl Strasbourg, Leicester City Art Gallery, Museo de Bahia Brazil, Nat Gallery Victoria Melbourne, Museum of Contemporary Art Helsinki, Royal Acad, Power Art Gallery Sydney Aust, Ferens Art Gallery Hull, City Art Galleries Sheffield, Chantrey Bequest, The Tate Gallery, Christchurch Kensington, The Long Term Credit Bank of Japan, Andersen Consulting, Ashikaga Bank of Tokyo, Zeneca, Bolton Art Gallery, The Financial Times, M A M, Ladbrokes, Huddersfield Art Gallery, Barings Asset Management, Tetrapak UK, Albert E Sharp, Deutsche Morgan Grenfell, Crown Commodities, Stanhope plc, St Anne's Coll Oxford; *One-Man Exhibitions* incl: Liberia Abril Madrid 1957, Roland Browse & Delbanco 1960, 1961, 1963, 1965 and 1968, Hoya Gallery London 1974, Acme Gallery 1978, from Landscape (Kettle's Yard Cambridge, Ferens Art Gallery Hull, Bede Gallery Jarrow) 1982–84, Work on Paper (Nicola Jacobs Gallery London) 1983, Reflections After Las Meninas (tour) 1987, Royal Acad of Arts Diploma Galleries London 1987, Hatton Gallery Newcastle 1988, Mead Gallery Warwick Univ 1988, Hansard Gallery Southampton 1988, Spacex Gallery Exeter 1988, Infaust Gallery Hamburg 1989, Infaust Gallery Shanghai 1989, Blasón Gallery London 1991, Artspace London 1992, 1994 and 1995, RWA Bristol 1993, On Memory and Reflection (nat touring exhbn starting at Barbican and subsequent museums in Exeter, Ayr, Dublin, Newcastle, Sheffield, Newport and Bolton) 1994–95, Art First London 1997 and 1999, Pueblo Landscapes Royal Acad 2000, Trees Stephen Lacey Gallery 2000, Re-Appearances St Anne's Coll Oxford 2000, Osborne Samuel Gallery London 2007, Victor Pasmore Gall Harrow Sch 2009, Fine Art Soc 2010, Kings Place Gall London 2010, ACME Studios 2010, 8 Large Paintings (two-person show with Peter Brook, The Gallery in Cork Street London) 2011; *Group Exhibitions* incl: Ashmolean Museum Oxford 1957–72, Br Painting 1952–77 (Royal Acad of Arts London) 1977, Walker Art Gallery Liverpool 1980, Hayward Annual (Hayward Gallery London) 1980 and 1982, Nine Artists (Helsinki, touring) 1983, Three Decades 1953–83 (Royal Acad of Arts London) 1983, 30 London Painters (Royal Acad of Arts London) 1985, Whitechapel Open (Whitechapel Art Gallery London) 1981–83, 1987 and 1994, The Romantic Tradition in Contemporary British Painting (Madrid, Murcia, touring) 1988, 8 Contemporary Br Artists (Galerie Sapet Valeree France) 1988, Le Paysage Contemporaine 1991/92 (touring Belgium, France), Creative Quarters Museum of London 2001, Royal Acad (annually), Royal West of England Acad Bristol, London Gp, Richmond Hill Gall, St Paul's Crypt London, Carlow Centre for Contemporary Art Ireland, Open Exhibition – The London Group (Menier Gallery) 2009, ING The Discerning Eye Exhibition (Mall Galleries) 2009, 30 Years of Eigse Art 2010, St Paul's in the 21st Century 2010, Acme Open Studios 2013, Osborne Samuel – 4 Contemporary Artists 2013, 'On London' The London Group 2014, Acme Open Studios 2014, Acme Robinson Road Open Studios 2015; *Prizes* RCA Travelling Scholarship 1955, RCA Drawing Prize 1955, Perth International Biennale 1973, Bayer Int Painting 1973, South East Arts Assoc Painting 1975, GLC Painting 1981, John Moores Minor Painting 1982; scholarships: Spanish Govt 1956, Abbey Minor 1956, Abbey Premier 1982, Lorne 1982–83; Greater London Arts Assoc 1977, Arts Cncl GB Award 1978, RA Picture of the Year 1996 (for Korn Ferry); *Style*— Anthony Whishaw, Esq, RA; ✉ c/o The Royal Academy, Burlington House, London W1V 0DJ (website www.anthonywhishaw.com)

WHISHAW, Ben; *b* 14 October 1980, Hitchin, Herts; *Educ* Samuel Whitbread Community Coll Shefford, RADA; *Career* actor; *Theatre* incl: title role in Hamlet (Old Vic) 2004, The Seagull (RNT) 2006, Cock (Royal Court Theatre) 2009, Peter and Alice (Noel Coward Theatre) 2013, Mojo (nominated Best Actor in a Play WhatsOnStage Awards, 2014), Bakkhai (Almeida Theatre); *Film* incl: Enduring Love 2004, Layer Cake 2004, Perfume: The Story of a Murderer 2006, I'm Not There 2007, Brideshead Revisited 2008, Bright Star 2009, The Tempest 2010, Richard II 2012 (Leading Actor BAFTA 2013), Cloud Atlas 2012, Skyfall 2012, The Zero Theorem 2013, Teenage 2013, Days and Nights 2014, The Muse (short) 2014, Lilting 2014, In the Heart of the Sea 2015, The Danish Girl 2015, Spectre 2015, The Lobster (nominated Best Supporting Actor Award British Ind Film Awards 2015); *Television* incl: Nathan Barley 2005, Criminal Justice 2008 (Best Actor International Emmy 2009), The Hour 2011–12, The Hollow Crown 2012, London Spy 2015; *Style*— Mr Ben Whishaw; ✉ c/o Christian Hodell, Hamilton Hodell, 20 Golden Square, London W1F 9JL

WHISTON, John; *Educ* Edinburgh Acad, Balliol Coll Oxford (BA); *Career* BBC: joined as gen trainee 1983, asst prodr BBC Music & Arts 1985–87 (worked on progs incl Timewatch, Bookmark and Omnibus), prodr BBC Music & Arts 1987–94 (sr prodr The Late Show, prodr Edinburgh Nights), head of Youth and Entertainment Features 1994–97; dir of progs: Yorkshire Tyne-Tees TV 1998–2001, Granada Content North 2001–02; dir of Drama, Kids and Arts Granada 2002–; prodr progs for BBC Music & Arts incl: Naked Hollywood (BAFTA Best Documentary), Absurdistan (BFI Grierson Best Documentary Award), Archive Productions progs (incl: The Lime Grove Story, A Night with Alan Bennett, TV Hell, Granadaland, Cops on the Box, A Night in with David Attenborough); other progs incl: The Mrs Merton Show, The Royle Family, Rough Guides, The Travel Show, The Big Trip, The Sunday Show, Kicking & Screaming, Great Railway Journeys, The Sunday Show, Before They Were Famous, Dennis Pennis, themed nights incl Weird Night and George Best Night; currently responsible for Granada drama progs incl: Coronation Street, Emmerdale, Heartbeat, A Touch of Frost, Poirot, Prime Suspect, Miss Marple, William & Mary, Life Begins, The Royal, Where the Heart Is, Vincent, Jericho, Cracker, Blue Murder, The South Bank Show and progs for children; *Style*— John Whiston, Esq

WHITAKER, Claire; OBE (2015); *Career* lending offr Natwest Corporate Banking Unit 1986–89, business affrs exec Decca Records 1989–90, dir of devpt Southbank Centre 1990–92, dir Africa '95 1992–96, dir Serious (music prodrs) 1996–; dir London Jazz Festival 1996–, chair Royal Cwlth Soc 2013– (tstee 2007–), chair Artworks (Paul Hamlyn Fndn special initiative) until 2015, tstee Caine Prize for African Writing 1996–; *Style*— Mrs Claire Whitaker, OBE; ✉ Serious, 51 Kingsway Place, Sans Walk, Clerkenwell, London EC1R 0LU (☎ 020 7324 1880)

WHITAKER, Baroness (Life Peer UK 1999), of Beeston in the County of Nottinghamshire; Janet Alison Whitaker; da of Alan Harrison Stewart, and Ella, *née* Saunders; *Educ* Nottingham HS for Girls, Girton Coll Cambridge (major scholar, BA), Bryn Mawr Coll (Farley grad fell, MA), Harvard Univ (Radcliffe fell); *Career* commissioning ed André Deutsch Ltd 1961–66, speechwriter to chm Health and Safety Cmmn 1976, head of gas safety HSE 1983–86, head of nuclear safety admin HSE 1986–88, head of health and safety Dept of Employment 1988–92, head of sex equality 1992–96, memb Employment Tbnls 1995–2000, conslt CRE and Cwlth Secretariat 1996–99, memb Immigration Complaints Audit Ctee 1998–99; vice-chair All-Pty Gp on Gypsies, Roma and Travellers, vice-chair All Pty Gp on Race and Communities, vice-chair Assoc Parly Gp on Design and Innovation; memb: EU Select Ctee Sub-Ctee on Educn, Social Affrs and Home Affrs 1999–2003, Jt Ctee on Human Rights 2000–03, Jt Parly Ctee on the Draft Corruption Bill 2003, Friends Provident Ctee of Reference 2000–08, Jt Parly Ctee on Draft Bribery Bill 2009; chair Camden Racial Equality Cncl 1999, chair Working Men's Coll 1998–2001 (fell 2010–), dep chair Ind Television Cmmn 2001–03, chair Dept For Educn Stakeholder Gp on gypsy, traveller and Roma educn 2013–, pres Advsy Cncl on educn of Roma and other travellers 2014–; memb: Advsy Cncl Transparency Int (UK) 2001–09, Cncl ODI 2003–07, Advsy Panel UNA-UK, Bd Br Inst of Human Rights, Design Cmmn; tstee UNICEF UK 2003–09; patron: Runnymede Tst, Br Stammering Assoc, Student Partnerships Worldwide; pres South Downs Soc 2012–16, pres Newhaven Historical Soc 2016–; patron Br Humanists Assoc; non-exec dir Tavistock and Portman NHS Tst 1997–2001; FRIBA 2013; *Recreations* travel, hill walking, music, art, theatre; *Clubs* Reform; *Style*— The Lady Whitaker; ✉ House of Lords, London SW1A 0PW

W

WHITAKER, Justine Claire; *née* Barrett; da of David Brian Barrett, of Sutton-in-Craven, N Yorks, and Mary, *née* Greenwood; *b* 11 May 1970, Keighley, N Yorks; *Educ* South Craven Sch N Yorks, Craven Coll Skipton (Student of the Year 1988, Dip), St James's Univ Hosp Leeds, Univ of Manchester (Dip), Univ of Bradford (MSc); *m* 14 Oct 2000, Richard Lawrence Kidd Whitaker; 1 s (William Alexander Kidd b 18 Jan 2003), 1 da (Charlotte Alice b 19 Jan 2006); *Career* St James's Univ Hosp Leeds: staff nurse 1992–95, research nurse 1995–96, lyphoedema nurse 1996–98, Macmillan lymphoedema clinical nurse specialist 1998–2001; Macmillan lymphoedema clinical nurse specialist East Lancs Hosp NHS Tst 2001–07, ind nurse and owner Northern Lymphology 2007–; sr lectr Dept of Nursing Univ of Central Lancs 2007–; memb Cncl Macmillan Cancer Relief; memb: RCN 1989, Nursing and Midwifery Cncl 1992; *Awards* Nurse of The Year 2007, Innovations in Cancer Nursing 2007, Nursing Standard Gold Award Assoc of Colls; Vascular Nursing – Lymphoedema; numerous articles in nursing jls; *Recreations* mountain biking, sailing, garden, indulging in my children and husband; *Style—* Mrs Justine Whitaker; ✉ Northern Lymphology-Forest of Bowland Treatment Centre, Dunnow Hall, Slaidburn, N Clitheroe, Lancashire BB7 3AD (☎ 01200 446471, e-mail justine@northernlymphology.com, website www.northernlymphology.com); Nursing Department, University of Central Lancashire, Preston Lancashire PR1 2HE (☎ 01772 893628, e-mail jcwhitaker@uclan.ac.uk)

WHITAKER, Patrick James; s of John Henry Foord Whitaker, of The Garden House, Dunorlan Farm, Tunbridge Wells, Kent, and Anne Jennifer, *née* Cheveley; *b* 9 April 1965; *Educ* Garth Hill Comp, Berkshire Coll of Art & Design (RSA art bursary, BTEC), St Martin's Sch of Art (BA); *Career* fndr designer Whitaker Malem (with Keir Malem, *qv*) 1988– (annual collections of hand crafted leatherwear for specialist int retail); launched new line of male and female leather torsos (with Adel Roostein) 1995; appearances on TV and subject of press profiles in quality fashion magazines, fashion lectr at various colleges of art and design incl visiting lectr RCA 1999–2000; memb Br Cncl and Br Embassy mission to promote Br fashion, lecture and set Acad project Vilnius Lithuania; cmmns for: Givenchy Haute Couture 1997, Valentino Haute Couture 1997, Tommy Hilfiger Red Label 1998, Tommy Hilfiger 1999–2000, Hussein Chalayan collection 2009, Giles Deacon collection 2010, Allen Jones (outfit for Kate Moss Project) 2012; special assignments incl: body sculptures for re-opening of Bauhaus Dessau, outfit for Naomi Campbell in Vauxhall advertising campaign 1993, collaboration with sculptor Allen Jones 1999–, piece for permanent collection Museum of Leather Craft Northampton 2000, collection for Alma Home launch 2000, R&D for Gucci collection 2000, cmmn by Allen Jones for new sculpture Waiting on Table (exhibited Royal Acad Summer Exhibition); private cmmns for: Mick Jagger, Cher, Pamela Anderson, Gloria Estefan, Janet Jackson, Jerry Hall, Bono, George Michael, Madonna, Jon Bon Jovi, Spice Girls, Steven Tyler, Allen Jones (major sculpture cmmn 2008); film cmmns incl: Mortal Kombat 1995, The Changeling 1995, Die Another Day 2002, Tomb Raider 2 2003, Troy 2004, Aeon Flux 2005, Harry Potter and the Goblet of Fire 2005, Eragon 2006, Casino Royale 2006, Harry Potter and the Order of the Phoenix 2007, Batman: The Dark Knight 2008, Speed Racer 2008, Robin Hood 2010, Clash of the Titans 2010, Captain America: The First Avenger 2011, Jack the Giant Killer 2012, Cloud Atlas 2012 (asst designer), 300: Rise of an Empire 2014, Jupiter ascending 2015 (costume fx designer), Avengers: Age of Ultron 2015, Pan 2015, Wonder Woman 2017 (creative supervisor for costume armour); exhibitions: Unlaced Grace (Banbury Museum and nat tour) 1994–95, Inside Out (Design Museum London) 2000, Personal Space Br Cncl Show (and commn, NY, Milan, London) 2000, Art 2001 (with Jibby Beane, exhibited Chair sculpture) 2001, Tokyo Designers Week (Br Cncl exhibit Living Britain) 2001, Designing 007: Fifty Years of Bond Style (Barbican) 2012; new studio/residence Garden House (with Heyhurst & Co Architects, nominated RIBA Channel 4 Grand Designs House Of The Year 2016); finalist Smirnoff Fashion Awards 1985, nominated British Fashion Awards 1992; *Recreations* film collection; *Style—* Patrick Whitaker, Esq; ✉ Whitaker Malem, The Garden Studio, 27 Buckingham Road, London N14 DG (☎ and fax 020 7923 7887, website www.whitakermalem.co.uk)

WHITAKER, Steven Dixon; s of late George Dixon Whitaker, and late Elsie Whitaker; *b* 28 January 1950; *Educ* Burnley GS, Churchill Coll Cambridge (MA); *m* Tereska Anita Christiana; 1 s (Alexander Steven George), 1 da (Emma Louise); *Career* called to the Bar Middle Temple 1973 (bencher 2010–14, currently memb); Master of the Supreme Court (Queen's Bench Div) 2002–07, Sr Master of the Sr Courts (Queen's Bench Div) and Queen's Remembrancer 2007–14; memb Civil Procedure Rules Ctee 2002–08; gen ed White Book 2007–14, chief advsy ed Atkin's Court Forms 2008–14; Freeman City of London 2007; *Recreations* horses, music, poetry, the arts; *Style—* Steven Whitaker, Esq; ✉ e-mail whitakersd@gmail.com

WHITBOURN, Dr Philip Robin; OBE (1993); s of Edwin Arthur Whitbourn (d 1953), of Sevenoaks, Kent, and Kathleen, *née* Sykes; *b* 10 March 1932; *Educ* Sevenoaks Sch, UCL (PhD); *m* 10 Jan 1959, Anne Pearce, da of Peter Melrose Marks (d 1938), of Glasgow; 1 da (Katherine b 1960), 1 s (James b 1963); *Career* architect; Sir Edwin Cooper RA and Partners 1955–58, Stewart Hendry and Smith 1958–60, Fitzroy Robinson Partnership 1960–66, Historic Bldgs Div GLC 1966–86; English Heritage: joined 1986, divnl architect London Region 1988–92, dir South Region 1992–94, chief architect Conservation Gp 1992–95; sec ICOMOS UK (Int Cncl on Monuments and Sites) 1995–2002; sec to Tstees INTACH (UK) Tst (Indian Nat Tst for Art and Cultural Heritage) 1995–2002; pres Royal Tunbridge Wells Civic Soc 1995–2005 (chm 1969–70, 1972–73, 1978–80 and 1990–91), memb Southwark Diocesan Advsy Ctee for the Care of Churches 1973–97, vice-pres Kent Fedn of Amenity Socs 2009–; FRIBA 1968, FSA 1984; *Clubs* Tunbridge Wells Cricket (vice-pres); *Style—* Dr Philip Whitbourn, OBE, FSA; ✉ Rosaville Lodge, 40 Beulah Road, Tunbridge Wells, Kent TN1 2NR (☎ 01892 523026)

WHITBURN, Vanessa Victoria; OBE (2014); da of Victor Donald Whitburn (d 1988), and Eileen, *née* Wellington (d 2004); *Educ* Mount St Mary's Convent Sch Exeter, Exeter Coll of FE, Univ of Hull (BA); *Career* BBC: studio mangr Broadcasting House and Bush House London 1974–76, asst floor mangr TV Drama Television Centre 1976–77 (work incl The Onedin Line), prodr Radio Drama Pebble Mill 1977–83 (work incl The Archers) sr prodr Radio Drama Pebble Mill 1983–88 (prodr/dir numerous plays and classic serials for Radio 3 and 4); prodr Brookside (Mersey Television for Channel Four) 1988–90, rejoined BBC as prodr/dir BBC TV Pebble Mill 1990–91, ed The Archers (BBC Radio 4) 1991–2013 (numerous awards incl Sony Award, Royal Variety Club Silver Heart, 2 Mind Mental Health Media Awards and 3 Television and Radio Industries Club Awards), exec prodr of radio drama BBC Midlands 1995–2013, ed Ambridge Extra 2011–13; freelance drama prodr/dir, conslt Radio Drama and Trg; fndr memb Mgmnt Bd Theatre Foundry 1985; memb Radio Acad; has also directed stage, radio and TV drama prodns for various groups incl Derby Playhouse and WGBH Boston; conslt for ODA on Ndiga Nacio (Kenyan radio soap opera), for SABC (S Africa) and for Midwest Radio Theater Workshop Missouri USA, memb Advsy Bd Nat Audio Theatre Festivals USA; hon doctorate Univ of Hull; *Books* The Archers – The Official Inside Story (1996); *Style—* Ms Vanessa Whitburn, OBE

WHITBY, Mark; s of George Whitby, MBE, FRIBA (d 1972), of London, and Rhona Carmian, *née* Butler; *b* 29 January 1950; *Educ* Ealing GS for Boys, King's Coll London (BSc); 1 s by prev partnership (Alex b 25 Sept 1982); m 19 Jan 1991, Janet, *née* Taylor; 2 da (Harriet b 29 Feb 1992, Katherine b 28 Oct 1996), 2 s (Ralph b 24 May 1993, Chad b 19 Jan 1999); *Career* fndr and dir Whitbybird 1983–2009, dir Davies Maguire & Whitby 2009–, chm WME 2011–; engrg projects throughout Europe incl: British Embassy Berlin, British Embassy Dublin, York Millennium Bridge, Peterborough Millennium Bridge, Lancaster Millennium Bridge, Igus Factory Cologne, Olivetti Research Centre Bari, Stock Exchange Berlin, Merchants Bridge Manchester (ISE Special Award, Millennium Design Product 1998) Mappa Mundi Museum Hereford, King's Fund HQ London, Sadlers Wells Theatre London, PGI Cummins Factory Kent, The National Rowing Museum Henley-on-Thames, 40 Grosvenor Place, Heathrow Terminal 2 and 3, new Docklands campus for Univ of East London; govr Building Centre Tst 1997–; chm Urban Design Alliance 2001–02; chm SEEDA Sustainability and Urban Renaissance Sector Gp 2002–04, memb Energy Foresight Panel 2003–04, dir Ownpower Ltd; FICE 1992 (pres 2001–02), FREng 1996, Hon FRIBA 1999; *Media* Secrets of Lost Empires (1996 and 1999), The Wobbly Bridge – A Tale of Over-Arching Ambition (2001); *Recreations* children, 20th Century engineering history, canoeing (memb Br Canoeing Team 1968 Olympics); *Style—* Mark Whitby, Esq, FREng, FICE, Hon FRIBA; ✉ Keys Heath, Cambridge Road, Hitchin, Hertfordshire SG4 0JU

WHITE, Alan; *b* 14 April 1955, Salford; *Educ* Salford GS, Univ of Warwick (LLB); *m* Gillian; 4 c; *Career* Audit Dept Arthur Andersen 1976–79, gen mangr finance Sharp Electronics 1979–85, gp finance dir N Brown Gp plc 1985–99, gp finance dir Littlewoods plc 1999–2002, chief exec N Brown Gp plc 2002–; *Recreations* tennis, squash, skiing, season ticket holder at Manchester United; *Style—* Mr A White; ✉ N Brown Group plc, Griffin House, 40 Lever Street, Manchester M60 6ES (☎ 0161 236 8256, 0161 238 2662)

WHITE, Andrew; QC (1997); s of Peter White, of Dorset, and Sandra Jeanette, *née* Lovelace (d 1988); *b* 25 January 1958; *Educ* UC Cardiff (LLB); *m* 1987, Elizabeth Denise, da of Thomas Rooney; 2 s (Harry George b 1988, Alexander Thomas b 1991); *Career* called to the Bar Lincoln's Inn 1980 (Hardwick scholar 1977, Megarry scholar 1979), bencher 2003; in practice 1981–, head of chambers 2011–; Liveryman Bakers' Co 2015–; *Publications* The Encyclopaedia of Forms and Precedents (contrib Building and Engineering, 5 edn); *Recreations* farming, sailing, music; *Style—* Andrew White, QC; ✉ 1 Atkin Building, Gray's Inn, London WC1R 5AT (☎ 020 7404 0102, fax 020 7405 7456)

WHITE, Air Vice Marshal Andrew David (Andy); CB; s of Edward Jethro White, and Margaret Campbell, *née* Lockhart; *b* 2 January 1952; *Educ* Wallington GS, Loughborough Univ, RAF Coll Cranwell, JSDC; *m* 11 Oct 1975, Christine Ann, da of Douglas Spratt; 2 s (Robert James b 2 April 1980, Stuart Richard b 9 March 1982); *Career* cmmnd RAF 1970; pilot 17 Sqdn RAF Brüggen, Tactical Weapons Unit RAF Brawdy and RAF Chivenor 1980–82, weapons instr 20 Sqdn RAF Brüggen 1982–84, Flight Cdr 14 Sqdn 1984–85, staff offr Attack/Ops Branch HQAAFCE 1985–88, staff offr to Dir of PR (RAF) MOD 1988–90, OC XV Sqdn RAF Laarbruch 1991–92, OC IX Sqdn RAF Brüggen 1992–94, personal staff offr to Chief of Air Staff MOD 1994–96, Station Cdr RAF Cottesmore 1996–99, OC Tri-National Tornado Trg Estab 1996–99, AO Plans/ HQ Strike Cmd 1999–2002, COS Ops HQ Strike Cmd 2002–03, AOC No 3 Gp 2003–06; ceo Nat Security Inspectorate 2006–10; non-exec dir Nat Air Traffic Servs 2006–13; chm of govrs Cottesmore Co Primary Sch 1996–99; GSM (Clasp) Iraq; *Recreations* golf, DIY, skiing, IT; *Clubs* RAF; *Style—* Air Vice Marshal Andrew White, CB

WHITE, Bruce Balfour; s of Robert White (d 1985), and Anne Elizabeth, *née* Balfour; *b* 12 October 1961, Perth, Scotland; *Educ* Univ of Dundee (LLB); *m* 1 Oct 1988, Alice, *née* Grant; 1 da (Rosie b 12 Nov 1990), 2 s (Toby b 1 June 1992, Angus b 23 Sept 1994); *Career* trainee slr Dorman Jeffrey & Co 1984–86; Linklater & Paines (now Linklaters): asst slr 1986–95, ptnr 1995–, head global projects 2005–; memb PPP Forum; memb Law Soc; *Recreations* reading, rugby, cricket, skiing; *Style—* Bruce White, Esq; ✉ Linklaters, 1 Silk Street, London EC2Y 8HQ (☎ 020 7456 2000, fax 020 7456 2222, e-mail bruce.white@linklaters.com)

WHITE, Prof Sir Christopher John; kt (2001), CVO (1995); s of Gabriel Edward Ernest Francis White, CBE (d 1988), of London, and Elizabeth Grace, *née* Ardizzone (d 1958); *b* 19 September 1930; *Educ* Downside, Courtauld Inst of Art, Univ of London (BA, PhD), Univ of Oxford (MA); *m* 14 Dec 1957, Rosemary Katharine Alice, da of Gordon Paul Desages (d 1960), of London; 2 da (Arabella Elizabeth b 1959, Clarissa Grace b 1961), 1 s (Sebastian Gabriel b 1965); *Career* asst keeper Dept of Prints and Drawings British Museum 1954–65, dir Messrs P and D Colnaghi London 1965–71, curator of graphic arts Nat Gallery of Art Washington DC 1971–73, dir of studies Paul Mellon Centre for Studies in British Art London 1973–85, assoc dir Yale Center for British Art New Haven CT 1973–85, dir Ashmolean Museum 1985–97; visiting curator Courtauld Gallery 2011; fell Worcester Coll Oxford 1985–97, prof of the arts of the Netherlands Univ of Oxford 1992–97; dir Burlington Magazine 1981–; tstee: V&A 1997–2004, Michael Marks Charitable Tst 1997–, Mauritshuis The Hague 1999–2008; memb Ctee of Tstees Nat Art Collections Fund 1998–2005; FBA 1989; *Books* Rembrandt and His World (1964), The Flower Drawings of Jan van Huysum (1965), Rubens and His World (1968), Rembrandt as an Etcher (1969, 2 edn 1999), Rembrandt's Etchings: A Catalogue Raisonné (jtly, 1970), Dürer: The Artist and his Drawings (1972), English Landscape 1630–1850 (1977), Dutch Pictures in the Collection of HM The Queen (1982, 2 edn 2015), Rembrandt in Eighteenth-century England (ed, 1983), Rembrandt (1984), Peter Paul Rubens: Man and Artist (1987), Drawing in England from Hilliard to Hogarth (jtly, 1987), Old Master Drawings from the Ashmolean Museum (jtly, 1992), The Dutch and Flemish Drawings at Windsor Castle (jtly, 1994), Anthony van Dyck: Thomas Howard, The Earl of Arundel (1995), Dutch, Flemish and German Paintings in the Ashmolean Museum (1999), The later Flemish Pictures in the Collection of HM The Queen (2007), Dutch and Flemish Drawings in the Victoria & Albert Museum (jtly, 2014); *Recreations* music, travel; *Style—* Prof Sir Christopher White, CVO, FBA; ✉ 34 Kelly Street, London NW1 8PH (☎ 020 7485 9148); Shingle House, St Cross, Harleston, Norfolk IP20 0NT (☎ 01986 782264)

WHITE, David Vines; s of Peter Vines White (d 1999), and Sheila, *née* Chatterton (d 2010); *b* 27 October 1961, Glasgow; *Educ* Kelvinside Acad, Marlborough, Pembroke Coll Cambridge (MA), Courtauld Inst of Art (MA); *Career* research asst Coll of Arms 1988–95, Rouge Croix Pursuivant 1995–2004, Somerset Herald 2004–; chm Heraldry Soc 2006–09 (memb Cncl 2000–), memb Cncl Br Record Soc 1998–, hon vice-pres Cambridge Univ Heraldic and Genealogical Soc 2002–, tstee Marc Fitch Fund 2008–, hon genealogist Royal Victorian Order 2010–; *Clubs* Travellers; *Style—* David White, Esq; ✉ College of Arms, Queen Victoria Street, London EC4V 4BT (☎ and fax 020 7248 1766, e-mail somerset@college-of-arms.gov.uk)

WHITE, Rt Rev Frank; s of John Edward White (d 1996), and Mary Ellen, *née* Nicholls (d 1989); *Educ* St Cuthbert's GS Newcastle upon Tyne, Consett Tech Coll, Univ of Wales Inst of Science and Technol (BScEcon), Univ of Wales Cardiff (Dip Social Science), Univ of Nottingham (DipTheol), St John's Coll Nottingham (Dip Pastoral Studies); *m* 1982, Alison Mary, da of Prof Keith Rodney Dumbell; *Career* dir Youth Action York 1971–73, detached youth worker Manchester Catacombs Tst 1973–77, asst curate St Nicholas' Durham 1980–84, sr curate St Mary and St Cuthbert Chester-le-Street 1984–87, full time hosp chaplain Durham HA 1987–89, vicar St John the Evangelist Birtley 1989–97, rural dean Chester-le-Street 1993–97, archdeacon of Sunderland 1997–2002, bishop of Brixworth 2002–10, asst bishop of Newcastle 2010–; hon canon Durham Cathedral 1997–2002, hon canon Peterborough Cathedral 2002–10, hon canon St Nicholas Cathedral Newcastle 2010–; proctor in convocation Gen Synod C of E 1987–2000; *Recreations* birdwatching, walking, motor cars, theatre, football, history and local studies; *Style—* The Rt Rev Frank White; ✉ The Bishop's Office, 29 Moor Road South,

Newcastle-upon-Tyne NE3 1PA (✆ 0191 285 2220, e-mail bishopfrank@newcastle.anglican.org)

WHITE, Hon Alderman Dr Frank Richard; JP (1968); s of Arthur Leslie White (d 1944), and Edna Phylis Jackson, *née* Meade (d 1976); *b* 11 November 1939, Eccles, Lancs; *Educ* Bolton Tech Coll; *m* 28 Jan 1967, Eileen, da of Frank Crook of Bolton; 2 s (John Richard Alexander b 1 Sept 1968, Christopher Niel b 10 July 1973), 1 da (Elizabeth Caroline b 30 July 1970); *Career* MP (Lab) Bury and Radcliffe 1974–83, parly sec Dept of Industry 1975–76, govt whip 1976–79, oppn spokesman church affrs 1979–83; chm: NW Lab MPs 1979–83, All-Pty Paper Industry Gp 1979–83; memb Select Ctee Employment 1979–83 (presented Home Workers Bill), oppn whip 1980–82, dir trg GMB Trade Union 1988–2000; dir: N Manchester Business Link, Bolton Literacy Tst; chair Community Legal Partnership; mayor of Bolton 2005–06; memb: Bolton Town Cncl 1963–74, 1986–90 and 1994–2012, Gtr Manchester CC 1973–75, Gtr Manchester Police Authy 1997–2003, Bolton Cabinet Cncl for Social Inclusion and Community Safety 2001–08; dir Lancs Cooperative Devpt Assoc Ltd 1984–, area dir United Natwest Co-op 1993–2002; chm Bolton Magistrates' Bench 1992–95, chair Bolton Age UK 2009–13, chair Bolton Community Radio 96.5FM 2004–12; vice-pres East Lancs Railway Preservation Soc 1983–2005; pres Bolton United Servs Veterans' Assoc 1988–2012; memb: IMS 1966, IPM 1971; Hon Alderman; hon fell Bolton Univ 1993; hon degree Bolton Univ 2010; *Recreations* history, walking, caravanning, Richard III supporter; *Clubs* Tonge Cricket, Tonge Lab (life memb 2013); *Style*— Hon Alderman Dr Frank R White, JP; ✉ 23 Dovedale Road, Breightmet, Bolton, Lancashire BL2 5HT (✆ 01204 527888, e-mail frankwhite39@virginmedia.com)

WHITE, Geoffrey; s of John Trevor White, and Henrietta Sheena White; *b* 5 January 1961, Glasgow; *Educ* Merchiston Castle Sch, Univ of Stirling; *m* Dana Catherine White; 2 da (Matilde Alice, Isobella Henrietta); *Career* previous sr mgmnt roles with: Thomas Tilling plc, BTR plc, Dee Corporation plc, Asda plc; dir and ceo Lonrho plc 2007–14, dir and ceo Fastjet plc (formerly Rubicon plc) 2012–14, dir Fidelity Bank 2013–, ceo Agility 2014–; *Clubs* 5 Hertford, Lansdowne; *Style*— Geoffrey White, Esq; ✉ 29 Garrick House, Carrington Street, London W1J 7AF

WHITE, Sir George Stanley James; 4 Bt (UK 1904), of Cotham House, Bristol; s of Sir George Stanley Midelton White, 3 Bt (d 1983, md Bristol Aeroplane Co, and ggs of Sir George White, 1 Bt, pioneer of Electric Street Traction, fndr first English aeroplane factory and responsible for introduction of Bristol Biplanes and Monoplanes), and Diane, Lady White; *b* 4 November 1948; *Educ* Harrow; *m* 1 (m dis 1979); 1 da (Caroline Morwenna); m 2, (m dis); 1 s ((George) Philip James), 1 da (Kate Elizabeth); m 3, Joanna, da of Kazimierz Stanley Migdal; *Heir* s, Philip White; *Career* conslt horologist; pres: Gloucestershire Soc 1993, Br Horological Inst 2001–02; chm: Bristol and Glos Archaeological Soc 1992–95, Advsy Bd Bristol Cars Ltd 2011–15; memb: Glos Diocesan Advsy Ctee for Faculties and the Care of Churches 1985– (clocks advsr to the Dio 1986–), Cncl Nat Tst 1998–2004, Advsy Bd Frazer-Nash Research Ltd 2012; parish clerk St Mary the Virgin Aldermanbury 2009–; High Sheriff Avon 1989, JP 1991–95; Master Worshipful Co of Clockmakers 2001 (Keeper of the Collection 1988–), Brother Worshipful Co of Parish Clerks 2009; FSA; *Books* English Lantern Clocks (1989), Tramlines to the Stars (1995), The Clockmakers of London (1999), Sundials: the Recent Work of Joanna Migdal (2009), Commissioning a Sundial (2010); *Publications* for aeronautical resumé www.bristolcars.co.uk; *Style*— Sir George White, Bt, FSA

WHITE, Graham Peter; *b* 28 May 1955, London; *Educ* Haberdashers' Aske's, St Catherine's Coll Oxford (MA); *Career* admitted slr 1978; Slaughter and May: ptnr 1987–2008, head of commercial real estate 1997–2008, latterly exec ptnr; *Style*— Graham White, Esq

WHITE, Prof Ian Hugh; s of Oliver Morrow White (d 1997), and Emily Greenaway, *née* Lowry; *b* 6 October 1959; *Educ* Belfast Royal Acad, Jesus Coll Cambridge (MA, PhD); *m* 13 Aug 1983, Margaret Rosemary, *née* Hunt; 1 da (Emma Rosemary b 17 May 1990), 1 s (James Robert Samuel b 4 Dec 1992); *Career* fell Jesus Coll Cambridge 1984–90 (research fell 1983–84), asst lectr Engrg Dept Univ of Cambridge 1984–90, prof of physics Univ of Bath 1990–96, prof of optical communication systems Univ of Bristol (head Dept of Electrical and Electronic Engrg 1998–2001), Van Eck prof of engrg Univ of Cambridge 2001–, master Jesus Coll Cambridge 2011–; Leverhulme research fell Royal Soc 1995–96; author of numerous contribs on semiconductor optoelectronic compartments, optical communications and photonics; FIEE 1994, CEng 1994, FREng 2006, FIEEE 2005; *Recreations* church, music; *Style*— Prof Ian White; ✉ Jesus College, Cambridge CB5 8BL (✆ 01223 339440, fax 01223 339304, e-mail ihw3@cam.ac.uk)

WHITE, Ian Shaw; s of Frank White (d 2008), and Joan, *née* Shaw, of May Hill, Glos; *b* 30 July 1952, Caerleon; *Educ* Bromsgrove, Churchill Coll Cambridge (MA); *m* 1, 18 Oct 1980, Susan Elizabeth (d 1989), da of Capt Alan Francis Bacon, of Purley, Surrey; 2 s (Duncan b 1985, Gordon b 1988); m 2, 28 March 1992, Barbara Jolanda, da of Maj Wladyslaw Arzymanow (d 1968); 2 s (Howard b 1994, Bernard b 1996); *Career* ptnr W Greenwell and Co 1984–86; dir: Greenwell Montagu 1986–88 (head of res 1987–88), Kleinwort Benson Securities 1988–93, Robert Fleming Securities 1993–97, TT International 1997–98, True Research Limited 1999–; chartered FCSI; *Recreations* travel, philosophy, family, politics; *Style*— Ian White, Esq; ✉ 22 Blomfield Road, Little Venice, London W9 1AD (✆ 020 7286 4360); True Research Limited, 4th Floor, 33 Cavendish Square, London W1G 0PW (✆ 07813 656749, fax 020 7691 9726, e-mail ian@trueresearch.co.uk)

WHITE, Advocate Jonathan; *Career* conslt Ogier; dir Jersey Finance Ltd; chm Durrell Wildlife Conservation Tst; memb: Law Soc of England and Wales 1981, Jersey Law Soc 1986, STEP; *Style*— Jonathan White, Esq; ✉ Ogier, Ogier House, The Esplanade, St Helier, Jersey JE4 9WG (✆ 01534 504472, e-mail jonathan.white@ogier.com)

WHITE, Mark Jonathan; *b* 10 June 1960, London; *Educ* Univ of Wolverhampton (BA), Coll of Law, KCL (LLM); *Career* admitted slr 1985; slr Eversheds 1985–93, gp co sec and slr Rotork plc 1993–99, co sec Enterprise Oil plc 2001–02 (dep co sec 1999–2001), gp co sec and counsel Wolseley plc 2002–07, gen counsel and co sec Compass Gp plc 2007–; fee-paid memb Upper Tbnl (Tax and Chancery Chamber); memb Law Soc; *Style*— Mark J White, Esq; ✉ Compass Group plc, Compass House, Guildford Street, Chertsey, Surrey KT16 9BQ (✆ 01932 573000, fax 01932 569956, e-mail mark.white@compass-group.co.uk)

WHITE, Michael; s of Albert Ernest White (d 1979), and Doris Mary, *née* Harvey; *b* 4 April 1955; *Educ* Langdon Sch, Univ of Oxford (MA), Inns of Court Sch of Law; *Career* called to the Bar Middle Temple (Harmsworth scholar); chief music critic Independent on Sunday, broadcaster and librettist, columnist Daily Telegraph, music critic New York Times; presenter: Best of 3 (BBC Radio 3), Opera in Action (BBC Radio 3), The Sound Barrier (BBC Radio 4); *Opera Librettos* The Adjudicator, Touristen Dachau; *Books* Wagner for Beginners, Collins Guide to Opera and Operetta, Introducing Wagner; *Recreations* travel, composition, other people's dogs; *Style*— Michael White, Esq; ✉ 16 Willow Road, Hampstead, London NW3 1TJ (e-mail mjwcritic@gmail.com)

WHITE, Michael Charles; s of Henry Wallis White (d 1967), of St Just, Cornwall, and Kay, *née* Wood (d 1957); *b* 21 October 1945; *Educ* Bodmin GS, UCL (BA); *m* 2 Feb 1973, Patricia Vivienne, da of (Harold) Lawrence Gaudin; 3 s (Samuel Wallis b 21 Sept 1974, Joseph Lawrence b 11 Aug 1976, Henry John b 7 Dec 1978); *Career* reporter: Reading Evening Post 1966–70, London Evening Standard 1970–71; The Guardian: sub ed, feature writer and diarist 1971–76, parly sketchwriter 1977–84, Washington corr 1984–88, assoc ed 1989–, political ed 1990–2006, asst ed (politics) 2006–; columnist Health Service Jl 1977–84 and 1992–; memb NUJ 1966–; Granada TV Sketchwriter of the Year 1982, House Magazine Political Writer Award 2003; fell UCL 2002; *Clubs* Garrick; *Style*— Michael White, Esq; ✉ The Guardian, Kings Place, 90 York Way, London N1 9GU (✆ 020 3353 2000, e-mail michael.white@guardian.co.uk)

WHITE, Peter; *b* June 1947, Winchester; *m* Jo; 2 da (Fiona (fostered), Cathy), 2 s (Tony, Robin); *Career* broadcaster; first totally blind person to produce reports for TV news; Sony Speech Broadcaster of the Year 2001 *Television* ed and presenter Same Difference (3 series, Channel 4) 1987–89, presenter and prodr Link (magazine prog on disability, Central TV) 1989–91, People First (three documentaries on disability, Channel 4) 1992 and 1993, presenter Facing South (bi-media phone-in strand, BBC South and BBC Local Radio) 1992–95 *Radio* BBC Radio Solent: gen reporter and presenter of progs on disability 1971–83, presenter morning current affairs and phone-in prog 1983–87 and 1992–95, presenter Saturday morning show 1989–; BBC Radio 4: author autobiographical talks series 1987–96, presenter and interviewer No Triumph, No Tragedy 1993, 1994, 1999, 2000, 2001 and 2003, Barking or Biting? (on the Disability Rights Cmmn) 2001, From Rags to Rights (history of disability in the UK) 2000, reg presenter In Touch 1979– (occasional presenter since 1974–79); deviser and presenter It's Your Round (BBC) 1993–94; disability affairs corr BBC 1995–; reg broadcaster on disability issues, progs incl: Today, The World at One, PM, The World Tonight, Newsbeat, Hayes Over Britain, 5 Live; presenter: You and Yours, Call You and Yours, Pick of the Week; reporter: Woman's Hour, Paralympics Atlanta 1996, Paralympics Sydney 2000; *Books* Issues (series for schs, 1989), See It My Way (autobiography, 1999); *Recreations* soccer, cricket; *Style*— Peter White, Esq; ✉ Broadcasting House, London W1A 1AA

WHITE, Peter Roland; s of Norman Leonard White (d 1993), and Gene Elwin, *née* McGrah (d 2012); *b* 9 July 1945, Birmingham; *Educ* Bournville Boys' Tech Sch, Univ of Birmingham (BDS); *m* 1, 23 March 1968 (m dis 1980), Elizabeth Susan, da of Thomas Colin Graty, of Leigh Sinton Worcs; 2 s (Gordon Michael White b 6 Aug 1970, Adam Edward White b 12 Jan 1973), 1 da (Frances Elizabeth Graty b 8 Nov 1968); m 2, 20 Dec 1980 (m dis 1997), Elisabeth Anne, da of Rev Fred Haworth; *Career* conslt oral surgn; Dudley Rd Hosp Birmingham 1968, Birmingham Dental Hosp 1969–70, Wordsley Hosp Stourbridge 1970–71, Univ of Manchester Dental Sch 1971–73, St Luke's Hosp Bradford 1973–74, Liverpool Dental Hosp and Broadgreen Hosp 1974–77; conslt oral surgn Pennine Healthcare Tst (formerly NW Regnl Health Authy then Manchester Area Health Authy then North Manchester Healthcare Tst) 1977–2006, clinical dir Rochdale Healthcare Tst 1992–93, dep med dir Rochdale Healthcare Tst 1994–2000; pres Nat Hosps Gp BDA 2002–03; postgrad tutor Rochdale and Oldham 1989–94 (Rochdale 1980–87); memb numerous NHS local ctees; publications in learned jls; life memb BDA 2005 (pres E Lancs E Cheshire Branch 1995); FDSRCS (Eng) 1971, FBAOMS 1977–2007 (memb 1971–77), memb Manchester Med Soc 1979–2007 (pres Odontological Section 1990); *Recreations* music, genealogy, bridge, walking; *Style*— Peter R White, Esq

WHITE, (Alan) Robert; s of Peter Derek White (d 2000), and Margaret, *née* Macmillan (d 2011); *b* 15 July 1965, Camblesforth, N Yorks; *Educ* Univ of Southampton (BSc); *Career* trainee Cosworth Engrg 1987–88; Cosworth Racing: devpt engr Indy engines 1988–97, chief engr Formula 1 engines 1997–2003; Renault F1 team (engines): tech dir 2004–05, dep md (tech) 2005–; *Style*— Robert White, Esq; ✉ Renault Sport F1, 1–15 Avenue President Kennedy, 91170 Viry-Chatillon, France (✆ 00 33 670 03 44 40, e-mail rob.white@renaultsportf1.com)

WHITE, Prof Robert J; s of Dennis H White, of Witney, Oxon, and Betty M, *née* Bird (d 1997); *b* 14 August 1963, Harrow, Middx; *Educ* John Lyon Sch Harrow, The Queen's Coll Oxford (scholar, BA), Nat Inst for Medical Research London (PhD); *Children* 1 s (Oliver b 7 Dec 1990), 1 da (Miranda b 27 Sept 1994); *Career* postdoctoral positions Univ of Cambridge 1990–95; Univ of Glasgow: lectr in biochemistry and molecular biology 1995–99, Jenner research fell Lister Inst of Preventive Medicine 1996–2001 (memb 2001–), prof of gene transcription 1999–; memb Editorial Bd BMC Molecular Biology 2004–, author of more than 50 pubns in learned jls; memb: Educn and Trg Ctee Fedn of Cancer Socs 2004–, Molecules, Genes and Cells Funding Ctee Wellcome Tst 2004–; memb: British Assoc for Cancer Research 1999–, European Assoc for Cancer Research (memb Exec Ctee 2003–); Young Scientist Award British Assoc for Cancer Research 1999, Merit Award Int Jl of Oncology 1999, Young Cancer Researcher Award European Assoc for Cancer Research 2003, Tenovus Medal 2004; FRSE 2004, FMedSci 2005; *Books* RNA Polymerase III Transcription (1998), Gene Transcription: Mechanisms and Control (2000); *Recreations* running; *Style*— Prof Robert White; ✉ Department of Biology, University of York, Heslington, York YO10 5DD

WHITE, Prof Robert Stephen; s of James Henry White, of Uley, Glos, and Ethel Gladys, *née* Cornick; *b* 12 December 1952; *Educ* Market Harborough Comp, West Bridgford Comp, Emmanuel Coll Cambridge (senior scholar, MA, bachelor scholar, PhD); *m* Helen Elizabeth, da of Dennis J Pearce; 1 s (Mark James b 1979), 1 da (Sarah Rosemary b 1981); *Career* guest investigator Woods Hole Oceanographic Instn USA 1977, 1988 and 1990, research asst Dept of Geodesy and Geophysics Univ of Cambridge 1978, postdoctoral scholar Woods Hole Oceanographic Instn USA 1978–79; Univ of Cambridge: research fell Emmanuel Coll 1979–82, NERC research fell Dept of Earth Scis 1979–81, sr asst in research 1981–85, asst dir of research 1985–89, fell St Edmund's Coll 1988–, prof of geophysics 1989–, acting head Dept of Earth Scis 1991 and 1993; Cecil & Ida H Green scholar Scripps Instn of Oceanography Univ of Calif San Diego 1987; awarded Stichting Fund for Sci Tech and Research Schlumberger Ltd 1994; George P Woollard Award Geological Soc America 1997; fell American Geophysical Union, FGS (Bigsby Medal 1991), FRS 1994; *Publications* author of numerous articles in international journals; *Style*— Prof Robert White, FRS; ✉ Bullard Laboratories, Madingley Road, Cambridge CB3 0EZ (✆ 01223 337187, fax 01223 360779)

WHITE, Roger; s of Geoffrey White, of Tetbury Upton, Glos, and Zoe, *née* Bowler; *b* 1 September 1950; *Educ* Ifield GS, Christ's Coll Cambridge (BA), Wadham Coll Oxford; *Career* Hist Building Div GLC 1979–83, sec Georgian Gp 1984–91, exec sec Garden History Soc 1992–96, contrib ed House & Garden 1995–2015, curator Nicholas Hawksmoor and the Replanning of Oxford (RIBADC, Ashmolean Museum) 1997–98, co-curator Europe and the English Baroque: English Architecture 1660–1715 (V&A) 2009; visiting res fell Yale Center for British Art 1990; pres Oxford Univ Architectural Soc 1975–76; memb: Ctee Painswick Rococo Garden 1985–94, Chiswick House Advsy Panel 1991–2007, Pell Wall Preservation Tst 1993–98; Chicheley Lecture All Souls Coll Oxford 1999, Hugh Shirreff Lecture Historic Houses Assoc 2011; FSA 1986; *Publications* John Vardy (in The Architectural Outsiders, 1985), Georgian Arcadia: Architecture for the Park and Garden (exhbn catalogue, 1987), The Architectural Evolution of Magdalen College (1993), Nicholas Hawksmoor and the Replanning of Oxford (exhbn catalogue, 1997), The Architectural Drawings of Magdalen College (2001), Chiswick House and Gardens (2001), Witley Court (2003, 2 edn 2008), Belsay Hall (2005), Oxford Sketchbook (with Graham Byfield, 2005), A Life of Frederick, Prince of Wales 1707–1751 (ed, 2007), Holkham Hall (2010), Kent and the Gothic Revival (in William Kent, Designing Georgian Britain 2013); *Recreations* looking at old buildings; *Style*— Roger White, Esq, FSA; ✉ 142 Weir Road, London SW12 0ND

WHITE, Roger John Graham; s of Alfred James White (d 1976), and Doris Elizabeth, *née* Robinson (d 1973); *b* 30 April 1940; *Educ* Tiffin Sch; *m* 18 June 1966, Elizabeth, da of Tom Lionel Greenwood, of Esher, Surrey; 2 s (Graham b 1968, Andrew b 1970), 1 da (Katherine b 1977); *Career* articled clerk Knox Cropper CAs; KPMG: joined 1962, sr mangr 1970, tax ptnr 1974, sr tax ptnr UK 1981–98, chm KPMG Int Tax Ctee 1990–94, conslt 1998–; memb: professional and industry tax ctees, Bd and Ops Ctee 1988–98; lectr and writer on tax matters; Income and Corporation Taxes Act 1988: appointed by Lord Chllr to membership of Tbnl under section 706 Income and Corporation Taxes Act (ICTA) 1988, appointed by Chllr of the Exchequer to the Advsy Panel under section 765 ICTA 1988; FCA 1962, FTII 1970; *Books* The Trading Company (1978), Purchase of Own Shares (1983), Peats to KPMG – Gracious Family to Global Firm (2004); *Recreations* bridge, gardening, books; *Clubs* Addington Soc (chm 1991–93), Reform; *Style*— Roger White, Esq; ✉ Courtlands, 20 Grange Court, Walton on Thames, Surrey KT12 1JD (☎ 01932 246474, e-mail rjgande@ukwhites.com); KPMG, 8 Salisbury Square, London EC4Y 8BB (☎ 020 7311 1000 or 020 7311 6732, fax 020 7311 6701, e-mail roger.jg.white@kpmg.co.uk)

WHITE, Sandra; MSP; *b* 17 August 1951; *Educ* Garthamlock Sr Secdy Sch Glasgow, Cardonald Coll, Glasgow Technical Coll; *Career* formerly clerkess; cncllr Renfrew DC 1989–96, positions incl: gp whip 1992–96, dep spokesperson on housing 1992–96, memb Appeals Sub-Ctee (industrial disputes), memb JCC manual workers, memb standing ctees on planning, leisure, housing, environmental services, general purposes; cncllr Renfrewshire Cncl 1995–, positions incl: gp whip 1995–, spokesperson on property and construction 1995–, dep spokesman on corporate services, memb JCC on manual workers, memb JCC on staff, memb Civic's Functions and the Housing Services Sub-Ctees, memb standing ctees on housing, leisure services, property and construction, corporate services; MSP (SNP): Glasgow 1999–2011, Glasgow Kelvin 2011–; SNP: memb 1983–, sec, social convenor, press offr, conf delegate, Nat Cncl delegate, Nat Assembly delegate, memb Local Govt Ctee; fndr memb Foxbar Tenants Assoc, fndr memb Seedhill Summer Play Scheme, former memb Hawkhead Community Cncl, JP 1992–95; *Style*— Mrs Sandra White, MSP

WHITE, Sharon; *Career* slr; Stephenson Harwood: joined 1988, ptnr 1997–, chief exec 2009–; *Style*— Ms Sharon White; ✉ Stephenson Harwood, 1 Finsbury Circus, London EC2M 7SH

WHITE, Sharon; *Career* DG Public Spending HM Treasy until 2013, second perm sec HM Treasy 2013–15, chief exec Ofcom 2015–; *Style*— Ms Sharon White; ✉ Ofcom, Riverside House, 2a Southwark Bridge Road, London SE1 9HA

WHITE, Stephen Frank; s of Sir Frank White, of London, and Anne Rowlandson, *née* Howitt; *b* 29 September 1955; *Educ* Eton, Univ of Bristol (BA); *Career* accountant Price Waterhouse and Co 1977–81, with Phillips and Drew 1981–83, Hill Samuel Investment Management Ltd 1983–85; dir F & C Investment Management Ltd 1985–; Liveryman Worshipful Co of Merchant Taylors; ACA; *Recreations* opera, gardening, walking; *Clubs* Brooks's; *Style*— Stephen F White, Esq; ✉ c/o F & C Management Ltd, Exchange House, Primrose Street, London EC2A 2NY (☎ 020 7628 8000)

WHITE, Prof Stephen Leonard; s of William John (Jack) White (d 1980), and Edna, *née* McGuckin (d 2009); *b* 1 July 1945, Dublin, Ireland; *Educ* Trinity Coll Dublin (entrance exhibitioner, fndn scholar, BA), Univ of Glasgow (PhD), Univ of Oxford (MA, DPhil), Trinity Coll Dublin (LittD); *m* 7 April 1973, Ishbel, *née* MacPhie; 1 s (Alexander b 21 Dec 1987); *Career* various temporary and visiting appts: Open Univ, Univ of Strathclyde, Balliol Coll Oxford, Univ of Naples, Inst of Applied Politics Moscow, Res Sch of the Social Sciences ANU, Inst of Advanced Studies Vienna; sr assoc memb Inst of Central and E European Studies Univ of Glasgow; Dept of Politics Univ of Glasgow: lectr 1971–85, reader 1985–91, prof 1991–, head of dept 1992–98; pres Br Assoc for Slavonic and E European Studies 1994–97; founding academician Acad of Social Sciences 1999, FRSE 2002, FBA 2010; *Books* incl: Political Culture and Soviet Politics (1979), Britain and the Bolshevik Revolution (1980), The Origins of Détente (1985), The Bolshevik Poster (1988), Russia Goes Dry: Alcohol, State and Society (1996), Russia's New Politics: The Management of a Postrevolutionary Society (2000), The Soviet Political Elite from Lenin to Gorbachev (with E Mawdsley, 2000), Communism and its Collapse (2001), Putin's Russia and the Enlarged Europe (jtly, 2006), Party Politics in New Democracies (jtly, 2007), Understanding Russian Politics (2011), Identities and Foreign Policies in Russia, Ukraine and Belarus (with V Feklyunina 2014); *Recreations* cinema, theatre, reading, travel; *Style*— Prof Stephen White; ✉ Department of Politics, University of Glasgow, Glasgow G12 8RT (☎ 0141 330 5352, fax 0141 330 5071, e-mail s.white@socsci.gla.ac.uk)

WHITE, Stewart Dale; s of Theo Jeffrey White (d 1979), of Sydney, Aust, and Mary Jean, *née* Stewart; *b* 23 July 1951; *Educ* Newington Coll, St Andrew's Coll Univ of Sydney (BA, LLB), Downing Coll Cambridge (LLM); *m* 20 Sept 1980, Elisabeth Mary Hargreaves, da of Geoffrey John Bolton (d 1968), of Eton Coll; 1 da (Victoria b 1 July 1982), 1 s (Andrew b 1 Aug 1983); *Career* admitted slr: NSW 1976, England and Wales 1979; sr assoc Allen Allen and Hemsley Sydney 1979–83; ptnr: Blake Dawson Waldron Sydney 1983–88, Denton Hall Burgin and Warrens London 1988–94, Ashurst Morris Crisp 1994–99, gp public policy dir Vodafone Gp 1999–2005, chm Bell Pottinger Public Affairs 2005–; memb Telecom Bd Int Telecommunication Union 2001–, dir UK-Japan 21st Century Gp 2002–; former cncllr Section on Business Law of Int Bar Assoc and fndr chm Communications Law Ctee of Int Bar Assoc; chm: Standing Ctee Media and Communications Lawasia 1986–92, Legal Symposium ITU COM 1989, Regulatory and Economic Symposium ASIA TELECOM '93 and '99; advsr to governmental and private sector entities in telecommunications industry in Europe, Middle East and Asia; appointed expert to Econ and Social Ctee of EC to advise on matters incl Green Papers on Satellite Policy and Mobile Communications and Cmmn's proposed Directives on Digital Short Range Radio and High Definition TV; memb Advsy Ctee TELECOM '87 and TELECOM '91, Strategy Summit TELECOMS '95, '99 and 2003; memb: Law Soc, Int Bar; *Publications* Vol 39 Butterworth's Encylopedia of Forms and Precedents on Telecommunication (ed), EC Telecommunications Law (European Practice Library Chancery, fndr conslt ed), Satellite Communications in Europe: Law and Regulation (jt author); *Recreations* swimming, sailing, walking, bridge, opera; *Clubs* Australian, Royal Sydney Yacht Squadron, Bembridge Sailing, Royal Thames Yacht, Henley Royal Regatta, Leander, Australian Jockey, Royal Sydney Golf, Sydney Cricket Ground; *Style*— Stewart White, Esq

WHITE, Tony; s of Richard Charles White (d 1989), and Dorothy Maud Dempster White; *b* 27 August 1947; *Educ* Eastbrook Secdy Modern Sch (represented Essex in athletics), East Ham Tech Coll (finalist Letraset Student awards); *m* 3 April 1971, Patricia Margaret, da of Charles Felton; 2 da (Sarah Jane b 8 June 1972, Anna Louise b 23 Sept 1973); *Career* dir and animator; head of design Halas & Batchelor: writer and dir Quartet (first prize Chicago Film Festival), A Short Tall Story (represented GB in int animation festivals, used by UN to promote peace), Jackson Five TV series; dir the Ink Thief children's mixed-media TV drama series (Animus Entertainments/Yorkshire-Tyne Tees TV); films with Richard Williams incl: A Christmas Carol (Academy award), The Pink Panther Strikes Again (D&AD award); prodr, dir and animator Hokusai – An Animated Sketchbook (Br Academy award); fndr Animus Productions (films incl TV specials Cathedral and Pyramid), fndr Animus Entertainments (films for TV and multi-media projects); lectured extensively in the US, Europe and UK; FSIA; *Books* The Animator's Workbook (Phaidon Press, 1988); *Style*— Tony White, Esq; ☎ 020 7490 8234, fax 020 7490 8235

WHITE, Victoria Alexandra; da of Graeme Ross, and Iris, *née* Cunningham; *b* 1 March 1972, Newcastle-upon-Tyne; *Educ* Univ of Sussex (BA); *m* 1999, Peter; 2 s (Arthur Inigo George b 23 June 2003, Sebastian Edmund b 1 July 2007); *Career* dep ed B magazine until 2000; Company: dep ed 2000–04, ed 2004–; memb ETC Ctee PPA; BSME Ed of the Year 2012; *Recreations* cinema, golf, skiing, travel; *Style*— Mrs Victoria White; ✉ Company, Hearst Magazines UK, 33 Broadwick Street, London W1F 9EP (Twitter @companyedvic)

WHITE-SPUNNER, Lt Gen Sir Barnabas William Benjamin (Barney); KCB (2011), CBE (2002); s of Benjamin Nicholson (Tommy) White-Spunner (d 1986), and Elizabeth (Biddy) White-Spunner (d 2010); *b* 31 January 1957; *Educ* Eton, Univ of St Andrews (MA); *m* 29 April 1989, Amanda, da of David Faulkner; 2 da (Laetitia b 1989, Florence b 1998), 1 s (Christy b 1991); *Career* cmmnd Blues and Royals 1979, dep ldr Br Chinese Taklamakan Expdn 1993, mil asst to Chief of Defence Staff 1994–96, CO Household Cavalry Regt 1996–98, dep dir Defence Policy MOD 1998–2000, cdr 16 Air Assault Bde 2000–02, cmd NATO Operation Harvest Macedonia 2001, cmd Kabul Multi National Bde 2002, Chief Jt Force Ops 2003–05, COS HQ Land Command 2005–07, GOC 3 (UK) Div 2007–09, GOC Multi Nat Div (SE) Iraq 2008, Cdr Field Army 2009–11, Col Commandant Hon Artillery Co 2010–13, Col Commandant Royal Yeomanry 2011–; Hon Col: Kent and Sharpshooters Yeomanry 2008–11, Tayforth Univs OTC 2009–13; chm Grand Military Race Ctee 2011–; ed Baily's Hunting Directory 1996–2006, corr The Field 1992–2000; exec chm Countryside Alliance 2012–15, currently ptnr Burstock LLP; chm CAFOD From Poverty to Opportunity 2013–; Hon Legionnaire (1st Class) French Foreign Legion 2002, Legion of Merit USA 2010; *Books* Baily's Hunting Companion (1994), Our Countryside (1996), Great Days (1997), Horse Guards (2006), Of Living Valour (2015; *Recreations* hunting, central Asia, fishing; *Clubs* Turf, Pratts; *Style*— Lt Gen Sir Barney White-Spunner, KCB, CBE; ✉ e-mail info@burstock.io

WHITEFORD, Dr Eilidh MacLeod; MP; da of Douglas Dodson Whiteford, of Macduff, Banffshire, and Kathleen, *née* MacLeod; *b* 24 April 1969, Aberdeen; *Educ* Banff Acad, Univ of Glasgow (MA, PhD), Univ of Guelph Canada (MA); *Career* lectr and academic devpt offr Univ of Glasgow 1999–2001, co-ordinator Scottish Carers' Alliance 2001–03, campaigns mangr Oxfam Scotland 2003–09; MP (SNP) Banff & Buchan 2010–; *Style*— Dr Eilidh Whiteford, MP; ✉ House of Commons, London SW1A 0AA (☎ 020 7219 7005, e-mail eilidh.whiteford.mp@parliament.uk)

WHITEHALL, Jack Peter Benedict; *b* 7 July 1988, London; *Educ* Marlborough; *Career* comedian and actor; stand-up shows incl: Nearly Rebellious 2009, Learning Difficulties 2010, Let's Not Speak of This Again 2011; television appearances incl: 8 Out of 10 Cats, Would I Lie to You, Mock the Week, Never Mind the Buzzcocks, Argumental, A League of Their Own (regular panelist 2012–), Live at the Apollo, Fresh Meat (as actor), Bad Education (as actor and writer); King of Comedy Br Comedy Award 2012; *Style*— Mr Jack Whitehall; ✉ c/o HJ PR, 19 Nassau Street, London W1W 7AF

WHITEHEAD, Dr Alan; MP; *b* 15 September 1950; *Educ* Isleworth GS, Univ of Southampton (BA, PhD); *m* 1 Dec 1979, Sophie Wronska; 1 s, 1 da; *Career* dir Outset 1979–83 (dep dir 1976–79), dir BIIT 1983–92, ldr Southampton City Cncl 1984–92, prof of public policy Southampton Inst (now Southampton Solent Univ) 1992–97; MP (Lab) Southampton Test 1997–; Parly under-sec of state Tport, Local Govt and the Regions 2001–02; chair: All-Pty Ports Gp 1998–2001, Parly Renewable and Sustainable Energy Gp 2003–15; co-chair Parly Sustainable Resource Gp 2003–15, sec Br Polish Parly Gp 1997–2001 and 2003–15; memb: Regnl Policy Cmmn (The Millan Cmmn) 1995–96, House of Commons Select Ctee for Environment, Tport and the Regions 1997–99, Dept for Constitutional Affrs Select Ctee 2002–10, Standards and Privileges Select Ctee 2005–, Energy and Climate Change Select Ctee 2007–15, Environmental Audit Select Ctee 2010–15; shadow min for generation and transmission Dept for Energy and Climate Change 2015–; vice-pres Local Govt Assoc 1997–98; *Style*— Dr Alan Whitehead, MP; ✉ House of Commons, London SW1A 0AA (☎ 020 7219 6338 or 020 7219 5517 (researcher), e-mail alan@alan-whitehead.org.uk)

WHITEHEAD, Andrew; *Educ* Leeds GS, Keble Coll Oxford (BA), Univ of Warwick (MA); *Career* BBC: political corr World Service 1988–92, Delhi corr 1993–97, presenter The World Today 1998–2001, ed The World Today 2002–; memb editorial collective of History Workshop jl; Asia Broadcasting Union Prize 1993, Bronze Award NY Festival 1998; *Style*— Andrew Whitehead, Esq; ✉ BBC World Service, BBC Broadcasting House, Portland Place, London W1A 1AA (☎ 020 7557 3874, e-mail andrew.whitehead@bbc.co.uk)

WHITEHEAD, Dr Anthony William; s of Stanley Kenneth Whitehead (d 2002), and Margaret Mary, *née* Welford (d 1973); *b* 22 May 1950, Derby; *Educ* Bemrose GS Derby, QMC London (BSc, PhD), RNC Greenwich (MSc); *m* 11 Sept 1976, Lynette Florence, *née* Talmey; 1 s (Jonathan William b 27 Oct 1979), 1 da (Rosalind Mary b 29 May 1982); *Career* research engr Nat Nuclear Corp 1975–77, research scientist Admiralty Marine Technol Establishment Teddington MOD 1977–85, project mangr Director General Submarines Bath MOD 1985–91, head Atomic Energy Tech Unit Dept of Energy 1991–92, head Nuclear Industries Tech Unit DTI 1992–99, dep dir Nat Measurement System DTI 1999–2001, head Science Policy Unit Home Office 2001–03, dir Sci and Soc Office of Sci and Innovation 2003–07, head Sci in Govt Govt Office for Sci 2007–11, dir governance and policy Instn of Engrg and Technol 2011–14; CEng 1979, memb Fédération Européenne d'Associations Nationales d'Ingénieurs (FEANI) 1991, FINucE 1991, FIMechE 1997, FIET 2011; *Style*— Dr Anthony Whitehead; ✉ e-mail a.w.whitehead@btinternet.com

WHITEHEAD, David; OBE (2011); s of Prof Thomas Paterson Whitehead, of Leamington Spa, Warwicks, and Doreen Grace, *née* Whitton; *b* 31 May 1952; *Educ* Warwick Sch, Univ of Birmingham, Birmingham Poly (BA), Avery Hill Coll of FE (PGCE); *m* Mary Teresa, da of Denis McGeeney; 1 s (Thomas David b 18 June 1981), 1 da (Rachel Brigid b 27 March 1984); *Career* Oyez Ltd, Fyffes Gp Ltd, Br Poultry Fedn, dir of policy Br Ports Fedn, dir Br Ports Assoc; chm Euro Sea Ports Orgn 2001–04; dir Ecoports Fndn, dir Sea and Water Ltd; memb: UKTI Ports Advsy Gp, Greenwich Forum, Cardiff Univ Industrial Advsr Gp; *Recreations* swimming, trying to play guitar, being outdoors; *Clubs* Athenaeum; *Style*— David Whitehead, Esq, OBE; ✉ British Ports Association, Carthusian House, 12 Carthusian Street, London EC1M 6EZ (☎ 020 7260 1780, fax 020 7260 1784, e-mail david.whitehead@britishports.org.uk)

WHITEHEAD, Dr James Sebastian; s of Stephen Richard Whitehead, and Mary Shelagh, *née* Harrison; *b* 21 February 1969, York; *Educ* Stonyhurst Coll, Hertford Coll Oxford (MA), Univ of Stirling (MPhil), Univ of Manchester (PhD, Charles Herford Award); *m* 2007, Nicola Mary Searle, *née* Hinton; 2 da (Ignatia Mary Alice b 2008, Chiara Maria Grace b 2010); *Career* asst master Radley Coll 2000–04, head of English Downside Sch 2004–05, dir of studies Downside Sch 2005–07, second master Worth Sch 2007–14, head master Downside Sch 2014–; chair Headmasters of the Schools of the English Benedictine Congregaton; memb Univs Sub-Ctee HMC; memb: ASCL, HMC 2014; *Publications* Thomas Hardy and Englishness (in Thomas Hardy in Context, ed P Mallett, 2004); *Recreations* cricket, golf, reading, skiing, walking; *Clubs* RSA, East India, Lansdowne; *Style*— Dr James Whitehead; ✉ Downside School, Stratton-on-the-Fosse, Radstock, Bath BA3 4RJ (☎ 01761 235101, e-mail jwhitehead@downside.co.uk, website www.downside.co.uk, Twitter @DownsideHM)

WHITEHEAD, Laurence Andrew; s of Francis Stafford Whitehead (d 1998), and Agnes Mary Wishart (d 1997); *b* 28 November 1944, Salisbury, Wilts; *m* Linette, *née* Dell; 1 da (Lucy b 1981), 1 s (David b 1984); *Career* acting warden Nuffield Coll Oxford; dir Blackrock Latin American Investment Tst plc 2003–; sr proctor Univ of Oxford 2011–12; *Style*— Laurence Whitehead, Esq; ✉ Nuffield College, New Road, Oxford OX1 1NF

WHITEHEAD, Neil Anthony; s of H Whitehead and P J Whitehead, *née* Gripe; *b* 7 February 1956; *Educ* King's Sch Gloucester, Kingston Poly (BA 3-D Design); *m* Fiona, da of J B Mackie; 1 da (Amelia b 7 Oct 2000, with Judith Page); *Career* designer; formerly with Murdoch Design and Jeremy Farmer; Fitch plc 1984–99, dir Rodney Fitch & Co 1999–2003: successively assoc dir, dir Retail Div, creative dir then head of retail design, sr dir in jt charge of London Gp; fndr and ceo Ashleycarterwhitehead Ltd 2003–; fndr dir SOLUS plc; clients incl: Kingfisher, BT, BSkyB, Unilever, Wyevale plc, Gadget Shop, Blu (Italy), Alto (Sweden), Ford, Dyrup (Denmark); various appearances on design progs for BBC TV incl Colour in Design and History of Retail Design (both BBC2), conf presentations at various indust events; Design Week Award (Exhbn Environment) 1995, Environment Award 1998; memb Mktg Soc, MCSD, fell Int Real Estate Fedn (FIABCI); *Sporting Achievements* W of England hockey, rugby, athletics under 19 1972–74; played for Br Polytechnic's rugby team 1976–78; capt Kingston Poly RFC (won BSPA Cup 1977); played 1st team Richmond RFC 1980–86, winner Middx Sevens 1983, also played for Middx 1981–85; *Recreations* all sports including tennis and rugby; *Clubs* Richmond RFC, Raffles, Bluebird; *Style*— Neil Whitehead, Esq

WHITEHEAD, (Godfrey) Oliver; CBE; *b* 9 August 1941; *Educ* Univ of Bradford (BSc), London Business Sch; *m* Stephanie; 4 c; *Career* John Laing plc: various engrg and line mgmnt roles 1963–83, exec dir 1983–86; exec dir AMEC plc 1986–89, chief exec Babcock Int plc 1989–93; Alfred McAlpine plc: chief exec 1993–2003, chm 2002–07, ret; pres Ringway Devpt plc 1989–2002 (chm 1987–89); chm: ITNET plc 2004–05, Minerva plc 2006–11, Norland Managed Services Ltd 2008–11, Silver Estates Ltd 2012–15, ret; non-exec dir: PSA 1989–91, Appleshaw Ltd 2003–09; past pres Smeatonian Soc of Civil Engrs; chm of tstees Charles Newman Meml Fund 2003–; Col and CO Engr and Logistics Staff Corps 1984–2007; Master Worshipful Co of Paviors 2007–08 (Liveryman 1986); CEng, FICE; *Style*— Oliver Whitehead, Esq, CBE

WHITEHEAD, Stephen; *Career* former gp communications dir Prudential plc, currently chief exec Assoc of the Br Pharmaceutical Industry; *Style*— Stephen Whitehead, Esq; ✉ Association of the British Pharmaceutical Industry, 7th floor, Southside, 105 Victoria Street, London SW1E 6QT

WHITEHILL, Sally Hellena; *b* 6 November 1978, Grantham, Lincs; *Educ* Oakham Sch Rutland (Jerwood scholar), Thacher Sch Calif (ESU scholar), Downing Coll Cambridge (MA), London Coll of Printing; *Career* Capitol Hill 2000, ESU 2001–03, agent Media Div Curtis Brown Gp Ltd 2003–07, founding dir Best of Brits Film Festival 2007–; memb: BAFTA/LA, Hollywood Radio and TV Soc, Personal Mangrs' Assoc; exec memb Int Ctee Women in Film; Skillset fellowship United Talent Agency Beverly Hills 2007; *Recreations* reading, theatre, film, running; *Style*— Ms Sally Whitehill

WHITEHORN, Katharine Elizabeth; CBE (2014); da of Alan Drummond Whitehorn (d 1980), and Edith Marcia, *née* Gray (d 1982); *Educ* Blunt House, Roedean, Glasgow HS for Girls, Newnham Coll Cambridge (MA); *m* 4 Jan 1958, Gavin Tudor Lyall (d 2003), s of Joseph Tudor Lyall; 2 s (Bernard b 1964, Jake b 1967); *Career* publisher's reader 1950–53, teacher Finland 1953–54, grad asst Cornell Univ 1954–55, Picture Post 1956–57, Woman's Own 1958, The Spectator 1959–61; columnist The Observer 1960–96 (assoc ed 1980–88), agony aunt Saga magazine 1997–; dir: BR Airports Authy 1972–77, Nationwide Building Society 1983–91, Nationwide Anglia Estate Agents 1987–90; memb: Latey Ctee on Age of Majority 1965–67, BBC Advsy Gp on Social Effects of Television 1971–72, Cncl RSM 1982–85; rector Univ of St Andrews 1982–85; vice-pres The Patients' Assoc 1983–96; voted Woman that Makes a Difference by International Women's Forum 1992; Hon LLD Univ of St Andrews 1985, Hon DLitt London Guildhall Univ 2000; memb: NUJ, Media Soc; *Books* Cooking in a Bedsitter (1960), Roundabout (1961), Only on Sundays (1966), Whitehorn's Social Survival (1968), Observations (1970), How to Survive in Hospital (1972), How to Survive Children (1975), Sunday Best (1976), How to Survive in the Kitchen (1979), View from a Column (1981), How to Survive your Money Problems (1983), Selective Memory (2007); *Clubs* RSM, ESU; *Style*— Ms Katharine Whitehorn, CBE; ✉ 14 Provost Road, London NW3 4ST (e-mail kathlondon@gmail.com)

WHITEHOUSE, Prof David John; s of Joseph Whitehouse (d 1989), of Wolverhampton, and Alice Gertrude, *née* Roberts (d 1985); *b* 15 October 1937; *Educ* Univ of Bristol (BSc), Univ of Leicester (PhD), Univ of Warwick (DSc); *m* 17 July 1965, Ruth Lily Epsley, da of William Pannell; 1 da (Anne Frances b 14 Jan 1969), 1 s (Steven Charles b 6 April 1971); *Career* devpt engr Switchgear Wolverhampton 1958–61, research engr Rank Taylor Hobson Leicester 1961–68, chief engr Rank Precision Industries 1968–78; Univ of Warwick: prof of mech engrg 1978, sr fell SERC 1986, dir Centre for Micro Engrg and Metrology 1981, prof of engrg science/chief scientist 1990, prof of engrg science (research) 1997–2002, emeritus prof Sch of Engrg 2002–; conslt prof Tech Univ of Harbin (PRC) 1997–, guest prof Univ of Tianjin (PRC) 1997–; author of 250 tech and scientific papers; IMechE Joseph Whitworth Prize 1971, IMechE James Clayton Prize 1979, Mendeleav Inst Leningrad Commemorative Medallion 1981 and 1982, Champion of Metrology 1998, Nat Physical Laboratory Metrology for World Class Manufacture Lifetime Contrib Award, American Soc of Precision Engrg Lifetime Achievement Award 2002 (cited as Father of Digital Metrology), Gen Pierre Nicolau Award Int Acad of Prodn Engrg 2012; Hon DSc Univ of Huddersfield 2006; fell: CIRP 1974, ISO, BSI, Japan Soc for Precision Engrg (JSPE), American Soc for Precision Engrg (ASPE), Inst of Prodn and Control, Inst of Control and Instrumentation, Inst of Mgmnt Engrs; FInstP, FIEE, FIET; *Books* Mean Line of Surface Texture (1965), Nano Technology (1991), Handbook of Surface Metrology (1994), Optical Methods in Surface Metrology (1996), Surfaces and their Measurement (2002), Handbook of Surface and Nanometrology (2003, 2 edn 2010); *Recreations* swimming, weight lifting, classical music; *Style*— Prof David Whitehouse; ✉ 171 Cromwell Lane, Burton Green, Coventry CV4 8AN (☎ 024 7647 3558, e-mail djwhitehous@sky.com); School of Engineering, University of Warwick, Coventry CV4 7AL (☎ 024 7652 3154, fax 024 7647 1457)

WHITEHOUSE, Dr David Robert; s of Derick William Whitehouse, of Birmingham, and Anne Valmai, *née* Mallet; *b* 7 January 1957; *Educ* Duddeston Manor Sch, Univ of Manchester (BSc, PhD); *m* 3 April 1982, Jillian Dorothy, da of Bernard Carey, of Preston; 1 s (Christopher David b 2 May 1985), 2 da (Lucy Claire b 8 June 1987, Emily Kate b 3 June 1991); *Career* Nuffield Radio Astronomy Laboratories Jodrell Bank 1978–82, Space Science Laboratory UCL 1982–85, conslt ed Space magazine 1987–91, space technol conslt, writer and broadcaster 1985–88, former science corr BBC (joined 1988); numerous articles published in int press and academic jls; pres Soc for Popular Astronomy 1995–98; asteroid 1987 DW5 renamed Whitehouse 2006; European Internet Journalist of the Year 2002–03, Arthur award for space communication 2005, several Netmedia awards; FRAS 1979; *Books* The Moon: A Biography (2001), The Sun: A Biography (2005), One Small Step: The Inside Story of Space Exploration (2009), Galileo (2009); *Recreations* mountaineering, music; *Style*— Dr David Whitehouse; ✉ website www.davidwhitehouse.com

WHITEHOUSE, Prof (Julian) Michael Arthur; s of Arthur Arnold Keer Whitehouse (d 2003), of Olney, Bucks, and Kathleen Ida Elizabeth, *née* Elliston (d 1989); *b* 2 June 1940; *Educ* Queens' Coll Cambridge (MA, MB BChir), St Bartholomew's Hosp of London (MD); *m* 10 April 1965, Diane France, da of Dr Raymond Maximillien Theodore de Saussure (d 1972); 1 s (Michael Alexander de Saussure b 1966) 2 da (Fiona Geraldine b 1968, Vanessa Caroline b 1972); *Career* hon conslt physician, sr lectr and acting dir Dept of Med Oncology Bart's 1976, subsequently prof of med oncology and hon conslt physician Southampton Univ Hosps and dir CRC Wessex Med Oncology Unit Southampton until 1997, dean Charing Cross and Westminster Med Sch 1997, vice-princ (undergrad med) Imperial Coll Sch of Med 1997–2000, ret, emeritus prof of med oncology ICSM; visiting prof: Univ of Boston 1981, Christchurch Clinical Sch of Med NZ 1986; former vice-pres European Soc of Med Oncology; chm: UICC Clinical Oncology Ctee, Jt Cncl for Clinical Oncology RCP and RCR until 1998, Educn and Trg Bd EORTC, Med Studies Ctee Univ of London, Cncl Paterson Research Inst Christie Hosp Manchester until 2002; non-exec dir W Middlesex Univ NHS Tst until 2000; past memb Cncl: CRC, GMC (Univ of London); ed Haematological Oncology until 1996; chm and memb Fitness to Practice Panels GMC until 2015; govr City of London Sch; govr St Swithun's Sch Winchester until 2015; Freeman City of London, Liveryman Worshipful Soc of Apothecaries; FRCP 1979, FRCR 1992, FRCPEd 1994, FMedSci 2000; *Books* CNS Complications of Malignant Disease (1979), A Pocket Consultant in Clinical Oncology (1989), Investigation and Management (with Christopher J Williams, 1984–85), Recent Advances in Clinical Oncology (1982 and 1986), Cancer – the Facts (with Maurice Slevin, 1996); *Recreations* writing, the sea, travelling; *Clubs* Athenaeum; *Style*— Prof Michael Whitehouse; ✉ 25 Chilbolton Avenue, Winchester, Hampshire SO22 5HE

WHITEHOUSE, Sarah Alice; QC (2014); *née* Norman; da of Rev Canon William Beadon Norman, and Beryl, *née* Welch; *b* 13 January 1961; *Educ* Felixstowe Coll Suffolk, Univ of St Andrews (MA, pres Univ Debating Union, pres Univ Cons Assoc), Univ of Westminster (pro exam in law), Inns of Court Sch of Law; *m* 15 Oct 1988, Andrew Timothy Brian, s of late Brian Paul Whitehouse; 1 da (Elizabeth Julia b 30 Dec 1992), 1 s (Mark Paul b 3 July 1997); *Career* National Westminster Bank plc 1983–85, sr mangr Fuji International Finance Ltd 1985–90, asst dir Barclays De Zoete Wedd Ltd 1990–91; Parly candidate (Cons) Warley W 1992; memb Lincoln's Inn 1991–, barr 1993–, Treasy counsel 2006–, sr Treasy counsel 2014–; *Publications* contrib: Fraud, Millington and Sutherland Williams on the Proceeds of Crime, EU Law and Criminal Practice; *Recreations* riding, walking, music; *Clubs* Carlton (assoc memb); *Style*— Ms Sarah Whitehouse, QC; ✉ 21 Nottingham Road, London SW17 7EA (☎ 020 8767 8029); 6KBW, 21 College Hill, London EC4R 2RP

WHITELAW, Prof Andrew George Lindsay; s of Dr Robert George Whitelaw, DL, of 64 Garvock Hill, Dunfermline, Scotland, and Cicily Mary, *née* Ballard; *b* 31 August 1946; *Educ* George Watson's Coll Edinburgh, King's Coll Cambridge (MA, MB BChir, MD); *m* 1, 7 Sept 1968 (m dis 1990), Sara Jane, da of Capt Jack Sparks (d 1979), of Peaslake, Surrey; 1 s (Benjamin Cameron b 12 May 1972), 2 da (Nicola Jane b 26 Dec 1970, Rebecca Catrin b 18 April 1974); m 2, 4 Aug 1990, Marianne, da of Dr Otto Thoresen, of Horten, Norway; 1 s (Thomas Thoresen b 31 Oct 1990); *Career* specialist paediatric training at Gt Ormond St and in Toronto 1972–79, conslt neonatologist and hon sr lectr Royal Postgrad Med Sch Hammersmith Hosp 1981–90, prof of paediatrics Univ of Oslo 1995–98 (assoc prof 1990–95), prof of Neonatal Med Univ of Bristol 1998–; memb Nuffield Cncl on Bioethics Fetus and Newborn 2003–06; pres Neonatal Soc 2006–09; FRCP 1988; *Publications* The Very Immature Infant Under 28 Weeks Gestation (with Cooke, 1988); over 150 original research articles and 50 review articles mostly on the diagnosis, mechanisms, prevention and treatment of neonatal brain injury; *Recreations* music, mountains, theatre; *Style*— Prof Andrew Whitelaw; ✉ Neonatal Neuroscience, Level D, St Michael's Hospital, Bristol BS2 8EG (e-mail andrew.whitelaw@bristol.ac.uk)

WHITELAW, Dr Douglas Dixon; s of George Whitelaw (d 1983), of Glasgow, and Jean, *née* Forrester (d 1986); *b* 4 March 1952; *Educ* HS of Glasgow, Univ of Glasgow (BSc, MSc, PhD); *m* 31 Dec 1974, Elspeth Martin, da of John Campbell; 2 s (Fraser Martin b 9 Nov 1981, Lindsay Elder b 21 Sept 1987); *Career* Wellcome Trust research fell Univ of Glasgow 1975–80, sr scientist Int Lab for Research on Animal Diseases (ILRAD) Nairobi Kenya 1980–88, EC sr research fell Univ of Glasgow 1989–90; Br Cncl: dep dir/sci offr Australia and NZ 1990–93, asst dir rising to dir Enugu Nigeria 1993–94, dir Kano Nigeria 1994–95, dep dir (sci) Korea 1996–2000, conslt 2000–; author of over seventy pubns in int scientific jls; *Recreations* music, golf, cricket; *Clubs* Nairobi, Royal Over-Seas League; *Style*— Dr Douglas Whitelaw

WHITELEY; *see also:* Huntington-Whiteley

WHITELEY, Julian Peter; s of Gen Sir Peter Whiteley, GCB, OBE, DL, and Nancy, *née* Clayden; *b* 15 March 1957; *Educ* Sherborne, Royal Naval Engineering Coll Plymouth (BSc), Univ of Cambridge (PGCE), Univ of Nottingham (MBA); *m* 1982, Elizabeth Anne, da of Vice-Adm Sir John Forbes, KCB; 3 da (Gemma b 10 May 1984, Kirstie b 13 March 1986, Laura b 10 May 1989); *Career* offr RN 1975–81; asst master physics Rugby Sch 1981–83, head of physics Sherborne Sch 1986–93 (asst master 1984–85), dep headmaster St Paul's Sch São Paulo 1993–97, headmaster Taunton Sch 1997–; *Recreations* sailing, windsurfing, reading, classic cars, theatre, foreign travel, entertaining; *Clubs* São Paulo Yacht, Yealm Yacht; *Style*— Julian Whiteley, Esq; ✉ Taunton School, Staplegrove, Taunton, Somerset TA2 6AJ (☎ 01823 349224, fax 01823 349201)

WHITELEY, Lucinda; *b* 4 October 1961; *Educ* St Hilda's Sch Whitby, Univ of Newcastle upon Tyne (BA); *m* Michael Watts; 2 da; *Career* prodn co-ordinator Longman Video 1983–84; prog mangr: Children's Channel 1984–86, LWT 1986; head of prog planning Children's Channel 1987–88, ed Early Morning Television Service Channel 4 Television 1988–92 (launched The Big Breakfast), freelance prodr 1993, commissioning ed children's progs Channel 4 Television 1993–97 (progs incl Wise Up, Coping With..., Hollyoaks, Ant and Dec Unzipped, Terry Pratchett's Discworld), sr vice-pres Prodn Polygram Visual Programming 1997–99 (progs incl Maisy), freelance exec prodr 1999–2000, dir Novel Entertainment 2001– (TV progs incl Fimbles, Roly Mo Show and Horrid Henry, stage show Horrid Henry: Live and Horrid, radio show Rockit's Pocket and Horrid Henry's Radio Show, game Horrid Henry's Missions of Mischief); vice-chair Second World Summit on Television for Children 1998; memb Bd BAFTA; *Awards* 7 BAFTAs, 3 Emmys, 2 Prix Jeunesse Awards, RTS Award, Peabody Award, Prix Europa, British Animation Award; *Style*— Ms Lucinda Whiteley; ✉ e-mail lucinda@novelentertainment.co.uk

WHITELOCKE, Rodger Alexander Frederick; s of Leslie W S Whitelocke (d 1955), of Bulstrode Park, Jamaica, and Ruth, *née* Hopwood; descendant of Sir James Whitelocke b 1570 (and Family Tree in Plantagenet Roll Exeter Vol) and Bulstrode Whitelocke, Keeper of the Great Seal b 1605 (s Sir James); *b* 28 February 1943; *Educ* Taunton Sch, Univ of London, Bart's (MB BS), Univ of London (PhD); *m* 28 July 1973 (m dis 2000), Eleonora Valerie, da of Professor W F Maunder; 1 da (Katherine b 1978), 2 s (Nicholas b 1979, James b 1984); *Career* house surgn Bart's 1969–70, research on prostaglandins in ocular inflammation Inst of Ophthalmology 1971–73 (PhD London), sr resident surgical offr Moorfields Eye Hosp 1976, sr registrar Bart's 1977–80; conslt ophthalmic surgn St Bartholomew's Hosp 1980–2008 (head of dept, clinical dir and sr surgn), conslt ophthalmologist Royal Marsden Hosp London 1983–; past hon conslt St Luke's Hosp for Clergy, visiting prof of visual scis City Univ London 1988–91; govr Voluntary Hosp of St Bartholomew 2006–; Withers Prize 1968, Royal Soc of Medicine Prize in Ophthalmology 1976; Freeman City of London, Liveryman Worshipful Co of Barbers (Hon Curator); FRCS, FRCOpth; *Publications* numerous clinical pubns and chapters in medical text books on subjects incl the treatment of diabetic retinopathy by laser, ocular oncology, sickle cell eye disease and prostaglandins in ocular inflammation; *Recreations* music, antiques, travel, gardening; *Clubs* Athenaeum, The Fountain, Bart's and the London Boat (past pres), Henley 100; *Style*— Rodger Whitelocke, Esq; ✉ Westwood, Heather Drive, Sunningdale, Berkshire SL5 0HR; 144 Harley Street, London W1G 7LD (☎ 020 7935 3834)

WHITEMAN, Prof John Robert; s of Robert Whiteman, and Rita, *née* Neale; *b* 7 December 1938; *Educ* Bromsgrove Sch, Univ of St Andrews (BSc), Worcester Coll Oxford (DipEd), Univ of London (PhD); *m* 8 Aug 1964, Caroline Mary, da of Oswald B Leigh (d 1941); 2 s (Angus b 1967, Hamish b 1969); *Career* sr lectr RMCS Shrivenham 1963–67; asst prof: Univ of Wisconsin USA 1967–68, Univ of Texas at Austin 1968–70; Brunel Univ 1970–: reader numerical analysis 1970–76 (on leave Richard Merton Gäst prof Univ of Münster FRG 1975–76), prof of numerical analysis and dir Brunel Inst of Computational Mathematics 1976–2014, head Dept of Mathematics and Statistics 1982–90, vice-princ 1991–96, Univ distinguished prof 2004–; visiting prof: Univ of Pisa 1985, Univ of Kuwait 1986, Texas A and M Univ USA 1986, Univ of Stuttgart 1990, Univ of Texas at Austin 1996; distinguished research fell Univ of Texas at Austin 1997–2012; Brunel and Ravenscroft Lectr 2004; dir ESAFORM (European Scientific Assoc for Forming Processes) 1995–2004; memb: SERC Mathematics Ctee 1981–86, SERC Sci Bd 2000–, Amersham Deanery Synod C of E; chm: SERC Sci Bd Educn and Trg Panel 1991–92, Cncl IMA 1996–2004 (vice-pres 2002–04); non-exec dir Langdale Owners plc 2004–; Freeman City of London 1979, Liveryman Worshipful Co of Glass Sellers 1979 (asst to the Ct, renter warden 2002, prime warden 2003, master 2004, chm of tstees Charity Fund 2008–); hon doctorate Univ of West Bohemia 1995; FIMA 1970, CMath 1991; *Books* numerous pubns on numerical solution of differential equations (particularly finite element methods) incl: The Mathematics of Finite Elements and Applications vols 1–10 (ed 1973–2000), Finite Elements: An Introduction to the Method and Error Analysis (2010), Numerical Methods for Partial Differential Equations (ed journal); *Recreations* walking, swimming, golf, tennis, orchestral music, church bell ringing; *Style*— Prof John Whiteman; ✉ Institute of Computational Mathematics, Brunel University, Uxbridge, Middlesex UB8 3PH (☎ 01895 265185, fax 01895 269732, e-mail john.whiteman@brunel.ac.uk)

WHITEMAN, Prof Peter George; QC (1977); s of David Whiteman (d 1988), and Betsy Bessie, *née* Coster (d 2003); *b* 8 August 1942; *Educ* Warwick Secdy Modern Sch, Leyton Co HS, LSE (LLB, LLM); *m* 24 Oct 1971, Katherine Ruth, da of Gershon Ellenbogen (d 2009); 2 da (Victoria Elizabeth b 1975, Caroline Venetia b 1977); *Career* lectr Univ of London 1966–70; called to the Bar Lincoln's Inn 1967 (bencher 1985); recorder of the Crown Court 1982–, dep High Court judge 1994–, jt head of chambers; memb Bar Cncl; memb Faculty of Laws Univ of Florida 1977–, prof of Law Univ of Virginia 1980–; attorney and cnsllr NY State 1982; visiting prof: Univ of Virginia 1978, Univ of Calif Berkeley 1980; legal advsr Ctee Unitary Tax Campaign (UK) 1982–1996; memb Editorial Bd Virginia Jl of Int Law 1982–; author numerous articles in learned jls; pres and chm Dulwich Village Preservation Soc 1987–97, memb Advsy Ctee The Dulwich Estate Scheme of Mgmnt 1988–97, chm Dulwich Jt Residents Ctee 1991–97; memb: Consultative Ctee Dulwich Picture Gallery 1990–97 (memb Campaign Cabinet 2010–), Patrons' Ctee Royal Acad of Arts 2010–; FRSA 1976; *Books* Whiteman on Income Tax (1988), Whiteman on Capital Gains Tax (1988), British Tax Encyclopedia (1988); *Recreations* writing, jogging, hill walking, croquet, opera and theatre; *Style*— Prof Peter G Whiteman, QC; ✉ Hollis Whiteman Chambers, 1–2 Laurence Pountney Hill, London EC4R 0FU (☎ 020 7933 8855)

WHITEMAN, Ven Rodney David Carter; s of Leonard Archibald Whiteman (d 1955), and Sybil Mary, *née* Morshead (d 1990); *b* 6 October 1940; *Educ* St Austell GS Cornwall, Ely Theological Coll; *m* 28 Oct 1969, Christine Anne, da of Edward Thomas James Chelton, of Cheltenham, Glos; 1 da (Rebecca Mary De Mornay b 1972), 1 s (James Rodney Charles b 1975); *Career* ordained Birmingham Cathedral: deacon 1964, priest 1965; curate All Saints Kings Heath 1964–70; vicar: St Stephen Rednal 1970–79, St Barnabas Erdington 1979–89; rural dean of Aston 1981–89, hon canon Birmingham Cathedral 1985–89, priest in charge Cardynham with Helland 1989–94, hon canon of Truro Cathedral 1989–2006, archdeacon of Bodmin 1989–2000, archdeacon of Cornwall 2000–06, archdeacon emeritus 2006–; *Style*— The Ven Rodney Whiteman; ✉ 22 Treverbyn Gardens, St Austell, Cornwall PL25 3AW (☎ 01726 879043)

WHITEMORE, Hugh John; s of Samuel George Whitemore (d 1987), and Kathleen, *née* Fletcher (d 1996); *b* 16 June 1936; *Educ* Judd Sch Tonbridge, King Edward VI Sch Southampton, RADA; *m* 1, July 1961 (m dis 1976), Jill, *née* Brooke; m 2, May 1976 (m dis 1994), Sheila, *née* Lemon; 1 s (Tom b 1976); m 3, May 1998, Rohan McCullough; *Career* playwright; stage plays: Stevie 1977, Pack of Lies 1983, Breaking the Code 1986, The Best of Friends 1988, It's Ralph 1991, A Letter of Resignation 1997, Disposing of the Body 1999, God Only Knows 2001, As You Desire Me (from Pirandello) 2005, The Last Cigarette (with Simon Gray) 2009, A Marvellous Year for Plums 2012; films incl: 84 Charing Cross Road (Royal Film Performance) 1987, Jane Eyre 1995; many TV plays and dramatisations incl: A Dance to the Music of Time (Channel 4) 1997, The Gathering Storm 2002 (Emmy for Outstanding Writing, Writer's Guild of America Award, Peabody Award), Into the Storm 2009, contribs to The Wednesday Play, Armchair Theatre and Play for Today; visiting prof in broadcast media Univ of Oxford 2003–04; FRSL 1999, Hon FKC; *Recreations* music, movies, reading; *Style*— Hugh Whitemore, Esq; ✉ 67 Peel Street, London W8 7PB

WHITEN, Prof (David) Andrew; *Educ* Univ of Sheffield (BSc), Univ of Bristol (PhD); *Career* SSRC res fell Univ of Oxford 1972–75; Univ of St Andrews: lectr 1975–90, reader 1990–97, prof of evolutionary and developmental psychology 1997–2000, Wardlaw prof of psychology 2000–; F M Bird visiting prof Emory Univ 1996, Br Acad res reader 1999–2001, Leverhulme major research fell 2003–06, Royal Soc Leverhulme Tst sr research fell 2006–07, elected fell Cognitive Science Soc 2013; Jean-Marie Delwart Int Scientific Prize Royal Belgian Acad of Sciences 2001, Rivers Medal RAI 2007, Osman-Hill Medal Primate Soc of GB 2010, Sir James Black Prize and Medal Royal Soc of Edinburgh 2013, Senior Prize for Public Engagement Royal Soc of Edinburgh 2014; Hon DSc Heriot-Watt Univ 2015, Hon DUniv Univ of Stirling 2016; FBPsS 1991, FBA 2000, FRSE 2001; *Publications* incl: Machiavellian Intelligence II (with R W Byrne, 1997), Cultures in Chimpanzees (with J Goodall et al, in Nature, 1999), The Second Inheritance System of Chimpanzees and Humans (in Nature, 2005), Culture Evolves (with R A Hinde, C B Stringer and K N Laland, 2012); *Style*— Prof Andrew Whiten; ✉ Centre for Social Learning and Cognitive Evolution, School of Psychology and Neuroscience, University of St Andrews, St Andrews, Fife KY16 9JU (☎ 01334 462073, fax 01334 463042, e-mail a.whiten@st-and.ac.uk, website www.st-andrews.ac.uk/profile/aw2 and https://risweb.st-andrews.ac.uk/portal)

WHITER, John Lindsay Pearce; s of Nugent Whiter (d 1966), and Jean Dorothy, *née* Pearce (d 2003); *b* 10 May 1950; *Educ* Eastbourne GS; *m* 5 July 1975, Janet Dulcie Sarah, da of Dr Kenneth Oswald Albert Vickery (d 2010); 2 s (Timothy b 1976, William b 1989), 1 da (Nancy b 1979); *Career* sr ptnr (London) Mazars (formerly Neville Russell) 1992–93 (ptnr 1977–88, managing partner (London) 1988–92), chief fin offr Benfield Gp Ltd 1994–2009; chm Argenta Syndicate Mgmnt Ltd 2009–; non-exec dir: Cooper Gay Swett & Crawford 2009–; chm and tstee Oasis Charitable Tst 2010–; Freeman City of London, Bishopsgate Ward; memb: Guild of Freeman of the City of London, Worshipful Co of Chartered Accountants in England and Wales, Worshipful Co of Insurers; FCA 1973, FInstD, FRSA; *Recreations* opera, music, Chelsea FC, family; *Clubs* City of London, RAC; *Style*— John Whiter, Esq; ✉ Hasilwood House, 62 Bishopsgate, London EC2N 4AW (☎ 020 7826 4002)

WHITEREAD, Rachel; CBE (2006); da of Thomas Whiteread (d 1988), of London, and Pat, *née* Lancaster (d 2003); *b* 20 April 1963; *Educ* Brighton Poly (BA), Slade Sch of Art UCL (DipHe in sculpture); *m* Marcus Taylor; *Career* artist and sculptor; involved in teaching on various postgrad and undergrad courses; Hon DLitt Brighton Poly 1998; *Solo Exhibitions* incl: Carlile Gall London 1988, Ghost (Chisenhale Gall London) 1990, Arnolfini Gall Bristol 1991, Karsten Schubert Ltd London 1991, Rachel Whiteread Recent Sculpture (Luhring Augustine Gall NY) 1992, House (E London) 1993, Basel Kunsthalle (Switzerland) 1994, ICA Philadelphia (USA) 1995, ICA Boston (USA) 1995, Rachel Whiteread: Shedding Life (Tate Gall Liverpool) 1996–97, Reina Sofia (Madrid) 1997, Water Tower Project (Public Art Fund, NY) 1998, Anthony d'Offay Gall London 1998, Rachel Whiteread (Luhring Augustine NY) 1999, Holocaust Memorial (Judenplatz Vienna) 2000, Fourth Plinth Project (Trafalgar Square London) 2001, Rachel Whiteread (Serpentine Gallery London and Scot Nat Gallery of Modern Art Edinburgh) 2001, Deutsche Guggenheim Museum (Berlin, touring exhibition) 2001, Haunch of Venison London 2002, Room 101 (V&A) 2003, Koyanagi Gall Tokyo 2003, Luhring Augustine NY 2003, MOMA Rio de Janeiro Brazil and Sao Paolo Brazil 2003–04, Kunsthaus Bregenz Austria 2005, Embankment (Turbine Hall Tate Modern) 2005, Rachel Whiteread (Donnaregina Museum of Contemporary Art Naples), Rachel Whiteread (Galleria Lorcan O'Neill Rome) 2006 and (Centro Arte Contemporaneo Malaga) 2007, Rachel Whiteread: Bibliography (Luhring Augustine NY) 2006, Rachel Whiteread August Seeling Prize Exhibition (Lehmbruck Museum Duisburg) 2007, Rachel Whiteread (Gagosian Gallery LA) 2008, Rachel Whiteread: Place (Museum of Fine Arts Boston) 2008, Rachel Whiteread: drawings (Hammer Museum LA, Nasher Sculpture Centre Dallas and Tate Britain) 2010; *Selected Group Exhibitions* incl: Whitworth Young Contemporaires Manchester 1987, Riverside Open London 1988, Whitechapel Open London 1989, Deichtorhallen Hamburg 1989–90, British Art Show (touring) 1990, Karsten Schubert Ltd London 1990, Metropolis (Martin-Gropius Bau Berlin) 1991, Broken English (Serpentine Gall) 1991, Gp Show (Luhring Augustine NY) 1991, Turner Prize Exhibition (Tate) 1991 and 1993, Double Take (Hayward and Kunsthalle Vienna) 1992, Documenta IX (Kassel Germany) 1992, Carnegie International (USA) 1995, Br Pavillion Venice Biennale 1997, Skulpture Projekte (Münster Germany) 1997, Sensation: Young British Artists from the Saatchi Collection (Royal Acad of Arts and Touring 1999) 1997, Wounds (Moderna Museet Stockholm) 1998, Displacements: Miroslaw Balka, Doris Salcedo, Rachel Whiteread (Art Gall of Ontario Toronto) 1998, Towards Sculpture (Fundacao Calouste Gulbenkian Lisbon) 1998, REAL/LIFE: New British Art (Tochigi Prefectural Museum of Fine Arts Japan and touring) 1998, Claustrophobia (IKON Gall Birmingham and touring) 1998, Le Musée à l'heure anglaise: Sculptures de la collection du British Council 1965–1998 (Musée des Beaux-Arts de Valenciennes) 1999, House of Sculpture (Modern Art Museum of Fort Worth Texas) 1999, Sincerely Yours (Astrup Fearnley MOMA Oslo) 2000, Le temps vite (Centre Georges Pompidou Paris) 2000, La forma del mondo/la fine del monde (Padiglione d'arte contemporanea Milan) 2000, Shadow of Reason (Galleria d'Arte Moderna Bologna Italy) 2000, The Language of Things (Kettles Yard Cambridge), Double Vision (Galerie fuer Zeitgenössische Kunst Leipzig), Public Offerings (Museum of Contemporary Art LA), Century City (Tate Modern London) 2001, Lost and Found 2 (Kulturhuset Stockholm) 2001, Electrify Me! (Friedrich Petzel Gall NY) 2001, Double Vision (Galerie für Zeitgenosaische Kunst Leipzig) 2001, Public Offerings (MoCA LA) 2001, Collaborations with Parkett; 1984 to Now (MoMA NY) 2001, Beautfiul Productions: Art to Play, Art to Wear, Art to Own (Whitechapel Gall London) 2001, Wall & Whiteread (Kukje Gall Seoul) 2002, To Be Looked At (MOMA NY) 2002, Sphere: Loans for the Inivisible Museum (Sir John Soane's Museum London) 2002, The Photogenic: Photography Through its Metaphors in Contemporary Art (ICA Philadelphia) 2002, Conversation?: Recent Acquisitions of the Van Abbemuseum (The Factory, Acad of Fine Arts Athens) 2002, The Physical World: An Exhibition of Painting and Sculpture (Gagosian Gall NY) 2002, Beautiful Productions: Parkett Collaborations and Editions since 1984 (Irish MOMA Dublin) 2002, Thinking Big: Concepts for 21st Century British Sculpture (Peggy Guggenheim Collection Venice) 2002, Blast to Freeze: British Art in the 20th Century (Kunstmuseum Wolfsberg and Les Abattoirs Toulouse) 2002, Days Like These (Tate Britain London) 2003, The Snow Show (Lapland, Finland) 2004, Scultura Leggera – Light Sculpture (Vicenza), Rachel Whiteread: Sculpture (Gagosian Gall London) 2005, Part Object Part Sculpture (Wexner Center for the Arts Ohio State Univ) 2005–06, Out of Line: Drawings from the Collection of Sherry and Joel Mallin (Herbert F Johnson Museum of Art Cornell Univ) 2005–06, Eccentric Modern (Fndn To-Life Inc Exhibition Space NY) , Art of Chess (Gary Tatintsian Gall Moscow), Pure (Sean Kelly NY) 2006, The Great Collections: The Guggenheim (Kunsthalle Bonn), More Than the World: Works from the Astrup Fearnley Collection (Astrup Fearnley Museet for Moderne Kunst Oslo), New Dimensions (John Berggruen Gall San Francisco) 2006–07, Responding to Khan: A Sculpture Conversation (Yale Univ Art Gall) 2007; *Awards* The Elephant Trust 1989, GLA Prodn Grant 1989, nominated Turner Prize 1991, DAAD Stipendium Berlin 1992, winner Turner Prize 1993, Venice Biennale Award for Best Young Artist 1997, Nord LB Art Prize 2004, August Seeling Sculpture Prize 2007; *Style*— Ms Rachel Whiteread, CBE; ✉ c/o Gagosian Gallery, 6–24 Britannia Street, London, WC1X 9JD (☎ 020 7841 9960, fax 020 7841 9961, website www.gagosian.com)

WHITFIELD, Hugh Newbold; s of Rev George Joshua Newbold Whitfield, of Exmouth, Devon, and Audrey Priscilla, *née* Dence; *b* 15 June 1944; *Educ* Canford Sch, Gonville & Caius Coll Cambridge and Bart's Med Coll London (MA, MChir); *m* Penelope Joy, da of William Craig; 2 s (Angus Hugh Newbold b 18 April 1976, Alastair James Newbold b 14 Jan 1981); *Career* cmmnd RAMC 1967–74; various house jobs Bart's, res fell Inst of Urology 1974–76; Bart's: chief asst Dept of Urology 1976–79, conslt urologist 1979–93, clinical dir Dept of Urology and dir Lithotripter Unit 1991–93; reader in urology and dir Stone Unit Inst of Urology 1993–2001, conslt urologist Central Middx Hosp 1993–2000, conslt urologist Battle Hosp Reading 2001–; civilian conslt advsr in urology to Army; ed Br Jl of Urology 1993–2002; former memb Nat Youth Orch of GB; memb: BMA 1968, Br Assoc of Urological Surgns 1974; FRCS 1972, FRSM 1975; *Books* Textbooks of Genito-Urinary Vols I and II (ed with W F Hendry, 1985, 2 edn, ed with W F Hendry, R S Kirby, J W Duckett, 1998), Urology: Pocket Consultant (1985), Genitourinary Surgey (ed 5 edn vols I-III, 1992); *Recreations* music, country pursuits, golf; *Clubs* Garrick; *Style*— Hugh Whitfield, Esq; ✉ Royal Berkshire Hospital, London Road, Reading, Berkshire RG1 5AN (☎ 0118 987 5111, e-mail hugh.whitfield@rbbh-tr.nhs.uk); 43 Wimpole Street, London W1G 8AE (☎ 020 7935 3095, fax 020 7935 3147, e-mail hughwhitfield@urologylondon.fsnet.co.uk)

WHITFIELD, June; CBE (1998, OBE 1985); da of John Herbert Whitfield (d 1955), and Bertha Georgina, *née* Flett (d 1982); *b* 11 November 1925; *Educ* Streatham Hill HS, RADA; *m* 1955, Timothy John Aitchison (d 2001), s of Cdr J G Aitchison, OBE; 1 da (Suzy b 4 June 1960); *Career* actress; stage debut ASM Pinkstring & Sealing Wax (Duke of York's) 1944; *Theatre* incl: Ace of Clubs (Cambridge Theatre and tour) 1950, South Pacific 1951, Penny Plain 1951, See You Later 1951, Love from Judy (Saville) 1952, From Here and There (Royal Court) 1955, Jack and the Beanstalk (Chichester 1982, Bath 1985, Guildford 1986), An Ideal Husband (Chichester) 1987, Over My Dead Body (Savoy) 1988, Babes in the Wood (Croydon 1990, Plymouth 1991, Cardiff 1992), Cinderella (Wimbledon) 1994, Bedroom Farce (Aldwych) 2002, Chichester Christmas Concert 2002, On the Town (musical, Coliseum) 2007; *Television and Radio* incl: Take It From Here 1953–60, Hancock 1956, Benny Hill 1961, Dick Emery 1973, subject of This is Your Life 1976 and 1995, Happy Ever After (5 series) 1974–78, Terry and June (9 series) 1979–87, The News Huddlines 1984–99, French and Saunders 1988, Cluedo 1990, Absolutely Fabulous! 1992–

94, 2001 and 2003 (specials 1996 (two), 2002, 2004 and 2012–13 (three)), Huddlines, Variety Special, A Pocket Full of Rye 1994, Whats My Line 1994 and 1995, At Bertram's Hotel 1995, Common as Muck 1996, The 4.50 from Paddington 1996, Family Money 1997, Tom Jones 1997, All Rise for Julian Clary 1997, Funny Women 1997, Nemesis (Radio 4), Like They've Never Been Gone (Radio 2) 1999 and 2001; The Undiscovered Casebook of Sherlock Holmes (Radio 2) 1999, '99 News Huddlines (1999), Catherine Cookson's The Secret (TV film) 1999, The Last of the Blonde Bombshells 1999, Mirror Ball (BBC) 2000, The News Huddlines 2000; Miss Marple (Radio 4): Murder at the Vicarage 1993, The Caribbean Mystery 1997, The Mirror Cracked 1998, A Murder is Announced 1999, The Body in the Library 1999, The Moving Finger 2001, They Do it With Mirrors 2001, Sleeping Murder 2001, Huddlines (Radio 4) 2001 and 2002, Like They've Never Been Gone (Radio 4) 2001 and 2002, Coming up for Air 2002, The Kumars at No 42 2003, Call My Bluff 2003 and 2004, BBC Worldwide Festival 2003, Gloria Hunniford Show 2003, 9 Floors 2003, Father Gilbert 2003, The Royal 2004, The Sound of Music 2004, Father Gilbert 2004, NFI Tribute 2004, Hitchhiker's Guide to the Galaxy 2005, Midsomer Murders 2005 Miss Marple By The Pricking of my Thumbs 2005, Last of the Summer Wine 2005–06, Bob the Builder (voice-over) 2006, Not Talking (Radio 3) 2006, Loose Ends (Radio 4) 2006, Hitchhiker's Guide to the Galaxy (Radio 5) 2006, South Bank Show 2007, Last of the Summer Wine 2007–08, The Dinner Party (Radio 4) 2007, Green Green Grass 2007–08, Harley Street 2008, Dr Who 2009, Coronation Street (ITV) 2010, A Monstrous Vitality (BBC Radio 4) 2011, A Month of June (Radio 4) 2012, Boomers (BBC) 2014, Max & Alec (BBC Radio 4) 2014, EastEnders (BBC 1) 2015, Apocalypse Slough (Sky 1) 2015, Miss Marple (BBC Radio 4) 2015; presenter We'll Meet Again 2009–10; *Film* Carry on Nurse 1958, Spy with the Cold Nose 1966, The Magnificent Seven Deadly Sins 1971, Carry on Abroad 1972, Bless This House 1972, Carry on Girls 1973, Romance with a Double Base 1974, Not Now Comrade 1975, Carry On Columbus 1992, Jude the Obscure 1995; *Recordings* Up Je T'aime, Wonderful Children's Songs, June Whitfield at the BBC (audio tape), The School at Thrush Green (audio book); *Awards* Variety Club Joint Personality Award 1979, The Comedy Awards: Lifetime Achievement Award 1994, Women in Film and TV 1998; TRIC Special Award 1999; 'Talkies' Oustanding Achievement Award 1999; *Books* ...and June Whitfield (autobiography, 2000), June Whitfield – At A Glance (2009); *Style—* Miss June Whitfield, CBE; ✉ c/o Maureen Vincent, United Agents Ltd, 12–26 Lexington Street, London W1F 0LE (☎ 020 3214 0800, website www.unitedagents.co.uk)

WHITFIELD, Dr Michael; s of Arthur Whitfield (d 1990), and Ethel, *née* Woodward (d 1986); *b* 15 June 1940; *Educ* King's Sch Chester, Univ of Leeds (BSc, PhD); *m* 31 July 1961, Jean Ann (d 1984), da of Stanley Beige Rowe (d 1964); 3 da (Katherine b 1962, Clare b 1964, Juliet b 1965), 1 s (Benjamin b 1968); *Career* res scientist CSIRO Fisheries and Oceanography Sydney Australia 1964–69, dir Marine Biological Assoc Plymouth 1987–99 (sr princ res scientist 1970–87), dir Plymouth Marine Laboratory 1994–95 (dep dir 1988–94); hon prof Univ of Plymouth 1995–2008; pres Challenger Soc for Marine Sci 1996–98, vice-pres Sir Alister Hardy Fndn for Ocean Sci 1992–99, vice-pres Marine Biological Soc of the UK 2000–; Hon DSc Univ of Göteborg 1991, Hon DSc Univ of Plymouth 2001; FRSC, FGS; *Books* Ion-selective Electrodes for the Analysis of Natural Waters (1970), Marine Electro Chemistry (1981), Tracers in the Ocean (1988), Light & Life in the Sea (1990), Aquatic Life Cycle Strategies (1999); *Recreations* hill walking, photography, watching wildlife; *Style—* Dr Michael Whitfield; ✉ The Marine Biological Association of the UK, The Laboratory, Citadel Hill, Plymouth PL1 2PB (e-mail mikewhit@btinternet.com)

WHITFIELD, Patrick John; s of Albert Victor Whitfield (d 1978), and Rose Anna, *née* Maye (d 1971); *b* 7 November 1931; *Educ* Wandsworth Sch, King's Coll London, St George's Hosp Med Sch (MB BS, LRCP); *m* 23 July 1955, Doris Eileen, da of Herbert Nelson Humphries (d 1962); 2 da (Roseanne Louise (Mrs Paul Roblin) b 8 Sept 1968, Natalie Anne b 17 Nov 1975); *Career* jr hosp appts 1958–64, trained at Regnl Plastic Surgery Centre Queen Mary's Univ Hosp; sr registrar: seconded Plastic Surgery Centre Oxford 1966, Queen Mary's Univ Hosp 1967–72 (seconded to Paris, Rome, NY); conslt plastic surgn: Westminster Hosp and SW Thames RHA 1972, Royal London Hosp Tst 1996–; recognised teacher in plastic surgery Univ of London (Westminster and Charing Cross Hosps), Plastic Surgery Section RSM 1973–81 (hon sec, memb Cncl, vice-pres, pres), memb Res Ctee Br Assoc of Plastic Surgns 1974–77, hon sec Br Assoc of Aesthetic Plastic Surgns 1977–83; memb: Br Assoc of Plastic Surgns 1972, Br Assoc of Aesthetic Plastic Surgns 1978 (fndr); FRSM 1968, FRCS; *Books* Operative Surgery (contrib); *Recreations* golf, scuba-diving, tennis, art appreciation; *Clubs* Athenaeum, Royal Wimbledon Golf; *Style—* Patrick Whitfield, Esq; ✉ 3 Coombe Neville, Warren Road, Kingston upon Thames, Surrey KT2 7HW (☎ 020 8949 4344)

WHITFIELD, Prof Roderick; s of late Prof John Humphreys Whitfield, and Joan, *née* Herrin, ARCA; *b* 20 July 1937, Oxford; *Educ* King Edward's Sch Birmingham, SOAS Univ of London, St John's Coll Cambridge (MA), Princeton Univ (MFA, PhD); *m* 1, 11 July 1963 (m dis 1983), Dr Frances Elizabeth, da of Prof Richard Charles Oldfield; 2 da (Martha-Ming b 1965, Tanya b 1967), 1 s (Aldus b 1970); m 2, 25 Aug 1983, Prof Youngsook Pak; *Career* Offr Cadet Jt Serv Sch for Linguists RAF 1955–57, PO RAFVR 1957, Flying Offr RAFVR; res assoc and lectr Princeton Univ 1964–66, res fell St John's Coll Cambridge 1966–68, asst keeper 1st class Dept of Oriental Antiquities Br Museum 1968–84, prof of Chinese and East Asian art Univ of London and head Percival David Fndn of Chinese Art 1984–93, Percival David chair of Chinese and East Asian art SOAS Univ of London 1993–2002 (prof emeritus 2002–); research fell Dunhuang Acad 1999–, Shaw lectr Nat Univ of Singapore 2009; memb Cncl Oriental Ceramic Soc 1984–93; sr ed Jl of Korean Art and Archaeology 2008–12; Ip Yee Memorial Medal Oriental Ceramic Soc of Hong Kong 1990; fell Palace Museum Beijing 2003–, fell Gansu Provincial Museum 2008–; fell Royal Asiatic Soc 1999–; Ma Ma Charitable Fndn visiting prof, Univ of Hong Kong 2015–; *Books* In Pursuit of Antiquity (1969), The Art of Central Asia, The Stein Collection at the British Museum (3 vols, 1982–85, Chinese Translation vol 1 2014), Treasures From Korea (ed 1984), Korean Art Treasures (ed 1986), Caves of the Thousand Buddhas (1990), Fascination of Nature: Plants and Insects in Chinese Painting and Ceramics of the Yuan Dynasty 1279–1368 (1993), The Problem of Meaning in Early Chinese Ritual Bronzes (ed, 1993), Dunhuang, Caves of the Singing Sands: Buddhist Art from the Silk Road (2 vols, 1995), The Arts of Central Asia: the Pelliot Collection in the Musée Guimet (collaborative translator, 1996), The Golden Age of Chinese Archaeology (contrib, 1999), Exploring China's Past: New Discoveries and Studies in Archaeology and Art (jt ed and translator, 2000), Cave Temples of Mogao: Art and History on the Silk Road (jt author, 2000, 2nd ed 2015), La Sérinde, Terre d'échanges (contrib, 2000), Handbook of Korean Art: Earthenware and Celadon (jt author, 2002), Handbook of Korean Art: Buddhist Sculpture (jt author, 2002), Handbook of Korean Art: Folk Paintings (ed, 2002), New Perspectives on China's Past: Chinese Archaeology in the Twentieth Century (contrib, 2004), Compassion and Fascination (contrib, 2004), Korean True-View Landscape Paintings by Chong Son (1676–1759) (jt trans and ed, 2005), Long Life: Festschrift in honour of Roger Goepper (contrib, 2006), Anthology of Research on Spring Festival on the River (in Chinese, contrib, 2007), Il Celeste Impero: Dall' Esercito di Terracotta alla Via della Seta (contrib, 2008), China at the Court of the Emperors: Unknown Masterpieces (contrib, 2009), The Printed Image in China: From the 8th to the 21st Centuries (contrib, 2010), What Makes a Masterpiece? (contrib, 2010), Catalogue of the Wou Lien-Pai Museum of Chinese Art (jt author, 2011), Bridges to Heaven: Essays on East Asian Art in Honor of Professor Wen C Fong (contrib, 2011), Collected Works of Korean Buddhism Vol IX: Collection of Chinese Poetry of the Great Monks of Korea (ed and jt trans, 2012), New Perspectives on Qing Ming Shanghetu (contrib, 2012), Lost Generation: Qing Loyalists and the Formation of Modern Chinese Culture (jt ed, 2012); *Style—* Prof Roderick Whitfield; ✉ 7 St Paul's Crescent, London NW1 9XN (e-mail rw5@soas.ac.uk)

WHITFIELD, Susan Margaret; da of Sir James Bottomley, KCMG, and Barbara, *née* Vardon (d 1994); sis of Peter Bottomley, MP, *qv*; *b* 23 November 1946; *Educ* Westonbirt Sch, New Hall Cambridge (MA); *m* 1; 3 da (Kitty b 1971, Charlotte (Mrs Nightingale) b 1973, Felicity (Mrs Murphy) b 1973); m 2, 1982, Robert Whitfield, s of Charles Kershaw Whitfield; 1 da (Poppy b 1983), 1 s (Jack b 1985); *Career* biology and sci teacher: Brooklands Co Secdy Sch 1968–69, Aylesbury HS 1969–72, The Misbourne Sch 1978–79, St Paul's Girls' Sch 1980–91; headmistress Notting Hill and Ealing HS (GDST) 1991–2008; pres Schoolmistresses and Governesses Benevolent Instn 2009–; govr Westonbirt Sch Glos 2008–; educnl and environmental interests; involved with Multiple Births Fndn; Freeman the Worshipful Co of Drapers; assoc memb Inst of Biology; *Recreations* family, gardening; *Style—* Mrs Susan Whitfield; ✉ Coombe Head, Tresham, Wotton-under-Edge, Gloucestershire GL12 7RW

WHITING, Alan; s of late Albert Edward Whiting, and late Marjorie Irene, *née* Rodgers; *b* 14 January 1946; *Educ* Acklam Hall Secdy GS Middlesbrough, UEA (BA), UCL (MSc); *m* 17 Aug 1968, Annette Frances, da of late James Kitchener Pocknee; 2 da (Alison Jane b 8 March 1976, Claire Louise b 17 Dec 1979), 2 s (Matthew Peter b 27 June 1977, Paul Michael b 11 Nov 1982); *Career* res assoc and asst lectr UEA 1967–68, cadet economist HM Treasy 1968–69, economic asst Dept of Econ Affairs and Miny of Technol 1969–70; economist: Euro Free Trade Assoc Geneva 1970–72, CBI 1972–73; DTI: econ advsr 1974–78, sr econ advsr 1979–83, Industrial and Commercial Policy Div 1983–85, under sec Economics Div 1985–88, Econ Mgmnt and Educn Div 1989, Fin and Resource Mgmnt Div 1989–92, Financial Services Div 1992; HM Treasy: under sec Securities and Investment Services Gp 1992–95, dep dir Financial Regulation 1995–97; exec dir regulation and compliance London Metal Exchange 1997–2004, chm and md Merlan Financial 2004–; dir Nymex (Europe) Ltd 2005–07, dir Nymex London Ltd 2008–09; chm: Gibraltar Financial Services Cmmn 2011–14 (dir 2005–11), NYSE/EURONEXT/Liffe 2012–14 (dir 2006–12); dep chm: Cncl The Mortgage Code Register of Intermediaries 1998–99, Mortgage Code Compliance Bd 2000–06; dir: Banking Code Standards Bd 2005–09, Lending Standards Bd 2009–14, ICE Futures Europe 2013–; *Books* The Trade Effects of EFTA and the EEC (jtly, 1972), The Economics of Industrial Subsidies (ed, 1975); *Recreations* building, gardening, sport, music; *Clubs* Bracknell Lawn Tennis, Mill Ride Golf (Ascot); *Style—* Alan Whiting, Esq; ✉ e-mail alan@whiting87.freeserve.co.uk

WHITING, (David) John; CBE (2016, OBE 2008); s of Peter Whiting (d 1992), and Isabel Whiting (d 2002); *b* 20 March 1951, Hull, E Yorks; *Educ* Hymers Coll Hull, Victoria Univ of Manchester (BSc); *m* 20 Aug 1977, Susan Barbara (Sue), da of Gwyn Jones (d 2001), and Joan Jones (d 2013); 3 da (Carolyn, Helen, Fiona); *Career* tax ptnr Price Waterhouse (now PricewaterhouseCoopers LLP) 1984–2009 (joined 1972), tax policy dir Chartered Inst of Taxation 2009–13, tax dir Office of Tax Simplication 2010–; First Tier Tax Tbnl 2009–13; non-exec dir HM Revenue and Customs 2013–, memb Bd Revenue Scotland 2015–; Tax Personality of the Year 2001, Tax Writer of the Year 2004, Lifetime Achievement Award 2009, CIOT Cncl Award 2014; memb: ICAEW 1975, Chartered Inst of Taxation 1978 (pres 2001–02); *Publications* Mirrlees Review of UK Taxation (contrib, 2008); frequent author of articles in professional and general press on taxation matters; *Recreations* family life, DIY, history, Fairport Convention, watching cricket; *Clubs* MCC; *Style—* John Whiting, Esq, CBE; ✉ Office of Tax Simplification, 1 Horse Guards Road, London SW1A 2HQ (e-mail john.whiting@ots.gsi.gov.uk)

WHITLAM, Michael Richard; CBE (2000); s of Richard William Whitlam (d 1971), and Mary Elizabeth, *née* Land (d 1983); *b* 25 March 1947, Normanton, Yorks; *Educ* Morley GS, Tadcaster GS, Coventry Coll of Educn, Univ of Warwick (CertEd), Cranfield Inst of Technol (MPhil); *m* 24 Aug 1968, Anne Jane, da of William McCurley (d 1987); 2 da (Rowena b 1971, Kirsty b 1973); *Career* former teacher Ripon Co GS; asst govr 1969–74: HM Borstal Hollesley Bay, HMP Brixton; dir: Hammersmith Teenager Project Nat Assoc of Care and Resettlement of Offenders, UK Ops Save The Children Fund 1978–86 (former dep dir); chief exec Royal Nat Inst for the Deaf 1986–90, DG British Red Cross Soc 1991–99, ceo Mentor Fndn International (preventing substance abuse among young people) 1999–2001 (conslt 2001–02), chief exec Int Agency for the Prevention of Blindness (IAPB) 2002–05; dir: Charity Appointments 1994–2000, MW Solutions for Charity 2005–; chm: London Intermediate Treatment Assoc 1979–82, Nat Intermediate Treatment Assoc 1980–83, Sound Advantage plc 1989–90, ACENVO 1988–91 (chm Policy Ctee 1994–99); special advsr Russam GMS 2004–16; memb: Exec Cncl Howard League 1974–84, Community Alternative Young Offenders Ctee NACRO 1979–82, Exec Cncl Nat Children's Bureau 1980–86, Bd REACH 1996–2000; former pres Strategic Planning Cmmn, pres Int Fedn of Red Cross and Red Crescent Socs 1997–99, chair Chalker Fndn for Africa 2007–16, memb Bd Prisoners Abroad, tstee dir Watford FC Community Educn Tst 2008–, tstee/dir Church Mission Soc 2011–16, memb Parochial Church Cncl 2011–; *Recreations* painting, walking, keeping fit, family activities, opera, management of the voluntary sector, member St Giles Church, theatre, coordinating the Ickenham Link with Rukiga in Uganda; *Style—* Michael Whitlam, Esq, CBE; ✉ Solutions for Charity, 40 Pepys Close, Ickenham, Uxbridge, Middlesex UB10 8NY (☎ and fax 01865 678169, e-mail m.whitlam@btinternet.com)

WHITLEY, Edward Thomas; s of John Caswell Whitley, of Hamsey, and Shirley Frances, *née* Trollope; *b* 6 May 1954; *Educ* Harrow, Univ of Bristol (BSc); *m* 15 June 1984, Hon Tara Olivia Chichester-Clark, da of Baron Moyola, PC, DL (Life Peer, d 2002); 1 s (James Edward Dawson b 17 Nov 1997); *Career* Price Waterhouse & Co 1976–81, Cazenove & Co 1981–2001 (ptnr 1988–2001), chief exec International Financial Services London (IFSL) 2001–08; dir Henderson Strata Investments plc 1990–2005, chm The St Julian's Estate Ltd 2009–; chm Financial Services Sector Advsy Gp 2005–06; tstee: Restoration of Appearance and Function Tst (RAFT) 1999–2011, World Trade Center Disaster Fund 2001–06; pres S Derry Wildfowl and Game Preservation Soc; memb ICAEW 1980, FCSI 2010; *Style—* Edward Whitley, Esq; ✉ Old Vicarage, Wilmington, near Polegate, East Sussex BN26 5SW

WHITLOCK, Max Antony; s of Brian Whitlock, and Madeleine, *née* Smith; *b* 13 January 1993, Hemel Hempstead, Herts; *Educ* Longdean Secdy Sch Herts; *Career* gymnast; achievements incl: 2 Silver medals (team and pommel horse) and Bronze medal (horizontal bar) Cwlth Games 2010, Gold medal (team) European Championships 2012, 2 Bronze medals (team and pommel horse) Olympic Games 2012, Gold medal (floor), Silver medal (all around) and Bronze medal (pommel horse) European Championships 2013, 2 Gold medals (floor and pommel horse) and Bronze medal (all around) Olympic Games 2016; *Recreations* cinema, music, travel; *Clubs* S Essex Gymnastics; *Style—* Mr Max Whitlock; ✉ c/o James Cook, Professional Sports Group, The Coach House, 2 Heath Road, Weybridge, Surrey KT13 8AP (☎ 07725 165052, email james@profsports.com, website www.profsports.com, Twitter @maxwhitlock1)

WHITMARSH, Martin Richard; s of Kenneth Whitmarsh, and Betty Whitmarsh; *b* 29 April 1958, Lyndhurst, Hants; *Educ* Portsmouth Poly (BSc); *m* 1986, Deborah Ann; 1 da (Harriet b 1988), 1 s (Edward b 1992); *Career* British Aerospace (now BAE Systems): joined as structural analysis engr 1980, rising to manufacturing dir 1988–89; McLaren

W

Gp: head of ops 1989, md McLaren Racing 1997–2004, chief operating offr 2004–, ceo McLaren Racing F1 Team 2009–, team princ Vodafone McLaren Mercedes F1 Team 2009–, dep chm McLaren Automotive Ltd 2010–; chm Formula One Teams Assoc (FOTA) 2010–; Hon LLD Univ of Portsmouth 2009, Hon DTech Univ of Southampton 2009; CEng; *Clubs* Br Racing Drivers (BRDC); *Style*— Martin Whitmarsh, Esq; ✉ McLaren Racing, McLaren Technology Centre, Chertsey Road, Woking, Surrey GU21 4YH (☎ 01483 261000)

WHITMORE, Sir John Henry Douglas; 2 Bt (UK 1954), of Orsett, Co Essex; s of Col Sir Francis Henry Douglas Charlton Whitmore, 1 Bt, KCB, CMG, DSO, TD (d 1962, maternal gs of Sir William Cradock-Hartopp, 3 Bt, while his paternal grandmother was Lady Louisa Douglas, eldest da of 5 Marquess of Queensberry); *b* 16 October 1937; *Educ* Eton, RMA Sandhurst, RAC Cirencester, Esalen Inst CA; *m* 1, 1962 (m dis 1969), Ella Gunilla, da of Sven A Hansson, of Danderyd, Sweden; 1 da; *m* 2, 1977 (m dis 2007), Diana Elaine, da of Fred A Becchetti, of Calif, USA; 1 s; *Heir* s, Jason Whitmore; *Career* retired Br and European champion racing driver, subsequently businessman, currently mgmnt and sports psychologist (also concerned with psychology of int relations) and lectr in leadership, corp social responsibility, environmental sustainability and psycho-spiritual devpt; conslt to EU on driver educn; chair Performance Consits Int Ltd; author of books on the mental aspects of sport, life and work; Hon PhD Univ of E London, Hon PhD Florida Christian Univ; *Books* Coaching for Performance, Need Greed or Freedom, Mind Games – Tennis, Superdriver, The Winning Mind; author of articles in professional jls, motoring columnist Daily Telegraph; *Recreations* skiing; *Clubs* British Racing Drivers; *Style*— Sir John Whitmore, Bt; ✉ e-mail johnwhitmore@performanceconsultants.com, website www.performanceconsultants.com

WHITNEY, John Norton Braithwaite; CBE (2008); s of Dr Willis Bevan Whitney, and Dorothy Anne, *née* Robertson; *b* 20 December 1930; *Educ* Leighton Park Sch Reading; *m* 9 June 1956, Roma Elizabeth (former dancer with London Festival Ballet), da of Gp Capt Isaac Hodgson; 1 da (Fiona b 17 Nov 1958), 1 s (Alexander b 31 Jan 1961); *Career* radio prodr 1951–64; fndr: Ross Radio Productions Ltd 1951, Autocue Ltd 1955, Radio Antilles 1963; fndr dir Sagitta Productions 1968–82; dir: Consolidated Productions (UK) Ltd 1980–82, Satellite TV plc 1982; md: Capital Radio 1973–82, Really Useful Gp Ltd 1989–90 (chm 1990–95); DG Ind Broadcasting Authy 1982–89, dir Friends Provident Life Office 1982–2002, chm Friends Provident Stewardship Ctee 1985–1999, non-exec chm Trans World Communications plc 1991–94, non-exec chm Friends Provident Ethical Investment Tst plc 1994–; chm: Sony Pace National Bowl 1991–95, Radio Joint Audience Research (RAJAR) Ltd 1992–2002, Sony Radio Awards 1992–98, Advsy Ctee Proven Global Rights Fund 1993–2004, The Radio Partnership 1996–99, Caspian Publishing 1996–2002, Forever Broadcasting plc 1999–2004, Friends Provident Charitable Fndn 2002–, RADA 2003–07; non-exec dir VCI plc 1995–98; fndr Recidivists Anonymous Fellowship Tst 1962, co-fndr and chm Local Radio Assoc 1964, chm Assoc Ind Radio Contractors 1973–75 and 1980, dir Duke of York's Theatre 1979–82, memb Bd RNT 1982–94; Royal Coll of Music: memb Centenary Devpt Fund (formerly Appeal Ctee) 1982–94, chm Media and Events Ctee 1982–94; memb: Cncl Royal London Aid Soc 1966–90, Cncl Fairbridge Drake Soc (formerly Drake Fellowship) 1981, Intermediate Technol Gp 1982–85, Films TV and Video Advsy Ctee Br Cncl 1983–89, Industry and Commerce Liaison Ctee Royal Jubilee Tsts 1986–89 (memb Admin Cncl of Tsts 1981–85), Bd Open Coll 1987–89, Cncl for Charitable Support 1989–93, Bd City of London Sinfonia 1994–2001; chm of tstees: Soundaround (nat sound magazine for the blind) 1981–2001 (life pres 2000), Artsline 1983–2000 (life pres 2001); tstee Venture Tst 1982–86, patron MusicSpace Tst 1990, tstee Hospital Broadcasting Assoc 1993–; govr: English Nat Ballet (formerly London Festival Ballet) 1989–91, Performing Arts and Technol Sch 1992–2001; vice-chm Japan Festival 1991 (chm Japan Festival Media Ctee 1991–92), tstee Japan Festival Educn Tst 1992–2003; vice-pres: Cwlth Youth Exchange Cncl 1982–85, RNID 1988–2004; pres: London Marriage Guidance Cncl 1983–90, TV and Radio Industries Club 1985–86 (companion 1979–); chm: Theatre Investment Fund 1990–2001, Br American Arts Assoc 1992–95, RADA 2003 (chm Cncl 2003–07); chm of tstees Friends Provident Charitable Fndn 2004–06; hon memb BAFTA, FRTS (vice-pres 1986–89), fell Radio Acad 1997, Hon FRCM, FRSA; *Books* To Serve the People (memoir, 2013); *Recreations* chess, photography, sculpture; *Clubs* Garrick, Whitefriars; *Style*— John N B Whitney, Esq, CBE; ✉ 5 Church Close, Todber, Dorset DT10 1JH (☎ 01258 820534, e-mail john@johnwhitney.co.uk)

WHITNEY, Dr Paul Michael; s of John Henry Whitney (d 1980), of Bexhill, and Irene, *née* Tither; *b* 4 May 1948; *Educ* Judd Sch Tonbridge, Aston Univ (BSc, PhD (Physical Chemistry)), Cranfield Sch of Mgmnt (MBA); *m* 1971, Melanie Jane, da of Gordon E A Hounslow; 1 da (Natasha Louise b 12 March 1973), 2 s (Benjamin Paul b 10 Nov 1974, Jonathan Mark b 20 Sept 1977); *Career* paper mill tech mangr Courtaulds/CDC Swaziland 1974–79 (research chemist/mgmnt trainee 1972–74), with Industrial and Commercial Finance Corp (now 3i plc) 1980–83; CIN Management Ltd: venture capital dir 1984, venture capital md 1985, chm 1988–93, chief exec 1988–93; chm NatWest Private Equity and chief exec NatWest Investment Management Ltd 1993–96, chief exec Sun Life Asset Management Ltd 1996–98, chm and chief exec Parallel Ventures Managers Ltd 1998–; non-exec dir Phytopharm plc; *Recreations* windsurfing, motor sports; *Clubs* RAC; *Style*— Dr Paul Whitney; ✉ Parallel Ventures Managers Ltd, 49 St James's Street, London SW1A 1JT (☎ 020 7600 9105, fax 020 7491 3372)

WHITTAKER, Craig; MP; s of Frank Whittaker, and Marjorie Whittaker; *b* 30 August 1962, Radcliffe, Lancs; *Educ* Belmont State HS NSW Australia; *Children* 1 s (Lee David Neil b 8 May 1987), 2 da (Sophie Jane b 12 April 1990, Bethannie Marie b 13 June 1994); *Career* retail gen mangr 1980–2009; MP (Cons) Calder Valley 2010–; PPS to the Immigration Min Home Office 2015–; memb Educn Select Ctee 2010–15, co-chair All Pty Parly Gp Street Children 2011–, chair All Pty Parly Gp Looked After Children & Care Leavers 2012–15, chair All Pty Parly Gp Fostering & Adoption 2012–15; *Style*— Craig Whittaker, Esq, MP; ✉ House of Commons, London SW1A 0AA (☎ 020 7219 7031, fax 020 7219 1054, e-mail craig.whittaker.mp@parliament.uk, website www.craigwhittakermp.co.uk); constituency office: Unit 7, Brookfoot Business Park, Elland Road, Brighouse, West Yorkshire HD6 2SD (☎ 01484 711260, fax 01484 718288)

WHITTAKER, (Rosemary) Jane; da of Robert Charnock Whittaker, of Blackpool, Lancs, and Betty, *née* Howard; *b* 27 February 1955; *Educ* Queen Mary's Sch Lytham, Univ of Manchester (LLB); *m* 6 Aug 1987, Colin Michael Brown; *Career* articled clerk Manchester (admitted slr 1978), slr International Computers Ltd (ICL) 1982–88, ptnr Macfarlanes slrs 1988–; chair Cons Lawyers' Assoc 1995–98; memb: Law Soc (memb Cncl 1995–, chair Equal Opportunities Ctee 1996–99), Assoc of Women Slrs (chair 1994–95); *Books* The Role of Directors in the European Community (1992); *Recreations* swimming, theatre, entertaining and cooking; *Style*— Ms Jane Whittaker; ✉ Macfarlanes, 10 Norwich Street, London EC4A 1BD (☎ 020 7831 9222, fax 020 7831 9607)

WHITTAKER, (Alan) Mark; s of Alan Whittaker, of Darwen, Lancs, and Jean, *née* Almond; *b* 17 April 1957; *Educ* John Ruskin HS Croydon, Univ of Durham (BA); *Children* 1 da (Daisy Ella May b 17 March 1998), 1 s (Jack Louis Mark b 14 Nov 2000); *Career* grad trainee Thomson Regnl Newspapers Newcastle upon Tyne 1979, reporter Lancashire Evening Telegraph 1980–82, BBC Radio Lancashire 1983–86, BBC Radio West Midlands 1986–88; presenter: Newsbeat BBC (Radio 1) 1988–96, Costing the Earth (Radio 4) 1994, Kershaw and Whittaker (Radio 5 Live) 1994–95, You & Yours (Radio 4) 1996–2002, Pick of the Week (Radio 4) 1998–2002, The World Today (World Service) 2003–12, One Planet (World Service) 2004–10, World Business Report 2012–, Business Matters 2013–; Reporter of the Year Sony Award (Bronze) 1995; *Recreations* hiking, football, public houses; *Clubs* Blackburn Rovers FC, Kidderminster Harriers, Selborne Soc, Friends of Real Lancashire, Pitshanger FC; *Style*— Mark Whittaker, Esq; ✉ 200 Meadvale Road, Ealing, London W5 1LT (☎ 020 8810 4757)

WHITTEMORE, Prof Colin Trengove; s of Hugh Ashcroft Whittemore (d 1983), of Mollington, Chester, and Dorothea, *née* Nance (d 2008); *b* 16 July 1942; *Educ* Rydal Sch, Harper Adams Agric Coll, Univ of Newcastle upon Tyne (BSc, PhD, DSc, NDA); *m* 24 Sept 1966, Christine, da of John Leslie Featherstone Fenwick (d 1964), of Corbridge, Northumberland; 3 da (Joanna b 1970, Emma b 1976, Rebecca b 1985), 1 s (Jonathan b 1974); *Career* lectr in agric Univ of Edinburgh 1970–78, head of Animal Prodn Advsy and Devpt E of Scotland Coll of Agric 1978–84, head Animal Sci Div Edinburgh Sch of Agric 1984–90; Univ of Edinburgh: prof of animal prodn 1984–90, head Dept of Agric 1989–90, prof of agric and rural economy 1990–2007, head Inst of Ecology and Resource Mgmnt 1990–2000, postgrad dean 2002–2007, emeritus prof 2007–; Sir John Hammond Prize, RASE Gold medal, Mignini Oscar and David Black award for scientific contribs and res; pres BSAS 1998; FRSE; *Books* Practical Pig Nutrition (with F W H Elsley, 1976), Lactation (1980), Pig Production (1980), Pig Science (1987), The Science and Practice of Pig Production (1993, 3 edn 2006), A Kindly Winter (2010), An Innocent Abroad (2011), A Living from the Edinburgh Countryside (2012), Curling Through Two-Hundred Years of Penicuik Curling Club: Rivalry and Good Fellowship (2014), Newlands (2014); *Recreations* skiing, horses; *Clubs* Farmers'; *Style*— Prof Colin Whittemore, FRSE; ✉ e-mail colin.whittemore@btinternet.com

WHITTING, HE Ian Robert; OBE (2011); *m* Tracy Gallagher; 2 da; *Career* FCO 1972–74, Moscow 1975–76, Tunis 1976–78, press attaché Athens 1980–83, FCO 1983–85, second sec (chancery) Moscow 1985–88, FCO 1988–90, first sec EU and economic Dublin 1990–94, dep head of mission and consul Abidjan 1994–97, conference media coordinator Commonwealth Heads of Government Meeting, G8 and EU Presidency FCO 1997–98, dep head Africa Equatorial Dept Sec of State's Special Rep to the Great Lakes Region FCO 1998–2002, head EU (Bilateral) Dept FCO 2002–03, dir of EU and econ affrs and subsequently dep head of mission and consul gen Athens 2003–08, ambass to Iceland 2008–12, ambass to Montenegro 2013–; *Style*— HE Mr Ian Whitting, OBE; ✉ c/o FCO (Podgorica), King Charles Street, London SW1A 2AH

WHITTINGDALE, Rt Hon John Flasby Lawrance; OBE (1990), PC (2015), MP; s of John Whittingdale (d 1974), and Margaret Esmé Scott, *née* Napier; *b* 16 October 1959; *Educ* Winchester, UCL (BSc); *m* 1990 (m dis 2008), Ancilla Campbell Murfitt; 1 s (Henry John Flasby b 26 May 1993), 1 da (Alice Margaret Campbell b 20 Dec 1995); *Career* head of political section Cons Res Dept 1982–84, special advsr to sec of state for Trade and Indust 1984–87, mangr NM Rothschild 1987, political sec to Rt Hon Margaret Thatcher as PM 1988–90 and mangr of her private office 1990–92; MP (Cons): Colchester S and Maldon 1992–97, Maldon and Chelmsford E 1997–2010, Maldon 2010–; PPS to Eric Forth, MP (min of state DfEE) until 1996, memb Parly Health Select Ctee 1993–97, oppn whip 1997–98, oppn frontbench spokesman on Treasy affrs 1998–99, PPS to Ldr of the Oppn 1999–2001, shadow sec of state for trade and industry 2001–02, shadow sec of state for culture, media and sport 2002–03, shadow sec of state for agriculture, fisheries and food 2003–04, shadow sec of state for culture, media and sport 2004–05, memb Exec Cons 1922 Ctee 2005–2006, chm Parly Culture Media and Sport Select Ctee 2005–, chm Jt Ctee on Privacy and Injunctions 2011–12, sec of state for culture, media and sport 2015–; sec Cons Parly Home Affairs Ctee 1992–94, Parly memb Bd Cons Pty 2006–10, vice-chm Cons Parly 1922 Ctee 2006–; memb Selsdon Gp; FRSA 2009; *Clubs* Essex; *Style*— The Rt Hon John Whittingdale, OBE, MP; ✉ House of Commons, London SW1A 0AA (☎ 020 7219 3557, fax 020 7219 2522, e-mail john.whittingdale.mp@parliament.uk)

WHITTINGHAM, Michael (Mike); s of Francis Sadler Whittingham (d 1972), of London, and Jean Mary, *née* Tarlton (d 1989); *b* 11 June 1954; *Educ* Alleyn's Sch Dulwich, Univ of Leicester (BA, MA), Loughborough Univ (PGCE); *m* Christine Paterson, da of Alexander McMeekin; *Career* athletics coach; memb Herne Hill Harriers; represented: London Schs, English Schs, Surrey Co, Southern Cos, Br Univs, 25 GB caps (400m hurdles, 800m, 4 x 400m); best performances: semi-final Euro Indoor Championships 1981, fourth Cwlth Games 1982; nat sr event coach 400m 1990– (jr event coach 400m hurdles 1987–88), exec dir Scottish Inst of Sport 2006– (overseen the most successful cycle for Scottish sport); coached athletes incl: Jon Ridgeon, Roger Black (Silver medal 1996), Kriss Akabusi (Bronze medal 1992), John Regis, Marcus Adam, Christine McMeekin, Jacqui Parker, Mark Richardson, Mark Hylton, Maria Akara, Nicola Sanders 2004–06 (Bronze medallist World Championships 2005, Gold medallist Cwlth Games 2006); also coached World Championship 4x400m team 1991 (Gold medal) and Olympic 4x400m team 1996 (Gold medal); Post Office Counters Coach of the Year 1992; lectr Univ of Lyon 1978–80, teacher 1980–85, dir of sport and physical educn Univ of Reading 1985–88, head of leisure servs Waverley BC 1988–92, Direction Sportive (sports mgmnt & devpt co) 1992–, dir of tech servs UKSport 2003–, exec dir Scottish Inst of Performance Sport 2006–, dir of high performance and Inst of Sport 2010– (inst progs won 3 Olympic/Paralympic medals Sochi Winter Olympics 2014); radio commentator BBC Radio and BBC World Service 1991–, broadcaster for OBS London Olympics 2012; Minister's nominee on Regnl Cncl Sports Cncl 1993–96; expert advsr: UK Sports Cncl, UK Sports Cncl Lottery Unit; conslt IAAF; mediation specialist, facilitation specialist and executive coach; memb Bd Winning Scotland Fndn; fundraiser Cancer Research Tst; Winston Churchill fell 1990; memb: Inst of Leisure Amenity Mgmnt, BASC, Nat Tst, UK/SA Initiative, Winning Students Advsy Bd, Br Curling Bd, SportScotland Bd; *Recreations* languages, piano, reading, arts, natural history, recreational sport, sea kayaking, skiing, gardening, music; *Style*— Mike Whittingham, Esq; ✉ Rhodens, The Green, Sands, Farnham, Surrey GU10 1LL (☎ 07791 688845)

WHITTINGTON, Prof Geoffrey; CBE (2001); s of Bruce Whittington (d 1988), and Dorothy Gwendoline, *née* Gent (d 1996); *b* 21 September 1938; *Educ* Sir Roger Manwood's GS, Dudley GS, LSE, Fitzwilliam Coll Cambridge, Univ of Cambridge (ScD); *m* 7 Sept 1963, Joyce Enid, da of George Smith (d 1963); 2 s (Alan Geoffrey b 1972, Richard John b 1976); *Career* res posts Dept of Applied Economics Cambridge 1962–72, fell Fitzwilliam Coll Cambridge 1966–72; prof of accountancy and finance: Univ of Edinburgh 1972–75, Univ of Bristol 1975–88; Univ of Bristol: head of Dept of Economics 1981–84, dean Faculty of Social Sciences 1985–87; PriceWaterhouseCoopers prof of fin accounting Univ of Cambridge 1988–2001 (emeritus prof 2001–), fell Fitzwilliam Coll Cambridge 1988–, hon prof Univ of Sussex 2014–; professorial res fell ICAS 1996–2001, sr research assoc Judge Business Sch Cambridge 2006–; memb: MMC 1987–96, Accounting Standards Bd 1994–2001 and 2006–09, Advsy Body on Fair Trading in Telecommunications 1997–98, Int Accounting Standards Bd 2001–06, Academic Panel CMA 2014–; Founding Societies' Centenary Award ICAEW 2003; Hon DSc Univ of Edinburgh 1998, Hon DUniv Univ of Sussex 2014; FCA 1973 (ACA 1963); *Books* Growth Profitability and Valuation (with A Singh, 1968), The Prediction of Profitability (1971), Inflation Accounting (1983), The Debate on Inflation Accounting (with D Tweedie, 1984), The Elements of Accounting (1992), Profitability, Accounting Theory and Methodology (2007); *Recreations* music, walking, visual arts; *Clubs* Athenaeum; *Style*— Prof Geoffrey Whittington, CBE; ✉ Fitzwilliam College, Cambridge CB3 0DG (e-mail gw12@cam.ac.uk)

WHITTLE, Lindsay; AM; *b* Caerffili; *Career* ldr Caerffili County Borough Cncl 1999–2004 and 2008–11, memb Nat Assembly of Wales (Plaid Cymru) S Wales E 2011–; *Style*—

Lindsay Whittle, Esq, AM; ✉ Ty Watkyn, 4A Church Road, Abertridwr, Caerphilly CF83 4DL

WHITTLE, Prof Martin John; *b* 6 July 1944; *Educ* William Grimshaw Secdy Modern Sch London, Southgate Tech Coll London, Univ of Manchester Med Sch (MB ChB, FRCOG, MD); *Career* house physician then house surgn Manchester Royal Infirmary 1972–73; clinical tutor Univ Hosp of S Manchester 1976–77, research fell LAC-USC Med Center Women's Hosp Los Angeles Calif 1978–79, conslt obstetrician Queen Mother's Hosp Glasgow and conslt gynaecologist Royal Samaritan Hosp for Women Glasgow 1982–91, dir of fetal med Univ Dept of Midwifery Queen Mother's Hosp Glasgow 1986–91; Univ of Birmingham: prof of fetal med Birmingham Women's Hosp 1991–2006, dir Div of Reproductive & Child Health 1998–2003, associate dean (Educn) 2004–06, emeritus prof 2006–; clinical co-dir NCC-WCH RCOG 2006–09; memb: Scientific Advsy and Pathology Ctee RCOG 1983–86, Working Gp on Infertility Servs in Scotland 1989–90, MRC Working Pty on Phenylketonuria 1991–92, Subspecialist Bd RCOG 1989–92, Birthright/RCOG Research Ctee 1991, RCOG Working Pty on Down's Screening 1992; chm Standing Jt Ctee RCOG and RCR 1993–96 (memb 1987–90, vice-chm 1990–93), fell Cncl RCOG 1997–2002; chm Antenatal Sub-Gp Nat Screening Ctee 2000–05; memb Editorial Bd: Prenatal Diagnosis 1990–; hon medical offr Jubilee Sailing Tst 2010–; hon chair Medical Advsy Ctee Jubilee Sailing Tst 2011–; memb: Blair Bell Research Soc, Perinatal Club, Int Fetoscopy Working Gp, Gynaecological Visiting Soc; FRCPGlas 1987 (MRCPGlas 1985), FRCOG 1988; *Books* Prenatal Diagnosis in Obstetric Practice (with Prof J M Connor, 1989, 2 edn 1995), Fetal Medicine: Basic Science and Clinical Practice (with C H Rodeck, 1999, 2 edn 2009); author of various book chapters and numerous articles; Just Another Trip (novel, 2015); *Recreations* flying (PPL), keen sailor, scuba-diving, enjoying classical music and art; *Style*— Prof Martin Whittle; ✉ e-mail mwhittle@doctors.org.uk

WHITTOW, Hugh John; s of Jack Whittow, and Marion Whittow; *b* 20 March 1951, Haverfordwest, Pembrokeshire; *Educ* Haverfordwest GS; *m* 1984, Lesley Grant; 2 da; *Career* reporter: Western Telegraph Haverfordwest 1968–71, Western Daily Press Bristol 1971, South Wales Echo Cardiff 1971–73, London Evening News 1973–78, Daily Star 1978–82, The Sun 1982–87; dep ed Daily Star 1987–2001, launch ed Daily Star Sunday 2002–03; Daily Express: dep ed 2003–11, ed 2011–; memb Editor's Code of Practice Ctee; Freeman of Haverfordwest 1998; *Recreations* family, skiing, rugby, golf, walking our dog Darcey on Newgale Beach, horse racing; *Style*— Hugh Whittow, Esq; ✉ Daily Express, Northern and Shell Building, 10 Lower Thames Street, London EC3R 6EN (✆ 020 8612 7000, fax 020 8612 7766)

WHITTY, Prof Geoffrey James (Geoff); CBE (2011); s of Frederick James Whitty (d 1981), and Kathleen May, *née* Lavender (d 1968); *b* 31 December 1946; *Educ* Latymer Upper Sch, St John's Coll Cambridge, Inst of Educn Univ of London (DLit); *Career* teacher secondary schs 1969–73, lectr Univ of Bath 1973–80, lectr KCL 1981–84, prof and dean Bristol Poly 1985–89, Goldsmiths' prof Goldsmiths Coll London 1990–92; Inst of Educn Univ of London: Karl Mannheim prof 1992–2000, dir 2000–10, dir emeritus 2011–; prof: Univ of Bath 2011–13, Bath Spa Univ 2014–, Univ of Newcastle Australia 2014–; Lady Plowden Meml Medal 2009; Hon DEd UWE 2001, Hon EdD Hong Kong Inst of Educn 2012; hon fell Coll of Teachers 2001; FRSA 1999, FAcSS 2002, fell American Educnl Research Assoc (AERA) 2015; *Books* Society, State and Schooling (jtly, 1977), Sociology and School Knowledge (1985), State and Private Education (jtly, 1989), Specialisation and Choice in Urban Education (jtly, 1993), Devolution and Choice in Education (jtly, 1998), Teacher Education in Transition (jtly, 2000), Making Sense of Education Policy (2002), Education and the Middle Class (jtly, 2003), Research and Policy in Education (2016); *Recreations* travel, reading, politics, football; *Clubs* Athenaeum; *Style*— Prof Geoff Whitty, CBE; ✉ e-mail g.whitty@ucl.ac.uk

WHITTY, Baron (Life Peer UK 1996), of Camberwell in the London Borough of Southwark; (John) Lawrence Whitty; PC (2005); s of Frederick James Whitty (d 1981), and Kathleen May Whitty (d 1967); *b* 15 June 1943; *Educ* Latymer Upper Sch, St John's Coll Cambridge; *m* 1, 11 Jan 1969 (m dis 1986), Tanya Margaret, da of Tom Gibson, of South Shields; 2 s (Hon Michael Sean b 1970, Hon Daniel James b 1972); m 2, 1 June 1993, Angela, da of James Forrester, of Glasgow; *Career* Hawker Siddeley 1962; Civil Serv 1965–70, Miny of Aviation, UKAEA, Miny of Technol; Economics Dept TUC 1970–73, nat research and political offr GMB (formerly Gen and Municipal Workers Union) 1973–85, gen sec Lab Pty 1985–94 (Euro sec 1994–97); a Lord in Waiting (Govt whip) 1997–98, Parly under-sec of state Dept for Environment, Food and Rural Affrs (formerly DETR) 1998–2005; chair Consumer Focus 2006–10; memb: Bd Ofwat 2006, Bd Environment Agency 2006–12; memb: Lab Pty (Islington, Greenwich, Dulwich, Battersea, Peckham, Westminster S, N Dorset), Fabian Soc; Friends of the Earth; *Recreations* swimming, walking, theatre; *Style*— The Lord Whitty

WHITWORTH, John Vincer; s of Hugh Hope Aston Whitworth, MBE (d 1996), of Strawberry Hill, Middlesex, and Elizabeth, *née* Boyes (d 1959); *b* 11 December 1945; *Educ* Royal HS Edinburgh, Merton Coll Oxford (MA, BPhil), Univ of Edinburgh; *m* 2 Aug 1975, Doreen Ann, da of Cecil Roberts; 2 da (Eleanor Ruth b 1 Jan 1984, Catherine Rebecca b 20 March 1987); *Career* poet; teacher of: English Colchester English Studies Centre 1970–71, business studies and economics Centre of Economic and Political Studies 1971–82 (exec dir until 1982); reviewer Poetry Review and The Spectator, poetry broadcast on BBC TV 1994 and 1995; *Awards* Alice Hunt Bartlett Award of the Poetry Soc 1980, South East Arts Award 1980, Observer Book of the Year (for Poor Butterflies) 1982, Barbara Campion Meml Prize 1983, prizewinner National Poetry Competition 1984, Cholmondeley Award for Poetry 1988; *Books* Unhistorical Fragments (1980), Poor Butterflies (1982), Lovely Day for a Wedding (1985), Tennis and Sex and Death (1989), The Faber Book of Blue Verse (ed, 1990), Landscape With Small Humans (1993), The Complete Poetical Works of Phoebe Flood (1996), From the Sonnet History of Modern Poetry (illustrated by Gerald Mangan, 1999), Writing Poetry (2001), The Whitworth Gun (2002), Being the Bad Guy (2007); *Recreations* cooking, playing with my daughters, suffering with the England cricket team, rearing guinea-pigs; *Style*— John Whitworth, Esq; ✉ 20 Lovell Road, Rough Common, Canterbury, Kent CT2 9DG (✆ 01227 462400)

WHORWELL, Prof Peter James; s of Arthur Victor Whorwell, of Canterbury, and Beryl Elizabeth, *née* Walton; *b* 14 June 1946; *Educ* Dover Coll, Univ of London (BSc, MB BS, PhD, MD); *Career* conslt physician and prof of med Univ of Manchester 1981–; dir S Manchester Functional Gastrointestinal Diseases Serv, med advsr Int Fndn for Functional Gastrointestinal Disorders, memb Euro Expert Panel for Functional Gastrointestinal Disorders, med conslt to many pharmaceutical cos; numerous pubns on gastrointestinal diseases; memb: Br Soc Gastroenterology, American Gastroenterology Assoc; MRCS, FRCP; *Style*— Prof Peter Whorwell; ✉ Academic Department of Medicine, Wythenshawe Hospital, Manchester M23 9LT (✆ 0161 291 5813, e-mail peter.whorwell@manchester.ac.uk)

WHYMAN, Erica; OBE (2013); da of Michael Whyman, of Walton-on-Thames, Surrey, and Jacqueline, *née* Patrick (d 2003); *b* 27 October 1969, Harrogate, Yorks; *Educ* Wadham Coll Oxford (BA), Bristol Old Vic Theatre Sch, Ecole Philippe Gaulier Paris; *Career* theatre dir; assoc prodr Tricycle 1997–98, assoc dir English Touring Theatre 1998–2000, artistic dir Southwark Playhouse 1999–2001 (Peter Brook Empty Space Award), artistic dir and chief exec Gate Theatre 2001–04, chief exec Northern Stage 2005–; prodns incl: A Shadow of a Boy (RNT), The Birthday Party (Sheffield Crucible); prodns for Northern Stage: A Doll's House, Ruby Moon, Our Friends in the North, A Christmas Carol, Oh What a Lovely War (nat tour), Who's Afraid of Virginia Woolf; awarded John S Cohen bursary for dirs; fell Clore Leadership Prog; *Style*— Ms Erica Whyman, OBE; ✉ Northern Stage, Barras Bridge, Newcastle upon Tyne NE1 7RH (✆ 0191 242 7210, fax 0191 242 7257, e-mail ewhyman@northernstage.co.uk)

WHYTE, Andrew Malcolm Dorrance; s of Rev Canon Malcolm Dorrance Whyte (d 2003), of Tarleton, Lancs, and Margaret, *née* Aindow (d 1983); *b* 4 June 1960; *Educ* Merchant Taylors' Crosby, Univ of Manchester (BA); *m* July 1987, Michele Rose, da of late Anthony Wickett; 1 s (James b 10 May 1989), 1 da (Leah b 4 Nov 1992); *Career* general sec Univ of Manchester Students' Union 1982–83, vice-pres Education NUS 1985–86, youth rights offr British Youth Cncl 1986–88, media and Parly liaison mangr Barnardo's 1988–91, dep dir of Corp Affrs News Int plc 1991–96, external affrs advsr Shell International Ltd 1996–98, head of PR BBC Broadcast 1998–2000, head of corporate and public relations BBC 2000–05, exec dir advocacy and communications Arts Cncl England 2006–09, dir of communications DEFRA 2009–10, dir of communications FCO 2010–11, dir of new ways of working DEFRA 2011–12, dir Kingsnorth Communications 2012–14, head of external and internal relations FCA 2014–15, dir of communications FCA 2015–; cncllr London Borough of Redbridge 1990–94; memb: Labour Party, Bd Thames Reach Housing Assoc 1998–2014; tstee Media Tst 2001–08; memb Cncl RTS 2004–07; MIPR 1992; FRSA 2006; *Recreations* spending time with my family, football (lifelong supporter of Liverpool FC), reading, politics and current affairs; *Style*— Andrew Whyte, Esq; ✉ 13 Bluebell Road, Ashford, Kent TN23 3NW (✆ 07703 107613, e-mail amdwhyte@hotmail.co.uk)

WHYTE, Prof Moira Katherine Brigid; OBE (2014); da of Maurice Whyte, and Anne Whyte; *b* 25 September 1959, Bath; *Educ* Univ of London (BSc, MB, BS, PhD); *m* 18 June 1988, David Grossman; 2 s (William, Thomas); *Career* Sir George Franklin prof of medicine, head Dept of Infection and Immunity and head Academic Unit of Respiratory Medicine Univ of Sheffield, prof of respiratory medicine and dir MRC Centre for Inflammation Res Univ of Edinburgh 2014–, Sir John Crofton prof of respiratory medicine and head Edinburgh Med Sch 2016–; FRCP, FRCPE, FERS, FMedSci; *Style*— Prof Moira Whyte, OBE; ✉ Professor of Respiratory Medicine, Director of the MRC/UoE Centre for Inflammation Research, The University of Edinburgh, The Queen's Medical Research Institute, 47 Little France Crescent, Edinburgh, EH16 4TJ (✆ 01312 426656 (secretary), Fax: 01312 426578)

WICKENS, Prof Alan Herbert; OBE (1980); s of Leslie Herbert Wickens (d 1986), of Birmingham, and Sylvia Amelia, *née* Hazelgrove (d 1968); *b* 29 March 1929; *Educ* Ashville Coll Harrogate, Loughborough Univ of Technol (DLC, DSc), Univ of London (BSc); *m* 1, 12 Dec 1953, Eleanor Joyce Waggott (d 1984); 1 da (Valerie Joanne b 1958); m 2, 2 July 1987, Patricia Anne McNeil, da of Willoughby Gervaise Cooper, of Dawlish; *Career* res engr: Sir W G Armstrong Whitworth Aircraft Ltd 1951–55, Canadair Ltd Montreal 1955–59, A V Roe & Co Ltd 1959–62; BR: Res Dept 1962–68, dir of advanced projects 1968–71, dir of res 1971–84, dir of engrg devpt and res 1984–89; Dept of Mechanical Engrg Loughborough Univ of Technol: industrial prof 1972–76 and 1992–2013, prof of dynamics 1989–92; visiting prof Manchester Met Univ 1998–2001, visiting prof Loughborough Univ 1992–2012; writer of various pubns on dynamics of railway vehicles, high speed trains and railway technol; jt winner Macrobert award 1975; pres Int Assoc of Vehicle System Dynamics 1981–86, hon fell Derbyshire Coll of Higher Educn 1984, chm Office of Research and Experiment Union Internationale de Chemin de Fer Utrecht 1988–90; hon memb Int Assoc for Vehicle System Dynamics 2001; Hon DTech CNAA 1978, Hon Dr Open Univ 1980, Hon DTech Univ of Loughborough 2006; MAIAA 1958, MRAeS 1963, FIMechE 1971, FREng 1980; *Books* Fundamentals of Rail Vehicle Dynamics (2003); *Recreations* gardening, travel, music; *Clubs* RAF; *Style*— Prof Alan Wickens, OBE, FREng; ✉ Ecclesbourne Farmhouse, Idridgehay, Belper, Derbyshire DE56 2SB (✆ 01773 550368)

WICKENS, Mark; s of Robert Wickens, of Berkhamsted, Herts, and Pat Wickens; *b* 23 November 1959; *Educ* Dr Challoner's GS Amersham, Kingston Poly (BA); *m* Anne; 2 da (Hannah b 20 Jan 1992, Polly b 27 May 1995); *Career* formerly design gp head Michael Peters Gp (clients incl: Bass, BA, ITV, Seagram), fndr Wickens Tutt Southgate 1989 (clients incl: Britvic, Smithkline Beecham, Unilever), fndr Brandhouse 1999 (clients incl: Diamond Trading Co, GlaxoSmithKline, Unilever); memb D&AD; 3 Design Effectiveness Awards, 4 Design Week Awards, D&AD Silver Award; FRSA;; *Publications* Total Branding by Design (contrib), First Choice: The World's Leading Designers Discuss Their Work; *Recreations* jazz guitar and cooking; *Style*— Mark Wickens, Esq; ✉ Brandhouse, 10A Frederick Close, London W2 2HD (✆ 020 7262 1707, fax 020 7262 1512, e-mail mw@brandhouse.co.uk)

WICKENS, Prof Michael; s of Dennis R Wickens (d 1967), and Edith (d 1993); *b* 2 September 1940; *Educ* LSE (BSc Econ, MSc Econ); *m* 1964, Julia Ruth, *née* Parrott; 1 da (Sarah Louise b 1965), 2 s (Stephen Michael b 1967, Matthew Dennis Roden b 1969); *Career* prof of economics: Univ of Southampton 1979–90, London Business Sch 1990–93, Univ of York 1993–, prof of economics Cardiff Business Sch 2008–; special advsr House of Lords Ctee on the Monetary Policy Ctee 1999–2001, special advsr House of Lords Economic Affrs Ctee 2001–, chm HM Treasy Academic Panel 1991–98, memb Shadow Monetary Policy Ctee 2010–; managing ed The Economic Jl 1996–2004, assoc ed for numerous academic jls; conslt IMF 2000–; memb: Econometric Soc 1964–, Royal Economic Soc 1969– (memb Exec Ctee 2006–); Houblon-Norman fell Bank of England 1994, Erskine fell Univ of Canterbury 2001; *Publications* Exercises in Econometrics (with P C B Phillips, 1978), Handbook of Applied Econometrics (with M H Pesaran, 1997), Macroeconomic Theory: A Dynamic General Equilibrium Approach (2008, 2 edn 2012); various articles in learned jls; *Recreations* music, golf; *Clubs* Fulford Golf; *Style*— Professor Michael Wickens; ✉ Department of Economics and Related Studies, University of York, Heslington, York YO1 5DD (✆ 01904 433764, fax 01904 433575, e-mail mike.wickens@york.ac.uk)

WICKER-MIURIN, Fields; OBE (2007); da of Warren Jake and Marie Peachee Wicker; *b* 30 July 1958, USA; *Educ* Univ of Virginia (BA cum laude), Johns Hopkins Univ Sch of Advanced Int Studies (MA), l'Institut d'Etudes Politiques Paris, Jagiellonian Univ Kraków; *m* Dr P Miurin; *Career* mangr Southern Europe Philadelphia National Bank 1982–89, ptnr and head of European financial servs practice Strategic Planning Associates 1989–94, dir of fin and strategy London Stock Exchange 1994–97, ptnr, vice-pres and head of global financial markets AT Kearney 1998–2000, chief operating offr and ptnr Vesta Capital Advsrs Ltd 2000–02, co-fndr and ptnr Leaders' Quest 2002–; non-exec dir: United Business Media plc 1998–2004, Savills plc 2002–10 (chair Audit Ctee), Royal London Gp 2003–06 (chair Investment Ctee), D Carnegie & Co AB 2003–07, CDC Gp 2004–14 (chair Devpt Impact Ctee), BNP Paribas 2011– (memb Audit Ctee), Miny of Justice (memb Nominations Ctee) 2013–15, SCOR Se 2013– (memb Risk, Strategy and Nomination and Remuneration Ctees), Control Risks Gp 2016– (memb Audit, Nominations and Remuneration Ctees), Dept for Culture, Media and Sport 2016– (chm Audit and Risk Ctee); sr ind dir BILT Paper 2011– (chair Remuneration and Nomination Ctee, chair CSR Ctee); memb: Technol Advsy Ctee NASDAQ NY 2000–05, Exec Bd DTI 2002–08 (chair Investment Ctee 2002–06), Panel of Experts of Economic and Monetary Affrs Ctee AM Ctee European Parl 2002–06, Advsy Cncl Batten Sch of Leadership and Public Policy Univ of Virginia 2011–; tstee: London International Festival of Theatre 1997–2004, Arts & Business 1998–2001, London Musici 2000–03, Brogdale Tst 2002–04; memb Cncl Tate Membs 2000–06; memb Cncl KCL 2002–11 (chair Audit Ctee); lectr and publishes on a range of business and leadership related subjects; World Economic Forum

Global Leader for Tomorrow, TED talk, Euromoney Top 50 Women in Finance, one of Time Magazine's 14 Europeans to shape the future of Europe, Top 40 Women in Reinsurance Intelligent Insurer 2014 and 2015; memb, FORUM; FRSA 1997, FKC; *Recreations* horses, nature, music, great conversations; *Clubs* Athenaeum (memb Investment Ctee), Lansdowne; *Style*— Mrs Fields Wicker-Miurin, OBE, FKC; ✉ Leaders' Quest, 11 Worple Way, Richmond-upon-Thames, Surrey TW10 6DG

WICKHAM, Prof Christopher John; s of Cyril George Wickham (d 1992), and Katharine Brenda Warington, née Moss; *b* 18 May 1950; *Educ* Millfield, Univ of Oxford (BA, DPhil); *m* 1990, Prof Leslie Brubaker, da of Prof Robert Brubaker; *Career* Univ of Birmingham: lectr 1977–87, sr lectr 1987–89, reader then prof 1993–2005; Chichele prof of medieval history Univ of Oxford 2005–; memb Lab Pty; FBA 1998; *Books* Early Medieval Italy (1981), The Mountains and the City (1988), Social Memory (with James Fentress, 1992), Land and Power (1994), Community and Clientele (1998), Legge, Pratiche e Conflitti (2000), Courts and Conflicts (2003), Framing the Early Middle Ages (2005); *Recreations* politics, travel; *Style*— Prof Chris Wickham; ✉ All Souls College, Oxford OX1 4AL (☎ 01865 279379)

WICKHAM, David Ian; s of Edwin and Betty Wickham; *Educ* St Olave's GS Orpington, S London Coll; *Career* served Fiji, Hong Kong, Caribbean and USA with Cable & Wireless plc 1977–87, various sr mgmnt positions Mercury Communications and Cable & Wireless Communications Ltd 1987–97, chm Gemini Cable Systems Ltd 1998, chief exec Cable & Wireless Global Network 1998–99, chm IsionAG 2001, chief exec Energis plc 2001–02; chm: Singlehurst Consulting 2002–, Telecom Direct Ltd 2003–07, YAC Ltd 2003–07, CCC plc 2004–07, Synchronica plc 2005–07, French Connections Ltd 2008–14, Juice Ltd 2008–14, mhub Ltd 2014–; MInstD 1998; *Recreations* golf, theatre; *Clubs* London Golf; *Style*— David Wickham, Esq; ✉ Mhub Ltd, 3rd Floor, 26 Finsbury Square, London EC2A 1DS (☎ 07800 020202, e-mail david.wickham@singlehurst.com)

WICKHAM, Rt Rev Robert James; *see:* Edmonton, Bishop of

WICKRAMASINGHE, Prof (Nalin) Chandra; s of Percival Herbert Wickramasinghe, of Sri Lanka, and Theresa Elizabeth, née Soysa; *b* 20 January 1939, Colombo, Sri Lanka; *Educ* Royal Coll Colombo, Univ of Ceylon, (BSc), Univ of Cambridge (MA, PhD, ScD); *m* 5 April 1966, (Nelum) Priyadarshini, da of Cecil Eustace Pereira; 1 s (Anil Nissanka b 1970), 2 da (Kamala Chandrika b 1972, Janaki Tara b 1981); *Career* fell Jesus Coll Cambridge 1963–73, prof and head Dept of Applied Mathematics and Astronomy UC Cardiff 1973–88, dir Inst of Fundamental Studies and advsr to Pres of Sri Lanka 1982–84; prof of applied maths and astronomy Univ of Wales 1988–2006; fndr dir Cardiff Centre for Astrobiology 2000–10, dir Buckingham Centre for Astrobiology 2011–; visiting prof of physics Univ of W Indies Mona Kingston 1994, hon prof Glamorgan Univ 2007–10, hon prof Univ of Buckingham 2011–, visiting prof Peradeniya Univ Sri Lanka 2014–, visiting by fell Churchill Coll Cambridge 2016; co-author with Prof Sir Fred Hoyle of a series of books on cosmic theory of life 1978–88; Powell Prize for English Verse Trinity Coll Cambridge 1962, Int Dag Hammarskjöld Gold Medal for Science 1986, Scholarly Achievement Award Inst of Oriental Philosophy Japan 1988, Soka Gakkai Int Peace and Culture Award 1993, Int Sahabdeen Award for Science 1996, John Snow Lecture Medal Assoc of Anaesthetists of GB and Ireland 2004; Hon Dr Soka Univ Tokyo 1996, Hon DSc Ruhana Univ Sri Lanka; FRAS, FRSA, FIMA; conferred title of Vidya Jyothi (Sri Lankan Nat Honour) 1992; *Books* Interstellar Grains (1967), Light Scattering Functions (1973), Lifecloud (with F Hoyle, 1978), Diseases from Space (1979), Evolution from Space (1981), Space Travellers (1981), From Grains to Bacteria (1984), Living Comets (1985), Archaeopteryx (1986), Cosmic Life Force (1988), The Theory of Cosmic Grains (1991), Our Place in the Cosmos (1992), Mysteries of the Universe and Life (with D Ikeda, 1994), Glimpses of Life, Time and Space (1994), Life on Mars? The Case for a Cosmic Heritage (with F Hoyle, 1997), Astronomical Origins of Life: Steps Towards Panspermia (2000), Cosmic Dragons: Life and Death of a Planet (2001), A Journey with Fred Hoyle (2005), Comets and the Origin of Life (with J T Wickramasinghe and W M Napier, 2009), A Destiny of Cosmic Life – Chapters in the Life of an Astrobiologist (2014), Where Did Life Come From? (2015), The Search for our Cosmic Ancestry (2015), Vindication of Cosmic Biology (2015); *Recreations* photography, poetry, history of science, gardening; *Style*— Prof Chandra Wickramasinghe; ✉ 24 Llwynypia Road, Lisvane, Cardiff CF4 5SY (☎ 029 2075 2146, mobile 07778 389 243, e-mail ncwick@gmail.com, website www.profchandra.org)

WICKREMASINGHE, Dr Nelisha; da of A Wickremasinghe, and A Wickremasinghe, née Amarasingham; *b* 24 January 1969, Sri Lanka; *Educ* Univ of Sussex (BA), Univ of Kent (MA), Ashridge Business Sch (DProf), Inst of Family Therapy (PGDip); *Children* 2 s (Saul b 26 Dec 1998, Jude b 6 April 2007); *Career* addiction cnsllr: Arlington House Camden 1991–92, Alcohol Recovery Project 1992–93; day prog mangr Milton House Islington 1993–96, addiction servs mangr Thames Gateway NHS Tst 1996–2002, fndr and dir Archiamma Organic Food and Restaurant 2000–05, regnl dir Common Purpose 2005–09; dir The Dialogue Space 2008–, dir Harthill Consulting 2009–10; memb Bd: Food Standards Agency 2004–07, Avon & Somerset Probation Serv 2004–05; AA Rosette for Culinary Excellence 2004–05, Somerset Life Food and Drink Award winner Most Distinctive Local Menu 2005; *Style*— Dr Nelisha Wickremasinghe; ✉ The Dialogue Space (☎ 07854 168015, e-mail nelisha@thedialoguespace.co.uk)

WICKS, Caroline Philippa (Pippa); da of Brian Cairns Wicks, of Bucks, and Judith Anne Wicks; *b* 18 December 1962; *Educ* Lady Verney HS High Wycombe, Haileybury, St Hugh's Coll Oxford (open scholar, Irene Shringley zoology scholar, MA), London Business Sch (Dip Corp Fin); *Career* Bain & Co mgmnt conslts: assoc conslt 1984–86, conslt 1987–90, mangr 1990–91; Courtaulds Textiles plc: business devpt mangr 1991–93, fin dir 1993–99; ceo FT Knowledge (a div of Pearson plc) 1999–2003, princ AlixPartners 2003–; non-exec dir: Arcadia plc 2001–02, Ladbrokes plc (formerly Hilton Gp) 2004–; *Recreations* reading, squash, tennis, wine, theatre, travel, antiques; *Style*— Mrs Pippa Wicks

WICKSTEAD, Prof Myles Antony; CBE (2006); *b* 7 February 1951; *Educ* Blundell's, Univ of St Andrews (MA), Univ of Oxford (MLitt); *m* 1990, Shelagh, né Paterson; 1 s (Edward Graeme b 30 May 1996), 1 da (Kathryn Natasha b 3 March 1999); *Career* Miny of Oversea Devpt 1976–79, asst private sec Office of the Lord Privy Seal 1979–1980, asst to UK exec dir World Bank Washington 1980–84, princ ODA 1984–88, private sec to min for Oversea Devpt 1988–90, head European Community and Food Aid Dept ODA 1990–93, head Br Devpt Div in E Africa (Nairobi) 1993–97, co-ordinator UK White Paper on Int Devpt 1997, UK alternate exec dir World Bank 1997–2000, cnsllr (devpt) Washington DC 1997–2000, ambass to Ethiopia 2000–04, head of secretariat Cmmn for Africa 2004–05; visiting prof of int relations King's College London; tstee/memb Bd: Baring Fndn, Advsy Cncl Wilton Park, Int Inspiration, Enterprise for Development, Joffe Charitable Tst, Restless Development; *Books* Aid and Development: A Brief Introduction (2015); *Style*— Professor Myles Wickstead, CBE; ✉ The Manor House, Great Street, Norton sub Hamdon, Somerset TA14 6SJ (☎ 01935 881385)

WIDDUP, (Stanley) Jeffrey; s of Terence Widdup (d 1985), of Farnham Royal, Bucks, and Barbara Widdup (d 1995); *b* 10 July 1951; *Educ* Haileybury, Inns of Court Sch of Law; *m* Aug 1981, Janet, da of late Jack Clark; 1 s (Jack b 17 Jan 1983); *Career* called to the Bar Gray's Inn 1973; head of chambers 1981–, asst recorder of the Crown Court 1993–99, recorder 1999–; *Recreations* golf, growing vegetables; *Clubs* Bramley Golf, Bigbury Golf, Guildford County; *Style*— Jeffrey Widdup, Esq; ✉ Stoke House, Leapale Lane, Guildford, Surrey GU1 4LY (☎ 01483 539131, fax 01483 300542)

WIDE, His Hon Charles Thomas; QC (1995); s of late Nicholas Scott Wide, and Ruth Mildred Norton, née Bird, of Felpham, W Sussex; *b* 16 April 1951; *Educ* The Leys Sch Cambridge, Univ of Exeter (LLB); *m* 1979, Hon Ursula Margaret Bridget Buchan, da of 3 Baron Tweedsmuir (d 2008); 1 da (Emily Susan b 10 June 1982), 1 s (Thomas Nicholas Buchan b 20 March 1984); *Career* called to the Bar Inner Temple 1974 (bencher 2011), recorder of the Crown Court 1995–2001 (asst recorder 1991–95), circuit judge 2001–11, resident judge Northampton Crown Court 2003–11, sr circuit judge 2011–16, ret; standing counsel HM Customs & Excise (Crime) Midland & Oxford Circuit 1989–95, standing counsel Inland Revenue (Crime) Midland & Oxford Circuit 1991–95; memb Criminal Procedure Rule Ctee 2004–12; reader Diocese of Peterborough 2007–; *Recreations* fell walking and beekeeping; *Clubs* Travellers; *Style*— His Hon Charles Wide, QC

WIELD, (William) Adrian Cunningham; s of Captain Ronald Cunningham Wield, CBE, RN (d 1981), of Chudleigh, S Devon, and Mary, née Macdonald (d 1991); *b* 19 February 1937; *Educ* Downside; *m* 8 June 1979, Benedicte, da of Poul Preben Schoning (d 1984), of Copenhagen, Denmark; 1 da (Isobel b 1980), 1 s (Alexander b 1983); *Career* 2 Lt Duke of Cornwall LI 1955–57; stockbroker; ptnr W Mortimer 1967–68; dir: EB Savory Milln (later SBCI Savory Milln) 1985–88 (ptnr 1968–85), Albert Sharp & Co 1988–98; ptnr Brian C Regan Chartered Accountants 2001–05; chm: Northgate Unit Tst 1983–86, Reed Brook Ltd 1993–94, Boisdale plc 1995–2015, Scientific Detectors Ltd 2001–02; non-exec dir: Buzzacott Investment Management Co 1990–94, Boisdale Bishopsgate 2002–15; memb London Stock Exchange 1959–88; *Books* The Special Steel Industry (published privately, 1973); *Recreations* golf, shooting, sailing; *Clubs* Reform; *Style*— Adrian Wield, Esq; ✉ North Lodge, Barton-on-the-Heath, Moreton-in-Marsh, Gloucestershire GL56 0PL (☎ 01608 674572, e-mail adrian.wield@btinternet.com)

WIELER, Anthony Eric; s of Brig Leslie Frederic Ethelbert Wieler, CB, CBE, JP (d 1965), of Hambledon, Surrey, and Elisabeth Anne, née Parker (d 1984); *b* 12 June 1937; *Educ* Shrewsbury, Trinity Coll Oxford (MA); *Career* Nat Serv 1958–60, 2 Lt 7 Duke of Edinburgh's Own Gurkha Rifles (in 1967 organised the appeal which raised £1.5m for Gurkha Welfare Tsts); joined L Messel & Co, memb London Stock Exchange until 1967, sr investment mangr Ionian Bank Ltd until 1972; fndr chm: Anthony Wieler & Co Ltd 1972–89, Anthony Wieler Unit Trust Management 1982–89; dir: Lorne House Trust IOM 1987–2001, Arbuthnot Fund Managers Ltd 1988–89, English Trust Co Ltd (i/c Investment Mgmnt Div) 1992–97, Kermesse Fund Ltd 2001–04; non-exec dir MTT (EU) Ltd 2012–; project dir Economic Surveys Thailand 1999, Turkey and Greece 2000; assoc dir Albert E Sharp & Co 1989–92; currently: business conslt SE Asia and Pacific Rim; fndr Oxford Univ Modern Pentathlon Assoc 1957 (organised first match against Cambridge), chm Hambledon PC 1965–76, initial subscriber Centre for Policy Studies 1972 (memb Wider Ownership Sub-Ctee), fndr One Million Club for XVI Universiade, memb and tstee numerous other charities particularly concerning Nepal, memb Br-Nepal Soc and Br-Nepal C of C (vice-chm 2004–08, chm 2008–10, vice-pres 2010–), co-chair Nepal Fair (London trade fair) 2008, memb Cncl for Foreign Chambers of Commerce London; advsr South London Coll 2011–15, hon advsr The Br Coll Kathmandu 2012–; memb Surrey Cncl Order of St John 1974–2004, dep pres St John Ambulance Surrey until 2004; hon sec AIIM 1974–88; MCSI 1993–; OStJ; awarded Gorkha Daksin Bahu by HM King of Nepal 1998; *Clubs* Royal Overseas League; *Style*— Anthony Wieler, Esq; ✉ The New Stable Cottage, Feathercombe, Hambledon, Godalming, Surrey GU8 4DP (☎ and fax 01483 860200, mobile 07831 353968, e-mail aewieler@hotmail.com)

WIGAN, Sir Michael Iain; 6 Bt (UK 1898), of Clare Lawn, Mortlake, Surrey, and Purland Chase, Ross, Herefordshire; s of Sir Alan Lewis Wigan, 5 Bt (d 1996), and Robina, da of Lt-Col Sir Iain Colquhoun of Luss, 7 Bt, KT, DSO, LLD; *b* 3 October 1951; *Educ* Eton, Exeter Coll Oxford; *Family* 1 s by Lady Alexandra Hay (Ivar Francis Grey de Miremont Wigan b 25 March 1979); *m* 1, 1984 (m dis 1985), Frances, da of late Flt Lt Angus Barr Faucett; *m* 2, 1989, Julia Teresa, eldest da of John de Courcy Ling, CBE, MEP; 3 s (Fergus Adam b 30 April 1990, Thomas Iain b 24 May 1993, Finnbarr Frederick b 17 Sept 1997), 1 da (Lilias Margaret b 9 March 1992); *Heir* s, Fergus Wigan; *Books* Scottish Highland Estate (1991), Stag at Bay (1993), The Last of the Hunter Gatherers: Fisheries Crisis at Sea (1998), Grimersta: The Story of a Great Fishery (2001), The Salmon: The Extraordinary Story of the King of Fish (2013); *Recreations* literature, deer stalking, fly fishing; *Style*— Sir Michael Wigan, Bt; ✉ Borrobol, Kinbrace, Sutherland KW11 6UB

WIGDORTZ, Brett Harris; OBE; *b* 9 October 1973, Long Branch USA; *Educ* Univ of Richmond, Univ of Hawaii; *Career* mgmnt conslt McKinsey & Co until 2002, fndr and ceo Teach First 2002–; *Books* Success Against The Odds (2014); *Style*— Brett Wigdortz, Esq, OBE; ✉ Teach First, 4 More London Place, London SE1 2AU

WIGGIN, William David (Bill); MP; s of Sir Jerry Wiggin, TD, and Rosie, née Orr (now Mrs Dale Harris); *b* 4 June 1966; *Educ* Eton, Univ Coll of N Wales Bangor (BA); *m* 3 July 2001, Camilla Jane, da of Donald Chilvers; 1 da (Rosie Jessica b 26 Aug 2001), 2 s (Jack William b 31 Dec 2004, Toby Donald Alfred b 27 March 2006); *Career* trader: Rayner Coffee Int 1989–91, Mitsubishi 1991–92, UBS 1992–95; assoc dir Dresdner Kleinwort Benson 1995–98, mangr Commerzbank 1998–2001; MP (Cons) Leominster 2001–; asst whip 2010–; memb Select Ctee: Welsh, Transport, Local Government and the Regions; *Clubs* Annabel's, Hurlingham, Rankin (Leominster); *Style*— Bill Wiggin, Esq, MP; ✉ House of Commons, London SW1A 0AA; Constituency Office, 8 Corn Street, Leominster, Herefordshire HR6 8LR (☎ 01568 612565)

WIGGINS, Sir Bradley Marc; kt (2013), CBE (2009, OBE 2005); s of Gary Wiggins (d 2008), the cyclist, and Linda Wiggins; *b* 28 April 1980, Ghent, Belgium; *m* 5 Nov 2004, Catherine; 1 s (Ben Michael b 26 March 2005), 1 da (Isabella Mary b 9 Nov 2006); *Career* cyclist; achievements incl: Gold medal individual pursuit Jr World Track Championships 1997, Silver medal team pursuit Cwlth Games 1998 (memb England team), Gold medal Madison Nat Track Championships 1999, Silver medal team pursuit World Championships 2000, Bronze medal team pursuit Olympic Games Sydney 2000, European Pursuit Champion 2001, Silver medal team pursuit World Championships 2001, Silver medal individual pursuit and Silver medal team pursuit Cwlth Games 2002 (memb England team), Gold medal individual pursuit and Silver medal team pursuit World Championships 2003, European Derny Champion 2003, Gold medal individual pursuit, Silver medal team pursuit and Bronze medal Madison Olympic Games Athens 2004, Gold Medals 4km individual pursuit and team pursuit Track World Championships 2007, Gold medals 4km individual pursuit, team pursuit and Madison Track World Championships Manchester 2008, Gold medals individual pursuit and team pursuit Olympic Games Beijing 2008, Br Nat Time Trial Champion 2009, fourth Tour de France 2009, winner Tour de France 2012, Gold medal time trial Olympic Games 2012, Gold medal team pursuit Olympic Games 2016; professional road debut 2002; memb: La Française des Jeux team 2002–04, Credit Agricole team 2004–05 (incl Giro d'Italia 2005), Cofidis team 2006–07 (incl Tours de France 2006 and 2007), Team High Road 2008–10, Team Sky 2010– (team ldr); BBC Sports Personality of the Year 2012; *Style*— Sir Bradley Wiggins, CBE; ✉ Twitter @bradwiggins

WIGGINS, Prof David; s of late Norman Wiggins, OBE, and Diana, née Priestley (d 1995); *b* 8 March 1933; *Educ* St Paul's, BNC Oxford (MA); *m* 1, 1968 (m dis), Hideko Ishiguro; *m* 2, 1980 (m dis), Jennifer Hornsby; 1 s (Peter Joshua Wiggins b 1987); *m* 3, 2010, Phillida Gili; *Career* asst princ Colonial Office 1957–58, Jane Eliza Procter visiting fell Princeton Univ 1958–59, lectr then fell New Coll Oxford 1959–67, prof of philosophy Bedford Coll London 1967–80, fell and praelector in philosophy Univ Coll Oxford 1981–89, prof of philosophy Birkbeck Coll London 1989–93, Wykeham prof of logic Univ of

Oxford 1994–2000; visiting appts: Stanford Univ 1964 and 1965, Harvard Univ 1968 and 1972, All Souls Coll Oxford 1973, Princeton Univ 1980, Findlay visiting prof Boston Univ 2001; Leverhulme fell 2001–04; author of various articles in learned jls; memb: Ind Cmmn on Tport 1973–74, Central Tport Consultative Ctee 1977–79; chm Tport Users Consultative Ctee for SE 1977–79; pres Aristotelian Soc 2000–01 (hon life memb 2014); memb London Tport and Amenity Assoc; Dr (hc) Univ of York 2005; hon fell BNC Oxford 2011; foreign memb American Acad of Arts and Sciences (1992); FBA 1978; *Books* Identity and Spatio Temporal Continuity (1967), Truth, Invention and the Meaning of Life (1978), Sameness and Substance (1980, 2 edn 2001), Needs, Values, Truth (1987, 3 edn 2002), Sameness and Substance Renewed (2002), Ethics: Twelve Lectures on the Philosophy of Morality (2006), Solidarity and the Root of the Ethical (2008); *Style—* Prof David Wiggins, FBA; ✉ New College, Oxford OX1 3BN

WIGGLESWORTH, Mark; *Career* assoc conductor BBC Symphony Orch 1991–93; music dir: Opera Factory 1991–94, The Premiere Ensemble, BBC Nat Orch of Wales 1996–2000; princ guest conductor Swedish Radio Orch 1998–2001; debut: Glyndebourne Festival Opera 2000, ENO 2001, ROH 2002; guest conductor: LPO, LSO, Salzburg Festival, Berlin Philharmonic, Royal Concertgebouw, Oslo Philharmonic, Santa Cecilia of Rome, Ochestra Filarmonica della Scala Milan, Chicago Symphony, Philadelphia Orch, Minnesota Orch, San Francisco Symphony, Los Angeles Philharmonic Orch, Israel Philharmonic, Welsh Nat Opera, Cleveland Symphony, Toronto Symphony, Montreal Symphony, New York Philharmonic, Hollywood Bowl, Sydney Symphony, BBC proms; *Style—* Mark Wigglesworth, Esq; ✉ c/o Askonas Holt, Lincoln House, 300 High Holborn, London WC1V 7JH (☎ 020 7400 1700, fax 020 7400 1799)

WIGGLESWORTH, Richard; *b* 9 June 1983, Blackpool, Lancs; *Educ* Kirkham GS Lancs; *Career* professional rugby player (scrum half); Sale Sharks 2002–10 (winners Parker Pen Shield 2005, Guinness Premiership 2006), Saracens 2010–; England: 12 caps, debut v Italy 2008, also rep at Under 18, Under 19, Under 21 (Six Nations Grand Slam 2004) Saxons (Churchill Cup 2007) level; *Style—* Richard Wigglesworth, Esq; ✉ Saracens, Allianz Park Stadium, Greenlands Lane, London NW4 1RL

WIGGLESWORTH, Prof Sarah; MBE (2003), RDI (2012); *Educ* Camden Sch for Girls, Univ of Cambridge (MA, DipArch); *Partner* Prof Jeremy Till, *qv*; *Career* architect; fndr Sarah Wigglesworth Architects 1994–; projects incl: Stock Orchard St Islington 2001 (Civic Tst Award 2001, RIBA Award 2004, RIBA Sustainability Award 2004), Chelsea Flower Show Pavilion 2002 (RHS Silver Medal), Mossbrook Sch Sheffield 2005 (RIBA Award 2005, RIBA Yorks White Rose Award 2005), Siobhan Davies Dance Studios London 2006 (RIBA Award 2006), Sandal Magna Community Primary Sch Wakefield 2010 (Gold Award, Building of the Year and Sustainability Award RIBA Northern Networks Awards 2011); prof of architecture Univ of Sheffield 1998– (estab PhD by Design); author and ed of many books and articles; Fulbright fell (with Prof Jeremy Till) 1991; FRSA; *Style—* Prof Sarah Wigglesworth, MBE, RDI; ✉ Sarah Wigglesworth Architects, 10 Stock Orchard Street, London N7 9RW (☎ 020 7607 9200, fax 020 7607 5800, website www.swarch.co.uk)

WIGHT, Robin Alexander Fairbairn; s of William Fairbairn Wight (d 1972), of Alwoodley, Leeds, and Olivia Peterina, *née* Clouston (d 1988); *b* 5 June 1938; *Educ* Dollar Acad, Magdalene Coll Cambridge (MA); *m* 27 July 1963, Sheila Mary Lindsay, da of James Forbes (d 1963), of Edinburgh; 1 da (Catriona Mary Susan b 1965), 3 s (James William Fairbairn b 1966, Alasdair Robin Forbes b 1968, Douglas Clouston Fullerton b 1973); *Career* ptnr Coopers & Lybrand CAs 1971–96; Coopers & Lybrand Scotland: regnl ptnr 1977–95, exec chm 1990–96; chm Arville Holdings 1981–2010; FCA 1976 (CA 1978); *Recreations* golf, watching rugby, skiing, business, bridge; *Clubs* RAC; *Style—* Robin Wight, Esq; ✉ 22 Regent Terrace, Edinburgh EH7 5BS (☎ 0131 556 2100)

WIGLEY, Bob; *b* 4 February 1961; *Educ* Exeter Sch, Univ of Bath; *Career* Merrill Lynch: joined 1996, co-head of corporate broking 2000, co-head of UK investment banking 2001, global co-head of telecom and media investment banking 2002, chm EMEA corporate banking 2003, chm EMEA 2004–09; currently chm: NetOTC Holdings Sarl, Stonehaven Search LLP, First Global Trust Bank, Tantalum Corp plc; memb Court Bank of England 2006–09; chm: Employers and Educn Taskforce 2006–09, Hibu plc 2009–14, Expansys plc 2009–14, Skrill Hldgs plc 2010, Green Investment Bank Cmmn 2010; non-exec dir Qatar Financial Centre Authy 2011; PM's ambass for UK business; memb Cncl Royal Coll of Music 2013; visiting fell Univ of Oxford, chm Oxford Univ Centre for Corporate Reputation, hon fell Univ of Cambridge Judge Business Sch; past Master Worshipful Co of Int Bankers; hon doctorate Univ of Bath; FCA; *Style—* Bob Wigley, Esq; ✉ Gordian Knot, Lansdowne House, 57 Berkeley Square, London W1J 6AB (☎ 020 7850 0345, fax 020 7855 0818, e-mail bob@bobwigley.co.uk)

WIGLEY, Baron (Life Peer UK 2011), of Caernarfon in the County of Gwynedd; Rt Hon Dafydd Wynne Wigley; PC (1997); s of Elfyn Edward Wigley; *b* 1 April 1943; *Educ* Caernarfon GS, Rydal Sch Colwyn Bay, Univ of Manchester; *m* Elinor, da of Emrys Bennett Owen, of Dolgellau; 3 s (2 s decd), 1 da; *Career* industl economist; with: Ford Motor Co 1964–67, Mars Ltd 1967–71, Hoover Ltd 1971–74; MP 1974–2001, AM (Plaid Cymru) Caernarfon 1999–2003; candidate Euro Parl 1994; vice-chair All Pty Disablement Gp House of Commons 1992–2001; Nat Assembly for Wales: Plaid Cymru shadow fin min 2001–03, memb N Wales Ctee 1999–03, memb Econ Devpt Ctee 2000–03, memb Culture Ctee 2001–03, chair Audit Ctee 2002–03; pres Plaid Cymru 1981–84 and 1991–2000; vice-pres Fedn of Industrial Devpt Authorities; hon fell Univ Coll of North Wales Bangor 1994; Hon LLD Univ of Wales 2002; *Books* An Economic Plan for Wales (1970), O Ddifri (1992), Dal Ati (1993), A Democratic Wales in a United Europe (1995), A Real Choice for Wales (1996), Maen ir Wal (2001); *Style—* The Rt Hon the Lord Wigley

WIGLEY, Dr Dale Brian; *Educ* Univ of Bristol (PhD); *Career* postdoctoral work Univ of Leicester and Univ of York, lectr then reader Univ of Oxford 1993–2000, researcher ICRF (now Cancer Research UK) 2000–; FRS 2004; *Style—* Dr Dale Wigley; ✉ Cancer Research UK, London Research Institute, Clare Hall Laboratories, Blanche Lane, South Mimms, Potters Bar EN6 3LD

WIGLEY, (Francis) Spencer; s of Frank Wigley (d 1970), Dep Cmmr Police Fiji, and Lorna, *née* Wattley; gf Sir Wilfrid Wigley, Chief Justice Leeward Islands, WI; *Educ* Dean Close Sch, Univ of Nottingham (BA), Henley Business Sch; *m* 1969, Caroline, *née* Jarratt; 2 s (Francis b 1972, Edward b 1973); 1 da (Elizabeth b 1979); *Career* admitted slr 1967; Rio Tinto plc: gen counsel 1976–83, sec and dir of corp servs 1983–92; Bass plc: sec and gen counsel 1992–2000, memb Bd Exec Ctee 1995–2000, personnel dir 1997–2000, chm Pension Funds 2001–05; tstee, dir and hon sec Shakespeare's Globe 2001–12, tstee Flavel Centre Dartmouth 2005–13, tstee Dartmouth Museum 2015–; govr: Amesbury Sch 1983–95 (chm 1987–93), Cranleigh Sch 1989–98 (chm Prep Sch 1991–96); *Recreations* sailing, sporting activities, music; *Clubs* RAC, Cruising Assoc, Royal Dart Yacht, Dartmouth Golf; *Style—* Spencer Wigley, Esq; ✉ Watersmeet, Swannaton Road, Dartmouth TQ6 9RL (☎ 01803 832355, e-mail spencer@mffernhurst.net)

WIGNALL, Michael Thomas; s of Alan Wignall, of Preston, and Catherine, *née* Dunn; *b* 23 May 1967, Preston, Lancs; *Educ* St Cuthbert Mayne Preston, Preston Coll; *m* 19 July 2015, Johanna Bethan, *née* Cole; 1 s (Matthew Jay b 3 March 1998); *Career* jr sous chef Heathcotes Longridge 1987–89 (2 Michelin stars); head chef: The Old Beams Waterhouses 1993–95 (1 Michelin star), Waldo's Cliveden 1996–98 (1 Michelin star, 4 AA rosettes), Michael's Nook Grasmere 1998–2002 (1 Michelin star, 4 AA rosettes); exec head chef The Devonshire Arms N Yorks 2002–07 (1 Michelin star, 4 AA rosettes), head chef Michael Wignall at The Latymer Pennyhill Park Hotel & Spa 2007–15 (2 Michelin stars, 5 AA Rosettes 2012), exec chef Gidleigh Park Hotel 2016–; chef CSSG Charity Dinner India 2013, pop-up restaurant Food & Art Additions Stockholm 2013, pop-up restaurant Selfridges 2014, creative dir Café Football, exec conslt chef Abode hotels (Canterbury, Exeter, Manchester and Chester); judge Masterchef the Professionals (BBC) 2013–14; best dessert under 21s and best overall entrant Salon Culinaire 1986, winner Northwest Chefs Circle 1987, Best Chef of the Year Northern Hospitality Awards 2007, Best Restaurant Newcomer of the Year Good Food Guide 2009, 7 out of 10 Good Food Guide 2009, winner for SW Britain's Best Dish (ITV), number 25 in the Square Meal Top 50 Restaurants in the UK, within top 50 San Pellegrino Top 100 UK Restaurants; involved with Bobby Moore Bowel Cancer Charity 2014 and 2015; *Books* Great British Chefs, Britain's Best Dish; *Recreations* wakeboarding, snowboarding, heliboarding, downhill mountain biking, lotus sport, photography, surfing; *Clubs* Quayside Wakeboard (Mytchett); *Style—* Michael Wignall, Esq; ✉ Gidleigh Park Hotel, Chagford, Newton Abbott TQ13 8HH (☎ 01647 433578, email michaelwignall@gidleigh.co.uk)

WIGODER, Hon Charles Francis; s of Baron Wigoder, QC (Life Peer, d 2004), and Yoland, *née* Levinson; *b* 2 March 1960; *Educ* Univ of Kent; *m* Elizabeth; 1 s (Benjamin b 1990), 3 da (Natasha b 1992, Clarissa b 1995, Emily b 1999); *Career* qualified CA KPMG 1984; head of corp fin and devpt Carlton Communications plc then Quadrant Gp plc 1985–88, fndr The Peoples Phone Co plc 1988 (sold 1996), currently exec chm Telecom Plus plc (joined 1998); *Recreations* bridge; *Clubs* Annabel's, Cercle de l'Union Interalliée; *Style—* The Hon Charles Wigoder; ✉ Telecom Plus plc, Network HQ, 508 Edgware Road, The Hyde, London NW9 5AB

WILBY, David Christopher; QC (1998); s of Alan Wilby, of Addingham, W Yorks, and late June, *née* Uppard; *b* 14 June 1952; *Educ* Roundhay Sch Leeds, Downing Coll Cambridge (MA); *m* 23 July 1976, Susan Christine, da of Eric Arding (d 1977), of Bardsey, W Yorks; 3 da (Victoria b 1981, Christina b 1983, Charlotte b 1987), 1 s (Edward b 1985); *Career* called to the Bar Inner Temple 1974 (bencher 2002); practising barr North Earstern Circuit, recorder 2000–, dep High Court judge 2008–; memb: Exec Ctee Professional Negligence Bar Assoc 1995–2009, Bar Cncl 1996–99, Judicial Studies Bd 2005–09; chm Bar Conf 2000, past chm Bar, judge Criminal Injuries Compensation CIC/TS 2007, arbitrator PLC Arbitration 2015; ed: Professional Negligence and Liability Law Reports 1995–, Professional Negligence Key Cases 1999–; memb: Cwlth Lawyers Assoc 1995–, Int Assoc of Defense Counsel 1998–; assoc memb American Bar Assoc 1996–; *Publications* Atkin's Court Forms (ed, Health and Safety Section, 2002, 3 edn 2010), The Law of Damages (2003, 3 edn 2010), Munkman on Employers Liability (2006, 16 edn 2013); *Recreations* golf, watching association and rugby football, being in France; *Clubs* Pannal Golf, Royal Cinque Ports Golf, Moortown Golf, Royal Over-Seas League; *Style—* David Wilby, Esq, QC; ✉ Old Square Chambers, 10–11 Bedford Row, London WC1R 4BU (☎ 020 7269 0300); Park Lane Plowden Chambers, 19 Westgate, Leeds LS1 2RD (☎ 0113 228 5000, e-mail david.wilby.qc@gmail.com)

WILBY, James Jonathon; s of late Geoffrey Wilby, of Ossett, W Yorks, and Shirley, *née* Armitage; *b* 20 February 1958; *Educ* Sedbergh, Univ of Durham, RADA; *m* 25 June 1988, Shana Louise, da of late Garth John Loxley Magraw; 3 s (Barnaby John Loxley b 9 Nov 1988, Nathaniel Jerome b 4 Feb 1996, Jesse Jack b 18 May 2001), 1 da (Florence Hannah Mary b 18 Oct 1992); *Career* actor; *Theatre* incl: Another Country (Queen's Theatre) 1983, As You Like It (Manchester Royal Exchange), Jane Eyre (Chichester Festival Theatre), The Tempest (Chichester Festival Theatre), The Common Pursuit (Lyric) 1988, The Trial (Young Vic) 1993, A Patriot for Me (RSC) 1995, Helping Harry (Jermyn Street Theatre) 2001, Don Juan (Lyric) 2004, On Emotion (Soho Theatre) 2008, The Consultant (Theatre 503) 2011, Less Than Kind (tour) 2012, The Second Mrs Tanqueray (Rose Theatre) 2012, Dead Sheep (Park Theatre); *Television* for BBC incl: Tell Me That You Love Me 1991, Adam Bede 1991, Mother Love 1992, You Me And It 1993, Lady Chatterley's Lover 1993, Crocodile Shoes 1994, Witness Against Hitler 1995, The Woman in White 1997, The Dark Room 1999, The Zoo 2014; other credits incl: Dutch Girls 1985, A Tale Of Two Cities 1989, The Treasure Seekers 1997, Trial and Retribution 2000, Bertie and Elizabeth 2002, Island at War 2003, Sparkling Cyanide 2003, Jericho 2005, Miss Marple 2006, Little Devil 2006, Lewis (ITV) 2007, The Last Viceroy (Channel 4) 2007, Impact Earth (Channel 4) 2007, Clapham Junction (Channel 4) 2007, A Risk Worth Taking 2008, Poirot 2009, Midsummer Murder 2010, New Tricks (ITV) 2012, The Best Possible Taste (ITV) 2012, Ripper Street, The Great Train Robbery – A Copper's Tale, Law and Order UK, Endeavour, Strike Back (Sky); *Film* incl: Maurice 1987, A Summer Story 1988, A Handful of Dust 1988, Immaculate Conception 1991, Howards End 1991, Une partie d'Échec 1994, Regeneration 1997, Tom's Midnight Garden 1998, An Ideal Husband 1999, Cotton Mary 1999, Gosford Park 2002, De-Lovely 2004, C'est Gradiva qui vous appelle 2006, Shadows in the Sun 2008; *Awards* Venice Film Festival Best Actor Award (for Maurice) 1987, Bari Film Festival Best Actor Award (for A Handful of Dust) 1988, Screen Actors Guild Outstanding Performance by a Cast in a Motion Picture (for Gosford Park) 2001; *Style—* James Wilby; ✉ c/o Sue Latimer, ARG, 4A Exmoor Street, London W10 6BD (☎ 020 7436 6400, fax 020 7436 6700)

WILBY, Peter John; s of Lawrence Edward Wilby (d 1981), and Emily Lavinia, *née* Harris (d 1995); *b* 7 November 1944; *Educ* Kibworth Beauchamp GS, Univ of Sussex (BA); *m* 5 August 1967, Sandra, da of Alfred James, of Derby; 2 s (David Paul b 29 Dec 1971, Michael John b 1 Oct 1973); *Career* educn corr: The Observer 1972–75 (reporter 1968–72), New Statesman 1975–77, Sunday Times 1977–86; educn ed The Independent 1986–89; Independent on Sunday: home ed 1989–91, dep ed 1991–95, ed 1995–96; New Statesman: books ed 1997–98, ed 1998–2005; media columnist New Statesman 2005–07, contributing ed Observer Sports Monthly 2005–08, media columnist Guardian 2007–09, columnist New Statesman 2007–; Media Commentator of the Year The Comment Awards 2011, Ted Wragg Award for sustained contribution to educn journalism Educn Journalism Awards 2013; Hon DLitt Univ of Leicester 2010; *Books* Parents' Rights (1983), Eden (2006); *Recreations* reading, lunching, cooking; *Style—* Peter Wilby, Esq; ✉ 51 Queen's Road, Loughton, Essex IG10 1RR (e-mail peter.wilby@gmail.com)

WILCOX, Claire; da of S W Wilcox, of London, and M J, *née* Smith; *b* 7 October 1954, London; *Educ* Godolphin and Latymer Sch London, Univ of Exeter (BA), Camberwell Sch of Art (BA); *m* 6 June 1992, Dr J F Stair; 2 da (Elizabeth Rose b 3 April 1991, Katherine Hattie b 29 June 1993); *Career* V&A: curator 1999–2004, sr curator 2004– (exhibitions incl: Radical Fashion 2001, Vivienne Westwood 2004, The Golden Age of Couture 2007, Alexander McQueen Savage Beauty 2015); prof in fashion curation London Coll of Fashion Univ of the Arts London; *Publications* Handbags (1999), Radical Fashion (2001), Vivienne Westwood (2004), The Golden Age of Couture: Paris and London 1947–57 (2007), The V&A Gallery of Fashion (2013), Alexander McQueen (2016); *Style—* Ms Claire Wilcox; ✉ V&A South Kensington, Cromwell Road, London SW7 2RL (☎ 020 7942 2000, website www.vam.ac.uk); literary agent David Godwin www.davidgodwinassociates.com

WILCOX, Prof Helen Elizabeth; *née* Boulton; da of James T Boulton, and Margaret H, *née* Leary; *b* 14 April 1955, Nottingham; *Educ* Nottingham Girls' HS, Univ of Birmingham (BA, Hughes Prize), St Anne's Coll Oxford (DPhil); *m* 29 July 1978, Allan F C Wilcox; 2 s (Thomas b 1984, Joseph b 1987); *Career* lectr in English literature Univ of Liverpool 1979–91, prof of English literature Univ of Groningen 1991–2006, prof of English Bangor Univ 2006– (head Sch of English Literature 2012–); dir Inst for Medieval and Early Modern Studies Univs of Aberystwyth and Bangor 2009–13; visiting prof: Univ of Santiago de Compostela, Nat Univ Singapore, Barnard Coll NY, Univ of Massachusetts

W

Amherst; Univ of Groningen Ubbo Emmius Award 2005, Dissertation Supervisor of the Year Bangor Univ 2012; FRSL 1999, fell English Assoc 2007, FRSA 2013, FLSW 2015; *Publications* incl: Her Own Life: Autobiographical Writings by Seventeenth-Century English Women (1989), Women and Literature in Britain 1500–1700 (1996), The English Poems of George Herbert (2007), 1611: Authority, Gender and the Word in Early Modern England (2013), Shakespeare's All's Well That Ends Well (2016), English: the Journal of the English Association (co-ed 2007–14, advsy ed 2014–); author of over 100 articles and book chapters; *Recreations* music (piano, cello, singing), swimming, walking in Snowdonia; *Style*— Prof Helen Wilcox; ✉ School of English Literature, Bangor University, Gwynedd LL57 2DG (☎ 01248 382109, fax 01248 382102, e-mail helen.wilcox@bangor.ac.uk)

WILCOX, Baroness (Life Peer UK 1996), of Plymouth in the County of Devon; Judith Ann Wilcox; da of John Freeman, of Plymouth, Devon, and Elsie Freeman; *b* 31 December 1939; *Educ* St Mary's Convent Wantage, Univ of Plymouth; *m* 1, 1961 (m dis 1986), Keith Davenport, s of Harold Cornelius Davenport, of Plymouth, Devon; 1 s (Hon Simon b 1963); m 2, 1986, as his 2 w, Sir Malcolm George Wilcox, CBE (d 1986), s of late George Harrison Wilcox; *Career* fndr Channel Foods Ltd Cornwall 1984–89, chm and md Pecheries de la Morinie 1989–91, chm Morinie et Cie France 1991–94; memb House of Lords Euro Select Ctee (Environment, Public Health and Consumer Affrs) 1996–, memb EU Sub-Ctee 1997–2000, memb House of Lords Select Ctee (Sci and Technol) 2000–02, vice-chair Fisheries Gp 2004–10, patron Corp Governance Gp 2004–10, vice-chair Consumer Affrs and Trading Standards Gp 2009–10, memb Tax Law Review Ctee, memb Select Ctee on Extradition Law 2014–; oppn whip 2002–05; oppn spokesman House of Lords: Treasy 2003–05, Cabinet Office 2005–06, trade and industry/ business, enterprise and regulatory reform 2006–08, energy and climate change 2008–10; Parly under-sec of state Dept for Business, Innovation and Skills 2010–, min of business innovation and skills House of Lords 2010–12, min of intellectual property 2010–12; memb Cncl for Europe 2012– (ctees: PACE, Equality, Rules); currently pres Nat Fedn of Consumer Gps; memb Bd: Automobile Assoc 1991–99, Port of London Authy 1993–2000 (vice-chm 2000–02); chm Nat Consumer Cncl 1990–96; former: memb Local Govt Commission, memb Bd Inland Revenue, memb PM's Citizen's Charter Advsy Panel, chm Citizen's Charter Complaints Task Force; non-exec dir: Carpetright plc 1997–, Cadbury Schweppes plc 1997–2006, Johnson Services plc 2003–; vice-pres The Girl Guides Assoc, chm of tstees Community of St Mary the Virgin Wantage, patron Nat Lobster Hatchery Padstow, govr Imperial Coll 2006; Hon DSc Univ of Plymouth; memb Governing Body Inst for Food Research 1998–2002; FRSA, Hon FCGI; *Recreations* walking, sailing, calligraphy, bird watching, film, theatre; *Clubs* Athenaeum, St Mawes Sailing; *Style*— The Rt Hon Lady Wilcox; ✉ House of Lords, London SW1A 0PW

WILD, Damian Paul Derek; s of Derek Wild (d 2005), and Valerie Wild; *b* 30 December 1969; *Educ* Univ of Central England (BA); *m* 8 May 1999, Nicola Taylor; 1 s (Louis b 31 Aug 2004), 1 da (Ella b 20 March 2006); *Career* reporter then chief reporter Public Finance 1993–97, freelance journalist CNN and South China Morning Post 1997–98; Accountancy Age: news ed 1999–2000, ed 2000–05; Incisive Media (formerly VNU Business Pubns): gp ed-in-chief business and finance titles 2006–08, publisher 2008–09; ed Estates Gazette 2009–; *Books* Decades (series co-author, 1998); *Recreations* travel; *Style*— Damian Wild; ✉ Estates Gazette, 1 Procter Street, London WC1V 6EU (e-mail damian.wild@estatesgazette.com)

WILD, Jonathan; s of John William Howard Wild, CO (RAF), of Poole, Dorset, and Madeleine Clifford Wild; *b* 4 August 1951; *Educ* Woking GS for Boys, UCL (BSc, DipArch); *m* 1, 27 April 1979 (m dis 2005), Jacqueline Ann, da of Roland Oliver Cise, of Walton-on-Thames, Surrey; 1 s (Nicholas James b 1980), 1 da (Anna Louise Julie b 1969); m 2, 4 Dec 2009, Maureen Rosemary Willmott-Wild, *née* McCammond; *Career* chartered architect; dir MoJo Architecture, Design, Development Ltd, sole princ Wild Alliance; RIBA, ARB; *Recreations* motor sport, music, travel, design; *Style*— Jonathan Wild; ✉ MoJo Architecture, Design, Development Limited, MoJo Studio, 38 Albany Road, Fleet, Hampshire GU51 3PT (☎ 01252 675699)

WILD, (John) Robin; s of John Edward Brooke Wild (ka 1943), of Scarborough, N Yorks, and Teresa, *née* Ballance; *b* 12 September 1941; *Educ* Sedbergh, Univ of Edinburgh (BDS), Univ of Dundee (DPD); *m* 31 July 1965, (Eleanor) Daphne, da of Walter Gifford Kerr (d 1975), of Edinburgh; 2 da (Alison b 1967, Rosemary b 1977), 1 s (Richard b 1978 d 2003); *Career* princ in gen dental practice Scarborough 1965–71, dental offr E Lothian CC 1971–74, chief admin dental offr Borders Health Bd 1974–87, regnl dental postgrad advsr SE Regnl Ctee for Postgrad Med Educn 1982–87, dir of studies (dental) Edinburgh Postgrad Bd for Med 1986–87, chief dental offr Scottish Office Home and Health Dept 1993–97 (dep chief dental offr 1987–93), dir of dental servs Scotland NHS 1993–97, chief dental offr Dept of Health 1997–2000, conslt in dental public health Dumfries and Galloway Health Bd 2005–07; hon sr lectr Univ of Dundee 1993–; pres Cncl of European Chief Dental Offrs 1999–2001, vice-pres Cwlth Dental Assoc 1997–2003, chm Scottish Cncl Br Dental Assoc 1985–87; chm: Scottish Borders Justices Ctee 2000–05, District Courts Assoc 2002–04; memb Judicial Cncl for Scotland 2007–09, memb Disciplinary Panel Inst and Faculty of Actuaries 2001–; JP (Ettrick and Lauderdale) 1982–2011; FFICS, fell Br Dental Assoc, FDSRCSE; *Recreations* restoration and driving of vintage cars, music, gardening; *Clubs* RSM, Frontline; *Style*— Robin Wild, Esq; ✉ Braehead House, St Boswells, Roxburghshire TD6 0AZ

WILDASH, HE Richard James; LVO; s of Arthur Ernest Wildash, of London, and Sheila Howard, *née* Smith; *b* 24 December 1955; *Educ* St Paul's, Corpus Christi Coll Cambridge (MA); *m* 29 Aug 1981, (Elizabeth) Jane, da of Peter Edward Walmsley, of Bebington; 2 da (Joanna Helen b 1987, Bethany Jane b 1996); *Career* entered HM Dip Serv 1977; served: E Berlin 1979, Abidjan 1981, FCO 1984, Harare 1988, FCO 1992, New Delhi 1994; dep high cmmr Kuala Lumpur 1998, high cmmr to Cameroon 2002–06 (concurrently non-resident ambass to Central African Repub, Chad, Equatorial Guinea and Gabon), high cmmr to Malawi 2006–09, ambass to Angola 2010–14 (concurrently non-resident ambass to Sao Tome and Principe), dep head of mission British Embassy Saudi Arabia 2014–; memb Chartered Inst of Linguists; FRGS, FLS, FZS; *Recreations* music, literature, the country; *Clubs* Civil Service Club; *Style*— Mr Richard Wildash, LVO; ✉ Flat 5, 26 Medway Street, London SW1P 2BD (☎ 020 7222 8092, e-mail wildash@tusker.co.uk)

WILDBLOOD, (Christopher) Michael Garside; MBE (2000); s of late Richard Garside Wildblood, of Ouseburn, N Yorks, and Rita Muriel, *née* Jellings; *b* 9 October 1945, Leeds; *Educ* Rugby, Corpus Christi Coll Cambridge (MA, Dip Arch); *m* 30 July 1971, Anne Somerville, da of late Alun Roberts, of Radyr, Glamorgan; 1 s (Thomas Garside b 1976), 3 da (Shân Catherine Somerville b 1978, Jane Somerville b 1987, Rachel Somerville b 1989); *Career* chartered architect; ptnr and princ Wildblood Macdonald, Chartered Architects 1975–2012 (conslt 2012–); chm: RIBA Leeds Soc of Architects 1985–87, RIBA Yorks Region 1985–86; vice-chm RIBA Enterprises Ltd 1998–2002; pres W Yorks Soc of Architects 1993–95; RIBA; *Recreations* golf, choral singing, watercolour painting; *Clubs* Alwoodley Golf, Old Rugbeian Golfing Soc; *Style*— Michael Wildblood, Esq, MBE; ✉ Hammonds, Lower Dunsforth, North Yorkshire YO26 9SA

WILDBLOOD, His Hon Judge Stephen Roger; QC (1999); s of Fred Roger John Wildblood, of Shropshire, and Patricia Ann Mary, *née* Greenwood (d 1965); *b* 18 August 1958; *Educ* Millfield, Univ of Sheffield (LLB); *m* 2003, Emma Jane; 3 s (Benedict b 11 Nov 1985, Samuel b 10 Dec 2004, Jacob b 2 July 2007), 3 da (Sarah b 16 May 1988, Sophie, Anna b 28 July 2008 (twins)); *Career* called to the Bar 1980, asst recorder 1997–2000, recorder 2000–07, dep High Court judge 2004–, circuit judge 2007–; *Publications* Financial Provision in Family Matters (with Eaton), Butterworths Family Law Service (contrib), Butterworths Encyclopaedia of Forms and Precedents (contrib); *Recreations* running, cycling, reading; *Style*— His Hon Judge Wildblood, QC; ✉ Bristol Civil Justice Centre, Redcliff Street, Bristol BS1 6GR

WILDE, Malcolm James; s of Malcolm John Wilde, and Irene Doris, *née* Rickwood; *b* 9 October 1950; *Educ* Bishopshalt Sch; *m* 1 Sept 1973, (Helen) Elaine, da of John Bartley, and Doris Bartley; 2 da (Joanne Caroline b 6 July 1976, Julia Felicity b 10 Feb 1981), 1 s (Alastair James Rory b 27 Feb 1987); *Career* mangr Western American Bank (Europe) Ltd 1970–75, vice-pres Crocker National Bank 1975–77; dir: Guinness Mahon Holdings Ltd, Guinness Mahon & Co Ltd 1977–87; md: British & Commonwealth Merchant Bank plc 1987–92, Standard Bank 1992–2006 (chief exec Asia), ceo Asia INTL FCStone Inc 2006–15, exec chm EMEA & Asia INTL FCStone Inc 2015–; *Recreations* golf, sport generally, opera, antique furniture; *Clubs* Piltdown Golf, RAC, Royal Ashdown Forest Golf, Tanglin, Hong Kong; *Style*— Malcolm Wilde, Esq; ✉ Clayton Manor, Underhill Lane, Clayton, West Sussex BN6 9PJ (e-mail malcolm.wilde@intlfcstone.com)

WILDING, His Hon Judge Keith; s of Sidney Wilding (d 1999), and Lilian Maud, *née* Stocken (d 2005); *b* 9 February 1953, London; *Educ* London Nautical Sch, Coll of Law London; *m* 21 July 1973, Jane Catherine, *née* Flanagan; 2 da (Katherine Helen Jane b 18 Feb 1982, Elizabeth Sarah Alice b 12 Feb 1986); *Career* admitted slr 1977; district judge 2002 (dep district judge 1991), circuit judge (South Eastern Circuit) 2013–;; *Recreations* cinema, cricket, golf, reading, rugby; *Clubs* Old Albanian Rugby Football; *Style*— His Hon Judge Wilding; ✉ The Family Court, Cassiobury House, 11–19 Station Road, Watford, Hertfordshire WD17 1EZ

WILDING, Prof Richard David; OBE (2013); s of Dr Malcolm Wilding, of Warks, and Christine Mary Wilding, of Aphion Les Bains, France; *b* 8 May 1965, Sheffield; *Educ* Pricethorpe Coll, Univ of Sheffield (BSc), Univ of Warwick (PhD); *m* 1990, Janice Caroline Lowe; 1 s (b 1991), 1 da (b 1994); *Career* prodn mangr Steetley Brick & Concrete Products Ltd 1987–89, systems engr IMI Refiners Ltd 1989–91; Warwick Manufacturing Gp Univ of Warwick: fell 1991–93, sr fell 1993–97, princ fell 1997–98; Cranfield Sch of Mgmnt Centre for Logistics and Supply Chain Mgmnt Cranfield Univ: lectr 1998–2000, sr lectr 2000–02, dir of in-company progs 2002–04, dir of customised progs 2004–06, chair in supply chain risk mgmnt 2006–10, chair and full prof of supply chain strategy 2010–; visiting prof RMIT Australia 2008–10; co-chm Ldrs in Supply Chain UK 2012– (memb Exec Ctee 2010–); fndr, author and prodr Supply Chain Podcast; various consultancy positions with UK and overseas companies, visiting lectureships, conference chairmanship and editoral bd work; vice-patron Beds Garden Carers 2012–; Distinguished Service Award for Thought Leadership and Service to Supply Chain Mgmnt European Supply Chain Distinction Award 2008, Individual Contribution Award European Supply Chain Excellence Award 2010, Viscount Nuffield Silver Medal for Achievement in Design and Production Inst of Engrg & Technol 2013; Liveryman Worshipful Co of Carmen, Freeman City of London 2013; FCILT 1992 (tstee and dir Bd 2011–, chm 2015–), FIET 1993, FHEA 2003 (formerly Inst of Learning and Teaching in HE (fell 2001)), FCIPS 2014; *Publications* chapters in books and articles in learned jls incl British Journal of Management, International Journal of Physical Distribution and Logistics Management, European Journal of Marketing, Journal of Marketing Management, Supply Chain Management and FT; *Recreations* walking, elliptical cross training, cleaning cars (car detailing), very amateur magician, BBQs, supporting local church; *Style*— Prof Richard Wilding, OBE; ✉ Cranfield School of Management, Cranfield, Bedford MK43 0AL (☎ 01234 751122, website www.richardwilding.info, podcast www.supplychainpodcast.info)

WILDMAN, David Aubrey; s of late Ronald Wildman, and late Bridget, *née* Cotter; *b* 4 July 1955; *Educ* Denbigh HS, Luton Coll; *m* 11 Oct 1975, Gillian, da of late Edward Close, of Richmond, N Yorks; 1 s (Philip b 1986), 1 da (Sophie b 1992); *Career* Chase Manhattan Bank 1973–75, Mobil Oil Co 1975–80; gp ceo 1988–: General & Medical Securities Ltd, General & Medical Finance plc, General & Medical Insurance Ltd, ProAmica Ltd; *Recreations* classic cars, theatre, fine art, family life; *Style*— David A Wildman, Esq; ✉ 41 Turnstone House, City Quay, London E1W 1AE (e-mail david.wildman@generalandmedical.com)

WILDSMITH, Brian Lawrence; s of Paul Wildsmith, of Yorks, and Annie Elizabeth Oxley (d 1984); *b* 22 January 1930; *Educ* De La Salle Coll, Slade Sch of Fine Art UCL (DFA); *m* 1955, Aurélie Janet Craigie, da of Bernard Ithurbide (d 1957); 1 s (Simon), 3 da (Clare, Rebecca, Anna); *Career* freelance artist 1957–, prodn design, illustrations, titles and graphics for first USA-USSR Leningrad film co prodn of the Blue Bird, artist and maker of picture books for young children; Brian Wildsmith Museum opened in Izu, Japan 1994; other one-man shows incl: Diamaru Museum Tokyo 1996 and 1997, Tenmaya-Yonagoshinmachi, Nagoya Mitsukoshi and Fukui City Art Museum, Kyoto Museum 2000, Okazaki Museum for Children 2001, Tokyo Fuji Museum and Japanese tour 2003, Japan Exhbn 2003, Taiwan Exhbn 2004 (touring 2004–05), Fantasia From a Fairyland (travelling exbn, over 1,350,000 visitors) 2003–05; various one-man shows in Japan 2001: incl Yokhama Kanagawa, Mihara Hiroshina, Nakano Tokyo, Fukuoka; lecture tours: USA, Canada, South Africa, Japan, Australia, NZ; winner: Kate Greenaway medal 1962, Kate Greenaway Medal Commendation 1963, Lewis Carroll Shelf Award 1966, Soka Gakkai Educnl medal 1988, The Ushio Culture award 1991, Tokyo Fuji Art-Museum Gold Medal 2003; *Books* ABC (1962), The Lion and the Rat (1963), The North Wind and the Sun (1964), Mother Goose (1964), 123 (1965), The Rich Man and the Shoemaker (1965), The Hare and the Tortoise (1966), Birds (1967), Animals (1967), Fish (1968), The Miller, the Boy, and the Donkey (1969), The Circus (1970), Puzzles (1970), The Owl and the Woodpecker (1971), The Twelve Days of Christmas (1972), The Little Wood Duck (1972), Squirrels (1974), Pythons Party (1974), Blue Bird (1976), The True Cross (1977), What The Moon Saw (1978), Hunter and his Dog (1979), Animal Shapes (1980), Animal Homes (1980), Animal Games (1980), Animal Tricks (1980), Seasons (1980), Professor Noah's Spaceship (1980), Bears Adventure (1981), Cat on the Mat (1982), The Trunk (1982), Pelican (1982), Apple Bird (1983), The Island (1983), All Fall Down (1983), The Nest (1983), Whose Shoes (1984), Toot Toot (1984), Daisy (1984), Give a Dog a Bone (1985), What A Tale (1986), My Dream (1986), Goats Trail (1986), Giddy Up (1987), If I Were You (1987), Carousel (1988), The Christmas Story (1989), The Snow Country Prince (1990), The Cherry Tree (1991), The Princess and The Moon (1991), Over the Deep Blue Sea (1992), The Easter Story (1993), The Tunnel (1993), Noah's Ark (1994), Saint Francis (1995), The Creation (1995), Katie and the Dream-Eater (in collaboration with HIH Princess Takamado, 1996), Brian Wildsmith's Wonderful World of Words (1996), Joseph (1997); in collaboration with Rebecca Wildsmith: Look Closer, Wake Up, Wake Up, What Did I Find, Whose Hat Was That (1993), Tug, Tug Footprints in the Snow (1996); Exodus (1998), The Bremen Town Band (1999), The Seven Ravens (2000), If Only (2000), How Many (2000), Not Here (2000), Knock Knock (2000), My Flower (2000), Jesus (2000), Mary (2002), A Christmas Journey (2003), The Christmas Crib – A Nativity Pop Up (2003); *Recreations* piano; *Style*— Brian L Wildsmith, Esq; ✉ 11 Castellaras le Vieux, 333 Allee du Domaine, 06370 Mouans-Sartoux, Alpes-Maritimes, France (☎ 00 33 4 9375 2411)

WILDSMITH, Prof John Anthony Winston (Tony); s of Winston Wildsmith (d 1978), and Phyllis, *née* Jones (d 2000); *b* 22 February 1946, Newent, Glos; *Educ* King's Sch Gloucester, Univ of Edinburgh Med Sch (MB, ChB, MD); *m* 1969, Angela Fay, *née* Smith; 3 da (Kathryn b 1972, Clare b 1973, Emma b 1976); *Career* early career: Royal Infirmary

Edinburgh/Univ of Edinburgh, various trg posts in anaesthesia; conslt anaesthetist/sr lectr Royal Infirmary Edinburgh 1977–95 (with year at Brigham and Women's Hosp Boston USA 1983–84, clinical dir of anaesthetics, intensive care and operating theatres 1992–95); new chair of anaesthesia Univ of Dundee and hon conslt anaesthetist Tayside Univ Hosps NHS Tst 1995–2007, prof emeritus Univ of Dundee 2006–; pres: Scottish Soc of Anaesthetists 2003–04, History of Anaesthesia Soc 2008–10; hon archivist Royal Coll of Anaesthetists 2012–15 (memb Cncl 1997–2007); memb Editorial Bd Br Jl of Anaesthesia 1987–2008; FRCA, FRCPEd, FRCSEd, FDSRCS; *Publications* jt ed: Principles and Practice of Regional Anaesthesia (1991, 4 edn 2013), Induced Hypotension (1991), Conduction Blockade for Postoperative Analgesia (1991), Anaesthesia for Vascular Surgery (2000); author of numerous papers on special interests, especially regional anaesthesia, and guideline documents on dental anaesthesia and conscious sedation; *Recreations* golf, wine, travel, model railways; *Clubs* RAC, Royal Burgess Golfing Soc; *Style*— Prof Tony Wildsmith; ✉ 6 Castleroy Road, Broughty Ferry, Dundee DD5 2LQ

WILES, Eric Allen; s of Arthur Wiles (d 2004), of Brandesburton, E Yorks, and Doris May, *née* Grantham (d 1978); *b* 12 December 1956, Beverley; *Educ* Hornsea Sch, Univ of Warwick (BA); *m* 9 June 1984, Carole Anne, da of Montague Carl Henry Docwra; 1 da (Olivia Alexandra b 5 Aug 1994), 1 s (Lucas Alexander b 30 April 2001); *Career* chartered accountant/tax conslt; trainee Binder Hamlyn 1978–82, Thornton Baker 1982–84, tax conslt Deloitte Haskins & Sells 1984–86; HSBC Asset Finance (UK) Ltd: tax mangr 1986–88, sr mangr Customer Serv 1988–91, fin controller 1991–93, sr mangr Business Devpt 1993–97; business devpt mangr HSBC Rail (UK) Ltd 1997–2010, head of finance Eversholt Rail (UK) Ltd 2010–13, md Wiles-Capella Ltd 2014–; chm Bd for Chartered Accountants in Business 1999–2000, vice-chm Members Servs 2004–08, memb Cncl ICAEW 1994–2011; memb Corp Worcester Coll of Technol 1997–2012 (chm 2000–12); chm RoSPA 2011–13 (treas 2004–09, vice-chm 2009–11), tstee Asthma UK 2003–12 (treas 2005–12); assoc FIMA 1979, assoc Chartered Inst of Taxation 1985, FCA 1992 (ACA 1982), FRSA 1995; *Recreations* gardening, travel, historical studies; *Style*— Eric Wiles, Esq; ✉ The Chapel, Chapel Lane, Upton Snodsbury, Worcestershire WR7 4NH (☎ 01905 381270)

WILES, Prof Paul; CB (2005); *b* 24 December 1944; *Educ* LSE, Trinity Hall Cambridge; *Career* res fell Inst of Criminology Univ of Cambridge 1970–72; Univ of Sheffield: lectr 1972–76, sr lectr 1976–88, prof of criminology 1988–99; dir of research, devpt and statistics and chief scientific advsr Home Office 1999–2010, Govt chief social scientist 2007–10, chief Govt social researcher and head Govt Social Research 2010–; visiting prof of criminology Univ of Oxford; author of various scientific papers and books; fell Wolfson Coll Oxford; *Style*— Prof Paul Wiles, CB

WILEY, Francesca; QC (2015); *Educ* Trinity Coll Oxford (MA); *Career* called to the Bar (Gray's Inn) 1996; *Recreations* cinema, music, reading, skiing, travel, walking; *Style*— Ms Francesca Wiley, QC; ✉ 1 Garden Court, Temple Avenue, London EC4Y 9BJ

WILEY, (William) Struan Ferguson; s of John Nixon Wiley (d 1968), and Muriel Isobel, *née* Ferguson (d 1969); *b* 13 February 1938; *Educ* Fettes, Univ of New Hampshire USA; *m* 1, 25 Jan 1964 (m dis 1977), Margaret Louise, da of Ian Graham Forsyth, of Crinan, Scotland; 2 da (Sarah b 1964, Anna b 1969), 1 s (Fergus b 1966); *m* 2, 21 Dec 1977, Rosemary Anne, da of Sir John Cameron, OBE, of Cowesby, N Yorks; *Career* Nat Serv 2 Lt 10 Royal Hussars 1956–58, TA 1958–68, Lt Queens Own Yorks Yeo 1958–68; dir: Chunky Chicks (Nichols) Ltd 1962, Sterling Poultry Prods Ltd 1965, Ross Poultry Ltd 1970, Allied Farm Foods Ltd 1970, Imperial Foods Ltd 1975; chm and md Ross Poultry and Ross Buxted Nitrovit Ltd 1977; chm: J B Eastwood Ltd 1978, J Lyons Catering Ltd 1981, Normand Ltd 1981, Embassy Hotels Ltd 1983, Almear Ltd 1995–2000, Food for Thought (UK) Ltd 1996–98; asst md J Lyons & Co Ltd 1981–90, dir Allied-Lyons plc 1986–90, Normand Motor Gp Ltd (and chief exec) 1990–94; non-exec dir: Golden Lay Eggs UK Ltd, Wembley Stadium Ltd, John Clark (Holdings) Ltd 1996–2013, Stadium Group plc 1996–2006 (chm 2000–06), Blackpool Pleasure Beach Ltd 1996–2009; non-exec chm: Kingsbury Group plc 1995–97, Mayfair Taverns Ltd 1996–98, United Vegetables Ltd 1997–2005; chm Br Poultry Breeders and Hatcheries Assoc 1976; memb: Governing Body Houghton Poultry Res Station 1974–82, Grand Cncl Hotel Catering Benevolent Assoc 1983, Leisure Industries Ctee NEDC 1987, Strategy Ctee Retail Motor Industry Fedn 1990–94; winner Poultry Industry Mktg Award 1977; Freeman: City of London 1980, Worshipful Co of Poulters 1981; *Recreations* golf, shooting, collecting old golf clubs; *Clubs* Cavalry and Guards, Woodhall Spa Golf, Sunningdale Golf, Sr Golfers Soc, Seacroft Golf; *Style*— Mr Struan Wiley; ✉ Old Rectory, Withcall, Louth, Lincolnshire LN11 9RL (☎ and fax 01507 343218, e-mail wiley@withcall.prestel.co.uk)

WILFORD, Michael James; CBE (2001); s of James Wilford (d 1964), and Kathleen, *née* Baulch (d 1964); *b* 9 September 1938; *Educ* Kingston Tech Sch, Northern Poly Sch of Architecture London (DipArch), Regent Street Poly Planning Sch; *m* 24 Sept 1960, Angela; 3 da (Karenna Jane b 1962, Jane Anne b 1970, Anna Patricia b 1973), 2 s (Carl Adrian b 1963, Paul Newton b 1966); *Career* architect; sr asst with: James Stirling and James Gowan 1960–63, James Stirling 1963–65; assoc ptnr James Stirling and Partners 1965–71, ptnr James Stirling Michael Wilford and Associates 1971–92 (sole practitioner 1992–93), sr ptnr Michael Wilford and Partners 1993–2001, sr ptnr Michael Wilford Architects 2001–; projects incl: Engrg Faculty Univ of Leicester (RIBA Nat Award and Reynold Aluminium Award 1964), History Faculty Univ of Cambridge (RIBA Nat Award 1970), Staatsgalerie Stuttgart (various German awards 1987–88), Clore Gallery addition to the Tate Gallery (RIBA Regnl and Nat Awards 1988), Tate Gallery Liverpool (RIBA Nat Award 1989), Sci Library Univ of Calif Irvine (Hon Award American Inst of Architects 1990, ALA/AIA Award of Excellence for Library Architecture 1995), B Braun Melsungen AG prodn plant Melsungen (various German awards 1993), Music Acad Stuttgart (RIBA Nat Educn Category Award and Sunday Times/RIBA Stirling Prize 1997), Temasek Poly Singapore (Singapore Inst of Architects Award for Best Educn Bldg and ICI Silver Award for Use of Colour in a Bldg 1998), Sto Ag Communications Bldg and HQ/prodn plant Weizen (RIBA Euro Award 1999), The Lowry Salford (Royal Fine Art Cmmn Bldg of the Year 2001, RIBA Regnl Award 2001, Civic Award 2002), Br Embassy Berlin (RIBA Euro Award 2001), B Braun Melsungen World HQ (various German awards 2001), Land of Baden Wurttemberg History Museum Stuttgart 2002, Peace Palace Library and Acad The Hague 2007, Music Sch Trossingen Germany 2007, Landesbank of Baden-Wurtemberg office building Karlsruhe Germany 2007, STO AG Visitor Centre Weizen Germany 2008, Br Embassy Tbilisi 2010, Peace Palace Visitor The Hague 2012, Braun manufacturing plant Penang Malaysia 2012, STO AG logistics expansion Weizen Germany 2012; visiting critic to many Schs of Architecture at home and abroad since 1968 (external examiner since 1978); tutor AA 1969–73; visiting prof: Rice Univ Houston 1980–88, Graham Wills visiting prof Univ of Sheffield 1980–91, Univ of Cincinnati 1990–92, Charles Davenport visiting prof Yale Univ 1994–95; memb: Educn and Professional Devpt Ctee RIBA 1979–81, Advsy Ctee Dresden Schloss and Museums 1995–96; chm of assessors RIBA Awards 1987, 1989, 1991, 1992 and 2001; assessor: Cardiff Bay Opera House Competition 1994, Buchanan Street Urban Competition Glasgow 1997, Aarhus City Art Museum Competition Denmark 1997, Kleiner Schlossplatz Competition Stuttgart 1999, European Central Bank HQ Frankfurt Competition 2003–04, Hessiches Landesmuseum Darmstadt Competition 2003–04, Central Salford Urban Design Competition 2004, Freiburg Univ Library Competition 2006; lectures and addresses at numerous architectural confs worldwide; Hon DLit Univ of Sheffield 1989, Hon DSc Newcastle Univ Aust 1993, Hon DLitt Univ of Salford 2002, Hon DSc Univ of Leicester 2011; hon memb Bund Deutscher Architekten BDA 1997; hon fell American Inst of Architects 2006; memb: Singapore Inst of Architects, Inst of Arbitrators, RIBA, FRSA; *Publications* subject of various pubns incl: The Museums of James Stirling and Michael Wilford (1990), James Stirling Michael Wilford and Associates Buildings and Projects 1975–92 (1994), Wilford-Stirling-Wilford (1996); *Recreations* earth moving, landscape design; *Style*— Michael Wilford, Esq, CBE; ✉ Michael Wilford Architects, Lone Oak Hall, Chuck Hatch, Hartfield, East Sussex TN7 4EX (☎ 01892 770980, fax 01892 770040, e-mail michaelwilford@michaelwilford.com)

WILKES, Prof (Francis) Michael; s of Francis Wilkes, of Dudley, Staffs, and Cecilia Josephine, *née* Grealey; *b* 9 November 1941; *Educ* St Philip's GS Birmingham, Univ of Birmingham (BSocSc, PhD); *m* Vivienne Mary, da of Alfred William Ernest Sawyer; 3 s (John Francis, David James (twins) b 19 Oct 1972, Stephen Mark b 9 March 1977); *Career* prof of business investment and mgmnt Univ of Birmingham 1991–2002 (emeritus prof 2002–, formerly lectr then sr lectr with secondments to Aston Univ Birmingham and Northwestern Univ USA), chllr Birmingham City Univ 2009–10; memb (Lib Dem) Birmingham City Cncl 1984–92 and 2000–12 (hon alderman 2012–); memb Fulbright Scholars' Assoc; Lord Mayor of Birmingham 2009–10; *Books* Management of Company Finance (with J M Samuels, 1971, 6 edn 1995), Capital Budgeting Techniques (2 edn, 1983), Mathematics for Business Finance and Economics (1994, 2 edn 1998), Financial Management and Decision Making (with J M Samuels and R E Brayshaw, 1998); *Style*— Hon Alderman Michael Wilkes; ✉ e-mail mwi8327963@aol.com

WILKES, Roderick Edward; s of Ernest Lawrence Wilkes (d 1987), of Staffordshire, and Sabra Whitehouse Johnson (d 2008); *b* 26 February 1945; *Educ* Kingshill Sch Secdy Modern for Boys Wednesbury, Wednesbury Coll of Commerce (HND, DipM); *m* 28 March 1970, Marie, da of Harold Page; 1 s (James Edward b 6 June 1972), 1 da (Victoria Louise b 6 May 1974); *Career* Guest Keen & Nettlefolds Ltd 1960–70, commercial conslt GKN Sankey Ltd 1970–73, mktg dir Morlock Industries Ltd 1973–84, gp mktg dir Ellison Circlips Gp 1984–86, sr md RFS 1987–94 (gen mangr 1986–87), md Phoenix Metal Products Ltd 1994–2003, chm Gray Page Ltd 2003–, chief exec CIM 2007–11 (formerly nat chm); nat chm Specialist Ceilings and Interiors Assoc; tstee RoSPA, vice-pres Jubilee Sailing Tst; Pres's Award CIM; Hon DBA Univ of Wolverhampton 2013; FRSA, FCAM, FIOD, FCIM, FCMI; *Recreations* theatre, swimming, travel, DIY; *Clubs* Leander Rowing, Lords Taverners; *Style*— Roderick E Wilkes, Esq; ✉ Monmoor Farm, Eardington, Bridgnorth, Shropshire WV16 5LA (☎ 01746 763076)

WILKIE, Agnes; da of Peter B Wilkie, and Margaret E, *née* McCracken; *Educ* Hamilton Acad, Univ of Strathclyde (BA); *Career* editorial asst D C Thomson 1976–77, journalist The Scottish Farmer 1977–79, features ed Horse and Hound 1979–80; Scottish Television: news prodr 1981–92, head of features and entertainment 1992–2006; head of int devpt TRC Media 2006–09, creative industry dir Northern Film & Media 2009–12, dep dir Baltic Centre for Contemporary Art 2012–; BAFTA Scotland awards: Best Entertainment Prog 1997, Best Special Interest Prog 1997; shortlisted: Best Short Film BAFTA 2004, Best Drama Prix d'Or 2004, Best Drama Prix Italia 2005; memb NUJ 1977–; *Recreations* sailing, running, riding, books, cinema, theatre, shopping, driving fast, climbing mountains in order to see views; *Style*— Ms Agnes Wilkie; ✉ Northern Film & Media, Studio 3, Hoults Estate, Walker Road, Newcastle upon Tyne NE6 1AB (☎ 0191 275 5960, e-mail agnes@northernmedia.org)

WILKIE, Prof Andrew Oliver Mungo; s of Douglas Robert Wilkie, FRS, and June Rosalind, *née* Hill; *b* 14 September 1959; *Educ* Westminster (Queen's scholar), Trinity Coll Cambridge (open scholar, exhibitioner, MA), Merton Coll Oxford (Geoffrey Hill Spray Prize, Flora Medical Student Award, BM BCh, MA), RCP London (DCH), Univ of Oxford (DM); *m* 24 June 1989, Jane Elizabeth, *née* Martin; 2 s (Oscar Brook Douglas b 17 Feb 1997, Fergus John Mungo b 26 Oct 1998); *Career* clinical geneticist; SHO at various hosps London and Bristol 1984–87, MRC trg fell MRC Molecular Haematology Unit and hon registrar Inst of Molecular Medicine John Radcliffe Hosp Oxford 1987–90, sr registrar Gt Ormond St Hosp for Sick Children London 1990–91, clinical research fell in dysmorphology Inst of Child Health 1991, sr registrar Inst of Medical Genetics Univ Hosp of Wales Cardiff 1992–93, hon conslt in clinical genetics Dept of Medical Genetics Churchill Hosp Oxford and Oxford Craniofacial Unit John Radcliffe Hosp 1993–, Wellcome Tst advanced research fell Inst of Molecular Medicine 1993–95, Wellcome Tst sr research fell in clinical science Weatherall Inst of Molecular Medicine 1995–2003, prof of genetics Univ of Oxford 2000–03, Nuffield prof of pathology Nuffield Div of Clinical Lab Sciences Univ of Oxford 2003–; chm Oxford Genetics Knowledge Park 2004–07 (co-chm 2002–04); Nuffield Cncl on Bioethics: memb Working Party on the Genetics of Mental Disorders 1996–98, memb Working Party on Genes and Behaviour 2000–02; author of numerous articles on human genetics of malformation and concept of the selfish testis in peer-review jls and chapters in books; memb Editorial Bd: Jl of Medical Genetics 1994–98, Human Genetics 1998–2011, Human Molecular Genetics 2002–09, Human Mutation 2005–14, PLoS Genetics 2010–, Philosophical Transactions of the Royal Soc B 2013–16; memb: Advsy Bd Encyclopedia of the Human Genome 2000–03, Ctee Genetical Soc 1996–99; memb: Br Soc of Human Genetics/Clinical Genetics Soc 1985–, Assoc of Physicians of GB and I 1997–, European Molecular Biology Organization 2006–, Science Advsy Ctee Genomics England 2013–; Oon Int Prize in Preventive Medicine Downing Coll Cambridge and Cambridge Univ Medical Sch 2002; FRCP 1998 (MRCP 1986), FMedSci 2002, FRSB 2013, FRS 2013; *Publications* numerous peer-reviewed articles in learned jls especially concerning the genetics of craniofacial malformations and identifying selfish selection mechanism in the testis; *Recreations* ornithology, wild camping, mountains, visual arts, cricket; *Style*— Prof Andrew Wilkie; ✉ Weatherall Institute of Molecular Medicine, John Radcliffe Hospital, Headington, Oxford OX3 9DS (☎ 01865 222619, fax 01865 222500, e-mail andrew.wilkie@imm.ox.ac.uk)

WILKINS, Jon Matthew; s of Keith Wilkins, of High Wycombe, Bucks, and Ros Wilkins (d 1994); *b* 29 November 1966, High Wycombe, Bucks; *Educ* Royal GS High Wycombe, Plymouth Poly (BSc); *m* 1 Aug 1998, Lara, *née* South; 2 s (Max, Alfie b 2007 (twins)); *Career* Granada Television 1988–90, MTV Europe 1990–92, Walt Disney Co 1992–94, strategy dir BMP DDB 1994–97, md PHD 1997–2000, founding ptnr Naked Communications 2000; memb MRS; MIPA, MInstD; *Recreations* sport, music; *Clubs* Chelsea FC (season ticket), Soho House; *Style*— Jon Wilkins, Esq; ✉ Naked Communications, 159–173 St John Street, London EC1V 4QJ (☎ 020 7336 8084, fax 020 7336 8009, mobile 07779 623806, e-mail jon@nakedcomms.com)

WILKINS, Baroness (Life Peer UK 1999), of Chesham Bois in the County of Buckinghamshire; Rosalie Catherine Wilkins; da of Eric Frederick Wilkins (d 1974), and Marjorie Phyllis Elizabeth, *née* Hockey (d 1973); *b* 6 May 1946; *Educ* Univ of Manchester; *Partner* Maria Brenton (civil partnership 2006); *Career* researcher and presenter The Link Programme (Central TV) 1975–88, freelance video and documentary presenter and prodr 1988–96; memb: Central Health Services Cncl 1974–76, BBC General Advsy Cncl 1976–78, Prince of Wales's Advsy Gp on Disability 1982–90; pres Coll of Occupational Therapists 2003–08; retired House of Lords 2015; The Snowdon Award 1983; *Style*— The Baroness Wilkins; ✉ House of Lords, London SW1A 0PW (☎ 020 7219 8522)

W

WILKINSON, Andrew John Owen; s of John Wilkinson, and Anne, *née* Mennie; *b* Liverpool; *Educ* St Edward's Coll Liverpool, Jesus Coll Oxford (MA, BCL); *m* 21 Sept 1991, Juliet, *née* Morris; 2 da (Alice Isabel b 12 Jan 1996, Imogen Grace b 31 May 2000), 1 s (Hal James Oliver 25 Nov 1997); *Career* called to the Bar 1983, admitted slr 1987; Clifford Chance 1985–1998, Cadwalader Wickersham & Taft LLP 1998–2007 (memb Mgmnt Ctee and managing ptnr 2000–07); md Goldman Sachs 2007–; memb editorial bd of several legal pubns; Legal Business Lawyer of the Year 2004, Restructuring Team of the Year Lawyer Awards 2005; sponsor and supporter Almeida Theatre; memb: Insolvency Lawyers Assoc, Int Bar Assoc; co-chair Insolvency Sub-ctee European High Yield Assoc; fell Soc of Practitioners of Insolvency; Insolvency of Banks: Managing the Risks, Insolvency Law (co-author), various chapters in Tolley's Insolvency; *Recreations* tennis, opera, theatre, piano; *Clubs* RAC, Blackwell Golf, Campden Tennis; *Style*— Andrew Wilkinson, Esq

WILKINSON, Prof Brian; *b* 1938; *Educ* King's Coll Durham (BSc Civil Eng, BSc Geology, Lebur Prize), Univ of Manchester (PhD), Univ of Durham (DSc); *Career* engr Babtie Shaw & Morton Glasgow 1961–63, lectr Dept of Civil Engrg Univ of Manchester 1963–69, sr engr Water Resources Bd Reading 1969–74, sr princ hydrologist Severn Trent Water Authy Birmingham 1974, head Communications Gp and research co-ordinator Water Research Centre Medmenham 1979–84 (head Water Resources Div 1974–79), prof of civil engrg and head of dept RMCS Shrivenham 1984–85, prof of civil engrg and dep dean Cranfield Univ Shrivenham 1985–88, head Wallingford Lab and dir Inst of Hydrology 1988–94, dir Centre for Ecology and Hydrology UK NERC 1994–99; visiting prof: Univ of Reading 1989–2005, Univ of Newcastle 1995–2005; dir Oxford Vacs Ltd 1997–99; sr conslt Solutions to Environmental Problems (StEP) 1999–, former head UK Delgn World Meteorological Orgn's Cmmn for Hydrology; former chm: UK Govt Interdepartmental Hydrology Ctee, Int Hydrological Prog Ctee UK UNESCO, UK Environmental Change Network Ctee; former memb: Royal Soc/Fell of Engrg UK Ctee of Int Decade for Natural Disaster Reduction, Br Ctee Int Assoc of Hydrogeologists, Terrestrial and Freshwater Science and Technol Bd NERC, Land Ocean Interaction Study Science Planning Gp and Steering Ctee, UK GEWEX Forum, Canadian GEWEX Science Advsy Panel, GEWEX Int Scientific Steering Ctee, NERC Terrestrial and Freshwater Science and Technol Bd, UK UNESCO Sustainable Devpt Ctee, ICE Environment Sustainability Bd, Panel EC 5 Year assess of RTD Environment and Sustainable Devpt Sub Programme; memb Expert Gp EU 2002 Monitoring of European Research Area; fndr memb EurAqua (Euro Network of Fresh Water Research Orgns); convenor IHAS Symposium Macromodelling of the Hydrosphere Japan 1993, UK rep to Science Cmmn UNESCO Gen Conference, project co-ordinator Ind Review Gp Brent Decommissioning Project 2007–, advsr Safety, Health and Environment Ctee Transport for London 2007–10; author numerous papers in ac jls; Fell Russian Acad of Natural Sciences 1997; CEng 1967, CGeol 1967, FICE 1984, FCIWEM 1984, FGS 1990; *Recreations* classical music, violin, viola, archaeology, shukokai karate black belt; *Style*— Professor Brian Wilkinson; ✉ Solutions to Environmental Problems (StEP), Millfield House, High Street, Leintwardine, Craven Arms SY7 0LB (e-mail gb.wilk@dsl.pipex.com)

WILKINSON, Charles Edmund; s of Dr Oliver Charles Wilkinson (d 1987), and Sheila Muriel, *née* McMullan (d 1997); *b* 6 June 1943; *Educ* Haileybury and ISC, Clare Coll Cambridge; *m* 1, 1967, Gillian Margaret, *née* Alexander; 2 da (Claire b 10 March 1972, Juliet b 13 June 1973); m 2, 2007, Constance Adele Elizabeth, *née* West; *Career* slr; sr ptnr Blyth Dutton 1980–91 (ptnr 1974), ptnr Lawrence Graham (following merger) 1991–2005, ret; chm: Doric Nimrod Air One Ltd, Doric Nimrod Air Three Ltd; dir: Doric Nimrod Air Two Ltd, Premier Energy and Water Tst plc, Landore Resources Ltd; Freeman City of London; memb Law Soc; *Clubs* Brooks's, Cavalry & Guards, City, Hurlingham, Royal Thames Yacht; *Style*— Charles Wilkinson, Esq; ✉ Birchwood House, Rue de la Hougue, Castel, Guernsey GY5 7EA (✆ 01481 255351, e-mail cewilkinson@birchwood.gg)

WILKINSON, Christopher John (Chris); OBE (2000); s of Maj Edward Anthony Wilkinson, of Welwyn Garden City, Herts, and Norma Doreen, *née* Trevelyan-Beer; *b* 1 July 1945; *Educ* St Albans Sch, Regent Street Poly Sch of Architecture (DipArch, RIBA); *m* 3 April 1976, Diana Mary, da of Alan Oakley Edmunds, of Limpsfield Chart, Surrey; 1 da (Zoe b 1978), 1 s (Dominic b 1980); *Career* princ founding dir Wilkinson Eyre Architects (formerly Chris Wilkinson Architects) 1983–; previous employment with Richard Rogers and Ptnrs, Michael Hopkins Architects and Foster Assocs; visiting prof: IIT Chicago 1998, Harvard GSD 2004; cmmr English Heritage 2007–11 (memb Urban Panel 2000–); memb Advsy Cncl Steel Construction Inst 1998–2000; chm: RIBA Region Awards 1996, 2000 and 2001, Aluminium Awards 1997, RA Works Ctee 2007–11; design patron Civic Tst Awards 2009–; memb RIBA Honours Awards Panel 2005 and 2006; works exhibited: Royal Acad Summer Exhbn (annually) 1986–88, 1991, 1995–97 and 2002–16, The Architecture Fndn 1992 and 1995, Tokyo Design Centre 1995, New Works Future Visions Sao Paolo 1997, New Urban Environments Tokyo 1998, Millennium Products 2000, Great Expectations Exhbn 2001, New Connections: The Jubilee Line Extension and Urban Regeneration 2001, Bridging Art and Science Science Museum 2001 (solo exhbn), Reflections Venice Biennale 2004, Reflectionist Destinations at Wapping Project (solo exhbn), Skin and Bones exhbn LA, Tokyo and London, Union of Architects St Petersburg 2008, Contemporary Architecture in Westminster 2009, V&A British Design Innovation in the Modern Age 2012, Supertall (Skyscraper Museum NY) 2011–12, Practical Utopias (AIA Centre NY) 2013–14, Lookout: Architecture with a View (Basel Switzerland) 2013–14, The Brits Who Built the Modern World RIBA 2014, Thinking through Drawing: Chris Wilkinson RA (Royal Acad) 2015, Thinking through Drawing (British School in Rome) 2016; projects incl: Stratford Market Depot and Stratford Station for Jubilee Line Extension, Dyson HQ Malmesbury, Magna Centre Millennium Project Rotherham, South Quay Footbridge, Hulme Arch, Challenge of Materials Gall, Making of Modern World Gall and Wellcome Wing exhbn at the Science Museum, Explore at Bristol, Gateshead Millennium Bridge, Nat Waterfront Museum Swansea, Empress State Building Redevelopment Earls Court, Alpine House Kew Gardens, Mary Rose Museum Portsmouth, John Madejski Acad Reading, Guangzhou IFC Guangzhou, King's Waterfront Arena and Conf Centre Liverpool, Earth Sciences Dept Univ of Oxford, Humanities Dept Queen Mary's Univ of London, Gardens by the Bay Singapore, Apraksin Dvor St Petersburg, Arundel Great Court redevelopment London, Basketball Arena Building for London 2012 Olympics, Hauser Forum Univ of Cambridge, Media City Footbridge Salford, The Forum Univ of Exeter, Siemens Urban Sustainability Centre The Crystal in Royal Victoria Docks, Splashpoint Worthing, Maggies Centre Oxford, Battersea Power Station, The Gas Holder Triplets King's Cross, Crown Sydney, Dyson Research Design and Development Building and Lightning Café Dyson Campus Malmesbury, 150 Leadenhall St EC3; Hon DLitt Univ of Westminster 2001, Hon Dr Oxford Brookes Univ 2007; FCSD, RA 2007, Hon FAIA 2007; *Awards* Eric Lyons Award 1993, CSD Designer of the Year 1996, Royal Acad AJ/Bovis Grand Award 1997, 39 RIBA Awards, 7 BCI Awards, 33 Structural Steel Awards, FT Architectural Award 1997, 39 Civic Tst Awards, AIA Award 1998, 2000, 2001, 2002 and 2003, FX Designer of the Year 2001, Stirling Prize for Architecture 2001 and 2002, CTBUH Best Tall Building Asia and Australasia 2011, World Building of the Year WAF 2012, RIBA Lubetkin Prize 2012 and 2013, RIBA Int Award 2012 and 2013, Sports Building of the Year WAF 2013; *Books* Supersheds (1991), Supersheds II (1995), Bridging Art and Science (monograph, with Jim Eyre, 2001), Wilkinson Eyre Bridges (2004), Wilkinson Eyre Destinations (2005), Exploring Boundaries (2007), Tectonics: A Building for Earth Sciences at Oxford (2010), Wilkinson Eyre Architects/ Works (2015), The Sketchbooks of Chris Wilkinson (2015); *Recreations* golf, painting, travel, olive farm in Tuscany; *Clubs* Chelsea Arts, FABS; *Style*— Chris Wilkinson, Esq, OBE, RA; ✉ 52 Park Hall Road, West Dulwich, London SE21 8BW (✆ 020 8761 7021); Wilkinson Eyre Architects Ltd, 33 Bowling Green Lane, London EC1R 0BJ (✆ 020 7608 7900, fax 020 7608 7901, e-mail c.wilkinson@wilkinsoneyre.com)

WILKINSON, Clive Victor; *b* 26 May 1938; *Educ* Four Dwellings Secdy Modern Sch; *m* 7 Oct 1961, (Elizabeth) Ann; 2 da; *Career* Birmingham City Cncl: cncllr 1970–84, ldr 1973–76 and 1980–82, ldr of oppn 1976–80 and 1982–84; dir NEC Birmingham 1973–84, fin and commercial dir Birmingham Rep Theatre 1983–87; chm Cncl for Small Industries in Rural Areas 1977–80; dep chm: AMA 1974–76, Redditch Devpt Corp 1977–81; chm: Sandwell DHA 1986–94, Wolverhampton Health Care NHS Tst 1995–98, W Midlands Regnl Office NHS Exec 1998–2001; chair Birmingham and Solihull Heartlands NHS Trust until 2010; non-exec dir FSA 2001–07; memb: Devpt Cmmn 1977–86, Electricity Consumers Cncl 1977–80, Audit Cmmn 1987–96, Black Country Devpt Corp 1989–92, Local Govt Cmmn 1992–95, Midlands Industrial Assoc 1978– (chm 1980–88); chm: Birmingham Civil Housing Assoc 1979–2011, Customer Servs Ctee Severn Trent Regnl Office of Water Servs 1990–; memb Cncl Univ of Birmingham 1974–84, tstee Bournville Village Tst 1982–; Hon Alderman City of Birmingham 1984; *Recreations* soccer; *Style*— Clive Wilkinson

WILKINSON, Craig; s of Ian Wilkinson, and Anne Wilkinson; *b* 18 January 1973; *Educ* LLB; *m* June 1999, Lucy; *Career* Business Advsy Services Price Waterhouse 1994–98, Bank of Scotland 1998–2000, Rothschild 2000–02, Lloyds Devpt Capital 2001–08, md LDC (Asia) Ltd 2009–; hon treas HKVCA; ACA; *Clubs* China, Hong Kong FC, London Caledonian; *Style*— C Wilkinson, Esq; ✉ LDC Asia Ltd, 26/F, 8 Queen's Road Central, Hong Kong (✆ 00852 3416 4400, fax 00852 3416 4001, e-mail cwilkinson@ldc.com.hk)

WILKINSON, Dr David George; s of George Arthur Wilkinson (d 1978), and Barbara Mary, *née* Hayton (d 1995); *b* 8 March 1958; *Educ* Aylesbury GS, Hymers Coll Hull, Univ of Leeds (BSc, PhD); *m* 16 Nov 1991, Qiling Xu; *Career* postdoctoral research Fox Chase Cancer Center Philadelphia 1983–86; Nat Inst for Medical Research London: postdoctoral research 1986–88, gp leader 1988–2000, head Div of Developmental Neurobiology 2000–15, head Genetics and Devpt Gp 2000–15; sr gp ldr Francis Crick Inst 2015–; memb EMBO 2000, FMedSci 2000; *Publications* In Situ Hybridization (1992); author of approx 120 research papers in scientific jls; *Recreations* natural history, music, poetry; *Style*— Dr David Wilkinson; ✉ The Francis Crick Institute, Mill Hill Laboratory, The Ridgeway, Mill Hill, London NW7 1AA (✆ 020 8816 2404, fax 020 8816 2523, e-mail david.wilkinson@crick.ac.uk)

WILKINSON, Glen Alexander Low; s of Cdr James Henry Wilkinson, of Gosport, Hants, and Alexia Menny, *née* Low; *b* 2 September 1950; *Educ* Churcher's Coll Petersfield, Univ of Birmingham Med Sch (MB ChB); *m* (m dis); 3 da (Rebecca b 9 Feb 1978, Angela b 9 March 1979, Laura b 19 May 1986), 1 s (Matthew James b 11 Feb 1988); *Career* sr registrar in cardiothoracic surgery W Midlands RHA 1985–88, sr fell (actg instr) in cardiothoracic surgery Univ Hosp Washington Seattle 1986–87, retired conslt cardiothoracic surgn Sheffield HA and Northern Gen Hosp; memb Soc of Cardiothoracic Surgns of GB and I 1986; FRCS 1978; *Recreations* model railway running and collecting, model boat building, photography, fly fishing; *Style*— Glen Wilkinson, Esq; ✉ 21 Mayfield Heights, Brookhouse Hill, Sheffield S10 3TT (✆ 0114 229 5202, e-mail glen.wilkinson@dsl.pipex.com)

WILKINSON, Jonathan Peter (Jonny); CBE (2015, OBE 2004, MBE 2003); *b* 25 May 1979, Frimley, Surrey; *Educ* Pierrepont Sch, Lord Wandsworth Coll; *Career* former rugby union player (fly half); with Newcastle Falcons RUFC 1998–2009 (winners Tetley's Cup 2001), Rugby Club Toulonnais 2009–14 (winners Heineken Cup 2013 and 2014, top 14 winners 2014), ret; England: 91 caps, scored 1179 points (English record), debut v Ireland 1998 (youngest England player since 1927), capt 2003, winners Six Nations Championship 2000, 2001, 2003 (Grand Slam 2003) and 2011, record holder most points in one test 35 points v Italy 2001 and most points in championship season 89 points 2001, ranked no 1 team in world 2003, winners World Cup Aust 2003 (leading points scorer), finalists World Cup France 2007, ret 2011; British and Irish Lions: memb squad tour to Aust 2001 (record holder most points in one test 18 points) and NZ 2005, world record points scorer of all time (currently 5007 total points); world record holder most drop goals 31; Int Players' Player of the Year 2002 and 2003, IRB Player of the Year 2003, BBC Sports Personality of the Year 2003, induction into Rugby Players Assoc Hall of Fame 2015; md Fineside Ltd; Freedom City of Newcastle upon Tyne 2004, Freedom Town of Bandol 2012, Freedom City of Toulon 2014; Hon DCL Northumbria Univ 2004, Hon DUniv Surrey 2009; *Books* Lions and Falcons (2002), My World (2004), How to Play Rugby My Way (2005), Tackling Life (2008), Jonny: My Autobiography (2011); *Recreations* playing guitar and piano, speaking and reading French and Spanish; *Style*— Jonny Wilkinson, Esq, CBE; ✉ website www.jonnywilkinson.com

WILKINSON, Rev Canon Keith Howard; s of Kenneth John Wilkinson, of Leicester, and Grace Winifred, *née* Bowler; *b* 25 June 1948; *Educ* Beaumont Leys Coll Leicester, The Gateway GS Leicester, Univ of Hull (BA), Emmanuel Coll Cambridge (Lady Romney Exhibitioner, MA), Westcott House Cambridge; *m* 27 Aug 1972, Carolyn, da of Lewis John Gilbert (d 1985), of Wokingham; 2 da (Rachel b 1979, Claire b 1979); *Career* head of religious studies Bricknell HS 1970–72, head of faculty (humanities) Kelvin Hall Comprehensive Sch Kingston upon Hull 1972–74; ordained: deacon 1976, priest 1977; asst priest St Jude Westwood Peterborough 1976–79, educn offr to the church Peterborough 1977–79, asst master and chaplain Eton Coll 1979–84, sr chaplain and head of religious studies Malvern Coll 1984–89 (sr tutor 1988–89), headmaster Berkhamsted Sch 1989–96, headmaster The King's Sch Canterbury 1996–2007, sr chaplain Eton 2008–; hon canon Cathedral Church of Christ Canterbury; chm Soc of Sch Masters and Sch Mistresses 1998–; FRSA 1994; *Recreations* films, music, drama, ecology, walking, buildings; *Clubs* East India; *Style*— The Rev Canon Keith Wilkinson

WILKINSON, Dr Laura Margaret; da of William Low Wilkinson, of Ayr, and Dorothy, *née* Smith; *Educ* Ayr GS, Wellington Sch Ayr, Univ of Glasgow (MB ChB); *Career* house offr in med then surgery Gartnavel Gen/Western Infirmary Glasgow 1984–85, SHO in gen med Monklands Dist Gen Hosp Airdrie 1985–87; Gartnavel Gen/Western Infirmary Glasgow: registrar then sr registrar in radiology 1987–93, conslt radiologist W of Scotland Breast Screening/Western Infirmary 1993–2007, conslt radiologist W of Scotland Breast Screening/Royal Alexandra Hospital Paisley 2007–, regnl advsr radiology W of Scotland 2008–12; Royal Coll of Radiologists: W of Scotland Jr Forum rep 1991–95, memb Scottish Standing Ctee 1991–95, chm Exec Jr Radiologists Forum 1993–95, Training Accreditation Ctee 2002–06, external advsr 2012–; sec Jr Forum Euro Assoc of Radiology 1995–96; chm and head of trg West of Scotland Sub-Ctee in Radiodiagnosis 1998–2002; external advsr Scottish Acad 2012–; FRCR 1992; *Clubs* RAF; *Style*— Dr Laura Wilkinson; ✉ Laigh Monkcastle, Dalry Road, Kilwinning KA13 6PN (✆ 01294 833161); West of Scotland Breast Screening Centre Glasgow, Royal Alexandra Hospital Paisley (✆ 0141 572 5833)

WILKINSON, Nigel Vivian Marshall; QC (1990); s of John Marshall Wilkinson (d 1993), of East Horsley, Surrey, and Vivien, *née* Gwynne-James (d 2009); *b* 18 November 1949; *Educ* Charterhouse, ChCh Oxford (Holford exhibitioner, MA); *m* 20 April 1974, Heather Carol (Rt Hon Lady Justice Hallett, DBE, *qv*), da of late Hugh Victor Dudley Hallett; 2 s (James b 4 June 1980, Nicholas b 20 April 1982); *Career* called to the Bar Middle Temple 1972 (bencher 1997); Astbury scholar 1972, memb Midland & Oxford circuit 1972–, recorder of the Crown Court 1992–, dep judge of the High Court 1997–; head Temple Garden Chambers 2008–; dep chm Cricket Cncl Appeals Ctee 1992–96; *Recreations* sport and entertainment; *Clubs* Garrick, MCC, I Zingari, Invalids CC, Armadillos CC, Vincent's

(Oxford), Butterflies CC, Rye, Hon Co of Edinburgh Golfers; *Style*— Nigel Wilkinson, Esq, QC; ✉ Temple Garden Chambers, 1 Harcourt Buildings, Temple, London EC4Y 9DA (☎ 020 7583 1315, website www.tgchambers.com)

WILKINSON, Vice Adm Peter John; CB (2010), CVO (2007); s of Sir Philip Wilkinson (d 2007), and Eileen, *née* Malkin (d 1991); *b* 28 May 1956; *Educ* Royal GS High Wycombe, St David's Coll Lampeter Univ of Wales (BA); *m* 12 Dec 1981, Tracey Kim, da of Eric Ward (d 1998); 2 da (Katherine Alice b 1989, Hilary Frances b 1991); *Career* RN: qualified in subs 1980, jr appts 1980–87, submarine command course 1987–88, CO HMS Otter 1988–89, CO HMS Superb 1991–92, CO HMS Vanguard 1994–96, Captain 2 Submarine Sqdn 1999–2001, dir RN Serv Conditions 2001–03, dir RN Life Mgmnt 2003–04, DG Human Resources (RN) and Naval Sec 2004–05, Defence Servs Sec 2005–07, DCDS (Personnel) 2007–10, ret; chm Seafarers UK 2010–; pres RN FA, hon vice-pres FA 2004–10, nat pres Royal Br Legion 2012–16; memb Cncl Forces Pension Soc 2011– (chm Cncl 2015–), patron Loch Class Frigates Assoc 2012–, patron Soldier on Charity 2012–16; Clerk Worshipful Co of Cooks 2011–; hon fell Univ of Wales Trinity St David 2013; FCIPD 2003; *Recreations* gardening, walking, watching all sports; *Clubs* Army and Navy (dir 2016–); *Style*— Vice Adm Peter Wilkinson, CB, CVO; ✉ Leach Building, Whale Island, Portsmouth, Hampshire PO2 8BY (☎ 023 9262 5542, fax 023 9262 5100)

WILKINSON, Sally Ann; da of Derek George Wilkinson (d 1978), of London, and Kathleen Mary Patricia, *née* O'Callaghan (d 1989); *b* 1 November 1953, London; *Educ* Westonbirt Sch, Watford Coll of Technol (HND); *Career* trainee exec Image Makers Ltd 1973, account exec Crawford Heard Ltd 1974, divnl press offr Thorn Domestic Appliances 1975–78, account exec rising to creative dir Kingsway Rowland 1978–89, divnl md The Rowland Co 1990–92, md SAW Associates 1993–94 and 1995–, dep gen mangr Edelman Worldwide London 1994–95, md Brook Wilkinson 1996–, managing ptnr the firm 2001–, head of corp affrs Merlin Entertainments plc 2004–; memb: Inst of Mktg 1978, Assoc of Women in PR 1990, Guild of PR; MInstD, FRSA; *Recreations* theatre, music, interior design, writing, art and antiques; *Clubs* Guards, Soho House; *Style*— Miss Sally Ann Wilkinson; ✉ the firm, Building 3, Chiswick Park, Chiswick High Road, London W4 5YA (☎ 020 8899 6110, mobile 07774 415372, e-mail saw@thefirmcomms.com)

WILKS, Jonathan Paul (Jon); CMG (2012); s of Douglas Edwin Ian Wilks, and Veronica Kay, *née* Mills; *b* 30 September 1967, Callow End, Worcs; *Educ* Durham Univ (BSc, MA), St Antony's Coll Oxford (MPhil); *m* 30 April 2015, Hon Patricia Marie Haslach; *Career* diplomat; FCO: joined 1989, asst desk offr Iran ME Dept 1990–91, Arabic language trg London 1991–92 and Cairo 1992–93, second sec (political and press and public affrs) Khartoum 1993–96, first sec (economic) Riyadh 1996–99, secondment as Iraq analyst Cabinet Office 2002–03, dep head Br Office Baghdad 2003, dep head (political) Iraq Policy Unit 2004–05, dep head Security Policy Gp 2005–07, regnl Arabic spokesperson Dubai 2007–09, dep head of mission Baghdad 2009–10, ambass to Yemen 2010–11, higher command and staff course Shrivenham 2012, UK special rep to the Syrian Oppn 2012–13, UK special rep for Syria 2014, ambass to Oman 2014–; Iraq Reconstruction Medal 2014; FRGS 1996; *Recreations* horse racing, music; *Clubs* Travellers, Nat Liberal; *Style*— Mr Jonathan Wilks, CMG; ✉ c/o Foreign and Commonwealth Office, King Charles Street, London SW1A 2AH

WILKS, Prof Stephen Robert Mark; s of Gordon Wilks (d 1993), and Florence, *née* Wilson (d 2008); *b* 2 January 1949, Newcastle upon Tyne; *Educ* Buckhurst Hill Co HS, City of Westminster Coll, Lancaster Univ (BA), Victoria Univ of Manchester (PhD); *m* 2 Oct 1976, Philippa Mary, *née* Hughes; 3 da (Susannah b 13 June 1979, Laura b 22 Nov 1980, Verity b 19 June 1985); *Career* with Fryer Whitehill & Co Chartered Accountants 1968–72; Univ of Liverpool: lectr then sr lectr Dept of Political Theory and Instns 1978–89, reader in political theory and instns 1989–90; Univ of Exeter: prof of politics 1990–2013 (prof emeritus 2013–), head Dept of Politics 1992–95 and 2003–04, ESRC sr research fell 1995–96, dep vice-chllr 1999–2002 and 2004–05; visiting prof Faculty of Law Univ of Kyoto 1989; memb: Cncl ESRC 2001–05 (chair Strategic Research Bd 2002–05), Competition Cmmn 2001–09, Competition Appeal Tbnl 2011–; FCA 1978 (ACA 1971); *Publications* Industrial Policy and the Motor Industry (1984, 2 edn 1988), Industrial Crisis: A Comparative Study of the State and Industry (ed with Kenneth Dyson, 1985), Comparative Government-Industry Relations: Western Europe, the United States and Japan (ed with Maurice Wright, 1987), Comparative Competition Policy: National Institutions in a Global Market (ed with Bruce Doern, 1996), In the Public Interest: Competition Policy and the Monopolies and Mergers Commission (1999), Reforming Public and Corporate Governance: Management and Market in Australia, Britain and Korea (ed with Byong-Man Ahn and John Halligan, 2002), The Political Power of the Business Corporation (2013); also author of numerous book chapters, articles, reports, working papers and reviews; *Recreations* walking, wine, gardening, tea; *Style*— Prof Stephen Wilks; ✉ Newlands, Millhayes, Stockland, East Devon EX14 9DG

WILLACY, Michael James Ormerod; CBE (1989); s of James Willacy (d 1977), and Majorie Winifred, *née* Sanders; *b* 7 June 1933; *Educ* Taunton Sch; *m* 1, Merle Louise, da of Johannes Schrier, of Denia, Spain; 2 s (Richard b 1962, Peter b 1969), 1 da (Jennifer b 1963); m 2, Victoria Stuart, da of Cecil Stuart John, of Mobberley, Cheshire; 3 s (James b 1985, Michael b 1986, David b 1990), 1 da (Elizabeth b 1988); *Career* gen mangr Shell UK Materials Services 1983–85, dir HM Govt Central Unit on Purchasing 1985–90, purchasing advsr HM Treasy 1991–92; md Michael Willacy Associates Ltd 1991–2011; chm Macclesfield C of C 1981–83, fndr chm Macclesfield Business Ventures 1982–83; Old Tauntonian Assoc: gen sec 1978–91, pres 1988–89, vice-pres 1989–; chm St Dunstan's Abbey Sch for Girls 1997–2004, govr Taunton Sch 1993–2008, hon vice-pres Plymouth Coll 2005–; FCIPS; *Recreations* golf, travel, gardening; *Clubs* Bigbury Golf (chm 2007–10); *Style*— Michael Willacy, Esq, CBE; ✉ 2 Erme Park, Ermington, Ivybridge, Devon PL21 9LY (☎ 01548 831014, e-mail michael.willacy914@btinternet.com)

WILLATS, Stephan; *b* 17 August 1943; *Educ* Ealing Sch of Art; *m* Stephanie Willats; *Career* artist; ed and publisher Control magazine 1965–, pt/t lectr 1965–72, dir The Centre for Behavioural Art 1972–73, DAAD fell W Germany 1979–80, convenor Art Creating Society Symposium Museum of Modern Art Oxford 1990; *Solo Exhibitions* incl: Visual Automatics and Visual Transmitters (MOMA Oxford) 1968, The Artist as an Instigator of Changes in Social Cognition and Behaviour (Gallery House London) 1973, Coding Structure and Behaviour Parameters (Gallery Banco Bresco Italy) 1975, Allitudes within Four Relationships (Lisson Gallery London) 1976, Questions About Ourselves (Lisson Gallery) 1978, Concerning our Present Way of Living (Whitechapel Art Gallery) 1979, Berlin Wall Drawings (Galerie Rudiger Schottle Munich) 1980, Mens en Omgeving De Beyard Centram voor beeldende Kanst (Breda Holland) 1981, Meta Filler and Related Works (Tate Gallery) 1982, Inside the Night (Lisson Gallery) 1983, Doppelgänger (Lisson Gallery) 1985, City of Concrete (Ikon Gallery Birmingham) 1986, Concepts and Projects Bookworks (Nigel Greenwood Books, London) 1987, Between Objects and People (Leeds City Art Gallery) 1987, Secret Language (Cornerhouse Gallery Manchester) 1989, Mosaics (Galerie Kaj Forsblom Helsinki) 1990, Multiple Clothing (ICA) 1993, Museum Mosaic (Tate Gallery London) 1994, Random Life (Victoria Miro Gallery London) 1994, Living Together (Tramway Glasgow) 1995, Writing On The Wall (Galerie Kaj Forsblom Helsinki) 1995; *Group Exhibitions* incl: Kinetic Art (Hayward Gallery) 1970, Art as Thought Process (Serpentine Gallery London) 1974, Social Criticism and Art Practice (San Francisco Art Inst) 1977, La Parola e le Imagine (Commune di Milano) 1979, Sculpture in the Twentieth Century (Whitechapel Art Gallery London) 1981, New Art at the Tate Gallery (Tate Gallery) 1983, Eye Level (Van Abbemuseum Eindhoven) 1986, 100 years of British Art (Leeds City Art Gallery) 1988, The New Urban Landscape (World Fin Centre NYC) 1990, Excavating the Present (Kettle Yard Gallery Cambridge) 1991, Instruction and Diagrams (Victoria Miro Gallery London) 1992, Visione Britannica (Valentina Moncada Rome Italy) 1994, Temples (Victoria Miro Gallery London) 1995, Ideal Standard Summertime (Lisson Gallery London) 1995; works in public collections incl: Art Museum Zurich, Scottish Nat Gallery of Modern Art Edinburgh, Tate Gallery London, Arts Cncl of GB, V&A, British Museum, Museum of Contemporary Art Utrecht Holland, Stichting Volkshuisvesting in de Kunst Den Haag Holland, Van Abbe Museum Eindhoven Holland, Stadtische Galerie Stuttgart; *Style*— Stephan Willats, Esq

WILLCOCKS, Lt-Gen Sir Michael Alan; KCB (2000, CB 1997), CVO (2009); s of Henry Willcocks (d 2001), and Georgina Bernadette, *née* Lawton (d 1989); *b* 27 July 1944; *Educ* St John's Coll, RMA Sandhurst, Univ of London (BSc); *m* 10 Dec 1966, Jean Paton, da of James Burnside Paton Weir (d 1967); 1 s (Julian b 20 June 1968), 2 da (Jessica b 28 April 1971, Hannah b 26 Feb 1976); *Career* cmmnd RA 1964, serv Malaya, Borneo, UK, Germany 1965–72; instr: RMA Sandhurst 1972–74, Staff Coll 1975–76; MOD 1977–79, Comd M Battery RHA 1979–80, Staff Coll Directing Staff 1981–82, CO 1 Regt RHA 1983–85, DACOS HQ UKLF 1985–87, Asst COS Intelligence/Ops HQ UKLF 1988, Cmd RA 4 Armd Div 1989–90, RCDS 1991, ACOS Land Operations Joint War HQ Gulf War (and aftermath) 1991, Dir Army Plans and Programme 1991–93, DG Land Warfare 1993–94, COS Allied Command Europe Rapid Reaction Corps 1994–96, COS Land Component of Peace Implementation Force (IFOR) Bosnia-Herzegovina 1995–96, Asst CGS 1996–99, Dep Cmd (Ops) Stabilization Force (SFOR) Bosnia-Herzegovina 1999–2000, UK mil rep NATO and EU 2000–01; Hon Col IRHA 1999–2006, Col Cmdt RA 2000–05, Representative Col Cmdt RA 2004–05; former Gentleman Usher of the Black Rod, Serjeant-at-Arms House of Lords and sec to the Lord Great Chamberlain 2001–09, ind reviewer Press Complaints Cmmn 2009–12, sr advsr C5 Captial 2009–11, dir IKOS CIF Ltd 2010–; European-Atlantic Gp 1994–; cmmr: Royal Hosp Chelsea 1996–99, The Pilgrims 2002–; vice-pres Turville Park Cricket Club 2005–, hon memb Kennel Club 2006–; tstee Lifeline Energy 2006–13; Hon DLitt Univ of Hull; Knight Cdr Sacred Military Constantinian Order of St George 2006; Meritorious Service Medal USA 1996 and 2000, Pingat Jasa Malaysia medal 2006; *Books* Airmobility and the Armoured Experience (1989); *Recreations* books, music, fishing, shooting, sailing; *Clubs* Beefsteak, National Liberal, Pitt, Saints and Sinners; *Style*— Lt-Gen Sir Michael Willcocks, KCB, CVO; ✉ c/o The National Liberal Club, Whitehall Place, London SW1A 2HE

WILLESDEN, Bishop of 2001–; Rt Rev Peter Alan (Pete) Broadbent; *b* 31 July 1952; *Educ* Merchant Taylors' Northwood, Jesus Coll Cambridge (MA), Univ of Nottingham (DipTh), St John's Coll Nottingham (DPS); *m* 1974, Sarah; 1 s (Simon b 13 Nov 1978); *Career* ordained deacon 1977, priest 1978; asst curate: St Nicholas Durham City 1977–80 (concurrently asst chaplain HM Remand Centre Low Newton), Emmanuel Hornsey Rd Holloway 1980–83; Bishop of Stepney's chaplain for mission 1980–89; Anglican chaplain to the Poly of N London 1983–89 (concurrently hon curate St Mary Islington), vicar Trinity St Michael Harrow 1989–94, archdeacon of Northolt 1995–2001; memb London Diocesan: Synod 1985–, Bishop's Cncl 1988–89 and 1991–, Fin Ctee 1991–2001; chm London Diocesan Bd for Schs 1996–2002, chm Memralife Gp 2009–; memb Gen Synod (Proctor in Convocation London) 1985–2001; chm Gen Synod: Business Ctee 1999–2000 (Sub-Ctee 1996–98), Elections Review Gp 1996–2000; memb Gen Synod: Panel of Chairmen 1990–92, Standing Orders Ctee 1991–95, Standing Ctee 1992–98, Appointments Sub-Ctee 1992–95; memb Dioceses Cmmn 1989–92, Diocesan rep on Crown Appts Cmmn 1990 and 1995; memb: Central Bd of Fin 1991–95 and 1996–98 (memb Exec Ctee 1991–95), Cncl Wycliffe Hall 1991–94, Archbishops' Advsy Gp on Fin Mgmnt and the Expectations of the Church 1993–98; chm Vacancy in See Ctees Regulation Working Pty 1991–93; memb: C of E Evangelical Cncl 1984–95, London Diocesan Evangelical Cncl 1985–, Open Synod Gp Ctee 1994–2000, Evangelical Gp in Gen Synod Ctee 1996–2000, Archbishops' Cncl 1999–2000, Urban Bishops Panel 2001–; asst ed Anvil (theol jl) 1984–86; contrib: Third Way, Church of England Newspaper; Lab cncllr London Borough of Islington (chm Devpt and Planning Ctee) 1982–89; chm: London Boroughs Tport Ctee 1986–89, London Road Safety Ctee 1987–89; dep chm London Planning Advsy Ctee 1985–89, vice-chm Planning and Tport Ctee Assoc of London Authorities 1985–89; tstee Church Urban Fund 2002–10; memb S Eastern Regnl Planning Conf 1986–89; London Borough of Harrow: co-opted memb Educn Ctee 1990–96, chm Standing Advsy Cncl on RE 1990–95, ind memb Standards Ctee 2002–10; chm Family Action Info and Rescue 1981–84; dir Spring Harvest 1998–; memb Central Govening Body City Parochial Fndn 1999–2003; chair St John's Coll Nottingham Cncl 2002–10; memb: Lab/Co-op Pty, ASTMS 1980–84, NUPE 1984–89; *Books* Hope for the Church of England? (contrib chapter The Political Imperative, 1986), Uncage the Lion (contrib, 1990), Church and Society in the 1990s (contrib 1990), Politics and the Parties (contrib chapter A Labour Party View, 1992), Restoring Faith in Politics (contrib, 1996); *Recreations* football (lifelong supporter of Tottenham Hotspur FC), theatre and film, railways, real ale, National Trust, popular music from the 1950s to the present day; *Style*— The Rt Rev the Bishop of Willesden; ✉ 173 Willesden Lane, Brondesbury, London NW6 7YN (☎ 020 8451 0189, fax 020 8451 4606, e-mail bishop.willesden@btinternet.com)

WILLETT, Keith Malcolm; CBE (2016); *b* 9 September 1957, Shoreham-by-Sea, Sussex; *Educ* Charing Cross Hosp Med Sch (MB BS); *Career* prof of orthopaedic trauma surgery Univ of Oxford, nat clinical dir for trauma care Dept of Health 2009–12, nat dir for acute care NHS Eng 2012–; chair Injury Minimisation Prog for Schools (NHS charity); LRCP, FRCS (MRCS), FRCSEd; *Style*— Prof Keith Willett, CBE

WILLETTS, Baron (Life Peer UK 2015), of Havant in the County of Hampshire; Rt Hon David Lindsay Willetts; PC (2010); s of John Roland Willetts, and Hilary Sheila Willetts; *b* 9 March 1956; *Educ* King Edward's Sch Birmingham, ChCh Oxford (BA); *m* 1986, Hon Sarah Harriet Ann Butterfield, *qv*, da of Baron Butterfield (Life Peer, d 2000); 1 da, 1 s; *Career* research asst to Nigel Lawson MP 1978; HM Treasy 1978–84: energy policy 1978–79, public expenditure control 1980–81, private sec to fin sec 1981–82, monetary policy 1982–84; memb PM's Downing Street Policy Unit 1984–86, dir of studies Centre for Policy Studies 1987–92, conslt dir Cons Research Dept 1987–92; MP (Cons) Havant 1992–2015; PPS to Sir Norman Fowler 1993–94, asst whip 1994–95, Lord Cmmr of HM Treasy 1995, Parly under sec Office of Public Serv 1995–96, Paymaster-Gen 1996; oppn front bench spokesman on employment 1997–98, shadow sec for educn and employment 1998–99, shadow sec for social security 1999–2001, shadow sec of state for work and pensions 2001–05, shadow sec of state for trade and industry 2005, shadow sec of state for educn and skills 2005–09, shadow min for univs and skills 2009–10, min for univs and science 2010–14; memb Cons Pty Policy Bd 2001–03, memb Governing Body Inst of Govt 2008–; visiting fell Nuffield Coll Oxford 1998–2006, visiting prof Cass Business Sch 2005–10, visiting prof KCL 2015–, hon fell Nuffield Coll Oxford 2015–; memb: Lambeth, Southwark and Lewisham FPC 1987–90, Parkside HA 1988–90, Social Security Advsy Ctee 1989–92; non-exec dir: Retirement Security Ltd 1988–94 (chm 1991–94), Electra Corporate Ventures Ltd 1989–94; dir Konigswinter UK 2007–; sr policy advsr Punter Southall 2005–09; writer and broadcaster; govr Ditchley Fndn, exec chair Resolution Fndn 2015–; memb: Cncl Inst for Fiscal Studies, Global Aging Cmmn 1999–2009; *Publications* Modern Conservatism (1992), Civic Conservatism (1994), Blair's Gurus (1996), Why Vote Conservative? (1997), Welfare to Work (1998), After the Landslide (1999), Browned-off: What's Wrong with Gordon Brown's Social Policy (2000), Tax Credits: Do They Add Up? (2002), Left Out, Left Behind (2003), Old Europe? Demographic Change and Pension

W

Reform (2003), Conservatives in Birmingham (2008), The Pinch: how the baby boomers took their children's future and why they should give it back (2010), Eight Great Technologies (2013), Robbins Revisited (2013), Higher Education, Who Benefits? Who Pays? (2015); *Clubs* Hurlingham, Garrick; *Style*— The Rt Hon the Lord Willetts; ✉ House of Lords, London SW1A 0PW (☎ 020 7219 3575)

WILLI, Prof Andreas Jonathan; s of Thomas Willi, and Ina Willi-Plein; *b* 17 December 1972, Altstätten, Switzerland; *Educ* Humanistisches Gymnasium Basel, Univ of Basel (Georg-Peter-Landmann Prize), Univ of Lausanne, Univ of Fribourg, CCC Oxford (Charles Oldham grad scholar, DPhil); *m* 17 Sept 2005, Helen Kaufmann; *Career* visiting research investigator Univ of Michigan Ann Arbor 1995–96; Univ of Basel: oberassistent in Latin philology 2001–02, oberassistent in Greek philology 2002–04; membro scientifico dell'Istituto Svizzero di Roma 2004–05, Diebold prof of comparative philology Univ of Oxford 2005–, fell Worcester Coll Oxford; memb: American Philological Assoc 1995–, Classical Assoc of the Middle West and South (CAMWS) 1995–, Philological Soc 1998–; Hellenic Fndn Award 2002; *Books* The Language of Greek Comedy (ed, 2002), The Languages of Aristophanes (2003), Sikelismos: Sprache, Literatur und Gesellschaft im griechischen Sizilien (2008), Laws and Rules in Indo-European (co-ed, 2012); *Style*— Prof Andreas Willi; ✉ Worcester College, Oxford OX1 2HB

WILLIAMS, Her Hon Judge (Jean) Adele; DL (Kent 2016); da of David James Williams (d 1975), and Dorothy May, *née* Rees (d 2006); *b* 28 July 1950, Carmarthenshire, S Wales; *Educ* Llanelli Girls' GS, UCL (LLB); *m* 20 Sept1975, His Hon Andrew Patience QC ; 1 da (Louise Angharad Adèle b 5 Aug 1981), 1 s (David William Andrew b 23 Aug 1984); *Career* called to the Bar Gray's Inn 1972; practising barr 1972–2000, circuit judge 2000–, resident judge Canterbury Crown Court 2008–; hon recorder of Canterbury 2016–; *Recreations* cinema, theatre, conversation; *Style*— Her Hon Judge Williams, DL; ✉ Canterbury Combined Court Centre, Chaucer Road, Canterbury, Kent CT1 1ZA (☎ 01227 819200)

WILLIAMS, Prof Adrian Charles; s of Geoffrey Francis Williams, OBE, of Aberystwyth, and Maureen, *née* Wade; *b* 15 June 1949; *Educ* Epsom Coll, Univ of Birmingham (MB ChB, MD); *m* 19 April 1980, Linnea Marie, da of Gerald Olsen, of Colorado, USA; 1 da (Sarah b 1981), 2 s (Alec b 1984, Henry b 1986); *Career* visiting fell NIH 1976–79, registrar Nat Hosp London 1979–81, conslt neurologist Queen Elizabeth Hosp Birmingham 1981–, Bloomer prof of clinical neurology Univ of Birmingham 1988–; memb Assoc Br Neurologists; FRCP 1986; *Recreations* sailing, skiing, gardening; *Style*— Prof Adrian Williams; ✉ 25 Farquhar Road, Edgbaston, Birmingham B15 3RA (☎ 0121 454 2633); Department of Neurology, Queen Elizabeth Hospital, Edgbaston, Birmingham B15 2TT (☎ 0121 627 2106)

WILLIAMS, Alan; *b* 1 July 1943; *m* 1; 1 da (Amanda Williams b 27 April 1972), 1 s (Simon Williams b 11 Aug 1977); m 2, 16 April 2008, Lisa Carol; *Career* sr press offr HM Treasy 1972–74, ed British Business 1974–79, chief info offr DTI 1979–86; The Post Office: controller of public affrs 1986–93, dir of PR 1993–95, memb Post Office Exec Bd and gp corporate affrs dir 1995–2003, memb Bd Parcelforce 1995–99; ptnr AWRailways 2003–; chm Esk Valley Railway Development Co 2003–; memb: Design Panel Br Railways Bd 1985–94, Bishop Line Community Rail Partnership 2004–; regular writer and commentator on political and safety issues surrounding tport; assoc Instn of Railway Signal Engrs 1986, pres Railway Study Assoc (LSE) 1998–99, vice-pres Railfuture 2015–; *Books* Railway Signalling (edns since 1963), Not the Age of the Train (1983), Two Centuries of Railway Signalling (2008); *Recreations* driving motor cars and steam engines very fast!; *Clubs* Reform; *Style*— Alan Williams, Esq; ✉ Moorland House, Staintondale, North Yorkshire YO13 0EW (☎ 01723 871984, e-mail awrailways@aol.com)

WILLIAMS, Prof Alan; CBE (1995); s of Ralph James Williams (d 1942), and Muriel, *née* Lewis; *b* 26 June 1935; *Educ* Cyfarthfa GS Merthyr Tydfil, Univ of Leeds (BSc, PhD); *m* 30 July 1960, Maureen Mary, da of Sydney Bagnall, of Leeds; 3 s (Christopher b 1964, Nicholas b 1967, Simon b 1971); *Career* Univ of Leeds: Livesey prof in fuel and combustion sci and head of Dept of Fuel and Energy 1973–2000, dean of engrg 1991–94, research prof 2000–; memb: DTI Advsy Ctee on Coal Research 1991–96, DTI Energy Advsy Panel 1993–96; memb OST Technol Foresight Energy Panel 1994–99; former pres and hon sec Inst of Energy, ed Jl of the Energy Inst 2004–09; CChem, CEng, FRSC, FEI, FIGEM, FIGasE, FRSA, FREng; *Publications* Combustion of Liquid Fuel Sprays, Combustion and Gasification of Coal; author of 650 papers in jls and conference proceedings; *Style*— Prof Alan Williams, CBE, FREng; ✉ Energy Research Institute, University of Leeds, Leeds LS2 9JT (☎ 0113 233 2507, fax 0113 246 7310, e-mail fueaw@leeds.ac.uk)

WILLIAMS, Prof Alan Lee; OBE (1973); *b* 29 November 1930; *Educ* Roan Sch Greenwich, Ruskin Coll Oxford; *Career* RAF Signals 1949–51; pt/t messenger Nat Fire Serv 1944–45, cncllr Greenwich BC 1951–53, nat youth offr Lab Pty 1955–62, chm BNC World Assembly of Youth 1960–66, head of UNA Youth Dept 1962–66, memb Cncl of Europe and Parly Assembly WEU 1966–70, ldr UK Delgn to Fourth Ctee UN Gen Assembly 1969; MP (Lab): Hornchurch 1966–70, Hornchurch and Havering 1974–79; PPS to sec of state for Def 1969–70 and 1974–76, PPS to sec of state for NI 1976–79, ldr Parly Delgn to N Atlantic Assembly 1974–79, chm PLP Def Ctee 1976–79; dep dir Euro Movement 1972–79, DG ESU 1979–86, chm Peace Through NATO 1983–92, dir Atlantic Cncl 1992–, pres Atlantic Treaty Assoc 2000–04; chm CSIS Euro Working Gp Washington DC 1974–91; memb: Cncl RUSI 1974–78, Tri-Lateral Cmmn 1976–2000, FO Advsy Ctee on Disarmament and Arms Control and Advsy Ctee PRO 1977–81; chm: Tport on Water 1974–, City Coll 1987–, Cedar Centre 1988–2008, Toynbee Area Housing Assoc 1993–99, Majlish Home Care Service 2004–, William Beveridge Fndn 2006, Mid Atlantic Club 2006; memb: Bd Attlee Fndn 1987–89, Cncl Toynbee Hall 1992– (warden and chief exec 1987–92); Freeman: City of London 1969, Co of Watermen and Lightermen 1952 (hon ct asst 2010); fell Queen Mary & Westfield Coll London 1994 (visiting prof 2003–); DLitt (hc) Schiller Int Univ; FRSA 1987; Golden Laurel Branch Award (Bulgaria) 2002; *Publications* Radical Essays (1966), Europe or the Open Sea (1971), Crisis in European Defence (1973), The European Defence Initiative: Europe's Bid for Equality (1985), The Decline of the Labour Party and the Fall of the SDP (1989), Prospects for a Common European Foreign and Security Policy (1995), NATO's Future in the Balance: Time for a Rethink? (1995), International Terrorism: Failure of International Response (1995), NATO and European Defence: A New Era of Partnership (1996), WEU: a Challenge for NATO (1997), NATO's 'Strategy for Securing the Future' (1999), Does NATO Have a Future? (2002), The Two Duffers go to War (jtly, 2011); *Clubs* Reform, Pilgrims, Mid Atlantic, ESU Dartmouth House; *Style*— Prof Alan Lee Williams, OBE; ☎ 020 8463 9394, e-mail a.leewilliams@btinternet.com

WILLIAMS, Alan Peter; s of late Ronald Benjamin Williams, of Lindfield, W Sussex, and Marcia Elizabeth, *née* Lister; *b* 27 October 1944, Cairo; *Educ* Merchant Taylors' Northwood, Univ of Exeter (LLB, capt cricket XI, editor Univ Newspaper); *m* 21 Sept 1968, Lyn Rosemary, da of late Reginald Ewart Campling; 1 da (Laura Kate Elisabeth b 3 April 1974); *Career* articled clerk Burton Yeates & Hart 1966–67; Dentons (and predecessor firms) 1967–2005: articled clerk 1967–68, admitted slr 1969, ptnr 1972–2003, opened Hong Kong office 1976; conslt DLA Piper (UK) LLP 2005–08; memb Publishing Law Gp Publishers' Assoc 1983–2009; dir Nat Youth Music Theatre 1990–2002, memb Cncl Shakespeare's Globe; memb Ct of Assts Worshipful Co of Pewterers; memb: Law Soc 1969, Richard III Soc; FRSA; *Books* Clark's Publishing Agreements (contrib, 9 edn), International Media Liability (by JohnWiley, contrib), Intellectual Property The New Law (jtly); Digital Media: Contracts, Rights and Licensing (jtly), Press, Printing and Publishing, chapter in Halsbury's Laws of England (jtly), Digital Media Contracts (jtly), Drafting Agreements for the Digital Media Industry (jtly); *Recreations* cricket, music, walking, photography, theatre; *Clubs* MCC, Groucho, Whitefriars, City Law, Inner Magic Circle (assoc memb); *Style*— A P Williams, Esq; ✉ Turret House, Old Place, Lindfield, West Sussex RH16 2HU (☎ 020 7247 3738, e-mail alanwilliams06@gmail.com)

WILLIAMS, Prof (Gruffydd) Aled; s of William Ernest Williams (d 1976), and Gwendolen, *née* Hughes (d 1992); *b* 20 January 1943, Denbigh; *Educ* Llangollen GS, UC of N Wales Bangor (BA, PhD); *m* 1 July 1972, Brid Éimear; 2 s (Gruffudd Owain b 21 May 1973, Siôn Ynyr b 17 May 1982), 1 da (Brid Gwenllian b 22 Jan 1975); *Career* asst lectr Dept of Welsh UC Dublin 1965–70, successively lectr, sr lectr and reader Dept of Welsh Univ of Wales Bangor 1970–95, prof of Welsh Univ of Wales Aberystwyth 1995–2008 (now emeritus prof); Sir Ellis Griffith Prize Univ of Wales 1988, Mrs L W Davies Bursary Univ of Wales 1988, Br Acad Sir John Rhys Meml lectr 2010; *Publications* Ymryson Edmwnd Prys a Wiliam Cynwal (1986), The Cambridge History of Literary Criticism, Vol 2: The Middle Ages (contrib, 2005), Dyddiau Olaf Owain Glyndwr (2015, Welsh Book of the Year (Creative Non-Fiction) 2016); author of numerous articles on medieval and renaissance Welsh literature; *Style*— Prof Aled Williams; ✉ Bronafon, Dolau, Bow Street, Aberystwyth, Ceredigon (☎ 01970 820664, e-mail gawilliams1@btinternet.com); Department of Welsh, Old College, King Street, Aberystwyth, Ceredigon SY23 2AX (☎ 01970 622135, fax 01970 622976, e-mail gaw@aber.ac.uk)

WILLIAMS, Prof Allan Peter Owen; s of Thomas Williams (d 1995), of Cardiff, and Hilda Marie Williams (d 1983); *b* 14 October 1935; *Educ* Eastbourne GS, Univ of Manchester (BA), Birkbeck Coll London (MA, PhD); *m* 25 July 1959, Rosella, da of Maj Honorio Jose Muschamp d'Assis Fonseca (d 1984); 2 da (Hélène b 1963, Roselyne b 1967), 1 s (Edmond b 1965); *Career* res exec (later res gp head) Marplan Ltd 1960–63; City Univ Business Sch: lectr 1963–74, sr lectr 1974–83, reader 1983–88, prof 1988–2001 (emeritus prof 2001–), dep dean 1996–2001; City Univ: dir Centre for Personnel Res and Enterprise Devpt 1978–2001, pro-vice-chllr 1987–93, head Dept of Business Studies 1993–96; dir Organisation Surveys Ltd 1966–69, conslt psychologist Civil Serv Selection Bd 1966–80; hon treas Br Psychological Soc 1971–74 (chm occupational psychology section 1979–80), memb Army Personnel Res Ctee MRC 1983–94, chm Personnel Psychology Panel APRC 1987–94, chm Mgmnt History Research Gp 2008–15; memb Bd of Dirs: Int Assoc of Applied Psychology 1990–2006, Br Acad of Mgmnt 1990–98; tstee: T Ritchie Rodger Res Fund 1984–, City Centre for Charity Effectiveness 2008–; fndr Liveryman Worshipful Co of Mgmnt Conslts; FBPsS 1979, CPsychol 1988, FBAM 1995, FAcSS 2009, fell Int Assoc of Applied Psychology 2010; *Books* The Role and Educational needs of Occupational Health Nurses (1982), Using Personnel Research (1983), Changing Culture: New Organisational Approaches (1989 and 1993), The Competitive Consultant (1994), Managing Change Successfully (2002), The Rise of Cass Business School: The Journey to World Class (2006), The Fifteenth Anniversary of ABS: 1992–2007 (2007), The History of UK Business and Management Education (2010), Occupational Psychology, Management Education and Consultancy: A Fifty-Year Narrative for Academics Striving to Manage their Careers in a Competitive Climate (2016); *Recreations* lawn tennis, photography, philately, bibliophile, golf; *Clubs* Barnet Lawn Tennis, Old Fold Manor Golf; *Style*— Prof Allan Williams; ✉ Cass Business School, City University London, 106 Bunhill Row, London EC1Y 8TZ

WILLIAMS, Brian Edward; s of Edward Clement Williams (d 2010), and Christine Edith, *née* Jones; *b* 28 April 1959; *Educ* Framlingham Coll Suffolk; *m* 16 Dec 1989, Deborah Jane, *née* Dingley; 2 s (Charles Edward Dingley b 2 Feb 1991, Edward Roger b 10 Feb 1994), 1 da (Lucinda Catherine b 21 Aug 1992); *Career* hotelier; Forte Hotels 1976–85: food & beverage mangr Imperial Torquay 1980–82, food & beverage mangr Dubai International 1982–85; Mandarin Oriental Hotel Group 1985–2003: food & beverage mangr Oriental Kuala Lumpur 1985–86, mangr Mandarin Hong Kong 1990 (resident mangr 1986–89), gen mangr Mandarin Oriental Macau and Hotel Bella Vista Macau 1991–94, gen mangr The Ritz London 1994–95, gen mangr Mandarin Oriental Hyde Park 1996–2000, vice-pres devpt Mandarin Oriental Hotel Gp EMEA until 2003; chief exec Scotsman Hotel Gp 2003–06, md Swire Hotels 2006–; *Recreations* skiing, golf, tennis, wine; *Style*— Brian Williams, Esq

WILLIAMS, Prof Brian Owen; CBE (2011); s of William Wood Williams (d 1988), of Kilbarchan, Scotland, and Joan Scott, *née* Adam; *b* 27 February 1947; *Educ* Kings Park Sch Glasgow, Univ of Glasgow (MD, MB, ChB); *m* 3 Dec 1970, Martha MacDonald, da of James Carmichael (d 1974), of Glasgow; 2 da (Jennifer b 1976, Linzie b 1978); *Career* maj RAMC 32 Scot Signal Regt TA 1976–83; conslt geriatrician Victoria Infirmary Glasgow 1976–79, sr lectr Univ of Glasgow 1979–82, conslt in admin charge W Glasgow Geriatric Med Serv 1982– (clinical dir 1993–), hon sr clinical lectr Univ of Glasgow 1982–; author of over 100 pubns on health care of the elderly; pres RCPSGlas 2006–09, past pres Br Geriatrics Soc, vice-pres (medical) RCPSGlas 2001–03 (past hon sec), past hon sec Scottish Royal Colls; memb: BMA, Scottish Soc of Physicians; Hon DSc Glasgow Caledonian Univ 2007; FRCP (London), FRCPGlas, FRCPEd, Hon Fell Royal Coll Speech and Language Therapy, FCPS (Pakistan), FRCPI, FRACP 2007; *Books* Practical Management of the Elderly (with Sir Ferguson Anderson, 4 edn, 1983, 5 edn, 1988); *Recreations* swimming, writing, hill walking; *Style*— Prof Brian Williams, CBE; ✉ 15 Thorn Drive, High Burnside, Glasgow G73 4RH (☎ 0141 634 4480); Gartnavel General Hospital, 1053 Great Western Road, Glasgow G12 0YN (☎ 0141 211 3167, fax 0141 211 3465)

WILLIAMS, Bryn Dwyfor; *b* 6 June 1977, Denbighshire; *Educ* Ysgol Uwchradd Glan Clwyd Llanelwy, Coleg Llandrillo Cymru; *Career* chef; formerly: Criterion (under Marco Pierre White), sous chef (under Michel Roux, Jr, *qv*) Le Gavroche, Patisserie Millet Paris, Hotel Negresco Nice 2001, Orrery Restaurant London; currently chef-prop Odette's London; television appearances incl: Great British Menu (BBC 2) 2006 and 2007, Saturday Kitchen (BBC 1), Something for the Weekend (BBC 2), Market Kitchen, Cegin Bryn (S4C) 2012; patron Gwledd Conwy Feast; *Books* Bryn's Kitchen (2011); *Style*— Bryn Williams, Esq; ✉ Odette's, 130 Regent's Park Road, London NW1 8XL (☎ 020 7586 8569, Twitter @brynodettes)

WILLIAMS, Dr Caroline Ann; da of Maurice Henry Jackson, of Portsmouth, Hants, and Dorothy, *née* Ludlow; *b* 2 March 1954; *Educ* Convent of the Cross Sch Waterlooville, St Hugh's Coll Oxford, Univ of Southampton (LLB); *m* 17 March 1973, Richard David Brooke Williams (d 2007), 1 s of Gp Capt Richard David Williams, CBE, of Hants; 1 da (Rowena b 27 June 1982), 1 s (Richard David b 6 Aug 1987); m 2, 7 Sept 2013, Laurence Colin Alster; *Career* admitted slr 1978; Blake Lapthorn: ptnr 1981–2000, conslt 2000–12; consult and non-exec dir of various companies; chm: Portsmouth Area Ctee Hampshire Incorporated Law Soc 1993–95, Univ of Portsmouth 1995–99, Portsmouth Historic Dockyard 2003–12, Hampshire Econ Partnership 2003–10, B C Capital Ltd 2003–, Biocontrol Ltd 2005–13; non-exec dir and dep chm Ampliphi Biosciences Corp 2011–13; non-exec dir Nat Museum of the Royal Navy 2011–, non-exec dir HMS Victory Preservation Tst 2012–; govr: Univ of Portsmouth 1993–2002, Portsmouth HS 1995–1999, Portsmouth GS 2003–05; govr and vice-chm Portsmouth Coll of Art Design and FE 1989–94; memb: Industrial Advsy Bd Portsmouth Univ Business Sch 1991–99, SE Regnl Cncl CBI 1996–2003, Bd SE England Devpt Agency 1998–2003, Industrial Advsy Bd Wessex Inst of Technol 2001–05, Bd Portsmouth City Growth 2004–05, Hants Senate 2008–10, Partnership for Urban S Hants Jt Ctee 2009–10, Int Women's Forum 2009–11;

Hon LLD Univ of Portsmouth 2002; memb Law Soc 1978; FRSA 1995; *Publications* A Practical Legal Guide to Occupational Pension Schemes (with Philip Harwood-Smart, 1993); *Recreations* sailing, walking; *Style*— Dr Caroline Williams; ✉ 27 St Catherine's Road, Hayling Island, Hampshire PO11 0HF (e-mail caroline.williams365@gmail.com)

WILLIAMS, Christopher; s of Henry Edward Williams (d 1957), of Bristol, and Beatrice May, *née* Somers (d 1990); *Educ* Colston's Sch Stapleton Bristol, St Cuthbert's Society Univ of Durham (BA); *Career* W & T Avery Ltd Soho Foundry Birmingham 1964–69, md Frenchay Transport Group 1969–; chm Frenchay Community Health Cncl 1980–81 (memb 1976–81, vice-chm 1978–80), chm Frenchay HA 1990–91 (memb 1981–91), chm Frenchay Healthcare NHS Tst 1992–98 (chm designate 1991–92, assoc non-exec dir 1998–); memb: NHS Nat Fire Policy Advsy Gp 1993–98, Standing Fin and Capital Ctee NHS Tst Fedn 1993–99, Cncl NHS Tst Fedn 1994–97; Northavon DC: cncllr (Cons) 1976–96, chm Fin and Gen Purposes Ctee 1980–90, chm of Cncl 1986–88, ldr Cons Gp 1991–96; chm Bd of Govrs Frenchay Park Hosp Sch 1978–94, dir Bristol/Avon Groundwork Tst 1990–96; fell Inst of Tport Admin 1992 (memb 1985); *Recreations* music, reading, travel; *Style*— Christopher Williams, Esq

WILLIAMS, Colin Campbell; s of Graham Williams (d 1942), and Eleanor, *née* Cuthbert (d 1988); *b* 9 February 1942, Woking, Surrey; *Educ* Uppingham, Magdalen Coll Oxford, UCLA; *m* 1975, Gerlinda, *née* Ackerl; 1 s (Alexander b 20 May 1979), 1 da (Sophie b 21 June 1981); *Career* fndr Wogen plc 1972–; chm Uppingham Sch 1999–2009; hon steward Westminster Abbey 1992–2012; *Recreations* bicycling; *Clubs* Boodles; *Style*— Colin Williams, Esq; ✉ Wogen plc, 4 The Sanctuary, London SW1P 3JS (☎ 020 7222 2171, fax 020 7222 5862, e-mail cwilliams_private@wogen.com)

WILLIAMS, (Alun) Craig; MP; s of Thomas David Williams, and Andrea Joan, *née* Richardson; *b* 7 June 1985, Welshpool; *Educ* Welshpool HS, N Shropshire Coll; *m* 5 May 2013, Clare Helena, *née* Bath; 1 s (David Charles b 20 April 2012), 1 da (Amelia Mary b 13 Feb 2016); *Career* Cardiff City Cncl 2008–15, MP (Cons) Cardiff N 2015–; *Recreations* cinema, music, walking, rugby; *Clubs* County, United and Cecil; *Style*— Craig Williams, Esq, MP; ✉ House of Commons, London SW1A 0AA (☎ 02920 733225, e-mail craig@craigwilliams.wales, Twitter @Craig4CardiffN)

WILLIAMS, David; *Career* co-fndr and chief exec Avanti Communications Gp plc; *Style*— David Williams, Esq; ✉ Avanti Communications Group plc, Cobham House, 20 Black Friars Lane, London EC4V 6EB

WILLIAMS, Prof David Franklyn; s of Henry Williams (d 1975), and Margaret, *née* Morgan (d 1975); *b* 18 December 1944; *Educ* Univ of Birmingham (BSc, PhD, DSc); *Children* 3 s (Adrian David b 1972, Jonathan Philip b 1974, Christopher Stephen b 1977); *Career* Univ of Liverpool: joined staff 1968, prof of clinical engrg 1984–2007, conslt scientist Royal Liverpool Univ Hosp 1990–2007, pro-vice-chllr 1997–2000, emeritus prof 2008–; dir UK Centre for Tissue Engrg 2004–07, prof and dir of int affrs Wake Forest Inst of Regenerative Medicine USA 2008–; sr Fulbright scholar and visiting prof Clemson Univ USA 1975–76, guest prof Tsinghua Univ Beijing 2007–, visiting prof Christiaan Barnard Dept of Cardiothoracic Surgery Univ of Cape Town 2008–, visiting prof Univ of NSW Sydney 2008–, chair prof of biomedical materials engrg Taipei Medical Univ 2010–; scientific advsr Euro Cmmn; author of 32 books and over 300 scientific pubns, ed-in-chief Biomaterials; Clemson Award US Soc for Biomaterials 1982, Winter Award Euro Soc for Biomaterials 1996, Fndrs Award US Soc for Biomaterials 2007, Chapman Medal Inst of Materials 2007, Gold Medal Acta Biomaterialia 2012; MAE; FIM, FIPSM, FREng 1999, fell American Inst for Medical and Biological Engrg, foreign fell Indian Nat Acad of Engrg 2014; *Books* Essential Biomaterials Science (2014); *Clubs* Athenaeum; *Style*— Prof David Williams, FREng; ✉ 1 Sheffield Place, Winston-Salem, NC 27104–2046, USA (☎ 00 1 336 671 8895, e-mail dfwillia@wfubmc.edu)

WILLIAMS, Dr David Frederick; s of Frederick Sefton Williams (d 2001), and Dorothy, *née* Banks; *b* 21 September 1951, Preston, Lancs; *Educ* Hutton GS Preston, Univ of Reading (BSc, PhD); *m* 16 Nov 1985, Jeannie Elizabeth, *née* Rickards; 2 da (Rebecca Jo-Anne b 25 May 1983, Sylvana Daisy b 11 Oct 1986), 1 s (Jonathan Richard Walter b 28 Feb 1996); *Career* lectr Dept of Geography Univ of Reading 1977–78, Clyde Surveys (formerly Fairey Surveys) 1978–82, NERC 1982–89, head UK Earth Observation Prog Br Nat Space Centre (BNSC) DTI 1989–96, head of strategy and int rels European Orgn for the Exploitation of Meteorological Satellites (EUMETSAT) Darmstadt 1996–2006, DG BNSC 2006–10; UK Space Agency: acting chief exec 2010–11, chief exec 2011–12; gp exec info sciences CSIRO Australia 2012– (exec dir Nat Facilities and Collections 2012–); tstee and memb Bd of Dirs Nat Space Centre Leicester 2006–12, chm European Space Agency 2011–12, memb Int Acad of Astronautics 2012–; *Recreations* football, rugby, gardening, renovation, farming; *Style*— Dr David Williams; ✉ CSIRO, 5 Julius Avenue, North Ryde, NSW 2113, Australia (☎ 0061 2 9490 5621)

WILLIAMS, Emrys; *b* 18 January 1958; *Educ* Slade Sch of Art (Boise Travelling scholar, Robert Ross scholar, BA), Stewart Powell Bowen fellowship 1983; *Career* artist in residence: Mostyn Art Gallery Llandudno 1983, South Hill Park Arts Centre and Wilde Theatre Bracknell 1985; *Solo Exhibitions* Andrew Knight Gallery Cardiff 1984, Pastimes Past (Wrexham Arts Centre) 1984, The Welsh Mountain Zoo (South Hill Park Arts Centre, Bracknell) 1985, Off Season – Winter Paintings (Oldham Art Gallery) 1985, Lanchester Poly Gallery Coventry 1986, Benjamin Rhodes Gallery London 1986, 1989 and 1991, Wrexham Arts Centre 1990; *Group Exhibitions* incl: Clwyd Ten (Wrexham Arts Centre) 1981, Thorugh Artists Eyes (Mostyn Art Gallery, Llandudno) 1982, John Moores Liverpool Exhibition XIII 1982–83, Serpentine Summer Show II (Serpentine London) 1983, Pauline Carter & Emrys Williams (Chapter Gallery) Cardiff 1984, John Moores Liverpool Exhibition XIV 1985, Group 56 (Bratislava Czechoslovakia) 1986, David Hepher and Emrys Williams (Castlefield Gallery) Manchester 1987, Big Paintings (Benjamin Rhodes Gallery) 1988, Ways of Telling (Mostyn Art Gallery, Llandudno) 1989, Group 56 (Glynn Vivian Museum, Swansea), 1990; *Work in Public Collections* Contemporary Art Soc of Wales, Arthur Andersen & Co, Glynn Vivian Art Gallery and Museum Swansea, Govt Art Fund, Clwyd County Cncl, Clwyd Fine Art Trust, Metropolitan Museum of Art NY; numerous works in private collections in Britain and USA; *Awards* minor prize John Moores Liverpool Exhibition 1983, third prize Royal Nat Eisteddfod of Wales 1985, third prize Royal Over-Seas League London (Wardair Travel prize to Canada) 1988, Welsh Arts Cncl award for travel to Normandy 1988, Welsh Arts Cncl award for travel to Germany 1991; *Style*— Emrys Williams, Esq

WILLIAMS, Faynia Roberta; *née* Jeffery; da of Michael Manuel Jeffery (d 1968), and Sally Caroline, *née* Stone (d 1968); *b* 10 November 1938, London; *Educ* Brighton and Hove HS, RADA (Dip), Univ of London (BA), Nat Film Sch, Univ of Westminster, St Antony's Coll Oxford (DPhil pending); *m* 1, 1961, Michael Brandis Williams (d 1968), s of Walter Williams; 2 da (Sabra Mildred b 1964, Teohna Eloise b 1966); m 2, 1975, Richard Arthur Crane, s of Rev Robert Bartlett Crane (d 1996); 2 s (Leo Michael b 1977, Samuel Richard b 1979); *Career* theatre and opera director, BBC prodr and dir drama and documentary features, and film maker; fell in theatre: Univ of Bradford 1974–78, Lancaster Univ 1978; Granada TV artist in residence and visiting prof Univ of Calif 1984, tutor and lectr Univ of Sussex 1996–; memb: Equity 1959 (chair CTS Ctee), Cncl Directors' Guild of GB (chair 1998–99); hon pres Dramatic Theatre Ctee Int Theatre Inst; Freedom City of London 1959; FRSA; *Theatre* first professional appearance Stephen Joseph's Theatre in the Round (with Harold Pinter and Alan Ayckbourn) 1958–60; contract artist MGM USA 1960–61; first directed The Oz Trial (Oxford Playhouse) 1971; asst dir Tadeusz Kantor 1973; artistic dir: Oxford Free Theatre 1972–74, Oxford Arts Festival 1973, Bradford Theatre in the Mill 1974–78, Brighton Theatre 1980–85 and 2009–, Tron Theatre Glasgow 1983–84, Univ of Essex Theatre 1985–89; freelance dir: Royal Court, Fortune, Bush, Young Vic, Barbican, Royal Albert; theatres abroad incl USSR, Poland, Aust, Sweden, USA, Budapest 1993, NT Romania 1991 and NT Mongolia 2001; prodns incl: Brothers Karamazov (with Alan Rickman, Edinburgh Int Festival 1981, Fortune Theatre London and USSR), King Lear (RSC/RNT Acter Co USA), Body of a Woman (Brighton Festival) 1999; dir and designer: Mothers Shall Not Cry (Millennium Cmmn, Royal Albert Hall Promenade Opera) 2000, The Tenderland (by Aaron Copeland, Barbican) 2002; dir The First Domino (Brighton Festival) 2009 (Best Theatre Performance Award 2009), dir I Am A Warehouse (Brighton Festival) 2010 and (Brighton) 2014, dir Dancing with Demons (V&A London and Brighton Festival) 2011 and (Br Cncl tour S America) 2014, dir GOGOL (Brighton Festival) 2012, dir Black Venus Brighton Festival 2013 (Shoreditch Town Hall 2014), Vlad the Impaler (Brighton Festival) 2015; *Television* incl: Signals, Channel 4 arts documentaries 1990; *Radio* prodr BBC Radio Drama 1992– incl: Moscow Stations (starring Tom Courtenay, nominated Radio Times Award) and Vlad the Impaler (starring John Hurt, nominated Sony Award); prodr and presenter BBC Radio Documentary Features 1993–; interviews incl: Joan Littlewood, Pina Bausch, Peter Stein, Patrice Chèreau, Peter Sellars, Dame Iris Murdoch and Ariel Dorfman; also Movers and Shakers (feature series, Radio 3), Bausch of Wuppertal (Radio 3 and World Service), Moscow Art Theatre Centennial Feature (Radio 3) 1997, Who Massacred the Innocents? (Radio 4) 2000, The Love of 3 Colonels (Radio 4) 2002, Filling the Void (Radio 4) 2004, Theatre in the Round (Radio 4) 2006, Theatre at the Frontline (Radio 4) 2010, The Gospel According to Joan (Radio 3) 2014; *Film* 2 shorts: Sleepy, Prelude; *Awards* incl: 9 Edinburgh Festival Fringe First Award; nominated: Best Dir for Satan's Ball London Critics' Award 1977, Best Dir for Brothers Karamazov 1981, Best Theatre Performance 2009, 2012 and 2013, Outstanding Production 2015; *Publications* Russian Plays (by Richard Crane; trans, 2011); *Recreations* the sea, travel to lesser-known places; *Clubs* Groucho; *Style*— Ms Faynia Williams, FRSA; ☎ 07900 088191, e-mail brightontheatre@gmail.com

WILLIAMS, Sir Francis Owen Garbett (Frank); kt (1999), CBE (1987); s of Owen Garbett Williams, of Liverpool; *b* 16 April 1942; *Educ* St Joseph's Coll Dumfries; *m* 1974, Virginia Jane (d 2013), da of Raymond Berry, of Marlow, Bucks; 3 c; *Career* md Williams Grand Prix Engrg Ltd; Helen Rollason Award BBC Sports Personality of the Year 2010; *Clubs* British Racing Drivers'; *Style*— Sir Frank Williams, CBE; ✉ Williams Grand Prix Engineering Ltd, Grove, Wantage, Oxfordshire (☎ 01235 777700)

WILLIAMS, Prof Frederic Ward (Fred); s of Prof Sir Frederic Calland Williams (d 1977), and Gladys, *née* Ward (d 2004); *b* 4 March 1940; *Educ* St John's Coll Cambridge (MA, ScD), Univ of Bristol (PhD); *m* 1, 11 April 1964, Jessie Anne Hope (d 2007), da of Rev William Wyper Wilson (d 1988); 2 s (Frederic b 21 Aug 1968, David b 11 Feb 1970); m 2, 8 Nov 2008, Ann Bull; *Career* asst engr Freeman Fox and Partners 1964; lectr in civil engrg: Ahmadu Bello Univ Nigeria 1964–67, Univ of Birmingham 1967–75; prof of civil engrg: Univ of Wales Inst of Science and Technol 1975–88, Cardiff Sch of Engrg Cardiff Univ 1988–2011 (head Div of Structural Engrg 1988–98, on leave of absence 2001–04), prof Dept of Bldg and Construction City Univ of Hong Kong 2001–04, ret; emeritus prof Cardiff Univ 2012–; fndr chm Cardiff Advanced Chinese Engrg Centre 1993–; guest prof Shanghai Jiao Tong Univ 1997–, guest prof Univ of Science and Technol of China 1999–; conslt to: NASA, British Aerospace; author of numerous papers in jls; FIStructE 1985, FREng 1999; *Recreations* hill walking; *Style*— Prof Fred Williams, FREng; ✉ 34 Silk Close, Lee, London SE12 8DL (e-mail fred@williamstube.com)

WILLIAMS, Gerard; s of Frank Williams, of Manchester, and Margaret Rose, *née* Lockwood; *b* 9 July 1959; *Educ* Manchester HS of Art, Manchester Poly, Brighton Poly; *Career* artist; res fell Henry Moore Inst 1997; visiting tutor: Goldsmiths Coll London 1998–2002, West Dean Col Edward James Fndn Sussex; *Solo Exhibitions* Interim Art 1986 and 1990, Anthony d'Offay Gallery 1989, Galleria Franz Paludetto Turin 1990, Patrick de Brock Gallery Antwerp 1991, Todd Gallery London 1993, Galerie 102 Düsseldorf 1993, Aldebaran, Baillargues France 1993, Galerie du Tableau Marseille 1994, The Showroom (London) 1994, Galerie 102 (Düsseldorf) 1996, Medieval Modern (London) 2002; *Group Exhibitions* incl: Whitechapel Open 1985, 1986, 1987 and 1988, Summer Show (Anthony d'Offay Gallery) 1988, That Which Appears is Good, That Which is Good Appears (Tanja Grunert Gallery Cologne) 1988, Home Truths (Castello di Rivara) 1989, Richard Wentworth Grenville Davey Gerard Williams (Sala Uno Rome) 1989, Its a Still Life (Arts Cncl of GB, touring) 1989–91, Leche Vitrines (Le Festival ARS Musica Brussels) 1990, TAC 90 (Sala Parpallo/Diputacion de Valencia, touring) 1990, Realismi (Galleria Giorgio Persano Turin, Ileana Toynta Contemporary Art Centre Athens) 1990, What is a Gallery? (Kettles Yard Univ of Cambridge) 1990, Maureen Paley Interim Art 1990–91, Anni Novanta (Bologna, Cattolica and Rimini) 1991, Lithuanian Artists Assoc Symposium 1991, Koji Tatsuno: 03.91 (Palais Galliera Paris) 1991, Made for Arolsen (Museumverein Arolsen Germany) 1992, Rencontres No 1 (Assoc La Vigie Nimes France) 1992, In House, Out House (Unit Seven London) 1993, Five British Artists (Patrick de Brock Gallery Antwerp) 1993, The East Wing Collection (Courtauld Inst London) 1993–96, Escale a Marseille (Tour du Roy Rene Marseille) 1994, Sous Reserve de Modification (Montpellier France) 1994, Seeing the Unseen (Nvisible Museum, London) 1994, Arte Inglese d' Oggi (Turin Galleria Civica di Modena Italy) 1994–95, Taking Form (The Fruitmarket Gallery Edinburgh) 1995, A Matter of Facts (Städtische Ausstellungshalle Münster) 1996, Good News (102 Galerie Düsseldorf) 1996, Williams & Williams (Bains Douches de la Plaine Marseille) 1997, When Ever (Gt Garden St Synagogue London) 1997, Craft (Richard Salmon, London and Kettles Yard Univ of Cambridge, Aberystwyth Arts Centre) 1997 and 1998, Echo (Pavillion der Volksbühne, Berlin) 1997, Infra-Slim Spaces (Univ of Kiev Ukraine) 1997, Over the Top (Ikon Gallery Birmingham, on tour) 1998–99, Furniture (Richard Salmon London and John Hansard Gallery Univ of Southampton) 1999, Sampled: fabric in sculpture (Henry Moore Inst Leeds) 1999, Modular Loops (Parker's Box NY) 2000, Stockholm Art Fair 2001, Bring and Buy (Transit Space London) 2002, Frankfurt Art Fair 2002; *Publications* author of numerous publications, incl: Technique Anglaise – Current Trends in British Art (1991), Asterides – Artists Residencies Catalogue (1993), Carnet de Bord – Artists Residencies 92–96 (1996), T2K (BA Textiles graduation catalogue Goldsmiths Coll London, 2000), Postgraduate Textiles (graduation catalgoue Goldsmiths Coll London, 2001), Invisible London (2001); *Style*— Gerard Williams, Esq; ✉ 175 Swaton Road, London E3 4EP (☎ 020 7515 2739, mobile 079 7353 0533, e-mail gerardwilliams@hotmail.com)

WILLIAMS, Prof Glynn Anthony; s of Idris Merrion Williams (d 1996), of Bayston Hill, Salop, and Muriel Elizabeth, *née* Purslow (d 1953); *b* 30 March 1939, Shrewsbury, Salop; *Educ* Wolverhampton GS, Wolverhampton Coll of Art (NDD), Rome scholar; *m* 6 July 1963 (m dis 2000), Heather, da of Cyril Woodhall (d 1952); 2 da (Victoria b 2 Jan 1964, Sophie b 7 Aug 1967); *Career* regular exhibitor of sculpture 1967– (represented by Bernard Jacobson Gallery London), currently emeritus prof of sculpture Royal Coll of Art; has exhibited internationally, represented GB in the third Kotara Takamura Exhibition in Japan; work in nat and int public collections incl Tate Gallery, Nat Portrait Gallery and V&A; cmmns incl: Henry Purcell Meml (Victoria Street London), Gateway of Hands (Chelsea Harbour London), Lloyd George Meml (Parliament Square) 2007; author of articles on sculpture published in various art magazines and art reviewer for TLS; tstee Forest of Dean Sculpture Trail 2012; memb Subject Panel CNAA; Prix de Rome 1961, hon fell Wolverhampton Poly 1989; FRCA, FRBS 1992, FRSA 1996;

Recreations music, crossword puzzles, cooking; *Clubs* Chelsea Arts; *Style*— Prof Glynn Williams; ✉ Bernard Jacobson Gallery, 28 Duke Street, St James, London SW1Y 6AG (e-mail glynn.williams@rca.ac.uk, website glynnwilliams.co.uk)

WILLIAMS, Prof Gordon; s of Charles Williams, of Anfield, Liverpool, and Marjorie Gerard, *née* Bradborn (d 1984); *b* 27 June 1945; *Educ* Bishop Vesey's GS Sutton Coldfield, UCH Med Sch (MB BS), MS Univ of London 1988, FRCS; *m* 1 (m dis 1989), Susan Mary Gubbins; 2 da (Katherine Louise b 1970, Victoria Mary b 1972); m 2, 20 Sept 1989 (m dis 2005), Clare, da of (Montgomery) Derek Sanderson (d 1976); *Career* conslt urologist and transplant surgn Hammersmith Hosp and hon sr lectr Imperial Coll Sch of Med at Hammersmith Hosp (Royal Postgraduate Med Sch until merger 1997) 1978–2007, dean St Paul's Millennium Med Sch Addis Ababa 2007–08, medical dir Addis Ababa Fistula Hosp 2009–; visiting surgn: Syria, Burma, Poland; James IV prof of surgery RCSEd 2005; external examiner Univ of Addis Ababa; numerous pubns on urology, urological cancer, impotence and diseases of the prostate; former chm NW Thames Urologists; former memb Cncl: Br Assoc of Urological Surgns, Int Soc of Urology, Euro Soc of Urology, Euro Transplant Soc; memb Bd of Chairmen Int Soc of Urology, pres Urology Section Royal Soc of Med 2002, chm Jt Ctee for Higher Surgical Training 2003–07; Albert Schweitzer Award Int Soc of Urology 2006, St Peters Medal Br Assoc of Urological Surgeons 2008; memb Worshipful Soc of Apothecaries 1984, Freeman City of London 1985; FRCSEd 2001, FRCSGlas 2004, hon memb Br Assoc of Urological Surgeons 2008; *Recreations* travel, Indian food; *Style*— Gordon Williams, Esq; ✉ e-mail gorwilliams@yahoo.com

WILLIAMS, Graham John; s of Hubert John Williams (d 1976), and Marguerite Madeleine Williams; *b* 24 April 1943; *Educ* Cranleigh, Univ of Edinburgh, INSEAD Fontainebleau (MBA); *m* Valerie Jane, *née* Dopson; 2 s (Alex b 23 Sept 1973, Nicholas b 21 March 1989), 1 da (Sara b 13 April 1992); *Career* articled clerk C F Middleton & Co CAs 1962–67, CA Coopers & Lybrand 1967–68, INSEAD 1968–69; Charterhouse Group: product mangr 1969, exec UK Venture Capital 1970–74, dir Charterhouse SA Paris 1975–79; dep md (and jt fndr) Barclays Development Capital Ltd 1979–84; Hays plc: fin dir 1984–2003, involved in MBO 1987 and subsequent listing 1989, dir 1992–2003; non-exec dir Acal plc 2003–; MICAS 1967; *Recreations* golf, tennis, sailing, skiing, swimming, squash; *Clubs* Old Cranleighans, Walton Heath Golf, RAC; *Style*— Graham Williams, Esq

WILLIAMS, Hugh; *see:* Bonneville, Hugh Richard

WILLIAMS, Huw Rhys Charles; s of David Charles Williams (d 1984), of Llanelli, Carmarthenshire, and Glenys Margaret, *née* Williams (d 2012); *b* 4 January 1954; *Educ* Llanelli GS, Jesus Coll Oxford (MA); *m* 22 Jan 1994, Kathleen Mary, da of Capt Melville Desmond John Hooper, master mariner (d 1990), of Penarth, Vale of Glamorgan; 1 step s (Martin John Rees); *Career* admitted slr 1978; princ asst slr Mid Glamorgan CC 1984, ptnr and lead ptnr public law Geldards LLP (previously Edwards Geldard) Cardiff, Derby, Nottingham and London 1988– (joined 1987, vice-chm 2007–); treas Wales Public Law and Human Rights Assoc 1999–2005; sec Wales Millennium Centre 1998–2013 (jt sec 2013–), memb Ct and Cncl then tstee Nat Museum of Wales 2003–10, tstee Nat Library of Wales 2010–; memb Law Soc (memb Planning and Environment Law Ctee 2003–16, memb Wales Ctee 2004–11 and 2016–), chair Public Law Wales (Wales Public Law and Human Rights Assoc) 2015–; *Recreations* art and architecture, naval history, scuba diving; *Clubs* Oxford and Cambridge, Cardiff and County; *Style*— Huw Williams, Esq; ✉ Geldards LLP, Dumfries House, Dumfries Place, Cardiff CF1 4YF (☏ 029 2023 8239, fax 029 2023 7268, e-mail huw.williams@geldards.co.uk)

WILLIAMS, Hywel; MP; s of Robert Williams (d 1976), of Pwllheli, and Jennie Page, *née* Williams; *b* 14 May 1953; *Educ* Ysgol Glan y Mor Pwllheli, UCW Cardiff (BSc), UCW Bangor (CQSW); *m* 1, 3 Sept 1977 (m dis 1998), Sian; 3 c (Gwenno Hywel b 16 Jan 1979, Elin Hywel b 15 Aug 1982, Angharad Hywel b 3 Oct 1983); m 2, 16 Dec 2010, Dr Myfanwy Davies; 1 s (Owain Gruffydd Hywel b 16 May 2013); *Career* social worker: Social Services Dept Mid Glamorgan CC 1974–76, Social Services Dept Gwynedd CC 1976–84 (pt/t memb Out of Hours team 1985–90); aproved social worker 1984; Welsh Office funded project worker Welsh medium devpts N and W Wales Practice Centre UCW Bangor 1991–93, head N and W Wales Practice Centre UCW Bangor 1991–93; freelance lectr, conslt and author in social work and social policy 1994–2001; CCETSW (Central Cncl for Educn and Trg in Social Work) Cymru: memb Welsh Ctee 1989–92, chair Welsh Language Sub-Ctee 1989–92; MP (Plaid Cymru) Caernarfon 2001–, memb Speaker's Panel of Chairmen, memb Welsh Affrs Ctee, memb Science and Technol Ctee, memb House Works of Art Ctee; *Publications* Social Work in Action in the 1980s (contrib, 1985), Geirfa Gwaith Cymdeithasol/A Social Work Vocabulary (compiler and ed, 1988), Geirfa Gwaith Plant/Child Care Terms (gen ed, 1993), Gwaith Cymdeithasol a'r Iaith Gymraeg/Social Work and the Welsh Language (contrib and co-ed, 1994), Llawlyfr Hyfforddi a Hyfforddiant/An Index of Trainers and Training (compiler and co-ed, 1994), Gofal – Pecyn Adnoddau a Hyfforddi Gofal yn y Gymuned yng Nghymru/Gofal – A Training and Resource Pack for Community Care in Wales (contrib and co-ed, 1998), Siarad yr Anweleding/Speaking the Invisible (contrib, 2002); *Style*— Hywel Williams, Esq, MP; ✉ House of Commons, London SW1A 0AA (☏ 020 7219 5021)

WILLIAMS, James Christopher; s of Arthur Williams, and Joan, *née* Walton; *Educ* Judd Sch Tonbridge, Central Sch of Speech and Drama; *Career* theatre executive; stage mangr 1977–81, prodn mangr 1982–88, exec dir Method & Madness (formerly Cambridge Theatre Co) 1988–98, dir and fndr Vocaleyes 1997–98 (dir 1998–2016, chm 1999–2003), exec dir Hampstead Theatre 1998–2003, chief exec Theatre of Comedy Co Ltd 2004–; dir: Hampstead Theatre Prodns Ltd 1998–2004, Inmidtown 2010–14; memb Camden Business Bd 2012–15; chm Audio Describers Assoc 1997–99 (founding gp); memb Cncl TMA 1995–2001 (memb Industrial Relations Ctee 1994–2015, memb Fin Ctee 1996–2001); memb Soc of London Theatre 2010– (memb Employment Strategy Ctee 2010–); tstee Cambridge Youth Theatre 1989–94; *Recreations* travel, property renovation, theatre, films; *Style*— James Williams, Esq; ✉ Theatre of Comedy Company Ltd, Shaftesbury Theatre, 210 Shaftesbury Avenue, London WC2H 8DP

WILLIAMS, Jan; OBE (2003); *b* 2 December 1954; *Educ* Llwyn-y-Bryn Secdy Modern Swansea, Univ of Wales (BA, MA), Univ of Aberdeen (Postgrad Cert in Health Economics), Cardiff Business Sch Univ of Wales (MBA); *m* ; 1 c; *Career* higher clerical offr trainee W Glamorgan HA 1979–80, nat admin trainee DHSS 1980–82, asst unit administrator rising to sr administrator W Glamorgan HA 1982–86, asst unit gen mangr Gwent HA 1986–88, unit gen mangr E Dyfed HA 1988–92; chief exec: Llanelli/Dinefwr NHS Tst 1992–95, W Glamorgan HA 1996, Iechyd Morgannwg Health 1996–99, Bro Taf HA 1999–2003; prog dir Review of Health and Social Care in Wales 2002–03, chief exec National Leadership and Innovation Agency for Healthcare 2005–; author of published papers in Health Services Jl, Nursing Management Jl and Nursing Times; memb Cncl Acas 1998–2003, memb Cncl and tstee Techniquest 2003–; CIHM 2003; *Style*— Jan Williams, OBE

WILLIAMS, (Hon) Jennifer Mary (Jenny); da of Baron Lord Donaldson of Lymington, PC (Life Peer, d 2005), and Dame (Dorothy) Mary Donaldson, GBE, JP (d 2003); sis of Hon Michael Donaldson, *qv*; *b* 26 September 1948; *m* 1970, Mike Williams, CB, *qv*; 3 s; *Career* under sec Privatisation & Strategy PSA 1991–93, head of Railways Privatisation & Regulation Directorate Dept of Tport 1993–96, head Local Govt Fin Policy Directorate DETR 1996–98, dir Business Tax Div Inland Revenue 1998–2000, DG Judicial Gp Lord Chllr's Dept 2000–04, chief exec Gaming Bd for GB 2004–05, cmmr and chief exec Gambling Cmmn 2005–15; memb Bd: Greyhound Regulatory Bd 2015–, Fundraising Regulator 2016–; memb Advsy Bd UNLV Int Center for Gaming Regulation 2016–; non-exec dir: Morley Coll 1993–2000, Northumbrian Water Gp plc 2004–; memb Bd Nat Campaign for the Arts 2004–07, vice-chair and tstee The Connection at St Martin's 2004–16; *Style*— Mrs Jenny Williams; ✉ e-mail jenny.williams@mj-w.net

WILLIAMS, John; AO (1987); *b* 24 April 1941, Australia; *Educ* Accademia Musicale di Siena Italy (scholarship), Royal Coll of Music; *Career* guitarist; taught by father from age 4, later studied with Andrés Segovia, USA and Japan debuts 1963; appeared with many Br orchs and at many Br festivals, toured extensively in Europe, N and S America, Soviet Union, Far E and Australia; one of the first classical musicians to appear at Ronnie Scott's jazz club, fndr memb of popular music gps SKY 1979–84 and John Williams and Friends 1983–, formed contemporary music ensemble Attacca 1991 (with whom toured UK and Australia 1992), tours with Harvey and John Etheridge; artistic dir and music advsr South Bank Summer Music Festival 1984–85, artistic dir Melbourne Arts Festival Australia 1987; work written for him by composers incl: Leo Brouwer, Peter Sculthorpe, Stephen Dodgson, André Previn; performed with orchs incl: Royal Philharmonic, LSO, City of Birmingham Symphony, English Chamber, Australian Chamber, Bournemouth Sinfonietta, Acad of St Martin-in-the-Fields, all other major Br orchs; appeared at venues incl: Queen Elizabeth Hall, Royal Festival Hall, Barbican Hall, Symphony Hall Birmingham, Fairfield Hall, Salle Pleyel Paris, Hong Kong Cultural Centre (inaugural concerts 1989), NEC Birmingham (10th Anniversary concert, with CBSO); appeared at festivals incl: BBC Proms, Cheltenham, Chichester, Exeter, Cardiff, Perth and Adelaide Festivals Aust, Toronto Int Guitar Festival, South Bank Latin American Festival, Lichfield, St Albans, Melbourne Arts Festival; performed European première of Nigel Westlake's Antarctica (for guitar and orch) with LSO under Kent Nagano Barbican Hall 1992; numerous TV appearances incl LWT South Bank Show documentary on life and work; past performances with Julian Bream, Paco Peña, Itzhak Perlman, André Previn, John Dankworth, Cleo Laine, Inti Illimani, etc; *Recordings* major guitar works and numerous concertos incl John Williams plays The Movies, The Magic Box; El Diablo Suelto – Venezuelan Guitar Music, The Ultimate Guitar Collection, Places Between (with John Etheridge); *Style*— John Williams, Esq, AO; ✉ c/o Askonas Holt, Lincoln House, 300 High Holborn, London WC1V 7JH (☏ 020 7400 1751, e-mail info@askonasholt.co.uk)

WILLIAMS, John Charles Wallis; s of Peter Alfred Williams (d 1997), of Menston, W Yorks, and Mary, *née* Bower (d 1990); *b* 12 December 1953; *Educ* St Peter's Sch York, The Queen's Coll Oxford (MA); *m* 28 June 1980, Wendy Irene, da of Harold Doe (d 2013); 2 da (Sarah b 1984, Clare b 1988); *Career* advertising exec J Walter Thompson Co 1975–86, PR exec Valin Pollen Ltd 1986–90 (head res and planning 1988–90, asst md 1989–90); Fishburn Hedges: fndr dir 1991–2013, md 1995–99, chm 1999–2001, non-exec dir 2001–05, sr advsr 2005–10, strategic planning dir 2011–12, chm public affrs 2012–13; princ John Williams and Assocs 2001–07; dep chair ChildLine 2001–06, chm Tomorrow's Company 2004–09 (tstee 2003–09), memb Bd Business in the Community 2002–, cmmr Charity Cmmn 2005–10, chm Richmond Theatre Prodns 2006–14, chm Tourism SE 2009–12, Executive Mentoring 2013–, vice-chair Assoc of Chairs 2014–, charities advsr Royal Bank of Canada 2014–15, tstee Inst of Business Ethics 2015–; FRSA; *Recreations* politics watching, US TV, popular music, Chelsea FC, cities with trams; *Style*— John Williams, Esq; ✉ e-mail john@williams-network.com, Twitter @ChiswickJohn

WILLIAMS, John Fagan; s of Frank Thomas Williams, and Margaret, *née* Fagan; *b* 7 January 1948; *Educ* Rishworth Sch; *m* 1, Lynne, *née* Boothby; 1 da (Kate); m 2, Rita, *née* Mason; *Career* local, regional and nat newspaper journalist 1967–76; fndr Staniforth Williams PR consultancy 1976–86, fndr jt md Mason Williams PR consultancy 1986– (over 28 awards for business excellence 1988–); fndr and ceo: Muse Group 2002, Grandstand Entertainment Int 2003; memb Bd PRCA 1994; FIPR 1979, FInstD 1990; *Sporting Achievements* int sports car racing driver (Europe and USA) 1981–90, eighth place World Sports Car Championship 1989, Champion Lamborghini Int Trophy 1997; *Recreations* race driving, sailing, music; *Clubs* British Racing Drivers', RAC; *Style*— John Williams, Esq

WILLIAMS, John Llewellyn; CBE (1999); s of David John Williams (d 1948), of Dronfield, nr Sheffield, and Anne Rosamund, *née* White; *b* 24 January 1938; *Educ* Christ's Hosp, Guy's Hosp Dental Sch London (BDS, LDS RCS, Evelyn Sprawson Prize), Guy's Hosp Med Sch London (MB BS); *m* 1960, Gillian Joy, *née* Morgan; 3 da (Amanda Jill (Mrs Henderson) b 1962, Jacqueline Mary (Mrs Lytton) b 1963, Anne-Marie (Mrs Wood) b 1970); *Career* formerly sr registrar Westminster Hosp, Queen Mary's Roehampton and UCH; conslt oral and maxillofacial surgn: St Richard's Hosp Chichester, Southlands and Worthing Hosps, St Luke's Hosp Guildford; hon conslt: Queen Mary's Hosp Roehampton, King Edward VII Hosp Midhurst; formerly hon civilian conslt Cambridge Mil Hosp Aldershot, hon clinical tutor UMDS; memb: Cncl RCS 1993–2001 (dean Faculty of Dental Surgery 1995–98, vice-pres 1997–99), GDC 1995–98, Ct of Patrons RCS 2005; sec-gen Euro Assoc of Cranio-Maxillofacial Surgery (pres 1998); chm Nat Confidential Enquiry into Perioperative Deaths 1999–2003; vice-chm Acad Med Royal Colls 1996, pres Br Assoc of Oral and Maxillofacial Surgeons 2000 (vice-pres 1999); memb: Jt Conslts Ctee 1989–98, Clinical Outcomes Gp Dept of Health 1993–99, Clinical Standards Advsy Gp 1994–99, Nat Inst for Clinical Excellence 1999–; chm: Med Devices Agency Dept of Health 2001–04, Cmmn on Safety of Devices MHRA 2004–09 (non-exec dir 2009–); dir MHRA (Medicines & Healthcare Products Regulatory Agency) 2009; Downs Surgical Prize Br Assoc of Oral and Maxillofacial Surgns 1995, John Tomes Medal BDA 1998, Colyer Gold Medal 2000; memb: BDA, BMA, Br Assoc of Maxillofacial Surgns, Euro Assoc of Cranio-Maxillofacial Surgery; Int Assoc of Oral and Maxillofacial Surgery: memb Bd 2001–, pres-elect 2003–05, pres 2005–07, chm IAOMS Fndn 2007–; hon fell American Assoc of Oral and Maxillofacial Surgeons 1998, hon fell Aust and NZ Assoc of Oral and Maxillofacial Surgeons 2005; FDSRCS, FRCSEd 1991, FRCS 1996, FDS RCS(Ed) (ad hominem) 2000, FRCA 2002; *Books* Maxillofacial Injuries (2 vols, ed, 2 edn 1995), 50 Years of IAOMS: Development of the Specialty (2012); *Recreations* horticulture (contrib National Gardens Scheme), skiing, sailing (RYA race training instructor), chasing good wine!; *Clubs* Royal Yachting Assoc, Hayling Island Sailing, RHS, Oral Surgery Club of GB; *Style*— John Llewellyn Williams, Esq, CBE; ✉ Cookscroft, Bookers Lane, Earnley, Chichester, West Sussex PO20 7JG (☏ 01243 513671, e-mail williams.cookscroft330@btinternet.com)

WILLIAMS, Dr John Peter Rhys; MBE (1977); s of Peter Rhys Jervis Williams, of Bridgend, and Margaret, *née* Rhodes; *b* 2 March 1949; *Educ* Bridgend GS, Millfield, St Marys Hosp Med Sch (MB BS, MRCS, LRCP); *m* 10 May 1973, Priscilla, da of Michael Parkin, of Buxton, Derbys; 3 da (Lauren b 1977, Anneliese b 1979, Francine b 1981), 1 s (Peter b 1987); *Career* conslt orthopaedic surgn Princess of Wales Hosp Bridgend 1986–2004, ret; Br jr tennis champion 1966, 55 Welsh International rugby caps 1969–81, memb Br Lions tour NZ 1971 and South Africa 1974; memb Br Orthopaedic Assoc, FRCSEd; *Books* JPR Autobiography (1977), JPR Given the Breaks – my life in rugby (2006); *Recreations* all sports especially squash, tennis, rugby; *Clubs* Lord's Taverners; *Style*— Dr John Williams, MBE; ✉ Llansannor Lodge, Llansannor, Cowbridge, South Glamorgan CF71 7RX (☏ 01446 772590, mobile 07790 993948)

WILLIAMS, John Thomas; MBE (2008); s of John T Williams, of South Shields, and Margaret, *née* Patterson; *b* 20 August 1958, South Shields, Tyne and Wear; *Educ* Mortimer Road Sch South Shields, S Shields Marine & Tech Coll, Westminster Catering Coll (City and Guilds); *Family* 1 da (Sabrina b 27 Nov 1985), 1 s (Jeremy b 21 Dec 1989);

Career commis chef Percy Arms Hotel Northumberland 1974–75, chef de cuisine Royal Roof Restaurant The Royal Garden Hotel London 1975–84, pt/t commis chef Ma Cuisine Restaurant March-Sept 1982, chef dir Restaurant le Crocodile London 1984–86, head chef Claridge's 1986–93, maitre chef de cuisine The Berkeley Hotel London 1994–95, maitre chef de cuisines Claridge's 1995–2004, exec chef The Ritz 2004–; exec chm Royal Acad of Culinary Arts GB; memb: Académie Culinaire de France, Wine Guild of UK; Hotel Catey Award for Outstanding Contribution 2008, Tatler Lifetime Achievement Award 2013; hon fell Thames Valley Univ 2005; memb Worshipful Co of Cooks; Freedom of City of London 2007; Chevalier de l'Ordre du Merite Agricole, disciple Le Conseil Magistral de Disciples d'Auguste Escoffier 2007; *Recreations* golf, cooking; *Style*— John Williams, Esq, MBE; ✉ The Ritz, 150 Picadilly, London W1J 9BR

WILLIAMS, Dame Josephine (Jo); DBE (2007, CBE 2000), DL (Cheshire); da of Frank Heald (d 2002), and Catherine Margaret, *née* Hatcher (d 1997); *b* 8 July 1948, Fishpool, Notts; *Educ* Keele Univ (BA, Dip); *m* 27 May 1980, Robert Williams; 2 step s (Andrew Lindon b 10 April 1968, Paul Gareth b 16 Dec 1978); *Career* social worker incl many mgmnt posts 1971–91; dir of social servs: Wigan MBC 1992–97, Cheshire CC 1997–2002; chief exec Mencap 2003–08, chair Care Quality Cmmn 2011–13; tstee: EveryChild, Dartington Hall Tst; pres Assoc of Dirs of Social Servs 1999–2000; Hon DLitt Keele Univ 2009; CCMI 2006, FCGI 2009; *Recreations* running, ballet, cooking, family and friends; *Style*— Dame Jo Williams, DBE, DL

WILLIAMS, Dr Juliet Susan Durrant; CBE (2009); da of Robert Noel Williams (d 1972), of Gower, W Glamorgan, and Frances Alice, *née* Durrant (d 1995); *b* Brackley, Northants; *Educ* Leeds Girls HS, Cheltenham Ladies' Coll, Bedford Coll London (BSc), Hughes Hall Cambridge (PGCE, Lacrosse blue); *Career* ed Macmillan & Co (publishers) 1966–68, asst ed The Geographical Magazine 1968–73, md Readers Union Gp of Book Clubs 1973–79, chief exec Marshall Cavendish Mail Order 1979–82, md Brann Direct Marketing 1982–88, dir The BIS Gp Ltd 1985–91, chief exec Bd Mktg Communications Div BIS 1988–91, chief exec Strategic Management Resources 1991–; chm: Waddie & Co Ltd 1996–98, Alden Gp Ltd 2004–07; chm SW of England RDA 2002–09, memb Bd Visit Britain; memb Industrial Devpt Advsy Bd DTI, memb Bd Acad of Sustainable Communities; ceo Vital Partnerships Grad Sch of Educn Univ Bristol 2012–15; chair Bd of Govrs Univ of St Mark and St John 2012–15; Hon Dr Oxford Brookes Univ 2005, Hon Dr Univ of Gloucestershire 2010; FRGS 1970, MInstM 1975; *Recreations* labrador retrievers, the countryside, motor sport; *Style*— Dr Juliet Williams, CBE; ✉ Treeton Cottage, Abbotskerswell, Newton Abbot, Devon TQ12 5PW (☎ 01626 361655); Strategic Management Resources, Longridge, Abbotskerswell, Newton Abbot, Devon TQ12 5PW (mobile 07831 097946, e-mail juliet@strategic-management-resources.co.uk)

WILLIAMS, Laurence Glynn; s of Hugh Williams (d 1988), and Ruby, *née* Lawrence; *b* 14 March 1946, Liverpool; *Educ* Liverpool Poly (BSc), Aston Univ (MSc); *m* 30 Oct 1976 (m dis 1997), Lorna Susan Rance; 1 da (Laura Elizabeth b 16 Oct 1978), 1 s (James Laurence b 16 Sept 1980); *Career* design engr Nuclear Power Gp 1970–71, nuclear engr Central Electricity Generating Bd 1973–76; HSE: joined Nuclear Installations Inspectorate 1976, nuclear inspr 1976–78, princ nuclear inspr 1978–86, superintending inspr 1986–91 (involved with audit of safety Sellafield 1986, BNFL regulatory inspr Sellafield 1989), dep chief inspr 1991–95, head Nuclear and Major Hazards Policy Div 1995–98; HM chief inspr of nuclear installations and dir Nuclear Safety Directorate 1998–2005, dir nuclear safety, security and environment Nuclear Decommissioning Authy 2005–08, currently prof of nuclear safety and regulation Sch of Computing, Engrg and Physical Sciences Univ of Central Lancs; chair: Int Nuclear Regulators Assoc 2000–02, Int Atomic Energy Agency Cmmn on Safety Standards 2000–05; memb: Safety Review Gp European Bank for Reconstruction and Devpt (former advsr), Chernobyl Sarcophagus Int Advsy Gp, Western European Nuclear Regulators Assoc; pres: Jt Convention on Safety of Spent Fuel Mgmnt, Safety of Radioactive Waste Mgmnt; CEng 1976, FIMechE 1991, FINucE 1998, FREng 2004; *Recreations* motorcycling, cycling, keeping fit, music, theatre, supporting Liverpool FC; *Style*— Laurence Williams, Esq, FREng

WILLIAMS, Sir Lawrence Hugh; 9 Bt (GB 1798), of Bodelwyddan, Flintshire; s of Col Lawrence Williams, OBE, JP, DL (d 1958), by his 2 w and 1 cous once removed, Elinor, da of Sir William Williams, 4 Bt, JP, DL; suc half-bro Sir Francis John Watkin Williams, 8 Bt, QC, JP (d 1995); *b* 25 August 1929; *Educ* RNC Dartmouth; *m* 1952, Sara Margaret Helen, 3 da of Prof Sir Harry Platt, 1 Bt, MD, MS, FRCS; 2 da (Emma Louise (Lady Suffield) b 1961, Antonia Margaret (Mrs Antonin Leif Peter Markutza) b 1963); *Heir* none; *Career* cmmnd RM 1947; served in: Korea 1951, Cyprus 1955, Near East 1956; Capt 1959, ret 1964; Lt Cdr RNXS 1965–87; farmer; chm Parciau Caravans Ltd 1964–, underwriting memb Lloyd's 1977–96; High Sheriff Anglesey 1970; *Clubs* Army and Navy, RNSA; *Style*— Sir Lawrence Williams, Bt; ✉ Parciau, Marianglas, Anglesey LL73 8PH

WILLIAMS, Mark; MP; *b* 24 March 1966; *Educ* Richard Hale Sch, UCW Aberystwyth, Univ of Plymouth; *Career* dep head Ysgol Llangors 2000–; Parly candidate (Lib Dem): Monmouth 1997 and 2000 (by-election), Ceredigion 2001; MP (Lib Dem) Ceredigion 2005–; Lib Dem spokesman on: schools 2005–06, Wales 2006–; memb Welsh Affrs Select Ctee 2005–, chair Backbench Lib Dem Ctee on Constitutional and Political Reform 2010–12, chair Backbench Lib Dem Ctee on Wales 2012–; memb: NASUWT, Greenpeace; *Style*— Mark Williams, Esq, MP; ✉ House of Commons, London SW1A 0AA

WILLIAMS, Mark; MBE (2004); *b* 21 March 1975, Wales; *Career* professional snooker player 1992–; ranked 1 in world 2000 and 2003; tournament winner: Benson & Hedges Championship 1994, Grand Prix 1996, Regal Welsh Open 1996 and 1999, British Open 1997, Irish Open 1998, Benson & Hedges Masters 1998 and 2003, Liverpool Victoria UK Championship 1999, Thailand Masters 1999 and 2002, Grand Prix 2000, Embassy World Championship 2000 and 2003 (runner-up 1999), UK Championship 2002, China Open 2002; *Clubs* golf, cars; *Style*— Mark Williams, Esq, MBE

WILLIAMS, Martyn Elwyn; MBE (2012); *b* 1 September 1975, Pontypridd, Mid Glamorgan; *Career* rugby union player (flanker); club: Pontypridd until 1999, Cardiff RFC 1999–2003, Cardiff Blues 2003– (capt until 2005); Wales: 98 caps, debut v Barbarians 1996, memb World Cup squad 2007; memb British and Irish Lions touring squad Australia 2001, NZ 2005 and S Africa 2009; *Books* Magnificent Seven; *Style*— Mr Martyn Williams, MBE; ✉ c/o Cardiff Blues, Cardiff Arms Park, Westgate Street, Cardiff, CF10 1JA

WILLIAMS, (John) Michael; MBE (1997); s of George Keith Williams (d 1980), and Joan Doreen, *née* Selby (d 1969); *b* 15 October 1942; *Educ* Cheltenham Coll, Worcester Coll Oxford (MA); *m* 17 Oct 2008, Susan Mary Bentley, *née* Ashby; *Career* admitted slr 1967; Cooper Sons Hartley & Williams: ptnr 1969–2000, conslt 2001–; pres: E Midlands Assoc of Law Socs 1996–97 and 2003–04, Buxton & High Peak Law Soc 1997–2003 (sec 1984–97 and 2003–); memb Cncl Law Soc 2015–; conductor Buxton Musical Soc 1968–, organist St John's Buxton 1985–, dir Buxton Arts Festival Ltd 1993–2015 (vice-pres 2015–), memb Panel of Music Advsrs to NW Arts 1995–2002, vice-patron Buxton Opera House 2013– (vice-chm 1978–2004, chm 2004–13); Archbishop of Canterbury's Cranmer Award for Worship 2016; *Recreations* music, cricket; *Style*— Michael Williams, Esq, MBE; ✉ 132 Lightwood Road, Buxton, Derbyshire SK17 6RW (☎ 01298 24185); Cooper Sons Hartley & Williams, 25 Market Street, Chapel-en-le-Frith, High Peak, Derbyshire SK23 6HS (☎ 01298 812138)

WILLIAMS, Michael Duncan; s of Harry Duncan Williams, of Oxford, and Irene Pamela, *née* Mackenzie; *b* 31 March 1951; *Educ* Oundle, Trinity Hall Cambridge (MA); *Career* vice-pres and UK sr credit offr Bank of America NT and SA 1973–89, dir: SFE Bank Ltd, Banque SFE 1988–89; dep gen mangr credit Nomura Bank Int plc 1989–93, dir Credit Risk Mgmnt Swiss Bank Corporation 1993–94, dir Risk Mgmnt European Bank for Reconstruction and Development 2002–11 (head Portfolio Mgmnt 1994–2001); hon treas: FISA, The International Rowing Fedn; dir Br Rowing Ltd 1989–2014 (hon life vice-pres 2014–), steward Henley Royal Regatta; *Recreations* rowing, golf, classic cars; *Clubs* Leander, London Rowing (pres 2005–15, vice-pres 2015–); *Style*— Michael Williams, Esq

WILLIAMS, Michael John; s of Stanley Williams, and Phyllis Mary, *née* Wenn; *b* 23 July 1948; *Educ* William Ellis Sch London, Univ of Liverpool (BA); *m* 1, 1971 (m dis 1996), Carol; 2 da (Stella b 1983, Amy b 1988); m 2, 2000, Melanie Powell; 1 s (Edmund b 2001), 1 da (Hero b 2007); *Career* graduate trainee Liverpool Daily Post & Echo 1970–73, features sub ed and news sub ed Birmingham Evening Mail 1973–75, home news sub ed The Times 1975–78, asst to editorial dir Thames & Hudson Book Publishers 1978–79; New Society magazine: diary ed and feature writer 1979–84, dep ed 1984–86; features ed Today newspaper 1986; The Sunday Times: dep news ed 1986–87, news ed 1987–89, asst ed (news) 1989–90, managing ed (news) 1990–92, managing ed (features) 1993–94; The Independent: exec news ed 1994–96, exec ed 1996–99; dep ed Independent on Sunday 1999–2007, readers' ed The Independent 2007–09, sr lectr School of Journalism Univ of Central Lancs 2008–; *Books* British Society (1984), Britain Now Quiz (1985), Society Today (1986), On the Slow Train (2010), On the Slow Train Again (2011), Steaming to Victory (2013), The Future of Quality News Journalism (ed with Peter Anderson 2014), The Trains Now Departed (2015); *Recreations* riding the great trains of the world, exploring Baroque churches; *Style*— Michael Williams, Esq; ✉ 35 Rochester Road, Camden Town, London NW1 9JJ (e-mail michael@michaelwennwilliams.co.uk)

WILLIAMS, Michael Lodwig (Mike); CB (2003); s of John Leslie Williams, of Cardiff, and Eileen Mary, *née* Sanders; *b* 22 January 1948, Newport, Gwent; *Educ* Wycliffe Coll, Trinity Hall Cambridge (MA), Nuffield Coll Oxford; *m* 1970, Jenny Mary Williams, *qv*, *née* Donaldson; 3 s; *Career* Miny of Fin Lusaka 1969–71; HM Treasy: joined in 1973, seconded to Price Waterhouse 1980–81, dir of industry 1992–97, ret 2003; chief exec UK Debt Management Office 1998–2003; memb Bd Euroclear UK and Ireland Ltd 1998–2002 and 2004–13; govt debt and cash mgmnt conslt 2003–; *Style*— Mike Williams, Esq, CB; ✉ website www.mj-w.net

WILLIAMS, Michael Roy; s of Edgar Harold Williams, and Joyce, *née* Smith; *b* 29 March 1947; *Educ* Selhurst GS, Univ of Exeter (BA); *m* 14 Jan 2012, Kin Tak Au (civil partnership converted 14 Jan 2015); *Career* UCMDS trainee Unilever plc/prod mangr Bird's Eye Foods 1969–72, account dir Leo Burnett advtg 1972–78, dir Geers Gross plc 1978–86, md Geers Gross UK 1978–86, dir Charles Barker plc 1986–89, chief exec Ayer Ltd 1986–90, dir Ayer Europe 1986–90, chm and ceo Serendipity Brand Makers Ltd 1990–, ptnr Serendipity Brand Makers Sydney Aust 1999–; *Novels* Alex Laid Bare (2006), The Accident That Waited to Happen (2007); *Recreations* writing, films, music, windsurfing, travel, France, SE Asia, Australia, wine, tennis; *Style*— Michael R Williams, Esq; ✉ Serendipity Brand Makers, Studio 1, 37–45 Myrtle Street, Chippendale, NSW 2008, Australia (☎ 00 61 2 9310 4599)

WILLIAMS, His Hon Judge Nicholas Michael Heathcote; QC (2006); s of late Sir Edgar Trevor Williams, and Gillian (Lady Williams), *née* Gambier-Parry; *b* 5 November 1954; *Educ* Marlborough, St Catharine's Coll Cambridge (Briggs scholar, MA); *m* 19 Dec 1987, Corinna Mary, da of late David Mitchell, and Barbara Mitchell; 2 s (Benjamin b 1988, Joshua b 1990), 1 da (Rebecca b 1993); *Career* RMA Sandhurst 1977, Lt Royal Green Jackets 1977–80; called to the Bar Inner Temple 1976, practising barrister 1980–2014, recorder (South Eastern Circuit) 2000, circuit judge (South Eastern Circuit) 2014–; *Recreations* reading, looking at paintings, skiing, cricket; *Clubs* Rifles Officers, MCC; *Style*— His Hon Judge Heathcote Williams, QC; ✉ Woolwich Crown Court, 2 Belmarsh Road, London SE28 0EY

WILLIAMS, Air Cdre Nigel; CBE (2005); s of Philip George Williams (d 1997), and June Dorothy, *née* Graves (d 2000); *b* 3 February 1951, Lincs; *Educ* Bentley GS Calne; *m* 9 June 1973, Barbara *née* Bellas; *Career* dir air traffic control ops HQ Military Air Traffic Ops 1996–97, OC London Air Traffic Control Centre West Drayton 1997–99; HQ Strike Command: dir Air Traffic Control Progs and Fin 1999–2003, Air Cdre Ops Support 2002–03, AO Battlespace Mgmnt 2003–06, sr air traffic mgmnt conslt HQ NATO 2006–10; pres Daedalus Soc; NATO Kosovo Medal 1999, Operational Serv Medal with Clasp for Afghanistan 2002, Operational Serv Medal with Clasp for Iraq 2003; Queen's Golden Jubilee Medal 2002; *Recreations* classic cars, property devpt, cycling, computing; *Style*— Air Cdre Nigel Williams, CBE; ✉ Mulberry House, Bests Lane, Sutton Veny, Wiltshire BA12 7AU (☎ 01985 840226, e-mail nbjwilliams@btinternet.com)

WILLIAMS, (Henry) Nigel; s of David Ffrancon Williams (d 1984); *b* 20 January 1948; *Educ* Highgate Sch, Oriel Coll Oxford; *m* Suzan Harrison; 3 s (Ned, Jack, Harry); *Career* author; memb: Amnesty, Index; FRSL; *Awards* Somerset Maugham Award 1979, Plays & Players Award 1980, BAFTA Award (for screenwriting) 1986 and 1994, International Emmy 2001, Emmy and Golden Globes Awards (for Elizabeth I) 2006; *Novels* My Life Closed Twice (1977), Jack Be Nimble (1980), Star Turn (1985), Black Magic (1986), Witchcraft (1987), The Wimbledon Poisoner (1990), They Came from SW19 (1992), East of Wimbledon (1993), Two and a Half Men in a Boat (1993), Scenes from a Poisoner's Life (1994), From Wimbledon to Waco (1995), Stalking Fiona (1997), 40 Something (1999), Hatchett and Lycett (2002), Unfaithfully Yours (2013); *Plays* Double Talk (Square One Theatre) 1976, Class Enemy (Royal Court then touring) 1978, Trial Run (Oxford Playhouse) 1980, Line 'Em (NT) 1980, Sugar and Spice (Royal Ct) 1980, WCPC (Half Moon) 1982, My Brother's Keeper (Greenwich Theatre) 1985, Country Dancing (RSC Stratford) 1986, Nativity (Tricycle Theatre London) 1989, Lord of the Flies (adaptation of William Golding's novel, RSC) 1995, Harry & Me (Royal Ct Theatre) 1997, The Last Romantics (Greenwich Theatre) 1997, My Face (NT Cottesloe) 2004; *Television and Film* Talking Blues (BBC) 1977, Real Live Audience (BBC) 1977, Baby Love (BBC) 1981, Johnny Jarvis (BBC) 1983, Charlie (Central) 1984, Breaking Up (BBC) 1986, Kremlin Farewell (BBC 2) 1990, Centrepoint (Channel Four) 1990, The Wimbledon Poisoner (BBC 1) 1994, The Last Romantics (TV film, BBC 2) 1997, Witchcraft (BBC) 1997, Skallagrigg (Montreal Film Festival, BBC), The Canterville Ghost (Paramount), Dirty Tricks (ITV) 2000, Bertie & Elizabeth (ITV) 2001, Elizabeth I 2005, Wodehouse at War 2013; *Radio* HR (BBC Radio 4 comedy series) 2009–13; *Recreations* swimming, walking; *Style*— Nigel Williams, Esq, FRSL; ✉ c/o Judy Daish Associates, 2 St Charles Place, London W10 6EG (☎ 020 8964 8811, fax 020 8964 8966)

WILLIAMS, Nigel Phillip; *b* 9 May 1956; *Educ* LSE (BSc Econ); *m* Oct 1999, Antoinette, da of Prof Karl-Ernst Baron Pilars de Pilar, and Petra, *née* von Johnston; 1 da (Victoria b 2 Dec 2004), 1 s (Charles b 4 Oct 2009); *Career* W Greenwell & Co 1977–78, assoc memb Grieveson Grant & Co 1978–84, md William Cooke Lott & Kissack Ltd 1984–90, advsr Czechoslovenska Obchodni Banka 1990–91, chm Mgmnt Bd Creditanstalt Investment Co 1991–96, currently managing ptnr Royalton Partners, chm City Parking Gp Poland; chm Bd: CertAsig Hldgs Luxembourg, Lester Brewster Meml Fndn 2003; memb: SBE 1978, SE 1983; *Recreations* golf, sailing, skiing; *Clubs* Turf, Brook (NY), Carlton, Royal Thames Yacht, Engadine Golf; *Style*— Nigel Williams, Esq; ✉ Royalton Partners SA, 3, Avenue Monterey, L-2163, Luxembourg (☎ 0035 22 647 0320, fax 0035 22 647 0321, e-mail nigel@royalton-partners.com)

WILLIAMS, Prof Sir Norman Stanley; kt (2015); s of Julius Williams (d 1998), and Mable, *née* Sundle (d 1978); *b* 15 March 1947; *Educ* Roundhay Sch Leeds, Univ of London (MB BS, MS); *m* Linda, da of Reuben Feldman, of London; 1 da (Charlotte b 1979), 1 s (Benjamin b 1983); *Career* res fell UCLA 1980–82, sr lectr in surgery Leeds Gen Infirmary

W

1982–86 (res fell 1977–78, lectr 1978–80), winner Patey Prize 1978, Fulbright scholar 1980, Moynihan fellowship 1985; Barts and The London Sch of Med and Dentistry: house surgn and physician 1970–71, surgical registrar 1971–76, prof of surgery 1986–, head Div of Surgery Clinical Neuroscience and Intensive Care 1998–2003; author of numerous chapters and papers on gastroenterological disease; pres IA (Ileostomy and Internal Pouch Support Gp) 1992–2008, chm UKCCCR Sub-Ctee on colorectal cancer 1997–2001, pres Euro Digestive Surgery 1997, memb Cncl RCS 2005–, chm Academic and Research Bd RCS 2006–, pres Soc of Academic and Research Surgery 2009–11; vice-chm Editorial Ctee British Jl of Surgery 1992–2001; memb Editorial Bd: Int Jl of Colorectal Disease, Jl of Surgical Oncology; Sir Alan Parks visting prof 2002, G B Ong visiting prof 2004; John Goligher lectr 2002, Zachary Cope lectr 2003, Hunterian Oration 2011; jt winner Bupa Prize for Medically Illustrated Textbook 1995, Nessim Habif Prize for Surgery 1995, Worshipful Soc of Apothecaries Galen Medal in Therapeutics 2002, Cutlers Surgical Prize 2011; memb: Br Soc of Gastroenterology, Surgical Res Soc, Assoc of Surgeons, Int Surgical Gp; FRCS 1975 (pres 2011–14), FMedSci, hon fell American Surgical Assoc 2008, hon fell American Coll of Surgeons 2013, FRCP 2013, FRCPEd 2013, FRCA 2014, FRCSI 2014, Hon FDS 2014; *Books* Surgery of the Anus, Rectum and Colon (jt author), Colorectal Cancer (ed), Bailey & Love's Short Practice in Surgery (jt ed); *Recreations* long distance swimming, theatre, cinema; *Style—* Prof Sir Norman Williams

WILLIAMS, Olivia; *b* 26 July 1968, London; *Educ* Newnham Coll Cambridge, Bristol Old Vic Theatre Sch; *m* 2003, Rhashan Stone; 2 da (Esmé Ruby b 6 April 2004, Roxana May b 7 April 2007); *Career* actress; *Theatre* Richard III (RSC) 1995, Love's Labour's Lost (Olivier Theatre and RNT) 2003, The Hotel in Amsterdam (Donmar Warehouse) 2003, The Changeling (Barbican Theatre) 2006, In A Forest, Dark and Deep (Vaudeville Theatre) 2011; *Television* incl: Emma 1996, Agatha Christie: A Life in Pictures 2004, Krakatoa: The Last Days 2006, Damage 2007, Miss Austen Regrets 2008, Dollhouse 2009–10; *Film* incl: The Postman 1997, Rushmore 1998, The Sixth Sense 1999, Born Romantic 2000, Peter Pan 2003, Valiant 2005, Tara Road 2005, Flashbacks of a Fool 2008, Broken Lines 2008, An Education 2009, Sex & Drugs & Rock & Roll 2010, The Ghost 2010 (Best Br Actress in a Supporting Role London Critics' Circle Award 2011); *Style—* Ms Olivia Williams; ✉ c/o Independent Talent Group Ltd, 40 Whitfield Street, London W1T 2RH

WILLIAMS, Owen John; s of Owen John Williams (d 1975), of St Clears, Dyfed, and Dilys Williams (d 2001); *b* 17 May 1950, Carmarthen, Wales; *Educ* Ysgol Abermâd Aberystwyth, Harrow, UC Oxford (MA), Birkbeck Coll London (MA); *m* 1, 2 March 1984 (m dis 1997), Mary Evans; 1 da (Olivia Jane b 23 Dec 1986); m 2, 7 Sept 2012, Valerie Pittman, *née* Chacksfield; *Career* called to the Bar Middle Temple 1974; chm O J Williams Ltd Group of Cos 1975–2004; Parly candidate (Cons): Ceredigion and Pembroke North 1987 and 1992, Carmarthen West and South Pembrokeshire 1997; Euro Parly candidate: Mid and West Wales 1989, Wales 1999 and 2004; Nat Assembly for Wales candidate: Meirionnydd Nant Conwy 1999, Ceredigion 2003; pres Carmarthen West and South Pembrokeshire Cons Assoc 2004–07; non-exec memb East Dyfed HA 1990–95; pres St Clears Sr Citizens' Assoc; memb Hon Soc Cymmrodorion; Lloyd's underwriter 1978–; *Recreations* horse racing and breeding, rugby, country music; *Clubs* Carlton; *Style—* O J Williams, Esq; ✉ 9 Bedford Row, London WC1R 4AZ (☎ 020 7489 2727, fax 020 7489 2828)

WILLIAMS, Rt Rev Paul Gavin; *see:* Southwell and Nottingham, Bishop of

WILLIAMS, Sir Paul Michael; kt (2011), OBE (2000), DL (S Glamorgan 2010); *b* 25 June 1948, Wales; *Career* DG Dept of Health and Social Services Welsh Govt 2008–11, registrar St John Cymru 2012– (Bailiff of St David's 2014–); UK pres IHM 2002–05; non-exec dir Natural Resources Wales 2012; tstee: St John Cymru, Royal Voluntary Service 2012, Royal Masonic Benevolent Instn 2012; High Sheriff S Glamorgan 2007–08; hon fell Cardiff Met Univ 2010; hon doctorate Univ of S Wales 2013; DMS, CIHM, CCMI, FRSA; KStJ 2016 (CStJ 2011, OStJ 2009); *Recreations* fly fishing, travel, art, music, gardening; *Clubs* Cardiff and County, Army and Navy; *Style—* Sir Paul Williams, OBE, KStJ, DL; ✉ e-mail pgmw@btinternet.com

WILLIAMS, (John) Peter; *b* 29 June 1953; *Educ* Kingston GS, St John's Coll Cambridge (MA); *m* 1980, Geraldine Mary, *née* Whelan; 1 s (Dominic b 1982), 2 da (Frances b 1984, Caroline b 1987); *Career* Thomson McLintock 1975–79, Grindlays Bank 1979–82; Daily Mail and General Tst 1982–2011 (fin dir 1991–2011); non-exec dir: IBIS Media VCT 2006–14, Hays Gp 2015–; sr ind dir Perform Gp plc 2011–, syndicator Cambridge Assesment 2011–; tstee Royal Acad 2011–; FCA 1989 (ACA 1979); *Recreations* hockey, golf, philately; *Style—* Peter Williams, Esq; ✉ 15 Bullingham Mansions, Pitt Street, London W8 4JH

WILLIAMS, (William) Peter; MBE (2007); s of William Edgar Williams (d 1983), of Canterbury, Kent, and Gladys Mary, *née* Thomas (d 1985); *b* 21 September 1933; *Educ* King Edward GS Totnes, Cotham GS Bristol; *m* 1, 1960 (m dis 1986); 2 s, 4 da; m 2, 1986, Jo Taylor Williams, da of Alexander Thomas Taylor, of Timaru, NZ; 1 da; *Career* journalist with Bristol Evening Post and BBC Radio in South West 1954–64, reporter/newsreader Day by Day Southern Television 1964–65, reporter and prodr This Week (later TV Eye) Thames Television 1965–79, reporter Panorama and presenter/exec prodr Open Secret BBC 1979–82, controller of factual progs TVS 1982–92; md: Studio Z 1992–98, Peter Williams Television 1992–; prodr Just Williams series of documentaries, originated The Human Factor series for ITV; awards incl: Test Tube Explosion 1983 (runner up Prix Italia), Just Williams – The Mercenaries 1984 (San Francisco Golden Gate Award), The Human Factor – Boy on a Skateboard 1985 (Asia Broadcasting Union Premier Documentary Award), Unit 731 – Did the Emperor Know? 1985 (San Francisco Golden Gate Award, Gold Medal NY Int Film and TV Festival 1986), Charlie Wing 1990 (RTS Best UK Regnl Prog, Rheims Euro TV Festival Best Documentary 1991), Ambulance! (Indies Best Regnl Prog 1995), Pandemic (winner Toronto Int Documentary Festival 2000); chm: CTFM Radio 1999–2004, Viridor Credits Environmental Trust (Kent) 2007–, New Marlowe Theatre Tst 2009–; pres Optimists Club 1988–2004; pres Canterbury Festival 2007– (chm 1986–2007); dir: E Kent Enterprise Agency 1987–2001, Technology East Kent 2001–10, Brett Environmental Tst 2001–06; fndr memb United for Local Television (ULTV) 2007; tstee Kent Community Fndn 2012–; RTS Lifetime Industry Achievement Award 2002; Hon Freedom of City of Canterbury 2001; Hon MA Univ of Kent at Canterbury 1992, Hon DLitt Univ of Kent 2012; hon fell Canterbury Christ Church Univ 2004; *Books* Winner Stakes All, McIndoe's Army, Unit 731 – The Secret of Secrets; *Recreations* theatre, music, tennis; *Clubs* Kent CCC (life memb); *Style—* Peter Williams, Esq, MBE; ✉ Boughton-under-Blean, Faversham, Kent; business (☎ and fax 01227 751171, e-mail peter@pwtv.co.uk)

WILLIAMS, Sir Peter Michael; kt (1998), CBE (1992); *b* 22 March 1945, Warrington; *Educ* Hymers Coll Hull, Trinity Coll Cambridge (MA, PhD); *m*; 1 s (b 1978); *Career* Mullard research fell Selwyn Coll Cambridge 1969–70, univ lectr Dept of Chemical Engrg and Chemical Technol Imperial Coll London 1970–75, fell St John's Coll Oxford 1988–2000, fell Imperial Coll London 1997, master St Catherine's Coll Oxford 2000–02, chllr Univ of Leicester 2005–10; VG Instruments Gp 1975–82 (dep gp md 1979–82), Oxford Instruments plc 1982–99 (chm 1991–99); chm: PPARC 1994–99, The Oxford Partnership 1995–97, Isis Innovation Ltd 1997–2001, NPL Mgmnt Ltd 2002–14, Engrg and Technol Bd 2002–06; non-exec dir: Taube Hodgson Stonex Ptnrs Ltd 1997–2000, Advent VCT & VCT2 plc 1998–2004, GKN plc 2001–10, WS Atkins 2004–11, Kromek plc 2015– (also chm); lectures and presentations incl: Royal Soc 'Zeneca' 1994, UK Innovation 1995, Duncan Davies Medal 1999, R&D 1999; chm of trustees Nat Museum of Science and Industry 1996–2002; Guardian Young Businessman of the Year 1986, Glazebrook Medal Inst of Physics 2006; hon fell: UCL, Selwyn Coll Cambridge, St Catherine's Coll Oxford; Hon DSc: Univ of Leicester, Nottingham Trent Univ 1995, Loughborough Univ 1996, Brunel Univ 1997, Univ of Wales 1999, Univ of Sheffield 1999, Univ of Warwick 1999, Univ of Salford 2003, Univ of Staffordshire 2004, City Univ 2007, Univ of Hull 2010, Univ of Bedford 2010; FREng 1996, FRS 1999 (vice-pres and treas 2007–12), FInstP (pres 2000–02), Hon FIChemE 2003, Hon FIEE 2004 (FIEE), Hon FIMC 2006, Hon FIMechE 2008; *Recreations* hiking, skiing, music, collecting wine; *Style—* Sir Peter Williams, CBE, FRS, FREng

WILLIAMS, Peter Rhys; s of Rhys Morgan Williams (d 1979), and Barbara Marion, *née* Pead (d 2003); *b* 30 December 1955, Cardiff; *Educ* Cathedral Sch Llandaff, King's Coll Taunton (exhibitioner), Univ of Exeter, Univ of Warwick, Coll of Law Guildford, UWE; *m* 10 Nov 1984, Anne Marcelle, *née* Ebery; 3 s (Thomas John Rhys b 24 Oct 1988, Henry George Rhys b 17 June 1991, Edward Morgan Rhys b 15 Feb 1993); *Career* slr and slr-advocate; ptnr Burges Salmon 1987–10 (articled clerk 1980–82), ptnr Michelmores LLP 2012–; past vice-chm Nat Trainee Slrs Gp 1982, former govr The Downs Sch Wraxall; Blundell lectr; fell Br Inst of Agric Conslts, memb Law Soc; FCIArb, Hon RICS; Scammell, Densham & Williams Law of Agricultural Holdings (ed); contrib to: Halsbury's Laws (vol on agric), Agricultural Law, Tax and Finance, Encyclopaedia of Forms and Precedents (vol on agric), Dispute Resolution, Farm Cottages; *Style—* Peter Williams, Esq; ✉ Michelmores LLP, Broad Quay House, Broad Quay, Bristol BS1 4DJ (☎ 0117 906 9300, e-mail peter.williams@michelmores.com)

WILLIAMS, Dr Peter Richard; s of Calvert Percy Halliday Williams, of Christchurch, Dorset, and Joan Lillian, *née* Cook; *b* 13 July 1946; *Educ* Bedford Modern Sch, Univ of Oxford, Univ of Saskatchewan, Univ of Reading (BA, MSc, PhD); *m* 2 Dec 1972, Esther May, da of Louis Van Der Veen, of Saskatoon, Saskatchewan, Canada; *Career* res fell: Univ of Birmingham 1975–80, Australian Nat Univ 1980–83; dep dir Inst of Housing 1986–88 (asst dir 1980–86), prof of housing mgmnt and dir Centre for Housing Mgmnt and Devpt Univ of Wales Cardiff 1989–94 (visiting fell 1994–95), dep DG Cncl of Mortgage Lenders 1994–2006, conslt 2006–; currently exec dir Intermediary Mortgage Lenders Assoc, chm Urban Residential Ltd and memb Bd Belmont Green Ltd; currently departmental fell Dept of Land Economy Univ of Cambridge; formerly memb Bd Housing Corp, memb Min of Housing, Planning and Construction's Housing Sounding Bd 1991–99; formerly memb Editorial Bd: Housing Studies, Roof Magazine; gen ed Housing Practice book series; formerly: memb Bd Tai Cymru (Housing for Wales), chm Housing Mgmnt Advsy Panel for Wales, chm Housing Studies Assoc; memb: RGS, Inst Br Geographers, Chartered Inst of Housing; *Books* Urban Political Economy (author and ed, 1982), Social Process and The City (ed, 1983), Conflict and Development (ed, 1984), Gentrification and The City (author and ed, 1986), Class and Space (author and ed, 1987), Home Ownership (co-author, 1990), Safe as Houses (co-author, 1991), Directions in Housing Policy (ed, 1997), Surviving or Thriving? Managing change in housing organisations (co-author, 1998), Housing in Wales: The Policy Agenda in an Era of Devolution (co-author, 2000), UK Housing Review (co-author, 2016); *Recreations* walking, punting, cricket, travel, rugby; *Clubs* Dittons Skiff and Punting, Thames Punting, Harlequins RFC, Middlesex CCC; *Style—* Dr Peter Williams; ☎ 020 8390 3264

WILLIAMS, Sir (Robert) Philip Nathaniel; 4 Bt (UK 1915), of Bridehead, Co Dorset; JP (1992), DL (Dorset 1995); s of Sir David Philip Williams, 3 Bt, DL (d 1970), by his 2 w, Elizabeth, Lady Williams, DL (d 2010); *b* 3 May 1950; *Educ* Marlborough, Univ of St Andrews (MA); *m* 1979, Catherine Margaret Godwin, da of Canon Cosmo Gabriel Rivers Pouncey (d 2006); 1 s (David b 1980), 3 da (Sarah b 1982, Margaret b 1984, Clare b 1987); *Heir* s David Williams; *Career* landowner (2500 acres); *Clubs* MCC; *Style—* Sir Philip Williams, Bt, DL; ✉ Bridehead, Littlebredy, Dorchester, Dorset DT2 9JA (☎ 01308 482232)

WILLIAMS, Prof Rhys Watcyn; s of Rev Morgan John Williams, and Barbara, *née* John; *b* 24 May 1946; *Educ* The Bishop Gore Sch Swansea, Jesus Coll Oxford (MA, DPhil); *m* Kathleen, da of William Henry Gould, of Bournemouth; 2 s (Daniel b 1978, Thomas b 1982); *Career* tutorial res fell Bedford Coll London 1972–74, lectr in German Univ of Manchester 1974–84; Univ of Wales Swansea (formerly Univ Coll Swansea): prof of German 1984–2008, dean Faculty of Arts 1988–91, pro-vice-chllr 1997–2008, emeritus prof 2008; pres: Int Carl Einstein Soc 1988–92, Conf of Univ Teachers of German 2002–05; hon fell Swansea Univ 2010; *Books* Carl Sternheim, A Critical Study (1982); *Style—* Prof Rhys Williams; ✉ 48 Derwen Fawr Road, Sketty, Swansea SA2 8AQ (☎ 01792 297835, e-mail r.w.williams@swan.ac.uk)

WILLIAMS, Prof Richard Andrew; OBE (2009); s of Henry Lewis Williams, of Worcester, and Jean Hazel, *née* Lewis; *b* 26 April 1960, Worcester; *Educ* Kings Sch Worchester, Imperial Coll London (BSc, PhD); *m* 1989, Jane Margaret, *née* Taylor; 1 da (Hannah-Rose), 1 s (Timothy); *Career* Univ of Manchester: dep warden Moberly Hall 1986–89, warden Moberly Hall 1989–90, lectr in chemical engrg UMIST 1986–92, sr lectr in chemical engrg UMIST 1992–93; prof of minerals engrg Univ of Exeter 1993–98; Univ of Leeds: prof of chemical engrg and info systems Keyworth Inst of Manufacturing 1999–2006, prof of mineral and process engrg 1999–2008, dir BNFL in particle science and technol alliance 2000–06, head Dept of Mining and Mineral Engrg 2001–03, pro-vice chllr for enterprise and knowledge transfer and int strategy 2005–10, pro-vice chllr for int partnerships 2010–11; pro-vice chllr and head Coll of Engrg and Physical Sciences Univ of Birmingham 2011–15, prof of energy and mineral resources Univ of Birmingham 2011–15, vice-chllr and princ Heriot-Watt Univ 2016–; dir: Manufacturing Technology Centre (Ansty) 2011–15, Alta Innovations 2012–15, Alta Birmingham China (Guangzhou) 2012–15, CBI W Midlands 2013–15; hon prof of chemical engrg Univ of Manchester and UMIST 1993–98, visiting prof Camborne Sch of Mines Univ of Exeter 1999–2004, visiting prof Sch of Materials Science and Engrg Univ of NSW 2006–, visiting prof Chinese Acad of Sciences, hon prof Southeast Univ Nanjing 2014–, hon prof Taylors Univ Kuala Lumpur 2014–; res dir Virtual Centre for Industrial Process Tomography consortium Univs of Exeter, Leeds and Manchester 1996–2007; fndr: Disperse plc, Industrial Tomography Systems plc, Structure Vision Ltd, Dispersia Ltd; convenor Int Ctee Univs Scotland; tstee Carnegie Fndn 2016–; Inst of Electical Engrg Abrose Fleming Medal and Premium 1993, Beilby Gold Medal and Prize 1997, Isambard Kingdom Brunel Lectureship 1998, Noel E Webster Medal 2001, Royal Acad of Engrg Silver Medal 2003, Belgian and Int Trade Fair for Technological Innovation Gold Medal 2007, Int Warsaw Invention Show Silver Medal 2007, Thomas Edison Innovation Award 2007, EPSRC RISE Scholar 2014–; MSCI 1986, CEng 1988, FIMMM 1994, FMES 1995, FIChemE 1995, FREng 2000 (vice-pres 2005–08 and 2015–), CSci 2004, FRSA 2005, MIoD 2005, foreign fell Australian Acad of Technological Science and Egrg 2008; *Publications* Particle Deposition and Aggregation Measurement, Modelling and Simulation (1995), Process Tomography Principles, Techniques and Applications (1995), Recent developments in manufacturing emulsions and particulate products using membranes (with G T Vladisavljevi?, in Advances in colloid and interface science 113); *Recreations* travel, contemporary fine art, wine, mentoring energy entrepreneurs; *Clubs* Athenaeum; *Style—* Prof Richard A Williams, OBE, FREng, FTSE; ✉ Heriot-Watt University, Edinburgh EH14 4AS

WILLIAMS, Richard Charles John; s of Herbert Charles Lionel Williams (d 1957), and Barbara Dorothy, *née* Moenich; *b* 19 October 1949; *Educ* Highgate Sch, London Coll of Printing (DipAD); *m* Agnieszka Wanda, da of Zygmunt Jan Skrobanski; 1 da (Mary Barbara Daisy b 31 July 1981), 1 s (Peter Crispin John b 4 April 1986); *Career* asst designer Industrial Design Unit Ltd 1973–74, sr designer J Sainsbury Ltd 1974–77, dir of packaging Allied International Designers 1977–86, co-fndr/md Design Bridge 1986–96, co-fndr Williams Murray Hamm 1997–; exec memb DBA 1989–90, memb D&AD, memb Design Cncl 2005–; FRSA, FCSD; *Recreations* motor sports; *Style*— Richard Williams, Esq; ✉ Williams Murray Hamm, 10 Dallington Street, London EC1V 0DB (✆ 020 3217 0000, fax 020 3217 0002)

WILLIAMS, Prof Richard James Willson; OBE (2010), TD; s of Ernest James Williams, of Downend, Bristol, and Eleanor Mary Willson Williams, *née* Rickard; *b* 5 February 1949; *Educ* Bristol GS, Univ of Birmingham (MB ChB, Marjorie Hutchings prize in psychiatry), Dip; *m* 21 May 1971, Janet May, da of Ronald Phillip Simons (d 1990); 2 da (Anna May b 12 July 1975, Katharine Alice Jane b 21 Nov 1977), 1 s (James Christopher Willson b 13 Aug 1981); *Career* house physician Selly Oak Hosp Birmingham 1972–73, house surgn Worcester Royal Infirmary 1973, registrar in psychiatry S Glamorgan AHA 1974–77 (sr house offr in psychiatry 1973–74), sr registrar in child and adolescent psychiatry S Glamorgan AHA and Welsh Nat Sch of Med 1977–80, conslt child and adolescent psychiatrist 1980– (Avon AHA 1980–82, Bristol and Weston HA 1982–91, United Bristol Healthcare NHS Tst 1991–98, Gwent Community Health NHS Tst 1998–99, Gwent Healthcare NHS Tst 1999–2009, Aneurin Bevan Univ Health Bd 2009–14) 1998–99), prof of mental health strategy Univ of Glamorgan (now Univ of S Wales) 1998–2014 (ret), emeritus prof of mental health strategy Univ of S Wales 2014–; dir NHS Health Advsy Serv 1992–96, dir Drugs Advsy Serv 1992–96, special professional advsr on child and adolescent mental health Welsh Govt 1999–2010, scientific advsr on the psychosocial and mental healthcare of people affected by disasters to the dir of emergency preparedness Dept of Health 2007–12; Univ of Bristol: clinical teacher in mental health 1980–89, clinical lectr in mental health 1989–94, hon sr lectr in mental health 1994–98, govr Inst of Child Health 1988–94, memb Ct 1990–93; sr fell Health Servs Mgmnt Centre Univ of Birmingham 1996–99; asst ed Jl of Adolescence 1990–97 (memb ed Bd 1997–), co-ed Child and Adolescent Psychiatry Section Current Opinion in Psychiatry 1993–; hon prof: of child and adolescent mental health Univ of Central Lancashire 2006–11, Robert Gordon Univ 2009–12, Humanitarian and Conflict Response Inst Univ of Manchester 2012–; memb Bd of Examiners for Dip in the Medical Care of Catastrophes Worshipful Soc of Apothecaries of the City of London 1998– (chair and convener (chief examiner) 2012–); RCPsych: memb Cncl 1986–90, 1993–99 and 2001–05, chm S Western Div 1996–99, dir of conferences 2001–07, chm Welsh Div 2002–06, memb Central Exec Ctee 2005–07, lead offr Disaster Mgmnt 2008–14; chm Assoc for the Psychiatric Study of Adolescents 1987–93; memb: Assoc for Child Psychology and Psychiatry 1978–, Assoc for Professionals in Servs for Adolescents 1979–, Assoc of Univ Teachers of Psychiatry 1989–, Br Paediatric Assoc 1987–96, Acad of Royal Colls in Wales 2002–08 (vice chm 2003 and 2006–08, chm 2004–06); DPM 1976, MHSM 1994, MInstD 1994, FRCPCH 1997 (MRCPCH 1996), FRSM 1992, Hon FRCPsych 2014 (FRCPsych 1990, MRCPsych 1976); *Publications* The APSA Register of Adolescent Units (5 edn 1990), A Concise Guide to the Children Act 1989 (1992), A Unique Window on Change (1993), Comprehensive Mental Health Services (1994 and 1995), Clinicians in Management (1994 and 1995), Suicide Prevention (1994), Comprehensive Health Services for Elderly People (1994), Drugs and Alcohol (1994), Guiding Through Change (1994), Together We Stand (1995), A Place in Mind (1995), The Substance of Young Needs (1996), Making a Mark (1996), Safeguards for Young Minds (1996, 2 edn 2004), Heading for Better Care (1996), Addressing the Balance (1997), Voices in Partnership (1997), Forging New Channels (1998), Promoting Mental Health in a Civil Society (2001), Deaths of Detained Patients in England and Wales (2001), Child and Adolescent Mental Health Services (2005); *Recreations* walking on Bodmin Moor, licensed radio amateur, military history, preserved steam railways; *Clubs* Athenaeum, IOD; *Style*— Prof Richard Williams, OBE, TD; ✉ Welsh Institute for Health and Social Care, University of South Wales, Lower Glyntaff Campus, Pontypridd CF37 1DL (e-mail richard.williams@southwales.ac.uk)

WILLIAMS, Richard Wayne; s of David Victor Williams (d 1964), and Sarah Irene, *née* Jones; *b* 13 June 1948; *Educ* Ystalyfera GS Swansea, UC Wales Aberystwyth (LLB), Univ of London (LLM); *m* 7 Sept 1974, Linda Pauline, da of Cecil Ernest Elvins; 2 s (Rhodri Christopher Wyn b 18 Jan 1982, Robin Owen Wyn b 12 Sept 1985); *Career* admitted slr 1973; ptnr Ince & Co 1978–2001 (conslt 2001–); visiting prof Dept of Law Univ of Wales Swansea; speaker at conferences on shipping matters UK and abroad; conslt on shipping matters to UN agencies and other int bodies; memb: Baltic Exchange, London Maritime Arbitrators Assoc; memb Law Soc; *Books* Limitation of Liability for Maritime Claims (1986, 3 edn 1998); *Recreations* archaeology, reading, travel; *Style*— Richard Williams, Esq; ✉ Ince & Co, International House, 1 St Katharine's Way, London E1W 1AY

WILLIAMS, Dr Rob; *b* 21 January 1985, Taplow, Bucks; *Educ* Sir William Borlase Sch Marlow, UCL (BSc), Birkbeck Coll London (PhD); *Career* rower; achievements incl: Bronze medal (lightweight quad) World Championships 2007, Gold medal (lightweight four) World Championships 2010, Bronze medal (lightweight four) World Championships 2011, Silver medal (lightweight four) Olympic Games 2012; *Clubs* London Rowing; *Style*— Dr Rob Williams

WILLIAMS, Robert James; s of late Capt Thomas Edwin Williams, MBE, of Lutterworth, Leics, and Joan Winifred, *née* Nelson; *b* 20 September 1948; *Educ* King Edward VII Sch Sheffield, UC Oxford (BA); *m* 29 July 1972, Margaret, da of late Charles Neville Hillier, of Guernsey, CI; 2 da (Katherine b 6 Aug 1979, Caroline b 24 Aug 1983); *Career* Linklaters & Paines: articled clerk 1971–73, asst slr 1973–81, Hong Kong Office 1978–80, ptnr 1981–93; non-exec dir: Edinburgh UK Smaller Companies Tracker Tst plc 1994–, The Law Debenture Corporation plc 2005– (exec dir 1993–2004); memb City of London Slrs' Co 1980; memb Law Soc 1973; *Recreations* swimming, walking, eating, sleeping; *Style*— Robert J Williams, Esq

WILLIAMS, Roderick Gregory Coleman; s of Adrian John Williams, of Headington, Oxford, and Norma-Rose Alesia, *née* Coleman; *b* 19 November 1965, London; *Educ* Christ Church Cathedral Sch Oxford, Haberdashers' Askes Sch, Magdalen Coll Oxford (BA), Inst of Educn London (PGCE), GSM; *m* 23 July 1988, Miranda Jane, *née* Clasen; 2 da (Josephine Alice b 19 Feb 1995, Cara Elizabeth b 7 Jan 1997), 1 s (Finlay Maxwell b 23 June 2000); *Career* opera singer (baritone); dir of choral studies Tiffin Sch Kingston upon Thames 1988–91; Opera North: title role in Don Giovanni, The Count in Le nozze di Figaro, Figaro in Il barbiere di Siviglia, Ned Keene in Peter Grimes; Scottish Opera: Marcello in La bohème, Lord Byron in Sally Beamish's Monster (world premiere); other roles incl: Papageno in Die Zauberflöte (ENO), Schaunard in La bohème (ROH), The Second Mrs Kong (Royal Festival Hall), title role in Pilgrim's Progress (Philharmonia Orch, Sadler's Wells) 2008; BBC Proms: Vision of St Augustine with BBC Nat Orch Wales 2005, The Ring Dance of the Nazarene, soloist first night 2013, soloist last night 2014; numerous recordings incl Vaughan Williams, Berkeley and Britten operas and English song; as composer has had work premiered at The Purcell Room, The Wigmore and Barbican Halls and work premiered on BBC Radio 3; Kathleen Ferrier Award (second prize) 1994, Great Grimsby Singing Competition 1992, Lilli Boulanger Award 1996; *Style*— Roderick Williams, Esq; ✉ c/o Ingpen and Williams, 7 St George's Court, 131 Putney Bridge, London SW15 2PA (✆ 020 8874 3222, e-mail jg@ingpen.co.uk)

WILLIAMS, Rev Canon (John) Roger; s of Sir Gwilym Tecwyn Williams, CBE (d 1989), and Kathleen Isobel Rishworth, *née* Edwards (d 1989); *b* 6 October 1937; *Educ* Denstone Coll, Lichfield Theol Coll, Westminster Coll Oxford (DipTh, MTh); *Career* ordained Lichfield

Cathedral: deacon 1963, priest 1964; asst curate: Wem 1963–66, St Peter's Collegiate Church Wolverhampton 1966–69; rector Pudleston-cum-Whyle with Hatfield and priest i/c Stoke Prior Humber and Docklow Hereford 1969–74, vicar Christ Church Fenton Stoke-on-Trent 1974–81, rector Shipston-on-Stour with Honington and Idlicote 1981–92, rural dean Shipston 1983–90, hon canon Coventry Cathedral 1990–2000 (canon emeritus 2000–), rector of Lighthorne, vicar of Chesterton and vicar of Newbold Pacey with Moreton Morrell 1992–2000, priest-in-charge Denstone with Ellastone and Stanton 2000–05, master St John's Hosp Lichfield 2005–11, ret; chaplain to High Sheriff of Warks 1987–88, 1991–93 and 1997–98; *Recreations* art, architecture, travel; *Style*— The Rev Canon Roger Williams; ✉ 3 Curborough Road, Lichfield, Staffordshire WS13 7NG (✆ 01543 419339)

WILLIAMS, Roger Hugh; CBE (2013); s of Morgan Glyn Williams (d 1984), and Eurlys Williams (d 1984); *b* 22 January 1948, Crickhowell, Powys; *Educ* Christ Coll Brecon, Selwyn Coll Cambridge (MA); *m* 28 April 1973, Penelope; 2 c; *Career* farmer 1969–; co cncllr Powys 1981–2001, MP (Lib Dem) Brecon and Radnorshire 2001–15; memb and vice-chm Powys TEC; chm Brecon Beacons Nat Park 1989–93, memb Devpt Bd for Rural Wales 1991–99; supporter: Campaign for Protection of Rural Wales, Brecknock Wildlife Tst; memb: NFU (county chm), Farmers' Union of Wales, CLA; *Recreations* walking, sport, nature conservation; *Style*— Roger Williams, Esq, CBE; ✉ House of Commons, London SW1A 0AA (✆ 020 7219 8145, fax 020 7219 1747, e-mail williamsr@ parliament.uk, website www.rogerwilliams.org.uk)

WILLIAMS, Prof Roger Stanley; CBE (1993); s of Stanley George Williams, and Doris Dagmar, *née* Clatworthy; *b* 28 August 1931; *Educ* St Mary's Coll Southampton, London Hosp Med Coll (MB, MD, LRCP); *m* 1, 8 Aug 1954 (m dis 1977), Lindsay Mary, *née* Elliott; 2 s (Robert b 8 March 1956, Andrew b 3 Jan 1964), 3 da (Anne b 5 March 1958, Fiona b 24 April 1959 d 1996, Deborah b 12 July 1961); *m* 2, 15 Sept 1978, Stephanie Gay, da of Gp Capt Patrick de Laszlo (d 1980); 2 da (Clemency b 28 June 1979, Octavia b 4 Sept 1983), 1 s (Aidan b 16 May 1981); *Career* Capt RAMC 1956–58; jr med specialist Queen Alexandra Hosp Millbank 1956–58, med registrar and tutor Royal Postgraduate Med Sch 1958–59, lectr in med Royal Free Hosp 1959–65, conslt physician Royal S Hants and Southampton Gen Hosp 1965–66, dir Inst of Liver Studies and conslt physician King's Coll Hosp and Med Sch 1966–96, prof of hepatology KCL 1994–96, dir Inst of Hepatology UCL and hon conslt physician UCL Hosps 1996–2011, medical dir Inst of Hepatology Fndn for Liver Research 2010–, dir Inst of Hepatology London 2011–; dir Int Office Royal Coll of Physicians; memb scientific gp on viral hepatitis WHO Geneva 1972, med dir Fndn for Liver Research 1974–, memb Advsy Gp on Hepatitis DHSS 1980–96 (memb Transplant Advsy Panel 1974–83), memb Clinical Standards Advsy Ctee Dept of Health 1994–; attended Melrose meml lecture Glasgow 1970, Goulstonian lecture RCP 1970, Searle lecture American Assoc for Study of Liver Disease 1972, Fleming lecture Glasgow Coll of Physicians and Surgns 1975, Sir Arthur Hurst meml lecture Br Soc of Gastroenterology 1975, Skinner lecture Royal Coll of Radiologists 1978, FitzPatrick lecture RCP 2006; Distinguished Serv Award Br Assoc for the Study of the Liver 2003, Sr Achievement Award American Soc of Transplantation 2004, Hans Popper Lifetime Achievement Award Int Liver Congress Hong Kong 2008, ILTS Distinguished Service Award 2011; Sir Ernest Finch visiting prof Sheffield 1974, hon conslt in med to Army 1988–98; Hans Sloane fell RCP 2004–08; memb: RSM (sec of section 1962–71), Euro Assoc for Study of the Liver (sec and treas 1968–71, pres 1984, hon pres 2008); pres Br Soc of Gastroenterology 1989–90, UK rep Select Ctee of Experts Organ Transplantation 1989–93, second vice-pres RCP 1991–93, chm Cons Med Soc; Freeman City of London, Liveryman Worshipful Soc of Apothecaries; hon fell UCL 2008; FKC 1992; Hon FACP, Hon FRCPI, FRCP (MRCP), FRCS, FRCPEd, FRACP, FMedSci; *Books* ed: Fifth Symposium on Advanced Medicine (1969), Immunology of the Liver (1971), Artificial Liver Support (1975), Immune Reactions in Liver Diseases (1978), Drug Reactions and the Liver (1981), Variceal Bleeding (1982), The Practice of Liver Transplantation (1995), International Developments in Health Care: A Review of Health Systems in the 1990s (1995), Critical Care in Acute Liver Failure (e-book, jt ed with Julia A Wendon, 2013); author of over 2,500 scientific papers, review articles and book chapters; *Recreations* tennis, sailing, opera; *Clubs* Athenaeum, Saints and Sinners, Royal Yacht Sqdn, Royal Ocean Racing; *Style*— Prof Roger Williams, CBE; ✉ Brickworth Park, Whiteparish, Wiltshire (✆ 01794 884553); Institute of Hepatology London, Foundation for Liver Research, 69–75 Chenies Mews, London WC1E 6HX (✆ 020 7255 9830, fax 020 7380 0405); private medical consultations: Kings International Private Patient Services (✆ 020 7346 3192, e-mail R.WilliamsPatients@researchinliver.org.uk)

WILLIAMS, Roy Samuel; OBE (2008); s of Roy Samuel Williams, Sr, and Gloria, *née* Kiffin; *b* 5 January 1968; *Educ* Henry Compton Sch, City and East London Coll, Kingsway Coll, Rose Bruford Coll (BA); *Career* playwright; *Theatre* No Boys Cricket Club (Theatre Royal Stratford East), Starstruck (Tricycle Theatre), Lift Off (Royal Court Theatre), Clubland (Royal Court Theatre), Fallout (Royal Court Theatre), Local Boy (Hampstead Theatre), The Gift (Birmingham Rep Theatre), Souls (Theatre Centre), Sing Yer Heart Out for the Lads (RNT), Night & Day (Theatre Venture), Josie's Boys (Red Ladder); *Television* BBC: Offside, Bredrens, Babyfather; *Radio* BBC: Homeboys, Tell Tale; *Awards* for Starstruck: John Whiting Award 1997, Alfred Fagon Award 1997, EMMA Award 1999; The George Devine Award 2000 (for Lift Off), Evening Standard Charles Wintour Award for Most Promising Playwright 2001 (for Clubland), BAFTA Best Schools Drama Award 2002 (for Offside); *Publications* Starstruck & The No Boys Cricket Club – Two Plays (1999), The Gift (2000), Clubland (2001), Sing Yer Heart Out for the Lads (2002), Roy Williams Plays 1 – The No Boys Cricket Club/Starstruck/Lift Off (2002), Fallout (2003); *Style*— Roy Williams, Esq, OBE

WILLIAMS, Russ; s of Henry Thomas Williams, and Patricia Primrose Williams; *Career* broadcaster; journalist and presenter Southern Sound 1983, mangr and sr presenter Metro FM 1987–90, presenter Capital Radio 1990–93; Virgin Radio: host Breakfast Show 1993–98, host Mid Morning Show 1998–; sports presenter: Sky Sports 1993–98, ITV Sports 1998–; Best Breakfast Show Sony Radio Awards 1997, Best On-Air Competition Sony Radio Awards 1998, Best Int Breakfast Show NY Radio Awards 1998; *Books* Football Babylon (1996), The Russ and Jono Breakfast Experience (1997), Football Babylon II (1998); *Recreations* football, golf, horses (owner); *Clubs* Tottenham Hotspur; *Style*— Russ Williams, Esq; ✉ MPC Entertainment, 15/16 Maple Mews, Maida Vale, London NW6 5UZ (✆ 020 7624 1184, fax 020 7624 4220, e-mail mpc@mpce.com)

WILLIAMS, Sally Ann; *b* 31 October 1962; *Educ* Cardiff Poly, NCTJ qualified journalist; *Career* journalist Essex County Newspapers 1983–85, head of newsroom The Post Office Nat HQ 1990–94 (joined The Post Office 1985), dep md (London) Countrywide Porter Novelli Ltd (formerly Countrywide Communications Ltd) 1994–; *Style*— Ms Sally Williams; ✉ Countrywide Porter Novelli Ltd, 31 St Petersberg Place, London W2 4LA (✆ 020 7853 2222, fax 020 7584 6655)

WILLIAMS, Shaun Peter; s of Peter Williams of Salisbury, and Gillian, *née* Collier; *b* 14 October 1961; *Educ* Canford Sch, Univ of Lausanne, Univ of Kent (BA); *m* 4 Nov 2006, Dr Karen Lock; *Career* sr reporter Salisbury Journal 1985–87; BBC TV 1987–94: grad prodn trainee, dir and prodr of various progs (incl Newsnight, Inside Story, Crimewatch, Film 90/91, Holiday); sr prodr The Sunday Programme 1994–95; PACT: dep chief exec 1995–98, chief exec 1998–2001; dir of corp affrs Carlton Communications plc 2001–02, dir of corp affrs Guardian News & Media Ltd 2002–; *Style*— Shaun Williams, Esq; ✉ Guardian News & Media Ltd, 90 York Way, London N1 9GU (✆ 020 7837 2332)

WILLIAMS, Sian Mary; da of John Price Williams, and Katherine, *née* Rees; *b* 28 November 1964; *Educ* Eastbourne Grammar and High Sch, Oxford Brookes Univ (BA), Univ of Westminster (MSc); 3 s (Joss Philip b 19 Oct 1991, Alex John b 30 Jan 1994, Seth Michael Woolwich b 7 Oct 2006), 1 da (Eve Rose Woolwich b 5 March 2009); *Career* BBC local radio trg scheme 1987–88, reporter and prodr BBC Radio Merseyside 1988–90, output ed and special events studio prodr World at One, PM and World This Weekend BBC Radio 4 1990–97, presenter BBC News 24 1997–99, newsreader BBC 1 1999–, special corr BBC 6 O'Clock News 1999–2001, presenter BBC Breakfast 2001–12, presenter National Treasures 2011–, co-host Saturday Live (BBC Radio 4) 2012–, presenter BBC Olympic Breakfast 2012, presenter BBC Sunday Morning Live 2013–15, presenter Radio 4 series 2014–, main news anchor Channel 5 2016–; pres Television and Radio Industries Club 2008–10; Best Presenter/Reporter Television and Radio Industries Club 2012 and 2013; fell Univ of Cardiff; *Books* Rise: Surviving and Thriving After Trauma (2016); *Recreations* walking, wine, cinema, running, writing; *Style*— Ms Sian Williams; ✉ c/o Knight Ayton Management, 29 Gloucester Place, London W1U 8HX (✆ 020 7831 4400)

WILLIAMS, Stanley Killa; JP (2005); s of Jack Killa Williams (d 1972), and Gwyneth Mary, *née* Jenkins (d 1995); *b* 2 July 1945; *Educ* Bromsgrove Sch, Merton Coll Oxford (MA), Coll of Law (Herbert Ruse Prize); *m* 15 July 1972, Dheidre Rhona, *née* Westerman; 1 da (Esther Catrin b 22 Dec 1975), 1 s (Justin Gareth Killa b 22 July 1977); *Career* slr Devon CC 1969–74 (trainee slr 1966–68), asst county sec Oxon CC 1974–80, dep co sec and slr Rowntree Mackintosh plc 1980–89; BTR plc: co sec and slr 1989–93, gp commercial attorney 1993–96; dir of legal affrs and co sec BSI 1997–2005, chm BSI Retirement Tst 2000–; Law Soc: memb 1969–, dir of Trg, Commerce and Industry Gp 2003–05, memb Cncl 2005–13, chm Commerce and Industry Gp 2005–06, memb Scrutiny Ctee 2006–07, memb Membership Bd 2007–08, memb Audit Ctee 2008–13; non-exec dir Corgi Tst 2005–06; chm York Ebor Round Table 1985–86; Pensions Mgmnt Inst Tstee Dip 2002; *Recreations* theatre, opera, travel, squash, golf, skiing; *Clubs* RAC; *Style*— Stanley Williams, Esq; ✉ e-mail killawilliams@hotmail.co.uk

WILLIAMS, Steffan Rhys; s of Malcolm Williams, and Nan Williams; *b* 1967, Geneva; *Educ* Lincoln Coll Oxford (MA, Rugby blue); *m* Janice; 1 da (Rosa), 1 s (Dylan); *Career* Citigate Dewe Rogerson 1995–98, Thomson Reuters 1998–2000, Capital MSL 2001–13, Finsbury 2014–15, Porta Communications plc 2016–, Newgate Communications 2016–; memb Devpt Ctee Legatum Inst 2014–; chm PRCA 2016–; advsr Iraq Britain Business Cncl 2014–; memb Devpt Ctee Swansea Univ 2015–; tstee Lincoln Coll Old Members 2010–, tstee Nat Botanic Garden of Wales 2015–; *Recreations* rugby, theatre, skiing, fly fishing, hill walking, squash, film, cigars; *Clubs* Garrick, Buck's, Vincent's (Oxford), Goblin (Oxford); *Style*— Steffan Williams, Esq; ✉ Porta Communications, Sky Light City Tower, 50 Basinghall Street, London EC2V 5DE (✆ 020 7680 6500)

WILLIAMS, Stephen; *b* 11 October 1966; *Educ* Mountain Ash Comp, Univ of Bristol; *Career* sometime tax conslt, formerly with PricewaterhouseCoopers and Grant Thornton; cnllr (Lib Dem): Avon CC 1993–96, Bristol City CC 1995–99 (ldr Lib Dem Gp 1995–97); MP (Lib Dem) Bristol W 2005–15 (Parly candidate (Lib Dem) Bristol W 2001); dir Watershed Arts Centre; memb: WWF, Amnesty Int, Nat Tst, Friends of the Earth; *Style*— Stephen Williams, Esq; ✉ House of Commons, London SW1A 0AA

WILLIAMS, Stephen Geoffrey (Steve); s of A E Williams, of Ilford, Essex; *b* 31 January 1948; *Educ* Brentwood Sch, KCL (LLB); *m* 1972, Susan Jennifer, da of Denis F Cottam; 1 s (Thomas b 8 August 1981); *Career* slr tax planning and commercial depts Slaughter & May 1972–75; ICI plc: slr legal dept 1975–84, asst co sec 1985–86; Unilever plc: jt sec, general counsel and chief legal offr 1986–2010; sr advsr Spencer Stuart and Associates 2011–; non-exec dir: Bunzl plc 1994–2004, Arriva plc 2005–10, Croda Int plc 2010–; sr ind dir Whitbread plc 2008–, dir Eversheds LLP 2011–, dep chm Moorfields NHS Tst 2012–; chair De La Warr Pavillion Tst 2008–, memb Bd Leverhulme Tst 2011–; memb: Law Soc, Company Law Ctee Law Soc, Companies Ctee CBI; FRSA; *Recreations* contemporary art, professional football, 20th century fiction, cinema, swimming; *Clubs* 2 Brydges Place, RAC, Banana Splitz; *Style*— Steve Williams, Esq

WILLIAMS, Suzanne (Suzi); da of Bryan Wynn Williams, of Liverpool, and Hilda Dorothy Williams; *b* 16 September 1971, Liverpool; *Educ* Wirral County GS for Girls, Univ of Bristol (BA); *Career* brand mgmnt Procter & Gamble 1990–97, head Global Mktg BBC 1997–99, strategy conslt KPMG 1999–2001, head of brand Orange 2001–2003/4, commercial devpt dir Capital Radio, gp mktg and brand dir BT 2006–2016; currently non-exec dir AA plc; tstee Help Musicians, non-exec dir The Patrons Lunch Events Ltd; Best Female Mktg Ldr Women In Mktg Awards 2012, Sponsorship Personality of the Year Hollis Awards 2012; fell Mktg Soc of GB; *Recreations* motorsport, music, travel, interior design; *Style*— Ms Suzi Williams; ✉ The AA plc, 90 Long Acre, London WC2E 9RA (Twitter @suziwilliamsldn)

WILLIAMS, Venetia Mary; da of John Williams, of Herefordshire, and Patricia, *née* Rose; *b* 10 May 1960, London; *Educ* Downe House Sch Newbury, Sch of St Clair Penzance; *Career* racehorse trainer 1995–; trained winners of: Grand National (Aintree), King George VI Chase (Kempton), Hennessy Gold Cup (Newbury), Welsh Grand Nat (Chepstow, twice), Scottish Champion Hurdle (Ayr), Ascot Chase, Cleeve Hurdle (Cheltenham, 3 times), Grand Annual Chase, Coral Cup, Pertemps Final Hurdle and Festival Plate Chase (3 times) (all Cheltenham Festival), Ormonde Stakes (Group 3, Chester, with first flat runner); *Style*— Miss Venetia Williams; ✉ Aramstone, Kings Caple, Hereford HR1 4TU (✆ 01432 840646, e-mail venetia.williams@virgin.net, website www.venetiawilliams.com)

WILLIAMS, Victoria Kirstyn (Kirsty); CBE (2013), AM; da of Edward G Williams, and Pamela, *née* Hall, of Llanelli, Carmarthenshire; *b* 19 March 1971; *Educ* St Michael's Sch Llanelli, Univ of Manchester and Univ of Missouri (BA); *m* 16 Sept 2000, Richard Rees; 3 da (Angharad b 25 Sept 2001, Carys b 21 May 2004, Rachel b 5 April 2006); *Career* former mktg and PR exec, former memb Nat Assembly Advsy Gp; memb Nat Assembly for Wales (Lib Dem) Brecon & Radnorshire 1999–; Nat Assembly for Wales: chair Health and Social Services Ctee 1999–2003, chair Standards Ctee 2003–; dep pres Lib Dem Wales 1997–99, Lib Dem business mangr and spokesperson on enterprise, transport and education until 2008, ldr Welsh Lib Dems 2008–16, shadow min for environment, sustainability and rural affrs 2010–11, shadow min for health and social care 2011–16, cabinet sec for educn 2016–; *Publications* Politics in 21st Century Wales; *Recreations* helping out on the family farm, spending time with family, shopping; *Style*— Ms Kirsty Williams, CBE, AM; ✉ National Assembly for Wales, Cardiff Bay, Cardiff CF99 1NA (✆ 0300 200 749, e-mail Kirsty.Williams@assembly.wales, website kirstywilliams.org.uk)

WILLIAMS OF BAGLAN, Baron (Life Peer UK 2010), of Neath Port Talbot in the County of Glamorgan; Dr Michael Charles Williams; s of Emlyn Glyndwr Williams (d 1991), of Baglan, Port Talbot, and Mildred May, *née* Morgan; *b* 11 June 1949, Bridgend, Glamorgan; *Educ* Sandfields Comp Sch Port Talbot, UCL (BSc), SOAS Univ of London (MSc, PhD); *m* 1, 25 May 1974 (m dis 1984), Margaret Rigby; 1 da (Rhiannon Esmee Helena b 29 July 1978); m 2, 30 Aug 1992, Isobelle Mary, da of John Jaques (d 1978); 1 s (Benedict Rhys b 5 May 1993); *Career* dir Human Rights UN Cambodia 1992–93, dir of info UN Protection Force (UNPROFOR) Zagreb 1994–5, sr fell IISS 1995–8, dir UN Office for Children and Armed Conflict NY 1999–2000, special advsr to the Foreign Sec 2000–05, dir ME and Asia UN NY 2005–06, UN special coordinator on Middle East 2006–07, UK special rep on Middle East and special projects 2007–08, UN under sec-gen and special coordinator for Lebanon 2008–11; conslt: UNHCR, Cncl of Euro, EC; sr fell 21st Century Tst; memb: IISS 1990, Cncl RIIA 2000, ICA, BBC World Service Tst 2005–08; int tstee BBC 2011–; govr SOAS, memb Cncl Univ of Swansea; distinguished visiting fell Royal Inst of Int Affrs 2011; Cdr Order of the Cedars Lebanon; *Publications* Communism, Religion and Revolt in Banten (1990), Vietnam at the Crossroads (1992), Civil-Military Relations and Peacekeeping (1998); *Recreations* reading (especially history), travel; *Clubs* Athenaeum; *Style*— The Lord Williams of Baglan; ✆ 020 7219 5353, e-mail williamsmc3@parliament.uk

WILLIAMS OF CROSBY, Baroness (Life Peer UK 1993), of Stevenage in the County of Hertfordshire; Prof Shirley Vivian Teresa Brittain Williams; PC (1974); da of Prof Sir George Catlin and the writer, Vera Brittain (Mrs Catlin); *b* 27 July 1930; *Educ* Somerville Coll Oxford, Columbia Univ; *m* 1, 1955 (m dis 1974), Prof Bernard Williams; 1 da (Hon Rebecca Clare); m 2, 1987, Prof Richard E Neustadt (decd); *Career* contested (Lab): Harwich 1954 and 1955, Southampton Test 1959; MP (Lab) Hitchin 1964–74, Hertford and Stevenage 1974–79; MP (SDP) Crosby 1981–83 (by-election, converted Cons majority of 19,272 to SDP one of 5,289); PPS to Min of Health 1964–66, Parly sec Miny of Lab 1966–67; Min of State: Educn and Sci 1967–69, Home Office 1969–70; oppn spokesman on: Social Serv 1970–71, Home Affrs 1971–73, Prices and Consumer Protection 1973–74; Sec of State Prices and Consumer Protection 1974–76, Sec of State Educn and Sci and Paymaster Gen 1976–79; Lib Dem ldr House of Lords 2001–04; cmmr Int Cmmn on Nuclear Non-proliferation and Disarmament 2008–10; chm Fabian Soc 1980 (gen sec 1960–64), memb Lab NEC 1970–81, pres SDP 1982–88 (co-fndr 1981); prof of elective politics Kennedy Sch of Govt Harvard Univ 1988–1996; pres Br-Russia Soc and East-West Centre 1996–2001, co-pres RIIA 2001–06; memb: Bd International Crisis Gp 1976–2005, Advsy Cncl to Sec-Gen UN Fourth World Women's Conference 1995, Comité des Sages Euro Cmmn 1995, Educn Devpt Center Newton MA 1992–2000, Bd Nuclear Threat Initiative 2001–; tstee Century Fndn (New York); memb: Int Advsy Ctee Cncl on Foreign Relations NY 1992–2006, Bd Rand Europe 1996–2002, Overseers Ctee JFK Sch of Govt Harvard Univ; dir Project Liberty 1990–97; chm of judges UK Teaching Awards 2007–11; visiting fell Nuffield Coll Oxford 1966–74; Godkin lectr Harvard Univ 1979, Janeway lectr Princeton Univ 1990, Regents lectr Univ of Calif Berkeley 1991, Darwin lectr Univ of Cambridge 1995, Strathclyde lectr 1995, Dainton lectr Br Library 1995, emeritus lectr Notre Dame Univ 2001; hon fell: Somerville Coll Oxford, Newnham Coll Cambridge; *Books* Politics is for People (1981), A Job to Live (1985), God and Caesar (2003), Climbing the Bookshelves (2009); *Television* Shirley Williams in Conversation (series, 1980), Women in the House (1997); *Radio* Snakes and Ladders (BBC Diary, 1996); *Recreations* hill walking, swimming, music; *Style*— The Rt Hon Baroness Williams of Crosby, PC; preferred style: Shirley Williams; ✉ House of Lords, London SW1A 0PW (✆ 020 7219 5850, fax 020 7219 1174)

WILLIAMS OF ELVEL, Baron (Life Peer UK 1985), of Llansantffraed in Elvel in the County of Powys; Rt Hon Charles Cuthbert Powell Williams; CBE (1980), PC (2013); s of Dr Norman Powell Williams, DD (d 1943), and Muriel de Lérisson (d 1979), da of Arthur Philip Cazenove; *b* 9 February 1933; *Educ* Westminster, ChCh Oxford (MA), LSE; *m* 1 March 1975, Jane Gillian, da of Maj Gervase Edward Portal (d 1960); *Career* British Petroleum Co Ltd 1958–64, Bank of London and Montreal 1964–66, Eurofinance SA Paris 1966–70, Baring Brothers & Co Ltd 1970–77 (md 1971–77), chm Price Cmmn 1977–79, md Henry Ansbacher & Co Ltd 1980–82, chief exec Henry Ansbacher Holdings plc, chm Henry Ansbacher & Co Ltd 1982–85, dir Mirror Group Newspapers plc 1985–92; *Clubs* Reform, MCC, Beefsteak; *Style*— The Rt Hon the Lord Williams of Elvel, CBE; ✉ House of Lords, London SW1A 0PW

WILLIAMS OF OYSTERMOUTH, Baron (Life Peer UK 2013), of Oystermouth in the City and County of Swansea; Rt Rev Rowan Douglas Williams; PC (2002); s of Aneurin Williams, and Dephine Williams; *b* 14 June 1950, Swansea; *Educ* Dynevor Sch Swansea, Christ's Coll Cambridge; *m* Jane; 2 c (Rhiannon, Pip); *Career* lectr in theology Coll of the Resurrection Mirfield 1975–77; ordained priest 1978; dean Clare Coll Cambridge and lectr in theology Univ of Cambridge 1984–86, Lady Margaret prof of divinity Univ of Oxford 1986–92, bishop of Monmouth 1992–2002, archbishop of Wales 1999–2002, archbishop of Canterbury 2002–12; Master Magdalene Coll Cambridge 2013–; chllr Univ of S Wales 2014–; FBA 1990, FRSL 2003; Royal Victorian Chain 2012; Order of Friendship Russion Fedn 2010; *Books* The Wound of Knowledge (1979), Resurrection (1982), The Truce of God (1983), Beginning Now: Peacemaking Theology (with Mark Collier, 1984), Arius, Heresy and Tradition (1987, 2 edn 2001), The Making of Orthodoxy (ed, 1989), Teresa of Avila (1991), Open to Judgement (sermons, 1994), Sergii Bulgakov: Towards a Russian Political Theology (1998), On Christian Theology (essays, 2000), Lost Icons: Reflections on Cultural Bereavement (2000), Christ on Trial (2000), Newman's Arians of the Fourth Century (ed, 2001), Love's Redeeming Work (ed, 2001), Poems of Rowan Williams (poetry, 2001), Ponder These Things (2002), Writing in the Dust (2002), Silence and Honey Cakes (2003), Dwelling of the Light (2003), Anglican Identities (2004), Grace and Necessity (2005), Why Study the Past? (2005), Tokens of Trust (2007), Wrestling with Angels (2007), Headwaters (poetry, 2008), Dostoevsky: Language, faith and fiction (2008), Crisis and Recovery (ed, 2010), A Silent Action (2011), The Lion's World (2012), The Edge of Words (2014), On Augustine (2016), The Tragic Imagination (2016); *Recreations* music, fiction; *Style*— The Rt Hon the Lord Williams of Oystermouth, PC; ✉ House of Lords, London SW1A 0PW

WILLIAMS-WYNNE, William Robert Charles; JP (Gwynedd 1974); s of late Col John Francis Williams-Wynne, CBE, DSO, JP (d 1998), and late Margaret Gwendolin, *née* Roper (d 1991); *b* 7 February 1947; *Educ* Packwood Haugh, Eton; *m* 18 Oct 1975 (m dis 2006), Hon Veronica Frances, da of Baron Buxton of Alsa, KCVO, MC, DL (Life Peer), *qv*, of Stiffkey, Norfolk; 3 da (Chloë b 14 Oct 1978, Leonora b 20 Oct 1980, Rose b 17 Feb 1983); *Career* Williams Wynne Farms 1969, Mount Pleasant Bakery 1983–99, Bronze Age 1998; JP 1974; chm: X Foxes Ltd 1992, Merioneth CLA 1996–99, Europa Club 1997–2004, Wales HHA 1999–2004, TASC 2002, Photonictherapy Ltd 2003; dir ACT Ltd 1997–2006; contested Gen Elections as Cons candidate for Montgomery 1974, RWAgS, Cncl RASE, chm WASEC, cmmr Nat Parks 1983–88, memb Prince of Wales Ctee 1983–88; FRICS 1972, ARAgS 2002, MICM 2006; *Recreations* flying; *Clubs* Pratts; *Style*— William Williams-Wynne, Esq; ✉ Williams Wynne, Tywyn, Gwynedd LL36 9UD (✆ 01654 710101/2, fax 01654 710103, e-mail www@wynne.co.uk)

WILLIAMSON, Sir (Robert) Brian; kt (2001), CBE; *b* 16 February 1945; *Educ* Truro Sch, Trinity Coll Dublin (MA); *m* June 1986, Diane Marie Christine de Jacquier de Rosée; *Career* PA to Rt Hon Maurice Macmillan MP (later Viscount Macmillan) 1967–71, ed Int Currency Review 1971; Gerrard Group: md Gerrard & National Holdings plc 1978–89, chm GNI Ltd 1985–89, chm Gerrard Group plc (formerly Gerrard & National Holdings plc) 1989–98; chm LIFFE 1998–2003 (dir 1981–88, non-exec chm 1985–88); memb British Invisible Exports Cncl 1985–88 (memb European Ctee 1988–90), memb Bd SIB (now FSA) 1986–98, memb Ct Bank of Ireland 1990–98 (dir Bank of Ireland British Holdings 1986–90); dir: Fleming Int High Income Investment Tst plc 1990–98, NASDAQ Int Bd 1993–98, MT Unit Tst Managers Ltd 1996–2000, HM Publishers Holdings Ltd 1996–99, Barlows plc 1997–98, Politeia 1999–, MLoop plc 2002, HSBC Holdings plc 2002–, Templeton Emerging Markets Investment Fund 2002–03, Resolution plc 2005–08 (chm 2004–05), Liv-Ex Ltd 2005–, Open Europe Ltd (formerly Vote No) 2005–08, NYSE Euronext 2007–13, Climate Exchange plc 2007–10, Waverton Investment Mgmnt (formerly J O Hambro Investment Mgmnt Ltd) 2010–15, Aggregated Micropower (AMP) Holdings plc 2012–, Edenbero-Tst Corporation Ltd 2012–; chm: Fleming Worldwide Investment Tst 1998 (dep chm 1996–98), Electra Private Equity plc (formerly Electra

Investment Tst) 2000–10 (dir 1994–2010), MT Fund Mgmnt Ltd 2000–; sr advsr Fleming Family and Ptnrs 2003–09; govr at large Nat Assoc of Securities Dealers (USA) 1995–98 (chm Int Markets Advsy Bd 1996–98), memb Governing Cncl Centre for Study of Financial Innovation 2000–, memb Supervisory Bd Euronext NV 2002–07; chm: Armed Forces Advsy Co 2002–09, Advsy Bd Armed Forces Common Investment Fund 2002–09; dir River and Rowing Museum Henley 1992–94; dir St George's House Tst (Windsor Castle) 1998– (memb Cncl 1996–2002), tstee St Paul's Cathedral Fndn 1999–2006, memb Cncl St George's Chapel Windsor Castle 2002–, memb ROH Devpt Ctee 2004–09, pres St Moritz Tobogganing Club 2009–14, tstee Winston Churchill Meml Tst 2009–, memb ROH Fndn Advsy Cncl 2009–, memb City of London Lord Maryor's Appraisal Panel 2009–, tstee Fallon Family Bd 2012–; Parly candidate (Cons): Sheffield Hillsborough 1974, Truro 1976–77; cmmnd HAC 1975; HM Lt City of London 2003; Freeman City of London 1994; FRSA 1991; *Clubs* Pratt's, White's, Flyfishers', Kildare Univ (Dublin), The Brook (NY); *Style—* Sir Brian Williamson, CBE

WILLIAMSON, Prof Edwin Henry; s of Henry Williamson (d 1977), and Renée, *née* Clarembaux; *b* 2 October 1949; *Educ* Univ of Edinburgh (MA, PhD); *m* 5 March 1976, Susan Jane, *née* Fitchie; 2 da (Louise b 2 Sept 1982, Phoebe b 28 Sept 1985); *Career* jr lectr in Spanish TCD 1974–77, lectr in Spanish Birkbeck Coll Univ of London 1977–90, Forbes prof of Hispanic studies Univ of Edinburgh 1990–2003, King Alfonso XIII prof of Spanish studies Univ of Oxford and fell Exeter Coll Oxford 2003–; visiting prof: Univ of São Paulo 1997, Stanford Univ 1999; Brettschneider visiting scholar Cornell Univ 2006; memb Assoc of Hispanists of GB and I 1974; Cdr Order of Isabel La Católica (Spain); The Half-Way House of Fiction: Don Quixote and Arthurian Romance (1984, 2 edn 1986), El Quijote y los Libros de Caballerías (1991), The Penguin History of Latin America (1992), Borges: A Life (2004); *Recreations* theatre, cinema, art, hillwalking; *Style—* Prof Edwin Williamson; ✉ Exeter College, Oxford OX1 3DP (☎ 01865 270476, e-mail edwin.williamson@exeter.ox.ac.uk)

WILLIAMSON, Rt Hon Gavin Alexander; CBE (2016), MP; *b* 25 June 1976; *Educ* Raincliffe Sch Scarborough, Scarborough Sixth Form Coll, Univ of Bradford (BSc); *m* Joanne; 2 da (Annabel, Grace); *Career* MP (Cons) Staffs S 2010–, PPS to Rt Hon Hugo Swire, MP, *qv*, 2011–12, PPS to Rt Hon Patrick Mcloughlin, MP, *qv* 2012–13, PPS to Rt Hon David Cameron, MP, Prime Minister, *qv* until 2016, Parly sec to the Treasy and chief whip 2016–; *Style—* The Rt Hon Gavin Williamson, CBE, MP; ✉ House of Commons, London SW1A 0AA

WILLIAMSON, Hazel Eleanor; QC; *see:* Marshall, Hazel Eleanor (Her Hon Judge Marshall)

WILLIAMSON, John Peter; s of John William Stephen Williamson (d 1979), of Camberwell, London, and Ellen Gladys, *née* Naulls (d 2002); *b* 19 January 1943, Amersham, Bucks; *Educ* Addey and Stanhope GS, Hackney Tech Coll, Thames Poly and many courses for professional qualifications; *m* 17 Oct 1964, Dorothy Shirley Esther, da of Leonard Frederick Farmer, of Blackheath, London; 2 s (Earl John Grant b 1975, Craig Stephen b 1980); *Career* engr mangr Production Dept Rolex Watch Co 1960–63 (fndr Rolex Sports Club, fndr Rolex Rocketry Soc); jt md and fin controller Dynamic Reading Inst 1968–69, int instr in speed reading, memory, mind maps (original concept creator 1958) and mind training techniques (unofficial world speed reading record holder 1967–68), fndr chm BIM Younger Mangr Assoc 1969–70, gp fin controller, co sec and asst md Hunter-Print Gp plc 1971–74, asst to company controller ITT/STC 1975 (responsibility for 26 Divs); corp planner; UK chm: Investigations, Operational Reviews and Computer Audits (mangr 1976–80), ITT Bd (USA); conslt: C E Heath & Co insurance brokers, Liberty Life, Trident Life, Sun Life Unit Services, Coll of Taxation; princ: Williamson Scrap & Waste Dealers 1951–56, Williamson Light Vehicle Manufacturers 1951–56, The Fun Weaponry Co (mfrs) 1953–59, Williamson's Professional Private Tuition Training 1968–74, Williamson Business Consultancy and Turnaround Specialists 1968–74, Williamson & Co Chartered Accountants 1973–2003, J P Williamson and Co Chartered Accountants 1981–86; partner Williamson of Peckham (watchmakers and jewellers) 1954–64, partner Williamson Property Mgmnt 1963–68, UK dir Odin Security & Surveillance 1963–2003; md: Prestige MicroSystems 1976–2002, Guardian Financial Services (Guardian Ind plc) 1983–2004; princ and md: Guardian Ind Property Services 1983–93, Guardian Ind Wills & Trusts 1994–2000, Guardian Ind Executors 1994–2000, Guardian Ind Publishing Corp 1995–99, Guardian Ind Gp Int 1995–2000, Guardian Ind General Insurance Services 1995–2003, Guardian Ind Finance Corp 1995–2003, Guardian Ind Business Transfer Services 1996–2001, Guardian Ind Eagles 1996–2002, Guardian Ind Network Mktg 1996–2002, Guardian Ind Corp Services 1996–2002, Audits Inc 1996–2002, Guardian Ind Debt and Arbitration Services 1996–2003, GIANTS Corp 1996–2003, The Operational Audit Corp 1997–2000, Guardian Ind Taxation Solutions 1997–2001, Guardian Ind Strategic Planners 1997–2002, GIMAPS 1997–2002, Guardian Ind Health and Wealth 1999–2001, Guardian Ind Communications Corp 1999–2001, Local Business Magnets 2012–, Reputation Vigilante 2012–, Gnu Local Directories 2012–; pres Retail Display Secrets Ltd 2008–, md and fndr Super Guerilla Ltd 2015–; conslt and coach: The Wealth Coach 1983–, The Wealth Coach Ltd 2003–, WOW! Windows, Display & Design 2004–; team ldr: The Product Factory 2005, Traffic Sch (online) 2007, co-leader Guerrilla Marketing Coach Certification Prog 2006–07; licensed credit broker; fndr chm SE London Micro-Computer Club (SELMIC) and conslt to several local and nat computer clubs 1975–80, co fndr Assoc of London Hobby Computer Clubs 1980; chm SE London Area Soc of Chartered Accountants 1992–93; memb: ICA SIB Vetting Panel, Main Ctee, Ethics and Regulation Review Panel and London Business Bd London Soc of Chartered Accountants, Regional Ctee Life Insurance Assoc 1993–94, Million Dollar Round Table (top 2 per cent of fin advsrs in world), LIA Achievement Forum Inner Circle (top 39 fin advsrs in UK), Nat Assoc of Commercial Fin Brokers; assoc memb Corp of Fin Brokers; fndr memb I Fin Planning 1987; United Cultural Convention Peace Prize 2008; only British copywriter to be honoured by admission to American Writers and Artists Inst Wall of Fame 2009; Freeman City of London 1986; memb: Inst of Internal Auditors (examiner 1978), PIA, FIMBRA, Life Insurance Assoc; FSA, FCA, CInstSMM, MCIM, FInstD, MIMgt, MIIM, MLIA (Dip), ALIMA (Dip), ACFB; *Books* author: ITT/STC EDP Audit Manual, Marketing Wealth Secrets Course (2008), The Hunter Print Value-added Tax Manual; creator of the 'Warpspeed Learning Systems', fndr of the 'Juji-Kiri Success Achievement System', author and fndr of The Wealth Coach systems and publications; creator: 'Rainmaker Masterclass', Super Guerilla Programmes, Super Guerilla Mastermind Gps; co-author: Guerilla Marketing On the Front Lines (2008), Retail Display Secrets Program (2008), Retail Display Secrets Introductory Course (2008), Immortal Business Mentors Program (2009), The College of Taxation Course Manuals for Income Tax, Corporation Tax, Capital Gains Tax, Inheritance Tax and Estate Planning, Build Your Own Millionaire Professional Practice (programme, 2015); novels: The Eggcentrics 1 – Death and Treasure (2014), The Eggcentrics 2 – Die Spy Die (2015); *Recreations* computers, reading, shooting, martial arts, grand master of 'The Knowledge' (onibujindo, onibujitsu), applied psychology, success achievement methodologies, wealth coaching, business development, writing, copywriting, internet marketing; *Style—* J P Williamson, Esq; ✉ c/o PO Box 56, Eltham, London SE9 1PA (☎ 020 8850 4195, e-mail john@thewealthcoach.com or jpwilliamson@freeuk.com, website www.thewealthcoach.com, www.johnwilliamson.today, www.wordsorcery.com)

WILLIAMSON, Sir (George) Malcolm; kt (2007); s of George Williamson (d 1969), and Margery Williamson; *b* 27 February 1939; *Educ* Bolton Sch; *m* Hang Thi Ngo; 1 s, 1 da; 1s and 1 da by previous marriage; *Career* Barclays Bank plc: various roles 1957–85, regnl gen mangr 1983–85; memb PO Bd and md Girobank plc 1985–89; Standard Chartered plc: gp exec dir 1989–91, md 1991–93, gp chief exec 1993–98; pres and ceo Visa International 1998–2004; chm: CDC Gp plc 2004–09, Nat Australia Gp Europe Ltd 2004–12, Clydesdale Bank plc 2004–12, Signet Jewellers 2005–12, Friends Life Gp 2009–, NewDay Gp Ltd 2010–; non-exec memb Gp Bd Nat Bank of Australia; dep chm/chm Britannic Gp plc, dep chm/chm Resolution plc 2002–08; non-exec dir: National Grid Gp plc 1995–99, G4S plc 2004–08, Nat Bank of Australia 2004–12, JPMorgan Cazenove Holdings 2005–10; chm: Prince's Youth Business Int (formerly Youth Business Int Advsy Bd) 2005–, Cass Business Sch Strategy & Devpt Bd 2008–; memb Bd of Tstees Int Business Leaders Forum 2006–10, chm Governing Cncl CSFI 2012–; FCIB, CIMgt; *Recreations* mountaineering, running, chess, walking, cycling; *Clubs* Rucksack, Manchester Pedestrian; *Style—* Sir Malcolm Williamson

WILLIAMSON, Mark David; *b* 29 December 1957, Aberdeen; *Educ* Milnerton HS Cape Town, Univ of Cape Town; *m* Fiona; 2 da (Amy, Emily); *Career* articled clerk rising to audit sr KPMG Aiken & Peat Cape Town 1977–84, audit sr rising to audit mangr KPMG Peat Marwick SE Region 1984–94, gp chief accountant then gp financial controller Simon Gp plc 1994–2000, chief financial offr Int Power plc 2003– (gp financial controller 2000–03); non-exec dir Imperial Tobacco; memb Inst of CA SA; *Recreations* tennis, walking, travel, good food; *Style—* Mark Williamson, Esq; ✉ International Power plc, Senator House, 85 Queen Victoria Street, London EC4V 4DP (☎ 020 7320 8631, fax 020 7320 8650, e-mail mark.williamson@iprplc-gdfsvez.com, website www.iprplc-gdfsvez.com)

WILLIAMSON, Prof Mark Herbert; OBE (1994); s of Herbert Stansfield Williamson (d 1955), and Winifred Lilian, *née* Kenyon (d 1990); *b* 8 June 1928; *Educ* Groton Sch Mass USA, Rugby, ChCh Oxford (DPhil); *m* 5 April 1958, Charlotte Clara Dallas, OBE (1997), da of Hugh Macdonald (d 1958); 1 s (Hugh b 1961), 2 da (Emma b 1963, Sophia b 1965); *Career* demonstrator in zoology Univ of Oxford 1952–58, with Scottish Marine Biological Assoc Edinburgh 1958–62, lectr in zoology Univ of Edinburgh 1962–65, prof (fndr and head of Dept) Dept of Biology Univ of York 1965–; FIBiol 1966; *Books* Analysis of Biological Populations (1972), Ecological Stability (1974), Island Populations (1981), Quantitative Aspects of Biological Invasions (1987), Biological Invasions (1996); *Recreations* natural history, walking; *Style—* Prof Mark Williamson; ✉ Midgley House, Spring Lane, Heslington, York YO10 5DX; Department of Biology, University of York, York YO10 5DD (☎ 01904 328737, fax 01904 328505, e-mail mw1@york.ac.uk)

WILLIAMSON, Matthew; *b* 23 October 1971, Manchester; *Educ* Central St Martin's Coll of Art; *Career* fashion designer; accessories designer Monsoon 1994–96; Matthew Williamson (own fashion house): founded 1997, reg exhibitor at fashion shows worldwide, launched lifestyle range 2002, flagship London store opened 2004, launched MW Matthew Williamson 2011; Moët and Chandon Fashion Tribute London Fashion Week 2005, Red Carpet Designer of the Year Br Fashion Award 2008; *Style—* Mr Matthew Williamson; ✉ Matthew Williamson Ltd, 46 Hertford Street, London W1J 7DP (☎ 020 7491 6220, e-mail matthew@matthewwilliamson.co.uk, website www.matthewwilliamson.com)

WILLIAMSON, Nigel; s of Neville Albert Williamson, decd, and Ann Maureen Kitson; *b* 4 July 1954; *Educ* Chislehurst and Sidcup GS, UCL; *m* 1976, Dr Magali Patricia; 2 s (Adam b 1977, Piers b 1978); *Career* ed: Tribune 1984–87, Labour Party News 1987–89, New Socialist 1987–89; The Times: political corr and columnist 1989–90, diary ed 1990–92, home news ed 1992–95, Whitehall corr 1995–96; contrib ed: Uncut, Songlines; freelance music writer for other pubns incl The Times and The Guardian 1996–; *Books* The SDP (1982), The New Right (1984), The Rough Guide to World Music (1999, contrib), Journey Through the Past: The Stories Behind the Songs of Neil Young (2002), The Uncut Collector's Guide to Bob Dylan (ed, 2003), The Rough Guide to Bob Dylan (2004), Rough Guide to the Blues (2006), Rough Guide to Led Zeppelin (2007), Rough Guide to the Best Music You've Never Heard (2008), Straight Ahead Guide to Led Zeppelin (2014), Straight Ahead Guide to Bob Dylan (2014); *Recreations* cricket, music, gardening, modern fiction; *Style—* Nigel Williamson, Esq; ✉ Long Tilings, Hever Lane, Hever, Kent TN8 7ET (☎ 01959 571127, e-mail nigelwilliamson@compuserve.com)

WILLIAMSON, Dr Paul; OBE (2016); s of Peter Williamson (d 2003), of London, and Mary Teresa, *née* Meagher (d 2005); *b* 4 August 1954; *Educ* Wimbledon Coll, UEA (BA, MPhil, LittD); *m* 11 Aug 1984, Emmeline Mary Clare, da of James Mandley (d 1983); 1 s (Joseph James b 29 Nov 1999); *Career* V&A: asst keeper Dept of Sculpture 1979–89, acting keeper Dept of Sculpture 1989, chief curator Sculpture Collection 1989–2001, sr curator 1995–98, keeper of sculpture, metalwork, ceramics and glass 2001–16, dir of collections 2004–07, emeritus keeper and hon sr research fell 2016–; memb: Wells Cathedral West Front Specialist Ctee 1981–83, Wall Paintings Sub-Ctee Cncl for the Care of Churches 1987–90, Ctee Br Acad Corpus of Romanesque Sculpture in Br and Ireland 1990–97, Lincoln Cathedral Fabric Cncl 1990–2001, Bd of Tstees Stained Glass Museum Ely 2005–09; memb Exhbn Organising Ctee: English Romanesque Art 1984, Age of Chivalry 1987, Gothic: Art for England 2003; expert advsr on sculpture Reviewing Ctee on the Export of Works of Art 1989–2016, foreign advsr to Int Center of Medieval Art 1991–94; memb Consultative Ctee: The Sculpture Jl 1997–, The Burlington Magazine 2003–; Lansdowne visiting prof Univ of Victoria BC 2001, Diskant lectr Philadelphia Museum of Art 2001; Guild Burgess of Preston 1972; FSA 1983 (memb Cncl 1997–2003, vice-pres 1999–2003), FRHistS 2011; *Books* An Introduction to Medieval Ivory Carvings (1982), Catalogue of Romanesque Sculpture in the Victoria and Albert Museum (1983), The Medieval Treasury: The Art of the Middle Ages in the Victoria and Albert Museum (ed, 1986, 3 edn 1998), The Thyssen-Bornemisza Collection: Medieval sculpture and works of art (1987), Northern Gothic Sculpture 1200–1450 (1988), Early Medieval Wall Painting and Painted Sculpture in England (ed with S Cather and D Park, 1990), Gothic Sculpture 1140–1300 (1995), European Sculpture at the Victoria and Albert Museum (ed, 1996), Netherlandish Sculpture 1450–1550 (2002), Wonder: Painted Sculpture from Medieval England (ed with S Boldrick and D Park, 2002), Medieval and Renaissance Stained Glass in the Victoria and Albert Museum (2003), Gothic: Art for England 1400–1547 (ed with R Marks, 2003), Medieval and Renaissance Treasures from the V&A (ed, 2007), Medieval Ivory Carvings: Early Christian to Romanesque (2010), Object of Devotion: Medieval Alabaster Sculpture from the Victoria and Albert Museum (ed, 2010), Medieval Ivory Carvings 1200–1550 (with G Davies, 2014); author of numerous articles and book reviews in The Burlington Magazine and others; *Recreations* wine, travel; *Style—* Dr Paul Williamson, OBE, FSA; ✉ e-mail pwilliamson302@gmail.com

WILLIAMSON, Philip Nigel; s of Leonard James Williamson, and Doris, *née* Chapell; *b* 23 September 1948; *Educ* Mill Hill Sch, Univ of Newcastle upon Tyne (BA, BArch); *m* 27 May 1983, Victoria Lois, da of Joseph Samuel Brown, of Clwyd, N Wales; 2 s (Nicholas James b 1984, Christopher Patrick b 1988); *Career* architect; chm and md: PNW Design Ltd (architects and interior designers) 1985–, PNW Properties Ltd 1985–; RIBA; *Recreations* sailing, music, winter sports; *Clubs* Royal Lymington Yacht; *Style—* Philip Williamson, Esq; ✉ Lower Pennington Farmhouse, Lower Pennington Lane, Lymington, Hampshire SO41 8AL (☎ 01590 672699)

WILLIAMSON, Phillippa; *Career* ceo Serious Fraud Office; *Style—* Mrs Phillippa Williamson; ✉ Serious Fraud Office, Elm House, 10–16 Elm Street, London WC1X 0BJ

WILLIAMSON, Raymond MacLeod; s of James Carstair Williamson (d 1974), and Marion, *née* Campbell (d 1998); *b* 24 December 1942, Glasgow; *Educ* HS of Glasgow, Univ of Glasgow (MA, LLB); *m* 4 April 1977, Brenda, da of Frederick Hamilton; 1 da (Dr Rachel MacLeod Williamson b 27 April 1979), 1 s (Donald Kerr Williamson b 19 Sept 1981); *Career* admitted slr 1968; MacRoberts: apprentice slr 1966–68, slr 1968–71, ptnr 1971–2006, sr ptnr 2000–06; pt/t employment judge 2003–15; memb Ctee European Employment Lawyers Assoc 1998–2007; ret; memb Law Soc of Scotland (memb Cncl 1990–96, convenor Employment Law Ctee 1990–2006); dean Royal Faculty of Procurators in Glasgow 2001–04; hon pres Scottish Int Piano Competition, hon pres Nat Youth Choir of Scotland, chm Westbourne Music, former chm Royal Scottish Nat Orch, former vice-chm RSAMD; govr HS of Glasgow 1987–2015; Lord Provost of the City of Glasgow Award for Culture 2010; Freeman City of Glasgow, memb Incorporation of Gardiners, memb Merchants House of Glasgow, Lord Dean Guild of the City of Glasgow 2013–15; FRSAMD; *Recreations* music; *Clubs* Glasgow Art, Western (Glasgow); *Style—* Raymond M Williamson, Esq; ✉ 11 Islay Drive, Newton Mearns, Glasgow G77 6UD (☎ 0141 639 4133, e-mail rwilliamson1942@gmail.com)

WILLIAMSON, Prof Robin Charles Noel; s of James Charles Frederick Lloyd Williamson (d 1970), of Hove, E Sussex, and Helena Frances, *née* Madden (d 1984); *b* 19 December 1942; *Educ* Rugby, Univ of Cambridge and Bart's Med Sch (BA, BChir, MA, MB MChir, MD); *m* 21 Oct 1967, Judith Marjorie, da of Douglas John Bull (d 1982), of London; 3 s (Richard b 1968, Edward b 1970, James b 1977); *Career* house surgn Bart's 1968, surgical registrar Royal Berks Hosp Reading 1971–73, sr surgical registrar Bristol Royal Infirmary 1973–75, clinical and res fell surgery Mass Gen Hosp and Harvard Med Sch 1975–76; Univ of Bristol: lectr in surgery 1977, conslt sr lectr in surgery 1977–79, prof of surgery 1979–87; prof of surgery and conslt surgeon Hammersmith Hosp and Imperial Coll Sch of Med at Hammersmith Hosp (Royal Postgraduate Sch of Med until merger 1997) 1987–2009 (dir of surgery 1987–95, deanery tutor in surgery 2008–12, dir Fndn Training Prog Imperial Coll Healthcare NHS Tst 2009–12), anatomy demonstrator Imperial Coll (Charing Cross) 2009–; chair London Clinic 2012– (memb Bd of Tstees 2010–), memb Jt Advsy Bd Weill Cornell Med Qatar 2014–; RSM: assoc dean 2001–02, dean 2002–06, emeritus dean 2006–08, pres 2008–10, chm Retired Fells Soc 2013–; visiting prof of surgery: Perth 1983, South Africa 1985, Boston 1985, Lund 1985, Melbourne 1986, Hong Kong 1987, San Francisco 1989, Brisbane 1989, Singapore 1994, Hamburg 1999; sec gen World Assoc of Hepatopancreatobiliary Surgery 1990–94 (treas 1986–90); pres: Pancreatic Soc of GB and I 1984–85, Int Hepatopancreatobiliary Assoc 1996–98 (sec-gen 1994–96), Assoc of Upper Gastrointestinal Surgns 1996–98, Assoc of Surgns of GB and I 1998–99 (chm Scientific Ctee 1994–97), European Soc of Surgery 1998, James IV Assoc Surgery 2002–05; co-sec Br Jl of Surgery Soc 1983–91, sr ed Br Jl of Surgery 1991–96, ed HPB 1999–2003, ed in chief HPB Surgery 2006–11; Hallett prize RCS 1970, Arris and Gale lectr RCS 1977–78, Moynihan fell Assoc of Surgns of GB and I 1979, Hunterian prof RCS 1981–82, Res Medal Br Soc of Gastroenterology 1982, Finlayson lectr RCS Glasgow 1985, Sir Gordon Bell lectr RACS (NZ) 1988, Bengt Ihre Medal Swedish Soc of Gastroenterology 1998, Wilson Wang lectr Prince of Wales Hosp Hong Kong 2000, Simpson-Smith lectr Charing Cross Hosp 2001, Stuart lectr RSM and RCS(Ed) 2007, Farndon Memorial lectr Soc of Academic and Research Surgery, Stevens lectr RSM 2011, Hunterian Soc lectr 2011, lectr Medical Soc of London 2013; Hon DScMed Mahidol Univ Thailand 1994; hon fell Royal Coll of Surgns of Thailand 1992; FRCS 1972, FRCS(Ed) ad hominem 2009; *Books* Colonic Carcinogenesis (jtly, 1982), General Surgical Operations (jtly, 1987), Emergency Abdominal Surgery (jtly, 1990), Surgical Management (jtly, 1991), Gastrointestinal Emergencies (jtly, 1991), Scott: An Aid to Clinical Surgery (jtly, 5 edn 1994, 6 edn 1998), Upper Digestive Surgery: Oesophagus, Stomach and Small Intenstine (jtly, 1999), Surgery (jtly, 2001), Surgery: Core Principles and Practice (jtly, 2016); *Recreations* travel, lighthouses, military uniforms and history; *Clubs* Oxford and Cambridge; *Style—* Prof Robin Williamson; ✉ The Barn, 88 Lower Road, Gerrards Cross, Buckinghamshire SL9 8LB (☎ 01753 889816, e-mail robin.williamson@btinternet.com); Department of Surgery, Imperial College School of Medicine, Hammersmith Hospital, Du Cane Road, London W12 0NN (e-mail r.williamson@imperial.ac.uk)

WILLIAMSON, Prof Stephen; s of Donald Williamson (d 1986), and Patricia Kathleen Mary, *née* Leyland (d 1997); *b* 15 December 1948; *Educ* Burnage GS Manchester, Imperial Coll of Science and Technol London (scholar, BSc, PhD, DSc, Sylvanus P Thompson prize); *m* 19 Dec 1970, Zita, da of Philip Mellor (d 1975); 1 s (Samuel Thurston b 1975), 2 da (Rebecca Anne b 1977, Lucy Frances b 1981); *Career* lectr in engrg Univ of Aberdeen 1973–81, reader in engrg Imperial Coll London 1985–89 (sr lectr 1981–85), prof of engrg Univ of Cambridge 1989–97, fell St John's Coll Cambridge 1990–97, tech dir Brook Hansen 1997–2000, prof of electrical engrg UMIST (now Univ of Manchester) 2000– (head of dept 2002–); FIEE 1988, FCGI 1990, FIEEE 1995, FREng 1995; *Recreations* gardening, reading; *Style—* Prof Stephen Williamson, FREng; ✉ School of Electrical and Electronic Engineering, University of Manchester, PO Box 88, Manchester M60 1QD (☎ 0161 200 4683, fax 01484 429726, e-mail steve.williamson@manchester.ac.uk)

WILLIAMSON, Prof Timothy; s of Colin Fletcher Williamson (d 1983), and Karina, *née* Side (now Mrs Angus McIntosh); *b* 6 August 1955, Uppsala, Sweden; *Educ* Leighton Park Sch Reading, Henley GS, Balliol Coll Oxford (Henry Wilde Prize, BA), ChCh Oxford (sr scholar, MA, DPhil); *m* 1, 24 March 1984 (m dis 2003), Elisabetta, da of Silvio Perosino; 1 da (Alice b 14 June 1993), 1 s (Conrad b 9 Sept 1996); m 2, 14 Feb 2004, Ana, da of Milan Mladenovi?; 1 s (Arno Nathan b 14 Jan 2005); *Career* lectr in philosophy Trinity Coll Dublin (MA ad eundem gradum) 1980–88, CUF lectr in philosophy Univ of Oxford and fell and praelector in philosophy UC Oxford 1988–94, prof of logic and metaphysics Univ of Edinburgh 1995–2000, Wykeham prof of logic Univ of Oxford 2000–, fell New Coll Oxford 2000–; visiting fell Dept of Philosophy Australian Nat Univ 1990 and 1995; visiting prof: Dept of Linguistics and Philosophy MIT 1994, Dept of Philosophy Princeton Univ 1998–99; Erskine visiting fell Dept of Philosophy and Religious Studies Univ of Canterbury NZ 1995, Nelson distinguished prof Univ of Michigan 2003, Townsend visitor Univ of California Berkeley 2006, Tang Chun-I visiting prof Chinese Univ of Hong Kong 2007, Nelson visiting prof Univ of Michigan 2013; Gaos chair Universidad Nacional Autónoma de México 2006; pres Mind Assoc 2006–07, vice-pres Br Logic Colloquium 2007–; Leverhulme major research fell 2009–12; memb: Aristotelian Soc 1986 (pres 2004–05), American Philosophical Assoc 1998; foreign memb Norwegian Acad of Science and Letters 2004, foreign hon memb American Acad of Arts and Sciences 2007; FRSE 1997, FBA 1997; *Books* Identity and Discrimination (1990, 2 edn 2013), Vagueness (1994), Knowledge and its Limits (2000), The Philosophy of Philosophy (2007), Williamson on Knowledge (contrib, 2009), Modal Logic as Metaphysics (2013); *Recreations* conventional behaviour; *Style—* Prof Timothy Williamson, FRSE, FBA; ✉ New College, Oxford OX1 3BN (☎ 01865 279555, fax 01865 279590, e-mail timothy.williamson@philosophy.ox.ac.uk)

WILLIS, Antony Martin Derek; s of late Thomas Martin Willis, and Dawn Marie, *née* Christensen; *b* 29 November 1941, Marton, New Zealand; *Educ* Wanganui Collegiate Sch Wanganui NZ, Victoria Univ Wellington NZ (LLB); *m* 1, 10 Feb 1962 (m dis), Diane Elizabeth, da of late Frederick Willis Gorton (d 1987); 3 da (Kirsty Elizabeth b 13 April 1963, Sara Jane b 7 June 1966, Nicola Mary b 6 Nov 1968); m 2, 12 April 1975, Diana Alice Cockburn, da of Robert Dermot McMahon Williams, of Redhill, Surrey; 1 s (Matthew William Dermot b 22 Aug 1988), 2 da (Charlotte Emily Christensen b 5 Jan 1978, Joanna Catherine Dalrymple b 7 Dec 1981); *Career* slr, later barr and mediator; Perry Wylie Pope & Page NZ 1967–70, Coward Chance London 1970–87 (managing ptnr 1987); Clifford Chance (merged firm of Coward Chance with Clifford Turner): jt managing ptnr 1987–88, sr litigation ptnr 1989–96; ind mediator 1998–; called to the Bar Middle Temple 2004, practising barr and mediator 2004–; fndr chm Slrs' Pro Bono Gp (now LawWorks) 1997–2001; Distinguished Fellow Int Acad of Mediators (US); memb: American Arbitration Assoc, NZ Law Soc; accredited mediator Centre for Dispute Resolution; former chm PIM Sr Mediators; memb CPR Inst for Dispute Resolution NY; chm Cncl Wycombe Abbey Sch 1999–2009; Freeman City of London 1975, Liveryman Worshipful Co of Slrs; FCIArb; *Recreations* motorcars, music, family; *Clubs* Reform, Wellington; *Style—* Antony Willis, Esq; ✉ Flat 16, 60–61 Cheyne Walk, London SW3 5LX; Brick Court Chambers, 7–8 Essex Street, London WC2R 3LD (☎ 020 7520 9975, mobile 07885 886662, fax 020 7379 3558, e-mail tony.willis@brickcourt.co.uk)

WILLIS, John Edward; s of Baron Willis (Life Peer; d 1992), and Audrey Mary, *née* Hale; does not use courtesy style of Hon; *Educ* Eltham Coll, Fitzwilliam Coll Cambridge (MA), Univ of Bristol (Postgrad Cert in Radio, Film and TV); *m* 1972, Janet, da of Kenneth Sperrin; 1 s (Thomas b 1975), 1 da (Beth b 1978); *Career* researcher ATV Network Ltd 1969–70; Yorkshire Television: researcher 1970–74, prodr/dir 1975–82, controller of documentaries and current affrs and ed First Tuesday 1983–88; Channel Four Television: controller of factual progs 1988–89, dep dir of progs 1990–92, dir of progs 1993–97; md United Film & Television Productions (UFTP) 1997–2001, md LWT 2001–02, vice-pres Nat Programmes WGBH Boston 2002–03, dir BBC Factual and Learning 2003–06 (memb BBC Creative Bd 2004–06), chief exec and creative dir Tinopolis 2006–; memb Bd Channel 5 1997–2001; external ombudsman The Guardian 2006–; visiting prof Univ of Bristol 1998–; tstee: Future Lab 2007–, Disasters and Emergency Ctee 2008–; chm BAFTA (tstee 2007–), FRTS 1993; *Awards* incl: BAFTA Best Documentary, Prix Jeunesse and RTS Outstanding Achievement as a Dir Awards for Johnny Go Home 1976, Int Emmy, RTS Best Investigative Journalism and Matthew Trust Award for The Secret Hospital 1979, Prix Futura and Broadcasting Critics' Prize for Alice: A Fight for Life 1983, Special Jury Award San Francisco for The Chinese Geordie 1983, 12 int environmental awards for Windscale: The Nuclear Laundry (co-dir) 1983, John Grierson Best Documentary Award for From the Cradle to the Grave 1987, RTS Silver Medal 1988, Cyril Bennett Award for Creative Contrib to TV RTS 2001; *Books* Johnny Go Home (1975), Churchill's Few (1983); *Style—* John Willis, Esq

WILLIS, Prof John Raymond; s of John Vindon George Willis, of Bicester, Oxon, and Loveday Gwendoline, *née* Parkin; *b* 27 March 1940; *Educ* Southall GS, Imperial Coll London (BSc, ARCS, PhD, DIC), Univ of Cambridge (MA); *m* 3 Oct 1964, Juliette Louise, da of Horace Albert Edward Ireland (d 1979); 3 da (Estelle b 1966, Lucy b 1967, Charlotte b 1969); *Career* asst lectr Imperial Coll London 1962–64, res assoc Courant Inst NY 1964–65, asst dir of res Univ of Cambridge 1968–72 (sr asst 1965–67), prof of applied mathematics Univ of Bath 1972–94, prof of theoretical solid mechanics Univ of Cambridge 1994–2000, prof of mathematics Univ of Bath 2000–01, prof of theoretical solid mechanics Univ of Cambridge 2001–07 (emeritus prof 2008–); ed-in-chief Jl of the Mechanics and Physics of Solids 1982–92 (jt ed 1992–2006); memb: SRC Mathematics Ctee 1975–78, SERC Mathematics Ctee 1984–87, Int Congress Ctee, Int Union for Theoretical and Applied Mechanics 1982–90; Timoshenko Medal American Soc of Mech Engrs 1997, Prager Medal Soc for Engrg Science 1998, EUROMECH Solid Mechanics Prize 2012; foreign assoc US Nat Acad of Engrg 2004, foreign assoc French Acad of Sciences 2009; FIMA 1966, FRS 1992; *Recreations* music, swimming; *Style—* Prof John Willis, FRS; ✉ Department of Applied Mathematics and Theoretical Physics, Centre for Mathematical Sciences, Wilberforce Road, Cambridge CB3 0WA (☎ 01223 337890, fax 01223 765900)

WILLIS, (Adrian) Peter; s of William Stanley Willis, and Ruth Enid, *née* Tomlinson; *b* 25 December 1966; *Educ* Buxton Coll Derbys; *Career* reporter The Sun 1988–89, columnist Daily Star 1989–90; The Sun: reporter 1990–92, dep showbusiness ed 1992–94, ed TV features and news 1994–95, ed Superguide 1995–97; The Daily Mirror: ed The Look 1997–98, features ed 1998–99, asst features ed 1999–2002, assoc ed then dep ed 2002–12, weekday ed 2012–; commended Br Press Awards 2001, winner Newspaper Awards Colour Supplement of the Year 1999, 2000 and 2001; creator and prodr The Pride of Britain Awards 1999– (televised ITV 2000–); memb NUJ 1985–, life memb Newspaper Press Fund; *Publications* Paul McKenna's Hypnotic Secrets (1995); *Recreations* marathon running; *Clubs* Met Bar, Davys; *Style—* Peter Willis, Esq; ✉ The Daily Mirror, 1 Canada Square, Canary Wharf, London E14 5AP (☎ 020 7293 3000, fax 020 7293 3834, e-mail p.willis@mgn.co.uk)

WILLIS, Very Rev Robert Andrew; DL (Kent 2011); s of Thomas Willis, of Kingswood, Bristol, and Vera Rosina, *née* Britton (d 1985); *b* 17 May 1947; *Educ* Kingswood GS, Univ of Warwick (BA), Worcester Coll Oxford (DipTh), Cuddesdon Theol Coll; *Career* ordained: deacon 1972, priest 1973; curate: St Chad's Shrewsbury 1972–75, vicar choral Salisbury Cathedral and chaplain to Cathedral Sch 1975–78, team rector Tisbury 1978–87, chaplain Cranborne Chase Sch and RAF Chilmark 1978–87, rural dean of Chalke 1982–87, vicar of Sherborne with Castleton and Lillington 1987–92, chaplain Sherborne Sch for Girls 1987–92, canon and prebendary of Salisbury Cathedral 1988–92, rural dean of Sherborne 1991–92, dean of Hereford 1992–2001, dean of Canterbury 2001–; proctor in convocation 1985–92 and 1994–; chm Deans' and Provosts' Conf 1999–2002, chm Deans' Conf 2002–; memb: Cncl Partnership for World Mission 1990–2001, C of E Liturgical Cmmn 1994–98, Cathedral Fabric Cmmn for England 1994–2006; memb Cncl Univ of Kent 2003–; govr: Cranborne Chase Sch 1985–87, Sherborne Sch 1987–92; chm of govrs: Hereford Cathedral Sch 1993–2001, King's Sch Canterbury 2001–; hon fell Canterbury Christ Church Univ 2004; sub dean Order of St John of Jerusalem 1999 (sub chaplain 1991); Freeman City of Canterbury 2008; Hon DD Yale Univ 2009, Hon DCL Univ of Kent 2011; FRSA 1993, FGCM 2006; KStJ 2009 (CStJ 2001), Cross of St Augustine 2012; *Books* Hymns Ancient and Modern (contrib, 1983), The Choristers' Companion (jtly, 1989), Common Praise (contrib, 2000), New English Praise (contrib, 2006), Sing Praise (contrib, 2011); *Recreations* music, literature, travel; *Clubs* Oxford and Cambridge; *Style—* The Very Rev Robert Willis, DL; ✉ The Deanery, The Precincts, Canterbury CT1 2EP (☎ 01227 762862, fax 01227 865222)

WILLIS, Robert George Dylan (Bob); MBE (1982); s of Edward Woodcock Willis (d 1982), and Anne Margaret, *née* Huntington (d 1997); *b* 30 May 1949; *Educ* King Edward VI Royal GS Guildford; *Children* 1 da (Katie-Anne b 1984); *Career* former professional cricketer, currently broadcaster and journalist; capt: Warwickshire 1980–84, England 1982–84; 90 tests for England, record number of wickets for England on retirement (325); cricket commentator Sky Sports; *Books* co-author of nine cricket books; *Recreations* opera, classical music, wine, real ale; *Clubs* MCC, Surrey CCC, Warwickshire CCC, Melbourne CC, Royal Wimbledon Golf, CAMRA; *Style—* Bob Willis, Esq, MBE; ✉ 2 Capatus House, 73 Mortlake High Street, London SW14 8HL

WILLIS OF KNARESBOROUGH, Baron (Life Peer UK, 2010), of Harrogate in the County of North Yorkshire; (George) Philip Willis; s of George Willis (d 1977), and Hannah Willis (d 1955); *b* 30 November 1941; *Educ* Burnley GS, City of Leeds Carnegie Coll (CertEd), Univ of Birmingham (BPhil); *m* 25 May 1974, Heather, *née* Sellars; 1 da (Rachel Helen b 14 June 1975), 1 s (Michael Paul b 1 Jan 1980); *Career* with Leeds LEA 1963–97, dep head teacher W Leeds Boys' HS 1973–77, head teacher Ormesby Sch Cleveland 1977–82, head teacher John Smeaton Community Sch 1983–97, MP (Lib Dem) Harrogate and Knaresborough 1997–2010; Lib Dem spokesman on further, higher and adult educn 1997–99; Lib Dem shadow min: for educn and employment 1999–2001, for educn and skills 2001–05; chair Science and Technol Select Ctee 2005–07, chair Innovation, Univs, Sci and Skills Select Ctee 2007–10, memb House of Lords Sci and Technol Ctee 2010–15; ldr Harrogate BC 1990–97 (cncllr 1988–99), cncllr and dep ldr N Yorkshire CC 1993–97; memb SHA 1977–97; chm Assoc of Medical Research Charities 2010–15, pres Assoc of Colls Charitable Tst 2010–15, chair Yorks and Humber Collaborations for Leadership in Applied Health Research and Care (CLAHRC) 2014–; conslt: Health Education England 2013–, Nursing and Midwifery Cncl 2015–; memb Cncl: Nat Environment Research Cncl 2011–, Fndn for Sci and Technol 2011–; Hon DSc Univ of Salford 2013; *Publications* Quality with Compassion: the future of nursing education (2012), Raising the Bar: Shape of Caring (2015); *Recreations* soccer (Leeds United); *Style*— The Lord Willis of Knaresborough

WILLMAN, John Romain; s of John Sydney Willman (d 1993), and Millicent Charlotte, *née* Thornton (d 1999); *b* 27 May 1949; *Educ* Bolton Sch, Jesus Coll Cambridge (MA), Westminster Coll Oxford (CertEd); *m* 1 April 1978, Margaret, da of Dr John Shanahan (d 1981), of Maida Vale; 1 s (Michael b 1982), 2 da (Kate b 1984, Claire b 1987); *Career* asst teacher Brentford Sch for Girls Middx 1972–76, fin researcher Consumers' Assoc 1976–79, ed of Taxes and Assessment (jls of Inland Revenue Staff Fedn) 1979–83, pubns mangr Peat Marwick Mitchell & Co 1983–85, gen sec Fabian Soc 1985–89, freelance writer and journalist, ed Consumer Policy Review 1990–91; Financial Times: public policy ed 1991–94, features ed 1994–97, consumer industries ed 1997–2000, banking ed 2000–01, chief ldr writer and assoc ed 2002–06, UK business ed 2006–09, editorial conslt 2009–; specialist advsr Treasy Select Ctee 2011–15, specialist advsr Parly Cmmn on Banking Standards 2012–13; Medical Journalism Financing Healthcare Prize 1998, Business Journalist of the Year 2001, Best Banking Submission Business Journalism Awards 2002; visiting research fell Social Market Fndn 1997, sr research fell Policy Exchange 2009; assoc IPPR 1990–91; *Books* Make Your Will (1989), Labour's Electoral Challenge (1989), Sorting out Someone's Will (1990), Which? Guide to Planning and Conservation (1990), Work for Yourself (1991), Labour and the Public Services (1994), Lloyds TSB Tax Guide (14 edn, 2000), A Better State of Health (1998), Innovation & Industry (2010); *Recreations* walking, theatre, opera; *Style*— John Willman, Esq; ☎ 07767 301225

WILLMAN, Prof Paul; *Educ* St Catharine's Coll Cambridge (MA), Trinity Coll Oxford (DPhil, MA); *m* Kathleen Pickett; *Career* res offr Nat Union of Bank Employees 1977–78; Imperial Coll London: lectr in industrial rels 1978–83 (tenure 1981); London Business Sch: lectr 1984–88, assoc prof 1988–91, prof of organisational behaviour and industrial rels 1991–2000, govr 1996–99; Univ of Oxford: Sir Norman Chester sr res fell Nuffield Coll 1989, fell Balliol Coll 2000–06, prof Saïd Business Sch 2000–06, ed-in-chief Human Relations 2001–06; prof of mgmnt LSE 2006–; memb Editorial Bd: CUP Mgmnt Studies 1985–95, Business Strategy Review 1990–92 and 1996–2000, Br Jl of Industrial Rels 1994–98; memb ACAS Arbitration Panel 1988–; memb: Industrial Rels Res Assoc, Int Industrial Rels Res Assoc, Br Univs Industrial Rels Assoc, Euro Gp for Organisational Studies, Soc for the Advancement of Socio-Economics, Acad of Mgmnt, Cncl Advsy Conciliation and Arbitration Service 2014–; *Publications* Fairness, Collective Bargaining and Incomes Policy (1982), Power, Efficiency and Institutions: A Critical Appraisal of the Markets and Hierarchies Paradigm (jt ed, 1983), Innovation and Management Control: Labour Relations at BL Cars (jtly, 1985), The Car Industry: Labour Relations and Industrial Adjustment (jtly, 1985), Technological Change, Collective Bargaining and Industrial Efficiency (1986), The Limits to Self Regulation: Ten Years of the Health and Safety at Work Act (jtly, 1988), Union Business: Trade Union Organisation and Financial Reform in the Thatcher Years (jtly, 1993), Traders: Risks, Decisions and Management in Financial Market (2004), Understanding Management – The Social Science Foundations (2014); numerous articles in learned jls, contributions to edited collections and published cases; *Recreations* county churches, dogs; *Style*— Prof Paul Willman; ✉ London School of Economics and Political Sciences, Houghton Street, London WC2A 2AE (☎ 020 7955 6739, e-mail p.willman@lse.ac.uk)

WILLMORE, Prof (Albert) Peter; s of Albert Mervyn Willmore (d 1957), and Kathleen Helen, *née* O'Rourke (d 1987); *b* 28 April 1930; *Educ* Holloway Sch London, UCL (BSc, PhD); *m* 1, 1962 (m dis 1972), Geraldine Anne; 2 s (Nicholas b 1963, Andrew b 1964); m 2, 6 Aug 1972, Stephanie Ruth, da of Leonard Alden, of Surrey; 1 da (Lucy b 1973), 1 s (Ben b 1976); *Career* res fell, lectr, reader then prof of physics UCL 1957–72, prof of space res Univ of Birmingham 1972–; Tsiolkowsky Medal USSR 1987; FRAS 1960, memb Bd of Tstees Int Acad of Astronautics 1996; *Recreations* ancient history, music, sailing; *Style*— Prof Peter Willmore

WILLMOT, Prof Derrick Robert; s of Jack Willmot (d 1982), and Olive, *née* Yarnall (d 1986); *b* 29 April 1947; *Educ* Chesterfield Boys' GS, UCL and UCH London (BDS, LDS), Univ of Sheffield (PhD); *m* 9 Jan 1971, Patricia Marie, da of Robert Creighton (d 1998), of San Luis, Menorca, Spain; 2 s (Mark b 1973, Andrew b 1974); *Career* dental house surgn Royal Portsmouth Hosp 1970, gen dental practitioner Ashbourne Derbyshire 1971, sr registrar UCH 1979 (registrar 1977); conslt orthodontist: Chesterfield Royal Hosp 1984–92, Charles Clifford Dental Hosp Univ of Sheffield 1992–2010; clinical dir dental servs CSUHT 1995–2000; Univ of Sheffield: clinical dean Sch of Clinical Dentistry 2000–02, head Dept of Oral Growth and Devpt 2001–05, emeritus prof 2010–; dean Faculty of Dental Surgery RCS England 2008–11 (memb Bd 1994–97 and 2003–11, vice-dean 2005–07); sec Conslt Orthodontists Gp 1989–94 (chm 2000–03), dental advsr Med Protection Soc 1992–; chm SAC in Orthodontics and Paediatric Dentistry 1995–98; memb Round Table 1972–87: Ashbourne, St Albans, Chesterfield; chm NE Derbys Music Centre 1986–90, memb Chesterfield Scarsdale Rotary Club 1988– (pres 2001–02); vice-chm Bd of Govrs Chesterfield Sch 1988–92, pres S Yorks BDA 1992–93; FDS 1978, DDO 1980, MOrthRCS 1987; *Recreations* fly fishing; *Clubs* Flyfishers, RSM; *Style*— Prof Derrick Willmot; ✉ e-mail d.willmot@sheffield.ac.uk, website www.ferndaledental.co.uk

WILLMOTT, Rt Rev Trevor; *see:* Dover, Bishop of

WILLOTT, Jenny; da of (William) Brian Willott, CB, and Alison Willott; *b* 29 May 1974; *Educ* Wimbledon HS, Uppingham Sch, Univ of Durham, LSE; *m* May 2009; 2 s (b July 2010 and Feb 2013); *Career* conslt Adithi NGO India 1995, memb fundraising team Oxfam 1996, head of office for Lembit Opik MP 1997–2000, researcher Lib Dem Gp Welsh Assembly 2000–01, administrator Barnardos Dewen Project 2001, head of advocacy UNICEF UK 2001–03, area mangr Victim Support S Wales 2003–05; MP (Lib Dem) Cardiff Central 2005–15 (Parly candidate (Lib Dem) Cardiff Central 2001); cncllr (Lib Dem) Merton BC 1998–2000; *Style*— Ms Jenny Willott; ✉ House of Commons, London SW1A 0AA (☎ 020 7219 8418, e-mail jenny.willott.mp@parliament.uk, website www.jennywillott.com)

WILLOTT, Robert Graham; s of William Arthur Willott (d 1968), and Vera Joanna, *née* Ashton (d 2008); *b* 9 March 1942, London; *Educ* Hitchin GS; *m* 1, 1968, Patricia Ann (d 1981); 2 da (Sian Elizabeth b 1971, Carys Ann b 1973); m 2, 2002, Carolyn Mary; *Career* Pawley & Malyon CAs: articled clerk 1959–65, mangr 1965–68, ptnr 1968–69; Haymarket Publishing Ltd: ed Accountancy Age 1969–72, publisher 1972–75, dir 1975–76; ICAEW: sec Parly and Law Ctee 1976–78, tech dir 1978–81; Touche Ross (formerly Spicer and Pegler, Spicer & Oppenheim): ptnr 1981–91, i/c Client Devpt Unit 1981–86, fndr and ptnr i/c West End Practice 1987–91, memb Nat Exec 1985–86 and 1988; Willott Kingston Smith and Kingston Smith: ptnr 1991–99, conslt 1999–2001; dir: Cheviot Capital Ltd 1985–98, Fintellect Ltd 1991–, Fintellect Publishing Ltd 2000–, Results Business Consulting Ltd 1997–2007, The Telephone Preference Service Ltd 1999–2006, Save the Children (Sales) Ltd 2000–04, Dare Digital Ltd 2000–10, ILG Digital Ltd 2003–07, Blockley Mystery Plays Ltd 2003–12; special prof Univ of Nottingham Business Sch 1992–2007; ICAEW: past memb Parly and Law Ctee, past memb Company Law Sub-Ctee; past special advsr DTI; chm Initial Working Pty and advsr to Design Business Assoc 1985–97; dir and hon treas The Direct Marketing Association (UK) Ltd 1996–2001, memb Mgmnt Ctee Blockley Cooperative Assoc Ltd 2007–12; tstee and hon treas Save the Children Fund 1999–04, chm Blockley Heritage Soc 2012–15 (tstee 2007–15, vice-pres 2015–16), tstee Read Easy UK 2013–14; memb Mktg Soc; FCA (1976, ACA 1965); *Publications* Going Public (ed 1971–73), Current Accounting Law and Practice (1976–85 and 1992–2000), Guide to Price Controls 1977–78 (1977), The Purchase or Redemption by a Company of its Own Shares (Tolley's, jtly 1982), How Advertising Agencies Made Their Profits (1984–90), Financial Performance of Marketing Services Companies (annual, ed 1991–2001, conslt ed 2002–), The Encyclopaedia of Current Accounting Law and Practice (2000–), Marketing Services Financial Intelligence (ed 2001–), New Media Agencies Financial Intelligence (ed, 2001–), Rebuilding Blockley (2010), Shop (jtly, 2015); *Style*— Robert Willott, Esq; ✉ Vine House, High Street, Blockley, Gloucestershire GL56 9ET (☎ 01386 700361, e-mail rgwillott@fintellect.com)

WILLOUGHBY, Holly Marie; *b* 10 February 1981, Brighton, E Sussex; *Educ* Burgess Hill Sch for Girls, Coll of Richard Collyer Horsham; *m* 4 Aug 2007, Dan Baldwin, *qv*; 1 s (Harry James b 11 May 2009), 1 da (Belle b 14 April 2011); *Career* television presenter; presenter: Xchange 2000–04, CBBC at the Fame Academy (BBC) 2002–03, X-perimental (BBC) 2003, Ministry of Mayhem (subsequently Holly & Stephen's Saturday Showdown, ITV) 2004–06 (Best Children's Television Presenter BAFTA 2006), Stars in Their Eyes Kids (ITV) 2004, Feel the Fear (ITV) 2005, Dancing on Ice (ITV) 2006–11, Streetmate (ITV) 2007, The Xtra Factor (ITV) 2008–09, Celebrity Juice (ITV) 2008–, This Morning (ITV) 2009– (Best Daytime Prog Nat Television Award 2014), The Voice (BBC) 2012–13, Surprise Surprise (ITV) 2012–; *Books* School for Stars series 2012–; *Style*— Ms Holly Willoughby; ✉ c/o Claire Dundas & Emily Page, James Grant Media Ltd, 94 Strand On The Green, Chiswick, London W4 3NN

WILLOUGHBY DE BROKE, 21 Baron (E 1491); (Leopold) David Verney; DL (Warks) 1999; s of 20 Baron Willoughby de Broke (d 1986, descended from the 1 Baron, who was so cr by Henry VII after being on the winning side at Battle of Bosworth Field (1485), and was 4 in descent from 4 Baron Willoughby de Eresby), and Rachel, *née* Wrey (d 1991); *b* 14 September 1938; *Educ* Le Rosey, New Coll Oxford; *m* 1965 (m dis 1989), his kinswoman Petra, 2 da of Col Sir John Aird, 3 Bt, MVO, MC, and Lady Priscilla Heathcote-Drummond-Willoughby (yr da of 2 Earl of Ancaster); 3 s (Rupert Greville b 1966, John Mark b 1967, Edmund Peyto b 1973); *Heir* s, Rupert Verney; *Career* chm: S M Theatre Ltd 1991–, St Martin's Magazines plc 1992–, Compton Verney Opera and Ballet Project 1992–; pres Heart of England Tourist Bd 1996–; patron Warks Assoc of Boys' Clubs 1991–; FRGS 1993; *Clubs* Pratt's, All England; *Style*— The Rt Hon Lord Willoughby de Broke, DL; ✉ Ditchford Farm, Moreton-in-Marsh, Gloucestershire GL56 9RD

WILLS, Sir David James Vernon; 5 Bt (UK 1923), of Blagdon, Co Somerset; s of Sir John Vernon Wills, 4 Bt, KCVO, TD, JP (d 1998); *b* 2 January 1955; *m* July 1999, Paula Katherine Burke, o da of Dr Peter Holmes, of Sittingbourne, Kent; *Heir* bro, Anthony Wills; *Career* farmer and landowner; memb Cncl Royal Bath & West and Southern Countries Soc 1982; memb Soc of Merchant Venturers 1991; *Recreations* field sports; *Style*— Sir David Wills; ✉ Estate Office, Langford Court, Bristol BS40 5DA (☎ 01934 862498, fax 01934 863019)

WILLS, Baron (Life Peer UK 2010), of North Swindon in the County of Wiltshire and of Woodside Park in the London Borough of Barnet; Rt Hon Michael Wills; PC (2008); *b* 20 May 1952; *Educ* Haberdashers' Aske's Elstree, Clare Coll Cambridge (BA); *m* 19 Jan 1984, Jill, *née* Freeman; 3 s (Thomas b 11 Dec 1984, Joe b 22 Aug 1987, Nicholas b 19 Dec 1993), 2 da (Sarah b 12 Dec 1988, Katherine b 10 July 1998); *Career* joined HM Dip Serv 1976, third sec FCO London 1976–77, second sec and labour attaché Br High Cmmn New Dehli 1977–80; prodr Weekend World (LWT) 1982–84 (researcher 1980–82), prodr/dir and md Juniper Productions (ind TV prodn co) 1985–97, MP (Lab) Swindon N 1997–2010; House of Commons: Parly under-sec of state: DTI 1999–2000, DfEE 2000–01, Lord Chllr's Office 2001–02, Parly under sec of state Home Office 2002–07, min of state Miny of Justice 2007–10; advsr to Shadow Cabinet 1985–97, gen election media advsr Lab trade and industry team 1992; dir Campaign for Fair Taxes 1992–95; *Style*— The Rt Hon the Lord Wills; ✉ House of Lord, London SW1A 0PW

WILLS, Nicholas Kenneth Spencer; s of late Sir John Spencer Wills (d 1991), of Battle, E Sussex, and Elizabeth Drusilla Alice Clare Garcke (d 1995); *b* 18 May 1941, Windsor, Berks; *Educ* Rugby, Queens' Coll Cambridge (MA); *m* 1, 1973 (m dis 1983), Hilary Ann Flood; 2 s, 2 da; m 2, 1985, Philippa Trench Casson; 1 da; *Career* articled clerk and qualified accountant on audit duty Binder Hamlyn 1963–67, investment analyst then investment mangr Morgan Grenfell 1967–70; chm: Argus Press Hldgs plc 1974–83, Electrical Press plc 1974–83, Initial plc 1979–87, BET Building Services Ltd 1984–87, Onslow Commercial and Trading 1994–2002; dep chm National Mutual Home Loans 1994–96; md: Birmingham & District Investment Tst plc 1970–91, Electrical & Industrial Investment plc 1970–91, Nat Electric Construction plc 1971–91; BET plc: dir 1975–92, md 1982–91, chief exec 1985–91, chm 1991–92; dir: St George Assurance Co Ltd 1974–81, Bradbury Agnew and Co Ltd 1974–83, National Mutual Life Assurance Society 1974–85, Colonial Securities Tst Co Ltd 1976–82, Cable Tst Ltd 1976–77, Globe Investment Tst plc 1977–90, Boulton and Paul plc 1979–84, Drayton Consolidated Tst plc 1982–92, National Westminster Bank plc (City and West End Advsy Bds) 1982–91, American C of C (UK) 1985–2000 (vice-pres 1988–2000), United World Colleges (International) Ltd 1987–95 (fin dir 1987–93), National Mutual Life Assurance Soc 1991–2002 (dep chm 1992–99, chm 1999–2002, chm Supervisory Bd 2002–07), Hitchin Priory Ltd 1992–2002 (dep chm 1994–99, chm 1999–2002), Tribune Tst plc 1992–2004, Manchester Trading & Commercial LLC 1995–2002, Toye & Co plc 1996–2013, ret, SMC Gp plc 1999–2009, IQ-Ludorum plc 2000–04, Solid Terrain Modeling Inc 2000–10, Archial Gp plc 2009–10; memb: Cncl CBI 1987–92 (memb Overseas Ctee 1987–91, Public Expenditure Task Force 1988, Economic Affairs Ctee 1991–96), Cncl Business in the Community 1987–92, Advsy Bd Fishman-Davidson Center for the Study of the Service Sector Univ of Pennsylvania 1988–92, Advsy Bd Charterhouse Buy-Out Funds 1990–98, Cncl Industrial Soc 1991–97; Prince's Youth Business Tst: memb Advsy Cncl 1988–2004, hon treas 1989–92, memb Investment Ctee 1992–98; chm: Involvement and Participation Assoc 1991–96, Mgmnt Ctee Cambridge Review of Int Affairs 1998–2003 (memb Advsy Bd 1999–2004); tstee Int Fedn Keystone Youth Orgns (IFKYO) 1988–2004, chm IFKYO Int Tstees 1990–2004; treas and churchwarden Church of St Bride Fleet St 1978–2001; govr Haberdashers' Aske's Schs Elstree 1989–97 (chm Girls' Sch Ctee 1994–97); memb PCC St Mary the Virgin Great Milton; hon memb Clan McEwan; memb Ct of Assts Worshipful Co of Haberdashers 1981 (Jr Warden 1987–89, Master 1997); hon fell Queens' Coll Cambridge 1990, hon fell Centre of Int Studies Cambridge 2000; CIMgt, FCT, FRSA; *Recreations* trying to farm in the Highlands, snow shoeing; *Clubs* White's, RAC, Beaver Creek; *Style*— Nicholas Wills, Esq; ✉ The Great House, Great Milton, Oxfordshire OX44 7PD

WILMOT-SMITH, Richard James Crosbie; QC (1994); s of John Patrick Wilmot-Smith (d 1993), and Rosalys Vida, *née* Massy (d 2002); *b* 12 May 1952; *Educ* Charterhouse, Univ

W

of N Carolina (John Motley Morehead scholar, AB); *m* 1978, Jenny, da of Richard William Castle; 2 da (Antonia b 12 Nov 1981, Claudia b 23 July 1984), 1 s (Freddie b 12 April 1986); *Career* called to the Bar Middle Temple 1978 (Benefactors law scholar, bencher 2003); recorder of the Crown Court 2000– (asst recorder 1994–2000); tstee Free Representation Unit 1997–; *Recreations* cricket; *Clubs* Kent CCC; *Style*— Richard Wilmot-Smith, Esq, QC; ✉ 39 Essex Street, London WC2R 3AT (✆ 020 7832 1111, e-mail richardws@39essex.co.uk)

WILSHAW, Sir Michael; kt (2000); *Career* princ Mossbourne Community Acad London until 2012, HM chief inspr of educn, children's services and skills Ofsted 2012–; *Style*— Sir Michael Wilshaw; ✉ Ofsted, Piccadilly Gate, Store Street, Manchester M1 2WD

WILSHER, Roy Andrew; OBE (2007), QFSM (2013); s of Kenneth Wilsher, and Valerie Wilsher; *b* 9 March 1963, Barnet; *Educ* Arnos Comp Enfield, South Bank Univ; *m* 28 June 1986; 2 s; *Career* London Fire Brigade: joined 1981, asst cmmr 2002–03; Herts Fire and Rescue Serv: dep chief fire offr 2004–05, chief fire offr 2005–; memb Ct Univ of Herts; tstee Herts in Trust charity; dir Chief Fire Offrs' Assoc 2011 (memb 2004); ceo Herts PCC 2013; Fire Serv Long Serv and Good Conduct Medal 2002, Queen's Jubilee Medal 2002, Queen's Diamond Jubilee Medal 2012; MIFireE 1990, CEng 2000, Cert IoD 2015; *Recreations* rugby, football, keep fit, reading; *Style*— Roy Wilsher, Esq, OBE, QFSM; ✉ Hertfordshire Fire and Rescue Service, Old London Road, Hertford, Hertfordshire SG13 7LD (✆ 01992 507501, e-mail roy.wilsher@hertscc.gov.uk)

WILSON, Prof Sir Alan Geoffrey; kt (2001); s of Harry Wilson (d 1987), of Darlington, Co Durham, and Gladys, *née* Naylor (d 1990); *b* 8 January 1939; *Educ* Queen Elizabeth GS Darlington, Corpus Christi Coll Cambridge (MA); *m* 17 April 1987, Sarah Caroline Fildes; *Career* scientific offr Rutherford Laboratory 1961–64, res offr Inst of Economics and Statistics Univ of Oxford 1964–66, mathematical advsr Miny of Tport 1966–68, asst dir Centre for Environmental Studies 1968–70; Univ of Leeds: prof of urban and regnl geography 1970–2004 (emeritus prof 2004–), chm Bd of Arts, Economics and Social Studies and Law 1984–86, pro-vice-chllr 1989–91, vice-chllr 1991–2004; DG for HE DfES 2004–06, master CCC Cambridge 2006–07, prof of urban and rgnl systems UCL 2007–; chair Arts and Humanities Research Cncl 2007–13, chair Home Office Science Advsy Cncl 2013–, chair Lead Expert Gp Foresight Future of Cities Project Govt Office for Science 2013–; memb Oxford City Cncl 1964–67, memb and vice-chm Kirklees AHA 1979–81, vice-chm Dewsbury DHA 1982–86; memb ESRC 2000–04; chm NHS Complaints Review Ctee 1993, memb Northern and Yorkshire RHA 1994–96; Fndr's Medal Royal Geographical Soc 1992; Hon DSc Pennsylvania State Univ 2002, Hon DEd Leeds Metropolitan Univ 2004, Hon DUniv Bradford 2004, Hon LLD Univ of Leeds 2004, Hon LLD Univ of Teesside 2006, Hon DSocSci KCL 2010; hon fell: UCL 2003, CCC Cambridge 2004; AcSS 2000; FBA 1994, FCGI 1997, CGeog 2001, FRS 2006; *Books* Entropy in Urban and Regional Modelling (1970), Catastrophe Theory and Bifuration (1981), Geography and the Environment (1981), Modelling the City: Performance, Policy and Planning (jtly, 1994), Intelligent GIS, Location Decisions and Strategic Planning (jtly, 1996), Complex Spatial Systems (2000), Knowledge Power (2010), The Science of Cities and Regions (2012), Urban Modelling (ed, 5 vols); *Recreations* reading, writing; *Clubs* Athenaeum; *Style*— Prof Sir Alan Wilson, FBA, FRS; ✉ Centre for Advanced Spatial Analysis, University College London, 90 Tottenham Court Road, London W1T 4TG (✆ 020 3108 3901, e-mail a.g.wilson@ucl.ac.uk)

WILSON, Rt Rev Dr Alan Thomas Lawrence; *see:* Buckingham, Bishop of

WILSON, Brig Alasdair Allan; OBE (1987); s of George Allan Wilson (d 1963), and Isobel Fraser, *née* Burgess (d 2013); *b* 12 April 1947; *Educ* Bury GS, RMA Sandhurst, RMCS Shrivenham (BSc), Army, Navy and NATO Staff Colls; *m* 14 Aug 1971, Allison May, *née* Muir; 2 s (Archie Douglas Allan, Alexander James Allan); *Career* 2 Lt RE 1967, Army Staff Coll 1978, RN Staff Coll Greenwich 1979, OC 7 Field Sqdn RE 1981–83, Cdr 33 Engr Regt 1986–88, Chief Engr ME Gulf War 1990–91, NATO Defence Coll Rome 1995, Chief Civil Affrs Bosnia 1995–96, Cdr 107 (Ulster) Bde 1996–98, ACOS HQ North NATO 1998–2001; sec RE Offrs Widows Soc, church warden All Saints Dickleburgh, lay chm Dickleburgh PCC; GSM NI 1971, Gulf War Medal 1991, Bosnia Medal 1996, Kosovo Medal 2000, Queen's Golden Jubilee Medal 2002, Cumulative Service Medal; pres RBL Dickleburgh, chm Dickleburgh PCC, chm Norfolk County Priory Gp of St John; FICE 2002; MStJ 2015; *Books* History of the Royal Engineers 1980–2000 (2012); *Recreations* golf, singing, shooting, croquet, gardening; *Clubs* Army and Navy; *Style*— Brig Alasdair Wilson, OBE; ✉ The Old Rectory, Dickleburgh, Diss, Norfolk IP21 4NN (✆ 01379 740561, mobile 07762 954207, e-mail aawilson@compuserve.com)

WILSON, Alastair James Drysdale; QC (1987); s of Alastair Robin Wilson, ERD, of Sudbury, Suffolk, and Mary Damaris, *née* Dawson; *b* 26 May 1946; *Educ* Wellington, Pembroke Coll Cambridge; *Children* 1 s, 2 da; *Career* called to the Bar Middle Temple 1968, recorder 1996–; *Recreations* gardening, restoring old buildings, treasure hunting at boot fairs; *Clubs* Norfolk; *Style*— Alastair Wilson, Esq, QC; ✉ Rainthorpe Hall, Tasburgh, Norfolk NR15 1RQ (✆ 01508 470 618); Hogarth Chambers, 5 New Square, Lincoln's Inn, London WC2A 3RJ (✆ 020 7404 0404, e-mail awilsonqc@clara.net)

WILSON, Andrew Norman; s of Lt-Col Norman Wilson (d 1985), and Jean Dorothy, *née* Crowder (d 2003); *b* 27 October 1950; *Educ* Rugby, New Coll Oxford (MA, Chllr's Essay Prize, Ellerton Theol Prize); *m* 1, 1971 (m dis 1989), Katherine Dorothea Duncan-Jones, *qv*; 2 da; m 2, 1991, Dr Ruth Guilding; 1 da (b 23 March 1998); *Career* author; asst master Merchant Taylors' Sch 1975–76, lectr St Hugh's Coll and New Coll Oxford 1976–81; literary ed: The Spectator 1981–84, Evening Standard 1990–97; columnist Evening Standard 1990–; FRSL 1981; *Books* The Sweets of Pimlico (1977, John Llewellyn Rhys Meml Prize 1978), Unguarded Hours (1978), Kindly Light (1979), The Laird of Abbotsford (1980, John Llewellyn Rhys Meml prize 1981), The Healing Art (1980, Somerset Maugham Award 1981), Who Was Oswald Fish? (1981), Wise Virgin (1982, W H Smith Literary Award 1983), The Life of John Milton (1983), Scandal (1983), Hilaire Belloc (1984), How Can We Know? (1985), Gentlemen in England (1985), Love Unknown (1986), Stray (1987), The Lion and the Honeycomb (1987), Penfriends from Porlock (1988), Tolstoy (1988, Whitbread Biography Award), Incline Our Hearts (1988), The Tabitha Stories (1988), Eminent Victorians (1989), C S Lewis (1990), A Bottle in The Smoke (1990), Daughters of Albion (1991), Jesus (1992), The Rise and Fall of the House of Windsor (1993), The Vicar of Sorrows (1993), Hearing Voices (1995), A Watch in the Night (1996), Paul: The Mind of The Apostle (1997), Dream Children (1998), God's Funeral (1999), The Victorians (2002), Iris Murdoch As I Knew Her (2003), London: A Short History (2004), My Name is Legion (2004), A Jealous Ghost (2005), After the Victorians (2005), Betjeman (2006), Our Times (2008); *Clubs* Travellers, Beefsteak; *Style*— A N Wilson, FRSL; ✉ 5 Regent's Park Terrace, London NW1 7EE

WILSON, Dr Ashley John; s of late John Wilson, of Harton, South Shields, Tyne & Wear, and Gladys Wilson; *b* 2 November 1950; *Educ* South Shields GS, Bedford Coll, Univ of London (BSc), Univ of York (DPhil); *m* 1, 2 Jan 1976, Sheila, da of James Mather, of South Shields, Tyne & Wear; m 2, 4 July 1998, Hazel Louise, da of Robert Burrows, of York, N Yorkshire; *Career* dir Centre for Cell and Tissue Res Univ of York 1980–, tech dir Carafiltration Ltd; ed Procedures in Electron Microscopy 1993–; memb: Br Humanist Assoc, Nat Secular Soc; active memb and sec York Humanist Gp, fell Royal Microsopical Soc; MIBiol 1975, CBiol 1979; *Books* An Atlas of Low Temperature Scanning Electron Microscopy (1984), Foams: Chemistry, Physics and Structure (1989), Resins for Light and Electron Microscopy (1992); *Recreations* singing, wine tasting, architectural history, badminton; *Style*— Dr Ashley J Wilson

WILSON, Rt Hon Brian David Henderson; PC (2003); s of late John Forrest Wilson, and Marion, *née* McIntyre; *b* 13 December 1948; *Educ* Dunoon GS, Univ of Dundee (MA), Univ Coll (Dip Journalism Studies); *m* 1981, Joni, *née* Buchanan; 1 da, 2 s; *Career* publisher and founding ed West Highland Free Press 1972–; MP (Lab) Cunninghame N 1987–2005; oppn front bench spokesman: on Scot Affrs 1988–92, on citizen's rights and open govt 1992, tport 1992–94 and 1995–96, on trade and industry 1994–95; memb Lab Pty election planning team 1996–97; min for: educn and industry Scottish Office 1997–98, trade 1998–99; min of state Scottish Office 1999–2001, min of state FCO 2001, min of state for Industry and Energy 2001–03, PM's special rep on overseas trade 2003–05; chair Wilson Review of Scottish Exporting 2014; chm Airtricity UK 2005–08, chm Harris Tweed Hebrides 2007–, chm Havana Energy 2010–; dir: Celtic plc 2005–, AMEC Nuclear 2005–14; visiting prof: Glasgow Caledonian Univ 2007–12, Strathclyde Univ 2015–; chm Britain's Energy Coast West Cumbria 2009–14; UK business ambass 2013–; contrib to: The Guardian, Daily Telegraph, The Scotsman; dir Cuba Studies Tst 2007–; first winner Nicholas Tomalin Meml Award 1975, Spectator Parliamentarian of Year Awards 1990, IOD UK Global Dir of the Year 2011; hon fell Univ of the Highlands and Islands 2009; FSA Scot; *Books* Celtic: a century with honour (1988), Official History of Celtic (2013), Remembering Sam; the Life and Times of Sam Galbraith (2016); *Clubs* Soho House, Archerfield, Stoke Park; *Style*— The Rt Hon Brian Wilson; ✉ Cnoc na Meinn, Mangersta, Isle of Lewis HS2 9EY (e-mail brianwilson@mangersta.net)

WILSON, Catherine (Kate); da of Gerald Wilson, and Margaret Wilson; *b* Edinburgh; *Educ* Univ of Oxford (BA); *Career* rights mangr Faber & Faber 1986–88, rights dir Reed Children's Books 1988–93, publisher and md Macmillan Children's Books 1993–2005, md Scholastic 2005–09, fndr and md Nosy Crow Ltd 2010–; memb: Publisher's Assoc, Ind Publishers Guild; *Recreations* books, my children, books and books; *Style*— Ms Kate Wilson; ✉ Nosy Crow, The Crow's Nest, 10A Lant Street, London SE1 1QR

WILSON, Catherine Mary; OBE (1996); da of Arthur Thomas Bowyer (d 1998), of Nettleham, Lincs, and Kathleen Edith May, *née* Hawes (d 1993); *b* 10 April 1945; *Educ* Windsor County GS; *m* 1968, Peter John Wilson, s of Henry Wilson; *Career* museum and gallery asst City and County Museum Lincoln 1964–72, curator Museum of Lincolnshire Life 1972–83, asst dir recreational servs Lincs Co Cncl 1983–91, dir Norfolk Museums Service 1991–98, museums conslt and lectr 2000–; memb Bd: Museums and Galleries Cmmn 1993–2000, Museums Trg Inst 1994–99, Assoc of Ind Museums 2000–05, Railway Heritage Ctee 2001–10, E Midlands Regnl Ctee Heritage Lottery Fund 2002–08; pres Soc for Lincs History and Archaeology 2006–10; FMA, FSA 1989, FRGS 1998; *Books* Lincolnshire's Farm Animals (2012); *Recreations* steam engines, industrial archaeology, local history; *Style*— Mrs Catherine Wilson, OBE, FSA

WILSON, Charles; *Career* with Procter and Gamble 1986, conslt OC&C Strategy Consultants 1987–91, dir Abberton Associates 1991–98, exec dir (branches, supply chain, strategy and systems) Booker plc 1998–2000, md Booker Cash and Carry (part of Iceland Group plc) 2000–01, exec dir (strategy, property, supply chain and systems) Arcadia Group plc 2001–03, exec dir (property, IT and supply chain) Marks and Spencer plc 2004–05, ceo Booker 2005–; *Style*— Charles Wilson, Esq

WILSON, Ven Christine Louise; da of Ronald Arthur Bravery, and Dinah Sylvia, *née* Bradley (d 2011); *b* 26 March 1958, Brighton, E Sussex; *Educ* Margaret Hardy Secdy Modern Brighton, Southern Diocese Ministerial Trg Scheme; *m* 27 March 1976, Alan Ronald Wilson; 3 da (Emma Louise b 14 Oct 1978, Sarah Ruth b 14 March 1980 d 2009, Elizabeth Rachel b 22 Jan 1985); *Career* ordained: deacon 1997, priest 1998; curate Henfield with Shermanbury and Woodmancote 1997–2002, team vicar Hove 2002–08, vicar Goring-by-Sea 2008–10, archdeacon of Chesterfield 2010–16, dean of Lincoln 2016–; memb Gen Synod C of E 2011–15, regional rep House of Bishops 2013–16; chair Cornerstone Community Centre 2002–08, chair Brunswick Community Devpt Center 2002–08, chair Peak Centre 2010–16; non-exec dir: Ecclesiastical Insurance Office plc, Ecclesiastical Insurance Gp 2012–; *Recreations* gardening, travel, entertaining; *Style*— The Very Rev the Dean of Lincoln; ✉ The Old Vicarage, Church Street, Baslow, Bakewell DE45 1RY (✆ 01246 583023, e-mail archchesterfield@derby.anglican.org)

WILSON, Corri; MP; *Career* MP (SNP) Ayr, Carrick and Cumnock 2015–; *Style*— Ms Corri Wilson, MP; ✉ House of Commons, London SW1A 0AA

WILSON, David Thomas Monti; *b* 30 July 1963, London; *Educ* Forest Sch London, Univ of Southampton (LLB), Coll of Law London; *m* Claire Amanda, *née* Laws; 2 s (Hugo, Henry); *Career* admitted slr: England and Wales 1987, Hong Kong 1987; former litigation ptnr Simmons & Simmons; Goldman Sachs Int: former European divnl head of compliance, currently md and sr counsel; memb Audit Ctee Law Society 2006–10; tstee UK Retirement Fund; chair Multi Acads Tst – Excalibur Acads Tst Wiltsm chair pro bono ctee City Law soc 1994–97, govr Forest Sch Essex; memb: Glyndebourne Festival Soc, Advsy Bd NSPCC 1994–97; Freeman City of London, Liveryman City of London's Slrs' Co; memb RGS; *Recreations* music, golf, travel; *Clubs* Athenaeum, Hurlingham, Woking, Shuttlecock; *Style*— David Wilson, Esq; ✉ Goldman Sachs International, Peterborough Court, 133 Fleet Street, London EC4A 2BB

WILSON, Derek; *b* 26 September 1963; *Educ* Todmorden GS, Leeds Sch of Architecture (BA), N London Sch of Architecture (DipArch); *m* 1998; *Career* architect; formerly with: John S Taylor Chartered Architects Todmorden, Archer Boxer Partners Hatfield; dir HOK Sport (formerly Lobb Partnership London) 1993– (joined 1989), former head of design and overlay London Organising Ctee for the Olympic Games (LOCOG), currently dir of own practice; projects incl: Alfred McAlpine Stadium Huddersfield 1992–98 (RIBA Building of the Year 1995), Reebok Stadium Bolton 1995–98 (British Construction Industry Building of the Year 1998), Sydney Olympics Overlay 1998–99, Arsenal FC new stadium 1999–2000 and 2004–06, masterplan London 2012 Olympic Games bid 2003–06, orgn of London 2012 Olympic Games, Le Havre FC new stadium 2010, England 2018 World Cup bid, Sochi 2014 Olympic Games; advsr Everton FC; memb Ctee: BSI, Central European Norms (CEN) for Standards in Spectator Facilities, Advsy Gp on Temporary Structures (AGOTS); contrib to magazine articles and published books; memb Bd Football Licensing Authy; RIBA 1990, ARB 1990; *Recreations* footballer, supporter Burnley FC; *Style*— Derek Wilson, Esq

WILSON, Des; s of Albert H Wilson (d 1989), of Oamaru, NZ, and Ellen, *née* Hoskins; *b* 5 March 1941; *Educ* Waitaki Boys' HS NZ; *m* 1 (m dis 1984); 1 s (Timothy), 1 da (Jacqueline); m 2, 24 May 1985, Jane, *née* Dunmore, of Brighton; *Career* columnist: The Guardian 1968–71, The Observer 1971–75; ed Social Work Today 1976–79, dep ed The Illustrated London News 1979–81; dir Shelter 1967–71, memb Nat Exec Nat Cncl for Civil Liberties 1971–73, head public affrs RSC 1974–76; chm: CLEAR 1982–90, Friends of the Earth 1983–86, Citizens Action 1984–90, Campaign for Freedom of Info 1984–90; Lib Pty: pres 1986–87, memb Fed Exec 1988–89, dir Gen Election Campaign Lib Democrats 1990–92; vice-chm public affrs worldwide Burson Marsteller 1993–94; dir of corp and public affairs BAA plc 1994–2000; non-exec dir: Ingenious Media 2000–02, Earls Court and Olympia Gp 2001–04; memb Bd Br Tourist Authy 1997–2003; public affrs advsr MCC 2001–, memb Mgmnt Bd and chm Corp Affrs and Mktg Advsy Ctee ECB 2003–04; memb: English Sports Cncl 2000–02 (sr vice-chm 1999–2002, chm Lottery Panel 1999–2002), UK Sports Cncl 2000–02; *Books* I Know it Was the Place's Fault (1970), Des Wilson's Minority Report – A Diary of Protest (1973), So You Want to Be a Prime Minister: A Personal View of British Politics (1979), The Lead Scandal (1982), Pressure: The A to Z of Campaigning in Britain (1984), The Environmental Crisis (ed, 1984), The Secrets File (ed, 1984), The Citizen Action Handbook (1986), Battle for Power: Inside the

Alliance General Election Campaign (1987), Swimming With the Devilfish: Under the Surface of Professional Poker (2006), Ghosts at the Table (2007); novels: Costa del Sol (1990), Campaign (1992), Private Business, Public Battleground (2002), Memoirs of a Minor Public Figure (2011), Growing Old – the Last Campaign (2014); *Style*— Des Wilson, Esq; ✉ 422 Harold Road, Hastings, East Sussex TN35 5HG

WILSON, (Robert) Gordon; s of Robert George Wilson, of Glasgow; *b* 16 April 1938; *Educ* Douglas HS, Univ of Edinburgh (BL), Univ of Dundee (LLD); *m* 1965, Edith Margaret Hassall; 2 da; *Career* MP (SNP) Dundee East Feb 1974–87; SNP: nat sec 1964–71, vice-chm 1972–73, sr vice-chm 1973–74, dep ldr Parly Gp 1974–79, chm 1979–90, vice-pres until 1997, former treas spokesman; slr; rector Univ of Dundee 1983–86, memb Ct Univ of Abertay Dundee until 1997; chm Marriage Counselling (Tayside) 1989–92, memb Church and Nation Ctee Church of Scotland 2000–03, dir Dundee Age Concern 2001–05, clerk Congregational Bd St Aidans Church and Broughty Ferry New Kirk Dundee 2003–06, chm of tstees SOLAS (Centre for Public Christianity) 2010–13, memb Bd Dundee CAB 2011, dir Options for Scotland 2013; *Publications* SNP: The Turbulent Years 1960–90, Pirates of the Air – the Story of Radio Free Scotland, Scotland: The Battle for Independence 1990–2014; *Recreations* reading, writing; *Style*— Mr Gordon Wilson; ✉ 48 Monifieth Road, Broughty Ferry, Dundee DD5 2RX (☎ 01382 779009, e-mail gordonwilson10@blueyonder.co.uk)

WILSON, Guy Edward Nairne Sandilands; s of John Sandilands Wilson (d 1963), and Penelope Ann, *née* Fisher-Rowe (d 2007); *b* 10 April 1948; *Educ* Heatherdown Sch, Eton, Univ of Aix-en-Provence; *m* 20 Oct 1979, (Marianne) Susan (d 2006), da of James Drummond D'Arcy Clark; 2 s (John b 1984 d 1998, Hugh b 27 Aug 1986); *Career* CA; Ernst & Young: joined 1967, ptnr 1979–2008, seconded to HM Treasy 1989–92; memb Bd Fresnillo plc 2008–; FCA, MSI; *Recreations* cricket, golf, tennis, squash, football, gardening; *Clubs* City of London, Brooks's, MCC, IZ, Arabs, Royal St George's Golf, Berkshire Golf, Luffness New Golf; *Style*— Guy Wilson, Esq

WILSON, Guy Murray; s of Capt Rowland George Wilson (d 1950), and Mollie, *née* Munson (d 1987); *b* 18 February 1950; *Educ* New Coll Oxford (MA), Univ of Manchester (Dip Art Gallery and Museum Studies); *m* 28 Oct 1972, Pamela Ruth, da of Alan Robert McCredie, OBE, of Yorkshire; 2 s (John b 1976, David b 1986), 2 da (Rebecca b 1978, Elizabeth b 1983); *Career* Royal Armouries HM Tower of London: keeper of edged weapons 1978–81, dep master 1981–88, master of the armouries 1988–2002; chm Int Ctee of Museums and Collections of Arms and Military History 2002–10; memb: Br Cmmn for Mil History, Arms and Armour Socs of GB and Denmark, Advsy Ctee on Hist Wreck Sites 1981–99; Liveryman Worshipful Co of Gunmakers 1990, Liveryman Worshipful Co of Armourers and Brasiers 2000; FSA 1984, FRSA 1992; *Books* Treasures from The Tower of London (jtly, 1982), The Royal Armouries in Leeds: The Making of a Museum (jtly, 1996), The Vauxhall Operatory: A Century of Inventions before the Scientific Revolution (2009); numerous articles and papers on arms and armour and military history; *Recreations* walking, reading, singing; *Clubs* Rotary Club of Harrogate Brigantes; *Style*— Mr Guy Wilson, FSA; ✉ Yeoman's Course House, Thornton Hill, Easingwold, York YO61 3PY (☎ 01347 868126, e-mail guy@wilson4004.freeserve.co.uk)

WILSON, Dr Ian; *b* 1964, Belfast; *Educ* Univ of Ulster (DPhil); *Career* composer; written over150 pieces incl concertos, orchestral pieces, string quartets, piano trios, chamber and vocal works; work performed by: Nat Symphony Orch of Ireland, BBC Nat Symphony Orch of Wales, Ulster, Belgrade Philharmonic and Norwegian Radio Orchs, London Mozart Players, Irish Chamber Orch, Vanbrugh, Vogler and Endellion Quartets, Psappha, Gemini and Concorde ensembles; work performed at festivals incl: BBC Proms, Int Soc for Contemporary Music World Music Days, Venice Biennale, Cheltenham, Brighton, Bath, Ultima Oslo (winner composition 1991); Hamelin (chamber opera) 2001–02 (performed Germany and Ireland 2003); dir Sligo New Music Festival 2003–11, assoc composer Ulster Orch 2010–13; Composition Prize Ultima Festival Oslo (for Running, Thinking, Finding) 1991, Macauly Fellowship Arts Council Ireland 1992; AHRB research fell Univ of Ulster 2000–03; Macaulay fell Arts Cncl of Ireland 1992; elected to Aosdana 1998; *Style*— Dr Ian Wilson; ✉ e-mail enquiries@ianwilson.ie, website www.ianwilson.ie

WILSON, Dame Jacqueline; DBE (2008, OBE 2002); da of late Harry Aitken, and Margaret, *née* Clibbens; *b* 17 December 1945, Bath; *Educ* Coombe Girls' Sch, Carshalton Tech Coll; *m* 1965 (m dis), William Millar Wilson; 1 da; *Career* children's author; journalist Jackie magazine D C Thomson Dundee 1963–65 (also gave name to magazine); most borrowed author from public libraries in the UK 2003 and 2004; has sold more than 35 million books in the UK; shortlisted Author of the Year British Book Awards 2003; Children's Laureate 2005–07; chllr Univ of Roehampton 2014; hon doctorate: Univ of Dundee, Univ of Winchester, Univ of Bath, Univ of Roehampton, Kingston Univ; *Books* incl: The Story of Tracy Beaker (1991, adapted for TV (5 series) 2002, adapted for radio), The Suitcase Kid (1992, Children's Book Award 1993), The Bed and Breakfast Star (1994, adapted for radio, Young Telegraph/Fully Booked Award 1995, shortlisted Carnegie Medal 1995), Double Act (1995, Gold Award (winner 9–11 years category and overall winner) Nestlé Smarties Book Prize 1995, shortlisted Carnegie Medal 1995, shortlisted Best Children's Book Writers' Guild Award 1995, Children's Book Award 1996, shortlisted Young Telegraph/Fully Booked Award 1996, screenwriter TV adaptation 2002 (Best Children's Fiction Award RTS 2003)), Bad Girls (1996, shortlisted Carnegie Medal 1996, adapted for stage 2003), Girls in Love (1997, adapted for TV 2003), The Lottie Project (1997, adapted for stage 1999, shortlisted Children's Book Award 1998), Girls Under Pressure (1998, shortlisted Children's Book Award 1999), Girls Out Late (1999), The Illustrated Mum (1999, adapted for TV 2003, shortlisted Carnegie Medal 1999, shortlisted Whitbread Children's Book Award 1999, Children's Book of the Year British Book Awards 2000, Guardian Children's Fiction Prize 2000, shortlisted Children's Book Award 2000), Lizzie Zipmouth (2000, Gold Award (6–8 years category) and Kids' Club Network Special Award Nestlé Smarties Book Prize 2000), Vicky Angel (2000), The Dare Game (2000, adapted for radio, adapted for stage), Dustbin Baby (2001, shortlisted W H Smith Award for Children's Literature 2002), Girls in Tears (2002, Children's Book of the Year British Book Awards 2003), Secrets (2002, shortlisted The Book I Couldn't Put Down Blue Peter Book Award 2003), The Worry Website (2002), Lola Rose (2003), Midnight (2003), Best Friends (2004, shortlisted Red House Children's Book Award 2005), The Diamond Girls (2004), Clean Break (2005), Love Lessons (2005), Candyfloss (2006), Starring Tracy Beaker (2006), Jacky Daydream (2007), Kiss (2007), Totally Jacqueline Wilson (2007), My Sister Jodie (2008), Cookie (2008), My Secret Diary (2009), Hetty Feather (2009, adapted for theatre 2014 (nominated Olivier Award 2015), adapted for TV 2015), Little Darlings (2010), The Longest Whale Song (2010), Lily Alone (2011), Sapphire Battersea (2011), The Worst Thing About My Sister (2012), Emerald Star (2012), Queenie (2013), Diamond (2013), Paws and Whiskers (2014), Opal Plumstead (2014), Butterfly Club (2015); *Clubs* Ivy; *Style*— Dame Jacqueline Wilson, DBE; ✉ c/o David Higham Associates Ltd, 7th Floor, Waverley House, 7–12 Noel Street, London W1F 8GQ (☎ 020 7434 5900, e-mail dha@davidhigham.co.uk, website www.davidhigham.co.uk)

WILSON, James; *Educ* Magdalene Coll Cambridge; *Career* slr; sr ptnr Ince & Co LLP 2008– (joined as trainee 1983); dir Maritime London; *Style*— James Wilson, Esq; ✉ Ince & Co LLP, International House, 1 St Katharine's Way, London E1W 1AY

WILSON, Jane; *b* Newcastle-Upon-Tyne; *Educ* Newcastle Poly (BA), Goldsmiths Coll London (MA); *Career* artist, in partnership with twin sister Louise Wilson, *qv*; prof of art Wolverhampton Univ 2013–15, sr tutor Moving Image Royal Coll of Art 2015; Hon DCL Univ of Northumbria 2002; *Two-Person Exhibitions* since 2000 incl: Turner Prize (Tate Gallery) 1999–2000, Stasi City & Crawl Space (MIT List Visual Arts Centre Cambridge Massachusetts) 2000, Bernier/Eliades Athens 2000, Star City (303 Gallery New York) 2000, Las Vegas, Graveyard Time (Dallas Museum of Art Texas) 2000, Kunst-Werke Berlin 2002, Centro de Fotografia Salamanca Spain 2003, Lisson Gallery London 2003, A Free and Anonymous Movement (Pori Art Museum Finland) 2004, Umea Bildmusset Sweden 2004, Fondazione Davide Halevim Milan 2004, Erewhon (303 Gallery NY) 2004, Bergen Art Museum Norway 2004, Socrates Sculpture Park NY 2004, De Appel Amsterdam 2004, The New Brutalists (Lisson Gallery London) 2005, Sealander (Haunch of Venison Gallery Zurich) 2006 and (New Art Gallery Walsall) 2007–08, Spiteful of Dream, Jane and Louise Wilson (Quad Gallery Derby) 2008–09, Jane and Louise Wilson (303 Gallery NY) 2008, Musée d'Art Contemporain de Montreal Canada 2009, Talbot Rice Gallery Edinburgh 2009, Unfolding the Aryan Papers (BFI Gallery London) 2009, EMPAC Troy NY 2010, Jane and Louise Wilson (Helga de Alvear Madrid) 2010, Suspending Time (Calouste Gulbenkian Fndn Lisbon) 2010, Tempo Suspenso (CGAC Santiago de Compostela Spain) 2010–11, John Hansard Gallery Southampton 2011, Dundee Contemporary Arts 2012, The Toxic Camera (Whitworth Art Gallery Manchester) 2012–13, Jane and Louise Wilson (303 Gallery NY) 2013, False Positives/ False Negatives (Paradise Row Gallery London) 2013, Imperial Measure (C Nichols Project LA) 2014, Undead Sun (Imperial War Museum London) 2014, Future Present (Emmanuel Hoffman Fndn The Schaulager Basel) 2015, Festival Della Memoria Ercolano (Museo Archeological Virtuale (MAV)) 2016, Jane and Louise Wilson (Middlesbrough Institute of Modern Art (MIMA)) 2016, Sealander (Focus Gallery The Getty LA) 2017; *Group Exhibitions* since 2005 incl: Space is the Place (Cranbrook Art Museum Bloomfield Hills Michigan) 2006, Out of Time (Museum of Modern Art NY) 2006, Serpentine Gallery Marathon London 2006, Double Vision (Deutsche Bank NY) 2007, Temptation of Space (Louis Vuitton Paris) 2007, Crossing Walls (Centro Atlantico de Arte Moderno Canary Palms Spain) 2007, Sounding the Subject (MIT List Visual Arts Center Cambridge Massachusetts) 2007, Quad Gallery Derby 2008, Sharjah Biennial 9 UAE (2009), Of Other Spaces (Columbus College of Art & Design Columbus) 2009, The Science of Imagination (Ludwig Museum Budapest) 2010, Centro de Artes Visuais Coimbra Portugal 2010, Star City – The Future Under Communism (Nottingham Contemporary) 2010, ALIAS: Photomonth in Krakow Poland 2011, A Plot for a Biennial (Sharjah Biennial 10 UAE) 2011, Critique and Crisis: Art in Europe Since 1945 (Deutsches Historisches Museum Berlin) 2012, Stanley Kubrick (LACMA LA) 2012–13, Tomorrow Was Already Here (Tamayo Museum Mexico City) 2012–13, The Toxic Camera (Int Film Festival Rotterdam) 2013, Ja Natuurlijk (Gemeentmuseum The Hague) 2013, Interiors (Stuart Shave Modern Art London) 2014, Ruin Lust (Tate Britain) 2014, A Thousand Doors (Gennadius Library and Gardens Athens) 2014, Art Basel Film Program 2014, Conflict, Time, Photography (Tate Modern) 2014, History is Now: 7 Artists Take on Britain (Hayward Gallery London) 2015, BP Walkthrough British Art (Tate Britain) 2015, And There Was Time (Fundacion Helga de Alvear Caceres Spain) 2015, From the Ruins (601 Artspace NY) 2015, Undead Sun (Doclisboa) 2016, Fireflies in the Night (Stavros Niarchos Cultural Center) 2016, Summer Exhibition (RA) 2016, Daydreaming...with Stanley Kubrick (Somerset House London) 2016, SeMA Biennale (Mediacity Seoul Korea) 2016; *Style*— Ms Jane Wilson; ✉ Moving Image Studio, Royal College Of Art, Unit 1, 1–11 Howie Street, London SW11 4AS (☎ 001 212 255 121); Galeria Helga de Alvear, Doctor Fourquet 12, ES-28012 Madrid

WILSON, Prof Janet Ann; da of Henry Donald Wilson (d 1991), of Edinburgh, and Margaret Penuel MacGregor, *née* Robertson (d 2005); *b* 10 November 1955, Haddington, E Lothian; *Educ* George Watson's Ladies' Coll Edinburgh, Univ of Edinburgh Med Sch (BSc, MB ChB, MD, Ellis Prize in Paediatrics); *m* 1, 1987 (m dis 1996), Mark Nicholas Gaze, s of John Owen Gaze; 1 s (Donald John b 1991); m 2, 17 Nov 2012, Christopher Goulding; *Career* house offr: in gen med Eastern Gen Hosp Edinburgh 1979–80, in gen surgery The Royal Infirmary Edinburgh 1980; demonstrator in anatomy Univ of Edinburgh 1980–81, SHO in gen surgery Dept of Clinical Surgery Univ of Edinburgh 1981–82, lectr/ sr registrar in otolaryngology City and Asociated Hosps Edinburgh 1987–92, conslt otolaryngologist and hon sr lectr Royal Infirmary Glasgow 1992–95, prof of otolaryngology, head and neck surgery Univ of Newcastle upon Tyne 1995–; pres: Otorhinolaryngological Research Soc 2002–04 (hon sec 1990–94), North of England Surgical Soc 2006–07, Laryngology and Rhinology Section RSM 2008–09, Harveian Soc of Edinburgh 2014, Br Laryngological Assoc 2014; chair Academic Cncl Br Academic Conference Otolaryngology 2006–09; memb Cncl RCSEd 1995–2000; hon sec ENT-UK Br Assoc of Otorhinolaryngologists 2008–11; European Rhinologic Soc Prize 1986, Br Academic Conf ORL Research Prize 1987, Angell James Prize 1988, Royal Soc of Med Downs Prize 1989, Lionel Coll Meml Fellowship 1990, Ernest Finch visiting prof Sheffield 1996, Univ of London Yearsley lectr 1999, Robert Owen lectr 2001, Kleinsasser lectr 2006, Scott Otology Soc Guthrie lectr 2010, BMA Jobson Horne Prize 2011, Semon Lecture Univ of London 2016; memb: European Rhinologic Soc 1986, Scottish Otolaryngological Soc 1987, Br Soc of Otolaryngologists 1987, Caledonian Soc of Gastroenterology 1989, BMA 1989, Br Soc of Gastroenterology 1992, Br Voice Assoc 1997, Harveian Soc (Edinburgh) 1999; FRCS, FRCSEd, hon fell Royal Coll of Speech and Language Therapists; *Books* Stell and Maran's Head and Neck Surgery (jt author, 4 edn); also 10 book chapters and over 200 scientific papers; *Recreations* performing arts, the company of friends; *Style*— Prof Janet A Wilson; ✉ Oak House, 1 Jesmond Dene Road, Newcastle upon Tyne NE2 3QJ (☎ 0191 284 0251); Department of Otolaryngology, Head and Neck Surgery, University of Newcastle upon Tyne, Freeman Hospital, Newcastle upon Tyne NE7 7DN (☎ 0191 223 1086, fax 0191 223 1246, e-mail j.a.wilson@ncl.ac.uk)

WILSON, Dr Jean Lesley; da of late Alan Herbert Wilson, and Beryl, *née* Wagstaff; *b* 2 August 1945; *Educ* King Edward VI HS for Girls Edgbaston (fndn scholar), Newnham Coll Cambridge (MA, PhD, Clothworkers' exhibitioner, Charles Oldham Shakespeare scholar); *m* 1972, Prof Norman Hammond, *qv*, s of William Hammond; 1 s (Gawain Jonathon Curle b 2 Dec 1975), 1 da (Deborah Julian Curle b 13 Sept 1982); *Career* lectr in English Univ of Edinburgh 1970–72, fell King's Coll Cambridge 1972–75, adjunct prof of English Boston Univ 1994–2007; pres Church Monuments Soc 2013; FSA 1980; *Books* Entertainments for Elizabeth I (1980 and 2008), The Archaeology of Shakespeare (1995, winner Archaeology Book of the Year Award 1996); author of numerous articles in jls and newspapers; *Recreations* needlework; *Style*— Dr Jean Wilson, FSA; ✉ Wholeway, Harlton, Cambridge CB23 1ET (☎ 01223 262376, e-mail jlw29@cam.ac.uk)

WILSON, John; s of Thomas Wilson (d 1993), and Elizabeth, *née* Murray; *b* 28 November 1956, Falkirk; *Educ* Camelon HS Falkirk, Coatbridge Coll, Univ of Glasgow (MA); *m* 27 Aug 1982, Frances McGlinchey; 1 da (Janine b 2 March 1991); *Career* coachbuilder W Alexanders Co Ltd 1972–82, project mangr Castlemilk Housing Involvement Project 1987–94, dir Glasgow Cncl of Tenants Assoc 1994–97, sr economic devpt offr Poverty Alliance 1998–99, fieldwork mangr Poverty Alliance 1999–2001, dir Scottish Low Pay Unit 2001–07; MSP (SNP) Central Scotland 2007–16; memb: RSPB, Historic Scotland, Nat Tst Scotland, Unite; *Style*— John Wilson, Esq; ✉ Merson, Greenfoot, Glenboig, Lanarkshire ML5 2QE (☎ 01236 873282, e-mail johnwilsonscot@hotmail.com)

WILSON, Prof Judith Elizabeth; da of H Perkins (d 1965), of Northants, and Margaret Joan Margrave; *b* 28 May 1950, Northampton; *Educ* Northampton HS, Univ of London; *m* 1969, Fergus Wilson; 2 da (Samantha, Tanya); *Career* property owner; owner of 675 houses in Kent; maths teacher Kent 1971–92, dep headteacher Southlands Sch 1987–92;

W

prof Imperial Coll Business School; *Style*— Prof Judith Wilson; ✉ The Limes, Heath Road, Boughton Monchelsea, Maidstone, Kent ME17 4HS (e-mail fergus.wilson@btopenworld.com)

WILSON, Justin Boyd; s of Keith Ronald Wilson, and Lynne Wilson; *b* 31 July 1978; *Educ* Birkdale Sch; *Career* motor racing driver; began racing Cadet Karts 1987, fifth Formula A Br Championship 1994, third Renault Grand Prix Buckmore Park 1994, winner race Formula Vauxhall Jr Winter Series 1994, winner Formula Vauxhall Challenge Cup 1995, third Formula Vauxhall Jr Championship 1995, third Formula Vauxhall Winter Series 1995 (Best Newcomer), second Formula Vauxhall Championship (Paul Stewart Racing) 1996, fourth Formula Vauxhall Championship (Paul Stewart Racing) 1997, winner Formula Palmer Audi Championship 1998, eighteenth FIA Int Formula 3000 Championship 1999, fifth FIA Int Formula 3000 Championship 2000, winner FIA Int Formula 3000 Championship 2001 (first Br winner, record number of points and podiums), fourth Telefonica World Series by Nissan 2002; Formula One Grand Prix: debut 2003 (test driver Jordan 2001), Minardi then Jaguar 2003; Champ Car World Series Conquest Racing 2004; BRDC Chris Bristow Trophy 1995, finalist McLaren Autosport BRDC Young Driver of the Year Award 1995 and 1998, Gold Star BRDC 2001; *Clubs* BRDC; *Style*— Justin Wilson, Esq; ✉ website www.justinwilson.co.uk

WILSON, Keith Drummond; s of Gordon Drummond Wilson (d 2005), of Maldon, Victoria, Aust, and Heather, *née* Lindsay (d 1994); *b* 18 July 1960; *Educ* The King's Sch Parramatta, Royal Melbourne Inst of Technol; *m* 12 July 1990, Pamela Elizabeth, da of John Angus Mackay (d 2006); 2 da (Elizabeth Rose b 1993, Olivia Catherine b 1996); *Career* news reporter The Herald Melbourne 1979–83, features ed The News and Travel International (TNT) London 1983; Amateur Photographer: news ed 1984–85, dep tech ed 1985–87, features ed 1987–88; launch ed What Camera? 1988–89; ed: Amateur Photographer 1989–98, Photo Technique 1993–95; gp ed IPC Photographic titles 1994–98; ed Crime Weekly 1999, launch ed Voice (for Scottish Telecom) 1999, ed Outdoor Photography 2000–07, gp ed Black & White Photography 2001–05, editorial dir GMC Publications 2005–11, fndr and ed Wild Planet Photo Magazine 2013–16; mangr Photo Panel Euro Imaging & Sound Assoc 1995–97; FRGS; *Books* Focus On Photography (1994), AVA Guide to Travel Photography (2004), Viewfinder (2005); *Recreations* photography, hill walking, cricket, cooking, cinema; *Style*— Keith Wilson, Esq; ✉ Wild Planet Photo Magazine (☎ 07976 610829, e-mail ozkeith@hotmail.com)

WILSON, Louise; *b* Newcastle-Upon-Tyne; *Educ* Duncan of Jordanstone Coll of Art Dundee (BA), Goldsmiths Coll London (MA); *Career* artist, in partnership with twin sister Jane Wilson, *qv*; visiting prof of art Wolverhampton Univ 2013–15, head of photography Univ of Northumbria 2015; Hon DCL Univ of Northumbria 2002; *Two-Person Exhibitions* since 2000 incl: Turner Prize (Tate Gallery) 1999–2000, Stasi City & Crawl Space (MIT List Visual Arts Centre Cambridge Massachusetts) 2000, Bernier/Eliades Athens 2000, Star City (303 Gallery New York) 2000, Las Vegas, Graveyard Time (Dallas Museum of Art Texas) 2000, Kunst-Werke Berlin 2002, Centro de Fotografia Salamanca Spain 2003, Lisson Gallery London 2003, A Free and Anonymous Movement (Pori Art Museum Finland) 2004, Umea Bildmusset Sweden 2004, Fondazione Davide Halevim Milan 2004, Erewhon (303 Gallery NY) 2004, Bergen Art Museum Norway 2004, Socrates Sculpture Park NY 2004, De Appel Amsterdam 2004, The New Brutalists (Lisson Gallery London) 2005, Sealander (Haunch of Venison Gallery Zurich) 2006 and (New Art Gallery Walsall) 2007–08, Spiteful of Dream, Jane and Louise Wilson (Quad Gallery Derby) 2008–09, Jane and Louise Wilson (303 Gallery NY) 2008, Musée d'Art Contemporain de Montreal Canada 2009, Talbot Rice Gallery Edinburgh 2009, Unfolding the Aryan Papers (BFI Gallery London) 2009, EMPAC Troy NY 2010, Jane and Louise Wilson (Helga de Alvear Madrid) 2010, Suspending Time (Calouste Gulbenkian Fndn Lisbon) 2010, Tempo Suspenso (CGAC Santiago de Compostela Spain) 2010–11, John Hansard Gallery Southampton 2011, Dundee Contemporary Arts 2012, The Toxic Camera (Whitworth Art Gallery Manchester) 2012–13, Jane and Louise Wilson (303 Gallery NY) 2013, False Positives/False Negatives (Paradise Row Gallery London) 2013, Imperial Measure (C Nichols Project LA) 2014, Undead Sun (Imperial War Museum London) 2014, Future Present (Emmanuel Hoffman Fndn The Schaulager Basel) 2015, Festival Della Memoria Ercolano (Museo Archeological Virtuale (MAV)) 2016, Jane and Louise Wilson (Middlesbrough Institute of Modern Art (MIMA)) 2016, Sealander (Focus Gallery The Getty LA) 2017; *Group Exhibitions* since 2005 incl: Space is the Place (Cranbrook Art Museum Bloomfield Hills Michigan) 2006, Out of Time (Museum of Modern Art NY) 2006, Serpentine Gallery Marathon London 2006, Double Vision (Deutsche Bank NY) 2007, Temptation of Space (Louis Vuitton Paris) 2007, Crossing Walls (Centro Atlantico de Arte Moderno Canary Palms Spain) 2007, Sounding the Subject (MIT List Visual Arts Center Cambridge Massachusetts) 2007, Quad Gallery Derby 2008, Sharjah Biennial 9 UAE (2009), Of Other Spaces (Columbus College of Art & Design Columbus) 2009, The Science of Imagination (Ludwig Museum Budapest) 2010, Centro de Artes Visuais Coimbra Portugal 2010, Star City – The Future Under Communism (Nottingham Contemporary) 2010, ALIAS: Photomonth in Krakow Poland 2011, A Plot for a Biennial (Sharjah Biennial 10 UAE) 2011, Critique and Crisis: Art in Europe Since 1945 (Deutsches Historisches Museum Berlin) 2012, Stanley Kubrick (LACMA LA) 2012–13, Tomorrow Was Already Here (Tamayo Museum Mexico City) 2012–13, The Toxic Camera (Int Film Festival Rotterdam) 2013, Ja Natuurlijk (Gemeentmuseum The Hague) 2013, Interiors (Stuart Shave Modern Art London) 2014, Ruin Lust (Tate Britain) 2014, A Thousand Doors (Gennadius Library and Gardens Athens) 2014, Art Basel Film Program 2014, Conflict, Time, Photography (Tate Modern) 2014, History is Now: 7 Artists Take on Britain (Hayward Gallery London) 2015, BP Walkthrough British Art (Tate Britain) 2015, And There Was Time (Fundacion Helga de Alvear Caceres Spain) 2015, From the Ruins (601 Artspace NY) 2015, Undead Sun (Doclisboa) 2016, Fireflies in the Night (Stavros Niarchos Cultural Center) 2016, Summer Exhibition (RA) 2016, Daydreaming...with Stanley Kubrick (Somerset House London) 2016, SeMA Biennale (Mediacity Seoul Korea) 2016; *Awards* Barclays Young Artist Award 1993, DAAD Scholarship 1999, nominated for Turner Prize 1999, IASPIS International Artist's Studio Program in Sweden (residency in Stockholm) 2000; *Style*— Ms Louise Wilson

WILSON, Mark Simon; s of Dennis Lionel Wilson, of Great Missenden, Bucks, and Elizabeth, *née* Jones; *b* 10 June 1961, Rugby, Warks; *Educ* Chesham HS, Univ of Birmingham, Coll of Law; *m* 30 Aug 1986, Helen Louise, *née* Swierczek; 2 s (Thomas Ludwik Edward b 19 Jan 1991, Nicholas Mark b 28 Mar 1997), 1 da (Anna Beth b 11 Feb 1993); *Career* slr; articled clerk Kidd Rapinet 1983–85, ptnr Freeth Cartwright 1990–99 (slr 1985–90), fndr ptnr Cartwright King 2000–15, ptnr Richard Nelson LLP 2015–; memb: Law Soc 1985, Serious Fraud Assoc 2001; *Recreations* motor racing, mountain biking, skiing, sailing; *Clubs* BARC; *Style*— Mark Wilson, Esq; ✉ Richard Nelson LLP, Priory Court, 1 Derby Road, Nottingham NG9 2TA (☎ 0845 216 2000, e-mail mark.wilson@richardnelsonllp.co.uk)

WILSON, Brig Sir Mathew John Anthony; 6 Bt (UK 1874), of Eshton Hall, Co York, OBE (Mil 1979, MBE Mil 1971), MC (1972); s of Anthony Thomas Wilson (d 1979), by his 1 w Margaret (d 1980), formerly w of Vernon Motion and da of late Alfred Holden; suc unc, Sir (Mathew) Martin Wilson, 5 Bt 1991; *b* 2 October 1935; *Educ* Trinity Coll Sch Port Hope; *m* 1962, Janet Mary, er da of late Edward Worsfold Mowll, JP, of Walmer; 1 s (Mathew Edward Amcotts b 1966), 1 da (Victoria Mary b 1968); *Heir* s, Mathew Wilson; *Career* Brig King's Own Yorks LI, ret 1983; exec dir Wilderness Fndn (UK) 1983–85; pres and ceo Dolphin Voyaging Inc 1995–; *Books* Taking Terrapin Home: A Love Affair with a Small Catamaran (1994), The Bahamas Cruising Guide with the Turks and Caicos Islands (1997), The Land of War Elephants. Travels Beyond the Pale: Afghanistan, Pakistan, and India (2003); *Clubs* Lakota; *Style*— Brig Sir Mathew Wilson, Bt, OBE, MC

WILSON, Dr Michael Anthony; s of Charles Kenneth Wilson (d 1995), and Bertha, *née* Poppleton (d 1987); *b* 2 June 1936; *Educ* Roundhay Sch, Univ of Leeds (MB ChB, DObstRCOG); *m* 1, 24 Jan 1959 (m dis 2011), Marlene; 2 s (Mark Edward b 3 May 1960, Ian Gregory b 2 May 1962); m 2, 15 April 2012, Beryl May Hunt; *Career* princ in GP Strensall N Yorks 1961–96; pres Yorks Regnl Cncl BMA 1975–79, chm Gen Med Servs Ctee 1984–90 (dep chm 1979–84); dir: BMA Servs Ltd 1987–2000, BMA Pension Fund 1992–2000 (also chm of tstees); memb: Standing Med Ctee to DHSS 1967–69 and 1978–90 (dep chm 1986–90), Cncl BMA 1977–90 and 1992–2000, GMC 1989–2003 (assoc 2003–06), Advsy Bd Med Protection Soc 1990–97, Code of Practice Authy Assoc of Br Pharmaceutical Industry 1990–2013, NHS Clinical Standards Advsy Gp 1991–93, Jt Conslts Ctee 1991–97; vice-pres BMA 2001 (fell 1979–); FRCGP; *Recreations* travel, Rotary, golf; *Clubs* East India, Rotary (York), Ampleforth Coll Golf; *Style*— Dr Michael Wilson; ✉ Court Ash, Woodacre Crescent, Bardsey, Leeds LS17 9DQ (☎ 01937 572381)

WILSON, Michael Sumner; CBE (2012); s of Cdr Peter Sumner Wilson, AFC (d 1993), and Margaret Kathleen, *née* Letchworth (d 1996); *b* 5 December 1943; *Educ* St Edward's Sch Oxford; *m* 5 June 1975 (m dis), Mary Dorothy Wordsworth, da of John Alexander Drysdale (d 1986); 1 da (Amanda Wordsworth Sumner b 12 March 1976); *Career* Equity & Law 1963–68, Abbey Life 1968–71; Hambro Life/Allied Dunbar: broker mangr 1971–73, exec dir 1973–76, main bd dir 1976–82, jt dep md 1982–84, jt md 1984–88, gp chief exec 1988–90; jt fndr dir St James's Place Gp 1991–, jt life pres St James's Place plc 2012– (chief exec 1991–2004, chm 2004–11), chm St James's Place Unit Trust Group 1997–2011, chm St James's Place Fndn 2012–; dir BAT Industries 1989–90, non-exec dir Vendôme Luxury Group plc 1993–98, non-exec dir RIT Capital Ptnrs plc 2013; chm Mental Health Fndn 1996–2000, tstee MQ: Transforming Mental Health 2010–; *Recreations* tennis, racing; *Style*— Michael Wilson, Esq, CBE; ✉ 42 Eaton Place, London SW1X 8AL; St James's Place plc, Spencer House, 27 St James's Place, London SW1A 1NR (☎ 020 7514 1907, fax 020 7514 1952)

WILSON, Michael W C; *b* 15 August 1955, Belfast; *Educ* Queen's Univ of Belfast (LLB, Cert); *Career* admitted slr NI 1978; managing ptnr Elliott Duffy Garrett; pres Slrs' Disciplinary Tbnl 2003–11 (memb 1998–2011); chm Health and Personal Social Services Disciplinary Panel 2005–; chm NI Branch R3 (Assoc of Business Recovery Professionals) 2006–; protector Building Change Tst 2009–; MSPI 1993, licensed insolvency practitioner 1993, FABRP 2000; *Clubs* Belvoir Park Golf, Bredagh GAC; *Style*— Michael Wilson, Esq; ✉ Elliott Duffy Garrett, Royston House, 34 Upper Queen Street, Belfast BT1 6FD (☎ 028 9024 5034, fax 028 9024 1337)

WILSON, Prof Nairn Hutchison Fulton; CBE (2004); s of William Fulton Wilson (d 2000), of Kilmarnock, Ayrshire, and Ann Hutchison, *née* Stratton (d 2011); *b* 26 April 1950; *Educ* Strathallan Sch, Univ of Edinburgh (BDS), Univ of Manchester (MSc, PhD); *m* 1; 2 da (Kirsty b 1972, Shona b 1976 d 1997); m 2, 12 April 1982, Margaret Alexandra, *née* Jones; 1 da (Hannah b 1983), 1 s (Iain b 1984); *Career* lectr in restorative dentistry Univ of Edinburgh 1974–75; Univ of Manchester: lectr 1975–82, sr lectr 1982–86, prof of restorative dentistry 1986–2001, pro-vice-chllr 1997–99, dean and clinical dir Univ Dental Hosp of Manchester 1992–95; KCL: dean and head Dental Inst (at Guy's, King's Coll and St Thomas's Hosps) 2001–12, prof of restorative dentistry 2001–11, dep vice-princ (health) 2009–12, hon prof of dentistry 2012–; non-exec dir North Manchester NHS Healthcare Tst 1994–97; pres: Br Assoc of Teachers of Conservative Dentistry 1992, Section of Odontology Manchester Medical Soc 1993–94, Br Soc for Restorative Dentistry 1994–95, Academy of Operative Dentistry European Sec 1998–2000, Educational Research Gp Int Assoc Dental Research 1998–2000, European Fedn of Conservative Dentistry 2003–05, Section of Odontology RSM 2008–09, Met Branch Br Dental Assoc 2012–13, Royal Odonto-Chirurgical Soc of Scotland 2013–14; Br Dental Assoc: pres-elect 2014–15, pres 2015–16, patron Benevolent Fund 2015–16; ed: Jl of Dentistry 1986–2000, Quintessentials of Dental Practice 2003–08, ed Primary Dental Jl 2016– (chm Editorial Bd until 2016); chm Editorial Bd Dental Practice; dean Faculty of Dental Surgery Royal Coll of Surgns of Edinburgh 1995–98; fndr tstee Manchester Dental Educn Tst 1993–2001; tstee: Oral and Dental Research Tst 1995– (chm and dir 2003–09), Oral Health Fndn (formerly Br Dental Health Fndn) 2013–, Nat Examination Bd for Dental Nurses 2014–; chm: Manchester Dental Educn Centre 1995–2000, Jt Ctee for Specialist Training in Dentistry 1998–99 and 2007–10, Specialist Trg Advsy Ctee for Dentistry 1999–2003, British Dental Eds Forum 2004–09, Cncl of Heads and Deans of Dental Schs 2006–08; pres GDC 1999–2003, pres Section of Odontology RSM 2008–09; registrar UK Public Health Register 2012–15, professional strategic exec European Fedn of Periodontology 2013–, dir Medical and Dental Defence Union of Scotland 2016–; patron Dental Wellness Tst 2011–; pres KCL Assoc 2012–14; external govr Univ of Portsmouth 2012–, dir Univ of Portsmouth Servs Ltd 2016–; College Medal RCS(Ed) 2001, George M Hollenback Meml Prize Acad of Operative Dentistry 2002, John Tomes Medal Br Dental Assoc 2011 (life memb), Dentistry Lifetime Contribution Award 2012, Outstanding Contribution to Dentistry Dentistry Scotland Awards 2012; DSc (hc) Univ of Portsmouth 2010; hon fell Hong Kong Coll of Dental Surgery, hon fell Faculty of Dental Surgery RCS Ireland; fell: American Coll of Dentists, Acad of Dental Materials, Pierre Fauchard Acad, Br Soc for Restorative Dentistry, HE Acad, KCL, Oman Dental Coll; memb: Acad of Operative Dentistry, American Acad of Restorative Dentistry; DRD RCS(Ed), fell FGDP(UK), FDS RCS(Ed), Hon FDS RCS(Eng) 2010, hon FRCPSGlas; *Publications* author of approx 270 scientific papers, author/ed of approx 55 textbooks; *Recreations* various; *Clubs* Strathallian; *Style*— Prof Nairn Wilson, CBE; ✉ 1 Oak Park, Alderley Edge, Cheshire, SK97GS (☎ 01625 586702, e-mail nairn.wilson@btinternet.com)

WILSON, Nicholas; s of Vernon Wilson (d 1971), and Dorothy, *née* Wood (d 1996); *b* 20 June 1945, Northumberland; *Educ* BSc; *m* 10 June 1969, Mary Anne, *née* Bellwood; 2 s (Christopher b 7 May 1972, Alexander b 10 June 1976); *Career* chm: Qatar Investment Fund plc, Epicure Qatar Opportunities Hldgs Ltd, Alternative Investment Strategies plc 2001– (dir 1997–), Beresford Gabler Securities Ltd; non-exec dir Epic Special Opportunities plc; *Style*— Nicholas Wilson, Esq; ✉ e-mail nickwilson@manx.net

WILSON, Nick; s of Stanley Wilson (d 1981), and Dorothy Wilson, of Winchester; *b* 21 April 1949; *Educ* Buxton Coll, Univ of Manchester (BA); *m* Sept 1984, Annie; 3 da (Sadie b 7 March 1986, Abigail, Zoe (twins) b 26 March 1989), 1 s (Bradley b 29 May 1995), 1 step s (Robin b 31 Oct 1974); *Career* dir and prodr children's progs BBC 1975–84, ed children's progs TV-am 1984–87 (devised Wide Awake Club, Wacaday and Are You Awake Yet?), ed children's and youth progs Granada TV 1988–89, dir of progs The Children's Channel 1993–94, ptnr Clear Idea Television 1989– (prodr numerous progs incl Top Banana, Hitman & Her and Coast to Coast), dir of children's progs Channel 5 Broadcasting 1996–2011, children's media conslt/writer 2011–, fndr nickwilson.tv Ltd 2013–; memb: BAFTA, RTS; *Awards* BAFTA nomination for Best Children's Factual Prog 1986, TRIC Award for Best Children's Prog 1987, Chicago Children's Film Festival Best Short Drama (for Snobs); *Recreations* tennis, fly fishing, family; *Clubs* BAFTA; *Style*— Nick Wilson; ☎ 07802 456081, e-mail nickwilson.tv@btconnect.com

WILSON, Nicola; *Career* equestrian; achievements incl: champion Scottish Open 2009, 2010, 2011 and 2014, Gold medal (team) European Championships 2009, Gold medal (team) Alltech World Equestrian Games 2010, Bronze medal (team) European Eventing Championships 2011, Silver medal (team) Olympic Games 2012; *Style*— Ms Nicola

Wilson; ✉ c/o Wallace PR & Communications, The Granary, Church End, Great Rollright, Oxfordshire OX7 5RX

WILSON, Patrick (Pat); s of Brig E W G Wilson, CBE, MC (d 1971), of Selkirk, and Edith Margaret, *née* Smith; *b* 6 June 1931, Selkirk; *Educ* Loretto, Edinburgh Coll of Agric; *m* 22 Nov 1955, Elizabeth Mary; 3 da (Rosemary (Mrs Nicoll) b 30 Aug 1957, Wendy (Mrs Busby) b 14 Sept 1959, Tessa (Mrs Searle) b 17 March 1963), 1 s (Randal b 22 April 1961); *Career* landowner; farmer: Perthshire 1953–, Sutherland and Wester Ross 1960–; chm and dir of several cos, chm Glenleven Estates, md Aberuchill 1981–2005; sr ptnr: Pat Wilson Farms, Pat Wilson Sporting Enterprises, Pat Wilson Farms Blackpark and Kinlochwe; former Scotland chm Br Deer Soc (fndr chm Central Scotland branch), fndr chm of first deer mgmnt gps; memb: Scottish Landowners Fedn, NFU of Scotland; standard bearer Royal Burgh of Selkirk 1955; *Recreations* stalking, shooting, fishing; *Clubs* R&A, Flyfishers, Royal Perth Golfing Soc and County and City, Royal and Ancient Golf Club of St Andrews; *Style*— Pat Wilson, Esq; ✉ Blackpark Lodge, Logiealmond, Perth PH1 3JB (✆ 07831 135748, fax 01738 583707)

WILSON, Paul; OBE (2004); s of Thomas William Wilson (d 1947), of Newcastle upon Tyne, and Gladys Rawden, *née* Scaife (d 1989); *b* 2 August 1947; *Educ* Univ of Northumbria and Univ of London (Dip Nursing), Univ of Northumbria and CNAA (DMS), Henley Management Coll and Brunel Univ (MBA); *Career* registered mental nurse St Nicholas Hosp Newcastle upon Tyne 1965–68, head of nursing in intensive therapy (formerly staff nurse) Royal Victoria Infirmary Newcastle upon Tyne 1970–74 (registered gen nurse 1968–70), mangr of night nursing services W Sector Hosps Northumberland HA 1974–76, staff offr to area nursing offr Merton Sutton and Wandsworth Area HA 1976–77, divnl nursing offr Roehampton Health Dist 1977–82, dir policy and planning Maidstone HA 1985–87 (chief nursing offr 1982–85), gen mangr Mental Health Services Greater Glasgow Health Bd 1987–91, dir of health care contracting Lothian Health Bd 1994–95 (dir of operations 1991–94), dir NHS Tsts NHS in Scotland Management Executive 1994–95, currently exec nurse dir NHS Lanarkshire; *Recreations* cats, children, Moi, food, travel, music; *Style*— Paul Wilson, OBE

WILSON, Prof Pelham Mark Hedley; s of John Leonard Wilson (d 1972), and Dilys Winifred Pugh, *née* Taylor (d 2012); *b* 29 April 1952, Bromley, Kent; *Educ* St Paul's, St John's Coll Cambridge; *m* 22 Aug 1992, Sibylle Cornelia, da of Erich Hennig (d 2003); 3 c (Constanze b 20 June 1993, Tobias b 13 Sept 1995, Alexia b 5 April 1998); *Career* fell Jesus Coll Cambridge 1977–81, fell Trinity Coll Cambridge 1981–; Univ of Cambridge: asst lectr 1980–85, lectr 1985–96, reader in algebraic geometry 1996–2001, prof of algebraic geometry 2001–; ScD Univ of Cambridge 1998; *Books* Curved Spaces (2007), Dirichlet Branes and Mirror Symmetry (jtly, 2009); numerous papers in scientific jls; *Style*— Prof Pelham Wilson; ✉ Trinity College, Cambridge CB2 1TQ

WILSON, Peter; MBE (2013); s of Charles Wilson, of Sherborne, Dorset, and Fiona, *née* Perkins; *b* 15 September 1986, Dorchester; *Career* sport shooter; achievements incl: Gold medal (individual) World Cup 2011, Gold medal (individual) World Cup 2012 (world record), Gold medal (individual) Olympic Games 2012; hon doctorate Bournemouth Univ 2014; *Style*— Mr Peter Wilson, MBE; ✉ Twitter @wilpex

WILSON, Peter Stafford; MBE (2000), DL (Norfolk 2008); s of Sir Geoffrey Wilson, and Judy Chamberlain, *née* Trowbridge; *b* 12 January 1951; *Educ* St Albans Sch Washington DC, Westminster, Exeter Coll Oxford; *m* 1, (m dis); m 2, 1980 (m dis), Patricia Clare; 2 s (Alexander, Tim), 1 da (Nichola); *Career* dir Bush Theatre London 1975–76; assoc dir Lyric Theatre Hammersmith 1980–83; ind prodr 1983–; credits incl: The Woman in Black, Stephen Daldry's An Inspector Calls, The Railway Children (Waterloo Station), Broken Glass, Rowan Atkinson at the Atkinson; chief exec: PW Productions Ltd 1983–, HM Tennent Ltd 1988–90, Norwich Theatre Royal 1992–; dir/prodr Mobil Touring Theatre 1985–; chair HighTide Festival Prodns; memb Bd: Propeller, Curve (Leicester); *Recreations* tennis, swimming, sailing, diving, bicycling; *Style*— Peter Wilson, Esq, MBE, DL; ✉ PWP Limited, 80–81 St Martin's Lane, London WC2N 4AA (✆ 020 7395 7580, fax 020 7240 2947, e-mail p.wilson@theatreroyalnorwich.co.uk)

WILSON, Rebecca; da of Stephen Wilson, of Norwich, and Sharon Wilson; *b* 6 December 1967, Norwich; *Educ* Hewett Sch Norwich, Christ's Coll Cambridge (BA), UCL (MA); *m* Oct 2000, Geoff Dyer; *Career* publishing dir of non-fiction Weidenfeld & Nicolson 1997–2001, dep ed Modern Painters 2002–04, ed ArtReview 2004–06, head of devpt Saatchi Online and ed Saatchi Online's daily magazine 2006–13, chief curator and dir Art Advisory Saatchi Art 2013–; *Style*— Ms Rebecca Wilson; ✉ The Saatchi Gallery, 77 Eaton Square, London SW1W 9AW (✆ 020 7811 5007, e-mail rebeccawilson10@gmail.com, website www.saatchigallery.com)

WILSON, Richard; OBE (1994); s of John Boyd Wilson (d 1975), and Euphemia, *née* Colquhoun (d 1960); *b* 9 July 1936; *Educ* Greenock HS, RADA; *Career* actor/director; rector Univ of Glasgow 1996–98; *Theatre* lead roles in Operation Bad Apple, An Honourable Trade, May Days, Normal Service (Hampstead Theatre), Waiting for God (Manchester Royal Exchange); Edinburgh Traverse: title role in Uncle Vanya, Vladamir in Waiting for Godot; Stephen Feeble in The Weekend (tour and West End), Kabak in Occupations (Stables Theatre Manchester); Dr Rance in What the Butler Saw (RNT) 1995; as dir Royal Court: Women Laughing, God's Second In Command, Other Worlds, Heaven and Hell, A Wholly Healthy Glasgow, Toast, Four, Mr Kolpert, Nightingale and Chase, I just Stopped By To See The Man; Royal Exchange Manchester: The Lodger, Women Laughing (Best New Play Manchester Evening News, Writers' Guild of GB Award for regnl theatre), An Inspector Calls, A Wholly Healthy Glasgow; Hampstead Theatre: Imagine Drowning (John Whiting Award), President Wilson in Paris, Lenz; Bush Theatre: View of Kabul, Commitments; also Prin (Lyric Hammersmith and Lyric Shaftesbury), Simply Disconnected (Chichester) 1996, Tom and Clem (Aldwych) 1997, Where Do We Live (Royal Court), Under the Whaleback (Royal Court) 2003; *Television* BBC: One Foot in the Grave (6 series), One Foot in the Algarve, The Vision Thing, Unnatural Pursuits, Fatherland, Normal Service, Tutti Frutti, The Holy City, Poppyland, Life as We Know it, In the Red, Life Support; Granada/Actor: Cluedo, Sherlock Holmes; YTV/Actor: High and Dry, Room at the Bottom, Emmerdale Farm; Under the Hammer, The Other Side of Paradise (Central/Grundy), Inspector Morse (Zenith), Mr Bean (Thames), Selling Hitler (Euston), The Woman I Love (HTV), Murder by the Book (TVS), Walking the Plank (Yorkshire), Sweeney, Only When I Laugh (4 series), Victorian Scandals, Sharp Intake of Breath (2 series), My Good Woman (3 series), Crown Court, Gulliver's Travels (Channel 4) 1996, Duck Patrol (LWT) 1997, High Stakes (ITV), Father Ted (Hat Trick), Born and Bred (BBC) 2003; dir BBC: Changing Step (winner Best Feature BANFF TV), A Wholly Unhealthy Glasgow, Under the Hammer, Remainder Man, Commitments; *Film* actor: Soft Top Hard Shoulder, Carry on Columbus, A Dry White Season, How to get ahead in Advertising, Fellow Travellers, Prick up your Ears, Whoops Apocalypse, Passage to India, Women Talking Dirty, Watch that Man; *Awards* British Comedy Award for Top TV Comedy Actor 1991, BAFTA Award for Light Entertainment 1991 and 1993, Scottish BAFTA for Best TV Actor 1993; *Recreations* squash, swimming and eating; *Clubs* RAC, Groucho, Garrick; *Style*— Richard Wilson, Esq, OBE; ✉ c/o Conway van Gelder Ltd, 18–21 Jermyn Street, London SW1Y 6HP (✆ 020 7287 0077, fax 020 7287 1940)

WILSON, Richard Henry; s of Arthur Wilson, and Ivy Wilson; *b* 1953; *Educ* London Coll of Printing, Hornsey Coll of Art (Dip AD), Univ of Reading (MFA); *m* Miyako Narita; 2 c (Aldo Ziranek Wilson, Yma Ziranek Wilson); *Career* artist; DAAD artist in residence Berlin 1992–93; contrib to numerous art pubns, work in various public and private collections; also musician (co-fndr and performer Bow Gamelan Ensemble 1983–91); Henry Moore fell Univ of East London 2002–04, visiting prof Univ of East London 2005; memb Artistic Record Ctee Imperial War Museum; Hon Dr Univ of Middlesex 2008; RA 2006; *Solo Exhibitions* incl: 20:50 (Matt's Gallery London) 1987, One Piece at a Time (installation inside Tyne Bridge Newcastle) 1987, Art of Our Time (Saatchi Collection and Royal Scot Acad Edinburgh) 1987, Leading Lights (Brandts Kunsthallen Odense Denmark) 1989, Sea Level (Arnolfini Gallery Bristol) 1989, She Came in Through the Bathroom Window (Matt's Gallery London) 1989, High-Tec (MOMA Oxford) 1989, Take Away (Centre of Contemporary Art Warsaw 1990, Saatchi Gallery 1991), Lodger (Galerie Valeria Belvedere Milan) 1991, Swift Half and Return to Sender (Galerie de l'Ancienne Poste Calais) 1992, Drawings (Künstlerhaus Bethanien Berlin) 1993, Matt's Gallery London 1994, Butler Gallery Kilkenny Castle Ireland 1994, LA/UK Festival Museum of Contemporary Art Los Angeles 1994, Galerie Klaus Fischer Berlin 1995, Galerie Valeria Belvedere Milan 1996, Room 6 Channel View Hotel Towner Art Gallery Eastbourne 1996, Formative Processes Gimpel Fils London 1996, Jamming Gears Serpentine Gallery 1996, In Zwickau Germany 1998, Over Easy (public art work) 1999, Xmas Tree (Tate Gallery) 1998–99, Hung Drawn Quartered (Tel Aviv) 1999, Pipe Dreams (Architectural Assoc), Slice of Reality (N Meadow Sculpture Project Millennium Dome) 2000, Structurally Sound (Ex Teresa Arte Actual Mexico City) 2000, Turbine Hall Swimming Pool (Clare Coll Mission Church London) 2000, Set North for Japan (Echigo Tsumari Project Niigata Prefecture Japan) 2000, Set North for Japan (Gimpel Fils London) 2001, A Sculpture for the Millennium Square (Leeds) 2001, Final Corner (permanent work, World Cup Project Fukuroi City Japan) 2002, Irons in the Fire (Mappin Gallery Sheffield) 2002–, Leeds Metropolitan Gallery 2002, Talbot Rice Gallery Edinburgh 2002, Irons in the Fire (Wapping Project London) 2003, Butterfly (Wapping Project London) 2003 and (Centre for Sculpture Bury) 2014, Rolling Rig (De La Warr Pavilion Bexhill-on-Sea) 2003, Caveau (Palazzo delle Papesse Contemporary Art Centre Sienna) 2003, Solo (Program Gallery London) 2004, Queen & Gantry (Storey Gallery Lancaster) 2005, Curve Gallery Barbican 2006, 5 Piece Kit (Matthew Bown Gallery London) 2006, Richard Wilson (Edinburgh Festival) 2008, Folkestone Triennial 2008, Force Quit (Worksprojects Bristol) 2009, 20:50 (Sulaymanyah Iraq) 2009 and (Saatchi Gallery London) 2010, Matthew Bown Gallery Berlin 2010, House of the Nobleman London 2010; *Group Exhibitions* incl: Up a Blind Alley (Trigon Biennale Graz Austria) 1987, Hot Live Still (Plymouth Art Centre) 1987, High Rise (São Paulo Bienal Brazil 1989, UK and USSR 1990), All Mod Cons (Edge Biennale Newcastle) 1990, Heatwave (Serpentine Gallery London) 1992, Galleria Mazzocchi Parma Italy 1992, Sydney Biennale 1992, Museet for Samtidskunst Oslo 1993, Private Kunstwerk Berlin 1993, The Boatshow (Cafe Gallery London) 1993, Time Out Billboard Project London 1993, Sendezeit: A Space without Art (Alexanderplatz Berlin) 1993, Tachikawa Public Art Project Tokyo 1994, Art Unlimited: Artists' Multiples (South Bank touring) 1994, Negev Desert Symposium Israel 1995, Contemporary Art Soc Drawing Show 1995, Nomad: Six European Sculptors (Städtische Ausstellungshalle Münster) 1996, Art-itecture: Ten Artists (Museum of Contemporary Art Barcelona) 1996, Islands (Nat Museum of Contemporary Art Canberra Australia) 1996, Dexion 50th Anniversary Sculpture Cmmn (NEC Birmingham) 1997, 54 x 54 (Times Building London) 1999, The Office of Misplaced Events (Temporary Annexe Lotta Hammer London) 1999, Structurally Sound (Ex Teresa Arte Actual Mexico City) 2000, Field Day (Taipei Fine Art Museum Taipei) 2001, Double Vision (Galerie fur Zeitgenossischekunst Leipzig) 2001, Close Encounters of the Art Kind (V&A) 2001, Multiplication (touring exhbn with Br Cncl) 2001–03, Thinking Big: 21st Century Br Sculpture (Peggy Guggenheim Collection Venice) 2002, Groove (Huddersfield Art Gallery) 2002, Independence (South London Art Gallery) 2003, Bad Behaviour (Longside Gallery Yorkshire Sculpture Park) 2003, Wings of Art (Stadt Aachen – Ludwig Forum für Internationale Kunst) 2003–04, 'Marks' in Space (Usher Gallery Lincoln) 2004, Galleria Fumagalli Bergamo 2004, Break Neck Speed (Yokohama Triennal) 2005, RA Summer Exhbn 2006, 2007, 2010, 2013 and 2014, Butterfly (Platform China Beijing) 2006, This will not happen without you (Locus and tour) 2007, Objects of Art (Matthew Bown Gallery) 2007, R Wilson (Galleria Fumagalli Italy) 2007, Meter's Running (Pula) 2007, Bank Job, Viaggio in Italy (Palazzo Fabroni Pistoia) 2010, Taps, Improvisations (with Paul Burwell, Matt's Gallery London) 2010, RA Now 2012, Encounters RA (Asia and Qatar) 2012/13, The Fabricated Object (Summaria Lunn Gallery) 2012/13 and (Ha Gamle Prestegard Norway) 2013, Bow Gamelan Ensemble Estuary Show (Docklands Museum) 2013, Lane 61 (Aichi Triennial Nagoya Japan) 2013, 1513 A Ship's Opera (Thames Festival) 2013, Exploding Utopias (Laure Genillard Gallery) 2013, No Formulas (Chelsea Space) 2013, The World Turned Upside Down (Meade Gallery) 2013, Bunny Smash (Museum of Contemporary Art Tokyo) 2013/14, Whitstable Festival 2014, Making It (Longside Gallery Yorkshire Sculpture Park and Mead Gallery) 2015; *Permanent Works* Rock'n'hole (Lincoln City and Archeological Museum) 2005; *Public Work* Turning the place Over (Year of Culture Liverpool) 2007, Hang on a minute lads I've got a great idea (De la Warr Pavilion Bexhill) 2012 and (Peninsula Hotel Hong Kong) 2015; *Sculpture Commissions* Square the Block (LSE) 2009, Shack Stack (St James's devpt Chelsea dock) 2010, Slipstream (Terminal 2 Heathrow) 2014; *Awards* Boise travel scholarship 1977, Arts Cncl minor award 1977, Gtr London Arts Project award 1978, 1981 and 1989, RSA award 1996, The Architectural Assoc Maeda Visiting Artist Award 1998, Paul Hamlyn Fndn Award to Visual Artists 2002–05, The Marsh Award for Excellence in Public Art 2014; *Publications* Richard Wilson (2001), Richard Wilson (2005); *Style*— Richard Wilson, RA; ✉ 44 Banyard Road, London SE16 2YA (✆ 020 7231 7312); c/o Michelle D'Souza Fine Art

WILSON, Rob; MP; *Career* former advsr to David Davis MP, cncllr (Cons) Reading BC 1992–96 and 2003–06; MP (Cons) Reading E 2005– (Parly candidate (Cons) Carmarthen W and Pembrokeshire S 2001), shadow min for HE 2007–; *Style*— Rob Wilson, Esq, MP; ✉ House of Commons, London SW1A 0AA

WILSON, Sir Robert Peter; KCMG (2000); s of Alfred Wilson (d 1951), and Dorothy Eileen Wilson, MBE, *née* Mathews (d 1991); *b* 2 September 1943, Carshalton, Surrey; *Educ* Epsom Coll, Univ of Sussex (BA), Harvard Business Sch (AMP); *m* 7 Feb 1975, Shirley Elisabeth, da of George Robson, of Hunmanby, N Yorks; 1 s (Andrew), 1 da (Nicola); *Career* asst economist Dunlop Ltd 1966–67, economist Mobil Oil Co Ltd 1967–70; Rio Tinto Gp (Rio Tinto Zinc Gp until 1997): joined 1970, md A M and S Europe Ltd 1979–82, head of planning and devpt RTZ plc 1982–87, main bd dir 1987–2003, chief exec RTZ Corporation plc 1991–97, exec chm Rio Tinto plc 1997–2003, exec chm Rio Tinto Ltd 1998–2003; chm Riverstone Energy Ltd 2013–16; non-exec dir: CRA Ltd (Australia) 1990 (unified with RTZ 1995, renamed Rio Tinto Ltd 1997), Boots Company plc 1991–98, BP plc 1998–2002, Diageo plc 1998–2003, The Economist Gp 2002–09 (non-exec chm 2003–09), BG Gp plc 2002–12 (non-exec chm 2004–12), GlaxoSmithKline plc 2003–14; sr advsr Morgan Stanley 2012–14; chm Int Cncl for Mining and Metals 2002–03; tstee Camborne Sch of Mines 1993–99, patron Centre for Energy, Petroleum and Mineral Law and Policy Univ Dundee 2010–; Hon DSc: Univ of Exeter 1993, Univ of Birmingham 2002, Univ of Sussex 2004; Hon LLD Univ of Dundee 2001; CIMgt 1991, FRSA 1999; *Recreations* theatre, opera; *Style*— Sir Robert Wilson, KCMG; ✉ e-mail robert@wilsonrp.com

WILSON, Ruth; *b* 13 January 1982, Ashford, Surrey; *Educ* Notre Dame Sch, Esher Coll, Univ of Nottingham, LAMDA; *Career* actress; *Television* Jane Eyre 2006, Capturing Mary 2007, A Real Summer 2007, The Doctor Who Hears Voices 2008, The Prisoner 2009, Small Island 2009, Luther 2010–13, The Affair 2014 (Outstanding Actress In A Drama

Series Golden Globes 2015); *Theatre* Philistines (RNT) 2007, A Streetcar Named Desire (Donmar Warehouse) 2009 (Best Supporting Actress Olivier Award 2009), Through a Glass Darkly (Almeida) 2010, Anna Christie (Donmar Warehouse) 2011 (Best Actress Olivier Award 2012), The El. Train (Hoxton Hall) 2013; *Film* Anna Karenina 2012, The Lone Ranger 2013, Saving Mr Banks 2013, Suite Francaise 2013, Locke 2013; *Style—* Ms Ruth Wilson; ✉ c/o Troika, 10a Christina Street, London EC2A 4PA

WILSON, Sally-Ann; da of G E Wilson, and Barbara June, *née* Griffin; *b* 16 June 1959, Ashford, Kent; *Educ* Thomas Peacock Sch Rye, Univ of E Anglia (BA, MPhil); *m* 2003, Alistair Richard (Dick) Meadows; *Career* former prodr/dir BBC and Anglia TV; Public Media Alliance (formerly Cwlth Broadcasting Assoc (CBA)): worldview project dir 2001–10, sec-gen 2010–14, ceo 2014–; Hon DBA Univ of Bedfordshire; *Publications* Operation Survival: A Celebration of People and Nature in Scotland (1996); *Recreations* history, walking, natural history; *Style—* Ms Sally-Ann Wilson; ✉ The Public Media Alliance, Room 1.80, DEV, UEA, Norwich NR4 7TJ (e-mail sally-ann@publicmediaalliance.org)

WILSON, Sammy; MP, MLA; *b* 4 April 1953; *Career* teacher; cncllr E Belfast CC 1981–; memb NI Assembly (DUP): Belfast E 1998–2003, Antrim E 2003–; MP (DUP) Antrim E 2005– (Parly candidate (DUP): Strangford 1992, Antrim E 2001); memb NI Policing Bd 2001–05; *Style—* Sammy Wilson, Esq, MP, MLA; ✉ House of Commons, London SW1A 0AA

WILSON, Simon; *Career* jewellery designer/retailer; co-fndr (with Nicky Butler) Butler and Wilson Antiquarius Market King's Road Chelsea 1968, opened flagship shop Fulham Rd 1974, cmmnd to design Christmas light display for Regent Street 1979–80 and 1980–81, Export Dept opened 1983, cmmnd to design exclusive range for Giorgio Armani 1984, second shop opened South Molton St 1985, joined London Designer Collections (first show Olympia) and opened concession at Harrods 1986, opened second concession at Jaeger Regent St 1987, shops opened West Hollywood Calif, Glasgow and at Selfridges 1988, major restrospective exhbn celebrating 21st anniversary 1989, subject of book Rough Diamonds (author Vivienne Becker) 1990, launched extended accessory line (belts and handbags) 1991, retail ops extended to Heathrow Airport 1992, joined QVC home shopping channel 1993, cmmnd to design exclusive range for tourists visiting Tower of London 1994; *Style—* Simon Wilson, Esq; ✉ Butler & Wilson, 189 Fulham Road, London SW3 6JN; Butler & Wilson, 20 South Molton Street, London W1K 5QY

WILSON, Stephen Richard Mallett (Sam); MBE (2016), DL (Suffolk 2006); s of Dr Peter Remington Wilson (d 1997), of Taunton, and Kathleen Rosemary Hough, *née* Mallett (d 1988); *b* 12 October 1941; *Educ* Uppingham, Clare Coll Cambridge (MA), Coll of Law Guildford; *m* 1969, Marycita Jane, da of Gwynn Craven Hargrove; 2 da (Gemma Harriet b 11 April 1972, Alexandra Jane b 17 Jan 1974), 1 s (Thomas William Gwynn b 1 Sept 1979); *Career* articled clerk Simmons & Simmons (admitted 1966); ptnr: Westhorp Ward & Catchpole 1968–89, Birkett Westhorp & Long 1989–95, Birketts 1995–2000 (conslt 2000–06); non-exec chm Boydell & Brewer Group Ltd (publishers) until 2015; pres Suffolk & N Essex Law Soc 1988 (sec 1980–88), formerly clerk to Gen Cmmrs of Income Tax (Stowmarket Div); Law Soc: memb 1964–, memb Cncl 1990–2001, chm Standards & Guidance Ctee 1996–99, chm Professional Standards Appeals Panel 1996–2008, memb Adjudication Panel 2001–08; tbnl judge HM Cts and Tbnls Service 1999–2014, chm St John Cncl Suffolk 1999–2004, chm St Elizabeth Hospice Ipswich 2008–12, chm Northgate Fndn Ipswich 2012–14; FRSA 1999–2005; *Recreations* walking, bridge; *Clubs* Garrick; *Style—* Sam Wilson, Esq, MBE, DL; ✉ c/o Birketts LLP, 24–26 Museum Street, Ipswich, Suffolk IP1 1HZ (☎ 01473 232300)

WILSON, Stuart Robert; s of Alasdair Ian Wilson, of Glasgow, and Joyce Mary, *née* MacCallum; *b* 20 February 1966, Glasgow; *Educ* Jordanhill Coll Sch Glasgow, Nat Film and Television Sch; *Partner* Victoria Clare Beattie; 1 da (Ava Ceileir Beattie-Wilson b 23 May 2008); *Career* production sound mixer; Scottish Film Trg Tst Technician Trg Scheme 1986–87; memb: Assoc of Motion Picture Sound (AMPS) 1997, BAFTA 2006, European Film Acad (EFA) 2009, AMPAS 2013; *Film* incl: The Land Girls 1998, In This World 2002 (nominated Best Technical Innovation in Sound BIFA Award 2002), 24 Hour Party People 2002, The Dreamers 2003, 9 Songs 2004, The Constant Gardener 2005 (nominated Best Sound BAFTA 2006), Marie Antoinette 2006, Harry Potter and the Order of the Phoenix 2006, Eastern Promises 2007 (Best Overall Sound Canadian Acad Award 2007), The Fantastic Mr Fox 2008, Harry Potter and the Deathly Hallows Parts 1 and 2 2009 (Best Sound Critics Choice Award 2011, nominated Best Sound BAFTA 2012), War Horse 2010 (nominated Best Achievement in Sound Mixing Acad Award 2012, nominated Best Sound BAFTA 2012, nominated Best Sound Critics Choice Award 2012), George Harrison Living in the Material World 2011 (nominated Outstanding Sound Mixing Emmy Award 2011), Skyfall 2012 (nominated Best Achievement in Sound Mixing Acad Award 2013, nominated Best Sound BAFTA 2013), Cinderella 2013, Star Wars: The Force Awakens 2015; *Publications* articles in jls incl: Sound & Picture Magazine, Line Up Magazine, Resolution Magazine; *Recreations* cinema, music, reading, travel, walking, yoga; *Style—* Stuart Wilson, Esq; ✉ c/o Sue Greenleaves, Independent Talent Group, Whitfield Street, London W1T 2RH (☎ 020 7636 6565)

WILSON, Sir (Robert James) Timothy (Tim); kt (2011), DL (Herts 2011); s of John Wilson (d 2004), of Leeds, and Joan Pendleton, *née* Roddis (d 1987); *b* 2 April 1949, Leeds; *Educ* Temple Moor Sch Leeds, Univ of Reading (BSc), Lancaster Univ (MA), Walden Univ (PhD); *m* 8 Jan 1972, Jacqueline, *née* Hinds; 2 da (Joanna Louise b 9 May 1982, Catherine Elizabeth b 2 Jan 1985); *Career* lectr Leeds Poly 1972–84, dir of studies Cranfield Univ 1984–87, asst dir Leicester Poly 1987–91, dep dir Hatfield Poly 1991–92; Univ of Hertfordshire: pro-vice-chllr 1992–2003, vice-chllr 2003–10, emeritus prof 2011–; author of over 40 pubns on operational research and educnl mgmnt 1982–2002; memb Bd: E of England Devpt Agency (EEDA) 2003–09, HEFCE 2005–11, Raffles Univ Singapore 2007–11, Unite Gp plc 2010–, Univ of Law Ltd 2012–15; tstee Gordon House Hospice Letchworth 2012–; England RFU: staff coach 1984–89, A-list referee 1991–94; pres Letchworth Golf Club 2012–15 (Capt 2001); Hon DEd Univ of Plymouth 2012, Hon DEd Univ of Hertfordshire 2013, Hon DSc London South Bank Univ 2015; FRSA 2008; *Recreations* rugby union, golf, dog walking; *Style—* Sir Tim Wilson, DL; ☎ 07770 746480, e-mail wilson.pendleton@gmail.com; University of Hertfordshire, College Lane, Hatfield, Hertfordshire AL10 9AB

WILSON, Prof Timothy Hugh; s of Hugh Walker Wilson (d 1965), and Lilian Rosemary, *née* Kirke (d 2007); *b* 8 April 1950; *Educ* Winchester, Mercersburg Acad USA, Corpus Christi Coll Oxford (MA), Warburg Inst Univ of London (MPhil), Univ of Leicester; *m* 12 May 1984, Jane, da of Francis George Lott (d 2001), and Anne Josephine Lott (d 1996); 2 s (Alastair James Johnnie b 11 June 1983, David George Lorenzo b 15 March 1992), 1 da (Julia Annie Jane b 17 Sept 1986); *Career* res asst National Maritime Museum 1977–79, asst keeper Dept of Medieval and Later Antiquities British Museum 1979–90, keeper of Western Art Ashmolean Museum 1990–2013, Barrie and Deedee Wigmore research keeper Dept of Western Art Ashmolean Museum 2013–; prof of the arts of the Renaissance Univ of Oxford 2010–; tstee Radcliffe Tst; fell: Villa I Tatti Florence 1984, Balliol Coll Oxford 1990, Royal Soc of Painter Printmakers 1990, Accademia Raffaello Urbino 2003, Accademia Pietro Vannucci Perugia 2008, Frick Center for the History of Collecting NY 2012; FSA 1989; *Publications* Flags At Sea (1986, 2 edn 1999), Ceramic Art of the Italian Renaissance (1987), Maiolica: Italian Renaissance Ceramics in the Ashmolean Museum (1989, 2 edn 2003), Le Maioliche Rinascimentali nelle Collezioni della Fondazione Cassa di Risparmio di Perugia (jtly, 2006–07), Italian Renaissance Ceramics: A Catalogue of the British Museum Collection (jtly, 2009); contrib to books and exhbn catalogues, various articles in specialist jls on Renaissance ceramics and related subjects; *Style—* Prof Timothy Wilson, FSA; ✉ Balliol College, Oxford OX1 3BJ; Department of Western Art, Ashmolean Museum, Oxford OX1 2PH (☎ 01865 278041, e-mail timothy.wilson@ashmus.ox.ac.uk, website www.ashmus.ox.ac.uk/contact/staffpages/?pid=386)

WILSON, Valerie; *Educ* Cowley Girls GS St Helens, Univ of Hull (BA), Univ of Edinburgh (MSc), Univ of Sheffield (EdD); *m* ; 3 s; *Career* teacher in various secdy schools 1966–72, tutor Edinburgh Univ Centre for Continuing Educn 1978–85, princ conslt Int Trg Services Ltd 1986–90, dir Stirling Univ Mgmnt Devpt Unit 1991–94, prog mangr Scot Cncl for Research in Educn 1994–97, princ researcher Scot Office Educational Research Unit 1997–99, dir Scottish Cncl for Research in Educn 1999–2002, dir SCRE Centre Univ of Glasgow 2002–04, hon sr research fell Univ of Glasgow 2004–16; memb Scot, Br and European Educational Research Assoc; author of various research reports, articles and chapters in books; FIPD 1989; *Recreations* memb reading group, hill walking; *Style—* Dr Valerie Wilson; ✉ e-mail valerie.wilson11@btinternet.com

WILSON OF CULWORTH, Rt Hon Lord; Rt Hon Sir Nicholas Allan Roy Wilson; kt (1993), PC (2005); s of late (Roderick) Peter Garratt Wilson, and late (Dorothy) Anne, *née* Chenevix-Trench; *b* 9 May 1945; *Educ* Bryanston, Worcester Coll Oxford (BA); *m* 14 Dec 1974, Margaret, da of Reginald Frank Higgins (d 1986); 1 s (Matthew b 1977), 1 da (Camilla b 1981); *Career* called to the Bar Inner Temple 1967; practised Western Circuit, recorder of the Crown Court 1987–93, QC 1987, judge of the High Court of Justice (Family Div) 1993–2005, Lord Justice of Appeal 2005–11, Justice of the Supreme Court of the UK 2011–; pres Family Mediators Assoc 1998–2013; Hon Dr Staffordshire Univ 2004; hon fell Worcester Coll Oxford 2008; *Style—* The Rt Hon Lord Wilson of Culworth; ✉ The Supreme Court of the United Kingdom, Parliament Square, London SW1P 3BD

WILSON OF DINTON, Baron (Life Peer UK 2002), of Dinton in the County of Buckinghamshire; Sir Richard Thomas James Wilson; GCB (2001, KCB 1997, CB 1991); s of Richard Ridley Wilson (d 1982), and Frieda Bell Wilson, *née* Finlay (d 1980); *b* 11 October 1942, Cardiff; *Educ* Radley, Clare Coll Cambridge (MA, LLM); *m* 25 March 1972, Caroline Margaret, da of Rt Hon Sir Frank Lee, GCMG, KCB (d 1971); 1 s (Hon Tom b 10 March 1979), 1 da (Hon Amy b 16 Feb 1981); *Career* called to the Bar Middle Temple 1965; private sec Bd of Trade 1969–71 (asst princ 1966–), princ Cabinet Office 1971, asst sec Dept of Energy 1977 (joined Dept 1974), team leader privatisation of Britoil 1982, promoted to princ estab and fin offr (under sec) 1982, mgmnt and personnel office Cabinet Office 1986, economic secretariat (dep sec) Cabinet Office 1987–90, dep sec HM Treasy 1990–92, permanent sec DOE 1992–94, permanent under sec of state Home Office 1994–97, Sec to the Cabinet and Head of the Home Civil Service 1998–2002; master Emmanuel Coll Cambridge 2002–12 (life fell 2012–); non-exec chm C Hoare & Co 2006–16; non-exec dir: Xansa plc 2003–07, British Sky Broadcasting Gp plc 2003–13; chm Cncl Radley Coll 2004–10 (memb 1995–2010), chm Prince's Teaching Inst 2005–09; *Clubs* Brooks's; *Style—* The Lord Wilson of Dinton, GCB; ✉ Emmanuel College, St Andrew's Street, Cambridge CB2 3AP

WILSON OF TILLYORN, Baron (Life Peer UK 1992), of Finzean in the District of Kincardine and Deeside and of Fanling in Hong Kong; Sir David Clive Wilson; KT (2000), GCMG (1991, KCMG 1987, CMG 1985); s of Rev William Skinner Wilson (d 1942), and Enid, *née* Sanders (d 1997); *b* 14 February 1935; *Educ* Trinity Coll Glenalmond, Keble Coll Oxford (scholar, MA), Univ of Hong Kong, Columbia Univ NY (visiting scholar), Univ of London (PhD); *m* 1 April 1967, Natasha Helen Mary, da of late Bernard Gustav Alexander; 2 s (Hon Peter Michael Alexander b 31 March 1968, Hon Andrew Marcus William b 21 June 1969); *Career* Nat Serv The Black Watch (RHR) 1953–55; HM Dip Serv: joined SE Asia Dept FO 1958, third sec Vientiane 1959–60, language student Hong Kong 1960–62, third then second sec Peking 1963–65, first sec Far Eastern Dept 1965–68, resigned 1968; ed The China Quarterly (Contemporary China Inst SOAS Univ of London) 1968–74; rejoined HM Dip Serv 1974, Cabinet Office 1974–77, political advsr to Govr of Hong Kong 1977–81, head S Euro Dept FCO 1981–84, asst under sec of state responsible for Asia and the Pacific FCO 1984–87, Govr and C-in-C of Hong Kong 1987–92; memb: Bd Br Cncl 1993–2002 (chm Scottish Ctee 1993–2002), Cncl CBI Scotland 1993–2002, PM's Advsy Ctee on Business Appts 2000–09 (chm 2008–09); chm Scottish and Southern Energy plc (formerly Scottish Hydro-Electric plc) 1993–2000, dir Martin Currie Pacific Trust plc 1993–2003; chllr Univ of Aberdeen 1997–2013; master Peterhouse Cambridge 2002–08, dep vice-chllr Univ of Cambridge 2005–08; pres: Bhutan Soc of the UK 1993–2008, Hong Kong Soc 1994–2012, Hong Kong Assoc 1994–2015; vice-pres RSGS 1996–; chm of tstees Nat Museums of Scotland 2002–06 (tstee 1999–2006); chm: Scottish Peers Assoc 2000–02 (vice-chm 1998–2000), Cncl Glenalmond Coll 2000–05 (memb 1993–2005), Advsy Cncl St Paul's Cathedral 2009–; memb Carnegie Tst for the Universities of Scotland 2000–16, tstee Scotland's Churches Tst (formerly Scotland's Churches Scheme) 1999–2002 and 2008–15, vice-pres Scotland's Churches Tst 2015–; registrar Order of St Michael and St George 2001–10, Lord High Cmmr Gen Assembly of the Church of Scotland 2010 and 2011; Burgess of Guild City of Aberdeen 2004; hon fell Keble Coll Oxford 1987, hon fell Peterhouse Cambridge 2008; Hon LLD: Univ of Aberdeen 1990, Univ of Abertay Dundee 1995, Chinese Univ of Hong Kong 1996; Hon DLitt: Univ of Sydney 1991, Univ of Hong Kong 2006 and 2011; Dr (hc) Univ of Edinburgh 2011; FRSE 2000 (pres 2008–11); KStJ 1987; *Recreations* hillwalking, theatre, reading; *Clubs* Alpine, New (Edinburgh), Royal Northern and Univ (Aberdeen); *Style—* The Rt Hon the Lord Wilson of Tillyorn, KT, GCMG, FRSE; ✉ House of Lords, London SW1A 0PW

WILSON-JOHNSON, David Robert; s of Harry Kenneth Johnson, of Irthlingborough, Northants, and Sylvia Constance, *née* Wilson; *b* 16 November 1950; *Educ* Wellingborough Sch, Br Inst of Florence, St Catharine's Coll Cambridge (BA), RAM; *Career* baritone; Royal Opera House Covent Garden debut We Come to the River 1976, Paris Opera debut Die Meistersinger 1989, US debut with Cleveland Orch 1990, NY debut with NY Philharmonic 1992; dir Ferrandou Summer Singing Sch 1986–; prof of singing Amsterdam Conservatorium 2004–; ARAM 1984, FRAM 1988; *Performances* at Covent Garden incl: Billy Budd 1982 and 1995, L'Enfant et les Sortilèges 1983 and 1987, Boris Godunov 1984, Die Zauberflöte 1985, 1986 and 1987, Turandot 1987, Madam Butterfly 1988, St François d'Assise (title role) 1988 (winner Evening Standard Award for Opera); others incl: Eight Songs for a Mad King (Paris) 1979, Last Night of the Proms 1981 and 1986, Count Heribert in Die Verschwörenen (Schubert, BBC Proms) 1997; Paris Opera incl: Die Meistersinger, Die Zauberflöte, Billy Budd, Messiaen (Amsterdam, Brussels, Lyon, NY, Edinburgh Festival); Netherlands Opera incl: Punch and Judy (Birtwistle) 1992, Von Heute Auf Morgen (Schoenberg) 1995, The Nose (Shostakovich) 1996, Oedipe (Enescu's) 1996; festival appearances at: Glyndebourne, Edinburgh, Bath, Bergen, Berlin, Geneva, Graz, Holland, Hong Kong, Jerusalem, NYC, Orange, Paris, Salzburg, Vienna; *Recordings* incl: Schubert Winterreise, Schoenberg Ode to Napoleon, La Traviata, Lucrezia Borgia, Mozart Masses from King's College, Haydn Nelson Mass, Belshazzar's Feast, Elgar The Kingdom, Berlioz L'Enfance du Christ, Tippett The Ice Break, Bach Cantatas and B Minor Mass; *Films* The Midsummer Marriage (Sir Michael Tippett), The Lighthouse (Sir Peter Maxwell Davies), Or Shall We Die (Michael Berkeley/Richard Eyre); *Recreations* swimming, slimming, gardening, growing walnuts at house in the Lot; *Style—* David Wilson-Johnson, Esq; ✉ Prinsengracht 455, 1016 Amsterdam, Netherlands (☎ +31 20 772 8104); Impulse Art Management, PO Box 15401, 1001 MK Amsterdam, Netherlands (☎ +31 20 626 6944, e-mail jumbo@ferrandou.org)

WILSON-SMITH, Christopher; QC (1986); s of Roy Seaton Wilson-Smith (d 1993), and Jane, *née* Broderick (d 1948); *b* 18 February 1944; *Educ* Borstal Institution in Swiss Alps, Michael Hall Rudolph Steiner Sch, Cncl of Legal Educn; *m* 6 Jan 1996, Marian; 4 c from previous m (Andrew b 4 Aug 1967, James b 1 May 1969, Johanaa b 1 June 1972, Benjamin b 28 Oct 1982); *Career* called to the Bar Gray's Inn 1965 (bencher 1996); recorder of the Crown Court (civil and crime) 1977; called to the NSW Bar Australia 2000; memb: Common Law Bar Assoc, Professional Bar Assoc, Assoc of Personal Injury Lawyers, SIA; former chm Hoe Bridge Prep Sch; *Recreations* my children and grandchildren, golf, bridge, my new wife; *Clubs* Mark's, Woking Golf; *Style—* Christopher Wilson-Smith, Esq, QC; ✉ Harlsbury Hook Heath Avenue, Woking GU22 0HH; Outer Temple Chambers, 222 Strand, Temple, London WC2R 1BA (☎ 020 7353 6381, fax 020 7583 1786)

WILTON, (James) Andrew Rutley; s of Herbert Rutley Wilton, and Mary Cecilia Buckerfield; *Educ* Dulwich Coll, Trinity Coll Cambridge; *Career* asst keeper: British Art Walker Art Gallery Liverpool 1965–67, Dept of Prints and Drawings British Museum 1967–76; curator Prints and Drawings Yale Center for British Art New Haven 1976–80, asst keeper Dept of Prints and Drawings British Museum 1980–85; Tate Gallery: curator Turner Collection The Clore Gallery 1985–89, keeper of the British Collection 1989–97, keeper and sr research fell 1998–2002; visiting research fell Tate Britain; hon curator of Prints and Drawings Royal Acad of Arts; Hon Liveryman and Hon Curator Worshipful Co of Painter-Stainers; FSA, Hon RWS, FRSA; *Books* Constable's English Landscape Scenery (1976), The Wood Engravings of William Blake (1976), British Watercolours 1750–1850 (1977), Turner in Switzerland (with John Russell, 1977), William Pars: Journey through the Alps (1979), The Life and Work of J M W Turner (1979), Turner Abroad (1982), Turner in his Time (1987), Five Centuries of British Painting (2002), Turner as Draughtsman (2006); author of numerous exhibition catalogues; *Recreations* music, walking, architecture, food; *Clubs* Athenaeum, Chelsea Arts, London Sketch; *Style—* Andrew Wilton, Esq; ✉ e-mail awilton1@btinternet.com

WILTON, Christopher Edward John; CMG (2003); s of late Sir John Wilton, KCMG, KCVO, MC, of Chichester, W Sussex, and Lady (Maureen) Wilton; *b* 16 December 1951; *Educ* Tonbridge, Univ of Manchester (BA); *m* 31 July 1975, Dianne, *née* Hodgkinson; 1 da (Caroline Victoria b 16 Jan 1981), 1 s (Richard Charles b 30 March 1984); *Career* prodn supervisor Esso Petroleum 1975–77, joined FCO 1977, second sec then first sec Bahrain 1978–81, FCO 1981–84, first sec Tokyo 1984–88, seconded to Cabinet Office 1988–90, cnsllr (commercial) Riyadh 1990–94, consul-gen Dubai 1994–97, FCO 1997–98, rgnl md GEC (latterly BAE Systems) 1998–2000, ambass to Kuwait 2002–05, ret; Middle East advsr Royal Bank of Scot 2005–08, Middle East advsr Selex Sensors and Aviation Systems 2005–08, chair Advsy Cncl London Middle East Inst 2006–08, memb Exec Ctee Arab Br C of C 2006–10, advsr de Mellow & Co Wealth Mgmnt 2012–15; co-chm Kuwait-Br Friendship Soc 2006–13, Middle East advsr EMCIIS 2008–12; currently: dir DCW Conslts Ltd, Middle East advsr Group4/Securicor, exec dir BlueSea UK Ltd; vice-chm DTZ plc 2009–11; chair Bd of Tstees Raleigh Adventurous Trg Charity until 2012, memb Bd of Tstees Wallacea Tst, chm Bd of Tstees Rosemary Fndn Hospice at Home Charity 2014–; Chevalier d'Honneur Chaîne des Rotisseurs; *Recreations* cooking, walking, piano, deserts; *Clubs* Athenaeum; *Style—* Christopher Wilton, Esq, CMG; ✉ c/o The Athenaeum, 107 Pall Mall, London SW1Y 5ER

WILTON, Dame Penelope; DBE (2016, OBE 2004); *b* Scarborough; *m* 1, 1974 (m dis 1984) Daniel Massey; m 2, 1990 (m dis 2001), Sir Ian Holm, *qv*; *Career* actress; *Theatre* NT: The Philanderer, Betrayal, Sisterly Feelings, Man and Superman, Much Ado About Nothing, Major Barbara, The Secret Rapture, Piano, Landscape; Greenwich Theatre: Measure for Measure, All's Well that Ends Well, The Norman Conquests; Royal Court: The Philanthropist, West of Suez; Nottingham Playhouse: King Lear, Widowers House; other credits incl: The Cherry Orchard (Lyceum Theatre Edinburgh), The Seagull (Chichester), Bloomsbury (Phoenix), The Deep Blue Sea (Almeida and Apollo), Andromache (The Old Vic), Vita and Virginia (Ambassadors), Moon Light (Pinter Festival), Landscape (Gate Theatre Dublin), Cherry Orchard (RSC), The Chalk Garden (Donmar Warehouse) 2008 (Best Actress Evening Standard Theatre Award 2008); *Television* Mrs Warren's Profession 1972, The Song of Songs 1973, The Pearcross Girls, King Lear 1975, The Widowing of Mrs Holroyd 1976, Pasmore, The Norman Conquests 1978, Othello 1981, Country 1981, The Tale of Beatrix Potter 1982, Ever Decreasing Circles 1984–89, The Monocled Mutineer 1986, Screaming 1992, The Borrowers 1992–93 (2 series), The Deep Blue Sea 1994, Madly in Love, Landscape, This Could Be the Last Time, Talking Heads (Nights in the Garden of Spain) 1998, Alice Through the Looking Glass 1998, Wives and Daughters 1999, The Whistle-Blower 2001, Bob & Rose 2001, Victoria & Albert 2001, Lucky Jim 2003, Doctor Who 2005 and 2008, Five Days 2007, Half Broken Things 2007, The Passion 2008, Downton Abbey 2010–, South Riding 2011, North by Northamptonshire 2011–12, The Girl 2012; *Films* incl: Joseph Andrews 1977, French Lieutenant's Woman 1981, Clockwise 1986, Cry Freedom 1987, Blame it on the Bellboy 1992, The Secret Rapture 1993, Carrington 1995, Tom's Midnight Garden 1999, Iris 2001, Calendar Girls 2003, Shaun of the Dead 2004, Pride and Prejudice 2005, Match Point 2005, The History Boys 2006, The Best Exotic Marigold Hotel 2011; *Style—* Dame Penelope Wilton, DBE

WILTON, Rosalyn Susan; *née* Trup; *b* 25 January 1952; *Educ* Univ of London (BSc); *Career* dir: GNI Ltd 1982–84, Drexel Burnham Lambert Ltd 1984–90; Reuters Ltd: sr vice-pres 1990–92, non-exec dir 1990–99, md Transaction Products 1992–99, memb Exec Ctee 1998–99; ceo Hemscott plc 1999–2006, chm IPREO Inc 2006–; sr advsr: 31 2007–11, Providence Equity Ptnrs 2011–; dir London Int Financial Futures Exchange 1985–90; non-exec dir: LIFFE 1984–90, Scottish Widows plc 1997–2000, Optos plc 2007–; *Style—* Mrs Rosalyn Wilton

WINCH, Prof Donald Norman; s of Sidney Winch, and Iris May, *née* Button; *b* 15 April 1935; *Educ* Sutton GS, LSE (BSc Econ), Princeton Univ (PhD); *m* 5 Aug 1983, Doreen Alice, *née* Matthews; *Career* visiting lectr Univ of Calif Berkeley 1959–60, lectr in economics Univ of Edinburgh 1960–63; Univ of Sussex: lectr 1963–66, reader 1966–69, prof of the history of economics 1969–, dean Sch of Social Scis 1968–74, pro-vice-chllr arts and social studies 1986–89; pubns sec Royal Econ Soc 1971–2016; vice-pres Br Acad 1993–94; Hon DLitt Univ of Sussex 2006; FBA 1986, FRHistS 1987; *Books* Classical Political Economy and Colonies (1965), James Mill: Selected Economic Writings (1966), Economics and Policy (1969), The Economic Advisory Council (with S K Howson, 1976), Adam Smith's Politics (1978), That Noble Science of Politics (with S Collini and J Burrow, 1983), Malthus (1987), Riches and Poverty (1996), Wealth and Life (2009); *Recreations* gardening; *Style—* Prof Donald Winch; ✉ University of Sussex, Falmer, Brighton, East Sussex BN1 9QN (☎ 01273 678634, fax 01273 625972, e-mail d.winch@sussex.ac.uk)

WINCHESTER, Dean of; *see:* Atwell, Very Rev James Edgar

WINCKLESS, Sarah; da of Bob Winckless, and Valerie Hart; *b* 18 October 1973, Reading, Berks; *Educ* Tiffin Girls' Sch Kingston upon Thames, Millfield, Fitzwilliam Coll Cambridge (Netball, Rowing, Athletics and Basketball blues); *Career* amateur rower; memb Cambridge Univ Women's Boat Club 1995–97 (pres 1996–97), sr int debut 1998; achievements incl: Silver medal single sculls World Univ Games 1998, ninth place double sculls Olympic Games Sydney 2000, Bronze medal double sculls Olympic Games Athens 2004, winner quadruple sculls World Cup 2005 and 2006, Gold medal quadruple sculls World Championships 2005 and 2006, Olympic Games Beijing 2008; chair Br Olympic Assoc Athletes' Cmmn 2010–14; leadership coach and motivational speaker; patron Scottish Huntington's Disease Assoc; Helen Rollason Award for Inspiration The Sunday Times and Sky Sports Women of the Year 2013; *Style—* Miss Sarah Winckless; ✉ 11 Shepherds Close, Henley, Buckinghamshire SL6 5LY (☎ 07788 458925, e-mail winckls@aol.com or sarah@sarahwinckless.com)

WINDEATT, Prof Barry Alexander Corelli; s of Edwin Peter Windeatt, and Queenie, *née* Rusbridge; *b* 5 April 1950; *Educ* Sutton GS Surrey, St Catharine's Coll Cambridge (MA, PhD, LittD); *Career* research fell Gonville & Caius Coll Cambridge 1974–78, fell Emmanuel Coll Cambridge 1978– (dir of studies in English 1979–98, keeper of rare books 1997–, vice-master 2013–); Cambridge Univ: asst lectr in English 1983–87, lectr in English 1987–95, reader in medieval literature 1995–2001, prof of English 2001– (chm English Faculty 1997–99, chair New Building for Cambridge English Ctee 1999–2005); *Publications* Chaucer's Dream-Poetry: Sources and Analogues (ed and trans, 1982), Geoffrey Chaucer, Troilus and Criseyde: A New Edition of The Book of Troilus (ed, 1984), The Book of Margery Kempe (trans, 1985), Chaucer Traditions (ed with Ruth Morse, 1990), The Oxford Guides to Chaucer: Troilus and Criseyde (1992), English Mystics of the Middle Ages (ed, 1994), Geoffrey Chaucer, Troilus and Criseyde: A New Translation (trans, 1998), The Book of Margery Kempe (ed, 2000), Troilus and Criseyde (ed, 2003), Julian of Norwich, Revelations of Divine Love: A New Translation (trans, 2015), Julian of Norwich, Revelations of Divine Love (ed, 2016); author of articles and reviews on medieval literature; *Recreations* other people's gardens, garden history, opera, explorations with Pevsner; *Style—* Prof Barry Windeatt; ✉ Emmanuel College, Cambridge CB2 3AP (☎ 01223 334214, e-mail baw1000@cam.ac.uk)

WINDER, Robert James; s of Herbert James Winder (d 1984), of London, and Mary, *née* Dalby; *b* 26 September 1959; *Educ* Bradfield Coll, St Catherine's Coll Oxford (BA); *m* 1989, Hermione, *née* Davies; 2 s (Luke b 1993, Kit b 1995); *Career* on staff Euromoney 1982–86, The Independent 1986– (literary ed until 1995, occasional contrib 1995–), dep ed Granta Publications 1997–99, Culture ed Independent on Sunday 2000–01; *Books* No Admission (1988), The Marriage of Time and Convenience (1994), Hell for Leather: A Modern Cricket Journey (1996), Bloody Foreigners: The Story of Immigration to Britain (2004), The Final Act of Mr Shakespeare (2010), Open Secrets (2010), The Little Wonder: 150 Years of Wisden (2013), Half-Time: The Glorious Summer of 1934 (2015); *Recreations* reading, writing, sport; *Style—* Robert Winder, Esq; ✉ 125 Elgin Crescent, London W11 2JH (☎ 020 7727 0640)

WINDLE, Prof Alan Hardwick; s of Stuart George Windle (d 1979), and Myrtle Lilian, *née* Povey (d 1960); *b* 20 June 1942; *Educ* Whitgift Sch, Imperial Coll London (BSc (Eng), ARSM, Bessemer medal, RSA Silver medal), Trinity Coll Cambridge (PhD, ScD); *m* 14 Sept 1968, Janet Susan, da of Dr Claude Morris Carr (d 2004), and Lorna, *née* Christopherson (d 1997); 3 da (Emma Rachel b 16 Oct 1969, Lucy-Clare b 17 June 1971, Rosemary Joy b 9 July 1976), 1 s (Roy Dudley Andrew b 22 Feb 1973); *Career* ICI research fell 1966–67, lectr in metallurgy Imperial Coll London 1967–75; Univ of Cambridge: lectr in materials science 1975–92, fell Trinity Coll 1978– (tutor 1983–91), prof of materials science 1992–2013 (emeritus prof 2014–), acting dir Melville Lab for Polymer Synthesis 1993–94, head Dept of Materials Science and Metallurgy 1995–2000; exec dir Cambridge-MIT Inst 2000–03, vice-pres Inst of Materials 2001–, dir Pfizer Inst for Pharmaceutical Materials Science 2006–; Rosenhain medal Inst of Metals 1987, Swinburne medal and prize Plastics and Rubber Inst 1992, Founders' Medal Polymer Physics Gp of the Inst of Physics, RSC and Inst of Materials 2007, Royal Soc Armourers and Braziers Medal 2007; govr The Whitgift Fndn 1997–2001, chm of tstees Mission Aviation Fellowship Europe 2001–03, cmmr The Royal Cmmn for the Exhbn of 1851 2001–10; Liveryman Worshipful Co of Founders 2011; fell American Physical Soc 2001, foreign memb Indian Acad of Sciences 2007; FIM 1992, FInstP 1997 (MInstP 1971), FRS 1997; *Books* A First Course in Crystallography (1978), Liquid Crystalline Polymers (with Prof A M Donald, 1992, 2 edn with Dr S Hanna and Prof A M Donald, 2006); *Recreations* flying light aircraft, model engineering; *Style—* Prof Alan Windle, FRS; ✉ Department of Materials Science and Metallurgy, University of Cambridge, Charles Babbage Road, Cambridge CB3 0FS (☎ 01223 334321, e-mail ahw1@cam.ac.uk)

WINDLE-TAYLOR, Paul Carey; s of Dr Edwin Windle-Taylor, CBE (d 1990), and Diana, *née* Grove (d 1987); *b* 25 November 1948; *Educ* Mill Hill Sch, Emmanuel Coll Cambridge (MA, MB BChir), St Thomas' Hosp London, MBA; *m* 1, 1973 (m dis); m 2, 1996; *Career* conslt otolaryngologist; FRCS; *Recreations* fly fishing, fine wines; *Clubs* Flyfishers'; *Style—* Paul C Windle-Taylor, Esq; ✉ e-mail pcw-t@dial.pipex.com

WINDSOR; *see also:* Royal Family section

WINDSOR, Dame Barbara; DBE (2016, MBE); da of John Deeks, and Rose, *née* Ellis; *b* 6 August 1937; *Educ* Our Lady's Convent London, Aida Foster's Stage Sch; *m* 2000, Scott Mitchell; *Career* actress; began career aged 13 in pantomime, subsequently toured singing in cabaret (incl Ronnie Scott Band); numerous appearances on chat and quiz shows; Freeman City of London 2010; *Theatre* incl: Love from Judy (West End debut), Fings Ain't Wot They Used to Be (Garrick), Oh, What a Lovely War (Broadway), Come Spy with Me (Whitehall, with Danny La Rue), Marie Lloyd in Sing A Rude Song (Garrick), The Threepenny Opera (with Vanessa Redgrave), The Owl and the Pussycat, Carry on London (Victoria Palace), A Merry Whiff of Windsor (one woman show, UK and world tour), Maria in Twelfth Night (Chichester Festival Co), Calamity Jane (nat tour), Kath in Kenneth William's prodn of Entertaining Mr Sloane (Lyric Hammersmith), The Mating Game, Miss Adelaide in Guys and Dolls (tour), Kath in first nat tour of Entertaining Mr Sloane (nominated Martini Regional Theatre Award for Best Actress), God in Spamalot; *Pantomime* numerous appearances incl: Babes in the Wood (Palladium), Fairy Godmother in Cinderella (Orchard Dartford) 1995–96; *Television* incl: Dreamers Highway, The Jack Jackson TV Show, Six Five Special, The Rag Trade (BBC), subject of This Is Your Life (Thames), Obituary Show (Channel Four), One Foot in the Grave (BBC), Peggy Mitchell in EastEnders 1994–2010 (Lifetime Achievement Award Br Soap Awards 2009), host Funny World (BBC) 1996, subject of Hall of Fame (BBC), Star for a Night (BBC), The Kumars at No 42 (BBC), subject of Who Do You Think You Are? (BBC) 2007; *Films* incl: Sparrers Can't Sing, Carry on films (first Carry on Spying 1964), Lost, Too Hot to Handle, Flame in the Street, On the Fiddle, Hair of the Dog, Chitty Chitty Bang Bang, A Study in Terror, Comrades, The Boyfriend, Double Vision, Cor Blimey, Alice In Wonderland; *Radio* numerous incl Fancy A Bit; *Albums* Barbara Windsor; numerous incl single Sparrers Can't Sing (top 30 hit); *Books* Laughter and Tears of a Cockney Sparrow, All of Me (2000); *Style—* Dame Barbara Windsor, DBE; ✉ Barbara Windsor MBE, Sauce E Limited, 7 Devonshire Mews West, London, W1G 6QE

WINDSOR, Dean of; *see:* Conner, Very Rev David John

WINDSOR, Dr Malcolm; OBE (2004); s of Leonard George Windsor, and Nancy, *née* Cordy; *Educ* Univ of Bristol (PhD); *m*; 2 da; *Career* industry res placement Cadbury-Schweppes Ltd 1955–62, res fell Univ of Calif 1966–68, memb Res Inst UK (MAFF Torry Res Stn) 1968–75, memb Chief Scientist's Gp MAFF 1975–84, on secondment Cabinet Office 1981, sec N Atlantic Salmon Conservation Orgn (NASCO) 1984–; chair EC int evaluation of first EC-funded prog of Fisheries and Aquaculture R&D, cmmnd by the EU to carry out an independent review of its Science and Technology Agreement with NZ 2013; UK scientist rep at int fisheries meetings and confs; chm Duddington Village Cons Soc; appointed Buckland Fndn prof 2014; CChem, FRSC; *Publications* author of one book and approximately 45 published papers; *Recreations* walking, jazz, bread making, conservation; *Style—* Dr Malcolm Windsor, OBE; ✉ 1 Duddington House Courtyard, Edinburgh EH15 1JG

W

WINDSOR, Stuart James; s of E J Windsor (d 1965), and Gwendoline Knott (d 1979); *b* 26 May 1946; *Educ* Chace Sch; *m* 1, Oct 1971 (m dis 2005); 3 s (Alexander b 3 Nov 1976, Miles b 4 Jan 1985, Freddie b 26 Dec 1988); m 2, June 2006, Harriet Hepburn; 1 da (Lily Katie b 28 Dec 2007); *Career* photographer; journalist until 1970, Fleet St photographer 1970–78 (Times, Sun, Observer, Daily Mail); photographic projects incl: coast to coast trip of America documenting lifestyles, rock and pop projects incl Rolling Stones Hyde Park concert, living with Kabre Tribe in N Togo (as part of Nat Geographic anthropological educnl field trip), project in Galapagos Islands, coverage of Mount Kinabalu Borneo climb; created photographic template for iconic P&O flag logo; solo exhibition of retrospective work Embankment Gallery; contrib to magazines and books on numerous travel and architectural topics, major rock and pop archive sale Bonhams, picture library contains 100,000 worldwide images, produces masterclasses on photographic and visual arts subjects, documented Polish Lifestyles in 360 Intactive Digital Images, created virtual 360 tour Last Night of the Proms BBC TV, 360 digital coverage Nobel Peace Prize Oslo, estab digital photo library Capital City Pictures devoted to London, creative ed Bond Street Magazine, dir of photography IPIX UK, photographic conslt Brooklands Museum; curator Private View exhibition (Brooklands Museum); creative dir: Universal 360, Sutton-Windsor Assocs, 360x360; *Books* Images of Egypt, France and French Lifestyles, Australia – This Beautiful Land, Dream Machines – BMW, The Arts – A History of Expression in the 21st Century; *CD-ROM* French Experience, Brooklands Museum Private View (print collection); *Recreations* travel, family, classic motoring, photography, cycling; *Style*— Stuart Windsor, Esq; ✉ 37 Baalbec Road, Highbury, London N5 1QN (✆ 07834 360999, e-mail stuart@stuartwindsor.com, website www.stuartwindsor.com)

WINEARLS, Prof Christopher Good; s of late Capt James Robert Winearls, and late Sheila, *née* Boardman; *b* 25 September 1949; *Educ* Diocesan Coll Rondebosch Cape Town, Univ of Cape Town (MB ChB), Univ of Oxford (DPhil); *m* 6 Dec 1975, Beryl Claire, da of late Dr Wilmer Edward George Butler, of Cairns, Queensland, Aust; 4 s (James b 1979, Alastair b 1982, Stuart b 1985, Robert Frederick Good b 1991); *Career* sr lectr in med Royal Postgrad Med Sch London 1986–88, conslt nephrologist Oxford Kidney Unit Oxford Radcliffe Hosp 1988– (chm Oxford Kidney Unit Tst Fund 1995–2015); censor RCP 2001–03; Rhodes scholar 1972; clinical vice-pres Renal Assoc of GB 2004–07; sr research fell Jesus Coll Oxford 2005–15 (emeritus fell 2015–), princ examiner in medicine Univ of Oxford 2007–12; Osler Medal Royal Coll of Physicians 2005; FRCP (London); *Publications* Oxford Textbook of Clinical Nephrology (ed, 2005, 4 edn 2015); *Recreations* sailing, photography; *Style*— Prof Christopher Winearls; ✉ The Oxford Kidney Unit, The Churchill, Oxford University Hospital, Oxford OX3 7LE (✆ 01865 225804, fax 01865 225773)

WINETROUBE, Assoc Prof Simon; s of Warren Winetroube, of Hull, and Leonore, *née* Fink (d 1997); *b* 5 April 1961, E Yorks; *Educ* Univ of Warwick (LLB), Chester Sch of Law, Univ of Lancaster (MA), Chartered Inst of Marketing (Cert), Univ of Cambridge/ Royal Soc of Arts (DipTEFLA); *m* 11 April 1999 (m dis 2014), Csilla Eszter, *née* Homolya; 2 s (Lewis Lee b 24 Dec 2003, Vincent Leonard b 10 Sept 2005); *Career* mgmnt trainee Northern Foods Ltd 1985–87, teacher of English UK and Spain 1987–90; Br Cncl: joined 1992, sr teacher Thailand 1992–94, regnl devpt offr Vietnam 1994–95, project mangr Hungary 1996–97, English and educn offr Russia 1998–2001, dep dir Ethiopia 2001–04, mangr Middle East Change Prog 2005–07, dir Qatar 2007–12; dir Curtin English Curtin Univ 2012–, memb Academic Bd Cutin Coll 2012–, memb Ctee Univ English Colls Australia; memb Advsy Cncl Nat ELT Accreditation Scheme (NEAS) 2014–; ed: Press Ahead (Ahademiai Kiado) Budapest 1997–, Business Reader Kereskedelmi Vendeglatoiporu Foiskola (KVIF) Press 1997–; founding fell Br Inst for English Language Teaching; *Recreations* marathon runner, squash player, amateur actor, rugby league player for Northern Dairies, Hull, Univ of Warwick, Univ of Lancaster, and Nottingham Crusaders (also represented Notts); *Clubs* Doha Rugby, South Perth Rugby League, Applecross Tennis; *Style*— Assoc Prof Simon Winetroube; ✉ 53A Reynolds Road, Mount Pleasant, Perth, WA 6153, Australia (e-mail simon.winetroube@curtin.edu.au)

WINKELMAN, Joseph William; s of George William Winkelman (d 1956), and Cleo Lucretia, *née* Harness (d 1978); *b* 20 September 1941; *Educ* Keokuk HS (pres of graduating class), Univ of the South Sewanee TN (BA, pres of graduating class), Wharton Sch of Fin Univ of Pennsylvania, Ruskin Sch of Drawing Univ of Oxford (Cert Fine Art); *m* 8 Feb 1969, Harriet Lowell, da of Gaspard D'Andelot Belin (d 2003), of Cambridge, MA; 2 da (Alice Mary b 21 March 1973, Harriet Lowell b 28 May 1974); *Career* secondary sch master for US Peace Corps Tabora Sch Tanzania 1965–66; memb Bd of Dirs Bankside Gallery London 1986–95 and 2002–06, chm Nat Assoc of Blood Donors 1994–95, govr Windmill First Sch Oxford 1994–98; artist; working mainly in relief and intaglio printmaking, handmaking own autographic prints; artist in residence St John's Coll Oxford 2004; work in public collection: Tate Gallery, V&A Museum, Royal Collection, Science Museum, Museum of London, Guildhall Library, Ashmolean Museum, Fitzwilliam Museum, Russian State Collection, Nat Museum of Wales, Royal West of England Acad, Musee d'Art Contemporian, Lahti Museum Finland, Iowa City Art Museum, Bowes Art Museum Barnard Castle, Victoria Art Gallery Bath, British Library London, Bodleian Library Oxford, work in public collection Library of Congress (Washington DC); hon fellowship: Printmakers' Cncl 1988, Oxford Art Soc 1993, RWS 1996; prizes: Int Miniature Print Exhibitions Cadaques Spain 1982 and Seoul Korea 1982, Royal W of Eng Acad Bristol for painting 1985; Lothrop Prize Print Club of Albany NY 1998, Center for Contemporary Printmaking Norwalk Conn 2001 and 2003; pres Royal Soc of Painter-Printmakers (RE) 1989–95; fell Royal Soc of Painter-Printmakers 1982 (assoc 1979), memb Royal Soc of Br Artists 1980–82, academician Royal West of England Acad (RWA) 1989–2006 (assoc 1983–89); *Publications* Illustrations for Sewanee Poems (by Richard Tillinghast, 2009); *Recreations* gardening, hill walking, theatre; *Clubs* Oxford Univ Yacht; *Style*— Joseph Winkelman, Esq; ✉ The Hermitage, 69 Old High Street, Headington, Oxford OX3 9HT (✆ 01865 762839, e-mail joe@winkelman.co.uk, website www.winkelman.co.uk)

WINKLEY, Sir David Ross; kt (1999); s of Donald Joseph Winkley, and Winifred Mary (d 1997); *b* 30 November 1941, Birmingham; *Educ* King Edwards Sch Birmingham (state scholar), Selwyn Coll Cambridge (exhibitioner, MA), Wadham Coll Oxford (DPhil); *m* Dr Linda Mary, *née* Holland; 1 da (Katherine J N b 23 June 1971), 1 s (Joseph D D b 15 June 1973); *Career* memb Centre for Contemporary Cultural Studies Univ of Birmingham 1964–66, dep head Perry Common Sch 1968–71, head Grove Sch Handsworth Birmingham 1974–96, fndr and pres National Primary Tst 1987–2006; fndr and tstee Children's Univ, fndr and chair Health Exchange 2008–; non-exec dir and vice-chair Heart of Birmingham Teaching Primary Care Tst 2002–13; hon prof Univ of Birmingham 1999–, hon prof Univ of Warwick 2005–; DLitt Univ of Birmingham 1999, Hon DUniv Univ of Central England 2000; fell Nuffield Coll 1981–83, hon fell Wadham Coll Oxford 2007–; memb RSM; *Publications* Diplomats and Detectives (1986), Handsworth Revolution (2002), The Philosophy Group (2010), Life Cycle (2012), Mr Worsley (2013); author of over 60 articles on various learned subjects; *Recreations* writing fiction, philosophy, playing piano especially Bach and modern jazz; *Style*— Sir David Winkley

WINKLEY, Leo; *b* 18 June 1971; *Educ* Cranleigh Sch, Lady Margaret Hall Oxford (MA), Open Univ (MEd); *m* 2003, Jules Winkley; 2 da (Tabitha b 5 Dec 2003, Dorothea b 12 Nov 2008), 1 s (Ivo b 27 Dec 2005); *Career* head of religious studies and asst housemaster Ardingly Coll 1994–99, head of religious studies Cheltenham Ladies' Coll 1999–2004; Bedales Sch Hants: dep head 2004–09, acting head 2009, managing head 2009–10; headmaster St Peter's Sch York 2010–; *Style*— Leo Winkley, Esq; ✉ St Peter's School, York YO30 6AB

WINKLEY, Dr Linda Mary; da of Reginald Bertram Holland (d 1984), and Vera Mary, *née* Mills; *b* 1 June 1942; *Educ* King Edward's HS for Girls Edgbaston, Univ of Birmingham (MB ChB, DPM, DCH, DRCOG); *m* 22 July 1967, David Ross Winkley, s of Donald Winkley, of Sutton Coldfield, W Midlands; 1 da (Katherine b 23 June 1971), 1 s (Joseph b 15 June 1973); *Career* in gen practice 1967–70, trained in adult psychiatry Warnford Hosp Oxford 1970–72, sr registrar Midland Trg Scheme in Child Psychiatry 1973–75, conslt child psychiatrist Selly Oak Hosp Birmingham 1976–2010, regnl speciality clinical tutor in child psychiatry 1989–99 (developed child psychotherapy servs in Midlands and set up course for psychotherapeutic work with children 1980), clinical dir Children's Hosp Birmingham 1993–94; conslt child and adolescent psychiatrist Newbridge House; memb Client Gp Planning Team, chm Children's Mental Health Promotion Sub-Ctee W Midlands, chm Div of Child Health and Paediatrics Selly Oak Hosp 1988–93; fndr memb and treas W Midlands Inst of Psychotherapy; memb: ACPP 1973, APP 1985; MACP 1986, FRCPsych 1989; *Publications* Emotional Problems in Children and Young People (1996); *Recreations* theatre, music, tennis; *Style*— Dr Linda Winkley; ✉ Newbridge House, 147 Chester Road, Streetly, West Midlands B74 3NE (✆ 0121 580 8362)

WINKWORTH, Jane; *b* 1948; *Educ* St Christopher Sch Letchworth, Kingston Sch of Art; *Career* shoe designer, artist and painter; fndr French Sole 1989, currently md and creative dir French Sole and London Sole USA; *Recreations* ballet, opera, theatre, the arts, fashion, life in LA; *Style*— Ms Jane Winkworth; ✉ 46 Markham Square, Chelsea, London SW3 4XA (✆ 020 7581 4128); Chestnut Cottage, Chobham, Surrey GU24 8EF (✆ 01276 856733); 1105 Idahoe Avenue, Santa Monica, CA 90403, USA (✆ 00 1 310 319 1658, e-mail jane@frenchsole.com)

WINKWORTH, Peter Leslie; s of Francis William Harry Winkworth (d 1975), and Ruth Margaret Llewellin, *née* Notley (d 1998); *b* 9 August 1948; *Educ* Tonbridge; *m* 16 June 1973, Tessa Anne, da of Sir Alexander Warren Page (d 1993); 2 da (Victoria (Mrs Lowrie) b 1975, Jessica (Mrs Muddle) b 1978), 1 s (Piers b 1976); *Career* racehorse breeder, formerly licensed racehorse trainer and merchant banker; dir: Close Brothers Ltd 1977–2007, Close Brothers Gp plc 1984–2007, Arkstar Ltd 1984–88, Clifford Brown Group plc 1987–93, Jackson-Stops & Staff Ltd 1990–92, Winterflood Securities Ltd 1993–2007; FCA, ATII, FCSI; *Recreations* golf, horse racing, rhododendrons; *Clubs* East India; *Style*— Peter Winkworth, Esq; ✉ Merton Place Stud, Dunsfold, Surrey GU8 4NP (e-mail peter@pwinkworth.com)

WINNICK, David Julian; MP; *b* 26 June 1933; *Educ* LSE; *Career* memb: Willesden Cncl 1959–64, Brent Cncl 1964–66; MP (Lab): Croydon S 1966–70, Walsall N 1979– (Parly candidate (Lab): Harwich 1964, Croydon Central Oct 1974, Walsall 1976); memb Select Ctees on: Race Relations and Immigration 1969–70, Environment 1980–83, Home Affrs 1983–87 and 1997–, Procedure 1989–97; co-chm Br-Irish Inter-Parly Body 1997– (vice-chm 1993–97), vice-pres APEX 1983–88; chm UK Immigrants Advsy Service 1984–90; *Style*— David Winnick, MP; ✉ House of Commons, London SW1A 0AA

WINSER, Kim; OBE (2006); *Educ* Purbrook Park GS; *Career* formerly divnl dir Marks and Spencer; chief exec Pringle of Scotland 2000–05, chief exec Aquascutum 2006–09, chm Agent Provocateur 2009–11, special advsr Net-A-Porter 2011–12, fndr and ceo Winser London Ltd 2012–; ind non-exec dir The Hongkong and Shanghai Hotels Limited 2014–; advsr 3i 2009–11, special advsr White Cloud Capital 2010–; contrib Forbes 2013–; tstee Nat History museum 2013–; patron: Prince's Tst, breast cancer charities; Hon DLitt Heriot-Watt Univ Edinburgh; *Style*— Dr K L Winser, OBE

WINSER, Dr Nigel de Northop; s of Robert Stephen Winser, of Kintbury, Berks, and Anne, *née* Carrick; *b* 4 July 1952, Kisumu, Kenya; *Educ* Bradfield Coll, Poly of Central London; *m* 17 July 1982, Shane, da of Arthur James Wesley-Smith, of Sheffield; 1 s (Philip b 1984), 1 da (Kate b 1987); *Career* Royal Geographical Soc: field dir Mulu Sarawak expedition 1976, expedition offr 1978 (expeditions carried out in Karakoram Pakistan, Kora Kenya, Wahiba Oman, Kimberley Aust, Temburong Brunei, Mkomazi Tanzania, Badia Jordan, Indian Ocean), estab Expedition Advsy Centre 1980, asst dir and head of exploration 1988, dep dir 1991–2005, i/c Shoals of Capricorn prog Indian Ocean 1998–2002; exec dir Earthwatch Inst (Europe) Oxford 2005–08, exec vice-pres Earthwatch Int 2008–15; currently field science conslt 2015–; ambass Earthwatch Europe 2015–; Winston Churchill travel fell 1977–78, exploration fell commoner Corpus Christi Coll Cambridge 1990; memb Field Studies Cncl 1999–2005, memb Advsy Bd Durrell Inst of Conservation and Ecology Univ of Kent 2016–; fndr: Sponsor Our Species 1992, Geographical Observatories Prog 1994; tstee: Project Urquhart 1993–, Mount Everest Foundation 1995–2002, Friends of Conservation (UK) 1996–2002, Gino Watkins Memorial Foundation 1996–2003, Andrew Croft Memorial Fund 2000–06, Global Canopy Prog 2000–10, Greencard Tst 2004–09, Oxford Univ Expeditions Cncl 2006–10, MEF Everest 50th Ctee; patron Br Schs Exploring Soc 2008; assoc memb Il Ngwesi Maasai Community Gp Ranch Kenya 2005 (hon elder 2014–); judge Tusk Trust Africa Conservation Awards 2012–; RGS Patrons Gold Medal for leadership of Oman Wahiba Sands project 1988, Explorers Club of NY Citation of Merit 1989, Mrs Patrick Ness Award for expdn leadership 1977, Mungo Park Medal Royal Scottish Geographical Soc 1995; Hon DSc Univ of Westminster 2006; memb Common Room Green Coll Oxford 2006, assoc memb St Cross Coll Oxford 2007; hon conservation fell ZSL 2013–; *Books* Sea of Sands and Mists (1989), contributing ed History of World Exploration (1991); *Recreations* fly fishing, field photography, expedition art, organising life-science lectures (Winser Dialogue); *Clubs* Alpine, Geographical, Rainforest, James Caird, Desert Dining, Just Artists and Travellers, Flyfishers'; *Style*— Dr Nigel Winser; ✉ The Old Forge, Brook End, Chadlington, Oxfordshire OX7 3NF (✆ 01608 676042, mobile 07495 469941, e-mail nigel@winserdialogue.com, Twitter @nigelwinser)

WINSKEL, Prof Glynn; s of Thomas Francis Winskel, and Helen Juanita, *née* McCall; *Educ* Univ of Cambridge (MA, ScD), Univ of Oxford (MSc), Univ of Edinburgh (PhD); *Career* res scientist Carnegie-Mellon Univ PA 1982–84; Univ of Cambridge: lectr 1984–88, fell King's Coll 1985–88, reader 1987–88, prof of computer sci 2000–, fell Emmanuel Coll 2000–; Univ of Aarhus Denmark: prof of computer sci 1988–2000, dir Res Centre BRICS (Basic Res in Computer Sci) 1994–2000; memb Academica Europaea 2011; *Books* The Formal Semantics of Programming Languages – An Introduction (1993); *Recreations* running, swimming, sup-boarding, art; *Style*— Prof Glynn Winskel; ✉ University of Cambridge Computer Laboratory, JJ Thompson Avenue, Cambridge CB3 0FD (✆ 01223 334613, fax 01223 334678)

WINSLET, Kate Elizabeth; CBE (2012); da of Roger Winslet, and Sally Winslet; *b* 5 October 1975; *m* 1, Nov 1998 (m dis 2001), Jim Threapleton; 1 da (Mia b 2000); m 2, May 2003 (m dis), Sam Mendes, *qv*; 1 s (Joe b 2003); m 3, 2012, Ned Rocknroll; 1 s (Bear b 2013); *Career* actress; *Theatre* What the Butler Saw 1994; *Television* incl: Dark Season 1991, Anglo-Saxon Attitudes 1992, Get Back 1992, Casualty 1993, Mildred Pierce 2011 (Best Actress in a Mini-Series Emmy Award 2011, Best Performance by an Actress In A Mini-series or Motion Picture Made for Television Golden Globe 2012); *Film* incl: Heavenly Creatures 1994 (Best Foreign Actress NZ Film and TV Critics' Awards, Best Br Actress Awards London Film Critics' Circle and Empire magazine), Sense and Sensibility 1995 (Best Supporting Actress Screen Actors' Guild, BAFTA Award, Oscar and Golden Globe nominations), Jude 1996, Hamlet 1996 (Best Br Actress Empire Magazine Awards, Evening Standard Award), Titanic 1997 (Best European Actress European Film Acad, Film Actress of the Year Variety Club of GB, Empire Magazine Award, Oscar, Golden

Globe and Screnn Actors Guild nominations), Hideous Kinky 1998, Holy Smoke 1999, Quills 2000, Enigma 2001, Iris 2001 (Oscar, BAFTA and Golden Globe nominations), The Life of David Gale 2003, Finding Neverland 2004 (BAFTA nomination), Eternal Sunshine of the Spotless Mind 2004 (Best Br Actress Awards London Film Critics' Circle and Empire magazine, Oscar, BAFTA and Golden Globe nominations), Romance & Cigarettes 2005, Little Children 2006 (Best Actress Golden Globe, BAFTA Award, Screen Actors' Guild and Oscar nominations 2007), All the King's Men 2006, Flushed Away (voice) 2006, The Holiday 2006, The Reader 2008 (Best Supporting Actress Golden Globe 2009, Best Supporting Actress Screen Actors Guild Awards 2009, Best Leading Actress BAFTA 2009, Best Actress Acad Award 2009, Best Actress European Film Awards 2009), Revolutionary Road 2008 (Best Actress Golden Globes 2009), Carnage 2011, Contagion 2011, Labor Day 2013 (nominated Best Actress Golden Globes 2014), Divergent 2014; Best Int Actress Goldene Kamera Award 2001, Actress of the Year London Film Critics' Circle 2009; *Style*— Miss Kate Winslet, CBE; ✉ c/o Dallas Smith, United Agents Ltd, 12–26 Lexington Street, London W1F 0LE (☎ 020 3214 0800, fax 020 3214 0801, website www.unitedagents.co.uk); c/o Hylda Queally, CAA, 2000 Avenue of the Stars, Los Angeles, CA 90067, USA (☎ 001 424 288 2000, fax 001 424 288 3671)

WINSOR, Sir Thomas Philip (Tom); kt (2015), WS (1984); s of late Thomas Valentine Marrs Winsor, and late Phyllis Margaret, *née* Bonsor; *b* 7 December 1957, Broughty Ferry, Dundee; *Educ* Grove Acad Broughty Ferry, Univ of Edinburgh (LLB), Univ of Dundee (Dip); *m* 1989 (m dis 2012); 2 da; *Career* admitted slr Scotland 1981, England & Wales 1991, Notary Public Scotland 1981; gen practice Dundee 1981–83, asst slr Dundas & Wilson CS 1983–84, asst slr Norton Rose 1984–91, ptnr Denton Hall 1991–99, Rail Regulator and Int Rail Regulator 1999–2004 (chief legal advsr and gen counsel Office of the Rail Regulator 1993–95), ptnr White & Case LLP 2004–12, HM chief inspr of constabulary 2012–; ind reviewer of police offr and staff remuneration and conditions for the Home Sec 2010–12; memb: Law Soc of Scotland, Law Soc of England & Wales, Int Bar Assoc, Univ of Dundee Petroleum and Mineral Law Soc (pres 1987–89), Soc of Scottish Lawyers in London (pres 1987–89); *Publications* Taylor and Winsor on Joint Operating Agreements (with MPG Taylor, 1989), Legal Lines and the Right Side of the Tracks (articles in Modern Railways Magazine 1996–99 and 2005–09); articles in books, newspapers and learned jls on oil and gas, electricity and railways law and regulation; *Recreations* family, literature, theatre, opera, music, cycling, Scottish constitutional history, law, the works of Robert Burns; *Style*— Sir Thomas Winsor, WS; ✉ HM Inspectorate of Constabulary, Global House (6th Floor), 89 Eccleston Square, London SW1

WINSTANLEY, Dr Charles Jeffery; TD (1991), JP (1993), DL (Gtr London 1997); s of Jeffery Winstanley, and Elisabeth Winstanley; *b* 6 March 1952, s of Jeffery Thomas Winstanley (d 2001), and Elisabeth Anne Kelson, *née* Miller (d 2011); *Educ* Wellington, RMA Sandhurst, Henley Mgmnt Coll, Brunel Univ (MBA, DBA), Army Staff Coll; *m* 20 June 1987, Columbine Halcyon, da of Maj Gen Patrick Hobart, DSO, OBE, MC; 1 da (b 1993), 1 s (b 1995); *Career* offr Br Army (16/5 Lancers 1970–76, Royal Yeomanry 1977–93); product mangr Purex Corp 1977–79, account mangr French Gold Abbott 1979–81, account dir Davidson Pearce plc 1981–87, md CJW Mktg Ltd 1987–2001; chair: Panel GMC 2000–07, Norfolk Probation Bd 2001–06, NHS Lothian 2007–13, Edinburgh Leisure 2010–15, Scottish Police Pension Bd 2015–, Bd Acad of Med Royal Colls 2016–; non-exec dir: Norfolk & Norwich Univ Hosp NHS Tst 1999–2006, MOD 2010–14, Scottish Govt 2010–13, UK Supreme Court 2011–; UK memb and rgnl chm Nat Consumer Cncl for Postal Servs (Postwatch) 2002–08, memb Asylum & Immigration Tbnl 2003–, memb Tbnl Disciplinary Panel 2014–; *Recreations* family, running, sailing, fly fishing, reading history; *Style*— Dr Charles Winstanley, TD, JP, DL; ☎ 07836 752352, e-mail cjwinstanley@aol.com

WINSTON, Prof Brian Norman; s of Reuben Winston (d 1989), of Wembley, and Anita, *née* Salamons (d 1983); *b* 7 November 1941; *Educ* Kilburn GS, Merton Coll Oxford (MA); *m* 1978, Adèle, da of Aleck Jackson; 1 da (Jessica b 1979), 1 s (Matthew b 1983); *Career* freelance journalist 1974–; researcher/prodr Granada TV 1963–66, prodr/dir BBC TV 1966–69, prodr/dir Granada TV 1969–72, lectr Bradford Coll of Art 1972–74, res dir Dept of Sociology Univ of Glasgow 1974–76, head of gen studies Nat Film & TV Sch Beaconsfield 1974–79, prof and head of film studies Tisch Sch of the Arts NY Univ 1979–86 (visiting prof of film 1976–77), dean Sch of Communications Pennsylvania State Univ 1986–92, prof and dir Centre for Journalism Studies Univ of Wales Coll of Cardiff 1992–97, head Sch of Communication and Creative Industries Univ of Westminster 1997–2002; Univ of Lincoln: dean Faculty of Media and Humanities 2002–05, pro-vice-chllr 2004–06, prof of communications 2006–07, Lincoln prof 2007–; produced The Third Walker (starring William Shatner and Colleen Dewhurst) Canada 1976; winner Emmy for documentary script writing for Heritage: Civilization and the Jews part 8 (WNET-TV, NY); chair Welsh Film Cncl 1995–97, govr BFI 1994–2001; *Books* Dangling Conversations – The Image of the Media (1973), Dangling Conversations – Hardware Software (1974), Bad News (1976), More Bad News (1980), Misunderstanding Media (1986), Working with Video (with Julia Keydel, 1986), Claiming the Real (1995 and 2008), Technologies of Seeing (1996), Media, Technology and Society (1998), Fires Were Started (1999), Lies, Damn Lies and Documentaries (2000), Messages: Free Expression, Media and the West from Gutenburg to Google (2005); *Recreations* cooking; *Style*— Prof Brian Winston; ✉ University of Lincoln, Brayford Pool, Lincoln LN6 7TS (☎ 01522 886871, e-mail bwinston@lincoln.ac.uk)

WINSTON, Baron (Life Peer UK 1995), of Hammersmith in the London Borough of Hammersmith and Fulham; Robert Maurice Lipson Winston; s of Lawrence Winston (d 1949), of London, and Ruth, *née* Lipson; *b* 15 July 1940; *Educ* St Paul's, Univ of London (MB BS); *m* 8 March 1973, Lira Helen, da of Simon Joseph Feigenbaum (d 1971), of London; 2 s (Hon Joel, Hon Benjamin), 1 da (Hon Tanya); *Career* sr res accoucheur The London Hosp 1965, sr lectr Inst of Obstetrics and Gynaecology 1975–81, visiting res prof Catholic Univ of Leuven Belgium 1976–77, conslt obstetrician and gynaecologist Hammersmith Hosp 1978–2005 (sr res fell 1975–78), prof of gynaecology Univ of Texas San Antonio 1980–81, reader in fertility studies Royal Postgrad Med Sch 1981–86, prof of fertility studies Univ of London 1986–2005, dean Inst of Obstetrics and Gynaecology Imperial Coll Sch of Med at Hammersmith Hosp (Royal Postgraduate Med Sch until merger 1997) 1995–98, vice-chm Div of Paediatrics Obstetrics and Gynaecology Imperial Coll Sch of Med, dir of NHS R&D Hammersmith Hosps Tst 1999–2005, prof emeritus Imperial Coll London 2005– (prof of sci and society 2008–); chllr Sheffield Hallam Univ 2001–; author of over 300 scientific papers on reproduction; chm Br Fertility Soc 1990–93 (fndr memb); pres: Int Fallopius Soc 1987–88, Progress All-Pty Parly Gp for Res In Reproduction 1991; memb House of Lords Select Ctee on Sci and Technol 1997– (chm 1999–2001); memb Bd Parly Office for Sci and Technol 1999– (vice-chm 2006–); pres Br Assoc for the Advancement of Sci 2005; memb Cncl Engr and Physical Sci Res Cncl 2007–; TV presenter: Your Life in their Hands (BBC) 1979–87, Making Babies (BBC) 1996–97, The Human Body (BBC) 1998, The Secret Life of Twins (BBC) 1999, The Superhuman (BBC) 2000, Threads of Life (BBC), Human Instinct (BBC), The Human Mind (BBC) 2003, Child of Our Time (BBC), Story of God (BBC) 2005, Child Against All Odds (BBC) 2006, Superdoctors (BBC) 2008; radio presenter Robert Winston's Musical Analysis (BBC Radio 4) 2009; memb: Cncl ICRF (now Cancer Research UK) 1997–2004, Bd Lyric Theatre Hammersmith 1997–2005; chm Cncl Royal College of Music 2007–; Cedric Carter Medal Clinical Genetics Soc 1992, Victor Bonney Prize Royal Coll of Surgns of Eng 1993, Chief Rabbinate Open Award for Contributions to Society 1993, Gold Medal Royal Soc for Health, Michael Faraday Gold Medal Royal Soc 1999, Gold Medal BMA Medicine in the Media 1999, Edwin Stevens Medal RSM 2003, Maitland Medal Inst of Engineers 2004, Al-Hammadi Medal RCSEd 2005, Peer of the Year 2008; hon fell Queen Mary & Westfield Coll London 1996, memb Cncl Univ of Surrey 2008–; Hon DSc: Univ of St Andrews, Univ of Strathclyde, Salford Univ, Cranfield Univ, UMIST, Oxford Brookes Univ, Univ of Sunderland, Univ of Middlesex, Lancaster Univ, Univ of Exeter, Queen's Univ Belfast, TCD, UEA, Univ of Auckland; FRCP, FRCOG, FRSA, FMedSci, FRCSEd, FRCPSGlas, FIBiol, Hon FREng; *Books* Reversibility of Sterilization (1978), Tubal Infertility (1981), Infertility – A Sympathetic Approach (1986), What We Know About Infertility (1987), Getting Pregnant (1989), Infertility, a postgraduate handbook (1993), Making Babies (1996), The IVF Revolution (1999), The Superhuman (2000), Human Instinct (2002), The Human Mind (2003), What Makes Me Me (2005, Aventis Prize), The Story of God (2005), Child Against All Odds (2006), It's Elementary (2007), Evolution Revolution (2009); *Recreations* theatre, music, skiing, wine, broadcasting; *Clubs* Athenaeum, Garrick, MCC; *Style*— The Rt Hon Lord Winston; ✉ 11 Denman Drive, London NW11 6RE (☎ 020 8455 7475); Imperial College London, Hammersmith Hospital, Du Cane Road, London W12 0HS (☎ 020 8383 2183, fax 020 8749 6973, car 078 3663 9339, e-mail r.winston@imperial.ac.uk)

WINSTONE, Ray; *b* 19 February 1957; *Educ* Edmonton County Sch, Corona Sch London; *Career* actor; *Theatre* incl: What a Crazy World We're Living In, QR's & Al's Clearly State, Hinkerman, Mr Thomas, Some Voices 1994, Dealer's Choice 1995, Pale Horse 1995, To the Green Fields and Beyond (Donmar Warehouse) 2001, The Night Heron (Royal Court) 2002; *Television* incl: Scum, Sunshine Over Brixton, Mr Right, Minder, Fox, The Lonely Hearts Kid, A Fairly Secret Army, Bergerac, Robin of Sherwood, Father Matthew's Daughter, Pulaski, Blore, Playing For Time, Palmer, Mr Thomas, Absolute Hell, Paint, Underbelly, Birds of a Feather, Black and Blue, Get Back I & II, Between the Lines, Nice Town, Murder Most Horrid, The Negotiator, Casualty, Space Precinct, The Ghost Busters of East Finchley, Kavanagh QC, Sharman, Thief Takers II, Macbeth on the Estate, Our Boy, Births, Marriages and Deaths, Tough Love, Lenny Blue, Henry VIII, Great Expectations 2011, Moonfleet 2013; *Films* incl: Scum 1979, That Summer 1979, Quadrophenia 1979, All Washed Up 1981, Tank Malling 1989, Ladybird Ladybird 1994, Nil By Mouth (BIFA Award for Best British Actor 1998) 1997, Face 1997, Dangerous Obsession 1997, Final Cut 1997, Martha Meet Frank, Daniel and Laurence 1998, Woundings 1998, The War Zone 1999, Agnes Browne (formerly The Mammy) 1999, Fanny & Elvis 1999, Five Seconds to Spare 1999, Love Honour and Obey 2000, Sexy Beast 2001, Last Orders 2001, Ripley's Game 2002, Bouncer 2002, Cold Mountain 2003, King Arthur 2004, Beowulf 2007, Indiana Jones and the Kingdom of the Crystal Skull 2008, 44 Inch Chest 2009, Sex & Drugs & Rock & Roll 2010, Edge of Darkness 2010, 13 2010, London Boulevard 2010, Rango 2011, Hugo 2011, Elfie Hopkins 2012, Snow White and the Huntsman 2012, The Sweeney 2012, Lords of London 2014, Noah 2014; *Recreations* supporting West Ham United FC; *Style*— Ray Winstone, Esq; ✉ c/o Creative Artists Management Ltd, 1st Floor 55–59 Shaftesbury Avenue, London W1D 6LD

WINTER, Henry; s of John Winter, of London, and Valerie, *née* Denison; *b* 18 February 1963, London; *Educ* Westminster, Univ of Edinburgh (MA), London Coll of Printing (Cert); *m* 25 Jan 1992, Catriona, *née* Elliott; 1 s (Toby b 28 March 1997), 1 da (Electra b 11 Nov 2000); *Career* sports journalist The Independent 1986, football corr Daily Telegraph 1994–2015, chief football writer The Times 2015–; football columnist Sunday Telegraph 2009–15; contrib: Sky Sports, BBC TV and Radio, ITV, TalkSPORT; author and after dinner speaker; Kenny Dalglish (1997 and 2010), John Barnes (1999), Steven Gerrard (2006), FA Confidential (2008), Fifty Years of Hurt (2016); *Recreations* running, visiting war museums, choral music; *Style*— Henry Winter, Esq; ✉ literary agent: David Luxton Associates, 23 Hillcourt Avenue, London N12 8EY (☎ 020 8922 3942); The Times, 1 London Bridge Street, London SE1 9GF (☎ 020 7782 5000)

WINTER, Canon Prof (David) Michael; OBE (2005); s of David Winter (d 1989), and Nanette, *née* Wellsteed; *b* 10 November 1955, Launceston, Cornwall; *Educ* Peter Symonds Coll Winchester, Wye Coll London (BSc), Open Univ (PhD); *m* 11 Aug 1979, Hilary Susan, *née* Thomas; 1 da (Emily Rowan b 24 March 1990), 1 s (Benedict Thomas David b 14 April 1993); *Career* res asst: Open Univ 1978–80, Univ of Exeter 1980–82; res offr Univ of Bath 1983–87, dir Centre for Rural Studies RAC Cirencester 1987–93, reader then prof Cheltenham and Gloucester Coll of HE 1993–2001, prof of rural policy and dir Centre for Rural Res Univ of Exeter 2002–; cmmr Cmmn for Rural Communities 2006–13, memb Governing Body Rothamsted Research 2014–; vice-pres Community Cncl of Devon 2008–13, memb Science Advsy Cncl DEFRA 2009–11; lay canon Exeter Cathedral 2008–; Agriculture: People and Policies (jt ed, 1986), The Voluntary Principle in Conservation (jtly, 1990), Church and Religion in Rural England (jtly, 1991), Rural Politics (1996), What is Land for? (jt ed, 2009); *Recreations* gardening, hedge-laying, walking, church, music, family; *Clubs* Athenaeum; *Style*— Canon Prof Michael Winter, OBE; ✉ Centre for Rural Policy Research, University of Exeter, Amory Building, Rennes Drive, Exeter EX4 4RJ (☎ 01392 263837, e-mail d.m.winter@ex.ac.uk)

WINTER, Peter John; s of Jack Winter (d 1983), and Ursula, *née* Riddington (d 2011); *b* 10 July 1950, Thornton Heath, Croydon; *Educ* Trinity Sch Croydon, Wadham Coll Oxford (scholar, MA), Univ of Reading (PGCE); *m* 20 Oct 1979, (Jennifer) Adwoa, da of Cobbina Kessie and Georgina Taylor; 1 da (Tiffany Akua Ampomah b 1983), 1 s (Matthew Jack Kofi b 1986); *Career* asst teacher Latymer Upper Sch 1973–79 (master i/c 1st XI cricket), head of modern languages Magdalen Coll Sch Oxford 1979–86 (master i/c hockey); Sevenoaks Sch: head modern languages 1986–89, housemaster Int Centre 1987–93; headmaster King Edward's Sch Bath 1993–2002, head Latymer Upper Sch 2002–12; memb HMC 1993–2012 (memb Academic Policy Sub-Ctee 1996–2001, chm SW Div 2000–01), inspr Ind Schs Inspectorate (ISI); *Recreations* Chelsea FC, music, travel, reading, golf, test match cricket, tennis (Club de Magalas), pétanque, France; *Style*— Peter Winter, Esq; ✉ 20 Oyster Wharf, 18 Lombard Road, London SW11 3RJ (☎ 020 7228 1195, mobile 07447 007736, e-mail pjsw1134@gmail.com); 60 Rue de la Cite, 34480 Magalas, France (☎ 0033 04 6728 2544)

WINTER, Richard Thomas; s of Thomas Alfred Baldwin Winter, of Warks, and Ruth Ethel, *née* Newbury; *b* 6 March 1949; *Educ* Warwick Sch, Univ of Birmingham (LLB), Stanford Grad Sch of Business; *m* Dorothy Sally, da of Peter Hancock Filer; 2 da (Hannah Louise b 2 Sept 1990, Fiona Ruth b 5 Aug 1992); *Career* articled clerk and asst slr Eversheds 1971–75, slr Fisons plc 1975–78, ptnr Eversheds 1981–94 (joined 1978, managing ptnr London office 1991); InterContinental Hotels Gp plc (formerly Bass plc then Six Continents plc): dir of gp legal affrs Bass plc 1994–2000, dir Bass Brewers Ltd 1997–2000, gp co sec and gen counsel Six Continents plc 2000–03, dir Six Continents Retail Ltd 2000–02, exec ctee memb, exec vice-pres (corp servs), gen counsel and co sec InterContinental Hotels Gp plc 2003–09; md International Hotel Intelligence Ltd 2010–; chm GH Property Mgmnt Services Ltd 2010–15; dir Britannia Holdings Ltd (Britvic) 2003–05; former memb Law Soc, former memb Competition Law Panel CBI; *Recreations* gym, trekking, shooting, sailing, skiing, theatre, opera; *Clubs* Royal Ocean Racing, Solway Yacht, Roehampton; *Style*— Richard Winter, Esq; ✉ International Hotel Intelligence Limited, 10 Wilbraham Place, London SW1X 9AA (☎ 07808 098777)

WINTER-SCOTT, Rosemary Geraldine; OBE (2014); *b* 14 January 1961, Plymouth; *Educ* Univ of Durham (BSc, PGCE); *Career* geography teacher Abbotsford Comp Sch 1984–

87, pt/t geography lectr Guildford Coll of Technol 1986–88, head of geography St Teresa's Sch Sunbury on Thames 1987–88, dep mangr Courtaulds Conventry Trg Centre 1988–91, trg and devpt co-ordinator Birmingham Trg and Enterprise Cncl 1991–94, sr mangr HR and business devpt Leics Trg and Enterprise Cncl 1994–97, managing assessor Investors In People Scotland 1997, dir/chief exec Investors in People Scotland 1997–2003, asst dir Learning Devpt and Careers Scottish Exec Health Dept 2003–04, head Employability and Skills Div Scottish Govt Dept for Lifelong Learning 2009, head of learning connections Scottish Govt Dept for Lifelong Learning 2009, accountant in bankruptcy and agency chief exec Scottish Govt 2009–; memb Bd Skills for Health 2002–04; memb Bd Assoc of Chief Execs 2010–, chair Int Assoc of Insolvency Regulators 2012–; govr Counden Court Sch and Community Coll Coventry 1989–94, tstee Laurance David Wellwood Scott Tst 2001–12, memb Bd Jordanhill Sch 2007–13 (convenor and chair 2008–13); memb CIPD; FInstD 2010; *Publications* How to Become an Investor in People (jtly, 1995); *Style*— Mrs Winter-Scott, OBE; ✉ Accountant in Bankruptcy, 1 Pennyburn Road, Kilwinning, North Ayrshire KA13 6SA

WINTERBOTTOM, Prof Michael; s of Allan Winterbottom (d 1982), of East Budleigh, Devon, and Kathleen Mary Winterbottom (d 1990); *b* 22 September 1934; *Educ* Dulwich Coll, Pembroke Coll Oxford (MA, DPhil); *m* 1, 31 Aug 1963 (m dis 1983), Helen, da of Harry Spencer (d 1977), of Willenhall, Staffs; m 2, 20 Sept 1986, Nicolette Janet Streatfeild Bergel, da of Henry Shorland Gervis (d 1968), of Sherborne, Dorset; 2 s (Peter, Jonathan); *Career* lectr in Latin and Greek UCL 1962–67, fell and tutor in classics Worcester Coll Oxford 1967–92 (reader in classical languages 1990–92), Corpus Christi prof of Latin Univ of Oxford 1993–2001 (emeritus prof 2001–), fell CCC Oxford 1993–2001 (emeritus fell 2001–); Dr (hc) Besançon 1985; FBA 1978; *Books* Quintilian (ed 1970), Ancient Literary Criticism (with D A Russell, 1972), Three Lives of English Saints (1972), The Elder Seneca (ed and translated, 1974), Tacitus, Opera Minora (ed with R M Ogilvie, 1975), Gildas (ed and translated 1978), Roman Declamation (1980), The Minor Declamations Ascribed to Quintilian (ed with commentary, 1984), Sopatros the Rhetor (with D C Innes 1988), Cicero De Officiis (ed, 1994), William of Malmesbury Gesta Regum Anglorum Vol i (ed with R A B Mynors and R M Thomson, 1998), William of Malmesbury Saints' Lives (ed with R M Thomson, 2002), Quintilian Book 2 (ed with T Reinhardt, 2006), William of Malmesbury Gesta Pontificum Anglorum Vol 1 (ed, 2007), William of Malmesbury Commentary on Lamentations (ed with R M Thomson, 2011), The Early Lives of St Dunstan (ed with M Lapidge, 2012), William of Malmesbury On Lamentations (translated, 2013), William of Malmesbury The Miracles of the Blessed Virgin Mary (ed, with R M Thomson, 2015); *Recreations* walking, travel, geology; *Style*— Prof Michael Winterbottom, FBA; ✉ 53 Thorncliffe Road, Oxford OX2 7BA

WINTERFLOOD, Brian Martin; MBE (2012); s of Thomas George Winterflood (d 1978), of Uxbridge, Middx, and Doris Maud, *née* Waddington; *b* 31 January 1937; *Educ* Frays Coll Uxbridge; *m* 10 Oct 1966, Doreen Stella, da of Albert Frederick McCartney, of London; 2 s (Guy b 2 April 1970, Mark b 8 March 1973), 1 da (Sarah b 9 July 1974); *Career* messenger Greener Dreyfus & Co (Stockbrokers) 1953–55; Nat Serv 1955–57; Bisgood Bishop & Co: joined 1957, ptnr 1967, dir 1971 (Co inc), jt md 1981 (co taken over by County NatWest Investment Bank 1986), non-exec dir 1986; exec dir County NatWest Bank 1986–88; Winterflood Securities: fndr 1988, md 1988–99, ceo 1999–2000, chm 2001–02, non-exec chm 2002–09, life pres 2009–; dir Union Discount plc 1991–93 (taken over by Close Brothers 1993), memb Bd Close Brothers Group plc 1995–2002; fndr memb Quoted Companies Alliance (QCL, formerly The City Group for Smaller Companies (CISCO)) 1992–2000 (memb Exec Ctee 1992–96, pres 2010), chm WINS Guilts 1994; non-exec dir Monument Securities 2002–06; memb: Ctee October Club 1990–2002, City Disputes Practitioners Panel 1994–2000, AIM Advice Appeals Ctee 1995–98, Non FTSE 100 Working Pty Ctee 1996–98, Secondary Markets Ctee 1996–98, Ctee ProShare 1998–2003, jt chm Advsy Bd EASD UK 2000–01; chm PYBT USM Initiative 1989–92, pres Security Industry Mgmnt Assoc (SIMA) 2004; pres REMEDI (Rehabilitation and Med Res Tst) 1989–2007 (vice-pres 2007–10, patron 2010–13); vice-pres Save the Children 2004–09, dep chm Lord Mayor Appeal 2004; govr Reeds Sch 2002–07 (pres Reeds Sch Appeal 1997–98, hon vice-pres 2007); tstee London Stock Exchange Benevolent Fund 1995, involved with Winterflood Theatre City of London Sch 2008; memb: Boost (City Life) Appeal 2001–02, Heart of the City 2002–, Ctee Lord Mayor's Appeal 2014–15 and 2015–16; patron: Wealth Mgmnt Variety Club (formerly APCIMS) 2015–, Museum of London 2015–, Nat History Museum 2015–; PriceWaterhouse Coopers plc Achievement Award 1994, APCIMS (Assoc Private Client Investment Mangrs Soc, now Wealth Mgmnt Variety Club) Award 2000, Lifetime Achievement Award SIMA 2008, Lifetime Achievement Award Variety Club 2008; memb Order of St George 2002; memb Guild of Int Bankers 2002; Freeman City of London 2002, Liveryman Int Bankers 2007 (memb Ct); FSI 1997 (MSI 1996), FRSA 2001; *Recreations* family, work, travel; *Clubs* City of London; *Style*— Brian Winterflood, MBE; ✉ Winterflood Securities Ltd, The Atrium Building, Cannon Bridge, 25 Dowgate Hill, London EC4R 2GA

WINTERS, Prof (Leonard) Alan; CB (2012); s of Geoffrey Walter Horace Winters, of Ipswich, Suffolk, and Christine Agnes, *née* Ive; *b* 8 April 1950; *Educ* Chingford Co HS, Univ of Bristol (BSc), Univ of Cambridge (MA, PhD); *m* 3 May 1997, Zhen Kun Wang; 2 da (Victoria b 1972, Catherine b 1973), 1 s (Oliver b 1998); *Career* jr research offr rising to research offr Dept of Applied Economics Univ of Cambridge 1971–80, lectr in economics Univ of Bristol 1980–86, economist World Bank 1983–85, prof of economics UCNW Bangor 1986–90, prof of economics Univ of Birmingham 1990–94, research mangr World Bank 1997–99 (div chief of int trade 1994–97), prof of economics Univ of Sussex 1999–, dir Research Dept World Bank 2004–07, chief economist DfID 2008–11; chm Global Devpt Network 2011–, memb Economic and Social Research Cncl 2015–; research fell Centre for Economic Policy Research; ed: World Bank Economic Review 2003–04, World Trade Review 2008–; assoc ed: Economic Jl 1992–97, Jl of Common Market Studies; former chm English Folk Dance and Song Soc; *Books* An Econometric Model of The Export Sector: The Determinants of British Exports and Their Prices (1981), International Economics (1985, new edn 1991), Europe's Domestic Market (1988), Eastern Europe's International Trade (1994), Trade Liberalisation and Poverty: A Handbook (2001), Regional Integration and Development (2003); *Recreations* music, cricket, walking; *Style*— Prof L Alan Winters, CB; ✉ School of Business, Management and Economics, University of Sussex, Falmer, Brighton BN1 9SL (✆ 01273 678332, fax 01273 673563, e-mail l.a.winters@sussex.ac.uk)

WINTERSGILL, Matthew William; s of Harold Heap Wintersgill (d 1973), of Bedford, and Patricia, *née* Gregory (d 2001); *b* 12 July 1949; *Educ* Stratton Sch, Canterbury Sch of Architecture; *m* 16 Sept 1978, Sara Neill, da of Gerald Bradley (d 1970), and Sheila Neill (d 1985), of London; *Career* architect; Powell and Moya 1973–78 (incl: Cripps Bldg project for Queen's Coll Cambridge, Sch for Advanced Architectural Studies Bristol, Nat West Bank Devpt Shaftesbury Ave London), Thompstone Harris Design Assocs 1978–80, ptnr Wintersgill LLP 1980– (formerly Thompstone Wintersgill Faulkner, then Wintersgill & Faulkner); work projects for: BAA, Bowater Corp, BP Oil Int, The Science Museum, Reuters, Prudential Assurance Co, IVECO Ford Truck Ltd, The Post Office, Nat West Bank, Rank Leisure, FCO; memb W End Soc of Architects; registered memb ARCUK (now ARB) 1974, RIBA 1975; *Recreations* drawing, swimming, travel, walking; *Style*— Matthew Wintersgill, Esq; ✉ Wintersgill LLP, 91–93 Farringdon Road, London EC1M 3LN (✆ 020 7269 6624, e-mail matthew.wintersgill@wandmarchitects.net, website www.wandmarchitects.net)

WINTERSON, Jeanette; OBE (2006); *b* 27 August 1959; *Educ* Accrington Girls' HS, St Catherine's Coll Oxford (BA); *Career* author; prof of new writing Univ of Manchester 2012–; *Books* Oranges Are Not the Only Fruit (1985, BBC TV adaptation 1990), The Passion (1987), Sexing The Cherry (1989), Written on the Body (1992), Art and Lies (1994), Art Objects (critical essays, 1995), Gut Symmetries (1997), The World and Other Places (short stories, 1999), The Power Book (2000), The King of Capri (for children, 2003), Lighthousekeeping (2004), Weight (novella, 2005), Tanglewreck (for children, 2006), The Stone Gods (2007), The Battle of the Sun (for children, 2009), The Lion, The Unicorn and Me (for children, 2009), Why Be Happy When You Could Be Normal (memoir, 2011), The Day Light Gate (2012), The Gap of Time (2015), 12 Days of Christmas (short stories, 2016), Land – An Exploration (with Antony Gormley, 2016); *Theatre* The Power Book (performed at NT, 2002); *Film* Great Moments in Aviation (1992); *Television* Ingenious (BBC 1) 2009; *Awards* Whitbread First Novel award 1985, John Llewelyn Rhys prize 1987, Commonwealth Writers' award 1988, E M Forster award (American Acad of Arts and Letters) 1989, Golden Gate San Francisco Int Film Festival 1990, Best Drama Euro TV Festival 1990, FIPA D'Argent Cannes 1991, BAFTA Best Drama 1991, Prix Italia 1991, International Fiction Award Festival Letteratura Mantova 1998, Arts and Libraries Award USA 2013, Stonewall Award 2013, Rapallo Carige Int Fiction Award Italy 2014; *Recreations* the garden, opera, my sports car; *Style*— Ms Jeanette Winterson, OBE; ✉ website www.jeanettewinterson.com; c/o Caroline Michel, PFD, 34–43 Russell Street, London WC2B 5HA

WINTERTON, Sir Nicholas Raymond; kt (2002), DL (Cheshire 2006); s of Norman H Winterton (d 1971), of Longdon Green, Staffs, and Veronica Cecil, *née* Cole (d 1975); *b* 31 March 1938, Leamington Spa, Warks; *Educ* Rugby; *m* 1960, (Jane) Ann Winterton, *qv*, da of J R Hodgson, of Sutton Coldfield; 2 s (Robert b 1960, Andrew b 1964), 1 da (Sarah b 1970); *Career* Nat Serv 2 Lt 14/20 King's Hussars 1957–59; sales exec trainee Shell-Mex and BP Ltd 1959–60, sales and gen mangr Stevens and Hodgson Ltd 1960–80; cncllr Warwickshire CC 1967–1972 (dep chm County Educn Ctee 1970–72, chm Co Youth Serv Sub-Ctee 1969–72); Parly candidate (Cons) Newcastle-under-Lyme 1969 (by-election) and 1970, MP (Cons) Macclesfield 1971–2010 (by-election); chm: Anglo-Danish Parly Gp 1992–2010, All-Pty Parly Media Gp 1992–2000, All-Pty Parly Br-Falkland Islands Gp 1997–2010, All-Pty Parly Br-Bahamas Gp, All-Pty Parly Br-Austria Gp 1997–2010; jt chm Br-Taiwan Parly Gp 1992–2010; vice-chm: Anglo Swedish Parly Gp 1992–2010, All-Pty Parly Road Transport Study Gp 1997–2000, Anglo South Pacific Gp 1997–2010, All-Pty Parly Clothing and Textiles Gp 1997–2010; chm House of Commons Procedure Ctee 1997–2005; memb Select Ctees: Modernisation of the House of Commons 1997–2010, Social Servs 1979–90, Standing Orders 1981–2010; chm Health Ctee 1991–92; memb: Exec Ctee Anglo Austrian Soc 1987–2000 (chm 1998–2000), House of Commons Chm's Panel 1986–2010, 1922 Exec Ctee 1997–2010 (vice-chm 1922 Ctee 2001–05, treas 2005–10), Exec Ctee CPA (UK Branch) 1997–2010, Fin and Gen Purposes Ctee 2001–06 (jt treas 2004–07), Inter-Parly Union (UK Branch) Exec Ctee 2001–10; treas Inter-Parly Union (UK Branch) 2007–09; non-exec dir Emerson International Inc; vice-pres: Nat Assoc of Master Bakers, Confectioners and Caterers 1992–2010, Royal Coll of Midwives 1993–; memb Imperial Soc of Knights Bachelor; Hon Freeman Borough of Macclesfield 2002; Freeman City of London 1981, Liveryman (1981) and former Upper Bailiff (1997–98) Worshipful Co of Weavers; Order of Brilliant Star with Grand Cordon (Repub of China) 2008; *Recreations* rugby football (spectator), squash, tennis, walking, reading, cinema, skiing; *Clubs* Cavalry and Guards', Old Boys and Park Green (Macclesfield), Lighthouse; *Style*— Sir Nicholas Winterton, DL

WINTERTON, Rt Hon Dame Rosie; DBE (2016), PC (2006), MP; *Educ* Doncaster GS, Univ of Hull (BA); *Career* asst to John Prescott MP 1980–86, Parly offr London Borough of Southwark 1986–88, Parly offr Royal Coll of Nursing 1988–90, md Connect Public Affairs 1990–94, head John Prescott's Private Office 1994–97; MP (Lab) Doncaster Central 1997–, min of state Dept of Health 2003–07, min of state Dept of Tport 2007–08, min of state Dept for Work and Pensions 2008–09, regnl min for Yorks and The Humber 2008–10, min of state Dept for Communities and Local Govt and Dept for Business, Innovation and Skils 2009–10, shadow ldr of the House and oppn chief whip 2010–16, oppn chief whip 2016–; Parly sec Lord Chllr's Office 2001–; PLP rep on Lab Pty Nat Policy Forum 1997–2001, ldr Leadership Campaign Team 1998–99, chair Tport and Gen Worker's Parly Gp 1998–99; memb: Intelligence and Security Ctee 2000, Standing Ctee of Transport Bill 2000; *Recreations* sailing, reading; *Clubs* Intake Social, Doncaster Catholic, Doncaster Trades and Labour; *Style*— The Rt Hon Dame Rosie Winterton, DBE, MP; ✉ House of Commons, London SW1A 0AA (e-mail rosie.winterton.mp@parliament.uk; Constituency Office, Trades and Labour Club, 19 South Mall, Frenchgate, Doncaster DN1 1LL (✆ 01302 326297)

WISBECH, Archdeacon of; *see:* Rone, Ven Jim

WISDOM, Julia Mary; da of Dennis Wisdom (d 1985), and Rosemary Jean, *née* Cutler; *b* 24 September 1958; *Educ* Cranborne Chase Sch, Bryanston, King's Coll London (BA); *Career* commissioning ed of crime fiction Victor Gollancz Ltd until 1993, publishing dir HarperCollins Publishers Ltd 2002– (editorial dir 1994–2001); memb Crime Writers' Assoc 1987; *Recreations* music, travel, reading; *Style*— Ms Julia Wisdom; ✉ HarperCollins Publishers Ltd, 77–85 Fulham Palace Road, London W6 8JB (✆ 020 8741 7070, fax 020 8307 4440)

WISE, Prof Christopher (Chris); *b* 1956; *Educ* BSc; *Career* structural engineer; Ove Arup and Partners (London, Sydney and San Francisco): joined 1979, dir 1992–99, bd dir until 1999; co-fndr Expedition Engineering 1999–; projects incl: Stockley Park Building B3 (Construction Industry Award 1989), Century Tower Tokyo (IStructE Special Award 1991), Cranfield Inst of Technol Library (Construction Industry Award 1993), Channel 4 New HQ London (RIBA Award 1995), Barcelona Bullring, Commerzbank New HQ Frankfurt (Construction Industry Award 1997), American Air Museum Duxford (Construction Industry Award 1997, Stirling Prize for Architecture 1998), Carré d'Art de Nimes, Broadwick House Soho, Terminal 5 Heathrow Airport, Gardermoen Airport Oslo, Torre de Collserola Barcelona (Premio Alacantara Award 1993), Northbank Footbridge Stockton-upon-Tees, South Dock Bridge London, Millennium Bridge London, Chiswick Park Footbridge London, Ellis Park Athletic Stadium Johannesburg, Malaysian Nat Stadium Kuala Lumpur, Courts of Justice Bordeaux, Law Courts Antwerp, Nat Assembly of Wales Cardiff, Munstead Water Tower Godalming (RIBA Award 1994), New Children's Hospital Stanford CA, Intesa Sanpaolo Tower Turin; prof of civil engrg design Imperial Coll London 1998–2005, Davenport prof Yale Univ Sch of Architecture 2006, dir Royal Designers Summer Sch 2006–12, prof of civil engrg design UCL 2012–15; external examiner AA; memb: Design Cncl 2005–11; Silver Medal Royal Acad of Engrg 2007, Gold Medal IStructE 2012, Gold Medal ICE 2012; MIStructE, RDI 1998, Hon FRIBA 2002, FREng, FRSA; *Style*— Prof Chris Wise, RDI; ✉ Expedition Engineering, Morley House, First Floor, 320 Regent Street, London W1B 3BB (✆ 020 7307 1000, fax 020 7307 1001, website www.expedition.uk.com)

WISE, Prof Richard; s of A R James Wise (d 1993), and Joan Wise (d 2004); *b* 7 July 1942, Prestbury, Cheshire; *Educ* Burnage HS, Univ of Manchester (MB ChB, MD); *m* 16 Feb 1979, Dr Jane Marion Symonds, da of R C Symonds, of Sedbergh; 1 s (Peter Richard b 1970 d 1989), 1 da (Katherine b July 1972); *Career* conslt and dir W Midlands Antibiotic Res Laboratory Dudley Rd Hosp Birmingham 1974, hon prof Univ of Birmingham 1995 (reader in clinical microbiology 1985–95); scientific advsr House of Lords Select Ctee 1997–98 and 1999–, civilian conslt to the Army, advsr European Centre for Disease

Control; non-exec dir: Centre for Applied Microbiology and Research 1997–2000 (chm Scientific Ctee), Health Protection Agency 2003–07; chm Specialist Advsy Ctee on Antimicrobial Resistance Dept of Health 2001–07, memb Nat Expert Panel on New and Emerging Infections; pres British Soc Antimicrobial Chemotherapy 1999–2001; author of numerous pubns on antibiotic resistance; vice-chair: Herefordshire Nature Tst 2007–10, W Midlands Campaign for the Protection of Rural England 2009–12; FRCP, FMedSci, FRCPath; *Recreations* viticulture, gardening, flying; *Clubs* East India, Herefordshire Aero; *Style—* Prof Richard Wise

WISEMAN, Dr Martin Jeremy; s of Leslie Wiseman, of Faversham, Kent, and Sonia Wiseman, *née* Linder; *b* 18 April 1953; *Educ* King's Sch Canterbury, Guy's Hosp Med Sch (MRCP); *m* 5 May 1979, Jane Carol, da of Dennis Bannister, of Bournemouth, Dorset; 2 da (Jessica b 1982, Anna b 1985), 1 s (Daniel b 1987); *Career* research fell Metabolic Unit Guy's Hosp 1981–86, head Nutrition Unit Dept of Health 1986–99, md (nutrition and regulatory affairs) Burson-Marsteller 1999–2000; visiting prof of human nutrition Univ of Southampton 1994–, hon sr lectr in nutrition and public health LSHTM 1994–, med advsr World Cancer Research Fund 2001–; author of publications on diabetes, nutrition and kidney disease; memb: Diabetes UK, Nutrition Soc; FRCP, FRCPath; *Recreations* gastronomy, travel, family, Times crossword; *Style—* Dr Martin Wiseman; ☎ 020 8778 7597, e-mail mjwiseman@ntlworld.com

WISEMAN, Prof (Timothy) Peter; s of Stephen Wiseman (d 1971), of Manchester, and Winifred Agnes Wiseman; *b* 3 February 1940; *Educ* Manchester Grammar, Balliol Coll Oxford (MA, DPhil); *m* 15 Sept 1962, (Doreen) Anne, da of Harold Williams, of Atherton, Lancs; *Career* reader in Roman history Univ of Leicester 1973–76 (lectr in classics 1963–73), visiting prof of classics Univ of Toronto 1970–71, prof of classics Univ of Exeter 1977–2001 (emeritus prof 2001–), chm Br Sch at Rome 2002–07; vice-pres Br Acad 1992–94, pres: Roman Soc 1992–95, Jt Assoc of Classical Teachers 1998–99, Classical Assoc 2000–01; Hon DLitt Durham 1988; FSA 1977, FBA 1986; *Books* Catullan Questions (1969), New Men in the Roman Senate (1971), Cinna the Poet (1974), Clio's Cosmetics (1979), Catullus and His World (1985), Roman Studies (1987), Death of an Emperor (1991), Talking to Virgil (1992), Historiography and Imagination (1994), Remus: A Roman Myth (1995), Roman Drama and Roman History (1998), The Myths of Rome (2004), Unwritten Rome (2008), Remembering the Roman People (2009), Ovid: Times and Reasons (jtly, 2011), The Death of Caligula (2013), The Roman Audience (2015), How Old Is Exeter? (2016); *Style—* Prof Peter Wiseman; ✉ Department of Classics, Amory Building, University of Exeter, Exeter EX4 4RJ (☎ 01392 724195, fax 01392 724377)

WISHART, John MacKeand (Jock); s of Thomas Wishart, of Dumfries, and Marion Jane MacKeand Hood, BEM; *b* 6 February 1953; *Educ* Dumfries Acad, Univ of Durham (BA, pres Union and Univ Boat Club); *m* 28 July 1984, Deborah Jane, da of Wilfred Preston; 1 s (Gregory John MacKeand b 16 Sept 1986), 1 da (Laurie Isla b 3 May 1991); *Career* PA to gp sales and promotions dir Lillywhites 1974–78, sales dir Ravelle Wrightweights 1978–80, conslt 1980–84; Hill and Knowlton: assoc dir 1984–89, sponsorship dir 1989–91, conslt 1991–; dir: Transoceanic Adventures 1996–99, Polar Adventures Ltd 2002–; head of public rels Rugby World Cup 1991, memb Organising Ctee World Corporate Games London 1992; memb London Int Sport 1994–, fndr memb Top 100 Club; sporting achievements: GB rowing rep World Jr Championships, winner Br Univ Championship medals for rowing, canoeing and weightlifting, rowing rep Scotland, finalist Wyfolds Cup Henley Royal Regatta 1978 and 1979, America's Cup challenger Newport RI 1980, past holder Round Britain Powerboat Record 1989, winner all major trophies Cowes Week IOW during period 1983–2002, Br Dragon Boat champion 1989, 1990, 1992, 1996 and 1998, fourth place Dragon Boat World Championships 1990, European champion 1993 and 1995, winner Br Skiffing Championships 1991, 1993 and 1999; navigator of Freedom (winner 12m World Championship Cowes IOW 2001); memb Br Polar Team (first men to walk unsupported to N Geomagnetic pole) 1992, organiser Ultimate Challenge (largest ever party and first televised trek to N Magnetic Pole) 1996, rowed Atlantic 1997, holder Powered Circumnavigation of the World record 1998, capt London-Paris rowing record team 1999, ldr Shackleton's Steps expdn 2000, organiser Polar Race 2003–13, London2Paris rowing challenge 2008 and 2010, ldr Row to the Pole expdn 2011, ldr Wooden Spoon Arctic Rugby Challenge 2015; RSGS Mungo Park Medal 2012; vice-pres Palatinate Assoc (Univ of Durham Old Boys); govr Sportaid; memb Exec Ctee Univ of Durham; *Recreations* sailing, dragon boat paddling, rowing, skiing, rugby; *Clubs* Leander, Mosimann's, Boisdales, Molesey Boat (capt 1978), Remenham, Royal Canoe, Royal Hong Kong Yacht, Tamesis, Skiff, London Corinthian Sailing, Thames Sailing, Kingston Royals Dragon Boat (chm 1987–95), Upper Thames Sailing; *Style—* Jock Wishart, Esq; ✉ 18 Neville Road, Kingston upon Thames, Surrey KT1 3QX (☎ 020 8549 1457, e-mail jockwish@aol.com, websites www.jockwishart.co.uk and www.arcticrugbychallenge.com)

WISHART, Martin; s of George Wishart, and Georgia, *née* Leask; *b* 29 August 1969, Edinburgh, Scotland; *Educ* Broughton HS; *m* 2003, Cecile, *née* Auvinet; 2 da (Clara b 29 Oct 2006, Amy b 25 April 2008); *Career* proprietor and chef Restaurant Martin Wishart Edinburgh 1999– (4 AA Rosettes, Michelin star), head chef Martin Wishart at Loch Lomond (Michelin star 2011–); hon doctorate Univ of Edinburgh 2012; *Recreations* motorsport, sailing; *Style—* Martin Wishart, Esq; ✉ Restaurant Martin Wishart, 54 The Shore, Edinburgh EH6 6RA

WISHART, Peter (Pete); MP; s of Alex Wishart (d 1982), of Dunfermline, and Nan Irvine, *née* Lister; *b* 9 March 1962; *Educ* Queen Anne HS, Moray House Coll of Educn; *m* 1990; 1 c (Brodie b 1991); *Career* community worker 1984–85; musician with Runrig 1985– (5 Top 40 hits, sold over 1 million albums: 4 Gold albums UK, 1 Gold album Denmark, 1 Platinum album Scot); MP (SNP): N Tayside 2001–05, Perth and N Perthshire 2005–; SNP House of Commons spokesperson on home affrs, culture, media and sport until 2015, shadow ldr of the House 2015–, chair Scottish Affrs Select Ctee 2015–; dir Fast Forward Positive Lifestyles; memb Campaign Ctee Scotland Against Drugs; memb Performing Rights Soc 1991–; *Recreations* music, hill walking; *Style—* Peter Wishart, Esq, MP; ✉ 17–19 Leslie Street, Blairgowrie, Perthshire PH10 6AH (☎ 01250 876576); 63 Glasgow Road, Perth PH2 0PE (☎ 01738 639598, e-mail wishartp@parliament.uk)

WISHART, Dr Ruth (Mrs R McLeod); da of John Wishart (d 1960), and Margaret, *née* Mitchell (d 1989); *b* 27 August 1945; *Educ* Eastwood Sr Secdy Sch, Open Univ (BA); *m* 16 Sept 1971, Roderick McLeod, s of Roderick McLeod (d 2004); *Career* women's ed Scottish Daily Record; asst ed: Sunday Mail, Sunday Standard, The Scotsman; currently: freelance columnist and broadcaster, chair Dewar Arts Awards, memb Bd Creative Scotland; Hon DUniv Stirling 1994; *Recreations* theatre, concerts, galleries, community magazine, events; *Style—* Dr R Wishart; ☎ 0143 684 2134, e-mail ruth@kilcreggan.demon.co.uk

WISNER, George John; s of George Phillip Wisner, and Lillian Florence, *née* Butler; *b* 1 June 1949; *Educ* Haverstock Hill Sch, Chelsea Sch of Art; *m* 26 March 1977 (m dis 2000); 2 da (Alice Willow b 29 Dec 1977, Shelley Rose b 11 Feb 1980); *Career* set designer; BBC: apprentice carpenter 1965–70, design asst 1971–74, designer 1974–80, head of design Open Univ Prodn Centre 1988–91, host visitor Liaison Dept BBC TV Centre London 1990–91; BBC prodns designed incl: Day in the Death of Joe Egg, The Gambler by Dostoyevsky, The Prime of Miss Jean Brodie, The Grand Inquisitor, End Game, Macbeth, Miss Julie, numerous children's progs; ptnr: Blakesley Gallery 1991–97, Cactus 1994–; memb: BAFTA, RSA; selected best apprentice in UK by City & Guilds to represent UK at Int Apprentice Competition Brussels 1969, Sir Herbert Mole Meml Medal Chelsea Sch of Art 1969; FRSA 1987; *Recreations* cycling, swimming, walking; *Style—* George Wisner, Esq; ✉ Kirby House, High Street, Blakesley, Towcester, Northamptonshire NN11 8RE

WISZNIEWSKI, Adrian Ryszard; s of Witold Eugene Wiszniewski, of Renfrew, Glasgow, and Elspeth Mary, *née* Hyland; *b* 31 March 1958; *Educ* Mackintosh Sch of Architecture, Glasgow Sch of Art (BA, postgrad Dip); *m* 11 May 1985, Diane Lennox, da of Ronald Alexander Foley, of Nairn; 2 s (Max Tristan Charles b 26 June 1987, Louis Lennox Highland b 6 Nov 1993), 1 da (Holly b 21 April 1990); *Career* artist; work in painting, printmaking, ceramics, tapestry, neon, sculpture, writing, film, furniture design, intriors; solo exhibitions in London, Belgium, Australia and Japan; also exhibited in several important int gp exhibitions and surveys throughout the world; theatre (writer): GBH (The Girl, the Boy and the Hag) 2007, La Befana 2009, Foundation Stone (Amber) 2010; Mark Rothko Scholarship 1984, Lord Provost Award (Glasgow) for Visual Arts 1999; ARSA; *Books* For Max (1988), A Man Tied-Up in His Own Composition (1996), GBH (The Girl, the Boy and the Hag); *Style—* Adrian Wiszniewski, Esq; ✉ Calder Mews, Main Street, Lochwinnoch, Renfrewshire PA12 4AH

WISZOWATY, Nick; s of Jozef Wiszowaty (d 1975), and Joan, *née* Roberts; *Educ* Tomlinscote Sch Camberley; *m* 6 Aug 1994, Katie, da of Christopher Taylor; *Career* with Matthew Freud Associates 1987–90, latterly Freud Communications; holder commercial pilot licence; *Recreations* family; *Clubs* Wentworth; *Style—* Nick Wiszowaty, Esq

WITCHELL, Nicholas N H; s of late William Joseph Henshall Witchell, and Barbara Sybil Mary, *née* MacDonald (decd); *b* 23 September 1953; *Educ* Epsom Coll, Univ of Leeds (LLB); *m* Maria F Staples; 2 da; *Career* joined BBC News 1976, reporter NI 1979–81, reporter London 1981–83, Ireland corr 1984; presenter: 6 O'Clock News 1984–89, BBC Breakfast News 1989–94; corr Panorama 1994, diplomatic corr BBC 1995–98, royal and diplomatic corr BBC 1998–; vice-pres Queen Elizabeth's Fndn, patron Queen Alexandra Hosp Home, dir Normandy Meml Tst Ltd; FRGS; OStJ; *Books* The Loch Ness Story (1974, 1975, 1982 and 1989); *Clubs* Reform; *Style—* Nicholas Witchell; ✉ BBC News, BBC Broadcasting House, London W1A 1AA

WITCOMB, Roger; OBE (2015); s of Canon Cyril Witcomb (d 1983), and Jo Witcomb, *née* Newman, of Salisbury, Wilts; *b* 5 May 1947; *Educ* Eton, Merton Coll Oxford (BA), Nuffield Coll Oxford (MPhil); *m* 1970, Marian, da of Maj Frank Stone; 2 s (Mark b 1977, Edward b 1980); *Career* economist Bank of England 1970–71, fell econ Churchill Coll Cambridge, fell and dir of studies in econs Gonville & Caius Coll Cambridge 1974–79, res offr Dept of Applied Econs Univ of Cambridge, various mgmnt positions at BP 1980–89, fin dir National Power plc 1996–2000, conslt Saxton Bampfylde Hever plc 2001–2002, sr advsr Actis Capital Partners 2002–07; non-exec dir: Anglian Water Services 2002–06, Andrews & Ptnrs Ltd 2005–11, Anglian Water Gp 2006–10; tstee Opportunity Int UK 2004–14; govr Univ of Winchester 2004–11 (chair 2006–11); memb Competition Cmmn 2009–14 (chair 2011–14), panel chair and non-exec dir Competition & Markets Authy 2014–; *Recreations* cricket, golf, singing; *Style—* Roger Witcomb, Esq; ✉ The Old Plough, Barton Stacey, Winchester SO21 3RH (☎ 01962 761780, mobile 07880 712248, e-mail roger@oldplough.com)

WITHERIDGE, Rev John Stephen; s of Francis Edward Witheridge (d 1988), and Joan Elizabeth, *née* Exell (d 1999); *b* 14 November 1953; *Educ* St Albans Sch, Univ of Kent at Canterbury (BA), Christ's Coll Cambridge (MA); *m* 1975, Sarah Caroline, da of Rev Peter Phillips; 2 da (Charlotte b 1978, Harriet b 1981), 2 s (George b 1983, Henry b 1986); *Career* curate Luton Parish Church 1979–82, head of religious studies and asst chaplain Marlborough Coll 1982–84, chaplain to the Archbishop of Canterbury 1984–87, conduct (sr chaplain) Eton Coll 1987–96, headmaster Charterhouse 1996–2013; assoc sr memb Wadham Coll Oxford 2014–16, hon chaplain and assoc sr memb Christ Church Oxford 2016–; govr: Brambletye Sch 2009–12, Clifton Coll 2009–13; FRHistS 2013; *Publications* Frank Fletcher: A Formidable Headmaster (2005), Excellent Dr Stanley: The Life of Dean Stanley of Westminster (2013); author of various articles and reviews; *Recreations* theatre, biography, gardening, grandchildren; *Style—* The Rev John Witheridge; ✉ Minster Cottage, Charlbury, Oxfordshire OX7 3PR

WITHEROW, John Moore; *b* 20 January 1952; *Educ* Bedford Sch, Univ of York (BA), Univ of Cardiff (Dip Journalism); *m* 1985, Sarah Linton; 2 s, 1 da; *Career* trainee Reuters London and Madrid 1977–80, home and foreign corr The Times 1980–83; The Sunday Times: defence corr 1984–85, diplomatic corr 1985–87, focus ed 1987–89, foreign ed 1989–92, managing ed (news) 1992–94, ed 1994–2013; ed The Times 2013–; visiting fell Said Business Sch Oxford; hon doctorate Univ of York; *Books* The Winter War: The Falklands (with Patrick Bishop, 1982, 2 edn 2012), The Gulf War (1993); *Recreations* skiing, sailing, tennis; *Clubs* Soho House, Ivy, Campden Hill Tennis, Hurlingham; *Style—* John Witherow, Esq

WITHEROW, Ross O'Neill; s of late Cecil John Witherow, of Cape Town, South Africa, and late Millicent Frances, *née* Wilson; *b* 2 January 1945, Pretoria, SA; *Educ* Bedford Sch, UCH Med Sch London (Grenfell student scholar, MB BS, MS, Eschmann prize); *m* 1, 1977 (m dis 1982), Michelle, *née* Heimsoth; 1 s (Alexander Guy O'Neill b 2 March 1981); m 2, 1990 (m dis 2005), Bridget Margaret Rossiter, da of Michael Christopher Alfred Codrington; 1 s (Thomas Edward b 12 Oct 1991), 1 step s (Peter Goodman Rossiter b 27 Aug 1983); *Career* house offr: UCH London 1968, Addenbrooke's Hosp Cambridge 1968–69; ship's surgn Union Castle Line 1969–70, SHO UCH 1971, registrar in surgery Edgware Gen Hosp 1972, sr registrar in gen surgery UCH 1974–75 (registrar 1973), postgrad res fell in urology Univ of Calif San Francisco 1976–77 (lectr 1978), lectr and hon sr registrar in urology London Hosp 1978–79, resident asst surgn St Paul's Hosp 1979–80, conslt urological surgn St Mary's Hosp London and clinical sr lectr (recognised teacher) Univ of London 1981–2007 (now emeritus conlst urological surgn); memb: Br Assoc of Urological Surgns 1981, Societé Internationale d'Urologie 1982; FRCS 1973, FRSM 1979, FEBU 1992; *Books* Surgical Infection (1977), Genito-Urinary Surgery (contrib, 1985), Diagnosis and Management of Male Erectile Dysfunction (contrib, 1992), Atlas of Urologic Surgery (contrib, 1998); *Recreations* skiing, golf, opera, cooking, sailing; *Clubs* Royal Thames Yacht; *Style—* Ross Witherow; ✉ 50 Ferryman's Quay, London SW6 2UT (☎ 020 7371 9167)

WITHERS, Prof Philip John; s of David Withers (d 1970), and Shirley Davis, *née* Stone; *b* 11 May 1963, Wales; *Educ* Kingsmead Comp Wiveliscombe, Taunton Sch, Trinity Hall Cambridge (BA), Univ of Cambridge (PhD); *m* 28 July 1990, Lindsey Jayne, *née* Owen; 1 da (Chloë Elizabeth b 25 Jan 1994), 2 s (David b 24 June 1996, Peter b 8 Aug 1999); *Career* research fell Darwin Coll Cambridge 1988–91, lectr in materials sci and metallurgy Univ of Cambridge 1989–98, prof of materials sci Univ of Manchester 1998–; dir BP Int Centre for Advanced Materials 2012–; Materials Sci and Technol prize Fedn of European Materials Socs 1999, Rosenhain medal and prize Inst of Materials 2001, Royal Soc Wolfson merit award holder 2002–07, Royal Soc Armourers and Brasiers Medal 2010, Queen's Anniversary Prize for Higher and Further Education (for new techniques in x-ray imaging of materials critical for power, transport and other key industries) 2012–14; FIMMM, CEng 2004, FREng 2005, FRAes; *Publications* An Introduction to Metal Matrix Composites (with T W Clyne, 1993), Introduction to the Characterisation of Residual Stresses by Neutron Diffraction (with M T Hutchings, T M Holden and T Lorentzen, 2005); over 400 pubns in jls; *Recreations* cricket, football, golf, photography; *Style—* Prof Philip Withers; ✉ Director of the BP International Centre for Advanced Materials, Pariser Building, The University of Manchester, Manchester M13 9PL(☎ 0161 306 4282, e-mail philip.withers@manchester.ac.uk)

WITHERS, Roger Dean; s of Frederick Charles Withers (d 1975), of Bradfield, Berks, and Norah, née Butler (d 2005); b 15 August 1942, Bradfield, Berks; m 17 Aug 1963, Patricia Margaret, née Fenn; 1 s (Alexander Roger b 11 June 1975); Career assoc conslt Booz, Allen and Hamilton Int 1968–73, divnl dir Ladbrokes plc 1973–86, md Bass Leisure Machine Services 1987–97, dir Bass Leisure 1992–98; chm: Bass Leisure South Africa 1995–99, Littlewoods Leisure 1999–2000, Arena Leisure plc 2001–06, Playtech plc 2006–13, Sportech plc 2011–, Safecharge Ltd 2014–; nat pres BACTA (British Amusement Catering Trade Association) 1993–95, dir Business in Sport and Leisure 2001–05; MInstD 1974; Recreations shooting, classic cars, travel, food and wine; Clubs Oriental; Style— Roger Withers, Esq; ✉ Sportech Inc, 101 Wigmore Street, London W1U 1QU

WITHINGTON, Neil Robert; s of Derek Henry Withington (d 1986), of Manchester, and Audrey, née Whittle; b 6 September 1956, Manchester; Educ William Hulme's GS Manchester, BNC (exhibitioner, MA, BCL); Family 2 da (Emma Louise Gordon b 15 March 1990, Polly Claire b 31 July 1992); Career called to the Bar Middle Temple 1981 (Harmsworth scholar); lectr Osgoode Hall Law Sch Toronto 1979–80, visiting prof Univ of Oklahoma Law Sch 1980, barr 28 St John Street Manchester 1981–86, sr lawyer ICI Pharmaceuticals 1986–90, sr lawyer ICI Millbank 1990–93, sr lawyer BAT Industries plc 1993–95, asst gen counsel BAT (Holdings) 1996–98, legal dir and gen counsel British American Tobacco plc 2000– (dep gen counsel 1998–2000); memb Worshipful Co of Tobacco Pipe Makers and Tobacco Blenders; Publications incl Horvath v The Queen: Reflections on the Doctrine of Confessions (1980); Recreations golf, theatre, wine; Clubs Burhill Golf, Wimbledon Park Golf, Oxford and Cambridge; Style— Neil Withington, Esq; ✉ British American Tobacco plc, Globe House, 4 Temple Place, London WC2R 2PG (✆ 020 7845 1480, fax 020 7845 2181, e-mail neil_withington@bat.com)

WITTS, Air Cdre Jeremy John; DSO (1991); b 18 June 1950; Educ Marlborough GS (RAF Scholar), RAF Coll Cranwell, RAF Staff Coll Bracknell, Birkbeck Coll London (MSc); Career served Vulcan B2 bomber force Cyprus and UK to 1978, two tours Bucaneer S2 RAF Laarbruch Germany, Sqdn Leader 1979, staff appt Tornado GR1 Project Office HQ Strike Command 1984–86, contingency planner (Harrier and Jaguar) HQ 1 Gp, Wing Cdr 1987, MOD appt Flight Safety 1 (RAF) Inspectorate of Flight Safety, Cdr 31 Sqdn RAF Brüggen Germany 1989–92, Cdr Tornado GR 1/1A Sqdn Dahran Gulf War 1991, appt MOD Air Force Plans and Programmes 1992–94, Gp Capt 1994, exec offr (NATO) to USAF 4-star Cdr Allied Air Forces Central Europe (AIRCENT) Ramstein Germany (also Sr RAF Staff Offr and Sr Nat Rep), Cdr RAF Northolt 1997–99, ADC to HM The Queen 1998–99, Cdr Tornado GR1 Detachment Solenzara Corsica (during Kosovo crisis) 1999, Air Cdre 1999, Equipment Support (Air) Dir of Ops (Fixed Wing) 2000–02, UK air attaché and asst def attaché Washington DC 2002–05, dir of fin and admin Univ Coll Sch 2005–; FRAeS; Style— Air Cdre J J Witts, DSO, FRAeS, RAF (Ret)

WIX, Jonathan; s of Harold Wix, of London, and Bernice Beare-Rosenberg, of Durban, South Africa; b 3 November 1951; m 1977, Carolyn; 1 s (James b 1983), 1 da (Amelia b 1986); Career hotelier; dir: North Bridge Investments Ltd, White Elephant Preservation Co Ltd, WEPC SA, Wix Gp; Recreations skiing, shooting; Clubs RAC; Style— Jonathan Wix, Esq; ✉ fax 01943 850745

WOFFENDEN, Kenneth John (Ken); s of James Harold Woffenden (d 1991), of Wilmslow, Cheshire, and Agnes, née Grisenthwaite (d 1976); b 22 October 1954; Educ Manchester Grammar, Pembroke Coll Cambridge (fndn scholar, MA, Ziegler Law Prize), Coll of Law Guildford; m 2 July 1983, Glesni Myfanwy, da of Gwynfor Thomas Davies (d 2013), and Gwenllian Letitia Glenys (d 2015); 3 da (Catherine b 28 Oct 1987, Emily b 18 Oct 1989, Alice b 24 Oct 1997), 1 s (Thomas b 8 April 1993); Career Simmons & Simmons: articled clerk 1977–79, admitted slr 1979, asst slr Corp Dept 1979–84, ptnr Corp Dept 1984–2003, admitted slr Hong Kong 1986, head Corp and Banking Gp Hong Kong 1987–90, ptnr Corp Dept 1990–95 (head of Gp 1994–95), managing ptnr Hong Kong office 1995–97, managing ptnr Corp Dept 1999–2004; Stevens & Bolton LLP: joined 2004, head Corp and Commercial Dept 2006–11, managing ptnr 2012–; memb: Law Soc of England and Wales; Recreations music, cricket, family life; Clubs RAC, Hong Kong; Style— Ken Woffenden, Esq

WOLF, Martin Harry; CBE (2000); s of Edmund Wolf (d 1997), of London, and Rebecca, née Wijnschenk (d 1993); b 16 August 1946; Educ UCS, Corpus Christi Coll Oxford (open scholar, MA), Nuffield Coll Oxford (MPhil); m Aug 1970, Alison Margaret (Baroness Wolf of Dulwich), da of late Herbert Kingsley Potter, of Newbury, Berks; 2 s (Jonathan Thomas b 24 Jan 1975, Benjamin Jacob b 11 Jan 1977), 1 da (Rachel Janet b 11 June 1985); Career World Bank: joined Young Professional programme 1971, Office of vice-pres for East Africa 1972–74, sr economist India Div 1974–77, memb core team World Devpt Report 1977–78, sr economist Int Trade and Capital Flows Div 1979–81; dir of studies Trade Policy Res Centre 1981–87; Financial Times: joined 1987, chief economics leader writer and assoc ed 1990–96, chief economics commentator and assoc ed 1996–; conslt to various orgns, advsr and rapporteur to Eminent Persons Gp on World Trade 1990 (winner New Zealand 1990 Commemoration Medal); visiting fell Nuffield Coll Oxford 1999–2007; memb: Nat Consumer Cncl 1987–93, Awards Ctee American Express Bank Review Essay Competition 1994, Cncl Royal Economic Soc 1991–96, UK Govt Ind Cmmn on Banking 2010–11; jt winner Wincott Fndn Sr Prize for excellence in financial journalism 1989 and 1997, RTZ David Watt Meml Prize 1994, Accenture Decade of Excellence Business Journalist of the Year Awards 2003, Newspaper Feature of the Year Award Workworld Media Awards 2003, Award for Advocacy of Responsible Capitalism First magazine 2005, Journalism Prize Fundacio Catalunya Oberta 2006, runner-up Foreign Press Assoc's Financial Story of the Year 2007, AMEC Lifetime Achievement Award Workworld Media Awards 2007, second Royal Statistical Soc's Statistical Excellence in Journalism Award (print and online journalism category) 2008, Commentator of the Year Business Journalist of the Year Awards, included in Prospect and Foreign Policy magazines' list of 100 leading public policy intellectuals (voted 38th) 2008, Ludwig-Erhard-Preis fuer Wirtschaftspublizistik (Ludwig Erhard Prize for economic commentary) Ludwig Erhard Fndn 2009, placed 15th in Foreign Policy's list of the Top 100 Global Thinkers 2009, Commentariat of the Year Comment Award 2009, Hans Möller Medaille Müncher Volkswirte Alumni Club 2009, Award for Columns in Newspapers Best in Business Journalism Competition Soc of American Business Eds and Writers 2009 (jtly), shortlisted Columnist of the Year, Specialist Journalist of the Year and Journalist of the Year Br Press Awards 2010, Radio Prog of the Year Wincott Award 2010 (for The Economy on the Edge (BBC Radio 4 and World Service)), Overseas Press Club of America Prize for best commentary on int news in any medium, 37th in Foreign Policy's list of Top Global Thinkers for 2010, shortlisted for Business Journalist of the Year British Press Award 2011, 55th in Foreign Policy's list of Top Global Thinkers for 2011, 32nd Ischia Int Journalism Prize 2012, James Cameron Award for Journalism 2012, Overseas Press Club of America Prize for best commentary on int news in any medium 2013; special prof Univ of Nottingham 1993–2011, hon prof Univ of Nottingham 2011–; hon fell: Oxford Inst for Economic Policy 2005–, CCC Oxford 2006, Nuffield Coll Oxford 2010, KCL 2012; distinguished hon fell European Intl Business Academy 2012; DLitt (hc) Univ of Nottingham 2006, DSc (hc) LSE 2006, DSc (hc) Univ of Warwick 2009, DLitt (hc) Kingston Univ 2010, DLitt (hc) Macquarie Univ 2012; Publications incl: Textile Quotas against Developing Countries (with Donald B Keesing, 1980), India's Exports (1982), Costs of Protecting Jobs in Textiles and Clothing (1984), Global Implications of the European Community's Programme for Completing the

Internal Market (1989), Meeting the World Trade Deadline: Path to a Successful Uruguay Round (1990), The Resistible Appeal of Fortress Europe (1994), Why Globalization Works (2004), Fixing Global Finance (2008, 2 edn 2010), The Shifts and the Shocks (2014); Recreations theatre, opera, reading; Clubs Reform; Style— Martin Wolf, Esq, CBE; ✉ Financial Times, 1 Southwark Bridge, London SE1 9HL (✆ 020 7873 3673/3421, e-mail martin.wolf@ft.com)

WOLFE, Anthony James Garnham; s of Herbert Robert Inglewood Wolfe (d 1970), and Lesley Winifred, née Fox (d 2003); b 30 August 1952; Educ Haileybury, Univ of Bristol (BSc); m 4 Sept 1982, Ommar Aung, da of Lionel Aung Kwa Takwali (d 1956); Career chartered accountant; London and Hong Kong Offices Peat Marwick Mitchell 1974–81, GT Mgmnt London and Hong Kong Offices 1981–91, Signature Financial Group 1992–94, Cogent 1994–2004; FCA; Recreations rugger, golf, travel, real tennis, walking; Clubs Royal Wimbledon Golf, Royal Tennis Court; Style— Anthony Wolfe, Esq; ✉ c/o Cofunds, 1 Minster Court, Mincing Lane, London EC3R 7AA

WOLFE, Dr Catherine Ann; b 15 May 1969; Educ Univ of Cambridge (MA, PhD), m Michael Peter Desmond O'Donoghue; Career registered trade mark attorney; ptnr Boult Wade Tennant 2009–; fell Inst of Trade Mark Attorneys 2008 (first vice-pres 2010–12, pres 2012–14); Style— Dr Catherine Wolfe; ✉ Boult Wade Tennant, Verulam Gardens, 70 Gray's Inn Road, London WC1X 8BT (e-mail cwolfe@boult.com, website www.boult.com)

WOLFE, Gillian Anne; CBE (2005, MBE 1995); da of Noel Henry Humphrey (d 1984), and Anne, née Nicholls (d 1981); b 25 March 1946; Educ Sydenham Girls' Sch, Central Sch of Art, Univ of London (BEd); m 1974, Dr Kenneth Maurice Wolfe, s of Henry Wolfe; 1 s (Theodore Henry b 8 March 1982), 1 da (Eleanor Henrietta b 27 Sept 1989); Career teacher London 1974–84; dir of learning and public affrs Dulwich Picture Gallery 1984–2015; specialist advsr to Clore Fndn 1998–, Learning Panel advsr to HHA 2009–, chair Public Education Ctee RIBA 2015–; cmmr Cmmn for Architecture and the Built Environment (CABE) 2000–03; tstee: Historic Royal Palaces 2002–05, CABE Educn Fndn 2002–06, Brighton Pavillion and Museums Fndn 2010–15, Charleston Tst 2010–15, Arts4Dementia 2011–, RIBA Br Architects Tst Bd 2014–, Mary Roxburgh Tst 2016–; chair DCMS/DfES Advsy Ctee on Built Environment Educn 2003–05; memb: Exec Ctee Nat Heritage 1997–2002, Advsy Panel Attingham Tst survey on educn in the historic built environment 2002–04; specialist advsr to RHS 2003–07, expert advsr to the Heritage Lottery Fund 2005–12; judge Museum of the Year Awards 1998–2001; memb: Museums Assoc, Soc of Authors 1997–; hon doctorate St Norbert Coll USA 2006, hon doctorate Canterbury Christ Church Univ 2014; Awards NACF Award for Educn 1987, Museum of the Year Award for Educn 1988, Euro Museum of the Year Award Special Commendation 1989, Sandford Awards 1990, 1995 and 2000, Prudential Award for Visual Arts 1991, Sainsbury's Arts Educn Award 1993, Interpret Britain Award 1994, Unigate/Age Resource Award 1997, Southwark Achievement Award 1998, Sandford Award (Decade Review) 2000, Interpret Britain Award 2000, Royal Soc of Public Health Award 2012; Books eight children's art books 1997–2012; book awards: Gulbenkian 1992, Parent Choice USA 2002, English Assoc 2006–07; Recreations gardens, dance; Style— Mrs Gillian Wolfe, CBE; ✉ e-mail gillian.wolfe@btinternet.com

WOLFE, John Henry Nicholas; s of Herbert Robert Inglewood Wolfe (1970), and Lesley Winifred, née Fox; b 4 June 1947; Educ Eastbourne Coll, St Thomas' Hosp Univ of London (MB BS, MS); m 1, 23 June 1973 (m dis 1990), Jennifer, da of Geoffrey Sutcliffe; 3 s (Robert, Owen, Matthew), 2 da (Tara, Roshean); m 2, 1 Oct 1994, Dorothy Carey; Career res fell Harvard Med Sch Brigham Hosp 1981–82, sr registrar St Thomas' Hosp 1982–84, Hunterian prof RCS 1983; conslt surgn: St Mary's Hosp Med Sch 1984, Royal Postgrad Med Sch Hammersmith Hosp, Edward VII Hosp for Offrs; chm Euro CME; vice-pres European Div of Vascular Surgery 1999–2001; pres: European Bd of Vascular Surgery 2001–04, Vascular Soc of GB and I 2005–06 (memb Cncl), European Soc of Vascular Surgery 2007–08 (chm Vascular Advsy Ctee); pres World Fedn of Vascular Surgery 2012–13, memb Speciality Bd and Cncl Assoc of Surgns; hon memb: Vascular Soc of S Africa, Br Soc of Vascular Technologists, Vascular Soc of India, Swiss Vascular Soc, Assoc of Surgeons of India, German Vascular Soc, European Assoc of Vascular Surgical Trainees, Australasian Vascular Soc, Soc of Vascular Surgery (USA); memb Editorial Bd European Jl of Vascular Surgery; Freeman City of London 2007; FRGS; Books Vascular Surgery (ed 1985, 1989), ABC of Vascular Diseases (1992); Recreations sailing, sculpture, rudimentary pond management; Clubs RSM, RORC, RGS; Style— John Wolfe, Esq; ✉ 6 Cleveland Avenue, London W4 1SN (e-mail jwolfe@uk-consultants.co.uk)

WOLFE, Richard John Russell; s of late Maj John Claude Frank Wolfe, of Surrey, and Betty Doris, née Hopwood; b 15 July 1947; Educ Ackworth Sch; m 1, 28 Nov 1970 (m dis 1977), Lorraine Louise Hart; 1 da (Pandora b 12 July 1976); m 2, 23 July 1994, Irene Mehmet; Career mgmnt trainee NM Rothschild and Son Ltd 1964–68, investment dealer British and Continental Bank 1968–72, fund mangr Hill Samuel and Co Ltd 1972–75, corporate fin offr NM Rothschild and Sons Ltd 1976–80, first vice-pres and head of real estate fin UK Security Pacific Nat Bank 1980–90, md and head of Euro real estate Bankers Trust Co 1990–92, fin conslt 1992–; tstee: Inlight Tst, Truemark Tst 1994–; AIB 1978; Books Real Estate Finance (contrib 1988); Recreations choir singing, swimming, training, study of ancient civilisations; Style— Richard Wolfe, Esq; ✉ Shieling Hall, Langley, Kent ME17 3JZ; Queen Victoria Street, London EC4N 4SA

WOLFENDALE, Prof Sir Arnold Whittaker; kt (1995); s of Arnold Wolfendale (d 1963), and Doris, née Hoyle (d 1983); b 25 June 1927, Rugby, Warks; Educ Stretford GS, Univ of Manchester (BSc, PhD, DSc); m 1952, Audrey, da of Arnold Darby (d 1968); 2 s (twins, Colin and David); Career prof of physics Univ of Durham 1965–92 (now emeritus); Astronomer Royal 1991–95; Home Office, Civil Defence, later regnl scientific advsr 1958–81, chm N Region Manpower Service Cmmn's Job Creation Programme 1975–78; pres: Royal Astronomical Soc 1981–83, Antiquarian Horological Soc 1993–, European Physics Soc 1999–2001; chm: Cosmic Ray Cmmn of IUPAP 1982–84, Astronomy and Planetary Science Bd SERC 1988–94 (memb SERC 1988–94); pres Durham Univ Soc of Fells 1988–94; Freeman Worshipful Co of Clockmakers 1991, Hon Freeman Worshipful Co of Scientific Instrument Makers 1993; Hon DSc: Bucharest Univ, SW Bulgaria Univ, Potchefstroom Univ, Lód? Univ, Univ of Central Lancs, Univ of Teeside, Univ of Newcastle upon Tyne, Open Univ, Paisley Univ, Lancaster Univ, Univ of Durham, Univ of Bolton, Univ of Turku; Univ of Turku medal 1987, Observatory medal Armagh 1992, Marian Smoluchowski medal Poland 1992, Harrison Medal Worshipful Co of Clockmakers 2006; Bakerian lecture and prize Royal Soc 2002; foreign fell: Nat Acad of Sciences of India 1990, Indian Nat Sci Acad 1991, Tata Inst of Fund Research Bombay; foreign assoc Royal Soc of South Africa; FRS, FInstP (pres 1994–96), FRAS; Recreations gardening, travel; Style— Prof Sir Arnold Wolfendale, FRS; ✉ Physics Department, University of Durham, South Road, Durham DH1 3LE (✆ 0191 334 3580, fax 0191 334 3585, e-mail a.w.wolfendale@durham.ac.uk)

WOLFF, Ben; s of Herbert Wolff, of London, and Doris Wolff; b 31 August 1966, London; m 7 Sept 2006, Gillian, née Rough; Career songwriter, prodr and DJ; memb (with Andy Dean, qv) The Boilerhouse Boys 1985–; written, produced and remixed for artists incl Paul Weller, Donna Summer, Gabrielle, Texas, Shaznay Lewis, Chaka Khan, The Stereophonics, Sarah McLachlan, A Tribe Called Quest, Pop Will Eat Itself and Joss Stone; involved in the discovery and signing of artists incl Bush, Lily Allen and Joss Stone; over 20 million credited sales to date, writer of numerous soundtracks for TV and cinema campaigns; co-fndr (with Andy Dean, *qv*) Society Supper Club, ambass Krug; *Style—* Ben Wolff, Esq

WOLFF, Prof Heinz Siegfried; s of Oswald Wolff (d 1968), of W Germany, and Margot, *née* Saalfeld; *b* 29 April 1928; *Educ* City of Oxford Sch, UCL (BSc); *m* 21 March 1953, Joan Eleanor Mary (d 2014), da of Charles Heddon Stephenson, MBE (d 1968); 2 s (Anthony b 1956, Laurence b 1961); *Career* head Div of Biomedical Engrg Nat Inst for Med Res 1962–70 (joined 1954), head Div of Bioengineering Clinical Res Centre 1970–83, dir Brunel Inst for Bioengineering Brunel Univ 1983–95 (emeritus prof 1995–), dir Huntleigh Research Inst Brunel Univ 2003–; chm: Life Science Working Gp ESA 1976–82, Microgravity Advsy Ctee ESA 1982–91, Microgravity Panel Br Nat Space Centre 1986–87; fndr Nat Care4Care Scheme 2010; vice-pres: REMAP 1995–, Disabled Living Fndn 1997–, Coll of Occupational Therapists 1989–; bd dir Edinburgh Int Science Festival 1992–; presenter TV series incl: BBC TV Young Scientist of the Year 1968–81, Royal Inst Christmas Lectures 1975, The Great Egg Race 1978–86, Great Experiments which Changed the World 1985–86; introduced Give and Take Care (nat scheme for the reciprocal caring of the elderly in their own homes by society) 2014 (awarded £1m by Innovate UK to implement nationally via Give&TakeCare CIC); Harding Award Action Research 1989, Edinburgh Medal for Services to Science and Society 1992, Donald Julius Goen Prize IMechE 1994, Keith Medal for Innovation Royal Scottish Soc of Arts 1996 and 2001; Hon Doctorate: Open Univ 1993, De Montfort Univ 1995, Middlesex Univ 1999, Oxford Brookes Univ 1999, Brunel Univ 2003; fell UCL 1987; memb: Biological Engrg Soc, Ergonomics Res Soc; Hon FRCP 1999, FIBiol, FIEE, FBES, FRSA; *Books* Biological Engineering (1969); *Recreations* working, dignified practical joking; *Style—* Prof Heinz Wolff; ✉ Heinz Wolff Building, Brunel University, Uxbridge, Middlesex UB8 3PH (☎ 01895 266922, e-mail heinz.wolff@brunel.ac.uk, website www.giveandtakecare.co.uk)

WOLFFE, Andrew John Antony; s of Antony Curtis Wolffe, MBE, of Gatehouse-of-Fleet, and Alexandra Lorna, *née* Graham; *b* 6 July 1964; *Educ* Kirkcudbright Acad, Edinburgh Coll of Art (BA); *Career* graphic designer; creative dir Tayburn Design 1986–98; designed Royal Mail Burns commemorative stamps 1995; dir Wolffe & Co Ltd 1998–; tstee Edinburgh Photography Gallery Tst 1991–, dir Edinburgh Sculpture Workshop 2006–; MSTD; *Recreations* fly fishing; *Style—* Andrew Wolffe, Esq; ✉ Wolffe & Co (☎ 01556 504100, e-mail andrew@wolffeandco.com)

WOLFSON, David; QC (2009); s of District Judge Bernard Wolfson, of Liverpool, and Rosalind, *née* Libman; *b* 19 July 1968; *Educ* King David HS Liverpool, Yeshivat Hakotel Jerusalem, Selwyn Coll Cambridge (exhibitioner, coll scholar, Squire scholar, MA, Stuart of Rannoch Award); *m* 2 April 1995, Louise, da of Jeff Durkin; 1 s (Samuel Levi b 16 Dec 2002), 2 da (Zara Michal b 1 Nov 2004, Abigail Yona b 4 Sept 2007); *Career* called to the Bar Inner Temple 1992 (major scholarship 1992, Inns of Court scholarship 1992); barr specialising in commercial law; bencher Inner Temple 2016–; dir Bar Mutual Indemnity Fund Ltd 2004–; memb Commercial Bar Assoc 1992–; tstee: Jewish Chronicle Tst, Univ of Cambridge Jewish Soc 2014–; chm of govrs Kerem Sch 2012–; *Publications* Bank Liability and Risk (contrib, 1995), Banking Litigation (contrib, 1999), Arbitration in England (contrib, 2013); author of articles in legal jls incl: All England Litigation Review, New Law Jl, Jl of Int Banking Law, Jl of Int Banking & Financial Law, Int Insurance Law Review, Commercial Lawyer; *Recreations* travel, wine, learning 'lishma'; *Clubs* 67 Pall Mall; *Style—* David Wolfson, Esq, QC; ✉ One Essex Court, Temple, London EC4Y 9AR (☎ 020 7583 2000, fax 020 7583 0118, e-mail david.wolfson@oeclaw.co.uk)

WOLFSON OF ASPLEY GUISE, Baron (Life Peer UK, 2010), of Aspley Guise in the County of Bedfordshire; (Hon) Simon Adam Wolfson; s of The Lord Wolfson of Sunningdale, *qv*; *b* 27 October 1967, London; *Educ* Radley, Trinity Coll Cambridge; *m* Eleanor, da of William Shawcross, CVO, *qv*; *Career* Next plc: joined 1991, retail sales dir 1993, Next Directory 1995, memb Bd 1997–, md Next Brand 1999, chief exec 2001–; *Style—* The Lord Wolfson of Aspley Guise; ✉ Next plc, Desford Road, Enderby, Leicester LE19 4AT

WOLFSON OF MARYLEBONE, Baroness; Estelle Wolfson; da of Nathan Feldman (d 1976), and Annette, *née* Martin (d 2014); *b* 30 April 1945; *Educ* Hasmonean GS for Girls, St Godric's Coll (RSA English/RSA Commerce); *m* 1, 1966, Michael Jackson FCA (d 1985); 1 da (Antoinette b 23 Mar 1971), 1 s (Edward b 21 Oct 1976); m 2, 1991, Baron Wolfson (Life Peer, d 2010); *Career* philanthropist; estab Lord Leonard and Lady Estelle Wolfson Fndn 2012; tstee: Wolfson Fndn 1992–2012, Wolfson Family Tst 1992–2012, Royal Coll of Physicians, RSM, Global eHealth Fndn; patron Royal Coll of Surgeons; Yeoman Worshipful Co of Apothecaries, Freedom of the City of London 2013; hon fell: Emmanuel Coll Cambridge, KCL, Univ Coll London, Imperial Coll London, Royal Albert Hall 2013; *Recreations* meeting people, walking, travel; *Style—* The Lady Wolfson of Marylebone; ✉ The Lord Leonard and Lady Estelle Wolfson Foundation, Alexander House, 3 Shakespeare Road, London N3 1XE

WOLFSON OF SUNNINGDALE, Baron (Life Peer UK 1991), of Trevose in the County of Cornwall; Sir David Wolfson; kt (1984); s of Charles and Hylda Wolfson; *b* 9 November 1935; *Educ* Clifton, Trinity Coll Cambridge (MA), Stanford Univ (MBA); *m* 1, 1962 (m dis 1967), Patricia Elizabeth (now Baroness Rawlings (Life Peer), *qv*), da of Louis Rawlings; m 2, 1967, Susan E, da of Hugh Davis; 2 s (Hon Simon Adam (now The Lord Wolfson of Aspley Guise (Life Peer), *qv*), b 1967, Hon Andrew Daniel b 1969), 1 da (Hon Deborah Sarah b 1973); *Career* Great Universal Stores plc: joined 1960, dir 1973–78 and 1993–2000, chm 1996–2000; sec to shadow cabinet 1978–79, chief of staff Political Office 10 Downing St 1979–85; chm: Alexon Group plc (formerly Steinberg Group plc) 1982–86, Next plc 1990–98 (non-exec dir 1989–98); non-exec dir: Stewart Wrightson Holdings plc 1985–87, Compco Holdings plc 1995–2003, Body Metrics Ltd 2000–02, Avocet Capital Mgmnt Ltd 2001–02, Fibernet Group plc 2001–; hon fell Hughes Hall Cambridge 1989; Hon FRCR 1978, Hon FRCOG 1989; *Recreations* golf, bridge; *Clubs* Portland, Sunningdale, Woburn Golf; *Style—* The Rt Hon Lord Wolfson of Sunningdale; ✉ House of Lords, London SW1A 0PW

WOLLASTON, Dr Sarah; MP; *b* 17 February 1962, Woking, Surrey; *Educ* KCL; *m* Adrian; 3 c; *Career* forensic medical examiner Devon and Cornwall Police 1996, GP Chagford Health Centre 1999–2010, GP trainer and teaching jr doctors and medical students Peninsula Medical Sch 2001–10; MP (Cons) Totnes 2010–; memb Health Select Ctee 2010–; MRCGP 1992; *Style—* Dr Sarah Wollaston, MP; ✉ House of Commons, London SW1A 0AA

WOLLENBERG, (J) Richard; *Career* Cardiff Property plc: dir 1980–, chief exec 1981–, chm 1989–; exec dir Campmoss Property Co Ltd, non-exec dir Galileo Resources plc; *Style—* Richard Wollenberg, Esq; ✉ Cardiff Property plc, 56 Station Road, Egham, Surrey TW20 9LF

WOLPERT, Prof Lewis; CBE (1990); *b* 19 October 1929; *Educ* Univ of the Witwatersrand (BSc), Imperial Coll London (DIC, fell 1996), KCL (PhD); *m* (m dis); 2 s, 2 da; *Career* civil engr 1951–54: SA Cncl for Scientific and Industrial Research, Israel Water Planning Dept; career changed to cell biology 1954, reader in zoology Dept of Zoology at KCL 1964, prof of biology as applied to med Royal Free & Univ Coll Med Sch (formerly Middx Hosp Med Sch) 1966–; visiting lectr Collège de France Paris, emeritus prof UCL 2004; TV presenter for Antenna (BBC2) 1988–89, various interviews and documentaries for Radio 3; memb American Philosophical Soc 2002; Scientific Medal of the Zoological Soc 1968, Royal Soc Michael Faraday Award 2000; Christmas Lectures Royal Instn 1986, Radcliffe Lectures Univ of Warwick 1990, The Medawar Lecture Royal Soc 1998; Hon DSc: CNAA 1992, Univ of Leicester 1996, Univ of Westminster 1996, Univ of Bath 1997; Hon DUniv Open Univ 1998; hon fell UCL 1995, foreign memb Polish Acad of Arts & Scis 1998; fell Imperial Coll London 1996, FKC 2001; Hon MRCP London 1986; FRS 1980, FRSL 1999; *Books* A Passion for Science (jtly, 1989), The Triumph of the Embryo (1991), The Unnatural Nature of Science (1992), Passionate Minds (1997), Principles of Development (1998), Malignant Sadness – The Anatomy of Depression (1999), Six Impossible Things Before Breakfast: The evolutionary origins of belief (2006), How We Live and Why We Die: The Secret Lives of Cells (2009), You're Looking Very Well – The Surprising Nature of Getting Old (2011); *Recreations* cycling, tennis; *Style—* Prof Lewis Wolpert, CBE, FRS; ✉ Department of Cell & Development Biology, University College London, Gower Street, London WC1E 6BT (☎ 020 7679 1320, e-mail l.wolpert@ucl.ac.uk)

WOLSTENHOLME, Andrew William Lewis; OBE (2009); s of Michael Ashmore Wolstenholme, and Vivien Wolstenholme; *b* 5 March 1959, London; *Educ* Univ of Southampton (BSc), RMA Sandhurst, INSEAD Business Sch; *m* 1987, Caroline Barnes-Yallowley; 5 s; *Career* served Br Army: Royal Engrs (SSLC) and The Queen's Royal Irish Hussars (SSC) 1978 and 1981–84; OVE Arup and Ptnrs London 1984–96 (dir Project Mgmnt Gp Hong Kong 1993–96); BAA plc 1996–2009: dir of capital projects BAA, prog dir Terminal 5 Heathrow, gp construction dir; md Balfour Beatty Mgmnt then dir of innovation and strategic capability Balfour Beatty Gp plc 2009–11, chief exec Crossrail 2011–; non-exec dir Defence Equipment and Services Bd MOD 2014–, chair Construction Leadership Cncl 2015–; dir Inst of Cancer Research 2005–11, memb Cncl Eastbourne Coll 2009–15; Hon DSc 2014; FICE 2010, memb RICS 2012, FREng 2013; *Publications* Never Waste a Good Crisis; *Recreations* watercolour painting, cooking, opera, tennis, walking, ukulele; *Style—* Andrew Wolstenholme, Esq, OBE; ✉ Crossrail Ltd, 25 Canada Square, Canary Wharf, London E14 5LQ (☎ 020 299 9299, e-mail andrewwolstenholme@crossrail.co.uk)

WOMBELL, Paul; s of Clifford Wombell, and Katherine Wombell; *Educ* Armthorpe HS Doncaster, St Martin's Sch of Art (BA); *m* Patricia Coral Wombell; *Career* administrator Midland Gp Nottingham 1983–86, dir Impressions Gallery York 1986–94, dir The Photographers' Gallery London 1994–2005; quest curator Photo Int Rotterdam 1994, memb Selection Ctee Photo Works in Progress Rotterdam 1997–98, conf organiser Ten Stories About Photography V&A 1998, master World Press Photo Rotterdam 2000, judge Amnesty Int Media Awards London 2001–02; memb jury: Prix de Rome Amsterdam 1996, Photographers Assoc of the Netherlands 1998; memb: Int Advsy Panel Fotofest Houston 1989–, Int Advsy Panel Aperture NY, Advsy Bd Encyclopedia of 20th Century Photography 2000; visiting prof Univ of Sunderland 2002–; *Books* Battle: Passchendaele 1917 (1981), The Globe (1989), Photovideo: Photography in the Age of the Computer (1991), Sportscape: The Evolution of Sports Photography (2000), Blink (co-ed, 2002); *Style—* Paul Wombell, Esq; ✉ 238 Brick Lane, London E2 7EB

WOMBWELL, Sir George Philip Frederick; 7 Bt (GB 1778), of Wombwell, Yorkshire; s of Maj Sir Philip Wombwell, 6 Bt, MBE (d 1977); *b* 21 May 1949; *Educ* Repton; *m* 1974, (Hermione) Jane, eldest da of Thomas S Wrightson, of Leyburn, N Yorks; 1 s (Stephen Philip Henry b 1977), 1 da (Sarah Georgina b 1980); *Heir* s, Stephen Wombwell; *Career* farmer; *Style—* Sir George Wombwell, Bt

WOMERSLEY, Prof David John; s of John Crossley Womersley, of Woodstock, Oxon, and Joyce, *née* Nesbitt; *b* 29 January 1957, South Shields, Tyne & Wear; *Educ* Strode's Sch Egham, Trinity Coll Cambridge (BA, PhD), DLitt (Oxon, 2015); *m* 11 Sept 1982, Carolyn Jane, *née* Godlee; 1 s (James Rupert Lister b 23 Oct 1986), 2 da (Katharine Jane Bland b 3 Nov 1988, Rachel Alice Lodge b 5 March 1992); *Career* Drapers' Co research fell Pembroke Coll Cambridge 1981, lectr Sch of English Univ of Leeds 1983, fell and tutor in English Jesus Coll Oxford 1984, Thomas Warton prof of English literature Univ of Oxford 2002–; sr proctor Univ of Oxford 2001–02; govr: Dragon Sch Oxford 1998–2010, Harrow Sch 2001–16; FRHistS 1997, fell English Assoc 2003, FBA 2009; *Books* The Transformation of the Decline and Fall of the Roman Empire (1988), Religious Scepticism: Contemporary Responses to Gibbon (1997), Augustan Critical Writing (1997), Gibbon: Bicentenary Essays (ed, 1997), Edmund Burke, Pre-Revolutionary Writings (1998), Restoration Drama: An Anthology (2000), A Companion to English Literature from Milton to Blake (ed, 2000), Gibbon and the 'Watchmen of the Holy City': The Historian and his Reputation, 1776–1814 (2002), Samuel Johnson, Selected Essays (2003), Cultures of Whiggism (ed, 2005), Divinity and State (2010); also produced edns of Edward Gibbon's The Decline and Fall of the Roman Empire and Reflections on the Fall of Rome, Literary Milieux (ed, 2008), Boswell's Life of Johnson (ed, 2008), Swift's Gulliver's Travels (2012), James II (2015), E W Montagu, Reflections on the Rise and Fall of the Ancient Republicks (ed, 2015); *Recreations* wine, yachting, cooking, dogs; *Clubs* Athenaeum, Saintsbury; *Style—* Prof David Womersley; ✉ St Catherine's College, Oxford OX1 3UJ (☎ 01865 271714, e-mail david.womersley@ell.ox.ac.uk)

WOMERSLEY, (John) Michael; s of John Basil Womersley (d 1979), of Yorks, and Ann Patricia, *née* Allured; *b* 18 February 1960; *Educ* King Edward's Sch Bath, Oxford Poly (HND); *m* 4 May 1991, Susanne Jayne, da of John Maurice George Garrard (d 1996), and Sue, *née* Mullins; 2 s (Oliver Peter b 25 Oct 1995, Richard John b 13 Jan 1999), 1 da (Rebecca Kate b 15 Aug 2000); *Career* asst mangr (Reading) British Transport Hotels 1981, commis chef Gidleigh Park 1982–84, sauce chef de partie Le Manoir aux Quat'Saisons 1984–86, successively legumier, commis patissier then baker L'Esperance Marc Meneau 1986–87, fish chef de partie Les Pres D'Eugenie Michel Guerard 1987, sr sous chef Cliveden Hotel 1988–89, head chef Lucknam Park Hotel 1989–95, chef proprietor Three Lions Restaurant Stuckton 1995–; memb Académie Culinaire de Grand Bretagne; fell Masterchefs of GB 2004; *Awards* first prize Yorkshire Fine Wine Competition 1990, third prize Mouton Cadet Competition 1992, first prixe Prix des Deux Cartes 1994; finalist Pierre Tatinger Competition 1993; Lucknam Park Hotel awards: County Restaurant of the Year Good Food Guide 1990, 4 AA red stars and 3 red rosettes 1991–, Ackerman clover 1991–95, Hotel of the Year Exec Travel and Utell 1991, Michelin star 1992–95; Three Lions awards: Michelin Red M 1996, 3 stars AA Guide, Hampshire Achiever of the Year Good Food Guide 1996, Hampshire Commended Restaurant of the Year 2001, Nat Newcomer of the Year Good Hotel Guide 2002, Hampshire Restaurant of the Year Good Food Guide 2006; *Recreations* advanced diver, skiing, golf, Tai Chi; *Style—* Michael Womersley, Esq; ✉ Three Lions Restaurant, Stuckton, Fordingbridge, Hampshire SP6 2HF (☎ 01425 652489, fax 01425 652144, e-mail the3lions@btinternet.com)

WOMERSLEY, Sir Peter John Walter; 2 Bt (UK 1945), of Grimsby, Co Lincoln; JP (1991); s of late Capt John Walter Womersley (ka 1944), and gs of Rt Hon Sir Walter Womersley, 1 Bt, PC (d 1961); *b* 10 November 1941; *Educ* Charterhouse, RMA Sandhurst; *m* 1968, Janet Margaret, da of Alastair Grant; 2 s, 2 da; *Heir* s, John Womersley; *Career* serv Regular Army, Offr Cadet at Sandhurst until 1962, 2 Lt King's Own Royal Border Regt 1962, Lt 1964, Capt 1966, ret 1968; human resources serv mangr SmithKline Beecham 1993–97 (personnel offr 1968–72, personnel mangr 1972–93), conslt specialising in job evaluation 1997–99; MIPM; *Books* Collecting Stamps (with Neil Grant, 1980); *Recreations* breeding rare poultry, motor racing photography; *Style—* Sir Peter Womersley, Bt; ✉ Broomfields, 23 Goring Road, Steyning, West Sussex BN44 3GF

WOO, (Dr) Sir Po-Shing; kt (1999); s of Seaward Woo, OBE, JP, and Woo Ng Chiu Man; *b* 19 April 1929, Hong Kong; *Educ* La Salle Coll Hong Kong, KCL (LLB); *m* 25 Sept 1956, Woo Fong Shuet Fun (Lady Helen Woo); 4 s (Nelson, Wilson, Jackson, Dawson), 1 da (Carmen); *Career* admitted slr England and Hong Kong 1960, NP 1966, admitted

W

slr and barr Australia 1983; fndr and conslt Woo Kwan Lee & Lo Slrs & Notaries Hong Kong; dir: Celtime Ltd, Deroston Ltd, Eastern Delegate Ltd, Fong Fun Co Ltd, Fong Fun Enterprises Ltd, Fukuki Co Ltd, Helene Court Ltd, Jetfun Investment Ltd, Jumbo Concord Investment Ltd, Kailey Enterprises Ltd, Oriental Eagle Investment Ltd, Sun Hung Kai Properties Ltd, Tobofaith Ltd, Wise Town Ltd; memb Exec Ctee Hong Kong Discharged Prisoners' Aid Soc 1966, urban cncllr 1967–71, memb Bd of Mgmnt Chinese Perm Cemeteries 1973–83, memb Bd of Review Inland Revenue 1978–81, dir Hong Kong Tuberculosis Chest and Heart Diseases Assoc 1983–88 (hon legal advsr 1983–2000), patron Woo Po Shing Gallery of Chinese Bronze Shanghai Museum 1996–, patron Sir Po-Shing Woo Auckland Observatory 1998–; hon voting memb: Hong Kong Jockey Club, Po Leung Kuk Advsy Bd (dir 1977–78), Tung Wah Gp of Hosps (dir 1955–56, advsr 1956–57); legal advsr Chinese Gold and Silver Exchange Soc, dir and legal advsr Shun Tak Fraternal Assoc (registered sch mangr and ctee memb Seaward Woo Coll 1975), hon pres and legal advsr S China Athletic Assoc, vice-pres Hong Kong Woo's Clan General Assoc Ltd; fndr: Woo Po Shing Medal in Law Univ of Hong Kong 1982, Woo Po Shing Overseas Summer Sch Travelling Scholarship Univ of Hong Kong 1983, Po-Shing Woo Charitable Fndn 1994, Woo Po Shing Chair of Chinese and Comparative Law City Univ Hong Kong 1995; memb Bd of Tstees Univ of Hong Kong 1996–2002 (Staff Terminal Benefits Scheme 1996–2002, Staff Provident Fund 1996–2002, Staff Retirement Scheme 1996–2002), memb Cncl Univ of Hong Kong 1997–2000; recipient: world fellowship Duke of Edinburgh's Award, hon professorship Nankai Univ Tianjin China, Hon LLD City Univ Hong Kong; memb: Inst of Admin Mgmnt, Inst of Trade Mark Agents; fell Hong Kong Mgmnt Assoc 2000; FCIArb, FBIM, FIMgt, FKC; Chevalier de l'Ordre des Arts et des Lettres (France) 2004; *Recreations* travelling, antiques (including Chinese paintings, bronze and ceramic), racehorse owner (including Hong Kong Derby winner 'Helene Star' and 'Helene Mascot'); *Clubs* Hong Kong, Hong Kong Jockey, RAC (UK); *Style—* Sir Po-Shing Woo

WOOD, Alistair Angus; LVO (2012), MBE (1992); s of late Ronald Angus Wood, and Adrienne Chester, *née* Hartridge; *b* 24 August 1953, Tenterden, Kent; *Educ* Ardingly, RMA Sandhurst, Univ of Aberdeen (MLitt); *m* 7 July 1979, Anna Caroline, *née* Parry; 1 da (Sophie Katharine b 11 Aug 1984), 2 s (Hugo Edward Angus b 29 Oct 1987, Angus Peter Emrys b 22 April 1992); *Career* regular cmmn The Blues and Royals 1974, regular army 1974–93, advsr to Cmmr of the Metropolis 1994–97, advsr to Royal Bafokeng Administration Repub of South Africa 1999–2000, advsr to Govt of Sierra Leone 2000–02, advsr to Transitional Islamic State of Afghanistan 2003–04, private sec to HRH Princess Alice, Duchess of Gloucester 2004, private sec to TRH The Duke and Duchess of Gloucester 2004–12, chief exec UK Flagship 2012–13; chm Commonwealth Argosy Ltd 2013–; advsr Ridley Eye Fndn 2010–; dep commandant Aberdeenshire ACF 1999–2000; tstee St John of Jerusalem Eye Hosp 2007–12; Freeman City of London 2007, Liveryman Worshipful Co of Stone Masons 2008; *Recreations* scuba diving, international relations, military history; *Clubs* Cavalry and Guards; *Style—* Alistair Wood, Esq, LVO, MBE

WOOD, Anne; CBE (2000); *Educ* Bingley Trg Coll Yorks; *Career* early career as teacher and prodr at Yorkshire Television and TV-Am; fndr and creative dir Ragdoll Prodns 1984–; prodns incl: Rosie and Jim (ITV) 1990–2000, Brum (BBC) 1991–2001, Tots TV (ITV) 1993–98, Open a Door (BBC) 1994–2003, Teletubbies (BBC) 1997–99, Boohbah (ITV) 2003–05, What Makes Me Happy (Channel 5) 2005, Blips (ITV) 2005–06, In the Night Garden (BBC) 2007–08, Tronji (BBC) 2009, The Adventures of Abney and Teal (BBC) 2011–12, Dipdap (BBC) 2011–12; Outstanding Contrib in Children's Television and Film BAFTA Special Award 2000, Harvey Lee Award for Outstanding Contrib to Broadcasting Br Press Guild Award 2007; hon degree Univ of Birmingham 2013; FRTS 1998; *Style—* Ms Anne Wood, CBE; ✉ Ragdoll Productions Ltd, 9 Timothy's Bridge Road, Stratford Enterprise Park, Stratford-upon-Avon, Warwickshire CV37 9NQ

WOOD, Dr Anthony James (Tony); s of Harry Wood (d 1961), of Lowestoft, Suffolk, and Elizabeth Ann, *née* Calvert (d 1975); *b* 20 November 1938; *Educ* Lowestoft GS, Univ of Nottingham (BSc), Univ of London (PGCE), Univ of Southampton (PhD); *m* 1960, Marion Christine, da of Basil Archie Paine; 1 s (David Anthony b 10 July 1964), 2 da (Susan Nicola b 7 Oct 1965, Wendy Michelle b 23 March 1976); *Career* physics teacher Fairham Comp Nottingham 1961–62, Instr Lt RN 1962–67, sr lectr Weymouth Coll of Educn 1969–73 (lectr 1967–69), princ lectr and head Mathematics Div Northampton Coll of Educn 1973–75, dean Faculty of Mathematics and Business Nene Coll Northampton 1975–84 (dean Blackwood Hodge Mgmnt Centre 1981–84), chief exec Luton Coll of HE 1989–93 (dir 1985–93, Leverhulme research fell 1985–86), vice-chllr and chief exec Univ of Luton 1993–98 (vice-chllr emeritus 1998–2006), educational conslt 1998–; vice-chllr emeritus Univ of Beds 2006– (hon sr research fell 2011–); chm Bedfordshire Family Practitioners' Ctee 1989–90; chm and non-exec dir: Bedfordshire FHSA 1990–94, Bedfordshire HA 1994–2000; external examiner Univ of Southampton 1978–83; dir: Putteridge Bury Ltd 1989–98, HE Business Enterprises 1991–93, HE Quality Cncl 1992–93; memb: European Fndn for Mgmnt Devpt 1981–98, Access Courses Recognition Gp CNAA 1987–92, Instns Ctee CNAA 1989–92, Ctee for Degree Awarding Powers HE Quality Cncl 1992–93, R&D Ctee NW Thames RHA 1993–94, CVCP 1993–98, Univs Liaison Ctee Anglia and Oxford RHA 1994–96; chm Standing Conference of Princs and Dirs of Colls and Insts of HE 1990–93; govr and tstee English Speaking Union 2011–15 (pres Ouse Valley branch 2012– (chm 2006–12)); FIMA 1975, CMath 1992; *Publications* Involving Parents in the Curriculum (1976), Curriculum Enrichment for Gifted Children (1979), Quicksilver Maths series (1982), Hedgehoppers series (1986), The Effects of Speaking and Listening Activities on Primary School Performance: An Empirical Research Study (2013), Speak Listen and Learn: Teaching Resources for Ages 7–13 (2015); *Recreations* home and family; *Style—* Dr Tony Wood; ✉ Five Farthings, 34 Church End, Biddenham, Bedford MK40 4AR (☎ 01234 349395, fax 01234 325835, e-mail tony.wood@redrobin.me.uk)

WOOD, Prof Bernard Anthony; s of Anthony Frederick Wood, of Budleigh Salterton, Devon, and late Joan Faith, *née* Slocombe; *b* 17 April 1945; *Educ* King's Sch Gloucester, Middx Hosp Med Sch Univ of London (BSc, MB BS, PhD); *Children* 1 s (Nicholas b 1970), 2 da (Penny b 1972, Hannah b 1986); *Career* Univ of London: lectr 1973–75, sr lectr 1975–78, reader 1978–82, SA Courtauld prof 1982–85; Derby prof of anatomy Univ of Liverpool 1985–97, dean Faculty of Med Univ of Liverpool 1996–97; Henry R Luce prof of human origins George Washington Univ 1997–2006, Univ prof of human origins George Washington Univ 2006–; pres Anatomical Soc of GB and Ireland 1996–98, past pres Primate Soc of GB, vice-pres Royal Anthropological Inst, past sec Br Assoc of Clinical Anatomists; *Publications* Human Evolution (1978), Major Topics in Primate and Human Evolution (1986), Koobi Fora Hominid Cranial Remains (1991), Wiley-Blackwell Encyclopedia of Human Evolution (2011); papers on human origins; *Recreations* English saltglaze stoneware, opera; *Style—* Prof Bernard Wood; ✉ Center for the Advanced Study of Human Paleobiology, Science and Engineering Hall, 800 22nd Street NW Suite 6000, Washington DC 20052, USA (☎ 00 1 202 994 6077, fax 00 1 202 994 6097, e-mail bernardawood@gmail.com)

WOOD, Charles Anthony; OBE (1996); s of Anthony Mewburn Wood (d 1994), of Chiddingstone, Kent, and Margaret Kathleen, *née* Stordy; *b* 20 November 1938; *Educ* Downside, Pembroke Coll Oxford (MA); *m* 10 Oct 1964, Susan Mary, da of Henry Anderson, MBE (d 1975), of Wallingford, Oxon; 3 s (Robert b 1969, Francis b 1979, Jonathan b 1982), 1 da (Juliette b 1971); *Career* Phillips & Drew 1962–71, L Messel & Co 1971–86; dir: Lehman Brothers Securities 1986–96, Greig Middleton & Co Ltd 1996–97, Old Mutual Asset Managers (UK) Ltd 1997–2002 (vice-pres Int Ops), Standard Life Equity Income Tst plc 2003–14 (chm 2006–), Cazenove Capital Mgmnt Pension Tstee Ltd 2005–15; chm: London and Quadrant Housing Tst Staff Benefits Plan 2006–10, Northcliffe Tstees Ltd 2007–14; memb Ctee Open Univ 2015–; chm New Islington and Hackney Housing Assoc 1984–95; AIIMR, MSI; *Books* Wood: A Family of Kent (2015); *Recreations* houses, gardens; *Clubs* City of London, Alpine; *Style—* Charles Wood, Esq, OBE; ✉ 14 Compton Terrace, London N1 2UN (☎ 020 7226 4056, e-mail charlesawood@btinternet.com)

WOOD, Charles Gerald; s of John Edward Wood, and Catherine Mae *née* Harris; *b* 6 August 1932, Guernsey, Channel Islands; *Educ* Chesterfield GS, King Charles I Sch Kidderminster, Birmingham Coll of Art; *m* 1954, Valerie Elizabeth Newman; 1 s (John Charles b 1954), 1 da (Katrina b 1959); *Career* dramatist, screenwriter and writer for television and radio 1963–; 1949–63: soldier (17–21st Lancers), scenic artist, layout artist and stage mangr, cartoonist (The Stage, The Globe and Mail Toronto), Bristol Evening Post; memb Drama Panel SW Arts 1970–72, conslt Nat Film Devpt Fund 1980–82, memb Cncl BAFTA 1990–93; FRSL 1984; *Theatre* plays incl: Cockade (Evening Standard Award), Dingo, Don't Make Me Laugh, Meals on Wheels, Fill the Stage with Happy Hours, H or Monologues at Front of Burning Cities, Tie Up the Ballcock, Welfare, The Garden, Veterans (Evening Standard Award), The Script, Jingo, Red Star, Has Washington Legs, Across From the Garden of Allah, Man Beast and Virtue (Pirandello), The Mountain Giants (Pirandello) 1993, The Tower (Dumas) 1995, Tumbledown 2012, Hotel Gallipoli 2013; *Television* plays: Not At All, Traitor in a Steel Helmet, Drill Pig, Prisoner and Escort, Drums Along the Avon, Mutzen Ab!, A Bit of a Holiday, A Bit of a Family Feeling, A Bit of Vision, A Bit of an Adventure, Death or Glory Boy, The Emergence of Antony Purdy Esq, Love Lies Bleeding, Do As I Say!; series: Don't Forget to Write, My Family and Other Animals (adaption), The Settling of the Sun, Sharpe's Company, Sharpe's Regiment, Sharpe's Waterloo, Mute of Malice, Briefs Trooping Gaily, Monsignor Renard (episode 3); documentaries: Last Summer By the Sea; *Radio* 1962–72: Prisoner and Escort, Cowheel Jelly, Next to Being a Knight; The Fireraisers (Max Frisch) 2004, The Conspiracy of Sèvres 2006; *Film* incl: The Knack, Help, How I Won the War, The Long Day's Dying, The Charge of the Light Brigade, The Bed Sitting Room, Cuba, Red Monarch, Puccini, Wagner, Tumbledown (Prix Italia RAI Prize, Best Single Play BAFTA, Best Single Play RTS, Best Single Play BPG), An Awfully Big Adventure (Beryl Bainbridge), A Breed of Heroes (Alan Judd, nomination for BAFTA), England My England (John Osborne), Iris (with Richard Eyre, nomination for BAFTA and Christopher Award NY, Humanitas Prize LA), The Other Man (with Richard Eyre); *Publications* incl: Cockade, New English Dramatists 8, Dingo, H, Veterans, Man Beast and Virtue (Pirandello), The Mountain Giants (Pirandello), The Tower (Dumas); *Style—* Charles Wood, Esq; ✉ c/o Sue Rodgers, Oxford House, 76 Oxford Street, London W1D 1BS (☎ 020 7636 6565)

WOOD, Christopher Joseph; s of Alan Joseph Wood, of St Albans, Herts, and Kay, *née* Wong; *b* 19 July 1969, St Albans, Herts; *Educ* Verulam Sch St Albans, St Albans Coll, Univ of Middlesex (BA), Inst of Direct Mktg (IDM Dip), CIM (Dip), MRS (Dip); *m* 16 Sept 1995, Sarah Louise, *née* Franks; 3 da (Emily b 3 Nov 1998, Hannah b 8 July 2001, Beth b 16 July 2003); *Career* mktg asst Don Greswell 1990–91, various roles rising to account dir Wunderman Cato Johnson 1993–98, dir of consumer mktg and special events rising to dir of brands Hilton Int 1998–2000, gp account dir Digitas Europe Inc 2000–01, sales and mktg dir Conran Restaurants 2001–05, md Toptable 2005–10, md Open Table 2010–; *Style—* Christopher Wood, Esq; ✉ Open Table, 15 Worship Street, London EC2A 2DT (e-mail cwood@opentable.com)

WOOD, David Bernard; OBE (2004); s of Richard Edwin Wood (d 1987), and Audrey Adele Whittle, *née* Fincham; *b* 21 February 1944; *Educ* Chichester HS for Boys, Worcester Coll Oxford (BA); *m* 1, 1966 (m dis 1970), Sheila, *née* Dawson; m 2, Jan 1975, Jacqueline, da of Prof Sydney William Stanbury; 2 da (Katherine b 1976, Rebecca b 1979); *Career* actor, writer, composer, playwright, theatre dir and prodr; West End acting credits incl: Hang Down Your Head and Die 1964, Four Degrees Over 1966, After Haggerty 1970, Jeeves 1975; film acting credits incl: If... 1968, Aces High 1976, North Sea Hijack 1980, Longitude 2000; dir: WSG Prodns Ltd/Whirligig Theatre 1966–2011, Verronmead Ltd 1982–2006, W2 Prodns 1995–2011; chair Action for Children's Arts 1998–, acting chair The Story Museum 2011–; *Publications* many plays published by Samuel French incl: The Owl and the Pussycat Went to See (1968), The Plotters of Cabbage Patch Corner (1970), The Gingerbread Man (1977), The Selfish Shellfish (1983), The See-Saw Tree (1987), Save the Human (1990); children's books incl: The Operats of Rodent Garden (1984), The Discorats (1985), Playtheatres (1987), Sidney the Monster (1988), Happy Birthday Mouse (1990), Save the Human (1990), Baby Bear's Buggy Ride (1993), Theatre for Children: Guide to Writing, Adapting, Directing and Acting (1997); Pop-up Theatre: Cinderella (1994), Bedtime Story (1995), The Magic Show (1995), Mole's Summer Story (1997), Silly Spider (1998), Mole's Winter Story (1998), Funny Bunny's Magic Show (2000), The Phantom Cat of the Opera (2000), The Toy Cupboard (2000), Under the Bed! (2006), Mole's Bedtime Story (2006), The Queen's Handbag (2006, specially written to celebrate the Queen's 80th birthday, performed in Buckingham Palace Gardens and broadcast live by BBC 1), Jack and the Baked Beanstalk (2007), A Present for Father Christmas (2008), Cinderella (2010), Scary Mary (2012), The Porridge Pincher (2012); stage adaptations of: Helen Nicoll and Jan Pie?kowski's Meg and Mog (1980), HRH The Prince of Wales' The Old Man of Lochnagar (1986), Roald Dahl's The BFG (1991), The Witches (1992), Enid Blyton's Noddy (1993), More Adventures of Noddy (1995), Dick King-Smith's Babe, the Sheep-Pig (1997), Roald Dahl's The Twits (1999), Eric Hill's Spot's Birthday Party (2000), Philippa Pearce's Tom's Midnight Garden (2000), Roald Dahl's Fantastic Mr Fox (2001), Roald Dahl's James and the Giant Peach (2001), Philip Pullman's Clockwork (2004), Roald Dahl's Danny the Champion of the World (2004), Ronda and David Armitage's The Lighthouse Keeper's Lunch (2006), Judith Kerr's The Tiger Who Came to Tea (2008), Roald Dahl's George's Marvellous Medicine (2009), Sam McBratney's Guess How Much I Love You (2010), Michelle Magorian's Goodnight Mister Tom (2011, Best Entertainment and Family Olivier Award 2013), L P Hartley's The Go-Between (Best Musical Prodn UK Theatre Award 2012), Roald Dahl's The Magic Finger (2014); film screenplays: Swallows and Amazons (1974), Back Home (1989); *Recreations* conjuring (memb Magic Circle), collecting old books; *Style—* David Wood, Esq, OBE; ✉ c/o Casarotto Ramsay Ltd, Waverley House, 7–12 Noel Street, London W1F 8GQ (☎ 020 7287 4450, fax 020 7287 9128)

WOOD, Rear Adm David John; CB (1998); s of John Herbert Wood (d 1982), and Nesta, *née* Jones (d 2007); *b* 12 June 1942; *Educ* St Paul's Sch, BRNC Dartmouth, RNEC Manadon (BSc(Eng)); *m* 1966, Hilary Jolly; 2 s (Thomas b 1971, Charles b 1972), 1 da (Anna b 1974); *Career* with RN; various Fleet Air Arm appts incl HMS Ark Royal and Sea Vixen and Wessex Sqdns 1965–73, Aircraft Support MOD 1973–76, Air Engr Offr Lynx Intensive Flying Trials Unit 1976–77, Army Staff Course 1978, Aircraft Procurement MOD (PE) 1979–81, Naval Sec's Dept MOD 1981–84, on staff FO Naval Air Command 1984–86, NATO Def Coll Rome 1986–87, asst dir for EH101 Project MOD (PE) 1987–89, dir Aircraft Support Policy (Navy) MOD 1989–91, dir Maritime Projects MOD (PE) 1991–95, DG Aircraft (Navy) 1995–98, defence aviation conslt 1998–; tstee Bishop's Palace Wells 2010– (vice-chm 2012–, chm 2013–); FRAeS 1993 (memb Cncl 1996); *Recreations* cross country walking and running, choral singing, supporting local church; *Style—* Rear Adm David Wood, CB; ✉ Ministry of Defence, Whitehall, London SW1A 2HB

WOOD, His Hon David Russell; s of Christopher Russell Wood (d 1987), of Riding Lea, Northumberland, and Muriel Wynne Wood; *b* 13 December 1948; *Educ* Sedbergh, UEA (BA); *m* 24 Feb 1979, Georgina Susan, da of Maj Dudley Buckle; 2 s (John Dudley Russell b 4 June 1980, Robert James Russell b 12 May 1985), 1 da (Rose-Ann Florence b 19 May 1982); *Career* called to the Bar Gray's Inn 1973, recorder of the Crown Court 1990–95 (asst recorder 1984–90), circuit judge (NE Circuit) 1995–2014, ret; past pres Cncl of Circuit Judges; *Recreations* country pursuits, tennis, piano; *Clubs* Northern Counties (Newcastle upon Tyne); *Style*— His Hon David Wood

WOOD, Derek Alexander; CBE (1995), QC (1978); s of Alexander Cecil Wood, and Rosetta, *née* Lelyveld; *b* 14 October 1937; *Educ* Tiffin Sch Kingston upon Thames, UC Oxford (BCL, MA); *m* 1, 9 Aug 1961 (m dis 2001), Sally Teresa Scott Wood; 2 da (Jessica Susan b 27 Oct 1965, Rebecca Lucy b 7 Sept 1968); m 2, 2001, Barbara Kaplan, *née* Spector; *Career* called to the Bar Middle Temple 1964 (bencher 1986, treas 2006); recorder of the Crown Court 1985–2002; princ St Hugh's Coll Oxford 1991–2002 (now hon fell); Dept of the Environment: memb Advsy Gp on Commercial Property Devpt 1975–78, memb Working Gp on New Forms of Social Ownership in Housing 1976, memb Property Advsy Gp 1978–94, chm Review of Rating of Plant and Machinery 1991 and 1996–98; chm: Standing Advsy Ctee on Trunk Rd Assessment Dept of Tport 1986–94, Working Pty on Code of Practice for Commercial Leases in England and Wales 1995, Bar Standards Bd Review of Bar Vocational Course 2005, Pupillage 2009, CPU 2010; drafted Univ of Oxford's Code of Statutes 2000–04; memb Cncl London Borough of Bromley 1975–78; dep chm Soc of Labour Lawyers 1978–91, chm Chislehurst Constituency Lab Pty 1972–76 and 1979–84, cncllr London Borough of Bromley 1975–78; memb Governing Cncl RICS 2003–06; chm: Oxfordshire Community Fndn 1995–2001, Attlee Fndn 2004–10 (tstee 2002–10); govr Quintin Kynaston Sch 2003–; hon fell UC Oxford 2002; hon fell Central Assoc of Agric Valuers 1988, Hon RICS 1991; FCIArb 1993; *Books* Leasehold Enfranchisement and Extension (ed, part of Halsbury's Laws of England series), Handbook of Arbitration Practice (jt ed, 1987, 2 edn 1993, 3 edn 1998); contrib to various works on property law; *Recreations* music; *Clubs* Athenaeum, RAC, Architecture; *Style*— Derek Wood, Esq, CBE, QC; ✉ Falcon Chambers, Falcon Court, London EC4Y 1AA (☎ 020 7353 2484, fax 020 7353 1261)

WOOD, Edmund Michael; s of George Lockhart Wood (d 1959), and Joan, *née* Halsey (d 2004); *b* 7 September 1943; *Educ* Maidwell Hall, Eton; *m* 6 Nov 1971, Elizabeth Anne, da of Sqdn Ldr Robert Roland Patrick Fisher (d 1991); 2 da (Sarah Georgina b 10 July 1974, Anne Louise b 15 Sept 1977); *Career* chartered accountant 1967; articled to Singleton Fabian & Co 1963; ptnr: Singleton Fabian Derbyshire & Co 1969–74, Binder Hamlyn 1974–98, Arthur Andersen 1994–98; currently conslt specialising in personal fin planning Mercer & Hole London and St Albans and dir Mercer & Hole Tstees Ltd 1998–; dir: Lee Valley Water Co 1982–90, BH Matheson Investment Management 1987–97; chm Hitchin Deanery Synod 1991–99; dir Richard Shuttleworth Tstees (chm 2014–); tstee: Rands Educn Fndn 1980 (chm 1992–), Sir Malcolm Stewart Bt Gen Charitable Tst 1997–, St Albans Diocesan Bd of Finance 2010–; FCA 1974 (ACA 1968); *Recreations* fishing, shooting, golf, gardening; *Style*— Edmund M Wood, Esq; ✉ The Old Rectory, Holwell, Hitchin, Hertfordshire SG5 3SP (☎ 01462 712228); Mercer & Hole, 72 London Road, St Albans, Hertfordshire AL1 1NS (☎ 01727 869141, fax 01727 869149)

WOOD, Gareth Haydn; s of Haydn William George Wood, and Joyce, *née* Jenkins; *b* 7 June 1950; *Educ* Pontypridd Boys' GS, Royal Acad of Music; *Career* memb RPO 1972–2005 (chm until 1994), composer of many pieces for brass bands incl Butlins Youth 1977 and Nat 4 Section 1980; cmmns incl: Overture Suffolk Punch (RPO), Festivities Overture (Philharmonia Orch), fanfares (100 years of the Financial Times), fanfare (150 years of Cunard), Sinfoniettas 2, 3 and 4 (Nat Youth Orch of Wales), Fantasy of Welsh Song (Welsh Prom Concerts), test-piece (European Brass Band Championships) 1992, The Land of Magic and Enchantment (40th anniversary of Pembs Nat Park), Fanfare for a New Beginning (opening of Kravis Centre W Palm Beach), Cardiff Bay Overture (Cardiff Bay Devpt Corp) 1993, Toduri (600th anniversary of City of Seoul), Halifax Diptych (Halifax Building Society), Poems within a Prayer (Robert Tear (tenor)), Bass Concerto No 1 (Wiltshire Youth Orch) 1995, Bass Concerto No 2 (Yehudi Menuhin Sch) 1997, Bass Concerto No 3 (Wiltshire Youth Orch), Fields of Amaranth (Bromley Youth Chamber Orch), Adagio for Strings (RPO), A Wiltshire Symphony (W Wilts Youth Wind Band), Trombone Concerto (Nat Youth Brass Band of Wales) 1999, 2nd Trumpet Concerto (Camarthen Youth Band) 2000, Concerto for Harp and Brass Band (Nat Youth Band of Wales) 2001, Waterless Seas for 6 Harps 2002, Time Machines (Bromley Youth Orch) 2002, The Caudlron (Bromley Youth Orch) 2003, Forbidden Gates (Royal Acad of Music) 2003, Rivers of Light (Royal Acad of Music) 2003, Legends of the Bear (Nat Youth Wind Band of Wales) 2004, Concerto for Percussion and Wind Band (Nat Youth Wind Band of Wales) 2006, Concerto for Tenor Horn and Brass Band (Nat Youth Brass Band of Wales) 2006, Actaeon (Buy As You View Band) 2007, A Simple Gift (Bromley Youth Orch) 2007, Each Side of Midnight (Eton Sch) 2007, An Ireland Adventure (Three Counties Wind Band) 2007, Brass Triumphant (for 125th anniversary of Cory Band) 2009, Artemis for six harps 2009, fanfare for the 50th birthday of The Duke of York (Royal Philharmonic Orch) 2010, Bedivere for trumpet and six harps 2010, fanfare for the opening of the Welsh Parliament 2011, In Olde Times (for four harps) 2011, Helvetia (for Cory Band) 2011, Sea Dogs (for Welsh Amateur Music Assoc) 2011, string quartet (for Mavron Quartet) 2012, Santa's Stressful Day (for Royal Welsh Coll of Music and Drama) 2012, Deep (for double bass and orch for Dulwich Coll) 2013, fanfare and processional for the installation of the chllr of the Univ of S Wales 2014, Rum and Laverbread (for Camerata Wales) 2014, Tuba Concerto (for Royal Welsh Coll of Music and Drama) 2015, Fanfare for our Youth (for the 70th Anniversary of the Nat Youth Orchestra of Wales) 2016; ARAM; *Style*— Gareth Wood, Esq; ✉ 52c Granville Park, Lewisham, London SE13 7DX

WOOD, Dr Graham Allan; s of William Wales Wood, of Glasgow, and Ann Fleming, *née* Blackwood; *b* 15 August 1946; *Educ* Hillhead HS, Univ of Glasgow (BDS), Univ of Dundee (MB ChB), Univ of Mexico (Dip Cleft Lip and Palate Surgery); *m* 23 Nov 1970, Lindsay, da of Alfred Balfour; 1 da (Nicola b 1975), 1 s (Alexander b 1985); *Career* gen dental practice 1968–70, house offr and sr house offr Glasgow Dental Hosp 1970–71, registrar in oral and maxillofacial surgery Canniesburn and Victoria Infirmary Hosps 1971–72, dental surgeon Int Grenfell Assoc 1972–73, registrar in oral and maxillofacial surgery Queen Elizabeth Hosp Birmingham 1973–74, sr registrar in oral and maxillofacial surgery N Wales 1979–83 (conslt 1983–95), conslt oral and maxillofacial surgn Canniesburn Hosp Glasgow 1995–2001, conslt oral and maxillofacial surgn Southern Gen Hosp Glasgow 2001–10, hon clinical sr lectr Univ of Glasgow 1995–2010, locum regnl conslt in oral medicine and lectr Sch of Dentistry Belfast 2011–; clinical prof in oral and maxillofacial surgery Univ of Texas 1990–2000; examiner Int Assoc of Oral and Maxillofacial Surgery (IAOMS) 2015–, fell Int Bd for Certification of Specialists in Oral and Maxillofacial Surgery (IBCSOMS) 2015–; memb: BMA, BDA; FDS RCPSGlas 1973, FRCSEd 1985, fell Br Assoc of Oral and Maxillofacial Surgns 1983, life fell Int Assoc of Oral and Maxillofacial Surgeons 1990, FDSRCS 2000, FDSRCS (Eng) 2000, FDSRCS (Ed) 2004; *Books* Cryosurgery of the Maxillofacial Region Vol II (contrib, 1986), Textbook of General & Oral Surgery (contrib, 2003); *Recreations* golf, squash, sailing, hill walking, skiing (formerly Canadian ski patroller); *Clubs* Oral Surgery Club of GB (pres), Kilmalcolm Golf, Glasgow Golf, Kilmalcolm Tennis; *Style*— Dr Graham A Wood; ✉ Cambro, Gryffe Road, Kilmalcolm, Renfrewshire PA13 4BB; Regional Maxillofacial Unit, Southern General Hospital, 1345 Govan Road, Glasgow G51 4TF (☎ 0141 232 7540)

WOOD, His Hon Judge Graham Nash; QC (2002); s of Benjamin Leslie Wood (d 1994), and Valerie, *née* Crone (d 2006); *b* 21 May 1957, Liverpool; *Educ* Liverpool Coll, Univ of Leeds (LLB); *m* 11 Feb 1984, Janet Helen, *née* Winstanley; 3 s (Matthew b 5 April 1986, Timothy b 11 Oct 1988, Joshua b 12 Aug 1991); *Career* called to the Bar Middle Temple 1979 (bencher 2010); barr 1979–2011, asst recorder 1996, recorder 2000, dep High Court judge 2010, circuit judge (Northern Circuit) 2011– (sr circuit judge 2014–); legal assessor GMC 2009–11; dep chllr Dioceses of Liverpool and Chester 2003–; chm of govrs Liverpool Coll 2009–12, reader C of E; *Recreations* sailing, skiing, travel, writing; *Style*— His Hon Judge Graham Wood, QC; ✉ Liverpool Civil and Family Court, 35 Vernon Street, Liverpool, Merseyside L2 2BX

WOOD, Graham Stuart; s of Edward and Janet Wood, of London; *b* 7 September 1965; *Educ* Central St Martin's Sch of Art (BA, MA); *m* 1995, Sophia, da of Leif Einarsson; *Career* co-fndr Tomato 1991 (design consultancy covering corp identity, creative direction, interactive/digital, TV and film titles, commercials/video direction, music, publishing, lecturing, exhibitions etc), exec creative dir Visual Communication JWT NY 2006–, head of Art JWT London 2009–, became freelance 2012, co-fndr Studio Heiss 2013; clients, brands and projects incl: Nike, Adidas, Reebok, Scott Walker, Levis, Unilever, JBO, Shell, Malcolm McLaren, Sony, Microsoft, 4AD, Samsung, Nine Inch Nails, Orange, Ford, Porsche, Lexus, Subaru, The Cocteau Twins, Electrolux, Philips, RCA, Rough Trade, Selfridges, Sketch Bar and Restaurant, MTV, VH1, Kiss FM, Procter & Gamble, Bacardi, Smirnoff, MAC Cosmetics, Dead Can Dance, the Guardian newspaper, Macy's, BBC, Channel 4, Science Museum, Reeves & Mortimer (Randall & Hopkirk), Helly Hansen, Pepsi, Sunglass Hut, Radisson Hotels, Simple Shoes, DeBeers, Tesco, Underworld, Converse; memb: Panel of Judges BBC Design Awards 1996, Exec D&AD 1996–98 (Pres's Lecture 1997); workshops, talks, performance and consultancies at colleges and institutions worldwide incl: Glastonbury, Univ of Cambridge, RCA, Hyper Island, RISD, SVA, Cooper Union, Konstfack Stockholm, art/govt progs in Tokyo/ Sapporo, events in Ireland, France, Germany, The Netherlands, Denmark, Norway, Sweden, SA, Taiwan, Japan, Australia, S America, US and Canada; interviewed by/ work featured by: BBC, ITV, Channel 4, Wallpaper Magazine, The Times, Guardian, Independent, Observer, Telegraph, Vanity Fair, Vogue, Wired, GQ, Idea, Creativity, Communication Arts, Shots, Campaign, Lurzers, Creative Review, Grafik, Baseline, U&LC, Print and others; *Exhibitions* incl: V&A and MOMA permanent collection, MOCA (San Francisco), BFI Collection, onedotzero, Barbican, Whitechapel Gallery, La Foret Tokyo, Parco Tokyo, Moderna Museet Stockholm, Jacobson Howard Gallery NY, LEA Gallery London, Scarlett Gallery Stockholm, AIGA Design Archives; *Awards* incl: AICP/ MOMA, D&AD Pencils, Webby (People's Choice and Honoree), FWA, Cannes Lions, BIMA, One Show, Tokyo Type Directors, BBC Design Awards, Charleston Film and Video Festival, Epica D'Or, XYZ Digital Typography, Studio of the Year, etc; *Books* tomato; process (1996), tomato; bareback (1999), Tycho's Nova (2001), Gasbook, Real and Imaginary Flowers; *Style*— Graham Wood, Esq; ✉ 16 Westbury Road, Beckenham, Kent BR3 4DD (☎ 07791 672279, e-mail grahamwood7@gmail.com)

WOOD, Sir Ian Clark; GBE (2016, CBE 1982), kt (1994); s of John Wood (d 1986) and Margaret, *née* Clark (d 1981); *b* 21 July 1942; *Educ* Robert Gordon's Coll Aberdeen, Aberdeen Univ (BSc); *m* 1970, Helen, *née* Macrae; 3 s; *Career* chm John Wood Group plc 1982–2012 (chief exec 1982–2006), chm J W Holdings Ltd; jt chm Oil and Gas Industry Leadership Team, memb Government Oil & Gas Industry Task Force (now PILOT) until 2006, chm Oil & Gas Technology Centre (OGTC); chllr Robert Gordon Univ 2004–; business ambass for Scot 2001; chm Cmmn on Developing Scotland's Young Workforce, ldr appointed by UK govt Review Maximising UKCS Oil & Gas Recovery, chm The Wood Fndn, chm Opportunity North East (ONE); memb Scottish Sea Fisheries Cncl 2007–, memb PILOT; fell Scottish Qualifications Authy 1997; Hon LLD Aberdeen 1984, Hon DBA Robert Gordon Univ 1998, Hon DTech Glasgow Caledonian Univ 2002, Hon DEng Heriot Watt Univ 2012, Hon DSc Univ of Strathclyde 2013; Fscotvec 1994, FCIB 1998, FRSE 2000, FRSA; *Awards* Grampian Industrialist of the Year 1978, Young Scottish Businessman of the Year 1979, Scottish Free Enterprise 1985, Scottish Business Achievement Award Tst (jtly) 1992, Corporate Elite Leadership Award (Services) 1992, Alick Buchanan-Smith Meml Award for Personal Achievement 1995, Corporate Elite World Player Award Business Insider 1996, entered into Entrepreneurial Exchange Hall of Fame 2002, CEO of the Year Business Insider/PwC Scotland Insider Awards 2003, Glenfiddich Spirit of Scotland Award for Business 2003, Entrepreneurial Exchange Philanthropist of the Year Award 2008, Offshore Energy Centres Hall of Fame Houston 2009, Energy Inst Cadman Medal 2010, Scottish Cncl for Devpt and Industry President's Award 2011, Oil & Gas UK Lifetime Achievement Award 2012, Wallace Award American Scottish Fndn 2012, Broadwalk UK Chm of the Year Award 2012, Royal Medal RSE 2013, Lifetime Achievement Award Northern Star Business Awards 2014, Oil Council Lifetime Achievement Award 2014, Bacon Award for Philanthropy 2015; *Recreations* tennis, art, family; *Style*— Sir Ian Wood, GBE; ✉ JW Holdings Ltd, Blenheim House, Fountainhall Road, Aberdeen AB15 4DT (☎ 01224 619842)

WOOD, Jake Dylan; *b* 12 July 1972, London; *m* 2001, Alison Murray; 1 da (Amber b 2005), 1 s (Buster b 2008); *Career* actor; *Television* incl: May to December, Only Fools and Horses, Murder in Mind, Press Gang, London's Burning, Sean's Show, Inspector Morse, One Foot in the Grave, Red Dwarf, A Touch of Frost, The Bill, Sea of Souls, Doc Martin, The Wilsons, Max Branning in EastEnders (BBC 1) 2006– (Best On-Screen Partnership Br Soap Award 2012 (jtly)); *Style*— Mr Jake Wood; ✉ c/o Jo Edwards, Conway Van Gelder Grant Ltd, 3rd Floor, 8–12 Broadwick Street, London W1F 8HW (☎ 020 7287 0077)

WOOD, James; s of Peter Ley Wood, and Elizabeth Gillian Wood; *b* 27 May 1953, Barton-on-Sea; *Educ* Nadia Boulanger Paris, Univ of Cambridge (organ scholar), Royal Acad of Music; *Career* composer and conductor; prof of percussion Darmstadt Int Summer Courses 1982–94; fndr and dir: New London Chamber Choir, Centre for Microtonal Music London, Critical Band; conductor: BBC Symphony Orch, London Sinfonietta, Ensemble Inter Contemporain, l'Itinéraire, Musikfabrik, Champ d'Action, Netherlands Wind Ensemble, Percussion Group The Hague, Belgian Radio Philharmonic, Kraków Radio Orch, Tokyo Philharmonic Choir, Netherlands Chamber Choir; cmmns for: Arditti Quartet, the King's Singers, Electric Phoenix, Amadinda Percussion Group Budapest, Duo Contemporain, Robert Van Sice, Nouvel Ensemble Moderne, Percussions de Strasbourg, New Music Players, BBC and IRCAM; cmmns BBC Proms: Oreion 1989 (conducted BBC Symphony Orch), Two men meet, each presuming the other to be from a distant planet (for Steven Schick and Critical Band) 1995; recordings incl: Stoicheia, Ho Shang Yao, Choroi Kai Thaliai, Rogosanti, Incantamenta, Two men meet, each presuming the other to be from a distant planet, Venancio Mbande talking with the trees, Phainomena; reconstruction Gesualdo Sacrae Cantiones Liber Secundus 2008–11; Gemini fellowship 1993, Arts Foundation Fellowship 1995/6, Holst Foundation Award, ECHO Klassik Prize for Choir Recording of the Year (for Gesualdo Sacrae Cantiones Liber Secundus – Harmonia Mundi) 2013; *Recreations* gardening, hiking, cooking; *Style*— James Wood, Esq; ✉ e-mail james.wood@gmx.net, website www.choroi.net

WOOD, James Alexander Douglas; QC (1999); s of Lt-Col Alexander Blythe Wood, TD, and Cynthia Mary, *née* Boot; *b* 25 June 1952; *Educ* Haileybury, Univ of Warwick (LLB); *m*; 2 s (Nathan b 1988, Tommy b 1990); *Career* called to the Bar Middle Temple 1975, recorder 1999–; memb: int mission of lawyers to Malaysia 1982, panel of inquiry into

W

visit of Leon Brittan to Univ of Manchester Students Union in March 1985; defending in many terrorism cases incl Operation Crevace and the transatlantic airline bomb plot; has appeared in many miscarriage of justice cases incl the Birmingham Six and Bridgewater Four Appeals; *Books* The Right of Silence, the Case for Retention (1989); *Recreations* travel, painting, the enhancement of civil liberties and the enforcement of civil rights; *Style*— James Wood, QC, Esq; ✉ Doughty Street Chambers, 54 Doughty Street, London WC1N 2LS (☎ 020 7404 1313, fax 020 7404 2283)

WOOD, James Maitland; QC (2013); s of James Wood (d 2013), and Dorothy Mary Wood (d 2014); *b* 25 January 1966, Warks; *m* 13 March 1993, Joné Martinez Gomez; 2 s (Inigo b 12 April 2002, Alejandro b 10 Sept 2004); *Career* called to the Bar: UK 1989, St Lucia 2007, Anguilla 2014; sr crown prosecutor CPS Birmingham 1992–2000 (team ldr 1998–2000); Cornwall St Chambers (formerly 6 Fountain Court): tenant 2000–07 and 2014–, door tenant 2007–14; Offices of Director of Public Prosecutions St Lucia 2007–08, dir of regnl law Revision Centre Anguilla 2008–14; hon AG for: Montserrat 2008–11, Anguilla 2011–14; gen counsel Br Indian Ocean Territory 2014–, princ legal advsr Br Antarctic Territory 2014–16, AG Br Antarctic Territory 2016–; memb Br Inst of Int and Comparative Law; *Recreations* diving, swimming with sharks, cooking, cycling; *Style*— James Maitland Wood, Esq, QC; ✉ Cornwall Street Chambers, 85–87 Cornwall Street, Birmingham B3 3BY (☎ 0121 233 7500, e-mail clerks@cornwallstreet.co.uk, website www.cornwallstreet.co.uk)

WOOD, Jane Caroline; da of Duncan Patrick (d 1983), and Kathleen, *née* Smith (d 1959); *b* 17 August 1943; *Educ* Putney HS for Girls, Lucy Cavendish Coll Cambridge (MA); *m* 1, 1962 (m dis 1987), Christopher Wood; 1 da (Caroline b 1963), 2 s (Adam b 1965, Benjamin b 1966 d 2014); m 2, 1996, Edward Russell-Walling; *Career* Secker & Warburg: asst to Barley Alison 1982–83, ed 1983–85, exec ed 1985–87; ed dir Arrow Books 1987–90, ed dir MacMillan Ltd 1990–94; Orion Books: publishing dir 1994–2007; publisher Quercus 2007–; *Recreations* reading, theatre, cinema, music, walking; *Style*— Ms Jane Wood; ✉ Quercus Publishing, Carmelite House, 50 Victoria Embankment, London EC4Y 0DZ (e-mail jane.wood@querusbooks.co.uk)

WOOD, Joanna Harriet; da of John Harvey Pinches, and Rosemary Vivian, *née* Bidder; *b* 3 July 1954; *Educ* Queensgate Sch London; *m* 1, 19 Dec 1997, Hon Edward Wood; 1 da (Leonora Sarah Clare Wood b 11 Aug 1982); m 2, 22 Dec 1995, Charles Louis Frederick Godfrey Hansard; 1 da (Harriet Louisa b 24 Feb 1997); *Career* PA to Chief of Personnel UN Geneva 1974–76, interior design apprentice Asprey's 1976–79, fndr interior design co Joanna Trading Ltd 1980– (IDFX Best Interior Design Practice 2010, Design et al Best Bathroom Design 2010, winner Design and Architecture Awards 2012 and 2013), prop furnishings and accessories shop Joanna Wood Ltd 1985–; clients incl: Sir David Frost, Lady Rothermere, Hon and Mrs Nigel Havers, John Reid, Jim Henson, Sotheby's, Rothmans Int, Theatre of Comedy, The New York Times, The Garrick Club, Richemont, AELTC; co-owner: Lewis & Wood fabrics and wall coverings, Lawson Wood upholstered furniture, Phillips & Wood lighting; chm Auction of Promises NSPCC, patron Cancer Research, treas Pimlico Road Assoc, hon memb Cncl NSPCC, fundraiser Nat Osteoporosis, memb Fundraising Dinner Exec Ctee Plantlife; fell Br Inst of Interior Design (BIID); RIBA; *Recreations* country pursuits, theatre, ballet, travel; *Style*— Joanna Wood; ✉ Joanna Wood Ltd, 7 Bunhouse Place, London SW1W 8HU (☎ 020 7730 0693, fax 020 7730 4135, website www.joannatrading.co.uk)

WOOD, John; s of Barrie Wood, and Rita Wood; *b* 18 June 1969, Hong Kong; *Educ* City of Norwich Sch, Norwich Sch of Art, Bath Coll of HE (BA); *Partner* Nicola Moore; 1 da (Amber Maya b 4 Dec 2006); *Career* artist; in partnership with Paul Harrison, *qv*; *Exhibitions* incl: The British Art Show 5 2000, Twenty Six (Drawing and Falling Things) (Chisenhale Gallery London) 2002, Sudden Glory (CCAC Inst Calif) 2002, Gwangju Biennale Korea 2002, Monitor: Volume One (Gagosian Gallery NY) 2002, Performing Bodies (Tate Modern London) 2002, A Century of Artists' Film in Britain (Tate Modern) 2003, Hundredweight (FA Projects London) 2003, Selected Works (MOMA NY) 2004, Selected Works (MIT Boston) 2004, Irreducible (Wattis Inst California Coll of the Arts) 2005, To Be Continued (Helsinki Kunsthalle) 2005, Mixed Doubles (Carnegie Museum of Art) 2005, Five Rooms (Ludwig Museum Budapest) 2006, Le Mouvement des Images (Centre Pompidou Paris) 2006, Smart Art (Kunsthalle Osnabruck) 2006, MAM 05 (MORI Art Museum) 2007, Breaking Step (Salon Belgrade) 2007, Echo Room (Alcala 31 Madrid) 2007, I Am Making Art (Centre d'Art Contemporain Geneva) 2007, Dimensionen (Galerie Von Bartha Garage Switzerland) 2008, Tongue-twister (Vera Cortes Art Agency Lisbon) 2008, Something and something and something else (The Lowry Manchester) 2008, Contemporary Art Museum Houston 2009, Ikon Gallery Birmingham 2009, Chateau de Rocheschouart France 2009, Vera Cortes Art Agency Lisbon 2009, Von Bartha Garage Basel 2009, Studiotrisorio Rome 2009, Rewind (Foundation de Lavache Qui Rit Lons France) 2010, Remote Viewing (Pacific Design Centre LA) 2010, Answers to Questions (Univ of Calif Santa Barbara) 2010, John Wood and Paul Harrison (Gallery Ho Marseille) 2010, Deadpan Pacific Design Centre LA 2010, Super 8 (Christopher Grimes Gallery Santa Monica) 2011, Borde Astronauts on the Moon (Gallery Martine Aboucaya Paris) 2011, 12 From Number 10 (Whitechapel Gallery London) 2012, Things That Happen (Carroll/Fletcher London) 2012, Slapstick (Kunstmuseum Wolfsberg Germany) 2013, Super 8 (Museum of Modern Art Rio de Janeiro) 2013, Revealed (Ulster Museum Belfast) 2013, Witnessing the Wilderness (Wimbledon Space) 2013, Private Utopia (British Council Touring Japan: Tokyo Station Gallery, Itami City Museum of Art, Kochi Museum of Art, Okayama Museum of Art) 2014, Works from the Berge Collection (Real Circulo Artistico de Barcelona) 2014, John Wood and Paul Harrison (Museo de Antioquia Medellin Columbia) 2014, Diamonds Always Come in Small Packages (Kunstmuseum Luzern Switzerland) 2015, Un Nouveau Festival (Centre Pompidou Paris) 2015, Some Things Are Hard To Explain (ICC Tokyo) 2015, Erdkunde (Bristol Museum and Art Gallery) 2015, Eppur Si Muove, Art and Technology a Shared Sphere (Mudam Luxembourg) 2015; *Publications* Answers to Questions (2010), Nothing Special (2012); *Style*— John Wood, Esq

WOOD, Prof John Vivian; CBE (2007); s of Vivian Wood (d 1996), of Oxford, and Lois, *née* Hall; *b* 10 September 1949; *Educ* St Lawrence Coll Ramsgate, Univ of Sheffield (BMet, Mappin Medal), Univ of Cambridge (PhD), Univ of Sheffield (DMet); *m* 1976, Alison, da of Cyril Lee; 1 s (Thomas b 1987), 1 da (Mary b 1988); *Career* Goldsmiths jr res fell Churchill Coll Cambridge 1974–78, lectr/sr lectr Open Univ 1978–89, Cripps prof of materials engrg and head of dept Univ of Nottingham 1989 (dean of engrs 1998–2001), chief exec Cncl for the Central Labs of the Res Cncls (seconded) 2001–07, princ Faculty of Engrg Imperial Coll London 2007–08 (sr int rels advsr 2008–10); visiting scholar Univ of Kyoto Japan; chm: Office of Sci & Technology's Foresight Panel on Materials 1997–2001, European Strategy Forum for Research Infrastructures 2005–08, Jt Info Systems Bd 2006–10, European Research Area Bd 2008–12; chair Global Research Data Alliance 2013–; dir: M4 Technologies Ltd 1995–, Diamond Light Source Ltd 2002–07, Spectrum 2003–07, Maney Publishing 2003–12, BioNano Consulting 2008–; conslt: Karl Storz GmbH Germany 1994–2001, Metal Powders Div GKN 1994–98, Osprey Metals Ltd 1987–96, Fibre Technology Ltd 1981–2001, Powdrex Ltd 1983–2001, Applied Microsurgical Res 1984–88, London & Scandinavian Metallurgical Co 1984–99; Inst of Materials: memb Cncl 1997–2002, President's Advsy Bd 1997–2000, memb Strategy Panel 1997–2000, chm Materials Processing Science Ctee 1987–96, memb Particulate Engrg Ctee 1987–2001, memb Publications Ctee 1979–87, chm PM 89 1987–89, chm of Tech Ctee PM 90 1987–90; chair European Research Area Bd 2008–12, chair Int Network for Access to Scientific Publications 2009–15, sec-gen Assoc of Cwlth Univs 2010–, chair Research Info Network 2012–; Grunfeld Medal and Prize Inst of Metals 1986, Ivor Jenkins Award Inst of Materials 2000, William Johnson Gold Medal 2001; chm and fndr Stables Tst, reader C of E; Liveryman Worshipful Co of Founders 1996, Freeman City of London 1996; Hon DSc Univ of Cluj-Napoca Romania 1994, hon doctorate A R Rahman Univ Chennai 2014, Hon DSc Krame Nkrumah Univ Ghana 2015; CEng, CPhys; FIM 1990, FREng 1999, FInstP 2000; Citizen of Honour City of Cluj-Napoca Romania, Credited Offr Order of Merit (Germany) 2010; *Publications* author of over 240 scientific publications and 17 patents; *Recreations* serious contemporary chamber and instrumental music, trees, fungi, affordable wine; *Clubs* Foundation Universitaire Brussels; *Style*— Prof John Wood, CBE, FREng; ✉ Association of Commonwealth Universities, Woburn House, Tavistock Square, London WC1H 9HF (e-mail john.wood@acu.ac.uk)

WOOD, Jonathan Richard (John); s of Norman Richard Wood (d 2009), and Mildred Patricia, *née* Smith (d 2010); *b* 12 October 1948; *Educ* Blundell's, Fitzwilliam Coll Cambridge (MA), Univ of London (MA); *m* 6 Aug 1982, Alison Lesley, *née* Birtwistle; 2 s (Edward b 11 July 1985, James b 29 Aug 1992), 1 da (Rebecca b 30 Jan 1988); *Career* admitted slr 1974; VSO Zambia 1967–68, ptnr Herbert Smith 1982–2007; memb Bd Charity Cmmn 2008–14, memb Advsy Ctee on Business Appts 2015–; Freeman City of London; *Books* A Practitioner's Guide to Contentious Trusts and Estates (co-author, 2002), International Succession (co-ed, 4 edn 2015); *Recreations* cricket, early 20th century literature, Scottish history; *Clubs* Reform, MCC; *Style*— Jonathan Wood, Esq; ✉ Herbert Smith, Exchange House, Primrose Street, London EC2A 2HS (☎ 020 7374 8000, fax 020 7374 0888, e-mail john.wood@herbertsmith.com)

WOOD, (William) Lawson; s of Robert Wood (d 1985), and Barbara, *née* Dougal; *b* 5 October 1953; *Educ* Eyemouth Secdy Sch, Newcastle Poly; *m* 31 Dec 1994, Lesley Anne, da of Dennis Richard Orson (d 1976); 3 c (Emma Victoria Watts b 3 Sept 1967, Lindsay Wood b 26 March 1977, Jamie Wood b 2 Feb 1979); *Career* photographer, author and illustrator; prop Ocean Eye Films (underwater photographic co) 1992–, clients incl: Br Airways, American Express, Thomson Worldwide, Daily Express and tourism offices worldwide; feature writer and correspondent: Dive Magazine, Scuba World, Sport Diver, 35mm Photographer, Tauchen Magazin (Germany), Aquanaut Magazin (Germany), Duiken (Norway), Sport Diver (SA); fndr memb Marine Conservation Soc, fndr and chm St Abbs & Eyemouth Marine Nature Reserve (first and only in Scotland) 2000–, chm Eyemouth and District Devpt Tst, vice-chm Berwickshire Dive Tourism Assoc; conslt: Marinescape, Deep Sea World (Scotland and China), Struik Int Holdings, New Holland Publishers, Readers' Digest, Condensed Books, Eyemouth Marine Interpretive Centre; HSE approved part IV commercial diver 1996, HSE approved sub aqua club diving instr 1996; memb: Marine Conservation Soc 1978, British Sub Aqua Club, Br Soc of Underwater Photographers, Bureau of Freelance Photographers, Eyemouth Town Community Cncl; hon memb Scottish Sub Aqua Club 1974; Northburn Caravan Park: grounds mangr 1971–83, jr ptnr 1974–83, gen mangr and sr ptnr 1986–92; co dir Aiksop Ltd 1974–83; diving offr on board Lady Jenny III (Red Sea) 1983–86; ptnr and md Eyemouth Holiday Park 1998–2002, ptnr Churches Hotel 2000–02; FRPS 1996, FBIPP 1997, FRGS 1998; *Awards* Jt Round Table and Rotary Int Award For Marine Conservation 1981, East of Scotland Devpt Bd Award for Marine Conservation 1982, Marine Conservation Soc Award for Marine Conservation 1983, winner of numerous underwater photographic competitions 1973–, incl: Scottish Nat Champion (5 times), Irish Open, gold medals in Camera beneath the Waves, Brighton Int, World Championships (Antibes), BBC Wildlife Photographer of the Year; *Books* incl: Lawson Wood Marine Photographer (1994), Exploring the Deep (jtly, 1994), Eyemouth in Old Picture Postcards Vol I (1995), History of Eyemouth Railway Company (1995), History of Eyemouth Lifeboat (1996), The Dive Sites of the Cayman Islands (1996), Diving and Snorkelling Guide to the Seychelles (1996), The Dive Sites of Cozumel and the Yucatan (1997), Diving and Snorkelling Guide to Scotland (1997), Eyemouth in Old Picture Postcards Vol II (1997), Berwick-upon-Tweed in Old Picture Postcards (1998), Top Dive Sites of the World (jtly, 1998), Top Dive Sites of the Caribbean (1999), Diving the Caribbean (1999), The Dive Sites of the Bahamas (1999), Diving and Snorkelling Guide to Bermuda (1999), The Dive Sites of Malta, Gozo and Comino (jtly, 1999), Adventure Divers Handbook (jtly, 1999), The Diver Guide to St Abbs and Eyemouth (1999), The Dive Sites of the Virgin Islands (2000), Diving and Snorkelling Guide to Trinidad and Tobago (2000), The Berwickshire Coast (2000), Top Dive Sites of the Indian Ocean (jtly, 2000), Caribbean Reef Fishes and Invertebrates (jtly, 2000), Scapa Flow (2001), Diving Guide to British Isles and Northern Europe (jtly, 2001), Scotland's Atlantic Coast (2002), Mediterranean Reef Fish and Invertebrates (2002), The Great Borders Flood of 1948 (2002), The Eight Minute Link (2002), The Diver Guide to Scotland's Atlantic Coast (2002), Mediterranean Reef Fishes and Invertebrates (2002), Shipwreck City (2003), World's Best Dives (jtly, 2003), Shipwrecks of the Cayman Islands (2004), The World's Best Wrecks (jtly, 2004), The Bull and the Barriers (2004), Pocket Guide to Cayman Islands Shipwrecks (2005), World's Best Coral Reefs (jtly, 2005), Sea Fishes and Invertebrates of the North Sea and English Channel (2008), Old St Abbs and Coldingham (2009), Old Eyemouth and Burnmouth (2009), Diving Guide to Scapa Flow (2 edn, 2009), Dive Guide to the Cayman Islands (2010), History of the Eyemouth Railway (2012), World's Best Tropical Dive Destinations (2012), Underwater Photography (2012), Dive The World's Best Destinations (2013), Shore Diving Guide to Cayman Brac (2013), The Heighmooth Herrin' (2013); *Recreations* scuba diving, reading, writing, music, theatre, films; *Style*— Lawson Wood, Esq; ✉ Churches Hotel, Albert Road, Eyemouth, Berkwickshire (☎ 01890 750401, mobile 07702 092054, e-mail lawsonwood@hotmail.com, website www.lawsonwood.co.uk)

WOOD, Leanne; AM; da of Jeffrey Wood, of Penygraig, Rhondda, and Avril, *née* James; *b* 13 December 1971, Llwynypia, Rhondda; *Educ* Tonypandy Comp Sch, Univ of Glamorgan (BA), Cardiff Univ (Dip); *Partner* Ian Brown; 1 da (Cerys Amelia Wood b 28 Jan 2005); *Career* probation offr Mid Glamorgan Probation Serv 1997–2000, political researcher to Jill Evans MEP 2000–01, pt/t lectr for Social Work Dip Cardiff Univ 2000–03, chair Cwm Cynon Women's Aid 2001– (support worker 2001–02), memb Nat Assembly for Wales (Plaid Cymru) S Wales Central 2003–, ldr Plaid Cymru 2012–; cncllr Rhondda Cynon Taf Local Authy 1995–99; co-chair Nat Assoc of Probation Offrs (NAPO) 1998–2000; chair Cardiff Stop the War Coalition 2003–04; *Publications* Making Our Communities Safer (2008), A Greenprint for the Valleys (2011); *Style*— Ms Leanne Wood, AM; ✉ National Assembly for Wales, Cardiff Bay, Cardiff CF99 1NA

WOOD, Dr (Kathryn) Louise; da of Prof Graham Charles Wood, FEng, FRS, of Bolton, Lancs, and Freda Nancy, *née* Waithman; *b* 10 February 1963; *Educ* Smithills GS Bolton, Univ of Edinburgh (BSc, Ellis Prize in Physiology), Univ of London (PhD); *Career* Medicines Control Agency (now Medicines and Healthcare products Regulatory Agency) Dept of Health: scientific offr Pharmacovigilance Unit 1990–92, co-ordinator Co Liasion Unit Pharmacovigilance Unit 1992–93, co-ordinator Medical Dictionary for Drug Regulatory Affrs (MedDRA, formerly MEDDRA) Project 1993–96 (memb MedDRA Mgmnt Bd Maintenance and Support Services Org 1998–2002), strategic devpt co-ordinator Post-Licensing Div 1996–99, mangr and dir GP Research Database Div 1999–2004, dir Mgmnt Bd 2001–04, head of innovation and industry R&D rels R&D Directorate 2004–09, dep dir and head of NHS research infrastructure and industry rels R&D Directorate 2009–12, dep dir and head of research infrastructure and growth R&D Directorate 2012–16 (secondment as dir of policy and public affrs Assoc of Medical

Research Charities 2015–16), dir Research & Development Dept of Health 2016–; chair UK Clinical Research Collaboration Industry Road Map Gp 2005, co-chair Ministerial Industry Strategy Gp Clinical Res Working Gp 2005–14, co-chair Healthcare Technol Co-operative Working Gp 2005–06; EU rep and sec Medical Terminology Expert Working Gp Int Conference on Harminisation 1995–97, convenor Nat Inst for Health Research (NIHR) NHS/Biopharmaceutical Industry R&D Leadership Forum 2010–14; hon fell Faculty of Pharmaceutical Medicine 2010; *Publications* author of pubns on central control of gastric physiology, med terminology and the GP Research Database; *Recreations* travel, dining out, swimming; *Style*— Dr Louise Wood

WOOD, Maj-Gen Malcolm David; CBE (2002, MBE 1988); s of Stanley Andrew Wood (d 1992), and Elisie Blackley, *née* Stamper; *b* 14 May 1953, Hampton Court, Surrey; *Educ* Hampton GS, RMA Sandhurst, St John's Coll Cambridge; *m* 13 Aug 1977, Nora Ann; 3 da (Katherine b 1981, Joanna b 1985, Rachel b 1988); *Career* cmmnd RAOC 1973; promoted: Lt-Col 1991, Col 1995, Brig 1997, Maj-Gen 2003; chm Army Football Assoc; mentioned in despatches 1993, Queen's Commendation for Valuable Service 1996; *Recreations* supporter Burnley FC; *Style*— Maj-Gen Malcolm Wood, CBE

WOOD, (Gregory) Mark; *b* 25 July 1953; *m* 1953, Susan; 3 c; *Career* chartered accountant; Price Waterhouse 1974–79, Commercial Union 1979–83, Barclays 1983–88, B&C 1988–90, MAI (New York) 1990–93, md insurance, fin services and retail businesses AA 1993–97, chief exec Sun Life and Provincial Holdings plc/AXA UK 1997–2001, exec dir Prudential plc and chief exec Prudential UK and Europe 2001–05; dep chm and chm Gen Insurance Ctee ABI 1999–2001, chm Govt Property Crime Reduction Action Team 2000–01; dep chm NSPCC 2002– (tstee 1999–); chm of govrs Amesbury Sch 2002–; FCA, MSI; *Recreations* skiing, tennis, golf, classical music, jazz; *Style*— Mark Wood, Esq

WOOD, Mark William; s of Joseph Hatton Drew Wood (d 1997); *b* 28 March 1952; *Educ* Gillingham GS, Univ of Leeds (BA), Univ of Warwick (MA), Univ of Oxford (CertEd); *Children* 1 da (Phoebe Elizabeth b 1989), 1 s (Rupert William Caspar b 1991); *Career* Reuters: corr Vienna 1977–78, corr E Berlin 1978–81, corr Moscow 1981–85, chief corr W Germany 1985–87, Euro ed 1987–89, ed-in-chief 1989–2000, exec dir 1990–96, md Reuters Content Partners 2000–02, chm Reuters Television 1992–2002; ITN: non-exec dir 1993–2002, non-exec chm 1998–2002, exec chm 2002–03, chm and chief exec 2003–09; dir Future plc 2009–10, ceo Future UK 2010–, ceo Future plc 2011–14, ceo Ten Alps plc 2014–; dir: Citywire 2002–, Future plc 2014–, Ten Alps plc 2014–; chm Meteor GmBH Germany 2000–02; memb: Library and Information Cmmn 1995–2000 (chm 1998–2000), Cncl for Museums, Libraries and Archives 2000– (dep chm 2002–03, chm 2003–08); *Recreations* History, opera, tennis, skiing, Spurs; *Clubs* Garrick; *Style*— Mark Wood, Esq; ✉ Ten Alps plc, Portland House, Bressenden Place, London SW1E 5BH (e-mail markwwood@googlemail.com)

WOOD, Sir Martin Francis; kt (1986), OBE (1982), DL (Oxon 1985); s of Arthur Henry Wood (d 1964), of Oxon, and Katharine Mary, *née* Cumberlege (d 1974); *b* 19 April 1927; *Educ* Gresham's, Trinity Coll Cambridge (MA), Imperial Coll London (BSc); *m* 26 May 1955, Kathleen Audrey, da of Rev John Howard Stanfield; 1 s (Jonathan Altham b 30 Sept 1956), 1 da (Patience Elizabeth b 12 Sept 1960 d 2007), 2 step c (Robin David b 3 May 1950, Sarah Margaret b 17 Nov 1951); *Career* Nat Serv NCB 1945–48, mgmnt trainee NCB 1954–55, sr research offr Clarendon Lab Physics Dept Univ of Oxford 1955–69, fell Wolfson Coll Oxford 1965–88 (hon fell 1988); hon pres Oxford Instruments Ltd (fndr 1959, chm until 1983, dep chm following flotation 1983–2014); pres Farm-Africa, fndr The Earth Tst (formerly Northmoor Tst), fndr Oxford Tst, former chm Oxford Economic Partnership, fndr Sylva Fndn 2009; author of numerous articles in professional jls and deliverer of lectures UK and abroad; jt winner Mullard Award Royal Soc 1982; Hon DSc Cranfield Inst of Technol 1983, Hon DTech Loughborough Univ of Technol 1985, Hon DEng Univ of Birmingham 1996, Hon DSc Univ of Nottingham 1996, hon fell Cardiff Univ 1998, Hon DUniv Open Univ 1999, Hon DSc Oxford Brookes Univ 2000, hon student Christ Church Oxford 2003, Hon DCL Univ of Oxford 2004, Hon DUniv Univ of York 2004; hon fell UMIST 1989; Hon FREng 1994, FRS 1987 (memb Cncl 1995–2000); Order of the Rising Sun 3rd Class (Japan) 2008; *Recreations* inventions, forestry and walking; *Style*— Sir Martin Wood, OBE, FRS, DL; ✉ Oxford Instruments plc, Tubney Woods, Abingdon, Oxfordshire OX13 5QX

WOOD, Michael Murray; s of Kenneth Wood (d 2015), and Isobel, *née* Murray (d 2006); *b* 28 March 1955, Edinburgh; *Educ* Loretto, Univ of Edinburgh; *m* 6 Sept 1980, Barbara Ann, *née* Lennard; 1 da (Louise Kathryn b 21 July 1984), 2 s (Andrew Constable Murray b 12 May 1987, Struan Lennard Muir b 26 July 1990); *Career* admitted slr 1979; Simpson & Marwick: ptnr 1981–2007, conslt 2007–15; pt/t sheriff 2006–; *Recreations* golf, curling, reading history, family; *Clubs* Merchant Co, Renaissance Golf, Luffness Golf; *Style*— Michael Wood, Esq; ✉ Kittlestane, Links Road, Longniddry, East Lothian EH32 0NJ (☎ 01875 852243, e-mail kittlestane@gmail.com)

WOOD, Mike; *Career* MP (Lab) Batley and Spen 1997–2015; *Style*— Mike Wood, Esq; ✉ House of Commons, London SW1A 0AA (☎ 020 7219 3000, e-mail woodm@parliament.uk)

WOOD, Neil Timothy; MBE (2006); s of Roy Edward Wood, and Jean Margaret Rose Wood; *b* 27 February 1965, London; *Educ* Bristol Univ (BSc); *m* 20 Oct 2006, Lara Johanna Kruger, *née* Swanepoel; *Career* ptnr Deloitte & Touche LLP 2002–; fin dir London 2012 Ltd 2003–06, chief fin offr London Organising Ctee of the Olympic Games and Paralympic Games Ltd (LOCOG) 2005–13; FCA 1989; *Style*— Neil Wood, Esq, MBE; ✉ Deloitte and Touche LLP, 1 New Street Square, London EC4A 3BZ (☎ 020 7936 3000)

WOOD, Nicholas Andrew Vicary; s of Charles Stephen Wood, (d 1965), and Celia Patty Wood, *née* Underwood (d 1959); *b* 31 January 1943; *Educ* Lewes Co GS, Queen Elizabeth's Sch Crediton; *m* 8 July 1972 (m dis 2000), Mary Kristina, da of Donald Bernard Naulin, of Williamsburg, Virginia; 2 da (Olivia Marian Vicary b 17 Oct 1984, Genevieve Anna Cordelia b 11 Oct 1987); *Career* called to the Bar Inner Temple 1970, bencher of the Inner Temple 1990; recorder 1993–2013 (asst recorder 1987–93); Ordnance Survey 1960–61, Meridian Airmaps Ltd 1961–62, commercial artist, designer, copywriter 1962–67; *Recreations* people, places, art, music, transport; *Style*— Nicholas Wood, Esq; ✉ Treasury Office, Inner Temple, London EC4Y 7HL (e-mail nwoodevon@btinternet.com)

WOOD, Prof Nicholas William; s of William Wood; *Educ* Univ of Birmingham (MB ChB), Univ of Cambridge (PhD); *m* Sonia Gandhi; *Career* Inst of Neurology: formerly sr lectr then reader then prof of clinical neurology, Galton prof of genetics 2009–; vice dean for research Faculty of Brain Sciences UCL; hon conslt physician Nat Hosp for Neurology and Neurosurgery, sr investigator Nat Inst of Health Research 2008 and renewed 2013, Nat Inst of Health Research Neuroscience prog dir UCL Hosps 2012–; FRCP 2000 (MRCP 1989), FMedSci 2004, fell American Neurological Assoc 2012; *Publications* author of numerous peer-reviewed articles in the field of neurogenetics; *Style*— Prof Nicholas Wood; ✉ Institute of Neurology, Queen Square, London WC1N 3BG (☎ 020 3448 4255, fax 020 7278 5616)

WOOD, Robin Lee Knoyle; s of Wilfred Knoyle (Tim) Wood (d 1973), and Marylee Wood (d 1985); *b* June 1950, Trowbridge, Wilts; *Educ* Lincoln Sch, US Int Univ Cal Western San Diego (int scholar, BA), UCL (research scholar, MSc); *m* March 1975, Olympia Alice, *née* Ramirez; 2 da (Emily Alice b Nov 1979, Lora Marylee b Jan 1986); *Career* ed Marshall Cavendish 1974–80; HarperCollins: ed 1980–90, publishing dir Leisure Books 1990–93, md Gen Refererence Div 1993–95, md Gen Reference and Collins Dictionaries Divs 1995–97, memb UK Exec Bd; md Adult Div Dorling Kindersley 1997–2000, publisher BBC Books BBC Worldwide Ltd 2000–04, freelance conslt 2004–05, chief exec Chrysalis Books Gp plc 2005, chm Anova Books Gp Ltd 2005–14 (chief exec 2005–08), chm Motovun Gp of Int Publishers 2015– (dir (2014–); non-exec dir Third Millennium Information Ltd 2005–15, non-exec dir Pavilion Books 2014–15; chm Independent Publishers Guild 2011–13 (dir 2009–); *Clubs* Two Brydges; *Style*— Robin Wood; ✉ Pavilion Books Group Ltd, 1 Gower Street, London WC1E 6HD (☎ 020 7462 1500, website www.pavilionbooks.com)

WOOD, Hon Mr Justice; Sir Roderic Lionel James Wood; kt (2004); s of Lionel James Wood (d 1969), and Marjorie, *née* Thompson; *b* 8 March 1951; *Educ* Nottingham HS, Lincoln Coll Oxford (MA); *Career* called to the Bar Middle Temple 1974 (bencher 2001); QC 1993, recorder 1997–2002 (asst recorder 1994–97), circuit judge (SE Circuit) 2002–04, judge of the High Court of Justice (Family Div) 2004–, family liaison judge for Wales 2007–12; jt chm Barristers Clerks Liaison Ctee 1994–95; chm Bar Professional Conduct Ctee 1999–2000 (vice-chm 1997–98), vice-chm Family Legal Aid and Fees Ctee 1995–98; memb: Family Law Bar Assoc 1988–2002, Bar Cncl 1993–95; memb Editorial Bd Longman Practitioner's Child Law Bulletin 1993–94; *Recreations* music, theatre, travel; *Style*— The Hon Mr Justice Roderic Wood

WOOD, Roger Nicholas Brownlow; s of Reginald Laurence Charles and Jean Olive Wood; *b* 21 July 1942; *Educ* Sherborne, Northwestern Univ USA; *m* 1, 1966, Julia Ellen, *née* Mallows (d 2013); 2 da; m 2, Malainak Thongma; *Career* with ICL UK Ltd 1962–89 (dir 1987–89), md STC Telecoms Ltd 1989–91, gp vice-pres NT Europe SA 1991–93; md: Northern Telecom UK Ltd 1991–93, Matra Marconi Space UK Ltd 1993–96, Automobile Assoc 2002–04; dir: Centrica plc 1996–2004, Radiotronica Espagna Spa 1991–93, Inst of Adavanced Motorists 2003, Paypoint plc 2004–, Reliance Ltd 2006–; memb: Parly Space Ctee 1993–96, UK Industry Space Ctee 1993–96; MInstD; FIMgt 1984, FBCS 1991; *Recreations* music, Provençe, aviation, Thai culture; *Clubs* Molesey Boat; *Style*— Roger Wood, Esq; ✉ 16 Albany Reach, Queens Road, Thames Ditton, Surrey KT7 0QH (e-mail Ryemead@onetel.com)

WOOD, Roger Norman Alexander; s of Adrian Theodore Wood (d 1992), of Bristol, and Doreen Mary, *née* Gordon-Harris; *b* 13 September 1947; *Educ* The Leys Sch Cambridge, Univ of Bristol (BSc); *m* 1971, Mary Thomasine Howard, da of Howard Reginald Thomas; 1 s (Alexander b 1973), 2 da (Emily b 1975, Joanna b 1976); *Career* Guthrie Corp Ltd 1972–81, United City Merchants plc 1981–86, Burmah Castrol plc 1986–91, George Wimpey plc 1991–94, Automotive Products Group Ltd 1995–96, dir Wineworld London plc 1997–2012, 100 Gp of Finance Directors 1986–94; chm: Leybourne Securities Ltd 1986–, CV Pharma Ltd 2013–; non-exec chm: Gartmore Monthly Income Trust plc 1993–2002, Premier Asset Mgmnt plc 2001–07, Gartmore Distribution Tst plc 2002–06; non-exec dir: Gartmore Value Investments plc 1990–93, Mid Kent Holdings plc 1996–2001, Fundamental Data Ltd 2000–08; govr Cheltenham Ladies' Coll; Liveryman Worshipful Co of Chartered Accountants; FCA; *Recreations* golf, tennis, opera; *Clubs* Oriental, West Hill Golf, Tanglin, Seremban Int Golf, Woking Golf, Royal Cinque Port Golf, Thurlestone Golf; *Style*— Roger Wood, Esq; ✉ High Leybourne, Hascombe, Godalming, Surrey GU8 4AD (☎ 01483 208559, mobile 07778 213337, e-mail roger.leybourne@btinternet.com)

WOOD, Ronald (Ronnie); *b* 1 June 1947; *m* 1; 1 s (Jesse); m 2, 2 Jan 1985 (sep), Jo Howard; 1 s (Tyrone b 1983), 1 da (Leah b 1978); *Career* guitarist; played: bass guitar in The Jeff Beck Group 1968–69, guitar in The Faces 1969–75, The Rolling Stones 1975–; has played with: Bo Diddley (toured as The Gunslingers), Rod Stewart (with The Faces), Muddy Waters, Jerry Lee Lewis and others; albums with Jeff Beck Gp: Truth (1968), Beck-Ola (1969, reached UK no 39); albums with The Faces: First Step (1970, UK no 45), Long Player (1971, UK no 31), A Nod's As Good As A Wink...To A Blind Horse (1971, UK no 2), Ooh La La (1973, UK no 1), Coast To Coast Overtures And Beginners (live, 1974, UK no 3); signed solo record contract with CBS Records 1978; albums with The Rolling Stones: Black And Blue (1976, UK no 2), Love You Live (live, 1977, UK no 3), Some Girls (1978, UK no 2), Emotional Rescue (1980, UK no 1), Tattoo You (1981, UK no 2), Still Life (American Concert 1981) (1982, UK no 4), Undercover (1983, UK no 3), Rewind 1971–1984 (compilation, 1984, UK no 23), Dirty Work (1986, UK no 4), Steel Wheels (1989, UK no 2), Flashpoint (live, 1991, UK no 6), Voodoo Lounge (1994, UK no 1), Bridges to Babylon (1997, UK no 6), No Security (1998), Forty Licks (2002); solo albums: I've Got My Own Album To Do (1974), Now Look (1975), Gimme Some Neck 1979, Slide On This (1992), Slide On Live (1993), Not for Beginners (2001), I Feel Like Playing (2010); concert films: Let's Spend the Night Together (dir Hal Ashby) 1983, Flashpoint (film of 1991 Steel Wheels Tour) 1991; DJ Absolute Radio 2010–; Outstanding Contribution Classic Rock Awards 2009, Rising Star/Radio Personality of the Year Award 2011, Best Specialist Music Prog Sony Radio Acad Silver Award 2012, 4 Sony nominations; Haleyon Fine Artist Prague; *Style*— Ronnie Wood, Esq; ✉ c/o Monroe Sounds, 5 Church Row, Wandsworth Plain, London SW18 1ES

WOOD, Sarah; OBE (2016); *Career* fundraising and devpt offr The Old Vic 2002–03, lectr in American studies Univ of Sussex 2004–05, co-fndr and chief executive Unruly 2006–; assoc lectr and course convenor Univ of Cambridge 2012–; *Style*— Ms Sarah Wood, OBE; ✉ Unruly, 42–46 Princelet Street, London E1 5LP

WOOD, HE Sir (James) Sebastian Lamin; KCMG; *b* 6 April 1961; *Career* diplomat; second then first sec Bangkok 1986–89, Security Policy Dept FCO 1989–91, first sec UKREP Jt Liaison Gp Hong Kong 1992–96, Security Policy Dept then UN Dept FCO 1996–98, princ private sec to Cabinet Sec 1998–2000, Weatherhead Centre for Int Affrs Harvard Univ 2000–01, political counsellor Washington 2001–05, dir Asia Pacific FCO 2005–08, secondment Rolls-Royce Gp 2008–09, ambass to China 2010–15, ambass to Germany 2015–; *Style*— HE Sir Sebastian Wood, KCMG

WOOD, His Hon Judge Simon Edward; s of late Walter Scott Wood, and Shirley, *née* Bittermann; *b* 23 October 1958, North Shields, Tyne and Wear; *Educ* Chorister Sch Durham, Royal GS Newcastle upon Tyne, Univ of Newcastle upon Tyne; *m* 9 June 1984, Catherine Mary, *née* Walton; 4 s (Charles E b 29 March 1989, Frederick J G b 13 May 1991, Hugo F T b 28 Feb 1994, Edwin H C b 21 Oct 1996); *Career* called to the Bar Middle Temple 1981 (Harmsworth scholar); in practice North Eastern Circuit 1981–2008, asst recorder 1998, recorder 2000, circuit judge (North Eastern Circuit) 2008– (Sunderland County Court 2008–10, Newcastle upon Tyne County Court 2010–); memb Northern Sinfonia Chorus 1983–, tstee Northern Sinfonia Tst 2007–13 (chm 2011–13); govr Royal GS Newcastle upon Tyne 1999–2009; dep chllr Diocese of Newcastle 2013–; NE circuit rep Cncl of HM Circuit Judges 2015–; *Publications* Charlesworth and Percy on Negligence (co-ed, 10 edn 2001, 11 edn 2006, 12 edn 2010); *Recreations* music; *Style*— His Hon Judge Simon Wood; ✉ The Law Courts, Quayside, Newcastle upon Tyne NE1 3LA (☎ 0191 201 2000)

WOOD, William James; QC (1998); s of late Sir Frank Wood, KBE, CB, and Lady Wood, *née* Wilson; *Educ* Dulwich Coll, Worcester Coll Oxford (BA, BCL), Harvard Law Sch (Kennedy scholar, LLM); *m* 1986, Tonya Mary, *née* Pinsent; *Career* called to the Bar 1980, memb Bar Tonga 2000; accredited mediator 1999; *Recreations* skiing, tennis, fishing; *Style*— William Wood, Esq, QC; ✉ Brick Court Chambers, 7–8 Essex Street, London WC2R 3LD (☎ 020 7379 3550, fax 020 7379 3558)

WOOD, William Jeremy (Jerry); s of Maj Peter Alexander Wood, RA, and Gwendoline Marion, *née* Hebron; *b* 2 June 1947; *Educ* Liverpool Coll, Univ of Manchester (BSc); *m* 17 March 1973, Judienne, da of Anthony Bridgett, of London; 1 da (Alexis (Lekki) b 1981); *Career* Euro prod mktg mangr Avon Overseas Ltd 1973–79, conslt PE Consulting

W

Group 1979–82, Euro strategic mktg dir Schering Plough Corporation 1983–85, bd dir Bell Pottinger Financial Ltd (formerly Lowe Bell Financial Ltd) 1986–99, md Bell Pottinger First Financial 1996–2002, bd dir Bell Pottinger Communications 2000–02, mktg and communications conslt 2002–; dir Hill Street Investments plc, chm Equity for Growth (Securities) Ltd; dir Inst of Certified Book-keepers (ICB); *Recreations* golf, skiing, travel; *Clubs* RAC; *Style*— Jerry Wood, Esq; ✉ Hornbeam, 19 Pelhams Walk, Esher, Surrey KT10 8QA (☎ and fax 01372 467277, e-mail wjw@uk2.net)

WOOD, His Hon Judge William Rowley; QC (1997); s of Dr B S B Wood, of Lymington, Hants, and Mrs E C Wood; *b* 22 March 1948; *Educ* Bradfield, Univ of Oxford; *m* 22 Sept 1975, Angela, *née* Beatson Hird; 1 s (Sam b 11 May 1977), 2 da (Alice b 3 Sept 1979, Lucy b 23 Nov 1982); *Career* called to the Bar Gray's Inn 1970, recorder of the Crown Court, circuit judge (Midland Circuit) 2002–06, circuit judge (South Eastern Circuit) 2006–; head of Chancery and Commercial Gp, chm Birmingham Diocesan Advsy Ctee, memb Official Referees' Bar Assoc; *Recreations* skiing, sailing, tennis, literature; *Style*— His Hon Judge Wood, QC

WOOD OF ANFIELD, Baron (Life Peer UK 2011), of Tonbridge in the County of Kent; Dr Stewart Martin Wood; s of Brian Wood, of Bidborough, Kent, and Gisela, *née* Schon; *b* 25 March 1968, Tunbridge Wells, Kent; *Educ* Judd Sch Tonbridge, UC Oxford (MA), Harvard Univ (Fulbright scholar, PhD); *m* 1998, Camilla Bustani; 2 s (Luca, Matias); *Career* Univ of Oxford: jr res fell St John's Coll 1995–96, fell in politics Magdalen Coll 1996–; memb Cncl of Economic Advsrs HM Treasy 2001–07, special advsr (foreign policy, culture, NI, media and sport) to Rt Hon Gordon Brown, MP (as PM) 2007–10, dir of communications to Rt Hon Ed Miliband, MP (leadership campaign) 2010, strategic advsr to Rt Hon Ed Miliband, MP, *qqv*, (as Ldr of HM Oppn) 2010–15; Shadow Cabinet min without portfolio 2010–15; conslt on BBC documentaries 1992–99, co-fndr and co-dir Nexus 1996–2000; chair UN Assoc (UK) 2016–; memb Bd English Stage Co 2008–, cmmr Marshall Aid Commemoration Cmmn 2016–; memb: Lab Pty 1995, Co-operative Pty 2010, Community 2010; *Publications* Options for Britain: A Strategic Policy Review (1996), Varieties of Capitalism (contrib, 2001); *Recreations* film, cricket, football, alt-country music; *Style*— The Lord Wood of Anfield; ✉ House of Lords, London SW1A 0PW (☎ 020 7219 5854, e-mail stewart.wood@parliament.uk)

WOODALL, Pamela Diane; da of Ronald Albert Woodall, and Margaret, *née* Williams (d 1989); *b* 21 June 1954; *Educ* Solihull HS for Girls, Univ of Manchester (BA), LSE (MSc); *Career* Govt Econ Serv 1975–79, head of statistics The Economist 1979–83, economist Bank of America 1983–85, economics ed The Economist 1993– (economics corr 1985–93); Wincott Fndn Award for sr financial journalist (jtly) 2006, Best Economic Journalist Business Journalist of the Year Awards 2006, Rybeynski Prize (jtly) Soc of Business Economists 2006; *Recreations* skiing, mountain hiking, gardening; *Style*— Ms Pam Woodall; ✉ The Economist, 25 St James's Street, London SW1A 1HG (☎ 020 7830 7050, e-mail pamwoodall@economist.com)

WOODBRIDGE, Dr Anthony Rivers; s of John Nicholas Woodbridge (d 1991), and Patricia Madeleine, *née* Rebbeck (d 1996); *b* 10 August 1942, Belfast; *Educ* Stowe, Trinity Hall Cambridge (MA); *m* 29 Sept 1976, Lynda Anne, da of Charles Henry Nolan (d 1992); 1 s (Christian b 30 March 1978); *Career* admitted slr 1967; ptnr Woodbridge & Sons Uxbridge 1969, sr ptnr Turberville Woodbridge Uxbridge 1983–97, sr ptnr The Woodbridge Partnership 1997–2009, conslt slr Thomas A Deegan 2011–; co sec: Abbeyfield Uxbridge Soc Ltd 1974–96 (vice-chm 1996–98), Burr Brown International Ltd 1992–96; admin Uxbridge Duty Slr Scheme 1983–91, clerk Cmmrs Income Tax 1985–2009; govr Fulmer Sch Bucks 1984–2003 (chm of govrs 1988–96), memb Hillingdon Health Authy 1990–92; chm: Hillingdon Community Health NHS Tst 1992–94, Harrow and Hillingdon Healthcare NHS Tst 1994–2001, Stoke Mandeville Hosp NHS Tst 2001–02, Hillingdon Hosp NHS Tst 2002–05; tstee Hillingdon Partnership Tst 1995–2003 and 2011– (chm 2014–); hon slr: Hilllingdon Samaritans 1973 (now hon legal advsr), Age Concern Hillingdon 1989–; memb Ct Brunel Univ 1995– (now life memb); memb Law Soc 1967; Hon DUniv Brunel Univ 2000; FIoD 1999; *Recreations* walking, cycling, touring, bridge; *Style*— Dr Anthony R Woodbridge, FIoD; ✉ 16 Fairfield Park Road, Fairfield Park, Bath, Avon BA1 6JN (☎ 01225 329650, mobile 07802 414590, e-mail tonywoodbridge@hotmail.com)

WOODBRIDGE, Dr Margaret Anne; *née* Yelloly; da of Samuel Webster Yelloly (d 1976), and Rowena Emily, *née* Bull (d 1989); *b* 7 June 1934; *Educ* Queen Margaret's Sch, Univ of St Andrews (MA), Univ of Liverpool (MA), Univ of Leicester (PhD); *m* 20 July 2004, Robin Woodbridge (d 2010); *Career* lectr Univ of Leicester Sch of Social Work 1966–72, lectr LSE 1973–76, head Dept of Applied Social Studies Goldsmiths Coll London 1976–86, prof of social work and dir of social work educn Univ of Stirling 1986–91, prof of social work Brunel Univ and the Tavistock Clinic 1991–93, hon prof Tavistock Clinic 1994–; chm Tavistock Inst of Med Psychology 2000–04; chm Social Work Educn Ctee Jt Univ Cncl 1988–91, memb Central Cncl for Educn and Training in Social Work 1989–92; *Books* Social Work Theory and Psychoanalysis (1985), Social Work and the Legacy of Freud (1989), Learning and Teaching in Social Work (1994); *Recreations* classical music, harpsichord; *Style*— Dr Margaret Woodbridge; ✉ 51 The Cloisters, Pegasus Grange, Whitehouse Road, Oxford OX1 4QQ

WOODCOCK, Anthony Douglas Henry; s of Douglas Henry Woodcock (d 1982), and Doreen, *née* Wade; *b* 22 November 1951; *Educ* Brecon Boys GS, Cardiff Univ (BMus); *m* 26 June 1981, Virginia, da of Ralph Harrison; 1 s (Thomas b 20 May 1983); *Career* music offr Welsh Arts Cncl 1974–77, asst dir South East Arts 1977–84, gen mangr City of London Sinfonia 1984–86, gen mangr St David's Hall Cardiff 1986–88, chief exec Royal Liverpool Philharmonic Soc 1988–91, md Bournemouth Orchestras 1991–98, pres Oregon Symphony 1998–2003, pres Minnesota Orchestra 2003–07, pres New England Conservatory 2007–; completed $115 million capital campaign, created new orchestral prog with Hugh Wolff, opera devpt with Stephen Lord and Luretta Bybee; new initiatives: Sistema Fellows, Entrepreneur Musicianship; memb Music Ctee Welsh Arts Cncl, memb cmmnd team (for Welsh Arts Cncl) to review BBC Welsh Symphony Orch; former dir Assoc of Br Orchs, former chm and sec Music Offrs Gp Regnl Arts Assoc, former chm cmmnd team (for Scottish Arts Cncl) to review work of Royal Scottish Orch, former artistic dir Swansea Festival; memb Bd: WGBH (Boston), Boston Children's Chorus, From the Top, Boston Public Schs Art Advsy Bd, Bay Chamber Concerts (Maine), Portland Youth Philharmonic; Royal Philharmonic Soc Award for Educn, Sainsbury's Award for Educn; *Recreations* tennis, reading, blogging; *Clubs* Algonguin; *Style*— Anthony Woodcock, Esq; ✉ New England Conservatory, 290 Huntington Avenue, Boston, MA 02115, USA

WOODCOCK, Prof Ashley; OBE (2006); s of Arthur Woodcock (d 2009), of Stoke-on-Trent, Staffs, and Vera, *née* Jones (d 1973); *b* 13 April 1951; *Educ* Univ of Manchester (BSc, MB ChB, MD); *m* 3 Aug 1974, Fiona Marilyn, da of Raymond Griffiths, of Gwaun-Cae Gurwen, Dyfed; 1 da (Hannah Vera b 1982), 2 s (Daniel Ashley b 1984, (Benjamin) George b 1986); *Career* specialist physician Gen Hosp Bandar-Seri-Begawan Brunei 1977–79; jr dr Brompton Hosp, Nat Heart Hosp, Hammersmith Hosp and St James Hosp 1979–86, conslt physician Manchester Royal Infirmary 1986–88, conslt physician Univ Hosp of S Manchester 1988–, prof of respiratory med Univ of Manchester 1999–, head Inst of Inflammation and Repair 2011–13, head Nat Inst for Health Research (NIHR) Clinical Research Facility Univ Hosp of S Manchester; chm Clinical Section European Respiratory Soc, pres Br Thoracic Soc; chair Montreal Protocol Medical Technical Options Ctee 1995–2015, co-chair Montreal Protocol Technical Economic Assessment Panel 2014–; FRCP 1992 (MRCP 1977), FMedSci 2008; *Recreations* golf, dog-walking; *Clubs* Hale and Aberdyfi Golf; *Style*— Prof Ashley Woodcock, OBE; ✉ North West Lung Centre, University Hospital of South Manchester, Southmoor Road, Manchester M23 9LT (☎ 0161 291 5870)

WOODCOCK, Nigel; s of Barry Woodcock, of Chesterfield, Derbys, and Monica Ann, *née* Redfern; *b* 17 June 1958; *Educ* Chesterfield Sch, Leamington Coll, QMC London (BSc(Econ)), London Business Sch, Warwick Business Sch (MBA), Harvard Business Sch; *m* Anneliese, *née* Roughton-Skelton; 2 da (Jane b 11 Aug 1980, Catherine b 18 Sept 1993), 2 s (Thomas b 27 June 1985, Robert b 21 June 1988); *Career* national NHS admin trainee NE Thames RHA 1980–81, asst hosp administrator The London Hosp Mile End 1982, asst hosp administrator Whittington Hosp Islington 1983, dep hosp sec The London Hosp Whitechapel 1986 (asst hosp sec 1983–85), dir of facilities N Herts HA 1986–88, unit gen mangr Lister Hosp Stevenage (N Herts HA) 1988–90; chief exec: W Cumbria Health Care NHS Tst 1993–2000 (unit gen mangr under W Cumbria HA 1990–92), (actg chief exec) N Lakeland Healthcare NHS Tst 2000–01, N Cumbria Mental Health and Learning Disabilities NHS Tst 2001–03, N Cumbria PCT 2003–08, Nigel Woodcock Consulting Ltd 2008–; assoc lay memb NHS Tower Hamlets Clinical Commissioning Gp 2015–16; chm Accelerate CIC 2014–; *Recreations* cricket, soccer, fell-walking, skiing; *Clubs* Derbyshire CCC,Surrey CCC; *Style*— Nigel Woodcock, Esq; ✉ e-mail: nigel@nigelwoodcock.co.uk

WOODCOCK, Thomas; CVO (2011, LVO 1996), DL (2005); s of Thomas Woodcock (d 1999), and Mary, *née* Woodcock (d 2006); *b* 20 May 1951; *Educ* Eton, Univ of Durham (BA), Darwin Coll Cambridge (LLB); *m* 11 July 1998, Lucinda Mary Harmsworth King; *Career* called to the Bar Inner Temple 1975 (bencher 2010); Rouge Croix Pursuivant 1978–82, Somerset Herald of Arms 1982–97, Norroy and Ulster King of Arms 1997–2010, garter princ King of Arms 2010–, genealogist Order of the Bath 2010–; advsr on naval heraldry 1996–, inspr of regtl colours and RAF badges 2010–; chm Harleian Soc 2004–, pres Lancashire Parish Register Soc 2004–; FSA; *Books* Oxford Guide to Heraldry (with John Martin Robinson, 1988), Dictionary of British Arms Medieval Ordinary (Vol I, ed with D H B Chesshyre, 1992, Vol II, ed with Hon Janet Grant and Ian Graham, 1996, Vol III, ed with Sarah Flower, 2009, Vol IV, ed with Sarah Flower, 2014), Heraldry in National Trust Houses (with John Martin Robinson, 2000); *Clubs* Travellers, Beefsteak, Pratt's; *Style*— Thomas Woodcock, Esq, CVO, DL, FSA; ✉ College of Arms, 130 Queen Victoria Street, London EC4V 4BT (☎ and fax 020 7236 3634)

WOODCRAFT, Tess; da of Alf Woodcraft (d 1981), and Peggy Woodcraft (now Mrs Perry); *b* 17 June 1948, Chelmsford, Essex; *Educ* Chelmsford Co HS, Univ of Leeds (LLB); *m* 3 June 2005, Alan Fountain; 1 s (Jack Woodcraft b 28 Feb 1980), 1 da (Billie Woodcraft b 23 July 1984); *Career* equalities offr NALGO 1978–87, journalist BBC and Channel 4 1987–89, chief exec Kids Club Network 1989–93, head of communication Islington Cncl 1993–94, dir Centre for Strategy and Communication 1995–; cmmr: Equal Opportunities Cmmn 1999–2005, Charity Cmmn for England and Wales 2005–09; *Style*— Ms Tess Woodcraft

WOODFORD, Neil; CBE (2013); *Educ* Univ of Exeter (BSc), London Business Sch; *Career* fund mangr Eagle Star 1987–88, currently head of investment Invesco Perpetual (joined 1988); *Style*— Neil Woodford, Esq, CBE; ✉ Invesco Perpetual, Perpetual Park, Perpetual Park Drive, Henley-on-Thames, Oxfordshire RG9 1HH

WOODFORD, Peggy Elizabeth Lainé (Mrs Aylen); da of Ronald Curtis Woodford, OBE (d 1970), and Ruth Mahy, *née* Lainé (d 1987); *b* 19 September 1937; *Educ* Guernsey Ladies' Coll, St Anne's Coll Oxford (MA); *m* 1 April 1967, Walter Stafford Aylen, QC, *qv*, s of Rt Rev Charles Arthur William Aylen (d 1972); 3 da (Alison b 1968, Frances b 1970, Imogen b 1974); *Career* writer; Italian govt res scholar Rome 1960–61, script and res asst BBC TV 1962–63, sr tutor Sixth Form Coll Reading 1964–67; Cadbury's/Nat Tst Short Story Award 2010; memb: Authors' Licensing and Collecting Soc 1982, Soc of Authors 1985, RSL; *Books* incl: Abraham's Legacy (1963), Mozart (1964), Schubert (1969), Please Don't Go (1972), Backwater War (1975), The Real Thing (1977), Rise of the Raj (1978), See You Tomorrow (1979), You Can't Keep Out the Darkness (1980), The Girl with a Voice (1981), Love Me Love Rome (1984), Misfits (1984), Monster in our Midst (1988), Out of the Sun (1990), Blood and Mortar (1994), Cupid's Tears (1995), On the Night (1996), Jane's Story (1998), One Son is Enough (2006), Please Don't Go (2007), Backwater War (2010), See You Tomorrow (2010); *Style*— Miss Peggy Woodford; ✉ 24 Fairmount Road, London SW2 2BL (☎ 020 8671 7301, fax 0870 131 8529, e-mail peggywoodford@talktalk.net, website www.peggywoodford.com); Literary Agent: Laura Morris Literary Agency, 21 Highshore Road, London SE1 5AA (☎ 020 7732 0153, e-mail laura.morris@lmlit.co.uk)

WOODFORD, Stephen William John; s of John Wilfred Stephen Woodford, of Trowbridge, Wilts, and Barbara, *née* Wood; *b* 11 February 1959; *Educ* Tomlinscote Sch Frimley, City Univ (BScEcon)); *m* 30 April 1988, Amelia Wylton, da of Wylton Dickson; 2 s (William Nicholas b 3 Aug 1989, Miles Wylton John b 31 July 1992), 2 da (Katherine Sophie Genevieve b 6 Aug 1997, Matilda Elizabeth b 28 Nov 2002); *Career* grad trainee Nestle Co Ltd 1980–82, account mangr Lintas Advertising 1982–85, account dir Waldron Allen Henry & Thompson 1985–89, account dir rising to gp account dir WCRS 1989–91, dep md Leo Burnett 1991–94; WCRS: client servs dir 1994–95, md 1995–99, ceo 1999–2006; chm and chief exec DDB London 2006–; pres IPA 2003–05; tstee Changing Faces, pres Nat Advertising Benevolent Soc; *Recreations* family, riding, swimming, the countryside; *Style*— Stephen Woodford, Esq

WOODGATE, Antony John (Tony); s of Bartlett George Woodgate (d 2002), and Charlotte, *née* Woerz (d 2015); *b* 11 May 1960, Melbourne, Aust; *Educ* Monash Univ Melbourne (BSc, LLB), Univ of Cambridge (LLM), Birkbeck Coll Univ of London; *m* 15 July 1995, Alison Coleman; 1 s (Michael b 10 July 1995), 1 da (Stephanie b 8 Aug 1998); *Career* admitted slr Victoria, Aust 1984, Eng and Wales 1989; Simmons and Simmons: joined 1986, ptnr 1991–; chm Slrs European Gp 1997–98; PLC EC and UK Competition Law Manuals (contrib); *Recreations* hiking, swimming; *Style*— Tony Woodgate, Esq; ✉ Simmons & Simmons, CityPoint, One Ropemaker Street London EC2Y 9SS (e-mail tony.woodgate@simmons-simmons.com)

WOODHEAD, (George) Melvyn Walker; s of George Wilson Woodhead (d 1999), of Wakefield, and Irene, *née* Walker (d 1987); *b* 11 July 1939, Wakefield, W Yorks; *Educ* Silcoates Sch Wakefield; *m* 24 Sept 1965, Susan, *née* Stevenson; 2 s (Mark Stephen b 22 July 1970, David Melvyn b 27 Feb 1976); *Career* Nat Serv 3/7 Queen's Own Hussars 1958–60; family haulage business 1960–62, sales negotiator Hepper & Sons 1962–64, asst to dir Evans of Leeds 1964–65, estab Woodhead Investments Ltd (property co) 1965; various local awards for refurbishment works; *Recreations* shooting, motoring, coin and art collecting; *Style*— Melvyn Woodhead, Esq; ✉ The Palms, 481 Barnsley Road, Sandal, Wakefield, West Yorkshire WF2 6BP (☎ 01924 256294, fax 01924 256755); Woodhead Investments Limited, Woodhead House, 8–10 Providence Street, Wakefield WF1 3BG (01924 374720, fax 01924 291901)

WOODHEAD, Robin George; s of Walter Henry Woodhead (d 1976), of Zimbabwe, and Gladys Catherine Woodhead, of Johannesburg, SA; *b* 28 April 1951; *Educ* Mount Pleasant Sch Salisbury Rhodesia, Univ Coll of Rhodesia and Nyasaland (LLB); *m* 1, 28 June 1980 (m dis 1992), Mary Fitzgerald, da of Fergus Hamilton Allen, CB, of Berks; *m* 2, 9 June 2010, Christian Ravina (civil partnership converted 4 June 2015); *Career* chm International Petroleum Exchange of London Ltd, md Premier Man Ltd, dir E D & F Man International Ltd 1981–86; chm and chief exec National Investment Group plc and chief exec National Investment Holdings plc 1986–91, chief exec London Commodity Exchange 1992–97, md Sotheby's Europe 1997–98, chief exec Sotheby's Europe 1998–99, chief exec Sotheby's Europe & Asia 2000–06, chief exec Sotheby's Int 2006–08, chm Sotheby's Int 2008–, chm Hofesh Shechter 2008–; chm David Rattray Meml Tst 2007–; govr and dep chm South Bank Centre 2004–; memb Law Soc 1978; *Recreations* riding, Zululand farmer; *Style*— Robin Woodhead, Esq; ✉ Sotheby's, 34–35 New Bond Street, London W1A 2AA (☎ 020 7293 5000, fax 020 7293 5969)

WOODHOUSE, Charles Frederick; CVO (1998), DL (2007); s of Wilfrid Meynell Woodhouse (d 1967), of Chester Row, London, and Margaret (Peggy), *née* Kahl; *b* 6 June 1941; *Educ* Marlborough, McGill Univ Montreal, Peterhouse Cambridge (MA); *m* 25 Jan 1969, Margaret Joan, da of Thomas Wheatcroft Cooper (d 1991), of Hulland Ward, Derbys; 2 da (Rachel b 11 Nov 1969, Philippa b 1 Nov 1971), 1 s (Timothy b 6 Dec 1973); *Career* admitted slr; ptnr Farrer & Co 1969–99 (conslt 1999–2001); slr to HRH The Duke of Edinburgh 1983–2001; legal advsr CCPR 1971–99; chm: The Cheviot Tst 1991–97, Rank Pension Plan Trustee Ltd 1992–2001; dir Santos USA Corp 1995–2002; hon legal advsr Cwlth Games Cncl for Eng 1983–2007, chm Sports Dispute Resolution Panel (now Sports Resolution UK) 1997–2007, pres Br Assoc for Sport and Law 1997–2000; chm Rural Regeneration Cumbria 2002–06, dir Lowther Castle and Gardens Tst 2006–11, dir Cumbria Vision 2006–08; tstee: LSA Charitable Tst 1989–2016, Yehudi Menuhin Meml Tst 1998–2002, Cumbria Community Fndn 2002–08, Hospice at Home Carlisle and N Lakeland 2003–10, Athletics Fndn 2004–15, Mulberry Tst; memb Royal Parks Review Gp 1993–96; pres Guildford CC 1989–2002, hon life vice-pres Surrey Championship; govr: Nelson Thomlinson Sch Wigton 2003–11, St Bees Sch Cumbria 2004–08; *Recreations* cricket, golf, writing, gardens and trees; *Clubs* MCC, Oxford and Cambridge, Worplesdon Golf, Surrey CCC, Free Foresters, Hawks' (Cambridge), Silloth-on-Solway Golf, Mungrisdale Writers Group; *Style*— Charles Woodhouse, Esq, CVO, DL; ✉ Quarry Hill House, Mealsgate, Cumbria CA7 1AE (☎ 01697 371225, e-mail cfwoodhouse@btinternet.com)

WOODHOUSE, Prof John Robert; s of Horace Woodhouse, and Iris Evelyn, *née* Pewton; *b* 17 June 1937; *Educ* King Edward VI GS Stourbridge, Hertford Coll Oxford (MA, DLitt), Univ of Pisa, Univ of Wales (PhD); *m* 5 Aug 1967, Gaynor, *née* Mathias; *Career* Nat Serv RAF 1955–57; asst lectr in Italian Univ of Aberdeen 1961–62, Br Cncl scholar Scuola Normale Superiore Pisa 1962–63, asst lectr then lectr UCNW Bangor 1963–66, lectr then sr lectr Univ of Hull 1966–73; Univ of Oxford: lectr in Italian 1973–89, fell St Cross Coll 1973–84, lectr Jesus Coll 1973–89, lectr St Edmund Hall 1975–89, lectr Brasenose Coll 1976–89, fell Pembroke Coll 1984–89 (supernumerary fell 1991–), fell Magdalen Coll 1990–2001 (emeritus fell 2001–), Fiat Serena prof of Italian studies 1989–2001 (emeritus prof 2001–); corresponding fell: Accademia Letteraria dell'Arcadia 1982, Accademia della Crusca 1991, Commissione per i testi di lingua Bologna 1992; fell: Huntington Library Calif 1986, Newberry Library Chicago 1988; Old Dominion fndn fell Harvard Univ 1969–70, founding fell Centro Studi Dannunziani Pescara 1979, sr research fell Center for Medieval and Renaissance Studies UCLA 1985; memb: Exec Ctee Soc for Italian Studies 1979–85 and 1989–95, Ctee Modern Humanities Res Assoc 1984–94 (hon life memb 1994, pres 2008), Exec Ctee Soc for Study of Medieval Languages and Literature 1998–2003; ed (Italian) Modern Language Review 1984–94, memb Editorial Bd Italian Studies Jl 1987–91; fndr chm Oxford Italian Assoc 1990–2010; govr Br Inst of Florence 1991–2001; Serena Medal of the British Academy 2002; FRSA 1983, FBA 1995; Cavaliere Ufficiale al Merito della Repubblica Italiana 1991; *Books* incl: Italo Calvino – a reappraisal and an appreciation of the trilogy (1968), V Borghini 'Storia della nobiltà fiorentina' (ed, 1974), Baldesar Castiglione – a reassessment of the Cortegiano (1978), G D'Annunzio 'Alcyone' (ed, 1978), G Rossetti 'Lettere familiari' (jt ed, 1983), Idem 'Carteggi' (jt ed, Vol I 1984, Vol II 1988, Vol III 1992, Vol IV 1996, Vol V 2001, Vol VI 2006) The Languages of Literature in Renaissance Italy (jt ed, 1988), From Castiglione to Chesterfield: The Decline in the Courtier's Manual (1991), Dante and Governance (ed, 1997), Gabriele D'Annunzio, Defiant Archangel (1998), Gabriele D'Annunzio, Arcangelo ribelle (1999), Gabriele D'Annunzio tra Italia e Inghilterra (2003), Il Generale e il Comandante: Ceccherini e D'Annunzio a Fiume (2004), L'Ottavo Giurato: Giuseppe Sovera con D'Annunzio a Fiume (2008); *Recreations* gardening; *Style*— Prof J R Woodhouse; ✉ Magdalen College, Oxford OX1 4AU

WOODING, Dr Neil Rhys; s of Desmond Frank Roydon Wooding, of Newport, and Gillian Mary, *née* Evans; *b* 23 October 1960, Newport; *Partner* Nick McNeill; 1 da (Ruby Anne Rhys Lessels b 22 July 1993); *Career* asst regnl mangr (Wales and SW) NACRO 1986–89, equal opportunities advsr Cardiff City Cncl 1989–92, head Equality Unit NHS Wales 1992–99, dir of HR and organisational devpt Bro Taf HA 1999–2003, dir NHS Centre for Equality and Human Rights 2003–05, dir Public Service Mgmnt Wales 2005–; equal opportunities cmmr for Wales Equal Opportunities Cmmn 2002–07, Wales cmmr Cmmn for Equality and Human Rights (CEHR) 2006–09; int consultancy: Office of the Chief Justice of Ghana 2009, Human Rights Law Network India 2009; non-exec dir: Chwarae Teg Wales Ltd 1996– (chair 2001), SE Wales Race Equality Cncl 1997–; co-chair Stonewall Cymru 2001–, memb Bd Stonewall UK 2002–, tstee and memb Bd Nat AIDS Tst 2002– (chair All-Wales HIV Reference Gp 1999–2003); vice-chair Welsh Food Alliance 1999–2003, memb Bd Health Living Centre New Opportunities Fund; govr Dyffryn Comp Sch Newport 1997–2003; fell Nat Centre for Public Policy, FCIPD; *Publications* incl: Two Centuries of British Penal Development (1985), An Evaluation of Career Development Opportunities for Women in Local Government (1989), Promoting Equality inside the National Health Service: A Best Practice Guide (1992), A Good Practice Guide to Flexible Working (1994, 2 edn 2003), Managing Careers in General Practice across Wales (1997), A Study of Race and Health Issues inside the Health Service in Wales (1998), The Organisational Construction of Fairness (2003), Undertaking Equality Impact Assessment within Public Service (2005), Promoting Workforce Engagement (2006), Engaged Leadership: The New Public Service Managerialism (2006), Telling Stories: Developing Organisational Narratives (2007), Thought Leading Others (2008), Becoming Co-Creational (2009), Using Appreciative Inquiry (2010); *Style*— Dr Neil Wooding; ✉ Ty Newydd, 9 Bucklewood, Bayfields, Chepstow, Monmouthshire NP16 6DX (☎ 01291 627983); Public Service Management Wales, 1st Floor, Fynnon Las, Ilex Close, The Orchards, Llanishen, Cardiff CF14 5EZ (☎ 029 2068 1201)

WOODING, Roy; s of Raymond Wooding (d 1957), and Elsie, *née* Lyons; *b* 11 October 1953; *Educ* Mexborough Co Secdy Sch; *m* 16 October 1976, Angela, da of George Jones; 1 da (Rachael Emma b 27 Sept 1978); *Career* professional photographer; M T Walters & Associates Ltd 1970–84, fndr ICS Photography 1984–; awarded BIPP Yorkshire Regions Industrial/Photographer of the Year 2003, 2005, 2006, 2007and 2008, 1 Silver BIPP Int Prints Award 2002 and 3 Bronze BIPP Int Prints Awards 2001; judge: BIPP A&Q Panel, Br Professional Photography Awards 2004–08; FBIPP 1982 (yst then in indust category, assoc BIPP 1976); *Books* contrib photographs to Photography Year Book (1983); *Recreations* skiing, spinning, fishing, theatre; *Style*— Roy Wooding, Esq; ✉ 20 Farmoor Close, Harlington, Doncaster, South Yorkshire DN5 7JP (☎ 01709 896237); ICS Photography, The Studio, 20 Far Moor Close, Harlington, Doncaster, South Yorkshire DN5 7JP (☎ 01709 896868, e-mail roy@icsphotography.co.uk, website www.icsphotography.com)

WOODLEY, Leonard Gaston; QC (1988); *Educ* Univ of London; *Career* called to the Bar Inner Temple 1963 (bencher), memb Bar Trinidad and Tobago; recorder 1989–2000; head of chambers 8 King's Bench Walk 1988–2000; cases incl: Mangrove Trial (Notting Hill Riot), Bristol Riot (St Paul's), Brixton Riot, Newham Seven Trial, Privy Cncl appeals; chm Laudat Inquiry into Mental Health, counsel Scarman Inquiry; memb Royal Cmmn on Long Term Care for the Elderly; memb Exec NCCL/Liberty; fndr Leonard Woodley Scholarship; friend ROH, memb Globe Theatre, patron Plan UK; *Clubs* MCC, Globe Lawn Tennis (life memb); *Style*— Leonard Woodley, Esq, QC

WOODMAN, Prof Anthony John; s of John Woodman (d 1988), and Alma Clare, *née* Callender (d 1982); *b* 11 April 1945; *Educ* Ushaw Coll Durham, King's Coll Newcastle upon Tyne, Univ of Durham (BA), King's Coll Cambridge (PhD); *m* 21 July 1977, Dorothy Joyce, da of Gordon Charles Monk (d 1970); 2 s (David b 1981, John b 1983); *Career* reader in Latin literature Univ of Newcastle upon Tyne 1979–80 (lectr in classics 1968–79); prof of Latin: Univ of Leeds 1980–84, Univ of Durham 1984–2004; Gildersleeve prof of classics Univ of Virginia 2004–; visiting prof Princeton Univ 1989–90, visiting fell Univ of Wisconsin/Madison 1995, visiting Gildersleeve prof of classics Univ of Virginia 2003–04; *Books* Quality and Pleasure in Latin Poetry (jtly, 1974), Velleius Paterculus: the Tiberian Narrative (1977), Creative Imitation and Latin Literature (jtly, 1979), Velleius Paterculus: the Caesarian and Augustan Narrative (1983), Poetry and Politics in the Age of Augustus (jtly, 1984), Past Perspectives: Studies in Greek and Roman Historical Writing (jtly, 1986), Rhetoric in Classical Historiography (1988), Tacitus: Annals IV (jtly, 1989), Author and Audience in Latin Literature (jtly, 1992), Tacitus and the Tacitean Tradition (jtly, 1993), Tacitus: Annals III (jtly, 1996), Latin Historians (jtly, 1997), Tacitus Reviewed (1998), Traditions and Contexts in the Poetry of Horace (jtly, 2002), Tacitus: The Annals (2004), Sallust: Catiline's War, The Jugurthine War, Histories (2007), The Cambridge Companion to Tacitus (2009), Latin Historiography and Poetry in the Early Empire: Generic Interactions (jtly, 2010), From Poetry to History: Selected Papers (2012), Catullus: Poems, Books, Readers (jtly, 2012), Agricola (jtly, 2014), Lost Histories: Selected Fragments of Roman Historical Writers (2015); *Style*— Prof A J Woodman; ✉ Department of Classics, Cocke Hall, PO Box 400788, University of Virginia, Charlottesville, VA 22904, USA (☎ 00 1 434 924 3008)

WOODROFFE, Simon; OBE (2006); *b* 14 February 1952; *Career* entreprenuer, businessman and public speaker; over 30 years in entertainment business; fndr prodn companies based in London and LA designing rock 'n' roll stages for artistes such as Rod Stewart, The Moody Blues, Stevie Wonder and events such as Live Aid; org financing and distribution Nelson Mandela, Amnesty Int and Prince's Tst concerts; tv prodn deals incl Japan's No 1 show Hit Studio International; fndr and creative driving force behind the YO! brand incl YO! Sushi, YOTEL and YO! Home; public speaker and performer Edinburgh Festival 2004; recorded album with The Blockheads 2003–04; Emerging Entrpreneur of the Year 1999, London Entrepreneur of the Year 1999, UK Group Restaurateur of the Year 2000, Best Venue (Retailer's Retailer of the Year Awards) 2001, Design and Art Direction Award (The Catey Awards) 2000; *Publications* The Book of YO! (2000); *Style*— Simon Woodroffe, OBE; ✉ YO! Company (☎ 07957 292165, e-mail nick@yo.co.uk, website www.yo.co.uk)

WOODROW, Dr Arabella Thomasine; *née* Morris; da of Michael Henry Carlile Morris (d 1987), of Basingstoke, Hants, and Margaret Joyce, *née* Flannery (d 1984); *b* 31 March 1954; *Educ* Queen Anne's Sch Caversham, Lady Margaret Hall Oxford (BA, DPhil); *m* 15 Dec 1979, Richard Erskine Woodrow, s of Cyril Erskine Woodrow (d 1960), of Scarborough; *Career* wine merchant; sales rep Harveys of Bristol 1979–84, Wine and Spirit Educn Tst dip 1981, Vintners scholarship from Vintners Co 1983, sales rep Christopher & Co Ltd 1984–85, wine buyer Cooperative Wholesale Soc 1986–99, wine buying dir Forth Wines Ltd 1999–2001, wine projects conslt Halewood Int 2002–03, freelance conslt 2003, business devpt mangr Myliko Wines 2003–07, wine trading mangr Morrison's Supermarkets 2007–12, dir of wine Broadland Wineries Ltd 2013–; memb: Inst of Masters of Wine 1986–, Wine Devpt Bd 1986–92, Wine Standards Bd 1990–99 (bd dir 2003–06); Freeman City of London 1995, Liveryman Worshipful Co of Vintners 2003; MW 1986; *Books* Wines Of The Rhone Valley; *Recreations* marathon running, triathlon, cookery, wine tasting, orienteering; *Style*— Dr Arabella Woodrow; ✉ Heights Farm, Banks Lane, Riddlesden, Keighley, West Yorkshire BD20 5PS (☎ 01535 611701, e-mail atwoodrow@druidpark.freeserve.co.uk)

WOODROW, William Robert (Bill); s of Geoffrey William Woodrow (d 2015), and Doreen Mary, *née* Fasken (d 2013); *b* 1 November 1948; *Educ* Barton Peveril GS, Winchester Sch of Art, St Martin's Sch of Art, Chelsea Sch of Art (Higher Dip Fine Art); *m* 12 Nov 1970, Pauline, da of John Neville Rowley; 1 s (Harry), 1 da (Ellen); *Career* sculptor; winner Anne Gerber award Seattle Museum of Art 1988; chair Roche Court Educnl Tst New Art Centre Salisbury 2011–; tstee: Tate Gallery 1996–2001, Imperial War Museum 2003–11; govr Univ of the Arts London 2003–08; RA 2002; *Exhibitions* numerous solo exhibitions in Europe, Australia, USA and Canada since 1972 incl: Fool's Gold (Duveen Galleries Tate Gallery London, later Darmstadt) 1996, Regardless of History Fourth Plinth Trafalgar Square London 2000–01, The Beekeeper (South London Gallery, Mappin Art Gallery Sheffield) 2001, Waddington Galleries London 2006 and 2008, Brood (The Great Hall Winchester) 2007, Lullin & Ferrari Zurich 2008, Waddington Custot Galleries London 2011, Lullin and Ferrari Zurich 2012, Royal Acad of Arts 2013; group exhibitions incl: Br Sculpture in the 20th Century Whitechapel Art Gallery 1981, Biennale of Sydney 1982, Aperto 82 Venice 1982, XII Biennale of Paris 1982, New Art at the Tate Gallery 1983, Transformations São Paulo (also Rio de Janeiro, Mexico City, Lisbon) 1983, Int Survey of Recent Painting and Sculpture New York 1984, Skulptur im 20 Jahrhundert Basle 1984, ROSC '84 Dublin 1984, Space Invaders toured Canada 1985, The Br Show toured Aust 1985, Carnegie Int Pittsburgh 1985, Entre el objeto y la imagen toured Spain 1986, Painting and Sculpture Today Indianapolis 1986, Br Art of the 1980's Stockholm and Tampere 1987, Documenta 8 Kassel 1987, Starlit Waters Tate Liverpool 1988, British Now Montreal 1988, GB-USSR Kiev Moscow 1990, Metropolis Berlin 1991, XXI São Paulo Bienal 1991, Arte Amazonas (Rio de Janeiro, Brasilia, Berlin, Dresden and Aachen) 1992–94, Collaborative Works (with Richard Deacon, Chisenhale Gallery London) 1993, Contemporary Br Art in Print Edinburgh and Yale 1995, Un Siecle de Sculpture Anglaise (Paris) 1996, Sexta Bienal de la Habana (Cuba) 1997, Forjar el Espacio (Las Palmas de Gran Canaria, Valencia, Calais) 1998–99, Bronze Holland Park London 2000, Field Day Sculpture from Britain (Taipei Fine Arts Museum Taiwan) 2001, Blast to Freeze: British Art in the 20th Century (Kunstmuseum Wolfsburg and Les Abbatoirs Toulouse) 2002–03, Turning Points: 20th Century British Sculpture (Tehran Museum of Contemporary Art) 2004, Eldorado (MUDAM Luxembourg) 2006, Sculpture in the Close (Jesus Coll Cambridge) 2007, Punk – No One is Innocent (Kunsthalle Wien) 2008, Modern British Sculpture (RA London) 2011; *Museum Collections* incl: Arts Cncl GB, Br Cncl, Imperial War Museum, Kunsthaus Zurich, Malmö Konsthall, MOMA NY, Nat Gallery of Canada, Rijksmuseum Kröller-Müller, Tate Gallery, Br Museum, Br Library; *Books* The Sculpture of Bill Woodrow (by Julia Kelly and Jon Wood, 2013); *Style*— W R Woodrow, Esq, RA; ✉ e-mail bill@billwoodrow.com

WOODS, David Victor; *b* 7 May 1958; *Educ* Skegness GS, Selwyn Coll Cambridge (MA), Coll of Law Guildford; *Career* admitted slr 1982; articled clerk Hill & Perks Slrs 1980–82; ptnr: Eversheds 1987–2001 (chm Nat Commercial Practice Gp 1993–98), Greenwoods Slrs LLP 2001–; notary public 2011–; *Style*— David Woods, Esq

WOODS, Margaret Rose (Meg); da of Douglas Edward Woods (d 1989), and Agnes Mary, *née* Low; *b* 19 April 1952, Johannesburg; *Educ* Univ of the Witwatersrand Johannesburg (BComm), Univ of Cape Town (MBA, Gold Medallist (first woman)); *Career* chartered fin analyst (CFA); dir of investment research Mathison and Hollidge Johannesburg 1977–

W

85 (first woman broking member Johannesburg Stock Exchange 1979), global equity analyst Donaldson Lufkin & Jenrette New York 1985–86, global/Asian equity portfolio mangr HSBC Asset Mgmnt London 1987–94, head Asia Pacific Equities Friends Provident Asset Mgmnt London 1994–97, head Global Equities Sun Life of Canada Asset Mgmnt 1998–99, head UK Equities Colonial First State Investments London 1999–2000, fndr ptnr Veritas Investment Management LLP 2000–; hon fell Cancer Research UK; Rising Star Business Award S Africa 1978, PAM Awards Investment Performance Growth Portfolios London 2009 and 2011, PAM Awards Investment Performance Defensive Portfolios London 2010; memb CFA Inst 1991; *Recreations* violin, opera, travel, walking, gardening; *Clubs* Glyndebourne; *Style*— Ms Margaret Woods; ✉ Veritas Investment Management LLP, 90 Long Acre, London WC2E 9RA (☎ 020 3740 8354, e-mail mwoods@veritasinvestment.co.uk, website www.veritasinvestment.co.uk)

WOODS, Michael John; s of Dr L H Woods, and Margery, *née* Pickard; *Educ* Bradfield; *m* 15 Jan 1966, Carolyn Rosemary, da of William Tadman, of Roborough, N Devon; 1 s (Nicholas John b 13 Aug 1967), 1 da (Jennifer Sarah Rosemary (Mrs Monks) b 29 May 1969); *Career* Nat Serv 1 Bn Royal Fus (serv Suez Crisis) 1955–57; trainee exec Mecca Ltd 1957–63; dir: Silver Blades Ice Rink Ltd 1963–70, Mecca Catering 1968–, Mecca Leisure Ltd 1973–; asst md: Mecca Bingo Social Clubs 1972–80, Mecca Leisure Ltd 1979–85; chm: Mecca Agency International 1983–85, Ison Bros (Newcastle) Ltd 1983–85, Pointer Motor Co 1983–85, Scot Automatic Printing 1983–85; md: Mecca Leisure Speciality Catering Div 1985–91, Speciality Catering Div Europe 1989–91; dir Saddle and Sirloin Restaurant Ltd 1991–97; self employed catering conslt 1991–, gp catering exec Apollo Leisure (UK) Ltd 1993–96; memb: Exec Bd Variety Club of GB 1985–2001, Cncl Actors' Charitable Tst, Hotel and Catering Benevolent Assoc, TICC 2000; tstee Ralph and Meriel Richardson Fndn 2003–; Freeman City of London 1998; FInstD 1965–2001, FIH (FHCIMA 1989); *Recreations* squash, swimming, shooting (clay and pheasant), fishing (sea trout); *Clubs* MCC (1985–2015); *Style*— Michael Woods, Esq; ✉ Glendale, Farley Green, Albury, Guildford, Surrey, GU5 9DL (☎ 01483 202472)

WOODS, Philip Dudley; s of John Webster-Woods (d 1991), and Dora Helen Davies, *née* Rushworth (d 2010); *b* 23 December 1950, Liverpool; *Educ* Birkenhead Sch, Liverpool Law Sch; *m* 6 March 1976, Jane, *née* Kalbraier; 2 s (Simon Maxwell Dudley b 27 May 1980, Jonathan Dudley b 12 Aug 1983); *Career* admitted slr: Eng and Wales 1974, Hong Kong 1975; asst slr: Percy Hughes & Roberts 1974–75, Deacons 1975–81; ptnr: Wilkinson & Grist 1981–89, Eversheds Alexander Tatham 1989–94 (chm Nat Intellectual Property Gp), Philip Woods & Co 1994–97, Hill Dickinson LLP 1997–2011 (head of intellectual property and IT); special counsel Spruson & Ferguson (Asia) Pte Ltd Singapore (formerly Ella Cheong Spruson & Ferguson) 2011–15, intelligent property, IT and media conslt 2015–; founding memb Intellectual Property Lawyers' Orgn (TIPLO), assoc memb Chartered Inst of Patent Agents, assoc memb Inst of Trade Mark Attorneys; *Recreations* wine, classic cars, reading, walking; *Clubs* Hong Kong, Oriental, Hong Kong Jockey, Royal Hong Kong Yacht, Hong Kong Cricket, Old Boys and Park Green, Foreign Correspondents (Hong Kong), Tanglin, Singapore Cricket; *Style*— Philip Woods, Esq; ☎ 07960 483585, e-mail woodiessg@hotmail.co.uk

WOODS, Richard; *Educ* Winchester Sch of Art, Slade Sch of Art; *Career* artist; Delfina Studio Award 2002; Freeman City of Chester; *Solo Exhibitions* Hales Gallery London 1994, Renovation & Customisation (Cristinerose NY) 2000, Modern Art Inc London 2000, Griedervon Puttkamer Berlin 2001, Deitch Projects NY 2002, V&A 2003; *Group Exhibitions* incl: The Galleries Royal Acad 2002; *Collections* Saatchi Collection London, ARKEN Museum of Contemporary Art Denmark, Frank Cohen Collection Cheshire, Arts Cncl; *Style*— Richard Woods, Esq

WOODS, Robert; CBE; *Career* The Peninsular and Oriental Steam Navigation Company (P&O): joined 1971, memb Bd 1996–, gp md P&O Nedlloyd Container Ltd 1997–2003, exec chm P&O Ports 2002–, chief exec 2004–06; non-exec dir John Swire & Sons 2002–; pres Chamber of Shipping 2002–04; *Style*— Robert Woods, Esq, CBE

WOODWARD, Dame Barbara Janet; DCMG (2016, CMG 2011), OBE (1999); da of Arthur Claude Woodward (d 1992), and Rosemary Monica Gabrielle, *née* Fenton; *b* 29 May 1961, Stowmarket, Suffolk; *Educ* Univ of St Andrews (MA), Yale Univ (MA); *Career* diplomat; Cabinet Office European Fast Stream, seconded to FCO EU Directorate (incl on 1992 EU Presidency) 1991–93, joined FCO 1994, second later first sec (Commercial/Political) Moscow 1994–98; FCO: Agenda 2000 Negotiating Team EU Dept 1998–99, head EU Enlargement Section 1998–99, dep head Human Rights Policy Dept 2001–03; political cnsllr later min and dep head of mission Beijing 2003–09, int dir UK Border Agency 2009–11, DG (Economic and Consular) FCO 2011–15, ambass to China 2015–; *Style*— HE Dame Barbara Woodward, DCMG, OBE; ✉ c/o FCO (Beijing), King Charles Street, London SW1A 2AH

WOODWARD, Bethany; da of Timothy Woodward, and Georgina Woodward; *b* 26 December 1992, Ringwood, Hants; *Partner* Lee Doran; *Career* Paralympic athlete; achievements incl: Gold medal (400m) World Championships 2011, Silver medal (200m) and Bronze medal (4x100m relay) Paralympic Games 2012; *Clubs* Southampton Athletics; *Style*— Miss Bethany Woodward; ✉ website www.bethanywoodward.com, Twitter @bethywoodward; c/o Eric Shirley (☎ 07823 880230, e-mail info@esteamathleteagency.co.uk, website www.esteamathleteagency.co.uk)

WOODWARD, Christopher Haldane; s of William Haldane Woodward, of Wirral, Cheshire, and Audrey Woodward; *b* 18 November 1946; *Educ* Calday Grange GS, Univ of Birmingham (BSocSc), Manchester Business Sch (MBA); *m* 9 Aug 1969, Frances Maria, da of Richard Alan Beatty, of Edinburgh; 1 s (Matthew b 1974), 2 da (Rosalind b 1976, Charlotte b 1980); *Career* grad trainee and economist mktg asst GKN 1968–70, mktg mangr GKN Farr Filtration 1970–72, mktg exec Guthrie Corporation 1974–75, mktg and devpt exec Tay Textiles 1976–77 (gp mktg and planning controller 1978–79), Cape Insulation Ltd 1979–82 (mktg mangr, nat sales mangr, sales and mktg dir); mktg dir: Euro Uniroyal Ltd 1982–86, 3i plc 1986–94; md Total Communications 1994–; dir: Mascord Ltd,Planalytics Assocs Ltd; *Recreations* opera, theatre, music, art; *Clubs* RAC; *Style*— Christopher Woodward, Esq; ✉ Total Communications (☎ 01825 724030)

WOODWARD, Sir Clive; kt (2004), OBE (2002); *b* 6 January 1956, Ely, Cambs; *Educ* HMS Conway Anglesey, Loughborough Univ (BA); *Career* rugby union coach and former player; played for: Loughborough Univ, Harlequins, Leicester Tigers, Manly (Aust); England: 21 caps 1980–1984, 4 tries, debut v Ireland, winners Grand Slam 1980; memb Br Lions touring squads to South Africa 1980 and NZ 1983; career as coach: Manly (Aust), Henley 1990–94, London Irish 1994–97, Bath (conslt coach), England U21 1994–97, head coach England 1997–2004 (winners Six Nations Championship 2000, 2001 and 2003 (Grand Slam 2003), unbeaten against South Africa, Aust and NZ autumn series 2002, ranked no 1 team in world 2003, unbeaten against NZ and Aust summer tour 2003, winners World Cup Aust 2003), head coach Br Lions tour to NZ 2005, performance dir Southampton FC 2005–06, dir of elite performance BOA 2006–12; memb Bd Leicester Tigers 2007–; Coach of the Year Sports England 2004; *Style*— Sir Clive Woodward, OBE

WOODWARD, Derek Richard; s of James Norman Woodward, of Hull, and Mary, *née* Dennison; *b* 17 September 1958; *m* 1991, Finuala, da of Patrick and Kay McDonald, of Dublin; 2 s (Ciaran b 16 Feb 1995, Daniel b 18 Nov 1997), 1 da (Olivia b 24 Nov 2001); *Career* asst co sec: Eagle Star 1984–90, BAT Industries plc 1990–98, co sec Allied Zurich plc 1998–2001, head of secretariat Centrica plc 2001–08, gp co sec Thomas Cook Gp plc 2008–; memb: ICSA; FCIS; *Recreations* family life, cycling, keeping fit; *Style*— Derek Woodward, Esq

WOODWARD, Gerard Vaughan; s of Reginald Llewelwyn Woodward (d 1991), and Sylvia, *née* Walsh (d 1981); *b* 4 December 1961; *Educ* St Ignatius Coll London, Falmouth Sch of Art, LSE (BSc, Maurice Freedman Prize); *m* 1983, Suzanne Jane, da of Robin Anderson; 1 s (Corin b 8 June 1995), 1 da (Phoebe b 28 April 2000); *Career* freelance artist 1985–89, freelance writer 1989–; prof in creative writing Bath Spa Univ 2004–; memb Soc Authors 1992–; FRSL; *Poetry* The Unwriter and Other Poems (1989, Eric Gregory Award), Householder (1991, Poetry Book Soc Choice, Somerset Maugham Award, shortlist J L Rhys Prize Mail on Sunday), After the Deafening (1994, Poetry Book Soc Choice), Island to Island (1999), We Were Pedestrians (2005), The Seacunny (2012); *Novels* August (2002, shortlist Whitbread First Novel Award), I'll Go to Bed at Noon (2004, shortlist Man Booker Prize for Fiction), A Curious Earth (2007), Nourishment (2010); *Short Stories* Caravan Thieves (2008); *Recreations* chess, playing the piano, pathology; *Style*— Prof Gerard Woodward; ✉ Rogers, Coleridge and White, 20 Powis Mews, London W11

WOODWARD, His Hon Judge Nicholas Frederick; s of Frederick Cyril Woodward, and Joan Woodward; *Educ* Wellingborough Sch, Trent Poly (BA); *m* (m dis); 1 s; *Career* barr 1976–2001, asst recorder 1998–2000, recorder 2000, circuit judge (Wales & Chester Circuit) 2001–; *Clubs* Chester City; *Style*— His Hon Judge Nick Woodward; ✉ The Court Service, Chester Crown Court, The Castle, Chester CH1 2AN

WOODWARD, Sarah Wendy Boston; da of Edward Woodward (d 2009), and Venetia Mary, *née* Battine; *b* 3 April 1963; *Educ* Moria House Sch Eastbourne, RADA (Bancroft Medal); *m* Patrick Michael Joseph Toomey; 2 da (Milly b 6 Dec 1997, Nell b 20 Sept 2002); *Career* actress; *Theatre* RSC: Henry V, Love's Labour's Lost, Hamlet, Richard III, Camille and Red Noses 1984–85, Murder in the Cathedral 1993–94, Rosaura in The Venetian Twins, Miranda in The Tempest 1993–94, Rosaline in Love's Labour's Lost 1995; Birmingham Repertory: Charley's Aunt, The Winter's Tale; other theatre incl: Artist Descending a Staircase (King's Head, Duke of York), The Rape of Lucrece (Almeida), Romeo and Juliet, Arms And The Man (Regent's Park Open Air Theatre), Angelus From Morning 'Til Midnight (Soho Poly), Build On Sand (Royal Court), Talk of the Devil (Bristol Old Vic), London Assurance (Chichester Theatre, Royal Haymarket), Schism in England (NT), Anne Danby in Kean (Old Vic, Toronto) 1990–91, Rose Jones in The Sea (RNT) 1991–92, Wild Oats (RNT) 1995, Connie Wicksteed in Habeas Corpus (Donmar Warehouse) 1996, Kitty in Tom & Clem (Aldwych) 1997, Charlotte in The Real Thing (Donmar Warehouse, Albery, Broadway) 1999–2000, Presence (Royal Court) 2001, Liaisons Dangereuses (Playhouse) 2003, Much Ado About Nothing (Globe) 2004, Susan in A Woman in Mind (Salisbury Playhouse) 2005, Adriana in A Comedy of Errors (Globe) 2006, Titania in A Midsummer Night's Dream and Lady Macbeth in Macbeth (both Regents Park Open Air Theatre) 2007, Monica in Present Laughter (RNT) 2008, Mistress Ford in The Merry Wives of Windsor (Globe) 2008, Miriam in Snake in the Grass (Print Room) 2011, Charlotta in The Cherry Orchard (RNT) 2011, Bea in Jumpy (Royal Court) 2011, Love and Information (Royal Court) 2012, Vanessa in Bracken Moor (Tricycle Theatre) 2013; *Television* incl: The Bill (LWT), Gems (Thames), The Two of Us (LWT), Sherlock Holmes (Granada), Poirot (Thames), Casualty (BBC), The Inspector Pitt Mysteries (Ardent) 1998, Final Demand (BBC) 2002, Doctors, Kingdom, New Tricks, Law and Order 2009, DCI Banks 2010, Loving Miss Haito (BBC), Outnumbered (BBC) 2012; *Radio* incl: Scuttling Off (Radio 4) 1988, 84 Charing Cross Road (World Service) 1991; *Film* The House of Angelo 1999, Doctor Sleep 2001, I Capture the Castle 2001, Bright Young Things 2003; *Awards* Clarence Derwent Award for Artist Descending a Staircase 1989, nominated for Best Newcomer Shakespeare Globe Awards 1994, Olivier Award for Best Performance in a Supporting Role (Tom & Clem) 1997, nominated for Tony Award for Best Featured Actress (The Real Thing) 2000; *Recreations* all sports, poker (winner Fulham Open Hold 'em Championship Trophy 1994), blackjack; *Style*— Miss Sarah Woodward

WOODWARD, Rt Hon Shaun Anthony; PC (2007); s of Dennis George Woodward, and Joan Lillian, *née* Nunn; *b* 26 October 1958; *Educ* Bristol GS, Jesus Coll Cambridge (MA); *m* 2 May 1987, Camilla Davan, da of Rt Hon Sir Tim Sainsbury, *qv*; 1 s (Tom b 1989), 3 da (Ella b 1991, Olivia b 1993, Kate b 1996); *Career* BBC TV journalist: researcher That's Life 1982–85, reporter and prodr Newsnight 1985–87, sr prodr Panorama 1987–89, editor That's Life 1990; dir of communications Cons Pty 1990–92, professorial fell Queen Mary & Westfield Coll London 1992–96; MP: (Cons) Witney 1997–99, (Lab) Witney 1999–2001, (Lab) St Helens 2001–; shadow min for London regeneration, the regions and tport until Dec 1999 (when resigned from Cons Pty and joined Lab Pty), Parly under sec of state NI 2005–06, min for creative industries and tourism DCMS 2006–07, sec of state for NI 2007–10, shadow sec for NI 2010–11; memb Jt Ctee on Human Rights 2001–; chm: Ben Hardwick Meml Fund 1984–93 (tstee 1993–97), Oxford Student Radio 1995–97; tstee: Childline 1997–2005 (dep chm 1993–97), Marine Stewardship Cncl 1998–2001, Human Dignity Tst 2012–; vice-pres St Helen's Millennium Centre 2001–; memb Fndn Bd RSC 1998–, memb Fundraising Cncl Southwark Cathedral 2011–, hon chair Hamptons Int Film Festival 2013–, dep chm LAMDA 2013–, chm LAMDA Capital Campaign 2013–; fell Harvard Univ Inst of Politics at John F Kennedy Sch of Govt 1994; *Books* Tranquillizers (with Ron Lacey, 1983), Ben – the Story of Ben Hardwick (with Esther Rantzen, *qv*, 1984), Drugwatch (with Sarah Caplin, 1985); *Recreations* opera, architecture, gardening, reading, travel; *Style*— The Rt Hon Shaun Woodward; ✉ House of Commons, London SW1A 0AA (☎ 020 7219 2680, e-mail woodwardsh@parliament.uk)

WOODWARD, Stephen James; s of Wesley James Woodward (d 1968), and Margery, *née* Gill (d 1978); *b* 25 May 1950; *Educ* King's Sch Rochester, W London Business Sch (BA); *m* 24 March 1973, Alison Linda, da of Robert Epps; 3 s (Paul James, David Robert, Michael Stephen); *Career* sponsored business undergrad De La Rue Co 1968–72, product exec Nestle Co 1972–75, sr product mangr Carnation Co 1975–78, mktg dir Seagram UK 1978–87, gp dir Lowe Howard-Spink advtg 1987–89; chief exec: Brands Div Michael Peters Group plc 1989–90, Ayer Group UK 1990–93 (responsible for founding DP&A Direct Mktg); chm: DP&A Ltd 1993–2002, Moonriver Group Ltd 1995–2007, Vertomis (Pty) Ltd 2008–; dir: Sportsglobal Ltd 2008–, Woody Investments Ltd, Aesop Agency 2010–, Ralph & Co 2010–, MyRuby Ltd 2008–; fndr ptnr Mulberry VAlue Practitioners LLP 2014–; memb Mktg Gp of GB, Solus Club 2012–; fell Mktg Soc (chm 1994–95); Officier L'Ordre des Coteaux de Champagne; *Books* Understanding Brands – By Ten People Who Do (1991), Branding In Action (1993); *Clubs* Croham Hurst Golf (capt 2004); *Style*— Stephen Woodward, Esq

WOODWARD, William Charles (Bill); QC (1985); s of Wilfred Charles Woodward, of Nottingham, and Annie Stewart, *née* Young; *b* 27 May 1940; *Educ* Nottingham HS, St John's Coll Oxford (BA); *m* 1965, Carolyn Edna, da of Francis Doughty Johns, of Kent; 1 da (Rebecca b 1966), 2 s (William b 1968, Fergus b 1974); *Career* called to the Bar Inner Temple 1964; memb Midland Circuit, marshall to late Sir Donald Finnemore, head Ropewalk chambers 1987–95, recorder 1989–2010, dep judge of the High Court 1997–2010; pres Mental Health Review Tbnl 2000–10; judge Court of Appeal St Helena 2002–13; special prof Univ of Nottingham 1998–2010; memb: Law Advsy Ctee Univ of Nottingham, Bar European Gp, Br Horological Inst; fndr memb: Nottingham Medico Legal Soc, East Midlands Business and Property Bar Assoc; *Recreations* sporadic cookery, serendipity, windsurfing in calm conditions; *Clubs* Pre-War Austin Seven, Notts United Services; *Style*— W C Woodward, Esq, QC; ✉ Ropewalk Chambers, 24 The

Ropewalk, Nottingham NG1 5EF (☎ 0115 947 2581, fax 0115 947 6532, e-mail wcwqc@ropewalk.co.uk)

WOOLDRIDGE, Michael James (Mike); OBE (2002); s of James Wooldridge (d 1996), and Eveline Betty, *née* Carter (d 2013); *b* 24 July 1947; *Educ* Bournemouth Sch for Boys, Harlow Tech Coll (later NCTJ Cert); *m* 1974, Ruth Kyre Holliday, da of Canon Keble Thomas (d 1992), and Gwyneth Thomas (d 2004); 3 c (Beth b 1977, Simon b 1978, Sophie b 1981); *Career* reporter Eastern Counties Newspapers 1965–68, VSO Uganda 1968–69; with the BBC 1970–: World Service News 1970–78, reporter Radio News 1978–82, East Africa corr 1982–89, Southern Africa corr 1989–90, religious affrs and community rels corr 1990–96, S Asia corr 1997–2001, world affrs corr 2001–; memb NUJ 1965; *Books* VSO in Action (1978), War Wounds (on Sudan, contrib 1988), The Day That Shook The World (contrib, 2001); *Recreations* family pursuits, walking, music, travel; *Style—* Mike Wooldridge, OBE; ✉ c/o BBC World Affairs Unit, 3rd Floor, Broadcasting House, London W1A 1AA

WOOLDRIDGE, Sarah Margaret Chappell; da of Leonard Walter Andrews Chappell, and Constance, *née* Doyle; *Educ* Braeside Sch Buckhurst Hill, La Nouvelle Roseraie Vevey, Mrs Hoster's Secretarial Coll; *m* 1, 1973 (m dis 1978), Antonio Lourenço; 1 s (Jorge Antonio Chappell Lourenço); m 2, 1980, Ian Wooldridge (d 2007); *Career* IMG dealing with VIP events, speakers and publishing (joined as PA to Mark McCormack 1966); supporter of cancer and dyslexia charities; *Recreations* Cons Pty, cooking, swimming, watching sport; *Clubs* Virgin Active, Kensington; *Style—* Mrs Ian Wooldridge; ✉ IMG, Building Six, Chiswick Park, London W4 5HR (☎ 020 8233 5000, mobile 07802 956225, e-mail sarah.wooldridge@img.com)

WOOLER, Stephen John; CB (2005); s of Herbert G Wooler, of Bedford, and Mabel Wooler; *b* 16 March 1948; *Educ* Bedford Modern Sch, UCL (LLB); *m* 5 Oct 1974, Jonquil Elizabeth, *née* Wilmshurst-Smith; 1 s (Charles Robert Alexander b 31 Jan 1980), 1 da (Stephanie Grace Alexandra b 20 Nov 1981); *Career* called to the bar Gray's Inn 1969, in practice 1969–73, master of the bench Gray's Inn 2008; Office of DPP: joined 1973, asst dir of public prosecutions 1982, seconded to Law Officers' Dept 1983, chief crown prosecutor (N London) 1987–89; seconded to Law Officers' Dept 1989, dep legal sec to Law Officers 1992–99, HM Chief Inspr to CPS 1999–2010, Asst Boundary Cmmr 2011–13; memb: Advsy Bd Inst of Criminal Law UCL 2009, Lord Chllr's Advsy Sub-Ctee for Bucks 2012–14, Financial Reporting Cncl Case Mgmnt Ctee 2013–, Lord Chllr's Advsy Ctee for Thames Valley 2014, Advsy Gp to the Victims' Cmmr 2014–; ind memb NI Legal Services Cmmn 2014–15, ind memb Legal Services Agency for NI 2015–; *Recreations* campanology, rugby, walking, garden; *Style—* Stephen Wooler, Esq, CB

WOOLF, Prof Anthony Derek; s of Douglas Langton Woolf (d 2000), of Woodford, Essex, and Kathorn Beth Woolf, *née* Pearce (d 1980); *b* 12 June 1951; *Educ* Forest Sch, London Hosp Med Coll (BSc, MB BS); *m* 4 Dec 1975, Hilary Ann, da of Ronald Ruddock-West (d 1978); 1 da (Sarah Louise b 1979), 1 s (Richard Thomas b 1981); *Career* sr registrar Royal Nat Hosp for Rheumatic Diseases and Bristol Royal Infirmary 1983–87, conslt rheumatologist Royal Cornwall Hosp Truro 1987–2014, clinical dir NIHR Clinical Research Network Southwest Peninsula 2014; hon prof of rheumatology: Univ of Exeter Medical Sch, Peninsula Coll of Medicine and Dentistry Plymouth 2014; author of papers on rheumatology, med educn, viral arthritis and osteoporosis; ed Best Practice and Research Clinical Rheumatology, memb Advsy Bd Annals of Rheumatic Diseases, chair Global Alliance for Musculoskeletal Health, chair Arthritis and Musculoskeletal Alliance (ARMA); past pres European Bd of Rheumatology; Yeoman Worshipful Soc of Apothecaries; FRCP 1994 (MRCP 1979); *Books* Osteoporosis: A Clinical Guide (1988, 1990 and 1998), How to Avoid Osteoporosis: A Positive Health Guide (1989), Osteoporosis: A Pocket Book (1994, 2 edn 2002), Osteoporosis: An atlas of investigation and management (2008); *Style—* Prof Anthony Woolf; ✉ Bone and Joint Research Group, Knowledge Spa, Royal Cornwall Hospital, Truro TR1 3HD (☎ 01872 256438, e-mail anthony.woolf@nhs.net)

WOOLF, David; s of Raymond Woolf (d 1997), of Newcastle upon Tyne and London, and Valerie Belle, *née* Robins (d 1954), of Plymouth; *b* 27 January 1945; *Educ* Clifton; *m* 19 June 1977, Vivienne Barbara, er da of Dr David Perk, of Johannesburg (d 1994); 2 s (James b 31 Jan 1979, John b 26 April 1982); *Career* trainee Keyser Ullman 1963–64, chartered accountant Chalmers Impey 1965–69, PA to Chm Corob Holdings 1969–71, fndr and chief exec Citygrove gp of companies (early developer of retail and leisure parks) 1971–2005; currently advsr to various family companies; chm Int Co-operation Ctee World Ort 2010– (tstee 2004–12); FCA 1969 (prize for 10th place 1967); *Recreations* digital art, theatre, opera, sailing, travel; *Clubs* Royal Southampton Yacht; *Style—* David Woolf, Esq; ☎ 020 7486 4198, e-mail davidwoolflondon@icloud.com

WOOLF, Dame Fiona; DBE (2015, CBE 2002); *née* Swain; da of R H A (Dick) Swain (d 1981), and Margaret, *née* Hart; *b* 11 May 1948, Edinburgh; *Educ* Keele Univ (BA); *m* 28 April 1990, Nicholas Woolf; 1 step-da (Elizabeth Woolf b 1973), 1 step-s (Christopher Woolf b 1977); *Career* admitted slr; asst slr Coward Chance 1973–78, ptnr McKenna & Co (now CMS Cameron McKenna) 1981–2004 (asst slr 1978–81, now ptnr); pres Law Soc 2006–07; memb Competition Cmmn 2005–13; Sherrif of London 2010–11, Lord Mayor of London 2013–14; sr fell Kennedy Sch of Govt Harvard Univ 2001–02; tstee Sci Museum 2015–, tstee Raleigh Int; hon pres Aldersgate Gp; memb Law Soc 1973; *Publications* Global Transmission Expansion: Recipes for Success (2003); *Recreations* historic buildings, music, museums, walking, wood turning; *Clubs* RAC, East India (hon memb); *Style—* Dame Fiona Woolf, DBE; ✉ City of London Corporation, Guildhall, London EC2P 2EJ

WOOLF, Baron (Life Peer UK 1992), of Barnes in the London Borough of Richmond; Sir Harry Kenneth Woolf; CH (2015), kt (1979), PC (1986); s of late Alexander Woolf, and late Leah, *née* Cussins; *b* 2 May 1933; *Educ* Fettes, UCL (LLB); *m* 1961, Marguerite, da of late George Sassoon; 3 s (Hon Jeremy Richard George b 26 Aug 1962, Hon Andrew James David b 18 June 1965, Hon Eliot Charles Anthony b 29 July 1967); *Career* Nat Service cmmnd 15/19 Royal Hussars 1954, Capt Army Legal Service 1955; called to the Bar Inner Temple 1954 (bencher 1976), recorder of the Crown Ct 1972–79, jr counsel Inland Revenue 1973–74, first Treasy jr counsel in common law 1974–79, judge High Ct (Queen's Bench Div) 1979–86, presiding judge SE Circuit 1981–84, Lord Justice of Appeal 1986–92, Lord of Appeal in Ordinary 1992–96, Master of the Rolls 1996–2000, Lord Chief Justice 2000–05; held inquiry into prison disturbances 1990–91, conducted inquiry Access to Justice 1994–96, chm Review of the Working Methods of the European Court of Human Rights 2005, chm Woolf Ctee into ethical business conduct in BAE Systems plc – the Way Forward 2007–08; memb: Senate of Bar and Bench 1981–85, Bowman Ctee 1996–97, Int Advsy Cncl on Law and Justice World Bank 2001–06; special advsr and chair Conflict Mgmnt Advsy Gp CEDR 2005–, mediator and arbitrator Blackstone Chambers 2005–; chm: Lord Chllr's Advsy Ctee on Legal Educn 1987–90, Middx Justice's Advsy Ctee 1987–90, Bd of Mgmnt Inst of Advanced Legal Studies 1986–93, Butler Tst 1992–96 (pres 1996–), St Mary's Hosp Special Tstees 1993–97, Advsy Cncl on Public Records 1996–2000, Magna Carta Tst 1996–2000, Financial Mktg Law Reform Ctee; pres: Law Teachers Assoc 1985–90, Jt Ctee for Jewish Social Services 1988–2000, W London Magistrates' Assoc 1987–92; govr Oxford Centre for Hebrew Studies 1988–93 (emeritus 1993), pro-chllr Univ of London 1994–2005, chm Cncl UCL 2005–08, chllr Open Univ Israel 2006–15 (hon fell 2015); visitor: UCL 1996–2000, Nuffield Coll Oxford 1996–2000, Downing Coll Cambridge 2006; visiting prof UCL 2005–, hon prof of Law Chinese Univ Hong Kong; hon memb: Public Soc of Teachers of Law 1988–, Ct Univ of London 1993–94; Lifetime Award Law Scribes of America, Centenary Award Chartered Inst of Arbitrators 2015, Rings of Tolerance; Hon LLD: Univ of Buckingham, Univ of Bristol, Univ of London and Anglia, Manchester Metropolitan Univ, Univ of Hull 2001, Cambridge Univ 2006, Valpariso Univ; Hon DSc Cranfield Univ 2001, Hon DCL Univ of Oxford 2004; Freeman Newcastle upon Tyne 2006; hon fell: Univ of Leeds, UCL; chartered arbitrator 2006; Hon FBA 2000, Hon FRSM 2012, Hon FCIArb 2015; *Publications* Protecting the Public: the new challenge (Hamlyn lecture, 1990), Declaratory Judgement (ed jtly, 2 edn 1993), De Smith Woolf & Jowell: Judicial Review of Administrative Action (ed jtly, 5 edn, 1995), Pursuit of Justice (2008); *Clubs* Garrick, Athenaeum, RAC; *Style—* The Rt Hon the Lord Woolf, CH

WOOLFE, Richard; s of Julian Woolfe, of Hove, Sussex, and Laurel, *née* Mendell; *b* 14 August 1962, Brighton, E Sussex; *Educ* Brighton Coll, Manchester Poly (BEd); *m* 10 April 1988, Hilary, *née* Berg; 1 da (Elise b 26 May 1989), 1 s (Daniel b 25 July 1991); *Career* md Real TV 1996–97, ed Entertainment Dept Granada TV 1998–99, head of entertainment Planet 24 Prodns 1999–2001, dir of television Living TV 2001–06, dir of progs Sky One, Two and Three 2006–08, channel controller Five 2009–10, creative dir Prizeo.com 2011–15, md Woolfetv 2012–, broadcast and televisionproduction and training conslt; Argos Consumer Journalist of the Year 1991, Channel of the Year Broadcast Digital Awards 2004 (for Living TV), Industry Player of the Year Edinburgh Int TV Festival 2005, Entertainment Channel of the Year Broadcast Digital Awards 2008 (for Sky One); memb: BAFTA, RTS; *Recreations* reading, wine; *Clubs* The Ivy, Soho House; *Style—* Richard Woolfe, Esq

WOOLFENDEN, (Kenneth) Alan; s of Frederick John Woolfenden (d 1971), and Mary, *née* Duff; *b* 25 July 1950; *Educ* N Manchester GS for Boys, Univ of Liverpool (MB ChB); *m* 1 April 1972, Susan Irene, da of Alan Eaton, of Manchester; 1 s (Jonathan Frederick b 12 Dec 1980); *Career* conslt urological surgn Royal Liverpool Univ Hosp Tst 1985–, clinical dir of urology Royal Liverpool and Broadgreen Univ Hosp Tst; hon lectr Dept of Surgery Faculty of Med Univ of Liverpool; dir Sr Registrar Trg Mersey Region; memb Cncl: Br Assoc of Urological Surgns, Liverpool Med Inst; memb Exec Cncl Mersey Region for Kidney Research; memb BMA 1973, FRCS 1978, FEBU 1992; *Style—* Alan Woolfenden, Esq; ✉ Riverside, Manorial Road, Parkgate, South Wirral, Cheshire CH64 6QW (☎ 0151 336 7229); 57 Rodney Street, Liverpool L1 9ER (☎ 0151 709 2079)

WOOLFENDEN, Christian; s of Ian Woolfenden, and Jane Elizabeth, *née* Walker; *b* 16 December 1978, Lancs; *Educ* Hutton GS, Hutton Grammar Sixth Form, Univ of Liverpool (BSc); *m* 25 July 2009, Elizabeth Clare, *née* Williams; *Career* Procter & Gamble: finance analyst 2000–03, mktg mangr 2003–08; global brand dir Bacardi 2008–11, chief mktg offr Paddy Power plc 2011–14, md Paddy Power plc 2014–15, chief mktg offr Lyst 2015–; FCMA 2003, memb Mktg Soc 2003; *Recreations* shooting, skiing, walking, climbing, fly fishing, surfing; *Style—* Christian Woolfenden, Esq; ✉ Lyst, 48 Hoxton Square, London N1 6PB (☎ 020 7874 9153, e-mail christian.woolfenden@gmail.com)

WOOLFSON, Dr Gerald; s of late Joseph Samuel Woolfson, and late Lilian Woolfson; *b* 25 March 1932; *Educ* Milton Sch Bulawayo and Zimbabwe, Univ of Cape Town (MB); *m* 1, 1955, Sheila Charlaff; 2 s (David b 1955, Adrian b 1965), 1 da (Karen b 1959); *m* 2, 1978, Lynne, *née* Silver; 1 s (Alexander b 1978); *Career* conslt psychiatrist Hammersmith and St Mary's Hosp Gp, hon sr lectr RPMS; FRSM, FRCP, FRCPsych; *Recreations* chess, doodling; *Style—* Dr Gerald Woolfson; ✉ 62 Wimpole Street, London W1G 8AJ (☎ 020 7935 3400, fax 020 7935 1414, e-mail geraldwoolfson@gmail.com, website www.geraldwoofson.co.uk)

WOOLFSON, Prof Michael Mark; s of Maurice Woolfson (d 1956), and Rose, *née* Solomons (d 1999); *b* 9 January 1927; *Educ* Hackney Downs Sch, Wellingborough GS, Jesus Coll Oxford (MA), UMIST (PhD, DSc); *m* 19 July 1951, Margaret, da of Dr Mayer Frohlich; 2 s (Mark b 1954, Malcolm b 1957), 1 da (Susan b 1960); *Career* HG 7 Northants Bn 1942–44, Nat Serv cmmnd 2 Lt RE 1947–49; res asst Cavendish Laboratory Cambridge 1952–54, ICI res fell Cambridge 1954–55, reader in physics UMIST 1961–65 (lectr 1953–61), currently emeritus prof Univ of York (prof of theoretical physics 1965); former pres Yorks Philosophical Soc; hon fell Jesus Coll Oxford 1999; FInstP, FRAS, FRS; *Books* Direct Methods in Crystallography (1961), An Introduction to X-Ray Crystallography (1970, 2 edn 1997), The Origin of the Solar System: The Capture Theory (1989), Physical and Non-Physical Methods of Solving Crystal Structures (1995), An Introduction to Computer Simulation (1999), The Origin and Evolution of the Solar System (2000), Planetary Science (2002, 2 edn 2013), Mathematics for Physics (2006), The Formation of the Solar System: Theories Old and New (2007, 2 edn 2013), Everyday Probability and Statistics: Health, Elections, Gambling and War (2008), Time, Space, Stars and Man: The Story of the Big Bang (2009), Materials, Matter and Particles: A Brief History (2010), On the Origin of Planets: By Means of Natural Simple Processes (2010), The Fundamentals of Imaging: From Particles to Galaxies (2012), Resonance: Applications in Physical Science (2014), Time and Age: Time Machines, Relativity and Fossils (2015); *Recreations* writing; *Style—* Prof Michael Woolfson, FRS; ✉ 61 Thackrah Court, Squirrel Way, Leeds LS17 8FQ (☎ 0113 469 2343); Department of Physics, University of York, York YO10 5DD (☎ 01904 432230, fax 01904 432214)

WOOLHOUSE, Prof Mark Edward John; OBE (2002); s of Prof John G Woolhouse, of Coventry, and R Carolyn, *née* Harrison; *b* 25 April 1959, Shrewsbury; *Educ* Queen Elizabeth's GS Ashbourne, Tiffin Sch Kingston, Univ of Oxford (BA), Univ of York (MSc), Queen's Univ Kingston Ontario (PhD); *m* 24 July 2004, Dr Francisca Mutapi; 1 da (Nyasha Ruth b 4 Nov 2006); *Career* research fell Dept of Biological Sciences Univ of Zimbabwe 1985–86, research fell Dept of Biology Imperial Coll London 1986–89, research fell Dept of Zoology Univ of Oxford and visiting research fell Blair Research Labs Zimbabwe 1989–97, prof of infectious disease epidemiology Sch of Biological Sciences Univ of Edinburgh 1997–; author of more than 200 pubns in scientific jls; Wright Medal Br Soc for Parasitology 2002; FRSE 2004, FMedSci 2010; *Recreations* walking, fly fishing; *Style—* Prof Mark Woolhouse, OBE; ✉ Centre for Immunity, Infection and Evolution, Ashworth Laboratories, King's Buildings, University of Edinburgh, Charlotte Auerbach Road, Edinburgh EH9 3FL (☎ 0131 650 5456)

WOOLLAMS, Christopher John; s of late George James Woollams, and Phyllis Joan, *née* Cox; *b* 4 July 1949; *Educ* Watford Boys' GS, St Peter's Coll Oxford (MA); *m* 1 (m dis); 3 da (Catherine Louise b 1978 d 2004, Georgina Clair b 1983, Stephanie Marie b 1986), 1 s (Benjamin Henry b 1995); m 2, Amphorn Wollams; 1 s (Harry James b 2009); *Career* fndr and chm Spiral Cellars Ltd 1980–91, dir Ogilvy and Mather London 1980–83, md Publicis 1984, chm Ted Bates Group London 1985 (Euro and Worldwide Bd dir 1986), chm Fitness in Home Ltd 1986–91, chief exec WMGO Group plc 1987–95, chief exec BDP Int 1998–, chm Health Issues Ltd 2002–, fndr and ceo CANCERactive; ed icon magazine; Freeman City of London; Lord of Pembury (manorial title); *Publications* Everything You Need to Know to Help You Beat Cancer (2002), The Tree of Life (2003), Oestrogen – the killer in our midst (2004), Cancer – your first 15 steps (2004), Conventional Cancer Cures – What's the Alternative? (2005), The Rainbow Diet – and how it can help you beat cancer (2009), The Secret Source of Your Good Health (2013), Integrated Cancer and Oncology News (icon); *Recreations* flying, golf, wine, writing, chess, skiing; *Clubs* RAC, Confrerie de Tastevin, Palm Hills (Thailand), Marketors, Royal Mougins (France); *Style—* Chris Woollams; ✉ e-mail chris@canceractive.com

WOOLLARD, Jessica Elizabeth Clare; da of William Woollard, and Isobel, *née* MacLeod; *Educ* St Paul's Girls' Sch, Univ of Manchester (BA); *Career* literary agent; dir Toby Eady Associates Ltd 1995–2005, literary agent The Marsh Agency 2006–; memb Soc of

W

Authors, memb Soka Gakkai Int (SGI-UK); *Recreations* travel, live music, books; *Style*— Ms Jessica Woollard; ⊠ The Marsh Agency, 50 Albemarle Street, London W1S 4BD (☎ 020 7297 4310, fax 020 7495 8961, e-mail jessica@marsh-agency.co.uk)

WOOLLEY, David Rorie; QC (1980); s of Albert Walter Woolley, of Wallingford, Oxon, and Ethel Rorie, *née* Linn; *b* 9 June 1939; *Educ* Winchester, Trinity Hall Cambridge (MA); *Career* called to the Bar Middle Temple 1962 (bencher 1988); recorder of the Crown Court 1982–94, inspr DOE Inquiry into Nat Gallery 1984; Liveryman Worshipful Co of Coopers; *Publications* Town Hall and the Property Owner (1965), Environmental Law (jtly, 2000, 2 edn 2009), History of the Middle Temple (jtly, 2011), Pataudi Nawab of Cricket (contrib, 2013); *Recreations* opera, real tennis, mountaineering; *Clubs* MCC; *Style*— David Woolley, Esq, QC; ⊠ Landmark Chambers, 180 Fleet Street, London EC4A 2HG (☎ 020 7430 1221)

WOOLLEY, Dr Paul Kerrison; s of Robert Charles Woolley (d 1979), and Hilda Kerrison, *née* Barnsley (d 2003); *b* 9 November 1939; *Educ* King Edward VI Sch Birmingham (Fndn Scholar), Univ of York (BA, DPhil); *m* 31 July 1976, Penelope Ann, da of Albert Ewart Baines; 2 s (Nicholas Kerrison *b* 26 Oct 1977, Robert Ewart *b* 10 June 1980); *Career* ptnr Murray & Co Birmingham 1965–67 (joined 1959), Esmée Fairbairn lectr in fin Univ of York 1971–76, specialist advsr House of Lords Ctee on EEC 1975–76, advsr IMF Washington DC 1980–83 (economist 1976–78, sr economist 1978–80); dir 1983–87: Baring Brothers & Co Ltd, Baring Investment Management, Baring International Investment Management, Baring Quantitative Management; ptnr Grantham Mayo Van Otterloo & Co Boston 1987– (dir 1998–2003), fndr and chm GMO Woolley Ltd London 2000–06 (md 1987–2000), chm GMO Europe 2003–06; sr fell The Paul Woolley Centre for the Study of Capital Market Dysfunctionality LSE 2007–, adjunct prof The Paul Woolley Centre for Capital Market Dysfunctionality Univ of Technol Sydney Aust 2007–, established The Paul Woolley Initiative for the Study of Capital Market Dysfunctionality Univ of Toulouse France 2007–15; author of various articles in academic and fin jls; hon prof Univ of York 2006–16 (hon fell 2003–06); memb Birmingham Stock Exchange 1964–67; Liveryman Worshipful Co of Broderers 1998– (Master 2010–11); Hon DUniv Univ of Technol Sydney 2011; *Recreations* walking, travel; *Clubs* Reform, City University; *Style*— Dr Paul Woolley; ⊠ London School of Economics, Houghton Street, London WC2A 2AE (☎ 020 7955 7477)

WOOLLEY, Prof Robert Peter; s of John S Woolley and Joan Grace Woolley; *b* 8 January 1954; *Educ* Eastbourne Coll, Royal Coll of Music, Inst of Educn Univ of London; *m* Sept 1982, Susan Jane, da of Michael Carrington; 2 da; *Career* harpsichordist, fortepianist, organist and conductor; concerts in UK, USA, Japan and throughout Europe since 1973, regular BBC and World Serv broadcaster, taught in Austria and Portugal, prof of harpsichord and historical performance RCM 1985–, memb Purcell Quartet; vice-chair of the jury Prague Spring Int Harpsichord Competition 2005; *Recordings* incl: Purcell – Complete Harpsichord Works, music by Handel, Frescobaldi, D Scarlatti, J S Bach, C P E Bach, Poglietti, Bohm, Sweelinck: complete keyboard works (in progress), Blow; *Recreations* walking, reading, architecture, photography; *Style*— Prof Robert Woolley; ⊠ Royal College of Music, Prince Consort Road, London SW7 2BS (☎ 020 7589 3643, rwoolley@rcm.ac.uk); e-mail info@woolleys.org.uk

WOOLLEY, Trevor Adrian; CB (2007); s of Harry George Woolley (d 1974), and Doreen Vera Woolley, *née* O'Hale (d 1961); *b* 9 August 1954; *Educ* Latymer Upper Sch Hammersmith, Peterhouse Cambridge (MA); *Career* MOD: admin trainee 1975–80, princ 1980–86, private sec to sec of the Cabinet 1986–89, dir of Procurement Policy 1989–93, head of Resources and Progs (Army) 1993–96, head of Resources and Progs (Prog Devpt) 1996–97, asst under-sec of state (Systems) 1997–98, DG Resources and Plans 1998–2002, cmd sec Land Command 2002–03, fin dir 2003–09, chief of corporate servs, defence equipment and support 2010–12, DG resources, defence equipment and support 2011; non-exec dir Oil and Pipelines Agency 2012–; lay memb Hounslow Clinical Commissioning Gp 2013–, memb Advsy Cncl on the Nat Archives 2014–; govr Latymer Upper Sch 1991–2014; *Books* Unnatural Selection – 50 Years of England Test Teams (2015); *Recreations* cricket, golf, walking; *Clubs* MCC; *Style*— Trevor Woolley, Esq, CB; ⊠ e-mail trvrwool@aol.com

WOOLLISCROFT, Andrew (Andy); s of John Woolliscroft, and Sheila, *née* Andersen; *b* 16 December 1955; *Educ* Adams' GS Wem, South Bank Poly London; *Partner* Zara Kane; 2 s (Samuel James Ishmael *b* 4 May 2000, Joshua Flynn Alexander *b* 6 Feb 2003); *Career* music agent: Bron Agency 1979–81, The Station Agency 1981–90, Primary Talent International 1990–; clients incl: Lou Reed, David Byrne, Patti Smith, John Cale, Ryuichi Sakamoto, The Proclaimers, Ron Sexsmith, The Sisters of Mercy; former clients incl: Thompson Twins, Tears For Fears, Julian Cope, OMD, Cocteau Twins, PIL, The Jesus & Mary Chain, Everything But The Girl, Björk, INXS, Spice Girls, Joe Jackson; *Recreations* golf, photography, family; *Style*— Andy Woolliscroft, Esq; ⊠ Primary Talent International, 10–11 Jockey's Fields, London WC1R 4BN (☎ 020 7400 4500, fax 020 7400 4501)

WOOLNER, Nigel; MBE (2016); s of Leonard Woolner (d 1987), of London, and Ida, *née* Chamberlain (d 1985); *b* 22 April 1940; *Educ* Latymer Upper Sch, Regent Street Poly Sch of Architecture (DipArch); *m* 1973, Carol Ann, *née* Smith; 2 s (Alexander *b* 27 Nov 1974, Thomas *b* 5 Aug 1979), 1 da (Philippa *b* 12 June 1977); *Career* architect; Chapman Taylor Partners: joined 1960, ptnr 1973–2005, dir 2005–07, conslt 2007–; major architectural projects incl: The Ridings Wakefield, The Market Place Bolton, The London Pavilion Piccadilly Circus, The Glades Bromley, The Exchange Putney, 172–182 Regent Street London, The Exchange Ilford, Priory Meadow Hastings, N1 Islington, Liberty Romford, Shires Leicester, Whitefriars Canterbury; professional practice examiner Architectural Assoc 1980–2011; Br Cncl of Shopping Centres: memb Bd 1996–2001, memb Awards Ctee 1996–2011, chm Awards Ctee 2001–05; fell Soc of Architect Artists 1990–; pres Bedford Park Soc 2005– (chm 1981–98), chm RSA House Panel 2000–05, memb Cncl RSA 2001–05; tstee Mills Williams Fndn 1995– (chm 2005–); Royal Coll of Music: chm Estates Ctee 2004–14, memb Cncl 2004–14; memb Orange Tree Theatre Building Ctee 2008–; govr Latymer Upper Sch 1985–2012; BCSC Award for Outstanding Serv 2005, Sceptre Lifetime Achievement Award 2008; memb RIBA, FRSA, FRCM 2015; *Books* ICSC Illustrated Architectural Guide to Vienna (with Carol Woolner, 1989), ICSC Illustrated Architectural Guide to Brussels (with Carol Woolner, 1994), 2nd ICSC Illustrated Architectural Guide to Vienna (with Carol Woolner, 1995), Venetian Sketchbook (2006), Illustrated Guide to Liverpool (with Carol Woolner, 2008); *Recreations* watercolour painting, exhibitions, Bedford Park Festival, Attendi Gallery, Royal Soc of Arts, Susie Baynham and Gallery Three, theatre, opera; *Clubs* Architecture, The Bond (pres 2005–06), Garrick; *Style*— Nigel Woolner, Esq, MBE, Dip Arch, RIBA, FRSA, FRCM; ⊠ 27 Queen Anne's Grove, Bedford Park, London W4 1HW (☎ 020 8994 4711, e-mail nwoolner@chapmantaylor.com)

WOOLRICH, John; *b* 3 January 1954; *Educ* Univ of Manchester (BA), Lancaster Univ (MLitt); *Career* composer; Northern Arts fell Univ of Durham 1982–85, composer in residence Nat Centre for Orchestral Studies London 1985–86, visiting lectr Goldsmiths Coll London 1986–87, composer in assoc Orch of St John's Smith Square 1994–95, lectr in music Royal Holloway Univ of London 1994–98, dir The Composers Ensemble 1989–, concerts dir Almeida Theatre 1999–, assoc artistic dir Aldeburgh Festival 2005–10 (guest artistic dir 2004), artistic assoc Birmingham Contemporary Music Gp 2004–, artistic dir Dartington Int Summer Sch 2010–13; visiting fell Clare Hall Cambridge 1999–2001, prof of music Brunel Univ 2010–13, artistic dir Mirepoix Musique 2013–; Hon FTCL; *Major works* Ulysses Awakes 1989, The Ghost in the Machine 1990, Viola Concerto 1993, Oboe Concerto 1996 (world première BBC Proms 1996), In The House of Crossed Desires 1996, Cello Concerto 1998, Violin Concerto 2008, Falling Down 2009, Capriccio 2009, Pluck from the Air 2013, To the Silver Bow 2014, The Voices 2014; *Style*— John Woolrich, Esq; ⊠ Faber Music, Bloomsbury House, 74–77 Great Russell Street, London WC1B 3DA

WOOLRIDGE, Jeremy Frederick; CBE (1998), DL (West Midlands); s of James Woolridge (d 1974), and Jean, *née* Crombie (d 2007); *b* 28 December 1944, Wolverhampton, W Midlands; *Educ* Tettenhall Coll, Univ of Manchester (BSc); *m* 30 Sept 1972, Susan, *née* Richards; 1 da (Angela Helen *b* 20 Nov 1975), 1 s (Christopher James *b* 11 March 1980); *Career* B E Wedge Ltd: joined Engrg Dept, gen mgmnt 1969, rising to md then chm 1987–; regnl chm CBI W Midlands 1994–96, past chm UK Galvanizers' Assoc, pres European Gen Galvanizers' Assoc, past vice-pres Engrg Employers' Fedn (past pres W Midlands branch); chm of govrs Tettenhall Coll 2005; High Sheriff W Midlands 2000–01; *Recreations* walking, growing orchids, supporting Wolverhampton Wanderers FC; *Clubs* Rotary Club (Wolverhampton); *Style*— Jeremy Woolridge, Esq, CBE, DL; ⊠ B E Wedge Holdings Ltd, Stafford Street, Willenhall, West Midlands WV13 1RZ (☎ 01902 630311, fax 01902 368078, e-mail jeremy.woolridge@wedge-galv.co.uk)

WOOLTON, 3 Earl of (UK 1956); Simon Frederick Marquis; also Baron Woolton (UK 1939), Viscount Woolton (UK 1952), and Viscount Walberton (UK 1956); s of 2 Earl of Woolton (d 1969, s of 1 Earl of Woolton, CH, PC, JP, DL, chm Lewis's and associated cos, min of Food 1940–43, min of Reconstruction and memb War Cabinet 1943–45, lord pres Cncl 1945 and 1951–52, chllr of Duchy of Lancaster 1952–55, chm Cons Pty 1946–55) by his 2 w (Cecily) Josephine, er da of Sir Alastair Penrose Gordon-Cumming 5 Bt (subsequently Countess Lloyd George of Dwyfor); *b* 24 May 1958; *Educ* Eton, Univ of St Andrews (MA); *m* 1, 30 April 1987 (m dis 1997), Hon Sophie, o c of 3 Baron Birdwood, *qv*; 3 da (Lady Olivia Alice *b* 16 April 1990, Lady Constance Elizabeth *b* 14 Oct 1991, Lady Claudia Louise *b* 3 March 1995); *m* 2, 28 Oct 1999, (Mary) Carol, da of Peter Davidson; *Heir* none; *Career* merchant banker S G Warburg & Co Ltd 1982–88, Woolton Elwes Ltd 1994–2000, New Boathouse Capital Ltd 2000–08, Quayle Munro Ltd 2008–, Quayle Munro Hldgs plc 2011–; tstee: Woolton Charitable Tst, Titsey Fndn, Balcarres Heritage Tst, Keats Shelley Meml Assoc; govr Tonbridge Sch; Liveryman Skinners Co; *Clubs* Royal and Ancient (St Andrews), White's, Brooks's, MCC, Swinley Forest Golf; *Style*— The Rt Hon the Earl of Woolton; ⊠ Clune Lodge, Tomatin, Inverness-shire IV13 7XZ

WOOSNAM, Ian Harold; OBE (2007, MBE 1992); s of Harold Woosnam, and Joan Woosnam; *b* 2 March 1958; *Educ* St Martins Modern Sch; *m* 12 Nov 1983, Glendryth, da of Terrance Mervyn Pugh; 1 s (Daniel Ian *b* 5 Feb 1985), 2 da (Rebecca Louise *b* 16 June 1988, Ami Victoria *b* 10 Sept 1991); *Career* professional golfer 1976–; tournament victories: News of the World under 23 match play 1979, Cacharel under 25 Championship 1982, Swiss Open 1982, Silk Cut Masters 1983, Scandinavian Enterprise Open 1984, Zambian Open 1985, Lawrence Batley TPC 1986, 555 Kenya Open 1986, Hong Kong Open 1987, Jersey Open 1987, Cepsa Madrid Open 1987, Bell's Scottish Open 1987 and 1990, Lancome Trophy 1987 and 1993, Suntory World Match-Play Championship 1987 and 1990, Volvo PGA Championship 1988, Carrolls Irish Open 1988 and 1989, Panasonic European Open 1988, Mediterranean Open 1990 and 1991, Monte Carlo Open 1990, 1991 and 1992, Epson Grand Prix 1990, US F & G Classic 1991, US Masters 1991, PGA Grand Slam of Golf 1991, Murphy's English Open 1993, Air France Cannes Open 1994, British Masters 1994, Johnnie Walker Classic 1996, Heineken Classic 1996, Scottish Open 1996, German Open 1996, Volvo PGA Championship 1997, Hyundai Motor Masters 1997, Cisco World Match Play Championship 2001; team events: Ryder Cup 1983, 1985 (winners), 1987 (winners), 1989 (winners), 1991, 1993, 1995 (winners), 1997 (winners), 2002 (non-playing vice-capt) and 2006 (capt, winners), Dunhill Cup 1985, 1986, 1988, 1989, 1990, 1991, 1993, and 1995, World Cup 1980, 1982, 1983, 1984, 1985, 1986, 1987 (team and individual winner), 1990, 1991 (individual winner), 1992, 1993, 1994, 1996, 1997 and 1998; finished top European Order of Merit 1987 and 1990, ranked number 1 Sony World Rankings 1991; *Recreations* snooker, water skiing, sports; *Style*— Ian Woosnam, Esq, OBE; ⊠ c/o IMG, McCormack House, Burlington Lane, London W4 2TH (☎ 020 8233 5300, fax 020 8233 5301)

WOOTTON, Adrian; s of Ronald Oliver Wootton, and Unity Wootton; *b* 18 May 1962; *Educ* UEA (BA, MA); *m* 1986, Karen Sarah Goodman; *Career* dir Bradford Playhouse 1986–89, founding dir Broadway Media Centre Nottingham 1989–93, acting dir BFI and head BFI Exhibition 1993–2002, ceo Film London 2003–; ceo Br Film Cmmn 2011–; dir: Shots in the Dark, Internet Crime, Mystery and Thriller Festival Nottingham 1991–2001; co-dir: Crime Scene, Festival of Crime and Mystery Genre, Nat Film Theatre 2000–; co-curator: Soundtracking, Festival of Popular Music and Cinema Sheffield 1999–2000; foreign conslt Noir in Festival Italy 1999–; advsr: London Film Festival 2003– (dir 1996–2002), Venice Film Festival 2004–; chair Sensoria Film and Music Festival Sheffield; memb Bd Creative Skillset Craft and Technical Bd 2011–; visiting prof of film and media Norwich Univ of the Arts 2012–; hon doctorate in the arts Norwich Univ of the Arts 2012, hon doctorate UEA 2014; memb: BAFTA, European Film Acad; *Publications* 100 Great Detectives (contrib, 1992), Celluloid Jukebox (jt ed, 1995), Black Friday & Selected Stories by Goodis (ed, 2006); contrib to The Guardian and various arts magazines; *Recreations* film, literature, music, theatre; *Clubs* Groucho, Soho House; *Style*— Adrian Wootton, Esq; ⊠ Film London, Suite 6.10, The Tea Building, 56 Shoreditch High Street, London E1 6JJ (website www.filmlondon.org.uk, Twitter @aojwFL_BFC)

WOOTTON, Prof David; s of Rev Canon R W F Wootton (d 1984), and Joan, *née* Earls; *b* 15 January 1952; *Educ* Peterhouse Cambridge (MA, PhD), Balliol Coll Oxford; *Partner* Dr Alison Mark; 2 c from previous m (Lisa *b* 30 April 1976, Thomas *b* 26 August 1985); *Career* prof of humanities Univ of Victoria Canada 1989–94, dean of arts Brunel Univ 1996–98, prof of history Queen Mary & Westfield Coll London 1998–2004, anniversary prof of history Univ of York 2004–; FRHistS 1986; *Publications* The Invention of Science (2015) and numerous other books and articles; *Style*— Prof David Wootton; ⊠ Department of History, University of York, Heslington, York YO10 5DD (email david.wootton@railhead.com)

WOOTTON, Sir David Hugh; kt (2013); s of James Wootton, and Muriel Wootton; *b* 21 July 1950, Bradford; *Educ* Bradford GS, Jesus Coll Cambridge (BA, MA); *m* 23 April 1977, Elizabeth Rosemary, da of Peter Knox; 2 da (Alexandra *b* 1978, Sophie *b* 1981), 2 s (James *b* 1979, Christopher *b* 1985); *Career* ptnr Allen & Overy 1979–2015; memb Law Soc 1975; Alderman for the Ward of Langbourn in the City of London, Sheriff City of London 2009–10, Lord Mayor City of London 2011–12; pres City of London Branch IOD, memb Bd TheCityUK; chllr City Univ 2011–12; chair: Northern Ballet, Local Partnerships; tstee Nat Opera Studio, steward Henley Royal Regatta, govr Bradford GS; Liveryman: Worshipful Co of Fletchers (former Master), City of London Slrs Co (former Master), Worshipful Co of Clockmakers, Worshipful Co of Glaziers (Sr Warden), Worshipful Co of Bowyers (memb Ct of Assts), Worshipful Co of Information Technologists (Master), Worshipful Co of Woolmen (memb Ct of Assts), Guild of Freemen (Master); hon Liveryman Worshipful Co of Security Professionals, memb Ct of Assts Co of Watermen and Lightermen; *Recreations* opera, rowing; *Clubs* Leander, Hawks' (Cambridge), Oxford and Cambridge, London Rowing, Athenaeum, East India; *Style*— Sir David Wootton; ⊠ City of London Corporation, Members' Room, Guildhall, London EC2P 2EJ (e-mail dhwootton@gmail.com)

WOOTTON, Robert John (Bob); s of William Robert Wootton (d 1987), of Marlow, Bucks, and Linda Rosalie, *née* Gyton; *b* 30 June 1955; *Educ* Oundle, UCL; *Career* trainee media exec Lintas Ltd 1974–81, successively trainee media exec, head of TV then assoc media dir Wight Collins Rutherford Scott Ltd 1981–85, media dir HDM Horner Collis Kirvan Ltd then Griffin Bacal Ltd 1985–94, ptnr De Saulles Associates media consultancy 1994–96, dir of media and advtg ISBA 1996–; MIPA 1986; *Recreations* active and passive participation in music, cookery, food and wine, mycology; *Style*— Bob Wootton, Esq

WORAM, Terence Annesley; s of Victor Henry Woram (d 1940), and Helena Mary, *née* Cox (d 1992); *b* 23 June 1933, Mutare, Zimbabwe; *Educ* Christian Brothers Coll Kimberley, Univ of Cape Town (BArch); *m* 14 Oct 1961, Patricia Eileen, da of Frederick Leslie Lawrence; 1 s (Michael Desmond b 27 Aug 1962, d 22 May 1980), 3 da (Catherine Ann b 17 Jan 1964, Frances Mary b 21 May 1965, Joanna Helen b 2 May 1967); *Career* Pallet and Price Salisbury Rhodesia 1953–56, Harrison and Abramovitz NY 1956–59, Trehearne Norman Preston and Ptnrs London 1960–64; ptnr: BL Adams Partnership London 1964–69, Green Lloyd and Adams London 1969–79; sr ptnr Terence Woram Associates 1979–; architectural awards: Richmond Soc 1983, Europa Nostra 1986, Aylesbury Soc 1988, Richmond Conservation-Design Awards 1993; rep cricket: combined SA Univs XI 1955, USA All Stars XI v W Indies 1958, Club Cricket Conf 1964; hon life memb Middx Cricket Bd; RIBA; *Recreations* cricket, travel, old Hollywood films; *Clubs* MCC (life memb), Richmond CC (hon memb), York House Soc (past chm); *Style*— Terence Woram, Esq; ✉ 48 Lebanon Park, Twickenham, Middlesex TW1 3DG

WORCESTER, Dean of; *see:* Atkinson, Very Rev Peter Gordon

WORCESTER, Bishop of 2007–; Rt Rev Dr John Inge; s of Geoffrey Inge (d 1959) and Elsie, *née* Hill (d 1968); *b* 26 February 1955, Folkestone, Kent; *Educ* Kent Coll Canterbury, Univ of Durham (BSc, MA, PhD), Keble Coll Oxford (PGCE), Coll of the Resurrection Mirfield; *m* 8 July 1989, Denise, *née* Longenecker (d 2014); 2 da (Eleanor b 17 Feb 1999, Olivia b 19 May 2004); *Career* ordained: deacon 1984, priest 1985; asst chaplain Lancing Coll 1984–86, sr chaplain Harrow Sch 1989–90 (jr chaplain 1986–89), vicar St Luke's Church Wallsend 1990–96, canon residentiary Ely Cathedral 1996–2003 (vice-dean 1999–2003), bishop of Huntingdon 2003–07; chair Cncl Archbishop's Examination in Theology 2012–, lead bishop on cathedrals and church buildings 2014–; tstee Common Purpose 2005–11 (tst protector 2011–); patron Worcs CCC 2007–; Hon DLitt Univ of Worcester 2011; Lord High Almoner 2013; *Publications* A Christian Theology of Place (2003), Living Love (2007); *Clubs* Athenaeum, Farmers; *Style*— The Rt Rev the Bishop of Worcester

WORCESTER, Prof Sir Robert Milton; KBE (2005), DL (Kent 2004); s of late C M Worcester, and late Violet Ruth Worcester; *b* 21 December 1933; *Educ* Univ of Kansas (BSc); *m* 1, 1958 (m dis), Joann, *née* Ransdell; 2 s; m 2, 1982, Margaret Noel, *née* Smallbone; *Career* conslt McKinsey & Co 1962–65, chief financial offr Opinion Research Corporation 1965–68; Market & Opinion Research International (MORI) Ltd: fndr 1969, md 1969–94, chm 1973–2005; pres World Assoc for Public Opinion Research 1983–84; int dir and chm Public Affrs Res Advsy Bd Ipsos Gp 2006–08, memb Advsy Bd GovNet 2008–; founding co-ed International Jl of Public Opinion Research1992–; visiting prof of govt LSE 1992– (govr 1995–, memb Cncl 1995–2005, hon fell 2005); chllr Univ of Kent 2006–; visiting prof: City Univ 1990–2002, Strathclyde Univ 1996–2001; hon prof: Univ of Kent 2002–, Univ of Warwick 2005–; memb: Ct Middlesex Univ 2001–, Cncl Univ of Kent 2002–; non-exec dir Medway Maritime Hospital NHS Tst 2002–04; pres Environmental Campaigns Ltd 2002–06, pres Inst of Business Ethics 2010–; vice-pres: European-Atlantic Group, Int Social Science Cncl UNESCO 1989–94, RSWT 1995–, Royal Soc for Nature Conservation 1995–, UNA 1999–; tstee: Magna Carta Tst 1995–, World Wide Fund for Nature (UK) 1988–94, Wildfowl and Wetlands Tst 2002–08; chm Pilgrims Soc 1993–2010 (vice-pres 2010–); govr Ditchley Fndn, ESU 2004–11; cmmr US-UK Fulbright Cmmn 1995–2005; co-chm Jamestown 400 Commemoration Br Ctee 2004–07, chm Magna Carta 2015 800th Anniversary Ctee 2010–; memb: Camelot Advsy Panel for Corporate Responsibility 2006–11, Advsy Bd European Business Jl, Nat Consumer Cncl 2002–06, Advsy Cncl Inst of Business Ethics 2004–, Advsy Bd Media Standards Tst 2006–; non-exec dir Kent Messenger Gp 2004–08, chm Maidstone Radio Ltd (CTR 105.4 fm) 2004–06; Kent ambass (appointed by Kent CC) 2003–, patron MRS 2012; Helen Dinerman Award World Assoc for Public Opinion Res 1996; Hon DSc Univ of Buckingham 1998, Hon DLitt Univ of Bradford 2001, Hon DUniv Middx 2001, Hon LLD Univ of Greenwich 2002, Hon DCL Univ of Kent 2006, Hon DCL Univ of Warwick 2012, Hon DLaws Richmond American Int Univ in London 2009; hon fell KCL 2007; Freeman City of London 2001; fell Market Res Soc 1997–, FRSS 2004–; *Books* Political Communications (co-ed, 1982), Political Opinion Polling: an International Review (ed, 1983), Private Opinions, Public Polls (co-author, 1986), Consumer Market Research Handbook (co-author, 3 edn 1986), We British (co-author, 1990), British Public Opinion (1991), Typically British (co-author, 1991), Dynamics of Societal Learning about Global Environmental Change (co-ed, 1992), The Millenial Generation (co-author, 1998), Explaining Labour's Landslide (co-author, 1999), The Next Leaders (co-author, 1999), Facing the Future (co-author, 2000), How to Win the Euro Referendum Lessons from 1975 (2000), The Big Turn-Off (co-author, 2000), Explaining Labour's Second Landslide (co-author, 2001), The Wrong Package (co-author, 2001), Explaining Labour's Landslip (co-author, 2005), Explaining Cameron's Coalition: How It Came About, An Analysis of the 2010 British General Election (co-author, 2011); *Recreations* choral music, gardening, castles; *Clubs* Reform, Beefsteak, Walbrook, The Brook NY; *Style*— Prof Sir Robert Worcester, KBE, DL; ✉ Ipsos MORI, 79–81 Borough Road, London SE1 1FY (☎ 020 7347 3000, fax 020 7347 3017, e-mail rmworcester@yahoo.com)

WORDSWORTH, Barry; s of Ron Wordsworth, and Kathleen, *née* Collins; *b* 20 February 1948; *Educ* Glyn GS, RCM (fndn scholar, Tagore Gold Medal, Watnet/Sargent Conducting Prize); *m* 1971, Ann, *née* Barber; 1 s (Benedict b 1984); *Career* princ conductor: Sadlers Wells Royal Ballet 1973–84, BBC Concert Orchestra 1989–2006 (conductor laureate 2006–); music dir: Brighton and Hove Philharmonic (and princ conductor) 1989–, Birmingham Royal Ballet 1990–, Royal Ballet Covent Garden 1990–95 and 2007–; Evening Standard Ballet Award for outstanding artistic achievement 1993; Hon DLitt Univ of Brighton 1996, Hon DUniv Central England 2004; RSM 1981, Hon FTCL 2006; *Recreations* cooking, swimming; *Style*— Barry Wordsworth, Esq; ✉ c/o Wray Armstrong, IMG, 616 Chiswick High Road, London W4 8AJ (☎ 020 8233 5800, fax 020 8233 5801)

WORDSWORTH, Prof (Bryan) Paul; s of Victor Pargiter Wordsworth, of Banstead, Surrey, and Dora Mary, *née* Beach; *b* 4 April 1952, Salisbury; *Educ* Whitgift Sch, Westminster Medical Sch Univ of London (MB BS); *m* 11 April 1981, Christine; 1 da (Megan Elizabeth b 9 Sept 1983), 2 s (Thomas William Heyford b 3 Nov 1985, Andrew Timothy b 10 Dec 1988); *Career* house physician and surgn Westminster Hosp 1975–76, SHO Mayday Hosp Croydon 1976–77, medical registrar Mayday Hosp and Croydon Chest Clinic 1977–78, registrar in rheumatology Middlesex Hosp 1979–80; Univ of Oxford: sr registrar in rheumatology/rehabilitation Nuffield Orthopaedic Centre 1980–87, research fell Nuffield Dept of Pathology 1983–85, research fell Nuffield Dept of Medicine 1987–92, clinical reader in rheumatology Nuffield Dept of Medicine, prof of rheumatology 1998–; governing body fell Green Templeton Coll Oxford 1992– (academic tutor then sr tutor 1995–2000, dean 2014–16); memb: Br Soc for Rheumatology, RSM, Br Assoc for Rheumatology and Rehabilitation, UK Skeletal Dysphasia Gp; govr Whitgift Sch 2014–; Michael Mason Prize Br Soc for Rheumatology 1992, Heberden Medal Br Soc for Rheumatology 2012; FRCP 1996 (MRCP 1978); Clinical and Biochemical Disorders of the Skeleton (jtly, 2005, 2 edn 2015), Association Scan of 14,500 SNPs in Four Diseases Identifies Autoimmunity Variants (jtly, 2007), Identification of multiple risk variants for ankylosing spondylitis through high-density genotyping of immune-related loci (jtly, 2013); *Recreations* cricket, gardening; *Clubs* Middleton Stoney Cricket, Old Whitgiftian Assoc; *Style*— Prof Paul Wordsworth; ✉ Tollgate Cottage, Lower Heyford, Bicester, Oxon OX25 5PE; Nuffield Orthopaedic Centre, Windmill Road, Headington, Oxford OX3 7LD (☎ 01865 741155, e-mail paul.wordsworth@ndorms.ox.ac.uk)

WORLEY, (Edward) Michael; CBE (1998), JP (1972); s of Sidney Clifford Worley (d 1963), and Mary Hilda (d 1968), da of Alfred Johnson, co-fndr Chad Valley Toy Co; *b* 29 March 1936; *Educ* Uppingham, Downing Coll Cambridge (MA); *m* 21 May 1966, Ann, *née* Bailey; 2 s (Andrew b 2 April 1971, Thomas b 14 June 1973), 1 da (Rachel b 5 March 1979); *Career* Steel Co of Wales Ltd (Port Talbot) 1957–62; William King Ltd (West Bromwich): joined 1962, md 1963–, chm 1973–; Unquoted Companies' Gp: chm Taxation Ctee 1979–2004, chm Exec 1993–2011, hon life pres Inst for Family Business 2013–; dep chm Wesleyan Assurance Soc 1993–2007 (dir 1980–2007); non-exec dir Birmingham Regnl Office Barclays Bank plc 1987–92; chm Sandwell TEC 1990–95, memb Cncl Birmingham Chamber of Industry and Commerce 1984–90, memb Bd Black Country Development Corp 1987–98, non-exec dir Black Country C of C and Industry 2001–04; pres: Nat Assoc of Steel Stockholders (now Nat Assoc of Steel Service Centres (NASS)) 1988–90, Fédération Internationale des Associations de Négociants en Aciers, Tubes et Métaux (FIANATM) 1995–97, Groupement Européen des Entreprises Familiales (GEEF, now Europe Family Businesses (EFB)) 2004–07; memb: Birmingham Diocesan Bd of Fin 1980–91, W Midlands Regnl HA 1982–93 (vice-chm 1990–93); tstee: Former United Birmingham Hosps Tst Funds 1998–2000, Birmingham Eye Fndn 1999–; chm Birmingham Botanical Gardens & Glasshouses 1981–99, govr Sandwell Coll 1988–2005; High Sheriff W Midlands 1997–98; Liveryman Worshipful Co of Founders; *Books* co-author: Regional Government (1968), Freedom to Spend (1971), Passing On (1973); *Recreations* gardening, sailing, reading; *Clubs* Buckland (Birmingham); *Style*— Michael Worley, Esq, CBE; ✉ William King Ltd, Atlas Centre, Union Road, West Bromwich, West Midlands B70 9DR (☎ 0121 500 4153, fax 0121 500 0453, e-mail michael.worley@williamking.co.uk)

WORRALL THOMPSON, Antony; s of Michael Worrall Thompson, and Joanna Brenda, *née* Duncan; *b* 1 May 1951; *Educ* King's Sch Canterbury, Westminster Coll (HND); *m* 1, 1975, Jill, *née* Thompson; m 2, 1983 (m dis), Militza Jane Hamilton, da of Hugh Miller; 2 s (Blake Antony Cardew, Sam Michael Hamilton); m 3, 7 Sept 1996, Jacinta Shiel; 1 s (Toby Jack Duncan), 1 da (Billie-Lara); *Career* chef; food and beverage mangr Coombe Lodge Hotel Essex 1972, head chef and mangr Golden Fleece Restaurant Brentwood 1972; head chef: Ye Olde Logge Brentwood 1974, Adriatico Restaurant Woodland Green 1976, Hedges Restaurant South Woodford 1977, Brinkley's Restaurant Fulham Rd 1978–79 (with 6 month sabbatical to France), Dan's Restaurant Chelsea 1980; Ménage à Trois: chef and patron Knightsbridge 1981, opened in Bombay 1983, opened New York 1985, opened in Melbourne 1986, sold 1988 (retains all consultancies); chef and patron Avoirdupois Kings Road 1984, opened Mise-en-Place Limited 1986, purchased KWT Foodshow 1988; chef and patron: One Ninety Queen's Gate 1989–97, Bistrot 190 1990–97, dell'Ugo 1992–97, Zoë 1992–97, Drones 1995–97, Woz Cafe Restaurant 1997–99, Wiz Restaurant 1998–2001, Bistrorganic 1999–2000, Notting Grill 2002–09, Kew Grill 2004–, The Greyhound Free House & Grill 2005–, The Lamb 2006–09, Barnes Grill 2006–09, Windsor Grill 2007–14, Windsor Larder 2008–13; md Simpsons of Cornhill plc 1993–97; columnist Daily Express and Sunday Express, capt quiz team on Question of Taste (Radio 4), appearances on various TV shows incl: Ready Steady Cook (BBC) 1995–2006, resident chef Food and Drink (BBC) 1997–2002, The Weakest Link (winner) 2002 and 2005, I'm a Celebrity – Get Me Out of Here 2003, Emmerdale 2008, presenter Saturday Kitchen (BBC) 2003–06, presenter Saturday Cooks! (ITV) 2006–07, presenter Christmas Cooks (ITV) 2006, presenter Daily Cooks Challenge (ITV) 2008–12; pres Real Food Campaign; patron: Middle White Pig Breeders Soc, Forest, North Yorks Smallholder Soc, Child Bereavement Charity, New British Welfare Tst; FHCIMA; *Awards* Meilleur Ouvrier de Grande Bretagne 1987 (life title), winner Mouton Rothschild menu competition 1988; *Books* The Small and Beautiful Cookbook (1984), Supernosh (1993), Modern Bistrot Cooking (1994), 30-Minute Menu (1995), Ready Steady Cook (with Brian Turner, 1996), The ABC of AWT (1998), Raw (autobiography, 2003), Food and Drink Cookbook (2002), 100 Best Recipes of Food and Drink (2002), Healthy Eating for Diabetes (2003), Little Book of Meat (2003), Antony Worrall Thompson's GI Diet (2005), Antony Worrall Thompson's Top 100 Beef Recipes (2005), Real Family Food (2005), The GI Diet Made Simple (2006), Antony's Weekend Cookbook (2006) Barbecues and Grilling (2006), The Diabetes Weight Loss Diet (2008), The Peoples Cookbook (2007), Saturday Cooks Cookbook (2008), The Sweet Life (2008), Fast Family Food (2008), Antony Makes It Easy (2010), The Essential Diabetes Cookbook (2010), Slow Cooking (2011), The Essential Low Fat Cookbook (2011); *Recreations* wine, antiques, art, interior design, gardening, sport, classical music, travel, pigs; *Clubs* Groucho; *Style*— Antony Worrall Thompson, Esq; ✉ e-mail antony@awtrestaurants.com, website www.awtonline.co.uk and www.awtrestaurants.com; The Greyhound Freehouse, Gallowstree Road, Rotherfield Peppard, Oxon RG9 5HT (☎ 01189 722227, e-mail greyhound@awtrestaurants.com); c/o Limelight Management, 10 Filmer Mews, 75 Filmer Road, London SW6 7JF (☎ 020 7384 9950, e-mail limelight.management@virgin.net, website www.limelightmanagement.com);

WORRICKER, Julian; *Educ* Epsom Coll, Univ of Leicester; *Career* radio presenter; staff reporter BBC Radio Leicester 1985–88, TV presenter BBC Midlands Today 1988–89, news ed Radio Leicester 1989–91, presenter Radio Five 1991–94; BBC Radio Five Live: joined as newsreader and reporter 1994, presenter Weekend Breakfast Prog and Nationwide 1994–98 (Sony Gold Radio Award 1997), presenter breakfast prog 1998–2003 (Sony Gold Radio Award 1999 and 2002, Best Radio Prog TRIC Awards 1999), presenter Worricker Prog 2003–06; BBC Radio 4: presenter You and Yours 2006–13, presenter Any Answers 2013–; also presenter BBC News 24, BBC World Serv and BBC Radio 4; *Style*— Julian Worricker, Esq

WORSLEY, Francis Edward (Jock); OBE (2002); s of Francis Arthur Worsley, and Mary, *née* Diamond; *b* 15 February 1941; *Educ* Stonyhurst, Sorbonne; *m* 12 Sept 1962, Caroline Violet, da of James Hamilton Grey Hatherell (d 1968); 2 s (Richard, Edward), 2 da (Miranda, Joanna); *Career* chm: The Financial Training Co Ltd 1972–91, Lloyd's Members' Agency Services Ltd 1994–2014; dir Lautro 1990–94; non-exec dir: The Cleveland Trust plc 1993–99, Reece plc 1994–98, Brewin Dolphin Holdings 2003–14, Accident Exchange Group plc 2004–06; memb Building Societies Cmmn 1991–2002; pres ICAEW 1988–89 (memb Cncl until 1996); complaints cmmr FSA (formerly SIB) 1994–2001; chm Cancer Research Campaign 1998–2002; Freeman: City of London, Worshipful Co of Chartered Accountants (Master 1992–93); FCA 1964; *Recreations* golf, wine, cooking; *Style*— F E Worsley, Esq, OBE, FCA; ✉ Brewin Dolphin Securities, 12 Smithfield Street, London EC1A 9BD

WORSLEY, His Hon Judge Paul Frederick; QC (1990); s of Eric Worsley, MBE, GM, and Sheila Mary, *née* Hoskin; *b* 17 December 1947, East Sheen, Surrey; *Educ* Hymers Coll Hull, Mansfield Coll Oxford (MA); *m* 14 Dec 1974, Jennifer Ann Avery, JP, da of late Ernest Avery; 1 s (Nicholas b 6 Sept 1975), 1 da (Charlotte b 26 Feb 1977); *Career* called to the Bar Middle Temple 1970 (Astbury scholar, bencher 1999, reader 2015); practising barr North Eastern Circuit 1970–2006, recorder Crown Ct 1987–2006 (asst recorder 1983–87), circuit judge (South Eastern Circuit) 2006–07, sr circuit judge Old Bailey 2007–16; additional judge Grand Court Cayman 2016–; memb Parole Bd 2007–13, course dir Judicial Studies Bd 2007–15; govr: Scarborough Coll 1997–2011, Leeds Girls' HS 2001–

W

05, Leeds GS 2005–08; tstee Stephen Joseph Theatre 2012–15; Freeman Worshipful Co of Coopers 2007, Freeman City of London, Freeman Worshipful Co of the Staple of Merchants of England (York); *Recreations* Spy prints, opera, croquet, dogs, collecting Georgian silver; *Clubs* Athenaeum; *Style*— His Hon Judge Paul Worsley, QC; ✉ Central Criminal Court, Old Bailey, London EC4M 7EH

WORSLEY-TAYLOR, Annette Pamela; MBE (2002); da of Sir John Godfrey Worsley-Taylor, 3 Bt (d 1952), and Anne, *née* Paget (now Anne, Lady Jaffray); *b* 2 July 1944; *Educ* Downham Sch Hatfield Heath; *m* Nov 1997, Anthony Sheil; *Career* fndr London Designer Collections 1975 (dir 1976–93); conceived, launched and organised London Designer Show 1991–92, organised and marketed London Fashion Week, fndr memb British Fashion Cncl 1983 (memb exec 1987–2000); *Recreations* fashion, design, music, theatre; *Style*— Ms Annette Worsley-Taylor, MBE; ✉ 3/57 Drayton Gardens, London SW10 9RU (✆ 020 7835 0222)

WORSWICK, Dr Richard David; *b* 22 July 1946; *Educ* Magdalen Coll Sch Oxford, New Coll Oxford (MA, DPhil); *m* 1970, Jacqueline Brigit Isobel, *née* Adcock; 3 da (Helen b 1975 d 2004, Catherine b 1978, Isobel b 1981); *Career* res asst SRC Dept of Inorganic Chemistry Univ of Oxford 1972–73, res product mangr Boots Co plc 1973–76; Harwell Laboratory UK Atomic Energy Authy: Mktg and Planning 1976–85, head Res Planning 1985–88, head Environmental and Med Sciences Div 1988–90; dir of Process Technol and Instrumentation AEA Industrial Technology 1990–91, Govt Chemist 1991–2002, chief exec Laboratory of the Govt Chemist (DTI Agency) 1991–96, chief exec LGC (Holdings) Ltd 1996–2005; memb Science and Technol Research Cncl 2013–, memb Cncl Science and Technol Facilities Cncl 2013–; chm: University Diagnostics Ltd 1997–2007, Pipeline Devpts Ltd 1998–2002, Promochem Ltd 2001–07, Cobalt Light Systems Ltd 2009–; dep chm LGC Group Holdings plc 2005–07; UK Entrepreneur of the Year (business products and servs) 2003; FRSC 1991; *Books* LGC: The Making of a Company (2011); *Recreations* listening to music, playing the violin, walking; *Style*— Dr Richard Worswick; ✉ Cobalt Light Systems Ltd, 174 Brook Drive, Milton Park, Abingdon, Oxfordshire OX14 4SD (e-mail richard.worswick@cobaltlight.com)

WORTH, Peter Herman Louis; s of Dr L H Worth (d 1982), and Ruth, *née* Niemeyer (d 1967); *b* 17 November 1935; *Educ* Marlborough, Trinity Hall Cambridge (MA, MB BChir), Middx Hosp Med Sch; *m* 8 Feb 1969, Judith Katharine Frances, da of Arthur Girling (d 1959), of Langham, Essex; 1 s (Hugo b 1970), 1 da (Anna b 1972); *Career* conslt urological surgn: UCH 1976, St Peter's Hosps 1976, Middx Hosp 1984 (now UCL Hosps), King Edward VII Hosp 1993; memb: Br Assoc of Urological Surgns, RSM; FRCS 1967; *Books* contrib chapters on urology in several medical textbooks; *Recreations* classical music, skiing, gardening; *Style*— Mr Peter Worth; ✉ Broad Eaves, Mill Lane, Broxbourne, Hertfordshire EN10 7AZ (✆ 01992 462827, e-mail peter.worth2@ntlworld.com)

WORTHEN, Prof John; s of Frederick Morley Worthen, and Dorothy Geach, *née* Barrett, of Northwood, Hartland and Bournemouth; *b* 27 June 1943; *Educ* Merchant Taylors' Sch, Downing Coll Cambridge (BA), Univ of Kent (MA. PhD); *m* 1983, Cornelia Linda Elfriede, da of Prof Helmut Rumpf; *Career* instructor Univ of Virginia 1968–69, jr res fell Univ of Edinburgh 1969–70; Univ Coll of Swansea: lectr in English 1970–85, sr lectr in English 1985–90, prof of English 1990–93; prof of D H Lawrence studies Univ of Nottingham 1994–2003; ind writer and biographer 2003–; *Books* D H Lawrence – The Early Years 1885–1912 (1991), The Gang: Coleridge, the Wordsworths and the Hutchinsons in 1802 (2001), D H Lawrence: The Life of an Outsider (2005), Robert Schumann: Life and Death of a Musician (2007), T S Eliot: A Short Biography (2009), The Cambridge Introduction to Samuel Taylor Coleridge (2011), The Life of William Wordsworth: A Critical Biography (2014); author of numerous pubns on D H Lawrence; *Recreations* music; *Style*— John Worthen; ✉ 386 Glenalmond Avenue, Cambridge CB2 8DY

WORTHINGTON, District Judge Adrian Joseph; s of Dennis Bernard Worthington, of Didsbury, Manchester, and Moya, *née* Owens; *b* 3 April 1958, Didsbury; *Educ* St Gregory's RC GS Manchester, Univ of Nottingham (BA), Coll of Law Chester; *m* Susie; 2 s (Joseph, Benedict), 1 da (Caitlin); *Career* Darlington & Parkinson Slrs: articles 1980–82, asst slr 1982–86, ptnr 1986–99; district judge (SE Circuit) 1999–; assessor Law Soc Family Law Panel 1999; memb: Law Soc Child Care Panel 1992–99, Legal Aid Ctee 1992–99 (chm 1996–99); memb N J Stag/Walnuts Alumni 1979–; *Recreations* football, walking, swimming, wine, film, computers; *Style*— District Judge Worthington; ✉ e-mail legalade@gmail.com

WORTHINGTON, Charles; MBE (2006); *Career* int hair stylist; owner and creative dir Charles Worthington salons; estab a portfolio of London salons, launched award-winning product ranges; twice winner British Hairdresser of the Year; involved with numerous charitable causes incl Look Good...Feel Better; *Books* City Hair, Big Date Hair, Holiday Hair, Big Day Hair; *Style*— Charles Worthington, Esq, MBE; ✉ 7 Percy Street, London W1T 1DQ (✆ 020 7299 8853, fax 020 7636 4531)

WORTHINGTON, Greville; s of Ben Worthington (d 1984), and Valerie, *née* Lawson, da of Sir Ralph Henry Lawson, 4 Bt; *b* 22 November 1963, Newcastle; *Educ* Ampleforth, Univ of Edinburgh; *m* 2 Sept 1995, The Hon Sophia Mary (Sophie), *née* Stapleton-Cotton, da of 5 Viscount Combermere (d 2000); 1 da (Io Bluebell b 20 March 1996), 2 s (Cy Benjamin b 23 Sept 1998, Rex Michael b 13 March 2002); *Career* M&G Fund Mgmnt 1988–92, dir Catterick Racecourse 1989–; judge Turner Prize 2002; tstee Henry Moore Fndn 1996–2013, tstee Yorks Sculpture Park 1999– (chm 2013–); sec Bamboo Soc; KM 1996; *Publications* Here & Now: Experiences in Sculpture (2001), Damien Hirst: Printmaker (2010), Keith Coventry: Black Bronze White Slaves (2012), Tim Walker: Dreamscapes (2013), 'Milk Snatcher' – The Thatcher Drawings by Gerald Scarfe (2015); *Recreations* contemporary art, bamboo collecting; *Style*— Greville Worthington, Esq; ✉ The Church of Saint Paulinus, Brough Park, Richmond, North Yorkshire DL10 7PJ

WORTHINGTON, Ian Alan; OBE (1999); s of Alan Worthington, of Stockport, and Bette, *née* Wright; *b* 9 August 1958, Stockport, Cheshire; *Educ* Stockport Sch Mile End; *Career* diplomat; FCO 1977–2014 (ret): Finance Dept 1977–78, third sec (scientific) Moscow 1980–82, mgmnt offr Lusaka 1982–85, press facilities offr News Dept 1985–88, second sec (commercial) Seoul 1988–91, dep head of mission Vilnius 1991–92, second sec (political) Kingston 1992–95, head Trade Office then consul gen Ekaterinburg 1995–98, inspr/reviewer Mgmnt Consultancy Servs 1998–2001, head of trade and investment Berlin 2001–06, ambass to Dominican Republic 2006–09 (concurrently non-resident ambass to Haiti), sabbatical (genealogy) 2010–14; *Recreations* family history, scuba diving; *Style*— Mr Ian A Worthington, OBE

WORTHINGTON, John; MBE (2016); s of Brig Roger Fraser Worthington (d 1984), and Mary, *née* Smith (d 1990); *b* 8 August 1938, London; *Educ* Gresham's, Architectural Assoc (travelling scholar, Holloway travelling scholar, AADipl), Univ of Philadelphia (MArch), Univ of Calif Berkeley; *m* 1963, Susan Mary, da of late Air Chief Marshal Sir John Davis; 1 s (Nicholas Fraser b 22 Dec 1969), 1 da (Samantha Jane b 27 June 1973); *Career* served Royal Enniskillen Fusiliers Berlin and Wuppertal 1957–59; architect: Alex Gordon & Partners 1964–65, Thompson, Berwick, Pratt & Partners Vancouver 1967–68, Ahrends, Burton & Koralek London 1969–70; res conslt Home Office 1970–71, fndr JFN Associates 1971–73, fndr ptnr Duffy Lange Giffone Worthington (now Duffy Eley Giffone Worthington) 1973–2010, external dir URBED 1975–78, ptnr DEGW 1976–90; prof of architecture and dir Inst of Advanced Architectural Studies Univ of York 1992–97, Graham Willis professorship Univ of Sheffield 2003–08, visiting prof Chalmers Univ of Technol Gothenburg 2000–03, visiting scholar Pembroke Coll Cambridge 2005–10, professorial fell Univ of Melbourne 2006–10; dir Acad of Urbanism 2009–14; chm CABE/RIBA Building Futures 2002–05, dep chm Regeneration Through Heritage 1994–2005; cmmr Ind Transport Cmmn 2011–; patron and past pres Urban Design Group; memb Bd London Thames Gateway Urban Devpt Corp 2004–09; Harkness fell Commonwealth Fund 1965–67; Hon DSc Univ of Reading 2016; Hon FRIBA 1998, FRSA; *Books* Office Planner (conslt ed and contrib, 1976), Planning Office Space (with Duffy and Cave, 1976), Industrial Rehabilitation (with Eley, 1984), Fitting Out the Workplace (with Konya, 1988), Reinventing the Workplace (1997, 2 edn 2005), Managing the Brief for Better Design (with Blyth, 2000, 2 edn 2010); contrib to numerous pubns; *Recreations* sailing, travel, walking; *Style*— John Worthington, MBE

WORTHINGTON, Nick; s of David Worthington, of Stoke Abbott, Dorset, and Bridgit, *née* Petter; *b* 19 October 1962; *Educ* Fitzharry's Comp Abingdon, Banbury Sch of Art and Design, St Martin's Sch of Art (BA); *Career* advtg copywriter; trainee TBWA London 1984, Symington & Partners London 1984–86, Jenner Keating Becker London 1986–88, Bartle Bogle Hegarty London 1988–96, Abbott Mead Vickers BBDO 1996–; winner numerous advtg awards incl 2 Gold Lions Cannes (for Levi's 501); motor cycle racer, BMCRC & KRC 250cc champion 1991; *Recreations* motorcycle racing; *Clubs* Br Motorcycle Racing; *Style*— Nick Worthington, Esq; ✉ Abbott Mead Vickers BBDO Ltd, 151 Marylebone Road, London NW1 5QE (✆ 020 7616 3500, fax 020 7616 3600)

WORTON, Prof Michael John; CBE (2014); s of William Asquith Worton (d 1973), and Nan Scott Elliot, *née* Little (d 2008); *b* 20 July 1951, Luanshya, Zambia; *Educ* Dumfries Acad, Univ of Edinburgh (MA, Gold Medal, F C Green Prize, PhD); *Career* lectr in French Univ of Liverpool 1976–80; UCL: lectr in French language and literature 1980–90, sr lectr in French 1990–94, prof of French 1994–98, vice-provost and Fielden prof of French language and literature until 2013 (ret); HE advsr Br Cncl; former non-exec dir Whittington Hosp NHS Tst; chair Heritage Without Borders; memb Cncl RADA, govr Conservatoire of Dance and Drama, memb Cncl of Mgmnt CARA, chair Strategic Directions Ctee Paris Sciences et Lettres; President's Medal Br Acad; Officier des Palmes Académiques, Medal of Honoured Worker in HE of the Repub of Kazakhstan, Chevalier de la Légion d'Honneur 2011; *Books* Intertextuality: Theories and practices (ed and introduced with Judith Still, 1990, reprinted 1993), Tournier: La Goutte d'or (1992, reprinted 1995), René Char: The Dawn Breakers/Les Matinaux (ed, introduced and translated, 1992), Textuality and Sexuality: Reading theories and practices (ed and introduced with Judith Still, 1993), Michel Tournier (ed, 1995), Typical Men (2001), Women's Writing in Contemporary France (2002), National Healths (2004), Liberating Learning: Widening Participation (ed and introduced with Patrick Derham, 2010), French Studies in and for the 21st Century (ed with Philippe Lane, 2011); also author of numerous book chapters, and of articles and reviews in learned jls; *Recreations* hill walking, theatre, opera; *Style*— Prof Michael Worton, CBE; ✉ mobile: ✆ 07919 110718, e-mail m.worton@ucl.ac.uk

WOSNER, John Leslie; s of Eugen Wosner, of London, and Lucy, *née* Chajes; *b* 8 June 1947; *Educ* Hasmonean GS, Univ of Sheffield (BA); *m* 17 March 1974, Linda Jose, da of Abraham Freedman; 1 da (Dina b 1975), 2 s (Jeremy b 1979, Daniel b 1982); *Career* articled clerk and mangr Arthur Andersen 1969–73, Tax Consultancy Div Harmood Banner CA's 1973–74; Pannell Kerr Forster: tax mangr 1974–76, ptnr 1976–2005, head Home Counties Tax Dept 1986–90, ptnr i/c Luton 1990–92, managing ptnr 1992–98, chm 1999–2005; conslt 2005–; Freeman City of London; ATII, FCA; *Recreations* history, reading, football, country walks; *Clubs* Travellers; *Style*— John Wosner, Esq

WOTTON, John Prier; s of (Arthur) John Wotton (d 1989), of Branscombe, Devon, and Persis Rubena, *née* Spearing; *b* 7 May 1954, Hounslow, Middx; *Educ* Latymer Upper Sch, Jesus Coll Cambridge (MA); *m* 1976, Linde Diana, *née* Lester; 2 da (Ruth b 1983, Sophie b 1988), 1 s (Tom b 1985); *Career* admitted slr 1978; ptnr Allen & Overy LLP 1984–2007 (joined 1976, conslt 2007–12); Law Soc: chm European Gp 2003–04, chm EU Ctee 2008–10, dep vice-pres 2009–10, vice-pres 2010–11, pres 2011–12, chm Educn and Trg Ctee 2012–15; memb Co-operation and Competition Panel for NHS-funded Services 2008–14, memb Panel Competition Cmmn 2013–4, external expert Monitor 2014–, Inquiry chair Panel Competition & Markets Authy 2014–; govr: Edward Latymer Fndn until 2015, Latymer Upper Sch; tstee Fauna & Flora Int, chm Kent Historic Buildings Ctee CPRE; *Recreations* cricket, gardening, music, conservation; *Clubs* Travellers, MCC; *Style*— John Wotton, Esq; ✉ Goddards Green, Angley Road, Cranbrook, Kent TN17 3LR (✆ 01580 715507, e-mail jpwotton@gmail.com)

WRACK, Matt; s of Robert Wrack (d 2003), and Winifred, *née* Town; *b* 23 May 1962, Manchester; *Career* joined London Fire Brigade 1983, gen sec Fire Brigades Union 2005–; *Style*— Matt Wrack, Esq; ✉ The Fire Brigades Union, Bradley House, 68 Coombe Road, Kingston upon Thames KT2 7AE (✆ 020 8541 1765, fax 020 8546 5187)

WRAGG, Lawrence de Villamil; eld s of Arthur Donald Wragg (d 1966), of Buxton, Derbys, and Lilia Mary May, *née* Adcock (d 1990); *b* 26 November 1943; *Educ* Rendcomb Coll, Univ of Bristol (BA), Sorbonne (Dip), Manchester Business Sch (MBA); *m* 1971 (m dis 2003), Aureole Margaret Willoughby Fowler; 2 da (Isabel (Mrs Richard Turkington) b 1977, Helen b 1988), 1 s (David b 1979); *Career* merchant banker; systems analyst National Data Processing Service 1968–69, mgmnt conslt Price Waterhouse Assocs 1969–72, exec dir Chemical Bank Int (formerly London Multinational Bank Ltd) 1974–82, dir Charterhouse Bank 1982–86, exec dir and head of capital markets Standard Chartered Merchant Bank 1987–88, dep chm Ketton Securities 1990–; chm: Lawrence Wragg Assocs Ltd 1989–, Proscyon Ptnrs Ltd 1990–2003; fndr and dir GBRW Ltd 1995–99, jt fndr and dir PXS Ltd 1997–2009; chm London Banks Composite Currency Ctee 1980–84; visiting lectr Manchester Business Sch 1980–82; memb Assoc of MBAs 1974–2013; CPRE: chm Cambridge City and S Cambs Ctee 1998–2000, chm Cambs Branch 1999–2001, nat vice-chm 2000–05, nat tstee and chm E of England Region 2005–10, chm Nominations Ctee 2010–13; memb Bd Nat Cambridgeshire 2016–; chm: The Ickleton Soc 1982–99, Cambridge Univ Musical Soc 2003 (memb 1999–); vice-chm: Ickleton PC 1988–90, Cam Valley Forum 2002–10; memb Fowlmere PC 2010– (vice-chm 2011–14, chm 2013–); hon treas Cncl Royal Musical Assoc 2006–11; tstee Musica Britannica 2006–11, tstee Handel Inst 2007–; chm of govrs Duxford Sch 1985–90; asst organist St Clement's Eastcheap 1987–89; AMBA 1974, MSI 1993, FRSA 1994; *Books* Composite Currencies (1984), Economist Guide to Eurobonds (contrib, 1990); *Recreations* music, mountaineering, skiing, running, opera; *Clubs* London Mountaineering (treas 1980–2003, pres 2003–06), Eagle Ski; *Style*— Lawrence Wragg, Esq; ✉ Clifton House, High Street, Fowlmere, Cambridgeshire SG8 7ST (✆ 01763 208729, e-mail ldevw@aol.com)

WRAGG, William; MP; *b* 11 December 1987, Stockport; *Educ* Univ of Manchester (BA, PGCE); *Career* MP (Cons) Hazel Grove 2015–; *Style*— William Wragg, Esq, MP; ✉ House of Commons, London SW1A 0AA

WRAXALL, Sir Charles Frederick Lascelles; 9 Bt (UK 1813), of Wraxall, Somerset; s of Sir Morville William Lascelles Wraxall, 8 Bt (d 1978), and Irmgard Wilhelmina Maria, *née* Schnidrig; *b* 17 September 1961; *Educ* Archbishop Tenison's GS Croydon; *m* 1983, Lesley Linda, da of William Albert Allan; 1 s (William Nathaniel Lascelles b 3 April 1987), 1 da (Lucy Rosemary Lascelles b 8 Oct 1992); *Heir* s, William Wraxall; *Career* civil servant DHSS 1978–80, trainee auditor Woolworths Pty Cape Town 1980–81, trainee accountant British Steel Corporation 1982–87, asst accountant Morgan Stanley Int 1987–; *Recreations* choral singing, football, stamp collection; *Style*— Sir Charles Wraxall, Bt

WRAY, Edward James; s of Philip Wray, and Brenda Margaret, *née* Collett; *b* 27 March 1968, Coulsdon, Surrey; *Educ* Tonbridge, Worcester Coll Oxford (MA); *m* 1 Nov 2003, Catherine May, *née* Pickering; 1 da (Amelia Rose Catherine b 10 Oct 2005); *Career* Shell

UK Ltd 1987–91, vice-pres Debt Capital Markets J P Morgan 1991–99; Betfair: co-fndr and dir 1999–, chief exec 1999–2003, chm 2006–; chief exec: TSE (Int) Ltd 2003–06, Betfair Aust 2006–07; Ernst & Young UK Emerging Entrepreneur of the Year 2002, Sharp Edge Entrepreneurs' Entrepreneur 2007; *Recreations* golf, sailing, food and wine; *Style—* Edward Wray, Esq; ✉ Betfair, The Waterfront, Hammersmith Embankment, Winslow Road, London W6 9HP (✆ 020 8834 8205, fax 020 8834 8010, e-mail edward.wray@betfair.com)

WRAY, Nigel; *b* 9 April 1948; *Educ* Mill Hill Sch, Univ of Bristol (BSc); *Career* chm: Fleet Street Letter plc 1976–90, Burford Holdings plc 1988–2001; non-exec chm Wilink plc; non-exec dir: Carlton Communications plc 1976–97, Singer and Friedlander plc 1986–2001, Peoples Phone 1989–96, Carlisle Holdings plc 1994–98, Chorion plc (formerly Trocadero plc) 1995–, Saracens plc 1995–, SkyePharma plc 1995–2000, Grantchester plc 1996–99, Columbus Group plc 1996–2000, Nottingham Forest plc 1997–99, Domino's Pizza Gp Ltd 1997–, Hartford plc 1998–2000, Safestore plc 1999–, Seymour Pierce Gp plc 2000–, Electric Word plc 2000–, Invox plc 2000–, Extreme Gp Ltd 2002–, Healthcare Enterprise Gp 2004–07, Prestbury Investment Holdings, Urbium; *Recreations* all sport (played rugby for Hampshire), cinema, musicals, reading a bit; *Style—* Nigel Wray, Esq

WRENCH, Peter Nicholas; s of Cyril Wrench (d 1991), and Edna Mary, *née* Bray; *b* 5 April 1957; *Educ* Clitheroe Royal GS, Royal Holloway Coll London (BA); *m* 1978, Pauline Jordan; 2 da (Jessica b 1983, Harriet b 1984); *Career* Home Office: joined 1980, private sec to Perm Sec 1987–88, Immigration and Nationality Dept 1988–93, Organised and International Crime Directorate 1993–2000, dep DG immigration and nationality 2000–03; dir of resettlement Prison Serv 2003–05, dir of strategy and asssurance Nat Offender Mgmnt Serv (NOMS) 2005–07, head of simplification project UK Border Agency until 2010; memb: Fitness to Practise Ctee Gen Pharmaceutical Cncl 2010– (dep chair 2015–), Equitable Life Payment Scheme Independent Review Panel HM Treasy 2011–, Interviewing Panel Judicial Appointments Cmmn 2012–, Planning, Resources and Performance Ctee Bar Standards Bd until 2015, Audit Ctee Office of the Immigration Services Cmmr, Review Body Judicial Conduct Investigations Office (formerly Office for Judicial Complaints), Independent Appeals Body PhonepayPlus, Panel Health and Care Professions Cncl 2014–, Disciplinary Tbnl CILEx Regulation 2015–; ind assessor of student finance appeals and complaints BIS and Welsh Govt 2015–; tstee RoadPeace 2014–; *Publications* Saint Dominic's Flashback: Van Morrison's Classic Album, Forty Years On (2012); *Recreations* obscure music, family, friends, edenontheline.co.uk, co-owner Tom Thumb Theatre Margate; *Style—* Peter Wrench, Esq

WREXHAM, Bishop of 2012–; Rt Rev Peter Malcolm Brignall; s of Charles V Brignall, and Marie E, *née* Stilz; *b* 5 July 1953, London; *Educ* Finchley Catholic HS, Barnet Coll of FE, Univ of Wales Swansea (Dip); *Career* ordained: deacon 1977, priest 1978; deacon St David's Mold 1977–78, asst priest Blessed Sacrament Connah's Quay 1978–79, asst priest Our Lady Star of the Sea Llandudno 1979–80, chaplain UC of N Wales Bangor 1979–84, asst priest St David and St Patrick Haverfordwest 1984–85, parish priest Parish of Knighton and Presteigne 1985–89, parish priest Our Lady and St James Bangor 1989–99, dean Cathedral of Our Lady of Sorrows Wrexham 1999–2012; chaplain: Bangor NHS Hospitals 1980–84, Carmelite Monastery Presteigne 1985–89, Bangor NHS Hospitals 1998–99, Wrexham NHS Hospitals 1999–2012; memb: Cncl Coll of Health Care Chaplains 1998–2008, Historic Churches Ctee for Wales and Herefordshire 2000–12, Liturgy Ctee Bishops' Conference 2010–12; govr and tstee Churches Tourism Network Wales 2008–; *Recreations* food and cooking from source to plate, strolling with a purpose (natural history, historic routes, visiting antiquities, etc), listening to classical music, learning to sign (BSL); *Style—* The Rt Rev the Bishop of Wrexham; ✉ Bishop's House, Sontley Road, Wrexham LL13 7EW (✆ 01978 262726, fax 01978 354257)

WREY, Benjamin Harold Bourchier; s of Maj Christopher Bourchier Wrey, TD (d 1976), and Ruth, *née* Bowden (d 2009); *b* 6 May 1940; *Educ* Blundell's, Clare Coll Cambridge (MA); *m* 19 Feb 1970, (Anne) Christine Aubrey Cherry, da of Col Christopher B Stephenson (d 1970); 1 da (Tanya b 20 Jan 1971); *Career* Pensions Advsy Dept Legal & General Assurance Society Ltd 1963–66, investment analyst Hambros Bank Ltd 1966–69; Henderson Global Investors Ltd (formerly Henderson plc): joined 1969, dir 1971–, jt md 1981–82, dep chm 1983–92, chm 1992–2004; dir: Henderson Electric & General Investment Tst plc 1977–2000, Henderson American Capital & Income Tst 1996–99, CCLA Investment Mgmnt Ltd 1998–2005; chm Institutional Fund Managers Assoc 1996–98, chm Charities Official Investment Fund 2005–09 (tstee 1998); former memb Fin Practitioners Panel City Disputes Panel, former memb Ctee Assoc of Investment Trust Companies (dep chm 1999–2002), memb Investment Ctee Univ of Cambridge Assistants Pension Scheme 2004–; memb: Advsy Cncl Nat Opera Studio 1996–2006, Cncl Br Heart Fndn 2003–10 (chm Investment Ctee 2003–10); *Recreations* shooting (represented Univ of Cambridge, Co of London, England and GB teams in full-bore target rifle shooting in UK and overseas, winner Bisley Grand Aggregate 1966 and 1969, runner up HM The Queen's Prize 1963 and 1977), alpine walking, fishing, ballet and opera; *Clubs* Boodle's, City of London, Hurlingham; *Style—* Benjamin Wrey, Esq; ✉ 8 Somerset Square, Addison Road, London W14 8EE (✆ 020 7603 4023)

WRIGGLESWORTH, Baron (Life Peer UK 2013), of Norton on Tees in the County of Durham; Sir Ian William Wrigglesworth; kt (1991); s of Edward Wrigglesworth, of Stockton on Tees; *b* 8 December 1939; *Educ* Stockton GS, Stockton Billingham Tech Coll, Coll of St Mark and St John Chelsea; *m* 1967, Patricia Susan, da of Hugh L Truscott; 2 s, 1 da; *Career* PA to Sir Ronald Gould as gen sec NUT 1966–68, head Co-op Pty Res Dept 1968–70, press and public affrs mangr Nat Giro 1970–74, divnl dir Smiths Industries plc 1975–2000; MP (Lab and Co-op 1974–81, SDP 1981–87) Thornaby, Teesside Feb 1974–83, Stockton South 1983–87; PPS: to Alec Lyon when Min of State Home Office 1974, to Roy Jenkins when Home Sec 1974–76; sec Manifesto Gp within Lab Party 1976–81, vice-chm Lab Econ Fin and Taxation Assoc 1976–81, oppn spokesman Civil Service 1979–81, SDP home affrs spokesman Nov 1982-May 1983, SDP econ and industrial affrs spokesman 1983–87, Alliance trade and industry spokesman 1987; chm: UK Land Estates Ltd 1995–2009, Prima Europe Ltd 1996–98, Government Policy Consultants Ltd (GPC) 1998–2000; dep chm John Livingston & Sons Ltd 1987–95; dir: CIT Holdings Ltd 1987–2003, Northern Devpt Co 1993–99; chm: Northern Region CBI 1992–94, Newcastle Gateshead Initiative 1999–2004, Baltic Centre for Contemporary Arts 2005–09, Port of Tyne 2005–12; govr Univ of Teesside 1993–2002; Freeman City of London, Liveryman Worshipful Co of Fndrs; *Recreations* walking, skiing, music; *Clubs* Reform, Groucho; *Style—* The Lord Wrigglesworth, kt; ✉ House of Lords, London SW1A 0PW (✆ 020 7219 8743, e-mail wrigglesworthi@parliament.uk)

WRIGHT, Alexander Andrew (Alex); s of Nicholas Wright, and Margaret Joan Wright; *b* 9 August 1965, London; *Educ* Winchester, Sidney Sussex Coll Cambridge (exhibitioner, MA); *m* 2005 (m dis 2011), Alison Ruth Webster; m 2, 31 May 2014, Mara Violato; *Career* commissioning ed CUP 1988–95, sr ed SPCK 1995–97, sr commissioning ed Blackwell Publishers 1997–99, dir SCM Press 2000–02, exec ed I B Tauris & Co Ltd 2003–; occasional journalist The Guardian; memb: Soc for Study of Theology 1993, Soc for the Study of Christian Ethics 1995, American Acad of Religion 1995, External Advsy Panel Faculty of Divinity Univ of Oxford 2001–, Classical Assoc 2005; memb Editorial Bd Political Theology 2003–15; *Books* Why Bother with Theology? (2002), Meanings of Life (2005), Exploring Doubt (2016); *Recreations* cinema, contemporary fiction, contemporary painting, running, hill walking, writing, medieval history, Italy and its culture, Norfolk; *Style—* Alex Wright, Esq; ✉ 73 Lime Walk, Headington, Oxford OX3 7AD (✆ 01865 682735, mobile 07989 333459); I B Tauris & Co Ltd, 6 Salem Road, London W2 4BU (✆ 020 7243 1225, fax 020 7243 1226, e-mail awright@ibtauris.com)

WRIGHT, Andrew Paul Kilding; OBE (2001); s of Harold Maurice Wright (d 1983), and Eileen Mary, *née* Kilding; *b* 11 February 1947; *Educ* Queen Mary's GS Walsall, Univ of Liverpool (BArch); *m* 10 Oct 1970, Jean Patricia, da of Alfred John Cross; 2 da (Hannah b 1973, Sarah b 1985), 1 s (Samuel b 1976); *Career* architect; Sir Basil Spence Glover & Ferguson 1973–78, chm Law & Dunbar-Nasmith 1999–2001 (assoc 1978–81, ptnr 1981–2001); Inverness Architectural Assoc: memb Cncl 1981–90, pres 1986–88; memb: Cncl RIBA 1988–94 and 1995–97, Ecclesiastical Architects and Surveyors Assoc 1989–; Royal Incorporation of Architects in Scotland: memb Cncl 1985–94 and 1995–99, pres 1995–97 (vice-pres 1986–88), membership convener 1992–94, convenor Conservation Working Gp 1994–95; delg Architects Cncl of Europe 1995–96, dir Bd of Glasgow 1999 Festival Co Ltd 1996–2003, Sec of State appointed Bd memb Ancient Monuments Bd for Scotland 1996–2003, cmmr Royal Fine Art Cmmn for Scotland 1997–2005; diocesan architect Dio of Moray Ross and Caithness 1988–98, architectural advsr Holyrood Progress Gp Scottish Parliament Corporate Body 2000–04, Conservation advsr Highland Buildings Preservation Tst 2001–13, hon architectural advsr Scottish Redundant Churches Tst 1996–; memb: Conservation Advsy Panel Hopetoun House Preservation Tst 1997–2007 (co-chair 2005–07), Church of Scotland Ctee on Artistic Matters 1999–2005, Saltire Soc Art in Architecture Awards Panel 2001–06, Historic Environment Advsy Cncl for Scotland 2003–09 (vice-chair 2003–06, chair Working Gp on Heritage Protection Legislation), Panel for the Fundamental Review of Historic Scotland Scot Exec 2003–04, Post Completion Advsy Gp Scottish Parl 2004–06, Conservation Ctee Nat Tst for Scotland 2007–11, Nat Casework Ctee Scottish Civic Tst 2011–, Historic Scotland Advsy Ctee 2012–15, Historic Scotland Transition Advsy Bd 2013–15; external examiner Robert Gordon Univ 1998–2003; tstee: Clan Mackenzie Charitable Tst 1998–, Cawdor Maintenance Tst 2010–, Cawdor Heritage Charity 2011–, Scottish Lime Centre Tst 2011–, Knockando Woolmill Trust 2015–; founding fell Inst of Contemporary Scotland; RIBA, PPRIAS, FRSA, FSA Scot; *Recreations* music, industrial heritage, fishing; *Style—* Andrew P K Wright, Esq, OBE, PPRIAS; ✉ Andrew P K Wright Chartered Architect and Heritage Consultant, 16 Moy House Court, Forres, Moray IV36 2NZ (✆ 01309 676655, e-mail andrew@andrewpkwright.co.uk)

WRIGHT, Dr Anne Margaret; CBE (1997); da of Herbert Holden (d 1973), of Kent, and Florence, *née* Kelly (d 1980); *b* 27 July 1946; *Educ* Holy Trinity Ind GS Bromley, KCL (Merchant Taylors' Co exhibition, William Henry Gladstone exhibition, BA, Lillian M Faithfull prize, Early English Text Soc prize, George Smith studentship, Inglis studentship, PhD); *m* 25 July 1970, Martin Wright, s of Robert Wright (d 1981), of London; 1 da (Amy Laura b 1982); *Career* lectr in English Lancaster Univ 1969–71, lectr rising to reader in modern English studies Hatfield Poly 1971–84, registrar for Arts and Humanities CNAA 1984–86, dep rector (academic) Liverpool Poly 1986–90, vice-chllr Univ of Sunderland (formerly Sunderland Poly) 1990–98, chief exec Univ for Industry 1998–2001, educnl conslt 2001–; chm: Sunderland Common Purpose 1990–97, Cmmn on Univ Career Opportunity 1993–98, Nat Lottery Cmmn 2005–13, Sch Teachers' Review Body 2008–11, Youth Music Theatre 2009–11; dir: The Wearside Opportunity 1991–93, Northern Sinfonia 1991–96, Northern Arts Bd 1991–95, Higher Educn Quality Cncl 1992–97, Wearside TEC 1993–98, Open Learning Fndn 1993–95; memb: Further Educn Funding Cncl 1992–96, Hong Kong Univ and Poly Grants Ctee 1992–2003, Cncl for Industry and HE 1994–99, NE C of C Cncl 1995–98, CBI Regnl Cncl 1996–98, Equal Opportunities Cmmn 1997–98, Armed Forces Pay Review Body 2002–08, Bar Standards Bd 2012–, Nursing and Midwifery Cncl 2013–; DL (Co of Tyne & Wear) 1997–2001; FRSA 1991, CCMI 1999– (CIMgt 1994, memb Bd of Companions); *Books* Literature of Crisis 1910–1922, Harley Granville Barker (critical biography in Modern British Dramatists 1900–1945, 1982), Tom Stoppard (critical biography in Dictionary of Literary Biography, 1982), Bernard Shaw's Saint Joan (1984); various publications on Shaw, Lawrence, T S Eliot and others; *Recreations* theatre, opera, the Arts; *Style—* Dr Anne Wright, CBE; ✉ Apartment 10, 206 Regents Park Road, London NW1 8AQ (✆ 020 7586 4707)

WRIGHT, Dr Anthony Wayland (Tony); s of Frank Wright, and Maud Wright; *b* 11 March 1948; *Educ* Kettering GS, LSE (BSc(Econ)), Harvard Univ (Kennedy scholar), Balliol Coll Oxford (DPhil); *m* 21 July 1973, Moira Elynwy, da of Edmor Phillips; 3 s (and 1 s decd); *Career* lectr in politics UCNW Bangor 1973–75, lectr, sr lectr then reader in politics Sch of Continuing Studies Univ of Birmingham 1975–92; MP (Lab): Cannock and Burntwood 1992–97, Cannock Chase 1997–2010; PPS to the Lord Chancellor 1997–98; prof of govt and public policy UCL 2010–; jt ed Political Quarterly; chm S Birmingham Community Health Cncl 1983–85, parent govr St Laurence Church Schs Northfield Birmingham 1989–92; hon prof Univ of Birmingham; *Books* Who Do I Complain To? (1997), Why Vote Labour? (1997), Socialisms: Old and New (1996), The New Social Democracy (jt ed, 1999), The British Political Process (ed, 2000), British Politics: A Very Short Introduction (2003); *Recreations* tennis, football, secondhand bookshops, walking, gardening; *Style—* Dr Tony Wright

WRIGHT, Bruce; *b* 8 May 1944; *Educ* Battersea GS, Univ of Leicester (BA, MA); *Career* financial controller Mars Confectionery 1978–81, fin dir Courage 1981–85, with Grand Metropolitan plc 1986–87, fin dir Meyer International plc 1987–97; interim fin dir: B&Q 1998, Allied Carpets 1998–99, Marks & Spencer Ventures 2000, First Choice Holidays plc 2001, Kwik-Fit Holdings plc 2002, Chubb plc 2003; ACIS 1971; *Style—* Bruce Wright, Esq; ✉ Bruval, Fairmead, Duffield Park, Stoke Poges, Slough, Berkshire SL2 4HY

WRIGHT, Christopher Norman; CBE (2005); s of late Walter Reginald Wright, and Edna May, *née* Corden; *b* 7 September 1944; *Educ* King Edward VI GS Louth, Univ of Manchester (BA), Manchester Business Sch; *m* 1, 15 March 1972 (m dis 1999), Carolyn Rochelle (Chelle), da of Lloyd B Nelson, of California, USA; 2 s (Timothy b 1973, Thomas b 1974), 1 da (Chloe b 1978); m 2, July 2003, Janice Anne Stinnes, *née* Toseland; 1 da (Holly b 1991); *Career* operator Univ and Coll Booking Agency Manchester 1965–67, formed Ellis Wright Agency (with Terry Ellis) 1967, changed name to Chrysalis 1968, chm 1985–, became international music publishing, film and radio gp Chrysalis Group plc, sold to BMG Rights 2011; chm QPR FC 1996–2001, chm and majority shareholder London Wasps RFC 1996–2008, chm and majority shareholder Digital Rights Gp 2004–13, chm Chysalis Vision 2015–; *Books* One Way or Another (autobiog. 2013); *Recreations* tennis, breeding racehorses, food and wine; *Clubs* Turf; *Style—* Christopher Wright, Esq, CBE; ✉ Chris Wright Consultancy, First Floor Suite, 181B High Street Kensington, London W8 6SH (✆ 020 7221 2382)

WRIGHT, Prof Crispin James Garth; *b* 21 December 1942; *Educ* Birkenhead Sch Cheshire, Trinity Coll Cambridge (exhibitioner, MA, PhD), ChCh Oxford (BPhil, DLitt); *m* Catherine; 2 s (Geoffrey, Arthur); *Career* jr research fell Trinity Coll Oxford 1967–69, lectr Balliol Coll Oxford 1969–70, lectr UCL 1970–71, research fell All Souls Coll Oxford 1971–78, Bishop Wardlaw prof Univ of St Andrews 1997–2008 (prof of logic and metaphysics 1978–2008), prof of philosophy Univ of Michigan Ann Arbor 1987–94 (James B and Grace J Nelson prof 1992–94), prof of philosophy NYU 2008–; visiting appts: lectr Univ of Pennsylvania 1983, prof Princeton Univ 1985–86, research prof in the Humanities Univ of Queensland 1989, fell Magdalen Coll Oxford 1991, prof Columbia Univ 1997–, global distinguished prof NY Univ 2002–; dir Northern Inst of Philosophy Univ of Aberdeen 2009–; prize fell All Souls Coll Oxford (by examination) 1969–71,

W

Fulbright scholar 1985–86, British Academy Research Readership 1990–92, Leverhulme personal research prof 1998–2003; FBA 1992, FRSE 1996, FAAAS 2012; *Books* Wittgenstein on the Foundations of Mathematics (1980), Frege's Conception of Numbers as Objects (1983), Realism: Meaning and Truth (1986), Truth and Objectivity (1992), The Reason's Proper Study (with R L V Hale, 2001), Rails to Infinity (2001), Saving the Differences (2003); *Style—* Prof Crispin Wright, FBA, FRSE, FAAAS

WRIGHT, Daphne; da of late Claud William Wright, and late Alison Violet, *née* Readman; *Educ* St Mary's Wantage; *Career* sec and editorial asst Chatto & Windus 1976–77, ed Hutchinson 1977–83, editorial dir Quartet 1983–84, Bellew Publishing 1984–86; winner Tony Godwin Meml Tst award 1980; chm Crime Writers' Assoc 2000–2001; memb: Crime Writers' Assoc 1989, Soc of Authors 1990; *Books* as Natasha Cooper: Festering Lilies (1990), Poison Flowers (1991), Bloody Roses (1992), Bitter Herbs (1993), Rotten Apples (1995), Fruiting Bodies (1996), Sour Grapes (1997), Creeping Ivy (1998), Fault Lines (1999), Prey to All (2000), Out of the Dark (2002), A Place of Safety (2003), Keep Me Alive (2004), Gagged and Bound (2005), A Greater Evil (2007), A Prisoned Mind (2008); as Clare Layton: Clutch of Phantoms (2000), Those Whom the Gods Love (2001); as N J Cooper: No Escape (2009), Lifeblood (2010), Face of the Devil (2011), Vengeance in Mind; *Recreations* reading, entertaining, talking; *Style—* Ms Daphne Wright; ✉ c/o Gregory & Company, 3 Barb Mews, London W6 7PA

WRIGHT, David; s of Kenneth William Wright, of Telford, Salop, and Heather, *née* Wynn; *b* 22 December 1966, Telford, Salop; *Educ* Wrockwardine Wood Comp, New Coll Telford, Wolverhampton Poly (BA); *m* 1 June 1996, Lesley; *Career* cncllr Oakengates Town Cncl 1989–2000 (sometime chm), cnclIr Wrekin DC 1989–97; worked on housing strategy Sandwell MBC 1988–2001; MP (Lab) Telford 2001–15; memb Unite; MCIH 1994; *Recreations* watching local football, exploring historic towns and cities; *Clubs* Wrockwardine Wood and Trench Labour, Dawley Social; *Style—* David Wright, Esq; ✉ House of Commons, London SW1A 0AA (☎ 020 7219 8331, fax 020 7219 1979, e-mail wrightda@parliament.uk)

WRIGHT, David Alan; OBE (1983); s of Herbert Ernest Wright, and Ivy Florence, *née* Welch; *b* 27 May 1942; *Educ* Surbiton GS, Univ of Birmingham (BSS); *m* 1966, Gail Karol, *née* Mesling; 4 s, 1 da; *Career* VSO Chad 1963, info offr BOT 1964, entered FCO 1965, asst private sec to min of state FO 1966–68, MECAS 1968–70, Baghdad 1970–73, Doha 1973–76, on secondment to DHSS 1976–78, FCO 1978–80, Durban 1980–83, Baghdad 1983–87, FCO 1987–92 (head Communications Dept 1988–90, Info Systems Div (Resources) 1990–92), consul-gen Atlanta 1992–97, ambass and consul-gen Qatar 1997–2002, jt head PROSPER HR Directorate FCO 2002–; cncllr Guildford BC 2003– (chair of licensing 2003–07, memb Exec 2007–12, dep ldr 2011–12), vice-chair Surrey Hills Bd 2005–, memb Surrey Probation Bd 2006–09, chair Surrey Save Credit Union 2011–; *Recreations* jogging, sailing, pottery, travel, music; *Clubs* Royal Over-Seas League; *Style—* David Wright, Esq, OBE; ✉ c/o Foreign & Commonwealth Office, Old Admiralty Building, London SW1A 2AH

WRIGHT, Sir David John; GCMG (2002, KCMG 1996, CMG 1992), LVO (1990); s of John Frank Wright, of Wolverhampton; *b* 16 June 1944; *Educ* Wolverhampton GS, Peterhouse Cambridge; *m* 3 Feb 1968, Sally Ann Dodkin; 1 s (Nicholas b 1970), 1 da (Laura b 1973); *Career* HM Dip Serv: third sec 1966, third later second sec Tokyo 1966, second later first sec FCO 1972, École Nationale d'Administration Paris 1975, first sec Paris 1976, private sec to Sec of Cabinet 1980, cnsllr (econ) Tokyo 1982, head of Personnel Servs Dept FCO 1985, dep private sec to HRH The Prince of Wales 1988–90; ambass Seoul 1990–94 (cmmr-gen UK Pavilion at Taejon Expo 1993), dep under sec for Asia, Americas, Africa and Trade Promotion FCO 1994–96, ambass Tokyo 1996–99, chief exec Br Trade Int 1999–2002, ret; vice-chm Barclays Capital 2003–11, vice-chm Barclays PLC 2011–; non-exec dir Balfour Beatty PLC 2003–07; non-exec dir AEA Technology 1994–95; chm of tstees Daiwa Fndn 2001–09, vice-pres China Br Business Cncl 2003–10, chm UK-Korea fndn 20016–12; chm govrs The Perse Sch (Cambridge) 2009–; memb Bd UK-Japan 21st Century Gp 2009–; Hon LLD: Univ of Wolverhampton 1997, Univ of Birmingham 2000; Grand Cordon of the Rising Sun (Japan) 1998; *Recreations* cooking, military history, golf; *Clubs* Garrick, Travellers, Saintsbury; *Style—* Sir David Wright, GCMG, LVO

WRIGHT, Dermot John Fetherstonhaugh; s of late J W Wright, of West Wittering, W Sussex, and late Dorothy, *née* Fetherstonhaugh; *b* 5 August 1944; *Educ* Wellington, Trinity Coll Cambridge (MA); *m* 1, 1969 (m dis 1992), Patricia Fergie; 2 da (Emma, Louise); m 2, 1992, Bridget Bovill; 1 da (Eleanor), 2 s (Francis, Charles); *Career* called to the Bar Inner Temple 1967, currently head of chambers, recorder SE Circuit; chm James Peek Tst (charity); govr W Wittering Primary Sch Sussex; *Recreations* yachting, playing piano, golf; *Clubs* W Wittering Sailing, Barnacle Cruising (pres); *Style—* Dermot Wright, Esq

WRIGHT, Gerald; s of William Arthur Reginald Wright (d 1967), and Olive Annie Neal Wright (d 1995); *b* 9 September 1935; *Educ* Monmouth Sch, Queens' Coll Cambridge (MA); *m* 1959, Elizabeth Ann, da of Dr William Edward Harris (d 1974), of Llandaff; 3 s (Jeremy, Mathew, William); *Career* Nat Serv 2 Lt Welch Regt 1954–56; dir Lintas London 1972–73, chm Lintas Scandinavia 1973–74, dep chm and md Lintas London 1974–80, md Thresher and Co Ltd 1980–81; Whitbread & Co: mktg dir (UK) 1981–82, chm Nat Sales Div 1982–83; chm and chief exec Lintas London 1983–89, regnl dir Eastern Europe, Austria and Switzerland Lintas Worldwide 1989–94, dir Posmark Ltd 1994–96, conslt Harris Wright & Associates 1994–, chm Popa Ltd 1997–98, dir Marketing Soc 1998–2000; fell Marketing Soc 2002–; *Recreations* reading, opera, walking, rugby, cricket, bridge, travel; *Clubs* Reform, Solus; *Style—* Gerald Wright, Esq; ✉ 4 Sovereign House, Royal Parade, Chislehurst, Kent BR7 6SN (☎ 020 8295 2755, e-mail gwright.4s@sky.com)

WRIGHT, Dr Helen Mary; *née* Kendal; da of Gordon Kendal, of Alyth, Perthshire, and Patricia, *née* Foggo; *b* 22 August 1970; *Educ* James Gillespie's HS Edinburgh, Lincoln Coll Oxford (MA, PGCE), Univ of Leicester (MA), Univ of Exeter (EdD); *m* 9 Jan 1993, Brian, s of Geoffrey Wright; 1 s (Harry McGregor b 3 June 2003), 2 da (Caitlin McGregor b 27 Oct 2006, Jessica McGregor b 9 Dec 2009); *Career* French and German teacher Reed's Sch Cobham 1993–95, head of dept Bishop's Stortford Coll 1995–97, head of dept and dep housemistress St Edward's Sch Oxford 1997–2000, headmistress Heathfield Sch Ascot 2001–03 (dep head 2000), headmistress St Mary's Calne 2003–12, headmistress Ascham Sch Sydney 2013–14, int educn advsr and speaker 2014–; teacher-educator and PGCE mentor 1997–2000; IB examiner and sr examiner (Higher Level) 1999–2009, ISI Inspector 2000–12; ed: ISMLA newsletter 1997–2000, Francophonie 1999–2002; academic conslt Scholastic Books 1998–2001, memb Oxford Today Ed Advsy Bd 2011–; memb: Assoc for Language Learning (ALL) 1993–, Ind Schs' Modern Languages Assoc (ISMLA) 1995– (also memb Ctee and patron), ASCL (SHA) 2000–12 (memb Cncl 2009–12), GSA 2001– (memb Cncl 2009–12, pres 2011), Bd ESU Scotland 2014–, Advsy Bd Figr (formerly Obrussa) 2014–, Bd Global Trails 2015–, Bd Changing the Chemistry 2015–, Cncl Malvern Coll 2015–; vice-chair Ind Schs Cncl 2011–12, assoc LSC Educn 2014–, Bd advsr Daneshill Prep Sch 2015–, UK and int educn advsr William Clarence Educn 2016–; memb Oxford Univ Soc Bd 2008– (dep chair 2016–); FRSA 2003, MInstD 2009; *Publications* Dr Behr-Sigel: A monk of the Eastern Church (trans), Learning through Listening (2004), Decoding Your 21st Century Daughter (2013), Powerful Schools: how schools can be drivers of social and global mobility (2016); numerous articles and reviews 1993–; *Recreations* reading, studying, travelling, gardening, jam-making, walking; *Clubs* Caledonian, Belgravia; *Style—* Dr Helen Wright

WRIGHT, Iain; MP; *b* 9 May 1972, Hartlepool; *Educ* Manor Comp, UCL; *Career* early career as accountant, worked for One NorthEast regnl devpt agency; MP (Lab) Hartlepool 2004– (by-election), PPS To Rosie Winterton, MP (as Min of State for Health) 2005–06; chair All Pty Parly Gp on Road Safety 2005–07, memb Modernisation of the House of Commons Ctee 2006–07, memb Public Accounts Ctee 2006–07; Parly under-sec of state Dept for Communities and Local Govt 2007–09, Parly under-sec of state for 14–19 reform and apprenticeships 2009; *Recreations* supporting Hartlepool FC; *Style—* Iain Wright, Esq, MP; ✉ House of Commons, London SW1A 0AA

WRIGHT, Ian; CBE (2015); s of late Peter Wright, and late Gladys, *née* Green; *b* 4 April 1958; *Educ* Desborough Sch Maidenhead, St Catharine's Coll Cambridge (MA); *m* 23 Dec 1987, Judith, da of Eric Gilboy, of Dean, Cumbria; 1 s (Iain), 1 da (Katie); *Career* pres Cambridge Student Union 1980–81, political organiser SDP 1981–85, PR conslt 1985–94, head of PR BHI 1994–97, dir of communications Boots The Chemists 1997–2000, dir of communications Diageo plc 2000–04, dir of corp relations Diageo plc 2004–14, DG Food and Drink Fedn 2015–; vice-pres SDP 1989–91, advsr to successive Lib Dem ldrs 1994–99 and 2005–; tstee: Children on the Edge 2010–, WAVE Tst 2015–; pres CIPR 2001; *Books* Reviving the Centre (with Roger Fox, 1989); numerous articles in nat media and other pubns; *Recreations* cricket, football, rugby, gardening, walking; *Style—* Ian Wright, CBE; ✉ ian.moatfarm@gmail.com

WRIGHT, Ian James; s of James Wilson Wright (d 1987), of Wishaw, and Dorothy, *née* Ormerod (d 1961); *b* 28 May 1948; *Educ* Liverpool Coll of Art (BA), RCA (MA); *m* 1976, Glenda, da of William Laverick Tindale; 3 s (Stewart James b 1978, Steven William b 1981, James Lewis b 1987); *Career* Kinneir Calvert Tuhill Design Consultants 1973–75; design dir: The Jenkins Gp 1975–1997, Cobalt Consultancy 1997–98 (formerly The Jenkins Group); fndr and design dir Air Design until 2011, Creative Communications; *Style—* Ian James Wright, Esq; ✉ 61 Warren Road, Chingford, London E4 6QR (☎ 020 8529 5373)

WRIGHT, Rt Hon Jeremy; PC (2010), QC (2010), MP; *b* 24 October 1972; *Educ* Taunton Sch, Trinity Sch NY, Univ of Exeter; *m* Yvonne; 1 da (Stephanie b 15 May 2005), 1 s (Elliott b 9 Dec 2010); *Career* called to the Bar Inner Temple 1996; MP (Cons): Rugby and Kenilworth 2005–10, Kenilworth and Southam 2010–; memb Constitutional Affrs Select Ctee 2005–07, opposition whip 2007–10, govt whip 2010–12, Lord Cmmr HM Treasy 2010–12, Parly under-sec of state for justice 2012–14, Attorney-Gen for England and Wales 2014–; chm All-Party Gp on Dementia 2007–10; *Style—* The Rt Hon Jeremy Wright, QC, MP; ✉ c/o Caroline Pickering, House of Commons, London SW1A 0AA (website www.jeremywrightmp.co.uk)

WRIGHT, Jerry; s of Gerald Wright, of Chislehurst, Kent, and Elizabeth, *née* Harris; *b* 28 October 1960, Beckenham, Kent; *Educ* Eltham Coll, Univ of Bristol (BA); *m* 15 July 1989, Ann Clare, *née* Faller; 1 s (Christopher James Faller b 14 April 1995), 1 da (Charlotte Elizabeth Faller b 29 June 1997); *Career* business gp dir Homecare and Personal Wash Lever Brothers Ltd 1993–97, sr corp strategist Unilever plc 1997–99, category dir Hair and Laundry Care IC SE Asia 2000–01, regnl brand dir Omo Greater Asia 2002–03, business unit head Birds Eye 2003–04, mktg and innovation dir Birds Eye 2005–06, business and mktg conslt 2007–08, chief exec Audit Bureau of Circulations Ltd 2008–15; global pres Int Fedn of ABCs 2010–14 (sec 2014–15); churchwarden St Bride's Church Fleet St 2010–, tstee St Bride's Fndn 2010– (vice-chm 2016–); Liveryman Worshipful co of Marketors 2008; *Recreations* rugby, cricket, music (especially opera), travel, food and drink, bridge, reading, crosswords; *Clubs* Reform, Solus; *Style—* Jerry Wright, Esq; ✉ e-mail jerrywwright@yahoo.co.uk

WRIGHT, Joe; *b* 1971, London; *Career* film dir; *Film* incl: Pride & Prejudice 2005, Atonement 2007, The Soloist 2009, Hanna 2011, Anna Karenina 2012; *Style—* Joe Wright, Esq; ✉ c/o Independent Talent Group, 40 Whitfield Street, London W1T 2RH

WRIGHT, (Ivor) John; s of Ivor Glynn Wright (d 1978), and Rosetta Amelia, *née* Forshow; *b* 22 June 1968, Clatterbridge, Wirral; *Educ* Univ of Glamorgan (BA); *Children* 1 da (Niamh Elizabeth b 27 Nov 2003); *Career* md Toyota/Lexus Europe, Saatchi & Saatchi 1994–2007 (previously md Saatchi & Saatchi London), Deutsche Bank 2001–02, Creativity, Innovation and Business Consultancy 2008, fndr Achilles Consulting Ltd 2008–09, dir Strategic Business Devpt McCann EMEA 2009–; MIPA, memb Mktg Soc; *Recreations* travel, food and wine; *Clubs* Solus, Soho House; *Style—* John Wright, Esq

WRIGHT, Karen Jocelyn Wile; da of Louis David Wile (d 1972), and Grace Carlin Wile (d 1998); *b* 15 November 1950; *Educ* Princeton HS, Brandeis Univ (BA), Univ of Cambridge (MA), London Business Sch (MSc); *m* 23 May 1981, Richard Bernard Wright, s of Bernard Gilbert Wright; 2 da (Louisa Karen b 17 April 1985, Rebecca Katherine b 21 Oct 1986); *Career* fndr and prop Hobson Gallery Cambridge 1975–84, Bernard Jacobson Gallery Cork St 1985, worked on Victor Willing catalogue Whitechapel Art Gallery 1986; Modern Painters magazine: fndr with Peter Fuller 1987, asst ed 1987–89, managing ed 1989–91, ed then ed-at-large 1991–; fndr (with David Bowie, Sir Tim Sainsbury and Bernard Jacobson) 21 Publishing 1998; AICA 1988; *Books* The Penguin Book of Art Writing (ed with Martin Gayford, 1998), Colour for Kosovo (ed with Daphne Astor, 1999), The Grove Book of Art Writing (2000), Writers on Artists (2002), Colour (2004); *Recreations* art, tennis, skiing, reading, relaxing with the teenagers; *Clubs* Groucho; *Style—* Mrs Karen Wright

WRIGHT, Malcolm; s of Alan Trevor Hurd Wright, and Patricia Anne Wright; *b* 29 May 1952; *Educ* St Peter's Sch York, Univ of Durham (BA), NCTJ (Dip Journalism); *m* 1981 (m dis 2010), Alison Cameron, da of Allan Cameron Walker; 2 da (Joanne Sarah b 7 June 1984, Grace Flora b 29 March 1989), 1 s (Samuel Allan b 28 Jan 1987); *Career* journalist; regnl newspaper journalist Keighley News, Yorkshire Evening Press and Northern Echo 1974–1980, freelance journalist The Guardian 1980–85, sr lectr in journalism Darlington Coll 1985–89; ITV Tyne Tees: joined as prodr and dir 1989, ed Current Affairs 1995, head of features 1996, controller of features 1997, head of network features 1998–2001, head of new media 2001–04; md ITV SignPost 2005–; vice-chm CODEWORKS Centre of Digital Excellence; founding dir Northern Film and Media; memb Labour Pty; *Awards* RTS Best Regnl Programme 1990 (for Mystery of the Derbyshire) and 1993 (for WarGames), British Environment and Media Awards Best Regnl Programme and RTS Special Award for Investigative Journalism 1992 (for Children of the Bomb), NY Film and TV Festival Best Factual finalist 1995 (for The Black File), San Francisco Golden Spire 1997 (exec prodr An Angel Passes By), Broadband Br Champion 2003, IVCA Clarion 2005, Disability Equality Employer of the Year 2005, National Reading Hero 2009, RADAR Human Rights Award for Doing IT Differently 2009, RTS Best Online Prodn 2010; Joining up the Dot.coms (2001); *Recreations* guitar, piano, crosswords, birdwatching; *Style—* Malcolm Wright, Esq; ✉ e-mail malcolm.wright@itv.com

WRIGHT, Dr Martin; s of Clifford Kent Wright (d 1969), of Sheffield, and Rosalie, *née* Mackenzie (d 1967); *b* 24 April 1930; *Educ* Repton, Jesus Coll Oxford (MA), LSE (PhD); *m* 26 July 1957, Louisa Mary (Lisa), da of John Osborne Nicholls (d 1974), of Yoxall, Staffs; 3 s (Edward b 1960, James b 1961, William b 1963), 2 da (Sophie b 1960 d 1993, Ellie b 1968); *Career* librarian Inst of Criminology Cambridge 1964–71, dir Howard League for Penal Reform 1971–81, information/policy devpt offr Victim Support 1985–94, consIt on mediation 1994–; vice-chair Restorative Justice Consortium 2001–07, sec European Forum for Victim/Offender Mediation and Restorative Justice 2002–06; visiting research fell Sch of Legal Studies Univ of Sussex 1995–2007, sr res fell Faculty of Health and Life Sciences De Montfort Univ 2007–; chm Lambeth Mediation Serv 1989–92; memb: Br Society of Criminology, Howard League for Penal Reform, Centre for Crime and Justice Studies, Conflict Research Soc; European Forum for Restorative Justice Award 2012; hon fell Inst of Conflict Resolution Sofia 2005, hon dip Polish Centre for Mediation Warsaw; *Books* The Use of Criminology Literature (ed, 1974), Making Good: Prisons, Punishment and Beyond (1982, reprinted 2008), Mediation and Criminal Justice: Victims, Offenders and Community (jt ed with B Galaway, 1989), Justice for Victims and Offenders: A Restorative Response to Crime (1991, 2 edn 1996), Restoring Respect for Justice: a Symposium (1999, trans into Polish 2005 and Russian 2007, 2 edn 2008), Civilising Criminal Justice: An International Agenda for Penal Reform (jt ed, 2013); *Recreations* suggesting improvements; *Style*— Dr Martin Wright; ✉ 19 Hillside Road, London SW2 3HL (☎ 020 8671 8037, e-mail martinw@phonecoop.coop, website www.martinwright.eu)

WRIGHT, Sir (John) Michael; kt (1990); s of Prof John George Wright (d 1971), and Elsie Lloyd, *née* Razey (d 1955); *b* 26 October 1932; *Educ* The King's Sch Chester, Oriel Coll Oxford (MA); *m* 25 July 1959, Kathleen Esther Gladys Wright, JP, da of Frederick Arthur Meanwell, MM (d 1945); 2 da (Elizabeth b 1961, Katharine b 1963), 1 s (Timothy b 1965); *Career* Nat Serv RA 1951–53, 2 Lt 1952, Lt 1953, TA 1953–56, TARO 1956–; called to the Bar Lincoln's Inn 1957 (bencher 1983, treas 2003), recorder of the Crown Court 1974–90, QC 1974, ldr SE Circuit 1981–83, chm Bar 1983–84 (vice-chm 1982–83), legal assessor RCVS 1984–90, judge of the High Court of Justice (Queen's Bench Div) 1990–2003, presiding judge SE Circuit 1995–98; chm of govrs Reigate GS 2004–08, chm of tstees Thalidomide Tst 2008–11 (tstee 1998–2011); hon fell Oriel Coll Oxford 2000; *Style*— Sir Michael Wright; ✉ Angel Shades, Angel Street, Petworth, West Sussex GU28 0BG

WRIGHT, Prof Michael Thomas; s of William George Wright (d 1985), and Lily May, *née* Turner; *b* 11 April 1947; *Educ* Sheldon Heath Sch Birmingham, Aston Univ (BSc, PhD); *m* 29 Aug 1970, Patricia Eunice, da of Stanley Douglas Cox; 1 da (Rebecca Michelle b 19 Sept 1977); *Career* apprentice EPE Co Birmingham 1963–68, res engr Redman Heenan Froude Worcs 1969–76, engrg dir Linear Motors Ltd Loughborough 1976–78, tech dir NEI Peebles Ltd Edinburgh 1978–82, engrg dir GEC Large Machines Rugby 1982–85, Molins plc 1985–90 (md Tobacco Div then gp md); Aston Univ: prof and head Dept of Mechanical and Electrical Engrg 1990–92, chm Aston Business School 1992–93, sr pro-vice-chllr 1994–96, vice-chllr 1996–2006, dir Aston Science Park Ltd 1997–2007; non-exec chm The 600 Group plc 1993–2006, non-exec dir ERA Technology 1994–2003, dir Birmingham Technology Ltd 1997–2006; governing dir Scot Engrg Trg Scheme Glasgow 1978–82; chair W Midlands HE Educn Assoc 2003–06; IEE Student Paper Award 1970, IEEE Petrochemical Indust Author Award 1981, IEE Power Div Premium for published work 1983; FIEE 1981, sr memb IEEE (USA) 1981, FREng 1988, FIMechE 1989, FRSA 1989, CMath 1994, FIMA 1994, CCMI 1997; *Style*— Prof Michael Wright, FREng; ✉ School of Engineering and Applied Science, Aston University, Aston Triangle, Birmingham B4 7ET (☎ 0121 204 4884, e-mail m.t.wright@aston.uk)

WRIGHT, Prof Sir Nicholas Alcwyn; kt (2006); s of Glyndwr Alcwyn Wright (d 1980), and Hilda Lilian, *née* Jones (d 1978); *b* 24 February 1943; *Educ* Bristol GS, Univ of Durham (MB BS), Univ of Newcastle upon Tyne (MD, PhD, DSc), Univ of Oxford (MA); *m* 1966, Vera, da of George Matthewson; 1 da (Claire Louise b 8 Aug 1968), 1 s (Graeme Alcwyn b 18 Dec 1969); *Career* Univ of Newcastle upon Tyne: demonstrator in pathology 1966–71, research fell 1971–74, lectr in pathology 1974–76, sr lectr 1976–77; Univ of Oxford: clinical reader in pathology 1977, Nuffield reader 1978, fell Green Coll 1979–80; dir of histopathology Hammersmith Hosp 1980–96, dean Royal Postgrad Med Sch (Imperial Coll Sch of Med following merger 1997) 1996–97; Imperial Coll Sch of Med at Hammersmith Hosp: vice-princ for research 1996–2001, dep princ 1997–2001; warden Barts and the London Queen Mary's Coll of Med and Dentistry 2001–11, head of tumour biology Barts Cancer Inst 2012–; Cancer Research (UK): dir Histopathology Unit 1988–2011, dir of clinical research 1991–96; chm Research for Health Charities Gp 1994; memb Cncl: Royal Coll of Pathologists 1982–96, Br Soc of Gastroenterology 1986– (pres 2003–04); pres Pathological Soc of GB and Ireland; Hon DSc: Univ of Herts, Univ of Durham, Univ of Bristol, Aston Univ; Hon MD Univ of St Andrews, Hon LLD Univ of Dundee 2012; hon fell Faculty of Medicine Imperial Coll London; FRCPath 1986, FMedSci 1998, FRCS 1999, FRCP 2001 (MRCP 1998); books and journal articles on tumour development; *Recreations* rugby football, cricket, squash, military history, cooking; *Clubs* Athenaeum; *Style*— Prof Sir Nicholas Wright; ✉ Centre of Tumour Biology, Barts Cancer Institute, Charterhouse Square, London EC1M 6BQ (☎ 020 7882 3575, e-mail n.a.wright@qmul.ac.uk)

WRIGHT, Capt Nicholas Peter (Nick); CVO (2010, LVO 1994); s of Lt Cdr Edward Wright (d 2001), and Peggy, *née* Askew (d 1993); *b* 11 November 1949, London; *Educ* Ampleforth, BRNC Dartmouth; *m* 1976, Venetia Ruth, *née* Berthon; 3 da (Serena Elizabeth b 10 July 1981, Sophie Victoria b 20 Nov 1985, Camilla Rose b 29 Oct 1990), 1 s (Charles Simon b 15 Nov 1983); *Career* RN: HM ships Whitby and Diomede 1969–73, Flag Lt to Flag Offr Medway 1973–75, HMS Norfolk 1976–77, Allied Forces Northern Europe Oslo 1978–80, HMS Lowestoft 1980–82, asst sec to Second Sea Lord 1982–84, staff BRNC Dartmouth 1985–87, HMS Illustrious 1985–87, sec to Flag Offr Portsmouth 1989–91, JSDC RNC Greenwich 1991, HM Yacht Britannia 1992–94, sec to ACNS 1995–97, CSO Personnel to Flag Offr Naval Aviation 1998–2000, sec to Dep SACLANT Virginia 2000–02, ret RN 2002; private sec to HRH The Princess Royal 2002–; tstee Wardour Chapel Tst 2014; Yr Bro Trinity House 2013; *Recreations* squash, cricket, tennis, skiing; *Clubs* Jesters; *Style*— Capt Nick Wright, CVO, RN; ✉ Buckingham Palace, London SW1A 1AA

WRIGHT, Rt Rev Prof Nicholas Thomas (Tom); s of Nicholas Irwin Wright, of Morpeth, Northumberland, and Rosemary, *née* Forman; *b* 1 December 1948; *Educ* Sedbergh, Exeter Coll Oxford (MA, DPhil, DD, Rugby Fives half blue), Wycliffe Hall Oxford; *m* 14 Aug 1971, Margaret Elizabeth Anne, da of Frank Albert Fiske; 2 s (Nicholas Julian Gregory b 9 June 1974, Oliver Thomas Irwin b 1 March 1981), 2 da (Rosamund Sarah Margaret b 17 March 1976, Harriet Elizabeth Ruth b 9 Feb 1979); *Career* ordained: deacon 1975, priest 1976; Merton Coll Oxford: jr res fell 1975–78, jr chaplain 1976–78; fell and chaplain Downing Coll Cambridge 1978–81, asst prof of New Testament lit McGill Univ Montreal 1981–86, hon prof Diocesan Coll Montreal 1981–86, fell, tutor and chaplain Worcester Coll Oxford 1986–93, univ lectr in theol Univ of Oxford 1986–93, canon theologian Coventry Cathedral 1992–99, dean of Lichfield 1993–99, canon theologian of Westminster 2000–03, 94 Bishop of Durham 2003–10, research prof of New Testament and early Christianity Univ of St Andrews 2010–; memb: Doctrine Cmmn C of E 1979–81 and 1989–95, Int Anglican Doctrinal Cmmn 2001–05, Lambeth Cmmn 2004; fell Inst for Christian Studies Toronto 1992–; memb: Soc of Biblical Lit 1982, Soc of New Testament Studies 1988; conslt and participant in numerous documentaries on Jesus and early Christianity incl: The Lives of Jesus 1996, Jesus Then and Now 1996, Heart of the Matter 1997, The Jesus Files 1998, Son of God 2001, The Apostles 2001, John Meets Paul 2002, Spring Journey 2004, Resurrection 2004, Evil 2005; poetry: Easter Oratorio (music by Paul Spicer, 2000), Advent Oratorio (music by Paul Spicer, 2009); participant in The Brains Tst 1999 and 2001; devised and presented numerous broadcast services 1995–2001; Br Acad Burkitt Medal for Biblical Studies 2014, Hon DD: Univ of Aberdeen 2001, Nashotah House 2006, Wycliffe Coll Toronto 2006, Univ of Durham 2007, Univ of St Andrews 2009, Univ of Northumbria 2010, Univ of London 2010, St Mary's Seminary and Univ Baltimore 2012, Iniv of Fribourg 2014, Univ of the South Tennessee 2015, Huron Coll Ontario 2015; Hon DLitt Gordon Coll 2003; Hon fell Downing Coll Cambridge 2003, Hon fell Merton Coll Oxford 2004; FRSEd 2014; *Books* Small Faith, Great God (1978), The Work of John Frith (1983), The Epistles of Paul to the Colossians and to Philemon (1987), The Glory of Christ in the New Testament (1987), The Interpretation of the New Testament 1861–1986 (1988), The Climax of the Covenant (1991), New Tasks for a Renewed Church (1992), The Crown and the Fire (1992), The New Testament and the People of God (1992), Who Was Jesus? (1992), Following Jesus (1994), The Lord and His Prayer (1996), Jesus and the Victory of God (1996), The Original Jesus (1996), For All God's Worth (1997), What St Paul Really Said (1997), Reflecting the Glory (1997), The Meaning of Jesus: Two Visions (with Marcus J Borg, 1999), The Way of the Lord (1999), The Myth of the Millennium (1999), Romans and the People of God (with S K Soderlund, 1999), Holy Communion for Amateurs (1999), The Challenge of Jesus (2000), Twelve Months of Sundays (3 vols, 2000, 2001 and 2002), Mark for Everyone (2001), Luke for Everyone (2001), Matthew for Everyone (2 vols, 2002), Paul for Everyone: Galatians and Thessalonains (2002), Paul for Everyone: The Prison Letters (2002), John for Everyone (2002), Romans (in New Interpreter's Bible, vol 10, 2002), The Meal Jesus Gave Us (2002), Paul for Everyone: 1 Corinthians (2003), Paul for Everyone: 2 Corinthians (2003), The Resurrection of the Son of God (2003), Quiet Moments (2003), Hebrews for Everyone (2003), Paul for Everyone: The Pastoral Letters (2003), For All the Saints? Remembering the Christian Departed (2003), Paul for Everyone: Romans (2004), The Scriptures, the Cross, and the Power of God (2005), Paul: Fresh Perspectives (2005), Scripture and the Authority of God (2005), Dictionary for Theological Interpretation of Scripture (jt ed, 2005), Judas and the Gospel of Jesus (2006), Evil and the Justice of God (2006), Simply Christian (2006), The Resurrection of Jesus: John Dominic Crossan and N T Wright in Dialogue (2006), The Cross and the Colliery (2007), Acts for Everyone (2007), Surprised by Hope (2008), Jesus: the Final Days (with Craig A Evans, 2008), Anglican Evangelical Identity (with J I Packer, 2008), Justification (2009), Lent for Everyone – Luke (2010), Virtue Reborn (2010), Lent for Everyone – Matthew (2011), Early Christian Letters for Everyone (2011), Revelation for Everyone (2011), The New Testament for Everyone (2011), Simply Jesus (2011), Lent for Everyone – Mark (2012), How God Became King (2012), The Case for the Psalms (2013), Paul and the Faithfulness of God (2013), Pauline Perspectives (2013), Creation, Power and Truth (2013), Surprised by Scripture (2014), Paul and his Recent Interpreters (2015), The Paul Debate (2015), Simply Good News (2015), God in Public (2016), The Day the Revolution Began (2016); *Recreations* music, poetry, golf; *Clubs* New (Edinburgh); *Style*— The Rt Rev Prof N T Wright; ✉ Hilton Cottage, Balbuthie, Elie

WRIGHT, Patrick Michael McKee; s of Ronald Cecil McKee Wright, (d 1973), of Westerham, Kent, and Mary Beatrice, *née* Minnitt (d 1995); *b* 8 October 1942; *Educ* Aldenham (head of sch, cricket and hockey capt); *m* 1969, Judy Theresa, da of Rodney Perry; 1 da (Rebecca Beatrice b 1972), 1 s (Alexander David McKee b 1976); *Career* mgmnt trainee Unilever 1960–63; sales and mktg dir Allen Lane Penguin Press/Longman 1970–73, md Penguin Books NZ 1973–78, gp dir sales and mktg Penguin Gp 1978–90, vice-chm Penguin Canada 1980–90, chm Penguin India 1986–90, chm Penguin Netherlands 1986–90, dir int devpt Penguin Gp 1987–90, chief exec Hodder & Stoughton 1990–93, md British Museum Co 1994–2001; non-exec dir W W Norton 1993–2014; vice-chm Book Marketing Cncl 1986–87, memb Br Library Publishing Advsy Bd 2002–07 (chm 2003–07); tstee Family Welfare Assoc 1997–2003, govr Froebel Coll 2003–06, memb Fin and Gen Purposes Ctee Univ of Roehampton 2004–10, govr Southville Jr Sch 2009– (vice-chm 2011–15, chm 2015–); vol Reading Help 2008–14; FRSA 2001; *Style*— Patrick Wright; ☎ 07879 884429

WRIGHT, Peter; s of Nigel Wright, and June, *née* Oxnam; *b* 13 August 1953; *Educ* Marlborough, Clare Coll Cambridge; *m* 3 Aug 1974, Dorothy; 3 s (Ben b 9 Sept 1981, William b 25 May 1987, Edward b 21 Sept 1990), 1 da (Alice b 30 March 1984); *Career* reporter Evening Post – Echo Hemel Hempstead 1975–78; Daily Mail: reporter 1979, asst news ed 1979–85, assoc news ed (foreign) 1985–86, asst features ed 1986–88, ed Femail 1988–91, asst ed (features) 1991–92, assoc ed 1992–95, dep ed 1995–98; ed Mail on Sunday 1998–2012, ed emeritus Associated Newspapers 2012–; *Style*— Peter Wright, Esq; ✉ Associated Newspapers, Northcliffe House, 2 Derry Street, Kensington, London W8 5TT

WRIGHT, His Hon Judge Peter Malcolm; s of His Hon Judge Malcolm Wright, QC, MBE (d 1959), and Peggy, *née* Prince, BEM (d 1980); *b* 5 June 1948; *Educ* Kingswood Sch Bath, Trinity Hall Cambridge (MA); *m* 26 April 1975, Eleanor Charlotte Madge, da of Lisson Palmer Madge, and Eleanor Madge, of Kendal, Cumbria; 1 da (Eleanor Louisa b 2 Feb 1979), 1 s (Edward Malcolm b 1 June 1981); *Career* VSO (Dakar, Senegal) 1967–68; called to the Bar Middle Temple 1974; legal assessor to Nursing and Midwifery Cncl 1990, recorder of the Crown Court 2000–06 (asst recorder 1998–2000), circuit judge 2006–; vice-chm Appeal Ctee CIMA 2000–06; tstee Lambeth Palace Library 2002–, memb Lambeth Partnership; govr Kingswood Sch Bath 1999–2016; *Recreations* music, walking, sailing, family life, retriever training; *Style*— His Hon Judge Peter Wright; ✉ Watford County Court, Cassiobury House, 11–19 Station Road, Watford WD17 1EZ (☎ 01923 699403)

WRIGHT, Peter Michael; s of late Dudley Cyril Brazier Wright, of Finchley, London, and Pamela Deirdre, *née* Peacock; *b* 6 March 1954; *Educ* Highgate Sch, RCM (Organ exhibitioner, ARCM, LRAM), Emmanuel Coll Cambridge (organ scholar, MA); *Career* sub organist Guildford Cathedral 1977–89, asst music master Royal GS Guildford 1977–89, organist and dir of music Southwark Cathedral 1989–, hon lay canon Southwark Cathedral 2014–; conductor: Edington Festival 1984–90, Guildford Chamber Choir 1985–94, Surrey Festival Choir 1987–2001; several recordings as organist and conductor released; RCO: memb Cncl 1990–97, hon sec Cncl 1997–2002, vice-pres 2003–05 and 2008–, pres 2005–08; memb Cathedral Organists' Conference; FRCO, FRSCM 2011, Hon FGCM; *Recreations* opera, theatre, travel, reading; *Style*— Peter Wright, Esq; ✉ 52 Bankside, Southwark, London SE1 9JE (☎ 020 7261 1291); Southwark Cathedral, London Bridge, London SE1 9DA (☎ 020 7367 6703, fax 020 7367 6725, e-mail peter.wright@southwark.anglican.org)

WRIGHT, Sir Peter Robert; kt (1993), CBE (1985); s of Bernard Wright (d 1981), and Hilda Mary, *née* Foster (d 1973); *b* 25 November 1926, Highgate, London; *Educ* Bedales, Leighton Park Sch Reading; *m* 1954, Sonya Hana, da of Yoshi Sueyoshi (d 1931); 1 s (Jonathan), 1 da (Poppy); *Career* dancer Ballets Jooss and Sadler's Wells Theatre Ballet 1947–55, ballet master Sadler's Wells Opera Ballet and teacher Royal Ballet Sch 1955–58, ballet master Stuttgart Ballet 1960–63, guest prodr BBC TV 1963–65, freelance choreographer and prodr 1965–69, assoc dir Royal Ballet 1970–76, dir Sadler's Wells Royal Ballet (relocated and renamed The Birmingham Royal Ballet in 1990) 1976–95 (dir laureate 1995–); special prof Sch of Performance Studies Univ of Birmingham 1990–; pres Benesh Inst of Choreology; vice-pres: Myashthenia Gravis Assoc, Royal Acad of Dance; Hon DMus Univ of London 1990, Hon DLitt Univ of Birmingham 1994; fell Birmingham Conservatoire of Music 1991; *Productions* noted for prodns of 19th century classical ballets incl The Sleeping Beauty, Swan Lake, Giselle, The Nutcracker, and Coppélia, for most major cos in Europe, The Royal Ballet, Birmingham Royal Ballet, Dutch and Canadian Nat Ballets, Royal Winnipeg Ballet, The Houston Ballet, Ballet de Rio de Janeiro, Stuttgart Ballet, Bavarian State Opera Ballet, Vienna State Opera Ballet, Star Dancers Ballet Tokyo, Ballet of the Colon Theatre Buenos Aires, Royal Swedish Ballet, Ballet de Santiago, Staatsballett Karlsruhe, Australian Ballet, Hungarian State Ballet, Sarasota Ballet; *Own Creations* The Mirror Walkers, The Great Peacock, A Blue Rose, Dance Macabre, Summertide, Namouna, Designs for Dancers, Quintet, Summer's Night, El Amor Brujo; *Awards* Standard Award for Most Outstanding Achievement in Ballet 1981, John Newson Award for Greatest Contribution to Sadler's Wells Royal Ballet

1988, Queen Elizabeth II Coronation Award Royal Acad of Dance 1990, Digital Premier Award 1991, Critics Circle Award for Distinguished Contribution to the Arts 1995, Nat Dance Award for Outstanding Achievement 2004, Critics Circle Centenary Award for Services to the Arts (Dance) 1913–2013 2013; *Recreations* music, theatre; *Style*— Sir Peter Wright, CBE; ✉ Flat 5 Wedderburn House, 95 Lower Sloane Street, London SW1W 8BZ

WRIGHT, Air Marshal Sir Robert Alfred; KBE (2004), AFC (1982); *b* 10 June 1947; *m* Maggie; 1 s, 1 da; *Career* joined RAF 1966, served 8 Sqdn Bahrain, served 17 (F) Sqdn RAF Brüggen 1971–75, qualified weapons instr 1975, joined Tactical Weapons Unit RAF Brawdy 1975, fighter weapons instr (exchange duty) US Navy 1976, Flight Cdr 208 Sqdn 1979, RAF Staff Coll 1982, served Operational Requirements Div MOD 1982–84, memb Directing Staff RAF Staff Coll 1984–87, cmd IX Sqdn RAF Brüggen 1987–89, Personal Staff Offr to Chief of the Air Staff MOD 1989–91, Station Cdr RAF Brüggen 1992–94, ACOS Policy & Plans NATO HQ High Wycombe 1994–95, Air Cdr Ops HQ Strike Command 1995–97, Mil Advsr to High Rep Sarajevo 1997–98, COS to Air Memb for Personnel and Dep C-in-C Personnel & Trg Command RAF Innsworth 1998–2000, ACOS Policy & Requirements (NATO appt) SHAPE 2000–02, UK Mil Rep NATO and EU 2002–; controller RAF Benevolent Fund 2007–, pres Naval 8/208 Sqdn Assoc; FRAeS 1997, FCMI 2006; *Recreations* golf, tennis, skiing; *Clubs* RAF; *Style*— Air Marshal Sir Robert Wright, KBE, AFC, FRAeS, FCMI

WRIGHT, Rosalind; CB (2001), QC (2006); *Educ* St Paul's Girls' Sch, UCL (LLB); *Career* called to the Bar Middle Temple 1964 (bencher 2001); in practice 2 Crown Office Row 1965–69; DPP: legal asst rising to sr legal asst 1969–81, asst dir South Div 1981–83, head Fraud Investigation Gp London 1983–87; SFA: head of prosecutions 1987–93, gen counsel and exec dir 1993–97; dir Serious Fraud Office 1997–2003; complaints cmmr London Metal Exchange 2010–; Middle Temple rep Bar Cncl 1998–2003 (chm Employed Bar Ctee 2002–03); chm Assoc to Combat Fraud in Europe 2001–03, chair Fraud Advsy Panel 2003–14, memb Regulatory Bd ACCA 2012–, memb European Anti-Fraud Office 2005–12 (chair 2005–07), memb Exclusion Ctee European Investment Bank 2012–; non-exec memb: Legal Services Gp DTI 2002–10, Bd OFT 2003–07, Inslovency Service Steering Bd 2006–12; vice-chm Jewish Assoc for Business Ethics 2003–; *Recreations* theatre, music, enjoying my children's achievements; *Style*— Mrs Rosalind Wright, CB, QC

WRIGHT, Simon James; *Educ* Imperial Coll London (BSc), KCL (PGCE); *Career* MP (Lib Dem) Norwich S 2010–15; ceo Nelson's Journey 2015–; *Style*— Simon Wright, Esq; ✉ Nelson's Journey, Smiles House, Octagon Business Park, Hospital Road, Little Plumstead, Norfolk NR13 5FH (website www.nelsonsjourney.org.uk)

WRIGHT, Stephen; *Educ* King's Sch Macclesfield, Queens' Coll Cambridge (BA, Volleyball half blue), Univ of Cambridge (PGCE); *m* Penny; 3 c; *Career* teacher Woolverstone Hall Sch, head of history Framlingham Coll (also housemaster), dep head Judd Sch Tonbridge 1994–98, headmaster Borden GS 1998–2004, headmaster Merchant Taylors' Sch Northwood 2004–; sec Kent and Medway Grammar Schs' Assoc, memb Kent Secdy Strategy Gp, memb Exec Secdy Heads' Forum; *Recreations* vegetable gardening, village cricket, theatre, opera; *Style*— Stephen Wright, Esq; ✉ Merchant Taylors' School, Sandy Lodge, Northwood, Middlesex HA6 2HT

WRIGHT, Dr Stephen Geoffrey; s of Stanley and Betty Wright, of Stoke-on-Trent; *b* 31 May 1944; *Educ* Longton HS, King's Coll Hosp Sch of Med London (MB BS); *m* 1, Jennifer Lynn, da of Francis T Clay (d 1998); 2 s (Matthew Stephen b 13 April 1979, Alexander Francis Stanley b 16 June 1982); m 2, Caroline Eveleigh, da of Anthony R Newman, OBE (d 2005); *Career* jr med posts in UK and Nigeria, sr lectr London Sch of Hygiene and Tropical Med and hon conslt Physician Hosp for Tropical Diseases 1980–95, assoc prof of med Coll of Med King Saud Univ Riyadh Saudi Arabia 1985–88, consltg physician Hosp for Tropical Diseases UCL Hosp Tst 1995–; hon physician King Edward VII's Hosp for Offrs London; FRCP 1991; *Books* Hunter's Tropical Medicine (assoc ed, 7 edn 1991); *Recreations* sport, gardening, music; *Style*— Dr Stephen Wright; ✉ Private Consulting Rooms, Emmanuel Kay House, King Edward VII Hospital, 37a Devonshire Street, London W1G 6QA (☎ 07973 536857 (appointments), fax 020 7467 4375, e-mail stephenwright1@doctors.org.uk)

WRIGHT, Sir Stephen John Leadbetter; KCMG (2006, CMG 1997); s of John Henry Wright, CBE (d 1984), and Joan, *née* Harvey (d 1993); *b* 7 December 1946; *Educ* Shrewsbury School, The Queen's Coll Oxford (BA); *m* 1, 1970 (m dis 2000); 1 da (Charlotte b 1977), 1 s (James b 1979); m 2, 2002, Elizabeth Abbott, da of F M B Duncan, MRCVS; *Career* HM Dip Serv: joined 1968, third sec Havana 1969–71, second sec FCO 1972–75, first sec (Br Info Servs) NY 1975–80, first sec UK Perm Rep to EC Brussels 1980–84, first sec FCO 1984–85, cnsllr Cabinet Office London 1985–87, cnsllr New Delhi 1988–91, cnsllr UK Perm Rep to EU Brussels 1991–94, dir (EU Affrs) FCO 1994–97, min Br Embassy Washington 1997–99, dir (Wider Europe) FCO 1999–2000, dep under sec FCO 2000–03, ambass to Spain 2003–07 (concurrently non-resident ambass to Andorra), ret Dip Serv; ceo Int Financial Servs London 2008–10; sr advsr: TheCityUK 2010–11, The Good Governance Gp 2008–14, Mitsui and Co Europe plc 2011–; *Recreations* rowing, music, art; *Clubs* London Rowing, Leander; *Style*— Sir Stephen Wright, KCMG; ✉ e-mail stephenjlwright@gmail.com

WRIGHT, Thomas Jeremy; s of Keneth Thomas Wright, and Eileen Ruth, *née* Broderick; *b* 18 September 1957; *Educ* Royal Russell Sch Croydon, Kingston Poly (BA, DipArch); *Family* 1 da (Lucy Wills-Wright b 20 Oct 1988); m, 22 June 2002, Carol Anne, da of Edward Mazgay; 1 da (Alice Mazgay b 8 May 2003); *Career* architect; dir of architecture Atkins 1991–, designer Burj Al Arab Dubai (world's tallest hotel) 1993; RIBA 1982; *Recreations* sailing; *Style*— Thomas Wright, Esq; ✉ Atkins, Woodcote Grove, Ashley Road, Epsom, Surrey KT18 5BW (☎ 01372 752064, e-mail tom.wright@atkinsglobal.com)

WRIGHT, Timothy Edward; s of Benjamin Wright, and Anne Wright; *b* 17 February 1960; *Educ* St Edmund's Sch Canterbury, Sunderland Poly (BA); *m* 1995, Michaela Hoskier, da of Peter Wordie, CBE; 2 s (Caspar b 6 Jan 1996, Tobias b 5 Jan 2002), 2 da (Fenella 8 May 1997, Rebecca 13 Nov 1999); *Career* Longman Publishing Gp: Euro sales manager 1984–90, int sales dir 1990–94; sales and mktg dir Churchill Livingstone Med Publishers 1994–98, chief exec Edinburgh Univ Press 1998–; chm Scottish Publishers Assoc 2001–04, dir Independent Publishers Guild 2001– (chm 2006–08); memb: Book Devpt Cncl of Publishers Assoc 1994–98, Scottish Arts Cncl Arts Project Ctee 1999–2002, Int Bd Publishers Assoc 2002–08, Cncl Academic and Professional Publishers, Cncl UK Publishers Assoc 2007–13; vice-chm The Book Trade Charity, tstee BTBS 2007–16; dir St Mary's Music Sch Edinburgh 2000–04, govr Ardvreck Sch Crieff 2015–; *Recreations* shooting, fishing, cricket, classical music; *Clubs* MCC, Farmers'; *Style*— Timothy Wright, Esq; ✉ The Tun, Holyrood Road, 12 Jackson's Entry, Edinburgh EH8 8PJ (e-mail timothy.wright@eup.ed.ac.uk)

WRIGHT, Tom Charles Kendal Knox; CBE (2007); s of David Wright, and Penelope Wright; *b* 22 February 1962; *Educ* Marlborough, Ealing Coll (BA), Inst of Mktg (DipM), DipMRS; *m* 1986, Charlotte, *née* Mudford; 1 da (Louise); *Career* gp marketing mangr Anchor Foods 1989–95, devpt dir Carlsberg-Tetley 1995–96, sales marketing dir Center Parcs UK 1996–99, md Saga Holidays and dir Saga Gp 1999–2002, chief exec VisitBritain 2002–09, chief exec Age UK Gp 2009–; chm Br Gas Tst 2009–13, chm Fuel Poverty Advsy Gp 2015–; Soc of Ticket Agents and Retailers 2002–15; tstee: Imperial War Museum 2004–12, Royal Green Jackets Museum 2012–, Imperial War Museum Devpt 2013–, Leeds Castle Fndn 2015–; *Recreations* running, walking, history; *Style*— Tom Wright, Esq, CBE

WRIGHT OF RICHMOND, Baron (Life Peer UK 1994), of Richmond upon Thames in the London Borough of Richmond upon Thames; Sir Patrick Richard Henry Wright; GCMG (1989, KCMG 1984, CMG 1978); s of Herbert Wright (d 1977), of Wellington Coll, and Rachel, *née* Green (d 2000); *b* 28 June 1931; *Educ* Marlborough, Merton Coll Oxford; *m* 1958, Virginia Anne, step da of Col Samuel John Hannaford (d 1983), and da of Irene Hannaford, MBE (d 2006); 2 s (Hon Marcus b 1959, Hon Angus b 1964), 1 da (Hon Olivia (Hon Mrs McDonald) b 1963); *Career* Nat Serv Lt RA; entered Foreign Serv 1955; served: Beirut, Washington, Cairo, Bahrain; private sec (overseas affrs) to PM 1974–77; ambass: Luxembourg 1977–79, Syria 1979–81; dep under sec FCO 1982–84, ambass Saudi Arabia 1984–86, perm under sec FCO and head Dip Serv 1986–91; dir: Barclays plc 1991–96, Unilever plc 1991–99, De La Rue plc 1991–2000, BP plc 1991–2001, BAA plc 1992–98; memb Security Cmmn 1993–2002; chm: RIIA 1995–99, Home-Start Int 2004–07; govr: Ditchley Fndn 1986–2011, Wellington Coll 1991–2001; House Magazine Award for Parly Speech of the Year 2004; hon fell Merton Coll Oxford 1987; FRCM 1994; KStJ 1990 (memb Cncl Order of St John 1991–97); *Clubs* Oxford and Cambridge; *Style*— The Lord Wright of Richmond, GCMG; ✉ House of Lords, London SW1A 0PW

WRIGHTSON, Prof Keith Edwin; s of Robert Wrightson (d 1968), and Evelyn, *née* Atkinson (d 1987); *b* 22 March 1948; *Educ* Dame Allan's Boys' Sch Newcastle, Fitzwilliam Coll Cambridge (Reddaway Scholar, Sr Scholar, MA, PhD); *m* 19 Aug 1972, Eva Mikusová, da of Jozef Mikus; 1 s (Nicholas Mikus b 6 Aug 1982), 1 da (Eliska Anne b 13 April 1989); *Career* research fell in history Fitzwilliam Coll Cambridge 1972–75, lectr in modern history Univ of St Andrews 1975–84; Univ of Cambridge: univ lectr in history 1984–93, reader in English social history 1993–98, prof of social history 1998–99; Jesus Coll Cambridge: fell 1984–99, dir of studies in history 1990–98, hon fell 2008; prof of history Yale Univ 1999–; visiting prof: Univ of Toronto, Univ of Alberta, Northumbria Univ, Univ of Newcastle; pres N America Conference on Br Studies 2013–15 (vice-pres 2011–13); memb Editorial Bd: Social History 1979–, Law and History 1982–89, Continuity & Change 1985–90, The Seventeenth Century 1985–, Rural History 1989–, Jl of Br Studies 2009–; Canadian Cwlth fell 1983–84; hon prof Univ of Durham; Hon DLitt Univ of Durham 2011, Hon DLitt Newcastle Univ 2013; FRHistS 1986, FBA 1996; *Books* Poverty and Piety in an English Village. Terling 1525–1700 (with David Levine, 1979, 2 edn, 1995), English Society 1580–1680 (1982, 2 edn 2003), The World We Have Gained (co-ed, 1986), The Making of an Industrial Society. Whickham 1560–1765 (with David Levine, 1992), Earthly Necessities: Economic Lives in Early Modern Britain (2000), Ralph Tailor's Summer: A scrivener, his city, and the plague (2011); also author of numerous essays and articles on English social history; *Recreations* modern jazz; *Style*— Prof Keith Wrightson, FBA; ✉ Department of History, Yale University, PO Box 208324, New Haven, Connecticut 06520–8324 (☎ 203 432 7248, fax 203 432 7587)

WRIGHTSON, Sir (Charles) Mark Garmondsway; 4 Bt (UK 1900), of Neasham Hall, Co Durham; s of Sir John Wrightson, 3 Bt, TD, DL (d 1983), and Hon Lady Wrightson (d 1998); *b* 18 February 1951; *Educ* Eton, Queens' Coll Cambridge; *m* 1975, Stella, da of late George Dean; 3 s (Barnaby, James, William); *Heir* s, Barnaby Wrightson; *Career* called to the Bar Middle Temple 1975; dir Hill Samuel Bank Ltd 1984–96; Close Brothers Corporate Finance Ltd: md 1996–99, chm 1999–2006; non-exec dir: Tees Valley Regeneration Ltd 2002–08, British Vita plc 2004–05, Amlin plc 2006–15, Domino Printing Sciences plc 2007–15; formerly: chm Corporate Finance Ctee London Investment Banking Assoc, memb Panel on Takeovers and Mergers; chm of tstees Bowes Museum 2008–; Liveryman Worshipful Co of Haberdashers; *Style*— Sir Mark Wrightson, Bt

WRIGLEY, Prof Christopher John (Chris); s of Arthur Wrigley (d 1999), of Shipton Gorge, Dorset, and Eileen Sylvia, *née* Herniman (d 2008); *b* 18 August 1947, Woking, Surrey; *Educ* Kingston GS, UEA (BA), Birkbeck Coll London (PhD); *m* 11 Sept 1987, Margaret, da of late Anthony Walsh; *Career* lectr in economic history Queen's Univ Belfast 1971–72, reader in economic history Loughborough Univ 1984–88 (lectr 1972–78, sr lectr 1978–84); Univ of Nottingham: reader in economic history 1988–91, prof of modern Br history 1991–2012, head Sch of History and Art History 2000–03, emeritus prof of modern Br history 2012–; ed The Historian 1993–98; Historical Assoc: memb Cncl 1980–2008, a vice-pres 1992–95, dep pres 1995–96, pres 1996–99; Lab History Soc: memb Exec Ctee 1983–2005, vice-chm 1993–97, chm 1997–2001, vice-pres 2012–; memb Cncl Economic History Soc Cncl 1983–92, 1994–2000 and 2002–08, a vice-pres Royal Historical Soc 1997–2001; chm Loughborough Lab Pty 1977–79 and 1980–85 (treas 1973–77), exec memb Loughborough Trades Cncl 1981–86, memb Consultative Cncl Arkwright Soc 2011–12 (tstee 2012–); Leics cncllr 1981–89 (ldr of Lab Gp 1986–89), Charnwood borough cncllr and dep ldr Lab Gp 1983–87; Parly candidate: (Lab) Blaby 1983, (Lab and Co-op) Loughborough 1987; Hon LittD UEA 1998; FRHistS; *Books* David Lloyd George and The British Labour Movement (1976), A J P Taylor – A Complete Bibliography (1980), A History of British Industrial Relations Vol 1 1875–1914 (ed, 1982), Vol 2 1914–1939 (ed, 1986), and Vol 3 1939–79 (ed, 1996), William Barnes – The Dorset Poet (1984), Warfare Diplomacy and Politics (ed, 1986), Arthur Henderson (1990), Lloyd George and the Challenge of Labour (1990), On the Move (jt ed, 1991), Lloyd George (1992), Challenges of Labour (ed, 1993), British Trade Unions 1945–95 (ed, 1997), The First World War and the International Economy (ed, 2000), British Trade Unions Since 1933 (2002), Winston S Churchill: A Biographical Companion (2002), A Companion to Early Twentieth Century Britain (ed, 2003), The Emergence of European Trade Unionism (jt ed, 2004), A J P Taylor: Radical Historian of Europe (2006), Churchill (2006), The Second Labour Government (jt ed, 2011), The Industrial Revolution: Cromford, The Derwent Valley and the Wider World (ed, 2015); *Recreations* swimming, walking; *Style*— Prof Chris Wrigley; ✉ School of History, University of Nottingham, Nottingham NG7 2RD (e-mail chris.wrigley@nottingham.ac.uk)

WRIGLEY, Prof Sir Edward Anthony (Tony); kt (1996); s of Edward Ernest Wrigley (d 1953), and Jessie Elizabeth, *née* Holloway (d 1976); *b* 17 August 1931; *Educ* King's Sch Macclesfield, Univ of Cambridge (MA, PhD); *m* 2 July 1960, Maria Laura, da of Everhard Dirk Spelberg (d 1968); 3 da (Marieke b 1961, Tamsin b 1966, Rebecca b 1969), 1 s (Nicholas b 1963); *Career* William Volker res fell Univ of Chicago 1953–54, lectr in geography Univ of Cambridge 1958–74; Peterhouse Cambridge: fell 1958–79, tutor 1962–64, sr bursar 1964–74, hon fell 1997; Hinkley visiting prof Johns Hopkins Univ 1975, Tinbergen visiting prof Erasmus Univ Rotterdam 1979, prof of population studies LSE 1979–88, sr res fell All Souls Coll Oxford 1988–94; Univ of Cambridge: prof of economic history 1994–97, master Corpus Christi Coll 1994–2000; co dir Cambridge Gp for the History of Population and Social Structure 1974–95; memb Inst for Advanced Study Princeton 1970–71, pres Manchester Coll Oxford 1987–96, pres British Acad 1997–2001 (treas 1989–95); laureate Int Union for the Scientific Study of Population 1993, Fndr's Medal RGS 1997, Leverhulme Medal Br Acad 2005; Hon DLitt: Univ of Manchester 1997, Univ of Sheffield 1997, Univ of Bristol 1998, Univ of Oxford 1999, Univ of Leicester 1999; Hon DSc Univ of Edinburgh 1998, Hon DScSocSci Queen Mary 2004; hon fell LSE 1997; FBA 1980; *Books* Industrial Growth and Population Change (1961), English Historical Demography (ed, 1966), Population and History (1969), Nineteenth Century Society (ed, 1972), Towns in Societies (ed with P Abrams, 1978), Population History of England (with R S Schofield, 1981), Works of Thomas Robert Malthus (ed with D Souden, 1987), People, Cities and Wealth (1987), Continuity, Chance and Change (1988), English Population History (with R S Davies, J Oeppen and R S Schofield, 1997), Poverty, Progress and Population (2004), Energy and the English Industrial Revolution (2010), The Early English Censuses (2011), The Path to Sustained Growth (2016); *Recreations* gardening; *Style*— Prof Sir Tony Wrigley, FBA; ✉ 13 Sedley Taylor Road, Cambridge CB2 8PW (☎ 01223 247614)

WRIGLEY, (William) Matthew; s of Rev William Vickers Wrigley (d 1998), of Rillington, N Yorks, and Margaret, *née* Hunter (d 2006); *b* 3 July 1947; *Educ* Westminster (Queen's scholar), King's Coll Cambridge (scholar, MA); *m* 17 July 1971, Susan Jane, da of Thomas Pratt; *Career* admitted slr 1972; ptnr: Biddle & Co London 1975–78, Dibb Lupton Broomhead Leeds 1978–96, Wrigleys Leeds 1996–; cncllr N Yorks CC 1985–89; memb Law Soc 1972; *Style*— Matthew Wrigley, Esq; ✉ Wrigleys, 19 Cookridge Street, Leeds LS2 3AG (☎ 0113 244 6100, fax 0113 244 6101, e-mail matthew.wrigley@wrigleys.co.uk)

WRONG, Henry Lewellys Barker; CBE (1986); s of Henry Arkel Wrong, and Jean, *née* Barker; *b* 20 April 1930; *Educ* Trinity Coll Univ of Toronto (BA); *m* 18 Dec 1966, Penelope Hamilton, da of Mark Richard Norman, CBE, of Much Hadham, Herts; 2 s (Mark Henry b 1967, Sebastian Murray b 1971), 1 da (Christina Jocelyn b 1970); *Career* admin Met Opera NY 1952–64; dir: programming Nat Arts Centre Ottawa 1964–68, Festival Canada Centennial Prog 1967, dir Barbican Centre for the Arts 1970–90, Euro Arts Fndn 1990–; chm: ADAPT 1988–96, Spencer House (London) 1990–94, LSO 1990–; tstee: ROH 1989–95, Henry Moore Fndn 1990–2007 (memb Advsy Ctee 2007–), Royal Fine Arts Cmmn 1995–2003; conslt Rothermere Inst for American Studies Oxford 2000; memb RSA 1988 (fell Arts Ctee); Liveryman Worshipful Co of Fishmongers 1987; Hon DLitt City Univ 1985; Offr Class Order of Merit (France) 1985, Hungarian Medal of Culture 1989, Centennial medal Canada 1967; *Clubs* White's, Badminton and Racket (Toronto); *Style*— Henry Wrong, Esq, CBE; ✉ Yew Tree House, Much Hadham, Hertfordshire SG10 6AJ (☎ 01279 842106)

WROTTESLEY, 6 Baron (UK 1838); Sir Clifton Hugh Lancelot de Verdon Wrottesley; 14 Bt (E 1642); s of Hon Richard Wrottesley (d 1970), and Georgina, now Mrs Jonathan Seddon-Brown; suc gf (5 Baron, sixteenth in descent from Sir Walter Wrottesley, a chamberlain of the Exchequer under Edward IV and himself third in descent from Sir Hugh de Wrottesley, KG (one of the original members of the Order), who fought with the Black Prince at Crécy) 1377; *b* Aug 1968, Dublin; *Educ* Eton, Univ of Edinburgh, Royal Military Acad Sandhurst; *m* 14 July 2001, Sascha, da of Urs Schwarzenbach; 3 s (Hon Victor Ernst Francis de Verdon b Jan 2004, Hon Magnus Vivian Otto de Coughton b June 2006, Hon Luca Urs Richard de la Wyke b March 2011) 1 da (Hon Isla Astrid Florence b Dec 2014); *Heir* s, Hon Victor Wrottesley; *Career* patron of three livings; dir: Natural Burial Co, FromVineyardsDirect, Br Bobsleigh & Skeleton Assoc; conslt: Noble Rot Fine Wine Portfolio Management, Torrance Yachts; *Clubs* White's, Turf, St Moritz Tobogganing, Corviglia Ski, Skinner's Guild, St Moritz Bobsleigh; *Style*— The Rt Hon the Lord Wrottesley; ✉ New Quadrant Partners, Ltd, 22 Chancery Lane, London WC2A 1LS

WU, Prof Duncan; s of Spencer Yin-Cheung Wu, of Sydney, Aust, and Mary, *née* Sadler; *b* 3 November 1961, Woking, Surrey; *Educ* Woking GS for Boys, Woking Sixth Form Coll, St Catherine's Coll Oxford (BA, DPhil); *m* 1, 5 Dec 1997 (m dis 2008), Caroline Beatrice, *née* Carey; m 2, 7 June 2011, Catherine Payling, MBE; *Career* British Acad postdoctoral research fell 1991–94, prof of English Univ of Glasgow 1999–2000 (reader 1995–99); Univ of Oxford: lectr in English 2000–03, prof of English language and literature 2003–08, fell St Catherine's Coll; prof Georgetown Univ USA 2008–; pres Charles Lamb Soc 2012; memb: Soc of Authors 1993–, British Assoc for Romantic Studies 1995–, German Soc for the Study of English Romanticism 1999–; tstee: Charles Lamb Soc 1991–, Keats-Shelley Meml Assoc 1995–; contrib to newspapers and jls incl: The Independent, The Guardian, New Statesman and Society, Daily Telegraph, TLS, PN Review; fell English Assoc 2003, FRSA 2009; *Books* Wordsworth's Reading 1770–1799 (1993), Wordsworth: A Selection of his Finest Poems (ed with Stephen Gill, 1994), Romanticism: An Anthology (1994, 4 edn 2012), Six Contemporary Dramatists: Bennett, Potter, Gray, Brenton, Hare, Ayckbourn (1995), Romanticism: A Critical Reader (1995), Wordsworth's Reading 1800–1815 (1996), William Wordsworth: The Five-Book Prelude (1997), Women Romantic Poets: An Anthology (1997), A Companion to Romanticism (1998), William Hazlitt, The Plain Speaker: Key Essays (1998), The Selected Writings of William Hazlitt (9 vols, 1998), Making Plays: Interviews with Contemporary British Dramatists and Directors (2000), Wordsworth: An Inner Life (2002), British Romanticism and the Edinburgh Review: Bicentenary Essays (ed with Massimiliano Demata, 2002), Blackwell Essential Literature Series (9 vols of poetry, 2002), Metaphysical Hazlitt: Bicentenary Essays (ed with Uttara Natarajan and Tom Paulin, 2005), New Writings of William Hazlitt (2007), Hazlitt: The First Modern Man (2008), Poetry of Witness: The Tradition in English (2014), All that is worth remembering: Selected Essays of William Hazlitt (2014), 30 Great Myths about the Romantics (2015); *CD-ROM* Romanticism: The CD-ROM (ed with David Miall, 1998); *Recreations* jazz, classical music, books and manuscripts, monster trucks; *Style*— Prof Duncan Wu; ✉ c/o Charlie Viney, 23 Erlanger Road, Telegraph Hill, London SE14 5TF

WULSTAN, Prof David; s of Rev Norman B Jones (d 1948), and (Sarah) Margaret, *née* Simpson (d 1973); *b* 18 January 1937; *Educ* Royal Masonic Sch, Coll of Tech Birmingham, Magdalen Coll Oxford (BSc, ARCM, MA, BLitt); *m* 9 Oct 1965, Susan Nelson, da of Frank Nelson Graham (d 1963); 1 s (Philip Richard James b 1969); *Career* fell and lectr Magdalen Coll Oxford 1964–78, visiting prof Univ of Calif Berkeley 1978, statutory lectr UC Cork 1979–80 (prof of music 1980–83), Gregynog prof of music UC Wales 1983–92, research prof Univ of Wales Aberystwyth 1992–; hon prof Univ of Wales 2010; dir The Clerkes of Oxenford 1964–; consltg ed Spanish Academic Press; memb Cncl Plainsong and Mediaeval Music Soc 1964–; numerous recordings and appearances for TV and radio, appearance at festivals, recordings of incidental music for TV and cinema, composer of church music; memb Soc for Old Testament Studies, memb Prayer Book Soc; hon fell St Peter's Coll Oxford 2008, fell Royal Soc of Musicians; *Publications* Gibbons Church Music (Early English Church Music) Vol 3 (1964) and Vol 27 (1979), Anthology of English Church Music (1968), Play of Daniel (1976), Coverdale Chant Book (1978), Sheppard, Complete Works (1979), Tudor Music (1985), Musical Language (1991), The Emperor's Old Clothes (2001), The Compilation of the Cantigas of Alfonso el Sabio (2001), The Rhythmic Organisation of the Cantigas de Santa Maria (2001), The Poetic and Musical Legacy of Heloise and Abelard (ed and contrib, 2003), Music from the Paraclete (2004), The Play of Daniel (revised edn 2008), Keep to the Lesbian Feet: Sappho, Horace, Guido and the Renaissance Sapphic (2009), A Pretty Paella: The Alfonsine Cantigas de Santa Maria and their connexions with other repertories (2009), The Rest is Silence: Speculations About Caedmon's Hymn (2009), St Peter's Chant Book (2011); articles in: Canterbury Dictionary of Hymnology (2014), Liber Amicorum Gerardo Huseby (2014), Listen Again: A New History of Music (2015), The Letter of St Bernard and the Tract on the Revision of the Cistercian Antiphoner (2015); many other editions, articles and reviews in Music and Letters, Journal of Plainsong and Medieval Music, Early Music, English Historical Review, Journal of Theological Studies, Journal of Semitic Studies, Iraq, Cantigueiros, al-Masaq, The Consort, Faith and Worship, Prayer Book Society Journal, Mapping the Medieval Mediterranean, SOTS Booklist; *Recreations* food and drink, bemoaning the loss of the English language, Aikido, Self Defence (instructor); *Style*— Prof David Wulstan; ✉ Hillview Croft, Lon Tyllwyd, Llanfarian, Aberystwyth, Cardiganshire SY23 4UH (☎ 01970 617832)

WULWIK, His Hon Judge Peter David; s of Eddie Wulwik (d 2007), and Mona, *née* Moss (d 1990); *b* 15 September 1950, London; *Educ* St Marylebone GS, Univ of London (LLB), Cncl of Legal Educn; *m* 6 April 1975, Joanna, *née* Rosenberg; 2 s (Stephen b 20 Oct 1979, Benjamin b 11 Aug 1981), 1 da (Philippa b 29 April 1984); *Career* called to the Bar Gray's Inn 1972; recorder 2000–04 (asst recorder 1995–2000), circuit judge 2004–, princ judge consumer credit appeals First Tier Tbnl 2009–14, princ judge estate agents' appeals First Tier Tbnl (Gen Regulatory Chamber), judge Upper Tbnl (Administrative Appeals Chamber) 2009–, and judge Upper Tbnl (Tax and Chancery Chamber) 2014–; pt/t chm: London Rent Assessment Panel and Leasehold Valuation Tbnl 1999–2004, Consumer Credit and Estate Agents Appeals Panel 2003–; pres Consumer Credit Appeals Tbnl 2008–09; contrib: Bennion's Consumer Credit Law Reports 1990–2000, Goode's Consumer Credit Reports 2000–04; *Recreations* reading, theatre, classical music, antique fairs, playing bridge, tennis, golf, watching Tottenham Hotspur FC; *Clubs* Radlett Lawn Tennis and Squash; *Style*— His Hon Judge Wulwik

WURTZEL, David Ira; s of late Paul Bernard Wurtzel, of LA, Calif, and Shirley Lorraine, *née* Stein; *b* 28 January 1949; *Educ* Univ of Calif Berkeley (BA), QMC London (MA) Fitzwilliam Coll Cambridge (MA); *Career* called to the Bar Middle Temple 1976 (bencher 2001); arts corr The Diplomat 1989–98, sr lectr City Univ, conslt ed Counsel magazine, contrib to various legal pubns; *Books* Thomas Lyster, A Cambridge Novel (1983); *Recreations* theatre, opera, travelling abroad, taking exercise, architecture, conservation; *Style*— David Wurtzel, Esq; ✉ City Law School, 4 Gray's Inn Place, London WC1R 5DX

WYATT, Prof Derrick Arthur; QC (1993); s of Iris Ross, and step s of Alexander Ross; *Educ* Alsop HS Liverpool, Emmanuel Coll Cambridge, Univ of Chicago Law Sch; *Career* lectr in law Univ of Liverpool 1971; called to the Bar 1972; fell Emmanuel Coll Cambridge 1975; fell St Edmund Hall Oxford 1978–2009 (emeritus fell 2009–), prof of law Univ of Oxford 1996–2009 (emeritus prof of law 2009–, visiting prof of law 2009–); *Publications* European Union Law (2000), Wyatt and Dashwood's European Union Law (2006, 2 edn 2011); *Recreations* walking; *Style*— Prof Derrick Wyatt, QC; ✉ St Edmund Hall, Oxford OX1 4AR (e-mail derrick.wyatt@seh.ox.ac.uk); Brick Court Chambers, 7–8 Essex Street, London WC2R 3LD (☎ 020 7379 3550, fax 020 7379 3558)

WYATT, Hon Petronella Aspasia; da of Baron Wyatt of Weeford (Life Peer, d 1997), and Veronica, *née* Racz; *Educ* St Paul's Girls' Sch, UCL (BA); *Career* reporter Daily Telegraph 1990–94, feature writer and columnist Sunday Telegraph 1994–97, asst ed and columnist The Spectator 1997–98, subsequently dep ed The Spectator; interviewer for Daily Telegraph and Mail on Sunday; lectr in USA 1999–; *Books* Father, Dear Father (1999); *Recreations* opera, singing, yoga, riding; *Clubs* Home House; *Style*— The Hon Petronella Wyatt; ✉ mobile 07836 256636

WYATT, (Alan) Will; CBE (2000); s of Basil Wyatt, of Oxford, and Hettie Evelyn, *née* Hooper; *b* 7 January 1942; *Educ* Magdalen Coll Sch Oxford, Emmanuel Coll Cambridge (BA); *m* 2 April 1966, Jane Bridgit, da of Beauchamp Bagenal (d 1959), of Kitale, Kenya; 2 da (Hannah b 1967, Rosalind b 1970); *Career* reporter Sheffield Morning Telegraph 1964–65, sub ed BBC Radio News 1965–68; BBC TV: prodr 1968 (programmes include Robinsons Travels, B Traven – A Mystery Solved, Late Night Line Up, The Book Programme), head presentation programmes 1977–80, head documentary features 1981–87, head features and documentaries gp 1987–88, md Network Television 1991–96 (asst md 1988–91); chief exec BBC Broadcast 1996–99; chm ToniandRosi Films Ltd 2011–; dir: BBC Enterprises 1991–94, UKTV (jt venture channels of BBC Worldwide Ltd and Flextech plc) 1997–99; chm Ctee on Violence in TV Programmes BBC 1983 and 1987; pres Royal Television Soc 2000–04 (vice-pres 1997–2000), vice-pres Euro Broadcasting Union 1998–2000; prodr/dir Toni and Rosi (documentary film, BBC 4) 2012; author of newspaper articles on broadcasting; dir: Coral Eurobet 2000–02, Vitec Gp 2002–11, Racing UK Ltd 2004–11 (chm 2008–11), Racecourse Media Gp (formerly Racecourse Media Services Ltd) 2006–11 (chm 2008–11); chm Human Capital Ltd 2001–08, Goodwill Assocs (Media) Ltd 2003–13; tstee Br Video History Tst (dir 1990–92), vice-chm Shadow Racing Tst 2003–06, tstee Services Sound and Vision Corp 2007–13, chm Teaching Awards Tst 2008–13; tstee Welsh Nat Opera 2013–; govr: London Inst (now Univ of the Arts London) 1989– (chm 1999–2007), Nat Film and Television Sch 1990–96 and 1998–2000, Magdalen Coll Sch Oxford 1999–2006; FRTS 1992; *Books* The Man Who Was B Traven (1980), The Fun Factory (2003); contrib to: Masters of the Wired World (1999), Proceedings of the Royal Institution vol 69; *Recreations* walking, horse racing, opera, theatre; *Clubs* Garrick, Century; *Style*— Will Wyatt, Esq, CBE; ✉ Abbey Willows, Rayford Lane, Middle Barton, Oxfordshire OX7 7DD (e-mail will.wyatt@btinternet.com)

WYBAR, Linda; *née* Clough; da of Thomas Smith Clough (d 2001), and Mary Bath, *née* Fenwick; *b* 21 June 1959, Blyth, Northumberland; *Educ* Blyth GS, Univ of Hull (BA, PGCE), Open Univ (MA); *m* 1, 7 Aug 1981, Flavio Romano Walker; 2 s (Benjamin Richard, Thomas Daniel (twins) b 21 April 1989); m 2, 25 Aug 1995, Geoffrey Stewart Wybar; *Career* teacher Rede Sch Strood 1981–82, Highworth Sch Ashford 1982–86, head of English Norton Knatchbull Boys' GS Ashford 1986–92, dep head Highsted GS Sittingbourne 1992–99, headteacher Tunbridge Wells Girls' GS 1999–; chm Kent and Medway GS Assoc 2004–; *Recreations* reading modern fiction, theatre-going, wine tasting, relaxing in Cornwall; *Clubs* Lansdowne; *Style*— Mrs Linda Wybar; ✉ Tunbridge Wells Girls' Grammar School, Southfield Road, Tunbridge Wells, Kent TN4 9UJ (☎ 01892 520902, fax 01892 536497, e-mail admin@twggs.kent.sch.uk)

WYBREW, John Leonard; s of late Leonard Percival Wybrew, of Radlett, Herts, and late May Edith Wybrew; *b* 27 January 1943; *Educ* Bushey GS, Sir John Cass Coll; *m* 1, 1967 (m dis 1990), Linda Gillian, da of Wing Cdr John James Frederick Long, of Lyminge, Kent; 1 s, 2 da; m 2, 2002, Denise Holloway, da of late Robert Ellis, of Burwardsley, Cheshire; *Career* life mangr and actuary Time Assurance Soc 1971–72, gen mangr and dir: Windsor Life Assurance Co Ltd 1972–76 (md 1976–, chm 1988–90 and 1992–2005), World-Wide Assurance Co Ltd 1972–76 (dir 1982–2004); chm Windsor Investment Mgmnt 1986–90, chm Windsor Tst Mangrs 1986–90, md Windsor Gp Ltd; pres and ceo British-American Life Assurance Co Pte Singapore 1990–92, non-exec dir Aberdeen Asset Mgmnt 2001–05, chm TES Gp Ltd 2008–13, dir Guardian Assurance 2012–, dir Ark Life Assurance Repub of Ireland 2014–; memb Ctee of Mgmnt Family Assurance Soc 1987–90 and 1998–2010; Liveryman Worshipful Co of Actuaries; FIA; Officier Commandeur de la Confrérie des Chevaliers du Tastevin; *Recreations* fly fishing, sailing, reading, golf, travel; *Clubs* Tanglin, Oriental, Annabel's; *Style*— John Wybrew, Esq; ✉ Castle View, Castle Street, Holt, Clwyd LL13 9YL (☎ 01244 677339)

WYKE, Prof John Anthony; s of Eric John Edward Wyke (d 1979), and Daisy Anne, *née* Dormer (d 1997); *b* 5 April 1942; *Educ* Dulwich Coll, St John's Coll Cambridge (scholar, MA, VetMB, coll prizes), Univ of London (PhD); *m* 1968, Anne Wynne, da of John Mitchell; 1 s (Robert Andrew b 1977); *Career* postdoctoral res Univ of Washington and Univ of Southern Calif 1970–72, head Tumour Virology Lab ICRF Labs 1976–83 (scientific staff 1972–76), head ICRF Labs Bart's 1983–87 (asst dir 1985), dir Beatson Inst for Cancer Res 1987–2002, dir Scottish Cancer Fndn 2002– (chair 2002–10); dir Assoc for Int Cancer Research 2003–; emeritus prof Univ of Glasgow 2002– (visiting prof 1991–2002), memb Cncl Royal Veterinary Coll 2008–12; tstee RSE Scotland Fndn 2012–; fell Leukemia Soc of America 1970–72; hon fell Univ of Glasgow 2004; FRSE 1989, FMedSci 1998, Hon FRCVS 1999 (MRCVS 1967); *Recreations* hill walking, skiing, gardening; *Style*— Prof John Wyke, FRSE

WYKES, Prof Dame Til; DBE (2016); *Educ* Congleton GS for Girls, Univ of Nottingham (BSc), Univ of Sussex (DPhil), Univ of London (MPhil); *Career* research fell Univ of Sussex 1977–78; Inst of Psychiatry KCL: scientific offr MRC Social Psychiatry Unit 1978–83, hon lectr 1980–86, lectr Psychology Dept 1986–91, sr lectr 1991–96, clinical research

W

co-ordinator 1992–, reader in clinical psychology 1997–99, prof of clinical psychology and rehabilitation 1999–, dir Service User Research Enterprise 2001–, vice-dean of research 2010–14; hon consit clinical psychologist Bethlem and Maudsley Special HA (now Tst) 1990– (hon conslt clinical psychologist 1988–90), dir Centre for Recovery in Severe Psychosis Maudsley Hosp 1998–; dir NIHR Clinical Research Network Mental Health 2003–15; Inst of Psychiatry, Psychology and Neurosci, KCL, vice-dean of res 2010–15, vice-dean psych and systems sci 2015–, dir NIHR Clinical Res Network Mental Health 2003–15, CRN Nat Specialty Lead for Mental Health 2015–; visiting prof Harvard Univ 2011–15; ed Jl of Mental Health 2002–; memb Neurosciences, Clinical Trial and EU Directives Bds and Chronic Fatigue Syndrome Research Strategy Gp MRC 2002–; May Davidson Award Br Psychological Soc 1995; memb Soc for Research in Psychopathology USA; FBPsS 1995 (memb Investigations Ctee 1995–99), CPsychol, FAcSS 2006, fell Acad of Cognitive Therapy US 2014, FMedSci 2016; *Publications* Violence and Health Care Workers (ed, 1994), Aggression and Violence in General Practice (jtly, 1995), Outcome and Innovation in the Psychological Treatment of Schizophrenia (jtly, 1998), A Dictionary of Statistics for Psychologists (jtly, 1999), Psychosocial and Pharmacological Rehabilitation for Schizophrenia (jt ed, 2002), Cognitive Remediation Therapy for Schizophrenia: Theory and Practice (jtly); *Style—* Prof Dame Til Wykes, DBE

WYLD, David John Charles; s of John Hugh Gilbert Wyld, TD, and Helen Selina, *née* Leslie Melville (d 1946); *b* 11 March 1943; *Educ* Harrow, ChCh Oxford (MA); *m* 1, 19 Dec 1970 (m dis), Sally, da of Ellis Morgan, CMG, of Hay-on-Wye, Herefords; 2 s (Barnaby b 1972, Jonathan b 1973); m 2, 20 June 1987, Caroline Mary, da of Walter Ronald Alexander, CBE, of St Andrews, Fife; 3 da (Charlotte b 1988, Alexandra b 1989, Rachel b 1991); *Career* called to the Bar 1968, admitted slr 1974; practising slr Linklaters & Paines 1974–79, ptnr Macfarlanes 1981–2004; sec gen Int Law Assoc 1993–, pres London Slrs' Litigation Assoc 1992–94, chm City of London Law Soc 2001–04; memb Law Soc 1974; *Recreations* reading, walking, golf; *Clubs* Garrick, Hon Co of Edinburgh Golfers, MCC, Berkshire Golf; *Style—* David Wyld, Esq; ✉ David Wyld & Co, Fleet House, 8–12 New Bridge Street, London EC4V 6AL (☎ 020 7583 7920, fax 020 7583 7921)

WYLDBORE-SMITH, William Francis; DL (Wilts 2003); s of John Henry Wyldbore-Smith (d 1982), of Scaynes Hill, W Sussex, and Tighnabruaich, Argyll, and Robina, *née* Ward (d 1993); *b* 15 January 1948; *Educ* Marlborough; *m* 1974, Prisca Faith, da of Rev Peter Nourse (d 1992); 1 da (Philippa b 1977); *Career* admitted slr 1972; ptnr: Osborne Clarke 1977–85, Wood Awdry and Ford 1986–2008, Thrings LLP 2008–13; pres Glos and Wilts Law Soc 2004–05; chm Brunel SEN Mutli Academy Tst, vice-chm Wiltshire Community Fndn; involved with various county and other volunteer orgns incl: Community First Youth Action Wilts, Wilts Victorian History Soc, Uplands Educational Tst, Wilts Community Resolution Scrutiny Panel, Marlborough Coll Fndn, West Country River Tst; memb: Law Soc, Soc of Tst and Estate Practitioners (STEP); Under Sheriff Wilts 1987–2005, High Sheriff Wilts 2013–14; Liveryman Worshipful Company of Musicians; *Recreations* gardening, shooting, reading; *Clubs* Brooks's; *Style—* W F Wyldbore-Smith, Esq, DL; ✉ Bremhill Manor, Calne, Wiltshire SN11 9LA

WYLIE, Alexander Featherstonhaugh; *see:* Kinclaven, The Hon Lord

WYLIE, Andrew; s of Craig Wylie, and Angela, *née* Fowler; *b* 4 November 1947, NY; *Educ* St Paul's, Harvard Coll (AB); *m* 1980, Camilla, *née* Carlini; 2 s (Nikolas Anton b 1970, Marco Matteo b 1985), 1 da (Alexandra Winthrop b 1994); *Career* fndr and pres The Wylie Agency NY 1980 and London 1996; memb Cncl on Foreign Rels; *Recreations* swimming, running, bicycling, tennis; *Clubs* Harvard, Knickerbocker (NY), River, Southampton, Bathing Corp (Southampton), Meadow (Southampton); *Style—* Andrew Wylie, Esq; ✉ The Wylie Agency LLC, 250 West 57th Street, Suite 2114, New York, NY 10107, USA (☎ 001 212 246 0069, fax 001 212 586 8953)

WYLIE, Prof John Cleland Watson; s of George Stewart Wylie (d 1966), of Belfast, and Phyllis Ann, *née* Watson (d 2006); *b* 6 July 1943; *Educ* Methodist Coll Belfast, Queen's Univ Belfast (LLB, LLD), Harvard Univ (LLM); *m* 22 Sept 1973, Gillian Lindsey, da of Eric Sidney Edward Gardner, of London; 1 s (Nicholas George b 1977), 1 da (Emma Louise b 1979); *Career* lectr in law Queen's Univ Belfast 1965–71, Frank Knox fell Harvard 1966–67; Cardiff Univ: sr lectr 1972–76, reader 1976–79, prof of law 1979–2009, dean Faculty of Law 1980–83, pro-vice-chllr 1990–93, head Cardiff Law Sch 1991–96, emeritus prof of law 2009–; ed: N Ireland Legal Quarterly 1970–76; dir: Professional Books Ltd 1981–87, Butterworth (Ireland) Ltd 1987–2005; land law conslt: Trinidad and Tobago Govt 1978–83, N Ireland Office 1980–90, A & L Goodbody Slrs 1992–, Irish Law Reform Cmmn 2001–08, Irish Dept of Justice, Equality and Law Reform 2004–, NI Law Cmmn 2007–10; memb Legal Studies Bd CNAA 1984–87, pres SPTL 1994–95, chm Ctee of Heads of Univ Law Schs 1993–94; Hon LLD Univ of Limerick; *Books* Irish Land Law (1975, 5 edn 2013), Irish Conveyancing Law (1978, 3 edn 2005), A Casebook on Equity and Trusts in Ireland (1985, 2 edn 1998), Land Laws of Trinidad and Tobago (1986), Irish Landlord and Tenant Law (1990, 3 edn 2014), Irish Conveyancing Statutes (1994, 2 edn 1999), The Law and Taxation of Trusts (co-author, 2007), The Land and Conveyancing Law Reform Act 2009: Annotations and Commentary (2009), Irish Landlord and Tenant Acts: Annotations, Commentary and Precedents (2015); *Recreations* reading, swimming, gardening; *Style—* Prof John Wylie; ✉ Pengethley House, Peterstow, Ross-on-Wye, Herefordshire HR9 6LN (☎ 01989 730240, mobile 07792 800327, fax 01989 730427, e-mail profjohnwylie@gmail.com)

WYLLIE, Andrew; CBE (2015); s of Kenneth David Wyllie, and Margaret Emily Wyllie; *b* 24 December 1962, Romford, Essex; *Educ* Dunfermline HS, Univ of Strathclyde, London Business Sch; *m* Jane; 1 da; *Career* md Taylor Woodrow Construction Ltd 2001–05, chief exec Costain Gp plc 2005–; non-exec dir Scottish Water 2009–; memb Construction Cncl CBI; fell Br American Project, FICE (vice pres 2015–), FIoD, CCMI, FREng 2009; *Style—* Andrew Wyllie, Esq, CBE; ✉ Costain Group plc, Costain House, Vanwall Business Park, Maidenhead, Berkshire SL6 4UB (☎ 01628 842444, fax 01628 842554, website www.costain.com)

WYLLIE, Gordon Malcolm; WS (1982); s of Thomas Smith Wyllie, of Dallas House, Troon, and Margaret Hutton Gordon Malcolm; *b* 20 July 1951; *Educ* Dunoon GS, Univ of Glasgow (LLB); *Career* law apprentice McGrigor Donald Glasgow 1972–74, head Executry Dept Strathern & Blair WS Edinburgh 1974–77, notary public, ptnr Biggart Baillie 1980–2012 (sr law asst 1977–80, head of charity and private client 1997–2012), ptnr Bird Semple Private Client Slrs 2012–14; clerk: Grand Antiquity of Glasgow 1984–2015, Trades House of Glasgow and sister bodies 1987–2004, Gen Cmmrs of Income Tax Glasgow North 1990–2009 (depute 1983) and Glasgow South 1992–2009; dir: Bailford Trustees Ltd until 2012, Albertas Inst 2014–15; memb Grand Antiquity Soc of Glasgow (pres 2000–01); sec Trades Hall of Glasgow Building Preservation Tst 1987–2005; deacon: Incorporation of Hammermen of Edinburgh 1996–99, Bonnetmakers and Dyers of Edinburgh 2003–09 (clerk 2009–); memb Incorporations of Tailors and Bonnetmakers and Dyers of Glasgow and Hammermen of Irvine (hc); visitor Maltmen of Glasgow 2012–13; Boxmaster of Convenery of Trades of Edinburgh 2000–03, Deacon Convener of the Trades of Edinburgh 2003–06; govr Trades Maiden Hosp of Edinburgh 1996–, chm Britannia Panopticon Music Hall Tst 1998–2007, govr Scottish Grant-Making Trusts Forum 2008–10, chm Edinburgh West End Community Cncl until 2013; chm Tst and Succession Ctee Law Soc of Scotland 2005–; chm and co-ordinator Incorporated Trades of Edinburgh 450th Anniversary of Convenery Exhibition 2012; memb: Royal Faculty of Procurators in Glasgow 1980–, Euro Cmmn Gp of Experts on Succession and Wills in the UK 2005–08, Soc of Tst and Estate Practitioners, Soc of Antiquaries of Scotland, Soc for Promotion of Hellenic Studies, Int Bar Assoc, Action Medical Research (chm in Scotland 2003–), St Andrew's Soc of Glasgow, Merchant Co of Edinburgh; fndr and fell Inst of Contemporary Scotland until 2014; Freeman City of Glasgow, Burgess of Edinburgh; Hon Dr Univ of Glasgow; MStJ; *Recreations* history, music and the arts generally, architecture and design, country dancing, country walks; *Clubs* Scottish Arts (Edinburgh), Western (Glasgow); *Style—* Gordon M Wyllie, Esq, WS; ✉ 22 Hanover Street, Edinburgh EH2 2EP (e-mail gordon.m.wyllie@gmail.com)

WYMAN, Peter Lewis; DL (2014), CBE (2006); s of late John Bernard Wyman, MBE, of Sharpthorne, W Sussex, and late Joan Dorethea, *née* Beighton (d 2013); *b* 26 February 1950; *Educ* Epsom Coll; *m* 16 Sept 1978, Joy Alison, da of late Edward George Foster, of Horsted Keynes, W Sussex; 1 s (John b 1985), 1 da (Gemma b 1988); *Career* chartered accountant; articled clerk Ogden Parsons & Co and Harmood Banner 1968–73; PricewaterhouseCoopers (formerly Deloitte Haskins & Sells and then Coopers & Lybrand): mangr 1974–78, ptnr 1978–2010, head of tax 1993–98, head of external relations 1998–2000, head of regulatory policy 2003, head of professional affrs 2004–09, global ldr for public affrs and regulatory matters 2008–10; sr advsr Albright Stonebridge Gp LLC 2010–15, princ Peter Wyman Private Clients 2010–15; chm Sir Richard Sutton Ltd 2011– (dir 2010–); chm Care Quality Cmmn 2016–; Coopers & Lybrand: memb Partnership Bd 1997–98, memb Partnership Cncl 1997–98, memb Residuary Body 1998–2010; memb Ctee London Soc of Chartered Accountants 1981–90 (chm 1987–88); ICAEW: chm Faculty of Taxation 1991–95, memb Cncl 1991–2009, chm Educn and Training Directorate 1995–99, memb Exec Ctee 1996–2003, vice-pres 2000–2001, dep pres 2001–02, pres 2002–03, chm Outstanding Achievement Award Selection Panel 2011–14; chm Professional Standards Office 1999–2000, chm Financial Reporting Advsy Bd Review Gp 2010–11, Advsy Bd Pasco Risk Mgmnt 2010–13, memb Bd and chm Audit Ctee Companies House 2011–16, chm Yeovil District Hosp 2011–16, memb Supervisory Bd Focal & Co 2011–14; special advsr on deregulation and taxation to Parly Under Sec of State for Corp Affairs 1993–94, external overseer Contribs Agency/Inland Revenue Jt Working Prog 1995–97; chm Consultative Ctee of Accountancy Bodies 2002–03, dep chm Financial Reporting Cncl 2002–03, chm Financial Trade Assoc Tax Forum 2008–10; memb: Deregulation Task Force 1994–97, Regulation of the Accountancy Profession Implementation Working Pty 1999–2001, Panel on Takeovers and Mergers 2002–03, Review of the Regulation of the Accountancy Profession Steering Gp 2002–04, Corp of London EU Advsy Gp 2004–09, Audit Ctee RSA 2005–11, Int Fedn of Accountancy Bodies 2006–09 (memb Transnational Auditors Ctee and Planning and Finance Ctee); chm Somerset Community Fndn 2009–2015 (dir 2002–04), memb Devpt Advsy Cncl Inst of Economic Affrs 2011–13; dir: Hestercombe Garden Tst 2010–11 (also chm Finance Ctee), City of London Sinfonia 2011–15; govr: Aylwin Girls Sch Southwark 2001–06 (chm 2003–06), Harris Bermondsey Acad 2006–07; tstee Five Bridges Sch 2002–05; memb Cncl Univ of Bath 2003–06 and 2009– (treas 2011–), memb Advsy Bd BPP Business Sch 2010–12; Freeman: City of London 1988, Worshipful Co of Chartered Accountants 1988 (Sr Warden 2005–06, Master 2006–07, Almoner 2011–14); ICAEW Award for Outstanding Acheivement 2006, Accountancy Age Award for Outstanding Industry Contribution 2008; FCA 1978 (ACA 1973), FRSA 1993 (memb Audit and Risk Ctee 2005–11); Deputy Lieutenant of Somerset 2014; *Recreations* my family's genealogy, twentieth century history, equestrian sports, gardening, music; *Style—* Peter L Wyman, Esq, CBE, DL; ✉ Plainsfield Court, Plainsfield, Over Stowey, Somerset TA5 1HH (☎ 07711 776128); Flat 1, Priory House, 3 Burgon Street, London EC4V 5DR (e-mail peterwyman@btinternet.com)

WYN-ROGERS, Catherine; da of Geoffrey Wyn Rogers, and Helena, *née* Webster; *b* 24 July 1954; *Educ* St Helena HS for Girls Chesterfield, RCM (fndn scholar, ARCM, Dame Clara Butt Award); *Career* mezzo-soprano; studied with Meriel St Clair, Ellis Keeler, Diane Forlano; concerts with: Vienna Philharmonic, RIAS Kammerchor, Bach Choir, Royal Choral Soc, Huddersfield Choral Soc, RPO, English Chamber Orch, Bournemouth Symphony Orch, Royal Liverpool Philharmonic Orch, Philharmonia, City of Birmingham Symphony Orchs, Three Choirs Festival, Aldeburgh Festival, The Sixteen, English Concert, Acad of Ancient Music, BBC Symphony Orch (BBC Proms, incl Last Night soloist 1995); opera cos appeared with: Scottish Opera, Welsh Nat Opera, Opera North, ENO, Salzburg Festival; Royal Opera House roles incl: Mrs Sedley in Peter Grimes, First Norn and Erda in Wagner's Ring Cycle, Sosostris in The Midsummer Marriage; also worked with: Bernard Haitink, Andrew Davis, Sir Charles Mackerras, Richard Hickox, Mark Elder, Roger Norrington; pres Derby Bach Choir 1995, patron Amadeus Choir of Toronto; *Recordings* Haydn's Harmoniemesse (with Winchester Cathedral Choir under David Hill), John Gay's Beggar's Opera, Teixeira's Te Deum and Bach's Christmas Oratorio (with The Sixteen and Orch for Collins Classics), Mozart's Vespers (with Trevor Pinnock), Vaughan Williams' Serenade to Music (with Roger Norrington), Elgar's The Dream of Gerontius (EMI), Graham Johnson's Complete Schubert Edition (Hyperion), Britten A Charm of Lullabies orchestrated by Colin Matthews (Northern Sinfonia under Steuart Bedford); *Recreations* drawing, painting; *Style—* Ms Catherine Wyn-Rogers; ✉ c/o Askonas Holt Ltd, Lincoln House, 300 High Holborn, London WC1V 7JH

WYNDHAM, Henry Mark; s of Hon Mark Wyndham, OBE, MC, and Anne, *née* Winn; *b* 19 August 1953; *Educ* Eton, Sorbonne; *m* 21 Dec 1978, Rachel Sarah, da of Lt-Col Leslie Francis Gordon Pritchard, MBE, TD (d 1977); 3 s (Ned b 1983, Leo b 1985, William b 1988); *Career* Christies International 1974–87 (dir 1983–87), fndr Henry Wyndham Fine Art 1987; chm: Sotheby's UK 1994–, Sotheby's Europe 1997–; expert BBC Antiques Road Show 1987–97; fell Pierpont Morgan Library NY; chm Arts and Library Ctee MCC 1993–98; tstee: Glyndebourne Opera, Prince of Wales Drawing Schools; memb: Patrons of British Art Tate Gallery (memb Ctee 1993–96), Sir George Beaumont Gp Nat Gallery, Dilettanti Soc, MCC Ctee 1987–98; former govr Thomas Coram Fndn, ambass Orbis, tstee Turner Art Gallery Eastbourne 2014–; Liveryman Worshipful Co of Goldsmiths; *Recreations* cricket, soccer, golf, tennis, travelling, shooting and fishing, looking at pictures, films, music, opera, gardening; *Clubs* White's, MCC (memb Ctee 1994–98), Pratt's, Saints and Sinners, Pilgrims, Grillions, Aberdino, Marks; *Style—* Henry Wyndham, Esq; ✉ The Old Rectory, Southease, Lewes, East Sussex BN7 3HX; Sotheby's, 34–35 New Bond Street, London W1A 2AA (☎ 020 7293 5057, fax 020 7293 5065)

WYNFORD, 9 Baron (UK 1829); John Philip Robert Best; only s of 8 Baron (d 2002); *b* 23 November 1950; *Educ* Radley, Keele Univ (BA), RAC Cirencester; *m* 10 Oct 1981, Fenella Christian Mary, only da of Capt Arthur Reginald Danks, MBE, TD (d 1996), and Hon Serena Mary (d 1998), da of 4 Baron Gifford; 1 da (Hon Sophie Hannah Elizabeth b 1985), 1 s (Hon Harry Robert Francis b 9 May 1987); *Heir* s, Hon Harry Best; *Career* ARICS land agency div 1979; Wynford Eagle Ptnrs (administering family estate): exec ptnr 1981–2002, sole prop 2002–10, exec ptnr 2010–; MRICS; *Recreations* music, reading, silviculture, claret; *Style—* The Rt Hon the Lord Wynford, MRICS; ✉ The Manor, Wynford Eagle, Dorchester, Dorset DT2 0ER (☎ 01300 320763)

WYNFORD-THOMAS, Prof David; s of Richard David Thomas (d 1991), of Barry, S Glamorgan; *b* 28 February 1955; *Educ* Welsh Nat Sch of Med (MB BCh, PhD, DSc); *Career* house offr posts in med and surgery 1978–79, asst lectr in pathology Univ of Wales Coll of Med (UWCM, formerly Welsh Nat Sch of Med) 1979–80, Wellcome research fell UWCM 1980–82, NIH post doctoral fell Dept of Molecular, Cellular and Developmental Biology Univ of Colorado Boulder 1982–83; Dept of Pathology UWCM: lectr 1984–86, sr lectr Cancer Biology Unit 1986–88, reader in tumour biology 1988–92, prof and head of dept 1992–; chm Div of Clinical Laboratory Sciences UWCM 2001–05, dean of medicine Cardiff Univ 2005–; external expert Institut National de la Santé et de la Recherche Médicale (INSERM) 2000–; pres: UK Branch European Tissue Culture Soc 1996–2000, Exec Ctee European Thyroid Cancer Network 1996–; memb: MRC Molecular and Cellular Med Grants Ctee 1992–96, Exec Ctee UK Molecular Biology and Cancer Network 1992–, MRC Molecular and Cellular Med Bd 1998–2002, MRC Leukaemia Steering Ctee 1998–2002, MRC Cross-Bd Clinical Trials Ctee 1998–2002, Cancer Research Campaign Grants Ctee 2000–05, Steering Ctee Nat Generic Tumour Bank 2001–, UK Govt Advsy Ctee on Genetic Manipulation 2001–03; subject ed (molecular and cellular pathology) Br Jl of Cancer 1995–, memb Editorial Bd Jl of Pathology 1992–2002; hon memb Assoc Française de Chirurgie Endocriniene; FRCPath 1996 (MRCPath 1989), FMedSci 2003; *Publications* Thyroid Tumours – Molecular Basis of Pathogenesis (with E D Williams, 1989); also 132 research articles and 16 book chapters; *Recreations* foreign languages, travel; *Style*— Prof David Wynford-Thomas; ✉ Dean's Office, School of Medicine, Cardiff University, Cardiff CF14 4XN (☎ 029 2074 2020)

WYNN, Cdr Andrew Guy; LVO (1984); yr s of Lt Cdr Hon Charles Wynn, RN, and Hon Hermione Willoughby, da of 11 Baron Middleton; *b* 26 November 1950, Birdsall, Yorks; *Educ* Eton, Gonville & Caius Coll Cambridge (MA); *m* 1, 1978 (m dis 1987), Susanjane, *née* Fraser-Smith; 1 s (Alexander Charles Guy b 1980); *m* 2, 1988, Shelagh Jean MacSorley, yr da of Prof I K M Smith, of Wallingford, Oxon; *Career* Lt Cdr RN, Equerry to HRH The Duke of Edinburgh 1982–84, Dep Supply Offr HMS Ark Royal 1984–86, Cdr RN, Offr Policy Section 1987–88; bursar Eton Coll 1998–2011 (sch bursar 1988–98); memb Exec Ctee Ind Schs Bursars' Assoc 2001–06, memb Cncl Old Etonian Tst 2009–; chm Schs and Univs Polo Assoc 1996–98 (sec 1991–96), tstee Manifold Tst 2011–, govr Elms Sch 2012–, tstee Hereford Cathedral Perpetual Tst 2015–; *Publications* HMS Ark Royal: The Ship and Her Men (with D Smith, 1987); *Recreations* shooting, fishing, photography, DIY; *Style*— Cdr Andrew Wynn, LVO, RN; ✉ Pixley Gate, Pixley, Ledbury, Herefordshire HR8 2RB (☎ 01531 670072)

WYNN, Terence; MEP (Lab) North West England; s of Ernest Wynn (d 1979), and Lily, *née* Hitchen (d 1976); *b* 27 June 1946; *Educ* Leigh Tech Coll, Riversdale Marine Coll, Univ of Salford (MSc); *m* 7 March 1967, Doris, da of Ernest Ogden (d 1971); 1 s (David Mark b 4 March 1968), 1 da (Terry Joanne b 20 Nov 1970); *Career* trg exec MTA 1985–89; councillor Wigan MBC 1979–90; MEP (Lab): Merseyside E 1989–94, Merseyside E and Wigan 1994–99, NW England 1999–; chm Euro Parly Budgets Ctee; *Recreations* reading, theatre, jogging, golf, music, rugby league; *Style*— Terence Wynn, Esq, MEP; ✉ Lakeside, Alexandra Park, Prescot Road, St Helens WA10 3TT (☎ 01744 451609, fax 01744 29832, e-mail terry_wynn.labour@virgin.net)

WYNN OWEN, Phil; CB (2008); s of Emrys Wynn Owen (d 2005), and Ruth Wynn Owen (d 2005); *b* 10 June 1960; *Educ* Maidstone GS, UC Oxford (MA), London Business Sch (MBA); *m* 1989, Elizabeth Mary, *née* Fahey; 3 s (Michael b 30 Dec 1990, Andrew b 28 April 1993, Thomas b 19 May 1995); *Career* civil servant; HM Treasy: trainee 1981–83, asst private sec to Chllr of the Exchequer 1984–86, princ Industry and Competition Policy 1986–88, princ Funding and Monetary Policy 1990–91, private sec to Perm Sec 1991–93, Treasy alternate dir Euro Investment Bank 1994–96, team ldr Tport Team 1993–96, team ldr Tax and Budget Team 1996, team ldr Tax Policy Team 1997–99, dir Fin Sector 2003; latterly DG for strategy and pensions Pensions Client Gp Dept for Work and Pensions; dir Regulatory Impact Unit Cabinet Office 1999–2003; *Recreations* family, cricket, gym, swimming, golf; *Clubs* MCC, Leigh Cricket (Kent), Hilden Leisure; *Style*— Phil Wynn Owen, Esq, CB

WYNN-EVANS, Charles Andrew; s of Anthony Wynn-Evans, of Kenilworth, Warks, and Margaret Wynn-Evans; *b* 12 December 1967, Leamington Spa, Warks; *Educ* King Henry VIII Sch Coventry, Univ of Bristol (LLB), Coll of Law Chester, Merton Coll Oxford (BCL); *m* 31 May 1997, Alex McColl; 1 da (Catherine b 3 Aug 1999), 1 s (David b 26 April 2002); *Career* admitted slr 1992; ptnr Dechert LLP (formerly Titmuss Sainer & Webb) 1997– (joined as trainee slr 1990); memb: Law Soc, City of London Slrs Co; *Recreations*

family, cricket, allotment gardening, watching Welsh rugby, politics; *Style*— Charles Wynn-Evans, Esq; ✉ Dechert LLP, 2 Serjeants' Inn, London EC4Y 1LT (☎ 020 7775 7545, fax 020 7775 7335, e-mail charles.wynn-evans@dechert.com)

WYNNE, Ian; *b* 30 November 1973; *Career* canoeist; memb Royal Canoe Club; achievements incl: Silver medal K1 500m and Bronze medal K2 1000m European Championships 2004, Bronze medal K1 500m Olympic Games Athens 2004; World record holder solo kayak crossing of the English Channel 2008; formerly sr technical coach GB Canoeing Olympic Team, currently lead coach Br Canoeing Olympic Devpt Prog; *Style*— Ian Wynne, Esq; ✉ British Canoeing, National Water Sports Centre, Adbolton Lane, West Bridgford, Nottingham NG12 2LU

WYNNE-MORGAN, David; s of Col John Wynne-Morgan (d 1989), and Marjorie Mary (Marcie), *née* Wynne (d 1992); *b* 22 February 1931; *Educ* Bryanston; *m* 1 (m dis), Romaine Chevers, *née* Ferguson; 2 s (Nicholas b 1956, Adrian b 1957); *m* 2 (m dis), Sandra, *née* Paul; *m* 3, 26 June 1973, Karin Elizabeth, da of Daniel Eugene Stines; 2 s (Jamie b 1975, Harry b 1980); *Career* journalist: Daily Mail 1951–54, Daily Express 1954–57; fndr Partnerplan PR (sold to Extel Group 1980); dir John Player, British Genius Exhbn 1978; chm Hill and Knowlton (UK) Ltd 1984–92, EMEA pres and chief exec Hill and Knowlton 1990–94 (chm Worldwide Exec Ctee 1992–94); co-fndr WMC Communications 1995–2007 (sold to Pelham PR), fndr and 50% owner Bell Pottinger Asia 2010– (Asian PR Consultancy of the Year Award), pres Bell Pottinger Financial and Corporate 2013–; dir Horsham Corporation 1995–97; chm Marketing Group GB 1989–91; played squash for Wales 1953–56; memb Cncl Lord's Taverners 1990–95 (chm Commercial Ctee 1992–94); MIPR; *Books* autobiography of late Pres Gamal Abdel Nasser (serialised Sunday Times), biography of Pietro Annigoni (serialised Daily Express), I Norman Levy; *Recreations* cricket, tennis, riding, squash; *Clubs* Turf, Annabel's, Mark's, Harry's Bar, Queen's, The Brook; *Style*— David Wynne-Morgan, Esq; ✉ Falkland House, Painswick, Gloucestershire GL6 6QN

WYNNE-PARKER, Michael; s of David Boothby Wynne-Parker (d 1955); *b* 20 November 1945, Cromford, Derbyshire; *Educ* Lady Manners Sch; *m* 1, 1975 (m dis 1991) Jennifer Lubbock; 2 da (Sarah Ruth Isabella b 1978, Fiona Alice Elizabeth b 1981); *m* 2, 1995 (m dis 2001) Mandana Farzaneh; *Career* fndr and pres Introcom Int (31 countries); former dir: Introcom Jordan Ltd, Esma Auto Estonia Ltd, Exclusive Tours of Estonia; conslt to various public and private cos and govt mins and charities; chm: Flame Gp Int 2012, Regal Recreation and Resorts Ltd 2012; special advsr Mafous Fndn 2012; ESU: former pres S Asia, vice-pres Sri Lanka, Nepal and India, former govr; fndr patron Pensthorpe Waterfowl Tst, patron St George Fndn Estonia, patron George Kimlov Soc; tstee: A Heart for Russia Fndn 2005–, ESU Sri Lanka Educnl Tst, Mencap City Fndn (fndr tstee and govr), Imperial Palestine Orthodox Soc Estonian Branch 2014, The Russian Orthodox Dio in GB and I 2014–; friend of Pushkin House London; fell Atlantic Cncl of the UK; fndr: Knockie Stalking Club, United Charities Unit Tst (formerly Mencap Unit Tst); chm: Br Forces Fndn Inaugural Ball 1999, Guild of Travel and Tourism 1999–, ESU of Sri Lanka Millennium Appeal 2000–, Cwlth Sambo Assoc 2013–; patron: Estonia-Finnish Symphony Orch 1999–, The Queen Elizabeth Castle of Mey Tst Scotland 2012– (vice-pres 2015); pres Commonwealth Sambo Assoc; former vice-chm Norfolk Beagles; life memb: Royal Soc of St George, Sri Lanka Friendship Assoc (fndr memb), Norfolk Naturalist Tst; memb: Br Forces Fndn Exec Club 2000, Royal Soc for Asian Affrs, Salisbury Gp, The Pilgrims, Great Britain-Russia Soc, Imperial Orthodox Palestine Soc Moscow 2012–; Knight Commander of the Military and Hospitaller Order of St Lazarus of Jerusalem 1980; *Books* Bridge over Troubled Water (1988), The Mandana Poems and Others (1998), Reflections in Middle Years (2005), Wilson Lutara – A man of Africa (2007), We Shall Fly – A Life of Tony Wadlow (2009), If My Table Could Talk (2011); *Recreations* field sports, travelling, gardens, books; *Clubs* Buck's, Mark's, Crockfords, Annabel's, Aspinall's, Puffin's (Edinburgh), Cavalry & Guards; *Style*— Michael Wynne-Parker, Esq; ✉ Introcom International Ltd, 23 Berkeley Square, London, W1H 6HE (☎ 01603 721942, e-mail info@introcominternational.com)

W

Y

YACOUB, Prof Sir Magdi Habib; OM (2014), kt (1991); *b* 16 November 1935; *Educ* Cairo Univ (MB BCh); *Career* rotating house offr Cairo Univ Hosp 1958–59, surgical registrar Postgrad Surgical Unit Cairo Univ 1959–61; resident surgical offr: London Chest Hosp 1962–63, Brompton Hosp May-Oct 1963; surgical registrar London Chest Hosp 1963–64, rotating sr surgical registrar Nat Heart and Chest Hosps 1964–68, instr and asst prof Section of Cardiovascular Surgery Univ of Chicago 1968–69; Harefield Hosp: conslt cardiac surgn 1969–92, dir of med research and educn 1992–; conslt cardiac surgn Nat Heart Hosp 1973–89, Br Heart Fndn prof of cardiothoracic surgery Nat Heart and Lung Inst Royal Brompton NHS Tst 1986–; special envoy to NHS 2002; hon conslt Royal Free Hosp Med Sch London and King Edward's Coll of Med Lahore Pakistan, hon prof of surgery Univ of Sienna Italy and hon prof of cardiac surgery Charing Cross and Westminster Hosp Med Schs London; ed: Annual in Cardiac Surgery, Current Opinion in Cardiology: Coronary Artery Surgery; memb various Editorial Bds incl: Jl of Cardiac Surgery, Current Opinion in Cardiology, Transplantation, Cardiovascular Pharmacology and Therapeutics; various visiting professorships and named/guest lectures incl: The Bradshaw Lecture RCP London 1988, honoured guest lecture Assoc of American Thoracic Surgns Washington DC 1991, Frances Rather Seybold lectr and visiting prof Texas Children's Hosp Houston 1992, The Tudor Edwards Lecture RCP London 1992, visiting prof and O T Clagett lectr Mayo Clinic Rochester Minnesota 1993, visiting prof in cardiac surgery and Hubbard lectr Brigham and Women's Hosp Boston Mass 1994, Claude S Beck visiting lectr Univ Hosps of Cleveland Ohio 1994, Stikeman visiting prof McGill Univ Montreal 1994, visiting prof Hartford Hosp Hartford Connecticut 1994, 17th Leonard Abrahamson Meml Lecture Dublin 1995; Clement Price Thomas Award RCS (England) 1989, Ambuj Nath Bose Prize RCP 1992; memb: Soc of Thoracic Surgns of GB and Ireland, Br Cardiac Soc, RSM, German Soc of Thoracic and Cardiac Surgery, German Cardiac Soc, Scandinavian Soc of Thoracic Surgns, Japanese Soc of Surgns, Int Soc of Thoracic and Vascular Surgery, Euro Soc of Cardiothoracic Surgns, Thai Soc of Cardiothoracic Surgns, Egyptian Soc of Cardiology, South African Soc of Cardiology, Cardiac Soc of Australia and NZ, Pakistan Cardiac Soc, Indian Soc of Cardiothoracic Surgns; fell American Coll of Cardiology; Hon DSc: Brunel Univ 1985, American Univ at Cairo 1989, Loughborough Univ 1990, Keele Univ 1995; Hon MCh Univ of Cardiff 1986, Hon PhD Univ of Lund 1988; FRCS, FRCS(Ed), FRCS(Glas) 1961, MRCS, LRCP (London) 1966, MRCP 1986, Hon FRCP 1990, FMedSci 1999, FAMS 1999, FRS 1999; *Style*— Prof Sir Magdi Yacoub, OM, FRS; ✉ The Magdi Yacoub Institute, Heart Science Centre, Harefield, Middlesex UB9 6JH

YAFFÉ, Paul; s of David Yaffé (d 1976), of Manchester, and Dinah Pash; *b* 21 April 1946; *Educ* Delamere Forest Sch, Cheetham Secdy Sch; *m* 21 June 1967, Janis Andrea, da of Eric Brown; 2 s (Mark Daniel b 22 July 1968, Adam James b 23 Oct 1972); *Career* portrait photographer 1961–; worked in family photographic firm, opened own studio in Southport 1967, began operations in Spain 1999, estab Yaffé Fusion Art SL 2005, numerous exhibitions UK and abroad, lectr on photography and modern promotional methods in photography; chm Judging Panel BIPP (portraiture, wedding and theatrical photography) 1978 (memb 1974, dep chm 1976), chm Admissions and Qualifications Bd BIPP 1983–87 (dep chm 1980); fell Master Photographers Assoc 1981, hon PFP Norwegian Fame Assoc, 4 times memb Kodak Gold Circle; memb Professional Photographers Assoc of America; FBIPP 1972, FRPS 1979, FRSA, MIMgt 1993; *Style*— Paul Yaffé, Esq; ✉ Yaffé Fusion Art SL, Marbella, Andalucia, Spain (☎ 0034 951 406 809, e-mail paul@yaffefusionart.com, website www.yaffefusionart.com, Facebook /yaffefusionartspain)

YAMAUCHI, Mara Rosalind; *née* Myers; da of Norman Myers, of Oxford, and Dorothy, *née* Myers; *b* 13 August 1973, Oxford; *Educ* St Anne's Coll Oxford, LSE (MSc); *m* 26 Oct 2002, Shigetoshi Yamauchi; *Career* former diplomat and athlete, now coach, speaker and writer; joined FCO 1996, second sec Tokyo 1999–2002, first sec Japan Section then HR Dept FCO 2003–06; athletic achievements incl: Bronze medal 10,000m Cwlth Games 2006, first Osaka Marathon 2008, sixth Marathon Olympic Games 2008, second London Marathon 2009; Achilles medal 2005 and 2007; *Recreations* reading, cooking, theatre, mountain-walking, travel; *Clubs* Harrow Athletics, Thames Hare and Hounds Athletics; *Style*— Mrs Mara Yamauchi; ✉ c/o British Athletics, Athletics House, Central Boulevard, Blythe Valley Park, Solihull, West Midlands B90 8AJ (website www.britishathletics.org)

YANOWSKY, Zenaida; *b* France; *Career* ballet dancer; with Opera National de Paris Ballet 1991–94, principal Royal Ballet 2001– (joined 1994); Silver Medal Varna 1991, Gold Medal European Young Dancers Competition 1993, Gold Medal Jackson Int Ballet Competition 1994; *Performances* incl: Odette, Odile, Sugar Plum Fairy, Myrtha, Raymonda Act III, Agon, The Bride in Les Noces, lead nymph in L'Après-midi d'un faune, Lilac Fairy, Carabosse, Gamzatti, Empress Elizabeth, The Siren in Prodigal Son, Symphony in C, Serenade, Monotones II, Concerto, Sinfonietta, The Four Temperaments; featured in dance films Duet (Channel 4) and The Sandman (Channel 4); *Style*— Ms Zenaida Yanowsky; ✉ c/o The Royal Ballet, Royal Opera House, Covent Garden, London WC2E 9DD

YARNOLD, Elizabeth (Lizzy); MBE (2014); *b* 31 October 1988, Kent; *Career* skeleton racer; achievements incl: Bronze medal World Championships 2012, winner Skeleton World Cup 2014, Gold medal Winter Olympic Games 2014, World Champion 2015, European Champion 2015; *Style*— Ms Lizzy Yarnold, MBE; ✉ c/o British Skeleton, Sports Training Village, University of Bath, Bath BA2 7AY; website www.lizzyyarnold.com, Twitter @theyarnold

YARNOLD, Prof John Robert; s of Neville Eric Yarnold, and Anne-Marie, *née* Elkan; *Educ* Taunton's Sch Southampton, Middx Hosp Med Sch (BSc, MB BS); *Career* house offr: the Middlesex Hospital radiotherapy & oncology 1973; house physician north Middlesex hosp 1973–74; Locum post-registration house physician central Middlesex hosp 1974; registrar, the Middlesex hosp radiotherapy & oncology 1974–76, locum snr registrar the Middlesex hosp, radiotherapy & oncology 1976–77; lectr: Middlesex Hosp Med Sch 1978–80, snr lectr & hon conslt in Radiotherapy & Oncology the Inst of Cancer Res & The Royal Marsden hosp 1980–93; Inst of Cancer Research reader 1993, prof of clinical oncology 2002–11; chair Breast Clinical Studies Gp Nat Cancer Research Inst 2001–; Rohan Williams Medal Pt II (final) 1977, hon life fell RACR 1996, President's Medal RCR 1999, George Edelstyn Mem lectr 2003, Klaus Breuer Medal 2007, Lifetime Achievement Award Euro Soc Radiotheraoy & Oncology 2015; MRCP 1974, FRCR 1977; *Recreations* music, tennis; *Style*— Prof John Yarnold; ✉ Royal Marsden Hospital, Downs Road, Sutton, Surrey SM2 5PT (☎ 020 8661 3388, e-mail jyarnold@icr.ac.uk)

YARNTON, David Nigel; *b* 25 February 1959, London; *Educ* St Peters Coll Adelaide, South Australian Inst of Technol, Australian Inst of Mgmnt (Cert), Univ of New England (Dip), Monash Univ Centre for Retail Studies; *m* Sally; 1 s (Edward), 1 da (Ella); *Career* Stanley Tools 1979–82, mangr Victoria Sidchrome Pty Ltd 1982–84, Victorian sales mangr British Paints Pty Ltd 1984–86, nat sales and mktg mangr Action Hi-Tech Pty Ltd 1986, md IAD Pty Ltd 1987–95, dir of sales and mktg Nintendo Australia Ltd 1995–2003, gen mangr Nintendo UK 2003–13; md Global Talent Gp 2012–, dir EyesOnAthletes 2012–, dir Gfinity Ltd 2015–, chm UKIE Esports 2015–, dir Truconversion 2016–; dir Australian Toy Assoc 2000, dir Interactive Entertainment Assoc of Australia 2002, memb Bd and chm Edinburgh Interactive Festival 2004–, memb Bd UKIE 2005–, dir and memb Bd GfK Charttrack 2007–12, memb UK Cncl for Children's Internet Safety 2009, fndr and chm Br Inspiration Awards 2010–; assoc Australian Inst of Mgmnt 1984, fell Australian Inst of Co Dirs 1990; *Publications* Dinosaurs, Technology, Media and Sport; *Clubs* Home House, MCC, Henley RFC; *Style*— David Yarnton, Esq; ✉ Church House, Binfield Road, Shurlock Row, Berkshire RG10 0QJ; Global Talent Group, PO Box 8192, Reading, Berkshire RG6 9QB

YARROW, Sir Alan Colin Drake; kt (2016); *b* 27 June 1951; *Career* ptnr Grieveson Grant 1981–89 (joined 1972); Kleinwort Benson Gp: head of UK institutional sales 1989, head of global distribution 1992, md Kleinwort Benson Securities 1994, memb Bd 1995; global head of equities and memb Mgmnt Bd Dresdner Kleinwort Benson 1995–2000, vice-chm Dresdner Kleinwort 2000–09 (former chm Dresdner Kleinwort Ltd and Dresdner Kleinwort Securities Ltd and dir Dresdner Kleinwort Asia), chm Chartered Inst for Securities and Investment 2009–, chm Kleinwort Benson Gp 2010–; non-exec chm Complinet Gp Ltd 2002–; dir Turquoise Servcies Ltd 2010–, dir Fixnetix 2010–; chm London Investment Banking Assoc (LIBA), vice-pres BBA 2004–; Lord Mayor of London 2014–; chllr City Univ London 2014–; memb: Exchange Markets Gp London Stock Exchange, Takeover Panel, FSA Practitioner Panel 2004–; FSI; *Recreations* golf, tennis, bridge; *Clubs* City, Boodle's, Hurlingham, Royal Wimbledon Golf; *Style*— Sir Alan Yarrow; ✉ e-mail alan.yerrow@cisi.org

YASS, Catherine; *b* 12 May 1963, London; *Educ* Slade Sch of Fine Art London (BA), Hochschule der Künste Berlin, Goldsmiths Coll London (MA); *m* Chris Kul-want; 1 da (Ennathea); *Career* artist; fell Central St Martins Sch of Art 2002– (memb Arts and Humanities Research Bd 2002–05); *Solo Exhibitions* Tavistock Centre for Psychotherapy London 1991, Laure Genillard London 1992, Guy's Cliffe (Herber Percy Gallery Warks) 1994, Chair (Viewpoint Photography Gallery Salford) 1994, Spectators (Aspex Gallery Portsmouth) 1995, Steel (Ffotogallery Cardiff) 1996, Stall (Laure Genillard London) 1996, Stage (Cell Space Barbican Centre London) 1997, Grave (Portfolio Gallery Edinburgh) 1997, Invisible City (Mizuma Art Gallery Tokyo) 1998, Baths (Sabine Schmidt Cologne) 1998, Galeria dels Angels Barcelona 1998, Baths (The Pool Central Club Hotel London) 1999, Project Space Galeri Wang Oslo 1999, Br Cncl Exhbn Space Prague 1999, i8 Gallery Reykjavik 2000, Synagogue (Art in Sacred Spaces) (Congregation of Jacob London) 2000, New Art Gallery Walsall 2000, Jerwood Gallery London 2001, Star (Br Cncl touring exhbn India) 2001, Cinema India: The Art of Bollywood (V&A London) 2002, Descent (asprey jacques London) 2002, Alison Jacques Gallery London 2004, Centro Atlantico de Arte Moderno Gran Canaria 2005, Herzliya Museum of Modern Art Israel 2005, Art Basel Unlimited Basel Art Fair 2005, Foam Photography Museum Amsterdam 2005, Galerie Lelong NY 2006, Khalil Sakakini Cultural Centre Ramallah 2006, Alison Jacques Gallery London 2008, High Wire (Centre for Contemporary Arts Glasgow and tour) 2008 and (Fondazione Sandretto De Rebaudengo Italy) 2010, The China Series (Stedelijk Museums Hertogenbosch) 2009, Desent (Saint Louis Art Museum) 2009, Afloat (Galeria Estiarte Madrid) 2009, Flight (Harn Museum Univ of Florida) 2009, De Lar Warr Pavillion Bexhill on Sea 2011; *Selected Group Exhibitions* Explorations of the Environment: Landscape Redefined (Barbara Gillman Gallery Miami) 2000, Light x 8 (Jewish Museum NY) 2000, Eat, Fuck, Die (Platform London) 2000, 10th India Triennale Delhi 2001, The gallery: UNCOVERED (Univ of Essex) 2001, No World Without You. Reflections of Identity in New British Art (Herzliya Museum Tel Aviv) 2001, Read Only Memory (Mead Gallery Warwick Arts Centre) 2001, Double Agent. Catherine Yass (Sir William Dunn Sch of Pathology Oxford) 2001, Multiplication: Artists' Multiples, Artists Multiplied (Br Cncl touring exhbn) 2001, Wetterling Gallery Sweden 2002, Tate Modern Collection (Tate Modern London) 2002, Glass Box Project: Catherine Yass (ARTLAB 16 at ICSTM London) 2002, The Ink Jetty (Neon Gallery) 2002, The City That Never Was: Fantastic Architecture in Western Art (touring exhibition) 2003, Wetterling 25-ars jubileum (Wetterling Gallery Stockholm) 2003, Some Things We Like... (aspreyjacques London) 2003, Up Close and Personal (Nottingham Castle Drawing With Light Int Photography Festival) 2003, Interior View: Artists explore the language of architecture 2004, WOW (Henry Art Gallery Seattle) 2004, Les Grande Spectacles (Museum der Moderne Salzburg) 2005, In Progress (Locarno Int Film Festival) 2005, Art Futures (Contemporary Art Soc Bloomberg SPACE London) 2005, New Territories (Cultuurcentrum Brugge Belgium) 2006, Summer Exhibition (Royal Acad London) 2006, Dual Realities (fourth Seoul Int Media Biennale) 2006, In The Society of London Ladies (La Nuit Blanche Miss China Beauty Room Paris) 2006, Seoul Int Photography Festival 2006, Hyper Design (sixth Shanghai Biennale) 2006, Dateline Israel: Recent Photography and Video (Jewish Museum NY) 2007, Urban Landscapes: Emancipation and Nostalgia (David Winton Bell Gallery Providence) 2007, Sleeping and Dreaming (Deutsches Hygene-Museum Dresden) 2007, Weather Report Climate Change and Visual Arts (Centro Atlántico de Art) 2007, Summer Exhibition (Royal Acad London) 2007, Bare Life (Museum on the Seam Isreal) 2007, Parallax (Fieldgate Gallery London) 2008, Turned On (Alan Cristea Gallery London) 2008, Dateline Israel (Jewish Museum of Maryland) 2008, Eastern Standard: Western Artists in China (Mass MoCA North Adams Mass) 2008, Passing Thoughts & Making Plans London 2009, Learning Modern (Sch Art Inst of Chicago) 2009, There Goes the Neighbourhood (Cleveland MoCA) 2009, The Photographic Object (The Photographers Gallery London) 2009, Eastern Standard: Western Artists in China (Mass MoCA) 2009, Courage (Contemporary Art from the Fondazione Sandretto de Rebaugdengo Italy) 2010; *Work in Public Collections* Arts Cncl of England, Biblioteca Albertina Leipzig, Br Cncl

Collection London, Delfina Entrecanales London, Dundee City Cncl, Govt Art Collection London, Jewish Museum NY, Laing Art Gallery Newcastle, Nat Museum and Galleries of Wales Cardiff, New Art Gallery Walsall, Public Art Devpt Tst London, Royal Mail London, Royal Pump Rooms Royal Leamington Spa, Scottish Nat Gallery of Modern Art Edinburgh, Tate Gallery London; *Awards* Glen Dimplex Award Irish Museum of Modern Art Dublin 1999, Sci-Art Wellcome Tst 2000, Year of the Artist Award Arts Cncl of England 2000, 10th India Triennale Award New Delhi 2001, shortlisted Turner Prize 2002, Wellcome Tst Award 2002; *Style*— Ms Catherine Yass; ✉ Alison Jacques Gallery, 16–18 Berners Street, London W1T 3LN (e-mail info@alisonjacquesgallery.com, website www.alisonjacquesgallery.com)

YASS, Irving; CB (1993); s of Abraham Yass (d 1961), and Fanny, *née* Caplin (d 1980); *b* 20 December 1935; *Educ* Harrow Co GS, Balliol Coll Oxford (BA); *m* 14 Aug 1962, Marion Ruth, da of Benjamin Leighton (d 1979); 1 da (Catherine b 1963), 2 s (David b 1965, Michael b 1966); *Career* asst princ Miny of Transport and Civil Aviation 1958, private sec to jt parly sec 1960, princ HM Treasy 1967–70, asst sec DOE 1971, sec Ctee of Inquiry into Local Govt Fin 1974–76; Dept of Transport 1976–: under-sec fin 1982–86, dir tport policy for London 1987–94; dir of planning and tport Government Office for London 1994–95, dir policy London First 1995–2008 (policy advsr 2008), ind conslt 2008–; *Style*— Irving Yass, Esq, CB

YASSUKOVICH, Stanislas Michael; CBE (1991); s of Dimitri Yassukovich, and Denise Yassukovich; *b* 5 February 1935; *Educ* Deerfield Acad Mass, Harvard Univ; *m* Diana Veronica, da of Ralph Obre Crofton Townsend; 2 s (Michael, Nicholas), 1 da (Tatyana); *Career* served US Marine Corps 1957–61; White Weld & Co: joined in Zurich 1961, London 1962, gen ptnr NY 1969, md London until 1973; EuroBanking Co Ltd London: md 1973, dep chm 1983–85; chm: Merrill Lynch Europe Ltd 1985–91, Cayzer Continuation PCC Ltd 2004–, S M Yassukovich & Co Ltd; non-exec chm: Flextech plc 1989–97 (dep chm 1997–2000), Park Place Capital Ltd 1991–, Henderson Euro Tst plc 1992–2008, Easdaq 1997–2000, Manek Investment Mgmnt Ltd 1998–; vice-chm Bristol & West plc 1991–99; dep chm: ABC International Bank plc 1993–2008, ABC International Bank Ltd 1985–2008, SW Water plc 1997–99 (non-exec dir 1992–99); non-exec dir: Mossiman's Ltd 1989–98, Tradepoint Financial Networks plc 1997–99, Telewest Communications 2000–03, Fortis Investments SA 2006–09; a dep chm Stock Exchange 1986–89, chm The Securities Assoc 1987–91; chm City Disputes Panel 1994–98; *Recreations* hunting, polo; *Clubs* White's, Buck's, The Brook (USA), Travellers (Paris); *Style*— Stanislas Yassukovich, Esq, CBE

YATES, Brian Douglas; s of Bertram Yates (d 1993), and Barbara, *née* Wenham (d 1984); *b* 1 May 1944; *Educ* Uppingham, Clare Coll Cambridge (MA), London Business Sch (MBA); *m* 1971, Patricia, da of Arthur Hutchinson, DFC, of Dublin; 1 s (Justin b 1976); *Career* various engrg appointments with Molins, RHP Bearings, Thorn EMI and Dexion; dir: Morris Material Handling Ltd 1988–2002, Euroconsumer Publications Ltd 1992–2014, Trading Standards Services Ltd 1992–2014; Consumers' Assoc: memb Cncl 1986–2014, chm Business Ctee 1989–1997, chm Cncl 1994–2007; memb: Northampton BC 1979–83, Hants CC 1985–89, Heathrow Airport Consultative Ctee 1992–, Fitness to Practice Panels GMC 2001–12, Immigration Appeal Tbnl 2003–14, Fitness to Practice Panel NMC 2009–, Appeals Ctee Law Society of Scotland 2014–; public memb Network Rail 2008–11; ombudsman for Estate Agents Cncl 1999–2005, Insolvency Licensing Ctee ICAEW 2007–13, chm Probate Ctee ICAEW 2013–; Eur Ing, CEng, MIM, FRSA; *Recreations* real and lawn tennis, orienteering, ski touring; *Clubs* Athenaeum, Royal Over-Seas League, Hatfield House Tennis, Harpenden Lawn Tennis, Lunar Soc of Birmingham; *Style*— Brian Yates, Esq; ✉ 19 Park Avenue South, Harpenden, Hertfordshire AL5 2DZ (☎ 01582 768484, fax 01582 767989); Consumers' Association, 2 Marylebone Road, London NW1 4DF (☎ 020 7770 7877, fax 020 7770 7650, e-mail brian.yates@which.net)

YATES, David; *b* 8 October 1963; *Educ* Univ of Essex, Georgetown Univ Washington DC; *Career* television and film dir; *Television* incl: The Bill 1994–95, Tale of Three Seaside Towns 1995, The Sins 2000, The Way We Live Now 2001 (Best Drama Serial BAFTA), State of Play 2003 (Best Directorial Achievement in Television Movie/Serial Directors Guild of GB 2003), The Young Visiters 2003, Sex Traffic 2004, The Girl in the Café 2005; *Film* incl: Harry Potter and the Order of the Phoenix 2007, Harry Potter and the Half-Blood Prince 2009, Harry Potter and the Deathly Hallows: Part 1 2010, Harry Potter and the Deathly Hallows: Part 2 2011; *Style*— Mr David Yates; ✉ c/o Elinor Burns, Casarotto Marsh Limited, Waverley House, 7–12 Noel Street, London W1F 8GQ

YATES, Prof (Anthony) David; s of Cyril Yates, and Violet Ethel, *née* Man; *b* 5 May 1946; *Educ* Bromley GS, St Catherine's Coll Oxford (David Blank exhibitioner, MA, Frank Alan Bullock prize), Coll of Law Guildford; *m* 1 (m dis 1989), Carolyn Paula, *née* Hamilton; 3 da (Sarah Olivia Ann, Katherine Lucy Hannah, Rachel Jane Louise); m 2, Susanna Margaret, *née* McGarry; *Career* Univ of Hull: asst lectr in law 1969–72, dep warden Morgan Hall of Residence 1969–70, warden Newholme Student Residence 1970–72; Univ of Bristol: lectr in law 1972–74, dep warden Wills Hall of Residence 1972–74, visiting lectr 1974–75; Univ of Manchester: lectr in law 1974–76, warden Chandos Hall of Residence UMIST 1975–76, sr lectr in law 1976–79, princ Dalton Hall 1976–80 (pt/t 1979–80), visiting prof 1979–80; Univ of Essex: chm Dept of Law 1979–83, dean Sch of Law 1979–84, Fndn prof of law 1979–87, pro-vice-chllr 1985–87, visiting prof 1987–89; ptnr Baker & McKenzie 1987–2001 (chief operating offr 1998–2001), warden Robinson Coll Cambridge 2001–; govr Coll of Law 2001–12 (dep chm 2005–09, chm 2009–12); visiting prof of law Univ of NSW 1985, Parsons visiting fell Univ of Sydney 1985, adjunct prof of law Univ of Sydney 2007–15; Law Soc of Eng and Wales: memb Cncl 1992–97, memb Trg Ctee 1993–97, chm Legal Practice Course Bd 1995–97, chm Working Party on review of Legal Practice Course 1996; memb Ctee City of London Law Soc 1993–98, memb Trg and Educn Ctee Slrs' Regulation Authy 2013–15; memb: Advsy Ctee for Law Trg Within the Office American Bar Assoc 1988–2001, Advsy Bd Orientation in American Law Prog Univ of Calif 1990–2012, Advsy Ctee Centre for Advanced Legal Studies Univ of Leuven Belgium 1994–2012; Public Housing Law ed Encyclopaedia of Social Welfare Law 1973–80, gen ed The Professional Lawyer 1991–93; memb: Advsy Bd Urban Law and Policy 1978–, Editorial Bd Review of International Business Law 1988–95, Editorial Bd Jl of Contract Law 1988–; LLD (hc) Univ of Law; Freeman City of London 1993; memb Law Soc 1969; *Publications* Exclusion Clauses in Contracts (1978, 2 edn 1982), Leases of Business Premises (1979), Landlord and Tenant Law (with A J Hawkins, 1981, 2 edn 1986), Standard Business Contracts (with A J Hawkins, 1986), The Carriage of Goods by Land, Sea and Air (ed-in-chief and contrib, 1993), The Carriage of Goods by Land and Air (with Malcolm Clarke, 2004, 2 edn 2008); also author of numerous articles in various jls; *Recreations* opera, food and wine, rugby football; *Clubs* Oxford and Cambridge, RSA; *Style*— Prof David Yates; ✉ Robinson College, Cambridge CB3 9AN (☎ 01233 339100)

YATES, Prof (William) Edgar; s of Douglas Yates (d 1955), and Doris, *née* Goode (d 1990); *b* 30 April 1938, Hove, E Sussex; *Educ* Fettes, Emmanuel Coll Cambridge (MA, PhD); *m* 6 April 1963, Barbara Anne, da of Wolfgang Fellowes (d 1984); 2 s (Thomas b 1971, Paul b 1975); *Career* 2 Lt RASC 1957–58; lectr in German Univ of Durham 1963–72, prof of German Univ of Exeter 1972–2001 (dep vice-chllr 1986–89, prof emeritus 2001–), Germanic ed Modern Language Review 1981–88, ed Nestroyana 1992–2009 (jtly with U Tanzer 2002–09); Österreichisches Ehrenkreuz für Wissenschaft und Kunst 1. Klasse 2001; memb: Modern Humanities Res Assoc (memb Ctee 1980–2015), Eng Goethe Soc (memb Cncl 1984–2009), Int Nestroy Soc (memb Cncl 1986–, vice-pres 1997–), Viennese Shakespeare Soc (vice-pres 1992–2002); chm of govrs Exeter Sch 1994–2008; corresponding fell Austrian Acad of Sciences 1992; FBA 2002; *Books* Grillparzer: A Critical Introduction (1972), Nestroy: Satire and Parody in Viennese Popular Comedy (1972), Humanity in Weimar and Vienna: The Continuity of an Ideal (1973), Tradition in the German Sonnet (1981), Nestroy (ed Stücke 12–14 1981–82, Stücke 34 1989, Stücke 18/I 1991, Stücke 22 1996, Stücke 17/II 1998, ed with J Hein Stücke 2 2000, ed with P Haida Nachträge I-II 2007), Viennese Popular Theatre (ed with J R P McKenzie,1985), Grillparzer und die europäische Tradition (ed with R Pichl and others, 1987), Schnitzler, Hofmannsthal, and the Austrian Theatre (1992), Nestroy and the Critics (1994), Vom schaffenden zum edierten Nestroy (ed, 1994), Theatre in Vienna: A Critical History, 1776–1995 (1996), Nestroys Reserve und andere Notizen (ed, 2000, revised edn 2003), Nestroy in München (with B Pargner, 2001), Der unbekannte Nestroy (ed, 2001), Bei die Zeitverhältnisse noch solche Privatverhältnisse (ed, 2001), Hinter den Kulissen von Biedermeier und Nachmärz (ed with H C Ehalt and J Hein, 2001), From Perinet to Jelinek: Viennese Theatre in its Political and Intellectual Context (ed with A Fiddler and J Warren, 2001), Briefe des Theaterdirektors Carl Carl und seiner Frau Margaretha Carl an Charlotte Birch-Pfeiffer (ed with B Pargner, 2004), Theater und Gesellschaft im Wien des 19.Jahrhunderts (ed with U Tanzer, 2006), Bin Dichter nur der Posse: Johann Nepomuk Nestroy, Versuch einer Biographie (2012); Festschrift, The Austrian Comic Tradition (ed J R P McKenzie and L Sharpe, 1998); *Recreations* theatre, opera, French wine; *Style*— Prof W E Yates, FBA; ✉ 7 Clifton Hill, Exeter EX1 2DL (☎ 01392 254713, e-mail w.e.yates@cliftonhill.co.uk)

YATES, Janty; da of Lt-Col Denys Ainsworth Yates, and Margaret, *née* Tyrer; *Educ* Highgrove Sch Ashford, Katinka Coll of Dress Design London; *Career* costume designer for film and television; *Television* Comic Strip 1991–92, Cracker 1993, Bliss (film) 1994, Karaoke 1996; *Film* costume asst: Quest for Fire 1981, Oxford Blues 1984, Dance with a Stranger 1985, Sour Sweet 1985; costume supervisor The Commitments 1991; costume designer: Bad Behaviour 1993, The Englishman Who Went Up a Hill But Came Down a Mountain 1995, Jude 1996, Welcome to Sarajevo 1997, The Man Who Knew Too Little 1997, Plunkett and Macleane 1999, With or Without You 1999, Gladiator 2000 (Academy Award Best Costume Design 2001, Las Vegas Film Critics Award Best Costume Design, BAFTA nomination for Best Costume Design), Hannibal 2001, Charlotte Gray 2001, Enemy at the Gates 2001, De-Lovely 2003, Kingdom of Heaven 2005, Miami Vice 2006, American Gangster 2007, Body of Lies 2008, Robin Hood 2010, Prometheus 2012, The Counselor 2012, The Vatican (portrait) 2013, Exodus 2013, The Martian 2014; *Recreations* riding, swimming, walking, gardening, film, theatre, 19th and 20th century art, reading, travel, scuba diving; *Style*— Ms Janty Yates; ✉ c/o Independent Talent Agency, Oxford House, 76 Oxford Street, London W1D 1BS (☎ 020 7034 2141)

YATES, Prof John Gordon; s of Thomas Edgar Yates (d 1973), and Mabel, *née* Price (d 1983); *b* 7 February 1937; *Educ* Dagenham County HS, SE Essex Tech Coll (BSc), Imperial Coll London (PhD, DIC); *m* 10 Sept 1960, Anne Elizabeth, da of Charles Henry Kersey; 1 s (Nicholas James b 7 Dec 1968); *Career* res technologist BP Chemicals 1962–64; UCL: lectr Dept of Chemical Engrg 1964–76, sr lectr 1976–84, reader in chemical technol 1984–90, prof of chemical engrg 1990, dean Faculty of Engrg 1991–93, Ramsay meml prof and head Dept of Chemical Engrg 1996–2003, Ramsay meml prof emeritus 2003–; external examiner in chem engrg Heriot-Watt Univ; memb Int Advsy Gp Swedish Strategic Res Prog in Multi-Phase Flow; Freeman City of London, Liveryman Worshipful Co of Engineers; DSc (Eng) London 1984; FRSC 1976, FIChemE 1992, FREng 1999; *Publications* Fundamentals of Fluidized-bed Chemical Processes (1983); over 120 publications in scientific literature and conf proceedings; *Recreations* music, literature, visual arts, astronomy, cooking; *Style*— Prof John Yates, FREng; ✉ 33 Parkside, London NW7 2LJ (☎ 020 8906 1896, fax 020 8906 1896, mobile 07530 485653, e-mail john@jgyates.fsnet.co.uk)

YATES, Roger Philip; s of Eric Yates, of Warrington, and Joyce Mary, *née* Brown; *b* 4 April 1957; *Educ* Boteler GS Warrington, Worcester Coll Oxford (BA), Univ of Reading; *m* 1, 7 Sept 1985 (m dis 1998), Kim Patricia, da of Anthony Gerald Gibbons, of Abinger, Surrey; 3 s (Max b 1987, Jeremy b 1989, Robert Alexander b 1992); m 2, 26 April 2003, Catriona MacLean; 1 da (Helena Rose b 2002); *Career* joined GT Mgmnt Ltd 1981, dir GT Mgmnt (UK) Ltd 1984–88, dir GT Mgmnt plc 1986–88, investment dir GT Unit Managers Ltd 1988; dir and chief investment offr Morgan Grenfell Investment Mgmnt 1988–94, dir Morgan Grenfell Asset Mgmnt 1991–94; dir and chief investment offr: LGT Asset Mgmnt plc 1994–98, Invesco Europe 1998–99; md Henderson Global Investors 1999–, ceo Henderson Gp plc (formerly HHG plc) 2003–; non-exec dir IG Gp Hldgs plc 2006–; *Recreations* golf, skiing, tennis; *Style*— Roger Yates, Esq

YATES-ROUND, Jeremy Laurence; s of Joseph Laurence John Yates-Round (d 2012), and Ellen Clancy, *née* Yapp; *b* 27 February 1961, Tunbridge Wells, Kent; *Educ* Tunbridge Wells Tech HS, West Kent Coll; *m* 27 April 1985, Theresa Tamara, *née* Britneff; 3 s (Joseph Laurence b 17 June 1991, Alexander William b 12 Sept 1993, Timothy James b 17 April 1996); *Career* export sales rep Hodder & Stoughton 1981–85, sales mangr William Collins 1985–89; Harper Collins Publishers: sales dir 1990–97, dep md Religious Div 1997–2000; md Sutton Publishing Ltd 2001–07, md UK and Europe Haynes Publishing plc 2009–; *Recreations* active memb of local church, listening to and playing music, football; *Style*— Jeremy Yates-Round, Esq; ✉ Haynes Publishing plc, Sparkford, Somerset BA22 7JJ (☎ 01963 440635, fax 01963 440001, e-mail jyates-round@haynes.co.uk)

YEA, Philip Edward; s of John Alfred William Yea (d 1971), and Elsie Beryl, *née* Putman; *b* 11 December 1954; *Educ* Wallington HS for Boys, Brasenose Coll Oxford (MA); *m* 5 Dec 1981, Daryl, da of William Anthony Walker; 2 s (William b 24 May 1984, Daniel b 6 Dec 1986), 1 da (Georgina b 20 Feb 1992); *Career* Perkins Engines Ltd 1977–80, Moteurs Perkins SA France 1980–82, Foursquare Div Mars Ltd 1982–83, Guinness plc 1984–88 (dir of business devpt United Distillers Group 1987–88), fin dir Cope Allman Packaging plc 1989–91 (joined 1988), fin dir Guinness plc 1993–97 (rejoined 1991), gp fin dir Diageo plc (following merger with Grand Metropolitan plc) 1997–99, md (private equity) Investcorp International 1999–2004, chief exec 3i Gp plc 2004–09; non-exec dir: William Baird plc 1995–99 (dep chm 1999), Manchester United plc 1999–2004 (sr non-exec dir and chm Audit Ctee), Halifax plc 1999–2001, HBOS plc 2001–04, Vodafone Gp plc 2005–, bwin.party digital entertainment plc 2014–16, Rocket Internet SE 2014–15, Computacenter 2015–; Aberdeen Asian Smaller Cos Investment Tst plc 2014–; sr ind dir Vodafone 2015–, chm Greene King plc 2016–; tstee Br Heart Fndn 2008–15 (chm Bd of Tstees 2009–15), ind dir and tstee Bd Francis Crick Inst 2011–; FCMA 1982, FRSA 1993, CIMgt 2000; *Recreations* family, cinema; *Style*— Philip Yea, Esq

YEATES, Andrew; *b* 27 September 1957; *m*; 2 c; *Career* admitted slr 1981; contracts mangr Thames Television and Thames Television International 1981–87, company lawyer Phonographic Performance Ltd 1987–88; Channel Four Television: prog acquisition exec 1988–89, sr prog acquisition exec 1989–90, head of acquisitions and business affrs 1991–94, corporation sec and head of rights 1994–99; DG BPI 2000–04 (dir legal affairs 1999–2000), gen counsel The Educational Recording Agency Ltd 2005–, intellectual property advsr Professional Publishers Assoc 2005–; dir: Br Copyright Cncl 2008–, The BRIT Sch; memb Law Soc; Liveryman Worshipful Co of Haberdashers; *Recreations* theatre, music; *Style*— Andrew Yeates; ✉ The Educational Recording Agency Ltd, 60 Gray's Inn Road, London WC1X 8LU (☎ 020 7837 3222, fax 020 7837 3750, e-mail ayeates@era.org.uk)

YELLAND, David Ian; s of John Michael Yelland, of York, and Patricia Ann, *née* McIntosh; *b* 14 May 1963, Harrogate, Yorks; *Educ* Brigg GS Lancs, Lanchester Poly Coventry (BA), Harvard Business Sch (AMP); *m* 1, 19 Jan 1996, Tania Farrell (d 2006); 1 s (Max David Farrell b 1998); m 2, 11 Dec 2010, Charlotte Elston; 1 da (Louisa Francesca Rose b 2012); *Career* graduate trainee journalist Company Sch Hastings Westminster Press 1984–85, jr reporter Bucks Advertiser Gerrards Cross 1985–87, news and industrial reporter Northern Echo Darlington 1987–88, journalist North West Times and Sunday Times Manchester 1988, city reporter Thomson Regnl Newspapers London 1988–90, NY corr The Sun 1993 (city ed 1990–93); New York Post: business ed 1993–96, dep ed 1996–1998; ed The Sun 1998–2003, vice-pres News Corp 2003–04, vice-chm Weber Shandwick 2004–06, ptnr Brunswick Gp LLP 2006–; *Books* The Truth About Leo (2010); *Recreations* graduate trainee journalist Company Sch Hastings Westminster Press 1984–85, jr reporter Bucks Advertiser Gerrards Cross 1985–87, news and industrial reporter Northern Echo Darlington 1987–88, journalist North West Times and Sunday Times Manchester 1988, city reporter Thomson Regnl Newspapers London 1988–90, NY corr The Sun 1993 (city ed 1990–93); New York Post: business ed 1993–96, dep ed 1996–1998; ed The Sun 1998–2003, vice-pres News Corp 2003–04, vice-chm Weber Shandwick 2004–06, ptnr Brunswick Gp LLP 2006–; tstee Action of Addiction 2011–; *Clubs* Savile, RAC, Royal Soc of Arts; *Style*— David Yelland, Esq; ✉ Brunswick Group LLP, 16 Lincoln's Inn Fields, London WC2A 3ED

YELLOWLEES, Prof Lesley Jane; CBE (2014, MBE 2005); *Educ* St Hilary's Girls' Sch Edinburgh, Univ of Edinburgh (BSc, PhD); *m* Peter, 1 s (Mark), 1 da (Sarah); *Career* Univ of Edinburgh: demonstrator 1986–89, lectr 1989–2005, prof of inorganic electrochemistry 2005–, vice-princ, head Coll of Science and Engrg; FRSC 2005 (pres 2012–14), FRSE 2012; *Style*— Prof Lesley Yellowlees, CBE, FRSE; ✉ College Office, Science and Engineering, Weir Building, Max Born Crescent, The King's Building, West Mains Road, Edinburgh EH9 3BF

YELTON, His Hon Judge Michael Paul; s of Joseph William Yelton (d 1998), and Enid Hazel Yelton (d 2006); *b* 21 April 1950; *Educ* Colchester Royal GS, CCC Cambridge (MA); *m* 1973, Judith Sara, *née* Chaplin; 1 da, 2 s; *Career* called to the Bar 1972, in practice 1973–98, recorder 1996–98 (asst recorder 1992–96), circuit judge (SE Circuit) 1998–; dir of studies in law CCC Cambridge 1977–81; *Books* Fatal Accidents, a practical guide to compensation (1998), Martin Travers, an appreciation (jtly, 2003), Trams, Trolleybuses, Buses and the Law (2004), Anglican Papalism (2005), Peter Anson (2005), Alfred Hope Patten and the Shrine of Our Lady of Walsingham (2006), Empty Tabernacles (2006), Anglican Church Building in London 1915–1945 (jtly, 2007), Alfred Hope Patten: His life and times in pictures (2007), West Mon (jtly, 2008), The Twenty One (2009), Blackwells of Earls Colne (2009), An Anglo-Catholic Scrapbook (2010), The South India Controversy (2010), Bedwas and Machen UDC (2010), Gelligaer (2011), Butterworth's New Law Guide to the Family Procedure Rules (jtly, 2011), Caerphilly (2013), Anglican Church Building in London 1946–2012 (jtly, 2013); *Recreations* reading, ecclesiology, football, transport; *Style*— His Hon Judge Yelton; ✉ Cambridge County Court, 197 East Road, Cambridge CB1 1BA

YENTOB, Alan; *b* 11 March 1947; *Career* BBC: joined as gen trainee 1968, prodr/presenter BBC Radio and External Broadcasting 1968–69, asst dir Arts Features TV 1969–73, prodr and dir Omnibus strand BBC2 1973–75, fndr ed Arena arts strand BBC2 1978–85, head of music and arts BBC TV 1985–87, controller of BBC2 1988–93, controller of BBC1 1993–96, dir of progs BBC TV 1996–97, dir of television BBC TV (also i/c BBC1, BBC2, Online and digital servs except news) 1997–2000, dir of drama, entertainment and children's 2000–04, creative dir 2004–; chm ICA 2002– (memb Advsy Ctee); govr The South Bank Bd Ltd 1999–; tstee: Architecture Fndn, Kids Company, Timebank 2001–; hon fell: RCA, RIBA; fell: BFI 1997, RTS; *Programmes* Arena documentaries incl: The Orson Welles Story, Billie Holiday – The Long Night of Lady Day, The Private Life of the Ford Cortina, My Way, The Chelsea Hotel; responsible for progs, films and series for BBC2 incl: The Late Show, Oranges Are Not The Only Fruit, The Snapper, Truly Madly Deeply, Have I Got News For You, Absolutely Fabulous, Rab C Nesbitt, Troubleshooter, Pandora's Box, Video Diaries, live relays of operas Tosca and Stiffelio, opera series The Vampyr; for BBC1 incl: introduction of Monday episode of EastEnders, re-introduction of Sunday afternoon family serial (incl Just William and The Borrowers), Leonardo series (writer and presenter), Imagine series (presenter); *Awards* incl: Best Arts Series Br Academy Awards for Arena 1982, 1983 and 1984, Best Arts Series Broadcasting Press Guild Awards for Arena 1985, Gold Award NY Film Festival and Int EMMY for Omnibus film The Treble 1985, Programming Supremo of the Year Broadcast Prodn Awards 1997; *Style*— Alan Yentob, Esq; ✉ BBC Television Centre, Wood Lane, London W12 7RJ (☎ 020 8743 8000)

YEO, Diane Helen; da of Brian Harold Pickard, FRCS, and late Joan Daisy, *née* Pickard; *b* 22 July 1945; *Educ* Blackheath HS, Univ of London, Institut Francais de Presse; *m* 30 March 1970, Timothy Stephen Kenneth Yeo, MP, *qv*, s of Dr Kenneth John Yeo; 1 s (Jonathan, *qv*, b 1970), 1 da (Emily b 1972); *Career* BBC Radio prodn 1968–74, dir clearing house scheme Africa Educnl Tst 1974–79, head of fundraising Girlguiding UK 1979–82, dir appeals and public rels YWCA 1982–85, chief exec Inst of Fundraising 1985–88, charity cmmr for Eng and Wales 1989–95, chief exec CLIC Sargent 1995–2001, exec dir UK for UNHCR 2001–03, chief exec Muscular Dystrophy Campaign 2003–05, chief exec Chelsea and Westminster Health Charity 2005–08, chm 151 Proprietors Ltd 2009–; conslt Diane Yeo Assocs 2003–, chair Arts Educnl Schs 2004–13; chair: Charity Standards Ctee 1991–94, Advsy Ctee on Trusteeship 1993–95, Advsy Ctee to Home Secretary on Volunteering 1995–96; memb: Nathan Ctee on Effectiveness and the Voluntary Sector 1989–90, Planning for Partnership Ctee 1995–96, Cncl and Audit Ctee Advtg Standards Authy 1997–, Fundraising Regulation Advsy Gp/Cabinet Office 2001–04, Advsy Cncl NCVO 1997–, Review Ctee Assoc of NHS Charities 2006–08; patron CANCERactive 2004–, memb Ct of Govrs Univ of Westminster 2008–, chair SOS Westminster 2010–, chair ETAT (Encouragement Through the Arts and Talking) 2014–, memb Mgmnt Bd Repeat Street Cinema 2015–; ambass Save the Children 1986; Charity Accounts Award 2001, Local Campaigner of the Year Award 2011; Paul Harris fell 2000; fell Inst of Fundraising 1983, FRSA 1989; *Recreations* piano, tennis, photgraphy; *Clubs* RSA, Sandwich Tennis; *Style*— Mrs Diane Yeo; ✉ diyeo@outlook.com

YEO, Jonathan; s of Tim Yeo, MP, *qv*, and Diane Yeo, *qv*, *née* Pickard; *b* 18 December 1970; *Educ* Westminster, Univ of Kent (BA); *m* m 2006, Shebah Ronay; 2 da (Tabitha b 2003, Yasmin b 2007); *Career* artist; self-taught, specialising in portraits and collages; cmmnd by House of Commons as Britain's first Election Artist to paint the three main political pty ldrs 2001; exhbns incl: The Outsiders (Lazarides Gallery London), Contemporary Display (Nat Portrait Gallery), 400 Years of British Portraiture (Philip Mould), BP Portrait Award (Nat Portrait Gall), Jonathan Yeo's Sketch book (solo exhbn, Eleven) 2006, The Naked Portrait (Scottish Nat Gall) 2007, Blue Period (solo exhbn, Lazarides Gallery) 2008, The Outsiders (282 Bowery NY) 2008 and (New Art Gallery Walsall) 2009, Porn in the USA (solo exhbn, Lazarides LA) 2010, You're Only Young Twice (solo exhbn, Larazides) 2011, I've Got You Under My Skin (solo exhbn, Circle Culture Berlin) 2012, Jonathan Yeo Portraits (touring solo exhbn, Nat Portrait Gallery, The Lowry Manchester and The Laing Art Gallery) 2013, Exposure 2015 (Circle Culture Gallery, Hamburg); cmmns incl: HRH The Duke of Edinburgh, Rt Hon Tony Blair, Lord Lloyd Webber, Erin O'Connor, Dennis Hopper, Sir David Attenborough (for Royal Collection) 2010, Sir Michael Parkinson (for Nat Portrait Gall) 2010; portrait of Rupert Murdoch acquired by Nat Portrait Gallery 2006, collage portrait of Pres George W Bush acquired by Bibliotheque Nat de France 2008, HRH Duchess of Cornwall (for Clarence House) 2014; patron Lymphoma Soc; *Publications* Jonathan Yeo: Blue Period (2008), Jonathan Yeo: You're Only Young Twice (2011), The Many Faces of Jonathan Yeo (2013); *Clubs* Chelsea Arts, Groucho, Shoreditch House; *Style*— Jonathan Yeo, Esq; ✉ e-mail info@jonathanyeo.com, website www.jonathanyeo.com)

YEO, Timothy Stephen Kenneth (Tim); s of Dr Kenneth John Yeo (d 1979), and Norah Margaret Yeo; *b* 20 March 1945; *Educ* Charterhouse, Emmanuel Coll Cambridge; *m* 1970, Diane Helen, *qv*, da of Brian Harold Pickard; 1 s (Jonathan, *qv*, b 1970), 2 da (Emily b 1972, Claudia-Marie b 1993); *Career* chief exec Scope 1980–83; MP (Cons) Suffolk S 1983–2015 (Parly candidate (Cons) Bedwellty 1974); jt sec: Cons Backbench Fin Ctee 1984–87, Social Services Select Ctee 1985–88; PPS to Rt Hon Douglas Hurd 1988–90, Parly under sec Dept of Environment 1990–92, Parly under sec Dept of Health 1992–93, min of state Dept of Environment 1993–94 (resigned); oppn spokesman on environment and local govt 1997–98, shadow min Agriculture, Fisheries and Food 1998–2001, shadow sec of state for culture, media and sport 2001–02, shadow sec of state for trade and industry 2002–03, shadow sec of state for public servs, health and educn 2003–04, shadow sec of state for transport and the environment 2004–05; memb Select Ctee on Employment 1994–96, memb Treasy Select Ctee 1996–97, chm Environmental Audit Select Ctee 2005–10, chm Energy and Climate Change Select Ctee 2010–15; chm Univent plc 1995–2009, non-exec chm AFC Energy 2007–, non-exec chm Eco City Vehicles plc 2007–12, non-exec chm TMO Renewables Ltd 2010–14; non-exec dir: Genus plc 2002–04, Eurotunnel plc 2007–, ITI Energy Ltd; chm Energy 2050 Industrial Advsy Bd Univ of Sheffield; dir Worcester Engrg Co Ltd 1975–86, asst treas Bankers Trust Company 1970–73, treas Int Voluntary Service 1975–78, tstee Tanzania Devpt Tst 1980–95, chm Charities VAT Reform Gp 1981–88, chm Tadworth Ct Tst 1983–91, chm Cncl Victoria Univ Uganda 2011–; golf corr Country Life 1994–, golf columnist FT 2004–08; *Publications* Public Accountability and Regulation of Charities (1983), Green Gold (2010); *Recreations* skiing; *Clubs* Garrick, MCC, Royal and Ancient, Sunningdale Golf, Royal St George's Golf; *Style*— Tim Yeo, Esq; ✉ House of Commons, London SW1A 0AA (☎ 020 7219 3000)

YEOMAN, Angela Betty; OBE, DL; da of Harry James Newell, of Weston-super-Mare, and Mabel Elizabeth; *b* 26 April 1931; *Educ* Stonar Sch; *m* 1952, John Foster Yeoman (decd); 2 da (Sally Jane b 9 Dec 1953, Susan Kate b 13 July 1955), 2 s (David b 9 Feb 1958, John b 9 Feb 1961); *Career* chm Foster Yeoman Ltd 1988–2006; memb: Somerset Building Tst, Cncl Royal Bath and West; Liveryman Worshipful Co of Paviors, Freeman Worshipful Co of Watermen and Lightermen; High Sheriff Somerset 2000; hon fell Inst of Quarrying 1990; *Clubs* Sloane, Pony; *Style*— Mrs Angela Yeoman; ✉ Southfield House, Whatley, Frome, Somerset BA11 3JY (☎ 01373 836209, mobile 07771 647175, fax 01373 836020, e-mail ayeoman@btinternet.com)

YEOMAN, Martin; s of Arthur John Yeoman (d 1993), and Gladys Dorothy, *née* Illsley; *b* 21 July 1953; *Educ* RA Schs (Silver medal for drawing); *Children* 1 s (George Edward Conway b 9 Feb 1998); *Career* artist; occasional painting companion to HRH The Prince of Wales; RP; *Solo Exhibitions* Highgate Gallery 1986, Two Tours of the Middle East (Agnews) 1987, New Grafton Gallery 1990, The Queen's Grandchildren (National Portrait Gallery) 1993, Selected Works (Mompesson House National Trust) 1994, Christopher Wood Contemporary Art 1995, Yeoman's Yemen (British Council exhbn National Art Gallery Sana'a and John Martin of London) 1997, Paintings in the Holy Land (Alan Kluckow Fine Art) 2000, Hindustan to Malabar (Offer Waterman and Co) 2002, India (Indar Pasricha Fine Art) 2004; *Group Exhibitions* Royal Acad Summer Exhbn 1976–77, 1979–90 and 1992–96, Imperial Tobacco Portrait Award (National Portrait Gallery) 1981 and 1985, Six Young Artists (Agnews) 1985, Four Painters (New Grafton Gallery) 1987, The Long Perspective (National Trust Exhbn, Agnews) 1987, A Personal Choice (Fermoy Gallery) 1988, Salute to Turner (National Trust Exhbn, Agnews) 1989, The Order of Merit (National Portrait Gallery) 1992, The Last of the Tide (Queen's Gallery Buckingham Palace) 2015, BP Portrait Award (Nat Portrait Gallery) 2016; *Work in Collections* HM The Queen, HRH The Prince of Wales, Sir Brinsley Ford, Diocese of Birmingham, Baring Brothers, Grimsby Sch of Art, National Portrait Gallery, British Council, British Museum, Ruth Borchard Collection 2015; *Awards* David Murray Landscape scholar 1978, Richard Ford scholar 1979, Elizabeth Greenshield scholar 1980, Hamerson Purchase Prize 1984, Menana Joy Schwabe Prize 1996, Philip Soloman Drawing Prize 1998, The Ondaatje Prize for Portraiture 2002, Bill Turner Prize 2004, Woodhay Picture Gallery Prize for Drawing 2016, Doreen McIntosh Prize 2016; *Clubs* New English Art; *Style*— Martin Yeoman, Esq; ✉ e-mail info@martinyeoman.com, website www.martinyeomanfineartist.com

YEOMANS, Prof Julia Mary; da of Anthony Harold Hickling Yeomans (d 1990), and Edna Maud, *née* Lewis (d 2012); *Educ* Univ of Oxford (MA, DPhil); *m* 1990, Prof Peter John Hore; 4 da (Katie b 1987, Victoria b 1989, Rosie b 1992, Rebecca b 2001); *Career* postdoctoral research asst Cornell Univ, lectr Univ of Southampton, prof of physics Univ of Oxford, Pauline Chan fell in physics St Hilda's Coll Oxford (tutor 1983–); EPJE de Gennes Lecture Prize 2013; FInstP 2000, FRS 2013; *Recreations* running, tango, travel, walking; *Style*— Prof Julia Yeomans; ✉ Rudolf Peierls Centre for Theoretical Physics, 1 Keble Road, Oxford OX1 3NP

YEOMANS, Lucy; da of Harry Hammond Light Yeomans, and Margot, *née* Boyle (d 2003); *b* 1 November 1970; *Educ* Univ of St Andrews (MA); *Career* successively: arts ed rising to ed Boulevard magazine Paris, arts ed The European, features ed then dep ed Tatler, features dir Vogue; ed Harper's Bazaar (formerly Harpers & Queen) 2000–; FRSA; *Style*— Miss Lucy Yeomans; ✉ Harper's Bazaar, 72 Broadwick Street, London W1F 9EP (☎ 020 7439 5533)

YEOMANS, Richard David; s of Richard James Yeomans (d 1964), of Basingstoke, Hants, and Elsie Marian, *née* Winson; *b* 15 February 1943; *Educ* Hartley Wintney Co Secdy Modern Sch, Hants Coll of Agric, Shuttleworth Coll (NDA); *m* 6 April 1968, Doreen Ann, da of William Herring, of Aldershot, Hants; 1 da (Claire b 14 Dec 1972), 1 s (Jonathan b 24 Feb 1976); *Career* with Milk Mktg Bd 1965–71; Unigate plc: area mangr (tport) 1971, gen mangr (milk) 1975, latterly bd dir; md: Wincanton Transport Ltd 1978–, Wincanton Group Ltd 1982–91; ops dir Milk Marketing Bd 1994, chief exec Milk Marque 1996–98 (ops dir 1994–96); chm: TLS Range plc 1992–98, Blakes Chilled Distribution Ltd 1997–99, Pourshins plc 1998–2004; dir: Peninsula Milk Processors Ltd 1998–2001, Aim Hire Ltd 1998–2004; princ David Yeomans Associates 1991–; exec vice-chm Montagu Ventures 2000–06; memb: Tport Tbnl 1999–2013, Residential Property Tbnl Serv 1999–2008, SE Flood Defence Ctee 2000–02; Liveryman Worshipful Co of Carmen; CIMgt 1982, FCIT 1989, FRSA 1990; *Recreations* shooting, boats, gardening, photography, travel; *Clubs* RAC; *Style*— David Yeomans, Esq; ✉ 43 Lillybrook, Lyneham, Chippenham, Wiltshire SN15 4AA (☎ 07818 558310, e-mail richarddyeomans@btinternet.com); Casa das Flores, Arco da Calheta, Madeira

YEOWART, Geoffrey Bernard Brian; s of Brian Albert Yeowart (d 2011), and Vera Ivy, *née* Goring; *b* 28 March 1949; *Educ* Ardingly, Univ of Southampton (LLB), KCL (LLM); *m* 1, 1979, Patricia Eileen (d 2008), da of Oswald Anthony (d 1984); 1 da (Clare b 1980), 2 s (Thomas b 1983, Matthew b 1986); m 2, 2010, Frances Winifred, da of Rev Canon Gervase Markham, MBE, of Morland, Cumbria (d 2007); *Career* admitted slr 1975 (admitted Hong Kong 1982); ptnr: Durrant Piesse 1985–88, Hogan Lovells Int LLP (formerly Lovell White Durrant then Lovells LLP) 1988–2013 (conslt 2013–); memb: Bank of England's City Euro Gp 1998–2006, HM Treasury's Euro Business Advsy Gp 2000–

05, FMLC (Financial Markets Law Ctee) and HM Treasury Task Forces on Emergency Powers and Financial Sector Operational Disruption 2003, FMLC working parties on administration set-off and investment bank insolvency; dep chm Financial Law Ctee CLLS (City of London Law Soc) 1999–2013; memb of CLLS working parties on the Euro, corporate insolvency law, financial collateral, set-off, modernisation of Part VII CA 89, Banking Act 2009, registration of charges, European securities law, bank recovery and resolution, Scottish floating charges and English opinion letters; memb Editorial Bd: Jl of Int Banking and Financial Law, Law and Financial Markets Review; Distinguished Service Award City of London Slrs' Co 2003; memb Law Soc; *Books* Euro Guide on Legal Issues (1999), European Banking Law (contrib, 2 edn, 1999), Yeowart and Parsons on the Law of Financial Collateral (2016); *Recreations* sailing, reading; *Clubs* Royal Dart Yacht; *Style*— Geoffrey Yeowart, Esq; ✉ Hogan Lovells International LLP, Atlantic House, Holborn Viaduct, London EC1A 2FG (☎ 020 7296 2000, fax 020 7296 2001, e-mail geoffrey.yeowart@hoganlovells.com)

YHAP, Laetitia Karoline; da of Leslie Neville Yhap (d 1987), and Elizabeth, *née* Kogler; *b* 1 May 1941; *Educ* Fulham Co GS, Camberwell Sch of Arts and Crafts (NDD), Slade Sch of Fine Art (DFA); *m* 1963 (m dis 1980), Jeffrey Camp; 1 s (Ajax b 1984); partner Michael Rycroft (sep 2007); *Career* artist in oils; Leverhulme Res award (travel in Italy) 1962–63; first solo show Norwich Sch of Art 1964, Young Contemporaries FBA galleries and tour 1965, various showings with London Gp 1965–, three solo shows Piccadilly Gallery 1968, 1970 and 1973, solo summer show Serpentine Gallery 1975, Drawings of People (mixed exhibition, Serpentine Gallery London) 1975, John Moores (mixed exhibition) Liverpool, The British Art Show 1979, Art and The Sea (ICA and tour) 1981, Tolly Cobbold 1983, solo show Air Gallery London 1984, The Hard-Won Image (Tate Gallery) 1984, solo show touring The Business of the Beach (Laing Art Gallery Newcastle) 1988, Picturing People (Br Cncl Exhibition touring Far East) 1990, solo show Rye Art Gallery 1991, solo show Worthing Art Gallery and Museum 1992, Life at the Edge (The Charleston Gallery) 1993, solo show Bound by the Sea (Gymnasium Gallery Berwick-upon-Tweed) 1994, solo show Maritime Counterpoint (Boundary Gallery London) 1996, solo show In Monochrome (Gallery Lydd Library Kent) 1998, solo show The Story So Far (Hastings Tst) 1999, solo show Extemporizations (Hastings Tst) 2000, Being in the Picture – A Retrospective (Piers Feetham Gallery London) 2002, A Journey to the Beginning: Images and Distillations 1963–2000 (Piers Feetham Gallery London) 2011, Fishermen of Hastings Stade (De'Longhi Print Room Pallant House Chichester) 2013, All Hands – A Time Before Steel Boats, Tractors & Mobiles on the Stade (Stade Hall Hastings) 2015, Face to Face Portraits (from The Andrew Lambirth Collection) 2016; memb London Gp; *Recreations* badminton, concert-going, Tai Chi, Chinese calligraphy, choral singing; *Style*— Ms Laetitia Yhap; ✉ 12 The Croft, Hastings, East Sussex TN34 3HH (website www.axisartists.org.uk)

YIANGOU, Constantinos; s of Andreas Yiangou, and Pantelitsa Yiangou; *b* 28 August 1961, Nicosia, Cyprus; *Educ* Pancyprian Gymnasium Nicosia, St Mary's Hosp Med Sch London, Univ of London (BSc, MB BS); *m* 4 Oct 2008, Carrie, *née* MacIntyre; *Career* SHO St Mary's Hosp London, St Charles Hosp London, Mayday Hosp and Brook Gen Hosp 1988–91, registrar in gen and vascular surgery Hillingdon Hosp and Central Middx Hosp 1992–93, res fell and hon registrar Dept of Breast Surgery and Oncology Charing Cross Hosp 1993–95, specialist registrar in gen and breast surgery Charing Cross Hosp, Hemel Hempstead Hosp and Lister Hosp Herts 1995–99, conslt gen surgn specialising in surgical oncology, breast and endocrine surgery Queen Alexandra Hosp Portsmouth 1999–; Portsmouth Hosps NHS Tst: clinical dir of breast and endocrine surgery 2004–10, assoc med dir 2009–, chief of surgery and cancer 2010–16, former lead clinician for breast cancer and thyroid cancer; princ investigator for several breast cancer trials Portsmouth; hon sr lectr in surgery Univ of Portsmouth 2003–, instructor (ATLS and BSS courses) and trainer on sentinel lymph node biopsy RCS; research interests: mgmnt of early breast cancer, sentinel lymph node biopsy incl intra-operative analysis of sentinel lymph nodes in breast cancer, molecular prognostic markers of breast cancer, diagnosis of thyroid cancer; entered on GMC Specialist Register 1999; memb: Nat Breast Faculty, UK Breast Intergroup; dir Enhancing Health Ltd 2008–15; chm Wessex Thyroid Cancer Network 2016–, memb Wessex Cancer Alliance 2016–; Norman Plummer Meml Prize 1995, Ronald Raven Prize 1995, Simpson-Smith Travelling Fellowship 1996–97; memb: BMA 1987, Assoc of Breast Surgery 1999, Br Assoc for Cancer Surgery 1999, Br Assoc of Endocrine and Thyroid Surgeons 2007; FRCS (Eng) 1991, FRCS (gen surgn) 1999, fell Assoc of Surgns of GB and I 2005; *Publications* author several pubns in surgical and cancer jls on the diagnosis, treatment and molecular biology of breast cancer and on improving the accuracy of pre-operative diagnosis of thyroid cancer; *Recreations* horse and motor racing, music; *Style*— Mr Constantinos Yiangou; ✉ Department of Surgery, Queen Alexandra Hospital, Cosham, Portsmouth, Hampshire PO6 3LY (☎ 02392 286000)

YONACE, Dr Adrian Harris; JP (Dorset 1989); s of Dr Jack Yonace (d 1975), of Salford, and Bryna, *née* Fidler (d 2000); *b* 26 November 1943; *Educ* Manchester Grammar, Univ of Manchester, Univ of Nottingham (BMedSci, BM BS); *m* 9 March 1989 (m dis 2012), Maureen Wilson, da of Thomas Wilson Ramsay, of Gullane; 2 c (Tristan Jack, Giselle Isla (twins) b 23 Aug 1995); *Career* computer systems analyst IBM 1965–67, computer conslt 1967–70; house physician and house surgn Univ Depts Manchester Royal Infirmary 1976–77, lectr in psychiatry Royal Free Hosp Univ of London 1980–83, conslt and hon sr lectr Friern Hosp and Univ of London 1983–89; conslt psychiatrist: St Ann's Hosp Poole 1989–93 and 1997–99, Priory Hosps Gp 1993–97; hon clinical teacher Univ of Southampton 1996–99 (hon clinical res fell 1993–96); conslt psychiatrist in private practice 1993–; sole hons examiner MB ChB Jt London Med Schs 1984, examiner RCPsych 1993–98 (observer 1999–), sr examiner MB ChB Finals Univ of London 1987–90; memb Mental Health Review Tbnl 2000–; specialist expert to Quality Care Cmmn 2014–; sec E Dorset BMA 1993–95; Silver Dip Eng Bridge Union Teachers Assoc; JP Inner London Juvenile Bench 1985–89, Court chm Poole Bench 1989–99; govr (both) Bournemouth Grammar Schs 2006–; FRCPsych 1994 (MRCPsych 1983); *Publications* Morgagni's Letters (jl of RSM, 1984, presented to H of Med Section 1985); *Recreations* scrabble, bridge, golf, twins; *Style*— Dr Adrian Yonace, JP; ✉ Bournemouth Nuffield Hospital, 65 Lansdowne Road, Bournemouth, Dorset BH1 1RW (☎ 07973 601294)

YORK, Archdeacon of; *see:* Seed, Ven Richard Murray Crosland

YORK, Dean of; *see:* Jones, Very Rev Keith Brynmor

YORK, Col Edward Christopher; OBE (2015), TD (1978), DL (N Yorks, 1988); s of Christopher York (d 1999), and Pauline Rose Marie, *née* Fletcher (d 2007); *b* 22 February 1939, London; *Educ* Eton; *m* 28 April 1965, Sarah Ann, da of Maj James Kennedy Maxwell, MC (d 1980), of Buckby Folly, Northants; 1 s, 1 da; *Career* 1 Royal Dragoons (ret 1964), CO Queen's Own Yeomanry 1979–81, ADC (TAVR) to HM The Queen 1982–86; chm Thirsk Race Course Co Ltd 1995–2007, chm and md Hutton Wandesley Farms Co Ltd and others 1986–2014; RASE rep CLBA Cncl 1999–2002; memb: Cncl RASE (hon show dir 1992–96, pres 1997, chm Cncl 1998–2002, hon tstee 2003), N Yorks CLBA 1978–2005, Cncl Yorkshire Agric Soc 1970–99 (pres 1989), Bd Yorkshire Museum of Farming 1979–2001; vice-pres Northern Assoc of Building Socs 1994–2001; Col Cmdt Yeomanry 1994–99, chm Yorks and Humberside Reserve Forces Assoc 1997–2003, Hon Col The Queen's Own Yeo 1998–2003; chm: Royal Armouries Devpt Tst (Leeds) 1995–99, county chm N Yorks Scouts 1999–2008; vice-chm (Army) Cncl RFCAs 2001–04; county pres: Army Benevolent Fund 1999–2014, SSAFA 2003–14; chm Christopher Topham's Apprenticing Charity 1974–, patron Mind and York Dist 2009–15; High Sheriff N Yorks 1988, Vice Lord-Lt N Yorks 1999–2014; FRAgS 1998; *Clubs* Boodle's; *Style*— Col E C York, OBE, TD, DL; ✉ Hutton Wandesley Hall, York YO26 7NA (☎ home 01904 738240, office 01904 738755, fax 01904 738468, e-mail ecy@huttonwandesley.co.uk)

YORK, 97 Archbishop of 2005–; Most Rev and Rt Hon Dr John Tucker Mugabi Sentamu; PC (2005), DL; patron of many livings, the Archdeaconries of York, Cleveland and the East Riding, and the Canonries in his Cathedral; the Archbishopric was founded AD 625, and the Province comprises twelve Sees; s of late Rev John Walakira, and late Ruth Walakira, of Buganda, Uganda; *b* 10 June 1949, Kampala, Uganda; *Educ* Old Kampala Secdy Sch, Makerere Univ Kampala (LLB, pres Student Union, sec Christian Union), Law Devpt Centre (Dip Legal Practice), Selwyn Coll Cambridge (MA, PhD); *Career* Uganda 1971–74: legal asst to Chief Justice, Diocesan Registrar, Advocate High Court of Uganda; undergrad Univ of Cambridge 1974–76 (postgrad 1976–79), ordained 1979, asst chaplain Selwyn Coll Cambridge 1979, asst curate St Andrew Ham Common and chaplain HM Remand Centre Latchmere House 1979–82, asst curate St Paul Herne Hill 1982–83, priest i/c Holy Trinity and parish priest St Matthias Tulse Hill 1983–84, vicar of Holy Trinity and St Matthias Tulse Hill 1984–96, priest i/c St Saviour Brixton 1987–89, hon canon Southwark Cathedral 1993–96, bishop of Stepney 1996–2002, bishop of Birmingham 2002–05; memb: Convocation of Canterbury and Gen Synod C of E 1985–96, Bishop's Cncl and Southwark Diocesan Synod 1985–96, Southwark Diocesan Race Rels Cmmn 1986–89, Archbishop's Advsy Gp on Urban Priority Areas 1986–92, Young Offenders Ctee NACRO 1986–95, Standing Ctee Gen Synod C of E 1988–96 (chm Ctee for Minority Ethnic Anglican Concerns 1990–99), Health Advsy Ctee HM Prisons 1993–95; prolocutor Lower House of Convocation of Canterbury and an offr of the Gen Synod C of E 1994–96; advsr to the Home Office Inquiry into the murder of Stephen Lawrence 1997–99, chair Damilola Taylor Murder Review 2002–03, chair Living Wage Cmmn 2013–14; chair NHS Sickle Cell and Thalassaemia Nat Screening Programme 2001–13, govr Univ of Birmingham NHS Fndn Hosp 2002–04, tstee John Smith Institute until 2011, pres Youth for Christ 2004–, pres YMCA 2005–, tourism ambass Visit York 2010, sponsor Fairness Cmmn City of York Cncl 2011–12; memb House of Lords; chancellor: York St John Univ 2006–, Univ of Cumbria 2007; Midlander of the Year 2003, Cambridgeshire Top 10 Black and Asian Local and Historical Role Models Award 2006, Yorkshire Man of the Year 2007, Speaker of the Year 2007; Freeman City of London 2000, Freeman City of Montego Bay 2007; Hon Dr: Open Univ 2001, Birmingham City Univ 2008, Univ of York 2010; Hon DPhil Univ of Glos 2002; Hon DD: Univ of Birmingham 2003, Univ of Hull 2007, Univ of Cambridge 2008, Univ of Nottingham 2008, Wycliffe Coll Toronto 2009, Sewanee (Univ of the South) Tennessee 2010, Univ of London 2010, Univ of Aberdeen 2013, Univ Coll Huron Ontario 2013; Hon DL Univ of Sheffield, Hon LLD Univ of Leicester 2005, Hon DLL Univ of the West Indies 2007, Hon DCL Univ of Northumbria at Newcastle 2008, Hon LLD Teesside Univ 2009, Hon LLD Univ of Leeds 2010, Hon DTheol Univ of Chester 2009; hon fell Selwyn Coll Cambridge, hon fell St Margaret's Coll Dunedin, visiting fell Univ of Otago 2014, hon master bencher Gray's Inns of Ct; fell UC of Christ Church Canterbury, fell Queen Mary & Westfield Coll London; FRSA; *Style*— The Most Rev and Rt Hon the Lord Archbishop of York; ✉ Bishopthorpe Palace, Bishopthorpe, York YO23 2GE

YORK, Michael; OBE (1996); s of Joseph Gwynne Johnson, and Florence Edith May Chown; *b* 27 March 1942; *Educ* Hurstpierpoint Coll, Bromley GS, UC Oxford (MA); *m* 1968, Patricia Frances; *Career* actor; Chevalier de l'Ordre des Arts et des Lettres (France) 1995; *Theatre* Dundee Repertory Theatre 1964, Nat Theatre Co 1965; credits incl: Outcry (NY) 1973, Bent (NY) 1980, Cyrano de Bergerac (Santa Fe) 1981, Whisper in the Mind (Phoenix) 1991, The Crucible (NY) 1992, Someone to Watch Over Me (NY) 1993, Amadeus (Hollywood Bowl) 2006, Camelot (USA tour) 2007, Strauss Meets Frankenstein 2008; *Television* Jesus of Nazareth 1976, A Man Called Intrepid 1978, For Those I Loved 1981, The Weather in the Streets 1983, The Master of Ballantrae 1983, Space 1984, The Far Country 1985, The Four Minute Mile 1988, The Heat of the Day 1988, Till We Meet Again 1989, The Night of the Fox 1990, Fall From Grace 1994, Not of This Earth 1995, Danielle Steel's The Ring 1996, True Women 1997, The Ripper 1997, A Knight in Camelot 1998, Perfect Little Angels 1998, The Haunting of Hell House 2000, The Lot 2001, Curb Your Enthusiasm 2003, La Femme Musketeer, Crusader 2004, Icon 2005, The Simpsons 2006, The Four Seasons 2009; *Films* Accident 1966, The Taming of the Shrew 1967, Romeo and Juliet 1967, England Made Me 1971, Cabaret 1972, The Three Musketeers 1973, Murder on the Orient Express 1974, Conduct Unbecoming 1975, Logan's Run 1975, The Riddle of the Sands 1978, Success is the Best Revenge 1984, Dawn 1985, Vengence 1986, The Return of the Three Musketeers 1988, The Long Shadow 1992, Rochade 1992, Eline Vere 1992, Wide Sargasso Sea 1993, Discretion Assured 1993, The Shadow of a Kiss 1994, Gospa 1995, Goodbye America 1997, Austin Powers: International Man of Mystery 1997, One Hell of a Guy 1998, Wrongfully Accused 1998, The Omega Code 1999, Austin Powers: The Spy Who Shagged Me 1999, Borstal Boy 2000, Megiddo 2001, Austin Powers in Goldmember 2002, Moscow Heat 2004, Mika & Alfred 2008, The Mill and the Cross 2011; *Books* Travelling Player (autobiography, 1991), The Magic Paw Paw (1994), A Shakespearean Actor Prepares (2000), Dispatches from Armageddon (2002), Are My Blinkers Showing (2006); *Clubs* Bohemian (San Francisco); *Style*— Michael York, Esq, OBE

YORK-JOHNSON, Michael; *see:* York, Michael

YORKE, John; *Educ* Newcastle Univ; *Career* theatre dir until 1986; BBC: studio mangr then music and radio drama prodr 1986–94, script ed EastEnders then storyline conslt Casualty 1994–99, exec prodr EastEnders 2000–03, dep head of drama 2003; head of drama Channel 4 2003–04; BBC: controller of continuing drama and head of ind drama 2004–06, controller of drama prodn 2006–13, md Company Pictures 2013–; *Style*— John Yorke, Esq; ✉ Company Pictures, New London House, 172 Drury Lane (2nd Floor), London WC2B 5QR

YORKE, John; s of Gerald Yorke (d 1981), and Angela, *née* Duncan (d 1986); *b* 12 October 1938, London; *Educ* Eton, Trinity Coll Cambridge (MA); *m* 1, 4 July 1967, Jean, *née* Reynolds (d 1987); 2 da (Anabel b 18 Dec 1971, Sara b 5 April 1974); *m* 2, 26 Sept 1992, Julia, *née* Allen; *Career* accountant Peat, Marwick, Mitchell & Co 1965–70 (articled clerk 1962–65); financial dir Mallett & Son (Antiques) Ltd 1970–98, financial dir Arthur Millner Ltd 1998–2011; non-exec dir Alginate Industries Ltd 1972–80, tstee: Forthampton Tst 1975–, Abbey Lawn Tst 1985–; High Sheriff Hereford and Worcs 2007–08; FCA 1965; *Recreations* shooting, travel; *Clubs* Garrick; *Style*— John Yorke, Esq; ✉ Forthampton Court, Gloucester GL19 4RD (☎ 01684 292440, e-mail yorke@forthampton.com)

YOSHIDA, Miyako; Hon OBE (2007); da of Eiji Yoshida, of Tokyo, and Etsuko, *née* Fukuda; *Career* ballet dancer; with Sadler's Wells Royal Ballet (now Birmingham Royal Ballet) 1984–95, princ Royal Ballet 1995–; UNESCO Artist for Peace 2004; *Performances* incl leading roles in: Swan Lake, Sleeping Beauty, The Nutcracker, Giselle, Elite Syncopations, La Fille Mal Gardée, The Dream, Don Quixote, Paquita, Allegri Diversi, Theme and Variations, Concerto Barrocco, Les Sylphides, Divertimento No 15, Dance Concertantes, Symphony in 3 Movements, Choreartium, Five Tangos, Pavane pas de deux, Sylvia; *Awards* Prix de Lausanne 1983, Global Award 1989, Dance and Dancer magazine Dancer of the Year 1991, E Nakagawa Award 1995, A Tachibana Award 1996 and 2003, C Hattori Award 1998, Award from Minister of Educn 2001, Unesco Artist for Peace 2004, Japan Soc Award 2007, Purple Ribbon Medal 2007; *Recreations* reading, watching films; *Style*— Miss Miyako Yoshida, OBE; ✉ The Royal Ballet, Covent Garden, London WC2E 9DD (☎ 020 7240 1200)

Y

YOUNG, Andrew George; *b* 15 June 1949, Glasgow; *Educ* Hyndland Secdy Sch Glasgow, Univ of Glasgow; *m* Sara Victoria; 5 da, 1 s; *Career* sr conslt Demography Social Security and Pensions Policy Govt Actuary's Dept 1972–2009, Pensions Regulator 2009–; fell Inst and Faculty of Actuaries; *Style*— Andrew Young, Esq; ✉ 95 Stanford Road, Brighton BN1 5PR (☎ 01273 563443, e-mail agyoung101@yahoo.co.uk); The Pensions Regulator, Napier House, Trafalgar Place, Brighton BN1 4DW

YOUNG, Prof Andrew William; s of Alexander Young, of Heckington, Lincs, and Winnifred Doris, *née* Allen (d 2001); *b* 14 March 1950; *Educ* Bedford Coll London (BSc), Univ of Warwick (PhD), Univ of London (DSc); *m* 1977, Mavis Langham; 2 da (Alexandra b 1 Feb 1989, Josephine b 20 Nov 1994), 1 step s (Jeremy Langham b 25 March 1968); *Career* lectr Univ of Aberdeen 1974–76, lectr then reader Lancaster Univ 1976–89, prof of psychology Univ of Durham 1989–93, special appt MRC Scientific Staff Applied Psychology Unit Univ of Cambridge 1993–97, prof of neuropsychology Univ of York 1997–; pres Psychology Section BAAS 1997–98, chair Br Neuropsychological Soc 1998–2000, pres Experimental Psychology Soc 2004–05; co-organiser The Science of the Face exhbn Scottish Nat Portrait Gallery 1998 (exhbn also taken to Cardiff, Belfast and Newcastle upon Tyne); Br Psychological Soc: Cognitive Psychology Award 1994 (jtly), President's Award 1995, Book Award 2001 (jtly); Dr (hc) Univ of Liège 2000; CPsychol 1988, FBPsS 1988 (hon fell 2005), FBA 2001, AcSS 2004; *Publications* In the Eye of the Beholder: the Science of Face Perception (with Vicki Bruce , *qv*, 1998); also co-author of numerous articles and papers in learned jls; *Style*— Prof A W Young; ✉ Department of Psychology, University of York, Heslington, York YO10 5DD (☎ 01904 434370, e-mail awy1@york.ac.uk)

YOUNG, Anthony Elliott (Tony); s of Prof Leslie Young, of Esher, Surrey, and Ruth, *née* Elliott; *b* 20 December 1943; *Educ* Epsom Coll, St John's Coll Cambridge (MA, MB, MChir), St Thomas' Hosp Med Sch; *m* 6 July 1968, Dr Gwyneth Vivien Wright, da of Prof Eldred Walls, of Edinburgh; 3 s (Adam Elliott b 1974, Oliver Elliott b 1975, Toby Elliott b 1977); *Career* conslt surgn St Thomas' Hosp 1981–2006; med dir Guy's and St Thomas' NHS Tst 1993–97, conslt surgn King Edward VII Hosp London 1997–2010; pres Br Assoc of Endocrine Surgns 2003–05; memb BMA 1968, FRSM 1970, FRCS 1971; *Books* Vascular Malformations (1988), The Medical Manager (2003), Companion in Surgical Studies (2005), The Professor and Women (novel, 2014); *Recreations* writing, painting, reading; *Style*— Anthony Young, Esq; ✉ 63 Lee Road, Blackheath, London SE3 9EN (☎ 020 8852 1921, e-mail anthony.e.young@ntlworld.com)

YOUNG, Prof Archie; s of Archibald Young, TD (d 1996), of Glasgow, and Mary Downie, *née* Fleming (d 1995); *b* 19 September 1946; *Educ* Glasgow HS, Univ of Glasgow (BSc, MB ChB, MD); *m* 24 Dec 1973 (m dis 1995), Sandra, da of Archibald Clark (d 1969), of Glasgow; 1 da (Sula b 1979), 1 s (Archie b 1980); *Career* clinical lectr Univ of Oxford 1978–85, prof of geriatric med Royal Free Hosp Med Sch London 1988–98 (conslt physician 1985–88), prof of geriatric med Univ of Edinburgh 1998–; Prince Philip Medal Inst of Sports Med 1995; Scottish swimming int 1965–70 (British 1970), Scottish water polo int 1968; memb Incorporation of Tailors Glasgow; FRCPG 1985, FRCP 1989, FRCPEd 1999; *Publications* numerous publications on the effects of use, disuse, ageing and disease on human muscle and exercise physiology; *Recreations* physical; *Clubs* Junior Mountaineering Club of Scotland; *Style*— Prof Archie Young; ✉ Geriatric Medicine, University of Edinburgh, Edinburgh Royal Infirmary, 51 Little France Court, Edinburgh EH16 4SB (☎ 0131 242 6481)

YOUNG, David; s of Derek Young, of Solihull, and Audrey, *née* Darby; *b* 11 October 1959, Solihull, W Midlands; *Educ* Solihull Sch, UCL (LLB), Coll of Law London; *m* 1 (m dis), Margaret Anne, *née* Wood; 2 da (Alison Claire b 1 Jan 1990, Stephanie Helen b 21 May 1994); m 2, Janine Alison, *née* Taylor; 1 s (Samuel Ethan b 8 Oct 1999), 1 da (Taryn Rhiannon Isabella b 28 Feb 2004); *Career* slr Eversheds 1984– (ptnr 1993–); memb: Law Soc England & Wales, Law Soc Scotland; *Style*— David Young, Esq; ✉ Eversheds LLP, 115 Colmore Row, Birmingham B3 3AL (☎ 0845 497 9797, fax 0121 232 1900, e-mail davidyoung@eversheds.com)

YOUNG, David Ernest; CBE (2007); s of Harold Ernest Young (d 1971), and Jessie, *née* Turnbull (d 2009); *b* 8 March 1942; *Educ* King Edward VII Sch Sheffield, CCC Oxford (BA); *m* 1, 8 Feb 1964 (m dis), Norma, da of Alwyn Robinson (d 1979); 2 da (Wendy b 1965, Michele b 1968); m 2, 4 April 1998, Margaret, *née* Pilleau; *Career* asst princ Air Miny 1963, private sec to CAS 1968–70, private sec to Min of State for Def 1973–75, asst sec Central Policy Review Staff Cabinet Office 1975–77; John Lewis Partnership: joined 1982, md Peter Jones Sloane Square 1984–86, fin dir 1987, dep chm 1993–2002; non-exec dir: Ocado plc 2001–12, Orbit Gp Ltd 2013–; ind memb Steering Bd of Companies House 1988–93, memb Hansard Soc Cmmn on Regulation of Privatised Utilities 1996; chm HEFCE 2001–07; memb Cncl: Open Univ 1996–2001, Univ of Sheffield 2008–; tstee RAF Museum 1999–2005, hon treas Soil Assoc 2004–10, chm Textile Industry Children's Tst 2005–08; Hon DLitt Univ of Sheffield 2005, Hon DBA Univ of Beds 2008; *Recreations* walking, opera, theatre; *Clubs* Phyllis Ct Henley-on-Thames; *Style*— David Young, Esq, CBE

YOUNG, David John; s of John Anthony Young (d 2001), and Marjorie Ellen Young (d 1996); *b* 22 January 1951; *Educ* Merchant Taylors', Watford Coll (Dip Printing Mgmnt); *m* 1, 1978, Jennifer, *née* Hicks; 1 s (William Francis b 1 Aug 1981); m 2, 1996, Elizabeth, *née* Noble; 2 da (Tallulah Ellen b 9 Nov 1997, Ottilie Florence b 16 May 1999); *Career* md Thorsons Publishing Gp 1980–89 (prodn mangr 1970–80), divnl md HarperCollins Publishers 1989–96, md Little, Brown & Co (UK) 1996–2000, chief exec Time Warner Book Gp UK 2000–05, chm and ceo Hachette Book Gp 2006–13, dep ceo Hachette UK 2013–15, ceo Orion Book Gp 2013–15, ret; chm: Book Mktg Cncl 1986–88, Book Industry Supply Chain Gp 2003, World Book Day 2004; memb: Cncl Publishers' Assoc 1986–90 and 2002–05, Bd Assoc of American Publishers 2005–13 (chm 2011–12), Bd Scholastic Corp USA 2015–; pres Book Trade Benevolent Soc 2013–; memb Bd Tate Enterprises Ltd 2015–; *Recreations* wine, reading, gardening, learning Italian; *Clubs* Garrick, Club at the Ivy; *Style*— David Young; ✉ 5 Nightingale Road, Guildford, Surrey GU1 1ER (e-mail davidjohnyoung51@hotmail.com)

YOUNG, David Tyrrell; s of Tyrrell Francis Young (d 1998), and Patricia Morrison, *née* Spicer (d 1998); *b* 6 January 1938, London; *Educ* Charterhouse; *m* 11 Sept 1965, Madeline Helen Celia, da of Anthony Burton Capel Philips (d 1983), of Tean, Stoke-on-Trent; 3 da (Melanie Rosamond b 1969, Annabel Katharine b 1971, Corinna Lucy b 1974); *Career* TA 1 Regt HAC 1955–67, ret Capt 1967; trainee CA Gérard Van De Linde & Son 1955–60, audit mangr James Edwards Dangerfield & Co 1961–65; Spicer & Oppenheim (formerly Spicer & Pegler): audit mangr 1965–68, ptnr 1968–82, managing ptnr 1982–88, sr ptnr and int chm 1988–90; dep chm Touche Ross & Co 1990–93; chm: N Herts NHS Tst 1994–2000, C&G 1999–2006, Capita Syndicate Mgmnt 2001–10; dir Groupama Insurance 1993–2000, Asprey & Garrard 1993–2000, Wates City of London Properties plc 1994–2001, Nomura Bank International plc 1996–2010, Berks Hathaway International Insurance Ltd 1997–2014; memb Cncl ICAEW 1979–82; memb HAC; Freeman City of London, memb Ct Worshipful Co of Fishmongers (Prime Warden 1993–94), Liveryman Worshipful Co of CAs (Master 1999–2000); FCA, FRSA, Hon FCGI; *Recreations* golf; *Clubs* Royal Worlington Golf, Huntercombe Golf; *Style*— David T Young, Esq; ✉ Lovegrove Barn, Fieldside, Long Wittenham, Oxfordshire OX14 4QB (☎ 01865 407763, e-mail david@dandmyoung.plus.com)

YOUNG, Douglas John (Doug); s of John Edward Young, of Corby, Northants, and Barbara Maxwell, *née* Haldane; *b* 31 December 1967, Corby, Northants; *Educ* Laxton Sch Oundle, Pembroke Coll Cambridge (MA); *Career* BBC Books 1991–96, Headline Publishing 1996–2001, Transworld Publishing 2001–; *Recreations* scuba diving, snowboarding, cooking; *Clubs* Soho House; *Style*— Doug Young, Esq; ✉ Channel 4 Books, Transworld Publishing, 61–63 Uxbridge Road, London W5 5SA (☎ 020 8231 6649, fax 020 8576 2659, e-mail d.young@transworld-publishers.co.uk)

YOUNG, Prof Douglas Wilson; s of John Robert Young (d 1992), and Christina, *née* Martin (d 2014); *b* 15 January 1939; *Educ* Eastwood Sch Glasgow, Univ of Glasgow (BSc, PhD, Carnegie scholar); *m* 1971, Ruth Lilian, da of Brian Welch; 1 da (Janet Mary b 1973), 1 s (Malcolm John b 1976); *Career* research fell Harvard Univ 1963–65; Univ of Sussex: lectr in chemistry 1965–84, reader 1984–88, prof of chemistry 1988–2005 (emeritus 2005–); dir Sussex Centre for Biomolecular Design and Drug Devpt 1996–2005; visiting scholar Uppsala Univ 1985, visiting prof Univ of Nantes 1989; Royal Soc of Chemistry: chm Bio-organic Gp 1991–94, Tilden Lectr and Medal 1993–94, vice-pres Perkin Div 1995–97, Interdisciplinary Award 2003; author of over 170 books and articles; FRSC, FRSE 1996; *Recreations* listening to music, DIY, watching cricket; *Clubs* Sussex County Cricket; *Style*— Prof Douglas Young, FRSE; ✉ Department of Chemistry, University of Sussex, Falmer, Brighton, East Sussex BN1 9QJ (☎ 01323 890201, e-mail d.w.young@sussex.ac.uk)

YOUNG, (Russell) Francis; s of Canon (Cecil) Edwyn Young, CVO (Queen's chaplain, d 1988), of Hove, E Sussex, and Beatrice Mary, *née* Rees (d 2001); *b* 27 February 1953; *Educ* Radley, Blackpool Coll of Hotel Mgmnt (HND Catering and Hotel Admin); *m* 9 May 1981, Anne, da of Charles Edward Williams; 1 s (Edward Francis Charles b 30 May 1982), 1 da (Alexandra Anne Mary b 1 May 1985); *Career* hotelier; asst food and beverage mangr Grosvenor Hotel Chester 1975–76 (trainee mangr 1974–75), mangr HM King Hussein of Jordan's summer palace Aqaba Jordan 1975–78, food and beverage mangr Sandy Lane Hotel St James Barbados 1978–80; Marriott Corp 1980–84: dir of restaurant Hunt Valley Marriott Baltimore Maryland 1980–81, opened as food and beverage dir Longwharf Marriott Boston Massachusetts 1981–82 then London Marriott 1982–84; gen mangr Oakley Court Hotel Windsor 1985–86, gp ops dir Select Country Hotels 1986–87; restored semi-derelict vicarage and opened as prop The Pear Tree at Purton 1987– (National Westminster Bank Award for Business Devpt 1992 and RAC Blue Ribbon); chm Bd of Govrs Bradon Forest Sch 1993–2002; wine columnist The Swindon Evening Advertiser; clerk to the Master Innholders 2003–06; Freeman City of London, Liveryman Worshipful Company of Distillers; MI 1994; FIH; *Recreations* cricket, family, walking; *Clubs* Purton Cricket; *Style*— Francis Young, Esq; ✉ The Pear Tree at Purton, Church End, Purton, Swindon, Wiltshire SN5 4ED (☎ 01793 772100, fax 01793 772369, e-mail francis@peartreepurton.co.uk)

YOUNG, Prof Ian Robert; OBE (1986); s of John Stirling Young (d 1971), and Ruth Muir, *née* Whipple (d 1975); *b* 11 January 1932; *Educ* Sedbergh, Univ of Aberdeen (BSc, PhD); *m* 1956, Sylvia Marianne Whewell, da of Frederick George Ralph; 2 s (Graham John b 1958, Neil George b 1960), 1 da (Fiona Marianne b 1966); *Career* Hilger & Watts Ltd 1955–59, Evershed & Vignoles Ltd 1959–67, Evershed Power Optics Ltd 1967–76, EMI Central Research Laboratory 1976–81, sr research fell GEC Hirst Research Centre, vice-pres Res Picker International Inc Cleveland OH 1981–, visiting prof Imperial Coll Sch of Med at Hammersmith Hosp (Royal Postgrad Med Sch until merger 1997) 1983–2001, sr research fell Dept of Electrical and Electronic Engrg Imperial Coll 2004–; Duddell Medal Inst of Physics 1983, Gold Medal Soc of Magnetic Resonance in Med 1988, Silver Medal Soc of Magnetic Resonance 1994, Whittle Medal Royal Acad of Engrg 2004; Hon DSc Univ of Aberdeen 1992; pres Soc of Magnetic Resonance in Med 1991–92, hon memb Soc of Magnetic Resonance Imaging 1989; FIEE 1967, FREng 1988, FRS 1989, hon FRCR 1990, FInstP 1991; *Recreations* ornithology, golf, walking; *Style*— Prof Ian Young, OBE, FRS, FREng; ✉ High Kingsbury, Kingsbury Street, Marlborough, Wiltshire SN8 1HZ (☎ 01672 516126)

YOUNG, James Drummond (Jim); s of James Henry Young, of Glasgow, and Mary, *née* Moore (d 1988); *b* 26 February 1950; *Educ* Hutchesons' GS, Univ of Glasgow (LLB); *m* 26 Sept 1973, Gillian Anne, da of William Boyd, MBE; 1 da (Jennifer Anne b 9 Dec 1976), 1 s (Graham James b 7 Jan 1979); *Career* trainee McGrigor Donald & Co 1971–73, slr West Lothian DC 1975–77; ptnr: Moncrieff Warren Paterson 1979–85, McGrigor Donald 1985–2005; pt/t employment tbnl judge Scotland 2003–; memb Law Soc of Scot 1975 (memb Employment Ctee); *Recreations* golf, cricket, contemporary art; *Clubs* Clydesdale Cricket, Merchants of Edinburgh Golf, Archerfield Golf; *Style*— Jim Young, Esq; ✉ 5 Braid Hills Avenue, Edinburgh (☎ 0131 447 1951)

YOUNG, Prof John Braithwaite; s of Charles Braithwaite Young, and Elizabeth Eva, *née* Wilson; *Educ* Chesham HS, Middx Hosp Med Sch (MB BS), Open Univ (MSc, MBA); *Career* Bradford Hosps Tst: conslt geriatrician 1986–, clinical dir 1991–95; prof of elderly care medicine Univ of Leeds 2005–; memb R&D Ctee Stroke Assoc 1995–98, specialist med advsr Dept of Health 2001–07; involved in clinical research in stroke and community services for older people; Freeman scholarship in obstetrics and gynaecology 1977, Geriatric Med Insight Award 1989, Lady Illingworth Award 2008; FRCP 1994 (MRCP 1980); *Publications* author of 12 book chapters and over 200 articles in peer-reviewed jls; *Recreations* fell racing, endurance running, DIY, fly fishing; *Clubs* Bingley Harriers & Athletic; *Style*— Prof John Young; ✉ Department of Elderly Care, St Luke's Hospital, Bradford, West Yorkshire BD5 0NA (☎ 01274 383406, e-mail john.young@bthft.nhs.uk)

YOUNG, Sir John Kenyon Roe; 6 Bt (UK 1821), of Bailieborough Castle, Co Cavan; s of Sir John William Roe Young, 5 Bt (d 1981), by his 1 w, Joan Minnie Agnes, *née* Aldous (d 1958); *b* 23 April 1947, Wimbledon, London; *Educ* Hurn Ct Sch Christchurch, Napier Coll; *m* 1977, Frances Elise, only da of W R Thompson; 1 s (Richard Christopher Roe, b 14 July 1983), 1 da (Tamara Elizabeth Eve b 9 Nov 1986); *Heir* s, Richard Young; *Career* former hydrographic surveyor; purchasing mangr; *Recreations* fishing; *Style*— Sir John K R Young, Bt

YOUNG, John Robert Chester; CBE (1992); s of Robert Nisbet Young (d 1956), and Edith Mary, *née* Roberts (d 1981); bro of Louise Botting, CBE, *qv*; *b* 6 September 1937; *Educ* Bishop Vesey's GS, St Edmund Hall Oxford (MA); *m* 1963, Pauline Joyce (d 1997); 1 s, 1 da (and 1 s decd); *Career* ptnr Simon & Coates stockbrokers 1965–82; Stock Exchange: memb 1965–82, memb Cncl 1978–82, dir of policy and planning 1982–87; vice-chm Exec Bd Int Stock Exchange 1987–90; chief exec: Securities Assoc 1987–91, SFA 1991–93, SIB 1993–95 (non-exec dir 1996–97); memb Ethics Ctee Securities Inst 1996–2009 (hon fell 2003); non-exec dir: East Surrey NHS Tst 1992–96, Elderstreet Millennium Venture Capital Trust 1996–2007, Darby Group plc 1996–98; dep chm Lloyd's Cncl and chm Lloyd's Regulatory Bd 1997–2002 (nominated memb Cncl and Regulatory Bd 1996–2002), public interest dir The Financial Services Compensation Scheme 2000–03, lay memb Legal Services Consultative Panel Miny of Justice 2004–10; advsr Royal Sch for the Blind (Seeability) 1997–2001; England and British Lions rugby union player 1958–61; *Recreations* rugby, cooking, grandchildren; *Clubs* Vincent's (Oxford), Achilles; *Style*— J R C Young, Esq, CBE

YOUNG, Jonathan Piers; s of Peter Alan George Young, of Chudleigh, Devon, and Mavis Irene Young; *b* 23 September 1959; *Educ* Blundell's, Univ of Leicester (BA); *m* 1993, Caroline Margaret, o da of John Jervis Murray Bankes, of Hinton Ampner, Hants; 1 da (Henrietta b 1994), 1 s (Fergus b 1996); *Career* ed: Shooting Times and Country magazine 1986–90, The Field 1991–; Freeman City of London, Renter Warden Worshipful Co of Gunmakers; *Books* A Pattern of Wings (1989); *Recreations* shooting, fishing, amusing terriers; *Clubs* The Silkies; *Style*— Jonathan Young, Esq; ✉ The Field, Floor 2, Pinehurst

2, Pinehurst Road, Farnborough Business Park, Farnborough, Hampshire GU14 7BF (☎ 01252 555222 (extension 55220), e-mail jonathan.young@timeinc.com)

YOUNG, Prof Kenneth George (Ken); s of Henry George Young, of Christchurch, Hants, and Olive, *née* Heybeard; *b* 3 January 1943; *Educ* Brockenhurst GS, LSE (BSc, MSc, PhD); *Career* res offr LSE 1966–73, res fell Univ of Kent 1974–77, sr res fell Univ of Bristol 1977–79, sr fell Policy Studies Inst 1979–87, prof and dir Inst of Local Govt Studies 1987–89, head Sch of Public Policy Univ of Birmingham 1989–90, prof of politics and head Dept of Political Studies Queen Mary & Westfield Coll London 1990–92 (vice-princ 1992–98), dir ESRC UK Centre for Evidence Based Policy 2000–05; KCL: prof of public policy 2005–, dir Inst for the Study of Public Policy 2008–, head Dept of Political Economy 2010–13; FRHistS 1983, AMRaeS 1997, AcSS 2001; *Books* Local Politics and the Rise of Party (1975), Metropolitan London (1982), Managing the Post-Industrial City (1983), New Directions for County Government (1989), Local Government Since 1945 (1997); *Recreations* reading, travel; *Style*— Prof Ken Young; ✉ Department of Political Economy, King's College London, Strand, London WC2R 2LS (☎ 020 7848 2708, e-mail ken.young@kcl.ac.uk)

YOUNG, Kirsty; da of John Young, and Catherine Young; *b* 23 November 1968; *Educ* HS of Stirling; *m* Nick Jones, *qv*; 2 da (Freya, Iona); *Career* newsreader and news presenter BBC Radio Scotland 1990–93, news anchor (3 series of Kirsty) Scottish TV 1993–95; BBC TV: reporter Holiday (BBC 1) 1995–96, reporter Film 96 (BBC 1) 1996; news anchor: Channel 5 Broadcasting 1997–99, ITN 1999–2002, Five 2002–07; presenter Desert Island Discs (BBC Radio 4) 2006–, presenter Crimewatch (BBC 1) 2008–; supporter Centrepoint; *Awards* Most Outstanding Newcomer Royal Variety Club Awards 1997, Newsreader of the Year TRIC Awards 1998; *Recreations* reading, cookery, laughter, films; *Style*— Miss Kirsty Young

YOUNG, Lionel Henry; s of Patrick Young (d 1996), and Marjorie Young; *b* 9 June 1955; *Educ* Gresham's, Univ of Durham (BSc); *m*; 2 c; *Career* head of corporate transaction servs Deloitte; memb: Worshipful Co of Fishmongers, Worshipful Co of Turners; MSI, FCA; *Recreations* walking, theatre, dining; *Style*— Lionel Young, Esq; ✉ Deloitte & Touche LLP, Athene Place, 66 Shoe Lane, London EC4A 3BQ

YOUNG, Mal; s of Charles Young, of Liverpool, and Maria, *née* Williams; *b* 26 January 1957; *Educ* Liverpool Sch of Art (Dip Art & Design); *m* Aug 2014, Mari Wilson; 1 step da (Lily May); *Career* design mangr Littlewoods Orgn Ltd 1975–83; actor/singer 1983–84; Mersey TV Co 1984–96: design asst for Brookside (Channel 4), asst floor mangr and floor mangr 1986–91, prodr Brookside and dir Brookside Prodns 1991–95, series prodr Brookside 1995–96, devised and produced And the Beat Goes On (Channel 4); head of drama Pearson TV 1996–97 (exec prodr The Bill (ITV) and creator Family Affairs (Channel 5)), controller of drama series BBC TV 1997–2001 (responsible for EastEnders, Casualty, Holby City, Waking the Dead, Doctors, Murder in Mind, Judge John Deed, Down to Earth, Dalziel & Pascoe, Afternoon Plays, Grease Monkeys, Dr Who), controller Continuing Drama Series BBC 2001–04, dir of drama 19 Entertainment 2004–10, ind exec prodr 2010–; writer and prodr: Born in the USA (Fox), Austin Golden Hour (US TV pilot CW/Paramount) 2008; writer and exec prodr: If I Can Dream (Hulu) 2010, Desperate Scousewives (Channel 4) 2011–12; writer and creative conslt Sony Pictures Int TV 2012–, fndr and ceo Dynamo Prodns 2012–14, fndr and ceo Pool of Life Prodns, supervising prodr Sony Pictures TV/CBS 2016; writer and prodr: Young Americans pilot (ABC TV), Blocked pilot (NBC); exec prodr The Young & The Restless (CBS/Sony) 2016–; hon prof Glasgow Caledonian Univ 2014–; Huw Weldon meml lectr RTS 1999; Special Award for Creative Contribution to TV British Soap Awards 2004; memb: Writers Guild of GB, Writers Guild of America; *Books* Sinbad's Scrapbook (1996); *Recreations* big music fan, musician, telly addict from an early age; *Clubs* Soho House, BAFTA, RTS; *Style*— Mal Young, Esq

YOUNG, HE Marianne; *née* Darch; da of James Darch, and Andrea Darch; *b* 8 August 1971; *Educ* St Teresa's Sch, Wellington Coll, Univ of Warwick (BA), City Univ London (Postgrad Dip); *m* 24 Aug 2002, Barry Young; 2 da, 1 s; *Career* diplomat; grad trainee The Times 1994–95, staff ed then Asia ed Fairplay Gp Singapore 1995–2000, sr corr Fairplay Gp UK 2000–01; FCO: departmental report ed Press Office 2001–02, press offr Press Office 2002–03, head Great Lakes Section Africa Directorate 2003, head E Africa and Horn Section Africa Directorate 2004–05, head of communications Engaging with Islamic World Gp 2005–06, head External Political Section Br High Cmmn S Africa and dep high cmmr to Lesotho and Swaziland 2007–11, high cmmr to Namibia 2011–15, head Climate Diplomacy Unit Science and Innovation Climate Change Dept 2015–16, dep head Global Economic Issues Dept Economic Diplomacy Directorate 2016–; *Recreations* literature, photography, scuba diving; *Style*— Mrs Marianne Young; ✉ c/o Foreign & Commonwealth Office (Windhoek), King Charles Street, London SW1A 2AH

YOUNG, Mark; s of Raymond Young, of Shalford, Surrey, and Joan, *née* Coatsworth; *b* 4 May 1961; *Educ* King's Sch Tynemouth, ChCh Oxford (MA); *m* Sara, da of Derek Cavalier; 2 da (Charlotte b 21 April 1989, Lucy b 23 June 1992); *Career* early career William Collins 1983–88, Coopers and Lybrand Media Gp 1988–91, head of business affrs ITN 1991–93, chief asst to dep DG BBC 1993–94; BBC Worldwide: fin and commercial dir 1994, md BBC World, md Europe, the Middle East, India and Africa (EMEIA) 1998–, ceo and pres BBC Worldwide Americas 2001–, md global mktg brand devpt (GMBD) 2002–; dir Indian Broadcasting Fndn; FCMA 2001; *Recreations* travel, gardening; *Style*— Mark Young, Esq; ✉ BBC Worldwide, Woodlands, 80 Wood Lane, London W12 0TT (☎ 020 8433 3850, fax 020 8433 3848)

YOUNG, (Peter) Miles; s of Matthew Derek Young (d 1989), and Joyce Doreen, *née* Robson (d 1976); *b* 12 June 1954; *Educ* Bedford Sch, New Coll Oxford (MA); *Career* advertising; Lintas London 1976–79, Allen Brady & Marsh 1979–83, dir client service Ogilvy & Mather Ltd 1983–90; Ogilvy & Mather Direct Ltd: md 1990–92, dep chm and chief exec 1992–93, chm 1993–95; chm Ogilvy & Mather Asia/Pacific 1995–; ldr Westminster Cncl 1993–95 (memb 1986–87); chm: New Technology Ctee 1986–87, Environment Ctee 1987–90; Burdett-Coutts Fndn 1986, govr Harper Tst 1989–, vice-chm Conserve 1990, chm Bedford Prep Sch Ctee 1992–; MIPA 1990; *Recreations* gastronomy, walking, Balkan travel; *Clubs* Hong Kong, China (Hong Kong); *Style*— Miles Young, Esq; ✉ 1 Chatham Path, Hong Kong

YOUNG, Sir Nicholas Charles; kt (2000); s of Leslie Charles Young (d 1986), and Mary Margaret, *née* Rudman (d 1998); *b* 16 April 1952; *Educ* Wimbledon Coll, Univ of Birmingham (LLB), Coll of Law; *m* 1977, Helen Mary Ferrier, da of William Renwick Hamilton; 3 s (Edward b 1980, Alexander b 1982, Thomas b 1984); *Career* supervisor residential unit HM Prison Grendon Underwood 1974–75, slr Freshfields 1977–78 (articled clerk 1975–77), travelled Europe and Asia 1978–79, ptnr Turner Martin & Symes 1981–85 (joined as slr 1979), sec for devpt Sue Ryder Fndn 1985–90, dir of UK ops British Red Cross 1990–95 (Cabinet Office Top Mgmnt Prog 1993), chief exec Macmillan Cancer Relief 1995–2001, chief exec British Red Cross 2001–14; tstee: Monte San Martino Tst (also Chm), Disasters Emergency Ctee, Humanitarian Forum (also dep chm), Guidestar UK 2003–06; chm Judging Panel Asian Women of Achievement Awards; Freeman City of London 2007; memb Law Soc 1975; *Recreations* amateur drama, cricket, literature, sailing, theatre and cinema; *Clubs* Stumblers' Association; *Style*— Sir Nicholas Young

YOUNG, Paul A; s of Charles Young, and Valerie Bell, *née* Ford; *b* 28 July 1973, Barnsley, S Yorks; *Educ* Wellfield Comp Wingate, New Coll Durham (BTEC), Leeds Met Univ, RSM; *Career* chocolatier and patissier; under Marco Pierre White: pastry chef Criterion Brasserie London 1996–97, head pastry chef Titanic Restaurant London 1998–99, head pastry chef Quo Vadis London 1999–2001; product devpt chef Northern foods exclusively for Marks and Spencer Sheffield 2001–02, product mangr/developer Katie's Kitchen for Sainsbury's Harrow 2002–03, head pastry chef La Rascasse London 2003–04, head chef Cutting Edge Sch of Food and Wine Robertsbridge E Sussex 2004–05, chef teacher The Cookery Sch London 2004–05, conslt patissier The Serious Food Co 2004–05, conslt chocolatier for ind chocolate cos 2004–; dir, prop and master chocolatier Paul A Young Fine Chocolates 2005–; writer and reviewer 2004–; television appearances incl: Food and Drink (BBC 2), regular guest patissier/chef Great Food Live (UKTV Food) 2003–06, guest chocolate chef Taste (Sky One) 2005, regular chef and chocolate and patisserie expert on This Morning (ITV), Sunday Brunch (Channel 4), ITV Good Morning, BBC News, Bloomberg and NBC; co-organiser and participant 24 hour celebrity chef cook-a-thon Children In Need 2003 and 2004; Gold Award Acad of Chocolates 2005, 2007, 2008, 2009 and 2011 (latterly for Sea-salted Caramel and Original Hot Chocolate), Best Salted Caramel in the World and Best Dark Chocolate Truffle Int Chocolate Awards 2012, Special Award for Innovation in the Chocolate Industry Acad of Chocolate 2013, Best Salted Caramel in the World Int Chocolate Awards 2013; vice-pres Sick Children's Tst, ambass The Air Ambulance Service; fndr memb Bd Guild of Fine Chocolate 2013, Direct Cocoa; hon memb Bd Acad of Chocolate 2006; *Books* Theme: Chocolate (2009), Adventures with Chocolate (2009, Best Chocolate Book in the World and Best Chocolate Book in the UK Gourmand World Cook Book Awards 2010, shortlisted Andre Simon Book Awards 2010), How to Make Chocolates (2014); regularly featured in Delicious Magazine and BBC Good Food Magazine; *Recreations* dining out, music, design, interior design, yoga, food history, climbing, running, travelling, walking, fundraising; *Clubs* Black's, The Club at the Ivy, Soho House; *Style*— Paul A Young, Esq; ✉ Paul A Young Fine Chocolates, 33 Camden Passage, Islington, London N1 8EA; Paul A Young Fine Chocolates, 20 The Royal Exchange, Threadneedle Street, London EC3V 3LP; Paul A Young Fine Chocolates, 143 Wardour Street, London W1F 8WA; e-mail info@paulayoung.co.uk, website www.paulayoung.co.uk, Twitter @paul_a_young; c/o Nudge PR (www.nudgepr.co.uk)

YOUNG, Robert (Bob); s of Walter Horace Young (d 1963), of Wood Green, London, and Evelyn Joan, *née* Jennings (d 2009); *b* 27 March 1944; *Educ* The Boys' GS Tottenham, Magdalen Coll Oxford (MA); *m* 18 Dec 1965, Patricia Anne, da of Robert Archibald Cowin, of Hest Bank, Lancs; 2 s (Matthew b 1969, Alec b and d 1972), 1 da (Judith b 1974); *Career* dir Rolls-Royce Motors Diesel Div 1977–81, gp commercial dir Vickers plc 1981–83; on secondment from Vickers: memb Central Policy Review Staff Cabinet Office 1983, memb 10 Downing St Policy Unit 1983–84; md Crane Ltd 1985–88, chief exec Plastics Div McKechnie plc 1988–90; dir: Beauford plc 1990–92, Casindell Ltd mgmnt conslts 1993–94, PricewaterhouseCoopers 1993–2000; dir LECG Ltd 2000–04, princ Europe Economics 2004–14 (now special advsr); CBI: regnl cncllr W Midlands 1980–81, chm Salop 1981; memb: Monopolies and Mergers Cmmn 1986–92, Fulbright Cmmn 1994–2004; FInstD 1985–2000; *Recreations* music, photography, cats; *Clubs* Oxford and Cambridge; *Style*— Robert Young, Esq; ✉ Cragdale House, Victoria Street, Settle, North Yorkshire BD24 9HD (e-mail bobyoungbd24@gmail.com)

YOUNG, Prof Robert James Craig; s of Leslie William Young, and Mary, *née* Cunningham; *Educ* Exeter Coll Oxford (MA, DPhil); *Career* lectr in English rising to sr lectr Univ of Southampton 1979–89; Univ of Oxford: lectr 1989–96, reader in English lit and language 1996–99, prof of English and critical theory 1999–2005; fell Wadham Coll Oxford 1989; Julius Silver prof of English and comparative lit NYU 2005–, dean of arts and humanities NYU Abu Dhabi 2016–; founding ed Oxford Literary Review 1977–, ed Interventions: Int Jl of Postcolonial Studies 1997–; Br Acad res fell 1998–2000; fndn fell English Assoc; FRSA 2002, memb Academia Europaea 2005, corresponding fell Br Acad 2013; *Publications* incl: White Mythologies: Writing History and the West (1990), Colonial Desire: Hybridity in Culture, Theory and Race (1995), Postcolonialism: An Historical Introduction (2001), The Idea of English Ethnicity (2007), Empire, Colony, Postcolony (2015); *Recreations* photography, reading, writing; *Style*— Prof Robert Young; ✉ website www.robertjcyoung.com; English Department, New York University, 244 Greene Street, New York, NY 10003, USA (e-mail robertjcyoung@nyu.edu)

YOUNG, Sir Robin Urquhart; KCB (2002); s of Ian Urquhart Young, and Mary Hamilton, *née* West; *b* 7 September 1948; *Educ* Fettes, UC Oxford (open scholar, BA); *Career* DOE: joined 1973, various positions in housing and local govt fin, private sec to Parly Under Sec for Local Govt (Guy Barnett) 1976, to Housing Min (John Stanley) 1980 and successively to Secs of State (Patrick Jenkin, Kenneth Baker and Nicholas Ridley) 1985–89, worked in local govt fin 1981–85, under-sec housing 1988–89, under-sec environment policy 1989–91, headed team responsible for White Paper on the Environment 1990–91, head Local Govt Review Team 1991–92, head Local Govt Directorate 1992–94; dep sec and first dir Government Office for London 1994–97, head Econ and Domestic Affairs Secretariat Cabinet Office 1997–98, perm sec DCMS 1998–2001, perm sec DTI 2001–05; dep chm Dr Foster LLP 2005, chm Dr Foster Intelligence Ltd 2006–, chm Apex Communications 2006–; memb Bd East of England Int 2006–; *Style*— Sir Robin Young, KCB

YOUNG, Prof Stephen John; s of John Leonard Young (d 1994), and Joan Young; *b* 23 January 1951; *Educ* Univ of Cambridge (MA, PhD); *m* 1 (m dis); 2 da (Emma, Claire); m 2, Aug 1999, Sybille Wiesmann; *Career* UMIST: lectr Control Systems Centre 1978–79, Computation Dept 1979–84; Engrg Dept Univ of Cambridge: lectr 1984–94, reader in info engrg 1994, prof of info engrg 1994–, head Information Engrg 2002–09, sr pro-vice-chllr 2009–15; fell Emmanuel Coll Cambridge 1985–; tech dir Entropic Ltd 1995–99; architect Microsoft 1999–2001; author of numerous conf papers and articles in learned jls; memb Cncl: Univ of Cambridge, Royal Acad of Engrg; FIET, CEng, FREng, FRSA, FIEEE; *Recreations* music, ballet, film, travel; *Style*— Prof Stephen Young; ✉ Engineering Department, University of Cambridge, Trumpington Street, Cambridge CB2 1PZ (☎ 01223 332752, fax 01223 332662, e-mail sjy@eng.cam.ac.uk)

YOUNG, Sir Stephen Stewart Templeton; 3 Bt (UK 1945), of Partick, Co City of Glasgow; QC (2002); s of Sir Alastair Spencer Templeton Young, 2 Bt, DL (d 1963), and (Dorothy Constance) Marcelle (d 1964), da of Lt-Col Charles Ernest Chambers, and wid of Lt John Hollington Grayburn, VC; *b* 24 May 1947; *Educ* Rugby, Trinity Coll Oxford, Univ of Edinburgh; *m* 1974, Viola Margaret, da of Prof Patrick Horace Nowell-Smith (whose mother was Cecil, ggda of Most Rev Hon Edward Vernon-Harcourt, sometime Archbishop of York and yr bro of 3 Baron Vernon) by his 1 w Perilla (da of Sir Richard Southwell and who m subsequently, as his 2 w, Baron Roberthall); 2 s (Charles Alastair Stephen b 21 July 1979, Alexander David b 6 Feb 1982); *Heir* s, Charles Young; *Career* slr 1973, advocate 1977; Sheriff of: Glasgow and Strathkelvin 1984, North Strathclyde at Greenock 1984–2001; Sheriff Princ of Grampian, Highland and Islands 2001–12; *Style*— Sir Stephen Young, Bt, QC; ✉ Beechfield, Newton of Kinkell, Dingwall IV7 8AS

YOUNG, Timothy Mark Stewart (Tim); *b* 6 October 1951; *Educ* Eton, Magdalene Coll Cambridge (MA), Univ of Bristol (PGCE); *m* Dr Alison Keightley; 2 s; *Career* asst master Eton Coll 1975–83 and 1984–87, asst master Wanganui Collegiate Sch 1984, teacher of social sci Harvard Sch LA 1987–88, housemaster Eton Coll 1988–92, headmaster Royal GS Guildford 1992–2007; dir of educn Rank Fndn 2007–; HMC: memb Academic Policy Sub-Ctee 1996–98, tutor New Heads' Preliminary Trg Course 1996–2001, treas 1998–2001, hon assoc memb 2007–; *Style*— Tim Young, Esq; ✉ Cobbetts, Mavins Road, Farnham, Surrey GU9 8JS

YOUNG, Timothy Nicholas; QC (1996); s of William Ritchie Young, and Patricia Eileen, *née* Greig; *b* 1 December 1953; *Educ* Malvern Coll, Magdalen Coll Oxford (exhibitioner, BA, BCL); *m* 6 June 1981, Susan Jane, da of Wing Cdr Eamon St Brendan Kenny; 2 s (William Henry b 6 Oct 1983, Charles Frederick b 3 Jan 1986), 1 da (Frances Elizabeth b 26 July 1988); *Career* lectr in law St Edmund Hall Oxford 1976–80, called to the Bar Gray's Inn 1977, in practice at Commercial Bar 1978–; *Books* Voyage Charters (1993, 2 edn 2001); *Recreations* watching and playing cricket and golf, watching rugby, drawing and watercolours, music; *Clubs* RAC, Thebertons CC, Dulwich and Sydenham Golf; *Style*— Timothy Young, Esq, QC; ✉ 20 Essex Street, London WC2R 3AL (☎ 020 7583 9294, fax 020 7583 1341, e-mail tyoung@20essexst.com)

YOUNG, (Hon) Toby Daniel Moorsom; s of Baron Young of Dartington, by his 2 w Sasha; *b* 1963; *Educ* BNC Oxford, Harvard Univ, Trinity Coll Cambridge; *Career* journalist and author; *Books* How to Lose Friends and Alienate People (2001), The Sound of No Hands Clapping (2006), How to Set Up a Free School (2012), What Every Parent Needs to Know (2014); *Recreations* food and drink; *Style*— Toby Young

YOUNG, Sir William Neil; 10 Bt (GB 1769), of North Dean, Buckinghamshire; s of Capt William Elliot Young (ka 1942), and gs of Sir Charles Alban Young, 9 Bt, KCMG, MVO (d 1944); Sir Charles's w was Clara, da of Sir Francis Elliot, GCMG, GCVO (gs of 2 Earl of Minto, also Envoy Extraordinary and Min Plenipotentiary to the King of the Hellenes 1903–17); *b* 22 January 1941; *Educ* Wellington, RMA Sandhurst; *m* 1965, Christine Veronica, o da of Robert Boland Morley, of Buenos Aires; 1 da (Catherine Clare (Mrs Hugh E Powell) b 1967), 1 s (William Lawrence Elliot b 1970); *Heir* s, William Young; *Career* Capt 16/5 Queen's Royal Lancers, ret 1970; former stockbroker with: Phillips & Drew, James Capel & Co; former ptnr Watson & Co; md Kleinwort Benson International Investment (Pacific) Ltd 1982–85, dir Kleinwort Benson International Investment Ltd 1982–87, head of investment mgmnt Saudi International Bank 1987–91, int private banking (head of Middle East) Coutts & Co 1991–94; dir Middle East Barclays Private Bank Ltd 1994–1999; currently chm: New World Tst Ltd 2000–12, Napo Pharmaceuticals Inc 2002–14; dir Vector Fund Ltd; chm High Ham branch Royal Br Legion; govr: High Ham C of E Sch, Langport Cons Assoc; *Recreations* tennis, gardening; *Style*— Sir William Young, Bt; ✉ South End House, High Ham, Langport, Somerset

YOUNG, William Robert (Will); s of Robin Young, and Annabel Young; *b* 20 January 1979, Hungerford, Berks; *Educ* Wellington, Univ of Exeter (BA), Arts Educnl Sch Chiswick; *Career* singer, songwriter and actor; winner Pop Idol (ITV) 2002; albums: From Now On 2002, Friday's Child 2003, Keep On 2005, Let It Go 2008, The Hits 2009; singles: Anything Is Possible/Evergreen 2002, Light My Fire 2002 , Long and Winding Road/Suspicious Minds (with Gareth Gates) 2002, Don't Let Me Down/You & I 2002, Leave Right Now 2003, Your Game 2004, Friday's Child 2004, Switch It On 2005, All Time Love 2006, Who Am I 2006, Changes 2008, Grace 2008, Let It Go 2009; Brit Awards: Best Newcomer 2002, Best British Single (for Your Game) 2006; actor: Mrs Henderson Presents 2005 (film), The Vortex (Royal Exchange Theatre Manchester) 2007, Skins (E4) 2010, Bedlam (Living) 2011, Cabaret (Savoy Theatre) 2012 (Newcomer of the Year Whatsonstage Award 2013); ambass Prince's Trust 2002–; *Style*— Will Young, Esq; ✉ c/o 19 Management, 33 Ransomes Dock, 35–37 Parkgate Road, London SW11 4NP (☎ 020 7801 1919, fax 020 7801 1920)

YOUNG OF COOKHAM, Baron (Life Peer UK 2015), of Cookham in the Royal County of Berkshire; Rt Hon Sir George Samuel Knatchbull; 6 Bt (UK 1813), of Formosa Place, Berks; CH (2012), PC (1993); s of Sir George Young, 5 Bt, CMG (d 1960), by his w Elisabeth (herself er da of Sir Hugh Knatchbull-Hugessen, KCMG, who was in turn n of 1 Baron Brabourne); *b* 16 July 1941; *Educ* Eton, ChCh Oxford; *m* 1964, Aurelia, da of Oscar Nemon, and Mrs Nemon-Stuart, of Boars Hill, Oxford; 2 s, 2 da; *Heir* s, George Young; *Career* economist NEDO 1966–67, Kobler res fell Univ of Surrey 1967–69, memb Lambeth BC 1968–71, econ advsr Post Office Corp 1969–74, memb GLC (Ealing) 1970–73; MP (Cons): Ealing Acton Feb 1974–97, Hampshire NW 1997–2015; oppn whip 1976–79, under sec of state DHSS 1979–81, under sec of state DOE 1981–86, comptroller of HM Household (sr Govt whip) 1990, min of state for the environment 1990–92, min for housing and inner cities 1992–94, fin sec to the Treasy 1994–95, sec of state for tport 1995–97, shadow defence sec 1997–98, shadow ldr House of Commons 1998–2000 and 2009–10, ldr House of Commons and Lord Privy Seal 2010–12, chief whip 2012–14; chm Standards and Privileges Select Ctee 2001–10; tstee Guinness Tst 1986–90; *Books* Tourism, Blessing or Blight?, I'm Keeping Young; *Style*— The Rt Hon the Lord Young of Cookham, Bt, CH, PC; ✉ House of Commons, London SW1A 0AA (☎ 020 7219 6665)

YOUNG OF GRAFFHAM, Baron (Life Peer UK 1984), of Graffham in the County of West Sussex; David Ivor Young; CH (2015), PC (1984), DL (West Sussex 1999); s of late Joseph Young and his w, Rebecca; *b* 27 February 1932; *Educ* Christ's Coll Finchley, UCL (LLB, Capt London Univ Golf 1954); *m* 1956, Lita Marianne, da of Jonas Shaw; 2 da (Hon Karen Debra b 1957 m 1983, Rt Hon Sir Bernard Rix, *qv*, Hon Judith Anne (Hon Mrs Nathoo) b 1960); *Career* admitted slr 1956; chm Eldonwall Ltd 1961–74, dir Town & City Properties Ltd 1971–74; chm: Manufacturers Hanover Property Services 1974–80, Greenwood Homes Ltd 1976–82; dir Centre for Policy Studies 1979–82 (memb Mgmnt Bd 1977–82); special advsr: Dept of Industry 1979–82, Dept of Educn and Sci 1981–82; chm Manpower Servs Cmmn 1982–84, memb/chm NEDC 1982–89; min without portfolio 1984–85, sec of state for employment 1985–87, sec of state for trade and industry and pres of the Bd of Trade 1987–89, retired from Govt 1989; dep chm Cons Pty 1989–90; enterprise adviser to the PM 2010–15; dir Salomon Inc (and subsids) 1990–94; chm: Cable & Wireless plc 1990–95, Neoscorp Ltd 1997–, Pixology Ltd 1997–; dir: Young Assocs Ltd, Pixology Ltd, Chichester Festival Theatre Co Ltd, Acacia City Ltd, Autohit plc, Business for Sterling, Br Israel C of C, Convergys Inc, Elfin Systems Ltd, IndogoVision plc, Int Telecommunications Clearing Corps Ltd (Bermuda), Newhaven Mgmnt Services Ltd, Pere (UK) Ltd; chm: Br Orgn for Rehabilitation by Training (ORT) 1975–80, Admin Ctee World ORT Union 1980–84, Int Cncl of Jewish Social and Welfare Servs 1981–, EU-Japan Assoc 1991–97, Cncl UCL 1995–2005, London Philharmonic Tst 1995–98, W Sussex Econ Forum 1996–; pres: Jewish Care 1990–97, World ORT Union 1990–, IOD 1993–2013; chair Chichester Festival Theatre 1997–2013; Hon FRPS 1981; *Publications* The Enterprise Years (1990); *Recreations* music, book collecting, photography; *Clubs* Savile; *Style*— The Rt Hon Lord Young of Graffham, CH, PC, DL; ✉ Young Associates Ltd, 100 Marylebone Road, York Gate, Regent's Park, London NW1 5DX (☎ 020 7148 4737, e-mail young@youngassoc.com)

YOUNG OF HORNSEY, Baroness (Life Peer UK 2004), of Hornsey in the London Borough of Haringey; Margaret Omolola (Lola) Young; OBE (2001); da of Maxwell Fela Young (d 1994); *b* 1 June 1951, London; *Educ* Parliament Hill Comp Sch for Girls, New Coll of Speech and Drama London (Dip Dramatic Art, CertEd), Middx Univ (BA, PhD); *m* 1984, Barrie Birch, s of Ronald Birch; 1 s; *Career* clerical and admin work in public utilities 1969–71, residential social worker London Borough of Islington 1971–73, professional actor 1976–84, co-dir and trg and devpt mangr Haringey Arts Cncl (HAC) 1985–89, enterprise offr Faculty of Educn and Performing Arts Middx Univ 1989–91, freelance lectr and arts conslt 1989–91, lectr in media studies Thames Valley Univ 1990–92, lectr rising to prof of cultural studies Middx Univ 1992–2001, project dir Archives and Museum of Black Heritage 1997–2001, head of culture GLA 2002–04, currently freelance cultural conslt; visiting prof of cultural studies Univ of São Paulo 1998; chair: Cultural Diversity Advsy Ctee Arts Cncl 2000–01, Arts Advsy Ctee Br Cncl 2004–08, Nitro (formerly Black Theatre Co-operative) 2004–10, Cwlth Gp on Culture and Devpt; memb: Bd inIVA (Inst for Int Visual Arts) 1994–2001, Visual Arts Panel Arts Cncl of England 1996–98 (memb Educn and Trg Sub-Ctee 1996–99), Theatre Ctee Arts Cncl of England 2000, Steering Gp on English Heritage (DCMS cmmnd review) 2000–02, Bd Resource: Cncl for Museums, Archives and Libraries 2000–02, Bd RNT 2000–03, Blue Plaques Sub-Ctee English Heritage 2001–03, Bd South Bank Centre 2002–10, Advsy Gp on Audiences and Access Natural History Museum 2003–06, DCMS Advsy Gp on Museums 2004, EU Select Ctee 2010– (chair Sub-Ctee G on Social Policies and Consumer Protection 2010–); external assessor Cmmn for Racial Equality Race in the Media Awards 1991–94; cmmr Royal Cmmn on Historic Manuscripts 2000–01; patron: Autograph 1997–2001, Action Space 2007–, Josephine Wolf Tst 2007–; series advsy ed Critical Photography (Manchester Univ Press) 1992, memb Editorial Collective Feminist Review 1992–94, memb Editorial Bd Parallax: Jl of Meta-discursive Theory 1994–, advsy ed Oxford Art Jl 1994–, conslt Companion to Black British History 2002; chair Panel of Judges Orange Prize for Fiction 1999; numerous radio and TV broadcasts, delivered keynote address and lectures at confs worldwide; memb Mgmnt Ctee Post-Adoption Centre 2000–03; memb Bd of Govrs Middx Univ 2002–03; FRSA 2000; *Publications* Fear of the Dark: 'Race', Gender and Sexuality in Cinema; also numerous articles, essays and interview in newspapers and other jls; *Recreations* reading, walking, all arts; *Clubs* Hosp; *Style*— The Rt Hon the Lady Young of Hornsey, OBE; ✉ e-mail younglo@parliament.uk

YOUNG OF NORWOOD GREEN, Baron (Life Peer UK 2004), of Norwood Green in the London Borough of Ealing; Sir Anthony Ian Young; kt (2002); *b* 16 April 1942; *Educ* Harrow County GS; *m* 1, 1962 (m dis 1984), Doreen Goodman; 1 s, 2 da; *m* 2, 1985, Margaret Newnham; 1 s, 1 da; *Career* Nat Communications Union: gen sec 1989–95, jt gen sec 1995–98, sr dep gen sec 1998–2002; memb: Academic Cncl Wilton Park 1997–2005, Steering Bd Employment Tbnl 1997–2006, Gen Cncl TUC 1998–2002 (pres 2001–02), British N America Ctee 1999–; govr BBC 1998–2002, chm One World Broadcasting Tst 2002–10; govr Three Bridges Primary Sch 2002–; a Lord-in-Waiting to HM The Queen 2008–; *Style*— The Lord Young of Norwood Green; ✉ House of Lords, London SW1A 0PW

YOUNG OF OLD SCONE, Baroness (Life Peer UK 1997), of Old Scone in Perth and Kinross; Barbara Scott Young; da of George Young (d 1981), of Perth, Scotland, and Mary, *née* Scott (d 2001); *b* 8 April 1948; *Educ* Perth Acad, Univ of Edinburgh (MA), Univ of Strathclyde; *Career* chartered environmentalist 2005; sr admin Gtr Glasgow Health Bd 1973–78, dir of planning and devpt St Thomas' Health Dist 1978–79, dist gen admin NW Dist Kensington, Chelsea & Westminster AHA 1979–82, dist admin Haringey HA 1982–85, dist gen mangr Paddington & North Kensington HA 1985–88, dist gen mangr Parkside HA 1988–91, chief exec RSPB 1991–98 (vice-pres 2000–), chm English Nature 1998–2000, chief exec Environment Agency 2000–08, chair Care Quality Cmmn 2008–09, memb Climate Change Adaptation Ctee 2009–10, chief exec Diabetes UK 2010–15; chllr Cranfield Univ 2010–; vice-chair Bd of Govrs BBC 1998–2000; vice-pres Flora and Fauna Int 1998–, vice-pres Birdlife Int 1999–, pres Bedfordshire, Cambridgeshire and Peterborough Wildlife Tst 2001–, pres Br Tst for Ornithology 2005–13, chair designate Woodland Tst 2016–; memb: World Cncl Birdlife Int 1994–98, Ctee of Sec of State for Environment's UK Round Table on Sustainability 1995–2000, Cmmn on Future of the Voluntary Sector 1995–96, Ctee on the Public Understanding of Sci (COPUS) 1996–97; patron Inst of Environmental & Ecological Mgmnt 1993–; tstee: NCVO 1993–97, Public Mgmnt Fndn 1998–99, IPPR 2000–09; pres South Georgia Heritage Tst 2010–, patron LANTRA 2013–; pres Inst of Health Servs Mgmnt 1987–88 (dip 1971); hon memb Linnean Soc of London 2002; Hon DUniv: Stirling 1995, Hertfordshire 1997; Hon DSc Cranfield Univ 1998; Hon Degree: Univ of St Andrews 2000, Univ of Aberdeen 2000, Univ of York 2000, Open Univ 2001, Anglia Ruskin 2008, Univ of Gloucester 2009, Univ of Exeter 2010; hon fell Sydney Sussex Coll Cambridge 2000; AHSM 1971; *Recreations* cinema, gardening, dressage; *Style*— The Rt Hon Baroness Young of Old Scone; ✉ House of Lords, London SW1A 0PW

YOUNGER, Captain Sir (John) David Bingham; KCVO (2013, LVO 2007); s of Maj Oswald Bingham Younger, MC (d 1989), of Etal, Northumberland, and Dorothea Elizabeth, *née* Hobbs (d 1996); *b* 20 May 1939, Doune, Perthshire; *Educ* Eton, RMA Sandhurst; *m* 1 Dec 1962, Anne Rosaleen (d 2012), da of Lt-Col John Logan, TD, DL (d 1987); 2 da (Sarah Juliet (Mrs Peter Landale, DL) b 1964, Camilla Jane b 1966), 1 s (Mark Robert b 1972); *Career* Argyll and Sutherland Highlanders cmmnd 1959, Adj 1 Bn Borneo and Singapore 1965–67 (GSM Clasps Borneo and Malaysia), Directorate of Mil Ops MOD 1967–69, ret 1969; Scottish & Newcastle Breweries Ltd 1969–79, co-fndr and md Broughton Brewery Ltd 1979–94, dir Broughton Ales Ltd 1995–96; chm Bowman Ltd 2008–15; vice-pres Royal Highland and Agric Soc of Scotland 1994; chm: Scottish Borders Tourist Bd 1989–91, Peeblesshire Charitable Tst 1994–2014; sec Queen's Body Guard for Scotland (Royal Co of Archers) 1993–2007 (memb 1969–, Brig 2002–, Ensign 2010), pres SSAFA (Borders Area) 2006–; memb Argyll and Sutherland Highlanders Regtl Tst and Ctee 1985–92, pres Lowland Reserve Forces and Cadets Assoc 2006–14; dir Queen's Hall Edinburgh 1992–2001, chm Eastgate Theatre (Peebles) Ltd 2015–; tstee Chambers Instn 2012–15; chm of govrs Belhaven Hill Sch Dunbar 1988–94; River Tweed Cmmr 2002–16; HM Lord-Lt of Tweeddale 1994–2014 (DL 1987, Vice Lord-Lt 1992–94); MInstD 1984; *Recreations* the countryside; *Style*— Captain Sir David Younger, KCVO; ✉ Glenkirk, Broughton, Peeblesshire ML12 6JF (☎ 01899 830570, e-mail kirkurd.youngers@virgin.net)

YOUNGER, James Samuel (Sam); CBE (2009); s of Rt Hon Sir Kenneth Gilmour Younger (d 1976), of London, and Elisabeth Kirsteen, *née* Stewart (d 2003); *b* 5 October 1951; *Educ* Westminster, New Coll Oxford (BA); *m* 5 May 1984, Katherine Anne, da of Cyril Kenneth Spencer; 1 s (Edward Spencer Younger b 6 June 1986); *Career* asst ed Middle East International magazine 1972–78; BBC World Service: sr asst Central Current Affrs Talks 1979–84, sr prodr Current Affrs World Service 1984–85 (exec prodr 1985–86), asst head BBC Arabic Service 1986–87, head Current Affrs World Service in English 1987–89, head BBC Arabic Service 1989–92, controller Overseas Services 1992–94, dir of broadcasting 1994, md BBC World Service 1994–98; DG British Red Cross Soc 1999–2001, chm Electoral Cmmn 2001–08, chair Quality Assurance Agency for HE 2004–09, chief exec Shelter 2009, chief exec Charity Cmmn 2010–14, chief exec Bell Educnl Tst 2010; memb Cncl Advertising Standards Authy 2014–, public interest cncl observer Chartered Inst of Taxation 2015–, chair CILEx Regulation 2015–; dir Eng Touring Opera 1999–2010; patron Windsor Leadership Tst 1998–, govr Cwlth Inst 1998–2005, memb Cncl Univ of Sussex 1998–2007 (chair 2001–07), vice-chair VSO 2014–; *Recreations* choral singing, sport; *Style*— Sam Younger, CBE; ✉ 28 Rylett Crescent, London W12 9RL (☎ 020 8743 4449)

YOUNGER OF LECKIE, 5 Viscount (UK 1923); Sir James Edward George Younger; 5 Bt (UK 1911); s of 4 Viscount Younger of Leckie, KT, KCVO, PC (d 2003), and Diana Rhona, *née* Tuck; *b* 11 November 1955, Edinburgh; *Educ* Winchester, Univ of St Andrews (MA), Henley Mgmnt Coll (MBA); *m* 4 June 1988, Jennie, *née* Wootton; 2 da (Hon Emily Evelyn b 26 Sept 1990, Hon Alice Elizabeth b 25 Feb 1992), 1 s (Hon Alexander William George b 13 Nov 1993); *Heir* s, Hon Alexander Younger; *Career* personnel mangr Coats Patons plc 1979–84, conslt Angela Mortimer plc 1984–86, conslt Stephens Consultancies 1986–92, dir McInnes Younger 1992–94, HR dir UBS 1994–2004, dir Culliford Edmunds 2004–07, conslt Eban Ltd 2007–10; memb House of Lords 2010–, party whip House of Lords 2011–13, parly under-sec of state for business, innovation and skills 2013–14, min i/c Intellectual Property Office 2013–14, Lord in Waiting (Govt whip) 2015–; chm

Buckingham Cons Assoc 2006–10, chm Milton Keynes Cons Assoc 2011–13; memb Queen's Body Guard for Scotland (Royal Co of Archers); tstee: Kate Kennedy Tst, Globe Run; pres Highland Soc of London 2012–16, vice-pres War Widows' Assoc 2012–; memb Assoc of Cons Peers (ACP), MCIM 1993; *Recreations* sailing, shooting, tennis, running, cricket, skiing; *Clubs* White Hunter Cricket, MCC (assoc memb); *Style*— The Rt Hon the Viscount Younger of Leckie; ✉ The Old Vicarage, Dorton, Aylesbury, Buckinghamshire HP18 9NH (✆ 01844 238396, e-mail jeg.younger@virgin.net)

YOUNGSON, Prof George Gray; CBE (2009); s of Alexander Keay Youngson, MBE, of Glenrothes, Fife, and Jean Oneil, *née* Kelly; *b* 13 May 1949; *Educ* Buckhaven HS, Univ of Aberdeen (MB ChB, PhD); *m* 17 March 1973, Sandra Jean, *née* Lister; 2 da (Kellie Jane b 1973, Louise b 1975), 1 s (Calum Lister b 1981); *Career* Univ of Aberdeen: lectr in surgery 1979–82, res fell 1974–76, emeritus prof of paediatric surgery 2010; res in cardiothoracic surgery Univ of W Ontario 1977–79, clinical fell in paediatric surgery Hosp for Sick Children Toronto 1983, conslt paediatric surgn Royal Aberdeen Children's Hosp 1985–2010, co-chair MSN Children and Young People with Cancer in Scotland 2010–; hon prof of paediatric surgery Univ of Aberdeen 1999; tstee ARCHIE Fndn; FRCSEd 1977 (memb Cncl, vice-pres 2009–12), Hon FRCPE 2011; *Recreations* bagpipe music, sport (fishing, tennis, squash, golf); *Style*— Prof George Youngson, CBE; ✉ Birken Lodge, Bieldside, Aberdeen AB15 9BQ (e-mail ggyrach@abdn.ac.uk)

YOUNIS, Dr Farouk Mustafa; s of Mustafa Younis (d 2004), of Amman, Jordan, and Wasila Mahmoud Khader; *b* 1 March 1947; *Educ* Markaziyah All HS Baghdad, Baghdad Univ Med Sch (MB ChB); *m* 13 Sept 1975, Cynthia Karen, da of George Gadsby (d 1992), of Ilkeston, Derbys; 1 s (Sami Farouk b 15 Feb 1977); *Career* surgeon; started career in Palestinian refugee camps in Lebanon with Red Crescent Soc Med and Health Prog 1971–72; trg posts UK 1973–: casualty, gen surgery, orthopaedics, thoracic, vascular and urologic surgery; casualty post Chesterfield, gen surgery posts Harrogate, Barrow in Furness and Huddersfield, orthopaedics post Cambridge, kidney transplant and gen surgery post Royal Free Hosp London, gen and vascular surgery Chelmsford, conslt surgeon Whittington Hosp 1981–83, private surgical practice 1981–2015, ret; memb: BMA, RSM, Ind Doctors' Forum, Soc of Minimal Invasion Therapy; FRCS 1977, fell Assoc of Surgns of GB & I; *Recreations* golf, travel, chess, skiing; *Clubs* N Middx Golf, Southerts Golf; *Style*— Dr Farouk Younis; ✉ 4 Langton Avenue, London N20 9DB; 129 Harley Street, London W1G 6BA (✆ 020 8446 3778, e-mail farouky@aol.com)

YOUSAF, Humza; MSP; s of Muzaffar Yousaf, and Shaaista, *née* Bhutta; *b* 7 April 1985, Glasgow; *Educ* Univ of Glasgow (BSc); *m* 30 July 2010, Gail Lythgoe; *Career* parly researcher to: Bashir Ahmad, MSP 2007–09, Anne McLaughlin, MSP 2009–10, Rt Hon Alex Salmond, MSP, *qv*, 2010; MSP (SNP) Glasgow 2011–; media spokesman for Islamic Relief Scotland; alumnus US State Dept Int Visitor Leadership Prog 2008; Political Force of the Future 2010; min for Europe and Int Dev in scottish govt 2012–; *Recreations* football (keen Glasgow Celtic FC supporter); *Style*— Humza Yousaf, Esq, MSP; ✉ The Scottish Parliament, Edinburgh EH99 1SP (✆ 0131 348 6209, e-mail humza.yousaf.msp@scottish.parliament.uk)

YUASA, Takuo; *b* 27 July 1949; *Educ* Coll/Conservatory of Music Univ of Cincinnati (BMus), Vienna Hochschule für Musik (Dip); *m* 1982, Shigeko Takaoka; 1 da (Michika b 1984); *Career* conductor Gumma Symphony Orch 1984–88; princ guest conductor: BBC Scottish Symphony Orch 1989–93, Ulster Orch 1997–2005; UK debut 1988, Proms debut 1989; conducted orchs incl: Tonkünstlerorchester Vienna, Japan Philharmonic, Tokyo Met Symphony, Warsaw Nat Philharmonic, Polish Radio Nat Symphony, London Philharmonic, Yomiuri Nippon Symphony, Oslo Philarmonic, Ulster Orchestra, Bournemouth Symphony, Royal Liverpool Philarmonic, Hallé Orch, Hong Kong Philharmonic, Syndey Symphony, Berlin Symphony; venues incl: Vienna Konzerthaus, Royal Festival Hall, opening concert Glasgow Euro City of Culture Festival 1990, Sydney Opera House, Scottish Opera (Traviata), Berlin Philharmonic Hall, numerous others in UK, Japan, Scandinavia, Australia and Europe; assoc prof Tokyo Univ of the Arts 2008–; IUE Cultural Prize 2007; *Recordings* Rimsky-Korsakov's Sheherazade (with London Philharmonic Orch), Benjamin Britten's Four Sea Interludes and others (with Royal Liverpool Philharmonic Orch), Lorenzo Ferraro's La Nueva España (with Nat Symphony of Ukraine), Henryk Górecki's Symphony No 3 (with Adelaide Symphony) with Ulster Orch: James MacMillan's Veni Veni Emanuel, Michael Nyman's Piano Concerto, John Tavener's The Protecting Veil, Benjamin Britten's Cello Symphony, Philip Glass' Violin Concerto, Arvo Pärt's Tabula Rasa, Arnold Schoenberg's Verklärte Nacht, Anton Webern's Passacaglia, Edward MacDowell's Suites No 1 & 2, Akio Yashiro's Symphony, Alan Rawsthorne's Piano Concertos, Four Brahms Symphonies 2006, Four Schumann Symphonies 2007; *Style*— Takuo Yuasa, Esq

YVON, HE Christopher; *b* 11 November 1969, Stroud, Glos; *Educ* Marling GS Stroud; *m* Annette; 2 da (Hannah b 21 Aug 1989, Octavia b 14 June 2011), 1 s (Dylan b 29 June 1992); *Career* diplomat; Migration and Visa Dept FCO 1989–91, attaché Prague 1991–93, Hong Kong Dept FCO 1993–94, third sec Bangkok 1995, Nr East and N Africa Dept FCO 1995, second sec Port Louis 1999–2002, Human Rights Policy Dept FCO 2003–04, Int Orgns Dept FCO 2004–07, dep head Int Orgns Dept FCO 2007–10, ambass to Macedonia 2010–14, chargé d'affaires to Slovenia 2014–15, ambass and UK perm rep to the Cncl of Europe 2016–; *Recreations* cinema, cycling, snooker; *Clubs* Rileys (London Victoria), Granklub (Skopje); *Style*— Mr Christopher Yvon; ✉ c/o FCO (Ljubljana), King Charles Street, London SW1A 2AH (e-mail christopher.yvon@fco.gov.uk)

Y

Z

ZABLUDOWICZ, Anita; OBE (2016), *m* Poju Zabludowicz; 4 c; *Career* art collector and patronne; co-fndr Zabludowicz Collection; *Style—* Mrs Anita Zabludowicz, OBE; ✉ Zabludowicz Collection, 176 Prince of Wales Road, Chalk Farm, London NW5 3PT (☎ 020 7428 8945, fax 020 7428 8949, e-mail caragh@zabludowiczcollection.com, website www.zabludowiczcollection.com)

ZAHAWI, Nadhim; MP; *b* 2 June 1967, Baghdad, Iraq; *Educ* King's Coll Sch Wimbledon, UCL (BSc); *m* Lana; 3 c; *Career* European mktg dir Smith & Brooks Ltd until 2000, co-fndr and ceo YouGov plc 2000–10; cncllr London Borough of Wandsworth 1994–2006, MP (Cons) Stratford-on-Avon 2010–; *Publications* Masters of Nothing; *Style—* Nadhim Zahawi, Esq, MP; ✉ House of Commons, London SW1A 0AA (website www.zahawi.com, Twitter @nadhimzahawi)

ZAIWALLA, Sarosh Ratanshaw; *b* 27 September 1947, Mumbai; *Educ* Univ of Bombay (BCom, LLB); *Children* 1 da (Freya b 1981), 1 s (Varun b 1983); *Career* admitted slr 1978; fndr ptnr Gagrat & Co London 1978–82, sr ptnr Zaiwalla & Co Solicitors London 1982–; specialist in international commercial contracts and maritime disputes and immigration and nationality cases; memb: Law Soc, Maritime Arbitrators' Assoc, Baltic Exchange London, Int Court of Arbitration of Int C of C Paris, London Court of Int Arbitration (fndr memb), Indian Cncl of Arbitration Delhi, London Maritime Arbitrators' Assoc (supporting memb), Int Cmmn on Arbitration; chm Br Org of People of Indian Origin (BOPIO); pres Soc of Friends of the Lotus Children; jt convenor Asian Business Breakfast Club; Law Day Award for Unique Contrib to Int Arbitration Law Indian Cncl of Jurists 2003; Freeman City of London 1998; accredited mediator CEDR; FRSA; *Style—* Sarosh Zaiwalla, Esq; ✉ Zaiwalla & Co, Chancery House, 53–64 Chancery Lane, London WC2A 1QS (☎ 020 7312 1000, fax 020 7404 9473, e-mail sarosh.zaiwalla@zaiwalla.co.uk or saroshzaiwalla@hotmail.com, website www.zaiwalla.co.uk)

ZAKAY, Sol; *Career* chm and ceo Topland Gp plc, chm and ceo Topland Gp Hldgs Ltd, exec chm and ceo Topland Gp of Companies; *Style—* Sol Zakay, Esq; ✉ Topland Group, 105 Wigmore Street, London W1U 1QY (☎ 020 7493 3373, e-mail allisonm@topland.co.uk)

ZAKRZEWSKA, Prof Joanna Maria; da of Mieczyslaw Zakrzewski (d 1999), and Kazimiera Zakrzewska (d 2001); *b* 7 December 1949, London; *Educ* King's Coll Dental Sch London (BDS), Newnham Coll Cambridge (MB, BChir), Univ of Cambridge (MD); *m* 1984, Jan Ledochowski; 1 s (Konrad b 18 March 1985), 1 da (Krystyna b 18 Jan 1988); *Career* dental house offr King's Coll Hosp Dental Sch 1973, gen dental practice 1973–74, SHO St Mary's Hosp London and Eastman Dental Hosp 1974–75, dental clinical asst St Mary's Hosp 1975–77, supervisor in pathology Newnham Coll Cambridge 1978–79, house surgn Norfolk and Norwich Hosp 1980–81, SHO St Mary's Hosp London 1981–82; Eastman Dental Hosp: registrar in oral and maxillofacial surgery 1982–84, locum sr registrar in oral and maxillofacial surgery and oral med 1984–86, res fell and hon sr registrar in oral med 1986–89, conslt and hon sr lectr in oral med 1989–95; hon conslt Nat Hosp for Neurology and Neurosurgery 1989–, conslt oral physician UCL Hosps 1991–96, conslt and hon sr lectr Mortimer Market Dental Clinic and Camden & Islington NHS Tst 1991–2000; Inst of Dentistry Barts and the London and Queen Mary's Sch of Med and Dentistry: sr lectr and hon conslt in oral med clinical diagnostic and oral sciences 1996–2005, prof of pain in relation to oral med 2004–07; conslt Eastman Dental UCL Hosps 2007–, conslt Pain Mgmnt Centre UCLH NHS Tst 2015–; expert advsr for guidelines for trigeminal neuralgia American Acad of Neurology and European Fedn of Neurological Socs 2004–06, taskforce ldr special interest gp of orofacial pain Int Assoc for the Study of Pain on classification of orofacial pain 2002–05, chm Med Bd and tstee Trigeminal Neuralgia Assoc UK, memb Med Advsy Bd Trigeminal Neuralgia Assoc US, expert advsr to NICE on stereotactic radiosurgery for trigeminal neuralgia, lead investigator Int Drug Trial with Convergence; memb: BMA, RSM (memb Cncl Odontological Section 1994–95, memb Cncl Pain Section 2008–11, pres Pain Section 2014–15), Cncl Pain Medicine 2008–14, Int Assoc for the Study of Pain, Pain Soc UK, Assoc for Med Educn in Europe, Assoc for the Study of Med Educn, BDA (hosp gp pres 2007–08), Int Assoc for Dental Res, Oral Health Gp of Cochrane Collaboration, European Assoc of Oral Med, Br Soc for Oral Med (memb Cncl, treas and sec 1989–91, pres 1997–99), Soc of Authors, Int Headache Soc, Medical Women's Fedn; hon memb Polish Pain Soc 2015; FDSRCS 1980, FFDRCSI 1991, FHEA 2000, fell Faculty of Pain Medicine Royal Coll of Anaesthetists 2008; Officer Cross of the Order of Merit Poland 2009; Trigeminal Neuralgia (1995), Assessment and Management of Orofacial Pain (2002), Insights: Facts and Stories Behind Trigeminal Neuralgia (2006), Orofacial Pain (2009); over 100 pubns in peer-reviewed jls; *Recreations* gardening, travel; *Style—* Prof Joanna Zakrzewska; ✉ Oral Medicine, UCLH Eastman Dental Hospital, 256 Gray's Inn Road, London WC1X 8LD (☎ 020 3456 1195, e-mail j.zakrzewska@ucl.ac.uk, website www.ledochowski.eu)

ZAMOYSKI, Count Adam Stefan; s of Lt-Col Count Stefan Zamoyski, OBE, VM, LLD, Commander with Star Order of Polonia Restituta (d 1976) by his w Princess Elizabeth Czartoryska (d 1989); *b* 11 January 1949, New York; *Educ* Downside, The Queen's Coll Oxford; *m* 14 June 2001, Emma, da of Sir Patrick Sergeant , *qv*; *Career* historian and author; pres Fndn of St John of Jerusalem Warsaw 1997–2011, chm Czartoryski Fndn Kraków 2005–11; hon doctorate Polish Univ Abroad 2012; Freeman City of London 1992; FSA 2002, FRSA 2005, FRSL 2006, memb Literary Soc 2010; Order of Polonia Restituta 1982 (Offr 1997, Cdr 2007); *Books* Chopin, A Biography (1979), Paderewski (1981), The Polish Way (1987), The Last King of Poland (1992), The Forgotten Few (1995), Holy Madness (1999), 1812 (2004), Rites of Peace (2007), Warsaw 1920 (2008), Poland: A History (2009), Chopin: Prince of the Romantics (2010), Phantom Terror: The Threat of Devolution and the Repression of Liberty 1789–1848 (2014); *Clubs* Pratt's, Puffin's, Ognisko; *Style—* Count Adam Zamoyski; ✉ 12 Avenue Studios, Sydney Close, London SW3 6HW (☎ 020 7584 9053, e-mail adam@adamzamoyski.com); Lipsko Polesie 37, 22-400 Zamo??, Poland

ZANCANI, Prof Diego; s of Lattanzio Zancani (d 2006), and Edi Giovanna, *née* Silvestrini; *b* 10 May 1944, Castel San Giovanni, Italy; *Educ* Bocconi Univ Milan, Univ of Oxford (MA); *m* 1, 26 Sept 1970 (m dis 2001), Graziella Bernini; 3 s (Leonardo b 7 Aug 1973, Sandro b 30 May 1978, Fabio b 17 Feb 1980); m 2, 31 May 2003, Valentina, *née* Olivastri; *Career* asst lectr in Italian Univ of Reading 1969–73, lectr in Italian Univ of Liverpool 1973–79, reader and prof of Italian Univ of Kent 1979–95; Univ of Oxford: faculty lectr in Italian 1995–2004, fell and tutor in Italian Balliol Coll 1995–, dean Balliol Coll 2002–04, prof of Italian 2004–10, praefectus Holywell Manor 2004–10, emeritus fell Balliol Coll 2010–, fell Japan Soc for the Promotion of Science 2012; visiting prof: History of the Book Parma Univ 1991, Italian Philology Univ of Reading 1992, Univ of Perugia 1995, Dept of Romance Languages and Literature Harvard Univ 2000 and 2003, Comparative Lit Univ of Pavia 2008, Univ of Tokyo 2012; Deputazione di Storia Patria Province di Parma e Piacenza 1975; Commendatore dell'Ordine della Stella della Solidarietà Italiana (2006); *Publications* Gride e bandi del Seicento (1985), G C Croce: Dall'Emilia All'Inghilterra (jtly, 1991), A Cornazzano: La Tradizione Testuale (jtly, 1992); numerous chapters in books and articles in the field of Renaissance studies, history of the language and of food; *Recreations* reading, walking, cooking, mushroom hunting; *Style—* Prof Diego Zancani; ✉ Balliol College, Broad Street, Oxford OX1 3BJ

ZARNECKI, Prof Jan (John) Charles; s of Jerzy (George) Zarnecki, of London, and Anne Leslie, *née* Frith; *b* 6 November 1949, London; *Educ* Queens' Coll Cambridge (open exhibitioner, MA), UCL (PhD); *m* 1, 2 July 1976 (m dis 1994), Gillian Elizabeth, *née* Fairbanks; 1 da (Holly Clare b 27 Jan 1978), 1 s (Thomas Guy b 29 Sept 1979); m 2, 14 Nov 2009, Catherine Philomena, *née* O'Donoghue; *Career* research asst Mullard Space Sci Lab UCL 1974–79, sr systems engr Dynamics Gp Br Aerospace 1979–81; Unit for Space Scis Univ of Kent: sr experimental offr 1981–85, lectr 1985–87, sr lectr 1987–96, reader 1996–2000; reader in space and planetary scis then prof of space sci Planetary and Space Research Inst Open Univ 2000–13 (head Space Scis Research Gp Planetary and Space Sciences Research Inst), emeritus prof of space science Open Univ 2013–; sr visiting scientist Solar System Div European Space Research and Technol Centre European Space Agency 1999–2000; projects incl: involvement with Hubble Space Telescope, project mangr Giotto DIDSY comet Halley spacecraft experiment, princ investigator Surface Science Package and co-investigator Atmosphere Structure Instrument for Huygens probe/lander on Cassini mission to Saturn and Titan, princ investigator Ultraviolet Spectrometer Aurora/ExoMars lander, dep princ investigator PTOLEMY and co-investigator Multi-Purpose Surface and Sub-Surface Science Subsystem (MUPUS) on Rosetta lander; memb: Cncl Royal Astronomical Soc 1995–98 (vice-pres 2009–11), Solar System Working Gp European Space Agency 1995–98, European Space Sci Ctee European Sci Fndn 1997–2000, Cncl PPARC 2005–07 (memb Sci and Soc Advsy Gp 2003–07); dir Int Space Science Inst (ISSI) Bern, Switzerland 2013–; chair European Space Agency Solary System & Exploration Working Gp 2014–; memb Shareholder's Ctee Eurotunnel plc 2003–06; memb Bd Milton Keynes Gallery; 5 separate awards from NASA and ESA 1997–2005, Arthur C Clarke Award 2005, Gold Medal RAS 2014; author of over 200 scientific and tech pubns; CPhys, memb IAU, FInstP, FRAS (pres-elect 2015–16, pres 2016–18); *Recreations* watching football, cookery, films; *Style—* Prof John Zarnecki; ✉ Planetary and Space Sciences Research Institute, The Open University, Walton Hall, Milton Keynes MK7 6AA (☎ 01908 659599, fax 01908 858022, e-mail J.C.Zarnecki@open.ac.uk)

ZEFF, Jon; s of Brian Zeff, and Paula Zeff; *b* 23 May 1966, London; *Educ* Univ Coll Sch London, Univ of Warwick (BA); *m* 1996, Alison Beat; 1 s, 1 da; *Career* asst dir Dept of Trade and Industry 1995–98; Dept for Culture, Media and Sport: head of Nat Lottery Div 1999–2001, head of policy, innovation and delivery 2001–03, head of broadcasting policy 2003–08, dir of media 2008–; *Style—* Jon Zeff, Esq; ✉ Department for Culture, Media and Sport, 2–4 Cockspur Street, London SW1Y 5DH (☎ 020 7211 6463, e-mail jon.zeff@culture.gsi.gov.uk)

ZEIDMAN, His Hon Judge Martyn Keith; QC (1998); s of Abe Zeidman (d 1971), and Jennie, *née* Davis (d 2000); *b* 30 May 1952; *Educ* Univ of London (external LLB); *m* 1977, Verity, da of His Hon Aron Owen; 1 da (Annette b 24 June 1979), 1 s (Austin b 20 November 1981); *Career* called to the Bar 1974, asst recorder (SE Circuit) 1995–99, recorder 1999–2001, circuit judge 2001–; pres Mental Health Review Tbnl: Restricted Cases; chm Jewish Marriage Cncl; *Publications* A Short Guide to the Landlord and Tenant Act 1987 (1987), A Short Guide to the Housing Act 1988 (1988), Steps to Possession (1989), A Short Guide to the Courts and Legal Services Act 1990 (1990), A Short Guide to the Road Traffic Act 1991 (1991), Making Sense of the Leasehold Reform Housing and Urban Development Act 1993 (1994), Archbold Practical Research Papers on Law of Mistake, Self Defence (1998); *Recreations* family, studying Jewish religious texts, cycling; *Style—* His Hon Judge Zeidman, QC; ✉ Snaresbrook Crown Court, The Court House, Hollybush Hill, London E11 1QW

ZEIN, Andrew; *Educ* St Paul's, Univ of Bristol; *Career* film prodn asst 1991–93, projects mangr IPH Westhall Ltd 1993–95, conslt BBC Entertainment Gp 1995–96, BBC broadcast entertainment business mangr (planning and strategy) 1996–97; Tiger Aspect Prodns: business devpt mangr 1997, commercial dir 1998, jt md 2001, md 2002–; chm PACT (TV) 2004–05 (vice-chm 2002–03); *Style—* Andrew Zein, Esq

ZEKI, Prof Semir; *b* 8 November 1940; *Educ* UCL (BSc, PhD); *m* 1967, Anne-Marie Claire, *née* Blestel; 1 da (Isabelle b 24 June 1973), 1 s (Sebastian b 13 Jan 1977); *Career* res assoc St Elizabeth's Hosp Washington DC 1967–68, asst prof of anatomy Univ of Wisconsin 1968–69, Henry Head res fell Royal Soc 1975–80; UCL: asst lectr in anatomy 1966–67, lectr in anatomy 1969–75, reader in neurobiology 1980–81, prof of neurobiology 1981–, co-head Wellcome Dept of Cognitive Neurology 1996–2001, fell 2000–; visiting prof: Duke Univ Durham NC 1977, Institut für Medizinische Psychologie Ludwig Maximilians Univ Munich 1982–87, Univ of Calif Berkeley 1984, 2003 and 2006, Inst for Advanced Study Stanford Univ 2002; visiting lectr Univ of St Andrews 1985, assoc Neurosciences Res Prog NY 1985, visiting prof Université Libre de Bruxelles 1997–98; delivered numerous special lectures; memb: Bd of Advisors Beit Meml Tst 1984–89, Scientific Advsy Bd The Neurosciences Institute NY 1986–, Bd of Scientific Govrs Scripps Res Inst Calif 1992–, Bd of Govrs Int Brain Res Orgn (IBRO) 1993–98; chm Vision Res Working Pty Wellcome Tst 1987– (memb 1985–87); tstee Fight for Sight 1992–97, guarantor Brain 1994–; memb: Ctee of Honour Paris Decorative and Fine Arts Soc 1997–, Nat Sciences Cncl of France 1998–2002, Bd Scientific Govrs Low Temperature Physics Lab Technical Univ Helsinki; Hocart Prize Royal Anthropological Inst 1961, Minerva Fndn Prize California 1985, Prix Science Pour l'Art Louis Vuitton Moët Hennessy (LVMH) Paris 1991, Rank Prize in Opto-electronics 1992, Zotterman Prize Swedish Physiological Soc 1993, Electronic Imaging Award 2002, King Faisal Int Prize in Science King Faisal Fndn 2004, Erasmus Medal Academia Europaea 2008, Segerfalk Fndn Award 2009, Aristotle Medal World Fedn of

Psychiatry 2011, Rome Prize Atena Onlus 2012; assoc ed and memb Ed Bds of scientific jls; ed Philosophical Transactions of the Royal Society 1997–2004; exhibition Bianco su Bianco: Oltre Malevich (Pecci Museum of Contemporary Art Milan) 2011; memb Physiological Soc 1978, hon memb Italian Primatological Assoc 1988, memb Academia Europaea 1990, memb European Acad of Sciences and Arts Salzburg 1992, foreign memb American Philosophical Soc 1998, fndr memb Acad of Medical Sciences 1998; Hon DSc: Aston Univ 1994, Aberdeen Univ 2008, Athens Univ 2012; FRSM 1972, FZS 1980, MRI 1985, FRS 1990, FMedSci 1998; *Books* A Vision of the Brain (1993), La Quête de l'essentiel (with Balthus, 1995), Inner Vision (1999), Splendours and Miseries of the Brain (2009), La Bella e la Bestia: Arte e Nueroscienze (with L Lumer, 2011); author of papers and articles in scientific jls; *Recreations* reading (especially about the darker side of man), music (especially opera), deep sleep; *Clubs* Athenaeum, Garrick; *Style—* Prof Semir Zeki, FRS; ✉ Laboratory of Neurobiology, University College London, Gower Street, London WC1E 6BT (☎ 020 7679 7316, fax 020 7679 7316)

ZELLICK, Prof Graham John; CBE (2009), Hon QC (2010); s of Reginald Zellick (d 1993), and Beana, *née* Levey (d 2010); *b* 12 August 1948; *Educ* Christ's Coll Finchley, Gonville & Caius Coll Cambridge (MA, PhD), Stanford Univ Sch of Law (Ford Fndn fell); *m* 18 Sept 1975, Prof Jennifer Temkin, da of Michael Temkin (d 1993), of London; 1 s (Adam b 1977), 1 da (Lara b 1980); *Career* Queen Mary & Westfield Coll (formerly QMC) London: lectr in laws 1971–78, reader in law 1978–82, prof of public law 1982–88, dean Faculty of Laws 1984–88, head Dept of Law 1984–90, Drapers' prof of law 1988–91, sr vice-princ and actg princ 1990–91, prof of law 1991–98, princ 1991–98, emeritus prof of law 1998–, visiting prof of law 2007–12; Univ of London: senator 1985–94, dean Faculty of Laws 1986–88, dep chm Academic Cncl 1987–89, memb Cncl 1994–2003, vice-chllr and pres 1997–2003 (dep vice-chllr 1994–97); visiting prof of law Univ of Toronto 1975 and 1978–79, visiting scholar St John's Coll Oxford 1989, hon prof Sch of Law Univ of Birmingham 2004–11, distinguished visiting fell NZ Law Fndn 2010; called to the Bar Middle Temple 1992 (bencher 2001, reader 2013), assoc memb of chambers 3 Verulam Buildings Gray's Inn 1993–2010; ed: Euro Human Rights Reports 1978–82, Public Law 1981–86; memb Editorial Bd: British Jl of Criminology 1980–90, Public Law 1981–91, Howard Jl of Criminal Justice 1984–87, Civil Law Library 1987–91; chm: Tel Aviv Univ Tst Lawyers' Gp 1984–89, Prisoners' Advice and Law Serv 1984–89, Ctee of Heads of Univ Law Schs 1988–90, Legal Ctee All-Pty Parly War Crimes Gp 1988–91, E London Strategic Forum for Nat Educn and Trg Targets 1993–95, Criminal Cases Review Cmmn 2003–08; dep chm Justice Ctee on Prisoners' Rights 1981–83; memb: Jellicoe Ctee on Bds of Visitors of Prisons 1973–75, Cncl Howard League for Penal Reform 1973–82, Newham Dist Ethics Ctee 1985–86, Lord Chllr's Advsy Ctee on Legal Aid 1985–88, Data Protection Tbnl 1985–96, Lord Chllr's Advsy Ctee on Legal Educn 1988–90, Bd of Dirs and Exec Ctee Inst of Citizenship Studies 1991–93, Cncl City and East London Confedn for Med and Dentistry 1991–95, Bart's Med Coll 1991–95, Cncl of Govrs The London Hosp Med Coll 1991–95, Cncl Spitalfields Heritage Centre 1992–98, Cncl Ctee of Vice-Chllrs and Princs 1993–97, Main Bd E London Partnership 1994–95, Bd of Dirs UCAS 1994–97, Steering Ctee London HE Consortium 1999–2001, Bd London Competitive Advantage Prog 2000–01, Criminal Injuries Compensation Appeals Panel 2000–03, Competition Appeal Tbnl 2000–03, Criminal Justice Cncl 2003–06, Investigatory Powers Tbnl 2013–; electoral cmmr 2001–04; pres Valuation Tbnl for England 2009–15, ret (memb Service Bd 2009–); vice-chm Cncl Academic Study Gp for Israel and the Middle East 1995–2003; non-exec memb: S Thames RHA 1994–95, E London and City HA 1995–97; pres W London (Reform) Synagogue 2000–06 (chm Senate 2006–14); govr: Central London Poly 1973–77, Pimlico Sch 1973–77, UCS 1983–92, QMC (later Queen Mary & Westfield Coll) 1983–98, N London Poly 1986–89, Univ of Greenwich 1994–97, William Goodenough Tst 1997–2003, Tel Aviv Univ 2000–09; chm: Reform Club Conservation Tst 2003–13, Bd of Govrs Leo Baeck Coll 2005–06; tstee: William Harvey Research Inst 1995–2000, Samuel Courtauld Tst 1997–2003, Richmond American Int Univ in London 2002–06 (govr 1999–2003, chm 2005–06); patron Redress Tst 1993–; JP Inner London 1981–85; Freeman City of London 1992, Master Worshipful Co of Drapers 2009–10 (Freeman 1991, Liveryman 1995, memb Ct of Assts 2000–); Hon LHD NYU 2001, Hon LLD Richmond 2003, Hon LLD Univ of Birmingham 2006, Hon DLit Queen Mary London 2010; hon fell: Burgon Soc (Hon FBS) 2001 (patron 2009–16, pres 2016–), Gonville & Caius Coll Cambridge 2001, Heythrop Coll 2005, Leo Baeck Coll 2007; FRSA 1991, FRSM 1996, FInstD 1996–2003, CCMI (CIMgt) 1997, Hon FSALS 1997, FICPD 1998–2003, FAcSS 2000, Hon FRAM 2003; *Books* Prisons in Halsbury's Laws of England (4 edn 1974, with Sir Louis Blom-Cooper, QC), Justice in Prison (with Sir Brian MacKenna, 1983), The Law Commission and Law Reform (ed 1988); *Style—* Prof Graham Zellick, CBE, QC; ✉ 63 Hampstead Way, London NW11 7DN; Wykeham House, Wothorpe, Stamford PE9 3LS (e-mail graham.zellick@gmail.com)

ZENON, HE Alexandros N; *b* 28 January 1953, Limassol, Cyprus; *Educ* Larnaca Lyceum, Univ of Athens, Paris IV-Sorbonne Univ, Int Inst of Public Admin Paris (Dip); *m* Aliki Pascali; 1 da; *Career* Cypriot diplomat; attaché Cyprus Problem Div Miny of Foreign Affrs 1979–81, Office of the Min of Foreign Affrs 1981–82, 1 sec Rome 1982–89, dep head Cyprus Delegation Vienna 1989, cnsllr Political Affrs Div Miny of Foreign Affrs 1989–91, 1 cnsllr Paris 1991–96, ambass to The Netherlands 1996–2000, ambass to Italy, Switzerland, Malta and San Marino 2000–05; Miny of Foreign Affrs: dir EU and European countries 2005–06, acting perm sec 2006–07, perm sec 2007–08, high cmmr to the Ct of St James's 2008–; memb: ad hoc Ctee of Experts on Rgnl and Minority Languages in Europe Cncl of Europe Strasbourg 1990–93, Ctee of Government Experts for the 1954 Hague Convention on the Protection of Cultural Property in the Event of Armed Conflict Paris 1995–98, Admin Cncl Perm Ct of Arbitration The Hague 1996–2000; perm rep Orgn for the Prohibition of Chemical Weapons The Hague 1997–2000; Companion of the Nat Order of Merit of the Repub of Malta 2002, Order of the Repub Malta 2005, Cdr Order of Merit Hellenic Repub 2005, Grande Ufficiale Order of Merit Italy 2006, Grand Decoration of Honour in Gold with Star Austria 2007, Grande Ufficiale Order of Sant'Agata Repub of San Marino 2009 (Cdr 1989), Commandeur Ordre National du Merite French Repub 2010; *Publications* The Historical Evolution of the Athenian Parliament (1973), The Historical Evolution of the British Commonwealth (1974), Relations of Turkey with the Arab States (1979), American Military Facilities in Turkey (1980), Intercommunal Relations in Cyprus Between 1960–63 and the Attempt to Amend the Constitution (1994); *Style—* HE Mr Alexandros Zenon; ✉ High Commission for the Republic of Cyprus, 13 St James's Square, London SW1Y 4LB (☎ 020 7321 4112, e-mail highcommissioner@chclondon.org.uk, website www.mfa.gov.cy/highcomlondon)

ZEPHANIAH, Prof Benjamin Obadiah Iqbal; s of Valerie Ebanks; *b* 15 April 1958; *Career* poet; writer in residence: Africa Arts Collective City of Liverpool (1 year), Hay-on-Wye Literature Festival, Memphis State Univ Tennessee, Keats House, Tongji Univ Shanghai 2012; TV and radio presenter (incl Passport to Liverpool, Radio 4), actor in Peaky Blinders (BBC) 2013 and 2014; patron: Irie Dance Co, Market Nursery Hackney, VIVA! (vegetarian gp), Chinese Women's Refuge Gp, SARI (Sport Against Racism in Ireland); pres Penrose Housing Assoc (for ex-prisoners); shortlisted: creative artist in residence Univ of Cambridge 1986, prof of poetry Univ of Oxford, prof of poetry and creative writing Brunel Univ; subject of two C4 documentaries, toured Europe, Canada, USA and the Caribbean, regular appearances on TV and radio; *Films* Didn't You Kill My Brother (Comic Strip), Farendg; *Records* Big Boys Don't Make Girls Cry, Free South Africa (with The Wailers), Dub Ranting, Rasta, Us and Dem, Back to Roots, Belly of de Beast, Naked; *Plays* Playing the Right Tune, Job Rocking, Hurricane Dub (BBC Young Playwrights award 1988), Streetwise, Delirium, Mickey Tekka, Listen to Your Parents (Race in the Media awards 2001); *Films* Dread Poets Society (BBC);; *Books* Pen Rhythm, The Dread Affair, In a Liverpool, Rasta Time in Palestine, City Psalms, Talking Turkeys (1994), Funky Chickens (1996), Propa Propaganda (1996), Schools Out (1997), Face (1999), Bloomsbury Book of Love Poems (ed, 1999), Wicked World (2000), The Little Book of Vegan Poems (2001), Refugee Boy (2001), Too Black, Too Strong (2001), We Are Britain (2002), Gangsta Rap (2004), J is for Jamaica (2006), Teacher's Dead (2007), Kung Fu Trip (2011), When I Grow Up (2011), Liam (2012), To Do Wid Me (2013), Terror Kid (novel, 2014); *Style—* Prof Benjamin Zephaniah; ✉ c/o United Agents Limited, 12–26 Lexington Street, London W1F 0LE (☎ 020 3214 0800, fax 020 3214 0801, website www.unitedagents.co.uk)

ZETA JONES, Catherine; CBE (2010); da of David James Jones, of Swansea, S Wales; *m* 2000 (sep), Michael Douglas, the actor; 1 s (Dylan Michael b 2000), 1 da (Carys Zeta b 2003); *Career* actress; ambass NSPCC 2005–, patron Swansea Life Film Festival 2008–; *Theatre* incl: The Pyjama Game (Number One Tour), Annie, Bugsy Malone (West End), 42nd Street (West End), Street Scene (ENO), A Little Night Music (Walter Kerr Theatre NY) 2009; *Television* incl: Darling Buds of May 1991, Out of the Blue 1991, Cinder Path 1994, Return of The Native 1995, Titanic 1996; *Films* incl: Scheherazade 1990, Coup de Foudre, Splitting Heirs 1993, Blue Juice 1995, The Phantom 1996, The Mask of Zorro 1997, Entrapment 1998, The Haunting 1999, High Fidelity 2000, Traffic 2000, America's Sweethearts 2001, Chicago 2002, Sinbad: Legend of the Seven Seas 2003, Intolerable Cruelty 2003, The Terminal 2004, Ocean's Twelve 2004, The Legend of Zorro 2005, No Reservations 2007, Death Defying Acts 2007, The Rebound 2009, Lay the Favourite 2012, Rock of Ages 2012, Playing for Keeps 2012, Broken City 2013, Side Effects 2013, Red 2 2013; *Style—* Ms Catherine Zeta Jones, CBE; ✉ c/o Independent Talent Group, 40 Whitfield Street, London W1T 2RH

ZETLAND, 4 Marquess of (UK 1892); Sir Lawrence Mark Dundas; 7 Bt (GB 1762), DL (N Yorks 1994); also Earl of Ronaldshay (UK 1892), Earl of Zetland (UK 1838), and Baron Dundas (GB 1794); eldest s of 3 Marquess of Zetland, DL (d 1989), and Penelope, Marchioness of Zetland (d 2003); *b* 28 December 1937; *Educ* Harrow, Christ's Coll Cambridge; *m* 4 April 1964, Susan Rose, 2 da of late Guy Richard Chamberlin; 2 s (Robin Lawrence, Earl of Ronaldshay b 5 March 1965, Lord James Edward b 2 May 1967), 2 da (Lady Henrietta Kate (Lady Henrietta Stroyan) b 9 Feb 1970, Lady Victoria Clare (Lady Victoria Madel) b 2 Jan 1973); *Heir* s, Earl of Ronaldshay; *Career* late 2 Lt Grenadier Gds; landowner; dir Catterick Racecourse, chm Redcar Racecourse Ltd, pres Enhance Global Ltd; steward of the Jockey Club 1992–94, dir British Horseracing Bd 1993–97; *Recreations* tennis (lawn and Royal), squash, racing (racehorses Foggy Buoy, Tatiana and Malek); *Clubs* All England Lawn Tennis, Jockey; *Style—* The Most Hon the Marquess of Zetland, DL; ✉ The Orangery, Richmond, North Yorkshire DL10 5HE (☎ 01748 823222, mobile 07836 779869, e-mail zetland@aske.co.uk); Flat F, 17/18 Smith Street, London SW3 4EE (☎ 020 7730 7414)

ZIMMER, Prof Robert Mark; s of Norman Zimmer, NY, USA, and Lenore *née* Wasserman; *Educ* Churchill Coll Cambridge, MIT (SB), Columbia Univ NY (MA, MPhil, PhD); *m* 23 July 1983, Joanna Elizabeth Marlow, da of Thomas Gondris, of Ipswich, Suffolk; 2 s (Edmund b 31 Jan 1992, Sebastian b 14 August 1996); *Career* lectr: Columbia Univ 1982–85, Brunel Univ 1985–; currently head Dept of Computing Goldsmiths Univ of London and co-dir Goldsmiths Digital Studios; visiting scholar Dept of Sanskrit and Indian Studies Harvard Univ 1989; visiting prof: Univ of Ottawa 1989, Univ of Bristol 1997–98; published poetry and articles on mathematics, computer science, electrical engrg and 18th century Eng lit; *Recreations* food, books; *Clubs* Young Johnsonians; *Style—* Prof Robert Zimmer

ZIMMERMANN, Frank Peter; *b* 1965, Duisburg, Germany; *Career* violinist; studied with Valery Gradov, Sashko Gawriloff, Herman Krebbers; awarded Premio dell Accademia Musicale Chigiana Siena 1990, received Rheinischer Kulturpreis 1994, received Bundesverdienstkreuz 1 Klass der Bundesrepublik Deutschland; orchs appeared with incl: Philadelphia Orch, Chicago Symphony Orch, Boston Symphony Orch, The Cleveland Orch, Los Angeles Philharmonic, Staadtskapelle Dresden, Gustav Mahler Youth Orch, Berlin Philharmonic Orch, Gewandhausorchstra Leipzig, Munich Philharmonic, Bayerische Rundfunk, Vienna Philharmonic, Chamber Orch of Europe, Orchestre de Paris, Oslo Philharmonic Orch, Royal Concertgebouw Orch, Russian Nat Orch, NHK Symphony Orch, LSO, English Chamber Orch, The London Philharmonic, Philharmonia Orch, NY Philharmonic; conductors worked with incl: Lorin Maazel, Barenboim, Andrew Davis, Sir Colin Davis, Wolfgang Sawallisch, Dohnányi, Bernard Haitink, André Previn, Kurt Sanderling, Franz Welser-Möst, Mariss Jansons; special concerts incl: Mozart Sinfonia Concertante for Violin and Viola (with Tabea Zimmermann and English Chamber Orch) Buckingham Palace 1991, May Day concert Royal Albert Hall with the Berlin Philharmonic Orch (televised all over world); regular recital partners: Enrico Pace, Piotr Anderzewski, Emanuel Ax (all pianists); formed Trio Zimmermann (string trio) with Antoine Tamestit (viola player) and Christian Poltra (cellist); *Recordings* incl: Saint-Saëns Concerto No 3, Stravinsky Concerto, Ravel Tzigane, all Mozart Sonatas, all Prokofiev Sonatas, works by Berg/Stravinsky/Ravel (Edison Award 1992, Diapason d'Or de l'Année 1992), works by Debussy/Ravel/Janácek (with Alexander Lonquich, Diapason d'Or 1992), works by Groupe des Six (Edison Award 1994), Eugène Ysaÿe 6 Solo Sonatas (Prix Cecilia, ECHO/Deutscher Schallplattenpreis), Brahms Violin Concerto with Mozart Violin Concerto No 3 (with Berlin Philharmonic Orch and Wolfgang Sawallisch), Tchaikovsky Concerto and Prokofiev Concerto No 1 (with Berlin Philharmonic Orch and Lorin Maazel), Weill Violin Concerto (with Berlin Philharmonic Orch and Mariss Jansons), Ligeti Violin Concerto (with ASKO Ensemble and Reinbert de Leeuw), Tchaikovsky (with Oslo Philharminic Orch and Manfred Honeck), Bruch Concerto No 1 (with Royal Philharmonic Orch and Paavo Berglund), Busoni Concerto (with Orch Sinfonica Nazionale della RAI and John Storgards), Busoni Sonata No 2 (with pianist Enrico Pace), 6 violin sonatas by J S Bach (with Enrico Pace), Szymanowski Concertos (with Warsaw Philharmonic Orch and Antoni Wit), Britten Concerto (with Swedish Radio Symphony Orch and Manfred Honeck), Hindemith Concerto (with hr-Sinfonieorchester and Paavo Jarvi) and Sonatas by Hindemith (with Enrico Pace), Mozart violin concertos with the Kammerorchester des Symphonieorchesters des Bayerischen Rundfunks; *Style—* Frank Peter Zimmermann, Esq; ✉ c/o Jeroen Tersteeg, Nymus Artists, 34 Avenue de Beau Sejour, 1180 Brussels, Belguim (☎ 32 2 372 3005, fax 32 2 372 3006, e-mail jt@nymusartists.com)

ZINKIN, Peter John Louis; *b* 23 July 1953; *Educ* Winchester, Magdalene Coll Cambridge (BA), London Business Sch (MSc(Econ)); *Career* London Business Sch 1978–81; Balfour Beatty plc: various appts 1981–88, gp planning and devpt mangr 1988–91, chm Balfour Beatty Developments 1991– (dir Main Bd 1991–2015); cncllr London Borough of Barnet 2014–; govr Birkbeck Univ London; MCT; *Style—* Peter Zinkin, Esq; ✉ Balfour Beatty plc, 130 Wilton Road, London SW1V 1LQ (☎ 020 7216 6800, fax 020 7216 6950)

ZUCKERMAN, Prof Arie Jeremy; *Educ* Univ of Birmingham (BSc, MSc, DSc), Univ of London (MB BS, MD, DipBact, Univ Gold medal, Evans prize, A B Cunning prize, A B Cunning award); *m* 8 July 1951, Alice Adamson (d 2011); 1 s (Mark Adam), 1 da (Jane Nicola); *Career* Flt Lt then Sqdn Ldr RAF Med Branch 1959–62; first obstetric house surgn Royal Free Hosp 1957–58, casualty surgn and admissions offr Whittington Hosp London 1958–59 (house physician in gen med 1958), Med Branch RAF 1959–62,

Z

Epidemiol Res Lab Public Health Laboratory Serv 1960–62, secondment as hon registrar Dept of Pathology Guy's Hosp Med Sch 1962–63, sr registrar Public Health Laboratory Serv 1963–65; LSHTM: sr lectr Dept of Bacteriology and Immunology 1965–68, reader in virology 1968–72, prof of virology 1972–75, dir Dept of Med Microbiology 1975–88; prof of microbiology Univ of London 1975–, dean Royal Free Hosp Sch of Med 1989–98, princ and dean Royal Free and UC Med Sch UCL 1998–99; WHO: conslt on hepatitis 1970–2005, memb Expert Advsy Panel on Virus Diseases 1974–2005, dir Collaborating Centre for Ref and Res on Viral Hepatitis 1974–89, dir Collaborating Centre for Ref and Res on Viral Diseases 1990–2005; hon conslt virologist: N E Thames Regnl Blood Transfusion Centre 1970–94, Charing Cross Hosp 1982–96, Nat Blood Authy 1994–99; hon conslt microbiologist Royal Free Hosp 1989–99, non-exec dir Royal Free Hampstead NHS Tst 1990–99, dir Anthony Nolan Bone Marrow Tst 1989–2002, chm Hepatitis B Fndn UK 2006–11; memb: Cncl RCPath 1983–86, Bd Public Health Lab Serv 1983–89, Cncl Zoological Soc of London 1989–92, Cncl UCL 1995–2003; memb Dept of Health Advsy Gps on Hepatitis, AIDS, transfusion-transmitted viruses and liver diseases 1970–2011; ed: Jl of Medical Virology 1976–2015, Jl of Virological Methods 1979–2015; contrib to numerous learned jls; Stewart prize of the BMA 1981, James Blundell medal and award Br Blood Tranfusion Soc 1992; MRCS, DObstRCOG 1958, FRCPath 1977 (MRCPath 1965), FRCP 1982 (LRCP 1957, MRCP 1977), FMedSci 1998; *Books* Virus Diseases of the Liver (1970), Hepatitis-associated Antigen and Viruses (1972), Human Viral Hepatitis (2 edn, 1975), Hepatitis Viruses of Man (with C R Howard, 1979), A Decade of Viral Hepatitis (1980), Viral Hepatitis (ed, 1986), Principles and Practice of Clinical Virology (1987, 6 edn 2009), Viral Hepatitis and Liver Disease (ed, 1988), Recent Developments in Prophylactic Immunization (ed, 1989), Viral Hepatitis (ed, 1990, 4 edn 2013), Viral Hepatitis: Scientific Basis and Clinical Management (with H Thomas, 1993, 4 edn with H Thomas, S Locranini and A Lok, 2014), Molecular Medicine of Viral Hepatitis (with T J Harrison, 1996), Prevention of Hepatitis B in the newborn, children and adolescents (ed, 1996), Hepatitis B in the Asian-Pacific Region (ed, vol 1 1997, vol 2 1998, vol 3 1999), Diabetes and Viruses (ed with K Taylor, H Hyoty and A Toniolo, 2013); *Recreations* opera, classical music, painting; *Style*— Prof Arie Zuckerman; ✉ e-mail arie.zuckerman@ucl.ac.uk

ZUKERMAN, Pinchas; *b* 1948; *Educ* began musical training with father, Israel Conservatory (with Ilona Feher), Acad of Music Tel Aviv, Julliard Sch USA (scholar, studied with Ivan Galamian); *Career* musician; violinist, violist, teacher and conductor; as soloist performs with major orchestras worldwide; soloist and conductor with many maj orchs incl: New York Philharmonic, Boston Symphony, Los Angeles Philharmonic, Nat Symphony Orch and San Francisco, Montreal, Toronto and Ottawa Symphonies, Berlin Philharmonic, Philharmonia, Eng Chamber Orch, Israel Philharmonic; former music dir: South Bank Festival, St Paul Chamber Orch; princ guest conductor Dallas Symphony Orch's Int Music Festival 1990–93; artist dir Baltimore Symphony Orch's Summer Musicfest 1996–99; music dir Nat Arts Centre Orch Ottawa Canada 1999–; extensive recital tours with Marc Neikrug, chamber music collaborations with Itzhak Perlman, Daniel Barenboim, Ralph Kirshbaum; discography incl over 100 recordings widely representative of violin and viola repertoires; Hon DUniv Brown USA; *Awards* first prize Twenty-Fifth Leventritt Int Competition 1967, Achievement award Int Center in NY, King Solomon award America-Israel Cultural Fndn, Medal of Arts 1983, Isaac Stern Award for Artistic Excellence Nat Arts Awards 2002; *Style*— Pinchas Zukerman; ✉ c/o Kirshbaum Demler & Assoc Inc, 711 West End Avenue, Suite 5KN, New York, NY 10025, USA (☎ 00 1 212 2224843)